S0-CBP-631

Who's Who in the West®

Who's Who in the West®

2010

37th Edition

Including Alaska, Arizona, California, Colorado, Hawaii, Idaho, Montana, Nevada, New Mexico, Oregon, Utah, Washington, and Wyoming; and in Canada: The provinces of Alberta, British Columbia, and Saskatchewan, and the Northwest and Yukon Territories

MARQUIS
Who'sWho®

890 Mountain Avenue, Suite 300
New Providence, NJ 07974 U.S.A.
www.marquiswhoswho.com

Who's Who in the West®

Marquis Who's Who

For information, contact: Marquis Who's Who
890 Mountain Avenue, Suite 300
New Providence, New Jersey 07974
1-800-473-7020
west@marquiswhoswho.com
www.marquiswhoswho.com

WHO'S WHO IN THE WEST® is a registered trademark of Marquis Who's Who LLC.
Library of Congress Catalog Card Number 49-48186
International Standard Book Number 978-0-8379-0941-7 (Classic Edition)
International Standard Serial Number 0083-9817

Manufactured in the United States of America.

Table of Contents

Preface

Marquis Who's Who is proud to present the 2010 Edition of *Who's Who in the West,* our 37th compilation of biographical information on men and women of distinction whose influence is concentrated in the western region of North America, but may also be felt internationally.

This volume contains over 16,000 names from the western region of the United States including Alaska, Arizona, California, Colorado, Hawaii, Idaho, Montana, Nevada, New Mexico, Oregon, Utah, Washington, and Wyoming. Also included are the Canadian provinces of Alberta, British Columbia, and Saskatchewan, and the Northwest and Yukon Territories. In some instances, persons who do not reside in the western region of the United States or Canada have also been included as biographees. They appear in this edition because they have made significant professional or civic contributions to this region. Reviewed, revised, and amended, the 37th Edition offers current coverage of a broad range of Westerners based on position or individual achievement.

The individuals profiled in this volume represent virtually every important field of endeavor. Included are executives and officials in government, business, education, medicine, religion, the press, law, and other fields. This edition also includes significant contributors in such areas as contemporary art, music, and science.

Factors such as position, noteworthy accomplishments, visibility, and prominence in a field are all taken into account in making selections for the book. Final decisions concerning inclusion or exclusion are made following extensive discussion, evaluation, and deliberation.

Biographical information is gathered in a variety of manners. In most cases, we invite our biographees to submit their biographical details. In many cases, though, the information is collected independently by our editorial staff who use a wide assortment of tools to gather complete, accurate, and up-to-date information. Sketches researched by Marquis Who's Who will be followed by an asterisk (*).

While the Marquis Who's Who editors exercise the utmost care in preparing each biographical sketch for publication, in a publication involving so many profiles, occasional errors may appear. Users of this publication are urged to notify the publisher of any issues so that adjustments can be made.

All of the profiles featured in *Who's Who in the West* are available on www.marquiswhoswho.com through a subscription. At the present time, subscribers to *Who's Who on the Web* have access to all of the names included in all of the Marquis Who's Who publications, as well as many new biographies that will appear in upcoming publications.

We sincerely hope that this volume will be an indispensable reference tool for you. We are always looking for ways to better serve you and welcome your ideas for improvements. In addition, we continue to welcome your Marquis Who's Who nominations. *Who's Who in the West* and all Marquis Who's Who publications pay tribute to those individuals who make significant contributions to our society. It is our honor and privilege to present their profiles to you.

Key to Information

[1] STEELE, FLETCHER DAVID, [2] mechanical engineer; **[3]** b. Normal, Ill., Jan. 20, 1939; **[4]** s. Thomas William and Susan (Shobe) S.; **[5]** m. Julie Ann Walsh, Sept. 8, 1964; **[6]** children: Elizabeth Carter, Michael Thomas. **[7]** BSME, Purdue U., 1961; MS, U. Ill., 1965. **[8]** Registered profl. engr., Calif., NJ. **[9]** Asst. engr. Kelly, Kitching, Berendes & Brault, Engrs., Chgo., 1966-67, engr., 1967-71; sr. engr. Kelly, Kitching, Berendes & Brault, Internat., Chgo., 1971-78, mgr. fluids divsn. 1979-84, v.p. R & D, 1985-90; exec. v.p., Ryan Belle Co., San Francisco, Calif., 1990—. **[10]** Lectr. Drake U., 1995-97. **[11]** Contbr. articles to Jour. Biomech. Engring., Jour. Fluids Engring. **[12]** Asst. troop leader Boy Scouts Am., 1992—. **[13]** Lt. US Army, 1961-63. **[14]** Recipient Nat. Engring. award, 1975; Fulbright scholar, 1965. **[15]** Mem. ASME, NSPE, Fla. Mech. Engrs. Assn., Big Sand Lake Club. **[16]** Republican. **[17]** Roman Catholic. **[18]** Achievements include design of L16500 Workhorse rotar; patent for internal piston lock for hydraulic cylinders; research in linear regression analysis for large-lot engine data comparisons. **[19]** Avocations: cooking, running. **[20]** Home: 733 N Ottawa Rd San Francisco CA 94109 **[21]** Office: 1245 34th St San Francisco CA 94109*

KEY

[1] Name
[2] Occupation
[3] Vital statistics
[4] Parents
[5] Marriage
[6] Children
[7] Education
[8] Professional certifications
[9] Career
[10] Career-related
[11] Writings and creative works
[12] Civic and political activities
[13] Military
[14] Awards and fellowships
[15] Professional and association memberships, clubs and lodges
[16] Political affiliation
[17] Religion
[18] Achievements information
[19] Avocations
[20] Home address
[21] Office address
[*] Researched by Marquis Who's Who

Table of Abbreviations

The following is a list of some frequently used Marquis abbreviations:

A

A Associate (used with academic degrees)
AA Associate in Arts
AAAL American Academy of Arts and Letters
AAAS American Association for the Advancement of Science
AACD American Association for Counseling and Development
AACN American Association of Critical Care Nurses
AAHA American Academy of Health Administrators
AAHP American Association of Hospital Planners
AAHPERD American Alliance for Health, Physical Education, Recreation, and Dance
AAS Associate of Applied Science
AASL American Association of School Librarians
AASPA American Association of School Personnel Administrators
AAU Amateur Athletic Union
AAUP American Association of University Professors
AAUW American Association of University Women
AB Arts, Bachelor of
AB Alberta
ABA American Bar Association
AC Air Corps
acad. academy
acct. accountant
acctg. accounting
ACDA Arms Control and Disarmament Agency
ACHA American College of Hospital Administrators
ACLS Advanced Cardiac Life Support
ACLU American Civil Liberties Union
ACOG American College of Ob-Gyn
ACP American College of Physicians
ACS American College of Surgeons
ADA American Dental Association
adj. adjunct, adjutant
adm. admiral
adminstr. administrator
adminstrn. administration
adminstrv. administrative
ADN Associate's Degree in Nursing
ADP Automatic Data Processing
adv. advocate, advisory
advt. advertising
AE Agricultural Engineer
AEC Atomic Energy Commission
aero. aeronautical, aeronautic
aerodyn. aerodynamic
AFB Air Force Base
AFTRA American Federation of Television and Radio Artists
agr. agriculture
agrl. agricultural
agt. agent
AGVA American Guild of Variety Artists
agy. agency
A&I Agricultural and Industrial
AIA American Institute of Architects
AIAA American Institute of Aeronautics and Astronautics
AIChE American Institute of Chemical Engineers
AICPA American Institute of Certified Public Accountants
AID Agency for International Development
AIDS Acquired Immune Deficiency Syndrome
AIEE American Institute of Electrical Engineers
AIME American Institute of Mining, Metallurgy, and Petroleum Engineers
AK Alaska
AL Alabama
ALA American Library Association
Ala. Alabama
alt. alternate
Alta. Alberta
A&M Agricultural and Mechanical
AM Arts, Master of
Am. American, America
AMA American Medical Association
amb. ambassador
AME African Methodist Episcopal
Amtrak National Railroad Passenger Corporation
AMVETS American Veterans
ANA American Nurses Association
anat. anatomical
ANCC American Nurses Credentialing Center
ann. annual
anthrop. anthropological
AP Associated Press
APA American Psychological Association
APHA American Public Health Association
APO Army Post Office
apptd. appointed
Apr. April
apt. apartment
AR Arkansas
ARC American Red Cross
arch. architect
archeol. archeological
archtl. architectural
Ariz. Arizona
Ark. Arkansas
ArtsD Arts, Doctor of
arty. artillery
AS Associate in Science, American Samoa
ASCAP American Society of Composers, Authors and Publishers
ASCD Association for Supervision and Curriculum Development
ASCE American Society of Civil Engineers
ASME American Society of Mechanical Engineers
ASPA American Society for Public Administration
ASPCA American Society for the Prevention of Cruelty to Animals
assn. association
assoc. associate
asst. assistant
ASTD American Society for Training and Development
ASTM American Society for Testing and Materials
astron. astronomical
astrophys. astrophysical
ATLA Association of Trial Lawyers of America
ATSC Air Technical Service Command
atty. attorney
Aug. August
aux. auxiliary
Ave. Avenue
AVMA American Veterinary Medical Association
AZ Arizona

B

B Bachelor
b. born
BA Bachelor of Arts
BAgr Bachelor of Agriculture
Balt. Baltimore
Bapt. Baptist
BArch Bachelor of Architecture
BAS Bachelor of Agricultural Science
BBA Bachelor of Business Administration
BBB Better Business Bureau
BC British Columbia
BCE Bachelor of Civil Engineering
BChir Bachelor of Surgery
BCL Bachelor of Civil Law
BCS Bachelor of Commercial Science
BD Bachelor of Divinity
bd. board
BE Bachelor of Education
BEE Bachelor of Electrical Engineering

BFA Bachelor of Fine Arts
bibl. biblical
bibliog. bibliographical
biog. biographical
biol. biological
BJ Bachelor of Journalism
Bklyn. Brooklyn
BL Bachelor of Letters
bldg. building
BLS Bachelor of Library Science
Blvd. Boulevard
BMI Broadcast Music, Inc.
bn. battalion
bot. botanical
BPE Bachelor of Physical Education
BPhil Bachelor of Philosophy
br. branch
BRE Bachelor of Religious Education
brig. gen. brigadier general
Brit. British
Bros. Brothers
BS Bachelor of Science
BSA Bachelor of Agricultural Science
BSBA Bachelor of Science in Business Administration
BSChemE Bachelor of Science in Chemical Engineering
BSD Bachelor of Didactic Science
BSEE Bachelor of Science in Electrical Engineering
BSN Bachelor of Science in Nursing
BST Bachelor of Sacred Theology
BTh Bachelor of Theology
bull. bulletin
bur. bureau
bus. business
BWI British West Indies

C

CA California
CAD-CAM Computer Aided Design–Computer Aided Model
Calif. California
Can. Canada, Canadian
CAP Civil Air Patrol
capt. captain
cardiol. cardiological
cardiovasc. cardiovascular
Cath. Catholic
cav. cavalry
CBI China, Burma, India Theatre of Operations
CC Community College
CCC Commodity Credit Corporation
CCNY City College of New York
CCRN Critical Care Registered Nurse
CCU Cardiac Care Unit
CD Civil Defense
CE Corps of Engineers, Civil Engineer
CEN Certified Emergency Nurse
CENTO Central Treaty Organization
CEO chief executive officer
CERN European Organization of Nuclear Research
cert. certificate, certification, certified
CETA Comprehensive Employment Training Act
CFA Chartered Financial Analyst
CFL Canadian Football League
CFO chief financial officer
CFP Certified Financial Planner
ch. church
ChD Doctor of Chemistry
chem. chemical
ChemE Chemical Engineer
ChFC Chartered Financial Consultant
Chgo. Chicago
chirurg., der surgeon
chmn. chairman
chpt. chapter
CIA Central Intelligence Agency
Cin. Cincinnati
cir. circle, circuit
CLE Continuing Legal Education
Cleve. Cleveland
climatol. climatological
clin. clinical
clk. clerk
CLU Chartered Life Underwriter
CM Master in Surgery
CM Northern Mariana Islands
cmty. community
CO Colorado
Co. Company
COF Catholic Order of Foresters
C. of C. Chamber of Commerce
col. colonel
coll. college
Colo. Colorado
com. committee
comd. commanded
comdg. commanding
comdr. commander
comdt. commandant
comm. communications
commd. commissioned
comml. commercial
commn. commission
commr. commissioner
compt. comptroller
condr. conductor
conf. Conference
Congl. Congregational, Congressional
Conglist. Congregationalist
Conn. Connecticut
cons. consultant, consulting
consol. consolidated
constl. constitutional
constn. constitution
constrn. construction
contbd. contributed
contbg. contributing
contbn. contribution
contbr. contributor
contr. controller
Conv. Convention
COO chief operating officer
coop. cooperative
coord. coordinator
corp. corporation, corporate
corr. correspondent, corresponding, correspondence
coun. council
CPA Certified Public Accountant
CPCU Chartered Property and Casualty Underwriter
CPH Certificate of Public Health
cpl. corporal
CPR Cardio-Pulmonary Resuscitation
CS Christian Science
CSB Bachelor of Christian Science
CT Connecticut
ct. court
ctr. center
ctrl. central

D

D Doctor
d. daughter of
DAgr Doctor of Agriculture
DAR Daughters of the American Revolution
dau. daughter
DAV Disabled American Veterans
DC District of Columbia
DCL Doctor of Civil Law
DCS Doctor of Commercial Science
DD Doctor of Divinity
DDS Doctor of Dental Surgery
DE Delaware
Dec. December
dec. deceased
def. defense
Del. Delaware
del. delegate, delegation
Dem. Democrat, Democratic
DEng Doctor of Engineering
denom. denomination, denominational
dep. deputy
dept. department
dermatol. dermatological
desc. descendant
devel. development, developmental
DFA Doctor of Fine Arts
DHL Doctor of Hebrew Literature
dir. director
dist. district
distbg. distributing
distbn. distribution
distbr. distributor
disting. distinguished

div. division, divinity, divorce
divsn. division
DLitt Doctor of Literature
DMD Doctor of Dental Medicine
DMS Doctor of Medical Science
DO Doctor of Osteopathy
docs. documents
DON Director of Nursing
DPH Diploma in Public Health
DPhil, Doctor of Philosophy
DR Daughters of the Revolution
Dr. Drive, Doctor
DRE Doctor of Religious Education
DrPH Doctor of Public Health
DSc Doctor of Science
DSChemE Doctor of Science in Chemical Engineering
DSM Distinguished Service Medal
DST Doctor of Sacred Theology
DTM Doctor of Tropical Medicine
DVM Doctor of Veterinary Medicine
DVS Doctor of Veterinary Surgery

E

E East
ea. eastern
Eccles. Ecclesiastical
ecol. ecological
econ. economic
ECOSOC UN Economic and Social Council
ED Doctor of Engineering
ed. educated
EdB Bachelor of Education
EdD Doctor of Education
edit. edition
editl. editorial
EdM Master of Education
edn. education
ednl. educational
EDP Electronic Data Processing
EdS Specialist in Education
EE Electrical Engineer
EEC European Economic Community
EEG Electroencephalogram
EEO Equal Employment Opportunity
EEOC Equal Employment Opportunity Commission
EKG electrocardiogram
elec. electrical
electrochem. electrochemical
electrophys. electrophysical
elem. elementary
EM Engineer of Mines
EMT Emergency Medical Technician
ency. encyclopedia
Eng. England
engr. engineer
engring. engineering
entomol. entomological
environ. environmental
EPA Environmental Protection Agency
epidemiol. epidemiological
Episc. Episcopalian
ERA Equal Rights Amendment
ERDA Energy Research and Development Administration
ESEA Elementary and Secondary Education Act
ESL English as Second Language
ESSA Environmental Science Services Administration
ethnol. ethnological
ETO European Theatre of Operations
EU European Union
Evang. Evangelical
exam. examination, examining
Exch. Exchange
exec. executive
exhbn. exhibition
expdn. expedition
expn. exposition
expt. experiment
exptl. experimental
Expy. Expressway
Ext. Extension

F

FAA Federal Aviation Administration
FAO UN Food and Agriculture Organization
FBA Federal Bar Association
FBI Federal Bureau of Investigation
FCA Farm Credit Administration
FCC Federal Communications Commission
FCDA Federal Civil Defense Administration
FDA Food and Drug Administration
FDIA Federal Deposit Insurance Administration
FDIC Federal Deposit Insurance Corporation
FEA Federal Energy Administration
Feb. February
fed. federal
fedn. federation
FERC Federal Energy Regulatory Commission
fgn. foreign
FHA Federal Housing Administration
fin. financial, finance
FL Florida
Fl. Floor
Fla. Florida
FMC Federal Maritime Commission
FNP Family Nurse Practitioner
FOA Foreign Operations Administration
found. foundation
FPC Federal Power Commission
FPO Fleet Post Office
frat. fraternity
FRS Federal Reserve System
FSA Federal Security Agency
Ft. Fort
FTC Federal Trade Commission
Fwy. Freeway

G

GA, Ga. Georgia
GAO General Accounting Office
gastroent. gastroenterological
GATT General Agreement on Tariffs and Trade
GE General Electric Company
gen. general
geneal. genealogical
geog. geographic, geographical
geol. geological
geophys. geophysical
geriat. geriatrics
gerontol. gerontological
GHQ General Headquarters
gov. governor
govt. government
govtl. governmental
GPO Government Printing Office
grad. graduate, graduated
GSA General Services Administration
Gt. Great
GU Guam
gynecol. gynecological

H

hdqs. headquarters
HEW Department of Health, Education and Welfare
HHD Doctor of Humanities
HHFA Housing and Home Finance Agency
HHS Department of Health and Human Services
HI Hawaii
hist. historical, historic
HM Master of Humanities
homeo. homeopathic
hon. honorary, honorable
House of Dels. House of Delegates
House of Reps. House of Representatives
hort. horticultural
hosp. hospital
HS High School
HUD Department of Housing and Urban Development
Hwy. Highway
hydrog. hydrographic

I

IA Iowa
IAEA International Atomic Energy Agency
IBRD International Bank for Reconstruction and Development
ICA International Cooperation Administration

Education
ICU Intensive Care Unit
ID Idaho
IEEE Institute of Electrical and Electronics Engineers
IFC International Finance Corporation
IL, Ill. Illinois
illus. illustrated
ILO International Labor Organization
IMF International Monetary Fund
IN Indiana
Inc. Incorporated
Ind. Indiana
ind. independent
Indpls. Indianapolis
indsl. industrial
inf. infantry
info. information
ins. insurance
insp. inspector
inst. institute
instl. institutional
instn. institution
instr. instructor
instrn. instruction
instrnl. instructional
internat. international
intro. introduction
IRE Institute of Radio Engineers
IRS Internal Revenue Service

J

JAG Judge Advocate General
JAGC Judge Advocate General Corps
Jan. January
Jaycees Junior Chamber of Commerce
JB Jurum Baccalaureus
JCB Juris Canoni Baccalaureus
JCD Juris Canonici Doctor, Juris Civilis Doctor
JCL Juris Canonici Licentiatus
JD Juris Doctor
jg. junior grade
jour. journal
jr. junior
JSD Juris Scientiae Doctor
JUD Juris Utriusque Doctor
jud. judicial

K

Kans. Kansas
KC Knights of Columbus
KS Kansas
KY, Ky. Kentucky

L

LA, La. Louisiana
LA Los Angeles
lab. laboratory
L.Am. Latin America
lang. language
laryngol. laryngological
LB Labrador
LDS Latter Day Saints
lectr. lecturer
legis. legislation, legislative
LHD Doctor of Humane Letters
LI Long Island
libr. librarian, library
lic. licensed, license
lit. literature
litig. litigation
LittB Bachelor of Letters
LittD Doctor of Letters
LLB Bachelor of Laws
LLD Doctor of Laws
LLM Master of Laws
Ln. Lane
LPGA Ladies Professional Golf Association
LPN Licensed Practical Nurse
lt. lieutenant
Ltd. Limited
Luth. Lutheran
LWV League of Women Voters

M

M Master
m. married
MA Master of Arts
MA Massachusetts
MADD Mothers Against Drunk Driving
mag. magazine
MAgr Master of Agriculture
maj. major
Man. Manitoba
Mar. March
MArch Master in Architecture
Mass. Massachusetts
math. mathematics, mathematical
MB Bachelor of Medicine, Manitoba
MBA Master of Business Administration
MC Medical Corps
MCE Master of Civil Engineering
mcht. merchant
mcpl. municipal
MCS Master of Commercial Science
MD Doctor of Medicine
MD, Md. Maryland
MDiv Master of Divinity
MDip Master in Diplomacy
mdse. merchandise
MDV Doctor of Veterinary Medicine
ME Mechanical Engineer
ME Maine
M.E.Ch. Methodist Episcopal Church
mech. mechanical
MEd. Master of Education
med. medical
MEE Master of Electrical Engineering
mem. member
meml. memorial
merc. mercantile
met. metropolitan
metall. metallurgical
MetE Metallurgical Engineer
meteorol. meteorological
Meth. Methodist
Mex. Mexico
MF Master of Forestry
MFA Master of Fine Arts
mfg. manufacturing
mfr. manufacturer
mgmt. management
mgr. manager
MHA Master of Hospital Administration
MI Military Intelligence, Michigan
Mich. Michigan
micros. microscopic
mid. middle
mil. military
Milw. Milwaukee
Min. Minister
mineral. mineralogical
Minn. Minnesota
MIS Management Information Systems
Miss. Mississippi
MIT Massachusetts Institute of Technology
mktg. marketing
ML Master of Laws
MLA Modern Language Association
MLitt Master of Literature, Master of Letters
MLS Master of Library Science
MME Master of Mechanical Engineering
MN Minnesota
mng. managing
MO, Mo. Missouri
moblzn. mobilization
Mont. Montana
MP Member of Parliament
MPA Master of Public Administration
MPE Master of Physical Education
MPH Master of Public Health
MPhil Master of Philosophy
MPL Master of Patent Law
Mpls. Minneapolis
MRE Master of Religious Education
MRI Magnetic Resonance Imaging
MS Master of Science
MS, Ms. Mississippi
MSc Master of Science
MSChemE Master of Science in Chemical Engineering
MSEE Master of Science in Electrical Engineering
MSF Master of Science of Forestry

MSN Master of Science in Nursing
MST Master of Sacred Theology
MSW Master of Social Work
MT Montana
Mt. Mount
mus. museum, musical
MusB Bachelor of Music
MusD Doctor of Music
MusM Master of Music
mut. mutual
MVP Most Valuable Player
mycol. mycological

N

N. North
NAACOG Nurses Association of the American College of Obstetricians and Gynecologists
NAACP National Association for the Advancement of Colored People
NACA National Advisory Committee for Aeronautics
NACDL National Association of Criminal Defense Lawyers
NACU National Association of Colleges and Universities
NAD National Academy of Design
NAE National Academy of Engineering, National Association of Educators
NAESP National Association of Elementary School Principals
NAFE National Association of Female Executives
N.Am. North America
NAM National Association of Manufacturers
NAMH National Association for Mental Health
NAPA National Association of Performing Artists
NARAS National Academy of Recording Arts and Sciences
NAREB National Association of Real Estate Boards
NARS National Archives and Record Service
NAS National Academy of Sciences
NASA National Aeronautics and Space Administration
NASP National Association of School Psychologists
NASW National Association of Social Workers
nat. national
NATAS National Academy of Television Arts and Sciences
NATO North Atlantic Treaty Organization
nav. navigation
NBA National Basketball Association
NC North Carolina
NCAA National College Athletic Association
NCCJ National Conference of Christians and Jews
ND North Dakota
NDEA National Defense Education Act
NE Nebraska
NE Northeast
NEA National Education Association
Nebr. Nebraska
NEH National Endowment for Humanities
neurol. neurological
Nev. Nevada
NF Newfoundland
NFL National Football League
Nfld. Newfoundland
NG National Guard
NH New Hampshire
NHL National Hockey League
NIH National Institutes of Health
NIMH National Institute of Mental Health
NJ New Jersey
NLRB National Labor Relations Board
NM, N.Mex. New Mexico
No. Northern
NOAA National Oceanographic and Atmospheric Administration
NORAD North America Air Defense
Nov. November
NOW National Organization for Women
nr. near
NRA National Rifle Association
NRC National Research Council
NS Nova Scotia
NSC National Security Council
NSF National Science Foundation
NSTA National Science Teachers Association
NSW New South Wales
nuc. nuclear
numis. numismatic
NV Nevada
NW Northwest
NWT Northwest Territories
NY New York
NYC New York City
NYU New York University
NZ New Zealand

O

ob-gyn obstetrics-gynecology
obs. observatory
obstet. obstetrical
occupl. occupational
oceanog. oceanographic
Oct. October
OD Doctor of Optometry
OECD Organization for Economic Cooperation and Development
OEEC Organization of European Economic Cooperation
OEO Office of Economic Opportunity
ofcl. official
OH Ohio
OK, Okla. Oklahoma
ON, Ont. Ontario
oper. operating
ophthal. ophthalmological
ops. operations
OR Oregon
orch. orchestra
Oreg. Oregon
orgn. organization
orgnl. organizational
ornithol. ornithological
orthop. orthopedic
OSHA Occupational Safety and Health Administration
OSRD Office of Scientific Research and Development
OSS Office of Strategic Services
osteo. osteopathic
otol. otological
otolaryn. otolaryngological

P

PA, Pa. Pennsylvania
paleontol. paleontological
path. pathological
pediat. pediatrics
PEI Prince Edward Island
PEN Poets, Playwrights, Editors, Essayist and Novelists
penol. penological
pers. personnel
PGA Professional Golfers' Association of America
PHA Public Housing Administration
pharm. pharmaceutical
PharmD Doctor of Pharmacy
PharmM Master of Pharmacy
PhB Bachelor of Philosophy
PhD Doctor of Philosophy
PhDChemE Doctor of Science in Chemical Engineering
PhM Master of Philosophy
Phila. Philadelphia
philharm. philharmonic
philol. philological
philos. philosophical
photog. photographic
phys. physical
physiol. physiological
Pitts. Pittsburgh
Pk. Park
Pky. Parkway
Pl. Place
Plz. Plaza
PO Post Office

polit. political
poly. polytechnic, polytechnical
PQ Province of Quebec
PR Puerto Rico
prep. preparatory
pres. president
Presbyn. Presbyterian
presdl. presidential
prin. principal
procs. proceedings
prod. produced
prodn. production
prodr. producer
prof. professor
profl. professional
prog. progressive
propr. proprietor
pros. prosecuting
pro tem. pro tempore
psychiat. psychiatric
psychol. psychological
PTA Parent-Teachers Association
ptnr. partner
PTO Pacific Theatre of Operations, Parent Teacher Organization
pub. publisher, publishing, published, public
publ. publication
pvt. private

Q

quar. quarterly
qm. quartermaster
Que. Quebec

R

radiol. radiological
RAF Royal Air Force
RCA Radio Corporation of America
RCAF Royal Canadian Air Force
Rd. Road
R&D Research & Development
REA Rural Electrification Administration
rec. recording
ref. reformed
regt. regiment
regtl. regimental
rehab. rehabilitation
rels. relations
Rep. Republican
rep. representative
Res. Reserve
ret. retired
Rev. Reverend
rev. review, revised
RFC Reconstruction Finance Corporation
RI Rhode Island
Rlwy. Railway
Rm. Room
RN Registered Nurse
roentgenol. roentgenological
ROTC Reserve Officers Training Corps
RR rural route, railroad
rsch. research
rschr. researcher
Rt. Route

S

S. South
s. son
SAC Strategic Air Command
SAG Screen Actors Guild
S.Am. South America
san. sanitary
SAR Sons of the American Revolution
Sask. Saskatchewan
savs. savings
SB Bachelor of Science
SBA Small Business Administration
SC South Carolina
ScB Bachelor of Science
SCD Doctor of Commercial Science
ScD Doctor of Science
sch. school
sci. science, scientific
SCV Sons of Confederate Veterans
SD South Dakota
SE Southeast
SEC Securities and Exchange Commission
sec. secretary
sect. section
seismol. seismological
sem. seminary
Sept. September
s.g. senior grade
sgt. sergeant
SI Staten Island
SJ Society of Jesus
SJD Scientiae Juridicae Doctor
SK Saskatchewan
SM Master of Science
SNP Society of Nursing Professionals
So. Southern
soc. society
sociol. sociological
spkr. speaker
spl. special
splty. specialty
Sq. Square
SR Sons of the Revolution
sr. senior
SS Steamship
St. Saint, Street
sta. station
stats. statistics
statis. statistical
STB Bachelor of Sacred Theology
stblzn. stabilization
STD Doctor of Sacred Theology
std. standard
Ste. Suite
subs. subsidiary
SUNY State University of New York
supr. supervisor
supt. superintendent
surg. surgical
svc. service
SW Southwest
sys. system

T

Tb. tuberculosis
tchg. teaching
tchr. teacher
tech. technical, technology
technol. technological
tel. telephone
telecom. telecommunications
temp. temporary
Tenn. Tennessee
TESOL Teachers of English to Speakers of Other Languages
Tex. Texas
ThD Doctor of Theology
theol. theological
ThM Master of Theology
TN Tennessee
tng. training
topog. topographical
trans. transaction, transferred
transl. translation, translated
transp. transportation
treas. treasurer
TV television
twp. township
TX Texas
typog. typographical

U

U. University
UAW United Auto Workers
UCLA University of California at Los Angeles
UK United Kingdom
UN United Nations
UNESCO United Nations Educational, Scientific and Cultural Organization
UNICEF United Nations International Children's Emergency Fund
univ. university
UNRRA United Nations Relief and Rehabilitation Administration
UPI United Press International
urol. urological
US, USA United States of America
USAAF United States Army Air Force
USAF United States Air Force
USAFR United States Air Force Reserve
USAR United States Army Reserve
USCG United States Coast Guard
USCGR United States Coast Guard Reserve
USES United States Employment Service

USIA United States Information Agency
USMC United States Marine Corps
USMCR United States Marine Corps Reserve
USN United States Navy
USNG United States National Guard
USNR United States Naval Reserve
USO United Service Organizations
USPHS United States Public Health Service
USS United States Ship
USSR Union of the Soviet Socialist Republics
USTA United States Tennis Association
UT Utah

V

VA Veterans Administration
VA, Va. Virginia
vet. veteran, veterinary
VFW Veterans of Foreign Wars
VI Virgin Islands
vis. visiting
VISTA Volunteers in Service to America
vocat. vocational
vol. volunteer, volume
v.p. vice president
vs. versus
VT, Vt. Vermont

W

W West
WA, Wash. Washington (state)
WAC Women's Army Corps
WAVES Women's Reserve, US Naval Reserve
WCTU Women's Christian Temperance Union
we. western
WHO World Health Organization
WI Wisconsin, West Indies
Wis. Wisconsin
WV, W.Va. West Virginia
WY, Wyo. Wyoming

X, Y, Z

YK Yukon Territory
YMCA Young Men's Christian Association
YMHA Young Men's Hebrew Association
YM & YWHA Young Men's and Young Women's Hebrew Association
yr. year
YT Yukon Territory
YWCA Young Women's Christian Association
zool. zoological

Alphabetical Practices

Names are arranged alphabetically according to the surnames, and under identical surnames according to the first given name. If both surname and first given name are identical, names are arranged alphabetically according to the second given name.

Surnames beginning with De, Des, Du, however capitalized or spaced, are recorded with the prefix preceding the surname and arranged alphabetically under the letter D.

Surnames beginning with Mac and Mc are arranged alphabetically under M.

Surnames beginning with Saint or St. appear after names that begin Sains, and are arranged according to the second part of the name, e.g., St. Clair before Saint Dennis.

Surnames beginning with Van, Von, or von are arranged alphabetically under the letter V.

Compound surnames are arranged according to the first member of the compound.

Many hyphenated Arabic names begin Al-, El-, or al-. These names are alphabetized according to each biographee's designation of last name. Thus Al-Bahar, Neta may be listed either under Al- or under Bahar, depending on the preference of the listee.

Also, Arabic names have a variety of possible spellings when transposed to English. Spelling of these names is always based on the practice of the biographee. Some biographees use a Western form of word order, while others prefer the Arabic word sequence.

Similarly, Asian names may have no comma between family and given names, but some biographees have chosen to add the comma. In each case, punctuation follows the preference of the biographee.

Parentheses used in connection with a name indicate which part of the full name is usually omitted in common usage. Hence, Chambers, E(lizabeth) Anne indicates that the first name, Elizabeth, is generally recorded as an initial. In such a case, the parentheses are ignored in alphabetizing and the name would be arranged as Chambers, Elizabeth Anne.

However, if the entire first name appears in parentheses, for example, Chambers, (Elizabeth) Anne, the first name is not commonly used, and the alphabetizing is therefore arranged as though the name were Chambers, Anne.

If the entire middle name is in parentheses, it is still used in alphabetical sorting. Hence, Belamy, Katherine (Lucille) would sort as Belamy, Katherine Lucille. The same occurs if the entire last name is in parentheses, e.g., (Brandenberg), Howard Keith would sort as Brandenberg, Howard Keith.

For visual clarification:

Smith, H(enry) George: Sorts as Smith, Henry George
Smith, (Henry) George: Sorts as Smith, George
Smith, Henry (George): Sorts as Smith, Henry George
(Smith), Henry George: Sorts as Smith, Henry George

Who's Who in the West®

Biographees

AANESTAD, SAM, state legislator; m to Susan; children: three. BA, DDS, U. Calif., LA; MPA, Golden Gate U., 1991. California State Assemblyman, District 3, 1999-2002, vice chairman, Natural Resources Committee, 1999-2002, member, Budget, Health, Water Parks & Wildlife Committees, 1999-2002, California State Assembly; California State Senator, District 4, 2003-.Vchief surgery, Sierra Nevada Member Hosp, formerly; member, California Dent Association Coun on Legislature, 3 years; oral & maxillofacial surgeon, currently; youth soccer, football & baseball coach, currently; radio broadcaster, Nevada Union High Sch Football, currently. Alumnus of Year, Univ California Los Angeles, 98. California & America Dent Asns; Rotary Club Grass Valley; Butte-Sierra District Dent Soc (president, formerly). Republican. Office: State Capitol Rm 5061 Sacramento CA 94249-0001 Mailing: Dist 4 200 Providence Mine Rd Ste 108 Nevada City CA 95959-2900 Office Phone: 530-470-1846, 916-651-4004. Office Fax: 916-445-7750. Business E-Mail: Senator.Aanestad@senate.ca.gov.*

AARON, CYNTHIA G., judge; b. Mpls., May 3, 1957; d. Allen Harold and Barbara Lois (Perlman) A.; m. Craig D. Higgs, May 15, 1993. Student, Brandeis U., 1975-77; BA with honors and distinction, Stanford U., 1979; JD cum laude, Harvard U., 1984. Bar: Calif. 1984, U.S. Dist. Ct. (so. dist.) Calif. 1984, U.S. Ct. Appeals (9th cir.) 1984, U.S. Dist. Ct. (no. dist.) Calif. 1986, U.S. Dist. Ct. (ctrl. dist.) Calif. 1988, U.S. Supreme Ct. 1991. Rsch. asst. to Prof. Alan Dershowitz Law Sch. Harvard U., 1982-83; trial atty. Fed. Defenders San Diego, Inc., 1984-88; ptnr. Aaron & Cortez, 1988-94; U.S. magistrate judge U.S. Dist. Ct. (so. dist.) Calif., San Diego, 1994—. Instr. Nat. Inst. for Trial Advocacy, 1988—93; adj. prof. Calif. Western Sch. Law, San Diego, 1990—93; adj. prof. law sch. U. San Diego, 1993, 95. Bd. dirs. San Diego Vol. Lawyer Program, 2001—. Mem.: San Diego County Judges Assn. (bd. dirs., pres. 2001—02), Lawyers Club San Diego, City Club San Diego, Phi Beta Kappa. Office: US Dist Ct So Dist 940 Front St Ste 1185 San Diego CA 92101-8940

AARON, DAVID L., diplomat, author; b. Chgo., Aug. 21, 1938; m. Chloe W. Aaron; 1 child. BA, Occidental Coll., PhD (hon.); MA, Princeton U. With Fgn. Svc., 1962—, polit. and econ. officer Guayaquil, Ecuador; internat. rels. officer Dept. of State, 1964-66; polit. officer NATO, Paris, 1966; with Arms Control and Disarmament Agy.; sr. staff mem. Nat. Security Coun., 1972-74; legis. asst. Senator Walter F. Mondale, Minn., 1974-75; task force leader select com. intelligence U.S. Senate, 1975-76; dep. asst. to pres. for nat. security, 1977-81; v.p. Oppenheimer and Co., Inc., 1981-85; writer, lectr. Lantz-Harris Agy., 1985-93. Sr. advisor Mondale Presdl. Campaign, 1984; cons. 20th Century Fund, 1990-92, sr. fellow, 1992-93; bd. dirs. quest value dual purpose fund Oppenheimer Capital Corp.; amb., U.S. rep. Orgn. Econ. Cooperation and Devel., Paris, 1996.; presdl. spl. envoy for cryptography, 1996; undersec. internat. trade dept. Commerce, 1997-00; sr. internat. adv. Dorsey & Whitney, 2000-2003; sr. fellow, dir. Ctr. for Middle East Pub. Policy, RAND, 2003—. Author: State Scarlet, Agent of Influence, Crossing By Night; contbr. articles to profl. jours. Staff mem. Carter-Mondale Presdl. Campaign; bd. dirs. Atlantic Coun. Decorated Nat. Def. medal. Mem. Nat. Dem. Inst. Internat. Affairs (bd. dirs.), Coun. Fgn. Rels., Internat. League Human Rights (bd. dirs.), Authors Guild, Pacific Coun. on Internat. Policy. Office: RAND Corp 1776 Main St Santa Monica CA 90407-2138 Office Phone: 310-393-0411. E-mail: daaron@rand.org.

AARON, M. ROBERT, electrical engineer; b. Phila., Aug. 21, 1922; s. Edward A. and Beatrice A.; m. Wilma Spiegelman, Nov. 18, 1944; children: Richard (dec.), James. BSEE, U. Pa., 1949, MSEE, 1951. Research engr. Franklin Inst. Research Labs., Phila., 1949-51; with Bell Telephone Labs. Inc., Murray Hill, NJ, 1951-89, supr., 1954-68, dept. head, 1968-89; ret., 1989; cons., 1989—. Lectr., tchr. in field. Mem. adv. com. Whippany (N.J.) Sch. Bd., 1950's. Guest editor for tech. jours., 1971-99; contbr. articles to profl. jours., poems to various jours.; patentee in field. Tutor NAACP Program, Red Bank, N.J., 1966-68. Served to lt. (j.g.) USCG, 1942-45. Co-recipient computers and communications prize Found. for Computers and Communications Promotion, 1988. Fellow IEEE (mem. fin. bd. 1976-77, awards bd. 1987-89, 93, co-recipient Alexander Graham Bell medal 1978, Centennial medal 1984, Millenium medal 2000), Internat. Engring. Consortium; mem. Nat. Acad. Engring., IEEE Circuits and Systems Soc. (assoc. editor 1969-71, pres. 1973), IEEE Comm. Soc. (chmn. awards bd. 1975-79, 80-84, bd. govs. 1986-89, Meritorious Svc. award 1985, fellow evaluation 1992-96, disting. lectr. 1995, lifetime svc. award 1997, Christopher Columbus internat. telecomms. award 1999), Student Soc. for Stem Cell Rsch. (mem. adv. bd. 2004—, internet libr. named Robert Aaron Libr.), Internat. Myeloma Found. Home: 7900 E Dartmouth Ave Apt 61 Denver CO 80231-4265 E-mail: b.aaron@ieee.org.

ABARBANEL, GAIL, social services administrator, educator; b. LA, Apr. 17, 1944; d. Sam and Sylvia (Cramer) A.; m. Stephen P. Klein, Jan. 31, 1975. BA magna cum laude, UCLA, 1966; MSW, U. So. Calif., 1968. Lic. clin. social worker. Clin. social worker Mental Health Agy., LA, 1968-74; founder, dir. Rape Treatment Ctr. & Dept. Social Svcs. Santa Monica Hosp. Med. Ctr., LA, 1974—. Cons., educator in field. Contbr. articles to profl. jours. Bd. dirs. Clare Found., 1975-77; atty. gen. task force Violence Against Women Act, 1995-00; mem. Calif. Campus Sexual Assault Task Force, 2003; active Am. Cancer Soc., 1975-79, Child Trauma Coun., 1978-81, Sr. Health Ctr., 1981-87, Mayor's Transition Team, 2005. Recipient Gov.'s Victim Svcs. award, 1985, Pub. Affairs award Coro Found., 1985, Woman of Year Leadership award YWCA, 1980, 82, Status of Women award AAUW, 1978, Nat. Outstanding Achievement award Am. Cancer Soc., 1977, Disting. Citizen award L.A. County Bar Assn., 1988, Humanitarian award Nat. Conf. Christians and Jews, 1987, Soc. for Clin. Social Work award, 1989, DOJ award for Outstanding Svc., on Behalf of Vibtims of Crime, Pres. of U.S., 1991, Woman of Distinction award Soroptimist Internat., 1992, Excellence in Profl. Achievement Alumni award, UCLA, 1994, Outstanding Corp. Citizen award Pub. Rels. Soc. Am. La. chpt., 1997, Calif. Sexual Assault Investigators Assn. award, 1999, Pathfinder award Women Lawyers Assn., 2004; named Outstanding Alumni, U. So. Calif., 1979, one of Heroes of 1988 L.A. mag. Fellow Soc. Clin. Social Work; mem. NASW (Agy of Yr. award 1977, Social Worker of Yr. award 1995), Nat. Orgn. for Victim Assitance (Exemplary Program award 1995), Nat. Coalition Against Sexual Assault, Nat. Orgn. Victims Assistance, Phi Beta Kappa, Pi Gamma Mu. Office: Santa Monica-UCLA Med Ctr 1250 16th St Santa Monica CA 90404-1249

ABARBANEL, HENRY DON ISAAC, physicist, academic administrator; b. Washington, May 31, 1943; s. Abraham Robert and Selma Helen (Kintberger) A.; m. Gwen Lorita Lewis, May 27, 1965 (div. July 1974); m. Beth Leah Levine, Sept. 12, 1982; children: Brett Lillian, Sara Alexis. BS in Physics, Calif. Inst. Tech., 1963; PhD in Physics, Princeton U., 1966. Rsch. assoc. Stanford (Calif.) Linear Accelerator Ctr., 1967-68; asst. prof. physics Princeton (N.J.) U., 1968-72; physicist Theoretical Physics Dept. Fermi Nat. Accelerator Lab., Batavia, Ill., 1972-81; staff scientist Lawrence Berkeley Lab., 1979-82; rsch. physicist Marine Phys. Lab. Scripps Instn. Oceanography, La Jolla, Calif., 1983—; dir. Inst. for Nonlinear Sci. U. Calif. San Diego, La Jolla, 1986—, acting dir. Inst. for Nonlinear Sci., 1986, dir. Inst. for Nonlinear Sci., 1986—, prof. physics in residence, 1986-88, prof. physics, 1988—. Cons. Lockheed Palo Alto (Calif.) Rsch. Lab., 1990—; vis. scientist Ctr. Etudes Nucleaires Saclay, France, 1970, Stanford Linear Accelerator Ctr., 1971, 1975-76, Inst. Haute Études Sci., Bures-sur-Yvette, France, 1989, Inst. Applied Physics Acad. Scis. USSR, Gorky, 1990; adj. prof. physics U. Calif. San Diego, 1982; vis. prof. U. Calif., Santa Cruz, 1975-76, San Diego, 1982, 86, Japan Soc. for the Promotion Sci., 1976; vis. assoc. prof. Stanford U., 1975-76; lectr. dept. physics U. Calif., Berkeley, 1980; chmn. steering com. joint program in nonlinear sci. U. Calif.-NASA, 1987-88; lectr. U. Chgo., 1973, U. Calif., Berkeley, 1980; exchange scientist Landau Inst. for Theoretical Physics NAS, Moscow, Leningrad, 1977; mem. U.S. Physics Del. to People's Republic China, 1973; mem. JASON, 1974—, mem. steering com., 1985-88, participant, project leader; cons. T-div. Los Alamos (N.Mex.) Nat. Sci. Lab., 1980-84; mem. bd. visitors in physics Office Naval Rsch., 1987, mem. bd. visitors in phys. oceanography, 1989-91; mem. bd. tech. advisors Program in Global Climate Change Dept. Energy, 1990—; invited speaker numerous profl. meetings. Co-editor: Encyclopedia of Chaos, 1991; editor-in-chief Springer-Verlag Series in Nonlinear Sci., 1989—; sci. referee various physics jours. Mem. Planning Commn., Del Mar, Calif., 1989-92, mem. city coun., 1992—. NSF predoctoral fellow, 1963-66, NSF postdoctoral fellow, 1966-67, Woodrow Wilson fellow (hon.); grantee Defense Advanced Rsch. and Projects Agy., 1979-83, 83-84, 86-89, 86-91, U.S. Dept. Energy, 1981-83, Office Naval Rsch., 1983-88, NASA, 1986, 88-89, 90-91, Lockheed Palo Alto Rsch. Lab., 1991—, U.S. Army Rsch. Office, 1991-94. Mem. Am. Phys. Soc., Am. Geophys. Union, Soc. for Indsl. and Applied Maths. Office: U Calif San Diego Inst Nonlinear Science Ucsd Mc # 0402 La Jolla CA 92093

ABBAS, ABUL K., pathologist, educator; MBBS, All-India Inst. Med. Sci. Resident pathology Peter Bent Brigham Hosp., Boston; fellow pathology Harvard Med. Sch., Boston, from instr. to prof., prof., head immunology rsch. divsn.; prof. and chmn. Dept. of Pathology U. Calif., San Francisco, 1999—. Vis. sci. Divsn. Immunology Nat. Inst. Med. Rsch., London. Editor: Immunity, 1993—96; assoc. editor: The Jour. of Immunology, 1981—85, section editor:, 1987—91, assoc. editor: The Am. Jour. of Pathology, 1992—96, Immunity, 2002—; contbr. over 150 articles to profl. jours. Recipient Warner-Lambert/Parke-Davis award, Am. Soc. Investigative Pathology, 1987. Office: Univ Calif Box 0511 M M590B Dept Pathology San Francisco CA 94143-0511

ABBE, ALEXANDER, lawyer; b. Bethesda, Md., Mar. 16, 1972; BA with distinction, Swarthmore Coll., 1994; JD cum laude, Univ. Pa., 1994. Bar: Calif. 1999. Assoc. Richards, Watson & Gershon, LA. Editor (exec.): Univ. Pa. Law Rev.; contbr. articles to profl. jours. Named a Rising Star, So. Calif. Super Lawyers, 2006. Mem.: LA County Bar Assn., Phi Beta Kappa. Office: Richards Watson & Gershon 40th Fl 355 S Grand Ave Los Angeles CA 90071-3101 Office Phone: 213-626-8484. Office Fax: 213-626-0078. Business E-Mail: aabbe@rwglaw.com.

ABBE, CHARLES J., manufacturing executive; b. 1941; Sr. ptnr. McKinsey & Co., Inc., San Francisco; various sr. mgmt. positions Raychem Corp., 1989-96; v.p., gen. mgr. Santa Rosa divsn. Optical Coating Lab., Inc., 1996-98, dir., pres., CEO, 1998-2000, sr. v.p., sr. oper. officer, 2000; pres., COO JDS Uniphase Corp., San Jose, 2000—.

ABBOTT, BARRY ALEXANDER, lawyer; b. New Haven, Aug. 20, 1950; s. Harold and Norma (Kaufman) A.; 1 child, Anne Stewart. AB, Dartmouth Coll., 1972; JD, U. Fla., 1975; MBA, Stanford U., 1977. Bar: Fla. 1975, Calif. 1976, US Dist. Ct. (so. dist.) Fla. 1976, US Dist. Ct. (no. dist.) Calif. 1976, US Ct. Appeals (9th cir.) 1976, US Supreme Ct. 1979, DC 1985, NY 1986. Assoc. Morrison & Foerster, San Francisco, 1977-83, ptnr., 1983-94; dir. Howard Rice Nemerovski Canady Falk & Rabkin, San Francisco, 1994—2006, of counsel, 2006—; chief legal officer, dir. govt. rels., and corp. sec. Rex Group, San Francisco, 2006—. Adj. faculty mem. Boalt Hall Sch. Law, U. Calif., Berkeley, 1998; lectr. corp., comml. and fin. inst. law various orgns.; mem. Fed. Res. Bd. Consumer Adv. Coun., 1992-94, chmn. consumer credit com., 1993-94, mem. governing com. Conf. on Consumer Fin. Law; mem. Am. Coll. Consumer Fin. Svcs. Attys., 1995—, bd. regents, 1995-98, sec., 2002-05, treas., 2005-07. Co-author: Truth in Lending: A Comprehensive Guide; contbr. articles to profl. jours. Named one of Outstanding Young Men of Am., U.S. Jaycees, 1980. Fellow Royal Soc. Arts (Silver medal 1972); mem. ABA (chmn. young lawyers divsn. bus. law com. 1987-88, chmn. ins. products subcom. 1987-92, vice chmn. consumer fin. svcs. commn. 1995-96, active various coms.), Calif. Bar Assn. (vice chair fin. instns. com. 1991-92, chair 1992-93, mem. ins. law com. 1994-96, mem. bus. law sect. exec. com. 1996-99, treas. 1997-98, vice chair 1998-99), Fla. Bar Assn., D.C. Bar Assn., N.Y. State Bar Assn., San Francisco Bar Assn. (chmn. membership com. 1984-86, bd. dirs. 1982, 87-88, Merit award 1985, 2004), Commonwealth Club (Calif.), Barristers Club (bd. dirs. 1981-83, treas., pres. 1982), Order of Coif, Phi Beta Kappa, Phi Kappa Phi. Republican. Office: The Rex Group 101 California St Ste 1950 San Francisco CA 94111 also: Haward Rice Nemerovski Canady Falk Rabkin 3 Embacadero Ctr 7th Fl San Francisco CA 94111-4024 Office Phone: 415-434-1600.

ABBOTT, CHARLES FAVOUR, lawyer; b. Sedro-Wolley, Wash., Oct. 12, 1937; s. Charles Favour and Violette Doris Abbott; m. Oranee Harward, Sept. 19, 1958; children: Patricia, Stephen, Nelson, Cynthia, Lisa, Alyson. BA in Econs., U. Wash., Seattle, 1959, JD, 1962. Bar: Calif. 1962, Utah 1981, Wash. 2005. Law clk. Judge M. Oliver Koelsch, US Ct. Appeals (9th cir.), San Francisco, 1963; assoc. Jones, Hatfield & Abbott, Escondido, 1964; pvt. practice Escondido, 1964-77, Provo, Utah, 1983-93; of counsel Mueller & Abbott, Escondido, 1997—; ptnr. Abbott, Thorn & Hill, Provo, 1981-83, Abbott & Abbott, 1993—98; pres. Charles F. Abbott PC, 1998—; of counsel Abbott & Assoc., PC, 1998—. Presenter in field. Author: How to Do Your Own Legal Work, 1976, 2d edit., 1981, How to Win in Small Claims Court, 1981, How to Be Free of Debt in 24 Hours, 1981, How to Hire the Best Lawyer at the Lowest Fee, 1981, The Lawyer's Inside Method of Making Money, 1979, The Millionaire Mindset, 1987, How to Make Big Money in the Next 30 Days, 1989, Business Legal Manual and Forms, 1990, How to Make Millions in Marketing, 1990, Telemarketing Training Course, 1990, How to Form A Corporation in Any State, 1990, The Complete Asset Protection Plan, 1990, Personal Injury and the Law, 1997, Fen-Phen Fallout--The Medical and Legal Crisis, 1998; mem. editl. bd. Wash. Law Rev. and State Bar Assn. Jour., 1961-62; bd. editors Phen-fen Litigation Strategist, 1998-2000; contbr. articles to profl. jours. Pres. HHT Found. Internat., 2006—07. Mem. ATLA, Utah Bar Assn., Calif. Bar Assn., US Supreme Ct. Bar Assn., Wash. State Bar Assn. Office Phone: 801-426-6902. Business E-Mail: charles@abbott-abbott.com.

ABBOTT, DAVID L., agricultural products executive; BS, Univ. Vt. CEO Purina Mills, St. Louis; pres., CEO E-markets Inc., Ames, Iowa. Mem.: Nat. FFA Found. (bd. mem.), Am. Feed Ind. Assn. (past pres.). Office: E Markets Inc 807 Mountain Ave Berthoud CO 80513-1368

ABBOTT, HORACE PORTER, English literature educator; b. Balt., Nov. 21, 1940; s. Horace P. and Barbara Ann (Trueblood) A.; m. Anita Vaivods, June 25, 1966; children: Jason, Byram. BA, Reed Coll., Portland, Oreg., 1962; MA, U. Toronto, Ont., Can., 1964, PhD, 1968. From asst. prof. to assoc. prof. U. Calif., Santa Barbara, 1966-82, prof., 1982—2005, prof. emeritus, 2005—, chair English, 1983-87, 90, acting dean humanities and fine arts, 1992-94, acting dir. Interdisciplinary Humanities Ctr., 1999—2001. Lectr., instr. Yeats Summer Sch., Sligo, Ireland, 1989. Author: The Fiction of Samuel Beckett, 1973, Diary Fiction, 1984, Beckett Writing Beckett, 1996, The Cambridge Introduction to Narrative, 2002, 2nd edit., 2008; (poetry) Cold Certainties and Changes Beyond Measure, 1988; editor: On the Origin of Fictions, 2001. Pres. Foothill Preservation League, Santa Barbara, 1996-2004. Recipient William Stafford award Poetry Assn. Wash., 1977. Mem. MLA, Samuel Beckett Soc. (pres. 1962-64), Soc. for the Study of Narrative Lit., Soc. for Lit. Sci. and the Arts, Modernist Studies Assn. Office: U of Calif Dept English Santa Barbara CA 93106 Office Phone: 805-893-3791. Business E-Mail: pabbott@english.ucsb.edu.

ABBOTT, RICHARD LEE, physician; s. Joseph C. and Anne Abbott; m. Cecilia V. BrundelRe, June 19, 1971; children: Galen Alexander, Alison Abbott Chassin, Lauren Abbott Maucere. BS, Tufts U., Medford, Mass., 1967; MD, George Washington U., Washington, 1971. Diplomate Am. Bd. of Ophthalmology, 1978. Dir. corneal diseases Calif. Pacific Med. Ctr., San Francisco, 1985—95; prof., dir. cornea svc. U. Calif. San Francisco, 1995—2003, Thomas W. Boyden endowed chair, 2003—. Bd. dirs. Internat. Coun. Ophthalmology, San Francisco, That Man May See, Ophthalmic Found., 1998—, Tissue Banks Internat., 2001—; bd. dirs., chair of underwriting Ophthalmic Mut. Ins. Co., San Francisco, mem. FDA ophthalmic devices panel, 1994—2001, bd. chmn., 2009—. Author: (medical text book) Surgical Intervention in Corneal and External Diseases. Rsch. assoc. Francis I. Proctor Found.; pres. Pan Am. Assn. Ophthalmology Found., 2003—06; trustee Heed Soc. Fellows, 2001—; adv. capacity for ednl. activities Project ORBIS, NYC, 2003—. Capt. US Indian Pub. Health Svc., 1972—74, Gallup, N.Mex. Grantee Rsch. grantee, Fight for Sight, Inc, 1977—78; fellow Heed Ophthalmic fellow, Heed Found., 1977—78. Fellow: Am. Acad. Ophthalmology (licentiate; sec. 1995—, bd. trustees 1996—2001, sec. quality care 2002—08, sec., knowledge base devel. 2002—08); mem.: Pan Am. Assn. Ophthalmology (pres. 2007—09), Acad. Ophthalmologica Internat. (life), Am. Ophthal. Soc. (life). Independent. Avocations: travel, photography, tennis, hiking. Office: Univ California 10 Koret Way K301 San Francisco CA 94143 Office Fax: 415-502-7418. Business E-Mail: richard.abbott@ucsf.edu.

ABDUR-RAHIM, SHAREEF (JULIUS SHAREEF ABDUL-RAHIM), professional basketball coach, retired professional basketball player; b. Marietta, Ga., Dec. 11, 1976; s. William and Aminah Abdur-Rahim; m. Delicia (DeeDee) Abdur-Rahim; children: Jabri Shareef, Samiyah. Forward, guard Vancouver Grizzlies NBA, 1996—2001, Altanta Hawks NBA, 2001—03, Portland Trail Blazers, 2003—05; forward Sacramento Kings NBA, 2005—08, asst. coach, 2008—. Guest Jamie Foxx Show. Founder The Future Found., Rebound America (to raise funds for 9/11 victims), 2001. Recipient Gold medal, men's basketball, Summer Olympic Games, 2000; named NBA's Number 1 Good Guy, The Sporting News, 2004; named to All-Rookie First Team, NBA, 1997, Eastern Conf. All-Star Team, 2002. Achievements include being the third overall draft pick in the NBA Draft, 1996. Avocations: pool, collecting basketball jerseys, movies. Office: c/o Sacramento Kings Arco Arena One Sports Plz Sacramento CA 95834*

ABDY, PAMELA, film producer; b. Nov. 23, 1973; Grad., Emerson Coll., Boston, 1995. Receptionist Jersey Films, LA, asst. to Danny DeVito, 1996—99, pres. prodn.; v.p. prodn. Paramount Pictures, 2003—04, sr. v.p. prodn., 2004—06, exec. v.p. prodn., 2006—. Assoc.

prodr.: (films) Man on the Moon, 1999; co-prodr.: The Caveman's Valentine, 2001; exec. prodr.: How High, 2001; prodr.: Garden State, 2004, Babel, 2006. Office: Paramount Pictures 5555 Melrose Ave Los Angeles CA 90038

ABEL, ELIZABETH ANN, dermatologist; b. Hartford, Conn., Mar. 16, 1940; d. Frederick A. and Rose (Borovicka) Abel; m. Barton Lane; children: Barton F. Lane, Geoffrey Lane, Suzanne Lane Franklin. Student, Colby-Sawyer Coll., 1957-60; BS, Wash. Hosp. Ctr. Sch. Med. Tech., 1961, U. Md., 1965, MD cum laude, 1967. Diplomate Am. Bd. Dermatology. Intern San Francisco Gen. Hosp., 1967-68; resident in medicine, fellow in oncology U. Calif. Med. Ctr., San Francisco, 1968-69; resident in dermatology NYU Med. Ctr., 1969-72, chief resident, 1971-72, USPHS research trainee in immunology, 1972-73; dep. chief dept. dermatology USPHS Hosp., SI, NY, 1973-74; instr. clin. dermatology Columbia U. Coll. Physicians and Surgeons, NYC, 1974-75, Stanford (Calif.) U. Sch. Medicine, 1975-77, clin. asst. prof. dermatology, 1977-82, asst. prof. dermatology, 1982-90, clin. assoc. prof., 1990-96, clin. prof., 1996—. Asst. editor Jour. Am. Acad. Dermatology, 1993-98; mem. med. adv. bd. The Nat. Psoriasis Found., 1993-95. Contbr. articles to profl. sci. jours. Mellon Found. fellow, 1983, 87. Fellow Am. Acad. Dermatology; mem. N.Am. Clin. Dermatologic Soc., San Francisco Dermatologic Soc., Internat. Soc. Dermatology, Pacific Dermatologic Assn., Women's Dermatologic Soc., Noah Worcester Dermatologic Soc., Alpha Omega Alpha. Avocations: piano, golf, travel, reading. Office: California Skin Institute 525 South Dr, Ste 115 Mountain View CA 94040 Personal E-mail: eaabelmd@aol.com.

ABELE, GEORGE W., lawyer; b. Rockville Centre, NY, Oct. 16, 1963; BA in econ. with distinction, U. Va., 1985; JD, UCLA, 1990. Bar: Calif. 1990. Extern clk. Nat. Labor Relations Bd., Appeals Office, Washington; ptnr. Paul, Hastings, Janofsky & Walker LLP, LA, vice chmn. employment law dept. Mem.: L.A. County Bar Assn., Calif. State Bar Assn., ABA. Office: Paul Hastings Janofsky & Walker LLP 515 S Flower St 25th Floor Los Angeles CA 90071-2228 Office Phone: 213-683-6131. Office Fax: 213-627-0705. Business E-Mail: georgeabele@paulhastings.com.

ABELL, NANCY L., lawyer; b. LA, July 19, 1950; BA with honors, Pitzer Coll., 1972; JD, UCLA, 1979. Bar: Calif. 1979. Extern clk. to Hon. Shirley Hufstedler U.S. Ct. Appeals (9th cir.), 1978; ptnr. Paul, Hastings, Janofsky & Walker LLP, LA, 1986—, chairperson employment law dept. Bd. govs. Inst. Corp. Counsel, 1989—, chairperson, 1994-95; bd. advisors UCLA Sch. Law. Author: (with P.W. Cane) An Employer's Guide to the Americans with Disabilities Act, 1991, An Employer's Guide for Preparing Affirmative Action Programs. Bd. advisors UCLA Sch. Law. Fellow Coll. Labor and Employment Lawyers, Inc.; mem. ABA (mgmt. co-chair trial advocacy subcom., employee rights and responsibilities com., labor and employment law sect. 1991-94); Order of Barristers, Order of Coif. Office: Paul Hastings Janofsky & Walker LLP 515 S Flower St Fl 23 Los Angeles CA 90071-2300 Office Phone: 213-683-6162. Office Fax: 213-996-3162. Business E-Mail: nancyabell@paulhastings.com.

ABERCROMBIE, NEIL, United States Representative from Hawaii; b. Buffalo, June 26, 1938; s. G. Don and Vera June (Giersdorf) Abercrombie; m. Nancie Ellen Caraway, July 18, 1981. BA, Union Coll., 1959; MA, U. Hawaii, 1964, PhD in Am. studies, 1974. Mem. Hawaii Ho. Reps., 1974—86, Hawaii Senate, 1978—86, US Congress from 1st Hawaiian dist., 1986—87, 1991—, mem. resources com., armed svcs. com., nat. security com. Mem. Honolulu City Coun., 1988—90. Co-author: Blood of Patriots. Democrat. Office: US Ho Reps 1502 Longworth Ho Office Bldg Washington DC 20515-1101 also: Prince Kuhio Fed Bldg Rm 4104 300 Ala Moana Blvd Honolulu HI 96850 Office Phone: 202-225-2726. Office Fax: 202-225-4580. E-mail: neil.abercrombie@mail.house.gov.

ABERMAN, HAROLD MARK, veterinarian; b. Chgo., Aug. 5, 1956; s. Howard Oscar and Goldie Esther Aberman. BS, Purdue U., 1979, MSE, 1987, BSE, 1986, DVM, 1983. NIH postdoctoral fellow Purdue U., West Lafayette, 1983-87; dir. sci. and biol. affairs Howmedica div. Pfizer, Rutherford, 1987-99; pres. Applied Biol. Concepts, Los Alamitos, Calif., 1996—; dir. devel. Orthop. Rsch. Inst., Long Beach, Calif., 1999-2001, med. device cons., 2001—; dir. sci. affairs, global sci. program dir. Synthes Spine, West Chester, Pa., 2003—. Adj. prof. N.C. State U., Raleigh, 1988—, Miss. State U., Starkville, Miss., 1990—, Purdue U., 1991—. Contbr. articles to profl. jours. Mem. ASME, AVMA, Am. Animal Hosp. Assn., Ortho. Rsch. Soc., Soc. Biomechanics, Acad. Surg. Rsch. Jewish. Office: Applied Biol Concepts 12581 Silver Fox Rd Los Alamitos CA 90720-5234 also: Synthes Spine 1302 Wrights Ln E West Chester PA 19380 Office Phone: 610-719-5687. Personal E-mail: haroldabc@aol.com.

ABERNATHY, SHIELDS B., allergist, immunologist, internist; b. Bronxville, NY, Mar. 14, 1951; m. Leslie Abernathy; children: Amelia, Camille, Lant. BA, Ohio Wesleyan U., 1973; MS, Harvard U., 1975; MD, Med. Coll. Pa., 1979. Diplomate Am. Bd. Internal Medicine, Am. Bd. Allergy and Immunology, eligible Am. Preventive Medicine, Nat. Bd. Med. Examiners; Qualified Med. Examiner Calif.; Fed. Aviation Med. Examiner; ACLS Am. Heart Assn. Intern in internal medicine L.A. County/U. So. Calif. Med. Ctr., LA, 1979-80; resident in internal medicine Hosp. of Good Samaritan, LA, 1980-81; resident UCLA Wadsworth VA Med. Ctr., 1981-82, fellow allergy and immunology, 1982-84. Med. philanthropic facilitator, Philippines, 2000, India, 2001, Indochina, 2001, Amazon, 2002, Africa, 2004, Honduras, 2008, lectr., rschr. in field. Fellow Am. Coll. Allergy and Immunology, Am. Acad. Allergy and Immunology; mem. Am. Med. Health Assn., Am. Pub. Health Assn. (internat. health sect.). Office: 1050 Las Tablas Rd Ste 3 Templeton CA 93465-9792 Office Phone: 805-434-1000. E-mail: sabernats@sbcglobal.net.

ABICH, YVETTE M., lawyer; BA, Loyola Marymount U., 1990; JD, Loyola Law Sch., 1994. Bar: Calif., US Dist. Ct. Ctrl. Calif., US Ct. Appeals Ninth Cir. Sr. counsel Colantuono & Levin, LA; city atty.. Redevelopment Agy. counsel City of Barstow, Calif.; asst. city atty. Sierra Madre & Calabasas, Calif. Named a Rising Star, So. Calif. Super Lawyers, 2004—06; named an Amazing Woman, Mexican-Am. Bar Assn., 2003. Office: Colantuono & Levin 31st Fl 555 W 5th St Los Angeles CA 90013-1018 Office Phone: 213-533-4201. Office Fax: 213-533-4191. Business E-Mail: yabich@cllaw.us.

ABIDI, ASAD ALI, electrical engineer, educator; BSEE with honors, Imperial Coll. Sci. and Tech., London, 1976; MSEE, U. Calif., Berkeley, 1978, PhD in Elec. Engring., 1981. Mem. tech. staff Advanced LSI Devel. Lab. Bell Labs., Murray Hill, NJ, 1981—84; asst. prof. elec. engring. dept. UCLA, 1985—88, assoc. prof., 1988—93, prof., 1993—. Vis. faculty rschr. high-speed electronics dept. Hewlett Packard Labs., Palo Alto, Calif., 1989; adv. Teranetics, Santa Clara, Calif. Contbr. articles to sci. jours.; editor: IEEE Jour. Solid-State Cir., 1992—95; co-editor: Integrated Circuits for Wireless Communications, 1998. Recipient TRW award for Innovative Tchg., 1988, Design Contest award, Design Automation Conf., 1998. Fellow: IEEE (Donald G. Fink award 1997, Millennium medal 2000); mem.: NAE. Office: UCLA Dept Elec Engring Box 951594 53-141 Engr IV Los Angeles CA 90095-1594 Office Phone: 310-825-9490. Office Fax: 310-206-8495. E-mail: abidi@icsl.ucla.edu.

ABILDSKOV, J. A., cardiologist, educator; b. Salem, Utah, Sept. 22, 1923; s. John and Annie Marie (Peterson) A.; m. Mary Helen McKell, Dec. 4, 1944; children— Becky, Alan, Mary, Marilyn BA, U. Utah, 1944, MD, 1946. Diplomate Am. Bd. Internal Medicine. Intern Latter-day Saints Hosp., Salt Lake City, 1947-48; resident Charity Hosp. La., New Orleans, 1948-51; instr. Tulane U., New Orleans, 1948-54; asst. prof. to prof. SUNY-Syracuse, 1955-68; prof. medicine U. Utah, Salt Lake City, 1968—. Dir. Nora Eccles Harrison Cardiovascular Rsch. and Tng. Inst., Salt Lake City, 1970-94. Contbr. articles to profl. jours. Served to capt. USAR, 1954-56 Recipient Disting. Research award U. Utah, 1976 Fellow Am. Coll. Cardiology; mem. Assn. Am. Physicians, Am. Soc. Clin. Investigation (emeritus), Assn. Univ. Cardiologists (founding), Western Assn. Physicians, Venezuelan Cardiology Soc. (hon.), Cardiology Soc. Peru (corresponding) Republican. Mem. Lds Ch.

ABLESER, EDWARD, state legislator; b. Tarzana, Calif., Mar. 16, 1978; BA in Polit. Sci. and Chinese, Ariz. State U., 2000, M in Counseling Psychology, 2004. City affairs coord. Ariz. State U., Tempe, 1997—98, chief of staff to exec. v.p., 1998—99, faculty, tchr. asst., 2002—06; mental health counselor SW Behavioral Health Svcs., Phoenix, 2003—; senator from Ariz., 2006; mem. Dist. 17 Ariz. House of Reps., 2007—, mem. health & human svcs. com., environ. com. Asst. pastor Exchange Tempe Cmty. Ch.; bd. dirs. Boys & Girls Club, Tempe, 2004—. Recipient Dr. Martin Luther King Jr. award, City of Tempe, 2004. Mem.: City of Tempe C. of C. (mem. leadership prog. 2004—), League of Conservation Voters, Am. Fedn. State, County, & Municipal Employees, Tempe Kiwanis Club (bd. dirs. 2005—). Democrat. Office: Ariz House Reps Capitol Complex 1700 W Washington Rm 331 Phoenix AZ 85007 Office Phone: 602-926-4118. Office Fax: 602-417-3164. Business E-Mail: eableser@azleg.gov.*

ABLIN, RICHARD JOEL, immunologist, educator; b. Chgo., May 15, 1940; s. Robert Benjamin and Minnie Edith (Gordon) A.; m. Linda Lee Lutwack; 1 son, Michael David. AB, Lake Forest Coll., Ill., 1962, DSc (hon.), 2005; PhD in Microbiology, SUNY, Buffalo, 1967. Diplomate Am. Bd. Clin. Immunology and Allergy; cert. specialist in pub. health and med. lab. microbiology Nat. Registry Microbiologists of Am. Acad. Microbiology, Am. Soc. Clin. Pathology Bd. Registry. Grad. asst. dept. biology SUNY-Buffalo, 1963-65, rsch. asst., 1963, rsch. fellow, 1965-66; USPHS postdoctoral fellow dept. microbiology Sch. Medicine, lectr., lab instr., 1966-68; instr., rsch. asst. Rosary Hill Coll., 1965-66; rsch. cons. program med. edn. AID, Paraguay, 1968; dir. divsn. immunology Millard Fillmore Hosp. Rsch. Inst., Buffalo, 1968-70; head sect. immunology, renal unit Meml. Hosp. Springfield, 1970-73; dir. sect. immunobiology div. urology dept. surgery Cook County Hosp. and Hektoen Inst. Med. Rsch., Chgo., 1973-75, sr. sci. officer divsn. immunology, 1976-83; sr. mem. sci. staff, clin. immunologist Cook County Hosp., 1973-75; asst. prof. medicine So. Ill. U., 1971-73; assoc. prof. microbiology Univ. Health Sci. (Chgo. Med. Sch.), 1973-74; pres., dir. Robert Benjamin Ablin Found. for Cancer Rsch., Evergreen Park, Ill., 1979—; rsch. assoc. prof. urology, dir. immunology unit dept. urology SUNY, Stony Brook, 1983—89, mem. U. Senate, 1986—89, 1989—92, mem. U. Gov. Coms., 1984—92; acad. del. United U. Professions, 1986—88, 1988—90; dir. sci. investigation Tetragenex Pharms., Inc., Park Ridge, NJ, 1991—2003, consulting scientist, 2003—. Vis. rsch. prof. Coll. Medicine U. Ariz., Tucson, 2001-04; rsch. prof., interim dir., 2006-08; asst. dir., 2008-; grad. edn. program, dept. immunobiology and pathology Ariz. Coll. Medicine, Ariz. Cancer Ctr. and BIO5 Inst., Tucson, 2005—; organizer, presenter, instr., participant numerous nat. and internat. profl. meetings, symposia, seminars. Editor: Allergologia et Immunopathologia, 1980—84; contbg. editor, 1974—84; co-editor: Cancer Metastasis-Biology and Treatment, 2000—; contbg. editor: Seminars in Immunopathology and Oncology, Ill. Med. Jour., 1975—88, Cancer Watch, 2001—; adv. editor: Jour. Cancer, 1976—89, Jour. Translational Medicine, 2006—, Current Cancer Therapy Reviews, 2008—, assoc. editor: Low Temperature Medicine, 1975—, Jour. Investigational Allergology and Clin. Immunology (formerly Allergologia et Immunopathologia), 1985—95, Jour. Exptl. Therapeutics and Oncology, 2003—, Cancer Science, 2007—, mem. editl. adv. bd.: Med. Sci. Rsch., 1984—2000, Cancer Detection and Prevention, 2006—; mem. editl. bd. Medikon, 1974—80, Immunology and Allergy Practice, 1979—95, Tumor Diagnostik and Therapie, 1980—98, Am. Jour. Reproductive Immunology and Microbiology, 1980—91, Cellular and Molecular Biology, 1985—87, Chemistry Today, 1991—97, Early Pregnancy: Biology and Medicine, 1995—, Internat. Jour. Oncology, 1996—, Advances in Therapy, 1999—, Prostate Jour., 1999—2001, Bratislava Med. Jour., 1999—, Exptl. Biology and Medicine, 2000—06, UroOncology, 2000—, Annals Clin. and Lab.Sci., 2000—, Clin. and Applied Immunology Revs., 2001—07, Clin. and Vaccine Immunology (formerly Clin. and Diagnostic Lab. Immunology), 2002—07, Expert Rev. Anticancer Therapy, 2002—, Cancer Therapy, 2003—, Internat. Jour. Cancer Prevention, 2003—, Current Opinion in Oncology, 2005—, Biomarkers in Medicine, 2008—, Cancer Cell Internat., 2008—, Jour. Exptl. and Clin. Cancer Rsch., 2008—, Current Oncology, 1998—, dep. editor, 2007—; contbr. articles to profl. jours.; contbr., editor: chapters to books. Chief Sangamo Nation Y-Indian Guides, Springfield, 1972-73; mgr. Skokie Indians' Boys' Baseball, Ill., 1973-74, 77, 80, 81, bd. dirs., 1979-83, exec. v.p., 1981-82; mgr. Little League Three Villages, Setauket, N.Y., 1986; cubmaster N.W. Suburban coun. Boy Scouts Am., 1974-78, asst. scoutmaster, 1975-77; mem. exploring divsn. Suffolk County coun. Boy Scouts Am., 1985-88; pres., dir. Spirit of Chgo. Hockey Club Found., Evergreen Park, Ill., 1982—. Recipient Nat. Pres. Leader's Dist. Boy Scouts Am., 1975, 1st award for sci. excellence The Haakon Radge Found. Advanced Cancer Studies, 2007; named Cubmaster of Yr. Boy Scouts Am., 1977, Gold award Magister in Cryosurgery, Internat. Soc. Cryosurgery, 2007. Fellow: Assn. Clin. Scientists, Am. Coll. Cryosurgery (adv. bd. 1977—78, v.p. 1977—79, parliamentarian 1977—79, adv. bd. 1980—81, 1984—99), Am. Coll. Allergy and Immunology (bd. registry), Indian Cryogenics Coun. (hon.); mem.: AAAS, Anticancer Therapeutics and Oncology Soc., Am. Soc. Clin. Pathology, Metastasis Rsch. Soc., Am. Assn. Cancer Rsch., Am. Assn. Immunologists, Am. Soc. Microbiology, Assn. Med. Lab Immunologists, Brit. Assn. Surg. Oncology, Buffalo Collegium Immunology, Internat. Soc. Immunology Reprodn., N.Y. Acad. Scis., Soc. Exptl. Biology and Medicine, Soc. Leukocyte Biology, Soc. Protozoologists, Soc. Study Reprodn., Transplantation Soc., Cryoimmunotherapeutic Study Group (chmn.), Japan Soc. Low Temperature Medicine (hon.), Internat. Soc. Cryosurgery (hon.; pres. 1977—80, bd. dirs. 1980—, hon. life pres., Gold award, Magister in Cryosurgery 2007), Witebsky Ctr. Microbial Pathogenesis and Immunology, Sigma Xi, Phi Beta Kappa. Achievements include identification of prostate specific antigen, used as tumor marker in prostate cancer, and of human thymic specific antigen providing means for differentiation of thymic lymphocytes from other lymphoid cells and the development of antithymocyte globulin (selectively immunosuppressive for thymocytes) used in renal allograft (transplant) recipients; development of concept of cryoimmunotherapy for treatment of cancer. Office: Univ Ariz Coll Medicine Health Scis Ctr Dept Immunobiology 1501 N Campbell Ave PO Box 245221 Tucson AZ 85724-5221 Office Phone: 520-626-7755. Business E-Mail: ablinrj@email.arizona.edu, ablinrj@ix.netcom.com.

ABO, RONALD KENT, freelance/self-employed architect; b. Rupert, Idaho, July 10, 1946; s. Isamu and Ameria (Hachiya) A.; m. Lisa A. Wiesley; children: Tamiko N., Reiko D., Ryan A., Emily A., Ian Y. BArch, U. Colo., 1969. Lic. architect, Colo. Designer SLP & Ptnrs., Denver, 1968-71; dir. Community Design Ctr., Denver, 1971-72; assoc. Barker, Rinker, Seacat, Denver, 1972-76; pvt. practice Denver, 1976-80; pres. Abo Gude Architects, Denver, 1980-84, Ron Abo Architects, Denver, 1984-91, Abo Architects PC, Denver, 1991-94, Abo Copeland Architecture, 1995—2002, ACLP Architecture, Inc., 2002—04, The ABO Group, Inc., 2005—. Design instr., thesis advisor U. Colo., Denver. Prin. works include Morrison Horticultre Ctr., 1983 (W.O.O.D. Inc. citation 1983), Highland Square, 1982 (AIA citation 1983), Roxborough Elem. Sch., 1990, Tropical Discovery Ctr. Denver Zoo, 1992, New Denver Internat. Airport Concourse Bldgs., 1993, Nederland Middle/H.S., 1996, Julesburg Welcome Ctr., 1997, Rocky Mountain Mfg. Acad., 1998. Active Denver Comty. Leadership Forum, 1986, Colfax-on-the-Hill, 1988—, U. Colo. Alumni Bd., Workforce Devel. Bd., 1990—, Savid House. Recipient Design Excellence award W.O.O.D. Inc., Denver, 1982, Martin Luther King Bus. Social Responsibility award, 1998. Mem. AIA (bd. dirs., pres.-elect Denver chpt. 1990, pres. 1991, pres.-elect Colo. chpt. 1997, pres. 1998), Asian C. of C. (pres. 1998), Colo. Aikido Assn. (head instr. Denver Buddhist Temple Aikido), Lions Club (bd. dirs.). Democrat. Avocation: 5th degree black belt. Office: The Abo Group Inc 12600 W Colfax Ave Ste C200 Lakewood CO 80215-3758 Business E-Mail: ron@theabogroup.com.

ABOUD, PAULA, state legislator; b. Tucson, Mar. 20, 1950; BA in English, U. Ariz., 1972. Tchg. cert. Ariz. Dept. Edn. Prog. dir., coach Colby Coll., Waterville, Maine, 1984—92; property mgr. Masadi Investment Group, 1995—2001; mem. Dist. 28 Ariz. State Senate, 2006—, mem. edn. accountability & reform com., appropriations com. Mem.: Dems. of Greater Tucson (pres. 2001—04), Southern Ariz. Stonewall Dems. Democrat. Office: Ariz State Senate Capitol Complex 1700 W Washington Rm 314 Phoenix AZ 85007 Office Phone: 602-926-6252. Office Fax: 602-926-3429. Business E-Mail: paboud@azleg.gov. E-mail: paboud@msn.com.

ABRAHAMS, SIDNEY CYRIL, physicist, crystallographer; b. London, May 28, 1924; arrived in U.S., 1948; s. Aaron Harry and Freda (Cohen) A.; m. Rhoda Banks, May 1, 1950; children: David Mark, Peter Brian, Jennifer Anne. BSc, U. Glasgow, Scotland, 1946, PhD, 1949, DSc, 1957; Doctor honoris causa, U. Uppsala, Sweden, 1981, U. Bordeaux, 1997. Rsch. fellow U. Minn., Mpls., 1949-50; mem. staff MIT, Cambridge, 1950-54; rsch. fellow U. Glasgow, 1954-57; mem. tech. staff Bell Labs., Murray Hill, NJ, 1957-82; disting. mem. tech. staff AT&T Bell Labs., Murray Hill, 1982-88; Humboldt sr. scientist Inst. Crystallography, U. Tübingen, Germany, 1989-90, Guest scientist Brookhaven Nat. Lab., Upton, N.Y., 1957-90; vis. prof. U. Bordeaux, France, 1979, 90; Humboldt sr. scientist U. Tübingen, 1995; adj. prof. physics So. Oreg. U., 1990—. Mem. editl. bd. Rev. Sci. Instruments, 1963-65; co-editor Anomalous Scattering, 1975; editor World Directory of Crystallographers, 1977; editor-in-chief Acta Crystallographica, 1978-87; book rev. editor Ferroelectrics, 1975—. Recipient Sr. U.S. Scientist award, Alexander von Humboldt Found., 1989-90. Fellow AAAS, Am. Phys. Soc., Internat. Union Pure and Applied Chemistry (rep. interdivsnl. com. on nomenclature and symbols 1978-2004); mem. Am. Crystallographic Assn. (pres. 1968, mng. editor 1965-90), Royal Soc. Chemistry, Am. Inst. Physics (chmn. pub. policy com. 1981-91), Internat. Union Crystallography (chmn. commn. on crystallographic apparatus 1972-75, commn. on jours. 1978-87, commn. on crystallographic nomenclature 1978-2004), Sigma Xi (founding pres. S. Oreg. U. chpt. 1993-95). Avocations: photography, hiking. Home: 89 Mallard St Ashland OR 97520-7316 Office: So Oreg U Physics Dept Ashland OR 97520 Business E-Mail: sca@sou.edu.

ABRAM, DONALD EUGENE, retired federal judge; b. Des Moines, Feb. 8, 1935; s. Irwin and Freda Phyllis (Gibson) A.; m. Frances Jennette Cooley, Apr. 22, 1962; children: Karen Lynn, Susan Ann, Scott Alan, Diane Jennette. BS in Bus., U. Col., 1957, JD, 1963. Ptnr. Phelps, Fonda, Hays, Abram and Shaw (now Peterson & Fonda, PC), Pueblo, Colo., 1963-75; dist. judge Colo. 10th Jud. Dist., Pueblo, 1975-81; chief U.S. magistrate judge U.S. Dist. Ct. State of Colo., 1981-00; ret., 2000. Lectr. law in criminal procedure U. Denver Sch. of Law, 1983-90; adj. prof. sociology, instr. bus. law U. So. Colo., Pueblo, 1977-81. Mng. editor, bd. dir. Colo. Law Review, 1961-63. Vice chmn. Pueblo County Rep. Party, 1973-75; city councilman Pueblo, 1970-73; pres. Pueblo city coun., 1972-73, Pueblo Goodwill Industries, 1965, Pueblo United Fund, 1968; chmn. consolidation planning com. Pueblo County Sch. Dists. 60, 70, 1968-70; mem. gov's. milit. affairs adv. com., 1975-78; mem. gov's. commn. children and families, 1978-80. Lt. (j.g.) USN, 1957-60, capt. Res. ret. Recipient Disting. Svc. award Colo. Jaycee, 1970, Disting. Citizen Svc. award, Pueblo Rotary, 1975. Mem. Fed. Magistrate Judges Assn. (pres. 1990-91), Pueblo C. of C.(bd. dirs. 1972, chmn. edn. com. 1970-71), Colo. Bar Assn. (1st v.p. 1975-76), Nat. Coun. U. S. Magistrates (dir., officer 1984-89), Juvenile Judges Assn. Colo. (chmn. 1979-80), Colo. Navy League (state pres. 1976-78). Lutheran. Office: US Dist Ct US Courthouse C-566 1929 Stout St Denver CO 80294-1929

ABRAMOVITZ, MOSES, economist, educator; b. Bklyn., Jan. 1, 1912; s. Nathan and Betty (Goldenberg) A.; m. Carrie Glasser, June 23, 1937; 1 son, Joel Nathan. AB, Harvard U., 1932; PhD, Columbia U., 1939; PhD (hon.), Uppsala U., Sweden, 1985, U. Ancona, Italy, 1992. Instr. Harvard U., 1936-38; mem. research staff Nat. Bur. Econ. Research, 1938-69; lectr. Columbia U., 1940-42, 46-48; prof. econs. Stanford U., 1948—, Coe prof. Am. econ. history, exec. head dept.

econs., 1963-65, 71-74. Vis. prof. U. Pa., 1955; prin. economist WPB, 1942, OSS, 1943-44; econ. adviser to U.S. rep. on Allied Commn. on Reparations, 1945-46; econ. adviser to to sec.-gen. Orgn. for Econ. Coop. and Devel., 1962-63; vis. fellow All Souls Coll., Oxford, Eng., 1968 Author: Price Theory for a Changing Economy, 1939, Inventories and Business Cycles, 1950, The Growth of Public Employment in Great Britain, 1957, (with Vera Eliasberg) Thinking About Growth, 1989; also articles.; editor: Capital Formation and Economic Growth, 1955; mng. editor Jour. Econ. Lit., 1981-85. Served as lt. AUS, 1944-45. Recipient Nitti prize Accademia Nazionale Dei Lincei, Rome, 1990. Fellow Am. Acad. Arts and Scis., Am. Econ. Assn. (disting., pres. 1980), Am. Statis. Assn.; mem. Am. Econ. History Assn. (pres. 1991-92), Western Econ. Assn. (pres. 1988), Accademia Nazionale dei Lincei (fgn.), Phi Beta Kappa. Office: Stanford U Dept Econs Stanford CA 94305-6072

ABRAMS, ARTHUR JAY, retired physician; b. Camden, NJ, Apr. 9, 1938; s. Morris and Sophia Sarah (Kates) A.; m. Marianne Ritto Abrams, June 8, 1963; children: Suzanne Beth, Cheryl Lyn, Robert Dwight. BA, Rutgers U., Camden, NJ, 1959; MD, Hahnemann U., 1963. Diplomate Am. Bd. Dermatology. Intern Madigan Army Med. Ctr., Tacoma, 1963-64; resident, chief resident Letterman Army Med. Ctr., San Francisco, 1964-67; dermatologist, Far East cons. 249th Gen. Hosp. U.S. Army, Tokyo, 1967-69; asst. chief dermatologist Tripler Army Med. Ctr., Honolulu, 1969-70; staff dermatologist El Camino Hosp., Mountain View, Calif., 1970—2005; clin. prof. dermatology Stanford U. Med. Ctr., 1979—; dermatology cons. San Jose State U., Calif., 1994—; maj. U.S. Army, 1963-70. Mem. AMA, Calif. Med. Assn., Pacific Dermatol. Assn., San Francisco Dermatol. Soc. Avocations: volleyball, walking.

ABRAMS, FREDRICK RALPH, physician, clinical ethicist; b. NYC, June 18, 1928; s. David and Jane R. (Rein) A.; m. Alice Marilyn Engelhard, Nov. 25, 1949; children: Reid, Glenn, Hal. BA, Cornell U., 1950, MD, 1954. Diplomate Am. Bd. Ob-Gyn. Intern Letterman Army Hosp., San Francisco, 1954-55; pvt. practice gynecology Denver, 1962-96; ret.; resident Fitzsimons Army Hosp., Denver, 1956-59; prof. U. Colo. Grad. Sch. Pub. Affairs, Denver, 1987—; dir. biomed. ethics Ctr. for Health Ethics and Policy, U. Colo., 1987-92; commr. Govs. Commn. on Life and the Law, State of Colo., 1991—. Vis. prof. Iliff Sch. Theology; founder Ctr. for Applied Biomed. Ethics Rose Med. Ctr., Denver, 1982-87; assoc. med. dir. Colo. Found. for Med. Care, 1992—; Lectr. for pub. edn. in med. ethics; mem. Nat. Adv. Bd. on Ethics in Reproduction, 1995—; sr. rsch. assoc. Denver U. Ctr. Health Policy and Contemporary Affairs, with U. Colo. Med. Ctr. Bioethics & Humanities. Contbr. chpts. to book and articles to profl. jours.; author Doctors On Theedge:Will Your Doctor Break The Rules For You, 2006 Maj. U.S. Army, 1955-62, bd. mem. Acad. Lifelong Learning, WFE Quality Inst.-HospiceMetro Denver. Grantee Robert Wood Johnson, 1988-89, Colo. Trust, 1987-90, Rose Found., 1982-87, Issac Hays, MD and John Bell, MD award for Leadership in Med. Ethics and Professionalism, AMA, 2006. Mem. Internat. Soc. for Advancement of Humanistic Studies in Gynecology (past pres.), Denver Med. Soc. (past v.p.), Colo. Med. Soc., Am. Coll. Ob-Gyn. (past chmn. ethics com.). Avocations: sculpture, jewelry, fly fishing, poetry, gardening. Office Phone: 303-781-7730. Personal E-mail: frabrams@aol.com.

ABRAMS, HERBERT LEROY, radiologist, educator; b. NYC, Aug. 16, 1920; s. Morris and Freda (Sugarman) Abrams; m. Marilyn Spitz, Mar. 23, 1943; children: Nancy, John. BA, Cornell U., 1941; MD, Downstate Med. Ctr., NYC, 1946. Diplomate Am. Bd. Radiology. Intern L.I. Coll. Hosp., 1946—47; resident in internal medicine Montefiore Hosp., Bronx, NY, 1947—48; resident in radiology Stanford (Calif.) U. Hosp., 1948—51; practice medicine specializing in radiology Stanford U., Calif., 1951—67, mem. faculty Sch. Medicine, 1951—67, dir. divsn. diagnostic roentgenology Sch. Medicine, 1961—67, prof. radiology Sch. Medicine, 1962—67; Philip H. Cook prof. radiology Harvard U., 1967—85, now prof. emeritus, chmn. dept. radiology, 1967—80; prof. radiology Stanford U. Sch. Medicine, 1985—90, prof. emeritus, 1990—; clin. prof. U. Calif. Sch. Medicine, San Francisco, 1986—. Radiologist-in-chief Peter Bent Brigham Hosp., Boston, 1967—80; chmn. dept. radiology Brigham and Women's Hosp., Boston, 1981—85; radiologist-in-chief Sidney Farber Cancer Inst., Boston, 1974—85; R.H. Nimmo vis. prof. U. Adelaide, Australia; mem.-in-residence Ctr. for Internat. Security and Cooperation, Stanford U., 1985—; mem. radiation study sect. NIH, 1962—66; cons. to hosps., profl. socs. Author (with others): Angiocardiography in Congenital Heart Disease, 1956, Congenital Heart Disease, 1965, Coronary Arteriography: A Practical Approach, 1983, Brigham Guide to Diagnostic Imaging, 1986, Assessment of Diagnostic Technology in Health Care; editor: Abrams' Angiography, 3d edit., 1983; author: The President Has Been Shot: Confusion, Disability and the 25th Amendment, 1992, 1994, The History of Cardiac Radiology, 1996; mem. edit. bd.: Investigative Radiology, editor-in-chief, founder: Cardiovasc. and Interventional Radiology, 1978—88, Postgrad. Radiology, 1983—99. Named David M. Gould Meml. lectr., Johns Hopkins, 1964, William R. Whitman Meml. lectr., 1968, Leo G. Rigler lectr., Tel Aviv U., 1969, Holmes lectr., New Eng. Roentgen Ray Soc., Boston, 1970, Ross Golden lectr., N.Y. Roentgen Ray Soc., N.Y.C., 1971, Stauffer Meml. lectr., Phila. Roentgen Ray Soc., 1971, J.M.T. Finney Fund lectr., Md. Radiol. Soc., Ocean City, 1972, Aubrey Hampton lectr., Mass. Gen. Hosp., Boston, 1974, Kirklin-Weber lectr., Mayo Clinic, 1974, Crookshank lectr., Royal Coll. Radiology, 1980, Alpha Omega Alpha lectr., vis. prof., U. Calif. Med. Sch., San Francisco, 1961—65, W.H. Herbert lectr., U. Calif., Caldwell lectr., Am. Roentgen Ray Soc., 1982, Percy lectr., McMaster Med. Sch., 1983, Charles Dotter lectr., Soc. Cardiovasc. and Interventional Radiology, 1988, Philip Hodes lectr., Jefferson Med. Coll., 1988, David Gould Meml. lectr., Johns Hopkins U., 1991, Hymer Friedell lectr., Western Res. Sch. Medicine, 1993, Felix Fleischner Meml. lectr., Harvard Med. Sch., 1997, Charles Dotter Meml. lectr., Am. Heart Assn., 1998; fellow, Nat. Cancer Inst., 1950, Spl. Rsch. fellow, Nat. Heart Inst., 1960, 1973—74, Henry J. Kaiser sr. fellow, Ctr. for Advanced Study in Behavioral Sci., 1980—81. Fellow: Am. Coll. Cardiology, Am. Coll. Radiology, Royal Coll. Radiology (Gt. Britain) (hon.), Royal Coll. Surgery (Ireland) (hon.); mem.: NIH (working group on disability of U.S. pres. 1995—98, internat. blue ribbon panel radiation effects rsch. found. Hiroshima 1996, chmn. consensus panel on MRI), NAS (com. biol. effects of low-level ionizing radiation BEIR VII 1999—2005), Nat. Coun. Health Tech. Assessment, Soc. Chmn. Acad. Radiology Depts. (pres. 1970—71), Soc. Cardiovasc. Radiology (Gold medal 2000), Internat. Physicians for Prevention of Nuc. War (founding v.p., participant Nobel Peace prize 1985), N.Am. Soc. Cardiac Radiology (pres. 1979—80), Radiol. Soc. N.Am. (Gold medal 1995), Am. Soc. Nephrology, Am. Heart Assn., Inst. Medicine, Assn. Univ. Radiologists (Gold medal 1984), Alpha Omega Alpha, Phi Beta Kappa. Achievements include naming of Abrams conference room in radiology and Women's Hospital; development of Herbert L. Abrams annual lectures of Harvard Medical School. Office: Stanford U Sch Medicine 300 Pasteur Dr Stanford CA 94305-5105 Home: 620 Sand Hill Rd Apt 109G Palo Alto CA 94304 Business E-Mail: hlabrams@stanford.edu.

ABRAMS, J.J. (JEFFREY JACOB ABRAMS), television producer, scriptwriter; b. NYC, June 27, 1966; s. Gerald W. Abrams; m. Katie McGrath; children: Henry, Gracie, August. Attended, Sarah Lawrence Coll. Actor: (films) Six Degrees of Separation, 1993, Diabolique, 1996; prodr., writer, actor: Regarding Henry, 1991; exec. prodr., dir., writer: (TV series) Felicity, 1998—2002; Alias, 2001—06; Lost, 2004— (Emmy award for outstanding directing for a drama series, 2005, best TV series, drama, Producers Guild Am., 2006); exec. prodr., writer (TV series) Fringe, 2008; exec. prodr.: (TV series) What About Brian, 2006, Six Degrees, 2006, Boundaries, 2008; exec. prodr., writer: (films) Forever Young, 1992; prodr.: The Pallbearer, 1996; actor, prodr.: (films) The Suburbans, 1999, Cloverfield, 2008; writer, prodr.: Joy Ride, 2001; writer, dir. Mission: Impossible III, 2006; writer Gone Fishin', 1997; prodr., dir. Star Trek, 2009; writer: (screenplay) Armageddon, 1998. Named one of 100 People in Hollywood You Need to Know, Fade In mag., 2005, 100 Most Influential People, Time Mag., 2006, 100 Most Powerful Celebrities, Forbes.com, 2007, 50 Smartest People in Hollywood, Entertainment Weekly, 2007. Office: William Morris Agency 1 William Morris Place Beverly Hills CA 90212*

ABRAMS, JONATHAN, Internet company executive; BS in Computer Sci., McMaster U. Software engr. Bell-Northern Rsch. (now Nortel R&D); lead java scientist Nortel Computing Tech. Lab; software engr. Netscape Comm., 1996, CrossWorlds Software; founder, CTO HotLinks Network Inc., 1999—2001, CEO, 1999—2000, acting v.p. of engring., 1999; lead, engring. group Bitfone Corp., 2001; founder, CEO Friendster Inc., Sunnyvale, Calif., 2002—. Adv. bd. mem. Silicon Valley Assn. of Startup Entrepreneurs.

ABRAMS, MARC, lawyer, political organization worker; b. NYC, Mar. 23, 1957; s. Stephen Robert and Virginia Ornstein Abrams; 1 child, Lawrence Christopher. BA magna cum laude, Wesleyan U., Middletown, Conn., 1978; MA, JD, U. Mich., 1981. Bar: Conn. 1982, N.Y. 1986, D.C. 1987, Pa. 1987, Oreg. 1989, U.S. Dist Ct. (so. dist.) N.Y. 1986, U.S. Dist. Co. (ea. dist.) Pa. 1988, U.S. Dist. Ct. Mont. 1989, U.S. Cir. Ct. (3d, 4th and 9th cirs.), U.S. Dist. Ct. Oreg. 1989, U.S. Supreme Ct. Asst. prof. U. Oreg., 1981-83; exec. dir. Student Press Law Ctr., 1983-85; pvt. practice, 1985—2002; sr. asst. atty. gen. State of Oreg., 2002—. Talk show host KXL-AM, 2002—; commentator KATU-TV, 2005—. Co-author: Law of the Student Press, 1983, Confronting Wrongful Discharge Under Oregon and Washington Law, 1989. Vice chair Lane County (Oreg.) Dem. Ctrl. Com., 1981-82, Multnomah County (Oreg.) Dem. Ctrl. Com., 1991-92; mem. Oreg. Dem. State Ctrl. Com., 1981-82, 91—, Multnomah Edn. Svc. Dist. Bd., 1993-97, chmn., 1996-97; fin. chair Oreg. State Dem. Party, 1993-95, vice chair, 1994-97, chmn., 1997-99; mem. Portland Sch. Bd., 1995-2003, vice chair, 1998-2002; treas. Assn. State Dem. Chairs, 1998-99. Recipient Johnnie Phelps medal Vets. for Human Rights, 1995. Jewish. Office: 1162 Court St NE Salem OR 97301 Business E-Mail: marc.abrams@state.or.us.

ABRAMS, NORMAN, retired law educator, former academic administrator; b. Chgo., July 7, 1933; s. Harry A. and Gertrude (Dick) A.; m. Toshka Alster, 1977; children: Marshall David, Julie, Hanna, Naomi. AB, U. Chgo., 1952, JD, 1955. Bar: Ill. 1956, US Supreme Ct. 1967. Assoc. in law Columbia U., 1955-57; rsch. assoc. Harvard U., 1957-59; sec. Harvard-Brandeis Coop. Rsch. for Israel's Legal Devel., 1957-58, dir., 1959; mem. faculty law sch. UCLA, 1959—, prof. law, 1964—2005, prof. law emeritus, 2005—06, 2007—, co-dir. Ctr. for internat. and strategic studies, 1982-83, chmn. steering com., 1985-87, 88-89, assoc. dean law, 1989-91, vice chancellor acad. pers., 1991-2001, interim exec. vice chancellor, 1998, interim dean law, 2003—04, acting chancellor, 2006—07, prof. law emeritus, 2007—. Reporter for So. Calif. indigent accused persons study Am. Bar Found., 1963; cons. Gov. Calif. Commn. LA Riots, 1965, Pres.'s Commn. Law Enforcement and Adminstrn. Justice, 1966-67, Nat. Commn. on Reform of Fed. Criminal Laws, 1967-69, Rand Corp., 1968-74, Ctr. for Adminstrv. Justice, ABA, 1973-77, Nat. Adv. Commn. on Criminal Justice Stds., Organized Crime Task Force, 1976; spl. hearing officer conscientious objector cases Dept. Justice, 1967-68; vis. scholar Inst. for Advanced Studies, Hebrew U., summer, 1994; vis. prof. Hebrew U., 1969-70, 86, Bar Ilan U., 1970-71, 78, U. So. Calif., 1972, Stanford U., 1977, U. Calif., Berkeley, Calif., 1977; spl. asst. to U.S. atty. gen. Dept. Justice, 1966-67, prof.-in-residence Criminal Divsn., 1966-67. Author: (with others) Evidence, Cases and Materials, 7th edit., 1983, 8th edit., 1988, 9th edit., 1997, Federal Criminal Law and Its Enforcement, 1986, (with S. Beale), 2d edit., 1993, 3d edit, 2000, 4th edit., 2006, Anti-terrorism and Criminal Enforcement, 2003, 2nd edit, 2005, 3d edit., 2008; mem. editl. bd. Criminal Law Forum, 1990—, Jour. Nat. Security Law and Policy, 2004—. Chmn. Jewish Conciliation Bd., LA, 1975-81; bd. dir. Bet Tzedek, 1975-85, LA Hillel Coun., 1979-82, Shalhevet HS, 1998—2007; chmn. So. Calif. region Am. Prof. for Peace in Middle East, 1981-83; bd. dir. met. region Jewish Fedn., 1982-88, v.p. 1982-83; pres. Westwood Kehillah Congregation, 1985; mem. bd. Israeli studies program UCLA, 2007-. Mem. Internat. Soc. for Reform of Criminal Law (mem. exec. com. 1994—), Phi Beta Kappa. Office: UCLA Law School 405 Hilgard Ave Los Angeles CA 90095-9000 Office Phone: 310-794-4056. Business E-Mail: abrams@law.ucla.edu.

ABRAMS, WILLIAM F., lawyer; b. Indpls., Sept. 21, 1954; AB with honors, Stanford U., 1976; JD, U. Santa Clara, 1979. Bar: Calif. 1979, U.S. Dist. Ct. (all Calif. dist., Md., Del.), U.S. Tax Ct., U.S. Ct. Appeals (8th, 9th cir.), U.S. Supreme Ct. 1983. Past mem. Orrick, Herrington & Sutcliffe, San Francisco; ptnr. Intellectual Property practice, head IP Litigation team Pillsbury Winthrop Shaw Pittman, Palo Alto, Calif.; ptnr. Bingham McCutcheon LLP, Palo Alto, Calif., 2006—. Instr. Stanford Univ. Mng. editor Santa Clara Law Rev., 1978; contbr. articles to profl. jours.; frequent legal commentator in print & broadcast media. Bd. dir. Youth Law Ctr., San Francisco, Silicon Valley Campaign for Legal Svcs., Hear My Voice, Ann Arbor, Palo Alto Babe Ruth League. Recipient Human Biology Excellence in Advising award, 2004; named a No. Calif. Super lawyer, San Francisco Mag., 2004; named one of Silicon Valley's Top 300 Lawyers, San Jose Mag., 2001—04. Mem. ABA, Am. Intellectual Property Law Assn., State Bar Calif., Santa Clara County Bar Assn. (trustee), Fed. Cir. Bar Assn., Intellectual Property Owners Assn., INTA, Bar Assn. San Francisco, Assn. Bus. Trial Lawyers, William A. Ingram Inn of Ct. Office: Bingham McCutcheon LLP 1900 University Ave Palo Alto CA 94303 E-mail: bill.abrams@bingham.com.

ABRAMSON, LESLIE HOPE, lawyer; b. Queens, NY, 1943; 1 child, Laine. Grad., Queens Coll.; JD, UCLA. Bar: Calif. 1970. Lawyer L.A. County Pub. Defender's Office, 1970—77; pvt. practice, 1977—. Co-author: (with Richard Flaste) The Defense is Ready: My Life in Crime, 1997. Recipient award for outstanding trial atty., Criminal Cts. Bar Assn., 1985. Mem.: Calif. Attys. for Criminal Justice (pres.).

ABRAMSON, NORMAN, retired engineering educator, electronics executive; b. Boston, Apr. 1, 1932; s. Edward and Esther (Vaslavsky) Abramson; m. Joan Freulich, July 4, 1954; children: Mark David, Carin Lynn. AB, Harvard U., 1953; MA, UCLA, 1955; PhD, Stanford U., 1958. Asst. prof. to assoc. prof. Stanford U., Calif., 1958—65; vis. prof. U. Calif., Berkeley, 1965, Harvard U., Cambridge, Mass., 1965-66; prof. U. Hawaii, Honolulu, 1966-94, emeritus prof., 2005—; v.p. Aloha Networks, Inc., San Francisco, 1994-2001, SkyWare, Inc., San Francisco, 2002—06, bd. dirs. Vis. prof. MIT, 1981—82; cons. Internat. Telecom. Union, Geneva, UNESCO, Paris, UN Devel. Prog., NYC. Author: Information Theory and Coding, 1963; co-editor: Computer Communication Networks, 1973; editor: Multiple Access Communications, Foundations for Emerging Technologies, 1993. Recipient Tech. award, Rhein Found., 2000. Fellow: IEEE (Koji Kobayshi Computers and Comm. award 1995, Alexander Graham Bell medal 2007), Internat. Engring. Consortium, IEEE Info. Theory Soc. (Golden Jubilee award for Tech. Innovation 1998). Achievements include patents in field. Home: 521 Lake St San Francisco CA 94118-1216 Personal E-mail: norm@hawaii.edu.

ABRAVANEL, ALLAN RAY, lawyer; b. NYC, Mar. 11, 1947; s. Leon and Sydelle (Berenson) A.; m. Susan Ava Paikin, Dec. 28, 1971; children: Karen, David. BA magna cum laude, Yale U., 1968; JD cum laude, Harvard U., 1971. Bar: N.Y. 1972, Oreg. 1976. Assoc. Paul, Weiss, Rifkind, Wharton & Garrison, NYC, 1971-72, 74-76; fellow Internat. Legal Ctr., Lima, Peru, 1972-74; from assoc. to ptnr. Stoel, Rives, Boley, Fraser & Wyse, Portland, Oreg., 1976-83; ptnr. Perkins Coie, Portland, 1983—. Editor, pub. Abravanel Family Newsletter. Chair Oreg. Internat. Trade Com., Oreg. Dist. Export Coun. Mem.: ABA. Office: Perkins Coie LLP 1120 NW Couch St Portland OR 97209-4125 Office Phone: 503-727-2000. E-mail: aabravanel@perkinscoie.com.

ABREU, BOBBY (BOB KELLY ABREU), professional baseball player; b. Maracay, Venezuela, Mar. 11, 1974; 1 child, Emily Paola. Outfielder Houston Astros, 1996—97, Phila. Phillies, 1998—2006, NY Yankees, 2006—08, LA Angels of Anaheim, 2009—. Mem. Venezuelan nat. team World Baseball Classic, 2009. Recipient Silver Slugger award, 2004, Gold Glove award, 2005; named to Nat. League All-Star Team, Major League Baseball, 2004—05. Achievements include leading the National League in: triples (11), 1999; doubles (50), 2002; winning the Major League Baseball All-Star Home Run Derby, 2005. Office: LA Angels of Anaheim 2000 Gene Autry Way Anaheim CA 92806*

ABT, STEVEN R., civil engineer, educator; b. Cheyenne Wells, Colo. BCE, Colo. State U., 1973, MSCE, 1976, PhDCE, 1980. Hydraulics staff engr. Leonard Rice Engring., Denver, 1974-76; instr. Colo. State U., Ft. Collins, 1976-80, from asst. prof. to assoc. prof., 1980-88, prof., 1988—, exec. asst. dean, 1997—2004, interim dean, 2004—05. Cons., Ft. Collins, 1976—. Editor, co-editor Proceedings; contbr. more than 78 articles to profl. jour. 2d lt. C.E., US Army, 1973, major gen. USAR, 1973—. Fellow ASCE; mem. Transp. Rsch. Bd., Internat. Erosion Control Assn. Office: Colo State U Engring and Rsch Ctr Fort Collins CO 80523-1372 Office Phone: 970-491-8203. E-mail: sabt@engr.colostate.edu.

ABU-HADBA, WALID, computer software company executive; BS in Sys. Engring. and Bus. Adminstrn., MBA. Mgr. consulting Microsoft Consulting Svcs. Microsoft Corp., Redmond, Wash., 1991, practice mgr. Advanced Tech. Consulting Practice, gen. mgr. Microsoft Product Support Svcs. Americas, global developer support, gen. mgr. support svcs. Asia-Pacific, Japan, v.p. enterprise specialist sales Enterprise and Ptnr. Group, corp. v.p. Developer & Platform Evangelism Group, 2008—. Office: Microsoft Corp One Microsoft Way Redmond WA 98052-6399

ACAIN, MICHAEL P., lawyer; b. Harbor City, Calif., June 16, 1974; BA cum laude, Loyola Marymount Univ., 1996, JD, 1999. Bar: Calif. 1999, US Dist. Ct. So. Calif. Assoc., civil litigation practice McKay, Byrne & Graham, LA. Editor (exec.): Loyola of LA Entertainment Law Jour.; contbr. articles to profl. jours. Recipient Am. Jurisprudence award in criminal procedure; named a Rising Star, So. Calif. Super Lawyers, 2006. Mem.: ABA, State Bar Calif., LA County Bar Assn. Office: McKay Byrne & Graham Ste 603 3250 Wilshire Blvd Los Angeles CA 90010 Office Phone: 213-386-6900. Office Fax: 213-381-1762.

ACCURSO, FRANK JOSEPH, physician, educator; b. Mt. Vernon, NY, Mar. 9, 1947; s. Joseph and Elsie A.; m. Tanya Lynn Kleen, Apr. 25, 1971; children: Aron, David. BS, CCNY, 1968; MS, U. Colo., 1971; MD, Albert Einstein Coll. Medicine, NYC, 1974. Diplomate Am. Bd. Pediatrics, Am. Bd. Pediatric Pulmonology; cert. in pediatric critical care medicine. Instr. pediatrics U. Colo. Sch. Medicine, Denver, 1979-80, asst. prof. pediatrics, 1980-87, assoc. prof. pediatrics, 1987-95, prof. pediatrics, 1995—. Dir., Cystic Fibrosis Ctr., Denver, Co. Author: (with others) Alfa Clinical Series, 1994, Lange Medical Books, 1993, Marcel Dekker, 1989. Recipient Svc. award Cystic Fibrosis Found. local Denver chap., 1992, numerous clin., rsch., and tng. grants, 1986—; named to 5280 Magazine's Top Doctors, 1999. Mem. AAAS, Am. Thoracic Soc., Am. Pediatric Soc., Am. Acad. Pediatrics, Soc. Pediatric Rsch., Office: U Colo Childrens Hosp 1056 E 19th Ave # B395 Denver CO 80218-1007 E-mail: accurso.frank@tchden.org.

ACHAUER, BRUCE MICHAEL, plastic surgeon; MD, Baylor U., 1967. Intern San Francisco Gen. Hosp., 1967-68; resident in gen. surgery U. Calif., Irvine, 1970-74, rsch. in plastic surgery, 1974-76, adj. prof. surgery, 1994—; fellow in plastic surgery Queen Victoria Hosp., East Grinstead, U.K., 1976; pvt. practice U. Calif. Irvine Med. Ctr., Orange, 1977—; mem. staff St. Joseph Hosp., 1977—; mem. active staff Children's Hosp. of Orange County, 1977—; pvt. practice plastic surgery Orange. Mem. courtesy staff Med. Ctr. of GGG, 1985—; dir. Am. Bd. Plastic Surgery, 1995—. Fellow Am. Acad. Pediatrics; mem. AMA, Am. Assn. Plastic Surgeons, Am. Cleft Palate Assn., Am. Soc. for Surgery of Hand, Am. Soc. Plastic and Reconstructive Surgeons (sec. ednl. found.).

ACHTEL, ROBERT ANDREW, pediatric cardiologist, educator; b. Bklyn., May 5, 1941; s. Murray and Amelia (Elian) A.; m. Erica Noel Woods, Mar. 10, 1963; children: Bergen Alison, Roland Hugh. BA, Adelphi U., 1963; MD, U. Cin., 1967. Diplomate Am. Bd. Pediat. Cardiology. Lic. comml. pilot FAA. Intern Cin. Children's Hosp., 1967-68; resident in pediat. Yale U., 1968-69, fellow in pediat. cardiology, 1969-71; clin. instr. pediat. U. Calif., Davis, 1972-73, asst. prof., 1977-83, U. Ky., Lexington, 1976—79; dir. pediat. ICU Sutter Meml. Hosp., Sacramento, 1977-85, dir. pediat. cardiology, 1982—, chmn. instl. rev. com., 1981-85, 96—; chmn. dept. pediat. Mercy Hosp., Sacramento, 1981—83, dir. pediat. ICU, 1982-83, vice chmn. pediat., 1983—85; dir. Laurel Hills Devel. Ctr., 1985-89; vice chmn. pediat. Mercy Hosp., 1995—97, chmn. dept. pediat., 1997—2001; clin. prof. pediatrics (cardiology) Stanford U. Sch. Medicine, 2003—05; adj. assoc. prof. pediat. Lucile Children's Hosp., Standford, 2008—. Chmn. rsch. com. Sutter Inst. for Med. Rsch., 1989—98; trustee Sutter Hosps. Found., 1988—2000, mem. exec. com., 1988—2000, vice chmn., 1992—93; vice chmn. dept. pediat. Mercy Hosp., 1995—97; vice chmn. Access Care, 1994—95; med. dir. FastServe Med. Group, 1995—97; chmn. Mercy Hosp., 1997—; vice chmn. tech. adv. com. pediat. cardiology State of Calif., 1997—2001; CEO Access Care, 1993—97; chmn. regional instl. rev. bd. Sutter/CHS Ctrl., 1996; mem. quality assurance & pharmacy com. Omni Health Plan, 1996—99; lectr. Mooney Aircraft Pilots Assn., FAA; bd. dirs. Sutter North Med. Group, 2008—; aviation safety counselor FAA, 1998—, aviation counselor western divsn., 1996—; lectr. Exptl. Aircraft Assn.; clin. prof. pediat. cardiology Stanford U. Sch. Medicine, 2003—; bd. dirs. Sutter North Med. Group. Contbr. articles on aviation safety to cassette Pilots Audio Update; contbr. articles on cardiovasc. rsch. to profl. publs.; contbr. monthly editl. to Mooney Airplane Pilots Assn. Log. Bd. dirs. Sutter Meml. Hosp. Found., 1986-2000; bd. dirs. Sutter Found., 1989, trustee, 1989-2001. Maj. M.C., USAF, 1971-73. Grantee, U. Ky. Tobacco and Health Fsch. Found. Mem. Am. Heart Assn. (bd. dirs. Sacramento chpt., mem. couns. on congenital heart disease and atherosclerosis and cardiovasc. surgery, grantee), Am. Coll. Chest Physicians, Am. Acad. Pediat., S.W. Pediat. Cardiology Soc., So. Soc. Pediat. Rsch, Sutter North Med. group. Office: 5301 F St Ste 316 Sacramento CA 95819-3948 also: 440 Plumas Blvd Yuba City CA 95991 Office Phone: 916-451-9900, 530-749-3390. E-mail: drbobav02@prodigy.net, achtelr@sutterhealth.org, Rachtel@stanford.edu.

ACHTENBERG, ROBERTA, former federal official; b. LA, July 20, 1950; d. Louis and Beatrice A.; 1 child. AB, U. Calif., Berkeley, 1972; postgrad., U. Calif., San Francisco, 1972-73; JD, U. Utah, 1975. Bar: Calif., U.S. Dist. Ct. (no. dist.) Calif., U.S. Ct. Appeals (9th cir.). Exec. dir. Nat. Ctr. Lesbian Rights, 1989-90; asst. sec. fair housing and equal opportunity HUD, Washington, 1993-95, Sr. Adv. to Sec., 1995—; sr. v.p. pub. policy dept. San Francisco C. of C., 1995—. Mem. County Bd. Suprs., City and County of San Francisco; bd. dirs. Bay Area Air Quality Mgmt. Dist., 1991-93; trustee, Calif. State U. Mem. Order of Coir, Phi Beta Kappa. Office: San Francisco C of C Pub Policy Dept 235 Montgomery St 12th Fl San Francisco CA 94104

ACHTER, STEVE, state agency administrator; Assoc. city planner Maplewood, Minn.; dir. planning and cmty. devel. Platte County, Wheatland, Wyo.; planner Wyo. State Dept. Econ. Planning and Devel., 1979; mgr. Cmty. Devel. Block Grant Program, State of Wyo.; dir. investment ready cmtys. divsn. Wyo. Bus. Coun., Cheyenne. Office: Wyoming Business Council 214 W 15th St Cheyenne WY 82002 Home Phone: 307-778-2705; Office Phone: 307-777-2811. E-mail: sachte@state.wy.us.

ACKEL, RICK R., electronics manufacturing executive; Ptnr. Arthur Anderson LLP; v.p. fin., CFO Sanmina Corp., San Jose, Calif. Office: Sanmina Corp 2700 North 1st St San Jose CA 95134

ACKERMAN, MARSHALL, publishing executive; b. NYC, Jan. 22, 1925; s. Albert and Beatrice (Munstuk) A.; m. Carol Lipman, June 8, 1948; children: Stark, Scott, A. Marc. AB, Harvard U., 1949; MS in Journalism, Northwestern U., 1950. Dir. employee relations Gimbel Bros., NYC, 1950-51; account exec. Leonard Wolf & Assoc. (advt. agy.), NYC, 1951-54; with Rodale Press, Inc., 1954-91, exec. v.p., 1967-91, vice chmn. bd., 1978-91; pub. Prevention mag., 1977-86, Theatre Crafts mag., 1967-78, vice chmn., Western divsn., 1986-91; ind. cons. health food industry, health media, 1992—2002. Pres. bd. assocs. Cedar Crest Coll., Allentown, Pa., 1976—78, trustee, 1983—87; pres. Pa. Stage Co., Allentown, 1978—80; chmn. Santa Barbara chpt. Am. Inst. Wine and Food, 1998—2003. Charge de Presse, Confrerie de la Chaine des Rotisseurs, Bailliage de Santa Barbara, 1998-2003; Decorated Bronze Star, Purple Heart. Home and Office: 894 Toro Canyon Rd Santa Barbara CA 93108-1642 E-mail: mackermanm@aol.com.

ACOBA, SIMEON RIVERA, JR., state supreme court justice, educator; b. Honolulu, Mar. 11, 1944; s. Simeon R. and Martina (Domingo) A. BA, U. Hawaii, 1966; JD, Northwestern U., Chgo., 1969. Bar: Hawaii 1969, U.S. Dist. Ct. Hawaii, U.S. Ct. Appeals (9th cir.). Law clk. Hawaii Supreme Ct., Honolulu, 1969-70; housing officer U. Hawaii, Honolulu, 1970-71; dep. atty. gen. State of Hawaii, Honolulu, 1971-73; pvt. practice, Honolulu, 1973-80; judge 1st Circuit Ct. Hawaii, Honolulu, 1980-94, Intermediate Ct. Appeals Hawaii, Honolulu, 1994-2000; assoc. justice Hawaii Supreme Ct., 2000—. Atty. on spl. contract divsn. OSHA, Dept. Labor, Honolulu, 1975—77, Pub. Utilities divsn., State of Hawaii, 1976—77; campaign spending com. State of Hawaii, 1976; staff atty. Hawaii State Legislature, 1975; instr. criminal law Hawaii Pacific U., 1992—. Bd. dirs. Hawaii Mental Health Assn., 1975—77, Nuuanu YMCA, 1975—78, Hawaii Youth at Risk, 1990—91; mem. Gov.'s Conf. on Yr. 2000, Honolulu, 1970, Citizens Com. on Adminstrn. of Justice, 1972, State Drug Abuse Commn., 1975—76, Com. to Consider the Adoption of ABA Model Rules of Profl. Conduct, 1989—91, Judicial Edn. Com., 1992—93, Hawaii State Bar Assn. Jud. Adminstrn. Com., 1992—94, Permanent Com. Rules Penal Procedure and Cir. Ct. Rules, 1992—96; subcom. chmn. Supreme Ct. Com. Pattern Jury Instrns., 1990—91; mem. Hawaii Supreme Ct. Ad Hoc Com. Jury Master List, 1991—92; chair. Access to Justice Commn. Recipient Liberty Bell award, 1964. Mem.: Am. Judicature Soc. (mem. ct. security com. Hawaii chpt. 2006—, mem. awards com., Hawaii chpt. 2007—), Hawaii State Bar Assn., Hawaii Bar Assn. (dir. young lawyers sect. 1973, ethics award com. 2005—). Office: Hawaii Supreme Ct 417 S King St Honolulu HI 96813-2912

ACORD, LEA, dean; MS in Pediat. Nursing, U. Pitts., PhD in Higher Edn. Adminstrn. Asst. prof. Sch. of Nursing U. Pitts., 1972-81; exec. dir. Ill. Nurses Assn., 1981-88; dir., assoc. prof. Sch. of Nursing, U. Maine, 1988-95; dean, prof. Coll. of Nursing, Mont. State U., Bozeman. Contbr. articles to profl. publs. Recipient Peggy Mussehl award for excellence Mont. Nurses Assn., 1997, Jean McLean Nursing Edn. award Maine State Nurses Assn., 1994, Hartford Gerontol. Curriculum award Assn. of Colls. of Nursing, 1998. Mem. Sigma Theta Tau (dean's task force). Office: Mont State U Bozeman Coll Nursing PO Box 173560 Bozeman MT 59717-3560

ACOSTA, MARITONI A., lawyer; BA, UCLA, 1991; JD, Loyola Law Sch., 1994. Bar: Calif., cert.: (Family Law Specialist). Ptnr., head family law mediation dept. Feinberg, Mindel, Brandt, Klein & Kline, LA, 2000—. Named a Rising Star, So. Calif. Super Lawyers, 2004—06. Mem.: Santa Monica Bar Assn. (chmn. family law sect.), Philippine Am. Bar Assn. (bd. dir.). Office: Feinberg Mindel Brandt Klein & Kline Ste 900 12400 Wilshire Bldv Los Angeles CA 90025 Office Phone: 310-447-8675 ext 115. Office Fax: 310-447-8678. Business E-Mail: macosta@fmbklaw.com.

ACOVELLE, JOHN A., lawyer; BA cum laude, U. So. Calif., 1984; JD magna cum laude, Southwestern U., 1987. Bar: Calif. 1987, US Ct. Fed. Claims, US Dist. Ct. (ctrl. and so. dists.) Calif. Ptnr., leader Construction, Environ., Real Estate and Land Use Litig. Practice Group Sheppard, Mullin, Richter & Hampton, LLP, San Diego. Mem.: Am. Subcontractors Assn., Associated Gen. Contractors of Am., Associated Builders and Contractors, State Bar Calif. Office: Sheppard Mullin Richter Hampton Llp 12275 El Camino Real Ste 200 San Diego CA 92130-4092 Office Phone: 858-720-8934. Office Fax: 858-509-3691. E-mail: jyacovelle@sheppardmullin.com.

ACREE, CINDY, state legislator; m. Robert Acree; 3 children. Grad., Southern Meth. U., U. Denver Coll. Law. Pres. Protektmark LLC; mem. Dist. 40 Colo. House of Reps., 2008—. Former instr. U. Denver Coll. Law; chmn. Colo. Neurological Inst. Bd. Dirs. Pres. Aurora Citizens Adv. Budget Com.; dir. Cherry Creek Sch. Dist. Long Range Facilities Planning Com.; coord. Caridovascular Disease & Stroke Prevention Program, Colo. Dept. Pub. Health & Environ.; founding mem. Spalding Cmty. Found. Bd. Dirs.; appointed mem. Cardiovascular Health Coalition. Named Most Disting. Alumna, Cottey Coll., 2007. Mem.: Colo. Stroke Registry Adv. Bd. Republican. Achievements include establishment of Cindy Acree Hope award by Colorado Neurological Institute. Office: State House 200 E Colfax Denver CO 80203 Office Phone: 303-866-2944. Business E-Mail: cindy.acree.house@state.co.us.*

ACREE, G. HARDY, airport executive; Previous positions with Anchorage Internat. Airport, Alaska, Phila., Indpls., and Riverside/San Bernardino area airports; mgr., dep. dir. aviation Bush Intercontinental Airport, Houston, 1995—99; dir. Sacramento County Airport Sys., Sacramento Internat. Airport, Calif., 1999—. Office: Sacramento County Airport Sys Sacramento Internat Airport 6900 Airport Blvd Sacramento CA 95837 Office Phone: 916-874-0719. E-mail: Acreeh@saccounty.net.

ADAIR, ROD, state legislator; b. Durant, Okla., Nov. 19, 1953; m. Dana Adair; children: Lauren, Ian. BS in Polit. Sci., MS in Govt. Demographer Mexico Demographic Research (present); mem. edn. com., mem. rules com. N.Mex. State Senate, mem. Dist. 33 Sante Fe, 1996—. Served in the US Army, 1976—96. Republican. Office: PO Box 96 Roswell NM 88202-0096 also: State Capitol Rm 414D Santa Fe NM 87503 Office Phone: 505-986-4385, 505-627-8372, 505-986-4385. E-mail: rod.adair@state.nm.us, radair@dfn.com.*

ADAMEK, CHARLES ANDREW, lawyer; b. Chgo., Dec. 24, 1944; s. Stanley Charles and Virginia Marie (Budzban) A.; m. Lori Merriel Klein; children: Donald Steven, Elizabeth Jean. BA with honors, U. Mich., 1966, JD, 1969. Bar: Ill. 1969, Calif. 1978. Clk. U.S. Dist. Judge U.S. Fed. Cts., Chgo., 1969-71; assoc. atty. Lord Bissell & Brook, Chgo., 1971-77, ptnr., 1977-78, LA, 1978—2006, of counsel, 2007—. Mem. ABA, Ill. State Bar Assn., State Bar Calif., Nat. Assn. Railroad Trial Counsel(emeritus mem.). Roman Catholic. Avocations: banjo, hockey. Office: Lord Bissell & Brook 300 S Grand Ave Ste 800 Los Angeles CA 90071-3119 Home Phone: 818-790-3941; Office Phone: 213-687-6721. Business E-Mail: cadamek@lordbissell.com.

ADAMS, CHARLES FRANCIS, advertising and real estate company executive; b. Detroit, Sept. 26, 1927; s. James R. and Bertha C. (DeChant) A.; m. Helen R. Harrell, Nov. 12, 1949; children: Charles Francis, Amy Ann, James Randolph, Patricia Duncan. BA, U. Mich., 1948; postgrad., U. Calif., Berkeley, 1949; student additional study, Oxford U., 1996. With D'Arcy-MacManus & Masius, Inc., 1947-80, exec. v.p., dir., 1970-76, pres., chief operating officer, 1976-80; pres. Adams Enterprises, 1971—; exec. v.p., dir. Washington Office, Am. Assn. Advt. Agys., 1980-84. Chmn., CEO Wajim Corp., Detroit; past mem. steering com. Nat. Advt. Rev. Bd.; mem. mktg. com. US Info. Agy.; pres. Internat. Visitors Ctr. of the Bay Area, 1988-89. Author: Common Sense in Advertising, 1965, Heroes of the Golden Gate, 1987, California of the Year 2000, 1992, The Magnificent Rogues, 1999, Murder By The Bay, 2005, The Complete Geezer Guidebook, 2009-. Past chmn. exec. com. Oakland U. Mem. Am. Assn. Advt. Agys. (dir., mem. govt. rels. com.), Advt. Fedn. Am. (past dir.), Nat. Outdoor Advt. Bur. (past chmn.), Nat. Golf Links Am. Club (Southampton, LI), Olympic Club, The Family Club, Marks Club, London, Les Amdassadevrs, London, Theta Chi, hon. mem. Alpha Delta Sigma, (hon.). Republican. Roman Catholic. Home: 2240 Hyde St # 5 San Francisco CA 94109-1509 Office: 10 W Long Lake Rd Bloomfield Hills MI 48304-2707

ADAMS, DIRK STANDLEY, lawyer; b. Lynch, Nebr., May 19, 1951; s. Howard W. and Marilyn (Standley) A.; m. Anita Low, Feb. 14, 1984. BS, U. Tex., 1972; JD, Harvard U., 1976. Bar: N.Y. 1977, Calif. 1985. Ptnr. Sullivan, Johnson, Peters, Burns, Adams & Mullin, P.C., Rochester, N.Y., 1981-82; exec. v.p., treas., gen. counsel Suffolk County Fed. Savs & Loan Assn., Centereach, N.Y., 1982; ptnr. Phillips, Lytle, Hitchcock, Blaine & Huber, Rochester, 1982-83; sr. v.p., gen. counsel, corp. sec. Fed. Home Loan Bank of San Francisco, 1983—; pvt. practice Wilsall, Mont. Acting counsel Fed. Asset Disposition Assn., San Francisco, 1985-86. Bd. dirs. Vol. Legal Services Project, Inc., Rochester, 1983. Mem. ABA (com. savs. and loan assns. sect. corp., banking and bus. 1983—), Calif. Bar Assn. (fin. instns. com. 1985). Office: 729 Shields River Rd Wilsall MT 59086-9431 Office Phone: 406-578-2330. Business E-Mail: dirksadams@mcn.net.

ADAMS, EULA L., data storage executive; BS in Acctg., Morris Brown U.; MBA, Harvard Bus. Sch. bd. dirs. MasterCard Internat. Former ptnr. Deloitte and Touche; CEO Western Union, exec. v.p. and gen. mgr. Telesvcs. First Data Corp., Atlanta, 1991-98, pres. First Data Resources and Teleservices, 2000—03, exec. v.p., pres. First Data Merchant Svcs. subs., 1998—2003; v.p. global services Storage Technology Corp., Louisville, Colo., 2004—. Bd. dirs. Solidus Networks, Inc, NetBank, Inc. Named one of 50 Most Powerful Black Executives, Fortune mag., 2002. Office: 1 StorageTek Dr Louisville CO 80028 Office Phone: 303-673-5151.

ADAMS, FRANK, adult education educator, consultant; b. Cleve., Sept. 11, 1948; s. Frank Albin and Helen (Coleman) Kovacevic. BS in Bus. Adminstrn., Bowling Green State U., Ohio, 1970, MEd in Phys. Edn., 1978. Tech. writer Soldier Phys. Fitness Sch., Ft. Ben Harrison, Ind., 1983-85; edn. specialist Directorate of Tng. and Doctrine, Ft. Huachuca, Ariz., 1985-90, Dept. Tactics Intelligence Mil. Sci., Ft. Huachuca, 1990-93, 111th Mil. Intelligence Brigade, Ft. Huachuca, 1993-97; staff 112th Mil. Intelligence Brig. U.S. Army Intelligence Ctr., 1998—2003, staff, faculty devel. divsn., 2003—06, ret., 2006; tech. writer Software Device Divsn. Ilex Sys., 2006—07; tng. specialist Gen. Dynamics Info. Tech., 2007—. Mem. steering com. tng. and doctrine command, staff and faculty devel. divsn., El Paso, Tex., 1987. Co-author: (field manual) Physical Fitness Training, 1984, (Internet site) Total Fitness; contbr. articles to profl. jours. and local newspapers. Recipient Civilian Achievement medal Dept. Army, Ft. Huachuca 1993, Comdr.'s award, 1995, 2003, Superior Civilian Svc. award, 1999, 2006, Knowlton award, 2006. Mem. AAHPERD (life), Mil. Intelligence Corp. Avocations: internal martial arts, spiritual reading, reiki master-teacher. Home: 4838 Corte Vista Sierra Vista AZ 85635-5738 Office: Gen Dynamics Info Tech Sierra Vista AZ 85635

ADAMS, HAZARD SIMEON, retired language educator, writer; b. Cleve., Feb. 15, 1926; s. Robert Simeon and Mary (Thurness) A.; m. Diana White, Sept. 17, 1949; children: Charles Simeon, Perry White. AB, Princeton, 1948; MA, U. Wash., 1949, PhD, 1953. Instr. to asst. prof. Cornell U., 1952-56; asst. prof. U. Tex., 1956-59; vis. assoc. prof. Washington U., St. Louis, 1959; from assoc. prof. to prof. Mich. State U., 1959-64; Fulbright lectr. U. Dublin, 1962-63; prof. U. Calif.-Irvine, 1964-77, founding chmn. English dept., 1964-69; dean Sch. Humanities, 1970-72, vice chancellor acad. affairs, 1972-74; co-founder, co-dir. Sch. Criticism and Theory, 1975—77; sr. fellow, 1975-88; hon. sr. fellow, 1988—; prof. English and comparative lit. U. Wash., Seattle, 1977-97, Byron W. and Alice L. Lockwood prof. humanities, 1988-97, prof. emeritus, 1997—. Prof. English U. Calif., Irvine, 1990-94. Author: Poems by Robert Simeon Adams, 1952, Blake and Yeats: The Contrary Vision, 1955, 2d edit., 1969, The Contexts of Poetry, 1963, William Blake: A Reading of the Shorter Poems, 1963, Poetry: An Introductory Anthology, 1968, The Horses of Instruction, 1968, Fiction as Process, 1968, The Interests of Criticism, 1969, William Blake: Jerusalem, Selected Poems and Prose, 1970, The Truth About Dragons, 1971, Critical Theory Since Plato, 1971, 3d edit., 2005, Lady Gregory, 1973, The Academic Tribes, 1976, 2d edit., 1988, Philosophy of the Literary Symbolic, 1983, Joyce Cary's Trilogies, 1983, Critical Theory Since 1965, 1986, The Book of Yeats's Poems, 1991, Antithetical Essays, 1991, Critical Essays on William Blake, 1991, The Book of Yeats's Vision, 1995, The Farm at Richwood and Other Poems, 1997, Many Pretty Toys, 1999, Four Lectures on the History of Criticism in the West, 2000, Home, 2001, The Offense of Poetry, 2007, Academic Child: A Memoir, 2008; mem. editl. bd. Epoch, 1954—56, Tex. Studies Lit. and Lang., 1957—59, Studies in Romanticism, 1966—, Blake Studies, 1969—89, Modern Lang. Quar., 1977—84. Served to 1st lt. USMC, 1943-45, 51. Guggenheim fellow, 1974-75 Mem. Internat. Assn. Univ. Profs. English, Am. Conf. for Irish Studies, Phi Beta Kappa. Home: 3930 NE 157th Pl Lake Forest Park WA 98155-6730 Personal E-mail: HAdams3048@aol.com.

ADAMS, J. PHILLIP, oil industry executive; BA in Fin. and Acctg., Utah State U., 1978. With Brown and Davis, CPAs, 1978—80, Flying J. Airlines, Inc., Brigham City, Utah, 1980—, pres., CEO, 1992—. Office: Flying J Inc PO Box 150310 Ogden UT 84415-0310

ADAMS, JAMES FREDERICK, psychologist, academic administrator, educator; b. Andong, Korea, Dec. 27, 1927; s. Benjamin Nyce and Phyllis Irene (Taylor) A.; m. Carol Ann Wagner, Jan. 17, 1980; children— James Edward, Dorothy Lee Adams Vanderhorst, Robert Benjamin. BA In Psychology, U. Calif.-Berkeley, 1950; Ed.M. in Counseling and Psychology, Temple U., 1951; PhD in Exptl. Psychology, Wash. State U., 1959. Cert. psychologist, Wash., Pa.; lic. psychologist, Pa. Psychometrician Measurement and Research Ctr., Temple U., Phila., 1951-52; asst. prof. psychology Whitworth Coll., Spokane, Wash., 1952-55; teaching and research asst. State U. Wash., 1955-57; research assoc. Miami U., Oxford, Ohio, 1957-59; asst. prof. psychology Coll. Liberal Arts, Temple U., 1959-62, assoc. prof., 1962-66, prof., 1966-80, chmn. dept. counseling psychology, 1969-72; vis. prof. psychology Coll. Soc. Scis., U. P.R., Rio Piedras, 1963-64, Coll. Scis., Cath. U., Ponce, PR, 1971-72; chmn. dept. counseling psychology Coll. Edn., Temple U., 1973-77, coord. divsn. ednl. psychology, 1974-76; grad. dean, prof. psychology Grad. Coll., U. Nev., Las Vegas, 1980-85; acad. (sr.) v.p. Longwood Coll., Farmville, Va., 1985-86. Author: Problems in Counseling: A Case Study Approach, 1962, Instructors Manual for Understanding Adolescence, 1969; (exhbn. catalogue with J. D. Selig) Colonial Spanish Art of the Americas, 1976; (comml. pamphlet with C. L. Davis) The Use of the Vu-graph as an Instructional Aid, 1960; editor: Counseling and Guidance: A Summary View, 1965, Understanding Adolescence: Current Developments in Adolescent Psychology, 1968, 4th edit., 1980, Human Behavior in a Changing Society, 1973, Songs that had to be Sung (by B. N. Adams), 1979; contbr. chpts., articles, tests and book revs. to profl. publs. Donor James F. Adams Endowment Wash. State U., Pullman, 2003. Served to cpl. USMC, 1945—46. Recipient Alexander Meiklejohn award AAUP, 1984; James McKean Cattell Rsch. Fund grantee Miami U., Oxford, Ohio, 1958, Bolton Fund Rsch. grant Temple U., 1960, 62, Faculty Rsch. grant Temple U., 1961, 63, Commonwealth of Pa. Rsch. grant Temple U., 1969-72, Summer Rsch. fellow Temple U., 1979; U. Munich scholar, 1955; named James F. Adams scholarship U. Nev., Las Vegas. Fellow Am. Psychol. Assn. (divs. 26, 17); mem. Eastern Psychol. Assn., Western Psychol. Assn., Interam. Soc. Psychology, Sigma Xi, Psi Chi Avocation: Art collecting and restoring. Home: 130 Palacio Rd Corrales NM 87048-9648

ADAMS, JOHN M., library director; b. Chgo., June 10, 1950; s. Merlin J. and Esther (Bohn) A.; m. Nancy Ileen Coultas, June 12, 1970; 1 child, Arwen Lee BA in English, U. Ill., 1972, MLS, 1973. Grad. asst. U. Ill. Libr., Urbana, 1972-73; libr. reference Sherman Oaks Libr., LA, 1973-75; libr. philosophy dept. LA Pub. Libr., 1975-77, head gen. reading svc., 1977-78; dir. Moline Pub. Libr., Ill., 1978-83, Tampa-Hillsborough County Pub. Libr. Sys., Fla., 1983-91; dir., county libr. Orange County Pub. Libr., Calif., 1991—2007, dir.

emeritus Calif., 2007—. Dir. Tampa Bay Libr. Consortium, Fla., 1983-91, Santiago Libr. Sys., 1991—2007, chmn., 1999; mem. adv. com. on pub. librs. Online Computer Libr. Ctr., 1992-95; bd. govs. Am. Rsch. Ctr. in Egypt, 2003-06. Contbr. articles to profl. jours. Pres. Orange County chpt. Am. Rsch. Ctr. in Egypt, 2002—07; bd. dirs. Planned Parenthood Tampa, 1984. Recipient Frontier award ALA Mag., 1981; named Outstanding Young Man, Moline Jaycees, 1983. Mem. ALA (J.C. Dana award 1982, 93, 2004), Calif. Libr. Assn. (named Literacy Libr. of Yr. 2006), Calif. County Librs. Assn., Orange County C. of C. Avocations: music, tennis. Office: Orange County Pub Libr 1501 E Saint Andrew Pl Santa Ana CA 92705-4930 Office Phone: 714-566-3040. E-mail: jadams@irtc.net.

ADAMS, JOSEPH KEITH, lawyer; b. Provo, Utah, Apr. 3, 1949; s. Joseph S. and Marian (Bellows) A.; m. Myrle June Overly, Sept. 2, 1971; children: Derek J., Bret K., Stephanie, Julie K., Scott J., Laura. BA summa cum laude, Brigham Young U., 1973; JD, Harvard U., 1976. Bar: Utah 1976, U.S. Dist. Ct. Utah 1976, U.S. Tax Ct. 1983. Assoc. Van Cott, Bagley, Cornwall & McCarthy, Salt Lake City, 1976-82, shareholder, 1982-98; also bd. dirs. Van Cott, Bagley, et al, Salt Lake City, 1993-97, chmn. tax and estate planning sect., 1995-98; ptnr. Stoel, Rives, LLP, Salt Lake City, 1998—. Adj. faculty Brigham Young U. Law Sch., Provo, 1993. Co-author: Practical Estate Planning Techniques, 1990. Planned giving com. Restoration Cathedral Madeleine, Salt Lake City, 1991-93; pres. Utah Planned Giving Roundtable, Salt Lake City, 1994, Salt Lake City Estate Planning Coun.; planned giving com. U. Utah Hosp. Found., 1994; bd. dirs. Salt Lake C.C. Found., 1982-98; chair Salt Lake profl. adv. group LDS Philanthropies, mem. nat. planned giving com.; past stake pres. LDS Ch. David O. Mackay scholar Brigham Young U., 1967-73. Fellow Am. Coll. Trust and Estate Counsel; mem. ABA (real property, probate and trust sect.), Utah State Bar (past exec. com., past chmn. estate planning probate sect.), Harvard Alumni Assn. Utah (chair bd. dirs. 1980-90), Harvard Law Sch. Assn. Utah (vice chair). Republican. Mem. Lds Ch. Avocations: skiing, reading, golf. Office: Stoel Rives LLP 201 S Main St Ste 1100 Salt Lake City UT 84111-4904 Office Phone: 801-328-3131. Business E-Mail: jkadams@stoel.com.

ADAMS, KENNETH ROBERT, gaming analyst, writer, historian, consultant; b. Carson City, Nev., Sept. 8, 1942; s. Maurice Adams and Gertrude Aloha (Wilson) Burke; children: John Anthony, James Joseph. Prin. Ken Adams and Assoc., Sparks, Nev., 1990—. Coord. gaming history series of the oral history program U. Nev., continuing edns. gaming mgmt. program adv. com., 1988-97, chmn., 1988. Co-author: Playing the Cards That Are Dealt, 1992, Always Bet on the Butcher, 1994, War Stories, 1995, Dwayne Kling: Luck in the Residue of Design, 2001, Jeanne Hood: Whatever Will Help!, 2006; publ., assoc. editor: Nev. Gaming Almanac, 1991—, Nev. Gaming Directory, 1997—, The Adams Report. Chmn. mktg. com. Downtown Improvement Assn., 1994—, pres., 2001—; steering com., chmn. gaming com. Festival Reno, 1984-86; mem. adv. bd. Leadership Reno Alumni Assn., 1995-97. Mem. Internat. Platform Assn. Office: Ken Adams Ltd 210 Marsh Ave Ste 103 Reno NV 89509-1698 Office Phone: 775-322-7722. Personal E-mail: akenradams@aol.com.

ADAMS, KIRK, state legislator; b. Ariz. m. JaNae Adams; 6 children. BS in Bus. Adminstrn., U. Phoenix. Ptnr. The Adams Agy, Mesa, Apache Junction, Yuma; chmn. Dist. 19 Rep. Com., 2002—04; mem. Dist. 19 Ariz. House of Reps., 2006—, spkr. of the house, 2009—, mem. rules com. Mem. Maricopa Assn. Govt.'s Transp. Policy Rev. Bd. Bd. dirs. Mesa United Way, Maricopa County Indsl. Devel. Authority. Recipient Spirit of Mesa award, Mesa United Way, 2007, Courage for Children award, Ariz. Assn. Foster & Adoptive Parents, 2008, Freedom of Info. award, Ariz. Newspaper Assn., 2008; named Rep. of Yr., Ariz. C. of C. & Industry, 2007. Mem.: Nat. Fedn. Ind. Businesses (chair Ariz, leadership coun.). Republican. Office: Ariz House Reps Capitol Complex 1700 W Washington Rm 221 Phoenix AZ 85007 Office Phone: 602-926-5495. Office Fax: 602-417-3019. Business E-Mail: kadams@azleg.gov.*

ADAMS, LORETTA, marketing executive; b. Panama; BS in Internat. Mktg., Am. U., 1962; postgrad. in Econs., U. Panama, 1963-64. Mgmt. trainee Sears Roebuck & Co., Panama City, 1962-63, mgmt. pers., 1963-65; supr. internat. advertising projects Kenyon & Eckhardt Advertising, Inc., NYC, 1965-68; asst. rsch. dir. divsn. L.Am. and Far E. Richardson-Vicks Internat., Mexico City and Wilton, Conn., 1968-69, rsch. dir. divsn. Mex. and L.Am., 1969-75, mem. top mgmt. strategic planning team, 1975-78; founder, pres. Mkt. Devel., Inc., San Diego, 1978—. Contbr. articles to profl. jours. Mem. Am. Mktg. Assn., European Soc. for Opinion & Market Rsch., Advt. Rsch. Found., Coun. Am. Survey Rsch. Orgns., Market Rsch. Assn. Office: Market Devel Inc 600 B St Ste 1600 San Diego CA 92101-4584

ADAMS, MARK KILDEE, lawyer; b. Des Moines, Oct. 8, 1938; s. Walter Bunting and Regina (Kildee) A.; m. Helen von Bachmayr Larsen, May 22, 1982; 1 child, Kirsten. AB, Harvard U., 1960, JD, 1966. Bar: N.Mex. 1966, U.S. Dist. Ct. N.Mex. 1966, U.S. Ct. Appeals (10th cir.) 1970, U.S. Claims Ct., Zuni Pueblo Tribal Ct. Assoc. Rodey, Dickason, Sloan, Akin & Robb, Santa Fe, 1966-70, ptnr., 1970—, dir. Santa Fe office. Co-author: N. Mex. Environ. Law Handbook; author: Unitization of Solid Mineral Properties, 1982, Minimum Work Clauses in Mining Leases, 1976. Capt. U.S. Army, 1960-62. Mem. ABA, Albuquerque Bar Assn. (bd. dirs. 1976-78), Lawyers Club (officer 1980-84). Republican. Office: Rodey Dickason Sloan Akin & Robb PA 315 Paseo de Peralta Santa Fe NM 87501 Office Phone: 505-954-3903. Office Fax: 505-954-3942. Business E-Mail: mkadams@rodey.com.

ADAMS, SAM, Mayor, Portland, Oregon; b. Mont., 1963; BA in Political Sci., U. Oreg., 2002. Campaign mgr., chief of staff Mayor Vera Katz, Portland, Oreg., 1991—2003; commr. utilities Portland City Coun., 2004—08; mayor City of Portland, 2009—. Democrat. Achievements include first openly gay mayor of a major US city. Office: 1221 SW 4th Ave Rm 340 Portland OR 97204 Office Phone: 503-823-4120. E-mail: samadams@ci.portland.or.us.*

ADAMS, THOMAS MERRITT, lawyer; b. St. Louis, Sept. 27, 1935; s. Galen Edward and Chloe (Merritt) A.; m. Sarah McCardell Davis, June 6, 1959; children: Mark Merritt, John Harrison, William Shields, Thomas Bondurant. AB, Washington U., St. Louis, 1956, JD, 1960; postgrad., London Sch. Econs., 1957; LLM, George Washington U., 1966. Bar: Mo. 1960, Calif. 1971. Atty. SEC, Washington, 1964-66; asst. dir., asst. gen. counsel Investment Bankers Assn., Washington, 1966-68; pres. Transamerica Investment Mgmt., 1969-80; ptnr. Lanning Adams & Peterson, 1980—. Author: State and Local Pension Funds, 1968; contbr. articles to profl. jours. Chmn. Salina Cmty. Ambassador program, Kans., 1961. Served to capt. USAF, 1960-63. Decorated Air Force Commendation medal. Mem. Phi Beta Kappa. Episcopalian. Office: Lanning Adams & Peterson 11777 San Vicente Blvd #750 Los Angeles CA 90049-5067

ADAMS, WAYNE VERDUN, pediatric psychologist, educator; b. Rhinebeck, NY, Feb. 24, 1945; s. John Joseph and Lorena Pearl (Munroe) A.; m. Nora Lee Swindler, June 12, 1971; children: Jennifer, Elizabeth. BA, Houghton Coll., 1966; MA, Syracuse U., 1969, PhD, 1970; postgrad., U. NC, 1975. Diplomate Am. Bd. Profl. Psychology (hon.); lic. psychologist, NY, Oreg. Asst. prof. Colgate U., Hamilton, NY, 1970-75; chief psychologist Alfred I. DuPont Inst., Wilmington, Del., 1976-86; dir. divsn. psychology, dept. pediat. DuPont Hosp. for Children (formerly Alfred I. DuPont Inst.), Wilmington, 1987-99; mem. Del. Bd. Licensure in Psychology, 1983-86, bd. pres., 1986; assoc. prof. pediat. Thomas Jefferson Coll. Medicine, Phila., 1995-99; prof. psychology George Fox U., Newberg, Oreg., 1999—, chair grad. dept. clin. psychology, 2001—. Grant reviewer NIH, 1999—2006; vis. prof. Wuhan U., China, 2004, 06. Cons. editor Jour. Pediatric Psychology, 1980-83, guest reviewer, 1984—; co-author 5 nationally used psychol. tests in field; contbr. over 25 articles to profl. jours. Scholar, Fulbright Found., 2006—07. Fellow APA, Nat. Acad. Neuropsychology; mem. Soc. Pediatric Psychology, Del. Psychol. Assn. (exec. com. 1979-82, pres. 1981-82), Oreg. Psychol. Assn. Office: George Fox U Grad Dept Clin Psychology Box 6141 414 N Meridian St Newberg OR 97132-2697

ADAMS, WILLIAM B., chemical company executive; BA, Tex. Tech. U. CEO WBA Cons., Ltd., 1980-86; pres. and CEO Check Tech. Corp., 1986-88; exec. chmn. Printrak, Inc., 1989-91; chmn. bd. Chronimed, Inc., 1985-94; chmn. bd. and CEO Eco Soil Sys., Inc., San Diego, 1991—. Home: Eco Soil Systems PO Box 7740 Burbank CA 91510-7740

ADAMSON, ANDREW, film producer, film director, scriptwriter; b. Auckland, New Zealand, Dec. 1, 1966; 3 children. Computer animator The Mouse That Roared, Auckland, New Zealand, 1985—86; design dir., sr. animator Video Images Ltd., 1986—91; mem. Pacific Data Images, 1991. Tech. dir. (films) Toys, 1992, visual effects supr. Batman Forever, 1995, A Time to Kill, 1996, Batman & Robin, 1997, dir., voice Shrek, 2001 (Audience award, Karlovy Vary Internat. Film Festival, 2001, Best Feature Film, Brit. Acad. Film and TV Awards, 2001, Annie award, 2001), dir., writer, voice Shrek 2, 2004 (Hollywood Film award for Animation of Yr., 2004), exec. prodr., dir., writer The Chronicles of Narnia: The Lion, the Witch and the Wardrobe, 2005 (Camie award, Character and Morality in Entertainment Awards, 2006), exec. prodr., writer Shrek the Third, 2007, prodr., dir., writer The Chronicles of Narnia: Prince Caspian, 2008; exec. prodr.: (films) Ballast, 2008; dir.: Shrek in the Swamp Karaoke Dance Party, 2001. Recipient New Zealand Order of Merit, 2006; named one of 100 People in Hollywood You Need to Know, Fade Mag., 2005. Office: c/o United Talent Agy 9560 Wilshire Blvd Ste 500 Beverly Hills CA 90212

ADAMSON, GEOFFREY DAVID, reproductive endocrinologist, surgeon; b. Ottawa, Ont., Can., Sept. 16, 1946; came to U.S., 1978, naturalized, 1986; s. Geoffrey Peter Adamson and Anne Marian Allan; m. Rosemary C. Oddie, Apr. 28, 1973; children: Stephanie, Rebecca, Eric. BSc with honors, Trinity Coll., Toronto, Can., 1969; MD, U. Toronto, 1973. Diplomate Am. Bd. Ob-Gyn., Am. Bd. Laser Surgery; cert. Bd. Reproductive Endocrinology. Resident in ob-gyn. Toronto Gen. Hosp., 1973-77, fellow in ob-gyn., 1977-78; fellow reproductive endocrinology Stanford U. Med. Ctr., Calif., 1978-80; practice medicine specializing in infertility Los Gatos, Calif., 1980-84; instr. Stanford U. Sch. Medicine, 1980-84, clin. asst. prof. Calif., 1984-92, clin. assoc. prof., 1992—, clin. prof., 1995—; assoc. clin. prof. Sch. Medicine U. Calif., San Francisco, 1992—; founder, chmn., CEO Advanced Reproductive Care Inc., Palo Alto, Calif., 1997—. Tech. adviser WHO, 2003—. Editor: (textbook) Endoscopic Management of Gynecologic Disease, 1996, Modern Management of Endometriosis, 2005, Single Embryo Transfer, 2009; mem. editl. bd. Can. Doctor mag., 1977—83, Jour. Am. Assn. Gynecol. Laparoscopists, 1996—, Fertility and Sterility, 2000—03, mem. editl. adv. bd. Mid. East Fertility Soc., 2004—, mem. editl. bd. others; assoc. editor: Mid. E. Fertility Soc., 2004—. Recipient Spl. Congl. Recognition cert., US Congress, 2006; McLoughlin fellowship, Ont. Ministry of Health, 1977—78. Fellow ACS, Royal Coll. Surgeons Can., Am. Coll. Ob-Gyns.; mem. AAAS, AMA, Am. Assn. Gynecol. Laparoscopists (adv. bd., bd. trustees, sec., treas. 2002-03, v.p. 2003-04, exec. com. 2002-06, v.p. 2003-04, pres. 2004-05, past pres. 2005-06), Am. Soc. Reproductive Medicine (com. mem., bd. dirs. 1997-99, 2000-03, exec. com., 2002-04, v.p., 2005-06, pres. elect 2006-07, pres. 2007—08, past pres. 2008-09), Soc. Reproductive Endocrinologists (charter), Soc. Reproductive Surgeons (charter, bd. dirs., sec., treas., v.p., pres., past pres.), Soc. Assisted Reproductive Tech. (treas., dir., v.p., pres., past pres. bd. dirs. 1991-05), Nat. Coalition Oversight of Assisted Reproductive Technicians (vice-chair 2001-03, chair 2003-05), Internat. Com. Monitoring Assisted Reproductive Techs. (sec.-treas. 2005-), Internat. Fedn. Fertility Socs. (audit com. 2001—, bd. dirs. 2007—), Pacific Coast Reproductive Soc. (dir., sec., v.p., pres., past pres., bd. dir. 1991-2001), Pacific NW Ob-Gyn Soc. (hon. life), Pacific Coast Ob-Gyn. Soc., Soc. Gynecologic Surgeons, San Francisco Gynecol. Soc. (past pres.), Soc. for Gynecologic Investigation, Bay Area Reproductive Endocrinologists Soc. (founding pres., hon. life), Gynecol. Laser Soc., N.Y. Acad. Scis., Shufelt Gynecol. Soc., Peninsula Gynecol. Soc. (past pres.), World Endometriosis Rsch. Found. (founding bd. mem. 2005-), Calif. Med. Assn., San Mateo County Med. Assn., Santa Clara County Med. Assn. (Outstanding Achievement in Medicine award 2006), Am. Fedn. Clin. Rsch., Nat. Resolve (bd. dirs. 1991-01, sec., treas., Lifetime Svc. award 1999), Can. Assn. Interns and Residents (hon. life, pres. 1977-79, bd. dirs. 1974-79, rep. AMA resident physician sect. 1978-79, rep. Can. Med. Protective Assn. 1975-78, rep. Can. Med. Assn. 1975-78, Disting. Svc. award 1980), Profl. Assn. Interns and Residents Ont. (bd. dirs. 1973-76, v.p. 1974-75, pres. 1975-76), Royal Coll. Physicians and Surgeons Can. (com. exams. 1977-80), Ont. Med. Assn. (sec. interns and residents sect. 1973-74). Avocations: hiking, ice hockey, skiing. Office: 540 University Ave Ste 200 Palo Alto CA 94301-1929

ADAMSON, JOHN WILLIAM, hematologist; b. Oakland, Calif., Dec. 28, 1936; s. John William and Florence Jean Adamson; m. Susan Elizabeth Wood, June 16, 1960; children: Cairn Elizabeth, Loch Rachael; m. Christine Fenyvest, Sept. 1, 1989. BA, U. Calif., Berkeley, 1958; MD, UCLA, 1962. Cert. Am. Bd. Internal Medicine, 1970. Intern, resident in medicine U. Wash. Med. Ctr., Seattle, 1962-64, clin. and rsch. fellow hematology, 1964-67, faculty, 1969-90, prof. hematology, 1978-90, head divsn. hematology, 1981-89; pres. NY Blood Ctr., NYC, 1989-97; dir. Lindsley F. Kimball Rsch. Inst., NYC, 1989-98; exec. v.p. rsch., dir. Blood Rsch. Inst./Blood Ctr.Southeastern Wis., Milw., 1998—2007; prof., head, divsn. hematology Med. Coll. Wis.; clin. prof. medicine U. Calif. San Diego, 2007—. Josiah Macy Jr. Found. scholar, vis. scientist Nuffield dept. clin. medicine, U. Oxford, Eng., faculty medicine, 1976-77. Author papers in field, chpts. in books. With USPHS, 1967-69. Recipient Rsch. Career Devel. award NIH, 1972-77, Rsch. grant, 1976-95. Fellow AAAS; mem. Am. Soc. Hematology (pres. 1995-96), Soc. for the Advancement of Blood Mgmt. (pres. 2005-07), Assn. Am. Physicians, Am. Soc. Clin. Investigation, Western Assn. Physicians. Office: Moores UCSD Cancer Ctr 3855 Health Sciences Dr La Jolla CA 92093 also: UCSD Dept Medicine 9111-E 9500 Gilman Dr La Jolla CA 92093-9111 Office Phone: 858-822-6276. Office Fax: 858-822-6288. E-mail: jadamson@ucsd.edu.

ADCOCK, COREY J., construction executive; CFO American West Homes, Las Vegas, Nev., 1996—. Office: Ste 140 250 Pilot Rd Las Vegas NV 89119-3543

ADDICOTT, FREDRICK TAYLOR, botanist; b. Oakland, Calif., Nov. 16, 1912; s. James Edwin and Ottilia Katherine Elizabeth (Klein) A.; m. Alice Holmes Baldwin, Aug. 11, 1935; children: Donald James, Jean Alice, John Fredrick, David Baldwin. AB in Biology, Stanford U., 1934; PhD in Plant Physiology, Calif. Inst. Tech., 1939. Instr. to asst. prof. Santa Barbara (Calif.) State Coll., 1939-46; assoc. physiologist emergency rubber project USDA, Salinas, Calif., 1942-44; asst. prof. to prof. UCLA, 1946-60; prof. agronomy U. Calif., Davis, 1961-72, prof. botany, 1972-77, prof. emeritus, 1977—. Vis. prof. U. Adelaide, Australia, 1966, U. Natal, Pietermaritzburg, Republic South Africa, 1970. Author: Abscission, 1982; editor, author: Abscisic Acid, 1983; contbr. over 88 articles to profl. jours. Fulbright rsch. scholar Victoria U., N.Z., 1957, Royal Bot. Garden, U.K., 1976; vis. fellow Australian Nat. U., 1983. Fellow AAAS; mem. Am. Soc. Plant Physiologists (Charles Reid Barnes Life Membership award 1990), Australian Soc. Plant Physiologists, Bot. Soc. Am., Internat. Plant Growth Substance Assn., Internat. Soc. Plant Morphologists, South African Assn. Botanists. Avocations: backpacking, cabinet making. Office: UC Davis Dept Plant Biology 1002 Life Sciences Addition Davis CA 95616

ADDIS, ILANA BETH, obstetrician; b. 1971; BA, U. Chgo., 1992; MPH, U. Calif., 1996; MD, U. Ariz. Coll. Medicine, 1998. Cert. Obsterics and Gynecology. Assoc. dir. Divsn. Female Pelvic Medicine & Recovery Surgery; asst. prof., Obstetrics & Gynecology U. Ariz. Coll. Medicine. Mem. Planned Parenthood of Southern Ariz., Southern Ariz. Human Soc., Big Brothers/Big Sisters; vol. Shubitz refugee clinic. Named one of 40 Under 40, Tucson Bus. Edge, 2006; fellow Am. Coll. Obstetrics and Gynecology; women's health clinical rsch. fellowship, U. Calif. Mem.: Nat. Physicians Alliance, Am. Urogynecologic Assn. Office: University of Arizona College of Medicine PO Box 245017 1501 N Campbell Ave Tucson AZ 85724

ADDIS, THOMAS HOMER, III, professional golfer; b. San Diego, Nov. 30, 1945; s. Thomas H. and Martha J. (Edwards) A.; m. Susan Tera Buckley, June 13, 1966; children: Thomas Homer IV, Bryan Michael. Student, Foothill Jr. Coll., 1963, Grossmont Jr. Coll., 1965; degree in profl. golf mgmt. (hon.), Ferris State U., 1995. Head golf profl., mgr. Sun Valley Golf Course, La Mesa, Calif., 1966-67; head golf profl., dir. golf Singing Hills Country Club and Lodge, 1969-98; sr. v.p. Golfstar Mgmt., 1998-99; v.p. Full Swing Golf, San Diego, 1999-2000; pres. Medallion Golf Inc., 2000—06; exec. dir., CEO So. Calif. PGA, 2006—. Gen. chmn. Nat. Jr. Golf Championship, U.S. Golf Assn., 1973-89; cons. Nat. Golf Found. Far East, 1978-; pres. Nat. Golf Corp., 2001-; owner Rocky Mountain Chocolate Factory, Mammoth; spkr. in field; instr. Profl. Golfers Career Coll., 1999-2006. Contbr. articles to profl. jours. Dir. Cuyamaca Coll. Found., Burn Inst.Prokids Golf; mem. internat. golf com. Spl. Olympics. Mem. PGA (pres. San Diego chpt. 1978-79, pres. sect. 1980-82, pres. PGA Am. 1994-96, named Profl. of Yr. So. Calif. sect. 1979, 89, Horton Smith award So. Calif. sect. 1980-81, 89, PGA Golf Profl. of Yr. 1989, Nat. Horton Smith award 1981, nat. bd. dirs. 1986-88, rules com. 1986-90, championship com. 1986—, hon. life mem. So. Calif. sect. and San Diego PGA,), So. Calif. PGA Hall of Fame, PGA Golf Profl. hall of Fame, Nat. Golf Found. (Joe Graffis award 1988), Nat. Amputee Golf Assn. (hon.), San Diego Jr. Golf Assn. (pres. 1997-98, 2000-2003), Golf Collectors Soc. Office: Mammoth Chocolate & Confections 1115 Silverleaf Canyon Rd Beaumont CA 92223-8609 Office Phone: 858-775-7421. Personal E-mail: medalliongolf@aol.com.

ADDY, JO ALISON PHEARS, economist; b. Germany, May 2, 1951; d. William Phears and Paula Hubbard; m. Tralance Obuma Addy, May 25, 1979; children: Mantse, Miishe, Dwetri, Naakai. BA, Smith Coll., 1973; MBA, Adelphi U., 1975; postgrad., Stanford U., 1975—79; MPA, Harvard U., 2006. Econ. analyst Morgan Guaranty, NYC, 1973—75; economist Young Profls. Program, World Bank, Washington, 1979—80; asst. v.p., internat. economist Crocker Bank, San Francisco, 1980—85; asst. v.p., economist for money markets 1st RepublicBank, Dallas, 1985—87; prin. SEGI Internat., Dallas, 1987—91; pres. Unimed Ventures, Inc., 1991—95; mng. dir. Alsweb Bus. Advantage, 2000—; mem. adv. bd. Plebys Internat. LLC, 2003—. Lectr. in field. Docent Bowers Mus.; vice chmn. St. John's Sch. Com.; pres. Saddleback Valley chpt. Nat. Charity League. Office: 8 Palomino Trabuco Canyon CA 92679-4837 Business E-Mail: jo.addy@gmail.com.

ADELL, HIRSCH, lawyer; arrived in US, 1937; s. Nathan and Nachama (Wager) A.; m. Judith Audrey Fuss, Feb. 8, 1963; children—Jeremiah, Nikolas, Balthasar, Valentine. Student, CCNY, 1949—52; BA, UCLA, 1955, LLB, 1963. Bar: Calif. 1963. Adminstrv. asst. to State Senator Richard Richards, 1956-60; ptnr. Warren & Adell, LA, 1963-75, Reich, Adell & Cvitan (and predecessor firm), LA, 1975—. Gen. counsel Ctrl. Valley Trust, 2003—. Served with AUS, 1953-55. Mem. ABA (labor and employment law sect.) Home: 545 S Norton Ave Los Angeles CA 90020-4610 Office: Reich Adell & Cvitan 3550 Wilshire Blvd Ste 2000 Los Angeles CA 90010-2421 Home Phone: 213-384-1295; Office Phone: 213-386-3860. Business E-Mail: hirscha@rac-law.com.

ADELMAN, ANDREW A., city manager; 2 children. BS in Civil Engring., U. Calif., Berkeley, BS in Nuc. Engring., MS in Structural Engring.; cert. in mgmt., Harvard U. Registered profl. engr., Calif., Ariz., Nev. Engr. Impel Corp. and Quadrex Corp., San Francisco, 1979-81; lead engr. Cygna Corp., San Francisco, 1981-83; chief engr. Panel Clip/Lumberlok, Hayward, Calif., 1983-84; plans and permit divsn. mgr., chief plan check engr. City of Fremont, Calif., 1984-92; chief bldg. offcl., dep. dir. Dept. Planning Bldg. and Code Enforcement, City of San Jose, Calif., 1992-97; gen. mgr. dept. bldg. and safety City of L.A., 1997—. Adj. prof. engring. Saginaw Valley State Coll., Mich., 1982. Commr. Calif. Seismic Safety Commn., Calif. Hosp. Bldg. Safety Bd. Recipient numerous awards. Mem. Tau Beta Pi, Chi Epsilon, Delta Chi. Office: City LA Bldg & Safety Dept 201 N Figueroa St Rm 1000 Los Angeles CA 90012-2623 Office Phone: 213-482-6800.

ADELMAN, IRMA GLICMAN, economics professor; b. Cernowitz, Rumania, Mar. 14, 1930; came to U.S., 1949, naturalized, 1955; d. Jacob Max and Raissa (Ettinger) Glicman; m. Frank L. Adelman, Aug. 16, 1950 (div. 1979); 1 son, Alexander. BS, U. Calif., Berkeley, 1950, MA, 1951, PhD, 1955. Teaching assoc. U. Calif., Berkeley, 1955-56, instr., 1956-57, lectr. with rank asst. prof., 1957-58; vis. asst. prof. Mills Coll., 1958-59; acting asst. prof. Stanford, 1959-61, asst. prof., 1961-62; assoc. prof. Johns Hopkins, Balt., 1962-65; prof. econs. Northwestern U., Evanston, Ill., 1966-72, U. Md., 1972-78; prof. econs. and agrl. econs. U. Calif. at Berkeley, 1979-94; prof. emeritus, 1994—. Cons. divsn. indsl. devel. UN, 1962-63, AID U.S. Dept. State, Washington, 1963-72, World Bank, 1968—, ILD, Geneva, 1973—. Author: Theories of Economic Growth and Development, 1961, (with A. Pepelasis and L. Mears), Economic Development: Analysis and Case Studies, 1961, (with Eric Thorbecke) The Theory and Design of Economic Development, 1966, (with C.T. Morris) Society, Politics and Economic Development— A Quantitative Approach, 1967, Practical Approaches to Development Planning-Korea's Second Five Year Plan, 1969, (with C.T. Morris) Economic Development and Social Equity in Developing Countries, 1973, (with Sherman Robinson) Planning for Income Distribution, 1977-78, (with C. T. Morris) Comparative Patterns of Economic Growth, 1850-1914, 1987, (J. Edward Taylor) Village Economies: Design, Estimation and Application of Village Wide Economic Models, 1996, Institutions and Development Strategies: Selected Essays of Irma Adelman Vol. I, 1994, Vol. II, 1994. Decorated Order of the Bronze Tower (Korea); fellow Ctr. Advanced Study Behavioral Scis., 1970-71; named Women's Hall Fame U. Calif., Berkeley, 1994. Fellow Am. Acad. Arts and Scis., Econometric Soc., Royal Soc. Encouragement Arts, Mfg. and Commerce (Berkeley citation 1996); mem. Am. Econ. Assn. (mem. exec. com., v.p. 1969-71). Office: Univ Calif Dept Agr & Natural Resources 207 Giannini Hall Spc 3310 Berkeley CA 94720-3310

ADELMAN, MARC D., lawyer; b. 1950; BA, Western Ill. U.; JD, Western State U. Bar: Calif. 1978. Pvt. practice, San Diego. Mem. ABA, Calif. State Bar Assn. (pres.). Office: Ste 700 600 W Broadway San Diego CA 92101-3370

ADELMAN, RODNEY LEE, federal agency administrator; b. Washington, Sept. 21, 1950; s. Charles H. and Vivian Fern (Sleek) A.; widowed; 1 child. BS, U. Md., 1972. Staff Senator Robert P. Griffin, Mich., 1970-73; fin. mgr. labor mgmt. svcs. adminstrn. Dept. of Labor, 1973-78; budget officer Congress of Micronesia, 1978-79, Federated States Micronesia, 1979-80; dir. budget and grants mgmt. Trust Territory of the Pacific Islands, 1980-85; comptroller Def. Personnel Support Ctr. Def. Logistics Agy., 1985-86; dir. Washington Liaison Office, Juneau, Alaska, 1986-92; dep. asst. adminstr. Power Mktg. Liaison Office, 1992-96; Alaska power adminstr. Dept. of Energy, Juneau, 1996-99; CFO Internat. Boundary and Water Commn., El Paso, Tex.

ADELSMAN, JEAN (HARRIETTE ADELSMAN), newspaper editor; b. Indpls., Oct. 21, 1944; d. Joe and Beatrice Irene (Samuel) A. BS in Journalism, Northwestern U., 1966, MS in Journalism, 1967. Copy editor Chgo. Sun-Times, 1967-75, fin. news editor, 1975-77, entertainment editor, 1977-80, asst. mng. editor features, 1980-84; now mng. editor Daily Breeze, Torrance, Calif. Office: Daily Breeze 5215 Torrance Blvd Torrance CA 90503-4077

ADELSON, JAY STEVEN, Internet company executive; b. Sept. 7, 1970; BS in Comm., Boston Univ. Head, network ops. Netcom, 1993—96; founder Equinix; co-founder, ops. mgr., Palo Alto Internet Exchange Digital Equipment Corp., 1996—2003; co-founder, CEO Digg, 2004—; co-founder, chmn. Revision3 Corp., 2005—. Named one of 50 Who Matter Now, Business 2.0, 2007, The 100 Most Influential People in the World, TIME mag., 2008. Office: Digg Inc 3rd Fl 135 Mississippi St San Francisco CA 94107 Office Phone: 415-436-9638.

ADELSON, SHELDON GARY, hotel and gaming company executive; b. Dorchester, Mass., Aug. 4, 1933; m. Miriam Ochshorn, 1991; children: Adam Arthur, Matan Sarel. Student, CCNY. Paperboy; mortgage broker; investment adv.; fin. cons.; chmn., CEO Interface Group Inc., Needham, Mass., 1974; chmn., CEO, treas. Las Vegas Sands, Inc., 1989—; chmn., CEO Las Vegas Sands Corp., 2004—; founder COMDEX Trade Shows, 1991—95, Sands Expo & Convention Ctr., 1990—, Venetian Resort-Hotel-Casino, 1991—, Sands Macau, 2004—, Venetian Macau, 2007—, The Palazzo Resort Hotel Casino, 2008—. Guest spkr. U. New Haven, Harvard Bus. Sch., Columbia Bus. Sch., Tel Aviv U., Babson Coll. Mem., US Holocaust Meml. Coun. US Holocaust Meml. Mus., Washington. Named one of Forbes Richest Americans, 2006, World's Richest People, Forbes Mag., 2005, 2007, 2008, 25 Most Influential Republicans, Newsmax Mag., 2008. Jewish. Office: Venetian Resort Hotel Casino 3355 Las Vegas Blvd S Las Vegas NV 89109 Office Phone: 702-414-1000. Office Fax: 702-414-4884.

ADELSTONE, JEFFREY ALAN, accountant, tax law specialist, educator; b. LA, Feb. 15, 1947; s. James and Joyce S. (Waldman) Adelstone; m. E. Ruth Wilcox, Apr. 6, 1968; children: Kimberley, Stacey, Toni. BS, U. Ariz., 1969, MEd, 1971. CFP; cert. jr. coll. instr. Ariz., instr. Ariz. Dept. Real Estate, accredited Accreditation Coun. Accountancy, enrolled to practice IRS. Tchr. Tucson H.S., 1969—72; instr. Pima C.C., 1970—78; pres., owner Adelstone Fin. Svcs., Inc., Tucson, 1970—. Contbr. articles to profl. jours. Active Rep. Task Force. Named Nat. Acct. of Yr., 85, Ariz. Acct. Advocate of Yr., SBA, 1988. Mem.: Ctrl. Ariz. Soc. Enrolled Agts. (bd. dirs.), Internat. Assn. Fin. Planners, Inst. Cert. Fin. Planners, Registry Fin. Planning Practitioners, Nat. Fedn. Ind. Bus. (state dir. for Ariz. 1983—84), Tucson BBB, Ariz. C. of C., U.S. C. of C., Enrolled Agts. Practicing in Ariz. (state pres. 1987—88), Ariz. Soc. Practicing Accts. (state v.p. 1983—84, state pres. 1984—86, dir. cretid union, pres. Tucson chpt.), Nat. Assn. Enrolled Agts., Nat. Soc. Pub. Accts. (state dir. 1987—, mem. fed. taxation com.). Office: Adelstone Fin Svcs Inc 1580 N Kolb Rd Ste 1W Tucson AZ 85715-4931

ADIZES, ICHAK, management consultant, writer; PhD, Columbia U. Prof. Hebrew U., Jerusalem, Tel Aviv U., Stanford (Calif.) U., Columbia U., NYC, UCLA; founder, profl. dir. Adizes Inst., Santa Barbara, Calif., 1975—; acad. dean Adizes Grad. Sch. for Study of Change and Leadership, Santa Barbara, Calif. Lectr. in field. Author: Self-Management, 1975, How to Solve the Mismanagement Crisis, 1979, Corporate Lifecycles: How and Why Corporations Grow and Die and What to Do About It, 1988, Mastering Change; The power of Mutual Trust and Respect in Personal Life, Business and Society, 1992, The Pursuit of Prime, 1996, Managing Corporate Life Cycles, 1999, The Ideal Executive: Why You Cannot Be One and What to Do About It, 2004, Management/Mismanagement Styles: How to Identify A Style and What to Do About It, 2004, Leading the Leaders: How to Enrich Your Style of Management and Handle People Whose Style Is Different From Yours, 2004; contbr. articles to profl. jours., newspapers. Office: Adizes Inst 6404 Via Real Carpinteria CA 93013-1611 Office Phone: 805-565-2901. Fax: (805) 565-0741. E-mail: ichak@adizes.com.

ADKERSON, RICHARD C., mining executive; BA with honors, Miss. State U., 1969, MBA, 1970. Prof. acctg. fellow SEC, Washington, 1976-78; ptnr., mng. dir., head worldwide oil and gas practice Arthur Anderson & Co.; fin. mgmt. positions with Freeport-McMoRan Copper & Gold, New Orleans, 1989—92, CFO, 1992—97, pres., COO, CFO, 1997—2000, pres., CFO, 2000—03, pres., CEO Phoenix, 2003—07, CEO, 2007—; co-chmn. McMoRan Exploration Co. Trustee Nat. D-Day Mus.; v.p., bd. dir., mem. exec. com. Miss. State Univ. Found.; mem. adv. bd. Coll. Bus. & Ind. & Agribus. Inst., Miss. State Univ.; mem. Bus. Council New Orleans & River Region; mem. develop. bd. Fellowship Christian Athletes New Orleans; mem. exec. bd. adv. Ourso Coll., La. State Univ.; mem. Pres. Council Xavier Univ.; mem. bd. vis. M.D. Anderson Cancer Ctr.; mem. adv. bd. Crosby Arboretum. Office: Freeport McMoRan Copper & Gold Inc 1 N Ctrl Ave Phoenix AZ 85004

ADKINS, JEANNE M., state agency administrator; b. North Platte, Nebr., May 2, 1949; BA, U. Nebr. Journalist; mem. Colo. Ho. of Reps., 1988—99, chairwoman judiciary com., vice-chairwoman legal svcs. com., mem. fin. com., regional air quality control coun., state edn. accountability commn.; dir. policy and planning Colo. Dept. Edn.; dir. Colo. Student Loan Program, 2002—. Founding sec. Douglas County Econ. Devel. Coun., bd. dirs., 1988. Fellow Vanderbilt U. Govt., Gates fellow JFK Sch. Govt. State/Local Program, Toll fellow. Mem. Am. Soc. Newspaper Editors, Soc. Profl. Journalists, Suburban Newspaper Assn. Republican. Baptist. Office: CSLP 999 18th St Ste 425 Denver CO 80202

ADKINSON, THEODORE H., lawyer; b. Newport Beach, Calif., Apr. 2, 1968; BA, Colgate Univ., 1990; JD cum laude, Pepperdine Univ., 1993. Bar: Calif. 1993. Assoc., bus. environ. & marine litigation Keesal, Young & Logan, Long Beach, Calif., 2000—. Named a Rising Star, So. Calif. Super Lawyers, 2006. Mem.: LA County Bar Assn. (mem. exec. bd., internat. sect.), Long Beach Maritime Bar Assn. Office: Keesal Young & Logan PO Box 1730 400 Oceangate Long Beach CA 90801-1730 Office Phone: 562-436-2000. Office Fax: 562-436-7416. Business E-Mail: ted.adkinson@kyl.com.

ADLEMAN, LEONARD M., computer scientist, educator; b. San Francisco, Dec. 31, 1945; m. Lori Bruce, 1983; 3 children. BS, U. Calif., Berkeley, 1968; PhD in Computer Sci., U. Calif., 1976. Instr. math. MIT, Cambridge, 1976—77, asst. prof. math., 1977—79, assoc. prof. math., 1979—80; assoc. prof. U. So. Calif., LA, 1980—83, prof., 1983—85, Henry Salvatori prof. computer sci., 1985—. Asst. prof. math. RSA Data Security, 1983—. Recipient Koji Kobayashi Computers and Comm. award, IEEE, 2000, ACM Turing award, 2003, ACM Paris Kanallakis award, 1996, Alexander von Humboldt Fellowship and Disting. Alumnus award, 1995. Mem. NAE, NAS; fellow Am. Acad. Arts & Sciences Office: U So Calif Dept Computer Sci 941 West 37th Place Los Angeles CA 90089-0781 E-mail: adleman@usc.edu.

ADLER, ERWIN ELLERY, lawyer; b. Flint, Mich., July 22, 1941; s. Ben and Helen M. (Schwartz) A.; m. Stephanie Ruskin, June 8, 1967; children: Lauren, Michael, Jonathan BA, U. Mich., 1963, LL.M., 1967; JD, Harvard U., 1966. Bar: Mich. 1966, Calif. 1967. Assoc. Pillsbury, Madison & Sutro, San Francisco, 1967-73; assoc. Lawler, Felix & Hall, LA, 1973-76, ptnr., 1977-80, Rogers & Wells, LA, 1981-83, Richards, Watson & Gershon, LA, 1983—. Bd. dirs. Hollywood Civic Opera Assn., 1975-76, Children's Scholarships Inc., 1979-80 Mem. ABA (vice chmn. appellate advocacy com. 1982-87), Calif. Bar Assn., Phi Beta Kappa, Phi Kappa Phi. Jewish. Office: Adler Law Group 350 S Figueroa St Ste 557 Los Angeles CA 90071

ADLER, FRED PETER, retired electronics company executive; b. Vienna, Mar. 29, 1925; came to U.S., 1942, naturalized, 1947; s. Michael and Ellida (Bronner) A.; m. Alicia Gulkis, 1950; children: Michael Steven, Andrew David; m. Adrienne Wilcox, 1991. BSEE with honors, U. Calif., Berkeley, 1945; MSEE (Charles A. Coffin fellow), Calif. Inst. Tech., 1948, PhD magna cum laude, 1950. Elec. engr. GE Rsch. and Cons. Labs., 1945-47; project engr. Jet Propulsion Lab., 1950; with Hughes Aircraft Co., 1950-70, sr. staff physicist, dept. mgr., 1954-57, mgr. advanced planning, 1957-59, dir. advanced projects labs., 1959-61, v.p., mgr. space systems div., 1961-66, v.p., asst. group exec. Aerospace Group, 1966-70; pres. Nadgeco Ltd., 1970—73, chmn. bd., 1973-77; v.p., group exec. aerospace groups Hughes Aircraft Co., 1973-81, sr. v.p., pres. electro-optical and data sys. group, 1981-87; dir. Jefferson Ctr. for Character Edn., Monrovia, Calif., 1973-99, chmn. bd., 1988-99; ret., 1999. Co-author: text Guided Missile Engineering, 1959; also articles tech. jours. Fellow AIAA; mem. N.Y. Acad. Scis., Sigma Xi, Tau Beta Pi. Home: 10795 Woodbine St Apt 208 Los Angeles CA 90034 Personal E-mail: fredadler06@ca.rr.com, fredpeter12@yahoo.com.

ADLER, JEFFREY D., media consultant, management consultant; b. Cleve., July 10, 1952; s. Bennett and Edythe Joy (Eisner) A.; m. Colleen Ann Bentley, May 29, 1983 (div. 2006). BS in Journalism, Northwestern U., 1975. Porter, waiter, bartender Amtrak, Chgo., 1975-76; reporter Enterprise-Courier, Oregon City, Oreg., 1977, Las Vegas Sun, 1977-80, O.C. Daily Pilot, Costa Mesa, Calif., 1982-85; v.p. pub. affairs Englander Comm., Newport Beach, Calif., 1985-86; pres. Adler Wilson Campaign Svcs., Laguna Hills, Calif., 1990-95, Adler Pub. Affairs, Long Beach, Calif., 1987—. Chair bd. dirs. Pacific Pub. Radio (KKJZ-FM), Long Beach, 2002—06. Mem. Am. Assn. Polit. Cons. Democrat. Jewish. Office: Adler Pub Affairs 200 Pine Ave Ste 300 Long Beach CA 90802-3038 Home: 1995 Molino Ave #202 Signal Hill CA 90755 Office Phone: 562-435-5551. Business E-Mail: jeffadler@adlerpa.com.

ADLER, KENNETH GORDON, physician; s. Arnold and Carole Adler; m. Katherine Ann Schuppert, Mar. 3, 1990; children: Jenna, Maya. BS in Psychology, Duke U., Durham, NC, 1979; MD, U. Pa., Phila., 1983; M in Med. Mgmt., Tulane U., New Orleans, 2000; cert. in healthcare info. tech., U. Conn., 2005; student AMIA 10/10 Program, Oreg. Health Scis. U., 2006. Cert. in family medicine Am. Bd. Med. Specialties, 1986, profl. in healthcare info. sys. Healthcare Info. and Mgmt. Sys. Soc., 2008. Intern, resident Med. U. SC, 1983—86; physician Ariz. Cmty. Physicians, Tucson, 1998—, med. dir. info. tech., 2005—. Contbr. numerous articles to profl. jours. Office: Desert Star Family Health 5300 E Erickson Ste 108 Tucson AZ 85712 Office Fax: 520-547-5743.

ADLER, LOUISE DECARL, judge; b. 1945; BA, Chatham Coll., Pitts.; JD, Loyola U., Chgo. Bar: Ill., 1970, Calif., 1972. Practicing atty., San Diego, 1972-84; standing trustee Bankruptcy Ct. So. Dist. Calif., San Diego, 1974-79, chief bankruptcy judge, 1996—2001. Mem. editorial bd. Calif. Bankruptcy Jour., 1991-92. Fellow Am. Coll. Bankruptcy; mem. San Diego County Bar Assn. (chair bus. law study sect. 1979, fed. ct. com. 1983-84), Lawyers Club of San Diego (bd. dirs. 1972-73, treas. 1972-75, sec. 1972-74, v.p. 1974-75), San Diego Bankruptcy Forum (bd. dirs. 1989-92), Nat. Conf. Bankruptcy Judges (bd. dirs. 1989-91, sec. 1992-93, v.p. 1993-94, pres. 1994-95). Office: US Bankruptcy Ct 325 W F St Rm 2 San Diego CA 92101-6017 Office Phone: 619-557-5661.

ADLER, MICHAEL I., lawyer; b. San Francisco, May 10, 1949; BA in Polit. Sci. summa cum laude, UCLA, 1971, JD, 1976; MA, Columbia U., 1973. Bar: Calif. 1977. Extern to Hon. Matthew O. Tobriner Calif. Supreme Ct., 1975; law clerk to Hon. William B. Enright U.S. Dist. Ct. (so. dist.) Calif., 1976-77; mem. mitzlell Solberbery & Knubb, LA, 1977—97; ptnr. Lichter, Grossman, Nichols & Adler, Inc., LA, 1997—. Mem. entertainment law symposium com. UCLA, 1979—; instr. UCLA Extension, 1980. Woodrow Wilson fellow, 1972; Columbia U. Presdl. fellow, 1973. Mem. ABA, State Bar Calif., L.A. County Bar Assn., Beverly Hills Bar Assn., Phi Beta Kappa, Phi Eta Sigma. Office: Lichter Grossman Nichols & Adler Inc 9200 W Sunset Blvd Ph 1200 Los Angeles CA 90069-3607 E-mail: madler@lgna.com.

ADLER, ROBERT L., lawyer, utilities executive; b. NYC, Nov. 14, 1947; m. Sara M. Adler; 2 children. AB magna cum laude, Harvard U., 1969, JD cum laude, 1973. Bar: Calif. 1974. Exec. asst. Orange County Bd. Suprs., 1970-71; legis. asst. to mem. congress, 1973-74; pres., CEO Ray Wilson Co., 1985; mem. Munger, Tolles & Olson, LA, 1975—78, ptnr., 1978—2008; exec. v.p., gen. counsel Edison Internat., Rosemead, Calif., 2008—. Articles editor Harvard Law Rev., 1972-73. Mem. ABA, State Bar Calif., L.A. County Bar Assn., Phi Beta Kappa. Office: Edison Internat 2244 Walnut Grove Ave Rosemead CA 91770-3714

ADREANI, MICHAEL B., lawyer; b. Nashua, NH, Nov. 23, 1969; BA, Univ. Calif., Berkeley, 1993; JD, Northeastern Univ., 1997. Bar: Calif. 1998, US Dist. Ct. Ctrl., No., Ea., So. Calif. Assoc. to ptnr., bus. & comml. litigation Roxborough, Pomerance & Nye LLP, Woodland Hills, Calif., 1997—. Contbr. articles to profl. jours. Named a Rising Star, So. Calif. Super Lawyers, 2006. Mem.: ABA, LA County Bar Assn., Italian-Am. Bar Assn., Risk & Ins. Mgmt. Soc. Office: Roxborough Pomerance & Nye Ste 250 5820 Canoga Ave Woodland Hills CA 91367 Office Phone: 818-992-9999. Office Fax: 818-992-9991. Business E-Mail: mba@rpnlaw.com.

AEHLERT, BARBARA JUNE, health facility administrator; b. San Antonio, June 17, 1956; d. Bobby Ray and Ronella Su (Light) Mahoney; m. Dean A. Aehlert, Sept. 6, 1980; children: Andrea, Sherri. AA in Nursing, Glendale CC, Ariz., 1976; BS in Profl. Arts, St. Joseph's Coll., Windham, Maine, 1997. Cert. ACLS instr., BLS and PALS instr., emergency med. tng./paramedic instr. Gen. mgr. Hosp. Ambulance Svc., Phoenix, 1982-83; critical care nurse Samaritan Health Svcs., Phoenix, 1978-80, coord. patient transp., 1980-82, mgr. clin. programs, 1983-92; dir. emergency med. svcs. edn. EMS Edn. and Rsch., 1992-97; pres. S.W. EMS Edn. Inc., Glendale, Ariz., 1997—; dir. field tng. S.W. Ambulance, Mesa, Ariz., 2006—. EMS coord., City of Mesa Fire Dept., 2001-04. Author: (book) Emergency Med. Technician: EMT in action, 2008, ACLS Study Guide, 3d edit., 2007, ACLS Quick Review Study Cards, 2003, PALS Study Guide, 3d edit., 2006, ECGs Made Easy, 3d edit., 2006, ECGs Made Easy Study Cards, 2003, Mosby's Comprehensive Pediatric Emergency Care, 2005. Republican.

AFIFI, ABDELMONEM A., biostatistics educator, dean; b. El-Menia, Egypt, Aug. 7, 1939; came to U.S., 1960; s. Abdelaziz A. and Nazira (Afifi) A.; m. Beverly L. Coppage, June 30, 1962 (div. 1974); children: Osama A., Mostafa A.; m. Marianne H. Blimlinger, Mar. 4, 1977. BS in Math., Cairo U., 1959; MS in Stats., U. Chgo., 1962; PhD in Stats., U. Calif., Berkeley, 1965. Demonstrator math. dept. Cairo U., 1959-60; prof. biostats. Sch. Pub. Health UCLA, 1965—, dean Sch. Pub. Health, 1987—. Vis. asst. prof. U. Wis., Madison, 1965; pres. Western Consortium for Pub. Health, Berkeley, 1987—; stats. cons. numerous orgns., U.S. and abroad, 1965—. Author: Statistical Analysis, 1979, Computer Aided Multivariate Analysis, 3d edit, 1995; contbr. numerous sci. articles to jours. Fulbright scholar, 1960-64, guest scholar Internat. Inst. Systems Analysis, Laxenburg, Austria, 1974-75, 76-77. Fellow Am. Statis. Assn.; mem. Am. Pub. Health Assn. Democrat. Avocations: classical music, photography, travel. Office: UCLA Sch Pub Health PO Box 951772 Los Angeles CA 90095-1772

AFRASIABI, PETER R., lawyer; BA magna cum laude, UCLA; JD, Univ. So. Calif. Bar: Calif. Law clk. Judge Alicemarie Stotler, US Dist. Ct. Ctrl. Calif., Judge Ferdinand F. Fernandez, US Ct. Appeals Ninth Cir.; atty. O'Melveny & Myers LLP; ptnr., comml. litigation practice Turner, Green, Afrasiabi & Arledge LLP, Costa Mesa, Calif. Adj. prof. Chapman Univ. Sch. Law, 2001—; bd. dir. Legal Aid Soc. Orange County, 2001—05. Contbr. articles to profl. jours.; editor (articles): Univ. So. Calif. Law Rev. Mem. human rels. com. City of Costa Mesa, Calif., 2000—01. Recipient Public Counsel Advocate of the Year award, 2002, USC Paul Davis Meml. award, Public Interest Legal Found., 2006; named a Rising Star, So. Calif. Super Lawyers, 2006. Mem.: Fed Bar Assn. Orange County (bd. dir. 2004), Order of the Coif. Office: Turner Green Afrasiabi & Arledge Ste 850 535 Anton Blvd Costa Mesa CA 92626 Office Phone: 714-434-8743. Office Fax: 714-434-8756. Business E-Mail: pafrasiabi@turnergreen.com.

AGARD, DAVID A., biochemistry and biophysics educator; BS in Molecular Biology and Biochemistry, Yale U., New Haven, 1975; PhD in Chem. Biology, Calif. Inst. Tech., Pasadena, 1980. Postdoctoral rschr. dept. biochemistry and biophysics U. Calif., San Francisco, 1980, asst. prof., 1983—89, assoc. prof., 1989—92, prof. biochemistry and biophysics and pharm. chemistry, 1992—; postdoctoral rschr. Med. Rsch. Coun. Lab. of Med. Biology, Cambridge, England, 1981—82; asst. investigator structural biology Howard Hughes Med. Inst., 1986—89, assoc. investigator, 1989—92, investigator, 1993—. Mem. Comprehensive Cancer Ctr. U. Calif., San Francisco, chair grad. group biophysics, 1995—, dir. Inst. Bioengineering, Biotechnology and Quantitative Biomedical Rsch., San Francisco, Berkeley and Santa Cruz, 2001—02, sci. dir. Inst. Bioengineering, Biotechnology and Quantitative Biomedical Rsch., 2002—. Contbr. articles to sci. jours. Recipient Presdl. Young Investigator award, NSF, 1983—91, Sidhu Award for Outstanding Contbns. Crystallography, 1986. Mem.: NAS. Office: Dept Biochemistry & Biophysics U Calif San Francisco 600 16th St San Francisco CA 94143-2240 Office Phone: 415-476-2521. Office Fax: 415-476-1902. E-mail: agard@msg.ucsf.edu.

AGASSI, SHAI, alternative energy company executive, former application developer; b. Ramat-Gan, Israel, Apr. 19, 1968; s. Reuven Agassi; m. Nili Agassi; 2 children. BS in Computer Sci., Israel Inst. Tech. Founder TopTier Software, 1992—2001, Quicksoft Ltd., Quicksoft Media; CEO SAP portals SAP AG, Walldorf, Germany, 2001, dir. tech. & strategy, 2002—07, mem. exec. bd., 2002—07; founder, CEO Project Better Place, 2007—. Served in Israeli Def. Forces. Named one of The World's Most Influential People, TIME mag., 2009. Achievements include patents in field. Office: Better Place Hdqs 1070 Arastradero Rd Ste 220 Palo Alto CA 94304 Office Phone: 650-845-2800. Office Fax: 650-845-2850.*

AGNEW, JOHN A., science educator; b. Millom, Cumbria, England, Aug. 29, 1949; arrived in U.S., 1971; s. Herbert and Anne (MacPherson) A.; children: Katherine, Christine. BA, Exeter U., Eng., 1970; Cert. Edn., Liverpool U., Eng., 1971; MA, Ohio State U., 1973, PhD, 1976. From asst. prof. to prof. Syracuse (NY) U., 1975—96; prof. UCLA, 1996—, chair dept. geography, 1998—2002, chair global studies program, 2007—. Dir. social sci. program Syracuse U., 1981—88; vis. prof. U. Chgo., 1992, U. Cambridge, England, 1992, U. Iowa, 1995, Univ. Coll., London, 1996, U. Durham, 2003, Queen's U., Belfast, 2003, Emmanuel Coll., Cambridge, 2004; Hettner lectr. U. Heidelberg, 2000; Guggenheim fellow UCLA, 2003—04. Author: Place and Politics, 1987, The U.S. in World Economy, 1987, Rome, 1995, Geopolitics: Re-Visioning World Politics, 1998, 2d edit., 2003, Place and Politics in Modern Italy, 2002, Making Political Geography, 2002, Hegemony: The New Shape of Global Power, 2005 (Outstanding Academic Title, 2005, Globalization and Sovereignty, 2009; co-author: Mastering Space, 1995, The Geography of the World Economy, 1989, 5th edit, 2008, Berlusconi's Italy, 2008; editor: The City in Cultural Context, 1984, The Power of Place, 1989, Human Geography: An Essential Anthology, 1996, Political Geography: A Reader, 1997, American Space/American Place, 2002, Companion to Political Geography, 2002, The Marshall Plan Today: Model and Metaphor, 2004; co-editor Geopolitics, 1999-2009; mem. editl. bd. Polit. Geography, Nat. Identities, Global Networks, Scottish Geog. Jour., European Jour. Internat. Rels., Progress in Human Geography, Irish Geography, Internat. Polit. Sociology. Recipient Chancellor's award for Scholarly Achievement, Syveune U., 1996, Disting. scholarship award, Assn. Am. Geographers, 2006, Disting. Tchg. award, UCLA, 2007. Fellow: Royal Geog. Soc.; mem.: AAAS, N.Y Acad. Sci., Am. Polit. Sci. Assn., Coun. European Studies, Assn. Am. Geographers (v.p. 2007—08, pres. 2008—09). Office: UCLA 1255 Bunche Hl Los Angeles CA 90095-1524 Office Phone: 310-825-1713. Business E-Mail: jagnew@geog.ucla.edu.

AGOSTA, WILLIAM CARLETON, chemist, educator; b. Dallas, Jan. 1, 1933; s. Angelo N. and Helen Carleton (Jones) A.; m. Karin Solveig Engstrom, July 2, 1958; children— Jennifer Ellen, Christopher William. BA, Rice Inst., 1954; AM, Harvard U., Cambridge, Mass., 1955, PhD, 1957. NRC postdoctoral fellow Oxford U., England, 1957-58; Pfizer postdoctoral fellow U. Ill., Urbana, 1958-59; asst. prof. U. Calif., Berkeley, 1959-61; liaison scientist US Navy, Frankfurt, Germany, 1961-63; asst. prof. chemistry Rockefeller U., NYC, 1963-67, assoc. prof., 1967-74, prof., 1974-98, prof. emeritus, 1998—. Vis. prof. U. Innsbruck, 1995, Princeton U., 1996; cons. in field; officer Chiron Press, Inc., 1977-85; mem. NRC Associateship Programs Chem. Scis. Panel, 1997-2005. Author: Chemical Communication, 1992, Bombardier Beetles and Fever Trees, 1996, Thieves, Deceivers, and Killers, 2001; mem. editl. adv. bd. Jour. Organic Chemistry, 1984-88; contbr. articles to profl. jours. Bd. dirs. San Juan Cmty. Home Trust, 2003—06, pres., 2004—06; bd. visitors U. Wash. Sch. Medicine, Wash., 2006—09, mem. scholarship com. Wash., 2006—; mem. Noxious Weed Control Bd., San Juan County, Wash., 2002—, Housing Bank Commn., San Juan County, 2006—, vice chmn., 2008, chmn., 2009. John Angus Erskine fellow U. Canterbury, New Zealand, 1981 Fellow AAAS; mem. Chem. Soc. London, Am. Chem. Soc., Interam. Photochem. Soc., European Photochemistry Assn., Am. Soc. Photobiology, Internat. Soc. for Chem. Ecology, Phi Beta Kappa, Sigma Xi. Home: PO Box 1547 Friday Harbor WA 98250-1547 Office Phone: 360-378-0816. E-mail: agosta@u.washington.edu.

AGRAN, LARRY, mayor, lawyer; b. Chgo., Feb. 2, 1945; m. Phyllis Agran; 1 child, Ken. BA, U. Calif. Berkeley, 1966; JD with honors, Harvard U., 1969. Legal counsel Calif. State Senate Com. on Health and Welfare; lectr., legis. and pub. policy UCLA Sch. Law, Grad. Sch. Mgmt., U. Calif. Irvine; mem. Irvine City Coun., 1978—90; mayor City of Irvine, Calif., 1982—84, 1986—90; mem. Irvine City Coun., 1998—; mayor City of Irvine, 2000—. Office: 1 Civic Ctr Plz PO Box 19575 Irvine CA 92623-9575

AGUILAR, PEPE (JOSÉ AGUILAR), singer; b. San Antonio, 1968; s. Antonio Aguilar and Flor Silvestre; m. Aneliz Aguilera, 1995; 2 children. Singer: (albums) Recuerdame Bonito, 1992, 14 Anos 9 Meses, 1995, Cautiva y Triste, 1995, Chiquilla Bonita, 1995, Con Tambora, 1995, Que Bueno, 1995, Tambora, 1995, Por Mujeres Como Tu, 1998, Por el Amor de Siempre, 1999, Por una Mujer Bonita, 1999 (Grammy award, Best Mexican-Am. Music Performance, 2001), Con Banda Sinaloense, 2001, Con Tambora, 2001, Con Banda, 2002, Puras Rancheras, 2002, Y Tenerte Otra Vez, 2003, Con Mariachi, 2003, Con Orgullo Por Herencia, 2003, No Soy de Nadie, 2004, Puro Boleros, 2005, Con Todo el Corazon Te Canta, 2005, Baladas y Boleros, 2005, Tu Camino y El Mio, 2006, Mi Credo, 2006, Amor Con Amor Se Paga, 2006, Historias de Mi Tierra, 2006 (Grammy award, Best Mexican-Am. Album, 2007), Pepe Aguilar Live, 2007, 100% Mexicano, 2007 (Grammy award, Best Mexican-Am. Album, 2008), En Vivo, 2007, Juntos, 2008. Office: care Balboa Records 10900 Washington Blvd Culver City CA 90232-4025

AGUILAR, VALENTIN G., II, lawyer; BS, U. Calif., Riverside, 1991; JD, U. So. Calif., 1996. Bar: Calif. 1996, NJ 2001. Ptnr., comml. real estate practice Manatt, Phelps & Phillips LLP, LA. Named a Rising Star, So. Calif. Super Lawyers, 2006. Mem.: State Bar Calif., Philippine Am. Bar Assn. (bd. dir.), LA County Bar Assn. Office: Manatt Phelps & Phillips Ea Tower Trident Ctr 11355 W Olympic Blvd Los Angeles CA 90064 Office Phone: 310-312-4313. Office Fax: 310-312-4224. Business E-Mail: vaguilar@manatt.com.

AGUILERA, A. ERIC, lawyer; b. May 14, 1972; BA, Univ. Calif., Berkeley, 1994; JD, UCLA, 1997. Bar: Calif. 1997, US Dist. Ct. Ctrl., So., Ea. & No. Calif., US Ct. Appeals Ninth Cir. Assoc. Wood, Bohm & Francis LLP; ptnr., bus. litigation & employment law practice Bohm, Matsen, Kegel & Aguilera, Costa Mesa, Calif. Named a Rising Star, So. Calif. Super Lawyers, 2005—06. Mem.: ABA, Fed. Bar Assn., State Bar Calif., Orange County Bar Assn. Office: Bohm Matsen Kegel & Aguilera Ste 700 Park Tower 695 Town Ctr Dr Costa Mesa CA 92626 Office Phone: 714-384-6500. Office Fax: 714-384-6501.

AGUIRRE, AMANDA, state legislator; b. Aguaprieta, Sonora, Mex., Feb. 6, 1953; children: Amanda, Anibal Jr. BS in Chemistry, U. Sonora; MA, Calif. State U., LA, 1981. Exec. dir. Western Ariz. Health Edn. Ctr., 1991—2003; pres., CEO Regional Ctr. Border Health, Inc., Somerton, Ariz., 1991—, San Luis Walk-In Clinic, Inc., Yuma, Ariz., 2004—; mem. Dist. 24 Ariz. House of Reps., 2003—06, Ariz. State Senate, 2006—. Pres. Rio Colo. Commn. Co-founder Nuestros Niños Found.; mem. Good Neighbor Environment Bd., 2003—; mem. adv. com. Ariz. Ctr. Pub. Health Preparedness, 2005—. Recipient OHTLI award, Ministry Fgn. Affairs Mex., 2000, Border Health Hero award, Pan Am. Health Orgn., 2002, Outstanding Legis. Svc. award, County Supervisors Assn. Ariz., 2004, Cmty. Nutrition award, Ariz. Dietetic Assn., 2005; named Health Worker of Yr., US-Mex. Border Health Assn., 1999; named an Outstanding Ariz. Legislator, Ariz. Rural Health Assn., 2006. Democrat. Roman Catholic. Office: Ariz State Senate Capitol Complex 1700 W Washington Rm 314 Phoenix AZ 85007 Office Phone: 602-926-4139. Office Fax: 602-417-3184. Business E-Mail: aaguirre@azleg.gov.*

AHART, ALAN M., judge; b. 1949; AB, U. Calif., Berkeley, 1970; JD, SUNY, 1975; LLM, U. Pa., 1979. Judge U.S. Bankrupty Ct. Cen. Dist. Calif., LA, 1988—. Contbr. articles to profl. jours. Office: US Bankruptcy Ct Calif Edward R Roybal Bldg 255 E Temple St Ste 1382 Los Angeles CA 90012-3332

AHERN, JOSEPH A., television station executive; Pres., gen. mgr. WLS-TV, Chgo., 1996-97; sr. v.p., mng. dir. Walt Disney Internat., London, 1997-98; pres., gen. mgr. KGO-TV, San Francisco, 1998—. Office: KGO-TV 900 Front St San Francisco CA 94111-1450

AHLEM, LLOYD HAROLD, psychologist; b. Moose Lake, Minn., Nov. 7, 1929; s. Harold Edward and Agnes (Carlson) A.; m. Anne T. Jensen, Dec. 29, 1952; children: Ted, Dan, Mary Jo, Carol, Aileen. AA, North Park Coll., 1948; AB, San Jose State Coll., 1952, MA, 1955; Ed.D., U. So. Calif., 1962. Tchr. retarded children Fresno County (Calif.) Pub. Schs., 1953-54; psychologist Baldwin Park (Calif.) Sch. Dist., 1955-62; prof. psychology Calif. State U., Stanislaus (formerly Stanislaus State Coll.), Turlock, Calif., 1962-70; pres. North Park U., Chgo., 1970-79, dir., 1966-70; exec. dir. Covenant Village Retirement Center, Turlock, 1979-89; dir. spl. projects Covenant Retirement Communities, Chgo., 1989-93; dir. Emanuel Med. Ctr., Turlock, Calif., 1984-99, Merced Mut. Ins. Co., Atwater, Calif., 1993—2005; chmn. Capital Corp. of West, Merced, Calif., 1995—2002; ret. Author: Do I Have To Be Me, 1974, How to Cope: Managing Change, Crisis and Conflict, 1978, Help for the Families of the Mentally Ill, 1983, Living and Growing in Later Years, 1992; columnist Covenant Companion, 1972-90. Decorated comdr. Order of Polar Star Sweden. Mem. Assn. Colls. Ill. (vice chmn. 1975-79) Mem. Covenant Ch. Club: Rotary (Paul Harris fellow 1987). Home: 2125 N Olive C-11 Turlock CA 95382

AHLERS, GUENTER, physicist, researcher; b. Bremen, Germany, Mar. 28, 1934; came to U.S., 1951; s. William Carl and Ida Pauline (Cornelson) A.; m. June Bly, Aug. 24, 1964 BS in Chemistry, U. Calif., Riverside, 1959; PhD in Physical Chemistry, U. Calif., Berkeley, 1963. Mem. tech. staff Bell Labs., Murray Hill, NJ, 1963—78; prof. physics U. Calif., Santa Barbara, 1979—. Chair fundamental physics discipline working group NASA, 1998—99. Contbr. over 260 articles to profl. jours. Recipient Tenth Fritz London Memorial award, 1978, Alexander von Humboldt Senior U.S. Scientist award, 1989—90, Fluid Dynamics prize, Am. Phys. Soc., 2007. Fellow AAAS, Am. Phys. Soc. (Fluid Dynamics prize, 2007), Am. Acad. Arts & Sci.; mem. NAS. Office: U Calif Dept Physics Santa Barbara CA 93106 Home: 1051B Senda Verde Santa Barbara CA 93105 Business E-Mail: guenter@physics.ucsb.edu.

AHMANSON, HOWARD F., JR., philanthropist; b. 1950; s. Howard Fieldstead Ahmanson; m. Roberta Green Ahmanson, 1986; 1 child. BA in Econ., Occidental Coll., LA; MA in Linguistics, U. Tex., Arlington. Head, personal philanthropic orgn. Fieldstead Inst.; provides funds for Fullhart-Carnegie Mus. Trust, Drew U., Discovery Inst., Claremont Inst., St. James Episc. Ch., Calvin Coll., Am. Anglican Coun., Chalcedon Report, US Republican Party and many others. Author multiple articles appearing in The Los Angeles Times, Philanthropy, Religion and Liberty, and other publ. Mem. Republican state ctr. com.; chmn. California Ind. Bus. Pol. Action Com. (PAC). Named one of 25 Most Influential Evangelicals in America, TIME Magazine, 2005. Mem.: Coun. for Nat. Policy (bd. of gov. 1996—98), Claremont Inst. (bd. of dirs.), John M. Perkins Found. Office: The Ahmanson Found 9215 Wilshire Blvd Beverly Hills CA 90210 Office Phone: 310-278-0770.

AHMANSON, ROBERTA, philanthropist; b. Perry, Iowa, 1949; d. Earl and Virginia Green; m. Howard Ahmanson, 1986; 1 child. BA, Calvin Coll., Grand Rapids, Mich., 1972; MA in English, U. Mich., Ann Arbor. Religion reporter The Orange County Register; bd. advisors Claremont Inst.; bd. dirs. Inst. on Religion and Democracy; head, personal philanthropic orgn. Fieldstead Inst.; bd. dirs. Mus. Biblical Art, NYC. Author: (novels) Islam at the Crossroads. Named one of 25 Most Influential Evangelicals in America, Time Magazine. Presbyterian. Office: PO Box 19599 Irvine CA 92623 Office Phone: 310-278-0770, 949-474-1965. Business E-Mail: fieldstead@nonnobis.com. E-mail: info@theahmansonfoundation.org.

AHRENS, THOMAS J., geophysicist; b. Wichita Falls, Tex., Apr. 25, 1936; s. Eric and Therese Ahrens. BS in Geology-Geophysics, MIT, 1957; MS in Geophysics, Calif. Inst. Tech., 1958; PhD in Geophysics, Rensselaer Poly. Inst., 1962. Geophysicist Pan Am. Petroleum Corp., Menlo Park, Calif., 1958-59; geophysicist, head geophysics sect. Poulter Lab., Stanford Rsch. Inst., Pasadena, Calif., 1962-67; assoc. prof. Calif. Inst. Tech., 1967-76, W.M. Keck prof. earth scis., prof. geophysics, 1976—. Mem. earth. scis. adv. com. NSF, 1973-76, adv. com. divsn. earth scis., 1979-82; chmn. geophysics Gordon Rsch. Conf., 1974; convenor mineral physics workshop Am. Geophys. Union, 1988, chmn. Macelwane award com., 1992-94; vis. com. dept. terrestrial magnetism and geophys. lab. Carnegie Inst. Washington, 1989, dept. geology and geophysics Princeton U., 1990—, Max Planck Inst. Chemistry, Mainz, Germany, 1993—, divsn. phys. sci. U. Chgo., 1993—. Editor: AGU, Handbook of Physical Constants, Vol. I, II, III, 1995; assoc. editor Rev. Sci. Instruments, 1972-74, Jour. Geophys. Rsch., 1972-74; adv. editor Physics and Chemistry of Minerals, 1976—; mem. editl. bd. Surveys in Geophysics, 1984-94; contbr. more than 300 sci. papers to profl. publs. 1st lt. U.S. Army, 1959-60. Recipient Shock Compression Sci. award Am. Phys. Soc., 1995, Arthur L. Day medal Geol. Soc. Am., 1995, Barringer award Meteoritical Soc., 1997; Geochem. fellow Geochem. Soc. and Geochem. Soc. of Europe, 1998; asteroid named after him/Main Belt Asteroid --4739, Tomahrens, 1985 by discoverer Theodore Bowell. Fellow AAAS (Newcomb-Cleveland prize 1984), Am. Geophys. Union (Harry H. Mess medal 1996); mem. U.S. Nat. Acad. Sci. Achievements include patents in shock consolidation of cubic boron nitride with whiskers of silicon compounds; method for measuring fracture toughness of brittle media; polycrystalline diamond and method for forming same. Office: Calif Inst Tech Seismological Lab # 252-21 Pasadena CA 91125-0001

AHUJA, JAGDISH CHAND, mathematics professor; b. Rawalpindi, West Pakistan, Dec. 24, 1927; came to U.S., 1966, naturalized 1972; s. Nihal Chand and Ishwardai (Chhabra) A.; m. Sudarshan Sachdeva, May 18, 1955; children— Naina, Anita BA, Banaras U., 1953, MA, 1955; PhD, U. B.C., 1963. Sr. math. tchr. D.A.V. High Sch., Nairobi, Kenya, 1955-56; tchr. math. Tanzania, 1956-58; teaching asst. U. B.C., 1958-61, teaching fellow, 1961-63, stats. lab. instr., 1959-61, lectr. stats., 1961-63; asst. prof. math. U. Calgary, Can., 1963-66; assoc. prof. math. Portland State U., Oreg., 1966-69, prof. math. Oreg., 1969—. Contbr. articles to profl. jours.; referee profl. jours., reviewer profl. jours. Mem. Inst. Math. Stats. Home: 4016 Orchard Dr Lake Oswego OR 97035-2406 Office: Portland State U Dept Math PO Box 751 Portland OR 97207-0751 Office Phone: 503-725-3627. Business E-Mail: ahujaj@pdx.edu.

AIGNER, DENNIS JOHN, economics professor, consultant; b. LA, Sept. 27, 1937; s. Herbert Lewis and Della Geraldine (Balasek) A.; m. Vernita Lynne White, Dec. 21, 1957 (div. May 1977); children: Mitchell A., Annette N., Anita L., Angela D.; m. Gretchen Camille Bertolet, Dec. 22, 1992. BS, U. Calif.-Berkeley, 1959, MA, 1962, PhD, 1963. Asst. prof. econs. U. Ill., Urbana, 1962-67; from assoc. prof. to prof. U. Wis., Madison, 1967-76; prof., chmn. dept. econs. U. So. Calif., LA, 1976-88; dean grad. sch. mgmt. U. Calif., Irvine, 1988-97, prof. grad. sch. mgmt., 1988—2007, prof. emeritus, 2007—, assoc. dean sch. environ. sci. and mgmt. Santa Barbara, 1998-2000, acting dean, 2000-01, dean, 2001—05, adj. prof., 2005—07. Pres. Dennis Aigner Inc., L.A., 1978—; dir. Analysis Group Econs. Author: Introduction to Statistical Decision Making, 1968, Basic Econometrics, 1971; editor: Latent Variables in Socio-Economic Models, 1977; co-editor: Jour. Econometrics, 1972-91. Fulbright fellow Belgium, 1970, Israel, 1983, Bren fellow U. Calif. Santa Barbara, 1998-2005; NSF grantee, 1968-70, 70-72, 73-76, 79-81, 84-86. Fellow Econometric Soc.; mem. Am. Statis. Assn., Am. Econ. Assn. Office: Merage Sch Business Univ California Irvine CA 92697 Office Phone: 949-824-6229. Business E-Mail: djaigner@uci.edu.

AIKEN, ANN L., federal judge; b. Salem, Oreg., Dec. 29, 1959; m. James R. Klonoski; 5 children. MA in Polit. Sci., Rutgers U., New Brunswick, 1976; BS in Polit. Sci., U. Oreg., 1974, JD, 1979. Bar: Oreg. 1980, U.S. Dist. Ct. Oreg. 1981. Law clk. Pub. Defender Svcs., Inc., 1979-80, Office of Legal Counsel to Gov. of Oreg., 1979-80, Judge Edwin E. Allen; atty. Sahlstrom and Dugdale PC, 1980-82; chief clk. Oreg. Ho. of Reps., 1982-83; atty. Thorp, Dennett, Purdy, Golden and Jewett PC, 1983-88; judge Lane County Dist. Ct., Oreg., 1988-92, Lane County Circuit Ct., 1993-98, U.S. Dist. Ct., Eugene, Oreg., 1998—. Aaald staff Betty Roberts for U.S. Senate, 1974, Kulongoski for Gov., 1982; adminstv. asst. to Oreg. speaker pro tem Albert Densmore, 1974-75, Office of Rep. James Weaver, 1976; staff Weaver for Congress com., 1976, office clk., 1976-77; mem. adv. bd. Jr. League of Eugene; bd. visitors U. Oreg. Sch. of Law, 1997—; bd. dirs. Relief Nursery, 1989—, Roland K. Rodman Inn of Court (Eugene chap.), 1990—, Lane Co. Child Advocacy Ctr., 2000; mem Nat. Chldn's. Alliance, 1998—. Eagleton fellow, 1975-76, Health, Edn. and Welfare Pubs. Svc. Edn. fellow, 1975-76. Mem. Oreg. Circuit Ct. Judges' Assn., Oreg. Jud. Conf., Oreg. Women Lawyers Assn., Oreg. State Bar Assn., Am. Leadership Forum.

AIKENS, C(LYDE) MELVIN, anthropologist, educator, archaeologist; b. Ogden, Utah, July 13, 1938; s. Clyde Walter and Claudia Elena (Brown) A.; m. Alice Hiroko Endo, Mar. 23, 1963; children: Barton Hiroyuki, Quinn Yoshihisa. A.S., Weber Coll., 1958; BA, U. Utah, 1960; MA, U. Chgo., 1962, PhD, 1966. Curator U. Utah Mus. Anthropology, Salt Lake City, 1963—66; asst. prof. U. Nev., Reno, 1966—68; asst. prof. anthropology U. Oreg., Eugene, 1968—72, assoc. prof., 1972—78, prof., 1978—2000, prof. emeritus, 2000—, rsch. affil., dir. U. Oreg. Mus. Natural and Cultural History, 1996—2005. Author: Fremont Relationships, 1966, Hogup Cave, 1970, Great Basin Archaeology, 1978, The Last 10,000 Years in Japan and Eastern North America, 1981, From Asia to America: The First Peopling of the New World, 1990, Archaeology of Oregon, 1993; co-author: Prehistory of Japan, 1982, Great Basin Numic Prehistory, 1986, Early Human Occupation in Far Western North America, 1988; editor: Archaeological Studies Willamette Valley, 1975; co-editor: Prehistoric Hunter-Gatherers in Japan, 1986, Pacific Northeast Asia in Prehistory, 1992, Archaeological Researches in the Northern Great Basin, 1994, Early and Middle Holocene Archaeology of the Northern Great Basin, 2004. NSF research grantee, 1970, 73, 78-80, 84; NSF Sci. Faculty fellow Kyoto U., Japan, 1971-72; Japan Found. research fellow Kyoto U., 1977-78, Tokyo U., 1986. Fellow Am. Anthrop. Assn., AAAS; mem. Soc. for Am. Archaeology, Register Profl. Archaeologists. Home: 3470 McMillan St Eugene OR 97405-3317 E-mail: maikens@uoregon.edu.

AILMAN, CHRISTOPHER J., investment company executive; b. 1958; m. Robin Ailman; 3 children. BA in Bus. Econs., U. Calif., Santa Barbara, 1980. Chief investment officer Sacramento Employees Retirement Sys. and County of Sacramento; mgr. Wash. State Investment Bd.; chief investment officer Calif. State Tchrs. Retirement Sys. (CalSTRS), Sacramento, 2000—. Recipient Richard L Stoddard Award, 2003, Disting. Svc. award for Advancing Latinos in Am. Bus., New Am. Alliance, 2006, IFE Leadership Award; named Chief Investment Officer of Yr., Inst. Fiduciary Edn., 2000. Office: Calif State Tchrs Retirement Sys (CalSTRS) PO Box 15275 Sacramento CA 95851-0275 Office Phone: 800-228-5453. Office Fax: 916-229-3879.

AIONA, JAMES R., JR., Lieutenant Governor of Hawaii; b. Honolulu, June 8, 1955; m. Vivian Welsh; children: Makana, Ohulani, Kulia, Kaimilani. BA in Polit. Sci., U. of the Pacific; JD, U. Hawaii. Law clk. hon. Wendell K. Huddy Cir. Ct. Judge First Cir. Hawaii, 1981—82; dep. pros. atty. City and County Honolulu, 1982—85, dep. corp. counsel City Attys. Office, 1985—87, chief litigator, 1987—90; family ct. judge 1st Cir. State Hawaii, 1990—93, cir. ct. judge 14th divsn., 1993—96; adminstrv. judge Drug Ct. Program, 1996—98; ret., 1998; pvt. practice, 1997—2002; part-time family dist. ct. judge, 1999—2002; lt. gov. State of Hawaii, Honolulu, 2002—. Asst. basketball coach varsity boys St. Lous H.S.; vol. soccer coach AYSO; vol. youth baseball coach Makakilo-Kapolei; vol. judge H.S. mock trials competition State of Hawaii; bd. mem. The Salvation Army, Reid J.K. Richards Found., Youth At Risk Adv. Coun., Maryknoll Schs., 1995—98. Republican. Office: Ofice Lt Governor Executive Chambers Hawaii State Capitol Honolulu HI 96813 Office Phone: 808-586-0255. Office Fax: 808-586-0231. E-mail: ltgov@hawaii.gov.

AISENBERG, BENNETT S., lawyer; b. Feb. 17, 1931; s. Joseph Samuel and Minna Ruth (Cohan) A. BA, Brown U., 1952; JD, Harvard U., 1955. Bar: Mass. 1955, Colo. 1958, U.S. Dist. Ct. Colo. 1958, U.S. Ct. Appeals (10th cir.) 1958. Ptnr. Gorsuch, Kirgis, Denver, 1958-80; pvt. practice Denver, 1980—. Mem. Nat. Acad. Arbitrators, Colo. Trial Lawyers Assn. (pres. 1984-85), Denver Bar Assn. (trustee 1982-85, 86-89, pres. 1991-92), Colo. Bar Assn. (pres. 1998-99). Office: 1600 Broadway Ste 2350 Denver CO 80202-4921

AITKEN, ASHLEIGH E., lawyer; BA cum laude, Boston Coll., 1997; JD, Univ. So. Calif., 2002. Bar: Calif. Assoc., bus. litigation Morrison & Foerster, Irvine, Calif., 2005—. Commr. Cmty. Services Bd., Anaheim, Calif. Named Rising Star, So. Calif. Super Lawyers, 2005—06; Scholar, State Bar Calif. Leadership Acad., 2005. Mem.: Assn. Bus. Trial Lawyers, Celtic Bar Assn. (bd. dir.), State Bar Calif., Orange County Bar Assn. (bd. dir.), Orange County Women Lawyers (v.p.). Office: Morrison & Foerster 12th Fl 19900 MacArthur Blvd Irvine CA 92612 Office Phone: 949-251-7500. Office Fax: 949-251-0900. Business E-Mail: aaitken@mofo.com.

AITKEN, CHRISTOPHER R., lawyer; b. Orange, Calif., May 10, 1969; married; 3 children. BA, UCLA, 1992; JD, Univ. So. Calif., LA, 1996. Bar: Calif. 1997. Ptnr., civil trial practice Aitken Aitken & Cohn, Santa Ana, Calif. Bd. chmn. Laura's House. Named a Rising Star, So. Calif. Super Lawyers, 2006. Mem.: William P. Gray Inn of Ct., Assn. Bus. Trial Lawyers, Consumer Attorneys Calif., Orange County Trial Lawyers Assn., Hispanic Bar Assn., State Bar Calif., Orange County Bar Assn. Office: Aitken Aitken & Cohn 3 Imperial Promenade Ste 800 PO Box 2555 Santa Ana CA 92707-0555 Office Phone: 714-434-1424. Office Fax: 714-434-3600. Business E-Mail: chris@aitkenlaw.com.

AITKEN, WYLIE A., lawyer; b. Detroit, Jan. 4, 1942; AA, Santa Ana Coll., Calif. State Coll.Fullerton; LLB, Marquette U., 1965. Bar: Calif. 1966, U.S. Dist. Ct. (Ctrl. dist. Calif.). Founding ptnr. Aitken Aitken Cohn, Santa Ana, Calif. Assoc. editor: Marquette Law Review, 1963—65. Pres. State Trial Bar; bd. mem., advisor State of Calif. Task Force Court Facilities, Fed. Judicial Adv.; com. mem Ctrl. Dist.-Senator Feinstein; mem. nat. bd. dirs., trustee Am. Bd. Trial Advs. Recipient Best Lawyers in America, Franklin G. West award, Orange County Bar Assn., Rage for Justice-Lifetime Achievement award, Marquette U. Law Sch., Jurisprudence award, Anti-Defamation League OC/LB, Trial Lawyer of Yr., Hispanic Bar Assn.; named, Am. Bd. Trial Advs., Top Gun Trial Lawyer of Yr., OC Trial Lawyer Assn., Bus. Trial Lawyer of Yr., Southern Calif. Super Lawyer, Preeminent Lawyers of America; named one of Top 500 Lawyers in America, Law Dragon Mag., Top 100 Calif.'s Most Influential Lawyers, LA Daily Jour. Office: Aitken Aitken Cohn 3 MacArthur Pl Ste 800 Santa Ana CA 92707 Office Phone: 866-434-1424. Business E-Mail: wylie@aitkenlaw.com.

AIZLEY, PAUL, state legislator; b. Boston, Mass., 1936; m. Sari Aizley; stepchildren: Adrienne Poch, Jody Strasser, Sophia Rasile, David Phillips, Matthew Dillingham, Stephanie Cain; 1 stepchild, Jonathan Dillingham (dec.). BA, Harvard U., Cambridge, Mass.; MS, U. Ariz.; PhD, Ariz.State U. Chair UNLV Faculty Senate, 1971—73; asst. UNLV Presidents, 1973—78; pres. (statewide office) Nev. Faculty Alliance, 1984; dean (continuing edn. & summer term) UNLV, 1989—2002; founding chair Nev. Fair Housing, 1995; pres. Western Assn. of Summer Session Adminstrs., 1999—2000, UNLV Chapter, Nev. Faculty Alliance, 2007—08; mem. UNLV Pub. Safety Com.; co-found., former pres. & mem. CLASS! Publications, Inc.; mem. Dist. 41 Nev. State Assembly. Recipient Distinguished Svc. award, Western Assn. Summer Session Adminstrs., 1993. Democrat. Office: 401 South Carson St Room 4118 Carson City NV 89701 Home: 237 East Eldorado Ln Las Vegas NV 89123 Home Phone: 702-361-8262; Office Phone: 775-684-8821. Fax: 702-361-7472. Business E-Mail: paizley@asm.state.nv.us.

AKAKA, DANIEL KAHIKINA, United States Senator from Hawaii; b. Honolulu, Sept. 11, 1924; s. Kahikina and Annie (Kahoa) A.; m. Mary Mildred Chong, May 22, 1948; children: Millannie, Daniel, Gerard, Alan, Nicholas. BEdn, U. Hawaii, 1952, MEdn, 1966. Tchr., Hawaii, 1953-60; vice prin., then prin. Ewa Beach Elem. Sch., Honolulu, 1960-64; prin. Pohakea Elem. Sch., 1964-65, Kaneohe Elem. Sch., 1965-68; program specialist Hawaii Compensatory Edn., 1978-79, from 1985; dir. Office Economic Opportunity, Hawaii, 1971-74; spl. asst. human resources State of Hawaii, 1975-76; mem. US Congress from 2nd Hawaii Dist., 1977-90; US Senator from Hawaii, 1990—; chmn. US Senate Veterans Affairs Com., 2007—; mem. US Senate Armed Services Com., US Senate Banking Housing & Urban Com., US Senate Homeland Security & Govt. Affairs Com., US Senate Indian Affairs Com. Bd. dirs. Hanahauoli Sch., Honolulu; mem. Act 4 Ednl. Adv. Council, Library Adv. Council.; Trustee Kawaiahao Congl. Ch. Served with US Army, 1945—47, Asia Pacific, World War II. Recipient Lifetime Achievement award, U. Hawaii Founders Alumni Assn., 1999, Stan Suyat Meml. Leadership award, Asian Govt. Exec. Network, 2003, Stephen L. Jackstadt award, Hawaii Coun. Econ. Edn., 2003, Congressional Am. Spirit Medallion, Nat. D-Day Mus., 2004, George "Buck" Gillispie Congressional award meritorious svc., Blinded Am. Veteran Assn., 2004, Adam Smith award for excellence in econ. edu., Nat. Council on Econ. Edu., 2005; named Friend of Nat. Parks, Nat. Parks Conservation Assn., 2005. Mem. NEA, Musicians Assn. Hawaii. Democrat. Congregationalist. Office: US Senate 141 Hart Senate Office Bldg Washington DC 20510-0001 also: Prince Kuhio Fed Bldg 300 Ala Moana Blvd Rm 3-106 PO Box 50144 Honolulu HI 96850-4977 Office Phone: 202-224-6361, 808-522-8970. Office Fax: 202-224-2126, 808-545-4683. E-mail: senator@akaka.senate.gov.*

AKASOFU, SYUN-ICHI, geophysicist, educator; b. Nagano-Ken, Japan, Dec. 4, 1930; came to U.S., 1958, naturalized, 1986; s. Shigenori and Kumiko (Koike) A.; m. Emiko Endo, Sept. 25, 1961; children: Ken-Ichi, Keiko. BS, Tohoku U., 1953, MS, 1957; PhD, U. Alaska, 1961. Sr. research asst. Nagasaki U., 1953-55; research asst. Geophys. Inst., U. Alaska, Fairbanks, 1958-61, mem. faculty, 1961—, prof. geophysics, 1964—, dir. Geophys. Inst., 1986-99; dir. Internat. Arctic Rsch. Ctr., U. Alaska, Fairbanks, 1998—2007. Author: Polar and Magnetospheric Substorms (Russian edit. 1971), 1968, The Aurora: A Discharge Phenomenon Surrounding the Earth (in Japanese), 1975, Physics of Magnetospheric Substorms, 1977, Aurora Borealis: The Amazing Northern Lights, 1979, 2d edit., 2002, Exploring the Secrets of the Aurora, 2002, 2d edit., 2007; co-author: Sydney Chapman, Eighty, 1968, Solar-Terrestrial Physics (Russian edit. 1974); editor: Dynamics of the Magnetosphere, 1979; co-editor: Physics of Auroral Arc Formation, 1980—, The Solar Wind and the Earth, 1987,Space Sci. Revs.; mem. editl. bd. Planet and Earth Sci. Recipient Chapman medal Royal Astron. Soc., 1976, award Japan Acad., 1977, Japanese Fgn. Minister award, 1993; named Disting. Alumnus U. Alaska, 1980, Centennial Alumnus Nat. Assn. State Univs. and Land Grant Colls., 1987, Edith R. Bullock prize U. Alaska Fairbanks, 1997, Alaskan of Yr.-Denali award, 1999; named one of the most cited authors Am. Soc. Info. Sci., 1981, 2002, Order of Sacred Treas., Emperor of Japan, 2003. Fellow AAAS, Am. Geophys. Union (John Adam Fleming medal 1977); mem. Sigma Xi Achievements include having the University of Alaska's International Arctic Research Center building renamed in his honor. Home Phone: 907-479-2863; Office Phone: 907-474-6012. Business E-Mail: sakasofu@iarc.uaf.edu.

AKERLOF, GEORGE ARTHUR, economics professor; b. New Haven, June 17, 1940; s. Gosta Carl and Rosalie C. Akerlof; m. Janet Louise Yellen, July 7, 1978; 1 child, Robert. BA, Yale U., 1962; PhD, MIT, 1966; D Econs. (hon.), U. Zurich, Switzerland, 2000. Cassell prof. of money and banking London Sch. Econs., 1978-80; assist. prof. U. Calif., Berkeley, 1966—70, assoc. prof., 1970—77, prof., 1977—78, 1980—; sr. fellow Brookings Instn., Washington, 1994—. Bd. dirs. Nat. Bur. Econ. Rsch., 1997—; bd. editors Quar. Jour. Econs., 1983—, Am. Econ. Rev., 1983-90.; sr. advisor Bookings Panel Econ. Activity Author: An Economic Theorist's Book of Tales, 1984; co-author: Efficiency Wage Theories of Unemployment, 1988, (with Robert Shiller) Animal Spirits: How Human Psychology Drives the Economy, and Why It Matters for Global Capitalism, 2009; co-editor Jour. Econs. and Politics, 1990—; contbr. articles to profl. jours. Recipient Woodrow Wilson fellow, 1962—63, Cooperative fellow NSF, 1963—66, Fulbright fellow, 1967—68, Nobel Prize in Economics, 2001. Fellow Am. Acad. Arts and Scis.; mem. Am. Econ. Assn. (mem. exec. com. 1988-91, v.p. 1995), Can. Inst. Advanced Rsch. (assoc.), Russell Sage Round Table on Behavioral Econs. Office: U Calif Dept Econs 549 Evans Hall # 3880 Berkeley CA 94720-3880

AKEROYD, RICHARD G., JR., library director; BA, U. Conn.; MLS, U. Pitts., 1969. With U. Conn. Libr., Nat. Commn. Libr. & Info. Sci., Denver Pub. Libr.; state libr. Conn. State Libr., Hartford, 1986—97; dir. libr. programs Bill & Melinda Gates Libr. Found., 1997—2003; state libr. N.Mex State Libr., Santa Fe, 2004. Mem.: ALA, Western Coun. State Libraries, Coalition for Networked Info., Am. Soc. Info. Sci. Office: NMex State Libr 1209 Camino Carlos Rey Santa Fe NM 87507 Office Phone: 505-476-9762. Office Fax: 505-476-9761. E-mail: richard.akeroyd@state.nm.us.

AKESSON, NORMAN BERNDT, agricultural engineer, emeritus educator; b. Grandin, ND, June 12, 1914; s. Joseph Berndt and Jennie (Nonthen) A.; m. Margaret Blasing, Dec. 14, 1946; children: Thomas Ryan (dec.), Judith Elizabeth. BS in Agrl. Engring., N.D. State U., 1940; MS in Agrl. Engring, U. Idaho, 1942. Registered profl. engr., Calif. Rsch. fellow U. Idaho, 1940-42; physicist U.S. Navy, Bremerton, Wash., 1942-47; asst. prof. agrl. engring. U. Calif., Davis, 1947-56, assoc. prof., 1956-62, prof., 1962-84, prof. emeritus, 1984—; engring. cons., 1984—. Cons. United Fruit Honduras, 1959, Israel, 1968, WHO Mosquito Control, 1969-84, FAO Aircraft in Agr., 1971-84, Japan, 1972, Egypt, 1980, China, 1985, Can. Forest Svc. Herbicide Application, 1987, U. Fla. Aircraft Application Herbicides, 1987; chmn. expert com. on vector control equipment WHO, 1976; chmn. com. on aircraft for agr. Coun. for Agrl. Sci. and Tech., 1982; pres. Calif. Weed Control Conf., 1966. Author: The Use of Aircraft in Agriculture, 1974, Pesticide Application Equipment and Techniques, 1979, Aircraft Use for Mosquito Control, 1981; contbr. over 330 articles to profl. jours. Recipient research and devel. award FAO, 1973-74, research and devel. award WHO, 1978; Fulbright fellow, Eng. and East Africa, 1957-58. Fellow Am. Soc. Agrl. Engrs. (chmn. Pacific region 1965, dir. 1972-74, assoc. editor tech. publs. 1983-93); mem. ASTM (chair E35-22 1982-84), Am. Chemical Soc., Nat. Agrl. Aviation Assn., Calif. Agrl. Aviation Assn., Nat. Mosquito Control Assn., Entomol. Soc. Am., Weed Sci. Soc. Am. (editl. bd. 1968-70), Western Weed Soc. (hon.), Calif. Weed Sci. Soc. (hon.), Farmers Club (London), Sigma Xi, Phi Kappa Phi, Alpha Zeta, Alpha Gamma Rho. Republican. Home: 1515 Shasta Dr # 1515 Davis CA 95616-6691 Office: U Calif Bio-Agr Engring Dept Davis CA 95616-5294 E-mail: NbAkesson@ucdavis.edu.

AKIBA, LORRAINE HIROKO, lawyer; b. Honolulu, Dec. 28, 1956; d. Lawrence H. and Florence K. (Iwasa) Katsuyama. BS with honors, U. Calif., Berkeley, 1977; JD, U. Calif., San Francisco, 1981. Bar: Hawaii 1981, US Dist. Ct. Hawaii 1981, US Ct. Appeals (9th cir.) 1981, US Supreme Ct. 1986. Dir. State of Hawaii Dept. Labor and Indsl. Rels., 1995—2000; ptnr. Cades, Schutte, Fleming & Wright, Honolulu, 1981—94, McCorriston Miller Mukai and MacKinnon LLP, Honolulu, 2000—. Lawyer rep. 9th Cir. Jud. Conf., 1991-94; mem., past treas. Hawaii Inst. for CLE, Honolulu, 1987—. Chairperson attys. divsn. Aloha United Way, Honolulu, 1991, 04, statewide chairperson, 1995; mem. State of Hawaii Environ. Coun., Honolulu, 1990-94, chair, 1992; mem. city and county Honolulu Transp. Commn., 2005-. Named one of Outstanding Young Women Am., 1985, Hawaii's Best Bus. Lawyers, 2007; named Lawyer of Yr., Hawaii Women Lawyers', 1990. Mem. ABA, Hawaii Bar Assn., Hawaii Women Lawyers Assn., Hawaii Women Lawyers Found. (pres. 1988-92), Honolulu Club, Phi Beta Kappa. Office: McCorriston Miller Mukai MacKinnon LLP PO Box 2800 Honolulu HI 96803-2800 Office Phone: 808-529-7300. Business E-Mail: akiba@m4law.com.

AKIL, MARA BROCK, television writer and producer; b. LA, May 27, 1970; m. Salim Akil, 1999; 1 child. BA in Journalism, Northwestern U. Bd. mem. Ctr. Theatre Grp. (Mark Taper Forum and Ahmanson Theatre). Writer (TV series) South Central, 1994, Moesha, 1998 (SHINE award, 1999), writer, creator Girlfriends, 2000—07 (SHINE award, 2001), The Game, 2006—; prodr.: (TV series) The Jamie Fox Show, 1996; exec. prodr.(creator): Girlfriends, 2000—03, The Game, 2006. Named one of Top 25 Hottest Women in Urban Entertainment, Honey mag.; named to Top 100 Hottest People List, VIBE mag., Power 150, Ebony mag., 2008. Mem.: Delta Sigma Theta. Office: CW TV Network Hdqs 4000 Warner Blvd Burbank CA 91522 Office Phone: 818-977-2500. Office Fax: 818-954-7667.

AKINAKA, ASA MASAYOSHI, lawyer; b. Honolulu, Jan. 19, 1938; s. Arthur Yoshinori and Misako (Miyoshi) A.; m. Betsy Yoshie Kurata, Oct. 7, 1967; children— David Asa Yoshio, Sarah Elizabeth Sachie. BA magna cum laude, Yale U., 1959; postgrad. (Rotary Found. fellow), Trinity Coll., Oxford U., 1959-60, Yale Law Sch., 1960-61; LL.B., Stanford Law Sch., 1964. Bar: Hawaii 1964. Research asst. U.S. Senator Oren Long, Washington, 1961-62; pvt. practice law Honolulu, 1964—. Bd. visitors Stanford Law Sch., 1971-74. Mem. Am. Bar Assn., Hawaii State Bar Assn. (pres. 1977), Pacific Club Democrat. Episcopalian. Office: PO Box 1035 Honolulu HI 96808-1035

ALAILY, RIMA J., lawyer; b. Oak Park, Ill., Aug. 31, 1972; BA, Brown Univ., Providence, RI, 1994; JD, Harvard Univ., Cambridge, Mass., 1998. Bar: Washington 1999. Former law clerk Honorable Robert L. Eastaugh Alaska Supreme Court; assoc. atty., antitrust and trade regulation Heller Ehrman LLP, Seattle. Spkr. in field. Contbr. articles to numerous profl. jours. Recipient Richard E. Guggenhime award, Heller Ehrman LLP, 2003; named Wash. Rising Star, Super-Lawyer Mag., 2006.

ALARCÓN, ARTHUR LAWRENCE, federal judge; b. LA, Aug. 14, 1925; s. Lorenzo Marques and Margaret (Sais) A.; m. Sandra D. Paterson, Sept. 1, 1979; children— Jan Marie, Gregory, Lance BA in Polit. Sci., U. So. Calif., 1949, LLB, 1951. Bar: Calif. 1952. Dep. dist. atty. L.A. County, 1952—61; legal adv. to gov. State of Calif., Sacramento, 1961—62, exec. asst. to Gov. Pat Brown, 1962—64; chmn. Calif. parole bd., 1964; judge L.A. Superior Ct., 1964—78; assoc. justice Calif. Ct. Appeals, LA, 1978—79; judge US Ct. Appeals (9th cir.), LA, 1979—92, sr. judge, 1992—. Adj. prof. Southwestern U. sch. of law, LA, 1985—2004, Loyola Marymount sch. of law, 1993—94. Editor: U. So. Calif. Law Rev. With US Army, 1943—46, ETO. Decorated Bronze Star, Purple Heart; recipient Infantry badge, Expert Rifleman medal, Four Battle Stars, ETO Ribbon. Mem.: ABA, LA Bar Assn. Office: US Ct Appeals 9th Cir 1607 US Courthouse 312 N Spring St Los Angeles CA 90012-4701 also: US Ct Appeals 95 Seventh St San Francisco CA 94103 Office Phone: 213-894-2693.

ALARCÓN, RICHARD, councilman; m to Corina; children: Armando, Antonio, Claudia & Andrea. Tchr.; sr. mgmt. analyst Criminal Justice Planning Office, LA; sr. personnel analyst LA personnel dept. Occupl. Health & Safety Divsn.; San Fernando Valley coord. Mayor's Offic; councilman, Dist. 7 LA City Coun., 1993—98, 2007—, chmn. public works com., vice chmn. govt. efficiency com., mem. cmty. redevelopment & housing com.; senator, Dist. 20 Calif. State Senate, 1999—2006, chmn. labor and indsl. rels. com.; assemblyman Dist. 39 Calif. State Assembly, 2006—07. Founder Richard Alarcón's Young Senators, Gift of Christmas, George and Anne Lopez - Richie Alarcón C.A.R.E. Found.; adminstrv. dir. Cmty. Youth Gang Svc.; chmn. Ne Cmty. Action Project. Recipient Truman award for the Outstanding Elected Ofcl., Democratic Party of San Fernando Valley, 2005; named a Local Hero, Nation Mag., 2003. United Way; Mothers Against Drunk Driving; America Heart Assn.; Women's Care Cottage; Habitat for Humanity; Meet Each Need with Dignity. Democrat. Office: Dist Office 13630 Van Nuys Blvd Pacoima CA 91331 also: City Hall 200 N Spring St Rm 425 Los Angeles CA 90012 Office Phone: 213-847-7777, 818-756-9115. Office Fax: 213-847-0707, 818-756-9270.*

ALBEE, ARDEN LEROY, geologist, educator; b. Port Huron, Mich., May 28, 1928; s. Emery A. and Mildred (Tool) A.; m. Charleen H. Ettenheim, 1978; children: Janet, Margaret, Carol, Kathy, James, Ginger, Mary, George. BA, Harvard U., 1950, MA, 1951, PhD, 1957. Geologist U.S. Geol. Survey, 1950-59; prof. geology Calif. Inst. Tech., 1959—2002, prof. emeritus, 2002—; chief scientist Jet Propulsion Lab., 1978-84, dean grad. studies, 1984—2001, project scientist Mars Observer and Global Surveyor Missions, 1984—. Cons. in field, 1950; chmn. lunar sci. rev. panel NASA, 1972-77, mem. space sci. adv. com., 1976-84; mem. exam. bd. T.O.E.F.L. (Test of English as a Foreign Lang.), 1995-97; mem. Grad. Record Exam. Bd., 1995-98; mem. exec. com. Assn. Grad. Schs., 1995-97. Assoc. editor Jour. Geophys. Rsch., 1976-82, Ann. Rev. Earth Space Scis., 1978—; contbr. numerous articles to profl. jours. Bd. regents L.A. Chiropractic Coll., 1990-98. Recipient Exceptional Sci. Achievement medal NASA, 1976 Fellow Mineral Soc. Am. (assoc. editor Am. Mineralogist 1972-76), Geol. Soc. Am. (assoc. editor bull. 1972-89, councilor 1989-92), Am. Geophys. Union. Office: Calif Inst Tech Mail Code 150-21 Pasadena CA 91125-0001 E-mail: aalbee@gps.caltech.edu.

ALBERS, DOLORES M., secondary school educator; b. Lander, Wyo., June 2, 1949; AA, Casper Coll., 1969; BS, U. No. Colo., 1972; postgrad., U. N.C., U. Wyo., Chadron State. Lic. massage therapist Utah. Physical edn. instr. for grades K-12, 6th and 8th grade sci. tchr. Bent County Sch. Dist. 2, McClave, Colo., 1972-75; physical edn./health instr. Sweetwater County Sch. Dist. # 2, Green River, Wyo., 1972—. Mem. phys. edn. coun. Mid. and Secondary Schs., 1999—2003, chmn. phys. edn. coun., 2002—03. Mem., chmn. Green River Parks and Recreation Bd.; coord. Hoops for Heart; co-chmn. United Way Sweetwater County, 1999-2001. Named Tchr. of Yr., Ctrl. Dist., 1994—95, Nat. Assn. Sport and Phys. Edn., 1995. Mem. AAHPERD, AALR, ASCD/NFOIA, NEA, Wyo. Edn. Assn., Wyo. Assn. Health, Phys. Edn., Recreation and Dance (Tchr. of Yr. award 1994-95), Green River Edn. Assn., Nat. Assn. for Sport and Phys. Edn., Mid. and Secondary Sch. Phys. Edn. Coun. (chmn. 2002-03). Roman Catholic. Avocations: snowboarding, backpacking, woodworking, crewel, cross country skiing. Home: 1745 Massachusetts Ct Green River WY 82935-6229 Office: Green River HS 1615 Hitching Post Dr Green River WY 82935-5771 Office Phone: 307-872-4747.

ALBERTS, BRUCE MICHAEL, cell biologist, former foundation administrator; b. Chgo., Apr. 14, 1938; s. Harry C. and Lillian (Surasky) A.; m. Betty Neary, June 14, 1960; children: Beth L., Jonathan B., Michael B. AB in Biochemical Scis. summa cum laude, Harvard Coll., 1960; PhD in Biophysics, Harvard U., 1965. Postdoctoral fellow NSF Institut de Biologie Moleculaire, Geneva, 1965-66; asst. prof. dept. chemistry Princeton U., NJ, 1966-73, assoc. prof. dept. biochemical scis. NJ, 1971-73, Damon Pfeiffer prof. life scis. NJ, 1973-76; prof., vice chmn. dept. biochemistry and biophysics U. Calif., San Francisco, 1976-81, Am. Cancer Soc. Rsch. prof., 1981-85, prof., chmn., 1985-90, Am. Cancer Soc. Rsch. prof. of biochemistry, 1990-93, prof., biochem. and biophysics dept., 2005—; pres. NAS, Washington, 1993—2005, pres.-emeritus, 2005—; chmn. NRC, Washington, 1993—2005. Trustee Cold Spring Harbor Lab., 1972-75; adv. panel human cell biology NSF, 1974-76; adv. coun. dept. biochemical scis. and molecular biology Princeton U., 1979-85; chmn. vis. com. dept. biochemistry and molecular biology Harvard Coll., 1983-86; chmn. mapping and sequencing the human genome Nat. Rsch. Coun. Com., 1986-88; bd. sci. couns. divsn. arthritis and metabolic diseases NIH, 1974-78, molecular cytology study sect. 1982-86, chmn. 1984-86; program adv. com. NIH Human Genome Project, 1988-91; sci. adv. bd. Jane Coffin Childs Meml. Fund for Med. Rsch., 1978-85, Markey Found., 1984—, Fred Hutchinson Cancer Rsch. Ctr., Seattle, 1988—; com. mem. corp. vis. dept. biology MIT, 1978—, dept. embryology Carnegie Inst., Washington, 1983—; faculty rsch. lectr. U. Calif., San Francisco, 1985; sci. adv. com. Marine Biological Lab., Woods Hole, Mass., 1988—; bd. dirs. Genentech Rsch. Found., Fed. Am. Socs. for Experimental Biology; adv. bd. Bethesda Rsch. Labs. Life Tech. Inc., Nat. Sci. Resources Ctr., Smithsonian Inst., 1990—; com. mem. adolescence and young adulthood/sci. standards, Nat. Bd. Profl. Teaching Standards, 1991—; co-chair InterAcademy Council, Amsterdam, 2000-. Co-author: The Molecular Biology of the Cell, 1989; editor: Mechanistic Studies of DNA Replication and Genetic Recombination, 1980; editorial bd. Jour. Biological Chemistry, 1976-82, Jour. Cell Biology, 1984-87; assoc. editor Annual Reviews Cell Biology, 1984—; essay editor Molecular Biology of the Cell, 1991—; editor-in-chief, Science, 2008-; contbr. numerous articles to profl. jours. including Saunders Sci. Publ., Current Sci., Ltd. Trustee Gordon & Betty Moore Found., Carnegie Corp., NY; overseer Harvard U., 2001—07. Fellow NSF, 1960-65; recipient Eli Lilly award in biological chemistry Am. Chemical Soc., 1972, Baxter award for Disting. Rsch. in Biomedical Scis. Assn. Am. Med. Colls., 1992; named Lifetime Rsch. Prof. Am. Cancer Soc., 1980, Outstanding Vol. Coord. Calif. Sch. Vol. Partnership, 1993. Gairdner Found. Internat. award, 1995. Fellow AAAS; mem. NAS (commn. life scis. Nat. Rsch. Coun., chmn. 1988-93, adv. bd. Nat. Sci. Resources Ctr., Nat. Com. Sci. Edn. Standards and Assessment, com. mem. Nat. Edn. Support System for Tchrs. and Schs., U.S. Steel Found. award 1975), Am. Chemical Soc., Am. Soc. for Cell Biology (pres.-elect, pres. 2007), Am. Soc. for Microbiology, Genetics Soc. Am., Am. Soc. Biochemistry and Molecular Biology (councilor), Am. Philos. Soc., European Molecular Biology Orgn. (assoc.), Phi Beta Kappa. Office: UC San Francisco Dept Biochem & Biophysics 600 16th St San Francisco CA 94143

ALBERTS, CELIA ANNE, lawyer; b. Denver, May 3, 1953; d. Robert Edward and Barbara Ellen Alberts. BA in French, U. Colo., 1975, JD, 1979; LLM in Taxation, U. Denver, 1984. Bar: Colo. 1979, U.S. Dist. Ct. Colo. 1979, U.S. Ct. Appeals (10th cir.) 1979. Assoc. Dietze, Davis & Porter, Boulder, Colo., 1979-82; sole practice Boulder, 1983-84; assoc. Loser, Davies, Magoon & Fitzgerald, Denver, 1984-87; adj. prof. law U. Denver, 1988; v.p., sr. counsel Merrill Lynch, Denver, 1989-96; sole practice Golden, Colo., 1997—. Mem. ABA, Colo. Bar Assn., Denver Bar Assn. (estate/probate divs.), Bar Assn. Ohio, U.S. Supreme Ct., Avocations: sports, crafts, reading, music. Home and Office: 237 Lamb Ln Golden CO 80401-9426

ALBERTS, DAVID SAMUEL, physician, pharmacologist, educator; b. Milw., Dec. 30, 1939; m. Heather Alberts; children: Tim, Sabrina. BS, Trinity Coll., Hartford, Conn., 1962; MD, U. Va., 1966. Dir. clin. pharmacology Ariz. Cancer Ctr., Tucson, 1975—, prof. medicine and pharmacology, 1982—99, dir. cancer prevention and control, 1988—2005, dep. dir., 1989-96, assoc. dean rsch. Coll. Medicine, 1996—2002, acting chief hematology and oncology, 1998-99, Regent's prof. medicine, pharmacology and pub. health, 2004—, dir., 2005—; v.p. bus. devel. AMPLIMED, Tucson, 2003—05. External advisor U. Chgo. Cancer Ctr., 1993-98, Tulane U. Cancer Ctr., New Orleans, 1993-96, M.D. Anderson Cancer Ctr., Houston, 1994—2004, Norris Cotton Cancer Ctr., Hanover, 1995-2000, Lee Moffit Cancer Ctr., Tampa, 2003—; mem. bd. sci. counselors divsn. Cancer Prevention and Control, Nat. Cancer Inst., NIH, 1990-94, chmn. chemoprevention external com. divsn. cancer prevention, 1997-2001; chmn. gynecologic cancer com. S.W. Oncology Group, 1977-2001; mem. monitoring and adv. panel Nat. Prostate Lung-Colon-Ovary Cancer Study, NCI-NIH, 1994—; mem. oversight com. NCI Nat. Lung Cancer Screening Trial, 2002—; chmn. cancer prevention com. Gynecologic Oncology Group, 1995—; chmn. oncologic adv. com. U.S. FDA, 1982-84, spl. cons., 1984-86; mem. bd. sci. adv., Nat. Cancer Inst., NIH, 1999—; bd. dirs., Cancer Rsch. and Prevention Found., 1992—. Co-editor-in-chief Cancer Epidemiology, Biomarkers and Prevention, 2002—; assoc. editor Cancer Rsch., 1989-2002, Cancer Chemother. and Pharmacol., 1992—, Clin. Cancer Rsch., 1994-96, Neoplasia, 1998—; editor Fundamentals of Cancer Prevention, 2005; contbr. articles to over 500 to profl. jours., 90 book chpts.; inventor azamitosene and anthracene anticancer agts., tumorimeter, hypodermic needle with automatic retracting point; tropical DFMO; two step carcinogen/HIV chemical deactivation system; method and composition for deactivating HIV infected blood and anticancer drugs; amifostine reversal of platinum-induced neuropathy; measurement of lesion progression via mapping of chromatin texture features along progression curve. Grantee Nat. Cancer Inst., NIH, 1975—. Mem. Am. Soc. Clin. Pharmacology and Therapeutics, Am. Soc. Clin. Oncology (ACS Prevention award 1999), Am. Cancer Soc. Cancer Prevention, Am. Soc. Preventive Oncology (Disting. Achievement award 2004), Am. Assn. Cancer Rsch. (Jos. Burchenal clin. rsch. award 2003, Excellence in Cancer Prevention award 2004), Soc. Gynecologic Oncologists. Achievements include Listed by Sci. June 15, 2001 as 3rd highest NIH peer reviewed funded clin. rschr. in U.S. Office: Ariz Cancer Ctr 1501 N Campbell Ave Tucson AZ 85724-0001

ALBINO, JUDITH ELAINE NEWSOM, university president; b. Jackson, Tenn. m. Salvatore Albino; children: Austin, Adrian. BJ, U. Tex., 1967, PhD, 1973. V.p. acad. affairs and rsch, dean system grad. sch. U. Colo., Boulder, 1990-91; mem. faculty sch. dental medicine SUNY, Buffalo, 1972-90, assoc. provost, 1984-87, dean sch. arch. and planning, 1987-89, dean grad. sch., 1989-90; pres. U. Colo., Boulder, 1991-95, pres. emerita, prof. psychiatry, 1995-97; pres. Calif. Sch. Profl. Psychology Alliant Internat. U., San Francisco, 1997—2004; cons. Health Sci. Ctr., Univ. Colo., Denver, 2004—. Contbr. articles to profl. jours. Acad. Adminstrn. fellow Am. Coun. on Edn., 1983; grantee NIH. Fellow APA (treas., bd. dirs.); mem. Behavioral Scientists in Dental Rsch. (past pres.), Am. Assn. Dental Rsch. (bd. dirs.), Psychologists in Mgmt. (pres.). Personal E-mail: judithalbino@comcast.net.

ALBRECHT, RICHARD RAYMOND, retired manufacturing executive, lawyer; b. Storm Lake, Iowa, Aug. 29, 1932; s. Arnold Louis and Catherine Dorothea (Boettcher) A.; m. Constance Marie Berg, June 16, 1957; children: John Justin, Carl Arnold, Richard Louis, Henry Berg. BA, U. Iowa, 1958, JD with highest honors, 1961. Bar: Wash. 1961. Assoc. Perkins, Coie, Stone, Olsen & Williams, Seattle, 1961—67, ptnr., 1968—74; gen. counsel U.S. Dept. Treasury, Washington, 1974—76; v.p., gen. counsel, sec. Boeing Co., Seattle, 1976—81, v.p. fin., contracts and internat. bus., 1981—83, v.p., gen. mgr. Everett divsn., 1983—84; exec. v.p. Boeing Comml. Airplane Group, Seattle, 1984—97, sr. advisor, 1997—2000. Bd. dirs. Esterline Technologies Corp., 1997-2005, Wash. Dental Svc. Mem. bd. regents Wash. State U., 1997-2005. With AUS, 1955-58. Recipient Outstanding Citizen of Yr. award Seattle-King County Municipal League, 1968-69, Disting. Alumni award U. Iowa, 2002. Mem. ABA, Wash. State Bar Assn., Am. Judicature Soc., Order of St. John (officer 1992-99, comdr. 1999-04, knight 2004-), Order of Coif, Rainier Club, Broadmoor Golf Club, Wing Point Golf Club, Seattle Tennis Club, Sigma Nu, Omicron Delta Kappa, Phi Delta Phi Home: PO Box 10669 Bainbridge Island WA 98110 Office: Perkins Coie LLP 1201 3rd Ave Ste 4800 Seattle WA 98101-3099 Office Phone: 206-855-8896. Business E-Mail: dick@albrecht.net.

ALBRECHT, STAN LEROY, academic administrator, sociologist, educator; b. Fremont, Utah, July 13, 1942; s. Rex LeRoy and Alta (Taylor) A.; m. Joyce Van Wagoner; children: Sheri, Michael, Bryant, Rachelle, Stacia. BS, Brigham Young U., 1966; MA, Wash. State U., 1968, PhD, 1970. Asst. prof. Utah State U., Logan, 1970-74, exec. v.p., provost, 2000—05, pres., 2005—; assoc. prof. Brigham Young U., Provo, Utah, 1974-78, prof., 1978—, dean, 1988-89, acad. v.p., 1989. Vis. asst. prof. SUNY, Albany, 1973. Author: Social Psychology, 1981, 87, Divorce and Remarriage, 1980, Research Methods, 1984. Mem. Am. Sociol. Assn., Rural Sociol. Soc. (v.p. 1986). Democrat. Mem. Lds Ch. Avocations: hiking, fishing. Office: Utah State U 1420 Old Main Hill Logan UT 84322-1420 Home: 818 E Summit Dr Smithfield UT 84335

ALBRIGHT, THOMAS D., science foundation director, educator, researcher; BS in Psychology, U. Md.; MS in Psychology and Neuroscience, Princeton U.; PhD in Psychology and Neuroscience, Princeton U., NJ. Postdoctoral fellow Princeton U.; prof., dir. Vision Rsch. Ctr., Sloan-Swartz Ctr. for Theoretical Neurobiology at Salk Inst. for Biol. Studies, San Diego. Adj. prof. U. Calif., San Diego. Contbr. scientific papers, articles to profl. jours. Recipient McKnight Neuroscience Devel. award, 1991—93, investigator, Howard Hughes Med. Inst., 1997; rsch. fellowship, Sloan Found., 1989—91. Fellow: Am. Acad. Arts and Scis.; mem.: NAS (Recipient award for Initiatives in Rsch. 1995). Achievements include research in neuronal bases of visual perception, visually guided behavior and visual memory in primates. Office: Salk Inst Biological Studies PO Box 85800 San Diego CA 92186-5800 Office Phone: 858-453-4100. Business E-Mail: tom@salk.edu.

ALBRITTON, DANIEL LEE, atmospheric scientist; b. Camden, Ala., June 8, 1936; BS in Elec. Engring., Ga. Inst. Tech., 1959, MS in Physics, 1963, PhD in Physics, 1967. Dir. Aeronomy Lab. NOAA, Boulder, Colo., 1986—. Leader atmospheric chemistry project Climate and Global Change Program NOAA; co-chmn. sci. assessments of stratospheric ozone U.N. Environ. Programme; mem. sci. working group Intergovtl. Panel on Climate Change; lectr. in atm scis. and policy/sci. interface. Former mem. editl. adv. bd. Jour. Molecular Spectroscopy; former co-editor Jour. Atmospheric Chemistry; contbr. 150 articles to profl. jours. Recipient pres. rank svc. award, 1990, 97, 2001, gold medal Dept. Commerce, 1977, 93, sci. freedom and responsibility award AAAS, 1993, sci. assessments award Am. Meteorol. Soc., 1993, stratospheric ozone protection award EPA, 1994, UN environ. programme ozone award, 1995, Pacesetter award Boulder Daily Camera, 2001. Fellow Am. Phys. Soc., Am. Geophys. Union. Achievements include research in laboratory investigation of atmospheric ion-molecular reactions and theoretical studies of diatomic molecular structure, investigation of atmospheric trace-gas photochemistry, sci. advisor in ozone depletion and climate change policy. Office: NOAA Aeronomy Lab 325 Broadway St Boulder CO 80305-3328

ALCON, ELISEO LEE, state legislator; Veteran; mem. Dist. 6 N. Mex. House of Reps., 2009—. Democrat. Office: House of Representatives State Capitol North Rm 203CCN Santa Fe NM 87501 Home: Box 2134 Milan NM 87021 Home Phone: 505-285-6387; Office Phone: 505-986-4254. Personal E-mail: eliseoalcon@msn.com.

ALCOSSER, SANDRA BETH, English language educator, writer; b. Washington, Feb. 3, 1944; d. Karl Richard and Bernetta Elaine (Hutson) Weis; m. Philip Maechling, May 24, 1978. BA, Purdue U., 1972; MFA, U. Mont., 1982. Assoc. editor Mademoiselle Mag., NYC, 1966-69; workshop dir. Lower East Side Svc. Ctr., NYC, 1973-75; dir. Poets in the Park-Ctrl. Park, NYC, 1975-77; solo artist Nat. Endowment for the Arts, various, 1977-85; tchg. asst. U. Mont., Missoula, 1980-82; instr. to asst. prof. English La. State U., Baton Rouge, 1982-87; assoc. prof. English San Diego State U., 1987-89, dir. creative writing program, 1988-91, 99—, prof. English, 1990—; faculty affiliate U. Mont., Missoula, 1995—, Richard Hugo writer in residence, 2000—. Vis. prof. Southern U., Baton Rouge, 1983; writer-in-residence Glacier Nat. Park, Mont., 1978, U. Mich., Ann Arbor, 1994, poet laureate, State of Mont., 2005. Author: Each Bone a Prayerpoetry, 1982, A Fish to Feed All Hunger, 1986, (Associated Writing Program award for Poetry), Sleeping Inside the Glacier, 1997, Except by Nature, 1998 (Nat. Poetry Series selection, James Laughlin award Acad. Am. Poets, William Stafford Poetry award Pacific N.W. Booksellers, Larry Levin award Va. Commonwealth U.); author: (with others) The Central Park Book, 1977, Ariadne's Thread: A Collection of Contemporary Women's Journals, 1982, Introspections: American Poets on One of their Own Poems, 1997; editor The Pushcart Prize Anthology, 1989-91; mem. editorial bd. Poetry International, 1996; contbr. poems to profl. jours. Poetry fellow Nat. Endowment for the Arts, Wash., 1985, 91, COMBO fellow San Diego Arts Council, 1987, Bread Leaf fellow Middlebury Coll., Vermont, 1992, Creative Arts fellow Mont. Arts Council, Helena, Mont., 1993-94. Mem. Poets and Writers, Associated Writing Programs. Avocations: hiking, cross-country. Office: San Diego State Dept English & Comparative Lit San Diego CA 92182 E-mail: alcosser@mail.sdsu.edu.

ALDAVE, BARBARA BADER, lawyer, educator; b. Tacoma, Dec. 28, 1938; d. Fred A. and Patricia W. (Burns) Bader; m. Rafael Aldave, Apr. 2, 1966; children: Anna Marie Alkin, Anthony John. BS, Stanford U., 1960; JD, U. Calif., Berkeley, 1966. Bar: Oreg. 1966, Tex. 1982, US Supreme Ct. 2008. Assoc. law firm, Eugene, Oreg., 1967-70; asst. prof. U. Oreg., 1970-73, prof. Eugene, 2000—; vis. prof. U. Calif., Berkeley, 1973-74; from vis. prof. to prof. U. Tex., Austin, 1974-89, co-holder James R. Dougherty chair for faculty excellence, 1981-82, Piper prof., 1982, Joe A. Worsham centennial prof., 1984-89, Liddell, Sapp, Zivley, Hill and LaBoon prof. banking fin. and comml. law, 1989; dean Sch. Law, prof. St. Mary's U., San Antonio, 1989-98, Ernest W. Clemens prof. corp. law, 1996-98; Loran L. Stewart prof. corp. law, dir., Ctr. for Law and Entrepreneurship U. Oreg. Sch. Law, 2000—. Vis. prof. Northeastern U., 1985-88, 98, Boston Coll. 1999-2000, Cornell U., 2002; ABA rep. to Coun. Inter-ABA, 1995-99; NAFTA chpt. 19 panelist, 1994-96. Pres. NETWORK, 1985-89; chair Gender Bias Task Force of Supreme Ct. Tex., 1991-94; bd. dirs. Tex. Alliance Children's Rights, Lawyer's Com. for Civil Rights Under Law of Tex., 1995-2000; nat. chair Gray Panthers, 1999-2003; pres. Portia Project, 2003—; vice chair Mex. Am. Cultured Ctr., 2003—. Recipient Tchg. Excellence award U. Tex. Student Bar Assn., 1976, Appreciation awards Thurgood Marshall Legal Soc. of U. Tex., 1979, 81, 85, 87, Tchg. Excellence award Chicano Law Students Assn. of U. Tex., 1984, Hermine Tobolowsky award Women's Law Caucus of U. Tex., 1985, Ethics award Kugle, Stewart, Dent & Frederick, 1988, Leadership award Women's Law Assn. St. Mary's U., 1989, Ann. Inspirational award Women's Advocacy Project, 1989, Appreciation award San Antonio Black Lawyers Assn., 1990, Spl. Recognition award Nat. Conv. Nat. Lawyers Guild, 1990, Spirit of the Am. Woman award J. C. Penney Co., 1992, Sarah T. Hughes award Women and the Law sect. State Bar Tex., 1994, Ann. Tchg. award Soc. Am. Law Tchrs., 1996, Legal Svcs. award Mexican-Am. Legal Def. and Ednl. Fund, 1996, Woman of Justice award NETWORK, 1997, Ann. Peacemaker award Camino a la Paz, 1997, Outstanding Profl. in the Cmty. award Dept. Pub. Justice, St. Mary's U., 1997, Charles Hamilton Houston award Black Allied Law Students Assn. St. Mary's U., 1998, Woman of Yr. award Tex. Women's Polit. Caucus, 1998, award Clin. Legal Edn. Assn., 1998, Lifetime Achievement award Jour. Law and Religion, 1998, Harriet Tubman award African-Am. Reflections, 2002, Frohnmayer Pub. Svc. award, U. Oreg., 2009. Mem.: ABA (com. on corp. laws, sect. banking and bus. law 1982—88, Latin Am. law initiative coun. 2004—06), Oregon Law Sch. Alumni Assn. (Frohnmayer Award 2009), US-Mex. Bar Assn. (U.S. chair legal edn. com. 2005—08, bd. dirs. 2008—), Inter-Am. Bar Assn., Am. Bar Found. (life), Tex. Bar Found. (life), Stanford U. Alumni Assn., Order of Coif, Delta Theta Phi (Outstanding Law Prof award St. Mary's U. chpt. 1990, 1991), Omicron Delta Kappa, Iota Sigma Pi, Phi Delta Phi. Roman Catholic. Home: 86399 N Modesto Dr Eugene OR 97402-9031 Office: U Oreg Sch Law Eugene OR 97403-1221 Home Phone: 541-344-0555; Office Phone: 541-346-3985. Personal E-mail: balaw98@aol.com. Business E-Mail: aldave@uoregon.edu.

ALDEA, GABRIEL S., cardiothoracic surgeon, educator; b. Bucharest, Romania, Nov. 7, 1956; came to U.S., 1970; s. Adrian and Blanche (Fainaru) A.; m. Susan Arnold, May 8, 1988; children: Alexander, Daniel. BA in Biochemistry summa cum laude, Columbia Coll., 1977; MD, Columbia U., 1981. Diplomate Am. Bd. Surgery, Am. Bd. Thoracic Surgery, Nat. Bd. Med. Examiners. Resident in gen. surgery N.Y. Hosp., Cornell Med. Ctr., NYC, 1981—86, adminstrv. chief resident Dept. Surgery, 1985-86; cardiothoracic residency Dept. Cardiothoracic Surgery N.Y. Hosp., Cornell Med. Ctr. & Meml. Sloane Kettering Hosp., NYC, 1988-90; cardiovasc. rsch. fellowship Cardiovasc. Rsch. Inst.-U. Calif. San Francisco, 1986-88; asst. vis. surgeon in cardiothoracic surgery Boston U. Med. Ctr., 1990-98; assoc. vis. surgeon in thoracic surgery Boston City Hosp., 1990-98; thoracic surgeon Jamaica Plain VA Hosp., Boston; assoc. prof. cardiothoracic surgery Boston U. Sch. Medicine, 1990-98; chief adult cardiac surgery, prof. surgery U. Wash., Seattle, 1998—2002, prof. surgery, 2002—; cardiac surgeon N.W. Hosp., Seattle, 1998—, Puget Sound VA Hosp., Seattle, 1998—. Contbr. articles to profl. jours. and chpts. to books. Recipient Nat. Rsch. Svc. award in heart & vascular diseases NIH, 1986-88. Fellow New Eng. Oncologic Soc., Am. Surg. Assn.; mem. AAAS, AMA, ACS, Am. Coll. Chest Physicians, Am. Coll. Cardiology, Am. Heart Assn., Soc. for Thoracic Surgeons, Am. Assn. for Thoracic Surgery, Assn. Acad. Surgery, Mass. Med. Soc., Rsch. Assocs. Southwestern Oncology Group, Western Thoracic Assn., Am. Surgical Assn. Home: The Highlands Seattle WA 98177 Office: U Wash Dept Cardiothorasic Surgery PO Box 356310 Seattle WA 98195-6310 Office Phone: 206-543-3093.

ALDEN, JOHN W., lawyer; BS, Stanford U., 1955, MS, 1956, JD, 1959. Bar: Calif. 1960. Assoc. Pillsbury, Madison & Sutro, 1959-67; assoc. gen. counsel Occidental Petroleum Corp., LA, 1967—2004; ret., 2004. Office: Occidental Petroleum Corp 10889 Wilshire Blvd Ste 1500 Los Angeles CA 90024-4216 E-mail: john_w_alden@oxy.com.

ALDER, BERNI JULIAN, physicist, researcher; b. Duisburg, Germany, Sept. 9, 1925; came to U.S., 1941, naturalized, 1944; s. Ludwig and Ottilie (Gottschalk) A.; m. Esther Berger, Dec. 28, 1956; children: Kenneth, Daniel, Janet. BS, U. Calif., Berkeley, 1947, MS, 1948; PhD, Calif. Inst. Tech., 1951. Instr. chemistry U. Calif., Berkeley, 1951-54; theoretical physicist Lawrence Livermore Lab., Livermore, Calif., 1955-93; prof. dept. applied sci. U. Calif., Davis, 1987-93, prof. emeritus, 1993; van der Waals prof. U. Amsterdam, Netherlands, 1971; prof. associé U. Paris, 1972. G.N. Lewis lectr. U. Calif., Berkeley, 1984, Hinshelwood prof., Oxford, 1986, Lorentz prof., Leiden, 1990, Kistiakowsky lectr. Harvard U., 1990, Royal Soc. lectr., 1991. Author: Methods of Computational Physics, 1963; editor: Jour. Computational Physics, 1966-91. Served with USN, 1944-46. Recipient Boltzmann medal Internat. Union Pure and Applied Physics, 2001; Guggenheim fellow, 1954-55; NSF sr. postdoctoral fellow, 1963-64, Japanese Promotion of Sci. fellow, 1989; Berni J. Alder prize established by European Phys. Soc., 1999. Fellow: Am. Acad. Arts Scis., Am. Phys. Soc.; mem.: Rare Gas Dynamics Soc. (Grad lectr. 2000), Am. Chem. Soc. (Hildebrand award 1985), Nat. Acad. Scis. Republican. Jewish. Office: Lawrence Livermore Lab PO Box 808 Livermore CA 94551-0808 Office Phone: 925-422-4384. Business E-Mail: alder1@llnl.gov.

ALDERMAN, MINNIS AMELIA, psychologist, educator, small business owner; b. Douglas, Ga., Oct. 14, 1928; d. Louis Cleveland Sr. and Minnis Amelia (Wooten) A. AB in Music, Speech and Drama, Ga. State Coll., Milledgeville, 1949; MA in Supervision/Counseling Psychology, Murray State U., Ky., 1960; postgrad., Columbia Pacific U., L.A., 1987. Tchr. music Lake County Sch. Dist., Umatilla, Fla., 1949—50; instr. vocal/instrumental music, dir. band, orch., choral Fulton County Sch. Dist., Atlanta, 1950—54; instr. English, speech, debate, vocal and instrumental music Elko County Sch. Dist., Wells, Nev., 1954—59, dir. drama, band, choral and orchestra, 1954—59; tchr. English and social studies Christian County Sch. Dist., Hopkinsville, Ky., 1960; instr. psychology, counselor critic prof. Murray State U., Ky., 1961—63, U. Nev., Reno, 1963—67; owner Minisizer Exercising Salon, Ely, Nev., 1969—71, Knit Knook, Ely, 1969—, Minimimeo, Ely, 1969—, Gift Gamut, Ely, 1977—; prof. dept. fine arts Wassuk Coll., Ely, 1986—91, assoc. dean, 1986—87, dean, 1987—90; counselor White Pine County Sch. Dist., Ely, 1960—68; dir. Child and Family Ctr. Ely Indian Tribe, 1988—93. Contbr. articles to profl. jours. Dir. Family Resource Ctr. (Great Basin Rural Nev. Youth Cabinet), 1996—; bd. dir. band Sacred Heart Sch., Ely, 1982-99; active Gov.'s Mental Health State Commn., 1963-65, Nev. Hwy. Safety Leaders Bd., 1979-82, Ely Shoshone Tribal Youth Camp, 1991-92, Elys Shoshone Tribal Unity Conf., 1991-92, Tribal Parenting Skills Coord., 1991, White Pine Overall Econ. Devel. Plan Coun., 1992-2005; bd. dir. White Pine County Sch. Employees Fed. Credit Union, 1961-68, pres., 1963-68; 2d v.p. White Pine Cmty. Concert Assn., 1965-67, pres., 1967, 85—, treas., 1975-79, dr. chmn., 1981-85; chmn. bd., 1984; bd. dir. United Way, 1970-76, White Pine chpt. ARC, 1978-82; mem. Gov.'s Commn. on Status Women, 1968-74, Gov.'s Nevada State Juvenile Justice Adv. Commn., 1992-94; dir. White Pine Cmty. Choir, 1962—, Ret. Sr. Vol. Program, 1973-74, White Pine Legis. Coalition, 2002—; sec.-treas. White Pine Rehab. Tng. Ctr. for Retarded Persons, 1973-75, White Pine County Juvenile Problems Cabinet, 1994—, Gt. Basin chpt. Nev. Employees Assn., 1970-76; chmn. adv. coun. White Pine Sr. Ctr., 2005—; mem. Gov.'s Commn. on Hwy. Safety, 1979-81, Gov's. Juvenile Justice Program; vice-chmn. Gt. Basin Health Coun., 1973-75, Home Ext. adv. Bd., 1977-80; vice-chmn. White Pine Coun. on Alcoholism and Drug Abuse, 1975-76, chmn., 1976-77, White Pine County Bus. Coun., 1998—; dir. White Pine Coalition; grants author 3 yrs. Indian Child Welfare Act, State Hist. Preservation, Fair and Recreation Bd. Centennial Fine Arts Ctr.; originator Cmty. Tng. Ctr. Retarded People, 1972, Ret. Sr. Vol. Program, 1973-74, Nutrition Program Sr. Citizens, 1974, Sr. Citizens Ctr., 1974, Home Repairs Sr. Citizens, 1974, Sr. Citizens Crafters Assns., 1976, Inst. Current World Affairs, 1989, Victims of Crime, 1990-92, grants author Family Resource Ctr., 1995; bd. dirs. Family coalition, 1990-92, Sacred Heart Parochial Sch., dir. band, 1982-2000; candidate diaconal ministry, 1982-93; invited performer Branson Jubilee Nat. Ch. Choir Festival, Mo., Ely Meth. Ch. Choir, 1960-84; choir dir., organist Sacred Heart Ch., 1984—; Precinct reporter ABC News, 1966; bd. dir. White Pine Juvenile Cabinet, 1993—, Ely/East Ely Bus. Coun., 1997—, Econ. Devel. Bd., 1998—; chmn. adv. coun. White Pine Sr. Ctr., 2005—; bd. White Pine C. of C., 2000—; bd. dirs. Whtie Pine Mus., 2006—, sec. 2009-; pres. White Pine Sr. Adv. Coun., 2005—. Recipient Recognition rose, Alpha Chi State Delta Kappa Gamma, 1994, Recognition Rose, 2002, Perserving America's Treasures in the 21st Century, 2001; named scholar, Nat. Trust for Hist. Preservation, 2000; grantee, Nat. Trust for Historic Preservation, LA, 2000. Fellow Am. Coll. Musicians, Nat. Guild Piano Tchrs.; mem. NEA (life), UDC, DAR, Nat. Fedn. Ind. Bus. (dist. chair 1971-85, nat. guardian coun. 1985—, state guardian coun. 1987—), AAUW (pres. Wells br. 1957-58, pres. White Pine br. 1965-66, 86-87, 89-91, 93—, bd. dir. 1965-87, rep. edn. 1965-67, implementation chair 1967-69, area advisor 1969-73, 89-91), Nat. Fedn. Bus. and Profl. Women (1st v.p. Ely chpt. 1965-66, pres. Ely chpt. 1966-68, 74-76, 85—, bd. dir. Nev. chpt., 1st v.p. Nev. Fedn. 1970-71, pres. Nev. chpt. 1972-73, nat. bd. dir. 1972-73), White Pine County Mental Health Assn. (pres. 1960-63, 78—), Mensa (supr. testing 1965—), White Pine C. of C. (bd. dirs. 2000—), White Pine Nuc. Waste Assn., Lincoln Hwy. Assn. (bd. dirs., 2004—), Bus. Area Network Group, Delta Kappa Gamma (chpt. pres. 1968-72, 94-99, 2008-, state bd. 1967—, chpt. parliamentarian 1974-78, 99—, state 1st v.p. 1967-69, state pres. 1969-71, nat. bd. 1969-71, state parliamentarian 1971-73, 95—, chmn. state nominating com. 1995-97, chmn. bylaws com. 2003—, workshop presenter aging, itelligence and learning, San Francisco, 1995), White Pine Knife and Fork Club (1st v.p. 1969-70, pres. 1970-71, bd. dirs.), Soc. Descs. Knights Most Noble Order of Garter, Nat. Soc. Magna Charta Dames, Delta Kappa Gamma (SW regional conf. workshop presenter 1995), Nat. Assn. Parliamentarians. Office: 1280 E Aultman St Ely NV 89301 Office Phone: 775-289-2116. Home Fax: 775-289-5217.

ALDERMAN, WILLIAM FIELDS, lawyer; b. Hamilton, Ohio, 1945; AB summa cum laude, Miami U., 1967; JD, Yale U., 1970. Bar: Calif. 1971. Ptnr. Orrick, Herrington & Sutcliffe, San Francisco, 1976—. Ct. apptd. arbitrator, mediator, evaluator, 1988—. Contbr. articles to profl. jours. Dir. Lawyers Com. Civil Rights San Francisco Bay Area, 1985—95, St. Thomas More Soc. San Francisco, 1987—94, pres., 1993; dir. Bay Area Legal Aid, 1995—. Recipient Jr. Pro Bono award, Lawyers Com., 1996. Mem.: ABA, State Bar Calif., Bar Assn. San Francisco (chair audit com. 2002—04), Phi Beta Kappa. Office: Orrick Herrington Sutcliffe 405 Howard St Fl 7 San Francisco CA 94105-2680 Office Phone: 415-773-5700. Business E-Mail: walderman@orrick.com.

ALDERSON, SANDY (RICHARD LYNN ALDERSON), former professional sports team executive; b. Seattle, Nov. 22, 1947; s. John Lester and Gwenny (Parry) A.; m. Linda Lee Huff, Dec. 20, 1969; children: Catrin Gwennan, Bryn Garreth. BA, Dartmouth Coll., 1969; JD, Harvard U., 1976. Assoc. Farella, Braun & Martel, San Francisco, 1976-81; gen. counsel Oakland Athletics, Calif., 1981-83, v.p. baseball ops., 1983-93, pres., gen. mgr., 1993—95, 1997—98; exec. v.p., baseball ops. Major League Baseball, 1998—2005; CEO San Diego Padres, 2005—09. Dir. Major League Scouting Bur., Newport Beach, Calif. Served to lt. USMC, 1969-73, Vietnam*

ALDISERT, RUGGERO JOHN, federal judge; b. Carnegie, Pa., Nov. 10, 1919; s. John S. and Elizabeth (Magnacca) Aldisert; m. Agatha Maria DeLacio, Oct. 4, 1952; children: Lisa Maria, Robert, Gregory. BA, U. Pitts., 1941, JD, 1947. Bar: Pa. 1947. Gen. practice law, Pitts., 1947—61; judge Ct. Common Pleas, Allegheny County, 1961—68, U.S. Ct. Appeals (3d cir.), Pitts., 1968—84, chief judge, 1984—87, sr. judge Pitts., Santa Barbara, Calif., 1987—. Adj. prof. law U. Pitts. Sch. Law, 1964—87; faculty Appellate Judges Seminar, NYU, 1971—85, assoc. dir., 1979—85; chmn. Fed. Appellate Judges Seminar, 1972—78; mem. Pa. Civil Procedural Rules Com., 1965—84, Jud. Conf. Com. on Adminstrn. Criminal Law, 1971—77; chmn. adv. com. on bankruptcy rules Jud. Conf. U.S., 1979—84; vis. prof. univs. in U.S. and abroad, 1965—99; intensive lectures at univs in, Italy, Germany, France, Poland, Croatia and Serbia. Author: Il Ritorno al Paese, 1966—67, The Judicial Process, Readings, Materials and Cases, 1996, 2d edit., 1996, Logic for Lawyers: A Guide to Clear Legal Thinking, 1997, 3d edit., 1997, Opinion Writing, 1990, Winning on Appeal, 2003, Road to the Robes: A Federal Judge Recollects Young Years and Early Times, 2005; contbr. over 50 articles to profl. publs. Allegheny dist. chmn. Multiple Sclerosis Soc., 1961—68; pres. ISDA, Cultural Heritage Found., 1965—68; trustee U. Pitts., 1968—; mem. bd. visitors Pitts. Sch. Law, 1968—, chmn., 1969—99. Maj. USMC, 1942—46, with USMC, 1946—51. Recipient Outstanding Merit award, Allegheny County Acad. Trial Lawyers, 1964, Disting. Appellate Jurist award, 2005, Disting. Citizen of Carnegia Borough award, 2005. Mem.: Am. Law Inst., Italian Sons and Daus. Am. Fraternal Assn. (nat. pres. 1954—68), Omicron Delta Kappa, Phi Alpha Delta, Phi Beta Kappa. Democrat. Roman Catholic. Office: US Ct Appeals 120 Cremona Dr Ste D Santa Barbara CA 93117-5511

ALDRIDGE, LAMARCUS NURAE, professional basketball player; b. Dallas, July 19, 1985; s. Georgia Aldridge. Student in Corp. Comm., U. Tex., Austin, 2004—06. Draft pick Chgo. Bulls, 2006; forward Portland Trail Blazers, Oreg., 2006—. Named Big 12 Defensive Player of Yr., 2006; named to First-Team All-Big 12, 2006, NBA All-Rookie First Team, 2007. Mailing: Portland Trail Blazers Rose Quarter One Center Ct Ste 200 Portland OR 97227

ALDRIN, BUZZ, retired astronaut; b. Montclair, NJ, Jan. 20, 1930; s. Edwin Eugene and Marion (Moon) Aldrin; m. Beverly Van Zile, Dec. 19, 1975 (div. 1978); m. Jean Ann Archer, Dec. 1954 (div.); children: James Michael, Janice Ross, Andrew John; m. Lois Driggs Cannon, Feb. 14, 1988. BS, US Mil. Acad., 1951; attended, Squadron Officers Sch., Air U., Maxwell AFB, Ala.; ScD in Astronautics, MIT, 1963; ScD (hon.), Gustavus Adolphus Coll., 1967, Clark U., 1969, U. Portland, 1970, St. Peter's Coll., 1970; LittD (hon.), Montclair State Coll., 1969; HHD (hon.), Seton Hall U., 1970. Commd. officer USAF, 1951, advanced through grades to col.; served as fighter pilot in Korea with 51st Fighter Interceptor Wing, 1953; aerial gunnery instr. Nellis AFB, Nev.; flight comdr. 36th Tactical Fighter Wing, Bitburg, Germany; assigned to Gemini Target Office Air Force Space Sys. Divsn., LA; USAF Field Office, Manned Spacecraft Ctr.; selected for 3rd group of astronauts NASA, 1963; backup pilot Gemini IX; pilot Gemini XII orbital rendezvous space flight, Nov. 11-15, 1966; backup command module pilot Apollo VIII; lunar module pilot on first manned lunar landing Apollo XI; comdr. Aerospace Rsch. Pilots Sch., Edwards AFB, Calif., 1971-72; ret. NASA, 1971, USAF, 1972; with Ctr. for Aerospace Scis. U. N.D., Grand Forks, 1989. Sci. cons. Beverly Hills Oil Co., Inforex Computer Co., Laser Video Corp., Mut. of Omaha Ins.; founder, pres. Starcraft Enterprises Internat.(Starcraft Boosters, Inc.), 1988-; founder, chmn. ShareSpace Found. to promote affordable space tourism for all people, 1998-; bd. dirs. Neah Power Systems, 2007-; appointed to Commn. on the Future of US Aerospace Industry, 2002; lectr. in field. Author: Return to Earth, 1973, Men From Earth, 1989, Encounter with Tiber, 1996, The Return, 2000, (children's book) Reaching for the Moon, 2005; (TV appearances) The Fall Guy, 1985, Punky Brewster, 1986, Head of the Class, 1989, (voice) The Simpsons, 1994; (TV films) The Boy in the Plastic Bubble, 1976; (films) (voice) Fly Me to the Moon, 2008. Decorated DSM, Legion of Merit, DFC with oak leaf cluster, Air medal with 2 oak leaf clusters,DSM NASA, Exceptional Svc. medal, Group Achievement award; recipient Harmon Internat. Trophy, 1967, Presdl. medal of Freedom, 1969, Robert J. Collier Trophy, Robert H. Goddard Meml. Trophy, Horatio Alger award, 2005, NASA Amb. Exploration award, 2006; named to NJ Hall of Fame, 2007, numerous other awards. Fellow AIAA; mem. Nat. Space Soc. (chmn.), Soc. Exptl. Test Pilots, Royal Aero. Soc. (hon.), Sea Space Symposium; charter Internat. Acad. Astronautics (corr.), Sigma Xi, Tau Beta Pi. Clubs: Masons (33 degree). Shot down two MiG-15s during 66 combat mission in the Korean War; In November, 1966, established record over 7 hours and 52 minutes outside spacecraft in extra-vehicular activity on the Gemini XII orbital flight mission; On July 20, 1969, walked on moon along with Neil Armstrong during Apollo XI Mission, becoming the first two humans to set foot on another world. This heroic endeavor was witnessed by the largest worldwide television audience in history; In 1988 he legally changed name from Edwin E. Aldrin Jr.; In 1993, received US patent for permanent space station he designed.*

ALENIUS, JOHN TODD, retired insurance executive; b. Denver, Sept. 27, 1938; s. Robert and Elizabeth Frances (Todd) A.; m. Sandra Lee Mally, June 30, 1962; children: Constance, Mark, Patricia, William. BBA, Regis. Coll., 1961; postgrad., Havard U., 1971; MA in Mgmt., Webster Coll., 1979. Commd. USAF, 1962, advanced through grades to col., personnel mgr. Vietnam, 1966-67, Colorado Springs, Colo., 1962-67, systems mgr. San Antonio, 1971-75; with exchange duty Canadian Armed Forces, Ottawa, Ont., Can., 1975-77; various system mgmt. positions USAF, San Antonio, 1977-83, dir. logistic mgmt. systems Sacramento, 1983-85; v.p. info. systems Vision Service Plan, Sacramento, 1985-88, exec. v.p. ops., 1988-98, exec. v.p., 1998—2001. Mem. Soc. Info. Mgmt., Am. Mgmt. Assn. Republican. Roman Catholic. Avocations: fishing, golf. Office: California Vision Service Inc 3333 Quality Dr Rancho Cordova CA 95670-7985 Home: 18359 Emerald Oaks San Antonio TX 78259-3636

ALESI, TOMMY, musician; Mem. band BeauSoleil, 1976—. Albums include The Spirit of Cajun Music, 1976, Parlez Nous au Boire, 1984, Louisiana Cajun Music, 1984, Zydeco Gris Gris, 1985, Allons a Lafayette, 1986, Bayou Boogie, 1986, Bayou Cadillac, 1989, Live! From the Left Coast, 1989, Deja Vu, 1990, Cajun Conja, 1991, La Danse de la Vie, 1993, L'Echo, 1994, L'Amour ou la Folie, 1995 (Grammy award for Best Traditional Folk Album, 1997), Arc de Triomphe Two-Step, 1997, Looking Back Tomorrow, 2001, Gitane Cajun, 2004, Live in Louisiana, 2006, Live at the 2008 New Orleans Jazz & Heritage Festival (Grammy award for Best Cajun Album, 2009), Alligator Purse, 2009. Recipient Big Easy Entertainment award for Best Cajun Band, 2005. Office: care Rosebud Agy PO Box 170429 San Francisco CA 94117-0429

ALEXANDER, F. KING, academic administrator; b. Ky. BA in Polit. Sci., St. Lawrence U.; MS in Comparative Edn. Policy, Oxford U.; PhD in Higher Edn. Adminstrn., U. Wis., Madison. Mgr. Liberty Nat. Bank, Louisville; postdoctoral rschr., office of the provost U. Wis., Madison, vice chancellor for acad. affairs, lectr. ednl. adminstrn.; adminstr., mem. faculty U. Ill., Urbana-Champaign; pres. Murray State U., 2001—05, Calif. State U., Long Beach, 2006—. Found. fellow U. Oxford; faculty affiliate Cornell Higher Edn. Rsch. Inst., Inst. Govt. and Pub. Affairs. Contbr. articles to profl. jours. and publs. Office: Calif State U Long Beach BH 300 1250 N Bellflower Blvd Long Beach CA 90840-0006

ALEXANDER, GARY C., state legislator; b. Seattle, Aug. 6, 1944; m to Jacquie; children: five, five grandchildren. Commissioner, Olympia Port, 95-96; board member, Thurston Co Econ Develop Coun, formerly; budget analyst, Washington State Off Financial Management, formerly; Washington State Representative, District 20, 96-, vice chairman, Appropriations Committee, currently, member, Capital Budget, Health Care & Fish & Wildlife Legislature Oversight Committees, Joint Committee on Pension Policy, Tourism Develop Advisor Committee & Aging Coun for Coordinated Transportation, currently, Washington House Representative.Chief financial officer, Behavioral Health Resources, 96-. Kiwanis. Republican. Protestant. Office: State House Repr 407 John L O'Brien Bldg PO Box 40600 Olympia WA 98504 Office Phone: 360-786-7990. E-mail: alexande_ga@leg.wa.gov.

ALEXANDER, GEORGE JONATHON, lawyer, educator, dean; b. Berlin, Mar. 8, 1931; s. Walter and Sylvia (Grill) A.; m. Katharine Violet Sziklai, Sept. 6, 1958; children: Susan Katina, George Jonathon II. AB with maj. honors, U. Pa., 1953, JD cum laude, 1969; LLM, Yale U., 1965, JSD, 1969. Bar: Ill. 1960, NY 1961, Calif. 1974. Instr. law, Bigelow fellow U. Chgo., 1959-60; instr. internat. relations Naval Res. Officers Sch., Forrest Park, Ill., 1959-60; prof. law Syracuse U. Coll. Law, 1960-70, assoc. dean, 1968-69; prof. law U. Santa Clara Law Sch., Calif., 1970—, dir. Inst. Internat. and Comparative Law Calif., 1986—2004, disting. univ. prof. Calif., 1994-95, Elizabeth H. and John A. Sutro prof. law Calif., 1995—2005, pres. faculty senate Calif., 1996-97, dir. grad. programs, 1998-2001, co-dir., 2002; dean Santa Clara U., Calif., 1970—85, dean emeritus, 2005—; pvt. practice, 2004—. Dir. summer programs at Oxford, Geneva, Strasbourg, Budapest, Tokyo, Hong Kong, Beijing, Shanghai, Ho Chi Minh City, Singapore, Bangkok, Kuala Lumpur, Seoul, Munich, Sydney, 1986-2004; vis. prof. law U. So. Calif., 1963; vis. scholar Stanford (Calif.) U. Law Sch., 1985-86, 92; cons. in field. Author: Civil Rights, U.S.A., Public Schools, 1963, Honesty and Competition, 1967, Jury Instructing on Medical Issues, 1966, Cases and Materials on Space Law, 1971, The Aged and the Need for Surrogate Management, 1972, Commercial Torts, 1973, 2d edit. 1988, U.S. Antitrust Laws, 1980, Writing A Living Will: Using a Durable Power of Attorney, 1988, (with Scheflin) Law and Mental Disabilities, 1998; author, editor: International Perspectives on Aging, 1992; also articles, chpts. in books, one film. Dir. Domestic and Internat. Bus. Problems Honors Clinic, Syracuse U., 1966-69, Regulations in Space Project, 1968-70; ednl. cons. Comptroller Gen. US, 1977-2002; mem. Nat. Sr. Citizens Law Ctr., 1983-90, pres., 1986-90. With USN, 1953-56. US Navy scholar U. Pa., 1949-52; Law Bds. scholar, 1956-59; Sterling fellow Yale, 1964-65; recipient Ralph E. Kharas Civil Liberties award, Syracuse U. Sch. Law, 1970, Owens award as Lawyer of Yr., 1984, Disting. prof. Santa Clara Univ. Faculty Senate, 1994-95, 2000 award for outstanding contbns. to cause of civil liberties Freedom of Thought Found.; named Disting. Vis. Prof. Krems Danube U., Vienna, 2001. Mem. Internat. Acad. Law Mental Health (mem. sci. com. 1997-99), Calif. Bar Assn. (first chmn. com. legal problems of aging), Assn. Am. Law Schs., Soc. Am. Law Tchrs. (dir. 1979-2004, pres. 1979-80, Visionary Activist for Equality, Access and Diversity Throughout Law and Soc. award 2000), AAUP (chpt. pres. 1962), NY Civil Liberties Union (chpt. pres. 1965, dir., v.p. 1966-70), Am. Acad. Polit. and Social Sci., Order of Coif (chpt. pres. 2004-), Justinian Honor Soc., Phi Alpha Delta (chpt. faculty adviser 1967-70) Achievements include having the university law clinic renamed the Katharine and George Alexander Law Center in 2004.

ALEXANDER, GERRY L., state supreme court chief justice; b. Aberdeen, Wash., Apr. 28, 1936; BA, U. Wash., 1958, JD, 1964; LLD (hon.), Gonzaga U., 2005. Bar: Wash. 1964, U.S. Supreme Ct. 2000. Pvt. practice, Olympia, Wash., 1964—73; judge Wash. Superior Ct., Olympia, 1973—85, Wash. Ct. Appeals Divsn. II, Tacoma, 1985—95; justice Wash. Supreme Ct., Olympia, 1995—2000, chief justice, 2000—. Lt. US Army, 1958—61. Named Disting. Alumnus, U. Wash., 2000. Mem.: ABA, Statute Law Com., Washington Cts. Hist. Soc., Bench-Bar-Press (chair), Puget Sound Inn of Ct. (pres. 1996), Thurston-Mason County Assn. (pres. 1973), Wash. State Bar Assn., Am. Judges Assn. Office: Temple of Justice PO Box 40929 Olympia WA 98504-0929 Office Phone: 360-357-2029. E-mail: j_g.alexander@courts.wa.gov.

ALEXANDER, JANET COOPER, law educator; b. 1946; BA in English Lit. with distinction, Swarthmore Coll., 1968; MA in English, Stanford U., 1973; JD, U. Calif., Berkeley, 1978. Bar: Calif. 1978, DC 1980, US Dist. Ct. Cen. Dist. Calif. 1978, US Dist. Ct. No. Dist. Calif. 1982, US Dist. Ct. Ea. Dist. Calif. 1985, US Supreme Ct. 1987. Jud. clk. to Hon. Shirley M. Hufstedler US Ct. Appeals 9th Cir., 1978—79; jud. clk. to Hon. Thurgood Marshall US Supreme Ct., 1979—80; assoc. Califano, Ross & Heineman, Washington, 1980—82, Morrison & Foerster, San Francisco, 1982—84, ptnr., 1984—87; assoc. prof. law Stanford Law Sch., Calif., 1987—94, prof. Calif., 1994—2002, Frederick I. Richman prof. Calif., 2002—, Justin M. Roach, Jr. faculty scholar Calif., 1998—2002; prin. investigator Stanford Ctr. on Conflict and Negotiation, 1994—2002. Vis. prof. Toin U. of Yokohama, Japan, 1998. Alumni coun. Swarthmore Coll., 2001—, exec. com., 2003—, co-chair coll. advisory and support com., 2003—, acting chair, 2003; leadership coun. Castilleja Sch., Palo Alto, Calif., 2002—, athletic coun., 2002—, sch. assn. bd., 2002—03, co-chair parent edn., 2002—03, lead parent rep., 2002—03. Mem.: Am. Assn. Law Schools (sections on civil procedure, fed. courts, women and the law). Office: Stanford Law Sch Crown Quadrangle 559 Nathan Abbott Way Stanford CA 94305-8610 Office Phone: 650-723-2892. Business E-Mail: jca@stanford.edu.

ALEXANDER, JOHN DAVID, JR., college administrator; b. Springfield, Tenn., Oct. 18, 1932; s. John David and Mary Agnes (McKinnon) A.; m. Catharine Coleman, Aug. 26, 1956; children: Catharine McKinnon, John David III, Julia Mary. BA, Southwestern at Memphis, 1953; student, Louisville Presbyn. Theol. Sem., 1953—54; PhD, Oxford U., Eng., 1957; LLD, U. So. Calif., Occidental Coll., 1970, Centre Coll. of Ky., 1971, Pepperdine U., 1991, Albertson Coll. Idaho, 1992; LHD, Loyola Marymount U., 1983; LittD, Rhodes Coll., 1986, Pomona Coll., 1996. Assoc. prof. San Francisco Theol. Sem., 1957-65; pres. Southwestern at Memphis, 1965-69, Pomona Coll., Claremont, Calif., 1969-91. Am. sec. Rhodes Scholarship Trust, 1981—98; mem. commn. liberal learning Assn. Am. Colls., 1966—69, mem. commn. instl. affairs, 1971—74; mem. commn. colls. So. Assn. Colls. and Schs., 1966—69; mem. Nat. Commn. Acad. Tenure, 1971—72; bd. dirs. Children's Hosp., LA,

1994—2000, Wenner-Gren Found. for Anthrop. Rsch., 1995—2007; trustee Tchrs. Inst. and Annuity Assn., 1970—2002, Woodrow Wilson Nat. Fellowship Found., 1978—99, Webbs Schs., Calif., 1995—2004, Seaver Inst., 1992—, Fellows of Soc. Phi Beta Kappa, 1993—, v.p., 1998—; trustee Emeriti Retirement Health Care Inc., 2004—; bd. dirs. Webb Schs. Calif.; bd. overseers Huntington Libr., 1991—. Editor: The American Oxonian, 1997-2000, History of the American Rhodes Scholarships in History of Rhodes Trust, 2001, The Goddess Pomona, 2007. Pres. Am. Friends of Nat. Portrait Gallery (London) Found., 2004—. Decorated comdr. Order Brit. Empire; named Disting. Friend of Oxford U., 2000; Rhodes scholar, Oxford U., 1955—57. Fellow AAAS; mem. Soc. Bib. Lit., Soc. Religion in Higher Edn., Phi Beta Kappa Alumni in So. Calif. (pres. 1974-76), Century Club, Calif. Club, Bohemian Club, Athenaeum (London) Phi Beta Kappa, Omicron Delta Kappa, Sigma Nu. Office: Pomona Coll 333 N College Way Claremont CA 91711-4429 Personal E-mail: a.cadalex@verizon.net.

ALEXANDER, SHAUN, professional football player; b. Florence, Ky., Aug. 30, 1977; m. Valerie Alexander, May 18, 2002; 1 child, Heaven. BS in Mktg., U. Ala., 1999. Running back Seattle Seahawks, 2000—08, Washington Redskins, 2008. Co-author (with Cecil Murphey): Touchdown Alexander: My Story of Faith, Football, and Pursuing the Dreams, 2006. Founder The Shaun Alexander Found., 2000—. Recipient Bert Bell award, NFL, 2005, ESPY award, Best NFL Player, ESPN, 2006, ESPY award, Best Record Breaking Performance, 2006; named NFL MVP, AP, 2005, Offensive Player of Yr., 2005, First Team NFL All-Pro, 2005; named to Nat. Football Conf. Pro Bowl Team, 2003—05. Achievements include leading the NFL in: rushing touchdowns, 2001, 2005; total touchdowns, 2004, 2005; rushing attempts, rushing yards, points scored, 2005.

ALEXANDER, STEWART A., political organization worker; b. Newport News, Va., Oct. 1, 1951; s. Stewart Alexander and Ann E. McClenney; m. Freda Alexander (div.); 1 child; m. Vicki C. Alexander, 1999. Attended, Calif. State U., Dominguez Hills. Retail clk. Safeway; lic. gen. contractor Calif.; with Lockheed Aircraft, Burbank, Calif., 1980—81; warehouseman Inter-Am. Pub. Distbn. Corp., Commerce, Calif.; polit. activist Fla. Consumer Action Network, 1985—86, LI Citizens Campaign, NY; radio talk show host Sta. KTYM, Inglewood, Calif., 1986—89; automobile sales cons.; mem. state exec. com., membership and fundraising coord. Peace and Freedom Party, Calif., 2005—. Labor and industry chmn. NAACP, South Bay Br., Inglewood; US vice-presdl. candidate Socialist Party US, 2008; ind. mayoral candidate City of LA, 1988—89; lt. gubernatorial candidate Peace and Freedom Party, Calif., 2005. Served with USAFR, 1970—76. Socialist. Office: c/o Peace and Freedom Party PO Box 24764 Oakland CA 94623 Business E-Mail: stewartalexander4paf@ca.rr.com.

ALEXIS, GERALDINE M., lawyer; b. NYC, Nov. 3, 1948; d. William J. and Margaret Daly; m. Marcus Alexis, June 15, 1969; children: Marcus L., Hilary I., Sean C. BA, U. Rochester, 1971; MBA, JD, Northwestern U., 1976. Bar: Ill. 1976, Calif. 2001, U.S. Dist. Ct. (no. dist.) Calif. 1976, U.S. Dist. Ct. (no. dist.) Ill. 1976, U.S. Trial Bar 1985, U.S. Ct. Appeals (7th cir.) 1986, U.S. Ct. Appeals (5th cir.) 1996, U.S. Ct. Appeals (9th cir.) 2002. Law clk. to Hon. John F. Grady, justice U.S. Dist. Ct. (no. dist.) Ill., Chgo., 1976-77; assoc. Sidley & Austin, Chgo., 1977-79, 81-83, ptnr., 1983-2000; advisor U.S. Dept. Justice Office Legal Counsel, Washington, 1979-81; ptnr. McCutchen, Doyle, Brown & Enersen (now Bingham McCutchen LLP), San Francisco, 2001—. Mem.: ABA (co-chair fin. svcs. com. antitrust sect.). Democrat. Office: Bingham McCutchen LLP 3 Embarcadero Ctr San Francisco CA 94111

ALEXOPOULOS, NICOLAOS GEORGE, electrical engineer, educator, dean; b. Athens, Greece, Apr. 14, 1942; arrived in US, 1959; s. Yeoryeos A. and Efstathia (Yiannopoulou) A.; m. Sue B. Bunting, June 25, 1966; children: Efstathia Nicole, Christina Ariadne, Theodore Andrew. BSEE, U. Mich., 1965, MSEE, 1967, PhD in Elec. Engring., 1968. Asst. prof. elec. engring. UCLA, 1969-75, assoc. prof., 1975-81, prof., 1981—96, assoc. dean faculty affairs, 1986-87, chmn. dept., 1987—92; dean The Henry Samueli Sch. Engring. U. Calif., Irvine, 1997—, prof. elec. engring. and computer sci., 1997—. Pres. Phraxos R & D Corp., Santa Monica, Calif., 1986—; cons. aerospace industry, 1970—. Contbr. articles to profl. jours. NSF rsch. grantee, 1979—. Fellow: IEEE (S.E. Schelkunoff Prize, Best Paper award 1985, 1998, Orange County Sec. Engr. of Yr. 2001); mem.: NAE. Office: U Calif Irvine 305 Rockwell Engring Ctr Box 2700 Irvine CA 92697-2700 Office Phone: 949-824-6002. Office Fax: 949-824-7966. E-mail: alfios@uci.edu.

ALFARO, FELIX BENJAMIN, retired physician; b. Managua, Nicaragua, Oct. 22, 1939; came to U.S., 1945, naturalized, 1962; s. Agustin Jose and Amanda Julieta (Barillas) A.; m. Carmen Heide Meyer, Aug. 14, 1965; children: Felix Benjamin, Mark. Student (state scholar), U. San Francisco, 1958-59, 61-62; MD, Creighton U., 1967. Diplomate Am. Bd. Family Practice. Clk. Pacific Gas & Electric Co., San Francisco, 1960-61; intern St. Mary's Hosp., San Francisco, 1967; resident Scenic Gen. Hosp., Modesto, Calif., 1967-70; pvt. practice, Watsonville, Calif., 1971—2000; ret., 2000. Hon. staff Watsonville Cmty. Hosp., 1971—. Capt. M.C., U.S. Army, 1968-69. Fellow: Am. Acad. Family Practice; mem.: VFW, AMA, NRA, 38th Parallel Med. Soc. Korea, Santa Cruz County Med. Soc., Calif. Med. Assn. Republican. Roman Catholic.

ALFIDI, RALPH JOSEPH, retired radiologist, educator, researcher, administrator; b. Rome, Apr. 20, 1932; s. Luca and Angeline (Panella) A.; m. Rose Esther Senesac, Sept. 3, 1956 (div. 1991); children: Suzanne, Lisa, Christine, Katherine, Mary, John; m. Mariella Boller, Aug. 29, 1992. AB, Ripon Coll., Wis., 1955; MD, Marquette U., Milw., 1959. Intern Oakwood Hosp., Dearborn, Mich., 1959-60; resident, chief resident, A.C.S. fellow U. Va., 1960-63; practice medicine, specializing in radiology Cleve., 1965-2000; staff mem. Cleve. Clinic, 1965-78, head dept. hosp. radiology, 1968-78; dir. dept. radiology Univ. Hosps., Cleve., 1978-92; prof. radiology U. N.Mex., Albuquerque, 2000—03. Cons. VA Hosp., Cleve.; chmn. dept. radiology Case Western Res. U. Sch. Medicine, 1978-92; chmn. staff Cleve. Clinic Found., 1975-76; co-founder Steris Corp. Author: Complications and Legal Implications of Special Procedures, 1972, Computed Tomography of the Human Body: An Atlas of Normal Anatomy, 1977; editor: Whole Body Computed Tomography, 1977; contbr. articles to radiology jours. Served to capt., M.C. U.S. Army Res., 1963-65 Picker Found. grantee, 1969-70; NRC grantee, 1969-70 Mem. Radiol. Soc. N. Am., Am. Roentgen Ray Soc., Am. Heart Assn., Soc. Cardiovascular Radiology, Soc. Gastrointestinal Radiology, Soc. Computed Body Tomography (pres. 1977-78), Eastern Radiol. Soc., Cleve. Radiol. Soc. (pres. 1976-77), Las Campanas Club. Roman Catholic. Achievements include discovery of renal splanchnic steal syndrome: aka Alfidi's Syndrome; patents for nitinol. Home: 81 Calle Ventoso W Santa Fe NM 87506-0141

ALFONSO, FRANK A., lawyer; b. LA, May 1, 1970; BS, Calif. State Univ., LA, 1994; JD, Southwestern Univ., 1998. Bar: Calif. 1998. Assoc. Law Offices of C. Michael Alder, Beverly Hills, Calif. Contbr. articles to profl. jours. Named a Rising Star, So. Calif. Super Lawyers, 2006. Office: Law Offices of C Michael Alder 9308 Civic Ctr Dr Beverly Hills CA 90210

ALFORD, STEVE (STEVEN TODD ALFORD), men's college basketball coach; b. New Castle, Ind., Nov. 23, 1964; m. Tanya Frost; children: Kory, Bryce, Kayla. BS, Ind. U. Mem. gold-medal U.S. basketball team Olympic Games, LA, 1984; professional basketball player Dallas Mavericks, Golden St. Warriors; head coach Manchester (Ind.) Coll., 1992-95, U. Iowa Hawkeyes, 1999—2007, U. New Mexico, 2007—. Named Ind. Collegiate Conf. Coach of Yr., 1993, 94, 95. Office: U New Mexico Athletic Dept Albuquerque NM 87131

ALGRA, RONALD JAMES, dermatologist; b. Artesia, Calif., Feb. 23, 1949; s. Cornelius and Helena Joyce (De Boom) A.; m. Phyllis Ann Brandsma, July 31, 1970; children: Brian David, Stephanie Ann. BS in Chemistry, Calvin Coll., 1971; MD, Baylor Coll. Medicine, 1974; MBA, Pepperdine U., 1989. Diplomate Am. Bd. Dermatology. Intern Gen. Hosp. Ventura County, Ventura, Calif., 1974-75; resident in dermatology Baylor Coll. Medicine, Houston, 1975-78; pvt. practice Hawthorne, Calif., 1978-88; asst. med. dir. FHP, Inc., Fountain Valley, 1988-89, assoc. med. dir., 1990-91, med. dir., 1991-93, sr. med. dir., 1993, assoc. v.p. med. affairs, 1993-95; COO, horses, zebras & unicorns, Irvine, Calif., 1995-96; exec., med. dir. Providence Health Plans, Eugene, Oreg., 1996-98; med. dir. HealthCare Ptnrs. Ltd., Torrance, Calif., 1999-2000; v.p., med. dir. THIPA, Torrance, 2000—. Fellow: Am. Acad. Dermatology; mem.: Am. Coll. Physician Execs., Am. Med. Informatics Assn., Alpha Omega Alpha. Republican. Avocations: computers, photography, running, gardening, hiking. Office: TMCI 2355 Crenshaw Blvd Ste 150 Torrance CA 90501 Office Phone: 310-540-1070. Personal E-mail: rjalgr@socal.rr.com. Business E-Mail: ralgra@thipa.com.

ALHADEFF, DAVID ALBERT, economics professor; b. Seattle, Mar. 22, 1923; s. Albert David and Pearl (Taranto) A.; m. Charlotte Pechman, Aug. 1, 1948. BA, U. Wash., 1944; MA, Harvard U., 1948, PhD, 1950. Faculty U. Calif.-Berkeley, 1949-87, prof. bus. adminstrn., 1959-87, prof. emeritus, 1987—, assoc. dean Sch. Bus. Adminstrn., 1980-82, 85-86. Author: Monopoly and Competition in Banking, 1954, Competition and Controls in Banking, 1968, Microeconomics and Human Behavior, 1982; Contbr. articles to profl. jours., chpts. to books. Served with AUS, 1943-46. Recipient The Berkeley Citation U. Calif.-Berkeley, 1987. Office: Haas Sch Bus Berkeley CA 94720-0001 Home: 6 Manor Pl Menlo Park CA 94025-3714

ALI, LAILA, professional boxer; b. Miami Beach, Fla., Dec. 30, 1977; d. Muhammad and Veronica Porsche (Anderson) Ali; m. John McClain, Aug. 27, 2000 (div. 2005); m. Curtis Conway, July 22, 2007; 1 child, Curtis Muhammad stepchildren: Cameron, Kelton, Leilani. BBA, Santa Monica Coll. Owner and operator nail salon, Calif.; profl. trainer LA. Author: Reach!: Finding Strength, Spirit and Personal Power, 2002; instr. (with Sugar Ray Leonard) workout video, 2007, actress (TV series) Strong Medicine, 2003, (TV films) All You've Got, 2006; performer: Dancing with the Stars, 2007; host (TV series) American Gladiators, 2008—. Named Internat. Boxing Assn. Super Middleweight Champion, 2002, Women's Internat. Boxing Assn. Super Middleweight Champion, 2002, Internat. Women's Boxing Fedn. Super Middleweight Champion, 2002. Avocations: cooking, pilates. Mailing: She Bee Stingin' Inc Ste 47-432 20929 Ventura Blvd Woodland Hills CA 91364

ALINDER, MARY STREET, writer, educator; b. Bowling Green, Ohio, Sept. 23, 1946; d. Scott Winfield and McDonna Street; m. James Gilbert Alinder, Dec. 17, 1965; children: Jasmine, Jesse, Zachary. Student, U. Mich., 1964-65, U. N.Mex., 1966-68; BA, U. Nebr., 1976. Mgr. The Weston Gallery, Carmel, Calif., 1978-79; chief asst. Ansel Adams, Carmel, 1979-84; exec. editor, bus. mgr. The Ansel Adams Pub. Rights Trust, Carmel, 1984-87; freelance writer, lectr., curator, Gualala, Calif., 1989—; selector and writer biographies Focal Press Ency., 3d edit., 1993; ptnr. The Alinder Gallery, Gualala, 1990—; cultural expert U.S. State Dept., Guadalajara, Mexico, 2003. Curator Ansel Adams Centenial Celebration, 2002, Ansel Adams: 80th Birthday Retrospective, Friends of Photography, Carmel, Acad. Sci., San Francisco, Denver Mus. Natural History, Ansel Adams and the West, Calif. State Capitol, Sacto., 2001; co-curator One With Beauty, M.H. deYoung Meml. Mus., 1987, Ansel Adams: American Artist, The Ansel Adams Ctr., San Francisco; lectr. Nat. Gallery Art, Barbican Ctr., M.H. deYoung Meml. Mus., Stanford U., LA County Mus., U. Mich.; vis. artist and lectr. Nebr. Art Assn., 1997; Wallace Stegner meml. lectr. Peninsula Open Space Inst., Mountainview, Calif., 1998, Assn. Internat. Photographic Art Dealers, NYC, 1999, Cin. Art Mus., 2000, Eiteljorg Mus., Indpls., 2001, Internat. Wildlife Mus., Jackson Hole, 2003, Telluride Mountain Film Festival, Nev. Mus. Art, Reno, 2004, U. Tex., Austin, 2005, Manzanar Hist. Monument, 2006; Sierra Club Golden Keynote spkr.; faculty Stanford U., 2000. Author: Picturing Yosemite (Places), 1990, The Limits of Reality: Ansel Adams and Group f/64 (Seeing Straight), 1992, Ansel Adams, A Biography (Henry Holt), 1996, Mabel Dodge Luhan, 1997 (View-Camera), Ansel Adams: Milestone, 2002; (with others) the Scribner Encyclopedia of American Lives, 1998; co-author: Ansel Adams: An Autobiography, 1985; co-editor: Ansel Adams: Letters and Images, 1988; columnist Coast and Valley Mag., 1993-98, Ansel Adams: Political Landscape, Focal Ency. Photography, 1993; political landscape (Civilization), 1999; contbr. articles to profl. jours., popular mags. Business E-Mail: malinder@mcn.org, alinders@mcn.org.

ALIOTO, ANGELA MIA, lawyer; b. San Francisco, Oct. 20, 1949; m. Adolfo Veronese (dec. Sept. 1990); children: Angela Veronese, Adolfo Veronese, Joseph Veronese, Gian-Paolo Veronese. BA, Lone Mountain Coll., 1971; JD, U. San Francisco, 1983. Lawyer Alioto and Alioto, San Francisco, 1980—; mem. bd. supr. City and County of San Francisco, 1989—97, pres. bd. supr., 1993—95. Candidate for mayor City of San Francisco, 1991, 2003; first vice-chair Calif. State Dem. Party, 1991—93; co-chair Calif. del. Dem. Nat. Conv., 1992; mem. Golden Gate Bridge Dist., Outer-Continental Shelf Bd. Control; vice-chair San Francisco County Transp. Authority; mem. San Francisco Mental Health Bd. Author: Straight to the Heart. Chair bd. dir. Nat. Shrine St. Francis Assisi. Mem.: Soc. Profl. Journalists, Am. Trial Lawyers Assn., Bar Assn. San Francisco, NAACP (life), Dante Soc. Am. Democrat. Roman Catholic. Office: Alioto & Alioto 700 Montgomery St San Francisco CA 94111

ALIOTO-PIER, MICHELA, city supervisor; b. 1968; m. Thomas Pier; children: Nicholas, Giovanna, Valentina. BS in Anthropology, UCLA; student, Sophia U., Tokyo. Liaison, domestic policy adv. to v.p. Al Gore US Dept. Health & Human Svcs.; commr. San Francisco Port Commn., 2003—04; supr., Dist. 2 San Francisco Bd. Supervisors, 2004—, mem. govt. audits & oversight com., pub. safety com., city ops. & neighborhood svcs. com. Apptd. adv. bd. mem. Pres.'s Coun. on Disabilities, 1984; del. Lifetime Summit on Women, 1997, US-Japan Summit Conf. on Disabilities; mem. San Francisco Disaster Coun. Candidate from 1st Congl. Dist. Calif. House of Reps., 1996; candidate Sec. of State, Calif., 1998, Calif., 2002. Named one of Top 21 Up-and-Coming Women Leaders in the Country, Ms. Mag. Democrat. Office: City Hall 1 Dr Carlton B Goodlet Pl Rm 244 San Francisco CA 94102-4689 Office Phone: 415-554-7752. Fax: 415-554-7843. E-mail: Michela.Alioto-Pier@sfgov.org.*

ALIRE, CAMILA A., dean emerita, librarian, educator; BA in Hist. and Secondary Edn., Adams State Coll., Alamosa, Colo., 1970; MLS, U. Denver, 1974; EdD in Higher Edn. Adminstrn., U. Northern Colo., 1984. Dir. McCook Coll., Nebr., 1974—76; asst. to dean, instr. U. Denver Grad. Sch. Librarianship and Information Mgmt., 1980—84; dir. Learning Resource Ctr. Pikes Peak Cmty. Coll., Colorado Springs, 1984—89; asst. dir. instrn. and rsch. svcs. U. Colo. Auraria Libr., Denver, 1989—91, dean/dir. librs., 1991—97; dean, prof. Colo. State U. Librs., Ft. Collins, 1997—2001, dean emerita, 2001—; dean, prof. U. N.Mex. Librs., Albuquerque, 2002—06; dean emerita U. N.Mex. Libr., 2005—; interim exec. dir. Greater Western Libr. Alliance, 2007; adj. prof. Simmons Coll., Boston, San Jose State U. Sch. Libr. and Information Scis., Calif. Del. Colo. Gov.'s Conf. on Libr. and Information Svcs., 1991, White House Conf. on Libr. and Information Svcs., 1991; mem. diversity com. U. Colo., Denver, 1991—97, mem. Elizabeth Gee Meml. Lectureship award com., 1993—; mem. information and instrnl. tech. planning group Colo. State U., 1997—2002, mem. pres. diversity adv. com., 1997—2002; scholar-in-residence Chgo. Pub. Libr. Sys., 1999; mem. faculty dispute resolution adv. bd. U. N.Mex., 2002—, campus compact liaison, 2003—; bd. dirs. Spellbinders, 2002—, Colo. Coun. on Libr. Devel., Assn. for Rsch. Librs., Greater Western Libr. Alliance Bd. Co-author: (books) Serving Latino Communities, 2007, Academic Librarians as Emotionally Intelligent Leaders, 2007; editor: (book) Library Disaster Planning and Recovery Handbook, 2000; contbr. articles to profl. jours. Bd. dirs. Dennis Chavez Found., 2004—05, Trejo Found., 2003—. Recipient Univ. medal, U. Colo., 1998; named a Sr. fellow, Palmer Sch. Libr. and Information Studies, LI U., 1995; named one of 100 Most Influential Hispanics, Hispanic Bus. Mag., 1997. Mem.: ALA (pres.-elect 2008—09, pres. 2009—, exec. bd., nominating com. edn., Elizabeth Futas Catalyst for Change award 1997), N.Mex. Consortium Academic Librs., Assn. Rsch. Librs. N.Mex., Assn. Coll. and Rsch. Librs., Colo. Libr. Assn. (Exemplary Libr. Svcs. to Ethnic Populations award 1995, 1997), Nat. Assn. to Promote Libr. and Information Svc. to the Spanish-Speaking (nat. pres., Libr. of Yr. 1997), Mountain Plains Libr. Assn. (Legis. award 1995). Office: San Jose State U Sch Libr and Information Scis One Washington Sq San Jose CA 95192 Office Phone: 303-913-8341. Office Fax: 303-814-2724. Personal E-mail: calire@att.net.

ALIVISATOS, ARMAND PAUL, chemist, educator; b. Chgo., Nov. 12, 1959; BA in Chemistry, U. Chgo., 1981; PhD in Chem. Physics, U. Calif., Berkeley, 1986. Postdoctoral fellow AT&T Bell Labs., 1986-88; asst. prof. to assoc. prof. U. Calif., Berkeley, 1988-95, prof. chemistry, 1995—, vice chmn. dept. chemistry, 1995-98, Chancellor's prof., 1998—2001, prof. materials sci. and mineral engring., 1999—; dir. materials sci. divsn. Lawrence Berkeley Nat. Lab., 2002—08, assoc. lab. dir. physical scis., 2005—08, dep. dir., 2008—. Sci. dir. Molecular Foundry, Inorganic Structure Facility, Lawrence Berkeley Nat. Lab. 2006- Editor-in-chief Am. Chem. Soc. Jour., Nano Letters. Recipient Sustained Outstanding Sci. Rsch. in Materials Chemistry award Dept. Energy, 1997, Coblentz award, 1994, Colloid and Surface Chemistry ACS award, 2004, Eni Italgas prize for Energy and Environment, 2006, Disting. Alumni award U. Chgo., 2006; co-recipient Ernest Orlando Lawrence award for Materials Rsch. Dept. Energy, 2007, Kavli Distinguished Lectureship in Nanoscience, MRS, 2008; Larry and Diane Bock Chair in Nanotechnology, 2006. Fellow Am. Phys. Soc., Am. Acad. Arts & Scis., AAAS; mem. Am. Chem. Soc.(Colloid and Surface Chemistry award, 2004), Materials Rsch. Soc. (Outstanding Young Investigator award 1995), NAS. Office: Univ Calif Dept Chemistry D43 Hildegard Berkeley CA 94720

ALKIRE, JOHN D., lawyer, arbitrator, mediator; b. Seattle, Nov. 15, 1948; s. Durwood Lee and Dorys (Maryon) A.; m. Karen A. Heerensperger, May 6, 1994; children: Lauren M., Kevin G. Student, U. Calif., Berkeley, 1967-68; BA, Principia Coll., Elsah, Ill., 1970; JD, U. Wash., 1975. Bar: Wash. 1975, Washington 1977, U.S. Dist. Ct. (we. dist.) Wash., U.S. Ct. Appeals (4th, 9th and D.C. cirs.), U.S. Supreme Ct. Budget analyst Office Mgmt. and Budget, Seattle, 1970-72; law clk 9th cir. Honorable Eugene A. Wright, Seattle, 1975-76; assoc. Jones, Grey & Bayley, Seattle, 1976-77, Steptoe & Johnson, Washington, 1977-80, Perkins Coie, Seattle, 1980-85, ptnr., 1985—. Mem. ABA, Wash. State Bar Assn. Avocations: sports, baseball, travel, meditation. Office: Perkins Coie 1201 3rd Ave Fl 40 Seattle WA 98101-3029

ALKON, ELLEN SKILLEN, physician; b. LA, Apr. 10, 1936; d. Emil Bogen and Jane (Skillen) Bogen Rost; m. Paul Kent Alkon, Aug. 30, 1957; children: Katherine Ellen (dec.), Cynthia Jane, Margaret Elaine. BA, Stanford U., 1955; MD, U. Chgo., 1961; MPH, U. Calif., Berkeley, 1968. Diplomate Nat. Bd. Med. Examiners, Am. Bd. Pediat., Am. Bd. Preventive Medicine in Pub. Health. Chief sch. health Anne Arundel County Health Dept., Annapolis, Md., 1970-71; practice medicine specializing in pediat. Mpls. Health Dept., 1971-73, dir. MCH, 1973-75, commr. health, 1975-80; chief preventive and pub. health Coastal Region of Los Angeles County Dept. Health Svcs., 1980-81; chief pub. health West Area Los Angeles County Dept. Health Svcs., 1981-85; acting med. dir. pub. health Los Angeles County Dept. Health, 1986-87, med. dir. pub. health, 1987-93; med. dir. Coastal Cluster Health Ctrs. L.A. County Dept. Pub. Health Svcs., 1993-96, CEO, 1996-98, med. dir., 1998-2000; dir. Pub. Health Edn. Medicine, 2000—, Pub. Health Edn. Physician. Adj. prof. UCLA Sch. Pub. Health, 1981—; adminstr. vis. nurses svc., Mpls., 1975-80. Fellow Am. Coll. Preventive Medicine, Am. Acad. Pediat.; mem. So. Calif. Pub. Health Assn. (pres. 1985-86, 04), Minn. Pub. Health Assn. (pres. 1978-79), Am. Pub. Health Assn., Calif. Conf. Local Health Officers (pres. 1990-91), Calif. Ctr. for Pub. Health Advocacy (pres.

2002-03), Calif. Acad. Preventive Medicine (pres. 1988-92, 2003-05), Delta Omega. Office: Los Angeles County DHS 313 N Figueroa St Rm 227 A Los Angeles CA 90012 Office Phone: 213-250-8688. Business E-Mail: ealkon@ph.lacounty.gov.

ALKON, PAUL KENT, language educator; Grad., Phillips Acad., 1953; AB, Harvard U., 1957; PhD in English Lit., U. Chgo., 1962. Instr., asst. prof. English lit. U. Calif.-Berkeley, 1962-70; assoc. prof. U. Md., 1970-71; assoc. prof. English U. Minn., Mpls., 1971-73, prof., 1973-80; Leo S. Bing prof. English emeritus U. So. Calif., L.A., 2007—. Vis. prof. English, Ben Gurion U. of Negev, Israel, 1977-78 Author: Samuel Johnson and Moral Discipline, 1967, Defoe and Fictional Time, 1979, Origins of Futuristic Fiction, 1987, Science Fiction Before 1900, 1994, Winston Churchill's Imagination, 2006. Mem. Am. Soc. 18th Century Studies (pres. 1989-90), Société française d'Etude du 18ème Siècle, Churchill Ctr. (bd. acad. advisers). Home: 17 Masongate Dr Palos Verdes Peninsula CA 90274-1560

ALLAN, JAMES S., sales professional; b. Chgo. m. Linda Queenan; children: Scott, Mitch, Tyler, Amanda. BS, Gustavus Adolphus Coll.; MBA in Mktg., Ind. U. Dealer sales mgr. Xerox Channel Sales Orgn. Rear adm. USNR. Decorated Def. Superior Svc. medal, Def. Meritorious Svc. medal.

ALLAN, LIONEL M., director for-profit and non-profit companies, Legal and Business Advisor; b. Aug. 3, 1943; AB cum laude, U. Mich., 1965; JD, Stanford U., 1968; student, U. Paris. Bar: Calif. 1969, US Supreme Ct. 1972. Law clk. US Dist. Ct. (no. dist.) Calif., 1969—70; pres. Allan Advisors, Inc., bd. governance and legal cons. firm. Spkr. and writer in field of corp. and bd. governance law; sec. adv. com. San Jose Fed. Ct., 1969-85; mem. bd. visitors Stanford Law Sch., 1985-88; mem. com. comml. code State Bar Calif., 1974-77, corps. com., 1983-86; elected to Am. Law Inst., 1989; spkr. Stanford Dir. Coll., 2004-. Co-author: How to Structure the Classic Venture Capital Deal, 1983, Equity Incentives for Start-up Companies, 1985, Master Limited Partnerships, 1987. Bd. dirs. San Jose Mus. Art, 1983-87; trustee KTEH-TV Channel 54 Found., 1987-2002, chair, 1992-94; dir. NCCJ, 1995-2001, Harker Sch., 1998—, chair 2002-; dir. Villa Montalvo Arts Ctr., 1986-2000, chair, 1989-93. Served to capt. JAGC USAR, 1974. Mem. ABA (com. on small bus., chmn. internat. bus. subcom. 1985-88, chmn. small bus. com. 1989-93), Santa Clara Bar Assn. (chmn. fed. ct. sect. 1971, 77), Internat. Bar Assn., Nat. Assn. Corp. Dirs. (chair Silicon Valley Calif. chpt. 2004-06, CEO 2006-), San Jose/Silicon Valley C. of C. (dir.), Pi Sigma Alpha, Phi Sigma Iota, Phi Delta Phi. Office: NACD Silicon Valley Chpt PO Box 562 Los Gatos CA 95031-0562 Office Phone: 408-354-8854. Business E-Mail: lonallan@comcast.net.

ALLAN, WALTER ROBERT, lawyer; b. Detroit, Aug. 1, 1937; s. Walter Francis and Henrietta (Fairchild) A. AB, U. Mich., 1959, JD, 1962. Bar: Calif. 1964, U.S. Ct. Appeals (9th Cir.) 1964, U.S. Supreme Ct. 1972, U.S. Ct. Appeals (D.C. cir.) 1973, U.S. Ct. Appeals (5th cir.) 1977, U.S. Ct. Appeals (3d cir.) 1988. From assoc. to ptnr. Pillsbury, Madison & Sutro, San Francisco, 1963—98; sole practitioner Tiburon, Calif., 1998—. Office: PO Box 771 Belvedere Tiburon CA 94920-0771 Office Phone: 415-889-4048. Business E-Mail: walterallan@mac.com.

ALLAN, WILLIAM GEORGE, artist, educator; b. Everett, Wash., Mar. 28, 1936; BFA, San Francisco Art Inst., 1958. Instr. painting U. Calif., Davis, 1965-67, Berkeley, 1969; prof. art Calif State U., Sacramento, 1968—99, prof. art emeritus, 1999—. Exhibited in group shows at Carnegie Internat. Exhbn., Pitts., 1975, Continuing Surrealism, La. Jolla (Calif.) Mus. Art, 1971, Whitney Painting Ann., NYC, 1972, 70th Ann. Exhbn. Art Inst. Chgo., 1972, Indpls. Mus. Art Exhbn., 1972, Whitney Mus. Am. Art, NYC, 1973-74, Painting and Sculpture in Calif.: The Modern Era, San Francisco Mus. Modern Art, 1976, Chgo. Arts Club, 1978; represented in permanent collections at Dallas Mus. Art, San Francisco Mus. Art, Phila. Mus. Art, Whitney Mus. Am. Art, Mus. Modern Art, NYC. Named Academician, NAD, 1997. Office: Calif State U Sacramento Dept Art 6000 J St Sacramento CA 95819-2605

ALLARD, J., computer software company executive; b. Glens Falls, NY, Jan. 12, 1969; m. Rebecca Norlander. BA in Computer Sci., Boston U. Computer scientist Microsoft Corp., Redmond, Wash., 1991—, corp. v.p., chief XNA arch., v.p., design and develop. entertainment and devices divsn., corp. v.p. design and devel., entertainment and devices divsn., corp. v.p. design and devel. Entertainment and Devices Divsn., 2007—. Mem. World Econ. Forum Young Global Leader program. Named Disting. Alumnus, Boston U., 2003, Baby Bill, Business 2.0; named one of Top 35 Entertainment Execs Under 35, Hollywood Reporter, Most Powerful Men Under 38, Details. Avocation: bicycling. Office: Microsoft Corp 1 Microsoft Way Redmond WA 98052-6399

ALLARD, WAYNE (ALAN WAYNE ALLARD), retired US Senator from Colorado, veterinarian; b. Ft. Collins, Colo., Dec. 12, 1943; m. Joan Malcolm, Mar. 23, 1967; children: Christie, Cheryl. DVM, Colo. State U., 1968. Veterinarian, dir. Allard Animal Hosp.; mem. Colo. State Senate, 1983-90, US Congress from 4th Colo. Dist., Washington, 1991—97; US Senator from Colo., 1997—2009; deputy majority whip, 2003—09. Chmn. United Way; active 4-H Found. Recipient Charles A. Lory Public Svc. award, Colo. State U., 1999, Outstanding Legis. award, Home Care Assn. of Colo., Humane Legis. of Yr. award, Am. Humane Assn., 2001, Champion of Wheat award, Nat. Assn. Wheat Growers, 2003, Friend of Home Care, Home Care Assn. Colo., 2003. Mem. Am. Veterinary Med. Assn., Colo. Vet. Medicine Assn., Larimer County Vet. Medicine Assn. (past pres.), Bd. Vet. Practitioners (charter mem.), Am. Animal Hosp. Assn., Nat. Conf. State Legislatures (vice-chmn. human resources com. 1987—, health-care cost containment com.), Loveland C. of C., Republican. Office Phone: 202-224-5941, 970-461-3530. Office Fax: 202-224-6471, 970-461-3658.*

ALLBEE, SANDRA MOLL, real estate broker; b. Reading, Pa., July 15, 1947; d. Charles Lewars and Isabel May (Ackerman) Frederici; m. Thomas J. Allbee, Oct. 18, 1975 (div. 1987). Exec. sec. Hamburg (Pa.) State Sch. and Hosp., 1965-73; regional mgr. Am. Bus. Service Corp., Newport Beach, Calif., 1973-78; v.p. T.A.S.A., Inc., Long Beach, Calif., 1978-86; realtor Very Important Properties, Inc., Rolling Hills Estates, Calif., 1986-90, Re/Max Palos Verdes Realty, Rolling Hills Estates, Calif., 1990—. Bd. dirs., v.p. Nat. Coun. on Alcoholism, Torrance, Calif., 1987-96; pres. Rollingwood Homeowners Assn., Rolling Hills Estates, Calif., 1985-92. Named to Hall of Fame, ReMax, 2006. Mem. Palos Verdes Rep. Women's Club (bd. dirs. 1989-94). Office: Re Max Palos Verdes Realty 450 Silver Spur Rd Rancho Palos Verdes CA 90275-3595 Office Phone: 310-541-2474. Business E-Mail: sallbee@remaxpv.com.

ALLCHIN, JIM, information technology executive; Student, U. Fla., Stanford U., Ga. Inst. Tech.; D in Computer Sci. Prin. arch. Banyan Systems Inc., numerous positions mgmt. positions in develop. and mktg., sr. v.p., chief technology officer; with Microsoft Corp., Redmond, Wash., 1990—, sr. v.p. personal and bus. systems, 1996—99, sr. v.p., platforms group, 1999, group v.p. platforms group, 1999—2005, co-pres., platform products & svcs. divsn., 2005—07. Mem. Sr. Leadership Team, Bus. Leadership Team, Microsoft Corp., Redmond, Wash.

ALLDREDGE, LEROY ROMNEY, retired geophysicist; b. Mesa, Ariz., Feb. 6, 1917; s. Leo and Ida (Romney) A.; m. Larita Williams, Dec. 27, 1940; children— Carol, David Leroy, Joseph Leo, Gary Dean, Mark Evans, Janice, Luann. BS, U. Ariz., 1939, MS, 1940; M.Sc. in Engring, Harvard, 1953; PhD, U. Md., 1955. Instr. physics U. Ariz., 1940-41; fed. radio insp. FCC, Los Angeles, also Washington, 1941-44; radio engr. dept. terrestrial magnetism Carnegie Inst. of Washington, 1944-45; chief electricity and magnetism div. Naval Ordnance Lab., White Oak, Md., 1945-55; analyst operations research office Johns Hopkins, 1955-59; research geophysicist Coast and Geodetic Survey, Dept. Commerce, Washington, 1959-66; acting dir. Inst. Earth Scis., Environmental Sci. Services Adminstrn., Boulder, Colo., 1966; dir. Earth Scis. Labs., 1967-69, Earth Sci. Lab. Nat. Oceanographic and Atmospheric Adminstrn., 1969-73; research geophysicist U.S. Geol. Survey, 1973-88; gen. sec., dir. central bur. Internat. Assn. Geomagnetism and Aeronomy, 1963-75. Asso. editor: Jour. Geophys. Research, 1966-69. Mem. Am. Geophys. Union (sect. on geomagnetism and aeronomy 1950-56, v.p. sect. 1956-59, pres. sect. 1959-61, chmn. Eastern meeting com. 1962-66), Sigma Xi, Phi Kappa Phi. Mem. Ch. of Jesus Christ of Latter-day Saints. Home: 3310 Valencia Dr Idaho Falls ID 83404-7502

ALLECTA, JULIE, lawyer; b. Worcester, Mass., Oct. 28, 1946; BA magna cum laude, U. N. Mex., 1973, MBA magna cum laude, 1977, JD, 1977. Bar: M. Mex. 1978, D.C. 1984, Calif. 1985, U.S. Supreme Ct., U.S. Ct. Appeals, fifth & tenth cir. Office gen. counsel SEC, Washington, 1977—81; ptnr. Paul, Hastings, Janofsky & Walker LLP, San Francisco. Editl. bd. Arlen Mutual Fund Handbook, Bd. IQ. Mem.: Am. Law Inst. ABA Com. Continuing Profl. Edn. (faculty mem.), Mutual Fund Dir. Forum (adv. dir.), ABA-Bus. Law Sect. (com. fed. regulation securities, sub. com. investment co. & investment advisers). Office: Paul Hastings Janofsky & Walker LLP 55 Second St 24th Floor San Francisco CA 94105 Office Phone: 415-856-7000. Office Fax: 415-856-7106. Business E-Mail: julieallecta@paulhastings.com.

ALLEGRA, ANTONIA, editor, writer; b. San Francisco, Feb. 21, 1946; d. Carlo Louis and Antonette Delfina (Laiolo) Lastreto; m. John H. Griffin, Aug. 14, 1965 (div. Feb. 1983); children: John, Deanna, Paul; m. Donn L. Black, Apr. 14, 1996. Student, Harvard U., Cambridge, Mass., 1969-71, Santa Clara U., 1963-65; Culinary Degree, Ecole de Cuisine Gaston, LeNotre, Paris, 1978, Le Cordon Bleu, Paris, 1981. Food editor San Diego Tribune, 1982-88; dir. culinary programs Beringer Winery, St. Helena, Calif., 1988-91; dir. Symposium for Profl. Food Writers, 1989—; dir. adminstrn. and comm. liaison Culinary Inst. of Am., St. Helena, 1991-95; co-host Wine Valley Radio, St. Helena, 1995—; pres. Internat. Assn. of Culinary Profls., Louisville, 1997; editor-in-chief Appellation Mag., Napa, Calif., 1992-96; dir. Symposium for Profl. Wine Writers, 2004—; culinary dir. La Cocina Que Canta Cooking Sch., Rancho La Puerta, Tecate, Baja California, Mexico, 2004. Lectr./cooking demonstrator Seabourn/Radisson Cruises, 1975—93; profl. career & writing coach Culinary Coaches & Consultants Collaborative, 1998—, co-founder, 2004; Napa Valley onscreen tipster KRON/TV Bay Area Backroads, 2004—; judge various food competitions; panelist various food/wine confs.; spkr. in field; writing coach, career coach. Author: (book) Napa Valley: The Ultimate Winery Guide, 1993, introductions to books in field; editor-in-chief: Napa Valley mag., 2001—; contbr. articles to profl. jours. Recipient award for Best New Regional Mag. (Appellation), Western Pub. Assn., L.A., 1994, Maggie award for best visitor's mag. Western Pub. Assn., 2004; named Woman of Distinction in the Culinary Professions, U. Calif. San Diego Cancer Ctr., 1987. Mem. Internat. Assn. of Culinary Profls. (v.p. 1996-97, pres. 1997-98), Internat. Women's Forum West, Assn. of Food Journalists (v.p. 1987), Napa Valley Culinary Alliance (pres. 1988-89), San Francisco Profl. Food Soc. (bd. dirs. 1989-90), Les Dames d'Escoffier Internat. (pres. San Francisco chpt. 1992), Napa Valley Wine Libr. Assn., Sonoma County Culinary Guild, Women for WineSense, Internat. Women's Forum, Sigma Delta Chi, others. Avocation: cooking. Office: Antonia Allegra & Assocs PO Box 663 Saint Helena CA 94574-0663 Office Phone: 707-963-0777. Business E-Mail: antonia@fcs.net.

ALLEN, A. WILLIAM, III, (BILL), food service executive; CEO la Madeleine French Bakery and Cafe; pres. West Coast Concepts, 2004—05; CEO Outback Steakhouse (OSI Restaurant Partners), 2005—.

ALLEN, BARRY K., communications executive, human resources specialist; m. Linda Allen; 2 children. BA, U. Ky.; MBA with honors, Boston U. With Ind. Bell, 1974—85, Wis. Bell, 1985; pres., CEO Ameritech Pub., Inc., 1987—89, Wis. Bell, Inc., 1989—93, Ill. Bell, Inc., 1993; pres., COO Marquette Electronics, 1993—95; sr. v.p. Ameritech, 1995—97, exec. v.p., 1997—99; pres. SBC/Ameritech, 1999—2000, Allen Enterprises LLC, 2000—02; exec. v.p., chief human resources officer Qwest Comm. Internat., Denver, 2002—04, exec. v.p. ops., 2004—07. Bd. dirs. Harley Davidson Inc., Cobalt, Inc., Fiduciary Mgmt., Inc. Bd. mem. Greater Milw. Com., Boys and Girls Club Milw., Jr. Achievement Wis., Children's Hosp. Wis., United Way, Milw., Chgo. Capt. US Army, 1970—74. Recipient Grad. Sch. Bus. Disting. Alumnus award, Boston U., 1996; named to, Gatton Sch. Bus. Hall of Fame, 2001.

ALLEN, CAROLYN S., state legislator; b. Hannibal, Mo., Sept. 8, 1937; Mem. Dist. 28 Ariz. House of Reps., 1995—2002, majority leader, 2001—02; mem. Dist. 8 Ariz. State Senate, 2003—, chair healthcare & med. liability reform com., mem. vets. & mil. affairs com., commerce & econ. devel. com. Mem. World Affairs Coun., Coun. State Governments, Ariz. Commn. Med. Edn. & Rsch., Scottsdale Planning Commn., Scottsdale Visioning Com.; mem. exec. com. Nat. Conf. State Legislators. Active Arizonans for Cultural Devel.; exec. dir. Scottsdale Arts Ctr. Assn., 1987—88; mem. adv. coun. McDowell Sonoran Land Trust; mem. adv. bd. Scottsdale Found. Handicapped; bd. dirs. Morrison Inst. Pub. Policy; Planned Parenthood Ctrl. Ariz. Planned Parenthood. Mem.: Nat. Fedn. Grand Old Party Women, Ariz. Fedn. Grand Old Party Women Regents, Las Rancheras Grand Old Party Womens Club (founding mem.). Republican. Protestant. Office: Ariz House Reps Capitol Complex 1700 W Washington Off 303 Phoenix AZ 85007-2890 Office Phone: 602-926-4480. Office Fax: 602-417-3155. Business E-Mail: callen@azleg.gov.*

ALLEN, CHARLES RAYMOND, television station executive; Gen. mgr. KAET-Ariz. State U., Tempe. Office: KAET Ariz State U Stauffer Hall B-Wing PO Box 871405 Tempe AZ 85287-1405

ALLEN, CHARLES WILLIAM, mechanical engineer, educator; b. Newbury, Eng., July 24, 1932; s. Isaac William and Emily (Butler) A.; m. Rita Joyce Pembroke, Dec. 28, 1957; children: Malcolm Charles, Verity Simone. BS, U. London, 1957; MS, Case Inst. Tech., 1962; PhD, U. Calif., Davis, 1966. Design engr. Lear Siegler, Cleve., 1957-62; group leader Aerojet Gen., Sacramento, 1962-63; assoc. engring. U. Calif., Davis, 1965-66; assoc. prof. Calif. State U., Chico, 1966-71, prof. engring., 1971-88, prof. emeritus, 1988—, head mech. engring., 1976-79, 82-84. Vis. fellow U. Leicester, Eng., 1974; vis. lectr., rschr. U. Guadalajara, Mex., 1986, guest prof., 1997. Contbr. articles to profl. jours. Fellow NASA, 1967, 68, 69 Mem. ASME. Home: 1691 Filbert Ave Chico CA 95926-1777 Office: Calif State U Dept Mech Engring Chico CA 95629 Personal E-mail: charleswilliamallen@yahoo.com.

ALLEN, CLARENCE RODERIC, geologist, educator; b. Palo Alto, Calif., Feb. 15, 1925; s. Hollis Partridge and Delight (Wright) A. BA, Reed Coll., 1949; MS, Cal. Inst Tech., 1951, PhD, 1954. Asst. prof. geology U. Minn., 1954-55; mem. faculty Calif. Inst. Tech., 1955—, prof. geology and geophysics, 1964-91, prof. emeritus, 1991—; interim dir. Seismological Lab., 1965-67, acting chmn. division of geological scis., 1967-68. Phi Beta Kappa Disting. lectr., 1978; chmn. cons. bd. earthquake analysis Calif. Dept. Water Resources, 1965-74; chmn. geol. hazards adv. com. for program Cal. Resources Agy., 1965-66; mem. earth scis. adv. panel NSF, 1965-68, chmn., 1967-68, mem. adv. com. environmental scis., 1970-72; mem. U.S. Geol. Survey adv. panel to Nat. Center Earthquake Research, Calif. Cal. Mining and Geology Bd., 1969-75, chmn., 1975; mem. task force on earthquake hazard reduction Office Sci. and Tech., 1970-71; mem. Can. Earthquake Prediction Evaluation Council, 1983-88; vice-chmn. Nat. Acad. Sci. Com. on Advanced Study in china, 1981-85; chmn. geology sect. Nat. Acad. Sci., 1982-85, Com. on Scholarly Communication with People's Republic China, 1984-89, chmn., 1987-89; mem. Nat. Acad. Sci. Comm. on Phys. Scis., Math. and Resources; mem. Pres.'s Nuclear Waste Tech. Rev. Bd., 1989-97. Served to 1st lt. USAAF, 1943-46. Recipient G.K. Gilbert award seismic geology Carnegie Instn., 1960. Fellow Am. Geophys. Union, Geol. Soc. Am. (counselor 1968-70, pres. 1973-74), Am. Acad. Arts Scis.; mem. Nat. Acad. Scis., Earthquake Engring. Research Inst. (bd. dirs. 1985-88, Housner medal 2001), Seismological Soc. Am. (dir. 1970-76, pres. 1975-76, medal 1995), Nat. Acad. Engring., Phi Beta Kappa. Office: Calif Inst Tech Dept Geology Pasadena CA 91125-0001 Office Phone: 626-395-6904. Business E-Mail: allen@gps.caltech.edu.

ALLEN, D. EDGAR, state legislator; m. Pat Allen; 6 children. BA, Weber State Coll.; MD, U. Utah. Med. intern, resident Duke U., Durham, N.C.; pvt. practice in dermatology; assoc. clin. prof.; mem. Utah Senate, Dist. 18, Salt Lake City, 1998—; mem. human svcs. com., health and environ. com.; mem. health and human svcs. appropriations com. Contbr. articles to med. jours. Mem. Weber County Drug and Alcohol Mentoring Bd., Mental Health Mentoring Bd., Youth and Families with Promise Mentoring Bd.; past mem. exec. com. Utah State Dem. Party; bd. govs. Am. Legion Boys State. Mem. Am. Cancer Soc. (past pres. Weber County dist.), Weber County Med. Soc. (past pres.). Democrat. Home: 4317 Fern Dr Ogden UT 84403-3269 Fax: 801-627-0517.

ALLEN, DAVID RATCLIFF, management consultant, writer; b. Jonesboro, La., Dec. 28, 1945; s. Gordon Emmet Allen and Miriam Allen (Foster) Drummond; m. Kathryn Allen. BA, New Coll., Sarasota, Fla., 1968. Gen. mgr. Natural Landscape Co., LA, 1977-80; pres. Allen Assocs., LA, 1980-83; v.p. Insight Consulting Grp., Santa Monica, Calif., 1983; founder, pres. David Allen Co., Ojai, Calif., 1996—. Contbr. articles to profl. publs.; author: Getting Things Done: The Art of Stress-Free Productivity, 2001, Ready for Anything: 52 Productivity Principles for Work and Life, 2003. Named one of 50 Who Matter Now, CNNMoney.com Bus. 2.0, 2006. Avocations: Karate, music. Office: David Allen Co 1674 McNell Rd Ojai CA 93023

ALLEN, DEBBIE, actress, choreographer, dancer, television director; b. Houston, Jan. 16, 1950; d. Vivian Ayers; m. Win Wilford (div.); m. Norm Nixon; 2 children: Vivian, Norman, Jr. BA, Howard U. Appeared in Broadway musicals including Purlie, 1972, West Side Story (revival), Guys and Dolls, Raisin, Aint Misbehavin, Sweet Charity, 1986 (revival, Tony Award); appeared in (play) Sweet Charity, Los Angeles, 1985, choreographer Broadway prodn. Carrie, 1988; (TV spl.) Dancing in the Wings, 1985, (TV series) Fame, 1982-87 (3 Emmys for choreography), In the House, 1995; dir. TV series A Different World, 1988-92; dir. episodes TV series Family Ties; dir., producer films including The Fish That Saved Pittsburgh, 1979, Fame, 1980, Ragtime, 1981, JoJo Dancer, Your Life is Calling, 1986, Mona Must Die, 1994, Blank Check, 1994, Out-of-Sync, 1995, Everything's Jake, 1999, (TV movie) C Bear and Jamal (voice), 1996; star, dir., prod., co-writer, choreographer The Debbie Allen Special, ABC-TV, 1988; dir., choreographer Polly (mus. version Disney's Pollyanna), 1989; dir., appeared in CBS Stompin' at the Savoy, 1992; rec. album Special Look, MCA Records, 1989; dir. pilot and 1st episode NBC series The Fresh Prince of Bel Air, 1990; dir., choreographer NBC-Disney movie Polly II, 1990; choreographer of 63d Acad. Awards, 1991, 64th Acad. Awards, 1992, 65th Acad. Awards, 1993, 66th Acad. Awards, 1994; dir. (TV) Cool Women, 2000, (Broadway plays) Cat on a Hot Tin Roof, 2008. Mem. exec. com. dean's adv. bd. UCLA Sch. Theatre, Film and TV, 1993. Office: William Morris Agency 151 S El Camino Dr Beverly Hills CA 90212-2775

ALLEN, DELL K., industrial engineer; Dir. Wandell Graphics, North Logan, Utah. Mem. NAE. Office: Wandlell Graphics 610 E 2330 N North Logan UT 84341

ALLEN, DONALD VAIL, investment company executive, pianist; b. South Bend, Ind., Aug. 1, 1928; s. Frank Eugene and Vera Irene (Vail) A.; m. Betty Dunn, Nov. 17, 1956. BA magna cum laude, UCLA, 1972, MA, 1973. Pres., chmn. bd. dirs. Cambridge Investment Corp.;

music editor and critic Times-Herald, Washington; music critic L.A. Times. Transl. works of Ezra Pound from Italian into English; author of papers on the musical motifs in the writings of James Joyce; specialist in works of Beethoven, Chopin, Debussy, Liszt, and Scriabin; premiere performances of contemporary piano music; represented by William Matthews Concert Agy., NYC; selected by William Steinway and Sascha Greiner of Steinway Piano Co. as an exclusive Steinway concert artist. Pres. Funds for Needy Children, 1974-76; mem. Am. Guild Organists. Mem. Ctr. for Study of Presidency, Am. Mgmt. Assn., Internat. Platform Assn., Nat. Assn. Securities Dealers, Chamber Music Soc., Am. Mus. Natural History. Avocations: languages, music, travel, writing, financial market.

ALLEN, DOUGLAS D., horticulture and products company executive; b. 1943; Pres. Hines Nurseries; chmn. Hines Horticulture, Inc., Irvine, 1995-2000, chmn. bd. emeritus, dir., 2000—. Office: Hines Horticulture Inc 12621 Jeffrey Rd Irvine CA 92620

ALLEN, GERI A., composer, pianist; b. Detroit; m. Wallace Roney. BA in Jazz Studies and Piano, Howard U., 1979; MA in Ethnomusicology, U. Pitts., 1982. Asst. prof. music Howard U.; instr. New England Conservatory, New Sch., NYC; assoc. prof. jazz and contemporary improvisation U. Mich.; mem. Ornette Coleman Quartet, 1991—95; musical dir. Mary Lou Williams Collective. Performer: (albums) The Nurturer, 1992, Twenty-One, 1995, Sound Museum, 1996, With Every Breath I Take, 1998, The Gathering, 1998, Houdini/Buster Williams Trio, 2000, No Room for Argument, 2000, Lift Every Voice, 2000, The Detroit Experiment, 2002, Jazzpar Concerts 2003, 2003, American Song, 2003, The Life of a Song, 2004, Remember Love, 2005, Zodiac Suite: Revisited, 2006, Timeless Portraits and Dreams, 2006, Miles: Cool and Collected, 2007, and many others; composer: For the Healing of the Nations, 2006; actor: (films) Jazz, Kansas City, 1996. Recipient Keys to the City, Detroit, Cleve., Disting. Alumni award, Howard U., Disting. Prof. award, Spl. Achievement award, SESAC, Eubie Blake award, Cultural Crossroads Ctr., NYC, 1988, Lady of Soul award, Soul Train, 1995, Jazzpar prize, Denmark, 1996, Benny Golson award, Howard U. Jazz Ensemble, 2005, African Am. Classical Music award, Spelman Coll., 2007; fellow John Simon Guggenheim Meml. Found., 2008. Office: U Mich Sch Music Theater & Dance EV Moore Bldg 1100 Baits Dr Ann Arbor MI 48109-2085 Home: c/o Ora Harris Ross Clayton Prodns 5090 E Lakeshore Dr San Ramon CA 94582-4822 Office Phone: 415-388-8266, 734-764-5599. E-mail: RossClytn@aol.com, gaallen@umich.edu.

ALLEN, JEFFREY MICHAEL, lawyer; b. Chgo., Dec. 13, 1948; s. Albert A. and Miriam (Feldman) A.; m. Anne Marie Guaraglia, Aug. 9, 1975; children: Jason M., Sara M. BA in Polit. Sci. with great distinction and distinction in honors, U. Calif., Berkeley, 1970, JD, 1973. Bar: Calif. 1973, U.S. Dist. Ct. (no. and so. dists.) Calif. 1973, U.S. Ct. Appeals (9th cir.) 1973, U.S. Dist. Ct. (ea. dist.) Calif. 1974, U.S. Dist. Ct. (cen. dist.) Calif. 1977, U.S. Dist. Ct. (so. dist.) Calif., U.S. Supreme Ct.; solicitor Supreme Ct. Eng. and Wales; lic. real estate broker. Prin. Graves & Allen, Oakland, Calif., 1973—; solicitor Supreme Ct. Eng. and Wales. Tchg. asst. dept. polit. sci. U. Calif., Berkeley, 1970-73; lectr. St. Mary's Coll., Moraga, Calif., 1976-90; bd. dirs. Family Svcs. of East Bay, 1987-92, 1st v.p., 1988, pres., 1988-91; mem. faculty Oakland Coll. Law, 1996-98, 2004-; mem. panel arbitrators Alameda County Superior Ct. 1983-; arbitrator comml. arbitration panel Am. Arbitration Assn.; assoc. prof. U. Phoneix, 2004-, Calif. State U., East Bay, 2005-; solicitor Supreme Ct. Eng. and Wales, 2006. Mem. editorial bd. U. Calif. Law Rev., 1971-73, project editor, 1972-73; mem. Ecology Law Quar., 1971-72; contbr. articles to profl. jours. Mem. U.S. Youth Soccer Constl. Commn., 1997—98, U.S. Youth Soccer Bylaws Com., 1998—; mem. region 4 regional coun. U.S. Youth Soccer, 1996—99, chmn. mediation and dispute resolution com., 1999—2000; bd. dirs. U.S. Futsal Fedn., 2000—; treas. Hillcrest Elem. Sch. PTA, 1984—86, pres., 1986—88; past mem. GATE adv. com., strategic planning com. on fin. and budget, dist. budget adv. com., instructional strategy counsel Oakland Unified Sch. Dist., 1986—91; mem. Oakland Met. Forum, 1987—91, Oakland Strategic Planning Com., 1988—90; mem. adv. com. St. Mary's Coll. Paralegal Prog.; commr. Bay Oaks Youth Soccer, 1988—94; asst. dist. commr. dist. 4 Calif. Youth Soccer Assn., 1990—92, also bd. dirs., pres. dist. 4 competitive league, 1990—93, sec. bd. dirs., 1993—96, chmn. bd. dirs., 1996—99; chmn. U.S. Soccer dateabase mktg. com. Calif. Soccer Assn., 1997—99; bd. dirs. Montera Sports Complex, 1988—89, Jack London Youth Soccer League, 1988—94, Calif. Soccer Assn., 1996—99. Mem.: Law Soc. Eng. and Wales, Rotary (bd. dirs. Oakland 1992—94), Oakland C. of C., Assn. Conflict Resolution, Calif. North Referee Assn. (referee adminstr. dist. 4 1992—96, state bd. dirs. 1996—2000), U.S. Soccer Fedn. (nat. C lic. coach and state referee, state referee instr. and state referee assessor), Calif. Scholarship Fedn., U.S. Soccer Assn. (database mktg. com., constl. commn.), Alameda County Bar Assn. (past vice chmn. com. continuing edn., exec. com. alternative dispute resolution programs, panel mediator, arbitrator), Calif. Bar Assn. (mem. ADR com. 2001—04), ABA (chmn. subcom. on use of computers in real estate trans. 1985—86, chmn. real property com. gen. practice sect. 1987—91, mem. programs com. 1991—93, adv. coord. 1993—96, sect. coun. 1994—98, mktg. bd. 1996—98, mem. 1998—99, editor, columnist Tech. and Practice Guide 1998—, editl. bd. GP Solo 1999—, editor, columnist Tech. e Report 2002—, advisor to nat. counsel commrs. of uniform state laws, online form state laws drafting com. for electronic discovery). Avocations: reading, computers, photography, skiing, baseball. Office: Graves & Allen 436 14th St Ste 1400 Oakland CA 94612-2716 Office Phone: 510-839-8777. Personal E-mail: jallenlaw@aol.com. Business E-Mail: jallenlaw@gravesallen.com.

ALLEN, JOHN LOGAN, retired geographer; b. Laramie, Wyo., Dec. 27, 1941; s. John Milton and Nancy Elizabeth (Logan) Allen; m. Anne Evelyn Gilroy, Aug. 9, 1964; children: Traci Kathleen, Jennifer Lynne. BA, U. Wyo., 1963, MA, 1964; PhD (univ. grad. fellow 1964-67), Clark U., Worcester, Mass., 1969. Mem. faculty U. Conn., Storrs, 1967—2000, prof. geography, 1979—2000, head dept., 1976—94, dir. grad. program in geography, 1992—2000, mem. nat. exec. com. Faculty Athletic Rep. Assn., 1987—96; parliamentarian Faculty Athletic Rep. Assn., 1996—; prof., chair dept. geography U. Wyo., Laramie, 2000—08, emeritus prof., 2008—, bd. visitors, 2008—. Non-resident fellow Ctr. Great Plains Studies; scholar-in-residence Nat. Lewis and Clark Trail Interpretive Ctr. Author: Passage Through the Garden: Lewis and Clark and the Geog. Lore of the Am. N.W., 1975, Jedediah Smith and the Mountain Men of the Am. West, 1991, Lewis and Clark and the Images of the Am. N.W., 1991, Student Atlas of World Politics, 1991, 8th edit., 2007, 9th edit., 2009, Atlas of Economic Development, 1997, Atlas of Environmental Issues, 1997, Student Atlas of World Geography, 1998, 6th edit., 2009, Student Atlas of Anthropology, 2003; editor (ann. edits.): Environment, 1982—, Reshaping Traditions, 1994—; mem. editl. bd.: Jour. Hist. Geography, —, project dir., gen. editor: North Am. Exploration: A Comprehensive History, 3 vols., 1997—; contbr. articles articles to profl. jours., chapters to books. Pres. Mansfield Mid. Sch. Assn., Conn., 1979—80; active Mansfield Conservation Commn., Mansfield Planning and Zoning Commn.; vice chmn. Mansfield Zoning Bd. Appeals; mem. adv. bd. Nat. Lewis and Clark Bicentennial Commn., Nat. Lewis and Clark Interpretive Ctr. Recipient Meritorious Achievement award, Lewis and Clark Trail Heritage Found., 1976, Excellence in Tchg. award, U. Conn. Alumni Assn., 1987, Outstanding Contbn. award, U. Conn. Club, 1993, Oustandint Alumnus award, U. Wyo. Coll. Arts and Scis., 1999, Spl. Recognition award, U. Conn., 2000; GMC scholar, 1957—63, NSF Postdoctoral fellow, 1970—71. Fellow: Royal Geog. Soc., Am. Geog. Assn.; mem.: AAAS, Soc. History Discovery (nat. councilor), Western History Assn. (hon.), Soc. Historians Early Am. Republic, Assn. Am. Geographers, Masons, Elks, Phi Beta Kappa, Omicron Delta Kappa, Phi Kappa Phi. Democrat. Congregationalist. Home: 2703 Leslie Ct Laramie WY 82072-2979

ALLEN, JOSE R., lawyer; b. Panama, Sept. 8, 1951; arrived in US, 1956; s. Joseph R. and Grace A. (Osborne) A.; m. Irvenia E. Waters, July 20, 1986; 1 child, Jeffrey Richard Allen. BA, Yale U., 1973; JD, Boston Coll., 1976. Bar: Mass. 1977, Calif. 1986. Asst. atty. gen. Mass. Atty. Gen. Office, Boston, 1976-79; trial atty. US Dept. Justice, Washington, 1979-80, asst. sect. chief, 1980-82, sect. chief, 1982-85, chief, environ. def. sect., land, and natural resources divsn., 1981—84, chief, gen. litigation sect., land, and nat. resources divsn., 1984—85; of counsel Orrick, Herrington & Sutcliffe, San Francisco, 1985-88; ptnr., environment practice area Skadden, Arps, Slate, Meagher & Flom LLP, San Francisco, 1988—. Mem. adv. com. on environ. Practising Law Inst., NYC, 1992—; spkr. in the field. Contbr. articles in profl. jours. Bd. dirs. San Francisco Bay Area Lawyers' Com. Urban Affairs, 1990, Legal Aid Soc. San Francisco, 1993. Mem. ABA (mem. sect. on natural resources, energy and environ. law and lit. sect.), Bar Assn. San Francisco, Charles Houston Bar Assn., State Bar Calif. (mem. environ. law sect.). Office: Skadden Arps Slate Meagher & Flom LLP Four Embarcadero Ctr San Francisco CA 94111 Office Phone: 415-984-6442. Office Fax: 888-329-1260. Business E-Mail: jrallen@skadden.com.

ALLEN, KEITH W., actor, singer, songwriter; b. Chgo., Dec. 3, 1953; s. Grover Dean and Francis Lee (Grayson) A.; m. Lori Paulette Ferrari, June 30, 1989; 1 child, Kelly Marie. AA, Blackhawk East Coll., 1986. Chief exec. officer New Hope Films, Denver, 1987—. Producer soundtracks and actor Producers Group Studios, Colorado Springs, Colo., 1990—. Actor, songwriter singles, albums including Pools of Anger, 1990; appeared in opening acts for Lou Rawls, 1977-78, Willie Tyler & Lester, 1985, Don Rickels, 1977-78, Kenny Rogers, 1977-78, Pat Cooper, 1977-78, Joan Rivers, 1977-78, Jerry Lewis Telethon, 1977-78. With U.S. Army, 1972-73, Vietnam. Mem. Colo. Film Commn. Democrat. Methodist. Avocations: Karate (black belt), boxing, running, weightlifting, tennis. Office: New Hope Films Inc 4900 DTC Pky # 246 Denver CO 80237-2703

ALLEN, LARRY CHRISTOPHER, retired professional football player; b. LA, Nov. 27, 1971; m. Janelle Allen; children: Jayla, Loriana, Larry, Jr. Student, Butte Jr. Coll., Sonoma State U. Tackle Dallas Cowboys, 1994—2005, San Francisco 49ers, 2006—07; ret., 2008. Named to NFC Pro-Bowl team, 1995-2001, 2003-06, NFL all decade team, 1990's; Named NFL First Team All-Pro, 1996-01. Achievements include was the third player in NFL history to be selected to the Pro Bowl for more than one offensive line position, 1998; being a member of SuperBowl XXX Champion Dallas Cowboys, 1995.

ALLEN, LARRY GLENN, biology professor, department chairman; m. Teresa Diane Hoyle, Apr. 11, 1982; 1 child, Eric Keith. BA in Biology, Calif. State U., Fullerton, 1974; MA in Biology, Calif. State U., 1976; PhD in Biology, U. So. Calif., LA, 1980. Rsch. biologist U. Calif., Santa Barbara, 1980—82; prof. biology Calif. State U., Northridge, 1982—, biology chair, 2005—. Chmn., bd. govs. Ocean Studies Inst., Long Beach, Calif., 1986—. Author: (book) The Ecology of Marine Fishes: California and Adjacent Waters, 2006. Mem.: So. Calif. Acad. Scis. (life; gov. 1985—89), Am. Soc. Ichthyologists and Herpetologists (life; bd. govs. 2005—), We. Soc. Naturalists (life; pres. 2007). Democrat-Npl. Achievements include research in ecology of California marine fish. Avocations: fishing, golf, art. Home: 24738 Via Madera Calabasas CA 91302 Office: Calif State Univ 18111 Nordhoff St Northridge CA 91330-8303 Office Fax: 818-677-2034. Business E-Mail: larry.allen@csun.edu.

ALLEN, LOUIS ALEXANDER, management consultant; b. Glace Bay, NS, Oct. 8, 1917; s. Israel Nathan and Emma (Greenberg) A.; m. Ruth Graham, Aug. 24, 1946; children: Michael, Steven, Ace, Terry Allen Beck, Deborah Allen. BS cum laude, Wash. State U., 1941. Cert. mgmt. cons. Asst. to dean of men Wash. State U., Pullman, 1940-42; tng. supr. Aluminum Co. Am., Pitts., 1946-49; mgr. pers. adminstrn. Koppers Co. Inc., Pitts., 1949-53; dir. rsch. projects The Conf. Bd., NYC, 1953-56; dir. orgnl. planning Booz, Allen & Hamilton, Chgo., 1956-58; founder Louis Allen Assocs., Inc., Los Altos, Calif., 1958-92; ind. rschr., 1992-95. Lectr. on bus. mgmt. Stanford U., U. Chgo., NYU, Japan, China, Australia, Africa and Europe. Author: Improving Staff and Line Relationships, 1956, Preparing the Company Organization Manual, 1957, Organization of Staff Functions, 1958, Management and Organization, 1958, The Management Profession, 1964, Professional Management: New Concepts and Proven Practices, 1973, Time before Morning: Art and Myth of the Australian Aborigines, 1975, Making Managerial Planning More Effective, 1982, The Allen Guide for Management Leaders, 1989, Common Vocabulary for Management Leaders, 1989, The Louis Allen Leader's Handbook, 1995, The New Leadership, 1996; (mus. catalog) Australian Aboriginal Art, 1972; translated into Japanese, German, French, Finnish, Swedish, Dutch, Spanish, Portuguese, Bahasa; contbr. numerous articles and monographs to profl. jours. on mgmt., primitive art; exhibitor primitive art major mus. worldwide, 1969—. Maj. USAF, 1942-55, PTO. Decorated Legion of Merit; recipient McKinsey award Acad. Mgmt. Mem. Inst. Mgmt. Cons. (sr. assoc., regional pres. 1985). Achievements include first to fully classify human work into categories, a typology which facilities diagnosis and correction of organizational problems. Personal E-mail: laglaceby@aol.com.

ALLEN, MATTHEW ARNOLD, physicist; b. Edinburgh, Apr. 27, 1930; arrived in US, 1955, naturalized, 1961; s. William Wolff and Clara (Bloch) A.; m. Marcia Harriet Katzman, Sept. 15, 1957; children: Bruce William, Peter Jonathan, David Michael. BSc in Physics, U. Edinburgh, 1951; PhD in Physics, Stanford U., 1959. Rsch. assoc. Hansen Labs., Stanford (Calif.) U., 1959-61; rsch. mgr. tube div. Microwave Assocs., Burlington, Mass., 1961-65; radio frequency group leader Stanford Linear Accelerator Ctr., 1965-82, head accelerator physics dept., 1982-84, head klystron microwave dept., 1984-90, asst. dir. for elec. and electronic systems, 1989-90, assoc. dir. lab., 1990—2003, emeritus, 2003—. Cons. Microwave Assocs. Inc., 1965-71, Aerojet Gen., Azusa, Calif., 1959-62, Bechtel Corp., San Francisco, 1965-67; mem. tech. rev. com. Synchotron Radiation Rsch. Ctr., Hsinchu, Taiwan, 1985-98; chmn. U.S.A. Particle Accelerator Conf., 1991. Contbr. articles to profl. jours.; patentee in field. Commr. Environ. Planning Commn., Mountain View, Calif., 1971-74; councilman Mountain View City Coun., 1974-82; mayor City of Mountain View, 1977, 81; pres. Mountain View Community TV, 1989. Lt. British Army, 1953-55. Fellow IEEE (life), Am. Phys. Soc.; mem. IEEE Nuclear and Plasma Scis. Soc. (adminstrv. com. 1978-84, 98-2001), Dem. Club (bd. dirs. 1980-84), Sigma Xi. Democrat. Jewish. Avocations: skiing, running, tv producing. Home: 620 Sand Hill Rd # 318D Palo Alto CA 94304 Office: Stanford Linear Accelerator Ctr 2575 Sand Hill Rd Menlo Park CA 94025 Business E-Mail: mattmar@pacbell.net.

ALLEN, MICHAEL JOHN BRIDGMAN, language educator; b. Lewes, Eng., Apr. 1, 1941; came to U.S., 1966; m. Elena Hirshberg; children: William, Benjamin. BA, Oxford U., Eng., 1964, MA, 1966, DLitt, 1987; PhD, U. Mich., 1970. Asst. prof. UCLA, 1970-74, assoc. prof., 1974-79, prof. English, 1979—, disting. prof., 1994, assoc. dir. Ctr. for Medieval and Renaissance Studies, 1978-88, dir., 1988—93, 2003—04; v.p. Renaissance Soc. Am., 2004—06, pres., 2006—08. Editor Renaissance Quar., 1993—2001; faculty rsch. lectr. UCLA, 1998. Author: Marsilio Ficino: The Philebus Commentary, 1975, Marsilio Ficino and the Phaedran Charioteer, 1981, The Platonism of Marsilio Ficino, 1984, Icastes: Marsilio Ficino's Interpretation of Plato's "Sophist," 1989, Nuptial Arithmetic, 1994, Plato's Third Eye: Studies in Marsilio Ficino's Metaphysics and Its Sources, 1995, Synoptic Art: Marsilio Ficino on the History of Platonic Interpretation, 1998; co-author: Sources and Analogues of Old English Poetry, 1976, Marsilio Ficino: Platonic Theology, Vol. I, Books I-IV, 2001, Vol. 2, Books V-VIII, 2002, Vol. 3, Books IX-XI, 2003, Vol. 4, Books XII-XIV, 2004, Vol. 5, Books XV-XVI, 2005, Vol. 6, Books XVII-XVIII, 2006; co-editor: First Images of America, 1976, Shakespeare's Plays in Quarto, 1984, Sir Philip Sidney's Achievements, 1990, Marsilio Ficino: His Theology, His Philosophy, His Legacy, 2002. Recipient Eby award for disting. tchg. UCLA, 1977; Guggenheim fellow, 1977; disting. vis. scholar Ctr. for Reformation and Renaissance Studies, U. Toronto, 1997, Ludwig Maximilians U., Munich, 1999, Ariz. Ctr. for Medieval and Renaissance Studies, 2002. Mem.: Premio Internazionale Galileo Galilei, Commendatore Dell' Ordine Della Stella, Italy, Phi Beta Kappa (vis. scholar 2007—08). Office: UCLA 149 Humanities Bldg 405 Hilgard Ave Los Angeles CA 90095-1530 Business E-Mail: mjballen@humnet.ucla.edu.

ALLEN, PAUL GARDNER, professional sports team and computer company executive; b. Seattle, Jan. 21, 1953; s. Kenneth and Faye Allen. Student, Wash. State U. Co-founder Traf-O-Data Co., Seattle, 1972—73; progammer Honeywell Internat. Inc., Waltham, 1974—75; co-founder Microsoft Corp. (formerly Micro-Soft), Albuquerque, 1975; gen. ptnr. Microsoft Corp., 1975—77, v.p., 1977—81, exec. v.p. rsch. & new product devel., 1981—83, sr. strategy adv., 2000—; founder Asymetrix Corp., Bellevue, Wash., 1985, Starwave Corp., Bellevue, 1992; co-founder Interval Rsch. Corp., Palo Alto, Calif., 1992; founder Vulcan Prodns.; founder, chmn. Vulcan Inc., Seattle; CEO Vulcan Ventures, Bellevue, 1987—; owner, chmn. bd. Portland Trail Blazers, 1988—; owner, chmn. Seattle Seahawks, 1997—; chmn. Charter Comm. Inc., 1998—, Charter Investment, Inc., 1998—; owner TechTV; sponsor, funder SpaceShipOne Venture, Mojave, Calif., 2003; founder Allen Telescope Array, SETI Inst. U. Calif. Berkeley, 2004. Bd. dirs. Egghead Discount Software, Microsoft Corp., 1983—2000, Darwin Molecular, Inc.; founder Allen Inst. Brain Sci., 2003—, Allen Brain Atlas Initiative, Experience Music Project, Seattle, Sci. Fiction Mus. and Hall of Fame, Seattle, 2004—; ptnr. DreamWorks SKG. Exec. prodr.: (film series) The Blues. Founder Paul G. Allen Family Found. Recipient Spl. Recognition award, Soc. Neurosci., 2007; co-recipient (with Burt Rutan) Smithsonian's Nat. Air & Space Mus. trophy, 2005, Rave award for sci., WIRED Mag., 2007; named one of Top 15 Philanthropists in America, Top 200 Collectors, Artnews mag., 2004—, World's Richest People, Forbes mag., 1999—, Forbes' Richest Americans, 2006, The 100 Most Influential People in the World, TIME mag., 2007, 2008, The Most Influential People in the World of Sports, Bus. Week, 2007, 2008; named to Computer Mus. Hall of Fame. Mem.: NAE. Achievements include sponsoring and funding the record flights for SpaceShipOne, which won the Ansari X prize on Oct. 4, 2004; SpaceShipOne donated to Smithsonian Instn. on October 6, 2005. Avocation: Collecting impressionism, Old Masters, pop art, tribal art. Office: Vulcan Inc 505 5th Ave S Ste 900 Seattle WA 98104 also: Seattle Seahawks 12 Seahawks Way Renton WA 98056-1572 Office Phone: 425-453-1940, 206-342-2000. Office Fax: 206-342-3000.

ALLEN, RICHARD, computer software executive; Sr. accountant Coopers & Lybrand; controller Luff Exploration Co.; exec. vp. fin./adminstrn., CFP J.D. Edwards & Co. Office: JD Edwards & Co One Technology Way Denver CO 80237

ALLEN, RICHARD GARRETT, healthcare educator; b. St. Paul, July 8, 1923; s. John and Margaretta (Taggart) A.; m. Ida Elizabeth Vernon, July 5, 1944; children: Richard Garrett, Barbara Elizabeth, Julie Frances (dec.). BS cum laude, Trinity U., 1954; MHA, Baylor U., 1957; postgrad., Indsl. Coll. of Armed Forces, 1962, USAF Command and Staff Coll., 1962. Commd. 2d lt. Med. Svc. Corps USAF, 1948, advanced through grades to maj., 1961; served in U.S., Pacific, Germany; ret., 1964; asst. adminstr. U. Ala. Hosp. and Clinics; dir. Ctr. for Hosp. Continuing Edn., Sch. for Health Svcs., U. Ala., Birmingham, 1965-68; dir. edn. New Eng. Hosp. Assembly, Inc., New Eng. Ctr. for Continuing Edn., U. N.H., Durham, 1968-74; dir. Office Health Care Edn., 1970-74; exec. v.p. Edn. and Rsch. Found., San Francisco, 1974-77, Assn. West Hosps., 1974-77. V.p. health affairs M G & M Comm., Foster City, Calif.; pres. Calif. Coll. Podiatric Medicine; CEO Calif. Podiatry Hosp. and Outpatient Clinic, San Francisco, 1977-81; prof. health care adminstrn. St. Mary's Coll. of Calif., Moraga, 1982-85; cons. health care and edn., 1985—; owner Sleepy Hollow Books, 1985—; mem. Nat. Adv. Coun. on Vocat. Edn., 1969-71; also cons.; cons. Booz, Allen & Hamilton, Washington, Ops. Rsch., Inc., Silver Spring, Md., Republic of Korea Air Force Med. Svcs., Seoul, Bio-Dynamics, Inc., Cambridge, Mass., HEALTHSAT-Appalachia Cmty. Svcs. Network, Washington, 1980—. Pub.: Hosp.

Forum, San Francisco, 1974-77; contbr. articles to profl. jours. Decorated Air Force Commendation medal with oak leaf cluster. Fellow Am. Coll. Hosp. Adminstrs.; mem. Am. Soc. for Health Manpower Edn. and Tng., Am. Hosp. Assn., AAUP, Am. Soc. Hosp. Edn. and Tng. (pres. 1972), Am. Assn. Colls. Podiatric Medicine (pres. 1979-81), Sherlock Holmes Soc. London, Masons. Episcopalian. Home and Office: Sleepy Hollow Books 1455 Camino Peral Moraga CA 94556-2018 Personal E-mail: dick78@earthlink.net.

ALLEN, ROBERT EUGENE BARTON, lawyer; b. Bloomington, Ind., Mar. 16, 1940; s. Robert Eugene Barton and Berth R. A.; m. Cecelia Ward Dooley, Sept. 23, 1960 (div. 1971); children: Victoria, Elizabeth, Robert, Charles, Suzanne, William; m. Judith Elaine Hecht, May 27, 1979 (div. 1984); m. Suzanne Nickolson, Nov. 18, 1995. BS, Columbia U., 1962; LLB, Harvard U., 1965. Bar: Ariz. 1965, U.S. Dist. Ct. Ariz. 1965, U.S. Tax Ct., 1965, U.S. Supreme Ct. 1970, U.S. Ct. Customs and Patent Appeals 1971, U.S. Dist. Ct. D.C. 1972, U.S. Ct. Appeals (9th cir.) 1974, U.S. Ct. Appeals (10th and D.C. cirs.) 1984, U.S. Dist. Ct. N.Mex., U.S. Dist. Ct. (no. dist.) Calif., U.S. Dist. Ct. (no. dist.) Tex. 1991, U.S. Ct. Appeals (fed. cir.) 1992, U.S. Dist. Ct. (ea. dist.) Wis. 1995. Spl. asst. atty. gen., 1978; judge pro-tem Ariz. Ct. Appeals, 1984, 92, 99; Ptnr., dir. Allen, Price & Padden, Phoenix, 2000—. Nat. pres. Young Dems. Clubs Am., 1971-73; mem. exec. com. Dem. Nat. Com., 1972-73, Ariz. Gov.'s Kitchen Cabinet working on a wide range of state projects; bd. dirs. Phoenix Bapt. Hosp., 1981-83, Phoenix and Valley of the Sun Conv. and Visitors Bur., United Cerebral Palsy Ariz., 1984-89, Planned Parenthood of Ctrl. and No. Ariz., 1984-87, Ariz. Heart Found., 1998—, Cordell Hull Found. for Internat. Edn., 1996—; trustee Environ. Health Found., 1994-97, Friends of Walnut Canyon, 1991-94; bd. dirs. Ariz. Aviation Futures Task Force, chmn. Ariz. Airport Devel. Criteria Subcom.; Am. rep. exec. bd. Atlantic Alliance of Young Polit. Leaders, 1973-77, 77-80; trustee Am. Counsel of Young Polit. Leaders, 1971-76, 81-85; mem. Am. delegations to Germany, 1971, 72, 76, 79, USSR, 1971, 76, 88, France, 1974, 79, Belgium, 1974, 77, Can., 1974, Eng., 1975, 79, Norway, 1975, Denmark, 1976, Yugoslavia and Hungary, 1985; Am. observer European Parlimentary elections, Eng., France, Germany, Belgium, 1979, Moscow Congressional, Journalist delegation, 1989, NAFTA Trade Conf., Mexico City, 1993, Atlantic Assembly, Copenhagen, 1993. Contbr. articles on comml. litig. to profl. jours. Mem. ABA, Ariz. Bar Assn., Maricopa County Bar Assn., N.Mex. State Bar, D.C. Bar Assn., Am. Judicature Soc., Fed. Bar Assn., Am. Arbitration Assn., Phi Beta Kappa, Harvard Club. Democrat. Episcopalian. Home: 4610 North Borgatello Phoenix AZ 85018 Office Phone: 602-478-9933. Personal E-mail: allenfamily5330@yahoo.com.

ALLEN, RONALD CARL, commissioner, artist, consultant, former state senator, computer company executive; b. Salt Lake City, Mar. 25, 1953; s. Carl Franklin and Mary Jean (Benson) A.; m. Delia Ann Fordham, Nov. 15, 1974; children: Lisa, Cindy, Jeffrey. BS in Acctg., U. Utah, 1980, MA in Art History, 2004. Owner, bus. mgr. Alinco Mfg., Salt Lake City, 1977-79; adminstrv. supr. Am. Stores, 1978-89; owner, pres. Comics Utah Bookstores, 1984-86; pres. Cons. Svcs., 1989—2003; fire chief No. Tooele County Fire Dept., 1987-96; mem. Utah Senate, 1998—2005, Dem. whip, 2001—05. Adj. instr. Utah State U. Chmn., chief North Tooele County (Utah) Fire Dept., 1987—95; mem. nat. adv. bd. Utah Mus. Fine Arts. Recipient over 40 visual arts awards, 1981—. Mem., Tooele County C of C, Salt Lake Acting Co. (bd. mem.). Mem. Lds Ch. Avocations: photography, sailing, golf. Office: 160 E 300 S Salt Lake City UT 84111 Office Phone: 801-530-6716. Personal E-mail: rallen@vonallen.com.

ALLEN, RUSSELL G., lawyer; b. Ottumwa, Iowa, Nov. 7, 1946; BA, Grinnell Coll., 1968; JD, Stanford U., 1971. Bar: Calif. 1971. Ptnr. O'Melveny & Myers LLP, Newport Beach, Calif., 1975-2001; wealth advisor J.P. Morgan Chase & Co., Newport Beach, Calif., 2001—04. Trustee Grinnell Coll. Capt. JAGC, USAF, 1971-75. Fellow Am. Coll. Trust and Estate Counsel; mem. ABA (real property, probate and trust law and taxation sects.), Orange County Bar Assn. (estate planning, probate and trust sects.) Office: 2101 East Coast Hwy Ste 215 Corona Del Mar CA 92625 Office Phone: 949-760-4090. E-mail: Russ@russallenlaw.com.

ALLEN, SHARON, accounting firm executive; B in Acctg., U. Idaho, 1973, Ph.D (hon.) in Adminstrv. Sci., 2004. Mng. ptnr. Pacific Southwest practice Deloitte & Touche USA LLP, LA, 2003—, chmn. bd., 2003—. Mem. bd. United Way Greater LA; bd. mem. YMCA Met. LA; co-chair Nat. Campaign Com. Campaign for Idaho; bd. dirs. Malcolm Baldridge Found., Harvard U., John F. Kennedy Sch. Govt. Women's Leadership Coun.; chmn. bd. dirs. Independent Coll. So. Calif. (ICSC), 2003—; adv. bd. Coll. Bus. and Econ. Named Woman of the Yr., Fin. Woman's Assn., 2006; named one of Top 100 Most Influential People in 2003, Acctg. Today mag., 100 Most Powerful Women, Forbes Mag., 2006—08, The 100 Most Influential Women in NYC Bus., Crain's NY Bus., 2007. Mem.: LA Area C. of C. (bd. mem.). Office: Deloitte & Touche USA LLP Two Calif Plz 350 S Grand Ave Ste 200 Los Angeles CA 90071-3492 Office Phone: 213-688-0800. Office Fax: 213-688-0100.

ALLEN, SYLVIA TENNEY, state legislator; b. Ariz. m. Richard Allen; 5 children. Pres. Ariz. Eagle Forum, 1980—90; agent Integrity Realty, Snowflake, Ariz., 2005—; mem. Dist. 5 Ariz. State Senate, 2008—, vice chair retirement & rural devel. com., mem. edn. accountability & reform com., appropriations com. Navajo Country Rep. Chmn., 2002—05; pres. Freedom for America League, 2000—06. Bd. dirs. Mogollon Med. Found., 2003—06. Republican. Office: Ariz State Senate Capitol Complex 1700 W Washington Rm 307 Phoenix AZ 85007 Office Phone: 602-926-5219. Office Fax: 602-417-3005. Business E-Mail: sallen@azleg.gov.*

ALLEN, TED, television personality; b. 1965; life ptnr. Barry Rice. BA in Psychology, Purdue U.; MA in Journalism, NYU. Co-author: Things a Man Should Know About Marriage: A Groom's Guide to the Wedding and Beyond, 1999, Things a Man Should Know About Style, 1999, Things a Man Should Know About Sex, 2001, Things a Man Should Know About Handshakes, White Lies and Which Fork Goes Where, 2001, Queer Eye for the Straight Guy: The Fab 5's Guide to Looking Better, Cooking Better, Dressing Better, Behaving Better, and Living Better, 2004, (cookbooks) The Food You Want to Eat: 100 Smart, Simple Recipes, 2005; co-author and contbg. editor: Things a Man Should Know column Esquire mag., 1997—, contbg. author: Conde Nast Traveler, Travel & Leisure, GQ, Nat. Geog. Adventure, Self, Men's Jour., Women.Com, Chgo. Sun-Times; sr. editor and restaurant critic Chgo. mag., food and wine specialist (TV series) Queer Eye for the Straight Guy, 2003—, judge Top Chef, Bravo, 2007, Iron Chef America, host Uncorked: Wine Made Simple, 2007, Food Detectives, 2008—. Office: William Morris Agy One William Morris Pl Beverly Hills CA 90212

ALLEN, TERRENCE R., lawyer; b. Phila., 1967; BA cum laude, BS cum laude, Univ. So. Calif., 1989; JD, Univ. So. Calif., 1993. Bar: Calif. 1993. Ptnr., corp. law practice O'Melveny & Myers LLP, Newport Beach, Calif. Named a Rising Star, So. Calif. Super Lawyers, 2004—06.

ALLEN, TIM (TIMOTHY ALLEN DICK), actor, comedian; b. Denver, June 13, 1953; s. Gerald and Martha Dick; m. Laura Diebel, Apr. 7, 1984 (div. Mar. 2003); 1 child, Katherine; m. Jane Hajduk, Oct. 7, 2006; 1 child, Elizabeth. Grad., Western Mich. U., 1975. Appeared in numerous Showtime spls.; actor: (TV series) Home Improvement, 1991-99 (Emmy award nomination, Lead actor - comedy 1993), exec. prodr., 1996-99, also writer; (films) The Santa Clause, 1994; (voice) Toy Story, 1995, Meet Wally Sparks, 1997, Jungle 2 Jungle, 1997, For Richer or Poorer, 1997, (voice) Toy Story 2, 1999, Galaxy Quest, 1999, Who is Cletis Tout, 2001, Joe Somebody, 2001, Big Trouble, 2002, The Santa Clause 2, 2002, Christmas with the Kranks, 2004, The Shaggy Dog, 2006, Zoom, 2006, The Santa Clause 3: The Escape Clause, 2006, Wild Hogs, 2007; (TV films) (voice) Jimmy Neutron: You Bet Your Life Form, 2004, (TV spls.) Comedy's Dirtiest Dozen, 1988, exec. prodr. Men Are Pigs, 1991; author: I'm Not Really Here, 1996, Don't Stand Too Close to a Naked Man, 1994; TV guest appearances The Flying Doctors, 1985, The Drew Carey Show, 1995, The Front, 1996, Soul Man, 1997, The Larry Sanders Show, 1992, Spin City, 1996, (voice) The Adventures of Jimmy Neutron: Boy Genius, 2004; exec. com. TV series Home Improvement, 1991. Recipient Golden Globe, 1995, Favorite Comedy Actor People's Choice award, 1995,97, 98, 99, TV Guide award 1999; nominated for Golden Globe awards 1993, 94, 96, 97, Blockbuster Entertainment award 1998. Office: William Morris Agy 151 El Camino Dr Beverly Hills CA 90212 Address: care Messina Baker 955 S Carillo Dr Ste 100 Los Angeles CA 90048

ALLEN, WALTER RECHARDE, sociology educator; b. Kansas City, Mo., Feb. 3, 1949; s. Grady Lee and Freddie Mae (Clayton) Allen; m. Wilma Jean Sharber, Sept. 26, 1970 (dec.); children: Rena Marie, Binti Tamarra, Bryan Recharde. BA, Beloit Coll., Wis., 1971; MA, U. Chgo., 1973, PhD, 1975. Asst. prof. sociology U. NC, Chapel Hill, 1974-79; asst. prof. sociology, Afro-Am. and African studies U. Mich., Ann Arbor, 1979-84, assoc. prof. sociology, Afro-Am. and African studies, 1985-88, assoc. dir. Cen. for Afro-Am. Studies, 1987-89, dir. Nat. Study Black Coll. Students, 1979-89, prof. sociology Afro-Am. and African studies, 1989-91; prof. sociology UCLA, 1989, assoc. dir. Robert Wood Johnson clin. scholars program, Sch. Medicine, 1992—97, prof. grad. sch. edn. & info. studies, 2004—. Co-author: The Colorline and the Quality of Life, 1987, African American Education: Race Community, Inequality and Achievement-A Tribute to Edgar G. Epps, 2006, Higher Education in a Global Society: Achieving Diversity, Equity, and Excellence, 2006,; co-editor: (book) Beginnings: Development of Black Children, 1985, College in Black and White, 1991; (bibliography) Black Families, 1965-80, 1986. Recipient distinguished leadership award United Negro Coll. Fund, 1985; Rockefeller Found. fellow, 1982-83, Fulbright scholar, 1984, 86-87; named Allerton Lectr. U. Ill., 1988. Mem. Internat. Sociol. Assn., Am. Sociol. Assn. (coun. 1991-94), Am. Ednl. Rsch. Assn. (disting. scholar 1987, rsch. excellence award, 1993), Assn. Black Sociologists (pres. 1992, disting. career award 1995), Assn. Study Higher Edn. (spl. merit award 2002), Sociol. Rsch. Assn., Phi Delta Kappa. Baptist. Avocations: reading, travel, swimming, gardening. Office: UCLA Dept grad sch edn & info studies 405 Hilgard Ave Los Angeles CA 90095-1521 Office Phone: 310-206-7107. Personal E-mail: walterrallen@yahoo.com. Business E-Mail: wallen@ucla.edu.

ALLERY, KENNETH EDWARD, career officer; b. Holyoke, Mass., Mar. 3, 1925; s. Alfred Edward and Anne (Millen) A.; m. Constance DuFresne, June 22, 1946; children— Katherine Ann, Kenneth Scott, Bryan Keith, David Edward. BA, Park Coll., 1965; MS, George Washington U., 1969; grad., Air Command and Staff Coll., 1961, Nat. War Coll., 1969. Commd. 2d lt. U.S. Army Air Force, 1944; advanced through grades to brig. gen. U.S. Air Force, 1972; insp. with Insp. Gen. Team 17th Air Force; exec. officer, ops. officer 526th Fighter Interceptor Squadron, Ramstein Air Base, Germany, 1961; sr. Air Force adviser Oreg. Air N.G., Portland Internat. Airport, 1965-67; dir. ops. and tng. 1st Air Force, Stewart AFB, N.Y., 1967-68; mem. N.Am. br. Directorate Plans and Programs, Orgn. Joint Chiefs of Staff, 1969-71; asst. dep. chief of staff for plans Aerospace Def. Command, Ent AFB, Colo., 1971-72, N.Am. Air Def. Command/Continental Air Def. Command, 1972-73, asst. dep. chief of staff for ops., 1973-74; also dep. chief of staff for ops. Aerospace Def. Command; command insp. gen. NORAD/CONAD/ADC, 1974-76; ret.; asst. to v.p. Syscon Corp., Colorado Springs, 1976-85; founder Allery Enterprises, Inc., Colorado Springs, 1996—99; bus. devel. mgr. Litton Computer Services, Colorado Springs, 1985-96; strategic planner Ensign Devel., Colorado Springs, 1999—. Bd. govs. Nat. Coll., Colorado Springs, 1993-94. Decorated D.S.M., D.F.C., Air medal with 4 oak leaf clusters, Meritorious Service medal with oak leaf cluster, Air Force Commendation medal.

ALLISON, ANDREW MARVIN, church administrator; b. Long Beach, Calif., May 21, 1949; s. Howard C. and Wilma A. (Franks) A.; m. Kathleen L. Anderson, May 28, 1971; children: Rebecca, Nathan, Joanna, Spencer, Jacob, Camilla. AA, Glendale CC, Ariz., 1972; BA in History, Brigham Young U., Provo, Utah, 1974; PhD of Polit. Sci., Coral Ridge U., Jacksonville, Fla., 1993. Cert. secondary tchr., Ariz., Utah. Adminstrv. staff, editor Brigham Young U., Provo, Utah, 1972-74; adminstrv. asst. LDS Ch., Salt Lake City, 1977-79; prin., tchr. LDS Seminaries, Ariz.,Utah, 1974-77, 79-80; assoc. editor, art dir. Bookcraft Publs., Salt Lake City, 1983-85; dir. rsch. and publs. Nat. Ctr. for Constl. Studies, Salt Lake City, 1980-83, 85-91, chmn., pres. West Jordan, Utah, 1991-95; product devel. editor Deseret Book Co., Salt Lake City, 1995-96; supr. confidential applications LDS Ch., Salt Lake City, 1996-99, mgr. confidential records, 1999—2006, product mgr., mem. and statis. records, 2006—07; project mgr. Office First Presidency, 2007—. Adj. prof. polit. sci. George Wythe Coll., Cedar City, Utah, 1993—2006. Author: The Real Thomas Jefferson, 1982, The Real Benjamin Franklin, 1983, The Real George Washington, 1991; contbr. articles to profl. jours. Mem. West Jordan City Coun., Utah, 2000—03, mayor pro-tem, 2001. Mem.: Phi Kappa Phi.

ALLISON, MERLE LEE, geologist; b. Phila., Jan. 15, 1948; s. Merle Raymond and Lois Loretta (Lynch) A. BS, U. Calif., Riverside, 1970; MS, San Diego State U., 1974; PhD, U. Mass., 1986. Registered geologist, Calif. Oil & gas engr. Calif. Divsn. Oil & Gas, Inglewood, 1971-72; geologist Chevron Corp., San Francisco, 1974-79; consulting geologist Amherst, Mass., 1980-84; scientist II Jet Propulsion Lab.-NASA, Pasadena, Calif., 1981; geologist Sohio Petroleum-BP, Dallas & Houston, 1984-87; sr. geologist U. Utah Rsch. Inst., Salt Lake City, 1987-89; dir., state geologist Utah Geol. Survey, Salt Lake City, 1989—. Pres. Western Earth Sci. Techs. Inc., Casper, Wyo., 1988-93; chair Utah Geog. Info. Coun., Salt Lake City, 1992-93. Editor: Energy & Mineral Resources of Utah, 1991; contbr. articles to profl. jours. Press sec., mgr. Caprio for Congress, San Diego, 1972, 74; city precinct mgr. Unruh for Gov., Riverside, 1978; energy advisor Clifford for Congress, Houston, 1990. Mem. Am. Assn. Petroleum Geologists, Geol. Soc. Am., Soc. Profl. Well Log Analysts, Am. Geophys. Union, Rocky Mountain Assn. Geologists, Utah Geol. Assn., Assn. for Women Geoscientists, Wyo. Geol. Assn., Nev. Petroleum Soc. Achievements include research on geology of Ganymede; diplog interpretation, various of in-situ crustal structures. Home: 2724 Meadow Dr Lawrence KS 66047-3237 Office: Utah Geological Survey 1594 W North Temple # 3410 Salt Lake City UT 84116-3154

ALLRED, CLARK B., judge; b. Ogden, Utah, Mar. 10, 1951; BA, Utah State U., 1975; JD, Brigham Young U., 1978. Pvt. practice lawyer; part-time magistrate judge U.S. Dist. Ct., Vernal, Utah, 1997—. Mem. Utah State Bar Assn.

ALLRED, GLORIA RACHEL, lawyer; b. Phila., July 3, 1941; d. Morris and Stella Bloom; m. Peyton Bray; 1 child, Lisa; m. William Allred (div. Oct. 1987). BA, U. Pa., 1963; MA, NYU, 1966; JD, Loyola U., LA, 1974; JD (hon.), U. West LA, 1981. Bar: Calif. 1975, US Dist. Ct. (ctrl. dist.) Calif. 1975, US Ct. Appeals (9th cir.) 1976, US Supreme Ct. 1979. Ptnr. Allred, Maroko, Goldberg & Ribakoff (now Allred, Maroko & Goldberg), LA, 1976—. Former host KABC TalkRadio, LA. Co-author: (with Deborah Caulfield Rybak) Fight Back and Win: My Thirty-year Fight Against Injustice--and How You Can Win Your Own Battles, 2006; Contbr. articles to profl. jours. Pres. Women's Equal Rights Legal Def. and Edn. Fund, LA, 1978—, Women's Movement Inc., LA. Recipient Commendation award City of LA, 1986, Mayor of LA, 1986, Pub. Svc. award Nat. Assn. Fed. Investigators, 1986, Vol. Action award Pres. of US, 1986, Women of Distinction award Nat. Coun. on Aging, 1994, The Judy Jarvis Meml. award, 2001; Named to Millennium Hall of Fame, Nat. Assn. Women Bus. Owners, LA Chapter, 2000. Mem. ABA, Calif. Bar Assn., Nat. Assn. Women Lawyers, Calif. Women Lawyers Assn., Women Lawyers LA Assn., Friars Club (NYC), Magic Castle Club (Hollywood, Calif.) Office: Allred Maroko & Goldberg 6300 Wilshire Blvd Ste 1500 Los Angeles CA 90048-5217 Office Phone: 323-653-6530.

ALLVIN, PAUL G., communications educator; b. 1968; B in Journalism, U. Ariz., 1993. Exec. dir. Ariz. Students Assn.; dir. Comm. Gov. Janet Napolitano; interim v.p., External Rels. U. Ariz., assoc. v.p., Comm. Mem. U. Ariz. Commn. on Status of Women. Dir. Comm. Make-A-Wish-Found.; mem. Phoenix Day and Family Learning Ctr., Valley of the Sun Chpt. Named one of 40 Under 40, Tucson Bus. Edge, 2006. Mem.: Make A Wish Found., Kids Voting Ariz. Bd., Pub. Rels. Soc. of Am., Ariz. Students Assn. Office: University of Arizona University Services Bldg PO Box 21958 Tucson AZ 85721 Office Phone: 520-621-9017. Office Fax: 520-626-4121. Business E-Mail: pallvin@email.arizona.edu.

ALMSTEAD, SHEILA LOUISE, art gallery owner; b. Albuquerque, Apr. 8, 1955; d. Laurence and Ida Seif Bair; m. Arlington J. Almstead (div.); children: Stacy Lynne Fusilier, Michael Laurence, Christopher James, Jason Andrew. BSW summa cum laude, Our Lady of Lake U., San Antonio, 1991; MSW, Our Lady of Lake U., 1992. Case mgr. San Antonio State Hosp. & Bexar County Mental Health, 1991—95; dir. health care svcs. Brighton Gardens, San Antonio. Mem. select Edn. Reform Com., San Antonio, 1991; mental health cons. Monarch Apts., San Antonio, 1995; med. social worker Morningside Home Health, San Antonio, 1996—97; owner Zingaro, Glendale, Ariz., 2002—; juror wholesalecrafts.com, 2006—; juror ann. trade show Am. Craft Retailers Expo., 2007—, juror, 2008, Sun City Club. Gallery of Am. Art: Internat. Fine Craft. Vol. ct. adv. Ct. Apptd. Spl. Advs., San Antonio, 1989—91. Mem.: Craft Retailers Assn. for Tomorrow, Am. Craft Coun., Alpha Chi, Phi Theta Kappa. Democrat. Avocations: theater, travel, music, reading, art. Office: Zingáro Home Accents 5746 W Glendale Ave Glendale AZ 85301 Office Phone: 623-934-0999.

ALOU, FELIPE ROJAS, former professional baseball team manager; b. Santo Domingo, Dominican Republic, May 12, 1935; Player San Francisco Giants, 1958-62, Milw. Braves, 1964-65, Atlanta Braves, 1966-69, Oakland Athletics, 1970-71, NY Yankees, 1971-73, Montreal Expos, 1973, Milw. Brewers, 1974; asst. coach Montreal Expos, 1979-80, 84, mgr., 1992—2001; bench coach Detroit Tigers, 2002; mgr. San Francisco Giants, 2002—06. Named to Nat. League All-Star team Sporting News, 1966; named Nat. League Mgr. of Yr. Sporting News, 1994, Baseball Writers' Assn. Am., 1994.

ALPER, MARK D., biochemist; b. Bklyn., May 14, 1945; s. Samuel and Miriam (Grifffel) A.; m. Christine Hexem, June 6, 1975; children: Samuel Andrew, Elizabeth Laura. AB, Harvard Coll., 1967; PhD, U. Calif., Berkeley, 1973. Adj. prof. dept. molecular and cell biology U. Calif., Berkeley, 1974—, dep. dir. Ctr. Advanced Materials, Lawrence Berkeley Lab., 1983—, assoc. dir. materials sci. div., 1987—, prof. biochem. molecular and cell biology dept.; dep. divsn. dri. material scis. divsn. Lawrence Berkeley Nat. Lab. Cons. various textbook pubs. Editor: Polymers for Advanced Technologies, 1989—. Mem. Materials Rsch. Soc., Am. Chem. Soc. Office: U Calif Materials Sci Div Lawrence Berkeley Lab 1 Cyclotron Rd Berkeley CA 94720-0001

ALPERS, EDWARD ALTER, history professor; b. Phila., Apr. 23, 1941; s. Bernard Jacob and Lillian (Sher) A.; m. Ann Adele Dixon, June 14, 1963; children: Joel Dixon, Leila Sher. AB magna cum laude, Harvard U., 1963; PhD, U. London, 1966. Lectr. history Univ. Coll., Dar es Salaam, Tanzania, 1966-68; from asst. prof. to prof. history UCLA, 1968—, dean divsn. honors Coll. Letters and Sci., 1985-87, dean honors and undergrad. programs, 1987-96, chair dept history, 2005—. Author: Ivory and Slaves in East Central Africa, 1975; editor: Walter Rodney: Revolutionary and Scholar, 1982, History, Memory and Identity, 2001, Africa and the West, 2001, Sidis and Scholars: Essays on African Indians, 2004, Slavery and Resistance in Africa and Asia, 2005, Slave Routes and Oral Tradition in Southeastern Africa,

2005, Resisting Bondage in Indian Ocean Africa and Asia, 2006, Cross Currents and Community Networks: Encapsulating the History of the Indian Ocean, 2007; (newsletter) Assn. Concerned Africa Scholars, 1983-85; contbg. editor: Comparative Studies of South Asia, Africa and the Middle East, 1997—; bd. editors The American Historical Rev., 2002-05; contbr. articles to profl. jours. Fellow Ford Found., 1972-73, NEH, 1978-79, Fulbright Found., 1980; Conf. fellow Humanities Rsch. Ctr., Nat. Australia U., Canberra, 1998; Fundacao Calouste Gulbenkian grantee, Lisbon, Portugal, 1975. Mem. Am. Hist. Assn. (mem. com. Joan Kelly Meml. prize 1998-99, chair 2000), Africa Studies Assn. (bd. dirs. 1985-88, v.p. 1992-93, pres. 1993-94), Assn. Concerned Africa Scholars (bd. dirs. 1983-95), Alliance for Undergrad. Edn. (UCLA rep. 1987-95, co-chair 1989-92), Hist. Abstracts (adv. bd. 1994—). Office: UCLA Dept History Los Angeles CA 90095-1473 Home Phone: 310-454-3239; Office Phone: 310-825-1883. Business E-Mail: alpers@history.ucla.edu.

ALPERT, HERB, composer, recording artist, producer, painter; b. LA, Mar. 31, 1935; s. Louis and Tillie (Goldberg) A.; m. Sharon Mae Lubin, Aug. 5, 1956 (div.): children: Dore, Eden; m. Lani Hall. Co-owner, founder A&M Record Co., 1962-94, Rondor Music Internat., 1994—. Band leader, trumpeter, arranger producer music group Herb Alpert & The Tijuana Brass, 34 recs. including The Lonely Bull, Whipped Cream & Other Delights, Going Places, Rise, Under A Spanish Moon, Colors, 1999 (14 Platinum recs., 15 gold recs., 7 Grammy awards); prodr. Broadway shows, including Angels in America, Jelly's Last Jam, Seven Guitars. Founder Herb Alpert Found. Recipient Lifetime Achievement award, Rock and Roll Hall of Fame, 2006. Mem.: Calif. Horse Racing Bd. Office: c/o No Bull Inc 1414 6th St Santa Monica CA 90401-2510

ALPERT, JOSEPH STEPHEN, cardiologist, educator; b. New Haven, Feb. 1, 1942; s. Zelly Charles and Beatrice Ann (Kopsofsky) A.; m. Helle Mathiasen, Aug. 6, 1965; children: Eva Elisabeth, Niels David. BA magna cum laude, Yale U., 1963; MD cum laude, Harvard U., 1969. Diplomate internal medicine and cardiovasc. disease Am. Bd. Internal Medicine. Successively intern, resident in internal medicine, fellow in cardiovascular disease Peter Bent Brigham Hosp.-Harvard U. Med. Sch., Boston, 1969-74, dir. Samuel A. Levine cardiac unit, asst. prof. medicine, 1976-78; prof., dir. divsn. cardiovascular medicine U. Mass. Med. Sch., Worcester, 1978-92, vice-chmn. dept. medicine, 1990—, Edward Budnitz prof. of cardiovascular medicine, 1988-92; Robert W. and Irene P. Flinn prof. U. Ariz., 1992—, chmn. dept. medicine, 1992—2006, asst. to the dean Coll. Medicine, 2006—. Cons. West Roxbury VA Hosp., Boston, VA Med. Ctr., Tucson; sec., treas. med. staff U. Mass. Med. Ctr., 1979-81, pres. med. staff, 1981-82; bd. dirs. Am. Bd. Internal Medicine. Author: The Heart Attack Handbook, 1978, 3d edit., 1993, Cardiovascular Physiopathology, 1984; co-author: Manual of Coronary Care, 1977, 1980, 1984, 1987, 1993, 2000, Manual of Cardiovascular Diagnosis and Therapy, 1980, 1984, 1988, 1996, 2003, Valvular Heart Disease, 1981, 1987, 2000, Intensive Care Medicine, 1985, 2d edit., 1991, The Clinician's Companion, 1986, Modern Coronary Care, 1990, 2d edit., 1996, Diagnostic Atlas of the Heart, 1994, Cardiology for the Primary Care Physician, 1996, 3d edit., 2000, Primary Care of Native American Patients, 1999, American Heart Association's Clinical Cardiology Consult, 2001, 2006; editor-in-chief Current Cardiology Reports, 2001—05, Am. Jour. Medicine, 2005—; editor: Cardiology in Rev., 2001—05; assoc. editor Jour. History of Medicine and Allied Scis., 1977—80, editl. cons. Little, Brown & Co., Appleton-Century Crofts, mem. editl. bd. Am. Jour. Cardiology, 1985—, Archives Internal Medicine, 1987—, Heart and Lung, 1987—90, Geriatric Cardiovascular Medicine, 1988—89, Am. Jour. Noninvasive Cardiology, 1987—95, Am. Heart Jour., 1992—97, Internat. Jour. Cardiology, 1992—, European Heart Jour., 1995—, Heart Disease, 1999—2004, Cardiology, 1985—, assoc. editor, 1987—, editor-in-chief, 1991—2005, Am. Jour. Medicine, 2005—; contbr. articles to profl. jours. Lt. comdr. USNR, 1974—76. Recipient Gold medal U. Copenhagen, 1968, Edward Rhodes Stitt award San Diego Naval Hosp., 1976, George W. Thorn award Peter Bent Bingham Hosp., 1977, Outstanding Tchr. award U. Mass. Med. Sch., 1981, 86, 87, 90, U. Ariz. Med. Sch., 1995, 97-2002, 06; Fulbright scholar Copenhagen, 1963-64; USPHS-Mass. Heart Assn. fellow, 1971-72, NIH spl. rsch. fellow, 1972-73 Fellow and Master ACP, Fellow Am. Coll. Cardiology (jour. editl. bd. 1983-86, chmn. tng. dirs. com. 1991—, trustee 1996-2001, Gifted Tchr. award 2004), Am. Coll. Chest Physicians (gov. for Mass. 1983-85); mem. AAAS, Am. Heart Assn. (fellow coun. clin. cardiology, vice chmn. 1991-92, chmn. 1993-95, exec. com. 1986—, Disting. Achievement award 2001), Am. Assn. History of Medicine, Am. Fedn. Clin. Rsch., Assn. Univ. Cardiologists, New Eng. Cardiovascular Club, Assn. Profs. of Medicine, Danish Cardiology Assn. (hon.), Argentine Heart Assn. (fgn. corr.), Israeli Heart Soc. (hon.), Am. Clin. and Climatological Assn., Aesculapian Club, Phi Beta Kappa, Sigma Xi, Alpha Omega Alpha. Office: U Az Coll Medicine 1501 N Campbell Ave Tucson AZ 85724-5017 Office Phone: 520-626-6138. Business E-Mail: jalpert@email.arizona.edu.

ALQUIST, ELAINE KONTOMINAS, state legislator; b. Chgo. m. Alfred Alquist (dec.); children: Peter, Bryan White. BS in Math., MacMurray Coll., Jacksonville, Ill.; MA in Guidance and Counseling, Washington U. California State Assemblywoman, District 22, 97-2002; California State Senator, District 13, 2005-. Democrat. Greek Orthodox. Office: Dist 13 100 Paseo de San Antonio Ste 209 San Jose CA 95113 Office Phone: 408-286-8318. Business E-Mail: Senator.Alquist@sen.ca.gov.

ALSBORG, THOMAS C., electronics executive; BS acctg., Oral Roberts Univ.; MBA, Univ. Santa Clara. CPA. Mgmt. positions McDonald's Corp.; CPA Ernst & Young; fin. mgmt. positions Solectron Corp., 1995—2002; v.p., CFO Solectron Global Services, 2002—05; CFO SYNNEX Corp., Fremont, Calif., 2007—. Office: SYNNEX Corp 44201 Nobel Dr Fremont CA 94538-3178

ALSENTZER, WILLIAM JAMES, JR., lawyer; b. Ravenna, Ohio, Mar. 15, 1942; s. William J. Alsentzer and Vivian (Guy) Soash; children: Lesley Joan, Michelle Guy. AB, Duke U., 1964, JD, 1966. Bar: Del. 1966, U.S. Dist. Ct. Del. 1967, Ariz. 1980, U.S. Dist. Ct. Ariz. 1980. Assoc. Wilson & Lynam, Wilmington, Del., 1967-70; ptnr. Bayard, Brill & Handelman, Wilmington, 1970-79; v.p., gen. counsel Bapt. Hosps. and Health Systems, Phoenix, 1979-2000; legal counsel BHHS Legacy Found., Phoenix, 2000—. Mem. Maricopa County Bar Assn., Am. Health Lawyers Assn., Fedn. Def. and Corp. Counsel. Office: 2999 N 44th St Ste 530 Phoenix AZ 85018

ALSPACH, PHILIP HALLIDAY, manufacturing executive; b. Buffalo, Apr. 19, 1923; s. Walter L. and Jean E. (Halliday) A.; m. Jean Edwards, Dec. 20, 1947 (dec.); children: Philip Clough, Bruce Edwards (dec.), David Christopher; m. Loretta M. Hildebrand, Aug. 1982. B in Mech. Engring., Tulane U., 1944. Registered profl. engr., Mass., Wis., La. With GE, 1945-64, mgr. indsl. electronics divsn. planning, 1961-64; v.p., gen. mgr. constrn. machinery divsn. Allis Chalmers Mfg. Co., Milw., 1964-68; exec. v.p., dir., mem. exec. com. Jeffrey Galion, Inc., 1968-69; v.p. I.T.E. Imperial Corp., Springhouse, Pa., 1969-75; pres. E.W. Bliss divsn. Gulf & Western Mfg. Co., Southfield, Mich., 1975-79; group v.p. Katy Industries, Inc., Elgin, Ill., 1979-85; pres. Intercon Inc., Irvine, Calif., 1985—, also bd. dirs.; pres. Intercon Publ., Irvine, 1991—. Adv. bd. dirs. Diamond Stainless, Inc. Author: Swiss-Bernese Oberland, 1992, 4th edit., 2008; contbr. articles to profl. jours. Mem. pres.'s coun. Tulane U., 1982-90. Mem. IEEE, Soc. Automotive Engrs. (sr.), Soc. Mfg. Engrs., Internat. Forum Corp. Dirs., Inst. Dirs. (U.K.), Am. Mgmt. Assn., Chaîne des Rotisseurs (officier). Home: 23 Alejo Irvine CA 92612-2913 Office: Intercon Inc 2500 Michelson Dr Ste #125 Irvine CA 92612-1529

ALSUP, WILLIAM, judge; b. June 27, 1945; BS, Miss. State U., 1967; MPP, Kennedy Sch. Govt., 1971; JD, Harvard U., 1971. Bar: Miss. 1972, Calif. 1973. Law clk. to Hon. William O. Douglas U.S. Supreme Ct., 1971-72; mem. Morrison & Foerster, San Francisco, 1972-99; asst. to solicitor gen. US Dept. Justice, 1978-80; judge US Dist. Ct. (no. dist.) Calif., 1999. Law del. 9th Cir. Jud. Coun., 1993-96. Mem. Am. Coll. Trial Lawyers. Office: US Dist Ct No Dist Calif 450 Golden Gate Ave San Francisco CA 94102-3482 Office Phone: 415-522-2000.

ALTER, EDWARD T., former state treasurer; b. Glen Ridge, NJ, July 26, 1941; s. E. Irving and Norma (Fisher) A.; m. Patricia R. Olsen, 1975; children: Christina Lyn, Ashly Ann, Darci Lee. BA, U. Utah., 1966; MBA, U. Utah, 1967. CPA Calif., Utah. Sr. acct. Touche Ross & Co., LA, 1967—72; asst. treas. U. Utah, Salt Lake City, 1972-80; treas. State of Utah, Salt Lake City, 1981—2008. Mem. Anthony Com. on Pub. Fin., 1988—92, Utah State Rep. Ctrl. Com., 1981—; bd. dirs. Utah Housing Corp., Utah State Retirement Bd., pres., 1984—93, 2003—04; mem. NASDAQ Bd. Nominating Com. Sgt. USAR, 1958—66. Named to All-pro Govt. Team, City and State Mag., 1988, recipient Adminstr. of Yr. award Romney Inst. Pub. Mgmt., Brigham Young U., 2003, Tanya Grit award, Pub. Fin. NAST Debt Mgr. Network. Mem. AICPA, Nat. Assn. State Treas. (past sr. v.p., pres. 1987-88, Harlan E. Boyles Disting. Svc. award 2003, Jesse M. Uhruh award svc. to state treas. 1989), Utah Assn. CPAs (Outstanding CPA 2000), Utah Bond Club (pres. 1981-82), Delta Sigma Pi, Delta Phi Kappa. Republican.

ALTER, ROBERT BERNARD, literature educator, critic; b. NYC, Apr. 2, 1935; s. Harry and Tillie (Zimmmerman) A.; m. Judith Berkenbilt, June 4, 1961 (div. 1973); children: Miriam, Dan; m. Carol Cosman, June 17, 1973; children: Gabriel, Micha. BA, Columbia U., 1957; MA, Harvard U., 1958, PhD, 1962; LHD (hon.), Hebrew Union Coll., 1985. Instr., then asst. prof. English Columbia U., 1962-66; mem. faculty U. Calif.-Berkeley, 1967—, prof. Hebrew and comparative lit., 1969—, chmn. dept. comparative lit., 1970-73, 88-89, class of 1937 prof., 1989—; columnist Commentary mag., 1965-73, contbg. editor, 1973-86. Author: Rogue's Progress: Studies in the Picaresque Novel, 1964, Fielding and the Nature of the Novel, 1968, After the Tradition, 1969, Partial Magic: The Novel as a Self-Conscious Genre, 1975, Defenses of the Immagination, 1977, A Lion for Love, 1979, The Art of Biblical Narrative, 1981, Motives for Fiction, 1984, The Art of Biblical Poetry, 1985; co-editor: The Literary Guide to the Bible, 1987, The Invention of Hebrew Prose, 1988, The Pleasures of Reading in an Ideological Age, 1989, Necessary Angels, 1991, The World of Biblical Literature, 1992, Hebrew and Modernity, 1994, Genesis: Translation and Commentary, 1996, The David Story: A Translation with Commentary of 1 and 2 Samuel, 1999, Canon and Creativity, 2000, The Five Books of Muses: A Translation with Commentary, 2004, Imagined Cities, 2005, The Book of Psalms: A Translator with Commentary, 2007; contbg. editor: Tri Quarterly mag., 1975—. Recipient essay prize English Inst., 1965, Nat. Jewish Book award for Jewish thought, 1982, Present Tense award for Jewish thought, 1986, Bay Area Book Reviewers Transl. award, 1997, Koret Book award, 2005, PEN-USA Transl. award, 2005; Guggenheim fellow, 1966-67, 78-79, sr. fellow NEH, 1972-73, fellow Inst. for Advanced Studies, Jerusalem, 1982-83; scholar Nat. Found. for Jewish Culture, 1995. Fellow Am. Acad. Arts and Scis., Am. Philosoph. Soc.; mem. Council of Scholars of Library of Congress, Assn. Lit. Scholars and Critics (pres. 1996-97). Jewish. Home: 1475 Le Roy Ave Berkeley CA 94708-1911 Office: U Calif Dept Comp Lit 4408 Dwinelle Hall Berkeley CA 94720-2510 Business E-Mail: altcos@berkeley.edu.

ALTERSITZ, JANET KINAHAN, principal; b. Orange, NJ, May 19, 1951; d. Patrick Joseph and Ida (Ciamillio) K.; 1 child, Jacob. AA, County Coll. Morris, 1971; BA, Glassboro State Coll., 1973; MEd, Ariz. State U., 1980. Educator Washington (N.J.) Twp. Mid. Sch., 1974-77, Deer Valley Sch. Dist., Phoenix, 1977-82; asst. prin. Desert Sky Mid. Sch., Glendale, Ariz., 1983-86, prin., 1986—. Cons. and presenter in field. Mem. ASCD, NAASP (mid. level rep. 1993—), Nat. Mid. Sch. Assn., Western Regional Mid. Level. Assn. (program chmn. 1992), Ariz. Sch. Adminstrs. (sec., treas. 1989-90, pres. 1990-91), Cen. Ariz. Mid. Level. Assn. (bd. dirs. 1989—, exec. dir. 1994—), P.O.K. Democrat. Roman Catholic. Home: 4642 W Villa Rita Dr Glendale AZ 85308-1520 Office: Desert Sky Mid Sch 5130 W Grovers Ave Glendale AZ 85308-1300 E-mail: jaltersitz@ds.dvusd.org.

ALTMAN, DREW E., foundation executive; b. Boston, Mar. 21, 1951; s. George and Harriet A.; m. Pamela Koch; children: Daniel, Jessica. BA magna cum laude, Brandeis U., 1973; MA, Brown U., 1974; PhD in Polit. Sci., MIT, 1983. Postdoctoral fellow, rsch. assoc. Harvard U. Sch. Pub. Health, Boston, 1975-76, 78-80; prin. rsch. assoc. Codman Rsch. Group, Boston, 1976-80; spl. asst. office of adminstr. Health Care Fin. Adminstrn. Dept. HHS, Washington, 1979-81; v.p. Robert Wood Johnson Found., Princeton, NJ, 1981-86; commr. N.J. Dept. Human Svcs., Trenton, 1986-89; program dir. health and human svcs. The Pew Charitable Trusts, Phila., 1989-90; pres., CEO Henry J. Kaiser Family Found., Menlo Park, Calif., 1990—. Contbr. articles to profl. jours. Mem. Inst. of Medicine, Nat. Acad. of Soc. Ins., Assn. for Health Svcs. Rsch. Office: Henry J Kaiser Family Found 2400 Sand Hill Rd Menlo Park CA 94025-6941

ALTMAN, STEVEN R., telecommunications executive; BS magna cum laude, No. Ariz. Univ., 1983; JD cum laude, U. San Diego, 1986. Atty. Gray, Cary, Ware & Freidenreich, San Diego; corp. counsel Qualcomm, San Diego, 1989—92, v.p., gen. counsel, 1992—95, gen mgr. tech. licensing, 1995—96, sr. v.p., 1996—98, exec. v.p., 1998—2000, pres. tech. licensing, 2000—05, pres., 2005—. Bd. mem. Salk Inst.; mem. Amylin Pharms. Office: 5775 Morehouse Dr San Diego CA 92121-1714

ALTROCK, RICHARD CHARLES, astrophysicist; b. Omaha, Dec. 20, 1940; s. Raymond John and Ada Ann (Baumann) A.; m. Janice Carol Reed, Mar. 23, 1963 (div. 1977); children: Craig Edward and Christopher Raymond (twins); m. Sally K. Neidig, Mar. 10, 1979; children: Kristin Ann, Krystal Sara. BS in Physics and Math., U. Nebr., 1962; PhD in Astro-Geophysics, U. Colo., 1968. Air Force cert. aquisition profl. Rsch. asst. U. Nebr., Lincoln, 1959—61, teaching asst., 1962; mathematician U.S. Army Engrs., Omaha, 1962; grad. asst. High Altitude Obs., Boulder, Colo., 1963—67; astrophysicist Air Force Rsch. Lab., Nat. Solar Obs., Sunspot, N.Mex., 1967—, work unit mgr., 1976—2002, site mgr., 1999—; project mgr. Coronal Synoptic Program, 1976—; project scientist Solar Mass Ejection Imager Space Expt., USAF, 1986—91, co-investigator, 1991—, task scientist, 1999—2002, Air Force Office of Sci. Rsch. Guest investigator NASA Solar Maximum Mission, 1984-86; vis. research fellow U. Sydney, Australia, 1971-72. Editor: Solar and Stellar Coronal Structure and Dynamics, 1988; contbr. articles to profl. jours.; speaker in the field. Bd. govs. N.Mex. Civil Liberties Union, 1974-76 Recipient Sustained Superior Performance awards USAF, 1986-96, Quar. Sci. and Engring. Tech. Achievement award Air Force Systems Command, 1987; Woodrow Wilson fellow, 1962-63, High Altitude Obs. fellow, 1962-63; mem. Air Force Office of Sci. Rsch. Star Team, 1992-99. Fellow AAAS; mem. Internat. Astron. Union, Am. Astron. Soc., Am. Geophys. Union, ACLU, Sigma Xi, Pi Mu Epsilon, Phi Beta Kappa, Delta Phi Alpha, Phi Gamma Delta. Achievements include co-discovery of the bimodal nature of solar rotation in Fe XIV data, which varies from strongly-differential to rigid over a solar cycle; that CaXV emission in the solar corona is not isolated in hot knots, but is ubiquitous over large energetic chromospheric active regions; of the first evidence of possible wave signature in the variation of spectral line intensity over the lifetime of a granule; first ground-based, two-dimensional photoelectric observation of a transient in the emission-line corona; proof (with other) that ground-based observations of the solar corona could be effectively used to predict recurrent geomagnetic disturbances; demonstration that emission maxima in the corona follow an unbroken progression from the poles to the equator over approximately 18 years, thus implying the existence of overlapping solar activity cycles, (with other) of the existence of convective overshoot phenomenon in the solar atmosphere, (with other) of the lack of solar pole-equator temperature differences in the photosphere and low chromosphere that could explain solar oblateness signals; invention of a new method for obtaining source functions from solar equivalent-width data for weak photospheric lines; research on solar granulation and solar corona. Home: PO Box 645 Cloudcroft NM 88317-0645 Office: Nat Solar Obs Sunspot NM 88349

ALTSCHUL, DAVID EDWIN, record company executive, lawyer; b. NYC, Apr. 8, 1947; s. Norbert and Grace (Aderer) A.; m. Margaret Berne, July 4, 1969; children: Jonathan, Jared, Eric, Emily. BA summa cum laude, Amherst Coll., 1969; JD, Yale U., 1974. Bar: Calif. 1974. Law clerk U.S. Dist. Ct. Conn., Hartford, 1974-75; assoc. Tuttle & Taylor, Los Angeles, 1975-76, Pryor, Cashman, Sherman & Flynn, Beverly Hills, Calif., 1976-77, Hardee, Barovick, Konecky & Braun, Beverly Hills, 1977-79; prin. Rosenfeld, Kassoy & Kraus, Beverly Hills, 1979-80; dir. bus. affairs Warner Bros. Records, Inc., Burbank, Calif., 1980-83, v.p. bus. and legal affairs, 1983-88, sr. v.p. bus. and legal affairs, 1988-93, gen. counsel and sr. v.p. bus. affairs, 1993-95, vice chmn., gen. counsel, 1995—; co-chair, ptnr. Altschul & Olin LLP, Encino. Bd. dirs. Rec. Industry Assn. Am., Reprise! Broadway's Best in Concert, 1998-99, L.A. Jewish Fedn. Music Industry Divsn.; mem. Millenium Coun., Save Ams. Treasures, 1998—. Bd. dirs. Los Encinos Sch., Encinos, Calif., 1986-93, treas., 1986-87, pres., 1987-92; bd. dirs. People for the Am. Way, 1991—, vice chmn., 1996-97, chmn., 1998—; bd. dirs. People for the Am. Way Found., 1991—, bd. dirs. exec. com., 1993—; bd. dirs. San Fernando Valley Neighborhood Legal Svcs., Inc., 1989-90, Rock the Vote, 1997-98. Mem. Phi Beta Kappa. Democrat. Jewish. Avocations: photography, reading. Office: Altschul & Olin LLP 16133 Ventura Blvd Suite 1270 Encino CA 91436-2408 Office Phone: 818-990-1800. Office Fax: 818-990-1429. Business E-Mail: daltschul@altolinlaw.com.

ALVARADO, LINDA G., construction executive; b. Albuquerque, 1952; m. Robert L. Alvarado. BA in Econs., Pamona Coll., Claremont, Calif.; Doctorate (hon.), Dowling Coll. Founder, pres., CEO Alvarado Constrn., Inc., Denver, 1976—. Bd. dirs. Lennox Internat. Inc., 1987—, Pitney Bowes, 1992—, Pepsi Bottling Grp. Inc., 1999—, 3M, 2000—, Qwest Comm. Internat., Inc., 2000—; co-owner, ptnr. Colo. Rockies franchise, 1993—. Commr. White House Initiative for Hispanic Excellence in Edn.; chmn. bd. dirs. Denver Hispanic C. of C. Recipient Leadership award, Nat. Minority Supplier Devel. Coun., 1996, Frontrunner award, Sara Lee Corp., 2001, Horatio Alger award; named Revlon Bus. Woman of Yr., 1996, Bus. Woman of Yr., US Hispanic C. of C., 1996; named one of 100 Most Influential Hispanics in America, Hispanic Mag., 25 Best Latinos in Bus., 2008; named to Nat. Women's Hall of Fame, 2003, Colo. Women's Hall of Fame. Office: Alvarado Construction 1266 Santa Fe Dr Denver CO 80204-3546 Office Phone: 303-629-0783. Office Fax: 303-595-4354.

ALVARADO, PABLO, day laborer organizer, immigrant rights activist; b. El Salvador; married; 2 children. High Sch. teaching credential, Universidad de El Salvador, 1989. Prog. coord. Inst. of Popular Edn. of So. Calif., 1991—95; lead coord., day labor project Coalition for Humane Immigrant Rights, LA, 1995—2002; nat. coord. Nat. Day Laborer Organizing Network, LA, 2002—. Recipient Leadership for a Changing World award, 2004; named one of 25 Most Influential Hispanics, Time Mag., 2005. Office: National Day Laborer Organizing Network Ste 101 2533 W Third St Los Angeles CA 90057

ALVAREZ, FRED, lawyer; BA in Econs. with honors, Stanford U., 1972, JD, 1975. Served two successive presidentially appointed sub-Cabinet positions, Washington; commr. US EEOC, Washington, 1984—87; asst. sec. labor US Dept. Labor, Washington, 1987—89; ptnr. Pillsbury Madison & Sutro, nat. group mgr., Labor & Employment Litig. Group; ptnr. Wilson Sonsini Goodrich & Rosati, Palo Alto, Calif., chmn., Employment & Labor Law Dept. Fellow: Coll. Labor & Employment Lawyers; mem.: ABA-Litig. Sect. (mgmt. chmn. employment sub-com. class actions & derivative suites com.), Calif. State Bar Assn., Am. Employment Law Coun. (adv. bd., ann. conf. chmn. 1996, 1997), ABA (House Delegates), Bar Assn. San Francisco (pres. 2000), Am. Law Inst. Office: Wilson Sonsini Goodrich & Rosati 650 Page Mill Rd Palo Alto CA 94304-1050 Office Phone: 650-493-9300. Office Fax: 650-493-6881. Business E-Mail: falvarez@wsgr.com.

ALVAREZ, MANUEL V., state legislator; b. Clint, Tex., Jan. 23, 1941; m. Beverly Sue Alvarez; children: Gary, Estella. Student, Cochise Coll., Ariz. Employment svcs. mgr. Ariz. Dept. Econ. Security, 1969—2000; mem. Dist. 25 Ariz. House of Reps., 2003—07; mem. DIst. 25 Ariz. State Senate, 2008—, mem. vets. & mil. affairs com., pub. safety & human svcs. com. Mem. Cochise County Bd. Adjustment; past pres. Elfrida Elem. Sch. Bd. Served with US Army, 1962—65. Mem.: Douglas Area Dems., Vets. of Foreign Wars, Am. Legion, Bisbee Rotary Club, Elfrida Lions Club, Mule Mountain Dem. Club. Democrat. Roman Catholic. Office: Ariz State Senate Capitol Complex 1700 W Washington Rm 311 Phoenix AZ 85007 also: 4128 W Jefferson Rd Elfrida AZ 85610 Office Phone: 602-926-5895. Office Fax: 602-417-3025. Business E-Mail: malvarez@azleg.gov.*

ÁLVAREZ, RODOLFO, sociology educator, consultant; b. San Antonio, Oct. 23, 1936; s. Ramon and Laura (Lobo) A.; m. Edna Rosemary (Simons), June 25, 1960 (div. 1984); children: Ánica, Amira. Cert. European Studies, Inst. Am. Univ., Aix en Provence, France, 1960; BA, San Francisco State U., 1961; MA, U. Wash., 1964, PhD, 1966. Tchg. fellow U. Wash., Seattle, 1963—64; asst. prof. Yale U., New Haven, 1966—72; dir. Chicano Studies Rsch. Ctr. Univ. Calif. at Los Angeles, 1972—74, assoc. prof. sociology, 1972—80, prof., 1980, chair under grad. coun., 1995—97. Vis. lectr. Wesleyan Univ., Middletown, Conn., 1970; founding dir. Spanish Speaking Mental Health Rsch. Ctr., 1973-75. Author: Discrimination in Organizations: Using Social Indicators to Manage Social Change, 1979; Racism, Elitism, Professionalism: Barriers to Cmty. Mental Health, 1976; mem. editorial bd. Social Sci. Quar., 1971-86. Pres. ACLU So. Calif., 1980-81, sec., treas. 1999, pres. Westwood Dem. Club, Calif., 1977-78, v.p. 2003-2005; trustee Inst. for Am. Univ., Aix en Provence, France, 1968—; bd. dir. Mex. Am. Legal Def. and Ednl. Fund, 1975-79, 88-92; mem. adv. commn. on housing 1984 Olympic Organizing Com., 1982-84; chmn. bd. dir. Narcotics Prevention Assn., L.A., 1974-77; mem. bilingual adv. com. Children's TV Workshop, N.Y.C., 1979-82; candidate rep. Nat. Dem. Platform Com., Washington, 1976; alt. del. Nat. Dem. Conv., N.Y.C., 1976; bd. dir. Univ. Credit Union, 1985-92, chmn. strategic plan com., 1987-92. Sgt. USMC, 1954-57. Pres. Mgmt. Fellow U. Calif., 1994-95; recipient citation meritorious svc. for devel. of Nat. Fed. Offenders Rehab. and Rsch. Program, State of Wash., 1967. Mem.: Assn. Provencale Des Peterins Des Compostelle (bd. dirs.), Pacific Sociol. Assn. (mem. coun. 1979—83, 1987—89, v.p. 1991—93, pres. 1996—97), Soc. Study of Social Problems (bd. dir. 1982—87, pres. 1985—86), Am. Sociol. Assn. (mem. coun. 1982—85, chair person sect. racial and ethnic minorities 1989—90, assoc. editor Am. Sociol. Rev. 1989—91), Internat. Sociol. Honor Soc. (pres. 1976—79), Archtl. Rev. Bd. City of Santa Monica, Calif., Marines Meml. Club, Rotary Internat. (exec. aide 2005—06, dist. 5280), Westwood Village Rotary Club (pres. 2004—05). Office: UCLA Dept Sociology 405 Hilgard Ave Los Angeles CA 90095-1551 Office Phone: 310-392-5125. Business E-Mail: alvarez@soc.ucla.edu.

ALVORD, CHASE, lawyer; b. 1968; BA, Furman Univ., 1990; JD, Willamette Univ. Coll. Law, 1996. Bar: Wash. 1996. Counsel State Commodity Commn. First Amendment; atty., media and first amendment rights Tousley Brian Stephens PLLC. Contbr. articles to numerous profl. jours. Named Wash. Rising Star, SuperLawyers Mag., 2006. Office: Tousley Brain Stephens Ste 2200 1700 Seventh Ave Seattle WA 98101-1332

AMADEI, BERNARD PAUL, civil engineer, not-for-profit developer, educator; b. July 23, 1954; MSc in Civil Engring., U. Toronto, Can., 1979; PhD in Civil Engring., U. Calif., Berkeley, 1982. Prof. U. Colo., Boulder, 1982—; founder, pres. Engrs. Without Borders - USA, 2000—. Mem. US Com. for Rock Mechanics Nat. Rsch. Coun., 1990—94; cons. in field. Contbr. articles to profl. jours.; co-author: Rock Anisotropy and the Theory of Stress Measurements, 1983, Rock Stress and its Measurement, 1997. Recipient Manuel Rocha medal, Internat. Soc. Rock Mechanics, 1984, Schlumberger Lecture award, 1992, Colo. Bank One award for Outstanding Outreach Cmty. Svc., 2002, E-Achievement award, E-Town, 2003, Nayudamma award, Nayudamma Ctr. for Devel. Alternatives, India, 2005, Norm Augustine award, Am. Assn. Engring. Socs., 2005, Svc. award for Profl. Excellence, Rotary Internat., 2005, Hassib J. Sabbagh award for Excellence in Engring. Constrn., World. Fedn. Engring. Orgns., 2005, Gen. Palmer award, Am. Coun. Engring. Companies Colo., 2006, Hoover medal, 2007; co-recipient Heinz Found. award for Environment, 2007; named Engr. of Yr., Drexel U., Coll. Engring., 2008. Mem.: ASCE (chmn Rock Mechanics Com. 1990—94), Nat. Acad. Engring., Am. Rock Mechanics Assn. (co-founder, pres.). Office: Univ Colo Dept Civil Environ Archl Engring Office ECOT 546 Boulder CO 80309-0428 Office Phone: 303-492-7734. Office Fax: 303-492-7317. Business E-Mail: amadei@colorado.edu.

AMAN, KALLEY R., lawyer; BS, Portland State Univ., 1995, MS, 1997; JD, Lewis & Clark Sch. Law, 2000. Bar: Calif. 2001, Oreg. 2001, US Dist. Ct., Ctrl. Calif. Oreg. Assoc. Buchalter Nemer PC, LA. Editor: Jour. Small & Emerging Bus. Law; contbr. articles to profl. jours. Named a Rising Star, So. Calif. Super Lawyers, 2006. Office: Buchalter Nemer PC Ste 1500 1000 Wilshire Blvd Los Angeles CA 90017-2457 Office Phone: 213-891-0700. Office Fax: 213-896-0400. Business E-Mail: kaman@buchalter.com.

AMBROSE, DANIEL MICHAEL, publishing executive; b. Salem, Oreg., Nov. 1, 1955; s. Franklin Burnell and Jean Marie (Crakes) A.; m. Cynthia Barbara Friedman, Mar. 26, 1983; children: Robert Grant, Michael Bruce. BS in Polit. Sci., Lewis and Clark Coll., 1977. Mktg. mgr. Washington Monthly, 1978-79; advt. promotion mgr. Am. Film Mag., Washington, 1979-80, advt. mgr., 1980-81, advt. dir., 1981-83, Backpacker Mag., NYC, 1983-84; advt. salesman House Beautiful, Hearst Mag., NYC, 1984-85; corp. advt. dir. mag. div. Hearst Pub. Corp., NYC, 1985-87; pub. Fathers Mag., NYC, 1987-89; advt. dir. Cahners Pub. Co., NYC, 1989-92; pub. Child Mag. Network Women's Mag. div. N.Y. Times Co., NYC, 1992-94; mng. dir. ambro.com., NYC, 1994—, DeSilva & Phillips Media Investment Bankers, NYC, 1998—2003. Media cons., investments and sales, N.Y.C., 1994—; presenter Mag. Pubs. Am.; bd. mem. Guard Pub. Co., 2005—; bd. dirs. Kaboose, Inc. Contbr. articles on mag. mgmt. to Folio mag. Chmn. bd. Kidsports, 2002—03. Avocations: book collecting, skiing, triathlons.

AMELIO, GILBERT FRANK, venture capitalist, information technology executive; b. NYC, Mar. 1, 1943; s. Anthony and Elizabeth (DeAngelis) Amelio; m. Glenda Charlene Amelio; children: Anthony Todd, Tracy Elizabeth, Andrew Ryan stepchildren: Brent Paul Chappell, Tina LaRae Chappell. BS in Physics, Ga. Inst. Tech., 1965, MS in Physics, 1967, PhD in Physics, 1968. Tech. dir., co-founder Info. Sci., Atlanta, 1962—65; tech. staff Bell Telephone Labs., Murray Hill, NJ, 1968—71; various staff, managerial, and executive positions to divsn. v.p., gen. mgr. Fairchild Camera and Instrument Corp., Mountain View, Calif., 1971—83; pres. semiconductor products divsn. Rockwell Internat. Corp., Newport Beach, Calif., 1983—88, pres. comm. sys. Dallas, 1988—91; pres., CEO Nat. Semiconductor Corp., Santa Clara, Calif., 1991—96, chmn., 1991—96; chmn., CEO Apple Computer, Inc., Cupertino, Calif., 1996—97; prin. Aircraft Ventures, LLC, 1997—2004; chmn., CEO AmTech, LLC, 1999—2004; chmn. CEO Beneventure Capital, LLC, 1999—2005; sr. ptnr. Sienna Ventures, 2001—; pres., CEO Prexient Micro Devices, Inc., 2003—; co-founder, chmn., CEO Acquicor Tech. Inc., Irvine, Calif., 2005—. Chief exec. roundtable U. Calif., Irvine, 1985—89; nat. adv. bd. Ga. Inst. Tech., Atlanta, 1981—87, Ga. Inst. tech. Rsch. Inst., 1982—89; bd. dirs. Sematech, Emeryville, Calif., Chiron Corp., Pacific Telesis Corp., Apple Computer, AT & T Inc. (formerly SBC Communications, Inc.), Viaquo, Newport Opticom; chmn. Recticon, Pottstown, Pa., 1983—87; advisor Malaysia Multimedia Super Corridor; dir., trustee Am. Film Inst. Recipient Albert Einstein award for lifetime achievement in the tech. industry, Fla. Internat. U. Entrepreneur of Yr. award, Masara Ibuka Consumer Electronics award; named Silicon Valley CEO of Yr., 1993. Fellow: IEEE (chmn. subcom. 1974—81, Masaru Ibuka Consumer Electronics award 1991); mem.: Bus. Higher Edn. Forum, Nat. Assn. Mfrs. (bd. govs.), Electronic Industries Assn. (bd. govs.), Semiconductor Industry Assn. (bd. dirs. 1983—, vice-chmn. 1992, chmn. 1994). Republican. Roman Catholic. Achievements include patents in field. Office: Sienna Ventures 2330 Marinship Way Ste 130 Sausalito CA 94965

AMEMIYA, TAKESHI, economist, statistician; b. Tokyo, Mar. 29, 1935; s. Kenji and Shizuko A.; m. Yoshiko Miyaki, May 5, 1969; children: Naoko, Kentaro. BA, Internat. Christian U., 1958; MA in Econs., Am. U., 1961; PhD, Johns Hopkins U., 1964. Mem. faculty Stanford U., (Calif.), 1964-66, 68—, prof. econs. (Calif.), 1974-86, Edward Ames Edmonds prof. econs. Calif., 1986—. Lectr. Inst. Econ. Research, Hitotsubashi U., Tokyo, 1966-68; cons. Author books and articles; mem. editl. bd. profl. jours. Recipient U.S. Sr. Scientist award Alexander von Humboldt Found., Fed. Republic Germany, 1988; Ford Found. fellow, 1963; Guggenheim fellow, 1975; NSF grantee; fellow Japan Soc. for Promotion of Sci., 1989. Fellow Econometric Soc., Am. Acad. Arts and Scis., Am. Statis. Assn.; mem. Internat. Statis. Inst., Am. Econ. Assn., Inst. Math. Stats., Phi Beta Kappa. Home: 923 Casanueva Pl Stanford CA 94305-1001 Office: Stanford Univ Dept Econs Stanford CA 94305 E-mail: amemiya@stanford.edu.

AMEND, WILLIAM JOHN CONRAD, JR., physician, educator; b. Wilmington, Del., Sept. 17, 1941; s. William John Conrad and Catherine (Broad) A.; m. Constance Roberts, Feb. 3, 1962; children—William, Richard, Nicole, Mark BA, Amherst Coll., 1963; MD, Cornell U., 1967. Diplomate Am. Bd. Internal Medicine and Nephrology. Asst. clin. prof. U. Calif. Med. Ctr., San Francisco, 1974-76, assoc. clin. prof., 1977-82, prof. clin. medicine and surgery, 1982—2005, prof. emeritus medicine, 2005—; chief divsn. nephrology U. Calif., San Francisco, 1998—2003; physician Falmouth Med. Assocs. Contbr. articles to med. jours. Chmn. med. adv. com. No. Calif. Kidney Found., 1987-88; mem. stewardship com. 1st Presbyn. Ch., Burlingame, Calif., 1983, 84, elder, 1982-85, 93-96. Maj. U.S. Army, 1969-71. Simpson fellow, 1963; recipient Gift of Life award No. Calif. Kidney Found., 1993 Fellow: ACP; mem.: Amherst Coll. Alumni Fund (class agt. 1973-83, reunion chmn. 2003, class pres. 2003—). Avocations: golf, gardening, hiking. Home: 2860 Summit Dr Burlingame CA 94010-6257 Office: U Calif Med Ctr 3rd & Parnassus San Francisco CA 94143-0001

AMES, BRUCE NATHAN, biochemisty and molecular biology professor; b. NYC, Dec. 16, 1928; s. Maurice U. and Dorothy (Andres) A.; m. Giovanna Ferro-Luzzi, Aug. 26, 1960; children: Sofia, Matteo. BA, Cornell U., 1950; PhD, Calif. Inst. Tech., 1953. Chief sect. NIH, Bethesda, Md., 1962-67; prof. biochemistry and molecular biology U. Calif., Berkeley, 1968—, chmn. biochemistry dept., 1983-89. Mem. Nat. Cancer Adv. Bd., 1976-82. Research, publs. on bacterial molecular biology, histidine biosynthesis and its control, aging, mutagenesis, detection of environ. mutagens and carcinogens, genetic toxicology, oxygen radicals and disease. Recipient Flemming award, 1966, Rosensteil award, 1976, Felix Wankel award, 1978, John Scott medal, 1979, Corson medal, 1980, Mott prize GM Cancer Rsch. Found., 1983, Gairdner award, 1983, Tyler prize for environ. achievement, 1985, gold medal Am. Inst. Chemists, 1991, Glenn Found. Gerontology award, 1992, Roentgen prize Nat. Acad. Lincei, 1993, Lovelace award for excellence in environ. health rsch., 1995, Honda prize, 1997, Kehoe award, 1997, The U.S. Nat. Medal of Sci., 1998, Medal City of Paris, 1998, The Linus Pauling Inst. prize for health rsch., 2001, Lifetime Achievement award Abbott-ASM, 2001. Fellow Acad. Toxicol. Scis., Am. Acad. Microbiology, Gerontol. Soc. Am.; mem. NAS, Am. Soc. Biol. Chemists, Am. Soc. Microbiology (N.B. lectr. 1980, Abbott Lifetime Achievement award 2001), Environ. Mutagen Soc. (award 1977), Genetics Soc., Am. Assn. Cancer Rsch., Soc. Toxicology (Gustavus John Esselen award 1992), Am. Chem. Soc. (Eli Lilly award 1964), Royal Swedish Acad. Scis., Am. Acad. Arts and Scis. Office: Children's Hosp Oakland Rsch Inst 5700 Martin Luther King Jr Way Oakland CA 94609 Office Phone: 510-450-7625. Business E-Mail: bnames@berkeley.edu.

AMES, EDMUND DANTES, singer, actor, producer; b. Boston, July 9, 1927; s. David and Sarah (Saslavsky) Urick; m.; children— Sonja, Ronald, Linda BA in Theater and Cinema, UCLA, 1975. Owner, mgr. Monte Cristo Prodns., Beverly Hills, Calif.; lead baritone Ames Bros.; performances major cities U.S., 1950-60; rec. artist RCA Records, 1963—. Broadway appearances include Carnival; starring role in TV series Daniel Boone, 1963-68; starring roles in regional theatre include Fiddler on the Roof. Bd. dirs. Bowers Mus., Santa Ana, Calif. Recipient 6 Gold Records Office: ICM 8942 Wilshire Blvd Beverly Hills CA 90211-1934

AMHOWITZ, HARRIS J., lawyer, educator; b. NYC, Mar. 19, 1934; s. Samuel and Ruth Amhowitz; m. Melanie Leigh Gale; children: Jennifer Ann, Joshua Seth. AB, Brown U., 1955; LLB, Harvard U., 1961. Bar: N.Y. 1961, U.S. Supreme Ct. 1967. Law clk. to judge U.S. Dist. Ct. N.Y., 1961-63; assoc. Hughes Hubbard & Reed, NYC, 1963-69; gen. counsel Coopers & Lybrand, NYC, 1970-96, dep. chmn., 1991-95, mem. internat. exec. com., 1991-95; of counsel Hughes Hubbard & Reed, 1996—2003. Adj. prof. NYU Sch. Law, 1975-83; receiver, spl. master U.S. Dist. Ct., 1963-70; pres. bd. dirs. Prosher Group, Ltd., 1970-71; trustee Citizens Budget Commn., Inc., 1983-97. Lt. comdr. USN, 1955—58. Mem. Assn. Bar City N.Y. (spl. com. on lawyers' role in securities transactions 1975-77, com. profl. and jud. ethics 1983-86, com. profl. discipline 1987-91), Harmonie Club. Home: 5150 N Windsong Canyon Dr Tucson AZ 85749

AMIR, MICHAEL M., lawyer; BA, Univ. Calif., Santa Barbara, 1995; JD, Univ. Calif., Hastings, 1999. Atty. Gibson, Dunn & Crutcher LLP, LA, O'Brien, Zarian LLP, LA; co-founder, ptnr., bus. litigation, intellectual property practice Doll, Amir & Eley LLP, LA. Editor (sr. exec. project): Hastings Constitutional Law Quarterly. Named a Rising Star, So. Calif. Super Lawyers, 2005—06. Mem.: State Bar Calif., Assn. Bus Trial Lawyers. Office: Doll Amir & Eley LLP Ste 1106 1888 Century Park E Los Angeles CA 90067 Office Phone: 310-557-9100. Office Fax: 310-557-9101. Business E-Mail: mamir@dollamir.com.

AMMIANO, TOM, state legislator; b. NJ, Dec. 15, 1942; life ptnr.; 1 child. BA in Comm. Arts, Seton Hall U., 1963; MA in Spl. Edn., San Francisco State U., 1965. Stand-up comic, 1981—; tchr. disabled students program City Coll. San Francisco, 1991—, instr. AIDS peer edn., 1992—; San Francisco city supr. San Francisco Bd. Supt., 1994—, pres. bd. suprs., 1998—2002; mem. Dist. 13 Calif. State Assembly, 2008—. Community resource tchr. AIDS spl. edn. project San Francisco Unified Sch. Dist.; classroom tchr. educable mentally retarded; tchr. of English in Vietnam; with Camp Easter Seal and Rec. Ctr. for the Handicapped, San Francisco. Active Mission Coalition, Ethnic Minority Coalition, Bay Area Gay Liberation; organizer demonstrations resp. for including sexual orientation in tchr. hiring; founder Gay Tchrs. Coalition, Gay Lesbian Speakers Bur. in Schs.; mem. community group Project Ten; mem. San Francisco Bd. Edn., 1990—, pres. 1993, v.p. 1991; elected to San. Francisco Bd. Supt., 1994—. Democrat. Office: San Francisco Bd Suprs City Hall 1 Dr Carlton B Goodlett Pl San Francisco CA 94102-4603 also: Dist 13 455 Golden Gate Ave Ste 14300 San Francisco CA 94102 also: State Capitol Rm 2175 PO Box 942849 Sacramento CA 94249-0013 Office Phone: 415-557-3013, 916-319-2013. Office Fax: 415-557-3015, 916-319-2113. Business E-Mail: Tom.Ammiano@sfgov.org.*

AMMON, DONALD R., hospital administrator; BA in Bus., Walla Walla Coll., Washington; MBA, Andrews U., Berrien Springs, Mich. With Hinsdale Hospital, Hinsdale, Ill., 1964—67; adminstr. Adventist Health/Adventist Med. Center, Portland, Oreg., 1967—76, CEO, 1976—81; exec. v.p. Adventist Health, Roseville, Calif., 1981—99, pres., CEO, 1999—. Fellow: Am. Coll. of Healthcare Executives. Office: Adventist Health 2100 Douglas Blvd Roseville CA 95661

AMMON, JOHN RICHARD, anesthesiologist; b. NYC, 1948; MD, U. Pa., 1974. Cert. in anesthesiology. Intern Crozer Chester Med. Ctr., 1974—75; resident in anesthesiology Mass. Gen. Hosp., Boston, 1975—77; fellow in cardiac anesthesiology Stanford (Calif.) Med. Ctr., 1977—78; dir., v.p. Am. Bd. Anesthesiology, Phoenix, 1988—99; pvt. practice Valley Anesthesiology Ltd., Phoenix, 1999—. Mem.: Am. Soc. Anesthesiology, Alpha Omega Alpha. also: Am Bd Anesthesiology 4101 Lake Boone Trl Ste 510 Raleigh NC 27607-7506 Office: Valley Anesthesiology Consultants 1850 N Central Ave Ste 1600 Phoenix AZ 85004-4633

AMON, WILLIAM, lawyer, tax specialist; BS with honors, U. Santa Clara, JD with highest honors. CPA. Ptnr. Deloitte & Touche, LA, 1996—. Lectr. in field. Named one of North America's Top Tax Advisers, Internat. Tax Rev., 1998—2000. Mem.: LA Internat. Tax Forum, Entertainment Tax Inst., Am. Inst. CPA, ABA (tax com. for affiliated corporations), Calif. Bar Assn. Office: Deloitte & Touche Two California Plz 350 South Grand Ave Ste 200 Los Angeles CA 90071-3462 Office Phone: 213-688-3290. Office Fax: 213-673-6733. E-mail: wamon@deloitte.com.

AMORE, SHIRLEY C., library director; Dir. Sarasota County Libr. Sys., Fla., 1997—2000; exec. dir. cmty. svcs. Sarasota County, 2000—06; city libr. Denver Pub. Libr., 2006—. Mem. legis. com. Colo. Assn. Librs. Co-author: The Librarian's Guide to Partnerships, 1999. Office: Denver Pub Libr 10 W Fourteenth Ave Pky Denver CO 80204 Office Phone: 720-865-1711. Office Fax: 720-865-1785. E-mail: samore@denverlibrary.org.

AMOROSO, FRANK, retired communication system engineer, consultant; b. Providence, July 31, 1935; s. Michele and Angela Maria Barbara (D'Uva) A. BSEE, MSEE, MIT, 1958; postgrad., Purdue U., 1958—60, U. Turin, 1964—65. Registered profl. engr., Calif. Instr. elec. engring. Purdue U., West Lafayette, Ind., 1958—60; rsch. engr. Melpar Inc., Roxbury, Mass., 1959, MIT Instrumentation Lab., Cambridge, Mass., 1960, Litton Sys. Advanced Devel. Lab., Waltham, Mass., 1960—61; engr. Melpar Applied Sci. Divsn., Watertown, Mass., 1961; mem. tech. staff RCA Labs. David Sarnoff Rsch. Ctr., Princeton, NJ, 1962—64, Mitre Corp., Bedford, Mass., 1966—67; sr. applied mathematician Collins Radio Co., Newport Beach, 1967—68; comm. sys. engr. N.Am. Rockwell Corp., El Segundo, Calif., 1968—71, Northrop Electronics Divsn., Palos Verdes Peninsula, 1971—72; comm. sys. engr., sr. staff engr. Hughes Aircraft Co., Fullerton, 1972—89; ret., 1989; cons., developer, presenter ednl. seminars, 1989—; profl. mentor to writers, 2005—. Cons. Lincom, Inc., LA, 1994—96, Omnipoint Corp., Price Comms., 2004—; cons. client Sklar Comm. Engring., 1996—, Mascarell Microones, S.L., Tarragona, Spain; instr. continuing engring. edn. program George Washington U., San Diego, 1993; instr. ext. short courses UCLA, 1987—89, 1998—; cons. Mobile Elec. Tracking Sys., Boca Raton, Fla., 1992, Word Works, Newport Beach, Calif., 2003—. Co-author: (book) Power Amplifier Design, 2002. 1st lt. U.S. Signal Corps, 1961-62. Recipient Outstanding Achievement award RCA Labs., 1964; grad. study scholar Italian Govt., 1964-66. Mem. IEEE (sr., life, session organizer, reviewer sci. paper submissions, chmn. conf. on mil. com., presenter). Achievements include patents in field. Home and Office: Digital Data Modulation Studies 271 W Alton Ave Apt D Santa Ana CA 92707-4171 Office Phone: 714-557-1061.

AMOS, REED C., lawyer; b. Richmond, Va., Sept. 1973; BA, Brigham Young Univ., 1997; JD, Catholic Univ, 2000. Bar: Calif. 2001. Law clk. Office Internat. Affairs, Criminal Div., US Dept. Justice; assoc., criminal defense practice Sherman & Sherman plc, Santa Monica, Calif. Atty. Angel de la Communidad Fundacion, LA. Named a Rising Star, So. Calif. Super Lawyers, 2006. Mem.: Am.

Soc. Internat. Law, Nat. Coalition Concerned Legal Professionals. Office: Sherman & Sherman PLC 2115 Main St Santa Monica CA 90405 Office Phone: 310-399-3259. Office Fax: 310-392-9029.

AMOS, WALLY (FAMOUS AMOS), entrepreneur; b. Tallahassee, July 1, 1936; s. Wallace Sr. and Ruby Amos; m. Maria LaForey (div.); children: Michael, Gregory; m. Shirlee Ellis (div.); 1 child, Shawn; m. Christine Amos, 1979; 1 child, Sarah. Stockroom clk. Saks Fifth Ave., NYC, 1957-58, stockroom supr., 1958-61; mail room clk. William Morris Agy., NYC, 1961, sec., 1961-62, asst. agt., 1962; talent agt., 1962-67; ind personal mgr. LA, 1967-75; founder Famous Amos Chocolate Chip Cookie Corp., Hollywood, Calif., 1975-89, Wally Amos Presents: Chip and Cookie, Kailua, Hawaii, 1991—, UNCLE Noname Cookie Co., 1992—; chmn. Uncle Wally Cookie Co. Author: The Famous Amos Story: The Face That Launched a Thousand Chips, 1983, The Power In You: Ten Secret Ingredients for Inner Strength, 1988, Man with No Name: Turn Lemons Into Lemonade, 1994. Nat. spokesman Literacy Vols. of Am., 1979-. Served with USAF, 1953—57. Recipient Pres.' award for Entrepreneurial Excellence, 1986, Horatio Alger award 1987, Nat. Literacy Honors award 1990.

AMRON, DAVID M., dermatologist; b. Calcutta, India, Feb. 21, 1961; Attended, Musicians Inst., LA, Calif., 1985, U. Calif., LA, 1978—80; BA in Biology, U. Calif. at San Diego, La Jolla, 1982; MD, Albert Einstein Coll. Medicine, 1988. Diplomate Am. Bd. Dermatology, 1995. Resident, dept. medicine Cedars-Sinai Med. Ctr., LA, 1988-89; staff rsch. assoc., divsn. dermatology UCLA Sch. Medicine, Calif., 1989, postgraduate rsch. fellow, divsn. dermatology Calif., 1991; rsch. fellow sponsored by Dermatology Found. and Herbert Lab., under Ronald L. Moy, MD, LA, 1990; resident, divsn. dermatology U. Calif. at San Diego Med. Ctr., 1992-95; mem. staff Sherman Oaks Hosp., Calif., 1995—; private practice Mid Valley Dermatology, Sherman Oaks, Calif., 1995—99; co-owner Spalding Drive Cosmetic Surgery and Dermatology, Beverly Hills, Calif., 1999—, Beverly Hills Doctors Surgery Ctr., 1999—. Hospital appointments include Cedars-Sinai Med. Ctr. and Century City Hosp., LA; presenter in field. Contbr. articles to peer-reviewed jours., chpts. to books; featured on KCBS Channel 2 News, Fox Good Day LA., KCBS Women to Women, KCAL Channel 9 News, EXTRA, Inside Edition, ABC News and VH1, where Dr. Amron was filmed performing his famous "mini liposuction" live, highlighting his impressive results while speaking with the patient during the entire procedure; also been featured in numerous studies on dermatology and cosmetic surgery in various magazines and newspapers articles; demonstrated on TV the use of the V-Beam laser for the treatment of rosacea and broken capillaries; guitarist, singer, songwriter in several performing Jazz/Blues groups, 1980-; profl. guitar instruction, 1985-88. CPR instructor Am. Heart Assn.; baseball coach La Jolla Little Leaque, 1980—. Fellow Am. Soc. Laser Medicine & Surgery, Am. Acad. Dermatology, Am. Acad. Dermatologic Surgery, Am. Soc. Liposuction Surgery, Am. Soc. for MOHS Surgery; mem. Am. Soc. Dermatol. Surgery, AMA, LA County Med. Assn. Avocations: tennis, skiing, bicycling, photography, fishing, music composition, theater, travel, camping. Office: Spaulding Drive Cosmetics Surgery & Dermatology 120 Spalding Dr Ste 315 Beverly Hills CA 90212 Office Phone: 310-275-2467. Office Fax: 310-275-6651.

AMSEL, ERIC DAVID, psychology professor; b. Can. s. Arthur Amsel; m. Judith Gundersheimer Suben, May 28, 1989; 2 children. BA, McGill U., Montreal, Que., Can., 1979; MEd, Harvard U., Cambridge, 1980; PhD, Columbia U., NYC, 1986. Postdoctoral fellow Yale U., New Haven, 1985—87; asst. prof. U. Sask., Saskatoon, Canada, 1987—89, Vassar Coll., Poughkeepsie, NY, 1989—96, Weber State U., Ogden, Utah, 1996—98, assoc. prof., 1998—2003, prof. psychology, 2003—, chair dept. psychology, 2006—. Vis. prof. Clark U., Worcester, Mass., 2002—03. Contbr. articles to profl. jours., chapters to books; co-author: The Development of Scientific Thinking Skills, 1988; co-editor: Change and Development: Issues of Theory, Method and Application, 1997, Language, Literacy and Cognitive Development: The Development and Consequences of Symbolic Communication, 2002; assoc. editor: New Ideas in Psychology, 2005—. Bd. dirs. Treehouse Children's Mus., Ogden, 1997—, vice chair, 2000—03. Recipient US Prof. of Yr. award, Carnegie Found. for Advancement of Tchg. and Coun. for Advancement and Support of Edn., 2006. Mem.: Soc. Rsch. in Child Devel., Rocky Mountain Psychol. Assn., Jean Piaget Soc. (bd. dirs. 1991—94, 2003—06), Internat. Soc. for Study of Behavioral Devel., Cognitive Devel. Soc., Am. Psychol. Soc., Am. Ednl. Rsch. Assn., Phi Kappa Phi (pres. 2001—02). Avocations: golf, skiing. Office: Dept Psychology Weber State U Ogden Campus 1202 University Cir Ogden UT 84408-1202 Office Phone: 801-626-6658. Office Fax: 801-626-6275. E-mail: Eamsel@weber.edu.

AMUSSEN, SUSAN DWYER, history professor; b. NYC, Aug. 24, 1954; d. Robert Martin and Diane (Duke) Amussen. AB, Princeton U., 1976; MA, Brown U., 1977, PhD, 1982. Mellon postdoctoral fellow Cornell U., Ithaca, NY, 1982—83; asst. prof. history Conn. Coll., New London, 1984—91; prof., interdiciplinary studies The Union Inst. and U., 1990—2008; prof. Sch. Social Sci. and Humanities Arts, U. Calif., Merced, 2008—. Author: An Ordered Society: Gender and Class in Early Modern England, 1988, Caribbean Exchanges: Slavery and the Transformation of English Society, 1640-1700, 2007; contbr. articles to profl. jours. Fellow Shelby Cullom Ctr. Hist. Studies, Princeton U., 1988—91, The Huntington Libr., 2002—03, Yale Ctr. for Brit. Art, 2004; Alice Freeman Palmer fellow, Wellesley Coll., 1981—82. Mem.: Berkshire Conf. Women Historians (co-chair book prize com., chair article prize com., program chair), N.Am. Conf. on Brit. Studies (regional co-program chmn., regional pres, chair fellowship com.), Women in Hist. Profession (mem. coordinating com.), Am. Hist. Assn. Office: Sch Social Sci Humanities & Arts PO Box 2039 Merced CA 95344 Business E-Mail: samussen@ucmerced.edu.

AMYLON, MICHAEL DAVID, physician, educator; b. Providence, Apr. 30, 1950; s. Sidney Robert and Mary Elisabeth (Alexander) A. AB, Brown U., 1972; MD, Stanford U., 1976. Diplomate sub-bd. hematology/oncology Am. Bd. Pediatrics. Resident physician Stanford U. Hosp., Calif., 1976-79; post-doctoral scholar Stanford U., Calif., 1979-81, acting asst. prof. Calif., 1981-82, asst. prof. pediat. Calif., 1982-89, assoc. prof. pediat. Calif., 1989-2001; prof. pediatrics Stanford U. Sch. Medicine, Palo Alto, Calif., 2001—03, prof. emeritus pediatrics hematology/oncology. Dir. marrow transplant svc. Children's Hosp. at Stanford, Palo Alto, Calif., 1986—2003; coord. nat. rsch. clin. trials in treatment pediatric leukemia and lymphoma Pediatric Oncology Group, St. Louis, Chgo., 1986—2001. Contbr. articles to profl. jours. Bd. dirs. Touchstone Support Network, Palo Alto, 1982-98, Robert J. Sturhahn Found., Novato, Calif., 1986-93, Okizu Found., Novato, 1993—, Parents Helping Parents, 1998—2005; med. dir. No. Calif. Oncology Camp, Nevada City, 1986—. Recipient For Those Who Care award Sta. KRON, 1990, "Ronnie" award Ronald McDonald House, 1992-93, Koshland prize Peninsula Cmty. Found., 1995, J.C. Penney Golden Rule award, 1996, Alwin C. Rambar-James B.D. Mark award for excellence in patient care Stanford U. Sch. Medicine, 2002. Mem. Am. Acad. Pediatrics, Am. Soc. Clin. Oncology, Am. Soc. Hematology, Am. Soc. Pediatric Hematology/Oncology, Am. Soc. Blood and Marrow Transplantation. E-mail: amylon@stanford.edu.

ANAND, SURESH CHANDRA, physician; b. Mathura, India, Sept. 13, 1931; arrived in U.S., 1957, naturalized, 1971; s. Satchit and Sumaran Bai Anand; m. Wiltrud Anand, Jan. 29, 1966; children: Miriam, Michael. MB, BS, King George's Coll., U. Lucknow, India, 1954; MS in Medicine, U. Colo., 1962. Diplomate Am. Bd. Allergy and Immunology. Fellow pulmonary diseases Nat. Jewish Hosp., Denver, 1957-58, resident in chest medicine, 1958-59, chief resident allergy-asthma, 1960-62; intern Mt. Sinai Hosp., Toronto, Ont., Can., 1962-63, resident in medicine, 1963-64, chief resident, 1964-65, demonstrator clin. technique, 1963-64, U. Toronto fellow in medicine, 1964-65; rsch. assoc. asthma-allergy Nat. Jewish Hosp., Denver, 1967-69; clin. instr. medicine U. Colo., Denver, 1967-69; internist Ft. Logan Mental Health Ctr., Denver, 1968-69; pres. Allergy Assocs. & Lab., Ltd., Phoenix, 1974—. Mem. staff Bapt. Hosp., chmn. med. records com., 1987; mem. staff St. Joseph's Hosp., St. Luke's Hosp., Humana Hosp., John C. Lincoln Hosp., Good Samaritan Hosp., Phoenix Children's Hosp., Tempe St. Luke Hosp., Desert Samaritan Hosp., Mesa Luth. Hosp., Scottsdale Meml. Hosp., Chandler Regional Hosp., Ariz., Valley Luth. Hosp., Mesa, Ariz.; mem. staff. Phoenix Meml. Hosp., mem. med. com.; pres. NJH Fed. Credit Union, 1967—68; adj. assoc. prof. medicine Midwestern U., 2004—. Contbr. articles to profl. jours. Mem. citizens adv. bd. Camelback Hosp. Mental Health Ctr., Scottsdale, Ariz., 1974—80; mem. Phoenix Symphony Coun., 1973—90, Ariz. Opera co., Boyce Thompson Southwestern Arboretum, Ariz. Hist. Soc., Phoenix Arts Mus., Smithsonian Inst. Fellow: ACP, Am. Coll. Allergy and Immunology (pub. edn. com. 1991—94, aerobiology com., internat. com.), Am. Assn. Cert. Allergists, Am. Acad. Allergy (pub. edn. com.), Am. Coll. Chest Physicians (crit. care. com.); mem.: AMA, AAAS, Ariz. Found. Med. Care (bd. trustees 2009—), European Acad. Allergology and Clin. Immunology, Ariz. Thoracic Soc., Assn. Care of Asthma, Internat. Assn. Asthmology, World Med. Assn., NY Acad. Soc., Greater Phoenix Allergy Soc. (v.p. 1984—86, pres. 1986—88, med. adv. team sports medicine Ariz. State U.), West Coast Soc. Allergy and Immunology, Maricopa County Med. Soc. (bd. dirs. 1996—98, exec. com. 1996—98, pres.-elect 2002, pres. 2003, chmn. bd. census 2006), Ariz. Allergy Soc. (v.p. 1988—90, pres. 1990—91), Ariz. Med. Assn. (ctrl. dist. dir. 2006—), Internat. Assn. Allergy and Clin. Immunology, Scottsdalians Toastmasters, Nat. Geog. Soc., Phoenix Zoo, Ariz. Wild Life Assn., Village Tennis Club. Office: 1606 E Guadalupe Rd Tempe AZ 85283-3047 also: 4901 N 44th St Phoenix AZ 85018 also: 6553 E Baywood Ave Ste 201 Mesa AZ 85206-1754 also: 2248 N Alma School Rd Chandler AZ 85224-2488 Home Phone: 602-840-0924; Office Phone: 480-838-4296. Personal E-mail: sanand1@aol.com.

ANANG, AMMA CECILIA, dance company administrator; MFA in Dance, Mills Coll. Co-founder, mgr., costume designer, dancer, make-up artist Ocheami Dance Co., Seattle. Office: PO Box 31635 Seattle WA 98103-1635

ANASTASIO, MICHAEL R., science administrator; m. Ann Anastasio; children: Alison, Alexandra. B in Physics, Johns Hopkins U.; MA in Theoretical Nuclear Physics, PhD in Theoretical Nuclear Physics, SUNY, Stony Brook. Physicist, B-Divsn. Lawrence Livermore Nat. Lab., Calif., 1980, assoc. dir. def. and nuclear techs., dep. dir. strategic ops., dir., 2001—06, Los Alamos Nat. Lab. (LANL), N.Mex., 2006—; pres. Los Alamos Nat. Security, LLC, 2006—. Tchr. Brooklyn Coll., CUNY; rschr. Ctr. for Nuclear Studies, Saclay, France, Nuclear Rsch. Ctr., Julich, Germany; sci. advisor Dept. of Energy; chair Coun. for Nat. Security, Coun. for Strategic Ops. Recipient Weapons Recognition of Excellence award, Dept. of Energy, 1990. Mem.: Sigma Pi Sigma. Avocations: sports, cello. Office: Los Alamos Nat Lab PO Box 1663 Los Alamos NM 87545 Office Phone: 505-667-5101. Office Fax: 505-665-2679. E-mail: manastasio@lanl.gov.

ANATOL, KARL W. E., provost; BA in Speech and English, Andrews U.; MA in Interpersonal Communication, Purdue U.; PhD in Speech Communications, U. So. Calif. Dean of students Caribbean Union Coll., Trinidad, 1956-60; teaching asst. Purdue U., Lafayette, Ind., 1966-69; asst. prof. Calif. State U., Long Beach, 1969-73, assoc. prof., 1975-80, assoc. dean instrnl. support, 1978-82, acting dean sch. humanities, 1982-83, dean sch. humanities, 1983-89, acting dean sch. bus., 1988—, acting provost, 1989-90, provost, 1990—2002, sr. v.p. acad. affairs, 1989—2002. Chmn. speech communications Calif. State U., Long Beach, 1977-78, acting exec. dir. libr. & learning resources, 1983-84, mem. univ. extension svcs. adv. bd.; program producer Radio Sta. WBAA Purdue U., 1969; staff assoc. Gen. Motors Inst., Mich., 1973; mem. City of Long Beach Spl. Task Force on Ednl. Redevel.; mem. adv. bd. Global Edn. Program in So. Calif.; mem. bd. advisors Am. Inst. Fgn. Study; mem. ednl. cons. team Weyerhauser Corp. Author: Fundamental Concepts in Human communication, The Process of Group Communication, Strategies for Persuasive Communication, Organizational Communication: Behavioral Perspectives, Public Communication, The Process of Group Communication, Organizational Communication: Behavioral Perspectives, Effective Oral Communication for Business and Professions, Oral Communication in Business and the Professions; contbr. articles to profl. jours. Chmn. allocations com. United Way; nat. exec. dir. Phi Beta Delta.

ANAWALT, PATRICIA RIEFF, anthropologist, researcher; b. Ripon, Calif., Mar. 10, 1924; d. Edmund Lee and Anita Esto (Capps) Rieff; m. Richard Lee Anawalt, June 8, 1945; children: David, Katherine Anawalt Arnoldi, Harmon Fred. BA in Anthropology, UCLA, 1957, MA in Anthropology, 1971, PhD in Anthropology, 1975. Cons. curator costumes and textiles Mus. Cultural History UCLA, 1975-90, dir. Ctr. for Study Regional Dress, Fowler Mus. Cultural History, 1990—; trustee S.W. Mus., LA, 1978-92; rsch. assoc. The San Diego Mus. Man, 1980—, UCLA Inst. Archaeology, 1994—. Trustee Archaeol. Inst. Am., U.S., Can., 1983-95, 98—; traveling lectr., 1975-86, 1994-2000, Pres.'s Lectureship, 1993-94, Charles E. Norton lectureship, 1996-97; cons. Nat. Geog. Soc., 1980-82, Denver Mus. Natural History, 1992-93; apptd. by U.S. Pres. to Cultural Property Adv. Com., Washington, 1984-93; fieldwork Guatemala, 1961, 70, 72, Spain, 1975, Sierra Norte de Puebla, Mex., 1983, 85, 88, 89, 91. Author: Indian Clothing Before Cortés: Mesoamerican Costumes from the Codices, 1981, paperback edit., 1990; co-author: The Codex Mendoza, 4 vols., 1992 (winner Archaeol. Inst. Am. 1994 James Wiseman Book award), The Essential Codex Mendoza, 1996; mem. editl. bd. Ancient Mesoamerica; contbr. articles to profl. jours. Adv. com Textile Mus., Washington, 1983-87. Grantee NEH, 1990, 96, J. Paul Getty Found. 1990, Nat. Geog. Soc., 1983, 85, 88, 89, 91, Ahmanson Found., 1996; Guggenheim fellow, 1988. Fellow Am. Anthrop. Assn.; mem. Centre Internat. D'Etude Des Textiles Anciens, Am. Ethnol. Soc., Soc. Am. Archaeology, Soc. Women Geographers (Outstanding Achievement award 1993), Textile Soc. Am. (bd. dirs. 1992-96, co-coord. 1994 biennial symposium), Soc. Antiquaries, London. Avocations: ballet, reading, hiking. Office: Fowler Mus Cultural History Ctr Study Of Regional Dress Los Angeles CA 90095-0001 Business E-Mail: panawalt@arts.ucla.edu.

ANAYA, RICHARD ALFRED, JR., financial consultant; b. NYC, Dec. 19, 1932; s. Ricardo Martinez and Clara (Chamarro) A.; m. Ninette Calandra, Sept. 8, 1957; children: Suzanne, Richard J. BBA, CCNY, 1958. CPA, N.Y. Tax acct. C.I.T. Fin. Corp., NYC, 1964-67; asst. treas. Mut. Broadcasting System, Inc., NYC, 1967-72; treas. Host Internat., Inc. (N.Y.S.E.), Santa Monica, Calif., 1972-85; dir. fin. Windsor Fin. Corp, Encino, Calif., 1985; ind. cons. mergers and acquisitions A&I Investments, Inc, Century City, Calif., 1986-87, Anaya Assocs., Century City, Calif., 1987-90, CPA cons. mergers and acquisitions Woodlands Hills, Calif., 1990—. Founder retail store chain, Clear Connect Comms., LLC, 1995. Served with U.S. Navy, 1952-54. Mem. AICPA, Calif. State Soc. CPAs, N.Y. State Soc. CPAs. Roman Catholic. Home Phone: 818-222-2747; Office Phone: 818-222-2747. E-mail: anayaassociates@pacbell.net.

ANAYA, RUDOLFO, writer, educator; b. Pastura, N.Mex., Oct. 30, 1937; s. Martin and Rafaelita (Mares) A.; m. Patricia Lawless, July 23, 1966. BA, U. N.Mex., Albuquerque, 1963, MA, 1968; PhD (hon.), U. Albuquerque, 1982; PhD, Mary Crest Coll., 1984; LLD (hon.), U. N.Mex., 1996. Prof. U. N.Mex., Albuquerque, 1974—. Author: (novels) Bless Me Ultima, 1972 (Premio Quinto sol) Heart of Aztlan, 1976, Tortuga, 1979 (Before Columbus Found. award), Alburquerque, 1992 (Pen West award for fiction), Zia Summer, 1995, The Farolitos of Christmas, 1995, Jalamanta, 1996, Rio Grande Fall, 1996, Jemez Spring, 2005, Curse of The Chupacabra, 2006, (children's picture book) Maya's Children, 1997, Shaman Winter, 1999, Roadrunner's Dance, 2000, Elegy for Cesar Chavez, 2000, Farolitos for Abuelo, 2000, The Santero's Miracle, 2004, The First Tortilla, 2007, (young adult) Serafina's Stories, 2004; (short stories) The Man Who Could Fly, 2006. NEA fellow, Nat. Medal of Arts (lit.), 2001. Home: 5324 Canada Vista Pl NW Albuquerque NM 87120-2412 Office: U NMex English Dept Albuquerque NM 87131-0001

ANDARY, THOMAS JOSEPH, biochemist, researcher; b. Oct. 8, 1942; s. Joseph Boula and Marion (Schwifetti) A. BS, No. Mich. U., 1966, MA, 1968; PhD, Wayne State U., 1974. Instr. biology No. Mich. U., Marquette, 1967—69; rsch. assoc. physiology Wayne State U., Detroit, 1973—76; sr. rsch. scientist, mgr. coagulation rsch. Hyland Labs., Costa Mesa, Calif., 1976—83; dir. quality control Hyland Therapeutics, Glendale, Calif., 1983—90; dir. quality assurance and regulatory affairs Baxter/Hyland Divsn., Glendale, Calif., 1990—91, v.p. quality assurance and regulatory affairs, 1991—96, responsible head, 1993—96. Cons. in regulatory affairs/quality assurance to biopharmaceutical industry, 1996—; lectr. in field. Contbr. articles to profl. jours. Recipient NDEA fellowship, 1969—72. Mem.: Drug Info. Assn., Internat. Assn. Biol. Standardization, N.Y. Acad. Scis., Am. Chem. Soc., Parenteral Drug Assn., Sigma Xi (Rsch. award 1973). Roman Catholic. Home and Office: 531 N Canyon Blvd Monrovia CA 91016-1707

ANDEREGG, KAREN KLOK, business executive; b. Council Bluffs, Iowa; d. George J. and Hazel E. Klok; m. George F. Anderegg Jr., Aug. 27, 1970 (div. Dec. 1993); m. William Drake Rutherford, Jan. 2, 1994. BA, Stanford U., 1963. Copywriter Vogue Mag., NYC, 1963-72; copy editor Mademoiselle Mag., NYC, 1972-77, mng. editor, 1977-80; assoc. editor Vogue Mag., NYC, 1980-85; editor-in-chief Elle Mag., NYC, 1985-87; pres. Clinique USA, 1987-92; bus. cons. Portland, Oreg., 1993—. Bd. dirs. Oreg. Dental Svcs. Health Plans, EthicsPoint, Inc., NORDIC.

ANDERS, GEORGE CHARLES, journalist, writer; b. Chgo., Nov. 12, 1957; s. Edward and Joan Elizabeth (Fleming) Anders; m. Elizabeth Anne Corcoran, Aug. 27, 1988. BA in Econs., Stanford U., 1978. Nat. copyreader Wall St. Jour., NYC, 1978—81, Heard on the St. columnist, 1981—82, London bur. chief European edit., 1982—85, news editor, 1985—89, sr. spl. writer, 1988—2000; sr. editor Fast Company Mag., 2000—03; news editor Wall St. Jour., 2003—. Contbg. editor: SmartMoney mag., 1992—95; author: Merchants of Debt, 1992, Health Against Wealth, 1996, Perfect Enough, 2003. Recipient Janus award, Am. Mortgage Bankers Assn., 1987; co-recipient Pulitzer Prize for nat. reporting, 1997.

ANDERS, WILLIAM ALISON, aerospace and defense manufacturing executive; b. Hong Kong, Oct. 17, 1933; s. Arthur Ferdinand and Muriel Florence (Adams) A.; m. Valerie Elizabeth Hoard, June 26, 1955; children: Alan Frank, Glen Thomas, Gayle Alison, Gregory Michael, Eric William, Diana Elizabeth. BS, U.S. Naval Acad., Annapolis, 1955; MS in Nuclear Engring., U.S. Inst. Tech., Wright-Patterson AFB, 1962. Commnd. 2d lt. U.S. Air Force, 1955, pilot, engr., 1955-69; astronaut NASA-Johnson Space Ctr., Houston, 1963-69, Apollo 8, 1st lunar flight, 1968; exec. sec. Nat. Aero. and Space Council, Washington, 1969-72; commr. AEC, Washington, 1973-74; chmn. Nuclear Regulatory Commn., Washington, 1975-76; U.S. Ambassador to Norway, 1976-77; v.p., gen. mgr. nuclear energy products div. Gen. Electric Co., 1977-80, v.p., gen. mgr. aircraft equipment div. DeWitt, N.Y., 1980-84; sr. exec., v.p. ops. Textron Inc., Providence, R.I., 1984-89; vice chmn. Gen. Dynamics, St. Louis, 1990-91, chmn., CEO, 1991-93, chmn. bd. dirs., 1993-94; pres. Apogee Group. Chmn. Heritage Flight Mus. Trustee Battell Meml. Inst., Reno Air Races Unltd. Class, 1997-99. Maj. gen. USAFR, 1983-88, ret. Decorated various mil. awards; recipient Wright, Collier, Goddard and Arnold flight awards; co-holder several world flight records; named Disting. Grad., U.S. Naval Acad., 2000. Mem. Soc. Exptl. Test Pilots, Nat. Acad. Engring., Tau Beta Pi (Nat. Aviation Hall of Fame 2004). Office: Heritage Flight Mus PO Box 1630 Eastsound WA 98245

ANDERSEN, ERIK M., lawyer; b. Anaheim, Calif., July 26, 1972; BA, UCLA, 1998; JD summa cum laude, Boston Coll., 2001. Bar: Calif. 2002, US Dist. Ct. Ctrl. Calif., US Ct. Appeals Fourth & Ninth Cir. Law clk. Judge Lourdes G. Baird US Dist Ct. Ctrl. Calif., Judge Robert R. Beezer US Ct. Appeals Ninth Cir.; assoc. Paul, Hastings, Janofsky & Walker LLP; assoc., bus. litigation Payne & Fears LLP,

Irvine, Calif. Editor (solicitations): Boston Coll. Law Rev. Named Rising Star, So. Calif. Super Lawyers, 2006. Mem.: ABA, State Bar Calif., Order of the Coif. Office: Payne & Fears LLP Ste 1100 4 Park Plz Irvine CA 92614 Office Phone: 949-851-1100. Office Fax: 949-851-1212. Business E-Mail: ema@paynefears.com.

ANDERSEN, IB, performing company executive; b. Copenhagen, 1954; Prin. dancer NYC Ballet, 1980—90; tchr. various companies in Belgium, Norway, Japan, Can. and U.S., 1990—2000; artistic dir., leader artistic team Ballet Ariz., 2000—. Avocations: cooking, painting, music, poetry, literature. Office: Ballet Arizona 3645 E Indian Sch Rd Phoenix AZ 85018 E-mail: ib@balletaz.org.

ANDERSEN, NIELS HJORTH, chemistry professor, biophysicist, consultant, researcher; b. Copenhagen, Oct. 9, 1943; came to U.S. 1949; s. Orla and Inger (Larsen) A.; m. Sidnee Lee (div. 1986); children: Marin Christine, Beth Arkady; m. Susan Howell, July 21, 1987. BA, U. Minn., 1963; PhD, Northwestern U., 1967. Rsch. assoc and fellow Harvard U., Cambridge, Mass., 1966-68; asst. prof. U. Wash., Seattle, 1968-72, assoc. prof., 1972-76, prof., 1976—; prin. scientist ALZA Corp., Palo Alto, Calif., 1970-75. Cons. Genetic Systems, Seattle, 1984-86, Bristol-Myer Squibb, Princeton, N.J., 1984-95, Amylin Pharmaceutics, San Diego, 1992-2001 Receptron Corp., Mountain View, Calif., 1995—2001, Chiron, Seattle, 1997—2003. Mem. adv. bd. Biopolymers; contbr. articles to profl. jours. Recipient Teacher-Scholar award Dreyfus Found., 1974-79, Career Devel. award NIH, 1975-80. Mem. AAAS, Am. Chem. Soc., Am. Peptide Soc., Protein Soc. Democrat. Avocations: music, dulcimer playing. Office: U Wash Dept Chem PO Box 351700 Seattle WA 98195-1700 Office Phone: 206-543-7099. E-mail: andersen@chem.washington.edu.

ANDERSEN, RONALD MAX, health services researcher, educator; b. Omaha, 1939; s. Max Adolph and Evangeline Dorothy (Wobbe) Andersen; m. Diane Borella, June 19, 1965; 1 child, Rachel. BS, U. Santa Clara, 1960; MS, Purdue U., 1962, PhD, 1968. Rsch. assoc. Purdue U., West Lafayette, Ind., 1962—63; assoc. study dir. Nat. Opinion Rsch. Ctr., Chgo., 1963—66; rsch. assoc. U. Chgo., 1963—77, from assoc. prof. to prof. Grad. Sch. Bus., 1974—90, dir. Program in Health Adminstrn. and Ctr. for Health Adminstrn. Studies, 1980—90; Wasserman prof. dept. health svcs. and sociology UCLA, 1991—, prof. emeritus, 2004—, chmn. dept. health svcs., 1993—96, 2000—03. Com. mem. Agy. for Health Care Policy and Rsch., Rockville, Md., 1970—. Mem. editl. bd.: Health Adminstrn. Press, 1980—83, 1988—98, Med. Care Rsch. & Rev., 1994—; author: A Decade of Health Services, 1967, Two Decades of Health Service, 1976, Total Survey Error, 1979, Health Services in the U.S., 1980, Ambulatory Care and Insurance Coverage in an Era of Constraint, 1987, Training Physicians, 1994, Changing the U.S. Health Care System, 1996, 2001. Grantee, Agy. for Health Care Policy and Rsch, 1982, Robert Wood Johnson Found., 1983, Kaiser Family Found., 1983, WHO, 1990; fellow, NIH, 1960—62. Mem.: APHA, Assn. for Health Svcs. Rsch. (dir. 1981—83, 1997—99, Disting. Career award 1996), Assoc. Univ. Program in Health Adminstrn. (Baxter Allegiance prize 1999), Inst. Medicine NAS, Am. Sociol. Assn. (chmn. med. sociology sect. 1980—81, Disting. Med. Sociologist 1994). Roman Catholic. Home: 10724 Wilshire Blvd Apt 312 Los Angeles CA 90024-4453 Office: UCLA Sch Pub Health Los Angeles CA 90024 Office Phone: 310-206-1810. Business E-Mail: randevse@ucla.edu.

ANDERSON, ARTHUR SALZNER, publishing company and marketing executive; b. Boise, Idaho, Jan. 17, 1923; s. Howard Ballantyne and Mildred Ina (Salzner) A.; m. Janice Virginia Jacobsen, June 21, 1948; children: Roger Bruce, Gregory Bryan, Julie Janice Olsen, Lane Jacobsen, Margaret Virginia Ence, Heidi Gail Eldredge, Steven Jacobsen. BA, U. Utah, 1947. Sales promotion asst. Internat. Harvester Co., 1947-48, zone mgr., 1948-51; sr. v.p., dir., chmn. exec. com. Evans Communications, Inc., Salt Lake City, 1977-84, dir., chmn. exec. com., 1984-87, pres., 1984-87; chmn. bd. Panoram Prodns., 1977-82; pres. Deseret Book Co., 1975-80, dir., 1975-92; pres., chief exec. officer Anderson Mktg. Inc., Salt Lake City, 1987—. Author: By Example, 1961, You Can Do It, 2003. Vice-pres. Salt Lake Area United Fund, 1977-80; mem. governing bd. Primary Children's Med. Ctr., 1975-2001, vice chmn., 1981-83, chmn., 1983-92; bd. dirs. Osmond Found., 1982-83. Served with AUS, 1943-46. Mem. Utah Advt. Fedn. (pres. 1967-68), Sales and Mktg. Execs. Utah (pres. 1965-66) Mem. Lds Ch. Home: 2242 Kensington Ave Salt Lake City UT 84108-2310 Office: Anderson Marketing Inc 975 Woodoak Ln # 200 Salt Lake City UT 84117-7267

ANDERSON, AUSTIN GILMAN, economics research company consultant; b. Mpls. s. Clifford Hawkins and Katharine (Irving) A.; m. Marilyn Wheeler, Mar. 17, 1968; children: Guy, Alisa, Michael, Emily. BS, Stanford U., 1964, MBA, 1966. Systems analyst Jet Propulsion Lab., Pasadena, Calif., 1966-68; assoc. Econs. Rsch. Assoc., LA, 1968-72, sr. v.p., 1977-88, pres., chief exec. officer, 1988—; dir. rsch. Property Rsch. Corp., LA, 1972-73; prin. Levander, Partridge & Anderson, Beverly Hills, Calif., 1973-77; v.p. Econs. Rsch. Assocs., LA. Instr. Grad. Sch. Mgmt. UCLA, 1989, extension, 1987; bd. dirs. Crown Iron Works Co., Mpls., 1983—; mem. bd. counselors Sch. Urban and Regional Planning U. So. Calif., L.A., 1984-95; mem. bd. trustees Real Estate Investment Trust of Calif., 1994—. Mem. Urban Land Inst. Avocations: sculpting, golf. Office: Econs Rsch Assocs 10990 Wilshire Blvd Ste 1500 Los Angeles CA 90024-3917

ANDERSON, CARL WEST, retired judge; b. Monterey Park, Calif., Sept. 11, 1935; s. Carl Ejnar and Mary Madeline (West) A.; m. Margo Hart, Aug. 15, 1964; children: Thomas Hart, Marnie Marie. AB in Pol. Sci., U. Calif., Berkeley, 1957, LLB, 1962; LLM in Jud. Process, U. Va., 1992. Bar: Calif. 1963. Dep. dist. atty. Alameda County (Calif.) Dist. Atty., 1964-72, sr. dep. dist. atty., 1972-75; judge Alameda County Superior Ct., 1975-84; assoc. justice Calif. Ct. Appeals, 1st dist., divsn. 3, San Fransisco, 1984; presiding justice divsn. 4, San Francisco, 1987-97, adminstrv. presiding justice, 1987-97; ret., 1997. Pvt. judge, assoc. Am. Arbitration Assn. and alternative adjucication, 1997—; mem. appellate performance stds. com. Nat. Ctr. for State Cts. Commn., 1994-95. Pres. Piedmont (Calif.) Coun. Boy Scouts Am., 1987, 88, 93. Capt. USAR, 1957-74. Scholar U. Calif. Alumni Assn., 1953; fellow U. Calif. Sch. Law and Ctr. for Study Law and Soc., Germany, 1962-63. Fellow ABA (commn. stds. jud. adminstrn. 1992-93, appellate judges conf. exec. com. JAD 1992, 93, chair-elect 1995—, chair 1996-97), Coun. Chief Judges Cts. Appeal (pres. 1992-93). Avocations: tennis, gardening, golf. E-mail: justicecanderson@sprynet.com.

ANDERSON, CHARLES ARTHUR, retired science administrator; b. Columbus, Ohio, Nov. 14, 1917; s. Arthur E. and Huldah (Peterson) A.; m. Elizabeth Rushforth, Oct. 27, 1942; children: Peter C., Stephen E., Julia E. AB, U. Calif., Berkeley, 1938; MBA, Grad. Sch. Bus. Adminstrn., Harvard U., 1940; LHD, Colby Coll., 1975. Asst. prof. Grad. Sch. Bus. Adminstrn., Harvard U., Boston, 1945-48; v.p. Magna Power Tool Corp., Menlo Park, Calif., 1948-58; prof., asso. dean Stanford Grad. Sch. Bus., 1959-61; v.p. Kern County Land Co., San Francisco, 1961-64; pres. Walker Mfg. Co., Racine, Wis., 1964-66, J.I. Case Co., Racine, 1966-68; pres., chief exec. officer SRI Internat., Menlo Park, 1968-79. Bd. dirs. KRI Internat., Japan, Eaton Corp., Conoco, Owens-Corning Fiberglas, NCR, Boise Cascade, Saga; mem. adv. council Bus. Sch., Stanford, 1966-72, 74-79; mem. industry adv. council Dept. Def., 1971-73 Author (with Anthony) The New Corporate Director. Mem. Menlo Park Planning Commn. and City Coun., 1955-61, Govs. Commn. on Reorgn. Wis. State Govt., 1965-67; bd. dirs. Calif. State C. of C., 1972-77, Internat. House, U. Calif., Berkeley, 1979-90; bd. dirs. Lucile Salter Packard Children's Hosp., Stanford, 1979-95, chmn., 1992-94. With USNR, 1941-45. Recipient Exceptional Service award USAF, 1965 Mem. Palo Alto Club, Pacific-Union Club, Menlo Country Club. Presbyterian. Office: 555 Byron St Apt 207 Palo Alto CA 94301-2037 Personal E-mail: caacaa@pacbell.com.

ANDERSON, CHARLES WILLIAM, computer science educator; BS in Computer Sci., U. Nebr., 1978; MS in Computer and Info. Sci., U. Mass., 1982, PhD in Computer and Info. Sci., 1986. Sys. analyst AGNET U. Nebr., 1977-79; tchg. asst. U. Mass., 1979, rsch. asst., 1979-86, computer graphics cons., 1984-86; sr. mem. tech. staff GTE Labs., Waltham, Mass., 1986-90; asst. prof. computer sci. dept. Colo. State U., Ft. Collins, 1991-97, assoc. prof. computer sci., 1997—. Mem. program com. Eighth Internat. Workshop on Machine Learning, Constructive Induction, 1991, Fla. Artificial Intelligence Rsch. Symposium, 1991, 97, IEEE-Internat. Conf. on Neural Networks, 1993, IEEE Internat. Conf. on Tools with Artificial Intelligence, 1993, Neural Info. Processing Sys. Conf., 1994; NSF panel reviewer, 1994-96; lectr. in field. Mem. editl. bd. Neural Computing Surveys; reviewer or refereee for profl. jours. including Cognitive Sci. Jour., Computer and Software Engring., Connection Sci. Jour., IEEE Control Sys. Mag., IEEE Transaction on Biomed. Engring., Jour. Empirical Software Engring., Machine Learning, others; contbr. chpts. to books and articles to profl. jours. Grantee Am. Gas Assn., 1991-92, Colo. State U., 1992, NSF, 1992-95, 92-94, 95-96, 95-96, 96—. Mem. AAAI, IEEE Computer Soc. (mem. elections com. 1994-96), Assn. for Computing Machines, Internat. Neural Network Soc., Upsilon Pi Epsilon. Office: Colo State U Dept Computer Sci Fort Collins CO 80523-0001 E-mail: anderson@cs.colostate.edu.

ANDERSON, CHRIS W., editor-in-chief; b. 1961; married; 5 children. BS in Physics, George Washington U.; MA in Quantum Mechanics and Sci. Journalism, U. Calif., Berkely. Several editl. positions Science jour., Nature; editor The Economist, London, Hong Kong, NY, 1994—2001; editor-in-chief WIRED mag. Condé Nast Publs., 2001—. Regular spkr., participant World Econ. Forum, Davos, Switzerland; chief scientist Dept. of Transp.; rschr. Los Alamos Nat. Lab., Meson Physics Facility. Author: The Long Tail: Why the Future of Business Is Selling Less of More, 2006. Recipient Nat. Mag. award for Gen. Excellence, Am. Soc. Mag. Editors, 2007, 2009, Nat. Mag. award for Design, 2008, 2009; named one of The World's Most Influential People, TIME mag., 2007. Mem.: Young Presidents' Assn. (officer). Office: WIRED Ste 305 520 3rd St San Francisco CA 94107 Fax: 415-276-5150. E-mail: canderson@wiredmag.com.*

ANDERSON, CHRISTINE MARLENE, software engineer; b. Washington, Nov. 19, 1947; 2 children. BS in Math., U. Md., 1969. Mathematician Naval Oceanographic Office, Suitland, Md., 1969-71; sr. analyst, fgn. tech. divsn. Planning Rsch. Corp., Ohio, 1971-72; computer scientist USAF Avionics Lab., Wright-Patterson Air Force Base, Dayton, Ohio, 1971-74; sr. analyst USAF C3 Ctr., Cheyenne Mountain, Colorado Springs, Colo., 1974-76; chief computer tech. section USAF Wright Lab./Armament Directorate, Eglin Air Force Base, Fla., 1982-92; ADA 9X project mgr. Office Sec. Defense, 1987-94; chief software tech. br. Phillips Lab., Kirtland Air Force Base, N.Mex., 1992-93, chief, space soperations and simulation divsn.oftware rsch. ctr. N.Mex., 1993-96, dir. space and missiles tech. directorate N.Mex., 1996; mem. sr. exec. svcs., dir. space vehicles directorate Phillips Lab., Kirtland Air Force Base, Air Force Rsch. Lab., N.Mex., 1996—. Co-chmn. on Ada computer programming lang. Am. Nat. Standards Inst., 1989—; editor Ada standard Internat. Standards Orgn., 1991—. Co-author: Aerospace Software Engineering, 1991; contbr. articles to profl. jours. Recipient Engr. of the Year USAF Armament Lab., 1989, Software Engring. award Am. Inst. Aeronautics, 1991, Program Mgr. of the Year award USAF Armament Lab., 1992, Sec. of Defense medal for Meritorious Civilian Svc., 1996. Fellow AIAA (chair software systems tech. com. 1987-89, bd. dirs. 1989—, Aerospace Software Engring. award 1991).

ANDERSON, DANA K., real estate company executive; With Macerich Group, Santa Monica, Calif., 1965—, now COO, exec. v.p. Bd. dirs. Alvamar Devel. Corp., Goodrich 560 Corp. Office: Macerich Co 233 Wilshire Blvd Ste 700 Santa Monica CA 90401-1207

ANDERSON, DANA Z., physics educator; b. Chgo., Apr. 10, 1953; BSEE, Cornell U., 1975; PhD, U. Ariz., 1981. Rsch. assoc. U. N.Mex., 1980-81; rsch. fellow in physics Caltech, 1981-84, lectr. in physics, 1983-84; asst. prof. dept. physics U. Colo., Boulder, 1984-89, assoc. prof., 1989-95, prof., 1995—, dir. optical sci. and engring. program, 1998—, Glenn Murphy chair Coll. engring. and applied sci., 2005—. Mem. Joint Inst. Lab. Astrophysics, U. Colo., Nat. Inst. Stds. and Tech., 1984-85, fellow, 1985—; cons. Litton Industries Guidance and Control Sys. Divsn., 1981-82, Rockwell Internat. Corp. Marine Sys. Divsn., 1982-84. Editor: Neural Information Processing Systems, 1988; guest editor IEEE Jour. Quantum Electronics, 1987; editor Neural Info. Processing Sys., 1988; mem. series adv. bd. Computation and Neural Sys.; bd. editors Jour. Neural Networks; topical editor Optics Letters; contbr. articles to profl. jours. Alfred P. Sloan Rsch. fellow, 1986-90; recipient Presdl. Young Investigator award 1985, Alexander von Humboldt award, 2001. Fellow Optical Soc. Am. (R.W. Wood prize 1994), Am. Physical Soc. Office: U Colo Joint Inst Lab Astrophysics Boulder CO 80309-0001

ANDERSON, DAVID CORYELL, lawyer, automotive executive; b. Seattle, Apr. 7, 1953; s. George Robert and Margaret Louise (Barron) A.; m. Sharon Lee Pfeifer, Feb. 14, 1976; children: Nicholas, Kate, Patrick. AB, Harvard U., 1975; JD, Stanford U., 1979. Bar: Wash. 1979. Assoc. Foster, Pepper & Shefelman, Seattle, 1979-86, ptnr., 1986-93; v.p., corp. sec., gen. counsel Airborne Express Inc., Seattle, 1993; v.p., gen. counsel PACCAR Inc., Bellevue, Wash., 2004—. Mem.: Wash. State Bar Assn. (at-large mem. exec. com. 2006—07). Office: PACCAR Inc Law Dept PO Box 1518 Bellevue WA 98009 Office Phone: 425-468-7499. Office Fax: 425-468-8228. E-mail: dave.anderson@paccar.com.

ANDERSON, DAVID E., zoological park administrator; Student, Pfeiffer Coll., 1964-65; BS in Zoology/Psychology, Duke U., 1972, postgrad., 1973. Colony supervisor Primate Ctr. Duke U., Durham, N.C., 1972-77, asst. dir. Primate Ctr., 1977-78; curator of mammals San Francisco Zool. Gardens, 1978-81, gen. curator, 1981-87, assoc. dir., gen. curator, 1987-90, dir., 1990—. Tech. advisor Nature Conservancy La., 1987-90; animal tech. cons., mem. advisement com. La. State U.; mem. animal care com. Tulane U.; chmn. steering com. Madagascar Fauna Captive Propagation Group. Revs. editor Zoo Biology, 1982-88; contbr. articles to profl. publs. With USMC, 1965-69, Vietnam. Mem. Am. Assn. Zool. Parks and Aquariums (grad. mgmt. sch. 1982, ethics com., long range planning com., accreditation com., program chmn. Nat. Conf. 1981, others), Internat. Union Dirs. Zool. Gardens (captive breeding specialist group). Office: San Francisco Zool Gardens 1 Zoo Rd San Francisco CA 94132-1098

ANDERSON, DAVID J., biology professor; AB in Biochemical Scis., Harvard U., 1978; PhD in Cell Biology, Rockefeller U., 1983. Asst. prof. Calif. Inst. Tech., Pasadena, 1986—92, assoc. prof., 1992—96, prof., 1996—2004, Roger W. Sperry prof. biology, 2004—; asst. investigator Howard Hughes Medical Inst., 1989—92, assoc. investigator, 1992—97, investigator, 1997—. Contbr. articles to sci. jours. Recipient Presdl. Young Investigator award, NSF, Charles Judson Herrick award in Neuroanatomy, Am. Assn. Anatomists, W. Alden Spencer award in Neurobiology, Columbia U. Mem.: NAS, Am. Acad. Arts & Scis. Office: Divsn Biology 216-76 Calif Inst Tech Pasadena CA 91125 Office Phone: 626-395-8374. Office Fax: 626-564-8243. E-mail: mancusog@caltech.edu.

ANDERSON, DAVID LOUIS, academic administrator, history professor; b. Pampa, Tex., Aug. 10, 1946; s. Benjamin Louis and Ruby Lucille (Baird) A.; m. Helen Esther Fleischer, June 9, 1973; 1 child, Hope Mindy. BA cum laude, Rice U., Houston, 1968; MA, U. Va., 1971, PhD, 1974. Vis. asst. prof. history U. Mont., Missoula, 1974-75, 76-77, Tex. Tech. U., Lubbock, 1975-76; asst. prof. history Sam Houston State U., Huntsville, Tex., 1977-80; lectr. in history Calif. Poly. State U., San Luis Obispo, 1980-81; asst. prof. history U. Indpls., 1981-84, assoc. prof. history, 1984-90, prof. history, 1990—2004, dept. chair, 1988-2000, assoc. dean arts and scis., 1999—2001, dean arts and scis., 2001—04; dean univ. studies and programs Calif. State U. Monterey Bay, Seaside, 2004—07, prof. history, 2007—. Author: Imperialism and Idealism, 1985, Trapped By Success: The Eisenhower Administration and Vietnam, 1991 (Robert H. Ferrell Book prize Soc. for Historians of American Fgn. Rels. 1992), Shadow on the White House: Presidents and the Vietnam War, 1993, Facing My Lai, 1998, The Human Tradition in the Vietnam Era, 2000, The Columbia Guide to the Vietnam War, 2002 (Best of Best prize Am. Lib. Assn.), The Human Tradition in America Since 1945, 2003, The Vietnam War, 2005, The War That Never Ends: New Perspectives on the Vietnam War, 2007. V.p., bd. dir. Leadership Monterey Peninsula. Sgt. US Army, 1968—70. Decorated Commendation medal US Army, Bronze Star; named Ind. Prof. of the Yr., Coun. for Advancement and Support of Edn., 1991. Mem. Am. Hist. Assn., Orgn. Am. Historians, Soc. for Historians of Am. Fgn. Rels. (coun. mem. 1995-97, 2006-08, v.p. 2004, pres. 2005), Natividad Med. Found. (pres. bd. dirs.), Ft. Ord Alumni Assn. (adv. bd.). Avocation: magic. Office: Calif State U Monterey Bay 100 Campus Ctr Bldg 86C Seaside CA 93955-8001 Office Phone: 831-582-3818. Business E-Mail: david_anderson@csumb.edu.

ANDERSON, DAYNA, medical researcher; b. 1979; Rsch. specialist, Immunology Ariz. Respiratory Ctr. Mem. Prosoc philanthropy com. Mem. Susan G. Komen Breast Cancer Found., Catalina Coun. Boy Scouts Am. Spurs and Stars, Southern Ariz. Ctr. Against Sexual Assault. Named one of 40 Under 40, Tucson Bus. Edge, 2006. Achievements include published article in Jour. of Allergy and Clinical Immunology. Office: Arizona Respiratory Center PO Box 245030 1501 N Cambell Ave Ste 2349 Tucson AZ 85724-5030

ANDERSON, DON LYNN, geophysicist; b. Frederick, Md., Mar. 5, 1933; s. Richard Andrew and Minola (Phares) Anderson; m. Nancy Lois Ruth, Sept. 15, 1956; children: Lynn Ellen, Lee Weston. BS, Rensselaer Poly. Inst., 1955; MS, Calif. Inst. Tech., 1959, PhD, 1962; DSc (hon.), Rensselaer Poly. Inst., 2000. With Chevron Oil Co., Mont., Wyo., Calif., 1955—56; with Air Force Cambridge Research Center, Boston, 1956—58, Arctic Inst. N.Am., Boston, 1958; mem. faculty Calif. Inst. Tech., Pasadena, 1962—, assoc. prof. geophysics, 1964—68, prof., 1968—, dir. seismol. lab., 1967—89, Eleanor and John R. McMillan prof. of geophysics, 1990—. Prin. investigator Viking Mars Seismic Expt.; mem. various coms. NASA; chmn. geophysics rsch. forum NAS; chmn. Arthur L. Day award com. NSF, chmn. Geosci. adv. com., 1994; chmn. adv. bd. for Sch. of Earth Scis. Stanford U., 1995; mem. adv. com. Purdue U., U. Chgo., U. Tex., Stanford U., U. Calif. Berkeley, Carnegie Instn., Washington, U. Paris, Yale U., Rice U.; Consortium for High Pressure Rsch. U. Calif.-Riverside; co-founder Inc. Rsch. Insts. for Seismology. Assoc. editor Jour. Geophys. Rsch., 1965—67, Tectonophysics, 1974—77; editor: Physics of the Earth and Planetary Interiors, 1984—94. Recipient Exceptional Sci. Achievement award, NASA, 1977, Emil Wiechert medal, German Geophys. Soc., 1986, Crafoord prize, Royal Swedish Acad. Scis., 1998, Nat. medal of Sci., 1998; fellow Guggenheim, 1998, Sloan Found., 1965—67. Fellow: AAAS (pres. tectonophysics sect. 1971—72, chmn. Macelwane award com. 1975, mem. Bowie medal com. 1985, pres.-elect 1986—88, pres. 1988—90, chair 1994, James B. Macelwane award 1966, Bowie medal 1990), Geol. Soc. Am. (assoc. editor bull. 1971—, mem. Penrose medal com. 1989, mem. Arthur L. Day medal com. 1989—90, mem. long range planning com. 1990—, Arthur L. Day medal 1987), Am. Geophys. Union; mem.: NAS (chmh. seismology com. 1975, chmn. Geophysics Rsch. Forum 1984—86), Seismol. Soc. Am., Royal Astron. Soc. (Gold medal 1988), Am. Philos. Soc., Sigma Xi. Home: 669 Alameda St Altadena CA 91001-3001 Office: Calif Inst Tech Seismol Lab 252 21 Pasadena CA 91125-0001

ANDERSON, DONALD BERNARD, oil industry executive; b. Chgo., Apr. 6, 1919; s. Hugo August and Hilda (Nelson) A.; m. Patricia Gaylord, 1945 (dec. 1978); m. Sarah Midgette, 1980. BS in Mech. Engring, Purdue U., 1942. Vice pres. Hondo Oil & Gas Co. (formerly Malco Refineries, Inc.), Roswell, N.Mex.; vice pres. Hondo Oil & Gas Co. and subs. corps., Roswell, N.Mex., 1946-63; pres. Anderson Oil Co., Roswell, 1963—, Cotter Corp., 1966-70, chmn.

bd., 1966-74; founder, pres. Anderson Drilling Co., Denver, 1974—, pres., chmn. bd., 1977—. Curator fine arts, mem. acquisitions com. Roswell Mus. and Art Center, 1949-56, trustee, 1956-85, pres. bd., 1960-85, 87—, trustee, pres. 1987-90; bd. dirs. Sch. Am. Rsch., Santa Fe, chmn. bd., 1985-88, bd. dirs. 1989—; bd. dirs. Jargon Soc., Penland, N.C.; regent Ea. N.Mex. U., 1966-72; commr. Smithsonian Instn., Nat. Mus. Am. Art, 1980-88. Lt. USNR, 1942-46. Office: PO Box 1 Roswell NM 88202-0001

ANDERSON, DONALD H., energy executive; b. 1948; Grad., U. Colo., Boulder, 1970. Acct. Peat, Marwick, Mitchell Y Co., Denver, 1970—78, Western Crude Oil Inc., Denver, 1978—82; with Lantern Petroleum Corp., Denver, 1983—; chmn, pres., CEO Pan Energy, Houston; pres., vice-chmn. & CEO TransMontaigne Inc., Denver, 2000—06; chmn. TransMontaigne Partners LP, Denver, 2006—. Office: TransMontaigne Partners LP 1670 Broadway Ste 3100 Denver CO 80217-5660

ANDERSON, DONALD LLOYD, weapon systems consultant; b. Stoughton, Wis., Sept. 19, 1921; s. Carl Gustave and Bessie (Cook) A.; m. Augusta Neidermeier, Sept. 10, 1948; children: Anita Briggs, Cathrine Krakower, Christine Robertson. Student, U. Niagara, Niagara Falls, NY, 1960, U. Md., Sembach, Germany, 1963-64, City Coll., Riverside, Calif. Commd. USAF, 1940, advanced through grades to chief master sgt., 1963, supply supt., 1940-71; weapon systems specialist Dynalectron Corp., Norco, Calif., 1971-88, VSE Corona (Calif.), Inc., 1988-89, Dyncorp, Norco, Calif., 1989-92, cons., 1992—. Tutor Myra Linn Sch., Riverside, Calif., 1991—. Author: (tng. manual) Standard Missile Data Processing Manual, 1989, 92. Vol. info. specialist Parkview Hosp., Riverside, 1992-96; staff mem., vol. NCO Acad., March AFB, Calif., 1991-94; vol. Citizens Patrol, Riverside Police Dept.; mem. all svcs. honor guard Riverside Nat. Cemetery, 2001—. Decorated Bronze Star medal, Meritorious Svc. medal, USAF Commendation medal, Vietnam Gallantry Cross with gold palm. Mem. DAV, VFW, NCOAC (life), Bombard Soc., Phoenix Club.

ANDERSON, DOROTHY FISHER, retired social worker, psychotherapist; b. Funchal, Madeira, May 31, 1924; d. Lewis Mann Anker and Edna (Gilbert) Fisher (adoptive father David Henry Fisher); m. Theodore W. Anderson, July 8, 1950; children: Robert Lewis, Janet Anderson Yang, Jeanne Elizabeth. BA, Queens Coll., 1945; AM, U. Chgo., 1947. Diplomate Am. Bd. Examiners in Clin. Social Work; lic. clin. social worker, Calif.; registered cert. social worker, N.Y. Intern Cook County (Ill.) Bur. Pub. Welfare, Chgo., 1945-46, Ill. Neuropsychiat. Inst., Chgo., 1946; clin. caseworker, Neurol. Inst. Presbyn. Hosp., NYC, 1947; therapist, Mental Hygiene Clinic VA, NYC, 1947-50; therapist, Child Guidance Clinic Pub. Elem. Sch. 42, NYC, 1950-53; social worker, counselor Cedarhurst (N.Y.) Family Service Agy., 1954-55; psychotherapist, counselor Family Service of the Midpeninsula, Palo Alto, Calif., 1971-73, 79-86, George Hexter, M.D., Inc., 1972-83; clin. social worker Tavistock Clinic, London, 1974-75, El Camino Hosp., Mountain View, Calif., 1979; pvt. practice, 1978—92; ret., 1992. Cons. Human Resource Services, Sunnyvale, Calif., 1981-86. Hannah G. Solomon scholar U. Chgo., 1945-46; Commonwealth fellow U. Chgo., 1946-47. Fellow Soc. Clin. Social Work (Continuing Edn. Recognition award 1980-83); mem. NASW (diplomate). Avocations: sculpture, tennis, travel, drawing, pastels.

ANDERSON, DUANE, anthropologist; b. Norton, Kans., Nov. 21, 1943; s. Charles Raymond and Leta Marie (Stapp) A.; m. Carol Sue Haloin, Jan. 25, 1944; 1 child, Diana Sue Anderson. BA, U. Colo., 1965, MA, 1967, PhD, 1972. Dir. Sanford Mus. and Planetarium, Cherokee, Iowa, 1966-75; state archaeologist U. Iowa, Iowa City, 1975-86; exec. dir. Dayton (Ohio) Mus. Natural History, 1986-92; v.p. Sch. Am. Rsch., Santa Fe, 1992—; dir. Mus. Indian Arts & Culture, Santa Fe. Co-editor (author): The Cherokee Excavations, 1990, All That Glitters, 1999; editor: Legacy, 1999, When Rain Gods Reigned, 2002. Pres. Iowa Acad. Scis., Cedar Falls, 1983-84, Plains Anthropol. Soc., Lincoln, Nebr., 1985-86, Coun. for Mus. Anthropology, Arlington, Va., 1992-94; mem. exec. com. U. Iowa Mus. Natural History, 1977-86; mem., chair Iowa State Preserves Bd., Des Moines, 1976-86; bd. dirs. N.Mex. Mus. Natural History Found., Albuquerque, 1994-97. NDEA grad. fellow, 1970; grantee NSF, 1976-77, NEH, 1976, 80, 88. Mem. Am. Anthropol. Assn., Soc. Am. Archeology, Am. Assn. Mus. (sr. examiner, accreditation), Plains Anthropol. Soc. (pres. 1985-86), Coun. for Mus. Anthropology (pres. 1992-94), Ctrl. States Anthropol. Soc. (sec. 1987-90). Avocations: travel, jewelry making. E-mail: danderson@miaclab.org.

ANDERSON, EDWARD VIRGIL, lawyer; b. San Francisco, Oct. 17, 1953; s. Virgil P and Edna Pauline (Pedersen) A.; m. Kathleen Helen Dunbar, Sept. 3, 1983; children: Elizabeth D., Hilary J. AB in Econs., Stanford U., 1975, JD, 1978. Bar: Calif. 1978. Assoc. Pillsbury Madison & Sutro, San Francisco, 1978—, ptnr., 1987-94; chmn. mng. ptnr., mem. firm mgmt. com. Skjerven Morrill LLP, San Jose, 1994—2003; ptnr. Sidley Austin LLP, San Francisco, 2003—. Editor IP Litigator, 1995—; mem. bd. editors Antitrust Law Devel., 1983-86. Trustee Lick-Wilmerding H.S., San Francisco, 1980—, pres.; trustee Silicon Valley Law Found., 1995—; trustee, v.p. Hamlin Sch. for Girls, San Francisco, 1998—, v.p. Mem. ABA, Calif. Bar Assn., San Francisco Bar Assn., Santa Clara Bar Assn., City Club San Francisco, Stanford Golf Club, Phi Beta Kappa. Republican. Episcopal. Home: 330 Santa Clara Ave San Francisco CA 94127-2035 Office: Sidley Austin LLP Ste 5000 555 Calif St San Francisco CA 94104 Home Phone: 415-661-9473; Office Phone: 415-772-7420. E-mail: evanderson@sidley.com.

ANDERSON, ERIC, state legislator; Gen. contractor, real estate developer; mem. Dist. 1 Idaho House of Reps., Boise. Republican. Office: Dist Office 33 Match Bay Rd Priest Lake ID 83856-5049 also: Legis Services Office PO Box 83720 Boise ID 83720 Office Phone: 208-265-6316.*

ANDERSON, GAIL V., obstetrician, gynecologist; b. Pensacola, Fla., Oct. 3, 1925; s. Parke Pleasant and Sarada M. (Thompson) A.; m. Alice Harriet Midghall, Nov. 6, 1923; children: Gail V. Jr., David C., Jerrold B., Walter P., Mark S. BA, BS, Columbia Union Coll., 1949; MD, Loma Linda U., 1953. Diplomate Am. Bd. Ob-Gyn. Resident in ob-gyn. D.C. Gen. Hosp., Washington, 1954-55, Georgetown U. Hosp., Washington, 1955-56; chief resident in ob-gyn. D.C. Gen. Hosp., Washington, 1956-57; dir. ob-gyn. L.A. County/U. So. Calif. Med. Ctr., 1958-70; prof. ob-gyn. U. So. Calif. Sch. Medicine, LA, 1968—, prof., chmn. dept. emergency medicine, 1971—. Mem. South Pasadena Sch. Bd., 1971-77; cand. city coun. South Pasadena, 1980; dir. salerni Collegium, 1958-95, pres., 1992-93. With USN, 1943-46. Hartford Found. grantee, 1964. Fellow ACS, ACOG; mem. Am. Bd. Emergency Medicine (founder), Am. Coll. Emergency Physicians (charter). Republican. Avocations: tennis, golf, travel. Home: 217 Oaklawn Ave South Pasadena CA 91030-1828 Office: Univ So Calif Dept Emergency Medicine 1200 N State St Los Angeles CA 90033-1029

ANDERSON, GILLIAN LEIGH, actress; b. Chgo., Aug. 9, 1968; d. Edward and Rosemary Anderson; m. Errol Clyde Klotz, Jan. 1, 1994 (div. 1997); 1 child, Piper Maru; m. Julian Ozanne, Dec. 29, 2004 (div. July 2007); children: Oscar, Felix. BFA, DePaul U., 1990; grad., Goodman Theatre Sch., Chgo. Appeared on TV series, X-Files, 1993-2002 (Emmy award for Outstanding Lead Actress in a Drama Series, 1997, Golden Globe award for Best Actress in a Drama Series, 1997), Bleak House, 2005; stage appearance in Absent Friends, Manhattan Theatre Club, 1991 (Theatre World award 1991), The Philanthropist, Along Wharf Theater, 1992, The Vagina Monologues, 1999, 2000, What the Night is For, 2002-03, The Sweetest Swing in Baseball, 2004; appeared in films Three at Once, 1986, A Matter of Choice, 1988, The Turning, 1992, X-Files the Movie, 1998, The Mighty, 1998, Playing By Heart, 1998, Hellcab, 1998, Princess Mononoke, 1999, The House of Mirth, 2000 (British Independent Film award for Best Actress, 2000), A Cock and Bull Story, 2005, The Mighty Celt, 2005, The Last King of Scotland, 2006, Straightheads, 2007, How to Lose Friends & Alienate People, 2008, The X-Files: I Want to Believe, 2008; TV appearances Class of '96, 1993, Reboot, 1995, The Simpsons, 1997, Frasier, 1999, Harsh Realm, 1999.

ANDERSON, GORDON SUTHERLAND, periodontist; b. Chgo., Dec. 19, 1934; s. Donald Sutherland and Elsie Florence (Ferguson) A.; m. Marilynn LaVance Holm, Sept. 26, 1964; children: Lindsey Paige, Tracey Elisabeth. Student, Wheaton Coll., Ill., 1952-55; DDS, Northwestern U., Chgo., 1959; MSD, U. Wash., 1964. Pvt. practice periodontics, San Mateo, Calif., 1964-82, Grants Pass, Oreg., 1983—96; mayor City of Grants Pass, 1993—2001; mem. Oreg. Ho. of Reps., 2002—. Mem. Grants Pass City Coun., 1987-92, pres., 1989; pres. So. Oreg. Coun. Mayors, 1994, 96, 97; bd. dirs. Oreg. Mayors Assn., 1995-00, pres., 1999; pres. Nat. League of Cities, Christian Pub. Ofcls. Caucus, 1998-99. Lt. USN, 1959-61. Fellow Am. Coll. Dentists; mem. We. Soc. Peridontology (sec. 1975-77), Am. Dental Assn., Oreg. Dental Assn., Am. Acad. Peridontology, Oreg. Soc. Peridontists, Rogue Valley Dental Soc., Republican Mayor and Local Ofcls., Rotary. Republican. Christian. Avocations: skiing, golf, farming. Office: 1201 NE 7th St Ste E Grants Pass OR 97526-1451 also: 900 Court St North East H-490 Salem OR 97301

ANDERSON, HERBERT HATFIELD, lawyer, farmer; b. Rainier, Oreg., Aug. 2, 1920; s. Odin A. and Mae (Hatfield) A.; m. Barbara Stuart Bastine, June 3, 1949; children: Linda, Catherine, Thomas, Amy, Elizabeth, Kenneth BA in Bus. Adminstrn., U. Oreg., 1940; JD, Yale U., 1949. Exec. trainee U.S. Steel Co., San Francisco, 1940-41; assoc. Koerner, Young, McColloch & Dezendorf, Portland, Oreg., 1949—54; ptnr. Spears, Lubersky, Bledsoe, Anderson, Young & Hilliard, 1954-90, Lane, Powell, Spears & Lubersky, Portland, 1990—. Instr. law Lewis and Clark Coll., Portland, 1950-70. Mem. planning adv. com. Yamhill County, Oreg., 1974-82; bd. dirs. Emanuel Hosp., 1967—; bd. dirs. Flyfisher Found., 1972—, pres., 1972-84; bd. dirs. Multnomah Law Libr., 1958—, sec. 1962-68, 77-94, pres., 1964-74. Served to maj., parachute inf. U.S. Army, 1942-46, European Theater. Fellow Am. Bar Found. (chmn. Oreg. chpt. 1988—2008); mem. ABA (chmn. governing com. forum on health law 1984-89, chmn. standing com. on jud. selection, tenure and compensation 1978-80, Lawyer's Conf., exec. com. 1980-94, chmn. 1989-90, jud. adminstrn. divsn. coun. 1988-94, sr. lawyer's divsn. coun. 1987-89), Am. Judicature Soc. (bd. dirs. 1981-85), Soc. Law and Medicine, Nat. Health Lawyers Assn., Am. Acad. Hosp. Attys., Oreg. Soc. Hosp. Attys. (pres. 1984-85), Multnomah Bar Found. (bd. dirs. 1955—, pres. 1959-64, 87—2006), Nat. Bankruptcy Conf. (conferee 1964—, exec. com. 1976-79, chmn. farmer insolvency com. 1985-88), Nat. Assn. R.R. Trial Counsel, Oreg. Bar Assn. (del. to ABA 1966-68), Multnomah Bar Assn. (pres. 1955), Western States Bar Conf. (pres. 1967), Oreg. Asian Pear Coun. (pres. 1989-91), Multnomah Athletic Club, Michelbook Country Club, Flyfishers Oreg. Club (pres. 1972), Flyfisher Found. (pres. 1957-67), Willamette Amateur Field Trial Club (pres. 1968-72), Amateur Field Trial Clubs of Am. (trustee 2002-), 101st Airborne Divsn. Assn., Masons, Sigma Chi. Democrat. Lutheran. Home: River Meadow Farm 19289 SE Neck Rd Dayton OR 97114-7815 Personal E-mail: hhanderson@verizon.net.

ANDERSON, HERBERT W., consumer products company executive; b. Indpls., Oct. 1, 1939; BS in Bus. Mgmt., U. Wis. Sr. mgmt. positions McGraw-Edison, Eaton Cos.; corp. v.p., mgmt. info. svcs. Western Gear Corp.; v.p., info. rescource mgmt. Northrop Grumman Corp., 1984-90, corp. v.p., ctr. mgr., 1990-94, dep. gen. mgr., DSSD, 1994-95, corp. v.p., gen. mgr., DSSD, 1995-98, pres., CEO, Logicon, 1998—2001, corp. v.p., pres. Information Technology, 2001—04, corp. v.p., special projects, 2004. With U.S. Army 1958-61.

ANDERSON, HERSCHEL VINCENT, retired librarian; b. Charlotte, NC, Mar. 14, 1932; s. Paul Kemper and Lillian (Johnson) Anderson. Grad., Needham B. Broughton HS, Raleigh, NC, 1950; BA, Duke U., 1954; MS, Columbia U., 1959. Library asst. Bklyn. Public Library, 1954-59; asst. bookmobile librarian King County Public Library, Seattle, 1959-62; asst. librarian Longview (Wash.) Public Library, 1962-63; librarian N.C. Mus. Art, Raleigh, 1963-64; audio-visual cons. N.C. State Library, Raleigh, 1964-68; dir. Sandhill Regional Library, Rockingham, NC, 1968-70; asso. state librarian Tenn. State Library and Archives, Nashville, 1970-72; unit dir. Colo. State Library, Denver, 1972-73; state librarian S.D. State Library, Pierre, 1973-80; dir. Mesa (Ariz.) Public Library, 1980-99. Founding mem., chief officers State Libr. Agys., 1973—80, bd. dirs.; dir. Bibliog. Ctr. Rsch., Denver, 1974—80, v.p., 1977; founding mem. Western Coun. St. Librs., 1975—80, v.p., 1978, pres., 79; mem. libr. technician tng. adv. com. Mesa CC, 1982—85, mem. commn. excellence, 1993—2003; chmn. Serials On-Line Ariz. Consortia, 1985—86; mem. Ariz. Libr. Devel. Coun., 1991—93, Ariz. State Libr. Adv. Coun., 1998—, chair, 1999—; mem. Libr. Facilities Adv. Bd., Gilbert, Ariz., 1999—2006. Founding mem., treas. Maricopa County Libr. Coun., 1981—99, pres., 1983, 1993; mem. hist. preservation com. City of Mesa, 2000—06, chmn., 2005—06; mem. Valley Citizens League, 1991—; jr. warden St. Mark's Episcopal Ch., Mesa, 1985—87, vestryman, 1987—90, 1995—98, sr. warden, 1996—98, archivist, 2000—; del. ann. conv. Episcopal Diocese Ariz., 1989—92, 1994—98, mem. archives com., 1990—97, mem. Diosecan Coun. Episcopal, 1996—98; mem. steering com. N.E. Regional Parish, 1994—2004, chair Native Am. com., 1999—2004; sec., bd. dirs. Sunridge Homeowners Assn., 1980—90, La Maricpsa Villas VI Homeowners Assn., 1990—99; bd. dirs. La Maricpsa Vaillas VI Homeowners Assn., 2001—. With US Army, 1955—57. Recipient Emeritus Honors, Ariz. Libr. Friends, 1987. Mem.: ALA, Nat. Cowboy and Western Heritage Mus., Heard Mus., Mesa Hist. Soc., N.C. Literary and Hist. Assn., Nat. Trust for Hist. Preservation, Ariz. Hist. Found., Ariz. Libr. Assn. (mem. exec. com. 1986—87), Mountain Plains Libr. Assn. (pres. 1974, bd. dirs. 1974—77, 1986—87, Intellectual Freedom award 1979), S.D. Libr. Assn. (life Libr. of Yr. award 1977), Kiwanis (bd. dirs. Mesa 1981—86, v.p. 1983, pres. 1985—86), Phi Kappa Psi. Home Phone: 480-898-9441. E-mail: andersonvince@aol.com.

ANDERSON, HOLLY GEIS, health facility administrator, educator, commentator; b. Waukesha, Wis., Oct. 23, 1946; d. Henry H. and Hulda S. Geis; m. Richard Kent Anderson, June 6, 1969. BA, Azusa Pacific U., 1970. CEO Oak Tree Antiques, San Gabriel, Calif., 1975-82; pres., founder, CEO Premenstrual Syndrome Med. Clinic, Arcadia, Calif., 1982—, Lake Forest, Calif., 2006—, Breast Healthcare Ctr., 1986-89, Hormonal Treatment Ctrs., Inc., Arcadia, 1992-94; with Thyroid Ctr., 2001—. On-air radio personality Women's Clinic with Holly Anderson, 1990—; lectr. in field. Author: (audio cassette) What Every Woman Needs to Know About PMS, 1987, PMS Talk, 1989; (video cassette)The PMS Treatment Program, 1989. Mem. The Dalton Soc., Am. Hist. Soc. of Germans from Russia. Republican. Avocations: writing, genealogy, travel, hiking, boating. Office: PMS Treatment Clinic 150 N Santa Anita Ave Ste 755 Arcadia CA 91006-3148 also: PMS Treatment Clinic 26700 Towne Center Dr Foothill Ranch CA 92610 Office Phone: 626-447-0679. Personal E-mail: hra3@earthlink.net.

ANDERSON, JAMES, state legislator; b. Douglas, Wyo., Mar. 17, 1943; m. Pamela Anderson. BS in Edn., Chadron State Coll., 1996; postgrad., U. Wyo. Tchr.; logging and sawmill operator; precinct committeeman; mem. Dist. 2 Wyo. House of Reps., 1996—2000, Wyo. State Senate, 2000—. Mem. appropriations com. Wyo. State Senate, corps., elections and polit. subdivsns. Mem. Converse County Group Home. Mem. Nat. Coun. Tchrs. Math., NRA, Wyo. Reading Coun., Ducks Unltd., U. Wyo. Alumni, Glenrock C. of C. Republican. Protestant. Office: Wyo State Senate 213 State CapitolBldg Cheyenne WY 82002 also: 92 Running Dutchman Dr Glenrock WY 82637-9512 Office Phone: 307-777-7881. Office Fax: 307-777-5466. E-mail: jamesda1@msn.com.*

ANDERSON, J.C., oil and gas industry executive, rancher; b. Oakland, Nebr. Student, Midland Coll., Fremont, Nebr., 1949-51; BSc in Petroleum Engring., U. Tex., 1954. With Amoco Prodn. Co., various locations; chief engr. Amoco Can., Calgary, Alta., Canada, 1966-68; founder, chmn. bd., CEO Anderson Exploration Ltd., Calgary, 1968—2001; rancher Anderson Ranch; pvt. practice. With Counter-Intelligence Corps, U.S. Army, 1954-56. Mem. Assn. Profl. Engrs., Geologists and Geophysicists of Alta., Soc. Petroleum Engrs., Can. Soc. Petroleum Geologists. Office: Ste 239 132-250 Shawville Blvd SE Calgary AB Canada T2Y 2Z7 Office Phone: 403-256-7550. E-mail: husker@telus.net.

ANDERSON, JOEL, state legislator; m Kate; children: Mary, Maura, and Michael. BS in Fin., Calif. State Polytechnic U., Pomona. California State Assemblyman, District 77, 2006-.Founder, small business, formerly; works with direct mktg firm, curently. President, Intl Business Fraternity of Delta Sigma Pi. Republican. Office: Dist 77 500 Fesler St Ste 201 El Cajon CA 92020 Office Phone: 619-441-2322. Office Fax: 619-447-2327. Business E-Mail: Assemblymember.Anderson@assembly.ca.gov.

ANDERSON, JOHN ALBERT, physician; b. Ashtabula, Ohio, Jan. 25, 1935; s. Albert Gunnard Anderson and Martha Anetta (Bieshline) White; m. Nicole Jeanne Anderson, July 10, 1963; children: Carole, John-Marc, Christopher B. BS, U. Ill., 1958, MD, 1960. Diplomate Am. Bd. Pediat., Am. Bd. Allergy and Immunology. Intern U. Ill., 1960-61, resident in pediat. Chgo., 1961-62, U.S. Naval Hosp., Bethesda, Md., 1964-65; fellow in allergy and immunology Children's Hosp., Washington, 1967-69; mem. sr. staff Henry Ford Hosp., Detroit, 1969-99, dir. pediat. allergy fellowship program, 1969-77, dir. allergy and immunology program, 1977-99, head divsn. allergy and immunology, dept. pediatrics, 1977-99, chmn. dept. pediatrics, 1982-90; physician Vivra Asthma and Allergy, Tucson, 1999-2000; with Vivra Asthma and Allergy, Inc., 2000—02; physician Allergy and Asthma Ctr. Ariz., Tucson, 2001—03, Aspen Med. Ctr., Fort Collins, Colo., 2003—05, Allergy and Asthma Care Ariz. PLLC, Yuma, 2006—. Clin. prof. U. Mich., Ann Arbor, 1985—94; prof. pediat. Case Western Res. U., 1994—99; dir. Am. Bd. Allergy and Immunology, 1990—96, sec., 1995—96. Contbr. articles Contbr. more than 60 articles to profl. jours. Lt. comdr. USN, 1962-66. Fellow Am. Acad. Allergy, Asthma and Immunology (pres. 1990-91), Am. Acad. Pediat. (chmn. allergy sect. 1979-82), Am. Coll. Allergy, Asthma & Immunology, Mich. Allergy Soc. (pres. 1978-79); mem. Asthma and Allergy Found. Am. (dir. 1992-99, v.p. med. affairs 1992-95, v.p. rsch. 1995-99), Coun. Med. Splty. Socs. (bd. dirs. 1992-94), Am. Bd. Med. Specialists, Sci. Advisors Internat. Life Scis. (allergy sect. 1990-2003). Home: 1609 S 42d Ave Yuma AZ 85365 Office: Allergy and Asthma Care Ariz PLLC 2110 W 24th Ste C Yuma AZ 85364 Office Phone: 928-344-2300.

ANDERSON, JOHN DAVID, architect; b. New Haven, Dec. 24, 1926; s. William Edward and Norma Vere (Carson) A.; m. Florence A. Van Dyke, Aug. 26, 1950; children— Robert Stewart, David Carson. AB cum laude, Harvard U., 1949, MArch, 1952; LHD (hon.), U. Colo., 2006. Draftsman John K. Monroe, Architect, Denver, 1952-54; draftsman, designer, assoc. Wheeler & Lewis, Architects, Denver, 1954-60; pvt. practice Denver, 1960-64; ptnr. Anderson, Barker Rinker, Architects, Denver, 1965-69, A-B-R Partnership, Architects, Denver, 1970-75; prin., CEO Anderson Mason Dale P.C., Denver, 1975-96, sr. prin., 1997—. Vis. lectr. U. Colo., U. N.Mex., U. Nebr., U. Cape Town, Colo. State U., Plymouth Polytech., Eng.; chmn. Colo. Gov.'s Task Force on Removal of Archtl. Barriers, 1972-74; vice chmn. Colo. Bd. Non-Residential Energy Conservation Stds., 1978-80. Prin. works include: Front Range Community Coll., Westminster, 1977, Solar Energy Rsch. Inst., Golden, 1980 (award winning solar heated structures). Served with USNR, 1944-46. Recipient Bonfils Stanton Found. award, 2007. Fellow AIA (pres. Colo. chpt. 1967, Western Mountain region dir. 1995-97, Silver medal, 1984, Firm of Yr. award 1986 Western Mountain region); mem. AIA (Arch. of Yr. award 1987, pres. 1971, nat. v.p. 1999, 1st v.p. 2000, pres. 2001), Internat. Solar Energy Soc., Coun. Ednl. Facility Planners (internat.

chmn. energy com. 1980). Democrat. Congregationalist. Home: 57 S Rainbow Trail Evergreen CO 80439-8341 Office: Anderson Mason Dale Architects 3198 Speer Blvd Denver CO 80211 Business E-Mail: janderson@amdarchitects.com.

ANDERSON, JOHN EDWARD, diversified holding company executive, lawyer; b. Mpls., Sept. 12, 1917; s. William Charles and Myrtle (Grosvenor) A.; m. Margaret Stewart, Sept. 14, 1942 (dec.); children: Margaret Susan, Judith Grosvenor, John Edward, Deborah Lee (dec.), William Stewart; m. Marion Redding, Mar. 3, 1967. BS cum laude, UCLA, 1940; MBA with distinction (Baker scholar), Harvard U., 1942; JD cum laude, Loyola U., 1950. Bar: Calif. 1950; CPA, Calif. Acct. Arthur Andersen & Co., Los Angeles, 1945-48; since practiced in Los Angeles, Irvine; ptnr. Kindel & Anderson, 1953-85; CEO Topa Equities, Los Angeles, Calif. Dir. Mellon 1st Bus. Bank, Summit Health Ltd., Topa Equities, Ltd., Topa Mgmt. Co., Jas. D. Easton, Inc., Indsl. Tools, Inc., Topa Ins. Co. Trustee Claremont McKenna Coll.; trustee St. John's Hosp. and Health Center Found.; bd. dirs. YMCA Met., Los Angeles. Served to lt. USNR, 1942-45. Named one of Forbes Richest Americans, 2006. Mem. AICPA, ABA, State Bar Calif., Calif. Soc. CPAs, L.A. Country Club, Calif. Club, Eldorado Country Club (Palm Desert, Calif.), Outrigger Canoe Club (Honolulu). Presbyterian (elder). Office: Topa Equities Ste 1400 1800 Avenue Of The Stars Los Angeles CA 90067-4216 Office Phone: 310-203-9199. Business E-Mail: tcurtis@topa.com.

ANDERSON, JOHN RICHARD, entomologist, educator; b. Fargo, ND, May 5, 1931; s. John Raymond and Mary Ann (Beaulieu) A.; m. Shereen V. Erickson, Mar. 26, 1955; children: Scott F., Lisa K., Steven F. BS, Utah State U., 1957; MS, U. Wis., 1958, PhD, 1960. Asst. prof. entomology U. Calif.-Berkeley, 1961-66, assoc. prof., 1967-70, prof., 1970-93, prof. emeritus, 1993—, assoc. dean research, 1979-85. Trustee, past chmn. Alameda County (Calif.) Mosquito Abatement Dist., 1961-73, 79-93. Editoral bd.: Jour. Med. Entomology, 1968-72, Jour. Econ. Entomology, 1977-81, Thomas Say Found, 1968-72. Served with USN, 1950-54. Rsch. grantee; recipient Berkeley citation for Disting. Achievement, 1993. Fellow AAAS, Entomol. Soc. Am. (governing bd. 1987-90, C.W. Woodworth award Pacific br. 1988), Royal Entomol. Soc. (London); mem. Can. Entomol. Soc., Am. Mosquito Control Assn., Nat. Audubon Soc., Am. Mus. Natural History, Oreg. Nat. Resources Coun., Oreg. Nat. Desert Assn., High Desert Mus., Sierra Club, Trout Unlimited. Office: U Calif Dept Insect Biology Berkeley CA 94720-0001

ANDERSON, JON DAVID, lawyer; b. Wichita, Kans., Oct. 29, 1952; s. Charles Henry Anderson and Patricia (Vaughan) Ross; m. Leanne Winters, Dec. 20, 1973; children: Nicklas, Scott, Brandt, Chase, Barrett, Britten, Kieryn. BA, U. Wash., Seattle, 1974; JD, Brigham Young U., 1977. Bar: Calif. 1977. Assoc. Latham & Watkins, L.A., Newport Beach, Calif., 1977-84, ptnr. Newport Beach, Costa Mesa, 1985—, mng. ptnr. Costa Mesa, Calif., 1987-93, chmn. Teaches trial advocacy & coached mock trial teams Constl. Rights Found. Bd. dirs. Orange County Coun., Boy Scouts Am. Mem. Calif. Bar Assn., Orange County Bar Assn., Marbella Country Club. Republican. Ch. of Jesus Christ of Latter-day Saints. Avocations: skiing, baseball, golf. Office: Latham & Watkins 650 Town Center Dr 20th Fl Costa Mesa CA 92626-1925 Office Phone: 714-755-8217. Office Fax: 714-755-8290. E-mail: jon.anderson@lw.com.

ANDERSON, JOSHUA E., lawyer; BA, Univ. Chgo., 1997; JD, UCLA, 2000. Bar: Calif. 2000, US Dist. Ct. No. & Ctrl. Calif., US Ct. Appeals Ninth Cir. Assoc., bus. litigation practice Sidley Austin LLP, LA, 2000—. Named a Rising Star, So. Calif. Super Lawyers, 2007. Mem.: Phi Beta Kappa, Order of the Coif. Office: Sidley Austin LLP 555 W 5th St Los Angeles CA 90013 Office Phone: 213-896-6687. Office Fax: 213-896-6600.

ANDERSON, KENT TAYLOR, lawyer; b. Salt Lake City, June 24, 1953; s. Neldon Leroy and Vera Minnie (Taylor) A.; m. Ellis Anderson (div. June 1979); m. Tara Dayle, Apr. 30, 1982; 1 child, Claire Marie. BA, U. Utah, 1975; JD, Georgetown U., 1978. Bar: Utah 1978, Calif. 1987. Assoc. Jones, Waldo, Holbrook & McDonough, Salt Lake City, 1978-83, ptnr., 1983-84; v.p., gen. counsel Am. Stores Properties, Inc., Salt Lake City, 1984-86; v.p., gen. counsel, asst. sec. Am. Stores Co., Salt Lake City, 1987—; sr. v.p., gen. counsel, sec. Alpha Beta Stores, Inc., Anaheim, Calif., 1986-89; exec. v.p., gen. counsel, asst. sec. Am. Stores Co., Salt Lake City, 1989-93, exec. v.p., 1993—; gen. mgr. Am. Stores Properties, Inc., Salt Lake City, 1993-95, COO strategy and devel., mem. exec. coun., 1995—. Mem. staff Georgetown Law Jour., 1976-78. Mem. Utah Bar Assn., Calif. Bar Assn., Phi Beta Kappa. Office: Am Stores Properties Inc 1654 Mohawk Way Salt Lake City UT 84108-3312

ANDERSON, LAWRENCE OHACO, federal judge, lawyer; b. Phoenix, Sept. 7, 1948; s. Jack M. and Viola (Ohaco) A.; m. Aimee. BS, U. San Francisco, 1971; JD, Ariz. State U., Tempe, 1974. Bar: Ariz. 1975. Prosecutor City of Phoenix, 1973-75; assoc. Jack M. Anderson, Phoenix, 1975-78; sole practice Phoenix, 1978-90; judge Superior Ct. of Ariz., Phoenix, 1990-92, judge, criminal calender, 1992-95, judge, juvenile ct., 1995-98, magistrate judge, 1998—. Natl. Wheelchair Weightlifting Championship, Spokane, Wash., 1974; Victory Achievement Award, State of Ariz., 1990; Outstanding Citizens award, Nat. Counil on Disability, 1992. Mem. ABA, Assn. Trial Lawyers Am., Ariz. Trial Lawyers Assn. (bd. dirs. 1985-90). Republic. Roman Catholic. Avocations: fishing, sports. Office: 401 W Washington SPC11 Phoenix AZ 85003-2120

ANDERSON, LOUIE, comedian; b. Mpls., Mar. 24, 1953; Appeared in film Cloak & Dagger, 1984, Quick Silver, 1986, Ferris Bueller's Day Off, 1986, The Wrong Guys, 1988, Coming to America, 1988, Bebe's Kids, 1992, Mr. Wrong, 1996, Do It for Uncle Manny, 2002, Back by Midnight, 2002; (TV) Life with Louie (voice), 1995, The Louie Show, 1996; author: Dear Dad: Letters From an Adult Child, 1989; comedian: HBO Spl., host (TV series) Family Feud, 1999. Recipient Daytime Emmy, 1996. Office: ICM 8942 Wilshire Blvd Beverly Hills CA 90211-1934

ANDERSON, LYNN L., bank executive; B in Bus., U. Kans., JD. Various positions Frank Russell, 1987; chmn. Frank Russell Trust Co., Tacoma, Frank Russell Investment Mgmt. Co., Tacoma. Vice chmn. Frank Russell Co. Office: Frank Russell Co 909 A St Tacoma WA 98402 Office Phone: 253-439-3510.

ANDERSON, MARILYN WHEELER, English language educator; b. Tulsa, Mar. 18, 1946; d. Robert Leslie and Lola Madelene (Offutt) Wheeler; m. Austin Gilman Anderson, Mar. 17, 1968; children: Guy, Lisa, Michael, Emily. BA, Calif. State U., LA, 1968; MA, UCLA, 1972, Calif. State U., Dominguez Hills, 1989. Actress and dir., LA, 1977-83; cons. Redondo Beach (Calif.) Beach City Schs., 1981-83; prof. of English El Camino Coll., Torrance, Calif., 1986—. Fine arts com. mem. El Camino Coll., 1992—, affirmative action officer, 1995-96; presenter in field. Author: (textbook) Keys to Successful Writing, 1998, 4th edit., 2007; contbr. articles to profl. jours. Vol. 1736 House/Crisis Ctr., Hermosa Beach, Calif., 1985-86; bd. dirs. Brain Injury Rsch. Ctr., UCLA, 1998—, spkr. Calif. Coun. for Humanities, 2002, keynote spkr. Joint Symposium of Nat. and Internat. Neurotrauma Socs., 2002. Mem. MLA, Nat. Coun. Tchrs. of English, UCLA Alumni Assn. Democrat. Avocations: jogging, travel, hiking. Office: El Camino Coll 16007 Crenshaw Blvd Torrance CA 90506-0001 Business E-Mail: manderso@elcamino.edu.

ANDERSON, MARTIN CARL, economist; b. Lowell, Mass., Aug. 5, 1936; s. Ralph and Evelyn (Anderson) A.; m. Annelise Graebner, Sept. 25, 1965 AB summa cum laude, Dartmouth Coll., 1957, MS in Engring., MSBA; PhD in Indsl. Mgmt., MIT, 1962. Asst. to dean, instr. engring. Thayer Sch. Engring. Dartmouth Coll., Hanover, NH, 1959; research fellow Joint Ctr. for Urban Studies MIT and Harvard U., Cambridge, 1961-62; asst. prof. fin. Grad. Sch. Bus. Columbia U., NYC, 1962-65, assoc. prof. bus., 1965-68; sr. fellow Hoover Inst. on War, Revolution and Peace Stanford (Calif.) U., 1971—; spl. asst. to Pres. of U.S. The White House, 1969-70, spl. cons. for systems analysis, 1970-71, asst. for policy devel., 1981-82. Mem. Pres.' Fgn. Intelligence Adv. Bd., 1982-85, Pres.' Econ. Policy Adv. Bd., 1982-88, Pres.' Gen. Adv. Com. on Arms Control and Disarmament, 1987-93; pub. interest dir. Fed. Home Loan Bank San Francisco, 1972-79; mem. Commn. on Crucial Choices for Ams., 1973-75, Def. Manpower Commn., 1975-76, Com. on the Present Danger, 1977—. Author: The Federal Bulldozer: A Critical Analysis of Urban Renewal, 1949-62, 1964, Conscription: A Select and Annotated Bibliography, 1976, Welfare: The Political Economy of Welfare Reform in the U.S., 1978, Registration and the Draft, 1982, The Military Draft, 1982, Revolution, 1988, Impostors in the Temple, 1992, Reagan in his Own Hand, 2001, Reagan: A Life in Letters, 2003, Reagan's Path to Victory, 2004; columnist Scripps-Howard News Svc., 1993-94. Dir. research Nixon presdl. campaign, 1968; policy adviser Reagan presdl. campaign, 1976, 80; del. Rep. Nat. Conv., 1992-2000; policy adviser Dole Presdl. Campaign, 1996; sr. adviser Bush presdl. campaign, 1998-2000; trustee Ronald Reagan Presdl. Found., 1985-92; mem. Calif. Gov.'s Coun. Econ. Advisors, 1993-98, chmn. Congl. Policy Adv. Bd., 1998-2001. 2d lt. AUS, 1958-59. Mem. Mont Pelerin Soc., Phi Beta Kappa. Clubs: Bohemian. Office: Stanford U Hoover Instn Stanford CA 94305-6010

ANDERSON, N. CHRISTIAN, III, former newspaper publisher; b. Montpelier, Idaho, Aug. 4, 1950; s. Nelson C. and Esther Barbara Anderson; m. Sara Ann Coffenberry, Dec. 11, 1971 (div.); children: Ryan, Erica; m. Aletha Ann Yurewicz, May 3, 1986; children: Paul, Amanda. BA in Liberal Studies with honors, Ore. State U., 1972. From asst. city editor to city editor Albany (Oreg.) Democrat-Herald, 1972—75; mng. editor Walla Walla (Wash.) Union Bulletin, 1975—77; assoc. mng. editor Seattle Times, 1977—80; from editor to exec. v.p., assoc. publisher The Orange County Register, Santa Ana, Calif., 1980—94; pub. Gazette Telegraph, Colorado Springs, 1994—98; pub. & CEO Orange County Register, Santa Ana, 1999—2007; sr. v.p. Freedom Comm., Inc., Irvine, Calif., 1999; pres. & CEO Freedom Orange County Info., 2000—07; pres., metro divsn. Freedom Comm., Inc., Irvine, Calif., 2001—07. Instr. Calif. State U., Fullerton, 1983, Fullerton, 87; Pulitzer Prize juror, 87, 88, 96; exec. editor Freedom Newspapers, Inc., Irvine, Calif., 1990—94; exec. v.p., CEO Golden West Publ., Irvine, 1991—94; mem. adv. bd. Poynter Inst. for Media Studies, St. Petersburg, Fla., 1994—99, also past chmn. adv. bd.; former chmn. bd. dirs. New Directions for News, newspaper think tank; mem. nominating com. AP; bd. dirs. Robert C. Maynard Inst. for Journalism Edn.; editor-in-chief, pub. OC Post, 2006—. Past chmn. Orange County Bus. Com. for Arts; past mem., bd. dirs. Calif. First Amendment Coalition; bd. dirs. Santa Ana Rotary Found., 1984, Colorado Springs Fine Arts Ctr., 1994—98, Colorado Springs Non-Profit Ctr., 1994—98, Colorado Springs Sports Corp., 1994—98, Pike's Peak United Way, 1994—98, South Coast Repertory, Econ. Devel. Corp., Colorado Springs, chmn. bd., 1996; bd. trustees, past pres. South Coast Repertory, 2004—06; bd. trustees Orange County Comm. Found., St. Margaret's Episcopal Sch. Recipient George D. Beveridge award, Nat. Press Found., 1989; named Nat. Newspaper Editor of Yr., 1989, Calif. Newspaper Exec. of Yr., Calif. Press Assn., 1993, Pub. of Yr., Editor & Pub., 2007. Mem.: Calif. Soc. Newspaper Editors (founder, former bd. dirs. and pres.), Soc. Newspaper Design (co-founder), Am. Soc. Newspaper Editors (bd. dirs. 1996, treas. 1996, sec. 1997, v.p. 1998, pres. 1999).

ANDERSON, NANCY J., computer software company executive, lawyer; married. BA summa cum laude, St. Olaf Coll.; JD cum laude, Harvard U. Atty. employment discrimination law, Chgo.; mgr. European anti-piracy program Microsoft Corp., Paris, 1993, head anti-piracy program Redmond, Wash., 1997, corp. v.p., dep. gen. counsel Worldwide Sales Group, Legal and Corp. Affairs Dept., 2002—. Bd. trustees St. Olaf Coll.; exec. bd., past pres. Trade Devel. Alliance of Greater Seattle. Office: Microsoft Corp One Microsoft Way Redmond WA 98052-6399

ANDERSON, NED, SR., Apache tribal official; b. Bylas, Ariz., Jan. 18, 1943; s. Paul and Maggie (Rope) Anderson; m. Delphina Hinton; children: Therese Kay, Linette Mae, Magdalene Gail, Ned, Sean. AA, Ea. Ariz. Coll., 1964, AAS in Computer Sci., 1989; BS, U Ariz., 1967, JD, 1973. Field dir. Nat. Study Indian Edn. dept. anthropology U. Ariz., Tucson, 1968-70, dir. Jojoba Project, Office of Arid Land Studies, 1973-76; tech. asst. Project Head Start Ariz. State U., Tempe, 1970; ethnographer Smithsonian Instn., Washington, 1970-73; with Jojoba devel. project San Carlos Apache Tribe, Ariz., 1976-78, tribal councilman, 1976-78, 93-98, tribal chmn., 1978-86, gen. mgr. spl. housing projects, 1991-99, coord. Ctrl. Ariz. project, 1999—. Contbr. articles to profl. jours. Mem. affirmative action com. City of Tucson, 1975—76; mem. study panel NAS, 1975—76; mem. supervisory bd. Ariz. Justice Planning Commn., 1978; mem. county govt. study commn. State of Ariz., 1981—84; mem. reinvention mgmt. lab. workgroup Nat. Housing Improvement Program, 1995—96; mem. Indian adv. bd. Intergovernmental Pers. Program, 1978; mem. adv. bd. Am. Indian Registry Performing Arts, 1985, San Carlos Fish and Game Commn., 1975, chmn., 1976; pres. Intertribal Coun. Ariz., 1979—85, 1992; pres. bd. dirs. Ft. Thomas HS Unified Dist., 1977, clk., 1987, clk. bd. dirs., 1989; bd. dirs. Southwestern Indian Devel., Inc., 1971, Indian Enterprise Devel. Corp., 1976—78, San Carlos Lake Devel., 1994—98, We. Apache Constrn. Co., 1994—98, Apache Gold Resort Pub. Authority, 1997—99, vice chmn., acting chmn., 2002—03, chmn., 2004—07; mem. adv. bd. Gila Pueblo CC ext. Ea. Ariz. Coll., 1979, Indian Edn., Ariz. State U., Tempe, 1978—86, U. Ariz., Tucson, 1978—86; trustee Bacone Coll.; enterprise bd. chmn. Apache Gold Casino Resort, 2003—07. Recipient Outstanding CC Alumni award, Ariz. CC Bd./Ea. Ariz. Coll., 1982, Outstanding Coop. award, U.S. Secret Svc., 1984, Univ. Rels. award, AT&T, 1989; A. T. Anderson Meml. scholar, 1989. Mem.: Nat. Geog. Soc., Ariz. Acad., Globe C. of C., Nat. Tribal Chmn.'s Assn. (mem. bd. edn., mem. adv. bd. 1978—86), Phi Theta Kappa. Home Phone: 928-475-4205; Office Phone: 928-475-3832.

ANDERSON, NORMA V., state legislator; b. Elyria, Ohio, July 6, 1932; Student, Denver U., Jones Real Estate Coll. Owner, operator KBJ Stables; office mgr. Capitol Solar; supr. Time, Inc.; mem. Colo. Ho. of Reps., Dist. 30, 1986-98, Fin. & State Affairs Coms., Legis. Coun., Colo. Senate, Dist. 22, Denver, 1998—2006, Judiciary, Appropriations Coms., Legis. Coun., State Compensation Bd., Colo. Uninsurable Health Ins. Bd.; majority leader, chair Legis. Audit, Edn., Trans. & Energy Coms.; vice-chair Health, Environ., Welfare & Inst. Com., Legis. Audit Com., Judiciary Com., Assembly on Fed. Issues; chair Minority Caucus, Bus. Affairs & Labor Com.; mem. labor dept. State Adv. Coun.; exec. com., chair Energy & Trans.; co-chair Social Security Task Force, DC. Mem. state adv. coun. labor dept.; bd. dir. state compensation, regional transp. dist., Foothills Found.; mem. West Chamber; mem. numerious senate coms. including most recently jud. com., appropriations com. Vice-chair Health Environ. Welfare Insts.; bd. dirs. Foothills Found.; mem. budget com. R-1 Sch. Dist; exec. com. Nat. Conf. State Legis.; vice-chair Arapahow House; adv. bd. Drug Control Systems Improvement, Com. Corrections; mem. Am. Cancer Soc., Bear Creek Jr. Sports Assn., Great Outdoors Colo. Republican. Office: State Capitol 200 E Colfax Ave Ste 274 Denver CO 80203-1716 Office Phone: 303-866-4859. E-mail: norma.anderson.senate@state.co.us.

ANDERSON, PAM (PAMELA DENISE ANDERSON), actress; b. Ladysmith, BC, Can., July 1, 1967; d. Barry and Carol Anderson; m. Tommy Lee, Feb. 19, 1995 (div. Feb. 28, 1998); children: Brandon Thomas Lee, Dylan Jagger Lee; m. Robert James "Kid Rock" Ritchie, Aug. 3, 2006 (div. Feb. 1, 2007); m. Rick Salomon, Oct. 6, 2007 (annulled Mar. 24, 2008). Syndicated columnist Jane, 2002—, Marie Claire, 2002—, Can. Elle, 2002—; launched clothing line "The Pamela Collection", 2003—. Actor: (TV series) Home Improvement, 1991—93, Baywatch, 1992—97; actor, exec. prodr.: (TV series) V.I.P., 1998; actor(voice): Stripperella, 2003—04, Stacked, 2005—06; (TV films) Baywatch: River of No Return, 1992, Come Die with Me: A Mickey Spillane Mike Hammer Mystery, 1994, Baywatch: Forbidden Paradise, 1995, Naked Souls, 1996, Baywatch: Hawaiian Wedding, 2003, (guest appearances): (TV series) Charles in Charge, 1990, Married...with Children, 1990, 1991, Top of the Heap, 1991, Days of Our Lives, 1992, The Nanny, 1997, Home Improvement, 1997, Just Shoot Me, 2001, Less Than Perfect, 2002, (guest appearances, voice) Futurama, 1999,: (films) Snapdragon, 1993, Raw Justice, 1994, Naked Souls, 1995, Barb Wire, 1996, Scary Movie 3, 2003, Borat, 2006, Blond and Blonder, 2007, Superhero Movie, 2008, (music videos for) Aerosmith, Lit, Cinderella, Vince Neil, Bree Sharp, Methods of Mayhem, Jaz-Z, Kid Rock; author: (novels) Star, 2004. Activist PETA; participant Nat. Conf. Viral Hepatitis, Can. Liver Found.; founder Pamela Anderson Found.; grand marshall S.O.S. ride Am. Liver Found., 2002. Recipient Linda McCartney award for animal rights, 1999. Achievements include has appeared a record twelve times on the cover of Playboy.

ANDERSON, PAUL IRVING, management executive; b. Portland, Oreg., Mar. 23, 1935; s. William F. and Ruth M. (Sundquist) Anderson; m. Lorraine A. Franz, Nov. 21, 1959; children: Todd, Susan, Cheryl, Cynthia. BS, Oreg. State U., 1956. Various positions in mktg., sales and engring. mgmt. 3M Co., St. Paul, Boston, 1956—74, gen. mgr. Brussels, 1974—77, dir. group bus. planning St. Paul, 1977—79; sr. v.p., gen. mgr. Rayovac Corp., Madison, Wis., 1979—82; pres. Anderson Cons. Co., Madison, 1982—83; divsn. v.p. RCA Corp., Indpls., 1983—84; pres. Anderson & Assocs., La Costa, Calif., 1984—87; pres., CEO Electro-Imaging Advisors, Inc., La Jolla, Calif., 1987—93; CEO Strategic Catalysts Inc., La Jolla, 1993—2004. Mem.: Am. Mgmt. Assn., Nakoma Golf Club, Columbia Club (Indpls.), Madison Club. Sigma Tau, Pi Tau Sigma, Tau Beta Pi. Republican. Presbyterian.

ANDERSON, PAUL THOMAS, film director, film producer, scriptwriter; b. Studio City, Calif., June 26, 1970; 1 child (with Maya Rudolph) Pearl Attended, Emerson Coll., Boston. Writer, dir. (films) The Dirk Diggler Story, 1988, Cigarettes & Coffee, 1993, Sydney, 1996, Flagpole Special, 1998, Mattress Man Commercial, 2003, Blossoms & Blood, 2003, writer, dir., prodr. Boogie Nights, 1997 (Metro Media award, 1997, New Generation award, LA Film Critics Assn., 1997, Best New Filmmaker, Boston Soc. Film Critics, 1997), Magnolia, 1999 (Best Dir., Best Screenplay, Toronto Film Critics. Assn., 1999, Film of Yr., San Sebastian Internat. Film Festival, 2000, Golden Berlin Bear award, 2000), Punch-Drunk Love, 2002 (Best Dir., Toronto Film Critics Assn., 2002, Best Screenplay, Gijon Internat. Film Festival, 2002, Propeller of Motovun, 2003, Best Dir., Audience award, 2003, Best Dir., Best Original Screenplay, Ctrl. Ohio Film Critics Assn., 2003), There Will Be Blood, 2007 (Best Dir., LA Film Critics Assn., 2007, Best Screenplay, Best Dir., San Diego Film Critics Soc., 2007, Best Dir., Nat. Soc. Film Critics Assn., 2008), writer, dir. (TV films) SNL Fanatic, 2000; dir.: (TV films) Couch, 2003. Office: Endeavor Agy 9601 Wilshire Blvd 3rd Fl Beverly Hills CA 90212

ANDERSON, PETER MACARTHUR, retired lawyer; b. New Castle, Ind., July 15, 1937; s. Earl Canute and Catherine Elizabeth (Schultz) A.; m. Ann Warren Gibson, Sept.1, 1962; children: David, Karen. AB, Dartmouth Coll., 1959; LLB, Stanford U., 1962. Bar: Calif. 1963, Wash. 2009. Assoc. O'Melveny & Myers, LA, 1966-70, Bogle & Gates, Seattle, 1970-74, mem., 1974-99; ptnr. Preston Gates & Ellis, Seattle, 1999—2002, sr. counsel, 2003—05; ret. Co-chmn. equal employment law com. ABA, 1983-86. Mem. Ecumenical Commn. for Seattle Archdiocese, St. Petersburg-Seattle Sister Chs. Com. Capt. U.S. Army, 1963-65. Fellow Coll. Labor and Employment Lawyers; mem. Phi Beta Kappa. Roman Catholic. Home: 9200 SE 57th St Mercer Island WA 98040-5005

ANDERSON, R. JOHN, apparel executive; BCommerce, Univ. New South Wales, 1972. Mgmt. positions Johnson & Johnson, H.J. Heinz Co.; mgmt. positions through v.p. merchandising & product develop. Levi Strauss & Co., San Francisco, 1979—95; gen. mgr. Levi Strauss Canada, 1996—98; pres. Levi Strauss Canada & Latin Am., 1996—98; pres. Asia Pacific Levi Strauss & Co., San Francisco, 1999—2004; interim pres. Levi Strauss Europe, 2003—04; sr. v.p., pres. Asia Pacific & global sourcing Levi Strauss & Co., San Francisco, 2004—06, sr. v.p., COO, 2006, pres., CEO, 2006—. Office: Levi Strauss & Co Levi's Plz 1155 Battery St San Francisco CA 94111

ANDERSON, RACHAEL KELLER (RACHAEL KELLER), retired library director; b. NYC, Jan. 15, 1938; d. Harry and Sarah Keller; m. Howard D. Goldwyn; children: Rebecca Anderson, Michael Goldwyn, Bryan Goldwyn, David Goldwyn. AB, Barnard Coll., 1959; MS, Columbia U., 1960. Librarian CCNY, 1960-62; librarian Mt. Sinai Med. Ctr., NYC, 1964-73, dir. library, 1973-79; dir. Health Scis Libr. Columbia U., NYC, 1979-91, acting v.p., univ. libr., 1982; dir. Ariz. Health Scis. Libr., U. Ariz., Tucson, 1991-2001; assoc. dir. Ariz. Telemedicine Program, 1996—2001; ret., 2001. Bd. dirs. Med. Libr. Ctr. of N.Y., N.Y.C., 1983-91; mem. biomed. libr. rev. com. Nat. Libr. Medicine, Bethesda, Md., 1984-88, chmn., 1987-88; mem. bd. regents Nat. Libr. Medicine, 1990-94, chmn., 1993-94; pres. Ariz. Health Info. Network, 1995. Contbr. articles to profl. jours. Mem. Med. Libr. Assn. (pres.-elect 1996-97, pres. 1997-98, bd. dirs. 1983-86, 98-99), Assn. Acad. Health Scis. Libr. Dirs. (bd. dirs. 1983-86, 90-93, pres. 1991-92). E-mail: rachaela@ahsl.arizona.edu.

ANDERSON, RICHARD ERNEST, agricultural engineer, consultant, rancher; b. North Little Rock, Ark., Mar. 8, 1926; s. Victor Ernest and Lillian Josephine (Griffin) A.; m. Mary Ann Fitch, July 18, 1953; children: Vicki Lynn, Lucia Anita. BSCE, U. Ark., 1949; MSE, U. Mich., 1959. Registered profl. engr., Mich., Va., Tex. Commd. ensign USN, 1952, advanced through grades to capt., 1968, ret., 1974; v.p. Ocean Resources, Inc., Houston, 1974-77; mgr. maintenance and ops. Holmes & Narver, Inc., Orange, Calif., 1977-78; pres. No. Resources, Inc., Billings, Mont., 1978-81; v.p. Holmes & Narver, Inc., Orange, Calif., 1981-82; owner, operator Anderson Ranch, registered Arabian horses, Pony, Mont., 1982—; pres., dir. Carbon Resources Inc., Butte, Mont., 1983-88, Agri Resources, Inc., Butte, Mont., 1988-95, Anderson Holdings, Inc., Pony, Mont., 1995—. Trustee Lake Barcroft-Virginia Watershed Improvement Dist., 1973-74; pres. Lake Barcroft-Virginia Recreation Center, Inc., 1972-73. With USAAF, 1944-45. Decorated Silver Star, Legion of Merit with Combat V (2), Navy Marine Corps medal, Bronze Star with Combat V, Meritorious Service medal, Purple Heart; Anderson Peninsula in Antarctica named in his honor. Mem.: ASCE. Republican. Methodist. Office: Anderson Holdings Inc PO Box 266 Pony MT 59747-0266

ANDERSON, R(OBERT) GREGG, real estate company executive; b. St. Joseph, Mo., Oct. 3, 1928; s. Clarence William and Marie Louise (Newman) A.; m. Janice Kimrey, May 6, 2001; 1 child, Robert Gregg Jr. Student, U. Okla., 1948-49, U. Tulsa, 1950. Pres. Gregg Anderson Realty, San Diego, 1959-63; v.p. Trousdale Constrn. Co., LA, 1963-67; pres. Amfac Properties div. Amfac, Inc., Honolulu, 1967-69; v.p. Amfac, Inc., Honolulu, 1967-69, sr. v.p., 1969-74; pres., chmn. bd. Accent Enterprises, Inc., Amfac Communities, Inc., Amfac Silverado Corp., Neilson Way Corp., 745 Fort St. Corp., Cen. Oahu Land Corp., L.A. Environ. Structures, Inc., 1969-74; chmn. bd. West Maui Properties, Inc., 1969-74; v.p. Silverado Country Club & Resort, Inc., 1969-74; pres. Gregg Anderson Realty & Devel., Inc., 1974—, Villa Pacific Bldg. Co., 1980—; gen. ptnr. Rancho Vista Devel. Co., Palmdale, Calif., 1980—; pres. Videocable, Inc., Palmdale, 1984-87; gen. ptnr. ProRep Assocs., 1991—. Bd. dirs. Antelope Valley Bd. Trade, 1991—. With USNR, 1950-54. Named Builder of Yr., Calif. Bldg. Industry Assn., 1998; inductee Calif. Bldg. Industry Hall of Fame, 1999. Mem. Bldg. Industry Assn. (bd. dirs. 1984-94), Rotary (hon.), Kiwanis (hon.). Republican. Avocations: tennis, golf, bowling. Office: Rancho Vista Devel Co 3011 Rancho Vista Blvd Ste F Palmdale CA 93551-4823 Office Phone: 661-265-9895.

ANDERSON, ROBERT MARSHALL, retired bishop; b. SI, NY, Dec. 18, 1933; s. Arthur Harold and Hazel Schneider A.; m. Mary Artemis Evans, Aug. 24, 1960; children: Martha, Elizabeth, Catherine, Thomas. BA, Colgate U., 1955; STB, Berkeley Div. Sch., 1961, DD (hon.), 1977, Seabury Western Sem., 1978, Yale U., 1977. Ordained priest Episcopal Ch. Curate St. John's Ch., Stamford, Conn., 1961-63, vicar, 1963-67, assoc. rector, 1968-72; priest in charge Middle Haddan, Conn., 1963-67; rector, 1967-68; dean St. Mark's Cathedral, Salt Lake City, 1972-78; bishop Episcopal Diocese of Minn., Mpls., 1978-93; interim recotr Church of the Holy Spirit, Lake Forest, Ill., 1994-95; asst. bishop Diocese of L.A., 1995-98. Served with U.S. Army. Danforth fellow, 1959-60. Mem. Berkeley Alumni Assn. (pres. 1972-76). Clubs: Mpls, Minikahda. Democrat. Office: Diocese of LA PO Box 512164 Los Angeles CA 90051-0164 Home: 9 Cassis Dana Point CA 92629-4018

ANDERSON, RONALD DELAINE, education educator; b. Poplar, Wis., Aug. 25, 1937; s. Leslie A. and Linnea A. (Bergsten) A.; m. Sandra Jean Wendt, June 1, 1963; children— Debra Jean, Timothy James, Nathan David. BS, U. Wis., 1959, PhD, 1964. Asst. prof. edn. Kans. State U., Manhattan, 1964-65; mem. faculty U. Colo., Boulder, 1965—, prof. edn., 1971—2007, asso. dean edn., 1972-78, prof. emeritus, edn., 2007—; exec. dir. Easy Yoke Retreat Ctr., 2007—. Cons. to numerous ednl. agys. Author: Religion and Spirituality in the Public School Curriculum, 2004, Religion and Teaching, 2008; co-author: Developing Children's Thinking Through Science, 1970, Issues of Curriculum Reform, 1994, Local Leadership for Science Education Reform, 1995, Portraits of Productive Schools, 1995, Study of Curriculum Reform, 1996; contbr. articles to profl. jours. Program dir. NSF, 1989—90. Fulbright scholar, 1986-87, Fellow AAAS (chair edn. sect. 1998-99, mem. Assn. Coun. 2002-05); mem. Nat. Assn. Rsch. Sci. Tchg. (pres. 1975-76), Assn. Edn. Tchrs. in Sci. (pres. 1972-73), Nat. Sci. Tchrs. Assn., Phi Delta Kappa. Home: 4800 North Creek Rd Beulah CO 81023-9601 Office: Easy Yoke Retreat Ctr Beulah CO 81023

ANDERSON, ROSS CARL, Mayor, Salt Lake City, Utah, lawyer, human rights advocate; b. Logan, Utah, Sept. 9, 1951; s. E. LeRoy and Grace (Rasmussen) Anderson; 1 child, Lucas Craig Arment. BS in Philosophy magna cum laude, U. Utah, 1973; JD with honors, George Washington U., 1978. Bar: U.S. Dist. Ct. Utah 1978. Assoc. Berman & Giauque, Salt Lake City, 1978-80; v.p., ptnr. Berman & Anderson, Rooker Larsen Kimball & Parr, Salt Lake City, 1980-82; ptnr. Berman & Anderson, Salt Lake City, 1982-85; ptnr., v.p. Hansen & Anderson, Salt Lake City, 1986-89, Anderson & Watkins, Salt Lake City, 1989-92; pres. Anderson & Karrenberg, Salt Lake City, 1992-98, of counsel, 1999; mayor Salt Lake City, 2000—08; founder & pres. High Rd. for Human Rights Edn. Project, High Rd. for Human Rights Advocacy Project. Columnist: Enterprise, 1997—98, I-15 Mag., 2000—01, Catalyst, 2002—. Pres. bd. dirs. Citizens Penal Reform, 1991—94, Guadalupe Edni. Programs, Salt Lake City, 1985—96, 1997—99, ACLU Utah, 1980—85; bd. dirs. Common Cause Utah, 1987—89, Planned Parenthood Utah, 1979—83; mem. Salt Lake Com. Fgn. Rels., 1983—95; Dem. candidate for Congress Utah 2d Congl. Dist., 1996. Mem.: Utah State Bar Assn. Avocations: history, skiing. Home: 418 Douglas St Salt Lake City UT 84102-3231 Office: 438 E 200 S Salt Lake City UT 84111 Office Phone: 801-364-3564 ext. 117.

ANDERSON, STEPHEN HALE, federal judge; b. Salt Lake City, Jan. 12, 1932; m. Shirlee Gehring; 2 children. Student, Eastern Oreg. Coll. Edn., LaGrande, 1951, Brigham Young U., Provo, 1956; LLB, U. Utah, 1960. Bar: Utah 1960, US Claims Ct. 1963, US Tax Ct. 1967, US Ct. Appeals (10th cir.) 1970, U.S. Supreme Ct. 1971, US Ct. Appeals (9th cir.) 1972. Tchr. South H.S., Salt Lake City, 1956—57; trial atty. tax divsn. US Dept. Justice, 1960—64; ptnr. Ray, Quinney & Nebeker, 1964—85; judge US Ct. Appeals (10th cir.), Salt Lake City, 1985—2000, sr. judge, 2000—. Spl. counsel Salt Lake County Grand Jury, 1975; mem. Nat. Jud. Coun. State and Fed. Cts., 1992—96; chmn. fed.-state jurisdiction com. Jud. Conf. U.S., 1995—98; ad hoc. com. on bankruptcy appellate panels 10th Cir. Jud. Coun., 1995—97; com. mem. US Ct. Appeals (10th cir.). Editor (in chief): Utah Law Rev. With US Army, 1953—55. Mem.: Am. Bar Found., Salt Lake County Bar Assn. (pres. 1977—78), Utah State Bar (pres. 1983—84), U. Utah Coll. Law Alumni Assn. (trustee 1979—83, pres. 1982—83), Salt Lake Area C. of C. (bd.govs. 1984), Order of Coif. Office: US Ct Appeals 4201 Fed Bldg 125 S State St Salt Lake City UT 84138-1102

ANDERSON, THEODORE WILBUR, statistics educator; b. Mpls., June 5, 1918; s. Theodore Wilbur and Evelynn (Johnson) A.; m. Dorothy Fisher, July 8, 1950; children: Robert Lewis, Janet Lynn, Jeanne Elizabeth. BS with highest distinction, Northwestern U., 1939, DSc, 1989; MA, Princeton U., 1942, PhD, 1945; LittD, North Park U., 1988; PhD (honoris causa), U. Oslo, 1997; D (hon.), U. Athens, 1999. Asst. dept. math. Northwestern U., 1939-40; instr. math. Princeton U., 1941-43, rsch. assoc., 1943-45, Cowles Commn., U. Chgo., 1945-46; staff Columbia U., 1946-67, successively instr. math. stats., asst. prof., assoc. prof., 1946-56, prof., 1956-67, chmn. math. stats. dept., 1956-60, 64-65, acting chmn., 1950-51, 63; prof. stats. and econs. Stanford U., 1967-88, prof. stats. and econs. emeritus, 1988—. Dir. project Office Naval Rsch., 1950-82; prin. investigator NSF project, 1969-92, Army Rsch. Office project, 1982-92; vis. prof. math. U. Moscow, 1968; vis. prof. stats. U. Paris, 1968; vis. prof. econs. NYU, 1983-84; acad. visitor math. Imperial Coll. Sci. and Tech., U. London, 1967-68, London Sch. Econs. and Polit. Sci., 1974-75, U. So. Calif., 1989; C.G. Khatri Meml. lectr. Pa. State U., 1992; rsch. visitor Tokyo Inst. Tech., 1977; sabbaticant IBM Systems Rsch. Inst., 1984; rsch. assoc. Naval Postgrad. Sch., 1986-87; cons. RAND Corp., 1949-66; mem. com. on basic rsch. adv. Office Ordnance Rsch., Nat. Acad. Scis.-NRC, 1955-58; mem. panel on applied math. adv. Nat. Bur. Standards, 1964-65; chmn. com. on stats. NRC, 1961-63; mem. exec. com. Conf. Bd. Math. Scis., 1963-64; mem. com. on support rsch. in math. scis. NAS, 1965-68; mem. com. Pres.'s Statis. Socs., 1962-64; sci. dir. NATO Advanced Study Inst. on Discriminant Analysis and Its Applications, 1972. Author: An Introduction to Multivariate Statistical Analysis, 1958, 3d edit., 2003, The Statistical Analysis of Time Series, 1971, (with Somesh Das Gupta and George P.H. Styan) A Bibliography of Multivariate Statistical Analysis, 1972, (with Stanley Sclove) Introductory Statistical Analysis, 1974, An Introduction to the Statistical Analysis of Data, 1986, (with Jeremy D. Finn) The New Statistical Analysis of Data, 1996; editor: (with Krishna B. Athreya and Donald L. Iglehart) Probability, Statistics and Mathematics: Papers in Honor of Samuel Karlin, 1989, (with Kai Tai Fang) Statistical Inference in Elliptically Contoured and Related Distributions, 1990; (with K.T. Fang and I. Olkin) Multivariate Analysis and Its Applications, 1994; editor Anns. of Math. Stats., 1950-52; assoc. editor jour. Time Series Analysis, 1980-88; mem. adv. bd. Econometric Theory, 1985—, Jour. Multivariate Analysis, 1988—; mem. editl. bd. Psychometrika, 1954-72. Recipient R.A. Fisher award Pres.'s Statis. Socs., 1985, Disting. Alumnus award North Park Coll. and Theol. Sem., 1987, Minnehaha Acad., 1992, Award of Merit Northwestern U. Alumni Assn., 1989; named Wesley C. Mitchell Vis. Prof. Columbia U., 1983-84; Guggenheim fellow, 1947-48, fellow Ctr. for Advanced Study in Behavioral Scis., 1957-58; vis. scholar, 1972-73, 80; Sherman Fairchild disting. scholar Calif. Inst. Tech., 1980; vis. disting. prof. Norwegian Coun. Sci. and Indsl. Rsch. U. Oslo; Abraham Wald Meml. lectr., 1982; S.S. Wilks lectr. Princeton U., 1983, P.C. Mahalanobis Meml. lectr., 1985, S.N. Roy Meml. lectr. Calcutta U., 1985, Allen T. Craig lectr. U. Iowa, 1991, C.G. Khatri Meml. lectr. Pa. State U., 1992, George Zyskind Meml. lectr. Iowa State U., 1995. Fellow AAAS (chmn. sect. 1990-91), Am. Statis. Assn. (v.p. 1971-73, Samuel S. Wilks Meml. medal 1988, R.A. Fisher lectr. 1985), Econometric Soc., Royal Statis. Soc., Inst. Math. Stats. (pres. 1963), Am. Acad. Arts and Scis.; mem. NAS, Am. Math. Soc., Internat. Statis. Insts., Bernouilli Soc. for Math. Stats. and Probability, Norwegian Acad. Sci. and Letters (fgn.), Phi Beta Kappa. Achievements include research in multivariate statistical analysis, time series analysis, and econometrics. Home: 746 Santa Ynez St Stanford CA 94305-8441 Office: Stanford U Dept Stats Stanford CA 94305-4065 Home Phone: 650-327-5204; Office Phone: 650-723-4732. Business E-Mail: twa@stanford.edu.

ANDERSON, THOMAS A., state legislator; b. May 8, 1933; 5 children. BS in Chemistry, St. Benedict Coll., Atchison, Kans. Commd. USN, 1977, advanced through ranks to lt. comdr.; ret., 1997; comdg. gen. 1st brigade N.Mex. State Def. Force; v.p. Paradise Hills Civil Assn.; mem. consumer and pub. affairs, energy and natural resources, and enrolling and engrossing B coms. N.Mex. House of Reps., Santa Fe, state rep. dist. 29, mem. Dist. 29, 2002—. Republican. Office: State Capitol Rm 412C Santa Fe NM 87501 Office Phone: 505-986-4451. E-mail: kb5ysg@arrl.net.

ANDERSON, TOM, former Internet company executive; b. Oct. 13, 1975; BA in English and Rhetoric, U. Calif., Berkeley, 1997; M in Film-Critical Studies, UCLA, 2000. Mem. creative dept. Xdrive Technologies, Inc., asst. mktg. dept.; co-founder ResponseBase Mktg., LLC, 2002, MySpace.com, 2003, pres., 2003—09. Recipient Vanguard award, Prodrs. Guild America, 2009; co-recipient with Chris DeWolfe, Breakout of Yr., Webby award, Internat. Acad. Digital Arts and Scis., 2006; named one of The 100 Most Influential People in the World, TIME mag., 2006, with Chris Dewolfe, 25 Most Influential People in Web Music, Powergeek 25, 2007. Fellow: World Network Found. Achievements include MySpace.com being the most popular social networking website on the internet.*

ANDERSON, WAYNE CARL, global public affairs officer, retired corporate financial executive; b. Sheboygan, Wis., May 5, 1935; s. Chester Phillip and Mabel Mary A.; m. Joan Dorothy Staranick, May 18, 1963; children: David Wayne, Steven Michael, Karen Colleen. BS in Bus. Adminstrn., Upsala Coll., 1977. Cert. arbitrator, mediator. Dir. state govt. rels. Nabisco Brands Co., Parsippany, NJ, 1974-78, dir. fed. govt. rels., 1978-79, dir. govt. rels., 1979-81, v.p. govt. rels., 1981-84, v.p. govt. and cmty. rels., 1984-87, v.p. pub. affairs, 1987; non-lawyer exec. Evans Kitchel & Jenckes, P.C., 1988-89; pres., CEO Ariz. C. of C., 1990-95; exec. v.p. Americare, 1996-98; exec. emeritus Thunderbird--The Am. Grad. Sch. Internat. Mgmt., 1999—. Guest lectr. in field. Editl. adv. bd. Pub. Affairs in Rev., 1980; contbr. articles to profl. jours. Mem. Roseland (N.J.) Planning Bd., 1978—79, Roseland Citizens Adv. Com., 1977—78, Gov.'s Adv. Coun. on Quality, 1991—95, Gov.'s Commn. Econ. Devel., 1991—95, Ariz. Space Commn., 1992—2000, commr. emeritus, 1996; trustee State Govt. Rsch. and Edn. Found., 1981—82; bd. dirs. Ariz. Quality Alliance, 1992—95, NCCJ, Fiesta Bowl Com., Ariz. Econ. Forum, Philos. Soc. Ariz., 2001—04; statewide com. chmn. Superbowl XXX, 1995—96; chmn. adv. bd. NYU, Baruch Coll., U. N.Y.; pres. Grace Luth. Ch., Livingston, NJ, 1980—81, chmn. bd. elders, 1981—82, Redeemer Luth. Ch., Scottsdale, Ariz., 1997—98, 2005—, v.p., 1998—; trustee Evang. Luth. Synod, 2003—; pres. State Govtl. Affairs Coun.; bd. dirs. Luth. Schs. Am., 2006—; chmn. bd. Ariz. Investment Coun., 2007. With US Army, 1958—60. Mem. Internat. Jaycees (senator 1989—), U.S. Jaycees (nat. dir. 1964-65), Pub. Affairs Coun. (exec. com. 1986, bd. dirs. 1988—), Nat. Fgn. Trade Coun. (dir. 1986), State Govt. Affairs Coun. (past pres. 1978-79), Ford's Theatre (bd. govs.), Acad. Polit. Sci., Pub. Affairs Profls. Ariz. (founder 1987—), Thunderbird Am. Grad. Sch. Internat. Mgmt., Thunderbird Global Coun., Consular Corps Ariz.(hon.) E-mail: wayneanderson@cox.net.

ANDERSON, WILLIAM SCOVIL, classics educator; b. Brookline, Mass., Sept. 16, 1927; s. Edgar Weston and Katrina (Brewster) A.; m. Lorna Candee Bassette, June 12, 1954 (dec. Dec. 1977); children: Judith, Blythe, Heather, Meredith, Keith; m. Deirdre Burt, May 28, 1983. BA, Yale U., New Haven, Conn., 1950, PhD, 1954; AB, Cambridge U., Eng., 1952, MA, 1955. Prix de Rome fellow Am. Acad. in Rome, 1954-55; instr. classics Yale U., 1955-59; resident in Rome, Morse fellow, 1959-60; mem. faculty U. Calif., Berkeley, 1960-94, prof. Latin and comparative lit., 1966-94, prof. charge Intercollegiate Ctr. Classical Studies, 1967-68, chmn. classics, 1970-73. Rsch. prof. U. Melbourne, 1984; Robson lectr. Victoria Coll., Toronto, 1987; Blegen rsch. prof. Vassar Coll., 1989-90, vice chair comparative lit., 1990-93; vis. disting. prof. Fla. State U., spring 1995; Gail Burnett lectr. San Diego State U., 2001; vis. prof. Ohio State U., 2003; vis. Case prof. Ind. U., 2005. Author: The Art of the Aeneid, 1969, Ovid, Metamorphoses, Critical Text, 1977, Essays on Roman Satire, 1982, Barbarian Play: Plautus' Roman Comedy, 1993, Ovid's Metamorphoses 1-5 and 6-10 Text and Commentary, 1972, 2d edit., 1997, Why Horace?, 1998; co-editor (with L.N. Quartarone) Approaches to Teaching Vergil's Aeneid, 2002. With US Army, 1946—48, Korea. Recipient Berkeley citation, 1994; NEH sr. fellow, 1973-74. Mem.: Danforth Assocs., Am. Philol. Assn. (pres. 1977), Soc. Religions. Episcopalian. Office: Univ Calif Dept Classics Berkeley CA 94720 Business E-Mail: wsand@berkeley.edu.

ANDERSON, WILLIAM WALLACE, financial executive; b. Balt., Apr. 8, 1958; s. Joseph Merryman II and Ann Marie (Moran) Anderson; m. Marian A. Gannon, July 24, 1987; children: Ciara Ann, Deirdre Christine. BA in Acctg., U. West Fla., 1980. CPA, Md., Calif. Audit staff to supr. Coopers & Lybrand, Balt., 1980-85, audit mgr. Dublin, 1985-87, Sacramento, 1987—92; dir. acctg. Raley's Supermarkets, Sacramento, 1992—97, v.p., contr., 1992—97, exec. v.p., CFO, 1997—. Bd. dirs., CFO Food for Families, Sacramento, 1990—. Mem. AICPA. Avocations: travel, basketball, tennis. Office: Raleys Supermarkets 500 W Capitol Ave West Sacramento CA 95605

ANDRASICK, JAMES STEPHEN, transportation executive; b. Passaic, NJ, Mar. 27, 1944; s. Stephen Adam and Emily (Spolnik) A.; children: Christopher J., Gregory O.; m. Ginger Michael Simon, Feb. 22, 1997. BS, USCG Acad., 1965; MS, MIT, 1971. Commd. ensign USCG, 1965, advanced through grades to lt., 1968; assigned to Vietnam, 1967-68; sys. analyst Jamesbury Corp., 1970; corp. fin. and product devel. staffs Ford Motor Co., 1971-74; mgr. corp. devel. IU Internat. Corp., Phila., 1974-78; from v.p. planning, contr. to exec. v.p. C. Brewer & Co., Ltd., Honolulu, 1978-92, pres., 1992-2000; sr. v.p., CFO, treas. Alexander & Baldwin, Inc., Honolulu, 2000—02, exec. v.p., 2002; pres., CEO Matson Navigation Co., 2002—. Chmn. bd., mng. gen. ptnr. ML Macadamia Orchards LP, 1986-88; chmn. bd. HCPC, Olokele Sugar Co., Hawaiian Sugar and Transp. Coop., 1993-96; chmn. Hawaiian Sugar Planters Assn., 1992-93; bd. dirs. Wailuku Agribus. Co., C. Brewer Co., Ltd., Honolulu. Bd. dirs. Aloha United Way, Honolulu, 1983-89, Hawaii Opera Theater, 2001-03; treas., bd. dirs. ARC, Hawaii, 1983-94, 96-2002, chmn., 1989-90; bd. dirs. Hawaii Employers Coun., 1992-98, chmn., 1995-98; trustee UH Found., 1988-94, vice chmn., 1992-93, chmn., 1993-94; trustee Hawaii Maritime Ctr., 1993-98; bd. dirs. Coast Guard Found., 1997—, Honolulu Symphony, 2002-05; trustee Mills Coll., 2004-. Mem.: San Francisco Nat. Maritime Pk. Assn. (bd. dirs.), Standard Club. Office: Matson Navigation Inc 555 12th St Oakland CA 94607 Business E-Mail: jandrasick@matson.com.

ANDRASSY, KYRA E., lawyer; b. Fontana, Calif., Nov. 27, 1972; BA, Univ. Calif., San Diego, 1995; JD, Loyola Law Sch., 1998. Bar: Calif. 2000, US Dist. Ct. No., Ea., Ctrl. & So. Calif. Law clk. Judge John E. Ryan, US Bankruptcy Ct., 1998—2000; assoc., bus. & bankruptcy litigation Weiland, Golden, Smiley, Wang Ekvall & Strok LLP, Costa Mesa, Calif. Editor: Loyola Law Rev., 1997—98. Named a Rising Star, So. Calif. Super Lawyers, 2006. Mem.: Orange County Bar Assn., Orange County Bankruptcy Forum. Office: Weiland Golden Smiley Wang Ekvall & Strok Ste 950 Ctr Tower 650 Town Ctr Dr Costa Mesa CA 92626 Office Phone: 714-966-1000. Office Fax: 714-966-1002.

ANDRE, MICHAEL PAUL, physicist, educator; b. Des Moines, Apr. 25, 1951; s. Paul Leo and Pauline (Vermie) A.; m. Janice Joan Hanecak, Mar. 12, 1988. BA, Cen. U. Iowa, 1972; postgrad., U. Ariz., 1972-73; MS, UCLA, 1975, PhD, 1980; cert., Am. Bd. Radiology, 1999. Rsch. assoc. Inst. Atmospheric Physics, Tucson, 1972-73; mem. tech. staff Hughes Aircraft Co., LA, 1973-74; postgrad. researcher UCLA, 1974-77; cons. LA, 1975-84; med. radiologic physicist LACO/UCLA Olive View, LA, 1977-81; sr. radiation physicist Cedars-Sinai Med. Ctr., LA, 1979-84; chief med. physicist Dept. Vet. Affairs, San Diego, 1981—; prof. radiology, chief divsn.Physics and Engring. sch. medicine U. Calif., San Diego, 1981—; chief scientific officer Radco Corp., 1996—; chief med. officer Almen Labs., Inc., 1999—. Qualified expert Calif. Radiol. Health Dept., Berkeley, 1979—; chmn. Nat. Physics Conf., San Diego, 1984-89; mem. U.

Calif.-San Diego Cancer Ctr., 2004— Editor: Physics and Biology of Radiology, 1988, Investigative Radiology, 1990—, Acoustical Imaging vol. 28, 2007; guest editor: Internat. Jour. Imaging Sci. & Tech., 1997; contbr. articles to profl. jours. Mountain guide Sierra Club, L.A., 1977-80; dir. Ariz. PIRG, Tucson, 1973; mountain guide Am. Alpine Inst., Peru, 1987-90. Rsch. grantee U. Calif.-San Diego Found., 1989—, NIH, Nat. Cancer Inst., 1986—, VA, 1989—, U.S. Army, 1994—, Pfeiffer Rsch. Found., 2002—. Mem. Am. Assn. Physicists in Medicine, Am. Inst. Ultrasound in Medicine, San Diego Radiol. Soc., Am. Inst. Physics, Soc. Photo-Optical Inst. Engrs., Am. Coll. Radiology, Soc. of Breast Imaging. Avocations: auto racing, mountain climbing. Office: U Calif Dept Radiology 9114 La Jolla CA 92093 E-mail: mandre@ucsd.edu.

ANDREAS, CHRISTOPHER ERIC, lawyer; b. San Francisco, Dec. 15, 1963; s. Arthur Andreas. BA in English and History, Lewis & Clark Coll., Portland, Oreg., 1986; JD, San Francisco Law Sch., 1994. Bar: Calif. 1995, US Dist. Ct. No. Dist. Calif. Pvt. practice law, San Francisco, 1994—95; assoc. Brayton Purcell, Novato, Calif., 1995—2000, jr. ptnr., 2000—. Mem.: ACLU, Marin Trial Lawyers Assn., Bar Assn. San Francisco, Trial Lawyers for Pub. Justice, Consumer Attorneys of Calif. Office: Brayton Purcell 222 Rush Landing Rd Novato CA 94948-6169 Office Phone: 415-898-1555. Office Fax: 415-898-1247.

ANDREASEN, STEVEN W., lawyer; b. Salt Lake City, Sept. 17, 1948; BA, U. Utah, 1970, JD, 1974. Bar: Washington 1974. Mem. Davis Wright Tremaine, Seattle, 1974—. Comment Editor: Utah Law Review 1973-74. Mem. Seattle Estate Planning Coun., Order of Coif, Am. Coll. Trust and Estate Counsel. Office: Davis Wright Tremaine 1201 3rd Ave Ste 2200 Seattle WA 98101-3047

ANDREESSEN, MARC LOWELL, software company executive, internet innovator; b. Cedar Falls, Iowa, Apr. 26, 1971; m. Laura Arrillaga, 2006. BS in Computer Sci., U. Ill., Urbana-Champaign, 1993. With Enterprise Integration Technologies, 1993; co-founder Mosaic Comm. Corp. (now Netscape Comm. Corp.), Mountain View, Calif., 1994; v.p. tech. Netscape Comm. Corp., Mountain View, Calif., 1994-97, exec. v.p., 1997-99; chief tech. officer Am. Online Inc. (AOL), 1999; co-founder, chmn. Opsware Inc. (formerly Loudcloud), 1999—; chief tech. officer, co-founder Ning, Inc., 2004—. Bd. dirs. Facebook, Inc., 2008—. Named one of Top 50 People Under The Age of 40, TIME mag., 1994. Achievements include development of Mosaic graphical browser for the World Wide Web.*

ANDREOS, GEORGE PHILLIP, lawyer; b. Chgo., Jan. 20, 1935; s. Nicholas and Harriet (MacKenzie) A.; m. Beverly Chadwell, Aug. 28, 1965; children: Leslie, Linda, Darin, Craig. BA, U. Ill., 1957; JD, Calif. Western Sch. Law, San Diego, 1964. Bar: Calif. (so. dist., 9th cir.), 1965. Dep. city atty. City of San Diego, 1965-66; sole practitioner San Diego, 1966—. Contbr. articles to profl. jours. Bd. dirs. For Parents' and Kids' Sake, Poway, Calif., 1984-92. Capt. USMC, 1957-60. Mem. San Diego County Bar Assn. (treas. 1989, v.p. 1990, pres. 1991), Calif. Trial Lawyers Assn. (bd. govs. 1979-83), San Diego Trial Lawyers Assn. (bd. dirs. 1977-82, pres. 1981), Outstanding Trial Lawyer 1982), Consumer Attys. San Diego (bd. dirs. 2000—). Avocations: handball, hiking, avocado and grapefruit grower. Office: 11405 W Bernardo Ct Ste 203 San Diego CA 92127-1639 Fax: 858-675-8695. E-mail: GAndreos@aol.com.

ANDREW, JANE HAYES, non-profit organization executive; b. Phila., Jan. 1, 1947; d. David Powell and Vivian Muriel (Seager) Hayes; m. Brian David Andrew, June 14, 1977; 1 child, Kevin Hayes. AB, Barnard Coll., 1968; grad., Harvard Arts Adminstrn. Inst., 1972; MBA, U. Wash., 1994. Mgr. theater Minor Latham Playhouse, Barnard Coll., NYC, 1970-74; co. mgr. Houston Ballet, 1974-77, Ballet West, Salt Lake City, 1978-83; gen. mgr. Pacific N.W. Ballet, Seattle, 1983-87. Organizer non-profit consortium nat. ballet cos. and nat. presenting orgns., 1987; pres., exec. dir. Ballet/America, 1988-91; ind. cons. arts mgmt., 1991-94; dir. Found. for Internat. Understanding Through Students, 1995-97; panelist NEA Dance Program Presentors, 1987-88, 88-89, 89-90, Seattle Arts Commn. dance grants, 1989, 90; cons. Ariz. Arts Commn., Phoenix, 1985-86; com. mem. 25th Anniversary of World's Fair, Seattle, 1986-87; panelist NEA Local Programs, 1987; vol. Interlace H.S., 1997. Editor (directory) Philadelphia Cultural Orgns., 1977. Bd. dirs. Good Shepherd Adv. Bd., Seattle, 1985-87. Recipient Dorothy D. Spivack award Barnard Coll., 1972. Mem. Dance/USA (chmn. mgrs. coun. 1986). Home and Office: 7706 146th Ave NE Redmond WA 98052-4105

ANDREW, LOUISE BRIGGS, emergency physician, medical legal consultant; b. High Point, NC, May 6, 1951; d. Eugene Leroy Briggs Jr. and Maria Elizabeth (Brockmann) Miller; m. Clifford George Andrew, June 13, 1970 (div.); children: Galen Michael, Amalie Linnea; m. Theodore Edward Harrison, Oct. 26, 1987. MD, Duke U., Durham, NC, 1975; JD in Health Law, U. Md., 1991. Bar:; cert. in Emergency Medicine. Intern, fellow emergency medicine Duke U. Hosp., 1975—76; resident internal medicine Johns Hopkins Hosp., Balt., 1976—78, resident pulmonary intensive care, 1978; assoc. dir. emergency medicine Francis Scott Key Med. Ctr., Balt., 1976; assoc. dir. Ctr. Profl. Well Being, Durham; asst. prof. internal/emergency medicine Johns Hopkins U. Sch. Medicine, 1980—92; founder, consultant MDMentor.com, 1992—. Co-founder, past pres. Coalition & Ctr. for Ethical Med. Testimony, 2003. Contbr. articles to profl. jours., chapters to books; spkr. in field. Recipient Disting. Alumni award, Johns Hopkins Emergency Medicine Residency Prog., 2000. Fellow: Internat. Fedn. Emergency Medicine, Am. Coll. Emergency Physicians (life; sec. Md. chpt. 1982—86, mem. Med. Legal Com., Profl. Liability Task Force, chair Personal & Profl. Well-Being Com., Council Meritorious Svc. award 2002, James D. Mills Outstanding Contbn. to Emergency Medicine award 2005); mem.: ABA, AMA, AAUP, Emergency Medicine Residents' Assn. (charter mem.), Soc. Acad. Emergency Medicine, Soc. Internat. Advancement Emergency Medicine (co-founder 1989, sec. 1989—93, Founder's award 1995), Soc. Profl. Wellbeing, Nat. Health Lawyers Assn., Am. Med. Women's Assn., Am. Assn. Women Emergency Physicians (pres. 1987—89, bd. dirs. 1990—93, Leadership award 1989, Well-Being in Emergency Medicine award 1996). Achievements include being one of the first physicians in the country to be certified as a specialist in emergency medicine, and one of the first faculty members at Hopkins to teach this discipline. Avocations: piano, flute, singing, calligraphy, languages. Office: MDMentor 403 S Lincoln St Ste 4 51 Port Angeles WA 98362 Office Phone: 425-609-0039. Business E-Mail: mail@lbandrew.com.*

ANDREW, LUCIUS ARCHIBALD DAVID, III, bank executive; b. Mar. 5, 1938; s. Lucius Archibald David Jr. and Victoria (Rollins) A.; m. Susan Ott, June 1, 1963 (div. 1973); children: Ashley W., L.A. David IV; m. Phoebe Haffner Kellogg, Dec. 21, 1974; children: Gaylord M., Charles H., Matthew K., Louise K. BS, U. Pa., 1962; MBA, NYU, 1965. Asst. treas. The Bank of N.Y., NYC, 1962-68; instl. salesman Drexel, Harriman, Ripley, NYC, 1968-70; v.p., br. mgr. Drexel, Firestone, Inc., Chgo., 1970-72; ptnr., br. mgr. Fannestock & Co., Chgo., 1972-74; pres. N.E.A., Inc., 1975-85; dir. First Am. Bank Corp., Chgo., 1985—. Vice chmn. Viner's, Ltd., Sheffield, Eng., 1981-82; chmn. exec. com. Cert. Mfg. Co., Shelton, Wash., 1975-85. Trustee Brooks Sch.; past trustee Seattle Repertory Theatre; bd. dirs. Swedish Met. Ctr. Found. Mem. The Brook, Racquet and Tennis Club (N.Y.C.), Racquet Club (Chgo.), Rainier Club, Univ. Club, Golf Club (Seattle), Tennis Club (Seattle). Home: The Highlands Seattle WA 98177 Office: 200 1st Ave W Ste 400 Seattle WA 98119-4219

ANDREWS, DONALD L., performing arts company executive; Pres., CEO Utah Symphony, Salt Lake City. Office: Utah Symphony Maurice Abravanel Hall 123 W South Temple Salt Lake City UT 84101-1496

ANDREWS, FRED CHARLES, mathematics professor; b. Aylesbury, Sask., Can., July 13, 1924; s. Henry Marmaduke and Margaret (Van de Bogart) A.; m. Joyce Davenny, Apr. 5, 1944; children— Linda (Mrs. Pierre Dunn), David W. (dec.), Gail E.(Mrs. Gregory Crandell). BS in Math, U. Wash., 1946, MS in Math. Statistics, 1948; PhD, U. Calif., Berkeley, 1953; PhD (hon.), U. Tampere, Finland, 1985. Research asso. Applied Math. and Statistics Lab., Stanford, 1952-54; asst. prof. math., asso. statistician U. Nebr., 1954-57; asso. prof. math. U. Oreg., 1957-66; dir. U. Oreg. (Statistics Lab. and Computing Center), 1960-69, prof. math., 1966-89, prof. emeritus math., 1989—, head dept. math., 1973-80. Vis. statistician Math Centrum, Amsterdam, The Netherlands, 1963-64; Fulbright-Hays sr. lectr. U. Tampere, Finland, 1969-70; Fulbright-Hays sr. lectr. Univ. Coll., Cork, Ireland, 1976-77; Fulbright sr. lectr. U. Jordan, Amman, 1983-84 Contbr. articles to profl. jours. Pres. Met.-Civic Club, Eugene-Springfield, 1967-68; Trustee Oreg. Grad. Center, 1967-77. Served to lt. (j.g.) USNR, 1943-46. Fellow AAAS; mem. Sigma Xi. Office: U Oreg Dept Math Eugene OR 97403 Personal E-mail: faja@comcast.net.

ANDREWS, J. DAVID, lawyer; b. Decatur, Ill., July 5, 1933; s. Jesse D. and Louise Glenna (Mason) A.; m. Helen Virginia Migely, July 12, 1958; children: Virginia, Robert, Michael, Betsy. BA magna cum laude, U. Ill., 1955, JD with honors, 1960. Bar: Wash. 1961. Ptnr. Perkins Coie, Seattle, 1960-96, sr. counsel, 1997—. Trustee AEF Pension Fund, 1975—79; bd. visitors U. Puget Sound Law Sch., 1976—94, Ill. Coll. Law, 2005—08; bd. dirs. Am. Bar Endowment, 1981—94, Endowment for Equal Justice, 2004—; pres. Am. Bar Endowment, 1985—87, Wash. Law Fund, 1997—98; bd. dirs., pres Am. Bar Ins. Plans Cons., Inc., 1991—. Contbr. articles to profl. jours Bd. dirs. Leukemia Soc. Wash., 1984-99, pres. 1985-91; nat. bd. dirs. Leukemia Soc. Am., 1992-96. Capt. USAF, 1955-57. Fellow Am. Bar Found. (bd. dirs., former treas.), Am. Coll. Trial Lawyers; mem. ABA (ho. of dels. 1967-69, 75—, asst. treas. 1972-74, treas. 1975-79, bd. govs. 1975-79, fed. judiciary standing com. 1985-90), Wash. Bar Assn. (chmn. pub. rels. com. 1971-73), Seattle-King County Bar Assn., Am. Judicature Soc. (bd. dirs. 1985-89), Phi Beta Kappa, Phi Kappa Phi, Phi Eta Sigma. Home: 9413 SW Quartermaster Dr Vashon WA 98070-7081 Office: Perkins Coie 1201 3rd Ave Ste 4000 Seattle WA 98101-3029 Office Phone: 206-359-8423. Business E-Mail: dandrews@perkinscoie.com.

ANDREWS, RICHARD OTIS, former art gallery director, curator; b. LA, Calif., Nov. 8, 1949; s. Robert and Theodora (Hammond) A.; m. Colleen Chartier, Jan. 3, 1976; 1 child, Bryce. BA, Occidential Coll., LA, 1971; BFA, U. Wash., 1973, MFA, 1975. Tech. design cons., project dir. for artist George Baker, West Germany, Nebr. and Calif., 1975—78; project mgr. City of Seattle Arts Commn., 1978—80, arts in pub. pls. coord., 1980—84; dir., visual arts program Nat. Endowment for Arts, 1985—87; dir. Henry Art Gallery, U. Wash., Seattle, 1987—2008. Co-curator Art Into Life: Russian Constructivism 1914-1932; curator James Turrell: Knowing Light, 2003, Maya-Lin: Systematic Landscapes, 2006; cons. pub. art program devel., 1982-84; bd. trustees Assn. Art Mus. Dirs., 1997-2000. Author: Insights/On Sites, 1984, James Turrell: Sensing Space, 1992, Maya-Lin: Systematic Landscapes, 2006; editor Artwork/Network, 1984; contbg. editor Going Public, 1988. Mem. Seattle Arts Commn., 2004—; pres. Skystone Found., Flagstaff, Ariz. Recipient Howard S. Wright award, Seattle Arts Commn., 1996, Anne Focke Arts Leadership award, 2007. Mem.: AIA (hon.).

ANDREWS, ROBERT GOFF, pediatrician, educator; b. Mpls., Jan. 28, 1949; s. James Edward and Marie Adelaide (Jones) A.; m. Carol Ann Chellino, July 1, 1979; 1 child, Joseph Einar. AB, Amherst Coll., 1972; MD, U. Minn., 1976. Diplomate Am. Bd. Pediats., Am. Bd. Pediat. Hematology and Oncology, Nat. Bd. Med. Examiners. Intern in pediats. New Eng. Med. Ctr., Boston, 1976-77, resident in pediats., 1977-79; fellow in pediat. hematology and oncology U. Wash. Sch. Medicine and Fred Hutchinson Cancer Rsch. Ctr., Seattle, 1979-83; pediats. instr. Sch. Medicine U. Wash., Seattle, 1983-84, asst. prof. Sch. Medicine, 1984-90, assoc. prof. Sch. Medicine, 1990—; dir. transp. and stem cell biology Wash. Regional Primate Rsch. Ctr., Seattle, 2000—. Presenter more than 50 papers and abstracts at sci. and med. meetings. Contbr. more than 150 articles and abstracts to profl. jours. Grantee Am. Cancer Soc., 1979-80, among others; fellow Am. Cancer Soc., 1983-86. Office: Fred Hutchinson Cancer Rsch Ctr 1100 Fairview Ave N Seattle WA 98109-4417

ANDREWS, STEVEN R., lawyer; b. 1953; BA, JD, U. Nebraska. Clerk to Judge Donald R. Ross U.S. Ct. of Appeals Eighth Circuit; special asst. to dir. FBI; various positions including interim pres., CEO, v.p., gen. counsel & sec. Multigraphics, Inc. (formerly AM Internat., Inc.), Mt. Prospect, Ill., 1994—99; sr. v.p., gen. counsel, sec. PepsiAmericas, Inc. (formerly Whitman Corp.), Rolling Meadows, Ill., 1999—2001; sr. v.p., gen. counsel Shopko Stores, Green Bay, Wis., 2002—03, sr. v.p. law & human resources, 2003—06; sec., gen. counsel Insight Enterprises, Tempe, Ariz., 2007—. Office: Insight Enterprises 1305 W Auto Dr Tempe AZ 85284

ANDRUS, CECIL DALE, academic administrator, former United States Secretary of the Interior; b. Hood River, Oreg., Aug. 25, 1931; s. Hal Stephen and Dorothy (Johnson) A.; m. Carol Mae May, Aug. 27, 1949; children: Tana Lee, Tracy Sue, Kelly Kay. Student, Oreg. State U., 1948-49; LLD (hon.), Gonzaga U., U. Idaho, U. N.Mex., Coll. Idaho, Idaho State U., Whitman Coll. Mem. Idaho State Senate, 1961—66, 1969—70; state gen. mgr. Paul Revere Life Ins. Co., 1969-70; gov. State of Idaho, 1971-77, 87-95; sec. US Dept. Interior, Washington, 1977-81; chmn. Andrus Ctr. for Pub. Policy, Boise State U., Idaho, 1995—. Bd. dirs. Coeur d'Alene Mines, del. Dem. Nat. Conv. 1972, 76, 84, 88. Author: Cecil Andrus: Politics Western Style, 1998. Chmn. bd. trustees Coll. of Idaho, 1985-89; bd. dirs. Sch. Forestry, Duke U. Advanced from recruit to AT2 USN, 1951—55, Pacific Theatre. Decorated Korean Svc. medal; recipient Disting. Citizen award Oreg. State U., 1980, Collier County Conservancy medal, 1979, Ansel Adams award, Audubon medal, 1985, Statesman of the Yr. award Idaho State U., 1990, Torch of Liberty award B'nai B'rith, 1991, William Penn Mott award, Nat. Parks Conservation Assn., 2000; named Conservationist of Yr., Idaho Wildlife Fedn., 1972. Mem. Nat. Govs. Conf. (exec. com. 1971-72, chmn. 1976), Fedn. Rocky Mt. States (chmn. 1971-72), Idaho Taxpayers Assn. (bd. dirs. 1964-66), Nat. Wildlife Fedn. (dir. 1981-82, Conservationist of Yr. award, 1980), VFW (Man of Yr., 1959), Masons. Democrat. Lutheran. Office: Boise State U Andrus Ctr Pub Policy 1910 University Dr Boise ID 83725-0399 Mailing: Andrus Ctr Pub Policy PO Box 852 Boise ID 83701

ANELLO, MICHAEL M., federal judge; b. Miami, 1943; BA, Bowdoin Coll., 1965; JD, Georgetown U., 1968. Bar: DC 1969, Calif. 1972. Dep. city atty. San Diego City Atty.'s Office, 1972—73; ptnr. Wingert, Grebing, Anello & Brubaker, San Diego, 1973—98; judge San Diego Superior Ct., 1998—2008, US Dist. Ct. (so. dist.) Calif., 2008—. Active duty USMC, 1968—72, served in USMC Reserve, 1973—90. Office: US Dist Ct So Dist Calif 940 Front St San Diego CA 92101-8900 Office Phone: 619-557-5960.*

ANEMA-GARTEN, DURLYNN C., communications educator, counseling administrator, writer; b. San Diego, Dec. 23, 1935; d. Durlin L. Flagg and Carolyn L. Owen; m. Charles Jay Anema, May 5, 1955 (dec. 09061986); children: Charlynn Anema Raimundi, Charles Jay, Richard F.; m. Vernon Ray Garten, July 30, 1988. BA, Calif. State U., Hayward, 1968, MS, 1977; EdD, U. Pacific, Stockton, Calif., 1984; PhD, Trinity Theol. Sem., Evansville, Ind., 1994. Cert. Christian therapist; cert. life secondary tchr., life sch. adminstr., Calif. Columnist San Leandro Morning News, Calif., 1960-62; secondary tchr. San Leandro and Hayward Sch. Dists., 1970-75; sch. adminstr. Hayward and Lodi Sch. Dists., Calif., 1975-80; dir. lifelong learning U. Pacific, 1981-84, prof. comm., 1984-89; pvt. sch. cons., 1989—; pvt. Christian counselor, 1994—. Pres., bd. dirs. Valley Cmty. Counseling Svcs., Stockton, 1982-92; cons., assoc. Raphael Coun. Ctr., Sacramento, 1994-98; adj. prof. Western Theol. Sem., Sacramento, 1999-2001. Author: Don't Get Fired, 1978, Get Hired, 1979, Sharing an Apartment, 1982, Harriet Chalmers Adams, 2nd edit., 2004, Louise Arner Boyd, 2000, Ynez Mexia, 2005; co-author: California Yesterday and Today, 1984, Options, 1993. Pres., bd. dirs. San Leandro Libr., 1970—75; pres. Homeowners Assn. San Leandro, 1973—75, Homeowners Assn. Garden Valley, Calif., 1980—97; ch. counselor Good Samaritan Covenant Ch., 1993—98; pres., bd. dirs. Valley Mountain Regional Ctr., Stockton, Calif., 2000—05; bd. dirs. Children's Commn., San Joaquin County, Calif., 1986—92, Sr. Citizens Commn., Calaveras County, Calif., 1998, Valley Cmty. Counseling Svcs., 1982—89, 2006—. Recipient Susan B. Anthony award San Joaquin County Commn. on Women, 1989. Mem. Soc. Profl. Journalists, Soc. Christian Therapists, Nat. Writers Assn., Calif. Writers Club, Jamés Monroe PTA (life), Phi Kappa Phi, Phi Delta Kappa. Avocations: travel, hiking, bicycling, reading. Office: 401 Oakridge Ct Valley Springs CA 95252-9362 Office Phone: 209-772-2521. Business E-Mail: durverga@caltel.com.

ANG, ALFREDO HUA-SING, civil engineering educator; b. Davao, The Philippines, July 4, 1930; came to U.S., 1955; s. Tiong Ang and Khio Tan; m. Myrtle Mae Ang; children: Evelyn, Irene, James. BSCE, Mapua Inst. Tech., Manila, 1954; MS, U. Ill., 1957, Phd, 1959. Registered structural engr., Ill. From asst. prof. to prof. U. Ill., Urbana, 1959-65, prof., 1965-88, U. Calif., Irvine, 1988—. Cons. NRC, Washington, 1979—, Ea. Internat. Engrs., Lafayette, Calif., 1983-90, Internat. Civil Engring Cons., Berkeley, Calif., 1992—; sr. tech. adviser Kajima Corp., Tokyo, 1984—, Tokyo Elec. Power Svcs. Co., 1987—; MCA engr. Mobil Offshore Base. Author: Probability Concepts in Engineering Planning and Design, Vol. I, 1975, Vol. II, 1984; editor Jour. Structural Engring., 1986—; co-editor-in-chief Internat. Jour. Computational Structural Engring., 2000—; mem. editorial bd. Jour. Structural Mechanics, 1971-84, Structural Safety, 1982—, Probabilistic Engring. Mechanics, 1985—, Reliability Engring. and System Safety, 1992—, Internat. Jour. Structural Engring. and Mechanics, 1992—; contbr. numerous articles to profl. jours. Recipient Sr. Rsch. award Am. Soc. Engring. Edn., 1983, Disting. Rsch. award U. Calif.-Irvine Alumni Assn., 1993, Disting. Engring. Alumni award, U. Ill., 2003. Fellow ASME, ASCE (chmn. STD EXCOM, internat. dir. 1998—, rsch. prize 1968, State-of-Art award 1973, Freudenthal medal 1982, Newmark medal 1988, hon. mem. 1991, Ernest Howard award 1996), AIAA (assoc.); mem. NAE, Earthquake Engring. Rsch. Inst., Seismol. Soc. Am., Soc. Naval Architects and Marine Engrs., Internat. Assn. for Structural Safety and Reliability (pres. 1985-89, Rsch. prize 1993). Home: 5311 154th Ave SE Bellevue WA 98006-5151 Office: U Calif Dept Civil Engring Irvine CA 92697-0001 E-mail: ahang2@aol.com.

ANGEL, ARTHUR RONALD, lawyer, consultant; b. Long Beach, Calif., May 10, 1948; s. Morris and Betty Estelle (Unger) A.; 1 child, Jamie Kathryn. BA, U. Calif., Berkeley, 1969; JD, Harvard U., Cambridge, Mass., 1972. Bar: Mass. 1972, DC 1975, Okla. 1979, Calif. 2001, US Dist. Ct. (we. dist.) Okla. 1980, US Dist. Ct. (no. dist.) Okla. 1981, US Dist. Ct. (ctrl. dist.) Calif. 2001, US Supreme Ct. 1983. Atty. FTC, Washington, 1972—78; pvt. practice Oklahoma City, 1978—87; ptnr. Angel & Ikard, Oklahoma City, 1987—93; of counsel Abel, Musser Sokolosky & Assoc., LA, 1994—2000; ptnr. Carrick Law Group, LA, 2001—02; atty. Nagler & Assocs., LA, 2002—04. Mem. adv. panel on cardiovascular devices, Washington, 1979-82; cons. FTC, 1978-79; adminstrv. law judge Okla. Dept. Labor, 1999-2000; spl. mcpl. judge City of Oklahoma City, 1999-2001. Recipient Meritorious Service award FTC, Washington, 1978. Fellow: Inst. Law and Social Scis.; mem.: ATLA, Calif. Bar Assn., DC Bar Assn. Democrat. Jewish. Home: 1305 N Poinsettia Pl Los Angeles CA 90046 Personal E-mail: arthurangel@sbcglobal.net.

ANGEL, JAMES ROGER PRIOR, astronomer; b. St. Helens, Eng., Feb. 7, 1941; came to U.S., 1967; s. James Lee and Joan (Prior) A.; m. Ellinor M. Goonan, Aug. 21, 1965; children: Jennifer, James. BA, Oxford U., Eng., 1963, D.Phil., 1967; MS, Calif. Inst. Tech., 1966. From rsch. assoc. to assoc. prof. physics Columbia U., 1967-74; prof. astronomy U. Ariz., 1975—, prof. optical sci., 1984—, Regents prof., 1990—. Sloan fellow, 1970-74; hon. fellow St. Peter's Coll., Oxford

U.; MacArthur fellow, 1996. Fellow Royal Soc., Royal Astron. Soc., Am. Acad. Arts and Scis.; mem. NAS, Am. Astron. Soc. (v.p. 1987-90, Pierce prize 1976). Achievements include research on white dwarf stars, quasars, the search for extra-solar planetary systems, astronomical mirrors, telescopes and their instruments, and adaptive optics, concepts to cool the Earth from space and for large scale use of solar energy. Office: Univ Ariz Steward Obs Tucson AZ 85721-0001 Business E-Mail: rangel@as.arizona.edu.

ANGEL, JAN, state legislator; m. Lynn Williams; 2 stepchildren; 2 children. Attended, Colo. State U., U. Alaska; grad., Wash. State U., NYU Wagner Grad. Sch. Pub. Service. Banker, bus. owner, real estate; commr. Kitsap County, 2000—08; mem. Dist. 26 Wash. House of Reps., 2009—. Recipient Freedom Award, Kitsap Alliance of Property Owners, 2008, Award of Excellence in Pub. Service, Kitsap County Assn. of Realtors, 2005. Republican. Office: 420 John L O'Brien Bldg PO Box 40600 Olympia WA 98504 Office Phone: 360-786-7964. E-mail: angel.jan@leg.wa.gov.

ANGELOFF, DANN VALENTINO, brokerage house executive; b. Hollywood, Calif., Nov. 15, 1935; m. Jo Jeanne Ahlstrom, Sept. 26, 1964; children: Jennifer J., Dann V., Julie A. BS in Fin., U. So. Calif., 1958, MBA, 1963. Trainee Dean Witter & Co., Inc., LA, 1957-60; v.p. Dempsey-Tegeler & Co., Inc., LA, 1960-70; mng. dir. West Coast corp. fin. dept. Reynolds Securities, Inc., LA, 1970-76; pres., bd. dirs. The Angeloff Co., LA, 1976—. Bd. dirs. Softbrands Inc., Mpls., B.B. Micro-Cap Growth Fund, Rye, NY, Electronic Recyclers Internat., Fresno, Calif., Pub. Storage, Glendale, Calif., Nicholas-Applegate Fund, San Diego; chmn. bd. Marshall Ptnrs., U. So. Calif.; bd. dirs. Marshall Bd. Leaders, U. Southern Calif. Trustee U. So. Calif., 1979-86, univ. counselor; bd. dirs., chmn. Trojan Bd. Govs., 1990-92. Mem. Skull and Dagger, Cardinal and Gold, Calif. Club, Valley Hunt Club, San Marino City Club, Kappa Beta Phi. Office: The Angeloff Co 626 Wilshire Blvd Ste 727 Los Angeles CA 90017

ANGRESANO, JAMES, political economics professor; BS, Lehigh U., 1968; MBA, NYU, 1971; PhD in Econs., U. Tenn., 1981. Mktg. rsch. analyst, NYC, 1968—71; asst. prof. Am. Coll. Switzerland, 1972—74; asst. to assoc. prof. econs. Hampden-Sydney Coll., Va., 1980—91; adj. assoc. prof. econs. Sweet Briar Coll., 1984—91; tutor adult degree prog. Mary Baldwin Coll., 1985—; Fulbright scholar Varna U. Econs., Bulgaria, 1991—92; acad. coord. Civic Edn. Project, Czech Republic, 1992—93; vis. prof. econs. Prague U. Econs., Czech Republic, 1992—93; rsch. assoc. Ctr. Post-Soviet and East European Studies U. Tex., Austin, 1993—95; prof. polit. economy Albertson Coll. Idaho, Caldwell, 1995—. Vis. acad. Mansfield Coll., Oxford U., 1987; vis. scholar Inst. Econs., Budapest, Hungary, 1990; vis. fellow Stanford U. Hoover Instn., 1997; vis. prof. China Agrl. U., 2001, 02; vis. prof. internat. economy U. Trento, Italy, 2002, 03, 04, 05; sr. Fulbright specialist U. Cairo, 2003, 04, Houston U., 2007. Contbr. articles to profl. publs., chapters to books; author: The Political Economy of Gunnar Myrdal: An Institutional Basis for Transformation Policy, 1997, French Welfare State Reform: Idealism Versus Swedish, New Zealand and Dutch Pragmatism, 2007. Recipient US Prof. of Yr. award, Carnegie Found. for Advancement of Tchg. and Coun. for Advancement and Support of Edn., 2006. Mem.: European Cmty. Studies Assn., European Assn. Comparative Econ. Studies, Assn. Comparative Econs., Phi Kappa Phi. Office: Dept Polit Economy The Coll Idaho 2112 Cleveland Blvd Caldwell ID 83605 Office Phone: 208-459-5480. E-mail: jangresa@hotmail.com.

ANKA, PAUL, singer, composer; b. Ottawa, Ont., Can., July 30, 1941; came to US, 1959; s. Andrew Emile and Camilia (Tannis) A.; m. Anne Alison de Zogheb, Feb. 16, 1963 (div. Oct. 2000); children: Alexandra, Amanda, Alicia, Anthea, Amelia. Grad. high sch., Ottawa; Doctorate Music (hon.), St. Johns U., NYC, 1981. Owner, prin. Spanka Music Corp., 1958—, Flanka Music Corp., 1958—, Camy Prodns., Inc., 1961-66; owner Panka Musci, 2001—. Internat. performer, 1956—; films include The Longest Day, 1961 (also wrote title song), Girl's Town, Look in Any Window, Captain Ron, 1992, Ordinary Magic, 1993, Shake, Rattle and Rock!, 1994, Mr. Playback: An Interactive Movie, 1995, Mad Dog Time, 1996, 3000 miles to Graceland, 1999, TV film Perry Mason: The Case of the Maligned Mobster, 1991; TV appearances include Larry King Live, Barbara Walters, The View, Ed Sullivan Show, Danny Thomas, Perry Como, Johnny Carson, Dean Martin, Hollywood Palace, Open Mind, Atlantic City USA, Happy Birthday, America, 1976, Sinatra: The First Forty Years; appeared syndicated variety show, 1973; replacement in Broadway mus. What Makes Sammy Run?, 1954; appeared at Copacabana, NYC, Sands Hotel, Caesars Palace, Hilton Hotel, all Las Vegas, Caribe Hilton Hotel, San Juan, PR, Paladium, London, Olympia, Paris, Uris, NYC, Waldorf Astoria, NYC, Golden Nugget Hotels, Las Vegas and Atlantic City; participated San Remo Music Festival, 1964; recs. include My Way, 1968, (You're) Having My Baby, 1974, One Man Woman/One Woman Man, 1974, I Don't Like To Sleep Alone, 1975, (I Believe) There's Nothing Stronger Than Our Love, 1975, Times of Your Life, 1975, Anytime (I'll Be There), 1976, Happier, 1976, My Best Friend's Wife, 1977, Everybody Ought To Be in Love, 1977, Headlines, 1979, Both Sides of Love 1981, Walk a Fine Line, 1983, Songs, 1983, Italiano, 1987, In Vegas, 1995, Amigos, 1996, A Body of Work, 1998, Christmas, 2000, Live, 2001, Live in Las Vegas, 2002, Live & In Concert, 2003, Rock Swings, 2005, Classic Songs, 2007; wrote: (with Burt Bacharach) score for film Together?, 1979; composer Diana, 1957, Crazy Love, Lonely Boy, 1959, Put Your Head on My Shoulder, 1959, Time to Cry, 1959, The Longest Day, 1962, Ogni Volta, 1964, Do I Love You, 1971, Tonight Show theme music; others; also compositions for other artists including My Way for Frank Sinatra and She's A Lady for Tom Jones. Named 21st most successful artist in Billboards history., Entertainer of Yr., Internat. Gaming Assn., 1991, Songwriters Hall of Fame, Nat. Acad. Popular Music, 1991; named a Chevalier, Order of Arts & Letters, France, 1991; named an Officer, Order of Can., 2005; named to, Can. Music Hall of Fame, 1980, Hollywood Walk of Fame, Can. Walk of Fame, 2005. Mem. Broadcast Music, Inc. (22 songwriting awards: 18 for most performed songs, 4 for songs performed more than one million times). Clubs: Friars NYC. Eastern Orthodox. Achievements include being a holder of 15 gold records for million dollar world-wide sellers, and having to his credit more than 42 million single sales and over 900 songs. Office: William Morris Aby 1 William Morris Pl Beverly Hills CA 90212 also: Paul Anka Productions 5706 Corsa Ave Ste 200 Westlake Village CA 91362-4057 E-mail: fan@paulanka.com.

ANNAUD, JEAN-JACQUES, film director, producer, scriptwriter; b. Juvisy, France, Oct. 1, 1943; s. Pierre and Madeleine (Tripoz) A.; m. Monique Rossignol, 1970 (div. 1980); 1 child, Mathilde; m. Laurence Duval; 1 child, Louise. Student, Ecole Louis Lumière, Institut Des Hautes Etudes Cinematographiques, Paris, 1966; Lic. Lettres, The Sorbonne, Paris, 1967. Freelance film dir., screenwriter, Paris, 1967—. Sreenwriter, dir.: Black and White in Color, 1976 (Oscar award Best Fgn. Film 1977), Hot head, 1978, Quest for Fire, 1981, (César award 1982), Name of the Rose, 1986 (César award 1987, Donatello award), The Bear, 1988 (César award best dir. 1988), The Lover, 1991 (Best Dir. award Japan Critics Assn., 1992); screenwriter, dir., prodr.: Wings of Courage, 1994 (in IMAX 3D), Seven Years in Tibet, 1997 (Best Fgn. Film Gilde Filmpreis, Germany, 1998), Enemy at the Gates, 2000, Two Brothers, 2004, His Majesty Minor, 2006. Decorated commandeur Ordre des Arts et Lettres; recipient Grand Prix Nat. du Cinema, prix du Cinéma de L'Académie Française. Mem.: Inst. de France. Home: 9 rue Guénégaud 75006 Paris France also: Repérage SAS 10 rue Lincoln 75008 Paris France Office: ICM c/o Jeff Berg 10250 Constellation Blvd Los Angeles CA 90067 Office Phone: 33 140769411. Business E-Mail: jj@reperage-films.fr.

ANSCHUTZ, PHILIP F., communications and professional sports team executive; m. Nancy Anschutz; 3 children. BS, Univ. Kans., 1961. Dir. chair. QCC, 1993—; founder Anschutz Corp., Denver, 1965; dir. chair. Anschutz Co., Denver, 1991—; CEO, dir. Anschutz Corp., Denver, 1992—; dir. So. Pacific Rail Corp., San Francisco, 1988-96; chair. So Pacific Rail Corp., 1988-96; vice chmn. (merger with So Pacific Rail Corp) Union Pacific, San Francisco, 1996—; dir. Forest Oil Corp., 1995—, Qwest Comm., 1997—, chmn., 1997—2002; co-owner L.A. Kings, 1995—; owner L.A. Galaxy, 1996—; investor-operator Major League Soccer, 1995—; owner San Francisco Examiner, The Ind., Grant Printing Co., San Francisco, 2004—. Dir. Regal Entertainment Group. Recipient Disting. Svc. Citation, Kans. U., 1992, Horatio Alger award; named one of 200 Top Collectors, ARTnews Mag., 2004, 2006, Forbes Richest Americans, 1999—, World's Richest People, Forbes Mag., 1999—2007, The Most Influential People in the World of Sports, Bus. Week, 2007, 2008. Republican. Avocations: Collecting 19th and 20th century Am. art, especially Western, tennis, squash, running marathons.

ANSELL, BENJAMIN JESSE, physician; MD, UCLA, 1992. Diplomate Am. Bd. Internal Medicine. Intern UCLA Med. Ctr., 1992-93, resident, 1993-95; asst. clin. prof. UCLA, 1995—2001, assoc. clin. prof, 2001—; dir. UCLA Edn. Health; dir. Ctr. Primary Care Based Cardiovasc. Disease Prevention UCLA. Fellow. ACP, Am. Heart Assn. Office: UCLA Med Ctr 200 Med Plz Ste 365 Los Angeles CA 90095-0001

ANSELL, EDWARD ORIN, lawyer; b. Superior, Wis., Mar. 29, 1926; s. H. S. and Mollie (Rudnitzky) A.; m. Hanne B. Baer, Dec. 23, 1956; children: Deborah, William. BSEE, U. Wis., 1948; JD, George Washington U., 1955. Bar: D.C. 1955, Calif. 1960. Electronic engr. FCC, Buffalo and Washington, 1948-55; patent atty. RCA, Princeton, NJ, 1955-57; gen. mgr. AeroChem. Rsch. Labs., Princeton, 1957-58; patent atty. Aerojet-Gen. Corp., La Jolla, Calif., 1958-63, corp. patent counsel, 1963-82, asst. sec., 1970-79, sec., 1979-82, assoc. gen. counsel, 1981-82; dir. patents and licensing Calif. Inst. Tech., Pasadena, Calif., 1982-92; pvt. practice Claremont, Calif., 1992—; co-founder Gryphon Pharms., South San Francisco, 1993, Ciphergen BioSystems, Fremont, Calif., 1993. Adj. prof. U. La Verne (Calif.) Coll. Law, 1972-78; spl. advisor, task force chmn. U.S. Commn. Govt. Procurement, 1971 Editor: Intellectual Property in Academe: A Legal Compendium, 1991; contbr. articles to profl. publs. Recipient Alumni Svc. award George Washington U., 1975. Mem.: Am. Intellectual Property Law Assn., Ea. Bar Assn. LA County, LA Intellectual Property Law Assn., Assn. Univ. Tech. Mgrs., State Bar Calif. (exec. com. intellectual property sect. 1983—86), Athenaeum Club Pasadena, Univ. Club Claremont. Office: 427 N Yale Ave # 204 Claremont CA 91711 Home Phone: 909-625-1244; Office Phone: 909-621-1985. Personal E-mail: anselaw@verizon.net.

ANSELL, JULIAN S., urologist, educator; b. Portland, Maine, June 30, 1922; s. Jacob M. and Anna Gertrude (Fieldman) A.; m. Eva Ruth Ballin, June 17, 1951; children: Steven, Jody, Carol, Ellen, Peter. BA, Bowdoin Coll., 1946; MD, Tufts U., 1951; PhD, U. Minn., 1959. Intern in surgery U. Minn. Hosps., Mpls., 1951-52, resident in urology, 1952-54; NIH fellow U. Minn., Mpls., 1954, instr., 1956-59; asst. prof., head urology U. Wash., Seattle, 1959-62, assoc. prof., head urology, 1962-64, prof., chair urology, 1965-87, prof. urology, 1987-92, prof. emeritus, 1992—. Contbr. scientific papers pub. to profl. jour. Chair Post Grad. Seminar Am. Urological Assn., 1978; pres. Soc. Univ. Urologists, 1979; med. quality assurance commn. Wash. State, 1992—2005, chair., 2001. With US Army, 1943—46. Mem. Am. Alpine Club. Achievements include development of neonatal closure of exstrophy of bladder; urology residency objectives; research in renal sparing surgery in bilateral renal cancer; total body potassium in patients with urinary diversion; smoking as a cause of bladder cancer; discordant urinary defects in monozygotic twins; healing in infected and irradiated tissues; reflux and renal failure. Office: 3827 49th Ave NE Seattle WA 98105-5233

ANSETH, KRISTI S., tissue engineer, educator; b. ND; BS in Chem. Engring., Purdue U., 1992; PhD in Chem. Engring., U. Colo., 1994. Rsch. assoc. Purdue U., West Lafayette, Ind., 1995; rsch. fellow Mass. Inst. Tech., Cambridge, Mass., 1995—96; asst. prof. chem. engring. U. Colo., Boulder, Colo., 1996—98, Patten asst. prof. chem. engring., 1998—99, Patten assoc. prof. chem. engring., 1999—2002, asst. investigator Howard Hughes Med. Inst., 2000—; assoc. prof. surgery U. Colo. Health Sci. Ctr., Denver, 2000—; prof. chem. engring. U. Colo., Boulder, 2002—03, Tisone prof. chem. and biol. engring., 2003—, assoc. faculty dir. initiative in molecular biotech., 2003—, prof. (by courtesy), 2004—. Vis. rschr. Ecole Nationale Superieure de Chimie, Mulhouse, France, 1994. Recipient Career award, NSF, 1998—2002, First award, NIH, 1998—2003, Dow Outstanding New Faculty award, Am. Soc. Engring. Edn., 1999, Outstanding Young Investigator award, Materials Rsch. Soc., 2001, Curtis W. McGraw award, Am. Soc. Engring. Edn., 2003, Allan P. Colburn award, AIChE, 2003, Alan T. Waterman award, NSF, 2004, others; fellow, Am. Inst. Med. and Biol. Engring., 2001. Office: Dept Chem and Biol Engring ECCH 128 Univ Colo Boulder CO 80309-0424 Office Phone: 303-492-3147. Office Fax: 303-492-4341. E-mail: kristi.anseth@colorado.edu.

ANSON, FRED COLVIG, chemistry educator; b. LA, Feb. 17, 1933; m. Roxana Anson; children: Alison, Eric. BS, Calif. Inst. Tech., 1954; MS, Harvard U., 1955, PhD, 1957. Instr. chemistry Calif. Inst. Tech., Pasadena, 1957-58, asst. prof., 1958-62, assoc. prof., 1962-68, prof. chemistry, 1968—, chmn. divsn. chemistry and chem. engring., 1984-94. Contbr. numerous articles to profl. jours. Fellow J.S. Guggenheim Found., U. Brussels, 1964, Alfred P. Sloan Found., 1965-69; scholar Fulbright-Hays Found., U. Florence, Italy, 1972, A. von Humboldt Found., Fritz Haber Inst., Berlin, 1984, 86, 94; recipient award in Electrochemistry Am. Chem. Soc., 1994. Fellow Electrochem. Soc.; mem. AAAS, Nat. Acad. Sci., Am. Chem. Soc. (Award in Electrochemistry, 1994), Am. Electrochem. Soc., Internat. Soc. Electrochemistry, Soc. Electroanalytical Chemistry, Tau Beta Pi. Office: Calif Inst Tech Divsn Chemistry and Chem Engring Ms 127 72 Pasadena CA 91125-0001

ANSPAUGH, LYNN RICHARD, research biophysicist; b. Rawlins, Wyo., May 25, 1937; s. Solon Earl and Alice Henrietta (Day) A.; m. Barbara Anne Corrigan, Nov. 2, 1965 (div.); children: Gregory, Heidi; m. Larisa Fedorovna Kornushina, Sept. 27, 1993. BA, Nebr. Wesleyan U., 1959; M in Bioradiology, U. Calif., Berkeley, 1961, PhD, 1963. Biophysicist Lawrence Livermore (Calif.) Nat. Lab., 1963-74, group leader, 1974-75, sect. leader, 1976-82, div. leader, 1982-92, dir. Risk Scis. Ctr., 1992-95, dir. Dose Reconstruction program, 1995-96; rsch. prof. radiobiology divsn. Univ. Utah, Salt Lake City, 1997—. Tchr. extension U. Calif., Berkeley, 1966-69; lectr. San Jose (Calif.) State U., 1975; guest lectr. UCLA, Stanford U., U. Calif., Davis, 1992-96; faculty affiliate Colo. State U., Ft. Collins, 1979-83; cons. EPA, Washington, 1984-85, U. Utah, Salt Lake City, 1983-88, NAS/NRC, 1998, 2005; mem. U.S. del. UN Sci. Com. on Effects of Radiation, Vienna, 1987—; mem. Nat. Coun. on Radiation Protection and Measurements, 1989-2001, disting. emeritus mem., 2008-; mem. radiation adv. com. EPA, 1999-2005. Contbr. articles to profl. jours. AEC fellow, 1959-61; fellow NSF, 1961-63. Fellow Health Physics Soc. (pres. environ. radiation sect. 1984-85, pres. No. Calif. chpt. 1986-87); mem. AAAS, Internat. Union Radioecology, Radiation Rsch. Soc., Sigma Xi. Office: PO Box 77777 Henderson NV 89077 Office Phone: 702-616-0914. E-mail: LAnspaugh@aol.com.

ANTANITUS, DAVID J., career officer; b. LaSalle, Ill. BS in Math., U.S. Naval Acad., 1974. Commd. 2d lt. USN; various assignments including USS Parche (SSN 683), 1975-79; asst. dept. comdr. for readiness and tng. Comdr. Submarine Squadron Fourteen, Holy Loch, Scotland, 1979-82; exec. officer USS Boston (SSN 703), 1986-91; comdr. Pre-Commissioning Unit Hampton (SSN 767); program mgr. Deep Submergence Systems Program (PMS 395)/NAVSEA; vice-comdr., rear adm. Space and Naval Warfare Systems Command. Decorated Legion of Merit, Meritorious Svc. medal, Navy Commendation medal with four gold stars.

ANTENORI, FRANK R., state legislator; b. Scranton, Pa., May 3, 1966; m. Lesley Antenori; children: Frank III, Brodie. BS in Health Sci., Campbell U., Buies Creek, NC, 2000. Cert. paramedic U. Tex., 1992. Nuc. weapons specialist US Army, 1984—88, spl. forces operator, 5th spl. forces group, 1988—2004, team sgt., 3rd spl. forces group, 2000—04, ret., 2004; program mgr. Raytheon Missile Sys., Tucson, 2004—; mem. Dist. 29 Ariz. House of Reps., 2008—, vice chair transp. & infrastructure com., mem. govt. com., health & human svcs. com. Pres. Pima County Libr. Adv. Bd., 2007—. Mem.: NRA (life), Spl. Forces Assn., Assn. of US Army (life), Non-Commd. Officers Assn. (life), Vets. of Foreign Wars (life), Ariz. Citizen's Def. League, Am. Legion. Republican. Roman Catholic. Office: Ariz House Reps Capitol Complex 1700 W Washington Rm 307 Phoenix AZ 85007 Office Phone: 602-626-5683. Office Fax: 602-417-3147. Business E-Mail: fantenori@azleg.gov.*

ANTHONY, CARMELO, professional basketball player; b. NYC, May 29, 1984; 1 child, Kiyan. Student, Syracuse U., 2003. Forward NBA Denver Nuggets, 2003—. Mem. US Men's Sr. Nat. Basketball Team, Athens, Greece, 2004, Beijing, 08. Vol. Family Resource Ctr., Denver. Recipient Gold medal, men's basketball, Beijing Olympic Games, 2008; named NCAA Final Four Most Outstanding player, 2003, NBA Rookie of the Month (6 Times), 2003—04, USA Basketball Male Athlete of Yr., 2006; named one of All-NBA 3rd Team, 2006; named to All-Rookie 1st Team, NBA, 2004, Western Conf. All-Star Team, 2005, 2007, 2008. Achievements include member of the NCAA National Championship winning Syracuse Orangemen, 2003; tying the NBA record for points scored in one quarter (33), 2008. Office: Denver Nuggets 1000 Chopper Cir Denver CO 80204

ANTIN, DAVID, poet, critic; b. Bklyn., Feb. 1, 1932; s. Max and Mollie (Kitzes) A.; m. Eleanor Fineman, Dec. 16, 1961; 1 son, Blaise BA, CCNY, 1955; MA, NYU, 1966. Prof. visual arts U. Calif., San Diego, 1968—99, prof. emeritus visual arts, 2000—. Author: Definitions, 1967, Autobiography, 1967, Code of Flag Behavior, 1968, Meditations, 1971, Talking, 1972, Talking at the Boundaries, 1976, Tuning, 1984, Selected Poems 1963-73, 1991, What It Means to be Avant Garde, 1993, (with Charles Bernstein) A Conversation with David Antin, 2002, I Never Knew What Time it Was, U.C.Press, 2005, John Cage Uncaged is Still Cagey, Singing Horse Press, 2005; contbg. editor: Alcheringa, 1972-80, New Wilderness, 1979-; mem. editl. com. U. Calif. Press, 1972-76. Recipient Creative Arts award U. Calif., 1972; Herbert Lehman fellow NYU, 1966; Guggenheim fellow, 1976-77; NEH fellow, 1983-84, Getty Rsch. fellow, 2002. Home: PO Box 1147 Del Mar CA 92014-1147 Office: U Calif San Diego Visual Arts Dept La Jolla CA 92037 E-mail: dantin@ucsd.edu.

ANTIN, JONATHAN, hairstylist, entrepreneur; b. LA, Aug. 16, 1967; s. Michael and Brenda Antin; 1 child, Asher Jones. Attended, Fairfax Beauty Acad. Owner, hairstylist Jonathan Salon West Hollywood, Jonathan Salon Beverly Hills, 2004—. Released signature hair product line Jonathan Product, 2005. Actor: (TV reality show) Blow Out, 2004—; judge Miss Teen USA Pageant, 2004. Office: Jonathan Salon 901 Westbourne Dr West Hollywood CA 90069 also: Bravo c/o NBC Entertainment 3000 W Alameda Ave Burbank CA 91523 Office Phone: 310-855-0225. E-mail: salon@jonathanproduct.com.

ANTONIOU, ANDREAS, electrical engineering educator; b. Yerolakkos, Nicosia, Cyprus, 1938; immigrated to Can., 1969. s. Antonios and Eleni Hadjisavva; m. Rosemary C. Kennedy, 1964 (dec.); children: Anthony, David, Constantine, Helen BSc (hon.), U. London, 1963, PhD, 1966; doctorate (hon.), Nat. Tech. U. Athens, Greece, 2002. Mem. sci staff GEC Ltd., London, 1966; sr. sci. officer P.O. Rsch. Dept., London, 1966-69; sci. staff in R & D No. Electric Co., Ottawa, Ont., Canada, 1969-70; from asst. prof. elec. engring. to prof., dept. chmn. Concordia U., Montreal, Que., Canada, 1970-83; founding chmn. elec. and computer engring. dept. U. Victoria, Canada, 1983-90, prof., 1983—2003, prof. emeritus, 2003—. Author: Digital Filters: Analysis, Design, and Applications, 1979, 2d edit., 1993, Digital Signal Processing: Signals, Systems, and Filters, 2005; co-author: Two-Dimensional Digital Filters, 1992, Practical Optimization: Algorithms and Engineering Applications, 2007; contbr. articles to profl. jours. Recipient Chmn.'s award, B.C. Sci. Coun., 2000. Fellow: IEEE, Instn. Engring. Tech. (Ambrose Fleming premium

1969); mem. IEEE Sig. Proc. Soc. (Disting. Lectr. 2003-04), IEEE Cirs. Sys. Soc. (assoc. editor/editor-in-chief Trans. on Cirs. and Sys. 1983-87, bd. govs. 1995-97, gen. chair Internat. Symposium Cirs. and Sys. 2004, Golden Jubilee award 2000, Tech. Achievement award 2005, Disting. Lectr. 2006-07), IEEE (Canada Outstanding Engring. Educator Silver medal 2008), Assn. Profl. Engrs. and Geoscientists BC (councilor 1988-90). Greek Orthodox. Home: 4058 Jason Pl Victoria BC Canada V8N 4T6 Office: U Victoria Dept Elec & Computer Engring PO Box 3055 STN CSC Victoria BC Canada V8W 3P6 E-mail: aantoniou@ieee.org.

ANTONOVICH, MICHAEL DENNIS, county official; b. LA; m. Christine Hu; children: Michael Dennis, Jr., Mary Christine. BA, Calif. State U., LA, 1963, MA, 1967; secondary tchg. cert., Calif. State U., 1966; grad., Pasadena Police Acad., 1967; postgrad., Stanford U., 1968—70, Harvard U., 1984, postgrad., 1987. Cert. secondary tchr. 1966. Govt. and history instr. LA Unified Sch. Dist., 1966-72; Rep. whip Calif. State Assembly, 1976-78, assemblyman, 1972-78; mem. bd. suprs. 5th Dist. LA County, 1980—; mem. Gov. George Bush-Cheney State Steering Com., 2000, Bush-Cheney Re-election Com., 2004. Instr. Calif. State U., 1979, 85, Pepperdine U., 1979; trustee L.A. C.C.'s Dist., 1969-72. Mem. Tournament of Roses Com., Glendale Symphony, L.A. Zoo. Assn., South Pasadena Police Dept. Res., Good Shepherd Luth. Home for Retarded Children; mem. Met. Transp. Authority, 1993—, chmn., 1994-95; mem. L.A. County Transp. Commn., 1980-93, chmn., 1984, 92; chmn. Calif. State Rep. Party, 1985-86; mem. LA Coliseum Commn., South Coast Air Quality Mgmt. Dist.; presdl. appointee U.S. Del. to UN Internat. Conf. on Indo-Chinese Refugees, Geneva, 1989, Com. on Privatization, 1987-88, U.S.-Japan Adv. Com., 1984, J. Fulbright Fgn. Scholarship Bd., 1991-93; mem. adv. bd. Atty. Gen.'s Missing Children, 1987-88; mem. del. Rep. Nat. Com., 1972-76, 84-88, 92-96, 2000, mem. platform com., 1976, co-chmn. human resources com., elected chmn., county mayor, 1983, 87, 1991, 96, 2001, 06. With US Army, 1957—65, lt. col. Calif. State Mil. Res., 2004—. Recipient Pub. Ofcl. Yr., Nat. Fedn. Indian-Ams., 1989, Outstanding and Invaluable Svc. award Home Visitation Ctr., 1990, Brother's Keeper award Chaplain's Eagles, 1990, Responsible Citizen award Thomas Jefferson Rsch. Ctr., 1990, Outstanding Citizen award Internat. Footprint Assn., 1991, Recognition award Salvation Army, Leadership awards United Way, 1987, 91, 93, Hon. Svc. award PTA, 1991, San Fernando Valley Outstanding Leadership award Min.'s Fellowship and Focus 90s, 1991, Mental Health Assn. award of appreciation Antelope Valley Social Ctr., 1991, Recognition award MADD, 1992, Appreciation award Soc. Hispanic Profl. Engrs., L.A. chpt., 1992, awards Boy Scouts Am., 1992, 93, 2001, Recognition award Mex. Am. Correctional Assn., 1996, Outstanding Leader award SER/Jobs Progress, 2002, Michael D. Antonovich Open Space Preserve dedicated, 2002, Person of Yr. award Met. News-Enterprise, 2002, Counties Care Kids award Nat. Assn. Counties, 2003, Friend of Youth award Glendale Youth Alliance, 2003, Humanitarian award Castaic Area Town Coun., 2004, Calif. Commendation medal Calif. N.G., 2004, 7 Seals award Dept. Def./Employee Support of Guard and Res., 2004, Spirit of Lincoln award L.A. Lincoln Club, 2004, Disting. Civic award Western Diocese of Armenian Ch., 2004, Humanitarian award Iranian Am. Parents Assn. Beverly Hills, 2005, Foster Parent of Yr. award Hilltoppers Aux. Assistance League of So. Calif., 2005, Presdl. Vol. Svc. award Points of Light Found., 2005, others; Michael D. Antonovich Antelope Valley Courthouse dedicated in his honor, 2003; Michael D. Antonovich Reg. Pk. dedicated, 2003; named Man of Yr. Pasadena NAACP, 1999. Mem. County Suprs. Assn. Calif. (bd. dirs.), Phila. Soc., Glendale C. of C., Blue Key, Elks, Sigma Nu. Lutheran. Office: LA County 5th Dist 869 Hall of Adminstrn 500 W Temple St Los Angeles CA 90012-2713

ANTREASIAN, GARO ZAREH, artist, lithographer, educator; b. Indpls., Feb. 16, 1922; s. Zareh Minas and Takouhie (Daniell) A.; m. Jeanne Glascock, May 2, 1947; children: David Garo, Thomas Berj. BFA, John Herron Sch. Art, 1948; DFA (hon.), Ind. U.-Purdue U. at Indpls., 1972. Instr. Herron Sch. Art, Indpls., 1948—59, 1961—64; tech. dir. Tamarind Lithography Workshop, Los Angeles, 1960-61; prof. art U. N.Mex., 1964-87, chmn. dept. art, 1981-84; tech. dir. Tamarind Inst., U. N.Mex., 1970-72; vis. lectr., artist numerous univs. Bd. dir. Albuquerque Mus., 1980-90; printmaker emeritus Southern Graphics Coun., 1994; Fulbright vis. lectr. U. São Paulo and Found. Armando Alvares Penteado, Brazil, 1985. Prin. author: The Tamarind Book of Lithography: Art and Techniques, 1970; one-man shows include Malvina Miller Gallery, San Francisco, 1971, Marjorie Kauffman Gallery, Houston, 1975-79, 84, 86, U. Colo., Boulder, 1972, Calif. Coll. Arts & Crafts, Oakland, 1973, Miami U., Oxford, Ohio, 1973, Kans. State U., 1973, Atlanta Coll. Art, 1974, U. Ga., Athens, 1974, Alice Simsar Gallery, Ann Arbor, 1977-79, Elaine Horwich Gallery, Santa Fe, 1977-79, Mus. of N.Mex., Santa Fe, 1979, Robischon Gallery, Denver, 1984, 86, 90, Moss-Chumley Gallery, Dallas, 1987, Rettig-Martinez Gallery, Santa Fe, 1988, 91, 92, U. N.Mex. Art Mus., 1988, Albuquerque Mus., 1988, Louis Newman Gallery, L.A., 1989, Expositum Gallery, Mexico City, 1989, State U. Coll., Cortland, NY, 1991, Mus. Art, U. Ariz., Tucson, 1991, 2004, Indpls. Mus. Art, 1994, Ruschmon Gallery, Indpls., 1994, Mitchell Mus. Art, Vernon, Ill., 1995, Cline-Lewallen Gallery, Santa Fe, 1997, 2002, Anderson Gallery, Albuquerque, 1997, Fenix Gallery, Taos, NM State U., Las Crucis, 1998, Lewallen Gallery, Santa Fe, 2002, Cline Gallery, Scottsdale, 2002, 03, 04, Cline Fine Art, Scottsdale, Ariz., 2002, Gerald Peters Gallery, Santa Fe, 2005, Fresno Art Mus., 2005, others; exhibited group shows Phila. Print Club, 1960-63, Ind. Artists, 1947-63, White House, 1966, Nat. Lithographic Exhbn. Fla. State U., 1965, Library Congress, 1961-66, Bklyn. Mus., 1958-68, 76, U.S. Pavilion Venice Biennale, 1970, Internat. Biennial, Bradford, Eng., 1972-74, Internat. Biennial, Tokyo, 1972, City Mus. Hong Kong, 1972, Tamarind UCLA, 1985, Roswell Mus., 1989, Pace Gallery, 1990, Worcester (Mass.) Art Mus., 1990, Amon Carter Mus., Ft. Worth, 1990, Albuquerque Mus., 1991, 92, Art Mus. U. N.Mex., 1991, 92, 99, 2001, Norton Simon Mus., Pasadena, Calif., 1999, U. NH, 1999, Cline Fine Art, Scottsdale, Ariz., 2002, 03, Fenix Gallery, Taos, 2003, Fresno Mus. Art, 2005, Gerald Peters Gallery, Santa Fe, 2005; represented in permanent collections: Albuquerque Mus., Bklyn. Mus., Guggenheim Mus., NYC, Cin. Mus., Chgo. Art Inst., Ind. State Mus., Mus. Modern Art, NYC, Library of Congress, Met. Mus., NYC, NY Pub. Libr., Mus. Fine Arts, Santa Fe, also, Boston, Indpls., Seattle, Phila., San Diego, Dallas, Worcester Art Museums, Los Angeles County Mus., Roswell Mus. and Art Ctr., Tucson Mus., murals, Ind. U., Butler U., Ind. State Office Bldg., Smithsonian Inst., So. Ill. U., U. Nev., Cinn. Mus. Art, others. Combat artist with USCGR, World War II, PTO. Recipient Distinguished Alumni award Herron Sch. Art, 1972, N.Mex. Annual Gov.'s award, 1987; Grantee Nat. Endowment for Arts, 1983; fellow Nat. Acad. Design, NYC, 1993. Fellow NAD; mem. World Print Coun. (bd. dirs. 1980-87), Nat. Print Coun. Am. (co-pres. 1980-82), Coll. Art Assn. Am. (bd. dirs. 1977-80).

AOKI, MASANAO, economics professor; b. Hiroshima, Japan, May 14, 1931; came to U.S. 1956; BS, U. Tokyo, 1953, MS, 1955; PhD, UCLA, 1960; DSc, Tokyo Inst. Tech., 1966. Prof. elec. engring. and econs. UCLA, 1963-73, 75-81, 85-92; prof. U. Ill., 1973-75, U. Osaka, Japan, 1981-85. Author: Optimization of Stochastic Systems, 1967, 2d edit., 1989, State Space Modeling of Time Series, 1987, 2d edit., 1996, New Approaches to Macroeconomic Modelings: Evolutionary Stochastic Dynamics, Multiple Equilibria, and Externalities as Field Effects, Modeling Aggregate Behavior and Fluctuations in Economics, 2002, Reconstructing Macroeconomics: A Perspective of Statistical Physics and Combinational Stochastic Processes, 2007. Mem.: Soc. Econ. Dynamics and Control (pres. 1982—83), Soc. Instrument and Control Engring. Japan, Japanese Econ. Assn. Office: UCLA Dept Econs 405 Hilgard Ave Los Angeles CA 90095-1477 Home Phone: 310-472-1988; Office Phone: 310-825-2360. Business E-Mail: aoki@econ.ucla.edu.

APATOFF, MICHAEL JOHN, entrepreneur; b. Harvey, Ill., June 12, 1955; s. William and Frances (Brown) A; m. Monique Van Blitter, 2005; 1 child, Dante Madison. BA, Reed Coll., 1980. Chief legis. asst. to U.S. Congressman Al Ullman, Chmn. Ways and Means Com., Washington, 1978-80; spl. asst. to U.S. Congressman Tom Foley, Majority Whip, Washington, 1981-85; exec. v.p., COO Chgo. Merc. Exch., 1986-90; pres., COO Dresdner RCM Global Investors, San Francisco, 1991-98, fin. entrepreneur, 1999—. Office: 11 Edwards Ave Sausalito CA 94965 Personal E-mail: mapatoff@mac.com.

APATOW, JUDD, scriptwriter, television and film producer; b. Syosset, NY, Dec. 6, 1967; m. Leslie Mann; 1 child, Maude. Exec. prodr., writer (TV series) The Ben Stiller Show, 1992—93 (Emmy award for best writing, 1993), Freaks and Geeks, 1999—2000, co-exec. prodr., writer, dir. The Larry Sanders Show, 1992—98 (Cable ACE award, 1994, 1995), exec. prodr., writer, dir. Undeclared, 2001—02, prodr., writer (TV films) Life on Parole, 2003, Sick in the Head, 2003, (films) Knocked Up, 2007, assoc. prodr. Crossing the Bridge, 1992, exec. prodr., writer Heavy Weights, 1995, Celtic Pride, 1996; prodr.: (films) The Cable Guy, 1996, Anchorman: The Legend of Ron Burgundy, 2004; prodr.: (films) Talladega Nights: The Ballad of Ricky Bobby, 2006, Superbad, 2007; exec. prodr.: (films) Kicking & Screaming, 2005, American Storage, 2006, The TV Set, 2006; prodr., dir., writer (films) The 40 Year Old Virgin, 2005, prodr., writer Walk Hard: The Dewey Cox Story, 2007; author: (screenplays) Fun with Dick and Jane, 2005. Named one of Top 25 Entertainers of Yr. (with Apatow Gang), Entertainment Weekly, 2007, 50 Smartest People in Hollywood, 2007, The 100 Most Influential People in the World, TIME mag., 2008, The 100 Most Powerful Celebrities, Forbes.com, 2008. Office: United Talent Agy 9560 Wilshire Blvd Ste 500 Beverly Hills CA 90212

APFEL, GARY, lawyer; b. NYC, June 2, 1952; s. Willy and Jenny (Last) A.; m. Serena Jakobovits, June 16, 1980; children: Alyssa J., I. Michael, Alanna J., Stephen J., Alexander. BA, NYU magna cum laude, 1973; JD, Columbia U., 1976. Bar: N.Y. 1977, Calif. 1988, U.S. Dist. Ct. (so. and ea. dists.) N.Y. 1977, U.S. Dist. Ct. (cen. dist.) Calif. 1988, U.S. Ct. Appeals (9th cir.) 1988. Assoc. Sullivan & Cromwell, NYC, 1976-80, LeBoeuf, Lamb, Leiby & MacRae, NYC, 1980-84, ptnr., 1985-88, Kaye, Scholer, Fierman, Hays & Handler LLP, LA, 1988-97, Akin, Gump, Strauss, Hauer & Feld, L.L.P., LA, 1997—2000; chmn. bd. ELSA, Inc., 2000—01; co-mng. ptnr. LA office LeBoeuf, Lamb, Greene & MacRae LLP, 2001—, chmn. corp. dept. Kent scholar Columbia U., 1976. Mem. ABA, Calif. State Bar Assn. (bus. law sect. corps. com.), Phi Beta Kappa. Office: LeBoeuf Lamb Greene & MacRae 725 S Figueroa St Ste 3100 Los Angeles CA 90017 Office Phone: 213-955-7350. Office Fax: 213-955-7399. Business E-Mail: gapfel@llgm.com.

APFEL, JOSEPH H., optical engineer, research scientist; AB in Physics, U. Calif., Berkeley, 1954, MA in Physics, 1956, PhD in Physics, 1959. With Optical Coating Lab., Inc., Santa Rosa, Calif., 1961—, former dir. corp. rsch., former v.p., chief tech. officer, now part-time staff mem. Contbr. articles to sci. jours. Recipient Joseph Fraunhofer award and Robert M. Burley prize Optical Soc. Am., 1995. Office: Optical Coating Lab Inc 2789 Northpoint Pkwy Santa Rosa CA 95407-7397

APPELBAUM, FREDERICK RAY, oncologist; b. Canton, Ohio, Sept. 2, 1946; s. Samuel and Evelyn (Shapiro) A.; m. Janet Wynn Schwarz, Feb. 3, 1980; children: Jacob, David. AB, Dartmouth Coll., 1968; MD, Tufts U., 1972. Intern, resident U. Mich., Ann Arbor, 1972-74; clin. assoc. NIH, Bethesda, Md., 1974-76, investigator, 1976-78; asst. prof. Fred Hutchinson Cancer Rsch. Ctr., Seattle, 1978-83, assoc. prof., 1983-88, clin. rsch. mem., 1988—, dir. clin. rsch., 1993—; prof. med. oncology U. Wash. Sch. Medicine, Seattle, 1988—, dept. head divsn. med. oncology, 1998—. Mem. bd. sci. advisors Nat. Cancer Inst.; exec. dir., Seattle Cancer Alliance, 1998-. Assoc. editor: Blood, 1993-2002; editl. bd., Tumor, Leukemia, Am. Jour. Hematology, Video Jour. Oncology, Bone Marrow Transplantation, Hematological Oncology, Cancer Biotherapy and Radiopharmaceuticals, others; contbr. articles to profl. jours. Grantee NIH, 1980-. Mem. Am. Assn. for Cancer Rsch., Am. Soc. Clin. Oncology (bd. dirs. 1990-93), Am. Soc. Hematology (bd. councillors 1994-98). Am. Soc. Blood and Marrow Transplantation (bd. dir.), Internat. Soc. for Exptl. Hematology, Alpha Omega Alpha. Jewish. Office: Fred Hutchinson Cancer Rsch 1100 Fairview Ave N D5 310 PO Box 19024 Seattle WA 98109-1024 Personal E-mail: fappelba@fhcrc.org.

APPENZELLER, OTTO, neurologist, researcher; b. Czernowitz, Romania, Dec. 11, 1927; came to U.S., 1963; s. Emmanuel Adam and Josephine (Metsch) A.; m. Judith Bryce, Dec. 11, 1956; children: Timothy, Martin, Peter. MBBS, Sydney U., Australia, 1957, MD, 1966; PhD, U. London, 1963. Diplomate Am. Bd. Psychiatry and Neurology. Prof. U. N. Mex., Albuquerque, 1970-90; vis. prof. McGill U., Montreal, Canada, 1977; hon. rsch. fellow U. London, 1983; vis. scientist Oxygen Transport Program Lovelace Med. Found., Albuquerque, 1990-92; pres. N.Mex. Health Enhancement and Marathon Clinics Rsch. Found., Albuquerque, 1992—; prof. exptl. neurobiology Bogomoletz Inst. Ukrainian Acad. Sci., Kiev, 1995-2000. U.S.-India exch. scientist NSF, 1992; Fogarty internat. exch. scientist, Kiev, Ukraine, 1993; rsch. com. UNESCO Internat. Coun. Sports and Phys. Edn., 1978-99; ref. Med. Rsch. Coun. New Zealand, 1986-99, reviewer, 1988-99; participant individual health scientist exch. program Fogarty Internat. Ctr., NIH to A.A. Bogomoletz Inst. Physiology, Kiev, 1993. Author: The Autonomic Nervous System, 5th edit., 1997; co-author: Headache, 1984; editor: Pathogenesis and Management of Headache, 1976, Health Aspects of Endurance Training, 1978, Sports Medicine, 3d edit., 1988, Jour. Headache, 1975-77, Annals of Sports Medicine, 1984-88; translator: Neurologic Differential Diagnosis (M. Mumentaler), 2nd edit., 1992; vol. editor: Handbook of Clinical Neurology: The Autonomic Nervous System, Parts I and II, 1998-2000; mem. editl. bd. numerous med. jours. Grantee Diabetes Rsch. and Edn. Found., 1988, Inst. C. Mondino, U. Pavia, Italy, 1992, 95-96, 2000, NMHEMC Rsch. Found., 1992-2008. Fellow ACP (sr.), Am. Acad. Neurology (sr.), Royal Australasian Coll. Physicians (sr.). Achievements include discovery of disease affecting peripheral nerves of Navajo children, of release of opioids and endothelin in human circulatory system after exercise, of chronic neurodegenerative disease in human T-lymphotropic viral II (HTLV II) infection, of peptidergic innervation of blood vessels supplying blood to peripheral nerves in present day and ancient mummified tissues of neurologic dis. in mummy portraits, of neuropathy in chronic pulmonary disease and chronic mountain sickness of fossilized biological rhythm in ancient human teeth, and teeth of extinct archosaurs; of archived biologic rhythms in human and animal hair; of cerebral vasodilatation to nitric oxide as a measure of fitness for life at altitude, of Molecular Signature, of Chronic Mountain Sickness in the Andes and Himalayas; of biologic markers of susceptibility to chronic mountain sickness in healthy children of andean highlanders, leader of Mt. Everest rsch. expedition, 1987, Khachenjunga and Himalayas rsch. expedition, 1989, Stock Kangri rsch. expedition, 1992, Tso Moriri Lake (Ladakh) rsch. expedition, 1994, Cerro de Pasco rsch. expedition, 1997, 99-2000, 03, rsch. expedition Simen Mountains, Ethiopia, 2005, Korzok, Ladakh, 2006, 2007, Ethiopia, Bale Mountain, 2009. Business E-Mail: oarun@unm.edu. E-mail: ottoarun12@aol.com, o.appenzeller@comcast.net.

APPLEGATE, CHRISTINA, actress; b. L.A., Nov. 25, 1971; d. Robert Applegate and Nancy Priddy; m. Johnathon Schaech, Oct. 20, 2001 (div. Aug. 10, 2007). Actress: (films) Jaws of Satan, 1980, Streets, 1990, Don't Tell Mom the Babysitter's Dead, 1991, Across the Moon, 1994, Vibrations, 1995, Wild Bill, 1995, Mars Attacks!, 1996, Nowhere, 1997, Claudine's Return, 1998, The Big Hit, 1998, Jane Austen's Mafia!, 1998, Out in Fifty, 1999, The Giving Tree, 2000, Just Visiting, 2001, Sol Goode, 2001, The Sweetest Thing, 2002, Heroes, 2003, View from the Top, 2003, Wonderland, 2003, Grand Theft Parsons, 2003, Employee of the Month, 2004, Anchorman: The Legend of Ron Burgundy, 2004, Surviving Christmas, 2004, Tilt-A-Whirl, 2005, The Rocker, 2008; (TV series) Washingtoon, 1985, Heart of the City, 1985-86, Married...With Children, 1987-97, Jesse, 1998-2000, Samantha Who?, 2007- (TV movies) Grace Kelly, 1983, Heart of the City, 1986, Dance 'til Dawn, 1988, Prince Charming, 2001, Suzanne's Diary for Nicholas, 2005, (voice only) Farce of the Penguins, 2006; (TV appearances) Father Murphy, 1981, Charles in Charge, 1984, '85, Silver Spoons, 1985, All Is Forgiven, 1986, Still the Beaver, 1986, Amazing Stories, 1986, Family Ties, 1987, 21 Jump Street, 1987, Top of the Heap, 1991, Saturday Night Live, 1993, Pauly, 1997, Friends, 2002, (voice only) King of the Hill, 2004, Reno 911!, 2008; Off-broadway appearances include: Sweet Charity, 2005 (Theatre World award, 2005), Named Favorite Female TV Star, People's Choice Awards, 2009.

APPLEMAN, NATE, chef; m. Clarisse Appleman. Grad., Culinary Inst. Am., Hyde Park, NY. Cert. pizzaiolos Verace Pizza Napoletana Assn. Intern Maisonette, Cin.; with Brasa, Seattle, 1999; mgr. meat station Campton Place, San Francisco, 2001; exec. sous chef Tra Vigne, A16, San Francisco, 2003—05, chef de cuisine, co-owner, 2005—06, exec. chef, co-owner, 2006—. Recipient Rising Star Chef of Yr. award, James Beard Found., 2009; named one of San Francisco's Rising Stars, StarChefs.com, 2007, America's Best New Chefs, Food & Wine Mag., 2009; nominee Rising Star Chef of Yr. award, James Beard Found., 2007. Office: A16 2355 Chestnut St San Francisco CA 94123 Office Phone: 415-771-2216.

APPLETON, JAMES ROBERT, academic administrator, educator; b. North Tonawanda, NY, Jan. 20, 1937; s. Robert Martin and Emma (Mollnow) A.; m. Carol Koelsch, Aug. 8, 1959; children: Steven, Jon, Jennifer. AB in Social Sci., Wheaton Coll., 1958; MA, PhD, Mich. State U., 1965. Lectr. Mich. State U., East Lansing, 1969-72; assoc. dean students Oakland U., Rochester, Mich., 1965-68, dean student life, 1968-72, assoc. prof. behavioral scis., 1969-72, v.p., 1969-72; v.p. student affairs U. So. Calif., LA, 1972-82, v.p. devel., 1982-87; pres. Univ. Redlands, Calif., 1987—2005, chancellor, 2005—. Author: Pieces of Eight: Rights, Roles & Styles of the Dean; guest editor Nat. Assn. Student Pers. Adminstrs. Jour., 1971; contbr. articles to profl. jours. Bd. dirs. So. Calif. Ind. Colls.; bd. dirs., treas., mem. exe. com. Nat. Assn. Ind. Colls. and Univs.; mem. exec. com. Inland Empire Econ. Partnership; mem. nat. exec. com. Tuition Exch.; trustee San Francisco Presbyn. Sem., 1985-95. 1st lt. U.S. Army, 1958-60. Named One of 100 Emerging Young Leaders in Higher Edn., Am. Council Edn./Change, 1978; recipient Fred Turner award Nat. Assn. Student Personnel Adminstrs., 1980. Mem. NCAA (pres.'s commn.), Assn. Ind. Calif. Colls. & Univs. (govtl. rels. com.), Am. Assn. Higher Edn., Western Coll. Assn. (past pres.). Avocations: music, sports. Home: 1861 Rossmont Dr Redlands CA 92373-7219 Office: U Redlands 1200 E Colton Ave PO Box 3080 Redlands CA 92373-0999 E-mail: james_appleton@redlands.edu.

APPLETON, STEVEN R., electronics executive; b. Mar. 1960; BBA, Boise State U., 1982. Fab supr., prodn. mgr., dir. mfg., v.p. mfg. Micron Tech., Inc., Boise, Idaho, 1983—91, pres., COO, 1991—94, chmn., CEO, pres., 1994—. Chmn. Semiconductor Ind. Assn.; bd. dir. Nat. Semiconductor Inc.; mem. World Semiconductor Council. Trustee Boise State Univ.; mem. Idaho Bus. Council. Office: Micron Tech PO Box 6 8000 South Federal Way Boise ID 83707

APRIL, RAND SCOTT, lawyer; b. Bklyn., Feb. 10, 1951; s. Arthur and Muriel (Marmorstein) A. BA, Northwestern U., 1972; JD, Columbia U., 1975. Bar: N.Y. 1976, U.S. Dist. Ct. (so. and ea. dists.) N.Y. 1976, Calif. 1989. Assoc. Marshall, Bratter, Greene, Allison & Tucker, NYC, 1975-78, Gordon, Hurwitz, Butowsky, Baker, Weitzen & Shalov, NYC, 1978-81, Skadden, Arps, Slate, Meagher & Flom, NYC, 1981-83, ptnr., 1983—. Stone scholar Columbia U., 1974-75. Mem. Phi Beta Kappa. Avocation: skiing. Office: Skadden Arps Slate Meagher & Flom 300 S Grand Ave Los Angeles CA 90071-3109

APT, LEONARD, pediatric ophthalmologist; AB with highest honors, U. Pa., 1942; MD with highest honors, Jefferson Med. Coll., 1945. Diplomate Am. Bd. Pediat., Am. Bd. Ophthalmology. Intern Jefferson Med. Coll. Hosp., Phila., 1945-46; rsch. fellow in pathology-hematology, resident in pediat. Children's Hosp., Detroit, 1946-49, resident in pediat. Cin., 1949—50, Children's Med. Ctr., Boston, 1950-52, chief med. resident, 1952-53, asst. physician, 1953-55; resident in ophthalmology Wills Eye Hosp., Phila., 1955-57; first spl. fellow in pediat. ophthalmology NIH, Bethesda, and Children's Hosp., Washington, 1957—59; first fellow in Pediat. Ophthalmology

Wills Eye Hosp., Phila., 1959—61; from asst. prof. to prof. ophthalmology Sch. Medicine, UCLA, 1961—72, prof., 1972—; disting. prof. UCLA, 1993—; attending surgeon Jules Stein Eye Inst., UCLA, founding dir. divsn. pediat. ophthalmology, 1961—81, founder, 1966, dir. emeritus, 1981—, co-dir. ctr. to prevent childhood blindness, 2005—. Tchg. fellow in pediat. Harvard U. Med. Sch., Boston, 1950—52, instr. pediat., 1953—55; sr. physician radioisotope unit Boston VA Hosp., 1953—55; cons. pediat. ophthalmology Cedars-Sinai Med. Ctr., LA, St. John's Hosp., Santa Monica, Calif., Bur. Maternal and Child Health, Dept. Pub. Health Calif., Dept. Health, LA. Author: Diagnostic Procedures in Pediatric Ophthalmology, 1963; mem. editl. bd.: numerous med. jours.; contbr. articles to profl. jours., chapters to books. Founder L.A. Philharmonic Assn.; presdl. circle mem. L.A. County Mus. of Art; v.p. fin. UCLA Grunwald Ctr. for Graphic Arts, Hammer Mus.; bd. dirs. Royce Ctr. Cir., UCLA Performing Arts Dept.; bd. dirs. Cmty. Outreach Program UCLA Design for Sharing; founder John Wooden UCLA Athletic Ctr.; exec. coun. mem. UCLA Divsn. of Humanities; founder UCLA Acosta Athletic Tng. Complex; judge Wines of Am. Ann. Competition. 1st lt. M.C. US Army, 1943—46. Recipient F.T. Stewart Surgery prize, Jefferson Med. Coll., 1945, Arthur J. Bedell Resident Rsch. prize, Wills Eye Hosp., Phila., 1957, Disting. Alumnus Achievement award, Jefferson Med. Coll., 1992, 1st Escalon Sci. award, 1992, Hall of Fame Distinction award, Cin. Pediat. Hist. Soc., 1994, 1st Disting. Alumni award, Sch. Arts and Scis. U. Pa., 1995, Alumni Univ. Svc. award, UCLA, 1996, William Feinbloom 1st Disting. Achievement award, 1999, Profl. Achievement award, UCLA Med. Alumni Assn., 1999, 1st Disting. Achievement award, Ethicon Inc.-Johnson & Johnson Co., 1999, S. Rodman Irvine prize, Jules Stein Eye Inst., UCLA, 2005. Mem.: AMA, Am. Med. Writers Assn., Pacific Coast Oto-Ophthal. Soc., Internat. Strabismol. Assn., Am. Assn. Pediat. Ophthalmology and Strabismus (1st Disting. Achievement award 1996, Honor award 1995), Soc. Pediat. Rsch., Assn. for Rsch. Ophthalmology, Am. Ophthal. Soc., Am. Acad. Pediats. (Lifetime Achievement award 2000, Ann. Leonard Apt Lectureship named in his honor 2000), Am. Acad. Ophthalmology (Honor award 1968), L'Ordre Mondial des Gourmets Deguistaeurs, Confrerie de la Chaine des Rotisseurs, Internat. Wine and Food Soc., Shriner, Masons (32d deg.), Alpha Omega Alpha. Avocations: sports, art, theater, gourmet food, oenology. Office: UCLA Sch Medicine Jules Stein Eye Inst 100 Stein Plz Los Angeles CA 90095-7000 Office Phone: 310-277-8383, 310-825-3986. Office Fax: 310-206-3652.

APTED, MICHAEL DAVID, film director; b. London, Feb. 10, 1941; BA, Downing Coll., Cambridge, Eng., 1963. Pres. Directors Guild Am., 2003—; mem. bd. govs. Acad. Motion Picture Arts and Scis. (documentary br.), 2002—. Dir.: (films) Triple Echo, 1972, Stardust, 1974, The Squeeze, 1976, Agatha, 1977, Coalminer's Daughter, 1980 (DGA nominee), Continental Divide, 1981, Gorky Park, 1983, Kipperbang, 1983 (Brit. Acad. TV and Film award nominee), Firstborn, 1984, Critical Condition, 1986, Gorillas in the Mist, 1988, Class Action, 1990, Thunderheart, 1991, Blink, 1993, Nell, 1994, Extreme Measures, 1996, Always Outnumbered, 1998, The World Is Not Enough, 1999, Enigma, 2000, Enough, 2002, Lipstick, 2002, Amazing Grace, 2006; (play) Strawberry Fields, 1978 (BAFTA, Emmy award); (documentaries) 14 UP, 21 UP (Internat. Emmy), 28 UP (Brit. Acad. award, Internat. Emmy), 1985, Bring On the Night, 1984 (Emmy, Grammy awards), The Long Way Home, 1989, Incident at Oglala, 1991, 35 UP, 1992 (BAFTA award), Moving the Mountain, 1993 (IDA award), Inspirations, 1997, 42 Up, 1998, Me & Isaac Newton, 1999, Married in America, 2002, 49 Up, 2005, The Grand Finale, 2006, Married in America 2, 2006, The Power of the Game, 2006; (Brit. TV) Slattery's Mounted Foot, 1970 (Brit. Critics Best Play), The Mosedale Horshoe, 1971 (Brit. Critics Best Play), Another Sunday and Sweet F.A., 1972 (Brit. Critics Best Play), Follyfoot, 1972 (Best Children's Svcs.), Kisses at Fifty (Brit. Critics Best Play, SFTA Best Dir.), The Collection (Internat. Emmy), (Am. TV) Big Breadwinner Hog, 1969, The Lovers, 1970, Follyfoot, 1971, My Life and Times, 1991, Crossroads, 1992, New York News, 1995, Rome, 2005 (Outstanding Directorial Achievement in Dramatic Series Night Directors Guild Am., 2005).

APUAN, DENNIS, state legislator; b. Manilla, Phillipines, Oct. 30, 1964; Mem. Dist. 17 Colo. House of Reps., Denver, 2008—. Vice chmn. El Paso County Dem. Party. Former bus. adminstr. Broadmoor Cmty. Ch.; cmty. organizer Colo. Unity; regional dir. Colo. Progressive Coalition; former mem. U. Colo-Colo. Springs Diversity Strategic Planning Team; program dir. & chmn. Pikes Peak Justice & Peace Commn. Democrat. Office: State House 200 E Colfax Denver CO 80203 Office Phone: 303-866-3069. Business E-Mail: dennis.apuan.house@state.co.us.*

APUZZO, MICHAEL LAWRENCE JOHN, neurological surgeon; b. New Haven, 1940; BA, Yale U., 1961; MD, Boston U., 1965. Intern in neurosurgery Yale U.; resident in surgery McGill U., 1966; resident in neurosurgery Yale U., New Haven, 1967-73; prof. neurol. surgery, radiation oncology, biology and physics U. So. Calif. Sch. Medicine, LA. Editor Neurosurgery on-line; contbr. over 600 articles to profl. jours. Office: U So Calif Sch Medicine Ste 5046 1200 N State St Los Angeles CA 90033-1029 Office Phone: 323-442-3001. Business E-Mail: apuzzo@usc.edu.

AQUILINI, FRANCESCO, investment company executive, professional sports team executive; s. Luigi Aquilini. B in Bus. Adminstrn., Simon Fraser U.; MBA, UCLA. Mng. dir. Aquilini Investment Group, Vancouver, BC, Canada; co-owner Vancouver Canucks, 2004—06, owner, chmn., gov., 2006—. Chair, primary sponsor Italian Gardens, Hastings Park, Vancouver. Office: Vancouver Canucks 800 Griffiths Way Vancouver BC V6B 6G1 Canada also: Aquilini Investment Group Standard Bldg Ste 200 - 510 W Hastings St Vancouver BC V6B 1L8 Canada

AQUINO, HENRY J. C., state legislator; b. Honolulu, Hawaii, May 26, 1977; AAS in Justice Adminstrn., Honolulu Cmty. Coll., 1999; BA in Pub. Adminstrn., U. Hawaii, West Oahu, 2002; MA in Comm., Hawaii Pacific U., 2007. Stock & driver You & Me Naturally Inc., 1998—2002; security & adminstrn. officer Wackenhutt Corp., 2003, Outrigger, 2003, Ohana Hotels, 2003; dist. chmn. Hawaii Dem. Party, 2004—05, region chmn., 2005—07; mem. Dist. 35 Hawaii House of Reps., 2008—. Asst. dir. A.G.A.P.E Ministry of Hawaii-Pacific, 1993—; vol. Rep. Julie Duldulao Campaign Com., 1994; religious edn. tchr. Saint Joseph CCD, 1998—; mem. Waipahu Elemn. Sch. Cmty. Coun., 2007—. Mem.: Catholic Charities Hawaii (classroom 7 presentation specialist 2005—07), Oahu Santanians, Waipahu Cmty. Assn. (dir. 2005—07, program coord. 2007—), Leeward Oahu Lions Club. Democrat. Catholic. Office: State Capitol 415 S Beretania St Rm 310 Honolulu HI 96813 Office Phone: 808-586-6520. Office Fax: 808-586-6521. Business E-Mail: repaquino@capitol.hawaii.gov.

ARABIAN, ARMAND, arbitrator, mediator, lawyer; b. NYC, Dec. 12, 1934; s. John and Aghavnie (Yalian) A.; m. Nancy Arabian, Aug. 26, 1962; children: Allison Ann, Robert Armand. BSBA, Boston U., 1956, JD, 1961; LLM, U. So. Calif., LA, 1970; LLD (hon.), Southwestern Sch. Law, 1990, Pepperdine U., 1990, U. West LA, 1994, We. State U., 1997, Thomas Jefferson Sch. of Law, 1997, Am. Coll. Law, 2001. Bar: Calif. 1962, US Supreme Ct. 1966. Dep. dist. atty. LA County, 1962-63; pvt. practice law Van Nuys, Calif., 1963-72; judge Mcpl. Ct., LA, 1972-73, Superior Ct., LA, 1973-83; assoc. justice Calif. Ct. Appeal, LA, 1983-90, Supreme Ct. Calif., San Francisco, 1990-96. Adj. prof. sch. law Pepperdine U., 1996-98. Contbr. articles to profl. jours. 1st lt. US Army, 1956-58. Recipient Stanley Lintz Meml. award San Fernando Valley Bar Assn., 1986, Lifetime Achievement award San Fernando Valley Bar Assn., 1993, Outstanding Jurist of the Yr., Malibu Bar Assn., 1996, Mesrob Mashdots medal Aram I Catholicos, Beirut, Lebanon, 1999, Mekhitar medal Brotherhood in Venice, Italy, 1999, Gold medal of honor of Peter the Great, Russian Acad. Sci., 1999, Mekhitar Gosh medal Pres. of Armenia Robert Kocharian, 2001, St. James the Apostle medal Beatitude Torkom Manoogian, Jerusalem, 2001, Albert Einstein Gold medal of honor, Russian Acad. Natural Scis., 2003, Ellis Island Medal Honor award, 2004, St. Gregory the Illuminator medal Karekin II Catholicos Yerevan, Armenia, 2004, Women of LA Highlight award, 2005, Fernando award, 2006; Pappas Disting. scholar Boston U. Sch. Law, 1987; Justice Armand Arabian Resource and Comm. Ctrs. named in honor of Van Nuys and San Fernando Calif. Courthouses, 1999; named reception area in his honor Chatsworth Superior Courthouse, Los Angeles County, 2005. Fernando award Found. Inc. of the San Fernando Valley Ake. Republican. Office: Arms Providers Inc 6259 Van Nuys Blvd Van Nuys CA 91401-2711 Office Phone: 818-997-8900. Fax: 818-781-6002. Business E-Mail: honarabian@aol.com.

ARAMBULA, JUAN, state legislator; m Amy; children: Joaquin, Carmen, Diego, Miguel. BA in Comparative Lit., Harvard U., 1975; MA in Edni. Adminstrn./Policy Analysis, Stanford U., 1978; JD, U. Calif., Berkeley, 1981. Supr. Fresno County Bd. Supervisors, 1997-2004; California State Assemblyman, District 31, 2005-; chmn, Jobs, Econ Develop & the Econ; member, Budget, Education, Education Finance & the Teach Prof comts, currently. Mem. Fresno Unified Sch. Bd., 1987—96, pres., 1990, 1994; co-chair Fresno Regional Jobs Initiative. Rose An Vuich Award for Ethics in Leadership, 2002. Mem.: Fresno County Sch. Trustees Assn. (pres.), Calif. State Assn. Counties, Calif. Sch. Boards Assn. (mem. bd. dirs.). Democrat. Office: Hugh Burns State Bldg 2550 Mariposa Mall Ste 5031 Fresno CA 93721 also: Rm 6011 PO Box 942849 Sacramento CA 94240-0031 Office Phone: 916-319-2031, 559-445-5532. Office Fax: 559-445-6006, 916-319-2131. Business E-Mail: assemblymember.arambula@assembly.ca.gov.

ARANAS, PAULINE, law librarian, educator; BA, UCLA; JD, U. So. Calif.; MLIS, U. Calif., Berkeley. Reference libr. law libr. U. So. Calif. Gould Sch. Law, LA, 1984, assoc. dir., adj. assoc. prof. law, 1992, assoc. dean, COO, 2004—06, assoc. dean, dep. dir. law libr., 2006—; dir. Alyne Queener Massey Law Libr., Vanderbilt U. Law Sch., 1994—2002, asst. dean libr. and info. tech., assoc. prof. law; assoc. law libr. UCLA Sch. Law, 2002—04. Mem.: State Bar of Calif., Am. Assn. Law Libraries. Office: USC Gould Sch Law 699 Exposition Blvd, 210 Los Angeles CA 90017 Office Phone: 213-740-6482. Office Fax: 213-740-7179. E-mail: paranas@law.usc.edu.

ARANT, EUGENE WESLEY, lawyer; b. North Powder, Oreg., Dec. 21, 1920; s. Ernest Elbert and Wanda (Haller) A.; m. Juanita Clark Flowers, Mar. 15, 1953; children: Thomas W., Kenneth E., Richard W. BS in Elec. Engring, Oreg. State U., 1943; JD, U. So. Calif., 1949. Bar: Calif. 1950. Mem. engring. faculty U. So. Calif., 1947-51; pvt. practice LA, 1950—51; patent atty. Hughes Aircraft Co., Culver City, Calif., 1953-56; pvt. practice LA, 1957—2001, Lincoln City, Oreg., 2001—. Author: The Idea Business: Rules of the Game, 2005; contbr. articles in american bar journal. Mem. La Mirada (Calif.) City Coun., 1958-60; trustee Beverly Hills Presbyn. Ch., 1976-78. Served with AUS, 1943-46, 51-53. Mem. ABA, State Bar Calif. Democrat. Home: 100 NE Indian Shores Lincoln City OR 97367 Office: PO Box 269 Lincoln City OR 97367 Office Phone: 541-557-1716. E-mail: gwapat@charterinternet.com.

ARBER, DANIEL ALAN, hematologist, pathologist; b. Houston, Tex., May 16, 1961; s. Harry D. and Nancy R. Arber; m. Carol A. Park, Apr. 15, 2006. BS, Tex. A&M U., College Station, 1983; MD, U. Tex. Health Sci. Ctr., San Antonio, 1986. Diplomate in anatomic and clin. pathology Am. Bd. Pathology, 1991, in hematology Am. Bd. Pathology, 1993. Intern E.A. Conway Meml. Hosp. La. State U. Shreveport, Monroe, La., 1986—87; resident anatomic and clin. pathology Scott & White Clinic Tex. A&M U., Temple, Tex., 1987—91, asst. prof. pathology Scott and White Clinic, 1993—94; fellow hematopathology City Hope Nat. Med. Ctr., Duarte, Calif., 1991—93, staff pathologist, 1995—2002, dir. hematopathology and molecular pathology, 1997—2002; prof. pathology Stanford U., Stanford, Calif., 2002—, assoc. chmn. pathology, 2005—, interm dir., clin. pathology and anatomic pathology svc., 2007—. Author: Illustrated Pathology of the Bone Marrow, 2006; contbr. chapters to books, over 150 articles to profl. jours. Named to America's Top Doctors for Cancer, 2005, 2006, Best Doctors in Am., 2005—06. Mem.: Arthur Purdy Stout Soc. Office: Stanford Univ Pathology 300 Pasteur Dr H1507 Stanford CA 94306-5627

ARBIB, MICHAEL ANTHONY, neuroscientist, educator, computer scientist; b. Eastbourne, U.K., May 28, 1940; came to U.S., 1961; s. John R. and Helen (Arbib) A.; m. Prue Hassell, Dec. 29, 1965; children: Phillipa Jane, Benjamin Giles. BSc with honors, U. Sydney, 1960; PhD in Math., MIT, 1963. Mem. faculty Stanford (Calif.) U., 1965-70, assoc. prof. elec. engring., 1969-70; adj. prof. psychology, prof. computer and info. sci. U. Mass., Amherst, 1970-86, chmn. dept. computer and info. sci., 1970-75; dir. Ctr. for Systems Neurosci., 1974-86, dir. Cognitive Sci. Program, 1980-82, dir. Lab. Perceptual Robotics, 1982-86; prof. biomed. engring., neurobiology, psychology U. So. Calif., LA, 1986-94, prof. computer sci., elec. engring., 1986—, dir. Ctr. for Neural Engring., 1987-94, dir. USC Brain Project, 1994—, chair computer sci., 1999-2000, Fletcher Jones prof. computer sci., prof., 1999—. Vis. prof. U. Western Australia, Perth, 1974, 96, 99, 2000, Technion, Israel, 1975, Washington U., St. Louis, 1976, U. Edinburgh, 1976-77, U. Calif., Irvine, 1980; vis. scientist Inst. Cybernetics, Barcelona, spring 1985, Cognitive Scis. Inst., U. Calif., San Diego, 1985-86; vis. lectr. U. New South Wales, Australia, 1962, 65, 68, Mont. State U., summers, 1963, 65, Imperial Coll. London, 1964; Gifford lectr. in natural theology U. Edinburgh, Scotland, 1983; John Douglas French lectr. Brain Rsch. Inst., UCLA, 1993; lectr. tours to U.S., USSR, Japan, Australia and China. Author: Brains, Machines and Mathematics, 1964, 2d. edit., 1987, Theories of Abstract Automata, 1969, The Metaphorical Brain, 1972, Computers and the Cybernetic Society, 1977, 2d edit., 1984, In Search of the Person, 1985, The Metaphorical Brain 2, 1989; (with others) Topics in Mathematical System Theory, 1969, System Theory, 1974, Discrete Mathematics, 1974, Conceptual Models of Neural Organization, 1974, Arrows, Structures and Functors, 1975, Design of Well-Structured and Correct Programs, 1978, A Basis for Theoretical Computer Science, 1981, A Programming Approach to Computability, 1982, Algebraic Approaches to Program Semantics, 1986, The Construction of Reality, 1986, From Schema Theory to Language, 1987, An Introduction to Formal Language Theory, 1988, Neural Organization: Structure, Function, Dynamics, 1997, The Neural Simulation Language, 2002; editor: The Handbook of Brain Theory and Neural Networks, 1995, 2d edit., 2003, (with others) Algebraic Theory of Machines, Languages and Semigroups, 1968, Neural Models of Language Processes, 1982, Competition and Cooperation in Neural Nets, 1982, Adaptive Control of Ill-Defined Systems, 1983, Vision, Brain and Cooperative Computation, 1987, Dynamic Interactions in Neural Networks: Models and Data, 1988, Visuomotor Coordination: Amphibia, Comparisons, Models, and Robots, 1989, Natural and Artificial Parallel Computation, 1990, Visual Structures and Integrated Functions, 1991, Neuroscience: From Neural Networks to Artificial Intelligence, 1993, Neuroscience and the Person, 1999, Computing the Brain, A Guide to Neuroinformatics, 2001; contbr. articles to profl. jours. Mem. IEEE, AAAS, Soc. Neurosci. Office: U So Calif Brain Project Los Angeles CA 90089-2750

ARBUTHNOT, ROBERT MURRAY, lawyer; b. Montreal, Quebec, Can., Oct. 23, 1936; s. Leland Claude and Winnifred Laura (Hodges) A.; m. Janet Marie O'Keefe, Oct. 6, 1968; children: Douglas, Michael, Mary Kathleen, Allison Anne. BA, Calif. State U., San Francisco, 1959; JD, U. Calif., San Francisco, 1966. Bar: Calif. 1967, U.S. Dist. Ct. (no. and cen. dists.) Calif. 1967, U.S. Ct. Appeals (9th cir.) 1967, U.S. Supreme Ct. 1975. Assoc. trial lawyer Rankin & Craddick, Oakland, Calif., 1967-69; assoc. atty. Ericksen, Arbuthnot, Brown, Kilduff & Day, Inc., San Francisco, 1970-73, ptnr., 1973-80, chmn. bd., mng. dir., 1980—. Gen. counsel CFS Ins. Svcs., San Francisco, 1990—; pro tem judge, arbitrator San Francisco Superior Ct., 1990—; lectr. in field. Bd. regents St. Mary's Coll. High Sch., Berkeley, Calif., 1988-91. With U.S. Army, 1959-62. Recipient Honors plaque St. Mary's Coll. High Sch., 1989. Mem. Internat. Assn. of Ins. Counsel, No. Calif. Assn. of Def. Counsel, Def. Rsch. Inst., Assn. Trial Lawyers Am., San Francisco Lawyers Club. Avocation: boating. Office: Ericksen Arbuthnot Kicduff Et Al 111 Sutter St #575 San Francisco CA 94104 E-mail: eakdlsf@aol.com.

ARCE, PHILLIP WILLIAM, hotel and casino executive; b. NYC, June 25, 1937; s. Joseph F. and Margaret (Degnan) A.; m. Dorothy Fiss, June 25, 1966; children: Joseph, William, Serena. Student, U. Notre Dame, 1955-56; AA, San Diego Jr. Coll., 1958; student, San Diego State U., 1958-60, San Diego U., 1960-62, LaSalle Law Sch., 1963-65. Various positions Del Webb Corp., Las Vegas and Reno, Nev., Oahu, Hawaii, 1963-75; exec. Caesars Palace, Las Vegas, 1975-78; pres. Frontier Hotel, Las Vegas, 1978-84; corp. v.p., v.p. mktg., sr. v.p. Dunes Hotel & Country Club, Las Vegas, 1985-88; hotel and gaming specialist Arce Cons., Las Vegas, 1988—. Tchr. hotel div. U. Nev., Las Vegas, 1966-67, 1976-77 Mem. exec. com. Boulder Dam Area coun. Boy Scouts Am., 1976-88; vice chmn. United Way So. Nev., 1968-70; founder, chmn. Las Vegas Events, Inc., 1980-89; pres. Easter Seals Nev., 1974-76, pres. first nat. telethon, 1975; bd. dirs. Air Force Acad. Found., 1982-89. Served with USMC, 1962. Recipient Appreciation award Easter Seals, 1972, 73, United Way, 1975, Silver Beaver Boy Scouts Am., 1984, others. Mem. Am. Hotel and Motel Assn. (bd. dirs. 1979-82), Nev. Hotel and Motel Assn. (founder, pres. 1980, Hotelier of Yr. award 1981), Las Vegas C. of C. (dir. 1979-85, pres. 1984). Republican. Roman Catholic. Home: 4243 Ridgecrest Dr Las Vegas NV 89121-4949 Office Phone: 702-458-7327.

ARCHER, CRISTINA LOZEJ, research scientist; b. Como, Italy, Apr. 21, 1970; d. Alessandra Bonfanti; m. Scott Mckinley Archer, Nov. 4, 2000; children: Eva Julia children: Emma Tiffany, Clara Maria. MS, Politecnico di Milano, Italy, 1995, San Jose State U., Calif., 1998; PhD, Stanford U., Calif., 2004. Post doctoral scholar Stanford U., 2004—05; atmospheric modeler Bay Area Air Quality Mgmt. Dist., San Francisco, 2005—07; rsch. assoc. Carnegie Instn. Washington, Stanford, Calif., 2007—. Cons. asst. prof. dept. civil and environ. engring. Stanford U., 2005—. Contbr. articles to profl. jours. Recipient Best thesis in environ. field award, Regione Lombardia, Milano, Italy, 1995. Mem.: Am. Geophys. Union, Am. Meteorol. Soc. (assoc.). Roman Catholic. Achievements include research in first study on global wind power potential; discovery and study of an atmospheric vortex. Avocations: bicycling, beach, reading, knitting. Office: Carnegie Instn Washington Dept Global Ecology 260 Panama St Stanford CA 94305 Personal E-mail: lozej@stanford.edu.

ARCHER, RICHARD JOSEPH, lawyer; b. Virginia, Minn., Mar. 24, 1922; s. William John and Margaret Leanore (Duff) A.; m. Kristina Hanson, Jan. 29, 1977 (dec.); children: Alison P., Cynthia J. AB, U. Mich., 1947, JD, 1948. Bar: Calif. 1949, U.S. Supreme Ct. 1962, Hawaii 1982. Partner firm Morrison and Foerster, San Francisco, 1954-71, Sullivan, Jones and Archer, San Francisco, 1971-81, Archer Rosenak & Hanson, San Francisco, 1981-85, Archer & Hanson, San Francisco, 1985—. With USNR, 1942—45. Decorated Bronze Star. Mem. ABA, Am. Bar Found. (life), Am. Law Inst. (life). Home: 702 Petaluma Blvd South Apt 48 Petaluma CA 94952 Office Phone: 707-874-3438. Personal E-mail: archerdic@aol.com.

ARCHER, STEPHEN HUNT, economist, educator; b. Fargo, ND, Nov. 30, 1928; s. Clifford Paul and Myrtle Mona (Blair) A.; m. Carol Rosa Mohr, Dec. 29, 1951 (div. Feb. 1971); children: Stephen Paul, Timothy William, David Conrad; m. Lana Jo Urban, Sept. 23, 1972 (dec. Mar. 2003). BA, U. Minn., 1949, MS, 1953, PhD, 1958; postdoctoral student (Ford Found. grantee), U. Calif. at Los Angeles, 1959-60. Mgr. trader J.M. Dain Co., Mpls., 1950, account exec., 1952-53; instr. econs. U. Minn., Mpls., 1954-56; asst. prof. fin. U. Wash., Seattle, 1956-60, assoc. prof., 1960-65, prof., 1965-73, chmn. dept. fin., bus. econs. and quantitative methods, 1966-70; dean Grad. Sch. Adminstrn. Willamette U., Salem, Oreg., 1973-76, 83-85, prof., 1976-79, Guy F. Atkinson prof., 1979-96. Fulbright sr. lectr. Bocconi U., Milan, Italy, 1982; v.p. Hinton, Jones & Co., Inc., Seattle,

1969-70; cons. Wash. Bankers Assn., 1971-72, Weyerhaeuser Co., 1971, Bus.-Econs. Adv. & Research Inc., 1969-77, State of Oreg., 1984, 86, 88, 91; vis. prof. Manchester Bus. Sch., Manchester, Eng., 1990-91, Aomori (Japan) Pub. coll., 2000-01. Author: Introduction to Mathematics for Business Analysis, 1960, Business Finance: Theory and Mgmt, 1966, rev. edit., 1972, The Theory of Business Finance, 1967, 2d rev. edit., 1983, Portfolio Analysis, 1971, rev. edit., 1979, Introduction to Financial Management, 1979, rev. edit., 1983, Cases and Readings in Corporate Finance, 1988; editor Jour. Fin. and Quantitative Analysis, 1966-70, Economic Perspectives, Economica Aziendale, Jour. Bus. and Entrepreneurship. Served with USNR, 1950-52. Mem.: Phi Beta Kappa, Beta Gamma Sigma. Home: 520 SE Columbia River Dr Apt 425 Vancouver WA 98661-8035 Personal E-mail: sarcher75@comcast.net.

ARCHERD, ARMY (ARMAND A. ARCHERD), columnist, retired commentator; b. Bronx, NY, Jan. 13, 1922; m. Selma Archerd. Grad., UCLA, 1941, U.S. Naval Acad. Postgrad. Sch., 1943. With Hollywood bur. AP, 1945—2005; columnist Herald-Express, Daily Variety, 1953—2005. Master of ceremonies numerous Hollywood premieres, Acad. Awards shows; co-host People's Choice Awards shows. Served to lt. USN. Recipient awards Masquers, L.A. Press Club, Hollywood Fgn. Press Club, Newsman of Yr. award Publicists Guild, 1970. Mem. Hollywood Press Club (founder). Office: care Daily Variety 5700 Wilshire Blvd Ste 120 Los Angeles CA 90036-5804 Office Phone: 323-965-4431. Business E-Mail: aarcherd@reedbusiness.com, army.archerd@variety.com.

ARCHIBALD, JAMES DAVID, biology educator, paleontologist; b. Lawrence, Kans., Mar. 23, 1950; s. James R. and Donna L. (Accord) A. BS in Geology, Kent State U., 1972; PhD in Paleontology, U. Calif., Berkeley, 1977. Gibb's fellow dept. geology Yale U., New Haven, 1977-79, asst., then assoc. prof. dept. biology, 1979-83; curator of mammals Peabody Mus. Natural Hist., New Haven, 1979-83; assoc. prof., then prof. dept. biology San Diego State U., 1983—. Extensive field expeditions in Mont., Colo., N.Mex., Pakistan, and former USSR, 1973—. Author: A Study of Mammalia and Geology Across the Cretaceous-Tertiary Boundary, 1982, Dinosaur Extinction and the End of an Era: What The Fossils Say, 1996; contbr. over 100 articles to profl. jours. Past trustee San Diego Natural History Mus. Fellow Alcoa Found., U. Calif.-Berkeley, Fulbright fellow to Russia, 1996; Disting Lectr., grantee Paleontology Soc.; grantee Sigma Xi, Nat. Geog. Soc., NSF, Petroleum Research Found., San Diego State U. Mem. Soc. Vertebrate Paleontology, Geol. Soc. Am., Paleontol. Soc., Soc. Systematic Zoologists, Am. Soc. Mammalogists, Willi Hennig Soc., Soc. for Study of Evolution, Phi Beta Kappa Nu, Sigma Xi. Office: San Diego State U Dept Biology San Diego CA 92182 Business E-Mail: darchibald@sunstroke.sdsu.edu.

ARCHIBALD, SANDRA ORR, dean, political science professor, economist; b. Chgo., Apr. 23, 1945; d. Carson J. and Rita A. (Michalski) O.; children: Alison Jane, Jay Coleman. BA, U. Calif., Berkeley, 1967, MA, 1971; MS, PhD, U. Calif., Davis, 1984. Dir. planning, analysis Rockefeller Commn. on Critical Choices for Americans, NYC, 1974-75; asst. resource mgmt. U. Calif., Berkeley, 1975-78; asst. prof. applied econs. Food Rsch. Inst. Stanford U., Calif., 1983—91; assoc. dean, dir. grad studies Humphrey Inst. Pub. Affairs, U. Minn., 1993—97, adj. prof. Dept. Applied Econs., assoc. prof., 1992—97, prof., 1999—2002, assoc. dean academic affairs and rsch. programs, 2001—02, interim dean, 2002, dep. assoc. dean, 2002—03; assoc. vice provost faculty devel. U. Minn., 1998—2003; dean., prof. pub. affairs Daniel J. Evans Sch. Pub. Policy, U. Wash., 2003—. Cons. Environ. Protection Agy., Washington, 1975-77, Nat. Acad. Scis., Washington, 1981-82, Pacihi Gas & Electric Co., San Francisco, 1984-85. Co-author (with C.O. McCorkle) Management and Leadership in higher Education, 1982; contbr. numerous articles to profl. jours. Bd. dirs. Little League, Los Altos Hills, Calif., 1980. Mem. Am. Assn. Agrl. Econs., Western Assn. Agrl. Econs. Home: 655 Novak Ave N Stillwater MN 55082-1578 Office: Daniel J Evans Sch Pub Affairs U Wash 208 Parrington Hall, Box 353055 Seattle WA 98195-3055 Office Phone: 206-616-1648. E-mail: sarch@u.washington.edu.*

ARCINIEGA, TOMAS ABEL, university president; b. El Paso, Tex., Aug. 5, 1937; s. Tomas Hilario and Judith G. (Zozaya) Arciniega; m. M. Concha Ochotorena, Aug. 10, 1957; children: Wendy H. Heredia, Lisa Gannon, Judy Shackleton, Laura. BS in Tchr. Edn., N. Mex. State U., 1960; MA, U. N. Mex., 1966, PhD, 1970; postdoc., Inst. for Ednl. Mgmt., Harvard U., 1989. Asst. dean Grad. Sch. U. Tex.-El Paso, 1972-73; co-dir. Southwestern Schs. Study, U. Tex.-El Paso, 1970-73; dean Coll. Edn. San Diego State U., 1973-80; v.p. acad. affairs. Calif. State U., Fresno, 1980-83, pres. Bakersfield, 1983—. Prof. ednl. adminstrn. and supervision U. N.Mex., U. Tex.-El Paso, San Diego State U., Calif. State U., Fresno, Calif. State U., Bakersfield; cons. in edn. to state and fed. agys., instns.; USAID advisor to Dominican Republic U.S. Dept. State., 1967-68; dir. applied rsch. project U. N.Mex., 1968-69, dep. chief party AID Project, Colombia, 1969-70; cons. in field. Author: Public Education's Response to the Mexican-American, 1971, Preparing Teachers of Mexican Americans: A Sociocultural and Political Issue, 1977; co-author: Chicanos and Native Americans: The Territorial Minorities, 1973; guest editor: Calif. Jour. Tchr. Edn., 1981; editor Commn. on Hispanic Underrepresentation Reports, Hispanic Underrepresentation: A Call for Reinvestment and Innovation, 1985, 88. Trustee emeritus Carnegie Corp. N.Y.; trustee Ednl. Testing Svc., Princeton, N.J., The Aspen Inst.; bd. dirs. Math., Engring., Sci. Achievement, Berkeley, Calif.; mem. bd. dirs. Air U., Hispanic Scholarship Fund; mem. Am. Coun. on Edn.; founding mem., trustee Tomas Rivera Policy Inst.; dir. Civic Kern Citizens Effective Local Govt.; mem. adv. bd. Beautiful Bakersfield; advisor Jr. League Bakersfield. Vis. scholar Leadership Enrichment Program, 1982; recipient Legis. commendation for higher edn. Calif. Legislature, 1975-78, Meritorious Svc. award Am. Assn. Colls. Tchr. Edn., 1977-78, Meritorious Svc. award League United L.Am. Citizens, 1983, Svc. award Hispanic and Bus. Alliance for Edn., 1991, Pioneer award Nat. Assn. Bilingual Edn., 1994; named to Top 100 Acad. Leaders in Higher Edn. Change Mag., 1978, Top 100 Hispanic Influentials Hispanic Bus. Mag., 1987, 97. Mem. Am. Ednl. Rsch. Assn. (edtl. com. 1979-82), Am. Assn. State Colls. and Univs. (bd. dirs.), Hispanic Assn. Colls. and Univs. (bd. dirs.), Assn. Mexican Am. Educators (various commendations), Am. Assn. Higher Edn. (instl. rep.), Western Coll. Assn. (past pres.), Rotary, Stockdale Country Club, Bakersfield Petroleum Club. Democrat. Roman Catholic. Home: 30450 Palomar Vista Dr Valley Center CA 92082-4537

ARDANS, ALEXANDER ANDREW, veterinarian, educator, lab administrator; b. Ely, Nev., June 6, 1941; s. Jean Baptiste and Eleanora (Campbell) A.; m. Janice Gae Sanford, Dec. 23, 1961; children: Tamara Marie, Stephanie Marie, Melanie Alexandra, Angela Rosanne, Jeanette Alison. Student, U. Nev., 1959-61; BS, U. Calif., Davis, 1963, DVM, 1965; MS, U. Minn., St. Paul, 1969. Instr. Colo. State U., Ft. Collins, 1965-66, U. Minn., St. Paul, 1966-69; asst. prof., Sch. Vet. Medicine U. Calif., Davis, 1969-74, assoc. prof., 1974-80, prof., 1980—, chmn. dept. medicine, 1983-87; dir. Calif. Animal Health and Food Safety Lab Sys., Davis, 1987—. Recipient Outstanding Tchr. award U. Calif.-Davis Sch. Vet. Medicine, 1970, 73, Alumni award Sch. Vet. Med. U. Calif. Davis, 2000. Mem. Nat. Acad. Practitioners, AVMA, Am. Assn. Vet. Lab. Diagnosticians (Pope award 2000), Calif. Vet. Med. Assn., Conf. Rsch. Workers in Animal Disease. Republican. Roman Catholic. Avocations: swimming, fishing, hunting. Office: Univ Calif Sch Vet Medicine CAHFS Davis CA 95617 Home Phone: 530-758-9191; Office Phone: 530-752-8709. Business E-Mail: aaardans@ucdavis.edu.

ARENA, BRUCE, professional soccer coach; b. Bklyn., Sept. 21, 1951; m. Phyllis Arena; 1 child. Student, Nassau CC, NY, 1969-71; BS in Bus., Cornell U., 1973. Asst. lacrosse coach, asst. soccer coach Cornell U., Ithaca, NY, 1973-76; head soccer coach U. Puget Sound, Tacoma, 1976-78; head soccer coach, asst. men's lacrosse coach U. Va., Charlottesville, 1978-95; head coach DC United, Washington, 1995-98, US Nat. Soccer Team, Chgo., 1998—2006; sporting dir., head coach NY Red Bulls, 2006—07; head coach LA Galaxy, 2008—. Mem. U.S. nat. teams in both soccer and lacrosse and competed professionally in both sports; past chmn. ACC soccer coaches, ISAA Divsn. I nat. poll; "A" coaching lic. from U.S. Soccer Fedn.; mem. NCAA Divsn. I soccer com., 1989-95; head coach U.S. Olympic team 1996, U.S. World Cup Team 2002, 2006. Named ACC Coach of Yr., 1979, 84, 86, 88, 89, 91, South Atlantic Region Coach of Yr., 1982, 83, 87, nat. Coach of Yr. by Lanzera, 1993. Inducted into Cornell Athletic Field Hall of Fame, 1986, Long Island Lacrosse Hall of Fame, 1990. Named MLS Coach of Year, 1997. Achievements include career record of 295-58-32 (.808) in 18 yrs. at U. Va., leading U. Va. to NCAA titles in 1989, 91, 92, 93, 94, taking U. Va. to 6 of the last 7 NCAA semi-finals and 8 straight quarter finals, directing U. Va. to 15 straight NCAA tournament appearances (longest active streak in U.S.), Major League Soccer Cup Championships, 1996, 97, U.S. Open Cup Championship, 1996, World Cup quarterfinals 2002. Office: LA Galaxy The Home Depot Ctr 18400 Avalon Blvd Ste 200 Carson CA 90746

ARES, MANUEL, JR., biology professor, researcher; BS in biology, Cornell Univ., Ithaca, NY; PhD, U. Calif., San Diego, 1982; post doctorate studies, Yale Univ. Sch. Medicine. Asst. prof. U. Calif., Santa Cruz, 1987—98, prof., 1998—, chmn. Dept. Molecular Cell & Devel. Biology, 2000—02. Prin. investigator Ares Lab, Santa Cruz, Calif.; prof. Howard Hughes Med. Inst.

ARGUE, DON HARVEY, college president, minister; b. Winnipeg, Man., Can., July 12, 1939; came to U.S., 1948; s. Andrew Watson and Hazel Bell (May) A.; m. Patricia Jean Opheim, Sept. 23, 1961; children: Laurie, Lee, Jonathan. BA, Cen. Bible Coll., Springfield, Mo., 1961; MA, Santa Clara U., 1967; EdD, U. of the Pacific, 1969; postdoctoral study, Gordon-Conwell Theol. Sem., 1990, Regent Coll., Vancouver, Can., 1990. Ordained to ministry Assemblies of God, 1964. Pastor 1st Assembly of God, Morganville, Calif., 1965-67; dean of students/men Bethany Coll., Santa Cruz, Calif., 1967-69; asst. prof., dean of student life, dean of students Evangel Coll., Springfield, 1969-74; dean, v.p. North Cen. Bible Coll., Mpls., 1974-79; pres. North Ctrl. Bible Coll., Mpls., 1979—2002, Northwest Univ., 1998—. Gen. presbyter Assemblies of God, Springfield. Recipient Decade of Growth award Christianity Today, 1990. Mem. Nat. Assn. Evangs. (1st v.p.), Soc. for Pentecostal Studies (pres.), Rotary. Home: PO Box 579 Kirkland WA 98083-0579 Office: Northwest University 5520 108th Ave NE Kirkland WA 98033

ARGUEDAS, CRISTINA CLAYPOOLE, lawyer; b. 1953; BA, U. NH; JD summa cum laude, Rutgers U., 1979. Bar: Calif. Supreme Ct. 1979, US Dist. Ct., No. Dist. Calif. 1979, So. Dist. Calif. 1983, Ctrl. Dist. Calif. 1982, Ea. Dist. Calif. 1982, Dist. Ariz. 1991, US Ct. Appeals: Ninth Cir. 1980, Tenth Cir. 1985, US Supreme Ct. 1983, US Tax Ct. 1994. Dep. fed. defender US Dist. Ct. (no. dist.) Calif.; ptnr. Arguedas, Cassman & Headley (formerly Cooper, Arguedas & Cassman), Emeryville, Calif., 1982—. Lawyer rep. US Ct. Appeals (9th cir.) Jud. Conf.; adj. prof. Benjamin N. Cardozo Sch. Law, Yeshiva U., Boalt Hall Sch. Law. Named one of 50 Top Lawyers, Nat. Law Jour., 1998, 100 Most Influential Lawyers in America, 2006, The 50 Most Influential Women Lawyers in America, 2007, Top 10 Lawyers in Bay Area, San Francisco Chronicle, 2003, America's Leading Lawyers for Bus., Chambers USA, 2005. Fellow: Am. Coll. Trial Lawyers; mem.: ABA Sect. of Litigation Trial Advisory Bd., Bd. Western Ctr. on Law and Poverty, Am. Bd. Criminal Lawyers, Am. Inns of Ct. (master 1999—), Internat. Acad. Trial Lawyers, Calif. Attys. for Criminal Justice (past pres.). Office: Arguedas Cassman & Headley 803 Hearst Ave Berkeley CA 94710 Office Phone: 510-654-2000.

ARGUELLO, CHRISTINE MARIE, federal judge; b. Thatcher, Colo., July 15, 1955; BS, U. Colo., 1977; JD, Harvard U., 1980. Bar: Fla. 1980, Colo. 1985. Assoc. Valdes-Fauli, Cobb & Petry, Miami, 1980—85; sr. assoc. Holland & Hart, Colorado Springs, 1985—88, equity ptnr., 1988—91; cons. Profl. Fee Examiners, Inc., 1991—96, v.p. legal, 1996—97; dep. for states svcs. Colo. Atty. Gen.'s Office, 1999—2000; shareholder, mng. ptnr. Duncan Green Brown & Langeness, PC, 2003—04; chief dep. atty. gen. Colo. Atty. Gen.'s Office, 2000—02; ptnr. Davis, Graham & Stubbs LLP, Denver, 2004—06; mng. sr. assoc. counsel U. Colo., Boulder, 2006—08; judge US Dist Ct., Colo., 2008—. Assoc. to full prof. U. Kans. Sch. Law, 1991—99; vis. prof., adj. prof. U. Colo. Sch. Law, 1999—2002; vis. prof. U. Denver Coll. Law, 2003. Office: Alfred A Arraj US Courthouse 901 19th St Denver CO 80294-3589*

ARIYOSHI, GEORGE RYOICHI, lawyer, business consultant, former governor; b. Honolulu, Mar. 12, 1926; s. Ryozo and Mitsue (Yoshikawa) A.; m. Jean Miya Hayashi, Feb. 5, 1955; children: Lynn Miye, Todd Ryozo, Donn Ryoji. Student, U. Hawaii, 1944-45, 47; BA, Mich. State U., 1949; JD, U. Mich., 1952; LLD (hon.), Mich. State U., 1979, U. Philippines, 1975, U. Guam, 1975; HHD (hon.), U. Visayas, Philippines, 1977, U. Hawaii, 1986; LHD (hon.), Soka U., Japan, 1984. Bar: Hawaii 1953. Sole practice, Honolulu, 1953-70; mem. Ter. of Hawaii Ho. of Reps., 1954-58, State of Hawaii Senate, 1959-70, chmn. ways and means com., 1963-64, majority leader, 1965-66, majority floor leader, 1969-70; lt. gov. State of Hawaii, 1970-73, acting gov., 1973-74, gov., 1974-86; of counsel Kobayashi, Watanabe, Sugita, Kawashima & Goda, Honolulu, 1986-90; with JACL AJA Biennium, 1988; of counsel Watanabe, Ing & Komeiji LLP, Honolulu, 1990—; ptnr. Cole, Gilburn, Goldhaber & Ariyoshi Mgmt. Inc.; mnging. ptnr. Ariyoshi, Mills & Assocs.; dir. Daily Wellness Co., 1998, Accela, Inc., 1998; co-founder, chmn. Convergence CT, Inc.; chmn. CBI, Inc., 2004. Dir. Hawaiian Ins. & Guaranty, Ltd., 1966-70, First Hawaiian Bank, 1962-70, Honolulu Gas Co., Ltd. (Pacific Resources Inc.), 1964-70; bus. cons.; pres., CEO Cultured Tech., Inc.; pres. Aina Kamalii Corp. holding co. Mauna Kea Beach Hotel, Maui Prince Hotel, Hapuna Beach Prince Hotel, Hawaii Prince Hotel and golf courses; co-chmn. Asia-Pacific Cons. Group; bd. dirs. Pacific Internat. Ctr. for High Tech. Rsch.; mem. Japan-Hawaii Econ. Coun.; founder pres. Internat. Comml. Dispute Resolution. Author: With Obligation to All. Mem. adv. bd. Japan Found. Ctr. for Global Partnership; mem. Pres.'s Adv. commn. on Trade Policy and Negotiations; exec. bd. Aloha Coun. Boy Scots Am., 1970-72; pres. Pacific Basin Devel. Coun., 1980-81; bd. mgrs. YMCA, 1955-57; chmn., treas. Earth Cons. Inc.; hon. co-chmn. Japanese-Am. Nat. Mus.; trustee Japanese-Am. Inst. Mgmt. Sci., bd. dirs. Bishop Mus.; bd. govs. Japanese Cultrual Ctr. Hawaii; nat. committeeman Dem. Party Hawaii; adv. mem. Japan-Am. Cooperation in Space Project; chmn., bd. govs. East-West Ctr., 1986-2003. Served in US Army, 1945—46. Named Japanese-Am. of the Biennium, Japanese-Am. Citizens League, 1984; named one of Top 10 Legislators in Hawaii, Kiwanis, 1962; recipient Distinguished Alumni awards U. Hawaii, 1975, Distinguished Alumni awards Mich. State U., 1975, Silver Beaver award, Aloha Coun. Boy Scouts Am., 1977, Marco Polo award, Hawaii World Trade Assn., 1983, Japan's Order of Sacred Treasure 1st class, 1985, Emperor's Silver Cup award, 1986. Mem. ABA (ho. dels. 1969—), Hawaii Bar Assn. (pres. 1969), Hawaii Bar Found. (charter, pres. 1969—), Western Govs. Conf., (chmn.1977-78), Western Govs. Assn., (chmn. 1984-85); Clubs: Military Intelligence Service Vets (pres. 1968-69). Democrat. Office: Watanabe Ing & Komeiji 23rd Fl 999 Bishop St Honolulu HI 96813 Office Fax: 808-544-8399. E-mail: gariyoshi@wik.com.

ARKIN, MICHAEL BARRY, lawyer, arbitrator, writer; b. Washington, Jan. 11, 1941; s. William Howard and Zenda Lillian (Liebermann) A.; children and stepchildren: Tracy Renee, Jeffrey Harris, Marcy Susan, Chatom Callan, Michael Edwin, Samuel Hopkins, Brandon Maddox, Jessica Remaley, Brandi Remaley Arkin, Casey Remaley Arkin; m. Laura Dorene Haynes, Aug. 16, 1998. AA, George Washington U., 1961; BA in Psychology, U. Okla., 1962, JD, 1965. Bar: Okla. 1965, U.S. Ct. Claims 1968, U.S. Supreme Ct. 1968, Calif. 1970, U.S. Tax Ct. 1970, U.S. Ct. Appeals (3d, 5th, 6th, 9th, 10th cirs.) 1970, U.S. Dist. Ct. (cen. dist.) Calif. 1970, U.S. Dist. Ct. (so. dist.) Calif. 1970, U.S. Dist. Ct. (ea. dist.) Calif. 1987. Trial atty. tax divsn. U.S. Dept. Justice, 1965-68, appellate atty., 1968-69; ptnr. Surr & Hellyer, San Bernardino, Calif., 1969-79; mng. ptnr. Wied, Granby Alford & Arkin, San Diego, 1979-82, Lorenz Alhadeff Fellmeth Arkin & Multer, San Diego, 1982, Finley, Kumble, Heine, Underberg, Manley & Casey, San Diego, 1983; pvt. practice Sacramento and San Andreas (Calif.), 1984-86; ptnr. McDonough Holland & Allen, Sacramento, 1986-87; pvt. practice San Andreas, Calif., 1987—2002; chief trial counsel Calaveras County Child Protective Svcs., 1995—2002; ind. state hearing officer Calif. Spl. Edn. Hearing Office, McGeorge Sch. Law, U. Pacific, 2002—05. Judge pro-tem Calaveras County Consol. Cts., Calif., 1999-02; cons. in field. Author: History of the Bench and Bar of Calaveras County California, 1997—. Bd. dirs. San Bernardino County Legal Aid Soc., 1971-73, sec., 1971-72, pres., 1973; mem. Calaveras County Adv. Com. on Alcohol and Drug Abuse, 1985-94, pres., 1991-92; treas. Calaveras County Legal Assistance Program, 1987—; trustee Calaveras County Law Libr., 1987-98; bd. dirs. Mark Twain Hosp. Dist., 1990-03, treas., 1994—. Named to Hon. Order of Ky. Cols., 1967. Mem. ABA, Calif. Bar Assn. (Wiley F. Manuel pro bono pub. svc. award 1991), San Diego County Bar Assn., San Bernardino County Bar Assn. (bd. dirs., sec.-treas. 1973-75, pilot drug abuse program 1970), Calaveras County Bar Assn. (bd. dirs., v.p. 1988-90, pres. 1990-95), Am. Arbitration Assn. (arbitrator 1987—). Democrat. Jewish. Home: 1041 Angel Rd Corrales NM 87048 Personal E-mail: markin2500@aol.com.

ARLEDGE, CHARLES STONE, former aerospace executive, entrepreneur; b. Bonham, Tex., Oct. 20, 1935; s. John F. and Mary Madeline (Jones) A.; m. Barbara Jeanne Ruff, June 18, 1966; children: John Harrison, Mary Katherine. BS, Stanford U., 1957, MS (Standard Oil Co. Calif. scholar 1958), 1958, MBA, 1966. Engr. Shell Oil Co., Los Angeles, 1958-64; with Signal Cos., La Jolla, Calif., 1966-86, v.p., 1970-79, group v.p., 1979-83, sr. v.p., 1983-86; v.p. Aerojet Gen. Corp., La Jolla, Calif., 1986-90; ptnr. Signal Ventures, 1990—2004. Mem.: California; La Jolla Beach and Tennis. Republican. Presbyterian. Home: PO Box 957 Rancho Santa Fe CA 92067-0957

ARLIDGE, JOHN WALTER, retired utilities executive; b. Rochester, NY, Feb. 4, 1933; s. Harold Wesley and Grace Edith (Kempshall) A.; m. Sandra Marie Koswar, Feb. 4, 1955; children: James William, Edward John. BS, L.A. State Coll., 1962. Registered profl. engr., Calif., Nev., Utah. Comm. sys. engring. design and purchase City of L.A., 1961—62, power sys. resource planning R & D, 1962—74; asst. to v.p. Nev. Power Co., Las Vegas, 1974—82, v.p. resource planning and power dispatch, 1982—89, sr. v.p. govt. affairs, 1989—93; v.p., dir. Nev. Electric Investment Co., Las Vegas, 1982—89; cons. on energy resources and regulation Las Vegas, 1995—. Advisor electric-lignite sector Ministry Indusry and Trade, Warsaw, Poland, 1992-95; mem. Nev. Engr.'s Adv. Com. on Geothermal Devel., 1974-76, Nev. Solar Energy Devel. Adv. Group, 1976-86; mem. energy task force WEST, 1972-84, mem. energy engring. planning com., 1978; mem. advanced energy sys. divsnl. com. Electric Power Rsch. Inst., 1973-92; mem. We. Utility Group on Fed. Land, 1977; mem. endangered species subcom., rail issues group Edison Elec. Inst., 1977; cons. on air, land and water We. Regional Coun., 1977; mem. Nev. adv. bd. U.S. Bur. Land Mgmt., 1975-77, mem. adv. coun. Las Vegas dist., 1980-92; mem. rsch. adv. bd. U. Nev.; trustee Corp. Devel. Sci. Tech. Nev. Contbr. articles on energy resources to various publs. Mem. Nev. adv. bd. Nature Conservancy; mem. Sec. Energy's Nat. Coal Coun., 1988-93. With USMC, 1950-54. Mem. IEEE, Geothermal Resources Coun. (dir.), Utility Coal Gasification Assn. (chmn.), Internat. Solar Energy Assn., Nat. Coal Coun. (advisor to sec. energy), Pacific Coast Elec. Assn., So. Nev. Off-Road Vehicle Assn., Slurry Transp. Assn. (dir. 1979), Masons. Personal E-mail: jwarlidge@msn.com.

ARMISEN, FRED, actor; b. LI, NY, Dec. 4, 1966; Drummer Blue Man's Group, Chgo. Writer, dir. (films) Guide to Music and South by Southwest, 1998; actor: (films) Like Mike, 2002, Melvin Goes to Dinner, 2003, The Frank International Film Festival, 2003, Euro Trip, 2004, Anchorman: The Legend of Ron Burgundy, 2004, Wake Up, Ron Burgudy: The Lost Movie, 2004, Christmas on Mars, 2005, Deuce Bigalow: European Gigolo, 2005, Kiss Me Again, 2006, Griffin and Phoenix, 2006, Tenacious D in The Pick of Destiny, 2006, Deck the Halls, 2006, Fast Track, 2006, (voice) Aqua Teen Hunger Force

Colon Movie Film for Theaters, 2007, The Promotion, 2008, Baby Mama, 2008, The Rocker, 2008, Confessions of a Shopaholic, 2009; writer, dir. (TV series) Fred, 1999; actor: (TV series) Reverb, 1999, Late World with Zach, 2002, Saturday Night Live, 2002—, Crank Yankers, 2003—04, (voice) Squidbillies, 2005—08,; (TV films) Next!, 2002. Office: c/o Brillstein-Grey Entertainment 9150 Wilshire Blvd Ste 350 Beverly Hills CA 90212

ARMISTEAD, ROBERT ASHBY, JR., scientific research company executive; b. Roanoke, Va., Feb. 7, 1940; s. Robert Ashby and Lucille Denis (Owen) A.; m. Mona Thornhill, Dec. 26, 1965; children: Robert Ashby III, Wade Owen, Clay Thornhill. BS in Physics with highest honors, Va. Mil. Inst., 1962; MS in Physics, Carnegie Mellon U., 1963, PhD in Nuclear Sci. and Engring., 1966; MBA, U. Santa Clara, 1973. Physicist reactor divsn. Oak Ridge (Tenn.) Nat. Lab., 1964-67; nuclear weapons effects projecy officer Def. Atomic Support Agy., Washington, 1967-69; mgr. radiation physics Stanford Rsch. Inst., Menlo Park, Calif., 1969-77; pres., chmn. Advanced Rsch. and Applications Corp., Sunnyvale, Calif., 1977—. Chmn. Calif. innovation com. 1986 White House Conf. Small Bus. Contbr. articles to profl. jours.; patentee x-ray imaging. Bd. dirs. Bay Area Regional Tech. Alliance, VMI Found., bd. trustees. Capt. U.S. Army, 1967-69. Named Innovator of Yr., U.S. Small Bus. Adminstrn., 1987, San Francisco Innovation Person of Yr. Small Bus. Adminstrn., 1987; Spl. fellow Atomic Energy Commn., 1963-64, Oak Ridge Grad. fellow, 1965-66. Mem. Am. Electronics Assn. (mem. procurement com. 1986-87, bd. dirs. 1987-90, mem. exec. com. 1989-90), Nat. Innovation Network (bd. dirs.). Avocations: tennis, golf. Office: 352 E Java DR Sunnyvale CA 94089-1328

ARMSTRONG, CHARLES G., professional baseball executive, lawyer; b. Louisville, Aug. 31, 1942; m. Susan; children: Dorrie, Katherine, Chuck. BS, Purdue U., 1964; JD, Stanford U., 1967. Bar: Calif. Practice law Hill Farrer & Burrill, Calif., 1971—; pres. Seattle Mariners Baseball Team, 1983—, CEO, 1984. Served with USN, 1967-70 Office: Seattle Mariners Safeco Field PO Box 4100 Seattle WA 98104-0100

ARMSTRONG, DAVID MICHAEL, biology professor; b. Louisville, July 31, 1944; s. John D. and Elizabeth Ann (Horine) A.; children: John D., Laura C. Armstrong-Stone. BS, Colo. State U., 1966; MA in Teaching, Harvard U., 1967; PhD, U. Kans., 1971. From asst. prof. to prof. natural sci. U. Colo., Boulder, 1971-85, prof. ecology and evolutionary biology, 1993—, assoc. chair, 1997-99; sr. scientist Rocky Mountain Biol. Lab., Gothic, Colo., 1977, 79; resident naturalist Sylvan Dale Ranch, Loveland, Colo., 1984—; acting dir. Univ. Mus., 1987-88, dir., 1989-93. Cons. in field. Author: Distribution of Mammals in Colorado, 1972, Rocky Mountain Mammals, 1975, 87, Mammals of the Canyon Country, 1982; co-author: Mammals of the Northern Great Plains, Mammals of the Plains States, Mammals of Colorado. Mem. non-game adv. council Colo. Div. Wildlife, 1972-76, Colo. Natural Areas Council, 1975-80. Mem.: Colo. Wildlife Fedn. (bd. dirs. 2000—02), The Nature Conservancy (trustee Colo. chpt. 1989—99, 2002—, chair 1996—98), Rocky Mountain Biol. Lab. (trustee 1979—83), Southwestern Assn. Naturalists (editor 1976—80), Am. Soc. Mammalogists (editor 1981—87). Avocations: draft horses, conservation activities, writing. Office: U Colo Ecology and Evolutionary Biology PO Box 334 Boulder CO 80309-0334 Personal E-mail: mausmann@aol.com. Business E-Mail: david.armstrong@colorado.edu.

ARMSTRONG, ELIZABETH NEILSON, curator; b. Winchester, Mass., June 30, 1952; d. Douglas Byron and Ruth Mary (Publow) A.; m. Daniel Alexander Boone, Mar. 1, 1985; children: Olivia Armstrong Boone, Phoebe Elizabeth Boone. BA, Hampshire Coll., 1974; MA, U. Calif., Berkeley, 1982. Grants adminstr. NEH, Washington, 1976-79; rsch. asst. San Francisco Mus. Modern Art, 1979-81; cons. Lowie Mus. Anthropology, Berkeley, 1981-82; Nat. Endowment for Arts curatorial intern Walker Art Ctr., Mpls., 1982-83, asst. curator, 1983-86, assoc. curator, 1986-89, curator, 1989-96; sr. curator Mus. Contemporary Art, San Diego, 1996—. Mem. adv. bd. Capp Street Project, San Francisco, 1987; guest curator Ctr. for Book Arts, N.Y.C., 1989; panelist NEA, Washington, 1988, 89, Pew Charitable Trust, 1994; cons., reviewer Nat. Gallery Art, Washington, 1990. Author: First Impressions, 1989; author, editor: Tyler Graphics: The Extended Image, 1987, Jasper Johns: Printed Symbols, 1990, In the Spirit of Fluxus, 1993. Mem. adv. com. Minn. Percent for Art Program, St. Paul, 1987; bd. dirs. Artpaper, Mpls., 1989-93. Recipient govt. merit award for outstanding performance NEH, 1979; humanities grad. rsch. grantee U. Calif., 1981; fellow for mus. profls. Nat. Endowment for Arts, 1989. Mem. Print Coun. Am., Minn. Ctr. for Book Arts. Avocations: snorkeling, tennis, skiing. Office: San Diego Mus Contemporary Art 700 Prospect St La Jolla CA 92037-4228

ARMSTRONG, LLOYD, JR., academic administrator, physics professor; b. Austin, Tex., May 19, 1940; s. Lloyd and Beatrice (Jackson) A.; m. Judith Glantz, July 9, 1965; 1 son, Wade Matthew. BS in Physics, MIT, 1962; PhD in Physics, U. Calif., Berkeley, 1966. Postdoctoral physicist Lawrence Berkeley Lab., 1965-66, cons., 1976; sr. physicist Westinghouse Rsch. Labs., Pitts., 1967-68, cons., 1968-70; rsch. assoc. Johns Hopkins U., Balt., 1968-69, asst. prof. physics, 1969-73, assoc. prof., 1973-77, prof., 1977-93, chmn. dept. physics and astronomy, 1985-87, dean Sch. Arts and Scis., 1987-93; provost, sr. v.p. for acad. affairs U. So. Calif., LA, 1993—2005, prof. physics, 1993—, prof. edn., 2005—, Univ. prof., 2005—. Assoc. rsch. scientist Nat. Ctr. Sci. Rsch. (CNRS), Orsay, France, 1972—73; vis. fellow Joint Inst. Lab. Astrophysics, Boulder, Colo., 1978—79; program officer NSF, 1981—83, mem. adv. com. for physics, 1985—87, mem. visitors com. physics divsn., 1991; chmn. com. atomic and molecular scis. NAS/NRC, 1985—88, mem. bd. physics and astronomy, 1989—96; mem. adv. bd. Inst. for Theoretical Physics, Santa Barbara, Calif., 1992—96, chmn., 1994—95, Inst. Theoretical Atomic and Molecular Physics, Cambridge, Mass., 1994—97, Rochester Theory Ctr. for Optical Sci. and Engring., 1996—98. Author: Theory of Hyperfine Structure of Free Atoms, 1971; contbr. articles to profl. jours. Bd. dirs. So. Calif. Econ. Partnership, 1994—2000, Calif. Coun. Sci. and Tech., 1994—2005. NSF grantee, 1972-90; Dept. Energy grantee, 1975-82. Fellow Am. Phys. Soc., Coun. on Fgn. Rels., Pacific Coun. on Internat. Policy (bd. dirs. 1996-05), Inside Track Adv. Bd. Office: U So Calif 3470 Trousdale Pkwy WPH 701 Los Angeles CA 90089-4037 Office Phone: 213-740-7218. Business E-Mail: lloydarm@usc.edu.

ARMSTRONG, MARY M., insurance company executive; Various positions Safeco Corp., Seattle, 1973-94, v.p., chief info. officer, 1994—. Office: SAFECO Corp SAFECO Plaza Seattle WA 98185

ARMSTRONG, NELSON WILLIAM, JR., gaming company executive; b. Port Huron, Mich., Mar. 5, 1941; s. Nelson William and Kathryn J. (Clarke) A.; m. Judith A. Roth, Sept. 5, 1964; children: Nelson William III, Tad John. BA, Mich. State U., 1964—64. Acct. Gen. Motors Corp., Warren, Mich., 1964—66; in acctg. and fin. Consumers Power Co., Jackson, Mich., 1966—73; dir acctg. Ramada Inns, Inc., Phoenix, 1973—77, asst. contr., 1977—79, v.p. audit svcs., 1979—82, corp. contr., 1982—85, v.p. adminstrn., 1985—, v.p. audit and adminstrv. svcs., 1985—, v.p. corp. contr., 1987—90; v.p. adminstrn., sec. Aztar Corp., Phoenix, 1990. Office: aztar 207 Grandview Dr Ste 400 Fort Mitchell KY 41017-2762

ARMSTRONG, SAUNDRA BROWN, federal judge; b. Oakland, Calif., Mar. 23, 1947; d. Coolidge Logan and Pauline Marquette Brown; m. George Walter Armstrong, Apr. 18, 1982 BA, Calif. State U.-Fresno, 1969; JD magna cum laude, U. San Francisco, 1977. Bar: Calif. 1977, U.S. Supreme Ct. 1984. Policewoman Oakland Police Dept., 1970-77; prosecutor, dep. dist. atty. Alameda County Dist. Atty., Oakland, 1978-79, 80-82; staff atty. Calif. Legis. Assembly Com. on Criminal Justice, Sacramento, 1979-80; trial atty. Dept. Justice, Washington, 1982-83; vice chmn. U.S. Consumer Product Safety Commn., Washington, 1984-86; commr. U.S. Parole Commn., Washington, 1986-89; judge Alameda Superior Ct., 1989-91, U.S. Dist. Ct. (no. dist.) Calif., San Francisco, 1991—. Recipient commendation Calif. Assembly, 1980 Mem. Nat. Bar Assn., ABA, Calif. Bar Assn., Charles Houston Bar Assn., Black C. of C., Phi Alpha Delta Republican. Baptist. Office: US Dist Ct N Calif 1301 Clay St Rm 390C Oakland CA 94612-5217

ARMSTRONG, WILLIAM L., former senator; b. Fremont, Nebr., Mar. 16, 1937; s. William L. and Dorothy (Steen) A.; m. Ellen M. Eaton, July 15, 1962; children: Anne Elizabeth, William. Student, Tulane U., 1954-55, U. Minn., 1956. Pres. Sta. KPV1-TV, Pocatello, Idaho; mem. Colo. State Ho. of Reps., 1963—64; senator Colo., 1965—72; majority leader Colo. Senate, 1969—72; US repr., Dist 5 Colo., 1973—78; deleg. Rep. Nat. Convention, 1976, 1980; chmn. Rep. Policy Com., US Senate, 1978—90; US senator Colo., 1978—90; chmn. bd. Cherry Creek Mortgage Co., Denver; pres. Colo. Christian Univ., 2006—. Served US Army Nat. Guard, 1957—63. Mem. AP Broadcasters Assn. (dir. 1971-72, v.p. 1972) Office: Colo Christian Univ Beckman Ctr 8787 W Alameda Ave Lakewood CO 80226 Office Phone: 303-595-3828, 303-963-3350. Business E-Mail: warmstrong@ccu.edu.

ARNEY, REX ODELL, lawyer, state senator; b. Ashland, Ky., Jan. 11, 1940; s. Harold Leat and Frances (Odell) Arney; m. Marion Carroll Roberts, July 23, 1979; children: Dana, Jill, Michele, Ryan, Michael, Kelly, Emily. BA, U. Wyo., 1962, MA, 1963; JD, U. Ill., 1968. Bar: Wyo. 1968. Instr. Black Hawk Coll., Moline, Ill., 1963—65; ptnr. Redle, Yonkee & Arney, Sheridan, Wyo., 1968—; mem. Wyo. Ho. Reps., 1973—77; senator Wyo. Senate, 1977—88; gen. counsel, congressional liaison NEA, 1988—90; ptnr. Brown, Drew & Masey, Sheridan, Wyo., 1990—. Bd. dirs. Sheridan County YMCA, Sheridan County Hospice. Fellow: Am. Coll. Probate Counsel; mem.: ABA, Wyo. Bar Assn., Am. Trial Lawyers Assn., Am. Judicature Soc., Lions, Elks. Republican. Episcopalian. Office: Brown Drew Massey LLP 532 Val Vista Suite 107 Sheridan WY 82801

ARNOLD, DENNIS B., lawyer; b. Apr. 25, 1950; BA magna cum laude, SUNY Buffalo, 1972; JD, Yale U., 1975. Bar: Calif. 1976. Asst.-in-instrn. Yale Law Sch., New Haven, Conn., 1974-75; law clk. to Hon. Murray M. Schwartz U.S. Dist. Ct., Del., 1975-76; ptnr. Irell & Manella, 1980-88, Gibson, Dunn & Crutcher LLP, LA, 1988—. Adj. assoc. prof. law Southwestern U. Sch. Law, 1980-82; advisor Restatement of Law, 2d edit., Suretyship and Guaranty, Am. Law Inst., 1989-95. Contbr. articles to profl. jours. Mem.: ABA, Am. Coll. Real Estate Lawyers, Fin. Lawyers Conf. (bd. govs. 1986—89, 1992—95, 1996—99, pres. 1999—2000), L.A. County Bar Assn. (exec. com. commercial law and bankruptcy sect. 1987—90, exec. com. real property sect. 1987—92, steering com. real estate fin. subsect. 1987—, exec. com. commercial law and bankruptcy sect. 1996—99), State Bar Calif. (real property and bus. law sect. 1978—, standing joint com. anti-deficiency laws 1985—89), Am. Law Inst. Office: Gibson Dunn & Crutcher LLP 333 South Grand Ave Los Angeles CA 90071-3197

ARNOLD, FRANCES HAMILTON, chemistry educator; b. Pitts., July 25, 1956; d. William Howard and Josephine Inman (Routheau) A.; m. Andrew Evan Lange, Mar. 4, 1994; children: James Howard, William Andrew. BS magna cum laude, Princeton U., 1979; PhD in Chem. Engring., U. Calif., Berkeley, 1985. Postdoctoral U. Calif., Berkeley, 1985, Calif. Inst. Tech., Pasadena, 1986, asst. chem. engring., 1987-92, assoc. prof., 1992—96, prof. chem. engring & biochemistry, 1999, Dick and Barbara Dickinson prof. chemical engring. and biochemistry. Vis. assoc. chemistry U. Calif., Berkeley, 1986—87; ann. lectr. Advanced Ctr. Biochemical Engring. Univ. Coll., London, 1994; William Rauscher Lectr. in Chemistry Rensselaer Polytechnic Inst., 1996; Purves Lectr. in Chemistry McGill U., 1998; Lindsay Disting. Lectr. Tex. A&M, 2003; Merck-Frosst Invited Lectr. Biochemistry U. Alberta, 2003; Sir Robert Price Lectr. CSIRO, Melbourne, 2003; Lewis lectr. MIT, 2006; Walker lectr. Pa. State U., 2006; Kelly lectr. Purdue U., 2006; Cruickshank lectr. Gordon Rsch. Confs., 2008; Linnaeus lectr. Uppsala U., 2008; Steenbock lectr. U. Wis., 2008. Contbr. articles to profl. jours. Recipient Office Naval Rsch. Young Investigator award, 1988, NSF Presdl. Young Investigator award, 1989, Van Ness Award, Rensselaer Polytechnic Inst., 1994, Profl. Progress Award, AIChE, 2000, Food Pharms., and Bioengring. Divsn. award, 2005, Enzyme Engring. award, 2007, Excellence in Sci. award, Fedn. Am. Socs. for Exptl. Biology, 2007; grantee David and Lucile Packard fellow, 1989. Mem.: NAS, NAE, AAAS (Sci. Innovation Topical Lectr.), Inst. Medicine, Santa Fe Inst. (Sci. Bd.), Am. Inst. Medical and Biological Engring., Am. Soc. Microbiology, Protein Soc., Am. Inst. Chem. Engrs., Am. Chem. Soc. (David Perlman Lectr. Award, ACS Biochemical Tech. 2003, Francis P. Garvan-John M. Olin medal 2005, Carothers award, ACS Del. divsn. 2003), Tau Beta Pi, Phi Beta Kappa. Achievements include research in protein engineering, directed evolution, biocatalysis, biological circuit design, bioenergy, and evolutionary design methods applied to biological systems. Office: Calif Inst Tech Div of Chem & Chem Engring 228B Spalding Pasadena CA 91125-0001 Office Phone: 626-395-4162. Office Fax: 626-568-8743. E-mail: frances@cheme.caltech.edu.

ARNOLD, J. KELLEY, United States magistrate judge; b. Lewiston, Idaho, Oct. 3, 1937; m. Diane Louise Jenkins. Student, Wash. State U., 1955-58; LLB, U. Idaho, 1961. Bar: Wash. 1961. Dep. pros. atty. Pierce County, 1963-64; atty., 1965-82; judge Wash. Superior Ct. Pierce County, Tacoma, 1982-94; magistrate judge for western Wash., U.S. Dist. Ct., Tacoma, 1994—. With U.S. Army, 1961-63. Office: US Dist Ct 1717 Pacific Ave Rm 3409 Tacoma WA 98402-3234 Office Phone: 253-593-6751. Business E-Mail: kelley_arnold@wawd.uscourts.gov.

ARNOLD, JAMES RICHARD, chemist, educator; b. New Brunswick, NJ, May 5, 1923; s. Abraham Samuel and Julia (Jacobs) A.; m. Louise Clark, Oct. 11, 1952; children: Robert C., Theodore J., Kenneth C. AB, Princeton U., 1943, MA, 1945, PhD, 1946. Fellow Inst. Nuc. Studies, U. Chgo., 1946—47, faculty, 1948—55; NRC fellow Harvard U., 1947—48; faculty chemistry Princeton U., 1955—59; assoc. prof. chemistry U. Calif., San Diego, 1958—60, prof., 1960—92, Harold C. Urey prof., 1983—92, chmn. dept. chemistry, 1960—63. Assoc. Manhattan Project, 1943-46; dir. Calif. Space Inst., 1980-89, interim dir., 1996-97; prin. investigator Calif. Space Grant Consortium, 1989—; mem. various bds. NASA, 1959—; space sci. bd. NAS, 1970-74, com. on sci. and pub. policy, 1970-77. Mem. editl. bd. Ann. Rev. Nuclear Chemistry, 1972, Revs. Geophysics and Space Physics, 1972-75, Moon, 1972—; contbr. articles to profl. jours. Pres. Torrey Pines Elem. Sch. PTA, 1964-65; pres. La Jolla Dem. Club, 1965-66; nat. coun. World Federalists-U.S.A., 1970-72. Recipient E.O. Lawrence medal AEC, 1968, Leonard medal Meteoritical Soc., 1976, Kuiper award Am. Astron. Soc., 1993; asteroid 2143 named Jimarnold in his honor, 1980; Guggenheim fellow, India, 1972-73. Mem. NAS, AAAS, Am. Acad. Arts and Scis., Internat. Acad. Astronautics, Am. Chem. Soc., Fedn. Am. Scientists, Citizens for Global Solutions. Office: U Calif San Diego Dept Chemistry Code 0524 La Jolla CA 92093 Home Phone: 858-453-0232. Business E-Mail: jarnold@ucsd.edu.

ARNOLD, JEANNE ELOISE, anthropologist, educator; b. Cleve., 1955; d. Lawrence Fred and Marybelle Eloise Arnold. BA, U. Mich., 1976; MA, U. Calif., Santa Barbara, 1979, PhD, 1983. Prof. anthropology U. No. Iowa, Cedar Falls, 1984-88, UCLA, 1988—, assoc. dir. Inst. Archaeology, 1988-99. Vis. instr. anthropology Rice U., Houston, 1981; vis. prof. anthropology Oreg. State U., Corvallis, 1983-84; sr. archaeologist Infotec Rsch., Inc., Sonora, Calif., 1986-87; cons. in field. Author 4 books; contbr. more than 45 articles and revs. to profl. jours. and over 25 chpts. to books. Rsch. grantee NSF, 1988-91, 95-99, 98—; Rsch. and Ednl. grantee UCLA and Santa Barbara, 1977—. Mem. Soc. Am. Archaeology, Soc. Calif. Archaeology, Cotsen Inst. Archaeology (mem. editorial bd. 1988—), Sigma Xi, Phi Beta Kappa. Avocations: photography, films. Office: UCLA Dept Anthropology Box 951553 Haines Hall Los Angeles CA 90095-1553

ARNOLD, JOHN DAVID, management counselor; b. Boston, May 14, 1933; s. I. I. and Edith (Gordon) A.; children by previous marriage: Derek, Keith, Craig; m. Diane Summers, Sept. 1994. BA in Social Rels. cum laude, Harvard U., 1955. Prodn. supr., dealer svc. mgr. Arnold Stretch Mates Corp., Boston, 1957-59; asst. dir. manpower and orgn. devel. Polaroid Corp., Waltham, Mass., 1959-63; dir. internat. ops. Kepner-Tregoe & Assocs., Princeton, NJ, 1963-68; pres. John Arnold ExecuTrak Sys. Inc. and Corp. Breakthroughs! Inc., Boston, 1968—. Merger integration catalyst, conflict resolution/prevention counselor, conf. leader numerous firms; spkr. in field. Author: Make Up Your Mind, 1978, The Art of Decision Making, 1978, Shooting the Executive Rapids, 1981, How To Make the Right Decisions, 1982, Trading Up-A Career Guide: How To Get Ahead without Getting Out, 1984, How To Protect Yourself Against a Takeover, 1986, The Complete Problem Solver! A Total System of Competitive Decision Making, 1992, When the Sparks Fly: Resolving Conflict in Your Organization, 1993; contbr. articles to popular mags. V.p. programming, exec. com., bd. dirs. Orange County Philharm. Soc., 2001-04, bd. dirs. World Music, 1998-00; co-chmn. Laguna Beach Music Festival, 2003-06. 1st lt. U.S. Army, 1955-57. Avocations: skiing, squash, investments, music. Office: John Arnold ExecuTrak Sys and Corp Breakthroughs! Inc 32031 Point Pl Laguna Beach CA 92651-6862 Office Phone: 949-499-5400. Office Fax: 949-499-7608. Personal E-mail: chimo7@cox.net.

ARNOLD, MICHAEL NEAL, real property appraiser, consultant; b. Madera, Calif., June 6, 1947; s. John Patrick and Patricia (Neal) A.; m. Suzanne Elizabeth Badal, Aug. 31, 1968; children: C. Matthew Neal Arnold, Nathaniel T. Badal Arnold, Andrew T. White Arnold, Thomas A. Badal Arnold. BA in Geography, U. Calif., Santa Barbara, 1974. Cert. gen. appraiser St. Calif. Ptnr. Hammock, Arnold, Smith & Co., Santa Barbara, 1976—. Instr. Santa Barbara City Coll., 1980-85, 99. Contbr. articles to profl. jours. Coach AYSO, Santa Barbara, 1978—; cub master Boy Scouts Am., Santa Barbara, 1985; mem. vestry, parish coun. Trinity Ch. Mem. Royal Inst. Chartered Surveyors, Appraisal Inst., Vieja Valley Site Coun., Santa Barbara Coun. Real Estate Appraisers (founder, sec., speaker bur.), Appraisal Inst. (instr. 1990—, grader, com. chair, officer, chpt. pres.), Amateurs Club, Santa Barbara City Coll. (adv. coun. mem.). Episcopalian. Avocations: reading, walking, skiing, genealogy. Home: 792 Calabria Dr Santa Barbara CA 93105 Office: Hammock Arnold Smith & Co 215 W Figueroa St Fl 2 Santa Barbara CA 93101-3602 Home Phone: 805-687-4073; Office Phone: 805-966-0869. Business E-Mail: mnarnold@hascosb.com.

ARNOLD, ROBERT MORRIS, banker; b. Seattle, June 6, 1928; s. Lawrence Moss and Grace Elizabeth (Heffernan) A.; children: Grace Allen Arnold, Lauren McLellan Gorter. BA in Fin. and Bus. Adminstrn., Yale U., 1951; grad., Pacific Coast Sch. Banking, 1963. With Seattle-1st Nat. Bank, 1951, 1955—, v.p., 1965-73, mgr. nat. accounts dept., 1969-73, sr. v.p., mgr. corp. bus. devel., 1973-99, also bd. dirs. Bd. dirs. Seafirst Corp. Bank of Am. Bd. dirs. Centrum Found., Fred C. Hutchinson Cancer Rsch.; trustee Poncho; bd. dirs., exec. com., fin. com. Seattle Art Mus., also mem., joint founder its Contemporary Art Coun. Officer USNR, 1951-55. Mem. Am. Inst. Banking, Mcpl. League Seattle, Yale Assn. Western Wash., Newcomen Soc. (treas. Pacific N.W. com.), Seattle Golf Club, Seattle Tennis Club, Seattle Yacht Club, University Club (Seattle), Bohemian Club (San Francisco), Thunderbird Golf Club (Palm Springs, Calif.), O'Donnell Golf Club (Palm Springs), Mission Hills Country Club (Palm Springs). Home: 1535 Parkside Dr E Seattle WA 98112-3719 also: 50 Hilton Head Dr Rancho Mirage CA 92270-1607 Office: Robert Arnold Investments 1001 4th Ave Ste 4300 Seattle WA 98154-1192

ARNOLD, ROY GARY, academic administrator; b. Lyons, Nebr., Feb. 20, 1941; m. Jane Kay Price, 1963; children: Jana Lynn Hoffman, Julie Kay Salvi. BS with distinction, U. Nebr., 1962; MS, Oreg. State U., 1965, PhD in Food Sci. and Tech., 1967. Research and devel. project leader Fairmont Foods Co., Omaha, 1962-63; asst. prof. food sci. and tech. U. Nebr., Lincoln, 1967-71, assoc. prof., 1971-74, asst. dir. resident instrn., 1971-72, acting dir. resident instrn., 1972-73, prof., 1974-87, head dept. food sci. and tech., 1973-79, coordinator food protein research group, 1975-79, dean, dir. agrl. expt. sta.,

1980-82, vice chancellor inst. agr. and natural resources, 1982-87; dean Coll. Agrl. Scis. Oregon State U., Corvallis, 1987-91, provost, exec. v.p., 1991-2000; exec. assoc., dean Coll. Argl. Scis., Corvallis, 2000—. Del., devel. com. Imo (Nigeria) State U., 1981; mem. Ralston Purina Grad. Food Sci. Fellowship com., 1976-78, rev. team dept. food sci. U. Ill., 1979, adminstrv. site visit com. to Mid-Am. Internat. Agriculture Consortium Agy. for Internat. Devel. Morocco project, 1983, exec. com. agr. 2001 com. U. Nebr. Bd. Regents, 1982-83; program chmn. corn and sorghum industry research conf. Am. Seed Trade Assn., 1985. Mem. editorial bd. Jour. Dairy Sci., 1976-82, Jour, Agrl. and Food Chemistry, 1978-81; contbr. numerous articles to profl jours.; patentee in field. Mem. adminstrv. bd. St. Mark's United Meth. Ch., Lincoln, 1975-78, chmn. long range planning com., 1977-78, chmn. bldg. com. 1978-82. Grantee Nutrition Found., FDA, Nebr. Soybean Bd., Am. Soybean Assn. Research Found., Am. Egg Bd; Gen. Foods fellow, 1963-66. Fellow AAAS; mem. Inst. Food Technologists (nat. orgn. chmn. forward planning subcom. of exec. com. 1976-79, expert panel food safety and nutrition 1979-82, chmn. 1980-81, nominations and elections com. 1981-83, exec. com. 1985-88, 93-96, pres.-elect 1993-94, pres. 1994-95, William V. Cruess award 1980, Carl R. Fellers award 1998; Ak-Sar-Ben sect. past treas., sec., chmn.-elect, chmn. nat. councilor), Nat. Assn. Colls. and Tchrs. Agr., Univ. Assn. Adminstrv. Devel. (exec. com. 1973-74, 76-77, pres. 1978-79), MidAm. Internat. Agrl. Consortium (bd. dirs. 1982-87, chmn. 1986-87), N. Cen. Adminstrv. Heads Agr. (chmn.-elect 1985-86), Nat. Assn. State Univs. and Land Grant Colls. (divsn. agr. coun. adminstrv. heads agr. exec. com. 1985-87), Coll. Agr. Alumni Assn. (v.p. 1977-79), Innocents Soc. (pres. 1961-62), Sigma Xi (Nebr. chpt. sec. 1979-81), Phi Kappa Phi, Alpha Zeta, Gamma Sigma Delta (Nebr. chpt. past treas., sec., v.p., pres., Merit Tchg. award 1975), Phi Tau Sigma, FarmHouse Frat. (Doane award Nebr. chpt. 1962). Clubs: Crucibles (Lincoln). Office: Oreg State Univ 126 Strand Ag Hall Corvallis OR 97331-8521

ARNOLD, STANLEY NORMAN, management consultant, educator; b. Cleve., May 26, 1915; s. Morris L. and Mildred (Stearn) A.; m. Barbara Anne Laing, Aug. 31, 1946; 1 child, Jennifer Laing BS in Econs., U. Pa., 1937. Co-founder, exec. v.p. Pick-N-Pay Supermarkets, Cleve., 1937-51; exec. v.p., dir. Cottage Creamery Co., Cleve., 1937-51; dir. sales promotion div. Young & Rubicam, NYC, 1952-58; founder, pres. Stanley Arnold & Assocs., Inc., NYC, 1958—. Cons. Ford Motor Co., United Airlines, Gen. Electric, Nat. Cash Register, IBM, Philip Morris, Am. Express, Bank of America, DuPont, Goodyear, Quaker Oats, Readers Digest, Continental Can, Hunt Foods, Moet-Hennessy, Seagram, Pan Am, Chrysler Corp., Pillsbury, Coca Cola, Gen. Mills, Lever Bros., Exxon, Arco, Hallmark, others; mem. adv. bd. Bank of Palm Springs div. Bank of Calif. subs. Mitsubishi Corp., 1989—; vis. exec. prof. Freeman Sch. Bus., Tulane U., 1998—. Author: Tale of the Blue Horse, 1968; Magic Power of Putting Yourself Over with People, 1961; I Ran Against Jimmy Carter, 1977. Syndicated daily columnist, 1943-48. Architect of plan to install new office of v.p. in White House. Contbr. articles to profl. jours. Pres. Ind. Sch. Fund of N.Y.C., 1960-66; mem. fund raising com. U.S. Olympic Team, 1984. Founding mem. Nat. Businessmen for Humphrey, 1968, Nat. Citizens for Humphrey, 1968; candidate for Dem. nomination for v.p. U.S., 1972; chmn. White House Libr. Fund Raising Com., 1961-63; corp. sponsor for The Rose as Nat. Flower, 1983-86; nat. chmn. Golf's Tribute to Ike, 1980; mem. Clinton adv. com., 1991-92; mem. Bush For Pres. Com., 2000, 04; mem. Rep. Nat. Com., 2000—. Recipient Sales Exec. award Sales Exec. Club N.Y., 1965; Wisdom award of Honor Wisdom Soc., 1979 Mem.: Outrigger Canoe Club, La Quinta Fishing Club, Desert Riders Club, Seven Lakes Country Club, Les Amis D'Escoffier, Doubles Dutch Club (N.Y.C.). Home: 162 Desert Lakes Dr Palm Springs CA 92264-5521 also: 2895 Kalakaua Ave Honolulu HI 96815-4003 also: 375 Park Ave New York NY 10152-0002 Office: 162 Desert Lakes Dr Palm Springs CA 92264-5521

ARNOLD, TOM, actor, comedian, television producer; b. Ottumwa, Iowa, Mar. 6, 1959; s. Jack and Ruth (stepmother) A.; m. Roseanne, Jan. 20, 1990 (div. 1994); m. Julie Champnella, July 22, 1995 (div. 1999); m. Shelby Roos, 2002 (separated, August, 2006) AA, Indian Hills Cmty. Coll.; bachelor's degree, U. Iowa. Actor, co-exec. prodr. The Jackie Thomas Show, 1992-93, HBO Tom Arnold the Naked Truth I, II, III; dir. HBO's Roseanne Live from Minn.; exec. prodr. (TV series) Tom, 1994; actor, exec.prodr. (TV series) The Tom Show, 1997-89, Roseanne, 1988-97; actor, prodr: (films) The Kid and I, 2005; actor Backfield in Motion, 1991, Hero, 1992, Undercover Blues, 1993, Body Bags, 1993, True Lies, 1994, Nine Months, 1995, Big Bully, 1995, The Stupids, 1996, Carpool, 1996, (also co-prodr.) McHale's Navy, 1997, Touch, 1997, Austin Powers: International Man of Mystery, 1997, Hacks, 1997, (voice) Buster and Chauncey's Silent Night, 1998, Golf Punks, 1998, (voice) Hercules, 1998, Jackie's Back!, 1999, Arnold Schwarzenegger: Hollywood Hero, 1999, Blue Ridge Fall, 1999, Animal Factory, 2000, We Married Margo, 2000, Civility, 2000, Just Sue Me, 2000, Bar Hopping, 2000, Romantic Comedy 101, 2001, Exit Wounds, 2001, Lloyd, 2001, Fever Pitch, 2001, Ablaze, 2001, Hansel & Gretel, 2002, (voice) Dennis the Menace in Cruise Control, 2002, Children on Their Birthdays, 2002, Cradle 2 the Grave, 2003, After School Special, 2003, (voice) Goose!, 2004, Soul Plane, 2004, Happy Endings, 2005, Chasing Christmas, 2005, Three Wise Guys, 2005, (voice) Lola's Cafe, 2006, Oranges, 2007, Pride, 2007, The Great Buck Howard, 2008; guest appearances Veronica's Closet, 1999, Baywatch, 2000, Judging Amy, 2003, Hope & Faith, 2004, Life According to Jim, 2004 and others. Office: William Morris Agency care Michael Gruber 151 S El Camino Dr Beverly Hills CA 90212-2775*

ARNOLD-JONES, JANICE E., state legislator, state legislator; b. Ft. Bragg, NC, Mar. 20, 1952; m. John L. Jones; children: Robert, Mary Ellen. BA in Speech Communication, U. N.Mex., 1974. Inside sales GESCO, Albuquerque and Honolulu, 1974—78; acct. exec. KGU Radio, Honolulu, 1978—79, Athens Banner Herald-Daily News/WRFC Radio, 1980—81, Peters Prodns., 1981—82; v.p. Lightning Corp., 1982—87, Parallax, Inc., 1998—; mem. Dist. 24 N.Mex. House of Reps., Santa Fe, 2002—, 2002—. Mem.: Area Coach Adm. Am. Youth Soccer Orgn., Sandia H.S. Area Neighborhood Assn. Republican. Office: State Capitol Room 412C Santa Fe NM 87503 E-mail: jearnoldjones@aol.com.*

ARNON, STEPHEN SOULÉ, physician, research scientist; b. Oakland, Calif., Oct. 14, 1946; s. Daniel I. and Lucile S. Arnon; m. Joyce M. Meissinger, Aug. 24, 1985; children: Eric, Christina. AB, Harvard U., 1968, MPH, 1972, MD, 1973. Lic. physician Calif. Resident physician U. Colo. Hosps., Denver, 1973—75; med. epidemiologist Ctrs. for Disease Control, Atlanta, 1975—76, Berkeley, Calif., 1976—77; founder, chief infant botulism treatment and prevention program Calif. Dept. Public Health, Berkeley and Richmond, 1977—. Contbr. articles and book chpts. to profl. publs. Bd. dirs. Orinda (Calif.) Pks. and Recreation Found., Orinda, 1992—. Lt. comdr. USPHS, 1975—77. Recipient Jens Aubrey Westengard and John Houghton Taylor scholarships, Harvard Med. Sch., 1968—73, Wiley medal, U.S. Pub. Health Svc., 1998, Therapeutic Achievement award, Nat. Orgn. for Rare Disorders, 2004. Fellow: Am. Coll. Epidemiology, Infectious Disease Soc. Am. Achievements include creation and development of pub. svc. orphan drug Botulism Immune Globulin Intravenous (Human) BabyBIG (registered) for treatment of infant botulism; research in orphan drug development; medical and public health management of botulinum toxin if used as bioweapon. Office: Calif Dept Public Health 850 Marina Bay Pkwy Richmond CA 94804 Office Phone: 510-231-7600. Business E-Mail: stephen.arnon@cdph.ca.gov.

ARNOTT, ROBERT DOUGLAS, investment company executive; b. Chgo., June 29, 1954; s. Robert James Arnott and Catherine (Bonnell) Cameron; children: Robert Lindsay, Sydney Allison, Richard James, Diana Haikova. BA, U. Calif., Santa Barbara, 1977. V.p. Boston Co., 1977—84; pres., chief exec. officer TSA Capital Mgmt., LA, 1984—87; v.p., strategist Salomon Bros. Inc., NYC, 1987—88; mng. ptnr. First Quadrant Corp., Morristown, N.J., Pasadena, Calif., and London, 1988—96, First Quadrant, LP, Pasadena, London, Boston, 1996—2008, chmn., 2002—04; chmn., CEO Rsch. Affiliates, LLC, 2002—. Mem. adv. bd. EDHEC, 2008, mem. chmn.'s adv. coun. Chgo. Bd. Options Exch., 1989-94; bd. dirs. Internat. Faculty in Fin.; mem. product adv. bd. Chgo. Mercantile Exch., 1990-96; vis. prof. UCLA, 2001-03. Author: The Fundamental Index, 2008; editor: Asset Allocation, 1988, Active Asset Allocation, 1992, Handbook of Equity Style Management, 1997, Fin. Analysts Jour., 2002-06; mem. editl. bd. Jour. of Investing, 1990—, Jour. Portfolio Mgmt., 1984-2002, Jour. Wealth Mgmt., 1997—; contbr. articles to profl. jours. and chpts. to books. Mem. Inst. Internat. Rsch. (adv. bd. 1990-96), Assn. for Investment Mgmt. and Rsch., Inst. Quantitative Rsch. in Fin., Toronto Stock and Futures Exch. (adv. coun. 1992—). Avocations: motorcycling, astrophotography, billiards, sommelier, travel. Office: Rsch Affiliates 620 Newport Ctr Dr Ste 900 Newport Beach CA 92657 E-mail: arnott@rallc.com.

ARO, EDWIN PACKARD, lawyer; b. Colorado Springs, Colo., July 20, 1964; s. Harold William and Margaret (Packard) A. BA, Denver U., 1986; JD magna cum laude, Boston U., 1989. Bar: Colo. 1989, U.S. Dist. Ct. Colo. 1990, U.S. Ct. Appeals (10th cir.) 1990. Law clk. Hon. Richard P. Matsch, U.S. Dist. Ct. for Colo., Denver, 1989-90; ptnr. Holme, Roberts & Owen LLP, Denver, 1990—, Hogan & Hartson LLP, Denver. Adj. prof. U. Denver Coll. of Law, 1994-2006; mem. Boston U. Law Rev., 1987-89. Mem. Boston U. Law Rev., 1987-89. Mem. ABA, Colo. Bar Assn., Denver Bar Assn., Faculty of Fed. Advocates. Office: Hogan & Hartson LLP One Tabor Ctr 1200 17th St Ste 1500 Denver CO 80202 Office Phone: 303-899-7389. Business E-Mail: eparo@hhlaw.com.

ARO, GLENN SCOTT, environmental and safety executive; b. Balt., Jan. 18, 1948; s. Raymond Charles Sr. and Elizabeth Virginia (Coppage) A.; m. Marlene Rose Lefler, Jan. 8, 1972 (div. June 1987); children: Vincent Wade, Marlena Irene; m. Rosie Ann Lucero, Nov. 22, 1994. BS in Mech. Engring., Gen. Motors Inst., Flint, Mich., 1972; MBA in Fin., Wayne State U., 1980. Registered environmental assessor, Calif. From engr. to supr. GM, Detroit, Balt., L.A., 1966-84; environ. specialist New United Motor, Fremont, Calif., 1984-86; environ. engring. mgr. Def. Systems FMC Corp., San Jose, Calif., 1986-89; cons./exec. sales rep. Gaia Systems, Menlo Park, Calif., 1990; corp. environ. & safety mgr. Ampex Corp., Redwood City, Calif., 1990-92; gen. ops. mgr. Hughes Environ. Systems, El Segundo, Calif., 1992-98; corp. EHS and ethics mgr. Hughes Electronics Corp., El Segundo, Calif., 1998—2001; prin. GS Aro & Assocs., Auburn, Calif., 2002—; environ. mgr. E&J Gallo of Sonoma, Healdsburg, Calif., 2004—06; owner GS Aro & Assocs., Auburn, Calif., 2006—. Lectr. colls. and seminars Environ. Regulatory Issues, 1988—. Author: Developing a National Environmental Policy in a Global Market, 1989; contbd. articles to profl. jours. Panel mem. Toxics Awareness Project, San Francisco, 1989—; com. mem. Environ. Working Group, Sacramento, 1986-88. Mem. Peninsula Indsl. & Bus. Assn. (bd. dirs., v.p. 1988-91). Republican. Roman Catholic. Avocations: running, reading, travel, baseball, basketball. Home: 117 Palmyra St Auburn CA 95603 Home Phone: 530-886-0827; Office Phone: 530-320-9428. Personal E-mail: glennaro@hotmail.com.

AROESTY, SIDNEY A., medical diagnostic manufacturing company executive; b. Rochester, NY, Nov. 20, 1946; s. Albert S. and Marilyn Jo (Stolnitz) A.; m. Carol Jean Hopper, Dec. 31, 1970; children: Jason David, Michael Jonathan. BS, U. Rochester, 1972. Lab. supr. Strong Meml. Hosp., Rochester, 1971-73; dir. spl. determinations lab. Highland Hosp., Rochester, 1973-78; exec. v.p. Diagnostic Products Corp., LA, 1978-88, pres., 1988-94, sr. v.p., COO, 1997—, also bd. dirs. Contbr. articles to profl. jours. Sgt. USAF, 1967-71. Office: Diagnostic Products Corp 5700 W 96th St Los Angeles CA 90045-5597 Home: 13600 Marina Pointe Dr Unit 1215 Marina Del Rey CA 90292-9253 Home Phone: 585-586-3142; Office Phone: 310-645-8200. E-mail: saroesty@dpconline.com.

ARONOWITZ, JOEL ALAN, plastic and reconstructive surgeon; b. Memphis, Dec. 5, 1956; MD, Baylor Coll. Medicine, 1982. Intern in gen. surgery Baylor Coll. Medicine, 1982-83, resident in plastic surgery, 1983-87; attending plastic surgeon Cedars Sinai Med. Ctr., 1987—, vice chmn. plastic surgery divsn., 1997—2005, chmn. plastic surgery divsn., 2005—. Office: 8635 W 3rd St Ste 1090 Los Angeles CA 90048-6104 Office Phone: 310-659-0705.

ARONSON, SETH, lawyer; b. NYC, 1955; BBA, Ohio U., 1978; JD, Loyola U., 1981. Bar: Calif. 1981, US Dist. Ct. (Ctrl. Dist. Calif.) 1983, US Dist. Ct. (So. and No. Dist. Calif.) 1985, US Ct. Appeals (9th Cir.) 1985, US Supreme Ct. 1987, US Ct. Appeals (8th Cir.) 1989. Ptnr Practice Group of O'Melveny & Myers, LLP, LA, head office L.A. br., chmn. securities litig. Bd. overseer Loyola Law Sch., 2000—, bd. vistors, 2001—; lectr. and panelist on various litig. topics at programs by the ABA, LA County Bar Assn., Assn. Bus. Trial Lawyers, Practising Law Inst., Directors Roundtable, Nat. Bus. Inst., FBA, and UCLA Law Sch.; chmn. securities litigation practice group O'Melveny & Myers, LLP. Contbr. articles in profl. jours. Bd. advisors UCLA Sch. Pub. Policy and Social Rsch., 2001—; bd. dir. Ninth Cir. Historical Soc., 2000—, Legal Aid Found., LA, 1993—2000, pres., 1998—99; bd. dir. LA C. of C., 2003—. Mem.: Assn. Bus. Trial Lawyers (bd. gov. 1992—2002, pres. 2001—02), LA County Bar Assn. (mem. exec. com., litig. sect. 1999—2003, chair: complex courts com. 2000—05). Office: O'Melveny & Myers LLP 400 S Hope St Los Angeles CA 90071-2899 Office Phone: 213-430-6000. Office Fax: 213-430-6407. Business E-Mail: saronson@omm.com.

ARONZON, PAUL S., lawyer; b. LA, 1954; BA cum laude, Calif. State U., Northridge, 1976; JD, Southwestern U., 1979. Bar: Calif. 1979, DC 1995, NY 1996. Mng. dir., exec. v.p., co-head investment banking Imperial Capital, LLC, LA, 2006—. Office: Imperial Capital LLC 2000 Avenue of the Stars 9th Fl Los Angeles CA 90067 Office Phone: 310-246-3631. Business E-Mail: paronzon@imperialcapital.com.

ARREDONDO, PATRICIA, academic administrator, psychology professor; D in Counseling Psychology, Boston U.; LHD (hon.), U. San Diego. Prof. U. N.H., Boston U.; adj. prof. Tufts U.; faculty mem., exec. training program, Bus. Sch. Columbia U.; assoc. prof., div. psychology in edn. Ariz. State U., Tempe. Spkr. in field. Contbr. Founder, pres. Empowerment Workshops, Inc., Boston, 1985—; adv. bd. Boston Mgmt. Consortium, Police Acad. Training Com., Boston Diversity Steering Com.; pres. bd. Parents & Children's Services; founding mem., co-chair Latino Profl. Network; bd. dir. Mass. Sch. Profl. Psychology, Freedom House, Sankaty Head Found. Recipient Disting. Profl. Svc. award, Assn. Counselor Edn. & Supervision, Mentor award. Fellow: Soc. for Psychol. Study of Ethnic Minority Issues, Div 45, APA (former pres.); mem.: Assn. for Multicultural Counseling and Devel. (former pres.), Nat. Psychol. Assn. (pres.), Chicana/o Faculty & Staff Assn. (Ariz. State U.) (pres.), Am. Counseling Assn. (pres., Kitty Cole Human Rights award). Fluent in Spanish. Office: Ariz State Univ Coll of Edn Div of Psych & Edn Payne Hall Rm 446 PO Box 870211 Tempe AZ 85287-0211 Office Phone: 800-347-6647 ext. 232, 480-965-5909. Office Fax: 480-965-4400. E-mail: empow@aol.com, empower@asu.edu.

ARROTT, ANTHONY SCHUYLER, physics educator; b. Pitts., Apr. 1, 1928; s. Charles Ramsey and June (Scheffler) A.; m. Patricia Graham, June 6, 1953; children— Anthony Patterson, Helen Graham, Matthew Ramsey, Elizabeth BS, Carnegie Inst. Tech., 1948, PhD, 1954; M.Sc., U. Pa., 1950. Mem. faculty Carnegie Inst. Tech., Pitts., 1953-56; researcher Ford Motor Co., Dearborn, Mich., 1956-68; prof. physics Simon Fraser U., Burnaby, B.C., Can., 1968—. Contbr. articles to profl. jours. Bd. dirs. Sci. for Peace, Can., 1983-92, pres., 1988-90; exec. Vancouver Inst., 1985—, pres., 1991-92. Recipient Gold medal B.C. Sci. Council, 1983; fellow Allis Chalmers Corp., 1951-53, Guggenheim Found., 1963, Royal Soc. Can., 1983—. Fellow Am. Phys. Soc.; mem. Can. Assn. Physicists (Medal Achievement 1986). Office: Simon Fraser U Physics Dept Burnaby BC Canada V5A 1S6 Business E-Mail: arrott@sfu.ca.

ARROW, KENNETH JOSEPH, economist, educator; b. NYC, Aug. 23, 1921; s. Harry I. and Lillian (Greenberg) Arrow; m. Selma Schweitzer, Aug. 31, 1947; children: David Michael, Andrew. BS in Social Sci., CCNY, 1940; MA, Columbia U., 1941, PhD, 1951, DSc (hon.), 1973; LLD (hon.), U. Chgo., 1967, CUNY, 1972, Hebrew U. Jerusalem, 1975, U. Pa., 1976, Washington U., St. Louis, 1989; D. Social and Econ. Scis. (hon.), U. Vienna, Austria, 1971; LLD (hon.), Ben-Gurion U. of the Negev, 1992; D in Social Scis. (hon.), Yale U., 1974; D (hon.), Université René Descartes, Paris, 1974, U. Aix-Marseille III, 1985, U. Cattolica del Sacro Cuore, Milan, Italy, 1994, U. Uppsala, 1995, U. Buenos Aires, 1999, U. Cyprus, 2000; Dr.Pol., U. Helsinki, 1976; MA (hon.), Harvard U., 1968; DLitt, Cambridge U., Eng., 1985; LLD (hon.), Harvard U., 1999; PhD (hon.), Tel Aviv U., 2001; LLD (hon.), Hitotsubashi U., 2004. Rsch. assoc. Cowles Commn. for Research in Econs., 1947—49; asst. prof. econs. U. Chgo., 1948—49; acting asst. prof. econs. and stats. Stanford, 1949—50, assoc. prof., 1950—53, prof. econs., stats. and ops. rsch., 1953—68; prof. econs. Harvard, 1968—74, James Bryant Conant univ. prof., 1974—79; exec. head dept. econs. Stanford U., 1954—56, acting exec. head dept., 1962—63, Joan Kenney prof. econs. and prof. ops. rsch., 1979—91, prof. emeritus, 1991—. Economist Coun. Econ. Advisers, U.S. Govt., 1962; cons. RAND Corp., 1948—; Fulbright prof. U. Siena, 1995; vis. fellow All Souls Coll., Oxford, 1996; overseas rsch. fellow Churchill Coll., Cambridge, 1963—64, Cambridge, 1970, 73, 86. Author: Social Choice and Individual Values, 1951, Essays in the Theory of Risk Bearing, 1971, The Limits of Organization, 1974, Collected Papers, Vols. I-VI, 1983—85; co-author: Mathematical Studies in Inventory and Production, 1958, Studies in Linear and Nonlinear Programming, 1958, Time Series Analysis of Inter-industry Demands, 1959, Public Investment, The Rate of Return and Optimal Fiscal Policy, 1971, General Competitive Analysis, 1971, Studies in Resource Allocation Processes, 1977, Social Choice and Multicriterion Decision Making, 1985. Capt. US Army, 1942—46. Recipient Alfred Nobel Meml. prize in econ. scis., Swedish Acad. Scis., 1972, Kempé de Feriet medal, Info. Processing for Mgmt. Under Uncertainty, 1998, Medal, U. Paris, 1998, U.S. Nat. Medal of Sci. in Behavioral/Social Sci., 2004; fellow Social Sci. Rsch. fellow, 1952, Ctr. for Advanced Study in the Behavioral Scis., 1956—57, Guggenheim, 1972—73. Fellow: AAAS (chmn. sect. K 1983), NAS (mem. coun. inst. medicine 1990—93), Am. Fin. Assn., Am. Econ. Assn. (exec. com. 1967—69, pres. 1973, John Bates Clark medal 1957), Internat. Soc. Inventory Rsch. (pres. 1983—90), Econometric Soc. (v.p. 1955, pres. 1956), Am. Acad. Arts and Scis. (v.p. 1979—81, 1991—93), Am. Statis. Assn., Inst. Math. Stats.; mem.: Royal Soc. (fgn.), Game Theory Soc., Brit. Acad. (corr.), Pontifical Acad. Social Scis., Soc. Social Choice and Welfare (pres. 1991—93), Western Econ. Assn. (pres. 1980—81), Finnish Acad. Scis. (fgn. hon.), Inst. Ops. Rsch. and Mgmt. Sci. (pres. 1963, chmn. coun. 1964, Von Neumann prize 1986, Fellows' award), Am. Philos. Soc., Internat. Econs. Assn. (pres. 1983—86). Office: Stanford U Dept Econs Stanford CA 94305-6072 Home Phone: 650-327-3957; Office Phone: 650-723-9165. Office Fax: 650-725-5702. Business E-Mail: arrow@stanford.edu.

ARTHUR, JOHN M., editor; Grad., Stanford U. With Pittsburg Post-Dispatch, Calif., San Francisco Examiner; city editor to mng. editor Orange County Edit. LA Times, 1986—92, asst. nat. editor, 1992—93, editor San Fernando Valley Edit., 1993, mng. editor Valley, Orange County and Ventura edits., Times Nat. Edit., 1997, dep. Page 1 editor/nights, 2000—05, Page 1 editor, 2005—07, mng. editor, 2007—08, exec. editor, 2008—. Office: LA Times 202 W 1st St Los Angeles CA 90012

ARTHUR, MICHAEL ELBERT, financial advisor, lawyer; b. Seattle, Oct. 9, 1952; s. Theodore E. and Gladys L. (Jones) A.; m. Claire C. Meeker, Dec. 23, 1974; children: Christine, Conor, Austin. BA, U. Calif., Santa Barbara, 1974; JD, Stanford U., 1977. Ptnr. Miller Nash LLP, Portland, Oreg., 1977—2001; fin. advisor UBS Fin. Svcs.,

Portland, 2001—. Trustee Chiles Found. Home: 13535 NW Lariat Ct Portland OR 97229-7001 Office: UBS Financial Svcs 805 SW Broadway Ste 2600 Portland OR 97205-3365 Office Phone: 503-225-9211. Business E-Mail: mike.arthur@ubs.com.

ARUM, ROBERT, lawyer, sports events promoter; b. NYC, Dec. 8, 1931; s. Samuel and Celia (Baumgarten) Arum; m. Barbara Mandelbaum, July 2, 1960 (div. 1977); children: John, Richard, Elizabeth; m. Sybil Ann Hamada, Dec. 18, 1977 (div. 1991); m. Lovee Hazan Du Boef, Sept. 14, 1991. BA, NYU, 1953; JD cum laude, Harvard U., 1956. Bar: NY 1956. Atty. firm Root, Barrett, Cohen, Knapp & Smith, NYC, 1956—61; asst. U.S. atty., chief tax sect. U.S. Atty.'s Office, So. Dist. N.Y., 1961—64; ptnr. firm Phillips, Nizer, Benjamin, Krim & Ballon, NYC, 1964—72, Arum & Katz, NYC, 1972—79; chmn. Top Rank, Inc.; Promoter Ali-Frazier Super Fight II, 1974, Evel Knievel Snake River Canyon Jump, 1974, Ali-Norton World Heavyweight Championship, 1976, Monzon-Valdez World Middleweight Championships, 1976, 1977, Ali-Spinks Championships, 1978, Leonard-Duran Championships, 1980, 1989, Top Rank/ESPN Boxing Series, 1980—, Arguello-Pryor Championship, 1983, Moore-Duran Championship, 1983, Hagler-Duran Championship, 1983, Hagler-Hearns Championship, 1985, Hagler-Leonard Superfight Championship, 1987, Leonard-Hearns "The War" Championship, 1989—91, Holyfield-Foreman World Heavyweight Championship, 1991, Holyfield-Holmes World Heavyweight Championship, 1992, Foreman/Morrison Heavyweight Championship, 1993, De la Hoya/Whitaker, 1997, De la Hoya/Chavez, 1996, 1998, De la Hoya/Quartey, 1999, De la Hoya/Trinidad, 1999, De la Hoya/Mosely, 2000, Morales/Barrera, 2002, De la Hoya/Vargas, 2002. Named to Boxing Hall of Fame, 1999. Mem.: Friars Club. Home: 36 Gulf Stream Ct Las Vegas NV 89113-1354 Office: 3980 Howard Hughes Pkwy Las Vegas NV 89109-0992 E-mail: erroa@aol.com.

ARUNDEL, JAMES D., lawyer; b. Omaha, July 30, 1947; BA, U. Nebr., 1969; JD, U. Chgo., 1972. Bar: Nebr. 1972, Colo. 1981. Mng. ptnr. Kutak Rock, Denver. Mem. Nebr. State Bar Assn., Colo. State Bar Assn., Omaha Bar Assn., Denver Bar Assn., Phi Beta Kappa. Office: 1801 California St #3100 Denver CO 80202-2626

ARVESON, WILLIAM BARNES, mathematics professor; b. Oakland, Calif., Nov. 22, 1934; s. Ronald Magnus and Audrey Mary (Hichens) A.; m. Lee A. Kaskutas. BS in Math, Calif. Inst. Tech., 1960; MA, UCLA, 1963, PhD, 1964. Benjamin Peirce instr. Harvard U., 1965-68; lectr. dept. math. U. Calif., Berkeley, 1968-69, assoc. prof., 1969-74, prof., 1974—, Miller rsch. prof., 1985—86, 1999—2000. Author: An Invitation to C*-algebras, 1976, A Short Course in Spectral Theory, 2001, Noncommutative Dynamics and E-semigroups, 2003; assoc. editor: Duke Math. Jour, 1975-86, Jour. of Operator Theory, 1977-87, editor, 1987—; contbr. articles to math. jours. Served with U.S. Navy, 1952-55. John Simon Guggenheim fellow, 1976-77 Mem. Am. Math. Soc. (assoc. editor bulletin 1988-91), Edinburgh Math. Soc. (assoc. editor proceedings 1989—). Office: U Calif Dept Math Berkeley CA 94720-0001 Business E-Mail: arveson@math.berkeley.edu.

ARVIZU, DAN ELIAB, mechanical engineer; b. Douglas, Ariz., Aug. 23, 1950; s. Walter and Ella (Rodriguez) A.; m. Patricia Ann Brady, Feb. 23, 1980; children: Joshua, Angela, Elizabeth, Kayley, Tecia. BSME, New Mexico State U., 1973; MSME, Stanford U., 1974, PhD in Mech. Engring., 1981. Mfg. engring. asst. Texas Instruments, Dallas, 1969-72; mem. tech. staff Bell Telephone Labs., Denver, 1973-77; mem. solar thermal tech. staff Sandia Nat. Labs., Albuquerque, 1977-81, mem. solar photovoltaic tech. staff, 1981-86, supr. photovoltaic cell rsch., 1986-88, mgr. tech. transfer, 1988-91, dir. tech. transfer, 1991-93, dir. adv. energy tech., 1993-97, dir. materials and process scis., 1997-98; v.p. energy, environment and sys. group CH2M Hill, 1998-2000, sr. v.p. tech., 2001—05, chief tech. officer energy, environ. and sys. bus., 2002—05; chair energy working group CEO Coalition to Advance Sustainable Tech., 2002—; exec. dir. engery and tech. U. Chgo., 2004—; dir., chief exec. Nat. Renewable Energy Lab. (NREL), Golden, Colo., 2005—. Mem. tech. transfer steering com. Nat. Ctr. for Mfg. Scis., Ann Arbor, Mich., 1992; mem. tech. transfer mgrs. adv. bd. Nat. Tech. Transfer Ctr., Wheeling, W.Va., 1992—96; mem. commercialization adv. bd. Solar II Power Plant, Barstow, Calif., 1996—96; mem. adv. bd. U. Tex.-El Paso model Inst. Excellence Program, 1995—; chmn. indsl. adv. bd. ME Acad. N.Mex. State U., 1995—99, bd. dirs.; mem. com. to rev. DOE's renewable energy tech. program NRC, 1998—2000; mem. corp. adv. bd. Colo. Sch. Mines, 1999—; mem. nat. adv. bd. for Hispanic engr. nat. achievement award conf. HENAAC, 1999—, bd. dirs., 2000—, Nat. Sci. Bd., 2004—; mem. indsl. adv. group U. Tex. El Paso Coll. Engring., 1999—; mem. nat. coal coun. Dept. Energy, 1999—; adv. group G8 Task Force Renewable Energy, 2000—01; mem. Army Sci. Bd. Dept. of Def., 2001—; adv. Divsn. Engring. and Physical Sci. Comm. Nat. Acad. of Engring., 2001—; bd. adv. Greater Metro Denver Salvation Army, 2000—; mem. com. to review Dept. Energy concentrating solar power tech. NRC, 2002—; chair blue ribbon panel on sci. and engring. workforce diversity Coun. on Competition; chmn. Hispanic Nat. Achievement Award conf. Contbr. articles to profl. jours. Recipient Sel. Hispanic Engr. Nat. Achievement award Exec. Excellence, 1996; named Disting. Engring. Alumnus N.Mex. State U., 1988, 96, Ingeniero Eminente, 1990, Outstanding Achievement award Hispanic Alliance for Career Enhancement, 1997, named Rising Star in Sci. Albuquerque Tribune newspaper, 1989, One of top 20 Hispanic Scientists and Engrs. in Am., Hispanic Engr. Mag., 1998, One of 50 Most Important Hispanics in Am. in Tech. and Bus., Hispanic Mag., 2003, 2004. Mem. ASME (solar standards com. 1981-83, nat. lab. tech. transfer com. 1990-93), IEEE, IEEE Electronic Device Soc. (adminstrv. com. 1986-91), Am. Soc. Material Internat., Tech. Transfer Soc. Achievements include leadership of national laboratory negotiating teams that resulted in Department of Energy policy changes to improve U.S. Goverment/ Industry partnership agreements, management of research effort that developed 30 percent solar to electric conversion efficiency solar cell, and development of Sandia National Laboratory's technology transfer center including development of policy, maturation of technology, and formal partnerships between industry and laboratories. Office: CH2M Hill Energy Environment and Sys Bus Group 6060 S Willow Dr Greenwood Village CO 80111-5142 E-mail: darvizu@ch2m.com.

ARZBERGER, GUS, state legislator, retired farmer, rancher; m. Marsha Daniels; two children; two stepchildren. Student, Air Force U. Mem. Ariz. Ho. of Reps., 1985-88, Ariz. State Senate, 1989—, mem. natural resources com., mem. transp. com., mem. agr. and environment com., mem. appropriations com., mem. govt. reform com., others. Supporter S.E. Ariz. Food Bank Warehouse; active Ariz. Civil Air Patrol; bd. dirs. Cochise County Sheriff's Posse; pres. Willcox Dem. Club; Dem. precinct committeeman; ex-officio mem. Ariz. Aero. Bd. Infantry platoon sgt. U.S. Army, WWII, ETO. Mem. VFW (bd. dirs.), Farm Bur., Ariz. Cotton Growers, Ariz. Grain Growers, Cochise-Graham County Cattle Growers Assn., Willcox C. of C. and Agr., Gila Valley Econ. Devel. Assn., Willcox Elks Lodge (charter), Vets. Club (bd. dirs.). Democrat.

ASBECK, PETER MICHAEL, engineering educator; BSEE, MIT, Cambridge, 1969; PhD in Elec. Engring., MIT, 1975. With Sarnoff Rsch. Ctr., Princeton, NJ, Philips Lab., Briarcliff Manor, NY, Rockwell Internat. Sci. Ctr., 1978—91, prin. scientist high speed electronics and optoelectronics function, 1991; prof. elec. and computer engring. U. Calif., San Diego, 1991—. Contbr. articles to sci. jours. Fellow: IEEE (David Sarnoff award 2003); mem.: NAE. Achievements include development of heterojunction bipolar transistors, which amplify cell phone signals so they are strong enough to travel from a cell phone antenna to the closest cell phone tower; patents in field. Office: Dept Elec and Computer Engring U Calif San Diego Mail Code 0407 9500 Gilman Dr La Jolla CA 92093-0407 Office Phone: 858-534-6713. Office Fax: 858-534-2486. E-mail: asbeck@ece.ucsd.edu.

ASCHER, NANCY LOUISE, surgeon; b. Detroit, Mar. 15, 1949; d. Meyer S. and Beckie (Berger) A.; m. John. P. Roberts, Dec. 10, 1992; children: Becky, John. AB, U. Mich., 1970, MD, 1974; PhD, U. Minn., 1985. Instr. surgery U. Minn., Mpls., 1982-85, staff surgeon, dir. liver transplant, 1982-87, assoc. prof., 1987; prof. surgery U. Calif., San Francisco, 1988—, chief transplant svc., 1989—, prof., vice chmn., 1993—99, chmn., dept. surg., 1999—. Presenter in field. Contbr. articles to profl. jours. Bd. trustees The Bay Sch. of San Francisco. Schering scholar, 1979; recipient Koret Israel prize, 1993. Fellow Am. Coll. Surgeons (surg. forum com.); mem. AMA, AAAS, Am. Assn. Immunologists, Am. Soc. Transplant Surgeons (publs. and programs com., edn. com., chair edn. com., councilor-at-large, sec., pres 2001-2002), Am. Surg. Assn., Calif. Med. Assn., Minn. Surg. Soc. (scholar 1982), Mpls. Surg. Soc., San Francisco Med. Soc., Internat. Transplantation Soc. (sec. local orgn. com.), Soc. U. Surgeons, Soc. Clin. Surgery, Surg. Biology Club, Acad. Medicine Task Force, Pacific Coast Surg. Soc., Live Transplant Soc., Inst. Medicine, Phi Beta Kappa, Phi Kappa Phi, others. Office: UCSF Box 0104 505 Parnassus Ave San Francisco CA 94143-0104 E-mail: aschern@surgery.ucsf.edu.

ASH, CECIL P., state legislator; b. Mesa, Ariz., Nov. 21, 1948; m. Linda Ash; children: Adam, Allison, Jordan, Jacob, Daniel. BS in Psychol., Brigham Young U., 1973; JD, Ariz. State U., 1976. Atty. Ash & Reeb Law Firm, 1977—78; legal adv. Ariz. Dept. Pub. Safety, 1978—83; broker Gentry Realty, Inc., 1980—86; atty. pvt. practice, 1983—90; broker Help-U-Sell of Mesa, 1986—89; atty. Office Maricopa County Pub. Defender, 1990—95; precinct committeeman Rep. Party, 1994—2008; owner & mgr. ViewPoint RV & Golf Resort, 1995—2004; mem. Dist. 18 Ariz. House of Reps., 2008—. Rep. UN United Families Internat., 2005—07. Parent adv. coun. Franklin Jr. High Sch., 1997. Mem.: Sunrise Rotary Club. Republican. Office: Capitol Complex 1700 W Washington Rm 127 Phoenix AZ 85007-2890 Office Phone: 602-926-3160. Office Fax: 602-417-3151. Business E-Mail: cash@azleg.gov.*

ASH, LAWRENCE ROBERT, public health educator; b. Holyoke, Mass., Mar. 5, 1933; s. Lawrence Clifton and Alice (Sartini) A.; m. Luana Lee Smith, Aug. 4 1960; 1 child, Leigh I. BS in Zoology, U. Mass., 1954, MA in Zoology, 1956; PhD in Parasitology, Tulane U., 1960. Asst. parasitologist U. Hawaii, Honolulu, 1960-61; instr. Tulane U., New Orleans, 1961-65; med. parasitologist South Pacific Commn., Noumea, New Caledonia, 1965-67; asst. prof. pub. health UCLA Sch. Pub. Health, 1967-71, assoc. prof., 1971-75, prof., 1975-94, chmn. dept., assoc. dean, 1979-84, prof. emeritus, 1994—. Panelist U.S. Panel on Parasitic Diseases, U.S.-Japan Program, Washington, 1972-78, chmn., 1978-84; cons. Naval Med. Rsch. Unit # 2 Taipei, China, Manila, 1970-80. Sr. author: Atlas of Human Parasitology, 1980, 4th rev. edit., 1997, 5th rev. edit., 2007, Parasites: A Guide to Laboratory Procedures and Identification, 1987; co-author: Parasites in Human Tissues, 1995. NIH grantee, 1970-84. Fellow Royal Soc. Tropical Medicine and Hygiene; mem. Am. Soc. Tropical Medicine and Hygiene (councilor 1974-77), Am. Soc. Parasitologists (councilor 1972-75, 88-92, v.p. 1982-83). Home: 10400 Northvale Rd Los Angeles CA 90064-4332 Office: UCLA Sch Pub Health Los Angeles CA 90095-0001 Office Phone: 310-825-5234. Business E-Mail: larryash@ucla.edu.

ASH, ROY LAWRENCE, former federal official; b. LA, Oct. 20, 1918; s. Charles K. and Fay E. (Dickinson) A.; m. Lila M. Hornbek., Nov. 13, 1943; children— Loretta Ash Danko, James, Marilyn Ash Hanna, Robert, Charles. MBA, Harvard, 1947. Chief fin. officer Hughes Aircraft Co., 1949-53; co-founder Litton Industries, Inc., Beverly Hills, Calif., 1953-72, dir., 1953-72, pres., 1961-72; mem. bd. dirs. Bank America Corp., 1968—72, 1976—91; mem. Bank America, 1964—72, 1978—91; chmn. Pres.'s Adv. Coun. on Exec. Orgn., 1969-71; asst. to Pres. U.S.; dir. Office Mgmt. and Budget, Washington, 1973-75; chmn. bd., chief exec. officer AM Internat., 1976-81. Co-chmn. Japan-Calif. Assn., 1965-72, 80-81; mem. vis. com. Harvard U. Kennedy Sch. Govt., 1992—; mem. Bus. Roundtable, 1977-81. Vice chmn. Los Angeles Olympic Organizing Com., 1980-85, chmn. fin. com.; trustee Calif. Inst. Tech., 1967-72, Com. for Econ. Devel., 1970-72, 75—; dir. Los Angeles World Affairs Council, 1968-72, 78—, pres., 1970-72; chmn. adv. council on gen. govt. Rep. Nat. Com., 1977-80; chmn. L.A. Music Ctr. Opera Assn., 1988-93. From pvt. to capt. Army Air Corps, 1942-46. Mem. C. of C. U.S. (bd. dirs. 1979-85, chmn. internat. policy com. 1979-85), Calif. Club, Harvard Club.

ASHBURN, ROY, state legislator; b. Bakersfield, Calif., Mar. 21, 1954; children: Shelley, Shannon, Stacy, Suzy. Student, Coll. of Sequoias; BA in Pub. Adminstrn., Calif. State U., Bakersfield, 1983. Owner Roy Ashburn Signs, 1969—72; field rep. Supr. LeRoy Jackson, 1972—77; dist. rep. Congressman William Thomas, 1979—83; mem. Calif. State Assembly, Sacramento, 1996—2002; mem. Dist. 18 Calif. State Senate, Sacramento, 2002—. Vice chmn. Rev. and Taxation; mem. appropriations com. Calif. State Assembly, mem. transp. and housing com., mem. pub. employees and ret. com., vice chmn., senate select com. def. and aerospace industry, chmn. Republican. Roman Catholic. Office: State Capitol Rm 3060 Sacramento CA 94248 also: Dist 18 5001 California Ave Ste 105 Bakersfield CA 93309 Office Phone: 661-323-0443. Business E-Mail: senator.ashburn@sen.ca.gov.*

ASHDOWN, FRANKLIN DONALD, physician, composer; b. Logan, Utah, May 2, 1942; s. Donald and Theresa Marie (Hill) A. BA, Tex. Tech. U., 1963; MD, U. Tex., 1967. Chief of med. Holloman Air Force Base, New Mexico, 1971-73; chief of staff Gerald Champion Mem. Hosp., Alamogordo, N.Mex., 1976, 91, 92; pvt. practice Alamogordo, 1973—; pres. Otero County Concerts Assn., Alamogordo, 1985-94, Otero County Med. Soc., Alamogordo, 1986. Cons. N.Mex. Sch. for Visually Handicapped, Alamogordo, 1973—76. Composer of more than 100 published and recorded works. Bd. dirs. Otero County Mental Health Assn., Alamogordo, 1973-77, Flickinger Found. for Performing Arts, 1995; bd. trustees Gerald Champion Meml. Hosp., 1992. Mem. Gerald Champion Mem. Hosp., N.M. Med. Soc., Am. Soc. Internal Med., ASCAP (Standard Panel award 2000, 01, 02). Republican. Office: Franklin D Ashdown Md PO Box 221 Alamogordo NM 88311-0221 Home Phone: 505-437-8807; Office Phone: 505-437-4586. E-mail: fashdown@wayfarer1.com.

ASHFORTH, ALDEN, musician, educator; b. NYC, May 13, 1933; m. Nancy Ann Regnier, June 12, 1956 (div. 1980); children— Robyn Richardson, Melissa Adams, Lauren Elizabeth AB, B.Mus., Oberlin Coll, 1958; M.F.A., Princeton U., 1960, PhD, 1971. Instr. Princeton U., N.J., 1961; instr. Oberlin Coll., Ohio, 1961-65, N.Y.U., NYC, 1965-66, Manhattan Sch. Music, NYC, 1965; lectr. CUNY, NYC, 1966-67; asst. prof. music UCLA, 1967-72, assoc. prof. music, 1972-80, prof., 1980—98, prof. emeritus, 1998—. Coordinator electronic music studio, 1969-86. Composer numerous instrumental, vocal and electronic works including: Episodes (chamber concerto for 8 instruments), 1962, The Unquiet Heart (cycle for soprano and chamber orch.), 1968, Big Bang (piano-four hands) 1970, Byzantium (organ and electronic tape), 1971, Sailing to Byzantium (organ and electronic tape), 1973, Aspects of Love (song cycle), 1978, Christmas Motets (a cappella chorus), 1980, The Miraculous Bugle (flugelhorn and percussion), 1989, Palimpsests (organ), 1997; producer, recorder New Orleans Jazz including, New Orleans Parade: The Eureka Brass Band Plays Dirges and Stomps, 1952, Doc Paulins Marching Band, 1982, Last of the Line: The Eagle Brass Band, 1984; contbr. articles to profl. jours. and to New Grove Dictionary of Jazz. Office: UCLA Music Dept Los Angeles CA 90095-0001

ASIMOW, PAUL D., geophysicist, educator; AB summa cum laude in Geol. Scis., Harvard U., 1991; MS in Geology, Calif. Inst. Tech., Pasadena, 1993, PhD in Geology, 1997. Postdoctoral rsch. fellow Columbia U. Lamont-Doherty Earth Obs., Palisades, NY, 1997—99; asst. prof. geology and geochemistry Calif. Inst. Tech., Pasadena, 1999—2005, assoc. prof. geology and geochemistry, 2005—. Contbr. articles to sci. jours. Recipient CAREER award, NSF, 2003—; grantee Alfred P. Sloan Found. fellowship, 2003—05. Mem.: AAAS, Mineral. Soc. Am., Geochemical Soc. (F. W. Clarke medal 2003), Am. Geophys. Union (James B. Macelwane medal 2005). Office: Divsn Geol and Planetary Scis Calif Inst Tech Mail Code 170-25 Pasadena CA 91125 Office Phone: 626-395-4133. Office Fax: 626-568-0935. E-mail: asimow@gps.caltech.edu.

ASKANAS, MARK S., lawyer; b. 1960; m. Aynah V. Askanas. BA, U. Calif., Berkeley, 1982; JD, U. Calif., Davis, 1985. Bar: Calif. 1986. Assoc. Jackson, Lewis, Schnitzler & Krupman, San Francisco, 1988—93, ptnr., 1993—2001; sr. v.p. human resources, gen. counsel Ross Stores Inc., Pleasanton, Calif., 2001—. Office: Ross Stores Inc 4440 Rosewood Dr Bldg 4 Pleasanton CA 94588-3050

ASKIN, WALTER MILLER, artist, educator; b. Pasadena, Calif., Sept. 12, 1929; s. Paul Henry and Dorothy Margaret (Miller) A.; child from previous marriage, Nancy Carol Oudegeest; m. Elise Anne Doyle, Apr. 17, 1993. BA, U. Calif., Berkeley, 1951, MA, 1952; postgrad., Ruskin Sch. Drawing and Fine Art, Oxford. Asst. curator edn. Legion of Honor Mus., San Francisco, 1953-54; prof. art Calif. State U., LA, 1956-92; pub. Nose Press, Pasadena, 1984—; vis. artist Pasadena Art Mus., 1962-63, U. N.Mex., 1972, Calif. State U., Long Beach, 1974-75, Cranbrook Acad. Art, Mich., 1978, Ariz. State U., Tempe, 1979, Art Ctr. Athens Sch. Fine Arts, Mykonos, Greece, 1973, Kelpra Studio, London, 1969, 73; mem. Task Force Future Arts Edn., Coll. Bd., 2008—; presentation lithoran Ariz. State U. Alumni Portfolio Southern Graphics Coun. Nat. conf., Chgo., 2009. Chief reader Advanced Placement Program, Ednl. Testing Svc., 1982—85; chmn. visual arts panel Art Recognition and Talent Search Nat. Found. Advancement in Arts-Commn. on Presdl. Scholars; advanced placement studio art exam. com. Coll. Bd., 1985—96, chmn., 1992—96, mem. Commn. of Future of Advanced Placement Program, 1999—2001, mem. acad. coun., 1989—94, chair arts adv. com., 1987—93; bd. dirs. Internat. Assn. for Humor Studies, 1989; adj. prof. Ariz. State U., 1988—90; artist-in-residence Ragdale Found., Lake Forest, Ill., 1986, John Michael Kohler Art Ctr., Sheboygan, Wis., 1987, Hambidge Ctr. for Arts & Sci., Ga., 1991, Vt. Studio Colony, 1988, U. Dallas, 2001; co-dir. 1st Internat. Conf. on Humor in Art, Chateau de la Bretsche, Brittany, France, 1989, 92; vis. prof. Ariz. State U., Tempe, 2001; invited artist 12 lithos Hullaballoo in Winter in collaboration with Wayne Kimball, Brigham Young U., 2001; historian art alumni group U. Calif., Berkeley, 2001—; curator Jest for Fun Channel Islands Art Ctr., 2004; juror various exhibitions; mem. coll. bd. Nat. Task Force Arts in Edn., 2008; juror, Pasadena Soc. Artist 83rd Annual Exhbn., Brand Libr., Glendale, 2008; illustration Cheap Eats Marthas Minions Maoazine, Marthas Vineyard, 2008. One-man shows include Contemporary Art in Pasadena, 1960-74, Santa Barbara Mus. Art, 1966, Hellenic-Am. Union, Athens, Greece, 1973, Hank Baum Gallery, San Francisco, 1970, 74, 76, Ericson Gallery, NYC, 1978, Abraxas Gallery, Calif., 1979-81, Kunstlerhaus, Vienna, Austria, 1981, USIA, Yugoslavia, 1985-86, Fla. State U., Tallahassee, 1988, Lizardi/Harp Gallery, Pasadena, 1988, 91, 95, LA Valley Coll., 1989, Armory Ctr. for Arts, 1991, Taipei Mus. Art, 1998, Norton Simon Mus., 1999, Taipei Fine Arts Mus., 1999, Gertrude Herbert Art Inst., Ga., 1999, Schafler Gallery, Pratt Inst., Bklyn., 1999, Kittredge Gallery, U. Puget Sound, Tacoma, 1999, Cmty. Visual Art Assn., Jackson Hole, Wyo., 1999, Wayland Bapt. U., Plainview, Tex., 1999, Norton Simon Mus., 2000, Bradley U., Peoria, Ill., 2000, Brand Libr., Glendale, Calif., 2001, U. Dallas, 2001, Brigham Young U., 2002, Calif. State U., Channel Islands, 2002, Pasadena Playhouse Gallery, 2003, Floating Rock Gallery, Pasadena, 2004, Village Sq. Gallery, Montrose, 2005, LA City Coll., 2005, Painting Ctr., NY, 2006, Brattleboro Mus. and Art Ctr., Vt., 2006, Internat. Print Ctr. NYC, 2007; exhibitions include LA Met. Transit Authority, 2003, Gallery LeLong, NYC, 2003, N.W. Watercolor Soc., Art Inst. Seattle, 2004, Art of Humor Studio Channel Islands Art Ctr., 2004, Artful Jesters Painting Ctr., NYC, 2006, Brattleboro Mus. Art Ctr., Vt., 2006, Palm Desert El Paseo, 2006—, So. Graphics Coun., 2006—, Rocky Mt. Nat. Watermedia Exhbn., 2006, El Paso Invitational, Tex., 2006, Foothills Art Ctr., Golden, Colo., 2006, LA City Coll., 2006, Humor in Art, The Painting Ctr., NYC, 2007, Internat. Print Ctr. Screenprint

Exhbn., NYC, 2007, 10th Anniversary Show, Calif. State U. Channel Islands, 2007, 29 Artists, Burbank Art Ctr., 2007, others; author: A Briefer History of the Greeks, 1983, Another Art Book to Cross Off Your List, 1984, Modern Manifesto Match Game, 1998, Hidedous Headlines, 1998, Womsters and Foozlers, 1998, On Becoming an Artist, 1999, (calendar) Man, Dog, Bone Artists' Calendar; represented in permanent collections Norton Simon Mus., Pasadena, Getty Ctr. for the Arts, LA, Mus. Modern Art, NYC, Whitney Mus. Art, NYC, San Francisco Mus. Contemporary Art, Albright Knox Mus., Buffalo, LA County Mus. Art, working with Art, LA municipal exhbn. program, World Airports, 2005-06, Ink and Clay 33, Calif. Poly. Stamp U., Pomona, 2007, Traupling Print exhbn., Southern Graphics Coun., 20006-, Collection of Mus. of Tekas Rsch. U., 2005, Screen Prints, Internat. Print Ctr., NYC, 2007; others; contbr. articles to profl. jours. and mags. Trustee Pasadena Art Mus., 1963-68; bd. dirs. LA Inst. Contemporary Art., 1978-81, Pasadena Gallery Contemporary Arts; bd. govs. Baxter Art Gallery, Calif. Inst. Tech., 1980-86; bd. dirs. The Calif. Artist, Book Program, 1985-2000; dir. The Visual Humor Project, 1989—. Recipient Outstanding Prof. award Calif. State U., 1973, Artists award Pasadena Arts Coun., 1970, award 61st ann. exhbn. N.W. Watercolor Soc., 2001, Past Pres.' award 80th ann. exhbn. Nat. Watercolor Soc., 2000, Purchase prize 3d nat. print biennial Frederick R. Weisman Mus., Mpls., 2001; named Disting. Alumnus, Pasadena City Coll.; grantee Ruth G. Jansen Edn. Meml., Pasadena Arts Commn., 1990, Calif. State U., 2006; also over 50 awards in competitive exhbns. art. Mem.: Kauai Soc. Artists, So. Graphics Coun., LA Printmaking Soc. (pres. 2002—04, founding mem.), Nat. Watercolor Soc. (1st v.p. 1960), Coll. Art Assn. Am. Home and Office: PO Box D South Pasadena CA 91031-0120

ASMUS, JOHN FREDRICH, physicist; b. Pasadena, Calif., Jan. 20, 1937; s. William F. and Eleanor E. (Kocher) Asmus; m. Barbara Ann Flaherty, Feb. 23, 1963; children: Joanne M., Rosemary H. BSEE, Calif. Inst. Tech., 1958, MSEE, 1959, PhDEE and Physics, 1965. Head optical systems dept. Aero Geo Astro Corp., Alexandria, Va., 1960-64; head laser dept. Gulf Gen. Atomic, San Diego, 1964-69; research staff Inst. Def. Analyses, Arlington, Va., 1969-71; v.p., bd. mem. Sci. Applications, Inc., Albuquerque, 1971-73; lectr. U. Calif., Davis, 1974, research physicist, co-founder art and sci. center San Diego, 1973—. Co-dir. JASON nat. laser program study Office of Pres. of US; keynote spkr. Laser World Trade Fair, Munich, 2003, Munich, 05, Munich, 07; mem. editl. bd. Springer Verlag, Elsevier Pub.; cons. in field. Mem. editl. bd.: Jour. Cultural Heritage, 2004—; contbr. scientific papers to profl. jours. Decorated knight Holy Sepulchre of Jerusalem; recipient Rolex Laureate for Enterprise award for restoration Xian terra cotta warriors, Montes Rolex SA, 1990, Best Scholarly Article award, Soc. Tech. Com., 1988; named George Eastman lectr., Optical Soc. Am., 1994, Rank Prize mentor, 2004, winner, IBM Supercomputing Competition for Image Enhancement fo Mona Lisa, 1989; fellow, Oberlin Coll., 1990; Schlumberger fellow, 1959—60, Tektronix fellow, 1960—61, Getty fellow, 1989, Explorers Club fellow, 1997. Mem.: IEEE, Soc. Photo-Optical Instrumentation Engrs. (editl. bd. mem. 2002—), Venice Soc., Nat. Trust Hist. Preservation, Am. Inst. Conservation, Internat. Inst. Conservation Hist. and Artistic Works, Lasers Conservation Artworks (sci. bd. mem., hon. pres.), Bay Area Art Conservation Guild, Sigma Xi, Tau Beta Pi. Achievements include patents for metallic vapor laser; embedded pinch laser; plasma pinch annealing system; chemical decontamination with ultraviolet; research in laser, ultrasonic and computer image enhancement techniques to art conservation; laser cleaning to the field of paleontology, and revealed new features of da Vinci's Mona Lisa; restored Cremona Cathedral; restored California State Capital; restored White House mural; restored Venice Ducal Palace Sculpture; development of laser-robotic technique for the decontamination of the Hanford nuclear weapons facility of US Department of Energy; laser, flashlamp and pinchlamp systems for depainting stealth aircraft and decontaminating the JET TOKAMAK thermonuclear fusion reactor; laser system for branding bowhead whales at a distance. Home: 8239 Sugarman Dr La Jolla CA 92037-2222 Office: IPAPS 0360 U Calif San Diego 9500 Gilman Dr La Jolla CA 92093-5004 Business E-Mail: jfasmus@ucsd.edu.

ASOMUGHA, NNAMDI, professional football player; b. Lafayette, La., July 6, 1981; B in Bus. Mgmt., U. Calif., Berkeley, 2003. Defensive back Oakland Raiders, 2003—. Named 1st Team All-Pro, AP, 2008; named to Am. Football Conf. Pro Bowl Team, NFL, 2008. Office: Oakland Raiders 1220 Harbor Bay Pky Alameda CA 94502*

ASPAAS, JENNIFER, lawyer; b. Spokane, Wash., Nov. 9, 1968; BA, Univ. Wash., 1991; JD, Gonzaga Univ., 1996; LLM in Taxation, Univ. Wash., 1997. Bar: Wash. 1996, Ore. 2003. Former clerk US Bankruptcy Judge, Ea. Dist., Wash., 1997—98; assoc. atty., creditor bankruptcy; real estate foreclosure; real estate title Insurance; mortgage insurance; litig. Bishop, White & Marshall, P.S., Seattle, 1998—. Spkr. in field. Contbr. articles to numerous profl. jours. Named Seattle Rising Star, SuperLawyer Mag., 2006. Mem.: Seattle Bar Assn., ABA. Office: Bishop White and Marshall PS 1301 720 Olive Way Seattle WA 98101

ASPERGER, JAMES, lawyer; b. Fresno, Calif., 1953; BA with highest honors, U. Calif., Davis, 1975; JD, U. Calif., LA, 1978. Bar: Calif. 1978, DC 1980. Law clerk to Hon. Stanley Mosk Supreme Ct. Calif., 1978—79; law clerk to Hon. William H. Rehnquist US Supreme Ct., 1979—80; asst. US atty. Central Dist. Calif., 1983—93; dep. chief, major frauds sect. LA US Attorney's Office, 1987—90, chief, major frauds sect., 1990—93; ptnr. O'Melveny & Myers LLP, LA, mem. policy com., chair global enforcement and criminal defense group. Lectr. continuing legal education courses on criminal law, civil enforcement actions, and the RICO statute; bd. dir. Western Ctr. on Law and Poverty, 1997—, Office of Pub. Counsel, 1998—. Assoc. editor UCLA Law Review, 1976—77, editor-in-chief, 1977—78; contbr. articles to profl. jours. Recipient Alumni award for Academic Distinction, U. Calif., LA; named one of Top Trial Lawyers in So. Calif., LA Bus. Jour., 1999. Fellow: Am. Coll. of Trial Lawyers; mem.: Fed. Bar Assn. (bd. dir., LA Chpt. 1997—), ABA (former chair, West Coast White Collar Crime Com. 1998—2000, vice-chair, Nat. White Collar Crime Com. 2000—02), Assn. Trail Lawyers of Am., Order of Coif, Phi Beta Kappa. Office: O'Melveny & Myers LLP 400 S Hope St Los Angeles CA 90071-2899 Office Phone: 213-430-6491. Office Fax: 213-430-6407. Business E-Mail: jasperger@omm.com.

ASTIN, ALEXANDER WILLIAM, education educator; b. Washington, May 30, 1932; s. Allen Varley and Margaret L. (Mackenzie) A.; m. Helen Stavridou, Feb. 11, 1956; children: John Alexander, Paul Allen. AB, Gettysburg Coll., Pa., 1953, LittD (hon.), 1981; MA, U. Md., 1956, PhD, 1958; LLD (hon.), Alderson-Broaddus Coll., 1982, Whitman Coll., 1986; LHD, Chapman Coll., 1987, Am. Coll. Switzerland, 1989, SUNY, 1989; D of Pedagogy, RI Coll., 1987; DSc, Thomas Jefferson U., 1990; EdD (hon.), Merrimack Coll., 1993; LLD (hon.), Pepperdine U., 1993. Dep. chief psychology service USPHS Hosp., Lexington, Ky., 1957-59; dep. chief psychology research unit VA Hosp., Balt., 1959-60; research asso., dir. research Nat. Merit Scholar Corp., Evanston, Ill., 1960-64; dir. research Am. Council Edn., Washington, 1965-73; Allan M. Cartter prof. edn. UCLA, 1973—; pres. Higher Edn. Research Inst., Los Angeles, 1973—. Author: The College Environment, 1968, The Educational and Vocational Development of College, 1971, The Power of Protest, 1975, Preventing Students from Dropping Out, 1975, Four Critical Years, 1977, Maximizing Leadership Effectiveness, 1980, Minorities in American Higher Education, 1982, Achieving Educational Excellence, 1985, Assessment for Excellence, 1991, What Matters in College?, 1993, others. Trustee St. Xavier Coll., Chgo., Marjorie Webster Jr. Coll., Washington, Gettysburg Coll., 1983-86, Eckerd Coll., Fla., 1986-91. Recipient Disting. Research award Am. Personnel and Guidance Assn., 1965, Disting. Research award Nat. Assn. Student Personnel Adminstrs., 1976, Outstanding Service award Am. Coll. Personnel Assn., 1978, Lindquist award for outstanding research on college students Am. Ednl. Research Assn., 1983, Excellence in Edn. award Nat. Assn. Coll. Admissions Counselors, 1985, Outstanding Research award Am. Coll. Personnel Assn., 1985, Outstanding Service award Council of Ind. Colls., 1986, Outstanding Research award Assn. for Study of Higher Edn., 1987, Roll of Svc. award Nat. Assn. Student Fin. Aid Adminstrs., 1991, Extended Rsch. award AACD, 1992, Sidney Suslow award Assn. for Instl. Rsch., 1992; fellow Center Advanced Study Behavioral Sci. Fellow Am. Psychol. Assn., AAAS; mem. Am. Assn. Higher Edn. (dir.) Office: UCLA Grad Sch Edn Higher Edn Rsch Inst 3005 Moore Hall Box 951521 Los Angeles CA 90095-9000

ASTON, EDWARD ERNEST, IV, dermatologist; b. Jersey City, Jan. 14, 1944; m. Kirsten Anita Aston. BA, U. Md., 1968; MD, U. Md., Balt., 1969. Diplomate Am. Bd. Dermatology. Intern Orange County Med. Ctr., Orange, Calif., 1969—70; resident U. Calif., Irvine-Orange County Med. Ctr., Irvine, Calif., 1971—74; pvt. practice Fullerton Med. Clinic Dermatology, Calif., 1974—. Part-time assoc. clin. prof. U. Calif., Irvine, 2002—. Office: 301 W Bastanchury Rd Ste 220 Fullerton CA 92835-3424

ASURA, JOHN F., paper company executive; BA, U. Scranton; MBA, U. Pa. CFO Sunshine Biscuits, Inc., 1995-96; CFO Consumer Banking PNC Bank, 1997-98, CEO of credit card subsidiary, 1998-99; prin. Crossroads LLC, 2000; interim CEO, dir. Day Runner Inc., Irvine, Calif., 2000. Fulbright-Hayes grant U. Bonn.

ATCHESON, SUE HART, business educator; b. Dubuque, Iowa, Apr. 12; d. Oscar Raymond and Anna (Cook) Hart; m. Walter Clark Atcheson (div.); children: Christine A. Hischar, Moffet Zoe A.H. Silverman, Claye Williams. BBA, Mich. State U.; MBA, Calif. State Poly. U., Pomona, 1973. Cert. tchr. and adminstr. Instr. Mt. San Antonio Coll., Walnut, Calif., 1968-90. Bd. dirs. faculty assn. Mt. San Antonio Coll., mem. acad. senate, originator vol. income tax assistance; spkr. in field; lectr. in bus. mgmt. Calif. State Poly. U., Pomona, 1973—75; cons., trainer Joint Venture between Mt. San Antonio Coll. and County of Los Angeles Dept. Pub. Social Svcs., summer, 2001. Author: Fractions and Equations on Your Own, 1975. Charter mem. Internat. Commn. on Monetary and Econ. Reform; panelist infrastructure funding reform, Freeport, Ill., 1989. Mem. Cmty. Concert Assn. Inland Empire (bd. dirs.), Scripps Coll. Fine Arts Found.(bd. dirs. 2006-08, co-pres. 2006-08), Recyclers Club (pres. 1996).

ATKIN, J MYRON, science educator; b. Bklyn., Apr. 6, 1927; s. Charles Z. and Esther (Jaffe) A.; m. Ann Spiegel, Dec. 25, 1947; children— David, Ruth, Jonathan. BS, CCNY, 1947; MA, NYU, 1948, PhD, 1956. Tchr. sci. Ramaz H.S., NYC, 1948—50; tchr. elem. sch. sci. Great Neck Pub. Schs., NY, 1950—55; prof. sci. edn. Coll. Edn., U. Ill., Urbana, 1955—79, assoc. dean, 1966—70, dean, 1970—79; prof. Sch. Edn., Stanford U., Calif., 1979—2004, prof. emeritus, 2004—, dean, 1979—86. Cons. OECD, Paris, Nat. Inst. Edn.; mem. edn. adv. bd. NSF, 1973-76, 84-86, vice-chmn., 1984-85, sr. advisor, 1986-87; mem. Ill. Tchr. Certification Bd., 1973-76; Sir John Adams lectr. U. London Inst. Edn., 1980, vis. scholar com. scholarly commn. Nat. Acad. Scis., People's Republic China, 1987; math. sci. edn. bd. NRC, 1985-89, nat. com. sci. edn. standards and assessment, 1992-96, com. on sci. edn. K-12, 1996-2002, vice chair, 1998, chair, 1999-2002; invited lectr. Nat. Sci. Coun., Taiwan, 1989—; resident Rockefeller Found., Bellagio Ctr., 1999; nat. assoc., Nat. Acads. of Sci., 2001-. Author children's sci. textbooks. Served with USNR, 1945-46. Fellow: AAAS (v.p. sect. Q 73 1974); mem.: NAS (assoc.), Am. Ednl. Rsch. Assn. (exec. bd. 1972—75, chmn. govt. and profl. liaison com.), Coun. Elem. Sci. Internat. (pres. 1969—70), Sigma Xi (chmn. com. on sci., math. and engring. edn.). Office Phone: 650-450-3514. Business E-Mail: atkin@stanford.edu.

ATKIN, JERRY C., air transportation executive; b. 1948; m. Carolyn Jones; 4 children. Degree, Dixie Coll., 1969; BS, MBA, U. Utah; HHD (hon.), Dixie Coll., 1995. CPA, 1972—74; dir. fin. SkyWest Airlines, St. George, Utah, 1974—75, pres., CEO, 1975—91, chmn., pres., CEO, 1991—2007, chmn., CEO, 2007—. Bd. dir. Regence Blue Cross & Blue Shield of Utah, The Regence Group, Portland, Oreg., Zions Bancorporation, Regional Airlines Assn.; state bd. regents Utah Sys. Higher Edn., 1999—. Recipient Outstanding Young Businessman of Yr. award, St. George C. of C., 1981; named to Hall of Fame in Bus., Dixie State Coll., 1999. Office: SkyWest Inc 444 South River Rd Saint George UT 84790

ATKINS, HOWARD IAN, bank executive; b. NYC, Feb. 12, 1951; s. Maurice and Gertrude Atkins; m. Vivian Leslie Katz; children: Jacqueline, Naomi. BS in Math., CCNY, 1972; MS in Econs., Ohio State U., 1974. Fin. analyst Chase Manhattan Bank, NYC, 1974-78, global funding coord., 1978-80, global funding exec., 1980-82, area treasury exec., Europe, 1982-86, portfolio and funding exec., 1986-88, corp. treas., 1988—91, sr. v.p., 1991—96; v.p., CFO New York Life, 1996—2001; exec. v.p., CFO Wells Fargo & Co., San Francisco, 2001—05, sr. exec. v.p., CFO, 2005—. Treas. Blackstone Coop. Assn., N.Y.C. Mem. Bankers Assn. for Fgn. Trade (Washington), N.Am. Corp. Treasurers. Jewish. Avocations: tennis, skiing, chess. Office: Wells Fargo & Co 420 Montgomery St San Francisco CA 94163

ATKINS, TONI, former councilwoman; b. Va., Aug. 1, 1962; BA in Polit. Sci., Emory and Henry Coll. Policy analyst, staff reporter Councilwoman Christine Kehoe, Dist. 3, San Diego, 1993—2000; councilwoman, Dist. 3 San Diego City Coun., 2000—08, chairwomen Pub. Safety & Neighborhood Svcs. Com.; acting mayor City of San Diego, 2005. Staff mem., dir. clin. svcs. Womancare Health Ctr., Hillcrest, 1987—92. Bd. mem. San Diego River Conservancy. Recipient Doug Scott Award for Polit. Action, San Diego Dem. Club, Outstanding Support for Non-Profits in Affordable Housing Recognition; named Woman of Yr., San Diego Lesbian & Gay Pride, 1997. Democrat. Office: 1350 Front St STe 3024 San Diego CA 92101 Office Phone: 619-236-6633. E-mail: toniatkins@sandiego.gov.*

ATKINSON, GORDON C., lawyer; b. Kansas City, Mo., May 16, 1955; BA cum laude, Harvard Univ., 1977; JD, Univ. Chgo., 1981. Bar: NY 1982, Calif. 1986, US Dist. Ct. (so., ea. dist. NY, so., ea., no., ctrl. dist. Calif.). Assoc. Rogers & Wells, NYC, 1981—85; ptnr., litigation Cooley Godward, San Francisco, 1985—, vice chmn. litigation dept. Founder & past pres. Chgo. Law Found.; adj. prof. Univ. Calif., Hastings. Trustee San Francisco Day Sch.; past pres. & mem. exec. com. Sunny Hills Children's Garden. Mem.: ABA, Bar Assn. San Francisco, Calif. State Bar, NY State Bar Assn., Santa Clara County Bar Assn. Office: Cooley Godward Llp 101 California St Fl 5 San Francisco CA 94111-5800 Office Phone: 415-693-2088. Office Fax: 415-951-3699. Business E-Mail: atkinsongc@cooley.com.

ATKINSON, PERRY, broadcast executive, former political organization administrator; m. Peggy Atkinson; children: Jason, Andrew. Conservative radio talk show host & speaker; v.p. broadcasting Family Life Comm., Tucson; pres. UCB USA, Inc.; pres., gen. mgr. KDOV 91.7 FM, Medford, Oreg.; co-founder, v.p. Pacific Bible Coll., Medford, Oreg. Del. Rep. Nat. Conv., 1992, 1996, 2000; mem. Rep. Nat. Com. Western States Chmn.'s Assn., 1999—; chmn. Jackson County Ctrl. Com., 1996—98; vice chmn. Oreg. Rep. Party, 1996—98, chmn., 1999—2003. Office: TheDove Studios Ste E 1236 Disk Dr Medford OR 97501 Office Fax: 541-776-5368, 541-842-4334.

ATKINSON, RICHARD CHATHAM, academic administrator, cognitive scientist; b. Oak Park, Ill., Mar. 19, 1929; s. Herbert and Margaret Atkinson; m. Rita Loyd, Aug. 20, 1952; 1 dau., Lynn Loyd. Ph.B., U. Chgo., 1948; PhD, Ind. U., 1955. Lectr. applied math. and stats. Stanford (Calif.) U., 1956—57, assoc. prof. psychology, 1961—64, prof. psychology, 1964—80; asst. prof. psychology UCLA, 1957—61; dep. dir. NSF, 1975—76, acting dir., 1976, dir., 1976—80; chancellor, prof. cognitive sci. and psychology U. Calif., San Diego, 1980—95; pres. U. Calif. Sys., 1995—2003, pres. emeritus, 2003—. Author: (with others) Introduction to Psychology, 14th edit., 2003, Computer Assisted Instruction, 1969, An Introduction to Mathematical Learning Theory, 1965, Contemporary Developments in Mathematical Psychology, 1974, Mind and Behavior, 1980, Stevens' Handbook of Experimental Psychology, 1988. With AUS, 1954—56. Guggenheim fellow, 1967; fellow Ctr. for Advanced Study in Behavioral Scis., 1963; recipient Disting. Rsch. award Social Sci. Rsch. Coun., 1962, Vannevar Bush award, 2003. Fellow APA (Disting. Sci. Contbn. award 1977, Thorndike award 1980), AAAS (pres. 1989-90), Am. Psychol. Soc. (William James fellow 1985), Am. Acad. Arts and Scis.; mem. NAS, Soc. Exptl. Psychologists, Am. Philos. Soc., Nat. Acad. Edn., Inst. of Medicine, Cosmos Club (Washington), Explorers Club (N.Y.C.). Home: 6845 La Jolla Scenic Dr S La Jolla CA 92037-5738 Office: U Calif San Diego Rm 5320 Atkinson Hall La Jolla CA 92093-0436 Business E-Mail: RCA@ucsd.edu.

ATLAS, JAY DAVID, philosopher, consultant, linguist, educator; b. Houston, Feb. 1, 1945; s. Jacob Henry and Babette Fancile (Friedman) A. AB summa cum laude, Amherst Coll., Mass., 1966; PhD, Princeton U., NJ, 1976. Mem. common rm. Wolfson Coll., Oxford, England, 1978, 1980; vis. fellow Princeton U., 1979; rsch. assoc. Inst. for Advanced Study, Princeton, 1982-84; vis. lectr. U. Hong Kong, 1986; prof. Pomona Coll., Claremont, Calif., 1989—, chair dept. linguistics and cognitive sci., 2001—03, 2006—09, Peter W. Stanley prof. linguistics philosophy, 2003—. Sr. assoc. Jurecon, Inc., LA; lectr. 2d European Summer Sch. in Logic, Lang. and Info., 1990; examiner U. Edinburgh, Scotland, 1993, U. Groningen, Netherlands, 1991, 93-97, vis. rsch. prof., 1995, 2005; vis. prof. UCLA, 1988-95, Max Planck Inst. for Psycholinguistics, Nijmegen, Netherlands, 1997, 2005; vis. fellow Amherst Coll., 2004; honoree, conf. asserting, meaning & implying Pomona Coll., 2005; disting. scholar faculty linguistics U. Cambridge, 2006. Author: Philosophy Without Ambiguity, 1989, Logic, Meaning, and Conversation, 2005; contbr. articles to profl. jours., popular mags. Mem. Am. Philos. Assn., Linguistic Soc. Am., Phi Beta Kappa, Sigma Xi. Office: Pomona Coll 185 E 6th St Claremont CA 91711-4410 Office Phone: 909-621-8947. E-mail: jatlas@alumni.princeton.edu.

ATTEBERY, LOUIE WAYNE, language educator; b. Weiser, Idaho, Aug. 14, 1927; s. John Thomas Attebery and Tressie Mae (Blevins) Attebery Miller; m. Barbara Phyllis Olson, Dec. 31, 1947; children: Bobby Lou, Brian Leonard. BA, Coll. of Idaho, 1950; MA, U. Mont., 1951; PhD, U. Denver, 1961. Tchr. Middleton H.S., Idaho, 1949-50, Payette H.S., Idaho, 1951-52, Nyssa H.S., Oreg., 1952-55, East H.S., Denver, 1955-61; prof. English Albertson Coll. Idaho, Caldwell, 1961-99, holder Eyck-Berringer chair English, 1987-98, acting acad. v.p., 1983-84; pres. West Shore Press, 1998—. Vis. fellow Harvard U., Cambridge, Mass., 1993-94. Author: The College of Idaho, 1981-91, A Centennial History, 1991, Sheep May Safely Graze: A Personal Essay on Tradition and A Contemporary Sheep Ranch, 1993, The Most of What We Spend, 1998, Albertson College of Idaho: The Second Hundred Years, 1999, J.R. Simplot: A Billion the Hard Way, 2000; editor: Idaho Folklife: Homesteads to Headstones, 1985; editor Northwest Folklore, 1985-91; gen. editor U. Idaho Northwest Folklife series, 1991-2004. Trustee Idaho Hist. Soc., 1984-91, Coll. of Idaho, 2003—. With USN, 1945-46. Bruern fellow, U. Leeds, Eng., 1971—72. Mem. Western Lit. Assn. (exec coun. 1964-65), Assn. Lit. Scholars and Critics, 1995-. Methodist. E-mail: lattebery@collegeofidaho.edu.

ATTIYEH, RICHARD EUGENE, economics professor; b. Bklyn., Oct. 8, 1937; s. Semeer Mathew and Dorothy (Krentz) A.; m. Jessica Falikman, July 20, 1958; children: Michael Richard, Amy Lauren, Gregory Moss. BA, Williams Coll., 1958; PhD, Yale U., 1966. Staff economist Pres.'s Council of Econ. Advisers, Washington, 1961-62; asst. prof. econs. Stanford U., Palo Alto, Calif., 1962-64, Yale U., New Haven, 1964-67; from assoc. prof. to prof. U. Calif.-San Diego, La Jolla, 1967—, dean grad. studies and research, 1982-94, vice chancellor for rsch., dean grad. studies, 1994—, interim sr. vice chancellor acad. affairs, 1996-97. Mem. Grad. Record Examinations Bd., 1987-92, chmn., 1990; bd. dirs. Coun. Grad. Schs., 1990-93, chmn., 1992. Mem. Am. Econ. Assn., Assn. Grad. Schs. (pres. 1996), Calif. Biomed. Rsch. Assn. (bd. chmn. 1997-99), Calif. Soc. for Biomed. Rsch. (treas. 1998-99). E-mail: rattiyeh@ucsd.edu.

ATTWOOD, DAVID THOMAS, physicist, researcher; b. NYC, Aug. 15, 1941; s. David Thomas and Josephine (Banks) A.; divorced; children: Timothy David, Courtney Catherine, Kevin Richard; m. Linda Jean Geniesse, Aug. 3, 1991. BS, Hofstra U., 1963; MS, Northwestern U., 1964; D Engring. Sci., NYU, 1972. Physicist Lawrence Livermore Nat. Lab., Livermore, Calif., 1972-83, Lawrence Berkeley Nat. Lab., Berkeley, Calif., 1983—; sci. dir. Advanced Light Source, 1985—88; prof. in residence U. Calif., Berkeley, 1989—, founding chair applied sci. and tech. PhD program. Founder Ctr. for X-Ray Optics, Lawrence Berkeley Lab., 1983; assoc. dir. NSF EUV Sci. Tech. Ctr., 2003—. Author: Soft X-Rays and Extreme Ultraviolet Radiation: Principles and Applications, 2000; editor: (with B.L. Henke) X-Ray Diagnostics, (with J. Bokor) Short Wavelength Coherent Radiation, (with F. Zernike) Extreme Ultraviolet Lithography, (with W. Meyer-Ilse and T. Warwick) X-Ray Microscopy; reviewer numerous sci. jours.; contbr. numerous articles to profl. publs. Fellow: Optical Soc. Am.; mem.: AAAS, Am. Phys. Soc. Achievements include research on x-ray optics and microscopy, extreme ultraviolet lithography, synchrotron radiation, partially coherent x-rays, and laser-plasma interactions. Office: Lawrence Berkeley Nat Lab Ctr X-ray Optics Berkeley CA 94720

ATWATER, BRIAN F., geologist, educator; BS in Geology, Stanford U., Calif., 1973, MS in Geology, 1974; PhD, U. Del., 1980. Geologist US Geol. Survey, mem. Pacific NW Earthquake Hazards Team; affiliate prof. dept. earth & space scis. and quaternary rsch. ctr. U. Wash., Seattle. Guest rschr. U. Tokyo, Geol. Survey Japan. Contbr. articles to sci. jours.; assoc. editor: Quaternary Rsch., 1994—2001; author: The Orphan Tsunami of 1700, 2005. Named one of 100 Most Influential People, Time mag., 2005. Mem.: NAS. Office: Dept Earth & Space Scis U Wash Johnson Hall 070 Box 351310 Seattle WA 98195-1310 Office Phone: 206-553-2927. Office Fax: 206-553-8350. E-mail: atwater@u.washington.edu.

ATWATER, TANYA MARIA, marine geophysicist, educator; b. LA, Aug. 27, 1942; d. Eugene and Elizabeth Ruth (Ransom) A.; 1 child, Alyosha Molnar. Student, MIT, 1960-63; BA, U. Calif., Berkeley, 1965; PhD, Scripps Inst. Oceanography, 1972. Vis. earthquake researcher U. Chile, 1966; research assoc. Stanford U., 1970-71; asst. prof. Scripps Inst. Oceanography, 1972-73; U.S.-USSR Acad. Scis. exchange scientist, 1973; asst. prof. MIT, 1974-79, assoc. prof., 1979-80, research assoc., 1980-81; prof. dept. geoscis. U. Calif., Santa Barbara, 1980—. Chairperson ocean margin drilling Ocean Crust Planning Adv. Com.; mem. pub. adv. com. on law of sea U.S. Dept. State, 1979-83; mem. tectonics panel Ocean Drilling Project, 1990-93; Sigma Xi lectr., 1975-76. Sci. cons.: Planet Earth: Continents in Collision (R. Miller), 1983; contbr. articles to profl. jours. Sloan fellow, 1975-77; recipient Newcomb Cleveland prize AAAS, 1980; named Scientist of Yr. World Book Ency., 1980. Fellow Am. Geophys. Union (fellows com. 1980-81, 94-95, Ewing award subcom. 1980, McElwane award subcom. 1994), Geol. Soc. Am. (Penrose Conf. com. 1978-80); mem. AAAS, Assn. Women in Sci. Am. Geol. Inst., Nat. Acad. Scis., Phi Beta Kappa, Eta Kappa Nu. Office: U Calif Dept Geoscis Santa Barbara CA 93106

ATWOOD, CHARLES L., hotel and gaming company executive; b. Pascagoula, Miss., Dec. 29, 1948; s. George L. and Mary Frances (Lewis) A. BS, Univ. So. Miss., 1970; MBA in Fin., Tulane U., 1973. CPA, Tenn. Asst. to CFO NEI Properties, New Orleans, 1973—78; controller Canal Pl. Ventures, New Orleans, 1978—79; from sr. fin. analyst to v.p. Harrah's Entertainment, Inc., Las Vegas, 1979—96, v.p., 1996—2001, treas., 1996—2003, sr. v.p., CFO, 2001—06, vice-chmn., 2006—. Bd. dirs. Equity Residential Trust, 2003—, Harrah's Entertainment, Inc., 2005—08, 2008—. Pres. Annesdale Snowden Hist. Dist., Memphis, 1984; bd. dirs. Memphis Heritage, 1986—, Las Vegas C. of C., Las Vegas Performing Arts Ctr.; mem. Dean's advisory bd., U. Nev.-Las Vegas Bus. Sch. Mem.: AICPA. Republican. Office: Harrahs Entertainment Inc One Harrahs Ct Las Vegas NV 89119

ATWOOD, MARY SANFORD, writer; b. Mt. Pleasant, Mich., Jan. 27, 1935; d. Burton Jay and Lillian Belle (Sampson) Sanford; m. John C. Atwood III, Mar. 23, 1957. Author: A Taste of India, 1969. Mem. San Francisco/North Peninsula Opera Action, Suicide Prevention and Crisis Ctr., DeYoung Art Mus., Internat. Hospitality Ctr., Peninsula Symphony. Mem.: AAUW, St. Francis Yacht Club. Republican. Office: 40 Knightwood Ln Hillsborough CA 94010-6132 Office Phone: 650-343-6524.

AU, WHITLOW W.L., acoustician; b. Honolulu, July 31, 1940; s. Tai Hing and Violet (Chun) A.; m. Dorothy E. Wagner, Sept. 3, 1966; children: Wagner, WaiLani, Wesley, WaiNani. BS, U. Hawaii, 1962; MS, Wash. State U., 1964, PhD, 1970. Scientist Naval Command Control and Ocean Surveillance Ctr., San Diego, 1970-71, sr. scientist Kaneohe, Hawaii, 1971-93; chief scientist marine mammal rsch. project Hawaii Inst. Marine Biology, Kaneohe, 1993—. Author: Sonar of Dolphins, 1993; contbr. articles to profl. jours. Recipient Meritorious Civilian Svc. award USN, 1986. Fellow Acoustical Soc. Am. (tech. com. animal bioacoustics 1989—); mem. IEEE. Roman Catholic. Achievements include patents for broadband sonar signal processor and target recognition system, simulated echo transponder for training marine mammals, and marine mammal guidance device. Home: 251 Kakahiaka St Kailua HI 96734-3461 Office: Hawaii Inst Marine Biology PO Box 1346 Kaneohe HI 96744-1346

AUERBACH, ALAN JEFFREY, economist, educator; b. NYC, Sept. 27, 1951; s. William and Tess (Kasper) A.; m. Gay Cameron Quimby, June 25, 1978; children: Ethan, Andrew. BA, Yale U., 1974; PhD, Harvard U., 1978. Asst. prof. dept. econs. Harvard U., Cambridge, Mass., 1978-82, assoc. prof., 1982-83; assoc. prof. dept. econs. U. Pa., Phila., 1983-85, prof., 1985-94, chmn. dept., 1988-90, prof. Sch. Law, 1990-94; Robert D. Burch prof. of tax policy and pub. fin. U. Calif., Berkeley, 1994—, chmn. dept., 2001—02. Author: The Taxation of Capital Income, 1983 (David A. Wells prize); co-author: Dynamic Fiscal Policy, 1987, Macroeconomics: An Integrated Approach, 1995, Generational Accounting Around the World, 1999; editor: Corporate Takeovers, 1988, Mergers and Acquisitions, 1988, Fiscal Policy: Lessons from Economic Research, 1997; co-editor: Handbook of Public Economics, Vol. I, 1985, Vol. II, 1987, Vol. III, 2002, Vol. IV, 2002, Demographic Change and Fiscal Policy, 2001, Ageing, Financial Markets, and Monetary Policy, 2002, Toward Fundamental Tax Reform, 2005, Public Policy and the Income Distribution, 2006, Taxing Corp. Income in the 21st Century, 2007, Institutional Fed. Pub. Fin., 2009; editor Jour. Econ. Perspectives, 1995-96; editor Am. Econ. Jour.: Econ. Policy, 2007—. Fellow Am. Acad. Arts and Scis., Econometric Soc.; mem. Am. Econ. Assn. (exec. com. 1992-94, v.p. 1999), Phi Beta Kappa. Home: 110 El Camino Real Berkeley CA 94705-2823 Office: U Calif Berkeley Dept Econs 549 Evans Hall Berkeley CA 94720-3880 Business E-Mail: auerbach@econ.berkeley.edu.

AUERBACK, SANDRA JEAN, social worker; b. San Francisco, Feb. 21, 1946; d. Alfred and Molly Loy Auerback; m. Victor Schunman. BA, U. Calif., Berkeley, 1967; MSW, Hunter Sch. Social Work, 1972. LCSW. Clin. social worker Jewish Family Services, Bklyn., 1972-73, clin. social worker Hackensack, N.J., 1973-78; pvt. practice psychotherapy San Francisco, 1978—; dir. intake adult day care Jewish Home for the Aged, San Francisco, 1979-91. Mem.: NASW (bd. dirs. Bay Area Referral Svc. 1983—87, chmn. referral svc. 1984—87, state practice com. 1987—91, rep. to Calif. Coun. Psychiatry, Psychology, Social Work and Nursing 1987—95, chmn. 1989, regional treas. 1989—91, v.p. cmty. svcs. 1991—93, chmn. 1993, chair Calif. polit. action com. 1993—95, v.p. profl. stds. 2000—02, cert., v.p. prof. stds. 2006—), Mental Health Assn. San Francisco (trustee 1987—95). Office: 450 Sutter St San Francisco CA 94108-4206 Home: 1000 Northpoint 408 San Francisco CA 94109 Home Phone: 415-775-7855; Office Phone: 415-421-8230. Personal E-mail: sauerback@yahoo.com.

AUGUST-DEWILDE, KATHERINE, banker; b. Bridgeport, Conn., Feb. 13, 1948; d. Edward G. and Benita Ruth (Miller) Burstein; m. David deWilde, Dec. 30, 1984; children: Nicholas Alexander, Lucas Barrymore. AB, Goucher Coll., 1969; MBA, Stanford U., 1975. Cons. McKinsey & Co., San Francisco, 1975-78; dir. fin. Itel Corp., San Francisco, 1978-79; sr. v.p., CFO PMI Group, San Francisco, 1979-85, pres., CFO, 1988-91; CEO, pres. First Republic Thrift & Loan of San Diego, 1988-96; exec. v.p. First Republic Bank, San Francisco, 1987—96, sr. v.p., chief fin. officer, 1987—2007, pres. and COO, 2007—. Mem. policy adv. bd. Ctr. for Real Estate and Urban Econs., U. Calif., Berkeley, 1987—2000; bd. dirs. First Republic Bank, Trainer, Wortham & Co., Inc. Bd. dirs. San Francisco Zool. Soc., 1993-2001, vice-chair, 1995-2000; trustee Carnegie Found., 1999-2004, Town Sch. for Boys, San Francisco, 1999-2004, vice chmn., 2004-06; mem. adv. coun. Stanford U. Grad. Sch. Bus., 2003-; trustee Mills Coll., 2004-07. Mem. Women's Forum (bd. dirs.), Bankers Club, Belvedere Tennis Club, Villa Taverna. Home: 2650 Green St San Francisco CA 94123-4607 Office: First Republic Bank 111 Pine St San Francisco CA 94111-5602 Office Phone: 415-296-3707. Business E-Mail: kaugust@firstrepublic.com.

AUNG-THWIN, MICHAEL ARTHUR, history educator; b. Rangoon, Burma, 1946; BA, Doane Coll., 1969; MA, U. Ill., Urbana, 1971; PhD, U. Mich., 1976. Asst. prof. Asian history Elmira (N.Y.) Coll., 1980-87; assoc. prof. history No. Ill. U., DeKalb, 1987-95, dir. Ctr. S.E. Asian Studies, 1987-95; prof. Asian Studies U. Hawaii, Honolulu, 1995—. Vis. prof. Cornell U., 1981; vis. scholar Ctr. for S.E. Asian Studies, Kyoto, Japan. Contbr. articles to profl. jours. NEH fellow, 1977-80. Mem. Assn. for Asian Studies (bd. dirs. 1980-83, mem. S.E. Asia Coun.), Burma Studies Found. (sec.-treas.). Office: U Hawaii Sch Hawaiian Asian Studies 1890 E West Rd Honolulu HI 96822-2318 E-mail: aungthwin@hawaii.edu.

AURAND, CHARLES HENRY, JR., music educator; b. Battle Creek, Mich., Sept. 6, 1932; s. Charles Henry and Elisabeth Dirk (Hoekstra) A.; m. Donna Mae Erb, June 19, 1954; children: Janice, Cheryl, Sandra, Charles III, William. MusB, Mich. State U., 1954, MusM, 1958; PhD, U. Mich., 1971. Cert. tchr., Mich., Ohio. Asst. prof. music Hiram Coll., Ohio, 1958-60; dean, prof. music Youngstown State U., 1960-73; dean No. Ariz. U., Flagstaff, 1973-88, prof. music, 1988-94, prof. emeritus, 1994—. Chmn. Ariz. Alliance for Arts Edn., 1974-77; solo clarinetist Flagstaff Symphony; solo, chamber music and orch. musician, 1973-86; fine arts cons. Miami U. of Ohio, 1982 Author: Selected Solos, Methods, 1963; musician: Foothills Chamber Choir. Elder Presbyn. Ch., 1965; chmn. Boy Scouts Am., Coconino dist., 1974-78; bd. dir. Ariz. Com. Arts for the Handicapped, 1982-88, Flagstaff Symphony Orch., 1973-85, Flagstaff Festival of Arts, 1973-89, Sedona Chamber Mus. Soc., 1989-99, Sedona Med. Ctr., 1998-2002, Civic Orch. Tucson, 2003-04; conf. dir. Internat. Clarinet Soc., 1991; pres. Citizens for an Alt. Route, 1995-98; mem. Ariz. Town Hall, 1996-98; bd. dir. Sedona Med. Ctr. Found., 1998-2002; mem. Foothills Chamber Music Ensemble, Catalina Chamber Ensemble, 2004-; mem. Ariz. Town Hall, 1996-2002; solo clarinet Sonora Winds, 2002-05. 1st lt. USAF,1955-57 Recipient award of merit Boy Scouts Am., 1977; cert. appreciation John F. Kennedy Ctr. Performing Arts, 1985. Mem. SAR (pres. No. Ariz. chpt. 2000-02, pres. Ariz. Soc. 2003—, state pres. 2003-04, sec.-treas. Tucson chpt. 2007-), Am. Assn. Higher Edn., Ariz. Humanities Assn., Music Educators Nat. Conf., State Adminstrs. Music Schs. (chmn. 1971-73), Internat. Clarinet Soc./ClariNetwork Internat. (conf. dir. 1991), No. Ariz. U. Retirees Assn. (pres. 1997-98), Kiwanis (pres. 1984-85). Republican. Lutheran. Avocations: golf, tennis, bridge. Home: 37738 S Hill Side Dr Tucson AZ 85739-2221 Personal E-mail: cdaurand2@msn.com.

AUST, STEVEN DOUGLAS, biochemistry, biotechnology and toxicology educator; b. South Bend, Wash., Mar. 11, 1938; s. Emil and Helen Mae (Crawford) A.; m. Nancy Lee Haworth, June 5, 1960 (dec.); children: Teresa, Brian; m. Karen Hurley, July 16, 2004. BS in Agr., Wash. State U., 1960, MS in Nutrition, 1962; PhD in Dairy Sci., U. Ill., 1965. Postdoctoral fellow dept. toxicology Karolinska Inst., Stockholm, 1966; New Zealand facial exzema sr. postdoctoral fellow Ruakura Agrl. Rsch. Ctr., Hamilton, 1975-76; mem. faculty dept. biochemistry Mich. State U., East Lansing, 1967-87, prof., 1977-87, assoc. dir. Ctr. for Environ. Toxicology, 1980-85, dir. Ctr. for the Study of Active Oxygen, 1985-87; dir. biotech. ctr. Utah State U., Logan, 1987-91, prof. chem. biochemistry, 1987—. Dir. basic rsch. and tng. program Super Fund Nat. Inst. Environ. Health Scis., 1988-96; mem. toxicology study sect. NIH, 1979-83; mem. environ. measurements com., mem. sci. adv. bd. EPA, 1980-83; mem. toxicology data bank, mem. peer rev. com. Nat. Libr. Medicine, 1983-85; mem. Mich. Toxic Substance Control Commn., 1979-82, chmn., 1981-82; pres., founder Intech One-Eighty Corp., North Logan Utah, 1993-99, pres. 1999—; mem. adv. panel for metabolic biochemistry program NSF, 1998; mem. EPA/DOE/NSF/ONR Joint Program on Bioremediation, 1998. Contbr. articles to profl. jours. Recipient Nat. Rsch. Svc. award NIH, USPHS, Dupont Sci. and Engring. award, 1988, Alumni Achievement award Wash. State U., 1998, Gov.'s Sci. and Tech. medal, 2002, Univ. Outstanding Grad. Mentor award, 2003, Disting. Alumnus in Sci., Edn., Rsch. award Washington State U., 2007; named D. Wynne Thorne Rschr. of Yr., 2003; NRC Facial Eczema fellow Ruakura Agrl. Rsch. Ctr., Hamilton, 1975. Fellow Acad. Toxicology Scis., Oxygen Soc.; mem. Am. Soc. Biol. Chemists, Am. Soc. Pharmacology and Exptl. Therapeutics, Soc. Toxicology, Am. Chem. Soc. (Kenneth A. Spencer award 2004), Am. Soc. Microbiology Avocations: raising, training quarter horses, fly fishing. Office: Utah State U Chemistry and Biochemistr Logan UT 84322-4705 Home Phone: 208-852-3611; Office Phone: 435-797-2730. E-mail: sdaust@cc.usu.edu.

AUSTERMAN, ALAN, state legislator; b. Everett, Wash., May 23, 1943; m. Virginia Austerman; children: Carol, Dawn. Print shop owner, 1975-88; newspaper owner Kadiak Times, 1976-83; owner Austerman's Office Supply, 1979-88; owner hunting and fishing lodge, 1985-90; mem. Kodiak Island Borough Assembly, 1985-90, 92-94, Alaska House of Reps., 1994-2000; Rep. senator dist. C Alaska State Senate, 2001—03; fishery policy advisor State of Alaska, 2003—06; mem. Alaska House of Reps. from Dist. 36, Juneau, 2009—. Mem. legis. fin. com. Alaska House of Reps., chmn. legis. fisheries com.; chair Pacific Fisheries Legis. Task Force. Exec. dir. KICVB, 1993-94. Pres. bd. dirs. Kodiak Jaycees; co-founder Kodiak Alaska State Pks. Adv. Com.; police officer City of Kodiak; mem. Kodiak Island Borough Pks. and Recreation; mem. personnel bd. City of Kodiak; mem. Kodiak Sch. Budget Review Com., Cmty. Coll. Adv. Bd., Hosp. Adv. Bd., Kiwanis. Sgt. Alaska Army N.G. Mem. Kodiak Island Sportsman Assn., Kodiak Rodeo Assn. (co-founder), Ducks Unltd. (chmn.), Kodiak C. of C. (pres. bd. dirs.), Elks, NRA, Pioneers of Alaska, Toastmasters. Republican. Avocations: hunting, fishing, photography, hiking. Office: State Capitol Rm 434 Juneau AK 99801 also: Dist 36 305 Center Ave Ste 1 Kodiak AK 99615 Office Phone: 907-465-2487, 907-486-8872. Office Fax: 907-465-4956, 907-486-5264. Business E-Mail: representative_alan_austerman@legis.state.ak.us. E-mail: Alanaust@ptialaska.net.*

AUSTIN, H(ARRY) GREGORY, lawyer; b. NYC, Mar. 18, 1936; s. Harry Gregory and Pauline (Moore) Austin; m. Deanna Ruth Anderson, Nov. 28, 1970; children: Sabrina Elizabeth, Harry Gregory III, Anne Catherine. BE, Yale U., 1957, postgrad., 1958; JD, U. Mich., 1961; LLD (hon.), Lincoln U., 1976. Bar: Colo. 1961, U.S. Supreme Ct. 1974. Assoc. Holland & Hart, Denver, 1962—73, ptnr., 1977—2001, of counsel, 2002—; gen. counsel SBA, Washington, 1973—75; solicitor, gen. counsel U.S. Dept. Interior, Washington, 1975—77; dir. Rocky Mountain Pub. Broadcasting Network, 2004—; bd. dirs. Craig Hosp., Denver, 2008—. Trustee Colo. Legal Aid Found., Denver, 1984—91, chmn., 1988—91; mem. adv. com. Colo. Sec. of State, 1996—; bd. dirs. Children's Hosp., Denver, 1985—97, Denver Police Found., 2004—. 1st lt. USAR, 1957—64. Fellow: Am. Bar Found.; mem.: Denver Bar Assn., Colo. Bar Assn. (chmn. bus. entities subsect. bus. law sect. 1987—89, vice chmn. bus. law sect. 1989—91, chmn. 1991—93, chmn. partnership laws com. 1993—), Am. Law Inst., Metro Denver C. of C. (bd. dirs., sec. 1995—97). Republican. Office: Holland & Hart LLP 555 17th St Ste 3200 Denver CO 80202-3979 Business E-Mail: gaustin@hollandhart.com.

AUSTIN, JACOB (JACK AUSTIN), retired Canadian government official; b. Calgary, Alta., Can., Mar. 2, 1932; s. Morris and Clara Edith (Chetner) A.; m. Natalie Veiner Freeman, Apr. 2, 1978; children: Edith Clare, Sharon Jill, Barbara Joan. BA, LLB, U. B.C.; LLM, Harvard U.; postgrad., U. Calif., Berkeley; ScD in Social Sci., U. East Asia. Bar: B.C. 1958, Yukon 1966. Chief of staff to prime min., 1974-75; dep. min. energy, mines and resources, 1970-74; mem. Senate, 1975—2007; leader of the govt. in the Senate, 2003—06; min. of state, 1981-82; min. of state for social devel., 1982-84; ret. Sr. internat. adv. Stern Partners, Vancouver, Canada, 2007—; hon. prof. Inst. Asian Rsch., U. BC, 2008—. Mem. Vancouver Club. Liberal. Jewish. Office: 650 W Georgia St Ste 2900 Vancouver BC Canada V6B 4N8 Office Phone: 604-646-3786. Business E-Mail: jaustin@sternpartners.com.

AUSTIN, JOAN D., personal care industry executive; V.p., treas. A-dec Inc., Newberg, Oreg., 1963—; pres. Austin Industries, Newberg. Chmn. bd. Drug and Alcohol Treatment Ctr. at Springbrook N.W., Newberg. Mem. Internat. Women's Forum, Found. for Women's Resources Office: A-dec Inc 2601 Crestview Dr Newberg OR 97132-9529

AUTRY, ALAN, Former Mayor, Fresno, California, film company executive, actor, former professional football player; b. Shreveport, La., July 31, 1952; m. Kimberlee Autry; children: Lauren, Heather, Austin. BA, U. Pacific, 1975. Quarterback Green Bay Packers; founder & pres. Dirt Road Prodns.; CEO Autry Entertainment Group; mayor City of Fresno, Calif., 2001—08. Mem. Advisory Council on Historic Preservation; mem. strengthening communities secretarial adv. com. U.S. Dept. Commerce; mem. adv. bd., ed. standing comm. U.S. Conf. Mayors; bd. dirs. League Calif. Cities; mem. authority bd. Fresno County Transp.; founding bd. mem. Operation Clean Air, Regional Jobs Initiative. Actor: (films) Remember My Name, 1978, North Dallas Forty, 1979, Popeye, 1980, Southern Comfort, 1981, Roadhouse 66, 1984, O.C. and Stiggs, 1985, Brewster's Millions, 1985, House, 1986, At Close Range, 1986, Amazing Grace and Chuck, 1987, World Gone Wild, 1988; writer, prodr., dir., actor (TV films) The Legend of Jake Kincaid, 2002; actor: (TV series) Best of the West, 1982, Cheers, 1983, The Dukes of Hazzard, 1984, Newhart, 1986, St. Elsewhere, 1986, In the Heat of the Night, 1988—93, Grace Under Fire, 1995—96. Office: Autry Entertainment Group 9493 N Washington Rd Fresno CA 93720 Office Phone: 559-434-4358. E-mail: mayor@fresno.gov.*

AUWERS, LINDA S., lawyer; Grad., Stanford U.; PhD, Brandeis U.; JD, U. Houston Law Ctr. Prof. history Temple U.; atty. Schlanger, Cook, Cohn, Mills & Grossberg; v.p., asst. gen. counsel Compaq Computer Corp., Houston, 1995—99, v.p., assoc. gen. counsel, sec., 1999—2001, v.p., dep. gen. counsel, sec., 2001—02; sr. v.p., gen. counsel, sec. ABM Indus., San Francisco, 2003—. Mem.: Am. Corp. Counsel Assn. (mem. corp. & securities law com.), Am. Soc. of Corp. Secretaries (mem. public co. affairs com.). Office: Abm Industries Inc 420 Taylor St # 200 San Francisco CA 94102-1702

AVAKIAN, BRAD, state legislator; m to Debbie Avakian; children: Nathan & Claire. Oregon State Representative, District 34, 2002-2007; Oregon State Senator, District 34, 2007-. Named, Eagle Scout, Boy Scouts America. Democrat. Mailing: 900 Court St NE H-472 Salem OR 97301

AVALOS, JOHN, city supervisor; b. Wilmington, Calif. m. Karen Zapata; 1 child, Emiliano. BA in English Lit., with honors, U. Calif., Santa Barbara; M in Social Work, San Francisco State U., 1997. Educator, counselor San Francisco Conservation Corps, Columbia Park Boys & Girls Club, San Francisco; intern adult medicine & HIV/AIDS clinic Mission Neighborhood Health Ctr., San Francisco;

cmty. organizer Coleman Advocates Children & Youth, San Francisco; union organizer Justice for Janitors Campaign, Svc. Employees Internat. Union (SEIU Local 1877), San Francisco; legis aide to supr. Chris Daly San Francisco, 2005—08; supr., Dist. 11 San Francisco Bd. Supervisors, 2009—, chair budget & fin. com., mem. city & sch. dist. com., Transp. Authority. Pres. bd. dirs. Tchrs. 4 Social Justice; past pres. San Francisco People's Orgn.; past bd. dirs. Bernal Heights Neighborhood Ctr., San Francisco, Media Alliance; past mem. adv. com. OMI/Excelsior Beacon Ctr., Excelsior Boys & Girls Club. Recipient Amilcar Mayen Open Palm award, Dolores St. Housing Svcs., 2006, Bay Area Activists Leadership award, Coleman Advocates Children & Youth, 2007. Office: City Hall 1 Dr Carlton B Goodlett Pl Rm 244 San Francisco CA 94102 Office Phone: 415-554-6795. Office Fax: 415-554-6769. Business E-Mail: John.Avalos@sfgov.org.*

AVARY, ROGER ROBERTS (FRANK BRAUNER), film director, producer, writer; b. Flin Flon, Manitoba, Canada, Aug. 23, 1965; s. Edwin Roberts and Brigitte (Bruninghaus) A.; m. Gretchen Avary Student, Art Ctr.Coll. Design, Pasadena, Calif., 1985—88. Writer D'Arcy, Masius, Benton & Bowles, LA, 1989-90, J. Walter Thompson, LA, 1990—. Writer: (film) 99 Days, 1991, (with Mario Puzo) The Lorch Team, 1992, Silent Hill, 2006; writer, dir. (film): Killing Zoe, 1994 (Yubari Internat. Film Festival Best Film award, 1994, Mystfest Best Film award, 1994, Mystfest Critics prize, 1994, Cannes Prix Tres Spl. Best Film award, 1994), True Romance, 1993; exec. prodr. (film): The Last Man, 1999; writer, prodr., dir. (film): The Worm Turns, 1993, The Rules of Attraction (screenplay), 2002, Glitterati, 2004; co-writer, co-exec. prodr. (film): Beowulf, 2007; co-exec. prodr. (film): Boogie Boy, 1997; co-writer (film): Pulp Fiction, 1994 (L.A. Film Critics Assn. Best Screenplay award, 1995, N.Y. Film Critics Cir. Best Screenplay award, 1995, Boston Soc. Film Critics Best Screenplay award, 1995, Nat. Soc. Film Critics Best Screenplay award, 1995, Chgo. Soc. Film Critics Best Screenplay award, 1995, BAFTA Best Screenplay award, 1995, Acad. award best screenplay 1995), Hatchetman, 1995, (children's book) Marshall's Dreams, 1991, (music video) for the group The Go Go's song The Whole World Lost Its Head, 1994; writer, dir., prodr. (TV movie) Mr. Stitch, 1995, Odd Jobs, 1997; actor: Phantasm IV: Oblivion, 1998

AVERY, STEPHEN NEAL, playwright, writer; b. Hot Springs, Ark., Mar. 20, 1955; s. Leo A. Avery and Dedette Carol (Miles) Sullivan; m. Kathleen Annette Twin, Sept. 7, 1979. Free-lance reporter Hot Springs Sentinel-Record and New Era, 1970-73. Author: (plays) Hungry: 3 Plays, 1991, Because, 1991, Insidious, 1992, Burning Bridges, 1999; prodn. ptnr. (Moriah Films documentary) Ever Again, 2005, (southern poverty law ctr. documentary) Viva La Causa, 2008. Active US Holocaust Meml. Mus., 2001—; leadership coun. So. Poverty Law Ctr., 2002—; founding mem. The Nat. Campaign for Tolerance, 2002—; founders cir. Ark. State U./Mountain Home Cultural Arts Ctr., 2002—; active Simon Wiesenthal Ctr., 2002—, Beil Hashoah Mus. of Tolerance, 2003—; mem. scholarship com. Am. Indian Edn. Found., 2005—; mem. Internat. Rescue Com., 2004—, AmeriCares, 2004—, Friends of Sesame Workshop, 2005—; founding sponsor Martin Luther King, Jr. Nat. Meml., 2005—, Flight 93 Nat. Meml., 2006—; active Nat. Rep. Congl. Com., 2004—; hon. co-chair President's Dinner for George W. Bush, 2004, 2005; active Am. Jewish Com., 2003—, World Jewish Congress, pres. coun., 2005—. With USN, 1973—77. Recipient Congl. Order of Merit, 2006, 2007, Rep. Senatorial Am. Spirit medal (formerly the Rep. Senatorial Medal of Freedom), 2007, Nahum Goldmann Leadership award, World Jewish Congress, 2007; named to inclusion in Rep. Presdl. Honor Roll, chmn., exec. comm. Nat. Rep. Congl. Com., 2005. Mem.: Drama League, Theatre Comms. Group, Authors League Am., Dramatists Guild Inc., World Trade Ctr. Meml. Found. (charter), US Naval Inst., Americans for the Arts Action Fund (charter), Save Ellis Island (charter), Nat. Mus. Am. Indian (charter), Nat. D-Day Mus. (charter), Nat. Mus. Women in Arts, Nat. Trust Hist. Preservation, Habitat for Humanity Internat., Nat. Campaign Tolerance. Avocation: museum and gallery exhbns.

AVERY, SUSAN KATHRYN, electrical engineering educator, researcher; b. Detroit, Jan. 5, 1950; d. Theodore Peter and Alice Jane (Greene) Rykala; m. James Paul Avery, Aug. 12, 1972; 1 child, Christopher Scott. BS in Physics, Mich. State U., 1972; MS in Physics, U. Ill., 1974, PhD in Atmospheric Sci., 1978. Asst. prof. elec. engring. U. Ill., Urbana, 1978-83; fellow CIRES U. Colo., Boulder, 1982—, assoc. prof. elec. engring., 1985-92, assoc. dean rsch. and grad. edn. Coll. Engring., 1989-92, prof. elec. engring., 1992—, dir. CIRES, 1994—; sec. USNC/URSI NRC, 1994—. Adv. com. chair Elec. and Communications Div. NSF, Washington, 1991-93, adv. panel atmospheric scis. program, 1985-88, steering com. CEDAR program, 1986-87, adv. com. engring. directorate, 1991-93, vis. professorship, 1982-83; working group ionosphere, thermosphere, mesosphere NASA, Washington, 1991—; mem.-at-large USNC/URSI NRC, Washington, 1991-93, com. on solar-terrestrial rsch., 1987-90; trustee Univ. Corp. for Atmospheric Rsch., 1991—, vice chair bd. trustees, 1993, sci. programs evaluation com., 1989-91; working group on tides in mesosphere and lower thermosphere Internat. Commn. Meteorology of Upper Atmosphere, 1981-86; mesosphere-lower thermosphere network steering com. Internat. STEP Program, 1989—, equatorial mid. atmosphere dynamics steering com., 1990—. Contbr. articles to Radio Sci., Adv. Space Rsch., Jour. Atmosphere Terrestrial Physics, Jour. Geophys. Rsch., others. Recipient Faculty Award for Women, NSF, 1991, Outstanding Publ. award NCAR, 1990; faculty fellow U. Colo., 1994; vis. fellow Coop. Inst. for Rsch. in Environ. Scis., 1982-83. Fellow Am. Meteorological Soc. (com. on mid. atmosphere 1990—); mem. IEEE, Am. Geophys. Union (com. edn. and human resources 1988-92), Am. Soc. Engring. Edn., Sigma Xi. Achievements include research on the dynamics of the mesosphere, stratosphere and troposphere with emphasis on unifying observational analyses and theoretical studies, on wave dynamics including the coupling of the atmosphere/ocean and interactions between large-scale and small-scale motions, on the use of ground-based doppler radar techniques for observing the clear-air atmosphere and use of new signal processing algorithms for radar data analysis. Office: U Colo Cires Cb 216 Boulder CO 80309-0001

AVIS, GREGORY M., venture capitalist; BA cum laude, Williams Coll., 1980; MBA, Harvard Bus. Sch. With McDonald & Co.; founder, mng. ptnr. Summit Partners, Palo Alto, Calif., 1984—. Bd. dirs. Clontech Labs, Ditech Comm., IMPAC Med. Sys., Powerwave Technologies, RightNow Technologies; math teacher Eastside Coll. Preparatory Sch., Palo Alto. Bd. mem. Williams Coll.; bd. mem., chair Community Found. Silicon Valley; bd. mem. Nat. Outdoor Leadership Sch., James Irvine Found.; sr. fellow Am. Leadership Forum. Office: Summit Partners 499 Hamilton Ave Palo Alto CA 94301

AVNET, JONATHAN MICHAEL, motion picture company executive, film director; b. Bklyn., Nov. 17, 1949; m. Barbara Brody; children: Alexandra, Jacob, Lily. BA, Sarah Lawrence Coll., 1971; postgrad., U. Pa., 1967-69; student, Conservatory for Advanced Film Studies, 1972-73. Reader United Artists, LA, 1974; dir. creative affairs Sequoia Pictures, LA, 1975-77; pres. Tisch/Avnet Prodns., LA, 1977-85; chmn. Avnet/Kerner Co., LA, 1985—. Pres. Allied Communications, Inc. Dir., producer: (films) Fried Green Tomatoes (3 Acad. award nominations, 3 Golden Globes, Writers Guild Gladd best feature film award), The War; producer, writer, dir. (TV series) Call To Glory, 1984-85 (Golden Reel award), Between Two Women (1 Emmy award); producer, exec. producer: (motion pictures) Risky Business, 1983, Deal of the Century, 1983, Less Than Zero, 1987, Men Don't Leave, 1990, Three Musketeers, 1993, When a Man Loves a Woman, 1994, Mighty Ducks(all three), Miami Rhapsody, 1995, George of the Jungle, 1996, Red Corner, 1997, Inspector Gadget, 1999, Things You Can Tell Just by Looking at Her, 2000, Steal This Movie, 2000, Sky Captain and the World of Tomorrow, 2004, Land of the Blind, 2006, 88 Minutes, 2007; dir. (films) Righteous Kill, 2008; exec. producer: (movies of the week) No Other Love, 1979, The Burning Bed (8 Emmy nominations), 1984, Silence of the Heart, 1984, Do You Know the Muffin Man, 1989, Heatwave (4 Cable Ace awards, including Best Picture), 1990, Backfield in Motion, 1991, The Nightman, 1992, The Switch, 1993, For Their Own Goodothers, 1993, Naomi & Wynonna: Love Can Build a Bridge, 1995, Poodle Springs, 1998, My Last Love, 1999, A House Divided, 2000, Uprising, 2001, Conviction, 2005. Trustee L.A. County Opera. Am. Film Inst. fellow. Mem. Am. Film Inst., Dir.s Guild of Am., Writers Guild of Am., Acad. Motion Pictures Arts and Scis., Producers Caucus. Avocations: basketball, skiing, biking.

AVRIT, RICHARD CALVIN, defense consultant, career officer; b. Tilamook, Oreg., Feb. 18, 1932; s. Roy Calvin and Mary Louise (Morgan) A.; m. Alice Jane Tamminga, July 10, 1959; 1 dau., Tamra Jane. BS in Engring, U.S. Naval Acad., 1953; MS in Engring. Electronics, U.S. Naval Postgrad. Sch., 1960; postgrad., U.S. Naval War Coll., 1971-72. Commd. ensign U.S. Navy, 1953, advanced through grades to rear adm., 1979; served weapons dept. U.S.S. George K. Mackenzie, 1953-54; ops. dept. U.S.S. Willis A. Lee, 1954-57; comdg. officer U.S.S. Sumner County, 1960-63; project officer, staff of comdr. Operational Test and Evaluation Force, Key West, Fla., 1963-66; exec. officer U.S.S. Berkeley, 1966-68; ops. officer, AAW project officer Comdr. Cruiser Destroyer Florilla Nine, 1968-70; comdg. officer U.S.S. Sellers, 1970-71; mil. asst. for surface guns and missiles to asst. dir. Ocean Control Directorate, Def. Research and Engring., Office Sec. of Def., 1972-76; comdg. officer U.S.S. Harry E. Yarnell, 1976-78; chief of staff, comdr. Naval Surface Force U.S. Atlantic Fleet, 1978-79; project mgr. for Saudi Naval Expansion Program, Naval Material Command, Washington, 1979-82; dir. navy logistics plans Office Chief of Naval Ops., Washington, 1982-84; cons. Info. Spectrum, Inc., 1984-88; pres. Mil. Data Corp., Arlington, Va., 1989-91; small bus. cons., 1992—. Decorated D.S.M., Legion of Merit (3), Bronze Star with Combat V, Meritorious Service Medal (2). Mem. Naval Inst., IEEE. Methodist. Home: 4839 Keswick Ct Dumfries VA 22025-1084 Personal E-mail: dick.avrit@verizon.net.

AWAKUNI, GAIL, principal; BS, MS, U. Hawaii, Manoa; PhD, Union Inst. Tchr. Radford HS, Hawaii, Moanalua HS, Hawaii; cohort vice prin. Kalani HS, Hawaii, 1993—94; vice prin. Kailua HS, Hawaii, 1994—97; prin. Enchanted Lake Elementary, Hawaii, 1997—2000, James Campbell HS, Hawaii, 2000—. Recipient Hawaii HS Prin. of Yr., 2004, Nat. HS Prin. of Yr., Nat. Assn. Secondary Sch. Principals, 2005. Office: James Campbell High School 91-980 North Rd Ewa Beach HI 96706 Office Phone: 808-689-1200. Business E-Mail: gail_awakuni@notes.k12hi.us.

AWAKUNI, GENE I., academic administrator, psychologist; BA, MA, Univ. Hawaii, Manoa; PhD in psychol., Harvard Univ. Dir. counseling & psychol. svc. Univ. Calif., Irvine, asst. vice chancellor Santa Barbara; v.p. student affairs Calif. Poly., Pomona; vice provost, student affairs Stanford Univ.; chancellor Univ. Hawaii, West Oahu, 2005—. Co-author: Resistance to Multiculturalism: Issues and Interventions. Named one of 25 People for the Next 25 Years, Hawaii Bus. Mag., 2007. Mem.: Asian Pacific Americans in Higher Edn. (past pres.). Office: Univ of Hawaii West Oahu 96-129 Ala'Ike Pearl City HI 96782 Office Phone: 808-454-4750. Office Fax: 808-453-6076.

AWSCHALOM, DAVID DANIEL, physics professor; b. Baton Rouge, Oct. 11, 1956; s. Miguel and Evelyn A.; m. Nancy L. Kawalek, Aug. 6, 1988. BSc in Physics, U. Ill., Urbana-Champaign, 1978; PhD in Exptl. Physics, Cornell U., 1982. Exxon rsch. fellow Cornell U., Ithaca, NY, 1981—82; postdoctoral fellow IBM Watson Rsch. Ctr., Yorktown Heights, NY, 1982—83, rsch. staff mem., 1984—89, mgr. nonequilibrium physics dept., 1989—92; prof. physics U. Calif., Santa Barbara, 1991—, prof. elec. and computer engring., 2001—. Mem. NRC Panel on Magnetic Semiconductors, 1990, NRC Panel on Naval Rsch., 1991, NSF Ctr. Quantized Electronics Structures, 1992; dir. Ctr. Spintronics and Quantum Computation; assoc. dir. Calif. Nanosystems Inst.; seminar spkr. in field. Contbr. articles to profl. jours. Named James scholar U. Ill., 1976-78; recipient Lyman Physics prize U. Ill., 1978, IBM Outstanding Innovation award, 1987, Internat. Magnetism prize, Internat. Union of Pure and Applied Physics, 2003, Néel medal, 2003, Agilent Europhysics prize, European Phys. Soc., 2005. Fellow Am. Phys. Soc. (Oliver E. Buckley prize, 2005), Am. Acad. Arts & Scis., AAAS (Newcomb Cleveland prize, 2006); mem. Materials Rsch. Soc. (Outstanding Investigator prize 1992), NAS. Achievements include development and application of an ultrafast optical technique for exploring electronic and magnetic interactions in quantum systems; invented new time- and spatially-resolved magnetic spectroscopies using superconducting and optical devices. Office: U Calif Dept Physics Broida Hall 4125 Mail Code 9530 Santa Barbara CA 93106-9530 Office Phone: 805-893-2121. Office Fax: 805-893-4170. E-mail: awsch@physics.ucsb.edu.

AXINN, GEORGE HAROLD, rural sociology educator; b. Jamaica, NY, Feb. 1, 1926; s. Hyman and Celia (Schneider) A.; m. Nancy Kathryn Wigsten, Feb. 17, 1945; children: Catherine, Paul, Martha, William. BS, Cornell U., 1947; MS, U. Wis., 1952, PhD, 1958. Editorial asst. Cornell U. Geneva, N.Y., 1947; bull. editor U. Md., College Park, 1949; chmn. dept. rural communication U. Del., Newark, 1950; mem. faculty Mich. State U., East Lansing, 1953—, assoc. dir. coop. extension service, 1955-60; coordinator U. Nigeria program, 1961-65, prof. agrl. econs., 1970-85, prof. resource devel., 1985-95, prof. emeritus, 1996—, asst. dean internat. studies and programs, 1964-85; pres., exec. dir. Midwest Univs. Consortium for Internat. Activities, Inc., 1969-76, 1969-76. FAO rep. to Nepal, 1983-85, India and Bhutan, 1989-91; cons. World Bank, 1973-74, Ford Found., 1968, UNICEF, 1978, FAO, 1974, 87, 89, Govt. of India, 1988; vis. prof. Cornell U., Ithaca, N.Y., 1958-60, U. Ill., Urbana, 1969-70 Author: Modernizing World Agriculture: A Comparative Study of Agricultural Extension Education Systems, 1972, New Strategies for Rural Development, Rural Life Associates, 1978, FAO Guide Alternative Approaches to Agricultural Extension, 1988, Collaboration in International Rural Development - A Practitioner's Handbook (with Nancy W. Axinn), 1997; contbr. articles to various publs. Served with USNR, 1944-46. Recipient Outstanding Alumni award Cornell U. Coll. Agrl. and Life Sci., 1993; W.K. Kellogg Found. fellow, 1956-57. Home: The Fountains at La Cholla 2001 W Rudasill Rd #5211 Tucson AZ 85704 Home Phone: 520-544-4024. Business E-Mail: axinn@msu.edu.

AYALA, FRANCISCO JOSÉ, geneticist, educator; b. Madrid, Mar. 12, 1934; came to U.S., 1961, naturalized, 1971; s. Francisco and Soledad (Pereda) A.; m. Hana Lostakova, Mar. 8, 1985; children by previous marriage: Francisco José, Carlos Alberto. BS, Universidad de Madrid, 1954; MA, Columbia U., 1963, PhD, 1964; D honoris causa, Universidad de León, Spain, 1982, Universidad de Barcelona, 1986, Universidad de Madrid, 1986, U. Athens, Greece, 1991, U. Vigo, Spain, 1996, U. Islas, Baleares, Spain, 1998, U. Valencia, Spain, 1999, U. Bologna, Italy, 2001, U. Vladivostok, Russia, 2002, Masaryk U., Czech. Rep., 2003, U. Padua, Italy, 2006, Nat. U. de la Plata, Argentina, 2007; D. U. Warsaw, Poland, 2009, U. Salamanca, Spain, 2009. Research assoc. Rockefeller U., 1964-65; asst. prof. Providence Coll., 1965-67, Rockefeller U., 1967-71; assoc. prof. to prof. genetics U. Calif., Davis, 1971-87, disting. prof. biology Irvine, 1987-89, Donald Bren prof. of Biol. scis., 1989—, univ. prof., 2003—. Bd. dirs. basic biology NRC, 1982-91, chmn., 1984-91, mem. commn. on life scis., 1982-91; mem. nat. adv. coun. Nat. Inst. Gen. Med. Scis.; mem. exec. com. EPA, 1979-80; mem. adv. com. directorate sci. and engring. edn. NSF, 1989-91; mem. nat. adv. coun. for human genome rsch. NIH, 1990-93; mem. Pres. com. advisors sci. and tech., 1994-2001. Author: Human Evolution. Trails from the Past, 2007, Darwin's Gift to Science and Religion, 2007, Systematics and the Origin of Species. On Ernst Mayr's 100th Anniversary, 2006, Variation and Evolution in Plants and Microorganisms. Toward a New Synthesis 50 Years after Stebbins, 2000, Evolutionary and Molecular Biology: Scientific Perspectives on Divine Action, 1998, Population and Evolutionary Genetics, 1982, Modern Genetics, 1980, 2d edit., 1984, Evolving: the Theory and Processes of Organic Evolution, 1979, Evolution, 1977, Molecular Evolution, 1976, Studies in the Philosophy of Biology, 1974. Recipient medal Coll. de France, 1979, Mendel medal Czech Republic Acad. Scis., 1994, Hon. Gold medal Acad. Nat. dei Lincei, Rome, 2000, U.S. Nat. Medal of Sci. award 2001, gold medal Stazione Zoological Naples, 2003; Guggenheim fellow, Fulbright fellow. Fellow AAAS (Sci. Freedom and Responsibility award 1987, bd. dirs. 1989-93, pres.-elect 1993-94, pres. 1994-95, chmn. of bd. 1995-96, chmn. com. on health of sci. enterprise 1991—, mem. nat. coun. for sci. and edn. for phase II, project 2061 1990—), Am. Acad. Microbiology; mem. NAS (sect. population biology evolution and ecology chmn. 1983-86, councillor 1986-89, bd. dirs. Nat. Acad. Corp. 1990—), Am. Acad. Arts and Scis., Am. Soc. Naturalists (sec. 1973-76), Genetics Soc. Am., Am. Genetic Assn. (hon. life, Wilhelmine E. Key award), Ecology Soc. Am., Am. Philos. Soc., Soc. Study Evolution (pres. 1979-80), Royal Acad. Scis. Spain (fgn. mem.), Russian Acad. Natural Scis. (fgn. mem.), Mex. Acad. Scis. (fgn. mem.), Acad. Nat. dei Lincei (Rome) (fgn.), Serbian Acad. Scis. & Arts (fgn. mem.), Sigma Xi (William Proctor prize 2000, pres. 2003—). Home: 2 Locke Ct Irvine CA 92617-4034 Office: U Calif Dept Ecology & Evolution Irvine CA 92697-0001 Office Phone: 949-824-8293. Business E-Mail: fjayala@uci.edu.

AYALA, JOHN L., retired librarian, dean; b. Long Beach, Calif., Aug. 28, 1943; s. Francisco and Angelina (Rodriguez) Ayala; m. Patricia Marie Dozier, July 11, 1987 (dec. Jan. 19, 2001); children: Juan, Sara; m. Gloria Ann Aulwes, Dec. 28, 2002. BA in History, Calif. State U., Long Beach, 1970, MPA, 1981; MLS, Immaculate Heart Coll., LA, 1971. Libr. paraprofl. Long Beach Pub. Lib., 1963-70; libr. L.A. County Pub. Libr., 1971-72, Long Beach City Coll., 1972-90, assoc. prof., 1972-90, pres. acad. senate, 1985-87; dean, Learning Resources Fullerton Coll., 1990—2006, evening/weekend supr., 1997—99, adminstr. study abroad program, 2000—06, ret., 2006; interim dir. libr. & learning resources Compton Coll., 2006—07. Chmn. Los Angeles County Com. to Recruit Mexican-Am. Librs., 1971-74; mem. acad. senate Calif. Cmty. Colls., 1985-90; pres. Latino Faculty/Staff Assn., NOCCD, 1993-2000. Editor: Calif. Librarian, 1971. Served with USAF, 1966-68, Vietnam. U.S. Office Edn. fellow for libr. sci., 1970-71. Mem. ALA (com. mem. 1971—, Melvil Dewey award com. 1998—), Calif. Libr. Assn., REFORMA Nat. Assn. to Promote Spanish Speaking Libr. Svc. (founding mem., v.p., pres. 1973-76), Arnulfo Trejo Libr. of the Yr. Award 2001, from Reforma), Calif. State U.-Long Beach Alumni Assn. (treas. 2003—). Democrat. Roman Catholic. Home: 607 E Las Palmas Dr Fullerton CA 92835-1617 Office Phone: 310-900-1648 2170. Personal E-mail: jayala@fullcoll.edu.

AYALA, ORLANDO, computer software company executive; b. Bogota, Colombia; married; 4 children. BA in Mgmt. Info. Sys. With NCR Corp., Dayton, Ohio, 1981—91, product & sales mgr., 1985—88; sr. dir. Latin Am. region Microsoft Corp., Miami, 1991—95, sr. v.p., intercontinental region Redmond, Wash., 1995—98, sr. v.p., South Pacific & Amer. region, 1998—2000, group v.p., worldwide sales, mktg. & svc. group, 2000—03, sr. v.p., small & midmarket solutions & ptnr. group, 2003, now sr. v.p. Unlimited Potential Group. Office: Microsoft Corp One Microsoft Way Redmond WA 98052-6399

AYER, WILLIAM S., air transportation executive; m. Pam Ayer; 1 child. Degree, Stanford U.; MBA, U. Wash. From v.p. strategy and route planning to sr. v.p. ops. Horizen Air Industries, 1985—95, sr. v.p. ops., 1995; from v.p. mktg. and planning to pres. Alaska Air Group, Inc., Seattle, 1995—2003, chmn., pres., CEO, 2003—. Office: Alaska Air Group Inc 19300 Pacific Hwy South Seattle WA 98188

AYLING, HENRY FAITHFUL, editor, consultant, journalist, poet; b. Bklyn., Dec. 30, 1931; s. Albert Edward John and Mina Campbell McCurdy (Lindsay) A.; m. Julia Corinne Gornto, 1954; children: Campbell, Eben, Corey, Harry, Faith. AA, Lincoln Coll., 1951; BA, Grinnell Coll., 1953; MA, Columbia U., Calif. State U., Carson, 1984; 2 grad. teaching certs., Calif. State U., Carson, 1985. Asst to registrar Columbia U., NYC, 1958-59; supr. crew scheduling Pan Am World Airways, Jamaica, NY, 1959-62, supr. payload control, 1963-65; mgr. crew scheduling Seabd. World Airlines, Jamaica, 1962-63, 65-68, mgr. system control, 1968-80; mgr. ops. control Flying Tiger Line,

1980-84; instr. English. ESL Long Beach (Calif.) City Coll., 1984-85; mng. editor IEEE Expert, IEEE Computing Futures IEEE Computer Soc., Los Alamitos, Calif., 1985-90, editorial dir. Computer Soc. Press, 1990-93; writer, editor, cons., 1993—. Mem. editorial bd. Expert Mag., 1986-90, CamAm Programming Inc., 1987-88; columnist Mag. Design and Prodn. mag., 1988-89; contbr. articles to profl. mags. and tech. books; contbr. poetry to various mags. and anthologies. Bd. dirs. Playa Serena Home Owners Assn., Playa Del Rey, Calif., 1983-85. Recipient Maggie awards Western Publs. Assn., 1988-89, IEEE Computer Soc. Golden Core award, 1997. Avocations: music, fine arts. Home and Office: 78291 Allegro Dr Palm Desert CA 92211-1894 Personal E-mail: jcayling@msn.com.

AYRES, JANICE RUTH, social services administrator; b. Idaho Falls, Jan. 23, 1930; d. Low Ray and Frances Mae (Salem) Mason; m. Thomas Woodrow Ayres, Nov. 27, 1953 (dec. 1966); 1 child, Thomas Woodrow Jr. (dec.). MBA, U. So. Calif., 1952, M in Mass Comms., 1953. Asst. mktg. dir. Disneyland, Inc., Anaheim, Calif., 1954-59; gen. mgr. Tamasha Town & Country Club, Anaheim, Calif., 1959-65; dir. mktg. Am. Heart Assn., Santa Ana, Calif., 1966-69; state exec. dir. Nev. Assn. Mental Health, Las Vegas, 1969-71; exec. dir. Clark Co. Easter Seal Treatment Ctr., Las Vegas, 1971-73; mktg. dir., fin devel. officer So. Nev. Drug Abuse Coun., Las Vegas, 1973-74; exec. dir. Nev. Assn. Retarded Citizens, Las Vegas, 1974-75; assoc., cons. Don Luke & Assocs., Phoenix, 1976-77; program dir. Inter-Tribal Coun. Nev., Reno, 1977-79; exec. dir. Ret. Sr. Vol. Program, Carson City, Nev., 1979—. Chair sr. citizen summit State of Nev., 1996; apptd. by Gov. Guinn, Nev. Commn. Aging, 2001; presenter in field; apptd. del. by Gov. of Nev. White House Conf. on Aging, 2005; sec. to bd. dirs. Chinese Workers Mus. Am., 2008—; elected pres. Resun Corps. Assn., 2009. Del. White Ho. Conf. on Aging, 2005; bd. suprs. Carson City, Nev., 1992—; obligation bond com., legis. chair; commr. Carson City Parks and Recreation, 1993—; bd. dirs. Nev. Dept. Transp., 1993; active No. Corp. for Nat. and Cmty. Svc. by Gov., 1994, V&TRR Commn., 1993, re-appointed by Gov., 2005—, chair, 1995, vice-chair, chair pub. rels. com., bd. dirs. Hist. V&TRR Bd.; chair PR Cmty./V&RR Commn. Nev. Home Health Assn.; appointed liaison Carson City Sr. Citizens Bd., 1995; chair summit Rural Nev. Sr. Citizens, Carson City; pres. No. Nev. RR Found., 1996—; chair Tri-Co-RR Commn., 1995, Gov.'s Nev. Commn. for Corp. in Nat. and Cmty. Svc., 1997—, pres., 1998, Carson City Pub. Transp. Commn., 1998—; Carson City Commn. for Clean Groundwater Act, 1998—; chairperson Celebrate Svc. Conf. Americore, 2000; apptd. by Gov. of Nev. Commn. on Aging, 2001—; apptd. by Nev. Gov. New Nev. Commn. to Restructure the Historic V&T RR, 2002—; mem. Nev. Commn. on Aging, 2001—; apptd. rep. of gov. to Nev. Commn. Recruitment V&T RR, 2002; apptd. by Nev. Treas. Brian Krolicki Women's Commn. Fin., 2003—; re-appointed to commn. by Gov. Nev. Commn. for Nat. and Cmty. Svc., 2005—; apptd. del. to White House Conf. on Aging Nev. Gov., 2005; apptd. to bd. dirs. Chinese Workers Mus. Am. Constrn. Project, 2007; elec. sec., bd. dir. Chinese Workers Mus., 2008; corp. sec. Chem. Workers Mus. Am., 2008—. Recipient Gold award, Western Fairs Assn., 2000, Woman of Distinction award, Soroptimist, 2003, Carson City Optimist, 2003, Nat. Optimist Conv., Reno, Nev., 2003, Outstanding Svc. to Seniors Blue Star award, Sanford Ctr. on Aging, 2004, Outstanding Contbn. to Success of Women in Bus., Carson Valley Sorpotomists; named Woman of Distinction, Soroptimist Club, 1988, Oustanding Dir. of Excellence, Gov. State of Nev., 1989, Outstanding Nev. Women's Role Model, Nev. A.G., 1996, Woman of Distinction, Carson Valley Optimist, 2002, Nev.'s Outstanding Older Worker for Experience-Works, 2002, Oldest CEO in Nev., 2002, Outstanding Nev. Pvt. Citizen, Nev. Gov. Kenny Guinn, 2003, Outstanding Dir., Vol. Action Ctr., J.C. Penney Co., invitee to White Ho. for outstanding contbns. to Am.; named to White House Conf. on Aging as Gov. del., 2005. Mem.: AAUW (elected pres., Capital Br. 2009), Social Svc. Programs Sr. Advs., Nev. Sr. Corps. Assn. (elected pres. 2009), Nevada Assn. Denim Corks Dirs. (elected pres. 2008), Chinese Mus. Am. (sec., elec. sec., bd. dirs.), Nat. Assn. Ret. and Sr. Vol. Dirs., Inc. (pres. 2003, nat. pres. 2003—), Internat. Assn. Bus. Commentators, No. Nev. Railroad Found. (pres. 1996—, 2005—08), Am. Soc. Assn. Execs., Nev. Assn. Transit Svcs. (bd. dirs., legis. chmn.), Nev. Fair and Rodeo Assn. (pres.), Nat. Soc. Fund Raising Execs., Women in Radio and TV, Pub. Rels. Soc. Am. (chpt. pres., Outstanding 25 Yr. Svc. award 2004), Internat. Platform Assn., Am. Mktg. Assn. (bd. dirs. 1999—), Am. Mgmt. Assn. (bd. dirs.), Nat. Women's Polit. Caucus. Office: 3303 Butti Way Bldg 1 Carson City NV 89701 Office Phone: 775-687-4680 ext. 2. Business E-Mail: branded@rsvp.carson-city.nv.us.

AZAD, SUSAN STOTT, lawyer; BS, Oreg. State U., 1984; JD, UCLA, 1989. Bar: Calif. 1989. With Latham & Watkins, LA, 1989—, ptnr., 1997—. Mem. assocs. com. Latham & Watkins, LA, 1992—94, fin. com., 1995—97, ethics com., 2001—. Mem.: ABA, LA County Bar Assn. (litigation sect., former mem. jud. election evaluations com., former mem. Calif. and state bar ct. rules com.). Office: Latham Watkins 355 S Grand Ave Los Angeles CA 90071-1560 Home Phone: 818-790-7454; Office Phone: 213-485-1234. Business E-Mail: susan.azad@lw.com.

AZARIA, HANK, actor; b. NYC, Apr. 25, 1964; m. Helen Hunt, July 17, 1999 (div. Dec. 18, 2000). BA, Tufts U., 1987. Actor: (films) Cool Blue, 1988, Pretty Woman, 1990, Quiz Show, 1994, Now and Then, 1995, Heat, 1995, The Birdcage, 1996, Grosse Pointe Blank, 1997, Godzilla, 1998, Great Expectations, 1998, Homegrown, 1998, Celebrity, 1998, The Cradle Will Rock, 1999, Alligatropolis, 1999, Mystery Men, 1999, Mystery Alaska, 1999, Tuesdays With Morrie (Emmy award, 2000), 1999, C-Scam, 2000, America's Sweethearts, 2001, Bark, 2002, Along Came Polly, 2004, Dodgeball: A True Underdog Story, 2004, The Simpsons Movie (voice), 2007, Run Fatboy Run, 2007, Chicago (voice), 2008; (TV movies) Frank Nitti: The Enforcer, 1988, Tuesdays with Morrie, 1999, Fail Safe, 2000, Uprising, 2001; (TV appearances) Family Ties, 1988, Growing Pains, 1985, The Fresh Prince of Bel-Air, 1990, Babes, 1990, Herman's Head, 1991, Friends, 1994, 2001, 2002, 2003, Tales From the Crypt, 1995, If Not for You, 1995, Mad About You, 1996-97; voice characterizations The Simpsons (voice of Apu, Chief Wiggum, Moe Syzlak, and others), 1989— (Emmy award for animation voice-over, 1998, 2001, 2003), Beethoven, 1994, Spider-Man, 1995, Anastasia, 1997, Stressed Eric (also prodr.), 1998, Futurama, 1999, Bartok the Magnificent (also co-prod.), 1999, CyberWorld, 2000; actor, prodr., dir., writer: (film) Nobody's Perfect, 2004; exec. prodr.: (TV series) Imagine That, 2002; actor, prodr.: Huff, 2004-; broadway: Monty Python's Spamalot, 2005 (Theatre World award, 2005). Recipient: Light on the Hill award, Tufts U., 1999. Office: The Simpsons c/o Twentieth Television PO Box 900 Beverly Hills CA 90213

AZARNOFF, DANIEL LESTER, pharmaceutical executive, consultant; s. Samuel J. and Kate (Asarnow) A.; m. Joanne Stokes, Dec. 26, 1951; children: Rachel, Richard, Martin. BS, Rutgers U., 1947, MS, 1948; MD, U. Kans., 1955. Asst. instr. anatomy U. Kans. Med. Sch., 1949—50, rsch. fellow, 1950—52, intern, 1955—56, resident, Nat. Heart Inst. research fellow, 1956—58, asst. prof. medicine, 1962—64, assoc. prof., 1964—68, dir. clin. pharmacology study unit, 1964—68, assoc. prof. pharmacology, 1965—68, prof. medicine and pharmacology, 1968, dir. Clin. Pharmacology-Toxicology Ctr., 1967—78, Disting. prof., 1973—78, also prof. medicine, 1965—67, pres. Sigma Xi Club, 1968—69, clin. prof. medicine, 1982—96, prof. medicine, 1997—2007; Nat. Inst. Neurol. Diseases and Blindness spl. trainee Washington U. Sch. Medicine, St. Louis, 1958—60; asst. prof. medicine St. Louis U. Sch. Medicine, 1960—62; sr. v.p. worldwide R&D, G.D. Searle & Co., Skokie, 1978; pres. Searle R&D, Skokie, 1979—85, Azarnoff Assocs., Inc., Evanston, Ill., 1986—87, D.L. Azarnoff Assocs., So. San Francisco, Calif., 1987—; prof. pathology, clin. prof. pharmacology Northwestern U. Med. Sch., 1978—85; sr. v.p. clin. regulatory affairs Cellegy Pharms., San Francisco, 1998—2003; sr. v.p. clin. devel., pharmacology Congentus Pharms., 2006—; commr. Nat. Commn. on Orphan Diseases, 1985—87; chmn. bd. dirs. Alpha RX Corp., South San Francisco, Calif., 1992—94; clin. prof. med. Stanford U. Sch. Med., 1998—2002. Professorial lectr. U. Chgo., 1978-86; dir. Second Workshop on Prins. Drug Evaluation in Man, 1970; chmn. com. on problems of drug safety NRC-NAS, 1972-76; chmn. bd. dirs. Oread, Inc., Lawrence, Kans., 1998-99; CEO Cibus Pharms., Burlingame, Calif., 1996-97; cons. numerous govt. agys.; chmn. bd. dirs. Cibus Pharm., Inc., 1996-97; CEO, chmn. bd. dirs. Vitalsensor, Inc., 2004-05. Editor: Devel. of Drug Interactions, 1974-77, Yearbook of Drug Therapy, 1977-79; series editor: Monographs in Clin. Pharmacology, 1977-84; mem. editl. bd. Drug Investigation, Brit. Jour. Clin. Pharmacology, Clin. Pharmacol. Therapy, Clin. Pharmacokinetics, Clin. Drug Investigation, 1989—, others. Served with U.S. Army, 1945-46. Recipient Ginsburg award in phys. diagnosis U. Kanas. Med. Ctr., 1953, Outstanding Intern award, 1956, Ciba award for gerontol. rsch., 1958, Rectors medal U. Helsinki, 1968, Nathanial T. Kwit Meml. Disting. Svc. award Am. Coll. Clin. Pharmacology, 2002; named Disting. Med. Alumnus, U. Kans. Coll. Health Sci., 1995; John and Mary R. Markle scholar, 1964, William N. Creasy vis. prof. clin. pharmacology Med. Coll. Va., 1975; Bruce Hall Meml. lectr. St. Vincents Hosp., Sydney, 1976, 7th Sir Henry Hallett Dale lectr. Johns Hopkins U. Med. Sch., 1978; Fulbright scholar Karolinska Inst., Stockholm, 1968. Fellow ACP, N.Y. Acad. Scis., Am. Assn. Pharm. Scientists (Rsch. Achievement award in clin. scis. 1995), AAAS (chmn. elect pharm. sect. 2001, chmn. pharm. divsn. 2002-03); mem. AMA (vice chmn. coun. on drugs 1971-72, editl. bd. jours.), Am. Soc. Clin. Nutrition, Am. Nutrition Instn., Am. Soc. Pharmacology and Exptl. Therapeutics (chmn. clin. pharmacology divsn. 1969-71, mem. exec. com. 1966-73, 78-81, del. 1975-78, bd. publ. trustees), Am. Soc. Clin. Pharmacology and Therapeutics (Oscar B. Hunter Meml. award 1995), Am. Fedn. Clin. Rsch., Brit. Pharmacol. Soc., Ctrl. Soc. Clin. Rsch., Royal Soc. for Promotion Health, Inst. Medicine of Nat. Acad. Scis., Soc. Exptl. Biology and Medicine (councillor 1976-80), Internat. Union Pharmacologists (sec. clin. pharmacology sect. 1975-81, internat. adv. com. Paris Congress 1978), GPIA (blue ribbon com. on generic medicine 1990), Sigma Xi. Office: DL Azarnoff Assoc LLC 610 Edgewood Dr Rio Vista CA 94571 Office Phone: 707-374-2715. Business E-Mail: dan@azarnoffassociates.com.

AZIZ, KHALID, petroleum engineering educator; b. Bahawalpur, Pakistan, Sept. 29, 1936; arrived in US, 1952, naturalized; s. Aziz Ul and Rshida; m. Mussarrat Rizwani, Nov. 12, 1962; children: Natasha, Imraan. BS in Mech. Enging., U. Mich., 1955; BSc in Petroleum Engring., U. Alta., 1958, MSc in Petroleum Engring., 1961; PhD in Chem. Engring., Rice U., 1966; LLD honoris causa, U. Calgary, 2008. Jr. design engr. Massey-Ferguson, 1955-56; various position to asst. prof. petroleum engring. U. Alta., 1960-62; various positions, chmn. bd. Neotech. Cons. Ltd., 1972-85; mgr., dir. Computer Modelling Group, Calgary, Alta., 1977-82; various positions to chief engr. Karachi (Pakistan) Gas Co., 1958-59, 62-63; various positions to prof. chem. and petroleum engring. U. Calgary, 1965-82; hon. prof., 1994—2001; prof. petroleum enging. dept. Stanford U., Calif., 1982—2006, assoc. dean rsch. Sch. Earth Scis., 1983-86, chmn. petroleum engring. dept., 1986-91, 94-95, Otto N. Miller prof. in earth scis., 1989—2009, prof. energy resources engring. dept., 2006—. Co-author: Flow of Complex Mixtures in Pipes, 1972, Petroleum Reservoir Simulation, 1979; contbr. articles to profl. jours. Recipient Diploma of Honor, Pi Epsilon Tau, 1991, Killam Resident fellow U. Calgary, 1977, Blaise Pascal Earth Scis. medal 2005, Lifetime Achievement award Petroleum Soc. Can.; Chem. Inst. Can. fellow, 1974. Mem. AIME (hon.), European Assn. Geoscientists and Engrs., Soc. Petroleum Engrs. (disting. mem., Ferguson award 1979, Reservoir Engring. award 1987, Lester C. Uren award 1988, Disting. Achievement award for Petroleum Engring. Faculty 1990, hon. mem. 1996), Nat. Acad. Engring., Russian Acad. Natural Scis. (fgn.), European Acad. of Sci. (Blaise Pascal medal in Earth Scis., 2005). Muslim. Achievements include rsch. in multiphase flow of oil/gas mixtures & steam in pipes & wells, multiphase flow in porous media, reservoir modeling and optimization, natural gas engring., hydrocarbon fluid phase behavior. Office: Stanford U Dept Energy Resources Engring Stanford CA 94305-2220

AZZI, JENNIFER L., personal trainer, retired professional basketball player; b. Oak Ridge, Tenn., Aug. 31, 1968; d. James and Donna Azzi. Diploma, Stanford U., 1990. Basketball player Arvika Basket, Sweden, 1995—96, Viterbo, Italy, Orchies, France, San Jose Lasers, 1996—99, Salt Lake City Starzz, 1999—2002, San Antonio Stars, 2003—04; ret., 2004; owner Azzi Tng., Utah. Mem. Nat. Women's Basketball Team. Spokesperson Nat. Fitness Tour; bd. dirs. USA Basketball, 2005—08. Recipient gold medal, Goodwill Games, 1994, World Championship Qualifying team, 1993, U.S. Olympic Festival West Team, 1987, 2 gold medals, World Championship and Goodwill Games, 1990, bronze medal, Pan Am. Games, 1991, World Championship team, 1994, Wade Trophy, 1990, Kodak All-Am. 1st team, 1989, 1990, gold medal, U.S. Olympic Team, 1996; named Al-Pac 10 1st team, 1988, 1989, 1990, MVP, NCAA Final Four, 1990, NCAA West Region, 1990, Naismith Nat. Player Yr., 1990. Office: Azzi Tng 8589 S Mardi Gras Ln West Jordan UT 84088 Office Fax: 801-282-2725. Business E-Mail: info@azzitraining.com.

BAACK, BRET ROLYN, plastic surgeon; b. Albuquerque, July 27, 1958; s. Rolyn Ernest and Karen Lee (Engelbert) B.; m. Elena Lisa Sandoval, Feb. 14, 1987; children: Amy, David. BS in Chemistry, U. N.Mex., 1979, BA in Biology, 1979, MD, 1983. Diplomate Am. Bd. Plastic Surgery. From asst. to assoc. prof. U. N.Mex., 1990—. Fellow ACS; mem. Am Soc. Plastic and Reconstructive Surgeons (socioecon. com. 1993—), Alpha Omega Alpha, Phi Beta Kappa. Luth. Avocations: keyboards, golf. Office: Univ Hosp Dept Surg-ACC-2 2211 Lomas Blvd NE Albuquerque NM 87106-2745

BAARSMA, BILL, Mayor, Tacoma; b. Tacoma, Wash, 1942; s. Connie and Clarence; m. Carol Baarsma, 1998; children: Bill Jr., Katya. BA in Polit. Science, U. Puget Sound, 1964; MA in Govt., D Pub. Adminstrn. Prof., bus. & pub. adminstrn. U. Puget Sound; mem. Tacoma City Coun., 1992—99; mayor City of Tacoma, Wash., 2002—. Mem. City of Tacoma's Redistricting Com., 1980. Mem.: Mayors Against Illegal Guns Coalition, Tacoma Urban League. Democrat. Office: 747 Market St Ste 1200 Tacoma WA 98402-3766 Business E-Mail: bbaarsma@cityoftacoma.org.*

BAAS, JACQUELYNN, museum director, art historian; b. Grand Rapids, Mich., Feb. 14, 1948; BA in History of Art, Mich. State U.; PhD in History of Art, U. Mich. Registrar U. Mich. Mus. Art, Ann Arbor, 1974-78, asst. dir., 1978-82; editor Bull. Museums of Art and Archaeology, U. Mich., 1976-82; chief curator Hood Mus. Art, Dartmouth Coll., Hanover, NH, 1982-84, dir., 1985-89, U. Calif. Berkeley Art Mus. and Pacific Film Archive, 1989—99, emeritus dir., 1999—, interim dir., 2007—08; program dir. Awake: Art and Buddhism, 1999—2004. Collaborating curator 6th Gwangju Biennale, 2006; interim dir. Mills Coll. Art Mus., 2008-09; cons. in field; organizer exhbns.; ind. art historian; lectr. in field. Author: Smile of the Buddha: Eastern Philosophy and Western Art, 2005; co-editor: Buddha Mind in Contemporary Art, 2004; contbr. articles and essays to jours. and books; co-editor: Learning Mind: Experience into Art. Mem. Internat. Assn. Art Critics, Coll. Art Assn. Am. Address: PO Box 5 The Sea Ranch CA 95497-0005 Office Phone: 510-406-4455.

BABAUTA, JUAN NEKAI, former governor; b. Saipan, No. Mariana Islands, Sept. 7, 1953; s. Santiago Miyasaki and Carmen (Nekai) B.; m. Diana Chong BS, MA, Ea. N.Mex. U., 1976; MS, U. Cin., 1979. Health planner TTPI Dept. Health Services, Saipan, 1977; dep. exec. dir. No. Mariana Islands State Health Planning & Devel. Agy., Saipan, 1979; exec. dir. Saipan, 1980-86; senator No. Mariana Islands Legis., Saipan, 1986—90; resident rep. to US Commonwealth of No. Mariana Islands, Saipan, 1990—2002, gov., 2002—06. Co-chmn. 902 Covenant Negotiation team; instr. No. Marianas Coll., Saipan, 1986. Chmn. bd. regents No. Marianas Coll., 1982-83, 84-86; chmn. Bd. Edn., Saipan, 1982-83, 84-86; mem. Med. Profession Licensing Bd., Saipan, 1983-86, Nat. State Bd. Edn., Saipan, 1982-86. Mem. Phi Kappa Phi. Republican. Roman Catholic. Avocation: reading.

BABAYANS, EMIL, financial planner; b. Nov. 9, 1951; arrived in U.S., 1969; s. Hacob and Jenik (Khatchatourian) B.; BS, U. So. Calif., 1974, MS, 1976. CLU; cert. fin. planner. Pres. Babtech Internat., Inc., Sherman Oaks, Calif., 1975—85; sr. ptnr. Emil Babayans & Assocs., Pasadena, Calif., 1985—. Mem.: Million Dollar Round Table, Am. Soc. CLU and Chartered Fin. Cons., Internat. Assn. Fin. Planners, Inst. Cert. Fin. Planners, Nat. Assn. Life Underwriters, Am. Mgmt. Assn. Armenian Orthodox. Office: 301 N Lake Ave Ste 920 Pasadena CA 91101 Home Phone: 818-366-2160. Personal E-mail: embco@aol.com.

BABB, RICHARD RANKIN, gastroenterologist, educator; b. Wilmington, Ohio, 1934; BA, Stanford U., 1956, MD, 1960. Diplomate in internal medicine and gastroenterology Am. Bd. Internal Medicine. Intern U. Hosp. Boston, 1960—61; resident in medicine Mayo Clinic, Rochester, 1961—66; fellow in gastroenteorology Balt. Mercy Hosp., 1966—67; gastroenterologist Palo Alto Clinic, Calif., 1968—; clin. prof. medicine Stanford U., 1980—; pvt. practice. Fellow: ACP; mem.: Am. Soc. Gastroenterol. Endoscopy, Am. Gastroent. Assn. (Disting. Clinician award 2001). Office: Palo Alto Clinic 795 El Camino Palo Alto CA 94301 Office Phone: 650-321-4121. E-mail: babbr@pamf.org.

BABCOCK, BARBARA ALLEN, lawyer, educator; b. Washington, July 6, 1938; d. Henry Allen and Doris Lenore (Moses) Babcock; m. Thomas C. Grey, Aug. 19, 1979. BA, U. Pa., 1960; LLB, Yale U., 1963; LLD (hon.), U. San Diego, 1983, U Puget Sound, 1988. Bar: Md. 1963, DC 1964. Law clk. US Ct. Appeals, Washington, 1963; assoc. Edward Bennett Williams, 1964—66; staff atty. Legal Aid Agy., Washington, 1966—68; dir. Pub. Defender Svc. (formerly Legal Aid Agy.), 1968—72; asst. atty. gen. US Dept. Justice, 1977—79; assoc. prof. Stanford U., 1972—77, prof., 1977—, Ernest W. McFarland Prof. Law, 1986—97, Judge John Crown prof. law, 1997—2004, Judge John Crown prof. emerita, 2004—. Author (with others): Sex Discrimination and The Law: History, Theory and Practice, 1996; co-author (with Massaro): Civil Procedure: Problems and Cases, 2001; contbr. articles profl. jour. Recipient John Bingham Hurlbut Award for Excellence in Tchg., Stanford U., 1981, 1986, 1998, 2004, Margaret Brent Women Lawyers of Achievement Award, ABA, 1999. Democrat. Office: Stanford U Sch Law Stanford CA 94305

BABCOCK, LEWIS THORNTON, federal judge; b. Rocky Ford, Colo., Apr. 4, 1943; m. Judith S. Babcock; two children. BA cum laude, U. Denver, 1965, JD, 1968; LLM, U. Va., 1968. Ptnr. Mitchell and Babcock, Rocky Ford, Colo., 1968-76; atty. City of Las Animas, Colo., 1969-74, City of Rocky Ford, 1970-76; asst. dist. atty. 11th Jud. Cir., La Junta, Colo., 1973-76, dist. judge, 1978-83; judge Colo. Ct. Appeals, 1983-88, US Dist. Ct. Colo., Denver, 1988—2008, chief judge, 2000—07, sr. judge, 2008—. Escrow and loan closing agt. FHA, Rocky Ford, 1973-76. Bd. dirs. Colo. Rural Legal Svcs. Inc., 1974-76. With Colo. N.G., 1968-74. Named to Order St. Ives. Mem. ABA, Colo. Bar Assn., Denver Bar Assn., Colo. Bar Found., North Ind. Dist. Bar Assn. Office: US Dist Ct A273 Arraj US Courthouse 1929 Stout St Rm 236 Denver CO 80294-1929*

BABCOCK, WALTER CHRISTIAN, JR., membrane company executive; b. Oakland, Calif., Oct. 20, 1947; s. Walter Christian and Beatrice Alice (Sommerfield) B.; m. Jacqueline Ann Mills, Dec. 30, 1971; children: Jennifer Suzanne, Rebecca Christine. BS, U. Calif., San Diego, 1969; MS, U. Oreg., 1970, PhD, 1976. V.p. Rsch. Cons. and Design, La Jolla, Calif., 1970-71; rsch. chemist Bend (Oreg.) Rsch. Inc., 1976-81, dir. separations div., 1981-86, v.p., 1983-87, pres., 1987—, chief oper. officer, 1987-89, chief exec. officer, 1989—, pres. Bd. dirs. Consep Membranes, Bend. Contbr. articles to profl. jours. Bd. dirs. St. Charles med. Ctr., Bend, 1986. Mem. Am. Chem. Soc., N.Am. Membrane Soc., Oreg. Biotech. Assn. (bd. dirs. 1990-91). Republican. Avocations: sailing, horseback riding. Office: Bend Rsch Inc 64550 Research Rd Bend OR 97701-8599

BABCOCK-LUMISH, TERRY LYNNE, economic geographer; b. Miami, Fla., Mar. 30, 1976; d. Robert Malcolm and Saundra Ellen Lumish; m. Brian Christopher Babcock, June 20, 2001. BS, Carnegie Mellon U., Pitts., 1997; MPA, Ind. U., 1999; DPhil in Econ.

Geography, U. Oxford, Eng., 2004. Lilly cmty. assistance fellow Gov. Frank O'Bannon's Children's Environ. Initiative, Inpls., 1997—99; presdl. mgmt. fellow Coun. of Econ. Advisers, US Dept. of Treasury, Washington, 1999—2001; rschr. To V.P. Al Gore, Alexandria, Va., 2001—02; assoc. fellow Rothermere Am. Inst., Oxford, 2002—; pres. Islay Consulting LLC, Tucson, 2005—; Wertheim fellow labor and work life program Harvard Law Sch. Bd. dir. Truman Scholars Assn., Washington, 2002—05, Renaissance House. Bd. dirs. Women's Found. So. Ariz., Women's Transition Project. Recipient Sr. Leadership award, Carnegie Mellon U., 1997, Stephen Omer Lee award, 1996; named one of 40 Under 40, Tucson Bus. Edge, 2006; Presdl. Mgmt. fellow, 1999—2001, Harry S Truman scholar, 1996, Clarendon scholar, U. Oxford/Oxford U. Press, 2002—05. Mem.: Ariz. List, Assn. Am. Geographers, Ariz. Town Hall, Nature Conservancy, Tuscon Bus. Edge (named 40 under 40), Rotary Internat., Pi Alpha Alpha, Phi Kappa Phi, Phi Beta Kappa. Avocations: travel, hiking, gourmet cooking.

BABER, WALTER FRANKLIN, political science professor; b. Oklahoma City, Aug. 18, 1953; s. Eldon Clay and Evalena Baber; m. Carolyn Diane Pearson, Aug. 8, 1975; children: Katherine Ann, John Jay. PhD, U. NC, Chapel Hill, 1980; JD, U. San Diego, 1991; BA magna cum laude, Calif. State. U. Bar: Calif. 1990. Assoc. prof. Calif. State U., Long Beach, 2001—. Author: Deliberative Environmental Politics, Organizing the Future, (articles) Social Sci. Jour., Public Integrity, Natural Resources Jour., Kansas Jour. Law and Pub. Policy, Pub. Adminstrn. Quarterly, Jour. Mgmt. History, The Bureuacrat, Internat. Jour. Pub. Adminstrn. Mem.: Western Polit. Sci. Assn., Am. Polit. Sci. Assn. (life). Democrat. Unitarian-Universalist. Home: 17047 Abra Way San Diego CA 92128 Office: Calif State Univ 1250 Bellflower Blvd Long Beach CA 90840 Business E-Mail: wbaber@csulb.edu.

BABIUK, LORNE ALAN, virologist, immunologist, researcher; b. Canora, Sask., Can., Jan. 25, 1946; s. Paul and Mary (Mayden) Babiuk; m. Betty Lou Carol Wagar, Sept. 29, 1973; children: Shawn, Kimberley. BSA, U. SK, Saskatoon, 1967, MSc, 1969, DSc, 1987; PhD, U. BC, Vancouver, 1972; DSc in Infectious Diseases, Colo. State U., Ft. Collins, 2007. Postdoctoral fellow U. Toronto, Ont., Canada, 1972-73; asst. prof. Western Coll. Vet. Medicine, Saskatoon, SK, 1973-75, assoc. prof., 1975-79, prof., 1979—. Cons. Molecular Genetics, Mpls., 1980—84, Genentech, San Francisco, 1981—84, Ciba Geigy, Basel, Switzerland, 1984—91; assoc. dir. rsch. Vet. Infectious Disease Orgn., Saskatoon, 1984—93, dir., 1993—2007; v.p. rsch. U. Alberta, 2007—. Contbr. chapters to books, articles to profl. jours. Recipient award, Can. Soc. Microbiology, 1990, Am. Vet. Immunology, 1992, Xerox-Can. Forum, 1993, Emerging Sci. and Tech. award for innovation, 1995, Pfizer award in animal health, 1998, Nat. Merit award, 1998, Bill Snowden Meml. award, 2000, Saskatchewan Order of Merit, 2004, Saskatchewan Centennial medal, 2005, Officer of Order of Can., 2005, Centennial medal, Province of Saskatchewan, 2005, Prix Galien Can. Rsch. award, 2005. Fellow: Can. Acad. Health Scis., Royal Soc. Can., Infectious Disease Soc. Am. (chair Can. rsch. in vaccinology and biotech. 2001—07), Royal Coll. Physicians and Surgeons Can. (hon.); mem.: Internat. Soc. Antiviral Rsch., Soc. Gen. Microbiology, Can. Soc. Microbiology, Am. Soc. Virology, Am. Soc. Microbiology, Internat. Soc. Interferon Rsch. Achievements include 25 patents in field. Home: 2130 Haddow Dr Edmonton AB T6R 3C9 Canada Office: Vice Pres Rsch 3-7 University Hall Edmonton AB Canada T6G 2J9 Office Phone: 780-492-5353. Business E-Mail: lorne.babiuk@ualberta.ca.

BABULA, WILLIAM, dean, writer; b. Stamford, Conn., May 19, 1943; s. Benny F. and Lottie (Zajkowski) B.; m. Karen L. Gemi, June 19, 1965; children: Jared, Joelle. BA, Rutgers U., 1965; MA, U. Calif., Berkeley, 1967, PhD, 1969. Asst. prof. English U. Miami, Coral Gables, Fla., 1969-75, assoc. prof., 1975-77, prof., 1977-81, chmn. dept. Eng., 1976-81; dean of arts and humanities Sonoma State U., Rohnert Park, Calif., 1981—. Author: Shakespeare and the Tragicomic Archetype, 1975, Shakespeare in Production, 1935-79, 1981; (short stories) Motorcycle, 1982, Quarterback Sneak, 1983, The First Edsel, 1983, Ransom, 1983, The Last Jogger in Virginia, 1983, The Orthodontist and the Rock Star, 1984, Greenearth, 1984, Football and Other Seasons, The Great American Basketball Shoot, 1984, Ms. Skywriter, Inc., 1987; (plays) The Fragging of Lt. Jones (1st prize Gualala Arts Competition, 1983), Creatures (1st prize Jacksonville U. competition 1987), The Winter of Mrs. Levy (Odyssey Stage Co., New Play Series 1988), Nat. Playwright's Showcase, 1988, Theatre Americana, 1990 (James Ellis award), Basketball Jones, Black Rep of Berkeley, 1988, West Coast Ensemble, Festival of One Acts, 1992, Mark Twain Masquers, 9th Ann. Festival One Act Plays, 1994 (2d Place award), The Last Roundup, 1991 (Odyssey Stage Co.); (novels) The Bombing of Berkeley and Other Pranks (1st prize 24th Ann. Deep South Writers' Conf. 1984), St. John's Baptism, 1988, According to St. John, 1989, St. John and the Seven Veils, 1991, St. John's Bestiary, 1994, St. John's Bread, 1999; contbr. articles to profl. pubs. and short stories to lit. mags. Mem. Shakespeare Assn. of Am., Dramatists Guild, Assoc. Writing Programs, Mystery Writers Am., Phi Beta Kappa. Democrat. Episcopalian. Office: Sonoma State U Sch Arts and Humanities Rohnert Park CA 94928 Business E-Mail: william.babula@sonoma.edu.

BACA, EDWARD DIONICIO, consulting firm executive, retired military officer; b. Santa Fe, July 27, 1938; s. Ernest J. and Delphine (Garcia) B.; m. Rita Ann Hennigan, Apr. 12, 1957; children: Brian Edward, Brenda Anne, Karen Lynne, Mark Andrew, Michelle Marie, David William, Daniel Patrick Student, Coll. of Santa Fe, N.Mex. Nat. Guard's Officer Candidate Sch., 1962, Chem., Biol. and Radiol. Sch., 1965, US Command & Gen. Staff Coll., 1976; BS in Liberal Arts, SUNY, 1986; LLD (hon.), N.Mex. State U. Advanced through ranks to lt. gen. US Army N.G., 1994, retired, 1998; Administrv. asst. N.Mex. Army N.G., 1957-58, procurement-contracting staff, 1958-59, clk., traffic mgr., supply clk., 1959-62, field account clk., 1962, field auditor, 1962-64, air nat. guard insp., 1964, supply officer, 1966-69, supervisory auditor Army-air, 1969-71, logistics officer, 1971-75, comptr., 1975-77, mil. personnel mgmt. officer, 1977-81, command adminstrv. officer, 1981-83, adjutant gen. of N.Mex., 1983—94; chief Nat. Guard Bureau US Dept. Def., Washington, 1994—98; founder Baca Group Inc., Albuquerque, 1998—. Bd. dirs. Vietnam Vets. Chapel, Angel Fire, N.Mex.; past pres. St. Francis Sch. Bd., Santa Fe; mem. parish council St. John the Bapt. Cath. Ch., Santa Fe. Served with ARNG, 1983— Decorated Army Commendation ribbon, Meritorious Service medal, US Army Disting Svc. medal (2), USAF Disting. Svc. medal, Legion of Merit, Disting. Svc. medal US Dept. Def., Republic of Vietnam Cross of Gallantry with Palm Unit Citation, Vietnam Svc. medal, Norweigan Royal Order of Merit with Command, Army Res. Component Achievement medal with Silver Oak Leaf Cluster, Nat. Def. Svc. medal with One Bronze Svc. star, Armed Forces Res. medal with Two Hourglass Devices, Army Svc. Ribbon, Overseas Svc. Ribbon, Meritorious Unit Commendation; recipient N.Mex. Medal of Valor, Meritorious Service award Nat. Guard Assn., 1981, Outstanding Drug Demand Reduction Program award US Dept Def., Am. G.I. Forum Founders award Mem. Mil. Order of World Wars, Vietnam Vets., DAV, U.S. Nat. Guard, N.Mex. Nat. Guard, Assn. U.S. Army Democrat. Roman Catholic. Office: Baca Group 12212 Camelot Pl NE Albuquerque NM 87122 Office Phone: 505-858-1445. E-mail: edbaca@bacagroup.org.*

BACA, JIM, mayor; BSBA, U. N.Mex. Mayor City of Albuquerque, 1997—. Former dir. alcohol and beverage control State of N.Mex., press sec. to gov., commr. pub. lands; past asst. to mayor, gen. mgr. Rio Grande Conservancy Dist.; former dir. Fed. Bur. Land Mgmt.; nat. cons. pub. land and conservation issues. Served with USAF.

BACA, JOE, United States Representative from California; b. Belen, N.Mex., Jan. 23, 1947; m. Barbara Baca; children: Joe Jr., Jeremy, Natalie; 1 child, Jennifer. BS in Sociology, Calif. State U., LA, 1971. Co-owner Interstate World Travel, San Bernardino, Calif., 1989; formerly with cmty. rels. divsn. Santa Fe Railroad Yard GTE; mem. Calif. State Assembly, Sacramento, 1992—98, spkr. pro tempore, 1995—98; US senator from Calif., 1998—99, mem. rules com., vet. affairs com., pub. employment & ret. com., energy, utilities & comm. com., local govt. com.; mem. US Congress from 43rd (formerly 42nd) Calif. dist., Washington, 1999—, mem. agriculture & sci. com., fin. svcs. com., resources com. Mem. Blue Dog Coalition, Cancer Caucus, Goods Movement Caucus, Ho. Army Caucus, Mil. Vets. Caucus, Native Am. Caucus, Nursing Caucus, US-Mex. Congl. Caucus, Congl. Diabetes Caucus, Dem. Caucus Homeland Security Task Force, vice chair Immigration Task Force; founder, co-chair Congl. Sex & Violence in Media Caucus; chair, whip Congl. Hispanic Caucus; chair 110th Congress Am. Caucus. Trustee San Bernardino Valley Coll., 1979—83; founder youth edn. motivation prog. PTA; active St. Thomas More Parish, Rialto, Calif.; bd, dirs. Arrowhead United Way, Future Leaders of America, San Bernadino Valley Cmty. College, San Bernadino Valley Found. Youth Athletics, San Gorgonio Coun. Girl Scouts of America, San Bernadino Boys and Girls Club. Specialist E-4 82nd and 101st divsns. US Army, 1966—68, Vietnam. Named Legislator of Yr., Am. Legion, Minority Male of Yr., Greater Riverside Area Urban League; named a Citizen of Distinction, San Bernardino Area LWV, Disting. Citizen in Inland Empire, Boy Scouts of America; named an Outstanding Legislator, Calif. Rifle & Pistol Assn., 1995. Mem.: Nat. Assn. Latino Elected & Apptd. Officials (bd. dirs.), San Bernadino Kiwanis Club. Democrat. Office: US Ho Reps 328 Cannon Ho Office Bldg Washington DC 20515-0543 also: Ste 102 201 N E St San Bernardino CA 92401-1520

BACA, JOSEPH FRANCIS, retired judge; b. Albuquerque, Oct. 1, 1936; s. Amado and Inez (Pino) Baca; m. Dorothy Lee Burrow, June 28, 1969; children: Jolynn, Andrea, Anna Marie. BA in Edn., U. N.Mex., 1960; JD, George Washington U., 1964; LLM, U. Va., 1992. Asst. dist. atty. 1st Jud. Dist., Santa Fe, 1965-66; pvt. practice Albuquerque, 1966-72; dist. judge 2d Jud. Dist., Albuquerque, 1972-88; justice N.Mex Supreme Ct., Santa Fe, 1989—2002, chief justice, 1995-97; ret., 2002. Spl. asst. to atty. gen. Office of N.Mex Atty. Gen., Albuquerque, 1966—71. Bd. dirs. State Justice Inst., 1994—, vice chmn., 1999—; Dem. precinct chmn. Albuquerque, 1968; del. N.Mex Constl. Conv., Santa Fe, 1969. Recipient Judge of the Yr. award, People's Commn. Criminal Justice, 1989, Quincentennial Commemoration Achievement award, La Hispanidad Com., 1992, Luchando pro la Justicia award, Mex. Am. Law Students Assn. U. N.Mex Law Sch., 1993, J. William Fulbright Disting. Pub. Svc. award, George Washington U. Alumni Assn., 1994, Recognition and Achievement award, Commn. Opportunities for Minorities in the Profession, 1992, others; named one of 100 Most Influential Hispanics, Hispanic Bus. Mag., 1997, 1998. Mem.: ABA, N.Mex Hispanic Bar Assn. (Outstanding Hispanic Atty. award 2000), Santa Fe Bar Assn., Albuquerque Bar Assn., Am. Jud. Soc. (bd. dirs. 1999—), Scribes (bd. dirs. 1998—2006), Am. Law Inst., N.Mex Bar Assn. (Outstanding Jud. Svc. award 1998, Disting. Jud. Svc. award 2002), Hispanic Nat. Bar Assn. (Lincoln-Juarez award 2000), Alumni Assn. (pres. 1980—81), KC, Kiwanis (pres. Albuquerque chpt. 1984—85, dep. grand knight 1968). Roman Catholic. Avocation: reading. Office Phone: 505-821-6881. E-mail: jbaca01@msn.com.

BACAS, ANDREW R., data processing executive; BA, Yale U.; MS, NYU; MBA, Wharton Sch. V.p. Simmons & Co. Internat.; vice chmn., CEO ImageMAX Inc., Fort Washington, Pa.; with Key Prin. Ptnrs., San Francsico. Vis. faculty Assn. Corp. Growth. Former flight officer USN.

BACCIGALUPPI, ROGER JOHN, agricultural products executive; b. NYC, Mar. 17, 1934; s. Harry and Ethel (Hutcheon) B.; m. Patricia Marie Wier, Feb. 6, 1960 (div. 1978); children: John, Elisabeth, Andrea; m. Iris Christine Walfridson, Feb. 3, 1979; 1 child, Jason. BS, U. Calif., Berkeley, 1956; MS, Columbia U., 1957. Asst. sales promotion mgr. Maco Mag. Corp., NYC, 1956-57; merchandising asst. Honig, Cooper & Harrington, San Francisco and L.A., 1957-58, 1958-60, asst. dir. merchandising, 1960-61; sales rep. Blue Diamond Growers (formerly Calif. Almond Growers Exch.), Sacramento, 1961-64, mgr. advt. and sales promotion, 1964-70, v.p. mktg., 1970-73, sr. v.p. mktg., 1973-74, exec. v.p., 1974-75, pres., 1975-91; founder RB Internat., Sacramento, 1992—. Vice chmn., bd. dirs. Agrl. Coun. Calif., 1975-91; mem. U.S. adv. com. Trade Policy and Negotiations, 1983-2002; mem. Agrl. Policy Adv. Com., 2005—; mem. U.S. adv. bd. Rabobank Nederlands, 1988-91; mem. Calif. World Trade Commn., 1993-2001; mem. adv. coun. Nat. Ctr. for Food and Agr. Policy Resources for Future, 1990-99. Vice chmn. Calif. State R.R. Mus. Found.; bd. dirs. Cmty. Colls. Found.; vice chmn. Grad. Inst. Cooperative Leadership, 1986-87, chair, 1987-89; bd. dirs. Valley Vision, Inc., 1995-03, AgriNova Corp., 2004-. With AUS, 1957. Mem. Calif. C. of C. (chmn. internat. trade com. 1988-94, bd. dirs. 1988—, vice chmn. bd. 1992-94, chmn. bd. 1995, Sacramento Host Com. (chmn. 1997, 98), Calif. for Higher Edn., Grad. Inst. Coop. Leadership (chmn., trustee), Grocery Mfrs. Am., Inc. (bd. dirs. 1988-91), Sutter Club. Office: RB Internat 777 Campus Commons Rd Ste 200 Sacramento CA 95825-8343 Office Phone: 916-565-7411.

BACH, ROBERT J. (ROBBIE BACH), computer software company executive; b. Peoria, Ill., Dec. 31, 1961; m. Pauline Bach; 3 children. BA in Econ., U. NC, Chapel Hill, 1984; MBA, Stanford U., 1988. Fin. analyst Morgan Stanley & Co.; with Microsoft Corp., Redmond, Wash., 1988—, bus. ops. mgr., Microsoft Europe, 1990—92, v.p. mktg., desktop applications divsn., v.p., learning, entertainment, & productivity divsn., 1996—99, v.p., home and retail, 1999—2000, sr. v.p. games divsn., chief Xbox officer, 2000—05, pres. entertainment & devices divsn., 2005—. Co-leader Microsoft Consumer Leadership Team. Chmn.-elect Boys & Girls Clubs Am., 2008; chmn. Microsoft Giving Campaign, Bellevue Boys and Girls Club. Mem.: Entertainment Software Assn. (chmn.). Office: Microsoft Corp One Microsoft Way Redmond WA 98052-6399

BACHMAN, BRIAN RICHARD, former electronics executive; b. Aurora, Ill., Jan. 14, 1945; BS, U. Ill., 1967; MBA, U. Chgo., 1969. With Gen. Electric, Syracuse, N.Y., 1982-85, TRW, Schaumburg, Ill., 1985-87; pres. Gen. Semiconductor Industries, Tempe, Ariz., 1987-90; group gen. mgr. ITT Cannon, Santa Ana, Calif., 1990-91; v.p., group gen. mgr. Philips Semiconductor, Sunnyvale, Calif., 1991. Office: Philips Semiconductors 811 E Arques Ave Sunnyvale CA 94085-4523

BACHMAN, DAVID CHRISTIAN, orthopedic surgeon; b. Peoria, Ill., Apr. 11, 1934; s. Leland Alvin and Elsie May (Springer) B.; m. Betty June Foster, Sept. 9, 1956; children: Lynne Allison, Laura; m. Karen Jean McDaniel, Oct. 21, 2006. BA, Goshen Coll., 1958; MD, Northwestern U., 1962. Intern Cook County Hosp., Chgo., 1962-63; resident in orthopaedic surgery Northwestern U. Med. Sch., 1963-67; practice medicine specializing in orthopaedic surgery Chgo., 1967-80; practice specializing in ski injuries, 1980-93; with Mountain Med. Services, Telluride, Colo., 1982-87, Ouray Mountain Rescue Team, Inc., Ouray Med. Ctr., Ouray, Colo.; coroner Ouray County, Colo., 1982-93; mem. staffs Northwestern Meml. Hosp., Children's Meml. Hosp., Grant hosp., Chgo., 1967-80, Montrose Meml. Hosp., Colo., 1984-93; med. cons. Western Area U.S. Postal Svc. Dir. Ctr. for Sports Medicine, Northwestern U. Med. Sch., 1978-80; team physician Chgo. Bulls, Nat. Basketball Assn., 1967-80; asst. prof. dept. orthop. surgery Northwestern U. Med. Sch., 1967-80; syndicated columnist on sports medicine Dr. Jock, 1976-90; cons. Western area U.S. Postal Svc., 1996-97; sr. area med. dir. Western Area U.S. Postal Svc., 1997-2002, Pacific Arae U.S. Postal Svc., 2002-06, nat. med. adminstr. U.S. Postal Svc., 2006—. Author: (with Marilyn Preston) Dear Doctor Jock... The Peoples Guide to Sports and Fitness, 1980, (with others) The Diet That Lets You Cheat, 1983, (with Tod Bacigalupi) The Way it Was, 1990, (with Robert Pickering) The Use of Forensic Anthropology, 1996. Elder Presbyn. Ch., 1965—; rsch. assoc. anthropology dept. Denver Mus. Natural History, 1994-99. Mem. ACS, Am. Acad. Orthop. Surgery, Am. Orthop. Soc. for Sports Medicine, Phi Rho Sigma. Presbyterian. Home and Office: 849 W Golf Course Pl Green Valley AZ 85622 Office Phone: 520-388-5202. Business E-Mail: david.c.bachman@usps.gov.

BACHRACH, CHARLES LEWIS, advertising agency executive; b. NYC, Feb. 22, 1946; s. Herbert and Lilla Clare (Blumberg) B.; m. Lois Susan Davis, Sept. 12, 1968; 1 dau., Jennifer Leigh. BS, Ithaca Coll., NY, 1968. Assoc. producer MPO Sports Co., NYC, 1968-69; unit mgr. NBC, NYC, 1969; with Ogilvy & Mather, Inc., NYC, 1969—, sr. v.p. broadcast, 1978-83, dir. Network and Programming Dept; sr. v.p. network and programming Western Internat. Media, 1983-89, exec. v.p., 1989—; pres. Western Internat. Syndication, 1983—; sr. v.p., dir. network and program purchasing Rubin Postaer & Assocs., LA, 1990-92, exec. v.p., dir. media and resources and programming, 1992—. Vis. prof. Ithaca Coll. Sch. Communications; vis. lectr. New Sch.; guest lectr. UCLA, Calif. State, L.A., Marymount Coll.; guest commentator NPR, CNN, NBC. Contbr. articles to profl. publs. Judge Internat. Emmy Awards.; Lobbyist N.Y. State pvt. colls.; bd. dirs. Caption Ctr., 1992. Recipient Disting. Alumni award Ithaca Coll., 1980, Aid to Advt. Edn. award Am. Advt. Fedn., 1986, Media Maven award Advt. Age, 1996; named One of Top 100 Young People in Advt., 1985. Mem. AAAA (com. broadcast network and programming), TV Acad. Arts and Scis., L.A. Advt. Club (bd. dirs. 1989). Office: Rubin Postaer and Assocs 1333 2d St Santa Monica CA 90401-1100 Home: 3424 French Daisy St Las Vegas NV 89135-2824

BACKLAR, PATRICIA, education educator; Attended, Vassar Coll., 1950, McGill U., 1951, Yale U. Sch. Drama, 1953. Sr. scholar Oregon Health Scis. U.; rsch. assoc. prof. bioethics dept. philosophy Portland State U., adj. asst. prof. dept. psychiatry. Mem. Nat. Bioethics Adv. Commn., 1996—2001; co-chair, Multnomah CountyMental health Addictions Advisory Coun. 2005-; co-chair, Oreg. Advisory Com. Genetic Privacy & rsch., 2001-; ethics com. Oreg. State Hosp., 1990-, bd. dirs. Nat. Cmty. Mental Helthcare Coun., 1994-98. Author: The Family Face of Schizophrenia, 1994; co-author, co-editor: Ethics in Community Mental Health, 2002 contbr. articles to profl. jours. Office Phone: 503-725-3499. Business E-Mail: backlarp@pdx.edu.

BACKUS, GEORGE EDWARD, theoretical geophysicist; b. Chgo., May 24, 1930; s. Milo and Dora (Dare) B.; m. Elizabeth Evelyn Allen, Nov. 15, 1961 (div. 1971); children: Benjamin, Brian, Emily; m. Varda Esther Peller, Jan. 8, 1977 PhB, U. Chgo., 1947, BS in Math., 1948, MS in Math. and Physics, 1950-53, PhD in Physics, 1956; D honoris causa, Inst. de Physique de Globe, Paris, 1995. Jr. mathematician Inst. for Air Weapons, Chgo., 1951-53; physicist Project Matterhorn, Princeton, NJ, 1957-58; asst. prof. math. MIT, Cambridge, 1958-60; assoc. prof. geophysics U. Calif. San Diego, La Jolla, 1960-62, prof. geophysics, 1962-94, rsch. prof. geophysics, 1994-99, prof. geophys. emeritus, 1999—. Mem. vist. com. Institut de Physique du Globe de Paris, 1987; co-chmn. Internat. Working Group on Magnetic Field Satellites, 1983-90; chair acad. senate U. Calif., San Diego, 1992-93. Contbr. articles to profl. jours. Guggenheim Found. fellow, 1963, 71; Royal Soc. Arts fellow, London, 1970— Fellow Royal Astron. Soc. (Gold medal 1986), Am. Geophys. Union (John Adam Fleming medal 1986); mem. NAS (com. on grants and fellowships Day Fund 1974-79, com. on sci. and pub. policy 1971-74), Académie des Sciences (France), Am. Math. Soc., Math. Assn. Am., Soc. for Indsl. and Applied Math., Am. Geophys. Union. Avocations: skiing, swimming, bicycling, hiking, history. Office: IGPP U Calif San Diego La Jolla CA 92093-0225 Home Phone: 858-452-8972. E-mail: gbackus@ucsd.edu.

BACON, ROBERT L., state legislator; b. Galesburg, Ill., July 14, 1935; s. Harry C. and Florence Bacon; m. Bev; 1 child: Beth. BA, Ill. State U., Normal, 1957; MA, U. No. Colo., Greeley, 1961. Tchr., Chatsworth, Ill., 1956—59, Windsor, Colo., 1959—60, Ft. Collins, Colo., 1960—91; adj. prof. Front Range CC, Larimer Campus, 1992—97; mem. Dist. 53 Colo. House of Reps., Denver, 1997—2002; mem. Dist. 14 Colo. State Senate, Denver, 2004—. Mem. Poudre Sch. Dist. Bd. Edn., 1991—. Named Disting. Tchr. Tchr. Award Found., 1978; Freshman Legislator of Yr. Sierra Club, 1998; named to All State Sch. Bd. Colo. Assn. Sch. Bds., 1996; recipient Legislature Excellence award, 1998. Mem. Communities in Schs. (bd. dirs. 1995-). Democrat. Unitarian. Office: Colo State Capitol 200 E Colfax Denver CO 80203 Office Phone: 303-866-4841. Business E-Mail: bob.bacon.senate@state.co.us.*

BADASH, LAWRENCE, science history educator; b. Bklyn., May 8, 1934; s. Joseph and Dorothy (Langa) B.; children: Lisa, Bruce. BS in Physics, Rensselaer Poly. Inst., 1956; PhD in History of Sci., Yale U., 1964. Instr. Yale. U., New Haven, 1964—65, research assoc., 1965-66; from asst. to assoc. prof. U. Calif., Santa Barbara, 1966-79, prof. history of sci., 1979—2002, prof. emeritus, 2002—. Dir. summer seminar on global security and arms control U. Calif., 1983, 86, energy rsch. group, 1992, pacific rim program mem., 1993-95; cons. Nuclear Age Peace Found., Santa Barbara, 1984-90. Author: Radioactivity in Am., 1979, Kapitza, Rutherford, and the Kremlin, 1985, Scientists and the Development of Nuclear Weapons, 1995, A Nuclear Winter's Jale: Science & Polities in The 1980, 2009; editor: Rutherford and Boltwood, Letters on Radioactivity, 1969; Reminiscences of Los Alamos, 1943-45, 1980. Bd. dirs. Santa Barbara chpt. ACLU, 1971-86, 96—2008, pres., 1982-84, 96-98; nat. bd. dirs. Com. for a Sane Nuclear Policy, Washington, 1972-81; mem. Los Padres Search and Rescue Team, Santa Barbara, 1981-94. Lt. (j.g.) USN, 1956-59. Grantee, NSF, Cambridge, Eng., 1965-66, 69-72, 90-92, Am. Philos. Soc., New Zealand, 1979-80, Inst. on Global Conflict and Cooperation, Univ. Calif., 1983-87; J.S. Guggenheim fellow, 1984-85. Fellow AAAS (sect. mem. at large 1988-92), Am. Phys. Soc. (chmn. divsn. of history of physics 1988-89, exec. com. forum on physics and society 1991-93); mem. History of Sci. Soc. (founder West Coast chpt., chpt. bd. dirs. 1971-73, nat. coun. 1975-78). Democrat. Jewish. Avocation: backpacking. Office: Univ Calif Dept History Santa Barbara CA 93106-9410

BADEN, COLIN, apparel executive; b. Concord, Mass., Mar. 27, 1962; MArch, U. Ariz., 1986. Ptnr. Lewis Architects, Seattle, 1990—96; dir. design Oakley, Inc., 1996—97, v.p. design, 1997—99, pres., 1999—. Named one of Most Influential People in the World of Sports, Bus. Week, 2007. Office: Oakley Inc 1 Icon Foothill Ranch CA 92610

BADGLEY, PENN, actor; b. Balt., Nov. 1, 1986; Attended, Santa Monica City Coll. Actor(voice): (video game) Mario Golf 64, 1999, Mario Tennis, 2000,: (TV series) The Young and the Restless, 2000—01, Do Over, 2002—03, The Mountain, 2004—05, The Bedford Diaries, 2006, Gossip Girl, 2007—; (films) The Fluffer, 2001, Debating Robert Lee, 2004, John Tucker Must Die, 2006, Drive Thru, 2007, (guest appearance): (TV series) Will & Grace, 1999, Daddio, 2000, Bull, 2000, The Brothers Garcia, 2000, 2002, What I Like About You, 2002, The Twilight Zone, 2003. Nominee Young Artist Award, 2001. Avocations: surfing, snowboarding, skiing. Office: c/o Raw Talent 9615 Brighton Way, Ste 300 Beverly Hills CA 90210 also: c/o CESD Talent Agency Ste 130/135 10635 Santa Monica Blvd Los Angeles CA 90025

BADGLEY, THEODORE MCBRIDE, retired psychiatrist, neurologist; b. Salem, Ala., June 27, 1925; s. Roy Joseph and Fannie (Limbaugh) B.; m. Mary Bennett Wells, Dec. 30, 1945; children: Justice O'Neil, Jan Badgley, Mona Jean Covey, Jason Wells, James John, Mary Rose Bleier. Student, Occidental Coll., 1942-44; MD, U. So. Calif., 1949. Diplomate: Am. Bd. Psychiatry and Neurology. Intern Letterman Gen. Hosp., San Francisco, 1949-50, resident in psychiatry, 1950-53; commd. capt. M.C. U.S. Army, 1950, advanced through grades to lt. col., 1967; chief mental hygiene cons. service Ft. Gordon, Ga.; and asso. clin. prof. psychiatry and neurology Med. Coll. Ga., 1954-55; resident in neurology Walter Reed Gen. Hosp., Washington, 1955-57, asst. chief psychiatry service, 1957-59, chief psychiatry service, 1959-62, asst. chief dept. psychiatry and neurology, 1962-63, dir. edn. and tng. psychiatry, 1957-63; chief dept. psychiatry and neurology U.S. Army Gen. Hosp., Landstuhl, Germany, 1963-66; chief psychiatry outpatient dept. Letterman Gen. Hosp., 1966-67; ret., 1967; dir. Kern View Mental Health Center, Bakersfield, Calif., 1967-69; pvt. practice medicine specializing in med. and forensic neuropsychiatry Bakersfield, 1967-93; pres. Sans Doloroso Inst., Bakersfield, 1969-93. Lectr. community health service orgns., profl. confs., seminars. Contbr. articles to profl. jours. Fellow Am. Psychiat. Assn. (disting. life); mem. Kern County Psychiat. Soc. (pres. 1972-93), Kern County Med. Soc. (pres. 1981). Personal E-mail: mcbadge@juno.com.

BADIE, RONALD PETER, banker; b. Elizabeth, NJ, Dec. 13, 1942; s. R. Peter and Madeline E. (Knoop) B.; m. Fabiana Duclos; children: Tracey, Tamara, Tara, Gabrielle, Alexandra. BS, Bucknell U., 1964; MBA, NYU, 1971. Sr. v.p. Bankers Trust Co., NYC, 1979-86, mng. dir. LA, 1986-96; sr. mng. dir. Bankers Trust Co. Calif., LA, 1996-99; mng. dir. Deutsche Banc Alex Brown, 1999-2001, v. chmn., 2001—. Mem. adv. bd. Green Equity Investors II; vice chair Deutsche Bank Alex Brown, 2001. Mem. adv. bd. entrepreneurial studies program UCLA Sch. Mgmt., Stonington Capital Appreciation Fund. Republican. Home: 3747 Chevy Chase Dr La Canada Flintridge CA 91011-4163 Office: Deutsche Banc Alex Brown 300 S Grand Ave Los Angeles CA 90071-3109

BAER, RICHARD N., lawyer, telecommunications industry executive; b. Glen Cove, NY, Mar. 30, 1957; married; 2 children. BA, Columbia U., NYC, 1979; JD, Duke U., Durham, NC, 1983. Bar: NY 1984, Colo. Asst. dist. atty., Bklyn., 1983—88; staff atty. SEC, Washington, 1988; assoc. Rosenman & Colin, NYC, 1988—92; chmn. litig. dept. Sherman & Howard, Denver, 1992—2000; spl. legal counsel to chmn. and CEO Richard C. Notebaert Qwest Comm. Internat. Inc., Denver, 2001—02, exec. v.p., gen. counsel, 2002—, chief adminstrv. officer, 2008—. Office: Qwest Comm Internat Inc Legal Dept 1801 California St Denver CO 80202 Office Phone: 303-992-2811. Office Fax: 303-383-8444. E-mail: rich.baer@qwest.com.

BAER, WALTER S., think-tank executive; b. Chgo., July 27, 1937; s. Walter S., Jr. and Margaret S. (Mayer) B.; m. Miriam R. Schenker, June 18, 1959 (div. 1987); children: David W., Alan B.; m. Jeri Weiss, Oct. 23, 1988. BS, Calif. Inst. Tech., 1959; PhD (NSF fellow), U. Wis., 1964. Rsch. physicist Bell Telephone Labs., Murray Hill, NJ, 1964-66; White House fellow Washington, 1966-67; White House sci. adv. staff, 1967-69; cons. and sr. scientist RAND Corp., Santa Monica, Calif., 1970-81, dir. energy policy program, 1978-81; dir. advanced tech. Times Mirror Co., Los Angeles, 1981-89; deputy v.p. domestic rsch. RAND Corp., Santa Monica, Calif., 1990—2006; sr. fellow U. So. Calif., Annenberg Sch. Comm., LA, 2006—. Cons. UN, maj. U.S. corps, 1970—; dir. Aspen (Colo.) Cable TV Workshop, 1972-73, L.A. Ednl. Partnership; pres. KCRW Found., Santa Monica, Calif.; adv. bd. Columbia U. Inst. Tele-Info., U.S. Com. for Internat. Inst. Applied Systems Analysis; dir. Am. Tng. Internat.; mem. gov. coun. on info. tech. State of Calif. Author: Interactive Television, 1971, Cable Television: A Handbook for Decisionmaking, 1973, also articles; editor: The Electronic Box Office, 1974, wc/ RAND Cable Television Series, 1974; editorial bd.: Telecommunications Policy, 1976—, Internat. Ency. Communications. Mem. European Community Visitor, 1978. Recipient U. Wis. award for excellence in teaching, 1960; Preceptor award Broadcast Industry Conf., 1974— Fellow AAAS (chmn. Indsl. Sci. Sec. 1992-93); mem. IEEE (mem. com. on comm. and info. policy 1994—), Am. Phys. Soc., Internat. Inst. Communications, Sigma Xi. Office: U So Calif Annenberg Ctr Comm Los Angeles CA 90089-7725 Office Phone: 310-488-3444. Business E-Mail: wbaer@usc.edu.

BAERWALD, SUSAN GRAD, television broadcasting company executive producer; b. Long Branch, N.J., June 18, 1944; d. Bernard John and Marian Grad; m. Paul Baerwald, July 1, 1969; children: Joshua, Samuel. Degre des Arts and Lettres, Sorbonne, Paris, 1965; BA, Sarah Lawrence Coll., 1966. Script analyst United Artists, L.A., 1978-80; v.p. devel. Gordon/Eisner Prodns., L.A., 1980-81; mgr. mini-series and novels for TV, NBC, Burbank, Calif., 1981-82, dir. mini-series and novels for TV, 1982, v.p. mini-series and novels for TV, 1982-89; exec. producer NBC Prodns., 1989-95, Savoy Pictures TV, 1995-96, Citadel Entertainment, 1996-97; sr. lectr. Am. Film Inst., 1999. Producer (TV movies) Blind Faith, 1990, One Spl. Victory, 1991, Cruel Doubt, 1992, A Time to Heal, 1994, Inflammable, 1995 (TV miniseries) Lucky/Chances, 1990. Bd. dirs. The Paper Bag Players, N.Y.C., 1974—, Women in Film Found., 2000, Non-Profit Alliance W.O.M.E.N., Inc., 1998; vol. L.A. Children's Mus., 1978-80; mem. awards com. Scott Newman Found., 1982-84; bd. dirs. L.A. Goal, 1996—. Recipient Vol. Incentive award NBC, 1983. Mem. ATAS (bd. govs. 1993-97, nat. awards chmn. 1997-98), Am. Film Inst., Hollywood Radio and TV Soc.

BAESEL, STUART OLIVER, architect; b. Charlotte, NC, Feb. 5, 1925; s. Edward Franklin and Rose (Engel) B.; m. Betsey London Cordon, Nov. 23, 1949; children— Stuart Oliver, Betsey London, Cordon Telfair Student, U. N.C., 1940-42, Ecole des Beaux Arts, Fountainbleau, France, 1948; B.Arch., N.C. State U., 1950; M.Arch., Cranbrook Acad. Art, 1951. Architect A.G. Odell, Jr. & Assocs., Charlotte, 1951-55; architect-designer Skidmore, Owings, Merrill, NYC, 1955-59, LBC & W Assocs., Columbia, SC, 1959-65; dir. design J.N. Pease Assocs., Charlotte, 1965-72; mem. faculty Architecture Sch. Calif. State U., Pomona, 1972-74; prin. Stuart Baesel, Architect, Design Group, La Jolla, Calif., 1972—. Dir., sec. treas. Design World, Inc., Charlotte, 1968-72; dir., pres. Space Planning Assocs., Charlotte, 1966-72 Editor: Rev. Architecture, Columbia, S.C., 1962-65 Cons. Charlotte Planning Bd., 1954. Served with USAAF, 1943-46, PTO Recipient various profl. awards, including Honor award S.C. chpt. AIA, 1964, 65, 66, N.C. chpt. AIA, 1956, 66, 68, 69, 70, 72 Fellow AIA (bd. dirs. N.C.); mem. N.Y. Archtl. League, Phi Delta Theta Clubs: La Jolla Beach and Tennis. Episcopalian. Home: 303 Coast Blvd Unit 1 La Jolla CA 92037-4635 Office: PO Box 1237 La Jolla CA 92038-1237

BAEZ, JOAN CHANDOS, vocalist; b. SI, NY, Jan. 9, 1941; d. Albert V. and Joan (Bridge) B.; m. David Victor Harris, Mar. 1968 (div. 1973); 1 son, Gabriel Earl. Appeared in coffeehouses, Gate of Horn, Chgo., 1958, Ballad Room, Club 47, 1958-68, Newport (R.I.) Folk Festival, 1959-69, 85, 87, 90, 92, 93, 95, extended tours to colls. and concert halls, 1960s, appeared Town Hall and Carnegie Hall, 1962, 67, 68, U.S. tours, 1970—, concert tours in Japan, 1966, 82, Europe, 1970-73, 80, 83-84, 87-90, 93—, Australia, 1985; rec. artist for Vanguard Records, 1960-72, A&M, 1973-76, Portrait Records, 1977-80, Gold Castle Records, 1986-89, Virgin Records, 1990-93, Grapevine Label Records (UK), 1995-97, Guardian Records, 1995-97, European record albums, 1981, 83, award 8 gold albums, 1 gold single; albums include Gone From Danger, 1997, Rare, Live & Classic (box set), 1993, Dark Chords on a Big Guitar, 2003, Bowery Songs, 2005; author: Joan Baez Songbook, 1964, (biography) Daybreak, 1968, (with David Harris) Coming Out, 1971, And a Voice to Sing With, 1987, (songbook) An Then I Wrote, 1979. Extensive TV appearances and speaking tours U.S. and Can. for anti-militarism, 1967-68; visit to Dem. Republic of Vietnam, 1972, visit to war torn Bosnia-Herzegovina, 1993; founder, v.p. Inst. for Study Nonviolence (now Resource Ctr. for Nonviolence, Santa Cruz, Calif.), Palo Alto, Calif., 1965; mem. nat. adv. coun. Amnesty Internat., 1974-92; founder, pres. Humanitas/Internat. Human Rights Com., 1979-92; condr. fact-finding mission to refugee camps, S.E. Asia, Oct. 1979; began refusing payment of war taxes, 1964; arrested for civil disobedience opposing draft, Oct., Dec., 1967. Office: Diamonds & Rust Prodns PO Box 1026 Menlo Park CA 94026-1026 Office Phone: 650-328-0266.

BAGDIKIAN, BEN HAIG, journalist, educator; b. Marash, Turkey, Jan. 30, 1920; came to U.S., 1920, naturalized, 1926; s. Aram Theodore and Daisy (Uvezian) B.; m. Elizabeth Ogasapian, Oct. 2, 1942 (div. 1972); children: Christopher Ben, Frederick Haig; m. Betty L. Medsger, 1973 (div.); m. Marlene Griffith, 1983 AB, Clark U., 1941, LittD, 1963; LHD, Brown U., 1961, U. R.I., 1992. Reporter Springfield (Mass.) Morning Union, 1941-42; assoc. editor Periodical House, Inc., NYC, 1946; successively reporter, fgn. corr., chief Washington corr. Providence Jour., 1947-62; contbg. editor Saturday Evening Post, 1963-67; project dir. study of future U.S. news media Rand Corp., 1967-69; asst. mng. editor for nat. news Washington Post, 1970-71, asst. mng. editor, ombudsman, 1971-72; nat. corr. Columbia Journalism Review, 1972-74; prof. Grad. Sch. Journalism U. Calif., Berkeley, 1976-90, dean, Grad. Sch. Journalism, 1985-88, prof. emeritus, Grad. Sch. Journalism, 1990—. Keynote spkr. Coun. Europe Ministerial Conf. on Mass Media Policy, Kiev, Ukraine, 2005. Author: In the Midst of Plenty: The poor in America, 1964, The Information Machines: Their Impact on Men and the Media, 1971, The Shame of the Prisons, 1972, The Effete Conspiracy, 1972, Caged: Eight Prisoners and Their Keepers, 1976, The Media Monopoly, 1983, 6th edit., 2000, Double Vision: Reflections on My Heritage, Life and Profession, 1995, The New Media Monopoly, 2004; also pamphlets; contbr.: The Kennedy Circle, 1961; editor: Man's Contracting World in an Expanding Universe, 1959; mem. editl. bd. Jour. Investigative Reporters and Editors, 1980-88. Mem. steering com. Nat. Prison Project, 1974-82; trustee Clark U., 1964-76; bd. dirs. Nat. Capital Area Civil Liberties Union, 1964-66, Com. to Protect Journalists, 1981-88, Data Ctr., Oakland, Calif., 1990-97; pres. Lowell Mellett Fund for Free an Responsible Press, 1965-76; acad. adv. bd. Nat. Citizens Com. for Broadcasting, 1978—; judge Ten Most Censored Stories, 1976-98. Recipient George Foster Peabody award, 1951, Sidney Hillman Found. award, 1956, Most Perceptive Critic citation Am. Soc. Journalism Adminstrs., 1978, Career Achievement award Soc. Profl. Journalists, John and Catherine Zenger award, 1996, James Madison award ALA, 1998, Wayne Danielson award, U. Tex., 2005, Lifetime Achievement award Nat. Soc. Profl. Journalists, 2007, Nat. Conf., Free Press, Memphis, 2007; named to RI Journalism Hall of Fame, 1992; fellow Ogden Reid Found., 1956, Guggenheim fellow, 1961-62. Mem. ACLU. Fellowship named after him. Home: 25 Stonewall Rd Berkeley CA 94705-1414 Home Phone: 510-848-2226. Personal E-mail: benmar@berkeley.edu.

BAGLEY, JAMES W., semiconductor equipment company executive; b. Jan. 19, 1939; BS, MS, Miss. State U. With Tex. Instruments, 1966-79; sr. v.p. Applied Materials, Inc., 1979-87, pres., CEO, 1987-96; CEO Lam Rsch. Corp., Fremont, Calif., 1997—98, chmn., CEO, 1998—2005, exec. chmn., 2005—. Bd. dirs. KLA-Tencor, Kulicke & Soffa Industries, Teradyne, Micron Tech., Inc., Semi/SEMATECH. Office: 4650 Cushing Pkwy Fremont CA 94538-6401

BAGLEY, WILLIAM THOMPSON, lawyer; b. San Francisco, June 29, 1928; s. Nino J. and Rita V. (Thompson) Baglietto; m. Diane Lenore Oldham, June 20, 1965; children: Lynn Lorene, William Thompson, Walter William, Shana Angela, Tracy Elizabeth. AB, U. Calif., Berkeley, 1949, JD, 1952. Bar: Calif. 1953, U.S. Supreme Ct. 1967. Atty. Pacific Gas & Electric Co., 1952-56; assoc. Gardiner, Riede & Elliott, San Rafael, Calif., 1956-60; ptnr. Bagley Bernt & Bianchi, San Rafael, 1961-74; mem. Calif. Legis., 1961-74; chmn. Commodity Futures Trading Commn., Washington, 1975-79; ptnr. Nossaman, Guthner, Knox and Elliott, San Francisco, 1980—. Mem. Calif. Pub. Utilities Commn., 1983-86; mem. Calif. Transp. Commn., 1983-89, chmn., 1987-88. Bd. editors Calif. Law Rev., 1951-52. Bd. regents U. Calif., 1989-2002; trustee Marin Cmty. Found., 2004—; bd. dirs. Nat. Futures Assn., Calif. Coun. Environ. and Econ. Balance, Edmund G. Brown Inst. Govtl. Affairs, L.A.; chmn. bd. Calif. Rep. League, 1980-82. Recipient Freedom of Info. award Sigma Delta Chi, 1970, Golden Bear award Calif. Pk. Commn., 1973; named Most Effective Assemblyman, Capitol Press Corps, 1969, Legislator of Yr., Calif. Trial Lawyers Assn., 1970, Alumnus of Yr., U. Calif. Alumni Assn., 2002. Mem. ABA, Calif. State Bar Assn., Three Stooges Fan Club, Elks Club (life), Phi Beta Kappa, Alpha Tau Omega. Presbyterian. Home Phone: 415-453-3355; Office Phone: 415-398-3600.

BAHR, EHRHARD, Germanic languages and literature educator; b. Kiel, Germany, Aug. 21, 1932; came to U.S., 1956; s. Klaus and Gisela (Badenhausen) B.; m. Diana Meyers, Nov. 21, 1973; stepchildren: Gary, Timothy, Christopher. Student, U. Heidelberg, Germany, 1952-53, U. Freiburg, 1953-56; MS Ed. (Fulbright scholar), U. Kans., 1956-58; postgrad., U. Cologne, 1959-61; PhD, U. Calif., Berkeley, 1968. Asst. prof. German UCLA, 1968-70, assoc. prof., 1970-72, prof., 1972—2003, prof. emeritus, 2003—, chmn. dept. Germanic langs., 1981-84, 93-98, chair grad. council, 1988-89. Author: Irony in the Late Works of Goethe, 1972, Georg Lukacs, 1970, Ernst Bloch, 1974, Nelly Sachs, 1980, Weimar on the Pacific: German Exile Culture in Los Angeles and the Crisis of Modernism, 2007, papers back, 2008; editor: Kant, What is Enlightenment?, 1974, Goethe, Wilhelm, Meister's Apprenticeship, 1982, Goethe, Wilhelm, Meister's Journeyman Years, 1982, History of German Literature, 3 vols., 1987—88, 2nd edit., 1998—99, The Novel as Archive: The Genesis, Reception and Criticism of Goethe's Wilhelm Meisters Wanderjahre, 1988; co-editor: The Internalized Revolution: German Reactions to the French Revolution, 1789-1989, 1992; commentary Thomas Mann: Death in Venice, 1991, reprint, 2005, Goethe: Wilhelm Meister's Apprenticeship, 1982; contbr. articles to profl. jour. Recipient Disting. Teaching award UCLA, 1970, Humanities Inst. award, 1972, summer stipend NEH, 1978 Mem. MLA, Am. Soc. 18th Century Studies, Am. Assn. Tchrs. German, German Studies Assn. (pres. 1987-88), Lessing Soc., Goethe Soc. N.Am. (exec. sec. 1979-89, pres. 1995-97). Office: UCLA Dept Germanic Langs Los Angeles CA 90095-1539 Office Phone: 310-825-3955. Business E-Mail: bahr@humnet.ucla.edu.

BAHR, HOWARD MINER, sociologist, educator; b. Provo, Utah, Feb. 21, 1938; s. A. Francis and Louie Jean (Miner) B.; m. Rosemary Frances Smith, Aug. 28, 1961 (div. 1985); children: Bonnie Louise, Howard McKay, Rowena Ruth, Tanya Lavonne, Christopher J., Laura L., Stephen S., Rachel M.; m. Kathleen Slaugh, May 1, 1986; children: Alden Keith, Jonathan Andrew, Dmitry Michael, Anton Hinckley, Sergei David. BA with honors, Brigham Young U., 1962; MA in Sociology, U. Tex., 1964, PhD, 1965. Rsch. assoc. Columbia U., NYC, 1965-68; vis. lectr., summer 1968; lectr. in sociology NYU, 1967-68, Bklyn. Coll., CUNY, 1967; assoc. prof. sociology Wash. State U., Pullman, 1968-73, prof., 1972-73, chmn. dept. rural sociology, 1971-73; prof. sociology Brigham Young U., Provo, Utah, 1973—; dir. Family Rsch. Inst., 1977-83; fellow David M. Kennedy, 1992. Virginia F. Culter lectr., 1997; vis. prof. sociology U. Va., 1976-77, 84-85. Author: Skid Row: An Introduction to Disaffiliation, 1973, Old Men Drunk and Sober, 1974, Women Alone: The Disaffiliation of Urban Females, 1976, American Ethnicity, 1979, Sunshine Widows: Adapting to Sudden Bereavement, 1980, Middletown Families, 1982, All Faithful People: Change and Continuity in Middletown's Religion, 1983, Life in Large Families, 1983, Divorce and Remarriage: Problems, Adaptations and Adjustments, 1983, Social Science Research Methods, 1984, Recent Social Trends in the United States 1960-90, 1991, Dine' Bibliography to the 1990's, 1999, The Navajo as Seen By the Franciscans, 1898-1921: A Sourcebook, 2004; contbr. articles to profl. jours.; assoc. editor: Rural Sociology, 1978-83, Jour. Marriage and the Family, 1978-83. NIMH grantee, 1968-70, 71-73; NSF grantee, 1971-72, 76-80 Mem. Soc. Applied Anthropology, Rural Sociol. Assn., Soc. Sci. Study of Religion. Mem. Lds Ch. Office: Brigham Young U Dept Sociology 2021 JFSB Provo UT 84602 Home Phone: 801-222-9703; Office Phone: 801-422-6275. Business E-Mail: hmbahr@byu.edu.

BAIER, MARIA, Councilwoman; m. Christopher Baier; children: Elizabeth, Christiana. BA, Ariz. State U.; JD, U. Ariz. Bar: Ariz. Pub. info. officer Ariz. Atty. Gen. Office; ind. contractor San Francisco Examiner; speech writer, press officer & policy adv. Ariz. Govs. Office; conservation fin. & mktg. dir. Trust for Pub. Land Ariz. Field Office; pres. & CEO Valley Partnership, 2004—06; councilwoman, Dist. 3 Phoenix City Coun., 2008—. Chmn. Econ., Commerce & Sustainability Com.; vice chmn. Agricultural Protection Commn.; mem. Downtown, Aviation, Housing & Neighborhoods Coms., Growing Smarter Oversight Coun., Conservation Acquisition Bd. Bd. mem. Phoenix Zoo, Ariz. League of Conservation Voters, Ariz. Adv. Com. Trust for Pub. Lands Conservation Campaign. Office: 200 W Washington St 11th Fl Phoenix AZ 85003 Office Phone: 602-262-7441. Office Fax: 602-534-4190. Business E-Mail: council.district.3@phoenix.gov.*

BAILAR, BARBARA ANN, retired statistician; b. Monroe, Mich., Nov. 24, 1935; d. Malcolm Laurie and Clara Florence (Parent) Dezendorf; m. John Francis Powell (div. 1966); 1 child, Pamela; m. John Christian Bailar; 1 child, Melissa. BA, SUNY, 1956; MS, Va.

Poly. Inst., 1965; PhD, Am. U., 1972. With Bur. of Census, Washington, 1958-88, chief Ctr. Rsch. Measurement Methods, 1973-79, assoc. dir. for statis. standards and methodology, 1979-88; exec. dir. Am. Statis. Assn., Alexandria, Va., 1988-95; sr. v.p. for survey rsch. Nat. Opinion Rsch. Ctr., Chgo., 1995—2001. Instr. George Washington U., 1984-85; head dept. math. and stats. USDA Grad. Sch., Washington, 1972-87. Contbr. articles, book chpts. to profl. publs. Pres. bd. dirs. Harbour Sq. Coop., Washington, 1988-89. Recipient Silver medal U.S. Dept. Commerce, 1980. Fellow Am. Statis. Assn. (pres. 1987); mem. AAAS (chair sect. stats. 1984-85), Internat. Assn. Survey Statisticians (pres. 1989-91), Internat. Statis. Inst. (Pres.'s invited speaker 1983, v.p. 1993-95), Cosmos Club. Personal E-mail: babailar@aol.com.

BAILEY, CHAMP, professional football player; b. Folkston, Ga., June 22, 1978; m. Hanady Bailey; 1 child. Student, U. GA. Cornerback Washington Redskins, 1999—2003, Denver Broncos, 2004—. Recipient Bronko Nagurski award, 1998; named NCAA All-Am., 1998, First Team All-Pro, NFL, 2004—06; named to Nat. Football Conf. Pro Bowl Team, 2000—03, Am. Football Conf. Pro Bowl Team, 2004—07. Achievements include leading the NFL in: interception return touchdowns, 2005, interceptions, 2006, interception return yards, 2006. Office: c/o Denver Broncos 13655 Broncos Pkwy Englewood CO 80112

BAILEY, DAVID H., computer scientist; married; 4 children. BS in Math., Brigham Young U., 1972; PhD in Math., Stanford U., 1976. Computer scientist U.S. Govt., Fort Meade, Md., 1976-80, TRW/ESL, Inc., Sunnyvale, Calif., 1980-82, SRI Internat., Menlo Park, Calif., 1982-84, NASA Ames Rsch. Ctr., Moffett Field, Calif., 1984-98, Lawrence Berkeley Lab., Berkeley, Calif., 1998—. Mem. editl. bd, referee numerous profl. jours.; presenter in field; contbr. articles to profl. jours. Recipient Chauvenet prize Math. Assn. Am., 1993, Merten Hasse prize, 1993. Mem. IEEE Computer Soc. (Sidney Fernbach award 1993), Soc. Indsl. and Applied Math., Assn. for Computing Machinery. Office: Lawrence Berkeley Lab Mail Stop 50B 2239 Berkeley CA 94720-0001 E-mail: dhbailey@lbl.gov.

BAILEY, DAVID NELSON, pathology educator, dean, academic administrator; b. Anderson, Ind., June 21, 1945; s. Omer Nelson and Louise Genevieve (Hurst) B. BS with high distinction, Ind. U., 1967; MD, Yale U., 1973. Diplomate Nat. Bd. Med. Examiners, Am. Bd. Pathology (Clin. and Chem. Pathology). Clin. fellow dept. lab. medicine Yale U., 1973-75; asst. resident specializing in clin. pathology Yale-New Haven Hosp., 1975-76, chief resident specializing in clin. pathology, 1976-77; asst. prof. pathology U. Calif., San Diego, 1977-81, assoc. prof. pathology, 1981-86, prof. pathology, 1986—, head div. lab. medicine, 1983-89, 94-98, acting chmn., 1986-88, chmn. dept. pathology, 1988—99, 2000—01; dir. toxicology lab. U. Calif. Med. Ctr., San Diego, 1977—, dir. clin. labs., 1982-99, interim vice chancellor for health scis., dean, 1999-2000, 2006—, dep. vice chancellor for health scis., 2001—, dean for faculty/student matters, 2003—. Mem. editorial bd. Jour. Analytical Toxicology, 1979—, Clin. Chemistry Jour., 1983-93, Am. Jour. Clin. Pathology, 1991—; contbr. articles to profl. jours. Recipient Gerald T. Evans award Acad. Clin. Lab. Physicians and Scientists, 1993; Merit scholar Ind. U., 1963-65, Arthur R. Metz scholar, 1965-67. Mem. Calif. Assn. Toxicologists (pres. 1981-82), Acad. Clin. Lab. Physicians and Scientists (pres. 1988-89), Am. Assn. Clin. Chemistry, Am. Chem. Soc., Assn. Pathology Chmn. (sec.-treas. 1996-99), Phi Lambda Upsilon, Alpha Omega Alpha. Office: U Calif San Diego Sch Medicine 9500 Gilman Dr La Jolla CA 92093-0602 Office Phone: 858-822-5577. Business E-Mail: dnbailey@ucsd.edu.

BAILEY, EXINE MARGARET ANDERSON, soprano, educator; b. Cottonwood, Minn., Jan. 4, 1922; d. Joseph Leonard and Exine Pearl (Robertson) Anderson; m. Arthur Albert Bailey, May 5, 1956. BS, U. Minn., 1944; MA, Columbia U., 1945; profl. diploma, 1951. Instr. Columbia U., 1947-51; faculty U. Oreg., Eugene, 1951—, prof. voice, 1966-87, coordinator voice instrn., 1969-87, prof. emeritus, 1987—; faculty dir. Salzburg, Austria, summer 1968, Europe, summer 1976. Vis. prof., head vocal instrn. Columbia U., summers 1952, 59; condr. master classes for singers, developer summer program study for h.s. solo singers, U. Oreg. Sch. Music, 1988—, mem. planning com. 1998-99 MTNA Nat. Convention. Profl. singer, N.Y.C.; appearances with NBC, ABC symphonies; solo artist appearing with Portland and Eugene (Oreg.) Symphonies, other groups in Wash., Calif., Mont., Idaho, also in concert; contbr. articles, book revs. to various mags. Del. fine arts program to Ea. Europe, People to People Internat. Mission to Russia for 1990. Recipient Young Artist award NYC Singing Tchrs., 1945, Music Fedn. Club NYC hon. award, 1951; Kathryn Long scholar Met. Opera, 1945 Mem. Nat. Assn. Tchrs. Singing (lt. gov. 1968-72), Oreg. Music Tchrs. Assn (pres. 1974-76), Music Tchrs. Nat. Assn. (nat. voice chmn. high sch. activities 1970-74, nat. chmn. voice 1973-75, 81-85, NW chmn. collegiate activities and artists competition 1978-80, editorial com. Am. Music Tchr. jour. 1987-89), AAUP, Internat. Platform Assn., Kappa Delta Pi, Sigma Alpha Iota, Pi Kappa Lambda. Home: 17 Westbrook Way Eugene OR 97405-2074 Office: U Oreg Sch Music Eugene OR 97403 Office Phone: 541-343-5206.

BAILEY, LEONARD LEE, surgeon; b. Takoma Park, Md., Aug. 28, 1942; s. Nelson Hulburt and Catherine Effie (Long) B.; m. Nancy Ann Schroeder, Aug. 21, 1966; children: Jonathan Brooks, Charles Connor. BS, Columbia Union Coll., 1964; postgrad., NIH, 1965; MD, Loma Linda U., Calif., 1969. Diplomate Am. Bd. Surgery, Am. Bd. Thoracic Surgery. Intern Loma Linda U. Med. Ctr., 1969-70, resident in surgery, 1970-73, resident in thoracic and cardiovasc. surgery, 1973-74; resident in pediatric cardiovasc. surgery Hosp. for Sick Children, Toronto, Ont., Canada, 1974-75; resident in thoracic and cardiovasc. surgery Loma Linda U. Med. Sch., 1975-76, asst. prof. surgery, 1976-86, prof. surgery, 1986—2005, disting. prof. surgery, 2005—, dir. pediatric cardiac surgery, 1976—, chief divsn. cardiothoracic surgery, 1988-92, chair dept. surgery, 1992—2008; surgeon in chief Loma Linda U. Children's Hosp., 2008—. Mem. ACS, Am. Assn. Thoracic Surgery, Am. Surg. Assn., Am. Coll. Cardiology, Western Thoracic Surg. Assn., Soc. Thoracic Surgery, Western Soc. Pediatric Rsch., Internat. Soc. for Heart Transplantation, Am. Heart Assn., Internat. Assn. for Cardiac Biol. Implants, Am. Soc. for Artificial Internal Organs, Pacific Coast Surg. Assn., Western Assn. Transplant Surgeons, Internat. Soc. for Cardiovasc. Surgery, United Network for Organ Sharing, The Transplant Soc. Democrat. Adventist. Office: Loma Linda U Med Ctr and Children's Hosp 11175 Campus St Ste 21120 Loma Linda CA 92350-1700 Office Phone: 909-558-8744. Business E-Mail: lbailey@llu.edu.

BAILEY, ROBERT C., opera company executive; b. Metropolis, Ill., Dec. 28, 1936; m. Sally McDermott, July 13, 1958. BA in Speech, U. Ill., 1958, MA in English, 1960; BM in Applied Voice, Eastman Sch. Music, 1965; MM in Applied Voice, New Eng. Conservatory Music, 1969. Music prodr. Nat. Pub. Radio, Washington, 1971-73, dir. cultural programming, 1973-75; mgr. Western Opera Theatre, San Francisco, 1975-79; instr. arts mgmt. Golden Gate U., San Francisco, 1977-82; cons. arts mgmt. San Francisco, 1980-82; gen. dir. Portland Opera Assn., Oreg., 1982—; dir. Opera Am., 1995—2001. Cons. On-Site Program Nat. Endowment Arts, Washington, 1982—; judge Met. Opera Auditions, 1977—. Recipient Chevalier in the Order of Arts and Letters French Govt., 1999. Mem. Bohemian Club (San Francisco), City Club (Portland), Arlington Club, Rotary Club.

BAILEY, STEPHEN FAIRCHILD, retired museum director, ornithologist, birding tour guide; b. Stamford, Conn., Feb. 7, 1948; s. Edwin Montgomery and Frances (Sherman) B.; m. Karen Lynn Burtness, Aug. 18, 1971 (div. July 1987). BA in Biology magna cum laude, Beloit Coll., 1971; PhD in Zoology, U. Calif., Berkeley, 1978. Mus. dir. Pacific Grove (Calif.) Mus. of Natural Hist., 1992—2004; ret., 2004; birding tour guide Rockjumper Birding Tours, South Africa, 2005—. Collections mgr. for ornithology and mammalogy Calif. Acad. Scis., San Francisco, 1984-92; biol. cons., 1979-92; adj. prof. biology San Francisco State U., 1986—; tchr. Albany Adult Sch., Calif., 1979-85. Co-author Atlas of the Breeding Birds of Monterey County, 1993; co-author, photographer Audubon Society Master Guide to Birding 3 vols., 1983; regional editor Am. Birds, 1985-98; contbr. articles to profl. jours. Rsch. fellowship Christensen Rsch. Inst., Papua New Guinea, 1989. Mem. Am. Birding Assn. (elected), Ecol. Soc. Am. (life), Am. Ornithologists Union, Cooper Ornithol. Soc. (life), Pacific Seabird Group, Phi Eta Sigma, Phi Beta Kappa. Avocations: birding, travel, nature study, military history. Home: 4564 Valley West Blvd Apt C Arcata CA 95521 E-mail: sfbailey@reninet.com.

BAILEY, WILLIAM BRUCE See ROSE, AXL

BAILEY-SERRES, JULIA N., geneticist, educator; PhD, U. Edinburgh, Scotland, 1986. Postdoctoral fellow NIH, 1986—89; USDA individual postdoctoral fellow U. Calif., Berkeley, 1989—90, with Riverside, 1990—, prof. genetics, geneticist, Coll. Natural and Agrl. Sciences, Dept. Botony & Plant Science. F.C. Donders Chair in Plant Genomics Utrecht U., 2008—09; dir.,founder NSF, ChemGen IGERT (Integrative Grad. Edn. and Rsch. Trainee Program), U. Calif., Ctr. for Plant Cell Biology, Riverside, 2005. Co-recipient USDA Nat. Rsch. Initiative Discovery award for work on submergence tolerant rice, 2008. Fellow: AAAS. Achievements include with colleagues genetically engineering rice for resistance to diseases and flooding. Office: Dept Botany and Plant Sciences U Calif 2101 Batchelor Hall Riverside CA 92521 Office Phone: 951-827-3738. Office Fax: 951-827-4437. Business E-Mail: serres@mail.ucr.edu. E-mail: julia.bailey@ucr.edu.*

BAIN, C. RANDALL, lawyer; b. Greeley, Colo., Feb. 1, 1934; s. Walter Lockwood and Harriet Lucille (Stewart) B.; m. Joanne Berg, Aug. 4, 1956 (div.); children: Jennifer Harriet, Charles Alvin; m. Lois Jean Frazier, Feb. 1, 1973 (dec.); 1 child, Frazier; m. Anna Scalise, Dec. 16, 2000. BA, Yale U., 1955, LLB, 1960. Bar: Ariz. 1961, U.S. Dist. Ct. Ariz. 1961, U.S. Ct. Appeals (9th cir.) 1963, U.S. Supreme Ct. 1968, U.S. Ct. Appeals (fed. cir.) 1992. Ptnr. Brown & Bain, Phoenix, 1961—2003, pres., 1972—87, exec. v.p., 1987—96, of counsel, 2003—04, Perkins, Coie, Brown & Bain, 2004—. Adj. prof. law Ariz. State U. Sch. Law, 2000-01. Trustee Phoenix Country Day Sch., 1983-94; chmn. bd. dirs. Ariz. Audubon, 2003—. Fellow Am. Bar Found.; mem. ABA, Ariz. Bar Assn. (chmn. fee arbitration com. 1982-86), Am. Law Inst., Yale U. Law Sch. Alumni Assn. (exec. com. 1982-85, 93-97), Audubon Ariz. (chmn. bd. dirs. 2003-). Office: Perkins Coie Brown & Bain PA 2901 N Central Ave Ste 2000 Phoenix AZ 85012-2788

BAIN, CONRAD STAFFORD, retired actor; b. Lethbridge, Alta., Can., Feb. 4, 1923; came to U.S., 1946, naturalized, 1946; m. Monica Marjorie Sloan, Sept. 4, 1945; children: Kent Stafford, Mark Alexander, Jennifer Jean. Grad., Am. Acad. Dramatic Art, 1948. Founder Actors Fed. Credit Union, 1962. Broadway appearances include Candide, 1957, Lost in the Stars, 1958, Hot Spot, 1963, Advise and Consent, 1961, Twigs, 1971, Uncle Vanya, 1973, On Borrowed Time, 1991; off-Broadway appearances include The Iceman Cometh, 1957, Hogan's Goat, 1966, Scuba Duba, 1967, The Kitchen, 1968, Steambath, 1969, The Dining Room, Pasadena Playhouse, 1991, On Borrowed Time, 1992, Ancestral Voices, 1999; film appearances A Lovely Way to Die, 1967, Who Killed Mary Whats er Name, 1968, Up the Sand Box, 1970, C.H.O.M.P.S, 1979, Child Bride of Short Creek, 1982, Postcards from the Edge, 1990; Pasadena Playhouse The Dining Room, 1991; co-star: (TV) Maude, 1971-78; star: (TV) Diff'rent Strokes, 1978-86, Mr. President, 1987—. Served with Canadian Army, World War II. Mem. Actors Equity Assn. (councilor 1962-76), ANTA West (dir. since 1977) Clubs: Players (N.Y.C.). Home: Unit 183 900 E Stanley Blvd Livermore CA 94550-4235

BAIN, DONALD KNIGHT, lawyer; b. Denver, Jan. 28, 1935; s. Francis Marion and Jean (Knight) B.; divorced; children: Stephen A., Andrew K., William B. AB, Yale U., 1957; LLB, Harvard U., 1961. Bar: Colo. 1961. Assoc. Holme Roberts & Owen, Denver, 1961—67, ptnr., 1967—2004, chmn. exec. com., 1988-90, counsel, 2005—; chmn. Colo. Rep. Com., 1993-97. Bd. dirs. Fairmount Cemetery Co.; mem. grievance com. Colo. Supreme Ct., 1975-80, chmn., 1980. Trustee Denver Pub. Libr. Friends Found., 1978—96, Denver Found., 1989—95, chmn., 1993—95; trustee Berger Found., 1994—96; trustee, chmn. Colo. Coun. on Arts, 1999—2005; trustee Human Svcs., Inc., 1970—81, chmn., 1979—80; trustee Colo. Humanities Program, 1975—78; mem. Denver Pub. Libr. Commn., 1983—91; active Rep. Nat. Com., Washington, 1993—97; candidate for mayor City of Denver, 1987, 1991; bd. dirs. Rocky Mountain Corp. Pub. Broadcasting, 1975—83, Downtown Denver, Inc., 1977—2004, Denver Metro C. of C., 1998—, BigHornAction.org, 1999—2003, Auraria Found., 1986—, Legal Aid Found., Colo., 1999—2005, Auraria Higher Edn. Ctr., 1978—89, Denver Archtl. Found., 2002—; chmn. Auraria Higher Edn. Ctr., 1986—89. Fellow Royal Geog. Soc., Am. Coll. Trial Lawyers, Explorers Club; mem. ABA, Colo. Bar Assn., Denver Bar Assn., Colo. Yale Assn. (pres. 1974-76), Assn. Yale Alumni (bd. govs. 1982-85), Selden Soc., Am. Antiquarian Soc., Internat. Wine and Food Soc., Confrerie des Chevaliers du Tastevin, Western Stock Show Assn., Cactus Club, Denver Country Club, Mile High Club, Denver Law Club, Grolier Club, Yale Club, Colo. Mountain Club, Capitol Hill CLub, Univ. Club (Denver), Garden of Gods Club. Republican. Avocation: antiquarian book collecting. Home: 1201 Williams # 13C Denver CO 80218 Office: Holme Roberts & Owen LLP 1700 Lincoln St Ste 4100 Denver CO 80203-4541 Office Phone: 303-861-7000. Business E-Mail: don.bain@hro.com.

BAIN, WILLIAM JAMES, JR., architect; b. Seattle, June 26, 1930; s. William James and Mildred Worline (Clark) B.; m. Nancy Sanford Hill, Sept. 21, 1957; children: David Hunter, Stephen Fraser (dec.), Mark Sanford, John Worthington. BArch, Cornell U., 1953. Lic. 1st class architect, Japan, lic. architect in U.K., Wash. Consulting design ptnr. NBBJ (formerly Naramore, Bain, Brady & Johanson), Seattle. Mem. affiliate program steering com. Coll. Architecture and Urban Planning, 1969-71; organizer founding bd. dirs. Pacific N.W. Bank; lectr. U. Wash., Wash. State U., NYU, Harvard U., Cornell, Tech. Transfer Inst. Japan. Prin. works include U. Wash. South Campus, U.S. Pavilion at Expo '74 Worlds Fair, Honolulu Mcpl. Bldg., Two Union Square High-Rise Office Bldg., Four Seasons Olympic Hotel and Sun Mountain Lodge,, U.S. District Courthouse, Seattle, Bagley Wright Theater, Paramount Theater renovation, Saitama Prefecture Demonstration Housing, Japan, Pacific Place Retail Complex, others. Bd. dirs. Arts Fund, 1989—, Arboretum Found., 1971-; bd. dirs. Downtown Seattle Assn., 1980—, 1st vice-chmn., 1990-91, chmn., 1991-92; bd. dirs. Seattle Symphony Orch., 1974-87, pres., 1977-79, lifetime dir.; mem. adv. coun. Coll. Architecture, Art & Planning, Cornell U., 1987-91, 94—, vis. com. U. Washington, 1999—; archl. adv. to bd. dirs. Seattle Pub. Libr.; adv. bd. Mus. History and Industry, Arcade Mag.; Citizen's Adv. Bd., 1997. With C.E., U.S. Army, 1953-55. Recipient Cert. of Achievement Port of Whittier, Alaska, 1955, Disting. Alumnus award Lakeside Sch., 1985, Jim Richards Founders award, Outstanding Alumnus, 2004; named to Hall Fame, Nat. Assn. Indsl. and Office Pks., 2004. Fellow AIA (pres. Seattle chpt. 1969, chmn. N.W. regional student profl. fund 1971, pres. Wash. coun. 1974, co-commn. Seattle centennial yr., Seattle medal 1997, Hall of Fame, 2004), N.W. Regional Archtl. Found. (pres. 1975); mem. Royal Inst. Brit. Architects, Japan Inst. Architects, Seattle C. of C. (bd. dirs. 1980-83), Urban Land Inst., Pacific Real Estate Inst., N.W. Forum, Am. Arbitration Assn. (comml. panel 1975—), L'Ogive Soc., Seattle Athletic Club, Seattle Tennis Club, Town Hall (bd. dirs. 2002—), Rotary (bd. dirs. 1970-72, svc. found. bd. 1976-80), Lambda Alpha Internat. (Robert Filly award 2003), Phi Delta Theta. Clubs: Rainier, Wash. Athletic, Tennis (Seattle); University. Episcopalian. Home: 2033 1st Ave Seattle WA 98121-2132 Office Phone: 206-223-5120. Office Fax: 206-621-2333. Business E-Mail: bbain@nbbj.com.

BAINES, KEVIN HAYS, astronomer, planetary scientist; b. Norwalk, Conn., Feb. 11, 1954; s. Elliot A. and Martha Ellen (Ashcroft) B.; m. Jenine Bsharah, June 4, 1982; children: Emily Ansara, Christopher Lewis. BA, Amherst Coll., 1976; MA, Washington U., St. Louis, 1978, PhD, 1982. Resident rsch. assoc. NRC-JPL, Pasadena, Calif., 1982-84; rsch. scientist Jet Propulsion Lab. Calif. Tech. Inst., Pasadena, 1984—2003, prin. scientist, Jet Propulsion Lab., 2003—. Contbr. articles to profl. jours. Flight dir. Aero Assn. Calif. Tech. Inst., 1986, 99--, treas., 1987-99. Virgil I. Grissom Astronaut fellow Washington U., 1976-79. Mem. AAAS (planetary scis. divsn.). Republican. Achievements include research in determination of vertical cloud/haze structures of Uranus and Neptune; role of asteroid-impact generated sulfuric gases on dinosaur extinctions; first to detect the spectrally-identifiable discrete ammonia ice clouds in Jupiter; discover of lightning at the poles of Jupiter; determination of methane and ortho/para hydrogen above solar averages in Uranus and Neptune; near-infrared spectral imagery and analysis of the atmospheric cloud and compositional structures of Jupiter, Saturn and Titan from the Galileo, Cassini and New Horizons spacecraft; discovery of meteorological systems at depth of saturn; determination of the Co aboudavar on Titan; near-infrared imagery and spectroscopy of Venus surface from Galileo, Cassini and Venus Express spacecraft; near-infrared photometry of rings and satellites of Uranus and Saturn. Avocations: flight instructing, scuba diving. Home: 778 Forest Green Dr La Canada Flintridge CA 91011 Office Phone: 818-354-0481. Business E-Mail: kbaines@aloha.jpl.nasa.gov.

BAINTON, DOROTHY FORD, pathologist, educator; b. Magnolia, Miss., June 18, 1933; d. Aubrey Ratcliff and Leta (Brumfield) Ford; m. Cedric R. Bainton, Nov. 28, 1959; children: Roland J., Bruce G., James H. BS, Millsaps Coll., 1955; MD, Tulane U. Sch. of Medicine, 1958; MS, U. Calif., San Francisco, 1966. Postdoctoral rsch. fellow U. Calif., San Francisco, 1963-66, postdoctoral rsch. pathologist, 1966-69, asst. prof. pathology, 1969-75, assoc. prof., 1975-81, prof. pathology, 1981—, chair pathology, 1987-94, vice chancellor acad. affairs, 1994—2004; ret. Mem. Inst. of Medicine, NAS, 1990—. Grantee, NIH, 1968—98. Fellow AAAS, Am. Acad. Arts & Scis.; mem. FASEB (bd. dirs.), Am. Soc. for Cell Biology, Am. Soc. Hematology, Am. Soc. Histochemists and Cytochemists, Am. Assn. of Pathologists. Democrat. Address: 50 Ventura Ave San Francisco CA 94116 E-mail: dbainton@mac.com.

BAIR, STEVEN, state legislator; b. Blackfoot, Idaho, Apr. 9, 1958; m. Lori Bair; 5 children. Mem. Dist 28 Idaho House of Reps., 2006—. Republican. Mem. Lds Ch. Office: Capitol Annex PO Box 83720 Boise ID 83720-0054 also: 947 W 200 S Blackfoot ID 83221 Office Phone: 208-334-2475, 208-684-5209. Office Fax: 208-334-2125, 208-684-5209.*

BAIR, WILLIAM J., retired radiobiologist; b. Jackson, Mich., July 14, 1924; s. William J. and Mona J. (Gamble) B.; m. Barbara Joan Sites, Feb. 16, 1952; children: William J., Michael Braden, Andrew Emil. BA in Chemistry, Ohio Wesleyan U., 1949; PhD in Radiation Biology, U. Rochester, 1954. NRC-AEC fellow U. Rochester, 1949-50, rsch. assoc. radiation biology, 1950-54; biol. scientist Hanford Labs. of GE, Richland, Wash., 1954-56, mgr. inhalation toxicology sect., biology dept., 1956-65, Battelle Meml. Inst., 1965-68; mgr. biology dept. Pacific Northwest Nat. Labs., Richland, 1968-74, dir. life scis. program, 1973-75, mgr. biomed. and environ. rsch. program, 1975-76, mgr. environ. health and safety rsch. program, 1976-86, mgr. life scis. ctr., 1986-93, sr. advisor health protection rsch., 1993—2002; ret., 2002. Lectr. radiation biology Joint Ctr. Grad. Study, Richland, 1955-75; cons. to adv. com. on reactor safeguards Nuc. Regulatory Commn., 1971-87; mem. com. on plutonium toxicology; subcom. inhalation hazards, com. pathologic effects atomic radiation NAS, 1957-64, ad hoc com. on hot particles of subcom. biol. effects ionizing radiation NAS-NRC, 1974-76, vice-chmn. com. on biol. effects of ionizing radiation, BEIR IV Alpha radiation, 1985-88, battlefield radiation exposure com., 1997-99; chmn. task force on biol. effects of inhaled particles Internat. Commn. on Radiol. Protection, 1970-79, com. 2 on permissible dose for internal radiation, 1973-93, chmn. task group on respiratory tract models, 1984-93; mem. Nat. Coun. on Radiation Protection and Measurements, 1974-92, hon. mem., 1992-, com. on maximum permissible concentration of radionuclides for occupl. and nonoccupl. exposure, 1970-74, com. basic radiation protection criteria, 1975-93, chmn. ad hoc com. on hot particles, 1974, chmn. ad hoc com. internal emitter activities, 1976-77, com. on internal emitter stds., 1977-92, chmn. com. mgmt. of persons contaminated with radionuclides, 2004—, Lauriston S. Taylor lectr., 1997; radiation adv. com. and sci. adv. bd. EPA, 1993-99; founder, pres. Herbert M. Parker Found., 1987-94, bd. trustees, 1994-; cons. in field, 2002-. Author 200 books, articles, reports, chpts. in books. Mem. cmty. concerts bd. Kiwanis Internat.; mem. bd. mid-columbia Woodturners, South Ctrl. Washington Orchid Soc., Columbia Basin Flycasters, Ctrl. United Protestant Ch. With US Army, 1943—46. Decorated Bronze Star; recipient Combat Infantry Badge US Army, E.O. Lawrence Meml. award AEC, 1970, cert. of appreciation AEC, 1975, Alumni Disting. Achievement citation Ohio Wesleyan U, Tribute of Appreciation US Environ. Protection Agy., 1999. Fellow AAAS (life), Health Physics Soc. (life, bd. dirs. 1970-73, 83-86, pres. elect 1983-84, pres. 1984-85, Disting. Sci. Achievement award 1991, Herbert H. Parker award Columbia chpt. 1998, J.N. Stannard lectr. No. Calif. chpt. and Sierra Nev. chpt. 2004); mem. Internat. Commn. Radiological Protection, Radiation Rsch. Soc., Soc. Exptl. Biology and Medicine (vice chmn. N.W. chpt. 1967-70, 74-75), Sigma Xi. Achievements include research in in developing methods for studying health effects of inhaled radioactive aerosols; discovery of different behaviors of inhaled plutonium-238 and 239 oxides; research in deposition, retention and translocation of inhaled aerosols showing relevance of particle size to pulmonary dynamics; demonstrated carcinogenic effects of inhaled plutonium; and led international commission on radiological protection task group in developing a human respiratory tract model for inhaled radioactive materials. Avocations: wildlife photography, woodcarving, fly fishing, orchids, wood turning. Home: 578 Clermont Dr Richland WA 99352-1966

BAIRD, ALAN C., screenwriter; b. Waterville, Maine, Jan. 5, 1951; s. Chester A. and Beverly E. B. BA, Mich. State U., 1973. Pres. Souterrain Teeshirts, Nice, France, 1977-78; page NBC, NYC, 1979-80; producer, dir. Random Prodns., Hollywood, Calif., 1981; writer, producer Preview STV, NYC, 1982-83, Sta. KCOP-TV, Hollywood, 1983-84; writer Vidiom Prodns., Hollywood, 1985-95; screenwriter, 1995—. Author: ATS Operations, 1976, Writes of Passage, 1992, 9TimeZones.com, 1999; prodr. TV script Live at the Palomino, 1981; designer Screenwright Screenplay Formatting Software, 1985; writer TV scripts Night Court, 1986, 20/60, 1986, Golden Girls, 1986, Family Ties, 1986, Max Headroom, 1987, Dave's World, 1993, movie scripts Trading Up, 1988, Merlinsky, 1989, Eleven Thousand Virgins, 1994, The Fall in Budapest, 1997; play script Twisted Pair, 1998. Crisis counselor San Francisco Suicide Prevention, 1975; prodn. asst. March of Dimes Telethon, Hollywood, 1985; escort, host, vol. Verdugo Hills Hosp., 1994-96. Recipient Harvard Book prize Harvard U., Cambridge, Mass., 1969. Avocations: flying, running, scuba diving, parachuting, competitive driving.

BAIRD, BRIAN N., United States Representative from Washington; b. Chama, N.Mex., Mar. 7, 1956; m. Rachel Nugent; children: William, Walter. BS in Psych., U. Utah, 1977; MS, U. Wyo., 1980, PhD in Clin. Psych., 1984. Mem. faculty dept. psych. Pacific Luth. U., 1986—97; mem. US Congress from 3rd Wash. dist., 1999—, mem. transp. and infrastructure com., mem. budget com., mem. sci. com., mem. select com. on continuity in govt. Cons. clin. psychologist St. Charles Med. Ctr., 1994-96. Author: The Internship Practicum Handbook, Are We Having Fun Yet?. Mem.: Wash. State Psychol. Assn., APA. Democrat. Office: US Ho Reps 1421 Longworth Ho Office Bldg Washington DC 20515-0001 Office Phone: 202-225-3536.

BAIRD, LOURDES G., federal judge; b. 1935; BA with highest honors, UCLA, 1973, JD with honors, 1976. Asst. U.S. atty. U.S. Dist. Ct. (ctrl. dist.) Calif., LA, 1977-83; ptnr. Baird & Quadros, 1983-84, Baird, Munger & Myers, 1984-86; judge East L.A. Mcpl. Ct., 1986-87; adj. prof. law Loyola U., LA, 1986-90; judge L.A. Mcpl. Ct., 1987-88, L.A. Superior Ct., 1988-90; U.S. atty. ctrl. dist. Calif., 1990-92; U.S. atty. U.S. Dist. Ct. (ctrl. dist.) Calif., LA, 1990-92, judge, 1992—. Faculty civil RICO program Practicing Law Inst., San Francisco, 1984-85, western regional program Nat. Inst. Trial Advocacy, Berkeley, Calif., 1987-88; adj. prof. trial advocacy Loyola U., L.A., 1987-90. Recipient Silver Achievement award for the professions YWCA, 1994; named Woman of Promise, Hispanic Womens' Coun., 1991, Alumnus of Yr., UCLA Sch. Law, 1991. Mem. Mexican-Am. Bar Assn., Calif. Women Lawyers, Hispanic Nat. Bar Assn., UCLA Sch. Law alumni Assn. (pres. 1984).

BAIRD, PATRICIA ANN, physician, educator; b. Rochdale, Eng. arrived in Can., 1955; d. Harold and Winifred (Cainen) Holt; m. Robert Merrifield Baird, Feb. 22, 1964; children: Jennifer Ellen, Brian Merrifield, Bruce Andrew BSc in Biol. Sci. with honors, McGill U., 1959, MD, CM, 1963; DSc (hon.), McMaster U., 1991; D (hon.), U. Ottawa, 1991; LLD (hon.), Wilfrid Laurier U., 2000. Intern Royal Victoria Hosp., Montreal, Que., Canada, 1963-64; resident, fellow in pediat. Vancouver Gen. Hosp., B.C., Canada, 1964-67; instr. pediat. U. B.C., Vancouver, 1968-72, from asst. prof. to prof., 1972-94, Univ. Killam Disting. prof., 1994—; head dept. med. genetics Grace Hosp., Vancouver, 1981-89, Children's Hosp., Vancouver, 1981-89, Health Scis. Centre Hosp., 1986-89. Med. cons. B.C. Health Surveillance Registry, 1977-90; chmn. genetics grants com. Med. Rsch. Coun., Ottawa, Ont., Can., 1982-87, mem. coun., 1987-90; mem. Nat. Adv. Bd. on Sci. and Tech. to Fed. Govt., 1987-91; genetic predisposition study steering com. Sci. Coun. Can., 1987-90; chair Royal Commn. on New Reproductive Technologies, 1989-93, Premier's Coun. on Aging Sr. Issues, 2005-06; co-chair Nat. Forum Sci. and Tech. Couns., 1991; v.p. Can. Inst. for Advanced Rsch., 1991-2002, vice chmn. bd., 2002—; bd. dirs. Biomed. Rsch. Centre, 1986-89; bd. govs. U. B.C., 1984-90; temporary cons. WHO, 1999-2001, human genetics ELSI planning group, 2000-02, expert adv. panel on human genetics, 2002—03. Contbr. articles to med. jours. Decorated officer Order of Can., 2000, Order of B.C., 1992; recipient Commemorative medal for Confedn. of Can., 1992, Queen's Golden Jubilee medal, 2002. Fellow RCP Can., Royal Soc. Can., Can. Coll. Med. Geneticists (v.p. 1984-86); mem. Am. Soc. Human Genetics (chair nominating com. 1987-89), B.C. Med. Assn., Can. Med. Assn., Genetics Soc. Can., Genetic Epidemiology (adv. bd. 1991-94), Internat. Fedn. of Gyn. and Obs. (mem. ethics com. 1997-99). Avocations: skiing, bicycling, music. Address: 3267 Point Grey Rd Vancouver BC V6K 1B3 Canada Business E-Mail: pbaird@interchange.ubc.ca.

BAIRD, WILLIAM MCKENZIE, chemical carcinogenesis researcher, biochemistry professor; b. Phila., Mar. 23, 1944; s. William Henry Jr. and Edna (McKenzie) Baird; m. Elizabeth A. Myers, June 21, 1969; children: Heather Jean, Elizabeth Joanne, Scott William. BS in Chem., Lehigh U., 1966; PhD in Oncology, U. Wis., 1971. Postdoctoral fellow Inst. Cancer Rsch., London, 1971—73; from asst. to assoc. prof. biochemistry Wistar Inst., Phila., 1973—80; assoc. prof. medicinal chem. Purdue U., West Lafayette, Ind., 1980—82, prof., 1982—97, Glenn L. Jenkins prof. medicinal chem., 1989—97, dir. Cancer Ctr., 1986—97, faculty participant, biochemistry program Cancer Ctr., 1980—97; dir. environ. Health Sci. Ctr. Oreg. State U., Corvallis, 1997—2000, prof., dept. environ. and molecular toxicology, 1997—, prof. dept. biochemistry and biophysics, 1997—. Adv. com. on biochemistry and chem. carcinogenesis Am. Cancer Soc., 1983—86; mem. chem. pathology study sect. NIH, 1986—90. Assoc. editor: Cancer Rsch., 1986—98; contbr. articles to profl. jours. Grantee NCI. Mem.: AAAS, Soc. Toxicology, Environ. Mutagen Soc., Am. Soc. Biochemistry and Molecular Biology, Am. Chem. Soc., Am. Assn. Cancer Rsch., Internat. Soc. for Study of Xenobiotics. Office: Oreg State U Environ and Molecular Toxicology 1007 ALS Bldg Corvallis OR 97331-7301 Home Phone: 541-758-6491; Office Phone: 541-737-1886. Business E-Mail: william.baird@orst.edu.

BAJCSY, RUZENA KUCEROVA, computer science educator; b. Bratislava, Czechoslovakia, May 28, 1933; came to U.S., 1968; d. Felix and Marguita (Weisz) Kucerova; m. Sherman Frankel. MSEE, Slovak Technical U., Bratislava, 1957; PhD in Elec. Engrin., Slovak Tech. U., Bratislava, 1967; PhD in Computer Sci., Stanford U., 1972; PhD (hon.), U. Ljubljana, Slovenia, 2001. Instr. and asst. prof., dept. math. and computer sci. Slovak Tech. U., Bratislava, 1967-68; rsch. scientist artificial intelligience lab. Stanford U., Calif., 1968-72; prof. computer science U. Pa., Phila., 1972—2001, chair computer and info. sci. dept., 1985-90, founder, Grasp Lab.(Gen. Robotics and Active Sensory Perception Lab), 1978, dir. Grasp Lab.(Gen. Robotics and Active Sensory Perception Lab), 1985—2001; asst. dir., head NSF CISE directorate Computer Info. Sci. and Engring. Directorate (CISE), Washington, 1998—2001; dir. Ctr. Info. Tech. Rsch. in Interest of Soc. (CITRIS) U. Calif., Berkeley, 2001—04, dir.-emeritus Ctr. Info. Tech. Rsch. in Interest of Soc. (CITRIS), 2004—, prof. elec. engring. and computer sci., 2001—. Vis. scientist INRIA, France, 1979; vis. prof. U. Copenhagen, Denmark, 1984, 1988, U. Pisa, Italy, 1988; Forsythe lectr. Stanford U., 1989; President's Info. Technology Adv. Com. (PITAC), 2003-05; review panel chair, Carnegie Mellon U. Robotics Inst., 2005; mem. vis. com. on advanced technology, Nat. Inst. Standards and Technology, 2008-; cons. in field. Editor periodicals including Computer Vision; contbr. several articles to profl. jours.; contbr. chapters to books; served on several editl. bds. Recipient Computing Rsch. Associates Disting. Svc. award, 2003; named one of 50 Most Important Women in Sci., Discover Mag., 2002. Fellow IEEE, Assn. Computing Machinery (Allen Newell award, 2001, Disting. Svc. award, 2004), Am. Assn. for Artificial Intelligence, Am. Acad. Arts & Scis.; mem. NAE, Inst. Medicine NAS. Office: U Calif Coll Engring Elec Engring and Computer Scis 665 Soda Hall Berkeley CA 94720 Office Phone: 510-642-9423. Business E-Mail: bajcsy@eecs.berkeley.edu.

BAKA, GREGORY, acting attorney general; Grad., US Naval Acad., 1979; JD, U. San Francisco, 1989. Asst. US atty. Dist. No. Mariana Islands US Dept. Justice, 1997—2004; pvt. practice, 2004—06; asst. atty. gen. Commonwealth of No. Mariana Islands, 2006, dep. atty. gen., 2006—08, acting atty. gen., 2008—. Office: Office of Atty Gen Capital Hill Caller Box 10007 Saipan MP 96950

BAKALY, CHARLES GEORGE, JR., lawyer, mediator; b. Long Beach, Calif., Nov. 15, 1927; s. Charles G. Sr. and Doris (Carpenter) B.; m. Patricia Murphey, Oct. 25, 1952; children: Charles G. III, John W., Thomas B. AB, Stanford U., 1949; JD, U. S.C., 1952. Assoc. O'Melveny & Myers, LA, 1956-63, ptnr., 1963-94; mem. JAMS, LA, 2000—. Mem. Commn. on Calif. State Govt. Orgn. and Economy, 1991-94, President's Nat. Commn. on Employment Policy, 1992-94; mem. 9th Cir. Jud. Conf. Lawyer Del. Ch., 1984-87, mem. indigent def. panel, 1992-94; chmn. Calif. Dispute Resolution Adv. Coun., 1987-88; pres. Dispute Resolution Svcs. Bd. Dirs., Calif. Dispute Resolution Coun. Author: (with Joel M. Grossman) Modern Law of Employment Relationships, 1983, 2d edit. 1989; contbr. chpts. to books. Capt. JAG USMC, 1952—56. Named one of Top 50 Mediators in Calif., LA Daily Jour., 2004. Fellow Am. Coll. Trial Lawyers, Coll. Labor and Employment Lawyers, Internat. Acad. Mediators; mem. ABA (chmn. sect. labor and employment law 1981-82, sect. dispute resolution), L.A. County Bar Assn. (trustee, chmn. labor law sect. 1976-77, dispute resolution sect.), Lincoln Club (pres. 1989-91), Chancery Club, Valley Hunt Club (Pasadena, Calif.), Calif. Club (L.A.), Bohemian Club (San Francisco). Office: JAMS 707 Wilshire Blvd Ste 4600 Los Angeles CA 90017 Office Phone: 213-253-9758. Business E-Mail: cbakaly@jamsadr.com.

BAKER, ALTON FLETCHER, III, editor, publishing executive; b. Eugene, Oreg., May 2, 1950; s. Alton Fletcher Jr. and Genevieve B.; m. Wendy, Jan. 27, 1979; children: Benjamin A., Lindsay A. BA in Comms., Washington State U., 1972. Reporter Associated Press, 1972-79; asst. city editor The Register-Guard, Eugene, 1979-80, city editor, 1980-82, mng. editor, 1982-86, editor, 1986-87, editor, publisher, 1987—; pres. Guard Publishing Co., Eugene, 1987—. Pres. Cmty. Newspapers, Inc., Portland. Pres. YMCA, Eugene, 1989, United Way of Lane County, Eugene, 1985-01, Eugene Festival Musical Theatre, 1990-94. Mem.: Oreg. Newspaper Pubs. Assn. (pres. 1999), Eugene Country Club (pres. 1999). Avocation: golf. Office: Guard Publishing Co 3500 Chad Dr Eugene OR 97408-7348 Office Phone: 541-338-2318.

BAKER, ANITA, singer; b. Toledo, Jan. 26, 1958; m. Walter Bridgeforth, Jr., Dec. 24, 1988; 1 child, Walter Baker Bridgeforth. Mem. funk band Chapter 8, Detroit, 1978-80; receptionist Quin & Budajh, Detroit, 1980-82; ind. singer, songwriter, 1982—. Rec. artist: (with Chapter 8) I Just Wanna Be Your Girl, 1980, (solo albums) The Songstress, 1983, Rapture, 1986 (Grammy award for best rhythm and blues vocal performance 1987), Giving You the Best That I Got, 1988 (Grammy awards for best rhythm and blues song, 1988, best rhythm and blues performance, female, single, 1988, best album, 1989), Compositions, 1990 (Grammy award for best rhythm and blues performance, 1990), Rhythm of Love, 1994 (Grammy award nominee for best album 1995, best female vocal 1995, best song 1995); songs include No More Tears, Angel, Caught Up in the Rapture, Sweet Love (Grammy award best rhythm and blues song 1987), Same Ol' Love, You Bring Me Joy, Been So Long, No One in the World. Recipient Grammy award gospel, soul, best performance, duo, group, choir or chorus, 1987, NAACP Image award, best female vocalist and best album of yr.

BAKER, BRIDGET, broadcast executive; b. Alaska; m. Robert Cerny; 3 children. B in Polit. Sci., Pitzer Coll., Claremont, Calif. Aide to Ted Stevens, US Senate, Ala.; with NBC Universal, 1988—, mgr. HDTV, exec. v.p. cable distbn., pres. TV Networks Distbn., 2006—. Bd. mem. Women in Cable Telecom. Found.; head LA hub GE Women's Network. Bd. mem. Pitzer Coll. Recipient Lifetime Achievement award, Women in Cable Telecom., 2004; named one of The 100 Most Powerful Women in Entertainment, Hollywood Reporter, 2007. Office: NBC Universal 100 Universal City Plz Universal City CA 91608

BAKER, CHARLES E., lawyer; b. Dallas, June 1, 1957; BA in Econs., U. Cambridge, UK, 1978; JD, U. Toronto, 1981; MBA, U. Denver, 2001. Assoc. Fraser & Beatty, 1983—88, ptnr., 1988—93; dir. bus. devel. Ball Corp., Broomfield, Colo., 1993—95, dir. corp. compliance, 1994—97, sr. dir. bus. devel., 1995—99, assoc. gen. counsel, 1999—2004, gen. counsel, asst. corp. sec., 2004—05, v.p., gen. counsel, asst. corp. sec., 2005—. Mem.: Can. Bar Assn., Am. Corp. Counsel Assn., Law Soc. Upper Can., ABA, Colo. Bar Assn. Office: Ball Corp 10 Longs Peak Dr Broomfield CO 80021-2510 Office Phone: 303-460-2586. Office Fax: 303-460-2691. E-mail: cbaker@ball.com.

BAKER, CHARLES LYNN, management consultant; b. Dallas, Mar. 17, 1934; s. Leonard Allan and Nellie (Boals) B.; m. Joan Heverly, June 1, 1968; 1 child, Annette Lynn. BS in Internat. Rels. summa cum laude, Syracuse U., 1967; MA in Polit. Sci. cum laude, Auburn U., 1975. Commd. USAF, advanced through grades to col., dep. inspector gen. Washington, 1975—80, retired, 1980; mng. ptnr. T.Z. Assocs., Balt., 1980—83; pres. McDermott Internat. Trading A.G., Zurich, 1983—90; mng. dir. McDermott Internat. Gen. Svcs., Hong Kong, 1983—90; pres. Baker Assocs., Rancho Santa Fe, Calif., 1990—. Bd. dirs. T.Z. Assocs., Balt., Environ. Scis., San Diego, Broadleaf Industries, San Diego; adj. prof. U. Redlands Grad. Bus. Sch. Author: Strategic Planning, 1987. Pres. Redlands Ballet Co., 1987-89; chmn. Redlands Cultural Art Commn., 1988-2000 Mem. Am. C. of C. (v.p. Hong Kong br. 1984-86), Rotary (pres. Redlands chpt. 1989-90, bd. dirs. internat. chpt. in Hong Kong 1983-85, pres. Hong Kong chpt. 1984), Pres.'s Assn. (chmn. 1988-2004), Calif. Cultural Arts Commn. Republican. Episcopalian. Avocations: golf, tennis, reading. Office: Baker Assocs 16047 Via Galan Rancho Santa Fe CA 92091-4014 Office Phone: 858-759-0801.

BAKER, DIANE R.H., dermatologist; b. Toledo, Nov. 17, 1945; BS, Ohio State U., 1967, MD cum laude, 1971. Diplomate Am. Bd. Dermatology. Intern U. Wis. Hosp., Madison, 1971-72, resident in dermatology, 1972-74, Oreg. Health Sci. Ctr., Portland, 1974-76; pvt. practce, Portland, 1976—. Clin. prof. dermatology Oreg. Health Sci. U., 1986—; mem. med. staff Meridian Park Hosp., Tualatin, Oreg., 1981—; dir. Am. Bd. Dermatology, 1995—, v.p., 2001. Mem.: AMA (del. 1995—), Oreg. Dermatol. Soc., Am. Dermatol. Assn. (v.p. 2001), Am. Acad. Dermatology (v.p. 1990), Alpha Omega Alpha. Office: 1706 NW Glisan St Ste 2 Portland OR 97209-2225

BAKER, DONNA M., research and development company executive, lawyer; m. Bill Baker; 1 child, Patrick. BA, Loyola Marymount U.; MBA, JD, UCLA. Assoc. Morrison & Foerster LLP; ptnr. Burke, Williams & Sorensen, LLP; v.p., gen. counsel Gemological Inst. Am., 2001, sr. v.p., gen. counsel, 2001—06, acting pres., 2006, pres., 2006—. Mem.: North San Diego County Bar Assn., San Diego Bar Assn., Calif. State Bar Assn., ABA, Am. Corp. Counsel Assn. Office: Gemological Institute of America Robert Mouawad Campus 5345 Armada Dr Carlsbad CA 92008 Office Phone: 760-603-4000. Office Fax: 760-603-4080.

BAKER, EDWARD MARTIN, engineering and industrial psychologist; s. Harold H. and Paula B.; m. Shige Jajiki; 1 son, Evan Keith. BA, CCNY, 1962, MBA, 1964; PhD (Research fellow), Bowling Green State U., 1972. Human factors research engr. environ. and safety engring. staff Ford Motor Co., Dearborn, Mich., 1972-77, tech. tng. assoc. mgmt. and tech. tng. dept. Detroit, 1977-79, orgn. devel. cons., personnel and orgn. staff, 1979-81, statis. assoc., ops. support product quality office, 1981-83, statis methods mgr. Asia-Pacific and Latin-Am. automotive ops., 1983-87, dir. total quality planning, cons. and statis. methods corp. quality office, 1987—, dir. quality strategy and ops. support, 1990-92; sr. fellow Aspen Inst., Wye, Md., 1992-95. Deming scholars MBA program adv. bd. Fordham U., 1992—, adj. faculty MBA program, 1994—; cons. in field. Author: Scoring a Whole in One, 1999; contbr. articles to profl. jours.; editorial referee: Jour. Quality Tech, 1974-75, 77-81. Trustee W. Edwards Deming Inst., Washington, 1993-2003. Capt. US Army, 1964—67. Fellow Am. Soc. Quality (Brumbaugh award 1975, Craig award 1976, 79, 86, 88, Ishikawa medal 1995, Deming medal 1997). Home and Office: PO Box 5797 Scottsdale AZ 85261-5797 Personal E-mail: lifemap@ix.netcom.com.

BAKER, EDWIN STUART, retired computer consultant; b. Ottumwa, Iowa, Feb. 14, 1944; s. Edwin Moore and Geraldine Vivian (Irby) B; m. Wilma Jeanne Parker, 1968 (div. 1970). Student, Whitman Coll., 1962—64; BS, Oreg. State U., 1978. Programmer agrl. engring. dept. Oreg. State U., Corvallis, 1977-78, rsch. asst., 1979-83, sr. rsch. asst., 1984-89; measurement standards specialist Oreg. Dept. Agr., Salem, 1990-93. Cons. in field. Mem. IEEE, Assn for Computing Machinery, Am. Legion, DAV, NRA, VFW, 59ers Svc. Club. Avocations: photography, horses. Home: PO Box 370 Lebanon OR 97355-0370 Office: Oreg Dept Agr Measurement Standards Divsn Salem OR 97310-0001 Office Phone: 541-570-5905. Personal E-mail: esb@computer.org.

BAKER, KEITH MICHAEL, history professor; b. Swindon, Eng., Aug. 7, 1938; arrived in US, 1964; s. Raymond Eric and Winifred Evelyn (Shepherd) B.; m. Therese Louise Elzas, Oct. 25, 1961 (div. 1999); children— Julian, Felix, Nicholas; m. Jennifer Lauren Paley, May 18, 2008. BA, Cambridge U., 1960, MA, 1963; postgrad., Cornell U., 1960-61; PhD, U. London, 1964. Instr. history and humanities Reed Coll., 1964-65; asst. prof. European history U. Chgo., 1965-71, assoc. prof., 1971-76, prof., 1977-89, master collegiate div. social scis., 1975-78, assoc. dean coll., 1975-78, assoc. dean div. social scis., 1975-78, chmn. commn. grad. edn., 1980-82; chmn. Coun. Advanced Studies in Humanities and Social Scis., 1982-86; prof. European history Stanford U., 1989—, J.E. Wallace Sterling prof. in humanities, 1992—, chair dept. history, 1994-95; Anthony P. Meier family prof. humanities, dir. Stanford Humanities Ctr., 1995-2000, cognizant dean humanities, 2000—03; Jean-Paul Gimon dir. France-Stanford Ctr. for Interdisciplinary Studies, 2002—. Vis. assoc. prof. history Yale U., 1974; mem. Inst. Advanced Study, Princeton, NJ, 1979-80; vis. prof., dir. studies Ecole des Hautes Etudes en Scis.

Sociales, Paris, 1982, 84, 91; fellow Ctr. for Advanced Study in Behavioral Scis., Stanford U., Calif., 1986-87, Santora Humanities Ctr., 2005-06; vis. prof. UCLA, 1989; vis. fellow Clare Hall, Cambridge U., Eng., 1994; chair scholars com. Am. Com. on the French Revolution, 1989. Author: Condorcet: From Natural Philosophy to Social Mathematics, 1975, Inventing the French Revolution, 1990; prin. author: Report Commission on Graduate Education, U. Chgo., 1982; editor: Condorcet: Selected Writings, 1977, The Political Culture of the Old Regime: The Old Regime and the French Revolution, 1987, The Terror, 1994; co-editor Jour. Modern History, 1980-89, What's Left of Enlightenment?, 2001; contbr. chpts. to books. Decorated chevalier Ordre des Palmes Académiques; fellow, NEH, 1967—68; ACLS study fellow, 1972—73, Guggenheim fellow, 1979. Fellow AAAS, Am. Philos. Soc.; mem. Am. Hist. Assn. (com. on coms. 1991-94), Soc. French History Studies (co-pres. 2005), Am. Soc. for 18th Century Studies (v.p. 1999, pres. 2000-01), Internat. Soc. Eighteenth Century Studies (pres. 2007-). Office: Stanford Univ Dept History Stanford CA 94305-2024 Home Phone: 650-493-4970; Office Phone: 650-723-2791. Business E-Mail: kbaker@stanford.edu.

BAKER, MITCHELL, computer software developer, foundation administrator; AB in Asian Studies, U. Calif., Berkeley; JD, U. Calif. Boalt Hall Sch. Law, Berkeley, 1987. Corp. and intellectual property assoc. Fenwick & West LLP, 1990—93; assoc. gen. counsel Sun Microsystems, 1993—94, Netscape Comm. Corp., 1994—99; joined Mozilla.org, 1998, gen. mgr., 1999; pres. Mozilla Corp., subsidiary of Mozilla Found., 2005, CEO; pres. Mozilla Found., 2003—05, chmn., 2008—. Bd. dirs. Open Source Applications Found., 2002—, Mozilla Corp., Mozilla Found., 2003—; adv. bd. SpikeSource. Named one of 100 Most Influential People of 2005, Time mag., Most Influential Women in Technology, Fast Company, 2009. Office: Mozilla Corp 1981K Landings Dr Mountain View CA 94043-0801*

BAKER, ROBERT FRANK, molecular biologist, educator; b. Weiser, Idaho, Apr. 9, 1936; s. Robert Clarence and Beulah (Hulet) B.; m. Mary Margaret Murphy, May 29, 1965; children: Allison Leslie, Steven Mark. BS, Stanford U., 1959; PhD, Brown U., 1966. Postdoctoral rsch. assoc. Stanford (Calif.) U., 1966-68; asst. prof. dept. biol. scis. U. So. Calif., LA, 1968-72, assoc. prof., 1972-83, prof., 1983—, dir. molecular biology div., 1978-80, mem. Comprehensive Cancer Ctr., 1984—. Vis. assoc. prof Harvard U. Med. Sch., Boston 1975-76; mem. genetic study sect. NIH, Bethesda, Md., 1977-79, 82 Contbr. articles to profl. jours. Grantee NIH, NSF, 1968—. Mem. Am. Soc. Zoologists, Am. Soc. Microbiology, Sigma Xi. Avocations: amateur radio, electronics. Home: 607 Almar Ave Pacific Palisades CA 90272-4208 Office: U So Calif Dept Molecular Biology Mc 1340 Los Angeles CA 90089-1340 Office Phone: 213-740-5565. Business E-Mail: baker@molbio.usc.edu.

BAKER, ROBERT M.L., JR., academic administrator, research scientist; b. LA, Sept. 1, 1930; s. Robert M.L. and Martha (Harlan) Baker; m. Bonnie Sue Vold, Nov. 14, 1964; children: Robert Randall, Robert M.L. III, Robin Michelle Leslie Fell. BA summa cum laude, UCLA, 1954, MA, 1956, PhD, 1958. Cons. Douglas Aircraft Co., Santa Monica, Calif., 1954—57; sr. scientist Aeronutronic, Newport Beach, 1957—60; head Lockheed Aircraft Rsch. Ctr., West L.A., 1961—64; assoc. mgr. math. analysis Computer Scis. Corp., El Segundo, 1964—80; pres. West Coast U., LA, 1980—97. Faculty UCLA, 1958—72; dir. Internat. Info. Systems Corp., Pasadena, Transp. Scis. Corp., LA; appointee Nat. Accreditation Adv. Com. U.S. Dept. Edn., 1987—90. Author: An Introduction to Astrodynamics, 1960, 2d edit., 1967, Astrodynamics-Advanced and Applied Topics, 1967, 1987; editor: Jour. Astron. Scis., 1961—76, SCL. To maj. USAF, 1960—61. Recipient Dirk Brouwer award, 1976; named Outstanding Young Man of Yr., 1965. Fellow: AAAS, AAIA (assoc.), Brit. Astro. Soc., Meteoritical Soc., Am. Astro. Soc.; mem.: Am. Phys. Soc., Sigma Pi Sigma, Sigma Xi, Phi Beta Kappa. Achievements include seven patents in field. Office: Gravwave LLC 8123 Tuscany Ave Playa Del Rey CA 90293-7856 Home Phone: 310-823-4143; Office Phone: 310-823-4143, 310-666-0517. Business E-Mail: drrobertbaker@gravwavellc.com.

BAKER, ROLAND JERALD, finance educator; b. Pendleton, Oreg., Feb. 27, 1938; s. Roland E. and Theresa Helen (Forest) B.; m. Judy Lynn Murphy, Nov. 24, 1973; children: Kristen L., Kurt F., Brian H. BA, Western Wash. U., 1961; MBA, U. Mich., 1968. Cert. purchasing mgr., profl. contract mgr. Asst. dir. purchasing and stores U. Wash., Seattle, 1970-75; mgr. purchasing and material control Foss Launch & Tug Co., Seattle, 1975-79; faculty Shoreline C.C., 1972-79, 98—, Pacific Luth. U., 1977-79, Edmonds C.C., 1974-79; chmn. educators group Nat. Assn. Purchasing Mgmt., Tempe, Ariz., 1976-79, exec. v.p., 1979-98; pres. Nat. Assn. Purchasing Mgmt. Svcs., Tempe, Ariz., 1989-95; founder, owner Global Supply Chain Inst., LLC, Seattle, 2007—. Faculty Ariz. State U., Tempe, 1988-91; world bus. adv. Coun. Am. Grad. Sch. of Internat. Mgmt., Glendale, Ariz., 1994-98; adv. bd. blockbuy.com, Inc., 1999-01, Perfect.com., Inc., 2000-06; exec. v.p MyGroupbuy Inc., 2000-03, also bd. dirs.; mem. faculty Shoreline C.C., Seattle, 1998—. Author: Purchasing Factomatic, 1977, Inventory System Factomatic, 1978, Policies and Procedures for Purchasing and Material Control, 1980, rev. edit., 1992. With USN, 1961-70, comdr. Res., 1969-91. Recipient Disting. Achievement award Ariz. State U. Coll. Bus., 1997; U.S. Navy postgrad. fellow, 1967. Mem. Purchasing Mgmt. Assn. Wash. (pres. 1978-79), Nat. Minority Supplier Devel. Coun. (bd. dirs.), Am. Prodn. and Inventory Control Soc., Nat. Assn. Purchasing Mgmt. (exec. v.p. 1979-97), Nat. Contract Mgmt. Assn., Internat. Fedn. Purchasing and Materials Mgmt. (exec. com. 1984-87, exec. adv. com. 1991-98), Global Owner Supply Chain Inst., 2008-. Office: Shoreline CC 16101 Greenwood Ave N Seattle WA 98133-5667 Personal E-mail: g.baker206@comcast.net. Business E-Mail: jbaker@shoreline.edu.

BAKER, VALERIE L., federal judge; b. Mpls., June 25, 1949; d. Glen R. and Lorraine (Guselc) Baker. BA in English, U. Calif Santa Barbara, 1971, MA, 1972; JD, UCLA, 1975. Bar: Calif. 1975. Assoc. Overtich, Lyman & Prince, LA, 1975—77; asst. US atty. US Atty.'s Office Ctrl. Calif. dist., LA, 1977—80; assoc. Lillick, McHose & Charles, LA, 1980—82, ptnr., 1982—86; judge LA Mcpl. Ct., 1986—87, Superior Ct. (LA County) Calif., 1987—2007, US Dist. Ct. (Ctrl. dist.) Calif., 2007—. Del. 9th Cir. Jud. Conf., 1985. Mem.: Santa Monica Bar. Assn. (antitrust sect.), LA County Bar Assn., Bus. Trial Attys. Assn., Fed. Bar Assn., Pacific Palisades Tennis, Santa Monica Tennis. Office: US Dist Ct Ctrl Calif 312 N Spring St Los Angeles CA 90012 Office Phone: 213-984-1565. Office Fax: 213-894-2215.

BAKER, WARREN J(OSEPH), university president; b. Fitchburg, Mass., Sept. 5, 1938; s. Preston A. and Grace F. (Jarvis) B.; m. Carol Ann Fitzsimons, Apr. 28, 1962; children: Carrie Ann, Kristin Robin, Christopher, Brian. BS, U. Notre Dame, 1960, MS, 1962; PhD, U. N.Mex., 1966. Rsch. assoc., lectr. E. H. Wang Civil Engring. Rsch. Facility, U. N.Mex., 1962-66; assoc. prof. civil engring. U. Detroit, 1966-71, prof., 1972-79, Chrysler prof., dean engring., 1973-78, acad. v.p., 1976-79; NSF faculty fellow MIT, Cambridge, 1971-72; pres. Calif. Poly. State U., San Luis Obispo, 1979—. Mem. Bd. Internat. Food and Agrl. Devel., USAID, 1983-85; mem. Nat. Sci. Bd., 1985-94, Calif. Bus. Higher Edn. Forum, 1993-98; founding mem. Calif. Coun. on Sci. and Tech., 1989—; trustee Amigos of E.A.R.T.H. Coll., 1991-96; bd. dirs. John Wiley & Sons, Inc., 1993—; bd. gov. US-Mex. Found. Sci., 2008-; exec. com. Math. Engring. Sci. Achievement, Calif., 2008-; bd. regents The Am. Archtl. Found., 1995-97; co-chair Joint Policy Coun. on Agr. and Higher Edn., 1995—; mem. Bus.-Higher Edn. Forum, 2001—; exec. com. and co-chair Math. & Sci. Edn. and Sci. Tech., Engring. and Maths. Initiatives; bd. dirs. Westport Innovations, Inc., 2002-. Contbr. articles to profl. jours. Mem. Detroit Mayor's Mgmt. Adv. Com., 1975-76; mem. engring. adv. bd. U. Calif., Berkeley, 1984-96; bd. dirs. Calif. Coun. for Environ. and Econ. Balance, 1980-85, Soc. Mfg. Engrs. Edn. Found., 2001-, bd. dirs., 2003-05; steering com. Nat. Acad. Engring. CC Pathways, 2004-05; trustee Nat. Coop. Edn. Assn.; chmn. bd. dirs. Civil Engring. Rsch. Found., 1989-91, bd. dirs., 1991-94. Fellow Engring. Soc. Detroit, ASCE (chmn. geotech. divsn. com. on reliability 1976-78, civil engring. edn. and rsch. policy com. 1985-89); mem. NSPE (pres. Detroit chpt. 1976-77), Am. Soc. Engring. Edn., Am. Assn. State Colls. and Univs. (bd. dirs. 1982-84), Nat. Assn. State Univ. and Land-Grant Coll. (commn. on info. tech. 1995-, chair 2003-06, bd. dirs. 2003-07), Commn. U. Sci. and Maths. Tchr. Imperative, 2007-. Office: Calif Poly State U Office of Pres 1 Grand Ave San Luis Obispo CA 93407-1000 Office Phone: 805-756-6000. Business E-Mail: presidentsoffice@calpoly.edu.

BAKER, WILLIAM DUNLAP, lawyer; b. St. Louis, June 17, 1932; s. Harold Griffith and Bernice (Kraft) B.; m. Kay Stokes, May 23, 1955; children: Mark William, Kathryn X., Beth Kristie, Frederick Martin. AB, Colgate U., 1954; JD, U. Calif., Berkeley, 1960. Bar: Calif. 1961, Ariz. 1961, U.S. Supreme Ct. 1969. Practice in, Coolidge, 1961, Florence, 1961-63, Phoenix, 1963—; law clk. Stokes & Moring, 1960; spl. investigator Office Pinal County Atty., 1960-61, dep. county atty., 1961-63; partner McBryde, Vincent, Brumage & Baker, 1961-63; assoc. atty. Rawlins, Ellis, Burrus & Kiewit, 1963-65, partner, 1965-81; pres., atty. Ellis & Baker, P.C., 1981-84, Ellis, Baker, Lynch, Clark & Porter P.C., 1984-86, Ellis, Baker, Clark & Porter, P.C., 1986-89, Ellis, Baker & Porter, P.C., 1989-92, Ellis Baker & Porter Ltd., Phoenix, 1992-95, Ellis, Baker & Porter, P.C., Phoenix, 1995-99, Ellis & Baker, P.C., 1999—. Referee Juvenile Ct. Maricopa County Superior Ct., 1966-85 Contbr. articles to profl. jours. Mem. Gov.'s Adv. Coun., Phoenix, 1969-71, Ariz. Environ. Planning Commn., 1974-75; bd. dirs. Agri-Bus. Coun., 1978—, sec., 1978-82; pub. mem. State Bd. Accountancy, 1995-03, sec., 1998-99, treas., 1999-00, pres., 2000-02, law com., 2004-; mem. Nat. Assn. Bds. Accountancy, litig. com., 2001-03, nominating com., 2002-04; legal counsel Ariz. Com. Rep. Party, 1965-69, mem. exec. com., 1972-78; vice-chmn. Maricopa County Rep. Com., 1968-69, chmn., 1969-71; bd. dirs. San Pablo Home for Youth, 1964-72, pres., 1971; bd. dirs. Maricopa County chpt. Nat. Found. March of Dimes, 1966-71, campaign chmn., 1970; trustee St. Luke's Hosp., 1976-85, sec., 1978-82, chmn., 1982-85; bd. dirs. Luke's Men, 1971-80, pres., 1976-77; bd. dirs. Combined Health Resources, 1982-85, St. Luke's Health Sys., 1977-95, chmn., 1985-89; bd. dirs. St. Luke's Health Initiatives, 1995-2008, vice chair, 2000-02; bd. dirs., v.p. Ariz. Anglican Cursillo Movement, 1982-86, treas. 2005-06; Western dist. layman rep. Nat. Episcopal Cursillo Com., 1996-98; regional v.p. Colgate Alumni Corp., 1977-82; vice chancellor Episcopal Diocese Ariz., 1970-96, ch. atty, 1996-03; sr. warden Christ Ch. of Ascension, 1983-86, 2001-03, chancellor, 2004-2007; chancellor & sec. Christ Ch. Anglican, 2007-; bd. dirs. Ariz. Western Coun., Ltd., 2003-06; mem., chancellor Assn. AW Anglican Congregations, 2008-. Served to 1st lt. USAF, 1954-57. Mem. ABA, Nat. Water Resources Assn. (life, co-chmn. task force on reclamation law 1990-97, resolutions com. 1990-93, chmn. state caucus 1993—, mem. fed affairs com 2000-, chair water supply task force 2000—, Pres.'s award 1991), Ariz. Soc. CPAs (hon.), Ariz. Bar Assn., Calif. Bar Assn., State C. of C. (bd. dirs. 1988-92), Maricopa County Bar Assn., Flagstaff Golf Assn. (bd. dirs. 1992-93, 94-96, pres. 1994-95), Phoenix Country Club, Ariz. Srs. Golf Assn. (bd. dirs. 1990-, mem. chmn. 2005, sec., treas. 2006, v.p. 2007, pres. 2007-08), Sigma Chi, Phi Delta Phi. Anglican. Home: 1627 E Cactus Wren Dr Phoenix AZ 85020 Office: Ste 102 7301 N 16th St Phoenix AZ 85020 Business E-Mail: wdb@ellisbaker.com.

BAKER, WILLIAM MORRIS, cultural organization administrator; m. Robin Baker. BA in History, U. Va., 1961. With FBI, 1965-87-89-91, asst. dir. criminal investigative divsn., ret., 1991; dir. pub. affairs CIA, 1987-89; sr. v.p., dir. worldwide anti-piracy Motion Picture Assn., Encino, Calif., 1991-94, pres., COO, 1994—. Spkr. in field; guest lectr. Ctr. for Internat. Affairs Harvard U., Fed. Exec. Inst. U. Va. 1st lt. USAF, 1962-65. Named Disting. Exec. by U.S. Pres. George Bush, 1990; recipient Disting. Intelligence medal CIA, 1989, Edmund J. Randolph award U.S. Atty. Gen.'s 40th Ann. Awards Ceremony, 1992, U.S. Marshals Star for lifetime achievement in law enforcement, 1992. Avocations: reading, running, sailing, skiing, cooking.

BAKER, WILLIAM P. (BILL BAKER), former congressman; b. Oakland, Calif., June 14, 1940; m. Joanne Atack; children: Todd, Mary, Billy, Robby. Grad. in Bus. and Indsl. Mgmt., San Jose State Coll. Budget analyst State Dept. Fin., Calif.; assemblyman 15th dist. State of Calif., 1980-92; mem. of Congress from 10th Calif. dist., 1993-96; ptnr. Baker, Welch & Wiens, Alamo, Calif. Vice chmn. budget writing Ways and Means Com., 1984-91 Exec. v.p. Contra Costa Taxpayers Assn.; active Contra Costa County Farm Bur. With USCG Res., 1958-65. Republican. Office: Baker Welch & Wiens 3189 Danville Blvd Ste 200 Alamo CA 94507-1956

BAKER, ZACHARY MOSHE, librarian; b. Mpls., June 8, 1950; s. Michael Harry and Margaret Esther (Zanger) B. BA, U. Chgo., 1972; MA, Brandeis U., 1974; MA in LS, U. Minn., 1975. Head tech. svcs. Jewish Pub. Libr., Montreal, Que., Canada, 1981-87; asst. libr. Yivo Inst. for Jewish Rsch., NYC, 1976-80, assoc. libr., 1980-81, head libr., 1987-99; Reinhard family curator Judaica & Hebraica collections Stanford U. Librs., 1999—, head humanities & area studies, 2006—. Hist. cons. Que. Inst. Rsch. on Culture, Montreal, 1983; libr. cons. U.S. Holocaust Meml. Coun., Washington, 1984-85, Fla. Atlantic U., Boca Raton, 1994, Ariz. State U., Tempe, 1998. Contbg. author: From a Ruined Garden, 1983, 98; author, contbg. editor Toledot, 1978-82, Judaica Librarianship, 1983-2003, 2004-; editor: Yiddish Catalog and Authority File of the Yivo Library, 1990, Judaica in the Slavic Realm, 2003, Ira Nowinski, Photographer as Witness, 2004. Crown fellow Brandeis U., 1973-74; travel and rsch. grantee Andrew W. Mellon Found., 1997, Lucius N. Littauer Found., 1990, 94, 96, 98/ Mem. ALA, Assn. Jewish Librs. (pres. 1994-96), Assn. for Jewish Studies, Coun. Archives and Rsch. Libr. in Jewish Studies (pres. 1998-02), Phi Beta Kappa, Beta Phi Mu. Avocations: map and atlas collecting, current events, travel. Office Phone: 650-725-1054. Business E-Mail: zbaker@stanford.edu.

BAKKEN, GORDON MORRIS, law educator; b. Madison, Wis., Jan. 10, 1943; s. Elwood S. and Evelyn A. H. (Anderson) B.; m. Erika Reinhardt, Mar. 24, 1943; children: Angela E., Jeffrey E. BS, U. Wis., 1966, MS, 1967, PhD, 1970, JD, 1973. From asst. to assoc. prof. history Calif. State U., Fullerton, 1969-74, prof. history, 1974—, dir. faculty affairs, 1974-86. Cons. Calif. Sch. Employees Assn., 1976-78, Calif. Bar Commn. Hist. Law., 1985—; mgmt. task force on acad. grievance procedures Calif. State Univ. and Colls. Systems, 1975; mem. Calif. Jud. Coun. Com. Trial Ct. Records Mgmt., 1992-97. Author 11 books on Am. legal history; contbr. articles to profl. jours. Placentia Jusa referee coord., 1983. Russell Sag resident fellow law, 1971-72, Am. Bar Found. fellow in legal history, 1979-80, 84-85; Am. Coun. Learned Socs. grantee-in-ai d, 1979-80. Mem. Orgn. Am. Historians, Am. Soc. Legal History, Law and Soc. Assn., Western History Assn., Calif. Supreme Ct. Hist. Soc. (v.p.), Phi Alpha Theta (v.p. 1994-95, pres. 1996-97). Democrat. Lutheran. Office Phone: 714-278-3048. Business E-Mail: gbakken@fullerton.edu.

BAKKENSEN, JOHN RESER, lawyer; b. Pendleton, Oreg., Oct. 4, 1943; s. Manley John and Helen (Reser) B.; m. Ann Marie Dahlen, Sept. 30, 1978; children: Michael, Dana, Laura. AB magna cum laude, Harvard U., 1965; JD, Stanford U., 1968. Bar: Oreg. 1969, Calif. 1969, US Dist. Ct. Oreg. 1969. Ptnr. Miller, Nash, Wiener, Hager & Carlsen, Portland, Oreg., 1968-99; pvt. practice lawyer, arbitrator, mediator, spl. master and trustee. Lawyer del. 9th Cir. Jud. Conf., San Francisco, 1980-82. Author: (with others) Advising Oregon Businesses, 1979, Arbitration and Mediation, supplement, 2000, 2008. Past bd. dirs. Assn. for Retarded Citizens, Portland; advisor Portland Youth Shelter House; mem. and counsel to bd. dirs. Friends of Pine Mountain Observatory, Portland. Mem. ABA (forum on constrn. industry), Am. Arbitration Assn., Oreg. State Bar, Oreg. Assoc. Gen. Contractors (legal com. 1991, counsel to bd. dirs. 1992), Arbitration Svc. Portland, Inc. (arbitrator), Multnomah Athletic Club. Avocation: astronomy. Office Phone: 503-245-0385.

BAKKER, THOMAS GORDON, lawyer; b. San Gabriel, Calif., Aug. 18, 1947; s. Gordon and Eva Marie (Hoekstra) B.; m. Charlotte Anne Kamstra, Aug. 1, 1969; children: Sarah, Jonathan. AB in History, Calvin Coll., Grand Rapids, Mich., 1969; JD, U. Mich., 1973. Bar: Ariz. 1973, U.S. Dist. Ct. Ariz. 1973, U.S. Ct. Appeals (9th cir.) 1973. Staff reporter Ariz. Criminal Code Revision Com., Phoenix, 1973-75; asst. atty. gen. State of Ariz., Phoenix, 1975-77; staff atty. div. 1 Ariz. Ct. Appeals, Phoenix, 1977-79; assoc. Burch, Cracchiolo et al, Phoenix, 1979-80; from assoc. to ptnr. Olson, Jantsch, Bakker, Phoenix, 1980—. Vice chmn. tort and ins. practice sect. Appellate Advocacy Commn., 1982-83; judge pro tem div. 1 Ariz. Ct. Appeals, 1985, 92. Served with U.S. Army, 1969-71. Fellow Ariz. Bar Found. (founding fellow); mem. Ariz. Bar Assn., Maricopa County Bar Assn., Am. Health Lawyers Assn., Def. Rsch. Inst., Ariz. Assn. Def. Counsel 163. Mem. Christian Reformed Ch. Avocations: reading, golf, aerobics, fishing. Office: Olson Jantsch Bakker 7243 N 16th St Phoenix AZ 85020-5203 Office Phone: 602-861-2705. E-mail: tgb@ojbb.com.

BALABAN, LARRY A., entertainment company executive, producer, director; b. Nov. 1963; m. Sara Balaban; 1 child, Frankie. Pres. Virtual Reality Prodns., 1994—97, Mr. B Prodns., NYC; founding ptnr. Genius Products, Inc., 1998, cons., 1998—99, exec. v.p. mktg. & prodn., 1999, exec. v.p. prodn. & creative svcs.; pres. Pacific Entertainment Corp., San Diego, 2006—. Bd. dirs. Genius Products, Inc., 2001—04. Exec. prodr., writer, composer, dir. Baby Genius DVD series, exec. prodr., creator Little Tikes DVD series. Bd. dirs. Coalition for Quality Children's Media. Named one of 40 Under 40, License mag., 2003. Office: Pacific Entertainment Corp 2195 San Dieguito Dr #1 San Diego CA 92104

BALANDIN, ALEXANDER A., electrical engineer, educator; b. Nizhny Novgorod, Russia, Apr. 30, 1968; came to US, 1993; s. Alexei A. and Tania A. (Ovechkin) Balandin; m. Maria P. Spitsin, Jan. 12, 1996. BS in Applied Math., Moscow Inst. Physics & Tech., 1989, MS in Applied Physics, 1991; MSEE, U. Notre Dame, Ind., 1995, PhD in Elec. Engring., 1996. Rsch. asst. dept. elec. engring. U. Notre Dame, Ind., 1993-96; rsch. assoc. dept. elec. engring. Quantum Device Lab. U. Nebr., Lincoln, 1996-97; rsch. engr. dept. elec. engring. Device Rsch. Lab. UCLA, 1997-99; asst. prof. dept. elec. engring. U. Calif., Riverside, 1999-2001, assoc. prof. dept. elec. engring., 2001—05, prof. dept. elec. engring., 2005—, dir. Nano-Device Lab., 2000—, chair materials sci. and engring. program, 2007—. Recipient Career award, NSF, Young Investigator award, ONR, Regents Faculty award, U. Calif. Fellow AAAS; mem. IEEE, Am. Phys. Soc., Electrochem. Soc., Eta Kappa Nu. Achievements include development of nanophononics, quantum dots; research in flicker noise reduction in high-power transistors; thermal transport in nanostructures; optical properties of nanostructures; investigation of thermal properties of graphene. Office: Univ Calif Dept Elec Engring Riverside CA 92521-0425 Business E-Mail: balandin@ee.ucr.edu.

BALANIS, CONSTANTINE APOSTLE, electrical engineering educator; b. Trikala, Thessaly, Greece, Oct. 29, 1938; arrived in US, 1955; s. Apostolos G. and Erini (Vlahocostas) B.; m. Helen Jovaras, May 21, 1972; children: Erini, Stephanie. BSEE, Va. Tech. U., 1964; MEE, U. Va., 1966; PhDEE, Ohio State U., 1969; Doctorate (hon.), Aristotle U. Thessaloniki, Greece, 2004. Electronics engr. NASA, Hampton, Va., 1964-70; asst. professorial lectr. George Washington U. Extension, Hampton, 1968-70; vis. assoc. prof. dept. elec. engring. W.Va. U., Morgantown, 1970-72, assoc. prof., 1972-76, prof., 1976-83; prof. dept. elec. engring. Ariz. State U., Tempe, 1983-91, Regents' prof., 1991—, dir. Telecommunications Rsch. Ctr., 1988-99. Cons. Motorola Inc., Scottsdale, Ariz., 1984-94, Loral Def. Systems, Litchfield Park, Ariz., 1986-88, Gen. Dynamics, Pomona, Calif., 1986-87, Naval Air Warfare Ctr., Patuxent River, Md., 1977-90, Naval Surface Warfare Ctr., Dahlgren, Va., 1985-86, Nat. Radio Astronomy Observatory, Green Bank, W.Va., 1972-74; Boeing, Seattle, 1996, Rockwell Internat., Cedar Rapids, Iowa, 1997. Author: Antenna Theory: Analysis and Design, 1981, 3d edit., 2005, Advanced Engineering Electromagnetics, 1989; editor: Antennas and Propogation, Computational Electromagnetic Series; patentee in field. Recipient Halliburton Best

Rschr. award W.Va. U., 1983, Russ award for Rsch., Ohio U., 1984, Tchg. Excellence award Ariz. State U., 1988, Outstanding Grad. Mentor award, 1996-97; grantee NASA, Army Rsch. Office, NSF, Office Naval Rsch., Dept. of Energy, Dept. of Transp., Naval Air Warfare Ctr., Naval Surface Warfare Ctr., Motorola Inc., Gen. Dynamics, Boeing Helicopter Sys., Sikorsky Aircraft, Rockwell Internat., Boeing Helicopters, IBM, 1972—. Fellow (life) IEEE (Individual Achievement award region 6, 1989, Spl. Engring. Professionalism award Phoenix sect. 1992, Third Millennium award 2000, AP Soc. Chen-To Tai Disting. Educator award 2005); mem. Sigma Xi, Phi Kappa Phi, Eta Kappa Nu, Tau Beta Pi. Avocations: golf, jogging, tennis, bowling. Home: 3154 E Encanto St Mesa AZ 85213-6110 Office: Ariz State U Dept Elec Engring Tempe AZ 85287-5706 Office Phone: 480-965-3909. Business E-Mail: balanis@asu.edu.

BALDESCHWIELER, JOHN DICKSON, chemist, educator; b. Elizabeth, NJ, Nov. 14, 1933; s. Emile L. and Isobel (Dickson) B.; m. Marlene R. Konnar, Apr. 15, 1991; children from previous marriage: John Eric, Karen Anne, David Russell. B. Chem. Engring., Cornell U., 1956; PhD, U. Calif., Berkeley, 1959. From instr. to asso. prof. chemistry Harvard U., 1960-65; faculty Stanford (Calif.) U., 1965-71, prof. chemistry, 1967-71; chmn. adv. bd. Synchrotron Radiation Project, 1972-75; vis. scientist Synchrotron Radiation Lab., 1977; dep. dir. Office Sci. and Tech., Exec. Office Pres., Washington, 1971-73; prof. chemistry Calif. Inst. Tech., Pasadena, 1973-99, chmn. div. chemistry and chem. engring., 1973-78, now J. Stanley Johnson prof., prof. emeritus. OAS vis. lectr. U. Chile, 1969; spl. lectr. in chemistry U. London, Queen Mary Coll., 1970; vis. scientist Bell Labs., 1978; mem. Pres.'s Sci. Adv. Com., 1969—, vice chmn., 1970-71; mem. Def. Sci. Bd., 1973-80, vice chmn., 1974-76; mem. carcinogenesis adv. panel Nat. Cancer Inst., 1973—; mem. com. planning and instl. affairs NSF, 1973-77; adv. com. Arms Control and Disarmament Agy., 1974-76; mem. NAS Bd. Sci. and Tech. for Internat. Devel., 1974-76, ad hoc com. on fed. sci. policy, 1979, task force on synfuels, 1979, Com. Internat. Security and Arms Control, 1992-95—; mem. Pres.'s Com. on Nat. Medal of Sci., 1974-76, pres., 1986-88, Pres.'s Adv. Group on Sci. and Tech., 1975-76; mem. governing bd. Reza Shah Kabir U., 1975-79; mem. Sloan Commn. on Govt. and Higher Edn., 1977-79, U.S.-USSR Joint Commn. on Sci. and Tech. Coop., 1977-79; vice chmn. del. on pure and applied chemistry to China, 1978; mem. com. on scholarly communication with China, 1978-84; chmn. com. on comml. aviation security NAS, 1988—, mem. def. sci. bd. task force on 'operation desert shield', 1990-91, mem. com. on internat. security and arms control, 1991-94—; mem. rsch. adv. coun. Ford Motor Co., 1979-94—, mem. chem. and engring. adv. bd., 1981-83; vis. lectr. Rand Afrikaans U., Johannesburg, South Africa, 1987, Found. Rsch. and Devel., Pretoria, South Africa, 1989. Mem. editorial adv. bd. Chem. Physics Letters, 1979-83, Jour. Liposome Rsch., contbr. articles to profl. jours. Served to 1st lt. AUS, 1959-60. Sloan Found. fellow, 1962-64, 64-65; recipient Fresenius award Phi Lambda Upsilon, 1968, Tolman award ACS, 1989. Mem. NAS, Am. Chem. Soc. (award in pure chemistry 1967, William H. Nichols medal 1990), Council on Sci. and Tech. for Devel., Am. Acad. Arts and Scis., Am. Philos. Soc. Office: Calif Inst Tech Divsn Chemistry & Chem Engring # 127-72 Pasadena CA 91125-0001

BALDESSARI, JOHN ANTHONY, artist; b. National City, Calif., June 17, 1931; s. Anton and Hedvig B.; divorced; children: Annamarie, Antonio. BA, San Diego State U., 1953, MA, 1957; postgrad., Otis Art Inst., Chouinard Art Inst., LA, 1957-59. Asst. prof. U. Calif., San Diego, 1968-70; mem. faculty Calif. Inst. Arts, Valencia, 1970-85; prof. art U. Calif., LA. One-man shows include La Jolla Mus. Art, Calif., 1960, 66, Southwestern Coll., Chula Vista, Calif., 1962, 64, 75, Molly Barnes Gallery, LA, 1968, Richard Feigen Gallery, NYC, 1970, Eugenia Butler Gallery, LA, 1970, Galerie Konrad Fischer, Dusseldorf, Fed. Republic Germany, 1971, 73, Art and Project, Amsterdam, The Netherlands, 1971, 72, Galerie MTL, Brussels, 1972, 75, Antwerp, Belgium, 1974, Galeria Franco Toselli, Milan, Italy, 1972, 74, Jack Wendler Gallery, London, 1972, 74, Sonnabend Gallery, NYC, 1973, 75, 78, 79, 80, 81, 84, 86, 87, 90, 92, 94, 98, Galerie Sonnabend, Paris, 1973, 75, Inst. Modern Art, Brisbane, Australia, 1976, Inst. Contemporary Art, Sydney, Australia, 1976, Ohio State U., Columbus, 1976, Portland Ctr. for Visual Arts, Oreg., 1978, Whitney Mus. Am. Art., NYC, 1978, Inst. Contemporary Art, Boston, 1978, Mcpl. Van Abbemuseum, Eindhoven, The Netherlands, 1980, 81, Mus. Folkwang, Essen, Fed. Republic Germany, 1981, Rudiger Schötte Gallery, Munich, 1981, Albright-Knox Gallery, Buffalo, 1981, Contemporary Art Ctr., Cin., 1982, Contemporary Arts Mus., Houston, 1982, Samangallery, Genoa, Italy, 1975, 81, Margo Leavin Gallery, LA, 1984, 86, 88-89, 92, 95, 97, 2002, 2005, 2007, Douglas Drake Gallery, Kansas City, Mo., 1983, Marianne Deson Gallery, Chgo., 1983, Swain Sch. Design, New Bedford, Mass., 1983, Contemporary Arts Mus., Houston, Anderson Gallery, Richmond, Va., 1982, Galerie Peter Pakesch, Vienna, 1984, 86, Galerie-Laage Salomon, Paris, 1984, 88, Univ. Art Mus. U. Calif., Berkeley, 1986, Santa Barbara (Calif.) Mus. Art, 1986, Multiples Inc., NYC, 1986-87, Cen. Nat. D'Art Contemporain de Grenoble, 1987, Dart Gallery, Chgo., 1987, Lisson Gallery, London, 1988, Primo Piano, Rome, 1988, Palais des Beaux-Arts, Brussels,1988, Hanover, Kastner-Gesellschaft, 1989, Cirrus, LA, 1989, Centro de Arte Regina Sofia, Madrid, 1989, Cape Musée d'Art Contemporain, Bordeaux, Instituto Valenciano de Arte Moderno, Centro Julio Gonzàlez, Valencia, Spain, Lawrence Oliver Gallery, Phila., 1989, Galerie Meert Rihoux, Brussels, 1989, 92, Mus. Contemporary Art, LA, 1990, Galerie Crousel Robelin, BAMA, Paris, 1991, Galerie Weber, Alexander Y Cobo, Madrid, 1991, traveling to San Francisco Mus. Modern Art, Hirshorn Mus. and Sculputure Garden, Mus. Contemporary Art, San Diego, 1996, Witte de With, Rotterdam, 1998, Marian Goodman Gallery, NYC, 2002, 2004, 2006, various others; group shows include Richard Feigen Gallery, NYC, 1968, U. Calif. San Diego Art Gallery, 1968, Dwan Gallery, NYC, 1969, Eugenia Butler Gallery, Los Angeles, 1969, Hayward Gallery, London, 1969, 80, Jewish Mus., NYC, 1970, Moore Coll. Art, Phila., 1970, Sonnabend Gallery, NYC, 1972, 73, 74, 78, 80-81, 84, 86-87, 90, Contemporary Arts Mus., Houston, 1972, 78, San Francisco Art Inst., 1972, Galerie Sonnabend, Paris, 1973, Kennedy Ctr., Washington, 1974, Paula Cooper Gallery, NYC, 1975, 81, 89, LA County Mus. Art, 1973, 74, 81, 87, 2006, Sch. Visual Arts, NYC, 1977, Mus. Fine Arts, Houston, 1977, Inst. Contemporary Arts, Boston, 1978, High Mus. Art, Atlanta, 1980, Westkunst, Cologne, Fed. Republic Germany, 1981, 5th Internat. Biennale, Vienna, Austria, 1981, Stedelijk Mus., Amsterdam, The Netherlands, 1974, 81, Kestner-Gesellschaft, Hanover, Fed. Republic Germany, 1982, Albright-Knox Gallery, Buffalo, 1982, Multiples Inc., 1982, Donald Young Gallery, Chgo., 1990, Whitney Mus. Am. Art, NYC, 1969, 72, 76, 77, 78, 79, 83, 2001, 2002, 2004, 2006, 2008, Marianne Deson Gallery, 1983, 87, Douglas Drake Gallery, NYC, 1987, Mus. Modern Art, NYC, 1970, 71, 72, 75, 77, 89, 99, 2000, 2006, 2007, Art Inst. Chgo., 1979, 85, Mus. Contemporary Art, Chgo., 1969, 77, 79, 2005, 2007, Mus. Contemporary Art, Los Angeles, 1986-88, 2004, Holly Solomon Gallery, NYC, 1986-87, Hoffman Borman Gallery, Santa Monica, Calif., 1987, Mus. Modern Art, Toyama, Japan, 1987, Newport Harbor Art Mus., Newport Beach, 1969, 74, 87, 89, Barbara Krakow Gallery, 1987, Bank of Boston Art Gallery, 1987, Phoenix Art Mus., 1987, LA Mcpl. Art Gallery, 1987, Castello Di Rivoli, Torino, 1987, Bess Cutler Gallery, NYC, 1987, Marian Goodman Gallery, NYC, 1987, 88, 89, 90, LA Contemporary Exhbns., 1987, Museums Ludwig in den Rheinhallen der Kolner Messe, Cologne, Fed. Republic of Germany, 1989, Centre Georges Pompidou, 1989, 2005, 2006, Met. Mus. Art, NYC, 1989, Nat. Gallery Art, Washington, 2001, Venice Biennale, 2003, various others; represented in permanent collections, Mus. Modern Art, NYC, Stedelijk Mus., Amsterdam, Holland, Kunstmuseum, Basel, Switzerland, Australian Nat. Gallery, Mus. Contemporary Art, LA and Chgo., Whitney Mus. Am. Art, NYC, Met. Mus. Art, NYC, Houston Mus. Fine Art; contbr. articles to profl. jours., photographic reproductions to books; subject of numerous articles. Recipient Skowhegan medal, 1988, Oscar Kokoschaka prize, Austria, 1996, Gov.'s award for Lifetime Achievement in Visual Arts, Calif., 1997, Spectrum Internat. award for Photography, Found. Lower Saxony, Germany, 1999, Lifetime Achievement award, Americans for the Arts, 2005, Archives Am. Art medal, 2007, Biennial award Contemporary Art, Bonnefantenmuseum Maastricht, 2008; grantee Nat. Endowment for Arts, 1973, 74, 75; fellow Guggenheim Found., 1986. Fellow: Am. Acad. Arts and Scis.; mem.: AAAL. Office: Sonnabend Gallery 536 W 22nd St New York NY 10011-1108 also: Margo Leavin Gallery 812 N Robertson Blvd Los Angeles CA 90069-4929 Office: U Calif Dept Art 1100 Kinross Ave Ste 245 PO Box 951615 Los Angeles CA 90095

BALDRIDGE, KIM, science educator; BS in Math., Minot State U., ND, 1982; MA in Math., ND State U., 1985, PhD in Theoretical Chemistry, 1988. Joined San Diego Supercomputer Ctr., 1989, dir. integrative computational scis., 2002—; adj. prof. chemistry U. Calif., San Diego, 1997—. Hon. guest prof. U. Basel. Recipient award, Fulbright Found., 1997, Agnes Fay Morgan rsch. award, Iota Sigma Pi, 2000. Fellow: AAAS, Am. Phys. Soc. Office: San Diego Super Computer Ctr Dept Chemistry 9500 Gilman Dr La Jolla CA 92093-0505

BALDWIN, BRUCE GREGG, botany educator, researcher; b. San Luis Obispo, Calif., Oct. 24, 1957; s. Robert Lee and Sally Louise (Elrod) B. BA in Biol. Scis. with honors, U. Calif., Santa Barbara, 1981; MS in Botany, U. Calif., Davis, 1985, PhD in Botany, 1989. NSF postdoctoral fellow U. Ariz., Tucson, 1990-92; asst. prof. dept. botany Duke U., 1992-94; curator Jepson Herbarium U. Calif., Berkeley, 1994—, asst. prof. in residence dept. integrative biology, 1994-98, assoc. prof. in residence dept. integrative biology, 1998-2000, assoc. prof. dept. integrative biology, 2000—05, prof. dept. integrative biology, 2005—. Mellon vis. scholar Rancho Santa Ana Bot. Garden, 1994. Contbr. articles to profl. jours. and books, reviewer; chief editor Jepson Flora project, 1994—. Recipient NSF Nat. Young Investigator award, 1994; Calif. Acad. Scis. fellow, 1999—, McBryde fellow, Nat. Tropical Botanical Garden, 2007. Mem. Am. Soc. Plant Taxonomists (publicity com. 1993-96, coun. 2002-05), Calif. Bot. Soc. (pres. 2000-03), Soc. Systematic Biology (coun. 2004-). Achievements include research in plant systematics, phylogenetics, plant cytogenetics and chromosome evolution, plant speciation, California floristics, phytogeography, insular evolution. Home: 2408 Parker St Berkeley CA 94704-2812 Office: U Calif Berkeley Jepson Herbarium Dept Integrative Biology 1001 Valley Life Scis Bldg 2465 Berkeley CA 94720-2465 E-mail: bbaldwin@berkeley.edu.

BALDWIN, GARY LEE, electronics engineer, educator; b. El Centro, Calif., Oct. 12, 1943; s. Benjamin H. and Susan Virginia (Webster) B.; m. Lois D. Johnson, Sept. 4, 1965 (div. Oct. 1984); children: Christopher, Bryan; m. Virginia J. Wade, Apr. 27, 1991. BSEE, U. Calif., Berkeley, 1966, MSEE, 1967, PhD, 1970. Mem. tech. staff Bell Telephone Labs., Holmdel, N.J., 1970-78; dir. solid-state tech. lab. Hewlett-Packard Labs., Palo Alto, Calif., 1978; former acting asst. prof. Electrical Engineering U. of Calif., Berkeley; exec. dir. Gigascale Silicon Rsch. Ctr., 1999—2003; asst. dean for indsl. relations, Coll. of Engring. U. Calif., Berkeley; exec. dir. Ctr. for Information Technol. for the Interest of Society (CITRIS). Holder 7 U.S. patents. Fellow IEEE (pres. solid-state cirs. coun. 1986-89, editor Solid-State Circuits jour. 1983-86, contbr. numerous articles) Office: UC Berkeley 280 HMMB Berkeley CA 94720-1776

BALDWIN, GEORGE CURRIDEN, physicist, researcher; b. Denver, May 5, 1917; s. Harry Lewis and Elizabeth (Watson) B.; m. Winifred M. Gould, Apr. 27, 1952; children: George T., John E., Celia M. BA, Kalamazoo Coll., 1939; MA, U. Ill., 1941, PhD, 1943. Instr. physics U. Ill., Urbana, 1943-44; rsch. assoc. GE, Schenectady, NY, 1944-55, nuclear engr. Cin., 1955-57; reactor mgr. Argonne Nat. Lab., Ill., 1957-58; physicist Gen. Engring. Lab. GE, Schenectady, 1958-67; adj. prof. nuclear engring. and sci. Rensselaer Poly. Inst., Troy, NY, 1964-67, prof., 1967-77, prof. emeritus, 1977—; staff mem. Los Alamos Nat. Lab., N.Mex., 1975-87; vis. scientist, 1987—89; ret., 1987. Author: An Introduction to Nonlinear Optics, 1969, The Science Was Fun, 2006; contbr. articles on nuclear and radiation physics to sci. publs. Councilman, Niskayuna, NY, 1965-69; mem. Zoning Bd., 1969-77. Recipient Disting. Alumnus award Kalamazoo Coll., 1987. Fellow Am. Phys. Soc.; mem. AAAS, Phi Beta Kappa, Sigma Xi, Phi Kappa Phi, Gamma Alpha. Achievements include discovery of nuclear giant dipole resonance; research on gamma-ray lasers; discovery of 1776 Escalante inscription. Personal E-mail: geoc142857@msn.com.

BALDWIN, JOHN, legal association administrator, lawyer; b. Salt Lake City, Feb. 9, 1954; BA, U. Utah., 1977, JD, 1980. Bar: Utah 1980, U.S. Dist. Ct. Utah 1980, U.S. Ct. Appeals (10th cir.) 1984. Assoc. Jardine, Linebaugh, Brown & Dunn, Salt Lake City, 1980-82; asst. atty. gen. Utah Atty. Gen.'s Office, Salt Lake City, 1982-85; dir. Utah Divsn. Securities, Salt Lake City, 1985-90; exec. dir. Utah State Bar, Salt Lake City, 1990—. Adj. assoc. prof. mgmt. Eccles Sch. Bus., U. Utah. Mem. N.Am. Securities Adminstrs. Assn. (bd. dirs. 1987-90, pres. 1988-89), U. Utah Young Alumni Assn. (bd. dirs. 1987-90), U. Utah Beehive Honor Soc. (bd. dirs. 1993-97), U. Utah Alumni Assn. (bd. dirs. 1995-97). Office: Utah State Bar 645 S 200 E # 310 Salt Lake City UT 84111-3837 Office Phone: 801-531-9077. Business E-Mail: jbaldwin@utahbar.org.

BALDWIN, LIONEL VERNON, retired university president; b. Beaumont, Tex., May 30, 1932; s. Eugene B. and Wanda (Wiley) B.; m. Kathleen Flanagan, Sept. 3, 1955; children: Brian, Michael, Diane, Daniel. BS, U. Notre Dame, 1954; SM, MIT, 1955; PhD, Case Inst. Tech., 1959. Rsch. engr. Nat. Adv. Com. Aerosci., Ohio, 1957-59; unit head NASA, 1959-61; assoc. prof. engring. Colo. State U., 1961-64, acting dean Coll. of Engring., 1964-65, dean and prof. Coll. of Engring., 1966-84; pres. Nat. Tech. U., Ft. Collins, Colo., 1984—2000; ret., 2000. Served to capt. USAF, 1955-57. Recipient award for plasma rsch. NASA, 1964, Kenneth Andrew Roe award Am. Assn. Engring. Soc., 1996. Fellow Am. Soc. Engring. Edn. (chmn. engring. deans coun.); mem. ASME, IEEE, NSPE, Sigma Xi, Tau Beta Pi, Sigma Pi Sigma. Achievements include patentee apparatus for increasing ion engine beam density. Home: 1900 Sequoia St Fort Collins CO 80525-1540

BALDWIN, RANSOM LELAND, animal science educator; b. Meriden, Conn., Sept. 21, 1935; s. Ransom Leland and Edna (Thurrot) B.; m. Mary Ellen Burns, June 1, 1957; children: Ransom Leland VI, Cheryl Lee, Robert Ryan. BS, U. Conn., 1957; MS, Mich State U., 1958, PhD, 1963. Research asst. Mich. State U., East Lansing, 1957-61; from asst. to assoc. prof. U. Calif., Davis, 1963-70, prof., 1970—2001, prof. emeritus, 2001—. Assoc. editor Jour. Nutrition, 1971-73, 83—; contbr. research articles to profl. jours. Gugenheim fellow, Fulbright fellow, NSF fellow, U.S. NAS fellow, 1993; recipient Borden award, 1980, Am. Feed Mfrs. Assn. award, 1970. Fellow AAAS, Am. Soc. Nutrition, Am. Diary Sci. Assn., Sigma Xi Office: U Calif Dept Animal Sci One Shields Ave Davis CA 95616 Home: 1515 Shasta Dr Apt 2208 Davis CA 95616-6682 Office Phone: 530-752-1250. Business E-Mail: rlbaldwin@ucdavis.edu.

BALDWIN, ROBERT LESH, biochemist, educator; b. Madison, Wis., Sept. 30, 1927; s. Ira Lawrence and Mary (Lesh) B.; m. Anne Theodora Norris, Aug. 28, 1965; children: David Norris, Eric Lawrence. BA, U. Wis., 1950; D.Phil. (Rhodes scholar), Oxford U., Eng., 1954. Asst. prof., then asso. prof. biochemistry U. Wis., 1955-59; mem. faculty Stanford, 1959—, prof. biochemistry, 1964-98, prof. emeritus, 1998—, chmn. dept., 1989-94. Vis. prof. Collège de France, Paris, 1972, Tsinghua U., Beijing, 2002; mem. adv. panel biochemistry and biophysics NSF, 1974—76; mem. NIH study sect. molecular and cellular biophysics, 1984—88. Assoc. editor Jour. Molecular Biology, 1964-68, 75-79; mem. editl. bd. Trends Biochem. Sci., 1977-84, Biochemistry, 1984—2008, Protein Sci., 1992-97. Mem. award panel Searle Scholars, 1993—96, 1997—98; mem. adv. panel in biophysics Burroughs-Wellcome, 1995—2001. Recipient Wheland award U. Chgo., 1995, Merit award NIH, 1988; Guggenheim fellow, 1958-59. Fellow Am. Biophysics Soc. (coun. 1977-81, Founder's award 1999); mem. NAS, Am. Soc. Biol. Chemists (Merck award 1999), Am. Chem. Soc., Am. Acad. Arts and Scis., Protein Soc. (coun. 1993-95, Stein and Moore award 1992). Home: 1243 Los Trancos Rd Portola Valley CA 94028-8125 Office: Stanford Med Sch Dept Biochemistry Beckman Ctr Stanford CA 94305-5307 E-mail: baldwinb@stanford.edu.

BALES, ROYAL EUGENE, retired philosophy educator; b. Pratt, Kans., Sept. 23, 1934; s. Harold Thomas and Gladys (German) B.; m. Flossie Kathleen O'Reilly, Apr. 16, 1960; children— David Scott, Elizabeth Laurel B.Music Edn. cum laude, U. Wichita, 1956, MA, 1960; PhD, Stanford U., 1968. Tchr. music Kans. Pub. Schs., 1956-57, 59-60; instr. philosophy Menlo Coll., Atherton, Calif., 1962-69, prof., 1970-2000, prof. emeritus, 2000—, chmn. social scis. and humanities, 1971-74, dean liberal arts, 1974-79, provost, 1979-87, standing mem. president's adv. council, 1971-87. Vis. fellow Harris-Manchester Coll., Oxford U., 1994, 98; Wong vis. prof. Guangdong U. of Law and Bus., Guangzhou, China, 1999. Contbg. author: About Philosophy, 2006; contbr. articles to profl. jours. Pres. El Camino Youth Symphony Assn., 1985-87; hon. gov. Harris-Manchester Coll., Oxford, 1994—. Scholar and fellow U. Wichita, 1952-60, Stanford U., 1966-67; prin. investigator NSF, Menlo Coll./Stanford, 1971-72; Rsch grant Stanford-Warsaw Exchange, Poland, 1969-70. Mem. Am. Philos. Assn., Save The Bay Assn., Phi Mu Alpha Sinfonia. Democrat. Avocations: classical music, designing and constructing furniture. Home: 1255 Sherman Ave Menlo Park CA 94025-6012 Personal E-mail: bales.r@sbcglobal.net.

BALES, W. SCOTT, state supreme court justice; BA summa cum laude, Mich. State U., 1978; MA in Econ., Harvard U., 1980; JD magna cum laude, Harvard Law Sch., 1983. Clerk, Office of Solicitor Gen. U.S. Dept. of Justice, 1983; clerk to Judge Joseph T. Sneed U.S. Ct. of Appeals for Ninth Circuit, 1983—84; clerk to Justice Sandra Day O'Connor U.S. Supreme Ct., 1984—85; atty. Meyer, Hendricks, Victor, Osborn & Maledon, 1985—94; special investigative counsel, Office of Inspector Gen. U.S. Dept. of Justice, 1995—97, dep. asst. atty. gen., Office of Policy Develop., 1998—99; asst. U.S. atty. Dist. of Ariz., 1995—99; solicitor gen. Office of Ariz. Atty. Gen., 1999—2001; atty. Lewis and Roca LLP, 2001—05; justice Ariz. Supreme Ct., 2005—. Teaching fellow Harvard U., 1979—83; adjunct prof. of law Ariz. State U., 2001, U. Ariz., 2003—05. Bd. dirs. Ariz. Found. for Legal Services and Ed., 2004—05. Recipient Inspector General's award of merit, 1997, U.S. Atty. General's Disting. Svc. award, 1998, Found. for Justice award, 2005. Office: Ariz Supreme Ct 1501 W Washington Ste 402 Phoenix AZ 85007 Office Phone: 602-452-3528. Office Fax: 602-542-9484.

BALEY, VIRKO, composer, conductor, pianist; b. Ukraine, 1938; MusB, MusM, LA Conservatory Music and Arts. Founder, condr., music dir. Nev. Symphony Orch., Las Vegas; prof. composition U. Nev., Las Vegas, 1970—2000, disting. prof. composition, 2000—; artistic advisor, prin. guest condr. Kiev Camerata, Ukraine; prin. condr. Kiev Music Fest, Ukraine. Composer: Orpheus Singing, Jurassic Bird, Dreamtime, Treny; composer, co-prodr. (films) Swan Lake: The Zone, 1989, composer A Prayer for Hetman Mazepa. Recipient Shevchenko prize for Music, Govt. of Ukraine, 1996, Creative award, State of Nev. Regents, 1996, Acad. award in Music, AAAL, 2008; grantee Nat. Endowment Arts; Petro Jacyk Disting. Rsch. fellow, 2007. Mem.: ASCAP. Office: Dept Music U Nev Las Vegas 4505 Maryland Pkwy Box 455025 Las Vegas NV 89154-5025 also: c/o Troppe Note Publishing Inc Ste 308 1350 E Flamingo Rd Las Vegas NV 89119 Office Phone: 702-895-0813. E-mail: vbaley@ccmail.nevada.edu.

BALKANSKI, ALEXANDRE, investment company executive; B in Physics, Harvard U., M in Bus. Econs., PhD. Founder, pres. Diamond Devices, Inc.; pres, CEO C-Cube Microsystems, Milpitas, Calif.; gen. ptnr. Bench Mark Capital, Menlo Park, Calif., 2000—. Office: Bench Mark Capital 2480 San Hill Rd Ste 200 Menlo Park CA 94025

BALL, ALAN, screenwriter; b. Atlanta, 1957; Student in theater, Fla. State U. Founding mem., writer, actor, dir. Alarm Dog Rep. Playwright: The M Word, 1991, Five Women Wearing the Same Dress, 1993, Made For a Woman, Bachelor Holiday, Your Mother's Butt, The

Amazing Adventures of Tense Guy, All That I Will Ever Be, 2007; Screenwriter, co-prodr. (feature film) American Beauty, 1999 (Oscar for best screenplay 1999, Golden Globe for best screenplay motion picture 2000, Satellite award for best original screenplay 2000; best screenplay BFCA award, DGA award, ALFA award, SEFCA award and WGA Screen award 2000), The M Word, 2004; screenwriter, creator, exec. prodr. (tv series) Grace Under Fire, 1993; co-exec. prodr. (tv series) Cybill, 1995; exec. prodr., creator (tv series) Oh Grow Up, 1999; screenwriter, dir., exec. prod. (tv series) Six Feet Under, 2001-2005 (Emmy for outstanding director for a drama series 2002). Office: c/o Andrew Cannava United Talent Agy 9560 Wilshire Blvd Fl 5 Beverly Hills CA 90212-2401

BALL, LAWRENCE, retired physical scientist; b. Albion, NY, Aug. 10, 1933; s. Harold Witheral and Gladys (Gibbs) B.; m. Caroline Moran, June 21, 1957, (dec. April 9, 2006); children: Daniel Lawrence, Logan Edward, Stacey Laura Ball Lucero, Ryan Laird (dec.); m. Roberta J. Fisher, Sept. 2, 2007. Diploma, Williston Acad., 1952; BSME, Antioch Coll., 1957; MSc in Elec. Engring., Ohio State U., 1962. Engring. aid Wright Air Devel. Ctr., Dayton, Ohio, 1957-60; engr. Deco Electronics Inc., Boulder, Colo., 1962-66; sr. engr. Westinghouse Rsch. Labs., Boulder, 1966-73, Westinghouse Ocean Rsch. Lab., Annapolis, Md., 1973-74; program mgr. div. geothermal energy U.S. Dept. Energy, Washington, 1974-79, lab. dir. Grand Junction, Colo., 1979-93; ret., 1993; resident inspector Armstrong Cons., Inc., Grand Junction, Colo., 2000—. Pres. Liberty Cons. Co., Grand Junction, 1984—. Co-inventor coal mine communications; contbr. articles to profl. jours. Mem. various vol. fire depts., 1954—79, Boulder Res. Police, 1968—74; sr. patroller Nat. Ski Patrol Sys., Md., Colo., 1973—92; mem. Grand Junction Safety Coun., 1992—98; active Amateur Radio Emergency Svcs., 1995—2004, dist. emergency coord., 1997—99; bd. dirs. Colo. Head Injury Found., chpt. pres., 1989—91. Named Profl. Govt. Employee of Yr., Western Colo. Fed. Exec. Assn., 1991. Mem. Toastmasters Internat. (area gov. 1991-92, divsn. gov. 1992-93, Toastmaster of Yr. Western Colo. 1990, DTM & ATM-S 1994), West Slope Wheelman (charter bd. dirs. 1992-93), Western Colo. Amateur Radio Club, Inc. (pres. 1994-96, bd. dirs. 1996-2004), Black Ridge Comms. Site Users Assn. (charter bd. dirs. 1995-2006, sec. 1997-2001, sec., treas. 1999-2001). Avocations: fishing, scuba diving (divecon), woodworking, amateur radio (extra class), Bible archaeology. Business E-Mail: larryb33@bresnan.net.

BALL, ROBERT JEROME, classics educator; b. NYC, Nov. 4, 1941; s. William and Pauline Ball. BA, Queens Coll., 1962; MA, Tufts U., 1963; PhD, Columbia U., 1971. Asst. prof. classics U. Hawaii, Honolulu, 1971-76, assoc. prof., 1976-83, prof., 1983—. Cons. in field. Author: Tibullus The Elegist: A Critical Survey, 1983, Reading Classical Latin: A Reasonable Approach, 1987, 2d edit., 1997, Reading Classical Latin: The Second Year, 1990, 2d edit., 1998; editor: The Classical Papers of Gilbert Highet, 1983, The Unpublished Lectures of Gilbert Highet, 1998. Recipient Excellence in Teaching award U. Hawaii, 1979; Presdl. scholar U. Hawaii, 1985. Mem. Am. Philol. Assn. (Excellence in Teaching award 1981). Office: U Hawaii Dept European Langs Honolulu HI 96822 Home Phone: 808-941-1371; Office Phone: 808-956-4164. Business E-Mail: rball@hawaii.edu.

BALLARD, GLEN, composer; b. Natchez, Miss., May 1, 1953; Grad. with honors, U. Miss., 1975. Recs. include Glen Ballard, co-writer, prodr. for Jagged Little Pill (Grammy award for Best Rock Album, 1996, Grammy award for Album of Yr., 1996), Hold On, Release Me, Shadows and Light; composer: You Oughta Know (Grammy award for Best Rock Song, 1996), The Places You Find Love, One Step, What's On Your Mind, Why is this Girl Giving Me Fever, Dance Electric, Try Your Love Again, All I Need, You Look So Good in Love (Country Song of Yr., 1986), Man in the Mirror, Nightline, State of Attraction, Keep the Faith, I Wonder Why, Wall in Your Heart, When the World Ends, The Polar Express, 2004 (Grammy award, Best Song Written for Motion Picture, for Believe, 2006), others; composer for various artists including Al Jarreau, Earth, Wind & Fire, Sheena Easton, Celine Dion, K.T. Oslin, Jack Wagner, Michael Jackson, Wilson Phillips, Curtis Stigers, Dave Matthews Band, Goo Goo Dolls, Josh Groban, Shelby Lynne, Anastacia (Oscar nomination), music prodr. (films) Lean on Me, 1989, Navy Seals, 1990, Into the West, 1992, Never Been Kissed, 1999, Teaching Mrs. Tingle, 1999, Titan A.E., 2000, Bridget Jones's Diary, 2001, The Mummy Returns, 2001, Shallow Hal, 2001; exec. prodr.: (films) Trapped, 2002; writer, prodr. (films) Clubland, 1999. Office: Chasen & Co Ste 405 8899 Beverly Blvd Los Angeles CA 90048-2431 also: The High Window Hollywood CA 90028

BALLARD, MELVIN RUSSELL, JR., investment executive, church official; b. Salt Lake City, Oct. 8, 1928; s. Melvin Russell and Geraldine (Smith) B.; m. Barbara Bowen, Aug. 28, 1951; children: Clark, Holly, Meleea, Tamara, Stacey, Brynn, Craig. Student, U. Utah, 1946, 50-52. Sales mgr. Ballard Motor Co., Salt Lake City, 1950-54; investment counselor Salt Lake City, 1954-56; founder, owner, mgr. Russ Ballard Auto, Inc., Salt Lake City, 1956-58, Ballard-Wade Co., 1958-67; owner, mgr. Ballard Investment Co., Salt Lake City, 1962—; mem. Quorum of Twelve, 1979—. Gen. authority LDS Ch., Salt Lake City, 1976—; bd. dirs. Nate-Wade, Inc., Salt Lake City, Silver King Mines, Inc., Salt Lake City, Huntsmand Chem. Co., Salt Lake City; chmn. bd. dirs. Deseret Book Co., Salt Lake City; gen. ptnr. N & R Investment, Salt Lake City, 1958—, Ballard Investment Co., Salt Lake City, 1955—. Bd. dirs. Salt Lake Jr. Achievement, 1978-80; bd. dirs. Freedoms Found., 1978—, David O. McKay Inst. Edn., 1979—; active Coun. Twelve Apostles, 1979. 1st lt. USAR, 1950-57. Mem. Salt Lake Area C. of C. (gov. 1979—). Republican. Office: LDS Church 50 E North Temple Salt Lake City UT 84150-0002

BALLHAUS, WILLIAM FRANCIS, JR., former aerospace industry executive, engineer; b. LA, Jan. 28, 1945; s. William Francis Sr. and Edna A. Ballhaus; m. Jane Kerber; children from previous marriage: William Louis, Michael Frederick; stepchildren: Benjamin Joel, Jennifer Angela. BSME with honors, U. Calif., Berkeley, 1967, MS in Mech. Engring., 1968, PhD in Engring., 1971. Rsch. scientist U.S. Army Aviation R & D, Ames Rsch. Ctr., Moffett Field, Calif., 1971—78; chief applied computation aerodynamics br. NASA-Ames Rsch. Ctr., Moffett Field, 1979-80, dir. astronautics, 1980-84, dir. Moffett Field and Edward AFB, Calif., 1984-89; acting assoc. adminstr., aeronautics and space tech. NASA Hdqrs., Washington, 1988-89; v.p. rsch. tech. Martin Marietta Space Launch Sys., Denver, 1989-90, v.p., program dir. Titan IV Centaur ops., 1990; pres. Civil Space and Communications, Martin Marietta, Denver, 1990-93, Aero & Naval Sys., Martin Marietta, Balt., 1993-94; corp. officer, v.p. engring. & tech. Lockheed Martin Corp., Bethesda, Md., 1995—2000; pres. The Aerospace Corp., 2001—08, CEO, 2001—08. Mem. scientific adv. bd. Air Force, 1994-2001, co-chmn. 1996-99; mem. corp. Charles Stark Draper Lab.; adv. coun. Jet Propulsion Lab.; bd. dirs. Space Found. Contbr. articles on computational fluid dynamics to profl. jours. Mem. sci. and acad. adv. bd. U. Calif., 1987-92; mem. engring. adv. bd. U. Calif., Berkeley and Davis, U. Southern Calif., and UCLA, U. Md., MIT Aero and Astro Dept.; sr. coun. mem. NASA Alumni League.; chmn. govt. and edn. div. United Way of Santa Clara County, Calif., 1987; mem. Air Force Sci. Adv. Bd., 1994-; mem. Def. Sci. Bd.; mem. sci. adv. bd. NOAA. Capt. USAR. Decorated Presdl. Rank of Disting. Exec., 1985; recipient H. Julian Allen award NASA-Ames Rsch. Ctr., 1977, Arthur S. Flemming award Jaycees, Washington, 1980, Disting. Profl. Engring. Sci. and Tech. award NSPE, 1986, Disting. Exec. Svc. award Sr. Execs. Assn., 1989, Disting. Svc. medal NASA, 1989, Disting. Engring. Alumnus award U. Calif., Berkeley, 1989, Air Force Exceptional Civilian Svc. medal, Air Force Scroll Appreciation, Nat. Reconnaissance Office Gold medal, Sir Force Assn. Gen. Bernard A. Schriever award for space leadership, Peter B. Teets award for championing the advancement of nat.-security space, Nat. Def. Indsl. Assn. Fellow AIAA (pres. 1988-89, Lawrence Sperry award 1980), Royal Aero. Soc., Am. Astronautical Soc.; mem. NAE (councillor, 2004-07), Internat. Acad. Astronautics, Tau Beta Pi (named Eminent Engr. U. Calif. Berkeley chpt.). Roman Catholic.

BALLHAUS, WILLIAM LOUIS, engineering executive; s. William Francis Ballhaus and Susan Elizabeth Berghoff; m. Darrin Jennifer Mollett, Sept. 12, 1998; 2 children. BSME, UC Davis, 1989; MS in Aeronautics and Astronautics, Stanford U., 1990, PhD in Aeronautics and Astronautics, 1994; MBA, UCLA, 1998. Rsch. asst. Stanford Aerospace Robotics Lab., Palo Alto, Calif., 1989—94; program dir. and sys. engring. mgr. Hughes Space and Comm., El Segundo, Calif., 1994—98; dir. Boeing Satellite Systems, Integrated Satellite Factory Ops., 1999—2000; gen. mgr. Boeing Electron Dynamic Devices, Inc., Torrance, Calif., 2000—01, Boeing Satellite Systems, Sys. Products Group, 2001—02; sr. v.p. Boeing Satellite Systems, Sys. Engring., 2002—03; pres. mission solutions BAE Systems, San Diego, 2003, pres. Nat. Security Solutions, 2004, pres. Nat. Security Solutions for Electronics and Integrated Solutions Operating Group Nashua, NH, 2005—08; pres., CEO DynCorp Internat., Inc., Falls Ch., Va., 2008—. Mem. of the dean's coun. Loyola Marymount U., Coll. of Sci. and Engring., Westchester, Calif., 2002—; bd. dirs. US Geospatial Intelligence Found.; bd. advisors Geospatial 21. Fellow: Brit. Am. Project, AIAA (assoc.). Achievements include patents for interconnective transponder systems and methods. Office Fax: 972-929-2848.

BALLING, ROBERT C., JR., geography educator; b. 1952; Asst. prof. geography U. Nebr., 1979-84; mem. faculty Ariz. State U., 1985—, assoc. prof., prof.; dir. Office of Climatology. Lectr. greenhouse effect debate, Australia, New Zealand, Can., Kuwait, U.S. Author: The Heated Debate: Greenhouse Predictions Versus Climate Reality, 1992; contbr. articles to sci. jours. Office: Ariz State U PO Box 871508 Tempe AZ 85287-1508

BALLINGER, CHARLES KENNETH, information specialist; b. Johnstown, Pa., July 28, 1950; s. Delores Jean (Cool) B.; m. Deb C. Delger, Sept. 14, 1985. Programmer analyst Cowles Pub. Co., Spokane, Wash., 1975-78; systems analyst Old Nat. Bank, Spokane, 1978-82; software engr. ISC System, Spokane, 1982; micro computer analyst Acme Bus. Computers, Spokane, 1982-85; info. ctr. analyst Wash. Water Power Co., Spokane, 1985-92; office automation analyst EDS Corp., Spokane, 1992-96, software engr.-mini/micro, 1996-98, info. analyst for client-server human resources info. sys., 1998-2000, info. analyst for energy trading divsn., 2000—03, info. analyst, 2003—. Cons. IDP Co., Spokane, 1978—. Contbr. articles to profl. jours. Served with Signal Corps, U.S. Army, 1968-71. Mem. IEEE (assoc.), Spokane Heath Users Group (pres. 1979-83). Avocations: software development, motorcycling, boating, shooting, amateur radio. Home: 3810 S Havana St Spokane WA 99223-6006 Office: Avista Corp 1411 E Mission Ave MSC-28 Spokane WA 99201 Office Phone: 509-495-4559. Personal E-mail: ckballinger@comcast.net. Business E-Mail: cballinger@avistacorp.com.

BALLINGER, JAMES K., museum director; b. Kansas City, Mo., July 7, 1949; s. Robert Eugene and Yvonne (Davidson) B.; m. Linda Wegner, Apr. 14, 2008; children: Erin, Cameron BA in Am. History, U. Kans., 1972, MA in Art History, 1974. Gallery coordinator Tucson Art Ctr., 1973; registrar U. Kans. Mus. Art, Lawrence, 1973-74; curator collections Phoenix Art Mus., 1974-81, curator Am. art, 1974—2004, asst. dir., 1981, Sybil Harrington dir., 1982—, chief curator. Mem. Nat. Coun. Arts Nat. Endowment for the Arts, 2005—; lectr. in field. Author: (exhbn. catalogues) Beyond the Endless River, 1980, Visitors to Arizona 1846 to 1980, 1981, Peter Hurd, 1983, The Popular West, 1982, Thomas Moran, 1986, Frederick Remington, 1989. Bd. dir. Balboa Art Conservation Ctr., Phoenix Cmty. Alliance; adv. bd. Spencer Mus. Art, U. Kans.; mem. Maricopa Regional Arts and Cultural Task Force, 2003; mem. dean's coun. Herberger Coll. Fine Arts, Ariz. State U. Named Nonprofit Dir. of Yr., Org. Nonprofit Executives Ariz., 2004. Fellow: Western Assn. Art Mus., Assn. Am. Mus. Dirs. (pres. 2007—08); mem.: Central Ariz. Mus. Assn. (v.p. 1983). Avocations: hiking, basketball, travel. Office: Phoenix Art Mus 1625 N Central Ave Phoenix AZ 85004-1685 Mailing: Nat Endowment for the Arts 1100 Pennsylvania Ave NW Washington DC 20506-0001 Home: 322 W Holly Phoenix AZ 85003 Office Phone: 602-257-2123. E-mail: jim.ballinger@phxart.org.

BALLMER, STEVEN ANTHONY, computer software company executive; b. Farmington Hills, Mich., Mar. 24, 1956; s. Frederick and Beatrice (Dworkin) Ballmer; m. Connie Snyder, 1990; 3 children. BA/BS in Applied Math. and Econs., Harvard U., 1977; student, Stanford U. Asst. product mgr. Procter & Gamble Co., 1977—79; with Microsoft Corp., Redmond, Wash., 1980—, v.p. mktg., v.p. corp. staffs, sr. v.p. sys. software, exec. v.p. sales & support, 1992—98, pres., 1998—2001, CEO, 2000—. Bd. dirs. Microsoft Corp., 2000—, Accenture, 2001—06; bd. overseers Harvard U.; adv. coun. Stanford Bus. Sch. Named one of World's Richest People, Forbes Mag., 2006—, The 100 Most Influential People in the World, TIME mag., 2008. Avocations: exercise, jogging, basketball. Office: Microsoft Corp 1 Microsoft Way Redmond WA 98052-8300

BALMER, THOMAS ANCIL, state supreme court justice; b. Longview, Wash., Jan. 31, 1952; s. Donald Gordon and Elisabeth Clare (Hill) B.; m. Mary Louise McClintock, Aug. 25, 1984; children: Rebecca Louise, Paul McClintock. AB, Oberlin Coll., 1974; JD, U. Chgo., 1977. Bar: Mass. 1977, D.C. 1981, U.S. Dist. Ct. Mass. 1977, Oreg. 1982, U.S. Dist. Ct. Oreg. 1982, U.S. Ct. Appeals (9th cir.) 1982, U.S. Ct. Appeals (D.C. cir.) 1983, U.S. Supreme Ct. 1987. Assoc. Choate, Hall & Stewart, Boston, 1977-79, Wald, Harkrader & Ross, Washington, 1980-82; trial atty. antitrust divsn. U.S. Dept. Justice, Washington, 1979-80; assoc. Lindsay, Hart, Neil & Weigler, Portland, Oreg., 1982-84, ptnr., 1985-90, Ater Wynne LLP, Portland, 1990—93; dep. atty. gen. State of Oreg., Salem, 1993-97; ptnr. Ater Wynne LLP, Portland, 1997—2001; justice Oreg. Supreme Ct., Salem, 2001—. Adj. prof. of law Northwestern Sch. Law Lewis and Clark Coll., 1983-84, 90-92. Contbr. articles to law jours. Active mission and outreach com. United Ch. of Christ, Portland, 1984-87, Met. Svc. Dist. Budget Com., Portland, 1988-90; bd. dirs. Multnomah County Legal Aid Svc., Inc., 1989-93, chair 1992-93; bd. dirs. Chamber Music Northwest, 1997-2003, Classroom Law Project, 2000—, chair, 2007-, U.S. Dist. Ct. Hist. Soc., 2003-05, Oreg. Law Inst., 2005—. Mem. Oreg. Bar Assn. (chmn. antitrust sect. 1986-87, mem. fed. practice and procedure com. 1999-2001). Home: 2521 NE 24th Ave Portland OR 97212-4831 Office: Oreg Supreme Ct Supreme Ct Bldg 1163 State St Salem OR 97310 Office Phone: 503-986-5717. Business E-Mail: thomas.balmer@ojd.state.or.us.

BALMUTH, MICHAEL A., retail executive; With Bamberger's; exec. v.p., gen. mdse. mgr. Karen Austin Petites, 1986—88; sr. v.p., gen. mdse. mgr. Bon Marche, Seattle, 1988—89; joined Ross Stores, 1989, various positions including sr. v.p., gen. merchandise mgr., exec. v.p. merchandising, 1993-96, CEO, vice chmn., 1996—2005, CEO, vice chmn., pres., 2005—. Office: Ross Stores Inc 4440 Rosewood Dr Pleasanton CA 94588

BALOGH, ARISTOTLE N., information technology executive; BSEE and Computer Sci., Johns Hopkins Univ., MS in Elec. Engring. Computer Engring. Sr. engr., mgmt. positions SRA Corp., UPS's Roadnet Technologies, Westinghouse Electric Corp., Network Solutions; v.p. engring. VeriSign Inc., Mountain View, Calif., 1999—2002, sr. v.p., ops., infrastructure, 2002—06, exec. v.p., ops., infrastructure, 2006—07, exec. v.p., chief tech. officer, 2007; chief tech. officer Yahoo Inc., Sunnyvale, Calif., 2008—. Named one of Top 25 Chief Tech. Officers, InfoWorld mag., 2007. Office: Yahoo Inc 701 First Ave Sunnyvale CA 94089 Office Phone: 650-961-7500.

BALOGH, MARY, writer; b. Swansea, Wales, 1944; m. Robert Balogh; 3 children. BA in English Lang. and Lit., with honors, U. Wales, 1965. Cert. U. Wales, 1967. Tchr. Kipling HS, Saskatchewan, Canada, 1967—82, Windthorst HS, Saskatchewan, 1982—88. Author: (novels) A Masked Deception, 1985, The Double Wager, 1985, AChance Encounter, 1985, Red Rose, 1986, The Trysting Place, 1986, The First Snowdrop, 1986, The Wood Nymph, 1987, The Constant Heart, 1987, Gentle Conquest, 1987, Secrets of the Heart, 1988, An Unacceptable Offer, 1988, The Ungrateful Governess, 1988, Daring Masquerade, 1989, A Gift of Daisies, 1989, The Obedient Bride, 1989, Lady with a Black Umbrella, 1989, The Gilded Web, 1989, A Promise of Spring, 1990, Web of Love, 1990, The Incurable Matchmaker, 1990, Devil's Web, 1990, An Unlikely Duchess, 1990, A Certain Magic, 1991, Snow Angel, 1991, The Secret Pearl, 1991, The Ideal Wife, 1991, Christmas Beau, 1991, A Counterfeit Betrothal, 1992, The Notorious Rake, 1992, Beyond the Sunrise, 1992, A Christmas Promise, 1992, Deceived, 1993, A Precious Jewel, 1993, Courting Julia, 1993, Dancing with Clara, 1994, Tangled, 1994, Tempting Harriet, 1994, Dark Angel, 1994, Christmas Belle, 1994, Longing, 1994, Lord Carew's Bride, 1995, Heartless, 1995, The Famous Heroine, 1996, Truly, 1996, The Plumed Bonnet, 1996, Indiscreet, 1997, The Temporary Wife, 1997, Silent Melody, 1997, A Christmas Bride, 1997, Unforgiven, 1998, Thief of Dreams, 1998, Irresistible, 1998, The Last Waltz, 1998, One Night for Love, 1999, More than a Mistress, 2000, No Man's Mistress, 2001, A Summer to Remember, 2002, Slightly Married, 2003, Slightly Wicked, 2003, Slightly Scandalous, 2003, Slightly Tempted, 2004, Slightly Sinful, 2004, Slightly Dangerous, 2004, Simply Unforgettable, 2005, 2006, Simply Love, 2006, Simply Magic, 2007, Simply Perfect, 2008, The Ideal Wife, 2008, First Comes Marriage, 2009, Then Comes Seduction, 2009. Recipient Romantic Times Career Achievement award for Regency Short Stories, 1993. Office: c/o Random House 1745 Broadway New York NY 10019 E-mail: author@marybalogh.com.*

BALSWICK, JACK ORVILLE, social science educator; Asst. prof. sociology Wis. State U., 1967, U. Ga., 1968-71, assoc. prof., 1972-78, prof., 1978-82; prof. sociology and family devel. Fuller Theol. Sem., Pasadena, Calif., dir. rsch. marriage and family ministries. Author (with wife, Judith K. Balswick): The Family, 1989, Social Problems, 1990. Office: Fuller Theol Sem Dept Marriage and Family Mins 180 N Oakland Ave Sch Psycholo Pasadena CA 91182-0001

BALTIMORE, DAVID, microbiologist, educator, former academic administrator; b. NYC, Mar. 7, 1938; s. Richard I. and Gertrude (Lipschitz) B.; m. Alice S. Huang, Oct. 5, 1968; 1 dau., Teak. BA in Chemistry with high honors, Swarthmore Coll., Pa., 1960; postgrad., MIT, 1960—61; PhD, Rockefeller U., NYC, 1964. Postdoctoral rschr. MIT, Cambridge, Mass., 1964—65; research assoc. Salk Inst. Biol. Studies, La Jolla, Calif., 1965—68; from assoc. prof. microbiology to dir. MIT, Cambridge, Mass., 1968—82, founding dir. Whitehead Inst. Biomed. Rsch., 1982—90; pres. Rockefeller U., NYC, 1990—91, prof., 1990—94; pres. Calif. Inst. Tech., Pasadena, 1997—2006, pres. emeritus, 2006—, Robert Andrews Millikan prof. biology, 2006—. Bd. govs. Weizmann Inst. Sci., Israel; co-chmn. Commn. on a Nat. Strategy of Aids, 1986; ad hoc program adv. com. on complex genome, AIDS rsch. adv. coun. NIH, 1996, chair vaccine adv. com., 1997—2002; bd. dirs. MedImmune, Inc., 2003—. Mem. editorial bd. Jour. Molecular Biology, 1971-73, Jour. Virology, 1969-90, Sci., 1986-98, New Eng. Jour. Medicine, 1989-94; contbr. articles to profl. jours. Bd. govs. Weizmann Inst. Sci., Israel; bd. dirs. Life Sci. Rsch. Found. Recipient Gustav Stern award in Virology, 1970, Warren Triennial prize Mass. Gen. Hosp., 1971, Eli Lilly and Co. award in Microbiology and Immunology, 1971, Nat. Acad. Scis. US Steel award, 1974, Gairdner Found. award, 1974, Nobel prize in physiology & med., 1975, Nat. medal of Sci., 1999, Warren Alpert Found. prize, 2000, Sci. Achievement award, AMA, 2002, 2006. Fellow AAAS (pres.-elect 2006, pres. 2007-), Am. Med. Writers Assn. (hon.), Am. Acad. Microbiology; mem. NAS, Am. Acad. Arts and Scis., Inst. Medicine, Am. Philos. Soc., Pontifical Acad. Scis., Royal Soc. (Eng., fgn.), French Acad. Scis. (fgn. assoc.). Office: Calif Inst Tech Mail Code 147-75 1200 E California Blvd Pasadena CA 91125-0001

BALTZ, PATRICIA ANN (PANN), retired elementary school educator; b. Dallas, June 20, 1949; d. Richard Parks and Ruth Eileen (Hartschuh) Langford; m. William Monroe Baltz, Sept. 6, 1969; 1 child: Kenneth Chandler. Student, U. Redlands, 1967-68; BA in English Lit. cum laude, UCLA, 1971. Cert. tchr. K-8, Calif. Tchr. 4th grade Arcadia (Calif.) Unified Sch. Dist., 1972-74, 92—, substitute tchr., 1983-85, tchr. 3dr grade, 1985-87, tchr. 6th grade, 1987-90, tchr. 4th and 5th grade multiage, 1990—2005, ret., 2005. Sci. mentor tchr.

Arcadia Unified Sch. Dist., 1991-94; mentor Tech. Ctr. Silicon Valley, San Jose, Calif., 1991. Tchr. rep. PTA, Arcadia, 1980-93; mem. choir, children's sermon team, elder Arcadia Presbyn. Ch., 1980-93; chaperone, vol. Pasadena (Calif.) Youth Symphony Orch., 1988-90; vol. Am. Heart Assn., 1990-92. Recipient Outstanding Gen. Elem. Tchr. award, Outstanding Tchr. of the Yr. award Disney's Am. Tchr. Awards, 1993, Calif. Tchr. of Yr. award Calif. State Dept. Edn., 1993, Georgie award Girl Scouts of Am., 1993, The Self Esteem Task Force award L.A. County Task Force to Promote Self-Esteem & Personal & Social Responsibility, 1993, Profl. Achievement award UCLA Alumni Assn.; appid. to Nat. Edn. Rsch. Policies & Priorities Bd., U.S. Sec. Edn. Richard Riley; Pann Baltz Mission Possible Scholar named in her honor. Mem. NEA, Nat. Sci. Tchrs. Assn., Calif. Tchr. Assn., Arcadia Tchrs. Assn. Avocations: reading, singing, calligraphy, book-making, computers. Home: 1215 S 3rd Ave Arcadia CA 91006-4205

BALZHISER, RICHARD EARL, research and development company executive; b. Wheaton, Ill., May 27, 1932; s. Frank E. and Esther K. (Merrill Werner) B.; m. Christine Karnuth, 1951; children: Gary, Robert, Patricia, Michele. BS in Chem. Engring., U. Mich., 1955, MS in Nuclear Engring., 1956, PhD in Chem. Engring., 1961. Mem. faculty U. Mich., Ann Arbor, 1961-67; White House fellow, spl. asst. to sec. Dept. Def., Washington, 1967-68; chmn. dept. chem. engring. U. Mich., 1970-71; assoc. dir. energy, environ. and natural resources White House Office of Sci. and Tech., Washington, 1971-73; dir. fossil fuel and advanced systems Electric Power Rsch. Inst., Palo Alto, Calif., 1973-79, sr. v.p. R&D, 1979-87, exec. v.p. R&D, 1987-88, pres., chief exec. officer, 1988-96, pres. emeritus, 1996—. Bd. dirs. Reliant Energy, Electro Source, Aerospace Corp.; mem. adv. bd. Nat. Renewable Energy Lab.; mem. pres. com. on sci. and tech. energy studies I and II, Pres.'s Com. on Sci. and Tech. Energy Studies, 1997-99. Co-author: Chemical Engineering Thermodynamics, 1972, Engineering Thermodynamics, 1977. Mem. Ann Arbor City Coun., 1965-67, mayor pro tem, 1967. Named to Acad. All-Am., U. Mich. Football, 1952, Acad. All-Am. Hall of Fame, 2002. Mem. Nat. Acad. Engring. Lutheran. Office: Electric Power Rsch Inst 3412 Hillview Ave Palo Alto CA 94304-1344 Office Phone: 650-855-2141. Office Fax: 650-855-2090. Business E-Mail: rbalzhis@epri.com.

BAMBURG, JAMES ROBERT, biochemistry professor; b. Chgo., Aug. 20, 1943; s. Leslie H. and Rose A. (Abrahams) B.; m. Alma Y. Vigo, June 7, 1970 (div. Dec. 1984); children: Eric Gregory, Leslie Ann; m. Laurie S. Minamide, June 22, 1985. BS in Chemistry, U. Ill., 1965; PhD, U. Wis., 1969. Project assoc. U. Wis., Madison, 1968-69; postdoctoral fellow Stanford U., Palo Alto, Calif., 1969-71; from asst. to full prof. Colo. State U., Ft. Collins, 1971—, acad. coordinator cell and molecular biol. program, 1975-78, interim chmn. dept. biochemistry, 1982-85, 88-89, assoc. chmn., 1996—99, assoc. dir. neuronal growth and devel., 1986-90, dir. neuronal growth and devel., 1990—96, dir. molecular cell integrative neuroscience, 2002—, assoc. dir. integrated bio med. edn. sci. tech. grad. program, 2005—07. Vis. prof. MRC Molecular Biol. Lab., Cambridge, Eng., 1978-79, MRC Cell Biophysics Unit, London, 1985-86, Children's Med. Rsch. Inst., U. Sydney, Australia, 1992-93, U. Calif. San Diego, 1999-2000, Scripps Rsch. Inst., La Jolla, Calif., 2006-07; mem., chmn. NIH Biomed. Scis. Study Sect., Bethesda, Md., 1980-85; ad hoc mem. Physiol. Chem. Study Sec., 1997, Molecular Devel. Cell Neurosci., 1998-99, 2001, Cell Biol. Function, 2001-03; mem. adv. bd. Macromolecular Resources, 1999-2005, Boulder Lab. 3D Fine Structure, 1994-2005, Alaska Basic Neurosci. Program, 2000-07; mem. ZNS1 spl. emphasis panel, 2007. Contbr. articles to sci. jours.; mem. editl. bd. Cell Motil Cytoskel. Fellow NSF, 1964-65, Nat. Multiple Sclerosis Soc., 1969-71, J.S. Guggenheim Found., 1978-79, Fogarty Ctr., 1985-86, 92-93, W. Evans Vis. scholar U. Otago, N.Z., 1991; recipient Disting. Svc. award Colo. State U. 1989, 2005, Outstanding Adviser award, 1996, Scholar Impact award, Colo. State U. 2006. Mem. Am. Chem. Soc., Am. Soc. Cell Biology, Am. Soc. Biochem. Mol. Biol., Internat. Neurochem. Soc., Soc. for Neurosci., Sigma Xi (pres. CSU chpt. 1989), Am. Physiol. Soc. Home: 2125 Sandstone Dr Fort Collins CO 80524-1825 Office: Colo State U Dept Biochemistry Mrb Rm 235 Fort Collins CO 80523-1870 Business E-Mail: jbamburg@lamar.colostate.edu.

BANCEL, MARILYN, fund raising management consultant; b. Glen Ridge, NJ, June 15, 1947; d. Paul and Joan Marie (Spangler) B.; m. Rik Myslewski, Nov. 20, 1983; children: Carey, Roxanne. BA in English with distinction, Ind. U., 1969. Cert. fund raising exec. Ptnr. The Sultan's Shirt Tail, Gemlik, Turkey, 1969-72; prodn. mgr. High Country Co., San Francisco, 1973-74; exec. dir. East Bay Performance, Inc., 1976—79; pub. Bay Arts Rev., Berkeley, Calif., 1976-79; dir. devel. Oakland (Calif.) Symphony Orch., 1979-81; assoc. dir. devel. Exploratorium, San Francisco, 1981-86, dir. devel., 1986-91; prin. Fund Devel. Counsel, San Francisco, 1991-93; v.p. The Oram Group, Inc., San Francisco, 1993—. Co-chmn. capital campaign com. Synergy Sch., San Francisco, 1995-2000; adj. prof. U. San Francisco, 1993-2002. Author: Preparing Your Capital Campaign, 2000. Mentor Assn. Fundraising Profl. Mentor Program, 1994-. Fellow U. Strasbourg, France, 1968. Mem. Assn. Fundraising Profls. (bd. Golden Gate chpt. 1996-98, chmn. National Philanthropy Day, 2000, Outstanding Fundraising Exec. award 2002), Giving Inst., Devel. Execs. Roundtable, Phi Beta Kappa. Democrat. Avocation: gardening. Office: 328 Duncan St San Francisco CA 94131-2022 Office Phone: 415-821-2534. Business E-Mail: mbancel@oramgroup.com.

BANCROFT, JAMES RAMSEY, lawyer; b. Ponca City, Okla., Nov. 13, 1919; s. Charles Ramsey and Maude (Viersen) Bancroft; m. Jane Marguerite Oberfell, May 28, 1944. AB, U. Calif., Berkeley, 1940, MBA, 1941; JD, Hastings Coll. Law, 1949. Bar: Calif. 1950; CPA, Calif. With McLaren, Goode, West & Co., CPAs, San Francisco, 1946-50; ptnr. Bancroft, Avery & McAlister, San Francisco, 1950-86, of counsel, 1986-92; pres. Madison Properties, Inc., San Francisco, 1967-98, Adams Properties, Inc., 1969-79, Adams-Western Inc., 1969-78; chmn. bd. United Nuc. Corp., Falls Church, Va., 1972-82, UNC Resources, 1978-82, dir., 1984-85; chmn. bd. Madison Capital Inc., San Francisco, 1986-93, Adams Capital Mgmt. Co., 1987-88, pres., 1988—2004; mng. ptnr. Bancroft Investments, San Francisco, 1980—; owner, mgr. Bancroft Vineyard, 1982—; of counsel Bancroft & McAlister, San Francisco, 1986—99; dir., chmn. exec. com. Brown & Haley, Tacoma, 1999—. Former pres. Suisun Conservation Fund; former dir. Suisun Resource Conservation Dist.; former trustee Dean Witter Found., 1952-94; pres. Harvey L. Sorensen Found.; bd. dirs. Calif. Urology Found.; former dir. San Francisco Found. for Rsch. and Edn. Orthop. Surgery; trustee, former chmn. Pacific Vascular Rsch. Found. Lt. USNR, 1942-46. Mem. ABA, Confrérie des Chevaliers du Tastevin, Bohemian Club, Pacific Union Club, Order of Coif, Phi Beta Kappa. Office: 221 Main St Ste 440 San Francisco CA 94105-1913

BANDER, MYRON, physics professor, dean; b. Belzyce, Poland, Dec. 11, 1937; came to U.S., 1949, naturalized, 1955; s. Elias and Regina (Zielonka) B.; m. Carol Heimberg, Aug. 20, 1967. BA, Columbia U., 1958, MA, 1959, PhD, 1962. Postdoctoral fellow CERN, 1962-63; research assoc. Stanford Linear Accelerator Center, 1963-66; mem. faculty U. Calif., Irvine, 1966—, prof. physics, 1974—, dean phys. scis., 1980-86; chair dept. physics, 1992-95. Sloan Found. fellow, 1967-69 Fellow Am. Phys. Soc. Office: U Calif Irvine CA 92697-0001 Home Phone: 949-759-0232; Office Phone: 949-824-5945. Business E-Mail: mbander@uci.edu.

BANDOW, DOUGLAS LEIGHTON, editor, columnist, consultant; s. Donald E. and Donna J. B. AA, Okaloosa-Walton Jr. Coll., Niceville, Fla., 1974; BS in Econ., Fla. State U., 1976; JD, Stanford U., 1979. Bar: Calif. 1979 DC 1984. Sr. policy analyst Reagan for Pres. Com., LA, 1979-80, Arlington, Va., 1980, Office of Pres. Elect, Washington, 1980-81; spl. asst. to the Pres. for policy devel. White House, Washington, 1981-82; editor Inquiry Mag., Washington, 1982-84; sr. fellow Cato Inst., Washington, 1984—2005; nat. syndicated columnist Copley News Svc., San Diego, 1983—2005; v.p. Citizen Outreach, 2006—; Cobden fellow Inst. for Policy Innovation, 2006—; Bastiat scholar Competitive Enterprise Inst., 2007—; Taft fellow Am. Conservative Def. Alliance, 2007—; sr. fellow in internat. religious persecution Inst. Religion Pub. Policy, 2008—. Author: Unquestioned Allegiance, 1986, Beyond Good Intentions: A Biblical View of Politics, 1988, Human Resources and Defense Manpower, 1989, The Politics of Plunder: Misgovernment in Washington, 1990, The Politics of Envy: Statism as Theology, 1994, Tripwire: Korea and US Foreign Policy in a Changed World, 1996, Foreign Follies: America's New Global Empire, 2006; co-author: The Korean Conundrum: America's Troubled Relations with North and South Korea, 2004; editor: US Aid to the Developing World, 1985, Protecting the Environment, 1986; co-editor: The US-South Korean Alliance, 1992, Perpetuating Poverty, 1994; contbr. articles to periodicals. Recipient Nat. Young Am. award Boy Scouts Am., 1977, Freedom Leadership award Freedoms Found., Valley Forge, Pa., 1977, cert. for polit. and journalistic activities Freedoms Found., Valley Forge, Pa., 1979; named Man of Yr. NY State Coll. Reps., 1982. Mem. Calif. Bar Assn., DC Bar Assn, Chess Collectors Internat. Libertarian. Avocations: reading, antiques, travel. Business E-Mail: chessset@aol.com.

BANDURA, ALBERT, psychologist, educator; b. Mundare, Alta., Can., Dec. 4, 1925; arrived in U.S., 1949, naturalized, 1956; m. Virginia Varns; 2 children. BA, U. B.C., 1949, D.Sc. (hon.), 1979; MA in Psychology, U. Iowa, 1951, PhD in Psychology, 1952. Prof. psychology Stanford U., 1953—, David Starr Jordan prof. social sci. in psychology, 1973—. Author: (with R.H. Walters) Adolescent Aggression, 1959, (with R.H. Walters) Social Learning and Personality Development, 1963, Principles of Behavior Modification, 1969, Aggression, 1973, Social Learning Theory, 1977, Social Foundations of Thought and Action: A Social Cognitive Theory, 1986; editor: Psychological Modeling: Conflicting Theories, 1971, Self-Efficacy in Changing Societies, 1995, Self-Efficacy: The Exercise of Control, 1997. Recipient Disting. Lifetime Contbn. award, Soc. for Advancement of Behavior Therapy, 2001, Disting. Achievement Alumni award, U. Iowa, 2005, Lifetime Achievement award, Am. Acad. Health Behavior, 2006, Everett M. Rogers award, Norman Lear Ctr., 2007, Grawemeyer award, 2007; Guggenheim Found. fellow, 1972. Fellow: Ctr. Advanced Study in Behavioral Sci., Am. Acad. Arts and Scis.; mem.: APA (pres. 1974, Disting. Scientist award divsn. 12 1972, Disting. Sci. Contbn. award 1980, Outstanding Lifetime Contbn. award 2004), Am. Psychol. Found. (Gold medal award 2006), Can. Psychol. Assn. (hon. pres. 1999), Internat. Soc. Rsch. on Aggression (Disting. Contbn. award 1980), Western Psychol. Assn. (pres. 1980, Lifetime Achievement award 2003), Calif. Psychol. Assn. (Disting. Scientist award 1973, Lifetime Disting. Contbr. award 1998, Healthtrac award for disting. contbns. to health promotion 2002, McGovern medal for disting. contbn. to health promotion sci. 2004, Lifetime Achievement award for health promotion rsch. 2006), Inst. Medicine NAS, Am. Psychol. Soc. (William James award 1989, James Cattell award 2003). Office: Stanford U Dept Psychology Stanford CA 94305-2130 Office Phone: 650-725-2409. Business E-Mail: Bandura@stanford.edu.

BANERJEE, PRITH, computer company executive, computer engineering professor; b. India, July 17, 1960; married; 1 child. B Tech, Indian Inst. Tech., 1981; MSEE, Univ. Ill., 1982, PhD, 1984. Asst. prof. elec. & computer engring. Univ. Ill., 1985—89, asst. prof., 1989—93, prof., 1993—96; rsch. assoc. prof. Coordinated Sci. Lab. Univ. Ill., 1989—93, rsch. prof., 1993—96; dir. computational sci. & engring. Univ. Ill., 1994—96; dir. Ctr. for Parallel & Distributed Computing Northwestern Univ., 1996—, dept. chmn. & Walter Murphy prof. elec. & computer engring., 1998—2001, 2002—04; founder, pres., CEO AccelChip Inc., 2000—02, chief scientist, 2002—04; founder, chmn., chief scientist BINACHIP Inc., 2003—; disting. prof., dean Coll. Engring. Univ. Ill., Chgo., 2004—07; exec. v.p. rsch., dir. HP Labs Hewlett Packard Corp., Palo Alto, Calif., 2007—. Contbr. articles to profl. jours., chapters to books; author: Parallel Algorithms for VLSI Computed-Aided Design, 1994. Recipient Pres. of India Gold Medal, Indian Inst. Tech., 1981, Young Faculty Develop. award, IBM, 1986, Presdl. Young Investigators award, NSF, 1987, sr. rsch. award, Xerox, 1992, Frederick Emmons Terman award, Elec. Engring. div. ASEE, 1996. Fellow: IEEE (Taylor L. Booth Edn. award 2001), ACM, AAAS. Achievements include patents in field. Office: HP Labs 1501 Page Mill Rd Palo Alto CA 94304

BANERJEE, UTPAL, biology professor, research scientist; b. New Delhi; BS in Chemistry, St. Stephens Coll., New Delhi; M in Phys. Chemistry, Indian Inst. Tech.; PhD in Chemistry, Calif. Inst. Tech., post doctorate in Biology. Asst. prof. Univ. Calif., LA, 1988—94, prof., 1994—, chair Molecular Cell & Devel. Biology Dept. Prof. Howard Hughes Med. Inst. Named one of Best 20 Profs. of the Bruin Century, UCLA, 2000. Fellow: Am. Acad. Arts & Scis. Office: 1506D Gonda Neuroscience and Genetics Rsch Ctr 695 Charles Young Dr Los Angeles CA 90095-1761 Office Phone: 310-206-5439, 310-825-2980. E-mail: banerjee@mbi.ucla.edu.

BANGERTER, NORMAN HOWARD, building contractor, developer, former governor, Former Governor, Utah; b. Granger, Utah, Jan. 4, 1933; s. William Henry and Isabelle (Bawden) B.; m. Colleen Monson, Aug. 18, 1953; children: Garret, Ann, Jordan, Blair, Alayne, Adam, Erdman Jake (foster child). Student, U. Utah, 1956-57, Brigham Young U., 1951-55; PhD (hon.), U. Utah, Weber State U., So. Utah U., Dixie Coll. V.p. B and H Real Estate Co., West Valley City, Utah, 1970-82; pres. Bangerter and Hendrickson Co., West Valley City, 1970-82; v.p., sec. Dixie-Six Land Devel., West Valley City, 1970s and 80s; mem. Utah Ho. of Reps. from 51st Dist., 1975-85, majority leader, 1979-81, speaker, 1981-85; chmn. task force for alternative forms of govt. West Valley City, Utah, 1982; gov. State of Utah, 1985-93; pres. NHB Construction Co., South Jordan, Utah, 1983—. Bd. dirs. Blue Cross & Blue Shield, 1993—96. Chmn. Interstate Oil Compact Commn. Recipient Outstanding Legislator award VFW, 1981, Disting. Svc. award Home Bldg. Industry, Alumni Disting. Svc. award Brigham Young U.; named Outstanding Businessman West Valley C. of C., named one of Top Ten Am. Legislators, 1983. Mem. Nat. Govs. Assn. (exec. com. 1987), Western Govs. Assn. (chmn. 1986), Nat. Conf. State Legislators, VFW. Mem. Lds Ch. Home: 1130 Goldenrod Cir Saint George UT 84790-7512

BANK, ROY J., television producer; b. June 13, 1972; Grad. in Bus., U. Pa., Phila. Prodr. Nickelodeon, Reveille; head devel. and ops. Mark Burnett Prodns. Prodr.: (TV series) Wild & Crazy Kids, The Restaurant, 2003, The Casino, 2004; co-exec. prodr. (online game) Flushed Away Underground Adventure, 2006. Avocation: kayaking.

BANKS, BRITT D., lawyer; b. Ft. Collins, Colo., Aug. 21, 1961; BS cum laude, U. Denver, 1983; JD, U. Colo., 1988. Bar: Colo. 1989, US Dist. Ct. Dist. Colo. 1991, US Ct. Appeals 10th Cir. 1991. Law clerk to Hon. Oliver Seth US Ct. Appeals 10th Cir., 1988—89; atty. Holland & Hart, 1989—93; joined Newmont Mining Corp., Denver, 1993, assoc. gen. counsel, 1996—2001, sec., 2001—04, v.p., gen. counsel, 2001—06, exec. v.p. legal and external matters, 2006—. Mem.: Colo. State Bar. Office: Newmont Mining Corp 1700 Lincoln St Denver CO 80203

BANKS, ELIZABETH, actress; b. Pittsfield, Mass., Feb. 10, 1974; m. Max Handelman, July 5, 2003. Grad. magna cum laude, U. Pa., 1996; grad., Am. Conservatory Theater, San Francisco, 1998. Actress (films) Surrender Dorothy, 1998, Shaft, 2000, Wet Hot American Summer, 2001, Ordinary Sinner, 2001, Spider-Man, 2002, Swept Away, 2002, Catch Me If You Can, 2002, The Trade, 2003, Seabiscuit, 2003, Heights, 2005, Sexual Life, 2005, The Sisters, 2005, The Baxter, 2005, The 40 Year Old Virgin, 2005, Daltry Calhoun, 2005, Slither, 2006, Invincible, 2006, Spider-Man 3, 2007, Bill, 2007, Fred Claus, 2007, Definitely, Maybe, 2008, Meet Dave, 2008, Lovely, Still, 2008, Zack and Miri Make a Porno, 2008, W., 2008, Role Models, 2008, The Uninvited, 2009, (TV series) Scrubs, 2006—07, Wainy Days, 2007—08, (TV miniseries) Comanche Moon, 2008. Home: c/o Untitled Entertainment 1801 Century Park E Ste 700 Los Angeles CA 90067-2309

BANKS, JAMES ALBERT, research director, educator; b. Marianna, Ark., Sept. 24, 1941; s. Matthew and Lula (Holt) Banks; m. Cherry Ann McGee, Feb. 15, 1969; children: Angela Marie, Patricia Ann. AA, Chgo. City Coll., 1963; BE, Chgo. State U., 1964; MA (NDEA fellow 1966-69), Mich. State U., 1967, PhD, 1969; LHD (hon.), Bank St. Coll. Edn., 1993, U. Alaska, Fairbanks, 2000, U. Wis., Parkside, 2001, DePaul U., 2003, Lewis and Clark Coll., 2004, Grinnell Coll., 2006. Elem. sch. tchr. Joliet, Ill., 1965; tchr. Francis W. Parker Sch., Chgo., 1965—66; asst. prof. edn. U. Wash., Seattle, 1969—71, assoc. prof., 1971—73, prof., 1973—, chmn. curriculum and instrn., 1982—87, Russell F. Stark univ. prof., 2001—06, Kerry and Linda Killinger prof. diversity studies, 2006—; dir. Ctr. Multicultural Edn., Seattle, 1991; Spencer fellow Ctr. Advanced Study Behavioral Scis., Stanford, Calif., 2005—06. Vis. prof. edn. U. Mich., 1975, Monash U., Australia, Australia, 1985, U. Warwick, England, 1988, U. Minn., 1991; vis. lectr. U. Southampton, England, 1989; Harry F. and Alva K. Ganders disting. lectr. Syracuse U., 1989; Tyler eminent scholar chair Fla. State U., 1998; Carl and Alice Daeufer lectr. U. Hawaii, Manoa, 1999; Sachs lectr. Tchrs. Coll. Columbia U., 1996; disting. scholar lectr. Kent State U., 1978; Read disting. lectr. Kent State. U., 2005; 20th ann. faculty lectr. U. Wash., 2004—05; disting. scholar lectr. U. Ariz., 1979, Ind. U., 1983; vis. scholar Brit. Acad., 1983; com. examiners Ednl. Testing Svc., 1974—77; nat. adv. coun. on ethnic heritage studies, U.S. Office Edn., 1975—78, com. on fed. role in ednl. rsch. NAS, 1991-92, mem. com. on developing a rsch. agenda on edn. of ltd. proficient and bilingual students, 1995—97; mem. bd. on children, youth and families NRC and Inst. of Medicine/NAS, 1999—2005; 29th ann. faculty lectr. U. Wash., 2005; Tish disting. vis. prof. Tchrs. Coll. Columbia U., 2007. Author: Teaching the Black Experience, 1970, Teaching Strategies for the Social Studies, 1973, 5th edit., 1999, Teaching Strategies for Ethnic Studies, 1975, 7th edit., 2003, Multiethnic Education: Practices and Promises, 1977, An Introduction to Multicultural Education, 1994, 3d edit., 2002, Educating Citizens in A Multicultural Soc., 1997, 2d edit., 2007; author: (with Cherry Ann Banks) March Toward Freedom: A History of Black Americans, 1970, 2d edit., 1974, rev. 2d edit., 1978; author: Multiethnic Education: Theory and Practice, 1981, 4th edit., (new title) Cultural Diversity and Education: Foundations, Curriculum, and Teaching, 2001, 5th edit., 2006; author: (with others) Curriculum Guidelines for Multicultural Education, 1976, 5th edit., 2005; author: We Americans: Our History and People, 2 vols., 1982, Race, Culture, and Education: The Selected Works of James A. Banks, 2006; contbg. author Handbook of Complementary Methods in Education Research, 2006, Internat. Ency. of Edn., 1985, Handbook of Research on Teacher Education, 1990, Handbook of Research on Social Studies Teaching and Learning, 1991, Encyclopedia of Ednl. Rsch., 1992, Handbook of Research on the Education of Young Children, 1993, Review of Research in Education, vol. 19, 1993, Encyclopedia of Black Studies, 2005, Preparing Teachers for a Changing World, 2005, Handbook of Complementary Methods in Education Research, 3rd edit., —; editor: Black Self-Concept, 1972, Teaching Ethnic Studies: Concepts and Strategies, 1973; editor: (with William W. Joyce) Teaching Social Studies to Culturally Different Children, 1971; editor: Teaching the Language Arts to Culturally Different Children, 1971, Education in the 80's: Multiethnic Education, 1981; editor: (with James Lynch) Multicultural Education in Western Societies, 1986; editor: (with C. Banks) Multicultural Education: Issues and Perspectives, 1989, 6th edit., 2007; editor: Handbook of Research on Multicultural Education, 1995, 2d edit., 2004, Multicultural Education, Transformative Knowledge, and Action, 1996, Diversity and Citizenship Education: Global Perspectives, 2004; mem. editl. bd. Jour. of Tch. Edn., 1985—89, Coun. Interracial Books for Children Bull., 1982—92, Urban Edn., 1991—96, Race, Ethnicity and Education, 1998—, Tchrs. Coll. Record, 1998—2002, Multicultural Perspectives, 2000—03; contbr. articles to profl. jours; co-author: Handbook of Research in Social Studies Education, 2008, The Sage Handbook for Citizenship and Democracy, 2009, Just Schools: Pursuing Equality in Socties of Difference, 2008; editor: The Routledge International Companion to Multicultural Education, 2009. Recipient Outstanding Young Man award, Wash. State Jaycees, 1975, Outstanding Svc. in Edn. award, Seattle U. Black Student Union, 1985, Pres. award, Tchrs. of English to Speakers of Other Languages, 1998, Disting Career Rsch. award, Nat. Coun. for the Social Studies,

2001, Disting. Alumni award, Coll. Edn., Mich. State U., 2004, Mich. State U., 2005, medal, UCLA, 2005; named Tisch Disting. Vis. Prof., Tchrs. Colls. Columbia U., 2007; Spencer fellow, Nat. Acad. Edn., 1973—78, Kellogg fellow, 1980—83, Rockefeller Found. fellow, 1980, Ctr. Advanced Studies in Behavioral Sci. fellow, Stanford U., 2005—06. Mem. ASCD (bd dirs. 1976-79, Disting. lectr. 1986, Disting. scholar, lectr. 1994, 97), Nat. Acad. Edn. (bd. dirs. 2003—), Nat. Coun. Social Studies (bd. dirs. 1973-74, 80-85, pres. 1982, Disting. Career Rsch. in Social Studies award 2001), Internat. Assn. Intercultural Edn. (editl. bd.), Social Sci. Edn. Consortium (bd. dirs. 1976-79), Am. Ednl. Rsch. Assn. (com. on role and status of minorities in edn. rsch. 1992-94, publs. com. 1995-96, pres.-elect 1996-97, pres. 1997-98, exec. bd. 1998-99, Disting. scholar/rschr. on minority edn. 1986, Rsch. Review award 1994, Disting. Career Contbn. award 1996, Social Justice in Edn. award 2004), Phi Delta Kappa, Phi Kappa Phi, Golden Key Nat. Honor Soc., Kappa Delta Pi. Office: Ctr for Multicultural Edn Univ Wash Box 353600 110 Miller Hall Seattle WA 98195-3600 Office Phone: 206-543-3386. Office Fax: 206-543-1237. Business E-Mail: jbanks@u.washington.edu.

BANKS, MICHELLE, lawyer, retail executive; BA, JD, UCLA. Bar: Calif. 1988. Assoc. Morrison & Foerster; counsel Itochu Corp., Japan; in-house legal counsel Golden State Warriors Basketball Team; sr. corp. counsel The Gap Inc., San Francisco, 1999—2003, assoc. gen. counsel, 2003—05, v.p., assoc. gen. counsel, 2005—06, sr. v.p., gen. counsel, 2006—08, sr. v.p., gen. counsel, corp. sec., chief compliance officer, 2008—. Mem.: Assn. Corp. Counsel (chair exec. adv. council), Bar Assn. San Francisco, Bay Area Gen. Counsel, Gen. Counsel Roundtable, Minority Corp. Counsel Assn. (bd. dir.). Office: The Gap Inc 2 Folsom St San Francisco CA 94105

BANKS, PETER MORGAN, physics professor; b. San Diego, May 21, 1937; s. George Willard and Mary Margaret (Morgan) B.; children by previous marriage: Kevin, Michael, Steven, David.; m. Mary E. Stewart, Dec. 28, 2002; 1 child, Mark. MS in E.E, Stanford U., 1960; PhD in Physics, Pa. State U., 1965. Postdoctoral fellow Institut d'Aeronomie Spatiale de Belgique, Brussels, 1965-66; prof. applied physics U. Calif., San Diego, 1966-76; prof. physics Utah State U., 1976-81, head dept. physics, 1976-81; vis. assoc. prof. Stanford U., 1972-73, prof. elec. engring., 1981-90, dir. space, telecommunications and radiosci. lab., 1982-90, dir. ctr. for aeronautics and space info. systems, 1983-90; prof. atmospheres, oceans, and space sci. U. Mich., 1990-95, adj. prof., 1996-2000; dean Coll. Engring., U. Mich., 1990-95; pres. Earth Data Corp., 1985-86; pres., CEO Environ. Rsch. Inst. Mich., 1995-97, ERIM Internat., Inc., 1997-99; ptnr. XR Ventures, LLC, 2000—04; CEO Akonni Biosystems, Inc., 2003; pres. Inst. for the Future, Menlo Park, Calif., 2004—05; gen. ptnr. Red Planet Capital, LP, 2006—08, Astrolabs Ventures, LP, 2008—. Vis. scientist Max Planck Inst. for Aeronomie, Germany, 1975; pres. La Jolla Scis., Inc., 1973—77, Upper Atmosphere Rsch. Corp., 1978—82; chmn. NASA adv. com. on sci. uses of space sta., 1985—87; prin. investigator space shuttle experiments, 1982, 85, 91; mem. Jason Group, 1983—97; bd. dirs. Tecumseh Products Corp.; chmn. bd. trustees Consortium Internat. Earth Sci. Info. Networks, 1991—94; co-chmn. NRC Commn. on Phys. Scis., Math. and Applications, 1998—2000. Author: (with G. Kockarts) Aeronomy, 1973, (with J.R. Doupnik) Introduction to Computer Science, 1976; assoc. editor: Jour. Geophys. Research, 1974-77; assoc. editor: Planetary and Space Sci, 1977-83, regional editor, 1983-86; contbr. numerous articles in field to profl. jours. Mem. space sci. adv. council NASA, 1976-80. Served with U.S. Navy, 1960-63. Recipient Appleton prize Royal Soc. London, 1978, Space Sci. award AIAA, 1981, NASA Disting. Service medal, 1986; Alumni fellow Pa. State U., 1982 Fellow Am. Geophys. Union; mem. Internat. Union Radio Sci., Nat. Acad. Engring., Univs. Space Rsch. Assn. (chmn. and trustee 2002—), Cosmos Club. Episcopalian. Home: 5602 Newanga Ave Santa Rosa CA 95405 E-mail: pb2@sonic.net.

BANNER, BOB, television producer, director; b. Ennis, Tex., Aug. 15, 1921; s. Robert James and Viola (Culbertson) B.; m. Alice Jane Baird, Jan. 14, 1946; children— Baird Allen, Robert James, Charles Moore. BBA, So. Meth. U., 1943; MA, Northwestern U., 1948. Pres. Bob Banner Assocs., 1958—. Vis. prof. So. Meth. U. Dir. Garroway-at-Large, NBC-TV; producer, dir. Fred Waring Show, CBS-TV; dir. Omnibus; TV producer, pres., Bob Banner Assos.; TV shows include (series) The Uptown Comedy Club, It's Showtime at the Apollo, Garroway At Large, Fred Waring Show, Don Ho, Omnibus, Jr. Almost Anything Goes, Almost Anything Goes, Candid Camera, Carol Burnett Show, Garry Moore Show, Dinah Shore Chevy Show, Kraft Summer Music Hall, Solid Gold, Star Search, It's Showtime at the Apollo, The Uptown Comedy Club, Real Kids, Real Adventures; (spls.) Perry Como Holiday Spls., Carnegie Hall Salutes Jack Benny, Peggy Fleming Holiday Spl., Amazing Music Spls., Happy Birthday, George Gershwin, 1996, Julie & Carol at Carnegie Hall, Ford Motor Co.'s 75th Ann., Am. West of John Ford, A Spl. Sesame St. Christmas; spls. starring Bob Hope, Julie Andrews, Andy Williams; (movies) My Sweet Charlie, My Husband is Missing, Warning Shot, Journey from Darkness, The Darker Side of Terror, If Things were Different, Yes Virginia There Is A Santa Claus, 1991, Crash Landing, 1992, With Murder In Mind, 1992, The Sea Wolf, 1993. Recipicient 15 Emmy awards, 11 Christopher awards, 3 Peabody awards. Mem. Acad. of TV Arts and Scis. Presbyterian.

BARAN, PAUL, computer executive; b. Poland, Apr. 29, 1926; came to U.S., 1928; m. Evelyn Murphy, 1955; 1 child, David. BSEE, Drexel U., 1949; MS in Engring., UCLA, 1959; DSc in Engring. (hon.), Drexel U., 1997; PhD in Policy Analysis (hon.), RAND Grad. Sch., 2000. With Eckert-Mauchley Computer Co., 1949, Rosen Engring. Products Co., 1950-54; systems group Hughes Aircraft Co., 1955-59; with RAND Corp., 1959-64; co-founder Inst. for Future, 1968; founder CableData Assocs., 1972; co-founder Equatorial Comm., 1978-80; founder Packet Techs., 1980, Telebit, 1980, Metricom, Inc., 1985; founder, chmn. bd. Com21, Inc., Milpitas, Calif., 1992—. Trustee IEEE History Ctr., 2000—, Charles Babbage Found., 2000—; bd. dirs. Marconi Internat. Fellowship Found. Recipient Edwin H. Armstrong award, IEEE Comm. Soc., 1987, 1st Ann. award, ACM Spl. Interest Group in Comm., 1989, Fellowship award, Marconi Internat., 1991, Centennial 100 medal, Drexel U., 1992, Pioneer award, Electronic Frontier Found., 1993, Computers and Comm. Found. award, 1996, award, NAE, 1996, The Economist Innovation award, 2003, Fellow award, Computer History Mus., 2005, Silicon Valley Engring. Hall of Fame award, 2007, 2007 Nat. Medal Technology and Innovation; named Entrepreneur of Yr. Tech., Silicon Valley Bus. Jour., 1999; named to Nat. Inventors Hall of Fame, 2007. Fellow AAAS, IEEE (life, Alexander Graham Bell medal 1990, Centennial medal 2000, Internet award 2000), Franklin Inst. (2001 Bower award and prize achievement in sci. 2001). Achievements include design of first doorway gun detector; inventor digital packet switching; several patents for work on several new communication technologies in part based upon the concept of packets. Home: 83 James Ave Atherton CA 94027-2009 E-mail: paul@baran.com.

BARAN, PHIL S., chemistry professor; AA with honors, Lake Sumter Cmty. Coll., Fla., 1995; BS with honors Chemistry, NYU, 1997; PhD in Chemistry, Scripps Rsch. Inst., La Jolla, Calif., 2001. NIH postdoctoral fellowship Harvard U., Cambridge, Mass., 2001—03; asst. prof. chemistry Scripps Rsch. Inst., La Jolla, Calif., 2003—06, assoc. prof. chemistry with tenure, 2006—. Contbr. articles to profl. jours. Recipient Dean's Undergraduate Rsch. Fund award in Chemistry, NYU, 1996—97, George Granger Brown award for Excellence in Chemistry, 1996—97, NSF Pre-doctoral Fellowship award, Scripps Rsch. Inst., 1998—2001, Lesly Starr Shelton award for Excellence in Chemistry Grad. Studies, 2000, Hoffmann-La Roche award for Excellence in Organic Chemistry, 2000, Nobel Laureate Signature award for Grad. Edn. in Chemistry, Am. Chem. Soc., 2003, Nat. Fresenius award, 2007, GlaxoSmithKline Chemistry Scholar award, 2005—06, Amgen Young Investigator award, 2005, Roche Excellence in Chemistry award, 2005, DuPont Young Prof. award, 2005, AstraZeneca Excellence in Chemistry award, 2005, Eli Lilly Young Investigator award, 2005—06, NSF Career award, 2006—10, Beckman Young Investigator award, Beckman Found. Fellow, 2006—08, Pfizer award for Creativity in Organic Chemistry, 2006; Searle Scholar, 2005, Herman and Margaret Sokol Chemistry Fellowship, NYU, 1995—97, NYU Coll. Art and Sciences Scholarship, 1995—97, William and Sharon Bauce Family Found. Fellowship award, Scripps Rsch. Inst., 1997, BMS Unrestricted "Freedom to Discover" Grant, 2006—10, Alfred P. Sloan Found. Fellow, 2006—08. Achievements include patents in field. Office: Dept Chemistry Mail Drop BCC 169 Scripps Rsch Inst 10550 N Torrey Pines Rd La Jolla CA 92037 Office Phone: 858-784-7373. Office Fax: 858-784-7375. Business E-Mail: pbaran@scripps.edu.

BARBAGELATA, ROBERT DOMINIC, lawyer; b. San Francisco, Jan. 9, 1925; s. Dominic Joseph and Jane Zeffra (Frugoli) B.; m. Doris V. Chatfield, June 8, 1956; children: Patricia Victoria, Robert Norman, Michael Alan. BS, U. San Francisco, 1947, JD, 1950. Bar: Calif. 1950, US Supreme Ct. 1964. Pvt. practice, San Francisco, 1950—; judge pro-tem San Francisco County Superior Ct., 1992-95. Lectr. U. San Francisco Law Sch., Pacific Med. Center. Contbr. to legal jours. Served with USNR, 1943-46. Mem. Calif. State Bar, Calif. Trial Lawyers Assn. (lectr., v.p.), Am. Bd. Trial Advocates (nat. pres. 1981-82, Trial Lawyer of Yr. 1986-87, San Francisco chpt. Pres. Don E. Bailey Professionalism award 2003, Lifetime Achievement award 2004, 05), Assn. Trial Lawyers Am., San Francisco Trial Lawyers Assn. (Lifetime Achievement award 2003), Am. Coll. Trial Lawyers, Internat. Soc. Barristers, San Francisco Lawyers Club. Roman Catholic. Office: 195 Alhambra St San Francisco CA 94123

BARBAROSH, CRAIG A., lawyer; b. Bklyn., Aug. 13, 1967; BA, Univ. Calif., Santa Barbara, 1989; JD with distinction, Univ. of the Pacific, 1992. Bar: Calif. 1992, US Ct. Appeals (9th cir.). Extern law clk. Judge James N. Barr, US Bankruptcy Ct. ctrl. dist. Calif.; ptnr., co-chmn. Insolvency & Restructuring practice, office mng. ptnr. Pillsbury Winthrop Shaw Pittman, Orange County, Calif. Editor (articles): Univ. of the Pacific Law Rev. Recipient CLAY Lawyer of the Year award, Calif. Lawyer mag., 2001; named an Outstanding Young Bankruptcy Lawyer, Turnarounds & Workouts mag.; named one of Top 20 Lawyers Under Age 40, Daily Jour. Calif. Law Bus. Mem.: Am. Bankruptcy Inst., Calif. Bankruptcy Forum, Orange County Bankruptcy Forum, Orange County Bar Assn., Order of the Coif. Office: Pillsbury Winthrop Shaw Pittman 7th Fl 650 Town Center Dr Costa Mesa CA 92626 Office Phone: 714-436-6822. Office Fax: 714-436-2800. Business E-Mail: craig.barbarosh@pillsburylaw.com.

BARBER, GARY, motion picture company executive; Chief oper. officer Morgan Creek Prodns., LA; pres. Morgan Creek Internat., LA. Exec. prodr. (films) Midnight Crossing, 1988, Communion, 1989, Young Guns II, 1990, Pacific Heights, 1990, Robin Hood: Prince of Thieves, 1991, Freejack, 1992, White Sands, 1992, Stay Tuned, 1992, The Crush, 1993, Major League II, 1994, Ace Ventura, Pet Detective, 1994, Trial by Jury, 1994, Imaginary Crimes, 1994, Chasers, 1994, Silent Fall, 1994, Ace Ventura, When Nature Calls, 1995, Two if by Sea, 1996, Diabolique, 1996, Bad Moon, 1996, Wild America, 1997, Incognito, 1997, Major League: Back to the Minors, 1998, Wrongfully Accused, 1998, Keeping the Faith, 2000, Unbreakable, 2000, Out Cold, 2001, Bruce Almighty, 2003, 1 Love, 2003, Seabiscuit, 2003, The Legend of Zorro, 2005, Memoirs of a Geisha, 2005, Stick It, 2006; prodr. (films) True Romance, 1993, Shanghai Noon, 2000, The Count of Monte Cristo, 2002, Dragonfly, 2002, Reign of Fire, 2002, Abandon, 2002, Shanghai Knights, 2003, Mr. 3000, 2004, The Pacifier, 2005, The Hitchhiker's Guide to the Galaxy, 2005, Stay Alive, 2006, The Lookout, 2007, The Invisible, 2007.

BARBER, JAMES P., lawyer; b. Berkeley, Calif., Nov. 11, 1944; BA, U. Calif., Santa Barbara, 1967; JD, U. Calif., 1973. Bar: Calif. 1973. Ptnr. Hancock, Rothert & Bunshoft LLP, San Francisco, 1980—. Articles editor Hastings Law Jour., 1972-73. Mem. ABA, State Bar Calif., Bar Assn. San Francisco, Def. Rsch. Inst., Thurston Soc., Order of the Coif. Office: Hancock Rothert Bunshoft Llp 1 Market St Ste 2000 San Francisco CA 94105-1411

BARBER, JERRY RANDEL, retired medical device company executive; b. Killarney, W.Va., Sept. 23, 1940; s. Edward Clay and Nora (Mullins) B.; m. Carrolyn Rae Acree, June 9, 1964; 1 child, Alyssa Rae. BSChemE, W.Va. U., 1962; MSChemE, Ohio State U., 1964, PhD, 1968. Rsch. engr. Union Carbide Corp., South Charleston, W.Va., 1968-73, group leader rsch., 1973-77, assoc. dir. rsch., 1977-81, dir. rsch. Tarrytown, NY, 1981-89, dir. new bus. and tech. devel. Danbury, Conn., 1989-93; gen. mgr. Medisyn Techs., Corp., Las Vegas, Nev., 1993-94; mng. dir. Medisyn Techs. Ltd., Arklow, Ireland, 1994-97; exec. v.p. techs. McGhan Med. Corp., Santa Barbara, Calif., 1997-98; v.p. R&D, Mentor Corp., Irving, Tex., 1998-2000, Santa Barbara, Calif., 1999—2000, v.p. advanced devel., 2000—05, v.p. rsch., 2005—06. Mem. AIChE, Am. Acad. Sci., Sigma Xi. Democrat. Methodist. Home: 2785 Poli St Ventura CA 93003-1556 Office Phone: 805-653-7951. Personal E-mail: jrbarber7@aol.com.

BARBER, LLOYD INGRAM, retired university president; b. Regina, Sask., Can., Mar. 8, 1932; s. Lewis Muir and Hildred (Ingram) B.; m. Muriel Pauline MacBean, May 12, 1956; children: Muir, Brian, Kathleen, David, Susan, Patricia. BA, U. Sask., 1953, B in Comm., 1954; MBA, U. Calif., Berkeley, 1955; PhD, U. Wash., 1964; LLD (hon.), U. Alta., 1983, Concordia U., 1984; postgrad., U. Regina, 1993. Hon. chartered acct. Instr. commerce U. Sask., 1955-57, asst. prof., 1957-64, assoc. prof., 1964-65, prof., 1965-68, 74-76, dean commerce, 1965-68, v.p., 1968-74; pres. U. Regina, Sask., prof. adminstrn., 1976-90; dir. Sask. Inst. for Pub. Policy, 2003—. Indian claims commr. Govt. of Can., 1969-76, hon. lt. col.; spl. inquirer for Elder Indian Testimony, 1977-81; bd. dirs. Bank of N.S., 1976-03, The Molson Cos., 1977-2004, Teck-Cominco, N.W. Co. Ltd., 1990-02, Can. West Global Comm. Corp., Greystone Capital Mgmt. Inc.; cons. to bus. and govt.; hon. prof. Shandong U. Trustee Inst. Rsch. on Pub. Policy, 1972-79; bd. dirs. Indian Equity Found., 1978-79, Can. Scholarship Trust Fund, Regina United Way, 1977-79; past bd. dirs. Wascana Centre Authority; bd. dirs. Nat. Mus. Nature, Inst. Sask. Enterprise, Can. Polar Commn.; bd. dirs., past trustee Can. Scheneley Football Awards; adv. com. to Rector on pub. affairs award Concordia U., 1983; past mem. Northwest Territories Legis. Coun., 1967-70, Natural Sci. and Engring. Rsch. Coun. Officer Aboriginal Order of Can.; recipient Vanier medal, 1978; named hon. Sask. Indian Chief Little Eagle. Mem. Am. Inst. Pub. Adminstrn., Nat. Stats. Coun., Assn. Univs. and Colls. Can. (past pres.), Am. Econ. Assn., Can. Econ. Assn., Order of Can. (companion), Sask. Order of Merit, Assn. Commonwealth Univs. (coun.), Assinobia Club, Regina Beach Yacht Club, Masons. Mem. United Ch. Office: PO Box 510 Regina SK Canada S0G 4C0 Office Phone: 306-729-2336. Business E-Mail: barberl@uregina.ca.

BARBER, PHILLIP MARK, lawyer; b. Pitts., Apr. 7, 1944; s. Armour G. and Irene Estelle (Doyle) B.; m. Barbara Jean Jennings, Aug. 6, 1966 (div. Dec. 1981); children: Heather C., Jessica L., Melissa A.; m. Penelope Louise Constantikes, Apr. 15, 1989 (div. Nov. 1991). BA, U. Mich., 1966; JD, Harvard U., 1969. Bar: Idaho 1969, Calif. 1971, U.S. Ct. Appeals (9th cir.) 1974, U.S. Supreme Ct. 1977. Law clk. Supreme Ct. Idaho, Boise, 1969-70; assoc. Nossaman, Waters, Scott, Krueger & Riordan, LA, 1970-71; asst. atty. gen. State of Idaho, Boise, 1971-72; assoc. Elam, Burke, Jeppesen, Evans & Boyd, Boise, 1972-76, ptnr., 1977-81, Hawley, Troxell, Ennis & Hawley, Boise, 1981-99. Mem. select com. on bar examination Idaho Supreme Ct., 1973-74, select com. on appellate rules, 1976-77, standing com. 1977-84; mem. Idaho Code Commn., 1978-96. Contbr. articles to profl. jours. Chmn. rules com. Idaho Dem. Comm., 1976; chmn. Boise Area Econ. Devel. Coun., 1985-88; leadership coun., N.W. Policy Ctr., 1988-97; vice chmn. N.W. Bus. Coalition, 1987-89; mem. exec. com. Idaho Bus. Coun., 1986-94. Recipient Disting. Citizen award Idaho Stateman Newspapers, 1985. Mem. ABA, Idaho State Bar (exam. com. 1983-85), State Bar Calif., Boise Bar Assn., Boise Area C. of C. (bd. dirs. 1980-81, 83-88, pres., chmn. bd. 1985). Roman Catholic. Avocations: golf, skiing, photography. Home: 1196 Shenandoah Dr Boise ID 83712-7451 Office: 350 N 9th St # M-202 Boise ID 83702-5459

BARBO, DOROTHY MARIE, obstetrician, gynecologist, educator; b. River Falls, Wis., May 28, 1932; d. George William and Marie Lillian (Stelsel) B. BA, Asbury Coll., 1954, DSc (hon.), 1981; MD, U. Wis., 1958. Diplomate Am. Bd. Ob-Gyn. Resident Luth. Hosp. Milw., 1958-62; instr. Sch. Medicine Marquette U., Milw., 1962-66, asst. prof., 1966-67; assoc. prof. Christian Med. Coll. Punjab U., Ludhiana, India, 1968-72; assoc. prof. Med. Coll. Pa., Phila., 1972-87, prof., 1988-91, U. N.Mex., Albuquerque, 1991-99, prof. emerita, 1999—; med. dir. Women's Health Ctr., Albuquerque, 1991-99. Acting dept. chair Christian Med. Coll., Punjab U., 1970; dir. Ctr. for Mature Woman Med. Coll. Pa., 1983-91; examiner Am. Bd. Ob-Gyn, 1984-97; bd. dirs. Ludhiana Christian Med. Coll. Bd., choir mem., 2005—; bd. dirs. Colorado Springs., Colo., chair, 2005, Svc. Master Co. Ltd., Downers Grove, Ill., 1982-91; bd. trustees Asbury Coll., 1996-2006, vice chair bd. trustees, chair acad. com., chair presdl. search com., 2007. Co-author: Care of Post Menopausal Patient, 1985; editor: Medical Clinics of N.A., vol. 71, 1987; assoc. editor, contbg. author: Textbook of Women's Health, 1998; contbr. chpt. to book. Student chpt. sponsor Christian Med. and Dental Soc., Phila., 1973-93, trustee, 1991-95, pres., chair bd. trustees, 1997-99, chair com. for continuing med. and dental edn.; tchr., elder Leverington Presbyn. Ch., Phila., 1988-91; interviewer Readers Digest Internat. fellowships, Brunswick, Ga., 1982—; bd. dirs. Phila. chpt. Am. Cancer Soc., 1980-86, vol., 1984; leadership St. Stephens UMC, 2007-, lay leader, 2008. Named sr. clin. trainee USPHS, HEW, 1963-65, one of Best Woman Drs. in Am. Harper Bazaar, 1985. Fellow ACS (sec. Phila. chpt. 1990), ACOG, Am. Fertility Soc.; mem. Obstet. Soc. Phila. (pres. 1989-90), Phila. Colposcopy Soc. (pres. 1982-84), Philadelphia County Med. Soc. (com. chmn. 1989-90), Alpha Omega Alpha. Avocations: gardening, travel, collecting antiques.

BARBOSA, LEANDRO MATEUS, professional basketball player; b. Sao Paulo, Brazil, Nov. 28, 1982; Guard Palmieras, Brazil, 1999—2001, Baura Tilibra, Brazil, 2001—03, Phoenix Suns, 2003—. Mem. Brazilian Nat. Team, 2002—03. Recipient Sixth Man award, NBA, 2007; named Brazilian League Rookie of Yr., 2002. Office: Phoenix Suns 201 E Jefferson St Phoenix AZ 85004

BARBOUR, MICHAEL G(EORGE), botanist, educator, ecologist, consultant; b. Jackson, Mich., Feb. 24, 1942; s. George Jerome and Mae (Dater) B.; m. Norma Jean Yourist, Sept. 30, 1963 (div. 1981); m. Valerie Ann Whitworth, Jan. 25, 1987; children: Julie Ann, Alan Benjamin, Steven Allan Whitworth. BS in Botany, Mich. State U., 1963; PhD in Botany, Duke U., 1967. Asst. prof. botany U. Calif., Davis, 1967-71, assoc. prof., 1971-76, prof., 1976—, chmn., 1982-85, prof. environ. horticulture, 1993—; ptnr. Ecolabs Cons., Davis, 1969—. Vis. prof. botany dept. Hebrew U., Jerusalem, 1979-81; vis. prof. marine scis. dept. La. State U., Baton Rouge, 1984; vis. prof. plant biology dept. Complutense U., Madrid, 1999, U. de la Laguna, Canary Islands, 2003, botany dept. U. Evora, Portugal, 2006, U. Sassari, Italy, 2009 Co-author: Coastal Ecology, Bodega Head, 1973, Botany, Terrestrial Vegetation of California, 1977, 2d edit., 1988, 3rd. edit. 2008, Terrestrial Plant Ecology, 1980, 3d edit., 1998, North American Terrestrial Vegetation, 1988, 2d edit., 2000, California's Changing Landscapes, 1993, Plant Biology, 1998, An Introduction to Plant Biology, 3d edit., 2005. Fulbright Found. fellow Adelaide, Australia 1964, Evora, Portugal, 2005; Guggenheim Found. fellow, 1978; NSF rsch. grantee, 1968-78, MAB/NSF rsch. grantee, 1989-92, USDA rsch. grantee, 1992—. Mem. Ecol. Soc. Am., Brit. Ecol. Soc., Internat. Assn. Vegetation Sci., Sigma Xi. Democrat. Jewish. Office: U Calif Plant Scis Dept Davis CA 95616 Office Phone: 530-752-2956. Business E-Mail: mgbarbour@ucdavis.edu.

BARCHET, STEPHEN, obstetrician, gynecologist, retired military officer; b. Annapolis, Md., Oct. 25, 1932; s. Stephen George and Louise (Lankford) B.; m. Marguerite Joan Racek, Aug. 9, 1965. Student, Brown U., 1949—52; MD, U. Md., 1956. Diplomate Am. Bd. Ob-Gyn.; cert. physician exec. Commd. ensign M.C. USN, 1955, advanced through grades to rear adm., 1978; intern Naval Hosp., Chelsea, Mass., 1956-57, resident in ob-gyn., 1958-61, resident in gen. surgery Portsmouth, Va., 1957-58; fellow Harvard Med. Sch., 1959-60; obstetrician-gynecologist Naval Hosp., Naples, Italy, 1961-63, Portsmouth, NH, 1963-64, Beaufort, SC, 1964-66, Bremerton, Wash., 1967-70, chief ob-gyn. Boston, 1970-73; asst. head, tng. br. Bur. Medicine and Surgery, Washington, 1973, head, 1973-75; dep. spl. asst. to surgeon gen. USN, 1975; assoc. dean Sch. Medicine, Uniformed Svcs. U. Health Scis., Bethesda, Md., 1976-77, exec. sec. bd. regents, 1976-77; spl. asst. to surgeon gen. for med. dept. edn. and tng. Bur. Medicine and Surgery, Navy Dept., Washington, 1977-79, insp. gen., 1979-80; comdg. officer Naval Health Scis. and Edn. and Tng. Command, Nat. Naval Med. Ctr., Bethesda, 1977-79; asst. chief planning, resources BUMED, 1980-82; dep. surg. gen., dep. dir. naval medicine Dept. Navy, 1982-83; ret., 1983; with Pacific Med. Ctr., Seattle, 1985-91; cons. Mil. Health Care, Seattle, 1987—; prin. MSA Programs, Seattle, 1995—; mng. ptnr. Benefit Payment Solutions, 1998—; coord. Health Plan for Life, 2003—; corp. officer Abrige Co., Bellingham, Wash., 2007—. Clin. asst. prof. Boston U. Sch. Medicine, 1971—; alt. regent Nat. Libr. Medicine, Bethesda, 1977-79; asst. prof. health care scis. George Washington U. Sch. Medicine and Health Scis., Washington, 1978—; ex officio mem. grad. med. edn. nat. adv. com. HEW, 1978-79; chmn. med.-dental com. Intersvc. Tng. Rev. Orgn., Washington, 1977-79; chmn. Washington Med. Savs. Accounts Project, 1994; bd. dir. Hope Heart Inst., chmn. edn. com., 2004-06; Policy Coun. Wash. Health Found., 2006-08. Contbr. articles to med. jours. Sec. The Rainier Club, 1992—93; bd. dir. North Seattle C.C. Found., 1992—95. Decorated Bronze Star, others. Fellow Am. Coll. Obstetricians and Gynecologists, Am. Coll. Physician Execs.; mem. AMA, Assn. Mil. Surgeons U.S., Soc. Med. Cons. Armed Forces, Wash. State Med. Assn., King County Med. Assn., N.W. Mil. Health Benefit Assn. (exec. dir. 1991-94). Home and Office: 18601 SE 64th Way Issaquah WA 98027-8616

BARCON, BARBARA L., utilities executive; b. 1956; BA in Psychology, Calif. State U., San Diego; MBA, Calif. State U., Long Beach, 1984. V.p., CFO space & comm. Hughes Electronics Co.; CFO Boeing Satellite Sys.; CFO so. Calif. region AT&T Broadband; v.p. planning & analysis, fin. process excellence, CFO Space Tech. Sector Northrop Grumman Corp., LA, 2003; sr. v.p. Gores Group LLC, LA; v.p. fin., CFO Pacific Gas & Elec. Co., San Francisco, 2008—. Office: Pacific Gas & Elec Co 1 Market Spear Tower Ste 2400 San Francisco CA 94105-1126

BARDACH, SHELDON GILBERT, lawyer; b. Holyoke, Mass., Sept. 4, 1937; s. Arthur Everett and Ruth (Goodstein) B.; m. Martha Robson, June 7, 1970; 1 child, Noah Arthur. AB, Bklyn. Coll., 1958; JD, UCLA, 1961. Bar: Calif. 1962. Pvt. practice, Beverly Hills, Calif., 1962-67, Century City, Calif., 1967-85; sr. mem. Law Offices Sheldon G. Bardach, LA, 1969—. Bd. dirs. Mambo Films, Inc.; arbitrator L.A. Superior Ct., 1979—; gen. counsel Century Artists, Ltd.; mem. nat. and internat. panels arbitrators Am. Arbitration Assn. Bd. editors Law in Transition Quar., 1967; contbr. articles to profl. jours. Bd. govs. Studio Watts Workshop, 1963-71; founder, bd. dirs. UCLA Sch. Law, 1968. Recipient Lubin award Sch. Law UCLA, 1961, Bancroft-Whitney award UCLA Sch. Law,, 1961. Mem. ABA, Calif. Bar Assn., Beverly Hills Bar Assn. (bd. govs. varristers 1964-69), Am. Arbitration Assn., UCLA Law Sch. Alumni Assn. (bd. dirs. 1991-94), L.A. County Bar Assn., Assn. Trial Lawyers Am., Comml. Law League Am., Vikings of Scandia, Zeta Beta Tau, Phi Alpha Delta. Democrat. Jewish. Office: 18321 Ventura Blvd Ste 915 Tarzana CA 91356-4255

BARDACKE, PAUL, lawyer; b. Oakland, Calif., Dec. 16, 1944; s. Theodore Joseph and Frances (Woodward) B.; children: Julie, Bryan, Francheska, Chloe. BA cum laude, U. Calif.-Santa Barbara, 1966; JD, U. Calif.-Berkeley, 1969. Bar: Calif. 1969, N.Mex. 1970. Atty. Legal Aid Soc., Albuquerque, 1969; firm Sutin, Thayer & Browne, Albuquerque, 1970—91; atty. gen. State of N.Mex., Santa Fe, 1983—86; ptnr. Eaves, Bardacke, Baugh, Kierst & Kiernan, P.A., Albuquerque, 1991—2005, Sutin, Thayer & Browne, PC, 2005—. Adj. prof. N.Mex. Law Sch., Albuquerque, 1973—; mem. faculty Nat. Inst. Trial Lawyers Advocacy, 1978—83. Bd. dirs. All Faiths Receiving Home, Albuquerque; bd. dirs. Friends of Art, 1974-76, Artspace Mag., 1970-80; bd. trustees Albuquerque Cmty. Found., 2001-. Reginald Heber Smith fellow, 1969 Fellow Am. Coll. Trial Lawyers; mem. ABA, Calif. Bar Assn., N.Mex. Bar Assn., Am. Bd. Trial Advs. (pres. N.Mex. chpt. 1992-93). Democrat. Office: Sutin, Thayer & Browne PC PO BOX 1945 Albuquerque NM 87103 Office Phone: 505-883-2500.

BARDEM, JAVIER, actor; b. Las Palmas de Gran Canaria, Gran Canaria, Canary Islands, Spain, Mar. 1, 1969; s. Pilar Bardem. Attended, Escuela de Artes y Officios. Actor: (TV series) Segunda Ensenanza, 1986, El Dia por delante, 1989—90; (films) The Ages of Lulu, 1990, High Heels, 1991, Jamon, Jamon, 1992, Numbered Days, 1994, The Detective and Death, 1994, Mouth to Mouth, 1995, Dance with the Devil, 1997, Torrente, the Stupid Arm of the Law, 1998, Before Night Falls, 2000 (Nat. Bd. Review award for Best Actor, 2000), Without News From God, 2001, The Dancer Upstairs, 2002, Mondays in the Sun, 2002, Collateral, 2004, The Sea Inside, 2004 (European Film award for Best Actor, 2004), Goya's Ghosts, 2006, No Country for Old Men, 2007 (Best Supporting Actor, NY Film Critics Circle award, 2007, Best Supporting Actor, Boston Soc. Film Critics, 2007, 2007 Best Supporting Actor, Critics Choice award, Broadcast Film Critics Assn., 2008, Best Performance by an Actor in a Supporting Role in a Motion Picture, Golden Globe award, Hollywood Fgn. Press Assn., 2008, Outstanding Performance by a Male Actor in a Supporting Role, SAG, 2008, Outstanding Performance by a Cast in a Motion Picture, SAG, 2008, Best Supporting Actor, Brit. Acad. Film and TV Arts, 2008, Acad. award for Best Actor in a Supporting Role, 2008), Love in the Time of Cholera, 2007, Vicky Cristina Barcelona, 2008. Recipient Nat. Cinematography prize, Inst. Cinematography and Audiovisual Art, 2008. Achievements include first Spanish actor to be nominated for an Academy award. Office: c/o Fine Line Features 116 N Robertson Blvd Los Angeles CA 90048

BARDWICK, JUDITH MARCIA, management consultant; b. NYC, Jan. 16, 1933; d. Abraham and Ethel (Krinsky) Hardis; m. John Bardwick, III, Dec. 18, 1954 (div.); children: Jennifer, Peter, Deborah; m. Allen Armstrong, Feb. 10, 1984. BS, Purdue U., 1954; MS, Cornell U., 1955; PhD, U. Mich., 1964; D in Cmty. Leadership (hon.), Franklin U., Columbus, OHio, 2008. Lectr. U. Mich., Ann Arbor, 1964-67, asst. prof. psychology, 1967-71, assoc. prof., 1971-75, prof., 1975-83, assoc. dean, 1977-83; clin. prof. psychiatry U. Calif., San Diego, 1984—; pres. In Transition, Inc. (name changed to Judith M. Bardwick, PhD, Inc., 1991), La Jolla, Calif., 1983—. Mem. population rsch. study group NIH, 1971—75. Co-author: (book) Feminine Personality and Conflict, 1970; author: Psychology of Women, 1971, In Transition, 1979, The Plateauing Trap, 1986, Danger in the Comfort Zone, 1991, In Praise of Good Business, 1998, Seeking the Calm in the Storm, 2002, One Foot Out the Door, 2007 (named best human resources/organl. dynamics book, 2007); mem. editl. bd. Women's Studies, 1973—, Psychology Women Quar., 1975—; contbr. articles to profl. jours. Mem. social sci. adv. com. Planned Parenthood Am., 1973; health and human svcs. working group San Diego Found., 2003—07. Fellow: APA; mem.: Am. Psychosomatic Soc., N.Y. Acad. Scis., Midwest Psychol. Assn., Phi Beta Kappa. Avocations: travel, history, art. Home and Office: 1389 Caminito Halago La Jolla CA 92037-7165 Home Phone: 858-456-0063; Office Phone: 858-456-1443. Business E-Mail: jmbwick@san.rr.com.

BARGER, WILLIAM JAMES, management consultant, educator; b. LA, Nov. 1, 1944; s. James Ray and Aylene M. (Skinner) B.; m. Jane A. Cox, Jan. 30, 1988. BA, U. So. Calif., 1966; MA, Harvard U., 1970, PhD, 1972. Asst. prof econs. U. So. Calif., Los Angeles, 1971-76; v.p. Bank Am., Los Angeles, 1976-81; sr. v.p. Gibraltar Savs. Co., Beverly Hills, Calif., 1981-84, exec. v.p., 1984-88; pres. High Point Acad., Pasadena, Calif., 1995—2001; dir. Maxson Young Assocs., San Francisco, 1995—2004. Mem. Phi Beta Kappa.

BARHAM, WARREN SANDUSKY, horticulturist; b. Prescott, Ark., Feb. 15, 1919; s. Clint A. and Hannah Jane (Sandusky) B.; m. Margaret Alice Kyle, Dec. 27, 1940 (dec. 1997); m. Evelyn M. Csongradi, Dec. 5, 1998 (dec. 2003); children: Barbara E., Juanita S., Margaret Ann, Robert W. BS in Agr., U. Ark., 1941; PhD, Cornell U., 1950. Grad. asst. in plant breeding Cornell U., Ithaca, NY, 1942—45; assoc. prof. horticulture NC State U., Raleigh, 1949—58; dir. raw material R & D Basic Vegetable Products, Inc., Vacaville, Calif., 1958-76; prof. Tex. A&M U., College Station, 1976-82, head dept., 1976-80; v.p. Castle & Cook Technicultre, Watsonville, Calif., 1982-84; dir. watermelon R & D Tom Castle Seed Co., Morgan Hill, Calif., 1984-86; CEO Barham Seeds Inc., Gilroy, Calif., 1987—; v.p. Kyle and Barham LLC, La Quinta, Calif., 1996—. Cons. Basic Vegetable Products, Inc., Vacaville, 1976-78, U.S. AID, Central Am., 1977, Egypt and U.S., 1980-82, Gentry Foods & Gilroy Foods, 1978-93, Fed. Republic Germany Govt., Ethiopia, 1984; industry rep. adv. com. Onion Rsch. Program USDA, 1960-70. Contbr. articles to profl. jours. Bd. dirs., pres. Vacaville Sch. Bd., 1964-74. Sgt. USAF, 1942-45, ETO. Fellow Am. Soc. Hort. Sci. (pres. 1982, bd. dirs. 1979-83, fellows nominating com. 2002-04, chair 2004); mem. Sons in Retirement (bd. dirs. 1992-95, v.p. 1993, pres. 1994), Rotary Inernat. (bd. dirs. 1964), Elks Club. Achievements include development of 34 varieties and hybrids of processing onions, 15 triploid and 8 diploid hybrid watermelons, 2 cucumber varieties, 13 fresh market hybrid onions and 1 tomato variety.

BARISH, BARRY C., physics professor, researcher; b. Omaha; BA in physics, U. Calif., Berkeley, 1957; PhD in exptl. high energy physics, Berkeley, 1962. Maxine and Ronald Linde prof. physics Calif. Inst. Tech., Pasadena, 1991—; prin. investigator Laser Interferometer Gravitational-Wave Observatory (LIGO) project, 1994; dir. LIGO, 1997—; former chmn. commn. particles and fields Internat. Union Pure and Applied Physics (IUPAP), chmn. US liaison com.; co-chair High Energy Physics Adv. Panel subpanel; mem. bd. dirs. Nat. Sci. Bd., 2002—. Spkr. in field. Recipient Klopsteg award, Am. Assn. Physics Tchrs., 2002. Fellow: AAAS, Am. Physics Soc.; mem.: NAS. Achievements include research in high-energy neutrinos important in demonstrating the quark substructure of the nucleon; search for magnetic monopole predicted in theories of Grand Unification. Office: LIGO Lab Calif Inst Tech MS 18 34 Pasadena CA 91125 Office Phone: 626-395-3853. Office Fax: 626-793-9594. Business E-Mail: barish@ligo.caltech.edu.

BARKAN, DAVID M., lawyer; AB magna cum laude, Harvard U., 1987; JD, U. Calif., 1992. Bar: Calif. 1982. Law clk. to Hon. Fern M. Smith US Dist. Ct., No. Dist. Calif., 1992—93; prin. litig., Practice Group Leader Fish & Richardson PC, Redwood City, 2001—. Office: Fish & Richardson PC 500 Arguello St, Ste 500 Redwood City CA 94063 Office Fax: 650-839-5070, 650-839-5065. E-mail: barkan@fr.com.

BARKER, BOB (ROBERT WILLIAM BARKER), television personality; b. Darrington, Wash., Dec. 12, 1923; s. Byron John and Matilda Kent (Tarleton) B.; m. Dorothy Jo Gideon, Jan. 12, 1945 (dec. Oct. 1981). BA in Econs. summa cum laude, Drury Coll., 1947. Founder DJ&T Found., Beverly Hills, Calif., 1995. Host: (radio show) The Bob Barker Show; (TV series) Truth or Consequences, 1956-75, The Price is Right, 1972-2007, Bob Barker Fun and Games Show, 1978; (TV specials) Miss Universe Beauty Pageant, 1966-87, Miss U.S.A. Beauty Pageant, 1966-87, Pillsbury Bake-Off, 1969-85, Rose Parade, CBS, 1969-88; appeared in (TV appearances) Bonanza, 1960, The Nanny, 1994, Something So Right, 1996, 1997, Martial Law, 1998, (voice only)Futurama, 2000, Yes Dear, 2001, (voice only) Family Guy, 2001, The Bold and the Beautiful, 2002; (films) Happy Gilmore, 1996; co-author: (with Dibby Diehl) Priceless Memories, 2009 Served to lt. (j.g.) USNR, 1943-45. Recipient Emmy award for Best Audience Participation Host, 1981-82, 83-84, 86-87, 87-88, 89-90, 90-91, 91-92, 93-94, 94-95, 95-96, 99-00, 00-01, Lifetime Achievement Emmy award for Daytime Television, 1999, Carbon Mike award of the Pioneer Broadcasters. Mem. AGVA, AFTRA, Screen Actors Guild. inducted, Acad. of Television and Arts & Sciences Hall of Fame, 2004. Office: The Price is Right care CBS TV 7800 Beverly Blvd Los Angeles CA 90036-2112

BARKER, CLIVE, artist, film director and producer, scriptwriter; b. Liverpool, Eng., 1952; s. Len and Joan B. Student, U. Liverpool, Eng. Author: (plays) Incarnations (Frankenstein in Love, History of the Devil, Colossus), Forms of Heaven (Paradise Street, Subtle Bodies, Crazyface); (short story collection) Books of Blood I-VI (books IV, V, and VI released in U.S. as The Inhuman Condition, 1986, In the Flesh, 1986, Cabal; (TV movie) Saint Sinner, 2002; (novels) The Damnation Game, 1985, Weaveworld, 1987, Cabal, 1988, The Great and Secret Show, 1989, Imajica, 1991, The Thief of Always, 1992, Everville, 1994, Sacrament, 1996, A-Z of Horror, 1997, Galilee, 1998, The Essential Clive Barker, 1999, Coldheart Canyon, 2001; prodr. Hellraiser II: Hellbound, 1990, Candyman, 1992, Hellraiser III: Hell on Earth, 1992, Candyman II: Farewell to the Flesh, 1995, Hellraiser: Bloodline, 1996, Gods & Monsters, 1997, (Fox TV) Spirits and Shadows, 1997; writer and dir. (screenplays) Hellraiser, 1987, Nightbreed, 1990, Lord of Illusions, 1995, Art Exhibition, 1998, Clive Barker's Freaks, 1998, Undying, 2001. Home: Los Angeles CA Mailing: PO Box 691829 West Hollywood CA 90069

BARKER, DOUGLAS P., food products executive; b. 1935; With Sunkist Growers, Van Nuys, Calif., 1961-78, Sun World Internat. Inc., Bakersfield, Calif., 1978-81, 84—, Blue Anchor, Sacramento, Calif., 1981-84; internat. sales mgr. Primetime Internat., Coachella, Calif. Office: Primetime Internat 86705 Avenue 54 Ste A Coachella CA 92236-3814

BARKER, JEFF, state legislator; m to Victoria Barker; children: two. Oregon State Representative, district 28, 2002-.trooper, Oregon State Police; officer, detective, Sgt, lt, Portland Police Bureau; volunteer, Cooper Mountain Elem Sch, Errol Hassell Elem Sch, Mt View Mid Sch, Aloha HS; donor blood drives, America Red Cross. Member, America Legion Aloha Post 104, Marine Corps League, 1st Marine Div Association. Democrat. Mailing: 900 Court St NE H-491 Salem OR 97301 Office Phone: 503-986-1428. E-mail: rep.jeffbarker@state.or.us.

BARKER, LYNN M., management consultant; BS in Physics, MS in Physics, U. Ariz. Co-founder, pres. Valyn Internat., Albuquerque. Mem. Am. Phys. Soc., Soc. Exptl. Mechanics, Internat. Soc. Optical Engring., Aeriballistoc Range Assn., Sigma Pi Sigma, Pi Mu Epsilon, Phi Beta Kappa, Sigma Xi. Office: 301 Solano Dr SE Albuquerque NM 87108-2649

BARKER, ROBERT JEFFERY, financial executive; b. Glendale, Calif., Feb. 22, 1946; s. Albert and Margaret E. (Windle) B.; m. Ildiko Barker, Jan. 1, 1989; 1 child, Alexander A. BSEE, UCLA, 1968, MBA, 1970. Cert. mgmt. acctg. Cost analyst Lockheed, Sunnyvale, Calif., 1976-78; from cost acctg. supr. to fin. systems mgr. Monolithic Memories Inc., Sunnyvale, 1976-84; dir. fin. Waferscale Integration, Inc., Fremont, Calif., 1984-88, v.p. fin., CFO, 1988-94; CFO Micrel, San Jose, Calif., 1994, v.p. corp. bus. devel., 1999—. Bd. dirs., treas. Am. Electronics Assn. Credit Union, Santa Clara, Calif., 1988—, bd. chmn., 1991; dir. Monolithic Memories Integration Fed. Credit Union, Sunnyvale, 1977-84, pres. 1983-84. Dir. Vets. Task Force, Palo Alto, Calif., 1980-87, pres. 1987. Capt. USAF, 1970-74. Mem. Nat. Assn. Accts., Fin. Execs. Inst., Toastmasters (pres. 1986-87). Republican. Presbyn. Avocations: volleyball, jogging, sports. Home: 1 Winchester Dr Atherton CA 94027-4040

BARKIN, ELAINE RADOFF, composer; b. NYC, Dec. 15, 1932; m. George J. Barkin, Nov. 28, 1957; 3 children. BA in Music, Queens Coll., 1954, MFA in Composition, 1956; PhD in Composition and Theory, Brandeis U., 1971; Cert. in Composition and Piano, Berlin Hochschule Musik, 1957; studied with Karol Rathaus, Irving Fine, Boris Blacher, Arthur Berger. Lectr. in music Queens Coll., 1964-70, Sarah Lawrence, 1969-70; from asst. to assoc. prof. music theory U. Mich., 1970-74; from asst. prof. to prof. composition and theory U. Calif., LA, 1974-97. Vis. asst. prof. Princeton (N.J.) U., 1974; lectr. in field. Asst. to co-editor: Perspectives of New Music, 1963-85; composer String Quartet, 1969, Sound Play for violin, 1974, String Trio, 1976, Plein Chant, alto flute, 1977, Ebb Tide, 2 vibraphones, 1977, ...the Supple Suitor...for soprano and five players, 1978, (chamber mini opera) De Amore, 1980, Impromptu for violin, cello, piano, 1981, (theatre piece) Media Speak, 1981, At the Piano, piano, 1982, For String Quartet, 1982, Quilt Piece graphic score for 7 instruments, 1984, On The Way To Becoming for 4-track Tape Collage, 1985, Demeter and Persephone for violin, tape, chamber ensemble, dancers, 1986, 3 Rhapsodies, flutes and clarinet, 1986, Encore for Javanese Gamelan Ensemble, 1986, Out of the Air for Basset Horn and Tape, 188, To Whom It May Concern 4 track tape collage, reader and 4 players, 1989, Legong Dreams, oboe, 1990, Gamélange for harp and mixed gamelan band, 1992, Five Tape Collages, Open Space CD #3, 1993, "for my friends' pleasure," soprano and harp, 1994, numerous improvised group and duo sessions on tape; produced cassette and video: New Music in Bali, 1994; "touching all bases" for electronic bass, electronic percussion, and Balinese gamelan, 1996, e: an anthology (music, texts and graphics) 1975-95, "poem" for wind ensemble, 1999, (Chamber Music and Improvisations) Open Space CD #12, 2000, (CDs) Song for Sarah for Violin, 2001, Ballade for Violoncello, 2002, Tambellan, 2004, Open Space CD #16, 2004, Colors for mixed gamelan, 2004, Four Midi Pieces, 2005, Piano Suite, 2006, Violin Duos, 2007, Four Machine Pieces, 2007. Recipient Fulbright award, 1957, awards NEA, 1975, 79, awards Rockefeller Found., 1980, Meet the Composer award, 1994. Home: 12533 Killion St Valley Village CA 91607-1533

BARKIN, ELLEN, actress; b. NYC, Apr. 16, 1954; m. Gabriel Byrne, 1988 (div. 1993); children: Jack, Romey Marion; m. Ron Perelman, June 28, 2000 (separated Jan. 19, 2006) Student, CUNY; grad., Hunter Coll. Ind. theatrical, film actress, 1980—. Theatrical prodns. include Shout Across the River, 1980, Killings on the Last Line, 1980, Extremities, 1982; appeared on TV soap operas Search for Tomorrow; Actor: Up in Smoke, 1978, Diner, 1982, Daniel, 1983, Tender Mercies, 1983, Enormous Changes at the Last Minute, 1983, Eddie and the Cruisers, 1983, Harry and Son, 1984, The Adventures of Buckaroo Banzai in the Fifth Dimension, 1984, Terminal Choice, 1985, Down by Law, 1986, Desert Bloom, 1986, The Big Easy, 1987, Siesta, 1987, Made in Heaven, 1987, Sea of Love, 1989, Johnny Handsome, 1989, Switch, 1991, Man Trouble, 1992, Mac, 1993, This Boy's Life, 1993, Into the West, 1993, Bad Company, 1995, Wild Bill, 1995, Mad Dog Time, 1996, The Fan, 1996, Fear and Loathing in Las Vegas, 1998, Drop Dead Gorgeous, 1999, the White River Kid, 1999, Crime and Punishment in Suburbia, 2000, Mercy, 2000, Someone Like You, 2001, She Hate Me, 2004, Palindromes, 2004, Trust the Man, 2005, Ocean's Thirteen, 2007; (TV films) Kent State, 1981, We're Fighting Back, 1981, Parole, 1982, The Princess Who Had Never Laughed, 1984, Terrible Joe Moran, 1984, Act of Vengeance, 1986, Clinton and Nadine, 1988, Before Women Had Wings, 1997, Strip Search, 2004 Office: c/o Creative Artists Agy 9830 Wilshire Blvd Beverly Hills CA 90212-1804

BARKLEY, JOSEPH RICHARD, controller; b. Pa., Sept. 3, 1942; s. Joseph Harold and Rose Mary (Manger) B.; m. Diane Marie Bentivoglio, July 10, 1965; children: Christopher Michael, Patrick Joseph. BS Engring., U.S. Mil. Acad., 1965; MBA in Fin., Scranton U., 1975. Commd. 2d lt. U.S. Army, 1965, advanced through grades to maj., 1979, ret., 1979; fin. and analysis dir. Am. Express Corp., NYC, 1978-82; asst. controller ops. div. Ins. Corp. N.Am., Phila., 1982-83; dir fin., adminstr. Cigna Corp., Phila., 1983-86; v.p., controller facilities div. Chase Manhattan Bank N.A., NYC, 1986-88, v.p. controller Ins. Products Group, 1988—. Contbr. articles to profl. jours. Judge, Newtown Election Bd., 1980—; mem. Council Rock Sch. Br., 1983-87; mem. Newtown Planning Commn., 1982, chmn.,

1990. Decorated Combat Inf. Badge, Bronze Star. Mem. West Point Soc. Phila., Fin. Exec. Inst. Republican. Roman Catholic. Avocations: skiing, running, auto racing. Office: Imperial Bancorp PO Box 92991 Los Angeles CA 90009

BARLETT, JAMES EDWARD, data processing executive; b. Akron, Ohio, Jan. 1, 1944; s. Willard Paul and Pauline (Candlish) B.; m. Sue Patterson, June 20, 1964; 1 child, Jamie Catherine BA, U. Akron, 1967, MBA, 1971. Systems analyst B.F. Goodrich, Akron, Ohio, 1962-69; ptnr. Touche Ross & Co., Detroit, 1971-79; 1st. v.p., then sr. v.p. Nat. Bank Detroit, 1979-84; exec. v.p. ops. NBD Bancorp and Nat. Bank Detroit; exec. v.p. worldwide ops. and syss. MasterCard Internat. Corp.; pres., CEO Galileo Internat., Rosemont, Ill., 1994—, chmn., 1997—. Bd. dirs. TeleTech Holdings, Inc., Korn/Ferry Internat., Computer Communications Am., Detroit, Cirrus System, Inc., also vice chmn. Trustee Sta. WTVS-TV, Detroit, 1984—, Detroit Country Day Sch., 1984—. Served to 1st lt. U.S. Army, 1967-69, Vietnam Decorated Bronze Star, Army Commendation medal Mem. Am. Bankers Assn., Mich. Bankers Assn., Detroit Athletic Club, Econ. Club, Bloomfield Hills Country Club, Detroit Club, Bloomfield Open Hunt Club. Republican. Episcopalian. Avocations: jogging; reading. Office: Galileo 6901 S Havana St Centennial CO 80112-3805

BARLOW, CHARLES, oil company executive; CFO Sinclair Oil Corp., Salt Lake City. Office: Sinclair Oil Corp PO Box 30825 Salt Lake City UT 84130-0825

BARMORE, JAMES GILBERT, museum director, curator; b. Gary, Ind., May 27, 1956; s. William Jennings Barmore and Evangeline Louise (Blinn) Dunmire; m. Linda Grant, Mar. 7, 1981; 2 children, Garrett & Kaden BA in history summa cum laude, Western State Coll., Gunnison, Colo., 1979; MA in mus. sci., Tex. Tech U., 1983. Curatorial asst. Tex. Tech U. Mus., Lubbock, 1981-82; mus. technician Denali (Alaska) Nat. Pk. and Preserve, 1983; hist. preservation officer Matanuska-Susitna Borough, Palmer, Alaska, 1983; curator mus. collections Mo. Hist. Soc., St. Louis, 1983-86; curator collections Mus. History and Industry, Seattle, 1986—91; dir. Skagit County Historical Mus., La Conner, Wash., 1991—2000, Nev. State Mus., Carson City, 2000—; spkr. profl. conf. Contbr. articles to profl. jours. Rsch. scholar Western State Coll. Found., 1978; Recipient Individual Excellence award, Washington Mus. Assn., 2005. Mem. Am. Assn. Mus., Am. Assn. for State and Local History (program speaker 1989). Avocations: mountain climbing, backpacking, skiing, boating, bicycling. Office: Nevada State Mus 600 N Carson St Carson City NV 89701-4004 Home: 3292 Pleasant Hills Dr Reno NV 89523 Office Phone: 775-687-4810 ext 226. Office Fax: 775-687-4168. Business E-Mail: jbarmore@nevadaculture.org.

BARNA, LILLIAN CARATTINI, school system administrator; b. NYC, Jan. 18, 1929; d. Juan Carattini and Dolores Elsie Nieves (Alicea); m. Eugene Andrew Barna, July 1, 1951; children: Craig Andrew, Keith Andrew. AB, Hunter Coll., 1950; MA, San Jose State U., 1970. Tchr. N.Y.C. Sch. Dist., 1950—52, Whittier (Calif.) Sch. Dist., 1952—54, tchr. HS, 1954—56; tchr. presch. Long Beach and Los Gatos, Calif., 1958—67; supr. early childhood edn. San Jose (Calif.) Unified Sch. Dist., 1967—72, sch. adminstr., 1972—80, supt. schs., 1980—84, Albuquerque Pub. Schs., 1984—88, Tacoma Sch. Dist. 10, 1988—93; cons. in field; exec. dir. Large City Schs. Supts., 1993—. Recipient Sorptomist Internat. Woman of Yr. award, 1980, Western Region Puertorican Council Achievement award, 1980, Calif. State U. Outstanding Achievement in Edn. award, 1982, Woman of Achievement award, Santa Clara County Commn. on Status of Women/San Jose Mercury News, Disting. Alumni award, San Jose State U., Shero award, Am. Assn. Sch. Adminstrn., 2005; named Outstanding Sch. Dist. Supt., Wash. State; named to Hunter Coll. Hall of Fame. Mem.: LWV, Am. Assn. Sch. Adminstrs. (Disting. Leadership award, Shero award 2006), Assn. Calif. Sch. Adminstrs., Women Leaders in Edn., Pan Am. Round Table, Rotary Club Saratoga, Delta Zeta, Phi Kappa Phi. Office: Large City Schs Supt PO Box 2096 Saratoga CA 95070 Office Phone: 408-867-4190. E-mail: lcbels@aol.com.

BARNARD, KATHRYN ELAINE, nursing educator, researcher; b. Omaha, Apr. 16, 1938; d. Paul and Elsa Elizabeth (Anderson) B. BS in Nursing, U. Nebr., Omaha, 1960; MS in Nursing, Boston U., 1962; PhD, U. Wash., Seattle, 1972; DSc (hon.), U. Nebr., 1990. Acting instr. U. Nebr., Omaha, 1960-61, U. Wash., Seattle, 1963-65, asst. prof., 1965-69, prof. nursing, 1972—, assoc. dean, 1987-92, founding dir. Ctr. on Infant Mental Health and Devel., 2001—, Charles and Gerda Spence Endowed Prof. in Nursing, 2002—. Bd. dirs. Nat. Ctr. for Clin. Infant Programs, Washington, 1980- Chmn. rsch. com. Bur. of Community Health Svcs., MCH, 1987-89. Recipient Lucille Petry award Nat. League for Nursing, 1968, Martha Mae Eliot award Am. Assn. Pub. Health, 1983, Professorship award U. Wash., 1985 Fellow Am. Acad. Nursing (bd. dirs. 1980-82); mem. Inst. Medicine (Gustav O. Leinhard Award, 2002); mem. Am. Nurses Assn. (chmn. com. 1980-82, Jessie Scott award 1982, Nurse of Yr. award 1984), Soc. Research in Child Devel. (bd. dirs. 1981-87), Sigma Theta Tau (founders award in research 1987, Episteme Award, 2003). Democrat. Presbyterian. Home: 11508 Durland Ave NE Seattle WA 98125-5904 Office: University of Washington Family & Child Nursing Box 357920 Seattle WA 98195-7920

BARNARD, SUSAN, literature and language educator; BA, Pomona Coll., 1969; MA in Edn., U. Wash., Tacoma, 1997. Lang. arts, reading tchr. CHOICE Alternative H.S., Shelton, Wash., 1995—. Vol. Mason County Literacy, 1991—; bd. mem. Habitat Humanity Mason County, 1995—. Named Wash. Tchr. of Yr., 2006; finalist Nat. Tchr. of Yr., 2006. Office: CHOICE Alternative HS 807 W Pine Shelton WA 98584 Business E-Mail: sbarnard@sheltonschools.org.

BARNEA, URI N., rabbi, conductor, musician; b. Petah-Tikvah, Israel, May 29, 1943; came to U.S., 1971; s. Shimon and Miriam Burstein; m. Lizbeth A. Lund, Dec. 15, 1977; 2 children. Tchg. cert., Oranim Music Inst., Israel, 1966; postgrad., Hebrew U., Israel, 1969-71; MusB, Rubin Acad. Music, Israel, 1971; MA, U. Minn., 1974, PhD, 1977; D (hon.), Rocky Mountain Coll., 1999; MAHL, Hebrew Union Coll., 2007. Music dir. Jewish Cmty. Ctr., Mpls., 1971-73; condr. Youval Chamber Orch., Mpls., 1971-73; asst. condr. U. Minn. Orchs., Mpls., 1972-77; music dir., condr. Unitarian Soc., Mpls., 1973-78, Kenwood Chamber Orch., Mpls., 1974-78, Knox-Galesburg Symphony, 1978-83, Billings (Mont.) Symphony Soc., 1984—2004, Mont. Ballet Co., 1993, 1994, 1998—2005; asst. prof. Knox Coll., Galesburg, Ill., 1978-83; violinist, violist Yellowstone Chamber players, Billings, 1984—2004; violist Tri-City Symphony, Quad-Cities, 1983—84; condr. Cedar Arts Forum String Camp, Cedar Falls, Iowa, 1981—82; rabbi Temple B'nai Israel, Hattiesburg, Miss., 2007—. Guest condr., Ark., Calif., Colo., Fla., Ill., Iowa, Maine, Mich., Minn., Mont., Pa., SD, Va., Wis. European conducting debut, London, Neuchatel and Fribourg, Switzerland, 1986; Can. conducting debut No. Music Festival, North Bay, Ont., 1989; Violin Concerto, 1990; Russian conducting debut Symphony Orch., Kuzbass, Kemerovo, 1993; recordings include: W. Piston's Flute and Clarinet Concertos, Mario Lombardo's Oboe Concerto, two compact discs of Am. music; composer numerous compositions including String Quartet (1st prize Aspen Composition Competition 1976), Sonata for Flute and Piano, 1975 (Diploma of Distinction 26th Viotti Internat. Competition, Italy 1975), Ruth, a ballet, 1974 (1st prize Oberhoffer Composition Contest 1976). Music adv. panel Ill. Arts Coun., 1980-83; v.p. Cmty. Concert Assn., Galesburg, 1980-83; bd. dirs. Knox Coll. Credit Union, Galesburg, 1982-83, Radio Sta. KEMC, Billings, 1984—, Fox Theater Corp., Billings, 1984-86. Recipient Friend of the Arts title Sigma Alpha Iota, 1982, Mont. Gov. Arts award for the arts, 2003, The Tuney award 2004, The Freeman Lacey award 2004; Ill. Arts Coun. grantee, 1979; Hebrew U. Jerusalem scholar, 1972-74, Hebrew U. and Rubin Acad. Mus. scholar, 1969, 70; Individual Artist fellow Mont. Arts Coun., 1986. Mem. NEA (music adv. panel 1990-95), ASCAP. Home: 1104 Poly Dr Billings MT 59102-1834 Office Phone: 601-545-3871. Personal E-mail: u_barnea@yahoo.com, bnaiisrael901@gmail.com.

BARNES, CHARLES ANDREW, physicist, researcher; b. Toronto, Ont., Can., Dec. 12, 1921; came to U.S., 1953, naturalized, 1961; m. Phyllis Malcolm, Sept., 1950. BA, McMaster U., Hamilton, Ont., Can., 1943; MA, U. Toronto, 1944; PhD, Cambridge U., Eng., 1950. Physicist Joint Brit.-Canadian Atomic Energy Project, 1944-46; instr. physics U. B.C., 1950-53, 55-56; mem. faculty Calif. Inst. Tech., 1953-55, 56—, prof. physics, 1962-92; prof. emeritus physics, 1992—. Guest prof. Niels Bohr Inst., Copenhagen, 1973-74. Editor, contbr. to profl. books and jours. Recipient medal Inst. d'Astrophysique de Paris, 1986, Alexander von Humboldt U.S. Sr. Scientist award, Fed. Republic of Germany, 1986; NSF sr. fellow Denmark, 1962-63. Fellow AAAS, Am. Phys. Soc. Office: Calif Inst Tech 1201 E California Blvd Pasadena CA 91125-0001

BARNES, FRANK STEPHENSON, electrical engineer, educator; b. Pasadena, Calif., July 31, 1932; s. Donald Porter and Thedia (Schellenberg) B.; m. Gay Dirstine, Dec. 17, 1955; children: Stephen, Amy. BS, Princeton U., 1954; MS, Stanford U., 1955, PhD, 1958. Fulbright prof. Coll. Engring., Baghdad, Iraq, 1957-58; rsch. assoc. Colo. Rsch. Corp., Broomfield, 1958-59; assoc. prof. U. Colo., Boulder, 1959-65, prof. dept. elec. engring., 1965—, chmn. dept., 1964-81, faculty rsch. lectr., 1965, acting dean Coll. Engring. and Applied Sci., 1980-81, disting. prof., 1997—, dir. interdisciplinary telecom. program, 1971-75, 88-89, 1996-99; pres. Video Accessory Corp., Boulder, Colo., 2001—07. Disting. lectr. IEEE Elec. Device Soc., 1994-01. Regional editor Electronics Letters of Brit. Instn. Elec.Engrs., 1970-75; exec. editor Ann. Rev. Telecom. Bd. dirs. Accreditation Bd. Engring. and Tech., 1980-82. Recipient cert. of merit Internat. Comm. Assn., 1989, Meritorious Svc. award IEEE Edn. Soc., 1993, Leon Montgomery award Internat. Comm. Assn., 1994, Univ. Colo. Centennial Celebration Engring. Recognition award, 1994, Catalyst award Colo. Inst. Tech., 2004, Disting. Rschr. award Internat. Telecomm. Edn. and Rsch. Assn., 2006; fellow Internat. Engring. Consortium, 1995. Fellow AAAS, IEEE (editor Student Jour. 1967-70, mem. G-Ed Adcom 1970-77, v.p. publ. activities 1974-75, pres. device soc. 1974-75, ednl. activities bd. 1976-82, editor IEEE Transactions on Edn. 1988-94, mem. press bd. 1989-90, ednl. activities bd., cert. of merit, Centennial medal, Millennium medal 2000, Edn. Soc. Achievement award 2003); mem. NAE (Bernard M. Gordon prize 2004), Am. Soc. Engring. (Elec. and Computer Engring. Disting. Educator award 2002), Soc. Lasers in Medicine, Engrs. Coun. Profl. Devel. (dir. 1976-82, chmn. com. on advanced level accreditation 1976-78), Biolectromagnetics Soc. (bd. dirs. 1982-84, 96-98, pres. 2000-01), Engring. Info. (bd. dirs. 1984-90), ASCE (assoc. editor, Jour. Energy Engring. 2008-). Home: 225 Continental View Dr Boulder CO 80303-4516 Home Phone: 303-499-9144. Business E-Mail: frank.barnes@colorado.edu.

BARNES, GERALD RICHARD, bishop; b. Phoenix, June 22, 1945; Grad., St. Leonard Sem., Dayton, Ohio, Assumption-St. John's Sem., San Antonio. Ordained priest Archdiocese of San Antonio, 1975; aux. bishop Diocese of San Bernardino, Calif., 1992—95, bishop, 1995—, ordained bishop, 1995. Chmn. com. migration and refugee svcs. Nat. Conf. Cath. Bishops. Roman Catholic. Office: Diocese of San Bernardino 1201 E Highland Ave San Bernardino CA 92404-4607 Office Phone: 909-475-5110. Office Fax: 909-475-5155.

BARNES, KEITH LEE, electronics executive; b. San Francisco, Sept. 14, 1951; s. Arch Lee and Charlotte Mae (Sanborn) B.; m. Sharon Ann Tosaw, June 9, 1986; children: Allecia, Alexandra, Wyatt. BS, Calif. State U., San Jose, 1976. Mgr. engring. and mktg. Gould, Inc., Rolling Meadow, Ill., 1976-79; v.p., gen. mgr. Kontron Electronics, Mountain View, Calif., 1979-85; v.p. Valley Data Scis., Mountain View, 1985-86; pres., CEO Integrated Measurement Sys., Beaverton, Oreg., 1986-2000, chmn., CEO, 2000—. Bd. dirs. Data Io Corp., LWG, Inc., Clarity Visual Systems, Inc. Patentee in field. Bd. dirs. Am. Electronics Assn., 1992-93, chmn. Oreg. bd., 1993; trustee Oreg. Grad. Inst. for Sci. and Industry, 1996—; vice chair Oreg. Growth Account, 1998; regent U. Portland, 2000. Mem. IEEE, PGC. Republican. Roman Catholic. Office: Integrated Measurements Systems, Inc 5975 NW Pinefarm Pl Hillsboro OR 97124-8563

BARNES, RAY, state legislator; b. Lawrence, Mass., Sept. 8, 1936; m. Paula Barnes; 1 child, Kequette. Grad., Northrop Inst. Tech., Inglewood, Calif., 1964, De Anza Coll., Cupertino, Calif., 1980. Lic. pilot, pvt. investigator. Tech writer Intel Corp., 1976—84; ind. contractor, 1984—89; pvt. investigator, owner Eyes & Ears Detective Agy., 1989—2003; mem. Dist. 7 Ariz. House of Reps., 2003—, chair environ. com., mem. mil. affairs & pub. safety com. Chair Ariz. Rep. Assembly, 1985—. Christian missionary Republic of Haiti, 1968—71; active Scottsdale Worship Ctr. With security svc. command USAF, 1954—57, Japan. Mem.: NRA, Carefree Kiwanis Club. Republican. Office: Ariz House Reps Capitol Complex 1700 W Washington Rm 110 Phoenix AZ 85007 Office Phone: 602-542-5503. Office Fax: 602-417-3107. Business E-Mail: rbarnes@azleg.gov.*

BARNES, THOMAS G., law educator; b. 1930; AB, Harvard U., 1952; DPhil, Oxford U., 1955. From asst. prof. to assoc. prof. Lycoming Coll., Williamsport, Pa., 1956-60; from lectr. to prof. history U. Calif., Berkeley, 1960—, humanities rsch. prof., 1971-72, prof. history and law, 1974—2006, co-chmn. Canadian studies program, 1982—2006, co-dir. Canadian studies program, 2006—, emeritus prof. history and law, 2006—. Dir. legal history project Am. Bar Found., 1965-86; com. mem. on ct. records 9th Cir. Ct. Author: Somerset 1625-1640: A County's Government During the Personal Rule, 1961, List and Index to Star Chamber Procs., James I, 3 vols., 1975, Lawes and Libertyes of Massachusetts, 1975, Hastings College of Law: The First Century, 1978; mem. editl. bd. Gryphon Legal Classics Libr.; editor Pub. Record Office. Huntington Libr. fellow, 1960, Am. Coun. Learned Socs. fellow, 1962-63, John Simon Guggenheim Found. fellow, 1970-71. Fellow Royal Hist. Soc.; mem. Selden Soc. (councillor, state corr.), Assn. Canadian Studies (pres. 2001-03, past pres., 2003-05). Office: U Calif Sch Law 452 Boalt Hl Berkeley CA 94720-7200 Home Phone: 510-524-6602; Office Phone: 510-642-1780. Business E-Mail: barnest@law.berkeley.edu.

BARNES, W. MICHAEL, electronics executive; B in Indsl. Engring., M in Indsl. Engring., Tex. A&M U., PhD in Ops. Rsch., 1968. Expert cons. Asst. Postmaster Gen., Washington; corp. ops. rsch. staff Collins Radio Co. now Rockwell Internat., 1968-72; dir. fin. MOS/Components Divsn. Rockwell Internat., Newport Beach, Calif., 1972-73; contr. Rockwell's Collins Comm. Switching Sys. Divsn., 1973-74, Rockwell Electronic Sys. Group, Dallas, 1974-77; v.p., gen. mgr. Rockwell's Collins Comm. Switching Sys. Divsn., 1977-82; v.p. fin. Rockwell's Telecom. Group, 1982-85, v.p. mktg. and bus. devel., 1985-89; corp. v.p. bus. devel. and planning Rockwell Internat. Corp., 1989-91, sr. v.p. fin. and planning, CFO, 1991—2001. Vis. prof. computer scis. So. Meth. U.; instr. maintainability engring. U.S. Army Logistics Tng. Ctr., Red River Depot; bd. dir. Advanced Micro Devices, Archer Daniels Midland Co., A.O. Smith Corp. Named Disting. Alumni, Tex. A&M U. Coll. Engring., 1992 Mem. Coun. Fin. Execs. (chmn. conf. bd. 1996). Mailing: AMD Bd Directors 1 AMD Pl PO Box 3453 Sunnyvale CA 94088-3453

BARNETT, R(ALPH) MICHAEL, theoretical physicist, educational agency administrator; b. Gulfport, Miss., Jan. 25, 1944; s. Herbert Chester and Lisa Margaret (Kielley) B.; children: Leilani Pinho, Julia Alexandra, Russell Alan. BS, Antioch Coll., 1966; PhD, U. Chgo., 1971. Postdoctoral fellow U. Calif., Irvine, 1972-74; rsch. fellow Harvard U., Cambridge, Mass., 1974-76; rsch. assoc. Stanford (Calif.) Linear Accelerator Ctr., 1976-83; vis. physicist Inst. Theoretical Physics U. Calif., Santa Barbara, 1983-84; staff scientist Lawrence Berkeley Nat. Lab., 1984-89, sr. scientist and head particle data group, 1990—; co-dir. QuarkNet Ednl. Project, 1999—. V.p. Contemporary Physics Edn. Project, 1987-98, pub. info. coor. Am. Phys. Soc. Dvsn. of Particles and Fields, 1994-97; edn. coord. ATLAS experiment at CERN, Geneva; prodr. film: The Atlas Experiment, 2000. Author: Teachers' Resource Book on Fundamental Particles and Interactions, 1988, Review of Particle Physics, 1990, 6th edit., 2002, Particle Physics—One Hundred Years of Discoveries, 1996, Guide to Experimental Particle Physics Literature, 1993, 2d edit., 1996, The Charm of Strange Quarks, Mysteries and Revolutions of Particle Physics, 2000, (chart) Fundamental Particles and Interactions, 1987, 4th edit., 1999, World-Wide Web feature, The Particle Adventure, 1995, rev. edit. 2000, (CD ROM) The Quark Adventure, 2000. Fellow Am. Phys. Soc. (pub. info. coord. divsn. particles and fields 1994-97, taskforce on informing the public, chair-elect Calif. sect.), Am. Assn. Physics Tchrs. (v.p., sect. North Calif.). Achievements include research on the Standard Model and its extensions, including studies of nature and validity of quantum chromodynamics; analyses of neutral current couplings; calculations of the production of heavy quarks; predictions of properties and decays of supersymmetric particles and higgs bosons. Office: Lawrence Berkeley Nat Lab MS-50-308 1 Cyclotron Rd Berkeley CA 94720-0001

BARNHART, ARTHUR L., state official; State contr. Colo. Personnel and Gen. Support Svcs., Denver.

BARNHART, DOUGLAS EDWARD, construction company executive; b. Tex., Dec. 15, 1946; BSCE, Tex. Tech. U., 1969. V.p. C.E. Wylie Constrn. Co., San Diego, 1976-83; CEO Douglas E. Barnhart, Inc., San Diego, 1983—. Chmn. Calif. Contractor's State Lic. Bd.; commr. Calif. Uniform Pub. Constrn. Cost Acctg. Commn.; bd. dirs. San Diego Nat. Bank. Recipient Small Bus. Award for excellence, Bus./Industry award Greater San Diego Industry-Edn. Coun., 1994. Mem. Am. Arbitration Assn., Associated Gen. Contractors Am. (chmn., dir. Constrn. Apprenticeship Trust, dir. Constrn. Pension Trust, chmn. naval engring. com., vice-chmn. heavy indsl. divsn.), Associated Builders and Contractors, Lincoln Club San Diego, Soc. Mil. Engrs., San Diego Associated Gen. Contractors (pres. 1994). Home: PO Box 667 Poway CA 92074-0667 E-mail: cpernieano@debconstruct.com.

BARNHART, PHIL, state legislator; Chairman, Democratic Party of Lane Co, formerly; dep District attorney, Community Serv, formerly; Oregon State Representative, District 11, 2000-.Psychologist, currently; adjunct faculty, Univ Oregon; attorney, currently; president, Oreg Mental Health Assocs, Inc & Addiction Counseling & Education Servs, Inc, formerly; board member, Eugene 4J Sch, Oreg Bd Psychologist Examiners & Boys & Girls Clubs Emarald Valley, formerly. Eugene Rotary Club. Democrat. Mailing: 900 Court St NE H-383 Salem OR 97301 also: PO Box 71188 Eugene OR 97401

BARON, FREDERICK DAVID, lawyer; b. New Haven, 1947; m. Kathryn Green Lazarus; children: Andrew K. Lazarus, Peter D. Lazarus, Charles B. BA, Amherst Coll., 1969; JD, Stanford U., 1974. Bar: Calif. 1974, DC 1975, US Supreme Ct. 1978, US Dist. Ct. DC 1979, US Ct. Appeals (DC cir.) 1979, US Dist. Ct. (no. dist.) Calif. 1982, US Ct. Appeals (9th cir.) 1982. Counsel select com. on intelligence US Senate, Washington, 1975-76; spl. asst. to US atty. gen. Washington, 1977-79; asst. US atty. for DC, 1980-82; atty. Clark, Baron & Korda, San Jose, Calif., 1982-83; ptnr., chmn. employment practice Cooley, Godward, Kronish, Palo Alto, Calif., 1983—95, Cooley, Godward, Palo Alto, Calif., 1997—; assoc. dep. atty. gen., dir. Exec. Office for Nat. Security US Dept. Justice, 1995-96. Lectr. US Info. Svc., 1979-80; pres. bd. trustees Keys Sch., Palo Alto, 1983-87; bd. dirs. Retail Resources, Inc., 1987-88; mem. bd. vis. Stanford Law Sch., 2003-05; guest lectr. Stanford Bus. Sch., 2000—. Co-author, editor US Senate Select Com. on Intelligence Reports, 1975-76; also articles. Issues dir. election com. US Senator Alan Cranston, 1974, Gov. Edmund G. Brown Jr., 1976; mem. transition team Pres. Carter, 1976-77, Pres. Clinton, 1992; del. Calif. Dem. Conv., 1989-90; mem. credentials com. Nat. Dem. Conv., 2004. Mem. ABA, Calif. Bar Assn., DC Bar Assn., Santa Clara County Bar Assn., Univ. Club. Office: Cooley Godward LLP 5 Palo Alto Sq Palo Alto CA 94306-2122

BARON, ROBERT CHARLES, publishing executive; b. LA, Jan. 26, 1934; s. Leo Francis and Marietta (Schulze) Baron; m. Charlotte Rose Persinger, Nov. 29, 1986; stepchildren: Brett Persinger, Kristen

Fochner. BS in Physics, St. Joseph's U., Phila., 1956. Registered profl. engr., Mass. Engr. RCA, Camden, N.J., 1955-57, Computer Control Co., Framingham, Mass., 1959-61, program mgr. Mariner II and IV space computers, 1961-65, engring. mgr., 1965-69; worldwide systems mgr. Honeywell Minicomputer, Framingham, 1970-71; founder, pres., CEO Prime Computer, Framingham, 1971-75; pvt. practice Boston, 1976-83; founder and pres. Fulcrum Pub., Golden, Colo., 1984—. Bd. dirs. Prime Computer, Framingham, Mass., Alling-Lander, Cheshire, Conn., Oxion, Hugoton, Kans., Fulcrum Pub., Golden, Colo. Author: Digital Logic and Computer Operations, 1966, Micropower Electronics, 1970, America in the Twentieth Century, 1995, Footsteps on the Sands of Time, 1999, What Was It Like Orville: The Early Space Program, 2002, Hudson: The Story of a River, 2004, Pioneers and Plodders, 2004, To the Mountaintop, 2007; editor: The Garden and Farm Books of Thomas Jefferson, 1987, Soul of America: Documenting Our Past, 1942-1974, 1989, Colorado Rockies: The Inaugural Season, 1993, Thomas Hornsby Ferrill and the American West, 1996. Vice chmn. bd. dirs. Mass. Audubon Soc., Lincoln, 1980—85; bd. dirs. Rocky Mountain Women's Inst., Denver, 1987—90, Denver Pub. Libr. Friends Found., 1989—96, pres., 1994—96; trustee Lincoln Filene Ctr., Tufts U., Medford, Mass., 1982—84. Mem.: Hakluyt Soc., Western History Assn., Mass. Hist. Soc., Thoreau Soc., Am. Antiquarian Soc. (bd. dirs., chmn. 1993—2003), Internat. Wilderness Leadership Found. (bd. dirs. 1990—2008, chmn. 1994—2000, 2003—08), Explorer's Club, Grolier Club. Avocations: writing, reading, sports, gardening, collecting clocks. Office: Fulcrum Pub 4690 Table Mountain Dr Ste 100 Golden CO 80403 Business E-Mail: bob@fulcrum-books.com.

BARONDES, SAMUEL HERBERT, psychiatrist, educator; b. Bklyn., Dec. 21, 1933; s. Solomon and Yetta (Kaplow) B.; m. Ellen Slater, Sept. 1, 1963 (dec. Nov. 22, 1971); children: Elizabeth Francesca, Jessica Gabrielle; m. Louann Brizendine, Sept. 14, 2002. AB, Columbia U., 1954, MD, 1958. Intern, then asst. resident in medicine Peter Bent Brigham Hosp., Boston, 1958-60; sr. asst. surgeon USPHS, NIH, Bethesda, Md., 1960-63; resident in psychiatry McLean and Mass. Gen. hosps., Boston, 1963-66; asst. prof., then assoc. prof. psychiatry and molecular biology Albert Einstein Coll. Medicine., Bronx, NY, 1966-69; prof. psychiatry U. Calif., San Diego, 1969-86, prof., chmn. dept. psychiatry, dir. Langley Porter Psychiat. Inst. San Francisco, 1986-94, dir. Ctr. Neurobiology and Psychiatry, 1994—, Jeanne and Sanford Robertson Prof. Neurobiol. and Psychiatry, 1996—. Pres. McKnight Endowment Fund for Neurosci., 1989-98; sci. adv. com. Rsch. Am.; governing coun. Internat. Brain Rsch. Orgn., 1994-2000; bd. sci. counselors NIMH, 1997-2002, chair, 2000-02. Author: Molecules and Mental Illness, 1993, Mood Genes, 1998, Better Than Prozac, 2003; mem. editl. bd. profl. jours.; contbr. articles to profl. jours. Recipient Rsch. Career Devel. award USPHS, 1967, Elliott Royer award, 1989, P.H. Stillmark medal Estonia, 1989; Fogarty Internat. scholar NIH, 1979; J. Robert Oppenheimer lectr., 2000. Fellow AAAS, Am. Psychiat. Assn., Am. Coll. Neuropsychopharmacology; mem. Inst. Medicine Nat. Acad. Sci. Office: U Calif-San Francisco Langley Porter Psychiat Ins 401 Parnassus Ave San Francisco CA 94143-0984 Business E-Mail: barondes@cgl.ucsf.edu.

BARONE, ANGELA MARIA, artist, researcher; b. Concesio, Brescia, Italy, June 29, 1957; arrived in U.S., 1983; d. Giuseppe and Adelmina (D'Ercole) Barone. Laurea cum laude in geol. scis., U. Bologna, Italy, 1981; PhD in Marine Geology, Columbia U., 1989; cert. in profl. photography, N.Y. Inst. Photography, 1992; cert. in fine art painting and drawing, N. Light Art Sch., Cin., 1993. Collaborative asst. Marine Geology Inst., Bologna, 1981-83, Inst. Geology and Paleontology, Florence, Italy, 1982-83, Sta. de Geodynamique, Villefranche, France, 1982; grad. rsch. asst. Lamont-Doherty Geol. Obs., Palisades, NY, 1983-89, postdoctoral rsch. asst., 1989; postgrad. rschr. Scripps Instn. of Oceanography, La Jolla, Calif., 1990-92; artist San Diego, 1993—. Contbr. articles to profl. jours. Mem.: Am. Geophys. Union (co-pres. meeting session 1990), Nat. Mus. Women Arts (assoc.). Home: 4958 Rio Verde Dr San Jose CA 95118-2335

BARONI, MICHAEL L., lawyer; b. NYC, Dec. 26, 1967; m. Lisa Baroni. BA in English with honors, Boston Coll., 1990; JD, Hofstra U., 1993. Bar: NY 1994, Calif. 2001. Of counsel Jacobson & Colfin, NYC; in-house counsel Gen. Media, Inc., 1995—97; gen. counsel Henry Holt & Co., 1997—98; sr. atty. Metromedia Fiber Network Svcs., 1998—2000; in-house counsel PAIX.net (subsidiary of Metromedia), 1998—2003; gen. counsel, sec. BSH Home Appliances Corp., Huntington Beach, Calif., 2003—. Contbr. articles over 100 to profl. jour.; monthly columnist Inside Counsel Mag., 2007—08. Pers. bd. Town of Los Gatos, 2003; chmn. Legal Group Assn. Home Appliance Mfrs., 2007—; chmn. sect. product liability OC Bar Assn., Calif., 2006; adv. bd. In-House Counsel Super Conf., 2008; mem. Free and Accepted Masons. Recipient Profl. Excellence award, Hofstra U. Sch. Law, 1st Pl. prize, ASCAP; named Super Lawyer, 2007. Mem.: ABA, Assn. Corp. Counsel, State Bar Calif., NY State Bar Assn., Orange Co. Bar Assn. Conservative. Episcopalian. Office: BSH Home Appliances Corp Legal Dept 5551 McFadden Ave Huntington Beach CA 92649 Office Phone: 714-899-3506.

BARR, JAMES NORMAN, retired federal judge; b. Kewanee, Ill, Oct. 21, 1940; s. James Cecil and Dorothy Evelyn (Dorsey) B.; m. Trilla Anne Reeves, Oct. 31, 1964 (div. 1979); 1 child, James N. Jr.; m. Phyllis L. DeMent, May 30, 1986; children: Renae, Michele. BS, Ill. Wesleyan U., 1962; JD, Ill. Inst. Tech., 1971. Bar: Ill. 1972, Calif. 1977. Assoc. Pretzel, Stouffer, Nolan & Rooney, Chgo., 1974-76; claims counsel Safeco Title Ins. Co., LA, 1977-78; assoc. Kamph & Jackman, Santa Ana, Calif., 1978-80; lawyer pvt. practice Law Offices of James N. Barr, Santa Ana, 1980-86; judge U.S Bankruptcy Ct. Ctrl. Dist. Calif., Santa Anna, 1987—2006. Adj. prof. Chapman U. Sch. Law, 1996—2006. Lt. USN, 1962-67, Vietnam. Mem. Fed. Bar Assn. (Orange County chpt. bd. dirs. 1996-2000), Orange County Bar Assn. (cmty. outreach com.), Nat. Conf. Bankruptcy Judges, Orange County Bankruptcy Forum (bd. dirs. 1989—), Peter M. Elliott Inn of Ct. (founder, first pres. 1990-91), Warren J. Ferguson Am. Inn of Ct. (founder). Office Phone: 714-338-5470.

BARR, M.E. See BIGELOW, MARGARET

BARR, RONALD JEFFREY, dermatologist, pathologist; b. Mpls., Jan. 5, 1945; s. Maxwell Michael and Ethel Deana (Ring) B.; m. Ulla Elisabet Edstam; children: Anna, Jessica, Sara. BA, Johns Hopkins U., 1967, MD, 1970. Diplomate Am. Bd. Pathology, Am. Bd. Dermatology. Intern U. Calif., San Diego, 1970-71, resident in pathology, 1971-75, resident in dermatology Irvine, 1975-78, fellow in dermatopathology, 1975-78, asst. prof. dermatology, 1977-83, assoc. prof. dermatology and pathology, 1983-86, prof. dermatology and pathology, 1987—2005, dir. Dermatopathology Lab., 1979—2005, prof., chmn. dept. dermatology Davis, 1986-87, emeritus prof. dermatology and pathology. Bd. dirs. Am. Bd. Dermatology, 1989-1998, pres., 1997. Contbr. more than 10 chpts. to books. more than 140 articles to profl. jours. Lt. USN, 1971-73. Fellow Am. Soc. Dermatopathology (pres. 1988-89); mem. Internat. Soc. Dermatopathology, Internat. Com. for Dermatopathology (sec.-treas. 1987-91, pres. 1992-93). Office: Laguna Pathology Med Group S Coast Med Ctr 31872 Coast Hwy Laguna Beach CA 92651 Office Phone: 949-499-7288. E-mail: rjbarr@uci.edu.

BARR, ROSEANNE See ROSEANNE

BARR, SCOTT, state legislator; b. 1916; m. Dollie Mae Barr. Grain, cattle & timber producer; Wash. State Repr., 1977—82; Mem. Wash. State Senate from 7th Dist., 1982—93. Special Service award, Outstanding Leadership Agriculture in State & Region; National Recognition Award, Outstanding Achievements & Leadership Proper Use & Future Concern for Renewable Natural Resources. Grange Farm Bureau; Cattlemen's Assn.; State Wheat Growers' Assn. (pres., formerly); State Assn. Conservation Districts (pres., formerly); Wash. State Wheat Commn. (chmn., formerly); Lions (pres., formerly) Republican.

BARRACK, THOMAS J., JR., real estate investor, lawyer; BA, U. So. Calif., 1969; JD, U. San Diego Law Sch., 1972; LLD (hon.), Pepperdine U. Internat. fin. lawyer; pres. Dunn Internat. Corp., 1976; dep. under sec. US Dept. Interior, Washington; sr. v.p. E.F. Hutton & Co., NY; pres. Oxford Devel. Ventures Inc.; prin. Robert M. Bass Grp.; founder Colony Capital LLC, LA, 1991, chmn., CEO, 1991—. Bd. dirs. Continental Airlines Inc., Accor, First Republic Bank, Pub. Storage Inc. Named one of 400 Richest Ams., Forbes mag., 2006. Office: Colony Capital LLC 1999 Avenue of the Stars Ste 1200 Los Angeles CA 90067

BARRACLOUGH, JACK T., state representative; b. Salt Lake City, Sept. 15, 1927; m. Elaine Barraclough; children: Denise, Bruce, Jan, Doug, Glade, Garrett, Renae, Jared, Jackie(dec.). AA, Boise Jr. Coll., 1948; BS, U. Idaho, 1951. Hydrologist, 1951—63; rsch. project chief, hydrology, 1963—83; scientific specialist, hydrology, 1984—95; cons. hydrologist, 1984—2000; state rep. dist. 33A Idaho Ho. of Reps., Boise, 1996—, chair environ. affairs com., mem. resources and conservation com. Co-chair Environ. Common Sense Task Force, 1996—2000; mem. Idaho Tech. Com. on Hydrology; vice chair NCSL Environment Com., 1998—2000; chair NCSL, Sci. Energy and Environment Resources, 1996—98, Pacific Fisheries Legis. Task Force, 1996—2000; mem. Pacific Fishery Mgmt. Coun., 1998—2000. Chief Pensacola Vol. Fire Dept., 1958—63. Served USN, 1945—46. Mem.: Idaho Acad. Sci., Am. Water Resources Assn., Am. Geophys. Union, Am. Inst. Hydrology (cert. hydrologist 1983—2000), Civitans, Kiwanis (sec. 1958—63). Republican. Lds Ch. Office: State Capitol PO Box 83720 Boise ID 83720-0038

BARRASSO, JOHN ANTHONY, United States Senator from Wyoming, orthopedic surgeon; b. Reading, Pa., July 21, 1952; s. John A. and Louise M. (DeCisco) B.; m. Linda D. Nix, May 6, 1978 (div.); children: Peter, Emma. BS, Georgetown U., 1974, MD, 1978. Diplomate Am. Bd. Orthopaedic Surgeons. Resident Yale-New Haven Hosp., 1978-83; orthopedic surgeon Casper (Wyo.) Orthopaedic Assocs., 1983—; chief of staff Wyo. Med. Ctr., 2003—05; mem. Wyo. State Senate from Dist 27, 2002—07, mem. minerals, bus. & econ. devel. com., labor, health & social services com., 2003—05, chmn. transp., highways & mil. affairs com., 2005—07; US Senator from Wyo., 2007—; mem. US Senate Energy & Nat. Resources Com., 2007—, US Senate Environment & Pub. Works Com., 2007—, US Senate Fgn. Rels. Com., 2009—, US Senate Indian Affairs Com., 2007—09, vice chmn., 2009—. Del., Rep. Nat. Convention, 1992, 2004; leader, delegation to Rep. of China, RNC, 1994; fin. chair, Enzi for Senate, 1996. Health reporter on radio and TV, 1984—; health reporter for newspapers, 1991—. Pres. United Way of Natrona County, Wyo. Health Fairs.; emcee Jerry Lewis Labor Day Telethon, Wyo.'s K-2 TV. Recipient Wyo. Physician of the Yr. award, Medal of Excellence, Wyo. Nat. Guard, Legis. Svc. award, Veterans Fgn. Wars. Mem. Wyo. Med. Soc. (pres.), Nat. Assn. Physician Broadcasters (pres. 1988-89), Rep. Nat. Com.(treas. 1991-92) Republican. Office: US Congress 307 Dirksen Senate Office Bldg Washington DC 20510 also: 100 E B St Ste 2201 Casper WY 82601*

BARREN, BRUCE WILLARD (HRH THE DUKE DE SERRES), merchant banker; b. Olean, NY, Jan. 28, 1942; s. James Lee and Marion Frances (Willard) Barren; children: James Lee, Christina Roseanne. Student, Hun Sch. of Princeton, 1959; BS, Babson Coll., 1962; MS, Bucknell U., 1963; grad. cert., Harvard U., 1967, Cambridge U., 1968. Exec. v.p. Am. Extract Co., 1960—62; sr. cons. Price Waterhouse, NY, 1963—67; v.p. Walston & Co., Inc., NY, 1967—70; sr. v.p. Delafield Childs, Inc., NY, 1970—71; chmn. EMCO/Hanover Group Ltd., 1971—; sr. v.p. Goodway, Inc., 1972—73; pres. Park West Med. Group, Inc., 1980—81; CEO First Pacific Bank, 1984—85; exec. editor Mgmt. Gazette, 1988—98. Bd. dirs. various US and internat. cos., 1978-95; CEO Four Winds Enterprises Inc., San Diego 1985-87, F.W. Myers & Co., Rouses Point, NY, 1990-91; US rep. Transatlantic Bio-scis. Fund, London, 1988-91; lectr. exec. MBA program UCLA, 1988-98, U. SC Grad. Sch., Pepperdine Exec. MBA Program. Whittier Sch. Law, Chapman U. Sch. Law; vice chmn., CEO Hydro-Mill Co., Chatsworth, Calif., 1996-98; mem. Calif. Small Bus. Adv. Com., 1990-92; instr. loan documentation and valuation procedures Sanwa Bank, 1995-96; CEO, dir. Potomac Worldwide, 1998-00; chmn. Tech. Asset Mgmt. Ltd., Eng., 2000-01; chmn. exec. com. Sunnylife Global, Inc., 2005-06; vice chmn. audit and compensation coms. Elephant Talk Comm. Inc., 2008-; author, instr. CPA, CPE courses, Tex., Calif. and NY. Mem. editl. adv. bd. Prentice-Hall, 2001-02; contbr. more than 150 articles to profl. jours. including CFO, Contr. Alert, KPMG Banking Insider. Decorated Grand Cross Order of the Cross of Constantinople, 1985-2008; recipient numerous Disting. Svc. awards various govt. offcls., including The White House, US Congress, Ctrl. Am. Parliaments, Govt. of China, Disting. Alumni award, Hun, Princeton, 2005, named to Athletic Hall of Fame, 1999. Mem.: Am. Mgmt. Assn. (author, instr. 1991—92), L'Assn. des Familles D'Amours, Byzantine Heraldic Soc., Blue Book Social Registry (LA and S.W.), Order of Constantinople (dep. grand chancellor), St. Andrews Soc., Ordo Supremus Militaris Templi Hierosolymitani (a.k.a. Templars) (chevalier), Grand Sovereign Dynastic Hospitalier Order St. John Knights of Malta (knight comdr.), Mil. and Hospitalier Order St. Lazarus of Jerusalem (comdr.). Roman Catholic. Avocation: writing. Office: 11740-11 West Sunset Los Angeles CA 90049 Office Phone: 310-471-3735. Business E-Mail: bbarren@verizon.net.

BARRETT, BRUCE RICHARD, physics professor; b. Kansas City, Aug. 19, 1939; s. Buford Russell and Miriam Aileen (Adams) B.; m. Gail Louise Geiger, Sept. 3, 1961 (div. Aug. 1969); m. Joan Frances Livermore, May 21, 1979. BS, U. Kans., 1961; postgrad., Swiss Poly., Zurich, 1961-62; MS, Stanford U., 1964, PhD, 1967. Rsch. fellow Weizmann Inst. Sci., Rehovot, Israel, 1967—68; postdoctoral rsch. fellow, rsch. assoc. U. Pitts., 1968—70; asst. prof. physics U. Ariz., Tucson, 1970—72, assoc. prof., 1972—76, prof., 1976—, assoc. chmn. dept., 1977—83, mem. faculty senate, 1979—83, 1988—90, 1991—97, mem. tech. transfer com., 1996—97, 1998—99, mem. grad. coun., 1998—2000. Chmn. adv. com. Internat. Scholars, Tucson, 1985-96; program dir. nuc. theory Nat. Sci. Found., 1985-87; chmn. rsch. policy com. U. Ariz. Faculty Senate, 1993-94, 95-96; affiliate prof. U. Wash.-Seattle, 2000—; mem. adv. com. Nat. Inst. Nuc. Theory, 2005-08, chair adv. com., 2007-08. Woodrow Wilson fellow, 1961-62; NSF fellow, 1962-66; Weizmann Inst. fellow, 1967-68; Andrew Mellon fellow, 1968-69; Alfred P. Sloan Found. research fellow, 1972-74; Alexander von Humboldt fellow, 1976-77; Japan Soc. for Promotion of Sci. rsch. fellow, 1998; NSF grantee, 1971-85, 87—; Netherlands F.O.M. research fellow Groningen, 1980; recipient sr. U.S. scientist award (Humboldt prize) Alexander von Humboldt Found., 1983-85, 2007-08. Mem. Am. Phys. Soc. (outstanding referee 2008-)Fellow Am. Phys. Soc. (publs. com. divsn. nuclear physics 1983-86, program com. 1993-94, 2002-03, chmn. steering com. nuc. physics summer sch. 1996-98, mem. exec. com. four corners sect. 1998-2004, chair 2003, chmn. forum on internat. physics 2002, chmn. com. internat. sci. affairs 2003, mem. com. 2001-04, mem. Bonner prize selection com. 2006-2007; membership com. 2007-), Phi Beta Kappa (pres. Alpha Ariz. chpt. 1992, 2000-02, nat. senate 2000—), Sigma Pi Sigma, Omicron Delta Kappa, Beta Theta Pi. Office: U Ariz Dept Physics PO Box 210081 Tucson AZ 85721-0081 Office Phone: 520-621-2979. Business E-Mail: bbarrett@physics.arizona.edu.

BARRETT, CRAIG R., electronics company executive; b. San Francisco, Aug. 29, 1939; m. Barbara Barrett, 1985; 2 children. BS in Materials Sci., MS in Materials Sci., Stanford U., Palo Alto, PhD in Materials Sci., 1964. NATO postdoctoral fellow Nat. Physical Lab., England, 1964—65; from faculty to assoc. prof., dept. materials sci. and engring. Stanford U., 1965-74; with Intel Corp., Chandler, Ariz., 1974—, tech. develop mgr., 1974—84, v.p. components tech. and mfg. group, 1984—87, sr. v.p., gen. mgr. components tech. and mfg. group, 1987—90, exec. v.p., mgr. components tech., 1990—93, COO, 1993—97, pres., 1997—98, CEO, 1998—2005, chmn., 2005—. Bd. dirs. Intel Corp., 1992—, Qwest Comms. Internat. Inc., US Semiconductor Industry Assn., Silicon Valley Mfg. Group, TechNet; co-chmn. Bus. Coalition for Excellence in Edn., Nat. Innovation Initiative Leadership Coun.; chmn. Computer Systems Policy Project; bd. trustee US Coun. for Internat. Bus.; appointee to President's Adv. Com. for Trade Policy and Negotiations and the the Am. Health Information Cmty.; mem. Nat. Academies Com. on Prospering in the Global Economy of the 21st Century: An Agenda for Am. Sci. and Tech. Author: Principles of Engineering Materials, of over 40 tech. papers dealing with the influences of microstructure on the properties of materials. Bd. dirs. Nat. Forest Found., Achieve. Fulbright fellow, Danish Tech. U., Denmark, 1972. Mem.: NAE (chair 2004—08). Office: Intel Corp 2200 Mission College Blvd Santa Clara CA 95054-1537

BARRETT, CYNTHIA TOWNSEND, neonatologist; b. Santa Barbara, Calif., Sept. 8, 1937; d. George Barker and Elizabeth Louise (Magee) B. AB, Vassar Coll., 1958; MD, Harvard U., 1962. Diplomate. Am. Bd. Pediats. Intern, resident in pediats., pediat. chief resident U. Wash., 1962-66, fellow in physiology & biophysics, 1966-67; fellow in fetal cardiovascular physiology U. Calif., San Francisco, 1967-70; chief divsn. neonatology, assoc. prof. pediats. UCLA Sch. Medicine, 1970—. Mem. Internat. Newborn Intensive Care Soc., European Soc. Perinatal Rsch., Western Soc. Pediat. Rsch., Am. Thoracic Soc., Soc. Pediat. Rsch., Perinatal Rsch. Soc. Republican. Episcopalian. Home: 6778 Shearwater Ln Malibu CA 90265-4144 Office: UCLA Sch Medicine Dept Pediats Rm 12-467 Los Angeles CA 90095-0001 E-mail: cbarrett@mednet.ucla.edu.

BARRETT, DOROTHY, performing company executive; b. LA; d. Lester Arnold and Kathryn (Halverson) Silvera; m. Robert A.H. Cochrane, May 20, 1949 (div. Feb. 1965); 1 stepchild, Michele Cochrane Shaw. Student, LA C.C., 1937-38. Adminstr. Am. Nat. Acad. of Performing Arts, 1964—2000, dir., 2000—; founder, dir. Acad. Children's Workshop, 1964—. Produced, choreographed 52 Christmas shows; tchr. of dance Barrett Sch. of the Arts, North Hollywood, 1948, Am. Nat. Acad., Studio City, 1964—, tchr. of acting, 1964—; tchr. of speech UCLA Extension, West Hollywood, 1972. Actress, dancer: (motion pictures) A Damsel in Distress, 1937, The Great Waltz, 1938, Gone with the Wind, 1939, Frisco Sal, Wizard of Oz, 1939, Juke Box Soundies, 1942, Hot Money, 1944, Monsieur Beaucaire, 1945, The Imperfect Lady, 1947, Perils of Pauline, 1945, The Stork Club, 1945, Mildred Pierce, 1945, A Bell for Adano, 1945, Weekend at the Waldorf, 1945, Blue Skies, 1946, Connecticut Yankee in King Arthur's Court, 1947, California, 1947, Samson and Delilah, 1948, The Babe Ruth Story, 1948; (Broadway stage productions) Earl Carroll's Vanities, 1939, Buddy De Sylva's Louisiana Purchase, 1940, Billy Rose's Diamond Horseshoe, 1943, George Abbott's Beat the Band, 1942, others; (TV) co-star KTLA's Secrets of Gourmet, 1946; prodr., dir.: A Touch of Broadway, 1996, 97, (on tour) 1998, 99-2003; author: (poetry) Between the Bookends, 1942, The Tolucan, The Legal Journal, 1959, Valley Green Sheet & Van Nuys News; contbr. articles to jours. Active Am. Women's Vol. Svc., 1942. Named Miss Culver City, 1937; recipient award ARC, 1943, Humanitarian award for work with children City of LA, 1994, award of Merit or 52 Yrs. Tchg. Children's Theatre, Motion Picture Coun. Office: Am Nat Acad Performing Arts 10944 Ventura Blvd Studio City CA 91604-3340 Office Phone: 818-763-4431.

BARRETT, JAMES EMMETT, federal judge; b. Lusk, Wyo., Apr. 8, 1922; s. Frank A. and Alice C. (Donoghue) Barrett; m. Carmel Ann Martinez, Oct. 8, 1949; children: Ann Catherine Barrett Sandahl, Richard James, John Donoghue. Student, U. Wyo., 1940—42, LLB, 1949; student, St. Catherine's Coll., Oxford, Eng., 1945, Cath. U. Am., 1946. Bar: Wyo. 1949. Mem. firm Barrett and Barrett, Lusk, 1949—67; atty. Niobrara Sch. Dist., 1950—64; county and pros. atty. Niobrara County, Wyo., 1951—62; atty. Town of Lusk, 1952—54; atty. gen. State of Wyo., 1967—71; judge U.S. Foreign Intelligence Ct. of Review, 1979—85, US Ct. Appeals (10th Cir.), 1971, sr. judge, 1987—. Active Boy Scouts Am.; trustee St. Joseph's Children's Home, Torrington, Wyo., 1971—85; sec.-treas. Niobrara County Rep. Ctrl. Com. Cpl. US Army, 1942—45, ETO. Recipient Disting. Alumni award, U. Wyo., 1973, Profl. Excellence award, Ewing T. Kerr Inn of Ct., 2005. Mem.: VFW, Am. Legion, Order of Coif (hon. mem. Wyo. Coll. Law/U. Wyo. chpt.). Home Phone: 307-635-5148.

BARRETT, JANE HAYES, lawyer; b. Dayton, Ohio, Dec. 13, 1947; d. Walter J. and Jane H. Barrett BA, Calif. State U.-Long Beach, 1969; JD, U. So. Calif., 1972. Bar: Calif. 1972, US Dist. Ct. (cen. dist.) Calif. 1972, US Ct. Appeals (9th cir.) 1982, US Supreme Ct. Assoc. Lawler, Felix & Hall, LA, 1972—84; ptnr. Arter & Hadden, 1984—94, DLA Piper, 2002—06, Morrison Foerster, 2006—; mng. ptnr. Preston, Gates & Ellis, 1994—2002. Lectr. bus. law Calif. State U., 1973-75. Mem. adv. bd. Harriet Buhai Legal Aid Ctr., 1991-96, mem. bd. pub. counsel, 1996-98; pres. Pilgrim Parents Orgn. 1990-91; chmn. fin. Our Mother Good Counsel Sch.; bd. regents Loyola, HS, 2000-08; mem. adv. coun. Ctr. on Ethnic and Racial Diversity. Named Outstanding Grad. Calif. State U., Long Beach, 1988, Outstanding Alumnae Polit. Sci., 1993, So. Calif. Super Lawyer, LA Mag., 2003, 2004-07, Best Lawyer Am., 2006-07. Fellow Am. Bar Found.; mem. ABA (bd. govs. 1980-84, chmn. young lawyers divsn. 1980-81, com. on delivery of legal svcs. 1985-89, exec. coun. legal edn. and admissions sects. 1985-89, fin. sec. torts and ins. practice 1982-83, adv. mem. fed. judiciary com. 9th circuit rep. 2000-05, mem. minority and ethnic diversity bd., v.p. 1997—, Am. Bar Endowment 1999, bd. dirs. 1990—, sec. 1993-95, v.p. 1998-99, pres., 1999-00, bd. fellows young lawyers divsn. 1992—, del 9th cir. jud. conf., atty. del. US Dist. Ct. ctrl. dist. Calif. Atty. Conf. 2002-05, US Dist. Ct. Ctrl. Dist. Calif. (discipline com. 2004-07, chair sect. com., admissions com. 2005-07), 9th Cir. Atty. Conf. (del. 2005), Calif. State Bar (com. adminstrn. of justice, editl. bd. Calif. Lawyers 1981-84), Legion Lex (bd. dirs. 1990-93), Los Feliz Homeowners Assn. (bd. dirs.). Democrat. Office: Morrison Foerster 555 W 5th St Los Angeles CA 90013 Home Phone: 213-253-8659; Office Phone: 213-892-5377. Business E-Mail: jbarrett@mofo.com.

BARRETT, MICHAEL HENRY, civil engineer; b. Dove Creek, Colo., June 20, 1932; s. Frank Ace and Carrie Ethel (Snyder) B.; m. Barbara Jane Kreutz, Aug. 7, 1954; children: Robert, Mary, Bonnie, William. BS in Civil Engring, U. Colo., 1955, postgrad., 1955-64; MBA, U. Denver, 1979. Registered profl. engr., Colo., Calif., Fla., Wis., N.C., Minn., N.Mex., Utah. Design engr., then partner Ketchum & Konkel, Denver, 1955-69; pres. Ketchum, Konkel, Barrett, Nickel, Austin, Denver, 1969-79, chmn. bd., 1979-85, pres., chmn., 1986-88; prin., cons. Martin/Martin, 1988—2003, prin. emeritus, 2003—; pres. Gold Creek Devel. Corp., 2006—. Bd. dirs. Testing Cons., Inc., Martin Assoc. Group, Restruction Corp., Smart Skyways, Inc.; faculty U. Colo., 1963-64, U. Denver, 1968-69; lectr. Civil Def., 1962-68; cons. MMFX Steel Co., 2000—. Patentee in field. Exec. bd. Denver Area coun. Boy Scouts Am., 1970-, pres., 1974-75, area v.p., 1976-82, area pres., 1982; mem. Westminster Planning Commn., Colo., 1971-72; chmn. bd. dirs. Denver Boys, Inc. Served with USNR, 1951-54, USAR, 1955-63. Recipient Lincoln Arc Welding award, 1966, 68, award Am. Inst. Steel Constrn., 1969, Disting. Engring. Alumnus award U. Colo., 1984, Honor award Colo. Engring. Coun., 1984, Silver Beaver award Boy Scouts Am., 1977, Silver Antelope award, 1983. Fellow ASCE (life); mem. NSPE, Am. Concrete Inst., Soc. Exptl. Stress Analysis, Profl. Engrs. Colo. (pres. 1970), Am. Cons. Engrs. Coun. (life; 1st place award 1973, pres. Colo. chpt. 1982, Orley Phillips award 1992, com. of fellows 1993, peer reviewer 1984—, George Washington Leadership award 1998), Cert. Cons. Engrs. of Colo. (life), Structural Engrs. Assn. Colo., Am. Arbitration Assn., Harvard Bus. Sch. Club, Denver C. of C., Rotary (hon., bd. dirs. 1976-78). Office: Martin & Martin Inc 12499 W Colfax Ave Lakewood CO 80215 Office Phone: 303-431-6100. Business E-Mail: mbarrett@martinmartin.com.

BARRETT, REGINALD HAUGHTON, wildlife management educator; b. San Francisco, June 11, 1942; s. Paul Hutchison and Mary Lambert (Hodgkin) Barrett; m. Katharine Lawrence Ditmars, July 15, 1967; children: Wade Lawrence, Heather Elizabeth. BS in Game Mgmt., Humboldt State U., 1965; MS in Wildlife Mgmt., U. Mich., 1966; PhD in Zoology, U. Calif., Berkeley, 1971. Rsch. biologist U. Calif., Berkeley, 1970—71, acting asst. prof., 1971—72; rsch. scientist divsn. wildlife rsch. Commonwealth Scientific and Indsl. Rsch. Orgn., Darwin, Australia, 1972—75; from asst. prof. to prof. U. Calif., Berkeley, 1975—, George and Wilhelmina Goertz disting. prof. wildlife mgmt., 2002—. Author (with others): Report on the Use of Fire in National Parks and Reserves, 1977, Research and Management of Wild Hog Populations, Proceedings of a Symposium, 1977, Sitka Deer Symposium, 1979, Symposium on Ecology and Management of Barbary Sheep, 1980, Handbook of Census Methods for Birds and Mammals, 1981, Wildlife 2001: Populations, 1992; contbr. abstracts, reports to profl. jours. Recipient Outstanding Achievement award, Humboldt State U. Alumni Assn., 1986, Bruce R. Dodd award, 1965, Howard M. Wight award, 1966; Undergrad. scholar, Nat. Wildlife Fedn., 1964, NSF Grad. fellow, 1965—70, Union Found. Wildlife Rsch. grantee, 1968—70. Fellow: Calif. Acad. Sci., Explorers Club; mem.: AAAS, Orgn. Wildlife Planners, Calif. Bot. Soc., Am. Inst. Biol. Scis., Internat. Union Conservation Nature (life), Am. Soc. Mammalogists (life), Soc. Range Mgmt. (life), Australian Mammal Soc., Soc. Am. Foresters, Ecol. Soc. Am. (cert. sr. ecologist), Wildlife Soc. (pres. Bay Area chpt. 1978—79, pres. western sect. 1997—98, cert. wildlife biologist, R. F. Dasmann Profl. of the Yr. award western sect. 1989), Sigma Xi, Xi Sigma Pi. Episcopalian. Avocations: hunting, fishing, photography, camping, backpacking. Office: U Calif 137 Mulford Hall Berkeley CA 94720-3114 Office Phone: 510-642-7261. Business E-Mail: rbarrett@nature.berkeley.edu.

BARRETT, RONALD W., biopharmaceutical executive; PhD in Pharmacology, Rutgers U. Various positions to sr. v.p. Affymax Rsch. Inst., Palo Alto, Calif., 1989—99; co-founder, chief scientist XenoPort, 1999, CEO, 2001—. Recipient Newcomb-Cleve. prize, 1996-97. Office: XenoPort 3410 Central Expressway Santa Clara CA 95051 Office Phone: 408-616-7200. Office Fax: 408-616-7210.

BARRICKS, MICHAEL ELI, retinal surgeon; b. Chgo., Feb. 22, 1940; s. Arthur Goetz and Ruth (Zuckerman) B.; m. Zondra Dell Natman, Jan. 18, 1992; 1 child, Charleigh Ruth. BA, Harvard Coll., 1961; MD, U. Chgo., 1965; PhD, Stanford U., 1973. Diplomate Nat. Bd. Med. Examiners; lic. physician, Calif. Intern then resident in surgery Stanford (Calif.) U., 1965-67, postdoctoral fellow, 1967-72; resident, fellow in ophthalmology Bascom Palmer Eye Inst., Miami, Fla., 1972-76; fellow in retinal surgery U. Calif., San Francisco, 1976-77; asst. prof., dir. retina svc. U. Tex., San Antonio, 1977-78; retinal surgeon, dir. retina svc. Permanente Med. Group., Oakland, Calif., 1979—. Asst. clin. prof. U. Calif., San Francisco, 1980-92, assoc. clin. prof., 1993-2001, clin. prof., 2001--. Contbr. articles to profl. jours. Recipient Gold award Am. Acad. Pediatrics, Outstanding Physician award Kaiser Hosp., 1982, Cert. of Appreciation for Outstanding Teaching, U. Calif, San Francisco; Nat. scholar Fisher Body Craftsmans Guild; USPHS fellow Stanford U., 1967-70, Atholl McBean fellow Stanford Rsch. Inst., 1970-71. Fellow Am. Acad. Ophthalmology; mem. Permanente Ophthalmologic Soc. (pres. 1981), Vitreous Soc., Harvard Varsity Club, Crimson Key Soc. E-mail: michael.barricks@worldnet.att.net, mbarricks@comcast.net.

BARRIE, LEN, real estate developer, professional sports team executive; b. Kimberley, BC, Can., June 14, 1969; m. Kristy Barrie; children: Victoria, Tyson. Center Pitts. Penquins, 1994—95, LA Kings, 1999—2000, Fla. Panthers, 1999—2001; ret., 2001; ptnr. OK Hockey LLC; co-owner Tampa Bay Lightning, 2008—. Pres., CEO Bear Mountain Resort, Victoria, BC, Canada. Office: Bear Mountain Resort 1271 Bear Mountain Parkway Victoria BC V9B 6R3 Canada also: Tampa Bay Lightning Hockey Club St Pete Times Forum 401 Channelside Dr Tampa FL 33602 Office Phone: 250-391-6100. Office Fax: 250-391-6101.

BARRON, STEPHANIE, curator; AB, Barnard Coll., Columbia U., 1972; student, Harvard Inst. Arts Adminstrn., 1973; MA, Columbia U., 1974; postgrad., CUNY, 1975-76. Intern, curatorial asst. Solomon R. Guggenheim Mus., 1971-72; Nat. Endowment Arts intern in edn. Toledo Mus. Art, 1973-74; exhbn. coord. Jewish Mus., NYC, 1975-76; assoc. curator modern art L.A. County Mus. Art, 1976-80, curator Twentieth Century art, 1980-94, coord. curatorial affairs, 1993-96, sr. curator Twentieth Century art, 1995—, v.p. edn. and pub. programs, 1996—2003; chief curator Modern and Contemporary Art, 2002—. Lectr., panelist in field. Contbr. articles to profl. jours. Mem. art adv. panel IRS, 1996—; advisor U.S. Holocaust Mus., 1996—; trustee Scripps Coll., 1996—; mem. steering com. Villa Aurora, 1994—; mem. bd. Stiftung Mortizburg, Halle, Germany, 2005-, Magritte Assn., 2005-. Decorated Comdr.'s Cross Fed. Republic of Germany, Order of Merit (Germany), 2001; recipient George L. Wittenborn award ARLIS, 1991, award for best Am. exhbn. of yr. Assn. Internat. Critics Art, 1991, 97, Theo Wormland Kunstpreis, 1992, George L. Wittenborn award, 1992, Alfred H. Barr Jr. award Coll. Art Assn., 1992, E.L. Kirchner prize, Switzerland, 1997, First Pl. award Am. Assn. Art Mus., 1998, Hon. Mention, ARLIS, 1998; named Woman of Yr., Bus. and Profl. Women of UJA, Jewish Fedn., 1991, Friends of Tel Hashomer, 1991; Nat. Endowment of Arts fellow, 1986-87; John J. McCloy fellow in art, 1981. Fellow Am. Acad. Arts and Scis.; mem. Am. Assn. Mus., Internat. Mus. Modern Art (internat. com. mus.), Internat. Coun. Mus., Internat. Com. for Mus. and Collections of Modern Art, Art Table. Office: LA County Mus Art 5905 Wilshire Blvd Los Angeles CA 90036-4597 Office Phone: 323-857-6025. Business E-Mail: sbarron@lacma.org.

BARROW, THOMAS FRANCIS, artist, educator; b. Kansas City, Mo., Sept. 24, 1938; s. Luther Hopkins and Cleo Naomi (Francis) Barrow; m. Laurie Anderson, Nov. 30, 1974; children: Melissa, Timothy, Andrew. BFA, Kansas City Art Inst., 1963; MS, Ill. Inst. Tech., 1965. With George Eastman House, Rochester, NY, 1966-72, asst. dir., 1971-72; assoc. dir. Art Mus. U. N.Mex., Albuquerque, 1973-76, assoc. prof., 1976-81, prof., 1981—2001, Presdl. prof., 1985-90. Author: The Art of Photography, 1971; sr. editor: Reading into Photography, 1982; curator, photography: N.Mex, 2008; contbr. to Brit. Ency. Am. Art, 1973, A Hundred Years of Photographic History: Essays in Honor of Beaumont Newhall, 1975, Experimental Vision, 1994; forward The Valiant Knights of Daguerre, 1978; contbr. articles to profl. jours.; one-man shows include Light Gallery, N.Y.C., 1974-76, 79, 82, Amarillo Art Ctr., 1990, Andrew Smith Gallery, Santa Fe, 1992, Laurence Miller Gallery, N.Y.C., 1996, U. N.Mex. Art Mus., 1997, Richard Levy Gallery, Albuquerque, 2000; exhibited in group shows including Pace Gallery, N.Y.C., 1973, Hudson River Mus., Yonkers, N.Y., 1973, Internat. Mus. Photography, Rochester, 1975, Seattle Art Mus., 1976, Mus. Fine Arts, Houston, 1977, Retrospective exhbn. L.A. County Mus. Art, 1987—; represented in permanent collections Nat. Gallery Can., Mus. Modern Art, Getty Ctr. for Arts and Humanities, Ctr. for Creative Photography U. Ariz. Nat. Endowment for Arts fellow, 1971, 78. Business E-Mail: tfbarrow@unm.edu.

BARRY, JOHN MAYNARD, urologist; b. Winona, Minn., Mar. 14, 1940; MD, U. Minn., 1965. Intern SUNY, Syracuse, 1965-66; resident U. Oreg. Med. Sch., Portland, 1969-73; prof., chmn. urology Oreg. Health Sci. U., Portland, 1980—, dir. renal transplantation, 1976—, chmn. abdominal organ transplantation, 2000—02. Office: Oreg Health Sci U Divsn Urology 3303 SW Bond Ave Portland OR 97293

BARRY, PHILLIP OWEN, college president; b. Chgo., May 24, 1951; m. April Lee Rank, Nov. 21, 1971; children: Patrick, Collin. Diploma, Edgewater Hosp., 1971; AAS, Morraine Valley Community Coll., 1973; BS, Chgo. Med. Sch., 1975; M. Edn. Adminstrn., Wichita State U., 1978; PhD, Kans. State U., 1983. Registered radiologic technologist Am. Registry Radiologic Technologists. With health care Med. Ctrs., Chgo., 1971-75; with faculty Hutchinson (Kans.) C.C., 1975-80; dir. Labette C.C., Parsons, Kans., 1980-83, assoc. dean, 1983-85, dean, 1985-87; pres. Salem C.C., Carneys Point, N.J., 1987-92, Hawkeye C.C., Waterloo, Iowa, 1992-95, Mesalands C. C., Tucumcari, N.Mex. Mem. grad. faculty Kans. State U., Manhattan, 1984-87, Glassboro (N.J.) State U., 1989-92, Small/Rural Coll. commn., Washington, 1989-92, mem. editorial bd., 1989—. Author: Radiography of Facial Bones, 1979; contbr. articles to profl. jours.; researcher in field. Mem. multiple positions Boy Scouts Am., Kans. N.J., 1975-91, Salem County Youth Commn., 1989-91, Coun. County Colls., 1987—; chmn. Ducks Unltd., Parsons, 1981-86; vice chmn. Econs. Devel. Com., Salem County, N.J., 1988-91; mem. exec. com. Healthy Heart Coalition, Salem County, 1990-91; bd. dirs. Waterloo C. of C., 1993-95, Cedar Valley Econ. Devel. Corp., 1993-95; trustee Silos and Smokestacks, 1992-95. Recipient Disting. Svc. award Ducks Unltd., 1985. Mem. Am. Assn. Community and Jr. Colls. (Outstanding Community Coll. Alumni 1991), Greater Salem C. of C., Rotary, Kiwanis (exec. 1985-87), Jaycees (Outstanding Young Men of Am. 1981). Avocations: horticulture, pomology.

BARRY, STEVE, sculptor, educator; b. Jersey City, June 22, 1956; s. Thomas Daniel and Lorraine B. BFA, Sch. Visual Arts, NYC, 1980; MFA, Hunter Coll., NYC, 1984. Adj. lectr. Hunter Coll., 1984-89; full prof. U. N.Mex., Albuquerque, 1989—. Kohler Arts and Industry Residency, 1996; bd. dir. Albuquerque Ctr. Contemporary Arts. Exhbns. include Bklyn. Army Terminal, NYC, 1983, City Gallery, NYC, 1986, 90, Storefront for Art and Architecture, 1988, Artists Space, NYC, 1989, Santa Barbara Art Mus., 1990, Kohler Arts Ctr., Sheboygan, Wis., 1991, Hirshhorn Mus., Washington, 1990, Fla. State U., 1992, Contemporary Art Mus., Houston, 1992, CAFE Gallery, Albuquerque, 1993, Charolette Jackson, Santa Fe, 1993, Ctr. for Contemporary Arts, Santa Fe, 1994, U. Wyo. Art Mus., 1995, Site Santa Fe, 1996, Sheldon Art Mus., Lincoln, Nebr., 1997, U. N.Mex. Art Mus., Albuquerque, 1997, 2006, Cedar Rapids Mus. of Art, Iowa, 1998, Albuquerque Contemporary Art Ctr., 2000, Plan B, Santa Fe, 2000, Donkey Gallery, Albuquerque, 2004, U. N.Mex. Art Mus., 2006. Rsch. grantee Coll. Fine Arts N.Mex., 2002; grantee Clocktower Nat. Studio, 1985, NEA, 1986, 88, 90, NY State Coun. Arts, 1987, NY Found. Arts, 1988; recipient AVA award, 1990, Regents Lectureship award U. N.Mex., 2006. Home: PO Box 1046 Corrales NM 87048-1046 Office: U NMex Dept Art & Art History Albuquerque NM 87131-0001 Home Phone: 505-897-3902; Office Phone: 505-277-5861. Business E-Mail: sbarry@unm.edu.

BART, PETER BENTON, editor, film producer, writer; b. NYC, July 24, 1932; m. Leslie Cox; children: Colby, Dilys. BA, Swarthmore Coll., 1954; MA, London Sch. Econs., 1956. Staff reporter The Wall Street Jour., NYC, 1956-57, The N.Y. Times, NYC, 1957-67; v.p. Paramount Pictures, Los Angeles, 1967-74; pres. Bart Palevsky Prodn., LA, 1974-77, Lorimar Film Co., Los Angeles, 1977-82; sr. v.p., film producer Metro Goldwyn Mayer/United Artists, LA, 1982-85; v.p., editorial dir. Variety and Daily Variety, LA, 1989—, editor-in-chief. Author: Destinies, 1980, Thy Kingdom Come, 1983, Fade Out: The Calamitous Final Days of MGM, 1990; prodr.: (films) Fun with Dick and Jane, Islands in the Stream, Youngblood. Office: Variety 5900 Wilshire Blvd Ste 3100 Los Angeles CA 90036-5030

BARTH, DAVID KECK, retired wholesale distribution executive, consultant; b. Springfield, Ill., Dec. 7, 1943; s. David Klenk and Edna Margaret (Keck) B.; m. Dian Oldemeyer, Nov. 21, 1970; children—David, Michael, John. BA cum laude, Knox Coll., Galesburg, Ill., 1965; MBA, U. Calif., Berkeley, 1971. With data processing div. IBM Corp., Chgo., 1966; with No. Trust Co., Chgo., 1971-72; mgr. treasury ops., then treas. fin. services group Borg-Warner Corp., Chgo., 1972-79; treas. W.W. Grainger, Inc., Skokie, Ill., 1979-83, v.p., 1984-90; pres. Barth Smith Co., 1991—2001. Mem. faculty Lake Forest Grad. Sch. Mgmt., Ill., 1994—2006; bd. dirs. Indsl. Distbn. Group Inc., Atlanta. Served to lt. USNR, 1966-69. Mem. Econ. Club Chgo., Beta Gamma Sigma, Phi Delta Theta. Lutheran. Personal E-mail: davidbarth@sbcglobal.net.

BARTH, DELBERT SYLVESTER, environmental studies educator; b. Lawrenceburg, Ind., June 6, 1925; BS in Mil. Engring., U.S. Mil. Acad., 1946; MS in Nuclear Physics, Ohio State U., 1952; MS in Solid State Physics, Stevens Inst. Tech., 1960; PhD in Biophysics, Ohio State U., 1962. Health physics trainee Oak Ridge Nat. Lab., Tenn., 1947-49; asst. prof. dept. physics and chemistry U.S. Mil. Acad., West Point, N.Y., 1956-60; staff officer evaluation and planning sect. rsch. br. div. radiological health U.S. Pub. Health Svc., Dept. Health, Edn. and Welfare, 1960-61; investigator, staff officer experimental radiobiology program rsch. br. DRH, Rockville, Md., 1962-63; dir. bioenviron. rsch. program Southwestern Radiological Health Lab., U.S. Pub. Health Svc., Las Vegas, 1963-69; dir. bur. criteria and standards Nat. Air Pollution Control Adminstrn., DHEW, Durham, N.C., 1969-71; dir. Bur. Air Pollution Scis., Research Triangle Park, N.C., 1971, Nat. Environ. Rsch. Ctr., Research Triangle Park, 1971-72, Las Vegas, 1972-76; dep. asst. adminstr. health and ecological effects ORD U.S. Environ. Protection Agy., 1976-78; vis. prof. biophysics U. Nev., Las Vegas, 1978-82, sr. scientist environ. rsch. ctr., 1982-88, dir. environ. rsch. ctr., 1989-92, prof. environ. studies program, 1992-94; prof. emeritus environ. studies program, 1994—. Mem. sub-com. on environ. effects, mem. adv. com. to fed. radiation, mem. com. on hearing, bioaccoustics, biomechs.; chmn. adv. com. Nat. Air Quality Criteria; environ. monitoring advisor, mem. environ. com. ecological scis. divsn. Inst. Environ. Scis.; mem. Army Sci. Bd., 1984-90; mem. awards bd. EPA. Recipient PHS Disting. Svc. medal. Mem. AAAS, Sigma Xi. Office: U Nev Las Vegas Environ Studies Program 4505 S Maryland Pkwy Las Vegas NV 89154-9900

BARTH MENZIES, KAREN, lawyer; b. Dubuque, Iowa, Dec. 8, 1966; d. Henry Victor and Janet Marie Barth. BA, Colo. State U., 1989; JD, U. Calif., Davis, 1995. Bar: Calif. 1995, U.S. Dist. Ct. (ctrl. dist.) Calif. 1995, U.S. Dist. Ct. (so. dist.) Calif. 1999, U.S. Dist. Ct. (ea. and western dists.) Ark. 2003, U.S. Dist. Ct. (so. dist.) Ill. 2003, U.S. Dist. Ct. (ctrl. dist.) Ill. 2006, U.S. Dist. Ct. Colo. 2003, U.S. Dist. Ct. (ea. and no. dists.) Calif. 2006, U.S. Ct. Appeals (9th cir.) 1999, U.S. Ct. Appeals (5th cir.) 2005. Legal intern Colo. Atty. Gen.'s Office, Denver, 1993, Calif. Atty. Gen.'s Office, Sacramento, 1994; legal intern to Justice Davis, Calif. 3d Dist. Appellate Ct., Sacramento, 1994; legal intern Sacramento Dist. Atty.'s Office, Sacramento, 1995; shareholder Baum, Hedlund, Anstei, Goldman & Menzies and predecessor firms, LA, 1995—. Lectr. in field; lead coun., plaintiff's steering com. MDL 1574 Paxil Products liability litig. Contbr. articles to profl. jours. Named Calif. Lawyer of Yr., Calif. Mag., 2004, Lawyer of Yr., Lawyer's Weekly, 2004, So. Calif. Super Lawyer, 2005—07; named one of Top 40 Lawyers Under 40, Nat. Law Jour., 2005; finalist Consumer Atty. of Yr., CAOC, 2006. Mem. AAJ (step-toxic, environ., pharmacol. sect.), ABA (litig. sect., tort, trial and ins. sect.), State Bar of Calif., Nat. Assn. Women Lawyers, Consumer Attys. Calif., Trial Lawyers for Public Justice, LA Women Lawyers Assn., George McBurney Complex Litigation Inn of Ct. Avocations: rock climbing, diving, skiing, basketball, volleyball. Office: Baum Hedlund Anstei Goldman & Menzies 12100 Wilshire Blvd Ste 950 Los Angeles CA 90025-7107 Office Phone: 310-207-3233. Business E-Mail: kbmenzies@baumhedlundlaw.com.

BARTHOLD, STEPHEN W., veterinarian; BS in Vet. Sci., U. Calif., Davis, 1967, DVM, 1969; MS in Pathology, U. Wis., 1973, PhD in Pathology, 1974. Dir. Ctr. Comparative Medicine U. Calif., Davis, prof. pathology, joint appt. Sch. Medicine & Sch. Vet. Medicine. Mem.: NAS (mem. Inst. Medicine). Office: Ctr Comparative Medicine U Calif Davis County Rd 98 & Hutchinson Dr Davis CA 95616 also: U Calif Davis 1 Shields Ave Davis CA 95616 Office Phone: 530-732-7913, 530-752-1245. Business E-Mail: swbarthold@ucdavis.edu.

BARTLETT, ARTHUR EUGENE, real estate company executive; b. Glens Falls, NY, Nov. 26, 1933; s. Raymond Ernest and Thelma (Williams) Bartlett; m. Collette R. Bartlett, Jan. 9, 1955 (dec.); 1 child, Stacy Lynn; m. Nancy Sanders Bartlett, Feb. 12, 2005. Sales mgr. Forest E. Olson, Inc., 1960-64; co-founder, v.p. Four Star Realty, Inc., Santa Ana, Calif., 1964-71, v.p., sec., 1964-71; founder, pres. Comps, Inc., Tustin, Calif., 1971-81; co-founder, chmn. of bd., pres., CEO Century 21 Real Estate Corp., Tustin, 1980—; pres. Larwin Sq. LLC Shopping Ctr, Tustin, 1979—2002. Chmn. bd. dirs. United Western Med. Ctrs., 1981—87. Mem.: Internat. Franchise Assn. (v.p., bd. dirs. 1975—80, Hall of Fame 1987), Masons.

BARTLETT, DAVID CARSON, state legislator; b. New London, Conn., Feb. 2, 1944; s. Neil Riley and Susan Marion (Carson) B.; m. Barbara Hunting, July 14, 1973 (div. 1974); m. Janice Anne Wezelman, Feb. 11, 1979; children: Daniel Wezelman (dec.), Elizabeth Anne. Student, Wesleyan U., Middletown, Conn., 1962-64; BA, U. Ariz., 1966, MA, 1970; JD, Georgetown U., 1976. Teaching asst. U. Ariz., Tucson, 1967-69; program analyst U.S. Dept. Labor, Washington, 1970-76; assoc. Snell & Wilmer, Tucson, 1976-77; pvt. practice Tucson, 1976-79; assoc. Davis, Eppstein & Hall, Tucson, 1979-85; mem. Ariz. Ho. of Reps., Tucson, 1983-88, Ariz. State Senate, 1989-92; chief counsel for civil rights Ariz. Atty. Gen.'s Office, Tucson, 1993-99, spl. couns., 1999—2002. Democrat. Home: 3236 E Via Palos Verdes Tucson AZ 85716-5854

BARTLETT, DAVID FARNHAM, physics professor; b. NYC, Dec. 13, 1938; s. Frederic Pearson and Margaret Mary (Boulton) B.; m. Roxana Ellen Stoessel, Nov. 19, 1960; children: Andrew, Susannah, Christopher, Jennifer AB, Harvard U., 1959; AM, Columbia U., 1961, PhD, 1965. Instr. Princeton U., NJ, 1964-67, asst. prof. NJ, 1967-71; assoc. prof. physics U. Colo., Boulder, 1971-82, prof., 1982—2003, prof. emeritus, 2004—. Editor: The Metric Debate, General Relativity and Gravitation, 1989; contbr. articles to profl. jours. Fellow Am. Phys. Soc.; mem. Am. Assn. Physics Tchrs., Am. Geophys. Union., Am. Astronomical Soc. Democrat. Home: 954 Lincoln Pl Boulder CO 80302-7234 Office: U Colo Dept Physics PO Box 390 Boulder CO 80309-0390 Office Phone: 303-492-6960. Business E-Mail: david.bartlett@colorado.edu.

BARTLETT, JAMES LOWELL, III, investment company executive; b. Boston, May 26, 1945; s. James Lowell and Shirley Victoria (Wyatt) B.; m. Shannon Mara McMillion, May 4, 1979; children: James Lowell IV, Zachary Morgan, Matthew Wyatt. BS, U. Calif., Berkeley, 1967, MBA, 1968. Loan officer nat. div. Bank of Am., Los Angeles, 1968; fin. mgr. Psychology Today mag., Del Mar, Calif., 1969; pres. Forum Communications Corp.; pub. Cuisine, Politics Today, Volleyball mags., NYC, 1970-82; pres. Bartlett & Co., Santa Barbara, Calif., 1982—. Commr. Internat. Volleyball Assn., 1977-80 Mem. Lds Ch. Office: 5662 Calle Real Santa Barbara CA 93117-2317

BARTLETT, LEONARD LEE, retired communications educator, advertising executive; b. Mountain Home, Idaho, May 31, 1930; s. Harold Roberts and Alma Martina (Nixon) B.; m. Sue Ann Kipfer, Nov. 5, 1966; children: Jennifer, Deborah; children by previous marriage: Linda Lee, Cynthia, Nancy, Pamela, William Charles. BA, Brigham Young U., Provo, Utah, 1957, MA, 1989. Advt. mgr. Steiner Co., Chgo., 1957-59; sr. v.p. Marsteller Inc., Chgo., 1959-67; vice chmn. Cole & Weber, Inc., Seattle, 1966-84; chmn. Cole & Weber Calif., San Francisco, 1984-86, Los Angeles, 1986-87; assoc. prof. communications Brigham Young U., Provo, 1989-2000; ret., 2000. Acting chmn. dept. comms. Brigham Young U., Provo, 1995—96, chmn. dept. comm., 1996—97, asst. to pres. univ. comms., 1997—2000. Mem. Am. Assn. Advt. Agys. (chmn. Western region 1980, nat. bd. 1980-81). Republican. Mem. Ch. Jesus Christ of Latter-day Saints. Home: 1211 East 2080 North Provo UT 84604-2123 Personal E-mail: leebar30@comcast.net.

BARTLETT, ROBERT WATKINS, metallurgist, educator, consultant; b. Salt Lake City, Jan. 8, 1933; s. Charles E. and Phyllis (Watkins) B.; m. Betty Cameron, Dec. 3, 1954; children: John C., Robin Parmley, Bruce R., Susanne. BS, U. Utah, 1953, PhD, 1961. Registered profl. engr., Calif. Group leader ceramics SRI Internat., Menlo Park, Calif., 1964-67; assoc. prof. metallurgy Stanford U., Palo Alto, Calif., 1967-74; mgr. hydrometallurgy Kennecott Minerals Co., Salt Lake City, 1974-77; dir. materials lab. SRI Internat., Menlo Park, Calif., 1977-80; v.p. rsch. Anaconda Minerals Co., Tucson, 1980-85; mgr. materials tech. Idaho Sci. and Tech. Dept., Idaho Falls, 1985-87; dean Coll. Mines and Earth Resources, U. Idaho, Moscow, 1987-97. Dir. Idaho Geol. Survey, Moscow. Author approximately 100 rsch. publs. in metallurgy; 12 patents in field; 1 textbook. Served to lt. (j.g.) USN, 1953-56. Recipient Turner award Electrochem. Soc., 1965, McConnell award AIME, 1985. Mem. Nat. Acad. Engring., Metall. Soc. (pres. 1989, EPD lecturer 1997), Soc. Mining Engrs. (disting. mem., Wadsworth award 1996), Sigma Xi, Tau Beta Pi. Office: 2505 Loch Way El Dorado Hills CA 95762 Personal E-mail: bobnbettybartlett@sbcglobal.net.

BARTLETT, THOMAS ALVA, retired educational administrator; b. Salem, Oreg., Aug. 20, 1930; s. Cleave Wines and Alma (Hanson) B.; m. Mary Louise Bixby, Mar. 20, 1954; children: Thomas Glenn, Richard A., Paul H. Student, Willamette U., 1947—49, DCL (hon.), 1986; AB, Stanford U., 1951, PhD, 1959; MA, Oxford U., 1953; LHD (hon.), Colgate U., 1977, Mich. State U., 1978, Union Coll., 1979; DCL (hon.), Pusan Nat. U., 1985, U. Ala., 1983, U. North Ala., 2001; DHL (hon.), Am. U. Cairo, 2004. Mem. U.S. Permanent Mission to UN, 1956—63; advisor Gen. Assembly Dels., 1956—63; pres. Am. U., Cairo, 1963—69, Colgate U., Hamilton, NY, 1969—77, Assn. Am. Univs., Washington, 1977—82; chancellor U. Ala. Sys., 1982—89, Oreg. State Sys. of Higher Edn. Office, Eugene, 1989—94, SUNY, 1994—96; ret., 1996; interim pres. Am. U., Cairo, 2002—03. Mem. UAR-U.S. Ednl. Exch. Commn., 1966-69; mem. Task Force on Financing Higher Edn. in N.Y. State (Keppel Commn.), 1972-73; chmn. Commn. Ind. Colls. and Univs. N.Y., 1974-76; bd. dirs. Nat. Assn. Ind. Colls. and Univs., 1975-76; trustee Univs. Field Staff Internat., 1985-87; mem. NASA Comml. Space Adv. Com., 1988-90. Mem. nat. bd. examining Chaplains Episcopal Ch., 1978-91; trustee Gen. Theol. Sem., 1977-82, Am. U., Cairo, 1978-2002, vice chair 1998-2002; trustee U.S.-Japan Found., 1988-2001, chmn. 1996-2001; bd. mem. Internat. Assn. of Univs., 1995-2000; trustee Am. U. Kuwait, 2004—; chair World Affairs Coun. Oreg., 2009-. Rhodes scholar, Oxford U., 1953. Mem. Coun. Fgn. Rels., Century Assn., Ala. Acad. Honor, Phi Beta Kappa. Home: 1209 SW 6th Ave Apt 904 Portland OR 97204 Home Phone: 971-544-0175. Personal E-mail: t-mbartlett@att.net.

BARTLIT, FRED HOLCOMB, JR., lawyer; b. Harvey, Ill., Aug. 1, 1932; s. Fred Holcomb and Agnes Marie (Rahn) Bartlit; m. Jana Cockrell, Feb. 28, 1987. BS in Engring., US Mil. Acad., 1954; JD, U. Ill., 1960. Bar: Ill. 1960, US Ct. Appeals 7th cir. 1962, US Ct. Appeals 6th cir. 1969, US Ct. Appeals 10th cir. 1970, US Supreme Ct. 1970, US Ct. Appeals 8th cir. 1971, US Ct. Appeals 3rd cir. 1973, US Ct. Appeals 5th cir. 1978. Assoc. Kirkland & Ellis, Chgo., 1960—64, ptnr., 1964—93, Bartlit Beck Herman Palenchar & Scott LLP, Chgo., Denver, 1993—. Lectr. in field; mem. faculty Nat. Inst. Trial Advocacy, 1975—. Served US Army, 1954—58. Named one of America's Top Trial Lawyers -- Who They Are & Why They Win, Glasser LegalWorks, 1996, 100 Most Influential Lawyers, Nat. Law Mag., 1997, 2006. Fellow: Internat. Acad. Trial Lawyers, Am. Coll. Trial Lawyers; mem.: Chgo. Bar Assn., Ill. Bar Assn., Castle Pines Golf, Mid-Am., Glen View. Republican. Presbyterian. Office: Bartlit Beck Herman Palenchar & Scott LLP 1899 W Ynkoop St 8th Fl Denver CO 80202

BARTNICKI-GARCIA, SALOMON, microbiologist, educator; b. Mexico City, May 18, 1935; came to U.S., 1957; s. Israel Bartnicki and Refugio Garcia; m. Ildiko Nagy, Aug. 10, 1975; children— Linda Laura, David Daniel. Bacteriological Chemist, Inst. Politecnico Nacional, Mexico City, 1957; PhD, Rutgers U., 1961. Rsch. assoc. microbiology Rutgers U., 1961-62; mem. faculty U. Calif., Riverside, 1962—, prof. plant pathology and microbiology, 1971-94, prof. emeritus, 1994, rsch. prof., 1994-2000, chmn. dept. plant pathology, 1989-92, dir. grad. program in microbiology, 1997-2000; sci. rschr. Ctr. Scientific Investigation and Higher Studies Ensenada, Ensenada, Mexico, 2000—. Vis. prof. Organic Chemistry Inst., U. Stockholm, 1969-70; selected faculty rsch. lectr. U. Calif., Riverside, 1989. Author research and rev. papers. Grantee NIH, 1963-96, NSF, 1971-96. Fellow AAAS, Am. Phytopathol. Soc. (Ruth Allen award 1983); mem. Am. Soc. Microbiology, Mycol. Soc. Am. (Disting. Mycologist award 1994), Brit. Soc. Gen. Microbiology, Brit. Mycol. Soc. (hon.), Am. Soc. Biol. Chemists. Home: 3787 Elliott St San Diego CA 92106-1235 Office: U Calif Dept Plant Pathology Riverside CA 92521-0001 also: CICESE Ensenada Mexico Office Phone: 52-646-175-0513. E-mail: bart@citrus.ucr.edu.

BARTO, DEBORAH ANN, physician; b. West Chester, Pa., July 27, 1948; d. Charles Guy and Jeannette Victoria (Golder) B. BA, Oberlin Coll., Ohio, 1970; MD, Hahnemann U., Phila., 1974; Reiki III, N.W. Sch. Healing, Redmond, Wash., 2003. Cert. Reiki master. Intern, resident Kaiser Permanente Hosp., San Francisco, 1974-77; dir. med. oncology Evergreen Hosp., Kirkland, Wash., 1980-85, head oncology quality assurance, 1992-94; med. dir. Cmty. Home Health Care Hospice, Seattle, 1981-84. Hosp. ethics com. Evergreen Hosp., 1995-98, integrative care com., 1996-2001. Mem. Evergreen Women's Physicians, Reiki III. Democrat. Buddhist. Avocation: horseback riding. Office: 13115 121st Way NE Ste C Kirkland WA 98034

BARTO, NANCY K., state legislator; b. Chgo. m. Joe Barto; 3 children. Student, Ariz. State U. Chair Rep. Com., 2002—06; mem. Dist. 7 Ariz. House of Reps., 2006—, chair health & human svcs. com., mem. edn. com., judiciary com. Active Pureheart Christian Fellowship. Republican. Office: Ariz House Reps Capitol Complex 1700 W Washington Rm 112 Phoenix AZ 85007 Office Phone: 602-569-4742, 602-926-5766. Office Fax: 602-417-3011. Business E-Mail: nbarto@azleg.gov. E-mail: nancybarto2006@yahoo.com.*

BARTOK, MICHELLE, cosmetic company executive; b. Youngstown, Ohio, Feb. 18, 1961; d. Albert James and Judith Ann (Phillips) Bartok; m. John Anthony Garruto, Apr. 2, 1988 (div. 1997); children: Catherine Michelle, Gabrielle Bartok. BS in Physiol. Psychology, U. Calif., Santa Barbara, 1984. EMT, Calif. Asst. to phys. therapist Santa Barbara Phys. Therapy, 1983-84, Escondido Phys. Therapy, Calif., 1984-85; regional sales rep. Ft. Dodge Labs., San Francisco, 1985-87; owner North Coast Therapeutics, Oceanside, Calif., 1986—92; CEO Innovative Bioscis. Corp., Carlsbad, Calif., 1992—; owner Beaches Cafe Inc., Encinitas, Calif., 1999-2000. Tchr. Fashion Inst. Design and Merchandising, San Diego, LA, 2003—, U. Calif., Irvine, 2006—07, UC Irvine Branding, 2006—; naming com. coll of bus. deans list advisory bd. Calif. State U., San Marcos, 2005—. Recipient Entrepreneur award, San Diego Women, San Diego Bus. Jour., 2005, 2006, 60th So Biz Jour. award; named one of Fastest 100 Cos., San Diego Bus. Jour., 2005, 2006. Mem. Soc. Cosmetic Chemists, Beauty Industry West (pub. rels. dir. 1991-92, chair symposium 1996, named Entrepreneur of Yr., 2003), Internat. Spa and Fitness Assn. (edn. com. 2006, sponsor Ironman competition 1989, edn. com. 2005-06, mem. bd. edn.). Avocations: outrigger canoes, yoga, surfing. Home: 178 Grandview St Encinitas CA 92024-1009 Office Phone: 760-603-0772. Business E-Mail: michelle@innovativebodyscience.com.

BARTON, ALAN JOEL, lawyer; b. NYC, Sept. 2, 1938; s. Sidney and Claire (Greenfield) B.; m. Ann Rena Beral, Jan. 29, 1961; children: Donna Frieda Olsen, Brian Joseph. AB, U. Calif., Berkeley, 1960, JD, 1963. Assoc. Nossaman, Krueger & Marsh, LA, 1963—70, ptnr., 1970—80, Paul, Hastings, Janofsky & Walker, LLP, LA, 1980—2002, sr. counsel, 2002—; advisor Palatin capital Group, LLC, 2002—. Lectr. UCLA Sch. Law, 2001—; lectr. corp. and securities law U. Calif. Continuing Edn. Bar, 1980—; lectr. venture capital and securities law Practicing Law Inst., 1986—. Assoc. editor U. Calif. Law Rev., 1963. Dir. Ctr. for Study of Young People in Groups, L.A., 1988-2004, Planned Parenthood, L.A., 1999-2004; trustee Dubnoff Ctr. for Ednl. Therapy, North Hollywood, Calif., 1976-80. Mem. ABA (com. on fed. regulation of securities), Calif. Bar Assn. (com. on corps.), Order of Coif, The Calif. Club, Stem Cell Rsch. Oversight Com., Cedars-Sinai Med. Ctr. (2005-). Republican. Jewish. Avocations: movies, Torah study, contemporary art, tennis, travel. Office: Paul Hastings Janofsky & Walker LLP 515 S Flower St Fl 25 Los Angeles CA 90071-2300

BARTON, GERALD LEE, farming company executive; b. Modesto, Calif., Feb. 24, 1934; s. Robert Paul and Alice Lee (Hall) B.; m. Janet Murray, June 24, 1955; children: Donald Lee, Gary Michael, Brent Richard. BA with distinction, Stanford U., 1955. Owner, pres. Barton Ranch, Escalon, Calif., 1961—; v.p. R.P. Barton Mfg. Co., Escalon, 1963—86; chmn. bd. Diamond Walnut Growers Inc., 1976-81, chmn. emeritus, 1981—2005, pres., 1986-90; chmn. GoldRiver Orchards, 2004—. Chmn. Growers Harvesting Com., Modesto, 1976-77, Diamond-Sunsweet Co., Stockton, Calif., 1978-80, Sun Diamond Growers, Inc., 1980-81; bd. dirs. Calif. Fin. Holding Co., Stockton, Stockton Savs. Bank, 1996-1997; vice-chmn. Fed. Land Bank, Modesto, 1976-81; pomology rsch. adv. bd. U. Calif., Davis, 1968-74, Walnut Mktg. Bd., Sacramento, 1971-73, 77-2000; mem. Calif. Walnut Commn., 1987-99; agribus. adv. bd. U. Santa Clara, 1979-89; dir. Ross Hort. Found., Union Safe Deposit Bank, 2000-04; ext. adv. bd. San Joaquin County U. Calif. Chmn. bd. edn. Escalon Unified Sch. Dist., 1963—75; vice chmn. San Joaquin County Sch. Bds. Assn., 1965; trustee Yosemite Assn., 1999—2005, The Cortopassi Inst., 2004—07; elder Trinity United Presbyn. Ch., Modesto, 2002—05; bd. dirs. St. Joseph's Healthcare Corp., 1991—95; bd. dirs., v.p. Stanislaus River Flood Control Assn., 1965—. With US Army, 1956—58. Decorated Order of the Golden Walnut, 1990; named Outstanding Young Farmer in San Joaquin County C. of C., 1965, Farmer of Yr. Escalon C. of C., 1979; recipient U. Calif. Friend of Ext. award, 1992; named to San Joaquin County Agrl. Hall of Fame, 1993, Escalon Unified Sch. Dist. Hall Fame, 2006; recipient Disting. Svc. award Calif. Walnut Commn., 1998; named Co-op Farmer Yr. Agrl. Coun. Calif., 2001. Mem. Stanford U. Alumni Assn., Delta Chi. Republican. Presbyterian. Office: 22398 McBride Rd Escalon CA 95320-9637

BARTON, GREGORY MARK, Olympic athlete; b. Jackson, Mich., Dec. 2, 1959; BS in Mech. Engring., U. Mich., 1983. Olympic kayak racer, 1000 meter singles, LA, 1984; Olympic kayak racer, 1000 meter singles and doubles Seoul, Korea, 1988, Barcelona, 1992. Recipient Bronze medal 1000 meter kayak singles Olympics, L.A., 1984, Gold medal 1000 meter kayak singles Olympics, Seoul, 1988, Gold medal 1000 meter kayak doubles Olympics, Seoul, 1988, Bronze medal 1000 meter kayak singles Olympics, Barcelona, 1992.

BARTON, JOHN HAYS, law educator; b. Chgo., Oct. 27, 1936; s. Jay and Agnes (Heisler) B.; m. Julianne Marie Gunnis, June 13, 1959; children: John II, Robert, Anne, Thomas, David. BS, Marquette U., Milw., 1958; JD, Stanford U., Calif., 1968. Bar: DC 1969. Engr. Sylvania Electronic Def. Labs., Mountain View, Calif., 1961-68; assoc. Wilmer, Cutler and Pickering, Washington, 1968-69; George E. Osborne prof. emeritus Stanford U. Law Sch., Calif., 1969—. Vis. prof. U. Mich. Law Sch., 1981, Harvard Law Sch., 1988; vis. scholar dept. clin. bioethics, NIH, 2004-05. Author: Politics of Peace, 1981; co-author: Law in Radically Different Cultures, 1983 (Am. Soc. Internat. Law award 1984), International Trade and Investment, 1986, The Evolution of the Trade Regime: Politics, Law and Economics of the GATT and the WTO, 2006; co-editor Words over War, 2000. Past chair Nat. Genetic Resources Adv. Coun.; past mem. NAFTA Dispute Settlement Panel; former mem. NRC Com. Intellectual Property Rights in Knowledge Based Econ., 2000-03; chair Commn. Intellectual Property Rights UK Dept. Internat. Devel., 2001-02. Lt. (j.g.) USN, 1958-61. Rockefeller Found. fellow, 1976-77; recipient Jenny Lanjouw Meml. Prize U. Calif. Berkeley, 2007. Fellow Am. Assn. Advancement Sci.; mem. Am. Soc. Internat. Law. Home: 1340 Harwalt Dr Los Altos CA 94024-5815 Office: Stanford U Sch Law Stanford CA 94305 Business E-Mail: jbarton@stanford.edu.

BARTON, RICHARD N., computer company executive; BS in Indsl. Engring., Stanford U., 1989. Strategy cons. Alliance Consulting Group, 1989-91; with Microsoft Corp., Redmond, Wash., 1991-94; gen. mgr. traveler bus. unit, founder Expedia, a div. Microsoft Corp., Redmond, Wash., 1994—99; pres. CEO, dir. Expedia, Inc., Bellevue, Wash., 1999—2003; chmn., CEO Zillow, Seattle, 2004—. Bd. dirs. Netflix, Ticketmaster, InterActiveCorp (formerly USA Interactive), AtomShockwave, Inc., Avvo Inc.; venture ptnr. Benchmark Capital. Office: Zillow 999 3rd Ave Ste 4600 Seattle WA 98104 also: InterActiveCorp 527 W 18th St New York NY 10011-2822

BARTON, RUTH, retired language educator; b. Sweetwater, Tex., July 7, 1934; d. John William and Ruby Catherine (Templeton) Pendergrass; m. Tom K. Barton, Apr. 21, 1957 (dec. July 1997); children: Belle Barton Rosing (dec.), Elliott Marshall. BJ, U. Tex., 1955; MS, U. Wis., 1961, PhD, 1969. Reporter Ft. Worth (Tex.) Press, 1955-57; claims rep. Social Security, Detroit, 1958-59; prof. English Colo. Coll., Colorado Springs, 1964—2003; ret. Advisor Cutler Pubs., Inc., Colo. Coll., Colorado Springs, 1970—2003, dir. writing program, 1983-99; presenter in field, 1978-2001. Author: (with others) Power, Gender, Values, 1987, Biographical Dictionary of Contemporary Catholic American Writing, 1989. Ruth Barton award named in her honor, Cutler Publs., Inc., 1996, Gresham, Riley award, 1998. Mem. Soc. Literature and Sci., Children's Lit. Assn. (newsletter layout editor 1992-98). Avocations: making pottery, travel, watching wildlife. Home: 1210 Custer Ave Colorado Springs CO 80903-2611 E-mail: rbarton@colorado.college.edu.

BARTON, STANLEY FAULKNER, retired management consultant; b. Halesowen, Worcestershire, Eng., Dec. 30, 1927; came to U.S., 1957, naturalized, 1963; s. Lazarus and Alice (Faulkner) B.; m. Marion Brittain, Dec. 20, 1952; children: Carolyn Francesca, Andrea Elizabeth. B.Sc. (hons.), U. Birmingham, Eng., 1949; PhD, U. Birmingham, 1952. Group leader Naval Rsch. Establishment, Halifax, N.S., Can., 1953-56; project coord. Def. Rsch. Chem. Labs., Ottawa, Ont., Can., 1956-57; devel. engr. Procter & Gamble, Cin., 1957-58, R & D group leader, 1958-59, R & D sect. head, 1959-69; tech. dir. food products-natural resources ITT, NYC, 1969-76; sr. v.p. tech. and quality ITT Rayonier, Inc., Stamford, Conn., 1976-90; v.p., dir. Spectrum Internat. Assocs., Inc., Tucson, 1990-92; ret., 1992. Pres. Catalina Cons., 1990—. Mem. Am. Theater Organ Soc. Home and Office: Catalina Cons 4051 N Circulo Manzanillo Tucson AZ 85750-1879 Personal E-mail: stanb4051@comcast.net.

BARTON, WILLIAM E., construction company executive; BS in Acctg. and Fin., San Jose State U.; MBA, U. Santa Clara. Various positions including cash mgr., treas., contr. Granite Constrn. Inc., Watsonville, Calif., 1980—, v.p., CFO, sr. v.p., CFO, 1999—. Bd. dirs. various non-profit orgns., Santa Cruz County. Mem. Constrn. Fin. Mgmt. Assn., Fin. Execs. Inst. Office: Granite Constrn Inc PO Box 50085 Watsonville CA 95077-5085

BARTOSIC, FLORIAN, lawyer, educator; b. Danville, Pa., Sept. 15, 1926; s. Florian W. and Elsie (Woodring) B.; m. Eileen M. Payne, 1952 (div. 1969); children: Florian, Ellen, Thomas, Stephen; m. Alberta C. Chew, 1990. BA, Pontifical Coll., 1948; B.C.L., Coll. William and Mary, 1956; LL.M., Yale U., 1957. Bar: Va. 1956, U.S. Supreme Ct. 1959. Asst. instr. Yale U., 1956-57; assoc. prof. law Coll. William and Mary, 1957, Villanova U., 1957-59; atty. NLRB, Washington, 1956, 57, 59; counsel Internat. Brotherhood of Teamsters, Washington, 1959-71; prof. law Wayne State U., 1971-80, U. Calif., Davis, 1980-92; recalled to tchg., 1994-99; prof. emeritus law U. Calif., Davis, 1993—, dean law, 1980-90. Adj. prof. George Washington U., 1966-71, Cath. U. Am., 1960-71; mem. panel arbitrators Fed. Mediation and Conciliation Service, 1972—; hearing officer Mich. Employment Relations Commn., 1972-80, Mich. Civil Rights Commn., 1974-80; bd. dirs. Mich. Legal Services Corp., 1973-80, Inst. Labor and Indsl. Relations, U. Mich., Wayne State U., 1976-80; mem. steering com. Inst. on Global Conflict and Cooperation, 1982-83; mem. adv. bd. Assn. for Union Democracy Inc., 1980—, adv. coms. Calif. Jud. Council, 1984-85, 87; vis. scholar Harvard Law Sch., 1987, Stanford Law Sch., 1987; sr. rsch. scholar ILO, 1990-91; acad. visitor Oxford U., London Sch. Econs., 1991; mem. exec. bd. Pub. Interest Clearinghouse, 1988-90. Co-author: Labor Relations Law in the Private Sector, 1977, 2d edit., 1986; contbr. articles to law jours. Mem. ABA (sec. labor rels. law sect. 1974-75), Fed. Bar Assn., Am. Law Inst. (acad. mem. labor law adv. com. on continuing profl. edn.), Soc. Profls. in Dispute Resolution (regional v.p. 1979-80), Indsl. Rels. Rsch. Assn., Internat. Soc. Labor Law and Social Legis., Internat. Indsl. Rels. Assn., Lawyers Guild, ACLU (dir. Detroit chpt. 1976-77), Order of Coif (hon.), Scribes. Home: 235 Ipanema Pl Davis

CA 95616-0253 Office: U Calif Sch Law Mrak Hall Dr Davis CA 95616 Home Phone: 530-752-2889; Office Phone: 530-756-7615. Business E-Mail: fbartosic@ucdavis.edu.

BARTUS, RAYMOND THOMAS, neuroscientist, writer, pharmaceutical executive; b. Chgo., May 19, 1947; s. Frank A. and Katherine (Bogus) B.; m. Cheryl Marie Gyure, Feb. 11, 1967; children: Raymond T., Kristin Marie. BA, California State U. Pa., 1968; MS, N.C. State U., 1970, PhD, 1972. NRC postdoctoral fellow, research assoc. Naval Med. Rsch. Lab., Groton, Conn., 1972; scientist Parke-Davis Rsch. Labs., Ann Arbor, Mich., 1973-75, sr. scientist, 1975-78, Lederle Labs., Am. Cyanamid Co., Pearl River, NY, 1978-79, group leader neuroscience, dir. geriatric discovery program, 1979-88; sr. v.p. R & D, chief sci. officer Cortex Pharms. Inc., Irvine, Calif., 1988-91, interim pres., 1990, exec. v.p., chief oper. officer, 1991-92, chief sci. officer, 1988-92; sr. v.p. neurobiology Alkermes Inc., Cambridge, Mass., 1992-96, sr. v.p. preclin. R&D, 1996—2001; sr. v.p. Worldwide Life Sci. R&D, 2001—02; v.p., rsch. and devel. Ceregene Inc., San Diego, 2002—04, sr. v.p., COO, 2004—. Bd. dir. Net Met; prof. N.Y.U. Med. Ctr., 1979—; adj. prof. Tulane U., 1978—87, U. Calif., Irvine, Calif., 1988—92, Tufts U., 1992—. Editor-in-chief, founder, Neurobiology of Aging, 1980-89; contbr. articles on neurosci. to profl. jours. Fellow Am. Coll. Neuropsychopharmacology; mem. Alzheimers Assn. (sci. med. bd. 1986-92), Soc. Neurosci., N.Y. Acad. Sci., Brain Tumor Soc., Am. Assn. Pharm. Sci., Am. Soc. Pharmacology and Exptl. Biology. Office: Ceregene Inc 9381 Judicial Dr #130 San Diego CA 92121 Business E-Mail: rtbartus@ceregene.com.

BARTZ, CAROL ANN, Internet company executive; b. Winona, Minn., Aug. 29, 1948; m. William (Bill) Marr; children: Bill, Meredith, Layne BS in Computer Sci. with honors, U. Wis., 1971; DSc (hon.), Worcester Poly. Inst.; LittD (hon.), William Woods U., NJ Inst. Tech. With sales mgmt. dept. 3M Corp., Digital Equipment Corp., 1976-83; mgr. customer mktg. Sun Microsystems, Inc., 1983-84, v.p. mktg., 1984-87, v.p. customer svc., 1987-90, v.p. worldwide field ops., exec. officer, 1990-92; pres., CEO Autodesk, Inc., San Rafael, Calif., 1992—2006, exec. chmn., 2006—09; pres., CEO Yahoo! Inc., Sunnyvale, Calif., 2009—. Bd. dirs. Network Appliance Inc., 1995-, Autodesk Inc., 1996-2009, Cisco Systems, Inc., 1997-, Intel Corp., 2007-09, Yahoo! Inc., 2009-; mem. President's Export Coun., 1994, President's Coun. Advisors on Sci. and Tech.; adv. coun. bus. sch. Stanford U. Bd. dirs. U. Wis. Sch. Bus., Nat. Breast Cancer Rsch. Found., Found. for Nat. Medals Sci. and Tech.; mem. adv. coun. Stanford U. Bus. Sch.; mem. Com. of 200; adv. for women's health issues; former mem. Ark. of Gov.'s Econ. Summit, Little Rock; mem. Sec. of Edn.'s Commn. on Future of Edn., 2005. Recipient Donald C. Burnham Mfg. Mgmt. award Soc. Mfg. Engrs., 1994, Horatio Alger Award, 2000, named one of The 100 Most Influential Women in Business, San Francisco Bus. Times, 2004, 100 Most Powerful Women in the World, Forbes mag., 2005, World's 30 Most Respected CEOs, Barron's mag., 2005. Mem. Calif. C. of C. (bd. dirs.). Avocations: gardening, tennis. Office: Yahoo! Inc 701 First Ave Sunnyvale CA 94089*

BARZA, HAROLD A., lawyer; b. Montreal, Que., Can., July 28, 1952; came to U.S., 1969; s. Solomon A. and Evelyn (Elkin) B. BA, Boston U., 1973; JD, Columbia U., 1976. Bar: N.Y. 1977, Calif. 1978, U.S. Dist. Ct. (ctrl. dist.) Calif. 1978. Law clk. to Hon. Milton Pollack U.S. Dist. Ct. (so. dist.) N.Y., 1976-77; assoc. Munger, Tolles & Rickershauser, LA, 1978-81; ptnr. Gelles, Singer & Johnson, LA, 1982-83, Gelles, Lawrence & Barza, LA, 1983-87, Loeb & Loeb, LA, 1987-99, Quinn, Emanuel, Urquehart, Oliver and Hedges, LA, 1999—. Adj. prof. mass comm. law Southwestern U. Sch. Law, L.A., 1979-82; judge pro tem., L.A. Mcpl. Ct., 1985—. Mem. bd. editors Columbia Law Rev., 1975-76. Mem. steering com. Jewish Nat. Fund, L.A., 1983. James Kent scholar, 1974-76, Harlan Fiske Stone scholar, 1973-74. Mem. ABA (mem. com. on antitrust litigation), Los Angeles County Bar Assn. (trial lawyers, litigation and intellectual property sects.). Office: Quinn Emanuel Urquhart Oliver and Hedges 865 S Figueroa St Los Angeles CA 90017-2543 E-mail: hab@qeuo.com.

BASCH, DARLENE CHAKIN, clinical social worker; b. Bklyn., Oct. 12, 1954; d. Samuel Benedict and Vivian (Sidranski) Chakin; m. Loren Bernhardt Basch, May 31, 1982; children: Michael Oswald, Ethan Raphael. BS, Cornell U., 1976; M in Social Welfare, U. Calif., Berkeley, 1979. Lic. clin. social worker, Calif.; bd. cert. Diplomate Social Work. Cottage clin. supr. St. Vincent's Sch., San Rafael, Calif., 1979-83; program dir. Jewish Family and Children's Service, San Francisco, 1983-84, therapist, program dir. family life edn., 1985-87; pvt. psychotherapist Los Angeles, Calif., 1982—; clin. soc. worker Family Friends UCLA Med. Ctr., 1988-95. Lead interviewer trainer, interviewer resources advisor, debriefing cons. Spielberg's Survivors of the Shoah Visual History Found., L.A., 1994-98; founder Descs. of The Shoah, L.A., 1995—; tchr. Rosenberg's Integrative Body Psychotherapy, 1999—; freelance writer, 2000— Chmn. Generation-to-Generation, San Francisco, 1979-87; sec. Holocaust Library and Research Ctr., San Francisco, 1980-87; exec. com. mem. World Gathering of Holocaust Survivors, Jerusalem, 1980-81. Mem. NASW, Internat. Soc. Traumatic Stress Studies, Internat. Assn. Body Psychotherapy (exec. dir. 1994-97), Soc. Clin. Social Work. Avocations: singing, guitar, reading, walking, spirituality. Office: 6310 San Vicente Blvd Ste 350 Los Angeles CA 90048-5448 Home: 356 S Reeves Dr Beverly Hills CA 90212-4513

BASCH, REVA, information services company executive; b. Chgo., Aug. 1, 1947; d. Victor Hugo and Hertha (Levi) B.; m. Jerrald C. Shifman, Apr. 17, 1982. BA in English Lit. summa cum laude, U. Pa., 1969; MLS, U. Calif., Berkeley, 1971. Head libr. Cogswell Coll., San Francisco, 1971-72; tech. info. specialist Gilbert Assocs. Inc., Reading, Pa., 1973-79; tech. libr. NuTech, San Jose, Calif., 1980-81; rsch. assoc. Info. on Demand, Berkeley, Calif., 1981-82, asst. dir. rsch., 1982-83, dir. rsch., 1983-86, v.p., dir. rsch., 1985-86; software designer Mead Data Ctrl., Personal Computer Sys. Group, Menlo Park, Calif., 1986-88; pres. Aubergine Info. Svcs., The Sea Ranch, Calif., 1986—. Author: Secrets of the Super Searchers, 1993, Electronic Information Delivery: Ensuring Quality and Value, 1995, Secrets of the Super Net Searchers, 1996, Researching Online for Dummies, 1998, 2d edit., 2000; columnist Online mag., CyberSkeptic's Guide to Internet Rsch.; contbr. articles to profl. jours. Recipient award for best paper UMI/Data Courier, 1990, Online Champion award Dun & Bradstreet. Mem. Assn. of Ind. Info. Profl.(pres.1991-92), Spl. Librs. Assn., Assn. Info. and Dissemination Ctrs., So. Calif. Online Users Group. Avocations: online communications, reading, travel, cooking.

BASCOM, RUTH F., retired mayor; b. Ames, Iowa, Feb. 4, 1926; d. Frederick Charles and Doris Hays Fenton; m. John U. Bascom, June 14, 1950; children: Lucinda, Rebecca, Ellen, Thomas, Paul, Mary. BS, Kans. State U., Manhattan, 1946; MA, Cornell U., 1949. Tchr. Dickinson County Cmty. H.S., Kans., 1946-48, Nat. Coll. Edn., Chgo., 1949-51. Co-chair Cascadia High Speed Rail, 1995-98. Chair City and State Bicycle Com., 1971-83; chair Met. Park Bd., Eugene, 1972-82; bd. pres. Youth Symphony, 1962-68; city councilor City of Eugene, Oreg., 1984-92, coun. v.p., pres., 1988-90, mayor, 1993-97; v.p., pres. LWV, Eugene, 1967-69; chair Oreg. Passenger Rail Com., 2000-05; state bd. 1000 Friends of Oreg., 1999-05. Recipient Gold Leaf award Internat. Soc. Arboriculture, 1993, Parks Heroes award, 2007; dedicated Ruth Bascom Riverbank Trail Sys., 2003, Disting. Svc. award U. Oreg., 2007. Democrat. Congregationalist. Avocations: music, tree farm, bicycling. Home: 65 West 30th Ave #35912 Eugene OR 97405 E-mail: jbascomr@pacinfo.com.

BASELT, RANDALL CLINT, toxicologist; b. Chgo., Feb. 12, 1944; s. Benjamin Oliver and Vivian Marie (Rende) B.; m. Lana Mak, June 11, 1966; 1 child, David. BS in Chemistry, U. Ill., 1965; PhD in Pharmacology, U. Hawaii, 1972. Cert. Am. Bd. Forensic Toxicology, Am. Bd. Clin. Chemistry, Am. Bd. Toxicology, forensic alcohol supr., clin. toxicologist technologist, clin. chemist, clin. lab. toxicologist. Forensic toxicologist Office of Coroner, County of Orange, Calif., 1965-69; rsch. fellow dept. pharmacology U. Hawaii Sch. Medicine, Honolulu, 1969-72; NIH postdoctoral rsch. fellow Medizinisch-Chemisches Inst., U. Bern (Switzerland) Sch. Medicine, 1972-73; rsch. toxicologist Office of Coroner, San Francisco, 1973-75; chief toxicologist Office of Med. Examiner, Farmington, Conn., 1975-78; dir. toxicology and drug analysis lab. U. Calif. Med. Ctr., Sacramento, 1978-84; dir. Chem. Toxicology Inst., Calif., 1984—. Asst. prof. lab. medicine U. Conn. Health Ctr., Farmington, 1975-78; assoc. prof. pathology U. Calif. Sch. Medicine, Davis, 1978-84; cons. drug abuse USN, 1983—, USAF, 1984—; accredited lab. inspector Nat. Lab. Cert. Program, 1988—. Author: Disposition of Toxic Drugs and Chemicals in Man, 5th edit., 1999, Biological Monitoring Methods for Industrial Chemicals, 3d edit., 1997, Analytical Procedures for Therapeutic Drug Monitoring and Emergency Toxicology, 2d edit., 1987, (with M. Houts and R.H. Cravey) Courtroom Toxicology, 1980; editor 7 other books; founder, editor Jour. Analytical Toxicology, 1977—; mem. editl. bd. Jour. Forensic Scis., 1983—; contbr. articles to profl. jours. Mem. Am. Acad. Clin. Toxicology, Am. Assn. for Clin. Chemistry, Am. Indsl. Hygiene Assn., Calif. Assn. Toxicologists (past pres.), Internat. Assn. Forensic Toxicologists, Jour. Am. Med. Assn. (peer rev. com. 1985—), Soc. Forensic Toxicologists (bd. dirs. 1978-80, lab. survey com. 1982-83), Soc. Toxicology, Southwestern Assn. Toxicologists.

BASHA, EDWARD N., JR., grocery chain owner; CEO Bashas Inc., Chandler, Ariz., chmn. Dir. Pinnacle West Capital Corp. Recipient Disting. Svc. award, Nat. Art Edn. Assn., 1992. Office: Bashas Inc 22402 S Basha Rd Chandler AZ 85248

BASINGER, RICHARD LEE, lawyer; b. Canton, Ohio, Nov. 24, 1941; s. Eldon R. and Alice M. (Bartholomew) B.; m. Rita Evelyn Gover, May 14, 1965; children: David A., Darron M. BA in Edn., Ariz. State U., 1963; postgrad. Macalester Coll., 1968-69; JD, U. Ariz., 1973. Bar: Ariz. 1973, US Dist. Ct. Ariz. 1973, US Tax Ct. 1977, US Ct. Appeals (6th cir.) 1975, US Ct. Appeals (9th cir.) 1976, US Supreme Ct. 1977; cert. arbitrator, Assoc. law offices, Phoenix, 1973-74; pvt. practice, Scottsdale, Ariz. 1974-75; pres. Basinger & Assocs., P.C., Scottsdale, 1975-97; dep. Mohave County Atty. Cir. Divsn., 1997-2003, also bd. dirs. Contbr. articles to profl. jours. Bd. dirs. Masters Trail Ventures, Scottsdale, 1984-85, Here's Life, Ariz., Scottsdale, 1976-84; precinct committeeman Rep. Party, Phoenix, 1983-85, Kingman, 2003—; bd. dirs. Ariz. Coll. of Bible, 1992-93. salvation army, Mohave County Adv. Bd., 2005-08. NSF grantee, 1968-69. Mem. ABA, Ariz. Bar Assn., Ariz. State Horseman's Assn. (bd. dirs. 1984-86, 1st v.p. 1986), Mohave County Bar Assn., Kingman Mohave Lions Club (pres. 2004-05), Mohave Rep. Forum (v.p. 2003-07, pres. 2008-09), Western Saddle Club (bd. dirs. 1983-86, pres. 1985-86). Home and Office: Basinger Legal Svcs PLC 441 Astor Ave Kingman AZ 86409-3514 Home Phone: 928-692-9458; Office Phone: 928-692-4771. Office Fax: 928-692-7663.

BASKIN, RONALD JOSEPH, biophysicist educator, dean; b. Joliet, Ill., Nov. 25, 1935; s. Mack Robert and Evelyn Josephine (Rudzinski) B.; m. Lydia Olga Lendl, Mar. 29, 1957; children— Ronald James, Thomas William. AB, UCLA, 1957; MA, 1959, PhD, 1960. Asst. prof. biology Rensselaer Poly. Inst., Troy, NY, 1961-64; asst. prof. zoology U. Calif., Davis, 1964-67, assoc. prof., 1967-71, prof., 1971—, chmn. dept. zoology, 1971-78, assoc. dean coll. letters and sci., 1986-90. Mem. editorial bd. U. Calif. Press. Contbr. articles to sci. publs. Nat. Heart Inst. predoctoral fellow, 1957-60 Mem. Biophys. Soc., Soc. Cell Biology, Am. Physiol. Soc., N.Y. Acad. Scis., Sigma Xi. Office: Molecular & Cellular Biology Sect U Calif Davis CA 95616 Office Phone: 530-752-1554. E-mail: rjbaskin@ucdavis.edu.

BASKIN, SCOTT DAVID, lawyer; b. NYC, Oct. 24, 1953; s. George and Anne (Strauss) B.; m. Sherry Nahmias, Mar. 13, 1982; children: Jonathan, Felicia. BA, Stanford U., 1975; JD, Yale U., 1978. Bar: Calif. 1978, U.S. Dist. Ct. (ctrl., ea., so. and no. dists.) Calif. 1979, U.S. Appeals (2d and 9th cirs.) 1979. Law clk. Hon. Herbert Choy, 9th Cir. Ct., Honolulu, 1978-79; ptnr. Irell & Manella, Newport Beach, Calif., 1979—. Lectr. Calif. Continuing Edn. of the Bar, 1985—. Contbr. articles to profl. publs. Office: Irell & Manella 840 Newport Center Dr Ste 400 Newport Beach CA 92660-6323 Home Phone: 949-760-5139; Office Phone: 949-760-5239, 949-760-0991. Business E-Mail: sbaskin@irell.com.

BASKINS, ANN O'NEIL, lawyer, former computer company executive; b. Red Bluff, Calif., Aug. 5, 1955; m. Thomas C. DeFilipps. AB in Hist., Stanford U., 1977; JD, UCLA, 1980. Bar: Calif. 1980. Assoc. Crosby, Heafey, Roach & May, 1980—81; atty. Hewlett-Packard Co., Palo Alto, Calif., 1982—85, sr. atty., 1985—86, asst. sec., 1985—99, corp. counsel, 1986—99, corp. sec., 1999—2006, sr. v.p., gen. counsel, 2000—06. Mem.: ABA, Assn. Gen. Counsel, Am. Soc. Corp. Secs., Am. Corp. Counsel Assn.

BASOMBRIO, JUAN C., lawyer; b. 1964; BA in Polit. Sci., Univ. Houston, 1986; JD, Ind. Univ., 1989. Bar: Minn. 1989, Calif. 1991, US Supreme Ct. 1992. Ptnr.-in-charge So. Calif. office Dorsey & Whitney LLP, Irvine, Calif., 2001—03, ptnr. trial dept., 1998—, mem. policy com., 2003—05. Office: Dorsey & Whitney LLP 38 Technology Dr Irvine CA 92618-5310 Office Phone: 949-932-3650. Office Fax: 949-932-3601. Business E-Mail: basombrio.juan@dorsey.com.

BASS, CARL, computer software company executive; BA, Cornell U., 1978. Co-founder Ithaca Software; v.p. AECAD group, chief tech. officer, exec. v.p. Autodesk Ventures Autodesk Inc., San Rafael, Calif., 1994—99; chmn., pres., CEO buzzsaw.com, 1999—2001; exec. v.p. emerging bus. & chief strategy officer Autodesk Inc., 2001—02, sr. v.p. design solutions group, 2002—04, COO, 2004—06, pres., CEO, 2006—. Bd. dir. Serena Software, PowerLight Corp., iRise, McAfee, Inc., 2008—. Office: Autodesk Inc 111 McInnis Pkwy San Rafael CA 94903

BASS, CHARLES MORRIS, financial and systems consultant; b. Miami, Fla., Sept. 21, 1949; s. Benjamin and Ellen Lucille (Williams) Bass; children: Cheryl Ellen, Benjamin Charles. BA, U. Md., 1972; MS, Am. Coll., 1982. CLU. Chartered fin. cons. Group rep. Monumental Life Ins. Co., 1972—73; agt. Equitable Life Ins. Co., NY, 1973—76; ptnr. Bass, Bridge and Assocs., Columbia, Md., 1976—81; pres. Multi-Fin. Svc., Inc., Balt., 1981—83; gen. mgr. Mfrs. Fin. Group, Denver, 1983—85; ptnr. Regency Econometrics Group, Denver, 1985—; spkr. in field. Chmn. United Way Howard County, 1977—78; mem. Econ. Devel. Adv. Coun. Howard County, 1979—83. With USAF, 1968—71. Mem.: Columbia Bus. Exchange, Howard County Bus. Club, Howard County C. of C., Estate Planning Coun., Columbia Life Underwriters Assn. (pres. 1982), Gen. Agts. and Mgrs. Assn., Am. Soc. CLUs, Nat. Assn. Life Underwriters, Million Dollar Round Table. Methodist. Home and Office: 204 White Willow Ave Las Vegas NV 89123-1102

BASS, HAROLD NEAL, pediatrician, medical geneticist; b. Chgo., Apr. 14, 1939; s. Louis A. and Minnie (Schachter) B.; m. Phyllis Appell, June 25, 1961; children: Laura Renee, Alana Suzanne. Student, U. Ill., 1956—59; MS in Pharmacology, U. Chgo., 1963, MD, 1963. Diplomate Am. Bd. Pediat., Am. Bd. Med. Genetics, Nat. Bd. Med. Examiners. Intern Children's Meml. Hosp., Chgo., 1963-64, resident, 1964-65, chief resident, 1965-66, fellow in med. genetics, 1965-66; chief pediat. and profl. svcs. Norton AFB Hosp., Calif., 1966-68; attending pediatrician/med. geneticist Kaiser Permanente Med. Ctr., Panorama City, Calif., 1968—; dir. med. genetics prog. Kaiser Permanente Med. Care Program So. Calif., 1987—2003; clin. prof. pediat. and human genetics UCLA Med. Sch., 1970—. Pres. med. staff Kaiser Permanente Med. Ctr., 1989-2004; bd. dirs. So. Calif. Permanente Med. Group, 1998-04; adj. prof. biology Calif. State U., Northridge, 1995—. Contbr. articles to profl. jours. Mem. mayor's adv. com. San Fernando Valley, City of L.A., 1973-78. Capt. USAF, 1966—68. Founding Fellow Am. Coll. Med. Genetics, Western Soc. Pediat. Rsch., Brady Handgun Control, ACLU, Am. Soc. Human Genetics, Amnesty Internat. Democrat. Jewish. Avocations: civic affairs, music, writing. Home: 11922 Dunnicliffe Ct Porter Ranch CA 91326-1324 Office: Kaiser Permanente Med Ctr 13652 Cantara St Panorama City CA 91402-5497 Home Phone: 818-360-0154; Office Phone: 818-375-2073. Business E-Mail: harold.n.bass@kp.org.

BASS, KAREN, state legislator; b. LA, Oct. 3, 1953; divorced; children: one. BS in Health Svcs., Calif. State U., Dominguez Hills. Cert. Physician Asst. U. Southern Calif. California State Assemblywoman, District 47, 2005-, house spkr., 2008-; member, Approp, Bus & Prof, Higher Education, Human Serv, Select Comm LA Health Care Crisis comts, currently. Comm Coalition, Exec Director, 1990-; Univ of Southern California Sch of Med, Clinical Instr, 1986-. Democrat. Christian. Office: Dist 47 5750 Wilshire Blvd Ste 565 Los Angeles CA 90036 Office Phone: 323-937-4747. Office Fax: 323-937-3466. Business E-Mail: Assemblymember.Bass@assembly.ca.gov.

BASS, RONALD, screenwriter; b. LA, 1943; Screenplays include Code Name: Emerald, 1985, Black Widow, 1987, Gardens of Stone, 1987, (with Barry Morrow) Rainman, 1988 (Academy award best original screenplay 1988), Sleeping with the Enemy, 1991, (with Amy Tan) The Joy Luck Club, 1993; screenwriter, exec. prodr.: (with Al Franken) When a Man Loves a Woman, 1994, Dangerous Minds, 1995, (with Terry McMillan) Waiting to Exhale, 1995, My Best Friend's Wedding, 1997, What Dreams May Come, 1998, Stepmom, 1998, How Stella Got Her Groove Back, 1998, Entrapment, 1999, Snow Falling on Cedars, 1999, Passion of Mind, 1999, The Lazarus Child, 2004.

BASSETT, CAROL ANN, journalism educator, writer; b. Langley AFB, Va., Mar. 2, 1953; d. William Brainard and Genevieve (Rivaldo) B. BA summa cum laude in Humanities, Ariz. State U., 1977; MA in Journalism, U. Ariz., 1982. Ptnr. Desert West News, Tucson, 1985-90; freelance writer Tucson, 1980-95; freelance writer for mags. Missoula, Mont., 1995-98; mem. faculty Sch. Journalism U. Mont., Missoula, 1996-98; mem. faculty Sch. Journalism and Comm. U. Oreg., Eugene, 1998—. Author: Essays in American Nature Writing, 2000, American Nature Writing, 2001, A Gathering of Stones: Journeys to the Edges of a Changing World, 2002 (finalist Oreg. Book award 2003), Organ Pipe: Life on the Edge, 2004; editor Tucson Weekly, 1989-90; contbr. numerous articles to nat. and internat. mags. including N.Y. Times. Recipient 2d Place Gen. Reporting award Ariz. Press Club, 1987, Gold medal for best environ. documentary Houston Internat. Film Festival, 1990, 1st Place Gen. Reporting award Ariz. Press Club, 1992, Silver Medal for Energy Issues documentary, Houston Internat. Film Festival, 1992; co-recipient Alfred I. duPont Columbia award, 1984-85, First Place award Investigative Reporting, 1986, 1st Place Polit. Reporting, 1989, First Amendment Journalism award, 1986; grantee Fund for Investigative Journalism, 1985, 87, Corp. for Pub. Broadcasting, 1988, Oxfam Am., 1991. Address: Sch Journalism Univ Oreg Eugene OR 97403 Office Phone: 541-346-2033. Business E-Mail: cbassett@uoregon.edu.

BASSINGTHWAIGHTE, JAMES BUCKLIN, physiologist, educator, medical researcher; b. Toronto, Sept. 10, 1929; s. Ewart MacQuarrie and Velma Emeline B.; m. Joan Elizabeth Graham, June 18, 1955; children: Elizabeth Anne, Mary, Alan, Sarah, Rebecca. BA, U. Toronto, 1951, MD, 1955; postgrad., Med. Sch. London, 1957-58; PhD, Mayo Grad. Sch. Medicine U. Minn., Rochester, 1964. Intern Toronto Gen. Hosp., 1955-56; physician Internat. Nickel Co., Sudbury and Matheson, Ont., 1956-57; house physician Hammersmith Hosp., London; postgrad. Med. Sch. London, 1957-58; teaching asst. physiology U. Minn., Mpls., 1961-62; fellow Mayo Grad. Sch. Medicine, Rochester, Minn., 1958-64, instr., 1964-67, asst. prof., 1967-69, assoc. prof., 1969-72; vis. prof. Pharmacology Inst., U. Bern, Switzerland, 1970-71; asso. prof. bioengring. U. Minn., 1972-75; prof. physiology Mayo Grad. Sch. Medicine, 1973-75, prof. medicine, 1975; prof. bioengring., radiology and biomath U. Wash., Seattle, 1975—; dir. Ctr. for Bioengring., 1975-80; vis. prof. medicine and physiology McGill U., 1979-81; affiliate prof. physiology Limburg U., Maastricht, Netherlands, 1990—. Mem. study sect. NIH, 1970-74, 80-83, chmn., 2004; chmn. Biotech. Resources Adv. Com., 1977-79, chmn. 1st Gordon Rsch. Conf. on Water and Solute Transport in Microvasculature, 1976; chmn. workshop on metabolic imaging Nat. Heart, Lung and Blood Inst., 1985; bd. dirs. Nat. Space Biomed. Rsch. Inst., NASA, 2002—; adv. bd. mem. Burroughs Wellcome Fund, 2004—, co-chmn. interface in sci. program, 2006—; Lewellen-Thomas lectr., U. Toronto, 1991; Coulter lectr. U. N.C., 1995; Oxford lectr. Internat. Soc. Magnetic Resonance Medicine, 1996; mem. ednl. materials com. Whitaker Found., 1995-2005; CASI award com. Burrough Wellcome Fund, 2004—, chair, 2007—. Author: (with L.S. Liebovitch and B.J. West) Fractal Physiology, 1994; contbr. over 270 articles to profl. publs. Recipient NIH Rsch. Career Devel. award, 1964-74, Louis and Artur Lucian award McGill U., 1979, Witzig award Cardiovasc. Sys. Dyamics Soc., 1982, Faculty Achievement award for outstanding rsch. U. Wash. Coll. Engring., 1993; Edmund Hustinx chair Maastricht U., 1999. Fellow Biomed. Engring. Soc. (dir. 1971-74, pres. 1977-78, Alza award 1986, editor-in-chief Annals of Biomed. Engring. 1993-2001, assoc. editor 2002—, Disting. Svc. award 1999); mem. AAAS, NAE, Am. Heart Assn. (coun. on circulation 1976—), Biophys. Soc. (assoc. editor Biophys. Jour. 1980-83), Microcirculatory Soc. (mem. coun. 1975-78, 80-83, pres. 1990-91, Landis award 1995), Am. Physiol. Soc. (mem. circulation group, editl. bd. 1972-76, 79-83, mem. edn. com., chair cardiovasc. sect. 1995-96, Wiggers award 2005), Internat. Union Physiol. Scis. (U.S.A. nat. com. 1978-86, U.S. del. to assembly 1980, 83, 86, chmn. 1983-86, chmn. Commn. on Bioengring. and Clin. Physiology 1986-97, chmn. satellite to 30th Congress on Endothelial Transport 1986, co-chmn. satellite on microvascular networks 1989, chmn. satellite on Physiome Project 1997, com. on physiome 1997—), Nat. Acad. Engring. (mem. peer com. 2005—, chair 2006—, Russ award com. 2006-07). Achievements include research in cardiovascular physiology and bioengineering, biomathematics and computer simulation with emphasis on ion and substrate exchange in heart, fractals in physiology, integrative biology and originator of the Physiome Project. Home: 3150 E Laurelhurst Dr NE Seattle WA 98105-5333 Office: U Wash Dept Bioengring PO Box 35-5061 Seattle WA 98195-5061 Office Phone: 206-685-2005. Business E-Mail: jbb2@u.washington.edu.

BASSIS, MICHAEL STEVEN, academic administrator; b. NYC, Sept. 8, 1944; s. Lewis and Barbara (Fay) B.; m. Mary Suzanne Wilson, Dec. 27, 1977; children: Anne Elizabeth, Christina, Jessica, Nicholas. BA with honors, Brown U., 1967; MA, U. Chgo., 1968, PhD, 1974. Asst. dir. acad. potential project Brown U., 1966-67; rsch. assoc. Ctr. for the Study of the Acts of Man U. Pa., 1968; instr., asst. prof.-assoc. prof. dept. sociology and anthropology U. R.I., 1971-81, acting asst. dean Coll. Arts and Scis., 1977-78; assoc. Harvard U. Grad. Sch. Edn., 1980-81; assoc. dean faculty U. Wis., Parkside, 1981-85, assoc. prof. sociology, 1981-86, interim asst. chancellor ednl. svcs., 1985-86; v.p. acad. affairs Ea. Conn. State U., 1986-89; exec. v.p., univ. provost Antioch U., Yellow Springs, Ohio, 1989-93; pres. Olivet (Mich.) Coll., 1993-98; dean, warden New Coll., U. South Fla., Sarasota, 1998—2001; president Westminster Coll. of Salt Lake City, 2002—. Presenter in field. Author (with W.R. Rosengren) The Social Organization of Nautical Education: The U.S., Great Britain and Spain, 1976, (with R.J. Gelles and A. Levine) Sociology: An Introduction, 4th edit., 1991, Social Problems, 1982; editor Teaching Sociology, 1982-85; contbr. articles to profl. jours. NIMH grantee, 1967-71, Exxon Edn. Found. grantee, N.Y.C., 1975, Fund for Improvement of Post-Secondary Edn. grantee, Washington, 1978. Mem. Am. Sociol. Assn. (undergrad. edn. sect., membership com. 1979-81, coun. 1980, 82, 86-89, teaching resources group 1984-86, publs. com. 1985, chair 1987-88), Am. Assn. Higher Edn., Nat. Soc. Experiential Edn. Office: Office of the President Westminster College 1840 South 1300 East Salt Lake City UT 84105 E-mail: mbassis@westminstercollege.edu.

BASSO, ROBERT J., manufacturing engineer, inventor; Degree in Mech. Engring., Tufts Coll. Registered profl. engr., Calif. Founder, pres. Centry Design, Inc., San Diego. Recipient Project of Yr. award San Diego Engring. Soc., 1995, Eli Whitney Productivity award Soc. Mfg. Engrs. 1998. Achievements include patents for carbon graphite golf shafts and fishing rods; developed environmentally clean, high intensity ultraviolet curing equipment for painting finished products. Office: Century Design Inc 3635 Afton Rd San Diego CA 92123-2199

BASTIAANSE, GERARD C., lawyer; b. Holyoke, Mass., Oct. 21, 1935; s. Gerard C. and Margaret (Lally) B.; m. Paula E. Paliska, June 1, 1963; children: Elizabeth, Gerard. BSBA, Boston U., 1960; JD, U. Va., 1964. Bar: Mass. 1964, Calif. 1970. Assoc. Nutter, McClennen & Fish, Boston, 1964-65; counsel Campbell Soup Co., Camden, NJ, 1965-67; gen. counsel A&W Internat. (United Fruit Co.), Santa Monica, Calif., 1968-70; ptnr. Kindel & Anderson, Los Angeles, 1970—. Mem. ABA, Calif. Bar Assn., Mass. Bar Assn., Japan Am. Soc., Asia Soc., World Trade Ctr. Assn. Clubs: California (Los Angeles); Big Canyon Country (Newport Beach, Calif.). Home: 2 San Sebastian Newport Beach CA 92660-6828 Office: Kindel & Anderson 2030 Main St Ste 1300 Irvine CA 92614-7220

BASTIAN, STANLEY A., lawyer; b. Seattle, Apr. 3, 1958; BS, U. Oreg., 1980; JD, U. Washington, 1983. Bar: Washington 1983, Oreg. Law clk. to Hon. Ward Williams Washington State Ct. Appeals Divsn. I, 1984—85; asst. city atty. Criminal Divsn. Office of City Atty., Seattle, 1985—88; atty. Jeffers Danielson Sonn & Aylward PS, 1988—. Mem.: Am. Acad. Trial Attys., Oreg. State Bar, ABA, Washington State Bar Assn. (pres.-elect 2006—07, bd. gov. 2004—06), Chelan-Douglas County Bar Assn. (pres. 2004—05). Avocation: travel. Office: Jeffers Danielson Sonn & Aylward PS 2600 Chester Kim Rd Wenatchee WA 98801 Office Phone: 509-662-3685. Office Fax: 509-662-2452. E-mail: stanb@jdsalaw.com.

BATALOV, LEO, lawyer; b. Krasnoturinsk, Russia, June 29, 1971; BA summa cum laude, Whitman Coll., 1996; JD highest honors, Univ. Wash., 1999. Bar: Wash. 1999. Assoc. atty., asset securitization, secured lending, mergers & acquisitions, securities law Heller Ehrman LLP, Seattle, 2000—. Contbr. articles to numerous profl. jours. Named Seattle Rising Star, SuperLawyer Mag., 2006. Mem.: ABA, Seattle Bar Assn., Wash. Bar Assn. Office: Heller Ehrman LLP Ste 6100 701 Fifth Ave Seattle WA 98104-7098

BATCHMAN, THEODORE EARL, electrical engineering educator, researcher; b. Gt. Bend, Kans., Mar. 29, 1940; s. Jake T. and Dorothy E. (Bardwell) B.; m. Nancy L. Leatherman, Dec. 23, 1961; children: Teddie Suzanne, Timothy Brent, Tracey Nanette. BSEE, U. Kans., 1962, MSEE, 1963, PhD, 1966. Engr., sci. specialist LTV, Dallas, 1966-70; sr. lectr. U. Queensland, Brisbane, Australia, 1970-75; from asst. prof. to prof. elec. engring. U. Va., Charlottesville, 1975-88; prof., dir. Sch. Elec. Engring. and Computer Sci. U. Okla., Norman, 1988-95; dean Coll. Engring. U. Nev., Reno, 1995—2008, dir. renewable energy ctr., 2008—. Cons. Commonwealth of Va., Richmond, 1982-83, U.S. Army FSTC, Charlottesville, 1986-90; mem. adv. bd. Chromachron Technology Corp., Columbia, Md., 1988-90. Rsch. grantee NASA, 1978-84, NSF, 1979-84, HHS, 1984-85, Naval Rsch. Labs., 1987-88, U.S. Army, 1989-90, NSF EPSCOR, 1991-94. Fellow IEEE (life, mem. edn. activities bd. 2002-04, Achievement award 1998), Am. Soc. Engring. Edn., Optical Soc. Am., ASEE Republican. Methodist. Avocations: woodworking, model railroading, photography. Home: 12500 Fieldcreek Ln Reno NV 89511-6659 Office: U Nev Coll Engring Office Of Dean Reno NV 89557-0001 Office Phone: 775-682-6443. Business E-Mail: batch_t@unr.edu.

BATEMAN, JUSTINE, actress; b. Rye, NY, Feb. 19, 1966; d. Kent and Victoria B. Bateman; m. Mark Fluent, 2001; children Duke, Olivia. Owns design firm, LA, 2000. Appeared in TV series Family Ties, 1982-88; (TV films) Right to Kill?, 1985, First the Egg, 1985, Can You Feel Me Dancing?, 1986, In the Eyes of a Stranger, 1992, Primary Motive, 1992, Deadbolt, 1993, Terror in the Night, 1994, Another Women, 1994, A Bucket of Blood, 1995, The Hollywood Mom's Mystery, 2004; (films) Satisfaction, 1988, The Closer, 1990, Primary Motive, 1992, Beware of Dogs, 1993, The Night We Never Met, 1993, God's Lonely Man, 1996, Kiss & Tell, 1996, Highball, 1997, Say You'll Be Mine, 1999, The TV Set, 2006; guest appearances Lois & Clark, 1996, Men Behving Badly, 1996, Still Standing, 2004, 2005, Arrested Development, 2006; (TV miniseries) Out of Order, 2003. Office: Creative Artists Agency 2000 Avenue Of The Stars Los Angeles CA 90067-4700

BATEMAN, ROBERT MCLELLAN, artist; b. Toronto, Ont., Can., May 24, 1930; s. Joseph Wilbur and Ann (McLellan) Bateman; m. Suzanne Bowerman, June 1961; children: Alan, Sarah, John; m. Birgit Freybe, Aug. 1975; children: Christopher, Rob. BA in Geography with honors, U. Toronto, Can., 1954, LLD (hon.), 2007; postgrad., Ont. Coll. Edn., 1955; DSc (hon.), Carleton U., Ottawa, 1982, McGill U., Montreal, 1995; LLD (hon.), Brock U., St. Catherine, Ont., 1982, U. Guelph, Ont., 1984, Laurentian U., Sudbury, Ont., 1987, U. Victoria, B.C., 2003; D Letters for Fine Arts (hon.), McMaster U., Hamilton, Ont., Can., 1983; LittD (hon.), Lakehead U., Thunder Bay, Ont., 1986; DFA (hon.), Colby Coll., 1989, Northeastern U., 1991. Tchr. Nelson H.S., Burlington, Ont., 1958-63, 65-69; tchr. geography Nigeria, 1963-65; tchr. art Lord Elgin H.S., Burlington, Ont., 1970-76. One-man shows include Tryon Gallery, London, 1975, 79, Smithsonian Instn., 1987, Nat. Mus. Natural Sci., Ottawa, 1981-82, Everard Read Gallery, Johannesburg, South Africa, 2000; Retrospective Tour, USA, 2002-03, Gerald Peters Gallery, Santa Fe, 2004, Masters Gallery, Calgary, 2006, McMichael Can. Art Collection, 2007; also touring U.S. and Can., Can. Embassy, Tokyo, 1992; represented in permanent collections Govt. Ont. Art Collection, Toronto Bd. Trade, Hamilton Art Gallery, Leigh Yawkey Woodson Art Mus., Wausau, Wis., H.R.H. The Prince of Wales, H.R.H. Prince Phillip, The Late Princess of Monaco, Am. Artists Collection, Gilcrease Mus., Tulsa, Art Gallery of Greater Victoria; commd. World Wildlife Fund, 1971, Endangered Species Silver Bowl, 1971, Endangered Species Postage Stamp Series, 1976-81, Northern Reflections - Loon Family, 1981, Govt. Can. wedding gift to Prince of Wales, 1981, Can. Post Office, Royal Can. Mint-Platinum Polar Bear series, 1990, Nat. Capital commn. Canadiana Fund; subject of the Art of Robert Bateman, 1981, The World of Robert Bateman, 1985, Robert Bateman An Artist in Nature, 1990, Natural Worlds: Robert Bateman, 1996, Safari, 1998, Thinking Like a Mountain, 2000, Birds, 2002, Backyard Birds, 2005, Birds of Prey, 2007, Polar Worlds, 2008 Bd. dirs. Elsa Wild Animal Appeal, Toronto, 1975—; hon. dir. Long Point Bird Obs., Ont.; hon. chmn. Harmony Found., Ottawa. Decorated Queen Elizabeth Silver Jubilee medal Govt. of Can., 1977, Officer of Order of Can., 1984; recipient award of excellence Soc. Animal Artists, 1979, 80, 86, 90, Gov. Gen. award for conservation, Quebec City, Can., 1987, Lescarbot award Can. Govt., 1992, Rachel Carson award, 1996, Golden Plate award Am. Acad. Achievement, 1998; named Artist of Yr., Am. Artist Collection, 1980, Master Artist, Leigh Yawkey Woodson Mus., Wausau, Wis., 1982, Environ. Hero, Nat. Audubon Soc., 1998, others. Mem. Order B.C., Jane Goodall Inst. (bd. dirs.), Audubon Soc. (hon. life), Royal Can. Acad. Arts, Can. Wildlife Fedn. (hon. life), Sierra Club (hon. life), Kenya Wildlife Fund (hon. dir.), Sierra Legal Def. Fund (hon. dir.), Ecotrust (adv. coun.), Pollution Probe (adv. coun.). Personal E-mail: rb@gulfislands.com.

BATES, ALAN, state legislator; b. Seattle, Mar. 17, 1945; Oregon State Representative, District 5, 2000-04; Oregon State Senator, District 3, 2004-.Member, Eagle Point Sch Bd, 1990-2001. Democrat. Mailing: 900 Court St NE S-205 Salem OR 97301 also: 414 Westminster Dr Eagle Point OR 97524-9499 Office Phone: 503-986-1703. Fax: 503-986-1130. Business E-Mail: sen.alanbates@state.or.us. E-mail: rep.alanbates@state.or.us; repbates@internetcds.com.

BATES, CHARLES CARPENTER, oceanographer; b. Rockton, Ill., Nov. 4, 1918; s. Carl and Vera B.; m. Pauline Barta; children: Nancy, Priscilla, Sally. Grad. (Rector scholar 1936-39), DePauw U., 1939; MA, UCLA, 1944; PhD in Geol. Oceanography, Tex. A&M Coll., 1953. Geophys. trainee Carter Oil Co., 1939-41; spl. asst. to pres. Am. Meteorol. Soc., 1945-46; mem. survey phys. and geol. environment Bikini Atoll atomic bomb tests, 1946; with div. oceanography U.S. Navy Hydrographic Office, 1946- 57, dept. dir. div., 1953-57; environ. surveillance coord. Office Devel. Coord., Office Naval Rsch., 1957-60; chief underground nuclear test detection br. Advanced Research Projects Agy., Office Sec. Def., 1960-64; sci. and tech. dir. U.S. Naval Oceanographic Office, 1964-68; sci. adviser to comdt., also chief scientist Office R&S, USCG, 1968-79. V.p. Spectrum Internat. Assocs., 1986-88; mem. bd. experts Civil Service Examiners, 1954-60; mem. adv. com. postdoctoral awards for Fulbright grants NRC, 1957-60; mem. meteorology panel, space sci. bd. Nat. Acad. Sci., 1959-61; mem. Mcht. Marine Coun., 1968-71, Nat. Transp. Rsch. Bd., 1968-71; co-chmn. U.S.-Japan panel marine facilities U.S.-Japan Natural Resource Program, 1969-71. Author: Geophysics in Affairs of Man, 1982, 2nd edit., 2001, America's Weather Warriors, 1814-1985, 1986; numerous articles, reports in field. Served to capt. USAAF, 1941-45, lt. col. USAFR, 1941-65. Decorated Bronze Star; recipient U.S. Navy Meritorious Civilian award, 1962, U.S. Navy Superior Civilian Service award, 1969, U.S. Dept. Transp. Silver medal, 1973, gold medal, 1979. Mem. Am. Geophys. Union (chmn. com. interaction sea and atmosphere 1950, mem. council 1964-67), Soc. Exploration Geophysicists (council 1963-67, v.p. 1965-66, hon. mem. 1981), Am. Meteorol. Soc. (chmn. com. indsl. bus. and agrl. meteorology 1946-48), Am. Assn. Petroleum Geologists (President's award 1954), Am. Mgmt. Assn. (research and devel. council 1970-79), Sigma Xi. Home and Office: 501 S La Posada Cir Apt 388 Green Valley AZ 85614 Home Phone: 520-648-8339; Office Phone: 520-648-8339.

BATES, CRAIG DANA, curator, ethnographer, government official; b. Oakland, Calif., Aug. 2, 1952; s. Dana Raymond and June (Robinson) B.; m. Jennifer Dawn Bernido, May 12, 1973 (div. 1987); 1 child, Carson Dana. Park technician Nat. Park Svc., Yosemite National Park, Calif., 1973-76, Indian cultural specialist, 1976-80, asst. curator, 1980-82, curator ethnography, 1982—. Rsch. assoc. Santa Barbara (Calif.) Mus. Natural History, 1983—; cons. Calif. Indian exhbn. SW Mus., L.A., 1985, Culin exhbn. Bklyn. Mus., 1988-89, Lowie Mus. Anthropology, U. Calif., Berkeley, 1990. Co-author: (with Martha Lee) Tradition and Innovation: A Basket History of the Indians of the Yosemite Mono Lake Area, 1990; contbr. more than 100 articles on Am. Indian culture to profl. jours. Office: Nat Park Svc Yosemite Mus PO Box 577 Yosemite National Park CA 95389-0577

BATES, JAMES ROBERT, newspaper editor; b. Great Bend, Kans., Dec. 12, 1954; s. Robert Lane and Phyllis Fern (Koltermann) B.; m. Jennifer Petkus, Nov. 7, 1986. BS, U. Kans., 1977; postgrad., U. Colo., 1979-80. Copy editor Springfield (Mo.) Daily News, 1977-78; reporter Colo. Springs (Colo.) Sun, 1978-79, news editor, 1980-86; copy editor, asst. news editor Denver Post, 1986-87, news editor, 1987-89, exec. news editor, 1989—. Recipient design and editing awards Colo. Press Assn., Colo. AP, 1986—. Mem. Soc. Newspaper Design. Office: The Denver Post 1560 Broadway Denver CO 80202-5177

BATES, KATHY, actress; b. Memphis, June 28, 1948; d. Langdon Doyle and Bertye Kathleen (Talbot) Bates; m. Anthony Campisi, 1991 (div. 1997). BFA, So. Meth. U., 1969. Actor: (plays) Vanities, 1976, Semmelweiss, Crimes of the Heart, The Art of Dining, Goodbye Fidel, 1980, Chocolate Cake and Final Placement, 1981, 5th of July, 'night, Mother, 1983 (Tony nomination, Outer Critics Circle award), Two Masters: The Rain of Terror, 1985, Curse of the Starving Class, Frankie and Johnny in the Clair de Lune (OBIE award 1988), The Road to Mecca; (films) Taking Off, 1971, Straight Time, 1978, Come Back to the Five and Dime, Jimmy Dean, Jimmy Dean, 1982, Two of a Kind, 1983, Summer Heat, 1987, My Best Friend Is A Vampire, 1988, Arthur 2: On the Rocks, 1988, Signs of Life, 1989, High Stakes, 1989, Men Don't Leave, 1990, Dick Tracy, 1990, White Palace, Misery, 1990 (Acad. award for Best Actress 1990, Golden Globe award), At Play in the Fields of the Lord, 1991, Fried Green Tomatoes, 1991 (Golden Globe nomination, BAFTA nomination), The Road to Mecca, 1992, Prelude to a Kiss, 1992, Used People, 1992, A Home of Our Own, 1993, North, 1994, Curse of the Starving Class, 1994, Dolores Claiborne, 1994, Angus, 1995, Diabolique, 1996, The War at Home, 1996, Primary Colors, 1998, Swept from the Sea, 1998, Titanic, 1998, The Waterboy, 1998, Baby Steps, 1999, Dash and Lilly, 1999, My Life as a Dog, 1999, Bruno, 2000, Rat Race, 2001, American Outlaws, 2001, About Schmidt, 2002, Love Liza, 2002, Dragonfly, 2002, Around the World in 80 Days, 2004, The Bridge of San Luis Rey, 2004, 3 & 3, 2005, Rumor Has It, 2005, Failure to Launch, 2006, Relative Strangers, 2006, Bonneville, 2006, (voice) Charlotte's Web, 2006, (voice) Bee Movie, 2007, Fred Claus, 2007, (voice) Christmas Is Here Again, 2007, P.S., I Love You, 2007, The Golden Compass, 2007, The Family That Preys, 2008, The Day the Earth Stood Still, 2008, Revolutionary Road, 2008 (Ensemble Performance award Palm Springs Internat. Film Soc., 2009); (TV films) Johnny Bull, 1986, Murder Ordained, 1987, Roe vs. Wade, 1989, No Place Like Home, 1989, Hostages, 1993, Talking with, 1995, The West Side Waltz, 1995, The Late Shift, 1996, Annie, 1999, My Sister's Keeper, 2002, Warm Springs, 2005; (TV series) The Doctors, 1977, All My Children, 1984;(TV appearances) The Love Boat, 1978, St. Elsewhere, 1986, 87, China Beach, 1989, LA Law, 1989, 3rd Rock from the Sun, 1999, (voice) King of the Hill, 2001, Six Feet Under, 2003-05; dir. (TV films) Fargo, 2003; (films) Have Mercy, 2006; actor, dir. (TV films) Ambulance Girl, 2005; actor, exec. prodr. (films) The Ingrate, 2004 Recipient Mary Pickford award, Internat. Press. Acad., 2007. Office: c/o Susan Smith Susan Smith Co 1344 N Wetherly Dr Los Angeles CA 90069

BATES, MARCIA JEANNE, information scientist educator; b. Terre Haute, Ind., July 30, 1942; d. Robert Joseph and Martha Jane B. BA, Pomona Coll., 1963; MLS, U. Calif., Berkeley, 1967; PhD, U. Calif., 1972. Peace corps vol., Saraburi, Thailand, 1963-64, Nongkhai, Thailand, 1964-65; jr. specialist Inst. Libr. Rsch., U. Calif., Berkeley, 1968; acting instr. U. Calif., Berkeley, 1969-70; asst. prof. U. Md., College Park, 1972-76, U. Wash., Seattle, 1976-80, assoc. prof., 1980-81, U. Calif., LA, 1981—91, assoc. prof. and dean, 1991—2004, prof., dept. chmn. libr. and info. sci., 1993—95, prof. emeritus, 2004—. Cons. U.S. Libr. Congress, Washington, 1986, 91, 2002-03, Getty Art Hist. Info. Program, Santa Monica, Calif., 1988-91, Info. Access Co., Foster City, Calif., 1992-95; mem. editl. bd. Jour. of Asis &T, 1989—, Libr. Quar., 1993-2001. Co-author: For Information Specialists, 1992; editor: Encyclopedia of Library and Information Sciences; contbr. articles to profl. jours. and pubs. Recipient Distinguished Lectureship award N.J. Am. Soc. for Info. Sci., New Brunswick, 1991. Fellow AAAS (sect. T electorate nominating com. 1980-84, chmn. 1983-84, sect. T com. mem.-at-large, 2001-04), mem. ALA (Frederick G. Kilgour award, 2001), Am. Soc. Info. Sci. and Tech. (bd. dirs. 1973-74, Best Jour. Article Yr. award, 1980, 99, Rsch. award 1998, award of Merit 2005), Assn. Records Mgrs. Adminstrs., Calif. Libr. Assn. (mem. task force on future of Libr. profession, 1993-95), Phi Beta Kappa. Achievements include design of information systems and interfaces for search and subject access in information retrieval systems. Office: Grad Sch Edn & Info Studies UCLA 405 Hilgard Ave Los Angeles CA 90095-1520

BATES, ROBERT C., academic administrator; m. Wendy Bates. BS in Biology, Lewis & Clark Coll., 1966; MS in Bacteriology and Pub. Health, Wash. State U., 1969; PhD in Virology, Colo. State U., 1972. Asst. prof. Va. Poly. Inst. and State U., 1972—78, assoc. prof., 1978—85, prof., 1985—2002, assoc. dean for rsch., facilities and grad. studies, 1987—94, dean Coll. Arts and Scis., 1994—2002; provost, exec. v.p. Wash. State U., Pullman, 2002—. Contbr. chapters to books, articles to profl. jours. Mem.: AAAS, Am. Soc. for Virology, Am. Soc. Biol. Chemists, Sigma Xi. Office: Office of Provost Wash State Univ PO Box 641046 Pullman WA 99164-1046 Home Phone: 509-334-6652; Office Phone: 509-335-5582. Business E-Mail: bates@wsu.edu.

BATES, WILLIAM, III, lawyer; b. Phila., May 1, 1949; s. William and Elizabeth (Martin) B. BA, Yale U., 1971; JD, Stanford U., 1974. Bar: Calif. 1974, U.S. Dist. Ct. (no. dist.) Calif. 1976, U.S. Dist. Ct.

(ea. dist.) Calif. 1978, U.S. Dist. Ct. (ctrl. dist.) Calif. 1984, U.S. Ct. Appeals (9th cir.) 1986, U.S. Dist. Ct. (so. dist.) Calif. 1987, U.S. Supreme Ct. Law clk. to chief judge U.S. Dist. Ct. Conn., Hartford, 1974—75; assoc. McCutchen, Doyle, Brown & Enersen, San Francisco, 1975—81; ptnr. Bingham, McCutchen (formerly McCutchen, Doyle, Brown & Enersen), 1981—. Mem. bd. visitors Stanford Law Sch., 2003—06. Mem. ABA (mem. bus. bankruptcy com.), State Bar Calif. (chair rules of ct. com. 1979-80, mem. uniform comml. code com. 1985-88, mem. debtor/creditor rels. com. 1989-92), San Francisco Bar Assn. (chair comml. law and bankruptcy sect. 1991-92). Democrat. Episcopalian. Avocations: wine tasting, bicycling, travel. Office: Bingham McCutchen 1900 University Ave East Palo Alto CA 94303-2223 Office Phone: 650-849-4400. E-mail: bill.bates@bingham.com.

BATEY, SHARYN REBECCA, medical writer; b. Nashville, Apr. 19, 1946; d. Robert Thomas and Sue (Alred) B. BS in Pharmacy, U. Tenn., 1969, D of Pharmacy, 1975; MS in Pub. Health, U. S.C., 1984. Hosp. pharmacist Vanderbilt Hosp., Nashville, 1969—71, VA Hosp., Beckley, W.Va., 1971—72, Gainesville, Fla., 1972—73, Battle Creek, Mich., 1973—74; hosp. pharmacy resident VA Hosp., Memphis, 1974—76; psychopharmacy resident Menninger Found., Topeka, 1976—77; clin. pharmacist William S. Hall Psychiat. Inst., Columbia, SC, 1977—82; asst. prof. U. S.C. Coll. Pharmacy, Columbia, 1977—83, asst. prof. Sch. Medicine, 1981—83, assoc. prof. Coll. Pharmacy and Sch. Medicine, 1983—89, prof., 1989; chief clin. pharmacy svcs. and ednl. programs William S. Hall Psychiat. Inst., Columbia, 1982—89; clin. rsch. scientist Burroughs Wellcome Co., Research Triangle Park, NC, 1989—95; clin. program head Glaxo Wellcome, Inc., Research Triangle Park, 1995—97, sr. clin. rsch. program head, 1997—2001; dir., clin. devel. Elan Pharms., San Diego, 2001—02, sr. dir. clin. devel., 2003—05; dir. clin. rsch. ISTA Pharms., Irvine, Calif., 2005—06; prin. med. writer PAREXEL Internat., 2008—. Clin. drug rsch./drug devel. fellow U. N.C. and Burroughs Wellcome, Research Triangle Park, 1983-84; pharmacist cons. NIMH, Bethesda Md., 1983-84, Health Care Fin. Adminstrn., Balt., 1983-84. Author audio visual programs Psychotropic Medication Edn. Program for Adults, Adolescents and Children, 1978, 84, 88, 89; contbr. articles on psychopharmacology to profl. jours. Recipient Significant Achievement award Am. Psychiat. Assn., 1980, Sci. Exhibit award Am. Psychiat. Assn., 1981. Mem. Am. Coll. Clin. Pharmacy, Am. Soc. Hosp. Pharmacists (chmn. edn. and tng. working group of psychopharmacy spl. interest group 1983-85, chmn. elect 1985-86, chmn. 1986-87, past chmn. 1987-88, project leader psychopharmacy specialty recognition petition 1986-89, psychopharmacy fellow selection com. 1986-88, chmn. psychopharmacy spl. practice group 1989), S.C. Dementia Registry (pres. user policy coun. 1989). Avocations: travel, reading. Home: 2645 28th St San Diego CA 92104

BATEY, WILLIAM H., II, Mayor, Moreno Valley, California; m. Sherri Batey; 1 child, William. Current fire capt. City of Riverside, Calif.; councilman City of Moreno Valley from Dist. 5, 1996—98; mayor City of Moreno Valley, 1998—. Mem. Pub. Safety Com. Bd. mem. Moreno Valley Promise; rep. Riverside County Habitat Conservation Agy., Joint Powers Commn., Western Riverside Coun. of Govt.; coach Moreno Little League, Moreno Pop Warner Football. With USAF. Achievements include development of literacy program for Parks & Community Services After-School Program. Office: Moreno Valley City Hall 14177 Frederick St PO Box 88005 Moreno Valley CA 92552 Office Phone: 951-413-3000. Office Fax: 909-413-3750. Business E-Mail: williamb@moval.org.*

BATLIN, ROBERT ALFRED, retired newspaper editor; b. San Francisco, Aug. 24, 1930; S. Philip Alfred and Lavenia Mary (Barnes) B.; m. Diane Elise Giblin, July 4, 1956; children— Lisa, Philippa. BA, Stanford U., 1952, MA, 1954. Reporter San Bruno Herald, 1952-53; copy editor, then dept. editor San Francisco News, 1956-59; dept. editor San Francisco News-Call Bull., 1959-65; feature editor San Francisco Examiner, 1965-74, arts editor, 1974-85, asst. style editor, 1985-2001; copy editor San Francisco Chronicle mag., 2001—02, ret., 2002. Served with AUS, 1954-56. Mem. Soc. of Profl. Journalists. Home: 91 Fairway Dr Daly City CA 94015-1215

BATT, ANTHONY, Internet company executive; Mgr. Internet Pub. Time Inc.; pres. tech. and products AsiaConnect; founder Nat. Newspaper Radio and TV of Malaysia; chief tech. officer Metapa Inc. (now Greenplum); co-founder, pres. Buzznet, 2003—. Creative and tech. cons. Absolut Vodka, TBWA Chiat Day, Amp'dMobile; advisor Craigslist. Tech. bd. advisor Santa Monica Boys and Girls Club. Recipient Comm. Arts Award for Web Interface Design, 1997. Office: Buzznet 6464 Sunset Blvd 6th Fl Hollywood CA 90028 also: 555 Fifth Ave 14th Fl New York NY 10017 Office Phone: 213-252-8999, 212-918-0690. Office Fax: 323-466-0150.

BATTAGLIA, FREDERICK CAMILLO, physician; b. Weehawken, NJ, Feb. 15, 1932; m. Jane B. Donohue; children: Susan Kate, Thomas Frederick. BA, Cornell U., 1953; MD, Yale U., 1957; DSc (hon.), U. Ind. Diplomate Am. Bd. Pediat. Intern in pediat. Johns Hopkins Hosp., 1957—58; USPHS postdoctoral fellow biochemistry Cambridge (Eng.) U., 1958—59; Josiah Macy Found. fellow in physiology Yale U. Med. Sch., 1959—60; asst. resident, fellow in pediat. Johns Hopkins Hosp., 1960—61, resident, fellow, 1961—62; USPHS surgeon lab. perinatal physiology NIH, San Juan, 1962—64; asst. prof. Johns Hopkins Med. Sch., 1963—65; mem. faculty U. Colo. Med. Sch., Denver, 1965—, prof. pediat., prof. ob-gyn., 1969—2003, prof. pediat., ob-gyn. emeritus, 2003—, dir. divsn. perinatal medicine, 1970—74, chmn. dept. pediat., 1974—89. Attending pediatrician Children's, Denver Gen., Fitzsimons Gen. Hosps. Editor (assoc.): Pediatrics; med. progress contbg. editor Jour. Pediat., 1966—74, editl. bd. European Jour. Ob-Gybn., 1971—, assoc. Jour Perinatal, med. editor Biol. Neonate, 1979—; contbr. numerous articles to med. jours. Mem.: Inst. Medicine NAS, Soc. Exptl. Biology and Medicine, Internat. Congress Perinatal Medicine (pres. 1996), Am. Pediatric Soc. (pres. 1996, John Howland medal 2004), Soc. Gynecol. Investigation (coun. 1969—72), We. Soc. Pediatric Rsch. (pres. 1987—), Perinatal Rsch. Soc. (pres. 1974—75), Soc. Pediatric Rsch. (pres. 1976—77), Am. Gynecologic and Obstetric Soc., Am. Acad. Pediat. (E. Mead Johns award 1969), Assn. Am. Physicians, Sigma Xi, Phi Beta Kappa. Home: 2975 E Cedar Ave Denver CO 80209-3211 Office: Fitzsimons Bldg 260 MS F441 PO Box 6508 Aurora CO 80010 Office Phone: 303-724-0546. Business E-Mail: fred.battaglia@uchsc.edu.

BATTELLE, JOHN, journalist, educator, writer, entrepreneur; B, Univ. Calif., B, M, Univ. Calif., Berkeley. Co-founder editor Wired Magazine and Wired Ventures; founder, former chair, CEO Standard Media Internat. (SMI); band mgr. BoingBoing.net; publisher The Industry Standard and Standard.com; monthly columnist, Titans of Technology Business 2.0; founder, chmn. Federated Media Publishing Inc.; maintains daily Searchblog battellemedia.com. Vis. prof. Univ. Calif., Grad. Sch. Journalism, Berkeley, dir., bus. reporting program; founding exec. prodr. Foursquare Conf.; founder, exec. prodr. Web 2.0 conf.; cons. in field. Author: The Search: How Google and Its Rivals Rewrote the Rules of Business and Transformed Our Culture, 2005. Named Global Leader for Tomorrow, World Econ. Forum, Davos, Switzerland; named one of 50 Most Important People on the Web, PC World, 2007; finalist Entrepreneur of Yr., Ernst & Young. Office: Federated Media Publishing 2 Harrison St Fl 7 San Francisco CA 94105-1671 E-mail: jbat@battellemedia.com.

BATTEN, ALAN HENRY, astronomer; b. Tankerton, Kent, England, Jan. 21, 1933; emigrated to Can., 1959, naturalized, 1975; s. George Cuthbert and Gladys (Greenwood) B.; m. Lois Eleanor Dewis, July 30, 1960; children: Michael Henry John, Margaret Eleanor. BSc with 1st class honors, U. St. Andrews, Scotland, 1955, DSc, 1974; PhD, U. Manchester, Eng., 1958. Rsch. asst. in astronomy, jr. tutor St. Anselm Residence Hall, U. Manchester, 1958-59; postdoctoral fellow Dominion Astrophys. Obs., Victoria, B.C., Canada, 1959-61, mem. staff, 1961-91, assoc. rsch. officer, 1970-76, sr. rsch. officer, 1976-91, guest scientist, 1991—. Lectr. astronomy U. Victoria, 1961-64; guest investigator Vatican Obs., 1970, Inst. Astronomia y Fisica del Espacio, Buenos Aires, 1972; lectr. history U. Victoria, 2004-05; rsch. awards com. Craigdarroch, 2003-07. Author: Binary and Multiple Systems of Stars, 1973, Resolute and Undertaking Characters: The Lives of Wilhelm and Otto Struve, 1988; editor: Extended Atmospheres and Circumstellar Matter in Spectroscopic Binary Systems, 1973, Algols, 1989, Astronomy for Developing Countries, 2001; sr. author: Eighth Catalogue of the Orbital Elements of Spectroscopic Binary Systems, 1989; co-editor: The Determination of Radial Velocities and Their Applications, 1967; translator: L'Observation des Etoiles Doubles Visuelles par P. Couteau, 1981; contbr. articles to profl. jours. Pres. Willows Elem. Sch. PTA, Victoria, 1971-73; active Anglican Ch. Can. Diocesan Synod, B.C., 1966-68, 74; adv. coun. Ctr. Studies Religion and Soc., U. Victoria, 1993-2002, 2006-, chmn., 1997-2000. Recipient Queen's Silver Jubilee medal, Can., 1977; Erskine Vis. fellow, U. Canterbury, New Zealand, 1995. Fellow Royal Soc. Can. (convenor interdisciplinary sect. 1980-81, mem. coun. 1980-81), Royal Astron. Soc., Explorers Club; mem. Internat. Astron. Union (v.p. 1985-91, pres. commn. 30 1976-79, pres. commn. 42 1982-85, chmn. nat. orgn. com. XVII Gen. Assembly 1975-79), Royal Astron. Soc. Can. (pres. 1976-78, hon. pres. 1993-98, editor jour. 1981-88), Astron. Soc. Pacific (v.p. 1965-68), Can. Astron. Soc. (pres. 1972-74), Am. Astron. Socs., Ancient Soc. Coll. Youths. Anglican. Home: 2987 Westdowne Rd Victoria BC Canada V8R 5G1 Office: Dominion Astrophys Obs 5071 W Saanich Rd Victoria BC Canada V9E 2E7 Business E-Mail: alan.batten@nrc.gc.ca.

BATTERMAN, BORIS WILLIAM, physicist, educator, academic administrator; b. NYC, Aug. 25, 1930; children: Robert W., William E., Thomas A. Degree, Cooper Union Coll., 1949-50; student, Technische Hochschule, Stuttgart, Germany; SB, MIT, 1952, PhD, 1956. Mem. tech. staff Bell Tel. Labs., Murray Hill, NJ, 1956-65; assoc. prof. Cornell U., Ithaca, NY, 1965-67, prof. applied and engring. physics, 1967—, dir. Sch. Applied and Engring. Physics, 1974-78, dir. Synchrotron Radiation Lab. (CHESS), 1978-97, Walter S. Carpenter Jr. prof. engring., 1985—2001, Walter S. Carpenter Jr. prof. emeritus, 2002—. Mem. staff Lawrence Berkeley Lab., 1998—, Stanford Linear Accelerator Ctr., 1999—; mem. U.S.A. Nat. Com. Crystallography, NAS, 1969—72. Assoc. editor Jour. Crystal Growth, 1964—74. Fulbright scholar, 1953-54; Guggenheim fellow, 1971, Fulbright Hayes fellow, 1971, Alexander von Humboldt fellow, 1983. Fellow: AAAS, Am. Phys. Soc. Office: 150 Lombard St #603 San Francisco CA 94111 E-mail: bwb1@cornell.edu.

BATTISTA, RICHARD, chef, educator; Degree in Fin., Burdett Coll. Cert. Exec. Chef, Exec. Pastry Chef, Culinary Educator. Exec. chef LaBrioche Restaurant chain; chef instr. Watertown Sch. System; dir. food and beverage Fairmont Hotel chain; exec. pastry chef Sheraton Corp., Ritz-Carlton Hotels; dir. colleges of food Calif. Culinary Acad.; dean LA Culinary Inst.; dir. culinary arts Inst. Calif.-LA; pres. Profl. Culinary Inst., Campbell. Former pres., bd. chmn. Am. Culinary Fedn.-LA. Recipient Grand prize, Culinaire Philanthropique of NY. Office: Professional Culinary Inst 700 W Hamilton Ave Ste 300 Campbell CA 95008

BATTS, MICHAEL STANLEY, retired language educator; b. Mitcham, Eng., Aug. 2, 1929; s. Stanley George and Alixe Kathleen (Watson) B.; m. Misao Yoshida, Mar. 19, 1959; 1 dau., Anna. BA, U. London, 1952, BA with honors, 1953, LittD, 1973; PhD, U. Freiburg, Germany, 1957; MLS, U. Toronto, 1974. Mem. faculty U. Mainz, Germany, 1953-54, U. Basel, Switzerland, 1954-56; Mem. faculty U. Wurzburg, Germany, 1956-58; instr. German U. Calif., Berkeley, 1958-60; mem. faculty dept. German U. B.C., Canada, 1960-91, prof., 1967-91, head dept., 1968-80; ret., 1992. Author: Die Form der Aventiuren im Nibelungenlied, 1961, Bruder Hansens Marienlieder, 1964, Studien zu Bruder Hansens Marienliedern, 1964, Das Hohe Mittelalter, 1969, Das Nibelungenlied-Synoptische Ausgabe, 1971, Gottfried von Strasburg, 1971, A Checklist of German Literature, 1945-75, 1977, The Bibliography of German Literature: An Historical and Critical Survey, 1978, A History of Histories of German Literature, 1835-1914, 1993, Germanic Studies at Canadian Universities From the Beginning to 1995, 1998; editor: Seminar, 1970-80. Served with Brit. Army, 1947-49. Alexander von Humboldt fellow, 1964-65, 83; Can. Coun. Sr. fellow, 1964-65, 71-72; Killam fellow, 1981-82. Fellow Royal Soc. Can.; mem. Can. Assn. Univ. Tchrs. German (pres. 1982-84), Alcuin Soc. (exec. v.p. 1972-79, pres. 1979-80), Internat. Assn. for Germanic Studies (pres. 1990-95). Personal E-mail: msb@interchange.ubc.ca.

BAUCH, THOMAS JAY, financial consultant, retired lawyer, apparel executive; b. Indpls., May 24, 1943; s. Thomas and Violet (Smith) B.; m. Ellen L. Burstein, Oct. 31, 1982; children: Chelsea Sara, Elizabeth Tree. BS with honors, U. Wis., 1964, JD with highest honors, 1966. Bar: Ill. 1966, Calif. 1978. Assoc. Lord, Bissell & Brook, Chgo., 1966-72; lawyer, asst. sec. Marcor-Montgomery Ward, Chgo., 1973-75; spl. asst. to solicitor Dept. Labor, Washington, 1975-77; dep. gen. counsel Levi Strauss & Co., 1977-81, sr. v.p., gen. counsel, 1981-96, of counsel, 1996-2000; pvt. practice, Tiburon, Calif., 1996-2000; mng. dir. Hall Capital Ptnrs. LLC, San Francisco, 2000—. Cons. prof. Stanford U. Law Sch., Calif., 1997-04. Mem. U. Wis. Law Rev., 1964-66. Bd. dirs. Urban Sch., San Francisco, 1986-91, Gateway HS, San Francisco, 1996-2003, Charles Armstrong Sch., Belmont, Calif., 1998-2001, San Francisco Opera Assn., 1998-2001, Telluride Acad., 1996-2000, Corinthian Acad.; bd. visitors U. Wis. Law Sch., 1991-95. Mem. Am. Assn. Corp. Counsel (founding mem., bd. dirs. 1984-87), Bay Area Gen. Counsel Assn. (founding mem., chmn. 1994), Univ. Club, Villa Taverna Club, Corinthian Yacht Club, Order of Coif, San Francisco Yacht Club. Office: Offit Hall Capital Ptnrs One Maritime Plz Ste 500 San Francisco CA 94111 Office Phone: 415-288-0544. Business E-Mail: tbauch@hallcapital.com.

BAUCOM, SIDNEY GEORGE, lawyer; b. Salt Lake City, Oct. 21, 1930; s. Sidney and Nora (Palfreyman) B.; m. Mary B., Mar. 5, 1954; children: Sidney, George, John JD, U. Utah, 1953. Bar: Utah 1953. Pvt. practice, Salt Lake City, 1953-55; asst. city atty. Salt Lake City Corp., 1955-56; asst. atty. Utah Power and Light Co., Salt Lake City, 1956-60, asst. atty., asst. sec., 1960-62, atty., asst. sec., 1962-68, v.p., gen. counsel, 1968-75, sr. v.p., gen. counsel, 1975-79, exec. v.p., gen. counsel, 1979-89, dir., 1979-89; of counsel Jones, Waldo, Holbrook & McDonough, Salt Lake City, 1989—. Past chmn. Utah Coordinating Coun. Devel. Svcs., Utah Taxpayers Assn.; past pres. Utah State Fair Found.; past dir. Utah Power & Light Co., El Paso Electric Co., vice chmn. Mem. Alta Club, Lions, Phi Delta Phi Mem. Lds Ch. Home: 2248 Logan Ave Salt Lake City UT 84108-2715 Office: Jones Waldo Holbrook & McDonough 1500 Wells Fargo Bank Bldg 170 S Main St Salt Lake City UT 84101-1605 Home Phone: 801-583-1221; Office Phone: 801-521-3200. Business E-Mail: sbaucom@joneswaldo.com.

BAUCUS, MAX SIEBEN, United States Senator from Montana; b. Helena, Mont., Dec. 11, 1941; s. John and Jean (Sheriff) Baucus; m. Wanda Minge, Apr. 23, 1983; 1 child, Zeno. BA in Economics, Stanford U., 1964, LLB, 1967. Bar: DC 1969, Mont. 1972. Staff atty. Civil Aeronautics Bd., Washington, 1967-68; atty. Securities & Exchange Commn. (SEC), Washington, 1968-71, legal asst. to chmn., 1970-71; atty. George and Baucus, Missoula, Mont., 1971—74; mem. Mont. House of Reps., 1973-74, US Congress from 1st Mont. Dist., 1975—78; US Senator from Mont., 1979—; chmn. US Senate Fin. Com., 2001, 2001—03, 2007—, US Senate Environment & Pub. Works Com., 1993—95; vice chmn. Joint Com. on Taxation, 2007—; mem. US Senate Agrl. Nutrition & Forestry Com., US Senate Environment & Pub. Works Com. Bd. dirs. Congressional Award Found. Recipient Guardian of Small Bus. award, Nat. Fedn. Independent Bus., 1983—84, Bronze Symbol Svc. award, Nat. Pork Producers Coun., 1997, Legis. award, Nat. Rural Health Assn., 1999, Am. Fin. Leadership award, Fin. Services Roundtable, 2001, Wheat Leader of Yr. award, Nat. Assn. Wheat Growers, 2003, Cyber Champion award, Bus. Software Alliance, 2005. Mem.: Mont. Bar Assn., DC Bar Assn. Democrat. Avocation: motorcycling. Office: US Senate 511 Hart Senate Bldg Washington DC 20510-0001 also: District Office Ste 100 222 North 32nd St Billings MT 59101 Office Phone: 202-224-2651, 406-657-6790. Office Fax: 202-224-0515.*

BAUER, ALBERT, state legislator; m. Patricia Bauer; children: Sue, Jim, Nancy. Student, Clark C.C., 1948-54; BA in Polit Sci. and History, Portland State Coll., 1957; MEd, Oreg. State Coll., 1958. Tchr. La Ctr. Sch. Dist., 1958-61, Vancouver Sch. Dist., 1961-80; Dem. caucus chmn. Wash. Legislature, Olympia, 1977-80, mem., 1981—, senate v.p. pro tempore, 1986-87, senate Dem. floor leader, 1987-90, senate Dem. dep. leader, 1991-92, senate v.p. pro tempore, 1999-2000, mem. edn. com., mem. higher edn. com., mem. rules com., chair capital budget com., mem. ways and means com., mem. joint legis. audit and rev. com., 1989—, mem. joint com. on pension policy, 1994—, mem. gov.'s higher edn. task force, 1995-98. Mem. Salmon Creek Grange, Salmon Creek Meth. Ch. With USN. Recipient UN medal, Legislator of Yr. award Wash. State Sch. Prins., Betty Sharff Meml. award, HOSTS Corp., Personal Commitment to Improve Edn. award Phi Delta Kappa, Walter G. Turner award Wash. State Ednl. Svc. Mem. Am. Legion (Post 176), Kiwanis (Greater Vancouver). Democrat. Office: 406 Legislative Bldg Olympia WA 98504-0001

BAUER, ERNST GEORG, physicist, researcher; b. Schoenberg, Germany, Feb. 27, 1928; MS, U. Munich, 1953, PhD in Physics, 1955. Rsch. asst. U. Munich, 1955-58; head crystal physics br. Michelson Lab., China Lake, Calif., 1958-69; prof. Tech. U. Clausthal, Germany, 1969-96. Disting. rsch. prof. Ariz. State U., Tempe, 1993—. Author: (book) Elektronenbeugung, 1958. Recipient Gaede prize, German Vacuum Soc., 1988, Niedersachsenpreis, 1994, Innovation award, Berliner Elektronenspeicherring-Gesellschaft für Synchrotronstrahlung MBH, 2004. Fellow: Am. Vacuum Soc. (Welch award 1992), Am. Phys. Soc. (Davisson-Germer prize 2005); mem.: German Electron Microscopy Soc., Materials Rsch. Soc., Goettingen Acad. Sci. Achievements include development of a classification of the basic thin film growth modes, which is used worldwide today; invention of LEEM (Low Energy Electron Microscopy) a unique surface imaging method. Office: Ariz State Univ Dept Physics Tempe AZ 85287-1504 Office Phone: 480-965-2993. Business E-Mail: ernst.bauer@asu.edu.

BAUER, RANDY MARK, management training firm executive; b. Sept. 2, 1946; s. Ralph I. and Gloria P. Bauer; m. Sue Deliva, July 4, 1975; children: Sherri, Kevin. BS summa cum laude, Ohio State U., 1968; MBA, Kent State U., 1971. Auditor Peat Marwick Mitchell & Co., Cleve., 1971-72; mgmt. devel. specialist GAO, Denver, 1972-80; adj. prof. mgmt. Columbia Coll., Denver, 1979—. Pres. Leadership Tng. Assos., Denver, 1979—; condr. exec. devel. workshops U. Colo., Denver, 1979—. Recipient Best in 1976 award GAO. Mem. Am. Soc. for Tng. and Devel., Beta Gamma Sigma. Address: 10022 Oak Tree Ct Lone Tree CO 80124-9714 Office Phone: 303-706-9590.

BAUER, ROGER DUANE, chemistry professor, consultant; b. Oxford, Nebr., Jan. 17, 1932; s. Albert Carl and Minnie (Lueking) B.; m. Jacquelyn True, Aug. 10, 1956; children— Lisa, Scott, Robert. BS, Beloit Coll., 1953; MS, Kans. State U., 1957, PhD, 1959. Asst. prof. chemistry Calif. State U., Long Beach, 1959-64, assoc. prof., 1964-69, prof., 1969-92; dean Calif. State U. (Sch. Natural Scis.), 1975-88. Served with U.S. Army, 1954-56. USPHS fellow, 1966; Am. Coun. on Edn. fellow, 1971 Mem. Am. Chem. Soc., Radiation Rsch. Soc., Sigma Xi, Phi Lambda Upsilon. Home: 6320 E Colorado St Long Beach CA 90803-2202 Office: Calif State U Coll Natural Sci Long Beach CA 90840-0001 Office Phone: 562-985-8640. Business E-Mail: rdbauer@csulb.edu.

BAUGHN, WILLIAM HUBERT, former business educator and academic administrator; b. Marshall County, Ala., Aug. 27, 1918; s. J.W. and Beatrice (Jackson) B.; m. Mary Madiera Morris, Feb. 20, 1945; children: Charles Madiera, William Marsteller. BS, U. Ala., 1940; MA, U. Va, 1941, PhD, 1948. Instr. U. Va., 1942-43, asst. prof., 1946-48; assoc. prof., then prof. econs. and bus. adminstrn. La. State U., 1948-56; prof. U. Tex., 1956-62, chmn. fin. dept., 1958-60, assoc. dean Coll. Bus. Adminstrn., 1959-62; assoc. dir. Sch. Banking of

South, 1952-66; dean Coll. Bus. and Pub. Adminstrn. U. Mo., 1962-64; dean Coll. Bus. and Adminstrn. U. Colo., 1964-84, pres., 1985, acting chancellor, 1986-87; pres. U. Colo. System, Boulder, 1990-91. Pres. Am. Assembly Collegiate Schs. Bus., 1973-74; chmn. Big Eight Athletic Conf., 1970-71, 78-79, 86-87; dir. Stonier Grad. Sch. of Banking, Rutgers U., 1966-86; mem. council Nat. Collegiate Athletic Assn., 1983-86. Author: (with E.W. Walker) Financial Planning and Policy, 1961; editor: (with C.E. Walker) The Bankers' Handbook, 1966, (with C.E. Walker and T.I. Storrs) 3d rev. edit., 1988, (with D. R. Mandich) The International Banking Handbook, 1983. Served to 1st lt. USAAF, World War II; lt. col. Res. Office: U Colo System Boulder CO 80309-0001 also: 350 Ponca Pl #341 Boulder CO 80303-3802

BAULE, JOHN ALVIN, museum director, consultant; b. Dubuque, Iowa, July 20, 1948; s. Kenneth Edward and Edith (Stiles) B. BA in Math. and Physics summa cum laude, U. Dubuque, 1970; postgrad., Loras Coll., Dubuque, 1972—75, Coll. of St. Thomas, St. Paul, 1990; MA in History of Mus. Studies, SUNY, Oneonta, 1979. Dir. St. Lawrence County Hist. Assn., Canton, NY, 1976-86, Hennepin County Hist. Soc., Mpls., 1986-90; assoc. dir. Hist. Soc. Western Pa., Pitts., 1990-92; dir. Yakima (Wash.) Valley Mus., 1992—. Interpretive cons. Minn. Hist. Soc., Hennepin History Mus. and City of Mpls., 1992; mus. aid panelist N.Y. State Coun. on Arts, N.Y.C., 1983-86; grant reviewer Inst. Mus. Svcs., Washington, 1988-91; mem. long-range planning com. Am. Swedish Inst., Mpls., 1988-90; mem. St. Anthony Falls Heritage Bd., Mpls., 1988-90; founding chmn. Preservation Adv. Bd., Canton, 1978-82; trustee, mem. exec. com., workshop leader, spkr., sec. corp. Regional Conf. Hist. Agys., Manlius, N.Y., 1978-84, also others. Contbr. articles to profl. publs. Coord. 50th Anniversary Exhbn., Mpls. Aquatennial Assn., 1989; performer, treas. Grasse River Cmty. Theater, Canton, 1977-86; mem. citizens adv. group West River Parkway Task Force, Mpls., 1988-89; pres. Rivermill Townhomes Assn., 1987-90; chmn. entertainment div. 4th of July Cmty. Celebration Com., 1993—; trustee, mem. exec. com. Humanities Wash., 1998-. Recipient North Country citation St. Lawrence U., Canton, 1986, pub. commendation Hennepin County Bd. Commrs., 1990; fellow Bush Found., 1990. Mem. Am. Assn. for State and Local History, Am. Assn. Mus., Mid-Atlantic Mus. Conf., Midwest Mus. Conf., Wash. Assn. Mus., Rotary. Avocations: travel, theater, hiking. Home: 3513 Highview Dr Yakima WA 98902-1531 Office: Yakima Valley Mus 2105 Tieton Dr Yakima WA 98902-3766 Office Phone: 509-248-0747.

BAUM, CARL EDWARD, electrical engineer, researcher; b. Binghamton, NY, Feb. 6, 1940; s. George Theodore and Evelyn Monica (Bliven) B. BS with honors, Calif. Inst. Tech., 1962, MS, 1963, PhD, 1969; Dr.-Ing.E.h. (hon.), Otto-von-Guericke U., 2004. Commd. 2d lt. USAF, 1962, advanced through grades to capt., 1967, resigned, 1971; project officer Air Force Rsch. Lab. (formerly Phillips Lab.), Kirtland AFB, N.Mex., 1963-71, sr. scientist for electromagnetics, 1971—2005; disting. rsch. prof. dept. elect. and computer engring. U. N.Mex., Albuquerque, 2005—. Pres. SUMMA Found.; mem. Commn. B US Nat. Com., 1975—, Commn. E, 1982—, Commn. A, 1990—. Author: (with others) Transient Electromagnetic Fields, 1976, Electromagnetic Scattering, 1978, Acoustic, Electromagnetic and Elastic Wave Scattering, 1980, Fast Electrical and Optical Measurements, 1986, EMP Interaction: Principles, Techniques and Reference Data, 1986, Lightning Electromagnetics, 1990, Modern Radio Science, 1990, Recent Advances in Electromagnetic Theory, 1990, Scattering, 1992, Direct and Inverse Methods in Radar Polarimetry, 1992, (with A.P. Stone) Transient Lens Synthesis: Differential Geometry in Electromagnetic Theory, 1991; editor: (with H.N. Kritikos) Electromagnetic Symmetry, 1995, (with L. Carin and A.P. Stone) Ultra-Wideband, Short-Pulse Electromagnetics 3, 1997, Detection and Identification of Visually Obscured Targets, 1998, (with A.P. Stone and J.S. Tyo) Ultra-Wide and Short Pulse Electromagnetics 8, 2007, Scattering, 2002; contbr. articles to profl. jours. Recipient award Honeywell Corp., 1962, R & D award USAF, 1970, Harold Brown award Air Force Systems Command, 1990; Air Force Rsch. Lab. fellow, 1996; Electromagnetic pulse fellow. Fellow IEEE (Harry Diamond Meml. award 1987, Richard R. Stoddart award 1984, John Kraus Antenna award 2006, Electromagnetics Field award, 2007); mem. Electromagnetics Soc. (pres. 1983-85), Electromagnetics Acad., Sigma Xi, Tau Beta Pi. Roman Catholic. Home: 5116 Eastern Ave SE Apt D Albuquerque NM 87108-5618 Office: Univ New Mexico Dept Electrical and Computer Engineering MSC01 1100 1 Univ New Mexico Albuquerque NM 87131-0001 Personal E-mail: carl.e.baum@ieee.org.

BAUM, PHYLLIS GARDNER, retired travel management consultant; b. Ashtabula, Ohio, Dec. 13, 1930; d. Charles Edward Schneider and Stella Elizabeth (Schaefer) Gardner; m. Kenneth Walter Baum, Oct. 21, 1948 (div. July 1971); children: Deidre Adair, Cynthia Gail; m. Dennis Carl Marquardt, Sept. 22, 1979 (dec. 1991). Grad. high sch., Cleve. Am. Soc. Travel Agents. Travel cons. Fredo Travel Svc., Ashland, Ohio, 1960-66; sales mgr. Travelmart, Willoughby, Ohio, 1966-68, br. mgr. Mentor, Ohio, 1966-68, Diners Fugazy Travel, Sun City, Ariz., 1968-69; travel cons. Jarrett's Travel Svc., Phoenix, 1969-72; sr. cons. Loyal Travel, Phoenix, 1972-74; co-mgr. Phil Carr Travel, Sun City, 1974-77; tour ops. mgr. ASL Travel, Phoenix, 1978-79; owner, mgr. Travel Temporaries, Glendale, Ariz., 1979-2000, ret., 2000. Cons. and lectr. in field. Adv. bd. mem. Small Bus. Devel. Ctr., Phoenix, 1986-2000. Mem. Pacific Asia Travel Assn. Ariz. (bd. dirs. 1986—), Ariz. Women in Travel, NAFE, Altrusa. Republican. Avocations: music, travel, tatting, knitting, horseback riding. Home: 14332 W Banff Lane Surprise AZ 85379

BAUM, WILLIAM ALVIN, astronomer, educator; b. Toledo, Jan. 18, 1924; s. Earle Fayette and Mable (Teachout) B.; m. Marie Sjolseth, Aug. 04, 1945 (div. 1960); children Karen Marie, Martha Jean; m. Ester Bru, June 27, 1961. BA summa cum laude, U. Rochester, 1943; PhD magna cum laude, Calif. Inst. Tech., 1950. Physicist U.S. Naval Rsch. Lab., Washington, 1946-49; astronomer Mt. Wilson and Palomar observatories, Pasadena, Calif., 1950-65; dir. Planetary Rsch. Ctr., Lowell Obs., Flagstaff, Ariz., 1965-90; rsch. prof. astronomy dept. U. Wash., Seattle, 1990—97, rsch. prof. emeritus, 1998—. Adj. prof. astronomy Ohio State U., 1969-91; adj. prof. physics No. Ariz. U., 1973-91; rsch. prof. astronomy U. Wash., Seattle, 1990-97, prof. emeritus, 1998—; cons. physics, astronomy, optics; cons. U.S. Army Research Office, Durham, N.C., 1967-74; vis. prof. Am. Astronom. Soc., 1961-98; adv. com. Nat. Acad. Sci., 19 58-67; mem. optical instrumentation panel adv. Air Force, 1967-76; coms. and panels NSF and NASA Office Space Scis., 1967-91; mem. NASA Viking Orbiter Imaging Team, 1970-79, Hubble Space Telescope Camera Team, 1977-96. Contbr. articles to tech. publs. Served to lt., jr. grade USNR, 1943-46. Guggenheim fellow, 1960-61; Asteroid 4175 named Billbaum, 1990. Mem. Am. Astron. Soc. (chmn. div. planetary scis. 1976-77), Royal Astron. Soc., Astron. Soc. Pacific, Internat. Astron. Union, Phi Beta Kappa, Sigma Xi, Theta Delta Chi. Achievements include asteroid 4175 named "Billbaum" in his honor, 1990. Home: 2124 NE Park Rd Seattle WA 98105-2422 Office: U Wash Dept Astronomy Seattle WA 98195-1580 Business E-Mail: baum@astro.washington.edu.

BAUMAN, WINFIELD SCOTT, finance educator; b. Dayton, Ohio, Nov. 7, 1930; s. Carl Louis and Lillian Elizabeth (Limpert) B.; m. Shirlee Ann Madden, June 20, 1953; children: Dale, Kent, Kimberly, Van. BBA, Ross. Sch. Bus., U. Mich., Ann Arbor, 1953; MBA, U. Mich., Ann Arbor, 1954; DBA, Ind. U., Bloomington, 1961. Securities rsch. analyst Wells Fargo Bank, San Francisco, 1956-57; stock broker UBS Fin. Svcs., Palo Alto, Calif., 1957-58; asst. prof. fin. Coll. Bus. Adminstrn. U. Toledo, 1961-63, assoc. prof. fin., 1963-66; prof. fin. U. Oreg., Eugene, 1966-72, head dept. fin., 1969-72; prof. bus. adminstrn. Darden Grad. Sch. Bus. Adminstrn. U. Va., Charlottesville, 1972-81; prof. fin. No. Ill. U., DeKalb, 1981—2001, prof. emeritus, 2001—, chair dept. fin., 1981-90; adj. prof. Robinson Coll. Bus., Ga. State U., 2003—05. Hon. vis. prof. City U. Bus. Sch., London, 1995. Contbr. articles to profl. jours., chpt. to Handbook of Modern Finance, 2004. Pres. Western Fin. Assn., 1971-72; nat. bd. dirs. Inst. Quantitative Rsch. in Fn., 1973-82; trustee, v.p., treas. Bedford (Mich.) Pub. Sch. Bd. Edn., 1963-66; chmn. endowment fund investment com. U. Oreg., 1969-72. Capt. USAF, 1954-56. Mem. CFA Inst. (exec. dir. 1972-78), CFA Soc. (pres., Portland, Oreg. 1971-72, bd. dirs., Chgo. 1996-2000), Midwest Fin. Assn. (bd. dirs. 1984-87, 95-98), Fin. Mgmt. Assn., Beta Gamma Sigma. United Methodist. Avocations: boating, travel, swimming. Business E-Mail: wsbauman@umich.edu.

BAUMANN, RICHARD GORDON, lawyer; b. Chgo., Apr. 7, 1938; s. Martin M. and Harriet May (Granof) B.; m. Terrie Bemel, Dec. 18, 1971; children: Michelle, Alison. BS cum laude, U. Wis., 1960, JD, 1964. Bar: Wis. 1964, Calif. 1970, US Supreme Ct. 1973; bd. cert. creditors rights specialist. Congressional intern U.S. Senator Hubert H. Humphrey, 1959; assoc. firm Kohner, Mann & Kailas, Milw., 1964-69, Sulmeyer, Kupetz & Alberts, LA, 1969-73; mem. firm Sulmeyer, Kupetz, Baumann & Rothman, LA, 1973—2003, SulmeyerKupetz, LA, 2003—. Judge pro tem LA Superior Ct., 1980—. Assoc. editor Comml. Law Jour., 1991—. Fellow Comml. Law Found. (bd. dirs.); mem. Nat. Inst. on Credit Mgmt. (bd. dirs.), Am. Bd. Cert. (bd. dirs.), Acad. Comml. and Bankruptcy Law Specialists (bd. dirs.), Comml. Law League (pres. 1990-91, bd. govs. 1986-92, chmn. Western Region Mem. Assn. 1982-83). Office: 333 S Hope St 35th Fl Los Angeles CA 90071 Office Phone: 213-626-2311. Business E-Mail: rbaumann@sulmeyerlaw.com.

BAUMGARDNER, RANDY, state legislator; b. Bedford, Ind., 1956; m. Lori Baumgardner; 1 child, Matthew;children from previous marriage: Richard, Charlie(dec.) stepchildren: Elizabeth Gramm, Michael Gramm. Employee Colo. State Dept. Transp.; owner Baumgardner Cattle Co.; mem. Dist. 57 Colo. House of Reps., Denver, 2008—. Active N.Am. Water Conservancy, Denver Water Bd. Office: Colo State Capitol 200 E Colfax Denver CO 80203 Office Phone: 303-866-2949. Business E-Mail: randy.baumgardner.house@state.co.us.*

BAUMGARTNER, ANTON EDWARD, automotive sales professional; b. NYC, May 18, 1948; s. Hans and Carmen Maria (Figueroa) B.; m. Brenda Lee Lemmon, May 24, 1969 (div. 1990); 1 child, Anton Nicholaus; m. Virginia Thiele, 1992 (div. 2003); 1 child, Bree Alexandra; m. Christine Stieber, 2007. BS, Woodbury U., 1970. Sales mgr. Maywood Bell Ford, Bell, Calif., 1966-69, O.R. Haan, Inc., Santa Ana, Calif., 1969-72; pres. Parkinson Volkswagen, Placentia, Calif., 1972-77; exec. v.p. United Moped, Fountain Valley, Calif., 1975-82; pres. Automobili Intermeccanica, Fountain Valley, 1975-82; gen. mgr. Bishop (Calif.) Volkswagen-Bishop Motors, 1982-85, Beach Imports-Irvine Imports, Newport Beach, Calif., 1985-88; chmn. bd. Stan and Ollie Ins. Co., Santa Ana, Calif., 1989—92; exec. v.p. Asterism, Inc., 1992-96; chmn. Marich Acceptance Inland Empire, 1996—98; gen. mgr. Saturn Retail Enterprises, Anaheim, Calif., 1999—2005, Swedish Cars of Orange County, 2005—. Mem. faculty, Automotive World Congress, Detroit, 1980. Contbr. articles to weekly serial publs. Mem. Coachbuilders Assn. N.Am. (sec. 1975-78). Home: 29401 Port Royal Way Laguna Niguel CA 92677-7945 Office: Swedish Motorcars Orange County Santa Ana CA 92705 Office Phone: 949-347-8626. Personal E-mail: tbaumgartner@cox.net.

BAUMRIND, DIANA, research psychologist; b. NYC, Aug. 23, 1927; AB, Hunter Coll., 1948; MA, U. Calif., Berkeley, 1951, PhD, 1955. Cert. and lic. psychologist, Calif. Project dir. psychology dept. U. Calif., Berkeley, 1955-58; project dir. Inst. of Human Devel., 1960—, also rsch. psychologist and prin. investigator family socialization and devel. competence project. Lectr. and cons. in field; referee for rsch. proposals Grant Found., NIH, 1970—, NSF, 1970—. Contbr. numerous articles to profl. jours. and books; author 2 monographs; mem. editorial bd. Devel. Psychology, 1986-90, Parenting: Science and Practice, 2000—. Recipient Rsch. Scientist award, NIMH; grantee NIMH, 1955-58, 60-66, Nat. Inst. Child Health and Human Devel., 1967-74, MacArthur Found., Grant Found., 1967—. Fellow Am. Psychol. Assn., Am. Psychol. Soc. (G. Stanley Hall award 1988), Soc. Research in Child Devel. Office: U Calif Inst of Human Devel 1217 Tolman Hall Berkeley CA 94720-1691 Office Phone: 510-642-3603.

BAVASI, PETER JOSEPH, sports management executive; b. Bronxville, NY, Oct. 31, 1942; s. Emil Joseph and Evit E. (Rice) B.; m. Judith Marzonie, June 13, 1964; children: Patrick, Cristina. BA in Philosophy, St. Mary's Coll., Moraga, Calif., 1964. Minor league gen. mgr. L.A. Dodgers, 1964-68; dir. minor league ops. San Diego Padres, 1968-73, v.p., gen. mgr., 1973-76; pres., CEO Toronto Blue Jays, 1976-81; pres. Peter Bavasi Sports, Inc., Tampa, Fla., 1981-84; pres., COO Cleve. Indians, 1984-87; pres., CEO Telerate Sports and SportsTicker, Jersey City, 1987-94; pres. ESPN/SportsTicker, Jersey City, 1995-96; prin. Bavasi Sports Ptnrs., LLP, La Jolla, 2001—. Office: Bavasi Sports Ptnrs LLP 1001 Genter St Unit 3G La Jolla CA 92037-5531

BAWDEN, GARTH LAWRY, museum director; b. Truro, Eng., Dec. 31, 1939; s. Richard Thomas and Susan Elizabeth Olga (Lawry) B.; m. Margaret Ruth Greet, Dec. 21, 1963 (div. Mar. 1978); children: Michael Greet, Teona Mary, Kerenza Elizabeth; m. Elaine Louise Comack, Oct. 26, 1978; children: Jonathan Richard, Rebecca Lawry. Diploma in phys. medicine, West Middlesex Sch. Phys. Medicine, Isleworth, Eng., 1961; BA in Art History, U. Oreg., 1970; PhD in Anthropology, Harvard U., 1977. Assoc. in archaeology Harvard U., Cambridge, Mass., 1977-81, instr., 1980-85, asst., acting dir. Peabody Mus., 1980-85; assoc. prof. U. N.Mex., Albuquerque, 1985-91; prof. U. Mex., Albuquerque, 1991—; dir. Maxwell Mus. U. N.Mex., Albuquerque, 1985—. Dir. field research project Harvard U., Galindo, Peru, 1971-74, dir. field survey Peabody Mus., Saudi Arabian Archaeol. Survey, 1978-80; field supr. Cuntisuyu Project, Moquegua, Peru, 1983-86; dir. U. N.Mex. Acheol. Project, So. Peru, 1985—. Author: (with G. Conrad) The Andean Heritage, 1982; contbr. articles on archaeology to profl. jours. Fellow Woodrow Wilson, U. Oreg., 1970, Tinker, Harvard U., 1983. Mem. Soc. Am. Archaeology, Assn. Field Archaeology, Assn. Sci. Mus. Dirs., Current Anthropology (assoc.), Phi Beta Kappa, Sigma Xi. Home: 6 Applewood Ln NW Albuquerque NM 87107-6404 Office: Univ NMex Maxwell Mus Anthropology Albuquerque NM 87131-0001

BAXTER, JOHN DARLING, internist, endocrinologist, educator, health facility administrator; b. Lexington, Ky., June 11, 1940; s. William Elbert and Genevive Lockhart (Wilson) B.; m. Ethelee Davidson Baxter, Aug. 10, 1963; children: Leslie Lockhart, Gillian Booth. BA in Chemistry, U. Ky., 1962; MD, Yale U., 1966; DSc (hon.), U. Ky, 2004. Intern, then resident in internal medicine Yale-New Haven Hosp., 1966-68; USPHS research assoc. Nat. Inst. Arthritis and Metabolic Diseases, NIH, 1968-70; Dernham sr. fellow oncology U. Calif. Med. Sch., San Francisco, 1970-72, mem. faculty, 1972—, prof. medicine and biochemistry and biophysics, 1979—, dir., Metabolic Rsch. Unit, 1981—2000. Attending physician U. Calif. Med. Center, 1972-; dir. endocrine research Howard Hughes Med. Inst., 1976-81, investigator, 1975-81; chief div. endocrinology Moffitt Hosp., 1980-97; founder, dir. Calif. Biotechnology, Inc., 1982-1992; dir., chmn. SciClone scientific adv. bd., 1991-. Editor textbook of endocrinology and metabolism; Author research papers in field; mem. editorial bd. profl. jours. Recipient George W. Thorn Outstanding Investigator award, Howard Hughes Med. Inst., 1978, Disting. Alumni award U. Ky., 1980, Dautrebande prize for research in cellular and molecular biology, Belgium, 1985, Albion Bernstein award N.Y. Med. Soc., 1987, Edwin B. Astook award, US Endocrine Society, 1997; grantee NIH, Am. Cancer Soc., others. Mem. Am. Chem. Soc., Am. Soc. Hypertension, Am. Soc. Clin. Investigation, Am. Thyroid Assn., Assn. Am. Physicians, Am. Fedn. Clin. Research, Endocrine Soc., pres., 2002-2003, Western Assn. Physicians, Western Soc. Clin. Research, Inst. Medicine, NAS.

BAXTER, MARVIN RAY, state supreme court justice; b. Fowler, Calif., Jan. 9, 1940; m. Jane Pippert, June 22, 1963; children: Laura, Brent. BA in Economics, Calif. State U., 1962; JD, Hastings Coll. of Law, 1966. Bar: Calif. 1966. Dep. dist. atty. Fresno County, Calif., 1967-68; assoc. Andrews, Andrews, Thaxter & Jones, 1968-70, ptnr., 1971-82; apptd. sec. to Gov. George Deukmejian, 1983-88; assoc. justice Calif. Ct. Appeal (5th dist.), 1988-90, Calif. Supreme Ct., 1991—. Mem. Jud. Coun. of Calif., chmn. policy coord. and liaison com., 1996-; dir. emeritus Hastings Coll. of Law. Recipient Man of the Yr. award, Armenian Nat. Com., 1991, Armenian Professional Soc., 1993, Mentor award, Fresno County Young Lawyers Assn., 1996. Mem. Fresno County Bar Assn. (bd. dirs. 1977-82, pres. 1981), Calif. Young Lawyers Assn. (bd. gov. 1973-76, sec.-treas. 1974-75), Fresno County Young Lawyers Assn. (pres. 1973-74), Fresno County Legal Svcs., Inc. (bd. dirs. 1973-74), Fresno State U. Alumni Assn. (pres. 1970-71), Fresno State U. Alumni Trust Coun. (pres. 1970-75). Office: Calif Supreme Ct 350 Mcallister St San Francisco CA 94102-4712

BAXTER, RALPH H., JR., lawyer; b. San Francisco, 1946; AB, Stanford U., 1968; MA, Cath. U. Am., 1970; JD, U. Va., 1974. Bar: Calif. 1974. Chmn. Orrick, Herrington & Sutcliffe LLP, San Francisco, 1990—, ptnr., CEO, 1990—. Mem. adv. bd. Nat. Employment Law Inst.; spkr. in field. Author: Sexual Harassment in the Workplace: A Guide to the Law, 1981, Sexual Harassment in the Workplace: A Guide to the Law, 2d rev. edit., 1989, 1994, Manager's Guide to Lawful Terminations, 1983, Manager's Guide to Lawful Terminations, rev. edit., 1991; mem. editl. bd.: Va. Law Rev., 1973—74, mem. editl. adv. bd.: Employee Rels. Law Jour. Named one of 100 most influential lawyers, Nat. Law Jour., 1997, 2000, Calif. Lawyers of Yr., Calif. Lawyer Mag., 2003. Mem.: ABA-labor & employment law sect. (mgmt. co-chmn. com. employment rights & responsibilities in workplace 1987—90, com. EEO), Nat. Employment Law Inst. (adv. bd.), State Bar Calif., Employee Relations Law Jour. (editl. adv. bd.). Office: Orrick Herrington & Sutcliffe LLP The Orrick Building 405 Howard St San Francisco CA 94105 Office Phone: 415-773-5650. Office Fax: 415-773-5759. Business E-Mail: ralphbaxter@orrick.com.

BAXTER, RICHARD ALAN, plastic surgeon, educator; b. Covina, Calif., Oct. 10, 1955; MD, U. Calif., San Diego, 1983. Cert. Am. Bd. Plastic Surgery, 1992. Intern surgery Swedish Med. Ctr., Seattle, 1983—84, resident surgery, 1984—88; fellowship plastic surgery Oreg. Health Scis. U., Portland, 1988—90; pvt. practice Mountlake Terrace, Wash.; chief med. officer Calidora Skin Clinic. Clin. instr. plastic surgery U. Wash. Sch. Medicine. Fellow: ACS; mem.: King County Med. Soc., Wash. State Med. Assn., N.W. Soc. Plastic Surgeons, Internat. Soc. Aesthetic Plastic Surgery, Am. Soc. Aesthetic Plastic Surgery, Am Soc. Plastic Surgeons, Wash. Soc. Plastic Surgeons (past pres.). Office: Plastic Surgery Clinic 6100 219th St SW Ste 290 Mountlake Terrace WA 98043 Office Phone: 425-776-0880. E-mail: drbaxter@drbaxter.com.

BAY, MICHAEL BENJAMIN, film director; b. LA, Feb. 17, 1965; Grad., Wesleyan U. Dir. Got Milk/Aaron Burr TV commerical (Grand Prix Clio award for Commerical Dir. of Yr., Mus. of Modern Art award for Best Campaign of Yr.), various other TV commericals; (films) Bad Boys, 1995, The Rock, 1996, Bad Boys II, 2003; dir., prodr.: (films) Armageddon, 1998, Pearl Harbor, 2001, The Island, 2005, The Transformers, 2007 (Best Movie, MTV Movie Awards, 2008); prodr. (films) The Texas Chainsaw Massacre, 2003, The Amityville Horror, 2005, The Texas Chainsaw Massacre: The Beginning, 2006, The Hitcher, 2007. Named Commerical Dir. of Yr., Directors Guild Am., 1995; named one of 50 Most Powerful People in Hollywood, Premiere mag., 2005. Address: c/o Rob Carlson William Morris Agency One William Morris Pl Beverly Hills CA 90212

BAYDA, EDWARD DMYTRO, retired chief justice; b. Alvena, Sask, Can., Sept. 9, 1931; s. Dmytro Andrew and Mary (Bilinski) B. BA, U. Sask., 1951, LLB cum laude, 1953; LLD (hon.), 1989, LLD (hon.) (hon.), 2006. Bar: Sask. 1954; apptd. Queen's Counsel, 1966. Barrister, solicitor, Regina, Sask., 1953-72; sr. ptnr. Bayda, Halvorson, Scheibel & Thompson, 1966-72; justice Ct. Queen's Bench for Sask., Regina, 1972-74, Ct. Appeal for Sask., Regina, 1974-81; chief justice Sask., Regina, 1981—2006; ret., 2006. Roman Catholic. Home: 3000 Albert St Regina SK Canada S4S 3N7 Office Phone: 306-525-7204.

BAYLESS, BETSEY, state official; b. Phoenix; BA in Latin Am. Studies and Spanish, U. Ariz., 1966; MPA, Ariz. State U., 1974; DHL (hon.), U. Ariz., 2001. V.p. pub. fin. Peacock, Hislop, Staley & Given, Inc., Phoenix; asst. dir. Ariz. Bd. Regents; acting dir. dept. revenue State of Ariz., dir. dept. adminstrn., sec. of state, 1997—2003; dir. Ariz. Dept. Adminstrn., 2003—. Bd. suprs. Maricopa County, 1989-97, chmn. bd., 1992, 94, vice chair, 1997; mem. Ariz. Bd. Investment, 2003—; bd. dirs. Child Help Ariz.; mem. Nat.bd. dirs. U. Ariz. Coll. of Bus. and Pub. Adminstrn.; adv. bd. Ariz. State U. West. Bd. dirs. Xavier Coll. Preparatory Found., Charter 100, Valley Leadership Class VI, Ariz. Rep. Caucus, Ariz. Women's Forum, 4-H Found., Ariz. Cmty. Found.; mem. leadership bd. U. Ariz. Health Svcs.-Phoenix Campus. Named to Hall of Fame, Ariz. State U. Coll. Pub. Programs; recipient Disting. Citizen award U. Ariz. Alumni Assn., Woman of Yr. award Capitol chpt. Bus. and Profl. Women, Disting. Achievement award NEH Fellowship, Achievement award Nat. Assn. Counties, 1993, Citizen award Bur. Reclamation, 1993, Woman of Achievement award Xavier Coll. Preparatory, 1995. Mem. Phi Beta Kappa (Freeman medal 1966). Republican.

BAYLOR, DENIS ARISTIDE, neuroscientist, educator; b. Oskaloosa, Iowa, Jan. 30, 1940; s. Hugh Murray and Elisabeth Anne (Barbou) B.; m. Eileen Margaret Steele, Aug. 12, 1983; children: Denis Murray, Michael Randel; 1 stepchild, Michele Gonelli. BA in Chemistry magna cum laude, Knox Coll., 1961, DS (hon.), 1989; MD cum laude, Yale U., 1965. Post-doctoral fellow Yale Med. Sch., New Haven, 1965-68; staff assoc. NINDS, Bethesda, Md., 1968-70; USPHS spl. fellow Physiol. Lab. Cambridge U., England, 1970-72; assoc. prof. physiology U. Colo. Med. Sch., Denver, 1972—74, Stanford U., 1974-75, assoc. prof. neurobiology, 1975-78, prof. neurobiology, 1978—2001, chmn. dept. neurobiology, 1992-95; sr. sci. officer Howard Hughes Med. Inst., 2004—05; First Annual W.S. Stiles lecturer U. Coll., London, 1989; Jonathan Magnes lecturer Hebrew U., Jerusalem, 1990; Woolsey lectr. U. Wis., 1992; E. Hille lectr. U. Wash., 1995. Mem. NIH Visual Scis. Study Sect., 1984-88, chmn., 1986-88; vis. com. med. scis. Harvard U., 1987-93; chmn. Summer conf. on Vision FASEB, 1989; Wellcome vis. prof. U. Miami, 1995; mem. sci. adv. com. Alcon Rsch. Inst., 1994-99; mem. HHMI Sci. adv. bd. 1997-2003, Med. adv. bd. 1998-01; mem. sci. adv. bd. Found. Fighting Blindness, 1998—; trustee The Grass Found., 1995-99. Mem. editorial bd. Jour. Physiology, 1977-84, Neuron, 1988-93, Jour. Neurophysiology, 1989—, Visual Neurosci., 1990-93, Jour. Neurosci., 1991—; contbr. articles to profl. jours. Recipient Sinsheimer Found. award, 1975, Mathilde Solowey award, 1978, Kayser Internat. award Retina Rsch. Found., 1988, Golden Brain award Minerva Found., 1988, Merit award Nat. Eye Inst., 1990, Alcon Rsch. Inst. award, 1991; Rank Optoelectronics prize Rank Orgn., Eng., 1980; Proctor medal Assn. Rsch. Vision & Ophthalmology, 1986, Von Sallman prize in eye rsch., 1998. Fellow Am. Acad. Arts and Scis.; mem. NAS, Royal Soc. London, Phi Beta Kappa, Alpha Omega Alpha. Avocations: golf, woodworking. Office: 835 Esplanada Way Stanford CA 94305

BAYLOR, DON EDWARD, professional baseball coach, retired professional baseball player; b. Austin, Tex., June 28, 1949; s. George Edward and Lillian Joyce B.; m. Rebecca Giles, Dec. 12, 1987; 1 child by previous marriage, Don Edward. Student, Miami-Dade Jr. Coll., Fla., Blinn Jr. Coll., Brenham, Tex. Outfielder, designated hitter Balt. Orioles, 1970-76, Oakland Athletics, 1976, designated hitter, 1988; outfielder, designated hitter Calif. Angels, 1976-82, NY Yankees, 1982—86, Boston Red Sox, 1986-87; designated hitter Minn. Twins, 1987; hitting coach Milw. Brewers, 1990—91; mgr. Colo. Rockies, Denver, 1992-98, hitting coach, 2008—, Atlanta Braves, 1999; mgr. Chgo. Cubs, 2000—02; bench coach NY Mets, 2003—04; hitting coach Seattle Mariners, 2005. Author: (with Claire Smith) Don Baylor, Nothing But the Truth: A Baseball Life, 1989. Nat. sports chmn. Cystic Fibrosis Found. Recipient Silver Slugger award, 1983, 85, 86, Designated Hitter of Yr. award, 1985, 86, Roberto Clemente award, 1985; named Am. League's Most Valuable Player, 1979, Sporting News Player of Yr., 1979, Nat. League Mgr. of Yr. Sporting News, 1995, Baseball Writers Assn. Am., 1995; named to Am. League All-Star Team, 1979. Achievements include leading the American League in: hit-by-pitch at-bats, 1973, 75, 76, 78, 84-87; sacrifice flies (12), 1978; games (162), runs (120), RBI (139), 1979; member of the World Series Championship winning Minnesota Twins, 1987. Office: Colo Rockies Coors Field 2001 Blake St Denver CO 80205

BAYLOR, ELGIN GAY, former professional sports team executive, retired professional basketball player; b. Washington, Sept. 16, 1934; m. Elaine; 1 child, Krystle. Student, Albertson Coll. Idaho, Caldwell, 1954—55, Seattle U., 1955—57. Forward Mpls./LA Lakers, 1958—71; asst. coach New Orleans Jazz, 1974—76, head coach, 1976—79; exec. v.p., gen. mgr. LA Clippers, 1986—94, v.p. basketball ops., 1994—2008. Named MVP, NCAA Tournament, 1958, NBA Rookie of Yr., 1959, co-MVP, NBA All-Star Game, 1959, NBA Exec. of Yr., 2006; named to NBA All-Star Team, 1959-65, 67-70, All-NBA First Team, 1959-65, 67-69, Naismith Meml. Basketball Hall of Fame, 1977, NBA 35th Anniversary All-Time Team, 1980, NBA 50th Anniversary All-Time Team, 1996.

BAYSINGER, KARA, lawyer; b. St. Cloud, Minn., Aug. 26, 1966; BA in Polit. Sci., U. Mich., 1988; JD, Loyola U., 1994. Bar: Ill. 1994, Calif. 1999. Asst. to gen. counsel Provident Ins. Co., Waukegan, Ill., 1988—90; compliance analyst Benefit Trust Life Ins. Co., Lake Forest, Ill.; asst. v.p. legal and regulatory affairs Celtic Life Ins. Co.; dir.-counsel product approval & compliance Bankers Life and Casualty Co., 1994—97; spl. counsel ins. regulatory practice group Long & Levit LLP, 1997; ptnr. Sonnenschein Nath & Rosenthal LLP, San Francisco, vice chair Ins. Practice Group. Co-chair Calif. adv. bd. BizWorld. Mem.: Calif. Bar Assn., Ill. Bar Assn. Office: Sonnenschein Nath & Rosenthal LLP 525 Market St Ste 2600 San Francisco CA 94105-2734 Office Phone: 415-882-2475. Office Fax: 415-543-5472. Business E-Mail: kbaysinger@sonnenschein.com.

BEA, CARLOS TIBURCIO, federal judge; b. San Sebastian, Spain, Apr. 18, 1934; Student, Menlo Jr. Coll., 1950—51; BA, Stanford U., 1956, JD, 1958. Bar: Calif. 1959. Assoc. Dunne, Phelps & Mills, 1959—66, ptnr., 1967—75; prin., owner Carlos Bea Law Corp., 1975—90; judge San Francisco (Calif.) Superior Ct., 1990—2003, US Ct. Appeals, (9th cir.), San Francisco, 2003—. Office: US Ct Appeals 95 Seventh St San Francisco CA 94103 Office Phone: 415-355-8180.

BEA, ROBERT G., civil engineering educator; BS, U. Fla., 1959, MS, 1960. Sr. staff civl engr. Shell Oil Co., 1959-76; chief engr., v.p. Ocean Engring. Divsn., Woodward-Clyde Cons., 1976-81; v.p. PMB Sys. Engring., Inc., 1981-88; prof. dept. civil engring., naval arch. and offshore engring U. Calif., Berkeley, 1988—. Cons. prof. engring Stanford U., 1985-89. Recipient J. Hillis Miller Engring. award. Mem. ASCE (Croes medal, 1959), Nat. Acad. Engring. Achievements include projects and research in coastal, offshore and ocean engineering; development of methods to define design criteria for fixed and mobile offshor structures; development of guidelines for the requalifications and rehabilitation of marine structures and ships; evaluation of forces due to waves, currents, earthquakes, ice and sea floor slides; development of technology for evaluation of the dynamic response characteristics of marine foundations and structures. Office: U Calif 215 Mclaughlin Hall Berkeley CA 94720-1712

BEADLE, CHARLES WILSON, retired mechanical engineering educator; b. Beverly, Mass., Jan. 24, 1930; s. Thomas and Jean (Wilson) B.; m. Dorothy Elizabeth Struyk, May 5, 1956; children: Steven C., Sara E., Gordon S. BS, Tufts U., 1951; MSE, U. Mich., 1954; PhD, Cornell U., 1961. Registered mech. engr., Calif. Research engr. Gen. Motors Research Labs., Detroit, 1951-54, RCA Research Labs., Princeton, N.J., 1954-57; prof. mech. engring. U. Calif., Davis, 1961-91, ret., 1991. Contbr. articles to profl. jours. Fellow ASME. Home: 420 12th St Davis CA 95616-2023 Office: U Calif Davis Dept Mech Engring Davis CA 95616

BEAKE, JOHN, professional football team executive; m. Marcia Beake; children: Jerilyn, Chip, Christopher. Grad., Trenton State Coll., NJ; M degree, Pa. State U. Asst. coach Pa. State U., 1961-62, Kansas City Chiefs, NFL, 1968-74, New Orleans Saints, NFL, 1976-77; offensive coordinator Colo. State U., 1974-76; dir. profl. personnel Denver Broncos, NFL, 1979-83, dir. football ops., 1983-84, asst. gen. mgr., 1984-85, gen. mgr., 1985-98; v.p. adminstrn. Denver Broncos, 1998—. Office: Denver Broncos 13655 Broncos Pky Englewood CO 80112-4150

BEALL, BURTCH W., JR., architect; b. Columbus, Ohio, Sept. 27, 1925; s. Burtch W. and Etta (Beheler) B.; m. Susan Jane Hunter, June 6, 1949; children: Brent Hunter, Brook Waite. Student, John Carroll U., 1943; BArch, Ohio State U., 1949. Draftsman Brooks & Coddington, Architects, Columbus, 1949-51, William J. Monroe, Architects, Salt Lake City, 1951-53, Lorenzo Young, Architect, Salt Lake City, 1953-54; prin. Burtch W. Beall, Jr., Architect, Salt Lake City, 1954—. Vis. lectr. Westminster Coll., 1955; adj. prof. U. Utah, 1955-85, 92-97; treas. Nat. Coun. Archtl. Registration Bds., 1982-84. Restoration architect Salt Lake City and County Bldg; contbr. projects to: A Pictorial History of Architecture in America, America Restored, This Before Architecture. Trustee Utah Found. for Arch., 1985, pres., 1987-91; mem. Utah State Bd. Fine Arts, 1987-95, chmn., 1991-93; chmn. Utah State Capitol Adv. Com., 1986-90, Western States Art Fedn., Bd. trustees, 1991-94; mem. exec. residence com. State of Utah, 1991-97; mem. Utah: A Guide to the State Found. With USN, 1943-45. Recipient several merit and honor awards; Found. fellow Utah Heritage Found., 1985. Fellow AIA (jury mem. 2000-02, Utah Lifetime Achievement award, 2004); mem. Masons, Sigma Alpha Epsilon. Methodist. Home and Office: 4644 Brookwood Cir Salt Lake City UT 84117-4908

BEALL, DENNIS RAY, artist, educator; b. Chickasha, Okla., Mar. 13, 1929; s. Roy A. and Lois O. (Phillips) B.; 1 son, Garm. Student, Okla. City U., 1950-52; BA, San Francisco State U., 1956, MA, 1958. Registrar Oakland (Calif.) Art Mus., 1958; curator Achenbach Found. for Graphic Arts, Calif. Palace of the Legion of Honor, San Francisco, 1958-1965; asst. prof. art San Francisco State U., 1965-69, assoc. prof., 1969-76, prof. art, 1976-92; prof. emeritus, 1992—. Numerous one-man shows of prints, 1957—, including: Award Exhbn. of San Francisco Art Commn., Calif. Coll. Arts and Crafts, 1978, San Francisco U. Art Gallery, 1978, Los Robles Galleries, Palo Alto, Calif.; numerous group shows 1960— including Mills Coll. Art Gallery, Oakland, Calif., Univ. Gallery of Calif. State U., Hayward, 1979, Marshall-Meyers Gallery, 1979, 80, Marin Civic Ctr. Art Galleries, San Rafael, Calif., 1980, San Francisco Mus. Modern Art, 1985; touring exhibit U. Mont., 1987-91, An Inner Vision, Oysterponds Hist. Soc., Orient, N.Y., 1998, Modernism in Calif. Printmaking, Annex Gallery, Santa Rosa, Calif., 1998, The Stamp of Impulse, Worcester (Mass.) Art Mus., 2001, Haverford Coll., 2001, Palm Springs (Calif.) Desert Mus., 2003, Internat. Print Ctr., N.Y.C., 2003, Cummer Mus. Art and Gardens, Jacksonville, Fla., 2003, Tweed Mus. Art, U. Minn., Duluth, 2006, Pollock-Krasner House, East Hampton, NY, 2006, Eye on the Sixties, Saisset Mus. Santa Clara U., 2008; represented in numerous permanent collections including Libr. of Congress, Washington, Mus. Modern Art, N.Y.C., Nat. Libr. of Medicine, Washington, Cleve. Mus., Whitney Mus., Phila. Mus., U.S. embassy collections, Tokyo, London and other major cities, Victoria and Albert Mus., London, Achenbach Found. for graphic Arts, Calif. Palace of Legion of Honor, San Francisco, Oakland Art Mus., Phila. Free Libr., Roanoke (Va.) Art Ctr., Worcester (Mass.) Art Mus., Whitney Mus. Am. Art, Cleve. Mus., various colls. and univs. in U.S. Served with USN, 1947-50, PTO. Office: San Francisco State Univ Art Dept 1600 Holloway Ave San Francisco CA 94132-1722 Office Phone: 707-632-5124. E-mail: chu2kar@comcast.net.

BEALL, FRANK CARROLL, science director and educator; b. Balt., Oct. 3, 1933; s. Frederick Carroll Beall and Virginia Laura (Ogier) McNally; m. Mavis Lillian Holmes, Sep. 7, 1963; children: Amanda Jane Fee, Mark Walter Beall, Alyssa Joan Beall. BS, Pa. State U., 1964; MS, Syracuse U., 1966, PhD, 1968. Rsch. technologist U.S. Forest Products Lab., Madison, Wis., 1966-68; asst., then assoc. prof. Pa. State U., University Park, 1968-75; assoc. prof. U. Toronto, Can., 1975-77; scientist, mgr. Weyerhaeuser Co., Federal Way, Wash., 1977-88; Fred E. Dickinson chair in wood sci. and tech. U. Calif. Forest Products Lab., Richmond, 1997—, prof., dir., 1988—. Contbr. articles in wood and sci. tech.; patentee for wood forming method, method of measuring content of dielectric materials, vertical progressive lumber dryer, bond strength measurement of composite panel products, hybrid pultruded products and method for their manufacture, pultrusion method for condensation resin injection, others. Fellow Acoustic Emission Working Group (chmn. 1996-98), Internat. Acad. Wood Sci. (sec.-treas. 1996-2002, treas. 2002--); mem. ASTM (com. DO7 on wood, chmn. 1994-98), Internat. Union Forestry Rsch. Orgns. (coord. rsch. group physiomech. properties of wood and wood-based materials), Am. Soc. for Non-destructive Testing, Forest Products Soc. (pres. 2001-02), Soc. Wood Sci. and Tech. (pres. 1991-92). Office: U Calif Forest Products Lab 1301 S 46th St Richmond CA 94804-4600 E-mail: frank.beall@ucop.edu.

BEALL, JIM T., JR., state legislator; b. San Jose, 1952; m Pat; children: two step-sons. BA in Polit. Sci., San Jose State U. Member, San Jose City Council, 80-94; Santa Clara County Board of Supervisors, 96-; California State Assemblyman, District 24, 2006-; chair, Committee on Human Services, 2006-. Democrat. Office: Dist 24 100 Paseo De San Antonio Suite 300 San Jose CA 95113 Office Phone: 408-282-9820. Office Fax: 408-282-8927. Business E-Mail: Assemblymember.Beall@assembly.ca.gov.

BEAN, RUSSELL S., state legislator; m. Teri Bean; children: Annie, Matt. BS, ME, Northern Mont. Coll. Ranch hand, part owner Bean Ranch, Zimmer Ranch, Barrett Ranch, 1970—; Men's Housing Dir. Northern Mont. Coll., 1982—84; tchr., discipline officer, asst. prin. & athletic dir. East Helena Pub. Schs., 1984—2000; prin. & dist. supt. Augusta Pub. Schs., 2000—07; independent contractor bus., 2007—; mem. Dist. 17 Mont. House of Reps., 2008—. Republican. Office: Montana House of Representatives PO Box 200400 Helena MT 59620-0400 Mailing: PO Box 480 Augusta MT 59410-0480 Home Phone: 406-562-3616; Office Phone: 460-444-4800. Office Fax: 460-444-4825. Business E-Mail: russellbean@live.com.

BEAR, GREGORY DALE, writer, illustrator; b. San Diego, Aug. 20, 1951; s. Dale Franklin and Wilma (Merriman) B.; m. Astrid May Anderson, June 18, 1983; children: Erik William, Alexandra. AB in English, San Diego State U., 1973. Tech. writer, host Reuben H. Fleet Space Theater, 1973; freelance writer, 1975—. Author: Hegira, 1979, Psychlone, 1979, Beyond Heaven's River, 1980, Strength of Stones, 1981, The Wind From a Burning Woman, 1983, The Infinity Concerto, 1984, Blood Music, 1985, Eon, 1985, The Serpent Mage, 1986, The Forge of God, 1987, Eternity, 1988, Tangents, 1989, Heads, 1990, Queen of Angels, 1990, Anvil of Stars, 1992, Moving Mars, 1993 (Nebula award 1994), Songs of Earth and Power, 1993, Legacy, 1995, Slant, 1997, Dinosaur Summer, 1998 (Endeavor award 1999), Foundation and Chaos, 1998, Darwin's Radio, 1999 (Endeavor award 2000, Nebula award 2001), Rogue Planet, 2000, Vitals, 2002, Darwin's Children, 2003, Collected Short Stories of Greg Bear, 2003, Dead Lines, 2004; short stories: Blood Music (Hugo and Nebula awards), 1983, Hardfought (Nebula award), 1993, Tangents (Hugo and Nebula awards), 1987; editor: New Legends, 1995. Cons. Citizen's Adv. Council on Nat. Space Policy, Tarzana, Calif. Mem. Sci. Fiction Writers of Am. (editor Forum 1983-84, chmn. grievance com. 1985-86, v.p. 1987, pres. 1988-90). Avocations: book collecting, science, music, movies, history. Home: 506 Lakeview Rd Lynnwood WA 98037-2141

BEARD, FRANK, musician; b. Nov. 6, 1949; married; 2 children. Mem. band, musician ZZ Top, 1970—. Albums include First Album, 1970, Rio Grande Mud, 1972, Tres Hombres, 1973, Fandango, 1975, Tejas, 1976, The Best of ZZ Top, 1977, Deguello, 1979, El Loco, 1981, Eliminator, 1983, Afterburner, 1985, The ZZ Top Sixpack, 1988, Greatest Hits, 1992, One Foot in the Blues, 1994, Antenna, 1994, Rhythmeen, 1996, XXX, 1999, Mescalero, 2003, Live from Texas, 2008. Mem. Sports Car Club Am. inducted Rock and Roll Hall of Fame, 2004. Office: care Warner Bros Records 3300 Warner Blvd Burbank CA 91505-4632

BEARD, RONALD STRATTON, lawyer; b. Flushing, NY, Feb. 13, 1939; s. Charles Henry and Ethel Mary (Stratton) Beard; m. Karin Paridee, Jan. 24, 1991; children: D. Karen, Jonathan D., Dana K. BA, Denison U., 1961; LLB, Yale U., 1964. Bar: Calif. 1964, U.S. Ct. Appeals (9th cir.) 1980, U.S. Dist. Ct. (ctrl. dist.) Calif. 1964. Ptnr. Gibson, Dunn & Crutcher, LA, 1964—2001, mng. ptnr., 1991—97, chmn., 1991—2001. Bd. dir. Callaway Golf, Javo Beverage Co. Trustee Denison U., Granville, Ohio, 1975—, chmn., 1998—2003; mem. Constl. Rights Found., 1994—2006; mem. steering com. Calif. Minority Coun. Program, 1991—2001; bd. dir. Gov.'s Coun. Physical Fitness and Sports, 2005—. Mem.: Calif. Bar Assn., Coto de Caza Golf Club, Chancery Club, City Club. Avocations: sports, travel, golf. Home: 27442 Hidden Trail Rd Laguna Hills CA 92653-5876 Office Phone: 949-451-4089. Business E-Mail: beard@zeughausergroup.com.

BEARD, TIMOTHY R, career officer; b. Mansfield, Ohio, Apr. 12, 1944; m. Melissa Cary Martinez; children: Amanda, Emily, Sarah. Diploma, U.S. Naval Acad., 1966; MS in Aero. Engring., USAF Test Pilot Sch. Commd. ensign USN, 1966, advanced through grades to rear adm.; stationed on USS Forrestal VA-94; dept. head VA-176; with Bur. Naval Pers. Office Sec. Def.; dep. dir. programming OPNAV Staff; commdg. officer Attack Squadron 176, USS Midway Air Wing 5, USS San Diego, USS John F. Kennedy; asst. to dep. chief staff Marine Corps Aviation; comdr. Carrier Group 1 & Tng. Command U.S. Pacific Fleet, dep. comdr., chief staff, comdr., chief, 1998—. Decorated Dep. Superior Svc. Medal, Legion of Merit, Bronze Star, Meritorious Svc. Medal, 11 Strike/Flight Air Medals, others.

BEART, ROBERT W., JR., colon and rectal surgeon, educator; b. Kansas City, Mo., Mar. 3, 1945; s. Robert Woodward and Helen Elizabeth (Wamsley) B.; m. Cynthia Anne, Jan. 23, 1971; children: Jennifer, Kristina, Amy. AB, Princeton U., 1967; MD, Harvard U., 1971. Diplomate Am. Bd. Surgery, Am. Bd. Colon and Rectal Surgery. Intern U. Colo., 1971-72, resident, 1972-76; prof. surgery Mayo Clinic, Scottsdale, Ariz., 1976—87, U. So. Calif., LA, 1992—. Maj. USMC, 1972-83. Fellow Am. Soc. Colon and Rectal Surgery (pres. 1994). Office: 1441 Eastlake Ave Ste 7418 Los Angeles CA 90033 Office Phone: 323-865-3690.

BEATTY, JOHN CABEEN, JR., judge; b. Washington, Apr. 13, 1919; s. John Cabeen and Jean (Morrison) B.; m. Clarissa Hager, Feb. 8, 1943 (dec. Apr. 4 1996); children: John Cabeen III, Clarissa Jean; m. Virginia R. Campbell, May 10, 1997. AB, Princeton U., 1941; JD, Columbia U., 1948. Bar: Oreg. 1948. Pvt. practice law, Portland, Oreg., 1948-70; ptnr. Dusenbery, Martin, Beatty, Bischoff & Templeton, 1956-70, of counsel, 1985-96; judge Cir. Ct., Oreg., 1970-85, sr. judge Oreg., 1985—. Mem. Oreg. Bd. Bar Examiners, 1953-54; chmn. legis. com. Oreg. Jud. Conf., 1976-82; mem. Oreg. CSC, 1962-64, Oreg. Law Enforcement Coun., 1974-77; vice chmn. Oreg. Commn. Jud. Br., 1979-85; vice chmn. Oreg. Criminal Justice Coun., 1985-90. Author: D Day to VE Day, 1946, The Fourth Part of Gaul, 2004, Collected Poems, 1937—2007. Mem. legis. com. Nat. Sch. Bds. Assn., 1966-68, chmn. coun. large city sch. bds., 1967-68; counsel Dem. Party Oreg., 1956-58; co-chmn. Oreg. for Kennedy Com., 1968; bd. dirs. Portland Pub. Schs., 1964-70, chmn., 1967, 69; chmn. policy adv. com. on hazardous waste Dept. Environ. Quality, 1985-86; mem. Mayor's Spl. Rev. Commn., 1986; chmn. various adv. coms. Dept. Environ. Quality, 1987-89; chmn. tech. adv. com. Willamette River Basin Water Quality Study, 1990-94; chmn. city club study Oreg. Initiative and Referendum, 1994-95; chmn. Oreg. Initiative Com., 1996-2000. Capt. AUS, 1941-46, ETO. Decorated Bronze Star medal; recipient City Club of Portland award, 1967. Mem.: ABA, Oreg. Bar Assn., Oreg. Hist. Soc. (dir. 1973—92), City Club (past pres., bd.

govs.), Racquet Club. Address: apt 1029 2545 SW Tervilliges Blvd Portland OR 97201 Home Phone: 503-452-3358, 503-299-1029. Personal E-mail: jcbeatty@comcast.net.

BEATTY, MICHAEL L., lawyer; b. 1947; s. Herbert Francis and Lola (Stuewe) B.; m. Kathleen Murphy; children: Erin, Piper. BA, U. Calif., 1969; JD, Harvard U., 1972. Bar: Tex. 1972. Assoc. mem. Vinson and Elkins, 1972-74; prof. U. Idaho, 1974-79; vis. prof. law U. Wyo., 1980-81; atty. Colo. Interstate Gas Co., 1981-84, gen. counsel, 1984-85; with The Coastal Corp., Houston, 1985-93, exec. v.p., gen. counsel, 1989-93; with Akin, Gump, Strauss, Hauer & Feld LLP, Houston, 1993-98; prin. Michael L. Beatty & Assocs., P.C., Denver, 1998; ptnr. Beatty & Wozniak, P.C., Denver. Chief of staff Colo. Gov. Roy Romer, 1993—95. Office: Beatty & Wozniak PC 216 16th Str Ste 1100 Columbine Plc Denver CO 80202 Office Phone: 303-294-4499. Office Fax: 303-407-4494. Business E-Mail: mbeatty@bwenergylaw.com.

BEATTY, WARREN, actor, film director, film producer; b. Richmond, Va., Mar. 30, 1937; s. Ira O. and Kathlyn (MacLean) Beaty; m. Annette Bening, Mar.12, 1992; children: Kathlyn, Benjamin, Isabel, Ella Corrine. Student, Northwestern U., 1956, Stella Adler Theatre Sch., NYC, 1957. Actor: (films) Splendor in the Grass, 1961, The Roman Spring of Mrs. Stone, 1962, All Fall Down, 1962, Lilith, 1963, Mickey One, 1965, Promise Her Anything, 1965, Kaleidoscope, 1966, The Only Game in Town, 1969, McCabe and Mrs. Miller, 1971, $(Dollars), 1971, The Parallax View, 1974, The Fortune, 1975, Town and Country, 2001; actor, prodr. Bonnie and Clyde, 1967 (Acad. award nomination for Best Actor), Ishtar, 1987; actor, prodr., co-screenwriter Shampoo, 1975 (Acad. award nomination for best screenplay); actor, prodr., co-dir., co-screenwriter, Heaven Can Wait, 1978 (Acad. award nominations for Best Actor, Best Dir. and Best Screenplay); actor, dir., prodr., co-screenwriter, Reds, 1981 (Acad. award for Best Dir., 1981); actor, dir. Dick Tracy, 1990; actor, co-prodr., Bugsy, 1991; actor, prodr., writer Love Affair, 1994, Bulworth, 1998; exec. prodr. The Pick-Up Artist, 1987; actor: (TV appearances) Studio One, 1948, What's My Line, 1950, Vibe, 1997; appeared in Broadway play A Loss of Roses, 1960 Recipient Irving G. Thalberg Memorial award, Acad. Motion Picture Arts & Sciences, 1999, Am. Soc. of Cinematographers Bd. of Governors award, 2000, BAFTA Fellowship, 2002, Kennedy Ctr. Honors, John F. Kennedy Ctr. Performing Arts, 2004, Cecil B. DeMille award, Hollywood Fgn. Press Assn., 2007, Lifetime Achievement award, Am. Film Inst., 2008. Mem. Dirs. Guild Am. Democrat.

BEATUS, BRIAN J., lawyer; b. Queens, NY, Jan. 17, 1967; BSEE cum laude, Boston Univ., 1989, JD, 1993. Bar: NY 1992, DC 1992, Calif. 1999, Pa. (inactive), US Dist. Ct. (no. & ctrl. dist. Calif., ea. dist. Tex.), US Ct. Appeals (Fed., DC, 9th cir.). Ptnr., head Silicon Valley Intellectual Property dept. Pillsbury Winthrop Shaw Pittman, Palo Alto, Calif. Named one of Silicon Valley's Top 300 Lawyers, San Jose mag., 2003, Silicon Valley's Top Legal Eagles, 2004. Mem.: ABA, Am. Intellectual Property Law Assn. Office: Pillsbury Winthrop Shaw Pittman 2475 Hanover St Palo Alto CA 94304-1114 Office Phone: 650-233-4683. Office Fax: 650-233-4545. Business E-Mail: brian.beatus@pillsburylaw.com.

BEAUCHAMP, E(DWARD) WILLIAM, priest, lawyer, university administrator, management educator; b. Detroit, Mich., May 17, 1942; s. Edward F. and Marion K. Beauchamp. BS in Acctg., U. Detroit, 1964, MBA, 1966; postgrad., Mich. State U., 1966-71; JD, U. Notre Dame, 1975, MDiv, 1981; D (hon.), U. Notre Dame Australia, 2005. Bar: Mich. 1975; ordained priest Roman Cath. Ch., Holy Cross Order, 1982. Tchr., assoc. dir. admissions Alma (Mich.) Coll., 1966-71; ptnr. Goggin, Baker and Beauchamp, Alma, 1975-77; asst. prof. mgmt., adminstrv. asst. to exec. v.p. U. Notre Dame, South Bend, Ind., 1980-84, exec. asst. to pres., 1984-87, exec. v.p., 1987—2002; sr. v.p. Univ. Portland, Oreg., 2002—03, pres. Oreg., 2003—. Bd. dirs. Lumina Found. Recipient Wall St. Jour. award, 1964, Bernstein, Bernstein, Wile and Gordon award, 1963. Office: Univ of Portland 5000 N Willamette Blvd Portland OR 97203-5798

BEAUCHAMP, JESSE LEE (JACK BEAUCHAMP), chemistry professor; b. Glendale, Calif., Nov. 1, 1942; m. Patricia Margaret Beauchamp; children: Melissa Ann, Thomas Alton, Amanda Jane, Ryan Howell, Michael Andrew. BS with honors in Chemistry, Calif. Inst. Tech., 1964; PhD in Chemistry, Harvard U., 1967. Arthur Amos Noyes instr. in Chemistry Calif. Inst Tech., Pasadena, 1967-69, asst. prof. chemistry, 1969-71, assoc. prof. chemistry, 1971-74, prof. chemistry, 1974—2000, Mary and Charles Ferkel prof. chemistry, 2000—. Panelist chem. rsch. evaluation Directorate of Chem. Scis. Air Force Office of Sci. Rsch., 1978-81, adv. panelist high energy density materials, 1988-92; exec. com. advanced light source users, LBL, 1984-87; exptl. evaluation com. TRIUMPH, U. B.C., 1985-88; grad. fellow selection panel, NSF, 1986-89; postdoctoral selection panel NATO, 1987-89; mem. com. critical techs.: role of Chemistry and Chem. Engring. Nat. Rsch. Coun., 1991-92; chmn. com. on comml. aviation security Nat. Materials Adv. Bd., Nat. Rsch. Coun., 1994-97; mem. Nat. Materials Adv. Bd. (NRC), 1997-00; commr. White House commn. on aviation safety and security, 1996-97; mem. adv. bd. Inst. Atomic and Molecular Scis., Academica Sinica, Taiwan, 2004-. Mem. editl. adv. bd. Chemical Physics Letters, 1981-87, Jour. Am. Chem. Soc., 1984-87, Jour Physical Chemistry, 1984-87, Organometallics, 1989-92, Interat. Jour. Chemical Kinetics, 1990—, The Ency. Mass Spectrometry, 2000-. Woodrow Wilson fellow Harvard U., 1964-65, NSF grad. fellow, 1965-67; fellow Alfred P. Sloan Found., 1967-70; tchr.-scholar Camille and Henry Dreyfus, 1971-76; meml. fellow John Simon Guggenheim, 1976-77. Fellow AAAS; mem. NAS (com. chem. scis., chem. kinetics subgroup 1980-83), Am. Chem. Soc. (award in pure chemistry 1978, exec. com. divsn. physical chem., 1980-82, Peter Debye award in phys. chemistry 1999, Frank H. Field and Joe L. Franklin award 2003), Am. Assn. Mas. Spectometry, Aircraft Owners and Pilots Assn., Soc. Fellows Harvard U. Office: Calif Inst Tech Dept of Chemistry Noyes Lab 127 # 72 Pasadena CA 91125-0001

BEAUCHAMP, PATRICK L., distributing company executive; Prin., owner Beauchamp Distributing Co., Compton, Calif., 1984—. Office: Beauchamp Distributing Co 1911 S Santa Fe Ave Compton CA 90221-5306 Fax: 310-537-8641.

BEAUMONT, PAMELA JO, marketing professional; b. Valentine, Nebr., July 30, 1944; d. William Henry and Phyllis Faye (Zersen) (Mott) Bostrom; m. Fred H. Beaumont, Apr. 17, 1971 (div. May 1981). BS in Bus., U. Colo., 1966, MBA, 1968. Asst. product mgr. Ore-Ida Foods, Boise, Idaho, 1969-71, product mgr., 1971-73, sr. product mgr., 1973-75, gen. mgr. sales and mktg. services, 1975; v.p. consumer affairs Albertson's Inc., Boise, 1975-76, v.p. mktg., 1976-87; ptnr. Forrest/Beaumont & Andrus, Boise, 1987—; chair Garden City Urban Renewal Agy., 1995—. Home: 9304 N Pebble Falls Ln Boise ID 83714 Office: 4948 Kootenai St Ste 201 Boise ID 83705-2082 E-mail: pamb@spro.net.

BEAUPREZ, BOB (ROBERT L. BEAUPREZ), former congressman; b. Lafayette, Colo., Sept. 22, 1948; m. Claudia Beauprez; children: Joe, Jim, Melanie, John. BS, U. Colo., 1970. Ptnr. Boulder Valley Holsteins, Lafayette, Colo., 1970-89; pres. Indian Peaks, Inc., Lafayette, Colo., 1989—; pres., CEO, chmn. Heritage Bank, Louisville, 1990—; state chmn. Rep. State Ctrl. Com. of Colo., 1999—2002; mem. US Congress from 7th Colo. dist., 2003—07, mem. ways & means com. Pres. Ind. Bankers Colo., 1997-98, chmn. 1998, bd. dirs. 1993-99; vice chmn., policy devel. com. Ind. Com. Bankers Am., 2000-; mem. Rep. Nat. Com. Western State Chmn. Assn., 1999—. Republican.

BEAVER, WILLIAM HENRY, accounting educator; b. Peoria, Ill., Apr. 13, 1940; s. John W. and Ethel M. (Kostka) B.; m. Suzanne Marie Hutton, May 22, 1965; children: Marie, Sarah, David. BBA, U. Notre Dame, 1962, D (hon.), 1998; MBA, PhD, U. Chgo., 1965; D (hon.), Norwegian Sch. Econs., 1996. CPA, Ill. Asst. prof. U. Chgo., 1965—69; assoc. prof. acctg. Stanford U., 1969—72, prof., 1972—, Joan E. Horngren prof., 1977—. Adv. com. on corp. disclosure SEC, 1976-77; cons. Fin. Acctg. Stds. Bd., 1980-86 Author: Financial Reporting: An Accounting Revolution, 1981, 3d edit., 1998; editl. bd.: The Acctg. Rev., 1977-80, Jour. Acctg. Rsch., 1968—, Jour. Acctg. and Econs., 1978—, Fin. Analysts Jour., 1979-98; contbr. articles to profl. jours Recipient Lit. award Jour. Accountancy, 1978, Faculty Excellence award Calif. Soc. CPA, 1978, Graham and Dodd award Fin. Analysts Fedn., 1979, Notable Contbn. to Acct. Lit. award, 1969, 79, 83, Outstanding Rsch. award Inst. Quantitative Rsch. in Fin., 1981, Nat. Acctg. award Alpha Kappa Psi Found., 1982, Disting. Tchg. award Stanford U., 1985, Seminal Contbn. to Acctg. Lit. award, 1989, Outstanding Doctoral Tchg. award, 2005; named to Acctg. Hall of Fame, 1996 Mem. AICPA, Am. Fin. Assn., Am. Acctg. Assn. (v.p. 1981-83, pres. elect 1986-87, pres. 1987-88, disting. internat. lectr. in acct. award 1979, outstanding educator award 1990, Wildman award 1985), Fin. Acctg. Found. (trustee 1993-96), Fin. Svcs. Rsch. Initiative (co-dir. 1992-95) Home: 949 Wing Pl Palo Alto CA 94305-1028 Office: Stanford U Grad Sch Bus Stanford CA 94305

BEBOUT, ELI DANIEL, state legislator; b. Rawlings, Wyo., Oct. 14, 1946; s. Hugh and Dessie Bebout; m. Lorraine J. Tavares; children: Jordan, Jentry, Reagen, Taggert. BSEE, U. Wyo., 1969. With U.S. Energy Co., Riverton, Wyo., 1974-75; field engr. Am. Bechtel Corp., Green River, Wyo., 1975-76; pres. NUPEC Resources, Inc., Riverton, 1976-83, Smith-Collins Pharm. Inc., Riverton, 1983—88; cons. Nucor Inc., Riverton, 1984—2006; v.p. Nucor Drilling, Inc., Riverton, 1987—2001; pres. Nucor Oil & Gas, 1993—2006; mem. Wyo. House of Reps., 1987—2000, minority whip, 1993—94, majority fl. leader, 1997—98, house spkr., 1999—2000; mem. Dist. 26 Wyo. State Senate, 2007—. Bd. dirs. Wyo. Bank Corp.; bd. mem. United Bancorporation Wyo. Past chmn. Wyo. Bus. Alliance; Wyo. Heritage Found.; past chmn. Energy Coun. Republican. Greek Orthodox. Office: Nucor Inc PO Box 112 Riverton WY 82501 Address: 213 State Capitol Building Cheyenne WY 82002 Office Phone: 307-856-0375, 307-777-7881. Office Fax: 307-777-5466. E-mail: senbebout@wyoming.com.*

BECERRA, OCTAVIO, corporate executive chef; b. LA, Oct. 28, 1963; married. Fine arts and photography studies, Santa Monica Coll.; culinary apprenticeship, Joachim Splichal, Calif., Michelin-Star Restaurants, France, Spain. Corp. exec. chef Patina Group LLC, LA.

BECERRA, ROSINA MADELINE, social welfare educator; b. San Diego, Mar. 6, 1939; d. Ray and Ruth (Albanez) B. BA, San Diego State U., 1961, MSW, 1971; PhD, Brandeis U., 1975; MBA, Pepperdine U., 1981. Mathematician United Tech. Corp., Sunnyvale, Calif., 1962-63; with Peace Corps, Washington, 1963-65; probation officer San Diego County Probation Office, 1965-69; research assoc. Brandeis U., Waltham, Mass., 1973-75; assoc. prof. UCLA, 1975-81, prof., 1981—, acting dean, 1989-90, assoc. dean, 1986-89, 92, dean, 1992—, assoc. vice chancellor faculty diversity, 2002—. Author: Defining Child Abuse, 1979, Hispanic Veterans Seek Health Care, 1982, The Hispanic Elderly, 1984 (Choice Mag. Book award 1986); editor: Hispanic Mental Health, 1981; contbr. articles to profl. jours. Ford Found. award, 1980.

BECERRA, XAVIER, United States Representative from California, lawyer; b. Sacramento, Jan. 26, 1958; s. Manuel and Maria Teresa Becerra; m. Carolina Reyes, 1987; children: Clarisa, Olivia, Natalia. BA in Econs., Stanford U., 1980, JD, 1984. Staff atty. Legal Assistance Corp. Ctrl. Mass., 1984—85; dir. dist. office, adminstrv. asst. to Senator Art Torres Calif. State Senate, L.A., 1986; dep. atty. gen. State of Calif., Sacramento, 1987-90; mem. 59th dist. Calif. State Assembly, 1990—92; mem. US Congress from 30st Calif. Dist., 1993—2003, US Congress from 31st Calif. Dist., 2003—, US House Budget Com., US House Ways & Means Com.; vice chmn. US House Democratic Caucus, 2009—. Mem. Mex. Am. State Legislators Policy Inst., Congl. Children's Working Group, Congl. Hispanic Caucus, chair, 1997—98; vice-chair US-Korea Interparliamentary Exchange, Diabetes Caucus; co-chair Congl. Friends of Spain; mem. exec. com. Congl. Asian Pacific Am. Caucus; exec. sec. Dem. Study Grp. Steering Com. Mem. Hispanic Outreach Adv. Bd.; bd. dirs. Nat. PTA; mem. bd. regents Smithsonian Inst.; bd. dirs. Pitzer Coll., Close Up Found. Recipient Edn. award, Hispanic Heritage Found., 2007. Mem.: Assn. Calif. State Attys. & Adminstrv. Law Judges, Calif. Bar Assn., Mexican-Am. Bar Assn. Democrat. Roman Catholic. Avocations: reading, carpentry, golf. Office: US Congress 1119 Longworth Ho Office Bldg Washington DC 20515-0531 also: Dist Office Ste 560 1910 Sunset Blvd Los Angeles CA 90026

BECHTEL, RILEY PEART, engineering company executive; s. Stephen D. Jr. Bechtel. BA in Polit. Sci., Psychology, U. Calif., Davis, 1974; JD, Stanford U., 1979, MBA, 1979. Bar: Calif. 1979. With Bechtel Group, Inc., San Francisco, 1966—79, Thelen, Marrin, Johnson & Bridges, San Francisco, 1979—81; from exec. v.p. to chmn., CEO, dir. Bechtel Corp., 1987—96, chmn., 1996—, CEO, 1996—, dir., 1996—. Mem. Bus. Coun., Bus. Roundtable policy com; bd. dirs. Bechtel Corp., 1987—; bd. dirs., mem. internat. coun. J.P. Morgan Chase; adv. com. Stanford U. Grad. Sch. of Bus.; dean's adv. coun. Stanford Law Sch. Trustee Jason Found. for Edn. Named one of Forbes' Richest Americans, 2006. Fellow: Am. Acad. Arts and Scis.; mem.: Am. Soc. Corp. Execs. (conservation fund corp. coun.), Am. Soc. Civil Engrs. (hon.). Office: Bechtel Corp 50 Beale St PO Box 193965 San Francisco CA 94119-3965

BECHTEL, STEPHEN DAVISON, JR., retired engineering company executive; b. Oakland, Calif., May 10, 1925; s. Stephen Davison and Laura (Peart) Bechtel; m. Elizabeth Mead Hogan, June 5, 1946; 5 children. Student, U. Colo., 1943—44, DSc (hon.), 1981; BS, Purdue U., 1946, D (hon.) in Engring., 1972; MBA, Stanford U., 1948. Registered profl. engr., N.Y., Mich., Alaska, Calif., Md., Hawaii, Ohio, D.C., Va., Ill. Engring. and mgmt. positions Bechtel Corp., San Francisco, 1941-60, pres., 1960-73, chmn. of cos. in Bechtel group, 1973-80; chmn. Bechtel Group, Inc., 1980-90, chmn. emeritus, 1990—, Fremont Group, 1995—. Former chmn., mem. Bus. Coun., life-term counselor, past chmn. Conf. Bd. Trustee, mem., past chmn. bldg. and grounds com. Calif. Inst. Tech.; mem. pres.'s coun. Purdue U.; mem. adv. coun., bd. visitors Inst. Internat. Studies, Stanford; former charter mem. adv. coun. Stanford U. Grad. Sch. Bus. With USMC, 1943-46. Decorated officer French Legion Honor; recipient Disting. Alumnus award, Purdue U., 1964, Ernest C. Arbuckle Disting. Alumnus award, Stanford Grad. Sch. Bus., 1974, Outstanding Achievement in Constrn. award, Moles, 1977, Disting. Engring. Alumnus award, U. Colo., 1979, Chmn.'s award, Am. Assn. Engring. Soc., 1982, Kenneth Andrew Roe award, 2003, Washington award, Western Soc. Engrs., 1985, Herbert Hoover medal, 1980, Nat. Medal Tech., Pres. Bush, 1991, Golden Beaver award, 1992, Oxford Cup award, Beta Theta Pi, 1997, Engr. Distinction award, U. Colo., 2000; named Man Yr. Engring., News-Record, 1974; named one of Forbes' Richest Americans, 2006. Fellow AAAS; mem. ASCE (hon., engring. mgmt. award 1979, pres. award 1985, OPAL award for outstanding lifetime achievement in constrn. 2000), Inst. Chem. Engrs. (U.K., hon.); mem. AIME, NSPE (hon. chmn. Nat. Engrs. Week 1990), NAE (past chmn., Founder's award 1999), Calif. Acad. Scis. (hon. trustee), Am. Soc. French Legion Honor (bd. dirs., Disting. Achievement medal 1994), Royal Acad. Engring. (U.K., fgn.), Pacific Union Club, Bohemian Club, San Francisco Golf Club, Claremont Country Club, Cypress Point Club, Bear River Club (Utah), Wild Goose Club (Calif.), Chi Epsilon, Tau Beta Pi. Office: PO Box 193965 San Francisco CA 94119-3965

BECHTLE, ROBERT ALAN, artist, educator; b. San Francisco, May 14, 1932; m. Nancy Elizabeth Dalton, 1963 (div. 1982); children: Max Robert, Anne Elizabeth; m. Whitney Chadwick, 1982. BA, Calif. Coll. Arts and Crafts, Oakland, 1954, M.F.A., 1958; postgrad., U. Calif.-Berkeley, 1960-61. Graphic designer Kaiser Industries, Oakland, 1956-59; instr. Calif. Coll. Arts and Crafts, 1957-61, assoc. prof. to prof.; lectr. U. Calif.-Berkeley, 1965-66; vis. artist U. Calif.-Davis, 1966-68; assoc. prof. San Francisco State U., 1968-76, prof., 1976-99, prof. emeritus, 1999—. One-man shows Mus. of Art, San Francisco, 1959, 64, Berkeley Gallery, 1965, Richmond Art Ctr. (Calif.), 1965, U. Calif.-Davis, 1967, O.K. Harris Gallery, N.Y.C., 1971, 74, 76, 81, 84, 87, 92, 96, Berggruen Gallery, San Francisco, 1972, E.B. Crocker Art Mus., Sacramento, 1973, Univ. Art Mus., U. Calif.-Berkeley, 1979, O.K Harris Works of Art, N.Y.C., 1981, 84, 87; Daniel Weinberg Gallery, Santa Monica, 1991, Gallery Paul Anglim, San Francisco, 1991, San Francisco Mus. Modern Art, 1991, others; exhibited in group shows San Francisco Art Inst., 1966, Whitney Mus. N.Y.C., 1967, Milw. Art Ctr., 1969, Mus. Contemporary Art, Chgo., 1971, Serpentine Gallery, London, 1973, Toledo Mus. Art, 1975, San Francisco Mus. Modern Art, 1976, 1985, 2005, Pushkin Fine Arts Mus., Moscow, 1978, Pa. Acad. Fine Arts, Phila., 1981, San Antonio Mus. Art, 1981, Pa. Acad. Fine Arts, Phila, 1981, Calif. Palace of Legion of Honor, San Francisco, 1983, Mus. Contemporary Art, L.A., 1984, Univ. Art Mus., U. Calif., Berkeley, 1987, Whitney Mus., N.Y.C., 1991, Fine Arts Mus. San Francisco, 1995, Jaffe Baker Gallery, Boca Raton, Fla., 1997, Young U., Provo, Utah, others; represented in permanent collections Achenbach Found. for Graphic Arts, San Francisco, Chase Manhattan Bank, N.Y.C., E.B. Crocker Art Mus., Sacramento, Gibbes Art Gallery, S.C., High Mus. Art, Atlanta, Hunter Art Mus., Chattanooga, Library of Congress, Washington, Lowe Art Mus.-U. Miami, Coral Gables, Fla., Mills Coll., Oakland, Mus. Modern Art, N.Y.C., Met. Mus., N.Y.C., Neue Gal der Stadt Aachen, West Germany, Oakland Mus., San Francisco Mus. Modern Art, Univ. Art Mus.-U. Calif-Berkeley, Fine Arts Mus. of San Diego, Rose Art Mus., Brandeis U., Waltham, Mass., U. Nebr.-Lincoln, Whitney Mus., N.Y.C., Guggenheim Mus., N.Y.C. Served with U.S. Army, 1954-56. Recipient James D. Phelan award, 1965, Acad. award Am. Acad. Arts and Letters, 1995; named Nat. Academician, Nat. Acad. Design, 1993; Nat. Endowment for Arts grantee, 1977, 83, 89, Guggenheim grantee, 1986. Office: San Francisco State U 1600 Holloway Ave Dept Art San Francisco CA 94132-1722

BECHTOLSHEIM, ANDY (ANDREAS VON BECHTOLSHEIM), information technology executive; b. Germany, 1956; Grad., U. Germany; MS in Computer Engring., Carnegie Mellon U., Pitts., 1976; PhD student in Computer Sci. and Elec. Engring., Stanford U., Calif., 1977—82. Co-founder Sun Microsystems, Inc., Santa Clara, Calif., 1982, various roles including v.p. tech., chief arch., workstation product line, 1982—95, sr. v.p., chief arch. Network Sys., 2004—08, still hold part-time role in product design, 2008—; founder, pres. Granite Systems (acquired by Cisco Sys.), 1995—96; various positions including v.p. engring., v.p., gen. mgr., Gigabit Sys. Bus. Unit Cisco Sys., 1996—2003; co-founder Kealia, Inc. (acquired by Sun Microsystems), Palo Alto, Calif., 2001, pres., 2003—04; co-founder Arastra, Menlp Park, Calif., 2004; chmn., chief develop. officer Arista Networks, Inc. (formerly known as Arastra), Menlo Park, Calif., 2008—. Co-founder HighBAR Ventures, 1999. Co-founder Carnegie Mellon U. West Coast Campus, Mountain View, Calif. Recipient Stanford Entrepreneur Co. of Yr. award, Smithsonian Leadership award for Innovation; Fulbright Scholarship, German Nat. Merit Found. Scholarship. Mem.: NAE. Achievements include inventing the "Stanford University Network workstation" which eventually became the Sun-1 Workstation and was instrumental in launching other successful Sun products, including the SparcStation 1; the latest design will be a supercomputer to be named the Sun Constellation System that will compete for the title as the world's fastest when installation is completed in 2007. Office: Arista Networks Inc 275 Middlefield Rd Ste 50 Menlo Park CA 94025 Office Phone: 650-960-1300. Office Fax: 405-276-3804.

BECK, COLLEEN MARGUERITE, archaeologist; b. San Jose, Calif., Feb. 21, 1951; d. William Robert and Willa Rose (Moore) Beck; m. William Keith Kolb; children: William Logan Kolb, Alexa Rose Kolb. BA, U. Calif., Berkeley, 1973, MA, 1974, PhD, 1979. Dir. Agy. for Conservation Archaeology, Eastern N.Mex. U., Portales, 1980-83, asst. prof., 1983-84; rsch. assoc. Lowie Mus. Anthropology, Berkeley, 1985-89; asst. rsch. prof. Desert Rsch. Inst., Las Vegas,

1990-92, dep. dir. quaternary scis. ctr., 1992-98, assoc. rsch. prof., 1993-98, rsch. prof., exec. dir., 1999—. Postdoctoral fellow Carnegie Mus. Natural History, Pitts., 1979-80; mem. N.Mex. Hist. Preservatio Adv. Bd., Santa Fe, 1981-86; mem. San Joaquin County Historic Records Commn., Stockton, Calif., 1986-89. Author: Ancient Roads on the North Coast of Peru, 1979; editor: Views of the Jornada Mogollon, 1984; author articles. Mem. tech. adv. bd. Las Vegas Sch. Dist., 1994-96; mem. tech. adv. bd. Bur. Land Mgmt., 1995—. Las Vegas Historic Preservation Commn., 1996—. NSF fellow, 197-76; Tinker Found. grantee, 1974-77. Fellow Am. Anthropology Assn. (life); mem. Soc. for Am. Archaeology, Nev. Archaeology Assn. (bd. dirs. 1993—, pres. 1995—), Archaeo-Nev. Soc., Nat. Trust for Hist. Preservation, Inst. Andean Studies (life), Nev. State Mus. Hist. Soc. Avocation: piano.

BECK, DENNIS L., judge; b. Belen, N.Mex., Dec. 7, 1947; m. Christine T. Beck, Mar. 2, 1968. BA, Coll. William & Mary, 1969, JD, 1972. Bar: Calif. 1972, U.S. Dist. Ct. (ea. dist.) Calif. 1978, U.S. Ct. Appeals (9th cir.) Calif. 1978. Asst. dist. atty. Fresno (Calif.) County, 1972-78, 79-83, 1987-90; assoc. Crossland Crossland Caswell & Bell, Fresno, 1978-79; judge Kings County Superior Ct., Hanford, Calif., 1983-85; assoc. Thomas, Snell, et al., Fresno, 1985-87; magistrate judge U.S. Dist. Ct. (ea. dist.) Calif., Fresno, 1990—. Office: US Dist Ct 1130 O St Rm 3489 Fresno CA 93721-2201

BECK, EDWARD WILLIAM, lawyer; b. Atchison, Kans., Aug. 19, 1944; s. Russell Niles and Lucille Mae (Leighton) B.; m. Marshia Ablon, June 24, 1966; children: Michael Adam, David Gordon, Stephen Jared BA cum laude, Yale U., 1967; JD cum laude, Harvard U., 1972. Bar: Calif. 1972. Assoc. firm Pillsbury, Madison & Sutro, San Francisco, 1972-77; gen. counsel Pacific Lumber Co., San Francisco, 1977-86, sec., 1978-86, v.p., 1980-86, dir., 1985-86; v.p., gen. counsel, sec. Yamanouchi Consumer Inc. (formerly Shaklee Corp.), San Franciso, Pleasanton, Calif., 1986-87, sr. v.p., gen. counsel, sec., 1987—2004, exec. v.p., gen. counsel, sec., 2004; sr. v.p., gen. counsel, sec. Mervyn's LLC, 2005—08; pres., CEO D20PS Internat., Inc., 2008—09; exec. v.p., gen. cons., sec. 24 Hour Fitness Worldwide, Inc., 2009—. Bd. dirs. Yamanouchi Consumer Inc. (formerly Shaklee Corp.), mem. audit com., 2001—04. Trustee, mem. exec. com. San Francisco Conservatory Music, 1988—, co-chmn. acad. affairs com., 1989—91, chmn. presdl. search com., 1991, chair trustees and officers com., 1993—96, exec. vice chair, 1994—2008, vice chair, 2008—, chair conservatory 2006 com., 1996—99, chmn. maj. gifts com., 1999—2001, co-chmn. instl. advancement com., 1999—2001, mem. bldg. com., 2000—05, chair new conservatory com., 2004—06; mem. law com. United Way of Bay Area Campaign, 1991—2000, chmn., 1992. Mem. ABA, Calif. Bar Assn., San Francisco Bar Assn. (bd. dirs. 1991-94, nominating com. 1993), Bay Area Gen. Counsels Group (chmn. 1991), San Francisco C. of C. (leadership coun. 1987—, gen. coun., bd. dirs., exec. com. 1993-96), San Francisco Yale Alumni Assn. (schs. com.). Office: Mervyns LLC 22301 Foothill Blvd MS 4135 Hayward CA 94541-2771

BECK, GLENN, radio personality; b. Mt. Vernon, Wash., Feb. 10, 1964; m. Tania Beck; 4 children. Disc jockey WKCI-FM (KC101), Hamden, Conn.; talk radio host WELI, Hamden, Conn., The Glenn Beck Program, WFLA-AM, Tampa, Fla., 2000—02; nat. talk radio host The Glenn Beck Program, Premiere Radio Networks, 2002—; TV show host Glenn Beck on Headline News, CNN, 2006—08, Glenn Beck, Fox News Channel, 2009—. Founder, editor Fusion Mag., 2005. Author: The Real America.: Messages from the Heart and Heartland, 2003, An Inconvenient Book: Real Solutions to the World's Biggest Problems, 2007 (#1 NY Times bestseller), The Christmas Sweater, 2008 (#1 NY Times bestseller, #1 Publishers Weekly bestseller); host (polit. comedy tour) Beck '08: Unelectable, 2008, contbg. writer/host (morning talk show) ABC's Good Morning America, 2006—; regular segment 'At your Beck and Call' (TV series) The O'Reilly Factor. Recipient Marconi Radio award for Network Syndicated Personality of Yr., Nat. Assn. Broadcasters, 2008. Republican. Church Of The Latter Day Saints. Office: Premier Radio Networks 15260 Ventura Blvd Sherman Oaks CA 91403 E-mail: me@glennbeck.com.*

BECK, JOHN CHRISTIAN, physician, educator; b. Audubon, Iowa, Jan. 4, 1924; s. Wilhelm and Marie (Brandt) Beck. MD, McGill U., 1947, MSc, 1951, DSc (hon.), 1994; PhD (hon.), Ben Gurion U. of Negev, 1981. Diplomate Am. Bd. Internal Medicine (chmn., dir.). Intern Royal Victoria Hosp., Montreal, 1947—48, sr. asst. resident, 1948—49, physician-in-chief, endocrinologist, 1964—74; chmn. dept. medicine and dir. Univ. Clinic McGill U., 1964—74; prof. medicine U. Calif., San Francisco, 1974—79; dir. Robert Wood Johnson Clin. Scholars Program, 1973—78; prof. geriat. medicine and gerontology UCLA, 1979—, dir. academic geriat. resource ctr., 1984—90; dir. long term car gerontology ctr. UCLA/U. So. Calif., 1980—85; dir. Calif. Geriatric Edn. Ctr., 1987—97, emeritus dir., 1993—; dir. multicampus program in geriat. medicine and gerontology UCLA, 1979—93. Pres. Am. Bd. Med. Spltys.; vis. prof. numerous univs.; Simeone lectr. Brown U., 1977; John McCreary Meml. lectr. U. B.C., 1985; Bruce Hall Meml. lectr. Garvan Inst. Med. Rsch., U. NSW, Sydney, 1989; Allen T. Bailey Meml. lectr. U. Sask., Canada, 1989; delivered Chaikin Oration, Australian Acad. Tech. Scis. and Engring., 2004—; Froehlich vis. prof. Royal Soc. Medcine, England, 2006. Editl. bd. Jour. Clin. Endocrinology and Metabolism, Current Topics in Exptl. Endocrinology, Psychiatry in Medicine, Health Policy and Edn., Jour. Am. Bd. Family Practice, cons. editor Roche Lab. Series on Geriatrics and Gerontology. Recipient Lifetime award, Ben Gurion U. of Negev, Israel, 1985, Ann. Gerontology award in edn., Jewish Homes for the Aging, 1994, commendation, City of L.A., 1994. Master: ACP (Philips award 2003); fellow: AAAS, Am. Fedn. on Aging Rsch. (Irving S. Wright award 1991), Gerontol. Soc. Am. (mem. editl. bd. jour., Joseph T. Freeman award 1990, Donald P. Kent award 2001), Am. Geriat. Soc. (Milo F. Leavitt Meml. award 1988), Western Assn. Physicians, Internat. Soc. Neuroendocrinology, Assn. Am. Med. Colls., Can. Assn. Profs. Medicine (Ronald V. Christie award 1987), Can. Physiol. Soc., McGill Osler Reporting Soc. (sec.), Royal Soc. Can., Inst. Medicine, Internat. Soc. Endocrinology (sec.-gen.), Can. Soc. Clin. Investigation (pres.), Endocrine Soc. (v.p., chmn. postgrad. assembly), Am. Fedn. Clin. Rsch. (coun. East divsn.), Can. Med. Assn. (postgrad. edn. com.), Am. Diabetes Assn., Can. Diabetes Assn., Royal Coll. Physicians Can. (mem. coun., Duncan Graham award 1990), Royal Coll. Physicians London, Montreal Physiol. Soc., Laurentian Hormone Conf. (bd. dirs.), Am. Clin. and Climatol. Assn., Can. Med. Protective Assn., Soc. Exptl. Biology and Medicine (mem. editl. bd. jour.), Alpha Omega Alpha, Sigma Xi; mem.: Australian Acad. Technol. Scis. and Engring. (Chaikin Oration 2004), Assn. for Gerontology in Higher Edn. (Disting. Svc. Recognition award 2001). Office: 1562 Casale Rd Pacific Palisades CA 90272-2714 Fax: 310-454-1944. Business E-Mail: egebjcb@ucla.edu.

BECK, MARILYN MOHR, columnist; b. Chgo., Dec. 17, 1928; d. Max and Rose (Lieberman) Mohr; m. Roger Beck, Jan. 8, 1949 (div. 1974); children: Mark Elliott, Andrea; m. Arthur Levine, Oct. 12, 1980. AA, U. So. Calif., 1950. Freelance writer nat. mag. and newspapers, Hollywood, Calif., 1959-63; Hollywood columnist Valley Times and Citizen News, Hollywood, Calif., 1963-65; West Coast editor Sterling Mag., Hollywood, Calif., 1963-74; free-lance entertainment writer LA Times, Calif., 1965-67; Hollywood columnist Bell-McClure Syndicate, 1967-72; chief Bell-McClure Syndicate (West Coast bur.), 1967-72; Hollywood columnist NANA Syndicate, 1967-72; syndicated Hollywood columnist NY Times Spl. Features, 1972-78, NY Times Spl. Features (United Feature Syndicate), 1978-80, United Press abroad, 1978-80, Internat. Editors News and Features, Chgo. Tribune/NY Daily News Syndicate, 1980-97; columnist TV Guide, 1989—92, Creators Syndicate, 1997—. Creator, host Marilyn Beck's Hollywood Outtakes spls. NBC, 1977, 78; host Marilyn Beck's Hollywood Hotline, Sta. KFI, LA, 1975-77; Hollywood reporter Eyewitness News, Sta. KABC-TV, LA, 1981, (TV program) PM Mag., 1983-88; on-air corr. E! TV, 1993-99, CompuServe Entertainment Authority, 1994-96, eDrive Internet Authority, 1996-97, e!online Internet Hollywood Authority, 1997-2000, Compuserve, Netscape, 2000—, aeNTV.com, 2001-02; author: (nonfiction) Marilyn Beck's Hollywood, 1973, (novel) Only Make Believe, 1988; co-author: Unfinished Lives, What If...?, 1996. Recipient Citation of Merit LA City Coun., 1973, Press award Pub. Guild Am., 1974, Bronze Halo award So. Calif. Motion Picture Coun., 1982. Address: 4926 Delos way Oceanside CA 92056

BECK, PAUL E., state legislator; b. Mitchell, SD, Nov. 5, 1964; m. Rena Beck; children: Connor, Logan. BA in Tourism & Bus. Recreation, U. Colo., 1987. Builder Paul Beck Constrn., 1991—2000; home insp. Mountain Home Inspections, 2000—; chmn Carbon Co. Dems., 2002—05; mem Dist. 59 Mont. House of Reps., 2008—. Democrat. Office: Montana House of Representatives PO Box 200400 Helena MT 59620-0400 Mailing: PO Box 1315 Red Lodge MT 59068-1315 Home Phone: 406-425-2310; Office Phone: 406-444-4800. Office Fax: 406-444-4825. Business E-Mail: paul@beckforcarboncounty.com.

BECK, TOM, state legislator, rancher; b. Deer Lodge, Mont., Nov. 14, 1939; m. Kay Beck. Student, Mont. State U. Rancher; mem. Mont. Senate, Dist. 28, Helena, 1987—; chair legis. adminstrn. com.; mem. fin. and claims com., rules com., fish and game com.; mem. agr., livestock and irrigation com.; majority whip Mont. Senate, 1995. Chmn. Powell Hosp. Bd.; former Powell County Commr. Mem. Mont. Assn. Counties (pres.). Republican. Office: Capitol Sta Helena MT 59620

BECKER, CHRISTOPHER, educator, chef; Profl. chef; founder Calif. Sch. Culinary Arts, Pasadena, 1994—, Kitchen Acad., Hollywood, 2005—, Sacramento, 2006—. Mem.: Calif. Assn. Pvt. Postsecondary Schools (treas.). Office: Kitchen Academy Divsn Career Education Corp 521 E Green St Pasadena CA 91101-5221 Office Phone: 626-484-1652. Office Fax: 626-441-0592.

BECKER, DAVID KENNETH, pediatrician, educator; b. Jan. 23, 1967; MPH, U. NC Chapel Hill, 1996. Cert. Am. Bd. Pediat. Resident U. NC Chapel Hill, 1996—99; with Doctors Without Borders; asst. clinical prof. dept. pediat. U. Calif. San Francisco, 2001—, Bravewell fellow Osher Ctr. Integrative Medicine. Office: Dept Pediat Mt Zion U Calif San Francisco Box 1660 2330 Post St 320 San Francisco CA 94143-1660 Office Phone: 415-885-7478. Office Fax: 415-885-3790. Business E-Mail: beckerda@peds.ucsf.edu.

BECKER, DONALD PAUL, surgeon, neurosurgeon; b. Cleve., 1935; MD, Case Western Res. U., 1961. Diplomate Am. Bd. Neurol. Surgery. Intern U. (Cleve.) Hosps., 1961-62, resident in surgery, 1962-63, resident in neurol. surgery, 1963-67; fellow in neurosurgery NIH, Bethesda, Md., 1966; prof. UCLA Med. Ctr., 1967-71; prof., chmn. divsn. neurol. surgery Med. Coll. Va., Richmond, 1971-85; chief neurosurgery UCLA Med. Ctr., 1985—; prof., chmn. divsn. neurol. surgery Med. Coll. Va., Richmond, 1971-85. Mem. ACS, AMA. Office: UCLA Med Ctr Divsn Neurosurgery PO Box 957039 Los Angeles CA 90095-7039

BECKER, JOANN ELIZABETH, retired insurance company executive; b. Chester, Pa., Oct. 29, 1948; d. James Thomas and Elizabeth Theresa (Barnett) Clark; m. David Norbert Becker, June 7, 1969. BA, Washington U., St. Louis, 1970, MA, 1971. CLU, ChFC, FLMI/M, CFA. Tchr. Kirkwood (Mo.) Sch. Dist., 1971-73; devel. and sr. devel. analyst Lincoln Nat. Life Ins. Co., Ft. Wayne, Ind., 1973-77, systems programming specialist, 1977-79, sr. project mgr., 1979-81, asst. v.p., 1981-85, 2d v.p., 1985-88, v.p., 1988-91; pres., CEO The Richard Leahy Corp., Ft. Wayne, 1991-93; pres. Lincoln Nat. Corp. Equity Sales Corp, Ft. Wayne, 1993-94; v.p. portfolio mgmt. group Lincoln Nat. Investment Mgmt. Co., Ft. Wayne, 1994-97, dir. investment mgmt., sr. v.p., 1997—2000, ret., 2000. Contbr. articles to profl. jours. Bd. dirs. Ind. Humanities Coun., Indpls., 1991-96, treas., exec. com., 1994-95, devel. com., 1995-96; bd. dirs. Auburn Cord Duesenberg Mus., Ind., 1995-2000, devel. and exec. com., 1997-2000; bd. dirs. Priest Lake Mus., 2005—; pres. Priest Lake Mus. Assn., 2006—. Named Women of Achievement, YWCA, Ft. Wayne, 1986, Sagamore of Wabash, Gov. State of Ind., 1990. Fellow Life Mgmt. Inst. Soc. Ft. Wayne (pres. 1983-84, honors designation 1980); mem. Life Ins. Mktg. Rsch. Assn. (Leadership Inst. fellow, exec. com. 1993-94, fin. svcs. com. 1993-94), Am. Mgmt. Assn., So. Ariz. Watercolor Guild (chair fundraising com. 2006—), Ft. Wayne C. of C. (chmn. audit-fin. com. 1989-2000).

BECKER, NANCY ANNE, former state supreme court justice; b. Las Vegas, May 23, 1955; d. Arthur William and Margaret Mary (McLoughlin) Becker. BA, U.S. Internat. U., 1976; JD, George Washington U., 1979. Bar: Nev. 1979, D.C. 1980, Md. 1982, U.S. Dist. Ct. Nev. 1987, U.S. Ct. Appeals (9th cir.) 1987. Legis. cons. D.C. Office on Aging, Washington, 1979—83; assoc. Goldstein & Ahalt, College Park, Md., 1980—82; pvt. practice Washington, 1982—87; dep. city atty., prosecutor criminal div. City of Las Vegas, 1983; judge Las Vegas Mcpl. Ct., 1987—89, Clark County Dist. Ct., Las Vegas, 1989—99, chief judge, 1993—94; assoc. justice Nev. Supreme Ct., 1999—2006. Cons. MADD, Las Vegas, 1983—87. Contbr. articles to profl. jours. Pres. Clark County Pro Bono Project, Las Vegas, 1984—95. Mem.: NCCJ, Am. Businesswomen's Assn. (treas. Las Vegas chpt. 1985—86), Southern Nev. Assn. Women Attys. (past officer), Soroptimist Internat., Vietnam Vets. Am., Las Vegas and Latin C. of C. Mailing: PO Box 80332 Las Vegas NV 89180

BECKER, RALPH ELIHU, JR., Mayor, Salt Lake City, Utah; b. Washington, May 30, 1952; s. Ralph Elihu Becker and Ann (Watters); m. Nancy Becker, 1980; children: Will Watters, Derek James. Student, Lafayette Coll., 1970—71; BA in Am. Civilization, U. Pa., 1973; JD, U. Utah, 1978, MS in Geography and Planning, 1982. Bar: Utah 1978. Former ranger & firefighter Grand Canyon Nat. Park Svc.; v.p. Bonneville Associates, 1978—81; co-owner, prin., pres., chmn. Bear West, 1985—2006; spl. asst. to dir. Utah Dept. Natural Resources, 1981—83; dep. dir. & state planning coord. Utah Office of Planning and Budget, 1983—85; planning coord. & dept. dir. Governor's Office of Planning and Budget; mem. Utah House of Reps., 1996—2007, minority whip leader, 1999—2000, minority leader, 2001—02, 2005—07; mayor City of Salt Lake City, 2008—. Bd. mem. Salt Lake City Planning Commn., 1988—96, Pub. Utilities & Tech. Com., 1997—; mem. Exec. Appropriations Com., Polit. Subdivisions Com., Legislature Mgmt. Com., Transp. Com., Utah Constitutional Rev. Commn.; adj. prof. U. Utah Coll. Architecture and Planning, 1986—. Contbr. articles to clean air, solar energy law, pub. land, environ. planning to profl. jours. Cmty. mem. Memory Grove Oversight Com.; mem. Capitol Preservation Bd., Policy Consensus Initiative; chmn. Salt Lake City Zoning Rewrite Com.; steering com. mem. Envision Utah; regional adv. com. mem. Rocky Mountain Land Use Inst. Recipient Pub. Svc. award, Utah Assn. of Special Districts, 2004, Outstanding Leadership award, Utah Assn. of Energy Users, 2006, Going to Bat award, Utah Heritage Found., 2006; Flemming Fellow, Ctr. of Policy Alternatives, 1999, Fellow, Dem. Leadership Coun., 2000, Toll Fellow, Coun. State Govts., 2004. Fellow: America Inst. Cert. Planners; mem.: Utah State Bar (chmn. 1986—88), Am. Planning Assn. (pres. 1988—90, Outstanding Svc. award 1983, 1986, Outstanding Achievement award 1989). Democrat. Avocations: kayaking, hiking, backcountry skiing, river rafting, backpacking. Office: PO Box 145474 Salt Lake City UT 84114-5474 Office Phone: 801-535-7704. Business E-Mail: mayor@slcgov.com.*

BECKER, RANDI, state legislator; m. Bob Becker; children: Reena, Rhyan. Attended, Green River CC, Auburn, Wash., Highline CC, Des Moines, Wash. Former flight attendant, realtor & medical receptionist; former administr. surgical center, Puyallup, Wash.; co-devel. obesity surgical practice; formerly with Good Samaritan Hosp.; started several hosp.-owned clinics & urgent care center; mem. Dist. 2 Wash. State Senate, 2008—. Mem.: NRA, Wash. State Med. Mgrs. Assn., Wash. Horsemen, Inc. Republican. Avocations: fishing, hunting, horseback riding, gardening. Office: 115B Irv Newhouse Bldg PO Box 40402 Olympia WA 98504-0402 Office Phone: 360-786-7602, 800-562-6000 (toll free). Office Fax: 360-786-7819.

BECKER, STEPHEN A., physicist; b. Evanston, Ill., Sept. 11, 1950; s. John N. and Irene A. (Wlodarski) B.; m. Wendee M. Brunish, May 30, 1980. BA, Northwestern U., 1972; MS, Case Western Res. U., 1974; PhD, U. Ill., 1979. Rsch. and teaching assoc. U. Ill., Champaign, Ill., 1979—80; postdoctoral fellow Calif. Inst. Tech., Pasadena, 1980—82; tech. staff mem. Los Alamos Nat. Lab., N.Mex., 1983—. Contbr. articles to Astrophys. Jour. Recipient Recognition of Excellence award U.S. Dept. Energy, 1999, R&D 100 award, 1999, Def. Program Excellence award, 2000, Disting. Performance award, Los Alamos Lab., 2005. Mem. Am. Astron. Soc., Internat. Astron. Union. Roman Catholic. Office: Los Alamos Nat Lab PO Box 1663 Mail Stop T085 Los Alamos NM 87545 Office Phone: 505-667-8964. Business E-Mail: sab@lanl.gov.

BECKER, STEPHEN ARNOLD, museum administrator; b. Redwood City, Calif., Aug. 24, 1951; s. Leo H. and May B. (Goldberg) B.; m. Beverly Nichols-Fredotovich, July 31, 1977; 1 child, Joseph Nikola. Asst. curator mus. Ind. U., Bloomington, 1973-77, lectr. folklore dept., 1975-77; historian Sacramento History Ctr., 1977-78; dir. history divsn. County Pks. Dept., Riverside, Calif., 1979-85; asst. dir. Mus. Internat. Folk Art, Santa Fe, 1985-89; dir. Mus. Indian Arts and Culture/Lab. Anthropology, Santa Fe, 1989-95; pres., CEO, Turtle Bay Mus. and Arboretum, Redding, Calif., 1995-98; mus. cons. Redding, 1998-2000; deputy dir. devel. & external affairs Lindsay Wildlife Mus., Walnut Creek, Calif., 1998—; dir. external affairs Zeum Art and Tech. Ctr., San Francisco, 2000—. Mem. Am. Assn. Museums, Am. Folklore Soc. Office: 221 4th St San Francisco CA 94103-3116 E-mail: sbecker@zeum.org.

BECKER, WILLIAM WATTERS, theater producer; b. New Orleans, Apr. 1, 1943; s. Ralph Elihu and Ann Marie (Watters) B.; m. Joan A. Alper; children: Kirsten Anne, Gevry Danielle. BA, Dartmouth Coll., 1964, MBA, 1965; LLB, Harvard U., 1968. Staff atty., Reginald Heber Smith fellow Community Legal Assistance Office, Cambridge, Mass., 1968-69; ptnr. Landfield, Becker & Green, Washington, 1969-89, Breed, Abbott & Morgan, 1989-92; prin. William W. Becker, Chtd., Washington, 1993—2001. Gen. counsel, dir. Voice Found., N.Y.C., 1976-2001; assoc. gen. counsel John F. Kennedy Ctr. Performing Arts, Washington, 1977-93, gen. counsel, 1993-2001; gen. counsel Kennedy Ctr. Prodns., Inc., 1972-2001; dir. Greater Washington Bd. Trade, 1978-92, gen. counsel, 1981-85; chmn. ShowOnDemand.com, Inc., 2000—, TheaterDreams, Inc., 2000-, The Chgo. Theatre, 2004—, The Kodak Theatre, 2005—. Prodr.: (plays) The Dinner Party, 2001, Urinetown, 2002, Into the Woods, 2003, Good Vibrations, 2004. Home: 7252 Stagecoach Dr Park City UT 84098 Home Phone: 435-258-6300. E-mail: beckerw@theatredreams.com.

BECKERLE, MARY C., cell biologist, educator; BA, Wells Coll., 1976; PhD, U. Colo., Boulder, 1982. With U. Utah, 1986—, disting. prof. biology, adj. prof. oncological scis., Ralph E. and Willia T. Main Presdl. Endowed Chair in Cancer Rsch., 1999—; dep. dir., sr. dir. lab. rsch. Huntsman Cancer Inst. (HCI), Utah, exec. dir. Utah, 2006—. Mem. pub. affairs adv. com. Fedn. Am. Societies for Exptl. Biology, 1997; organizer Gordon Rsch. Conf. on Motile and Contractile Sys., Human Frontiers in Sci. Conf. Contbr. articles; mem. of several editl. bds., assoc. editor Molecular Biology of the Cell. Recipient Sr. Rsch. award, Am. Cancer Soc., Utah Governor's award for sci. and tech., 2001, Rosenblatt prize for excellence, U. Utah, 2007; named established investigator, Am. Heart Assn.; Guggenheim Fellow, 2000, Rothschild-Yvette Mayet award Scholar, Curie Inst. Paris, 2000. Fellow: Am. Acad. Arts & Scis.; mem.: Am. Soc. Cell Biology (pres. 2006, organizer of meetings). Office: Huntsman Cancer Inst 2000 Circle of Hope Salt Lake City UT 84112 Business E-Mail: mary.beckerle@hci.utah.edu.

BECKHAM, STEPHEN DOW, history educator; b. Marshfield, Oreg., Aug. 31, 1941; s. Ernest Dow and Anna Marie (Adamson) B.; m. Patricia Joan Cox, Aug. 26, 1967; children: Andrew Dow, Ann-Marie Catherine. BA, U. Oreg., 1964; MA, UCLA, 1966, PhD, 1969. Lectr. Long Beach (Calif.) State U., 1968-69; from asst. to assoc. prof. Linfield Coll., McMinnville, Oreg., 1969-77; from assoc. prof. to prof. Lewis and Clark Coll., Portland, Oreg., 1977-93, Pamplin prof. history, 1993—, named endowed chair in history, 1993—. Assoc. Heritage Rsch. Assoc., Eugene, Oreg., 1979—, USA Rsch. Author: Requiem for a People: The Rogue Indians and the Frontiersmen, 1971, 2nd edit., 1996, The Simpsons of Shore Acres, 1971, Coos Bay: The Pioneer Period, 1973, The Indians of Western Oregon: This Land Was Theirs, 1977, Land of the Umpqua: A History of Douglas County, Oregon, 1986; editor: Tall Tales from Rogue River, 1974, 2d edit., 1990, Lewis & Clark Coll., 1991, Many Faces: An Anthology of Oregon Autobiography, 1993, Seventy-Five Years of Buildings: Hoffman Construction Company, 1995, Lewis & Clark From the Rockies to the Pacific, 2002, The Literature of the Lewis & Clark Expedition, 2003, Astoria Column, 2004, Oregon Indians: Voices from Two Centuries, 2006, Stimson Lumber, 2009; contbr. numerous to profl. publs. Mem. bd. advisers Nat. Trust for Hist. Preservation, Washington, 1978-85; mem. State Adv. Com. on Hist. Preservation, Salem, Oreg., 1977-85; mem. Oreg. Geog. Names Bd., Portland, 1990-93; pres., bd. dirs. John and LeRee Caughey Found., L.A., 1985—; bd. dirs. Oreg. Hist. Soc., 1994-2003. Can. Govt. faculty enrichment fellow, 1985; recipient Ruth McBride Powers Preservation of Yr. award, 1986, Oreg. Prof. of Yr. award, 1992; Sears-Roebuck award, 1986. Mem. Am. Hist. Assn. (Asher Disting. Teaching award 1995), Am. Anthropol. Assn. Democrat. Baptist. Home: 1389 Hoodview Ln Lake Oswego OR 97034-1505 Office: Lewis and Clark Coll Portland OR 97219 Business E-Mail: beckham@lclark.edu.

BECKHAM, VICTORIA CAROLINE, singer, apparel designer; b. Herfordshire, Eng., Apr. 17, 1974; d. Anthony and Jacqueline Adams; m. David Beckham, July 4, 1999; children: Brooklyn Joseph, Romeo James, Cruz David. Attended, Laine Theatre Arts Coll., Epsom, England. Mem. The Spice Girls, 1994—2000; solo artist, 2000—04; designer VB Rocks Rock & Republic, 2004—06; creative dir. dVb Style, 2006—; designer Intimately Beckham, 2006, dVb Eyewear, 2006; jewelry and handbag designer Samantha Thavasa; designer evening gown collection, 2008. Runway model Maria Grochvogel, 2000, Roberto Cavalli, 2006; spokesmodel Roc-a-Wear clothing line, 2003, Marc Jacobs, 2008; Brit. amb. Dolce & Gabbana. Singer: (albums) Spice, 1996, Spiceworld, 1997, Forever, 2000, Victoira Beckham, 2001; featured in (films) Spice World, 1997, (documentaries) Victoria's Secrets, 2000, Being Victoria Beckham, 2002, The Real Beckhams, 2003, Victoria Beckham: Coming to America, 2007, appearances in (TV series) Ugly Betty, 2007, voice (video game) Spice World: The Game, 1998; author: (autobiography) Learing to Fly, 2001, (books) That Extra Half an Inch: Hair, Heels and Everything In Between, 2006; guest judge (TV series) Project Runway, 2008. Recipient (with The Spice Girls) 5 awards, Smash Hits Poll Winners Party, 1996, (with The Spice Girls) 2 awards, 1998, (with The Spice Girls) Best Dance Video, MTV Video Music award, 1997, (with The Spice Girls) MTV Video Music award, 1997, (with The Spice Girls) 2 Billboard awards, 1997, (with The Spice Girls) 4 Brit awards, 1997, (with The Spice Girls) London's Favorite Female Group award, Capital FM Awards, 1997, (with The Spice Girls) Capital Icon award, 2008, (with The Spice Girls) 4 MTV Europe Music awards, (with The Spice Girls) 3 World Music awards, (with The Spice Girls) Best Selling Brit. Album Act Around The World, Brit. Awards, 1998, (with The Spice Girls) Outstanding Contribution To The Brit. Music Industry, 2000, (with The Spice Girls) 3 Am. Music awards, 1998, Best Dressed Female award, Elle Mag., 2000, Best Dressed Internat. Female, 2003, Best Dressed Female Artist, Lycra Brit. Style Awards, 2003, (with The Spice Girls) Top Boxscore, Billboard Touring Awards, 2008; named Best Dressed Woman of Yr., Prima mag., 2002, 2003, Woman of Yr., Brit. Glamour Mag., 2007, Entrepreneur of Yr., 2007, (with The Spice Girls) Best Comeback, Sun Bizarre Awards, 2007, (with The Spice Girls) Best Band, Glamour Women of Yr. Awards, 2008, (with The Spice Girls) Best Live Return, Vodafone Live Music Awards, 2008. Office: dVb Style 33 Ransomes Dock 35-37 Parkgate Rd London SW114NP England*

BECKMANN, JON MICHAEL, publishing company executive; b. NYC, Oct. 24, 1936; s. John L. and Grace (Hazelton) B.; m. Barbara Ann Efting, June 26, 1965. BA, U. Pa., 1958; MA, NYU, 1961. Sr. editor Prentice-Hall Inc., Englewood Cliffs, NJ, 1964-68; v.p., editor Barre Pubs., Mass., 1970-73; pub. Sierra Club Books, San Francisco, 1973-94; pres. Beckmann Assocs. and Millennium Press, Sonoma, Calif., 1994—. Author: After-Dinner Drinks, 1998. Mem. Book Club of Calif. Office: Beckmann Assocs & Millennium Press 18185 7th St E Sonoma CA 95476-4797 Office Phone: 707-938-8194. E-mail: jonnytheb@vom.com.

BEDFORD, DANIEL ROSS, lawyer; b. Berwyn, Ill., Aug. 19, 1945; s. Fred Doyle and Nelda Elizabeth (Dittrich) B.; children: Ian, Kate. BS, Stanford U., 1967, JD, MBA, Stanford U., 1971. Bar: Calif. 1972. Assoc. Thelen & Marrin, San Francisco, 1971-78, ptnr., 1979-86, Orrick, Herrington & Sutcliffe, San Francisco, 1986—. Mem. ABA, Calif. Bar Assn., San Francisco Bar Assn., Am. Coll. of Investment Counsel. Democrat. Episcopalian. Office: 400 Sansome St San Francisco CA 94111-3304 Home: 320 Via Recodo Mill Valley CA 94941-4707

BEDFORD, OLIVIA CAJERO, state legislator; b. Tuscon; d. Bernardo and Carmen Cajero. Student, Pima Cmty. Coll., Tucson, U. Ariz. Mem. Dist. 27 Ariz. House of Reps., 2003—, mem. appropriations com., commerce com. Pres. Dems. of Greater Tucson; vice-chair Pima County Dem. Party; mem. Ariz. Tourism Adv. Coun., Ariz. Women's Caucus. Recipient Walk the Talk award, Ariz. Med. Assn., 2007. Mem.: Women in Govt., Nat. Assn. Latino Elected Officials, Hospitality Sales & Mktg. Assn. Internat., Tucson Mountain Assn., Gates Pass Area Neighborhood Assn. Democrat. Office: Ariz House Reps Capitol Complex 1700 W Washington Rm 338 Phoenix AZ 85007 Office Phone: 602-926-5835. Office Fax: 602-417-3027. Business E-Mail: ocajerob@azleg.gov.*

BEDIENT, PATRICIA M., paper company executive; BSBA, Oreg. State Univ. CPA. CPA Arthur Andersen, Portland, Oreg., ptnr., 1987—93, Boise, Idaho, 1993—99, mng. ptnr., head forest products practice Seattle, 1999—2002; v.p. strategic planning Weyerhaeuser Co., Federal Way, Wash., 2003—06, sr. v.p. fin. & strategic planning, 2006—07, exec. v.p., CFO, 2007—. Bd. dir. Alaska Air Group, Weyerhaeuser Co. Found. Trustee Oreg. State Univ. Found.; mem. adv. bd. Univ. Wash. Sch. Bus.; mem. San Francisco regional adv. bd. FM Global; past pres. City Club Portland; past bd. mem. World Forestry Ctr., Forest History Soc.; past mem. adv. com. Forest Rsch. Lab Oreg. State Univ.; past chmn. bd. regents St. Mary's Acad., Portland; past vice-chmn. Boise C. of C. Mem.: Am. Inst. CPAs, Wash. Soc. CPAs. Office: Weyerhaeuser 33663 Weyerhaeuser Way Federal Way WA 98063-9777

BEDSWORTH, WILLIAM W., judge; b. Long Beach, Calif., Nov. 21, 1947; m. Carolyn Kelly McCourt, Mar. 28, 1999. BA cum laude, Loyola U., LA, 1968; JD, U. Calif., Berkeley, 1971. Felony trial deputy, appellate atty., mng. atty. Orange County Dist. Atty.'s Office, Calif.; judge Orange County Superior Ct., 1986-97; assoc. justice 4th Appellate Dist., Calif. Ct. of Appeals, Santa Ana, 1997—. Adj. prof. Western State U. Coll. of Law, Chapman U. Sch. of Law, Orange, Calif., Calif. Jud. Coll., Berkeley. Author: What I Saw and Heard, 1996, A Criminal Waste of Time, 2003; author nationally syndicated column A Criminal Waste of Space; contbr. articles to profl. publs. Former bd. dirs. NCCJ, Orange County Bar Assn.; bd. dirs. Fair Share 502; goal judge Nat. Hockey League, 1993—. Named Judge of Yr., Hispanic Bar Assn., 1997. Mem. Assn. Orange County Dep. Dist. Atty. (past pres.). Avocations: softball, country music, ice hockey.

BEE, KEITH A., state legislator; b. Tucson, Dec. 5, 1965; Student, U. Ariz. Mem. Ariz. State Senate, 1992—, vice-chmn. fin. instns. and retirement, mem. health com., chmn. transp. com. Leader 4-H. Mem. Ariz. Assn. Pupil Trans. Republican. Address: 11171 E Escalante Rd Tucson AZ 85730-5604 E-mail: kbee@azleg.state.az.us.

BEE, ROBERT NORMAN, banker; b. Milw., Mar. 4, 1925; s. Clarence Olson and Norma Pern (Pitt) B.; m. Dolores Marie Cappelletti, Apr. 23, 1955; children: Diane, John, Leslie. PhB, Marquette U., 1949; BS in Fgn. Svc., Georgetown U., 1950, MA, 1955. With Dept. Treasury, various locations, 1950—65; fin. attache Stockholm, 1952—54, Ankara, Turkey, 1956—60; chief fin. affairs Am. embassy, Bonn, Germany, 1960—65; dep. dir. AID, Karachi, Pakistan, 1965—67; 1st. v.p. 1st Wis. Nat. Bank, 1967—71; sr. v.p. Wells Fargo Bank; also pres. Wells Fargo Internat. Investment Corp., San Francisco, 1971—78; mng. dir., CEO London (England) Interstate Bank Ltd., 1978—87; mng. dir. TSB Pvt. Bank Internat. SA, London, 1987—90; chmn. U.S. Fin. Adv. Svc., London, 1990—92, SAJ Investments Ltd., London, 1991—95; sr. advisor Porvenir Inc., San Francisco, 1998—2000; dir. Sunlink Corp., San Rafael, Calif., 2007—. Sr. fellow Ctr. Internat. Banking Studies, Charlottesville, Va. Chmn. World Affairs Coun. Milw., 1970-71; bd. dirs. Adam Smith Inst., London, chmn., 1985-87; chmn. Am. Soc. in London, 1986-87. With AUS, 1943-46. Recipient Bronze Star, 1945. Mem. Bankers Assn. for Fgn. Trade (pres. 1977-78). Home and Office: 1940 Vallejo St Apt 5 San Francisco CA 94123-4918 Office Phone: 415-931-7520. Personal E-mail: robnbee@comcast.net.

BEE, TIMOTHY S., state legislator; b. Tuscon, Ariz., June 20, 1969; m. Grace Bee; 6 children. Grad., U. Ariz., 1990. Owner Bee Brothers Printing, 1989—2001; ptnr. Bee Line Transp., 1987—; mem. Ariz. State Senate, 2001—, majority leader, 2003—06, pres., 2007—. Mem. Congl. Congress on Civic Edn. Mem.: Nat. Coun. State Legislators, Am. Legis. Exchange Coun. Republican. Office: Ariz State Senate Rm 204 1700 W Washington Phoenix AZ 85007 Office Phone: 602-542-5683. E-mail: tbee@azleg.state.az.us.

BEEBE, LYDIA I., oil industry executive; b. McPherson, Kans. m. Charles Doyle; 3 children. B, U. Kansas; JD, U. Kansas Sch. Law; MBA, Golden Gate U., San Francisco. Atty. and various legal and govt. affairs positions, including legis. rep. in Washington, tax lawyer and sr. mgr. tax dept. Chevron Corp., 1977—95, corp. sec., chief governance officer, 1995—. Sec., bd. dirs. Chevron Corp., sec., exec. com., sec., bd. nominating and governance com., mgr. corp. governance dept., sr. mgr., corp. governance and stockholder services; bd. dirs. Chevron Employees PAC, Coun. Instl. Investors, Soc. Corp. Secs. and Governance Profls., past chmn., corp. practices com. Past pres., bd. mem., mem. adv. bd. Profl. Bus. Women Calif.; mem. San Francisco Mcpl. Fiscal Adv. Com.; bd. dirs. Presidio Trust, 2003—08, chair fin. and audit com.; mem. Calif. Fair Employment and Housing Commn., 1991—99, chair, 1995—99; bd. dirs. Lincoln Club, No. Calif.; bd. governors Kans. U. Law Alumni; bd. trustees Nat. Jud. Coll., Golden Gate U. Recipient Breakthrough award, Profl. Bus. Women Calif., 1996; named Alumna of Yr., Golden Gate U., 2004; named one of Most Influential Businesswomen in the Bay Area, San Francisco Bus. Times, 1999—2008. Office: Chevron Corp Hdqs 6001 Bollinger Canyon Rd San Ramon CA 94583

BEEBE, MARY LIVINGSTONE, curator; b. Portland, Oreg., Nov. 5, 1940; d. Robert and Alice Beebe; m. Charles J. Reilly. BA, Bryn Mawr Coll., Pa., 1962; postgrad., Sorbonne, U. Paris, 1962—63. Apprentice Portland Art Mus., 1962—64, Boston Mus. Art, 1964—66; curatorial asst. dept. drawing Fogg Art Mus., Harvard U., Cambridge, Mass., 1966-68; prodr. Am. Theatre Co., Portland State U., Oreg., 1969—72; exec. dir. Portland Ctr. for Visual Arts, 1972—81; dir. Stuart Collection U. Calif., San Diego, 1981—. Cons. in field; lectr. in field; mem. art steering com. Portland Devel. Commn., 1977-80, New Denver Internat. Airport, 1990-97; bd. dirs. Henry Gallery, U. Wash., Seattle, 1977-80; project cons. Nat. Rsch. Ctr. for Arts, N.Y.C., 1978-79; bd. dirs. Western Assn. Art Museums, Art Mus. Assn. San Francisco, 1978-84; bd. dirs., trustee Art Matters Inc., N.Y.C., 1984-, Balboa Art Conservation Ctr., San Diego, 2001-; trustee Russell Found., 1982-94, bd. dirs., 1983-85; hon. mem. bd. dirs. Portland Ctr. for Visual Arts, 1981-88; mem. arts adv. bd. Centre City Devel. Corp., San Diego, 1982-94, U. Calif. San Francisco Mission Bay, 1999—, Indpls. Mus. Art, Art and Nature Pk. adv. bd., 2003-05, nat. adv. bd. Headlands Ctr. for the Arts, San Francisco; panel mem., cons. Nat. Endowment Arts; mem. adv. com. Port of San Diego, 1983-88, San Diego Design Ctr., 1987-88, ART/LA, 1987-94, Pearl Art Found., Portland, 1998-2000, inSITE94, inSITE97, inSITE00, inSITE03 and 05, San Diego, 1993-, Friends of Art and Preservation in Embassies Profl. Sculpture adv. com., Wash., 2003-; mem. pub. art adv. com. Harvard and Radcliffe, 1989-93, U. Wash., Seattle, 1989-96, Commn. for Arts and Culture, San Diego, 2003-; juror numerous art exhbns. Nat. Endowment Arts fellow, 1979. Author: Landmarks: Sculpture Commissions for the Stuart Collection at the University of California, San Diego, 2001; contbr. articles to profl. jours. Recipient Allied Professions award AIA, 1992, Nat. Honors award, 1994. Achievements include having the Stuart Collection featured on CBS Sunday Morning with Charles Kuralt, 1993. Office: U Calif San Diego Stuart Collection 9500 Gilman Dr La Jolla CA 92093-0010 Office Phone: 858-534-2117. Business E-Mail: mbeebe@ucsd.edu.

BEECHAM, WILLIAM R., newspaper editor; Bur. chief AP, Salt Lake City, 1982—. Office: 30 E 1st S Salt Lake City UT 84111-1930

BEENE, RICHARD STUART, newspaper editor; b. Knoxville, Tenn., June 11, 1951; s. William Wolbach and Julia (Swysgood) B.; m. Dianne Elise Klein, May 29, 1983; children: Lauren Elizabeth, Hannah Julia. BA in History, Ga. So. U., 1973. Reporter Fort Lauderdale (Fla.) Sentinel, 1978-80; state mgr. UPI, NYC, Miami & Atlanta, 1980-84, bur. chief Cairo, 1983; L.Am. corr. Dallas Times Herald, 1984-87; city editor L.A. Times, 1987-94; exec. editor Bakersfield (Calif.) Californian, 1994-98, pres., CEO, 1998—. Recipient Pulitizer, L.A. Times, 1995. Mem. Am. Soc. Newspaper Editors, Calif. Soc. Newspaper Editors, Sigma Delta Chi. Avocation: bicycle racing. Office: Bakersfield Californian 1707 Eye St Bakersfield CA 93301-5299

BEER, JAMES A., information technology executive, former air transportation executive; b. London; BS in Aero. Engring., London U.; MBA, Harvard U. With Anderson Consulting; fin. analyst Am. Airlines, 1991, mng. dir. corp. devel., mng. dir. internat. planning, v.p. fin. analysis and fleet planning, 1998—2000, treas., v.p. corp. devel., 2000—02, v.p. for Europe and Asia, 2002—03; sr. v.p., CFO AMR Corp. and Am. Airlines, 2003—06; CFO Symantec, Cupertino, Calif., 2006—. Office: PO Box 619616 Dallas TX 75261-9616 also: Symantec 20330 Stevens Creek Blvd Cupertino CA 95014

BEER, REINHARD, atmospheric scientist; b. Berlin, Nov. 5, 1935; came to U.S., 1963, naturalized, 1979; s. Harry Joseph and Elizabet Maria (Meister) B.; m. Margaret Ann Taylor, Aug. 11, 1960. B.Sc. with Honors, U. Manchester, Eng., 1956, PhD, 1960. Rsch. asst. physics U. Manchester, 1956-60, sr. asst. astronomy, 1960-63; sr. scientist Jet Propulsion Lab., Pasadena, Calif., 1963-70, group supr. tropospheric sci., 1970—2005, sr. rsch. scientist, 1985—, mgr. atmospheric and oceanographic scis. sect., 1990-92, flight team leader, 1997—, prin. scientist, 1999—. Vis. assoc. prof. astronomy U. Tex., Austin, 1974; vis. astronomer Kitt Peak Nat. Obs., 1979-81, Mauna Kea Obs., 1982-86; prin. investigator Tropospheric Emission Spectrometer NASA Earth Observing System, 1989—, airborne emission spectrometer program NASA, 1992-2003, group supr. Tropospheric Emission Spectrometry, 2005—06; co-investigator NASA Atlas 1 mission, 1992, Atlas 2, 1993. Author: Remote Sensing by Fourier Transform Spectrometry, 1992; contbr. articles to profl. jours. Hon. Turner and Newall fellow, 1961; recipient medal for exceptional sci. achievement NASA, 1974, NASA group achievement award for Pioneer Venus, 1980, Spacelab 3 ATMOS experiment and sci., 1986, group achievement award Tropospheric Emission Spectrometry, 2005, Exceptional Achivement medal NASA, 2008. Mem. AAAS, Am. Geophys. Union, Optical Soc. Am. Achievements include discovery of extra-terrestrial deuterium (heavy hydrogen), 1972, of carbon monoxide in Jupiter, 1975. Office: 183-601 Jet Propulsion Lab Pasadena CA 91109

BEESLEY, H(ORACE) BRENT, bank executive; b. Salt Lake City, Jan. 30, 1946; s. Horace Pratt and Mary (Brazier) B.; m. Bonnie Jean Matheson, Dec. 20, 1980; children: Laura Jean, Sarah Janice, Mary Roslyn, Amy Elizabeth, David Brent, Katherine Ann, Daniel Pratt. BA, Brigham Young U., 1969; MBA, JD, Harvard U., 1973. Bar: Utah 1973. Instr. U. Utah, Salt Lake City, 1973-81; ptnr. Ray, Quinney & Nebeker, Salt Lake City, 1977-81; dir. Fed. Savs. and Loan Ins. Corp., Washington, 1981-83; chmn., chief exec. officer Charter Savs. Corp., Jacksonville, Fla., 1983-86; pres., chief exec. officer Farm Credit Corp. Am., Denver, 1986-88; chmn., chief exec. officer Heritage Bank, St. George, Utah, 1988—. Bd. dirs. Fed. Home Loan Bank, Seattle, 1992-95, Savs. and Cmty. Bankers Am., 1992-96, Utah Heritage Found., 1978-81, Utah Arthritis Found., 1978-81; trustee So. Va. Coll., 1998-2002. Mem. Utah State Bar Assn., Alta Club, Entrada at Snow Canyon Country Club. Home: 1492 Kristianna Cir Salt Lake City UT 84103-4221 Office: 95 E Tabernacle St Saint George UT 84770-2307

BEEZER, ROBERT RENAUT, federal judge; b. Seattle, July 21, 1928; s. Arnold Roswell and Josephine (May) B.; m. Hazlehurst Plant Smith, June 15, 1957; children: Robert Arnold, John Leighton, Mary Allison. Student, U. Wash., 1946-48, 51; BA, U. Va., 1951, LLB, 1956. Bar: Wash. 1956, U.S. Supreme Ct. 1968. Ptnr. Schweppe, Krug, Tausend & Beezer, P.S., Seattle, 1956-84; judge pro tem Seattle Mcpl. Ct., 1962—76; judge US Ct. Appeals (9th cir.), Seattle, 1984-96, sr. judge, 1996—. Alt. mem. Wash. Jud. Qualifications Commn., Olympia, 1981-84 1st lt. USMCR, 1951-53 Fellow Am. Coll. Trust and Estate Counsel, Am. Bar Found.; mem. ABA, Seattle-King County Bar Assn. (pres. 1975-76), Wash. Bar Assn. (bd. govs. 1980-83) Clubs: Rainier, Tennis (Seattle). Office Phone: 206-553-0384. Business E-Mail: judge_beezer@ca9.uscourts.gov.

BEFFORT, SUE F. WILSON, state legislator; Mem. Dist. 19, N.Mex. State Senate, 1996-; Employment cons., currently. DA's Legislature Award; Nursing Legislature Award; Primary Care Legislature Award; Chamber of Commerce Tax, Econ Develop, Bus. Awards (3); Association Commerce & Industry Bus Star. Republican. Episcopalian. Mailing: State Capitol, Rm 415G Santa Fe NM 87503 E-mail: sue.wilsonbeffort@state.nm.us, sue.beffort@nmlegis.gov.*

BEGAM, ROBERT GEORGE, lawyer; b. NYC, Apr. 5, 1928; s. George and Hilda M. (Hirt) B.; m. Helen C. Clark, July 24, 1949; children— Richard, Lorinda, Michael. BA, Yale U., 1949, LL.B., 1952. Bar: N.Y. bar 1952, Ariz. bar 1956, U.S. Dist. Ct. Ariz. 1957, U.S. Ct. Appeals (9th cir.) 1958, U.S Supreme Ct. 1973. Assoc. firm Cravath, Swaine & Moore, NYC, 1952-54; spl. counsel State of Ariz., Colorado River Litigation in U.S. Supreme Ct., 1956-58; pres. Begam & Lewis PA, Phoenix. Author: Fireball, 1987, Long Life, 2008, 2 Novels. Pres. Ariz. Repertory Theater, 1960—66; trustee Atla Roscoe Pound Found.; bd. dirs. Boys Clubs of Met. Phoenix; bd. govs. Welzmann Inst. Sci., Rehovot, Israel; pres. Am. Com. for Welzmann Inst. of Sci., 1996—98, chmn. fin. resource devel., 2000—; v.p. Ariz. Theatre Co., 2006—07; bd. dirs. Phoenix Theater Ctr., 1955—60, 1987—92, Ariz. Theatre Co., 2001—. 1st lt. USAF, 1954—56. Fellow: Internat. Soc. Barristers; mem.: State Bar Ariz. (cert. specialist in injury and wrongful death litigation), Am. Bd. Trial Advocates (bd. dirs.), Western Trial Lawyers Assn. (pres. 1970), ATLA (pres. 1976—77, chmn. polit. action com. 1979—86), Phoenix Country Club, Yale Club (N.Y.C.). Avocations: writing, theater, golf. Office: Begam Lewis & Marks 111 W Monroe St Ste 1400 Phoenix AZ 85003-1787 Office Phone: 602-254-6071. Business E-Mail: rbegam@begamlaw.com.

BEGELMAN, MITCHELL CRAIG, astrophysicist, educator, writer; AB, AM, Harvard U., 1974; PhD, U. Cambridge, Eng., 1978. Asst. prof. dept. astrophys., planetary and atmospheric scis. U. Colo., Boulder, 1982-87, assoc. prof., 1987-91, prof., 1991—, assoc. chair, 1992-95, chmn., 1995-98, fellow Joint Inst. for Lab. Astrophysics, 1984—. Recipient Presdl. Young Investigator award, 1984, Sci. Writing award Am. Inst. Physics, 1996; Alfred P. Sloan Found. rsch. fellow, 1987-91; John Simon Guggenheim fellow, 1998-99. Fellow Royal Astron. Soc., Cambridge Phil. Soc.; mem. Am. Astron. Soc. (Helen B. Warner prize 1988). Office: U Colo Joint Inst Lab Astrophysics PO Box 440 Boulder CO 80309-0440

BEGICH, MARK P., United States Senator from Alaska, former mayor; b. Anchorage, Mar. 31, 1962; s. Nicholas Joseph and Pegge Begich; m. Deborah Bonito, 1990; 1 child, Jacob. Chair Alaska Student Loan Corp.; chmn. Anchorage Assembly, assemblyman, 1988—98; mayor City of Anchorage, 2003—08; US Senator from Alaska, 2009—. Founder Making a Difference Program; bd. mem. Boys and Girls Club, Spirit of Youth Found., Family Resource Ctr., Resource Devel. Coun. Named Friend of Edn., Anchorage Edn. Assn., Top Ofcl. Statewide, 1997, 2004. Mem.: NRA, Airforce Assn., Assn. US Army. Democrat. Office: PO Box 196650 Anchorage AK 99519 also: 825 Hart Senate Office Bldg Washington DC 20510 Office Phone: 907-343-7102, 202-244-3004. Office Fax: 907-343-7180.*

BEHNKE, CARL GILBERT, beverage franchise executive; b. Seattle, May 13, 1945; s. Robert Joseph and Sally (Skinner) B.; m. Renee Behnke; children: Marisa Winifred, Merrill West. BA, Princeton U., 1967; MBA, Harvard U., 1973. Adminstrv. asst. ALPAC Corp., Seattle, 1973—75, v.p., 1978—84, pres., bd. dirs., 1984—93; sales mgr. Pepsi Cola/7Up, Honolulu, 1974—76; chmn. bd. Skinner Corp.; pres. REB Enterprises, Seattle, 1993—. Bd. dirs. Sage Terrace Inc., The Commerce Bank of Wash., Northwestern Trust, Internat. Yogurt Co. Bd. dirs. Pres.'s Club, U. Wash., 1980-84, Jr. Achievement Puget Sound, 1981-, chmn. bd., 1988, United Way Wash., 1982-86; pres. Bellevue Boys and Girls Club, 1985-87; trustee U. Puget Sound, Patrons of N.W. Civic Cultural and Charitable Orgns., pres., 1990; chmn. bd. dirs. Eastside Performing Arts Ctr., 1987-90; chmn. bd. Seattle-King County Conv. and Visitors Bur., 1989; mem. exec. bd. Seattle Organizing Com./Goodwill Games, 1987; bd. dirs. Croquet Found. Am., Pacific N.W. Ballet. Named one of 100 Newsmakers of Tomorrow, Time Mag.-Seattle C. of C., 1978. Mem.: Wash. Athletic Club, Young Pres.'s Orgn., 7Up Bottlers Assn., Pepsi-Cola Bottlers Assn., Wash. State Soft Drink Assn., Nat. Soft Drink Assn., Puget Sound Croquet Club, Columbia Tower Club, Rainier Club, Men's Univ. Club, Ctrl. Park Tennis Club. Republican. Office: 601 Union St Ste 3016 Seattle WA 98101-3913 Home: 2325 91st Pl Ne Clyde Hill WA 98004-2411

BEHRENDT, JOHN CHARLES, geophysicist, researcher, writer; b. Stevens Point, Wis., May 18, 1932; s. Allen Charles and Vivian Eulaine B.; m. Donna Ebben, Oct. 6, 1961 (div.); children: Kurt Allen, Marc Russell; m. Laura Backus, May 16, 2004. Student, Cen. State Coll., Stevens Point, 1950-52; BS in Physics, U. Wis., Madison, 1954, MS in Geology, 1956, PhD in Geophysics, 1961. Cert. geophysicist, Calif. Asst. seismologist Arctic Inst. N.Am., Ellsworth Sta., Antarctica, 1956-58; rsch. assoc. U. Wis., Madison, 1958-64; rsch. geophysicist U.S. Geol. Survey, Denver, 1964—68, Liberia, West Africa, 1968-70, Denver, 1970-72; chief br. of Atlantic-Gulf of Mex. marine geology Woods Hole, Mass., 1974-77; research geophysicist, Antarctic coordinator U.S. Geol. Survey, 1977-95, geophysicist emeritus, 1995—; fellow Inst. Arctic and Alpine Rsch U. Colo., Boulder, 1996—2006, fellow emeritus, 2006—, rsch. scientist, 1996—. Frequent pub. spkr. on Antarctica and other rsch.; advisor U.S. Depts. State and Interior, Washington, 1977-2008; mem. U.S. del. to Antarctic Treaty Meetings, various countries, 1977-95, various working groups NAS-NRC; rsch. on Antarctica, earthquakes in ea. U.S., Rocky Mountain tectonics, Gt. Lakes geologic structure, Atlantic continental margin of N.Am. and West Africa. Author: Innocents on the Ice: A Memoir of Antarctic Exploration, 1957, 1998 (Colo. Book award for non-fiction 1999), The Ninth Circle: A Memoir of LIfe and Death in Antarctica, 1960-1962, 2005; contbr. more than 275 articles to profl. jours. Recipient Antarctic Svc. medal U.S. Dept. Def., 1966, Meritorious Svc. award Dept. Interior, 1992, Filice Ippolito Gold medal for Antarctic Rsch., Italian Antarctic Rsch. Program and Acad. Nazionale dei Linceia, 1999. Fellow: AAAS, Geol. Soc. Am., Explorers Club; mem.: Am. Polar Soc. (pres. 2006—), Soc. Exploration Geophysicists, Am. Geophys. Union. Avocations: photography, outdoor activities, music. Business E-Mail: behrendj@stripe.colorado.edu.

BEHRENS, BEREL LYN, physician, academic and health facility administrator; b. New South Wales, Australia, 1940; MB, BS, Sydney U., Australia, 1964. Diplomate Am. Bd. Pediatrics, Am. Bd. Allergy and Immunology. Intern Royal Prince Alfred Hosp., Australia, 1964; resident Loma Linda (Calif.) U. Med. Ctr., 1966-68, Henrietta Egleston Hosp. for Children, Atlanta, 1968—69, T.C. Thompson Children's Hosp., Chattanooga, 1969—70; faculty pediatrics Loma Linda U., 1970-72, with dept. pediatrics, 1972—, dean Sch. Medicine, 1986-91, pres., 1990—, Loma Linda U. Med. Ctr., 1999—; pres., CEO Loma Linda U. Adventist Health Scis. Ctr., 1997—. Office: 11175 Campus St Loma Linda CA 92354 E-mail: myhanna@ahs.llumc.edu.

BEHRENS, M. KATHLEEN, medical researcher; PhD in Microbiology, U. Calif., Davis. With Robertson Stephens Mgmt. Co., 1983—99, gen. ptnr., 1986-93; mng. dir. RS Investments, San Francisco, 1999—. Bd. dirs. Abgenix Inc., HealthTrio; mem. President's Coun. Advisors on Sci. and Tech. Mem. Nat. Venture Capital Assn. (pres. elect 1999—). Office: RS Investments 388 Market St San Francisco CA 94111 also: Abgenix Inc 7601 Dumbarton Cir Fremont CA 94555-3616

BEHRING, KENNETH E., professional sports team owner; b. Freeport, Ill., June 13, 1928; s. Elmer and Mae (Priewe) B.; m. Patricia Riffle, Oct. 16, 1949; children: Michael, Thomas, David, Jeffrey, Scott. Student, U. Wis., 1947. Owner Behring Motors, Monroe, Wis., 1953-56, Behring Corp., Ft. Lauderdale, Fla., 1956-72, Blackhawk Corp., Danville, Calif., 1972—, also chmn. bd. dirs.; owner Seattle Seahawks, NFL, 1988-97. Calif. land developer; mem. policy adv. bd. real estate and urban econs. U. Calif., Berkeley.; chmn. bd. dirs. Behring-Hofmann Ednl. Inst., Inc. U. Calif. Trustee U. Calif., Berkeley; regent St. Mary's Coll., Moraga, Calif., Holy Name Coll., Oakland, Calif.; hon. trustee Mt. Diablo Hosp. Found., Concord, Calif.; hon. chmn. Seattle Art Mus., Am. Cancer Soc., Muscular Dystrophy, Silverado Concours. Named Man of Yr. Boys Town Italy, Entrepreneur of Yr. INC mag. Mem. Am. Acad. Achievement (honoree 1989), Assn. Wash. Bus., Seattle Master Builders Assn., Blackhawk Club, Vintage Club, Seattle Yacht Club, Wash. Athletic Club. Office: Blackhawk Corp PO Box 807 Danville CA 94526-0807

BEIGHLE, DOUGLAS PAUL, aerospace transportation executive; b. Deer Lodge, Mont., June 18, 1932; s. Douglas Paul Beighle and Clarice Janice (Driver) Kiefer; m. Gwendolen Anne Dickson, Oct. 30, 1954 (dec. Jan. 1996); children: Cheryl, Randall, Katherine, Douglas J.; m. Kathleen Pierce, June 26, 2005 BS in Bus. Adminstrn., U. Mont., 1954; JD, U. Mont, 1958; LL.M., Harvard U., 1960. Bar: Mont. 1958, Wash. 1959, U.S. Supreme Ct. 1970. Assoc. Perkins & Coie, Seattle, 1960-67, ptnr., 1967-80; v.p. contracts Boeing Co., Seattle, 1980-81, v.p. contracts, gen. counsel, sec., 1981-86, sr. v.p., 1986-97; chief legal counsel Puget Energy, Inc., Bellevue, Wash., 1970-80, bd. dirs., 1981—2005, chair, 2002—05; exec. dir. Wash. State, U.S. West Comm., Denver, 1990-95. Bd. dirs. Washington Mut. Inc., Seattle, 1989-05, ret., 2005, Active Voice Corp., Seattle, 1997-01, Simpson Investment Co., Seattle, 1998-05; bd. dirs., chmn. KCTS-9 TV, 1996-05. Nat. bd. dirs. Jr. Achievement, Colorado Springs, 1981-95; bd. dirs. Greater Puget Sound Jr. Achievement, 1983—, Intiman Theatre, Seattle, 1991-93; trustee Mcpl. League Seattle, 1983-88, U. Mont. Found., Missoula, 1983-91, Mansfield Found., Missoula, 1990-95, Pacific Sci. Ctr., Seattle, 1992—, pres. 1996; trustee Arts Fund, Seattle, 1994—, chair, 1995-96. 1st lt. USAF, 1954-56. Harvard U. Law Sch. fellow, 1959 Mem. Wash. State Bar Assn. (chmn. adminstrv. law sect. 1979-80), Nat. Assn. Mfrs. (bd. dirs., regional vice chmn. 1988-93), Greater Seattle C. of C. (chair 1994-95), Rainier Club Seattle, Seattle Yacht Club. Republican. Presbyterian. Office: 1000 2nd Ave Ste 3700 Seattle WA 98104-1053

BEINFIELD, HARRIET, medical association administrator; b. Cleve., Oct. 15, 1946; d. Malcolm Sydney and Marjorie Koster Beinfield; m. Efrem Korngold, June 1980; children: Natasha Korngold, Shem Korngold, Bear Korngold. BA, New Sch. Social Rsch., NYC, 1968. Lic. Traditional Acupuncture Coll., Hatton, 1973. Cofounder Chinese Medicine Works, San Francisco, co-dir., 1973—; chinese herb formulator Kan Herb Co., Scotts Valley, Calif., 1992—2008. V.p. Terma Found., Half Moon Bay, Calif., 1998—; adv. bd. dir. Osher Ctr. Integrative Medicine, UCSF, San Francisco, 2001—; editl. bd. Alternative Therapies Health & Medicine, Boulder, Colo., 2001—. Explore: Jour. Sci. and Healing, Phila., 2005—; adv. bd. Haywood W. Burns Inst., San Francisco, 2003—; pres. Aku Project, Morristown, NJ, 2005—. Author: (book) Between Heaven and Earth: A Guide to Chinese Medicine; contbr. articles to profl. jours. Office: Chinese Medicine Works 1201 Noe St San Francisco CA 94114 E-mail: hbeinfield@gmail.com.

BEISTLINE, EARL HOOVER, mining consultant; b. Juneau, Alaska, Nov. 24, 1916; s. Ralph H. and Catherine (Krinach) B.; m. Dorothy Ann Hering, Aug. 24, 1946; children— Ralph Robert, William Calvin, Katherine Noreen, Lynda Marie. B. Mining Engring., U. Alaska, 1939, E.M., 1947, LL.D. (hon.), 1969. Mem. faculty U. Alaska, 1946-82, dean Sch. Mines, 1949-61, dean Coll. Earth Sci. and Mineral Industry, 1961-75, provost Coll. Earth Sci. and Mineral Industry, 1970-75, exec. officer no. region, 1970-73, dean Sch. Mineral Industry, 1975-82, dean emeritus, prof. mining engring. Sch. Mineral Industry, 1982—; mining cons. Served to maj. AUS, 1941-46. Fellow AAAS, Explorers Club; mem. NSPE, Am. Inst. Mining and Metall. Engrs., Mining and Metall. Soc. Am., Arctic Inst. N.Am., Am. Soc. Engring. Edn., N.W. Mining Assn., Alaska Mining Assn., Pioneers of Alaska. Home and Office: PO Box 80148 Fairbanks AK 99708-0148

BÉJAR, MARTHA, computer software company executive; BS cum laude, U. Miami; MBA, Nova Southeastern U.; grad., Advanced Mgmt. Program, Harvard U. With BellSouth Corp., Bell Comms. Rsch.; joined Nortel, 1989, gen. mgr. voice over IP solutions, gen. mgr. Network Access Divsn., pres. Caribbean and Latin America regions; corp. v.p. comm. sector Microsoft Corp., Redmond, Wash., 2007—. Bd. dirs. Nat. Ctr. for Women & Info. Tech. Named one of the top fifty Hispanic women in the US, Hispanic Inc. Bus. Mag., 2000, 20 Elite Women, Hispanic Bus. Mag., 2008. Office: Microsoft Corp One Microsoft Way Redmond WA 98052-6399

BEJCZY, ANTAL KÁROLY, research scientist and facility administrator; b. Ercsi, Hungary, Jan. 16, 1930; came to U.S., 1966; s. Jenö and Erzsébet (László) B.; m. Margit Tóth, Oct. 12, 1957. BSEE, Tech. U., Budapest, Hungary, 1956; PhD in Physics, Sci. U., Oslo, 1963. Univ. lectr. Sci. U., Oslo, 1963-66; rsch. scientist Norwegian Rsch. Coun., Oslo, 1963-66; sr. rsch. fellow Calif. Inst. Tech., Pasadena, 1966-69; mem. tech. staff Jet Propulsion Lab., Pasadena, 1969-79, tech. mgr., 1979-95, sr. rsch. scientist, 1985—2001, ret., 2001; cons., 2001—. Bd. dirs. Zoltán Bay Applied Scis. Found., Budapest, Hungary, 1993-99; affiliate prof. Washington U., St. Louis, 1983-. Contbr. articles on robotics and telerobotics to profl. jours.; assoc. editor Automatic Control Trans., 1982-85; mem. editl. bd. Jour. Robotic Sys., 1983—; patentee in field. Recipient Jean Vertut award Robotics Internat., 1987; NASA Exceptional Svc. medal, 1991. Fellow IEEE (life; Third Millenium Medal award 2000, Pioneer in Robotics and Automation award 2004, Disting. Svc. award 2007); mem. Robotics and Automation Soc. of IEEE (pres. 1986-87, adminstrv. com. 1991-99, AIAA Space Automationa and Robotics award 2007, Engring., Sci. and Tech. Hall of Fame inductee, 2007), Hungarian Acad. Engring. (hon.). Avocations: tennis, gardening, music. Office: Jet Propulsion Lab MS 198-219 4800 Oak Grove Dr Pasadena CA 91109-8001

BEJNAR, THADDEUS PUTNAM, law librarian; b. Carmel, Calif., Aug. 19, 1948; s. Waldemere and Katherine (Marble) B.; m. Susan Mavis Richards, Mar. 25, 1976 (div. Jan. 1986); m. Catherine Slade Baudoin, Apr. 10, 1988 (div. Apr. 1995). AB in Philosophy, U. So. Calif., 1971; JD, Georgetown U., 1978; MLIS, U. Tex., 1986. Bar: N.Mex. 1978, U.S. Dist. Ct. N.Mex. 1980, U.S. Ct. Appeals (10th cir.) 1981. Atty. Indian Pueblo Legal Svcs., Zuni, N.Mex., 1978-80; pvt. practice law Albuquerque, 1980-84; legal rsch. libr. U. N.Mex., Albuquerque, 1984-87; law libr. Supreme Ct. Law Libr. State of N.Mex., Santa Fe, 1987—2005; ref. libr. Socorro Pub. Libr., 2006—. Tchr. legal admisibility electronic records Advanced Legal Rsch. C.L.E., 1984-95; bd. dirs. Waldemere, Bejnar & Assocs., 1982-, Spectra Rsch. Inst., 1995-01. Author: Jurisdictional Guide to Jury Instructions, 1986; editor N.Mex. Jud. Conduct Handbook, 1989-93, Manual of Citation for the Ctrs. of the State of N.Mex., 1991-92, 2d edit., 1997; sr. editor N.Mex. Legal Forms, 1991-94. Chmn. N.Mex. del. White House Conf. Librs., 1991; chmn. N.Mex. Adv. Com. on Rules and Publs., 1992-96; ptnr. Legal Informatics, an internat. cons. firm, 1992-04; bd. dirs. N.Mex. Libr. Found., 1997-01. Lt. USAF, 1971-74. Mem. ALA (councilor 2000—07), Am. Assn. Law Librs., N.Mex. Libr. Assn., Spl. Libr. Assn. (pres. Rio Grande chpt. 2004-05), Adirondack Mt. Club, Order of Coif, Phi Kappa Phi, Phi Alpha Delta, Beta Phi Mu. Mem. Soc. Of Friends. Avocations: stamp collecting/philately, hiking. Home: Rt 2 Box 94 Socorro NM 87801 Office Phone: 575-835-1114. E-mail: thaddeus@bejnar.com.

BEKAVAC, NANCY YAVOR, retired academic administrator, lawyer; b. Pitts., Aug. 28, 1947; d. Anthony Joseph and ELvira (Yavor) Bekavac. BA, Swarthmore Coll., 1969; JD, Yale U., 1973. Bar: Calif. 1974, U.S. Dist. Ct. (cen. dist.) Calif. 1974, U.S. Dist. Ct. (no. dist.) Calif. 1975, U.S. Ct. Appeals (9th cir.) 1975, U.S. Dist. Ct. (so. dist.) Calif. 1976, U.S. Surpeme Ct. 1979, U.S. Ct. Appeals (8th cir.) 1981. Law clk. at large U.S. Ct. Appeals (D.C. cir.), Washington, 1973-74; assoc. Munger, Tolles & Rickershauser, LA, 1974-79, ptnr., 1980-85; exec. dir. Thomas J. Watson Found., Providence, 1985-87, cons., 1987-88; counselor to pres. Dartmouth Coll., Hanover, N.H., 1988-90; pres. Scripps Coll., Claremont, Calif., 1990—2007. Adj. prof. law UCLA Law Sch., 1982—83; mem. Calif. Higher Edn. Roundtable, 1996—; trustee Am. Coun. Edn., 1994—97; bd. dir. Electro Rent Corp. Author: (books) Imagining the Real Future, 1996. Bd. mgrs. Swathmore Coll., 1984—; trustee Wenner-Gren Found. Anthrop. Rsch., 1987—94; bd. trustees Am. Coun. Edn., 1994—97; chair Assn. Ind. Colls. and Univs., 1996—97. Recipient Human Rights award, LA County Commn. Civil Rights, 1984; fellow Woodrow Wilson fellow, Thomas J. Watson fellow, 1969. Mem.: WestEd. (bd. dir.), Women's Coll. Coalition, Am. Assn. Ind. Calif. Colls. and Univs. (chair 1996), Commn. on White House Fellowships (chmn., selection com. 1993—94), Seaver Found. (bd. dir.), Sierra Club. Avocations: hiking, reading, travel. Office Phone: 909-621-8148. E-mail: president@scrippscollege.edu.

BEKEY, GEORGE ALBERT, computer scientist, educator; b. Bratislava, Slovakia, June 19, 1928; arrived in U.S., 1945, naturalized, 1956; s. Andrew and Elizabeth Bekey; m. Shirley White, June 10, 1951; children: Ronald Steven, Michelle Elaine. BS with honors, U. Calif., Berkeley, 1950; MS, UCLA, 1952, PhD, 1962. Rsch. engr. UCLA, 1950-54; mgr. computer ctr. Beckman Instruments, LA and Berkeley, Calif., 1955-58; mem. sr. staff, dir. computer ctr. TRW Systems Group, Redondo Beach, Calif., 1958-62; mem. faculty U. So. Calif., LA, 1962—, prof. elec. and biomed. engring. and computer sci., 1968—2003, chmn. dept. elec. engring. systems, 1978-86, dir. Robotics Lab., 1983-98, chmn. computer sci. dept., 1984-89, dir. Ctr. for Mfg. and Automation Rsch., 1987-94, assoc. dean Sch. Engring., 1996-2001; adj. prof. engring. Calif. Poly. State U., San Luis Obispo, Calif., 2005—. Chair computer sci. Gordon Marshall, 1990—2002; cons. to govt. agys. and indsl. orgns. Author (with W. J. Karplus): Hybrid Computation, 1968; author: (with K. Goldberg) Robotics and Neural Networks, 1994; author: Autonomous Robots, 2005; co-editor: Hospital Information Systems, 1972, System Identification, 1983, Neural Networks and Robotics, 1993, Autonomous Underwater Robots, 1996, Robot Colonies, 1997, Distributed Autonomous Robotic Systems, 2000, Modeling and Simulation, Theory and Practice, 2003; editor-in-chief Autonomous Robots Jour., 1999—2006; founding editor: IEEE Trans. Robotics and Automation, mem. editl. bd.: 3 profl. jours.; contbr. articles to profl. jours. With US Army, 1954—56. Recipient Disting. Faculty award, 1977, Sch. Engring. Svc. award, U. So. Calif., 1990, Presdl. medallion, 2000, Engelberger prize in robotics, 2001, Alumni Achievement Academia, UCLA, 2005, Lifetime Achievement award, USC, 2008; scholar, Calif. Polytech. U. San Luis Obispo, 2005—. Fellow: IEEE (3d Millennium medal 2000), AAAS, Am. Assn. Artificial Intelligence, Am. Inst. Med. and Biol. Engring.; mem.: NAE, Biomed. Engring. Soc., Soc. Computer Simulation, Assn. Computing Machinery, IEEE Robotics and Automation Soc. (pres. 1996—97, Pioneer in Robotics and Automation award 2002, Disting. Svc. award 2004, Nat. Robotics award 2006), Tau Beta Pi, Eta Kappa Nu. Achievements include patents in field. Office: U So Calif Computer Sci Dept Los Angeles CA 90089-0781

BELFIORE, JOE, computer software company executive; m. Kristina Belfiore; children: Alexander, Piper, Sydney. Grad., Stanford U., 1990. Program mgr. Microsoft Corp., 1990, lead project mgr. user interface of Windows 95, group program mgr. Internet Explorer 4 and Windows 2000 user interface, product unit mgr. Windows User Experience, gen. mgr. Windows eHome Divsn., now corp. v.p. entertainment and devices. Office: Microsoft Corp One Microsoft Way Redmond WA 98052-6399

BELITZ, PAUL EDWARD, lawyer; b. Omaha, July 11, 1951; s. Edward Paul and Jo Anna Beverly (Brown) B.; m. Joanne Deborah Nilson, June 9, 1973; children: Nicholas P., Christopher T. BS with high distinction, U. Nebr., 1973; JD magna cum laude, Creighton U., 1976. Bar: Nebr. 1976, Colo. 1982. Assoc., then ptnr. Kutak Rock LLP, Omaha, 1976-81, ptnr. Denver, 1982—. Bd. dir. Fleischer Found., Scottsdale, Ariz., 1986—. Mem.: ABA, Denver Bar Assn., Colo. Bar Assn., Nebr. Bar Assn., Glenmoor Country Club (Cherry Hills Village, Colo. stategic planning com.). Avocations: reading, skiing, golf. Office: Kutak Rock LLP 1801 California St Ste 3100 Denver CO 80202 Office Phone: 303-297-2400. E-mail: paul.belitz@kutakrock.com.

BELL, C. GORDON, computer architect and engineer, entrepreneur, researcher; b. Kirksville, Mo., Aug. 19, 1934; s. Roy Chester and Lola Dolph (Gordon) Bell; m. Gwendolyn Kay Druyor, Jan. 3, 1959; 2 children. BSEE, MIT, 1956, MSEE, 1957; DEng (hon.), Worcester Polytechnic Inst., 1993. With Digital Equipment Corp., 1960—66, v.p., R&D, 1972—83; prof., computer sci. and elec. engring. Carnegie-Mellon U., 1966—72; founder Encore Computer, 1983; first asst. dir. NSF Computing Directorate, 1986—87; founding mem. Ardent Computer, 1986—88; v.p., R&D Ardent Computer (merged with Stellar), 1988—89; advisor Microsoft Corp., 1991—95, sr. researcher, media presence rsch. group San Francisco, 1995—. Led Nat. Rsch. and Edn. Network panel; chairing the cross-agy. govt. panel that led to the formation of the Internet; author First High Performance Computer and Comm Initiative; co-founder Computer Mus., Boston, 1979; founding bd. mem. Computer History Mus., Mountain View, Calif., 1999; bd. dir., tech. adv. bd. Cradle Tech., DiamondCluster Exchange, Dust Networks, Inc., Vanguard Group; founder, dir. Bell-Mason Group. Contbr. articles to profl. jours.; co-author: Computer Structures: Readings and Examples, 1971, Designing Computers and Digital Systems Using PDP-16 Register Transfer Modules, 1972, Computer Engineering, 1978, Computer Structures: Principles and Examples, 1982, High Tech Ventures: The Guide To Entrepreneurial Success, 1991; maintains MyLifeBits. Sponsor Gordon Bell prize (Assn. Computing Machinery/IEEE Conf. on Supercomputing), 1987—. Recipient AEA Inventor award for the greatest economic contribution to the New England region, Nat. Medal Tech., 1991, MCI Comm. Info. Tech. Leadership award for

Innovation, 1995; named Fellow, Computer History Mus., 2003; Fulbright Scholar, U. New South Wales, 1957—58. Fellow: IEEE (also Computer Pioneer) (Von Neumann medal 1992, Vladamir Karapetroff Eminent Member's award of Eta Kappa Nu 2001), Assn. for Computing Machinery, AAAS, Am. Acad. Arts and Sciences; mem.: NAS, NAE. Achievements include being the architect of various mini- and time-sharing computers (PDP's) and led the develop. of Digital Equipment Corp. VAX and VAX computing environ; patents in field. Avocations: bicycling, scuba diving, skiing, fishing. Office: Microsoft Corp 835 Market St Ste 700 San Francisco CA 94111 Office Fax: 415-778-8225, 425-936-7329. Business E-Mail: GBell@microsoft.com.

BELL, DRAKE (JARED DRAKE BELL), actor, singer; b. Orange County, Calif., June 27, 1986; s. Robin Dodson. Band mem. Drake Bell; owner Backhouse Records. Judge Miss Teen USA Pageant, 2006. Actor: (films) Drifting School, 1995, The Neon Bible, 1995, Jerry Maguire, 1996, Dill Scallion, 1999, High Fidelity, 2000, Perfect Game, 2000, Yours, Mine and Ours, 2005, Superhero Movie, 2008 (Choice Movie Breakout Male, Teen Choice Awards, 2008), College, 2008; (TV films) The Jack Bull, 1999, Dragonworld: The Legend Continues, 1999, Chasing Destiny, 2001; (TV series) The Amanda Show, 1999—2001, Drake & Josh, 2004—07 (Favorite TV Actor, Nickelodeon Kids' Choice Award, 2006, 2007, 2008); singer: (albums) Telegraph, 2005, It's Only Time, 2006. Office: Platform Pub Rels Inc 2666 N Beachwood Dr Los Angeles CA 90068

BELL, FRANK OURAY, JR., lawyer; b. San Francisco, Aug. 13, 1940; s. Frank Ouray Sr. and Clara Belle (McClure) Bell; m. Sherrie A. Levie, Mar. 29, 1981; children: Aimee, David;children from previous marriage: Carin, Laurie. AB, San Francisco State U., 1963; JD, U. Calif., San Francisco, 1966. Bar: Calif. 1966, U.S. Dist. Ct. (no. dist.) Calif. 1967, U.S. Ct. Appeals (9th cir.) 1967, U.S. Supreme Ct. 1973. Dep. atty. gen. Calif. State's Atty.'s Office, Sacramento, 1966-68; ptnr. Goorjian & Bell, San Francisco, 1968-70; chief asst. Fed. Pub. Defender's Office, San Francisco, 1970-82; dir. Calif. State Pub. Defender's Office, 1984-87; pvt. practice law San Francisco, 1982-84; sr. litig. assoc. Olimpia, Whelan & Lively, San Jose, Calif., 1987-89; pvt. practice San Mateo and Redwood City, Calif., 1989—. Mem.: Calif. Pub. Defenders Assn. (bd. dirs. 1986—87), San Mateo County Bar Assn. Democrat. Jewish. Office: 333 Bradford St Ste 270 Redwood City CA 94063 Office Phone: 650-365-8300. Business E-Mail: FrankBell@FrankBellLaw.com.

BELL, JEFF, former computer software marketing executive; BA in History and Spanish, Kenyon Coll.; MA in Internat. Econs., Johns Hopkins U.; MBA, U. Pa. Wharton Sch. Bus. Joined Ford Motor Co., 1989, dir. retail mktg. and e-business; v.p. mktg. comm. to v.p. product strategy Chrysler Group, 2001—06; corp. v.p. global mktg. Interactive Entertainment Bus. Microsoft Corp., 2006—08. Trustee Nat. Multiple Sclerosis Soc., Kenyon Coll. Recipient MediaPost Online All-Star Award, 2005; named Interactive Marketer of Yr., Advertising Age, 2005; named one of 21 Most Intriguing People in Mktg., min Magazine.

BELL, LARRY STUART, artist; b. Chgo., Dec. 6, 1939; s. Hyman David and Rebecca Ann (Kriegmont) B.; three children. Student, Chouinard Art Inst., LA, 1957-59. One man exhbns. include Stedelijk Mus., Amsterdam, 1967, Pasadena (Calif.) Art Mus., 1972, Oakland (Calif.) Mus., 1973, Ft. Worth Art Mus., 1975, Santa Barbara (Calif.) Mus. Art, 1976, Washington U., St. Louis, 1976, Art Mus. So. Tex., Corpus Christi, 1976, Erica Williams, Anne Johnson Gallery, Seattle, 1978, Hayden Gallery, MIT, Cambridge, Mass., 1977, Hudson River Mus., Yonkers, N.Y., 1981, Newport Harbor Art Mus., 1982, Marian Goodman Gallery, N.Y.C., 1982, Ruth S. Schaffner Gallery, Santa Barbara, Calif., Arco Ctr. Visual Arts, L.A., 1983, Unicorn Gallery, Aspen, Colo., 1983, Butler Inst. Am. Art, Youngstown, Ohio, 1984, Leigh Yawkey Woodson Art Mus., Wausau, Wis., 1984, Colorado Springs, Colo. Fine Arts Ctr., 1987, Cleve. Ctr. for Contemporary Art, Ohio, 1987, Mus. Contemporary Art, L.A., 1987, Am. Acad. and Inst. Arts and Letters, N.Y.C., 1987, Boise (Idaho) Gallery Art, 1987, Gilbert Brownstone Gallery, Paris, 1987, Braunstein/Quay Gallery, San Francisco, 1987, 89, Fine Arts Gallery, N.Mex. State Fairgrounds, 1987, Laguna Art Mus., Laguna Beach, Calif., 1987, High Mus. Art, Atlanta, 1988, Sena Galleries West, Santa Fe, 1989, Kiyo Higashi Gallery, L.A., 1989, 90, 94, 02, Musee D'Art Contemporain, Lyon, France, 1989, Contemporary Art Ctr., Kansas City, Mo., 1989, San Antonio Art Inst., 1990, New Gallery, Houston, 1990, Braunstein/Quay Gallery, San Francisco, 1990, Galerie Rolf Ricke, Koln, Fed. Republic Germany, 1990, Galerie Montenay, Paris, 1990, 95, The Works Gallery, L.A., 1990, Galerie Kammer, Hamburg, Germany, 1990, Tony Shafrazi Gallery, N.Y.C., 1991, Tucson Mus. Art, 1991, New Gallery, Houston, 1991, Janus Gallery, Santa Fe, 1992, Kiyo Higashi Gallery, L.A., 1992, 93, New Gallery, Houston, 1992, Tampa Mus. Art, 1992, Kiyo Higashi Gallery, L.A., 1993, 94, New Directions Gallery, Taos, N.M., 1993, Dartmouth St. Gallery, Albuquerque, 1994, Braunstein/Quay Gallery, San Francisco, 1994, Leedy/Voulkos Gallery, Kansas City, 1994, Kiyo Higashi Gallery, L.A., 1994, U. Wyo. Art Mus., Laramie, 1995, Denver Art Mus., 1995, Indigo Gallery, Boca Raton, Fla., 1995, Harwood Mus. U. N. Mex., Taos, 1995, Galerie Montenay, Paris, 1995, Joy Tash Gallery, Scottsdale, Ariz., 1996, Kiyo Higashi Gallery, L.A., 1996, Boulder Mus. Contemporary Art, 1996, Braunstein/Quay Gallery, San Francisco, 1996, Art et Industrie Gallery, N.Y.C., 1996, The Albuquerque Mus., 1997, The Reykjavik Mcpl. Art Mus., Iceland, 1997, Bergen (Norway) Kunstmus., 1998, Seljord (Norway) Art Assn., 1998, Wood Street Galleries, Pitts., 1999, Mus. Moderner Kunst Landkreis Cuxhaven, Otterndorf, Germany, 1999, Kiyo Higashi Gallery, 1999, Center Galleries, Detroit, 2000, Larry Bell Studio Annex/New Directions Gallery, Taos, N.Mex., 2000, Mus. Moderner Kunst Landkreis Cuxhaven, Otterndorf, Germany, 2000, New Gallery, Houston, 2001, Gallery Gan, Tokyo, 2001, Skovridder AS, Oslo, Norway, 2001, Roswell Mus. and Art Ctr., 2002, New Gallery, Houston, 2002, Off Main Gallery, Santa Monica, Calif., 2003, St. John's Coll., Santa Fe, 2003, Harwood Art Mus. U. N.Mex., Taos, N.Mex., 2004, Bernard Jacobson Gallery, London, U. Tenn., Chattanooga, 2005, Jacobson Howard Galllery, N.Y.C., 2005, Pace Wildenstein Gallery, N.Y.C., 2005, McClain Gallery, Houston, Alan Koppel Gallery, Chgo., 2005, Frank Lloyd Gallery, Santa Monica, Calif., 2006, Daniel Templon Gallery, Paris, 2006, Annandale Galleries, Sydney, 2006, Bernard Jacobson Gallery, London, 2007, Danese Gallery, NY, 2007, Haines Gallery, San Francisco, 2007, Frank Lloyd Gallery, Sanda Monica, 2008, Seiler and Mosseri-Marlio Gallery, Zurich, Switzerland, 2008, Logan Fine Arts, Houston, 2008, Galerie Daniel Templon, Paris, 2008, Bernard Jacobson Gallery, London, Harwood Mus. UNM, Taos, 2008, Taos Ctr. Arts, 2009; numerous group exhbns. including most recently Calif., 2000, Peggy Guggenheim Collection, Venice, Italy, 2000, Guggenheim Mus. Bilbao, Spain, 2000, La. Mus. Art, Humlebaek, Denmark, 2000, L.A. County Mus. Art, 2000, Solomon R.Guggenheim Mus., N.Y.,2001, Bernard Jacobson Gallery, London, 2001, Museu Serralves, Porto, Portugal, 2002, The Contemporary Mus., Honolulu, 2002, Yale U.Art Gallery, New Haven, Conn., 2002, Denver Art Mus., 2002, Gagosian Gallery, N.Y.C., 2002, Franklin Parrasch Gallery, N.Y.C., 2003, Gagosian Gallery, N.Y.C., 2002,Stephen Stux Gallery, N.Y.C., 2002, Harwood Mus. U. N.Mex., Taos, 2004, Bernard Jacobson Gallery, London, 2005, Sintra Mus. Modern Art, Portugal, 2003, Contemp.Art Ctr., New Orleans, 2003, Guggenheim Mus. Art, N.Y., 2003, MOCA, L.A., 2004, U. Pa., Phila., 2004, L.A. County Mus. Art, L.A., 2004, Miami Art Mus.,, 2004, Mus. Contemporary Art, San Diego, 2004, Marian Goodman Gallery, N.Y., 2004, Jacobson-Howard Gallery, N.Y., 2004, Frederick R. Weisman Art Mus., U. Minn., 2005, McNay Art Mus., San Antonio, 2005, Centro Cultural Belem, Lisboa, Portugal, 2005, Patricia Faure Gallery, Santa Monica, Calif., 2005, Chevron Gallery, Irvine, Calif., 2005, Las Vegas Art Mus., Nev., 2006, Ctr. George Pompidou, Paris, 2006, LACMA, L.A., 2006, Norton Simon Mus., L.A., 2006, Whitney Mus. Am. Art, NYC, 2006, 223 Art, Belgium, 2006, L&M Arts, NYC, 2006, Harwood Mus. ARt, Taos, N.Mex., 2007, Orange County Mus. Art, Newport Beach, Calif., 2007, Smithsonian Inst., Washington, 2007, Solomon R. Guggenheim Mus., NY, 2007, Kunstmuseum Liechte stein, Vaduz, Germany, 2007, Musee Nat. d'Art Moderne Ctr. Pompidou, Paris, 2007, Milw. Art Mus., 2008, William Turner Gallery, Santa Monica, Mus. Contemporary Art, Sydney, 2008, Mus. Contemporary Art, LA, 2008, Ackland Art Mus., UNC, Chapel Hill, 2008, Hirshhorn Mus. & Sculpture Garden, Washington, 2008, Kunsthaus, Zurich, Switzerland, 2009, others; represented in permanent collections including Nat. Collection Fine Arts, Musee de Art Contemporaine, Lyon, France, Mus. of Fine Arts, Santa Fe, N.Mex., Whitney Mus. Am. Art, N.Y.C., Laguna Gloria Mus., Austen, H & W Bechtler Gallery, Charlotte, Calif. Crafts Mus., San Francisco, Parrish Art Mus., Southampton, Tate Gallery, London, Gallery New South Wales, Australia, Albright-Knox Gallery, Buffalo, Art Inst. Chgo., Denver Art Mus., Dallas Mus. Fine Arts, Guggenheim Mus., Houston, L.A. County Mus., Victoria and Albert Mus., London, San Antonio Mus. Art, The Menil Collection, Houston, Mpls. Inst. Arts, Mus. Ludwig, Koln, Albuquerque Mus., Mpls. Inst. Arts, others; instr. sculpture, U. South Fla., Tampa, U. Calif., Berkeley, Irvine, So. Calif. Inst. of Architecture, Taos (N.Mex.) Inst. of Art, City of Albuquerque, Art in Pub. Places, 1999, Myers Devel. Co., 1999, Billingsley Co., Carrolton, Tex., Mus. Abteiberg, Monchengladbach, Germany, Centex Homes, South Coast Divsn., Brea, Calif., MOCA, LA, Calif., Great Eagle Devel. and Mgmt. Ltd., Hong Kong. Copley Found. grantee, 1962; Guggenheim Found. fellow, 1970; Nat. Endowment Arts grantee, 1975; recipient Gov.'s award for excellence in visual arts, N.Mex., 1990. Office Phone: 505-758-3062. Business E-Mail: bell@newmex.com.

BELL, LEE PHILLIP, television personality, producer; b. Chgo. d. James A. and Helen (Novak) P.; m. William Joseph Bell, Oct. 23, 1954; children: William J., Bradley, Lauralee. BS in Microbiology, Northwestern U., Evanston, Ill., 1950. With CBS-TV, Chgo., 1952-86; pres. Bell-Phillip TV Prodns., 1985—. Bd. dirs. William Wrigley, Jr. Co., Chgo. Bank Commerce, Phillips Flowers Inc. TV and radio shows include Lee Phillip Show, Chgo., from 1952, Lady and Tiger Show WBBM Radio, from 1962, WBBM TV from 1964; hostess Noon Break, numerous TV Spls. including Forgotten Children, The Rape of Paulette (nat. Emmy award, duPont Columbia award); Children and Divorce (Chgo. Emmmy award) co-creator: (with William Bell) The Young and the Restless CBS-TV daytime drama, 1973 (Emmy award); co-creator, exec. producer The Bold and the Beautiful, 1987—. Bd. dirs. United Cerebral Palsy, Chgo. Unlimited, Northwestern U. Hosp., Chgo. Heart Assn., Nat. Com. Prevention of Child Abuse, Mental Health Assn., Children's Home and Aid Soc., Salvation Army, Chgo., Family Focus; mem. Chgo. Maternity Ctr.; life mem. Northwestern U. Bd. Trustees. Recipient 16 Chgo. Emmys, Top Favorite Female award TV Guide mag., 1956, Outstanding Woman of Radio and TV award McCall's mag., 1957-58, 65, bd. govs. award Chgo. chpt. Nat. Acad. TV Arts and Scis., 1977, Achievement award, 2007, Emmy, 2007, William Booth award for community svc. Salvation Army, 1990; named Person of Yr. Broadcast Advt. Club, Chgo., 1980. Mem. Am. Women Radio and TV (Golden Mike award 1968, Broadcaster of Yr. 1993), Acad. TV Arts and Scis. (bd. dirs.), Chgo. chpt. Acad. TV Arts and Scis., Women's Athletic Club of Chgo., Comml. Club, Delta Delta Delta. Home: 9955 Beverly Dr Beverly Hills CA 90210 Office: CBS c/o Bold and Beautiful 7800 Beverly Blvd Los Angeles CA 90036-2188 Home Phone: 310-467-1932; Office Phone: 323-575-2812. Business E-Mail: markpinciotti@boldandbeautiful.tv.

BELL, MAXINE TOOLSON, state legislator; b. Logan, Utah, Aug. 6, 1931; d. John Max and Norma (Watson) Toolson; m. H. Jack Bell, Oct. 26, 1949; children: Randy J. (dec.), Jeff M., Scott Alan (dec.). AA in Libr. Sci., Coll. Southern Idaho; CSI, Idaho State U., 1975. Farmer; librarian Sch. Dist. 261, Jerome, Idaho, 1975-88; mem. Dist. 26B Idaho House of Reps., Boise, 1988—. Bd. dirs. Idaho Farm Bur., 1976-77; rep. western states American Farm Bur. Women, 1990-93, vice chmn., 1993; vice chmn. American Farm Bur., 1993-2005, chmn. appropriations com., 1999; mem. Jerome County Rep. Precinct Com., 1980-88; vice chmn. Idaho Health Systems Agy. Recipient Pres. medallion award, Idaho State U., 2005. Fellow: Coun. State Govt. Leadership Training. Republican. Home: 194 S 300 E Jerome ID 83338-6532 Office: Idaho State Legislature Capitol Annex PO Box 83720 Boise ID 83720-0038 Office Phone: 208-332-1000. Office Fax: 208-334-5397. Personal E-mail: mbell@magiclink.com. Business E-Mail: mhjbel@msw.com, mbell@house.idaho.gov.*

BELL, ROBERT CECIL, lawyer; b. San Francisco, June 1, 1951; s. Robert Elmer and Lillian Marie (Petrik) B. BJ, U. Nev., 1973; JD, U. Pacific, 1980. Bar: Nev. 1980, Colo. 1993, U.S. Dist. Ct. Nev. 1980, U.S. Bankruptcy Ct. 1981, U.S. Ct. Appeals (9th cir.) 1982, U.S. Supreme Ct., 1988. Investigator, legal asst. Washoe County Dist. Atty.'s Office, Reno, 1975-77; law clk. to presiding justice Washoe County Dist. Ct., Reno, 1980-81; sole practice Reno, 1981—. Judge pro tem Reno Mcpl. Ct., 1985—, Sparks Mcpl. Ct. 1986—; adminstrv. law judge, Reno; bd. dirs. Washoe Legal Svcs., Reno. Bd. dirs. March of Dimes, Reno, 1985—; mem. Supreme Ct. Hist. Soc. Mem. ABA, Washoe County Bar Assn., Assn. Trial Lawyers Am., Nev. Trial Lawyers Assn., Reno Rodeo Assn., Reno Air Races, U. Pacific McGeorge Sch. Law Alumni Assn. (bd. dirs. 1986—). Democrat. Lutheran. Avocations: photography, flying, skiing, golf, guitar. Office: 20 Winter St Reno NV 89503 Office Phone: 775-333-9977.

BELL, ROBERT JEFFREY, lawyer; b. LA, June 1, 1947; AB, U. Calif., Santa Cruz, 1969; JD summa cum laude, Loyola U., LA, 1976. Bar: Calif. 1976. Ptnr. Luce, Forward, Hamilton & Scripps, San Diego, mng. ptnr., 2004—. Chief note and comment editor: Loyola U. L.A. Law Rev., 1975-76. Mem. ABA, State Bar Calif. Office: Luce Forward Hamilton & Scripps LLP 600 W Broadway Ste 2600 San Diego CA 92101 E-mail: rbell@luce.com.

BELL, STOUGHTON, computer scientist, mathematician, educator; b. Waltham, Mass., Dec. 20, 1923; s. Conrad and Florence Emily (Ross) Bell; m. Mary Carroll O'Connell, Feb. 26, 1949 (div. 1960); children: Karen, Mark; m. Laura Joan Bainbridge, May 24, 1963 (div. 1979); children: Nathaniel Stoughton, Joshua Bainbridge; m. Edna Casman, June 25, 2001. Student, Harvard U., 1946-49; AB, U. Calif., Berkeley, 1950, MA, 1953, PhD, 1955. Mem. staff Sandia Corp., Albuquerque, 1955-66, div. supr., 1964-66; vis. lectr. U. N.Mex., 1957-66, dir. computing center, 1966-79, assoc. prof. math., 1966-71, prof. math. and computer sci., 1971-92, prof. emeritus, 1992—. Vis. lectr. N.Mex. Acad. Scis., 1965—. Co-author: (book) Linear Analysis and Generalized Functions, 1965, Introductory Calculus, 1966, Modern University Calculus, 1966, Mathematical Analysis for Modeling, 1999. With AUS, 1943—44. Mem.: Ops. Rsch. Soc. Am., Am. Statis. Assn., Soc. Indsl. and Applied Math., Math. Assn. Am., Am. Math. Soc., Assn. Computing Machinery (nat. lectr. 1972—74). Office: U NMex Computer Sci Dept Albuquerque NM 87131-1386 Home Phone: 505-256-9489. Business E-Mail: sto@cs.unm.edu.

BELL, W. DONALD, electronics executive; BSEE, U. AL. V.p., sales and mktg. Texas Instruments; pres and CEO Electronic Arrays (now NEC Microelectronics); sr. vp memory & microprocessors, mktg. v.p., exec. v.p. Am. Microsystems Inc.; exec. V.P. Kierulff Electronics, 1980-81, pres., 1981-86; pres and COO Docummun, Inc., 1986-88; pres., CEO, chmn. Bell Microproducts, San Jose, CA, 1988—. Mem. bd. dir. Sand Hill Capital, Eng. Leadership Bd. for the U. of AL. Disting. Eng. Fellow of U of AL. Office: Bell Microproducts 1941 Ringwood Ave San Jose CA 95131-1721

BELL, WILLIAM C., foundation administrator; BS in Biology and Behavioral Sci., Delta State U.; MS, Hunter Coll. Sch. Social Work. Former assoc. exec. dir. Miracle Makers, NYC; deputy commissioner of field svcs. and contract agy. case mgmt. NYC Administration for Children's Svcs., 1994—96, deputy commissioner div. of child protection, 1996—2002, commissioner, 2002—04; exec. v.p. child and family svcs. Casey Family Programs, 2004—06, pres., CEO, 2006—. Mem. Pew Commn. on Children in Foster Care; bd. dirs. Council on Social Work Ed.; mem. exec. com. Nat. Assn. of Public Child Welfare Administrators. Recipient Leadership Recognition award, Black Administrators in Child Welfare, Advocacy Merit award for Outstanding Leadership in Children's Svcs., Child Welfare League of Am., 2000, Betsey R. Rosenbaum award for Excellence in Public Child Welfare Admin., Nat. Assn. for Public Child Welfare Administrators, 2003. Office: Casey Family Programs 1300 Dexter Ave N Seattle WA 98109-3542

BELL, WILLIAM J., JR., television producer; b. 1963; s. William Joseph and Lee Phillip Bell; m. Maria Bell. Pres. Bell-Phillip TV Prodns. Inc., LA, Bell Dramatic Serial Co., LA. Trustee LA County Mus. Art, 2005—. Named one of Top 200 Collectors, ARTnews mag., 2006—08. Office: LA County Mus Art 5905 Wilshire Blvd Los Angeles CA 90036 Office Phone: 323-857-6000. Office Fax: 323-857-4702.

BELLAH, ROBERT NEELLY, sociologist, educator; b. Altus, Okla., Feb. 23, 1927; s. Luther Hutton and Lillian Lucille (Neelly); m. Melanie Hyman, Aug. 17, 1949; 4 children BA, Harvard U., 1950, PhD, 1955. Rsch. assoc. Inst. Islamic Studies McGill U., Montreal, Canada, 1955—57; with Harvard U., Cambridge, Mass., 1957—67, prof., 1966—67; mem. faculty dept. sociology U. Calif., Berkeley, 1967—97, Elliott prof. emeritus, 1997—. Author: Tokugawa Religion, 1957, Beyond Belief, 1970, The Broken Covenant, 1975 (Sorokin award Am. Sociol. Assn. 1976), (with Charles Y. Glock) The New Religious Consciousness, 1976, (with Phillip E. Hammond) Varieties of Civil Religion, 1980, (with others) Habits of the Heart, 1985, (with others) The Good Society, 1991, Imagining Japan, 2003, The Robert Bellah Reader, 2006. With U.S. Army, 1945-46 Fulbright fellow, 1960-61; recipient Harbison award Danforth Found., 1971, Nat. Humanities medal, 2000 Mem. Am. Acad. Arts and Scis., Am. Sociol. Assn., Am. Acad. Religion, Am. Philos. Soc Episcopalian. Office: U Calif Dept Sociology Berkeley CA 94720-1980

BELLEVILLE, PHILIP FREDERICK, lawyer; b. Flint, Mich., Apr. 24, 1934; s. Frederick Charles and Sarah (Adelaine) B.; m. Geraldean Bickford, Sept. 2, 1953; children: Stacy L., Philip Frederick II, Jeffrey A. BA in Econs. with high distinction and honors, U. Mich., 1956, JD, 1960, MS in Psychology CCU, 1997, PsyD, 2008. Bar: Calif. 1961. Assoc. Latham & Watkins, L.A., 1960-68, ptnr. L.A. and Newport Beach, Calif., 1968-98, chmn. litigation dept., 1973-80, ptnr. L.A., Newport Beach, San Diego, Washington, 1980-98, Chgo., 1983-98, NYC, 1985-98, London and San Francisco, 1990-98, Moscow, 1992-98, Hong Kong, 1995-98, Tokyo, 1995-98, Singapore, 1997-98, Silicon Valley, 1997-98; judge Los Angele and Orange County Superior Cts., 2007—. Mem. diversion evaluation com. Calif. Med. Bd., 2006—08; mem. evaluation com. State Bar Lawyer's Assistance Program, 2003—06, mem. oversight com., 2006—, vice chmn., 2007—08, chmn., 2008—. Past mem. So. Calif. steering com. NAACP Legal Def. Fund, Inc.; cmty. adv. bd. San Pedro Peninsula Hosp., 1980—88; bd. dirs. Harbor Interfaith, 2001—, chmn. bd., 2004—06, past pres., 2007—08; bd. dirs. House of Hope, 2004—, pres., 2006—. James B. Angell scholar U. Mich., 1955-56 Mem. ABA, State Bar Calif., LA County Bar Assn., Order of Coif, Portuguese Bend (Calif.) Club, Palos Verdes (Calif.) Golf Club, Caballeros, Phi Beta Kappa, Phi Kappa Phi, Alpha Kappa Psi Avocations: sports, art, antiques. Home Phone: 310-541-5256.

BELLO, MARIA ELANA, actress; b. Norristown, Pa., Apr. 18, 1967; 1 child, Jackson Blue McDermott. BS in Polit. Sci., Villanova U. Co-founder Harlem's Dream Yard Drama Project, 1992. Actress: (off-Broadway plays) include The Killer Inside Me, Small Town Gals With Big Problems, Urban Planning; film appearances include Maintenance, 1992, Permanent Midnight, 1998, Payback, 1999, Coyote Ugly, 2000, Duets, 2000, Sam the Man, 2000, China: The Panda Adventure, 2001, Auto Focus, 2002, 100 Mile Rule, 2002, The Cooler, 2003, Nobody's Perfect, 2004, Secret Window, 2004, Silver City, 2004, Assault on Precinct 13, 2005, A History of Violence, 2005, The Sisters, 2005, The Dark, 2005, Thank You for Smoking, 2006, World Trade Center, 2006, Flicka, 2006, The Jane Austen Book Club, 2007, Yellow Handkerchief, 2008, Downloading Nancy, 2008, The

Mummy: Tomb of the Dragon Emperor, 2008, Nothing Is Private, 2008; (TV films) The Commish: In the Shadow of the Gallows, 1995, Born in Brooklyn, 2001; (TV series) Mr. & Mrs. Smith, 1996, ER, 1997-98 (Screen Actors Guild award for outstanding performance by an ensemble in a drama series, 1997). Co-founder Dream Yard Drama Project for Kids, Harlem, NYC.

BELLOTTI, MIKE, college football coach; b. Concord, Calif. married; 1 child, Luke; children: Keri, Sean. BS with hon. in Phys. Edn., Univ. Calif. Davis, 1973. Wide receivers coach Univ. Calif. Davis; head coach Chico St. Univ., 1984—88; offensive coord. Univ. Oregon, 1989—95, head coach, 1995—. Named PAC-10 Coach of Yr., Sporting News, 2008. Office: Dept Athletics Univ Oregon Eugene OR 97403*

BELLUZZO, RICK E. (RICHARD), information technology and former computer software company executive; BS in Acctg., Golden Gate U. Various positions including gen. mgr. Laser Jet Divsn., Hewlett-Packard Co., exec. v.p.; CEO Silicon Graphics Inc., 1998—99; group v.p. Personal Svcs. and Devices Group, group v.p. consumer group Microsoft Corp., Redmond, Wash., 1999—2001, pres., COO, 2001—02; chmn. bd., CEO Quantum Corp., San Jose, Calif., 2002—. Mem. Sr. Leadership Team, Bus. Leadership Team, Microsoft Corp.; bd. dir. PMC-Sierra, JDS Uniphase. Bd. trustee Golden Gate Univ. Avocations: running, scuba diving, skiing. Office: Quantum Corp 1650 Technology Dr Ste 800 San Jose CA 95110-1382

BELNAP, DAVID F., journalist; b. Ogden, Utah, July 27, 1922; s. Hyrum Adolphus and Lois Ellen B.; m. Barbara Virginia Carlberg, Jan. 17, 1947. Student, Weber Coll., Ogden, 1940. Asst. city editor Seattle Star, 1945-47; bur. chief UP Assns., Helena, Mont., 1947-50, Honolulu, 1950-52; regional exec. Pacific N.W., 1952-55, dir. Latin Am. services, 1955-67; Latin Am. corr. L.A. Times, 1967-80, asst. fgn. news editor, 1980-93. Recipient Overseas Press Club Am. award for best article on Latin Am., 1970, Maria Moors Cabot prize, 1973 Mem. Overseas Press Club Am., LA Press Club, Am. Club of Buenos Aires, Phoenix Club of Lima (Peru). Home and Office: 1134 W Huntington Dr Arcadia CA 91007-6308

BEN-ASHER, M. DAVID, physician; b. Newark, June 18, 1931; s. Samuel Irving and Dora Ruth (Kagan) Ben-Asher; m. Bryna S. Zeller, Nov. 22, 1956. BA, Syracuse U., 1952; MD, U. Buffalo Sch. Med., 1956. Intern E.J. Meyer Mem. Hosp., Buffalo, 1956-57; resident Jersey City Med. Ctr., 1957-58; asst. chief med. service U.S. Army Hosp., Ft. McPherson, Ga., 1958-60; resident Madigan Gen. Hosp., Tacoma, 1960-62; chief gen. med. service Walson Army Hosp., Ft. Dix, NJ, 1962-64; attending staff St. Mary's Hosp., Tucson, 1964—; pvt. practice, 1964—. Bd. dir. Tucson Symphony, 1971-73; mem. Ariz. State Bd. Med. Examiners, 1978-88, joint bd. for regulation of physicians' assts., 1990-97; bd. trustees United Synagogue Am., 1981-87, nat. adv. bd., 1987-91. Fellow ACP; mem. AMA, Pima County Med. Soc. (bd. dir. 1971-77, pres. 1976), Ariz. Med. Assn., Am. Soc. Nephrology. Democrat. Avocations: health club, music, computers. Home: 3401 N Tanuri Dr Tucson AZ 85750-6735 Office: So Ariz Med Specialists 4733 N 1st Ave Tucson AZ 85718-5610 Office Phone: 520-888-3032.

BENAVENTE, DIEGO TENORIO, territorial legislator, former lieutenant governor; b. Saipan, No. Mariana Islands, Apr. 21, 1959; s. Roman Manahane Benavente and Dolores (Tenorio); m. J. Victoria Iniarte; children: Jacob, Diana, James, Dolores. Grad., Northern Mariana Islands Police Academy, 1977; student, College of S. Idaho. Mem. Dist. 1 No. Mariana Islands Commonwealth House of Reps., Saipan, 1990—2002, 2008—, spkr. of the house, 1996—2002; lt. gov. Commonwealth of No. Mariana Islands, Saipan, 2003—06. Republican. Roman Catholic. Office: No Mariana Islands Commonwealth Legis PO Box 500586 Saipan MP 96950 Office Phone: 670-664-8890. Business E-Mail: rep.benavented@cnmileg.gov.mp.

BENCIVENGO, CATHY ANN, lawyer; BA, Rutgers U., 1980, MA, 1981; JD magna cum laude, U. Mich., 1988. Bar: Calif. 1988, US Dist. Ct. (no., ea., so. Calif. dist.), US Ct. Appeals (9th, Fed. cir.), US Supreme Ct. Ptnr., co-chmn. Patent Litigation practice group DLA Piper Rudnick Gray Cary, San Diego. Adj. faculty Univ. San Diego Law Sch., 1999; judge pro tem San Diego County Small Claims Ct.; dir. San Diego Mediation Ctr., 1999—2000. Eagleton Inst. of Politics Fellow. Mem.: San Diego Bar Found. (dir.), ABA, Fed. Bar Assn., Fed. Cir. Bar Assn., San Diego County Bar Assn. (co-chmn. Intellectual Property sect. 1993—94, dir. 1996—98, treas. 1997, v.p. 1998, chmn., lawyer referral & info. svc.), Order of the Coif.

BENDER, BYRON WILBUR, linguistics educator; b. Roaring Spring, Pa., Aug. 14, 1929; s. Ezra Clay and Gertrude Magdalene (Kauffman) B.; m. Lois Marie Graber, Aug. 25, 1950; children: Susan Alice, Sarah Marie, Catherine Anne, Judith Lee, John Richard. BA, Goshen Coll., 1949; MA, Ind. U., 1950, PhD, 1963. Edn. specialist Trust Terr. of Pacific Islands, Majuro, Marshall Island, 1953-59, Saipan, Marianas Island, 1962-64; asst. prof. Goshen Coll., Ind., 1960-62; assoc. prof. linguistics U. Hawaii at Manoa, Honolulu, 1964-69, prof., 1969-99, chmn. dept., 1969-95, prof. emeritus, 2000—. Bd. dirs. U. Hawaii Profl. Assembly, Honolulu, 1978-88, 92-98, pres., 1982-88. Author: Spoken Marshallese, 1969, Linguistic Factors in Maori Education, 1971, (with others) Marshallese-English Dictionary, 1976; editor Oceanic Linguistics Spl. Publ., 1965-2007, Studies in Micronesian Linguistics, 1984, Oceanic Linguistics, 1991-2007; mng. editor Oceanic Linguistics, 1965-90, 2008—. Trustee Hawaii Pub. Employees Health Fund Bd., 1987-95; mem. U. Hawaii Bd. Regents, 2003-08. Recipient Merit awards U. Hawaii 1971, 76, 86. Mem. NEA (standing com. higher edn. 1985-89), Linguistic Soc. Am. (dir. Linguistic Inst. summer 1977, program com. 1987-89, parliamentarian 1994-97). Mem. Soc. Of Friends. Home: Apt 1504 6710 Hawaii Kai Dr Honolulu HI 96825-1548 Office: U Hawaii Dept Linguistics 1890 E West Rd Honolulu HI 96822-2318 Home Phone: 808-395-3269. Personal E-mail: bender@hawaii.rr.com. Business E-Mail: bender@hawaii.edu.

BENDER, CHARLES WILLIAM, lawyer; b. Cape Girardeau, Mo., Oct. 2, 1935; s. Walter William and Fern Evelyn (Stroud) Bender; m. Carolyn Percy Gavagan, June 20, 1961 (div. 1983); children: Theodore Marten, Christopher Percy; m. Betty Lou Port, May 5, 1983; stepchildren: Courtney Elizabeth, Cameron Ann. AB magna cum laude, Harvard U., 1960, LLB magna cum laude, 1963. Bar: Calif. 1965, U.S. Dist. Ct. (ctrl. dist.) Calif. 1965, U.S. Ct. Appeals (9th cir.) 1969, U.S. Supreme Ct. 1979, DC 1984. Assoc. O'Melveny & Myers, LA, 1965—71, ptnr., 1972—84, mng. ptnr., 1984—92, chmn., 1993—2001. Editor: Harvard U. Law Rev., 1961—62; articles editor:, 1962—63. Trustee LA Legal Aid Found., 1971, Lawyers' Com. for Civil Rights Under Law, Washington, 1985—2001; advisor campaign Alan Cranston for Senator, Calif., 1968, Calif., 1974, Calif., 1980; mgr. campaign Jess Unruh for Gov., Calif., 1970. With US Army, 1956—57. Fellow Sheldon Traveling, Harvard U., 1963—64. Democrat. Home: 2831 The Strand Hermosa Beach CA 90254-2400 Office: O'Melveny & Myers 400 S Hope St Los Angeles CA 90071-2899 Personal E-mail: cbender35@mac.com.

BENDER, JOHN C., paper company executive; BS, U.S. Naval Acad.; MSA, George Washington U. Indsl. engr. timer and wood products divsn. Boise Cascade Corp., Yakima, Wash., 1969, v.p. opers. Boise, sr. v.p. bldg. products, 1999—.

BENDER, MICHAEL LEE, state supreme court justice; b. NYC, Jan. 7, 1942; s. Louis and Jean (Waterman) B.; m. Judith Jones, Feb. 27, 1967 (div. Mar. 1977); children: Jeremy, Aviva; m. Helen H. Hand, Sept. 10, 1977; children: Maryjean Hand-Bender, Tess Hand-Bender, Benjamin Hand-Bender. BA in Philosophy, Dartmoutn Coll., 1964; JD, U. Colo., 1967. Bar: Colo. 1967, D.C. 1967, U.S. Supreme Ct. 1980. Pub. defender City and County Denver, 1968-71; assoc. regional atty. EEOC, 1974-75; supr. atty. Jefferson County Pub. Defender, 1975-77; divsn. chief Denver Pub. Defender, Denver, 1977-78; atty. Gibson, Dunn & Crutcher, LA, 1979-80; ptnr. Bender & Treece PC, Denver, 1983-93; pres., shareholder Michael L. Bender PC, 1993-97; justice Colo. Supreme Ct., 1997—. Adj. faculty U. Denver Coll. Law, 1981-86, chair. ABA Criminal Justice sect., Washington, 1990-91, NACD Lawyers Assistant Com., 1989-90, U. Colo. Sch. of Law, 2004; dir. Nat. Assn. Criminal Def. Lawyers, 1984-90; mem. practitioner's adv. com. U.S. Sentencing Com., 1990-91; mem. com. for Criminal Justice Act for Dist. Colo. U.S. Dist. Ct., 1991-93, domestic rels. reform com.; liaison mem. Colo. Pub. Edn. com., Ct. Svcs., 1998—, atty. regulation adv. com., 1998-99; co-chair civil justice com. Supreme Ct., 1998-; liaison Supreme Ct. Standing Com. Colo. Rules Profl. Conduct, 2003-; bd. mem. Int. for Advancement of Am. Legal System, 2006-. Contbr. articles to profl. jours. Bd. govs. Colo. Bar, 1989-91. Recipient Fireman award Colo. State Pub., 1990; Robert C. Heeney Meml. award Nat. Assn. Criminal Def. Lawyers, 1990; Named Vol. of Yr. Denver Bar Assn., 1988. Mem. Colo. Bar Assn. (ethics com. 1980—), ABA (chair criminal justice sect. 1990-91, criminal justice standards com. 1997—). Democrat. Jewish. Avocations: aerobics, skiing, bicycling, camping. Office: Colo Supreme Ct State Jud Bldg 2 E 14th Ave Fl 4 Denver CO 80203-2115

BENDER, RICHARD, dean, architect, educator; b. NYC, Jan. 19, 1930; s. Edward and Betty (Okun) B.; m. Sue Rosenfeld, Aug. 9, 1956; children: Michael, David. BCE, CCNY, 1951; MArch, Harvard U., 1956. Architect Walter Gropius, 1951-53, William Lescaze, 1958-60; with Town Planning Assocs., NYC, 1960-66, ptnr., 1961-66, prin., 1966—; pvt. practice Berkeley, 1966—. Lectr. Columbia U., N.Y.C., 1957-60; asst. prof. Cooper Union, 1961; prof., now prof. emeritus, architecture U. Calif., Berkeley, 1969—, chmn. dept., 1974-76; vis. prof. urban design and constrn., endowed vis. chair U. Tokyo, 1989—; dir. bldg. rsch. bd. Nat. Acad. Sci., 1974-80, mem. adv. bd. on the built environment; adv. panels HUD, Nat. Endowment Arts; mem. design rev. bd. City of San Francisco, U. Calif., J.P. Getty Trust; cons. univ campus planning U. Calif., Berkeley, 1972—95, U. Calif., San Diego, 1987-90, U. Calif., Davis, 1989-93, U. Calif., Santa Cruz, 1992-96, U. Calif., Merced, 2000-03, master plan Benesse Inst. of Arts, Naoshima Island, Japan, 1993-2000, master plan for MediaPolis, Taipei, Taiwan, 1997-2000 master plan for New Town Cergy-Pontoise, France, 1993-2000. Author: A Crack in the Rearview Mirror, 1973. Bd. dirs. Bridge Housing, San Francisco, 1980—; trustee Mills Coll., 1993-98. With U.S. Army, 1954-55. Home: 804 Santa Barbara Rd Berkeley CA 94707-2018 Office: U Calif Coll Environ Design Berkeley CA 94720-1839

BENDIX, HELEN IRENE, lawyer; b. NYC, July 24, 1952; d. Gerhard Max and Eva Gabriela (Sternberger) B.; m. John A. Kronstadt, Nov. 29, 1974. BA, Cornell U., 1973; JD, Yale U., 1976. Bar: Calif. 1976, D.C. 1978, U.S. Dist. Ct. D.C. 1980, U.S. Dist. Ct. (ctrl. dist.) Calif. 1986, U.S. Ct. Appeals (D.C. cir.) 1981, U.S. Ct. Appeals (9th cir.) 1987, U.S. Dist. Ct. (so. dist.) Calif. 1990. Law clk. to Hon. Shirley M. Hufstedler U.S. Ct. Appeals (9th cir.), LA, 1976-77; assoc. Wilmer Cutler & Pickering, Washington, 1977-79; asst. prof. law UCLA, 1979-80; from assoc. to ptnr. Leva Hawes Symington Martin & Oppenheimer, Washington, 1980-85; of counsel Gibson Dunn & Crutcher, LA, 1986-89; ptnr. Heller Ehrman White & McAuliffe, LA, 1989-96; sr. v.p., gen. counsel KCET Cmty. TV of So. Calif., 1996—; judge Mcpl. Ct. L.A. Jud. Dist., 1997-2000, Superior Ct. L.A., 2000—. Vis. prof. law UCLA, 1985-86; chair ADR com. L.A. Superior Ct., 2004-. Co-author: Moore's Federal Practice, Vols. X and XI, 1976, Vols. XII and XIII, 1979; contbr. articles to profl. jours. Violinist Palisades Symphony, Pacific Palisades, Calif., 1989—. Mem. European Union Ctr. of Calif., (mem. exec. adv. bd. 2003-05), Am. Law Inst., DC Bar Assn., Calif. State Bar Assn. (chair internat. law sect. 1990-91), Calif. Judges Assn., L.A. County Bar Assn. (past pres. dispute resolution svcs.), Jud. Coun. Calif. (mem. ad hoc com. on canon 6D 1998, working group on mediator ethics 2000, mem. access and fairness adv. com.), Chancery Club, Phi Beta Kappa. Office: Dept 18 111 N Hill St Los Angeles CA 90012-3014

BENE, STEVEN G., lawyer, game systems company executive; BS, Rice U.; JD, Stanford U. Bar: Calif. Joined Electronic Arts Inc., Redwood City, Calif., 1995, v.p., assoc. gen. counsel, 2003—04, v.p., acting gen. counsel, corp. sec., 2004, sr. v.p., gen. counsel, corp. sec., 2004—. Office: Electronic Arts Inc 209 Redwood Shores Pky Redwood City CA 94065

BENEDICT, BURTON, retired museum director, anthropologist; b. Balt., May 20, 1923; s. Burton Eli Oppenheim and Helen Blanche (Deiches) B.; m. Marion MacColl Steuber, Sept. 23, 1950; children: Helen, Barbara MacVean AB cum laude, Harvard U., 1949; PhD, U. London, 1954. Sr. rsch. fellow Inst. Islamic Studies, McGill U., Montreal, Que., Can., 1954-55; sociol. rsch. officer Colonial Office, London and Mauritius, 1955-58; sr. lectr. social anthropology London Sch. Econs., 1958-68; prof. anthropology U. Calif., Berkeley, 1968-91, prof. emeritus, 1991—, chmn. dept., 1970-71, dean social scis., 1971-74, dir. Hearst Mus. Anthropology, 1989-94; dir. emeritus Hearst Mus. Anthropology, 1994—. Dir. U. Calif. Study Ctr. for U.K. and Ireland, London, 1986-88 Author: Indians in a Plural Society, 1961; author and editor: Problems of Smaller Territories, 1967, (with M. Benedict) Men, Women & Money in Seychelles, 1982, The Anthropology of World's Fairs, 1983; contbr. numerous articles to profl. jours. Trustee East Bay Zool. Soc. Sgt. USAF, 1942-46. Recipient Western Heritage award Nat. Cowboy Hall of Fame, 1984; rsch. fellow Colonial Office, 1955-58, 60, U. Calif., Berkeley, 1974-75; grantee NEH, 1981-83. Fellow Royal Anthrop. Inst. (mem. coun. 1962-65, 67-68, 86-89), Am. Anthrop. Assn.; mem. Assn. Social Anthropologists of Brit. Commonwealth, Athenaeum Club (London) Avocations: museums, the zoo, birdwatching, collecting postcards, world fairs. Office: U Calif Berkeley Dept Anthropology Berkeley CA 94720-0001

BENEFIELD, DEBBIE, state legislator; Mem. Dist. 29 Colo. House of Reps., Denver, 2004—. Democrat. Office: Colo State Capitol 200 E Colfax Denver CO 80203 Office Phone: 303-866-2950. E-mail: debbie.benefield.house@state.co.us.*

BENET, LESLIE ZACHARY, pharmacologist, educator; b. Cin., May 17, 1937; s. Jonas John and Esther Racie (Hirschfeld) Benet; m. Carol Ann Levin, Sept. 8, 1960; children: Reed Michael, Gillian Vivia. AB in English, U. Mich., 1959, BS in Pharmacy, 1960, MS in Pharm. Chemistry, 1962; PhD in Pharm. Chemistry, U. Calif., San Francisco, 1965; PhD (hon.), Leiden U., Netherlands, 1995, U. Athens, 2005; PharmD (hon.), Uppsala U., Sweden, 1987; DSc (hon.), U. Ill., Chgo., 1997, Phila. Coll. Pharm. and Sci., 1997, LI U., 1999. Asst. prof. pharmacy Wash. State U., Pullman, 1965—69; asst. prof. pharmacy and pharm. chemistry U. Calif., San Francisco, 1969—71, assoc. prof., 1971—76, prof., 1976—, vice chmn. dept. pharmacy, 1973—78, chmn. dept. pharmacy, 1978—96, dir. drug studies unit, 1977—, dir. drug kinetics and dynamics ctr., 1979—98, chmn. dept. biopharm. scis., 1996—98. Mem. pharmacology study sect. NIH, Washington, 1977—81, chmn., 1979—81, 1986—88, mem. pharmacol. scis. rev. com., 1984—88; mem. generic drugs adv. com. FDA, 1990—94; mem. Sci. Bd., 1992—98; chair external rev. com. CBER, 1998, chair expert panel on individual equivalence, 1998—2000; mem. sci. adv. bd. SmithKline Beecham Pharms., 1989—92, Pharmetrix, 1989—92, Alteon, Inc., 1993—, TheraTech, Inc., 1993—96, Roche Biosci., 1998—2001, Pain Therapeutics, Inc., 1999—2003, UMD, Inc., 1999—2008, Silico Insights, Inc., 2000—, InforMedix, 2001—06, LifeCycle Pharma, 2004—08, Hurel Corp., 2004—, Co-Mentis, 2004—, Savient Pharm., 2004—07, Limerick BioPharma, 2005—, Panacea Biotech Ltd., 2006—, CNS Bio Pty Ltd., 2007—, Auspex Pharm., 2008—, Optina Biotech., 2008—, Viral Genetics, 2009—; chmn. bd. AvMax, Inc.; bd. dirs. Impax Pharmas., One World Health. Assoc. editor Pharmacology and Therapeutics, 1995—2000, editor Jour. Pharmacokinetics and Biopharmaceutics, 1976—98, mem. editl. bd. The Effect of Disease States on Drug Pharmacokinetics, 1976, Pharmacology, 1979—, Pharmacy Internat., 1979—82, Pharm. Rsch., 1983—95, Pharmacokinetic Basis for Drug Treatment, 1984, Pharmacokinetics: A Modern View, 1984, ISI Atlas of Sci.: Pharmacology, 1988—89, Integration of Pharmacokinetics, Pharmacodynamics and Toxicokinetics in Rational Drug Development, 1992, Clinical Applications of Mifepristone (RU486) and Other Antiprogestins, 1993, Pharm. News, 1994—98, AAPS Jour., 1999—, Molecular Interventions, 2000—, Chemistry and Pharm. Bull., 2000—, Drug Metabolism and Pharmacokinetics, 2002—, Current Drug Metabolism, 2004—, Giving Full Measure to Counter Measures, 2004, Expert Opinion on Drug Metabolism and Toxicology, 2005—; contbr. more than 490 articles to profl. jours. Apptd. Forum on Drug Devel. and Regulation, 1988. Recipient Disting. Tchr. award, 1972—73, Outstanding Faculty Mentorship award, 2001, Rsch. Achievement award in pharm. scis., Pharm. Sics. World Congress, 2004, Career Achievement award in oral drug delivery, Controlled Release Soc., 2004, Disting. Clin. Rsch. award, 2007; named ISI Highly Cited Rschr., 2003. Fellow: AAAS (mem.-at-large exec. com. pharm. scis. sect. 1978—81, 1991—95, chair 1996—97), Am. Assn. Pharm. Scientists (pres. 1986, treas. 1987, bd. dirs. 1988—93, Disting. Pharm. Scientist award 1989, Disting. Svc. award 1996, Wurster rsch. award in pharmaceutics 2000), Acad. Pharm. Scis. (chmn. basic pharmaceutics sect. 1976—77, mem.-at-large exec. com. 1979—83, pres. 1985—86, Rsch. Achievement award 1982); mem.: ISSX (councillor 1992—96, treas. 1998—99), AAUP, Japanese Soc. for Study of Xenobiotics (internat. hon. mem. 2007), Pharm. Scis. World Congress (Rsch. Achievement award 2004), Inst. Medicine of NRC (devel. & acquisition med. countermeasures against biol. warfare agts. 2002—04, chmn. com. accelerating rsch., mem., standing com. biodef. 2007—), Am. Assn. Colls. Pharmacy (bd. dirs. 1992—95, pres. 1993—94, Volwiler Rsch. Achievement award 1991), Am. Coll. Clin. Pharmacy, Drug Info. Assn., Internat. Pharm. Fedn. (bd. pharm. scis. 1988—, chair 1996—2000, Host-Madsen medal 2001), Generic Pharm. Industry Assn. (mem. blue ribbon com. on generic medicines 1990), Am. Soc. for Pharmacology and Exptl. Therapeutics, Am. Soc. Clin. Pharmacology and Exptl. Therapeutics (Rawls-Palmer award and lectureship 1995), Am. Pharm. Assn. (Higuchi Rsch. prize 2000), Am. Coll. Clin. Pharmacology (Disting. Svc. award 1988), Am. Found. for Pharm. Edn. (bd. dirs. 1987—, Disting. Svc. "Profile" award 1993), Inst. Medicine of NAS (forum on drug devel. and regulation 1988—94, chmn. com. on antiprogestins 1993, membership com. 1994—97, chmn. other health profns. sect. 1995—97, chmn. com. pharmacokinetics and drug interactions in elderly 1996—97, mem. Round Table R & D Drugs, Biologics & Med. Devices 1997—2000, bd. on health scis. policy 1999—2005, mem. forum on drug discovery, devel. and transl. 2005—), Sigma Xi, Phi Lambda Sigma, Rho Chi (Ann. Lecture award 1990). Office: U Calif San Francisco Dept Biopharm Scis 533 Parnassus Rm U68 San Francisco CA 94143-0446 Office Phone: 415-476-3853. Business E-Mail: leslie.benet@ucsf.edu.

BENEZRA, NEAL, museum director, curator; b. Oakland, Calif., Aug. 20, 1953; m. Maria Makela; 1 child, Ava. BA, U. Calif., Berkeley, 1976; MA, Stanford U., 1981, PhD, 1983; postgrad., German Acad. Exch. Svc., 1983. Coord. Anderson Collection, Atherton, Calif., 1980-83; asst. curator Des Moines Art Ctr., 1983-84, curator, 1984-85; assoc. curator The Art Inst. Chgo., 1985-86, curator, 1987-91, asst. dir. art and pub. programs, 1996, dep. dir., Frances and Thomas Dittmer curator modern and contemporary art, 2000—02; chief curator Hirshhorn Mus. and Sculpture Garden, Smithsonian Instn., Washington, DC, 1991—96, asst. dir. art & pub. progs., 1996—99; dir. San Francisco Mus. Modern Art, 2002—. Vis. lectr. U. Ill., Urbana-Champaign, 1988; vis. assoc. prof. U. Chgo., 1990; mem. Smithsonian Coun.; art adv. bd. mem. U. Calif., San Francisco; art adv. panel IRS, Dept. Treasury. Curator exhbn./author catalogue: Robert Arneson: A Retrospective, 1986, Ed Paschke: Paintings, 1989, Affinities and Intuitions: The Gerald S. Elliott Collection of Contemporary Art, 1990, Martin Puryear, 1991, Bruce Nauman, 1993-94, Stephen Balkenhol, 1995-96. Grad. fellow Stanford U., 1978-81, McCloy fellow in German art, 1984-85. Office: San Francisco Mus Modern Art 151 Third St San Francisco CA 94103-3159

BENFIELD, JOHN RICHARD, surgeon, educator; b. Vienna, June 24, 1931; arrived in U.S., 1938, naturalized, 1945; s. Richard and Charlotte Lola Benfield; m. Joyce A. Cohler, Dec. 22, 1963; children:

Richard L., Robert E., Nancy J. AB, Columbia U., 1952; MD, U. Chgo., 1955. Diplomate Am. Bd. Surgery, Am. Bd. Thoracic Surgery. Intern Columbia-Presbyn. Hosp., NYC, 1955-56; E.H. Andrews fellow in thoracic surgery U. Chgo., 1956-57; chief resident and instr. in surgery U. Chgo. Clinics, 1962-64, resident in surgery, 1956-57, 59-63; asst. prof. surgery U. Wis., 1964-67; asst. prof. UCLA, 1967-69, assoc. prof., 1969-73, prof., 1973-77, clin. prof., 1978-88; prof. surgery, chief cardiothoracic surgery, vice chmn. surgery U. Calif. Davis Med. Ctr., Sacramento, 1988-95, prof. surgery, chief thoracic surgery, 1995-98, prof. emeritus, 1998—; attending surgeon V.A. Martinez Med. Ctr., 1988-98; courtesy staff Kaiser Permanente Med. Ctr., Sacramento, 1988-98. James Utley prof. surgery, chmn. dept. surgery Boston U., 1977; chmn. surgery City of Hope Nat. Med. Ctr., Duarte, Calif., 1978-87; bd. dirs. Am. Bd. Thoracic Surgery, 1982-88; cons. U.S. Naval Med. Ctr., San Diego, 1968-88; mem. sr. staff VA Wadsworth Med. Ctr., LA, 1978-88. Editor Current Problems in Cancer, 1975-86; mem. editl. bd. Annals Thoracic Surgery, 1979-2001, assoc. editor, 1987-2001; mem. editl. bd. Annals Surg. Oncology, 1994-2000; contbr. articles to profl. jours., chpts. to books. Sec., trustee Univ. Synagogue, LA. Served as capt. M.C. U.S. Army, 1957-59, Korea. Grantee Life Ins. Med. Rsch., 1962-66, Am. Heart Assn., 1968-71, USPHS, 1971-92. Mem. ACS (bd. govs. 1982-88, 92-98), Am. Surg. Assn., Am. Assn. Thoracic Surgery, Am. Assn. Cancer Rsch., Am. Med. Writers Assn., Internat. Assn. Study Lung Cancer, Internat. Soc. Surgery, Calif. Med. Soc., Ctrl. Surg. Assn., LA Acad. Medicine, The Royal Soc. Medicine (Gt. Britain), The Transplantation Soc., Soc. Thoracic Surgeons (v.p. 1994-95, pres. 1995-96), Soc. Univ. Surgeons, Pacific Coast Surg. Assn. (v.p. 1995-96), Soc. Surg. Oncology, Am. Coll. Chest Physicians (pres. Calif. chpt. 1996-97), Western Thoracic Surgeons Assn. (pres. 1989-90), Internat. Surg. Soc., Thoracic Surgery Dirs. Assn. (pres. 1995-97), Thoracic Surgery Found. Rsch. and Edn. (pres. 2003-06). Office Phone: 310-294-7333. Personal E-mail: j.benfield@verizon.net.

BENFORD, GREGORY ALBERT, physicist, writer; b. Mobile, Jan. 30, 1941; s. James Alton and Mary Eloise (Nelson) Benford; m. Joan Abbe, Aug. 26, 1967; children: Alyson Rhandra, Mark Gregory. BS, U. Okla., 1963; MS, U. Calif., San Diego, 1965, PhD, 1967. Research asst. U. Calif., San Diego, 1964—67; postdoctoral fellow Lawrence (Calif.) Radiation Lab., 1967—69, research physicist, 1969—71; prof. physics U. Calif., Irvine, 1971—. Cons. in field. Author: (novels) If the Stars are Gods, 1977, In the Ocean of Night, 1977, The Stars in Shroud, 1978, Find the Changeling, 1980, Timescape, 1980 (Nebula award), Against Infinity, 1983, Across the Sea of Suns, 1984, Artifact, 1985, Heart of the Comet, 1986, In Alien Flesh, 1986, Great Sky River, 1987, Tides of Light, 1989, Beyond the Fall of Night, 1990, Chiller, 1993, Furious Gulf, 1994, Sailing Bright Eternity, 1995; author: (with Mark O Martin) A Darker Geometry, 1996; author: Foundation's Fear, 1997, Cosm, 1998, The Martian Race, Eater, 2000; author: (collections) Matter's End, 1994; editor: Far Futures, 1995; editor: (with Martin H. Greenburg) The New Hugo Winners Volume IV, 1997; editor: Nebula Awards Showcase 2000: The Year's Best SF and Fantasy Chosen by the Science Fiction and Fantasy Writers of America, 2000; editor: (with George Zebrowski) Skylife: Space Habitats in Story and Science, 2000; editor: Worlds Vast and Various, 2000, Deep Time, 1999, Cosm, 1999, Eater, 2000. Recipient Brit. Sci. Fiction award, 1981, Australian Ditmar award for internat. novel, 1981, John Campbell award for best novel, 1981, UN medal in Lit., 1993, Lord prize in Sci., 1994, Lord Found. prize, 1995; grantee Office Naval Rsch., 1975—, 1982—, Army Rsch. Orgn., 1977—82, Air Force Office Sci. Rsch., 1982—, Calif. Space Office, 1984—85; fellow Woodrow Wilson, 1963—64. Mem.: NASA Sci. Adv. Bd., Soc. Sci. Exploration, Sci. Fiction Writers Am. (Nebula award 1975, 1981), Royal Astron. Soc., Am. Phys. Soc., Phi Beta Kappa. Office: Univ California Physics Dept 4129 Frederick Reines Hall Irvine CA 92697-4575 Business E-Mail: gbenford@uci.edu.

BENGIER, GARY T., online company executive; BBA in Computer Sci., Kent State U.; M in Bus. Adminstrn., Harvard Bus. Sch. Sr. fin. mgmt. Kenetech Corp., Qume Corp.; sr. fin. officer Compass Design Automation; CFO Vxtreme, eBay, Inc., San Jose, CA. Office: EBay Inc 2125 Hamilton Ave San Jose CA 95125

BENHAM, JAMES H., state official; b. Twin Falls, Idaho, July 14, 1944; s. James Henry and Matilda (Riggs) B.; m. Ann Elizabeth McIntosh, Mar. 27, 1965; 2 children. BA in Polit. Sci., Idaho State U., 1990, MPA, 1992. From police officer to chief of police Pocatello (Idaho) Police Dept., 1988-94; U.S. marshal dept. justice U.S. Dist. Idaho, Boise, 1994—. Contbr. articles to profl. jours. Bd. dirs. Nat. Criminal Justice Assn., 1992-93. Mem. Idaho Peace Officers Assn. (pres. 1986), Idaho Chief of Police Assn. (pres. 1990-91), Pocatello Police Relief Assn., Lions, Phi Kappa Phi. Methodist. Avocations: golf, fishing, hunting, gardening, exercise. Office: US Marshal for Dist Idaho 550 W Fort St # 010 Boise ID 83724-0101

BENHAMOU, ERIC A., information technology company executive; MSEE, Stanford U.; diplome d'Ingenieur, Ecole Nationale Superieure d'Arts et Metiers, Paris; doctorate (hon.), Ben Gurion U. of Negev, Widener U., Western Govs. U., U. S.C. Project mgr., software mgr., design engr. Zilog, Inc.; v.p. Bridge Comm., 1981—87; CEO 3Com Corp., Santa Plz., Calif., 1990—2000, chmn., 1990—, palmOne, Inc., Milpitas, Calif., 1999—2007, CEO, 2001—03; chmn., CEO Benhamou Global Ventures, LLC., 2003—. Bd. dirs. Smart Valley Inc., Cypress Semiconductor, Legato, Santa Clara U. Sch. Bus., New Am. Found., Intransa, Atrica, INSEAD Sch. Bus., Stanford U. Sch. Engring., Ben Gurion U. of Negev; chair Am. Electronics Assn. Nat. Info. Infrastructure Task Force; apptd. to Pres. Info. Tech. Advisory Com., 1997, Joint High Level Adv. Panel US-Israel Sci. and Tech. Commn., 2003; adj. prof. INSEAD; vis. prof. Ben Gurion U. Recipient Pres. Environ. and Conservation Challenge award, 1992, Medaille Nessim Habif, Ecole Nat. Supérieure d'Arts, 1997, Fgn. Investment Jubilee award Israeli Prime Min. Benjamin Netanyahu, 1998, Ellis Island medal honor, 1998, David Packard Civic Entrepreneur award, 2007. Fellow: Internat. Engring. Consortium. Office: Palmone Inc 950 W Maude Ave Sunnyvale CA 94085-2801

BEN-HORIN, DANIEL, information technology executive; b. Queens, NY, Dec. 25, 1947; BA in Psychology, U. Chgo., 1969. Writer NY Times, The Nation, Harper's Weekly, Mother Jones, Redbook, and others; with Ariz. Republic; editor New Times, Phoenix; dir. Media Alliance, San Francisco, 1981—84; instr. journalism U. Calif., Santa Cruz; founder, pres. CompuMentor, 1987—. Spkr. in field. Named one of 50 Most Influential People in Nonprofit Sector, Nonprofit Times, 2004—07. Office: CompuMentor 435 Brannan St Ste 100 San Francisco CA 94107 Office Phone: 415-633-9300. Office Fax: 415-633-9400.

BENI, GERARDO, electrical engineer, educator; b. Florence, Italy, Feb. 21, 1946; came to U.S., 1970; s. Edoardo and Tina (Bazzanti) B.; m. Susan Hackwood, May 24, 1986; children: Catherine Elizabeth, Juliet Beatrice. Laurea in Physics, U. Firenze, Florence, Italy, 1970; PhD in Physics, UCLA, 1974. Research scientist AT&T Bell Labs., Murray Hill, NJ, 1974-77, Holmdel, NJ, 1977-82, disting. mem. tech. staff, 1982-84; prof. elec. and computer engring. U. Calif., Santa Barbara, 1984—91, dir. Ctr. for Robotic Systems in Microelectronics, 1985—91, prof. elec. engring. Riverside, 1991—, dir. multimedia lab. and studio, 1991—94, chmn. elec. engring. dept., 1997—98. Dir. Multimedia Lab & Studio, 1991—94. Founder, editor: Jours. Robotic Systems, 1983-2005 (Jour. of Yr. award 1984); editor: Recent Advances in Robotics, 1985, Vacuum Mechatronics, 1990; contbr. more than 170 articles to tech. jours. Fellow AAAS, Am. Physics Soc. Achievements include patents in field. Office: U Calif-Riverside Coll Engring Riverside CA 92521-0001 Business E-Mail: beni@ee.ucr.edu.

BENING, ANNETTE, actress; b. Topeka, May 29, 1958; m. J. Steven White, May 26, 1984 (div. 1991); m. Warren Beatty, March 12, 1992; children: Kathlyn Bening Beatty, Benjamin Beatty, Isabel Ashley Ira Beatty, Ella Corinne Beatty. Student, Mesa Coll.; theatre degree, San Francisco State U.; studied at Am. Conservatory Theatre. Bd. govs. Acad. Motion Picture Arts & Sciences, 2008—. Actress: (films) The Great Outdoors, 1988, Valmont, 1989, The Grifters, 1990 (Acad. Award nomination Best Supporting Actress 1990), Postcards from the Edge, 1990, Guilty by Suspicion, 1991, Regarding Henry, 1991, Bugsy, 1991, Love Affair, 1994, Richard III, 1995, The American President, 1995, Mars Attacks!, 1996, The Siege, 1998, American Beauty, 1999 (Acad. Award nomination for Best Actress), In Dreams, 1999, What Planet Are You From?, 2000, Open Range, 2003, Being Julia, 2004 (Named Best Actress Nat. Bd. Rev. Motion Pictures 2004, Golden Globe for Best Actress, 2005), Running with Scissors, 2006, The Women, 2008; (TV movies) Manhunt for Claude Dallas, 1986, Hostage, 1988, Mrs. Harris, 2005; (TV appearances) Miami Vice, 1987, Wiseguy, 1987, The Sopranos, 2004; (TV series) Liberty's Kids: Est. 1776, 2002; (stage appearances) Coastal Disturbances, 1986, (Tony award nomination 1986, Clarence Derwin award 1987, Theatre World award 1987), Spoils of War, 1988, Hedda Gabler, 1999 Recipient Star, Hollywood Walk of Fame, 2006, Bd. of Governors award, Am. Soc. Cinematographers, 2008. Avocation: scuba diving. Office: c/o Nancy Seltzer and Associates 6220 Del Valle Dr Los Angeles CA 90048

BENIOFF, MARC, Internet company executive; b. San Francisco, Sept. 25, 1964; BS in Bus. Admin., U. of Southern Calif., 1986. Founder Liberty Software, 1979; assembly lang. programmer Apple Computer, 1984; various leadership positions in sales, mktg. and prod. devel. Oracle Corp., 1996—99, sr. v.p. web/workgroup systems div., 1995—96, sr. v.p. mktg., 1996—99; founder, chmn., CEO Salesforce.com, Inc., 1999—, also bd. dir. Apptd. by Pres. George W. Bush as co-chairman President's Information Technology Advisory Com. (PITAC), 2003—; apptd. by Hawaiian Gov. Linda Lingle Citizens to Achieve Reform in Edn., 2003—; bd. dirs. Grand Central Communications, 2003—. Co-author: Compassionate Capitalism, 2004. Founder salesforce.com Found., 2000—. Recipient Promise of Peace award, Prime Min. of Israel Benjamin Netanyahu, Bridge award, HEAVEN (Helping Educate, Activate, Volunteer, and Empower via the Net), Excellence in Corp. Philanthropy award, Com. Encouraging Corp. Philanthropy, 2007; named Northern Calif. Entrepreneur of Yr., Ernst & Young, 2003, Alumni Entrepreneur of Yr., U. SC Marshall Sch. Bus., 2004, Entrepreneur of Yr., SunBridge, World Class Innovator, DEMO, 2005, Internat. CEO of Yr., Selling Power, Ernst and Young Entrepreneur of Yr., 2007; named one of Top 10 Entrepreneurs to Watch, Fortune, 25 people responsible for turning e-business around, BusinessWeek, 20 Most Influential People in the Industry, CRM Mag., Agenda Setters, Silicon.com, 50 Who Matter Now, CNNMoney.com Bus. 2.0, 2006, Top 100 Most Influential People in IT, eWEEK, 2007. Created an on-demand hosted Customer Relationship Management (CRM) solution that would replace traditional enterprise software technology which went public in June, 2004. Office: salesforce.com One Market St Ste 300 San Francisco CA 94105

BENJAMIN, KARL STANLEY, artist, educator; b. Chgo., Dec. 29, 1925; s. Eustace Lincoln and Marie (Klamsteiner) B.; m. Beverly Jean Paschke, Jan. 29, 1949; children: Beth Marie, Kris Ellen, Bruce Lincoln. Student, Northwestern U., 1943-46; BA, U. Redlands, 1949; MA, Claremont Grad. Sch., 1960. With dept. arts Pomona Coll., Claremont, Calif., 1979-97, Loren Barton Babcock Miller prof., artist-in residence, 1978-94, prof. emeritus, 1997—; prof. art Claremont Grad. Sch. Traveling exhbns. include New Talent, Am. Fedn. Arts, 1959, 4 Abstract Classicists, Los Angeles and San Francisco museums, 1959-61, West Coast Hard Edge, Inst. Contemporary Arts, London, Eng., 1960, Purist Painting, Am. Fedn. Arts, 1960-61, Geometric Abstractions in Am., Whitney Mus., 1962, Paintings of the Pacific, U.S., Japan and Australia, 1961-63, Artists Environment, West Coast, Amon Carter Mus., Houston, 1962-63, Denver annual, 1965, Survey of Contemporary Art, Speed Mus., Louisville, 1965, The Colorists, San Francisco Mus., 1965, Art Across Am, Mead Corp., 1965-67, The Responsive Eye, Mus. Modern Art, 1965-66, 30th Biennial Exhbn. Am. Painting, Corcoran Gallery, 1967, 35th Biennial Exhbn. Am. Painting, 1977, Painting and Sculpture in California: The Modern Era, San Francisco Mus. Modern Art, 1976-77, Smithsonian Nat. Collection Fine Arts, Washington, 1976-77, Los Angeles Hard Edge: The Fifties and Seventies, Los Angeles County Mus. Art, 1977, Corcoran Gallery, Washington, Cheney Cowles Mus., Spokane, 1980, Calif. State U., Bakersfield, 1982, Henry Gallery, U. Wash., 1982, U. Calif., Santa Barbara, 1984, LA Mcpl. Art Galleries, Barnsdall Park, 1986, Turning the Tide: Early Los Angeles Modernists, Santa Barbara Mus. Art, Oakland Mus., others, 1989-91, LA County Mus. Art, 1996, After Geometric Expression, LA Mus. Art, 2004, The Optic Nerve, Columbus, Ohio, Mus. of Art, 2006, Birth of the Cool, Orange County, Calif., Mus. of Art, 2006; rep. permanent collections, Whitney Mus., LA County Mus. Art, San Francisco Mus. Art, Santa Barbara, Calif., Mus. Art, Pasadena, Calif., Art Mus., Long Beach, Calif., Mus. Art, La Jolla, Calif., Mus. Art, Fine Arts Gallery San Diego, U. Redlands, Mus. Modern Art, Israel, Pomona Coll., Scripps Coll., Univ. Mus., Berkeley, Calif., Wadsworth Atheneum, Nat. Collection Fine Arts, Seattle Mus. Modern Art, Newport Harbor Mus., U. N.Mex. Mus. Art, Wash. State U., LA Mus. Contemporary Art, Houston Mus. Contemporary Art, Balt. Mus. Art, Chgo. Art Inst.; retrospective exhbn. covering yrs. 1955-87 Calif State U. at Northridge, 1989, retrospective exhbn. 1979-94, Pomona Coll., 1994, 450 year survey Calif. art Orange County Mus. Art, Newport Beach, 1998-99, LA County Mus., 2004, San Diego Mus. Art, 2004, Riverside Mus. Art, Calif., 2006, Columbus Mus. Art, Ohio, 2007. Served with USNR, 1943-46. Visual Arts grantee NEA, 1983, 89. Office: Pomona Coll Dept Arts 333 N College Way Dept Arts Claremont CA 91711-4429 also: Claremont Grad U Art Dept 251 E 10th St Claremont CA 91711-3913

BENJAMIN, LORNA SMITH, psychologist; d. Lloyd Albert and Esther Smith; children: Laureen, Linda. AB, Oberlin Coll., 1955; PhD, U. Wis., 1960. Lic. psychologist Utah, Wis. NIMH fellow dept. psychiatry U. Wis., 1958-62, clin. psychology intern, 1960-64, asst. prof., 1966-71, assoc. prof., 1971-77, prof. psychiatry, 1977-88; prof. psychology U. Utah, 1988—; founder, Interpersonal Reconstructive Therapy Clinic U. Utah Neuropsychiatric Inst. Adj. prof. psychiatry U. Utah, 1988-; rsch. assoc. Wis. Psychol. Inst., Madison, 1962-66. Author: Interpersonal Diagnosis and Treatment of Personality Disorders, 2003, Interpersonal Reconstructive Therapy: A Peronality Based Treatment Approach for Complex Cases, 2006; contbr. articles to profl. jours. Mem.: APA, Soc. Psychotherapy Rsch., Phi Beta Kappa. Office: Univ Utah Dept Psychology 380 S 1530 E Salt Lake City UT 84112-8934 Home Phone: 801-558-9504; Office Phone: 801-581-4463. Business E-Mail: lsb_3@msn.com.

BENJAMIN, STEPHEN ALFRED, pathologist, department chairman, educator, researcher; b. NYC, Mar. 27, 1939; s. Frank and Dorothy (Zweighaft) Benjamin; m. Barbara Larson, July 25, 1982; children: Jeffrey, Karen, Susan, Douglas. AB, Brandeis U., 1960; DVM, Cornell U., 1964, PhD, 1968. Diplomate Am. Coll. Vet. Pathologists. Fellow pathology Johns Hopkins U., Balt., 1966-67; asst. prof. comparative medicine M.S. Hershey (Pa.) Med. Ctr. of Pa. State U.; exptl. pathologist Inhalation Toxicology Research Inst., Albuquerque, 1970-77; prof. pathology, environ. health and radiol. health scis. Colo. State U., Ft. Collins, 1977—, dir. collaborative radiol. health lab., 1977-91, assoc. dean grad. sch., 1986-94, co-dir. ctr. for environ. toxicology and tech., 1991—, chmn. dept. microbiology, immnology and pathology, 2001—. Contbr. articles sci. articles to profl. mags. Mem.: Amer. Coll. Vet. Pathol., Soc. Toxicologic Pathology, Am. Vet. Med. Assn. Office: Colo State U Dept Pathology Ctr Environ Toxic Fort Collins CO 80523-0001

BENJAMIN, SUSAN SELTON, elementary school educator; b. NYC, June 3, 1946; m. Robert F. Benjamin, Nov. 30, 1968; children: Joshua, Alana. BS, Cornell U., 1968; MEd, Tufts U., 1969. Tchr. Wakefield (Mass.) Schs., 1969-73, Los Alamos (N.Mex.) Schs., 1973—, Piñon Elem. Sch., Los Alamos, N.Mex. Resource tchr. Montessori Sch. House, San Diego, 1986; tchr. U. N.Mex., Los Alamos, 1989, 90; cons. Activities Integrating Math. and Sci. (AIMS) Nat. Leadership, Fresno, Calif., 1992—. Chair leadership Hadassah, Los Alamos, 1991—. Named Outstanding Women of N.Mex., 1980, N.Mex. State Tchr. of Yr., 2002; recipient Presdl. award for excellence in math. tchg. N.Mex. State, 1990, 92, Leadership award Hadassah, 1996. Mem. Nat. Coun. Math. Tchrs. Avocations: hiking, travel, tennis, aerobics. Office: Piñon Elem Sch 90 Grand Canyon Los Alamos NM 87544

BENNET, MICHAEL FARRAND, United States Senator from Colorado; b. New Delhi, Nov. 28, 1964; s. Douglas Joseph and Susanne (Klejman) Bennet; m. Susan Diane Daggett, Oct. 25, 1997; 3 children. BA in History, Wesleyan U., Conn., 1987; JD, Yale U., 1993. Law clk. US Ct. Appeals (4th Cir.); asst. to dep. atty. gen. US Dept. Justice, 1995—97; mng. dir. Anschutz Investment Co., 1997—2003; chief staff to Mayor John Hickenlooper City of Denver, Denver, 2003—05; supt. Denver Pub. Schools, 2005—09; US Senator from Colo., 2009—; mem. US Senate Agrl. Nutrition & Forestry Com., 2009—, US Senate Banking Housing & Urban Affairs Com., 2009—, US Senate Homeland Security & Govt. Affairs Com., 2009—, US Senate Spl. Com. on Aging, 2009—. Democrat. Episcopalian. Office: US Senate 702 Hart Senate Office Bldg Washington DC 20510 also: 2300 15th St Ste 450 Denver CO 80202 Office Phone: 720-423-3300. Office Fax: 720-423-3318.*

BENNETT, ALAN B., research and development company executive, educator; b. Sacramento, Nov. 3, 1954; BS in Botany and Internat. Agrl. Devel., U. Calif., Davis, 1977; PhD in Plant Biology, Cornell U., 1982. Postdoctoral rsch. assoc. sect. plant biology Cornell U., Ithaca, NY, 1982—83; from asst. prof. to assoc. prof. dept. vegetable crops U. Calif., Davis, 1983—91, chair dept. vegetable crops, 1990—93, prof. dept. vegetable crops, 1991—, assoc. dean Coll. Agrl. and Environ. Scis., 1993—99; exec. dir. tech. transfer and rsch. adminstrn. U. Calif. Sys., 2000—. Office: U Calif-Davis Dept Vegetable Crops 101 Mann Lab Davis CA 95616

BENNETT, ALAN JEROME, electronics executive, physicist; b. Phila., June 13, 1941; s. Leon Martin and Reba (Perry) B.; m. Frances Kitey, June 16, 1963; children: Sarah, Rachel, Daniel. BA, U. Pa, 1962; MS, U. Chgo., 1963, PhD, 1965. Physicist R & D ctr. GE, Schenectady, N.Y., 1966-74, br. mgr. R & D ctr., 1975-79; dir. electronics lab. Gould Inc., Rolling Meadows, Ill., 1979-84; v.p. R & D Varian Assocs., Palo Alto, Calif., 1984-91; dir. program devel. Lawrence Livermore Nat. Lab., Livermore, Calif., 1992-96, dir. indsl. partnerships and commercialization, 1997—2003, mgr. program devel., lab. assoc., 2003—. Contbr. articles to profl. jours. Fellow NSF, 1963-65, 66. Mem. Phi Beta Kappa, Sigma Xi. Avocations: linguistics, amateur radio. Home: 233 Tennyson Ave Palo Alto CA 94301-3737 Personal E-mail: alanbennett@sbcglobal.net.

BENNETT, C. FRANK, molecular pharmacologist; b. Aztec, N.Mex., Nov. 1, 1956; s. Clarence Acie Bennett and Elizabeth Lavender (Fish) Taylor; m. Paula Marie Chamberland, May 17, 1986; children: Christopher Franklin, Nicholas Dean Paul. BS in Pharmacy, U. N.Mex., 1980; PhD, Baylor U., 1985. Registered pharmacist. Staff pharmacist Hermann Hosp., Houston, 1982-85; postdoctoral fellow Smith Kline & French Labs., Phila., 1985-87, assoc. sr. investigator, 1987-89; sr. scientist ISIS Pharm., Carlsbad, Calif., 1989-90, group leader, 1990—. Dir. inflammation program ISIS Pharm., Carlsbad, 1989—. Contbr. articles to profl. jours. Grantee NIH; recipient Bristol award in Pharmacy Bristol Labs., 1980. Mem. AAAS, Am. Soc. for Cell Biology, Rho Chi. Avocations: fishing, camping. Office: ISIS Pharm Inc 2292 Faraday Ave Carlsbad CA 92008

BENNETT, CHARLES FRANKLIN, JR., biogeographer, educator; b. Oakland, Calif., Apr. 10, 1926; s. Charles Franklin and Charlotte Louise (Normand) B.; m. Carole Ann Messenger, Nov. 30, 1947; 1 child, Ashley Lynn. PhD, UCLA, 1959. Instr. UCLA, 1959-60, asst. prof., 1960-65, assoc. prof., 1965-69, prof. biogeography, 1969—; prof. emeritus, 1993—. Cons. in field. Author: Human Influence on Zoogeography of Panama, 1968, Man and Earth's Ecosystems, 1976, Conservation of Natural Resources, 1983; contbr. articles to profl. jours. Guggenheim fellow, 1970-71. Fellow AAAS, Royal Geog. Soc.; mem. Ecol. Soc. Am., Assn. Tropical Biology, Soc. for Conservation Biology, Fauna and Flora Preservation Soc., Am. Inst. Biol. Scis. Avocation: collecting natural history books. Home: 317 S Anita Ave Los Angeles CA 90049-3805 Office: UCLA Dept Geography 405 Hilgard Ave Los Angeles CA 90095-9000 Business E-Mail: chasben@ucla.edu.

BENNETT, CHARLES LEON, vocational and graphic arts educator; b. Salem, Oreg., Feb. 5, 1951; s. Theodore John and Cora Larena (Rowland) B.; m. Cynthia Alice Hostman, June 12, 1976 (div.); m. Lynn Marie Toland, Aug. 12, 1977 (div.); children: Mizzy Marie, Charles David.; m. Christina M. Crawford, Dec. 19, 1987 (div.); m. Iris J. Perrigo, Mar. 17, 2001. AS in Vocat. Tchr. Edn., Clackamas C.C., 1977; AS in Gen. Studies, Linn Benton C.C., 1979; BS in Gen. Studies, Ea. Oreg. State Coll., 1994. Tchr. printing Tongue Point Job Corps, Astorial, Oreg., 1979-80; tchr., chmn. dept. Portland (Oreg.) Pub. Schs., 1980—2006; owner, mgr. printing and pub. co. Portland, 1981-87; ret., 2006. With AUS, 1970-72. Mem. NRA, Oreg. Vocat. Trade-Tech. Assn. (cept. chmn., pres. graphic arts divsn., Indsl. Educator of Yr. 1981-82), Oreg. Vocat. Assn. (Vocat. Tchr. of Yr. 1982-83), Graphic Arts Tech. Found., In-Plant Printing Mgmt. Assn., Internat. Graphic Arts Edn. Assn. (v.p. N.W. region VI), Oreg. Assn. Manpower Spl. Needs Pers., Oreg. Indsl. Arts Assn., Internat. Platform Assn., Nat. Assn. Quick Printers, Am. Vocat. Assn., Pacific Printing and Imaging Assn., Inplant Printing Mgmt. Assn., Portland Club Lithographers and Printing House Craftsmen. Republican. Home: 20295 S Unger Rd Beavercreek OR 97004-8884 Office: 546 NE 12th Ave Portland OR 97232-2719 Office Phone: 503-916-5100 x 2039. Personal E-mail: cbennett@bctonline.com. Business E-Mail: cbennett@pps.k12.or.us.

BENNETT, DICK, college basketball coach; b. Pitts., Apr. 20, 1943; m. Anne; children: Kathi, Amy, Tony. BS in phys. edn., Ripon Coll., 1965; MEd, UW-Stevens Point. Basketball coach West Bend (Wis.) HS, 1965-66; coach various Wis HS teams, 1966-76, UW-Stevens Point, 1976-85, UW-Green Bay, 1985-95, U. Wis., Madison, 1995—2000, Wash. St. U., Pullman, 2003—06. 1st team at U. Wis. (17-15) appeared in 1996 N.I.T.; 2d team (18-10) made 2d U. Wis. appearance in N.C.A.A. tournament in 50 yrs., put together sch.'s 1st 6-game winning streak since 1951. Named WSUC Coach of Yr., 1982, 1985, NAIA Coach of Yr., 1984, NAIA Area IV Coach of Yr., 1985, Mid-Continent Coach of Yr., 1990, 1992, NABC Dist. 11 Coach of Yr., 1992, 1994, Basketball Times Midwest Coach of Yr., 1994. Achievements include 21-yr. collegiate coaching record, 395-214 (.649). Office: Bohler Athletic Complex Wash State Univ Basketball PO Box 641602 Pullman WA 99164-1602

BENNETT, FRED GILBERT, lawyer; b. May 28, 1946; HBA magna cum laude, U. Utah, 1970; JD, U. Calif., 1973. Bar: Calif. 1974. Ptnr. Gibson, Dunn & Crutcher, LA, 1980-98; sr. ptnr. Quinn Emanuel Urquhart Oliver & Hedges, 1998—. Mem. nat. com. on arbitration U.S. Coun. for Internat. Bus., 1984—, chmn. western subcom., 1989—; comml. and constrn. arbitrator Internat. C. of C./Am. Arbitration Assn. Large Complex Case Panel; chmn. continuing edn. com. Am. Arbitration Assn. Large Complex Case Panel; bd. dirs. Am. Arbitration Assn. Mng. editor UCLA Law Rev., 1972-73. Named Outstanding U.S. Lawyer, Chambers U.S.A., 2003. Mem. ABA, Internat. Bar Assn., L.A. County Bar Assn., Phi Beta Kappa. Office: Quinn Emanuel Urquhart Oliver & Hedges 865 S Figueroa St Los Angeles CA 90017-2543

BENNETT, GERALD A., state legislator; Mem. Dist. 1 Mont. House of Reps., 2008—. Republican. Office: Montana House of Representatives PO Box 400200 Helena MT 59620-0400 Mailing: 784 Taylor Rd Libby MT 59923-8458 Home Phone: 406-293-7012; Office Phone: 406-444-4800. Office Fax: 406-444-4825. Personal E-mail: jbenhd1@hotmail.com.

BENNETT, KENNETH R., state official, former state senator; b. Tucson, Aug. 1, 1959; s. Archie Roy and Donna Lucille (Bulechek) B.; m. Jeanne Tenney Bennett, Mar. 13, 1982; children: Ryan, Dana, Clifton. BS, Ariz. State U., 1984. CEO Bennett's Oil Co., 1984—2006; mem. Ariz. State Senate from Dist. 1, Tucson, 1999—2007, pres., 2003—06; CEO GeoBio Energy, Inc., Seattle, 2008—; sec. state State of Ariz., Phoenix, 2009—. Mem. Ariz. State Bd. Edn., Phoenix, 1992-99, pres., 1996-97; Ariz. State Bd. for Charter Schs., Phoenix, 1994—, Governor's Task Force Edn. Reform, Phoenix, 1991-92. Mayor pro tempore City of Prescott (Ariz.), 1988; councilman City of Prescott (Ariz.), 1985-89; Mayor Pro Tempore City of Prescott (Ariz.), 1988, scoutmaster Boy Scouts of America, 1993—. Recipient Polly Rosenbaum award, Ariz. State Library, Archives & Pub. Records, 2007. Mem., Education Leaders Council, Washington; Ariz. St. Charter Sch. Bd. Republican. Mem. Lds Ch. Office: Office Secretary of State State Capitol 1700 W Washington Phoenix AZ 85007 Office Phone: 520-628-6583. Office Fax: 520-628-6938.*

BENNETT, MARK J., state attorney general; m. Patricia Tomi Ohara. BA summa cum laude in Polit. Sci., Union Coll., 1976; JD magna cum laude, Cornell U., 1979. Law clk. to Hon. Samuel P. King, Chief Judge US Dist. Ct. Hawaii; asst. US atty. Washington, 1980—82, Honolulu, 1982—90; litig. ptnr. McCorriston, Miller, Mukai & MacKinnon, LLP, Honolulu, 1991—2002; pro bono spl. dep. atty. gen., spl. asst. pros. atty. Hawaii State Ct.; atty. gen. State of Hawaii, Honolulu, 2003—. Instr. criminal and civil trial advocacy Atty. Gen.'s Adv. Inst., Washington; instr. U. Hawaii Sch. Law. Recipient Spl. Achievement award, US Atty. Gen., 1986. Mem.: Am. Coll. Trial Lawyers. Republican. Office: Office of Atty Gen 425 Queen St Honolulu HI 96813 Office Phone: 808-586-1500.*

BENNETT, PAUL GROVER, agribusiness executive; b. Ancon, Panama, Sept. 1, 1940; s. Arden Lamont and Mercedes (Reluz) B.; m. Diane Huarte, Dec. 17, 1967; children: Courtney, Kimberly, Christopher, Michael. BA, Northwestern U., 1962; MBA, Stanford U., 1968. Fin. analyst, rsch. supt. Std. Fruit Co. (Dole Food Co.), Limon, Costa Rica, 1968-70, rsch. dir. La Ceiba, Honduras, 1970-72, asst. gen. mgr. Guayaquil, Ecuador, 1972—73; v.p., regional contr. Castle & Cooke Foods (Dole Food Co.), San Francisco, 1973-74, v.p., gen. mgr. Davao, Philippines, 1974-76, Medellin, Colombia, 1977-78, Mauna Loa Macadamia Nut Corp., Hilo, Hawaii, 1978-81, pres., 1981-83; group v.p. diversified svcs. Inernat. Air Svc. Co. Ltd, Foster City, Calif., 1983-86; pres. Hawaiian Holiday Macadamia Nut co., Honolulu, 1986-89; sr. ptnr. Agricon Hawaii, Honolulu, 1989-91; pres., CEO Calif. Ammonia Co., Stockton, 1981-93; pres. Naturipe Berry Growers, Watsonville, Calif., 1993-96; pres., CEO Sakata Seed Am., Inc., Morgan Hill, Calif., 1997—. Dir. Am. Seed Trade Assn., Washington, 1999—, Asociacion Mexicana de Semilleros, Mexico City, 1999—2000; bd. dirs., 1st vice chmn. Agrl. Coun. of Calif., 1994—96; alt. dir. Calif. Strawberry Commn.; mem. adv. bd. Food and Agribus. Inst., St. Clara U.; bd. dirs. Calif. Agrl. Leadership Found., 2003—. Served to lt. comdr. USN, 1962—66. Mem.: Stanco, Stanford Alumni Assn., Phi Gamma Delta. Republican.

BENNETT, RANDY, men's college basketball coach; m. Darlene Bennett; children: Chase, Cade. Attended, Mesa CC, Ariz., 1980—82; BSc in Biology, U. Calif., San Diego, 1986. Asst. coach U. San Diego Toreros, 1985—86, asst. coach, recruiting coord., 1988—96; asst. coach U. Idaho Vandals, 1986—88; asst. coach, recruiting coord. Pepperdine U. Waves, 1996—99; asst. coach St. Louis U. Billikens, 1999—2001; head coach St. Mary's Coll. Gaels, 2001—. Named Co-West Coast Conf. Coach of Yr., 2008. Office: St Mary's Coll Basketball 1928 St Mary's Rd PO Box 5100 Moraga CA 94575*

BENNETT, ROBERT F., United States Senator from Utah; b. Salt Lake City, Sept. 18, 1933; s. Wallace F. Bennett; m. Joyce McKay; 6 children. BS, U. Utah, 1957. Staff positions US House Reps., US Senate, Washington; CEO Franklin Quest, Salt Lake City, 1984-90; senator from Utah, chief dep. whip, counsel to Rep. leader U.S. Senate, Washington, 1993—, ranking mem. agr. appropriations and fin. inst. subcom, 2007—, mem. joint econ. com., 2007—, mem. banking, housing, urban affairs com., appropriations com., ranking mem. rules com., 2007—. Mem. Rep. high tech. task force; lobbyist various orgns., Washington; head Dept. Transp.'s Congl. Liaison. Author: Gaining Control. Chmn. Education Strategic Planning Commn. Utah State Bd. Edn. (mem. Edn. Strategic Planning Com.). Recipient Light of Learning award for Outstanding Contbns. to Utah edn., 1989; named Entrepreneur of Yr. for Rocky Mtn. region INC. magazine, 1989. Republican. Office: US Senate 431 Dirksen Senate Ofc Bldg Washington DC 20510-0001 Office Phone: 202-224-5444.*

BENNETT, ROBERT R., telecommunications company executive; b. Apr. 19, 1958; BA in Econ. (with Honors), Denison U.; MBA, Columbia U. With The Bank of N.Y.; v.p., dir. fin. Telecom., Inc., 1987-90; prin. fin. officer Liberty Media Corp., Englewood, Colo., 1990, exec. v.p., CFO, exec. v.p., sec. & treas., 1995—97, CFO, 1996—97, CEO, 1997—2005, pres., 1997—2006, Discovery Holding Co., Englewood, Colo., 2006—. Bd. dirs. OpenTV Corp., UnitedGlobalCom, Inc., Ascent Media Group, Inc., Liberty Satellite & Technology, Inc., IAC/Interactive Corp., 2001—04, Starz Encore Group, Discovery Holding Co., 2006—, Sprint Nextel Corp., 2006—. Office: Discovery Holding Co 12300 Liberty Blvd Englewood CO 80112

BENNETT, STEPHEN M., former computer software company executive; b. Madison, Wis., Mar. 8, 1954; BA in Fin. and Real Estate, U. Wis., 1976. Various mgmt. positions GE Appliances, GE Med. and GE Supply; v.p. of Ams. GE Elec. Distbn. and Control; pres., CEO GE Capital Vendor Fin. Svcs., 1996—99, GE Capital e-Bus., 1999; exec. v.p., CEO GE Capital subs. of GE Corp., 1999—2000; CEO, pres. Intuit Inc., Mountain View, Calif., 2000—07. Bd. dirs. Sun Microsystems, Inc., 2004—.

BENNETT, THOMAS LEROY, JR., clinical neuropsychology educator; b. Norwalk, Conn., Sept. 25, 1942; s. Thomas LeRoy and Gertrude Upson (Richardson) B.; m. Jacqueline Beekman, Aug. 5, 1972; children: Dean, Shannon, Brian, Laurie. BA, U. N. Mex., 1964, MS, 1966, PhD, 1968. Diplomate Am. Bd. Profl. Neuropsychology (examiner, treas. 1993-96, 2001--, pres.-elect 1995-97, pres. 1997-99), Am. Bd. Forensic Examiners, Am. Bd. Profl. Disability Cons., Am. Bd. Profl. Psychology. Asst. prof. Calif. State U., Sacramento, 1968-70; assoc. prof., then prof. psychology and physiology Colo. State U., Ft. Collins, 1970-98, coord. exptl. psychology sect., 1978-81, 92-95, prof. emeritus, 1998—; pvt. practice neuropsychology Ft. Collins, 1981—. Mem. allied health staff Poudre Valley Hosp., Ft. Collins; clin. dir. Ctr. for Neurorehab. Svcs., Ft. Collins. Author: Brain and Behavior, 1977, The Sensory World, 1978, The Psychology of Learning and Memory, 1979, Exploring the Sensory World, 1979, Introduction to Physiological Psychology, 1982, The Neuropsychology of Epilepsy, 1992, Brainwave-R: Cognitive Strategies for Brain Injury Rehabilitation, 1997, Mild Traumatic Brain Injury, 1999, Psychology Video Teaching Modules: The Brain, 2d edit., 1997, Psychology Video Teaching Modules: The Mind, 2000; also articles and book chpts.; assoc. editor Rehab. Psychology, Archives of Clinical Neuropsychology; mem. editl. bd. Cognitive Rehab., Archives Clin. Neuropsychology, Jour. Head Injury, Bull. of Nat. Acad. Neuropsychology, Neuropsychology Rev., others. Elder Timnath Presbyterian Ch. Named Outstanding Grad. Educator for Coll. Natural Scis., 1998. Fellow APA, Nat. Acad. Neuropsychology (editl. bd. Bull., bd. dirs. 1993-95, conv. chmn. 1993, 94), Am. Psychol. Soc., Am. Coll. Profl. Neuropsychology (pres. 1997-99); mem. Am. Coll. Forensic Examiners, Psychonomic Soc., Rocky Mountain Psychol. Assn., Soc. for Cognitive Rehab., Nat. Head Injury Found. (provider's coun.), Colo. Head Injury Found. (provder's coun.), Internat. Neuropsychol. Soc., Colo. Neuropsychol. Soc., Sigma Xi (named Colo. State U. Honored Scientist 1996). Home: 213 Camino Real Fort Collins CO 80524-8907 Office: Ctr Novorehabilitation Svc K145 Robertson St Fort Collins CO 80524 Office Phone: 970-493-6667.

BENNETT, WILLIAM GORDON, casino executive; b. Glendale, Ariz., Nov. 16, 1924; Gen. mgr. Del Webb Corp., Las Vegas, 1965-70; with Western Equities Inc., Reno, Nev., 1971-78; chmn. Circus Circus Enterprises Inc., 1974-95, dir.; owner Sahara Hotel, Las Vegas, 1995—. Office: Sahara Hotel Casino 2535 Las Vegas Blvd S Las Vegas NV 89109-1123

BENNETT, WILLIAM JOHN (BILL BENNETT), radio personality, former United States Secretary of Education; b. Bklyn., July 31, 1943; s. F. Robert and Nancy (Walsh) Bennett; m. Mary Elayne Glover, May 29, 1982; children: John, Joseph. BA, Williams Coll., Williamstown, Mass., 1965, LLD (hon.), 1983; PhD, U. Tex., Austin, 1970; JD, Harvard Law Sch., 1971; LittD (hon.), Gonzaga U., 1982; HHD (hon.), Franklin Coll., Ind., 1982, U. N.C., 1984, George Washington U., 1985, Gallaudet Coll., 1985, The Citadel, 1986; LHD (hon.), U. N.H., 1982, Manhattan Coll., 1983, Elon Coll., 1984, Loyola Coll., Md., 1984, Assumption Coll., 1985, Yeshiva U., 1986, Cen. State U., Wilburforce, Ohio, 1987; LD (hon.), Williams Coll., 1983, U. Notre Dame, 1984. Asst. to pres. Boston U., 1972-76; exec. dir. Nat. Humanities Ctr., Research Triangle Park, NC, 1976-79, pres., dir., 1979-81; assoc. prof. NC State U., Raleigh, 1979-81, U. NC, 1979-81; chmn. NEH, Washington, 1981-85; sec. US Dept. Edn., 1985-88; dir. Office Nat. Drug Control Policy, Washington, 1989-90; co-dir. Empower America, Washington, 1993—2004; co-chmn. Nat. Commn. Civic Renewal, College Park, Md., 1996—98, Partnership for Drug-Free America, New York; host nat. syndicated radio prog. Bill Bennett's Morning in America, 2004—. Faculty mem. U. Southern Miss., U. Tex., Harvard U., U. Wis.; chmn. Am.'s for Victory Over Terrorism, 2002—; Washington fellow Claremont Inst., Calif., 2003—. Author, editor Schools Without Drugs, 1986, The De-Valuing of America: The Fight for Our Culture and Our Children, 1992, The Book of Virtues: A Treasury of Great Moral Stories, 1993, The Children's Book of Virtues, 1995, Moral Compass: Stories for a Life's Journey, 1995, Body Count: Moral Poverty...and How to Win America's War Against Crime and Drugs, 1996, Our Sacred Honor: Words of Advice from the Founders in Stories, Letters, Poems and Speeches, 1997, The Children's Book of Heroes, 1997, The Educated Child: A Parent's Guide from Preschool through Eighth Grade, 1999, The Death of Outrage: Bill Clinton and the Assault on American Ideals, 1999, The Broken Hearth: Reversing the Moral Collapse of the American Family, 2001, Virtues of Friendship and Loyalty, 2002, Why We Fight: Moral Clarity and the War on Terrorism, 2003, America: The Last Best Hope (Volume I): From the Age of Discovery to a World at War, 2006, America: The Last Best Hope (Volume II): From a World at War to the Triumph of Freedom, 2007, host (weekly talk show) Beyond the Politics (CNN), 2008—, contbg. writer Nat. Review Online, Nat. Review, Commentary. Republican. Roman Catholic. Office: Claremont Inst Ste E 937 W Foothill Blvd Claremont CA 91711 Office Phone: 909-621-6825. Office Fax: 909-626-8724.*

BENNETT, WILLIAM MICHAEL, internist, educator, nephrologist; b. Chgo., May 6, 1938; s. Harry H. and Helen A. (Kaplan) B.; m. Sandra S. Silen, June 12, 1977; four children. Student, U. Mich., 1956-59; BS, Northwestern U., 1960, MD, 1963. Diplomate Am. Bd. Internal Medicine, Am. Bd. Nephrology, Am. Bd. Clin. Pharmacology. Intern U. Oreg., 1963-64; resident Northwestern U., 1964-66; practice medicine specializing in internal medicine Portland, Oreg., Boston; mem. staff Mass. Gen. Hosp., 1969-70; asst. prof. medicine U. Oreg. Health Scis. Center, 1970-74, assoc. prof., 1974-78, prof. medicine and pharmacology, 1978-2000, ret., 2000. Author: Pharmacology and Management of Hypertension, 1994, Manual of Nephrology, 1990, Drug Therapy in Renal Failure, 1994; contbr. articles to med. jours. Served with USAF, 1967-69. Master ACP; mem. Am. Soc. Nephrology (pres. 1998-99), Transplantation Soc., Internat. Soc. Nephrology, Am. Soc. Pharmacology and Exptl. Therapeutics. Office: Legacy Good Samaritan Hosp Transplant Svcs 1040 NW 22d Ave Ste 480 Portland OR 97210 also: NW Renal Clinic 1130 NW 22d St Ste 640 Portland OR 97210 Office Phone: 503-413-6555. E-mail: bennettw@lhs.org.

BENNINGTON, CHESTER CHARLES, singer; b. Phoenix, Mar. 20, 1976; m. Samantha Bennington, Oct. 31, 1996 (div. 2005); 1 child, Draven Sebastian; m. Talinda Bentley; 1 child, Tyler Lee stepchildren: Jaime, Isiah. Lead vocalist Grey Daze, 1993—98, Linkin Park, 1999—, Dead By Sunrise, 2004—. Singer: (albums) Hybrid Theory, 2000, Meteora, 2003, Live in Texas, 2003, Minutes to Midnight, 2007, Road to Revolution Live at Milton Keynes, 2008, (songs) Crawling, 2000 (Grammy award for Best Hard Rock Performance, 2002), In the End, 2000 (MTV Video Music award for Best Rock Video, 2002), Somewhere I Belong, 2003 (MTV Video Music award for Best Rock Video, 2003), Breaking the Habit, 2003 (MTV Video Music award for Viewer's Choice, 2004), (with Jay-Z) Numb/Encore, 2004 (Grammy award for Best Rap/Sung Collaboration, 2006), What I've Done, 2007 (Top Modern Rock Track, Billboard Year-End Charts, 2007), Shadow of the Day, 2007 (MTV Video Music award for Best Rock Video, 2008). Recipient Best-Selling Rock Group award, World Music Awards, 2002, 2003, Favorite Alternative Artist award, Am. Music Awards, 2003, 2004, 2007, 2008; named Top Modern Rock Artist (with Linkin Park), Billboard Year-End Charts, 2001, 2004, 2007. Office: Linkin Park Machine Shop Recordings PO Box 36915 Los Angeles CA 90036

BENNION, JOHN WARREN, urban education educator; b. Salt Lake City, Nov. 25; s. M. Lynn and Katherine Bennion; m. Sylvia Lustig; children: Philip, Stanford, David, Bryan, Grant, Andrew. BS in Philosophy, English, U. Utah, 1961, MA in Edn. Adminstrn., 1962; PhD in Edn. Adminstrn., Ohio State U., 1966. Tchr. Granite High Sch., Salt Lake City, 1961-63; asst. instr. Ohio State U., Columbus, 1963-64, adminstrv. asst., 1965-66; adminstrv. intern Parma (Ohio) Sch. Dist., 1964-65; asst. supt. Elgin (Ill.) Pub. Schs., 1966-68; asst. prof. edn. adminstrn. Ind. U., Bloomington, 1968-69; supt. Brighton Cen. Schs., Rochester, N.Y., 1969-79, Bloomington (Minn.) Pub. Schs., 1979-80, Provo (Utah) Sch. Dist., 1980-85, Salt Lake City Schs., 1985-94; prof. urban edn., dir. Utah Edn. Consortium U. Utah, Salt Lake City, 1994—. Dir. Utah Urban Sch. Alliance, Salt Lake City; ednl. cons. Comprehensive Sch. Reform, Salt Lake City. Mem. ASCD, Assn. Early Childhood Edn., Am. Assn. Sch. Adminstrs. (Nat. Superintendent of Yr. award 1992, Disting. Svc. award 2002), Phi Delta Kappa, Rotary. Home: 4001 S 700 E Ste 230 Salt Lake City UT 84107-2522 also: 1684 Browning Ave Salt Lake City UT 84105-2704

BENNION, SCOTT DESMOND, physician; b. Casper, Wyo., July 26, 1948; s. Desmond and Wanda Bennion; m. Stephanie Dawn Bennion; children: Scott, Beau, Brandon. BS summa cum laude, U. Wyo., 1970, MS, 1972; MD, U. Utah, 1975. Diplomate Nat. Bd. Med. Examiners, Am. Bd. Internal Medicine, Am. Bd. Dermatology, Am. Bd. Dermatologic Immunology/Diagnostic and Lab. Immunology. Intern U. Rutgers Med. Sch., 1975-76, resident in internal medicine, 1976-78, chief resident dept. medicine, 1978; commd. 2d lt. U.S. Army, 1976, advanced through grades to col., 1991; resident in dermatology Fitzsimons Army Med. Sch., Denver, 1981-84, chief resident dermatology svc., 1984, chief dept. clin. investigations, 1994-96, chmn. lab. animal use and care com., 1994-96; asst. chief dermatology svc. 98th Gen. Hosp., Nuremburg, Germany, 1986, chief dept. health clinics, 1987-88; chief immunodermatology sect. dermatology svc. Fitzsimons Army MC, Aurora, Colo., 1989—96; command surgeon ARTASK, Kuwait, 1992; command surgeon joint task force Kuwait and Army Ctrl. Command-Forward, 1992; dermatology cons. to the Army Surgeon Gen., 1996-99; chief Troop Med. Clin. Fitzsimmons Army Garrison, 1996-99. Asst. clin. prof. dept. dermatology U. Colo. Health Sci. Ctr., 1992—99, assoc. prof. clin. dermatology, 1999—; assoc. prof. clin. medicine U. Wash. Med. Ctr. Contbr. chpts. to books: Military Dermatology, 1994, Secrets of Dermatology, 1996, 2d edit., 2000, 3rd edit., 2007, Dubois Lupus, 1997, also articles to profl. publs. Pres. Nuremburg Elem. Sch. PTSA; asst. cubmaster, cubmaster, chmn. Volksmarch com. Boy Scouts Am., 1986; pres. Foxridge Improvement Assn., 1992-01, pres., 1994-01; bd. dirs. Wyo. Make a Wish Found., 2000-; mem. Alcova Lake Area Bd., 2001-; trustee Casper Coll., 2000-, sec. to bd., 2002-04, treas. to bd., 2004-05, v.p. 2005—08, pres. 2009-; trustee Anam Chara Hospice, Denver, 2001. Named to Order of Mil. Med. Merit, 1987; named Cubmaster of Yr. Bavaria dist. Boy Scouts Am., 1987, Businessman of Yr., Nat. Rep. Congl. Com. Bus. Adv. Coun., 2001; recipient Legion of Merit award, 1999. Fellow: ACP, Am. Acad. Dermatology (mem. govt. medicine task force 1996—2000, Colo. Dermatology Soc. rep. to adv. bd. 1997—, mem. rev. bd. to adv. bd. 2000—, Wyo. Acad. Dermatology rep. to adv. bd.); mem.: Dermatology Found. Leadership Soc. (chmn. Wyo.), Ctrl. Wyo. Skin Clinic, Wyo. Acad. Dermatology (sec. 1999—2003, pres. 2003—), Soc. for Investigative Dermatology, Assn. Mil. Dermatologists (sec.-treas. 1990—96, guest editor jour. 1991, pres. 1998—99, Residents award 1984), Assn. Mil. Surgeons, Phi Kappa Phi. Avocations: skiing, diving. Home: 2800 Garden Creek Rd Casper WY 82601 Office: 2546 E 2nd St #400 Casper WY 82609 E-mail: sdbennion@aol.com.

BENNION, STEVEN D., former academic administrator; b. Salt Lake City; m. Marjorie Hopkins, 1963; 5 children. BA, Univ. Utah; MPA, Cornell Univ.; EdD, Univ. Wisc. Budget & acad. planner Univ. Wisc., 1972—82; pres. Snow Coll., Ephraim, Utah, 1982—89, Ricks Coll. (now Brigham Young Univ. -Idaho), Rexburg, Idaho, 1989—97, So. Utah Univ., Cedar City, 1997—2006.

BENOIT, JOHN J., state legislator; m. Sheryl Benoit; children: Benjamin, Sarah. AA, Riverside City Coll.; BS, Calif. State U., 1978; MA in Pub. Adminstrn., U. Calif., San Bernardino, 1993. Law enforcer; mem. Dist. 64 Calif. State Assembly, 2003—08; mem. Dist. 37 Calif. State Senate, 2009—. Mem. Desert Sands Unified Sch. Dist. Bd. Edn.; mem. budget com.; mem. rules com.; vice chair ins. com. Mem. United Way, 1989—. Republican. Roman Catholic. Office: Dist 37 73-710 Fred Waring Dr Ste 108 Palm Desert CA 92260 Office Phone: 760-568-0408. Office Fax: 760-568-1501.*

BENOLIEL, JOEL, lawyer; b. Seattle, June 11, 1945; s. Joseph H. and Rachel (Maimon) B.; m. Maureen Alhadeff, Mar. 1971; 1 child, Joseph D. BA in Polit. Sci., U. Wash., 1967, JD, 1971. Bar: Wash., US Dist. Ct. (we. dist.) Wash., US Ct. Appeals (9th cir.), US Mil. Ct. Appeals. Assoc. atty. MacDonald, Horgue & Bayless, Seattle, 1971-73, ptnr., 1973-78; v.p., gen. counsel Jack A. Benaroya Co., Seattle, 1978-84; ptnr. Trammell Crow Co., Seattle, 1985-87, Spieker Ptnrs., Bellevue, Wash., 1987-92; sr. v.p. law and real estate, gen. counsel Costco Wholesale Corp. (formerly Price Costco, Inc.), Issaquah, Wash., 1992—. Bd. dir. Overlake Sch., Redmond, Wash., 1995—, Congregation Ezra Bessaroth, Seattle, 1992-95. With US Army, 1968-74. Avocations: tennis, boating, skiing, reading fiction. Office: Costco Wholesale Corp 999 Lake Dr Issaquah WA 98027-5367*

BENSCH, KLAUS GEORGE, pathology educator; b. Miedar, Germany, Sept. 1, 1928; married; 3 children. MD, U. Erlangen, Germany, 1953. Diplomate: Am. Bd. Pathology. Intern U. Hosps. of Erlangen, 1953-54; resident in anat. pathology U. Tex./M.D. Anderson Hosp., Houston, 1954—56; instr. pathology Yale Med. Sch., 1958-61, asst. prof., 1961-64, assoc. prof., 1964-68; prof. pathology Stanford Med. Sch., 1968—, acting chmn. dept. pathology, 1984-85, chmn. dept. pathology, 1985-99, prof. emeritus, 2001—. Office: Stanford U Med Sch Dept Pathology 300 Pasteur Dr Palo Alto CA 94304-2203 E-mail: kbensch@stanford.edu.

BENSON, ANDREW ALM, biochemistry educator; b. Modesto, Calif., Sept. 24, 1917; s. Carl Bennett and Emma Carolina (Alm) B.; m. Ruth Carkeek, May 22, 1942 (div. 1969); children: Claudia Benson Matthews, Linnea; m. Dorothy Dorgan Neri, July 31, 1971. BS, U. Calif., Berkeley, 1939; PhD, Calif. Inst. Tech., 1942; Phil D h.c., U. Oslo., 1965; Docteur h.c., U. Paris, 1986. Instr. chemistry dept. U. Calif., Berkeley, 1942-43, asst. dir. Bio-organic group Radiation Lab., 1946-54; rsch. assoc. dept. chemistry Stanford U., 1944-45, Calif. Inst. Tech., 1945-46; assoc. prof. agrl. biol. chemistry Pa. State U., 1955-60, prof., 1960-61; prof.-in-residence biophys./physiol. chemistry UCLA, 1961-62; prof. Scripps Instn. Oceanography, U. Calif., San Diego, 1962-88, prof. emeritus, 1988—. Fulbright vis. prof. Agrl. Coll. Norway, 1951-52. Contbr. articles on biochem. rsch. on photosynthesis, lipids, coral metabolism, arsenic metabolism, methanol application in agr. to profl. jours. Trustee Found. for Ocean Rsch., San Diego, 1970-88; mem. adv. coun. The Costeau Soc., 1976—; mem. internat. adv. bd. Marine Biotech. Inst. Co. Ltd., Tokyo, 1990-98. Recipient Sugar Rsch. Found. award, 1950, Ernest Orlando Lawrence Meml. award, 1962, Rsch. award Supelco/Am. Oil Chemists Soc., 1987; Sr. Queen's fellow Australia, 1979; Eminent Scientist of RIKEN, Japan, 1995; named Hon. Citizen Alert Bay, B.C., Can., 1988. Fellow AAAS; mem. Am. Acad. Arts and Sci., NAS, Royal Norwegian Soc. Sci. and Letters, Am. Oil Chemists Soc., Am. Chem. Soc. (emeritus), Am. Soc. Plant Physiologists (Stephen Hales prize 1972), Am. Soc. Biochemistry and Molecular Biology, Inst. Marine Biology, Far East Br., Acad. Sci. Russia (hon.). Home: 6044 Folsom Dr La Jolla CA 92037-6711 Office: Scripps Instn Oceanography La Jolla CA 92093-0202

BENSON, BRUCE DAVEY, academic administrator, oil and gas company executive; b. Chgo., July 4, 1938; s. P. Bruce and Harriet (Fentress) Benson; m. Marcy Head Benson; children: James, David, Ann. BA in Geology, U. Colo., Boulder, 1964; postgrad., Colo. Sch. Mines, 1964—65; LHD (hon.), U. Colo., 2004. Field geologist Exxon, 1964; founder, pres. Benson Mineral Group, Inc., Denver, 1965—; pres. U. Colo., Denver, 2008—. Commr. Colo. Commn. on Higher Edn., 1985—89, chmn., 1986—89; chmn. bd. dirs., CEO, pres. US Exploration, Inc., 1997—2004; bd. dirs. Am. Land Lease Corp., 2000—; chmn. Gov.'s Blue Ribbon Panel for Higher Edn. for 21st Century, 2001—03; co-chair P-20 Edn. Coordinating Coun., 2007—. Fin. chmn. Colo. Rep. Com., Denver, 1984—87; trustee Boy Scouts Am., Denver, 1986—; pres., bd. trustees Berkshire Sch., Sheffield, Mass., 1986. Recipient Silver Beaver Award, Boy Scouts Am., 1996, Arthritis Found. Humanitarian Award, 1999, David S. D'Evelyn Award for Inspired Leadership, 1999, Ira C. Rothgerber Award, U. Colo., 2003. Mem.: Petroleum Club, Kans. Ind. Oil and Gas Assn., Rocky Mountain Assn., Soc. Econ. Paleontologists and Mineralogists, Geol. Soc. Am., Denver Athletic Club. Republican. Avocations: tennis, skiing, white water rafting, scuba diving. Office: Benson Mineral Group Inc 1560 Broadway Ste 1900 Denver CO 80202-5153 also: Office of Pres U Colo 1800 Grant St Ste 800 Denver CO 80203 Office Phone: 303-860-5600. Office Fax: 303-860-5610.

BENSON, DEE VANCE, federal judge; b. Salt Lake City, Aug. 25, 1948; s. Gilbert and Beryl Butler (Despain) B.; children: Angela, Natalie, Lucas, Katherine. BA, Brigham Young U., 1973, JD, 1976. Bar: Utah 1976, admitted to practice: US Dist. Ct. Utah 1976, US Ct. Appeals (10th Cir.) 1976, US Supreme Ct. 1984, US Ct. Appeals (5th Cir.) 1988. Ptnr. Snow, Christensen & Martineau, Salt Lake City, 1976-84; legal counsel Senate Judiciary Com., Washington, 1984-86; chief of staff Senator Orrin Hatch's Office, Washington, 1986-88; legal counsel US Senate Select Com., Washington, 1987; assoc. dep. atty. gen. US Dept. Justice, Washington, 1988, US atty. dist. Utah Salt Lake City, 1989-91; judge US Dist. Ct. Utah, Salt Lake, 1991—99, 2006—, chief judge, 1999—2006; judge Fgn. Intelligence Surveillance Ct. (FISC), 2004—. Legal counsel Iran-Contra Congl. Investigating Com., Washington, 1987. Contbg. author univ. law rev. Mem. ABA, Utah State Bar (com. on cts. and judges), Salt Lake County Bar Assn., Phi Alpha Delta. Mem. Lds Ch. Avocations: soccer, skiing, bicycling, basketball, running. Office: US Dist Ct 350 S Main St Ste 251 Salt Lake City UT 84101-2106*

BENSON, JOAN, musician, educator; b. St. Paul; d. John Raymond and Frances (Ostergren) B. MusM, U. Ill., 1952; performer's cert., Ind. U., 1953; pvt. studies with Edwin Fischer, Switzerland, 1953-57; pvt. studies with Fritz Neumeyer, Fed. Republic Germany, 1958-59; pvt. studies with Santiago Kastner, Portugal, 1960. Concert musician, worldwide, 1962—; lectr. early keyboard Stanford U., Palo Alto, Calif., 1970-76; asst. prof. U. Oreg., Eugene, 1976-82. Mem. artist faculty Aston Magna Acad., Mass., 1980, 82; adj. prof. U. Oreg., 1982—; artistic advisor Boston Clavichord Soc., 1996—. Albums: Repertoire, 1962, Music of C. P. E. Bach for Piano and Clavichord, 1972, Pasquini and Haydn on Clavichords of the Boston Museum of Fine Arts, 1982, Kuhnau and C.P.E. Bach on Clavichord, 1988; contbr. music notes to Titanic and Focus record labels; contbr. articles to internat. profl. jours. Recipient Kate Neil Kinley award. Mem. Am. Musicol. Soc. Home: 2795 Central Blvd Eugene OR 97403-2528 Business E-Mail: joanb@uoregon.edu.

BENSON, JON H., information technology executive; Grad. in Elec. Engring. V.p., gen. mgr. StorageTek overall tape bus. Sun Microsystems, Inc., v.p. engring. for virtual storage and tape solutions bus., sr. v.p. storage, 2007—. Mem. indsl. adv. bd. elec. and computer engring. Colo. State U., Ft. Collins. Achievements include patents in field. Office: Sun Microsystems Inc 4150 Network Cir Santa Clara CA 95054 Office Phone: 650-960-1300. E-mail: jon.benson@sun.com.

BENSON, MICHAEL T., academic administrator; m. Celia Barnes; 2 children. BA in Polit. Sci., Brigham Young U.; PhD in Modern Middle Ea. History, St. Antony's Coll. Mem. staff devel. office U. Utah, 1995—98, assoc. dir. major gifts, spl. asst. to pres. & sec., 1999—2002; pres. Snow Coll., Ephraim, Utah, 2002—06, Southern Utah U., Cedar City, Utah, 2006—. Cons. historian Harry S. Truman Presdl. Libr.; academic adv. Skirball Cultural Ctr., LA; instr. U. Utah; bd. adv. Marriott Libr.; adv. bd. U. Utah Internat. Studies. Author: Harry S. Truman and the Founding of Israel, 1997. Office: Office of President Southern Utah University 351 W University Blvd Cedar City UT 84720 Office Phone: 435-586-7700.

BENSON, ROBERT CRAIG, III, business consultant; b. Waukegan, Ill., May 27, 1944; s. Robert Craig II and Leona (Pollard) B.; m. Ree Ann Christensen, June 3, 1961; children: Bradley, Barry. BA in Bus. Adminstrn. and Math., Dakota Wesleyan U., Mitchell, SD, 1967. CPA, Cert. Mgmt. Cons. Supervising sr. Broeker Hendrickson & Co., St. Paul, 1967-70; ptnr. Sands Benson & Weinberg, St. Paul, 1970-73; mgr. Miller, McCollom & Co., Denver, 1973-74; mng. ptnr. Benson Wells & Co., Denver, 1974-84; pres. Am. Bus. Advisors, Denver, 1984—. Lectr. Ctr. for Leadership Devel., Kiev, Ukraine, 1998—; Opperman disting. alumni lectr. Dakota Wesleyan U., 2002. Contbr. articles to profl. jours. Bd. mem., chair Denver Youth for Christ, 1975-85; elder Cherry Hills Cmty. Ch., Highlands Ranch, Colo., 1982-87; bd. dirs. COMPA Food Bank, Denver, 1986-93, Global Connections Internat., 2000-2003, Project C.U.R.E., 2000-04, Dakota Wesleyan U., 2004—, Loveland Logic Inst., 1999—. Recipient Alumnus of Yr., Dakota Wesleyan U., 2006. Mem.: AICPA, Inst. Mgmt. Cons., Colo. Soc. CPAs (co-chmn. profession practice bd. 1981—82). Avocations: golf, teaching about God, bridge. Office: Am Bus Advisors Inc 6635 S Dayton Ste 210 Greenwood Village CO 80111 Business E-Mail: bob@abadvisors.com.

BENSON, ROBERT EUGENE, lawyer; b. Red Oak, Iowa, Apr. 7, 1940; s. Paul J. and Frances (Sever) B.; m. Ann Marie Lucke, July 20, 1968; children: Steven J., Robert J., Katherine A. BA, U. Iowa, 1962; LLB, U. Pa., 1965. Bar: Colo. 1965. Assoc. Holland & Hart, Denver, 1965—71, ptnr., 1971—2006, of counsel, 2007—. Adj. faculty U. Denver Coll. Law, 1992. Author: The Power of Arbitrators and Courts to Order Discovery in Arbitration, 1996, Application of the Pro Rata Liability, Comparative Negligence and Contribution Statues, 1994, Colorado Arbitration and Other ADR Law, 2006, CLE in Colorado, 2006; co-author: How to Prepare For, Take and Use a Deposition, 5th edit., 1994; mng. editor: Colorado Construction Law, 1999, 2003, 2005, 2007; contbr. articles to profl. jours. Capt. USAF, 1965-73. Mem. ABA, Colo. Bar Assn., Denver Bar Assn., Coll. Comml. Arbitrators. Democrat. Avocations: golf, skiing. Home: 5454 Preserve Pky N Greenwood Village CO 80121-2185 Office: Holland & Hart LLP 555 17th St Ste 3200 Denver CO 80202-3950 Home Phone: 303-770-3571; Office Phone: 303-295-8234. Business E-Mail: rbenson@hollandhart.com.

BENSON, SALLY M., atmospheric scientist; BA in Geology, Barnard Coll., 1977; MS, PhD in materials sci. and mineral engring., U. Calif, Berkeley, 1988. With Lawrence Berkeley Nat. Lab., 1977—, dir. earth scis. divsn., 1993—97, assoc. lab. dir. for energy scis., 1997—2001, dep. dir. ops., 2001—. Office: Lawrence Berkeley Nat Lab 1 Cyclotron Rd Bldg 50E Berkeley CA 94720 E-mail: smbenson@lbl.gov.

BENSON, SIDNEY WILLIAM, chemistry researcher; b. NYC, Sept. 26, 1918; m. Anna Bruni, 1986; 2 children. AB, Columbia Coll., 1938; A.M., PhD, Harvard U., 1941; Docteur Honoris Causa, U. Nancy, France, 1989. Rsch. asst. Gen. Electric Co., 1940; rsch. fellow Harvard U., 1941-42; instr. chemistry CCNY, 1942-43; group leader Manhattan Project Kellex Corp., 1943; rsch. scientist, div. 9 Nat. Rsch. Coun., 1944—46; asst. prof. U. So. Calif., 1943-48, assoc. prof., 1948-51, prof. chemistry, 1951-64, 76-89, disting. prof., 1986—, disting. prof. emeritus, 1989—, dir. chem. physics program, 1962-63; rsch. chemist Nat. Rsch. Coun., Divsn. 9, 1944—46; dir. dept. kinetics and thermochemistry Stanford Rsch. Inst., 1963-76; sci. dir. Hydrocarbon Rsch. Inst. U. So. Calif., 1977-90, sci. dir. emeritus, 1991—; rsch. assoc. dept. chemistry and chem. engring. Calif. Inst. Tech., 1957-58; vis. prof. UCLA, 1959, U. Ill., 1959; hon. Glidden lectr. Purdue U., 1961; vis. prof. chemistry Stanford U., 1966-70, 71, 73; mem. adv. panel phys. chemistry Nat. Bur. Standards, 1969-72, chmn., 1970-71; hon. vis. prof. U. Utah, 1971; vis. prof. U. Paris VII and XI, 1971-72, U. St. Andrews, Scotland, 1973, U. Lausanne, Switzerland, 1979. Frank Gucker lectr. U. Ind., 1984—; Brotherton prof. in phys. chemistry U. Leeds, 1984; cons. G.N. Lewis; lectr. U. Calif., Berkeley, 1989. Author: Foundations of Chemical Kinetics, 1960, rev. edit. 1982, Thermochemical Kinetics, 1968, 2d edit., 1976, Critical Survey of the Data of the Kinetics of Gas Phase Unimolecular Reactions, Reactions, 1970, Chemical Calculations, 3d edit., 1971, Atoms, Molecules and Chemical Reactions, 1972; founder, editor-in-chief Internat. Jour. Chem. Kinetics, 1967-83; mem. editl. adv. bd. Combustion Sci. and Tech., 1973-94, Oxidation Comms., 1978—, Revs. of chem. Intermediates, 1979-87, Hydrocarbon Letters, 1980-81, Jour. Phys. Chemistry, 1981-85; sci. adv. coun. Annales Medicales de Nancy, 1993-2002. Recipient cert. of Merit for War Work, NRC, 1946; Polanyi medal Royal Soc. Eng., 1986; faculty rsch. award U. So. Calif., 1984, Presdl. medal, 1986, Peter Kapitsa Gold Medal award Russian Acad. Natural Sci., 1997; Guggenheim fellow, 1950-51, Fulbright fellow, France, 1950-51, fellow NSF, 1957-58, 71-72; recipient citation Chem. Rev., 2000; nominated for Scientist of Yr. Internat. Biog. Ctr., Cambridge, Eng., 2002. Fellow AAAS, Am. Phys. Soc.; mem. NAS, Am. Chem. Soc. (Tolman medal 1977, Hydrocarbon Chem. award 1977, Langmuir award 1986, Orange County award 1986), Faraday Soc., Indian Acad. Sci., Phi Beta Kappa, Sigma Xi, Pi Mu Epsilon, Phi Lambda Upsilon, Phi Kappa Phi Home: 1110 N Bundy Dr Los Angeles CA 90049-1513 Office: U So Calif University Pk Mc 1661 Los Angeles CA 90089-0001

BENSON, STEPHEN R., editorial cartoonist; BA in Polit. Sci. cum laude, Brigham Young U., 1979. With Senate Rep. Policy Com., 1979-80; cartoonist The Ariz. Republic, Phoenix, 1980-90, 91—, The Morning-News Tribune, Tacoma, Wash., 1990-91. Author: Fencin' with Benson, 1984, Evanly Days, 1988, Back at the Barb-B-Cue, 1991, Where Do You Draw the Line?, 1992. Recipient Nat. Headliner award, 1984, 1st Place Best of the West, 1991, 92, 93, Pulitzer Prize finalist editorial cartooning, 1984, 89, 92, 94, Pulitzer Prize for editorial cartooning, 1993. Office: The Ariz Republic 200 E Van Buren St Phoenix AZ 85004-2238

BENTER, GEORGE H., JR., banker; b. 1942; BS, San Diego State U., 1963; MBA, UCLA, 1964. With Security Pacific Nat. Bank, 1964—, exec. v.p., 1986—, Security Pacific Corp. Dir. Whittaker Corp., L.A. Office: City National Corporation 400 N Roxbury Dr Beverly Hills CA 90210

BENTLEY, THOMAS ROY, retired language educator, writer; b. Belfast, No. Ireland, June 5, 1931; s. Thomas and Anne (Hill) B.; m. Joan M. Williams, Dec. 24, 1955; children: Kimberley, Shannon, Carolyn. BA, U. Toronto, 1960, MA, 1966; EdB, Ont. Coll., 1961; PhD, Meml. U., Nfld., Can., 1970. Assoc. dean edn. U. B.C., Vancouver, Can., 1973-77, head lang. edn., 1978-79, acting dean edn., 1979-81, prof. lang. edn., 1983-96, prof. emeritus, 1996—. Cons. to maj. cos. on comm. and transp. issues; co-founder Internat. Lifewriting Network. Author 4 books on English comms.; editor 12 books on Can. lit.; contbr. articles to profl. jours.; broadcaster numerous programs on radio and TV. Mem. Nat. Assn. Tchrs. English (chmn. internat. assembly 1981), Assn. Profs. Emeriti, Nat. Conf. for Rsch. in English, Can. Coun. Tchrs. English (editor, bd. dirs., 1975-78), Vancouver Club. Office: 5529 University Blvd Vancouver BC Canada V6T 1K5 Business E-Mail: roy.bentley@ubc.ca.

BENTON, ANDREW KEITH, academic administrator, lawyer; b. Hawthorne, Nev., Feb. 4, 1952; s. Darwin Keith and Nelda Lou Benton; m. Deborah Sue Strickland, June 22, 1974; children: Hailey Michelle, Christopher Andrew. BS in Am. Studies, Okla. Christian Coll., 1974; JD, Oklahoma City U., 1979. Bar: Okla. 1979, U.S. Dist. Ct. (we. dist.) Okla. (admitted to) 1982. Sole practice, Edmond, Okla., 1979-81, 83-84; ptnr. Benton & Thomason, Edmond, 1981—83; asst. v.p. Pepperdine U., Malibu, Calif., 1984—85, v.p., 1985—87, v.p. adminstrn., 1987—89, v.p. univ. affairs, 1989—91, exec. v.p., 1991—2000, pres., 2000—. Chmn. precinct, state conv. del. Okla. Reps., 1980. Mem.: Am. Coun. on Edn., Assn. of Ind. Calif. Coll. & Univ., Nat. Assn. Ind. Coll. & Univ., Okla. Bar Assn. (contbr. articles to ednl. community), ABA (chmn. subcom. emerging land use trends 1987—88, chmn. subcom. decisional trends 1988—90), Calif. Club, Jonathan Club. Republican. Mem. Ch. Of Christ. Office: Pepperdine U 24255 Pacific Coast Hwy Malibu CA 90263-0002

BENTON, AUBURN EDGAR, lawyer; b. Colorado Springs, Colo., July 12, 1926; s. Auburn Edgar and Ella Dot (Heyer) B.; m. Stephanie Marie Jakimowitz, June 8, 1951; children: Margrit Laura, Mary Ellen. BA, Colo. Coll., 1950; LLB, Yale U., 1953. Bar: Colo. 1953, U.S. Dist. Ct. Colo. 1953, U.S. Ct. Appeals (10th cir.) 1954. Assoc. Holme Roberts & Owen LLP, Denver, 1953-57, ptnr., 1957-91, of counsel, 1992—. Mem. Bd. Edn. Denver Pub. Schs., 1961-69; mem. Colo. Commn. Higher Edn., Denver, 1975-85; mem. Colo. Bd. Ethics, Denver, 1975-98; mem. Nat. Common Cause Bd., Washington, 1975-85; dir. soc. sci. found. U. Denver. Mem. Colo. Bar Assn., Denver Bar Assn., Cactus Club (Denver), Phi Beta Kappa. Democrat. Home: 901 Race St Denver CO 80206-3735 Office: Holme Roberts & Owen LLP 1700 Lincoln St Ste 4100 Denver CO 80203-4541

BENTON, DONALD MARK, state legislator, political organization chairman; b. Agua Dulce, Calif., Apr. 8, 1957; s. Arlis Redford and Dorothy Helen B.; m. Mary E. Enders, Nov. 6, 1982; children Jennifer Marie, Adam Carson, Bradly, Austin. AS, Coll. of the Canyons, Valencia, Calif.; BS in Bus. Mgmt. & Comm., Concordia U., Portland, Oreg. Founder, chief exec. officer Santa Clarita Temporaries, Inc., Newhall, Calif., 1979-83; dist. mgr. Farmers Ins. Group, LA, 1983-88; nat. sales trainer, speaker Nat. Cons. Svcs., Vancouver, Wash., 1988; founder, chief exec. officer The Benton Grp., 1988—; mem. Wash. Ho. of Reps., Olympia, 1994-96, Wash. Senate, Dist. 17, Olympia, 1996—; chair. Wash. Republican Party, 1998—2001; senator State of Wash. from 17th Dist., 1996—. Author: How To Start a Temporary Service, 1981; inventor aerovane. Clk., trustee Santa Clarita Community Coll. Dist., Valencia, Calif., 1981-88, pres. bd. trustees, 1985; pres. Santa Clarita Valley Jaycees, 1981-82; chmn. bd. dirs. Santa Clarita Valley unit ARC, 1983-86. Recipient resolution Calif. Assembly, 1981, ofcl. resolution L.A. County Bd. Suprvs., 1982, spl. recogition U.S. Congress, 1982, Outstanding Young Man award Santa Clarita Valley Jaycees, 1982. Republican. Address: Wash Senate 109-B Irving R Newhouse Bldg PO Box 40417 Olympia WA 98504-0417 E-mail: benton_do@leg.wa.gov.

BENTON, FLETCHER, sculptor; b. Jackson, Ohio, 1931; BFA, Miami U., Oxford, Ohio, 1956, DFA (hon.), 1993, Rio Grande U., 1994. Mem. faculty Calif. Coll. Arts and Crafts, 1959, San Francisco Art Inst., 1964-67; prof. art Calif. State U., San Jose, 1967-81, prof., 1981-86. One-man shows include, San Francisco Mus. Modern Art, 1965, Albright-Knox Mus., Buffalo, 1970, Galeria Bonino, N.Y.C., 1969, Galerie Francoise Mayer, Brussels, San Francisco Mus. Modern Art, 1970, London Arts Gallery, Detroit, 1970, Galeria Bonino, Buenos Aires, Estudio Actual, Caracas, Venezuela, 1970, Landry-Bonino Gallery, N.Y.C., 1972, Phoenix Mus. Art, 1973, Galeria Bonino, Rio de Janiero, 1973, Calif. State U.-Berkeley, 1973, Neuberger Mus., N.Y., 1974, Hirshhorn Mus., 1974, Phila. Art Alliance,

1974, Elvehejem Mus. Art, Wis., 1976, San Francisco Modern Mus. Art, 1976, Huntsville Mus. Modern Art, Ala., 1977, Alrich Mus. Contemporary Art, Conn., John Berggruen Gallery, San Francisco, 1978, 84, 89, 96, Am. Acad. and Inst. Arts and Letters, N.Y.C., 1979, Chgo. Arts Club, 1979, Milw. Art Ctr., 1980, Suermondt-Ludwig Mus., Asschen, Fed. Republic Germany, Klingspor Mus., Offenbach, Fed. Republic Germany, 1981, 96, Kunsthandlung Brigitte Haasner, Wiesbaden, Fed. Republic Germany, 1987, 92, 96, Sung Dem Fine Arts, Seoul, Korea, 1991, Dorothy Goldeen Gallery, Santa Monica, Calif., 1988, 93, Galerie Simonne Stern, New Orleans, 1990, 93, Riva Yares Gallery, Scottsdale, 1991, Miami U., Oxford, 1993, Gallery Camino Real, Boca Raton, Fla., John Berggruen Gallery, San Francisco, 1996, Klingspor Mus., Germany, 1996, Gallery Camino Real, Boca Raton, Fla., 1996, Galerie B. Haasner, Germany, 1996, Galerie Simonne Stern, N. Orleans, 1997, Frankfurt Art Fair, Germany, 1997, numerous others; group shows include San Francisco Art Inst., 1964, San Francisco Modern Mus. Art, 1964, Calif. Pal. of Legion of Honor, 1964, Whitney Mus. Am. Art, N.Y.C., 1967, 68, Los Angeles County Mus., 1967, Phila. Art Mus., 1967, Walker Art Ctr., Mpls., 1968, Art Inst. Chgo., 1968, Internat. Mus. Fine Arts, Osaka, Japan, 1970, Hayward Gallery, London, 1970, Stanford (Calif.) Mus., 1971, Am. Acad. and Inst. Arts and Letters, N.Y.C., 1981, Whitney Mus. Am. Art, N.Y.C., 1981, Oakland Mus., 1982, John Berggruen Gallery, 1983, Olympic Arts Festival, Los Angeles, France, Fed. Republic Germany, Eng., Norway, 1984, John Berggruen Gallery, 1985, 89, 92, Chapman Coll. (Calif.), 1985, The Adrich Mus. Contemporary Art, Conn., 1985, Centro de Arte Moderna, Lisbon, Portugal, 1986, Kunsthandlung Brigitte Haasner, Wiesbaden, Fed. Republic Germany, 1987, 88, Dorothy Goldeen Gallery, Santa Monica, Calif., 1988, AndreEmmerich Gallery, 1991, 92, Rio Grande (Ohio) U., 1994, Miami Art Mus., Oxford, Ohio, 1996, numerous others; major collections Euroclear Hdqs. Brussels, Belgium, 1993, Modernesstadt Cologne, 1993, Gothaer, Cologne, Top Gallant, 1994, Pauling, N.Y. Served with USN, 1949-50. Recipient Disting. Svc. award to arts Am. Acad. and Inst. Arts and Letters, 1979, Career award Ohioana Libr. Assn., 1994, Lifetime Achievement award, Internat. Sculpture Center, 2008; Pres.'s Scholar award San Jose State U., 1980. Office: Fletcher Benton Studio 250 Dore St San Francisco CA 94103-4308

BENTON, LEE F., lawyer; b. Springfield, Ohio, Feb. 18, 1944; AB, Oberlin Coll., 1966; JD, U. Chgo., 1969. Bar: Calif. 1970. Sr. counsel Cooley Godward Kronish LLP, Palo Alto, Calif.; strategic advisor Calif. Inst. for Quantitative Bioscience, UCSF, San Francisco. Teaching fellow Stanford Law Sch., 1969-70. Mem. Order Coif, Phi Beta Kappa. Office: Cooley Godward Kronish LLP 5 Palo Alto Sq 3000 El Camino Real Palo Alto CA 94306-2120 Home Phone: 650-321-8128; Office Phone: 650-843-5017. Business E-Mail: lbenton@cooley.com.

BENTON, ROBERT, film director, screenwriter; b. Waxahachie, Tex., Sept. 29, 1932; BA, U. Tex. Screenwriter: (with David Newman) There Was A Crooked Man, 1962, Bonnie and Clyde, 1967, What's Up Doc?, 1972, (with Mario Puzo and Tom Mankiewicz) Superman, 1978, The Ice Harvest, 2005; dir., writer: Bad Company, 1972, The Late Show, 1977, Kramer vs. Kramer, 1979 (Best Dir. Acad. award 1979, Best Screenplay Acad. award 1979), Still of the Night, 1982, Places in the Heart, 1984 (Best Screenplay Acad. award 1984), Nadine, 1987, Nobody's Fool, 1994, Twilight, 1998; dir.: Billy Bathgate, 1991, The Human Stain, 2003; co-exec. prodr.: The House on Carroll Street, 1988. Recipient Screen Laurel award, Writers Guild Am., West, 2007. Mem. Dirs. Guild Am.

BENTON-HARDY, LISA RENEE, psychiatrist, educator; BA, Stanford U., 1988; MD, U. Calif., San Francisco, 1992. Diplomate Nat. Bd. Med. Examiners, Am. Bd. Psychaiat. and Neurology. Intern U. Calif. Davis-East Bay, Oakland, CA, 1992-93; adult psychiatry resident Stanford (Calif.) U. Med. Ctr., 1993-96, child and adolescent psychiatry fellow, 1995-97; staff psychiatrist Alliance for Cmty. Care, San Jose, Calif., 1994—. Calif. Wellness Found. Violence Prevention Initiative acad. scholar, Stanford U. Med. Ctr., 1995-97; presenter in field. Contbr. articles to profl. jours., chpt. to book. Laughlin fellow Am. Coll. Psychiatrists, 1997. Mem. AMA, Am. Psychiat. Assn. (Program for Minority Rsch. and Tng. in Psychiatry mini-fellowship award 1996), Am. Acad. Child and Adolescent Psychiatry (Presdl. Scholar award 1996, Charter fellow, leadership award 1994), No. Calif. Psychiat. Soc. Office: Childrens Hosp Oakland Dept Psychiatry 747 52nd St Oakland CA 94609-1809

BENVENUTTI, PETER J., lawyer; b. Gulfport, Miss., June 24, 1949; s. Peter J. and Elizabeth Cullen (Beyer) B.; m. Lise A. Pearlman, May 31, 1974; children: Anna B., Jamie E., Amalia R. AB, Harvard U., 1971; JD, U. Calif., Berkeley, 1974. Bar: Calif. 1974, U.S. Dist. Ct. (no. dist.) Calif. 1974, U.S. Dist. Ct. (ea. dist.) Calif. 1977, U.S. Dist. Ct. (ctrl. and so. dists.) Calif. 1989, U.S. Dist. Ct. Ariz. 1990, U.S. Ct. Appeals (9th cir.) 1984. Assoc. Dinkelspiel & Dinkelspiel, San Francisco, 1974-80, ptnr., 1981-88, Heller, Ehrman, White & McAuliffe, San Francisco, 1988—; mng. ptnr. San Francisco Office, 1995-97. Bd. dirs. ARC, 1981-83. Mem. ABA, Bar Assn. San Francisco (pres. Calif. bankruptcy forum 1993-94, lawyer rep. 9th Cir. Jud. Conf. 1994—). Democrat. Home: 1147 Clarendon Cres Oakland CA 94610-1807 Office: Heller Ehrman White & McAuliffe 333 Bush St San Francisco CA 94104-2806 Office Phone: 415-772-6403. Office Fax: 415-772-6268. E-mail: pbenvenutti@hewm.com.

BERCAW, JOHN EDWARD, chemistry educator, consultant; b. Cin., Dec. 3, 1944; s. James Witherow and Mary Josephine (Heywood) B.; m. Teresa Diane Ingram, July 10, 1965; children— David Lawrence, Karin Elizabeth BS in Chemistry, N.C. State U., 1967; PhD in Chemistry, U. Mich., 1971. Postdoctoral U. Chgo., 1971-72; A.A. Noyes fellow Calif. Inst. Tech., Pasadena, 1972-74, asst. prof. chemistry, 1974-77, assoc. prof. chemistry, 1977-79, prof. chemistry, 1979-93, Centennial prof. chemistry, 1993—, Shell Disting. prof., 1985-90. Cons. Exxon Corp., Annandale, N.J., 1979— Fellow Am. Acad. Arts and Scis.; mem. NAS, AAAS, Am. Chem. Soc. (chmn. divsn. inorganic chemistry 1988-89, organometallic subdivsn. chair 1980, chmn. Gordon Rsch. Conf. on Organometallic Chemistry 1991, award in pure chemistry 1980, award in organometallic chemistry 1990, award for disting. svc. in inorganic chemistry 1997, George A. Olah award for hydrocarbon or petroleum chemistry 1999, Arthur C. Cope Scholar award 2000). Home: 1455 Afton St Pasadena CA 91103-2702 Office: Calif Inst Tech 1201 E California Blvd Pasadena CA 91125-0001

BERCH, REBECCA WHITE, state supreme court justice, lawyer; b. Phoenix, June 29, 1955; d. Robert Eugene and Janet Kay (Zimmerman) White; m. Michael Allen Berch, Mar. 9, 1981; 1 child, Jessica. BS summa cum laude, Ariz. State U., 1976, JD, 1979, MA, 1990. Bar: Ariz. 1979, U.S. Dist. Ct. Ariz., U.S. Ct. Appeals (9th cir.), U.S. Supreme Ct. Assoc., ptnr. McGroder, Tryon, Heller, Rayes & Berch, Phoenix, 1979-85; dir. legal rsch. and writing program Ariz. State U. Coll. Law, Tempe, 1986-91, 94-95; solicitor gen. State of Arizona, Phoenix, 1991-94, 1st asst. atty. gen., 1996—98; judge Ariz. Ct. Appeals, 1998—2002; justice Ariz. Supreme Ct., Phoenix, 2002—, vice chief justice, 2005—. Mem. Judicial Ethics Advisory Com., Bd. Certified Ct. Reporters, Arizona Supreme Ct. Com. on Examinations, Arizona Judicial Coll. Bd.; co-chair Arizona Appellate Practice Inst. Co-author: (Book) Introduction to Legal Method and Process, 1985, 2002, Teacher's Manual for Introduction to Legal Method and Process, 1992, 2002, Handling Complex Litigation, 1986; Bd. editors Jour. Legal Writing Inst., 1993—2002; contbr. articles to profl. jours. and newspapers. Bd. dirs. Tempe-Mesa chpt. ACLU, 1984—86, Homeless Legal Assistance Project, Phoenix, 1990—98. Recipient Outstanding Service award, Arizona Atty. General's Office, 1992, 1994, Outstanding Alumnus award, Ariz. State U. Coll. Law, 1999. Mem. Ariz. Women Lawyer's Assn. (Profl. Achievement award 2002), Ariz. State Bar Assn. Republican. Methodist. Avocations: reading, travel. Office: Ariz Supreme Ct 1501 W Washington St Phoenix AZ 85009-3831 Office Phone: 602-542-4535. Business E-Mail: Rberch@Azbar.org.

BERCOVICI, DAVID ANTHONY LEONARDO, geophysics educator, researcher; b. Rome, Sept. 18, 1960; came to U.S., 1964; s. Leonardo and Antonia (Maddison) B.; m. Julie Ann Jirikowic, Dec. 10, 1983; children: Sarah Kathryn, Hannah La'ia. BS, Harvey Mudd Coll., 1982; MS, UCLA, 1987, PhD, 1989. Rsch. asst. UCLA, 1985-89; postdoctoral fellow Woods Hole (Mass.) Oceanographic Instn., 1989-90; asst. prof. U. Hawaii, Honolulu, 1990-95, assoc. prof., 1995-99, prof., 1999—. Mem. Venus data analysis panel program NASA, Houston, 1992-93; NSF grand challenge panelist, Washington, 1993. Contbr. articles to Sci., Jour. Geophys. Rsch., Geophys. Rsch. Letters. Mem. U. Hawaii Profl. Assembly, Honolulu, 1990—. Named NSF Presdl. Young Investigator, 1994-99. Fellow Am. Geophys. Union (James B. Macelwane medal 1996, U. Hawaii Regents medal Excellence in Rsch.). Achievements include development of theories on how plate tectonics and continental drift are generated from thermal convection in the earth's mantle; development of theories on how buyoyant plumes in the mantle rise and evolve. Office: U Hawaii Dept Geology and Geophysics Honolulu HI 96822

BEREN, STEVE, Internet marketing professional; b. NYC, Sept. 9, 1951; married. Attended, City Coll. NY. Records specialist Bullivant, Houser, Bailey, 1996—2000; ops. mgr. Impex Devel., 2000—03; dir. prodn. ops. ShopLocal.com, Seattle, 2003—. Candidate, Wash. dist. 7 US House of Reps., 2006, 2008; mem. Christian Faith Ctr. Office: ShopLocal.com 1525 4th Ave Seattle WA 98101 Office Phone: 206-381-8520.

BERENATO, JOSEPH C., manufacturing executive; b. 1947; BS in Engring., U.S. Naval Acad.; MA in English, U. Va.; MBA in Fin., NYU. Various exec. mgmt. positions Mfrs. Hanover Trust Co.; v.p., CFO, treas. Ducommon Inc., LA, 1991-95, exec. v.p., COO, 1995-96, pres., 1996—, pres., CEO, 1997—, also bd. dirs. Office: Docommun Inc 23301 Wilmington Ave Carson CA 90745

BERENBAUM, MICHAEL GARY, theology educator; b. Newark, July 31, 1945; s. Saul Berenbaum and Rhea Kass; m. Linda Bayer, Aug. 25, 1968 (div. July 1992); children: Ilana, Lev; m. Melissa Patack, June 25, 1995; children: Joshua, Mira. Student, Jewish Theol. Sem., 1963—67, Hebrew U., 1965—66; AB in Philosophy, Queens Coll., 1967; postgrad., Boston U., 1967—69; PhD in Religion and Culture, Fla. State U., 1975; DD (honoris causa), Narazeth Coll., Rochester, NY, 1995; LHD (hon.), Dennison U., 2000. Instr. dept. philosophy and religion Colby-Sawyer Coll., 1969—71; adj. asst. prof. religion, Jewish chaplain Wesleyan U., 1973—80; assoc. professorial lectr. dept. religion George Washington U., 1981—83; opinion page editor Washington Jewish Week, 1983—86, acting editor, 1985; sr. scholar Religious Action Ctr., 1986—88; Hymen Goldman prof. theology Georgetown U., 1983—97; rsch. fellow U.S. Holocaust Meml. Mus., 1987—88, project dir., 1988—93, dir. U.S. Holocaust Rsch. Inst., 1993—97; pres., CEO Survivors of Shoah Visual History Found., 1997—99; prof. theology U. Judaism, 1998—; Ida E. King disting. vis. scholar of the Holocaust Richard Stockton Coll., 1999—2000; pres. Berenbaum Group, 1999—; dir. Sigi Ziering Inst.: Exploring Ethical and Religious Implications of the Holocaust, 2002—. Adj. prof. Judaic studies Am. U., 1987; assoc. dir.-Zachor Holocaust Resource Ctr., 1978; dep. dir. Pres. Commn. on Holocaust, 1979—80; vis. prof. Hebrew Studies U. Md., 1983; assoc. Gannett Ctr. Media Studies Columbia U. Author: The Vision of the Void: Theological Reflections on the Works of Elie Wiesel, 1979, reprinted as Elie Wiesel: God, The Holocaust and the Children of Israel, 1994, The World Must Know: The History of the Holocaust as Told in the U.S. Holocaust Museum, After Tragedy and Triumph, 2d edit., 1990, A Promise to Remember: The Holocaust in the Words and Voices of the Survivors, 2003; editor: From Holocaust to New Life, 1985, Witness to the Holocaust, 1997, The Holocaust and History: The Known, The Unknown, The Disputed and The Reexamined, 1998; co-editor: Holocaust: Religious and Philosophical Implications, 1989, Anatomy of the Auschwitz Death Camp, 1996, What Kind of God?, 1997, The Bombing of Auschwitz: Should the Allies Have Attempted It, 2001; mem. editl. bd.: Tikkun, Jour. Holocaust and Genocide Studies; contbg. editor: Sh'ma; editor: Together, 1986—89;: The Holocaust and History, 1998; co-editor: After the Passion Has Gone - American Religious Consequences, 2005; editor: Murder Most Merciful: Essays on the Ethical Conundrum Raised By Sigi Ziering's The Trial of Herbert Bierhoff, 2005; exec. editor: Encyclopaedia Judaica, 2006; editor: Not Your Father's Antisemitism, 2008. Recipient Simon Rockower Meml. award in Jewish journalism for Disting. Editl. Writing, Am. Jewish Press Assn., 1986, Disting. Coverage of Arts, 1987, Outstanding Informational Emmy award for One Survivor Remembers, 1995, Cable Ace award for One Survivor Remembers, 1996; fellow Ezra Styles, Yale U., 1979, Danforth Found. Underwood, 1976—77, George Wise, Tel Aviv U., 1974, Charles E. Merrill, Fla. State U., 1972—73. Fellow: Soc. Values in Higher Edn. Democrat. Jewish. Office Phone: 323-930-9325. E-mail: michael@berenbaumgroup.com.

BERENDT, PAUL, political organization worker; b. July 16, 1956; m. Beth Berendt. BA, Evergreen State Coll., 1987. Chmn. Wash. State Dem. Party, 1995—2006. Roman Catholic. Home: 1702 Sulenes Loop SE Olympia WA 98501-7042

BERENTSEN, KURTIS GEORGE, music educator, conductor; b. North Hollywood, Calif., Apr. 22, 1953; s. George O. and Eleanor J. (Johnson) B.; m. Jeanette M. Sacco, Aug., 1975 (div. 1977); m. Floy I. Griffiths, March 17, 1984; 1 child, Kendra Irene. MusB, Utah State U., 1975; MA in Music, U. Calif., Santa Barbara, 1986; cert. colloguy, Concordia Coll., 1996. Cert. cmty. coll. tchr., Calif., pub. tchr., Calif.; commd. minister Luth. Ch., Mo. Synod, 1996. Dir. music Hope Luth. Ch., Daly City, Calif., 1975—81; gen. mgr. Ostara Press, Inc., Daly City, 1975—78; condr. U. Calif., Santa Barbara, 1981—86; dir., condr. Santa Barbara Oratorio Chorale, 1983—85; dir. music 1st Presbyn. Ch., Santa Barbara, 1983—84, Goleta Presbyn. Ch., Calif., 1984—85; min. music Trinity Luth. Ch., Ventura, 1985—92, Christ Luth. Ch. & Sch., Little Rock, 1992—98; dir. choral music Concordia U., Portland, Oreg., 1998—; instr. Ventura Coll., 1987—88; music dir., condr. Gold Coast Cmty. Chorus, Ventura, 1988—92. Choir dir. Temple Beth Torah Jewish Community, Ventura, 1982-87; adj. prof. Pepperdine U., Malibu, Calif., 1988; chorus master Ventura Symphony Orch., 1987. Condr. oratorios Christus Am Oelberg, 1983, Elijah, 1984, Hymn of Praise, 1988, cantata Seven Last Words, 1979, 84, Paukenmesse, 1989, Mozart's Requiem, 1990, 05, Requiem-Fauré, 1991, 2002, Judas Messiah-Handel, 2007; soloist 15 major oratorio and opera roles, 1971-92, Nat. Anthem, L.A. Dodgers, 1989; dir. (with John Rutter) Gold Coast Community Chorus, Carnegie Hall, NYC., 1991, Tribute to America, Lincoln Ctr. Concert, NYC, 1991. Min. music, tchr. Christ Luth. Ch. and Sch., Little Rock, 1992—. First place winner baritone vocalist Idaho Fedn. Music Clubs, 1971, recital winner Utah Fedn. Music Clubs, 1974. Mem. Choral Condrs. Guild, Assn. Luth. Ch. Musicians, Am. Guild of English Handbell Ringers, Am. Choral Dirs. Assn., Music Educators Nat. Conf., Sigma Nu (sec., song leader 1973-75). Home and Office: 2811 NE Holman St Portland OR 97211-6067 Home Phone: 503-358-5878. Business E-Mail: kberentsen@cu-portland.edu.

BERESFORD, THOMAS PATRICK, psychology professor, alcohol/drug abuse services professional; b. Danville, Ill., Mar. 16, 1946; s. Thomas Edmund and Susan Elizabeth Beresford; m. Carol Ahmann, Aug. 22, 1970; children: Thomas Edward, Henry Francis, Charles Edmund. BA, Stanford U., 1969; MD, U. Colo., 1973; MA, Boston Coll., 1978. Diplomate Am. Bd. Psychiatry and Neurology. Resident, chief resident Cambridge Hosp.-Harvard Med. Sch., Cambridge, Mass., 1973-76; jr. assoc. in medicine Peter B. Brigham Hosp., Boston, 1976-78; clin. instr. Stanford (Ca.) U. Sch. Medicine, 1978-80; asst. prof. psychiatry Med. Coll. Wis., Milw., 1980-82; assoc. prof. psychiatry U. Tenn. Sch. Medicine, Memphis, 1982-86; assoc. prof., prof. psychiatry U. Mich. Med. Sch., Ann Arbor, 1986-92; prof. psychiatry U. Colo. Sch. Medicine, Denver, 1992—, now dir. psychiatry. Chief psychiatry VA Med. Ctr., Memphis, 1982-86; assoc. chair psychiatry U. Mich., 1986-88, sci. dir., Alcohol Rsch. Ctr., 1988-91; mem. numerous profl. coms.; presenter, cons. in field. Author: (poetry) The Pharos, 1979, Annals of Internal Medicine, 1981, (poetry) A Father's Handbook, 1982, Front Range, 1984, Handbook of Psychiatric Diagnostics Procedures, vol. I, 1984, editor vol. II, 1985; author: Liver Transplantation and the Alcoholic Patient, 1994, Neuropsychiatry: An Introductory Approach, 2001; editor: Alcohol and Aging, 1995; assoc. editor Psychiat. Medicine, 1981-92, Psychosomatics, 1982—; asst. editor, co-author numerous titles, contbr. numerous articles to profl. jours. Recipient Emanuel Friedman award U. Colo., 1972, Henry Russel award U. Mich., 1988; Stegner fellow Stanford U., 1978-79; rsch. grantee Nat. Inst. Alcohol Abuse and Alcoholism, 1986, ctr. grantee, 1988, tng. grantee, 1990, Dept. Vets. Affairs Tng. grantee, 1995. Fellow Acad. Psychosomatic Medicine, Am. Psychiat. Assn., Acad. Psychosomatic Medicine (Best Poster award 1991, Disting. Svc. award 1994, Ann. Rsch. award 2000), Rsch. Soc. on Alcoholism. Home: 6410 S Olathe St Aurora CO 80016-1034 Office: U Colo VA Med Ctr 116 Campus Box C 268-46 1055 Clermont St Denver CO 80220-3808 E-mail: thomas.beresford@uchsc.edu.

BEREUTER, DOUGLAS KENT, foundation administrator, former congressman; b. York, Nebr., Oct. 6, 1939; s. Rupert Wesley and Evelyn Gladys (Tonn) B.; m. Louise Meyer, June 1, 1962; children: Eric David, Kirk Daniel. BA, U. Nebr., 1961; M in City Planning, Harvard U., 1966, MPA, 1973. Urban planner HUD, San Francisco, 1965-66; dir. div. state and urban affairs Nebr. Dept. Econ. Devel., 1967-68, state planning dir., 1968-70; coord. fed.-state relations Nebr. State Govt., 1967-70, urban planning cons., 1971-78; assoc. prof. U. Nebr., 1971—73, Kansas St. U., 1971—78; mem. Nebr. Legislature, 1974-78, US House of Reps. from 1st Nebr. Dist., 1979—2004, mem. fin. svcs. com., mem. and vice chmn. internat. rels. com., vice chmn. intelligence com., mem. transp. and infrastructure com.; pres., CEO The Asia Found., San Francisco, 2004—. Mem. Nebr. State Crime Commn., 1969-71; chmn. standing com. urban devel. Nat. Conf. State Legislatures, 1977-78; mem. Nat. Agrl. Export Commn., 1985-86; bd. trustees Nat. Arbor Day Found., Lincoln; pres. NATO Parliamentary Assembly, 2003-04. Served as officer US Army, 1963-65. Mem. Coun. Fgn. Rels., Phi Beta Kappa, Sigma Xi. Republican. Lutheran. Office: The Asia Found PO Box 193223 San Francisco CA 94104

BERG, ALFRED OREN, epidemiology and family practice medicine educator; b. Wichita, Kans., July 3, 1949; BA, Tabor Coll., 1970; MD, Washington U., 1974; MPH, U. Wash., 1979. Prof., chair dept. U. Wash., 1979—. Assoc. editor Jour. Am. Bd. Family Practice, 1991—. Mem. Am. Acad. Family Physicians, NAS, Soc. Tchrs. Family Medicine, Inst. Medicine.

BERG, JEFFREY SPENCER, talent agency executive; b. LA, May 26, 1947; s. Dick Berg and Barbara Freedman; m. Denise Luria; 2 children. BA in English with honors, U. Calif., Berkeley, 1969. V.p., head lit. divsn. Creative Mgmt. Assocs., Los Angeles, 1969-75; v.p. motion picture dept. Internat. Creative Mgmt., Los Angeles, 1975-80, pres., 1980-85, chmn., CEO, 1985—. Dir. Josephson Internat., Inc., Marshall McLuhan Ctr. of Global Communication; bd. dirs. Oracle Corp., Am. Film Inst. Trustee U. Berkeley Found.; bd. govs. Music Ctr. L.A. County; pres. letters and sci. exec. bd. U. Calif. Berkeley; bd. vis. Anderson Grad. Sch. of Mgmt., UCLA. Recipient Cavaliere Ufficiale Order of Merit, Republic of Italy, 1991; named one of 50 Most Powerful People in Hollywood, Premiere mag., 2004—06. Mem. U. Calif. Berkeley Alumni Assn. Office: Internat Creative Mgmt 8942 Wilshire Blvd Beverly Hills CA 90211-1934

BERG, MADELAINE R., lawyer; b. Bklyn., Aug. 13, 1951; d. Gerald and Lorraine (Nodkin) B. BA, Bklyn. Coll., 1973, MFA, 1975; JD, Bklyn. Law Sch., 1980. Bar: NY 1981, US Dist. Ct. (so. dist.) NY 1981, Pa. 1992, US Dist. Ct. (ea. dist.) Pa. 1992, Ariz., 2007. Spl. counsel, environ. law practice area Stroock & Stroock & Lavan LLP, NYC, 1980—2006; private practice, environ. law, 2006—. Contbr. articles to profl. jours. Office: Madelaine R Berg Esq LLC 9040 N Flying Butte Fountain Hills AZ 85268

BERG, PAUL, biochemist, educator; b. NYC, June 30, 1926; s. Harry and Sarah (Brodsky) Berg; m. Mildred Levy, Sept. 14, 1947; 1 child, John. BS, Pa. State U., 1948; PhD (NIH fellow 1950-52), Western Res. U., 1952; DSc (hon.) (hon.), U. Rochester, 1978, Yale U., 1978, Washington U., St. Louis, 1986, Oreg. State U., 1989, Pa. State U., 1995. Postdoctoral fellow Copenhagen (Denmark) U., 1952—53; postdoctoral fellow Sch. Medicine, Washington U., 1953—54. Am. Cancer Soc. scholar cancer research dept. microbiology sch. medicine, 1954—57, from asst. to assoc. prof. microbiology, 1955—59; prof. biochemistry Sch. Medicine, Stanford (Calif.) U., 1959—, Sam, Lulu and Jack Willson prof. biochemistry, 1970—94, Robert W. Cahill prof. cancer rsch., 1994—2000, chmn. dept. sch. medicine, 1969—74, now Cahill prof. in cancer rsch. emeritus; and dir. emeritus, Beckman Ctr. for Molecular and Genetic Med., 2000—. Dir. Stanford U. Beckman Ctr. for Molecular and Genetic Medicine, 1985—2000, Affymetrix, 1993—, Nat. Found. Biomed. Rsch., 1994—; non-resident fellow Salk Inst., 1973—83; adv. bd. NIH, NSF, MIT; vis. com. dept. biochemistry and molecular biology Harvard U.; bd. sci. advisors Jane Coffin Childs Found. Med. Rsch., 1970—80; chmn. sci. adv. com. Whitehead Inst., 1984—90; bd. sci. adv. DNAX Rsch. Inst., 1981—; internat. adv. bd. Basel Inst. Immunology; chmn. nat. adv. com. Genome Project, 1990—92. Editor: Biochem. and Biophys. Research Communications, 1959—68; editl. bd.: Molecular Biology, 1956—69; contbr. to profl. jours. Trustee Rockefeller U., 1990—92. Lt. (j.g.) USNR, 1943—46. Recipient Eli Lilly prize biochemistry, 1959, V.D. Mattia award, Roche Inst. Molecular Biology, 1972, Henry J. Kaiser award for excellence in teaching, 1969, Disting. Alumnus award, Pa. State U., 1972, Sarasota Med. awards for achievement and excellence, 1979, Gairdner Found. annual award, 1980, Lasker Found. award, 1980, Nobel award in chemistry, 1980, NY Acad. Sci. award, 1980, Sci. Freedom and Responsibility award, AAAS, 1982, Nat. Medal of Sci., 1983, 7th Ann. Biotechnology Heritage award, Chem. Heritage Found., 2005, numerous disting. lectureships including Harvey lectr., 1972; named Calif. Scientist of Yr., Calif. Museum Sci. and Industry, 1963, Lynen lectr., 1977, Priestly lectrs., Pa. State U., 1978, Dreyfus Disting. lectrs., Northwestern U., 1979, Lawrence Livermore Dir.'s Disting. lectr., 1983, Linus Pauling lectr., 1993. Fellow: AAAS; mem.: NAS, Royal Soc. (elected fgn. mem. 1992), French Acad. Sci. (elected fgn. mem. 1981), Japan Biochem. Soc. (elected fgn. mem. 1978), Internat. Soc. Molecular Biology, Am. Philos. Soc., Am. Soc. Microbiology, Am. Soc. Cell Biology (chmn. pub. policy com. 1994—), Am. Soc. Biol. Chemists (pres. 1974—75), Am. Acad. Arts and Scis., Inst. Medicine. Office: Stanford Sch Medicine Beckman Ctr B-062 Stanford CA 94305-5301 E-mail: pberg@cmgm.stanford.edu.

BERG, PETER, actor; b. NYC, Mar. 11, 1964; m. Elizabeth Rogers, 1993 (div. 1996). Film appearances include Demonstrator, 1971, Miracle Mile, 1988, Heart of Dixie, 1989, Never on Tuesday, 1989, Shocker, 1989, Genuine Risk, 1991, Late for Dinner, 1991, Aspen Extreme, 1993, Fire in the Sky, 1993, Across the Moon, 1994, The Last Seduction, 1994, Girl 6, 1996, The Great White Hype, 1996, Cop Land, 1997, Dill Scallion, 1999, Corky Romano, 2001, Collateral, 2004, Smokin' Aces, 2006, Lions for Lambs, 2007; dir.: (films) Very Bad Things, 1998, The Rundown, 2003, Friday Night Lights, 2004, Hancock, 2008; actor, dir.: (TV series) Chicago Hope, 1994-98.

BERG, PHILIP, religious organization administrator; b. NYC, Aug. 20, 1929; s. Max and Ester (Reis) B.; m. Karen Mulnick, July 2, 1971. Rabbi, Mesifta Torah Vadaath, NYC, 1952; JD in Hebrew Law, Yeshiva Kol Yehuda, Tel Aviv, 1967. Spiritual leader Rsch. Ctr. Kabbalah Internat., LA, 1962—. Home: 83-84 115th St Jamaica NY 11418-1303 Office: Rsch Ctr Kabbalah Internat 1062 S Robertson Blvd Los Angeles CA 90035-1505

BERGEN, CANDICE, actress, writer, photojournalist; b. Beverly Hills, Calif., May 9, 1946; d. Edgar and Frances (Westerman) B.; m. Louis Malle, Sept. 27, 1980 (dec. 1995); 1 child, Chloe; m. Marshall Rose, June 15, 2000. Student, U. Pa. Model during coll. Actor (films) The Group, The Sand Pebbles, 1966, The Day the Fish Came Out, Live for Life, 1967, The Magus, 1968, Soldier Blue, The Executioner, The Adventurers, Getting Straight, 1970, The Hunting Party, 1970, Carnal Knowledge, 1970, 19 T.R. Baskin, 1971, 11 Harrowhouse, 1974, Bite the Bullet, The Wind and the Lion, 1975, The Domino Principle, The End of the World in Our Usual Bed in a Night Full of Rain, Oliver's Story, 1978, Starting Over, 1979, Rich and Famous, 1981, Gandhi, 1982, Stick, 1985, Miss Congeniality, 2000, Sweet Home Alabama, 2002, View from the Top, 2003, The In-Laws, 2003, Sex and the City: The Movie, 2008, The Women, 2008, Bride Wars, 2009; (TV films) Arthur the King, 1985, Murder by Reason of Insanity, 1985, Mayflower Madam, 1987, Shelley Duvall's Bedtime Stories, Vol. 7, 1993, Mary and Tim, 1996 (TV appearances) What's My Line, 1965, Coronet Blue, 1967, The Muppet Show, 1976, The Way They Were, 1981, 2010 (voice), 1984, Trying Times, 1987, Seinfeld, 1990, Images of Life: Photographs that have Changed the World, 1996, The Human Face (miniseries), 2001, Murphy Brown: TV Tales, 2002, Sex and the City, 2002; (TV series) Murphy Brown, 1988-98 (Emmy award, Leading Actress in a Comedy Series, 1989, 90, 92, 94, 95), Boston Legal, 2004-; (TV miniseries) Hollywood Wives, 1985, Trying Times, Moving Day; author Knockwood; photojournalist credits include articles for Life, Playboy; dramatist: (play) The Freezer (included in Best Short Plays of 1968).

BERGER, ADAM, Internet company executive; b. LA; m. Susan Berger. BS in Chem. Engring., U. Calif., Berkeley; MBA with distinction, Harvard Bus. Sch. With Procter & Gamble; cons. Boston Consulting Group., 1991—94; pres. Franklin Mint, Phila., 1994—98; CEO WeddingChannel.com Inc., LA, 1999—2006; chmn., CEO Spark Networks, Inc., LA, 2007—. Bd. dirs. PeopleSupport, Inc., 2003—, Spark Networks, Inc., 2006—. Office: Spark Networks Ste 800 8383 Wilshire Blvd Beverly Hills CA 90211 Office Phone: 323-658-3000. Office Fax: 323-658-3001.

BERGER, ALBERT, film producer; Grad., Tufts U.; student, Columbia U., NYC. Owner, mgr. Sandburg Theatre, Chgo.; script writer Paramount Pictures, v.p. devel. Marvin Worth Prodns.; co-founder Bona Fide Prodns., 1993—. Prodr.: (films) King of the Hill, 1993, Election, 1999, The Wood, 1999, Pumpkin, 2002, Cold Mountain, 2003, The Ice Harvest, 2005, Bee Season, 2005, Little Miss Sunshine, 2006 (Darryl F. Zanuck Prodr. of Yr. award in Theatrical Motion Pictures, Prodrs. Guild of Am., 2007), Little Children, 2006; exec. prodr.: Crumb, 1994, I Am Trying to Break Your Heart, 2002; (TV films) The Spree, 1998. Office: Bona Fide Prodns Ste 804 8899 Beverly Blvd Los Angeles CA 90048

BERGER, PAUL ERIC, artist, photographer; b. The Dalles, Oreg., Jan. 20, 1948; s. Charles Glen and Virginia (Nunez) B. BA, UCLA, 1970; M.F.A., SUNY-Buffalo, 1973. Vis. lectr. U. Ill., 1974-78; prof. art U. Wash.-Seattle, 1978—. Exhibited one-man shows of photographs, Art Inst. Chgo., 1975, Light Gallery, N.Y.C., 1977, Seattle Art Mus., 1980, Light Gallery, N.Y.C., 1982, Univ. Art Mus., Santa Barbara, Calif., 1984, Cliff Michel Gallery, 1989, Seattle Art Mus., 1990, Fuel Gallery, 1993, Galerie Lichtblick GFFK, Cologne, Germany, 1996, SOHO Photo, N.Y.C., 1999, Mus. Contemporary Photography, Chgo., 2003. NEA Photographer's fellow, 1979, NEA Visual Artist's fellow, 1986; recipient Artist's Commn., Wash. State Arts Commn., 1990. Mem. Soc. Photographic Edn., Mus. of Contemporary Photography. Office: U Wash Sch Art PO Box 353440 Seattle WA 98195-3440 E-mail: peberger@u.washington.edu.

BERGER, STANLEY ALLAN, mechanical and biomechanical engineering educator; b. Bklyn., Aug. 9, 1934; s. Jack and Esther B.; m. Anna Ofman, Jan. 30, 1966 (div. Aug. 1984); children: Shoshana, Maya; m. Beth Fain, March 23, 2008. BS, Bklyn. Coll., 1955; PhD, Brown U., 1959. Rsch. assoc. Princeton U., NJ, 1959-60; from lectr. to prof. U. Calif., Berkeley, 1961—2005, Montford G. Cook chair bioengring., 2005—. Cons. IBM, The Rand Corp., Lockheed Missiles and Space Co., Sci. Applications, Inc., Aluminum Co. Am. Author: Laminar Wakes, 1971; editor: Introduction to Bioengineering, 1996; contbr. articles to profl. jours. Fellow: AIAA, ASME (chair applied mechanics divsn. 1997—98), AAAS, Biomed. Engring. Soc., Am. Inst. Med. and Biol. Engring., Am. Phys. Soc. (chair divsn. fluid dynamics 2001—02). Office: U Calif Dept Mech Engring Berkeley CA 94720-1740 Home Phone: 510-526-8682; Office Phone: 510-642-5950. Business E-Mail: saberger@me.berkeley.edu.

BERGER, VICKI, state legislator; b. Salem, Oreg., Mar. 1949; m. Jerry Berger; 3 children. BA, U. Wyo., 1974. Member sch board, Salem-Keizer Sch District, 1988-92; Oreg State Representative, District 20, 2002-.Owner, West Salem Lazerquick, ret. Republican. Mailing: 900 Court St NE H-479 Salem OR 97301 Office Phone: 503-986-1420. E-mail: rep.vickiberger@state.or.us.

BERGER, WOLFGANG H., oceanographer, educator, geologist; b. Erlangen, Germany; came to U.S., 1961; MS in Geology, U. Colo., 1963; PhD in Oceanography, U. Calif., San Diego, 1968. Asst. prof. Scripps Inst. Oceanography U. Calif., La Jolla, Calif., 1971-74, assoc. prof., 1974-80, prof. oceanography, 1980—. Co-editor: Abrupt Climatic Change, 1987, Ocean Productivity, 1989, co-author: The Sea Floor, 1993. Co-chief scientist, Ocean Drilling Prog., Leg 130 (1990), Leg 175 (1997). Recipient Bigelow medal Woods Hole (Mass.) Oceanographic Inst., 1979, Huntsman medal Bedford Oceanographic Inst., Can., 1984, Humboldt award German Sci. Found., Bonn, Germany, 1986, Lady Davis fellow Hebrew U., 1986, Albert I medal, Paris, 1991, Balzan prize, 1993, Steinmann medal Geol. Vereingung, 1998, Francis P. Shepard medal, Soc. for Sedimentary Geology, 2001. Fellow AAAS, Am. Geophysical Union (Ewing medal 1988), Geol. Soc. Am.; mem. European Geophysical Soc., Academia Europaea (fgn.). Avocation: photography. Office: U Calif San Diego Scripps Inst Oceanography MS 0244 La Jolla CA 92093-0244

BERGESON, TERESA, school system administrator; b. Mass. BA in English, Emmanuel Coll., Boston, 1964; M in Counseling and Guidance, Western Mich. U., 1969; PhD in Edn., U. Wash. Tchr., sch. guidance counselor, Mass., Alaska, Wash.; exec. dir. Ctrl. Kitsap Sch. Dist., 1989-92, Wash. State Commn. on Student Learning, 1993—96; state supt. pub. instrn. Olympia, Wash., 1997—. V.p. Wash. Edn. Assn., 1981, pres., 1985—89. Mem.: Wash. Edn. Assn. (v.p. 1981—85, pres. 1985—89). Office: Old Capital Bldg 600 S Washington PO Box 47200 Olympia WA 98504-7200 Office Fax: 360-753-6712. E-mail: bergeson@ospi.wednet.edu.

BERGHEL, HAL L., columnist, inventor, consultant, lecturer, educator; b. Mpls., May 10, 1946; s. Oscar H. and Edna M. (Muller) B.; m. Margi Millard, May 7, 1983; children: David, Steven, Kevin. BA, U. Nebr., 1971, MA, 1973, MA, 1976, PhD, 1977. Asst. prof. mgmt. U. Nebr., Lincoln, 1979-80, asst. prof. computer sci., 1981-86; prof. computer sci. U. Ark., Fayetteville, 1986-99; prof., dir. Sch. Computer Sci. U. Nev., Las Vegas, 1999—2005, assoc. dean Coll. Engring., 2005—, dir. Cyber Security Rsch. Ctr., 2003, dir. Sch. Informatics, 2006—; dir. Internet Forensics Lab, 2000—, dir. identity theft and fin. fraud rsch. & ops. ctr., 2004—. Pres. Fourth Generation Cons., Lincoln, Nebr., 1980-84; founder, owner Berghel Net Cons. Group, 2003—; ptnr. BC Innovations Mgmt, 2008-. Contbr. numerous articles to profl. jours. Fellow IEEE (Disting. visitor 1994-97, 98-2000, 2004—, press. ops. com. 2004—, chpts. bd. 2005—, electronic products and svcs. com.), Assn. for Computing Machinery (dist. lectr. 1991-93, 96—, vice chair membership bd. 1996-2003, publs. bd. 1992-98, 2000-03, local activities bd. 1993-95, Disting. Svc. award 1996, Outstanding Contbn. award 2000, Lifetime Achievement award 2004); mem. Ark. Soc. for Computer and Info. Tech. (chair, bd. dirs. 1988-96). Office: Univ Nev Las Vegas Coll Engring Las Vegas NV 89154-4019

BERGIN, ALLEN ERIC, clinical psychologist, educator; b. Spokane, Wash, Aug. 4, 1934; s. Bernard F. and Vivian Selma (Kullberg) B.; m. Marian Shafer, June 4, 1955; children: David, Sue, Cyndy, Kathy, Eric, Ben, Patrick, Daniel, Michael. BS, Brigham Young U., 1956, MS, 1957; PhD, Stanford U., 1960. Diplomate Am. Bd. Profl. Psychology, 1969. Fellow U. Wis., Madison, 1960-61; prof. psychology and edn. Tchr. Coll., Columbia U., NYC, 1961-72; prof. psychology Brigham Young U., Provo, Utah, 1972-99, prof. emeritus, 1999—, dir. Values Inst., 1976-78, dir. clin. psychology, 1989-93. Assessment officer Peace Corps, Washington, 1961-66; cons. NIMH, Rockville, Md., 1969-75, 90; former pres. Soc. Psychotherapy Rsch., Assn. Mormon Counselors. Co-author: Changing Frontiers in Psychotherapy, 1972, A Spiritual Strategy for Counseling and Psychotherapy, 1997, 2d edit., 2005; co-editor: Handbook of Psychotherapy, 1971, 4th edit., 1994 (citation classic 1979), Handbook of Pyschotherapy and Religious Diversity, 2000, Casebook for a Spiritual Strategy, 2004; author: Eternal Values and Personal Growth, 2002. Bishop LDS Ch., Emerson, NJ, 1970-72, Provo, 1981-84, stake pres., 1992-1995, Church Ed. Mission, San Diego, 2002-03; mem. steering com. Utah Gov.'s Conf. on Families, Salt Lake City, 1979-80. Recipient Biggs-Pine award Am. Assn. Counseling and Devel., 1986, Maeser rsch. award Brigham Young U., 1986, exemplary paper award Templeton Found., 1996, Pfister award Am. Psychiat. Assn., 1998, Dising. Profl. Contbr. to Knowledge award Am. Psychol. Assn., 1998, Rsch. Ctr. award Soc. for Psychotherapy Rsch., 1998. Republican. Avocations: writing, travel.

BERGLUND, CARL NEIL, electronics company executive; b. Thunder Bay, Ont., Can., July 21, 1938; came to U.S., 1978; s. Anton Robert and Mary (Sideen) B.; m. Evelyn Jean McEvilla, Apr. 1, 1961; children: Cheryl Lynn, Gregory Neil (dec.), Carl Anton. BS with honors, Queen's U., Kingston, Ont., 1960; MS in Elec. Engring., MIT, 1961; PhD in Elec. Engring., Stanford U., 1964. Mem. tech staff Bell Labs., Murray Hill, N.J., 1964-66, supr. semicond. devices, 1966-72; mgr. electronic materials Bell No. Research, Ottawa, 1972-73; v.p. tech. Microsystems Internat., Ottawa, 1973-74; dir. silicon technology Bell No. Research, Ottawa, 1974-78; dir. tech. devel. Intel Corp., Aloha, Oreg., 1978-83; pres., chief exec. officer ATEQ Corp., Beaverton, Oreg., 1983-87; pres. Northwest Tech. Group, Tigard, Oreg., 1987—; prof. elec. engring. and applied physics Oreg. Grad. Inst., Beaverton, 1994—. Contbr. articles to profl. jours.; patentee (in field). Recipient Bacus award, SPIE, 1995, SEMI award, 2001. Fellow: IEEE; mem.: Electron Devices Soc. Home: 3135 NW Lacamas Dr Camas WA 98607-9147 Office: Northwest Tech Group PMB 138 Ste D-105 1901 NE 162d Ave Vancouver WA 98684-9346 E-mail: berglund@ece.ogi.edu.

BERGMAN, BARBARA E., law educator; BA, Bradley U., 1973; JD, Stanford Law Sch., 1976. Bar: Calif., DC, N.Mex. Law clk. to Judge Ben C. Duniway, 9th Cir.; atty. Wilmer, Cutler & Pickering, Washington; assoc. counsel Pres. Jimmy Carter; staff atty. Pub. Defender Svc., Washington; practiced labor law Bredhoff & Kaiser; prof. evidence/trial practice, advocacy and criminal procedure U. N.Mex., 1987—. Tchr. Nat. Inst. Trial Advocacy progs., Nat. Criminal Def. Coll., Inst. Criminal Def. Advocacy; team leader Nat. Inst. Trial Advocacy Nat. Prog., Boulder, Colo. Co-author: Every Trial Criminal Defense Resource Book, 1994, Wharton's Criminal Evidence, 15th edit.; editor: New Mexico Criminal Practice Manual, DC Criminal Jury Instructions, 4th edit.; contbr. articles to profl. jours. Recipient Richard S. Jacobson award, Roscoe Pound Found. Mem.: Nat. Assn. Criminal Def. Lawyers (past pres., has served as first v.p., second v.p., treas., sec., and bd. dir., past chair budget and investment coms., past co-chair Amicus Curiae Com., Robert C. Heeney award 2000). Office: UNM Sch Law MSC11 6070 Office 3115 1 University of New Mexico Albuquerque NM 87131-0001 Office Phone: 505-277-3304. Office Fax: 505-277-4594. E-mail: bergman@law.umn.edu.

BERGMAN, GEORGE MARK, mathematician, educator; b. Bklyn., July 22, 1943; s. Lester V. and Sylvia G. (Bernstein) B.; m. Mary Frances Anderson, Dec. 26, 1981; stepsons: Jeff Elam, Michael L. Anderson; children: Clifford I. and Rebecca N. Anderson-Bergman (twins). BA, U. Calif., Berkeley, 1963; PhD, Harvard U., 1968. Asst. prof. Dept. Math. U. Calif., Berkeley, 1967-72, assoc. prof., 1972-78, prof., 1978—. Contbr. articles to profl. jours. Mem. AAUP, ACLU, Am. Math. Soc. Democrat. Avocations: linguistics, dance. Office: U Calif Dept Math Berkeley CA 94720-3840

BERGMAN, MARILYN KEITH, lyricist, writer; b. Bklyn. d. Albert A. and Edith (Arkin) Katz; m. Alan Bergman, Feb. 9, 1958; 1 child, Julie Rachel. BA, NYU; MusD (hon.), Berklee Coll. Music, 1995, Trinity Coll., 1997. Lyricist, collaborator (with Alan Bergman) (numerous pop, theatrical and film score songs, TV themes) Bracken's World, 1969—70, The Sandy Duncan Show, 1972, Maude, 1972—78, Good Times, 1974—79, The Nancy Walker Show, 1976, The Dumplings, 1976, Alice, 1976—82, In the Heat of the Night, 1988—94, Brooklyn Bridge, 1991—93, The Powers That Be, 1993, TV film lyrics The Hands of Time (from Brian's Song), 1971, Queen of the Stardust Ballroom, 1975 (Emmy award for best dramatic underscore and best musical material, 1975, score only), Sybil, 1976 (Emmy award for best dramatic underscore 1976, 1976), Too Many Springs (from Hollow Image), 1979, theatrical scores Something More, 1964, Ballroom, 1978 (Grammy award nominee for best cast show album, 1979), The Lady and the Clarinet, 1980, feature film songs The Marriage Go-Round, from The Marriage Go-Round, 1960, Any Wednesday, from Any Wednesday, 1966, Make Me Rainbows, from Fitzwilly, 1967, (score) In the Heat of the Night, 1967, The Windmills of Your Mind, from the Thomas Crown Affair, 1968 (Acad. award for best song, 1968, Golden Globe award best original song, 1969), His Eyes, Her Eyes, from The Thomas Crown Affair, 1968, You Must Believe in Spring, from Young Girls of Rochefort, 1968, Maybe Tomorrow, from John and Mary, 1969, Tomorrow Is My Friend, from Gaily, Gaily, 1969, There's Enough to Go Around, 1969, A Smile, A Mem'ry and an Extra Shirt, from A Man Called Gannon, 1969, Sugar in the Rain, from Stiletto, 1969, What Are You Doing the Rest of You Life?, from The Happy Ending, 1969 (Acad. award nominee for best song, 1969), I Was Born in Love With You, from Wuthering Heights, 1970, Sweet Gingerbread Man, from The Magic Garden of Stanley Sweetheart, 1970, Nobody Knows, 1970, Move, from Move, 1970, Pieces of Dreams (Little Boy Lost), from Pieces of Dreams, 1970 (Academy award nominee for best song, 1970), The Costume Ball, from Doctors' Wives, 1971, All His Children, from Sometimes a Great Notion, 1971 (Acad. award nominee for best song, 1971), Rain Falls Anywhere It Wants To, from the African Elephant, 1971, The Summer Knows, from Summer of '42, 1971 (Grammy award nominee for song of the year 1972, 1972), A Face in the Crowd, from Le Mans, 1971, Marmalade, Molasses and Honey, from The Life and Times of Judge Roy Bean, 1972 (Acad. award nominee for best song, 1972), Love's the Only Game in Town, from Pete and Tillie, 1972, Molly and Lawless John, 1972, The Way We Were, from The Way We Were, 1973 (Grammy award for song of the year, 1973, Acad. award for best song, 1973, Golden Globe award for best original song, 1974, Grammy award for best original score, 1974), Breezy's Song, from Breezy, 1973, In Every Corner of the World, from Forty Carats, 1973, Summer Wishes, Winter Dreams, from Summer Wishes, Winter Dreams, 1973, Easy Baby, from 99 and 44/100%, 1974, There'll Be Time, from Ode to Billy Joe, 1975, Evening Sun, Morning Moon, from The Yakuza, 1975, I Believe in Love, from A Star is Born, 1976 (Grammy award nomination best original score, 1977), I'm Harry, I'm Walter, from Harry and Walter Go to New York, 1976, Hello and Goodbye, from Noon to Three, 1976, Bobby Deerfield, from Bobby Deerfield, 1977, The Last Time I Felt Like This, from Same Time Next Year, 1978 (Acad. award nominee for best song, 1978), The One and Only, from The One and Only, 1978, There's Something Funny Goin' On, from ...And Justice For All, 1979, I'll Never Say Goodbye, from The Promise, 1979 (Acad. award nominee for best song, 1979), Where Do You Catch the Bus for Tomorrow, from A Change of Seasons, 1980, Ask Me No Questions, from Back Roads, 1981, How Do You Keep the Music Playing?, from Best Friends, 1982 (Acad. award nominee for best song, 1982), Think About Love, 1982, Comin' Home to You, from Author! Author!, 1982, Tootsie, from Tootsie, 1982, It Might Be You, 1982 (Acad. award nominee for best song, 1982, Grammy award nominee for best original score, 1983), If We Were in Love, from Yes, Giorgio, 1982 (Acad. award nominee for best song, 1982), Never Say Never Again, from Never Say Never again, 1983, Papa, Can You Hear Me?, from Yentl, 1983 (Academy award nomination best song, 1983), The Way He Makes Me Feel, 1983 (Acad. award nominee for best song, 1983), Will Someone Ever Look at Me That Way?, 1983 (Acad. award best original score and Grammy award nomination for best original score, 1984, Acad. award nominee for best original song, 1983), Yentl, 1983 (Acad. award for best original score, 1983), Little Boys, from The Man Who Loved Women, 1983, Something New in My Life, from Mickey and Maude, 1984, The Music of Goodbye, from Out of Africa, 1985, I Know the Feeling, from The January Man, 1989, The Girl Who Used to Be Me, from Shirley Valentine, 1989 (Acad. award nominee for best song, 1989, Golden Globe nominee for best original song, 1990, Grammy award nominee, 1990), Welcome Home, from Welcome Home, 1989, Most of All You, from Major League, 1989, Dreamland, from For the Boys, 1991, Places That Belong to You, from The Prince of Tides, 1991, It's All There, from Switch, 1991, Moonlight, from Sabrina, 1995 (Acad. award nominee for best original song, 1996, Golden Globe nominee, Grammy nominee), The Best of Friends, from Bogus, 1996, Love is Where You Are, from At First Sight, pop songs You Don't Bring Me Flowers, 1978 (Grammy award nominee for song of the year, 1978), In the Heat of the Night, The Summer Knows, Nice 'N' Easy (Grammy award nominee for song of the year, 1960), Someone in the Dark, L.A. Is My Lady, After the Rain, I Was Born in Love With You, That Face, Look Around, I Love to Dance Like They Used to Dance, What Matters Most, One Day, A Child Is Born, Sleep Warm, Sentimental Baby, Live It Up, If I Close My Eyes, Yellow Bird, Like a Lover, Where Do You Start?, On My Way to You, Ordinary Miracles (Cable Ace award and Emmy award for best original song), A Ticket to Dream (Emmy Awd. for best song), albums Never Be Afraid for Bing Crosby, The Ballad of the Blues for Jo Stafford, 1999, Barbra Streisand: The Concert (Ace nominee for writing of a spl.). Recipient singers salute to songwriter award, Clooney Found., 1986, Aggie award, Songwriter's Guild, 1987; named to songwriters hall of Fame, 1980; grantee Am. Film Inst., 1976. Mem.: ASCAP (pres., chmn. bd. dirs. 1994—). Office: ASCAP 7920 Sunset Blvd Ste 300 Los Angeles CA 90046

BERGMAN, NANCY PALM, real estate investment company executive; b. McKeesport, Pa., Dec. 3, 1938; d. Walter Vaughn and Nellie (Sullivan) Leech; m. Donald Bergman; 1 child, Tiffany Palm Taylor. Student, Mt. San Antonio Coll., 1970, UCLA, 1989—93. Corporate sec. U.S. Filter Corp., Newport Beach, Calif., 1965—. Pres. Jaguar Research Corp., L.A. and Atlanta, 1971-; owner Environ. Designs, L.A., 1976—; pres. Prosher Corp., L.A., 1978-83; now pres., dir. Futura Investments, L.A.; CEO Rescor, Inc. Author: Resident Managers Handbook. Elder Beverly Hills Presbyn. Ch., 2006. Home: 1255 Benedict Canyon Dr Beverly Hills CA 90210 also: 23540 Tapatia Rd Homeland CA 92548 Office: PO Box 15246 Beverly Hills CA 90209

BERGMAN, ROBERT GEORGE, chemist, educator; b. Chgo., May 23, 1942; s. Joseph J. and Stella (Horowitz) Bergman; m. Wendy L. Street, June 17, 1965; children: David R., Michael S. BA in Chemistry cum laude, Carleton Coll., 1963, PhD (hon.), 1995; PhD, U. Wis., 1966. NATO fellow in chemistry Columbia U., NYC, 1966-67; Arthur Amos Noyes instr. chemistry Calif. Inst. Tech., Pasadena, 1967-69, asst. prof. chemistry, 1969-71, assoc. prof. chemistry, 1971-73, prof., 1973-77; prof. chemistry U. Calif., Berkeley, 1977—2002, Gerald E.K. Branch disting. prof. chemistry, 2002—, asst. dean Coll. Chemistry, 1987—91, 1996, 2005—07, Miller Rsch. prof. Berkeley, 1982-83, 93, 2003. Sherman Fairchild Disting. scholar Calif. Inst. Tech., 1984; mem. panel bioinorganic and metallobiochemistry study sect. NIH, 1977—80; cons. Union Carbide Corp., 1977—81, 1990—2001, E. I. DuPont de Nemours, 1982—85, Chevron Rsch. Co., 1983—89, Dow Chem. Co., 2001—02; disting. vis. prof. U. NC, Chapel Hill, 1999. Mem. editl. bd.: Chem. Revs., Jour. Am. Chem. Soc., Organometallics, Tetrahedron Publs., European Jour. Inorganic Chemistry; contbr. articles to profl. jours. Recipient Tchr. Scholar award, Camille and Henry Dreyfus Found., 1970—75, Excellence in Tchg. award, Calif. Inst. Tech., 1978, Merit award, NIH, 1991, E. O. Lawrence award for chemistry, Dept. Energy, 1993, Chem. Pioneer award, Am. Inst. Chemists, 2000, Technology Transfer award, Lawrence Berkeley Nat. Lab., 2004, T.W. Richards award, ACS Northeastern Sect., 2008; named Sr. Edward Franklin Lectr., Royal Soc. Chemistry, 2008; NIH fellow, 1964—66, Alfred P. Sloan Found. fellow, 1970—72, Guggenheim fellow, 1999. Mem.: NAS (Chem. Scis. award 2007), AAAS, Am. Chem. Soc. (Organometallic Chemistry award 1986, Arthur C. Cope scholar 1987, Edward Fahs Smith award 1990, Ira Remsen award 1990, Arthur C. Cope award 1996, Edward Leete award 2001, James Flack Norris award 2003, Northeastern Sect., T.W. Richards medal 2008), Phi Beta Kappa, Phi Lambda Upsilon, Sigma Xi (Monie Ferst award 2003). Home: 501 Coventry Rd Kensington CA 94707-1316 Office: U Calif Dept Chemistry Berkeley CA 94720-0001 Home Phone: 510-527-2937. E-mail: bergman@cchem.berkeley.edu.

BERGREN, SCOTT C., career officer; b. Mineola, NY; BA in Econ., Clemson U., 1970; student navigator tng., Mather AFB, Calif., 1970-71; student, Squadron Officer Sch., 1974; M in Polit. Sci., Auburn U., 1981; student, Air Command and Staff Coll., 1981, Air War Coll., 1990, Harvard U., 1996. Commd. 2d lt. USAF, 1970, advanced through grades to maj. gen., 1999, various F-4 Phantom assignments, 1971-76; air staff ops. officer programs and resources Air Staff Tng. program, Hdqs. USAF, Pentagon, Washington, 1976-77, asst. exec. officer to dep. chief staff programs/resources, 1976-77; instr., navigator and exchange officer 237th Operational Conversion Unit, RAFB Honington, Eng., 1977-80; dir. ops. force analysis div. then spl. asst. comdr. Hdqs. Tactical Air Command, Langley AFB, Va., 1981-85; comdr. 325th Tactical Tng. Wing's Aircraft Generation Squadron, Tyndall AFB, Fla., 1985-87, asst. dep. comdr. maintenance, 1985-87; dep. comdr. maintenance 33rd Tactical Fighter Wing, Eglin AFB, Fla., 1987-89; Air Univ. chair for chief staff of Air Force Maxwell AFB, Ala., 1990-91; various comdr. positions Nellis AFB, Nev., 1991-93; stationed at U.S. Ctrl. Command, MacDill AFB, Fla., 1994-96; vice comdr. San Antonio Air Logistics Ctr., Kelly AFB, Tex., 1996-97; comdr. 82d Tng. Wing, Sheppard AFB, 1997-99; dir. maintenance, dep. chief staff installations & logistics HQ/USAF, 1999-2000; comdr. Ogden Air Logistics Ctr., Hill AFB, Utah, 2000—. Decorated Silver Star, D.F.C. with silver oak leaf cluster, Purple Heart, Air medal with three silver oak leaf clusters and bronze oak leaf cluster, Small Arms Expert Marksmanship Ribbon, Rep. Vietnam Gallantry Cross with Palm, Rep. Vietnam Campaign medal. Office: Hill AFBM OO-ALC/CC 7981 Georgia St Hill AFB UT 84056-5824

BERK, BLAIR, lawyer; b. Fayetteville, NC, May 16, 1964; BA summa cum laude, MA summa cum laude, Boston U., 1987; JD, Harvard Law Sch., 1990. Bar: Calif. 1992. Ptnr. Tarlow & Berk P.C., L.A. Mem.: ABA, Nat. Assn. Criminal Def. Lawyers, Calif. Lawyers for Criminal Justice (co-chair seminars com. 1997—99, bd. govs. 1997—2004), Women Lawyers Assn. LA (co-chair crimnal law section 1996—99), Beverly Hills Bar Assn. (chair criminal law sect. 2001—), Phi Beta Kappa. Office: Tarlow & Berk PC 9119 Sunset Blvd Los Angeles CA 90069*

BERKLEY, JAMES DONALD, clergyman; b. Yakima, Wash., May 19, 1950; s. Donald William and Erma Ercile (Van Meter) B.; m. Deborah Milam, Aug. 18, 1974; children: Peter James, Mary Milam. BS, U. Wash., 1972; MDiv, Fuller Theol. Seminary, 1975, D Ministry, 1980. Intern First Presbyn. Ch., Yakima, Wash., 1971-73, Bel Air Presbyn. Ch., LA, 1973-75; asst. pastor Community Presbyn Ch., Ventura, Calif., 1975-78; sr. pastor Dixon (Calif.) Community Ch., 1978-85; sr. assoc. editor Leadership jour. Christianity Today Inc., Carol Stream, Ill., 1985-90, editor Your Church, 1990-94; sr. assoc. pastor First Presbyn. Ch., Bellevue, Wash., 1994—2002; nat. issues ministry dir. Presbyns. for Renewal, Bellevue, 2002—05; dir Presbyn. Action, Bellevue, 2005—. Author: Making the Most of Mistakes, 1987, Called into Crisis, 1988, The Dynamics of Church Finance, 2000, Essential Christianity, 2001; gen. editor: Preaching to Convince, 1986, Leadership Handbooks of Practical Theology, Vol. I, 1992, Vols. II and III, 1994; editor reNEWS, 1999—2005. Recipient 1st place award interview Evangelical Press Assn., 1991, 92. Republican. Avocations: bagpipes, hiking, golf, films, music. Home: 304 128th Ave NE Bellevue WA 98005-3242 Office: Presbyn Action 304 128th Ave NE Bellevue WA 98005 Office Phone: 425-637-7742. E-mail: jimberkley@msn.com.

BERKLEY, ROBERT JOHN, retired federal agency professional; b. Albion, Mich., Oct. 2, 1933; s. Paul Clifford and Ina Muriel (Burroughs) B.; m. Sharon Irene Haynes, Sept. 9, 1955 (div. 1965); children: Thomas Alan, Richard Jon, Luann Michele; m. Jacquelyn Jane (Lewis) Ballou, Jan. 14, 1966. AA, Jackson CC, Mich., 1953; BS in Police Adminstrn., Calif. State U., LA, 1962. Police officer City of Claremont, Calif., 1959-62, 63-66; investigator U.S. Civil Svc. Commn., Washington and L.A., 1962-63, 66-72; spl. agt. FAA, Seattle, 1972-99, office mgr., 1973-99, ret., 1999. Local chmn. Selective Svc. Bd., Wash., 1981-2001. Sgt. USMC, 1953-56, Korea. Mem. SAR (chpt. pres. 1989-90, state sec. 1989-91, state pres. 1992, Patriots medal 1990, Law Enforcement medal 1991, 92), Wash. State Genealogical Soc. (state rep. region #8 2004—), Local Area Geneal. Soc. (pres. 2006-), Am. Legion, Eastern Star (patron 1989-90), Masons (master 1984, life), Scottish Rite, Shriners. Avocations: computers, photography, camping, travel. Home: 644 Briarwood Ter East Wenatchee WA 98802-8326 Personal E-mail: r.berkley@verizon.net.

BERKLEY, SHELLEY (ROCHELLE LEVINE BERKLEY), United States Representative from Nevada, lawyer; b. NYC, Jan. 20, 1951; m. Lawrence Lehrner; 2 children. BA in Polit. Sci., U. Nev., Las Vegas, 1972; JD, U. San Diego Sch. Law, 1976. Counsel S.W. Gas Corp.; dep. dir. Nev. Commerce Dept.; mem. Nev. State Assembly, 1982—84; vice chair bd. regents Nev. Univ. and Cmty. Coll. Sys., 1990—98; v.p. govt. and legal affairs Sands Hotel, 1996—98; mem. US Congress from 1st Nev. dist., 1999—, mem. ways and means com. and vets.' affairs com. Bd. chair Nev. Hotel and Motel Assn.; nat. dir. Am. Hotel-Motel Assn.; del. White House Conf. on Tourism. Bd. trustees Sunrise-Columbia Hosp. and Med. Ctr., Las Vegas. Recipient Clark County Mother of Yr., 1994, Humane Legislator of Yr. award, Am. Humane Assn., 2000, Medal of Merit, Jewish War Vets. of the U.S.A., 2003, Outstanding Dem. of Yr., Paradise Democratic Club. Mem.: Women's Democratic Club Clark County, Clark County Bar Assn., US Bar Assn., So. Nev. Assn. Women Attys., Nev. State Bar Assn. Democrat. Jewish. Office: US House Reps 405 Cannon House Office Bldg Washington DC 20515 Office Phone: 202-225-5965. Office Fax: 202-225-3119. E-mail: shelley.berkley@mail.house.gov.

BERKLEY, STEPHEN M., entrepreneur, investor; b. NJ, 1944; s. Irving S. and Goldie A. Berkley; children: David, Michael. Student, London Sch. Econs., 1964-65; BA in Econs., Colgate U., 1966; MBA, Harvard U., 1968. Mgmt. cons. Boston Cons. Group, 1968, 71-73; mgr. strategic planning Potlatch Corp., 1973-77; v.p. bus. devel. Qume Corp. subs. ITT, Hayward, Calif., 1977-80, v.p., gen. mgr. memory products divs., 1980-81; v.p. mktg. Quantum Corp., Milpitas, Calif., 1981-83, chmn., CEO, 1987-92, chmn., 1992-93, 95-98; pres. Plus Devel. Corp., 1983-87, chmn., CEO, 1987-92; pres. The Rosewood Found., 1991—. Bd. dirs. Quantum Corp., Edify Corp., Splashcast Inc., 2006-, Hidden Harvest, 2005—, v.p. of bd., 2006—; chmn. Coactive Computing Corp.; instr. bus. and econs. East Carolina U., 1969-71. Served to lt. USNR, 1968-71. Mem. Corp. Planners Assn. (dir.), Harvard Bus. Sch. Club No. Calif., Los Altos Golf and Country Club, The Reserve Golf Club, Phi Beta Kappa. Avocations: golf, modern art, travel.

BERKNER, KLAUS HANS, laboratory administrator, physicist; b. Dessau, Anhalt, Germany, Mar. 2, 1938; came to U.S., 1948; s. Hans Otto and Sigrid Erika B. SB, MIT, 1960; PhD, U. Calif., Berkeley, 1964. NSF grad. fellowship U. Calif., Berkeley, 1960-61; NSF postdoctoral fellowship Culham, Eng., 1965-66; physicist Lawrence Berkeley (Calif.) Lab., 1964-79, sr. physicist, 1979—, deputy div. dir. accelerator and fusion research, 1982-84, acting div. dir., 1984-85, div. dir., 1985-91, assoc. lab. dir. for ops., 1991-94; dep. dir. ops., 1994—. Mem. Basic Energy Scis. Adv. Com., 1991-96, co-chair, 1993-96; mem. Fusion Energy Adv. Com., 1991-93. Contbr. over 100 articles on atomic physics, accelerators and fusion research to profl. jours. Fellow Am. Phys. Soc. Office: Lawrence Berkeley Nat Lab Dep Dir Ops 1 Cyclotron Rd Berkeley CA 94720-0001 E-mail: khberkner@lbl.gov.

BERKOWITZ, BOBBIE, medical educator; BS in Nursing, U. Wash., M of Nursing; PhD in Nursing Sci., Case We. Res. U. Chief nursing svcs. Seattle-King County Dept. Pub. Health, 1986—93; dep. sec. Wash. State Dept. Health, 1993—97; dir. Turning Point Nat. Program Office Robert Wood Johnson Found.; mem. faculty U. Wash. Sch. Nursing, Seattle, 1996—, prof. and chair dept. psychosocial and cmty. health Sch. Nursing, 1998—2004, alumni endowed prof. nursing, 2004—, dir. Ctr. for the Advancement of Health Disparities Rsch. Adj. prof. dept. health svcs. U. Wash. Sch. Pub. Health & Cmty. Medicine, Seattle; mem. Wash. State Bd. Health, 1988—93; apptd. by gov. Wash. Health Care Commn., 1990—92; bd. dirs. Hanford Environ. Health Found.; vice-chair, bd. dirs. QualisHealth; vice-chair The Pub. Health Found. Bd.; bd. trustees Group Health Cooperative, 2004—. Mem. editl. bd.: jour. Pub. Health Nursing, Am. Jour. Pub. Health, sr. assoc. editor: jour. Policy, Politics, & Nursing Practice, assoc. editor: jour. Nursing Outlook. Recipient Sch. Nursing Disting. Alumni award, U. Wash.; scholar, Ctrs. for Disease Control and Prevention's Pub. Health Leadership Inst., 1993—94. Fellow: Am. Acad. Nursing; mem.: NAS, Inst. Medicine (co-chair com. on pub. health performance monitoring). Office: U Wash Psychosocial and Cmty Health Box 357263 Seattle WA 98195-7263

BERKOWITZ, ETHAN A., lawyer, former state representative; b. San Francisco, Feb. 4, 1962; m. Mara Kimmel; children: Hannah, Noah. AB in Govt. and Econs with honors, Harvard U., 1983; MA in Philosophy and Polar Studies, Cambridge U., 1986; JD, U. Calif., 1990. Exporter United Exporters Co.; co-owner Snow City Cafe; ptnr. EZR Co.; dir. Inst. of the North; law clerk Alaska State Ct. of Appeals; enforcement officer US Antarctic Program, 1993—94; asst. dist. atty. Anchorage, 1993—93; owner Nunatak, LLC, 2001—. Mem. Alaska Ho. of Reps., 1996—2006, minority leader, 1999—2006; bd. dirs. Anchorage Econ. Devel. Corp., Exptl. Program to Stimulate Competitive Rsch. Mem. bd. dirs. Boys & Girls Club Anchorage, Spl. Olympics, Cmty. Dispute Resolution Ctr. Democrat. Avocations: hockey, fishing, travel, reading. Office: PO Box 91365 Anchorage AK 99509

BERKOWITZ, STEVEN, computer software company executive; Staff acct. J Herbert & Co, NYC, 1980-81, Paramount Pictures, NYC, 1981-83; fin. analyst Macmillan Pub., NYC, 1983-85, bus. mgr., 1985-88, v.p. fin., 1988-91; v.p. pub. MIS Press, NYC, 1991-94; pres., COO IDG Books Worldwide, Foster City, Calif., 1994—98, CFO, 1998—99; pres., CEO Intermap Systems, 1999—2001; pres., web properties IAC Search & Media (AskJeeves.com, now Ask.com, 2006), Oakland, Calif., 2001—03, pres., 2003—04, CEO, 2004—06; sr. v.p. internet unit, which includes MSN and Windows Live brands Microsoft Corp., Redmond, Wash., 2006—. Office: Microsoft Corp 1 Microsoft Way Redmond WA 98052-6399 Office Fax: 510-985-7400, 510-985-7412.

BERKUS, DAVID WILLIAM, venture capitalist; b. LA, Mar. 23, 1941; s. Harry Jay and Clara S. (Widess) B.; m. Kathleen McGuire, Aug. 6, 1966; children: Eric, Matthew, Amy. BA, Occidental Coll., 1962. Pres. Custom Fidelity Inc., Hollywood, Calif., 1958-74, Berkus Compusystems Inc., LA, 1974-81; pres., CEO, Computerized Lodging Sys. Inc. subs., LA, 1981-93; pres. Berkus Tech. Ventures, venture capital, LA, 1993—; mng. dir. worldwide lodging Sulcus Computer Corp., 1998-99; mng. ptnr. Kodiak Ventures, LP, LA, 1999—. Author: Better Than Money, 1994, Extending the Runway, 2006; author software Hotel Compusystem, 1979. Chmn. bd. Boy Scouts Am., San Gabriel Valley, 1986, v.p. area IV, 1993-94, pres. 1995-98, v.p. western region, 1998—; trustee Occidental Coll., LA Lt. USNR, 1963-72. Recipient Disting. award Merit, Boy Scouts Am., 1986, INC. mag. 500 award, 1986, Silver Beaver award Boy Scouts Am., 1988, Silver Antelope award, 1997, Dir. of Yr. award Forum for Corp. Dirs., 1999, Alumni Seal award Occidental Coll., 2000; inducted into hospitality industry Hall of Fame, 1998. Mem. Am. Hotel-Motel Assn., Audio Engring. Soc. (chmn. LA sect. 1973-74), Tech. Coast Angels (chmn. 2002-04). Achievements include first to develop artificial intelligence-based yield mgmt. sys. Office: 1430 Glencoe Dr Arcadia CA 91006-1909

BERKUS, JAMES, talent agent; Founder, pres. Leading Artists Agy. (now United Talent Agy.), 1981—91; pres., chmn. United Talent Agy., Beverly Hills, Calif., 1991—. Bd. advisors IFILM Corp., Hollywood. Mem. Santa Monica Mountains Conservancy, 2005—. Named one of 50 Most Powerful People in Hollywood, Premiere mag., 2004—06. Office: United Talent Agy 9560 Wilshire Blvd Fl 5 Beverly Hills CA 90212-2400 E-mail: berkusj@unitedtalent.com.

BERLAND, JAMES FRED, software company executive; b. Chgo., July 12, 1943; s. Samuel Jesse and Lillian (Singer) B. Student, Reed Coll., 1961-64, UCLA, 1964-66; student exec. mgmt. program, Harvard U., 1980. Photographer with Elson-Alexandre, 1970-73; freelance journalist, 1970-74; pub. affairs dir. Sta. KPFK-FM-Pacifica, LA, 1974-77; news dir., 1977-78; gen. mgr., v.p. Sta. KPFK-FM, Pacificia Found. Radio, 1978-84; pres., CEO News Wave Internat., Inc., LA, 1984-85; CEO, Berland Techs., Inc., LA, 1985—, Car-dReady Internat., Inc., 1998—. Mem. Calif. State Task Force on Telecom. Policy; active Californians for Pub. Broadcasting, chmn., 1980-81, pres., 1981-83; bd. dirs. Card Realty Internat. Mem. Assn. Calif. Pub. Radio Stas. (pres. 1980-82), Profl. Networking Group, CEO Club. Democrat. Office: 11242 Playa Ct Unit B Culver City CA 90230-6127 E-mail: Jim@berlandtech.com.

BERLEKAMP, ELWYN RALPH, mathematics professor; b. Dover, Ohio, Sept. 6, 1940; s. Waldo and Loretta Berlekamp; m. Jennifer Joan Wilson, Aug. 21, 1966; children: Persis, Bronwen, David. BSEE, MSEE, MIT, 1962, PhD in Elec. Engring., 1964. Asst. prof. U. Calif., Berkeley, 1964-66; mem. tech. staff Bell Labs., Murray Hill, NJ, 1966-71; prof. math. U. Calif., Berkeley, 1971—, assoc. chmn. of elec. engring. and computer sci. dept., 1975-77; pres. Cyclotomics, Berkeley, 1981-89, Axcom, Berkeley, 1989-90. Bd. dirs. AK Peters, Ltd.; chmn. bd. Math. Sci. Rsch. Inst., Berkeley, 1994—96, Internat. Computer Sci. Inst., Berkeley, 2000—03. Author: Key Papers in Coding Theory, 1974, Algebraic Coding Theory, 1984; co-author: Winning Ways, vols. 1 and 2, 1982, Mathematical Go, 1994, The Dots and Boxes Game, 2000; contbr. scientific papers, articles to profl. jours. Named Outstanding Young Elec. Engr., Eta Kappa Nu, 1971; fellow, Am. Assn. Advancement Sci., 2004. Fellow: IEEE (Best Rsch. Paper award 1967, Centennial medal 1984, Koji Kobayashi award 1990, Hamming award 1991), Info. Theory Soc. of IEEE (pres. 1973, Shannon award 1993); mem.: NAS, NAE, AAAS, Am. Math. Soc. (bd. govs. 1980—82), Am. Acad. Arts and Scis. Achievements include patents for algorithms and devices which corrects errors, erasures, and missed synchronization in communications and digital memory systems. Avocation: bicycling. Home: 120 Hazel Ln Piedmont CA 94611-4033 Office: 2039 Shattuck Ave 408 Berkeley CA 94704

BERMAN, BRUCE, entertainment company executive, television producer; b. NYC, Apr. 25, 1952; Grad., Calif. Inst. Arts Film Sch.; grad. magna cum laude in history, UCLA, 1975; JD, Georgetown U., 1978. Bar: Calif. 1978. Asst. to Jack Valenti Warner Bros., Burbank, Calif.; asst. to Peter Guber Casablanca Filmworks, 1979; asst. to Sean Daniel and Joel Silver Universal Pictures, 1979, v.p. prodn., 1982, Warner Bros., 1984, sr. v.p. prodn., 1988, pres. theatrical prodn., 1991-96, chmn., CEO Village Roadshow Pictures, 1998; pres. Worldwide Prodn., 1991-96. Founder Plan B Entertainment, 1996—. Office: Village Roadshow Pictures care Warner Bros Studios 3400 W Riverside Dr Ste 900 Burbank CA 91505-4639

BERMAN, DANIEL LEWIS, lawyer; b. Washington, Dec. 14, 1934; s. Herbert A. and Ruth N. (Abramson) B.; children: Priscilla Decker, Jane, Katherine Ann, Sara Mark, Heather, Melinda. BA, Williams Coll., 1956; LLB, Columbia U., 1959. Bar: N.Y. 1960, Utah 1962,

Wyo. 2004. Assoc. Chadbourne, Parke, Whiteside & Wolff, NYC, 1959-60; asst. prof. law U. Utah, 1960-62; pvt. practice Salt Lake City, 1962—, Berman & Savage PC, Salt Lake City, 1981—2008. Vis. prof. U. Utah, 1970, 74, 77; mem. Utah Coordinating Coun. Higher Edn., 1965-68; mem. Salt Lake County Merit Coun., 1974-80; mem. nominating commn. Utah Appellate Ct., 1999—2003. Trustee Salt Lake Art Ctr., 1978-80; Dem. candidate for U.S. Senate from Utah, 1980; mem. Utah Transit Authority, 1992-97. Mem. Am. Law Inst., Salt Lake Area C. of C. (bd. govs. 1976-79). Democrat. Jewish. Office: Berman & Savage PC 170 S Main Ste 500 Salt Lake City UT 84101-1660 Office Phone: 801-328-2200. Personal E-mail: dlb@bermansavage.com. Business E-Mail: dlb@bermanlaw-slc.com.

BERMAN, DAVID ALBERT, pharmacologist, educator; b. Rochester, NY, Nov. 4, 1917; s. Sam Moses and Anna (Newman) B.; m. Miriam Goodman, July 13, 1945; children: Shelley, Judith. BS, U. So. Calif., 1940, MS, 1948, PhD, 1951. Instr. U. So. Calif. Med. Sch., LA, 1952-54, asst. prof., 1954-58, assoc. prof., 1958-63, prof., 1963—93, Disting. emeritus prof., 1993. Contbr. articles to profl. jours. Mem. Calif. Rsch. Adv. Panel, San Francisco, 1970-82. Recipient Elaine Stevely Hoffman Achievement award, 1971, Merit award Am. Heart Assn., 1979, Faculty Achievement award Burlington No. Found., 1988, Tchg. award Kaiser Permanente, 1993, Kaiser Permanente Tchg. award, 1971, 75, 77, 79, 81, 83, 85, 87, 89, 90-93, 96-99, 03. Mem. Am. Soc. Pharmacology and Exptl. Therapeutics, Sigma XI, Phi Kappa Phi. Home: 3304 Scadlock Ln Sherman Oaks CA 91403-4912 Office: 2025 Zonal Ave Los Angeles CA 90089-0110 Office Phone: 323-442-1791. Business E-Mail: daberman@usc.edu.

BERMAN, GAIL, former film company executive, media company executive; b. Aug. 17, 1956; m. Bill Masters, 1980; 2 children. B in Theater, U. Md., 1978. Former exec. prodr. Comedy Channel, HBO; from v.p. TV to pres. and CEO Sandollar Prodns., 1991—97, advisor, 1997—98; founding pres. Regency TV, 1998—2000; pres. entertainment Fox Broadcasting Co., 2000—05; pres. Paramount Pictures, Hollywood, Calif., 2005—07; co-pres., co-founder BermanBraun, Santa Monica, 2007—. Recipient Lucy award, Women in Film, 2003; named one of 100 Most Powerful Women in Entertainment, Hollywood Reporter, 2003, 2004, 2005, 2006, 50 Most Powerful Women in Am Bus., Fortune Mag., 2003, 100 Most Powerful Women, Forbes mag., 2005—06. Office: BermanBraun 2900 W Olympic Blvd 3rd Fl Santa Monica CA 90404 Office Phone: 310-369-1000.

BERMAN, HOWARD LAWRENCE, United States Representative from California, lawyer; b. L.A., Apr. 15, 1941; s. Joseph Berman and Eleanor (Schapiro); m. Janis Gail Schwarz, 1979; children: Brinley Ann, Lindsey Rose. BA in Internat. Rels., UCLA, 1962, LLB, 1965. Bar: Calif. 1966. Vol. VISTA, Balt., San Francisco, 1966-67; assoc. Levy, Van Bourg & Hackler, LA, 1967-72; mem. Calif. State Assembly from 57th Dist., 1973—74, Calif. State Assembly from 43rd Dist., 1974—82; majority leader Calif. State Assembly from 43d dist., 1974—79; mem. US Congress from 26th Calif. Dist., 1982—2003, US Congress from 28th Calif. Dist., 2003—; chmn. US House Fgn. Affairs Com., 2008—; mem. US House Judiciary Com. Mem. Congl. Children's Working Grp.; bd. dirs. Ctr. for Law Public Interest; regional bd. mem. Anti-Defamation League. Pres. Calif. Fedn. Young Dems., 1967—69; mem. adv. bd. Jewish Fund for Justice. Recipient President's award, Nat. Music Pubs. Assn., 2007. Democrat. Jewish. Office: US Congress 2221 Rayburn Ho Office Bldg Washington DC 20515-0528 also: Dist Office 14546 Hamlin St Ste 202 Van Nuys CA 91411*

BERMAN, JEFF, Internet company executive; m. Melissa Berman. BA in Govt., Conn. Coll., 1993; JD, Yale U., 1996. Staff atty. Pub. Defender Svc. for DC, 1996—2001; chief counsel to US Senator Chuck Schumer, Washington, 2001—05; staff dir. Subcommittee on Adminstrv. Oversight and the Cts., Washington, 2001—05; sr. v.p. pub. affairs MySpace, 2006—08, exec. v.p. mktg. and content, 2008, pres. sales and mktg., 2008—. Adj. prof. Georgetown U. Law Ctr. Office: MySpace 1223 Wilshire Blvd, Ste 402 Santa Monica CA 90403-5400 Office Phone: 310-969-7400.

BERMAN, JENNIFER R., urologist; BA in Spanish and psychology, Hollins Coll., 1986; MS in human anatomy and physiology, U. Md. Sch. Medicine, 1988; MD, Boston U. Sch. Medicine, 1992. Resident in gen. surgery U. Md., 1994, resident in urology, 1998; fellow in urology/pelvic floor reconstructive surgery David Geffen Sch. Medicine, LA, 2001; former co-dir. (with sister Laura) Network Excellence in Women's Sexual Health, 1998—2004; co-dir. women's sexual health clinic Boston U. Sch. Medicine, masters med. sci. thesis advisor, 1998, instr. urology, 2000—01; dir. female sexual medicine ctr. UCLA, 2001—; asst. prof. urology UCLA Med. Ctr., 2001—; co-host (with sister Laura) Berman & Berman, Discovery Health Channel, 2004—. Vis. prof. U. Kan. Med. Ctr., 2002, Emory U., Atlanta, 2003; lectr. in field; mem. editl. bd. Healthgate Inc., Sexual Health Capsule and Comment; mem. sci. adv. bd. Quanlilife Pharm., Cellegy Pharm., Auxillum. Co-author (with sister Laura): For Women Only: A Revolutionary Guide to Overcoming Sexual Dysfunction and Reclaiming Your Sex Life, 2001, Secrets of the Sexually Satisfied Woman, 2005; contbr. articles to profl. jour. Recipient Rising Star Yr., Nat. Assn. Women Bus. Owners, 2002, Women of Action award, Israel Cancer Rsch. Fund, 2002, Women Who Make a Difference award, LA Bus. Jour., 2002, Outstanding Programming award, Cable Positive /TV Guide, 2003; named Women's Health Adv. Yr., Calif. Gov. Conf. Women, 2001. Mem.: AMA, Am. Urological Assn., Soc. Study Impotence, Sexual Medicine Soc. N. Am., Internat. Soc. Study Women's Sexual Health.

BERMAN, MICHAEL LEONARD, gynecologic oncologist; b. Washington, Mar. 11, 1942; s. Ben I. and Sylvia (Rogers) B.; m. June 21, 1964; children: Mara, Lisa, Deborah, Vicki. BS in Phys. Scis., U. Md., 1963; MD, George Washington U., 1967. Diplomate Am. Bd. Obstetrics and Gynecology; lic. physician, Calif. Resident in ob-gyn. George Washington U., Washington, 1968-69, Harbor Gen. Hosp., Torrance, Calif., 1971-74; NICHD clin. assoc. UCLA Sch. Medicine, 1969-71, acting asst. prof. ob-gyn., 1974-75, asst. prof. ob-gyn., 1975-77; asst. prof. and dir. divsn. gynecologic oncology U. Pitts./Magee Women's Hosp., 1977-81; assoc. prof. U. Calif.-Irvine Coll., Orange, 1981-90; prof. divsn. gynecologic oncology U. Calif.-Irvine Coll. Medicine, Orange, 1990—; dir. divsn. gynecologic oncology U. Calif.-Irvine Med. Ctr., Orange, 1981—90; clin. assoc. prof. U. Nev., Las Vegas, 1983-99. Cons. med. staff Saddleback Meml. Hosp., Laguna Hills, Calif., 1988—, U. Nev., Las Vegas, 1985-99, City of Hope Nat. Med. Ctr., Duarte, Calif., 1983-94; fellow in gynecologic oncology City of Hope Nat. Med. Ctr., Duarte, and UCLA Med. Ctr., 1974-76; attending physician Long Beach Meml. Med. Ctr./Women's Hosp., 1981—; lectr. in field; mem. carrier adv. com. Medicare, State of Calif., 1993—; cons. Health Care Fin. Adminstrn., others. Co-editor: Med. Tribune News, 1994—99; mng. editor: SGO Issues, 1990—91; reviewer Am. Jour. Obstetrics and Gynecology, Cancer, Gynecologic Oncology, Obstetrics and Gynecology, reviewer PDQ External Adv. Bd NIH, Nat. Cancer Inst., 1994—96; co-author: Bibliography of Chemical Kinetics and Collision Processes, 1969; contbr. numerous articles and abstracts to profl. jours., chapters to books. Recipient Physician's Recognition award AMA, 1990-93; Am. Cancer Soc. 2d yr. faculty clin. fellow, 1977-78, 1st yr. faculty clin. fellow, 1976-77, 2d yr. fellow, 1975-76, 1st yr. fellow, 1974-75; rsch. grantee NIH, 1987-90, 89-94, U.S. Biosci., 1989-91, Cetus, 1989-92, Gynecologic Oncology Group, 1989-94, Nat. Cancer Inst., 1991—. Fellow: ACOG (health econs. com. 1992—, mem. com. on coding and nomenclature 1997—99, chair com. coding and nomenclature 1999—2001); mem.: AMA, ACS, Gynecologic Oncology Group, Long Beach Obstetrics and Gynecology Soc., Internat. Gynecologic Cancer Soc., Am. Soc. Clin. Oncology, Am. Radium Soc., Western Assn. Gynecologic Oncologists (sec.-treas. 1981—86, pres. 1987), Soc. Gynecologic Oncologists (chair com./govt. rels. com. 1991—94, chair govt. rels. com. 1994—97, chair coding com. 1997—2000, pres.-elect 1999—2001, pres. 2001—02, past pres. 2002—), Dan Morton Soc., Phi Delta Epsilon, Alpha Omega Alpha. Office: Univ of Calif-Irvine Med Ct Dept Ob-Gyn 101 The City Dr S Bldg 23 Orange CA 92868-3201 Office Phone: 714-456-7974. E-mail: mlberman@uci.edu.

BERMAN, MYLES LEE, lawyer; b. Chgo., July 11, 1954; s. Jordan and Eunice (Berg) B.; m. Mitra Moghimi, Dec. 19, 1981; children: Elizabeth, Calvin, Justin. BA, U. Ill., 1976; JD, Chgo.- Kent Coll. of Law, 1979. Bar: Ill. 1980, Calif. 1987, U.S. Dist. Ct. (no. dist.) Ill. 1980, U.S. Dist. Ct. (ctrl. dist.) Calif. 1988, U.S. Dist. Ct. (no. and so. dist.) Calif., 2001, U.S. Supreme Ct. 1992. Asst. state's atty. Cook County State's Atty.'s Office, Chgo., 1980-82; pvt. practice Offices of Myles L. Berman, Chgo., 1982-91; pvt. practice, LA, 1988—. Founder Nat. Drunk Driving Def. Task Force; traffic ct. judge pro tem Beverly Hills Mcpl. Ct., 1990; traffic ct. judge pro tem Culver Mcpl. Ct., 1991; probation monitor State Bar Calif., 1992—; spkr. in field. Mem. editl. com.: Century City Lawyer, 1992; co-author: Driving Under the Influence Cases, California Criminal Law Procedure and Practice; author: DUI Trial Notebook; contbr. articles to profl. jours. Mem. ABA, NACDL, Los Angeles County Bar Assn., Century City Bar Assn. (chmn. criminal law sect. 1989, bd. govs. 1991—93, Outstanding Svc. award 1990, 92, 93, 94, Spl. Recognition 1994, treas. 1994, sec. 1995, v.p. 1996, pres.-elect 1997, pres. 1998-99, criminal law award for excellence 2001-02), Cyberspace Bar Assn., Calif. Dui Lawyers Assn. (specialist) Avocation: sports. Office: 9255 Sunset Blvd Ste 720 Los Angeles CA 90069-3304 also: #9 3075 E Thousand Oaks Blvd Westlake Village CA 91362 also: 4665 MacArthur Ct Ste 240 Newport Beach CA 92660 Office Phone: 310-273-9501. E-mail: duilaw@topgundui.com.

BERMAN, NEIL SHELDON, retired chemical engineering professor; b. Milw., Sept. 21, 1933; s. Henry and Ella B.; m. Sarah Ayres, June 3, 1962; children: Jenny, Daniel. BS, U. Wis., 1955; MS, MA, U. Tex., 1961, PhD, 1962. Engr. Std. Oil Co. Calif., LA, 1955-62; rsch. engr. E.I. DuPont Co., Wilmington, Del., 1962-64; from asst. prof. to prof. chem. engring. Ariz. State U., 1964-2000, prof. emeritus, 2000—, Grad. Coll. Disting. Rsch. prof., 1984-85; ret., 2000. Cons. air pollution, fluid dynamics; mem. Phoenix Air Quality Maintenance Area Task Force, 1976-77. Contbr. articles on fluid dynamics of polymer solutions, air pollution, thermodynamics and chem. engring. edn. to profl. jours. Served to capt. M.S.C. USAR, 1956-58. Recipient numerous grants for rsch. in fluid dynamics and air pollution. Fellow Am. Inst. Chem. Engrs. (chmn. Ariz. sect. 1978-79), AAAS, Ariz.-Nev. Acad. Sci. (corr. sec. 1981-88, pres.-elect 1988-89, pres. 1989-90); mem. ASME, Am. Chem. Soc., Am. Phys. Soc., Ariz. Coun. Engring. and Sci. Assns. (chmn. 1980-81), Soc. Rheology, Am. Soc. Engring. Edn., Am. Acad. Mechanics, Nat. Assn. State Acads. Sci. (mem.-at-large bd. dirs.), Sigma Xi, Tau Beta Pi, Phi Kappa Phi. Home: 418 E Geneva Dr Tempe AZ 85282-3731 Office: Ariz State U Dept Chem Engring Tempe AZ 85287-6006 Home Phone: 480-966-0290. Business E-Mail: neil.berman@asu.edu.

BERMAN, RICHARD P., lawyer; b. LA, Oct. 26, 1946; BA, U. Calif., 1968, JD, 1972. Bar: Calif. 1973. Mem. Law Office of Richard P. Berman, Fresno, Calif. Instr. criminal law Fresno City Coll., State Ctr. Peace Officers Acad., 1974—79; mem. adv. coun. sch. scis. Calif. State U., Fresno, 1986—98. Capt. med. svc. corps USAR, 1975—79. Master: Am. Inns of Ct.; mem.: Calif. Attys. Criminal Justice (mem., patron bd. govs. 1983—89, 1992—2001), Fresno Trial Lawyers Assn. (dir. 1979—85), Consumer Attys. Calif., Nat. Assn. Criminal Def. Lawyers (life), State Bar Calif. (mem. pub. affairs com. 1986—89), Fed. Bar Assn., Fresno County Bar Assn. (chmn. criminal law sect. 1982, 1984, mem. bench, bar and media com. 1990, dir. 1992—94, pres. 1994—95, mem. blue ribbon com. ct. coordination), Phi Alpha Delta. Office: 2333 Merced St Fresno CA 93721 Office Phone: 559-438-7425. Office Fax: 559-233-6947.

BERMAN, STEPHEN G., toy manufacturing executive; b. 1965; V.p., mng. dir. TH-Q Internat., Inc., 1991-95; co-founder, exec. v.p., sec. JAKKS Pacific Inc., Malibu, Calif., 1995-96, pres., COO, sec., dir., 1996—. Office: JAKKS Pacific Inc Ste 250 22619 Pacific Coast Hwy Malibu CA 90265-5080 Fax: (310) 317-8527.

BERMAN, STEVEN, Mayor, Gilbert, Arizona; BA, Ariz. State U., Tempe. Former sales & mgmt. Xerox, US West, Qwest; former chmn. Williams Gateway Airport Authority; councilman Gilbert Town Coun., 1987—93; mayor City of Gilbert, 1989—91, 2001—. Pres. Ariz. Mcpl. Water Users Assn., KC Ranch Home Owners Assn.; bd. mem. Greater Phoenix Econ. Coun., Maricopa Transp. Policy Com.; exec. bd. mem. Maricopa Assn. Govts., Ariz. League Cities and Towns. 2nd lt. US Army, 1971, capt. US Army, 1986. Mem.: NRA, Am. Legion, Gilbert Post 39, Mil. Order of World Wars, Apache Trails Chpt. Office: 50 E Civic Center Dr Gilbert AZ 85296 Office Phone: 480-503-6860. E-mail: mayor@ci.gilbert.az.us.*

BERN, HOWARD ALAN, biologist, researcher, science educator; b. Montreal, Que., Can., Jan. 30, 1920; m. Estelle Bruck, 1946; children: Alan, Lauren. BA, UCLA, 1941, MA, 1942, PhD in Zoology, 1948; D (hon.), U. Rouen, France, 1996; LLD (hon.), U. Hokkaido, Japan, 1994; DPhil (hon.), Yokohama City U., 1997; DSc (hon.), Toho U., Japan, 2001. Nat. Rsch. Coun. predoctoral fellow in biology UCLA, 1946—48; instr. in zoology U. Calif., Berkeley, 1948-50, asst. prof., 1950-56, assoc. prof., 1956-60, prof., 1960-89, prof. integrative biology, 1989-90, prof. emeritus, 1990—; rsch. endocrinologist Cancer Rsch. Lab., U. Calif., Berkeley, 1960—; chair group in endocrinology U. Calif., Berkeley, 1962-90, faculty rsch. lectr., 1988. Rsch. prof. Miller Inst. for Basic Rsch. in Sci., 1961; vis. prof. pharmacology U. Bristol, 1965-66, U. Kerala, India, 1967, Ocean Rsch. Inst., U. Tokyo, 1971, 86, U. P.R., 1973-74, U. Tel Aviv, 1975, Nat. Mus. Natural History, Paris, 1981, Toho U., Funabashi, Japan, 1982-84, 86-89, U. Hawaii, 1986, 91-93, Hokkaido U., 1992, 94, U. Fla., 1991-92; James vis. prof. St. Francis Xavier U., Antigonish, N.S., 1986; Walker-Ames prof. U. Wash., 1977; disting. visitor U. Alta., Edmonton, Can., 1981; John W. Cowper Disting. vis. lectr. SUNY, Buffalo, 1984; Watkins vis. prof. Wichita (Kans.) State U., 1984; vis. scholar Meiji U., Tokyo, 1986; internat. guest prof. Yokohama City U., Japan, 1988, 95; adv. com. on instl. rsch. grants Am. Cancer Soc., 1967-70; adv. com. Nat. Cancer Inst., 1975-79; adv. com. in endocrinology and metabolism NIH, 1978-79; mem. GM Cancer Rsch. Found., Sloan Medal Selection Com., 1984-85, Japan Internat. Prize in Biology Selection Com., 1987, 92, 96; guest of honor Internat. Symposium Amphibian and Reptilian Endocrinology and Neurobiology, Camerino, Italy, 2001, Jeju, Korea, 2003; lectr., spkr. in field Mem. editl. bd. Endocrinology, 1962-74, Gen. and Comparative Endocrinology, Revs. in Fish Biology and Fisheries, Jour. Exptl. Zoology, 1965-69, 86-89, Internat. Rev. Cytology, Neuroendocrinology, 1974-80, Cancer Rsch., 1975-78, Jour. Comparative Physiology B, 1977-84, Am. Zoologist, 1978-83, Acta Zoologica, 1982-96, Zool. Sci., Tokyo, 1984-2002; contbr. articles to profl. jours. Assoc. Nat. Mus. Natural History, Paris, 1980; adv. com. Contra Costa Cancer Rsch. Fund, 1984-98, Stazione Zoologica Anton Dohrn di Napoli, 1987-92. Recipient Disting. Tchg. award U. Calif., Berkeley, 1972, The Berkeley Citation, 1990, Disting. Svc. award Soc. Adv. Chicanos and Native Americans in Sci., 1990, Hatai medal Sci. Coun. Japan, 1998, Beverton medal Fisheries Soc. Brit. Isles, 2001, Outstanding Achievement award Am. Inst. Fishery Rsch. Biologists, 2003; Guggenheim fellow, 1951-52, NSF fellow U. Hawaii, 1958-59, fellow Ctr. for Advanced Study in Behavioral Scis., Stanford, 1960, NSF fellow Stazione Zoologica, Naples, 1965-66, Japan Soc. Promotion of Sci. Rsch. fellow U. Toyama, Japan, 1993. Fellow NAS, AAAS, Am. Acad. Arts and Scis., Indian Nat. Sci. Acad. (fgn.), Società Nazionale di Scienze Lettere e Arti Napoli (fgn.), Calif. Acad. Sci., Accademia Nazionale dei Lincei (fgn.), Am. Inst. Fishery Rsch. Biologists; mem. Soc. Integrative Comparative Biology (hon.; pres. 1967, Howard A. Bern Disting. Lectureship in comparative endocrinology 2002—), Am. Assn. Cancer Rsch., Am. Physiol. Soc., Endocrine Soc., Internat. Soc. Neuroendocrinology (coun. 1977-80), Exptl. Biology and Medicine (coun. 1980-83), Am. Soc. Molec. Marine Biol. Biotech., Western Soc. Naturalists, Japan Soc. Zootech. Sci. (hon.), Am. Fisheries Soc., Japan Soc. Comparative Endocrinology (hon.), Cosmos Club. Home: 1010 Shattuck Ave Berkeley CA 94707-2626 Office: U Calif Dept Integrative Biology Berkeley CA 94720-3140 Office Phone: 510-642-2940. Fax: 510-643-6264. Business E-Mail: bern@berkeley.edu.

BERNACCHI, RICHARD LLOYD, lawyer; b. LA, Dec. 15, 1938; s. Bernard and Anne B. BS with honors in Commerce (Nat. Merit Found. scholar), U. Santa Clara, 1961; LL.B. with highest honors (Legion Lex scholar, Jerry Geisler Meml. scholar), U. So. Calif., 1964. Bar: Calif. 1964. Assoc. Irell and Manella, LA, 1964-70, ptnr., 1970—; lectr. Am. Law Inst., 1972-73; lectr. data processing contracts and law U. So. Calif., LA, 1972, 78, 81. Co-chmn. Regional Transp. Com., 1970-72; mem. adv. bd. U. So. Calif. Computer Law Inst., 1979—, Ariz. Law and Tech. Inst., 1982-86; U. Santa Clara Computer and High Tech. Law Jour., 1982-90. Author: (with Gerald H. Larsen) Data Processing Contracts and the Law, 1974, (with Frank and Statland) Bernacchi on Computer Laaw, 1986; editor-in-chief U. So. Calif. Law Rev., 1962-64; adv. bd. Computer Negotiations Report, 1983-95, Computer and Tech. Law Jour., 1984-93, Computer Law Strategist, 1984-94. Capt. AUS, 1964—66, PTO. Mem. ABA (mem. adv. com. on edn. 1973-74, chmn. subcom. taxation computer sys. of sect. sci. and tech. 1976-78), L.A. Bar Assn., Computer Law Assn. (bd. dirs. 1973-86, chmn. preconf. symposium on law and computers 1974-75, West Coast v.p. 1976-79, sr. v.p. 1979-81, pres. 1981-83, adv. bd. 1986—), Internat. Bar Assn. (co-chmn. sect. on bus. law mem. com. on internat. tech. and e-commerce law 1995-98, steering com. 1998—), Am. Fedn. Info. Processing Socs. (mem. spl. com. electronic funds transfer sys. 1974-78), Order of Coif, Scabbard and Blade, Tech. Coast Angels, Beta Gamma Sigma, Alpha Sigma Nu. Office: Irell & Manella 1800 Avenue Of The Stars Los Angeles CA 90067-4276 Office Phone: 310-770-5608. Business E-Mail: dbernacchi@irell.com.

BERNARD, ALEXANDER, protective services official; b. LA, Apr. 23, 1952; s. Louis and Hannah (Bergman) Bernard; m. Diana LoRee Winstead, Dec. 17, 1976; children: Michael Alexander, Andrew Alexander. AA magna cum laude, L.A. Valley Coll., 1976; BS summa cum laude, Calif. State U., LA, 1989. Parking meter collector LA (Calif.) City Clk.'s Office, 1973—79; police officer LA (Calif.) Airport, LA, 1979—95, sgt. police svcs. divsn., 1995—2003; gen. mgr. Kern Law Enforcement Assn., Bakersfield, Calif., 2003—. Adv. com. Calif. Commn. Peace Officer Stds. and Tng., 1999—2004, vice chmn., 2001, chmn., 02, 2007—. Contbr. articles to profl. jours. Active Boy Scouts Am. Mem.: NRA (life), Ret. Peace Officers Assn. Calif. (bd. dirs. 2005—, pres. 2006—), LA Airport Peace Officers Assn. (pres. 1981—89, bd. dirs. 1992—94, pres. 1994—95), Fraternal Order Police, LA Airport Police Suprs. Assn. (v.p. 1997—98, pres. 1999—2003, v.p. 2003, bd. dirs.), Peace Officers Rsch. Assn. Calif. (chpt. pres. 1982—84, state bd. dirs. 1984—85, chpt. pres. 1985—87, state bd. dirs. 1987—2003, 1987—2003, ethnic rels. com. 1993—94, exec. com. 1994—2003, sec. 1999—2003, state bd. dir. 2006—08), Calif. Peace Officers Assn., Labor and Employment Rsch. Assn., Law Enforcement Alliance Am. (life), Internat. Police Assn. (life), Calif. Rifle and Pistol Assn. (life), Golden Key (life), Phi Kappa Phi (life). Republican. Avocations: travel, record collecting. Office: Kern Law Enforcement Assn 3417 Pegasus Dr PO Box 82516 Bakersfield CA 93380 Business E-Mail: kleagm@bak.rr.com.

BERNARD, EDDIE NOLAN, oceanographer; b. Houston, Nov. 23, 1946; s. Edward Nolan and Geraldine Marie (Dempsey) B.; m. Shirley Ann Fielder, May 30, 1970; 1 child, Elizabeth Ann BS, Lamar U., 1969; MS, Tex. A&M U., 1970, PhD, 1976. Geophysicist Pan Am. Petroleum Co., 1969; rsch. asst. oceanographic rsch. Tex. A&M U., College Station, Tex., 1969-70; rschr. NOAA, 1970-73, dep. dir. pacific marine environ. lab. Seattle, 1980-82, dir. hydrothermal vents program, fisheries oceanography program; rschr. Joint Tsunami Rsch. Effort, 1973-77; dir. Nat. Tsunami Warning Ctr., 1977-80, Pacific Marine Environ. Lab., Seattle, 1982—, chmn. Nat. Tsunami Hazard Mitigation Program, 1997—2004. Exec. com. Coop. Inst. for Marine Resource Studies and adv. bd. for Coll. of Oceanic and Atmospheric Sci., Oreg. State U., 2002—; adminstrv. bd. Joint Inst. Marine and Atmospheric Rsch. U. Hawaii; mem. adminstrv. bd. Joint Inst. for the Study Atomsphere and Oceans, U. Wash.; mem. Washington Sea Grant Steering Com., 1987-2003; sci. coun. Joint Inst. for Marine

Observations, Scripps Instn. of Oceanography, 1992—; exec. com. Cooperative Inst. Arctic Rsch. U. Alaska; advisor Japan Agy. for Marine-Earth Sci. and Tech., 2000—; head US del. first, second and third meetings internat. coordinating group Indian Ocean Tsunami Warning Sys.; affiliate prof. U. Wash. Editor: Tsunami Hazard: A Practical Guide for Tsunami Hazard Reduction, 1991, Developing Tsunami Resilient Communities, 2005; contbr. articles to profl. jours. Recipient Meritorious Presdl. Rank award, Pres. Clinton, 1993, Pres. G.W. Bush, 2002, Gold medal, US Dept. Commerce, 2004, 2005, Tsunami Soc. award, 2006; named Best of New Generation award, Esquire Mag., 1984. Mem. Am. Meteorological Soc., Internat. Union of Geodesy and Geophysics (chmn. Tsunami commn. 1987-95), Am. Geophys. Union, Oceanography Soc. Office: Pacific Marine Environ Lab 7600 Sand Point Way NE Seattle WA 98115-6349 Business E-Mail: eddie.n.bernard@noaa.gov.

BERNAU, SIMON JOHN, mathematics professor; b. Wanganui, New Zealand, June 12, 1937; came to U.S., 1969; s. Earnest Lovell and Ella Mary (Mason) B.; m. Lynley Joyce Turner, Aug. 11, 1959; children: Nicola Ann, Sally Jane. B.Sc., U. Canterbury, Christchurch, New Zealand, 1958, M.Sc., 1959; BA, Cambridge U., Eng., 1961, PhD, 1964. Lectr. U. Canterbury, 1964-65, sr. lectr., 1965-66; prof. math. U. Otago, Dunedin, New Zealand, 1966-69; assoc. prof. U. Tex., Austin, 1969-76, prof., 1976-85; prof., head math. dept. Southwest Mo. State U., Springfield, 1986-88; prof., chmn. dept. math. scis. U. Tex., El Paso, 1988-95; dean Coll. Sci. Calif. State Poly., Pomona, 1995—2002, prof. dept. math., 2002—. Researcher numerous publs. in field, 1964—; referee profl. jours., 1965—. Gulbenkian jr. research fellow Churchill Coll., Cambridge U., 1963-64 Mem. Am. Math. Soc. (reviewer 1965—), Math. Assn. Am., London Math. Soc. Office: Calif State Poly U Coll of Sci 3801 W Temple Ave Pomona CA 91768-2557 Home: 1322 Crown Way Paso Robles CA 93446

BERNHARD, HERBERT ASHLEY, lawyer; b. Jersey City, Sept. 24, 1927; s. Richard C. and Amalie (Lobl) B.; m. Nancy Ellen Hirschaut, Aug. 8. 1954; children: Linda, Alison, Jordan, Melissa. Student, Mexico City Coll., 1948; BEE, N.J. Inst. Tech., 1949; MA in Math., Columbia U., 1950; JD cum laude, U. Mich., 1957. Bar: Calif. 1958, U.S. Dist. Ct. (cen. dist.) Calif. 1958, U.S. Dist. Ct. (no., ea. and so. dists.) Calif. 1963, U.S. Ct. Claims 1966, U.S. Dist. Ct. (ea. dist.) Wis. 1982, U.S. Dist. Ct. (ea. and we. dists.) Ark. 1982, U.S. Dist. Ct. Nebr. 1982, U.S. Ct. Internat. Trade 1979, U.S. Tax Ct. 1969, U.S. Ct. Appeals (2d, 3d, 4th, 5th, 7th, 8th, 9th, 10th, 11th and D.C. cirs.) 1969, U.S. Supreme Ct. 1965. Research engr. Curtis-Wright Co., Caldwell, NJ, 1950-52, Boeing Aircraft Co., Cape Canaveral, Fla., 1952-55; assoc. O'Melveny & Myers, Los Angeles, 1957-62; ptnr. Greenberg, Bernhard, et al, Los Angeles, 1962-85, Jeffer, Mangels, Butler & Marmaro, Los Angeles, 1985—. Instr. math. U. Fla., Cape Canaveral, 1952-55; instr. elec. engring. U. Mich., Ann Arbor, 1955-57; referee L.A. Superior Ct., 1985—, arbitrator, 1988—, judge pro tem, 1988—; judge pro tem L.A. Mcpl. Ct., 1985—, Beverly Hills Mcpl. Ct., 1989—, Malibu Mcpl. Ct., 1994—. Contbr. articles to profl. jours. Chmn. adv. com. Skirball Mus., 1976-98; bd. overseers Hebrew Union Coll., 1976-98. With USAF, 1946-47. Recipient Disting. Achievement award N.J. Inst. Tech., 1998. Mem. Jewish Publ. Soc. (trustee 1986-96). Office: 78557 Alliance Way Palm Desert CA 92211-3069

BERNHARD, PETER C., lawyer, state agency administrator; b. Apr. 24, 1949; BA cum laude, Harvard Coll., 1971; JD, George Washington U., 1975. Bar: Nev. Bar Assn. 1975, Clark County Bar Assn., US Ct. Appeals Ninth Circuit, US Dist. Ct., Dist. Nev., US Supreme Ct. Atty./ptnr. Bernhard & Leslie; pres., stockholder Bernhard, Bradley & Johnson; chartered counsel Bullivant, Houser & Bailey PC. Mem., chair Nev. Commn. Ethics, 1999; chair Nev. Gaming Commn., 2001, 2003—. Mem.: ABA, Harvard Club Nev., Assn. Trial Lawyers Am. Office: Nev Gaming Commn 555 E Washington St Ste 2600 Las Vegas NV 89101 Office Phone: 702-650-6565. Office Fax: 702-650-2995.

BERNHARD, SANDRA, actress, comedienne, singer; b. Flint, Mich., June 6, 1955; d. Jerome and Jeanette B., 1 child. Stand-up comedienne nightclubs, Beverly Hills, Calif., 1974-78; films include Cheech and Chong's Nice Dreams, 1981, The King of Comedy, 1983 (Nat. Soc. Film Critics award), Sesame Street Presents: Follow That Bird, 1985, Track 29, 1988, Without You I'm Nothing, 1990, Hudson Hawk, 1991, Truth or Dare, 1991, Inside Monkey Zetterland, 1993, Dallas Doll, 1994, Unzipped, 1995, Catwalk, 1995, Plump Fiction, 1996, Somewhere in the City, 1997, Lover Girl, 1997, The Apocalypse, 1997, An Alan Smithee Film: Burn Hollywood Burn, 1997, I Woke Up Early the Day I Died, 1998, Exposé, 1998, Wrongfully Accused, 1998, Dinner Rush, 2000, Playing Mona Lisa, 2000, The Third Date, 2003; also appears in Heavy Petting, 1988, Perfect, 1985, The Whoopee Boys, 1986, Casual Sex?, 1988; stage appearances (solo) Without You I'm Nothing, 1988, Giving Till It Hurts, 1992, I'm Still Here...Damn It, 1998-99, Sandra Bernhard: Everything Bad and Beautiful, 2006; TV appearances (host) Living in America, 1990; regular guest The Richard Pryor Show, Late Night with David Letterman; TV series Instant Comedy with the Groundlings, The Hitchhiker, The Full Wax, Tales from the Crypt, Roseanne, Space Ghost Coast to Coast, The Larry Sanders Show, Clueless, Chicago Hope, Highlander, Comedy Central's The A-List, 1992-1993, Superman (voice), Ally McBeal, Hercules (voice), 1999, The Sandra Bernhard Experience (host), 2001-2002; (TV movies) Freaky Friday, 1995, The Late Shift, 1996; albums (co-author 8 songs) I'm Your Woman, 1985, Without You I'm Nothing, 1988, Excuses for Bad Behavior, Part I, 1994; books include Confessions of a Pretty Lady, 1988, Love Love Love, 1993, May I Kiss You On The Lips, Miss Sandra?, 1998.

BERNHEIMER, MARTIN, music critic; b. Munich, Sept. 28, 1936; came to U.S., 1940, naturalized, 1946; s. Paul Ernst and Louise (Nassauer) B.; m. Lucinda Pearson, Sept. 30, 1961 (div. Feb. 1989); children: Mark Richard, Nora Nicoll, Marina and Erika (twins); m. Linda Winer, Sept. 27, 1992. MusB with honors, Brown U., 1958; student, Munich Conservatory, 1958-59; MA in Musicology, NYU, 1961. Free-lance music critic, 1958—; contbg. critic N.Y. Herald Tribune, 1959-62; mem. music faculty NYU, 1959-62; contbg. editor Mus. Courier, 1961-64; temporary music critic N.Y. Post, 1961-65; N.Y. corr. Brit. Publ. Opera, 1962—65; L.A. corr., 1965—; corr. West Coast Brit. Opera Mag., 1965—; asst. to music editor Saturday Rev., 1962-65; mng. editor Philharmonic Hall Program, NYC, 1962-65; music editor, chief critic L.A. Times, 1965-96; N.Y. corr. Brit. Publ. Opera, 1997—. Mem. faculty U. So. Calif., 1966-71, music faculty UCLA, 1969-75, Calif. Inst. Arts, 1975-82, Calif. State U., Northridge, 1978-81, Rockefeller Program for Tng. of Music Critics; mem. Pulitzer Prize Music Jury, 1984, 86, 90; L.A. corr. for Swiss publ. Opernwelt, 1984—. Contbg. author New Groves Dictionary; contbr. liner notes for recordings; appearances on radio and TV, Met. Opera Broadcasts; contbr. articles to Vanity Fair, Music Quar., The Critic, Opera News, Mus. Am., Fin. Times, London, Sidewalk N.Y. (internet), others; N.Y. corr. Fin. Times and Opera mag.; lectr., moderator, essayist on Met. Opera Broadcast. Recipient Deems Taylor award ASCAP, 1974, 78, Headliners award, 1979, Pulitzer Prize for disting. criticism, 1982, Lifetime Achievement award Svc. to Music, Calif. Assn. Profl. Music Tchrs., 1990. Mem. Nat. Opera Inst. (ind. selection com. 1980), Pi Kappa Lambda (hon.). E-mail: mbern@earthlink.net.

BERNSTEIN, GERALD WILLIAM, management consultant, researcher; b. Boston, Nov. 25, 1947; s. Alan Irwin and Anne B.; m. Kathleen Ann Chaikin, Jan. 12, 1985. BS in Aero. Engring., Rensselaer Poly. Inst., 1969; MS in Engring., Stanford U., 1978. Transp. engr., dept. transp. State of NY, Albany, 1969-70; transp. planner Kennebec Regional Planning Com., Winslow, Maine, 1974-77; dir. transp. dept. SRI Internat., Menlo Park, Calif., 1979-95; v.p. BACK Mgmt. Svcs., San Francisco, 1995-98; mng. dir. Stanford Transp. Group, San Francisco, 1998—. Session chmn. aviation workshop NSF, 1985, 91, 99, 2002; profl. conf. chmn. Contbr. articles to profl. jours. Chmn. transp. com. Glenn Park Neighborhood Assn., San Francisco, 1982-85; dir. Balboa Terrace Neighborhood Assn., San Francisco, 1986-88; trustee Congregation Beth Israel-Judea, 1991-93. With U.S. Army, 1970-72. Recipient Cert. Appreciation City of Waterville, Maine, 1977. Mem. Am. Inst. Aeronautics and Astronautics (sr. mem.), Transp. Rsch. Bd. NRC (chmn. econs. and forecasting com.), Toastmasters Club (Menlo Park, pres. 1986). Democrat. Jewish. Avocations: flying, skiing. Office: Stanford Transp Group 236 W Portal Ave Ste 359 San Francisco CA 94127-1423 Business E-Mail: jerry@velocity-group.com.

BERNSTEIN, HAROLD SETH, pediatric cardiologist, molecular geneticist; b. NYC, Oct. 6, 1959; s. Wallace Carl and Naomi (Oldak) B.; m. Patricia Margaret Foster. AB, Harvard Coll., 1982; MPhil, CUNY, 1985, PhD, 1986; MD, Mt. Sinai Sch. Med., 1990. Diplomate Nat. Bd. Med. Examiners. Postdoctoral fellow div. med. & molecular genetics Mt. Sinai, NYC, 1986-88; intern U. Calif., San Francisco, 1990-91, resident in pediatrics, 1991-93; clin., rsch. fellow div. pediatric cardiology Cardiovascular Rsch. Inst., U. Calif., San Francisco, 1993—. Contbr. articles to profl. jours. Harvard Coll. scholar, 1980; NIH fellow in med. genetics, 1982-86, pediatric cardiology, 1993—; recipient Disting. Performance in Rsch. award Associated Med. Schs. N.Y., 1989, Achievement award for clin. excellence Upjohn, 1990. Fellow Am. Acad. Pediatrics; mem. AAAS, Am. Soc. Human Genetics, Am. Fedn. Clin. Rsch., Alpha Omega Alpha. Achievements include rsch. in cloning and sequencing of the first human CDNA encoding galactosidase A; first to identify molecular defect in the human galactosidase A gene resulting in Fabry Disease. Office: Univ Calif Div Pediatric Cardiology 505 Parnassus Ave, Box 0130 San Francisco CA 94143-0130

BERNSTEIN, LAWRENCE R., inorganic chemist, pharmaceutical chemist; b. LA, Dec. 23, 1955; s. Emil O. and Eleanor R. (Mordell) B.; children: Hannah L., Aaron A. AB, Harvard U., Cambridge, Mass., 1977, AM, 1978; PhD, Stanford U., Calif., 1985. Tutor in geol. sci. Harvard U., Cambridge, Mass., 1977-78; exploration geologist Brit. Petroleum, San Francisco, 1979-81; geologist U.S. Geol. Survey, Menlo Park, Calif., 1982-86; sr. rsch. scientist Yaskawa Co., Mountain View, Calif., 1990-92; rsch. dir. Terrametrix, Menlo Park, Calif., 1992—. Founder, dir., cons. GeoMed, Inc., Menlo Park, 1995-2000. Author: Minerals of the Washington, D.C. Area, 1980; patentee in pharma. field. Fed. Jr. fellow US Govt., 1973-77; John Harvard hon. scholar, 1976, 77. Mem. Mineral Soc. Am., Am. Soc. for Bone and Mineral Rsch., Am. Chem. Soc., Internat. Ctr. Diffraction Data (minerals editor 1992—), Phi Beta Kappa, Sigma Xi. Achievements include discovery of compounds to administer gallium and other metals orally for the treatment of cancer; discovery of promising new treatments for bacterial infections neuropathic pain and psoriasis. Home: 285 Willow Rd Menlo Park CA 94025-2711 Office: Terrametrix 285 Willow Rd Menlo Park CA 94025-2711 Home Phone: 650-322-9244; Office Phone: 650-324-3344. Personal E-mail: larry.b@earthlink.net.

BERNSTEIN, LESLIE, academic administrator, biostatistician, epidemiologist; BA, U. Calif., 1965; MS, U. So. Calif., 1978, PhD, 1981. Rsch. assoc. dept. preventive medicine U. So. Calif., LA, 1981-82, asst. prof. biostats./epidemiology, 1982-88, assoc. prof. biostats./epidemiology, 1988-91, prof. biostats./epidemiology, 1991—, sr. assoc. dean faculty affairs, 1996—2003, AFLAC Inc. chair in cancer rsch., 1997—, vice provost med. affairs, 2003—05. Sci. dir. U. So. Calif. Cancer Surveillance program, 1988—; mem. bd. sci. counselors Nat. Cancer Inst., 2001-06; mem. sci. adv. panel Calif. Gov., 1989-92; mem. sci. com. Internat. Soc. Study Esophageal Diseases, 1994—; chair adv. com. L.I. Breast Cancer Cancer Study, Columbia U., 1994-2000; chair external adv. com. Nurse's Health Study Harvard U., 1995—; sci. adv. com. Registry for Rsch. on Transplacental Carcinogenesis, U. Chgo., 1997—; external adv. com. No. Calif. Cancer Ctr., Hawaii Cancer Ctr., 1997—. Contbr. over 350 articles to profl. jours. Office: U So Calif/Norris Cancer Ctr Keck Sch Medicine 1441 Eastlake Ave 4449 Los Angeles CA 90033-0804 Business E-Mail: lbern@usc.edu.

BERNSTEIN, MICHAEL ALAN, history educator; b. 1954; BA in Econs. magna cum laude, Yale U., 1976, MA in Econs., 1978, MPhil in Econs., 1980, PhD in Econs., 1982. Instr. for the preliminary examinations in econs. Faculty Econs. and Politics, U. Cambridge, Eng., 1976-77; staff economist Office of Integrative Analysis Energy Info. Adminstrn., U.S. Dept. Energy, Washington, 1978; lectr. in econs. Mills Coll., Oakland, Calif., 1979; acting instr. econs. Yale U., 1980, asst. prof. history and associated faculty mem. dept. econs., 1982-87; asst. prof. history U. Calif., San Diego, 1987-88, assoc. prof. history, 1988-91, assoc. prof. history, associated faculty mem. dept. econs., 1991-2000, chair dept. history, 1992-2000, prof. history, 2000—. Chair undergrad. program com. and departmental rep. dept. history Princeton U., 1983-84, 85-86, mem. priorities com. on the budget, 1985-87; co-chair Columbia U. Seminar in Econ. History, 1985-86; dir. grad. studies in U.S. history dept. history U. Calif., San Diego, 1988-89, mem. chancellor's com. on the status of women, 1989-91, mem. rep. assembly of the acad. senate, 1990-92, chair undergrad. curriculum and advising com. dept. history, 1990-92, vice-chair dept. history, 1990-92, prin. investigator Calif. History-Social Sci. Project, 1994—, mem. adv. com. Office of Sexual Harassment Prevention and Policy, 1994—; mem. steering com. U. Calif. Intercampus Group in Econ. History, 1988—. Author: The Great Depression: Delayed Recovery and Economic Change in America, 1929-39, 1987, Japanese edit., 1991; co-editor (with D. Adler) Understanding American Economic Decline, 1994; mem. editl. bd. Jour. Econ. History, 1989-94; contbr. articles to profl. jours. Fulbright scholar Christ's Coll., Cambridge, Eng., 1976-77, Univ. Grad. fellow and Falk Found. fellow in econs. Yale U., 1977-81, ACLS fellow for studies in modern soc. and values, 1985, ACLS Postdoctoral fellow for sr. scholars, 1990, Andrew E. Mellon fellow Nat. Humanities Ctr., Research Triangle Park, N.C., 1990; Hoover scholar Herbert Hoover Presdl. Libr. Assn., West Branch, Iowa, 1991; recipient Grant-in-Aid, Econ. History Assn., 1982. Mem. Am. Econs. Assn., Am. Hist. Assn. (mem. com. on the Albert J. Beveridge Award and the John H. Dunning Prize 1991-93, chair 1993), Econ. History Assn. (com. on rsch. in econ. history 1994—), Orgn. Am. Historians (mem. Ellis Hawley Prize Organizing Com. 1994—), Am. Coun. Learned Socs. (mem. acad. adv. com. of the Am. studies program 1990—). Office: U Calif San Diego Dept History 0104 9500 Gilman Dr Dept 0104 La Jolla CA 92093-5004

BERNSTEIN, SANFORD IRWIN, biology professor; b. Bklyn., June 10, 1953; s. Harold and Adele Dorothy B.; m. Laurel Spear, July 10, 1983. BS, SUNY, Stony Brook, 1974; PhD, Wesleyan U., 1979. Rsch. fellow U. Va., Charlottesville, 1979-82; asst. prof. biology San Diego State U., 1983-85, assoc. prof., 1985-88, prof., 1988—. Assoc. dir. Molecular Biology Inst., 1987-92, dir. 1992-95; co-dir. DNA cert. program, 1983—, chair biology dept., 1995-2000, coord. joint-doctoral program in cell and molecular biology with U. Calif. San Diego, 2000—08; established investigatorship Am. Heart Assn., 1989-94; mem. grant rev. panels NIH, Am. Heart Assn. Mem. editl. bd. Devel. Biology, 1991-95, J. Muscle Rsch. and Cell Motility, 2006—; Rsch Letters Biochemist, 2008-; contbr. articles to profl. jours. Muscular Dystrophy Assn. fellow, 1979-82, grantee, 1984-2006; 2008-; grantee NIH, 1983—, NSF, 1997-2000. Mem.: AAAS, Am. Physiol. Soc., Biophys. Soc., Am. Soc. Biochemistry and Molecular Biology, Am. Soc. Cell Biology, Genetics Soc. Am., Sigma Xi. Achievements include research in developmental regulation of muscle gene expression in Drosophila, muscle protein isoform function, alternative RNA splicing. Office: San Diego State U Biology Dept and Molec Bio Inst San Diego CA 92182-4614 Business E-Mail: sanford.bernstein@sdsu.edu.

BERNSTEIN, SOL, cardiologist, educator; b. West New York, NJ, Feb. 3, 1927; s. Morris Irving and Rose (Leibowitz) B.; m. Suzi Maris Sommer, Sept. 15, 1963; 1 son, Paul. AB in Bacteriology, U. So. Calif., 1952, MD, 1956. Diplomate Am. Bd. Internal Medicine. Intern Los Angeles County Hosp., 1956-57, resident, 1957-60; practice medicine specializing in cardiology LA, 1960—; staff physician dept. medicine Los Angeles County Hosp./U. So. Calif. Med. Ctr., LA, 1960—, chief cardiology clinics, 1964, asst. dir. dept. medicine, 1965-72, med. dir., 1974-94; med. dir. central region Los Angeles County, 1974-78; dir. Dept. Health Svcs., Los Angeles County, 1978; assoc. dean Sch. Medicine, U. So. Calif., LA, 1986-94, assoc. prof., 1968—; med. dir. Health Rsch. Assn., LA, 1995—2005. Cons. Crippled Childrens Svc. Calif., 1965—. Contbr. articles on cardiac surgery, cardiology, diabetes and health care planning to med. jours. Served with AUS, 1946-47, 52-53. Fellow ACP, Am. Coll. Cardiology; mem. Am. Acad. Phys. Execs., Am. Fedn. Clin. Research, NY Acad. Sci., Am. Heart Assn., LA Soc. Internal Medicine, LA Acad. Medicine, Sigma Xi, Phi Beta Phi, Phi Eta Sigma, Alpha Omega Alpha. Home: 4966 Ambrose Ave Los Angeles CA 90027-1756 Home Phone: 323-666-8547. Business E-Mail: sol@hsc.usc.edu.

BERNSTEIN, WILLIAM, film company executive; b. NYC, Aug. 30, 1933; s. Philip and Sadie (Lazar) B.; m. Evelyn Pauline Schnur, Aug. 3, 1958; children: Marian Suzanne, Steven Laurence. BA, NYU, 1954; LLB, Yale U., 1959. Atty. United Artists Corp., NYC, 1959-67, v.p. bus. affairs, 1967-72, sr. v.p. bus. affairs, 1972-78; exec. v.p. Orion Pictures Corp., NYC, 1978-91, pres., chief exec. officer, dir., 1991-92; exec. v.p. Paramount Pictures Corp., LA, 1992—. Mem. ABA, Acad. Motion Picture Arts and Scis. Home: 282 Bentley Cir Los Angeles CA 90049-2414 Office: Paramount Pictures Corp 5555 Melrose Ave Los Angeles CA 90038-3197

BERRING, ROBERT CHARLES, JR., law educator, librarian, association administrator; b. Canton, Ohio, Nov. 20, 1949; s. Robert Charles and Rita Pauline (Franta) B.; m. Leslie Applegarth, May 20, 1998; children: Simon Robert, Daniel Fredrick. BA cum laude, Harvard U., 1971; JD, MLS, U. Calif.-Berkeley, 1974. Asst. prof. and reference libr. U. Ill. Law Sch., Champaign, 1974—76; assoc. libr. U. Tex. Law Sch., Austin, 1976—78; dep. libr. Harvard Law Sch., Cambridge, Mass., 1978—81; prof. law, law libr. U. Wash. Law Sch., Seattle, 1981—82, U. Calif., Boalt Hall Law Sch., Berkeley, 1982—, dean sch. library and info. scis., 1986—89, Walter Perry Johnson Prof. Law, 1998—, dir. law libr., interim dean, 2003—04. Mem. Westlaw Adv. Bd., St. Paul, 1984-91; cons. various law firms; mem. on Legal Exch. with China, 1983—, chmn., 1991-93.; vis. prof. U. Cologne, 1993. Author: How to Find the Law, 8th edit., 1984, 9th edit., 1989, Great American Law Revs., 1985, Finding the Law, 1999; co-author: Authors Guide, 1981; editor Legal Reference Svc. Quar., 1981—; author videotape series Commando Legal Rsch., 1989. Chmn. Com. Legal Ednl. Exch. with China, 1991—93. Robinson Cox fellow U. Western Australia, 1988; named West Publishing Co. Acad. Libr. of Yr., 1994. Mem. Am. Assn. Law Libraries (pres. 1985-86), Calif. Bar Assn., ABA, ALA, Am. Law Inst. Office: U Calif Law Sch Boalt Hl Rm 345 Berkeley CA 94720-0001 Business E-Mail: berringr@law.berkeley.edu.

BERRY, GLENN, artist, educator; b. Feb. 27, 1929; s. B. Franklin and Heloise (Sloan) B. BA magna cum laude, Pomona Coll., 1951, BFA (Honnold fellow); MFA, Sch. Art Inst. Chgo., 1956. Faculty Humboldt State U., Arcata, Calif., 1956-69, prof. art, 1969-81, emeritus, 1981—. One-man shows include Ingomar Gallery, Eureka, Calif., 1968, Ankrum Gallery, LA, 1970, Esther Bear Gallery, Santa Barbara, Calif., 1971, Coll. Redwoods, Eureka, 1989, Humboldt State U., Arcata, Calif., 1992, Morris Graves Mus. of Art, Eureka, Calif., 2000; exhibited in group shows at Palace of Legion of Honor, San Francisco, Pasadena Art Mus., Calif., Rockford Coll., Ill., Richmond Art Mus., Calif., Henry Gallery U. Wash., Seattle, Morris Graves Mus. Art, Eureka, 2000; represented in permanent collections Storm King Art Ctr., Mountainville, NY, Kaiser Aluminum & Chem. Corp., Oakland, Calif., Desert Mus., Hirshhorn Mus., Washington, others; mural Griffith Hall, Humboldt State U., 1978, 2005, Morris Graves Mus. Art, Eureka, Calif. Mem. Phi Beta Kappa. Home: PO Box 2241 Mckinleyville CA 95519 Home Phone: 707-677-3725.

BERRY, JOHN CHARLES, psychologist, academic administrator; b. Modesto, Calif., Nov. 29, 1938; s. John Wesley and Dorothy Evelyn (Harris) B.; m. Arlene Ellen Sossin, Oct. 7, 1978; children: Elise, John Jordan, Kaitlyn. AB, Stanford U., 1960; postgrad., Trinity Coll.,

Dublin, Ireland, 1960—61; PhD, Columbia U., 1967. Rsch. assoc. Judge Baker Guidance Ctr., Boston, 1965—66; psychology assoc. Napa State Hosp., Imola, Calif., 1966—67, staff psychologist, 1967—75, program asst., 1975—76; program dir. Met. State Hosp., Norwalk, Calif., 1976—77; asst. supt. Empire Union Sch. Dist., Modesto, 1977—93, dep. supt., 1993—. Contbg. author: Life History Research in Psychopathology, 1970. Mem.: Assn. Calif. Sch. Adminstrs., Am. Psychol. Assn., Sigma Xi. Home: 920 Eastridge Dr Modesto CA 95355-4672 Office: Empire Union Sch Dist 116 N Mcclure Rd Modesto CA 95357-1329

BERRY, KENNETH J., sociology educator; Prof. dept. sociology Colo. State U. Recipient Banner I. Miller award Am. Meteorol. Assn., 1994. Office: Colorado St Univ Dept Sociology B258 Clark Fort Collins CO 80523-0001

BERRY, PHILLIP SAMUEL, lawyer; b. Calif., 1937; s. Samuel Harper and Jean Mobley B.; children: David, Douglas, Dylan, Shane, Matthew; m. Carla Gilmer, Mar. 16, 2002. AB, Stanford U., 1958, LLB, 1961. Bar: Calif. 1962. Ptnr. Berry, Davis & McInerney, Oakland, Calif., 1968-76; owner Berry & Berry, Oakland, Calif., 1976—, pres., 1977—. Adv. com. Calif. Natural Resources, U. Calif., Berkeley; mem. Calif. State Bd. Forestry, 1974-86, vice-chmn., 1976-86. Trustee So. Calif. Ctr. for Law in Pub. Interest, 1970-87, Sierra Club Legal Def. Fund, 1975-90, Pub. Advs., 1971-86, chmn. bd., 1980-82; dir. Pacific Environment, 1997—. With AUS, 1961-67. Mem. ABA, Calif. State Bar Assn., Sierra Club (nat. pres. 1969-71, 91-92, v.p. conservation law 1971—, v.p. polit. affairs 1983-85, John Muir award), Am. Alpine Club. Office: 2930 Lakeshore Ave Oakland CA 94610-3614

BERRY, RICHARD LEWIS, information technology manager, writer, magazine editor, lecturer, programmer; b. Greenwich, Conn., Nov. 6, 1946; s. John William and Dorothy May (Buck) B.; m. Eleanor von Auw, June 7, 1968. BA, U. Va., 1968; MSc, York U., Can., 1972. Rsch. asst. MacMaster U., Hamilton, Ont., Canada, 1973-74; project engr. Intraspace Internat., Toronto, Ont., 1974-75; tech. editor Astronomy mag., Milw., 1976-78, editor, 1978-82, editor-in-chief, 1982-91; editor Telescope Making mag., Milw., 1978—91; editl. dir. Earth mag., 1990-91, cons., 1992; freelance writer, programmer, lectr., 1991—; editor Cookbook Camera Newsletter, 1994-99; founder, mng. ptnr. Digital Clarity Cons., 2003—. Mem. adv. bd. Global Network of Automatic Telescopes; com. chair Internat. Space Sta. Amateur Telescope Project, Astron. League, 2002—. Author: Build Your Own Telescope, 1985, Discover the Stars, 1987, (with others) The Star Book, 1984, Introduction to Astronomical Image Processing, 1991, AIP Image Processing Software, 1991, BatchPIX Image Processing Software, 1992, Choosing and Using a CCD Camera, 1992, The CCD Camera Cookbook, 1994, The Dobsonian Telescope: A Practical Manual for Building Large Aperture Telescopes, 1997, Handbook of Astronomical Image Processing, 2000; contbg. author: Robotic Observatories, 1989, ST6PIX Image Processing Software, 1992, CB245 Image Processing Software, 1994, Multi245 Image Compositing Software, 1995, QColor Color Synthesis Software, 1997, Astronomical Image Processing for Windows, 2000, 2d edit., 2004; editor: Telescope Optics, Design and Evaluation, 1988. Mem. adv. bd. Global Network of Automatic Telescopes; mem. Internat. Space Station Amateur Telescope com. Astron. League. Recipient Clifford-Holmes award Astronomy for Am., 1981, Dorothea Klumpke-Roberts award Astron. Soc. Pacific, 1990, Omega Centauri award Tex. Star Party, Clyde W. Tombaugh award Riverside Telescope Makers Conf., 1995, G. Bruce Blair award Western Amateur Astronomers, 1998, Leslie C. Peltier award Astron. League, 2001, Astron. League award, 2002; Asteroid 3684 Berry named in his honor by Internat. Astron. Union, 1990. Mem. Internat. Amateur Profl. Photoelec. Photometry, Internat. Dark Sky Assn., Am. Astron. Soc. Avocation: photography. Office Phone: 503-859-3030. E-mail: rberry@wvi.com.

BERRY, ROBERT EMANUEL, aerospace company executive; b. Atlantic City, July 4, 1928; s. Charles Allen and Anne Martha (Smith) B.; m. Dorothy Ellen Rohan, June 13, 1953; 1 child, Robert Emanuel Jr. BS in Econs./Gen. Sci., Manhattan Coll., 1953; MA in Econs., U. Pa., 1958. Instr. econs. Wharton Sch., Phila., 1956-57; mgr., engring. adminstr. GE, Phila., 1957-62; dir. advanced systems Philco-Ford Corp., Palo Alto, Calif., 1962-67, dir. Newport Beach ops. Newport Beach, Calif., 1967-69; pres., chmn. INTELCOM Industries, 1969-75; dep. dir. Dept. of Def., Washington, 1975-77; div. gen. mgr. Ford Aerospace, Palo Alto, 1977-90; pres. Space Systems/Loral, Palo Alto, 1990—99, chmn., 1999—. Mem. Space Systems & Technology Adv. Com., Washington, 1986—, Comml. Space Transp. Adv., Washington, 1991-93, U. San Francisco Telecommunications Adv. Bd., 1988—. Lt. USNR, 1953—62. Fellow: AIAA (Aerospace Comm. award 1996); mem.: IEEE (life). Office: Space Systems/Loral 3825 Fabian Way Palo Alto CA 94303-4604

BERRY, ROBERT WORTH, lawyer, retired military officer, educator; b. Ryderwood, Wash., Mar. 2, 1926; s. John Franklin and Anita Louise (Worth) Berry. BA in Polit. Sci., Wash. State U., 1950; JD, Harvard U., 1955; MA, John Jay Coll. Criminal Justice, 1981. Bar: DC 1956, US Dist. Ct. (DC) 1956, US Ct. of Appeals (DC cir.) 1957, US Ct. Mil. Appeals 1957, Pa. 1961, US Dist. Ct. (ea. dist.) Pa. 1961, US Dist. Ct. (ctrl. dist.) Calif. 1967, US Supreme Ct. 1961, Calif. 1967, US Ct. Claims 1975, Colo. 1997, US Dist. Ct. Colo. 1997, US Ct. Appeals (10th cir.) 1997, US Tax Ct. 1959. Rsch. assoc. Harvard U., Cambridge, Mass., 1955—56; atty. Office Gen. Counsel US Dept. Def., Washington, 1956-60; staff counsel Philco Ford Co., Phila., 1960-63; dir. Washington office Litton Industries, 1967-71; gen. counsel US Dept. Army, Washington, 1971-74, civilian aide to sec. army, 1975-77; col. US Army, 1978-87; prof., head dept. law US Mil. Acad., West Point, NY, 1978-86; ret. as brig. gen. US Army, 1987; mil. asst. to asst. sec. of army, Manpower and Res. Affairs Dept. of Army, 1986-87; asst. gen. counsel pub. affairs Litton Industries, Beverly Hills, Calif., 1963-67; chair Coun. of Def. Space Industries Assns., 1968; resident ptnr. Quarles and Brady, Washington, 1971-74; dir., corp. sec., treas., gen. counsel G.A. Wright, Inc., Denver, 1987-92, dir., 1987-2000; pvt. practice law Fort Bragg, Calif., 1993-96; spl. counsel Messner & Reeves LLC, Denver, 1997—2004. Bd. dirs. G.A. Wright Mktg., Inc., v.p./gen. counsel, 2001-; bd. dirs. Denver Mgmt. Svcs. Inc., v.p., gen. counsel, 2001—; foreman Mendocino County Grand Jury, 1995-96. With US Army, 1944-46, 1951-53, 1978-87. Decorated Bronze Star, Legion of Merit, Disting. Service Medal; recipient Disting. Civilian Service medal U.S. Dept. Army, 1973, 74, Outstanding Civilian Service medal, 1977. Mem. Am. Corp. Counsel Assn. (ACCA), Calif. Bar Assn., Pa. Bar Assn., Colo. State Bar Assn., Denver Bar Assn., DC Bar Assn., Internat. Masters of Gaming Law (affiliate mem.), Army-Navy Club, Army-Navy Country Club, Phi Beta Kappa, Phi Kappa Phi, Sigma Delta Chi, Lambda Chi Alpha. Protestant. Office: GA Wright Mktg Inc 10325 East 47th Ave Denver CO 80238 Office Phone: 303-333-4453. Business E-Mail: bobb@gawright.com.

BERRY, STEPHEN JOSEPH, reporter; b. Ft. Jackson, SC, May 2, 1948; s. Charles and Marjorie (Sheehan) Berry; m. Cheryl C. Berry, Nov. 24, 1973; 1 child, Stephen Richard. BA in Polit. Sci., U. Montevallo, 1970; MA, U. N.C. at Greensboro, 1984. Mem. staff Dothan (Ala.) Eagle, 1970—72, Greensboro (N.C.) News and Record, 1971—, Orlando (Fla.) Sentinel, 1989—96, The L.A. Times, 1996—. Recipient Pulitzer Prize, 1993, Pub. Svc. award, AP News Execs. Coun. Calif.-Nebr., 1998, 1st pl., Soc. Profl. Journalists Excellence award in sports reporting, 1994, Benjamin Fine award, 1985, N.C. Sch. Bell award, 1986. Mem.: Phi Alpha Theta. Home: 6527 Ellenview Ave West Hills CA 91307-2717 Office: LA Times Times Mirror Sq Los Angeles CA 90053

BERRY, WILLIAM BENJAMIN NEWELL, geologist, educator, former museum administrator; b. Boston, Sept. 1, 1931; s. John King and Margaret Elizabeth (Newell) B.; m. Suzanne Foster Spaulding, June 10, 1961; 1 child, Bradford Brown. AB, Harvard U., 1953, A.M., 1955; PhD, Yale U., 1957. Asst. prof. geology U. Houston, 1957-58; asst. prof. to prof. paleontology U. Calif., Berkeley, 1958—; prof. geology, 1991—; curator Mus. of Paleontology U. Calif., Berkeley, 1960-75, 87—, dir., 1975-87, chmn. dept. paleontology, 1975-87; marine scientist Lawrence Berkeley Lab., 1989—. Cons. U.S. Geol. Survey., Environ. Edn. to Ministry for Environ., Catalonia, Spain. Author: Growth of a Prehistoric Time Scale, 1968, revised edit., 1987, Principles of Stratigraphic Analysis, 1991; assoc. editor Paleoceanography; contbr. numerous articles on stratigraphic, paleontol. and environ. subjects to profl. jours.; editor publs. in geol. scis. Guggenheim Found. fellow, 1966-67 Fellow Calif. Acad. Scis.; mem. AAAS (pres. Pacific divsn. 2003—), Paleontol. Soc., Geol. Soc. Norway, Internat. Platform Assn., Explorers Club, Commonwealth Club Calif. Home: 1366 Summit Rd Berkeley CA 94708-2139 Office: U Calif Dept Earth/Planetary Scis McCone Hall Berkeley CA 94720 E-mail: bnberry@uclink4berkeley.edu.

BERRYHILL, BILL, state legislator; m. Triana Berryhill; children: William, Alexandra, Gabriela. Operator BB Vineyards, 1978—; mem. Dist. 27 Calif. State Assembly, 2008—. Bd. mem. Ceres Unified Sch. Dist., Calif.; mem. Greater Stockton C. of C., Stockton, Calif., Stanislaus County Farm Bur., Calif., San Joaquin County Farm Bur. Republican. Office: PO Box 942849 Rm 4009 Sacramento CA 94249-0022 also: 4557 Quail Lakes Dr Ste 3C Stockton CA 95207 Office Phone: 916-319-2026, 209-473-6972. Office Fax: 209-473-6977. E-mail: Assemblymember.Bill.Berryhill@assembly.ca.gov.*

BERSELL, SEAN DEVLIN, trade association executive; b. Miami, Fla., 1959; AB, Dartmouth Coll., Hanover, NH, 1981; JD, U. N.Mex. Sch. Law, 1985. Bar: Pa. 1985. Legis. counsel to US senator Pete V. Domenici, Washington, 1985-91; asst. dir. office legis. & congl. affairs Nat. Pk. Svc., Washington, 1991-93; various positions to sr. dir. pub. affairs AIChE, Washington, 1993-99; v.p. pub. affairs Entertainment Merchants Assn. (formerly Video Software Dealers Assn.), Encino, Calif., 1999—. Chair Media Coalition, 2006—08.

BERSHAD, NEIL JEREMY, electrical engineering educator; b. Bklyn., Oct. 20, 1937; BEE, Rensselaer Poly. Inst., 1958, PhD in Elec. Engring, 1962; MSEE, U. So. Calif., 1960. Mem. tech. staff Hughes Aircraft Co., Culver City, Calif., 1958—62, staff engr., 1964—69; prof. elec. engring. and computer sci. U. Calif., Irvine, 1966—94, prof. emeritus, 1994—. Contbr. more than 100 articles on communication theory, signal processing and adaptive filtering to profl. jours. 1st lt. USAF, 1962-65. Fellow IEEE (assoc. editor comm. jour., acoustics, speech and signal processing jour.). Office Phone: 949-824-6709. Business E-Mail: bershad@ece.uci.edu.

BERSI, ANN, lawyer; b. San Jose; BA, MA, San Diego State U.; JD, Calif. Western Sch. of Law; PhD in Higher Edn. Adminstrn., U. Conn. Bar: Calif. Past mem. law firms Morris, Brignone & Pickering, Lionel, Sawyer & Collins, Las Vegas; dir. employee rels. State of Nev., 1981-83; exec. dir. State Bar Nev., 1983-89; dep. dist. atty. civil divsn. Clark County Dist. Atty.'s Office, Las Vegas, 1995—2005. Past instr. pub. adminstrn. Pace U., N.Y.; legal counsel Clark County Sch. Dist. Bd. Trustees, Clark County Bd. Equalization, 1995-2005; mem. State Jud. Selection Commn., 2000—, Nev. Tax Commn., 2005— Mem. State Bar Nev. (pres. bd. govs. 1999-2000). Office: 5216 Painted Lakes Way Las Vegas NV 89149

BERSON, DAVID WILLIAM, economist; b. NYC, June 18, 1954; s. Norman and Judith George DeMille (Fineman) B.; m. Anne Marie Bradley, June 18, 1976; children: Sarah Bradley, Matthew Bradley. BA, Williams Coll., 1976; M in Pub. Policy, U. Mich., 1979, PhD, 1982. Jr. staff economist Coun. Econ. Advisers, Washington, 1979-80; instr. sch. bus. adminstrn. U. Mich., Ann Arbor, 1978-81; asst. prof. econs. Claremont McKenna Coll., Claremont, Calif., 1981-83; vis. scholar Fed. Res. Bank Kansas City, Mo., 1982-85; sr. fin. economist Wharton Econometric Forecasting Assocs., Phila., 1983-84, chief fin. economist, 1985-87; sr. economist U.S. League Savs. Insts., Washington, 1987, Fannie Mae, Washington, 1987-88, v.p., chief economist, 1989—2007; sr. v.p., chief economist & strategist The PMI Group, Inc., Walnut Creek, Calif., 2007—. Contbr. articles to profl. jours. Co-chair platform com., budget policy com. Calif. State Democratic Party, 1981-82. Pub. Policy fellow Inst. Pub. Policy Studies, U. Mich., 1976-79. Mem. Nat. Assn. Bus. Economists (bd. dirs. 1988—, chmn. fin. roundtable 1988—), Phila. Coun. Bus. Economists, Am. Econs. Assn., Nat. Economists Club. Avocations: rotisserie league baseball, electronics, reading, golf, softball, basketball. Office: The PMI Group Inc PMI Plz 3003 Oak Rd Walnut Creek CA 94597

BERTHELSDORF, SIEGFRIED, retired psychiatrist; b. Shannon County, Mo., June 16, 1911; s. Richard and Amalia (Morschenko) von Berthelsdorf; m. Mildred Friederich, May 13, 1945; children: Richard, Victor, Dianne. BA, U. Oreg., 1934, MA, MD, 1939. Intern U.S. Marine Hosp., Staten Island, NY, 1939-40; psychiat. intern Bellevue Hosp., NYC, 1940-41; psychiat. resident N.Y. State Psychiat. Hosp., NYC, 1941-42; research assoc. Columbia U. Coll. Physicians and Surgeons, NYC, 1942-43; asst. physician Presbyn. Hosp. and Vanderbilt Clinic, NYC, 1942-51; supervising psychiatrist Manhattan (N.Y.) State Hosp., 1946-50; asst. adolescent psychiatrist Mt. Sinai Hosp., NYC, 1950-52; psychiat. cons. MacLaren Sch. for Boys, Woodburn, Oreg., 1952-84, Portland (Oreg.) Pub. Schs., 1952-67; ret., 1984. Clin. prof. U. Oreg. Health Scis. Ctr., 1956—; tng. and supervising analyst Seattle Psychoanalytic Inst., 1970—. Author: Treatment of Drug Addiction in Psychoanalytic Study of the Child, Vol. 31, 1976, Ambivalence Towards Women in Chinese Characters and Its Implication for Feminism, American Imago, 1988, (with others) Psychiatrists Look at Aging, 1992. Bd. dirs., v.p. Portland Opera Assn., 1960-64, Portland Musical Co., 1987-92; bd. dirs. Portland Chamber Orch., 1964-70, 92-94, 96-97, exec., 1997-2003. Maj. USAF, 1943-46. Recipient Henry Waldo Coe award U. Oreg. Med. Sch., Portland, 1939, citation Parry Ctr. for Children, Portland, 1970, Child Advocacy award ORAPT, 1998. Fellow Am. Psychiat. Assn. (life), Am. Geriatrics Soc. (founding fellow); mem. Am. Psychoanalytic Assn. (life), Portland Psychiatrists in Pvt. Practice (charter, pres. 1958), Mental Health Assn. (bd. dirs., chmn. med. adv. com. 1952-60), Multnomah County Med. Soc. (pres.'s citation 1979), Oreg. Psychoanalytic Found. (founding mem.), Am. Rhododendron Soc. (bd. dirs., v.p. Portland chpt. 1956-58, Bronze medal and citation 1974), Am. Rhododendron Species Found. (bd. dirs. 1960-75), Phi Beta Kappa, Sigma Xi, Phi Sigma, Phi Mu Alpha. Avocations: farming, music. Personal E-mail: SiegfriedMD@aol.com.

BERTINELLI, VALERIE (VALERIE ANNE BERTINELLI), actress; b. Wilmington, Del., Apr. 23, 1960; m. Eddie Van Halen, Apr. 11, 1981 (div. Dec. 21, 2007); 1 child, Wolfgang. Student, Tami Lynn Acad. Artists, Calif. Owner Bertinelli, Inc.; spokesperson Jenny Craig, 2007-. Actress: (films) C.H.O.M.P.S., 1979, Ordinary Heros, 1986, Number One with a Bullet, 1987; (TV movies) Young Love, First Love, 1979, The Promise of Love, 1980, The Princess and the Cabbie, 1981, I Was a Mail Order Bride, 1982, The Seduction of Gina, 1984, Shattered Vows, 1984, Silent Witness, 1985, Rockabye, 1986, Pancho Barnes, 1988, Taken Away, 1989, In a Child's Name, 1991, What She Doesn't Know, 1992, Aladdin and His Magic Lamp, Murder of Innocence, 1993, The Haunting of Helen Walker, 1995, Two Mothers for Zachery, 1996, A Case for Life, 1996, Personally Yours, 2000, Crazy Love, 2003, Finding John Christmas, 2003; (TV spls.) The Secret of Charles Dickens, 1979, The Magic of David Copperfield; (TV series) One Day at a Time, 1975-84, Sydney, 1990, Cafe Americain, 1993-94, Touched By an Angel, 2001-03; (TV miniseries) I'll Take Manhattan, 1987, Night Sins, 1997; guest appearances include Apple's Way, 1974, The Hardy Boys/Nancy Drew Mysteries, 1978, Who Wants to be a Millionaire, 2001, Family Guy (voice), 2001, One Day at a Time Reunion, 2005; author: Losing It... And Gaining My Life Back One Pound At A Time, 2008 Office: William Morris Agy care Marc Schwartz 151 S El Camino Dr Beverly Hills CA 90212-2775

BERTOZZI, CAROLYN R., chemistry professor; b. Boston, 1966; AB in Chemistry summa cum laude, Harvard U.; PhD, U. Calif., Berkeley, 1993. Summer intern Bell Labs, 1987; predoc. fellow Office of Naval Rsch., 1988—91; postdoc. fellow U. Calif., San Francisco, prof. chemistry Berkeley, 1996—, Joel H. Hildebrand chair in chemistry, 1998—2000, T. Z. and Irmgard Chu disting. prof. Contbr. articles to profl. jours. including J. Org. Chem., Chem. and Biol., Biochem. Recipient MacArthur Found. award, 1999, Presdl. Early Career award in Sci. and Engring., 2000, Donald Sterling Noyce prize for excellence in undergrad. tchg., 2001, Irving Sigal Young Investigator award, Protein Soc., 2002. Fellow: Am. Acad. Arts and Sciences; mem.: NAS, Am. Chem. Soc. (Arthur C. Cope Scholar award 1999, Award in Pure Chemistry 2001). Office: U Calif Berkeley Chemistry Dept 820 Latimer Hall Berkeley CA 94720-0001 Office Phone: 510-643-1682. Office Fax: 510-643-2628. E-mail: bertozzi@cchem.berkeley.edu.

BERWICK, FRANCES, broadcast executive; b. U.K. Former dir., internat. distbn. Channel 4, England; sr. v.p., programming, production Bravo, 1996—2006, exec. v.p., programming, production, 2007—. Prodr.: (TV films) Cirque du Soleil: Alegria, 2001, Straight Talk, 2006; (TV series) Inside the Actors Studio, The Art of Influence, 1998, Queer Eye for the Straight Guy, 2003— (Emmy award for outstanding reality program, 2004), Boy Meets Boy, 2003, Celebrity Poker Showdown, 2004, Kathy Griffin: My Life on the D-List, 2005, Project Runway, 2004—06 (Inspiration award, LA Fashion Awards, 2007), 30 Even Scarier Movie Moments, 2006. Named one of The 50 Most Powerful Women in NYC, NY Post, 2007. Office: Bravo 3000 W Alameda Ave Ste 250 Burbank CA 91523

BERZON, MARSHA S., federal judge; b. Cin., Apr. 17, 1945; BA, Radcliffe Coll., 1966; JD, Boalt Hall Sch. Law, 1973. Bar: Calif. 1973, DC 1975. Clerk Judge James Browning, 9th Cir., 1973—74, Justice William Brennan, 1974—75; atty. Woll & Mayer, Washington, 1975—77, Altshuler, Berzon, Nussbaum, Berzon & Rubin, San Francisco, 1978—2000; judge US Ct. Appeals (9th cir.), 2000—; assoc. gen. counsel AFL-CIO, 1987—99. Lectr. U. Calif. Sch. Social Welfare, Berkeley, Calif., 1992, La. State U. Sch. of Law, 2003; practitioner-in-residence Cornell Sch. of Law, NY, 1994, Ind. U. Law Sch., 1998. Named Margaret Brent award, ABA, 2007. Mem.: Fed. Bar Assn., State Bar of Calif., DC Bar Assn., Am. Law Inst., Am. Bar Found. Office: US Ct Appeals 9th Cir 95 7th St San Francisco CA 94103-1526 Office Phone: 415-355-8160. Office Fax: 415-556-9491.

BESING, RAY GILBERT, lawyer, educator; b. Roswell, N.Mex., Sept. 14, 1934; s. Ray David and Maxine Mable (Jordan) B.; children: Christopher, Gilbert, Andrew, Paul. Student, Rice U., 1952—54; BA, Ripon Coll., 1957; postgrad., Georgetown U., 1957; JD, So. Meth. U., 1960. Bar: Tex. 1960. Ptnr. Geary, Brice, Barron, & Stahl, Dallas, 1960-74; sr. ptnr. Besing, Baker & Glast, Dallas, 1974-77; prin. Law Offices of Ray G. Besing, P.C., Dallas, 1977—96. Tchg. fellow Faculty Laws U. Coll. London, 2008-09, 2008-, lectr. in field, 1998—. Author: Who Broke Up AT&T?: From Ma Bell to the Internet, 2000-, The Intersection of Sherman Section 2 and the Telecommunications Act of 1996: What Should Congress Do?, 2005; mng. editor So. Meth. U. Law Jour., 1959-60. Pres. Dallas Cerebral Palsy Found., 1970; trustee Ripon Coll., 1969—76; mem. Tex. Gov.'s Transition Team on Telecom., 1982; mem. exec. coun. Episc. diocese Dallas, 1969—72; bd. dirs. Dallas Symphony, 1972, Dallas Theatre Ctr., 1971, Found. for Santa Fe C.C., 2001—03, Found. for Santa Fe Concert Assn., 1998—2001. Tex. Moot Ct. champion, 1958. Mem. Tex. Bar Assn., Dallas Bar Assn., Dallas Jr. C. of C. (v.p. 1964), Sigma Chi. Democrat. Episcopalian. Office Phone: 505-988-1553. E-mail: raybesing@nets.com.

BEST, MELVYN EDWARD, geophysicist; b. Victoria, BC, Can., Mar. 8, 1941; s. Herbert Best and Irene Jessie (Kelly) MacKenzie; m. Virginia Marie Pignato, July 19, 1970; children: Lisette Anne, Aaron Michael. BSc in Math. and Physics with honors, U. B.C., Vancouver, 1965, MSc in Physics, 1966; PhD in Theoretical Physics, MIT, 1970. Geophysicist mineral exploration Shell Can. Resources Ltd., Calgary, Alta., Canada, 1972-77, divsn. geophysicist minerals, 1980-82, mgr. petroleum engring. rsch., 1982-85; head non-seismic rsch. Royal

Dutch Shell Exploration and Prodn. Labs., The Hague, Netherlands, 1978-80; geophys. advisor Teknica Resource Devel. Ltd., Calgary, 1985-86; head basin analysis subdivision Atlantic Geoscience Ctr. Geol. Survey Can., Dartmouth, N.S., 1986-90, dir. Pacific Geosci. Ctr. Sidney, B.C., 1990-94, sr. rsch. scientist, 1994-97; geophys. cons. Bemex Consulting Internat., Victoria, B.C., 1997—; environ. geophys. Lockheed-Martin Corp., Edison, NJ, 2001—. Vis. lectr., rsch. assoc. dept. physics McGill U., Montreal, Que., 1970—72; mem. panel Jeanne d'Arc hydrocarbon resource assessment Can. Govt., 1987—90; mem. petroleum geology working group Office Energy R&D, 1987—92; mem. oil and gas com. Can. Nfld. Offshore Petroleum Bd., 1990—94, official Can. rep. coom. coordination joint prospecting for mineral resources in Asian offshore waters, 1992—94; sessional lectr. Sch. Earth and Ocean Scis. U. Victoria, 1995—, adj. prof. earth and ocean scis., 1998—; adj. prof. geology and geophysics U. Calgary, 1998—2004; part-time sr. geophysicist Lockheed Martin Corp., Edison, NJ, 2001—. Author: Resistivity Mapping and Electromagnetic Imaging, 1992; editor: (with J.B. Boniwell) A Geophysical Handbook for Geologists, 1989, (with T.P. Ng) Development and Exploitation Scale Geophysics, 1995; assoc. editor Bull. Can. Soc. Petroleum Geologists, 2004-07. Vol. lectr. Can. Coll. Chinese Studies, Victoria, B.C., 1995-99; vol. Victoria chpt. Habitat for Humanity, 1996-97. Recipient meritorious svc. award Can. Soc. Exploration Geophysicists, Calgary, 1996. Mem. Can. Soc. Exploration Geophysicists (chmn. continuing edn. com. 1982-85, mem. tech. com. 1985 conv., assoc. editor jour. 1986-93, 95-2003, editor jour. 1993-95), Soc. Exploration Geophysicists (prodn. and devel. geophysics com. 1985-88, geophys. rsch. com. 1988—, organizer workshop 1989, instr. continuing edn. 1985-2000, global affairs com. 2005—), Soc. Environ. and Engring. Geophysics (assoc. editor jour. 1995-97, 2000-02, editor 1997-2000, v.p. coms. 2003-05, gen. chmn. symposium on application geophysics to environ. and engring. problems meeting 2006, grant selection com., natural sci. and engring. rsch. coun. solid earth scis. 2006-08), Assn. Profl. Engrs., Geologists and Geophysicists Alta. (cert.), Assn. Profl. Engrs. and Geoscientists B.C. (cert.). Avocations: badminton, squash, tennis, hiking, sailing. Home and Office: Bemex Cons Internat 3701 Wild Berry Bend Victoria BC Canada V9C 4M7 Office Phone: 250-658-4225. Personal E-mail: best@islandnet.com.

BETHANCOURT, JOHN E., oil industry executive; b. Dallas, Nov. 12, 1951; BS in Petroleum U., Tex. A&M U., 1974. Field engr., then various engring. and mgmt. positions Getty Oil, Kilgore, Tex., 1974—84; area mgr. South Tex. Texaco U.S.A., Midland, Tex., 1984—89, asst. divsn. mgr. Midland producing divsn., 1989—91, asst. to mgmt. office of pres. and CEO White Plains, NY, 1991—93, mng. dir. bus. devel Mid. East/Far East divsn., 1993—96, v.p. bus. devel. internat. mfg. and mktg. divsn., 1996—97, v.p. corp. devel. upstream devel. orgn. Houston, 1997—2000, pres. prodn. ops., 2000—01, v.p., 2000—01; v.p. human resources ChevronTexaco Corp., San Ramon, Calif., 2001—03, exec. v.p. tech. & services, 2003—. Office: ChevronTexaco 6001 Bollinger Canyon Rd San Ramon CA 94583-2324

BETTENHAUSEN, MATTHEW ROBERT, state official, lawyer; b. Joliet, Ill., Aug. 6, 1960; s. Robert Theodore and E. Colleen Bettenhausen. BS summa cum laude in Acctg., U. Ill., 1982, JD cum laude, 1985. Bar: Ill. 1985. Assoc. Sonnenschein, Carlin, Nath & Rosenthal, Chgo., 1985; law clk. to judge Chgo., 1985-87; asst. U.S. atty. U.S. Dept. Justice, Chgo.; dep. gov. Criminal Justice and Pub. Safety State of Ill., 2000—03; dir. state & territorial coordination US Dept. Homeland Security, Washington, 2003—05; dir. Office of Homeland Security State of Calif., 2005—. Dep. chief Criminal Receiving and Gen. Crimes Sects. U.S. Attys. Office, dep. chief Organized Crime and Drug Enforcement Task Force, acting chief appeals, assoc. chief entire criminal divsn.; adj. prof. adv. trial advocacy and evidence John Marshal Law Sch., Chgo.; lectr. in field. Bd. dirs. Bicentennial of Constl. Commn., Tinley Park, Ill., 1985—. Recipient Civic award, C. of C. Tinley Park, 1985, scholarship, Nat. Inst. Trial Advocacy, 1987.

BETTINGER, MICHAEL JOHN, lawyer; b. Youngstown, Ohio, Aug. 31, 1958; s. John Arthur and Barbara Marion (Bowen) B. BS summa cum laude, St. Joseph's Coll., 1980; JD, U. Notre Dame, 1983. Bar: Ill. 1983, Calif. 1985, US Supreme Ct. 1990. Law clk. to Hon. John L. Coffey U.S. Ct. Appeals (7th cir.), Chgo., 1983-85; ptnr., head of intellectual property litig., mem. exec. com. Preston Gates & Ellis LLP, San Francisco. White scholar, Notre Dame Law Sch. Mem.: St. Thomas More Soc., State Bar of Ill., State Bar of Calif. Home: 29 Belvedere Ave Belvedere CA 94920-2420 Office: Preston Gates & Ellis LLP Ste 1700 55 Second St San Francisco CA 94105 Office Phone: 415-882-8002. Office Fax: 415-882-8220. Business E-Mail: mikeb@prestongates.com.

BETTINGER, WALTER W., II, investment company executive; b. Ohio, Nov. 29, 1960; m. Laura G. Bettinger (div.); 3 children; m. Teri Farnsworth. BBA summa cum laude in Finance and Investments, Ohio U., 1983; completed Gen. Mgmt. program, Harvard Bus. Sch. Joined pension dept. Westfield Cos., Medina County, Ohio, 1981; founder The Hampton Co. (acquired by The Charles Schwab Corp.), Bath Township, Ohio, 1983—95; gen. mgr. SchwabPlan, COO and then pres. Retirement Plan Services Enterprise The Charles Schwab Corp., 1995—2001, pres. corp. services divsn., 2001—04, exec. v.p., 2004—05, COO individual investor enterprise, 2004—05, pres. individual investor enterprise, 2005—07, pres., COO, 2007—08, pres., CEO, 2008—. Bd. dirs. The Charles Schwab Corp., 2008—. Exec. advisory bd. Ohio U. Coll. Bus.; chmn. Walter W. Bettinger II Charitable Found. Mem.: Am. Soc. Pension Actuaries, Nat. Defined Contribution Coun. (bd. dirs., exec. com.). Office: The Charles Schwab Corp 101 Montgomery St San Francisco CA 94104*

BETTINGHAUS, ERWIN PAUL, research scientist; b. Peoria, Ill., Oct. 28, 1930; s. Erwin Paul and Paula (Bretscher) B.; m. Carole Irma Overmier, Apr. 5, 1952; children: Karen Lee, Joyce Anne, Bruce Alan. BA, U. Ill., 1952, PhD, 1959; MA, Bradley U., 1953. Instr. Mich. State U., East Lansing, 1958-60, asst. prof., 1960-64, assoc. prof., 1964-69, prof., 1969-97, prof. emeritus, 1997—, chmn. dept. comm., 1972-76, dean Coll. Comm. Arts and Scis., 1976-96, dean emeritus, 1997—; dep. dir. AMC Cancer Rsch. Ctr., Denver, 1997—2002; sr. scientist Cooper Inst., 2002—05, assoc. v.p., 2003—05; sr. scientist Klein Buendel, Inc., 2005—. Vis. prof. U. Okla., 1970-71 Author: The Nature of Proof, 1971, Persuasive Communication, 1994. Mem. Nat. Cancer Adv. Bd., 1988-94. With U.S. Army, 1953-56. Mem. AAAS, APA, Internat. Comm. Assn. (pres. 1982), Am. Comm. Assn., Assn. for Edn. in Journalism, Assn. Comm. Adminstrn. (pres. 1991). Home: 2170 S Parfet Dr Lakewood CO 80227-1900 Office: 1667 Cole Blvd Ste 225 Golden CO 80401 Office Phone: 303-565-4341. Business E-Mail: ebettinghaus@kleinbuendel.com.

BETTISON, CYNTHIA ANN, museum director, archaeologist; b. St. Louis, Sept. 8, 1958; d. William Leslie and Barbara Ann (Yunker) B. BA in Anthropology and Biology, Pitzer Coll., 1980; MA in Anthropology, Eastern N.Mex. U., 1983; ABD in Anthropology, U. Calif., Santa Barbara, 1986, PhD in Anthropology, 1998. Cert. profl. archaeologist Archaeol. Stds. Bd., 2004. Asst. curator dept. anthropology U. Calif., Santa Barbara, 1988-89, curator dept. anthropology, 1990-91; dir. Western N.Mex. U. Mus., Silver City, 1991—. Co-dir. Western N.Mex. U. Archaeol. Field Sch., 1992, 94, 95; lectr. Western N.Mex. U., 1992, 93, adj. asst. prof. dept. social scis., 1994—; various archaeol. positions, 1981—. Contbr. articles to profl. jours. Recipient Conservation Assessment Program grant, 1994-95, NEH, 1994; Gila Nat. Forest grantee, 1992, 94, 95, Silver City Lodgers Tax Bd. grantee, 1992, Andrew Isabell Meml. Fund grantee U. Calif., 1990, SIMSE grantee, 1994-95, 95-96. Mem. AAUW, Am. Assn. Mus., Am. Anthrop. Assn., Am. Soc. Conservation Archaeology, N.Mex. Mus. Assn. (pres. 2002-04), Soc. for Am. Archaeology, Archaeol. Soc. N.Mex., N.Mex. Archaeol. Coun. (sec. 1993-94), Coun. Mus. Anthropology (sec. 1992-94), Assn. of Coll. and Univ. Mus. and Galleries (bd. dirs. 2004—, sml. mus. adminstrn. com. bd. mem.)), Mountain Plains Mus. Assn., Univ. Women's Club, Univ. Club, Optimist Club (sec. Silver City chpt. 1992), Silver City Rotary Club (v.p. 1999-2000, pres. elect 2000-2001, pres. 2001-2002, dist. 5520 asst. gov. 2002-04), Silver City Grant County C. of C., Chpt. BR PEO, Phi Kappa Phi.

BETTS, JAMES WILLIAM, JR., financial analyst, consultant; b. Oct. 11, 1923; s. James William and Cora Anna (Banta) B.; m. Barbara Stoke, July 28, 1951; 1 child, Barbara Susan (dec.). BA, Rutgers U., 1946; postgrad., New Sch. for Social Rsch., 1948—49; MA, U. Hawaii, 1957. With Dun & Bradstreet, Inc., 1946-86, svc. cons., 1963-64, reporting and svc. mgr., 1964-65, sr. fin. analyst Honolulu, 1965-86; owner Portfolio Cons. of Hawaii, 1979—. Cons. Saybrook Point Investments, Old Saybrook, Conn., 1979—; owner James W. Betts & Co., 1996—, Scrapbook Press, 2002—. Author: From Nowhere to Somewhere on a Round Trip Ticket, 2003, Strategy of the Baltimore & Ohio Railroad, 1930-1932, 2006, Quirky Tales of the Rails, 2009; contbr. articles to mags. With AUS, 1943. Mem. Am. Econ. Assn., Nat. Assn. Bus. Economists, Col. Henry Rutgers Soc., Internat. Inst. Forecasters, Western Econ. Assn. Internat., Transporation Rsch. Forum. Republican. Episcopalian. Home and Office: 1434 Punahou St #1028 Honolulu HI 96822-4740 Home Phone: 808-599-7817; Office Phone: 808-955-7817. Personal E-mail: kimorail@aol.com.

BETTS, JANET GNIADEK, lawyer; b. Chgo., Oct. 16, 1954; d. Henry M. and Betty Gniadek. BS in Dental Hygiene, Loyola U., Chgo., 1976; JD, Ill. Inst. Tech., Chgo., 1979; LLM in Taxation, Depaul U., Chgo., 1982. Bar: Ariz. 1980, U.S. Dist. Ct. Ariz. 1980, U.S. Tax Ct. Ariz. 1980, U.S. Ct. Appeals (9th cir.) Ariz. 1980. Assoc. Winston & Strawn, Phoenix, 1982-84, Streich, Lang, Weeks & Cardon, Phoenix, 1984-87; in-house counsel Brooker & Wake, Tempe, Ariz., 1987; ptnr. Gust Rosenfeld, Phoenix, 1987—99; of counsel Kutak Rock LLP, Omaha, 2000—04; mem. Jennings, Strouss & Solomon PLC, Phoenix, 2004—. Bd. dirs. Arrowhead Cmty. Bank. Past pres. ctrl div. Ariz. chpt. Am. Heart Assn., Phoenix, 1992-93, past chmn. bd. dirs. Ariz. chpt., 1994—95; bd. dirs. Ariz. Osteoporosis Coalition, Area Humane Soc., 1997-2003. Recipient Volunteer of the Year award, Amer. Heart Assn. (Ariz. affiliate), 1992-94, Fund-raising Event award, 1993-94, Devel. Chmn. award, 1992-93, Dir. Recognition award, 1991-92, Amer. Heart Assn. (Ctrl. divsn.), Polit. Excellence award, Ariz. Human Society, 2000, Mem. ABA, Ariz. Bar Assn., Maricopa County Bar Assn., Am. Heart Assn., Ariz. Humane Soc. (bd. dirs. 1997-2003). Republican. Avocations: hiking, mountain bike, golf. Office: Jennings Strouss Salmon Plc 201 E Washington St Fl 11 Phoenix AZ 85004-2385 Office Phone: 602-262-5927, 480-663-2162. E-mail: jbetts@jsslaw.com.

BETZ, A. LORRIS, pediatrician, educator; b. LaCrosse, Wis., Feb. 9, 1947; s. Alert L. and Charlotte M. (Kopp) B.; m. Ann C. Doyle, Aug. 30, 1968; children: Jennifer A., Bryan L. BS, U. Wis., 1969, MD., PhD, 1975. Intern pediatrics U. Calif., San Francisco, 1975, resident in pediatrics, 1975-79; asst. prof. pediatrics and neurology U. Mich., Ann Arbor, 1979-83, assoc. prof. pediatrics and neurology, 1983-87, prof. pediatrics, surgery, neurology, 1987—99, dir. neurosurg. rsch., surgery, 1987—99, assoc. dean for faculty affairs, 1993-97, interim dean Med. Sch., 1997—99; dean, sr. v.p. health sci. U. Utah Med. Sch., Salt Lake City, 1999—, sr. v.p. Cons. NIH, Bethesda, Md., 1985—. Editorial bd.: Jour. Neurochemistry, 1986-94; contbr. articles to Sci., Brain Rsch., Sci. Am., Stroke, Am. Jour. Physiology. Grantee, NIH, Univ. Mich., 1980—; named Established Investigator, Am. Heart Assn., Univ. Mich., 1981. Mem. Internat. Soc. Cerebral Blood Flow and Metabolism (bd. dirs. 1991—, sec. 1995—), Internat. Soc. Neurochemistry, Am. Physiol. Soc., Soc. for Pediatric Rsch., Am. Pediatric Soc., Phi Beta Kappa, Sigma Xi, Alpha Omega Alpha. Achievements include research in basic mechanisms that are responsible for moving nutrients and electrolytes between the blood and the brain of mammals, processes that produce brain injury following a stroke. Office: Health Sci Ctr Moran Eye Ctrs Fl 5 50 N Med Dr Salt Lake City UT 84132-0001

BEUERLEIN, STEVE TAYLOR, professional football player; m. Kristen Beuerlein; children: Taylor, Jake, Kailey. Profl. football player Oakland (Calif.) Raiders, 1989-91, Dallas Cowboys, 1991-93, Cardinals, 1993-95, Jacksonville, 1995; quarterback Carolina Panthers, Charlotte, 1996—2000, Denver Broncos, 2001—. Participant Pro Bowl, 1999. Office: 1701 Bryant St, Suite 100 Denver CO 80204

BEUTLER, LARRY EDWARD, psychologist, educator; b. Logan, Utah, Feb. 14, 1941; s. Edward and Beulah (Andrus) B.; children: Jana, Kelly, Ian David, Gail. BS, Utah State U., 1965, MS, 1966; PhD, U. Nebr., 1970. Diplomate Am. Bd. Clin. Psychology. Asst. prof. psychology Duke U., Ashville, NC, 1970-71; asst. prof. Stephen F. Austin State U., Nacogdoches, Tex., 1971-73; assoc. prof. Baylor Coll. Medicine, Houston, 1973-79; prof. U. Ariz., Tucson, 1979-90, U. Calif., Santa Barbara, 1990—, Pacific Grad. Sch. Psychology, Stanford U., Palo Alto, Calif., 2002—. Co-author: Systematic Treatment Selection, 1990, Guidelines for the Systematic Treatment of the Depressed Patient, 2000, Integrative Assessment of Adult Personality, 2003, Principles of Therapeutic Change That Work, 2006, others; editor Jour. Cons. Clin. Psychology, 1990-96, Psychology of Terrorism, 2007; editor Jour. Clin. Psychology, 1997—2004. Fellow APA (pres. divsn. psychotherapy, 1997, pres. divsn. clin. psychology, 2002), Am. Psychol. Soc.; mem. Soc. Psychotherapy Rsch. (pres. 1986-88). Home: 2620 Piedra Verde Ct Placerville CA 95667 Office: Pacific Grad School Of Psychology 405 Broadway St Redwood City CA 94063-3133 Home Phone: 530-642-1353. Business E-Mail: lbeutler@pgsp.edu.

BEVAN, MICHAEL J., immunologist, educator, researcher; PhD in Immunology, Nat. Inst. Med. Rsch., Mill Hill, London, 1972. Postdoctoral Salk Inst.; asst. to assoc. prof. biology Ctr. for Cancer Rsch. MIT; mem. dept. immunology Scripps Rsch. Inst., La Jolla, Calif.; investigator Howard Hughes Med. Inst., 1990—; prof. immunology U. Wash., Seattle, 1990—. Contbr. scientific papers, articles to profl. jours. Fellow: Royal Soc. London; mem.: NAS. Achievements include research in T lymphocyte development, homeostasis, and function. Office: Univ Wash Dept Immunology I 604 H HSC Box 357370 1959 NE Pacific St Seattle WA 98195 Office Phone: 206-685-3610. Office Fax: 206-685-3612. Business E-Mail: mbevan@u.washington.edu.

BEVAN, WILLIAM ARNOLD, JR., emergency physician; b. Sault St. Marie, Mich., June 23, 1943; s. William Arnold and Syneva Lois (Martin) B.; m. Martha Lynn Peterson, Dec. 29, 1973; children: Terry Eugene, Brian William, Patrick Jon. BS, U. Minn., 1966, MD, 1970. Diplomate Am. Bd. Family Practice, Am. Bd. Emergency Medicine. Intern U. Utah, 1970—71; family practitioner Vail Mountain Med. Profl. Corp., Vail, Colo., 1972—83; emergency physician Vail Valley Emergency Physicians, 1983—; dir. Vail Valley Med. Ctr., 1990—. Dir. Vail Valley Emergency Dept., 1992—, pres. med. staff, 1977; adviser Western Eagle County Ambulance Dist., 1983—. Trustee Shattuck St. Mary's Sch., Faribault, Minn., 1977—; football coach Battle Mountain H.S., Vail, 1978—; trustee, bd. dirs. Vail Christian H.S., 1998—, football coach; Eagle Scout. Named Man of Yr. Boy Scouts Am., 1966, 77, Physician of Yr. Vail Valley Med. Ctr., 2007. Fellow Am. Coll. Emergency Physicians; mem. AMA, Rocky Mountain Med. Soc., Colo. Med. Soc., U. Minn. Alumni Assn. (life). Republican. Lutheran. Home: 25 Cottonwood Rd Eagle CO 81631 Office: Vail Valley Emergency Dept 181 W Meadow Dr Vail CO 81657-5058 Mailing: Box 1143 Avon CO 81620 Home Phone: 970-949-7093; Office Phone: 970-476-8065. E-mail: williambevan@comcast.net.

BEVELACQUA, JOSEPH JOHN, physicist, researcher; b. Waynesburg, Pa., Mar. 17, 1949; s. Frank and Lucy Ann Bevelacqua; m. Terry Sanders, Sept. 4, 1971; children: Anthony, Jeffrey, Megan, Peter, Michael, Karen. BS in Physics, Calif. State Coll., Pa., 1970; postgrad., U. Maine, Orono, 1970—72; MS in Physics, Fla. State U., Tallahassee, 1974, PhD, 1976. Cert. radiol. shield survey engr.; diplomate Am. Bd. Health Physics, cert. health physicist; sr. reactor operator cert. Teaching/rsch. asst. U. Maine, 1970-72; tchg. and rsch. asst. Fla. State U., 1973-76; rsch. asst. NSF, 1975-76, rsch. assoc., 1976; nuc. engr. Bettis Atomic Power Lab., West Mifflin, Pa., 1973, sr. nuc. engr., 1976-78; ops. rsch. analyst US Dept. Energy, Oak Ridge, 1978-80, chief physicist advanced laser isotope separation program, 1980-83; sr. radiol. engr. Three Mile Island Sta.-Unit 2 GPU Nuc. Corp., Middletown, Pa., 1983-84, Three Mile Island emergency preparedness mgr., 1984-86, mgr. TMI-2 safety rev. group, 1986-89, dir. radiol. controls TMI-2, 1989; supt. health physics Point Beach Nuc. Power Plant Wis. Electric Co., Two Rivers, 1989-95; prodn. planning mgr. Point Beach Nuc. Plant, 1995—96; pres., CEO Bevelacqua Resources, Richland, Wash., 1993—; sr. radiol. controls tech. advisor USDOE-Office River Protection, Hanford, 1996—2005, acting dir. environ. divsn., 2000; assoc. AJC & Assocs. Inc., 2005—. Cons. US Dept. Energy Process Evaluation Bd. Isotope Separation, Washington, 1981—82; acting. asst. mgr. environ., safety, health, and quality US Dept. Energy-Office River Protection, Hanford, 2000. Author: Contemprary Health Physics: Problems and Solutions, 1995, Basic Health Physics: Problems and Solutions, 1999, Health Physics in the 21st Century, 2008, 20 health physics tng. manuals, 3 CD-ROMS; contbr. articles to profl. jours. Mem. Rep. Presdl. Task Force Nat. Rep. Senatorial Com. Recipient Outstanding Performance award, Dept. of Energy, 1982, 1996—2004, Profl. Excellence award, California U. of Pa., 2000; grantee, USAF, NSF, Von Humboldt fellow, U. Hamburg. Mem.: NRA (life), US Golf Assn., Am. Bd. Health Physics (vice chmn. comprehensive panel examiners 1990, chmn. 1991, nat. office mem.), Health Physics Soc., Profl. Reactor Operators Soc., Babcock and Wilcox Owners Group Emergency Preparedness, Nuc. Utility Coordinating Group Emergency Preparedness Implementation, Soc. Nuc. Medicine, NY Acad. Scis., Susquehanna Valley Health Physics Soc. (mem. exec. com.), Health Physics Soc. (Columbia chpt., mem. placement com. 1989—92, mem. nominating com. 1994—97), Am. Acad. Health Physics (mem. profl. devel. com. 1992—94, chmn. 1994, mem. nominating com. 1994—96), Math. Assn. Am., Am. Math. Soc., Am. Phys. Soc., Am. Nuc. Soc. (Ea. Wash. chpt., Silver cert. 2007), Soc. Physics Students, Oak Ridge Sportsman's Club, Tri Cities Ams. Ice Hockey Booster Club, Sigma Pi Sigma. Independent. Lutheran. Achievements include research in theoretical studies of light nuclei, few nucleon transfer reactions, radiation shielding, laser isotope separation, uranium enrichment, free electron lasers, neutron nuclei; symmetry violations in nuclei, grand unification theories, quark models of nuclear forces, neutrino interactions; nuclear fuel cycle, generation III and IV fission reactors, laser fusion, gravitational collapse of stars, beta dosimetry, internal dosimetry, health effects of ionizing radiation; nuclear reactor safety, accident analysis, fusion reactor safety, muon catalyzed fusion, health physics at fusion reactors, radon health effects and mitigation, radioactive and mixed waste management; applied health physics, internal and external dosimetry, dark matter, strange matter, symmetry violations in nuclei, cosmology, radiation effects during low earth orbit, lunar missions; planetary missions, quantum field theory, astrophysics, supersymmetry, quantum gravity, string theory, twister theory, muon colliders, neutrino dose equivalents, genetic approaches for cancer research; heavy ion cancer therapy, therapy applications using microbeams and nanotechnology; quantum chromodynamics, differential geometry, general relativity, gravitation, neutrino physics, neutrino dosimetry; special relativity, standard model of particle physics and radiation induced immune system activation; heavy ion therapy, radiotherapy using microbeams and nanotechnology. Avocations: golf, hockey, lacrosse, running, rock climbing. Home and Office: Bevelacqua Resources 343 Adair Dr Richland WA 99352-8563 Office Phone: 509-628-2240. Personal E-mail: bevelresou@aol.com.

BEVERIDGE, CRAWFORD W., information technology executive; BSc in Social Scis., U. Edinburgh; MSc in Indsl. Adminstrn., U. Bradford, Eng.; D (hon.), U. Edinburgh, Napier U., Edinburgh, Robert Gordons U., Aberdeen, Scotland. Human resources mgmt. positions Hewlett-Packard Co., Digital Equipment Corp., Analog Devices; v.p. corp. resources Sun Microsystems, Inc., 1985—91, exec. v.p. people and places, chief human resources officer Santa Clara, Calif., 2000, exec. v.p., chmn. Europe, Mid. East and Africa, Asia Pacific and the

Ams.; CEO Scottish Enterprise, Scotland, 1991—2000. Bd. dirs. Autodesk, Memec, Scottish Equity Ptnrs., Ltd. Recipient Comdr. of Order of Brit. Empire, 1995. Office: Sun Microsystems Inc 4150 Network Cir Santa Clara CA 95054 Office Phone: 800-555-9786. Office Fax: 650-960-1300, 408-276-3804.

BEWLEY, PETER DAVID, corporate director, investor; b. Atlantic City, Aug. 4, 1946; s. Philip Bessor and Gladys Elizabeth Bewley; m. Barbara L. Sell, June 1, 1968 (dec. June 25, 1971); 1 child, Peter David Jr.; m. Lee D. Catanese, Aug. 12, 1972; 1 child, Stephen Philip. BA in politics cum laude, Princeton U., 1968; JD, Stanford U., 1971. Bar: Calif. 1971, DC 1972, US Ct. Appeals DC cir. 1972, US Supreme Ct. 1976. Law clk. O'Melveny and Myers, LA; assoc. Wilmer, Cutler & Pickering, Washington, 1972-76; atty. Johnson & Johnson, New Brunswick, NJ, 1977—85, asst. gen. counsel, 1985—90, assoc. gen. counsel, 1990—94; sr. v.p., gen. counsel, sec. NovaCare, Inc., King of Prussia, Pa., 1994-98, The Clorox Co., Oakland, Calif., 1998—2005. Bd. dirs. Non Prescription Drug Mfrs. Assn., Washington, 1991-94, Access Worldwide Comm Inc., Boca Raton, Fla., 1998-2001, WD-40 Co., San Diego, 2005-. Mem. editl. bd. Food and Drug Law Jour., 1992-94. City councilman, Gladstone, NJ, 1993—94; vice chair bd. dirs. Children Now, chair fin. com.; exec. campaign adv. com. United Negro Coll. Fund of the Bay Area, 1998—2005; exec. com. bd. visitors Stanford Law Sch. Capt. USAF, 1971—72. Mem. Nat. Assn. Corporate Dirs., Order of Coif. Avocations: travel, skiing, reading.

BEYER, CASEY K., legislative staff member; b. Reno, Jan. 4, 1955; BA, U. Calif., Santa Barbara, 1978; MUP, San Jose U., 1984. Staff aide Rep. Ed Zschau, 1983-86; cons. to hi-tech cos. Silicone Valley, Calif., 1987-88; dist. dir. Rep. Tom Campbell, Campbell, Calif., 1989-92, 1996-97, chief of staff, 1997—; state adminstr. State Senator Tom Campbell, Campbell, 1993-95. Mem. exec. com. Tax and Fiscal Policy Joint Venture, 1994—, mem. working group, 1994—.

BEYER, ELIZABETH TERRY, state legislator; City councilor, City of Springfield; Oregon State Representative, District 12, 2002-,president, Hamlin PTA; member, Convention & Visitor Association Lane County; member, Springfield Edn Found; TransPlan advisor comt member, City Library Bd. Democrat. Address: PO Box 131 Springfield OR 97477 Office: 900 Court St NE H-277 Salem OR 97301 Office Phone: 503-986-1412. E-mail: terrybeyer@attbi.com, rep.terrybeyer@state.or.us.

BEYER, LEE LOUIS, state legislator; b. Norfolk, Nebr., June 4, 1948; s. Louis E. and Arlene (Henderson) B.; m. Elizabeth Terry Yates, July 26, 1969; children: Jonathan, Joshua, Megan. BS in Pub. Mgmt., U. Oreg., 1974. Exec. dir. Linn-Benton-Lincoln Manpower Consortium, Corvallis, Oreg., 1974-76; mgmt. analyst Oreg. State Exec. Dept., Salem, 1976-78; ops. mgr. Lane County Employment Tng. Dept., Eugene, Oreg., 1978-80; exec. dir. Eugene Pvt. Industry Coun., 1980-83; indsl. devel. mgr. City of Eugene, 1983-86; city councilor Springfield, 1986-93; mem. Oreg. Ho. of Reps., Salem, 1991-98; mem. house dem. whip Oreg. Senate, Salem, 1998—. Mem., chair Lane C.C. Vocat. Edn. Commn., Eugene, 1978-79, 83—; bd. dirs. Eugene/Springfield Visitor and Conv. Bur., Eugene, Eugene/Springfield Metro. Partnership, Eugene. Mem., chmn. Intergovtl. Met. Policy Com., Springfield, 1986—; pres., councilman City of Springfield, 1986—; mem., chair Springfield City Planning Commn., 1979-86, Springfield Budget Com., 1984—; Oreg. state rep., 1991—. With USAF, 1967-70. Democrat. Lutheran. Avocations: reading, fishing. Office: Oreg Senate S 306 State Capitol Salem OR 97310-0001

BEYER, RICHARD MICHAEL, manufacturing executive; b. NYC, Oct. 12, 1948; s. Thomas Robert Sr. and Madeline Frances B.; m. Nikki Cole Greene, Nov. 5, 1983; children: Laura, Christopher. BS in Russian, Georgetown U., 1970, MS in Russia, 1974; MBA, Columbia U., 1977. V.p. mktg. ITT, Raleigh, N.C., 1984-86, v.p., gen. mgr. PABX sys. divsn., 1986-87, Alcatel, Alexandria, Va., 1987-89; v.p., gen. mgr. Rockwell Internat., Downers Grove, Ill., 1989-93; pres. comm. & computing group Nat. Semiconductor Corp., Sunnyvale, Calif., 1993-95, exec. v.p., COO, 1995-96; pres., COO VSLI Tech. Inc., San Jose, Calif., 1996-98; pres., CEO FVC.COM, Inc., Santa Clara, Calif., 1999—2000; CEO Elantec Semiconductor, Inc., Irvine, Calif., 2000—02, Intersil Corp., Milpitas, Calif., 2002—08; chmn., CEO Freescale Semiconductor, Inc., Austin, Tex., 2008—. Bd. dirs. VLSI Tech., Inc., 1996-98, FVC.COM, Inc., 1999-2000, Elantec Semiconduxtor, Inc., 2000-02, Credence Systems Corp., 2003-08, Xceive Inc., 2006-08, Semiconductor Ind. Assn. Bd. dirs. San Jose Symphony, 1995—96, 2003—. 1st lt. USMC Res., 1970—73. Mem. Am. Electronics Assn. (bd. dirs. 1997-98). Republican. Methodist. Avocations: skiing, bicycling, reading, tennis, wine. Office: Freescale Semiconductor Inc 6501 William Cannon Dr W Austin TX 78735 Business E-Mail: rich.beyer@freescale.com.

BEYER, ROGER, state legislator; b. Oregon City, Oreg., Sept. 14, 1960; m to Barbara; children: Neil, Erin, Curt, Jeff & Carl. Member, Maple Sch Bd, 90-93, chairman, 92-93; Oregon State Representative, District 28, formerly, chairman, Commerce Subcomt on Bus, 97, chairman, Bus & Consumer Affairs, formerly, member, Agriculture & Forestry, Rules, Elections & Public Affairs Committees, formerly, Oregon House Representative; Oregon State Senator, District 15, 2001-02; Oregon State Senator, District 9, 2003-.Managing partner, Beyer Tree Farm, 83-. Clackamas-Marion Forest Protective Association (board director, 85-, vice president, 88-89, president, 89-90); NW Christmas Tree Association (board director, 84-91, vice president, 89-90, secy/treas, 87-89). Republican. Office: 900 Court St NE, S-217 Salem OR 97301 Office Phone: Capit: 503-986-1709. E-mail: rwbeyer@molalla.net.

BEYERS, WILLIAM BJORN, geography educator; b. Seattle, Mar. 24, 1940; s. William Abraham and Esther Jakobia (Svendsen) B.; m. Margaret Lyn Rice, July 28, 1968. BA, U. Wash., 1962, PhD, 1967. Asst. prof. geography U. Wash., Seattle, 1968-74, assoc. prof., 1974-82, prof., 1982—, chmn. dept. geography, 1991-95, 2005—08. Mem.: Western Regional Sci. Assn., Regional Sci. Assn., Assn. Am. Geographers. Home: 7159 Beach Dr SW Seattle WA 98136-2077 Office: U Wash Dept Geography PO Box 353550 Seattle WA 98195-3550 Home Phone: 206-935-6282; Office Phone: 206-543-5871. Fax: 206-543-3313. E-mail: beyers@u.washington.edu.

BEYLKIN, GREGORY, mathematician; b. St. Petersburg, Mar. 16, 1953; came to U.S., 1980; naturalized citizen, 1985; s. Jacob and Raya (Pripshtein) B.; m. Helen Simontov, 1974; children: Michael, Daniel. Diploma in Math., U. St. Petersburg, Leningrad, 1975; PhD in Math., NYU, 1982. Assoc. rsch. sci. NYU, 1982-83; mem. profl. staff Schlumberger-Doll Research, Ridgefield, Conn., 1983-91; prof. dept. applied math. U. Colo., Boulder, 1991—. Contbr. articles to profl. jours. Mem. Am. Math. Soc., Soc. for Indsl. and Applied Math., Soc. Exptl. Geophysicists. Office: U Colo Dept Applied Math 526 UCB Boulder CO 80309-0526 Business E-Mail: beylkin@boulder.colorado.edu.

BEZOS, JEFFREY PRESTON, mail order services company executive; b. Albuquerque, Jan. 12, 1964; s. Miguel and Jacklyn Bezos; m. Mackenzie Tuttle, 1993; 3 children. BS in Elec. Engring. & Computer Sci., summa cum laude, Princeton U., 1986; D in Sci. & Tech. (hon.), Carnegie Mellon U., 2008. With FITEL, NY, 1986—88, Bankers Trust Co., NY, 1988-90, v.p. NY, 1990, D.E. Shaw & Co., NY, 1990-94, sr. v.p. NY, 1992-94; founder Amazon.com Inc., Seattle, 1994—, chmn., 1994—, pres., 1994—99, 2000—, CEO, 1996—, treas., sec., 1996—97; founder Blue Origin, Seattle, 2000—. Bd. dirs. Amazon.com Inc., 1994—, Drugstore.com, 1998—. Named Person of Yr., TIME mag., 1999, Publishers Weekly mag., 2008; named one of 40 Under 40 Richest, Fortune, 2003, The 50 Who Matter Now, CNNMoney.com Bus. 2.0, 2006, 2007, Forbes' Richest Americans, 2005—, The World's Richest People, Forbes mag., 2006—, The 50 Most Important People on the Web, PC World, 2007, The World's Most Influential People, TIME mag., 2008, 2009, The Global Elite, Newsweek mag., 2008, America's Best Leaders, US News & World Report, 2008. Mem.: Phi Beta Kappa. Achievements include funding Blue Origin, builders of low cost vehicles that would send passengers into space on short flights; launching and landing Goddard, a first development vehicle in the New Shepard program at Blue Origin. Office: Amazon com Inc 1200 12th Ave S Ste 1200 Seattle WA 98144*

BHAGAT, NANCY, marketing executive; Bachelor's in bus. adminstrn. and polit. sci., Gettysburg Coll. With Schell/Mullaney, J. Walter Thompson; sr. v.p. global mktg. Computer Associates Internat.; chief mktg. officer Macromedia; v.p. sales and mktg., dir. integrated mktg. Intel Corp., 2005—. Named one of Best Marketers, BtoB Mag., 2008. Office: Intel Corp 2200 Mission Coll Blvd PO Box 58119 Santa Clara CA 95052-8119 Office Phone: 408-765-8080.

BHAGWAN, SUDHIR, computer industry and research executive, consultant; b. Lahore, West Pakistan, Aug. 9, 1942; came to U.S., 1963; s. Vishan and Lakshmi Devi (Arora) B.; m. Sarita Bahl, Oct. 25, 1969; children: Sonia, Sunil. BSEE, Punjab Engring. Coll., Chandigarh, India, 1963; MSEE, Stanford U., 1964; MBA with honors, Golden Gate U., 1977. Engr. Gaylor Products, North Hollywood, Calif., 1964-68, Burroughs Corp., Pasadena, Calif., 1968-70, engring. mgr. Santa Barbara, Calif., 1970-78, Intel Corp., Hillsboro, Oreg., 1978-81, chmn. strategic planning, 1981-82, gen. mgr., 1983-88; pres., exec. dir., bd. dirs. Oreg. Advanced Computing Inst., Beaverton, 1988-90; strategic bus. mgr. INTEL Corp., Hillsboro, Oreg., 1990-92, gen. mgr. bus. multimedia products, 1992-93, bus. area mgr., 1993-94, dir. internat. mktg., 1995-99; pres. Bhagwan Enterprises LLC, 2000—. Spkr. to high tech. industry, Oreg., 1988—; mem. organizing com. Distributed Memory Computing Conf., 1989—90, gen. chmn., 1990—91; chmn. computer tech. adv. bd. Oreg. Mus. Sci. and Industry, 1991—93; bd. advisors NSF (SBIR), Wellpartner; bd. dirs. SnapNames, Passport Online; mem. Portland Venture Group; mem. selection com. Portland Angel Network, 2002—. Cons. Oreg. Econ. Devel. Dept., 1988-91; bd. dirs. St. Mary's Acad., Portland, 1989-92. Mem. Am. Electronics Assn. (higher edn. com. Oreg. chpt. 1989-90, exec. com. 1990). Avocations: electronics, photography, tennis, art. Home: 13940 NW Harvest Ln Portland OR 97229-3653 E-mail: sbhagwan@att.net.

BHARTIA, PRAKASH, defense research management executive, educator; b. Calcutta, West Bengal, India, Jan. 6, 1944; arrived in Can., 1967, arrived in US, 2003, permanent resident, 2004; s. Benarshi Prasad and Bhagwati Devi (Chirimar) B.; m. Savitri Kanhai, Apr. 27, 1971; children: Sanjay Manish, Anil Manoj. B in Tech. with honors, Indian Inst. Tech., Bombay, 1966; MSc, U. Man., Winnipeg, Can., 1968, PhD, 1971. Assoc. prof. U. Regina, Sask., Canada, 1976, asst. dean Sask., 1975-77; def. scientist, chief R&D br. Nat. Defence, Ottawa, Ont., Canada, 1977—; head navigation sect. Defence Rsch. Establishment Ottawa, 1981-85; dir. R&D air Defence Hdqrs., Govt. of Can., Ottawa, 1985-86; dir. R&D commnications and space Nat. Defence, Govt. of Can., 1986-89; dir. sonar div. Defence Rsch. Establishment Atlantic, Halifax, 1989-91; dir. radar div. Defence Rsch. Establishment Ottawa, 1991—; chief Defence Rsch. Establishment Atlantic, 1992-97; dir.-gen. Def. Rsch. Establishment, Ottawa, 1997—2003; exec. v.p. Natel Engring. Co. Inc., Chatsworth, Calif., 2004—. Adj. prof. U. Ottawa, 1977-96, Daltech, 1997—; dir. Can. Microelectronics Centre, Kingston, 1986-88; mem. elec. engring. grant selection com. Natural Scis. and Engring. Rsch. Coun., Ottawa, 1990—, chmn. ind. chair evaluation com., Victoria, 1991; bd. dirs. Tradex Investment Funds, Ottawa, Canadian Ctr. Marine Communication. Author: Microstrip Antennas, 1980, Millimeter Wave Engineering and Applications, 1984, E Plane Integrated Circuits, 1987, Millimeter Wave Microstrip and Printed Circuit Antennas, 1990; author, editor: Microwave Solid State Circuit Design, 1988, Microstrip Lines and Slotlines, 1996, RF and Microwave Coupled Line Circuits, 1999, Microstrip Antenna Design Handbook, 2000; patentee in field. Mem. engring. adv. com. Queen's U., Kingston, 1989-92, chmn. bd., 1992. Decorated Order of Canada; recipient Queen's Golden Jubilee Medal. Fellow: IEEE, Can. Acad. Engrs., Royal Soc. of Can., Instn. Elec. and Telecomm. Engrs.; mem.: India Soc. Engrs., Eng. Inst. Can. Hindu. Home: 21026 Schoenborn St Canoga Park CA 91304 Office: Natel Engring Co Inc 9340 Owensmouth Ave Chatsworth CA 91311 Home Phone: 818-349-9617; Office Phone: 818-734-6511. Personal E-mail: bhartiaprakash@hotmail.com. Business E-Mail: pbhartia@natelengr.com.

BHATIA, PETER K., editor, journalist; b. Pullman, Wash., May 22, 1953; s. Vishnu N. and Ursula Jean (Dawson) B.; m. Elizabeth M. Dahl, Sept. 27, 1981; children: Megan Jean, Jay Peter. BA, Stanford U., 1975. Polit. reporter, asst. news editor Spokesman Rev., Spokane, Wash., 1975-77; news editor Dallas Times Herald, 1980-81; asst. news editor San Francisco Examiner, 1977-80, news editor, 1981-85, dep. mng. editor/news, 1985-87; mng. editor Dallas Times Herald, 1987-88; editor York Dispatch, York, Pa., 1988-89; mng. editor The Sacramento Bee, 1989-93; exec. editor The Fresno Bee, 1993; mng. editor The Oregonian, Portland, 1993-97, exec. editor, 1997—. Pulitzer Prize juror, 1992-93, 98-99; pres. Accrediting Coun. on Edn. in Journalism and Mass Comm., 2007—; bd. dirs. Am. Press Inst. Mem. adv. bd. Murrow Sch. Communication Wash. State U.; mem. new media adv. bd. Oreg. State U.; bd. chmn. Albertina Kerr Ctrs. for Children, 2001—02, found. chair, 2004—05; chmn. bd. St. John Fisher Sch., 2000—04; bd. trustees Jesuit HS, Portland, 2007—, St. Andrew Nativity Sch., Portland, 2007—. Mem.: Investigative Reporters and Editors, South Asian Journalists Assn. (Hall of Fame 2007), Nat. Assn. Minority Media Execs., Asian Am. Journalists Assn. (Journalism award 2007), AP Mng. Editors (bd. dirs. 1991—97), Am. Soc. Newspaper Editors (bd. dirs. 1997—, treas. 2000—01, sec. 2001—02, v.p. 2002—03, pres. 2003—04, chair awards bd. 2006), Stanford U. Alumni Assn. (bd. dirs. 1998—2001), Theta Delta Chi, Sigma Delta Chi. Office: The Oregonian 1320 SW Broadway Portland OR 97201-3499 Home Phone: 503-293-1006; Office Phone: 503-221-8393. Business E-Mail: pbhatia@news.oregonian.com.

BHAUMIK, MANI LAL, physicist; b. Calcutta, India, Jan. 5, 1932; came to U.S., 1959, naturalized, 1968; s. Gunadhar and Lolita (Pramanik) B. BS, U. Calcutta, 1951, MS, 1953; PhD, Indian Inst. Tech., 1958, DSc (hon.), 1995. Fellow UCLA, 1959—63; with Xerox Electro-Optical Sys., Pasadena, Calif., 1961—67, Northrop Corp. Labs., Hawthorne, Calif., 1968—71, dir. rsch., 1971—75; mgr. Laser Tech. Lab., Northrop Rsch. and Tech. Ctr., 1976—84, sr. staff scientist, 1984—86. Lectr. physics Calif. State U., Long Beach, 1967-69. Contbr. articles to profl. jours.; author: Code Name GOD, 2005, The Cosmic Detective, 2008; creator (animated TV series) Cosmic Quantum Ray. Fellow Am. Phys. Soc., IEEE. Achievements include patents in field. Office: Laser Tech Lab PO Box 24050 Los Angeles CA 90024-0050

BIAGI, RICHARD CHARLES, retail executive, real estate consultant; b. Crockett, Calif., Aug. 29, 1925; s. Louis Joseph and Angelina Antonette (Gambaro) B.; m. Emily Annette Gino, Aug. 7, 1949 (dec.); children: Sharon A. Biagi Juhnke, Sandra A. Biagi Ogden; m. Alice C. Mulder, Nov. 26, 1995. BSBA, U. Calif., Berkeley, 1950, cert. in real estate, 1956. Real estate analyst Safeway Stores inc., Oakland, Calif., 1953-58; real estate negotiator Lucky Stores Inc., San Leandro, Calif., 1958-60, div. real estate mgr., 1960-62, mgr. corp. real estate, v.p. corp. real estate mgr. Dublin, Calif., 1963-86; cons. real estate Alamo, Calif., 1986—. Served with USNR, 1943-46, PTO. Mem. Internat. Council Shopping Ctrs. (trustee 1971-76), U. Calif. Bus. Adminstrn. Alumni Assn. (pres. 1970), Calif. Bus. Properties Assn. (bd. dirs. 1972-92), Toastmasters (pres. San Leandro club 1959). Avocations: photography, bicycling, golf. Home (Winter): 75-335 St Andrews Ct Indian Wells CA 92210-7656

BIALOSKY, MARSHALL HOWARD, composer; b. Oct. 30, 1923; Student, Converse Coll., 1942-43, 46, Colo. Coll., 1948; MusB cum laude, Syracuse U., 1949; MusM, Northwestern U., 1950. Asst. prof. music Milton (Wis.) Coll., 1950-54; asst. condr. Milton Coll. Band, 1954; asst. prof. humanities and music U. Chgo., 1956-61; assoc. prof. music and humanities, condr. chorale SUNY, Stony Brook, 1961-64; prof., chmn. dept. fine arts Calif. State U., Dominguez Hills, 1964-77, founding chmn. dept. music, 1977-78, prof. dept. music, 1978-86, prof. emeritus dept. music, 1986—. Mem. Calif. State Coll. Employee Assn. Statewide Acad. Coun., 1968-71; mem. Calif. State Coll. Internat. Program Acad. Coun. and Exec. Com., 1967-73; bd. dirs. Monday Evening Concerts, L.A., 1966-77; dir. Saturday Conservatory Music, L.A. chpt., 1967-71; coord. humanities MA program Calif. State U., Dominguez Hills; composer-in-residence Chamber Music Conf. and Composer's Forum of the East, Bennington Coll., 1989. Performer various cities, radio stas. and schs; composer piano music including An Album for the Young, Five Western Scenes, mixed chorus including American Names, A Sight in Camp in the Daybreak Gray and Dim, Women's Chorus including American Poets Suite, At Last, Vocal Music including Two Songs to Poems of Howard Nemerov, folk songs, spirituals, Christmas music, music for wind instruments, string instruments, brass instruments, guitar and percussion instruments. Contbr. articles to jours. Fulbright award, 1954-56; Wurlitzer Found. grantee, 1979, N.Y.C. Meet-the-Composer grantee, 1984, 86; recipient Career Achievement award Profl. Fraternity Assn. Am., 1980. Mem. ASCAP (creative grant award 1976—), Coll. Music Soc., Am. Soc. Univ. Composers (nat. chmn. 1974-77), Nat. Assn. Composers U.S.A. (pres. 1978—), Soc. Composers Inc., Am. Assn. Choral Condr. Office: Nat Assoc Composer USA PO Box 49256 Los Angeles CA 90049-0256

BIANCHINI, GINA L., Internet company executive; b. 1972; BA in Polit. Sci., Stanford U., 1994, MBA. With CKS Group, Goldman Sachs & Co.; co-founder, pres. Harmonic Comm. (sold to Dentsu); co-founder, CEO Ning, Palo Alto, Calif., 2004—. Named one of 50 Who Matter Now, Business 2.0, 2007, Most Influential Women in Technology, Fast Company, 2009. Office: Ning Inc 735 Emerson St Palo Alto CA 94301-2411

BIANCO, JAMES A., research and development executive; b. Bronx, NY, July 26, 1956; married; 3 children. BS cum laude with honors, NYU, 1979; MD, Mt. Sinai Sch. of Medicine, 1983. Intern, then resident Mt. Sinai Med. Ctr., NYC, 1983-87; fellow in oncology U. Wash., Seattle, 1987-91, asst. prof. medicine, 1991-92; dir. bone marrow transplant program VA Med. Ctr., Seattle, 1990-92; asst. mem. Fred Hutchinson Cancer Rsch. Ctr., Seattle, 1991-92; pres., CEO Cell Therapeutics, Inc., Seattle, 1992—. Spkr. in field. Recipient Corp. Visionary award, Gilda's Club, Seattle, 2006. Mem. Alpha Omega Alpha. Achievements include profile in Bus. Week Mag., 2006. Avocations: cooking, guitar. Office: Cell Therapeutics Inc Cti 501 Elliott Ave W # 400 Seattle WA 98119-3908

BICE, SCOTT HAAS, dean, law educator; b. LA, Mar. 19, 1943; s. Fred Haas and Virginia M. (Scott) B.; m. Barbara Franks, Dec. 21, 1968. BS, U. So. Calif., 1965, JD, 1968. Bar: Calif. 1971. Law clk. to Chief Justice Earl Warren, 1968-69; asst. prof., assoc. prof., prof. law U. So. Calif., Los Angeles, 1969—, assoc. dean, 1971-74, dean Law Sch., 1980-2000, Carl Mason Franklin prof., 1983-2000, Robert C. Packard prof. law, 2000—; CEO Five B Investment Co., 1995—. Vis. prof. polit. sci. Calif. Inst. Tech., 1977; vis. prof. U. Va., 1978-79; bd.dirs. Western Mut. Ins. Co., Residence Mut. Ins. Co., Imagine Films Entertainment Co., Jenny Craig, Inc., Arena Pharms., Inc. Mem. editl. adv. bd. Calif. Lawyer, 1989-93; contbr. articles to law jours. Bd. dirs. LA Family Housing Corp., 1989-93, Stone Soup Child Care Programs, 1988—, LA Child Guidance Clinic, 2003; trustee Bice Passavant Found., 2000-, trustee Sigma Phi Epsilon Ednl. Foun., 2006-. Affiliated scholar Am. Bar Found., 1972-74. Fellow Am. Bar Found. (life); mem. Am. Law Inst. (life), Calif. Bar, Los Angeles County Bar Assn., Am. Law Deans Assn. (pres. 1997-99), Calif. Club, Chancery Club (treas. 2001-02, sec. 2002-03, v.p. 2003-04, pres. 2004-05), Econ. Roundtable, Twilight Club, Catalina Island Yacht Club (judge adv. 2002-07). Home: 787 S San Rafael Ave Pasadena CA 91105-2326 Office: Univ So Calif Sch Law Los Angeles CA 90089-0071 Home Phone: 626-441-2432; Office Phone: 213-740-4549. Business E-Mail: sbice@law.usc.edu.

BICHSEL, HANS, physicist, consultant, researcher; b. Basel, Switzerland, Sept. 2, 1924; came to U.S., 1951; s. Paul and Anna Maria Bichsel; m. Sue O. Greenwalt, Sept. 12, 1959; children: Elizabeth Christine, Joseph Oliver. MA, PhD, U. Basel, 1951. Rsch. asst. Princeton (N.J.) U., 1951-55; rsch. assoc. Rice U., Houston, 1955-57; asst. prof. physics U. Wash., Seattle, 1957-59; affiliate prof. physics U. Wash., Seattle, 1992—; assoc. prof., prof. radiology U. Wash., Seattle, 1969-80; asst. prof., assoc. prof. physics U. So. Calif., LA, 1959-68; assoc. prof. U. Calif., Berkeley, 1968-69. Cons. Internat. Commn. on Radiation Units, Bethesda, Md., 1970—, Los Alamos (N.Mex.) Nat. Lab., 1978-83, IAEA, Vienna, Austria, 1990—; vis. scientist Nat. Inst. Radiol., Scis., Chiba, Japan, 1991-96, U. Sherbrooke Med. Sch., Que., Can.; rschr. Relativistic Heavy Ion Collider, Brookhaven Nat. Lab., 1999—; referee Phys. Rev., Nuclear Instruments and Methods, Physics in Medicine and Biology, also others. Contbr. articles to profl. jours. Fellow Am. Phys. Soc.; mem. Swiss Phys. Soc. Achievements include research in heavy ion radiation therapy and statistics of interactions of radiations with matter. Home and Office: 1211 22nd Ave E Seattle WA 98112-3534 Home Phone: 206-329-2792; Office Phone: 206-543-4054. Personal E-mail: hbichsel@scientist.com. Business E-Mail: hbichsel@u.washinst.edu.

BICKART, THEODORE ALBERT, university president emeritus; b. NYC, Aug. 25, 1935; s. Theodore Roosevelt and Edna Catherine (Pink) B.; m. Carol Florence Nichols, June 14, 1958 (div. Dec. 1973); children: Karl Jeffrey, Lauren Spencer; m. Frani W. Rudolph, Aug. 14, 1982; 1 stepchild, Jennifer Anne Cumming. B Engring. Sci., Johns Hopkins U., 1957, MS, 1958, DEng, 1960; D Univ. (hon.), Dneprodzerzhinst State Tech. U, Ukraine, 1996. Asst. prof. elec. and computer engring. Syracuse (N.Y.) U., 1963-65, assoc. prof., 1965-70, prof., 1970-89, assoc. to vice chancellor for acad. affairs for computer resources devel., 1983-85, dean L.C. Smith Coll. Engring., 1984-89; prof. elec. engring., dean engring. Mich. State U., East Lansing, 1989-98; pres. Colo. Sch. Mines, Golden, 1998-2000. Vis. scholar U. Calif., Berkeley, 1977; Fulbright lectr. Kiev Poly Inst., USSR, 1981; vis. lectr. Nanjing Inst. Tech., China, 1981; hon. disting. prof. Taganrog Radio Engring. Inst., Russia, 1992—; fellow Accreditation Bd. for Engring. and Tch., Engring. Accreditation Commn., exec. com., 1998-2000; chmn. Engring. Workforce Commn., 1996-98; elected-mem. Johns Hopkins U. Soc. Scholars, 2001. Co-author: Electrical Network Theory, 1969, Linear Network Theory, 1981; contbr. numerous articles to profl. jours. Served to 1st lt. U.S. Army, 1961-63 Recipient numerous rsch. grants. Fellow IEEE (best paper awards Syracuse sect. 1969, 70, 73, 74, 77, chmn. com. on engring. accreditation activities 1996-98, bd. ednl. activities 1999, chmn. accreditation policy coun. 2001-2003, Meritorious Achievement award 2006, Meritorious Svc. citation 2006), Am. Soc. Engring. Edn. (v.p. 1997-99); mem. Am. Math. Soc., Assn. for Computing Machinery, Soc. for Indsl. and Applied Math., N.Y. Acad. Scis., Ukrainian Acad. Engring. Scis.), Internat. Higher Edn. Acad. Scis. (Russia), Internat. Acad. Informatics (Russia), Johns Hopkins U. Soc. Scholars., Johns Hopkins U. Alumni Assn. (Disting. Alumnus award), ABET (fellow) Avocations: bicycling, hiking, gardening, woodworking, model building. Home: 541 Wyoming Cir Golden CO 80403-0900 Home Phone: 303-277-0125. Personal E-mail: tabickart@comcast.net. Business E-Mail: tbickart@mines.edu.

BICKEL, PETER JOHN, statistician, retired educator; b. Bucharest, Romania, Sept. 21, 1940; arrived in U.S., 1957, naturalized, 1964; s. Eliezer and P. Madeleine (Moscovici) B.; m. Nancy Kramer, Mar. 2, 1964; children: Amanda, Stephen. AB, U. Calif., Berkeley, 1960, MA, 1961, PhD, 1963; PhD (hon.), Hebrew U. Jerusalem, 1988. Asst. prof. stats. U. Calif., Berkeley, 1964-67, assoc. prof., 1967-70, prof., 1970—2006, chmn. dept. stats., 1976-79, dean phys. scis., 1980-86, chmn. dept. stats., 1993-97; prof. emeritus, 2006. Vis. lectr. math. Imperial Coll., London, 1965-66; fellow J.S. Guggenheim Meml. Found., 1970-71, J.D. and Catherine T. MacArthur Found., 1984-89; NATO sr. sci. fellow, 1974; chmn. com. on applied and theoretical stats. NRC, 1998-2000, mem. bd. on math. scis., 2000—, chmn., 2000-03; chmn. sci. adv. coun. Stats. and Applied Math. Inst., NSF. Author: (with K. Doksum) Mathematical Statistics, 1976, 2d edit., 2000, (with C. Klaassen, Y. Ritov and J. Wellner) Efficient and Adaptive Estimation in Semiparametric Models, 1993; assoc. editor Annals of Math. Stats., 1968-76, 86-93, PNAS, 1996—2000, Bernouilli, 1996—, Statistica Sinica, 1996—2003; contbr. articles to profl. jours. Decorated comdr. Order Orange Nassau (Netherlands);J.D. and Catherine T. MacArthur Found. fellow, 1984-89. Fellow AAAS (chair sect. U 1996-97), Inst. Math. Stats. (pres. 1980), Am. Statis. Assn.; mem. NAS, Royal Statis. Soc., Internat. Statis. Inst., Am. Acad. Arts and Scis., Royal Netherlands Acad. Arts and Scis., Bernoulli Soc. (pres. 1990). Office: U Calif Dept Stats Evans Hall Berkeley CA 94720 Home Phone: 510-526-4055; Office Phone: 510-642-1381. Business E-Mail: bickel@stat.berkeley.edu.

BIDLACK, WAYNE ROSS, nutritional biochemist, toxicologist, food scientist; b. Waverly, NY, Aug. 12, 1944; s. Andrew L. Bidlack and Vivian Pearl Cowles Williams; m. Wei Wang. BS, Pa. State U., 1966; MS, Iowa State U., 1968; PhD, U. Calif., Davis, 1972. Postdoctoral fellow dept. pharmacology U. So. Calif., LA, 1972-74, asst prof. sch. medicine, 1974-80, assoc. prof., 1980-92, prof., 1992—, asst. dean student affairs, 1988-91, chmn. dept. pharmacology and nutrition, 1991-92; chmn. dept. food sci. and human nutrition Iowa State U., Ames, 1992-95; dean Coll. Agr. Calif. State Poly. U., Pomona, 1995—2007, prof. dept. human nutrition and food sci., 2007—. Assoc. editor Biochem. Medicine and Metabolic Biology, 1986-87; mem. editl. bd. Jour. Am. Coll. Nutrition, 1995—, Environ. Nutritional Interactions, 1996-2000, Toxicology, 2000-04. Chmn. Greater L.A. Nutrition Coun., 1982-83, So. Calif. Inst. Food Technologists, 1988-89, Toxicology and Safety Evaluation divsn. Inst. Food Technologists, 1989-90, food sci. communicator, 1986-90; chmn. Nat. Coun. Against Health Fraud, 1983-85; expert panel on foods and nutrition, 1989-93. Recipient Outstanding Tchr. Award, U. So. Calif. Sch. Medicine, 1987-88, Meritorious Svc. award Calif. Dietetic Assn., 1990, Disting. Achievement award So. Calif. Inst. Food Technologists, 1990, Bautzer Faculty award Calif. State U., 1998; fellow Inst. Food Technologists, 1998, Wang Family award Calif. State U., 2002. Mem. Soc. Toxicology (chair awards com. food safety sect. 1993-94, chair 1994-95), Calif. State Bd. Food and Agr., Nat. Golden Key Soc. (hon.), Gamma Sigma Delta. Republican. Avocations: golf, book collecting. Office: Calif State Polytech U Coll of Agrl 3801 W Temple Ave Pomona CA 91768-2557 Business E-Mail: wrbidlack@csupomona.edu.

BIDWILL, WILLIAM V., professional sports team executive; s. Charles W. and Violet Bidwill; m. Nancy Bidwill; children: William Jr., Michael, Patrick, Timothy, Nicole. Grad., Georgetown U. V.p. Ariz. Cardinals (formerly St. Louis Cardinals Football Team), co-owner, 1962-72, owner, 1972—, also chmn., 1972—, pres. Mem. NFL Broadcasting Com., NFL Bus. Ventures Com. Bd. trustees Bert Bell/Pete Rozelle Player Benefit Plan. Office: Ariz Cardinals PO Box 888 Phoenix AZ 85001-0888

BIELER, CHARLES LINFORD, zoo executive director emeritus, former development director; b. East Greenville, Pa., May 19, 1935; s. Frederick William and Emma May (Freed) B.; m. Judith L. Goodwin, Feb. 23, 1963; children: Stewart, Beatriz, Christina. BA, Gettysburg Coll., 1957. Dir. tng. Gen. Motors Corp., 1962-69; mem. staff Zool. Soc. San Diego, 1969—, exec. asst. to dir., 1972-73, dir., 1973-85, dir. devel., 1987—. Bd. dirs. San Diego Conv. and Visitors Bur., 1983-88, vice chmn., 1988, chmn., 1989. Bd. dirs. Mercy Hosp. Corp., 1988—. With U.S. Army, 1957-62. Recipient Gettysburg Coll. Disting. Alumni award, 1984 Fellow Am. Assn. Zool. Parks and Aquariums (pres. 1983-84) Home: 1915 Sunset Blvd San Diego CA 92103-1545 Office: San Diego Zoo PO Box 551 San Diego CA 92112-0551

BIENENSTOCK, ARTHUR IRWIN, physicist, educator, federal official; b. NYC, Mar. 20, 1935; s. Leo and Lena (Senator) Bienenstock; m. Roslyn Doris Goldberg, Apr. 14, 1957; children: Eric Lawrence, Amy Elizabeth(dec.), Adam Paul. BS, Poly. Inst. Bklyn., 1955, MS, 1957; PhD, Harvard U., 1962; PhD (hon.), Poly. U., 1998, Lund U., 2006. Asst. prof. Harvard U., Cambridge, Mass., 1963—67; mem. faculty Stanford (Calif.) U., 1967—, prof. applied physics, 1972—, vice provost faculty affairs, 1972—77, dir. synchrotron radiation lab., 1978—97, dir. Lab. for Advanced Materials, 2002—03, vice provost, dean rsch. and grad. policy, 2003—06, spl. asst. to the pres., 2006—; assoc. dir. sci. Office of Sci. and Tech. Policy, Washington, 1997—2001. Mem. U.S. Nat. Com. Crystallography, 1983—88; mem. sci. adv. com. European Synchrotron Radiation Facility, 1988—90, 1993—96; mem. com. condensed matter and materials physics NRC, 1996—97, mem. bd. chem. scis. and techs., 2001—03. Contbr. scientific papers to profl. jours. Bd. dirs. Calif. chpt. Cystic Fibrosis Rsch. Found., 1970—73, mem. pres.'s adv. coun., 1980—82; trustee Cystic Fibrosis Found., 1982—88. Recipient Sidhu award, Pitts. Diffraction Soc., 1968, Disting. Alumnus award, Poly. Inst. N.Y., 1977; NSF fellow, 1962—63. Fellow: AAAS, Am. Phys. Soc. (gen. councilor 1993—96, v.p. 2006, pres. elect 2007—, pres. 2008); mem.: Materials Rsch. Soc., Am. Crystallographic Assn. Jewish. Home: 967 Mears Ct Stanford CA 94305 Office: Bldg 160 Rm 223 Stanford CA 94305-2205 Office Phone: 650-723-8845. Business E-Mail: arthurb@stanford.edu.

BIENIAWSKI, ZDZISLAW TADEUSZ RICHARD, engineering educator, writer, consultant; b. Cracow, Poland, Oct. 1, 1936; came to U.S., 1978, naturalized; m. Elizabeth Hyslop, 1964; 3 children. Student, Gdansk Tech. U., Poland, 1954—58; BS in Mech. Engring., U. Witwatersrand, Johannesburg, South Africa, 1961, MS in Engring. Mechanics, 1963; PhD in Rock Engring., U. Pretoria, South Africa, 1968; DEng (hon.), U. Madrid, 2001. Prof. mineral engring. Pa. State U., Univ. Park, 1977—96, prof. sci., tech. & society, 1994-96, prof. emeritus, 1996—; pres. Bieniawski Design Enterprises, Prescott, Ariz., 1996—; Disting. prof. geol. engring. U. Madrid, Spain, 2001—. Vis. prof. U. Karlsruhe, Germany, 1972, Stanford U., 1985, Harvard U., 1990, Cambridge (Eng.) U., 1997; chmn. U.S. Nat. Com. on Tunneling Tech., 1984-85; U.S. rep. to Internat. Tunnel Assn., 1984-85. Author: Rock Mechanics Design in Mining and Tunneling, 1984, Strata Control in Mineral Engineering, 1987, Aiming High-A Collection of Essays, 1988, Engineering Rock Mass Classifications, 1989, A Tale of Three Continents, 1991, Design Methodology in Rock Engineering, 1992, Gaudeamus Igitur Poems, 1997, Alec's Journey, 1999, Beasts in the Onion Leaves and Renaissance Dialogues, 2006; editor: Tunneling in Rock, 1974, Exploration for Rock Engineering, 1976, Milestones in Rock Engring., 1996; contbr. over 200 articles to profl. jours. Recipient Mayor's Proclamation of City of State Coll. Bieniawski Day, 1983, Rock Mechanics Rsch. award, 1984, Disting. Toastmaster Internat. award, 1974; Bieniawski Auditorium at U. Madrid Sch. Mines named in his honor, 2003. Avocations: genealogy, cosmology, foreign policy. Home: The Ranch 3023 Sunnybrae Cir Prescott AZ 86303-5770

BIERBAUM, J. ARMIN, petroleum company executive, consultant; b. Oak Park, Ill., June 29, 1924; s. Armin Walter and Harriett Cornelia (Backmann) B.; m. Janith Turnbull, Apr. 17, 1948; children: Steve, Todd, Charles, Peter, Mark. BS, Northwestern U., 1945, MS, 1948. Project engr. Am. Oil Co., Ind., 1948-53; sales engr. Universal Oil Products Co., Des Plaines, Ill., 1953-56; tech. dir. Nat. Coop. Refinery Assn., McPherson, Kans., 1956-58; asst. plant mgr., treas., v.p., dir. Gen. Carbon & Chem. Corp., Robinson, Ill., 1958-61; cons. Williston, ND, 1962-64; v.p. ops. Midland Coops., Inc., Mpls., 1964-72; sr. v.p. ops. Tosco Corp., Los Angeles, 1972-77; pres., chief exec. officer Gary Energy Co., Englewood, Colo., 1977-79, U.S. Ethanol Corp., Englewood, 1979-82; cons., 1983—. Served with USNR, 1942-45. Mem. Am. Inst. Chem. Engrs., Sigma Xi, Phi Epsilon Pi. Office: 1609 Ridgecrest Dr Loveland CO 80537-9073

BIERBAUM, JANITH MARIE, artist; b. Evanston, Ill., Jan. 14, 1927; d. Gerald Percy and Lillian (Sullivan) Turnbull; m. J. Armin Bierbaum, Apr. 17, 1948; children: Steve, Todd, Chad, Peter, Mark. BA, Northwestern U., 1948; student, Mpls. Art Inst., 1964; postgrad., St. Paul Art Inst., 1969-70. Rsch. asst. AMA, Chgo., 1948-49; tchr. Chgo. high schs., 1949-51; freelance artist Larkspur, Colo., 1951—. Exhibited in group shows at Foot Hills Art Ctr., 1985, 86, 87, Palmer Lake (Colo.) Art Assn., 1986-87, 88-89, Gov.'s Mansion, Bismarck, N.D., 1960; oil painting appeared in 1989 Women in Art Nat. calendar pub. by AAUW. Recipient 1st Place Purchase award, U. Minn., Mpls., 1966, Coors Classic award, Coors Beer, Golden, Colo., 1987. Mem.: Colo. Artist Assn. Republican. Avocations: cross country skiing, swimming, hiking. Home and Office: 1609 Ridgecrest Dr Loveland CO 80537-9073

BIERSTEDT, PETER RICHARD, entertainment industry consultant, lawyer; b. Rhinebeck, NY, Jan. 2, 1943; s. Robert Henry and Betty Bierstedt; m. Carol Lynn Akiyama, Aug. 23, 1980 (div. Oct. 1995); m. Lieschen van Straaten, Aug. 11, 2000. AB, Columbia U., 1965, JD cum laude, 1969; cert., U. Sorbonne, Paris, 1966. Bar: N.Y. 1969, Calif. 1977, U.S. Supreme Ct. 1973. Atty. with firms in, NYC, 1969-74; pvt. practice cons. legal and entertainment industry, 1971, 75-76, 88—; with Avco Embassy Pictures Corp., LA, 1977-83, v.p., gen. counsel, 1978-80, sr. v.p., 1980-83, dir., 1981-83; gen. counsel New World Entertainment (formerly New World Pictures), LA, 1984-87, exec. v.p., 1985-87, sr. exec. v.p. Office of Chmn., 1987-88, also bd. dirs.; pres. subs. New World Prodns. and New World Advt. New World Pictures, 1985-88. Guest lectr. U. Calif., Riverside, 1976-77, U. So. Calif., 1986, 91, UCLA, 1987, 95-96; bd. dirs. New World Pictures (Australia) Ltd., FilmDallas Pictures, Inc., Cinedco, Inc. Exec. prodr. (home video series) The Comic Book Greats. Mem. Motion Picture Assn. Am. (dir. 1980-83), Acad. Motion Picture Arts and Scis. (exec. br.), LA Copyright Soc., ACLU. Democrat. Avocations: astronomy, literature, tennis, scuba diving. Office Phone: 323-667-2698. Business E-Mail: peter@bierstedt.com.

BIETER, DAVID H., Mayor, Boise, Idaho; m. Julia Bieter. BA in Internat. Studies cum laude, U. St. Thomas, St. Paul, 1982; JD, U. Idaho Coll. Law, Moscow, 1986. Bar: US Dist. Ct. Idaho 1986. Civil counsel Bonner County, Sandpoint; civil prosecuting atty., land-use specialist Ada County, Boise, 1989—99; mem. Idaho House of Reps., 1999—2004; mayor City of Boise, Idaho, 2004—. Ex-officio mem. Downtown Bus. Assn.; mem. Social Action Com. Catholic Charities; founder Boise Basque Choir; bd. mem. Basque Ctr., Basque Charities. Recipient Am. Jurisprudence award for labor law, Univ. Idaho Coll. Law. Office: 150 North Capitol Blvd Boise ID 83702 Mailing: PO Box 500 Boise ID 83701-0500 Office Phone: 208-384-4404, 208-384-4422. Office Fax: 208-384-4420. Business E-Mail: mayor@cityofboise.org.*

BIG BOI, See PATTON, ANTWAN

BIGELOW, MARGARET ELIZABETH BARR (M.E. BARR), retired botany educator; b. Elkhorn, Man., Can., Apr. 16, 1923; d. David Hunter and Mary Irene (Parr) Barr; m. Howard Elson Bigelow, June 9, 1956 (dec.). BA with honors, U. B.C., Vancouver, Can., 1950, MA, 1952; PhD, U. Mich., 1956. Rsch. attaché U. Montreal, Que., Can., 1956-57; instr. U. Mass., Amherst, 1957-65, asst. prof., 1965-71, assoc. prof., 1971-76, prof., 1976-89, prof. emerita, 1989—. Author: Diaporthales in N.A., 1978, Prodromus to Loculoascomycetes, 1987, Prodromus to Nonlichenized Members of Class Hymenoascomycetes, 1990; contbr. articles to profl. jours. With Can. Women's Army Corps, 1942—46. Mem. Mycol. Soc. Am. (v.p. to pres. 1980-82, editor 1975-80, Disting. Mycologist Award, 1993), Brit. Mycol. Soc., Am. Inst. Biol. Sci. (gen. chmn. ann. meeting 1986). Avocations: gardening, reading. Home and Office: 9475 Inverness Rd Sidney BC Canada V8L 5G8

BIGELOW, MICHAEL, film director, visual effects expert; BA, UCLA, 1982. With Dream Quest Images, Simi Valley, Calif., 1982—, tech. dir. comml. div., 1985-87, supr. motion control feature div., supr. visual effects. Comml. dir. Dept. Econ. Devel. Commonwealth of Va., 1988, also Leo/Burnett Advt. Agy. Works include: (commls.) Dodge Daytona Billboard, GE Achievement in Space, Black and Decker Hands (Clio award), Polaroid Worlds, Journey; (film features) The Fly, Nightmare on Elm Street III, Michael Jackson's Moonwalker (Smooth Criminal), Warlock, Predator, Short Circuit II, Nightmare on Elm Street IV: The Dream Master, Earth Girls are Easy, Real Men, The Abyss, Total Recall, Warlock, Deuce Bigelow: European Gigilo, 2005.

BIGGART, NICOLE WOOLSEY, dean; m. James Biggart; 1 child, Scott. BA, Simmons Coll., 1969; MA, U. Calif., Davis, 1977; PhD, U. Calif., Berkeley, 1981. Asst. prof. adminstrn. and sociology U. Calif., Davis, 1981—87, assoc. prof. mgmt. and sociology, 1987—90, prof., 1991—2002; Jerome J. and Elsie Suran chair in tech. mgmt. Grad. Sch. Mgmt., U. Calif., Davis, 2002—, dean, 2003—. Adv. bd. Sloan Found. social sci. rsch. coun. program on corp. as social instn., 1999—; mem. editl. bd. Orgn.: The Interdisciplinary Jour. of Orgn., Theory, and Soc., 1993—, Calif. Mgmt. Rev., 1993—. Co-author: (books) Governor Reagan, Governor Brown: Sociology of Executive Power, 1984, Enhancing Organizational Performance, 1997, The Changing Nature of Work, 1999; author: Charismatic Capitalism: Direct Selling Organizations in America, 1989; editor: Economic Sociology: A Reader, 2001. Mem.: Macro-Orgnl. Behavior Soc.

BIGGER, DAROLD F., religious studies educator; m. Barbara Bigger; children: Shannon (dec.), Hilary Catlett. BA in Theology, Walla Walla Coll., 1966, MSW, 1995; MDiv cum laude, Andrews U., 1970; PhD in Theology and Personality, Claremont Sch. Theology, 1978. Pastor Crestline (Calif.) Ch., La Sierra Univ. Ch., Riverside, Calif.; sr. pastor Walla Walla (Wash.) Coll. Ch., 1980-93, mem. religion and social work faculties, 1993, prof. religion, prof. social work. Rear adm. USNR. Disting. Svc. medal

BIGGS, ANDY, state legislator; m. Cindy Biggs; 6 children. B in Asian Studies, Brigham Young U.; MA in Polit. Sci., Ariz. State U.; JD, U. Ariz. Bar: Ariz., Wash., NM. Retired atty.; mem. Dist. 22 Ariz. House of Reps., 2003—, chair transp. & infrastructure com., vice-chair appropriations com., mem. ways & means com. Named #1 Friend of Taxpayer, Ariz. Fedn. Taxpayers; named a Friend of Liberty, Goldwater Inst. Republican. Office: Ariz House Reps Capitol Complex 1700 W Washington Rm 312 Phoenix AZ 85007 Office Phone: 602-926-4371. Office Fax: 602-417-3022. Business E-Mail: abiggs@azleg.gov.

BIGGS, JASON, actor; b. Pompton Plains, NJ, May 12, 1978; s. Gary and Angela Biggs; m. Jenny Mollen, Apr. 23, 2008. Student, NYU, Montclair State U. Actor: (films) Conversations With My Fahter, 1991, The Boy Who Cried Bitch, 1991, American Pie, 1999, Boys and Girls, 2000, Loser, 2000, Saving Silverman, 2001, American Pie 2, 2001, Prozac Nation, 2001, American Wedding, 2003, Jersey Girl, 2004, Guy X, 2005, Eight Below, 2006, Over Her Dead Body, 2008, My Best Friend's Girl, 2008; (TV series) Drexell's Class, 1991, As the World Turns, 1994—95; (Broadway plays) The Graduate, 2002. Office: c/o SFM 1122 S Robertson # 15 Los Angeles CA 90035

BILBRAY, BRIAN PATRICK, United States Representative from California; b. Coronado, Calif., Jan. 28, 1951; m. Karen Walker; children: Briana, Kristen, Patrick, Scott, Shannon. Grad., Southwestern Coll. Coun. mem. City of Imperial Beach, Calif., 1976—78, mayor Calif., 1978—84; mem. San Diego County Bd. Supervisors, 1984—94, US Congress from 49th Calif. dist., Washington, 1994—2000; mem US Congress from 50th Calif. dist., Washington, 2006—, mem. oversight & govt. reform com., sci. & tech. com. Co-chair nat. bd. advs. Fedn. Am. Immigration Reform; bd. dirs. San Diego Assn. Govts.; chair Criminal Justice Coun., San Diego Trolley Bd.; founder, pres. San Deigo Coun. on Literacy. Republican. Roman Catholic. Avocations: sailing, surfing, horseback riding. Office: US Ho Reps 2350 Rayburn Ho Office Bldg Washington DC 20515-0550

BILBRAY, JAMES HUBERT, Former United States Representative from Nevada, lawyer, consultant; b. Las Vegas, Nev., May 19, 1938; s. James A. and Ann E. (Miller) B.; m. Michaelene Mercer, Jan. 1960; children: Bridget, Kevin, Erin, Shannon Student, Brigham Young U.,

1957—58, U. Nev., Las Vegas, 1958—60; BA, Am. U., 1962; JD, Washington Coll. Law, 1964; D of Laws (hon.), U Nev. Las Vegas, 2001. Bar: Nev. 1965. Staff mem. Senator Howard Cannon U.S. Senate, 1960-64; dep. dist. atty. Clark County, Nev., 1965-68; mem. Lovell, Bilbray & Potter, Las Vegas, 1969-87, Nev. Senate, 1980-86, chmn. taxation com., 1983-86, chmn. interim com. on pub. broadcasting, 1983; mem. 100th-103rd Congresses from 1st Nev. dist., 1987-95; mem. fgn. affairs com., 1987-88; mem. house armed svs. com., mem. small bus. com., chmn. procurement, taxation and tourism subcom., 1989-95; ptnr. Alcalde & Fay, Arlington, Va., 1995; of counsel Kummer Kaempfer Bonner Renshaw & Ferrario, Las Vegas. Mem. subcoms. Africa, trade exports and tourism, select com. on intelligence, 1993-95; alt. mcpl. judge City of Las Vegas, 1987-89; del. North Atlantic Alliance, 1989-95; bd. visitors U.S. Mil. Acad., West Point, 1995-99, vice chmn., 1996-97; mem. adv. bd. Ex-Import Bank U.S., 1996-97; mem. adv. com. U.S. Nat. Security Policy, 2000-01; mem. Calif. Nev. High Speed Train Commn., 2005 Base Closing and Realignment Commn. Mem. bd. regents U. Nev. Sys., 1968—72; mem. Nat. Coun. State Govts. Commn. on Arts and Historic Preservation; mem. bd. visitors USAF Acad., 1991—93; mem. U.S. Nat. Security Policy Bd. Adv. Com., 2000—01, Calif. Nev. High Speed Train Commn., Base Closing and Rearmament Commn., Dem. Nat. Com., 1996—; Nev. chmn. Kerry for Pres., 2004; mem. Calif.-Nev. High Speed Train Commn., 2005—, US Base Closing Commn., 2005; mem. bd. govs. US Postal Svc., 2006—. Named Outstanding Alumnus U. Nev., Las Vegas, 1979, Man of Yr. Am. Diabetes Assn., 1989, Man of Yr. Haddassah (Nev.), 1990 Mem. Nev. State Bar Assn., Clark County Bar Assn., U. Nev.-Las Vegas Alumni Assn. (pres. 1964-69, Humanitarian of Yr. 1984), Rotary, Phi Alpha Delta, Sigma Chi, KC. Democrat. Roman Catholic. Office Phone: 702-792-7000.

BILGINSOY, CIHAN, economics professor; arrived in U.S., 1977; s. Sadi and Raika Bilginsoy; m. Gunseli Berik; children: Alev, Mehmet. BS, Mid. East Tech. U., Ankara, 1976; MS, U. Minn., 1979; PhD, U. Mass., 1986. Prof. econ. U. Utah, Salt Lake City, 1993—. Contbr. articles to profl. jours. Office: U Utah Dept Econ 1645 Central Campus Dr Room 308 Salt Lake City UT 84112 Office Fax: 801-585-5649. Business E-Mail: bilginsoy@economics.utah.edu.

BILLS, ROBERT HOWARD, political party executive; b. North Conway, NH, Jan. 13, 1944; s. Howard William and Mary Catherine (Jackson) B.; m. Donna Gail Florian; children: Emily Ida, Katherine Mary. Staff writer Weekly People Newspaper, Bklyn., 1970-74, Palo Alto, Calif., 1974-76; nat. sec. Socialist Labor Party, Sunnyvale, 1980—, mem. nat. exec. subcom., 1976-79. Office: Socialist Labor Party of Am PO Box 218 Mountain View CA 94042-0218 Home Phone: 650-969-4838. Business E-Mail: socialists@slp.org.

BILLUPS, CHAUNCEY, professional basketball player; b. Denver, Sept. 25, 1976; m. Piper Riley; children: Cydney, Ciara, Cenaya. Attended, U. Colo., Boulder, 1995—97. Guard Boston Celtics, 1997, Toronto Raptors, 1997-98, Denver Nuggets, 1998-00, 2008—, Minn. Timberwolves, Mpls., 2000—02, Detroit Pistons, 2002—08. Mem. US Sr. Men's Nat. Basketball Team, 2007. Recipient Gold medal, FIBA Americas Championship, 2007; named NBA Finals MVP, 2004; named to Ea. Conf. All-Star Team, NBA, 2006—08, We. Conf. All-Star Team, 2009. Achievements include being a member of the NBA Championship winning Detroit Pistons, 2004. Avocation: music. Office: Denver Nuggets 1000 Chopper Cir Denver CO 80204*

BING, STEVE, film producer; b. Mar. 31, 1965; s. Peter S. and Helen Bing; 1 child, Damien. Writer (films) Missing in Action, 1984, Missing in Action 2: The Beginning, 1985, Kangaroo Jack, 2003, (TV series) Married...With Children, 1987—97; prodr.: (films) Without Charlie, 2001, Night at the Golden Eagle, 2002, The Big Bounce, 2004; exec. prodr.: Get Carter, 2000; actor: The Dark Backward, 1991. Named one of 50 Most Powerful People in Hollywood, Premiere mag., 2005. Address: 1801 Avenue of the Stars #150 Los Angeles CA 90067

BINGAMAN, JEFF (JESSE FRANCIS BINGAMAN JR.), United States Senator from New Mexico; b. El Paso, Tex., Oct. 3, 1943; s. Jesse and Beth (Ball) B.; m. Anne Kovacovich, Sept. 13, 1968, 1 child. BA in Govt., Harvard U., 1965; JD, Stanford U., 1968; LittD (hon.), N.Mex.State U., 2008. Bar: N.Mex. 1968. Atty. Stephenson, Campbell & Olmsted, 1971-72; ptnr. Campbell, Bingaman & Black, Santa Fe, 1972-78; asst. atty. gen. State of N.Mex., 1969, atty. gen., 1979—82; US Senator from N.Mex., 1983—; chmn. US Senate Energy & Nat. Resources Com., 2001, 2001—03, 2007—; mem. US Senate Fin. Com., US Senate Health, Edn. Labor & Pensions Com., Joint Econ. Com. Served with USAR, 1968—74. Recipient Disting. Svc. award, Am. Dietetic Assn., 1997, Pub. Servant Outstanding award Excellence, 3Com Corp. & Consortium for Sch. Networking, 2000, Public Svc. award, Am. Chem. Soc., 2001, Congressional award, Small Bus. Coun. Am., 2001, Public Svc. award, Am. Assn. Public Health Dentistry, 2002, Capitol Dome award, Am. Cancer Soc., 2003, Outstanding Lifetime Achievement award, Friends of Nat. Inst. Dental and Craniofacial Rsch., 2003, Excellence in Public Svc. award, Am. Acad. Pediatrics, 2004, Joseph F. Boyle award for Disting. Pub. Svc., Am. Coll. Physicians, 2004, Disting. Cmty. Health Champion award, Nat. Assn. Cmty. Health Centers, 2005. Democrat. Meth. Office: US Senate 703 Hart Senate Bldg Washington DC 20510-0001 also: District Office Ste 101 119 East Marcy Santa Fe NM 87501 Office Phone: 202-224-5521, 505-988-6647. Office Fax: 202-224-2852. E-mail: senator_bingaman@bingaman.senate.gov.*

BINGHAM, H. RAYMOND, computer software company executive; b. Heber City, Utah, Oct. 18, 1945; s. Lyman Dunbar and Thora (Murdock) B.; m. Kristin Bernadine Allgood, Oct. 10, 1968; children: Ashley Dare, Derrick, Raymond, Erin Sloan, Adam Jay, Christopher Brian. BS, Weber State College, 1970; MBA, Harvard U., 1972. V.p. N_REN Internat., Peutie, Belgium, 1975-80; asst. treas. Marriott Corp., Bethesda, Md., 1980-81; mng. dir. Agrico Overseas Investment, Tulsa, Okla., 1981-85; exec. v.p., chief fin. officer Red Lion Hotels & Inns, Vancouver, Wash., 1985-93, Cadence Design Systems, Inc., San Jose, Calif., 1993-99, pres., CEO, 1999—. Bd. dirs. WTD Industries Inc., Portland. Bd. dirs. Oreg. Pub. Broadcasting Found., Portland, 1989—, Oreg. Symphony Assn., Portland, 1989—; mem. Harvard Bus. Sch. Assn. Oreg., Portland, 1985—. Mem. Urban Land Inst., Nat. Realty Inst., Fin. Execs. Inst. Republican. Mem. Lds Ch. Avocations: tennis, running, skiing. Home: 1 Bridal Ln Woodside CA 94062-2599 Office: Cadence Design Systems 2655 Seely Ave Bldg 5 San Jose CA 95134-1931

BINNIE, NANCY CATHERINE, retired nurse, educator; b. Sioux Falls, SD, Jan. 28, 1937; d. Edward Grant and Jessie May (Martini) Larkin; m. Charles H. Binnie. Diploma, St. Joseph's Hosp. Sch. Nursing, Phoenix, 1965; BS in Nursing, Ariz. State U., 1970, MA, 1974. Intensive care charge nurse Scottsdale (Ariz.) Meml. Hosp., 1968-70, coordinator critical care, 1970-71, John C. Lincoln Hosp., Phoenix, 1971-73; prof. nursing GateWay Community Coll., Phoenix, 1974-96; ret., 1996. Coord. part-time evening nursing programs Gateway Community Coll., 1984-97, interim dir. nursing, 1989, 91. Mem. Orgn. Advancement of Assoc. Degree Nursing, Practical and Assoc. Coun. Nursing Educators, Ariz. Coun. Nurse Educators. Avocations: gardening, golf, sewing. Personal E-mail: nbinnie@msn.com.

BINTLIFF, BARBARA ANN, library director, law educator; b. Houston, Jan. 14, 1953; d. Donald Richard and Frances Arlene (Appling) Hay; m. Byron A. Boville, Aug. 20, 1977 (dec. 2006); children: Bradley, Bruce. BA in Political Sci. with hon., Cen. Wash. U., Ellensburg, 1975; JD, U. Wash., Seattle, 1978, MLL, 1979. Bar: Wash. 1979, U.S. Dist. Ct. (ea. dist.) Wash. 1980, Colo. 1983, U.S. Dist. Ct. Colo. 1983. Atty., libr. Gaddis and Fox, Seattle, 1978-79; reference libr. U. Denver Law Sch., 1979-84; assoc. libr., sr. instr. Sch. Law U. Colo., Boulder, 1984-88, assoc. prof., libr. dir., 1989—2001, prof., dir. Law Libr., 2001—, Nicholas Rosenbaum prof. law, 2002—. Legal cons. Nat. Ctr. Atmospheric Rsch., Environ. and Societal Impacts Group, Boulder, 1980; vis. prof. U. Wash., Seattle, 1996, chair U. Colo. Boulder, Faculty Assembly, 2003-05. Co-author: Colorado Legal Resources: An Annotated Bibliography, 2004; co-editor, Public Services in Law Libraries: Evolution and Innovation in the 21st Century, 2007; editor: A Representative Sample of Tenure Documents for Law Librarians, 1988, 2nd edit., 1994, Chapter Presidents' Handbook, 1989, Representatives Handbook, 1990, Marketing Toolkit for Academic Law Libraries, 2004; assoc. editor: Legal Reference Svcs. Quarterly, Perspectives: Teaching Legal Research and Writing; co-editor: Public Services in the 21st Century Evolution and Innovation, 2007; contbr. articles to profl. jours. Recipient Boulder Faculty Assembly Excellence Svc. award, 2001, Calhoun Svc. award, U. Colo., 2002; named Disting. Alumnus, Ctrl. Wash. U., 2000. Mem. Am. Assn. Law Librs. (v.p./pres.-elect 2000-01, pres. 2001-02; Frederick Charles Hicks award 2005, Presdl. citation 2006, Spectrum article of Yr. 2007), Am. Law Inst. (elected), Colo. Assn. Law Librs. (pres. 1982), Southwestern Assn. Law Librs. (pres. 1987-88, 91-92). Episcopalian. Office: U Colo Law Sch 2450 Kittredge Loop Dr Rm 424 Boulder CO 80309-0402 Business E-Mail: barbara.bintliff@colorado.edu.

BIONDI, FRANK J., JR., entertainment company executive; b. NYC, Jan. 9, 1945; s. Frank J. and Virginia (Willis) B.; m. Carol Oughton, Mar. 16, 1974; children: Anne, Jane. BA, Princeton U., 1966; MBA, Harvard U., 1968. Assoc.-corp. fin. Shearson Lehman, Inc., NYC, 1970-71, Prudential Securities, NYC, 1969; prin. Frank J. Biondi Jr. & Assocs., NYC, 1972; dir. bus. analysis Teleprompter Corp., NYC, 1972-73; asst. treas., assoc. dir. bus. affairs Children's TV Workshop, NYC, 1974-78; dir. entertainment program planning Home Box Office, Inc., NYC, 1978, v.p. programming ops., 1979-82, exec. v.p. planning & adminstrn., 1982-83, pres., CEO, 1983, chmn., CEO, 1984; exec. v.p. entertainment bus. sector The Coca-Cola Co., 1985; chmn., CEO, Coca-Cola TV, 1986; pres., CEO Viacom Inc, NYC, 1987-96; chmn., CEO Universal Studios, Inc., Universal City, Calif., 1996-98; pres. Biondi Reiss Capital Mgmt., NYC, 1998—99; sr. mng. dir. WaterView Advisors LLC, Santa Monica, Calif., 1999—. Bd. dirs. The Bank of N.Y., 1995-2007, The Bank of NY Mellon, 2007-, Seagram Co. Ltd., Vail Resorts, Inc., USA Network Inc, Amgen, Inc., 2002-, Hasbro Inc., 2002-, Harrah's Entertainment, Cablevision Systems, 2005-, Seagate Technology, 2006-, Yahoo! Inc., 2008- Bd. dirs. Leake-Watts Svcs., Yonkers, N.Y., 1975, Mus. TV and Radio, N.Y.C., Claremont Grad. U., Princeton U. Mem. Princeton of N.Y. Club, Edgartown Yacht Club, Game Creek Club (Vail, Colo.).

BIRCH, MICHAEL, Internet company executive, application developer; b. 1970; m. Xochi Birch; 2 children. Attended, Imperial Coll. London, 1988—91. Co-founder BirthdayAlarm.com, 2001, Ringo-.com, 2003; co-founder, CEO Bebo Inc., San Francisco, 2005—. Spkr. in field. Office: Bebo, Inc 6th Fl 795 Folsom St San Francisco CA 94107

BIRCH, TOBEYLYNN, librarian; BA in Psychology, U. Calif.-Santa Cruz, 1972; MA in Librarianship, U. Denver, 1976. Acquisitions asst. UCLA, 1976—79; asst. libr. Calif. Sch. Profl. Psychology, LA, 1980—81, dir. libr., 1981; libr. Alliant Internat. U., Alhambra, Calif., 2001—04, systemwide dir. lib. svcs., 2004—. Mem. bd. dir. Statewide Calif. Elec. Libr. Consortium (SCELC), 2003—. Mem.: ALA (sec. Libr. Instrn. Roundtable 1985—86, v.p. 1987—87, pres. 1988—89), Assn. Mental Health Librs., Calif. Acad. and Rsch. Libr., Beta Phi Mu. Office: Alliant Internat U 1000 S Fremont Ave Unit 5 Alhambra CA 91803 Business E-Mail: tbirch@alliant.edu.

BIRD, ANDY, film company executive; BA with honors, U. Newcastle Upon Tyne, Eng., 1985. Breakfast show prodr. Piccadilly Radio, Manchester, England; with Music Box Virgin Broadcasting Co., London, head programming Radio Radio; various radio and TV positions, 1989—94; head Unique TV Unique Broadcasting, 1992; sr. v.p., gen. mgr. Turner Entertainment Networks Ltd. Time Warner, 1994—2000, pres. TBS Internat., 2000—04; pres. Walt Disney Internat., Burbank, Calif., 2004—. Office: Walt Disney Co 500 S Buena Vista St Burbank CA 91521-0001

BIRD, BRAD (PHILLIP BRADLEY BIRD), film director, writer, animator; b. Kalispell, Mont., Sept. 11, 1957; m. Elizabeth Canney; 3 children. With Walt Disney Co.; dir., screenwriter Warner Bros.; dir. Pixar Animation Studios, 2000—. Animator: (films) The Fox and the Hound, 1981; The Plague Dogs, 1982; writer Batteries Not Included, 1987; dir., writer The Iron Giant, 1999; dir., writer, actor (voice) The Incredibles, 2004 (Academy award for best animated feature film of yr., 2005); Ratatouille, 2007 (Best Screenplay, Boston Soc. Film Critics, 2007, Best Animated Film, Producers Guild Am., 2008, Best Animated Film, Brit. Acad. Film and TV Arts, 2008, Acad. award for Best Animated Feature Film, 2008); writer, dir. Jack-Jack Attack, 2005; exec. cons.: (TV films) The Simpsons Christmas Special, 1989; dir.: Do the Bartman, 1990; dir., writer, animation prodr.: (TV series) Amazing Stories, 1985; dir., exec. cons. The Simpsons, 1989; writer, creator Family Dog, 1993; exec. cons. The Critic, 1994; King of the Hill, 1997; exec. prodr.: The Making of The Incredibles, 2005, Vowellet: An Essay by Sarah Vowell, 2005, Mr. Incredible and Pals, 2005, One-Man Band, 2005, More Making of The Incredibles, 2005. Named one of 50 Smartest People in Hollywood, Entertainment Weekly, 2007. Office: Pixar Animation Studios 1200 Park Ave Emeryville CA 94608

BIRD, DAVID R., lawyer; b. June 7, 1949; BS, Brigham Young U., 1973, JD, 1977. Bar: Utah 1977, U.S. Ct. Appeals (10th Cir.) 1978, U.S. Dist. Ct. (Dist. Utah) 1977, U.S. Supreme Ct. 1987. Atty., shareholder environ., energy and natural resources dept. Parsons, Behle & Latimer, Salt Lake City. Spkr. in field. Co-author: Utah Environmental and Land Use Permits and Approval Manual, 1980, Brownfields Law and Practice, 2003, others. Bd. dirs. Utah Found.; trustee Barrick Mercer Gold Mine Found.; mem. workers compensation adv. coun. Labor Commn.; mem. environ. adv. coun. Salt Lake Valley Health Dept.; past chair legis. affairs com. Salt Lake Area C. of C. Mem.: ABA, Utah State Bar (mem. legis. affairs com. 1979—2001, chmn. water com. 1981—83, environ. law com. 1983—85, energy and natural resources sect. 1988—89, pres.-elect 2004, jud. coun., pres. 2005), Utah Mfrs. Assn. (mem. legis. com., environ. com.), Utah Mining Assn. (exec. com., tax com., environment com.), Boy Scouts Am., Phi Kappa Phi. Office: Parsons Behle & Latimer One Utah Ctr 201 S Main St Ste 1800 PO Box 45898 Salt Lake City UT 84145-0898 Office Phone: 801-532-1234. Office Fax: 801-536-6111. E-mail: dbird@pblutah.com.

BIRD, FORREST M., retired medical inventor; b. Stoughton, Mass., June 9, 1921; MD, PhD, ScD. Technical air tng. officer Army Air Corps; founder Bird Corp., Bird Space Tech. Corp., Sandpoint, Idaho. Trustee emeritus Am. Respiratory Care Found. Inventor Bird Universal Medical Respirator for acute or chronic cardiopulmonary care, 1958, "Babybird" respirator, 1970. Inductee Nat. Inventors Hall of Fame, 1995. Avocation: collector & pilot of 18 vintage flying aircraft. Office: Bird Space Tech Corp PO Box 817 Sandpoint ID 83864-0817

BIRD, LEWIS L., III, apparel executive; Fin. mgmt. position BayBanks, Inc., Ford Motor Co., AlliedSignal Inc., dir. bus. analysis and planning, 1998—99; v.p. fin. and ops. Gateway, Inc., 1999—2001; CFO Old Navy divsn. Gap Inc., 2001—03, COO North Am. divsn., 2003—05, exec. v.p. new bus. devel., 2005—06; pres. subsidiaries Nike, Inc., Beaverton, Oreg., 2006—. Office: Nike Inc One Bowerman Dr Beaverton OR 97005-6453 Office Phone: 503-671-6453.

BIRD, SUE (SUZANNE BRIGIT BIRD), professional basketball player; b. Syosset, NY, Oct. 16, 1980; d. Herschel and Nancy Bird. Grad. in Comm. Sci., U. Conn., 2002. Guard Seattle Storm, 2002—. Mem. USA Basketball Women's Sr. Nat. Team, 2002, Athens, Greece, 04, Beijing, 08. Recipient Wade Trophy, 2002, ESPY award, Best Female Coll. Athlete, ESPN, 2002, Honda award, Women's Coll. Basketball Player of Yr., 2002, Gold medal, FIBA World Championships, 2002, Gold medal, women's basketball, Athens Olympic Games, 2004, Beijing Olympic Games, 2008; named Naismith Player of Yr., 2002, AP Player of Yr., 2002; named to All-WNBA First Team, 2002, 2003, 2005, WNBA Western Conf. All-Star Team, 2002, 2003, 2007. Achievements include being a member of the NCAA Division 1 National Championship Team, University of Connecticut Huskies, 2000, 02; selected as the number 1 overall pick in the 2002 WNBA Draft. Office: Seattle Storm 351 Elliott Ave W Ste 500 Seattle WA 98119

BIRD, TERRY W., lawyer; b. LA, Feb. 11, 1946; BA, Stanford U., Calif., 1967; JD, UCLA, 1970. Bar: Calif. 1970. Law clk. Calif. Ct. Appeals (2nd dist.), 1970—72; asst. US atty., 1972—77; prin. atty. Bird, Marella, Boxer, Wolpert, Nessim, Drooks & Lincenberg, LA. Mem. 9th Cir. Jud. Conf. Magistrates Adv. Com., 1988—91, 9th Cir. Exec. Com., 1989—93, 9th Cir. Gender Bias Task Force, 1991—94, 9th Cir. Adv. Bd., 2002—05. Mem.: Am. Coll. Trial Lawyers, Inns of Ct. (pres. complex litig. 1993—94), Assn. Bus. Trial Lawyers (bd. dirs. 1991—93), LA County Bar Assn. (chmn. fed. cts. com. 1991—95), ABA (mem. white collar crime com.). Office: Bird Marella Boxer Wolpert Nessim Drooks & Lincenberg PC 23rd Fl 1875 Century Pk E Los Angeles CA 90067-2561 Office Phone: 310-201-2100. Office Fax: 310-201-2110.

BIRDSALL, CHARLES KENNEDY, electrical engineer; b. NYC, Nov. 19, 1925; s. Charles and Irene Birdsall; m. Betty Jean Hansen, 1949 (dec.); children: Elizabeth(dec.), Anne(dec.), Barbara, Thomas, John; m. Virginia Pletcher, Aug. 21, 1981. BS, U. Mich., Ann Arbor, 1946, MS, 1948; PhD, Stanford U., Calif., 1951. Various microwave amplifier projects Hughes Aircraft Co., Culver City, Calif., 1951—55; leader GE Microwave Lab., Electron Physics Group, Palo Alto, Calif., 1955-59; prof. elec. engring. U. Calif., Berkeley, 1959-91; prof. U. Calif., Grad. Sch., Berkeley, 1994—. Founder Plasma Theory and Simulation Group, 1967—; founder, chmn. Energy and Resources Group, 1972—74; cons. on fusion simulations Lawrence Livermore Lab. of U. Calif., 1960—86; prof. Miller Inst. Basic Rsch. in Sci., 1963—64; sr. vis. fellow U. Reading, England, 1976; rsch. assoc. Inst. Plasma Physics Nagoya (Japan) U., 1981; co-founder Nagoya (Japan) U., Undergrad. Program Computational Engring. Sci, 2000; Chevron vis. prof. energy Calif. Inst. Tech., 1982; area coord. phys. electronics/bioelectronics, 1984—86; lectr. Plasma Sch. Internat. Ctr. for Theoretical Physics, Trieste, Italy, 1985—99; vis. prof. Inst. Plasma Physics, Nagoya U., Fusion Theory joint U.S.-Japan, 2002, Gunma U., Kiryu, Japan, 2003; Intergovtl. Personnel Act AirForce Rsch. Lab., Albuquerque, 2002—. Author: (with W.B. Bridges) Electron Dynamics of Diode Regions, 1966, (with A.B. Langdon) Plasma Physics via Computer Simulation, 1985, 91, 93, 2002, 2005, (with S. Kuhn) Bounded Plasmas, 4 vols., 1994. With USNR, 1944—46. U.S.-Japan Coop. Sci. Program grantee, 1966-67; Fulbright grantee U. Innsbruck, 1991; recipient Berkeley Citation, 1991; first recipient (with A.B. Langdon) of Dawson award for pioneering plasma simulation, 2003. Fellow IEEE (1st recipient Plasma Sci. and Applications award June 1988), AAAS, Am. Phys. Soc.; mem. Plasma Theory and Simulation Group, Energy and Resourses Group, Internat. Ctr. for Theoretical Physics, Inst. Plasma Physics, Sigma Xi, Tau Beta Pi, Eta Kappa Nu. Achievements include being the co-originator many-particle plasma simulations in two and three dimensions using cloud-in-cell/particle-in-cell methods, 1966; holder 24 patents. Office: U Calif EECS Dept Cory Hall Berkeley CA 94720-1770 Office Phone: 510-643-6631. Business E-Mail: birdsall@eecs.berkeley.edu.

BIRGENEAU, ROBERT JOSEPH, academic administrator, physicist, researcher; b. Toronto, Ont., Can., Mar. 25, 1942; arrived in US, 1963; s. Peter Duffus and Isobel Theresa (Meehan) B.; m. Mary Catherine Ware, June 20, 1964; children: Michael, Catherine, Patricia, Michelle. BSc, U. Toronto, 1963; PhD in physics, Yale U., 1966. Vis. tchr. Benedict Coll., Columbia, SC, summer 1965; instr. dept. engring.

and applied sci. Yale U., New Haven, 1966-67; Nat. Research Council Can. postdoctoral fellow Oxford U., England, 1967-68; mem. tech. staff Bell Labs, Murray Hill, NJ, 1968-74, research head scattering and low energy, physics dept., 1975; guest sr. physicist Brookhaven Nat. Lab., Upton, NY, 1968—; vis. scientist RisNational Lab., Roskilde, Denmark, 1971, 79; prof. physics MIT, Cambridge, 1975—2000, Cecil and Ida Green prof. physics, 1982—2000, assoc. dir. Rsch. Lab. of Electronics, 1983-86, head solid state, atomic and plasma physics, 1987-88, head dept. physics, 1988-91, dean Sch. Sci., 1991-2000; pres., prof. physics U. Toronto, 2000—04; chancellor U. Calif., Berkeley, 2004—. Cons. Bell Labs., 1977-80, IBM Rsch. Labs., Yorktown Heights, NY, 1980-83, Sandia Nat. Labs., Albuquerque, 1985-92; mem. steering com. Panel on Neutron Scattering, NAS, 1977, mem. exec. com. Major Materials Facilities Com., 1984; co-chmn. Gordon Conf. on Quantum Solids and Fluids, 1979, Gordon Conf. on Condensed Matter Physics, 1986; mem. external adv. com. physics divsn. Los Alamos Nat. Lab, 1982-86; mem. policy and adv. bd. Cornell High Energy Synchrotron Source, 1980-84, chmn., 1983-84; mem. rev. panel on neutron scattering Dept. Energy, 1980, 82, mem. Basic Energy Sciences Adv. Com., 1991-94, chair Panel on Rsch. Reactors, 1996, Panel on Synchrotron Radiation Sources & Sci., 1997; mem. materials rsch. adv. com. NSF, 1989-90; mem. adv. coun. NEC Rsch. Inst., 1995-2000; mem. sci. policy com. Lawrence Berkeley Nat. Lab., 1997-2000; co-chair Polaroid Sci. and Tech. Bd., 1998-2001; mem. external adv. com. physics dept., Oxford U., 2000-; chair. vis. com. ETH Domain, Switzerland, 2002; mem. DOE Task Force on the Future of Sci. Programs, 2003. Contbr. articles to profl. jours.; assoc. editor for condensed matter physics, Physical Review Letters, 1980-83; mem. editorial bd. Physical Review B, 1987-89. Trustee Associated Univs., Inc., 1990-97, Boston Mus. Sci., 1992-2001, Brookhaven Sci. Assocs., 1997-2000, Univ. Health Network, 2000-, Royal Ont. Mus., 2000-, United Way Greater Toronto Campaign Cabinet, 2000-, Univs. Rsch. Assn., Inc., 2000-; bd. govs. Argonne Nat. Lab., 1992-2001; mem. physics fellow selection com. Sloan Found., 1995-2001; bd. dirs. St. Michael's Hosp., 2000-04. Recipient Yale Sci. and Engring. Alumni Achievement Award, 1981, Wilbur Lucius Cross Medal, Yale U., 1986, Bertram Eurgene Warren Award, Am. Crystal Assn., 1988, Magnetism Award, Internat. Union Pure and Applied Physics, 1997, Academic Leadership Award, Carnegie Corp. of NY, 2008; named 48th Richtmyer Meml. lectr, Am. Assn. Physics Tchrs., 1989, A.W. Scott lectr., Cambridge U., 2000. Fellow AAAS (exec. coun. 1992-94), Am. Phys. Soc. (Oliver E. Buckley prize com. 1981, 90-2001, Oliver E. Buckley Prize for Condensed Matter Physics 1987, Julius E. Lilienfeld award 2000), Am. Acad. Arts Sci. (membership com. 1989-92, Founders award 2006), Royal Soc. London, Royal Soc. Can, Inst. Physics; mem. NAS (fgn. assoc., 2004), Am. Philos. Soc. Roman Catholic. Avocations: landscaping, squash, basketball. Office: U Calif Office Chancellor 200 Calif Hall Berkeley CA 94720 Office Phone: 510-642-7464. E-mail: chancellor@berkeley.edu.

BIRK, DAVID R., lawyer, electronics executive; b. Altoona, Pa., 1947; m. Wilma Birk; children: Caitlin, Whitney, Leah, Carrie. BA, U. Fla., Gainesville, 1969; JD, Cornell U., Ithaca, NY, 1972. Bar: NY 1973. Assoc. Jacobs, Persinger & Parker, NYC, 1974-77; ptnr. Burstein & Marcus, White Plains, NY, 1977-80; sr. atty. Avnet, Inc., Great Neck, NY, 1980-89, gen. counsel, 1989—, sr. v.p., 1992—, corp. sec., 1997—. Bd. dirs. UAP Holding Corp., Greeley, Colo., 2007—. 1st lt. US Army, 1972—74. Named one of The State's 10 Most Influential Lawyers, Ariz. Bus. mag. Mem. NY State Bar (mem. corr. law com.), Assn. of Bar of City of NY (mem. profl. discipline com.). Avocation: rowing. Office: Avnet Inc 2211 S 47th St Phoenix AZ 85034-6403 Office Phone: 480-643-2000. E-mail: david.birk@avnet.com.

BIRK, IAN, lawyer; b. Seattle, Sept. 22, 1978; BA summa cum laude, Univ. Wash., 1997, JD, 2001. Bar: Wash. 2001. Assoc. atty. Keller Rohrback LLP, Seattle, Wash., 2001—. Contbr. articles to numerous profl. jours. Named Seattle Rising Star, SuperLawyer Mag., 2006. Mem.: ABA, Wash. Bar Assn. Office: Keller Rohrback LLP Ste 3200 1201 Third Ave Seattle WA 98101-3052

BIRKELBACH, ALBERT OTTMAR, retired oil industry executive; b. Oak Park, Ill., Feb. 22, 1927; s. August and Ann B.; m. Shirley M. Spandet, Aug. 21, 1948; children: J.A., Lisa M., Grace L. Birkelbach Boland, Ann C. Birkelbach. BSCh.E., U. Ill., 1949. Various engring., supervisory and mgmt. positions Globe Oil & Refining Co., Lemont, Ill., 1949-53, Anderson Prichard Oil Corp., Cyril, Okla., 1953-58, Signal Oil & Gas Co., Los Angeles, 1958-64; mng. dir. Raffinerie Belge de Petroles, Antwerp, Belgium, 1964-74; v.p. Occidental Petroleum Corp., London, Eng., 1972-74; cons. in field, 1974-75; pres. ATC Petroleum Inc., NYC, 1975-81, also dir.; pres. Amorient Petroleum Corp., Laguna Niguel, Calif., 1981-84; mgmt. cons., 1984-87. Served with USCG, 1945-47. Decorated knight Order Leopold Belgium). Home: 33957 N 66th Way Scottsdale AZ 85262 Address: 33957 N 66th Way Scottsdale AZ 85262-7231

BIRMINGHAM, RICHARD JOSEPH, lawyer; b. Seattle, Feb. 26, 1953; s. Joseph E. and Anita (Loomis) B. BA cum laude, Wash. State U., 1975; JD, Seattle U., 1978; LLM in Taxation, Boston U., 1980. Bar: Wash. 1978, Oreg. 1981, U.S. Dist. Ct. (we. dist.) Wash. 1978, U.S. Tax Ct. 1981. Ptnr. Davis Wright Tremaine, Seattle, 1982-93, 2008—; shareholder Birmingham Thorson & Barnett, P.C., Seattle, 1993—2008. Mem. King County Bar Employee Benefit Com., Seattle, 1986, U.S. Treasury ad hoc com. employee benefits, 1988—. Contbg. editor: Compensation and Benefits Mgmt., 1985—; contbr. articles to profl. jours. Mem. ABA (employee benefits and exec. compensation com. 1982—), Wash. State Bar Assn. (speaker 1984-86, tax sect. 1982—), Oreg. State Bar Assn. (tax sect. 1982—), Western Pension Conf. (speaker 1986), Seattle Pension Round table. Democrat. Avocations: jogging, bicycling, photography. Home: 3820 49th Ave NE Seattle WA 98105-5234 Office: Davis Wright Tremaine Ste 2200 1201 3rd Ave Seattle WA 98101 Business E-Mail: RBirmingham@BTBPC.com, richbirmingham@dwt.com.

BIRNBAUM, MILTON, laser physicist, educator, researcher; b. Bklyn., Nov. 27, 1920; s. Louis and Dora Birnbaum; m. Mildred C. Delott, Nov. 24, 1957; children: Robin Sue, David Michael. AB, Bklyn. Coll., 1942; MS, U. Md., 1948, PhD, 1953. Physicst Naval Rsch. Lab., Washington, 1945-53; asst. prof. physics Poly. Inst. Bklyn., 1955-57, assoc. prof., 1957-61; sr. scientist Aerospace Corp., El Segundo, Calif., 1961-86; rsch. prof. U. So. Calif., LA, 1986—. Mem. IEEE, Am. Phys. Soc.

BIRREN, JAMES EMMETT, research and development company executive; b. Chgo., Apr. 4, 1918; m. Elizabeth S., 1942; children: Barbara Ann, Jeffrey Emmett, Bruce William. Student, Wright Jr. Coll., 1938; BEd, Chgo. State U., 1941; MA, Northwestern U., 1942, PhD, 1947, ScD (hon.), 1985; postgrad., U. Chgo., 1950—51; PhD (hon.), U. Gothenberg, Sweden, 1983; LLD (hon.), St. Thomas U., Can., 1990. Tutorial fellow Northwestern U., 1941—42; rsch. asst. project for study of fatigue Office Sci. Rsch. and Devel., 1942; rsch. fellow NIH, USPHS, 1946—47; rsch. psychologist gerontology unit NIH, 1947—51; rsch. psychologist NIMH, 1951—53, chief sect. on aging, 1953—64; dir. aging program Nat. Inst. Child Health and Human Devel., Bethesda, Md., 1964—65; dir. Gerontology Ctr.; prof. psychology U. So. Calif., 1965—89, Disting. prof. emeritus, 1992—, dean Davis Sch. Gerontology, 1975—86, Brookdale Disting. scholar, 1986—90, dir. Inst. Advanced Study in Gerontology and Geriat., 1981—89; dir. Borun Ctr. Gerontol. Rsch. UCLA, 1989—93, assoc. dir. Ctr. on Aging, 1990—; emeritus prof. and dean gerantology U. Southern Calif., LA. Fellow Ctr. for Advanced Study in Behavioral Scis., Stanford, Calif., 1978-79; Green vis. prof. U. B.C., 1979; vis. scientist Cambridge (Eng.) U., 1960-61; Harold E. Jones meml. lectr. U. Calif., Berkeley, 1965; mem. LA County Bd. Suprs.' Com. on Aging, 1967-69; sr. fellow U. So. Calif. Urban Ecology Inst., 1968-70; mem. Dean's Coun., U. So. Calif., 1970-86; chmn. aging rev. com. Nat. Inst. Aging, 1974-75; program dir. Integration of Info. on Aging: Handbook Project, 1973-76; mem. steering com. Care of Elderly, Inst. of Medicine, 1976-77; bd. dirs. Sears Roebuck Found., 1977-80; chmn. life course prevention rsch. rev. com. NIMH, 1985-87; cons. Roche Seminars on Aging Series, 1980-82. Author: Psychology of Aging, 1964; editor: Handbook of Aging and the Individual, 1959, (with K.W. Schaie) Handbook of the Psychology of Aging, 1996, Encyclopedia of Gerontology, 1996, (with R.B. Sloane) Handbook of Mental Health and Aging, 1992; contbr. articles to books, profl. publs.; bd. collaborators: Gerontologia, 1956-89; asst. editor: Jour. Gerontology, 1956-61, assoc. editor 1961-63, editor-in-chief 1968-74, chmn. publs. com., 1975-78, adv. editl. bd., 1956-69; bd. adv. editors: Devel. Psychobiology, 1967-69; adv. editor: Jour. Human Devel., 1957-58. Mem. adv. com. and del. White House Conf. on Aging, 1995. With USNR, 1943-46; to scientist dir. USPHS Scientist Corps, 1947-65. Recipient award for rsch. on problems of aging CIBA Found., 1956, Stratton award Am. Psychopath. Assn., 1960, Sr. 65er award Dist. 65 Retail Workers and Dept. Store Union, Sr. 65er award AFL-CIO, 1962, medal for meritorious svc. USPHS, 1965, citation Am. Assn. Ret. Persons, 1970, Am. Pioneers in Aging award U. Mich., 1972, commendation for disting. contbns. to field of gerontology Mayor of LA, 1968, 74, Merit award Northwestern U. Alumni Assn., 1976, Creative Scholarship and Rsch. award U. So. Calif., 1979, Disting. Educator award Assn. Gerontology in Higher Edn., 1983, Eminent Svc. award Stovall Found., 1984, award of Distinction Am. Fedn. for Aging Rsch., 1986, Sandoz prize for rsch. on aging, 1989, Can. Assn. Gerontology award, 1990, Disting. Emeritus award U. So. Calif., 1992, Pres.'s award Am. Soc. on Aging, 1996, Disting. Career Contbn. to Gerontology award Gerontol. Soc. Am., 2002, Ollie Randall award Nat. Coun. on Aging, 2004, Hall of Fame award Am. Soc. on Aging, 2004; USPHS rsch. fellow, 1946-47. Fellow AAAS, Am. Geriat. Soc. (founding fellow Western divsn.), Am. Psychol. Assn. (Disting. Sci. Contbn. award 1968, chmn. membership com. 1969, Disting. Contbn. award Divsn. Adult Devel. and Aging 1978, pres. divsn. 1955-56, editor newsletter 1951-55), Gerontol. Soc. (pres. 1961-62, chmn. publs. com. 1974-77, award for meritorious rsch. 1966, Brookdale award 1980); mem. Am. Physiol. Soc., Internat. Assn. Gerontology (chmn. exec. com. 1966-69, chmn. program com. 1968-69), Psychonomic Soc., Western Gerontol. Soc. (dir. 1965-, pres. 1968-69), Golden Key Club, Skull and Dagger Club, Sigma Xi, Phi Kappa Phi. Office: 3640 Dragonfly Dr #208 Thousand Oaks CA 91360

BISCHEL, MARGARET DEMERITT, physician, consultant; b. Moorhead, Minn., Nov. 8, 1933; d. Connie Magnus Nystrom and Harriett Grace (Petersen) Zorner; m. Raymon DeMeritt, 1953 (div. 1958); 1 child, Gregory Raymon; m. John Bischel, 1961 (div. 1964); m. Kenneth Dean Serkes, June 7, 1974. BS, U. Oreg., Eugene, 1962; MD, U. Oreg., Portland, 1965. Diplomate Am. Bd. Internal Medicine, Nat. Bd. Med. Examiners. Resident, straight med. intern Los Angeles County/U. So. Calif. Med. Ctr., 1965-68, NIH fellow nephrology, 1968-70, asst. prof. renal medicine, 1970-74; asst. prof., instr. medicine U. So. Calif., 1968-74; instr. nephrology East L.A. City Coll., 1971-74; dir. med. edn. Luth. Gen. Hosp., Park Ridge, Ill., 1974-78, dir. nephrology sect., 1977-80, pres. med. staff, 1974-88; founding mem., med. dir., dir. med. svcs. Luth. Health Plan, Park Ridge, 1983-87; clin. assoc. prof. medicine Abraham Lincoln Sch. Medicine U. Ill., 1975-80; sr. cons. Parkside Assocs., Inc., Park Ridge, 1986-88; pvt. practice Chgo., 1974-88; physician Buenaventura Med. Clinic, Ventura, Calif., 1989-94, med. dir., 1992-94; prin. Apollo Managed Care Cons., Santa Barbara, Calif., 1988—. Trustee Luth. Health Care System, Park Ridge, 1986-90, Unified Med. Group Assn., Seal Beach, Calif., 1993-94; hon. lifetime staff mem. Luth. Gen. Hosp., Park Ridge; mem. formulary com. HealthNet, 1992-94, med. adv. com. TakeCare, 1993-94, quality assurance com. PacifiCare, 1993-94; mem. doctor's adv. network AMA, 1994-96; JCAHO advisor for behavioral health care providers, 2000—2006. Author: 40 books including Managing Behavioral Healthcare, 2d edit., 2006, 3rd edit., 2007, The Credentialing and Privileges Manual, 2d edit., 2005, 3rd edit., 2007, Medical Review Criteria Guidelines for Managed Care, 8th edit., 2006, 6th edit., 2007, 7the edit. 2008, 8th edit., 2009, Mng. Phys., Occupl., Speech Therapy and Rehab., 6th edit. 2008, 7th edit. 2009; editor: Med. Mgmt. Manual, Managed Care Bull.; Mem. editl. bd. Capitation Mgmt. Report, 1998-2006; contbr. chpts. to books and articles to profl. jours. Fellow: ACP (Calif. Gov.'s advisor 1993—95); mem.: Am. Coll. Physician Execs. Avocations: real estate, gardening. Office: Apollo Managed Care Cons 860 Ladera Ln Santa Barbara CA 93108-1626 Office Phone: 805-969-2606. Personal E-mail: mbischel@cox.net. Business E-Mail: mbischel@apollomanagedcare.com.

BISHOP, C. DIANE, state agency administrator, educator; b. Elmhurst, Ill., Nov. 23, 1943; d. Louis William and Constance Oleta (Mears) B. BS in Maths., U. Ariz., 1965, MS in Maths., MEd in Secondary Edn., 1972. Lic. secondary educator. Tchr. math. Tucson Unified Sch. Dist., 1966-86, mem. curriculum council, 1985-86, mem. maths. curriculum task teams, 1983-86; state supt. of pub. instrn. State of Ariz., 1987-95, gov.'s policy advisor for edn., 1995-97, dir. gov.'s office workforce devel. policy, 1996-2000; asst. dep. dir. Ariz. Dept. Commerce, 1997-2000; exec. dir. Gov.'s Strategic Partnership for Econ. Devel., 1997—2002; pres. The Vandegrift Inst., 2000—06; exec. dir. Maricopa Health Found., 2002—08; headmaster Scottsdale Preparatory Acad., 2008. Mem. assoc. faculty Pima C.C., Tucson, 1974-84; adj. lectr. U. Ariz., 1983, 85; mem. math. scis. edn. bd. NRC, 1987-90, mem. new standards project governing bd., 1991; dir. adv. bd. sci. and engring. ednl. panel, NSF; mem. adv. bd. for arts edn. Nat. Endowment for Arts. Active Ariz. State Bd. Edn., 1984-95, chmn. quality edn. commn., 1986-87, chmn. tchr. crt. subcom., 1984-95, mem. outcomes based edn. adv. com., 1986-87, liaison bd. dirs. essential skills subcom., 1985-87, gifted edn. com. liaison, 1985-87; mem. Ariz. State Bd. Regents, 1987-95, com. on preparing for U. Ariz., 1983, HS task force, 1984-85, bd. Ariz. State Community Coll., 1987-95, Ariz. Joint Legis. Com. on Revenues and Expenditures, 1989, Ariz. Joint Legis. Com. on Goals for Ednl. Excellence, 1987-89, Gov.'s Task Force on Ednl. Reform, 1991, Ariz. Bd. Regents Commn. on Higher Edn., 1992; mem. governing bd. Phoenix Union HS Dist. 2005—; mem. bd. dirs. Great Heart Prep. Acad., 2005-. Woodrow Wilson fellow Princeton U., summer 1984; recipient Presdl. Award for Excellence in Teaching of Maths., 1983, Ariz. Citation of Merit, 1984, Maths. Teaching award Nat. Sci. Research Soc., 1984, Distinction in Edn. award Flinn Found., 1986; named Maths. Tchr. of Yr. Ariz. Council of Engring. and Sci. Assns., 1984, named One of Top Ten Most Influential Persons in Ariz. in Field of Tech., 1998. Mem. AAUW, NEA, Nat. Coun. Tchrs. Math., Coun. Chief State Sch. Officers, Women Execs. in State Govt. (bd. dirs. 1993), Ariz. Assn. Tchrs. Math., Women Maths. Edn., Math. Assn. Am., Ednl. Commn. of the States (steering com.), Nat. Endowment Arts (adv. bd. for arts edn.), Nat. Forum Excellence Edn., Nat. Honors Workshop, Ariz. Bioindustry Assn. (bd. dirs. 1997—2008, sec. 2000—2008), Phi Delta Kappa. Republican.

BISHOP, DAVID, entertainment company executive; b. Camden, NJ, Oct. 23, 1954; s. Byron Benjamin and Doris Rose (Clark) B.; m. Jean Thelma Robinson, Sept. 8, 1984; 1 child, Caitlin Virginia. BA, Glassboro State U., 1980; MBA, St. Joseph's U., 1984. Sales mgr. SBI Video, Cherry Hill, N.J., 1978-85; v.p., sales MGM/United Artists, Culver City, Calif., 1985-91; pres., COO, Live Home Video, 1991-94; exec. v.p. MGM/UA Home Entertainment Worldwide, Santa Monica, Calif., 1994—96, pres., 1996—2000; pres., COO MGM Home Entertainment Group, 2000—05; pres., worldwide brand integration strategy Sony Pictures Entertainment, 2005—. Office: Sony Pictures Entertainment 10202 W Washington Blvd Culver City CA 90232

BISHOP, KATHRYN ELIZABETH, realtor, film producer, writer; b. Seattle, July 7, 1945; d. Wesley Thomas Bishop and Muriel (Robert) Leisher; divorced; 1 child, Zachary. BA, Wartburg Coll., 1966. Voice over talent Chgo. Bd. Edn. Radio Network, 1960-62; prodn. asst. Sta. CBS-TV, WBBM-TV, Chgo., 1961-63; disk jockey, engr., writer Sta. KWAR-FM, Waverly, Iowa, 1964-65; assoc. producer Bing Crosby Prodns. Inc., Chgo., 1966-69; producer Sedelmaier Films, Chgo., 1969-73; v.p., head prodn. Wakeford/Orloff Inc., LA, 1977-78; founder, owner Stiles-Bishop Prodns. Inc., LA, 1974—; co-founder, exec. prodr. The Colman Group Inc., LA, 1982-87; co-founder, co-owner Rapport Films, Inc., Hollywood, Calif., 1987-92; feature film prodr., 1992—. Co-author: (screenplay) Millionaire's Club; screenwriter: Cinnamon Bear. Mem. TV Acad. Arts and Scis., Dirs. Guild Am. Avocations: pottery, sailing, skiing. Office: Stiles-Bishop Prodns Inc 12652 Killion St Valley Village CA 91607-1535 Office Phone: 818-423-1503. Business E-Mail: kbishop9@earthlink.net.

BISHOP, LEAH MARGARET, lawyer; b. NYC, Nov. 2, 1954; d. Franklin Gerald and Evelyn (Fremed) B.; m. Gary M. Yale, Aug. 10, 1975; children: Elizabeth Yale, Rebecca Yale. BA summa cum laude, Brandeis U., 1975; JD, Columbia U., 1979. Bar: NY 1980, US Dist. Ct. (ea. and so. dists. NY) 1980, Calif. 1981, US Dist. Ct. (ctrl. dist. Calif.) 1981; cert. State Bar Calif. Bd. Legal Specialization (estate planning, trust and probate law). Law clk. to Hon. Edmund Palmieri US Dist. Ct. (so. dist. NY), 1979-80; assoc. O'Melveny & Myers, LA, 1980-87, ptnr., 1987—2006, Loeb & Loeb, LLP, LA, 2006. Named one of Top 100 Attys., Worth mag., 2006, 2007. Fellow Am. Coll. Trust and Estate Counsel; mem. LA County Bar Assn. (mem. exempt orgn. com.), Phi Beta Kappa. Democrat. Jewish. Office: Loeb & Loeb LLP Ste 2200 10100 Santa Monica Blvd Los Angeles CA 90067-4120 Office Phone: 310-282-2353. Office Fax: 310-919-3963. E-mail: lbishop@loeb.com.

BISHOP, LEO KENNETH, clergyman, educator; b. Britton, Okla., Oct. 11, 1911; s. Luther and Edith (Scovill) B.; m. Pauline T. Shamburg, Sept. 15, 1935; 1 dau., Linda Paulette. AB, Phillips U., 1932, LHD, 1958; MA, Columbia U., 1944; MBA, U. Chgo., 1957; LittD, Kansas City Coll. Osteopathy and Surgery, 1964. Assoc. min. Univ. Place Ch., Oklahoma City, 1932-35; min. First Ch., Paducah, Ky., 1935-41, Ctrl. Ch., Des Moines, 1941-45; dir. St. Louis office NCCJ, 1945-48, v.p., dir. ctrl. divsn. Chgo., 1949-63; dir. pub. affairs People-to-People, Kansas City, Mo., 1963-66; v.p. Chgo. Coll. Osteopathy, 1966-72; pres. Bishop Enterprises, Colorado Springs, Colo., 1972—, also lectr. Contbr. religious and ednl. jours.; Developed: radio series Storm Warning; TV series The Other Guy, 1954. Cons. Cmty. Social Planning Coun., Mayor's Race Rels. Com., YMCA, St. Louis; Am. del. Conf. World Brotherhood, Paris, 1950; bd. dirs. Am. Heritage Found. Recipient Most Useful Citizen award Paducah Jr. C. of C., 1937, Disting. Svc. award Dore Miller Found., 1958, Freedom Found. of Valley Forge award, 1961; named Chicagoan of Year, 1960. Mem.: Rotary, Union League, Winter Night. Home and Office: Montara Meadows A342 3150 E Tropicana Ave Las Vegas NV 89121

BISHOP, ROBERT, United States Representative from Utah; b. Kaysville, Utah, July 31, 1951; m. Jeralynn Hansen; children: Shule, Jarom, Zenock, Maren, Jashon. BA in Polit. Sci., U. Utah, 1974. Tchr. Box Elder High Sch., Brigham City, Utah, 1974—80, 1985—2002; tchr., debate coach Ben Lomond High Sch., Orden, Utah, 1980—85; mem. Utah House Reps., 1979-94, minority leader, 1990-92, spkr., 1992-94, contract lobbyist, 1995; state chmn. Utah Rep. Party, 1997—2001; mem. US Congress from 1st Utah dist., 2002—. Co-founder Western States Coalition; mem. Utah Speech Arts Assn., 1975—87, chmn., 1981—84; mem. Utah State Ctrl. Com., 1992; co-founder, mem. exec. bd. Western States Coalition, 1994; chair Utah State Convention, 1990. Mem. Brigham City Hist. Preservation Com., Brigham City Heritage Alliance Com.; chmn. Brigham City Cmty. Theater. Republican. Mem. Lds Ch. Office: US House Reps 124 Cannon House Office Bldg Washington DC 20515-4401 Office Phone: 202-225-0453.

BISHOP, ROBERT CALVIN, pharmaceutical company executive; b. LA, Jan. 13, 1943; s. Harold Eames and Mary Frances (Allen) B.; m. Susan Elizabeth Ogden, Nov. 18, 1966; children: John Ogden, James Allen, Bryan Hutchings. AB in Psychology, U. So. Calif., 1966, PhD in Biochemistry, 1976; MBA, U. Miami, 1981. Rsch. assoc. Hyland Labs., Glendale, Calif., 1966-69; cons. LA, 1970-75; program mgr. Am. Hosp. Supply Corp., Glendale, 1976-78, rsch. dir. Dade div. Miami, Fla., 1978-81, v.p. Evanston, Ill., 1981-85; pres. Allergan Med. Optics, Irvine, Calif., 1986-88; sr. v.p. Allergan Inc., Irvine, 1989; pres. Allergan Pharmaceuticals, Irvine, 1989-91, Allergan Therapeutics Group, 1991-92; pres., CEO, dir. AutoImmune, Inc.,

Pasadena, Calif., 1992—. Bd. dirs. MFS/Sun Life Series Trust & Compass Accts., Caliper Life Scis. Inc., Millipore Corp. Contbr. articles to profl. jours.; patentee in field. Bd. dirs. Eye Bank Assn. Am., Washington, 1988-90, Amyotropic Lateral Sclerosis Assn., LA, 1984-87, Quintiles Transitional Corp., 1994-2003, Optobionics Corp., 2003-07. With USAR, 1963—69. Mem. Annandale Golf Club (Pasadena, Calif.). Republican. Presbyterian. Avocation: golf. Home: 1199 Madia St Pasadena CA 91103-1961 Office: AutoImmune Inc 1199 Madia St Pasadena CA 91103

BISHOP, ROBERT R., computer company executive; BS in Math. Physics with honors, U. Adelaide; MS, NYU. Sr. exec. Digital Equip. Corp., 1968—82, Apollo Computer, Inc., 1982—86; pres. world trade corp. Silicon Graphics, Inc., 1986—95, non-executive chmn. bd., world trade corp., 1996—99, chmn., COO, 1995—, chmn. bd. dir., CEO, 1999—. Internat. adv. panel Multimedia Super Corridor, Malaysia; invited prof. Swiss Fed. Inst. Tech., Lausanne; adj. prof. Stockholm Sch. Econs.; lectr. U. St. Gallen, Wirtschafts Tech.; spkr. in field. Mem.: Govs. World Econ. Forum Info.Techs., World Intellectual Property Orgn., Industry Adv. Commn., Swiss Acad. Engring. Scis.

BISHOP, TILMAN MALCOLM, state legislator; b. Colorado Springs, Jan. 1, 1933; m. Pat Bishop, 1952; 1 son, Barry Alan (dec.). BA, MA, U. Northern Colo., Greeley, D (hon.), 1999. Adminstr., dir. student svcs. Mesa State Coll., Grand Junction, Colo., 1962-94; mem., pres. pro tem Colo. Senate, 1971-99, ret., 1999. Bd. dirs. Rocky Mountain Pub. Broadcasting TV, Colo. Duck Stamp Commn. Mem. World Series com. Nat. Jr. Coll. Baseball; elected commr. Mesa County, 2003-07; trustee El Pomar Found.; mem selection com. Colo. Sports Hall of Fame; elected bd. regents U. Colo., 2007—. With US Army. Mem. Elks, Lions. Republican. Methodist. Avocations: fishing, small game hunting. Home: 2255 Piazza Way Grand Junction CO 81506 Personal E-mail: tilmanmb@bresnan.net.

BISHOP, WILLIAM PETER, management consultant, rancher, musician; b. Lakewood, Ohio, Jan. 18, 1940; s. William Hall and Ethel Laverle (Evans) B.; m. Sarah Gilbert, Sept. 1, 1963. BA in Chemistry with honors (Nat. Merit scholar), Coll. Wooster, Ohio, 1962; PhD (NDEA fellow), Ohio State U., 1967. Resident research assoc. Ohio State U., 1967-69; mem. staff Sandia Labs., Albuquerque, 1969-75; head nuclear waste program NRC, Washington, 1975-78; dep. dir. environ. observation div. NASA, 1978-81, dep. dir. life scis. div., 1981-83; dep. asst. adminstr. satellites NOAA, 1983-85, acting asst. adminstr. satellites and info. services, 1985-87; v.p. SAIC, Washington, 1987-89; v.p. for rsch. Desert Rsch. Inst., Las Vegas, Nev., 1989-94; assigned to U.S. Dept. of Energy, 1995-99; pres. B-plus, Inc., Paonia, Colo., 1999—. Mem. Nat. Acad. Com. Earth Studies, 1989-91, Task Group on Priorities in Space Rsch., 1990-94; chair Adv. Commn. on Geoscis. NSF, 1994-97. Author articles in field. Trustee Keystone (Colo.) Ctr., 1986-95, Nev. Devel. Authority, 1989-95, Univ. Corp. for Atmospheric Rsch., 1991-97; bd. dirs. Opportunities Industrialization Ctrs., Albuquerque, 1974-75, Cave Rsch. Found., 1967-74; dir. Western Slope Environ. Resources Coun., 200-04. Recipient Meritorious Service award NRC, 1977; Spaceship Earth award NASA, 1981; Meritorious Service award U.S. Dept. Commerce, 1985, Spl. Act or Svc. awrad, U.S. Dept. Energy, 1999. Fellow Nat. Speleological Soc. (conservation editor bull. 1974-78), Am. Astron. Soc. (v.p. tech. 1987-88); mem. AAAS, Am. Meteorol. Soc., Rotary, Sigma Xi, Phi Lambda Upsilon. Personal E-mail: bplusinc@tds.net.

BISSELL, GEORGE ARTHUR, architect; b. LA, Jan. 31, 1927; s. George Arthur and Ruby Zoe (Moore) B.; m. Laurene Conlon, Nov. 21, 1947; children: Teresa Ann, Thomas Conlon, William George, Robert Anthony, Mary Catherine. BArch, U. So. Calif., 1953. Registered architect, Calif. Ptnr. Bissell Co., Covina, Calif., 1953-57, Bissell & Durquette, A.I.A., Pasadena, Calif., 1957-61; owner George Bissell, A.I.A., Laguna Beach, Calif., 1961-65; ptnr. Riley & Bissell, A.I.A., Newport Beach, Calif., 1965-72; pres. Bissell/August, Inc., Newport Beach, 1972-83, Bissell Architects, Inc., Newport Beach, 1983—. Bd. dirs. Newport Ctr. Assn., 1973-78, Lido Isle Community Assn., Newport Beach, 1985-87, Hamilton Cove Assn., 1991-92. With U.S. Mcht. Marine, 1944-46. Fellow AIA (pres. Orange County chpt. 1975, Calif. coun. 1978, nat. bd. dirs. 1980-83, Progressive Arch. award 1974, Nat. AIA Honor award 1978, 98, Merit award Calif. Coun. 1988, AIA Calif. Coun. Lifetime Achievement award 2000); mem. Newport Harbor Yacht Club, Lido Isle Yacht Club. Avocations: sailing, skiing, travel. Home: 108 Via Havre Newport Beach CA 92663-4905 also: Yacht Banshee Newport Beach CA 92663 Office: Bissell Architects 333A Shipyard Way Newport Beach CA 92663-Office Phone: 949-675-9901. E-mail: Bisarch@aol.com.

BISSELL, JAMES DOUGAL, III, motion picture production designer; b. Charleston, SC, Aug. 6, 1951; s. James Dougal Sr. and Elizabeth McPherson (Jones) B.; m. Teresa Ann Atkinson, June 1, 1974 (div. Sept. 1987); m. Martha Wynne Snetsinger, Oct. 22, 1995; children: James Dougal, Alexander Wynne, Elizabeth Wynne. BFA in Theatre, U. N.C., 1973. Art dir. various TV movies, LA, 1976-81; prodn. designer E.T. The Extra-Terrestrial, LA, 1981, Twilight Zone-The Movie, LA, 1982, The Falcon and The Snowman, Mexico City, 1983-84; prodn. designer, 2d unit dir. The Boy Who Could Fly, Vancouver, B.C., Canada, 1985, Harry and the Hendersons, LA, 1986; prodn. designer Someone to Watch Over Me, LA and NYC, 1986-87, Twins, LA and Santa Fe, 1988—. Visual cons. St. Elmo's Fire, Hollywood, 1984; title co-designer Amazing Stories, Hollywood, 1985; art dir. The Last Starfighter, Hollywood, 1983; prodn. designer, 2nd unit dir. Always, LA, Libby Mt., Epharata, Wash., 1989; prodn. designer Arachnophobia, Venezuela, Cambria, Calif., LA Prodn. designer Rocketeer, 1990, The Pickle, NYC and LA, Dennis the Menace, Chgo., 1992, Blue Chips, LA, Chgo., New Orleans, 1993, Jumanji, Vancouver, New Eng., 1994-95, Tin Cup, Tucson, Houston, 1995, My Fellow Americans, LA, Asheville, NC, The Sixth Day, 1999, Cats and Dogs, 2000, Confessions of a Dangerous Mind, 2002, Hollywood Homicide, LA, 2002; visual cons., 2d unit dir. 50 First Dates, LA, 2003, Ring II, LA, 2004, Good Night and Good Luck, LA, 2005 (Oscar nomination 2005, Satellite award 2005, 300 ADG nomination 2006), Spiderwick Chronicles, Montréal, 2006, Leatherheads, NC, SC. Mem.: Acad. Motion Picture Arts and Scis., Dir.'s Guild Am., Art Dir.'s Guild (past v.p.).

BISSELL, MINA J., lab administrator, biochemist; b. Tehran, Iran, May 14, 1940; Student, Bryn Mawr Coll., 1959-61; AB in Chemistry cum laude, Radcliff Coll., Cambridge, Mass., 1963; MA in Bacteriology and Biochemistry, Harvard U., Cambridge, Mass., 1965, PhD in Microbiology-Molecular Genetics, 1969. Milton rsch. fellow, 1969-70; Am. Cancer Soc. rsch. fellow, 1970-72; staff biochemist Lawrence Berkeley Nat. Lab. U. Calif., Berkeley, 1972-76, mem. sr. staff, 1976—, co-dir. div. biology and medicine Lab. Cell Biology, 1980—, dir. divsn., 1988-92, coord. life scis., 1989-91, assoc. lab. dir. bioscience, 1989, dir. life scis. divsn. Lawrence Berkeley Nat. Lab., 1992—, mem. faculty dept. comparative biochemistry, 1979—. Vis. prof. Kettering Inst., U. Cin. Med. Schs., 1986-88; disting. vis. scientist Queensland Inst. Med. Rsch., Brisbane, Australia, 1982; mem. coun. Gordon Rsch. Conf., 1991-94; George P. Peacock lectr. pathology U. Tex., Dallas, 1992; Dean's lectr. Mt. Sinai Med. Sch., N.Y.C., 1993; presenter numerous lectures, condr. symposia; keynote spkr. Gordon Conf. on Proteoglycans, 1994, others. Mem. editl. bd. and sect. editor In Vitro Cell and Devel. Biology Rapid Comm., 1986—; mem. editl. bd. Jour. Cellular Biochemistry, 1990-92; assoc. editor In Vitro Cellular and Devel. Biology, 1990—, Molecular and Cellular Differentiation, 1992—, Molecular Carcinogensis, 1993-97, Devel. Biology, 1993—, Cancer Rsch., 1994—, Breast Jour., 1994—; contbr. numerous articles to sci. jours. Recipient 1st Joseph Sadusk award for breast cancer rsch., 1985, Ernest Orlando Lawrence award Dept. Energy, 1996, Krakower award in Pathology, 2003, Discovery Health Channel Med. Honors, 2004; Fogarty sr. fellow NIH, Imperial Can. Rsch. Fund Labs., London, 1983-84, Guggenheim fellow, 1992-93,; honored by Susan G. Komen Breast Cancer Found. Fellow AAAS; mem. Am. Soc. for Cell Biology (mem. coun. 1989-91, Women in Cell Biology Career Recognition award 1993, pres. 1997), Internat. Soc. Differentiation (bd. dirs. 1990-96). The pioneer in postulating, and then proving that the extracellular matrix (ECM), the mass of fibrous and globular proteins that surrounds cells performs a critical role in dictating a tissue's organization and function. In 1981, Dr. Bissell formulated the concept of a "dynamic reciprocity." This communication scheme between the nucleus, the cells and their microenvironment suggests that signals are sent into the cell through ECM receptors which attach to the cell's outer skeleton and convey important information to the nucleus and the chromosomes. Office: Lawrence Berkeley Nat Lab Div Life Scis 1 Cyclotron Rd Ms 83 101 Berkeley CA 94720-8260 Business E-Mail: mjbissell@lbl.gov.

BITTERMAN, MARY GAYLE FOLEY, foundation executive; b. San Jose, Calif., May 29, 1944; d. John Dennis and Zoe (Hames) Foley; m. Morton Edward Bitterman, June 26, 1967; 1 child Sarah Fleming. BA, Santa Clara U., 1966; MA, Bryn Mawr Coll., 1969, PhD, 1971; PhD in Comml. Sci. (hon.), U. Richmond, 2008. Exec. dir. Hawaii Pub. Broadcasting, Honolulu, 1974-79; dir. Voice Am., Washington, 1980-81, Dept. Commerce, Honolulu, 1981-83, E.-W. Ctr. Inst. Culture, Comm., 1984-88; cons. pvt. practice, 1989-93; pres., CEO KQED, Inc., San Francisco, 1993—2002, The James Irvine Found., 2002—03; Dir. Osher Lifelong Learning Inst., 2003; pres. The Bernard Osher Found., 2004—. Vice chmn. TIDE 2000, Tokyo, 1984—93; adv. coun. mem. Stanford Inst. Econ. Policy Rsch. Prodr.: (film) China Visit, 1978; contbr. numerous articles on internat. telecomms. to various pubs. Bd. dir. Bank of Hawaii, Honolulu, Honolulu, 1994—, United Way, Honolulu, 1986—1993, World Affairs Coun., 1994-2002, McKesson Corp., San Francisco, 1995—1999, Bernard Osher Found., Barclays Global Investors, Bay Area Econ. Forum, Bay Area Coun., exec. com., 1994-2002; bd. dirs. Assn. Pub. TV Sta., 1994-2002, chmn. 2001-2002; trustee Am.'s Pub. TV Stas., 1997—2002, Santa Clara U., 2004-07; chmn. Kuakini Health System, 1991—1994; bd. dir. PBS, chmn. Recipient Candle of Understanding award Bonneville (Utah) Internat. Corp., 1985; named hon. mem. Nat. Fedn. Press Women, 1986; Doctor of Humane Letters (honoris causa), Dominican Coll. of San Rafael, 1999; Doctor of Public Svc. (honoris causa), Santa Clara U., 2003; Ralph Lowell award, 2007. Mem.: Pacific Forum, CSIS (bd. gov.), Commonwealth Club Calif. (bd. dir.), Nat. Acad. Pub. Admin. (fellow). Office: One Ferry Bldg Ste 255 San Francisco CA 94111 Address: 229 Kaalawai Pl Honolulu HI 96816-4435 Office Phone: 415-677-5946. Business E-Mail: mbitterman@osherfoundation.org.

BITTERMAN, MORTON EDWARD, psychologist, educator; b. NYC, Jan. 19, 1921; s. Harry Michael and Stella (Weiss) B.; m. Mary Gayle Foley, June 26, 1967; children— Sarah Fleming, Joan, Ann BA, NYU, 1941; MA, Columbia U., 1942; PhD, Cornell U., 1945. Asst. prof. Cornell U., Ithaca, N.Y., 1945-50; assoc. prof. U. Tex., Austin, 1950-55; mem. Inst. for Advanced Study, Princeton, N.J., 1955-57; prof. Bryn Mawr Coll., Pa., 1957-70, U. Hawaii, Honolulu, 1970—; dir. Békésy Lab. Neurobiology, Honolulu, 1991—2000. Author: (with others) Animal Learning, 1979; editor: Evolution of Brain and Behavior in Vertebrates, 1976; co-editor: Am. Jour. Psychology, 1955-73; cons. editor Jour. Animal Learning and Behavior, 1973-76, 85-88, Jour. Comparative Psychology, 1988-92. Recipient Humboldt prize Alexander von Humboldt Found., Bonn, W.Ger., 1981; Fulbright grantee; grantee NSF, Office Naval Research, NIMH, Air Force Office Sci. Research, Deutsche Forschungsgemeinschaft. Fellow Soc. Exptl. Psychologists (Warren medal 1997, E.R. Hilgard award 2004), Am. Psychol. Assn. (D. O. Hebb award 2001), AAAS; mem. Psychonomic Soc. Home: 229 Kaalawai Pl Honolulu HI 96816-4435 Office: Univ Hawaii Bekesy Lab of Neurobiology 1993 E West Rd Honolulu HI 96822-2321 Office Phone: 808-956-6987. Business E-Mail: jeffb@pbrc.hawaii.edu.

BITTERWOLF, THOMAS EDWIN, chemistry educator; b. New Orleans, Jan. 19, 1947; s. Alvin John and Naomi Mae (Hendrix) B.; m. Caroline Elizabeth Means, May 25, 1968; children: Heidi Elizabeth, Katharine Naomi. BS, Centenary Coll., 1968; PhD, W.Va. U., 1976. Commd. ensign USN, 1973, advanced through grades to comdr., 1987; instr. Naval Nuclear Power Sch., Orlando, Fla., 1973-77, U.S. Naval Acad., Annapolis, Md., 1977-82; resigned USN, 1982; asst. prof. U.S. Naval Acad., Annapolis, Md., 1982-85, assoc. prof., 1985-88; assoc. prof. chemistry U. Idaho, Moscow, 1988-91, prof. chemistry, dir. teaching enhancement, 1991-96, assoc. dean coll. letters scis., 1996-98; exit stds. commr. Idaho High Schs., 1998—. Contbr. articles to refereed jours. Mem. AAAS, Am. Chem. Soc., Royal Soc. Chemistry, Sigma Xi. Methodist. Avocation: theater. Home: PO Box 8188 Moscow ID 83843-0688 Office: U Idaho Dept Chemistry Moscow ID 83844-0001

BIVENS, DONALD WAYNE, lawyer, political organization administrator; b. Ann Arbor, Mich., Feb. 5, 1952; s. Melvin Donley and Frances Lee (Speer) Bivens; children: Jody, Lisa, Andrew. BA magna cum laude, Yale U., 1974; JD, U. Tex., 1977. Bar: Ariz. 1977, US Dist. Ct., Ariz. 1977, US Ct. Appeals (9th cir.) 1977, US Ct. Appeals (fed. cir.) 1984, US Supreme Ct. 1982. Ptnr. Bivens & Nore, PA, Phoenix, 1977, Meyer Hendricks & Bivens, PA, Phoenix, Snell & Wilmer LLP, Phoenix. Judge pro tem Maricopa County Superior Ct., Ariz., Ariz. Ct. Appeals, Phoenix, 1999—2000. Editor (note & comment editor): Tex. Law Review, 1976—77. Pres. Scottsdale Men's League, 1980—82; v.p., bd. dirs. Phoenix Symphony Assn., 1980—86; mem. adv. com. Ariz Theater Co., 1987—88; dir. Salvation Army, 2006—; pres. Ariz Young Dem., 1980—82; chmn. Ariz. Dem. Party, 2007—; sr. warden St. Barnabas on the Desert Episc. Ch., 2002—05; ch. atty. Episc. Diocese Ariz., 2005—; bd. dirs. Scottsdale Arts Ctr. Assn., 1981—84, Planned Parenthood Ctrl. and No. Ariz, 1989—92; adv. bd. Smithsonian Am. Art Mus., 2006—, Phoenix Sch. Law, 2006—. Recipient Consul Award, U. Tex. Sch. Law, 1977, 3 Outstanding Young Men Award, Phoenix Jaycees, 1981; named one of Top 50 Super Lawyers in Ariz., Law & Politics Mag., 2007. Mem.: ABA (chmn. computer litig. com. 1989—92, counsel mem. litig. sect. 1995—98, Ariz. state del., House Dels. 1999—2007, co-chmn. litig. sect. tech. com. 2002—05, co-chmn. litig. sect. resource com. 2005—07, bd. govs. 2007—), Am. Law Inst., Thurgood Marshall Inn Ct. (founding pres. 1992—93), Maricopa County Bar Assn. (chmn. Trial Adv. Inst. 1986—87, bd. dirs., pres. 1991—92, Mem. of Yr. 1998), Ariz. Trial Lawyers Assn., State Bar Ariz. (peer review com. 1992—, bd. govs. 1993—2000, pres. 1998—99), Ariz. Bar Found., Am. Bar Found. Democrat. Avocations: music, theater. Home: 6311 E Naumann Dr Paradise Valley AZ 85253-1044 Office: Snell & Wilmer LLP One Arizona Center Phoenix AZ 85004-2202 also: Ariz Dem Party 2910 N Central Ave Phoenix AZ 85012 Office Phone: 602-382-6549, 602-298-4200. E-mail: dbivens@swlaw.com, dbivens@azdem.org.*

BJORK, GORDON CARL, economist, educator; b. Seattle, Dec. 15, 1935; s. Gordon E. and Florence E. (Bloomberg) B.; m. Susan Jill Serman, Dec. 29, 1960; children: Katharine, Rebecca, Susannah, Anders. AB, Dartmouth Coll., 1957; BA (hon.), Oxford U., 1959, MA, 1963; PhD, U. Wash., 1963. Lectr. econs. U. B.C., Vancouver, Can., 1962-63; asst. prof. econs. Carleton U., Ottawa, Ont., 1963-64; assoc. prof. econs. Columbia U., NYC, 1964-68; pres. Linfield Coll., McMinnville, Oreg., 1968-74; prof. econs. Oreg. State U., Corvallis, 1974-75; Lovelace prof. econs. Claremont McKenna Coll., Claremont Grad. Sch., Calif., 1975—. Henry Walker disting. vis. prof. bus. enterprise U. Hawaii, 1985-86; vis. prof. econs. Nottingham (Eng.) U., 1990; mem. nat. adv. com. on environ. policy and tech. EPA. Author: Private Enterprise and Public Interest: The Development of American Capitalism, 1969, Life, Liberty and Property: The Economics and Politics of Land Use Planning and Environmental Control, 1980, Stagnation and Growth in the American Economy, 1985, The Way It Worked and Why It Won't: Structural Change and the Slowdown of U.S. Economic Growth, 1999. Lt. USCGR, 1960-68. Rhodes scholar, 1957; Battelle Inst. fellow, 1975 Mem. Phi Beta Kappa Republican. United Ch. of Christ. Home: 4609 Vista Buena Rd Santa Barbara CA 93110-1945 Office: Claremont McKenna Coll Dept Econs Claremont CA 91711 E-mail: gbjork@mckenna.edu.

BJORKLUND, NANCY BASLER, history professor; b. Santa Ana, Calif., Dec. 20, 1940; d. Herman Henry and Virginia Eleanor Basler; m. Lawrence Paul Bjorklund (div. Aug. 27, 1987); children: Julie, Kristen, David. BA, UCLA, 1962, MA, 1964; PhD, U. Calif., Irvine, 1987. Instr. Leeward Coll., Pearl City, Hawaii, 1971—72, Saddleback Coll., Mission Viejo, Calif., 1973—77, Rancho Santiago Coll, Santa Ana, 1974—84; tchg. assoc. and asst. U. Calif., Irvine, 1978—84; prof. history Fullerton Coll., Calif., 1984—. Contbr. articles to profl. jours. Chair bd. higher edn. and campus ministeries Meth. Ch., Calif.-Pacific Conf., 1999—2003. Grantee, U. Calif., Irvine, 1982, 1984. Mem.: Pacific Coast Conf. Brit. Studies, Nat. Endowment Humanities, Phi Beta Kappa. Methodist. Office: Fullerton Coll 321 E Chapman Ave Fullerton CA 92832 Business E-Mail: nbjorklund@fullcoll.edu.

BLACK, ARTHUR LEO, biochemistry educator; b. Redlands, Calif., Dec. 1, 1922; s. Leo M. and Maria A. (Burns) Black; m. Trudi E. McCue, Nov. 11, 1945; children: Teresa Townsend, Janet Carter, Patti Tleimat. BS, U. Calif., Davis, 1948, PhD, 1951. Faculty physiol. chemistry Sch. Vet. Medicine U. Calif. at Davis, 1951—, prof., 1962—, prof. emeritus, 1991—, chmn. dept. physiol. scis., 1968-75. Cons. NIH, 1970-72, U.S. Dept. Agr., 1977-80; chmn. Nutritional Scis. Tng. Com., 1971-72 Contbr. papers to profl. jours. Served to 1st lt. USAAF, 1943-46. Recipient Sci. Faculty award NSF, 1958; Acad. Senate Disting. Teaching award U. Calif., Davis, 1977; Research grantee NSF; Research grantee NIH, 1952— Fellow Am. Inst. Nutrition (Borden award 1963); mem. Am. Soc. Biol. Chemists, Am. Physiol. Soc., Am. Soc. for Nutritional Scis., Sigma Xi, Phi Beta Kappa, Phi Zeta. Home: 891 Linden Ln Davis CA 95616-1763 Office: U Calif Dept Molecular Bioscis Davis CA 95616

BLACK, BRUCE D., judge; b. Detroit, July 27, 1947; BA, Albion Coll., 1969; JD, U. Mich., 1971. Pvt. law practice, N.Mex., 1972—91; judge N.Mex. Ct. Appeals, 1991-96, US Dist. Ct. N.Mex., 1996—. Office: US Dist Ct NMex 106 Federal Pl Santa Fe NM 87501 Office Phone: 505-955-8830. Office Fax: 505-955-8835.

BLACK, BUD (HARRY RALSTON BLACK), professional baseball manager; b. San Mateo, Calif., June 30, 1957; s. Harry Black. BS in Fin., San Diego State U., 1979. Pitcher Seattle Mariners, 1981, Kans. City Royals, 1982—88, Cleve. Indians, 1988—90, 1995, Toronto Blue Jays, 1990, San Francisco Giants, 1991—94; pitching coach LA Angels of Anaheim, 1999—2006; mgr. San Diego Padres, 2006—. Office: San Diego Padres 9449 Friars Rd San Diego CA 92108

BLACK, DONNA RUTH, lawyer; b. Yuma, Ariz., Sept. 13, 1947; d. Roy Welch and Rosalie Edith (Harrison) B.; children: Gavin Lewis, Trevor Elias. BA in History with honors, U. Ariz., 1969; JD, UCLA, 1975. Bar: Calif. 1975, D.C. 1979, U.S. Dist. Ct. (ctrl. dist.) Calif., 1975, U.S. Dist. Ct. (no. dist.) Calif. 1987, U.S. Dist. Ct. (ea. dist.) Calif. 1989, U.S. Ct. Appeals (8th cir.) 1978, U.S. Ct. Appeals (9th cir.) 1983, U.S. Supreme Ct. 1994. Equity ptnr. Baker & Hostetler, LA, 1975-95; equity ptnr. Manatt, Phelps & Phillips, LA, 1995—. Author/editor: California Environmental Law Handbook. Mem. ABA (chmn. sect. natural resources, energy and environ. law, mem. nominating com. ho. of dels., chmn. sect. officers' conf. adv. com.), State Bar Calif., Los Angeles County Bar Assn., UCLA Law Alumni Assn. (bd. dirs. 1996—, v.p. 1998—, pres. 1999). Avocations: music, art, travel, poetry, writing. Home: 515 Dalehurst Ave Los Angeles CA 90024-2515

BLACK, FREDERICK A., prosecutor; b. July 2, 1949; s. John R. and Dorothy Black; m. Katie Black, Oct. 27, 1976; children: Shane, Shanthini, Sheena. BA, U. Calif., Berkeley, 1971; JD, Lewis and Clark Coll., 1975. Bar: Oreg. 1975, Guam 1976, U.S. Ct. Appeals (9th cir.) 1976. Dir. Office of Guam Pub. Defender, 1975-78; dep. dir. Office of Oreg. Fed. Defender, 1981-84; asst. U.S. atty. Dist. Guam and No. Mariana Islands, 1978-81, 84-89, 1st asst. U.S. atty., 1989-91; U.S. atty. Dept. Justice Dist. Agana, Guam and No. Mariana Islands, 1991—2003; sr. litigation counsel U.S. Attys Office, 2003—. Author: Oregon Search and Seizure Manual. Leader Boy Scouts Am. Recipient Spl. award Chief Postal Inspector, 1986, Drug Enforcement Adminstrn. award, 1986, 89. Mem. Guam Water Polo Team. Avocation: sailing. Office: US Atty's Office 108 Hernan Cortez Ave Ste 500 Hagatna GU 96910-5009

BLACK, GARY D., investment company executive; Grad., U. Pa.; MBA, Harvard U., 1988. Analyst Sanford C. Bernstein & Co., Alliance Bernstein, exec. v.p., head Instl. Asset Mgmt., 1999—2001; mng. dir. US Internat. And Third Party Bus. Goldman Sachs & Co., 2001—02; chief investment officer Global Equities Goldman Sachs Asset Mgmt., 2002—04; pres. Janus Capital Group Inc., Denver, 2004—05, chief investment officer, 2004—, CEO, 2006—. Office: Janus Capital Group Inc 151 Detroit St Denver CO 80206-4923 Office Phone: 303-333-3863. Office Fax: 212-642-8442. E-mail: gary.black@janus.com.

BLACK, JEFFREY M., professor (wildlife); b. Berea, Ohio, Jan. 28, 1959; s. Robert B. and Helen Black; m. Gillian C. Harmsworth; children: Abigail M., Nicholas B. BA, Hiram Coll., Ohio, 1982; PhD, U. Wales, Cardiff, UK, 1987, DSc, 2001. Prin. rsch. officer, unit head Wildfowl & Wetlands Trust, Slimbridge, England, 1989—97; adj. PhD supr. U. Oxford, Edward Grey Inst. Field Ornithology, Oxford, England, 1989—2001; post doctoral scholar U. Cambridge, Large Animal Rsch. Group Zoology, Cambridge, England, 1997—98; prof. Humboldt State U., Arcata, Calif., 1998—. Adj. MSc supr. U. Kent, Canterbury, England, 1992—95; rsch. cons. Directorate Nature Conservation, Trondheim, Norway, 1997—98; rsch. assoc. Arctic Inst., U. Tromso, Norway, 1998—2001. Author: (book) Wild Goose Dilemmas, Partnerships in Birds: the study of monogamy, Waterfowl Ecology. Recipient Young Alumni Outstanding Contbn. Humanity award, Hiram Coll., Ohio, 1995, Faculty Merit award, Humboldt State U., 1998, 1999, 2000. Mem.: Wildlife Soc., Animal Behavior Soc., Internat. Soc. Behavioral Ecology. Achievements include research in subtleties of life among Arctic geese, swans and ducks. Office: Wildlife Dept Humboldt State Univ 1 Harpst St Arcata CA 95521 Business E-Mail: jmb7002@humboldt.edu.

BLACK, MAX C., state legislator; b. Delta, Utah, July 2, 1936; s. William Ernst Black and Ella (Clark) B.; m. Clydene S. Black, June 29, 1961; children: Jeffrey, Gary, Wendi. BA in Bus., U. Utah, 1962. Underwriter Am. Agencies, Salt Lake City, 1962-67; field rep. USF&G Ins. Co., Boise, Idaho, 1967-75; agy. owner Black & Warr Ins. Agy., Boise, Idaho, 1975-91; mem. Dist. 15 Idaho House of Reps., 1993—. Pres. Boise Independent Agents, 1981, Idaho Profl. Agents, 1982 (bd. dirs. 1981-92, agent of the yr. 1981). Mem. Optomist Internat. Republican. Avocations: watch collecting, woodcarving. Home: 3731 Buckingham Dr Boise ID 83704 Office: State Capitol Bldg PO Box 83270 Boise ID 83720-0081 also: Dist 15 3731 Buckingham Dr Boise ID 83704 Office Phone: 208-375-2635. Office Fax: 208-332-1000, 208-375-8250. Business E-Mail: mblack@house.idaho.gov.*

BLACK, PETE, retired state legislator, educator; b. Ansbach, Germany, Sept. 16, 1946; came to U.S., 1948; s. Howard and Kadi (Fietz) B.; m. Ronda Williams, July 12, 1970; 1 child, Darin. BS, Idaho State U., 1975, MEd, 1998. Cert. elem. tchr. Tchr. Pocatello (Idaho) Sch. Dist., 1975—; mem. Idaho Ho. Reps., Boise, 1983-96, asst. minority leader, 1987-96; tech. tng. specialist Sch. Dist. 25, 1996—, info. officer, 2003—. Mem. edn. tech. coun.; mem. adv. coun. chpt. II ESEA. Bd. dirs. Arts for Idaho; mem. State Libr. Bd.; mem. Idaho Pers. Commn., Pocatello Civil Svc. Commn., Pocatello Parks and Recreation Bd. With USNR, 1964. Mem. NEA, Idaho Edn. Assn. (bd. dirs.), Idaho Libr. Assn., Idaho State U. Alumni Bd. Democrat. Home: 2249 Cassia St Pocatello ID 83201-2059 Office: Idaho House of Reps Statehouse Mail Boise ID 83720-0001 Home Phone: 208-237-1779; Office Phone: 208-235-3251. E-mail: blackcat1@cableone.net.

BLACK, ROBERT LINCOLN, pediatrician, educator; b. LA, Aug. 25, 1930; s. Harold Alfred and Kathryn (Stone) Black; m. Jean Wilmott McGuire, June 27, 1953; children: Donald J., Douglas L., Margaret S. AB, Stanford U., Calif., 1952, MD, 1955. Diplomate Am. Bd. Pediat. Intern Kings County Hosp., Bklyn., 1955—56; resident and fellow Stanford U. Hosp., 1958—62; practice medicine specializing in pediat. Monterey, Calif., 1962—. Clin. prof. Stanford U., 1962—; cons. Calif. Dept. Health, Sacramento, 1962—; mem. Calif. State Maternal, Child, Adolescent Health Bd., 1984—93. Author (with others): California Health Plan for Children, 1979. Mem. Monterey Peninsula Unified Sch. Bd., 1965—73, pres., 1968—70; mem. Mid-Coast Health Sys. Agy., Salinas, Calif., 1975—80, pres., 1979—80; bd. dirs. Lucile Packard Found. for Child Health, 2000—, Lyceum of Monterey Peninsula, 1963—, Carmel Bach Festival, Calif., 1972—81. With USAF, 1956—58. Fellow: Am. Acad. Pediat. (Child Advocacy award sr. sect. 2002); mem.: Physicians for Social Responsibility, Monterey County Med. Soc., Calif. Med. Assn., Inst. Medicine of NAS. Democrat. Home: 976 Mesa Rd Monterey CA 93940-4612 Office: 920 Cass St Monterey CA 93940-4507 Office Phone: 831-372-5841.

BLACK, SHANE, screenwriter; b. Pitts., Dec. 16, 1961; s. Paul and Patricia Ann B. Screenwriter: Lethal Weapon, 1987, The Monster Squad, 1987, Lethal Weapon 2, 1989, Lethal Weapon 3, 1992, Last Action Hero, 1993, Leathal Weapon 4, 1998; screenwriter, prodr.: The Last Boy Scout, 1991 (exec. prodr.), The Long Kiss Goodnight, 1996, AWOL, 1999 (exec. prodr.); screenwriter, dir.: Kiss Kiss, Bang Bang, 2005; actor: (films) Predator, 1987, Dead Heat, 1988, RoboCop 3, 1993, Night Realm, 1994, As Good as It Gets, 1997, We, the Screenwriter, 2002, The Boy Scout, 2002. Office: Endeavor 350 S Beverly Dr Beverly Hills CA 90212-4811

BLACK, W. L. RIVERS, III, lawyer; b. Biloxi, Miss., Sept. 2, 1952; s. William L. Jr. and Virginia B.; m. Lisa A. Paige, Feb. 25, 1981 (div.); children: Jordanna, Caitlin; m. Elaine K., Apr. 25, 1993; children: Aristide, Hallie. BPA, U. Miss., 1974, JD, 1977; LLM in Marine Law, U. Wash., 1982; LLM in Internat. Law, U. Brussels, 1983. Bar: Miss. 1977, U.S. Ct. Mil. Appeals 1980, Wash. 1982, U.S. Ct. Appeals (9th cir.) 1983, U.S. Ct. of Internat. Trade, 1998. Instr. U. Md., Scotland and Italy, 1978-81; ptnr. Lane Powell Spears Lubersky, Seattle, 1983-99, Cozen and O'Connor, Seattle, 2000—. Mem. editl. bd. Maritime Law Reporter. Mem. assoc. bd. Corp. Coun. for the Arts; mem. bd., Pacific Marine Rsch. With USN, 1977-81, Morocco, Scotland. Capt. JAGC, USNR, 1983—. Mem. Seattle-King Bar Assn. (chair maritime sect. 1987-88), Inter-Pacific Bar Assn. (chair maritime law com. 1994-96), Asia-Pacific Lawyers Assn. (chair maritime com. 1986-89), Maritime Law Assn. of U.S. (Proctor), Washington Athletic Club, Naval Club (London). Methodist. Avocation: sailing. Office: Cozen O Connor 1201 3rd Ave Ste 5200 Seattle WA 98101-3071 E-mail: rblack@cozen.com.

BLACK, WILFORD REX, JR., state legislator; b. Salt Lake City, Jan. 31, 1920; s. Wilford Rex and Elsie Isabell (King) B.; m. Helen Shirley Frazer; children: Susan, Janet, Cindy, Joy, Peggy, Vanna, Gayle, Rex. Locomotive engr. Rio Grande R.R., 1941-81; mem. Utah Senate, Salt Lake City, 1972-96, spkr. 3d House, 1975-76, majority whip, 1977-78, minority leader, 1981-90. Sec. Utah State Legis. Bd., United Transp.; chmn. bd. Rail Operators Credit Union, 1958—87. Mission pres. Rose Park Stake Mormon Ch. Rose Park Stake Mormon Ch.; high priest group leader Rose Park 9th Ward, 1980—83, 10th Ward, 1996—99; mem. Rose Park Stake High Coun., 1957—63. With USAR, 1942—45. Recipient various awards r.r. and legis. activities. Democrat. Office: 826 N 1300 W Salt Lake City UT 84116-3877

BLACKBURN, ELIZABETH HELEN, molecular biologist; b. Hobart, Australia, Nov. 26, 1948; d. Harold and Marcia; 1 child. BSc in BioChemistry, U. Melbourne, Australia, 1970, MSc in BioChemistry, 1972; PhD in Molecular Biology, U. Cambridge, Eng., 1975; PhD in Molecular and Cellular Biology, Yale U., New Haven, Conn., 1977; DSc (hon.), Yale U., 1991. Fellow in molecular and cellular biology Yale U., New Haven, 1975-77; fellow in biochemistry U. Calif., San Francisco, 1977-78, asst. prof., dept. molecular biology Berkeley, 1978—83, assoc. prof., dept. molecular biology, 1983—86, prof., dept. molecular biology, 1986—90, prof., dept. microbiology and immunology to Morris Herzstein prof. biology and physiology, dept. of biochemistry and biophysics San Francisco, 1990—, chair dept. microbiology and immunology, 1993-99. Coun. mem. President's Coun. on Bioethics, 2002—04; non-resident fellow Salk Inst.; faculty mem. Program in Biol. Sciences, U. Calif. San Francisco, Biomedical Sciences grad. PhD programs, U. Calif. San Francisco; program mem. U. Calif. San Francisco Comprehensive Cancer Ctr.; sci. adv. bd. mem. Genetics Policy Inst.; invited lectr. in field. Contbr. articles to profl. jours. Recipient Eli Lilly Rsch. award for microbiology & immunology, 1988, le Grand Prix Charles-Leopold Mayer, 1998, Gairdner Found. award, 1998, Australia prize, 1998, Keio Med. Sci. prize, 1999, Harvey prize, 1999, Assn. Am. Med. Coll. Baxter award, 1999, Passano award, Passano Found., 1999, Novartis-Drew award for biomed. sci., 1999, Rosenstiel award, 1999, Feodor Lynen award, 2000, Dickson prize for medicine, 2000, Medal of Honor, Am. Cancer Soc., 2000, G.H.A. Clowes Meml. award, Am. Assn. Cancer Rsch., 2000, Pezcoller Found. Internat. award for Cancer Rsch., 2001, Alfred P. Sloan Jr. prize, Gen. Motors Cancer Rsch. Found., 2001, Bristol-Myers Squibb award for disting. achievement in cancer rsch., 2003, Robert J. and Claire Pasarow Found. Med. Rsch. award, 2003, Dr A.H. Heineken prize for medicine, 2004, Benjamin Franklin medal for life scis., Franklin Inst., 2005, Genetics prize, Peter Gruber Found., 2006, Vanderbilt prize in biomedical sci., 2007, L'Oréal-UNESCO award for Women in Science, 2008; co-recipient Albert Lasker award for basic med. rsch., Lasker Found., 2006, Louisa Gross Horwitz prize, Columbia U., 2007, Medicine & Biomed. Rsch. prize, Albany Med. Ctr., 2008; named Calif. Scientist of Yr., 1999, Scientist of the Yr. Notable, Discover Mag., 2007; named one of 100 Most Influential People in the World, TIME mag., 2007. Fellow: AAAS, Am. Acad. Arts & Scis., Royal Soc. London; mem.: NAS (fgn. assoc.) (Molecular Biology award 1990), Inst. Medicine, Am. Acad. Microbiology, Genetic Soc. of America (bd. dirs. 2000—02), Am. Soc. Cell Biology (pres. 1998, E.B. Wilson medal 2001), Harvey Soc. NY. Achievements include discovery of structures called telomeres on the tips of chromosomes which hold them together; an enzyme called telomerase, the enzyme that restores the ends of chromosomes by replenishing telomeres, which are the protective caps that seal off these chromosome ends. Office: UCSF MC 2200 Genentech Hall 600 16th St San Francisco CA 94158-2517 Office Fax: 415-514-2913. E-mail: elizabeth.blackburn@ucsf.edu.

BLACKHAM, LEONARD MOYLE, state legislator; b. Mt. Pleasant, Utah, Aug. 26, 1949; m. Laura Bagley, Feb. 20, 1970; 6 children. AS, Snow Coll., 1969; BS, Utah State U., 1971. Turkey prodr. agrl. co-op bus.; mem. Utah Ho. of Reps., 1992-94, Utah Senate, Dist. 28, Salt Lake City, 1994—; majority whip, 1995-96; mem. legis. exec. appropriations com.; mem. legis. tax and revenue standing com. Chmn. bd. dirs. Moroni Feed Co.; bd. dirs. Norbest; mem. various coms. including energy, natural resources, agrl. standing. Past county commr. Republican.

BLACKMAN, LEE L., lawyer; b. Phila., Aug. 28, 1950; s. Harold H. and Mary Elizabeth Blackman; m. Kathryn M. Forte, Oct. 5, 1979; 1 child, Shane Forte. BA, U. So. Calif., 1973, JD, 1975. Bar: Calif. 1975, U.S. Dist. Ct. (ctrl. dist.) Calif. 1975, U.S. Ct. Appeals (9th cir.) 1977, U.S. Supreme Ct. 1980, U.S. Dist. Ct. (ea. dist.) Calif. 1984, U.S. Dist. Ct. (no. dist.) Calif. 1988, Hawaii 2005, U.S. Dist. Ct. Hawaii 2005, Ariz. 2008. Atty. Kadison, Pfaelzer, Woodard, Quinn & Rossi, LA, 1975-81, assoc., ptnr., 1981-87; ptnr. McDermott, Will & Emery, LA, 1987-2000; atty. pvt. practice, 2000—. Arbitrator LA Superior Ct., 1986—90; judge pro tem Superior Ct. State of Calif., 1986—92; spkr. in field. Mem. editl. adv. bd. Airport Noise Report, 1989—99; article editor: ABA Health Litig. Reporter, 1996—97. Mem.: State Bar Ariz., State Bar Hawaii, Legion Lex Inn of Ct. (master bencher 1989—2000), State Bar Calif. Office: 8035 E Corte Del Joven Tucson AZ 85750 E-mail: llblackman@aol.com.

BLACKMORE, PETER, computer company executive; MA, Trinity Coll., Cambridge. Mktg. dir. Rank Xerox UK, England; v.p. computing group for Europe Compaq (merged with HP), 1991—2000; sr. v.p. & gen. mgr. for N. Am. Compaq Computer Corp., 1999, sr. v.p. & gen. mgr. sales & services, 1999—2000, exec. v.p. sales & services, 2000—02; exec. v.p. enterprise sys. group Hewlett-Packard, Palo Alto, Calif., 2002—04, exec. v.p. customer solutions group, 2004; advisor to bd. dirs. StreamServe, Inc., 2004; exec. v.p., pres. worldwide sales, mktg. & tech. Unisys Corp., 2005—07; pres., COO UTStarcom, Inc., Alameda, Calif., 2007—08, pres., CEO, 2008—. Office: UTStarcom Inc 1275 Harbor Bay Pkwy Alameda CA 94502

BLACKSTOCK, JOSEPH ROBINSON, newspaper editor; b. LA, Dec. 8, 1947; s. Joseph Richard McCall and Doris Louise (Robinson) B.; m. Nancy Ruth Frederiksen, Feb. 9, 1974; children: Miriam, Susan, Cynthia, Catherine. BA, Calif. State U., LA, 1970, MA, 1977. Sports writer Monterey Park Californian, 1967-72; sports and news writer, mng. editor San Gabriel Valley Tribune, West Covina, Calif., 1972-89; exec. editor Pasadena (Calif.) Star-News, 1989-93; layout editor Riverside (Calif.) Press-Enterprise, 1993-98; asst. city editor Inland Valley Daily Bull., Ontario, Calif., 1998—. With USAR, 1970-78.

BLAHD, WILLIAM HENRY, nuclear medicine physician, director; b. Cleve., May 11, 1921; s. Moses and Rae (Lichtenstader) B.; m. Miriam Weiss, Jan. 29, 1971; children— Andrea Margery, William Henry, Karen Ruth. Student, Western Res. U., 1939-40, U. Ariz., 1940-42; MD, Tulane U., 1945. Diplomate Am. Bd. Nuclear Medicine (chmn. 1982, v.p. 1986-97, exec. dir. 1998-2003), Am. Bd. Internal Medicine (bd. govs. 1981). Resident in pathology and internal medicine VA Wadsworth Med. Ctr., 1948-52, ward officer metabolic rsch. ward, 1951-52, asst. chief radioisotope svc., 1952-56, chief nuclear medicine dept. LA, 1956-97, dir. nuclear medicine tng. program, 1997—; nuc. medicine residency program dir. Am. Bd. Nuc. Medicine, LA. Prof. dept. medicine U. Calif., Los Angeles; mem. ACGME residency rev. com. for nuclear medicine, 1979-97, chmn., 1991-97; mem. Joint Rev. Com. on Ednl. Programs in Nuclear Medicine Tech., 1986-93; mem. subcom. on naturally occurring and accelerator produced radioactive materials Com. on Interagency Radiation Rsch. and Policy Coordination, 1988-92; cons. nuclear medicine; mem. adv. com. on human uses radioisotopes Calif. Dept. Health Svcs.; mem. HEW Interagy. Task Force on Ionizing Radiation, 1978; dir. nuclear medicine Mt. Sinai Hosp., L.A., 1955-76, Valley Presbyn. Med. Ctr., Van Nuys, Calif., 1959-85, St. Joseph Hosp. Med. Ctr., Burbank, Calif., 1958-83. Author 3 textbooks on nuclear medicine. Contbr. numerous articles to med. jours. Served with U.S. Army, 1946-48. Grantee Muscular Dystrophy Assn. Am., 1965-69, Nat. Cancer Inst., 1973-76; recipient Lifetime Achievement award Wadsworth Physicians and Surgeons Alumni Assn., 2000, William H. Oldendorl Lifetime Achievement award West L.A. Med. Ctr., 2000. Fellow ACP, Am. Coll. Nuclear Physicians (bd. regents 1974-80); mem. AMA, Soc. Nuc. Medicine (trustee 1966-74, pres. 1977-78, Disting. Scientist award No./So. Calif. chpts. 1975, Disting. Sci. award We. Regional chpts. 1995, Disting. Pub. Svc. Career award Fed. Exec. Bd. L.A. 1998, Presdl. Disting. Svc. award 2000, 02), Health Physics Soc. (pres. So. Calif. chpt. 1964-66), Calif. Med. Assn. (sci. bd. 1975-81, chmn. adv. bd. nuclear medicine 1976-84), Am. Bd. Med. Spltys., COCERT, Soc. Exptl. Biology and Medicine, Los Angeles County, Calif. Med. Assns., We. Assn. Physicians, Am. Fedn. Clin. Rsch., Nat. Assn. VA Chiefs Nuclear Medicine (pres. 1985-87), We. Soc. Clin. Rsch., Alpha Omega Alpha. Office: Nuclear Med Dept VA Greater LA Healthcare 691/W115 11301 Wilshire Blvd Los Angeles CA 90073

BLAINE, DAVID (DAVID BLAINE WHITE), magician; b. Bklyn., Apr. 4, 1973; s. John Bukalo and Patrice Maureen White. Performed in TV spl. (also exec. prodr.) David Blaine: Street Magic, 1996, David Blaine: Magic Man, 1998, David Blaine: Premature Burial, 1999, David Blaine: Frozen in Time, 2000, David Blaine: Fearless, 2002, David Blaine: Vertigo, 2002, David Blaine: Above the Below, 2003, David Blaine: Drowned Alive, 2006, David Blaine: Shackled, 2006; actor: Celebrity, 1998, Mister Lonely, 2007; guest performances include TV programs Rosie O'Donnel Show, Late Night with Conan O'Brien, Howard Stern, Friay Night with Jonathan Ross, Louis, Marin and Michael, Before, During and After the Sunset, The Work of Director Mark Romanek; author (book) Mysterious Stranger, 2002. Jewish. Achievements include submerging himself in a water-filled sphere for 177 hours, more than 1 week, in New York City, 2006; setting the Guinness World Record for breath-holding with 17 minutes and 4 seconds, 2008.

BLAINE, DAVIS ROBERT, valuation consultant, investment banker; b. Gary, Ind., Oct. 30, 1943; s. Jack Davis and Virginia Sue (Mintzer) B.; m. Karen Ellen Levenson, Dec. 28, 1981; children: Davis Justin, Tristan D., Brittara K., Whitney K. BA, Dartmouth Coll., 1965; MBA, U. Mich., 1969. Founder, sr. v.p. Am. Valuation Cons., Chgo., 1971-78, chmn. bd., 1978; exec. v.p. Valuation Rsch., Chgo., 1978-80, pres. LA, 1980-83; sr. v.p. Arthur D. Little Valuation, Inc., Woodland Hills, Calif., 1983-87; owner, chmn. bd. Olesen, 1989-92; founder, mng. ptnr. Profls. Network Group, 1988—. Founder, chmn. bd. The Mentor Group Inc., L.A., 1981-; founder, pres. ICS Corp., Chgo., 1976-82, v.p. bd., 1982-87. Served to lt. (j.g.) USNR, 1966-68. Mem.: Beta Theta Pi. Office Phone: 818-597-3559. Business E-Mail: dblaine@thementorgrp.com.

BLAIR, ANDREW LANE, JR., lawyer, educator; b. Oct. 10, 1946; s. Andrew Lane and Catherine (Shaffer) B.; m. Catherine Lynn Kessler, June 21, 1969; children: Christopher Lane, Robert Brook. BA, Washington & Lee U., 1968; JD, U. Denver, 1972. Bar: Colo. 1972, U.S. Dist. Ct. Colo. 1972, U.S. Ct. Appeals (10th cir.) 1972. Assoc. Dawson, Nagel, Sherman & Howard, Denver, 1972-78; mem. Sherman & Howard LLC, Denver, 1978. Lectr. U. Denver Law Sch., 1980-83, U. Colo., Colorado Springs, 1984, U. Colo. Law Sch., Boulder, 1991. Author: Uniform Commercial Code sects. for Colorado Methods of Practice, 1982; contbr. articles to profl. jours. Mem. ABA, Colo. Bar Assn. Democrat. Methodist. Office: Sherman & Howard 633 17th St Ste 2900 Denver CO 80202-3665 E-mail: ablair@sah.com.

BLAIR, DONALD W., apparel executive; b. West Chester, Pa., Apr. 4, 1958; BS in Econs., U. Pa., Phila., 1980, MBA, 1981. CPA NY, 1982. Sr. acct. Deloitte, Haskins & Sells, 1981-84; sr. fin. analyst PepsiCo, Inc., 1984-85, v.p., planning Pizza Hut divsn., 1996-97; mgr. fin. planning Pepsi-Cola USA, 1985-86, group mgr. bus. planning, 1986-88; fin. dir. Pepsi-Cola New Eng., 1988-90, Pepsi-Cola Japan, Tokyo, 1990-92; v.p. fin. Pepsi-Cola Asia, Hong Kong, 1992-96; sr. v.p., fin. The Pepsi Bottling Group Inc., 1997-99; v.p., CFO Nike, Inc., Beaverton, Oreg., 1999—. Office: Nike Inc One Bowerman Dr Beaverton OR 97005-6453 Office Phone: 503-671-6453.

BLAIR, FREDERICK DAVID, interior designer; b. Denver, June 15, 1946; s. Frederick Edward and Margaret (Whitely) Blair. BA, U. Colo., 1969; postgrad., U. Denver, 1981—82. Interior designer The Denver, 1969-76, store mgr., 1976-80; v.p. Hartley Ho. Interiors, Ltd., Denver, 1980-83; pvt. practice Denver, 1983—. Com. mem. Ice Ho. Design Ctr., Denver, 1985—86, Design Directory Western Region, Denver, 1986; mem. edn. com. ASID Nat. Conf., Denver, 1991; coord. Amb. Vol. Program Denver Internat. Airport, 2000—; mgr. concierge & visitors ctr. Cherry Creek Shopping Ctr., Denver, 2003. Designs shown in various mags. Bd. dirs. One Day, Very Spl. Arts, 1993, Supporters Children, 1996—, mem. steering com., 1994, pres.-elect, 1996—97, pres., bd. dirs., 1999—; mem. Denver Art Mus., Nat. Trust Hist. Preservation, Hist. Denver. Recipient Aviation Ace Award, DIA, 2001. Mem.: Am. Soc. Interior Designers (co-chmn. com. profl. registration 1986, mem. edn. com. nat. conf. 1991, bd. dirs. Colo. chpt. 1990—, Humanist award 1997). Christian Scientist. Avocations: skiing, painting, tennis. Home Phone: 303-394-7972; Office Phone: 303-399-4305. Personal E-mail: rickblairdesign@aol.com.

BLAIR, M. WAYNE, lawyer; b. Spokane, Wash., Oct. 17, 1942; BS in Elec. Engr., U. Washington, 1965, JD, 1968. Bar: Wash. 1968. Mem. Wash. State Bd. for Jud. Adminstrn., 1995-2000. With USAF, 1968-72. Recipient Helen M. Geisness award, 1987, President's award, 1990. Mem. ABA (Ho. of Dels. 1988-91), Am. Judicature Soc.,

Washington State Bar Assn. (bd. govs. 1991-94, pres. 1998-99, Lifetime Service award, 2004), Seattle-King County Bar Assn. (trustee 1981-83, pres. 1987-88). Office: 5500 Bank of America Twr 701 5th Ave Seattle WA 98105-7097

BLAIR, ROBERT L., technology company executive; Dir. sales Precision Monolithics, Inc.; pres. SEMAG divsn. Xidex Corp.; sr. v.p. sales and ops. Logistix Corp.; v.p. ops. ESS Tech. Inc., Fremont, Calif., 1994-97, CEO, pres., bd. dirs. Office: 48401 Fremont Blvd Fremont CA 94538

BLAIRE, STEPHEN EDWARD, bishop; b. LA, Dec. 22, 1941; Grad., St. John's Sem., Camarillo, Calif. Ordained priest Archdiocese of LA, 1967, curia moderator, chancellor, 1986—90, aux. bishop, 1990—95; assoc. pastor St. Luke's Ch., Temple City, Calif.; tchr. Bishop Alemany HS, Mission Hills, Calif., prin., 1977—86; vice prin. Bishop Amat HS, La Puente, Calif.; ordained bishop, 1990; regional bishop Our Lady of the Angels, 1995—99; bishop Diocese of Stockton, Calif., 1999—. Mem.: US Conf. Cath. Bishops (pres. com. for ecumenical and inter-religious affairs). Roman Catholic. Office: Diocese of Stockton 1105 N Lincoln St Stockton CA 95203-2410 Office Phone: 209-466-0636. Office Fax: 209-941-9722.

BLAIS, ROBERT HOWARD, lawyer; b. Muskegon, Mich., May 14, 1955; BA with high honors, Mich. State U., 1977; JD cum laude, U. Notre Dame, 1980. Ptnr. Bogle & Gates, Seattle, 1988-93; shareholder Gores & Blais, Seattle, 1993—. Adj. prof. estate and tax planning Seattle U., 1982-83; chairperson Wash. State U. Planned Giving Adv. Bd., 1989-96. Mem. ABA, Wash. State Bar Assn. (real property, probate and trust coun. 1987-88), Seattle-King County Bar Assn., Estate Planning Coun. Seattle (pres. 1996-97), Am. Coll. Trust and Estate Counsel. Office: Gores and Blais 1201 3rd Ave Ste 4800 Seattle WA 98101-3266

BLAKE, CHARLES E., minister, bishop; b. Little Rock, Aug. 5, 1940; s. Junios Augustus and Lula (Champion) B.; m. Mae Lawrence Blake; children: Kimberly Roxanne, Charles Blake II, Lawrence Champion. BA, U.S. Internat. U., 1962; MDiv, ITC, Atlanta, 1965; DDiv, Calif. Grad Sch. Theology, 1982; ThD, Oral Roberts U., Tulsa, 1988. Ordained to ministry, Ch. of God in Christ, 1962. Interim pastor Marietta (Ga.) Ch. of God in Christ, 1963-64; co-pastor Greater Jackson Meml. Ch. of God in Christ, San Diego, 1965-69; pastor West Angeles Ch. of God in Christ, LA, 1969—; bishop First Jurisdiction of So. Calif., LA, 1985—; exec. bd. Bd. Regents, Oral Roberts U., Tulsa, 1986—, chmn. exec. com., 1991—; gen. bd. officer Gen. Bd. of Ch. of God in Christ Internat., 1988—; founding chmn. bd. dirs. C.H. Mason Theol. Sem.; exec. com. mem. bd. dirs. Interdenominational Theol. Sem. Mem. Charismatic Bible Ministries, Inc., Tulsa, 1987—, Network of Christian Ministries, 1987-91; adv. com. mem. Pentecostal World Conf.; founder, CEO Save Africa's Children; LA bd. mem. Azusa Centennial Celebration, 2006; chmn., founder LA Ecumenical Congress; mem. religious adv. com. Coun. Fgn. Rels. Author sermon anthology with over 500 original works. Recipient Whitney M. Young award, LA Urban League, 2000, Big Heart award, Greenlining Inst., William Booth award, Salvation Army, Humanitarian medal, Harvard Found., 2003, 2006 Trumpet award, Disting. Leadership award, African Presdl. Archives and Rsch. Ctr. Boston U., 2007; named to Power 150, Ebony mag., 2008. Achievements include having February 5, 2004 designated as Bishop Charles E. Blake Day by LA County Bd. Suprs. Office: West Angeles Ch of God Christ 3045 Crenshaw Blvd Los Angeles CA 90016-4264

BLAKE, D. STEVEN, lawyer; b. Saginaw, Mich., June 2, 1940; BA, Mich. State U., 1963; JD, U. Calif., Davis, 1971. Bar: Calif. 1972. Of counsel Downey Brand LLP, Sacramento, 1971—; arbitrator, mediator. Adj. prof. law U. Pacific, 1998-2000. Co-author: California Real Estate Finance and Construction Law, 1995. Mem. ABA (bus. law sect.), Am. Arbitration Assn. (arbitrator), State Bar Calif. (co-chair corp. com., sect., fin. instns. com., bus. law sect., panelist, presenter numerous seminars Calif. State Bar Continuing Edn. Bar 1981-91, co-chair corps. com. bus. law sect. 1997), Yolo County Bar Assn. Office: Downey Brand LLP 555 Capitol Mall Ste 1050 Sacramento CA 95814-4601 Office Phone: 916-444-1000.

BLAKE, PATRICK H., trucking executive; b. 1949; married; two sons. Dockman Consol. Freightways, 1969, exec. v.p. ops., 1994-99, pres., 1999-2000, CEO, 2000—; pres., CEO Consol. Freightways Corp., 2000—.

BLAKE, ROB, professional hockey player; b. Simcoe, Ont., Can., Dec. 10, 1969; m. Brandy Blake; 1 child, Jack. Defenseman LA Kings, 1989—2001, 2006—08, capt., 2007—08; defenseman Colo. Avalanche, 2001—06, San Jose Sharks, 2008—. Player NHL All-Star Game, 1994, 1999—2004; mem. Team Can., Olympic Games, Salt Lake City, 2003. Recipient James Norris Trophy, 1998; named to First All-Star Team, NHL, 1998, Second All-Star Team, 2000—02. Achievements include being a member of Stanley Cup Champion Colo. Avalanche, 2001; being a member of gold medal Canadian Hockey team, Salt Lake City Olympic Games, 2002. Office: San Jose Sharks 525 W Santa Clara St San Jose CA 95113

BLAKENEY, ALLAN EMRYS, Canadian government official, lawyer, educator; b. Bridgewater, NS, Can., Sept. 7, 1925; s. John Cline and Bertha (Davies) B.; m. Mary Elizabeth Schwartz, 1950 (dec. 1957); m. Anne Louise Gorham, May 1959; children: Barbara, Hugh, David, Margaret. BA, Dalhousie U., 1945, LLB, 1947, LLD (hon.); BA, Oxford U., 1949, MA, 1955; DCL (hon.), Mount Allison U.; LLD (hon.), York U., Toronto, U. Western Ont., London, 1991, U. Regina, 1993, U. Sask., 1995. Bar: N.S. 1950, Sask. 1951. Queen's counsel, 1961; sec. to govt. fin. office Govt. Sask., Canada, 1950-55; chmn. Sask. Securities Commn., 1955-58; ptnr. Davidson, Davidson & Blakeney, Regina, Sask., 1958-60, Griffin, Blakeney, Beke, Koskie & Lueck, Regina, 1964-70; premier of Sask., 1971-82; mem. Sask. Legislature, 1960-88; prof. Osgoode Hall Law Sch. York U., 1988—90; prof. U. Sask., 1990—. Leader of the opposition Sask. Legislature, 1970-71, 82-87; min. of edn., Sask., 1960-61, provincial treas., 1961-62, min. pub. health, 1962-64; mem. Royal Commn. on Aborginal Peoples, 1991-93. Decorated Officer Order of Can., Sask. Order of Merit; Rhodes scholar, Oxford U., 1948—49. Fellow Royal Soc. Can. Home: 1752 Prince of Wales Ave Saskatoon SK Canada S7K 3E5 Office: U Sask Coll Law 15 Campus Dr Saskatoon SK Canada S7N 5A6 Office Phone: 306-966-5881.

BLAKESLEE, SAM, state legislator; b. Calif. m Kara; children: three. Attended, Cuesta Cmty. Coll.; B in Geophysics, U. Calif., B in Geophysics, M in Geophysics, U. Calif., Berkeley; PhD, U. Calif., Santa Barbara. California State Assemblyman, District 33, 2005-; vice chairman, Public Employ, Retirement & Soc Sec; member, Agriculture, Budget, Budget Process, Util & Commerce comts, currently-.Blakeslee & Blakeslee Invest Firm, Strategic Budget Planner; Exxon, Research Scientist. Republican. Office: State Capitol Rm 4015 Sacramento CA 94249 also: Dist 33 1104 Palm St San Luis Obispo CA 93401 Office Phone: 916-319-2033, 805-549-3381. Office Fax: 916-319-2133, 805-549-3400. Business E-Mail: assemblymember.blakeslee@assembly.ca.gov.

BLANCH, HARVEY WARREN, chemical engineering educator; BS in Chem. Engring., U. Sydney, Australia, 1968; PhD, U. NSW, 1971. Lectr. Sch. of Biol. Technology U. NSW, 1971; asst. prof. dept. chem. engring. U. Del., 1974-77, assoc. prof., 1977-78; assoc. prof. dept. chem. engring. U. Calif., Berkeley, 1978-82, prof. dept. chem. engring., 1982—, chair dept. chem. engring., 1997—2001; sr. faculty scientist Lawrence Berkeley Nat. Lab., 1984—; assoc. dir. Marine Bioproducts Engring. Ctr., 1998—2004. Mem. numerous adv. bds. and panels in field, including NIH Cell Culture Ctr., 1991—, rsch. program com. Dept. Energy, Basic Energy Scis., 1993; numerous univ. coms.; cons. and lectr. in field. Author: (book) Biochemical Engineering, 1995; editor: Jour. Bioprocess Engring., 1986—, The Chem. Engring. Jour./Biochem. Engring. Jour., 1985—, (books) Applied Biocatalysis, 1991, Comprehensive Biotechnology, 1980-84, others; mem. editl. bd.: Biotechnology and Bioengring., 1990—, Advances in Biochem. Engring., 1992—; author more than 250 publs. in field; patentee in field. Fellow Internat. Inst. Biotechnology, Am. Inst. for Med. and Biol. Engring. (founder); mem. NAE, Am. Inst. Chem. Engrs. (recipient Food, Pharm. and Bioengring. Divsn. award 1996), Am. Chem. Soc. (Johnson award 1995, Enzyme Engring award 1997), Am. Soc. Engring. Edn. Office: U Calif/Berkeley Chem Engrg 420 Latimer Hall Berkeley CA 94720 Office Phone: 510-642-1387. E-mail: blanch@socrates.berkeley.edu.

BLANCHARD, CHARLES ALAN, lawyer, retired state senator; b. San Diego, Apr. 14, 1959; s. David Dean and Janet (Laxson) B.; m. Allison Major, 2001. BS, Lewis & Clark Coll., 1981; M of Pub. Policy, Harvard U., 1985, JD, 1985. Bar: Ariz. 1987, U.S. Dist. Ct. Ariz. 1988, U.S. Ct. Appeals (D.C. cir.) 1988, U.S. Ct. Appeals (9th cir.) 1988, U.S. Supreme Ct. 1994. Law clk. to hon. Harry T. Edwards, Washington, 1985-86; law clk. to hon. Sandra Day O'Connor U.S. Supreme Ct., Washington, 1986-87; assoc. ind. counsel Ind. Counsel James McKay, Washington, 1987-88; atty. Brown & Bain, P.A., Phoenix, 1988-97; state senator State of Ariz., Phoenix, 1991-95; dir. Office of Legal Counsel Office of Nat. Drug Control Policy, Washington, 1997-99; gen. counsel U.S. Army, 1999-2001; ptnr. Brown & Bain PA, Phoenix, 2001—04, Perkins Coie Brown & Bain PA, Phoenix, 2004—. Adj. prof. Ariz. State U. Coll. Law, 1996, 2003—; chmn. Senate Judiciary Com., Phoenix, 1991-93; Dem. candidate U.S. Congress, 1994; dir. homeland security State of Ariz., 2003; mem. regulatory rev. coun., Gov., 2004—. Contbr. articles to profl. jours. Bd. dirs. Luth. Vol. Corps., Washington, 1986-88, Florence (Ariz.) Immigrant and Refugee Rights Project, 1990-97, 2001-, Homeless Legal Assistance Project, Phoenix, 1992-97, Tempe Comty. Action Agy., 1994-97, ABA Com. on Immigration Law, 1996-98, ABA Com. on Substance Abuse, 1998-02, Childrens Action Alliance, Phoenix, 2005—, Ariz. Found. for Legal Svc. and Edn., 2005—; state committeeman Ariz. Dem. Party, Phoenix, 1991-97, 2005—07. Recipient Disting. Svc. award Ariz. Atty. Gen., 1992, Disting. Civilian Svc. award U.S. Army, 2001; Toll fellowship Coun. of State Govts., 1991; named Disting. Young Alumni Lewis and Clark Coll., 1987. Mem. ABA. Home: 1814 Palmcroft Dr NE Phoenix AZ 85007 Office: PO Box 400 Phoenix AZ 85001-0400 Home Phone: 602-254-5851; Office Phone: 602-351-8000. E-mail: cblanchard@perkinscoie.com.

BLANCHARD, JAY S., state senator; b. Des Moines, 1946; married; 3 children. PhD, U. Ga., 1979. With U.S. PO; tchr.; Dem. senator dist. 30 Ariz. State Senate. Mem. faculty U. Miss., U. Ky., U. Tex.; mem. fin., transp. and ethics coms. Ariz. State Senate, vice chair rules com.; cons. in field. Author, editor 5 books on tech.; contbr. chpts. to books, articles to profl. jours. With USMC, 1971-73. Mem. APA, Am. Ednl. Rsch. Assn., Internat. Reading Assn. Office: Ariz State Senate 1700 W Washington Phoenix AZ 85007-2890 E-mail: jblancha@azleg.state.az.us.

BLAND, DOROTHY ANN, construction executive, real estate agent; b. Black Township, Pa., Jan. 12, 1945; m. Jonathan Lee Sharp, Sept. 28, 1963 (dec. Dec. 31, 1979); children: Deborah, Todd, Wade; m. Brian C. Bland, Nov. 2, 1985; stepchildren: Paulette, Kelli. Lic. Real Estate Agent, Utah. Beauty coll. recruiter, sec. Continental Coll. of Beauty, Salt Lake City, 1968-72; exec. sec. Vaughn Hansen Assoc., Salt Lake City, 1973-82; v.p., co-owner Bland Bros., Inc., West Jordan, Utah, 1985—; co-owner Blands Sand & Gravel, Utah, 1990—. Real estate agent Preferred Properties, Salt Lake City, 1982-90, Mansell, Salt Lake City, 1990—. Avocations: golf, travel. Office: Bland Brothers Topsoil And Nursery PO Box 708250 Sandy UT 84070-8250

BLANDFORD, ROGER DAVID, science educator; b. Grantham, Eng., Aug. 28, 1949; s. Jack George and Janet Margaret (Evans) B.; m. Elizabeth Kellett, Aug. 5, 1972; children: Jonathan, Edward. BA, Magdalene Coll., Cambridge U., 1970; MA, PhD, Cambridge U., 1974. Rsch. fellow St. John's Coll., Cambridge U., 1973-76; asst. prof. astronomy Calif. Inst. Tech., Pasadena, 1976-79, prof., 1979-89, Richard Chace Tolman prof. theoretical astrophysics, 1989—; mem. Inst. Advanced Study, Princeton, 1974-75; Luke Blossom prof. particle astrophysics and cosmology Stanford U., 2003—, Pehong and Adele Chen dir. Kvali Inst. for Particle Astrophysics and Cosmology, 2003—. Contbr. articles to profl. publs. W.B.R. King scholar, 1967-70; Charles Kingsley Bye fellow, 1972-73; Alfred P. Sloan research fellow, 1980, Guggenheim fellow, 1988—. Fellow Royal Soc., Royal Astron. Soc. (Eddington medal 1999), Cambridge Philos. Soc.; mem. NAS, Am. Astron. Soc. (Warner prize 1982, Heineman prize 1998), Am. Acad. Arts and Scis. Office: PO Box 20450 MS29 Stanford CA 94309 Home: 820 Monte Rosa Dr Menlo Park CA 94025-6723 Office Phone: 650-926-2600. Business E-Mail: rdb3@stanford.edu.

BLANKENSHIP, EDWARD G., architect; b. Martin, Tenn., June 22, 1943; BArch, Columbia U., 1966, MSc in Arch., 1967; MLitt in Arch., Cambridge U., Eng., 1971. Sr. v.p. Landrum & Brown, Inc. Office: 218 Park Crest Dr Newport Beach CA 92657 Office Phone: 949-252-5214.

BLANKLEY, TONY, public relations executive, columnist, radio personality; b. London, 1948; m. Davis C. Lynda; 3 children. BA in Polit. Sci., UCLA; JD, Loyola Law Sch., LA. Bar: Calif. 1972. Prosecutor Calif. Atty. General's office, 1972—82; policy analyst and speechwriter Pres. Reagan Adminstrn., 1982—88; staff writer Congresswoman Bobbi Fiedler, 1988—90; press. sec. House spkr. Newt Gingrich US Congress, 1990—97; contbg. editor George Mag., 1997—99; weekly polit. columnist The Washington Times, 1999—2002, editl. page editor, 2002—07, now weekly columnist; exec. v.p. global public affairs Edelman, Washington, 2007—. Vis. sr. fellow in nat.-security comm. Heritage Found., Washington, 2007—. Actor: (films) The Harder They Fall, 1955; author: The West's Last Chance: Will We Win the Clash of Civilizations?, 2005, American Grit: What It Will Take to Survive and Win in the 21st Century, 2007; co-host (nat. syndicated pub. radio prog.) KCRW's Left, Right & Center, regular panelist (TV series) The Diane Rehm Show, The McLaughlin Group. Office: KCRW 1900 Pico Blvd Santa Monica CA 90405-1947 Office Phone: 202-636-2869.*

BLANTON, JOHN ARTHUR, architect, writer; b. Houston, Jan. 1, 1928; s. Arthur Alva and Caroline (Jeter) Blanton; m. Marietta Louise Newton, Apr. 10, 1954 (dec. 1976); children: Jill Blanton Milne, Lynette Blanton Rowe(dec.), Elena Diane. BA, Rice U., 1948, BS in Architecture, 1949. With Richard J. Neutra, LA, 1950-64; pvt. practice Manhattan Beach, Calif., 1964—. Lectr. UCLA Ext., 1967—76, 1985. Columnist: Easy Reader newspaper, 1994—96; contbr. articles to profl. jours. City commr. Bd. Bldg. Code Appeals, Manhattan Beach; chmn. Zoning Adjustment Bd., 1990, Planning Commn., 1993—99. With Signal Corps US Army, 1951—53. Recipient local and nat. awards (published internationally). Mem.: AIA (contbr. book revs. to jour. 1972—76). Office: John Blanton AIA Architect 1456 12th St # 4 Manhattan Beach CA 90266-6187 Office Phone: 310-546-1200.

BLANTZ, ROLAND C., nephrologist, educator; b. Portland, Oreg. BA in Humanities and Chem. Engring., Johns Hopkins U., Balt., 1961, MD, 1965. Diplomate Am. Bd. Internal Medicine, Am. Bd. Nephrology. Resident U. Colo. Med. Ctr., 1965—67; fellow U. Tex. Southwestern Med. Sch., 1969—72; chief nephrology VA San Diego Healthcare Sys., 1972—90; prof. nephrology U. Calif., San Diego, 1980—, head nephrology, hypertension, 1988—. Contbr. articles to profl. jours. Capt. USAF, 1967—69. Recipient William S. Middleton award, Dept. Vets. Affairs, 2006. Mem.: Coun. Am. Kidney Socs. (chair 2001—02), Josish Macy Found., Maritius Kidney Found. (Seldin award 2005), AAP, AFCR, ASCI, Am. Soc. Nephrology (pres. 2001—02). Office: Dept Medicine U Calif San Diego 9500 Gilman Dr #9111H La Jolla CA 92093 Office Phone: 858-552-7528. E-mail: rblantz@ucsd.edu.

BLASCHKE, TERRENCE FRANCIS, medicine and molecular pharmacology educator; b. Rochester, Minn., Oct. 4, 1942; s. Robert Elmer and Carmella Ann Blaschke; m. Jeannette F. Martin, June 8, 1968; children: Anne, John. BS in Math. cum laude, U. Denver, 1964; MD, Columbia U., 1968. Diplomate Am. Bd. Internal Medicine, Nat. Bd. Med. Examiners. Intern in medicine UCLA Ctr. for Health Scis., 1968-69, asst. resident, 1969-70; clin. assoc. metabolism br. Nat. Cancer Inst., NIH, Bethesda, Md., 1970-72; clin. rsch fellow div. clin. pharmacology dept. medicine U. Calif. Med. Ctr., San Francisco, 1972-74; asst. prof. medicine (clin. pharmacology) Stanford (Calif.) U. Sch. Medicine, 1974-81, asst. prof. pharmacology, 1978-81, assoc. prof. medicine (clin. pharmacology) and pharmacology, 1981-91, prof. medicine (clin. pharmacology)-molecular pharmacology, 1991—2006, prof. medicine and molecular pharmacology emeritus, 2006—, assoc. dean for med. student advising, 2002—06; v.p. Pharsight Corp., Calif., 2000—02. Bd. govs. Am. Bd. Clin. Pharmacology, 1990-92; vis. worker div. molecular pharmacology Nat. Inst. for Med. Rsch., London, 1980-81, Ctr. for Biopharm. Scis., U. Leiden and dept. med. info. scis. Erasmus U., The Netherlands, 1990; mem. Medi-Cal drug use rev. bd. Calif. Dept. Health Svcs., 1993-96; chmn. generic drugs adv. com. FDA, 1990-94, mem. nonprescription drugs adv. com., 2003-; mem. bd. sci. advisors Merck Sharp and Dohme Rsch. Labs., Rahway, N.J., 1986-90; mem. pharmacology study sect. NIH, 1979-83; faculty of medicine Moi U., El Doret, Kenya; vis. prof. Ctr. Drug Devel. Sci., Georgetown U., 1997-98; spl. govt. employee FDA, 1997-. Mem. editl. bd. Drug Therapeutics: Concepts for Physicians, 1978-81, Rational Drug Therapy, 1984-85, Clin. Pharmacology and Therapeutics, 1981—, Drug Interaction Facts, 1983-87, Drug Metabolism and Disposition, 1994-2000; assoc. editor Ann. Rev. Pharmacology and Toxicology, 1989—. Officer USPHS, 1970-72. Recipient faculty devel. award in clin. pharmacology Pharm. Mfrs. Assn. Found.; Burroughs-Wellcome scholar. Mem.: AAAS, ACP, Western Pharmacology Soc., Western Assn. Physicians, Western Soc. Clin. Investigation, Am. Fedn. Clin. Rsch., Am. Soc. Pharmacology and Exptl. Therapeutics (exec. com. clin. pharmacology divsn. 1986—89, chair clin. pharmacology divsn. 2002—03), Am. Soc. for Clin. Pharmacology and Therapeutics (chmn. liaison com. clin. pharmacology 1985—89, sci. program com. 1986—87, pres. 1988—89, assoc. sec.-treas. 1990—92, chmn. long range planning com. 1992—94, Rawls-Palmer award, Henry W. Elliott award), Phi Beta Kappa, Alpha Omega Alpha. Office: Stanford U Med Ctr Div Clin Pharmacology S-009 300 Pasteur Dr Stanford CA 94305-5130 E-mail: blaschke@stanford.edu.

BLASE, NANCY GROSS, librarian; b. New Rochelle, NY; d. Albert Philip and Elsie Wise (May) Gross; m. Barrie Wayne Blase, June 19, 1966 (div.); m. Charles M. Goldstein, July 25, 1999; 1 child, Eric Wayne. BA in Biology, Marietta Coll., Ohio, 1964; MLS, U. Ill., 1965. Info. scientist brain info. svc. Biomed. Libr., UCLA, 1965-66; libr. Health Sci. Libr., U. Wash., Seattle, 1966-68, Medlars search analyst, 1970-72, coord. Medline, 1972-79, head Natural Scis. Libr., 1979—. Mem. libr. adv. com. Elizabeth C. Miller Libr., Ctr. for Urban Horticulture, Seattle, 1986-90. Contbr. articles to profl. jours. Mem. Bet Chaverim, Seattle, pres., 1998—2000. NSF fellow interdept. tng. program for sci. info. specialists U. Ill., 1964-65. Mem.: Internat. Tng. in Comm. (pres. Pacific N.W. region 1994—95), Am. Soc. Info. Sci. (pres. personal computer spl. interest group 1993—94, chair constn. and bylaws com. 1994—97, chair med. informatics spl. interest group 1998—99, rsch. grantee Pacific N.W. chpt. 1984—85), Phi Beta Kappa (pres. U. Wash. chpt. 1993—97, pres. Puget Sound Assn. 2001—03, mem. com. on chpts. 2002—). Avocations: walking, reading. Home: 10751 Durland Ave NE Seattle WA 98125-6945 Office: U Wash Natural Scis Libr Box 352900 Seattle WA 98195-2900 Personal E-mail: nancy@blases.org. Business E-Mail: nblase@u.washington.edu.

BLASIER, ROBERT DALTON, JR., lawyer; b. Pitts., Feb. 27, 1945; s. Robert D. Blasier Sr.; m. Charlotte M. Blasier, Aug. 17, 1990; children: Matthew, Elizabeth. BS, Carnegie Inst. Tech., Pitts., 1967; JD, Harvard U., 1970. Bar: Calif 1971. Dep. dist. atty. Contra Costa County Office, Martinez, Calif., 1970-78; dir. enforcement Calif. Fair Polit. Practices Commn., Sacramento, 1978-84; prv. practice El

Dorado Hills, Calif. State Bar Calif. Avocations: golf, sailing. Office: 3600 Peidra Montana Rd El Dorado Hills CA 95762-9405 Office Phone: 916-933-7289. Office Fax: 916-933-7452. E-mail: bobblasier@aol.com.

BLATTER, FRANK EDWARD, travel company executive; b. Denver, Jan. 9, 1939; s. Anthony John and Irene Marie (Tobin) B.; m. Barbara E. Drieth, Sept. 6, 1959; children: Dean Robert, Lisa Kay Faircloth, Paul Kelly. BS, Regis U., Denver, 1961; grad., Colo. Sch. Banking, 1966, Sch. Bank Adminstrn., 1973. CPA, Colo. Acct. McMahon, Maddox & Rodriguez CPAs, Denver, 1960-63, United Bank Denver, 1963-65; with United Banks Colo., Inc., Denver, 1965-86; pres. Cath. Cmty. Svcs., Denver, 1987, Premiere Travel and Cruises, Denver, 1988—. Mem. nat. adv. coun. and devel. com., chmn. ann. funds coun. Regis U.; chmn. adv. coun. Camp Santa Maria; crusade chmn. Am. Cancer Soc., Denver. Mem. AICPA, Tax Execs. Inst. (past pres. Denver), Colo. Soc. CPAs, Fin. Execs. Inst. (dir.), Bank Adminstrn. Inst. (dir.), Arrowhead Golf Club. Roman Catholic. Office: 3900 S Wadsworth Blvd Ste 475 Denver CO 80235-2207

BLATTNER, MEERA MCCUAIG, computer scientist, educator; b. Chgo., Aug. 14, 1930; d. William D. McCuaig and Nina (Spertus) Klevs; m. Minao Kamegai, June 22, 1985; children: Douglas, Robert, William. BA, U. Chgo., 1952; MS, U. So. Calif., 1966; PhD, UCLA, 1973. Rsch. fellow in computer sci. Harvard U., 1973-74; asst. prof. Rice U., 1974-80; assoc. prof. applied sci. U. Calif.-Davis, Livermore, 1980-91, prof. applied sci., 1991-99, prof. emeritus, 2000—; pres. Color Wheel Creations, Las Vegas, Nev., 2001—05, Digital Touch Media, LLC, Las Vegas, 2004. Adj. prof. U. Tex., Houston, 1977—99; vis. prof. U. Paris, 1980; program dir. theoretical computer sci. NSF, Washington, 1979—80. Co-editor: (with R. Dannenberg) Multimedia Interface Design, 1992; contbr. articles to profl. jours. NSF grantee, 1977-81, 93-99. Mem. Assn. Computing Machinery, Computer Soc. of IEEE. Office: 8516 Glenmore Dr Las Vegas NV 89134 E-mail: meerakamegai@cox.net.

BLAU, ELIZABETH ANNE, restaurant executive; b. NYC, Aug. 31, 1967; BS in Govt., Georgetown U., Washington; MS in Restaurant Mktg., Cornell U. Sch. Hotel Admin., Ithaca, NY. Dir. devel. Le Cirque, NYC; chief confectioner, sr. mgr. Hand-Crafted Hilliards Candies, West Hartford, Conn.; scholarship program developer James Beard Found., NYC; co-owner The Butler Did It Catering, Washington; asst. catering dir. Blantyte Hotel, Lenox, Mass.; v.p. of restaurant development Mirage Resorts, Inc., Las Vegas. Avocations: hiking, climbing, horseback riding, skiing.

BLAU, HELEN MARGARET, pharmacology educator; b. London, May 8, 1948; (parents Am. citizens); d. George E. and Gertrude Blau; m. David Spiegel, July 25, 1976; children: Daniel Spiegel, Julia Spiegel. BA in Biology, York U., Eng., 1969; MA in Biology, Harvard U., 1970, PhD in Biology, 1975; Doctorate (hon.), U. Nijmegen, Netherlands, 2003. Predoctoral fellow dept. biology Harvard U., Cambridge, Mass., 1969-75; postdoctoral fellow div. med. genetics, dept. biochemistry and biophysics U. Calif., San Francisco, 1975-78; asst. prof. dept. pharmacology Stanford (Calif.) U., 1978-86, assoc. prof. dept. pharmacology, 1986-91, prof. dept. molecular pharmacology, 1991—99, prof. dept. microbiology and immunology, 2002—, chair dept. molecular pharmacology, 1997—2001, dir. gene therapy tech., 1997—, Donald E. and Delia B. Baxter prof., 1999—, dir. Baxter Lab. in Genetic Pharmacology, 2002—. Rolf-Sammet-Fonds vis. prof., U. Frankfurt, 2003; plenary talk on stem cells, Academic des Sci. della France at Pontifical Acad., the Vatican, Modern Biotech. Symposium, 2003; co-chmn. various profl. meetings; spkr. in field. Mem. editorial bd. 14 jours. including Jour. Cell Biology, Somatic Cell Molecular Genetics and Exptl. Cell Rsch., Molecular and Cellular Biology, Genes to Cells, Molecular Therapy; contbr. articles to profl. jours. Mem. ad hoc molecular cytology study sect. NIH, 1987-88; mem. five-yr. planning com genetics and teratology br. NICHHD/NIH, 1989. Recipient Rsch. Career Devel. award NIH, 1984-89, SmithKline & Beecham award, 1989-91, Women in Cell Biology Career Recognition award, 1992, Excellence in Sci. award FASEB, 1999, McKnight Endowment Fund for Neurosci. award, 2001; Mellon Found. faculty fellow, 1979-80, William H. Hume faculty scholar, 1981-84; grantee NIH, NSF, Ellison Med. Found., Muscular Dystrophy Assn., March of Dimes, 1978—; Yvette Mayent-Rothschild fellow for vis. profs. Inst. Curie, Paris, 1995. Fellow AAAS, Havard Overseers; mem. NAS (del. to China 1991), Internat. Soc. Differentiation (pres. 2002-04), Am. Soc. for Cell Biology (nominating com. 1985-86, program com. 1990), Soc. for Devel. Biology (pres. 1994-95), Inst. Medicine (coun. mem.) Nat. Acad. Scis., Am. Soc. Gene Therapy (bd. dirs. 1999-2002). Avocations: skiing, swimming, hiking, music, theater. Office: Stanford U Sch Medicine 269 Campus Dr CCSR 4215 Stanford CA 94305-5175 Fax: (650) 736-0080. E-mail: hblau@stanford.edu.

BLECHER, MAXWELL M., lawyer; b. Chgo., May 27, 1933; Degree, DePaul Univ.; LLB, Univ. So. Calif., 1955. Mem. Blecher & Collins P.C., Los Angeles. Mem. Nat. Commn. for Review of Antitrust Laws & Procedures, 1978—79. Contbr. articles to profl. jour. Fellow: Am. Bd. Trial Advocates, Am. Coll. Trial Lawyers; mem.: State Bar Calif., ABA (chmn. Private Antitrust Litigation Com. 1974—76, mem. Council 1976—77), Am. Judicature Soc., Assn. Bus. Trial Lawyers, Chancery Club, Com. Support Antitrust Laws, Fed. Bar Assn., L.A. County Bar Assn. Office: Blecher & Collins PC 20th Floor 611 W Sixth St Los Angeles CA 90017 Office Fax: 213-622-4222.

BLEICH, JEFFREY LAURENCE, lawyer, educator; b. Neubreuke, Germany, May 17, 1961; came to U.S., 1964; s. Charles Allen Bleich and Linda Sue Caplan; m. Rebecca Lee Pratt, Aug. 12, 1984; children: Jacob, Matthew, Abigail. BA in Polit. Sci., Amherst Coll., 1983; MA in Pub. Policy, Harvard U., 1986; JD, U. Calif., Berkeley, 1989. Bar: Calif. 1989, D.C. 1990, U.S. Ct. Appeals (D.C. cir.) 1990, U.S. Dist. Ct. (no. dist.) Calif. 1992, U.S. Ct. Appeals (4th cir.) 1993, U.S. Supreme Ct. 1993, U.S. Ct. Appeals (9th cir.) 1994. Law clk. US Ct. Appeals, Washington, 1989-90, US Supreme Ct., Washington, 1990-91; legal asst. Iran-U.S. Claims Tribunal, The Hague, 1991-92; ptnr. Munger, Tolles & Olson LLP, San Francisco, 1992—. Adj. prof. U. Calif., Berkeley, 1993—. Editor-in-chief Calif. Law Rev., Nat. Debt; columnist San Francisco Atty. Dir. White Ho. Youth Violence Initiative, 1999-2000, chair, Calif. State U., 2007-. Recipient Pro Bono Publico award, 1996, James Madison award Soc. Profl. Journalists, 1998, Learned Hand award, 2007; named Top 100 Lawyers in Calif., 2003-09, Atty. of Yr., Calif. Lawyer, 2007. Mem. ABA (amicus curiae com., chair), State Bar Calif. (pres. 2007-08), Bar Assn. San Francisco (pres.), Lawyers' Com. Civil Rights of San Francisco Bay Area (co-chair), Lawyers Com. Human Rights (bd. dirs. 1998—), Legal Aid Soc. (bd. dirs. 1998—), Barristers Club San Francisco (pres.), Am. Law Inst. Democrat. Avocations: short story writer, tennis, camping. Office: Munger Tolles & Olson 560 Mission St Fl 27 San Francisco CA 94105 Office Phone: 415-512-4000. Business E-Mail: jeff.bleich@mto.com.

BLEILER, STEVEN A., mathematician; s. Frank Wesley and Dorothy Louise Bleiler; children: Brittany Jane Newhouse, Allison Suzanne. PhD, U. Oreg., Eugene, 1981. Postdoctoral fellow U. Tex., 1981—84, 1985—86; vis. asst. prof. U. Utah, Salt Lake City, 1984—85, U. BC, Vancouver, Canada, 1986—88; prof. math. and stats. Portland State U., Oreg., 1988—; vis. prof. U. Melbourne, Australia, 1996—97. Math. and statis. cons. Random Precision, Portland, 1988—. Contbr. chapters to books, articles to sci. jours. Trustee Math. Scis. Rsch. Inst., Berkeley, Calif., 1991—95. Recipient John Elliot Allen award for Disting. Tchg., Portland State U., 1998, Disting. Tchg. award, Math. Assn. Am., 2003; Rsch. grants, NSF, 1986—2008. Mem.: Math. Assn. Am. (vis. lectr. 1991—95), Am. Math. Soc., Sigma Xi. Office: Portland State Univ Dept Math and Stats Portland OR 97202 Office Fax: 503-725-3661. Business E-Mail: bleilers@pdx.edu. E-mail: steve@randomprecision.org.

BLENCOWE, PAUL SHERWOOD, lawyer, private investor; b. Amityville, NY, Feb. 10, 1953; s. Frederick Arthur and Dorothy Jeanne (Ballenger) Blencowe; m. Mary Frances Faulk, Apr. 11, 1992; children: Kristin Amanda, Alison Michelle, Caitlin Emily. BA with honors, U. Wis., 1975; MBA, U. Pa., 1976; JD, Stanford U., 1979. Bar: Tex. 1979, Calif. 1989. Assoc. Fulbright & Jaworski, Houston, 1979-86, London, 1986-87, ptnr., 1988-89, Fulbright & Jaworski L.L.P., LA, 1989-2000, of counsel, 2000—. Editor: China's Quest for Independence: Policy Evolution in the 1970s, 1980; editor-in-chief Stanford Jour. of Internat. Law, 1978-79; contbr. articles on U.S. securities and corp. law to profl. jours. Mem. The Calif. Club, Phi Beta Kappa, Phi Kappa Phi, Beta Theta Pi. Office: Fulbright & Jaworski LLP 555 S Flower St Fl41 Los Angeles CA 90071 Office Phone: 213-892-9332. Business E-Mail: pblencowe@fulbright.com.

BLESSING-MOORE, JOANN CATHERINE, allergist, pulmonologist; b. Tacoma, Sept. 21, 1946; d. Harold R. and Mildred (Benson) Blessing; m. Robert Chester Moore; 1 child, Ahna. BA in Chemistry, Syracuse U., 1968; MD, SUNY, Syracuse, 1972. Diplomate Am. Bd. Pediatrics, Am. Bd. Allergy Immunology, Am. Bd. Pediatric Pulmonology. Pediatric intern, then resident Stanford U. Sch. Medicine, Palo Alto, Calif., 1972-75, allergy pulmonology fellow, 1975-77; co-dir. pediatric allergy pulmonology dept. Stanford U. Children's Hosp., Palo Alto, Calif., 1977-84; clin. asst. prof. dept. Allergy Immunology Respiratory Disease (AIR) Stanford U. Sch. Medicine, Palo Alto, Calif., 1977-84, co-dir. pediatric pulmonology lab., 1977-84; clin. asst. prof. dept. immunology Stanford U. Hosp., 1984—; allergist Palo Alto Med. Clinic, 1984-90; pvt. practice allergy immunology-pediatric-pulmonary Palo Alto, San Mateo, Calif., 1990—. Dir. ednl. program for children with asthma Camp Wheeze, Palo Alto, 1975-90; cons. FDA, Allergy Pulmonary Adv. Bd., 1992-97; cons. in field. Author handbooks, camp program manuals; co-editor jour. supplements; mem. edit. bd. Allergy jours.; contbr. articles to sci. publs. Fellow Am. Acad. Allery, Asthma, Immunology (various offices 1980—, joint task force parameters of care asthma and allergy 1989—, Outstanding fellow 1998, Women in Allergy award 2000), Am. Coll. Chest Physicians (com. mem. 1980—), Am. Coll. Asthma, Allergy and Immunology (mem. regent com. 1995-98); mem. Am. Thoracic Soc., Am. Lung Assn., No. Calif. Allergy Found. (bd. dirs., pres.), Peninsula Women's Assn., Santa Clara and San Mateo County Med. Soc. (bd. dirs. 1999-2004), Chi Omega. Republican. Presbyterian. Avocations: music, sailing, skiing, horseback riding, scuba diving. Office: 780 Welch Rd Ste 204 Palo Alto CA 94304-1518 also: Stanford Univ Hosp Dept Immunology Palo Alto CA 94304 Office Phone: 650-696-8236. Business E-Mail: j_blessingmoore@hotmail.com.

BLETHEN, FRANK A., newspaper publisher; b. Seattle, Apr. 20, 1945; BS in Bus., Ariz. State U. Pub. Walla Walla Union-Bulletin, Wash., 1975-79; exec. in circulation, advt., mktg. & labor Seattle Times Co., 1980—85, pub. & CEO circulation mgr., 1985—. Chmn. Walla Walla Union-Bull., Yakima (Wash.) Herald Republic, Blethen Maine Newspapers, Portland, Augusta, Waterville; pres. Blethen Corp. Mem. pres.' adv. bd. Wash. State U. and U. Wash.; campaign chair United Way King County, 1996, 97, bd. dirs., 1996; bd. dirs. Maynard Inst. for Minority Journalism Edn., 1994—. Recipient Pulitzer prize (3) for best newspaper reporting and investigative reporting, 1997, Nat. Reports, 1991, Ida B. Wells award for lifetime achievement in advancement of minority employment, 1997, Leadership Conf. on Civil Rights Chairperson's award for spl. merit, 1999, Edward R. Murrow award Wash. State U., 1998, Weldon B. Gibson Disting. Vol. award Wash. State U., 1998; named to Wash. State Hall of Journalistic Achievement, 1998. Mem. Nat. Assn. of Minority Media Execs., Am. Newspaper Pubs. Assn. (bd. dirs., chmn. telecomm. com.), Sigma Delta Chi. Office: Seattle Times PO Box 70 Seattle WA 98111 also: Seattle Times 1120 John St Seattle WA 98109

BLEWETT, ANDERS, state legislator; Mem. Dist. 21 Mont. House of Reps., 2008—. Democrat. Office: Montana House of Representatives PO Box 200400 Helena MT 59620-0400 Mailing: PO Box 2807 Great Falls MT 59403-2807 Home Phone: 406-231-8618; Office Phone: 406-444-4800. Office Fax: 406-444-4825. Business E-Mail: anders.blewett@gmail.com.

BLEWETT, KENNETH K., business executive; CEO Richardson & Ptnrs., Albuquerque. Office: Richardson & Ptnrs PO Box 3487 Albuquerque NM 87190-3487

BLEY, JOHN L., financial executive; BA in Econs. and Polit. Sci., Pacific Lutheran U., 1980; JD, MBA Willamette U., 1985. Atty. Graham & Dunn, 1985—88; dep. supr. banking Wash. State Div. Banking, 1988—91, supr. banking, 1991—93; dir. Wash. State Dept. Fin. Instns., Olympia, 1993—2002; CEO Integra Advisors, Seattle, 2002—. Office: Integra Advisors LLC 2801 Alaskan Way Ste 300 Seattle WA 98121-1128

BLICKENSDERFER, CHARLES THOMAS (TOM), state legislator, lawyer; b. Denver, June 21, 1957; m. Kristin Blickensderfer. BA in History, Colo. Coll.; JD, U. Denver. Atty.; lobbyist Colo. Arts Coun.; staff intern U.S. House of Reps., White House; mem. Colo. State Assembly, 1991-92, Colo. State Senate, 1992—, mem. joint legal svcs. com., mem. joint legis. coun. com., vice-chair svcs. com. Bd. mem. Inter Faith Task Force. Mem. Greenwood Village C. of C., South Metro C. of C., Littleton Bus. Assn., Colo. Chpt. Cities in Schs. Republican. also: 9 Parkway Dr Englewood CO 80110-4227

BLIGE, MARY JANE, singer; b. Yonkers, NY, Jan. 11, 1971; d. Cora Blige; m. Kendu Isaacs, Dec. 7, 2003; 3 stepchildren. Singer: (albums) What's the 411?, 1992, (NY Music award for Best R&B Album, 1993), My Life, 1994 (Billboard Music award for R&B Album of Yr., 1995), Mary Jane, 1995, Share My World, 1997 (Am. Music award for Favorite R&B Album, 1998, Soul Train Lady of Soul award for R&B Soul Album of Yr., 1998), Mary, 1999 (Soul Train Music award for Best R&B Album & Lady of Soul award for Album of Yr., 2000), The Tour, 1999, No More Drama, 2001, Dance For Me, 2002, Love & Life, 2003, The Breakthrough, 2005 (Favorite Album, Am. Music Awards, 2006, Billboard R&B Album of Yr., 2006, Best R&B Album, Grammy Awards, 2007, Best Album, Soul Train awards, 2007), Reflections: A Retrospective, 2006, Mary J. Blige and Friends, 2006, Growing Pains, 2007 (Grammy award for Best Contemporary R&B Album, 2009); (songs) I'll Do For You, 1991, Real Love, 1991 (Soul Train Music award for Best Female Single, 1993), I'll Be There for You/You're All I Need (with Method Man), 1995 (Grammy award for Best Rap Duo Performance, 1996, named one of 100 Greatest Videos Ever Made, MTV, 1999), Not Gon' Cry, 1996, No More Drama, 2001 (Best R&B Video, MTV Video Music awards, 2002), He Think I Don't Know, 2001 (Grammy award for Best Female R&B Vocal Performance, 2003), Whenever I Say Your Name (with Sting), 2003 (Grammy award for Best Pop Collaboration With Vocals 2004), Be Without You, 2005 (BET Video of Yr. award, 2006, Billboard R&B Song of Yr., Hot 100 Airplay Song of Yr., R&B Song Airplay of Yr., & Videoclip of Yr., 2006, Best Female R&B Vocal Performance & Best R&B Song, Grammy Awards, 2007, NAACP Image award for Music Video, 2007), (with Chaka Khan) Disrespectful, 2007 (Grammy award for Best Duo R&B Performance with Vocals, 2008), (with Aretha Franklin) Never Gonna Break My Faith, 2007 (Grammy award for Best Gospel Performance, 2008), (with Ludacris) Runaway Love, (BET award for Best Collaboration, 2007); actress: (films) Angel, 2001, Prison Song, 2001. Recipient Soul Train Music award for Best New Artist 1993, Best Debut R&B Artist & Rising Star award, NY Music Awards, 1993, Source award for R&B Artist of Yr., 1994, 1995, Heroes award, RIAA, 1999, Patrick Lippert award, Rock the Vote, 2001, Best Female R&B award, Black Entertainment TV (BET), 2001, 2006, Favorite R&B Female Artist, Am. Music Awards, 2003, 2006, Legend award, Vibe mag., 2005, 9 Billboard Music awards, including R&B Artist of Yr., Female R&B Artist of Yr., R&B Songs Artist & Album Artist of Yr., 2006, Female Artist award, NAACP Image Awards, 2007, Voice of Music award, ACAP Rhythm & Soul Music Awards, 2007.

BLINN, JAMES F., computer scientist; BS in Physics and Comm. Sci., U. Mich., 1970, MSE in Computer, Info., Control Engring., 1972; PhD in Computer Sci., U. Utah, 1978; DFA (hon.), Parsons Sch. Design, 1995. Graphics rsch. fellow Microsoft Corp., Redmond, Wash. External adv. bd. Geometry Ctr. Contbr. articles to profl. jours. Recipient service medal NASA, 1983, Siggraph Computer Achievement award, 1983; fellow MacArthur Found., 1991. Mem. IEEE (Outstanding Contbn. award 1989, writer column Computer Graphics and Application Jour.), NAE. Office: Microsoft Corp Graphics Rsch 1 Microsoft Way Redmond WA 98052-6399

BLITZ, STEPHEN M., lawyer; b. NYC, July 29, 1941; s. Leo and Dorothy B.; m. Ellen Sue Mintzer, Sept. 23, 1962; children: Catherine Denise, Thomas Joseph. BA, Columbia U., 1962, BS, 1963; LLB, Stanford U., 1966; MS in Acctg., U. Colo., 2001. Bar: Calif. 1967, U.S. Dist. Ct. (ctrl. dist.) Calif. 1967, Colo. 1996, Wis. 2004. Law clk. to judge U.S. Dist. Ct. (ctrl. dist.) Calif., 1966-67; ptnr. Gibson, Dunn & Crutcher, LA, 1967-96, Denver, 1996-2001; of counsel Fleishman & Shapiro, Denver, 2001—. Adj. prof. law U. West L.A. Sch. Law, 1978-80, dir. Pub. Counsel, 1981-83, 94-96. Bd. dirs. Colo. Preservation, Inc., 1999-2005. Mem. ABA, L.A. County Bar Assn. (exec. com. 1986-96, chmn. 1994-95, real property sect.), Colo. Bar Assn., Denver Bar Assn., Order of Coif, Beta Gamma Sigma. Office: Fleishman & Shapiro PC 1600 Broadway Ste 2600 Denver CO 80202-4926 Office Phone: 303-861-1000.

BLIZZARD, ALAN, artist; b. Boston, Mar. 25, 1939; s. Thomas and Elizabeth B. BFA, Mass. Coll. Art; MA, U. Ariz.; MFA, U. Iowa, 1963. Instr. in art U. Iowa; vis. asst. prof. art Albion Coll., U. Okla.; asso. prof. UCLA; now prof. painting Scripps Coll. and; Claremont Grad. Sch. Represented in permanent collections Bklyn. Mus., Met. Mus. Art, N.Y.C., Art Inst. Chgo., Denver Art Mus., La Jolla (Calif.) Mus. Art, Ashland U., Columbia U., McGeorge Sch. Law, Pomona Coll., Sacramento State U., Pitzer Coll., Fluor Corp., Kouri Capital Corp., N.Y.C., Crocker Mus. Art, Sacramento. Office: Scripps Coll Art Dept Claremont CA 91711

BLOCH, CLIFFORD ALAN, pediatric endocrinologist; b. Johannesburg, Republic of South Africa, May 13, 1953; came to U.S., 1984; s. Leonard E. and Audrey (Silver) B.; m. Natalie Cohen, Dec. 5, 1976; children: Tracy L., Jennifer K. B Medicine and Surgery, Witwatersrand U., 1976. Diplomate Am. Bd. Pediatrics (subbd. pediatic endocrinology). Med. and surg. intern U. Witwatersrand, Johannesburg, Republic of South Africa, 1977; med. officer S.A. Med. Corps, Johannesburg, 1978-79; pediatric resident U. Witwatersrand, 1980-83, cons. pediatrician, 1984; pediatric endocrine fellow U. Cin., 1984-87; asst. prof. Childrens Hosp. of Denver, 1987—; pediatric endocrinology, pediatrician Pediatric Endocrine Associates, Englewood, Colo. Contbr. articles to profl. jours. Served to capt. SAMC, 1983. Grantee U. Colo. (BRS), 1988, Childrens Hosp. Denver (kempe research ctr.), 1987. Fellow Am. Acad. Pediatrics; mem. Am. Diabetes Assn., Endocrine Soc., Pediatric Endocrine Soc., Western Soc. for Pediatric Research, Colo. Soc. for Endocrinology and Metabolism. Jewish. Discovered the link in 2007 between lavender oil and tea tree oils found in shampoos, soaps, and lotions can temporarily leave boys with large breasts. Home: 5791 S Havana Ct Englewood CO 80111-3927 Office: Pediatric Endocrine Associates 499 E Hampden Ave Suite 290 Englewood CO 80113-2792

BLOCH, PAUL, public relations executive; b. Bklyn., July 17, 1939; s. Edwin Lionel and Antoinette (Greenberg) B. B.B. Polit. Sci., UCLA, 1962. Publicist Rogers & Cowan, Beverly Hills, Calif., 1962-70, v.p., 1970-75, sr. v.p., ptnr., 1975-83, exec. v.p., sr. ptnr., 1983—, also vice chmn., co-chmn. Asst. Am. Cancer Soc., United Way, Am. Diabetes Assn., UNICEF, 1975—; adv. council Orange County Sheriff's Dept., 1980—. Served with U.S. Army, 1957. Recipient Les Mason award Publicity Guild Am., 1991. Mem. Publicists Guild of Am. (award for publicity campaign for Brian's Song 1972), Country Music Assn. Office: Rogers & Cowan 8687 Melrose Ave Ste G700 Los Angeles CA 90069-5721

BLOCK, BARBARA ANN, biology professor; b. Springfield, Mass., Apr. 25, 1958; d. Merrill and Myra (Winograd) B. BA, U. Vt., 1980; PhD, Duke U., 1986. Postdoctoral fellow U. Pa., Phila., 1986-88; asst. prof. organismal biology U. Chgo., 1988-93; asst. prof. biol. sci. Stanford U., 1993-97, assoc. prof., 1997—. Contbr. articles to profl. jours. Recipient Presdl. Young Investigator award NSF, 1989; MacArthur fellow, 1996, Pew Conservation fellow, 1997. Mem. AAAS, Am. Soc. Zoologists, Biophys. Soc. Democrat.

BLOCK, GENE DAVID, academic administrator, biologist, educator; b. NYC, Aug. 17, 1948; s. Philip and Roslyn (Klein) B.; m. Carol Sue Kullback, June 28, 1970. AB, Stanford U., 1970; MS, U. Oreg., 1972, PhD, 1975. NIH postdoctoral fellow Stanford U., 1975-78; asst. prof. U. Va., Charlottesville, 1978-83, assoc. prof., 1983-88, prof. biology, 1988—2007, prof. medicine, 1991—2007, dir. Biodynamics Inst., 1989-91; dir. NSF Biol. Timing Ctr. NSF Biol. Timing Ctr., Charlottesville, 1991—2002; Alumni Coun. Thomas Jefferson Prof. of Biology U. Va., Charlottesville, 1993—2007, v.p. rsch., 1993—2001, v.p., provost, 2001—07; chancellor UCLA, 2007—. Disting. prof. psychiatry and behavorial sci. UCLA, 2007—. Contbr. articles on biol. timing to profl. jours.; patentee in field. Home Phone: 310-825-9980; Office Phone: 310-825-2151.

BLOCK, KEITH, computer software company executive; BS in Info. Systems, Carnegie-Mellon U., Pitts., MS in Mgmt. Sr. cons. Booz, Allen and Hamilton, 1984—86; with Oracle Corp., Redwood City, Calif., 1986—, v.p. Ams. Consumer Packaged Goods consulting, group v.p. East Consulting, sr. v.p. N.Am. Comml. Consulting, exec. v.p. N.Am. Consulting, mem. exec. mgmt. com., 2001—, exec. v.p. N.Am., 2002—. Bd. trustees Concord Mus.; bd. visitors Carnegie-Mellon U. Office: Oracle Corp 500 Oracle Pky Redwood City CA 94065 Office Phone: 650-506-0024.

BLOCK, MARTY, state legislator; married. Attended Polit. Sci., Syracuse U.; BA in Polit. Sci./Edn., Ind. U.; JD in Law, DePaul U. Prof. San Diego State U., San Diego, dean; mem. San Diego Cmty. Coll. Dist., San Diego, San Diego County Bd. of Edn., San Diego; del. Dem. Nat. Conv., 1988, 1992, 1996, 2004; mem. Dist. 78 Calif. State Assembly, Calif., 2008—, asst. majority whip. Democrat. Office: State Capital Room 3132 PO Box 942849 Sacramento CA 94249 also: District Office 2nd Fl 7144 Broadway Lemon Grove CA 91945 Office Phone: 619-462-7878, 916-319-2078. Office Fax: 619-462-0078, 916-319-2178.*

BLOCK, MICHAEL KENT, economics and law professor, former government official; b. NYC, Apr. 2, 1942; s. Philip and Roslyn (Klein) B.; m. Carole Arline Polansky, Aug. 30, 1964 (div.); children: Robert Justin, Tamara Nicole; m. Olga Vyborna, Dec. 1, 1996. AB, Stanford U., 1964, A.M., 1969, PhD, 1972. Research analyst Bank of Am., San Francisco, 1965-66; research assoc. Planning Assocs., San Francisco, 1966-67; asst. prof. econs. U. Santa Clara, 1969-72; asst. prof. econs. dept. ops. research and adminstrv. sci. Naval Postgrad. Sch., Monterey, Calif., 1972-74, assoc. prof., 1974-76; research fellow Hoover Instn., Stanford U., 1975-76, sr. research fellow, 1976-87; dir. Center for Econometric Studies of Justice System, 1977-81; ptnr. Block & Nold, Cons., Palo Alto, Calif., 1980-81; assoc. prof. mgmt., econs. and law U. Ariz., Tucson, 1982-85, prof. econs. and law, 1989—; mem. U.S. Sentencing Commn., Washington, 1985-89; exec. v.p. Cybernomics, Tucson, 1991—2002; pres. Goldwater Inst. for Pub. Policy, Phoenix, 1992—2002; sr. policy adviser State of Ariz. Gov. Symington, 1996-97. Chair Basis Sch. Bd., 1998—; mem. Ariz. Residential Utility Consumer Bd., 1995-96, chmn. Ariz. Constl. Def. Coun., 1994-97, Ariz. Juvenile Justice Adv. Coun., 1996-97; seminar dir. Econ. Devel. Inst./World Bank, 1992-95; cons. in field. Author: (with H.G. Demmert) Workbook and Programmed Guide to Economics, 1974, 77, 80, (with James M. Clabault) A Legal and Economic Analysis of Criminal Antitrust Indictments:, 1955-80; contbr. articles to profl. publs. Fellow NSF, 1965, Stanford U. Fellow Progress and Freedom Found.; mem. Am. Econ. Assn., Phi Beta Kappa. Office: U Ariz Econ Dept McClelland Hl Rm 401 Tucson AZ 85721-0001

BLOCK, ROBERT N., federal judge; b. Boston, July 27, 1950; BA, U. Calif., LA, 1972; JD, U. Calif. Law Sch., LA, 1978. Apptd. magistrate judge cen. dist. U.S. Dist. Ct. Calif., 1995. Office: 1006 US Courthouse 312 N Spring St Los Angeles CA 90012-4701 Fax: 213-894-6860.

BLOCK, STEVEN MICHAEL, biophysicist, educator; b. Durham, NC, Oct. 4, 1952; s. Martin M. and Beate S. (Sondhelm) B.; m. Kathleen Ann Beasley, Aug. 15, 1985. BA with honors, Oxford U., 1974, MA in Physics, 1978; MA in Biology, U. Colo., 1982; PhD, Calif. Inst. Tech., 1985. Postdoctoral rschr. Stanford U., 1985—87, prof. applied physics and biol. scis. Calif., 1999—, sr. fellow Freeman Spogli Inst. Internat. Studies; lectr. Harvard U., Cambridge, Mass., 1987-91, assoc., 1991-93; fellow Rowland Inst., Cambridge, 1987-93; assoc. prof. Princeton U., NJ, 1994-98, prof., 1998—99. Contbr. articles to sci. jours.; mem. editl. bd.: The Scientist, 1986—97, Biophysical Jour., 1995. Fellow Am. Acad. Arts & Scis., AAAS; mem. Biophysical Soc. (mem. exec. bd. 1995-97, coun. mem. 1995-98, pres. 2005-06, Young Investigator award 1994), NAS, Sigma Xi. Jewish. Avocations: bluegrass banjo, alpine skiing. Office: Dept Biol Scis Stanford U Gilbert Hall 371 Serra Mall M/C5020 Stanford CA 94305-5020 Office Phone: 650-724-4046. E-mail: sblock@stanford.edu.

BLODGETT, ELSIE GRACE, elementary school educator, small business owner, property manager; b. Eldorado Springs, Mo., Aug. 2, 1921; d. Charles Ishmal and Naoma Florence (Worthington) Robison; m. Charles Davis Blodgett, Nov. 8, 1940; children: Carolyn Doyel, Charleen Bier, Lyndon, Daryl(dec.). Student, Warrensburg State Tchrs. Coll., Mo., 1939—40; BA, Fresno State Coll., Calif., 1953. Tchr. schs., Mo., 1940—42, Calif., 1947—72; owner, mgr. rental units, 1965—; exec. dir. San Joaquin County Rental Property Assn., Stockton, Calif., 1970—81; prin. Delta Rental Property Owners and Assoc., 1981—82; propr. Crystal Springs Health World, Inc., Stockton, 1980—86. Active PTA, Girl Scouts U.S., Boy Scouts Am., Vols. in Police Svc., 1993—2004; capt. Delaware Alpine Neighborhood Watch, 1994—2003; past bd. dirs. Stockton Better Bus. Bur.; bd. dirs. Stockton Goodwill Industries, 1994—2003. Named (with husband) Mr. and Mrs. Apt. Owner of San Joaquin County, 1977. Mem.: Nat. Apt. Assn. (state treas. women's divsn. 1977—79), Calif. Ret. Tchrs. Assn., Mil. Wives, DAV Aux., Stockton Zonta Lodge. Republican. Methodist. Home: 4350 St Andrews Dr Stockton CA 95219

BLODGETT, HARRIET, retired language educator; b. NYC, Sept. 4, 1932; d. Morris and Fannie (Cohen) Horowitz; m. William Edward Blodgett, Sept. 4, 1955; 1 child, Bruce. BA, Queens Coll., 1954; MA, U. Chgo., 1956; PhD, U. Calif., Davis, 1968. Lectr. in English and comparative lit. U. Calif., Davis, 1973-85, 86-87, lectr. in English Irvine, 1985-86; lectr. in English, humanities and women's studies Calif. State U., Sacramento, 1982-87; lectr. Calif. State U. Stanislaus, Turlock, 1989-92, asst. prof., then assoc. prof., 1992-98, prof., 1998—2005, prof. emerita, 2005. Lectr. Stanford U., U. Calif. Santa Cruz, 1988; vis. scholar Inst. for Rsch. on Women and Gender, Stanford U., 1983, affil., 1984-92. Author: Patterns of Reality: Elizabeth Bowen's Novels, 1975, Centuries of Female Days: Englishwomen's Private Diaries, 1988; editor, compiler: Capacious Hold-All: An Anthology, 1991; contbr. articles to profl. jours., chpts. to books. Mem. Phi Beta Kappa. Avocations: painting, gardening, reading. Home: 781 Mulberry Ln Davis CA 95616-3430 Personal E-mail: hblodget@dcn.org.

BLOEMBERGEN, NICOLAAS, physicist, researcher; b. Dordrecht, Netherlands, Mar. 11, 1920; arrived in U.S., 1952, naturalized, 1958; s. Auke and Sophia M. (Quint) Bloembergen; m. Huberta D. Brink, June 26, 1950; children: Antonia, Brink, Juliana. BA, Utrecht U., 1941, MA, 1943; PhD, Leiden U., 1948; MA (hon.), Harvard U., 1951, LHD (hon.), 2000; DSc (hon.), Laval U., 1987, U. Conn., 1988, U. Hartford, 1991, Moscow State U., 1997; LHD (hon.), U. Mass., Lowell, 1994, U. Ctrl. Fla., 1996, N.C. State U., 1998. Tchg. asst. Utrecht U., 1942—45; rsch. fellow Leiden U., 1948; mem. Soc. Fellows Harvard U., 1949—51, assoc. prof., 1951—57, Gordon McKay prof. applied physics, 1957—, Rumford prof. physics, 1974, Gerhard Gade univ. prof., 1980, prof. emeritus, 1990; prof. optics U. Ariz., 2001—. Vis. prof. U. Paris, 1957, U. Calif., 1965, Coll. de France, Paris, 1980, U. Ariz., 2001—; Lorentz guest prof. U. Leiden, 1973; Raman vis. prof., Bangalore, India, 79; Fairchild Disting. scholar Calif. Inst. Tech., 1984; hon. prof. Fudan U., Shanghai; Disting. vis. prof. CREOL U. Ctrl. Fla., 1995. Author: Nuclear Magnetic Relaxation, 1948, Nonlinear Optics, 1965, Enconters in Magnetic Resonance, 1996, Encounters in Nonlinear Optics, 1996; contbr. articles to profl. jours. Recipient Stuart Ballantine medal, Franklin Inst., 1961, Half Moon trophy, Netherlands Club N.Y., 1972, Nat. Medal of Sci., 1975, Lorentz medal, Royal Dutch Acad., 1978, Frederic Ives medal, Optical Soc. Am., 1979, von Humboldt sr. scientist award, Munich, 1980, Nobel prize in Physics, 1981, Dirac medal, U. New South Wales, Australia, 1983, Medal of Honor, Inst. Elec. and Electronic Engrs., 1983, Von Humboldt Sr. Scientist award, 1987, von Humboldt medal, Munich, 1989, Byvoet medal, U. Utrecht, 2001, Russell Varian prize, Euromar, 2005; fellow Guggenheim, 1957. Fellow: IEEE (Morris Liebmann award 1959), Am. Acad. Arts and Scis., Am. Phys. Soc. (Buckley prize for solid state physics 1958); mem.: NAE, Norwegian Soc. Scis. and Letters (fgn.), Paris Acad. Scis. (fgn. assoc.), Koninklyke Nederlandse Akademie von Wetenschappen (corr.), Indian Acad. Scis. (hon.), Optical Soc. Am. (hon.), Deutsche Akademie der Naturforscher Leopoldina, Am. Philos. Soc., Nat. Royal Dutch Acads. Scis. Office: Optical Scis Ctr Univ Ariz 1630 E Univ Blvd Tucson AZ 85721 Business E-Mail: nbloembergen@optics.arizona.edu.

BLOHM, KENNETH E., lawyer; b. Green Bay, Wis., 1956; s. Melvin A. and Ruth M. B.; m. Helen M. Marinak, Sept. 24, 1983. BA, U. Wis., 1977; JD, Harvard U., 1981. Bar: Calif. 1982, DC, NY, US Ct. Appeals (9th cir.) 1982. Law clk. US Ct. Appeals (9th cir.), San Francisco, 1981-82; assoc. Morrison & Foerster, San Francisco, 1982; ptnr. Latham & Watkins, San Francisco. Mem. ABA, Calif. Bar Assn., Phi Beta Kappa, Phi Kappa Phi. Office: Latham & Watkins 505 Montgomery St Ste 2000 San Francisco CA 94111 Office Phone: 415-395-8079. Office Fax: 415-395-8095.

BLOM, DANIEL CHARLES, lawyer, investor, retired insurance company executive; b. Portland, Oreg., Dec. 13, 1919; s. Charles D. and Anna (Reiner) B.; m. Ellen Lavon Stewart, June 28, 1952; children: Daniel Stewart (dec.), Nicole Jan Heath. BA magna cum laude, U. Wash., 1941, postgrad., 1941-42; JD, Harvard U., 1948; postgrad., U. Paris, 1954-55. Bar: Wash. 1949, U.S. Supreme Ct. 1970. Tchg. fellow speech U. Wash., 1941—42; law clk. to justice Supreme Ct. Wash., 1948—49; since practiced in Seattle; assoc. Graves, Kizer & Graves, 1949—51; gen. counsel Northwestern Life Ins. Co., 1952—54; ptnr. Case & Blom, 1952—54; assoc., ptnr., of counsel Ryan, Swanson & Cleveland, 1956—; exec. v.p., gen. counsel Family Life Ins. Co., 1964—85, spl. counsel, 1985—91. Vice chmn. Wash. Bd. Bar Examiners, 1970-72, chmn., 1972-75; mem. industry adv. com. Nat. Assn. Ins. Commrs., 1966-68; pres. Wash. Ins. Coun, 1971-73, gen. counsel, 1975-78; mediator Arbitration Forums, Inc. Editor Wash. State Bar Jour., 1951-52; assoc. editor The Brief, 1975-76; author: Life Insurance Law of the State of Washington, 1980, Banking and Insurance, Deregulatory Cross-Currents, 1985, Hostile Insurance Company Takeovers: New Frontier of the Law, 1990, Administrative Finality Under the Washington Insurance Code, 1991, Business and Professionalism, 1994, The Civility Problem, 1995, Technics and the Civilization of Law Practice, 1997, Varieties of Regulatory Experience, 1998, Legislative Review of Administrative Rules in the State of Washington: A Light that Failed?, 2003. Chmn. jury selection Wash. Gov.'s Writer's Day Awards, 1976; bd. dirs. Crisis Clinic; trustee Bush Sch., 1971-79, v.p., 1976-77; trustee, v.p. Frye Mus., Seattle, 1976-82, World Affairs Coun. Seattle, 1972-94, Friends of Seattle Pub. Libr., 1982-87; bd. visitors U. Wash. Libr., 1988-92, Friends of U. Wash. Librs., bd. dirs., 1991-95, pres., 1991-92. 2d lt. AUS, 1942-45, PTO. Decorated Bronze Star; Rhodes scholarship finalist, 1949. Fellow: Am. Bar Found.; mem.: ABA (vice chmn. com. on life ins. law, sect. tort and ins. pratice 1971—76, chmn. 1976—78, sect. program chmn. 1978—79, mem. coun. 1979—83, chmn. pub. rels. com. 1981—83, chmn. com. on profl. independence of the lawyer 1984—85, chmn. com. on scope and correlation 1985—86, policy coord. tort and ins. practice sect. 1986—90, del. ABA to Union Internat. des Avocats 1986—91, chmn. com. on handbook and bylaws 1987—88, chmn. hist. com. 1991—94), Fedn. Regulatory Counsel (dir. 1995—97, 2002—04), Found. UIA (coun. 1990—97), Am. Arbitration Assn., Am. Coun. Life Ins. (legis. com. 1982—85), Assn. Life Ins. Counsel, Am. Judicature Soc., N.Am. Found. for Internat. Legal Practice (pres. 1987—89, dir. 1987—95, chmn. 1990—95), Union Internat. des Avocats (v.p. 1987—92), Seattle Bar Assn., Wash. Bar Assn. (chmn. legal edn. liaison com. 1977—78, award of merit 1975), Harvard Assn. Seattle and Western Wash. (trustee 1976—77), Harvard Law Sch. Assn., Rainier Club, Tau Kappa Alpha, Phi Beta Kappa. Home: 100 Ward St # 602-3 Seattle WA 98109-5613 Office: Ryan Swanson & Cleveland 1201 3rd Ave Ste 3400 Seattle WA 98101-3034 Home Phone: 206-283-6258; Office Phone: 206-654-2280. Personal E-mail: blomdc@msn.com.

BLOOM, FLOYD ELLIOTT, internist, neuroscientist; b. Mpls., Oct. 8, 1936; s. Jack Aaron and Frieda (Shochman) B.; m. D'Nell Bingham, Aug. 30, 1956 (dec. May 1973); children: Fl'Nell, Evan Russell; m. Jody Patricia Corey, Aug. 9, 1980. AB cum laude, So. Meth. U., Dallas, 1956; MD cum laude, Washington U., St. Louis, 1960; DSc (hon.), So. Meth. U., 1983, Hahnemann U., 1985, U. Rochester, 1985, Mt. Sinai U. Med. Sch., 1996, Thomas Jefferson U., 1997, Washington U., 1998, The Scripps Rsch. Inst., 2005. Intern Barnes Hosp., St. Louis, 1960—61, resident internal medicine, 1961—62; rsch. assoc. NIMH, Washington, 1962—64; fellow depts. pharmacology, psychiatry and anatomy Yale Sch. Medicine, 1964—66, asst. prof., 1966—67, assoc. prof., 1968; chief lab. neuropharmacology NIMH, Washington, 1968—75, acting dir. divsn. spl. mental health, 1973—75; commd. officer USPHS, 1974—75; dir. Arthur Vining Davis Ctr. for Behavorial Neurobiology; prof. Salk Inst., La Jolla, Calif., 1975—83; dir. divsn. preclin. neurosci. and endocrinology Scripps Rsch. Inst., La Jolla, 1983—89, chmn. dept. neuropharmacology, 1989—2005, prof. emeritus, 2005—; editor in chief Sci. Mag., 1995—2000; founding CEO Neurome, Inc., LaJolla, Calif., 2000—06, chmn. bd., 2000—06, chief scientific officer, 2000—06. Mem. Pres. Commn. on Alcoholism, 1980—81, Nat. Adv. Mental Health Coun., 1976—80; chmn. sci. adv. bd. Pharmavene, Inc., 1994—98, Advancis Corp., 2000—07, Middlebrook Pharms., 2007—; mem. Rsch. Adv. Com. Gulf War Vets. Illnesses, 2005—, President's Coun. Bioethics, 2006—, Independent Citizens Oversight Com., 2007—, Calif. Inst. Regenerative Medicine; bd. dirs. Alkermes, Inc., Elan Pharmaceuticals. Author: (with others) Biochemical Basis of Neuropharmacology, 1971, 8th edit., 2002, (with Lazerson and Hofstadter) Brain, Mind and Behavior, 1984, (with Lazerson) 2d edit., 1988, (with C.A. Nelson) 3d edit., 2000, (with W. Young and Y. Kim) Brain browser, 1989; editor: Peptides: Integrators of Cell and Tissue Function, 1980, Progress in Brain Research, vol. 199, 1994, vol. 100, 1997, (with D.J. Kupfer) Neuro-Psychopharmacology: The Fourth Generation of Progress, 1994, Handbook of Chemical Neruoanatomy, 1997, The Primate Nervous System, 1997, vol. II, 1998, vol. III, 1999, (with Beal and Kupfer) The Dana Guide to Brain Health, 2003; co-editor: Regulatory Peptides, 1979-90, (with M. Randolph) Funding Health Sciences Research, 1990, The Best of the Brain from Scientific American, 2007; assoc. editor: Biological Psychiatry, 1993-95; editor-in-chief Science, 1995-2000, Brain Rsch., 2000-. Trustee Washington U., St. Louis, 1998—, chmn. nat. med. coun., 2000—. Recipient A. Cressy Morrison award NY Acad. Scis., 1971, A.E. Bennett award for basic rsch. Soc. Biol. Psychiatry, 1971, Arthur A. Fleming award Science mag., 1973, Mathilde Solowey award, 1973, Biol. Sci. award Washington Acad. Scis., 1975, Alumni Achievement citation Washington U., 1980, McAlpin Rsch. Achievement award Mental Health Assn., 1980, Lectr.'s medal College de France, 1979, Steven Beering medal, 1985, Janssen award World Psychiat. Assn., 1989, Passerow Found. award, 1990, Herman von Helmholtz award, 1991, Pythagora award, 1994, Presdl. award Soc. for Neurosci., 1995, Golgi prize U. Brescia, 1996, Meritorious Achievement award Coun. Biology Editors, 1999, Gold medal Soc. Biol. Psychiatry, 1997, Disting. Svc. award Am. Psychiat. Assn., 2000, Thomas William Salmon medal, NY Acad. Medicine for Psychiatry and Mental Hygiene, 2004, Dedman Coll. Disting. Grad. award, So. Meth. U., 2005, Rhoda and Bernard Sarnat Internat. prize in Mental Health, Inst. of Medicine of the Nat. Academies, 2005; Disting. Fellow Am. Psychiat. Assn., 1986; named Sci. of Yr. Achievement Rewards for Coll. Scientists, 1996. Fellow AAAS (bd. dirs. 1986-90, pres.-elect 2001, pres. 2002, chmn. bd. dirs. 2003), Am. Coll. Neuropsychopharmacology (coun. 1976-78, chmn. program com. 1987, pres. 1988-89, Hoch award 1998); mem. NAS (chmn. sect. neurobiology 1979-83, co-chair reports rev. com. 2004—, chair com. publs. 2007—), Inst. Medicine (coun. 1986-89, 93-95, Walsh McDermott medal 2004, Rhoda and Bernard Garnet award in Mental Health 2005), Am. Philos. Soc. (chmn. Lashley award com. 2001—), Am. Acad. Arts and Scis., Soc. Neurosci. (sec. 1973-74, pres. 1976, chmn. publs. com. 1999-2002), Am. Soc. Pharmacology and Exptl. Therapeutics, Am. Soc. Cell Biology, Am. Physiol. Soc., Am. Assn. Anatomists, Am. Neurol. Assn., Rsch. Soc. Alcoholism (chmn. program com. 1985-87, pres.-elect 1989-91, pres. 1991-93), Swedish Acad. Sci. (fgn. assoc. 1989). Home: 628 Pacific View Dr San Diego CA 92109-1768 Business E-Mail: fbloom@scripps.edu. E-mail: fbloom@bloomsciassocs.net.

BLOOM, GARY L., data processing executive; b. Sept. 1960; m. Judy Bloom. BS in Computer Sci., Calif. Poly. State U., San Luis Obispo. Various tech. positions IBM Corp., Chevron Corp.; various positions Oracle Corp., Redwood Shores, Calif., 1986—2000, v.p. mainframe and integration tech. divsn., 1992—96, v.p. massively parallel computing divsn., 1992—96, sr. v.p. product and platform techs. divsn., 1996—97, sr. v.p. woldwide alliances and techs. divsn., 1997, sr. v.p. sys. products divsn., 1997—98, exec. v.p. systems product, 1998—99, exec. v.p., 1999—2000; mem. bd. dir., pres., CEO Veritas Software Corp., Mountain View, Calif., 2000—, chmn. bd. dis., 2002—, also mem. exec. mgmt. com., mgmt. com., product devel. mgmt. com.; pres., vice chmn. Symantec (merged with Veritas), 2005—06. Serves on President's Cabinet Calif. Polytechnic State U., San Luis Obispo. Office Phone: 650-527-8000.

BLOOM, JACOB A., lawyer; b. Bklyn., Apr. 10, 1942; BA, Columbia U., 1963, LLB, 1966. Bar: Calif. 1968. Sr. ptnr. Bloom, Hergott, Diemer & Cook, LLP, Beverly Hills, Calif. Champion Moot Ct. Office: Bloom Hergott Diemer & Cook LLP 150 S Rodeo Dr Fl 3 Beverly Hills CA 90212-2410

BLOOM, JOSEPH D., psychiatrist, medical educator; MD, Albert Einstein Coll. Medicine. Diplomate in psychiatry and in forensic psychiatry Am. Bd. Psychiatry and Neurology. Intern Mt. Zion Hosp. and Med. Ctr., San Francisco; resident in psychiatry Harvard U.; chief psychiat. resident Southard Clinic Mass. Mental Health Ctr.; chief mental health unit Alaska Native Health Svc. USPHS; pvt. practice Anchorage; dir. cmty. psychiatry tng. program Oreg. Health Sci. U., Portland, 1977, chmn. dept. psychiatry, 1986-94, interim dean Sch. Medicine, 1993-94, dean Sch. Medicine, 1994-2001. Office: Oreg Health Scis U Sch Medicine 3181 SW Sam Jackson Park Rd Portland OR 97201-3011 Home Phone: 503-978-5156; Office Phone: 503-494-6689. E-mail: bloomj@ohsu.edu.

BLOOM, STEPHEN MICHAEL, magistrate judge, lawyer; b. San Francisco, June 10, 1948; s. Alan I. and Wilma (Morgan) B.; m. Rebecca J. Nelson, June 19, 1976; children: Benjamin Jacob, Molly Marie, John Robert. Student, Dartmouth Coll., 1966-68; BA in English, Stanford U., 1970; student, Calif. State U., Sacramento, 1973-74; JD, Willamette Coll. Law, 1977. Bar: Oreg. 1977, U.S. Dist. Ct. Oreg. 1979. Adminstrv. asst. Calif. Dept. Edn., Sacramento, 1973-74; atty. Joyce & Harding, Corvallis, Oreg., 1977-78; dep. dist. atty. Umatilla County, Pendleton, Oreg., 1978-79; atty. Morrison & Reynolds, Hermiston, Oreg., 1979-81, Kottkamp & O'Rourke, Pendleton, 1981—. Appointed U.S. magistrate, 1988. Bd. dirs. Edn. Svc. Dist., Pendleton, 1982-89. Lt. (j.g.) USN, 1970-72. Mem. ABA,

Oreg. Bar Assn., Rotary (pres. 1990-91, bd. dirs. 1991). Avocation: sailing. Office: US Dist Ct PO Box 490 Pendleton OR 97801-0490 Home: 2051 SW Rose Ln Portland OR 97201-8012

BLOOMFIELD, ARTHUR JOHN, music critic, writer; b. San Francisco, Jan. 3, 1931; s. Arthur L. and Julia (Mayer) B.; m. Anne Buenger, July 14, 1956; children: John, Cecily, Alison. AB, Stanford U., 1951. Music and art critic San Francisco Call-Bull., 1958-59, San Francisco News Call-Bull., 1962-65; co-music and art critic San Francisco Examiner, 1965-79; corr. Mus. Am. mag., 1958-61, 63-64, Opera mag., 1964-89; restaurant critic Focus mag., San Francisco, 1979-83; program note writer Mus. and Arts Records, 1996—. Author: The San Francisco Opera, 1923-61, 61, Fifty Years of the San Francisco Opera, 1972, Guide to San Francisco Restaurants, 1975, 77, The San Francisco Opera 1922-78, 1978, Arthur Bloomfield's Restaurant Book, 1987, Sunday Evenings with Pierre Monteux, 1997, 2006, The Gastronomical Tourist, 2002. With AUS, 1953-55. Home: 2229 Webster St San Francisco CA 94115-1820

BLUEMER, BEVAN, acrobatics company executive; b. 1970; married. Owner, ind. cons. Arbonne Internat.; owner, dir. Ariz. Acrobatics. Prog. facilitator GEARUP, Amphitheater High Sch.; dir. campus campaign, The Vagina Monologues. Mem. Beowolf Alley Theatre. Named one of 40 Under 40, Tucson Bus. Edge, 2006.

BLUESTONE, DAVID ALLAN, pediatrician; b. Pitts., Apr. 9, 1938; s. Sam Bluestone and Sarah Cohen Sager; m. Joan Sidlow, Oct. 12, 1957 (div. 1980); children: Daniel, Bradley, Deborah; m. Leslie Florence Widson Kaplan, May 26m 1983. BA, Hamilton Coll., 1959; MD, U. Pitts., 1963. Diplomate Am. Bd. Pediatrics. Pediatric intern Health Ctr. Hosps. U. Pitts., 1963-64; pediatric resident Children's Hosp., Pitts., 1964-65, LA, 1967-68; pediatrician Med. Arts Pediatric Med. Group, Inc., LA, 1968—. Lt. Med. Corps USNR, 1965-67. Fellow Am. Acad. Pediat.; mem. AMA, Calif. Med. Assn., Los Angeles County Med. Assn., L.A. Pediatric Soc., Phi Delta Epsilon (pres. L.A. Grad. Club 1982-83, assoc. regional gov. 1994—), Zeta Phi. Avocations: travel, photography. Office: Med Arts Pediatric Med Group Inc 6221 Wilshire Blvd Ste 215 Los Angeles CA 90048-5201

BLUHER, JOHN H., lawyer, diversified financial services company executive; BS, JD, U. Wyo. Sr. counsel SEC, Disnv. Enforcement, 1987—92; exec. v.p. & gen. counsel AIG Sun America, 1997—2001; sr. v.p. & global chief compliance officer Prudential Securities, 2001—02; gen. counsel, corp. sec. & dir. risk mgmt. Knight Trading Group, 2002—04; sr. v.p., gen. counsel & chief pub. affairs officer Janus Capital Group, Denver, 2004—, exec. v.p., mem. exec. com. & operating com., 2005—. Office: Janus Capital Group 151 Detroit St Denver CO 80206-4923 Office Phone: 303-333-3863. Office Fax: 303-639-6662.

BLUM, GERALD HENRY, retired retail executive; b. San Francisco, 1926; s. Abe and Mildred B.; children: Shelly, Todd, Ryan, Derek. AB, Stanford U., Calif., 1950. Mdse. trainee Emporium, San Francisco, 1950—51; with Gottschalks Inc. (formerly E. Gottschalk & Co., Inc.), Fresno, Calif., 1951—98; v.p. Gottschalks Inc., Fresno, 1954—63, exec. v.p., 1963—82, pres. and vice chmn., 1982—94, ret., 1995, bd. dirs. Bd. dirs. Fresno Conv. Bur., 1954—, pres., 1985-87; bd. dirs. BBB, Fresno, 1954-77, Blue Cross, Calif. 1972-85; chmn. C.A.R.E., Fresno County, 1957—, Eagle Scout Awards Banquet, 1993, Calif. State U. Bus. Coun., Fresno, 1997-98; adv. com. Fresno County Arts Ctr., 1982-85, bd. dirs., 1958-66, v.p. 1961, 88-94; mem. Area VII Calif. Vocat. Edn. Com., 1972-75, Mayor's Bi-Racial Com., 1968-69; founding v.p. Jr. Achievement, Fresno County, 1957-63; bd. dirs. Fresno Boys Club, 1958-62, Ctrl. Calif. Employers Coun., 1956-62, treas. 1958; bd. dirs. Fresno Philharm. Orch., 1954-58, Salvation Army, Fresno, 1956-67, Youth Edn. Svc., 1956-57, Fresno County Taxpayers Assn., 1954, San Joaquin Valley Econ. Edn. Project, 1953; bd. dirs., bus. adv. coun. Fresno City Coll., 1955-57; trustee Valley Children's Hosp., 1955-57, United Crusade, Fresno, 1952-62; adv. bd. Liberty Mut. Ins. Co., 1990-2001. Recipient Disting. Svc. award Fresno Jaycees, 1959; winner World's Championship Domino Tournament, 1969, 86, 88. Mem. Nat. Retail Fedn. (dir. 1978-94), Calif. Retailers Assn. (dir. 1964-94), Fresno C. of C. (dir. county, city 1955-57, Boss of Yr., Jr. C. of C. 1980), Retail Mmgt. Inst., U. Santa Clara (dir. 1986-98), Nat. Secs. Assn. (Boss of Yr. 1978), Fresno County Stanford U. Alumni Assn. (pres. 1952), Pres. Club of Calif. State U., Rotary (v.p. Fresno club 1962), Univ. Sequoia Sunnyside Club, Downtown Club (Fresno, pres. 1978). Personal E-mail: gblum2020@aol.com.

BLUM, JOAN KURLEY, retired not-for-profit fundraiser; b. Palm Beach, Fla., July 27, 1926; d. Nenad Daniel and Eva (Milos) Kurley; m. Robert C. Blum, Apr. 15, 1967 (dec. Apr. 2001); children: Christopher Alexander, Martha Jane, Louisa Joan. BA, U. Wash., 1948. Cert. fund raising exec. U.S. dir. Inst. Mediterranean Studies, Berkeley, Calif., 1962-65; devel. officer U. Calif., Berkeley, 1965-67; pres. Blum Assocs., Fund-Raising Cons., San Anselmo, Calif., 1967-92; ptnr. Philmark Australia, 1980—2001; pres. The Blums of San Francisco, 1992-2001, ret., 2001. Mem. faculty U. Calif. Extension, Inst. Fund Raising, S.W. Inst. Fund-Raising U. Tex., U. San Francisco, U.K. Vol. Movement Group, London, Australasian Inst. Fund Raising. Contbr. numerous articles to profl. jours. Mem. Marin County Civil Grand Jury, 2004—05. Recipient Golden Addy award Am. Advt. Fedn., Silver Mailbox award Direct Mail Mktg. Assn., Best Ann. Giving Time-Life award, others; decorated commdr. Sovereign Order St. Stanislas. Mem. Nat. Soc. Fund-Raising Execs. (dir.), Nat. Assn. of Hosp. Devel., Women Emerging, Rotary (pres., 2007—), Fund Raising Inst. (Australia), Tahoe Yacht Club. Office: 202 Evergreen Dr Kentfield CA 94904-2708 Business E-Mail: sugarblum@aol.com.

BLUM, RICHARD HOSMER ADAMS, foundation administrator, educator, writer; b. Ft. Wayne, Ind., Oct. 7, 1927; s. Hosmer and Imogene (Heino) B. AB with honors magna cum laude, San Jose State Coll., 1948; PhD, Stanford U., 1951. Rsch. dir. Calif. Med. Assn., San Francisco, 1956-58, San Mateo County (Calif.) Mental Health Service, San Mateo, 1958-60; lectr. Sch. Criminology, U. Calif., Berkeley, 1960-62; mem. faculty Stanford (Calif.) U., 1962-78, prof. dept. psychology, 1970-75, prof. dept. gynecology and obstetrics, 1982-97; mem. faculty Stanford (Calif.) U. Law Sch., 1975-78; chmn. bd. Am. Lives Endowment, Portola Valley, Calif., 1979—. Chmn. Internat. Rsch. Group on Drug Legis. and Programs, Geneva, 1969—78; pres. Bio-Behavioral Rsch. Group, Inc., Palo Alto, 1964—87; owner, operator Shingle Mill Ranch, 1964—; vis. fellow Wolfson Coll. U. Cambridge, 1984; vis. prof. social and polit. sci. U. Cambridge, 1997—98; dir. ethics program World Jurist Assn./World Peace Through Law Ctr., Washington, 2000—; dep. chmn. Commn. for the World Equity Ct.; prof. St. Josephs of Arimanthea Theol. Sem., Berkeley, Calif., China U. Polit. Sci. and Law, Beijing; officer Superior Ctr. Conservator for Health Care; guest prof. Northeastern U., Changchun; disting. vis. prof. Dalian U., China; pres. Knightsbridge Castle Found. Author: 30 books. Trustee Palace Mus. of the Last Emperor Puye, Manchuria, China. With U.S. Army, 1951-53, Korea. Decorated Bronze Star; recipient APA Presdl. citation. Fellow APHA (coun. sr. advisors), AAAS, Am. Psychol. Soc., Soc. Advanced Legal Studies (hon., life); mem. Archaeol. Inst. Am., Sigma Xi, Cosmos Club, Athenaeum Club, San Francisco Univ. Club. Unitarian. Home: PO Box 620482 Woodside CA 94062-0482

BLUM, ROBERT M., lawyer; b. NYC, July 12, 1954; BS cum laude, Northwestern U., 1975; JD, Duke U., 1978. Bar: Calif. 1978, US Dist. Ct. (No. Dist.) Calif., US Dist. Ct. (Ea. Dist.) Calif., US Dist. Ct. (So. Dist.) Calif. Ptnr. Thelen, Marrin, Johnson & Bridges, San Francisco; gen. counsel Thelen Reid & Priest LLP, San Francisco. Article & notes editor Adminstrv. Law Issue, Duke Law Jour., 1977—78; contbr. articles to profl. jours., chapters to books. Office: Thelen Reid & Priest LLP 101 Second St Ste 1800 San Francisco CA 94105-3601 Office Phone: 415-369-7277. Office Fax: 415-371-1211. Business E-Mail: rblum@thelenreid.com.

BLUM, SCOTT ALLEN, Internet company executive; b. San Jose, Calif., Jan. 3, 1964; m. Audrey Blum; 2 children. Student, Saddleback CC. Founder MicroBanks, 1985, Pinnacle Micro, 1987, Buy.com, Inc., Aliso Viejo, Calif., 1997, chmn., CEO, 1997—99; mng. ptnr. Think Tank Holdings, LLC, Jackson, Wyo., 1999—. Bd. dirs. TechSpace. Office: Buy dot com Inc 85 Enterprise Ste 100 Aliso Viejo CA 92656 also: ThinkTank Holdings LLC PO Box 8378 Jackson WY 83002 Office Phone: 949-389-2000. Office Fax: 949-389-2800.

BLUMBERG, GRACE GANZ, lawyer, educator; b. NYC, Feb. 16, 1940; d. Samuel and Beatrice (Finkelstein) Ganz; m. Donald R. Blumberg, Sept. 9, 1959; 1 child, Rachel. BA cum laude, U. Colo., 1960; JD summa cum laude, SUNY, 1971; LLM, Harvard U., 1974. Bar: N.Y. 1971, Calif. 1989. Confidential law clk. Appellate Divsn., Supreme Ct., 4th Dept., Rochester, NY, 1971-72; tchg. fellow Harvard Law Sch., Cambridge, Mass., 1972-74; prof. law SUNY, Buffalo, 1974-81, UCLA, 1981—. Reporter Am. Law Inst., Prins. of the Law of Family Dissolution, 2002. Author: Community Property in California, 1987, Community Property in California, rev. edit., 1999, 2003, Blumberg's California Family Code Annotated; contbr. articles to profl. jours. Office: UCLA Sch Law Box 951476 Los Angeles CA 90095-1476

BLUMBERG, MARK STUART, health service researcher, scientist, director; b. NYC, Nov. 16, 1924; s. Sydney N. and Mollie (Leshrowitz) B.; m. Luba Monasevitch, 1952; children: Bart David, Eve Luise; m. 2d Elizabeth R. Conner, 1974. Student, Johns Hopkins U., 1942-43, Harvard U., 1943-44, student Sch. Pub. Health, 1955, DMD, 1948, MD, 1950. Intern, children's med. service Bellevue Hosp., NYC, 1950-51; ops. analyst Johns Hopkins U. Ops. Research Office, Chevy Chase, Md., 1951-54; exchange analyst Army Ops. Research Group (U.K.), West Byfleet, Eng., 1953-54; staff Occupational Health Program, USPHS, Washington, 1954-56; assoc. ops. analyst to dir. health econs. program Stanford (Calif.) Research Inst., 1956-66; asst. to v.p. adminstrn. to dir. health planning, office of the pres. U. Calif., Berkeley, 1966-70; corp. planning advisor to dir. spl. studies Kaiser Found. Health Plan, Inc., Oakland, Calif., 1970-94; dir. Kaiser Found. Health Plan of Conn., Hartford, 1982-94, Kaiser Found. Health Plan Mass., 1987-94; cons. risk adjusted measures Oakland, 1994—; co-founder, sr. scientist TruRisk LLC, 1998—. Various times cons. Pan Am. Health Orgn., Calif. State Dept. Mental Hygiene, Carnegie Commn. on Higher Edn., various agys. HHS. Contbr. writings to profl. publs. Vol. Grenfell Med. Mission, Harrington Harbour, Que., Can., summer 1948; mem. tech. adv. com. AB 524 State of Calif., 1992—. Served with USNR, 1943-45; with USPHS, 1954-56. Mem. Ops. Research Soc. Am. (past mem. council, Health Applications sect.), Hosp. Mgmt. Systems Soc. (charter), Inst. of Medicine of Nat. Acad. Scis. Achievements include patents for computerized underwriting of group life and disability using medical claims data. Office Phone: 510-601-9536.

BLUMBERG, NATHAN(IEL) BERNARD, journalist, educator, writer and publisher; b. Denver, Apr. 8, 1922; s. Abraham Moses and Jeannette Blumberg; m. Lynne Stout, June 1946 (div. Feb. 1970); children: Janet Leslie, Jenifer Lyn, Josephine Laura; m. Barbara Farquhar, July 1973. BA, U. Colo., 1947, MA, 1948; D.Phil. (Rhodes scholar), Oxford U., Eng., 1950. Reporter Denver Post, 1947-48; assoc. editor Lincoln (Nebr.) Star, 1950-53; asst. to editor Ashland (Nebr.) Gazette, 1954-55; asst. city editor Washington Post and Times Herald, 1956; from asst. prof. to assoc. prof. journalism U. Nebr., 1950-55; asso. prof. journalism Mich. State U., 1955-56; dean, prof. Sch. Journalism, U. Mont., 1956-68, prof. journalism, 1968-78, prof. emeritus, 1978—; pub. Wood FIRE Ashes Press, 1981—. Vis. prof. Pa. State U., 1964, Northwestern U., 1966-67, U. Calif., Berkeley, 1970; Dept. State specialist in Thailand, 1961, in Trinidad, Guyana, Surinam and Jamaica, 1964 Author: One-Party Press?, 1954; The Afternoon of March 30: A Contemporary Historical Novel, 1984, also articles in mags. and jours.; co-editor: A Century of Montana Journalism, 1971; editor: The Mansfield Lectures in International Relations, Vols. I and II, 1979; founder: Mont. Journalism Rev, 1958—; editor, pub. Treasure State Rev., 1991—. Served with arty. U.S. Army, 1943-46. Bronze Star medal. Mem. Assn. Am. Rhodes Scholars, Brasenose Soc., Kappa Tau Alpha (nat. pres. 1969-70). Home: PO Box 99 Bigfork MT 59911-0099

BLUMENAUER, EARL, United States Representative from Oregon; b. Portland, Oreg., Aug. 16, 1948; m. Margaret Kirkpatrick; 2 children. BA, Lewis and Clark Coll., Portland, Oreg., 1970, JD, 1976. Asst. to pres. Portland State U., Oreg., 1971-73; mem. Oreg. State Ho. Reps., 1973-79, Multnomah County Bd. Commrs., Portland, Oreg., 1979-87; commr. pub. works City Coun., Portland, 1987-96; mem. US Congress from 3rd Oreg. dist., 1996—, mem. ways and means com., mem. budget com., mem. select com. on energy independence and climate change. Mem. Gov.'s Commn. Higher Edn., Oreg., 1990—91. Recipient Apgar award, Nat. Bldg. Mus., 2000, Nat. Bicycle Advocacy award, League of Am. Bicyclists, 2001; named Legislator of Yr., Am. Planning Assn., 1999; fellow German Marshall, 1995. Democrat. Avocations: bicycling, running. Office: 729 NE Oregon St Ste 115 Portland OR 97232 Office Phone: 202-225-4811. Office Fax: 503-230-5413.

BLUMENFELD, CHARLES RABAN, lawyer; b. Seattle, May 24, 1944; s. Irwin S. and Freda I. (Raban) B.; m. Karla Axell; children: David, Lisa. BA, U. Wash., JD, 1969. Bar: Wash. 1969, U.S. Dist. Ct. (we. dist.) Wash. 1969, U.S. Ct. Appeals (9th cir.) 1975, U.S. Supreme Ct. 1979, U.S. Dist. Ct. D.C. 1981, U.S. Ct. Appeals (D.C. cir.) 1981. Legis. counsel U.S. Senator Henry M. Jackson, Washington, 1969-72; ptnr. Bogle & Gates, Seattle, 1973-99, PerkinsCoie, Seattle, 1999—2007; assoc. v.p. alumni rels. U. Washington, Seattle, 2007—. Office: U Washington Alumni Assn 1415 NE 45th St Seattle WA 98105 Home Phone: 206-323-4868; Office Phone: 206-685-6929. Business E-Mail: cblumenfeld@u.washington.edu.

BLUMENFELD, ELI, lawyer; b. N.Y.C., May 17, 1933; s. William E. and Bessie (Rappaport) B.; m. Nancy Sue Greenberg, Dec. 2, 1973; children: Beth C., Robert K., Jennifer P., Whitney S., Kevin Jonathan. JD, UCLA, 1963. Bar: Calif., 1964. Dist. counsel IRS, Portland, Oreg. and L.A., 1964-69; mem. firm Mitchell, Silberberg & Knupp, L.A., 1969; acct., bus. mgr. Charles Goldring, Esq., L.A., 1962-64; sole practice, L.A., 1969—. Served with USN, 1951-55. Mem. ABA, Calif. Bar Assn., L.A. Bar Assn., Beverly Hills Bar Assn., Hillcrest Country Club, Vista Del Mar Pres. Club (v.p., 1979-81, chmn. bd., 1981-86, pres. 1986-93). Office: 468 N Camden Dr Ste 300 Beverly Hills CA 90210 Office Phone: 310-205-0800. Business E-Mail: eli517@aol.com.

BLUMENTHAL, GEORGE, academic administrator, astronomy and astrophysics professor; BS, U. Wis.-Milw.; PhD in Physics, U. Calif., San Diego. Faculty mem. U. Calif., Santa Cruz, 1972—, chair Astronomy and Astrophysics Dept., chair Academic Senate, 2001—03, acting chancellor, 2006—07, chancellor, 2007—; chair U. Calif. Academic Senate, 2004—05. Office: U Calif Santa Cruz 1156 High St Santa Cruz CA 95064-1077 E-mail: chancellor@ucsc.edu.

BLUMER, HARRY MAYNARD, architect; b. Stillwater, Okla., Aug. 27, 1930; s. Harry H. and Nona A. (Ftizpatrick) B.; m. C. Sue Linebaugh, Sept. 2, 1952; children: Eric W., Laura B., Martha L. BArch, Okla. State U., 1953; BS in Bus., Ariz. State U., 1976. Registered arch., Ariz., landscape arch., Ariz., arch., U.S. Govt.; cert. constrn. specifier, fallout shelter analyst, U.S. Dept. Def. Designer, draftsman Norman Byrd Architect, Oklahoma City, Okla., 1952, Overend & Boucher Architects, Wichita, Kans., 1953-54; archtl. designer, draftsman Louis G. Hesselden Architect, Albuquerque, 1956; project designer, planner, constrn. & contract adminstr. Flatow, Moore, Bryan & Fairburn Architects, Albuquerque, 1956-61; regional architect U.S. Forest Svc., Albuquerque, 1961-62; v.p. prodn. Guirey, Srnka, Arnold & Sprinkle, Phoenix, 1962-82; prin. arch. H. Maynard Blumer, FAIA, FCSI, Consulting Arch., Scottsdale, Ariz., 1982—. Lectr. architecture Ariz. State U., Tempe, 1968-69; rep. specifications consulting projects for various structures including Chandler Med. Office bldg., 1982, Ariz. State U. w. campus utility tunnel, 1986, Mayo Clinic consourse and parking structure, 1993, City of Tempe, Ariz. Comm. Tech. Ctr., 1997, numerous others; speaker in field. Contbr. articles to profl. publs. Bd. dirs., camping com., camp master plan design Maricopa County Coun. Campfire Girls, 1962-69; pres. N.Mex. Cactus and Succulent Soc., 1959-60; sec. Advancement Mgmt., Phoenix, 1972-73, dir., 1971-72; bd. govs. Amateur Athletic Union U.S., 1972-75, chmn. nat. conv. registration com., 1975; v.p. Ariz. Assn. Bd. MGrs., 1972-73, pres., 1973; treas. Pop Warner Football Assn., 1975; pres. parents club Scottsdale YMCA Judo Club, 1970-80; chairperson materials testing lab. citizens' rev. com. City of Phoenix, 1978, mem. arch. selection com., 1990, constrn. mediation panelist, 1995; commr. planning and zoning commn. Town of Paradise Valley, Ariz., 1994-97, mem. Hillside blding. rev. com. rotation, 1994—, mem. spl. use permit rev. com. rotation, 1994—; 1st lt. U.S. Army Corps Engrs., 1954-56, Korea. Recipient Valley Beautiful Citizens Coun. Cmty. Recognition award 1964, 68, Outstanding Use Masonry award, Ariz. Masonry Guild, 1968, Ariz. Aggregate Assn. Spl. Recognition award, 1986, Edn. Commendation award Constrn. Specifications Inst., 1980. Fellow AIA (Honor award Ctrl. Ariz. chpt. 1967, Oustanding Svc. to Profession award 1986), Constrn. Specification Inst. (Phoenix chpt., mem. chpt. fellows com. 1973—, roundtable chair, moderator 1981—, Pres.'s Disting. Svc. cert. 1968, Disting. Leadership plaque Phoenix chpt. 1968, Oustanding Profl. Mem. award, 1981, Pres.'s cert. Appreciation 1985, numerous others); mem. ASTM. Office: 8517 N 49th St Paradise Valley AZ 85253-2002

BOAHEN, KWABENA, bioengineering educator; BS in Elec. and Computer Engring., MS in Elec. and Computer Engring., Johns Hopkins U., Balt., 1989; PhD in Computation and Neural Systems, Calif. Inst. Tech., 1997. Asst. prof. depts. bioengineering and elec. engring. U. Pa., Phila.; assoc. prof. bioengineering Stanford U., Calif., 2006—. Contbr. articles to sci. jours. Recipient Faculty Early Career award, NSF, 2001, Young Investigator award, Office of Naval Rsch., 2002, NIH Dir.'s Pioneer award, 2006; grantee Packard Found. fellowship in Sci. and Engring., 1999—2004. Achievements include development of a silicon retina able to process images in the same manner as a living retina. Office: Brains in Silicon Stanford U Clark Ctr W3 1 318 Campus Dr W Stanford CA 94305-5441 Office Phone: 650-724-5633. Office Fax: 650-724-5791. E-mail: boahen@stanford.edu.

BOAL, DEAN, retired arts center administrator, educator; b. Longmont, Colo., Oct. 20, 1931; s. Elmer C. and L. Mildred (Snodgrass) B.; m. Ellen Christine TeSelle, Aug. 23, 1957; children: Brett, Jed. B.Music, B.Music Edn., U. Colo., 1953; M.Music, Ind. U., 1956; D. Musical Arts, U. Colo., 1959. Mem. faculty Hastings (Nebr.) Coll., 1958-60; head piano dept. Bradley U., Peoria, Ill., 1960-66; dean, pianist Peabody Conservatory, Balt., 1966-70; prof. piano, chair music SUNY, Fredonia, 1970-73; pres. St. Louis Conservatory, 1973-76; dir. radio sta. KWMU, St. Louis, 1976-78; v.p., gen. mgr. Sta. WETA-FM, Washington, 1978-83; dir. arts and performance programs Nat. Pub. Radio, Washington, 1982-89; pres. Interlochen (Mich.) Ctr. for the Arts, 1989-95; pres. emeritus, 1995—. Author: Concepts and Skills for the Piano, Book I, 1969, Book II, 1970, Interlochen: A Home for The Arts, 1998; contbr. articles to profl. jours. Mem. adv. bd U. Colo. Coll. Music, 1987-2000; trustee Alma Coll., 1992-95; bd. dirs., chmn. Peak Assn. of the Arts, 1998-2000. Served with U.S. Army, 1953-55. Woodrow Wilson teaching fellow, 1983-89; recipient Disting. Alumnus award in Profl. Music Univ. Colo., 1987. Mem. Eastern Public Radio Network (chmn. 1979-82), Coll. Music Soc., Pi Kappa Lambda, Mu Phi Epsilon, Phi Mu Alpha. Presbyterian.

BOAL, PETER CADBURY, performing company executive; b. Bedford, NY, Oct. 18, 1965; s. Richard Bradlee and Lyndall Elizabeth (Cadbury) B.; m. Kelly Cass, Aug. 15, 1992; 3 children: Sebastian Bradlee, Oliver, Sarah. Student, Sch. Am. Ballet, NYC, 1975-83, NY State Summer Sch. Arts, 1981-82. With corps de ballet NYC Ballet, 1983-87, soloist, 1987-89, prin., 1989—2005, Ballet Du Nord, Roubaix, France, 1988; artistic dir. Pacific NW Ballet, Seattle, 2005—. Performed in NYC Ballet's Balanchine Celebration, 1993, also Apollo, Divertimento from Le Baiser de la Fée, Harlequinade,

Trustee Profl. Children's Sch. Recipient Award Dance Mag., 1996, NY Dance and Performance award, 2000 Mem. Am. Guild Mus. Artists. Democrat. Avocation: skiing. Office: Pacific NW Ballet 301 Mercer St Seattle WA 98109

BOALER, JO, education educator; BSc in Psychology, U. Liverpool, Eng., 1985; MA in Math. Edn., London U., 1991, PhD in Math. Edn., 1996. Tchr. secondary sch. math., Camden, London, 1986—89; dep. dir. math. assessment project King's Coll., London U., 1989—93, lectr., rschr. on math. edn., 1993—98; assoc. prof. Stanford (Calif.) U., 2000—. Mem. Math. Edn. Study Panel; bd. dirs. Gender and Edn. jour. Mem.: Internat. Orgn. for Women in Math. Edn. Office: Stanford U Sch Edn 485 Lasuen Mall Stanford CA 94305-3096

BOARDMAN, CONNIE, former mayor, biologist, educator; BS, MS, Calif. State U., Long Beach. Prof. biology Cerriots C.C., Norwalk. Mem. econ. devel. com. Huntington Beach (Calif.) City Coun., mem. intergovernmental com., mem. animal care svcs. com., mem. comm. com.; alt. mem. Orange County Sanitation Dist.; coun. liaison Allied Arts Bd., Environ. Bd., Mobile Home Adv. Bd., Oakview Task Force, Sister City Assn.; mem. city coun. City of Huntington Beach, 2000—, mayor, 2002—03.

BOARDMAN, DAVID, editor; m. Barbara Winslow; children: Emily, Madeline. BS in Journalism, Northwestern U., 1979; M in Comm., U. Wash., 1983. Copy editor Football Weekly, Chgo., 1977-79; reporter Anacortes American, Wash., 1979-80, Skagit Valley Herald, Mt. Vernon, Wash., 1980-81; reporter, copy editor The News Tribune, Tacoma, 1981-83; copy editor The Seattle Times, 1983, editor, reporter, 1984, nat. editor, 1984-86, local news editor, 1986-87, asst. city editor, 1987-90, regional editor, 1990-96, metro. editor, 1997—, asst. mng. editor, 1997—2003, exec. editor, 2003—. Vis. faculty Poynter Inst. Media Studies, St. Petersburg, Fla. Recipient Goldsmith Prize in Investigative Reporting JFK Sch. Govt. Harvard U., 1993, Worth Bingham prize, 1993, Investigative Reporters and Editors award, 1993, AP Mng. Editors Pub. Svc. award, 1992, 1st place nat. reporting Pulitzer Prize, 1990, lead editor Pulitzer Prize in investigative reporting, 1997; finalist Pulitzer Prize, 1993, 98, 99, 2002, 03; juror Pulitzer Prizes, 1999-2000; fellow Japan-IBCC fellowship Ctr. Fgn. Journalists, 1995. Office: Seattle Times 1120 John St Seattle WA 98109 also: Seattle Times PO Box 70 Seattle WA 98111 E-mail: dboardman@seattletimes.com.

BOATRIGHT, CLYDE A., state legislator; b. Manzinolla, Colo., July 7, 1930; m. Karen Boatright. Student, U. Alaska. Enlisted USN, 1947, ret., 1967; realtor; mem. Idaho Senate, Dist. 2, Boise, 1994—. Mem. joint fin. and transp. coms., Idaho Senate. Former chair, bd dirs., North Idaho Fair. Mem. Shriners, Masons, Rathdrum (Idaho) C. of C., Coeur d'Alene (Idaho) C. of C. Republican. Office: State Capitol 700 W Jefferson St Boise ID 83720-0001

BOBEK, NICOLE, professional figure skater; b. Chgo., Aug. 23, 1977; Competitive history includes: mem. of 1st place team Hershey's Kisses Challenge, 1997, placed 13th in World Championships, 1997, 3rd in Nat. Sr., 1997, 2nd (team) U.S. Postal Svc. Challenge, 1996, 3rd (team) Hershey's Kisses Challenge, 1996, 10th place Centennial on Ice, 1996, 1st place Starlight Challenge, 1995, 3rd in World Championships, 1995, 1st in Nat. Sr., 1995, 2d place, World Pro Championship, 2000, 3d place, Canadian Open, 2001, numerous others. Champions on Ice Tour, 2000-. Avocations: dance, drawing, poetry, modeling, designing clothes. Office: USFSA 20 1st St Colorado Springs CO 80906-3624

BOBISUD, LARRY EUGENE, mathematics professor; b. Midvale, Idaho, Mar. 16, 1940; s. Walter and Ida V. (Bitner) B.; m. Helen M. Meyer, June 15, 1963. BS, Coll. of Ida., 1961; MA, U. N.M., 1963, PhD, 1966. Vis. mem. Courant Inst. Math. Scis. NYU, NYC, 1966-67; prof. math. U. Idaho, Moscow, 1967—2002, prof. emeritus, 2002—. Contbr. articles to profl. jours. Mem. Am. Math. Soc. Home: 860 N Eisenhower St Moscow ID 83843-9581 Office: Univ Idaho Dept Math Moscow ID 83844-1103 Business E-Mail: bobisud@uidaho.edu.

BOBRICK, STEVEN AARON, transportation executive; b. Denver, Apr. 11, 1950; s. Samual Michael and Selma Gertrude (Birnbaum) B.; m. M. Diane Boltz, Oct. 5, 1980. Attended, U. Colo., 1968-72. Registered apt. mgr. Owner Bobrick Constrn., Denver, 1969-72; with Bell Mtn. Sports, Aspen, Colo., 1972-75; mgr. Compass Imports, Denver, 1975-80, Aurora (Colo.) Bullion Exch., 1980-81; contr. Bobrick Constrn., Aurora, 1981-85; appraiser Aurora, 1985—; property mgr. Aurora (Colo) Cmty. Mental Health, 1989-98, active real estate and constrn., facilities mgr., 1989-98; exec. mgmt. asst. E-470 Pub. Hwy. Authority, 1998, mktg./pub. rels. web master, 1998-99; ops. dir. Northwest Pkwy Pub. Hwy. Authority, 1999—2007, Northwest Pkwy. LLC/Brisa, 2007—. Co-author: Are You Paying Too Much in Property Taxes, 1990. Coun. mem. City of Aurora, 1981-89; chmn. Explore Commercial Opportunities, Aurora, 1986-89, bd. dirs.; bd. dirs. Adam County Econ. Devel. Commn., Northglenn, Colo., 1985-89; vice chair Aurora Urban Renewal Authority, 1982-89; chmn. Aurora Enterprise Zone Found., 1991-94; bd. dirs. Aurora Community Med. Clinic, 1987-88, Aurora Cmty. Mental Health Ctr., 2001. Avocations: skiing, bicycling, exercise. Office: 3701 Northwest Pkwy Broomfield CO 80020 Personal E-mail: sbobrick@mindspring.com. Business E-Mail: sbobrick@nwpky.org.

BOBROW, MICHAEL LAWRENCE, architect; b. NYC, Apr. 18, 1939; s. Jack and Ruth (Gureasko) B.; m. Julia Dessery Thomas, Mar. 24, 1980; children by previous marriage: Elizabeth, Erica, David; 1 stepchild, Leslie Thomas. BArch, Columbia U., 1963. Registered arch. Calif. Sr. arch. Office Surgeon Gen./U.S. Air Force, Washington, 1963-66; dir. arch. Med. Planning Assoc., Malibu, Calif., 1966-72; founder, chmn., design ptnr. Bobrow/Thomas & Assocs., LA, 1972. Founder, coord. programs in health complex facilities design UCLA Grad. Sch. Arch. and Urban Planning, 1972-80; adj. prof. UCLA Grad. Sch. Pub. Health, deans adv. bd.; chmn. UCLA, Columbia U. Internat. Hosp. Design Competition; trustee Otis Coll. Art & Design; chmn. bd. Arts and Arch. Mag. Prin. works include City of Hope Nat. Med. Ctr., Cook County Hosp., Prototype Campus Calif. State U., Channel Islands, Motion Picture and TV Hosp., Cedars Sinai Med. Ctr., Otis Coll. Art & Design, VA L.A. Clinic, St. Lukes Med. Ctr., Camp Pendleton Naval Hosp., Shriners Hosp., UCLA Arroyo Bridge, Beckman Rsch. Lab., others; contbr. articles to profl. jours. Pres. The Friends of the Schindler House, L.A., 1978-79; dir. Am. Hosp. Assn. Ann. Design Inst.; chmn. strategic planning and design com. Westwood Village Bus. Improvement Dist.; chmn. Hosp. Coun. So. Calif. Seismic Design Inst., 1994. Named one of Outstanding Architects Under 40, Bldg. Design and Constrn. Mag., 1978; recipient Preservation award L.A. Conservancy to the Friends of Schindler House, 1982. Fellow AIA (co-chmn. com. on arch. for health spl. task force on capital reimbursement 1983—, Nat. and Regional Design awards); mem. Beverly Hills Tennis Club.

BOCHCO, STEVEN, screenwriter, television producer; b. NYC, Dec. 16, 1943; s. Rudolph and Mimi B.; m. Barbara Bosson, 1969 (div. 1997; 2 children; m. Dayna Kalins Aug. 12, 2000. BA, Carnegie Mellon U., 1996. Scriptwriter, editor, prodr. Universal Studios, LA, 1966-78; writer, prodr. MTM Enterprises, Studio City, 1978-85, Twentieth Century Fox, LA, 1985-87, Paramount Network TV, 1999—2004, Disney Touchstone TV, 2005—; chmn. CEO Steven Bocho Prodns., LA, 1987—. Writer: (films) (with Michael Cimino and Deric Washburn) Silent Running, 1972, (TV series) Ironside, 1967-75, Columbo, 1971-78, McMillan and Wife, 1971-76, Griff, 1973-74, Delvecchio, 1976-77, McMillan, 1977, Turnabout, 1979, (TV films) (with Harold Clements) The Counterfeit Killer, 1968, Double Indemnity, 1973, Uneasy Lies the Crown, 1990; writer, prodr.: (TV series) Bay City Blues, 1983-84, Griff, 1973-74, (TV mini series) Over There, 2005; (TV films) The Invisible Man, 1975, Richie Brockelman: Missing Twenty-four Hours, 1976, Lieutenant Schuster's Wife, 1972, Columbo: Uneasy Lies the Crown, 1990; writer, exec. prodr.: (TV series) Paris, 1979-80, (TV films) Vampire, 1979, prodr: (TV series) Capitol Critters, 1992, The Byrds of Paradise, 1994; co-creator, exec. prodr., writer: (TV series) Hill Street Blues, 1981-86 (Emmy award best drama series 1981, 82, 83, 84, Emmy award best writing in drama series 1981, 82, Golden Globe award best drama series 1982, 83), L.A. Law, 1986-87 (Emmy award best drama series 1987, 89, Emmy award best writing in drama series 1987, Golden Gobe award best drama series 1987, 88), Hooperman, 1987-89, Doogie Howser, M.D., 1989-93, Cop Rock, 1990, Civil Wars, 1991-93, NYPD Blue, 1993—2005 (Golden Globe award best drama series 1994, Outstanding Drama Series Emmy award, 1995), Murder One 1995-96, Total Security, 1997, Philly, 2001; exec. prodr.: (TV series) Public Morals, 1996, Brooklyn South, 1997-98, City of Angels, 2000, Commander in Chief, 2005-.

BOCHNER, STEVEN E., lawyer; BA, San Jose State, 1977; JD, Boalt Hall, U. Calif. Berkeley, 1981. Ptnr. Wilson Sonsini Goodrich & Rosati, Palo Alto, Calif., mem. exec. mgmt. com. & policy com. Guest instr.-venture capital & bus. law issues Stanford Grad. Sch. Bus., U. Calif., Berkeley, Haas Sch. Bus.; lectr. Stanford Law Sch.; lectr.-corp. & securities law U. Calif. Berkeley, Boalt Hall Law Sch. Co-author: Guide to the Initial Pub. Offering, 2004. Adv. com. on smaller pub. companies SEC, 2005—; mem. NASDAQ Listing & Hearing Rev. Coun., 1996—, co-chmn., 2005—; adv. bd. VentureOne; bd. dir. Joint Venture Silicon Valley Network. Office: Wilson Sonsini Goodrich & Rosati 650 Page Mill Rd Palo Alto CA 94304-1050 Office Phone: 650-493-9300. Office Fax: 650-493-6811. Business E-Mail: sbochner@wsgr.com.

BOCHY, BRUCE, professional baseball team manager; b. Landes de Boussac, France, Apr. 16, 1955; m. Kim B.; children: Greg, Brett. Catcher Houston Astros, 1978—80, NY Mets, 1982, San Diego Padres, 1983—87, third base coach, 1993-94, mgr., 1994—2005, San Francisco Giants, 2006—. Named Nat. League Mgr. of Yr., MLB, 1996, The Sporting News, 1996, 1998. Office: San Francisco Giants Pac Bell Park 24 Willie Mays Plz San Francisco CA 94107

BOCIAN, PETER, computer company executive; BA, Mich. State U., M in Acctg., 1982. Various mgmt. positions NCR Corp., Dayton, Ohio, 1983—2002, CFO, v.p. retail solutions divsn., 1999—2002, CFO retail and fin. group, 2002—03, v.p., fin., CFO, 2003—07; exec. v.p., CFO, chief adminstrv. officer Starbucks Corp., Seattle, 2007—08; exec. v.p., chief adminstrv. officer Hewlett Packard, Palo Alto, Calif., 2008—. Office: Hewlett Packard 3000 Hanover St Palo Alto CA 94304-1185

BOCK, S. ALLAN, physician, educator; b. Balt., Apr. 28, 1946; s. Sam and Charlotte Bock; m. Judith Lloyd, Oct. 19, 1985; children: Sam, Lea. AB, Washington U., 1968; MD, U. Md., 1972. Diplomate Am. Bd. Pediatrics, Am. Bd. Allergy and Immunology; lic. physician, Colo. Intern U. Md. Hosp., Balt., 1972-73; resident in pediatrics U. Colo. Med. Ctr., Denver, 1973-74, asst. prof. pediatrics; fellow in pediatric allergy and immunology Nat. Jewish Hosp. and Rsch. Ctr., Denver, 1974-76; assoc. clin. prof. pediatrics U. Colo. Health Scis. Ctr., Boulder, 1982-90, clin. prof. pediatrics, 1990—. Vol. physician Nat. Jewish Ctr. Immunology and Respiratory Medicine, 1976—; pediatric allergist Dept. Health and Hosps., 1976-84. Contbr. numerous articles to profl. jours. Recipient Jacob E. Finesinger prize for excellence in psychiatry, 1972, Outstanding vol. clin. faculty award Am. Acad. Allergy Asthma and Immunology, 1977. Fellow Am. Acad. Allergy and Immunology, Am. Acad. Pediatrics; mem. Alpha Omega Alpha. Avocations: skiing, hiking, biking, jazz. Office: Boulder Valley Asthma Allergy Clinic 3950 Broadway St Boulder CO 80304-1104 Office Phone: 303-444-5991.

BODANSKY, DAVID, physicist, researcher; b. NYC, Mar. 10, 1924; s. Aaron and Marie (Syrkin) B.; m. Beverly Ferne Bronstein, Sept. 7, 1952; children: Joel N., Daniel M. BS, Harvard U., 1943, MA, 1948, PhD, 1950. Instr. physics Columbia U., NYC, 1950-52, assoc., 1952-54; mem. faculty U. Wash., Seattle, 1954—, assoc. prof. physics, 1958-63, prof., 1963-93, prof. emeritus, 1993—, chmn. dept., 1976-84. Co-author: (with Fred H. Schmidt) The Energy Controversy: The Fight over Nuclear Power, 1976, (with others) Indoor Radon and Its Hazards, 1987, Nuclear Energy: Principles, Practices, and Prospects, 1996, 2d edit., 2004; editl. bd.: Rev. Sci. Instruments, 1967-69. With Signal Corps AUS, 1943-46. Sloan Rsch. fellow, 1959-63, Guggenheim fellow, 1966-67, 74-75. Fellow Am. Phys. Soc. (chair Panel on Pub. Affairs 1995), AAAS; mem. Am. Assn. Physics Tchrs., Am. Nuc. Soc., Health Physics Soc., Phi Beta Kappa. Achievements include research in nuclear physics, nuclear astrophysics and energy policy. Office: U Wash Dept Physics Seattle WA 98195-1560 Business E-Mail: bodansky@phys.washington.edu.

BODENSTEINER, LISA M., former utilities executive, lawyer; BS in Bus. Adminstrn. and Acctg., U. Nev., 1985; JD, Santa Clara U., 1989. Assoc. Thelen, Reid & Priest, 1994—96; assoc. counsel Calpine Corp., 1996—99, v.p., gen. counsel, 1999—2001, sr. v.p., gen. counsel, 2001—02, asst. sec., exec. v.p., gen. counsel, 2002—06.

BODKIN, HENRY GRATTAN, JR., lawyer; b. LA, Dec. 8, 1921; s. Henry Grattan and Ruth May (Wallis) B.; m. Mary Louise Davis, June 28, 1943; children: Maureen L. Dixon, Sheila L. McCarthy, Timothy Grattan. BS cum laude, Loyola Marymount U., Los Angeles, 1943, JD, 1948. Bar: Calif. 1948. Pvt. practice, Los Angeles, 1948-51, 53-95; ptnr. Bodkin, McCarthy, Sargent & Smith (predecessor firms), LA; of counsel Sullivan, Workman & Dee, LA, 1995—. Mem. L.A. Bd. Water and Power Commrs., 1972-74, pres., 1973-74; regent Marymount Coll., 1962-67; trustee Loyola-Marymount U., 1973-91, vice chmn., 1985-86. With USNR, 1943-45, 51-53. Fellow Am. Coll. Trial Lawyers; mem. Calif. State Bar (mem. exec. com. conf. of dels. 1968-70, vice chmn. 1969-70), California Club, Chancery Club (pres. 1990-91), Riviera Tennis Club, Tuna Club, Phi Delta Phi. Republican. Roman Catholic. Home: 956 Linda Flora Dr Los Angeles CA 90049-1631 Office: Sullivan Workman & Dee 800 S Figueroa St Fl 12 Los Angeles CA 90017-2521 Home Phone: 310-472-3441; Office Phone: 213-624-5544. E-mail: bodkin01@cs.com.

BODNEY, DAVID JEREMY, lawyer; b. Kansas City, Mo., July 15, 1954; s. Daniel F. and Retha (Silby) B.; m. Sarah Hughes; children: Christian Steven, Anna Claire, Daniel Martin. BA cum laude, Yale U., 1976; MA in Fgn. Affairs, U. Va., 1979, JD, 1979. Bar: Ariz. 1979, U.S. Dist Ct. Ariz. 1980, U.S. Ct. Appeals (9th cir.) 1980, U.S. Supreme Ct. 1983. Legis. asst., speechwriter U.S. Senator John V. Tunney, Washington, 1975-76; sr. editor Va. Jour. of Internat. Law, 1978-79; assoc. Brown and Bain PA, Phoenix, 1979-85, ptnr., 1985-90; gen. counsel New Times, Inc., Phoenix, 1990-92; ptnr. Steptoe & Johnson, LLP, Phoenix, 1992—, mng. ptnr., 2002—03. Vis. prof. Ariz. State U., Tempe, 1985, 94—. Co-author: Libel Defense Resource Center: 50-State Survey, 1982—. Bd. dirs. Ariz. Ctr. for Law in the Pub. Interest, Phoenix, 1983-90, pres., 1989-90; chmn. Yale Alumni Schs. Com., Phoenix, 1984-87; vice chmn. City of Phoenix Solicitation Bd., 1986-88, chmn., 1988-89; bd. dirs. Children's Action Alliance, 1995—, chmn., 2003-07, chmn.; adv. panel on Civil Liberties to White House Commn. on Aviation Safety and Security, 1997; bd. dirs. Ariz. region Anti-Defamation League, 2001—, v.p., 2004-06, chmn., 2006-; adv. coun. dir. Ariz. Ctr. Pub. Policy Recipient Cert. Merit, ABA. Mem. ABA (forum com. on communication law 1984—, concerned correspondents network com. 1979—), Ariz. Bar Assn. Clubs: Yale (bd. dirs. Phoenix club 1979—), Ariz. Acad., Maricopa County Bar Assn. Democrat. Office: Steptoe & Johnson Collier Ctr 201 E Washington St 1600 Phoenix AZ 85004 Business E-Mail: dbodney@steptoe.com.

BOEDER, THOMAS L., lawyer; b. St. Cloud, Minn., Jan. 10, 1944; s. Oscar Morris and Eleanor (Gile) B.; m. Carol-Leigh Coombs, Apr. 6, 1968. BA magna cum laude, Yale U., 1965, LLB, 1968. Bar: Wash. 1970, U.S. Dist. Ct. (We. Dist.) Wash. 1970, U.S. Dist. Ct. (Ea. Dist.) Wash. 1972, U.S. Ct. Appeals (9th Cir.) 1970, U.S. Supreme Ct. 1974, U.S. Ct. Appeals (D.C. Cir.) 1975, U.S. Ct. Appeals (10th Cir.) 1993. Litigation atty. Wash. State Atty. Gen., Seattle, 1970-72, antitrust div. head, 1972-76, chief, consumer protection and antitrust, 1976-78, also sr. asst. atty. gen. and criminal enforcement, 1979-81; ptnr., Litig. Practice Area Perkins Coie LLP, Seattle, 1981—. With US Army, 1968—70, Vietnam. Mem. ABA (antitrust sect.), Wash. State Bar Assn. (antitrust sect.), Phi Beta Kappa. Lutheran. Office: Perkins Coie LLP 1201 3rd Ave Fl 40 Seattle WA 98101-3029 Home Phone: 206-523-2795; Office Phone: 206-359-8416. Office Fax: 206-359-9416. Business E-Mail: tboeder@perkinscoie.com.

BOEHM, BARRY WILLIAM, computer science educator; b. Santa Monica, Calif., May 16, 1935; s. Edward G. and Kathryn G. (Kane) B.; m. Sharla Perrine, July 1, 1961; children: Romney Ann, Tenley Lynn. BA, Harvard U., 1957; PhD, UCLA, 1964; ScD (hon.), U. Mass., 2000. Programmer, analyst Gen. Dynamics, San Diego, 1955-59; head infosci. dept. Rand Corp., Santa Monica, 1959-73; chief scientist TRW Def. Sys. Group, Redondo Beach, Calif., 1973-89; dir. infosci. and tech. office Def. Advanced Rsch. Agy. Dept. Def., Arlington, Va., 1989-92, dir. software and computer tech. office, dir. def. rsch. and engring., 1992; TRW prof. software engring., dir. Ctr. for Software Engring. U. So. Calif., LA, 1992—. Co-chmn. Fed. Coordinating Coun. Sci., Engring. and Tech. High Performance Computing WG, Washington, 1989-91; chmn. DOD Software Tech. Plan WG, Arlington, 1990-92, NASA G & C/Infosystems Adv. Com., Washington, 1973-76; guest lectr. USSR Acad. Sci., 1970; chmn. bd. visitors Carnegie Mellon U. Software Engring. Inst., 1997—; chmn. USAF-Sci. Adv. Bd. Info. Tech. Panel, 1994-97, Army/DARPA Future Combat Systems Software Steering Com., 2001—, vis. prof. Chinese Acad. Sci., 2005. Author: ROCKET, 1964, Software Engineering Economics, 1981; co-author: Characteristics of Software Quality, 1978, Software Risk Management, 1989, Software Cost Estimation with COCOMO II, 2000, Balancing Agility and Discipline, 2004, Software Engineering: Barry W. Boehm's Contributions, 2007; co-editor: Planning Community Information Utilities, 1972, Foundations of Empirical Software Engineering, 2005, Value-Based Software Engineering, 2005, Unifying The Software Process Spectrum, 2005. Recipient Warnier prize Soc. Software Analysts, 1984, Freiman award Internat. Soc. Parametric Analysts, 1988, Award for Excellence Office of Sec. of Def., 1992. Fellow Internat. Coun. on Sys. Engring., Assn. for Computing Machinery (Disting. Rsch. award in Software Engring. 1997), NAE, AIAA (chair TC computers 1968-70, Info. Sys. award 1979), IEEE (gov. bd. computer sci. 1981-82, 86-87, H.D. Mills award 2000). Office: U So Calif Computer Sci Dept Los Angeles CA 90089-0781 Business E-Mail: boehm@sunset.usc.edu.

BOEHM, ERIC HARTZELL, information technology executive; b. Hof, Germany, July 15, 1918; came to U.S., 1934, naturalized, 1940; s. Karl and Bertha (Oppenheimer) Boehm; m. Inge Pauli, June 5, 1948 (dec.); children: Beatrice(dec.), Ronald James, Evelyn(dec.), Steven David. BA, Wooster Coll., Ohio, 1940, Litt.D. (hon.), 1973; MA, Fletcher Sch. Law and Diplomacy, 1942; PhD, Yale U., 1951. With Dept. Air Force, 1951-58; chmn., CEO BoehmGroup.com, 2006—; bd. dirs. ABC-CLIO, Santa Barbara, Calif., 1960—; pres. Internat. Sch. of Info. Mgmt., 1987-94. Chmn. bd. dirs. Internat. Acad. at Santa Barbara, 1970—2003; pub. Environ. Studies Inst., 1971—2003, Info. Inst., 1980—2003; cons. on bibliography, info. sys. Author: We Survived, 1949, 83, 2004; microfilm Policy-making of the Nazi Government, 1969; editor Historical Abstracts, 1955-83, cons., 1983; editor America: History and Life, 1964-83, cons., 1983; editor Bibliographies on International Relations and World Affairs, an Annotated Directory, 1965, Blueprint for Bibliography, a System for Social Sciences and Humanities, 1965, Clio Bibliography Series, 1973; co-editor Historical Periodicals, 1961, 2d edit., 1983-85; pub. Advanced Bibliography of Contents: Political Science, 1969, ART Bibliographies: Modern, 1972, Environ. Periodicals Bibliography, 1972; bd. advisors Info. Strategy, The Exec.'s Jour., 1984; contbr. articles to profl. jours. Bd. dirs. UN Assn., Santa Barbara, 1973-77, Santa Barbara's Adv. Bd. Internat. Relationships (Sister Cities), 1974, Friends of Public Library, Friends of U. Calif. at Santa Barbara Library; mem. affiliates bd. U. Calif.-Santa Barbara; vice chmn. New Directions Found., 1984-88; adv. bd. Nuclear Age Peace Found., 1985; chmn. BoehmGroup.com, 2003—. With USAAF, 1942-46. Recipient Disting. Alumnus award Wooster Coll., 1990. Mem. AAAS,

Am. Soc. Info. Sci., Assn. Bibliography in History (v.p. 1986, pres. 1987), Calif. Library Soc., Nat. Trust Historic Preservation, Santa Barbara Com. Fgn. Rels., Santa Barbara C. of C. (dir. 1980-84), Univ. Club, Rotary, Phi Beta Kappa. Home and Office: 800 E Micheltorena St Santa Barbara CA 93103-2220 Home Phone: 805-965-6266; Office Phone: 805-965-9889. Personal E-mail: eboehm1918@aol.com.

BOEHM, FELIX HANS, physicist, researcher; b. Basel, Switzerland, June 9, 1924; came to U.S., 1952, naturalized, 1964; s. Hans G. and Marquerite (Philippi) B.; m. Ruth Sommerhalder, Nov. 26, 1956; children: Marcus F., Claude N. MS, Inst. Tech., Zurich, 1948, PhD, 1951. Research assoc. Inst. Tech., Zurich, Switzerland, 1949-52; Boese fellow Columbia U., 1952-53; faculty Calif. Inst. Tech., Pasadena, 1953—, prof. physics, 1961—, William L. Valentine prof., 1985-94, William L. Valentine prof. emeritus, 1995—; Sloan fellow, 1962-64; NSF sr. fellow Niels Bohr Inst., Copenhagen, 1965-66, CERN, Geneva, 1971-72, Laue-Langevin Inst., 1980. Recipient Humboldt award, 1980, 84. Fellow Am. Phys. Soc. (Tom W. Bonner prize 1995); mem. Nat. Acad. Scis. Achievements include research on nuclear physics, nuclear beta decay, neutrino physics, atomic physics, muonic and pionic atoms, parity and time-reversal. Home: 2510 N Altadena Dr Altadena CA 91001-2836 Office: Calif Inst Tech Mail Code 161 33 Pasadena CA 91125-0001 E-mail: boehm@caltech.edu.

BOEHM, ROBERT FOTY, mechanical engineer, educator, researcher; b. Portland, Oreg., Jan. 16, 1940; s. Charles Frederick and Lufteria (Christie) B.; m. Marcia Kay Pettibone, June 10, 1961; children— Deborah, Robert Christopher BS in Mech. Engring., Wash. State U., Pullman, 1962, MS, 1964; PhD, U. Calif., Berkeley, 1968. Registered profl. engr., Calif. With Gen. Electric Co., San Jose, Calif., 1964-66; mem. faculty U. Utah, Salt Lake City, 1968-90, prof. mech. engring., 1976-90, chmn. dept., 1981-84; Nat. Sandia Labs., Albuquerque, 1984-85; prof. U. Nev., Las Vegas, 1990—, chmn. mech. engring. dept., 1990-96, univ. sys. sr. liaison to Dept. Energy, 1994-95, dir. rsch. Coll. Engring., 1999-2001. Mem. Utah Solar Adv. Com., Utah Energy Conservation and Devel. Coun., 1980-88; dir. Energy Rsch. Ctr., 1994—. Author: Design Analysis of Thermal Systems, 1987; editor: Direct Contact Heat Exchange, 1988, Developments in the Design of Thermal Systems, 1997; tech. editor Jour. Solar Energy Engring., 1980-84; contbr. articles to profl. jours. Named Utah Engring. Educator of Yr., Utah Engrs. Coun., 1988, Disting. Tchr., U. Utah, 1989; recipient UNLV Barrick Sr. Rsch. award, 1994. Fellow ASME; mem. ASHRAE, Am. Soc. for Engring. Edn., Internat. Solar Energy Soc., Corvair Soc. Am., Vintage Chevrolet Club Am., Sigma Xi. Home: 4999 Mesa View Dr Las Vegas NV 89120-1216 Office: U Nev Mech Engring Dept PO Box 454027 Las Vegas NV 89154-4027 E-mail: boehm@me.unlv.edu.

BOERSMA, P. DEE, conservation biologist, educator; b. Mt. Pleasant, Mich., Nov. 1, 1946; d. Henry W. and Vivian (Anspach) B. BS, Ctrl. Mich. U., 1969; PhD, Ohio State U., 1974; DSc (hon.), Ctrl. Mich. U., 2003. From asst. prof. to prof. zoology Inst. Environ. Studies U. Wash., Seattle, 1988—, assoc. dir. Inst. Environ. Studies, 1987—93, acting dir. Inst. Environ. Studies, 1990—91, adj. prof. women's studies, 1993—2007, prof. biology, 2003—, Wadsworth endowed chair in conservation sci., 2006—, acting chair biology, 2005—06; mem. sci. adv. com. for outer continental shelf Environ. Studies Program, Dept. Interior, 1980—83; prin. investigator Magellanic Penguin Project Wildlife Cons. Soc., 1982—. Evans vis. fellow U. Otago, New Zealand, 1995, Pew fellow in marine conservation, 1997-2000; naturalist Lindblad Expdns., 2001-04. Assoc. editor Ecological Applications, 1998-2001; exec. editor Conservation Mag., 2000—; contbr. articles to profl. jours. Mem. adv. U.S. del. to UN Status Women Commn., N.Y.C., 1973, UN World Status Women Commn., N.Y.C., 1973, UN World Population Conf., Romania, 1974; mem. Gov. Lowry's Task Force on Wildlife, 1993; sci. adv. EcoBios, 1985-95; bd. dirs. Zero Population Growth, 1975-82, Washington Nature Conservancy, 1995-98; adv. bd. Walt Disney World Animal Kingdom, 1993—, Island press, 1999-2007, Compass, 2000-04; bd. dirs. Peregine Fund, 1994-, Bullitt Found., 1996-00, Islandwood, 2000-04; mem. scholar diplomatic program Dept. State, 1977. Recipient Outstanding Alumni award Ctrl. Mich. U., 1978, Matrix award Women in Comm., 1983; named to Kellogg Nat. Leadership Program, 1982-85; recipient Top 100 Outsiders of Yr. award Outside Mag., 1987, Outstanding Centennial Alumni award Ctrl. Mich. U., 1993; sci. fellow The Wildlife Conservation Soc., 1982—, Aldo Leopold Leadership fellow, 2000-01. Fellow AAAS, Am Ornithol. Union (Elliott Coules award, 2008); mem. AAAS, Ecol. Soc. Am., Wilson Ornithol. Soc., Cooper Ornithol. Soc., Soc. Am. Naturalists, Soc. Conservation Biology (bd. govs. 1991-94, pres-elect 1995-97, pres. 1997-99, Disting. Svc. award 2006), Ecol. Soc. Am. (mem.-at-large 2003-06), Internat. Union Biol. Scis., Seattle Girls Sch. (Grace Hopper award, 2008), Gopher Brokers Club (pres. Seattle chpt. 1982-83). Office: U Wash Dept Biology PO Box 351800 Seattle WA 98195-1800 Business E-Mail: boersma@u.washington.edu.

BOGAARD, WILLIAM JOSEPH, mayor, lawyer, educator; b. Sioux City, Iowa, Jan. 18, 1938; s. Joseph and Irene Marie (Hensing) B.; m. Claire Marie Whalen, Jan. 28, 1961; children: Michele, Jeannine, Joseph, Matthew. BS, Loyola Marymount U., LA, 1959; JD with honors, U. Mich., 1965. Bar: Calif. 1966, U.S. Dist. Ct. (ctrl. dist.) Calif. 1966. Ptnr. Agnew, Miller & Carlson, LA, 1970-82; exec. v.p., gen. counsel First Interstate Bancorp, LA, 1982-96; vis. prof. securities regulation and banking Mich. Law Sch., Ann Arbor, 1996-97; lectr. securities regulation and corps. law sch. U. So. Calif., LA, 1997—99; mayor Pasadena, Calif., 1999—. Mem. Calif. Commn. on Jud. Nominees Evaluation, 1997-99. Capt. USAF, 1959—62. Mem. Calif. State Bar, Los Angeles County Bar Assn. (Corp. Counsel of Yr. award 1988). Avocations: jogging, french and spanish languages, hiking. Office: 100 N Garfield Ave Pasadena CA 91101-1726 Personal E-mail: w_j_b@msn.com. Business E-Mail: bbogaard@cityofpasadena.net.

BOGDEN, DANIEL G., former prosecutor; b. Huron, Ohio, 1956; BBA, Ashland U., 1978; JD, U. Toledo. Dep. dist. atty. Washoe County, 1987—90; asst. US atty. dist. Nev. US Dept. Justice, Las Vegas, 1990—2001, US atty., 2001—07. Recipient Outstanding Alumnus award, Ashland U. Alumni Assn., 2005.

BOGEN, ANDREW E., lawyer; b. LA, Aug. 23, 1941; s. David and Edith B.; m. Deborah Bogen, Oct. 10, 1970; children: Elizabeth, Michael. BA, Pomona Coll., Claremont, Calif., 1963; LLB, Harvard U, 1966. Bar: Calif. 1966. Assoc. Gibson, Dunn & Crutcher, LA, 1966-73, ptnr. corp. transactions and securities, 1973—. Mem. exec. com. Gibson Dunn & Crutcher, 1991—. Trustee Exceptional Children's Found., LA, 1976-89, Weingart Found., 1999—; bd. dirs. St. Anne's 1990— (chmn.). Office: Gibson Dunn & Crutcher 333 S Grand Ave Ste 4400 Los Angeles CA 90071-3197 Office Phone: 213-229-7000. Office Fax: 213-229-7520. Business E-Mail: abogen@gibsondunn.com.

BOGER, DALE L., chemistry professor; b. Hutchinson, Kans., Aug. 22, 1953; s. Lester W. and Elizabeth (Korkish) B. BS in Chemistry, U. Kans., 1975; PhD in Chemistry, Harvard U., 1980; PhD (hon.), U. Ferrara, 2000. Asst. prof. medicinal chemistry U. Kans., Lawrence, 1979-83, assoc. prof. medicinal chemistry, 1983-85; assoc. prof. chemistry Purdue U., West Lafayette, Ind., 1985-87, prof. chemistry, 1987-91; Richard and Alice Cramer chair chemistry, prof. Scripps Rsch. Inst., La Jolla, Calif., 1991—. Mem. Skaggs Inst. for Chem. Biology, 1996—; Smissman Lectr. U. Kans., 2000; Ross Lectr. Dartmouth Coll., 2002; Alder Lectr. U. Köln, 2005. Founding editor Bioorganic and Medicinal Chemistry Letters, 1990—, exec. editl. bd. mem. Tetrahedron Publications, 1990—. Recipient Career Devel. award NIH, 1983-88, American Cyanamide Academic award, 1989, A. R. Day award, 2000, Paul Janssen award for creativity in organic synthesis, 2002, Adrien Albert medal, Royal Soc. Chemistry, 2003; NSF fellow, 1975-78, Alfred P. Sloan fellow, 1985-89, Japan Promotion of Sci. Fellow, 1993; Searle scholar, 1981-84. Fellow AAAS, Am. Assn. Adv. Sci., Am. Acad. Arts and Scis.; mem. Am. Chem. Soc. (Arthur C. Cope scholar 1989, Aldrich award for creativity in organic synthesis 1999, Ernest Guenther award in chemistry of natural products, 2007, councilor, 1996-99, Medicinal Chemistry Divsn., awards com. mem. 1984-86, Long Range Planning Com., 1981-83), Internat. Soc. Heterocyclic Chemistry (Katritzky award in Heterocyclic Chemistry, 1997). Office: Dept Chemistry and Skaggs Inst for Chem Biology 10550 N Torrey Pines Rd BBC 483 La Jolla CA 92037-1000 Home: 8212 Caminito Maritimo La Jolla CA 92037-2233 Office Phone: 858-784-7522. Office Fax: 858-784-7550. Business E-Mail: boger@scripps.edu.

BOGGS, GIL, principal ballet dancer; b. Pensacola, Fla. m. Sandra Brown. Student with Robert Barnett, Atlanta Ballet. Prin. Atlanta Ballet, 1977-82; mem. corps be ballet Am. Ballet Theatre, NYC, 1982-84, soloist, 1984-87, 88-91, prin. dancer, 1991—99; dancer Twyla Tharp Dance Co., 1987-88; mgr. Golf Acad. Chelsea Piers, 2001; artistic dir. Colo. Ballet, Denver, 2006—. Repertoire includes La Bayadere, Brief Fling, Coppelia, Drink to Me Only With Thine Eyes, Theme and Variations, Donizetti Variations, Etudes, Fancy Free, Giselle, Manon, The Nutcracker, Rodeo, Romeo and Juliet, Swan Lake, La Sylphide, Tchaikovsky Pas de Deux, Sleeping Beauty, Requiem, Cinderella, BriefFling, Bum's Rush, Nine Sinatra Songs, The Catherine Wheel, Symphonic Variations, Undertow, others; dances works of Paul Taylor, Merce Cunningham, Mark Morris. Office: Colo Ballet 1278 Lincoln St Denver CO 80203 Office Phone: 303-339-1614. E-mail: gil@coloradoballet.org.

BOGGS, PAULA ELAINE, lawyer, beverage service company executive; b. Washington, May 2, 1959; d. Nathaniel Boggs Jr. and Janice C. (Anderson) Barber. BA, Johns Hopkins U., Balt., 1981; JD, U. Calif., Berkeley, 1984. Bar: Pa. 1986, DC 1988, Wash. 1992, US Dist. Ct. (we. dist. Wash.) 1988, US Ct. appeals (9th cir.) 1990, US Ct. Appeals (DC and fed. cirs.) 1995. Sr. law clk. Office of Army Gen. Counsel, Arlington, Va., 1984-85; spl. asst. Office of Dep. Under Sec. Dept. Army, Arlington, 1985-86; staff atty. White House Iran-Contra legal task force, Washington, 1987-88; asst. U.S. atty. (we. dist.) Wash. US Dept. Justice, Seattle, 1988-93; staff dir. adv. bd. investigative capability US Dept. Def., Arlington, 1994; ptnr. Preston, Gates & Ellis, Seattle, 1995—97; v.p. legal Dell Computer Corp., 1997—2002; exec. v.p. law & corp. affairs, gen. counsel, sec. Starbucks Corp., Seattle, 2002—. Mem. faculty Nat. Inst. Trial Advocacy, 1995; adj. prof. law U. Wash., Seattle, 1993. Vol. instr. presdl. classroom for young Ams., Washington, 1991; bd. dirs. ctrl. dist. YMCA, Seattle, 1991-93, Greater Seattle YMCA, 1995—; nat. chair Johns Hopkins U. Second Decade Soc., Balt., 1995-96. Recipient Sec. Def. award for Excellence William J. Perry, 1994; Presdl. svc. badge Pres. Ronald Reagan, 1988; Def. Meritorious Svc. award, 1987, Spl. Achievement award Dept. Justice, 1990, 91. Mem. ABA (ho. dels., litig. sect. co-chair bus. torts com., bus. crimes com., criminal justice sect. white collar crimes com., standing com. on constn. and bylaws), Nat. Bar Assn., Wash. State Bar Assn. (corrections com.), King County Bar Assn., Fed. Bar Assn., Wash. Women Lawyers (bd. dirs. 1991-93), Loren Miller Bar Assn. Avocations: running, bicycling, reading. Office: Starbucks Corp 2401 Utah Ave S PO Box 34067 Seattle WA 98124-1067

BOGGS, WILLIAM S., lawyer; b. Toledo, May 17, 1946; AB summa cum laude, Wittenberg U., 1968; JD cum laude, Harvard U., 1972. Bar: Calif., US Dist. Ct.(ctrl. & so. dists.) Calif., US Ct. Appeals (9th cir.), US Supreme Ct., All state & fed. cts. Calif. Ptnr. Gray, Cary, Ware & Freidenrich, San Diego, 1979, DLA Piper, San Diego. Spkr. in field. Contbr. articles to. profl. jour. Bd. trustee Found. of La Jolla High Sch.; bd. trustee Museum of Man, bd. dir., pres., 1996—98. Named Best Lawyers, 2007. Mem. ABA, San Diego County Bar Assn., Internat. Assn. Defense Counsel, Assn. Bus. Trial Lawyers, San Diego (emeritus bd mem., bd. of Govs. 1998-2000), Assn. So. Calif. Def. Counsel (bd dir. 1997-1998), Big Brothers San Diego County (bd. dir., pres. 1980-82, emeritus bd. mem.), Harvard Club San Diego, Def. Research Inst., master Louis M. Welsh Am. Inns of Ct. Office: DLA Piper 401 B St Ste 1700 San Diego CA 92101 Office Phone: 619-699-2758. Office Fax: 619-699-2701. Business E-Mail: william.boggs@dlapiper.com.

BOGREN, HUGO GUNNAR, radiology educator; b. Jönköping, Sweden, Jan. 9, 1933; came to U.S., 1970; s. Gunnar Hugo and Signe Victoria (Holmström) B.; m. Elisabeth Faxén, Nov. 1, 1956 (div. 1976); children: Cecilia, Niclas, Joakim; m. Gunilla Lady Whitmore, July 2, 1988. MD, U. Göteborg, Sweden, 1958, PhD, 1964. Diplomate Swedish Bd. Radiology. Resident, fellow U. Göteborg, 1958-64, asst. to assoc. prof. radiology, 1964-69; from assoc. prof. to prof. radiology and internal medicine U. Calif. Davis, Sacramento, 1972—. Vis. assoc. prof. U. San Francisco, 1970-71; vis. prof. U. Kiel, Fed. Republic Germany, 1980, cardiac magnetic resonance unit Royal Brompton Hosp. and Imperial Coll., London, 1986-87, 93-94, 2002-03; participant in med. aid fact finding mission, Bangladesh, 1992. Contbr. numerous articles to profl. jours., chpts. to books. Sr. Internat. Fogarty fellow NIH, London, 1986-87. Fellow Am. Heart Assn., Radiol. Soc., N.Am. Soc. Cardiac Imaging, Soc. Thoracic Radiology, Internat. Soc. Magnetic Resonance in Medicine, Soc. Cardiovasc. Magnetic Resonance, Soc. Cardiovasc. Computed Tomography, Swedish Assn. Med. Radiology; mem. Royal Gothenburg Sailing Club Sweden (hon.), Swedish Cruising Club, Rotary (del.). Lutheran. Avocations: ocean sailing, skiing, classical music. Office: U Calif Davis Med Ctr Div Diagnostic Radiology 4860 Y St Ste 3100 Sacramento CA 95817-2307 Office Phone: 916-734-6535. Personal E-mail: hugobogren@aol.com. Business E-Mail: hugo.bogren@ucdmc.ucdavis.edu.

BOGUSKY, ALEX, advertising executive; Formerly with Ryder & Schild, Miami, Fla.; art dir. Crispin Porter, Miami, 1989—92, creative dir., 1992—96; ptnr. Crispin Porter & Bogusky, 1996—, exec. creative dir., 1997—2005, chief creative officer, 2005—, co-chmn., 2008—. Judge Andy Awards, 2005. Co-author: The 9-Inch Diet, 2009; work featured in NY Times, Wall St. Jour., USA Today, Newsweek, TIME, Adweek, Brandweek, Advt. Age and Creativity mags. Named one of 50 Who Matter Now, CNNMoney.com Bus. 2.0, 2006; named to Hall of Achievement, Am. Advt. Fedn., 2002. Office: Crispin Porter & Bogusky LLC 3390 Mary St Ste 300 Miami FL 33133 also: 6450 Gunpark Dr Boulder CO 80301 Office Phone: 305-859-2070.

BOGY, DAVID B(EAUREGARD), mechanical engineering educator; b. Wabbaseka, Ark., June 4, 1936; s. Jesse C. and Dorothy (Duff) B.; m. Patricia Lynn Pizzitola, Mar. 28, 1961; children: Susan, Rebecca. BS, Rice U., 1959, MS, 1961; PhD, Brown U., 1966. Mech. engr. Shell Devel. Co., Houston, 1961-63; asst. prof. mech. engring. U. Calif., Berkeley, 1967-70, assoc. prof., 1970-75, prof., 1975—, chmn. dept. mech. engring., 1991-99, founder, dir. computer mechanics lab., William S. Floyd, Jr. Disting. prof., 1993—. Cons. IBM Rsch., 1972-83 Contbr. some 300 articles to profl. jours. Served with C.E. U.S. Army, 1961-62. Fellow ASME, IEEE; mem. NAE. Achievements include research in static and dynamic elasticity, fluid jets and mechanics of computer disk files and printers. Home: 8531 Buckingham Dr El Cerrito CA 94530-2533 Office: U Calif 6103 Etcheverry Hall Berkeley CA 94720-1740 Office Phone: 510-642-2570. Business E-Mail: dbogy@berkeley.edu.

BOHAN, MICHELLE, agent; married; 3 children. Agent William Morris Agy.; ptnr. talent dept. Endeavor Agy., 2005—. Involved with YouthAIDS, Habitat for Humanity. Named one of The 100 Most Powerful Women in Entertainment, Hollywood Reporter, 2005, 2006, 2007. Office: Endeavor Agy LLC 9601 Wilshire Blvd Beverly Hills CA 90210

BOHANNON, ROBERT H., diversified services company executive; married; 2 children. BBA, Kensington U. Head consumer credit bus. Marine Midland Bank; exec. v.p. ops. Mortgage Ins. Co. subs. GE Credit Corp.; pres., CeO ops. Travelers Experss subs. VIAD, Mpls., 1993; pres., CEO, chmn. Viad, Phoenix, 1996—; COO, 1996.

BOHLE, SUE, public relations executive; b. Austin, Minn., June 23, 1943; d. Harold Raymond and Mary Theresa (Swanson) Hastings; m. John Bernard Bohle, June 22, 1974; children: Jason John, Christine K. BS in Journalism, Northwestern U., 1965, MS in Journalism, 1969. Tchr. pub. high schs, Englewood, Colo., 1965-68; account exec. Burson-Marsteller Pub. Relations, Los Angeles, 1969-73; v.p., mgr. pub. relations J. Walter Thompson Co., Los Angeles, 1973-79; founder, pres. The Bohle Company, LA, 1979—; pres., CEO The Bohle Co., LA; former exec. v.p. Ketchum Comms., LA. Freelance writer, instr. comm. Calif. State U., Fullerton, 1972—73; instr. writing LA City Coll., 1975—76; lectr. U. So. Calif., 1979—. Contbr. articles to profl. jours. Dir. pub. rels. LA Jr. Ballet, 1971—72; pres. Panhellenic Advisers Coun. UCLA, 1972—73; mem. adv. bd. LA Valley Coll., 1974—75, Coll. Comm. Pepperdine U., 1981—85, Sch. Journalism U. So. Calif., 1987—95, Calif. State U., Long Beach, 1988—93; bd. visitors Medill Sch. Journalism Northwestern U., 1984—. Recipient Alumni Svc. award, Northwestern U., 1995; named charter mem., Hall of Fame; named to Hall of Achievement, Medill Sch. Journalism, 1997, 50 Top Women in PR, PR Week mag., 2001; Univ. scholar, Northwestern U., 1961—64, Panhellenic scholar, 1964—65. Fellow: Pub. Rels. Soc. Am. (del. nat. assembly 1980, bd. dirs. LA chpt. 1981—90, v.p. 1983, mem. exec. com. counselors Acad. 1984—86, pres. 1989, co-chmn. long-range strategic com. 1990, sec.-treas. 1990, pres.'s adv. coun. 1991, chmn. 1992, sec. Coll. Fellows 1993, vice chair 1994, del. nat. assembly 1994—96, chmn. 1995, Silver Anvil award 1990, 1994, Best Show award, Sabre award 2000, Best of Show Prisms award 2005, named in Top 100 Women in Gaming 2006); mem.: Accrediting Coun. Edn. Journalism and Mass Comms. (mem. accreditation coun. 2005—07), Women in Comm., World com., Worldcom PR Network, Shai-ai, Kappa Alpha Tau, Delta Zeta (Woman of the Yr. award 1993). Office: 1900 Avenue of the Stars # 200 Los Angeles CA 90067-4301 Office Phone: 310-785-0515 ext. 223. E-mail: sue@bohle.com.

BOHLINGER, JOHN C., Lieutenant Governor of Montana, former state legislator; b. Bozeman, Mont., Apr. 21, 1936; s. John and Aileen Bohlinger; m. Bette J. Bohlinger (dec. Jan. 2006); 6 children; m. Karen Seiler, Jan. 12, 2008. BA, U. Mont., 1959. Owner women's apparel store, 1961-92; mem. Mon. Ho. Reps. Dist. 14 & 94, 1993—98, Mont. State Senate, Dist. 7, Helena, 1998—2004; mem. local govt. com., pub. health, welfare and safety com.; mem. taxation com., vice chair ethics com.; lt. gov. State of Mont., 2005—. Past pres., chmn. bd. Yellowstone Arts Ctr.; bd. dirs. Billings Symphony Soc., St. Vincent de Paul Soc., Mont. State U. Billings Found., Yellowstone Treatment Ctr. Served with USMC, 1954-61. Mem. Billings Rotary Cub. Republican. Roman Catholic. Office: Office Lt Gov Capitol Station PO Box 200801 Helena MT 59620 Office Phone: 406-444-5665.*

BOHN, DENNIS ALLEN, engineering executive; b. Oct. 5, 1942; s. Raymond Virgil and Iris Elouise (Johnson) Bohn; m. Patricia Tolle, Aug. 12, 1986; 1 child, Kira Michelle. BSEE with honors, U. Calif., Berkeley, 1972, MSEE with honors, 1974. Engring. technician GE Co., San Leandro, Calif., 1964—72; R & D engr. Hewlett-Packard Co., Santa Clara, Calif., 1973; application engr. Nat. Semicondr. Corp., Santa Clara, 1974—76; engring. mgr. Phase Linear Corp., Lynnwood, Wash., 1976—82; v.p. R & D, ptnr. Rane Corp., Mukilteo, Wash., 1982—; founder Toleco Systems, Kingston, Wash., 1980. Editor: We Are Not Just Daffodils, 1975; contbr. poetry to Reason mag.; tech. editor Audio Handbook, 1976; contbr. articles to tech. jours.; columnist Polyphony mag., 1981—83. Suicide and crisis ctr. vol., Berkeley, 1972—74, Santa Clara, 1974—76. With USAF, 1960—64. Recipient Am. Spirit Honor medal, USAF, 1961, Math. Achievement award, Chem. Rubber Co., 1962—63. Mem.: IEEE, Audio Engring. Soc., Tau Beta Pi. Achievements include 3 patents in field. Office: Rane Corp 10802 47th Ave W Mukilteo WA 98275-5098 Business E-Mail: dennisb@rane.com.

BOHN, RALPH CARL, educational consultant; b. Detroit, Feb. 19, 1930; s. Carl and Bertha (Abrams) B.; m. Adella Stanul, Sept. 2, 1950 (dec.); children: Cheryl Ann, Jeffrey Ralph; m. JoAnn Olvera Butler,

Feb. 19, 1977 (div. 1990); stepchildren: Kathryn J., Kimberly J., Gregory E.; m. Mariko Tajima, Jan. 27, 1991; 1 child, Thomas Carl; 1 stepchild, Daichi Tajima. BS, Wayne State U., 1951, EdM, 1954, EdD, 1957. Instr. part-time Wayne State U., 1954-55, summer 1956; faculty San Jose (Calif.) State U., 1955-92, prof. div. tech., 1961-92, chmn. dept. indsl. studies, 1960-69, assoc. dean ednl. svc., 1968-70, dean continuing edn., 1970-92, prof. emeritus, 1992—; cons. Calif. State U. Sys., 1992—; cons. quality edn. sys. USAF, 1992-2000; dir. nat. program on non-collegiate sponsored instrn. Calif. State Univ. Sys., 1995—2000, Calif. State U. Inst., 1997—99; pres. Univ. Cons., 1994—. Guest faculty Colo. State Coll., 1963, Ariz. State U., 1966, U. P.R., 1967, 74, So. Ill. U., 1970, Oreg. State U., 1971, Utah State U., 1973, Va. Poly. Inst. & State U., 1973, U. Idaho, 1978; cons. U.S. Office Edn., 1965-70, Calif. Pub. Schs., 1960, Nat. Assessment Ednl. Progress, 1968-79, ednl. div. Philco-Ford Corp., 1970-73, Am. Inst. Rsch., 1969-83, Far West Labs for Ednl. Rsch. Devel., 1971-86; adv. bd. Ctr. for Vocat. and Tech. Edn., Ohio State U., 1968-74; dir. project Vocat. Edn. Act, 1965-67, NDEA, 1967, 68; co-dir. Project Edn. Profession Devel. Act, 1969, 70; mem. commn. coll. and univ. contracts Western Assn. Schs. and Colls. 1976-78, chmn. spl. com. on off-campus instrn. and continuing edn., 1978-88; chmn. continuing edn. accreditation visit U. Santa Clara, 1976; chmn. accreditation team Nellis AFB, Nev., 1992, 2002, U. Nev., Las Vegas, 2000, Nat. U., 2000, Oreg. State U., 2001, Golden Gate U., 2001; chmn. accreditation team to Yokusaka Naval Sta., Japan, 2000, Atsugi Naval Air Facility, Japan, 2000, Yokota Air Base, Japan, 2000, Camp Pendleton Marine Corps Base, 2001, 07, Naval Air Sta., Lamoore, 2002, Dyess AFB, 2003, Twentynine Palms Marine Corps. Base, Calif., 2003, eArmyU web-based degree programs U.S. Army, Washington, 2004, Camp Zama, Army, Tokyo, 2004, Iwakuni Marine Corps Air Sta., Japan, 2005, Osan AFB, Korea, 2005, Junsan AFB, Korea, 2005, Scott AFB, Ill., 2005, Offutt AFB, Nebr., 2005, Misawa AFB, Japan, 2006, US Army Command and Gen. Staff Coll. Coll., Kans., 2006, Sasebo Navel Fleet Base, Japan, 2006, Kitsap Naval Base, Washington, 2007, Wash. State Nat. Gurard, Tacoma, Wash., 2007, Quantities Marine Corps. Base, Va., 2008, H.M.Smith Marine Corps. Base, Honolulu, Hawall, 2008, Tinker Air Force Base, Okla. City, 2008, US Army Bas Ft Myer Va., 2009, Marine Corps Air Sta. Yuma Ariz., 2009; others; sr. cons. Global Partnership Devel. Calif. State U. Sys., 2000-03. Author: (with G.H. Silvius) Organizing Course Materials for Industrial Education, 1961, Planning and Organizing Instruction, 1976; (with A. MacDonald) Power-Mechanics of Energy Control, 1970, 2d edit., 1983, The McKnight Power Experimenter, 1970, Power and Energy Technology, 1989, Energy Technology: Power and Transportation, 1992; (with others) Basic Industrial Arts and Power Mechanics, 1978, Technology and Society: Interfaces with Industrial Arts, 1980, Fundamentals of Safety Education, 3d edit., 1981, Energy, Power and Transportation Technology, 1986; (with A. MacDonald) Energy Technology, Power and Transportation, 1991; editor (with Ralph Norman) Graduate Study in Industrial Arts, 1961; indsl. arts editor Am. Vocat. Jour., 1963-66; editor Jour. Indsl. Tchr. Edn., 1962-64. Lt. (j.g.) USCGR, 1951-53, capt. Res. ret. Recipient award Am. Legion, 1945; Wayne State U. scholar, 1953. Mem. NEA, Nat. Assn. Indsl. Tech. (bd. accreditation), Am. Indsl. Arts. Assn. (pres. 1967-68, Ship's citation 1971), Am. Coun. Indsl. Art Tchrs. Edn. (pres. 1964-66, Man of Yr. award 1967), Nat. Univ. Continuing Edn. Assn. (chair accreditation com. 1988-91), Nat. Assn. Indsl. Tchr. Educators (past v.p.), Calif. Indsl. Edn. Assn. (State Ship's citation 1971), Am. Drive Edn. Assn., Nat. Fluid Power Soc., Am. Vocat. Assn. (svc. awards 1966, 67), N.Am. Assn. for Summer Sessions (v.p. western region 1976-78), Luth. Acad. Scholarship, Calif. Employees Assn. (pres. San Jose State Coll. chpt. 1966-67), Western Assn. Summer Session Adminstrs. (newsletter editor 1970-73, pres. 1974-75), Calif. C. of C. (edn. com 1969-77), Industry-Edn. Coun. Calif. (bd. dirs. 1974-80), Sci. and Human Values, Inc. (bd. dirs. 1974-2003, chmn. bd. 1976-2002), Tahoe Tavern (bd. dirs. 1987-91, chmn. bd. 1988-90), Seascape Lagoon Homeowners Assn. (bd. dirs. 1988-95, chmn. 1989-95), Nat. Gold Key Honors Soc. (hon. life). Home and Office: 713 Clubhouse Dr Aptos CA 95003-5431 Personal E-mail: rmbohn@cruzio.com.

BOHNEN, ROBERT FRANK, hematologist, oncologist, educator; b. Huntington, NY, Jan. 3, 1941; s. Oscar and Sarah Leah (Piel) B.; m. Mollyn Villareal, June 20, 1965; children: Sharon Kay, Scott Owen David, Paul Alan. BS in Zoology, Syracuse U., 1961; MD, Columbia U., 1965. Diplomate Am. Bd. Internal Medicine, Am. Bd. Med. Oncology, Am. Bd. Hematology. Intern Buffalo (N.Y.) Gen. Hosp., 1965-66; resident in medicine SUNY, Buffalo, 1968-69, U. Utah, Salt Lake City, 1969-70, clin. hematology fellow, 1970-71, med. oncology fellow, 1971-72; physician hematology and med. oncology Cons. Med. Group, Carmichael and Roseville, Calif., 1972-91, Cancer Treatment Ctr. Merle West Med. Ctr., Klamath Falls, Oreg., 1991—. Instr. medicine and hematology/oncology U. Calif., Davis, Sacramento, 1973-77, asst. clin. prof. medicine and hematology/oncology, 1977-83; clin. instr. dept. family medicine Oreg. Health Scis. U., Portland, 1994—; sr. staff Mercy Am. River Hosp., Carmichael, Calif., Mercy San Juan Hosp., Carmichael, Roseville (Calif.) Cmty. Hosp.; courtesy staff Sutter Cmty. Hosp. Sacramento; active staff Merle West Med. Ctr., Klamath Falls; med. dir. Hospice Roseville, Calif.; prin. investigator No. Calif. Oncology Group Clin. Trials; med. adv. bd. Vis. Nurses Assn.; lectr. and presenter in field. Contbr. articles to profl. jours. Chmn. Greater Sacramento Cancer Coun. Clin. Trials Com./No. Calif. Oncology Group Outreach Com.; bd. dirs., sec. Greater Sacramento Cancer Coun.; chmn. profl. edn. com., bd. dirs. Tri-County chpt. Am. Cancer Soc.; soloist Sacramento Valley Concert Choir, Klamath Chorale; active Masterworks Chorus; cast mem. Linkville Players and Ross Ragland Theater Prodns., Klamath Falls, 1991—; choir dir. Sacred Heart Ch., Klamath Falls, 1992—2004. Med. Oncology fellow Am. Cancer Soc., U. Utah Med. Ctr., 1971-72. Mem. Am. Soc. Clin. Oncology, Phi Beta Kappa. Democrat. Roman Catholic. Avocations: musical theater, photography, choral singing and directing. Office: Cancer Treatment Ctr Merle West Med Ctr 2610 Uhrmann Rd Klamath Falls OR 97601-1123 Home Phone: 541-884-8932. Business E-Mail: rbohnen@mwmc.org.

BOHR, KEITH, Mayor, Huntington Beach, California; Grad., Ariz. State U., Tempe, 1987, Huntington Beach Citizen's Police Acad. Former mem. City of Huntington Beach Econ. Devel. Dept.; current real estate broker & cons.; councilman City of Huntington Beach, 2004—08, mayor, 2008—. Rep. Calif. Coastal Coalition Bd., Orange County Coastal Coalition, Pub. Cable TV Authority. Vol. CASA Ct. Appointed Spl. Advocates; chmn. Orangewood Children's Found. PALS; coun. liaison Environ. Bd., Fourth of July Bd., Specific Events Com., Pers. Commn., Youth Bd.; bd. mem. Comm. Com., Intergovernmental Rels. Com. Mem.: Sister City Assn. Huntington Beach, Huntington Valley Boys & Girls Club. Office: 2000 Main St Huntington Beach CA 92648 Office Phone: 714-536-5553. Business E-Mail: kbohr@surfcity-hb.org.*

BOK, DEAN, cell biologist, educator; b. Douglas County, SD, Nov. 1, 1939; s. Kryn Arie and Rena (Van Zee) B.; m. Audrey Ann Van Diest, Aug. 21, 1964; children: Jonathan, Jeremy, James. BA, Calvin Coll., 1960; MA, Calif. State U., Long Beach, 1965; PhD, UCLA, 1968. Sci. instr. Valley Christian High Sch., Cerritos, Calif.; prof. neurobiology and Dolly Green prof. ophthalmology UCLA; assoc. dir. Jules Stein Eye Inst., 1972—78. Wellcome vis. prof. biomed. scis., 1994; mem. Nat. Adv. Eye Coun., 1998—2002. Recipient disting. teaching awards UCLA, sr. sci. investigator award Rsch. To Prevent Blindness Inc., 1986, 95, Disting. Alumnus award Calif. State U., 1986, Calvin Coll., 1990; grantee Nat. Eye Inst., Nat. Retinitis Pigmentosa Soc.; William and Mary Greve internat. rsch. scholar Rsch. To Prevent Blindness Inc., 1982. Fellow AAAS; mem. Nat. Eye Inst. (bd. sci. counselors 1980-82, MERIT award 1987-96), Assn. Research in Vision and Ophthalmology (trustee 1978-82, Friedenwald award 1985, Alcon award 1985), Am. Soc. Cell Biology. Home: 2135 Kelton Ave Los Angeles CA 90025-5705

BOLDIN, ANQUAN, professional football player; b. Pahokee, Fla., Oct. 3, 1980; 1 child, Anquan Jr. Student in criminology, Fla. State Univ. Wide receiver Ariz. Cardinals, 2003—05. Named Offensive Rookie of Yr., AP, 2003; named to Nat. Football Conf. Pro Bowl Team, NFL, 2003, 2006, 2008. Achievements include leading the NFL in: receiving yards per game, 2005. Office: Ariz Cardinals PO Box 888 Phoenix AZ 85001-0888

BOLDT, WILLIAM GREGORY, academic administrator, consultant; b. Berkeley, Calif., Apr. 22, 1948; s. Alvin M. and Lucille Frances (Keefe) B.; m. Genene Lee Hutchins, Feb. 2, 1974; children: Kim, Kristin, Ryan. BS, U. Oreg., 1971, MS, 1975, EdD, 1980. Asst. prof. Oreg. State U., Corvallis, 1971-76, assoc. prof., 1980-86; asst. prof. U. Oreg., Eugene, 1976-80; dist. dir. Cornell U., Ithaca, N.Y., 1986-89, asst. dean coll. agriculture and life scis., 1989—; pres. Creative Mktg. Assocs., Ithaca, 1984; v.p. for univ. advancement Calif. Polytechnic State U., San Luis Obispo, Calif.; vice chancellor for univ. advancement U. Calif. Riverside, 2004—. Chair Cornell U. Mktg. Com., 1987-90, Oreg. State U. Mktg. Com., 1983-86. Author: Creative Marketing for Higher Education, 1990, Strategic Marketing for Higher Education, 1992, Marketing Your College, 1992, Fund Raising for Higher Education, 1992; editor Jour. of Extension, 1990. Pack master Cub Scouts Am., Cayuga Heights, Ithaca, 1991; trustee Tompkins County Libr., Ithaca, 1992. Recipient Outstanding Profl. award Oreg. Therapeutic Recreation Soc., 1980, Disting. Svc. award Nat. Assn. 4-H Agents, 1985, Excellence award SUNY, 1992. Mem. Epsilon Sigma Phi (Superior Performance award 1991, Nat. Mktg. Chair 1992). Office: Vice Chancellor Univ Adv Univ Calif Riverside 900 Univ Ave Riverside CA 92521

BOLES, RICHARD GREGORY, clinical geneticist, researcher; b. Pasadena, Calif., Apr. 8, 1961; s. Richard Eugene and Dorothy Mae (Martolio) B.; children: Scott, Philip, Henry, Caroline. BS in Biochemistry magna cum laude, U. Ariz., 1983; MD, UCLA, 1987. Diplomate Am. Bd. Pediatrics, Am. Bd. Med. Genetics. Pediatric intern, resident Harbor-UCLA Med. Ctr., Torrance, Calif., 1987-90; fellow in genetics Yale U., New Haven, 1991-93; asst. prof. pediatrics Sch. Medicine U. So. Calif., LA, 1993—2004, assoc. prof. pediats. Sch. Medicine, 2004—; attending physician Children's Hosp. of L.A., 1993—, dir. prenatal diagnosis ctr., 1997-99. Mem. sci. adv. bd. United Mitochondria Disease Found., 1996—2006; mem. profl. adv. bd. Cyclic Vomiting Syndrome Assn. U.S.A./Can., 1998—. English lang. editor Micro Structure Bull., Uppsala, Sweden, 1994-99; contbr. more than 50 articles to sci. jours. Grantee United Mitochondrial Disease Found., 1997, NIH, 2000-03, Nat. Alliance on Rsch. in Schizophrenia and Depression, 2005-06. Mem. Soc. Inherited Metabolic Disease, Am. Soc. Human Genetics, Phi Beta Kappa, Reflex Sympathetic Dystrophy Syndrome Assn., American RSDHope, 2007-08. Achievements include ongoing research projects in mitochondrial genetics, especially regarding testing modalities; research in mitochondrial disease and cycling vomiting syndrome. Office: Children's Hosp LA Box 90 4650 W Sunset Blvd Los Angeles CA 90027-6062 Office Phone: 323-361-2178. Business E-Mail: rboles@chla.usc.edu.

BOLES, ROGER, otolaryngologist; b. Oakland, Calif., Jan. 13, 1928; s. Albert and Julia B.; m. Marianna (Reeves), June 16, 1956; children: Martin Reeves, Melissa. BS, Stanford U., 1949; post grad., Denver U., 1950—52; MD, George Washington U., 1956. Diplomate Am. Bd. Otolaryngology, Am. Bd. Med. Splty. Intern Fitzsimmons Army Hosp., Denver, 1956—57; asst. resident through sr. clin. instr. Mich. U. Hosp., Ann Arbor, 1959—63, faculty dept. otorhinolaryngology, 1963—74, prof., 1973—74; prof., chmn. otolaryngology U. Calif. Sch. Medicine, San Francisco, 1974—2008; pres. med. staff U. Calif., San Francisco, 1982—83, prof. emeritus otolaryngology, 1998, ret., 1998. Cons. for otolaryngology to Surgeon Gen., USAF, 1975-85; mem. staff San Francisco Gen. Hosp., 1984—, Childrens Hosp. San Francisco (bd. dir. 1987-91); cons. in otolaryngology Va. Hosp., Ann Arbor, Wayne County Hosp., Eloise, Mich., So. Mich. Prison, Jackson Fed. Penitentiary, Milan, Mich., 1963-74, Letterman Gen. Hosp., Presidio of San Francisco, U.S. Naval Hosp., Oakland, Calif., 1974-93, Kaiser Hosp., Oakland, 1975, Va. Hosp., San Francisco; bd. dir. Council Med. Splty. Socs., 1981-82, sec., 1982-83; bd. dir. Am. Acad. Otolaryngology Head and Neck Surgery, 1981-88, coord. for continuing med. edn., 1980-83, pres., 1987; mem. Accreditation Coun. for Continuing Med. Edn., 1986-92, chmn., 1990; chmn. PEPP com., 1988-89, 90, vice chmn., 1989, residency rev. com. for otolaryngology; Marshall Hale Hosp., San Francisco, 1975-83, bd. dir., 1983-87; mem. Am. Bd. Med. Splty., 1984-89, exec. com., 1988-89; vis. prof. various universities; participant in conferences, conventions, workshops, seminars, inst. Contbg. chapters. to books, numerous reviews, articles, and abstracts to profl. lit. Served in MC, AUS., 1956-59. Fellow ACS (chmn. adv. coun. for otolaryngology 1977-80, adv. com. for continuing med. edn. 1982-83), Am. Laryngol. Assn.; mem. AMA (ho. del. 1975-82, bd. editors archives otolaryngology 1975-85, mem. reference com. on ins. and med. svc. 1978, adv. com. for continuing med. edn. 1981-87), AOA Hon. Med. Soc., Am. Acad. Opthalmology and Otolaryngology (assoc. sec. com. on continuing edn. 1974-80, chmn. manuals editorial com. 1977-80, mem. at large exec. com. div. otolaryngology 1977-78, mem. interspecialty cooperation com. coun. of med. splty. soc. 1986-88), Am. Acad. Facial Plastic and Reconstructive Surgery (co-chmn. standards com. 1977-80, med. edn. com. 1979-81—), Soc. Univ. Otolaryngologists (sec. treas. 1973-80, chmn. com. on under grad. curriculum 1969-74, mem. exec. council 1968-79, pres. 1978, 91), Council Acad. Soc., Assn. Am. Med. Coll., Assn. Acad. Dept. Otolaryngology (vice chmn. sub-com. Nat. Cancer Inst. liaison com. 1977-81, chmn. edn. nominating com. 1978-79), Am. Bronco-Esophagological Assn. (mem. coun. 1981-82), Am. Bd. Otolaryngology(bd. dir. 1974-91, exec. com. 1981-88, mem. various committees 1974-91, chmn. ad hoc com. for nomination process for membership on bd. dir. 1976-77, pres. 1986-88), Am. Council Otolaryngology (mem. sub-com. on hearing 1976-80, rsch. adv. com. 1977-81, pres. 1978-79), Am. Laryngol., Rhinological and Otolaryn. Soc. (mem. editl. bd. transactions 1978-88, mem. coun. 1982-88, pres. 1986-87, historian 1994—), Am. Soc. Neck and Head Surgery, Otosclerosis Study Group, Am. Tinnitus Assn. (sci. adv. bd. 1978-81), Pacific Coast Oto-Opthal. Soc., Soc. Med. Cons. to Armed Forces, Calif. Med. Assn. (program co-chmn. sect. on allergy and otolaryngology, neurology and otolaryngology 1977-78, chmn. adv. council of otolaryngology 1979-80), Calif. Otolaryn. Soc. (pres. 1978-80), U. Calif. San Francisco Sch. Medicine Alumni Faculty Assn. (pres. 1978-79), Am. Otological Soc., Am. Laryngol. Assn. (coun. 1983-84), San Francisco Med. Soc. (bd. dir. 1983-90, treas. 1989-90), Royal Coll. Surgeons in Ireland (hon.), U. Mich. Med. Ctr. Alumni Assn. (bd. gov. 1983), Gold Headed Cane Soc. (hon.), U. Calif. San Francisco Sch. Medicine. Home: PO Box 620203 Woodside CA 94062-0203 Office: Univ Calif San Francisco Dept Otolaryngology 400 Parnassus Ave # A-717 San Francisco CA 94143

BOLIN, VERNON SPENCER, microbiologist, consultant; b. Parma, Idaho, July 9, 1913; s. Thadeus Howard Bolin and Jennie Bell Harm; m. Helen Epling, Jan. 5, 1948 (div. 1964); children: Rex, Janet, Mark; m. Barbara Sue Chase, Aug. 1965; children: Vladimir, Erik. BS, U. Wash., 1942; MS, U. Minn., 1949. Tchg. asst. U. Minn., Mpls., 1943-45; rsch. assoc. U. Utah, Salt Lake City, 1945-50, fellow in surgery, 1950-52; rsch. virologist Jensen-Salsbery Labs., Inc., Kansas City, Mo., 1952-57; rsch. assoc. Wistar Inst., U. Pa., 1957-58; rsch. virologist USPHS, 1958-61; founder Bolin Labs., Phoenix, 1959—, also bd. dirs. Contbr. articles to profl. jours. Served with U.S. Army, 1931-33. Mem. N.Y. Acad. Scis., Phi Mu Chi. Home: 36629 N 19th Ave Phoenix AZ 85086-9143

BOLLAPRAGADA, RAMESH, information scientist, educator; arrived in U.S., 1991; s. Rajarao and Mangatayaru Dulla Bollapragada; m. Rama Bollapragada, Nov. 24, 1997. BEE, India, 1988, MS Control Systems, Engring., 1989; MBA, Carnegie Mellon U., Pitts., 1993, PhD, 1996. Sr. engr., Bangalore, India, 1989—91; mem. rsch. staff IBM, T.J. Watson Rsch. Ctr., Yorktown Heights, NY, 1994; mem. tech. staff Bell Labs, Lucent Technologies, Holmdel, NJ, 1996—2002; prof. Coll. of Bus., San Francisco State U., 2002—. Vis. prof. Adminstrv. Staff Coll. of India, Bella Vista Campus, Hyderabad, India, 2003, Hyderabad, 04, Ops. Rsch. Dept., Politecnico Di Torino, Italy, 2004, Sch. Computer Sci., Software Rsch. Inst., Carnegie Mellon U., Pitts., 2005, Helsinki Sch. Econs., 2005. Author: (exhibition (conference) INFORMS Conference in Atlanta (Wagner Prize Award presentation, 2003); contbr. articles to profl. jours, numerous exhibits for scientific conferences. Recipient Advanced Technologies Excellence award, Bell Labs, Lucent Technologies, 1999; William Larimer Mellon fellow, Carnegie Mellon U., 1991—96. Mem.: Inst. for Ops. Rsch. and Mgmt. Sci. Achievements include patents for methods and apparatus for analyzing and designing various network configuration scenarios. Personal E-mail: rbollapragada@yahoo.com. Business E-Mail: rameshb@sfsu.edu.

BOLLENBACH, STEPHEN FRASIER, retired hotel executive; b. LA, July 14, 1942; s. Walter and Betty (Mason) B.; m. Suzanne Weimer, Apr. 13, 1963 (div. Dec. 1969); m. Barbara May Christeson, Dec. 31, 1970; children: Christopher, Keat. BS in Fin., UCLA, 1965; MBA, Calif. State U., 1968. CFO D.K. Ludwig Group, NYC, 1977-80; chmn., CEO S.W. Savs. & Loan, Phoenix, 1980-82; sr. v.p. fin., treas. Marriott Corp., Washington, 1982-86; sr. v.p., CFO, dir. Holiday Corp., Memphis, 1986-90, Promus Cos., Memphis, 1990; exec. v.p., CFO Marriott Corp., Washington, 1992-93; pres., CEO Host Marriott Corp., Washington, 1993-95; sr. exec. v.p., CFO Walt Disney Co., Burbank, Calif., 1995-96; pres. Hilton Hotels Corp., Beverly Hills, Calif., 1996—2004, CEO, 1996—2004, co-chmn., CEO, 2004—07. Non-exec. chmn. KB Home, 2007-; bd. dirs. Time Warner Inc., 2001-, Macy's Inc., 2007-; lead dir., Am. Internat. Group, Inc. (AIG), 2008-; mem. adv. bd. CFO Mag., Boston. Office: KB Home 1099 Wilshire Blvd 7th Fl Los Angeles CA 90024

BOLLES, CHARLES AVERY, librarian; b. Pine Island, Minn., Aug. 10, 1940; s. Arthur Marston and Clarice Ione (Figy) B.; m. Marjorie Elaine Hancock, May 17, 1964; children: Jason Brice, Justin Brian. BA, U. Minn., 1962, MA in Libr. Sci., 1963, PhD in Libr. Sci., 1975. Catalog and serials librarian U. Iowa, Iowa City, 1964-67; asst. prof. Emporia (Kans.) State U., 1970-76, dir. Sch. Libr. Sci., 1978-80; dir. libr. devel. divsn. Kans. State Libr., 1976-78; state librarian State of Idaho, Boise, 1980—. Mem. ALA, Chief Officers State Libr. Agys., Western Coun. State Librs. (chmn. 1985-86, 98-99), Pacific N.W. Libr. Assn. (pres. 1990-91), Idaho Libr. Assn. Office: Idaho State Libr 325 W State St Boise ID 83702-6014

BOLTWOOD, RUSSELL LEWIS, lawyer, telecommunications industry executive; b. St. Louis, Apr. 15, 1963; s. Chester McBride and Joan Mary (Schnable) B. AB, U. Calif., Berkeley, 1986; JD, Golden Gate U., 1993. Assoc. atty. Davis, Reno & Courtney, San Francisco, 1993—96; corp. HR, risk mgr. Fritz Companies, Inc., San Francisco, 1996—97; gen. counsel, chief human resources officer UTStarcom, Inc., Alameda, Calif., 1997—. Vol. United Way, Oakland, 1987—. Mem. Am. Mensa, Commonwealth Club Calif., Toastmasters Internat. Avocations: music, backpacking, creative writing, composition of music. Home: 560 Elysian Fields Dr Oakland CA 94605-5010 Office: UTStarcom 1275 Harbor Bay Parkway Alameda CA 94502 Office Phone: 510-846-8800.

BOMES, STEPHEN D., lawyer; b. Providence, Jan. 15, 1948; s. Edward and Lillian L. (Dick) B.; m. Barbara Jean Thomas, Feb. 4, 1989; 1 child, Laura Alexandra. BS, Boston U., 1968; JD, U. Calif., Hastings, 1971; postgrad., Columbia U., 1974; LLM, NYU, 1975. Bar: Calif. 1972, N.Y. 1975, Fla. 1975, D.C. 1975, U.S. Dist. Ct. (no. and cen. dists.) Calif. 1972, U.S. Ct. Appeals (2d and 9th cirs.). Assoc. Milbank, Tweed, Hadley & McCoy, NYC, 1975-79, London, 1979-81; ptnr. Brobeck, Phleger & Harrison, San Francisco, 1981-93, Loeb and Loeb, LA, 1994-96, Heller Ehrman White & McAuliffe, LA, 1997—. Instr. NYU 1973-75; adj. asst. prof. CUNY, 1974; mem. Brazil Soc. No. Calif., Pan. Am. Soc. Author: The Dead Hand: The Last Grasp, 1976, (with W.F. Johnson) Real Estate Transfer, Development and Finance, Cases and Materials, 1975; co-editor: Commercial Agency and Distributions in Europe, 1992; contbr. chpts. to books. Trustee 1066 Found. NYU fellow, 1973-75; included in Euromoney's Guide to the World's Leading Banking Lawyers. Mem. L.A., Assn. of Bar of City of N.Y., Internat. Bar Assn., Jonathan Club. E-mail: sdbomes@aol.com, sbomes@hewm.com.

BOMMER, TIMOTHY J., magistrate judge, lawyer; b. Columbus, Ohio, Dec. 9, 1940; s. Thomas F. and Susan L. (Proper) B.; children: Breton J., Kevin A., Melissa K. BA, U. Wyo., 1963, JD, 1970. Bar: Wyo. 1970, Colo. 1970. Dep. county and pros. atty., 1970-74; magistrate judge U.S. Dist. Ct., Jackson, 1976—; sole practice Jackson, 1977—. Chmn. fee arbitration com. Wyo. State Bar, 1980-84; mem. Wyo. Jud. Nominating Commn., 1984-88. Mem. ATLA, Am. Bd. Trial Advocates. Republican. Episcopalian. Avocations: boating, hunting, fishing, skiing. Address: PO Box 1728 Jackson WY 83001-1728

BOMSE, STEPHEN V., lawyer; b. LA, Dec. 18, 1944; AB, Stanford U., 1964; LLB, Yale U., 1967. Bar: Calif. 1967. Assoc. Heller, Ehrman, White & McAuliffe, San Francisco, 1967—72, ptnr., 1972—, co-chair Antitrust & Trade Regulation Practice Group. Vis. prof. law Stanford U., 1988-89; rep. 9th Cir. Jud. Conf., 1980-82; gen. counsel No. Calif. ACLU, 1980—. Fellow: Am. Bar Found.; mem.: Assn. Bus. Trial Lawyers of No. Calif. (pres. 1994—95), Bar Assn. Calif., State Bar Calif., ABA, Am. Law Inst. Office: Heller Ehrman 333 Bush St San Francisco CA 94104-2878 Office Phone: 415-772-6142. Office Fax: 415-772-6268. E-mail: sbomse@hewm.com.

BONANNI, FABRIZIO, medical products executive; PhD in Chemistry, U. Florence; grad., Northwestern U. Inst. Internat. Mgmt., J.L. Kelloff Grad. Sch. Mgmt.; grad. Exec. Program in Mfg., Harvard U. Grad. Sch. Bus. Adminstrn. With Baxter Internat. Inc., Italy, 1974, v.p. quality and regulatory affairs Brussels, corp. v.p. regulatory and clin. affairs, corp. v.p. quality systems; sr. v.p. quality and compliance, corp. compliance officer Amgen, Inc., 1999—2003, sr. v.p. mfg., 2003—08, exec. v.p. ops., 2008—. Dir. Aastrom Biosciences, Inc. Trustee PR Sci., Tech. and Rsch. Trust, Mus. Contemporary Art, LA; bd. dirs. Calif. Healthcare Inst.; bd. trustees Calif. Sci. Ctr. Found. Office: Amgen Inc 1 Amgen Ctr Dr Thousand Oaks CA 91320-1799 Office Phone: 805-447-1000. Office Fax: 805-447-1010.

BONAPART, ALAN DAVID, lawyer; b. San Francisco, Aug. 4, 1930; s. Benjamin and Rose B.; m. Helen Sennett, Aug. 20, 1955; children: Paul S., Andrew D. AB with honors, U. Calif., Berkeley, 1951, JD, 1954. Bar: Calif. 1955, US Tax Ct. 1965, US Supreme Ct. 1971. Assoc. Bancroft & McAlister (formerly Bancroft, Avery & McAlister), San Francisco, 1959-62; ptnr. Bancroft & McAlister, San Francisco, 1962-93, Bancroft & McAlister, A Profl. Corp., 1993-99, Bancroft & McAlister LLP, 1999—2007, coun., 2007—. Past trustee Bancroft and McAlister Found.; mem. adv. com. Heckerling Estate Planning Inst., U. Miami, Fla., 1974-87, 92—, mem. faculty, 1974, 91-2000; past dir. Myrtle V. Fitchen Charitable Trust. Mem. ABA, Am. Coll. Trust and Estate Counsel, Bar Assn. State Bar Calif. (cert. in estate planning, probate and trust law Bd. Legal Specialization 1991-2006). Office: Bancroft & McAlister LLP Ste 200 300 Drake's Landing Rd Greenbrae CA 94904-3123 Office Phone: 415-464-8855 301. Business E-Mail: abonapart@bamlaw.com.

BOND, DAVID F., food products executive; With Deloitte & Touche, San Francisco, 1986-97, named ptnr., 1988; sr. v.p., fin. and control, chief acctg. officer Safeway, Inc., Pleasanton, Calif., 1997—. Office: Safeway Inc PO Box 99 Pleasanton CA 94566-0009

BONDAREFF, WILLIAM, psychiatrist, educator; b. Washington, Apr. 29, 1930; s. Leon and Gertrude; m. Rita Haber Kassoy, Jan. 2, 1988; children: Hyla, Sarah. BS in Zoology, George Washington U., 1951, MS in Zoology, 1952; PhD in Anatomy, U. Chgo., 1954; MD, Georgetown U., 1962. Diplomate Am. Bd. Psychiatry and Neurology with added qualifications in geriatric psychiatry. Rsch. assoc., instr. anatomy U. Chgo., 1955; rotating intern USPHS Hosp., Balt., 1962-63; resident in psychiatry Northwestern Meml. Hosp. Inst. Psychiatry, Chgo., 1978-80; asst. prof. anatomy Northwestern U., Evanston, Ill., 1963-65, assoc. prof., 1965-69, prof., 1969-78, chmn. dept. anatomy, 1970-78; prof. psychiatry and gerontology U. So. Calif., LA, 1981—; mem. staff U. So. Calif. Univ. Hosp., LA, 1991—; mem. attending staff L.A. County/U. So. Calif. Med. Ctr., LA, 1981—; mem. Hosp. Good Samaritan, LA, 1981-96; mem. staff Norris Cancer Hosp., 1987—; mem. attending staff Cedars-Sinai Med. Ctr., 2001—, emeritus, 2005—; dir. psychiatry USC Univ. Hosp., 2006—. Physician/cons. VA Hosp., Downey, Ill., 1969-80, Jewish Home for Aged, Reseda, Calif., 1981-90; vis. staff mem. medicine Passavant Pavilion Northwestern Meml. Hosp., 1972-80; dir. div. geriat. psychiatry U. So. Calif., 1981—; dir. U. So. Calif.-St. Barnabas Alzheimer Disease Ctr., 1985-2001; acting dir. dept. Gerontology Research Inst. Andrus Gerontology Ctr.-U. So. Calif., 1982; staff psychiatrist Los Angeles County Hosp., 1981—; past holder various com. offices Northwestern U. Editor Mechanisms of Aging and Devel., 1970—; assoc. editor Am. Jour. Anatomy, 1970-76; mem. editl. bd. Alzheimer Disease and Associated Disorders-An Internat. Jour., 1985-95, Neurbiology of Aging, 1980-94, The Jour. of Gerontology, 1981-84, Internat. Rev. Jour. of Psychiatry, 1988—, Jour. Alzheimer's Disease, 1997-2001; contbr. articles to profl. jours. Mem. sci. adv. bd. Alzheimer's Disease & Related disorders Assn. L.A., bd.dirs., 1989—; mem. rsch. rev. com. treatment, devel. and assessment Nat. Inst. Mental Health, 1987-92. Served with USPHS, 1955-63. USPHS fellow, 1955, U. Cambridge Clare Hall vis. fellow, 1980, Hughes Hall vis. fellow, 1988; scholar Allergy Found., 1960, U. Chgo., 1953; recipient Career Devel. award Nat. Inst. Neurol. Disease and Blindness, 1966-69, Sesquicentennial award Hobart and William Smith Colls., 1972, Sandoz prize Internat. Assn. Gerontology, 1983, Alzheimer Disease and Related Disorders Assn. award, 1984; Fulbright Lectr., U. Goteborg, Sweden, 1967-68. Fellow AAAS (councilor 1970-74), Am. Psychiat. Assn. (geriatrics task force 1981), Gerontol. Soc.; mem. Am. Assn. Anatomists (chmn. local com. ann. meeting 1969), Electron Microscope Soc. Am., Am. Soc. Cell Biology, Am. Acad. Neurology (chmn. neuroanatomical scis. sect. 1971-77), Soc. Neurosci., Assn. Anatomy Chmn. (councilor 1975-77), Am. Assn. Geriat. Psychiatry (program com. 1984-89, bd. dirs. 1985-89), So. Calif. Psychiat. Soc., Internat. Psychogeriat. Assn., Cajal Club, Cosmos Club, Sigma Xi. Office: U So Calif Sch Medicine HCC 4100 1520 San Pablo St Los Angeles CA 90033-1018 Office Phone: 323-442-6016. Business E-Mail: bondaref@usc.edu.

BONDS, BARRY (LAMAR), former professional baseball player; b. Riverside, Calif., July 24, 1964; s. Bobby and Pat Bonds; m. Susann Branco, Feb. 5, 1988 (div. Dec. 1994); children: Nikolai, Shikari; m. Liz Watson, 1998; 1 child, Aisha. BA in Criminal Justice, Ariz. State U., 1986. Outfielder Pitts. Pirates, 1986—92, San Francisco Giants, 1992—2007. Star: (Reality TV show) Bonds on Bonds, 2006. Founder Barry Bonds Family Found., 1993—. Recipient Gold Glove award, 1990—94, 1996—98, Silver Slugger award, 1990—97, 2000—04, Espy award, Best Baseball Player, 1994, 2002, 2004, Espy award, Best Male Athlete, 1994, Philanthropist of Yr. award, Nat. Conf. Black Philanthropy, 1999, Hank Aaron award, 2001—02, 2004; named Nat. League MVP, Baseball Writers' Assn. of Am., 1990, 1992—93, 2001—04, Maj. League Player of Yr., The Sporting News, 1990, 2001, 2004, Nat. League Player of Yr., 1990, 1991, Player of the Decade (1990's), Male Athlete of Yr., 2001; named one of The Most Influential People in the World of Sports, Bus. Week, 2007; named to All-Am. Team, Sporting News Coll., 1985, Nat. League All-Star Team, Maj. League Baseball, 1990, 1992—98, 2000—04, 2007. Achievements include holds the record for most home runs in a single season (73), 2001; became third player in MLB to hit 700 career home runs on Sept. 17, 2004; only mem. in 500/500 Club (HR/Steals); became MLB all-time leader in walks with 2,191 on July 4, 2004; led Nat. League in batting average, 2002 (.370), 2004 (.362); oldest player to win Nat. League MVP Award at 40 years old, 2004; holds MLB record with 7 league MVP awards; holds MLB record for consecutive seasons with 30+ Home Runs, 1992-2004; passing Hank Aaron for the all-time home run record by hitting his 756th on August 7, 2007, against the Washington Nationals. Avocations: golf, photography, music.

BONE, KEN, men's college basketball coach; b. Seattle, Wash., May 21, 1958; s. Walt Bone; m. Connie Bone; children: Kendra, Jenae, Chelsea. BA, Seattle Pacific U., 1983, MA in Athletic Adminstrn., 1993. Asst. coach Shorecrest HS, Wash., 1982—83, Calif. State U. Stanislaus Warriors, 1983—84, head basketball coach, 1984—85, Olympic Coll. Rangers, Bremerton, Wash., 1985—86; asst. coach Seattle Pacific U. Falcons, 1986—90, head basketball coach, 1990—2002; asst. coach U. Wash. Huskies, 2002—05; head basketball coach Portland State U. Vikings, 2005—09, Wash. State U. Cougars, 2009—. Named Dist. 8 Coach of Yr., Nat. Assn. Basketball Coaches, 2000, Co-Coach of Yr., PacWest Conf., 2000, Coach of Yr., Big Sky Conf., 2008. Office: Wash State Univ Athletics Bohler Athletic Complex Colo Ave PO Box 641602 Pullman WA 99164-1602 Office Phone: 509-335-0240. Business E-Mail: mens_basketball@wsu.edu.*

BONESTEEL, MICHAEL JOHN, lawyer; b. LA, Dec. 22, 1939; s. Henry Theodore Samuel Becker and Kathleen Mansfield (Nolan) B.; children: Damon Becker, Kirsten Kathleen; m. Susan Elizabeth Schaaf, June 1, 1980. AB in History, Stanford U., 1961; JD, U. So. Calif., 1966. Bar: Calif. 1967, U.S. Dist. Ct. (ctrl. and so. dists.) Calif. 1967, U.S. Ct. Appeals (9th cir.) 1967, U.S. Dist. Ct. (no. dist.) Calif. 1969, U.S. Dist. Ct. (ea. dist.) Calif. 1983, U.S. Supreme Ct. 1989. Assoc. Haight, Brown & Bonesteel, and predecessors, LA, 1967—71, ptnr., 1972—. Fellow Internat. Acad. Trial Lawyers, Am. Coll. Trial Lawyers; mem. ABA, State Bar Calif., Los Angeles County Bar Assn., Def. Rsch. Inst., Assn. So. Calif. Def. Counsel, Am. Soc. Most Venerable Order of Hospitaller St. John of Jerusalem, Hospitaller Order St. Lazarus of Jerusalem, Grand Priory of Am., Bel Air Bay Club, L.A. Country Club. Office: Ste 800 6080 Center Drive Los Angeles CA 90045-1574 Address: PO Box 45068 Los Angeles CA 90045-0068 Office Phone: 310-215-7100. E-mail: mbonesteel@hbblaw.com.

BONET, LISA (LILAKOI MOON, LISA MICHELLE BONEY), actress; b. San Francisco, Nov. 16, 1967; d. Allen and Arlene Boney; m. Lenny Kravitz, Nov. 19, 1987 (div. Apr. 1993); 1 child, Zoe; 2 children. Studied acting, Celluloid Actor's Studio, North Hollywood, Calif. Actress TV series The Cosby Show, 1984-87, A Different World, 1987-88, also appearances in The Cosby Show, 1987-91, Tales From the Darkside, St. Elsewhere, NBC-TV, The Two of Us (recurring role), New Eden, 1994; films include Angel Heart, 1987, Tales From the Darkside 2, 1991 Bank Robber, 1993, Dead Connection, 1994, Serpent's Lair, 1995, Enemy of The State, 1998, High Fidelity, 2000, Lathe of Heaven, 2002, Biker Boyz, 2003, Whitepaddy, 2006; dir. music videos Let Love Rule, 1988, The Gentleman Who Fell, 1993, Revelation Sunshine, 1999. Recipient Youth in Film award.

BONFIELD, ANDREW JOSEPH, tax practitioner; b. London, Jan. 26, 1924; came to U.S., 1946; s. George Willliam and Elizabeth Agnes B.; m. Eleanor Ackerman, Oct. 16, 1955; children: Bruce Ian, Sandra Karen. Federally authorized tax practitioner. Gen. mgr. Am. Cushion Co., LA, 1948-50, Monson Calif. Co., Redwood City, 1951-58; mfrs. mktg. rep. San Francisco, 1958-62; tax practitioner, bus. cons. Redwood City, 1963—, San Jose, Calif., 1963—, Los Gatos, Calif., 1963—, Kihei, Hawaii, 1986-98, Carmel, Calif., 1998. Past treas., dir. Northwood Park Improvement Assn.; exec. bd. Santa Clara County Coun. Boy Scouts Am., 1971—, past coun. pres., mem. Nat. coun.; mem. Santa Clara County Parks and Recreation Commn., 1975-81, 82-86, mem. County Assessment Appeals Bd., 1978-86, Hawaii Bd. Taxation Review, 1992-98; pres. Mission Soc. Enrolled Agts. With Brit. Royal Navy, 1940—46. Decorated King George VI Silver Badge; recipient Silver Beaver award, Vigil honor award Boy Scouts Am.; enrolled to practice before IRS. Mem. Nat. Assn. Enrolled Agts., Calif. Soc. Enrolled Agts., Hawaii Assn. Pub. Accts., Royal Can. Legion (past state parliamentarian, past state 1st vice comdr.), Rotary (pres. San Jose E. 1977-78, pres Kihei-Wailea 1993-94), Masons, Shriners. Home: 181 Hacienda Carmel Carmel CA 93923-7946 Office Phone: 831-625-7681. Personal E-mail: aebonfield@comcast.net.

BONGIORNO, JAMES WILLIAM, electronics executive; b. Westfield, NY, Apr. 2, 1943; s. Samuel Salvatore and Marjorie Ruth (Hardenburg) B. Student pub. schs. Profl. musician, 1961—65; engr. Hadley Labs., Pomona, Calif., 1965—66, Marantz Co., Woodside, NY, 1966—67; chief engr. Rectilinear Rsch. Corp., Bklyn., 1967—68; profl. musician, writer Popular Electronics, also Audio mag., 1968—71; dir. engring. Dynaco Inc., Phila., 1972, S.A.E. Inc., Los Angeles, 1973—74; founder, pres. Gt. Am. Sound Co. Inc., Chatsworth, Calif., 1974—77; founder, 1977; pres. Sumo Electric Co. Ltd., West Hollywood, Calif., 1977—82; ind. electronic cons. Lompoc, Calif., 1982—88; founder, pres. Spread Spectrum Techs., Inc., Lompoc, Calif., 1988—. Ind. electronic cons. Patentee class A audio amplifier, FM IF-detector. Recipient State of Art Design award, Stereo Sound mag., Tokyo, 1976, 1980, 2003, High End Audio Best of CES Show award, 2003. Mem. Audio Engring. Soc., Am. Fedn. Musicians. Republican. Home and Office: 716 N G St Apt 2 Lompoc CA 93436-4530 Home Phone: 805-740-9902; Office Phone: 805-740-9902. Personal E-mail: sstinc@earthlink.net.

BONIFACHO, BRATSA, artist; b. Belgrade, Yugoslavia, 1937; arrived in Can., 1973, naturalized, 1976. Student, Sumatovachka Sch. Art, Belgrade, 1957-59; BArch, MFA, U. Belgrade, 1965; postgrad., Acad. di Belle Arti, Italy, 1966-68, Atelier Kruger, West Germany, 1966-68. Tchr. painting and drawing Sch. Fine Arts, Belgrade, 1967-68; pvt. tutor, 1979-87. One-person shows Gallery Scollard, Toronto, 1978, Contemporary Art Gallery, Vancouver, 1979, Richmond Art Gallery, B.C., 1982, 93, 97, Burnaby Art Gallery, Vancouver, Can., 1982, Heffel Gallery Ltd., Vancouver, 1988, 90, 91, Quan-Schieder Gallery, Toronto, 1989, 90, Fran Willis Art Gallery, Victoria, B.C., Can., 1992, 93, 94, 95, 2000, Patrick Doheny Fine Art Gallery, Vancouver, 1992, 93, 94, Artropolis, 1993, Seattle Art Fair, 1993, Threshold Gallery, Vancouver, 1993, Bau-Xi Art Gallery, Vancouver and Toronto, 1995, 96, 99, 2001, 02, 03, 04, 09, Kimzey Miller Gallery, Seattle, 1996, Mus. History and Art, Anchorage, 1997, Galerija Progres, Belgrade, 2000, Contemporary Art Gallery, Zrenjanin, Yugoslavia, 2001, Gallery of the Matica Srpsick, Novi Sad, Yugoslavia, 2002, Foster/White Gallery, Seattle, 2004, 05, 08, 09, Gallery Bau-Xi, Toronto, 2009, Herringer Kiss Gallery, Calgary, Alta., 2009, Art Fair, Toronto, 2004, 05, 06, 07, Cologne Art Fair, Germany, 2005, Bau Xi Gallery, Vancouver, B.C., 2006, 2007, 2008, 2009; Art Fair, Toronto, 2006, 09, Gallery Bau-Xi, Toronto, 2006, 07; exhbn. Richmond Art Gallery, B.C., Foster/White Gallery, Seattle, 2006, 2008, juried group exhbns. in B.C., 1974-93; NY Art Fair, 2008, Toronto Art Fair, 2008, represented in numerous pub. and pvt. collections. Grantee, B.C. Arts Coun., 1996, 1998, 2000, Can. Coun., 1996, 1998, 1999; travel grantee, 2000, 2001, 2002, B.C. travel grantee, 1999. Office: PO Box 549 Sta A Vancouver BC Canada V6C 2N3 Office Phone: 604-254-1405. Business E-Mail: bonifacho@telus.net.

BONNELL, VICTORIA EILEEN, sociologist, educator; b. NYC, June 15, 1942; d. Samuel S. and Frances (Nassau) B.; m. Gregory Freidin, May 4, 1971. BA, Brandeis U., 1964; MA, Harvard U., 1966, PhD, 1975. Lectr. politics U. Calif., Santa Cruz, 1972—73, 1974—76, asst. prof. sociology Berkeley, 1976—82, assoc. prof., 1982—91, prof., 1991—. Chair Berkeley Ctr. for Slavic and East European Studies, U. Calif.-Berkeley, 1994-2000, dir. Inst. Slavic, East European, and Eurasian Studies, 2002-04. Author: Roots of Rebellion: Workers' Politics and Organizations in St. Petersburg and Moscow, 1900-1914, 1983; editor: The Russian Worker: Life and Labor Under the Tsarist Regime, 1983, (with Ann Cooper and Gregory Freidin) Russia at the Barricades: Eyewitness Accounts of the August 1991 Coup, 1994, Iconography of Power: Soviet Political Posters Under Lenin and Stalin, 1997, Identities in Transition: Eastern Europe and Russia After the Collapse of Communism, 1996, Beyond the Cultural Turn: New Directions in the Study of Society and Culture, 1999, (with George Breslauer) Russia in the New Century: Stability or Disorder, 2004, (with Thomas Gold) New Entrepreneurs of Europe and Asia: Russia, Eastern Europe and China, 2004; contbr. articles to profl. jours. Recipient Heldt prize in Slavic women's studies, 1991; AAUW fellow, 1979; Regents Faculty fellow, 1978, Fulbright Hays Faculty fellow, 1977, Internat. Rsch. and Exch. Bd. fellow, 1977, 88, Stanford U. Hoover Instn. nat. fellow, 1973-74, Guggenheim fellow, 1985, fellow Ctr. Advanced Study in Behavioral Scis., 1986-87, Pres.' Rsch. fellow in Humanities, 1991-92; grantee Am. Philos. Soc., 1979, Am. Coun. Learned Socs., 1976, 90-91. Mem.: Am. Assn. Advancement Slavic Studies, Am. Sociol. Assn. Business E-Mail: vbonnell@berkeley.edu.

BONNER, ROBERT CLEVE, lawyer; b. Wichita, Kans., Jan. 29, 1942; s. Benjamin Joseph and Caroline (Kirkwood) B.; m. Kimiko Tanaka, Oct. 11, 1969; 1 child, Justine M. BA magna cum laude, Md. U., 1963; JD, Georgetown U., 1966. Bar: D.C. 1966, Calif. 1967, Ct. Appeals (4th, 5th, 9th, 10th cirs.), U.S. Supreme Ct. Law clk. to judge U.S. Dist. Ct., LA, 1966-67; asst. U.S. atty. (ctrl. dist.) Calif. U.S. Dept. Justice, LA, 1971-75, U.S. atty., 1984-89; judge U.S. Dist. Ct. (ctrl. dist.) Calif., LA, 1989-90; ptnr. Kadison, Pfaelzer, et al, Los Angeles, 1975-84; dir. Drug Enforcement Adminstrn., Washington, 1990-93; ptnr. Gibson, Dunn & Crutcher LLP, LA, 1993—2001, 2005—07; commr. US Customs Svc., Washington, 2001—03, US Customs & Border Protection, US Dept. Homeland Security, 2003—05. Chair Calif. Commn. on Jud. Performance, 1997-99, co-chair, Calif. Lawyers for Bush-Cheney, 2000; sr. prin., Sentinel HS Group, 2008-, sr. prin. Sentinel HS Group 2008- Served to lt. comdr. JAGC, USN, 1967-70 Recipient Medallion of Merit award, Friendly Sons of St. Patrick, 2006. Fellow Am. Coll. Trial Lawyers, Fed. Bar Assn. (pres. Los Angeles chpt. 1982-83); mem. L.A. C. of C. (bd. dirs. 1999-2001), Calif. Bar Assn., DC Bar Assn. Republican. Roman Catholic. Office: Gibson, Dunn & Crutcher LLP 333 S Grand Ave Los Angeles CA 90071 Office Phone: 213-229-7000. Business E-Mail: robert.bonner@sentinelhs.com. E-mail: rbonner@gibsondunn.com.

BONNIE, SHELBY W., Internet company executive; b. 1964; married; 3 children. BS in Commerce with distinction, U. Va., 1986; MBA, Harvard U., 1990. With Morgan Stanley & Co.; mng. dir. Tiger Mgmt., 1990—93; co-founder CNET Networks, Inc., San Francisco, 1993, CFO, 1996-97; chmn., CEO CNET Networks Inc., San Francisco, 2000—06; COO CNET: The Computer Network, San Francisco, 1997-99. Bd. dirs. CNET Networks Inc, 1993—; chmn. Interactive Advertising Bur., 2001—03, chmn. emeritus, 2003—. Recipient The NY Ten award, 2003. Office Phone: 415-344-2000. Office Fax: 415-395-9207.

BONO MACK, MARY WHITAKER, United States Representative from California; b. Cleve., Oct. 24, 1961; d. Clay and Karen Whitaker; m. Sonny Bono, Feb. 1986 (dec. Feb. 5, 1998); children: Chesare Elan, Chianna Maria; m. Glenn Baxley, 2001 (div. 2005); m. Connie Mack, Dec. 15, 2007; stepchildren: Addison, Connie. BFA in Art History, U. So. Calif., 1984. Cert. personal fitness instr. Mem. US Congress from 45th (formerly 44th) Calif. dist., 1998—; mem. energy & commerce com. Bd. dirs. Palm Springs Internat. Film Festival; chair Congl. Salton Sea Task Force; vice-chair Entertainment Task Force, Travel & Tourism Task Force; founder Intellectual Property Promotion & Piracy Prevention Caucus; founder, co-chair Recording Arts & Scis. Caucus. Active DARE Program, Olive Crest Home Abused Children, Tiempos de Los Ninos. Named Woman of Yr., San Gorgonio chpt. Girl Scouts of America, 1993. Republican. Avocations: outdoor activities, computer technology. Office: US House of Reps 405 Cannon Ho Office Bldg Washington DC 20515-0545

BONVICINI, JOAN M., women's college basketball coach; b. Bridgeport, Conn., Oct. 10, 1953; Grad., So. Conn. State U., 1975. Coach Calif. State U., Long Beach, 1980-91; head coach U. Ariz., Tucson, 1992—. Spkr. basketball seminars and camps; mem. NCAA Rules com. Bd. dirs. Tucson Area Girl Scouts, Boys and Girls Club of Tucson. Named to Hall of Fame So. Conn. State U., 1989, Conn. Women's Basketball Hall of Fame, 1994, Hall of Fame Long Beach State U., 1996, Coach of Yr., NCAA, 1981, PAC-10, 1998. Mem. Women's Basketball Coaches Assn. (pres. 1988). Office: U Ariz 236 Mckale Ctr Tucson AZ 85721-0001

BOOCHEVER, ROBERT, federal judge; b. NYC, Oct. 2, 1917; s. Louis C and Miriam (Cohen) Boochever; m. Lois Colleen Maddox, Apr. 22, 1943 (dec.); children: Barbara K, Linda Lou, Ann Paula,

Miriam Deon; m. Rose Marie Borden, Aug. 31, 2001. AB, Cornell U., 1939, JD, 1941; HD (hon.), U. Alaska, 1981. Bar: NY 1944, Alaska 1947. Law clk. Nordlinger, Riegel & Cooper, 1941; asst. US atty. Juneau, Alaska, 1946—47; ptnr. firm Faulkner, Banfield, Boochever & Doogan, Juneau, 1947—72; assoc. justice Alaska Supreme Ct., 1972—75, 1978—80, chief justice, 1975—78; judge US Ct. Appeals (9th cir.), Pasadena, Calif., 1980; sr. judge US Ct. Appeals, Pasadena, 1986—. Mem. 9th cir. rules com. US Ct. Appeals, 1983—85, chmn. 9th cir. libr. com., 1995—2001; chmn. Alaska Jud. Coun., 1975—78; mem. appellate judges seminar NYU Sch. Law, 1975; mem. Conf. Chief Justices, 1975—79, vice chmn., 1978—79; mem. adv. bd. Nat. Bank of Alaska, 1968—72; guest spkr. Southwestern Law Sch. Disting. Lecture Series, 1992. Contbr. articles to profl. jours. Chmn. Juneau chpt. ARC, 1949—51, Juneau Planning Commn., 1956—61; mem. Alaska Devel. Bd., 1949—52, Alaska Jud. Qualification Commn., 1972—75; mem. adv. bd. Juneau-Douglas C.C. Capt. US Army, 1941—45. Recipient Disting. Alumnus award, Cornell U., 1989; named Juneau Man of Yr., Rotary, 1974, The Boochever & Bird Chair for Study and Tchg. of Freedom and Equality, U. Calif. Sch. Law, Davis, 2000. Fellow: Am. Coll. Trial Attys.; mem.: ABA, Am. Law Inst., Am. Judicature Soc. (dir. 1970—74), Juneau Bar Assn. (pres. 1971—72), Alaska Bar Assn. (pres. 1961—62), Alaskans United (chmn. 1972), Juneau C. of C. (pres. 1952, 1955), Altadena Town and County Club, Cornell Club L.A. Office: US Ct Appeals 125 S Grand Ave Rm 502 Pasadena CA 91109-1510 Home Phone: 626-577-9351; Office Phone: 626-229-7200. Business E-Mail: boochever@ca9.uscourts.gov.

BOOKIN, DANIEL HENRY, lawyer; b. Ottumwa, Iowa, Oct. 16, 1951; BA, U. Iowa, 1973; JD, Yale U., 1976. Bar: Calif. 1978. Law clk. U.S. Dist. Ct. (no. dist.) Calif., 1976-77; asst. U.S. atty. U.S. Dist. Ct. (so. dist.) N.Y., 1978-82; ptnr. O'Melveny & Myers, San Francisco, 1982—. Mem. bd. editors Yale Law Jour., 1975-76. Fellow Am. Coll. Trial Lawyers, Phi Beta Kappa. Office: O'Melveny & Myers Embarcadero Ctr W Tower 2 Embarcadero Ctr Ste 2800 San Francisco CA 94111-3903 Business E-Mail: dbookin@omm.com.

BOONSHAFT, HOPE JUDITH, public relations executive; b. Phila., May 3, 1949; d. Barry and Lorelei Gail (R ienzi) B. BA, Pa. State U., 1972; postgrad. Del. Law Sch, Kellogg Inst. Mgmt. Tng. Program writer Youth Edn., NYC, 1972; legal aide to judge Phila., 1975; dir. spl. projects Guiffre Med. Ctr., Phila., 1975; senatorial campaign fin. dir. Arlen Specter, Phila., 1975; presdl. campaign fin. dir. Jimmy Carter, Atlanta, 1976; fin. dir. Dem. Nat. Com., 1977—79; dir. devel. World Jewish Congress, NYC, 1978, Yeshiva U., LA, 1979; dir. comm. Nat. Easter Seal Soc., Chgo., 1979-83; CEO Boonshaft-Lewis & Savitch Pub. Rels and Govt. Affairs, LA, 1983-93; sr. v.p. Edelman Worldwide, 1993-95; exec. v.p. external affairs Sony Pictures Entertainement, LA, 1995—. Spl. adv. cmty. rels. The White House, 1977-80; guest lectr. U. Ill., 1982, May Co.'s Calif. Women in Bus. Bd. dirs. L.A. Arts Coun., Los Angeles County Citizens for Economy and Efficiency in Govt. Commn., Calif. Film Commn., Spkrs. Commn. Calif. Initiative. Home: 1967 Mandeville Canyon Rd Los Angeles CA 90049-2235 Office: Sony Pictures Entertainment 10202 Washington Blvd Culver City CA 90232-3119

BOOTH, FORREST, lawyer; b. Evanston, Ill., Oct. 31, 1946; s. Robert and Florence C. (Forrest) B.; m. Louise A. Hayes, June 14, 1980; 1 child, Kristin A. BA, Amherst Coll., 1968; JD, Harvard U., 1975. Bar: D.C. 1976, U.S. Ct. Appeals (D.C. cir.) 1976, Calif. 1977, U.S. Dist. Ct. (no. dist.) Calif. 1977, U.S. Ct. Appeals (9th cir.) 1977, U.S. Supreme Ct. 1979. Assoc. Graham & James, Washington, 1975-76, Mccutchen, Doyle, Brown & Emersen, San Francisco, 1976-78; ptnr. Hancock, Rothert & Bunshoft, San Francisco, 1978-89; sr. ptnr. Booth Banning LLP, San Francisco, 1990—; mem. Severson and Werson, San Francisco. Faculty mem. S.E. Admiralty Law Inst., Savannah, Ga., 1990; chmn. Pacific Admiralty Seminar, San Francisco, 1983-97; advisor U. San Francisco Maritime Law Jour., 1992—. Contbr. articles to profl. jours. Lt. USN, 1968-72, Vietnam. Best Lawyers in Am. Mem. Maritime Law Assn. U.S. (proctor), World Trade Club of San Francisco, Marine Club London, Assn. Average Adjusters U.K., St. Francis Yacht Club, Asia-Pacific lawyers assn., internat. bar assn., bar assn. San Francisco. Avocations: sailing, photography, skiing. Office: 1 Market St #1440 San Francisco CA 94105-1521 also: Severson & Werson Ste 2600 1 Embarcadero Ctr San Francisco CA 94111 Office Phone: 415-398-3344. Office Fax: 415-956-0439. Business E-Mail: fb@severson.com.

BOOTH, JOHN NICHOLLS, minister, writer, photographer; b. Meadville, Pa., Aug. 7, 1912; s. Sydney Scott and Margaret (Nicholls) B.; m. Edith Kriger, Oct. 1, 1941 (dec. Sept. 22, 1982); 1 child, Barbara Anne Booth Christie. BA, McMaster U., 1934; MDiv, Meadville/Lombard Theol. Sch., 1942; LittD, New Eng. Sch. Law, 1950. Ordained to ministry Unitarian Ch., 1942. Profl. magician, 1934-40; min. Unitarian Ch., Evanston, Ill., 1942-48, 1st Ch., Belmont, Mass., 1949-57, 2d Ch. (Now 1st Ch.), Boston, 1958-64, Unitarian Ch., Long Beach, Calif., 1964-71; interim pastor NYC, Gainesville, (Fla.), Detroit, 1971-73. Celebrity platform lectr. and performer on conjuring and mentalism, 1942-58; ministerial adviser to liberal students MIT, 1958-63; mem. books selection com. Gen. Theol. Library, Boston, 1960-63. Author: Super Magical Miracles, 1930, Magical Mentalism, 1931, Forging Ahead in Magic, 1939, Marvels of Mystery, 1941, The Quest for Preaching Power, 1943, Fabulous Destinations, 1950, Story of the Second Church in Boston, 1959, The John Booth Classics, 1975, Booths in History, 1982, Psychic Paradoxes, 1984, Wonders of Magic, 1986, Dramatic Magic, 1988, Creative World of Conjuring, 1990, Conjurians' Discoveries, 1992, The Fine Art of Hocus Pocus, 1995, Keys to Magic's Inner World, 1999, Extending Magic Beyond Credibility, 2001; contbr. articles to mags. and newspapers; photographer full length feature travel documentary films for TV, lecture platforms made in India, Africa, S.Am., Indonesia, South Seas, Himalayas; presented first color travelogue on TV in U.S. over NBC in N.Y.C., 1949; panel mem. radio program Churchmen Weigh The News, Boston, 1951-52; spl. corr. in Asia for Chgo. Sun-Times, 1948-49; by-line writer Boston Globe, 1954-66; producer, photographer motion pictures Heart of Africa, 1954, Golden Kingdoms of the Orient, 1957, Indonesia: Pacific Shangri La, 1957, Treasures of the Amazon, Ecuador and Peru, 1960, Adventurous Britain, 1962, South Seas Saga in Tahiti, Australia and New Guinea, summer 1966, The Amazing America of Will Rogers, 1970, Spotlight on Spain, 1975. Co-founder Japan Free Religious Assn., Tokyo, 1948; co-founder Mass. Meml. Soc., 1962, dir., 1962-64; organizer Meml. Soc. Alachua County (Fla.), 1972; pres. Long Beach Mental Health Assn., 1964-66; adv. coun. Fair Housing Found. Recipient John Nevil Maskelyne prize London Magic Cir., 1987; placed on former N.Y. Town Hall Travelogue Cinematographers Wall of Fame, 1967; named Disting. Alumnae Gallery of McMaster U.; lit. fellow Acad. Magical Arts, 1977, lifetime achievement fellow, 1990, masters fellow, 2001. Mem. Unitarian-Universalist Mins. Assn. (past dir.), Am. Unitarian Assn. (past com. chmn.), Unitarian Mins. Pacific S.W. Assn. (v.p.), Clergy Counseling Svc. So. Calif., Soc. Am. Magicians (inducted into Hall of Fame 1983), Magic Castle Hollywood, Internat. Brotherhood Magicians (hon. life), L.A. Adventurers Club (pres. 1983), Evanston (Ill.) Ministerial Assn. (pres. 1947-48). Achievements include having the first regularly scheduled TV series (Looking at Life) in U.S. by clergyperson, WBKB, Chgo., mid-1940s.

BOOTMAN, J. LYLE, pharmacy educator; BS, U. Ariz., 1974; MS, U. Minn., 1976, PhD, 1978; ScD, U. Sci. Phila., 2006. Clin. resident NIH; faculty Coll. Pharmacy, U. Ariz., 1978—, acting dean, 1987—90, dean, 1990—, founding & exec. dir. Health Outcomes and PharmacoEconomic Rsch. Ctr. Cons. and spkr. in field. Contbr. articles to profl. jours. Named one of the 50 most influential pharmacists in Am., The American Druggist, 1997; fellow Am. Found. for Pharm. Edn., Bush Found. Fellow Am. Assn. for Pharm. Scientists; mem. NAS Inst. Medicine, Am. Pharm. Assn. (trustee, pres. 1999-2000). Office: Coll Pharmacy Pulido Ctr PO Box 210202 Tucson AZ 85721 Office Phone: 520-626-1657. Office Fax: 520-626-0546. Business E-Mail: bootman@pharmacy.arizona.edu.

BOOZE, THOMAS FRANKLIN, toxicologist; b. Denver, Mar. 4, 1955; s. Ralph Walker and Ann (McNatt) B.; children: Heather N., Ian T. BS, U. Calif., Davis, 1978; MS, Kans. State U., 1981, PhD, 1985. Asst. instr. Kans. State U., Manhattan, 1979-85; consulting toxicologist Chevron Corp., Sacramento, 1985-92; sr. toxicologist URS/Radian Internat., Sacramento, 1992-2000; toxicologist Dept. Toxic Substances Control Calif. EPA, Sacramento, 2000—. Cons. field, Manhattan, Kans., 1981-83. Contbr. articles to profl. jours. Vol. Amigos de las Americas, Marin County, Calif., 1973, Hospice Care, Manhattan, 1985. Mem. Soc. Toxicology, Soc. Risk Analysis, Sigma Xi. Home: 8338 Titian Ridge Ct Antelope CA 95843-5627 Office: HERD 8810 CalCenter Dr Sacramento CA 95826 Business E-Mail: tbooze@dtsc.ca.gov.

BOOZER, CARLOS AUSTIN, JR., professional basketball player; b. Aschaffenburg, Germany, Nov. 20, 1981; s. Carlos Boozer; m. Cindy Boozer. BA in Sociology, Duke U., 2003. Forward Cleve. Cavaliers, 2002—04, Utah Jazz, 2004—. Mem. US Men's Sr. Nat. Basketball Team, Athens, Greece, 2004, Beijing, 08. Recipient Bronze medal, men's basketball, Athens Olympic Games, 2004, Gold medal, men's basketball, Beijing Olympic Games, 2008; named to Western Conf. All-Star Team, NBA, 2007, 2008. Achievements include being a member of the NCAA National Championship winning Duke University Blue Devils, 2001. Office: Utah Jazz 301 W South Temple Salt Lake City UT 84101

BORCHERDS, RICHARD EWEN, mathematics professor; b. Cape Town, South Africa, Nov. 29, 1959; BA, Cambridge U., England, 1981; PhD, Cambridge U., 1983. Rsch. fellow Trinity Coll., Cambridge, England, 1983-87; asst. prof. U. Calif., Berkeley, 1987-88, prof., 1993—; rsch. fellow Cambridge U., England, 1988-92, lectr., 1992-93, prof., 1996. Contbr. articles to profl. jours. including J. Alg., Adv. Math., Duke Math. J. Recipient Fields medal, 1998. Fellow: Royal Soc. Office: U Calif Dept Math 970 Evans Hall # 3840 Berkeley CA 94720-3840 Office Phone: 510-642-6550, 510-642-8464. Office Fax: 510-642-8204. E-mail: reb@math.berkeley.edu.

BORCHERS, ROBERT REECE, physicist, science administrator; b. Chgo., Apr. 4, 1936; s. Robert Harley and Rena Josephine (Reece) B.; m. Mary Bridget Hennessy, Nov. 26, 1960; children: Patrick Joseph, Anne Marie, Robert Edward BS in Physics, U. Notre Dame, 1958; MS in Physics, Math., U. Wis., 1959, PhD in Nuclear Physics, 1962. Prof. physics U. Wis., Madison, 1962—76, vice chancellor, 1976—77. U. Colo., Boulder, 1977—79; dep. assoc. dir. MFE Program Lawrence Livermore (Calif.) Nat. Lab., 1979—83, assoc. dir. computation, 1983—91, asst. to dir. for univ. rels., 1991—93; divsn. dir. advanced sci. computing NSF, Arlington, Va., 1993—2001; chief tech. officer Maui High Performance Computing Ctr., 2001—; CEO R.R. Borchers & Assocs., 2001—04; chief scientist CS Cubed Group, 2004—07. Mem. com. NSF, Washington, 1973-93, Nat. Acad. Sci., Washington, 1983-93. Editor Computers in Physics jour., 1987-91, chmn. editorial bd., 1991-95; contbr. numerous chpts. in books, articles on physics and computing. NSF postdoctoral fellow, 1964; A.J. Schmidt Found. fellow and scholar, 1954-60; Sloan Found. fellow, 1964-68; Guggenheim Found. fellow, 1970; recipient W.H. Kiekhofer Disting. Teaching award U. Wis., Madison, 1966; Centennial of Sci. Alumnus award U. Notre Dame, 1966 Fellow Am. Phys. Soc.; mem. IEEE Computer Soc. Avocations: golf, music. Office: MHPCC 550 Lipoa Ste 100 Kihei HI 96753 Business E-Mail: marquis@bborchers.com.

BORDA, DEBORAH, symphony orchestra executive; b. NYC, July 15, 1949; d. William and Helene (Malloy) B. BA, Bennington Coll., 1971; postgrad., Royal Coll. Music, London, 1972-73. Program dir. Mass. Coun. Arts and Humanities, Boston, 1974-76; mgr. Boston Musica Viva, Boston, 1976-77; gen. mgr. Handel and Haydn Soc., Boston, 1977-79, San Francisco Symphony, 1979-86; pres. St. Paul Chamber Orch., 1986-88; exec. dir. Detroit Symphony Orch., 1988-90; pres. Minn. Orch., Mpls., 1990-91; exec. dir. N.Y. Philharm., NYC, 1991-99; exec. v.p., mng dir. Los Angeles Philharmonic Assoc., 1999—. Office: Los Angeles Philharmonic Assn 135 N Grand Ave Los Angeles CA 90012

BORDA, RICHARD JOSEPH, retired insurance company executive; b. San Francisco, Aug. 16, 1931; s. Joseph Clement and Ethel Cathleen (Donovan) B.; m. Judith Maxwell, Aug. 30, 1953; children: Michelle, Stephen Joseph. AB, Stanford U., 1953, MBA, 1957. With Wells Fargo Bank, San Francisco, 1957-70, mgr., 1963-66, asst. v.p., 1966-67, v.p., 1967-70, exec. v.p. adminstn. San Francisco, 1973-85; asst. sec. Air Force Manpower Res. Affairs, Washington, 1970-73; vice chmn., chief fin. officer Nat. Life Ins. Co., Montpelier, Vt., 1985-90; chmn., chief exec. officer Sentinal Group Funds, Inc., 1985-90. Former pres. Air Force Aid Soc., Washington; mem. bd. internat. advisors Monterey Inst. Internat. Studies; govs. coun. Boys and Girls Club Monterey Peninsula; dir. Cmty. Found. Monterey County. Recipient Exceptional Civilian Svc. award, 1973, 95, Stanford Assocs. award. Mem. USMC Res. Officers Assn., Bohemian Club, Old Capital Club, Air Force Aid Soc. (disting. counselor), Phi Gamma Delta, Cypress Point Club. Republican. Episcopalian.

BORDALLO, MADELEINE ZEIEN (MRS. RICARDO JEROME BORDALLO), Delegate to United States House Representative from Guam; b. Graceville, Minn., May 31, 1933; d. Christian Peter and Mary Evelyn (Roth) Zeien; m. Ricardo Jerome Bordallo, June 20, 1953; 1 daughter, Deborah Josephine. Student, St Mary's Coll., South Bend, Ind., 1952; AA, St. Katherines Coll., St. Paul, 1953; AA hon. degree for community service, U. Guam, 1968. Presented in voice recital Guam Acad. Music, Agana., 1951, 62; mem. Civic Opera Co., St. Paul, 1952-53; mem. staff KUAM Radio-TV sta., Agana, 1954-63; freelance writer local newspaper, fashion show commentator, coordinator, civic leader, 1963; nat. Dem. committeewoman for Guam, 1964—2004; 1st lady of Guam, 1974-78, 81-85; senator 16th Guam Legislature, 1981-82, 19th Guam Legislature, 1987-88, 20th Guam Legislature, 1989-90, 21st Guam Legislature, 1991-92, 22nd Guam Legislature, 1993-94; Dem. Party candidate for Gov. of Guam, 1990; lt. gov. of Guam, 1994—2002; rep. from Guam to 108th-110th Congresses, 2002—, mem. armed svcs., resources and small bus. coms. Del. Nat. Dem. Conv., 1964, 68, 72, 76, 80, 84, 88-92, 96, 2000-04, pres. Women's Dem. Party Guam, 1967-69; rep. Presdl. Inauguration, Washington, 1965, 77, 85, 2005; del. Dem. Western States Conf., Reno, 1965, L.A., 1967, Phoenix, 1968, conf. sec., 1967-69; del. Dem. Women's Campaign Conf., Wash., 1965, Dem. Inauguration, 1992. Pres. Guam Women's Club, 1958-59; del Gen. Fedn. Women's Clubs Convs., Miami Beach, Fla., 1961, New Orleans, 1965, Boston, 1968; v.p. Fedn. Asian Women's Assn., 1964-67, pres., 1967-69, pres. 1996-98; pres. Guam Symphony Soc., 1967-73, del. convs., Manila, Philippines, 1959, Taipei, Formosa, 1960, Hong Kong, 1963, Guam, 1964, Japan, 1968, Taipei, 1973; chmn. Guam Christmas Seal Drive, 1961; bd. dirs. Guam chpt. ARC, 1963, sec., 1963-67, fund dr. chmn., 2000; pres. Marianas Assn. For Retarded Children, 1968-69, 73-74, 84—; bd. dirs. Guam Theatre Guild, Am. Cancer Soc.; mem. Guam Meml. Hosp. Vols. Assn., 1966—, v.p., 1966-67, pres., 1970-71; chmn. Hosp. Charity Ball, 1966; pres. Women for Service, 1974—, Beauty World Guam Ltd., 1981—, First Lady's Beautification Task Force of Guam, 1983-86; pres. Palace Restoration Assn., 1983—; nominee Dem. party for Gov. of Guam, 1990. Mem. Internat. Platform Assn., Guam Rehab. Assn. (assoc.), Guam Lytico and Bodig Assn. (pres. 1983-98), Spanish Club of Guam, Inetnon Famalaoan Club (pres. 1983-86), Guam Coun. of Women's Club (pres. 1993-95), Nat. Conf. Lt. Govs. (exec. com. 1998—). Democrat. Home: Watergate E 305 N 2510 Virginia Ave NW Washington DC 20037 Office Phone: 202-225-1188. Business E-Mail: madeleine.bordallo@mail.house.gov, roseanne.meno@mail.house.gov.

BORDEN, WESTON THATCHER, chemistry professor; b. NYC, Oct. 13, 1943; s. Martin L. and Doris (Weston) B.; m. Marcia E. Robbins, May 15, 1971 (div. 1987); children: Alice, Michael; m. Shelia R. Buxton, Mar. 1, 2002. BA, Harvard U., 1964, MA, 1966, PhD, 1968. Instr. Harvard U., Cambridge, Mass., 1968-69, asst. prof., 1969-73; assoc. prof. U. Wash., Seattle, 1973-77, prof., 1977—. Author: Modern Molecular Orbital Theory, 1975; editor: Diradicals, 1982; contbr. articles to profl. jours. Bd. dirs. Itteki Zendo Assn., 1995—. Fellow Fulbright Found., Sloan Found., Guggenheim Found., Japan Soc. for Promotion of Sci.; recipient Humboldt Scientist award. Mem. AAAS, Am. Chem. Soc. Buddhist. Avocation: traditional Japanese art. Office: U Wash Dept Chemistry Bg 10 Seattle WA 98195-0001 E-mail: borden@chem.washington.edu.

BORDY, MICHAEL JEFFREY, lawyer; b. Kansas City, Mo., July 24, 1952; s. Marvin Dean and Alice Mae (Rostov) B.; m. Marjorie Enid Kanof, Dec. 27, 1973 (div. Dec. 1983); m. Melissa Anne Held, May 24, 1987; children: Shayna Robyn, Jenna Alexis, Samantha Falyn. BA, Hamilton Coll., 1974; PhD, U. Kans., 1980; JD, U. So. Calif., 1986. Bar: Calif., 1986, US Dist. Ct. (cen. dist.) Calif., 1986, (so. dist.) Calif., 1987, US Ct. Appeals (9th cir.), 1986. Tchg. asst. biology U. Kans., Lawrence, 1975-76, rsch. asst. biology, 1976-80; post-doctoral fellow Johns Hopkins U., Balt., 1980-83; tchg. asst. U. So. Calif., LA, 1984-86; assoc. Thelen, Marrin, Johnson & Bridges, LA, 1986-87, Wood, Lucksinger & Epstein, LA, 1987-89, Cooper, Epstein & Hurewitz, Beverly Hills, Calif., 1989-93; ptnr. Jacobson, Runes & Bordy, Beverly Hills, 1994-96, Jacobson, Sanders & Bordy, LLP, Beverly Hills, 1996-97, Jacobson White Diamond & Bordy, LLP, Beverly Hills, 1997—2001, White, Bordy & Levey, LLP, LA, 2002—05, Bordy and Levey, LLP, LA, 2005—07, Michael J. Bordy, A PLC, 2007—08, Isaacman, Kaufman & Painter, A PC, 2008—. Bd. govs. Beverly Hills (Calif.) Bar Barristers, 1988-90, chair real estate law sect. 1998-2000, exec. com. 2000—; bd. govs. Cedars-Sinai Med. Ctr., LA, 1994—; bd. dirs. Sinai Temple, 1998-2003, Jewish Fedn., LA, 2004—; cabinet United Jewish Fund/Real Estate, LA, 1995—; exec. com. Moriah Soc. for U. Judaism, 2002--; planning com. Am. Cancer Soc., 1996-2000; active Guardians of the Jewish Home for the Aging, 1995—, Lawyers Against Hunger, 1995-2002, Fraternity of Friends, 1997-99. Pre-Doctoral fellow NIH, Lawrence, 1977-80, post-doctoral fellow Mellon Found., Balt., 1980-83; named one of Southern Calif. Super Lawyers, 2005—. Mem. ABA, State Bar Calif., LA County Bar Assn., Beverly Hills Bar Assn. (gov., barrister 1988-92, chair real estate sect. 1998-00), Profl. Network Group. Democrat. Jewish. Avocations: running, triathlons, reading. Office: Isaacman Kaufman & Painter 8484 Wilshire Blvd Ste 850 Beverly Hills CA 90211 Office Phone: 323-782-7700. Business E-Mail: mjbordy@ikplaw.com.

BOREL, JAMES DAVID, anesthesiologist; b. Chgo., Nov. 15, 1951; s. James Albert and Nancy Ann (Sieverson) B BS, U. Wis., 1973; MD, Med. Coll. Wis., 1977. Diplomate Am. Bd. Anesthesiology, Nat. Bd. Med. Examiners, Am. Coll. Anesthesiologists. Rsch. asst. McArdle Lab. for Cancer Rsch., Madison, Wis., 1972—73, Stanford U. and VA Hosp., Palo Alto, 1976—77; intern Cambridge Hosp., Mass., 1977—78; resident anesthesiology Peter Bent Brigham Hosp., Boston, 1978—80; fellow anesthesiology Ariz. Health Scis. Ctr., Tucson, 1980—81; assoc. anesthesiology U. Ariz. Coll. Medicine, Tucson, 1981—. Vis. anaesthetist St. Joseph's Hosp., Kingston, Jamaica, 1980; clin. fellow medicine Harvard Med. Sch., Boston, 1977-78; clin. fellow anesthesia Harvard Med. Sch., 1978-80; anesthesiologist Mt. Auburn Hosp., Boston, 1978-80; rsch. assoc. U. Ariz. Coll. Medicine, Tucson, 1980-81; rsch. assoc., 1980-81; active staff Mesa (Ariz.) Luth. Hosp., 1981—; courtesy staff Scottsdale (Ariz.) Meml. Hosp., 1982— Contbr. numerous articles to profl. jours Mem. AMA, AAAS, Ariz. Anesthesia Alumni Assn., Ariz. Soc. Anesthesiologists, Am. Soc. Regional Anesthesia, Can. Anesthetists' Soc., Internat. Anesthesia Rsch. Soc., Am. Soc. Anesthesiologists Office: Valley Anesthesia Consultant 1850 N Central Ave Ste 1600 Phoenix AZ 85004-4633 Office Phone: 602-262-8900.

BOREN, ROBERT REED, communications educator; b. Burley, Idaho, Nov. 8, 1936; s. Gilbert Reed Boren and Olive Chambers McBride; m. Marjorie Jean Dixon, Sept. 9, 1958; children: David, Michael, Elisabeth, Stephen. BA, Brigham Young U., 1958, MA, 1964; PhD, Purdue U., 1965. Instr. Purdue U., Lafayette, Ind.,

1959-61; asst. prof. Brigham Young U., Provo, Utah, 1961-67; assoc. prof. U. Mont., Missoula, 1967-71; prof. Boise (Idaho) State U., 1971—, chair, 1971-95; pres. Insight Cons., Boise, 1995—. Pres., bd. dirs. Salmon River Electric Coop. Author: The Human Transaction, 1975, Communication Behavior, 1975, Communication Experiments, 1975, Conducting the Council's Business, 1976, Wildflowers of the Sawtooth Mountains, 1979, Facilitator's Guide for Public Meetings, 1981, Effective Business Writing, 1985, Effective Communication, 1985, Effective Business Communication, 1986, Mountain Wildflowers of Idaho, 1989. Mem. Nat. Comm. Assn., Western States Comm. Assn. (v.p., pres. 1971-73, Disting. Svc. award 1998), Western Forensics Assn. (v.p., pres. 1968-70), Idaho Consumer Owned Utilities Assn., Snake River Power Assn. (bd. dirs., v.p., bd. dirs.), Phi Kappa Delta. Avocations: hiking, rafting, fishing, hunting. Home: HC 67 Box 742 Clayton ID 83227-9801 Office: Boise State U 1910 University Dr Boise ID 83725-0399 Business E-Mail: rboren@custertel.net.

BOREN, ROGER W., judge; b. Bingham Canyon, Utah, Sept. 11, 1941; m. Winifred A. Scott, Feb. 4, 1965; 6 children. BA, U. Calif., Berkeley, 1966; MA, San Jose State U., 1968; JD, UCLA, 1973. Bar: Calif. 1973, U.S. Dist. Ct. (ctrl. dist.) Calif. 1973. Dep. atty. gen. State of Calif., 1973-84; judge Mcpl. Ct., Newhall Jud. Dist., 1984—85; judge Superior Ct., L.A. County, Calif., 1985-87; assoc. justice 2 Appellate Dist., Calif. Ct. Appeals, LA, 1987-93, presiding justice, 1993—. Bd. dirs. Henry Mayo Newhall Meml. Hosp., 1985—. Mem. Lds Ch.

BORENSTEIN, DANIEL BERNARD, psychiatrist, educator; b. Silver City, N.Mex., Mar. 31, 1935; s. Jack and Marjorie Elizabeth (Kerr) B.; m. Bonnie Denice Ulland, June 11, 1967; 1 child, Jay Brian. BSChemE, MIT, 1957; MD, U. Colo., 1962. Diplomate Am. Bd. Psychiatry and Neurology. Intern U. Hosp. U. Ky., 1962-63; resident in psychiatry U. Colo. Med. Ctr., 1963-66; chief resident, psychiatry instr. U. Colo. Sch. Medicine, 1965-66; psychiatry instr. U. So. Calif. Sch. Medicine, 1966-67; asst. clin. prof. psychiatry UCLA Sch. Medicine, 1972-84, assoc. clin. prof., 1984-96, clin. prof., 1996—2008, hon. clin. prof., 2008—. Founder, dir. UCLA Mental Health Program for Physicians in Tng., 1980—84; clin. assoc. L.A. Psychoanalytic Soc. and Inst., 1967—71, pres. clin. assocs., 1970—71, faculty, 1973—83, sr. faculty, 1983—2005; pvt. practice medicine specializing in psychoanalysis and psychiatry, West L.A., 1966—; assoc. vis. psychiatrist UCLA Ctr. Health Scis., 1973—90; cons. Medicare Program, 1995—2005; examiner Am. Bd. Psychiatry and Neurology; reviewer various med. and psychiat. jours., 1991—. Author: Manual of Psychiatric Peer Review, 1985, Psychiatric Peer Review: Prelude and Promise, 1985; contbr. articles to profl. jours. Bd. dirs. L.A. Child Devel. Ctr., 1981—85, Found. Advancement Psychiat. Edn. and Rsch., 1991—2005, Coop. Am. Physicians/Mutual Protective Trust, 1994—. Lt. AUS, 1957—58. Recipient Disting. Clin. Prof. award, UCLA Sch. Medicine, 2006. Fellow: Am. Coll. Psychiatrists (com. on hon. fellowship 2002—05), Am. Psychiat. Assn. (life; mem. coun. area VI 1977—79, com. to rev. psychiat. news 1979—81, coun. area VI, dep. rep. assembly dist. brs. 1981—82, work group on competition and legis. 1981—83, nominating com. 1982—83, assembly liaison to peer rev. com. 1982—86, assembly rep. dist. brs. 1982—89, assembly liaison to fin. and mktg. com. 1986—87, assembly corr. group on subspecialization 1986—89, assembly liaison to coun. on econ. affairs 1987—89, med. student edn. com. 1987—90, bd. liaison jud. action commn. 1989—91, bd. trustees 1989—, com. managed care 1990—92, com. mem., bd. liaison to managed care com. 1992—99, bd. liaison econ. affairs coun. 1992—99, chmn. bd. ethics appeals, sec. 1995—97, v.p. 1997—99, pres.-elect 1999—2000, pres. 2000—01, chair med. dir. contract negotiating com. 2001, cons. bus. rels. com., chair nominating com. 2001—02, past pres. 2001—, bus. rels. com. 2002—05, fin. and budget com. 2003—06, elections com. 2008—, Disting. fellow); mem.: AMA (ho. dels., alt. 1998—2002, del. 2003—07), Am. Psychoanalytic Assn. (com. on confidentiality 1983—96, com. on govt. rels. and ins. 1983—2000), L.A. Psychoanalytic Soc. and Inst. (co-chmn. ext. divsn. 1973—74, chmn. peer rev. com. 1975—78, curriculum com. 1980—84), Calif. Psychiat. Assn. (exec. coun. 1977—79, 1981—95, chmn. jud. com. 1986—88, bd. trustees 1989—95, Spl. Recognition award 1995), Calif. Med. Assn. (ho. of dels. psychiat. splty. rep. 1979—84, com. on mental health and mental disabilities 1979—85, alt. del. ho. del. 1984—86, del. 1986—88, com. on mental health and mental disabilities 1987—88, bd. trustees 1992—2001, chmn. physicians benevolence oper. com. 1996—2001, chmn. bldg. com. 1999—2001), L.A. County Med. Assn. (chmn. mental health com. Bay dist. 1980—85, com. on substance abuse 1981—86, Bay Dist. bd. dirs. 1981—, Bay Dist. v.p. 1985—86, pres.-elect 1986—87, com. on well-being 1986—89, pres. 1987—88, exec. coun. 1988—91), So. Calif. Psychiat. Soc. (chmn. peer rev. com. 1974—77, exec. coun. 1976—89, ethics com. 1977—85, pres. 1978—79, chmn. fellowship and awards com. 1979—85, chmn. Commn. on Psychiatry and the Law 1980—81, Appreciation award 1979, 1st recipient Disting. Svc. award 1984, Outstanding Achievement award 1993, Outstanding Svc. citation 1975). Office: 151 N Canyon View Dr Los Angeles CA 90049-2721 Office Phone: 310-472-7386.

BORENSTEIN, LORNA M., information technology executive; married. Degree in Bus. summa cum laude, Am. Coll., London; BCL, McGill U., B in Common Law with honors. Lawyer Peterson & Ross, Chgo., Osler, Hosking & Harcourt, Toronto; asst. counsel Hewlett-Packard Ltd., Canada; v.p. Silverbow E-Commerce Inc.; v.p., gen. mgr. eBay Can.; v.p., gen. mgr. personals Yahoo! Inc., 2004—05, v.p. mktg. search and marketplace group, 2005, v.p, 2005—07; pres. Move Inc., Westlake Village, Calif., 2007—. Named one of Can.'s Power 50, 2002. Office: Move Inc 30700 Russell Ranch Rd Westlake Village CA 91362 Office Phone: 805-557-2300. Office Fax: 805-557-2680.

BORENSTEIN, MARK A., lawyer; b. Bklyn., June 26, 1951; BA, SUNY, Buffalo, 1973; JD, George Washington U., 1976; LLM, Georgetown U., 1978. Bar: Va. 1976, D.C, 1977, Calif. 1978. Law clk. to Hon. Irving Hill U.S. Dist. Ct. (cen. dist.), Calif., 1976-77; mem. Tuttle & Taylor, LA, 1978-2000, Shapiro, Borenstein & Dupont, Santa Monica, Calif., 2000—02, Overland & Borenstein, LA, 2002—. Lectr. U. So. Calif., 1980—82, vis. prof. law, 1997, adj. prof., 1999—. Exec. editor: George Washington Law Review, 1975-76. Inst. for Pub. Interest Representation Law fellow Georgetown U. Law Ctr., 1977-78. Mem. Phi Beta Kappa, Order of the Coif. E-mail: mborenstein@overlandborenstein.com.

BORESI, ARTHUR PETER, writer, educator; b. Toluca, Ill. s. John Peter and Eva Boresi; m. Clara Jean Gordon, Dec. 28, 1946; children: Jennifer Ann Boresi Hill, Annette Boresi Pueschel, Nancy Jean Boresi Broderick. Student, Kenyon Coll., 1943—44; BSEE, U. Ill., 1948, MS in Mechanics, 1949, PhD in Mechanics, 1953. Research engr. N. Am. Aviation, 1950; materials engr. Nat. Bur. Standards, 1951; mem. faculty U. Ill., Urbana, 1953—, prof. theoretical and applied mechanics and nuclear engring., 1959-79; prof. emeritus U. Ill. at Urbana, Urbana, 1979; Disting. vis. prof. Clarkson Coll. Tech., Potsdam, NY, 1968-69; NAVSEA research prof. Naval Postgrad. Sch., Monterey, Calif., 1978-79; prof. civil engring. U. Wyo., Laramie, 1979-95, head, 1980-94, prof. emeritus, 1995—. Vis. prof. Naval Postgrad. Sch., Monterey, Calif., 1986—87; cons. in field. Author: Approximate Solution Methods in Engineering Mechanics, 1991, 2d edit., 2002, Elasticity in Engineering Mechanics, 4th edit., 2000, Engineering Mechanics: Statics, 2001, Engineering Mechanics: Dynamics, 2001, Advanced Mechanics of Materials, 6th edit., 2002; contbr. articles to profl. jours. With USAAF, 1943—44, with US Army, 1944—46. Fellow: ASCE, ASME, Am. Acad. Mechanics (founding, treas.); mem.: Am. Soc. Engring. Edn. (Archie Higdon Disting. Educator award 1993). Office: 3310 Willett Dr Laramie WY 82072 Business E-Mail: boresi@uwyo.edu.

BORGATTA, EDGAR F., sociologist, educator; b. Milan, Sept. 1, 1924; came to U.S., 1929, naturalized, 1934; s. Edgar A. and Frances (Zinelli) B.; m. Marie Lentini, Oct. 5, 1946; children: Lynn, Kim, Lee. BA, NYU, 1947, MA, 1949, PhD, 1952. Cert. psychologist, N.Y., Vt., Wis. Instr. NYU, 1949-51, lectr., prof., 1954-59; lectr., rsch. assoc. Harvard U., 1951-54; social psychologist, asst. sec. Russell Sage Found., 1954-59; prof. sociology Cornell U., Ithaca, NY, 1959-61; Brittingham rsch. prof. U. Wis., Madison, 1961-72, chmn. dept. sociology, 1962-65, chmn. divsn. social studies, 1965-68; disting. prof. sociology Queens Coll., CUNY, 1972-77, prof Grad. Ctr., 1972-82, dir. Italian Social Sci. Ctr., 1972-77; rsch. CUNY Case Ctr. for Gerontol. Studies, 1978-81, dir. data svc., 1981-82; prof. sociology U. Wash., Seattle, 1981—93, chmn. dept., 1992—93, prof. emeritus, 1994—; dir Inst. on Aging U. Wash., Seattle, 1981-86. Cons. to bus. and govt., 1953-, Russell Sage Found., 1970-72; lectr., prof., adj. prof. sociology NYU, 1954-59; cons. editor Rand McNally & Co., 1961-74; chmn. bd. F.E. Peacock Pubs., Inc.; Nat. Inst. Gen. Scis.; spl. rsch. fellow, 1972. Editor: Research on Aging, Sociol. Methodology, Sociol. Methods and Research; co-editor: Handbook of Personality Theory and Research; editor-in-chief: Encyclopedia of Sociology, 2d edit.; contbr. articles to profl. jours. Fellow Am. Psychol. Assn., Am. Psychol. Soc.; mem. Psychometric Soc., Sociol. Rsch. Assn., Am. Sociol. Assn. (v.p. 1983), Pacific Sociol. Assn. (pres. 1985), Internat. Inst. Sociology (pres. 1984-89). Office: c/o Apt 1120 116 Fairview Ave N Seattle WA 98109 Office Phone: 206-254-1862. Business E-Mail: borgatta@u.washington.edu.

BORGMAN, LEON E., geologist; BS in Geol. Engring., Colo. Sch. Mines, 1953; MS in Math., U. Tex., Houston, 1959; PhD in Stats., U. Calif., Berkeley, 1962. Oceanographical engr. Shell Devel. Co., Houston, 1953-59; assoc. prof. stats. U. Calif., Davis, 1961-67, assoc. prof. engring. geosci. Berkeley, 1967-70; prof. geology and stats. U. Wyo., Laramie, prof. emeritus. Cons. Shell Devel. Co., Exxon Prodn. Rsch., Chevron Oil Field Rsch. Co., Continental Shelf Inst., Norway, Waterways Exptl. Sta., EPA, Navy Civil Engring. Lab.; tech. adv. UN. Contbr. articles to profl. jours., chpts. to books. Named Disting. lectr. Internat. Assn. Hydraulic Rsch., 1989. Mem. ASCE (tech. com. ocean engring. 1990—, Internat. Coastal Engr. award 1994), NAE, NAS (com. coastal flooding 1980-82), Am. Coun. Geostats. (gov. com. 1985-90). Office: U Wyo Geology Bldg Rm 1034 Laramie WY 82070

BORGNINE, ERNEST, actor; b. Hamden, Conn., Jan. 24, 1917; s. Charles B. and Anna (Boselli) B.; m. Rhoda Kemins, Sept. 2, 1949, (div. Aug. 29, 1958); m. Katy Jurado, Dec. 31, 1959 (div. June 3, 1963); m. Ethel Merman, June 27, 1964 (div. May 25, 1965); m. Donna Rancourt, June 30, 1965 (div. Jan 1, 1972); m. Tova Traesner, Feb. 24, 1973; 2 children. Student pub. schs., New Haven; student, Randall Sch. Dramatic Arts, Hartford, Conn. Actor: (plays) Mrs. McThing, Harvey, The Odd Couple, Hamlet, An Offer You Can't Refuse; (films) China Corsair, 1951, The Whistle at Eaton Falls, 1951, The Mob, 1951, From Here to Eternity, 1953, The Stranger Wore a Gun, 1953, Johnny Guitar, 1954, Demetrius and the Gladiators, 1954, The Bounty Hunter, 1954, Vera Cruz, 1954, Bad Day at Black Rock, 1955, Violent Saturday, 1955, Marty, 1955 (Acad. award for Best Actor, 1956), Run For Cover, 1955, Violent Saturday, 1955, The Square Jungle, 1955, Last Command, 1955, Jubal, 1956, The Catered Affair, 1956, The Best Things in Life Are Free, 1956, Three Brave Men, 1956, The Vikings, 1958, The Badlanders, 1958, Torpedo Run, 1958, Summer of the Seventeenth Doll, 1959, The Rabbit Trap, 1959, Man on a String, 1960, Pay or Die, 1960, Go Naked in the World, 1961, Barabba, 1961, McHale's Navy, 1964, The Flight of the Phoenix, 1966, The Oscar, 1966, Chuka, 1967, The Dirty Dozen, 1967, The Legend of Lylah Clare, 1968, Ice Station Zebra, 1968, The Split, 1968, The Wild Bunch, 1969, The Adventurers, 1970, Suppose They Gave a War and Nobody Came, 1970, A Bullet for Sandoval, 1970, Rain for a Dusty Summer, 1971, Hannie Caulder, 1971, Bunny O'Hare, 1971, Willard, 1971, The Poseidon Adventure, 1972, The Revengers, 1972, The Emperor of the North, 1973, The Neptune Factor, 1973, Law and Disorder, 1974, Sunday in the Country, 1974, Hustle, 1975, The Devil's Rain, 1975, Shoot, 1976, The Greatest, 1977, Convoy, 1978, Crossed Swords, 1978, The Day the World Ended, 1979, The Black Hole, 1979, Ravagers, 1979, The Double McGuffin, 1979, When Time Ran Out, 1980, Super Fuzz, 1981, High Risk, 1981, Escape from New York, 1981, Deadly Blessing, 1981, Young Warriors, 1983, Cane arrabbiato, 1984, Codename: Wildgeese, 1986, Skeleton Coar, 1987, Spike of Bensonhurst, 1988, The Big Turnaround, 1988, Real Men Don't Eat Gummi Bears, 1989, The Last Match, 1990, Soldier of Fortune, 1990, Tides of War, 1990, Any Man's Death, 1990, Mortal Passions, 1990, Mistress, 1992, Outlaws: The Legend of O.B. Taggart, 1994, Sprit of the Season, 1994, Captiva Island, 1995, Merlin's Shop of Mystical Wonders, 1996, (voice only) All Dogs Go to Heaven 2, 1996, McHale's Navy, 1997, Gattaca, 1997, 12 Bucks, 1998, (voice only) Small Soldiers, 1998, Me!, 1998, BASEketball, 1998, An All Dogs Christmas Carol, 1998, The Last Great Ride, 1999, Abilene, 1999, The Kiss of Debt, 2000, The Lost Treasure of Sawtooth Island, 2000, Castle Rock, 2000, Hoover, 2000, Whiplash, 2002, Crimebusters, 2003, The Long Ride Home, 2003, Barn Red, 2004, Blueberry, 2004, That One Summer, 2005, 3 Below, 2005, Rail Kings, 2005, Frozen Stupid, 2006, La Cura del gorilla, 2006, Oliviero Rising, 2007, Chinaman's Chance, 2008, Strange Wilderness, 2008, The Lion of Judah, 2009; (TV movies) Sam Hill: Who Killed Mr. Foster?, 1971, The Trackers, 1971, Legend in Granite, 1973, Twice in a LIfetime, 1974, Future Cop, 1976, Holiday Hookers, 1976, Fire!, 1977, The Ghost of Flight 401, 1978, Cops and Robin, 1978, All Quiet on the Western Front, 1979, Blood Feud, 1983, Carpool, 1983, Love Leads the Way: A True Story, 1984, Dirty Dozen: The Next Mission, 1985, Alice in Wonderland, 1985, Dirty Dozen: The Fatal Mission, 1988, Jake Spanner, Private Eye, 1989, Appearances, 1990, Mountains of Diamonds, 1991, Hunt for the Blue Diamond, 1993, Tierarztin Christine, 1993,Tierarztin Christine II: Die Versuchung, 1995, The Blue Light, 2004, The Trail to Hope Rose, 2004, A Grandpa for Christmas, 2007, Aces 'N' Eights, 2008; (TV mini-series) Jesus of Nazareth, 1977, The Last Days of Pompeii, 1984, Treasure Island in Outer Space, 1987, Oceano, 1989; (TV series) McHale's Navy, 1962-66, The Single Guy, 1995-97, Airwolf, 1984-86, (voice only) All Dogs Go to Heaven, 1996-97; (TV appearances) Captain Video and His Video Rangers, 1951, Goodyear Television Playhouse, 1951, Short Short Dramas, 1953, The Ford Television Theatre, 1954, Waterfront (2 episodes), 1954, Fireside Theatre, 1955, The O. Henry Playhouse,1957, Make room for Daddy, 1957, Navy Log, 1957, Wagon Train (5 episodes), 1957-62, Zane Gray Theatre, 1957-60, ShlitzPlayhouse of Stars, 1958, Frontier Justice, 1959, Laramie, 1959-60, General Electric Theatre (2 episodes), 1961-62, Blue Angels, 1961, Alcoa Premiere, 1962, Bob Hope Presents the Chrysler Theatre, 1966, Run For Your Life, 1966, Get Smart, 1968, Little House on The Praric (2 episodes), 1974, Future Cop (5 episodes), 1977 Love Boat (2 episodes), 1982, Magnum, P.I., 1982, Matt Houston, 1983, Masquerade, 1983, Highway To Heaven, 1986, Murder, She Wrote, 1987, Jake and the Fat Man, 1989, Home Improvement, 1992, The Commish (2 episodes), 1993-94, (voice only) The Simpsons, 1993, Pinky and the Brain, 1996, JAG, 1998 (voice only) SpongeBob SquarePants, 1999, Early Edition, 1999, Chicken Soup for the Soul, 2000, Walker, Texas Ramger, 2000, Touched By an Angel, 2002, 7th Heaven, 2002, Family Law, 2002, The District, 2003, ER (2 episodes), 2009; author: Ernie: the Autobiography, 2008. Active VA, across the country; served with USNR, 1935-1945, World War II. Recipient Calif. Commendation medal, 2007. Mem. Masons (33 degree). Lodges: Mason. Avocation: playing golf.

BORKO, HILDA, education educator; BA in Psychology, UCLA, 1971, MA in Philosophy of Edn., 1973, PhD in Ednl. Psychology, 1978. Elem. tchg. credential Calif., specialization in mental retardation U. So. Calif. Asst. and assoc. prof. Coll. Edn., Va. Poly. Inst. and State U., 1980—85; assoc. prof. Coll. Edn., U. Md., College Park, 1985—91, Sch. Edn., U. Colo., Boulder, 1991—94; prof. Sch. Edn. U. Colo., Boulder, 1994—. Co-author (with M. Eisenhart): (book) Designing Classroom Research: Themes, Issues, and Struggles, 1993 (Outstanding article award, 1992); contbr. articles to profl. jours. and chpts. to books. Recipient grants in field. Mem.: APA, Nat. Acad. Edn., Nat. Coun. for Tchrs. of Math., Invisible Coll. for Rsch. on Tchg., Am. Assn. Colls. of Tchr. Edn., Am. Ednl. Rsch. Assn. (pres. 2003—04), Pi Gamma Mu, Phi Beta Kappa, Phi Delta Kappa. Office: U Colo Sch Edn CB249 Boulder CO 80309 Office Phone: 303-492-8399.

BORMAN, FRANK, former astronaut, laser patent company executive; b. Gary, Ind., Mar. 14, 1928; s. Edwin Borman; m. Susan Bugbee; children: Fredrick, Edwin. BS, U.S. Mil. Acad., 1950; M. Aero. Engring., Calif. Inst. Tech., 1957; grad., USAF Aerospace Research Pilots Sch., 1960, Advanced Mgmt. Program, Harvard Bus. Sch., 1970. Commd. 2d lt. USAF, advanced through grades to col., 1965, ret., 1970; assigned various fighter squadrons U.S. and Philippines, 1951-56; instr. thermodynamics and fluid mechanics U.S. Mil. Acad., 1957-60; dir. Continental Airlines Holdings Inc. (formerly Tex. Air Corp.), Houston, 1992—; instr. USAF Aerospace Research Pilots Sch., 1960-62; astronaut Manned Spacecraft Ctr., NASA, until 1970; command pilot on 14 day orbital Gemini 7 flight, Dec. 1965; including rendezvous with Gemini 6; command pilot Apollo 8, 1st lunar orbital mission, Dec. 1968; sr. v.p. for ops. Eastern Air Lines, Inc., Miami, Fla., 1970-74, exec. v.p., gen. operations mgr., 1974-75, pres., chief exec. officer, 1975-85, chief exec. officer, 1975-86, chmn. bd., 1976-86; vice chmn., dir. Tex. Air Corp., Houston, 1986-92; chmn., CEO, pres. Patlex Corp., Las Cruces, N.Mex., 1993—; chmn. bd. Autofinance Group, Inc., Westmont, Ill.; Chm of Bd of Dir DBT OnLine Inc., Fort Lauderdale, 1996. Bd. dirs. Continental Airlines, Home Depot, Outboard Marine Corp. Co-auth.: (with Robert J. Serling) Countdown: An Autobiography of Frank Borman, 1988 Recipient Disting. Svc. award NASA, 1965, Collier trophy Nat. Aeros. Assn., 1968, Congl. Space Medal of Honor, Harmon Internat. Aviation trophy. Office: Patlex Corp 725 Leonard Bryan Aly Las Cruces NM 88007-9015

BORN, GEORGE HENRY, aerospace engineer, educator; b. Westhoff, Tex., Nov. 10, 1939; s. Henry and Lydia (Schulle) B.; m. Carol Ann Leslie, Mar. 21, 1992. BS, U. Tex., 1962, MS, 1965, PhD, 1968. Engr. Ling-Temco-Vought, Dallas, 1962-63; aerospace technologist Johnson Space Ctr., Houston, 1967-70; mem. tech. staff Jet Propulsion Lab., Pasadena, Calif., 1970-83; sr. rsch. engr. U. Tex., Austin, 1983-85; prof. aerospace engring. U. Colo., Boulder, 1985—, dir. Colo. Ctr. for Astrodynamics Rsch., 1985—. Contbr. articles to profl. jours. Recipient Exceptional Svc. medal NASA, 1980, Pub Svc. medal NASA, 1994. Fellow AIAA (Mechanics and Control of Flight award 1999), Am. Astronautical Soc. (Brouwer award 1998); mem. AAAS, NAE, Am. Geophys. Union, Oceanog. Soc., Inst. Navigation, Am. Meteorol. Soc., Am. Soc. Engring. Educators, Tau Beta Pi. Office: U Colo Campus Box 431 Boulder CO 80309-0431

BORNSTEIN, ELI, artist, sculptor; b. Milw., Dec. 28, 1922; dual citizen, U.S. and Can. m. Christina Girgulis; children: Sarah, Thea. BS, U. Wis., 1945, MS, 1954; student, Art Inst. Chgo., U. Chgo., 1943, Academie Montmartre of Fernand Leger, Paris, 1951, Academie Julian, 1952; DLitt, U. Sask., Can., 1990. Tchr. drawing, painting and sculpture Milw. Art Inst., 1943-47; tchr. design U. Wis., 1949; tchr. drawing, painting, sculpture, design and graphics U. Sask., Canada, 1950-90, prof., 1963-90, prof. emeritus, 1990—, head art dept., 1963-71. Painted in France, 1951-52, Italy, 1957, Holland, 1958; exhibited widely, 1943-; retrospective exhbn. (works 1943-64), Mendel Art Gallery, Saskatoon, 1965, one man shows, Kazimir Gallery, Chgo., 1965, 67, Saskatoon Pub. Libr., 1975, Can. Cultural Ctr., Paris, 1976, Glenbow-Alta. Inst. Art, Calgary, 1976, Mendel Art Gallery, Saskatoon, 1982, York U. Gallery, Toronto, 1983, Confedn. Ctr. Art Gallery, Charlottetown, P.E.I., 1983, Owens Art Gallery, Mt. Allison U., Sackville, N.B., 1984, Fine Arts Gallery, U. Wis.-Milw., 1984, Mendel Art Gallery, Saskatoon, 1996, Forum Gallery, NY, 2007; represented in numerous pvt. collections; executed marble sculpture now in permanent collection, Walker Art Ctr., Mpls., 1947; commns. include aluminum constrn. Sask. Tchr. Fedn. Bldg., 1956, structurist relief in painted wood and aluminum Arts and Sci. Bldg., U. Sask., 1958, structurist relief in enamelled steel Internat. Air Terminal, Winnipeg, Man., Can., 1962, four-part constructed relief Wascana Pl., Wascana Ctr. Authority, Regina, Sask., 1983, six panel structurist relief exterior Synchrotron-Can. Light Source Bldg., U. Sask, 2003, tripart hexaplane constrn. Internat. U., Bremen, Germany, 2006-07, U. Man., Winnipez, 2008; also structurist reliefs exhibited, Mus. Contemporary Art, Chgo., Herron Mus. Art, Indpls., Cranbrook Acad. Art

Galleries, Mich., High Mus., Atlanta, Can. House, Cultural Centre Gallery, London, 1983, Can. Cultural Ctr., Paris, 1983, Brussels, 1983, Bonn, 1984, Milw. Art Mus., 1984, Forum Gallery, NY, 2005-07, Internat. Art & Design Fair, Park Ave. Armory, NY, 2007, Forum Gallery, LA, 2008, Artropolis, Chgo., 2008; model of aluminium construction, 1956 and model version of structurist relief in 5 parts, 1962, now in collection, Nat. Gallery, Ottawa, Ont., model version of Wascana commn. aquired by Can. Ctr. for Arch., Montreal; others in numerous collections.; co-editor: Periodical Structure, 1958-59; founder, editor: The Structurist, ann. publ. 1960-72, biennial, 1972—; contbr. articles, principally on Structurist art to various publs. Recipient Allied Arts medal Royal Archtl. Inst. Can., 1968; hon. mention for 3 structurist reliefs 2d Biennial Internat. Art Exhbn., Colombia, S.Am., 1970. Sask. Order of Merit, 2008. Address: 3625 Saskatchewan Cres S Corman Park SK Canada S7T 1B7 Office: U Sask Box 378 RPO U Saskatoon SK Canada S7N 4J8 Office Phone: 306-966-4198. E-mail: eli.bornstein@usask.ca.

BORNSTEIN, JULIE ILENE, state agency administrator; b. San Diego, July 17, 1948; d. Leon and Pearl Bornstein; m. Steven J. Gordon, May 19, 1974; children: Loren, Brian. BA in Polit. Sci., UCLA, 1970, MA in Comm., 1971; JD, U. So. Calif., LA, 1974. Assoc. Labowe & Ventreso, LA, 1974-77; sr. ptnr. Bornstein & Gurewitz, LA, 1978-82; pvt. practice atty. Palm Desert, Calif., 1982-92; rep. 80th dist. Calif. State Assembly, Sacramento, 1992—94; chief of staff, chief dep. Office State Controller, Sacramento, 1997-99; dir. Calif. Dept. Housing and Cmty. Devel., Sacramento, 1999—. Bd. mem., pres. Women in Bus., LA, 1977—84; adj. prof. Coll. of Desert, Palm Desert, 1985—89, 1995—97, McGeorge Sch. Law, Sacramento, 1996—98; exec. bd., ctrl. com. Calif. Dem. Party, 1987—, mem. Women's Rules & Campaign Svcs. coms.; chair Calif. Dem. Women's Caucus; mem. Campaign Affordable Housing, Coachella Valley Housing Coalition, Desert AIDS Project, Palm Desert Civic Arts Com. Contbr. chapters to books to books. Active Jewish Fedn. Women's Divsn., Temple Isaiah. Mem.: Dem. Women's Assn. of the Desert. Democrat. Jewish. Office: Dept Housing and Cmty Devel 1800 Third St # 450 Sacramento CA 95814

BORNSTEIN, PAUL, medical educator, biochemist; b. Antwerp, Belgium, July 10, 1934; arrived in US, 1947, naturalized, 1952; s. Abraham and Mina (Ginsburg) B. BA, Cornell U., 1954; MD, NYU, 1958. Intern in surgery Yale-New Haven Hosp., 1958-59, intern in medicine, 1959-60, asst. resident in medicine, 1960-62; sr. fellow Arthritis Found. Pasteur Inst., Paris, 1962-63; rsch. assoc. NIH, Bethesda, Md., 1963-65, rsch. investigator, 1965-67; asst. prof. biochemistry and medicine U. Wash., 1967-69, assoc. prof., 1969-73, prof., 1973—2008, prof. emeritus Wash., 2008—, attending physician, 1968—. Mem. editl. bd. Jour. Biol. Chemistry, 1972-78, 80-85, Jour. Cell Biology, 1988-91, 94-97, Matrix Biology, 1993—2008; assoc. editor Arteriosclerosis, 1980-90, Collagen Related Rsch., 1981-88; contbr. articles to profl. jours. Served to sr. surgeon USPHS, 1963-67. Recipient Lederle Med. Faculty award USPHS, 1968, Rsch. Career Devel. award NIH, 1969, Macy Faculty Scholar award, 1975, Merit award NIH, 1989, Solomon Berson Alumni Achievement award NYU, 2004, Springer award ICCNS, 2008; Guggenheim fellow, 1985. Mem.: Internat. Soc. Matrix Biology (pres. 2001—03), Am. Soc. Matrix Biology (v.p. 2001—02, pres. 2002—03), Assn. Am. Physicians, Western Soc. Clin. Rsch., Am. Soc. Biol. Chemistry, Am. Soc. Clin. Investigation. Home: PO Box 219 Tesuque NM 87574 E-mail: bornsten@u.washington.edu.

BORODKIN, ALICE, state legislator; b. NYC; m to Arnold; children: Steven & Julie, one grandchild. State repr, 10th District, Colorado, formerly, member, Bus Affairs & Labor & Transportation & Energy Committees, currently; member, Denver Women's Comn, Women's Econ Develop Coun, Minority Bus Advisor Coun, Democratic Bus Coalition & Nat Women's Polit Caucus Metro Denver, currently.; Colorado State Representative, District 9, 2003-, member, Bus Affairs & Labor and Transportation & Energy Committees, currently, Colorado House Representative.Publ, Women's Bus Chronicle, Inc, currently. Small Bus Person of Year, Cherry Creek Chamber of Commerce, 97; Woman-Woned Bus of Year Award, Colorado Bus & Prof Women, 2000; Woman Entrepreneur of Year Award, Nat Found Women Legislature & SBA Office of Bus Ownership, 2000. Cherry Creek Chamber of Commerce; Women's Chamber of Commerce; Nat Association Women Bus Owners; Denver Metro Chamber; Alliance of Prof Women; Hispanic Chamber of Commerce. Democrat. Mailing: 200 E Colfax Room 271 Denver CO 80203 Office Phone: 303-866-2901. E-mail: alice.borodkin.house@state.co.us; aliceborodkin@qwest.net.

BOROWSKY, PHILIP, lawyer; b. Phila., Oct. 9, 1946; s. Joshua and Gertrude (Nicholson) B.; m. Judith Lee Goldwasser, Sept. 5, 1970 (div. 1996); children: Miriam Isadora, Manuel, Nora Jo; m. Victoria Culko Smith, Oct. 17, 2004. BA, UCLA, 1967; JD, U. San Francisco, 1973. Bar: Calif. Pres. and mng. ptnr. Cartwright, Slobodin, Bokelman, Borowsky, Wartnick, Moore & Harris, San Francisco, 1987-95; pres. Law Offices Philip Borowsky, Inc., San Francisco, 1996—2002; mng. ptnr. Borowsky & Hayes LLP, San Francisco, 2002—. Mem. faculty Practicing Law Inst., NYC, 1983-84; mem. adj. faculty Hastings Coll. Law, San Francisco, 1982-83, Am. Arbitration Assn., 1982—. Co-author: Unjust Dismissal and At-Will Employment, 1985; mem. bd. editl. cons. Bad Faith Law Update, 1986—2004. With US Army, 1968—70, Vietnam. Democrat. Office: Borowsky & Hayes LLP 100 Spear St STE 1640 San Francisco CA 94105-1571 Office Phone: 415-896-6800. Business E-Mail: philip.borowsky@borowsky.com.

BORSCH, FREDERICK HOUK, bishop; b. Chgo., Sept. 13, 1935; s. Reuben A. and Pearl Irene (Houk) B.; m. Barbara Edgeley Sampson, June 25, 1960; children: Benjamin, Matthew, Stuart. AB, Princeton U., 1957; MA, Oxford U., 1959; STB, Gen. Theol. Sem., 1960; PhD, U. Birmingham, 1966; DD (hon.), Seabury Western Theol. Sem., 1978, Gen. Theol. Sem., 1988; STD (hon.), Ch. Div. Sch. of Pacific, 1981, Berkley Div. Sch., New Haven, Conn., 1983. Ordained priest Episcopal Ch., 1960; curate Grace Episcopal Ch., Oak Park, Ill., 1960-63; tutor Queen's Coll., Birmingham, Eng., 1963-66; asst. prof. N.T. Seabury Western Theol. Sem., Evanston, Ill., 1966-69, assoc. prof. N.T., 1969-71; prof. N.T. Gen. Theol. Sem., NYC, 1971-72; pres., dean Ch. Divinity Sch. of the Pacific, Berkeley, Calif., 1972-81; dean of chapel, prof. religion Princeton U., 1981-88; bishop Episc. Diocese, LA, 1988—2002; interim dean Berkeley Div. Sch. at Yale, New Haven, 2002—03; prof. Lutheran Theol. Sem., Phila., 2003—. Vis. prof. Yale Div. Sch., 2003; rep. Faith and Order Commn., Nat. Coun. Chs., 1975-81; mem. exec. coun. Episc. Ch., 1981-88, Anglican Cons. Coun., 1984-88; chair bd. govs. Trinity Press Internat., 1989-2003; bd. adv. UCLA Sch. Pub. Policy & Social Rsch., 1998—, Ctr. for the Study Religion, Princeton U., 2000—; trustee Princeton U., 1998-2002. Author: The Son of Man in Myth and History, 1967, The Christian and Gnostic Son of Man, 1970, God's Parable, 1976, Introducing the Lessons of the Church Year, 1978, Coming Together in the Spirit, 1980, Power in Weakness, 1983, Jesus: The Human Life of God, 1987, Many Things in Parables, 1988, Christian Discipleship and Sexuality, 1993, Outrage and Hope, 1996; editor: Anglicanism and the Bible, 1984, The Bible's Authority in Today's Church, 1993, The Magic Word, 2001. Keasbey scholar, 1957-59 Fellow Soc. Arts, Religion and Contemporary Culture; mem. Am. Acad. Religion, Soc. Bibl. Lit., Studiorum Novi Testamenti Societas, Phi Beta Kappa Home: 2930 Corda Ln Los Angeles CA 90049-1105 E-mail: fhborsch@earthlink.net.

BORSTING, JACK RAYMOND, business administration educator; b. Portland, Oreg., Jan. 31, 1929; s. John S. and Ruth B.; m. Peggy Anne Nygard, Mar. 22, 1953; children: Lynn Carol, Eric Jeffrey. BA, Oreg. State U., 1951; MA, U. Oreg., 1952, PhD, 1959. Instr. math. Western Wash. Coll., 1953-54; teaching fellow U. Oreg., 1956-59; mem. faculty Naval Postgrad. Sch., 1959-80, prof. ops. research, chmn. dept., 1964-73, provost, acad. dean, 1974-80; asst. sec. def. (comptroller) Washington, 1980-83; dean Sch. Bus. U. Miami, Fla., 1983-88; Robert Dockson prof. and dean sch. bus. adminstrn. U. So. Calif., Los Angeles, 1988-94; E. Morgan Stanley prof. bus. adminstrn. and exec. dir. Ctr. for Telecomms. Mgmt./U. So. Calif. Marshall Sch. Bus., Los Angeles, 1994—2001, prof., 2002—05. Vis. prof. U. Colo., 1967, 69, 71; vis. disting. prof. Oreg. State U., 1968; bd. visitors Def. Sys. Mgmt. Coll., 1985-91, chmn., 1988-91; trustee Met Life Investor, 2000—, adv. bd. Naval Postgrad. Sch., 1982-86, 98—; bd. overseers Ctr. Naval Analysis, 1984-94; trustee Aerospace Corp., 1986-92, Inst. Def. Analysis, 1990-2003; bd. advisors Elec. Power Rsch. Inst., 1999—; bd. govs., lead gov. Am. Stock Exch., 2005—. Contbr. to profl. jours. Trustee Orthop. Hosp. Found., L.A., 1992—, chmn., 1996-98, chmn. bd. dirs. 1999-2002; trustee Rose Hills Found. 1996—, chmn. 2005; gov. Town Hall of Calif., 1988-94; mem. Army Sci. Bd., 2002—. Recipient Disting. Pub. Service medal Dept. Def., 1980, 82, Disting. Svc. award Oreg. State U., 1982; disting. alumni fellow U. Oreg., 2004. Fellow AAAS, Mil. Ops. Rsch. Soc. (bd. dirs. 1965-72, pres. 1970-71), Internat. Engring. Consortium, Informs; mem. Army Sci. Bd., Inst. Mgmt. Sci., Am. Statis. Soc., Ops. Rsch. Soc. Am. (mem. coun. 1969-79, sec. 1972-74, pres. 1975-76, Kimball medal 1982, Koopmans award 2000), Internat. Fedn. Ops. Rsch. Socs. (treas. 1980-88), Calif. Club, 100 Club LA, Old Capitol Club, Sigma Xi, Pi Mu Epsilon, Beta Theta Pi. Episcopalian. Office: Marshall Sch Bus DCC 217 USC Los Angeles CA 90089-0871 Home Phone: 760-346-5011; Office Phone: 213-740-0982.

BORTMAN, DAVID, lawyer; b. Detroit, Sept. 17, 1938; s. Erwin Arne and Miriam Elaine (Shapiro) B. BA, U. Mich., 1962, JD, 1965. Bar: Mich. 1965, Ill. 1971. Asst. prosecutor Wayne County, Detroit, 1965-71; staff atty. Fed. Defender, Chgo., 1971-73; trial atty. SEC, Chgo., 1974-77; sole practice Chgo., 1977-79; ptnr. Bortman, Meyer & Barasa, Chgo., 1980-90; pvt. practice LA, 1990—. Mem. Fed. Ct. Jury Instrns. Com., Chgo., 1984—85; mem. adv. bd. Air Force Office of Pub. Affairs. Chmn. telethon com. Muscular Dystrophy Assn., Chgo., 1984; pres. Met. Chgo. Air Force Cmty. Coun., 1985-88; mem. World Affairs Coun. Mem. ABA, ATLA, Acad. of TV Arts and Scis., State Bar Calif., Los Angeles County Bar Assn. (mem. lawyer referral com.), Beverly Hills Bar Assn. (entertainment law steering com.), Fed. Bar Assn. (bd. dirs. Chgo. chpt. 1985-90), Rotary, U. Mich. Club of L.A., U. Mich. Club of Chgo. (bd. govs. 1987-89), Union League of Chgo. (bd. dirs. 1986-89), Variety Club Children's Charities, Jonathan Club, Thalians Charity, West L.A. C. of C. (bd. dirs.), Century City C. of C. (bd. dirs., co-chmn. Entertainment Industry Coun.). Jewish. Home: 11908 Dorothy St Apt 102 Los Angeles CA 90049-5330 Office: 433 N Camden Dr #600 Beverly Hills CA 90210 Home Phone: 310-207-0673; Office Phone: 310-288-1980. Personal E-mail: davesq@earthlink.net.

BORWEIN, JONATHAN MICHAEL, mathematics professor; b. St. Andrews, Scotland, May 20, 1951; arrived in Can., 1963; s. David and Bessie (Flax) B.; m. Judith Diendre Scott Roots, Sept. 17, 1973; children: Rachel, Naomi, Tova. BA in Math. with honors, U. Western Ont., 1971; MSc, Jesus Coll. Oxford, 1972, DPhil, 1974; doctorate (hon.), U. Limoges, 1999. Postdoctoral fellow Dalhousie U., 1974-75, from asst. prof. to assoc. prof., 1976-82, lectr., rsch. assoc., 1975-76, assoc. prof., 1982-84, prof., 1984-93, Can. rsch. chair in distributed and collaborative tech. faculty computer sci., 2004—; from asst. prof. to assoc. prof. Carnegie-Mellon U., 1980-82; prof. U. Waterloo, 1991-93; Shrum prof. math. Simon Fraser U., Burnaby, B.C., 1993—2003, Can. rsch. chair in info. tech., 2001—03, dean sci. search com., 2003. French Nat. fellow Limoges, Prof. Invité, 1985; disting. vis. prof. Ctr. Math. Rsch., U. Montreal, 1986; Sr. Killam fellow Dalhousie U., 1987-88; visitor Technion, 1990; adj. prof. dept. math., stats. and computing sci. Dalhousie U., 1993-96; mem. math. grant selection com. Natural Scis. and Engring. Rsch. Coun., 1988-91, chmn., 1989-91, com. collaborative rsch. initiatives, 1992-96; mem. Simon Fraser Ctr. for Sys. Sci., 1992—, Simon Fraser U. Rsch. Coun., 1993; dir. Simon Fraser Ctr. Exptl. & Constructive Math., Burnaby, B.C., Can., 1993-2002; mem. WestGrid Exec. Com., 2000-05, chair 2003-04, exec. mem. at large external rels., 2004-05; chair Internat. Math. Union, 2002-; exec. com. Electronic Info. Comm., 2002-; mem. adv. com., author's panel C3.ca Assn. Inc., 2003-05, mem. bd., 2003-06, vice-chair, 2005-06, interim-chair, 2006, chair, exec., 2006-07; mem. Killam selection com., 2004-07, Senate Disciplinary Com., 2004-05, Math Awareness Com., 2004-05; mem. sci. com. Info Sci. Tech. Europe-Can., 2005-; adv. bd. Internat Ctr. Excellence Math. Edn., Melbourne, Australia, 2005-; dir. Atlantic Assn. Rsch. Math. Sci., 2006-; mem. selection com. Can. Sci. Engring. Hall of Fame, 2006-; mem. nat. adv. bd. Virtual Rschr. on Call, 2006-; leader rev. team Math. Rev. U. West Indies, 2006. Editor: (with P. Borwein) CMS Books in Mathematics, 1998-2004; assoc. editor: Set-Valued Analysis, 1992, ZOR: Mathematical Methods of Operations Research, 1994—, Ramanujan Jour., 1995, Experimental Mathematics, 1996—; mem. editl. bd. Jour. Convex Analysis, 1993—, Proc. Am. Math. Soc., 1998-2007; mem. editl. bd., hon. editor: Communications in Applied Nonlinear Analysis, 1994—; area editor: Dictionary of Theories, 1992—; editor: (with P. Borwein) CMS Series of Monographs and Advanced Texts, 1990-98; cons. editor for math. The Guinness Encyclopedia, 1989-90. Mem. collaborative rsch. grants com. NATO, 1997-1998, chair, 1998, phys. engring. sci. tech. panel, 1999-2000; mem. Can. Inst. for Sci. and Tech. Info. Bd., 1998—; active New Dem. Party, 1967—; mem. bd. govs. rep. Cans., 2004-07; mem. bd. trustees World Math. Knowledge Mgmt. Interest Group, 2005-. Recipient Atlantic Provinces Coun. on the Scis., Fraser medal for rsch. excellence, 1988; Ont. Rhodes scholar Jesus Coll., 1971-74, U.W.O. Faculty Assn. scholar, 1971, Albert O. Jeffrey scholar, 1969, Timkins Internat. Fund scholar, 1968; Australian Rsch. Grant Coun. fellow Australian Nat. U., Newcastle, 1988. Fellow Royal Soc. Can. (mem. J.M. Synge Selection Com. 2004-07), AAAS (Coxeter-James lectr. 1987, bd. dirs., rsch. com. 1985-88, chmn. constn. revision com. 1987-88); mem. Can. Math. Soc. (editl. bd., pres.-elect 1999-2000, pres. 2000-02, assoc. pub. books and rich media 2004-), Math. Assn. Am. (Chauvenet prize 1993, Merten M.H. prize 1993), Bulgarian Acad. Sci. (fgn. mem.). Business E-Mail: jborwein@cs.dal.ca.

BORYSENKO, JOAN, psychologist, biologist; b. Boston, Oct. 25, 1945; d. Edward and Lillian Zakon; children: Natalia, Justin, Andrei. BA in Biology, Bryn Mawr Coll., 1967; PhD, Harvard Med. Sch., 1972. Lic. psychologist. Asst. prof. anatomy and cellular biology Tufts U., 1973-78; instr. in medicine Harvard Med. Sch., Boston, 1981-88; pres., founder Mind/Body Health Scis., Boulder, Colo., 1988—. Author: Minding the Body, Mending the Mind, 1987, Guilt is the Teacher, Love is the Lesson, 1990, Fire in the Soul, 1993, (with Miroslav Borysenko) The Power of the Mind to Heal, 1994, Pocketful of Miracles, 1995, A Woman's Book of Life, 1996, Seven Paths to God, 1997, A Woman's Journey to God, 1999, Inner Peace for Busy People, 2001; others; mem. adv. bd. several jours. and Web sites in field. Achievements include pioneering work in the study of psychoneuroimmunology. Office: Mind/Body Health Scis 393 Dixon Rd Boulder CO 80302-9769 E-mail: luziemas@aol.com.

BOS, JOHN ARTHUR, retired aircraft manufacturing executive; b. Holland, Mich., Nov. 6, 1933; s. John Arthur and Annabelle (Castelli) B.; m. Eileen Tempest, Feb. 15, 1974; children: John, James, William, Tiffany. BS in Acctg., Calif. State Coll., Long Beach, 1971. Officer 1st Nat. Bank, Holland, Mich., 1954-61; dir. bus. mgmt. Boeing Commercial MD-80 and Mil. Airlift and Tanker Programs, Long Beach, 1962-99. CFO Classis of Calif. Reformed Ch. in Am., 1970-2003. Mem. Inst. Mgmt. Accts. (cert. mgmt. acct. 1979), Nat. Assn. Accts. Avocations: automobile marketing, golf, consulting. E-mail: bjabos@hotmail.com.

BOSCH, SAMUEL HENRY, diversified financial services company executive; b. Waupun, Wis., Dec. 24, 1934; s. Henry Samuel and Emma (Elgersma) B.; m. Corinne Marilyn Aardema, June 21, 1958; children: Michelle, Jonathan, David, Sara. BS in Physics, San Diego State U., 1961; MS in Physics, UCLA, 1962. Sr. rsch. engr. Gen. Dynamics, San Diego, 1962-69; mgr. mktg. Digital Equipment Corp., Maynard, Mass., 1969-77; dir. mktg. Sys. Engring. Lab., Ft. Lauderdale, Fla., 1977-79; mgr. mktg. Intel, Hillsboro, Oreg., 1979-81; dir. mktg. Metheus, Hillsboro, 1981-82; pres. ATM Techs., Beaverton, Oreg., 1982-86; pres., owner Peregrin Techs., Inc., Portland, Oreg., 1986—. Spkr. at industry confs. Contbr. articles to sci. jours. Served with U.S. Army, 1955-57. Mem. Concord Coalition, N.W. China Coun. Mem. Oreg. Hist. Soc. Republican. Mem. Christian Ref. Ch. Achievements include patent in ATM processing. Home: 20055 NW Nestucca Dr Portland OR 97229-2821 Office: Peregrin Techs Inc 14215 NW Science Park Dr Portland OR 97229 E-mail: boschs@peregrin.net.

BOSCH COBB, KAREN, library director; Assoc. county libr. Fresno County Pub. Libr., Calif., interim county libr., 2003—05, county libr. Calif., 2005—. Mem. adminstrv. coun. San Joaquin Valley Libr. Sys.; bd. mem. Heartland Regional Libr. Network. Mem.: Calif. Libr. Assn. (Mem. of Yr. award 2005). Office: Fresno County Pub Libr 2420 Mariposa St Fresno CA 93721 Office Phone: 559-488-3185. Office Fax: 559-488-1971. E-mail: Karen.BoschCobb@fresnolibrary.org.

BOSCO, DOUGLAS H., former Congressman, lawyer; b. Bklyn., July 28, 1946; married. BA in English, Willamette U., 1968, JD, 1971. Bar: Calif. Private practice, San Rafael, Calif., 1971—73; dir. Calif. Dept. Human Rels., 1973; exec. dir. Marin County Housing Authority, 1974—78; mem. Calif. State Assembly, 1978—82, US Congress from 1st Dist. Calif., 1983—91; of counsel Hanson Bridgett LLP, Larkspur, Calif. Past mem. Calif. Indsl. Welfare Commn., Calif. Judicial Nominations Comm. Bd. dirs. Marin County Housing Authority; bd. dirs. Marin County Consumer Protection Agy., Sonoma County Fair; fundraiser hosp. ship S.S. Hope; co-founder No. Calif. Emeritus Coll. for Sr. Citizens; mem. Calif. Wildlife Conservation Bd.; mem. Calif. State Assembly, 1978-81, Democratic caucus chmn., 1981. Democrat. Roman Catholic. Office: Hanson Bridgett LLP Ste 3E 80 Sir Francis Drake Blvd Larkspur CA 94939 Office Phone: 415-925-8400. Office Fax: 415-541-9366. Business E-Mail: dbosco@hansonbridgett.com.

BOSE, ANJAN, electrical engineering educator, academic administrator; b. Calcutta, India, June 2, 1946; s. Amal Nath and Anima (Guha) B.; m. Frances Magdelen Pavlas, Oct. 30, 1976; children: Rajesh Paul, Shonali Marie, Jahar Robert. B Tech with honors, Indian Inst. Tech., Kharagpur, 1967; MS, U. Calif., Berkeley, 1968; PhD, Iowa State U., 1974. Systems planning engr. Con Edison Co., NYC, 1968-70; instr., research assoc. Iowa State U., Ames, 1970-74; postdoctoral fellow IBM Sci. Ctr., Palo Alto, Calif., 1974-75; asst. prof. elec. engring. Clarkson U., Potsdam, N.Y., 1975-76; mgr. EMSD, Control Data Corp., Mpls., 1976-81; prof. elec. engring. Ariz. State U., Tempe, 1981-93; disting. prof. Wash. State U., Pullman, 1993—, dir. Sch. Elec. Engring. and Computer Sci., 1993-98, dean Coll. Engring. and Architecture, 1998—2005, regents prof., 2006—. V.p. Power Math Assocs., Tempe, 1981-84; program dir. power sys. NSF, Washington, 1988-89. Contbr. over 100 articles to engring. jours. Fellow: IEEE; mem.: Nat. Acad. Engring. Home Phone: 509-332-5114. Business E-Mail: bose@wsu.edu.

BOSKIN, MICHAEL JAY, economics professor; b. NYC, Sept. 23, 1945; s. Irving and Jean B.; m. Chris Dornin, Oct. 20, 1981. AB with highest honors, U. Calif., Berkeley, 1967, MA in Econs., 1968, PhD in Econs., 1971. Asst. prof. economics Stanford U., 1970-75, assoc. prof., 1976-78, prof., 1978—86, dir. Ctr. for Econ. Policy Rsch., 1981—88, Wohlford prof. economics, 1987-89, Tully M. Friedman prof. economics, 1993—; chmn. Coun. Econ. Advisors Exec. Office of the Pres., Washington, 1989-93; pres., CEO Boskin & Co., Menlo Park, Calif., 1993—. Vis. prof. Harvard U., Cambridge, Mass., 1977-78; disting. faculty fellow Yale U., 1993, scholar Am. Enterprise Inst., 1993—; rsch. assoc. Nat. Bur. Econ. Rsch., 1976—; sr. fellow Hoover Instn., Stanford U., 1993-; bd. dirs. Oracle Corp., 1994-, Exxon Mobil Corp., 1996-, Airtouch Comm., Inc., 1996-99, Vodafone Group PLC, 1999-2008; chmn. Congl. Adv. Commn. on the Consumer Price Index, 1995-97; advisor, cons. numerous govt. agencies, pvt. businesses. Author: Too Many Promises: The Uncertain Future of Social Security, 1986, Reagan and the Economy: Successes, Failures Unfinished Agenda, 1987, Frontiers of Tax Reform, 1996, Capital Technology and Growth, 1996, Toward a More accurate Measure of the Cost of Living, 1996; contbr. articles to profl. jours., popular media. Mem. several philanthropic bds. dirs. Faculty Rsch. fellow Mellon Found., 1973; recipient Abramson award for Outstanding

Rsch. Nat. Assn. Bus. Economists, 1987, Dean's award for Disting. Teaching, 1988, W.S. Johnson award for Contributions to free Enterprise, Nat. Fedn. Independent Bus., 1990, Pub. Servant of the Year award U Calif. Alumni Assn., 1990, Medal of the Pres. Italian Republic, 1991, Disting. Pub. Svc. award Stanford U., 1993, Disting. Teaching award Stanford U., 1998, Adam Smith prize Nat. Assn. Bus. Economists, 1998. Fellow Nat. Assn. Bus. Econs. (Presdl. medal Italian Republic, Adam Smith prie 1998). Avocations: tennis, skiing, reading, theater, golf. Office: Stanford U 213 HHMB Stanford CA 94305-6010 E-mail: boskin@hoover.stanford.edu.

BOSL, PHILLIP L., retired lawyer; b. Feb. 27, 1945; BA, U. Calif., Santa Barbara, 1968; JD, U. So. Calif., 1975. Bar: Calif. 1975. Ptnr. Gibson, Dunn & Crutcher LLP, LA, 1983—2005; ret., 2005. Mem. U. So. Calif. Law Rev., 1973-75. Officer USCG, 1969-72. Mem. ABA, LA County Bar Assn., Assn. Bus. Trial Lawyers, Securities Industry and Fin. Markets Assn. (compliance and legal divsn.), Nat. Futures Assn. (arbitrator), Financial Industry Regulatory Authority (arbitrator), Order of Coif. Home Phone: 562-597-2600; Office Phone: 213-713-4885. Personal E-mail: pbosl@earthlink.net.

BOSMAJIAN, HAIG ARAM, speech communication educator; b. Fresno, Calif., Mar. 26, 1928; s. Aram and Aurora (Keosheyan) B.; m. Hamida Just, Feb. 27, 1957; 1 child, Harlan. BA, U. Calif., Berkeley, 1949; MA, U. of Pacific, 1951; PhD, Stanford U., 1960. Instr. U. Idaho, Moscow, 1959-61; asst. prof. U. Conn., Storrs, 1961-65; prof. speech comm. U. Wash., Seattle, 1965—. Author: Language of Oppression (Orwell award), 1983: editor: Censorship, Libraries and the Law, 1983; Justice Douglas, 1980, Freedom of Speech, 1983, First Amendment in the Classroom Series, 1987: vol. 1, The Freedom to Read, 1987, vol. II, The Freedom of Religion, 1987, vol. III, Freedom of Expression, 1988, vol. IV, Academic Freedom, 1989, vol. V, Freedom to Publish, 1989, Metaphor and Reason in Judicial Opinions, 1992, The Freedom Not to Speak, 1999, Burning Books, 2006. Recipient Bicentennial of the Bill of Rights award Western States Communication Assn., 1991. Office Phone: 206-543-2660.

BOSSON, RICHARD CAMPBELL, state supreme court justice; b. Balt., Mar. 19, 1944; s. Albert D. and Elizabeth S. (Schaeffer) B.; m. Gloria Candelaria, Jan. 9, 1971; children: Christopher, Monica. BA, Wesleyan U., Middletown, Conn., 1966; JD, Georgetown U., 1969; M in Jud. Process, U. Va., 1998. Bar: Conn. 1969, N. Mex. 1970, US Dist. Ct. N. Mex. 1970; cert. soccer referee, 1992—. Atty. Legal Aid Soc. of Albuquerque, 1970-73; staff atty. Mexican Am. Legal Def. Fund, 1974, Latin Am. Tchg. Fellow, Fletcher Sch., Bogota, Colombia, 1975; chief of civil div. Atty. Gen. Office, Santa Fe, 1976-78; sr. ptnr. Bosson & Canepa P.A., Santa Fe, 1980—94; judge N.Mex. Ct. of Appeals, 1994—2002; justice N.Mex. Supreme Ct., 2002—, chief justice, 2005—. Mem. constl. revision commn., 1994—95; soccer referee Lead H.S. Candidate Dem. nomination for Atty. Gen of N. Mex., 1978. Reginald Heber Smith fellow. Mem. N.Mex. Trial Lawyers Assn. (bd. dirs. 1980-93), Nat. Assn. Bond Lawyers, Am. Trial Lawyers Assn. Office Phone: 505-827-4892. Business E-Mail: suprcb@nmcourts.com, supbbr@nmcourts.com.

BOSTROM, SUSAN L., marketing executive; b. 1960; 3 children. BS, U. Ill.; MBA, Stanford U. Acct. exec. AT&T Corp., 1982; with McKinsey & Co., Nat. Semiconductor; sr. v.p. global mktg. and strategic planning FTP Software; with Cisco Systems, Inc., San Jose, Calif., 1997—, v.p. Internet bus. solutions, 1998—2000, sr. v.p., 2000—07, chief mktg. officer worldwide govt. affairs, 2006—, exec. v.p., 2007—. Exec. sponsor women's initiative Cisco Systems, Inc., 2001—04. Bd. dirs. Varian Med. Systems, 2004—, Stanford Hospitals and Clinics; mem. adv. bd. Stanford Inst. Econ. Policy Rsch. Named one of Best Marketers, BtoB Mag., 2008. Office: Cisco Systems Inc 170 W Tasman Dr San Jose CA 95134

BOSWELL, JAMES DOUGLAS, medical research executive; b. Tulsa, Feb. 12, 1942; m. Pamela Scott; children: Megan, Melanie Student, U. Okla., 1960-61; BA, U. Tulsa, 1964, MA, 1966; PhD, Madison U., 2004. Indsl. relations rep. Trans World Airlines, 1966-68; dir. placement Skelly Oil Co., 1968-72, mgr. employee and pub. relations, 1972-75, gen. mgr. adminstrn., 1975-77; corp. mgr. human resources Getty Oil Co., 1977-81; v.p. employee and pub. relations L.A. Times, 1981-91; CEO House Ear Inst., LA, 1991—, trustee, 1995—. Bd. dirs. Employers Group; pres. Skelly Oil Found., Tulsa, 1974-78, Getty Oil Co. Found., 1978-79. Bd. dirs. L.A. Boys and Girls Club, v.p., 1985; bd. dirs. L.A. Theatre Ctr., 1988-90, L.A. chpt. ARC; bd. dirs. L.A. Jr. Achievement, 1982-91, vice chmn. human resources, 1986; fellow Nat. Health Found., 1992, San Marino Cmty. Ch. Found., 1992-95; mem. Econ. Round Table, 1993, sec.-treas., 1995-96. Mem. Am. Soc. Personnel Adminstrn., Am. Psychol. Assn., Newspaper Personnel Relations Assn., Am. Newspaper Assn. (labor and personnel relations com. 1982-91). Avocations: tennis, skiing, golf. Office: House Ear Inst 2100 W 3rd St 5th Fl Los Angeles CA 90057-1922 Home: 1123 S Orange Grove Blvd Pasadena CA 91105-3314

BOSWELL, SUSAN G., lawyer; b. El Paso, Tex., June 26, 1945; BA, U. Ariz., 1972, JD, 1976. Bar: Ariz. 1977, Nev. 1992. Dir. Tuscon (Ariz.) office Quarles, Brady, Streich, Lang, PC (formerly known as Streich & Lang P.C.), Phoenix, 1987—. Instr., faculty mem. Nat. Inst. Trail Advocacy, 1991; bd. vis. U. Ariz. Coll. of Law. Fellow Am. Coll. Bankruptcy; mem. State Bar of Ariz. (peer review com., assistance com.), Ariz. Women Lawyers Assn, Phi Kappa Phi. Office: Quarles Brady Streich Lang PC 1 S Church Ave Ste 1700 Tucson AZ 85701-1630

BOSWORTH, BRUCE LEIGHTON, school administrator, educator, consultant; b. Buffalo, Mar. 22, 1942; s. John Wayman and Alice Elizabeth Rodgers; children: David, Timothy, Paul, Sheri, Skyler. BA, U. Denver, 1964; MA, U. No. Colo., 1970; EdD, Walden U., 1984. Elem. tchr. Littleton (Colo.) Pub. Schs., 1964-67, 70-81; bldg. prin. East Smoky Sch. Divsn. 54, Valleyview, Alta., Can., 1967-70; pres., tchr. St. Michael's-of-the-Mountains Sch., Littleton, 1981—. Adoption cons. hard-to-place children; ednl. cons. spl. needs children Holy Name Parish. Mem. ASCD, Coun. Exceptional Children, Masons, Shriners, York Rite. Home and Office: PO Box 1154 Littleton CO 80160-1154 Home Phone: 303-781-0749. Personal E-mail: misterbura@yahoo.com.

BOSWORTH, KATE, actress; b. LA, Jan. 2, 1983; Actor: (films) The Horse Whisperer, 1998, Remember the Titans, 2000, The Newcomers, 2000, Blue Crush, 2002, The Rules of Attraction, 2002, Wonderland, 2003, Advantage Hart, 2003, Win a Date with Tad Hamilton, 2004, Beyond the Sea, 2004, Bee Season, 2005, Superman Returns, 2006, The Girl in the Park, 2007, 21, 2008; (TV series) Young Americans, 2000. Recipient Women in Hollywood Tribute award, Elle Mag., 2007. Mem.: Nat. Honor Soc. Office: United Talent Agy 5th Fl 9560 Wilshire Blvd Beverly Hills CA 90212

BOSWORTH, THOMAS LAWRENCE, architect, retired educator; b. Oberlin, Ohio, June 15, 1930; s. Edward Franklin and Imogene (Rose) B.; m. Abigail Lumbard, Nov. 6, 1954 (div. Nov. 1974); children: Thomas Edward, Nathaniel David; m. Elaine R. Pedigo, Nov. 23, 1974; stepchildren: Robert Haden Pedigo, Kevin Ian Pedigo. BA, Oberlin Coll., 1952, MA, 1954; postgrad., Princeton U., 1952-53, Harvard U., 1956-57; MArch, Yale U., 1960; PhD Honoris Causa (hon.), Kobe U., Japan, 2003. Draftsman Gordon McMaster AIA, Cheshire, Conn., summer 1957-58; resident planner Tunnard & Harris Planning Cons., Newport, RI, summer 1959; designer, field supr. Eero Saarinen & Assocs., Birmingham, Mich., 1960-61, Hamden, Conn., 1961-64; individual practice architecture Providence, 1964-68, Seattle, 1968—2004; ptnr. Bosworth Hoedemaker, Architecture and Planning, Seattle, 2004—; asst. instr. architecture Yale U., 1962-65, vis. lectr., 1965-66; asst. prof. R.I. Sch. Design, 1964-66, assoc. prof., head dept., 1966-68; prof. architecture U. Wash., Seattle, 1968-98, chmn. dept., 1968-72, dir. multidisciplinary program Rome, 1984-86, prof. emeritus, 1998—; chief architecture Peace Corps Tng. Program, Tunisia, Brown U., summers 1965-66. Vis. lectr. Kobe U., Japan, Oct., 1982, Nov., 1990, Apr., 1993, May, 1995, June, 1998; Pietro Belluschi disting. vis. prof. U. Oreg., 1996; dir. arch. in Rome program U. Wash., Rome, 1996, prof. 2000, 2003. Bd. dirs. N.W. Inst. Arch. and Urban Studies, Italy, 1983-90, pres., 1983-85; dir. Pilchuck Glass Sch., Seattle, 1977-80, trustee, 1980-91, adv. coun., 1993—; mem. Seattle Model Cities Land Use Rev. Bd., 1969-70, Tech. Com. Site Selection Wash. Multi-Purpose Stadium, 1970, Medina Planning Commn., 1972-74, steering adv. com. King County Stadium, 1972-74; chmn. King County (Wash.) Environ. Devel. Commn., 1972-74, King County Policy Devel. Commn., 1974-77; bd. dirs. Arcade Mag., 1988-2002, pres. 1988-2000; bd. mgrs. YMCA Camping Svcs., 1998-2002; adv. bd. U. Wash Rome Ctr., 1999—. With U.S. Army, 1954-56. Recipient 20 design awards; Winchester Traveling fellow Yale U., 1960, Assoc. fellow Ezra Stiles Coll. Yale U., Mid-career fellow in arch. Am. Acad. in Rome, 1980-81; vis. scholar Am. Acad., Rome, spring 1988, fall 2007. Fellow AIA (Seattle medalist 2003); mem. Monday Club (Seattle), Bohemian Club (San Francisco), Tau Sigma Delta. Home: 2411 25th Ave E Seattle WA 98112-2610

BOTCHAN, MICHAEL R., molecular biologist, biochemist; b. Bklyn., July 13, 1945; BA in Biology, NYU, 1967; PhD in Biophysics, U. Calif., Berkeley, 1972. Postdoctoral rsch. Cold Spring Harbor Lab., NY, 1972—74, sr. scientist, 1974—80; assoc. prof. dept. molecular biology U. Calif., Berkeley, 1980—94, prof. dept. molecular and cell biology, 1984—. Adj. assoc. prof. dept. microbiol. SUNY, Stony Brook, 1977—79; mem. adv. com. cell biology and microbiol. Am. Cancer Soc., 1978—81, mem. adv. com. nucleic acids and proteins, 1986—90, postdoctoral fellowship com. Calif. divsn., 1986—89; mem. virology study sect. NIH, 1986—91; mem. sci. adv. com. Damon Runyon-Walter Winchell Cancer Rsch. Fund, 1989—92, chmn. sci. adv. com., 1992; mem. sci. rev. bd. Howard Hughes Med. Inst. Contbr. articles to sci. jours.; mem. editl. bd.: Jour. Virology, 1984—90, Molecular and Cellular Biology, 1985—91, Oncogene, 1987—91; editor: Plasmid, 1986. Recipient NIH Merit award, 1987, 2004. Fellow: AAAS, Am. Acad. Arts & Scis.; mem.: NAS. Achievements include research in DNA virus transformation; eukaryotic DNA replication and transcription; recombination in somatic cells. Office: Dept Molecular and Cell Biology U Calif 401 Barker Hall Number 3204 Berkeley CA 94720-3204 Business E-Mail: mbotchan@berkeley.edu.

BOTELHO, BRUCE MANUEL, mayor, retired state attorney general; b. Juneau, Alaska, Oct. 6, 1948; s. Emmett Manuel and Harriet Iowa (Tieszen) Botelho; m. Guadalupe Alvarez Breton, Sept. 23, 1988; children: Alejandro Manuel, Adriana Regina. Student, U. Heidelberg, Federal Republic of Germany, 1970; BA, Willamette U., 1971, JD, 1976. Bar: Alaska 1976, U.S. Ct. Appeals (9th cir.) 1976, U.S. Supreme Ct. 1979. Asst. atty. gen. State of Alaska, Juneau, 1976—83, 1987—89, dep. commr., acting commr. Dept. of Revenue, 1983-86; mayor City, Borough of Juneau, 1988—91, 2003—, dep. atty. gen., 1991—94, 2003—; atty. gen. State of Alaska, 1994—2002. Chmn. Alaska Resources Corp., 1984—86; exec. com. Conf. of Western Attys. Gen., 1997—2002. Editor: Willamette Law Jour., 1975—76; contbr. articles to profl. jours. Pres. Juneau Human Rights Commn., 1978—80, Alaska Coun. Am. Youth Hostels, 1979—81, Juneau Arts and Humanities Coun., 1981—83; pres. S.E. Alaska Area Coun. Boy Scouts Am., 1991—93, 2001—05, commr. S.E. Alaska Area Coun., 1993—2000, exec. com. Gt. Alaska Coun., 2006—; pres. Juneau World Affairs Coun., 2000—; chmn. Gov.'s Conf. on Youth and Justice, 1995—96, Gov. Task Force on Confidentiality of Childrens Procs., 1998—2002; trustee Alaska Children's Trust, 1996—2000, Alaska Permanent Fund, 2000—02; co-chmn. Alaska Justice Assessment Commn., 1997—2002; active Commn. for Justice Across the Atlantic, 1999—; chmn. Alaska Criminal Justice Coun., 2000—02; fed. commr. Alaska Rural Jursice and Law Enforcement Commn., 2004—; Assembly mem. Borough of Juneau, 1983—86; chmn. adminstrv. law sect. Alaska Bar Assn., 1981—82; bd. dirs. Alaska Econ. Devel. Coun., 1985—87, Found. for Social Innovations, Alaska, 1990—93, Alaska Mcpl. League, 2003—; bd. mem. Alaska Immigration Justice Project, 2005—; bd. dirs. Tongass Futures Roundtable, 2006—. Recipient Silver Beaver award, Boy Scouts Am., 2000, Jay Rabinowitz Pub. Svc. award, Alaska Bar Assn., 2007; named Pro Bono Atty. of Yr., 2005. Mem.: Nat. Assn. Attys. Gen. (exec. com. 1998—2002). Democrat. Methodist. Avocation: dance. Office Phone: 907-506-5240. Business E-Mail: botelho@gci.net, mayor@ci.juneau.ak.us.

BOTSAI, ELMER EUGENE, architect, educator, retired dean; b. St. Louis, Feb. 1, 1928; s. Paul and Ita May (Cole) Botsai; m. Patricia L. Keegan, Aug. 28, 1955; children: Donald Rolf, Kurt Gregory; m. Sharon K. Kaiser, Dec. 5, 1981; 1 child, Kiana Michelle. AA, Sacramento Jr. Coll., 1950; AB, U. Calif., Berkeley, 1954; D of Architecture, U. Hawaii, 2000. Registered architect, Hawaii, Calif. Draftsman, then asst. to arch. So. Pacific Co., San Francisco, 1953-57; designer H.K. Ferguson Co., San Francisco, 1955; project arch. Anshen & Allen Arch., San Francisco, 1957-63; prin. Botsai, Overstreet & Rosenberg, Arch. and Planners, San Francisco, 1963—79, Elmer E. Botsai FAIA, Honolulu, 1979—; of counsel Groupe 70 Internat., 1998—2008; chmn. dept. arch. U. Hawaii, Manoa, 1976-80, dean Sch. Arch., 1980-90, prof., 1990-99, prof. emeritus, 2000—. Lectr. U. Calif., Berkeley, 1976, dir. Nat. Archtl. Accrediting Bd., 1972-73, 79; adminstrv. and tech. cons. Wood Bldg. Rsch. Ctr., U. Calif., 1985-90, mem. profl. preparation project com. at U. Mich., Ann Arbor, 1986-87; co-author water infiltration seminar series for Bldg. Owners and Mgr. Rsch. Ctr., 1986-87; chief investigator effects of Guatemalan earthquake for NSF and AIA, Washington, 1976; steering com. on structural failures Nat. Bur. Standards, 1982-84; chmn., dir. gen. svc. Adv. Com. State of Calif. Co-author: Architects and Earthquake, Rsch. Needs, 1976, ATC Seismic Standards for Nat. Bur. of Standards, 1976, Arch. and Earthquakes: A Primer, 1977, Seismic Design, 1978, Wood-Detailing for Performance, 1990, Wood as a Building Material, 2d edit., 1991; contbr. articles and reports to profl. jour.; prin. works include expansion of Nuc. Weapons Tng. Facility at Lemoore Naval Air Sta., Calif., LASH Terminal Port Facility Archtl. Phase, San Francisco, Incline Village (Nev.) Country Club, 1365 Columbus Ave. Bldg., San Francisco, modernization Stanford Ct. Hotel, San Francisco; monument area constrn. several Calif. cemeteries. With US Army, 1946—48. Recipient Cert. Honor Fedn. Archtl. Coll. Mex. Republic, 1984, Disting. Alumni award U. Hawaii, 2005; named to Wisdom Hall of Fame, 1998; NSF grantee for investigative workshop project, San Diego, 1974-80, Ernest H. Hara award for outstanding lifetime Svc. to the profession of Architecture, 1999, medal of hon. Am. Inst. Architects, Hawaii, 2003, Disting. Alumni award, U. Hawaii, 2005. Fellow AIA (bd. dir., 1966-71, treas. No. Calif. chpt. 1968-69, pres. 1971, nat. v.p., 1975-76, nat. pres. 1978, pres. Hawaii 1985); hon. fellow Royal Can. Inst. Arch., NZ Inst. Arch. (hon.), Royal Australian Inst. Arch. (1st arch., 1st Am.), La Societe de Arquitectos Mexicano; mem. Archtl. Sec. Assn. (hon.), Soc. Wood Sci. and Tech., Internat. Conf. Bldg. Ofcl. Home: 321 Wailupe Cir Honolulu HI 96821-1524

BOTTJER, DAVID JOHN, earth science and biology educator; b. NYC, Oct. 3, 1951; s. John Henry and Marilyn (Winter) B.; m. Sarah Ranney Wright, July 26, 1973. BS, Haverford Coll., 1973; MA, SUNY, Binghamton, 1976; PhD, Ind. U., 1978. NRC postdoctoral rsch. assoc. US Geol. Survey, Washington, 1978-79; asst. prof. dept. geol. sci. U. So. Calif., LA, 1979-85, assoc. prof. dept. geol. sci., 1985-91, prof. dept. earth sci., 1991—, prof. dept. biol. sci., 2003—, chair dept. earth sci., 2006—. Rsch. assoc. Los Angeles County Mus. Natural History, 1979—; vis. scientist Field Mus. Natural History, Chgo., 1986; Paleontol. Soc. Disting. lectr., 1992-93; mem. Nat. Sci. Found. panel on earth systems history, 1997-99; sr. fellow UCLA Ctr. for the Study of Evolution and Origin of Life, 2000; co-dir. USC-LACMNH Ctr. Chinese Fossil Discoveries, 2008-. Editor Palaios, 1989-96; assoc. editor Cretaceous Rsch., 1988-91; mem. editl. bd. Geology, 1984-89, 95-2000, Hist. Biology, 1988-93; co-editor Columbia U. Press Critical Moments and Perspectives in Paleobiology and Earth History (book series), 1990—; editor-in-chief Palaeo-3, 2000—. Recipient Disting. Scientist award, Ctr. for Study of Evolution and Origin of Life, UCLA, 2002. Fellow AAAS, Geol. Soc. Am., Geol. Soc. London, Paleontol. Soc. (pres. 2004-06); mem. Soc. Sediment Geology (pres. Pacific sect. 2001-02), Internat. Paleontology Assn. Office: U So Calif Dept Earth Scis Los Angeles CA 90089-0740 Office Phone: 213-740-6100. Business E-Mail: dbottjer@usc.edu.

BOUCEK, JENNY, professional basketball coach; b. Nashville, Dec. 20, 1973; B with high honors in Sports Medicine & Sports Mgmt., U. Va., 1997. Guard WNBA Cleve. Rockers, 1997; profl. basketball player Icelandic Basketball League; asst. coach WNBA Washington Mystics, 1999—2000, WNBA Miami Sol, 2000—02, WNBA Seattle Storm, 2003—05; advanced scout NBA Seattle SuperSonics, 2005—06; head coach WNBA Sacramento Monarchs, 2006—. Head coach WNBA Western Conf. All-Star Team, 2007. Named Atlantic Coast Conf. All-Star Team, 1994, GTE Academic All-Am., 1995, 96. Avocations: basketball, volleyball, tennis. Office: Sacramento Monarchs ARCO Arena One Sports Pky Sacramento CA 95834

BOUCHER, HAROLD IRVING, retired lawyer; b. Chico, Calif., June 27, 1906; s. Charles Augustus and Nina Eugenia (Knickerbocker) B.; m. Beula Blair Davis, Apr. 11, 1931. LLB, JD, U. Calif., Berkeley, 1930. Bar: Calif. 1930. Assoc. to adv. ptnr. Pillsbury, Madison & Sutro, Attys. at Law, San Francisco, 1934-93, ret. ptnr., 1993. Named to Order of British Empire Queen Elizabeth II of England, 1972. Fellow Am. Bar, Am. Coll. Probate (regent 1966), Am. Coll. Counsel (pres. 1967-68); mem. ABA, State Bar Calif., Old Capital Club.

BOUDART, MICHEL, chemical engineer, consultant, educator; b. Belgium, June 18, 1924; came to U.S., 1947, naturalized, 1957; s. Francois and Marguerite (Swolfs) B.; m. Marina D'Haese, Dec. 27, 1948; children: Mark, Baudouin, Iris, Philip. BS, U. Louvain, Belgium, 1944, MS, 1947; PhD, Princeton U., 1950; D honoris causa, U. Liège, U. Notre Dame, U. Nancy, U. Ghent. Research asso. James Forrestal Research Ctr., Princeton, 1950-54; mem. faculty Princeton U., 1954-61; prof. chem. engring. U. Calif., Berkeley, 1961-64, adj. prof. chem. engring., 1994—; prof. chem. engring. and chemistry Stanford U., 1964-80, Keck prof. engring., 1980-94, Keck prof. engring. emeritus, 1994—. Co-founder Catalytica, Inc.; Humble Oil Co. lectr., 1958; AIChE lectr., 1961; Sigma Xi nat. lectr., 1965; chmn. Gordon Rsch. Conf. Catalysis, 1962. Author: Kinetics of Chemical Processes, 1968, (with G. Djéga-Mariadassou) Kinetics of Heterogenous Catalytic Reactions, 1983; editor: (with J.R. Anderson) Catalysis: Science and Technology, 11 vols., 1981-96, (with Marina Boudart and René Bryssinck) Modern Belgium, 1990; mem. adv. editl. bd. Catal. Letters, 1989—, Catalysis Rev., 1968—, Jour. Molecular Catalysis, 1995—, Cattech, 1996—. Recipient Curtis-McGraw rsch. award Am. Soc. Engring. Edn., 1962, R.H. Wilhelm award in chem. reaction engring., 1974, Chem. Pioneer award Am. Inst. Chemists, 1991; Belgium-Am. Ednl. Found. fellow, 1948, Procter fellow, 1949; Fairchild disting. scholar Calif. Tech. Inst., 1995. Fellow AAAS, Am. Acad. Arts. and Scis., Calif. Acad. Scis.; mem. NAS, NAE, Am. Chem. Soc. (Kendall award 1977, E.V. Murphee award in indsl. and engring. chemistry 1985), Catalysis Soc., Am. Inst. Chem. Engrs., Chem. Soc., Académie Royale de Belgique (fgn. assoc.), French Nat. Acad. Pharmacy (fgn.). Home: 228 Oak Grove Ave Atherton CA 94027-2218 Office: Stanford U Dept Chem Engring Stanford CA 94305 Office Fax: 650-723-9780.

BOUGHEY, JAMES DENNIS, lawyer; b. Chgo., Nov. 20, 1943; s. William James and Helen Louise (Bybee) B.; m. Susannah Clark, Feb. 18, 1980 (div. June 1985); children: Lindsay, Conor; m. Martha J. Bodor, Sept. 3, 1989. BA, U. Mich., 1966; JD, U. Ill., 1969. Bar: Calif., US Dist. Ct. Calif., US Ct. Claims, US Ct. Internat. Trade, US Ct. Appeals (9th and 5th cirs.), US Supreme Ct. Assoc. Dorr, Cooper & Hays, San Francisco, 1970-74, ptnr., 1974-85, mng. ptnr., 1985-89, Boughey, Garvie & Busner, San Francisco, 1990—; ptnr. Wilson, Elser, Moskowitz, Edelman & Dicker LLP, San Francisco. Chmn. Cultural Affairs Commn., San Rafael, Calif. Mem. ABA, Calif. Bar Assn., Assn. Maritime Underwriters of San Francisco (assoc.), Average Adjuster Assn. of US (assoc.), Average Adjuster Assn. of UK (assoc.), Maritime Law Assn. of US, Hawaii State Bar Assn., Fed. Bar

Assn., Assn. Defense Counsel of No. Calif., Internat. Assn. Defense Counsel, Defense Rsch. Inst., Bar Assn. San Francisco, World Trade Assn. of San Francisco C. of C., World Trade Club of San Francisco, San Francisco Marine Exchange, Propeller Club of Port of Golden Gate. Avocations: scuba diving, boating. Home: 80 Oakmont Ct San Rafael CA 94901-1235 Office: Wilson, Elser, Moskowitz, Edelman & Dicker LLP 14 Fl 650 California St San Francisco CA 94108 Office Phone: 415-433-0990 3036. Office Fax: 415-434-1370. E-mail: bougheyj@wemed.com.

BOUGHTON, LESLEY D., library director; b. New Haven, Jan. 21, 1945; d. Robert and Marjorie (Anderson) D.; m. Charles E. Boughton, Sept. 5, 1964 (dec. 1991); children: Michael, James, Gregg. AB, Conn. Coll., 1971; MLS, So. Conn. State U., 1978. Dir. Platte County Library, Wheatland, Wyo., 1980-88, Carbon County Library, Rawlins, Wyo., 1988-93, Natrona County Pub. Library, Casper, Wyo., 1993—99; state libr. Wyo. State Libr., Cheyenne, 1999—. Mem. Gov's. Telecommunications Coun., Wyo., 1994—. Mem. ALA (chpt. councilor 1988, 91), Wyo. Library Assn. (pres. 1985, Disting. Svc. award 1991), Chief Officers of State Libr. Agys. Office: Wyo State Libr 516 S Greeley Hwy Cheyenne WY 82002 Office Phone: 307-777-5911. Business E-Mail: lbough@state.wy.us.

BOUKER, INA B., elementary school educator; b. Manokotak, Alaska; m. John Bouker. BA, Univ. Hawaii, Hilo. Tchr. Dillingham City Schools, Alaska, 1984—; now tchr. Dillingham Elem. Sch., Alaska. Named Alaska Tchr. of Yr., 2007; named one of Summit Educators of Yr., First Alaskans Inst., 2002. Mem.: Bristol Bay Native Corp. Office: Dillingham Elem Sch PO Box 170 Dillingham AK 99576 Business E-Mail: ina@dlgsd.org.

BOUKNIGHT, LON (J.A. BOUKNIGHT JR.), lawyer, retired utilities executive; b. Florence, SC, Apr. 9, 1944; s. J.A. and Frances Lea (Huff) B.; m. Deborah Anne Harmon, Jan. 3, 1981; children: Robert Harmon, Amanda Alison. BA in Hist., Wofford Coll., 1965; JD, Duke U., 1968. Bar: NC 1968, DC 1973. Ptnr. Tally, Tally & Bouknight, Fayetteville, NC, 1968-73, Newman & Holtzinger, P.C., Washington, 1973-94, Steptoe & Johnson, LLP, Washington, 1994—2005, chmn., 1998—2004; gen. counsel, exec. v.p. Edison Internat., Rosemead, Calif., 2005—08. Contbr. articles to pub. utilities jours. Mem. ABA (chmn. antitrust com. pub. utility law sect. 1985), Fed. Energy Bar Assn. Avocations: golf, baseball, reading.

BOULANGER, DONALD RICHARD, financial services executive; b. Berlin, NH, May 28, 1944; s. Romeo James and Jeanette A. (Valliere) B.; m. Wendy Elwell, Nov. 26, 1990 (div. Sept. 1996). BA, Harvard U., 1966, PhD, 1972. V.p. First Interstate Bank, LA, 1972-76, Kaufman and Broad, LA, 1976-80, sr. v.p. Los Angeles, 1983-89; v.p. Transam. Corp., San Francisco, 1981-83; exec. v.p. Far West Savs., Newport Beach, Calif., 1983; pres. Nat. Deposit Fin. Corp., Universal City, Calif., 1989—. Bd. dirs. Nat. Deposit Life Ins. Co., Phoenix, Citadel Holding Corp, Am. Stock Exch., Glendale, Calif. Republican. Roman Catholic. Avocation: scuba diving. Office: Nat Deposit Fin Corp 10 Universal City Plz North Hollywood CA 91608-1009

BOULDEN, JUDITH ANN, judge; b. Salt Lake City, Dec. 28, 1948; d. Douglas Lester and Emma Ruth (Robertson) Boulden; m. Alan Walter Barnes, Nov. 7, 1982; 1 child, Dorian Lisa. BA, U. Utah, 1971, JD, 1974. Bar: Utah 1974, U.S. Dist. Ct. Utah 1974. Law clk. to A. Sherman Christianson U.S. Cts., Salt Lake City, 1974; assoc. Roe & Fowler, Salt Lake City, 1975-81, McKay Burton Thurman & Condie, Salt Lake City, 1982-83; trustee Chpt. 7, Salt Lake City, 1976-82, Standing Chpt. 12, Salt Lake City, 1987-88, Standing Chpt. 13, Salt Lake City, 1979-88; sr. ptnr. Boulden & Gillman, Salt Lake City, 1983-88; U.S. Bankruptcy judge U.S. Cts., Salt Lake City, 1988—. Mem. Utah Bar Assn. Avocations: gardening, golf.

BOULEY, JOSEPH RICHARD, pilot; b. Fukuoka, Japan, Jan. 7, 1955; came to U.S., 1955; s. Wilfrid Arthur and Minori Cecelia (Naraki) B.; m. Sara Elizabeth Caldwell, July 6, 1991; children: Denise Marie, Janice Elizabeth, Eleanor Catherine, Rachel Margaret, David Caldwell, Caroline Minori. BA in English, U. Nebr., 1977; MAS, Embry Riddle Aeronautical U., 1988; grad., Fed. Law Enforcement Tng. Ctr., Artesia, N.Mex., 2003. Cert. master level athletics ofcl. USA Track and Field, 2001, level one official Internat. Fedn. Bobsled and Tobogganing, 2007. Commd. 2d lt. USAF, 1977, advanced through grades to maj., 1988, F-117A Stealth Fighter pilot Persian Gulf, 1991; ret. lt. col. USAFR, 2000; pilot United Airlines, 1992—. Ct. apptd. spl. advocate Office of Guardian Ad Litem, Salt Lake City, 1996-99. Decorated DFC, Air medal (4), Air Force Commendation medal (3), Air Force Achievement medal; recipient Alumni Achievement award U. Nebr., 1998; inducted into Air Force ROTC Hall of Fame, U. Nebr., 2003. Mem. VFW, Am. Legion, DFC Soc., Airline Pilots Assn., Red River Valley Fighter Pilots Assn., Aircraft Owners and Pilots Assn. Roman Catholic. Avocations: flying, golf, running, photography, skeleton. Home: 952 E Springwood Dr North Salt Lake UT 84054 Personal E-mail: balijo@aol.com.

BOULOS, PAUL FARES, civil and environmental engineer; b. Beirut, June 28, 1963; came to U.S., 1983; s. Fares and Marie-Rose (Abou Hadid) B. BS, Beirut U., 1985; BSCE, U. Ky., 1985, MSCE, 1986, PhD, 1989; advanced mgmt. program, Harvard Bus. Sch., 2003. Asst. prof. U. Ky., Lexington, 1990-91; dir. water distbn. tech. MWH Global, Broomfield, Colo., 1991—; pres., COO MWH Soft Inc., Broomfield, 1996—. Internat. hydraulic expert on over 200 municipal drinking water projects worldwide; cons. in field. Author KYPIPED: Comprehensive Network Analyzer, 1990, H2OMAP, H2ONET and InfoWater Distribution Modeling and Management, 1999, 9 authoritative engrng. textbooks; contbr. over 100 articles to profl. publs. Recipient Best Rsch. Paper award U.S. EPA, 1994, ASCE, 1996, AWWA, 2003, 2007; grantee NSF, 1987, Am. Water Works Rsch. Found., 1992. Mem. ASCE (treas. 1992), Am. Water Works Assn., Sigma Xi, Tau Beta Pi, Chi Epsilon (U.S. delegation to NATO Advanced Study Inst. 1993), Am. Acad. Water Resources Engrs.(hon), 2008, Lebanese Am. Found. (Pride Heritage award, 2008, Effis Island medal, 2009). Achievements include work on computer-assisted water quality and hydraulic network modeling. Home: 9971 Winona St Westminster CO 80031-2528 Office: 380 Interlocken Crescent Ste 300 Broomfield CO 80021

BOULOT, PHILIPPE, chef; b. Apr. 15, 1959; m. Susan Boulot. Grad., Jean Drouant Hotel Sch., Paris, 1978. With The Nikko, Paris, Four Seasons Inn on the Park, London, Four Seasons Cliff Hotel, San Francisco, The Mark Hotel, NYC; exec. chef The Heathman Restaurant, Portland, 1994—. Named Best Chef: Northwest/Hawaii, James Beard Found., 2001. Office: The Heathman Hotel 1001 SW Broadway at Salmon Portland OR 97205

BOUQUET, FRANCIS LESTER, physicist; b. Enterprise, Oreg., Feb. 1, 1926; s. Francis Lester and Esther (Johnson) B.; m. Betty Jane Davis, Sept. 26, 1979 (dec. Aug. 15, 1989); children: Tim, Jeffrey, Janet; stepchildren: John Perry, Peggy Korv. AA, U. Calif., Berkeley, 1948, BA, 1950; MA, UCLA, 1953. Physicist U.S. Radiol. Def. Lab., San Francisco, 1953-55; engr., mgr. Lockheed Aircraft Co., Burbank, Calif., 1955-74; physicist Jet Propulsion Lab., Pasadena, Calif., 1974-88; pres. Systems Co., Graham, Wash., 1988-93, FLB Assocs., Medford, Oreg., 1994—. Cons. in field. Author: Solar Energy Simplified, 1984, 4th edit., 1994, Radiation Damage in Materials, 1985, 3d edit., 1990, Radiation Effects on Electronics, 1986, 5th edit., 1995, Introduction to Materials Engineering, 1986, 3d edit., 1990, Introduction to Seals, O-Rings and Gaskets, 1988, 2d edit., 1992, Great Chefs of the Southwest Cookbook, 1988, rev. edit., 1989 (new title Chefs of the Southwest Cookbook), Radiation Effects on Teflon, 1989, Engineering Properties of Teflon, 1989, 2d edit., 1994, Radiation Effects on Kapton, 1990, Engineering Properties of Kapton, 1990, Lake Havasu Cookbook, 1990, Spacecraft Design-Thermal and Radiation, 1991, Solar Energy Technology, 1991, Practical Guide to Autos, 1992, Starting Your Business, vols. 1 & 2, 1992, Nuclear Energy Simplified, 1992, Introduction to Biological Radiation Effects, 1992, 2d edit., 1994, Successful Decision-Making, 1993, True Life Stories, 1994, Exoatmospheric and Space Travel, 1994, Engineers' Guide to Autos, 1994, Radiation Effects on Nonelectronic Materials Handbook, 1994. Elder 1st Presbyn. Ch., Van Nuys, Calif. 1970-81. Served with U.S. Army, 1944-46, with Signal Corps U.S. Army, 1951-52, PTO. Recipient Eagle Scout award Boy Scouts Am., 1940, Performance commendations Lockheed Aircraft Co., 1964, 66, Mgmt. Achievement Program award, 1973, 20 NASA awards, 1980-92; named to Honor Roll of Inventors, 1966. Mem. N.Y. Acad. Sci., Calif. Soc. Profl. Engrs., Nat. Soc. Profl. Engrs., IEEE (chmn. Los Angeles chpt. Nuclear and Plasma Scis. Soc. 1973-74), Am. Inst. Physics, AIAA, Nat. Mgmt. Assn., Air Force Assn., Lockheed Mgmt. Club, Caltech Mgmt. Club. Republican.

BOURGAIZE, ROBERT G., economist; BA, U. Wash., 1949. Bd. dirs., sr. v.p. Peoples Nat. Bank, Seattle; pres. Central Bank, N.A., Tacoma, University Place Water Co., Epsilon Econ. Inc. Mem. Nat. Assn. Bus. Economists, English-Speaking Union U.S.A. (nat. dir.), Royal Commonwealth Soc., Am. Waterworks Assn. (life), Pacific Northwest Writers Conf., Adam Smith Econ. Found., Adam Smith Soc. (founder 1976), Theta Chi. Office: 4201 B Bridgeport Way W University Place WA 98466-4304

BOURNE, HENRY R., pharmacology professor, department chairman, researcher; b. Danville, Va., Mar. 1, 1940; m.; three children. MD, Johns Hopkins U., 1965. Instr. in medicine U. Calif., San Francisco, 1971—72, asst. prof. medicine and pharmacology, 1972—75, assoc. prof. medicine and pharmacology, 1975—81, chief, div. of clinical pharmacology, 1980—83, sr. staff mem., Cardiovascular Rsch. Inst., 1980—, prof. medicine and cellular and molecular pharmacology, 1981—, prof., chair. dept. pharmacology, 1983—91, acting chair, dept. pharmacology, 1993—94. Editorial bd. Science, 1988—, Molecular Biology of the Cell, 1991—, UCSF Mag., 1992—, Current Biology, 1993—, Current Opinion in Cell Biology, 1994—, Sci. Perspectives, 1996—, Ency. Life Scis., 1997—. Recipient Merit award, NIH, 1990—91. Mem. AAAP, AAAS, NAS, Am. Assn. Cell Biology, Am. Soc. Pharmacology & Exptl. Therapeutics (Rawls-Palmer award, 1985), Am. Soc. Biol. Chemists, Inst. Medicine, Phi Beta Kappa, Alpha Omega Alpha. Office: Bourne Lab UCSF Box 2140 600 16th St San Francisco CA 94107 also: U Calif Box 0450 513 Parnassus Ave Med Sci 1212 San Francisco CA 94143-0450 Office Phone: 415-476-8162. Office Fax: 415-514-0169. E-mail: bourne@cmp.ucsf.edu.

BOURNE, LYLE EUGENE, JR., psychology professor; b. Boston, Apr. 12, 1932; s. Lyle E. and Blanche (White) H. BA, Brown U., 1953. Asst. prof. psychology U. Utah, 1956-61, assoc. prof., 1961-63; vis. assoc. prof. U. Calif., Berkeley, 1961—62, vis. prof., 1968—69; assoc. prof. psychology U. Colo., Boulder, 1963—65, prof., 1965—2001, prof. emeritus, 2002—, dir. Inst. Cognitive Sci., 1979—83, chmn. dept. psychology, 1983—91; clin. prof. psychiatry U. Kans. Med. Ctr., 1967—90. Vis. prof. U. Wis., 1966, U. Mont., 1967, U. Hawaii, 1969; cons. in exptl. psychology, VA, 1965-93. Author: Human Conceptual Behavior, 1966, Psychology of Thinking, 1971, Psychology: Its Principles and Meanings, rev. edits., 1976, 79 82, 85, Cognitive Processes, 1979, rev. edit., 1986, Psychology: A Concise Introduction, 1988, Psychology: Behavior in Context, 1998; acad. editor: Basic Concept Series, Learning-Cognition Series, Scott, Foresman Pub. Co., 1970-76, Charles Merill Co., 1980-84, Advanced Psychological Texts Series, Sage Publications, 1992—; editor Jour. Exptl. Psychology: Human Learning and Memory, 1975-80; cons. editor Jour. Clin. Psychology 1975-97, Jour. Exptl. Psychology: Learning, Memory and Cognition, 1984-92, Memory and Cognition, 1984-89. Recipient Rsch. Scientist award NIHM, 1969-74. Mem.: APA (coun. editors 1975—80, coun. reps. 1976—79, chmn. early awards com. 1978—79, bd. sci. affairs 1978—81, coun. reps. 1986—89, bd. sci. affairs 1989—92, pres. divsn. 3 1992, publ. and commn. bd. 1995—), Coun. Grad. Depts. Psychology (exec. bd. 1985—89), Soc. Gen. Psychology (pres. 2001), Rocky Mountain Psychol. Assn. (pres. 1987—88), Fedn. Behavioral Psychol. and Cognitive Scis. (v.p. 1994—95, pres. 1995—97), Soc. Exptl. Psychologists (chmn. 1987—88), Psychonomic Soc. (governing bd. 1976—81, chmn. 1980—81), Sigma Xi. Home: 785 Northstar Ct Boulder CO 80304-1088 Home Phone: 303-776-7511. Business E-Mail: lyle.bourne@colorado.edu. E-mail: lbourne@psych.colorado.edu.

BOURQUE, RAY, retired professional hockey player; b. Montreal, Que., Can., Dec. 28, 1960; m. Chris Bourque; children: Melissa, Christopher Ray. Defenseman Boston Bruins (NHL), 1979-2000, Colo. Avalanche, 2000—01. Mem. QMJHL All-Star 1st team, 1977-78, 78-79, NHL All-Star 1st team, 1979-80, 81-82, 83-84, 84-85, 86-87, 89-90, 93-94, 2nd team, 80-81, 82-85, 85-86, 88-89; player NHL All-Star game, 1981-86, 88-94. Recipient Calder NHL Rookie of Yr. trophy, 1980, Norris Outstanding Defenseman trophy, 1987, Frank J. Selke trophy, 1978-79, Emile (Butch) Bouchard trophy, 1978-79, James Norris Meml. trophy, 1986-87, 87-88, 89-90, 90-91, 93-94, King Clancy Meml. trophy, 1991-92; named to Sporting News All-Star 2nd team, 1980-81, 82-83, 85-86, 88-89, Sporting News All-Star 1st team, 1981-82, 83-84, 86-87, 87-88, 89-90, 93-94; inducted to Hockey Hall of Fame, 2004 Achievements include being a member of Stanley Cup Champion Colorado Avalanche, 2001.

BOUSKA LEE, CARLA ANN, nursing and healthcare educator; b. Ellsworth, Kans., Nov. 26, 1943; d. Frank J. and Christine Rose (Vopat) Bouska; m. Gordon Larry Lee, July 8, 1967. RN, Marymount Coll., Salina, Kans., 1964; BSN, U. Kans., 1967; MA, Wichita State U., 1972, EdS, 1975, M in Nursing, 1984; PhD, Kans. State U., 1988. RN, cert. family and adult nurse practitioner, health edn. specialist, advanced nurse adminstr. Staff, charge nurse Ellsworth (Kans.) County Vet. Meml. Hosp., 1964—65; critical, coronary, and surg. nurse Med. Ctr. U. Kans., Kansas City, 1966—67, Watkins Meml. Hosp. and Student Health Ctr., 1965—66; asst. dir., chief instr. Wesley Sch. Nursing, Wichita, Kans., 1967—74; asst prof., chair nurse clinician/practitioner dept. Wichita State U., 1974—84, asst. prof. grad. health adminstrn. program, 1984—92; assoc. prof., dir. nurse practitioner program Ft. Hays State U., Hays, Kans., 1992—95; assoc. prof., coord. postgrad. nursing studies Clark Coll., Omaha, 1995—, nursing health svcs. mgmt. and allied health, 1994—; cons., v.p. devel. GRCIs Industries, Inc., 1994—; coord. nurses continuing edn. Providers - Kans. Mo. Nurses Assn. EMT, physician asst. HCA; lectr. Wichita State U., 1972—74, mem. grad. faculty, 1993—95; cons. Hays Med. Ctr.-Family Healthcare Ctr., 1993—96, Baker U., Northeastern U., Boston; mem. adv. coun. Kans. Newman Coll.; mem. adv. bd. Kans. Originals, Kans. Dept. Econ. Devel. Project, Wilson; mem. grad. faculty U. Kans., 1993—95; rschr. in field; bd. advisors Who's Who in Am. Nursing; bd. rsch. advisors Internat. Biog. Ctr., Cambridge, England. Author (with Ig & Barrett): Fluids and Electrolytes: A Basic Approach, 1996; author: Delman's Fundamental and Advanced Nursing Skills, 2000, (poetry) Seasons: Marks of Life, 1991 (Golden Poet award, 1991); actor: (poetry) Winter Tree, 1995 (Internat. Poet of Merit award, 1995); author: (booklet) Czechoslovakian History, 1988 (honor room Czech Mus. and Opera House, Wilson); author: (and editor) History of Kansas Nursing, 1987; contbr. articles to profl. jours. Co-founder Kans. Nurses Found., pres., trustee, 1978—93; vol. ARC, 1967—92, bd. dirs., 1977—90; mem., rschr. Gov.'s Commn. Health Care, Topeka, 1990; vol., lectr. Am. Heart Assn., 1967—, Am. Cancer Soc., 1967—; chair Nat. Task Force on Core Competence of Nurse Practitioners, 1994—95; mem. State of Kans. health care agenda Kans. Pub. Health Assn., 1995; city coord. campaign Sec. State, 1986; election judge Sedgwick County, Kans., 1989—94. Recipient Tchr. award, Mortar Bd.; named Outstanding Cmty. Leader, Jaycees, Alumnus of Yr., Kans. U., 1979, Marymount Coll., 1987, Poet of the Yr., 1995; grantee Nurse Practitioner Tng. grantee, U.S. Health and Human Svcs., 1966—67. Fellow: Am. Acad. Nursing, Am. Acad. Nursing; mem.: Internat. Soc. Poets (disting.), Gt. Plains Nurse Practitioners Soc. (founder, pres. 1993—), Kans. Nurse Found. (pres., dir., dist. alt. rep. 1978), Kans. Alliance Advanced Nurse Practitioners (founder, pres. 1986—, pres., dir., dist. alt. rep. 1992), Kans. Nurses Assn. (bd. dirs., treas.), Nat. Commn. on Credentialing of Health Edn. Specialists, Am. Bus. and Profl. Women's Assn. (Hall of Fame 1999), Am. Acad. Nurse Practitioners, Nat. League Nursing, ANA (nat. and site visitor ANCC), Sigma Theta Tau (Internat. Woman of the Yr. 1998), Alpha Eta (pres. chpt.). Republican. Roman Catholic. Avocations: poetry, music, gardening, writing, sewing. Home: 1367 N Westlink Ave Wichita KS 67212-4238 Office: Holy Names College Dept Nursing 3500 Mountain Blvd Oakland CA 94619-1699 Fax: 510-436-1376. E-mail: lee@hnc.edu.

BOUSSO, RAPHAEL, physicist, educator; PhD, Cambridge U., 1998. Postdoctoral fellow Stanford U., Kavli Inst. Theoretical Physics, Santa Barbara; fellow physics dept. Harvard U., 2002—03; mem. faculty to assoc. prof. physics dept. U. Calif., 2003—. Fellow Radcliffe Inst., 2002—03. Contbr. articles to sci. jours.; author: A Covariant Entropy Conjecture, 1999, The Holographic Principle, 2002, Light Sheets and Bekenstein's Bound, 2003; author: (with J. Polchinski) The String Theory Landscape, 2004; co-author: Quantization of Four Form Fluxes and Dynamical Neutralization of the Cosmological Constant, 2000. Recipient NSF award, 2004; named one of Brilliant 10, Popular Sci. mag., 2002. Office: Ctr Theoretical Physics U Calif Dept Physics 366 LeConte Hall 7300 Berkeley CA 94720-7300 Office Phone: 510-643-9195. E-mail: bousso@lbl.gov.

BOUTROS, GEORGE F., investment banker; b. Beirut, 1960; married; 3 children. BS in Civil Engrng., U. Calif., Berkeley, 1983, MS in Structural Engrng., 1984; MBA, UCLA. Various positions to mng. dir., mergers and acquisitions Morgan Stanley, 1986—96; mng. dir., tech. group Deutsche Morgan Grenfell (DMG), 1996—99; co-head, global tech. banking, co-head, global mergers and acquisions Credit Suisse First Boston, San Francisco, mng. dir., co-chmn. global tech. group, 1999—. Named a Top Dealmaker, Dealmaker mag., 2006, Top Rainmaker for tech., 2007. Office: Credit Suisse First Boston Global Tech Group 650 California St San Francisco CA 94108 Office Phone: 415-249-2100.

BOVEN, DOUGLAS GEORGE, lawyer; b. Holland, Mich., Aug. 11, 1943; BSE, U. Mich., 1966, JD, 1969. Bar: Calif. 1970. Ptnr. Reed Smith LLP, San Francisco, 1989—. Arbitrator Fed. and Superior Ct. Panel of Arbitrators, 1980—; panelist Superior Ct. Early Settlement Program, 1987-. Mem. ABA (mem. bus. bankruptcy, Chpt. 11 and secured creditors coms.), Am. Bankruptcy Inst., Comml. Law League Am., State Bar Calif. (insolvency law and real estate sects.), Sonoma County Bar Assn., Bay Area Bankruptcy Forum, Bar Assn. San Francisco (comml. law and bankruptcy sect., mem. arbitrator fee disputes com. 1973—), Tau Beta Pi. Office: Reed Smith LLP Two Embarcadero Ctr Ste 2000 San Francisco CA 94111 Office Phone: 415-543-8700. Business E-Mail: dboven@reedsmith.com.

BOW, STEPHEN TYLER, JR., business executive; b. Bow, Ky., Oct. 20, 1931; s. Stephen Tyler Sr. and Mary L. (King) B.; m. Kathy O'Connor, July, 1982; children: Jerry, Jon; children by previous marriage: Sandra Bow Morris, Deborah Bow Goodin, Carol, Clara, Lisa. BA in Sociology, Berea Coll., Ky., 1953; grad. exec. program bus. adminstrn., Columbia U., 1976. CLU. With Met. Life Ins. Co., 1953-74, 76-89; agt. Lexington, Ky., 1953-55; sales mgr. Birmingham, Ala., 1955-58; field tng. cons., 1958-59; territorial field supr., 1959-60; dist. sales mgr. Frankfort, 1960-64, Lexington, 1964-66; exec. asst. field tng. NYC, 1966-67; regional sales mgr. NJ, 1967-72; agy. v.p., officer-in-charge Can. hdqrs., 1972-74; exec. v.p., chmn., chief exec. officer Capital Holding Corp., Louisville, 1974-76; officer-in-charge Midwestern hdqrs. Met. Life Ins. Co., Dayton, 1976-83, sr. v.p., officer-in-charge Western Hdqrs., 1983-89; chmn., CEO Southeastern Group, Inc., Louisville, 1993-94; pres., CEO Anthem Life of Ind., Indpls., 1993-95; chmn., CEO Anthem Life Ins. Cos., 1995-96; exec. v.p. Assoc. Ins. Cos., Inc., Indpls., 1993-96; chmn. Acordia of San Francisco, 1993-96; pres., CEO Delta Dental Ky., Louisville, 1989-94, Blue Cross and Blue Shield Ky., Louisville, 1989-93; vice chmn. DeHayes Group, 1996—; pres. Steve Bow and Assocs., Inc., 1996—; chmn. Victory Tech., Inc., 1998—. Past chmn. Dayton Power and Light Audit Com.; chmn. bd. dirs. Advice Co.; chmn. EBridge Techs. Past bd. dirs. San Francisco Visitors and Conv. Bur., 1985-87, Ind. Coll. of No. Calif., Bay Area Coun., Lindsey Wilson Coll.; mem. adv. bd. Hugh O'Brian Youth Found.; bd. dirs. Calif. Legis. Adv.

Commn. on Life and Health Ins., Metro United Way, Ky. Health Care Access Found., Greater Louisville Econ. Devel. Coun., Leadership Ky., Greater Louisville Fund for the Arts, Boy Scouts Am., Bay Area Boy Scouts Am., Bay Area Council, U. San Francisco, Ky. Home Mut., Ky. Forward, Asian Bus. League, McLaren Coll. Bus., My Old Ky. Home Coun.; mem. corp. council San Francisco UN Assn.; past mem. San Francisco Pvt. Industry Council; past chmn. United Negro Coll. Fund of San Francisco, 1985-86; mem. exec. com. bd. dirs., v.p. county ops. United Way of San Francisco Bay Area, 1985-87; vol. chmn. U.S. Savs. Bond Campaign, Bay Area, 1987; trustee Ky. Ind. Coll. Fund, Berea Coll.; chmn. bd. dirs. Advice Co. Recipient Outstanding Sales Mgmt. award N.Y. Sales Congress, 1972, Frederick D. Patterson award United Negro Coll. Fund San Francisco, 1986, Outstanding County Ops. Vol. award United Way of Bay Area, 1987, Bus. Appreciation award Jeffersontown, Ky. C. of C., 1993, Pres.'s award, 1993, Leadership award Internat. Women's Forum, Washington, 1993; named Citizen of Yr. Wright State U. Med. Sch., Dayton, 1982. Mem. Nat. Assn. Life Underwriters, Gen. Agts. and Mgrs. Assn., Calif. Bus. Roundtable, Nat. Assn. Corp. Dirs. (founder, former pres.), Calif. C. of C. (bd. dirs.), Ky. C. of C., Ky. Home Life Exec. Com., Am. Cancer Soc. Clubs: Lincoln of Northern Calif. Republican. Methodist. Avocations: golf, painting, reading. Office Phone: 916-652-7667. Business E-Mail: steve@adviceco.com.

BOWDEN, DOUGLAS MCHOSE, neuropsychiatric scientist, neuroinformaticist; b. Durham, NC, Apr. 7, 1937; s. Daniel Joseph and Charlotte (McHose) B.; m. Vivian Lee Bowden, 1966 (div. 2005); children: Dana, Julie, Carlos, Luis BA, Harvard U., 1959; MD, Stanford U., 1965. Staff assoc. NIMH, Bethesda, Md., 1966-69; asst. prof. psychiatry U. Wash., Seattle, 1969-73, assoc. prof. dept. psychiatry & behavioral scis., 1973-79, prof. psychiatry & behavioral scis., 1979—; core staff sci. Nat. Primate Rsch. Ctr., U. Wash., 1969—; from asst. dir. to assoc. dir. Regional Primate Rsch. Ctr., U. Wash., 1977-88, dir., 1988-94. Adj. assoc. prof. pharmacology U. Wash., 1975-79, adj. prof. pharmacology, 1979-88; rsch. fellow Japan Soc. Promotion of Sci., Japan Assn. Animal Sci., Tokyo, Tsukuba, Inuyama/Kyoto, Japan, 1989. Author: Neuronames (c) Neuroanatomical Nomenclature, 1992; editor: Aging in Nonhuman Primates, 1979; translator Traumatic Aphasia, its Syndromes, Psychology and Treatment, 1970, Primate Models of Human Neurogenic Disorders, 1976 Surgeon USPHS, 1966-69. Fellow Gerontol. Soc. Am.; mem. Soc. Neurosci. Office: U Wash Natl Primate Rsch Ct Box 357330 1705 NE Pacific St Seattle WA 98195-7330 Office Phone: 206-543-2456. Business E-Mail: dmbowden@u.washington.edu.

BOWEN, DEBRA LYNN, Secretary of State, California, former state legislator; b. Rockford, Ill., Oct. 27, 1955; d. Robert Calvin and Marcia Ann (Crittenden) Bowen; m. Mark Nechodom; 1 child. BA, Mich. State U., 1976; JD, U. Va., 1979. Bar: Ill. 1979, Calif. 1983. Assoc. Winston & Strawn LLP, Chgo., 1979-82, Washington, 1985-86, Hughes Hubbard & Reed, LA, 1982-84; sole practice LA, 1984-93; mem. Calif. State Assembly from 53rd dist., Sacramento, 1992—98, Calif. State Senate from 28th dist., Sacramento, 1998—2006; sec. state State of Calif., Sacramento, 2007—. Gen. counsel, State Employee's Retirement System Ill., Springfield, 1980-82; adj. prof. Watterson Coll. Sch. Paralegal Studies, 1985. Exec. editor Va. Jour. Internat. Law, 1977-78; contbr. articles to profl. jours. Mem. mental health law com. Chgo. Coun. Lawyers, 1980-82. Rotary Internat. fellow Internat. Christian U., Tokyo, 1975; Wigmore scholar Northwestern U. Sch. Law, Chgo., 1976; recipient James Madison Freedom of Info. award No. Calif. chpt. Soc. Profl. Journalists, 1995, Profile in Courage award, John F. Kennedy Libr. Found., 2008. Mem. Calif. Bar Assn. (exec. com. pub. law sect. 1990-94), Phi Kappa Phi. Democrat. Office: Office Sec State 1500 11th St Sacramento CA 95814

BOWEN, JAMES THOMAS, career officer; b. Mason City, Iowa, May 4, 1948; s. Stanley Thomas and Marilyn Louise (Ott) B.; m. Joyce Anne Kermabon, Sept. 10, 1977; 1 child, Steven James. BBA, U. Iowa, 1969; MS, U. So. Calif., LA, 1974. Cert. project mgmt. profl. Commd. 2nd lt. USAF, 1969, advance through grades to col., 1991; student pilot 3575th Pilot Tng. Wing, Vance AFB, Okla., 1969-70; co-pilot 773rd Tactical Airlift Squadron, Clark AFB, Phillipines, 1971; pilot 6594th Test Group, Hickam AFB, Hawaii, 1971-75; acquisition program mgr. Aeronautical Systems Div., Wright-Patterson AFB, Ohio, 1976-82; chief, standoff surveillance and attack systems HQ USAF, Rsch. Devel. and Acquistion, Pentagon, Va., 1984-87; chief, acquistion plans and programs br. Air Force Inspection and Safety Ctr., Norton AFB, Calif., 1988-90; dir. projects joint tactical autonomous weapons Aero. Systems Div., Wright-Patterson AFB, Ohio, 1990-91, dir. devel. and integration F-16, 1991-94; F-16 mgmt. dir. Ogden Air Logistics Ctr., Hill AFB, Utah, 1994-95; custom sys. program mgr. Hewlett Packard and Agilent Tech. Cos., Santa Rosa, Calif., 1996-2001; site mgr. Agilent Techs., Rohnert Pk., Calif., 2001—02, sr. program mgr., 2002—05; owner On Target Program Mgmt. Solutions Consulting Co., 2006—. Decorated Air medal USAF, 1972. Mem. Mil. Officers Assn. Am., Air Force Assn., Def. Systems Mgmt. Coll. Alumni Assn., Am. Mgmt. Assn., Ret. Officers Assn., Project Mgmt. Inst. Methodist. Avocations: skiing, deep sea fishing, golf.

BOWEN, JEWELL RAY, chemical engineering professor; b. Duck Hill, Miss., Jan. 9, 1934; s. Hugh and Myrtle Louise (Stevens) B.; m. Priscilla Joan Spooner, Feb. 4, 1956; children: Jewell Ray, Sandra L., Susan E. BS, MIT, 1956, MS, 1957; PhD, U. Calif., Berkeley, 1963. Asst. prof. U. Wis., Madison, 1963-67, assoc. prof., 1967—70, prof. chem. engring., 1970-81, chmn. chem engring. dept., 1971-73, 78-81, assoc. vice chancellor, 1972-76; prof. chem. engring. U. Wash., Seattle, 1981-2000, prof. emeritus, 2001—, dean coll. engring., 1981-96. Cons. in field; adviser NSF, Dept. Def.; vis. prof. Kyoto U. Internat. Innovation Ctr., 2002; bd. dirs. Inst. Dynamics of Explosions and Reactive Sys., 1989-2007, pres., 1989-95, treas., 1995-05. Contbr. articles to profl. jours.; editor: 7th-10th Internat. Colloquia on Dynamics of Explosions and Reactive Systems, 1979, 81, 83, 85, chmn. program com. 18th. Mem. Wash. High Tech. Coordinating Bd., 1983—87; bd. dirs. Wash. Tech. Ctr., 1983—87, interim exec. dir., 1989—91; bd. dirs. U. Wash. Retirement Assn., 2003—07, 1st v.p., 2004—05, pres., 2005—07. Recipient SWE Rodney Chipp award, 1995; NATO-NSF postdoctoral fellow, 1962-63, sr. postdoctoral fellow, 1968; Deutsche Forschungsgemeinschaft prof., 1976-77. Fellow AIAA, AAAS (com. on coun. affairs 1995-97, sect. chmn. 1996-97), Am. Soc. Engring. Edn. (deans coun. 1985-92, chmn. 1989-91, bd. dirs. 1989-94, 1st v.p. 1991, pres.-elect 1992, pres. 1993); mem. AIAA, AIChE, Am. Phys. Soc., Combustion Inst., Sigma Xi, Tau Beta Pi, Beta Theta Pi. Office: U Wash Dept Chem Engring PO Box 351750 Seattle WA 98195-1750 Home: 410 NE 70th St Apt 402 Seattle WA 98115-5476 Personal E-mail: bowen5324@comcast.net.

BOWEN, R. WILLIAM, lawyer; b. Montgomery, Ala., Feb. 17, 1953; BS, U. Va., 1975, JD, 1980. Bar: D.C. 1980, Calif. 1982. Mem. Luce, Forward, Hamilton & Scripps, San Diego; v.p. Gen-Probe Inc., 1997—, gen. counsel, 1997—, asst. sec., 1997—2002, sec., 2002—. Mem. ABA (litigation sect., securities litigation com., profl. liability com.). Office: 10210 Genetic Center Dr San Diego CA 92121 Office Phone: 858-410-8000.

BOWEN, RICHARD LEE, retired academic administrator, political scientist, educator; b. Avoca, Iowa, Aug. 31, 1933; s. Howard L. and Donna (Milburn) B.; m. Connie Smith Bowen, 1976; children: James, Robert, Elizabeth, Christopher; children by previous marriage—Catherine, David, Thomas. BA, Augustana Coll., 1957; MA, Harvard, 1959, PhD, 1967. Fgn. service officer State Dept., 1959-60; research asst. to U.S. Senator Francis Case, 1960-62; legis. asst. to U.S. Senator Karl Mundt, 1962-65; minority cons. sub-com. exec. reorgn. U.S. Senate, 1966-67; asst. to pres., assoc. prof. polit. sci. U. S.D., Vermillion, 1967-69, pres., 1969-76, Dakota State Coll., Madison, 1973-76; commr. higher edn. Bd. Regents State S.D., Pierre, 1976-80; Disting prof. polit. sci. U. S.D., 1980-85; pres. Idaho State U., Pocatello, 1985—2005, pres. emeritus, 2005—. Served with USN, 1951-54. Recipient Outstanding Alumnus award Augustana Coll., 1970; Woodrow Wilson fellow, 1957, Congl. Staff fellow, 1965; Fulbright scholar, 1957.

BOWER, ALLAN MAXWELL, lawyer; b. Oak Park, Ill., May 21, 1936; s. David Robert and Frances Emily Bower; m. Deborah Ann Rottmayer, Dec. 28, 1959. BS, U. Iowa, 1962; JD, U. Miami, Fla., 1968. Bar: Calif. 1969, U.S. Supreme Ct. 1979. Internat. aviation law practice, LA, 1969—; ptnr. Kern & Wooley, LA, 1980-85, Bronson, Bronson & McKinnon, LA, 1985-90, Lane Powell Spears Lubersky, LA, 1990-99, Bailey & Ptnrs., Santa Monica, Calif., 1999—. Contbr. articles to profl. publs. Mem. Lawyer-Pilots Bar Assn. Republican. Presbyterian.

BOWER, CHRISTOPHER JAMES, investment banker; b. Sterling, Ill., Mar. 5, 1957; s. William Joseph and Elsie Sandra (Sopko) B. BS in Acctg. and Fin., U. Colo., 1978; JD, U. San Diego, 1983. CPA, Calif. Mem. profl. staff Arthur Young and Co. Internat., Denver, 1978-79; founder, CEO & mng. dir. Pacific Corp. Group LLC, La Jolla, Calif., 1979—. Bd. dirs. Pacific Corp. Internat., LA; sec. Pacific Corp. Fin. Inc., La Jolla; chmn. Pacific Corp. Advisors, Inc., La Jolla, Pacific Corp. Valuation Inc., La Jolla, 1979—. Contbr. articles to profl. jours. Mem. AICPA, Calif. State Soc. CPAs. Office: Pacific Corp Group Inc Ste 200 1200 Prospect St La Jolla CA 92037-3608 Office Phone: 858-456-6000. Office Fax: 858-456-6018.

BOWER, CURTIS A., engineering executive; Sr. audit Price Waterhouse; audit mgr., spl. projects mgr. Caltex Petroleum; staff v.p., group controller Allied Signal; exec. v.p., CFO, treas. Parsons Corp., Pasadena, Calif., 1991—2006, vice.-chmn. bd. dirs., spl. asst. to the chmn. and CEO, 2006—. Office: Parsons Corp 100 W Walnut St Pasadena CA 91124-0001

BOWER, JANET ESTHER, writer, educator; b. National City, Calif., Apr. 14, 1943; d. Murvel and Esther Eva (Clark) Newlan; m. Robert S. Bower Jr., Nov. 23, 1968; children: Llance Clark, Esther Elizabeth. BA in History and Psychology, Calif. We. U., San Diego, 1965; MA in History, UCLA, 1966; MA in Edn., U.S. Internat. U., 1970. Std. jr. coll. credential, elem. credential, Calif. Instr., mem. adj. faculty San Diego CC Dist., 1969—, Grossmont/Cuyamaca Coll. Dist., El Cajon, Calif., 1973, 1997—2000, Palomar Coll. Dist., San Marcos, Calif., 1993, 1997—2007, Midlands Tech. Coll., Columbia, SC, 1995—96, Mira Costa Coll., 2001—07; ret., 2007. Adj. faculty mem. Nat. U., 1999-2005, Union Inst., 2000-04; hist. cons. pub. Contbg. author: Women in the Biological Sciences, 1997; contbr. articles to periodicals; pub. editor Friends of the Internat. Ctr. Newsletter, U. Calif., San Diego, 1984-85. Bd. dirs. Women of St. Paul's Episcopal Ch., San Diego, 1983-86, Oceanids, U. Calif., San Diego, 1980-85; mem. St. Andrews Episcopal Ch.; vol., docent Noyes House, Internat. Cmty., 2008. Grantee US Dept. Edn., 1968-69. Mem. Am. Hist. Assn., Calif. Hist. Soc., Project Wildlife (hon. life mem.), St. Andrew's Episcopal Ch, PEO (EE chpt. 2008), Globe Guilders of the Old Globe, San Diego. Republican. Avocations: cooking, travel. Personal E-mail: newbower@gmail.com. Business E-Mail: jbower@sdccd.net.

BOWER, ROBERT W., electrical engineer; BS in Physics with honors, U. Calif., Berkeley, 1962; MSEE, Calif. Inst. Tech., 1963, PhD in Applied Physics, 1973. Asst. mgr. MOS divsn. Hughes A.C., 1965-70; cons., 1970-75; from v.p. to pres. Mnemonics Inc., 1975-77; assoc. prof. dept. elec. sci. and engring. UCLA, 1977-78; mgr. bipolar device tech. Advanced Micro Devices Inc., 1979-85; prof. dept. elec. and computer engring. U. Calif., Davis, 1987—, prof. emeritus. Vis. scientist Tech. U. Munich, 1986-87; cons. TRW, Intel, Honeywell, GCA, AMD, Xerox, Hughes, Motorola, Datapoint, ITT, High Voltage Engring., Eurocil; presenter in field. Contbr. articles to profl. jours, chpts. to books; patentee in field. Recipient Ronald H. Brown Am. Innovator award U.S. Dept. Commerce, 1997; inductee Nat. Inventors Hall of Fame, 1997. Fellow IEEE; mem. NAE, Boehmische Phys. Soc., Phi Beta Kappa, Sigma Xi. Acheivements include research in development and invention of self assigned-gate ion-implanted MOS-FET, and establishment of ion implantation to fabricate semiconductor integrated circuits. Office: U Calif Davis Dept Elec/Computer Engring Davis CA 95616

BOWERING, GEORGE HARRY, writer, consultant, language educator; b. Penticton, BC, Can., Dec. 1, 1936; s. Ewart Harry and Pearl Patricia (Brinson) Bowering; m. Angela May Luoma, Dec. 14, 1962; 1 child, Thea Claire. Student, Victoria Coll., 1953—54; BA, U. B.C., 1960, MA, 1963; postgrad., U. Western Ont., 1966—67. Asst. prof. Am. lit. U. Calgary, Canada, 1963-66; writer in residence Sir George Williams U., Montreal, Que., 1967-68, asst. prof., 1968-71; prof. Simon Fraser U., Burnaby, B.C., 1972—2001; poet laureate of Can. Author: Mirror on the Floor, 1967, Autobiology, 1972, Flycatcher and Other Stories, 1974, Concentric Circles, 1977, A Short Sad Book, 1977, Protective Footwear, 1978, Another Mouth, 1979, Burning Water, 1980, A Place to Die, 1983, Caprice, 1987, Harry's Fragments, 1990, The Rain Barrel, 1994, Shoot!, 1994, Parents From Space, 1994, Piccolo Mondo, 1998, Diamondback Dog, 1998; poetry Points on the Grid, 1964, The Man in Yellow Boots, 1965, The Silver Wire, 1966, Rocky Mountain Foot, 1968, The Gangs of Kosmos, 1969, Touch, 1971, In the Flesh, 1973, The Catch, 1976, Particular Accidents: Selected Poems, 1981, Smoking Mirror, 1984, Kerrisdale Elegies, 1984, 71 Poems for People, 1985, Delayed Mercy, 1986, Sticks & Stones, 1989, Quarters, 1991, Urban Snow, 1992, George Bowering Selected, 1993, The Moustache, 1993, Blonds On Bikes, 1997; (poetry) His Life: A Poem, 2000, Baseball, 2003, Changing on the Fly, 2004, Vermeer's Light, 2006; (essays) The Mask in Place, 1982, A Way with Words, 1982, Craft Slices, 1985, Errata, 1988, Imaginary Hand, 1988, A Magpie Life, 2001, Cars, 2002, Left Hook, 2005; author: (history) Bowering's B.C., 1996, Egotists and Autocrats, 1999, Stone Country, 2003; editor Taking the Field: The Best of Baseball Fiction, 1990, 92, Likely Stories: A Postmodern Sampler, 1992, And Other Stories, 2001, (short stories) Standing On Richards, 2004, Baseball Love, 2006. Served with RCAF, 1954-57. Mem.: Assn. Can. TV and Radio Artists. Home: 4403 W 11th Ave Vancouver BC Canada Personal E-mail: bowering@sfu.ca.

BOWERS, MICHAEL THOMAS, chemistry professor; b. Spokane, Wash., June 6, 1939; s. John W. and Fae (Scott) B.; married, Feb. 8, 1964; children: Molly, Shelia, Melissa. BS, Gonzaga U., 1962; MS, U. Ill., 1964, PhD, 1966. Asst. prof. U. Calif., Santa Barbara, 1966-73, assoc. prof., 1973-76, prof. chemistry, 1976—. Faculty rsch. lectr. faculty senate U. Calif., Santa Barbara, 1994. Editor Internat. Jour. Mass Spectrometry, 1986—; contbr. over 300 articles to profl. jours.; editor 3 books in field; assoc. editor Jour. Am. Chem. Soc. 1st lt. U.S. Army, 1966-68. Guggenheim Found. fellow, 1994. Fellow AAAS, Am. Phys. Soc.; mem. Am. Chem. Soc. (assoc. editor jour. 1989—, Nobel laureate signature award 1989, Outstanding Achievement in Mass Spectrometry award 1996), Am. Soc. Mass Spectrometry (Disting. Contbn. award 2004), Internat. Mass Spectrometry Soc. (Thomson gold medal 1997). Roman Catholic. Avocations: golf, running. Office: U Calif Dept Chemistry Santa Barbara CA 93106 Office Phone: 805-893-2893. E-mail: bowers@chem.ucsb.edu.

BOWERS, PAUL D., transportation company executive; b. Rome, NY, Aug. 28, 1948; Dir. aviation Alaska Dept. Transp. and Pub. Facilities Statewide Aviation, Anchorage, 1995—. Office: Alaska Dept Transp and Pub Facilities Statewide Aviation 4111 Aviation Dr Anchorage AK 99502-1058

BOWERS, RUSSELL W., state legislator, sculptor, painter; b. Mesa, Ariz., Oct. 20, 1952; m. Donetta Bowers. Grad., Brigham Young U.; postgrad., Mesa C.C., Ariz. State U. Mem. Ariz. Ho. of Reps., 1993-97, Ariz. Senate, Dist. 21, Phoenix, 1996—; mem. edn. com., mem. family svcs. com.; mem. govt. and environ. stewardship com. Ariz. State Senate, vice-chmn. rules com. Republican. Address: 8831 E Quill St Mesa AZ 85207-9706 Fax: 602-542-4511. E-mail: rbowers@azleg.state.az.us.

BOWERS, TERREE A., lawyer; b. Shirley, Mass., Aug. 6, 1954; s. Thomas Allan and Virginia Ann (Wilson) B.; m. Constance Tasulis, Mar. 15, 1987; 3 children. BA with high honors, U. Tex., 1976, JD, 1979. Bar: Calif. 1979, US Dist. Ct. (ctrl. dist. Calif.), US Ct. Appeals (9th cir.). Legal clk. state affairs com. Tex. Senate, 1979; assoc. Adams, Duque & Hazeltine, LA, 1979-82; asst. US atty. Dept. Justice, LA, 1982-92; US atty. Ctrl. Dist. Calif., LA, 1992-94; legal coord. Internat. War Crimes Tribunal Yugoslavia, 1994—99; advisor Internat. War Crimes Tribunal-Rwanda, 1994—99; chief dep. City Atty.'s Office, LA, 1998—2005; ptnr. white collar crime practice grp. Howrey LLP, LA, 2005—. Mem. standing com. on discipline Fed. Dist. Ct. (Ctrl. Dist. Calif.); co-chair human rights subcommittee ABA Internat. Law Com.; bd. mem. Inner City Law Ctr.; adj. prof. internat. crime law seminars UCLA, 2000—02. Recipient Disting. Svc. award Atty. Gen., 1992, Nat. commendation Depts. Justice, Treasury and State. Mem. Phi Beta Kappa, Alpha Phi Omega, Friars, Omicron Delta Kappa, Goodfellow. Office: Howrey LLP Ste 1100 550 S Hope St Los Angeles CA 90071 Office Phone: 213-892-1882, 626-224-3900. Office Fax: 213-892-2300. E-mail: BowersT@howrey.com.

BOWIE, PETER WENTWORTH, judge, educator; b. Alexandria, Va., Sept. 27, 1942; s. Beverley Munford and Louise Wentworth (Boynton) B.; m. Sarah Virginia Haught, Mar. 25, 1967; children: Heather, Gavin. BA, Wake Forest Coll., 1964; JD magna cum laude, U. San Diego, 1971. Bar: Calif. 1972, DC 1972, US Dist. Ct. DC 1972, US Dist. Ct. Md. 1973, US Dist. Ct. (so. dist.) Calif. 1974, US Ct. Appeals (DC cir.) 1972, US Ct. Appeals (9th cir.) 1974, US Supreme Ct. 1980. Trial atty. honors program Dept. of Justice, Washington, 1971-74; asst. U.S. Atty. US Atty.'s Office, San Diego, 1974, asst. chief civil divsn., 1974-82, chief asst. US atty., 1982-88; lawyer rep. US Ct. Appeals (9th cir.) Jud. Conf., 1977-78, 84-87; judge US Bankruptcy Ct., San Diego, 1988—2006, chief judge, 2006—. Lectr. law Calif. Western Sch. Law, 1979-83; exec. com. 9th Cir. Judicial Conf., 1991-94; com. on codes of conduct Jud. Conf. of US, 1995-2003; advisor ABA Joint Commn. to Evaluate Model Code of Jud. Conduct, 2003-. Bd. dirs. Presidio Little League, San Diego, 1984, coach, 1983-84; alumni adv. bd. Sch. Law U. San Diego, 1998-2002. Lt. USN, 1964-68, Vietnam. Recipient Disting. Alumni award, U. San Diego Sch. Law, 2003. Mem. State Bar Calif. (hearing referee ct. 1982-86, mem. rev. dept. 1986-90), Fed. Bar Assn. (pres. San diego chpt. 1981-83), San Diego County Bar Assn. (chmn. fed. ct. com. 1978-80, 83-85), Assn. Bus. Trial Lawyers (bd. govs.), San Diego Bankruptcy Forum (bd. dirs.), Rotary Club, Phi Delta Phi. Republican. Mem. Unitarian Ch. Office: US Bankruptcy Court 325 West F St San Diego CA 92101-6017 Office Phone: 619-557-5158.

BOWKER, LEE HARRINGTON, sociologist, educator, writer; b. Bethlehem, Pa., Dec. 19, 1940; s. Maurice H. Bowker and Blanche E. Heffner; m. Nancy Bachant, 1966 (div. 1973); 1 child, Kirsten Ruth; m. Dee C. Thomas, May 25, 1975; children: Jessica Lynn, Gwendolyn Alice. BA, Muhlenberg Coll., 1962; MA, U. Pa., 1965; PhD, Wash. State U., 1972. Instr. in Sociology Lebanon Valley Coll., Annville, Pa., 1965-66, Allbright Coll., Reading, Pa., 1966-67; assoc. prof. Whitman Coll., Walla Walla, Wash., 1967-77; prof., assoc. dean U. Wis., Milw., 1977-82; dean grad. sch. and research Ind. (Pa.) U. of Pa., 1982-85; provost, v.p. Augustana Coll., Sioux Falls, SD, 1985-87; dean behavioral and social scis. Humboldt State U., Arcata, Calif., 1987-97, emeritus dean, prof. sociology, 1997—2006. Cons. various pubs., colls., univs. and state agys; expert witness. Author: Prison Victimization, 1980, Humanizing Institutions for the Aged, 1982, Masculinities and Violence, 1997, The Role of the Department Chair, revised edit., 1997, Ending the Violence, rev. edit., 1998; assoc. editor Pacific Sociol. Rev., 1975-78, Justice Quar., 1983-85, Criminal Justice Policy Rev., 1984-95; contbr. articles to profl. jours. Pres. Blue Mountain Action Coun., OEO, Walla Walla, 1969-71; dir. social therapy program, Wash. State penitentiary, Walla Walla, 1971-73; bd. dirs. Milw. Bur. Community Corrections, 1979-81, Sioux Falls Symphony, 1985, United Way of Humboldt County, 1988-91. Grantee NIMH

1973, 79, 81, Washington Arts Commn. 1972, Washington Office Community Devel. 1974, Fulbright Found. 1985, Nat. Retired Tchrs. Assn./Am. Assn. Retired Persons Andrus Fund. 1980; Law Enforcement Assistance Adminstrn. co-grantee, 1978. Mem.: Am. Soc. Criminology, Am. Sociol. Assn., Pacific Sociol. Assn. Home: 3513 H St Eureka CA 95503-5358 Personal E-mail: dtbandlhb@suddenlink.net.

BOWLEN, PAT (PATRICK DENNIS BOWLEN), professional sports team and holding company executive, lawyer; b. Prairie du Chien, Wis., Feb. 18, 1944; s. Paul Dennis and Arvella (Woods) B. BBA, U. Okla., 1966, JD, 1968. Bar: Alta. 1969. Read law Saucier, Jones, Calgary, Alta., Can., assoc., 1969-70; asst. to pres. Regent Drilling Ltd., 1970-71; pres. Batoni-Bowlen Enterprises Ltd., 1971-79, Bowlen Holdings Ltd., Edmonton, Alta., Can., 1979—; pres., chief exec. officer, owner Denver Broncos, 1984—. Named one of Most Influential People in the World of Sports, Bus. Week, 2008. Mem. Law Soc. Alta., Can. Bar Assn., Young Presidents Orgn., Edmonton Club Roman Catholic. Avocations: golf, skiing, surfing. Office: Denver Broncos 13655 Broncos Pkwy Englewood CO 80112-4150

BOWLES, DAVID STANLEY, engineering educator, consultant; b. Romford, Essex, Eng., June 30, 1949; m. Valerie Rosina Curd; children: Penny, Simon, Amy. BSc, City U., Eng., 1972; PhD, Utah State U., 1977. Registered profl. engr., Utah; cert. profl. hydrologist. Jr. civil engr. George Wimpey & Co., Hammersmith, London, 1967-72; rsch. asst. prof. Utah State U., Logan, 1976-80, rsch. assoc. prof., 1980-81, adj. rsch. assoc. prof., 1981-83, rsch. prof., 1983-85, prof., 1985—, assoc. dir., 1986-91, dir., 1992-96, Inst. for Dam Safety Risk Mgmt., 2000—. Vis. scientist Internat. Inst. Applied Systems Analysis, Laxenburg, Austria, 1979; br. mgr., engr. Law Engring., Denver, 1981-83; prin. Risk Assessment Cons. Engrs. and Economists (RAC), 1986—; mem. Australian Com. on Large Dams. Contbr. numerous articles to profl. jours. Bd. dirs. U.S. Soc. on Dams. Fellow ASCE, Am. Water Resources Assn.; mem. Soc. Risk Analysis, Am. Geophys. Union, Am. Inst. Hydrology, Assn. State Dam Safety Ofcls. Home: 1520 Canyon Rd Providence UT 84332-9431 Office: Utah Water Rsch Lab Utah State Univ Logan UT 84322-8200 Home Phone: 435-753-6004; Office Phone: 435-797-4010. E-mail: bowles@cache.net.

BOWLSBY, BOB, athletic director; b. Jan. 10, 1952; m. Candice Bowlsby; children: Lisa, Matt, Rachel, Kyle. BS, Moorhead State U., 1975; MS, U. Iowa, 1978. Asst. athletic dir. No. Iowa U., athletic dir., 1984-91, U. Iowa, Iowa City, 1991—2007, Stanford U., Calif., 2007—. Chair NCAA Divsn. I Mgmt. Coun., 1997-99; mem. NCAA Divsn. I Basketball com., 2000-03, chair, 2004-05. Chmn. Big Ten Championships and awards com.; chair NCAA Olympic Sports Liaison Com., NCAA/USOC liaison com., Olympics com. mem; bd. dirs. Iowa Games. Mem. Nat. Assn. Collegiate Dir. of Athletics (exec. com.). Office: Stanford U Stanford CA 94305-6150 Office Phone: 319-335-9435. E-mail: robert-bowlsby@uiowa.edu.

BOWLUS, BRAD A., health care company executive; BA in Bus., Calif. State U., Northridge; MBA, Pepperdine U. Regional dir. WellPoint Health Networks, Inc., Calif.; v.p., So. Calif. region PacifiCare Health Systems Inc., 1994-95, pres., CEO, dental, vision, divn., 1995-96, pres., CEO, Wash., 1996-97, pres., CEO, Calif., 1997—99, pres., CEO, Health Plan Div., 1999—. Bd. mem. several non-profit organs. Mem. Young Pres. Orgn. Office: PacifiCare Health Systems 5995 Plaza Dr Cypress CA 90630

BOWMAN, A. BLAINE, electronics executive; BS in Physics, Brigham Young U., Utah; MBA, Stanford U., Calif. Product engr. Motorola Semiconductor Products Divsn.; mgmt. cons. McKinsey and Co.; pres., CEO Dionex, Sunnyvale, Calif., 1977—. Office: Dionex PO Box 3603 1228 Titan Way Sunnyvale CA 94088-3603

BOWMAN, JEFFREY R., former fire chief; b. Akron, Ohio, Apr. 24, 1952; s. Roger Heath and Ruth Ann (Corrigan) B.; div.; children: Katie, Andrew, Brian. BS in Orgnl. Behavior, U. San Francisco, 1986. Firefighter Anaheim (Calif.) Fire Dept., 1973-75, paramedic, 1975-79, capt., 1979-83, battalion chief, 1983-85, div. chief, 1985-86, fire chief, 1986—2002, San Diego Fire Dept., 2002—06. Pres. bd. dirs. Anaheim Boys and Girls Club, 1988—; chmn. fundraising Boy Scouts Am., Anaheim, 1988. Mem. Internat. Assn. Fire Chiefs, Calif. Fire Chiefs Assn.

BOWMAN, JON ROBERT, magazine editor, film critic; b. Spokane, Wash., Nov. 9, 1954; s. Donald Ken and Carolyn Joyce (Crutchfield) B.; m. Geraldine Maria Jaramillo, Jan. 27, 1979 (div. Dec. 1985); m. Amy Farida Siswayanti, May 23, 1992 (div. Jan. 1994). BA, U. N.Mex., 1976. Reporter, arts editor, news editor N.Mex. Daily Lobo, Albuquerque, 1972-76; film critic Albuquerque Jour., 1974-76; reporter Alamogordo (N.Mex.) Daily News, 1976; sci. writer, editor Los Alamos (N.Mex.) Monitor, 1976-81; reporter, arts editor New Mexican, Santa Fe, 1981-86, film critic, 1987—; editor New Mexico Mag., Santa Fe, 1986—. Guest lectr. U. N.Mex., Coll. Santa Fe, 1976—. Author: (with others) Explore New Mexico, 1988, A New Mexico Scrapbook, 1990, Day Trip Discoveries: Selected New Mexico Excursions, 1993, The Allure of Turquoise, 1995; contbr. articles to mags. and newspapers; author salutes for Greer Garson, James Coburn, Ben Johnson, and John Huston for festivals honoring them. Vol. tchr. Albuquerque pub. schs., 1972-76; organizer film festivals Albuquerque and Santa Fe. 1972-91, benefits including Ctr. for Contemporary Arts, Santa Fe; program cons. Taos Talking Picture Festival, 1995—. Recipient Sci. Writing award AP, 1978, citation AP, 1979, others. Avocations: movies, baseball, travel. Office: NMex Mag Lew Wallace Bldg 495 Old Santa Fe Trl Santa Fe NM 87501-2750 Home: 119 La Placita Cir Santa Fe NM 87505-4008

BOWNE, MARTHA HOKE, editor, consultant; b. Greeley, Colo., June 9, 1931; d. George Edwin and Krin (English) Hoke; children: Gretchen, William, Kay, Judith. BA, U. Mich., 1952; postgrad., Syracuse U., 1965. Tchr. Wayne (Mich.) Pub. Schs., 1953-54, East Syracuse and Minoa Cen. Schs., Minoa, NY, 1965-68; store mgr. Fabric Barn, Fayetteville, NY, 1969-77; store owner Fabric Fair, Oneida, NY, 1978-80; prodr., owner Quilting by the Sound, Port Townsend, Wash., 1987—2000, Quilting by the Lake, Cazenovia, NY, 1981—. Organizer symposium Am. Quilters Soc.; founder, pres. Quilter's Quest confs., 1994—. Mem., pres. Minoa Library, 1960-75; mem. Onondaga County Library, Syracuse, 1968-71. Mem.: Am. Quilters Soc. (editor Am. Quilter mag. 1985—95). Avocations: reading, hiking, travel, bridge, Scrabble. Home: 478 Oden Bay Dr Sandpoint ID 83864-6499 E-mail: martyidaho@sandpoint.net.

BOWNESS, RICK (RICHARD GARY BOWNESS), professional athletics coach; b. Moncton, NB, Can., Jan. 25, 1955; s. Robert Swales and Thelma Mae (MacDonald) B.; m. Judith Mary Egan, July 23, 1977; children: Richard Egan, Jonathan Ryan, Kristen Ashley. Professional hockey player Atlanta Flames, NHL, 1975-77, Detroit Red Wings, NHL, 1977-78, St. Louis Blues, NHL, 1978-80, Winnipeg (Man.) Jets, NHL, 1980-82, asst. coach, 1983-87, head coach, 1988-89; player, coach Sherbrooke (Que.) Jets, Am. Hockey League, 1982-83; coach, gen. mgr. Moncton Hawks, Am. Hockey League, 1987-88; head coach, gen. mgr. Maine Mariners, Am. Hockey League, 1989-91; head coach Boston Bruins, NHL, 1991-92, Ottawa Senators, NHL, 1992-96, N.Y. Islanders, NHL, 1996-99; asst. coach Phoenix Coyotes, 1999—2004, interim head coach, 2004—.

BOW WOW, See MOSS, SHAD

BOXER, BARBARA, United States Senator from California; b. Bklyn., Nov. 11, 1940; d. Ira and Sophie (Silvershein) Levy; m. Stewart Boxer, 1962; children: Doug, Nicole. BA in Economics, Bklyn. Coll., 1962. Aide to Rep. John L. Burton US Congress, 1974—76; stockbroker, econ. rschr. NY Securities Firm, NYC, 1962-65; journalist, assoc. editor Pacific Sun, 1972-74; congl. aide to rep. 5th Congl. Dist. San Francisco, 1974-76; mem. US Congress from 6th Calif. Dist., 1983—93; chair US House Subcommittee on Govt. Activities & Transp. of House Govt. Ops. Com., 1990-93; US Senator from Calif., 1993—; chair US Senate Environment & Pub. Works Com., 2007—, US Senate Select Com. on Ethics, 2007—; mem. US Senate Fgn. Rels. Com., US Senate Commerce, Sci. & Transp. Com. Mem. Presdl. Advisory Commn. on Holocaust Assets in the US. Author (with Nicole Boxer): Strangers in the Senate: Politics and the New Revolution of Women in America, 1993; (with Catherine Whitney) Nine and Counting: The Women of the Senate, 2000, (with Mary-Rose Hayes) (novels) A Time to Run, 2005. Mem. Marin County Bd. Suprs., 1976-82, pres. 1980-81; mem. Bay Area Air Quality Mgmt. Bd., San Francisco, 1977-82, pres., 1979-81; bd. dirs. Golden Gate Bridge Hwy. and Transport Dist., San Francisco, 1978-82; pres. Dem. New Mems. Caucus, 1983. Recipient Open Govt. award Common Cause, 1980, Rep. of Yr. award Nat. Multiple Sclerosis Soc., 1990, Margaret Sanger award Planned Parenthood, 1990, Women of Achievement award Anti-Defamation League, 1990, Star Legis. award LA Women's Legis. Coalition, 1991, Elected Official of the Year Stonewall Democratic Club, 1997, Edgar Wayburn award Sierra Club, 1997, Demetris Bouhoutsos award Hellenic-Am. Coun. So. Calif., 1998, Pres. award for the Advancement of Women Nat. Assn. Women Lawyers, 1998, Alumnae of the Year, Bklyn. Coll., 1999, Reg. Elected Official of the Year Sacramento Area Coun. Governments., 1999, Vision award Highwood Online Girlsite, 1999, Pub. Servant award Nat. Orgn. on Fetal Alcohol Syndrome, 1999, Every Action Counts Congl. award Hadassah, 1999, Dorothy Donahoe Women of the Year Award, 1999, Spirit of Achievement Albert Einstein Coll. Med., 2000, Paul E. Tsongas award Lymphoma Rsch. Found. Am., 2000, Peter H. Behr award Friends of the River, 2000, Environmental Leadership award Calif. League of Conservation Voters, 2003. Mem.: Marin Community Video, Marin Nat. Women's Polit. Caucus, Marin Edn. Corps. Democrat. Jewish. Office: US Senate 112 Hart Senate Office Bldg Washington DC 20510-0001 also: District Office Ste 2240 600 B St San Diego CA 92101-4508 Office Phone: 202-224-3553, 619-239-3884. Office Fax: 619-239-5719.*

BOXER, LESTER, lawyer; b. NYC, Oct. 19, 1935; s. Samuel and Anna Lena (Samovar) B.; m. Frances Barenfeld, Sept. 17, 1961; children: Kimberly Brett, Allison Joy. AA, UCLA, 1955, BS, 1957; JD, U. So. Calif., 1961. Bar: Calif. 1962; U.S. Dist. Ct. (ctrl. dist.) Calif. 1962. Assoc. Bautzer & Grant, Beverly Hills, Calif., 1961-63; pvt. practice Beverly Hills, 1963-65, 69—; ptnr. Boxer & Stoll, Beverly Hills, 1965-69. Mem. Calif. Bar Assn., LA County Bar Assn., Beverly Hills Bar Assn. Office: 1801 Century Park E Ste 2513 Los Angeles CA 90067-4703 Office Phone: 310-553-3344.

BOXER, STEVEN G., physical chemistry educator; b. NYC, Oct. 18, 1947; m. Linda M. Boxer, 1977; children: Lisa, George. BS with honors, Tufts U., 1969; PhD Phys. and Phys. -organic Chemistry, U. Chgo., 1976. Asst. prof. chemistry Stanford U., 1976—82, assoc. prof. chemistry, 1982—86, prof. chemistry, 1986—, chmn. dept. physics, 1988—99, Camille and Henry Dreyfus prof. chemistry, 2000—. Lectr. and cons. in field. Recipient Presdl. Young Investigator award, 1984-89, Five- Coll. Lectr. in Chemistry, 1993, NIH Merit award, 1994-2004, Arthur C. Cope scholar award Am. Chem. Soc., 1995, Earle K. Plyler prize for Molecular Spectroscopy, 2008. Fellow: AAAS, Biophysical Soc., Am. Acad. Arts and Scis.; mem.: NAS, Am. Soc. Photobiology (Rsch. award 1992). Office: Stanford Univ Dept of Physics Stanford CA 94305-5080 Office Fax: 650-723-4817. Business E-Mail: sboxer@stanford.edu.

BOYAN, NORMAN J., retired education educator; b. NYC, Apr. 11, 1922; s. Joseph J. and Emma M. (Pelezare) B.; m. Priscilla M. Simpson, July 10, 1943; children: Stephen J. (dec.), Craig S., Corydon J. AB, Bates Coll., Lewiston, Maine, 1943; A.M., Harvard U., 1947, Ed.D., 1951. Instr. U.S. history Dana Hall Sch., Wellesley, Mass., 1946-48; research assoc. Lab. Social Relations, Harvard U., 1950-52; asst. prin. Mineola (N.Y.) High Sch., 1952-54; prin. Wheatley Sch., East Williston, N.Y., 1954-59; assoc. prof. edn., dir. student teaching and internship U. Wis., 1959-61; assoc. prof. edn. Stanford U., 1961-67; dir. div. ednl. labs. U.S. Office Edn., 1967-68, assoc. commr. for research, 1968-69; prof. edn. Grad. Sch. Edn., U. Calif., Santa Barbara, 1969-90, prof. emeritus, 1990—, dean, 1969-80; assoc. in edn. Grad. Sch. Edn., Harvard U., 1980-81; dir. Ednl. Leadership Inst. U. Calif., 1989-91. Vis. scholar Stanford U., 1974, 86; vis. prof. U. Ark. Program in Greece, 1977, Coll. Edn., Pa. State U., 1981, Faculty Edn. U. B.C., 1983, U. Alta., 1988, UCLA, 1991; cons. in field. Co-author: Instructional Supervision Training Program, 1978; mem. editl. bd. Harvard Edn. Rev, 1948-50, Jour. Secondary Edn, 1963-68, Jour. Edn. Rsch., 1967-82, Urban Edn, 1967-90; cons. editor, contbr. 5th edit. Ency. Ednl. Rsch., 1982; editor, contbr. Handbook Rsch. on Ednl. Adminstrn., 1988; contbr. articles to profl. jours. Served with USAAF, 1943-46. Recipient Shankland award for advanced grad. study in ednl. adminstrn., 1950, Roald F. Campbell Lifetime Achievement award U. Coun. for Ednl. Adminstrn., 1998. Mem. Am. Ednl. Rsch. Assn. (v.p. div. A 1978-80), Phi Beta Kappa, Phi Delta Kappa. Home: 1031A Calle Sastre Santa Barbara CA 93105-4439 Personal E-mail: nboyan@cox.net.

BOYCE, DAVID S., lawyer; b. Medina, NY, 1949; AB, Cornell U., 1971; MBA, U. Utah, 1973; JD with high honors, U. Fla., 1977; LLM in Taxation, Georgetown U., 1979. Bar: Calif. 1979; cert. tax specialist Calif. Bd. of Legal Specialization. Atty.-adv. Judge Howard A Dawson Jr, US Tax Ct., 1977—79; adj. prof. law Univ. San Diego, 1980—84; now adminstrv. ptnr. LA office Jones Day. Mem.: ABA, Am. Health Lawyers Assn., LA Bar Assn., Order of Coif. Office: Jones Day 555 S Flower St 50th Fl Los Angeles CA 90071 Office Phone: 213-243-2403. Office Fax: 213-243-2539. Business E-Mail: dsboyce@jonesday.com.

BOYD, BETTY ANN, state legislator; b. Manchester, Conn., Sept. 16, 1943; d. Rudolph and Bertha Johnson; m. Douglas; children: James, Kirsten. Attended, Upsala Coll., NJ. Dir. campaigns and devel. Caring Connection, Lutheran Office Govt. Ministry, Red Rocks Area Spl. Olympics; mem. Dist. 26 Colo. House of Reps., 2000—06; mem. Dist. 21 Colo. State Senate, 2006—, pres. pro tempore. Bd. dirs. Citizens for Lakewood's Future; chair Jefferson County Good News Coalition. Mem. Am. Assn. Univ. Women (past pres.). Democrat. Lutheran. Office: 200 E Colfax Rm 305 Denver CO 80203 Office Phone: 303-866-4857. Business E-Mail: betty.boyd.house@state.co.us.*

BOYD, CAROLYN PATRICIA, history professor; b. San Diego, June 1, 1944; d. Peter James and Patricia Mae (de Soucy) B.; m. Frank Dawson Bean, Jan. 4, 1975; children: Peter Justin Bean, Michael Franklin Bean. AB with great distinction and with honors in History, Stanford U., 1966; MA, U. Wash., 1969, PhD, 1974. Tchg. asst. dept. history U. Wash., 1970-71; from instr. to prof. dept. history U. Tex., Austin, 1973-95, prof. history, 1995-99, assoc. dean Grad. Studies, 1986-88, 90-92, chair history dept., 1994-99; dir. univ. honors program, assoc. prof. history U. Md., College Park, 1989-90; prof. history U. Calif., Irvine, 1999—, chair history dept., 2004—06, dean Grad. Divsn., 2006—08. Lectr. in field. Author: Praetorian Politics in Liberal Spain, 1979, La política pretoriana en el reinado de Alfonso XIII, 1990, Historia Patria: Politics, History and National Identity in Spain, 1875-1975, 1997, Spanish edit., 2000, Religion y politica en la Espana contemporanea, 2007; mem. editl. bd. Essays, 1992-95, Ayer, 2005-; author chpts. to books; contbr. articles to profl. jours. Recipient Summer award U. Tex. Rsch. Inst., 1997; Woodrow Wilson hon. fellow, 1966, Fulbright-Hays fellow, 1966-67, NDEA Title IV fellow, 1968-72, AAUW fellow, 1972-73, ACLS fellow, 1985; ACLS Grant-in-Aid, 1977, Am. Philos. Soc. grant, 1978, URI Rsch. grant, 1985, New Del Amo Program grant, 2000-02; fellow Woodrow Wilson Internat. Ctr. for Scholars, 2002-03. Mem. Am. Hist. Assn. (James Harvey Robinson prize com. 1992-94, John Fagg prize com. 2001-03), Soc. Spanish and Portugese Hist. Studies (gen. sec. 2000-04, mem. exec. com. 1978-80, 83-85, 96-98, chair local arrangements, program chmn. conf. 1987), Coun. European Studies, Internat. Inst. in Spain, Assn. Contemporary History. Office: Univ Calif Irvine Dept History Irvine CA 92697-3275 Business E-Mail: cpboyd@uci.edu.

BOYD, DAVID WILLIAM, mathematician, educator; b. Toronto, Ont., Can., Sept. 17, 1941; s. Glenn Kelvin and Rachael Cecilia (Garvock) B.; m. Mary Margaret Shields, Sept. 26, 1964; children: Deborah, Paul, Kathryn. BS, Carleton U., 1963; MA, Toronto U., 1964, PhD, 1966. Asst. prof. U. Alta., 1966-67, Calif. Inst. Tech., 1967-70, assoc. prof., 1970-71, U. B.C., Vancouver, Can., 1971-74, prof. math., 1974—, dept. head, 1986-89. Recipient E.W.R. Steacie Prize, 1978; I.W. Killam sr. research fellow, 1976-77, 81-82, Coxeter-James prize, 1979, Jeffery-Williams prize, 2001, CRM-Fields prize, 2005. Fellow Royal Soc. Can.; mem. Am. Math. Soc., Can. Math. Soc. Office: Univ BC Dept Math Vancouver BC Canada V6T 1Z2 Home Phone: 604-224-5107. E-mail: boyd@math.ubc.ca.

BOYD, DEAN WELDON, management consultant; b. Shreveport, La., July 15, 1941; s. Vernon Dean and Josie (Weldon) B.; m. Susan C. Wickizer; children: Jodie Boyd-Wickizer, Silas Boyd-Wickizer. BEE, MIT, 1963, MEE, 1965; PhD in Engring. Econ. systems, Stanford U., 1970. Rsch. engr. Jet Propulsion Lab., Pasadena, Calif., 1965-67; sr. decision analyst Stanford Rsch. Inst., Menlo Park, Calif., 1967-70; asst. prof. info. sci. U. Calif., Santa Cruz, 1970-75; mgr. cons. Cottage Grove, Oreg., 1975-77; founder Decision Focus, Inc., Mountain View, Calif., 1977-97, CEO, prin., pres., 1997; vice chmn. Talus Solutions (formerly Decision Focus Inc.), Mountain View, 1997—. Contbr. articles to profl. jours. Mem. Sch. Bd. South Ln. Sch. Dist., Cottage Grove, 1986—. Mem. Coun. Logistics Mgmt., Inst. Mgmt. Sci. Achievements include developing methodologies for logical selection of portfolios of interrelated activities.

BOYD, LANDIS LEE, agricultural engineer, educator; b. Orient, Iowa, Dec. 1, 1923; s. Harold Everett and Edith Elizabeth (Lauer) B.; m. Lila Mae Hummel, Sept. 7, 1946; children— Susan Lee, Barbara Edith, Shirley Rae, Carl Steven, Philip Wayne. BS in Agrl. Engring, Iowa State U., 1947, MS, 1948, PhD in Agrl. Engring. and Engring. Mechanics, 1959. Registered profl. engr., N.Y., Minn. Sr. research fellow Iowa State Coll., 1947-48, 54-55; from asst. prof. to prof. Cornell U., Ithaca, 1948-60, coordinator grad. instrn., 1958-64; engring. design analyst Allis-Chalmers Mfg. Co., Milw., 1962-63; mem. faculty U. Minn. at St. Paul, 1964-78, prof. agrl. enging., head dept., 1964-72, asst. dir. Agrl. Exptl. Sta., 1972-78, dir. Coll. Agr. Research Center; asso. dean Coll. Agr., Wash. State U., Pullman, 1978-85; exec. dir. Western Assn. Agrl. Expt. Sta. Dirs., Agrl. Expt. Sta. Colo. State U., Fort Collins, 1985-92, adj. prof. bioresource and chem. engring., 1985—. Vis. scholar Ctr. Study Higher Edn.; vis. faculty-in-residence, intern Office Vice Pres. for Research, U. Mich., 1968; (Fed. Exec. Inst.), 1975; Cons. FAO, La Molina, Peru, 1964, 69; part-time cons. in field, 1948— Supt. farm bldg. project N.Y. State Fair, 1956, 57. Served with USNR, 1943-45. NATO postdoctoral grantee, 1962; recipient Iowa 4-H Alumni Recognition award, 1968; profl. achievement citation in engring. Iowa State U., 1980; Japan Soc. Promotion of Sci. fellow, 1981, U. Tokyo Vis. Faculty fellow, 1993. Fellow Am. Soc. Agrl. Engrs. (grad. paper award 1949, MBMA award 1969, v.p.-regions 1970-73), Minorities in Agr., Natural Resources and Related Scis., Sigma Xi, Phi Kappa Phi, Gamma Sigma Delta, Alpha Epsilon, Kappa Sigma, Rotary (Paul Harris fellow, leader group study exch. to dist. 4850 in Argentina 1994). Methodist. Home and Office: 1725 Concord Dr Fort Collins CO 80526-1671

BOYD, LARRY C., information technology executive; married; 2 children. B in Polit. Sci., Stanford U., JD. Ptnr. Gibson, Dunn & Crutcher, 1985—99; sr. v.p. legal svcs. U.S. Ingram Micro Inc., Santa Ana, Calif., 2000—04, sr. v.p., sec., gen. counsel, 2004—. Mem.: ABA, Orange County Bar Assn., State Bar Calif. Office: Ingram Micro Inc 1600 E St Andrew Pl PO Box 25125 Santa Ana CA 92799-5125 Office Phone: 714-566-1000.

BOYD, MALCOLM, minister, writer; b. Buffalo, June 8, 1923; s. Melville and Beatrice (Lowrie) B.; life ptnr. Mark Thompson. BA, U. Ariz., 1944; B.D., Ch. Div. Sch. Pacific, 1954; postgrad., Oxford U., Eng., 1955; S.T.M., Union Theol. Sem., NYC, 1956; DD (hon.), Ch. Div. Sch. of Pacific, 1995. Ordained to ministry Episcopal Ch., 1955.

V.p., gen. mgr. Pickford, Rogers & Boyd, 1949-51; rector in Indpls., 1957-59; chaplain Colo. State U., 1959-61, Wayne State U., 1961-65; nat. field rep. Episcopal Soc. Cultural and Racial Unity, 1965-68; resident fellow Calhoun Coll., Yale U., 1968-71, assoc. fellow, 1971—; writer-priest in residence St. Augustine-by-the Sea Episcopal Ch., 1982-95. Lectr. World Council Chs., Switzerland, 1955, 64; columnist Pitts. Courier, 1962-65; resident guest Mishkenot Sha'ananim, Jerusalem, 1974; chaplain AIDS Commn. Episcopal Diocese L.A., 1989—; poet-in-residence Cathedral Ctr. of St. Paul, L.A., 1996—, hon. canon, 2002; mem. adv. bd. White Crane Inst., 2007. Host (TV) Sex in the Seventies, LA, 1975; author: Crisis in Communication, 1957, Christ and Celebrity Gods, 1958, Focus, 1960, rev. edit., 2001, If I Go Down to Hell, 1962, The Hunger, The Thirst, 1964, Are You Running with Me, Jesus?, 1965, rev. edit., 1990, 40th anniv. rev. edit., 2006, Free to Live, Free to Die, 1967, Book of Days, 1968, As I Live and Breathe: Stages of an Autobiography, 1969, The Fantasy Worlds of Peter Stone, 1969, rev. edit., 2008, My Fellow Americans, 1970, Human Like Me, Jesus, 1971, The Lover, 1972, When in the Course of Human Events, 1973, The Runner, 1974, The Alleluia Affair, 1975, Christian, 1975, Am I Running with You, God?, 1977, Take Off the Masks, 1978, rev. edit. 2007, Look Back in Joy, 1981, rev. edit., 2007, Half Laughing, Half Crying, 1986, Gay Priest: An Inner Journey, 1986, Edges, Boundaries and Connections, 1992, Rich with Years, 1993, Go Gentle Into That Good Night, 1998, Running with Jesus: The Prayers of Malcolm Boyd, 2000, Simple Grace: A Mentor's Guide to Growing Older, 2001, Prayers for the Later Years, 2002; plays Boy, 1961, Study in Color, 1962, The Community, 1964, others; editor: On the Battle Lines, 1964, The Underground Church, 1968, (with Nancy L. Wilson) Amazing Grace: Stories of Gay and Lesbian Faith, 1991; (with Chester Talton) Race and Prayer: Collected Voices, Many Dreams, 2003, (with J. Jon Bruno) In Times Like These--How We Pray, 2005, A Prophet in His Own Land: A Malcolm Boyd Reader, 2008; book reviewer: LA Times, 1979-85; contbg. editor, columnist Episcopal News; columnist Modern Maturity, 1990-2000; contbr. articles to popular mags. including Newsday, Parade, The Advocate, also newspapers. Active voter registration, Miss., Ala., 1963, 64; mem. Los Angeles City/County AIDS Task Force. Malcolm Boyd Collection and Archives established Boston U., 1973; recipient Integrity Internat. award, 1978, Union Am. Hebrew Congregations award, 1980, Lazarus Project award, 2002, Louie Crew award for svc. to gay and lesbian people, 2003, Giants of Justice award Clergy and Laity United for Econ. Justice, 2004, Unitas award, Union Theol. Sem., NYC., 2005, Lambda Lit. Found. Life Achievement award, 2008. Mem. Nat. Council Chs. (film awards com. 1965), P.E.N. (pres. PEN Ctr. U.S. West 1984-87), Am. Center, Authors Guild, Integrity, Nat. Gay Task Force, Clergy and Laity Concerned (nat. bd.), NAACP, Amnesty Internat., Episc. Peace Fellowship, Fellowship of Reconciliation (nat. com.). Episcopalian. Office: PO Box 512164 Los Angeles CA 90051-0164 Business E-Mail: malcolmboyd@ladiocese.org.

BOYD, WILLIAM S., hotel and gaming company executive; s. Sam A. and Mary Boyd; 3 children. JD, Univ. Nev., Las Vegas. Pvt. practice law, 1960—75; co-founder Boyd Gaming Corp., Las Vegas, 1974, chmn., pres., CEO, 1988—2007, exec. chmn., 2008—. Named one of Forbes' Richest Americans, 2006. Mem.: Am. Gaming Assn. (vice chmn.). Office: Boyd Gaming Corp 6465D S Rainbow Blvd Las Vegas NV 89118- Office Phone: 702-792-7200. Office Fax: 702-792-7313.

BOYD, WILLIAM SPROTT, lawyer; b. San Francisco, Feb. 12, 1943; s. R. Mitchell S. and Mary (Mitchell) B.; children: Mitchell Sagar, Sterling McMicking. AB, Stanford U., 1964, JD, 1971. Bar: Calif. 1972, U.S. Dist. Ct. (no. dist.) 1972, U.S. Ct. Appeals (9th cir.) 1972, U.S. Dist. Ct. (cen. dist.) Calif. 1974, U.S. Dist. Ct. (ea. dist.) Calif. 1976. Assoc. Brobeck, Phleger & Harrison, San Francisco, 1971-77, ptnr., 1977—, of counsel. Mem. Lawyers Com for Urban Affairs, San Francisco, 1979—; bd. dirs. San Francisco Legal Aid Soc., 1980-85. Lt. USNR, 1965-68, Vietnam. Mem. ABA, Calif. Bar Assn., San Francisco Bar Assn.

BOYDEN, JACLYNE WITTE, dean; BA, Calif. State U., Hayward, 1970; MBA, Golden Gate U., 1982. Dept. mgr. dept. biochemistry and biophysics U. Calif., San Francisco, 1980-82, dept. mgr. dept. medicine, 1982-84, coord. adminstrv. policies Office of Pres., 1984-85, asst. dir. Cardiovasc. Rsch. Inst., 1985-88, vice dean for Adminstrn. and Fin. Sch. Medicine, 1992—; assoc. dean for Adminstrn. SUNY Sch. Medicine, Stony Brook, 1988-92. Mem. Med. Group Mgmt. Assn., AAMC Group on Instnl. Planning (steering com. 1991-93), AAMC Group Bus. Affairs (chmn. profl. devel. com. 1996, mem. steering com. 1997—, nat. sec. 1997, chairperson-elect 1998, chair 1999).

BOYDSTON, JAMES CHRISTOPHER, composer; b. Denver, July 21, 1947; s. James Virgal and Mary June (Wiseman) B.; m. Ann Louise Bryant, Aug. 20, 1975. BA in Philosophy, U. Tex., 1971. Lutenist and guitarist Collegium Musicum, U. Tex., Austin, 1968-70; tchr. classical guitar Extension div. The New Eng. Conservatory of Music, Boston, 1972-73. Arranger music: S. Joplins, "The Entertainer," 1976; arranger/composer/performer cassette recording: Wedding Music for Classical Guitar, 1988; composer music: International Portraits for Classical Guitar, 1999, Baroque Suites 1-4, 2003; composer/performer/CD recording: Morsels for Classical Guitar, 2005; inventor classical guitar bridge-saddle, 1990; author original poetry included in: The World of Poetry Anthology, 1991. Avocations: astronomy, reading, building clavichords, camping. Home: 4433 Driftwood Pl Boulder CO 80301-3104

BOYER, CARL, III, not-for-profit developer, retired mayor, municipal official; b. Phila., Pa., Sept. 22, 1937; s. Carl Boyer Jr. and Elizabeth Campbell Timm; m. Ada Christine Kruse, July 28, 1962. Student, U. Edinburgh, Scotland, 1956-57; BA, Trinity U., 1959; MEd in Secondary Edn., U. Cin., 1962; postgrad., Calif. State U., Northridge, 1964-72. Tchr. Edgewood High Sch., San Antonio, Tex., 1959-60; libr. U. Cin., Cincinnati, Ohio, 1960-61; tchr. Eighth Avenue Elem. Sch., Dayton, Ky., 1961-62, Amelia High Sch., Amelia, Ohio, 1962-63; instr. Kennedy San Fernando Comm. Adult Sch., San Fernando, Calif., 1964-74, Mission Coll., San Fernando, 1971; tchr. San Fernando High Sch., San Fernando, Calif., 1963-98. Faculty chmn. San Fernando High Sch., dept. chmn.; cons. Sofia (Bulgaria) City Coun., 1991, Bandung Regency, Indonesia, 2003; key spkr. World Mayors' Conf., Jaipur, India, 1998. Author: Santa Clarita: The Formation and Organization of the Largest Newly Incorporated City in the History of Humankind, 2005; author, compiler 23 books on genealogy and family history; contbr. articles to profl. jours. Councilman City of Santa Clarita, Calif., 1987-98, mayor pro tem, 1989-90, 94-95, mayor, 1990-91, 95-96; mem. Nat. League Cities Internat. Mcpl. Consortium, 1992-98; mem. revenue and taxation com. League Calif. Cities, 1992-95; sec. Calif. Contract Cities Assn., 1992-93; trustee Santa Clarita C.C. Dist., 1973-81, pres., 1979-81; bd. dirs. Castaic Lake Water Agy., 1982-84, pres. Newhall-Saugus-Valencia Fedn. Homeowners Assn., 1969-70, 71-72; pres. Del Prado Condo. Assn., Inc., Newhall, Calif.; exec. v.p. Canyon County Formation Com.; chmn. Santa Clarita City Formation Com., 1987; pres. Santa Clarita Valley Internat. Program, 1991-97, 04-05, v.p., 2005-07, sec., 2007-; treas. Healing the Children Calif., 1994-96, pres., 1996-99, 03-05, nat. pres., 1999-00, vol. med. mission adminstr., 2000—. Mem. New Eng. Hist. Geneal. Soc. Democrat. Methodist. Avocations: travel, photography. Home: PO Box 220333 Santa Clarita CA 91322-0333

BOYER, HERBERT WAYNE, retired biochemist, biotechnology company executive; b. Pitts., July 10, 1936; m. Grace Boyer, 1959. BS in Biology and Chemistry, St. Vincent Coll., Latrobe, Pa., 1958, DSc (hon.) (hon.), 1981; MS, U. Pitts., 1960, PhD, 1963. Post-grad. study Yale U., 1963—66; mem. faculty U. Calif., San Francisco, 1966—, prof. microbiology, 1966—75, prof. biochemistry and biophysics, 1975—91, prof. biochemistry and biophysics emeritus, 1991—; co-founder, dir. Genentech, Inc., San Francisco, 1976—, v.p., 1976—90. Investigator Howard Hughes Med. Inst., 1976—83; bd. dir. Allergan, Inc., Irvine, Calif., 1994—, chmn. bd. dirs., 1998—2001, vice-chmn. bd. dirs., 2001—; bd. dir. Scripps Rsch. Inst. Mem. several editl. bds.; contbr. articles to profl. jours. Recipient V.D. Mattai award, Roche Inst., 1977, Albert and Mary Lasker award for basic med. research, 1980, Golden Plate award, Am. Acad. Achievement, 1981, Indsl. Rsch. Inst. Achievement award, 1982, Moet Hennessy-Louis Vuitton prize, 1988, Jerome H. Lemelson-MIT prize for excellence in invention and innovation, 1996, Nat. Tech. medal, 1989, Nat. Sci. medal, 1990, Perkin medal, Soc. Chem. Industry, 2007; co-recipient Swiss Helmut Horten Rsch. award, 1993; named to Calif. Inventor's Hall of Fame, 1985, Nat. Inventor Hall of Fame, 2001. Fellow: AAAS, Am. Acad. Arts and Scis.; mem.: NAS, Am. Soc. Biol. Chemists. Achievements include obtaining, with Stanley N. Cohen, first patent in the field of recombinant deoxyribonucleic acid (DNA), 1980.

BOYER, PAUL DELOS, biochemist, educator; b. Provo, Utah, July 31, 1918; s. Dell Delos and Grace (Guymon) Boyer; m. Lyda Mae Whicker, Aug. 31, 1939. BS, Brigham Young U., 1939; MS, U. Wis., 1941, PhD in Biochemistry, 1943; PhD (hon.), U. Stockholm, 1974, U. Minn., 1996, U. Wis., 1998. Asst. rschr. biochemistry U. Wis., 1939—43; Instr., research assoc. Stanford, 1943—45; from asst. prof. to prof. biochemistry U. Minn., 1945—56; Hill research prof. U. Minn. Med. Sch., 1956—63; prof. chemistry UCLA, 1963—89, dir. Molecular Biology Inst., 1965—83, dir. biotech. program, 1985—88, 1985-89, prof. emeritus, 1989—; chmn. biochemistry study sect. USPHS, 1962—67. Mem. U.S. Nat. Com. for Biochemistry, 1965—71. Editor: Ann. Rev. of Biochemistry, 1965—71; assoc. editor:, 1972—88; editor: Biochemical and Biophysical Research Communications, 1969—79, The Enzymes, 1970—; mem. editl. bd.: Biochemistry, 1969—76, Jour. Biol. Chemistry, 1978—83, 1987—; contbr. articles to profl. jours. Recipient McCoy award chem. rsch., 1976, Tolman award, 1984, Rose award, Am. Soc. Chemistry and Molecular Biology, 1989, UCLA medal, 1998; co-recipient Nobel prize for chemistry, 1997; fellow Guggenheim Found., 1955—56. Fellow: AAAS (v.p. biol. scis. 1985—88, council); mem.: NAS, Biophys. Soc., Am. Chem. Soc. (chmn., biochem. divsn. 1959—60, Enzyme Chemistry award 1955), Am. Soc. Biol. Chemists (pres. 1969—70, council mem.). Home: 1033 Somera Rd Los Angeles CA 90077-2625 Office: Dept Chem-Biochem Paul Boyer Hall 639 607 Charles E Young Dr E Box 951569 Los Angeles CA 90095-0001

BOYKO, EDWARD JOHN, internist, medical researcher; b. Bethlehem, Pa., Feb. 19, 1953; s. Edward and Mary (Levan) B.; m. Beth Welcome Alderman, Sept. 27, 1980; children: Eva Jane, Bryan Martin. BA, Columbia U., 1975; MD, U. Pitts., 1979; MPH, U. Wash., 1984. Intern, internal medicine U. Chgo. Hospitals and Clinics, Ill., 1979—80, resident, internal medicine Ill., 1980—82; fellow Robert Wood Johnson Scholars Program, U. Wash., Seattle, 1982-84; attending physician U. Colo., Denver, 1984—, asst. prof. medicine and preventive medicine, 1984—; asst. prof. dept. medicine U. Wash, 1989-92, assoc. prof, 1992—97, prof. medicine, 1997—; dir. Seattle Epidemiologic Rsch. and Info. Ctr. (ERIC); chief, gen. internal medicine sect. VA Puget Sound Health Care Sys. Spl. mem. NIH study sect., Washington, 1988; mem. Nat. Diabetes Data Group, NIDDK, 1992; adj. prof. dept. epidemiology, U. Wash. Contbr. articles to med. jours. Recipient Career Develop. award, Nat. Found. for Heitis and Colitis, 1986—89, U. Wash. Medicine/Ctr. of Excellence in Women's Health award for Outstanding Mentorship, 2004. Mem. Soc. Epidemiologic Rsch., Am. Diabetes Assn., Alpha Omega Alpha. Avocations: skiing, hiking. Home: 4551 NE 41st St Seattle WA 98105-5109 Office: VA Puget Sound Health Care Sys 111 M 1660 S Columbian Way Campus Box 358280 Seattle WA 98108 also: U Wash 1100 Olive Way Ste 1400 Seattle WA 98101 Office Phone: 206-764-2830. Office Fax: 206-764-2563. Personal E-mail: eboyko@u.washington.edu.

BOYLAN, MERLE NELSON, librarian, educator; b. Youngstown, Ohio, Feb. 24, 1925; s. Merle Nelson and Alma Joy (Kepple) B. BA, Youngstown U., 1950; M.L.S., Carnegie-Mellon U., 1956; postgrad., U. Ariz., 1950—51, Ind. U., 1952. Libr., Pub. Health Libr. U. Calif., Berkeley, 1956-58; sci. librarian U. Ariz., Tucson, 1958-59; engring. librarian Gen. Dynamics/Convair, San Diego, 1959-61, Gen. Dynamics/Astronautics, 1961-62; assoc. librarian Lawrence Radiation Lab., U. Calif., Livermore, 1962-64, library mgr., 1964-67; chief librarian NASA Ames Rsch. Ctr., Moffett Field, Calif., 1968-69; asso. dir. libraries U. Mass., Amherst, 1969-70, dir. libraries, Univ. librarian, 1970-72; dir. libraries U. Tex., Austin, 1973-77, U. Wash., Seattle, 1977-89, dir. emeritus, 1989—, prof. Sch. Librarianship, 1982-89; exec. bd. Amigos Bibliographic Council, 1974-77; mem. fin. com., governance com., user's council, computer service council Wash. Library Network, 1978—. Del. Gov.'s Conf. Librs. and Info. Svcs., 1979; sec. Texas State Bd. Libr. Examiners, 1974-77; mem. bibliographic networking and resource sharing advisory group Southwestern Libr. Interstate Coop. Endeavor, 1975-77; sec., chmn. exec. bd. Pacific N.W. Bibliographic Ctr., 1977-83; mem. com. centralzed acquisitions of libr. materials for internat. studies Ctr. for Rsch. Librs.; del. OCLC Users Coun., 1981-86. Sec. bd. trustees Littlefield Fund for So. History, 1974-77, Fred Meyer Charitable Trust; mem. adv. bd. Libr. and Info. Resources for Northwest, 1984-87. Mem. ALA, Assn. Coll. and Rsch. Librs. (legis. com. 1977-81), Assn. Rsch. Librs. (bibliographic control com. 1979-83), Spl. Librs. Assn., Am. Soc. Info. Sci., Beta Phi Mu. Home: 1354 Bellefield Park Ln Bellevue WA 98004-6854 Office: Univ of Wash Librs Suzzallo Libr Seattle WA 98195-0001 Home Phone: 425-453-9440.

BOYLE, ALAN, editor; b. Bernard, Iowa, Aug. 24, 1954; s. Orland and Irma Boyle; m. Tonia Boyle; children: Natalie, Evan. BA in English and Philosophy, Loras Coll., Dubuque, Iowa, 1976; MS in Journalism, Columbia U., NYC, 1977. Features editor Spokesman-Rev., Spokane, Wash., 1978—84; fgn. desk editor Seattle Post-Intelligencer, 1985—96; sci. editor MSNBC, Redmond, Wash., 1997—. Presenter in field. Author: (web coverage) MSNBC Space News (Space Journalism award, 06), (web log) Cosmic Log (Sci. Journalism award AAAS, 02, Communication award (Online/Internet), NAS, 2008). Mem.: Coun. Advancement Sci. Writing (bd. dirs. 2005—), Nat. Assn. Sci. Writers, Soc. Profl. Journalists (pres. western Wash. pro chpt. 2002—03), NW Sci. Writers Assn. (pres. 2005—08). Office: MSNBC 1 Microsoft Way Redmond WA 98052

BOYLE, BARBARA DORMAN, film company executive; b. NYC, Aug. 11, 1935; d. William and Edith (Kleiman) Dorman; m. Kevin Boyle, Nov. 26, 1960; children: David Eric, Paul Coleman. BA in English with honors, U. Calif., Berkeley, 1957; JD, UCLA, 1960. Bar: Calif. 1961, N.Y. 1964, U.S. Supreme Ct. 1964. Atty. bus. affairs dept, corp. asst. sec. Am. Internat. Pictures, LA, 1960-65; ptnr. Cohen & Boyle, LA, 1967-74; exec. v.p., gen. counsel, chief op. officer New World Pictures, LA, 1974-82; sr. v.p. prodn. Orion Pictures Corp., LA, 1982-85; exec. v.p. prodn. RKO Pictures, LA, 1986-87; pres. Sovereign Pictures, Inc., LA, 1988-92, Boyle and Taylor Prodns., 1993-99, Valhalla Motion Pictures, LA, 2000—03; chair film, TV and digital media dept. UCLA, 2003—. Lectr. in field. Exec. prodr. (film) Eight Men Out, 1987, Bottle Rocket, 1995, Campus Man; prodr. (films) Mrs. Munck, 1995, Phenomenon, 1996, Instinct, 1999; exec. prodr. The Hi Line, 1998; co-prodr. Phenomenon II, 2002; contbr. chpts. to books. Bd. dirs. UCLA Law Fund Com., L.A. Women's Campaign Fund; pres. Ind. Feature Project/West; founding mem. entertainment adv. coun. sch. law UCLA, co-chmn. 1979-80, co-chair, 2002-03. Named UCLA Law Sch. Alumni of Yr, 1999, Women in Film Crystal award, 2000. Mem. Acad. Motion Picture Arts and Scis. (exec. com.), Acad. TV Arts and Scis. (exec. com.), Women in Film (pres. 1977-78), Hollywood Women's Polit. Com., Calif. Bar Assn., N.Y. State Bar Assn. Office: UCLA Sch of Theater Film & TV 203 E Melnitz Box 951622 Los Angeles CA 90095-1622 Office Phone: 310-825-7741.

BOYLE, DAN, professional hockey player; b. Ottawa, Ont., Can., July 12, 1976; m. Amber Boyle, June 2008. Defenseman Fla. Panthers, 1999—2002, Tampa Bay Lightning, 2002—08, San Jose Sharks, 2008—. Named to West First All-Am. Team, NCAA, 1998, Second All-Star Team, NHL, 2007, NHL All-Star Game, 2009. Achievements include being a member of Stanley Cup Champion Tampa Bay Lightning, 2004. Office: San Jose Sharks 525 W Santa Clara St San Jose CA 95113*

BOYLE, DANNY, film director; b. Manchester, Eng., Oct. 20, 1956; Dir.: Shallow Grave, 1994 (Silver Seashell award San Sebastian Internat. Film Festival, best dir., 1994, Alexander Korda award, Brit. Acad. Awards, best Brit. film, 1994), Trainspotting, 1996 (Golden Space Needle award Seattle Internat. Film Festival, best dir., 1996, nominated Ind. Spirit award, Best Fgn. Film, 1997, nominated Alexander Korda award, Brit. Acad. Awards, best Brit. film, 1996, Bodil Festival award, best European film, 1996), A Life Less Ordinary, 1997, The Beach, 2000, Alien Love Triangle, 2002, Vacuuming Completely Nude in Paradise, 2001, Strumpet, 2001, 28 Days Later..., 2002, Millions, 2004, Sunshine, 2007, Slumdog Millionaire, 2008 (Best Dir. for Brit. Ind. Film Brit. Ind. Film Awards, 2008, Best Dir. Washington DC Area Film Critics Assn., 2008, African Am. Film Critics Assn., 2008, Satellite award for Best Dir. Internat. Press Acad., 2008, 2008 Best Dir., Critics' Choice award, Broadcast Film Critics Assn., 2009, Best Dir. - Motion Picture, Golden Globe award, Hollywood Fgn. Press Assn., 2009, Best Motion Picture - Drama, 2009, Best Dir., LA Film Critics Assn., 2009, Outstanding Directorial Achievement in Feature Film, Dirs. Guild America, 2009, Best Dir., Brit. Acad. Film and TV Arts, 2009, Acad. award for Best Directing, 2009); dir. (TV series): Inspector Morse, 1987, Mr. Wroe's Virgins, 1993; exec. prodr.: Twin Town, 1997; prodr.: Elephant, 1989 Republican. Office: c/o DGA 7920 W Sunset Blvd Los Angeles CA 90046-3300

BOYLE, JUDY, state legislator; Freelance writer; natural resource dir. US Rep. Helen Chenoweth-Hage; mem. Dist. 9 Idaho House of Reps., 2008—. Former leader 4-H Club; chmn. Pacific Legal Found. Idaho Adv. Bd.; v.p. Adams-Valley County Farm Bur.; mem. Ranchers-Cattlemen Action Legal Fund. Mem.: NRA (NRA Friends com.), Weiser River Cattlemen. Republican. Office: Capitol Annex PO Box 83720 Boise ID 83720-0054 also: PO Box 57 Midvale ID 83645 Office Phone: 208-334-2475, 208-631-2123. Office Fax: 208-334-2125, 208-355-3225. Business E-Mail: jboyle@house.idaho.gov.*

BOYLE, (CHARLES) KEITH, artist, educator; b. Defiance, Ohio., Feb. 15, 1930; Student, Ringling Sch. Art; B.F.A., U. Iowa. Prof. painting and drawing Stanford U., Calif., 1962-88. Group shows include Stanford U. Mus., 1964, San Francisco Mus. Art, 1965, Ann Arbor, Mich., 1965, Joslyn Art Mus., Omaha, 1970, San Jose Mus. Art, Calif., 1978; represented in permanent collections: San Francisco Mus. Art, Stanford U. Mus., Mead paper Corp., Atlanta, Nat. Fine Arts Collection, Washington, Oakland Mus., Continental Bank, Chgo., Seton Med. Ctr., Daily City, Calif., Schneider Mus., Ashland, Oreg. Grantee NEA, 1981-82, Pew Meml. Trust, 1986-87. Address: 507 Modoc St Reno NV 89509-3339

BOYLE, KEVIN RICHARD, lawyer; s. Richard E. and Janet E. Boyle. BA, Vanderbilt U., 1994; JD 1st in class, U. Ariz., 1997. Bar: Calif. 1997, DC 1999, U.S. Ct. Appeals (9th cir.) 1998, U.S. Dist. Ct. (ctrl., no. and so. dists.) Calif. 2001. Law clk. to Hon. Melvin Brunetti U.S. Ct. Appeals (9th cir.), Reno, 1997—98; assoc. Kirkland & Ellis, Washington, 1998—99; law clk. to Chief Justice William H. Rehnquist U.S. Supreme Ct., Washington, 1999—2000; atty. Greene, Broillet, Panish & Wheeler, Santa Monica, Calif., 2001—05; founding ptnr. Panish, Shea & Boyle, LA, 2005—. Named Top 100 Lawyers, Calif. Daily Jour. Office: Panish Shea & Boyle 11111 Santa Monica Blvd Ste 700 Los Angeles CA 90025 Office Phone: 310-477-1700. Business E-Mail: Boyle@PSandB.com.

BOYLE, LARRY MONROE, federal judge; b. Seattle, June 23, 1943; s. Thomas L. and Winona (Green) B.; m. Beverly Rigby, Jan 31, 1969; children: Brian, Jeffery, Bradley, David, Melissa, Layne. BSc, Brigham Young U., 1968; JD, U. Idaho, 1972. Bar: Idaho 1973, U.S. Dist. Ct. Idaho 1973. Atty. Hansen, Boyle, Beard & Martin, P.A., Idaho Falls, Idaho, 1973-86; dist. judge 7th Jud. Dist., Idaho Falls,

1986-89; judge U.S. Supreme Ct. Idaho, Boise, 1989-92; magistrate judge U.S. Dist. Ct. Idaho, Boise, 1992—, chief magistrate judge. Office: US Courthouse Box 040 550 W Fort St Boise ID 83724-0101

BOYLE, MICHAEL FABIAN, lawyer; b. Lynwood, Calif., Apr. 11, 1949; s. Erwin Francis Boyle and Phanelphia (Gibson) Brunkow; 1 child, Conor Francis; m. Judy Pettigrew, May 14, 1986. BA, San Diego State U., 1972; JD, U. Calif., 1975. Bar: Calif. 1975, US Dist. Ct. (no. dist.) Calif. 1975. Assoc. Connolley, Hothem & Flint, San Francisco, 1975-77; ptnr. Higgs, Fletcher & Mack, San Diego, 1978—2006, gen. counsel J.R. Filanc Constrn. Co., 2006-. Deans adv. com. Coll. Art & Letters, 2002—. Contbr. articles to profl. jours. Bd. dirs. San Diego Hospice Corp. Bd., 1989-91, mem. The Mayor and City Coun. Citizens Fin. Com., 1990. Capt. USAR, 1971-82. Mem. ABA, Calif. Bar Assn., San Diego County Bar Assn. (chmn. ins. com.), San Diego State Univ. Alumni Assn. (officer, bd. dirs. 1984-89), Construction Fin. Mgnt. Assn. (officer, bd. dirs. 1986-92), San Diego County Taxpayers Assn. (officer, bd. dirs. 1997) Democrat. Roman Catholic. Home: 13482 Caminito Carmel Del Mar CA 92014-3847 Office: 740 N Andreasen Dr Escondido CA 92029 Home Phone: 858-481-9388; Office Phone: 760-941-7130. Business E-Mail: mboyle@filanc.com.

BOYLEN, JIM, men's college basketball coach; b. East Grand Rapids, Mich., Apr. 18, 1965; m. Christine Boylen; children: Ashlen Clare, Layla Blue. B in Bus., U. Maine, 1987. Grad. asst. Mich. State U. Spartans, 1987—89, asst. coach, 1989—92, 2005—07; video coord. Houston Rockets, 1992—94, asst. coach, 1994—2003, Golden State Warriors, 2003—04, Milw. Bucks, 2004—05; head basketball coach U. Utah Utes, 2007—. Office: Univ Utah Athletics Dept 1825 E South Campus Dr Salt Lake City UT 84112-0900 Office Phone: 801-581-5451.*

BOYTER, CALE, film company executive; b. June 28, 1972; m. Melissa Boyter; 1 child. Student, Mont. State U. With Paradigm; asst. to sr. v.p. devel. New Line Cinema, LA. Exec. prodr.: (films) Dumb and Dumberer, 2003, Elf, 2003, Butterfly Effect, 2004, Boy-Next-Door, 2004, A Hist. of Violence, 2005, Wedding Crashers, 2005, Just Friends, 2005, Grilled, 2006, How to Eat Fried Worms, 2006. Office: New Line Cinema 116 N Robertson Blvd Los Angeles CA 90048-3103

BOZARTH, GEORGE S., historian, musicologist, musician; b. Trenton, NJ, Feb. 28, 1947; MFA, Princeton U., 1973; PhD, Princeton U., 1978. Prof. music history U. Wash. Dir. Brahms Archive, Seattle, Internat. Brahms Conf., Washington, 1983; co-artistic dir. Gallery Concerts, Seattle. Editor: Johannes Brahms, Orgelwerke, The Organ Works, Munich, G Henle, 1988, J.S. Bach Cantata, Ach Gott vom Himmel sieh darein, BWV2, Neue Bach Augabe, 1/16, 1981, 84, The Correspondence of Johannes Brahms and Robert Keller, 1996, Brahms Studies: Analytical and Historical Perspectives, 1990; contbr. articles to profl. jours. and vols. of studies. Fulbright-Hayes scholar to Austria, 1975-77; fellow ACLS, 1982; NEH Rsch. Conf. grantee, 1983; grantee Am. Philos. Soc., 1999. Mem. Am. Brahms Soc. (exec. dir.), Am. Musicol. Soc., Early Music Am., Classical Consort. Office: U Wash Sch Music PO Box 353450 Seattle WA 98195-3450

BOZDECH, MAREK JIRI, physician, educator; b. Wildflecken, Bavaria, Federal Republic Germany, Oct. 12, 1946; s. Jiri Josef and Zofia Jadwiga (Swiatecka) B.; m. Frances Barclay Craig, Dec. 22, 1967; children: Elizabeth, Andrew, Matthew. AB, U. Mich., 1967; MD, Wayne State U., 1972. Diplomate Am. Bd. Internal Medicine, Am. Bd. Med. Oncology, Am. Bd. Hematology. Intern and resident in internal medicine U. Wis. Hosps., Madison, 1972-75, dir. clin. hematology lab., 1978-82, dir. bone marrow transplantation, 1984-85; asst. prof. medicine U. Wis., Madison, 1978-84, assoc. prof. medicine, 1984-85; clin. fellow in hematology Moffitt Hosp. U. Calif., San Francisco, 1975-76, postdoctoral fellow in hematology Cancer Research Inst., 1976-78, research assoc. Cancer Research Inst., 1977-78, assoc. prof., 1985-89; dir. adult bone marrow transplantation U. Calif. Med. Ctr., San Francisco, 1985-89; chief oncology Kaiser Permanente Med. Ctr., Santa Rosa, Calif., 1989-91; pvt. practice specializing in oncology Hematology Redwood Regional Oncology Ct., Santa Rosa, 1991—. Contbr. articles to profl. jours. Scout leader Boy Scouts Am., Novato, Calif., 1985; bd. trustees Pacific Found. Med. Care, 1995—. Recipient Nat. Research Service award NIH, 1977-78; Wayne State U. scholar, 1971. Mem. ACP, Am. Soc. Hematology, Am. Soc. Clin. Oncology, Assn. No. Calif. Oncologists (bd. dirs. 1994-97), Sonoma County Med. Assn. (bd. dirs. 1994-96). Avocations: skiing, gardening, music, films, theater. Home: 50 La Placita Ct Novato CA 94945-1244 Office: Redwood Regional Oncology 121 Sotoyome St Ste 203 Santa Rosa CA 95405-4822 Personal E-mail: mbozdech@mindspring.com, mbozdech@yahoo.com.

BRACCO, LORRAINE, actress; b. Bklyn., Oct. 2, 1954; m. Daniel Guerard, 1979 (div. 1982); 1 child, Margaux; m. Harvey Keitel, 1982 (div. 1993); 1 child, Stella; m. Edward James Olmos, Jan. 28, 1994 (div. Mar. 1, 2002). Studied, Actors Studio; studied with Stella Adler, Ernie Martin, John Strasberg. Actress: (films) Duos sur canape, 1979, What Did I Ever Do to the Good Lord to Deserve a Wife Who Dinks in Cafes with Men?, 1980, Commissaire Moulin, 1980, Fais gaffe a la gaffe, 1981, A Complex Plot About Women, Alleys and Crimes, 1986, The Pick-Up Artist, 1987, Someone to Watch Over Me, 1987, Sing, 1989, The Dream Team, 1989, As Long as It's Love, 1989, Sea of Love, 1989, Goodfellas, 1990 (Acad. award nominee for best supporting actress 1990, LA Film Critics Assoc. award for best sup. actress, 1990), Talent for the Game, 1991, Switch, 1991, Medicine Man, 1992, Radio Flyer, 1992, Traces of Red, 1992, Being Human, 1994, Even Cowgirls Get the Blues, 1994, The Basketball Diaries, 1995, Hackers, 1995, Les Menteurs, 1996, Silent Cradle, 1997, Ladies Room, 1999, Tangled, 2000, Your Aura is Throbbing, 2000, Riding in Cars With Boys, 2001, Tangled, 2001, Death of a Dynasty, 2003, Max and Grace, 2004, My Suicidal Sweetheart, 2005; (TV movies) Scam, 1993, Getting Gotti, 1996, Lifeline, 1996, The Taking of Pelham One Two Three, 1998, Custody of the Heart, 2000, Sex in our Century, 2001, Dinner with the FoodFellas, 2006; (TV series) The Sopranos, 1999-2007,(Outstanding Performance by an Ensemble in a Drama Series, 2000, 2008); (TV appearances) Crime Story, 1986, Law & Order: Trial By Jury, 2005; (off-Broadway plays) Goose and Tom-Tom; (Broadway plays) The Graduate, 2002; dir. (films) AutoMotives, 2000; Author: On the Couch, 2006 Mem.: bd. of dir. Riverkeeper, NY Council for the Humanities. Office: First Artists Assoc 12 W 57th St #PH New York NY 10019-3900

BRACHMAN, RON, research and development company executive; BSEE, Princeton U.; MS, PhD, Harvard U. Rsch. v.p. AT&T Labs, 1986—2002; dir. info. processing tech. office U.S. Def. Advanced Rsch. Projects Agy., 2002—05; v.p. worldwide rsch. ops. Yahoo! Inc., NYC, 2005—. Co-author (with Hector Levesque): (textbook) Knowledge Representation and Reasoning, 2004. Fellow: Am. Assn. Artificial Intelligence (past pres.). Office: Yahoo Inc 701 1st Ave Sunnyvale CA 94089

BRACK, O. M., JR., language educator; b. Houston, Nov. 30, 1938; s. O. M. and Olivia Mae (Rice) B.; 1 child, Matthew Rice; m. Cynthia Alison Burns, May 22, 2004. Student, U. Houston, 1956-57; BA, Baylor U., Waco, Tex., 1960, MA, 1961; PhD, U. Tex., Austin, 1965. Asst. prof. William Woods Coll., 1964-65; asst. prof. English lit. U. Iowa, Iowa City, 1965-68, assoc. prof., 1968-73, dir. center textual studies, 1967-73; prof. English lit. Ariz. State U., Tempe, 1973—2008, prof. emeritus, 2008—. Chmn. 18th Century Short Title Catalogue Com., 1970-73; pres. Arete Publs., Ltd., 1976-81; Albert H. Smith Meml. lectr. bibliography Birmingham Bibliog. Soc., Eng., 1983; vis. fellow U. Oxford Wolfson Coll., 1986-87; mem. adv. bd. 18th-Century Brit. Periodical Subject Index, 1996—, Soc. for Textual Scholarship, 1998; bd. dirs. 18th-Century Short-Title Catalogue, Inc., 1999-2000. Author: Bibliography and Textual Criticism, 1969, Samuel Johnson's Early Biographers, 1971, Hoole's Death of Johnson, 1972, Henry Fielding's Pasquin, 1973, A Catalogue of the Leigh Hunt Manuscripts, 1973, The Early Biographies of Samuel Johnson, 1974, American Humor, 1977, Twilight of Dawn, 1987, Writers, Books and Trade, 1994, Samuel Johnson in New Albion, 1997, The Macaroni Person and the Concentrated Mind, 2004, A Commentary on Mr. Pope's Principles of Morality, or Essay on Man, 2004, The Devil Upon Crutches, 2005, Tobias Smollett, Scotland's First Novelist, 2007, Hawkin's Life of Samuel Johnson, 2009; textual editor: Works of Tobias Smollett, 1966—; gen. editor: Works of Tobias Smollett, 1973-86; editor: English Literature in Transition, 1981-82, mem. editl. com., 1982—91; editor: Studies in Eighteenth Century Culture, 1981-86; mem. editl. com.: Yale edit. Works of Samuel Johnson, 1977—; editl. cons. The Literature of England, Scott, Foresman & Co., 1977-79, Works of David Hume, Princeton U. Press, 1990-91, Oxford U. Press, 1995-97; asst. editor: Eighteenth-Century Bibliography, 1964-73, Books at Iowa, 1966-73; editor Eighteenth Century: A Current Bibliography, 1983-90; mem. editl. com.: Age of Johnson, 1985-2003, Rocky Mountain Rev. of Lang. and Lit., 1980-98, Clarissa Project, 1987-2000. Mem. Salvation Army Coun., South Mountain Corps, 1996-2002, chair, 1999-2002. Recipient Grad. Coll. Disting. Rsch. award, 1981—82, Rocky Mountains MLA Huntington Libr. award, 1986, Humanities Rsch. award, 1989—90, Faculty Achievement award, Ariz. State U. Alumni Assn., 1991; named Grad. Coll. Outstanding Mentor, 2000; grantee, Am. Philos. Soc., 1967, NEH, 1993—95, 1995—98, Huntington Libr., 2007—; fellow, 1978, Am. Coun. Learned Soc., 1979—80, Newberry Libr., 1982, Andrew W. Mellon Fund, Huntington Libr., 1994, Huntington Libr., 1996, 1997; scholar Disting. scholar, Phi Kappa Phi, 1975. Mem. MLA, Am. Soc. 18th Century Studies, East-Ctrl. Soc. 18th Century Studies, South Central 18th Century Soc. (pres. 1982-83), Western Soc. for 18th Century Studies (pres. 2000-01), Brit. Soc. 18th Century Studies, Rocky Mountain MLA, Bibliog. Soc. Am., Bibliog. Soc. U. Va., Bibliog. Soc. (London), Printing Hist. Soc., Am. Printing History Assn., Assn. for Scottish Literary Studies, Samuel Johnson Soc. So. Calif. (bd. dirs. 1989—, pres. 1994-95), The Lichfield Johnson Soc., The Johnson Soc. London, The Johnson Soc. Australian, Grolier Club, The Johnsonians (pres. 2001-02). Episcopalian. Business E-Mail: om.brack@asu.edu.

BRACKEN, THOMAS ROBERT JAMES, real estate investment executive; b. Spokane, Wash., Jan. 1, 1950; s. James Lucas and Frances (Cadzow) B.; m. Linda Jacobson, Sept. 9, 1972; children: Karl Forest, David Erskine. BS, Yale U., 1971; MBA, Columbia U., 1972. Sr. appraiser Prudential Ins., NYC, 1972-74, mgr. real estate NYC and Newark, 1974-76, assoc. gen. mgr. Seattle, 1977-78; v.p. First City Investments, Seattle, 1978-80; pres. Fenix, Inc., Seattle, 1980-86; v.p. Washington Mortgage Corp., Seattle, 1982-85, exec. v.p., 1986-88; sr. v.p. Pioneer Bank, Lynwood, Wash., 1985-86; pres.real estate financing USL Capital, San Francisco, 1988-97; sr. v.p. real estate fin. group Orix, USA, San Francisco, 1997-98; pres. Presidio Interfunding Corp., San Francisco, 1998-99; dir. L.J. Melody & Co., San Jose, Calif., 2000—03; mem. Crossbow Capital, LLC, Los Altos, Calif., 2000—; mng. dir. The Broe Cos., San Francisco, 2003—05; sr. v.p. Capmark Fin. Inc., San Francisco, San Jose, 2005—. Mem. Nat. Assn. Indsl./Office Parks (v.p. Seattle chpt. 1981-83), Yale Assn. Western Wash. (pres. 1984-86), Urban Land Inst., Mortgage Bankers Assn. Presbyterian. Avocations: running, sports. Office: Capmark Fin Inc 601 Montgomery St 15th Fl San Francisco CA 94111 Office Phone: 415-646-7712. Personal E-mail: tombracken@msn.com. E-mail: tom.bracken@capmark.com.

BRADBURY, BILL (WILLIAM CHAPMAN BRADBURY III), former state official; b. Chgo., May 29, 1949; s. William L. and Lorraine (Patterson) B.; m. Betsy Harrison (Sept. 1984); children: Abby, Zoe; m. Kathleen P. Eymann, June 7, 1986. Student, Antioch Coll., 1967-69. News reporter KQED-TV Newsroom, 1969-70; dir. pub. affairs Sta. KMPX-FM, San Francisco, 1970; mem. video prodn. group Optic Nerve, San Francisco, 1970-73; project dir. Coos Country TV, Bandon, Oreg., 1973-75; reporter, anchor Sta. KVAL-TV, Eugene, Oreg., 1975-76; news dir. Sta. KCBY-TV, Coos Bay, Oreg., 1976-78; prodr., writer, editor video news feature src. Local Color, Langlois, Oreg., 1978-79; field prodr. PM Mag., Sta. KGW-TV, Portland, Oreg., 1979-80; mem. Oreg. House Reps., Salem, 1980-84, Oreg. State Senate, Salem, 1984-95, pres., 1993-95; exec. dir. Sake of the Salmon, Gladstone, Oreg., 1995-99; sec. state State of Oreg., Salem, 1999—2009. Chmn. Western Legis. Conf., Coun. State Govs., 1991, mem. ocean resources com.; founder, former chmn. Pacific Fishery Legis. Task Force. Prodr. documentaries Gorda Ridge—Boom or Bust for the Oregon Coast?, The Tillamook Burn—From Ruin to Rejuvenation, Not Guilty by Reason of Insanity, Child as Witness, Local Color, Salmon on the Run, The First Perennial Poetic Hoohaw, TV Town Hall Meetings, Common Sense, also prodr. mktg. videos and commls. for polit. candidates, hosp. Democrat. Mem. Soc. Of Friends. Avocation: kayaking.*

BRADEN, GEORGE WALTER, II, sales executive; b. LA, Sept. 1, 1936; s. Paul Sumner and Evelyn Widney (Traver) B.; m. Trina Rose Thomas, July 3, 1964; children: Barbara Diane, Beverly Eileen Braden Christensen. BS, Calif. State U., 1963; grad. cert., U. So. Calif., 1990, Harvard U., 1991; postgrad., UCLA, 1990—; MBA, Chadwick U.; JA, Blackstone Law Sch. Mgr. western region vet. div. Bristol-Myers, Syracuse, N.Y., 1970-79; pres. Braden Sales Assocs. Internat., Apple Valley, Calif., 1980—. Mem. Friends of Hoover Inst., Stanford, Calif., Courtenay Soc. Powderham Castle Exeter, Devon, Eng., chmn.; charter mem. Rep. Presdl. Task Force, Washington, 1989—; commr. Rep. Presdl. Adv. Com., Washington, 1991—; active Nat. Rep. Senatorial Com. Capt. USMB, 1985-93, maj., 1993—. Recipient Presdl. order of Merit, Heritage Found., Rep. Presdl. award, 1994, Order of St. John, 1999; numerous awards Boy Scouts of Am.; named Lord of North Bovey, Lord of Newton Bushel. Mem. Am. Mktg. Assn., Tex. A&M U. Internat. Assn. of Agri-Bus., Curia Baronis Guild for Barons, Lords of Manor, Pres.'s Club, Order of St. John. Mem. Lds Ch.

BRADFORD, DAVID S., surgeon; b. Charlotte, NC, Oct. 15, 1936; m. Sharon Hale; children: David Mackay, Jennifer Sutherland, Tyler Speir. BA, Davidson Coll., 1958; MD, U. Pa., 1962. Diplomate: Am. Bd. Orthopaedic Surgeons. Intern in surgery Columbia-Presbyn. Med. Center, NYC, 1962-63, resident in gen. surgery, 1965-66; resident in orthopaedic surgery N.Y. Orthopaedic Hosp., Columbia-Presbyn. Med. Center, NYC, 1966-68, jr. Annie C. Kane fellow orthopaedic surgery, 1968-69; research trainee orthopaedics Nat. Inst. Arthritis and Metabolic Diseases, 1969-70; prof. orthopaedic surgery U. Minn. Hosps., Mpls., 1970-90, chief of spine surgery, 1984-90; dir. Twin Cities Scoliosis Spine Ctr., Mpls., 1984—90; prof., chmn. dept. orthopaedic surgery U. Calif., San Francisco, 1991—. Mem. bd. editors: Spine, Spine Journal, Spine Letter, AOA News, Clinical Orthopaedics and Related Rsch., Journal of Am. Academy of Orthopaedic Surgeons, Journal of Orthopaedic Rsch.; contbr. articles to profl. jours. Mem. AMA, Am. Acad. Orthopaedic Surgeons, Am. Orthopaedic Assn., Assn. Bone and Joint Surgeons (past pres.), Orthopaedic Rsch. Soc., Scoliosis Rsch. Soc. (past pres.), British Scoliosis Soc., European Spine Deformity Soc., Internat. Soc. Orthopaedic Surgery and Traumatology, N. Am. Spine Soc., Orthopaedic Rsch. & Educational Found., Scoliosis Rsch. Soc., Spine Arthroplasty Soc. Office: U of Calif San Francisco Dept Orthopedic Surgery MU-320W Box 0728 San Francisco CA 94143-0728 Office Phone: 415-476-2280.

BRADFORD, JOANNE K., Internet company executive; b. 1963; married; 2 children. BA in Journalism and Advertising, San Diego State U. Mgmt. tng. RH Macy, 1986; dist. sales mgr. Engring. News Record; acct. mgr. BusinessWeek mag. McGraw-Hill Cos., 1989, tech. mktg. mgr. BusinessWeek mag., v.p. sales Western region BusinessWeek mag., 1997, v.p. sales N. Am. Mktg. BusinessWeek mag.; v.p., chief media revenue officer MSN, Redmond, Wash., 2001—06; corp. v.p. global sales & trade mktg Microsoft Corp., Redmond, Wash., 2006—08; exec. v.p. nat. mktg. svcs. Spot Runner Inc., LA, 2008; sr. v.p., U.S. Revenue and Market Develop. Yahoo! Inc., Sunnyvale, Calif., 2008—. Recipient Chmn.'s award, Microsoft Corp., McGraw-Hill Excellence in Mgmt. award, BusinessWeek mag., 2000; named one of Media Up-and-Comers, BusinessWeek mag, Women to Watch, Advt. Age, 2003. Mem.: Interactive Advertising Bureau (bd. dirs.). Office: Yahoo! Inc 701 First Ave Sunnyvale CA 94089 Office Phone: 310-430-7900.

BRADFORD, LAURA KAY, state legislator, small business owner; b. Crookston, Minn., Jan. 9, 1957; d. Lawrence Charles and Phyllis Elaine (Thibodo) Sunsdahl; children: Elizabeth, Meredith, Preston. Student, Mesa State Coll., 1990-91. Lic. real estate agt. Pres. Pro-Safe Profl. Linens, Inc., Grand Junction, Colo., 1987-91, Bio-Dry Diaper, Grand Junction, 1991—; mem. Dist. 55 Colo. House of Reps., Denver, 2009—. Cons. State Dental Assisting of Colo., 1988-91, Mesa County Pub. Health, Grand Junction, 1990; mem. Colo. Women's Econ. Devel. Coun., 1995-2000. Inventor specialized linens, re-useable diaper. Deacon 1st Presbyn. Ch., Grand Junction, 1987-89. Mem. Nat. Fedn. Ind. Bus. Republican. Avocations: camping, sewing, fishing. Office: Pro Safe Products 830 1/2 S 7th St Grand Junction CO 81501 also: Colo State Capitol 200 E Colfax Denver CO 80203 Office Phone: 303-866-2583. Business E-Mail: laurabradford55@gmail.com.*

BRADLEY, CHARLES WILLIAM, podiatrist, educator; b. Fife, Tex., July 23, 1923; s. Tom and Mary Ada (Cheatham) B.; m. Marilyn A. Brown, Apr. 3, 1948 (dec. Mar. 1973); children: Steven, Gregory, Jeffrey, Elizabeth, Gerald. Student, Tex. Tech., 1940-42; D. Podiatric Medicine, Calif. Coll. Podiatric Medicine U. San Francisco, 1949, MPA, 1987, D.Sc. (hon.). Pvt. practice podiatry, Beaumont, Tex., 1950-51, Brownwood, Tex., 1951-52, San Francisco, San Bruno, Calif., 1952—; assoc. clin. prof. Calif. Coll. Podiatric Medicine, 1992-98. Chief of staff Calif. Podiatry Hosp., San Francisco; mem. surg. staff Sequoia Hosp., Redwood City, Calif.; mem. med. staff Peninsula Hosp., Burlingame, Calif.; chief podiatry staff St. Luke's Hosp., San Francisco; chmn. bd. Podiatry Ins. Co. Am.; cons. VA; assoc. prof. podiatric medicine Calif. Coll. Podiatric Medicine. Mem. San Francisco Symphony Found.; mem. adv. com. Health Policy Agenda for the Am. People, AMA; chmn. trustees Calif. Coll. Podiatric Medicine, Calif. Podiatry Coll., Calif. Podiatry Hosp.; mem. San Mateo Grand Jury, 1989. Served with USNR, 1942-45. Mem. Am. Podiatric Med. Assn. (trustee, pres. 1983-84), Calif. Podiatry Assn. (pres. No. div. 1964-66, state bd. dirs., pres. 1975-76, Podiatrist of Yr. award 1983), Nat. Coun. Edn. (vice-chmn.), Nat. Acads. Practice (chmn. podiatric med. sect. 1991-96, sec. 1996—), Am. Legion, San Bruno C. of C. (bd. dirs. 1978-91, v.p. 1992, bd. dir. grand jury assoc. 1990), Olympic Club, Commonwealth Club Calif., Elks, Lions. Home: 2965 Trousdale Dr Burlingame CA 94010-5708 Office: 560 Jenevein Ave San Bruno CA 94066-4408 E-mail: bradlee2@aol.com.

BRADLEY, DAVID T., state legislator; b. Seattle, Nov. 13, 1952; m. Debra D'Amore; children: Brian, Nathan, Sean, Brooke. BS in Psychology, U. Md., 1977; MS in Edn., Old Dominion U., Norfolk, Va., 1979; MBA, U. Phoenix, 1976. Cert. profl. counselor 1984, behavioral healthcare exec. 1989. Staff, dept. econ. security Palo Verde Hosp., Blythe, Calif., 1980—86; adminstr. Ramsey Canyon Hosp., Sierra Vista, Ariz., 1986—92; pres., exec. dir., CEO La Paloma Family Svcs., Tucson, 1993—; mem. Dist. 28 Ariz. House of Reps., 2003—. Vice-chair Pima County Dem. Party, 1993—94, chair, 2002; pres. Dems. of Greater Tucson, 1994—98, Behavior Healthcare Coalition Southern Ariz., 1999; mem. Cmty. Partnership Southern Ariz., 1999—2000. Coach Saharo Little League, 1986—96; active Vestry St. Michael & All Angels Ch. Served with USN, 1972—80. Mem.: Tuscon C. of C., Child Welfare League of America, Ariz. Cmty. Action Assn., Am. Legion, Tuscon Rotary. Democrat. Episcopalian. Office: Ariz House Reps Capitol Complex 1700 W Washington Rm 337 Phoenix AZ 85007 Office Phone: 602-926-3300. Office Fax: 602-417-3028. Business E-Mail: dbradley@azleg.gov.*

BRADLEY, DONALD EDWARD, lawyer; b. Santa Rosa, Calif., Sept. 26, 1943; s. Edward Aloysius and Mildred Louise (Kelley) B.; m. Marianne Stark, Apr. 22, 1990; children: Evan Patrick, Matthew Jordan, Andrea Phelps. AB, Dartmouth Coll., 1965; JD, U. Calif., San Francisco, 1968; LLM, N.Y.U., 1972. Bar: Calif. 1968, U.S. Dist. Ct.

(no. dist.) Calif. 1968, U.S. Ct. Appeals (9 cir.) 1968, U.S. Tax Ct. 1972, U.S. Ct. Claims 1973, U.S. Supreme Ct. 1981. Assoc. Pillsbury, Madison & Sutro, San Francisco, 1972-77, ptnr., 1978-84; mem. Wilson Sonsini Goodrich & Rosati, Palo Alto, Calif., 1984—, gen. counsel, ex office mem., bd. dirs. Mng. dir. Wilson Sonsini Goodrich & Rosati, Palo Alto, 1995—; adj. prof. Golden State U., San Francisco, 1973-82; pres., chmn. bd. dirs. Atty.'s Ins. Mut. Risk Retention Group, Honolulu, 1986-, mem., bd. dirs. Hastings Coll. Law, U. Calif., San Francisco. Capt. U.S. Army, 1969-70. Recipient Charles M. Ruddick award N.Y.U., 1972, award Bureau of Nat. Affairs, Washington, 1968. Mem. ABA, Internat. Bar Assn., Santa Clara Bar Assn., San Francisco Bar Assn., Internat. Tax Club. Office: Wilson Sonsini Goodrich & Rosati 650 Page Mill Rd Palo Alto CA 94304-1050 Office Phone: 650-493-9300. Office Fax: 650-493-6811. E-mail: dbradley@wsgr.com.

BRADLEY, GILBERT FRANCIS, retired bank executive; b. Miami, Ariz, May 17, 1920; s. Ever and Martha (Piper) B.; m. Marion Bebb, June 21, 1941; children: Larry Paul, Richard Thomas, Steven Ever. Grad., LaSalle Extension U., 1942, U. Wash., 1953; Advanced Mgmt. Program, Harvard U. With Valley Nat. Bank, Ariz., Miami, Globe, Clifton, Nogales and Phoenix, 1937—, pres. Phoenix, 1973-76, chmn. bd., chief exec. officer, 1976-82, ret., 1982, dir., vice chmn. exec. com., 1982—, Valley Nat. Corp., 1982—. Mem. adv. council Fed. Res. Bd., Comptroller of the Currency, Denver; instr. Am. Inst. Banking. Mem. Tucson Airport Authority, 1960—; mem. adv. council Ariz. State U. Sch. Bus., pres. dean's adv. council; dean's adv. council U. Ariz., Tucson. Served to capt. USAAF, 1942-45. Decorated D.F.C., Air medal with three oak leaf clusters. Mem. Ariz. Bankers Assn. (pres.), Assn. Res. City Bankers, Ariz. C. of C. (v.p., dir.), Tucson C. of C. (dir.), Better Bus. Bur. (dir.), Tucson Clearing House Assn. (past pres.), Navy League, Air Force Assn., Beta Gamma Sigma. Clubs: Masons, Rotary. Home: Apt 1102 7500 N Calle Sin Envidia Tucson AZ 85718-7349

BRADLEY, LAWRENCE D., JR., lawyer; b. Santa Monica, Calif., Feb. 19, 1920; s. Lawrence D. Bradley and Virginia L. Edwards; m. Joan Worthington, Feb. 1, 1945; children: Gary W., Brooks, Eric Scott. BS, USCG Acad., 1942; LLB, Stanford U. Law Sch., 1950. Bar: Calif. 1950, U.S. Dist. Ct. (ctrl. dist.) Calif. 1950, U.S. Dist. Ct. (so. dist.) Calif. 1967. Assoc. Pillsbury, Madison & Sutro, LA, 1950-59, ptnr., 1959—90; ret. ptnr. Pillsbury Winthrop Shaw Pittman LLP, 1990—. Lectr. admiralty and ins. law U. So. Calif., 1952-80. Pres. Stanford Law Rev., 1949-50; assoc. editor Am. Maritime Cases, 1990-2000. Mem. adv. bd. Tulane Admiralty Law Inst., 1990—. With USN, 1942-48; served to lt. comdr. Res. Mem. ABA, Calif. Bar Assn., Maritime Law Assn. U.S. (mem. exec. com. 1974-78, chmn. cruise line com. 1991-94), Inst. Navigation, Order of Coif, Calif. Club, Chancery Club, Calif. Yacht Club, San Diego Yacht Club, Propeller Club, Transpacific Yacht Club, Tutukaka South Pacific Yacht Club. Office: Pillsbury Winthrop Shaw Pittman LLP 725 S Figueroa St Ste 2800 Los Angeles CA 90017-5443 Home Phone: 310-472-4639; Office Phone: 213-488-7256.

BRADLEY, (R.) TODD, communications and computer company executive; b. Balt., Nov. 29, 1958; BSBA, Towson State U., Balt. V.p. Fed. Express; v.p., mng. dir. EMEA ops. AC Nielsen; various exec. positions to pres. NCH Promotional Svcs. subsidiary Dun & Bradstreet Corp., 1993—97; pres., CEO Transport Internat. Pool subsidiary of GE Capital Svcs., 1997—98; sr. v.p. Europe, Mid. East and Africa region Gateway Inc., San Diego, 1998—2001, sr. v.p. US consumer bus., 1999—2001; exec. v.p. global ops., 1999—2001; exec. v.p., COO Solutions Grp. Palm Inc., 2001—02, pres., COO Solutions Grp., 2002, CEO, Solutions Grp., 2001—03; CEO palmOne, Inc., Milpitas, Calif., 2003—05, adv., 2005; exec. v.p. personal systems grp. Hewlett-Packard Co., Palo Alto, Calif., 2005—. Bd. visitors Towson U. Office: Hewlett-Packard Co 3000 Hanover St Palo Alto CA 94304 Office Phone: 408-503-7000.*

BRADLEY, WALTER D., lieutenant governor, real estate broker; b. Clovis, N.Mex., Oct. 30, 1946; s. Ralph W. and M. Jo (Black) B.; m. Debbie Shelly, Sept. 17, 1977; children: Tige, Lance, Nicole, Kristin. Student, Eastern N.Mex. U., 1964—67. Supr. Tex. Instruments, Dallas, 1967—73; mgr., salesman Nat. Chemsearch, Irving, Tex., 1973—76; real estate broker, owner Colonial Real Estate, Clovis, 1976; real estate broker Realtors Assn. N.Mex., Clovis, N.Mex., 1976—; state senator Curry County, State of N.Mex., 1990—92; lt. gov. State of N.Mex., Santa Fe, 1995—2003; dir. comml. divsn. N.Mex. State Land Office, 2004; dir. bus. and govt. affairs Dairy Farmers Am., 2005—. V.p., bd. dirs. Clovis Indsl. Commn., 1983—86, pres. econ. devel., 1987; bd. dirs. United Way, Clovis, 1984—86, Curry County Blood Adv. Bd., Clovis, 1980—85; chmn. Curry County Reps., Clovis, 1984—88, Cosmos Soccer, Clovis, 1984. Recipient Leadership award, Albuquerque NAACP, 1997, Disting. Svc. award, N.Mex. Farm and Livestock Bur., 1997, Leadership Beautification award, Keep N.Mex. Beautiful, 2000, Mark Weidler Disting. Pub. Servant award, N.Mex. Petroleum Marketers Assn., 2000, Outstanding N.Mex. Small Bus. Supporter, N.Mex. Small Bus. Devel. Ctr., 1997, Outstanding Leadership award, N.Mex. Cattle Growers' Assn., 1996; named Man of Yr., Progressive Farmer Mag., 1998. Mem.: N.Mex. Jaycees, Curry County Jaycees, Clovis C. of C., Clovis Bd. Realtors (pres. 1982, 1993), Realtors Assn. N.Mex. (v.p., bd. dirs. 1982—85, v.p. 1987—88), Lions. Republican. Baptist. Home: 917 B Norris St Clovis NM 88101 Office Phone: 575-763-4528. E-mail: wbradley@dfamilk.com.

BRADLEY, WILLIAM STEVEN, art museum director; b. Salina, Kans., Aug. 20, 1949; s. William Bernard and Jane Ray (Gebhart) B; m. Kathryn Mann, Mar. 18, 1972; children: Kate, Christina, Megan, Emma, Drew. BA, U. Colo., 1971; MA, Northwestern U., 1974, PhD, 1981. Instr. Wells Coll., Aurora, N.Y., 1979-81; curator, asst. prof. Tex. Tech. U. and Mus., Lubbock, Tex., 1982-85; chief curator San Antonio Mus. Art, 1985-86; dir. Alexandria (La.) Mus. Art, 1987-92, Davenport (Iowa) Mus. Art, 1992—2001; asst. prof. art dept. Mesa State Coll., Grand Junction, Colo., 2006—. Vis. lectr. Cornell U., Ithaca, N.Y., 1980-81; cons. Am. Assn. Mus., Washington, 1989—. Author: Emil Nolde, 1986; editor: (catalog) Elemore Morgan, 1992, Emery Clark, 1989; reviewer Inst. Mus. Svcs., 1985-90. V.p. La. Assn. Mus., Baton Rouge, 1988, 90. Home: 576 1/2 Garden Grove Ct Grand Jct CO 81501-6908 Office: Mesa State Coll Art Dept 1100 North Ave Grand Junction CO 81501 Home Phone: 970-257-1785; Office Phone: 970-248-1073. E-mail: Wm549@aol.com, sbradley@mesastate.edu.

BRADSHAW, MURRAY CHARLES, musicologist, educator, composer; b. Hinsdale, Ill., Sept. 25, 1930; s. Murray Andrew and Marie (Novak) Orth; m. Doris Hogg (div.); children: Jean Marie, Murray Edward, Thomas Andrew; m. Sharon Ann Slitton, Apr. 19, 1997. MusM in Piano, Am. Conservatory Music, Chgo., 1955, MusM in Organ, 1958; PhD in Musicology, U. Chgo., 1969. Prof. UCLA, 1966—2004. Music critic Gary Post Tribune, Ind., 1962—64; chair dept. musicology UCLA, 1993—95. Author: The Origin of the Toccata, 1972, The Falsobordone, 1978, Francesco Severi, 1981, Girolamo Diruta The Transylvanian, 1984, Giovanni Luca Conforti, 1985, Gabriele Fattorini, 1986, Emilio d' Cavalieri, 1990, Conforti, "Breve et facile", 1999, Emilio de' Cavalieri, Rappresentatione di Anima, et di Corpo (1600), 2007; gen. editor: Musicological Studies and Documents and Miscellanea, 2000—; contbr. articles and reviews to profl. jours. Organist, choirmaster various chs., Ill., Ind., Calif., 1948—. With US Army, 1954—56. Grantee, Am. Philos. Soc., 1987; Travel grantee, NEH, 1994. Mem.: Am. Guild Organists, Am. Musicol. Soc. (pres. local chpt. 1979—81), Ctr. Medieval and Renaissance Studies. Avocations: walking, dance, bridge, languages. Home: 17046 Burbank Blvd Apt 3 Encino CA 91316-1830 Office: UCLA Dept Musicology 405 Hilgard Ave Los Angeles CA 90095-9000 Personal E-mail: mbrads3486@aol.com.

BRADSHAW, RALPH ALDEN, biochemistry educator; b. Boston, Feb. 14, 1941; s. Donald Bertram and Eleanor (Dodd) B.; m. Roberta Perry Wheeler, Dec. 29, 1961; children: Christopher Evan, Amy Dodd. BA in Chemistry, Colby Coll., 1962; PhD, Duke U., 1966. Asst. prof. Washington U., St. Louis, 1969-72, assoc. prof., 1972-74, prof., 1974-82; prof., chair dept. U. Calif., Irvine, 1982-93, prof., 1993—. Study sect. chmn. NIH, 1979, mem., 1975-79, 80-85; mem. sci. adv. bd. Hereditary Disease Found., 1983-87, ICN Nucleic Acids Rsch. Inst., 1986-87; rsch. study com. physiol. chem. Am. Heart Assn., 1984-86, mem. Coun. on Thrombosis, 1976-90; fellowship screening com. Am. Cancer Soc. Calif., 1984-87; chmn. adv. com. Western Winter Workshops, 1984-88; dir., chmn., mem. organizing com. numerous symposia, confs. in field including Proteins in Biology and Medicine, Shanghai, Peoples Republic of China, 1981, Symposium Am. Protein Chemists, San Diego, 1985, mem. exec. com. Keystone Symp. Mol. Cell. Biol., 1991-97, chmn., 1991-94, bd. dirs., 1997—, treas., 1997—; trustee Keystone Ctr., 1991-97; mem. exec. com. Internat. Union Biochem. Mol. Biol., 1991-97, U.S. Nat. Commn. Biochem., 1987-96, chmn., 1992-96; bd. dirs. Fed. Am. Soc. Exptl. Biology, 1992-96, v.p., 1994-95, pres., 1995-96. Mem. editl. bd. Archives Biochemistry and Biophysics, 1972-88, Jour. Biological Chemistry, 1973-77, 78-79, 81-86, assoc. editor, 1989-2002, Jour. Supramolecular Structure/Cellular Biochemistry, 1980-91, Bioscience Reports, 1980-87, Peptide and Protein Reviews, 1980-86, Jour. Protein Chemistry, 1980-90, IN VITRO Rapid Com. in Cell Biology, 1984—; editor Trends in Biochem. Scis., 1975-91, editor-in-chief, 1986-91, J. Neurochem, 1986-90, Proteins: Structure, Functions & Genetics, 1988-92; assoc. editor Growth Factors, 1989—; assoc. editor Protein Sci., 1990-92, 1997-2002, mem. editl. bd., 1992-2002; mem. editl. bd. Biotech. Appl. Biochem., 1995—; co-editor-in-chief Molecular Cell Biol.-Rsch. Comms., 1998-2002; editor-in-chief Molecular and Cellular Proteomics, 2000—; contbr. numerous articles to sci. jours. Recipient Young Scientist award Passano Found., 1976. Fellow AAAS; mem. Am. Chem. Soc. (Sect. award 1979), Am. Soc. Biochem. Molecular Biology (coun. 1987-90, treas. 1991-97), Am. Peptide Soc., N.Y. Acad. Scis., Protein Soc. (acting pres. 1986-87), Am. Soc. for Cell Biology, Soc. for Neuroscience, The Endocrine Soc., Am. Soc. Bone Mineral Rsch., Assn. Biomolecular Rsch. Facilities, Sigma Xi. Office: U Calif Irvine Coll Medicine Dept Physiol & Biophysics D238 Med Sci I Irvine CA 92697-4560

BRADSHAW, RICHARD ROTHERWOOD, engineering executive; b. Phila., Sept. 12, 1916; s. Joseph Rotherwood and Rosanna (Jones) B.; m. Audrey Grace Skinn, Oct. 3, 1940 (dec. Jan. 1981); children— Linda M., Barbara A., Vicki; m. Chanin Hale, Feb. 14, 1986. BS, Calif. Inst. Tech., 1939; MS, U. So. Calif., 1950. Pres. Richard R. Bradshaw, Inc., Van Nuys, Calif., 1946—, pres. br. office Honolulu. Contbr. articles to tech. jours., Important works include, Disneyworld Hotels, Orlando, Fla., U.S. embassy, Warsaw, Poland, U.S. Exhbn. Bldg., Moscow USSR, Taraara Hotel, Tahiti, Gulf Life Bldg., Jacksonville, Fla., Los Angeles City Airport. Recipient Alfred Lindau award Am. Concrete Inst., 1968, many others for structural design. Mem. ASCE, Internat. Assn. Bridges and Structural Engring., Am. Seismol. Soc., Cons. Engrs. Assn., Internat. Assn. Thin Shells, Am. Concrete Inst., Am. Arbitration Assn. Office: Richard R Bradshaw Inc 17300 Ballinger St Northridge CA 91325-2005

BRADSHAW, TERRY (TERRY PAXTON BRADSHAW), sports announcer, former professional football player; b. Shreveport, La., Sept. 2, 1948; m. Melissa Babich, 1972 (div. 1973); m. Jo Jo Starbuck, 1976 (div. 1983); m. Charlotte Hopkins, 1983 (div. 1999); children: Rachael, Erin. Grad., La. Tech. U. Quarteback Pitts. Steelers, 1970-84; sports analyst CBS Sports Inc NFL Today, 1987-94, Fox Sports, 1995—. Author, country and western singer, entertainer, appears in numerous commls., pub. speaker; author: It's Only a Game, 2001 (NY Times Best Selling Book), Keep It Simple, 2002 (NY Times Best Seller); actor: (films) Hooper, 1978, Smokey and the Bandit II, 1980, Cannonball Run, 1981, (voice) Robots, 2005, Failure to Launch, 2006, (TV series) Home Team with Terry Bradshaw, 1997; special guest appearances include Hardcastle and McCormick, 1985, The Sinbad Show, 1994, Blossom, 1994, Married with Children, 1995, 1996, Everybody Loves Raymond, 1997, (voice) King of Hill, 2000, Malcolm in the Middle, 2002, 8 Simple Rules...for Dating My Teenage Daughter, 2002, The Simpsons, 2005, Mad TV, 2005, several talk shows and others. Named Most Valuable Player, Super Bowl XIII, 1978, Super Bowl XIV, 1979, Most Favorite TV Sportscaster TV Guide, 1999; named to Pro Bowl, 1978, 79; inducted into Pro Football Hall of Fame, 1989; recipient Emmy award for sports studio analyst, 2000, 02; named Father of Yr. L.A., 2000; recipient Star on Hollywood Walk of Fame, 2001. Achievements include being the quarterback in Super Bowl wins of 1974, 75, 78, 79. Office: care Fox Network PO Box 900 Beverly Hills CA 90213-0900 also: Terry Bradshaw Enterprises Inc RR 1 Box 1033 Thackerville OK 73459-9742

BRADWAY, ROBERT, medical products executive; BA in Biology, Amherst Coll., Mass.; MBA, Harvard U. Positions through mng. dir. healthcare practice Europe Morgan Stanley, NYC & London, 1988—2006; v.p. ops. strategy Amgen, Inc., Thousand Oaks, Calif., 2006—07, exec. v.p., CFO, 2007—. Office: Amgen Inc 1 Amgen Ctr Dr Thousand Oaks CA 91320-1799 Office Phone: 805-447-1000. Office Fax: 805-447-1010.

BRADY, DONNA ELIZABETH, sales, marketing and performing company executive; d. Frank A. and Dorothy Eleanor (Munden) B. BA, Knox Coll., 1976. Stage mgr., lighting designer Dance Edn. Svcs., Inc., Northport, NY, 1973—86; coord. Am. Dance Festival Tech. Assistance Project, NYC, 1981—85; exec. dir. Performing Arts Resources, Inc., NYC, 1986—, also pres., bd. dirs.; fiscal/mktg. specialist Monterey Bay Aviation, 2002—05, dir. sales and mktg., 2005—07; dir. ops. OfficeStar Computer Tng. Ctr., 2007—. Project staff Tech. Assistance Group/TAG Found., Ltd., NYC, 1980-81; treas. NY Tech. Assistance Providers Network, 1995, 96, co-chair 1997; lighting designer, stage mgr. Solomons Co. Dance, 1978-81; asst. stage mgr. Pilobolus, 1978. Bd. dir. Artists Cmty. Fed. Credit Union, 1992-2001, sec., 1993-2000; bd. dir., treas. Acanthus Dance, 1997—. Mem. Am. Dance Guild (bd. dirs. 1980-87, treas. 1983-87). Office Phone: 831-324-0794. Personal E-mail: dbradypar@aol.com.

BRADY, MARY ROLFES, music educator; b. St. Louis, Nov. 26, 1933; d. William Henry and Helen Dorothy (Slavick) Rolfes; m. Donald Sheridan Brady, Aug. 29, 1953; children: Joseph William, Mark David, Douglas Sheridan, John Rolfes, Todd Christopher. Student, Stanford U., 1951—54, UCLA, 1967, U. So. Calif., 1972—73; pvt. studies with, Roxanna Byers, Dorothy Desmond, and Rudolph Ganz. Pvt. piano tchr., LA, 1955—; TV and radio performer. Pres. Jr. Philharm. Com. L.A., 1975-76; legis. coord., bd. dirs. Philharm. Affiliates, L.A., 1978-80. Life mem. Good Samaritan Hosp., St. Vincent Med. Ctr., L.A.; trustee St. Francis Med. Ctr., 1984-88; bd. dirs. Hollygrove-L.A. Orphans Home, Inc. Mem. Am. Coll. Musicians Club, Stanford Women's Club (past bd. dirs., pres. L.A. chpt. 1977—), The Muses, Springs Country Club.

BRADY, RODNEY HOWARD, diversified financial services and broadcast company executive, retired academic administrator, federal official; b. Sandy, Utah, Jan. 31, 1933; s. Kenneth A. and Jessie (Madsen) B.; m. Carolyn Ann Hansen, Oct. 25, 1960; children: Howard Riley, Bruce Ryan, Brooks Alan. BS in Acctg. with high honors, U. Utah, MBA with high honors, 1957; DBA, Harvard U., 1966; postgrad., UCLA, 1969-70; PhD (hon.), Weber State Coll., 1986, Snow Coll., 1991, Univ. Utah, 1997. Missionary Ch. Jesus Christ of Latter-day Saints, Great Britain, 1953-55; teaching assoc. Harvard U. Bus. Sch., Cambridge, Mass., 1957-59; v.p. Mgmt. Systems Corp., Cambridge, 1962-65, Center Exec. Devel., Cambridge, 1963-64, v.p., dir. Boston, 1964-65; v.p. Tamerand Reef Corp., Christiansted, St. Croix, V.I., 1963-65; v.p., dir. Am. Inst. Execs., NYC, 1963-65; v.p., mem. exec. com. aircraft div. Hughes Tool Co., Culver City, Calif., 1966-70; asst. sec. adminstrn. and mgmt. Dept. HEW, Washington, 1970-72; chmn. subcabinet exec. officers group of exec. br., 1971-72; exec. v.p., chmn. exec. com., dir. Bergen Brunswig Corp., Los Angeles, 1972-78; chmn. bd. Uni-mgrs. Internat., Los Angeles, 1974-78; pres. Weber State Coll., Ogden, Utah, 1978-85; pres., CEO Bonneville Internat. Corp., Salt Lake City, 1985-96, also dir.; pres., CEO Deseret Mgmt. Corp., Salt Lake City, 1996—. Bd. dirs. Amerisource Bergen Corp., 1st Security Bank Corp., 1985-2000, Mgmt. and Tng. Corp., Deseret Mut. Benefit Assn., chmn.; bd. dirs. Maximum Svc. Television, Inc., Intermountain Health Care Found., Nat. Assn. Broadcasters TV Bd., 1993-96; bd. advisors Mountain Bell Telephone, 1983-87; chmn. Nat. Adv. Com. on Accreditation and Instl. Eligibility, 1984-86, mem., 1983-87; chmn. Utah Gov.'s Blue Ribbon Com. on Tax Recodification, 1984-90; cons. Dept. Def., Dept. State, Dept. Commerce, HEW, NASA, Govt. of Can., Govt. of India (and indsl. firms), 1962—. Author: An Approach to Equipment Replacement Analysis, 1957, Survey of Management Planning and Control Systems, 1962, The Impact of Computers on Top Management Decision Making in the Aerospace and Defense Industry, 1966, (with others) How To Structure Incentive Contracts— A Programmed Text, 1965, My Missionary Years in Great Britain, 1976, An Exciting Start Along an Upward Path, 1978; contbr. articles to profl. jours. Mem. exec. com. nat. exec. bd. Boy Scouts Am., 1977—; chmn. nat. Cub Scout commn., 1977-81, pres. Western region, 1981-83, chmn. nat. ct. of honor, 1984-88; mem. adv. com. program for health sys. mgmt. Harvard U., 1973-78, mem. nat. adv. coun. U. Utah, 1971—, chairperson, 1974-76, nat. adv. bd. Coll. Bus., 1985—, chmn., 1989-93, mem. adv. com. Brigham Young U. Bus. Sch., 1972—; mem. dean's round table UCLA Grad. Sch. Mgmt., 1973-78; trustee Ettie Lee Homes for Boys, 1973-79; mem. gov. bd. McKay Dee Hosp., Ogden, Utah, 1979-87; bd. dirs. Utah Endowment for Humanities, 1978-80, Nat. Legal Ctr. for the Pub. Interest, 1991—, vice chmn., 1994-95, chmn., 1995-97, Utah Shakespeare Festival, 1992-2001, Ogden C. of C., 1978-83; bd. dirs. Utah Opera Co., 1997—, Utah Symphony Orch., 1985—. 1st lt. USAF, 1959-62. Recipient Silver Antelope award Boy Scouts Am., 1976; recipient Silver Beaver award Boy Scouts Am., 1979, Silver Buffalo award Boy Scouts Am., 1982, Disting. Alumni award U. Utah, 1990. Mem. Nat. Assn. TV Broadcasters (bd. dirs.), Am. Mgmt. Assn. (award 1969), L.A. C. of C. (tax structure com. 1969-70), Salt Lake Area C. of C. (bd. dirs. 1985-88), SAR (pres. Utah chpt. 1986-87), Sons of Utah Pioneers, Freedoms Found. at Valley Forge (nat. bd. dirs. 1986—), L.A. Country Club, Alta Club, Rotary, Phi Kappa Phi, Tau Kappa Alpha, Beta Gamma Sigma. Mem. LDS Ch. (past pres. L.A. stake). Office: Deseret Mgmt Corp Eagle Gate Tower 60 E South Temple Ste 575 Salt Lake City UT 84111-1016

BRAFF, ZACH, actor, director, scriptwriter; b. South Orange, NJ, Apr. 6, 1975; s. Hal and Anne Braff. BA in Film, Northwestern U., Evanston, Ill. Actor: (films) Manhattan Murder Mystery, 1993, Getting to Know You, 1999, Blue Moon, 2000, The Broken Hearts Club: A Romantic Comedy, 2000, Endsville, 2000, (voice) Chicken Little, 2005, The Last Kiss, 2006, The Ex, 2007; actor, dir., writer (films) Garden State, 2004 (Grammy Award for Best Compilation Soundtrack, 2005); actor: (TV series) Scrubs, 2001—; (TV films) My Summer as a Girl, 1994, (theatre) Macbeth, 1998, Romeo & Juliet, Twelfth Night, 2002. Achievements include directing and writing several short films including Lionel on a Sun Day; directing commercials and public service announcements.

BRAGDON, LYNN LYON, library administrator; b. Kansas City, Mo., Dec. 22, 1944; d. Chester Willard and Frances Helen (Bechtold) Lyon; m. James Albert Bragdon, Jr., June 16, 1969. BS in Edn., Ctrl. Mo. State U., Warrensburg, 1967; MLS, U. Okla., Norman, 1968. Rsch. libr. E.I. DuPont de Nemours, Wilmington, Del., 1968-72; asst. libr. North Cobb H.S., Marietta, Ga., 1972-74; head cataloging U. Miss. Med. Ctr., Jackson, 1975-76, assoc. dir. libr. ops., 1976-77; mgr. reference svcs. Miss. R & D Ctr., Jackson, 1977-79; chief libr. svc. VA Med. Ctr., Grand Junction, Colo., 1980-96, mgr. libr. sect., 1997—. Mem. governing bd. Pathfinders Regional Libr. System, 1985-2004; mem. regional adv. com. Midcontinental Regional Med. Libr. Program, Omaha, 1988-92; mentor new chiefs libr. svc. Dept. Vets. Affairs, Washington, 1992—. Mem. Jr. Svc. League, Grand Junction, 1984—, bd. dirs., 1986-94, 2002-05, sec., 1988-90, coord. park, 1991-94; active Western Colo. Mus., 1984-2000; asst. lay leader Meth. Ch., 1996-2000, chmn. evangelism com., 2004-06, mem. ch. coun., 2004-06, mem. lay leadership com., 2007—; mem., ex-officio Va. libr. adv. coun. Dept. Vet. Affairs, 2001-06. Recipient Med.

Informatics fellowship Nat. Libr. Medicine, 2002. Mem. Acad. Health Info. Profls. (disting.), Med. Libr. Assn., Colo. Coun. Med. Librs., Colo. Nat. Monument Assn. (v.p., bd. dirs. 1986-87, mem. bd. dirs. 1986-92), Grand Junction Gem and Mineral Soc. (libr. 1983), Western Colo. Botanic Soc., Grand Valley Rose Soc. Friends McEnnis Canyons nat. Conservation Area. Methodist. Avocations: travel, cross country skiing, music, golf, boating. Office: Library 142D VA Med Ctr 2121 North Ave Grand Junction CO 81501-6428 Home: 388 Rodell Dr Grand Junction CO 81507 Business E-Mail: lynn.bragdon@va.gov.

BRAGG, ROBERT HENRY, physicist, researcher; b. Jacksonville, Fla., Aug. 11, 1919; s. Robert Henry and Lilly Camille (McFarland) B.; m. Violette Mattie McDonald, June 14, 1947; children: Robert Henry, Pamela. BS, Ill. Inst. Tech., Chgo., 1949, MS, 1951, PhD, 1960. Assoc. physicist rsch. lab. Portland Cement Assn., Skokie, Ill., 1951-56; sr. physicist physics div. Armour Rsch. Found. Ill. Inst. Tech., Chgo., 1956-61; sr. mem., mgr. phys. metallurgy dept. Lockheed Palo Alto Rsch. Lab., Palo Alto, Calif., 1961-69; prof. materials sci. U. Calif., Berkeley, 1969-87, chmn. dept. materials sci. and mineral engring., 1978-81, prof. emeritus, 1987—. Faculty sr. scientist Lawrence Berkeley Lab., 1969-87, emeritus 1987—; mem. materials rsch. adv. com. NSF, 1982-86; program dir. div. materials rsch. U.S. Dept. Energy, 1981-82; cons. IBM, Siemens-Allis, NASA, NIH, NSF, NRC; vis. prof. Musashi Inst. of Tech., Tokyo, 1989, Howard U., 1979; del. 2d Edward Bouchet Internat. Conf., Accra, Ghana, 1990; rschr. Mich. U., Howard U., AT&T Collaborative Access Team, 1999. Contbr. articles to profl. jours. Pres. Palo Alto NAACP, 1967-68. With U.S. Army, 1943-46. Decorated Bronze star (2); recipient Disting. award No. Calif. sect. Am. Inst. Mining and Metall. Engrs., 1970, citation U. Calif., Berkeley, 1996; J. William Fulbright rsch. fellow, Nigeria, 1992-93. Fellow Nat. Soc. of Black Physicists; mem. AAUP, AAAS, Am. Phys. Soc., Am. Ceramics Soc. (chmn. No. Calif. sect. 1980), AIME (chmn. No. Calif. sect. 1970), Am. Carbon Soc., No. Calif. Coun. Black Profl. Engrs., Am. Crystallographic Assn., Sigma Xi, Tau Beta Pi. Democrat. Home: 2 Admiral Dr Ste 373 Emeryville CA 94608-1502 Office: U Calif Dept Materials Sci & Engring Berkeley CA 94720-0001 Personal E-mail: petebragg@aol.com.

BRAGINSKY, STANISLAV IOSIFOVICH, physicist, geophysicist, researcher; b. Moscow, Apr. 15, 1926; s. Iosif Samuilovich Braginsky and Khaya Nutovna Drikker; m. Maya Aronovna Boyarskaya, May 8, 1955; children: Galina, Leonid. Degree in engring. and physics, Moscow Inst. of Mechs., 1948; cand. sci. in physics and math., Inst. Atomic Energy, Moscow, 1953, DSc in Physics and Math., 1966. Sr. scientist I.V. Kurchatov Inst. of Atomic Energy, Moscow, 1948-78, O. Yu. Schmidt Inst. of Physics of the Earth, Moscow, 1978-88; geophysicist, researcher Inst. Geophysics/Planetary Physics UCLA, 1989—. Recipient Lenin prize for rsch. in plasma physics Acad. Sci. USSR, 1958, John Adam Fleming medal for rsch. in geomagnetism Am. Geophys. Union, 1993. Fellow Am. Geophys. Union. Achievements include development of two-temperature equations of plasma dynamics and theory of the pinch-effect in high power electrical discharges in gases; advancement of theory of hydromagnetic dynamo of the Earth and theory of geomagnetic secular variations. Office: UCLA Inst Geophys & Planetary Phys 405 Hilgard Ave Los Angeles CA 90095

BRAHAM, RAYMOND L., pediatric dentistry educator; came to the U.S., 1968; Grad., U. London, 1957; M in Pedodontics, cert. advanced tng., Boston U., 1970. Pvt. practice dentistry, London; chief resident pedodontics Winnipeg (Can.) Children's Hosp.; pedodontic triance Boston U. Sch. Grad. Dentistry, faculty; clin. prof. dentistry dept. pediat. Sch. Medicine U. Calif., San Francisco, clin. prof., assoc. chair clin. affairs pediat. dentistry, interim-dir. postgrad. program pediat. dentistry. Lectr. in field. Sr. author, editor: The Dental Implications of Epilepsy, 1976; editor: (with M.E. Morris) Handbook of pedoDontics-Clinical and Laboratory Techniques, 1975, Textbook of Pediatric Dentistry, 1980, Odontologia Pediatrica, 1984, Textbook of Pediatric Dentistry, 1985, 2nd edit., 1988; reviewer, cons. several nat. jours.; contbr. chpts. to books and articles to profl. jours. Fellow Am. Acad. Pediat. Dentistry, Am. Acad. Dentistry for the Handicapped (past pres.), Royal Soc. Health Eng., Royal Soc. Medicine London. Office: U Calif Sch Dentistry PO Box 438 San Francisco CA 94143-0001 Fax: 415-476-1499. E-mail: rbraham@itsa.ucsf.edu.

BRAHMA, CHANDRA SEKHAR, civil engineering educator; b. Calcutta, India, Oct. 5, 1941; came to U.S., 1963; s. Nalinia Kanta and Uma Rani (Bose) B.; m. Purnima Sinha, Feb. 18, 1972; children: Charanjit, Barunashish. B in Engring., Calcutta U., 1962; MS, Mich. State U., 1965; PhD, Ohio State U., 1969. Registered profl. engr. Calif., Utah, N.H., Tex., Wis. Asst. engr. Pub. Works Dept., Calcutta, 1962-63; rsch. asst. Mich. State U., East Lansing, 1963-65; teaching and rsch. assoc. Ohio State U., Columbus, 1965-69; project engr. Frank H. Lehr Assocs., East Orange, N.J., 1969-70; sr. soils engr. John G. Reutter Assocs., Camden, N.J., 1970-72; asst. prof. Worcester (Mass.) Poly. Inst., 1972-74; prin. soils engr. Daniel, Mann, Johnson & Mendenhall, Balt., 1974-79; sr. engr. Sverdrup Corp., St. Louis, 1979-80, cons., 1980—; prof. Calif. State U., Fresno, 1980—2002, prof. emeritus, 2002—. Cons. Expert Resources, Inc., Peoria Heights, Ill., 1981—, The Twining Labs., Inc., Fresno, 1982—, Law Offices Marderosian and Swanson, Fresno, 1985—, Law Offices Hurlbutt, Clevenger, Long and Vortmann, Visalia, Calif., 1988—, Tech. Adv. Svcs. for Attys., Blue Bell, Pa., 1992—. Author: Fundaciones y Mechanica de Suelos, 1986; contbr. articles to profl. jours. Head sci. judge Calif. Cen. Valleys Sci. and Engring. Fairs, Fresno, 1988-2002. Recipient Outstanding Prof. of Yr. award Calif. State U., 1989, Halliburton award Calif. State U., 1991, Calif. Ctrl. Valley Outstanding Profl. Engr. award Calif. Soc. Profl. Engrs., 1993, Disting. Svc. award, 1994, Claude C. Laval Jr. award Innovative Tech. and Rsch. Calif. State U., 1991, 92, Portrait of Success award KSEE 24, Fresno, Calif., 1997, Std. of Excellence award Tau Beta Pi, 1997, Outstanding Prof. award Tau Beta Pi, 1998, Outstanding Prof. award NSPE, 1998; Brahma St. named in City of Bakersfield, Calif., 1989; Fulbright scholar, 1984; Hugh B. William fellow, Assn. Drilled Shaft Contractors, 1986, others. Fellow ASCE (v.p. 1983-84, pres. 1984-85, Outstanding Engr. award 1985, Disting Svc. award, 1986, Outstanding Prof. award 1985, Edmund Friedman Profl. Recognition award 1993); mem. ASTM, Am. Soc. Engring. Edn. (AT&T Found. award 1991, Outstanding Tchg. award 1997, AT ANDT Found. award for excellence in tchg. and rsch. 1991), Rotary (chair Clovis club 1986—, chair pub. rels. 1987, chair youth svcs. 1989, bd. dirs. 1989). Democrat. Hindu. Avocations: swimming, tennis, music, reading. Home and Office: 561 Houston Ave Clovis CA 93611-7032 Home Phone: 559-323-0316; Office Phone: 559-323-0316. E-mail: chandrab@csufresno.edu, esbconsultant@netscape.net, chandrah.1@netzero.net.

BRAMMELL, STEPHEN HARRISON, lawyer; b. Ardmore, Okla., Dec. 5, 1957; m. Allison Brammell. BBA with distinction, U. Okla., 1979; JD, Georgetown U. Law Ctr., 1982. Bar: Okla. 1982, Tenn. 1988, Nev. 2003. Assoc. Conner & Winters, Tulsa, 1982—84; corp. staff atty. Harrah's Entertainment Inc., Las Vegas, 1984—87, sr. staff atty., 1987—97, v.p., assoc. gen. counsel, 1997—99, sr. v.p., gen. counsel, 1999—. Office: Harrah Entertainment Inc Legal Dept One Harrahs Ct Las Vegas NV 89119 Home: 1 Caesars Palace Dr Las Vegas NV 89109-8969 Office Phone: 702-407-6000. Office Fax: 702-407-6037. E-mail: sbrammell@harrahs.com.

BRAMMER, J. WILLIAM, JR., judge, lawyer; b. Des Moines, Iowa, Sept. 15, 1942; s. James W. and Mary Virginia (Steck) Brammer; m. Donna Crosby, June 20, 1964; children: Jill S., James W. III. BS, U. Ariz., 1964, JD, 1967. Bar: Ariz. 1967, U.S. Dist. Ct. Ariz. 1968, U.S. Ct. Appeals (9th cir.) 1970, U.S. Supreme Ct. 1970. Law clk. to judge Ariz. Ct. Appeals, Tucson, 1967—68; asst. atty. City of Tucson, 1968; from assoc. to ptnr. DeConcini, McDonald, Brammer, Yetwin & Lacy PC, Tucson, 1968—97; judge Ariz. Ct. of Appeals, Tucson, 1997—. Mem. com. exams. Ariz. Supreme Ct., Phoenix, 1977-84, chmn. 1982-84; mem. Commn. on Jud. Conduct, 2003—, chair, 2005—; mem. bd. govs. State Bar Ariz., 1995-97. Bd. visitors U. Ariz. Coll. Law, Tucson, 1981-84, 88—. Fellow: Ariz. Bar Found.; mem.: ABA, Law Coll. Assn. U. Ariz. (pres. 1990—91), Pima County Bar Assn. (pres. 1993—94), Morris K. Udall Inn of Ct. (pres. 2001—02). Office: Ariz Ct Appeals 400 W Congress St Ste 302 Tucson AZ 85701-1353 Office Phone: 520-628-6945. Business E-Mail: brammer@appeals2.az.gov.

BRAMSON, EDWARD J., electronics corporation and financial executive; b. 1952; Student, London U. V.p., mng. dir. Hillside Capital, 1976—; v.p. Ampex Corp., also dir. Office: Ampex Corp 401 Broadway, MS1101 Redwood City CA 94063-3126

BRANCA, JOHN GREGORY, lawyer, consultant; b. Bronxville, NY, Dec. 11, 1950; s. John Ralph and Barbara (Werle) B. AB in Polit. Sci. cum laude, Occidental Coll., 1972; JD, UCLA, 1975. Bar: Calif. 1975. Assoc. Kindel & Anderson, Los Angeles, 1975—77, Hardee, Barovick, Konecky & Braun, Beverly Hills, Calif., 1977—81; ptnr. Ziffren, Brittenham, Branca, Fischer, Gilsert, Lurie, Stiffelman, Cook, Johnson, Lande & Wolf LLP, LA, 1981—. Cons. N.Y. State Assembly, Mt. Vernon, 1978-82, various music industry orgns., L.A., 1981—. Editor-in-Chief UCLA-Alaska Law Rev., 1974-75; contbr. articles to profl. jours. Cons., bd. trustees UCLA Law Sch. Com., UCLA Athletic Dept., Occidental Coll., Musician's Assistance Program, 1995. Recipient Bancroft-Whitney award; named Entertainment Lawyer of Yr. Am. Lawyer mag., 1981. Mem. ABA (patent trademark and copyright law sect.), Calif. Bar Assn., Beverly Hills Bar Assn. (entertainment law sect.), Phi Alpha Delta, Sigma Tau Sigma. Avocations: art, antiques, music, real estate. Office: Ziffren Brittenham Branca Fischer Gilsert Lurie Stiffelman Cook Johnson Lande & Wolf LLP 1801 Century Park W Fl 9 Los Angeles CA 90067-6406

BRANCH, MICHELLE (MICHELLE JAQUET DESEVREN BRANCH), musician; b. Flagstaff, Ariz., July 2, 1983; d. David and Peggy Branch; m. Teddy Landau, May 23, 2004; 1 child, Owen Isabelle. With Maverick Records, Beverly Hills, Calif., 2001—. Musician: (albums) Broken Bracelet, 2000, The Spirit Room, 2001, Hotel Paper, 2003, Everything Comes and Goes, 2008; musician: (with The Wreckers) Stand Still, Look Pretty, 2006; musician: (singles) Everywhere, 2001, All You Wanted, 2001, Goodbye to You, 2003, Are You Happy Now?, 2003, Breathe, 2003; (with Santana) (singles) The Game of Love, 2002 (Grammy award for Best Pop Collaboration with Vocals, 03), (with The Wreckers) Leave the Pieces, 2006. Recipient Grammy award for Best New Artist, 2003. Office: Maverick Recording Co 3300 Warner Blvd Burbank CA 91505-4632

BRANCH, W. RIC, state legislator; b. Weiser, Idaho, Aug. 5, 1955; m. Cory Branch; children: LaBree, Ross, Victoria. Student, U. Idaho, We. Coll. Auctioneering. Cattle rancher; mem. Idaho Senate, Dist. 9, Boise, 1995—. Chair agrl. affairs com., 1994—; mem. commerce and human resources, local govt. and tax., and resources and environment coms.; mem. Washington County state com., 1988—. Bd. dirs., Idaho Rural Devel. Coun.; sch. bd. trustee, 1989-95. Recipient Friend of Agr. award, Farm Bur. Fedn., 1996. Mem. NRA, Farm Bur., Idaho Cattle Assn. (chair rsch. and edn. com.), Weiser River Cattle Assn. (bd. dirs.), Indian Mountain Grazing Assn. (v.p.), Fruitland (Idaho) C. of C., Fayette (Idaho) C. of C. Republican. Protestant. Office: State Capitol PO Box 83720 Boise ID 83720-3720

BRAND, MICHAEL, museum director; b. Australia, 1958; m. Tina Gomes Brand; 2 children. BA in Asian Studies, with honors, Australian Nat. U., Canberra, 1979; MA, Harvard U., 1982, PhD, 1987. Rsch. fellow Arthur M. Sackler Gallery Smithsonian Instn., 1987, co-dir. Mughal Garden Project Lahore, Pakistan, 1988—93; curator Asian art Mus. Art Rhode Island Sch. Design, 1985—87, Nat. Gallery of Australia, 1988—96; asst. dir. Queensland Art Gallery, Brisbane, Australia, 1996—2000; dir. Va. Mus. Fine Arts, Richmond, 2000—05, J. Paul Getty Mus., LA, 2005—. Co-author (with Glenn D. Lowry): Akbar's India: Art from the Mughal City of Victory, 1985. Office: J Paul Getty Mus 1200 Getty Ctr Dr Ste 1000 Los Angeles CA 90049-1679 Office Phone: 310-440-7330. E-mail: mbrand@getty.edu.

BRAND, VANCE DEVOE, astronaut, director; b. Longmont, Colo., May 9, 1931; s. Rudolph William and Donna (DeVoe) B.; m. Joan Virginia Weninger, July 25, 1953; children: Susan Nancy, Stephanie, Patrick Richard, Kevin Stephen; m. Beverly Ann Whitnel, Nov. 3, 1979; children: Erik Ryan, Dane Vance. BS in Bus., U. Colo., 1953, BS in Aero. Engring., 1960; MBA, UCLA, 1964; grad., U.S. Naval Test Pilot Sch., Patuxent River, Md., 1963; DSc (hon.), U. Colo., 2000. With Lockheed-Calif. Co., Burbank, 1960-66, flight test engr., 1961-62, traveling engr. rep., 1962-63, engring. test pilot, 1963-66; astronaut NASA Johnson Space Ctr., Houston, 1966-92, command module pilot Apollo-Soyuz mission, 1975, comdr. STS-5 Mission, 1982, comdr. STS 41-B Mission, 1984, comdr. STS-35 Mission, 1990; chief plans Nat. Aero-Space Plane Joint Program Office, Wright-Patterson AFB, Ohio, 1992-94; asst. chief flight ops. directorate DFRC NASA, Edwards, Calif., 1994-98, dep. dir. aerospace projects, 1998—2002, dir. aerospace projects, 2002—04, dep. assoc. ctr. dir. for programs, 2004—06, assoc. ctr. dir. programs, 2006—08. With USMCR, 1953-57. Decorated 2 Disting. Svc. medals NASA, 2 Exceptional Svc. medals, 3 Space medals; inducted into Internat. Space Hall of Fame, 1996, U.S. Astronaut Hall of Fame, 1997, Internat. Aerspace Hall of Fame, 2001. Fellow AIAA, Am. Astron. Soc., Soc. Exptl. Test Pilots.

BRANDEL, ROLAND ERIC, lawyer; b. Chgo., Nov. 30, 1938; s. Eric John and Louise Catherine (Covich) B.; m. Catherine Terry, July 3, 1963 (div. July 1970). BS in Econs., Ill. Inst. Tech., 1960; JD, U. Chgo., 1966; postgrad., Columbia U., 1970. Commd. ensign U.S. Navy, 1960, advanced through grades to lt. comdr., ret., 1970; clk. to chief justice Calif. Supreme Ct., San Francisco, 1966-67; sr. counsel, ptnr. Morrison & Foerster, 1967—. Vis. prof. law U. Calif., Berkeley, 1974-75; consumer adv. council Fed. Res. Bd., Washington, 1976-80; vis. com. U. Chgo. Law Sch., 1983-86, Golden Gate Law Sch., San Francisco, 1983—; study groups of EFT and Negotiable Instruments Sec. of State Adv. Commn., Washington, 1983-90; chmn. San Francisco Com. on Fgn. Relations, 2002-. Co-author: Law of EFT Systems, 1988, TIL: 4 Comp. Guide plus supplement, 1981-87, Community Reinvestment Act Manual, 1978, Financial Privacy Comp. Manual, 1979. Mem. Planning Commn. City of Berkeley, 1972-74; chmn. Waterfront Adv. Bd., Berkeley, 1973. Recipient Lifetime Achievement award, Calif. Bankers Assn., 2000, Am. Coll. Consumer Fin. Svcs. Lawyers, 2004, Bus. Law Sec, State Bar Calif., 2006. Mem. ABA (chmn. consumer fin. svcs. com. 2006, coun. bus. law 1982-86, 2002—06, chmn. ad hoc com. payment systems 1983-88), Inst. Marine Resources (adv.bd. 1983-86), Nat. Ctr. Fin. Svcs. (chmn. legal adv. com. 1985—, mng. com. 1983—), State Bar Calif. (chair bus. law sect., 1993-94, mem. 2006), Am. Coll. Consumer Fin. Svcs. (pres. 1999-2001), U. Chgo. Law Sch. Alumni (pres. 1968-94). Home: 58 Roble Rd Berkeley CA 94705-2838 Office: Morrison & Foerster 425 Market San Francisco CA 94105 Office Phone: 415-268-7093. E-mail: rbrandel@mofo.com.

BRANDENBERG, FRANK G., electronics executive; B in Indsl. Engring., Wayne State U., M in Ops. Rsch. Various Burroughs Corp., UNISYS Corp., 1987-97; pres., CEO EA Industries, Inc., 1997-99; corp. sr. v.p., group exec. elec. components & materials Litton Industries, Inc., Woodland Hills, Calif., 1999—. Office: Litton Industries Inc 21240 Burbank Blvd Woodland Hills CA 91367-6675

BRANDES, CHARLES H., investment company executive; BA, Bucknell U. Founder Brandes Investment Ptnrs., 1974, chmn. exec. com., mem. investment oversight com. Author: Internat. Value Investing: Making the Right Choice at the Right Price, 1996, Value Investing Today, 1997. Named one of 400 Richest Ams., Forbes mag., 2006. Office: Brandes Investment Ptnrs 11988 El Camino Real, Ste 500 PO Box 919048 San Diego CA 92191-9048

BRANDES, STANLEY HOWARD, anthropology educator, writer; b. NYC, Dec. 26, 1942; s. Emanuel Robert and Annette (Zalisch) B.; m. Jane Brandes; children: Nina Rachel, Naomi Clara. BA, U. Chgo., 1964; MA, U. Calif., Berkeley, 1969, PhD, 1971. Asst. prof. anthropology Mich. State U., East Lansing, 1971-75; asst. prof. anthropology U. Calif., Berkeley, 1975-78, assoc. prof., 1978-82, prof. anthropology, 1982—, chmn. dept., 1990-93, 97-99. Dir. Barcelona Study Ctr., U. Calif. and Ill., Spain, 1981-82, Mexico City Study Ctr., 1995-96, U. Calif. Author: Migration, Kinship and Community, 1975, Metaphors of Masculinity, 1989, Forth: The Age and the Symbol, 1985, Power and Persuasion, 1988, Staying Sober in Mexico City, 2002, Skulls to the Living, Bread to the Dead: The Day of the Dead in Mexico and Beyond, 2006; co-editor: Symbol as Sense, 1980. NIH fellow, 1967-71; NICHD Rsch. fellow, 1975-77; fellow John Carter Brown Libr., 1994; Am. Council Learned Socs. grantee, 1977 Fellow Am. Anthrop. Assn.; mem. Am. Ethnological Soc., Soc. for Psychol. Anthropology Office: U Calif Dept Anthropology Berkeley CA 94720-0001 Office Phone: 510-642-6945. Business E-Mail: brandes@berkeley.edu.

BRANDLER, JONATHAN M., lawyer; b. LA, Jan. 8, 1946; AB, U. Calif., Berkeley, 1967; JD, U. So. Calif., 1970. Bar: Calif. 1971. Ptnr. Hill, Farrer & Burrill LLP, LA. Lectr. Inst. Bus. Law, 1981-92. Mem. State Bar Calif. (labor law sect.), L.A. County Bar Assn. (labor law sect.). Office: Hill Farrer & Burrill LLP 1 California Plaza 300 S Grand Ave Ste 37 Los Angeles CA 90071-3110 E-mail: jbrandler@hfbllp.com.

BRANDON, KATHRYN ELIZABETH BECK, pediatrician; b. Sept. 10, 1916; d. Clarence M. and Hazel A. (Cutler) Beck; children: John William, Kathleen Brandon McEnulty, Karen (dec.). MD, U. Chgo., 1941; BA, U. Utah, 1937; MPH, U. Calif., Berkeley, 1957. Diplomate Am. Bd. Pediats. Intern Grace Hosp., Detroit, 1941-42; resident Children's Hosp. Med. Ctr. No. Calif., Oakland, 1953-55, Children's Hosp., LA, 1951-53; pvt. practice La Crescentia, Calif., 1946-51, Salt Lake City, 1960-65, 86—. Med. dir. Salt Lake City public schs., 1957-60; dir. Ogden City-Weber County (Utah) Health Dept., 1965-67; pediatrician Fitzsimmons Army Hosp., 1967-68; coll. health physician U. Colo., Boulder, 1968-71; student health physician U. Utah, Salt Lake City, 1971-81; occupational health physician Hill AFB, Utah, 1981-85; child health physician Salt Lake City-County Health Dept., 1971-82; cons. in field; clin. asst. U. Utah Coll. Medicine, Salt Lake City, 1958-64; clin. asst. pediatrics U. Colo. Coll. Medicine, Denver, 1958-72; active staff emeritus Primary Children's Hosp., LDS Hosp., and Cottonwood Hosp., 1960-67. Fellow APHA, Am. Pediat. Acad., Am. Sch. Health Assn.; mem. AMA, Utah Coll. Health Assn. (pres. 1978-80), Pacific Coast Coll. Health Assn., Utah Med. Assn., Salt Lake County Med. Soc., Utah Pub. Health Assn. (sec.-treas. 1960-66), Intermountain Pediat. Soc.

BRANDSTATER, MURRAY EVERETT, physiatrist; b. Hobart, Australia, Apr. 21, 1935; MB, BS, U. Melbourne, Australia, 1957. Cert. in Phys. Med. Rehab. Intern Box Hill Dist. Hosp., Melbourne, 1958; resident in internal medicine Alfred Hosp., Melbourne, 1959, 61-62; resident Royal Children's Hosp., Melbourne, 1960; rsch. in phys. med. rehab. Mayo Clinic, Rochester, Minn., 1964-68; prof. phys. med. rehab. McMaster U., Hamilton, Ont., Can., 1968-84; mem. staff Loma Linda (Calif.) U. Med. Ctr., 1984—; prof. phys. med. rehab. Loma Linda U., 1981—. Mem. AMA, AAEM, MRCP, RCPC. Office: Loma Linda Calif U Med Ctr 11406 Loma Linda Dr Rm 516 Loma Linda CA 92354 Office Phone: 909-558-6204. Business E-Mail: mbrandtstater@pol.net.

BRANDT, PHILIP H., federal judge; b. Juneau, AK, 1944; BA in Econs., Harvard U., 1966; JD, U. Wash., 1972. Atty. U.S. Dept. Justice and Fed. Maritime Commn., 1972-73; dep. prosecuting atty. Pierce County, Wash., 1973-75; dir. stds. project Wash. Gov.'s Com. on Law and Justice, 1975-76; with LeCocq, Simonarson, et al, 1976-86, Graham & Dunn, 1986-91; apptd. bankruptcy judge U.S. Dist. Ct. (we. dist.) Wash., 1991. Mem. 9th Cir. Bankruptcy Appellate Panel, 1998—. Capt. USNR, 1966-89. Mem. ABA, Wash. State Bar, Nat. Conf. Bankruptcy Judges, Tacoma-Pierce County Bar, King County Bar. Home: 700 Stewart St Seattle WA 98101-1271

BRANDT, R. SKIPPER, state senator; b. Grangeville, Idaho, May 26, 1964; m. Pia Brandt; 1 child, Nicolas. Student, U. Idaho, 1982. Mgr. Stites Ace Hardware; Rep. senator dist. 7 Idaho State Senate, 2000—. Mem. coun. City of Kooskia, Idaho, 1991-95; bd. dirs. Idaho County Sheriff's Posse, 1992-97, Clearwater Resource Coalition, 1994-97; mayor City of Kooskia, 1998—. Office: PO Box 296 Kooskia ID 83539 also: Idaho State Senate State Capitol 700 W Jefferson Boise ID 83720-0081 E-mail: skip@cybrquest.com.

BRANDT, RICHARD PAUL, communications and entertainment company executive; b. NYC, Dec. 6, 1927; s. Harry and Helen (Satenstein) Brandt; m. Helen H. Kogel, May 31, 1975; children: Claudia, David, Matthew, Thomas, Jennifer. BS with high honors, Yale U., 1948; PhD of Comm. Arts (hon.), Am. Film Inst., 2002. With Trans-Lux Theatres Corp., 1950-54, v.p., 1952-54; with Trans-Lux Corp., Norwalk, Conn., 1950—59, v.p., 1959-62, pres., 1962-80, chmn. bd., 1974—2003, CEO, 1974-92, chmn. emeritus, 2003—; dir. Am. Book-Stratford Press, Inc., 1962-87, Brandt Theatres, 1950—85, Presdl. Realty Corp., 1972—; founding gov. Ind. Film Importers & Distbrs. Am., 1959-63, bd. dirs., 1959-69; v.p., mem. exec. com. Theatre Owners Am., 1965—78; mem. bill of rights com. Council Motion Picture Orgns., 1963-65; bd. dirs. Film Soc. Lincoln Ctr., 1968-71; mem. N.Y. State Bus. Adv. Com. on Mgmt. Improvement, 1966-70. Bd. dirs. Trans-Lux Corp.; chmn. bd. Univ. Settlement Soc., 1964-66, hon. pres., bd. dirs., 1966-77; dir. Am. Theatre Wing, 1970-99, United Neighborhood Houses, 1968-73; bd. dirs., treas. Settlement House Employment Devel., 1969-72; trustee, mem. exec. com. Am. Film Inst., 1971—, vice chmn., 1980-83, chmn. bd., 1983-86, chmn. emeritus 1986—; trustee Mus. Holography, 1979-82; mem. Tony awards mgmt. com., 1986-98; founder Live Poets Soc., 1991—. Vice chmn. bd. Coll. of Santa Fe, 1987-98; trustee Maritime Ctr., Norwalk, 1991-92; treas. bd., exec. com. Coll. of Santa Fe, 1999-2004; bd. dirs. Taos Talking Pictures Festival, 1998-2003. Recipient Disting. Svc. award Coll. Santa Fe, 2004; named Exhibitor of Yr., ShoWest, 1984. Mem. Nat. Assn. Theatre Owners (dir. 1957-78, exec. com. 1965-78, Sherrill Corwin award 1983), Phi Beta Kappa, Sigma Xi. Office: Trans Lux Corp 2209 Miguel Chavez Rd Bldg A Santa Fe NM 87505

BRANN, ALTON JOSEPH, manufacturing executive; b. Portland, Maine, Dec. 23, 1941; s. Donald Edward and Marjorie Margaret (Curran) B. BA, U. Mass., 1969. Mgr. advanced programs Dynamics Research Corp., Wilmington, Mass., 1969-73; dir. engring. Litton Guidance & Control Systems, LA, 1973-79, dir. program mgmt., 1979-81, v.p. engring., 1981-83, pres., 1983-86; group exec. Navigation Guidance and Control Systems Group, Beverly Hills, Calif., 1986-88; sr. v.p. Components and Indsl. Products Group Litton Industries, Beverly Hills, 1988-90, pres., COO, 1990-92, CEO, 1992-94, chmn., 1994-96; chmn., CEO Western Atlas Inc., Beverly Hills, 1994-97, UNOVA Inc., Beverly Hills, 1997—. Trustee Mfrs. Alliance Productivity and Innovation, coun. fgn. diplomacy, U.S.-Russia bus. coun. Mem. IEEE (sr. mem.), Optical Soc. Am., L.A. World Affairs Coun., Town Hall of L.A. Avocations: skiing, sailing.

BRANNEN, JEFFREY RICHARD, lawyer; b. Tampa, Fla., Aug. 27, 1945; s. Jackson Edward and Tobiah M. (Lovitz) B.; m. Mary Elizabeth Strand, Nov. 24, 1972; 1 child, Samuel Jackson. BA in English, U. N.Mex., 1967, JD, 1970. Bar: N.Mex. 1970, U.S. Dist. Ct. N.Mex. 1970, U.S. Ct. Appeals (10th cir.) 1976, U.S. Supreme Ct. 1978. Law clk. N.Mex. State Supreme Ct., Santa Fe, 1970-71; from assoc. to pres., shareholder Montgomery & Andrews, pa, Santa Fe, 1972-93; pres. Jeffrey R. Brannen, P.A., Santa Fe, 1993—; of counsel Comeau, Maldegan, Templeman & Indall (formerly known as Carpenter, Maldegan, Templeman & Indall), Santa Fe, 1995—. Faculty Nat. Inst. Trial Advocacy, Hastings Ctr. for Trial & Appellate Advocacy, 1980-93; co-chmn. Pers. Injury Inst., Hastings, 1992. Mem. ABA, Am. Bd. Trial Advocates (N.Mex. pres. 1998), Assn. Def. Trial Attys. (state chmn. 1992—), Def. Rsch. Inst. (Exceptional Performance Citation 1989), N.Mex. Def. Lawyers Assn. (pres. 1989). Democrat. Avocations: skiing, soccer, fly fishing, travel. Office: 325 Pesco de Heralta Santa Fe NM 87501 Office Phone: 505-983-4429. Fax: (505) 982-4611. Business E-Mail: jrb@brannenlaw.net.

BRANSCOMB, LEWIS MCADORY, physicist, researcher; b. Asheville, NC, Aug. 17, 1926; s. Bennett Harvie and Margaret (Vaughan) B.; m. Margaret Anne Wells, Oct. 13, 1951 (dec. Oct. 1997); children: Harvie Hammond, Katharine C. Branscomb Kelley; m. Constance Mullin, July 3, 2005. AB summa cum laude, Duke U., 1945, DSc (hon.); MS, Harvard U., 1947, PhD, 1949; DSc (hon.), Poly. Inst. N.Y., Clarkson Coll., Rochester U., U. Colo., Western Mich. U., Lycoming Coll., U. Ala., Pratt Inst., Rutgers U., Lehigh U., U. Notre Dame; DEng (hon.), Colo. Sch. Mines, 1999; D Pub. Politics, Carnegie Mellon U., 2000; DSc (hon.), SUNY, Binghamton; LHD (hon.), Pace U. Instr. physics Harvard U., 1950-51; lectr. physics U. Md., 1952-54; vis. staff mem. Univ. Coll., London, 1957-58; chief atomic physics sect. Nat. Bur. Standards, Washington, 1954-60, chief atomic physics div., 1960-62; chmn. Joint Inst. Lab. Astrophysics, U. Colo., 1962-65, 68-69; chief lab. astrophysics div. Nat. Bur. Standards, Boulder, Colo., 1962-69; prof. physics U. Colo., 1962-69; dir. Nat. Bur. Standards, 1969-72; chief scientist, v.p. IBM, Armonk, NY, 1972-86, mem. corporate mgmt. bd., 1983-86; dir. sci. and tech. policy program Kennedy Sch. Govt., Harvard U., Cambridge, Mass., 1986-96, Albert Pratt pub. service prof., 1988-94; Aetna prof. pub. policy and corp. mgmt. Harvard U., Cambridge, Mass., 1994-96, prof. emeritus, 1996—; dir. Belfer Ctr. for Sci. and Internat. Affairs, 2001—; adj. prof. Sch. Internat. Rels. and Pacific Studies, U. Calif., San Diego, 2005—, disting. rsch. fellow, Inst. for Global Conflict and Cooperation, 2007—. Mem.-at-large Def. Sci. Bd., 1969-72; mem. high level policy group sci. and tech. info. Orgn. Econ. Coop. and Devel., 1968-70; mem. Pres.'s Sci. Adv. Com., 1965-68, chmn. panel space sci. and tech., 1967-68; mem. Nat. Sci. Bd., 1978-84, chmn., 1980-84; mem. Pres.'s Nat. Productivity Adv. Com., 1981-82; mem. standing com. controlled thermonuclear rsch. AEC, 1966-68; mem. adv. com. on sci. and fgn. affairs Dept. State, 1973-74; mem. U.S.-USSR Joint Commn. on Sci. and Tech., 1977-80; chmn. Com. on Scholarly Communications with the People's Republic of China, 1977-80; mem. tech. assessment adv. coun. Office of Tech. Assessment, U.S. Congress, 1990-95; chmn. Carnegie Forum Task Force on Teaching as a Profession, 1985-86; dir. Lord Corp., 1987-; mem. pres.'s bd. visitors U. Okla., 1968-70; mem. astronomy and applied physics vis. coms. Harvard U. 1969-83, bd. overseers, 1984-86; mem. physics vis. com. M.I.T., 1974-79; mem. Pres.'s Com. Nat. Medal Scis., 1970-72; bd. dir. Am. Nat. Standards Inst., 1969-72; trustee Carnegie Instn., 1973-90, mem. Carnegie Commn. on Sci., Tech. and Govt., 1988-93; trustee Poly. Inst. N.Y., 1974-78, Vanderbilt U., 1980-2003, Nat. Geog. Soc., 1984-01, Woods Hole Oceanographic Instn., 1985-92, 93-98, LASPAU, 2002-2003; chmn. Nat. Info. Infrastructure-2000 steering com. NRC, 1994-95; Harvie Branscomb disting. vis. prof. Vanderbilt U., 1999-2000; rsch. assoc. Scripps Instn. Oceanography U. Calif., San Diego, 2005—. Author: Empowering Technology, 1993, Confessions of a Technophile, 1995, Korea at the Turning Point, 1996, Investing in Innovation, 1998, Industrializing Knowledge, 1999, Taking Technical Risks, 2001, Making America Safer, 2002, Seeds of Disaster, Roots of Response, 2006; editor Rev. Modern Physics, 1968-73. Trustee Telluride Inst., 1996-97; mem. Commn. on Global Info. Infrastructure, 1995—. USPHS fellow, 1948-49; Jr. fellow Harvard Soc. Fellows, 1949-51; recipient Rockefeller Pub. Service award, 1957-58, Gold medal exceptional service Dept. Commerce, 1961, Arthur Flemming award D.C. Jr. C. of C., 1962, Samuel Wesley Stratton award Dept. Commerce, 1966, Career Service award Nat. Civil Service League, 1968, Vannevar Bush award, nat. Sci. Bd., 2001, Proctor prize Rsch. Soc. Am., 1972, Okawa prize in Info. and Telecomm., 1998, prize for Info. and Telecomms. Ohkawa Found., 1998, Centennial medal, Harvard U., 2002. Fellow Am. Phys. Soc. (chmn. divsn. electron physics 1961-68, pres. 1979), AAAS (dir. 1969-73, 1999-2003, William Carey lectr. medal 2008), Am Acad. Arts and Scis.; mem. NAS (coun. 1972-75, 98-2001), Nat. Acad. Engring. (Arthur Bueche award), Engring. Acad. Japan (fgn. assoc.), Russian Acad. Sci., Washington Acad. Scis. (Outstanding Sci. Achievement award 1959), Nat. Acad. Pub. Adminstrn., Am. Philos. Soc., Phi Beta Kappa, Sigma Xi (pres. 1985-86). Office: U Calif San Diego Grad Sch Internat Rels Pac Studies 9500 Gilman Dr #0519 La Jolla CA 92093-0519 Office Phone: 858-454-6871. Business E-Mail: lbranscomb@branscomb.org.

BRANTINGHAM, BARNEY, journalist, writer; b. Chgo., Feb. 26, 1932; s. Carl Brantingham and Frances Bell; m. Angela Mendez, Oct. 30, 1957 (div.); children: Barclay Carl, Frances, Wendy, Kenneth. Grad., U. Ill., 1954. Reporter Star Newspapers, Chicago Heights, Ill., 1957-59; editor San Clemente (Calif.) Sun-Post, 1959-60; reporter Santa Barbara (Calif.) News-Press, 1960—, columnist, 1977—. Commentator Sta. KTMS, Santa Barbara, 1989-91, Sta. KIST, Santa Barbara, 1991, SAM, 1990, 92; radio sta. feature and travel commentator KQSB, 1994-97; co-host Around the World with Arthur and Barney, Sta. KTMS, 1998, KEYT-AM, 1998-2003, Around the World, Sta. KZBN, 2003—; founding dir. Opinionated Traveler internet site www.opinionatedtraveler.com. Prodr. TV program Santa Barbara Traveler; author: The Pro Football Hall of Fame, 1988, Barney's Santa Barbara, 1989, Around Santa Barbara County with Barney, 1992; co-dir. The Opinionated Traveler Internet Site. With U.S. Army, 1955-57. Mem. Internat. Food, Wine and Travel Writers Assn. (dir. 1991-95), Am. Travel Media Assn. (bd. dirs.). Avocation: travel. Office: Santa Barbara News-Press PO Box 1359 Santa Barbara CA 93102-1359 Home Phone: 805-962-1156; Office Phone: 805-564-5105. Personal E-mail: barney163@cox.net. E-mail: bbrantingham@newspress.com.

BRANTINGHAM, PAUL JEFFREY, criminologist, educator; b. Long Beach, Calif., June 29, 1943; s. Charles Ross and Lila Carolyn (Price) Brantingham; m. Patricia Louise Matthews, Aug. 26, 1967; 1 child, Paul Jeffrey Jr. BA, Columbia U., 1965, JD, 1968; Diploma in Criminology, Cambridge U., 1970. Bar: Calif. 1969. Asst. prof. Fla. State U., Tallahassee, 1971-76, assoc. prof., 1976-77, Simon Fraser U., Burnaby, BC, Canada, 1977-85, prof., 1985—2005, Royal Can. Mounted Police Univ. prof. crime analysis, 2005—, assoc. dean faculty interdisciplinary studies, 1980-82; dir. spl. revs. Pub. Svc. Commn. Can., Ottawa, Ont., 1985-87. Editor: Juvenile Justice Philosophy, 1974, 2d edit., 1978, Environmental Criminology, 1981, 2d edit., 1991; author: Patterns in Crime. Recipient Eisenhower Watch award, Columbia U., 1966; Ford Found. fellow, 1969—70, Western Soc. Criminology fellow, 1996, Sr. fellow, Fraser Inst. Mem.: ABA, Western Soc. Criminology (v.p. 2000—01, pres. 2001—02, J.D. Lohman award 2003, Pres. award 2006, R.V.G ECCA Clarke Symposium award 2007), Soc. Reform Criminal Law, Can. Criminal Justice Assn., Acad. Criminal Justice Scis., Am. Soc. Criminology (chmn. nat. program 1978), Calif. Bar Assn. Home: 4680 Eastridge Rd North Vancouver BC Canada V7G 1K4 Office: Simon Fraser U Sch Criminol 8888 University Dr WMC 1632 Burnaby BC Canada V5A 1S6 Home Phone: 604-929-6910; Office Phone: 778-782-4175. Business E-Mail: branting@sfu.ca.

BRAS, RAFAEL LUIS, dean, engineering educator; b. San Juan, Oct. 28, 1950; s. Rafael and Amalia Antonia (Muniz) B.; m. Patricia Ann Brown, June 29, 1974; children: Rafael Edmundo, Alejandro Luis. BSCE, MIT, 1972, MSCE, 1974, DSc in Water Resources and Hydrology, 1975; Laurea (hon.), U. Perugia, Italy, 1991. Registered profl. engr., Mass., PR. Asst. prof. U. PR, Mayaguez, 1975—76; from asst. prof. hydrology to assoc. prof. MIT, Cambridge, Mass., 1976—82, prof., 1982—, head water resources and environ. engring. divsn., 1983—91, dir. Ralph M. Parsons Lab., 1983—91, dir. Minority Intro. to Eng. and Sci., 1987, William E. Leonhard prof. engring., 1988—95, head dept. civil and environ. engring., 1992—2001, Bacardi and Stockholm Water Founds. prof., 1995—2004, chair faculty, 2002—05, Edward A. Abdun-Nur prof. civil and environ. engring., 2004—08; assoc. dir. Ctr. for Global Change Sci., 1990—, dir. Terrascope Program, 2006—; dean Henry Samueli Sch. Engring., U. Calif., Irvine, 2008—. Vis. assoc. prof. U. Simon Bolivar, Caracas, Venezuela, 1982-83; vis. scholar Internat. Inst. Applied Sys. Analysis, Vienna, 1983; vis. prof. Iowa Inst. Hydraulic Rsch., U. Iowa, 1989-90; mem. adv. bd. engring. divsn. NSF, 1988-91; earth scis. and applications divsn. adv. subcom. NASA, 1990, sci. team TRMM mission, 1991-94, chair Earth Sys. Sci. and Applications Adv. Com., 1998-2002; sci. steering group GCIP-Global Energy and Water Cycle Experiment, 1991-95; adv. coun. for com. Nat. Insts. for Environment; mem. adv. com. civil engring. dept. Rensselaer Poly. Inst., 2000-02, Johns Hopkins U., 1998—,dept. civil and environ. engring. Cornell U., 2001—; mem. adv. coun. Princeton U., 1999—; mem. nominating com. Stockholm Water Prize, 1996-2004; mem. exec. com. Clarke Prize, 2002-04; mem. sci. com. Inter Poly. Sch., Milan, Italy, 2003-2006; vis. prof. Harvard U., 2001-2002; mem. com. New Orleans regional hurricane protection program, NAS, 2005—; mem. rels. com. UCAR, 2006—07; cons. in field; lectr. in field. Author: (with I. Rodriguez-Iturbe) Random Functions and Hydrology, 1985, 94, Hydrology: An Introduction to Hydrologic Science, 1990; editor: The World at Risk: Natural Hazards and Climate Change, 1993; editor Nonlinear Processes in Geophysics, 1996-2000; contbr. articles to profl. jours.; assoc. editor Water Resources Rsch., 1980-88, Jour. Geophys. Rsch.-Atmospheres, 1996-98; mem. editl. bd. Jour. Hydrology, Internat. Jour. Environ. Tech.; mem. editl. adv. bd. SERRA, 1998—. Recipient Walter L. Huber Civil Engring. prize, 1993, Giants in Sci. award Quality Edn. for Minorities Math., Sci. and Engring. Network, 2001, Albert Baez Jr. award and Outstanding Educator award Hispanic Engr. Nat. Achievement Awards Conf., 1999, MLK-MIT Leadership award, 2000, Clarke prize, 1998, Hispanic Engr. Nat. Achievement award hall of fame, 2003, AGU Lorenz Lecture, 2003; named to Top 100 Most Influential Hispanics, Hispanic Bus., 1997; Guggenheim fellow, 1982; P.R. Econ. Devel. Adminstrn. fellow; Horton lectr. AMS, 1999, Kisiel Disting. lectr., 2002, William Mong Disting. lectr. U. Hong Kong, 1999-2000, Boussinesq-KNAW lectr., 2005; NASA Pub. Svc. medal, 2002. Fellow: AMS, AAAS (mem. electorate nominating com. engring. sect. 2007—), ASCE (task com. 1996—97, Huber prize 1993, Simon W. Freese Environ. Engring. award 2008), Am. Meteorol. Soc. (Robert E. Horton lectr. award 1999), Am. Geophys. Union (chmn. bd. jous. editors 1984—88, chair budget and fin. 1990—94, pres. Hydrology sect. 2003—06, statutes and bylaws com. 2006—, assoc. editor, Horton award 1981, James B. Macelwane award 1982, Lorenz lectr. 2003, Hydrology Days award 2006, Horton medal 2007); mem.: Internat. Water Acad., U.S. Nat. Acad. Engring., Nat. Acad. Engring. Mex. (corr.), Soc. Presdl. Fellows Lectrs., Boston (Mass.) Soc. Civil Engrs., MIT Alumni Assn. (Bronze Beaver award 2005), Tau Beta Pi, Sigma Xi, Chi Epsilon. Roman Catholic. Office: U Calif Henry Samueli Sch Engring 305 Rockwell Engring Ctr Irvine CA 92697-2700 Office Phone: 949-824-6002. Office Fax: 949-824-7996. Business E-Mail: rlbras@uci.edu.

BRASHIER, KENNETH E., humanities educator; BA, U. Mo., 1987, U. Oxford, 1990; MA, Harvard U., 1993; PhD, U. Cambridge, 1998. Faculty mem. Reed Coll., Portland, Oreg., 1998—2003, assoc. prof. religion and humanities, 2003—. Recipient US Professors of Yr. Award for Outstanding Baccalaureate Coll. Prof., Carnegie Found. for Advancement of Tchg. and Coun. for Advancement and Support of Edn., 2006; grantee NEH Fellowship; Rhodes Scholar, Harry S Truman Scholar. Office: Reed Coll 3203 SE Woodstock Blvd Portland OR 97202-8199 Office Phone: 503-517-5065. E-mail: brashiek@reed.edu.

BRASS, ERIC PAUL, internal medicine and pharmacology educator, academic administrator; b. Bklyn., Sept. 3, 1952; s. Edward A. and Barbara B.; m. Kathy E. Sietsema, Sept. 3, 1994; children: Carl, Courtney, Alexander. BSChemE, Case Western Res. U., 1974, MSChemE, 1975, PhD in Pharmacology, 1979, MD, 1980. Diplomate Am. Bd. Internal Medicine. Resident in internal medicine U. Wash., Seattle, 1980-82, fellow in clin. pharmacology, 1982-83; asst. prof. medicine and pharmacology U. Colo., Denver, 1983-89; assoc. prof. medicine and pharmacology Case Western Res. U., Cleve., 1989-93; asst. dir. Calif. Clin Trials, 1993-94; prof., chair dept. medicine Harbor-UCLA Med. Ctr., 1994—2000; dir. Harbor-UCLA Ctr. Clin. Pharm., 2000—; prof. medicine David Geffen Sch. Medicine, UCLA, 1994—. Mem., chair FDA Nonprescription Drug Adv. Com., 1995—2001. Contbr. more than 130 articles to sci. jours. Recipient Faculty Devel. award Pharm. Mfrs. Assn. Found., 1985; NIH rsch. grantee, 1985, 88, 93. Mem. Am. Fedn. Clin. Rsch., Am. Soc. Pharmacology and Exptl. Therapeutics, Am. Soc. Clin. Pharmacology and Therapeutics (Young Investigator award 1987), Am. Soc. Clin. Investigation. Office: Harbor-UCLA Med Ctr 1124 W Carson St Torrance CA 90502-2004 Office Phone: 310-222-4050. Business E-Mail: ebrass@ucla.edu.

BRATTON, BILL (WILLIAM JOSEPH BRATTON), police chief; b. Boston, Oct. 6, 1947; m. Cheryl A. Fiandaca, 1986 (div.); 1 child, David; m. Rikki Jo Klieman, April 30, 1999 BS in Law Enforcement, Boston State Coll., postgrad.; grad. Sr. Execs. and Sr. Exec. Fellows Program, Harvard U.; grad., FBI Nat. Exec. Inst., New Eng. Inst. Law Enforcement Mgmt. Command Program, Police Exec. Rsch. Forum Sr. Mgmt. Inst. for Police. Exec. supt. Boston Police Dept., 1980—82, police commr., 1992-94; chief of police Mass. Bay Transp. Authority, 1983-86; supt. Met. Police Dept., Boston, 1986-90; chief N.Y.C. Transit Police Dept., 1990-92; police commr. N.Y.C. Police Dept., 1994-96; exec. v.p. First Security Consultants, NYC, 1996—98; pres., COO Carco Group Inc, St. James, NY, 1998—2001; cons. Kroll Associates, 2001—02; chief of police L.A. Police Dept., 2002—. Mem. exec. session of policing Kennedy Sch. Govt. Harvard U., 1985-92 mem. policing in 21st century work group Nat. Inst. Justice, Washington. Co-author (with Peter Knobler): Turnaround: How America's Top Cop Reversed the Crime Epidemic, 1998. Mem. Internat. Assn. Chiefs of Police (major cities chiefs group), Police Exec. Rsch. Forum (pres. 1994—). Roman Catholic. Office: Office of the Chief of Police 150 N Los Angeles St Los Angeles CA 90012

BRATTON, CHRISTOPHER ALAN, academic administrator, videographer, art educator; b. Akron, Ohio, July 3, 1959; s. William Raymond and Barbara Jean (Yerkey) B.; m. Dalida Maria Benfield, Oct. 7, 1994; children, Isadora and Joaquin BFA, Atlanta Coll. of Art, 1982; student, Whitney Ind. Study Program, 1984-86; MFA, U. Wis., Milw., 1994. Project dir. Rise and Shine Prodns., NYC, 1988-89; guest lectr. Sch. of Visual Arts, NYC, 1990, Sch. of the Art Inst., Chicago, Ill., 1990; vis. prof. ctr. for modern culture and media Brown U., Providence, 1991-92; faculty mem. Sch. of Art Inst., Chgo., 1992—2004, chmn. dept. video, 1993-95, chmn. dept. video, com. on exhbns. and events, instn-wide tech. initiative, 1997—98, chair dept. of film, video, and new media Chicago, Ill., 2000—01, dean undergraduate studies, 2002—04; pres. San Francisco Art Inst., Calif., 2004—. Guest lectr. in video prodn. SUNY at Old Westbury, 1986, Channel Four workshop, Derry Northern Ireland, 1986, seminars N.Y.U., panelist N.Y. Marxist Sch., Video, Edn. and Culture, N.Y.C., 1989, Literacy on the Table seminar, Video and Literacy, Bronx (N.Y.) Coun. on the Arts, 1989, Columbus in Context, Union Theol. Sem., N.Y., Mediactive Conf. Low Format Video and Media Edn., 1990; curator Teaching TV, Artists' Space, N.Y., 1990, vis. artist Hallwalls, Buffalo, Ednl. Video Ctr., N.Y.C., 1991, R.I. Sch. of Design, Providence, 1992, Gallery 400, Univ. Ill., Chgo., 1994; coord. producer Teaching TV, Deep Dish TV, 1992; presenter Hunter Coll. Roundtable on Media and Culture, N.Y.C., 1992, The Ctr. for 20th Century Studies, U. Wis., Milw., 1992; grants panelist NEA Regional fellowships, Film in the Cities, Mpls., 1993; panelist Guerilla TV, Ctr. for New TV, N.Y.C., 1993. Editor, curator: (videotape) Teaching TV, 1991; dir. (videotapes), Counterterror The North of Ireland, 1990, (Best Advocacy Work, The Atlanta Film and Video Festival 1991, Silver Apple, Oakland, Calif. Nat. Ednl. Film and Video Festival, Finalist Athens (Ohio) Festival) Framing the Panthers in Black and White (Am. Film Fest Red Ribbon, New Eng. Film and Video Fest Best Social Documentary, Australian Video Festival finalist, Hallwalls Festival of New Journalism, Buffalo, Jurors' award, Peoples Choice award The Global Africa Festival, Oakland, Calif., Spl. Jurors' award Black Maria Film and Video Fetival, East Orange, N.J., others), A Small War: The United States in Puerto Rico, 1995. Recipient fellowship in sculpture NEA, 1988, Citation Nat. Ednl. Film and Video Festival for Brooklyn, 1989, Bronze Apple for Walls and Bridges, 1990, Grand prize Internat. Youth Film and Video Festival, Warsaw for Brooklyn, 1990, Artist's Residency fellowship, Wesner Ctr. for Contemporary Art, Columbus, Ohio, 1993; grantee, Checkerboard Found., 1989, N.Y. State Coun. on the Arts, 1989, 91, J. Roderick MacArthur Found., 1989, NEA, 1990. Office: San Francisco Art Inst 800 Chestnut St San Francisco CA 94113 E-mail: president@sfai.edu.

BRATTSTROM, BAYARD HOLMES, biology professor; b. Chgo., July 3, 1929; s. Wilber LeRoy and Violet (Holmes) B.; m. Cecile D. Funk, June 15, 1952 (div. May 1975); children: Theodore Allen, David Arthur.; m. Martha Isaacs Marsh, July 8, 1982. BS, San Diego State Coll., 1951; MA, UCLA, 1953, PhD, 1959. Dir. edn. Natural History Mus., San Diego, 1949-51, asst. curator herpetology, 1949-51; assoc. zoology UCLA, 1954-56; research fellow paleoecology Calif. Inst. Tech., Pasadena, 1955; instr. biology Adelphi U., Garden City, NY, 1956-60; asst. prof. Calif. State U., Fullerton, 1960-61, assoc. prof., 1961-66, prof., 1966-94, prof. emeritus, 1994—. Co-owner Horned Lizard Ranch, Horned Lizard Press; rschr., author publs. in osteology, ecology, conservation, zoogeography of vertebrates, social behavior; hon. rsch. assoc. herpetology, vertebrate paleontology Los Angeles County Mus., 1961—; pres. Fullerton Youth Mus. and Natural Sci. Ctr., 1962-64, dir., 1962-66; assoc. prof. zoology UCLA, summers 1962-63; vis. prof. zoology Sydney U., Australia, 1978, U. Queensland, Brisbane, Australia, 1984; vis. rschr. James Cook U., Townsville, Australia, 1993-94; ecol. cons. to numerous govtl. agys. and pvt. corps. Author: The Talon Digs Deeply Into My Heart, 1974; co-author (with M.A. Brattstrom): Aussie Slang, 2000, A Field Guide To Poor Teaching. Recipient Disting. Teaching award Calif. State U., Fullerton, 1968, Dean's award for Outstanding Teaching and Rsch., 1992; Am. Philos. Soc. grantee to Mex., 1958, to Panama, 1959; NSF grantee, 1964-66; NSF fellow Monash U., Australia, 1966-67. Fellow AAAS (mem. coun. 1965-90), Herpetological League; mem. Am. Soc. Ichthyologists and Herpetologists (bd. govs. 1962-66, v.p. western div. 1965), Orange County Zool. Soc. (mem. bd. 1962-65, pres. 1962-64), So. Calif. Acad. Sci. (dir. 1964-67), Ecol. Soc. Am., Soc. for Study Evolution, Soc. Systematic Zoology, San Diego Soc. Natural History, Soc. Vertebrate Paleontology, Am. Soc. Mammalogists, Cooper Ornithol. Soc., Am. Ornithol. Soc., Am. Soc. Zoologists, Sigma Xi. Home: Horned Lizard Ranch PO Box 166 Wikieup AZ 85360

BRAUMAN, JOHN I., chemist, educator; b. Pitts., Sept. 7, 1937; s. Milton and Freda E. (Schlitt) B.; m. Sharon Lea Kruse, Aug. 22, 1964; 1 dau., Kate Andrea. BS, MIT, 1959; PhD (NSF fellow), U. Calif., Berkeley, 1963. NSF postdoctoral fellow UCLA, 1962-63; asst. prof. chemistry Stanford (Calif.) U., 1963-69, asso. prof., 1969-72, prof., 1972-80, J.G. Jackson-C.J. Wood prof. chemistry, 1980—, chmn. dept., 1979-83, 95-96, cognizant dean phys. scis., 1999—2003. Cons. in phys. organic chemistry; adv. panel chemistry divsn. NSF, 1974-78; adv. panel NASA, AEC, ERDA, Rsch. Corp., Office Chemistry and Chem. Tech., NRC; coun. Gordon Rsch. Confs., 1989-95, trustee, 1991-95. Mem. editl. adv. bd. Jour. Am. Chem. Soc., 1976-83, Jour. Organic Chemistry, 1974-78, Nouveau Jour. de Chimie, 1977-85, Chem. Revs., 1978-80, Chem. Kinetics, 1987-89, Accts. Chem. Rsch., 1995-97, 98-2001; bd. trustees Ann. Revs., 1995—, mem. editl. adv. bd.; dep. editor for phys. scis. Sci., 1985-2000, chair sr. editl. bd., 2000—. Alfred P. Sloan fellow, 1968-70, Guggenheim fellow, 1978-79; Christensen fellow Oxford U., 1983-84, Nat. Medal of Science award, 2002. Fellow AAAS (chmn. sect. 1996-97, mem.-at-large sect. 1997-99), Calif. Acad. Scis. (hon.); mem. NAS (home sec. 2003-07, 07-, Award in Chem. Scis. 2001), Am. Acad. Arts and Scis., Am. Philos. Soc., Am. Chem. Soc. (award in pure chemistry 1973, Harrison Howe award, 1976, R.C. Fuson award, 1986, James Flack Norris award 1986, Arthur C. Cope scholar, 1986, Linus Pauling medal 2002, J. Willard Gibbs medal 2003, exec. com. phys. chemistry divsn., com. on sci. 1992-97), Sigma Xi, Phi Lambda Upsilon. Home: 849 Tolman Dr Palo Alto CA 94305-1025 Office: Stanford U Dept Chemistry Stanford CA 94305-5080

BRAUN, DAVID A(DLAI), lawyer; b. NYC, Apr. 23, 1931; s. Morris and Betty Braunstein; m. Merna Feldman, Dec. 18, 1955; children: Lloyd Jeffrey, Kenneth Franklin, Evan Albert. AB, Columbia U., NYC, 1952, LLB, 1954. Bar: N.Y. 1955, Calif. 1974. Assoc. Ellis, Ellis and Ellis, NYC, 1954—56, Davis and Gilbert, 1956—57; ptnr. Pryor, Braun, Cashman & Sherman, 1957—73, Hardee, Barovick, Konecky & Braun, NYC, 1973, LA, 1974—81; pres., CEO Polygram Records, Inc., N.Y.C., 1980—81; counsel Wyman, Bautzer, Rothman, Kuchel & Silbert, LA, 1982—85; ptnr. Braun, Margolis, Burrill & Besser, LA, 1985—87; counsel Silverberg, Rosen, Leon & Behr, 1987—89, Silverberg, Katz, Thompson & Braun, 1989—91; spl. counsel Proskauer, Rose, Goetz & Mendelsohn, 1991—93; ptnr. Monasch Plotkin & Braun, 1993—94; pvt. practice, 1994—98; sr. counsel Akin, Gump, Strauss, Hauer & Feld, LLP, LA, 1998—2006. Adj. prof. U. So. Calif. Sch. Cinema-TV; guest lectr. UCLA Ext.; adv. com. Ctr. for Law, Media and the Arts, Columbia U. Sch. Law; internet adv. bd. mem. Nat. Inst. Entertainment and Media Law, Southwestern U. Sch. Law. Co-prodr.: (off-Broadway play) A Woman of Will, 2005. Bd. visitors Columbia Coll., 1980-86, Columbia Law Sch., 1992-94; bd. dirs. Reprise! Broadway's Best in Concert, Musician's Assistance Program, 1994-98, Tu 'Um EST Cmty. Drug Rehab. Ctr., Rock and Roll Hall of Fame, 1985-93. Recipient Service award, Grammy Foundation, 2008. Mem. Assn. of City of NY, LA County Bar Assn., Beverly Hills Bar Assn., Nat. Acad. TV Arts and Scis. (pres. NY chpt. 1972-73), NATAS, Am. Arbitration Assn., Columbia Coll. (John Jay award, 1981), Hollywood Radio and TV Soc. (bd. dirs. 1983-86), Sigma Chi, Phi Alpha Delta. Jewish. Home and Office: 1035 Alston Rd Santa Barbara CA 93108-2407 Office Phone: 805-969-6126. Personal E-mail: dbraun423@cox.net.

BRAUN, HARLAND W., lawyer; b. NYC, Sept. 21, 1942; BA, U. Calif., LA, 1964, JD, 1967. Bar: Calif. 1967, U.S. Dist. Ct. (Ctrl. Dist. Calif.) 1967, cert.: specialist in pvt. practice 1973. Dep. dist. atty., LA County, 1968—73; pvt. practice, 1973—. Mem. UCLA Law Rev., 1965—67. Mem. UCLA Law Review, 1965—67. Mem.: Am. Inn of Ct. (mem., criminal justice sect. organizing com.), LA County Bar Assn., Calif. Attys. Criminal Justice, Criminal Courts Bar Assn. Office: Harland W Braun PC 1880 Century Park E Ste 710 Los Angeles CA 90067-1608 Office Phone: 310-277-4777. Office Fax: 310-277-4045. E-mail: Harland@braunlaw.com.

BRAUNSTEIN, GLENN DAVID, physician, educator; b. Greenville, Tex., Feb. 29, 1944; s. Mervin and Helen (Friedman) B.; m. Jacquelyn D. Moose, July 5, 1965; children: Scott M. Braunstein, Jeffrey T. Braunstein. BS summa cum laude, U. Calif., San Francisco, 1965, MD, 1968. Diplomate Am. Bd. Internal Medicine, subsplty. endocrinology, diabetes, metabolism. Intern, resident Peter Bent Brigham Hosp., Boston, 1968-70; clin. fellow in medicine Harvard U. Med. Sch., Boston, 1969-70; clin. assoc., reproduction rsch. br. NIH, Bethesda, Md., 1970-72; chief resident in endocrinology Harbor Gen. Hosp. UCLA, 1972-73; dir. endocrinology Cedars-Sinai Med. Ctr., LA, 1973-86, chmn. dept. medicine, 1986—; asst. prof. medicine UCLA Sch. Medicine, 1973-77, assoc. prof., 1977-81, prof., 1981—, vice chair dept. medicine, 1986—. Cons. for AMA drug evaluations, 1990—; mem. internat. adv. com. Second World Conf. on Implantation and Early Pregnancy in Human, 1994; mem. endocrinologic and metabolic drugs adv. com. FDA, 1991-95, chmn., 1994-95, spl. advisor, 1995-2001, 04-, chmn., 2001-04; bd. mem. Am. Bd. Internal Medicine Endocrinology, Diabetes, Metabolism Subsplty., 1991-99, chmn., 1995-99, bd. dirs., 1995-99; bd. dirs. Am. Bd. Emergency Medicine 2002-06. Mem. editl. bd. Mt. Sinai Jour. Medicine, 1984-88, Early Pregnancy: Biology and Medicine, 1998, Am. Family Physician, 1995—, The Am. Jour. Medicine, 1996—, Clin. Endocrinology & Metabolism, 1978-80; assoc. editor Integrative Medicine: Integrating Allopathic, Alternative and Complementary Medicine, 1997-2000. Bd. dirs. Israel Cancer Rsch. Fund, 1991-94, Cedars-Sinai Med. Ctr., 1997-2003; mem. Jonsson Comprehensive Cancer Ctr., 1991—. Recipient Gold Headed Cane Soc. award U. Calif. San Francisco Med. Ctr., 1968, outstanding achievement and cmty. svc. award Anti-Defamation League, 1997, James R. Klinenberg Chair in Medicine, 2000—, Sherman M. Mellinkoff Faculty award UCLA Sch. Medicine, 2002; Merck scholar, 1968, Mosby scholar, 1968. Fellow ACP (mem. adv. com. to gov., So. Calif. region 1989—, credentials com. So. Calif. region 1993); mem. AAAS, Cross Town Endocrine Club (chmn. 1982-83), Endocrine Soc. (publs. com. 1983-89, long range planning com. 1986-87, recent progress hormone rsch. com. 1993-98, ann. meeting steering com. 1993-98, spl. programs com. 1998—, media adv. com. 1999-2005, chmn. 2002-05, Disting. Physician award 2006), Pacific Coast Fertility Soc. (pres. 1988), Western Soc. for Clin. Rsch., Am. Fedn. for Clin. Rsch., Am. Thyroid Assn., Am. Fertility Soc., Western Assn. Physicians (pres. 1998-99), North Am. Menopause Assn., Assn. Am. Physicians, Am. Soc. Clin. Investigations (mem. nominating com. 1989), Univ. Calif. San Francisco Sch. Medicine Alumni Faculty Assn. (regional v.p. so. Calif., mem. bd. dirs. Israel Cancer Rsch. Fund 1991-94), Phi Delta Epsilon, Alpha Omega Alpha. Office: Cedars Sinai Med Ctr Dept Med Pla Level Rm 2119 8700 Beverly Blvd Los Angeles CA 90048-1865 Office Phone: 310-423-5140. Business E-Mail: braunstein@cshs.org.

BRAUTIGAN, ROGER L., reserve career officer; BS, U. Ariz.; Master, U. Pacific. Platoon leader 22nd Replacement Battalion, Vietnam; tng., ops., and battalion exec. officer 91st Tng. Divsn.; mobilization plans officer Fort Ord; inspector general 125th Army Reserve Command; chief of tng., chief of ops. Office of the Chief Army Reserve, The Pentagon, Washington; sr. reserve advisor to commanding general US Army Europe, Seventh Army. Maj. gen. USAR. Decorated Legion of Merit with oak leaf cluster, Bronze Star, Meritorious Svc. medal with 3 oak leaf clusters.

BRAVERMAN, ALAN MICHAEL, Internet company executive; s. Berton and Elaine Braverman. BS, U. Ill., 1991—95. With eGroups.com, San Francisco, 1998—2000; tech. yahoo Yahoo.com, Santa Clara, Calif., 2000—01; CTO, co-founder Eventbrite (formerly Mollyguard), San Francisco, 2001—03, xoom.com, San Francisco, 2003—06, Geni, Inc., LA, 2006—. Office: Geni Inc 9255 Sunset Blvd Ste 727 West Hollywood CA 90069

BRAVERMAN, ALAN N., lawyer; b. Mass. BA, Brandeis U., 1969; JD, Duquesne U., 1975. Bar: D.C. 1976. Assoc. Wilmer, Cutler & Pickering, 1976-82, ptnr., 1983-93; exec. v.p., gen. counsel ABC, Inc., NYC, 1993-2000; deputy, gen. counsel The Walt Disney Co., Burbank, Calif., 2000—03, sr. exec. v.p. & gen. coun., 2003—. Office: ABC Inc 500 S Buena Vista St Burbank CA 91521-0922 Office Phone: 818-560-7896.

BRAVMAN, JOHN COLE, materials scientist, educator; b. NYC, July 24, 1957; s. Maurice Daniel and Ella Katherine (Mahnke) B.; children: Christopher Daniel, Matthew Donald. BS, Stanford U., 1979, MS, 1981, PhD, 1984. Engr. Fairchild Semiconductor, Palo Alto, Calif., 1979-84; asst. prof. Stanford U., 1985-91, assoc. prof., 1991-95, prof., 1995-99, v. provost, 1999—. Contbr. over 150 articles to sci. jours. Recipient Walter J. Gores Award for Teaching Excellence, Stanford U., 1989, Tau Beta Pi Award for Engring. Edn. Excellence, 1990, Bradley Stoughton Young Tchrs. award, ASM Internat., 1991. Mem. IEEE, Matls. Rsch. Soc., Am. Phys. Soc., ASM Internat., The Metall. Soc. Office: Stanford Univ Bldg 550 Stanford CA 94305

BRAVO, ADELE, elementary school educator; b. Calif. married; 2 children. BA in Social Work, Azusa Pacific Univ.; MEd student, Regis Univ. Tchr., 1990—, Whittier, Calif., Boulder Valley, Colo., Louisville (Colo.) Elem. Sch. Site coord. Summer Literacy Acad., 2000—, ESL Summer Sch., 2000—. Named Colo. Tchr. of Yr., 2006. Mem.: Luiseno Shoshone Indians. Office: Louisville Elem Sch 400 Hutchinson St Louisville CO 80027 Business E-Mail: adele.bravo@bvsd.org.

BRAVO, PAUL, professional soccer player; b. San Jose, Calif., July 19, 1968; Student, Santa Clara U. Midfielder San Francisco Bay Blackhawks, 1991, San Francisco Greek-Ams.; U.S. Open Cup champions, 1994; midfielder Monterey Bay Jaguars, 1995, San Jose Clash, 1996; advanced to play-offs, 1996; midfielder Colo. Rapids, Denver, 1997—; advanced to play-offs, 1997, 98.

BRAXTON, TONI, singer, actress; b. Severn, Md., Oct. 7, 1967; m. Keri Lewis; children: Denim Cole Braxton Lewis, Diezel Ky Braxton Lewis. Performer Toni Braxton: Revealed, Flamingo Hotel and Casino, Las Vegas, 2006—08. Albums Toni Braxton, 1993 (Favorite Soul/R&B Album, Am. Music Awards, 1995), Secrets, 1996 (Favorite Soul/R&B Album, Am. Music Awards, 1997), The Heat, 2000 (Favorite Soul/R&B Album, Am. Music Awards, 2001), Snow Flakes, 2001, More Than a Woman, 2002, Platinum & Gold Collection, 2004, Please, 2005, Libra, 2005, The Essential: Toni Braxton / The Best So Far, 2007, appeared in (films) Kingdom Come, 2000, contbr. Boomerang soundtrack, 1992, Secrets, 1997; performer: (Broadway Musical) Beauty and the Beast, 1998—99, Aida, 2003, (TV series) Dancing with the Stars, 2008. Nat. celebrity spokesperson Autism Speaks, 2007—. Recipient Best New Artist, Grammy Awards, 1994, 1994, 1995, 1997, 2001, 1997, Favorite New Adult Contemporary Artist, Am. Music Awards, 1994, Favorite New Soul/R&B Artist, 1994, Favorite Female Soul/R&B Artist, 1997, 2001, Aretha Franklin Soul Train award, 2000, BET Black Oscar, 2000. Office: c/o The Brokaw Co 9255 Sunset Blvd, Ste 804 Los Angeles CA 90069

BRAY, TIMOTHY J., orthopedist, surgeon; s. James Francis Bray and Eileen Zelma Davis; m. Kathy Lou Ulmer, Sept. 15, 1979; children: Brendon Francis, Kelly Lewis, Shannon Katherine. MD, U. Calif., Irvine, 1975, U. Guadalajara, Mex., 1975. Orthopaedic Surgeon U.C.San Francisoc, 1982. Orthop. surgeon Reno Orthop. Clinic, 1987—. Chief orthop. trauma Renown Med. Ctr., 1994—. Mem.: Am. Acad. Ortop. Surgeons, Orthop. Trauma Assn. (pres. 2007—). Achievements include design of Development of private practice trauma model. Office: Reno Orthop Clinic 555 N Arlington Reno NV 89503 Business E-Mail: bray@renoortho.com.

BRAZIER, ROBERT G., transportation executive; Student, Stanford U. With Airbone Aircraft Service Inc., 1953-63; v.p. ops. Pacific Air Freight Inc., 1963-68; sr. v.p. ops. Airbone Freight Corp., Seattle, 1968-73, exec. v.p., 1973-78, COO, 1973—, pres., dir, COO, 1978—. Office: Airborne Freight Corp PO Box 662 Seattle WA 98111-0662

BRAZIL, WAYNE D., federal judge; BA, Stanford U., 1966; MA, Harvard U., 1967, PhD, 1975; JD, U. Calif., Berkeley, 1975. Extern clk. to Hon. John J. Purchivo Calif. Superior Ct., 1973-74; extern clk. to Hon. Donald R. Wright Calif. Supreme Ct., 1975-78; with Farella, Braun & Martel, San Francisco; apptd. magistrate judge no. dist. U.S. Dist. Ct. Calif., 1984. Tchr. Vols. in Asia, 1966; tchr., counselor Upward Bound, U. Mass., 1968-69; vis. prof. law U. Ky., 1978; assoc. prof. law U. Mo., 1978-80; prof. law Hastings Coll., 1980-84. Contbr. articles to law jours. Capt. USAR, 1974. Mem. ABA, Am. Law Inst., Calif. Bar Assn., Phi Beta Kappa, Order of Coif. Office: Oakland Federal Courthouse 1301 Clay St Oakland CA 94612-5217 Fax: 510-637-3327.

BREAUX, JIMMY, musician; Mem. band BeauSoleil, 1976—. Albums include The Spirit of Cajun Music, 1976, Parlez Nous au Boire, 1984, Louisiana Cajun Music, 1984, Zydeco Gris Gris, 1985, Allons a Lafayette, 1986, Bayou Boogie, 1986, Bayou Cadillac, 1989, Live! From the Left Coast, 1989, Deja Vu, 1990, Cajun Conja, 1991, La Danse de la Vie, 1993, L'Echo, 1994, L'Amour ou la Folie, 1995 (Grammy award for Best Traditional Folk Album, 1997), Arc de Triomphe Two-Step, 1997, Looking Back Tomorrow, 2001, Gitane Cajun, 2004, Live in Louisiana, 2006, Live at the 2008 New Orleans Jazz & Heritage Festival (Grammy award for Best Cajun Album, 2009), Alligator Purse, 2009. Recipient Big Easy Entertainment award for Best Cajun Band, 2005. Office: care Rosebud Agy PO Box 170429 San Francisco CA 94117-0429

BREBER, PIERRE R., oil industry executive; b. 1964; BS, U. Calif., Berkeley, MS in Mech. Engring.; MBA, Cornell U., 1989. Fin. analyst MBA devel. program Chevron Corp., 1989, mgr. investor rels., mgr. fin. Europe upstream strategic bus. unit, comptroller internat. upstream, v.p. fin. Global Downstream, 2007—08, v.p., treas., 2009—. Office: Chevron Corp 6001 Bollinger Canyon Rd San Ramon CA 94583*

BRECHT, ALBERT ODELL, library and information technology administrator; b. Dallas, n, Nov. 19, 1946; BA in Govt. and Sociology, North Tex. State U., 1969; JD, U. Houston, 1972; LLM, U. Wash., 1973. Bar: Tex. 1972. Asst. law libr. U. So. Calif., LA, 1973-74, asst. law libr. in-charge Law Libr., 1975, lab libr., asst. prof. law, 1975-77, dir. Law Libr., 1977—, assoc. prof., 1977-79, prof., 1979—, interim dep. univ. libr. for ctrl. libr. sys., 1984-85, assoc. dean Law Libr. and Info. Tech., 1996—. Pres. Libraria Sodalitas, 1980; mem. Westlaw Acad. Adv. Bd., 1988-92. Author: (with A. Holoch and K. Pecarovich) Medical Malpractice Insurance and Its Alternatives: The Legal, Medical, and Insurance Literature—A Bibliography, 1975; contbr. articles and book revs. to profl. jours. Mem. Am. Assn. Law Librs. (audio-visual com. 1975, chmn. nominations com. 1978, recruitment com. 1975-76, placement com. 1979-81, cons. law librs. of correctional instns., chmn. program com. ann. meeting 1983, v.p. 1986-87, pres. 1987-88, moderator program on law librs. 1991), Spl. Librs. Assn., So. Calif. Assn. Law Librs. (v.p. 1974-75, pres. 1975-76, bd. dirs. 1978, chmn. com. on cons. for non-law librs. 1981). Office: U So Calif Law Libr University Park Los Angeles CA 90089-0001

BRECKENRIDGE, KLINDT DUNCAN, architect; b. Iowa City, Apr. 24, 1957; s. Jack Duncan and Florence (Kmiecik) B.; m. Nancy Ann Dernier, Apr. 19, 1986; children: Wilson Reid, Lauren Alessandra, Carson Duncan. BArch, U. Ariz., 1981. Registered architect, Ariz., Calif., Nev.; cert. NCARB. Architect Finical & Dombrowski, Tucson, 1981-84; pvt. practice Tucson, 1984—. Assoc. faculty Pima Community Coll. Bd. dirs., pres. Mirical Sq. Mem. AIA (treas. So. Ariz. chpt. 1997-99, pres. 1999-2000, state pres. elect 2003, com. arch. edn., pres.-elect). Democrat. Episcopalian. Avocation: running. Office: Brackenridge Group 700 N Stone Ave Tucson AZ 85705-8306 Home: 5960 N Moccasin Trl Tucson AZ 85750-0809 E-mail: breckenridge@breckenridgearch.com.

BRECKINRIDGE, JAMES BERNARD, optical scientist; s. Albert Coles and Catherine Rose (Wengler) B.; m. Ann Marie Yoder, July 24, 1965; children: Douglass E., John Brian. BS in Physics, Case Inst. Tech., 1961; MS in Optical Sci., U. Ariz., 1970, PhD in Optical Sci., 1976. Rsch. asst. Lick Obs., Mt. Hamilton, Calif., 1961-64; electron tube engr. Rauland Corp., Chgo., 1967; rsch. asst. Kitt Peak Nat. Obs., Tucson, full time, 1964-66, 68, 75-76, part time, 1969-74; mem. tech. staff Jet Propulsion Lab., Calif. Inst. Tech., 1976—2009, part-time faculty in applied physics, 1981—2008, mgr. optics sect., 1981-94, vis. assoc. faculty, 2009—; program mgr. for innovative imaging tech. and sys. Def. Program Office, 1994—99; leader NASA Team to Assess Optics Tech. in Former Soviet Union, 1992-97; program dir. advanced tech. and instrumentation, program dir. Nat. Radio Astronomy Obs., NSF, 1999—2002; chief technologist Astron. Search for Origins, NASA, 2002—07, exoplanet exploration program tech., 2008; vis. assoc. Grad. Lab. Aeronatics CALTECH, 2009—. Co-investigator NASA Spacelab 3; adv. com. NASA, NSF, Dept. Def.; staff mem. Hubble Space Telescope Failure Bd., 1990, tech. mgr. Hubble Space Telescope Camera Optics Repair; reader, history sci. and tech., Huntington Libr., San Marino, CA, 2007-. Contbr. 90 articles to jours. in field; 5 patents in field. Scoutmaster Boy Scouts Am.; mem. Soc of the Cin. in NJ. Fellow Optical Soc. Am. (bd. dirs.), Royal Astron. Soc., Internat. Soc. Optical Engring. (bd. govs., pres. 1994, George W. Goddard award 2003); mem. Am. Astron. Soc., Coun. Sci. Soc. Pres.'s (bd. dirs. 1996), Internat. Astron. Union, Internat. Congress on Optics (U.S. chair 1999-2001), Breckinridge Family Assn. (pres. 1999—2006). Achievements include research in space-based remote optical and infrared sensing instrumentation, interferometry, spectroscopy, image intensifiers and image analysis. Office: 4800 Oak Grove Dr Pasadena CA 91109 Home: 985 E California Blvd Ste 203 Pasadena CA 91106 Office Phone: 818-354-6785. Personal E-mail: jbreckin@earthlink.net. Business E-Mail: jbreckin@caltech.edu.

BREDT, DAVID SCOTT, neuroscience and physiology educator; b. Phila., May 12, 1964; s. Allen Bruce and Carol Emily (Segal) B. BA in Chemistry summa cum laude, Princeton U., 1986; PhD, Johns Hopkins U., 1992, MD, 1993. Post-doctoral fellow Lab. Solomon H. Snyder dept. neurosci. Sch. Medicine Johns Hopkins U., 1993; asst. prof. through prof. neurosci. and physiology U. Calif., San Francisco, 1994—. Author: (with others) Neuropeptide Functions in the Brain, 1991, Long Term Potentiation: A Current Debate of Issues, vol. 2, 1993, Biology of Nitric Oxide, 1992, Nitric Oxide: Brain and Immune System, 1993; editor Frontiers in Bioscience; contbr. articles to profl. jours. Recipient Michael A. Shanoff Meml. award Johns Hopkins U. Sch. Medicine, 1992, Rsch. Essay award Am. Acad. Neurology, 1993, Young Investigator award NSF, 1994—; Med. Scientist Tng. Program grantee, 1986-93; Klingenstein fellow, 1994—, McKnight fellow, 1994—. Mem. Phi Beta Kappa. Jewish. Office: U Calif Depts of Physiology 513 Parnassus Ave # 859 San Francisco CA 94122-2722

BREED, MICHAEL DALLAM, biology professor; b. Kansas City, Mo., Sept. 2, 1951; s. Laurence W. and Loree (Dallam) B.; m. Cheryl A. Ristig, Aug. 9, 1975. BA, Grinnell Coll., 1973; MA, U. Kans., 1975, PhD, 1977. Asst. prof. environ., population, organismic biology U. Colo., Boulder, 1977-83, assoc. prof., 1983-89, prof., 1989—, acting chmn. dept. anthropology, 1991-93, chmn. dept., 1986-90, 97-99, acting assoc. dean, 1991-93, chmn., dept. east asian lang. and civilizations, 2002—. Contbr. articles to sci. jours. Mem. Internat. Union for Study of Social Insects (pres. N.Am. sect. 1984, sec. gen. 1994—), Animal Behavior Soc., Internat. Bee Rsch. Assn., Entomol. Soc. Am. (officer sect. C 1992-95), Sigma Xi. Home: 700 Dahlia St Denver CO 80220-5112 Office: U Colo 334 UCB Boulder CO 80309 Office Phone: 303-492-7687. Office Fax: 303-492-8699. E-mail: Michael.Breed@Colorado.EDU.

BREEDEN, SHIRLEY, state legislator; b. Needles, Calif., 1955; children: Erik, Bryan, Jennifer. Attended Bus. Adminstr., CC of Southern Nev.; attended Continuing Edn. Program, U. Nev., Las Vegas; attended Personnel Mgmt. Issues, Clark County Sch. Dist. Professional Devel. Edn. Programs; attended, Leadership 2000. Ct. apptd. special adv.; mem. Clark County Dist. 5 Nev. State Senate, 2008—. Recipient proclamation from Nev. State Assemblyman Tick Segerblom for professional accomplishments & exemplary pub. svc., 2008; named Ct. Apptd. Adv. of the Year, 2006. Mem.: Nev. Alliance Ret. Americans, Ret. Pub. Employees Nev. Democrat. Office: 401 South Carson St Room 2131 Carson City NV 89701 Home: 291 Kershner Ct Henderson NV 89074 Home Phone: 702-456-6192; Office Phone: 775-684-1457. Fax: 702-463-1008. Business E-Mail: sbreeden@sen.state.nv.us.

BREEN, RICHARD F., JR., law librarian, educator; b. Providence, Aug. 1, 1940; s. Richard F. and Elizabeth (Hurlin) B.; children: Stephanie, Jonathan. AB in Econs., Dartmouth Coll., 1962; LLB, U. Maine, Portland, 1967; MLS, U. Oreg., 1973. Bar: Maine, N.H. Asst. dean U. Maine Sch. Law, Portland, 1967-70; with firm Tesreau and Gardner, Lebanon, NH, 1970-72; assoc. law libr., assoc. prof. law U. Maine Sch. Law, Portland, 1974-76; law libr., assoc. prof. law Willamette U. Coll. Law, Salem, Oreg., 1976-80, law libr., prof. law, 1980—, interim adminstrv. dean., law libr., 1986-87. Legal specialist to Albania for ABA Ctrl. and East European Law Initiative, 1995. Mem. U.S. Olympic Biathlon Tng. Team, 1963. Capt. USAR, 1962—64. Mem. Am. Assn. Law Librs., Casque and Gauntlet Sr. Soc. Democrat. Congregationalist. Avocations: cross country skiing, hiking. Office: Willamette U Law Libr 245 Winter St SE Salem OR 97301-3916 Office Phone: 503-370-6386. Business E-Mail: dbreen@willamette.edu.

BREEN, STEPHEN P., editorial cartoonist; b. LA, 1970; m. Cathy Breen; 4 children. BA in Polit. Sci., U. Calif., Riverside, 1992. Editl. cartoonist Asbury Park Press, Neptune, NJ, 1994—2001, San Diego Union-Tribune, 2001—. Author, illustrator (childrens' books) Stick, 2007, Violet The Pilot, 2008, cartoons pub. regularly in NY Times, USA Today, Newsweek, nationally syndicated by Copley News Svc. Recipient Pulitzer prize for editl. cartooning, 1998, 2009, Berryman award, Nat. Press Found., 2007, Nat. Headliner award, 2009, John Locher Meml. award, Assn. Am. Editl. Cartoonists, Charles M. Schulz award, Scripps Howard Found. Office: San Diego Union-Tribune 350 Camino de la Reina92 PO Box 120191 San Diego CA 92112-0191*

BREGA, CHARLES FRANKLIN, lawyer; b. Callaway, Nebr., Feb. 5, 1933; s. Richard E. and Bessie (King) B.; m. Betty Jean Witherspoon, Sept. 17, 1960; children: Kerry E., Charles D., Angie G. BA, The Citadel, 1954; LLB, U. Colo., 1960. Bar: Colo. 1960. Assoc. firm Hindry & Meyer, Denver, 1960-62, partner, 1962-75, dir., 1975; dir. firm Roath & Brega, Denver, 1975-89, Brega & Winters, Denver, 1989—2003, Lindquist & Vennum PLLP, Denver, 2004—. Lectr. in field; guest prof. U. Colo., U. Denver, U. Nev., others. Trustee Pres.'s Leadership Class, U. Colo., 1977—. Served with USAF, 1954-57. Named Colo. Super Lawyer, 2005—08; named one of Best Lawyers in Am., 1983, Best Lawyers in Colo. Since its Inception. Mem. Colo. Trial Lawyers Assn. (pres. 1972-73), Assn. Trial Lawyers Am. (gov. 1972-79), ABA, Am. Law Inst., Am. Bd. Trial Advs., Internat. Acad. Trial Lawyers, Internat. Soc. Barristers, Cherry Hills Country Club, Denver Athletic Club. Episcopalian. Home: 4501 S Vine Way Englewood CO 80110-6027 Office: Fairfield & Woods 1700 Lincoln St Ste 2400 Denver CO 80203-4524 Home Phone: 303-761-2077; Office Phone: 303-894-4438. Business E-Mail: cbrega@fwlaw.com.

BREGA, KERRY ELIZABETH, physician, researcher; b. Denver, Sept. 8, 1961; d. Charles Franklin and Betty Jean Brega. BA, U. Colo., 1983, MD, 1989. Diplomate Am. Bd. Spine Surgery, Am. Bd. Neurol. Surgery. Resident in neurosurgery U. Colo., Denver, 1990-95, asst. prof. neurosurgery, 1995—; dir. neurosurgery Littleton Adventist Hosp., Denver, 1998—; asst. prof. neurosurgery U. Colo., Denver, 1995—2005, assoc. prof. neurosurgery, med. dir. Stroke Ctr., 2006—, assoc. dir. neurosurg. residency tng. program, 2006—. Bd. dirs. Donor Alliance, Denver, 1994—. Mem. Am. Coll. Spine Surgery, Am. Assn. Neurol. Surgeons, Congress Neurol. Surgeons, Colo. Neurol. Soc., Alpha Omega Alpha. Office Phone: 303-315-1429.

BREGMAN, MARK, information technology executive; BS in Physics, Harvard Coll.; MS in Physics, PhD in Physics, Columbia U. Sr. mgmt. positions IBM Rsch. and IBM Japan, 1984—2000; CEO Airmedia Inc., 2000—01; exec. v.p. product ops. Veritas Software Corp., Mountain View, Calif., 2002—04, chief tech. officer, 2004, acting mgr., application and svc. mgmt. group, 2004; chief tech. officer Symantec Corp., Cupertino, Calif., 2004—06, exec. v.p., chief tech. officer. Bd. overseers Fermi Nat. Accelerator Lab. Mem. vis. com. Harvard U. Lib. Mem.: Am. Physical Soc., IEEE (sr.). Office: Symantec Corp 20330 Stevens Creek Blvd Cupertino CA 95014 Office Phone: 800-327-2232. Office Fax: 650-527-2908.

BREIGER, RONALD LOUIS, social sciences educator; b. NYC, Mar. 19, 1948; s. Lazarus H. and Lillian E. (Berman) Breiger; m. Linda Ruth Waugh, May 20, 1984; 1 child, David Luis Waugh-Breiger. AB, Brandeis U., 1966—70; PhD, Harvard U., 1970—75. Asst. prof. of sociology Harvard U., 1975—79, assoc. prof. of sociology, 1979—81; prof. of sociology Cornell U., Ithaca, 1981—95, dept. chmn., 1988—93, Goldwin Smith prof. sociology, 1995—2000; prof. of sociology U. of Ariz., 2000—. Vis. prof. U. of Lille-1, France, 2002. Editor: (jour.) Social Networks, 1998—2006; author: (collected works) Explorations in Structural Sociology (Harvard Studies in Sociology series); chair (symposium) Nat. Acad. Scis. workshop on Dynamic Network Models and Analysis. Fellow Ctr. for Advanced Study in the Behavioral Scis., 1985—86. Mem.: Nat. Sci. Found. (mem. sociology panel 1988—90), Sociol. Rsch. Assn., Internat. Network for Social Network Analysis (mem. exec. bd. 2003—, exec. bd. mem. 2003, Simmel award 2005), Am. Sociol. Assn. (exec. com., sect. on math. sociology 2000—02, chair sect. on math. sociology 2009—). Office: U Ariz Dept of Sociology Tucson AZ 85721-0027 Office Phone: 520-621-3531.

BREITHAUPT, BRENT HENRY, museum curator; b. Milw., Jan. 11, 1956; s. Henry G. Breithaupt and Ann M. (Kluge) Catalano; m. Vicki Ann Burton, Aug. 2, 1980. BS in Geology, U. Wis., Milw., 1978; MS in Geology, U. Wyo., 1981. Mus. asst. Milw. Pub. Mus., 1975-78; curatorial asst. Geol. Mus. U. Wyo., Laramie, 1980-81, dir., curator Geol. Mus., 1981—, instr. correspondence study, 1983—, instr. Sch. Extended Studies and Pub. Svc., 1986—. Spkr. in field. Contbr. articles to profl. jours. Mem. Paleontol. Soc., Soc. for Study of Amphibians and Reptiles, Am. Soc. Ichthyologists and Herpetologists, Herpetologists League, Colo.-Wyo. Acad. Scis., Colo.-Wyo. Assn. Mus., Soc. Vertebrate Paleontology (regional editor news bulletin 1985—), Wis. Geol. Soc. (v.p. 1976), Nat. Speleological Soc., Wyo. Geol. Soc., Sigma Xi. Avocations: fencing, running, nordic and alpine skiing, rock climbing, caving, soccer. Office: U Wyo The Geol Mus Laramie WY 82071-3006

BRELAND, SANDY ANN, broadcast executive, director; b. New Orleans, Sept. 7, 1962; d. John Jerry and Betty Joy (Johnson) B.; m. John David McNamara, Apr. 10, 1992; 1 child, Ryan David. BA in Comms., Loyola U., 1983. Prodr., assignment editor WWL Radio, New Orleans, 1984-88; asst. editor WWL-TV, New Orleans, 1989-94, news dir., 1994—2006, KTVK/KASW-TV, Phoenix, 2006—. Recipient George Foster Peabody award for coverage of Hurricane Katrina, 2006, Edward R. Murrow award for coverage of Hurricane Katrina, 2006, Alfred I. duPont-Columbia U. award for coverage of Hurricane Katrina, 2007. Mem. Loyola U. Pres. Coun., RTNDA, CBS News Dir. Caucus. Avocations: boating, reading to child, camping. Office: KTVK/KASW-TV 5555 N 7th Ave Phoenix AZ 85013

BREMER, RONALD ALLAN, genealogist, editor; b. Southgate, Calif., May 2, 1937; s. Carl Leonard and Lena Evelyn (Jury); children: Blindy, Ron, Trina, Rebecca, Jim, Melinda, Aaron, Serena, Lorrie, Jennie, Elizabeth, Hans, Adam, Rachel. Student, Los Angeles Trade Tech., Cerritos Coll., Am. U., Brigham Young U.; grad., Nat. Inst. Geneal. Rsch., 1961. Prof. genealogist, 1959—; research specialist Fam. Hist. Libr., Salt Lake City, 1969-72; profl. lectr. on genealogy Salt Lake City, 1973—; pres. The Ron Bremer Rsch. Inst. Lectr. in field. Author: World's Funniest Epitaphs, 1983; Compendium of Historical Sources, 1983; (with Bill Dollarhide) America's Best Genealogy Resource Centers, 1998; editor Genealogy Digest mag., Salt Lake City, 1983-84, Roots Digest, 1984-85. Personal E-mail: ronbremer@juno.com.

BREMS, DAVID PAUL, architect; b. Lehi, Utah, Aug. 10, 1950; s. D. Orlo and Gearldine (Hitchcock) B.; m. Johna Devey Brems; children: Stefan Tomas Brems, Beret Alla Brems. BS, U. Utah, 1973, MArch, 1975. Registered arch., Utah, Calif., Colo., Ariz., Wyo., N.Mex., Idaho, Mont., Tex., Wash., NCARB. Draftsman Environ. Assocs., Salt Lake City, 1971-73; draftsman/architect intern Environ. Design Group, Salt Lake City, 1973-76; architect/intern Frank Fuller AIA, Salt Lake City, 1976-77; prin. Edward & Daniels, Salt Lake City, 1978-83; pres. David Brems & Assocs., Salt Lake City, 1983-86; prin. Gillies, Stransky, Brems, Smith P.C., Salt Lake City, 1986—. Mem. urban design com. Assist, Inc., Salt Lake City, 1982—85, Salt Lake County Planning Commn., 1991—97, chmn., 1992—96; mem. Emigration Twp. Planning Commn., 1997—2007, chmn., 1997—99; mem. Emigration Masterplan Adv. Com., 1997—99; invited lectr. Wyo. Soc. Archs., 1992, sch. engring. U. Utah, 1993, 95, VA, 1993, Utah Soc. Archs., 1994, Utah Power and Light, 1994, WMR, 2006, UMR, 2007, others; juror U. Utah Grad. Sch. Architecture, 1975—, adj. prof., 1990—, mem. adv. com., 2000—; juror Utah Soc. Am. Planning Assn., 1994—, Sunstone Symposium, 1995, Contemporary Arts Group, 1995—, others. Pub. Firm Profile Intermountain Architecture, 1996, Web Mag., 1997; prin. works include solar twin homes Utah Holiday (Best Solar Design award), Sun Builder, Daily Jour., Salt Lake Tribune, Brian Head Day Lodge, Easton Aluminum, Four Seasons Hotel, Gore Coll. Bus., CMF Tooele, utah Regional Corrections Facility, St. Vincents De Paul Ctr., Steiner Aquatic Ctr., U. Utah Football Support Facility, Sports Medicine West, West Jordan Cmty. Water Park, Utah N.G. Apache Helicopter Hangar & Armory, Kashmitter I Residences, St. Thomas More Cath. Ch., Spanish Fork Cmty. Water Park, Natures Herbs, ABC Office Bldg. Divsn. of Natural Resources Bldg., Kashmitter II Residence, Litton Residence, Elliott Emigration Residence, Elliott Boulder Residence, Utah Olympic Speed Skating Oval for 2002 Olympics, Vis. Ctr. Grand Staircase Escalante Nat. Monument, Bennett Fed. Bldg., Utah Mus. Natural History, and others; ALTA Club mem., Great Salt Lake Yacht Club mem., Bear Lake Yacht Club mem., mem. Leadership Utah; mem. 2002 Olympic Energy and Water subcom., 1996—; mem. State of Utah Divsn. of Facilities Mgmt. Com. on Energy Efficient Architecture. Mem. Salt Lake City Bus. Advisory. Recipient awards Am. Concrete Inst., 1993, Chief Engrs. Honor award U.S. Army Corps Engrs., 1994; Bronze medalist Utah Summer Games, 1991, Silver medalist, 1992, Gold medalist, 1994, Design award Dept. Def., 1995, Blue Seal award, 1995, Outstanding Project award U.S. Dept. Def., 1995, Western Mountain Region Hon. Mention St. Thomas More, 1996, Solar Today award Sun award, Energy Uses News award Dept. Natural Resources, 1996, Western Mountain Region Merit award Bennet Fed. Bldg., 2003, Western Mountain Citation award, 2003, Jewish Cmty. Ctr. Holocaust Meml., 2003,Utah Heritage Found. award, others; named Best Pvt. Project by Intermountain Architecture, 1994, Salt Lake County Vol. of Yr. Salt Lake County Planning Commn., 1995, Best Recreation Project Intermountain Arch., 1995, award for Sahara Office Bldg., Ceramic Tiles of Italy, 2004, award Utah Masonry Coun. Fellow: AIA (chmn. Western Mountain Regiona honor awards 1983, pres. Salt Lake chpt. 1983—84, chmn. Western Mountain Region conf. 1986, pres. Utah Soc. 1987, chmn. Western Mountain Regional honor awards 1988, com. on design 1990—, juror Colo. West awards 1992, chmn. com. on environment AIA Utah 1993, chmn. Design for Life Workshop at Sundance 1993, Utah concrete masony assoc. Emigration Canyon home 2003, chair com. on design AIA 2006, Honor awards 1983, Merit awards 1983, 1985, Honor awards 1988, PCI award 1988, IFRAA award 1988, Merit awards 1988, 1993, IFRAA award 1994, Merit awards 1999, Steel Inst. award 2002, Honor award 2002, Sarnafil award 2002, Merit award 2003, Honor awards 2003, Nat. Concrete Masony award of excellence 2003, Heritage Found. awards 2003, Utah Bronze medal 2006, award Utah sect. IES for St. Thomas More, Utah 25 Yr. award for Emigration Passive Solar Twin Home, Sustainable Design Excellence Honor award 2007); mem.: Utah Energy Forum, Am. Solar Soc., Am. Solar Energy Soc., Utah Soc. Architects, Black Builder Mesa Water Assn. (sec.), Acorn Hills Water Assn. (trustee), Am. Planning Assn. (juror awards 1994), Illuminating Engring. Soc. (assoc.), Utah Open Lands (S.W. Utah br.), Salt Lake Olympic Com. (environ. adv. com.), Hobie Fleet 67 (commodore 1985—86). Home: 119 N Young Oak Rd Salt Lake City UT 84108-1601

BREMSER, GEORGE, JR., electronics executive; b. Newark, May 26, 1928; s. George and Virginia (Christian) B.; m. Marie Sundman, June 21, 1952 (div. July 1979); children: Christian Fredrick II, Priscilla Suzanne, Martha Anne, Sarah Elizabeth; m. Nancy Kay Woods, Oct. 27, 1983 (div. Feb. 1989); m. Betty Glover Lohse, Oct. 8, 1997 (dec. Mar. 2001). BA, Yale U., 1949; postgrad., U. Miami, 1959; MBA, NYU, 1962. With McCann-Erickson Inc., NYC, 1952-61, asst. gen. mgr. Bogota, Colombia, 1955, gen. mgr., 1955-57, account supr. NYC, 1958, v.p., mgr. Miami, Fla., 1959-61; with Gen. Foods Corp., White Plains, NY, 1961-71; v.p., gen. mgr. internat. div. Gen. Foods Europe, White Plains, NY, 1967; pres. Gen. Foods Internat., White Plains, 1967-71; group v.p. Gen. Foods Corp., White Plains, 1970-71; chmn., pres., chief exec. officer Texstar Corp., Grand Prairie, Tex., 1971-81; exec. v.p. Shaklee Corp., San Francisco, 1981-82; chmn., pres., chief exec. officer Etak Inc., Menlo Park, Calif., 1983-88, 96, chmn., 1989-96, 97—; chmn., pres., CEO Etak, Inc., Menlo Park, Calif., 1996-97, chmn., 1997-2000, CEO, 2000-01; bd. dir. Tele Atlas N.A., Inc., 2000—07, chief adminstrv. officer, 2001—02. Bd. dirs. PBI Industries Inc Trustee Union Ch., Bogota, 1956-57; Dem. county committeeman, Ridgewood, N.J., 1962-63; mem. New Canaan (Conn.) Town Council, 1969-73; founder, past pres. Citizens Com. for Conservation, New Canaan; mem. coun. Save the Redwoods League, 1987—. Served to 2d lt. USMC 1950-52, capt. Res. Mem. New Canaan Country Club, Brook Club, Yale Club (N.Y.C.), Block Island Club, Casino Club (Nantucket, Mass.), Explorers Club, Phi Beta Kappa, Beta Gamma Sigma, Beta Theta Pi. Home: Apt 3317 131 Embarcadero West Oakland CA 94607-3768 also: Mansion Beach Rd Block Island RI 02807 Office: Tele Atlas NA Inc 1700 Seaport Blvd Ste 150 Redwood City CA 94063 Office Phone: 650-385-2300 x2306. Business E-Mail: george.bremser@teleatlas.com.

BREN, DONALD L., real estate company executive; b. LA, 1932; married; 7 children. BA in Bus. Admin. and Econs., U. Wash., 1958, MBA. Founder, pres. Bren Co. (renamed Calif. Pacific Homes), Newport Beach, 1958—, Mission Viejo Co., Newport Beach, 1963—67; CEO Irvine Co., Newport Beach, 1977—, chmn. bd., 1998—. Established Donald Bren Sch. Environmental Sci. & Mgmt., U. Calif., Irvine Ranch Land Reserve Trust, 2005, Excellence in Edn. Enrichment Fund, 2006. Chmn. Donald Bren Found.; trustee Orange County Mus. Art, LA County Mus. Art, Calif. Inst. Tech., U. Calif. at Irvine Found., Uncommon Alliance Nature Conservancy, 1996—. Officer USMC, 1954—57. Recipient Semper Fidelis award, Marine Corps U. Found., 1998, Gen. Leonard F. Chapman medallion, 2003, Presdl. medal, U. Calif., 2004; named one of 50 Most Generous Philanthropists, Fortune Mag., 2005, BusinessWeek mag., 2006, World's Richest People, Forbes Mag., 2001—, Forbes Richest Americans, 1999—, 100 Most Influential People in So. Calif., LA Times, 2006. Fellow: Am. Acad. Arts & Scis. Avocations: sailing, skiing, tennis. Office: The Irvine Co 550 Newport Center Dr Newport Beach CA 92660-7011

BRENDEN, JOHN C., state legislator; m. Carol Brenden; children: Kim, Chris, Eric. BA in Polit. Sci./Philosophy, Concordia Coll, Moorhead, Minn., 1963; attended, U. Mont., Missoula, 1963; grad. studies, Adams State Coll., Alamosa, Colo., 1963—64, Pacific Luth. U., Parkland, Wash., 1964—65. Owner/operator Scobey/ Plentywood/ Sidney/ Williston, 1968—88, Brenden Farms, Scobey; real estate agt.; chmn. Mont. Rep. Party, 1983—87; mem. Governor's Office, Northwest Power Planning Coun., 1989—93, Mont. State Senate, 1993—94, mem. Dist. 18, 2008—. Republican. Office: Montana Senate PO Box 200500 Helena MT 59620-0500 Mailing: PO Box 970 Scobey MT 59263-0970 Home Phone: 406-783-5394; Office Phone: 406-444-4800. Office Fax: 406-444-4875.

BRENLY, BOB, professional sports team executive, broadcaster; Grad., Ohio U., 1977. Appeared as a catcher 1 All-Star game; catcher nine major league seasons San Francisco Giants; 3d baseman catcher Bobcats; mgr. Ariz. Diamondbacks, 2000—04. TV color analyst Ariz. Diamondbacks, broadcaster, Chgo. Achievements include became first rookie manager since 1997 to lead his team to the playoffs; Mgr. World Series Champion, 2001.

BRENNAN, CARRIE, principal; b. 1967; BA, Darthmouth Coll., Hanover, NH; MA, U. Ariz. Founding faculty mem. Catalina Foothills High Sch.; prin. City High Sch., Tucson. Co-dir. Southern Ariz. Writing Project's Tchr. Inst.; workshop instructor curriculum design and collaborative profl. devel.; chair Symposium on Sch. Improvement. Involved with Tucson Small Sch. Project. Named one of 40 Under 40, Tucson Bus. Edge, 2006. Office: City High School PO Box 2608 Tucson AZ 85702 Office Phone: 520-623-7223. Office Fax: 520-547-0680. Business E-Mail: carrie@cityhighschool.org.

BRENNAN, CIARAN BRENDAN, accountant, oil industry executive; b. Dublin, Jan. 28, 1944; s. Sean and Mary (Stone) B. BA with honors, Univ. Coll., Dublin, 1966; MBA, Harvard U., 1973; MS in Acctg., U. Houston, 1976. Lic. real estate broker, Calif.; CPA, Tex. Auditor Coopers & Lybrand, London, 1967-70, Price Waterhouse & Co., Toronto, Ont., Canada, 1970-71; asst. contr. Kerr-McGee Corp., Oklahoma City, 1976-80; contr. Cummings Oil Co., Oklahoma City, 1980-82; CFO Red Stone Energies, Ltd., 1982, Leonoco, Inc., 1982-87; treas., chief fin. officer JKJ Supply Co., 1983-87, Saturn Investments Inc., 1983-87, JFL Co., 1984-87, Little Chief Drilling &

Energy Inc., 1984-85; pres. Ciaran Brennan Corp., 1990—; CFO Nationwide Industries, 1991-93; mgr. of budget Mission Foods, 1996-98; contr. Hoffy Bacon, 1998—2001; ptnr. CiaranBrennan.com, 2001—; cons. SEC, Audit and Sarbanes - Oxley. Bd. dirs., cons. small oil cos.; adj. faculty Oklahoma City U., 1977-86; vis. faculty Ctrl. State U., 1977-86; cons., cons. in field. Contbr. articles to profl. jours. Mem. AICPA, Inst. Chartered Accts. Eng. and Wales, K.C. Republican. Roman Catholic. Office Phone: 562-650-7999. Personal E-mail: ciaranrb@aol.com.

BRENNEMAN, AMY, actress; b. New London, Conn., June 22, 1964; m. Brad Silberling, Sept. 30, 1995; children: Charlotte Tucker, Bodhi Russell. BA in Comparative Religion, Harvard U., 1987. Mem. Cornerstone Theater Co. Actress (films) Bye, Bye Love, 1995, Heat, 1995, Casper, 1995, Fear, 1996, The Jane Austen Book Club, 2007, 88 Minutes, 2007, Downloading Nancy, 2008, (TV series) Middle Ages, 1992, NYPD Blue, 1993—94, actress and co-creator Judging Amy, 1999—2005, actress Private Practice, 2007—, actress and co-creator (TV films) Mary Cassatt: An American Impressionist, 1999, Things You Can Tell Just By Looking at Her, 2000, Off the Map, 2003, Nine Lives, 2005, actress (plays) Saint Joan of the Stockyards, 1992, (off Broadway) The Learned Ladies, God's Heart, 1997, (plays) A Nervous Smile, 2006. Founder Cornerstone Theater Co., Conn. Address: Travel Entertainment 9171 Wilshire Blvd Ste 700 Beverly Hills CA 90211 also: PMK/HBH Pub Rels 8500 Wilshire Blvd Ste 700 Beverly Hills CA 90211 Office: Creative Artists Agency 2000 Avenue Of The Stars Los Angeles CA 90067-4700

BRENNEMAN, DELBERT JAY, lawyer; b. Albany, Oreg., Feb. 4, 1950; s. Calvin M. and Velma Barbara (Whitaker) B.; m. Caroline Yorke Allen, May 29, 1976; children: Mark Stuart, Thomas Allen. BS magna cum laude, Oreg. State U., 1972; JD, U. Oreg., 1976. Bar: Oreg. 1976, U.S. Dist. Ct. Oreg. 1977, U.S. Ct. Appeals (9th cir.) 1977. Assoc. Schwabe, Williamson, and Wyatt, Portland, Oreg., 1976-83, ptnr., 1984-92, Hoffman, Hart & Wagner, Portland, Oreg., 1993—. Spkr. Oreg. Self-Ins., 1978, 90; seminar instr. U. Oreg. Law Sch., Eugene, 1980. Mem. ABA, Oreg. State Bar Assn., Multnomah County Bar Assn. (spkr. 1983-84), Order of Coif, Multnomah Athletic Club, Propeller Club of U.S. (bd. dirs. 1983-85), Phi Kappa Phi, Beta Gamma Sigma. Office: Hoffman Hart & Wagner 1000 SW Broadway Fl 20 Portland OR 97205-3072 Home Phone: 503-292-4667; Office Phone: 503-222-4499. Personal E-mail: brennemans@gmail.com. Business E-Mail: djb@hhw.com.

BRENNER, DAVID ALLEN, academic administrator, medical educator; MD, Yale U. Resident Yale-New Haven Med. Ctr.; rsch. assoc. genetics and biochemistry branch Nat. Inst. of Arthritis, Diabetes, Digestive and Kidney Diseases, NIH; gastroenterology fellow U. Calif., San Diego, 1985; physician Veterans Affairs San Diego Healthcare Sys.; prof., chief Divsn. Digestive Diseases and Nutrition U. NC, Chapel Hill, 1993; vice chancellor health scis., dean Sch. Medicine U. Calif., San Diego, 2007—. Bd. dirs. AlphaOne Found., Alcoholic Beverage Med. Rsch. Found. Mem.: Am. Clin. and Climatological Assn., Am. Gastroenterological Assn. (chair Rsch. Policy Com.), Am. Coll. Physicians, Assn. Am. Physicians (sec.), Am. Soc. Clin. Investigation. Office: U Calif San Diego Sch Medicine 9500 Gilman Dr # 0602 La Jolla CA 92093-0602 Office Phone: 858-534-1501. E-mail: dbrenner@ucsd.edu.*

BRENNER, SYDNEY, molecular biologist, researcher; b. Germiston, South Africa, Jan. 13, 1927; naturalized, British citizen; s. Morris and Lena (Blacher) B.; m. May Woolf Balkind, 1952; 3 children; 1 stepchild. MSc, U. Witwatersrand, Johannesburg, South Africa, 1947, MB, BCh, 1951; DPhil, Oxford U., 1954; 10 hon. degrees. Postdoctoral fellow U. Calif. Berkeley; mem. sci. staff Med. Rsch. Coun., Cambridge, England, 1957-92, dir. lab. molecular biology, 1979-86, dir. molecular genetics unit, 1986-91; fellow King's Coll., Cambridge U., 1959—; hon. fellow Exeter Coll., Oxford U., 1985; rsch. scientist dept. medicine U. Cambridge Sch. Clin. Medicine, 1992-96; mem. staff Scripps Rsch. Inst., La Jolla, Calif., 1992-94; pres., dir. The Molecular Scis. Inst., La Jolla & Berkeley, Calif., 1996—2000; disting. rsch. prof. The Salk Inst. for Biol. Studies, UCSD, La Jolla, Calif., 2000—. Carter-Wallace lectr. Princeton U., 1966, 77; Gifford lectr. U. Glasgow, Scotland, 1978-79; Dunham lectr. Harvard U., 1984; hon. prof. genetic medicine U. Cambridge Clin. Sch., 1989-96; lectr. in field. Contbr. articles to sci. jours. Recipient Warren Triennial prize, 1968, William Bate Hardy prize Cambridge Philos. Soc., 1969, Albert Lasker Med. Rsch. award, 1971, Royal medal Royal Soc., 1974, Charles-Leopold Mayer prize French Acad., 1975, Gairdner Found. ann. award, 1978, Krebs medal FEBS, 1980, CIBA medal Biochem. Soc., 1981, Feldberg Found. prize, 1983, Rosenstiel award Brandeis U., 1986, Prix Louis Jeantet de Medecine, Switzerland, 1987, medal Genetics Soc. Am., 1987, Harvey prize Technion-Israel Inst. Tech., 1987, Hughlings Jackson medal Royal Soc. Medicine, 1987, Waterford Bio-Med. Sci. award Rsch. Inst. Scripps Clinic, 1988, Kyoto prize Inamori Found., 1990, Gairdner Found. Internat. award, Can., 1991, King Faisal Internat. prize, 1992, Disting. Achievement award Bristol-Myers Squibb, 1992, Albert Lasker award for Spl. Achievement in Medicine, 2000, Novartis Drew award in Biomed. Sci., 2001, Nobel Prize in Physiology or Medicine, 2002. Fellow Royal Soc. (Croonian lectr. 1986, Royal medal 1974, Copley medal 1991), AAS, IASc (hon.) RSE (hon.), Royal Coll. Physicians (Neil Hamilton Fairley medal 1985) Royal Coll. Pathologists (hon.); mem. Max-Planck Soc., Deutsche Acad. Natural Sci. Leopoldina (Gregor Mendel medal 1970), Am. Philos. Soc. (fgn.), Real Acad. Ciencias (Spain), Am. Acad. Arts and Scis. (fgn. hon.), NAS (U.S., fgn. assoc.), Royal Soc. South Africa (fgn. assoc.), Acad. Europa, Chinese Soc. Genetics (hon.), Assn. Physicians Gt. Brit. and Ireland (hon.); associé étranger, Académie des Scis.; corr. Scientifique Emérite de l'INSERM. Achievements include discovery of the existence of messenger RNA. Office: Salk Inst Biol Studies Univ Calif 9500 Gilman Dr La Jolla CA 92093-0346 E-mail: sbrenner@salk.edu.

BRES, PHILIP WAYNE, automotive executive; b. Beaumont, Tex., Mar. 6, 1950; s. Roland Defrance Bres and Edna Gene (Griffith) Seale; m. Janet Vivian Meyer, May 16, 1987; children: Rachel Elizabeth, Rebecca Claire. BA, Lamar U., Beaumont, Tex., 1972; MBA, Stephen F. Austin State U., 1973. Distbn. mgr., bus. mgmt. mgr. Mazda Motors of Am., Houston, 1973-75; analyst, cons. C.H. McCormack and Assocs., Houston, 1975-76; assoc. Frank Gillman Pontiac/GMC/Honda, Houston, 1976-79, David Taylor Cadillac Co., Houston, 1979-80; pres. Braintrust Inc., Houston, 1980-83; sales mgr. Mossy Oldsmobile, Inc., Houston, 1983-84; gen. mgr. Mossy Nissan/Ford, Bellevue, Wash., 1984-86; dir. ops. Mossy Co., Encinitas, Calif., 1986-91; gen. mgr. Performance Nissan, Duarte, Calif., 1991—. Seminar lectr. Rice U., Houston, 1980-83. Author: The Entrepreneurs Guide for Starting a Successful Business., 1982; contbr. (book) Business Planning for the Entrepreneur, 1983. Mem. Houston C. of C. (small bus. coun.), Opt Astron. Soc., Univ. Club, Phi Eta Sigma, Phi Kappa Phi.

BRESLAUER, GEORGE WILLIAM, political science educator; b. NYC, Mar. 4, 1946; s. Henry Edward and Marianne (Schaeffer) B.; m. Yvette Assia, June 5, 1976; children: Michelle, David. BA, U. Mich., 1966, MA, 1968, PhD, 1973. Asst. prof. polit. sci. U. Calif., Berkeley, 1971—79, assoc. prof., 1979—90, prof., 1990—, Chancellor's prof., 1998—2001, chmn. dept., 1993—96, chmn. Ctr. Slavic and East European Studies, 1982—94, dean social scis., 1999—2006, exec. v.p. and provost, 2006—. Vice chmn. bd. trustees Nat. Coun. Soviet and East European Rsch., Washington, 1988-91. Author: Khrushchev and Brezhnev as Leaders, 1982, Soviet Strategy in the Middle East, 1989, Gorbachev and Yeltsin as Leaders, 2002; editor: Can Gorbachev's Reforms Succeed?, 1990, Learning in U.S. and Soviet Foreign Policy, 1991, Russia in the New Century: Stability or Disorder?, 2001. Grantee Ford Found., 1982-84, Carnegie Corp., 1985-94, 97-99. Mem. Am. Assn. for Advancement Slavic Studies (bd. dirs., exec. com. 1990-93). Office: U Calif Dept Polit Sci 210 Barrows Hall Berkeley CA 94720-1950 Office Phone: 510-642-1961. Business E-Mail: bresl@berkeley.edu.

BRESLIN, ABIGAIL KATHLEEN, actress; b. NYC, Apr. 14, 1996; d. Michael and Kim Breslin. Actress (films) Signs, 2002, Raising Helen, 2004, The Princess Diaries 2: Royal Engagement, 2004, Keane, 2004, Chestnut: Hero of Central Park, 2004, Air Buddies, 2006, Little Miss Sunshine, 2006 (Best Young Actress, Critics Choice Award, Broadcast Film Critics Assn., 2007, Outstanding Performance by a Cast in a Motion Picture, SAG, 2007), The Ultimate Gift, 2006, The Santa Clause 3: The Escape Clause, 2006, No Reservations, 2007, Nim's Island, 2008, Kit Kittredge: An American Girl, 2008, (TV films) The Family Plan, 2005, (TV appearances) Hack, 2002, What I Like About You, 2002, Law & Order: Special Victims Unit, 2004, Navy NCIS: Naval Criminal Investigative Service, 2004, Ghost Whisperer, 2006, Grey's Anatomy, 2006, The View, 2006, MTV Video Music Awards, 2006, The Tonight Show with Jay Leno, 2006. Office: Envision Entertainment 8840 Wilshire Blvd Beverly Hills CA 90211-2606

BRESLOW, NORMAN EDWARD, biostatistics educator, researcher; b. Mpls., Feb. 21, 1941; s. Lester and Alice Jane (Philp) Breslow; m. Gayle Marguerite Bramwell, Sept. 7, 1963; children: Lauren Louise, Sara Jo. BA, Reed Coll., 1962; PhD, Stanford U., 1967; Doctorate (honoris causa), U. Bordeaux II, 2001. Trainee Stanford U., 1965—67; vis. research worker London Sch. Hygiene, 1967—68; instr. U. Wash., Seattle, 1968—69, asst. prof., 1969—72, assoc. prof., 1972—76, prof., 1976—, chmn. dept. biostats., 1983—93; statistician Internat. Agy. Research Cancer, Lyon, France, 1972—74. Mem. Hutchinson Cancer Ctr., Seattle, 1982—; statistician Nat. Wilms' Tumor Study, 1969—2003; cons. Internat. Agy. Rsch. Cancer, Lyon, 1978—79; assoc. prof. U. Geneva, 1994—2006. Co-author: (Scientific publ. nos. 32 and 82 on statistics in cancer rsch.) IARC, ISI (most highly cited publication in mathematical sciences for 1993-2003). Recipient Spiegelman Gold medal, APHA, 1978, Preventive Oncology Acad. award, NIH, 1978—83, Snedecor award, Com. of Pres.'s on Statis. Socs., 1995, R.A. Fisher lectr. award, 1995; named sr. U.S. Scientist, Alexander Humboldt Found., Fed. Republic of Germany, 1982; grantee rsch., NIH, 1984—; fellow sr. Internat., Fogarty Ctr., 1990. Fellow: AAAS, Royal Statis. Soc., Am. Statis. Assn. (com. on fellows 1996—2000, N. Mantel award 2002); mem.: Internat. Biometric Soc. (regional com. 1975—78, coun. 1994—2000, v.p. 2001, 2004, pres. 2002—03), Inst. Medicine-Nat. Acad. Scis., Internat. Statis. Inst. Avocations: ski mountaineering, hiking, bicycling. Office: Univ Wash Dept Biostatistics Seattle WA 98195-7232 Business E-Mail: norm@u.washington.edu.

BRESSAN, PAUL LOUIS, lawyer; b. Rockville Centre, NY, June 15, 1947; s. Louis Charles Bressan and Nance Elizabeth Batteley. BA cum laude, Fordham Coll., 1969; JD, Columbia U., 1975. Bar: N.Y. 1976, Calif. 1987, U.S. Dist. Ct. (so., ea. and no. dists.) N.Y. 1976, U.S. Dist. Ct. (no. and ctrl. dists.) Calif. 1987, U.S. Ct. Appeals (2d cir.) 1980, U.S. Supreme Ct. 1980, U.S. Ct. Appeals (1st and 4th cirs.) 1981, U.S. Ct. Appeals (11th cir.) 1982, U.S. Ct. Appeals (9th cir.) 1987, U.S Ct. Appeals (7th cir.) 1991, U.S. Dist. Ct. (ea. dist.) Calif. 1995; U.S. Dist. Ct. (so. dist.) Calif. 1997. Assoc. Kelley, Drye & Warren, NYC, 1975-84, ptnr. NYC and Los Angeles, 1984—2003; shareholder Buchalter Nemer, LA, 2003—. Served to lt. USNR, 1971-72. Named One of Outstanding Coll. Athletes of Am., 1969; Harlan Fiske Stone scholar Columbia Law Sch. Mem. ABA, Calif. Bar Assn., Phi Beta Kappa. Republican. Roman Catholic. Office: Buchalter Nemer 1000 Wilshire Blvd Ste 1500 Los Angeles CA 90017-2457 Office Phone: 213-891-5220. Business E-Mail: pbressan@buchalter.com.

BRESSLER, MARCUS NATHAN, engineer, consultant; b. Havana, Cuba, July 31, 1929; came to U.S., 1942; s. Isaac and Augustine (Draiman) B.; m. Sondra Kipnes, Nov. 7, 1954; children: Eric L., Lisa A., Karen J. Lee. B of Mech. Engring., Cornell U., 1952; MSME, Case Inst. Tech., 1960. Registered profl. engr., Tenn. Stress analysis engr. The Babcock & Wilcox Co., Barberton, Ohio, 1955-66; design engr. Lenape Forge, West Chester, Pa., 1966-70; mgr., product design and devel. engr. Taylor Forge, Cicero, Ill., 1970-71; supr. codes, standards and materials TVA, Knoxville, 1971-79, sr. engring. specialist, 1979-88; pres. M.N. Bressler, PE, Inc., Knoxville, 1988—. 1st lt. U.S. Army, 1952-54, capt. USAR, 1957. Fellow ASME (life fellow, mem. boiler and pressure vessel stds. com., bd. conformity assessment, bd. nuc. codes and stds., Century Medallion 1980, Bernard F. Langer Nuc. Codes and Stds. award 1992, J. Hall Taylor medal for pressure tech. codes and stds. outstanding contbns. 1996, Dedicated Svc. award 2001). Home: 13508 King Lake Trl Broomfield CO 80020-8141 Office Phone: 303-469-6660. Personal E-mail: mbresslerpe@juno.com.

BREST, PAUL A., law educator, foundation administrator; b. Jacksonville, Fla., Aug. 9, 1940; s. Alexander and Mia (Deutsch) B.; m. Iris Lang, June 17, 1962; children: Hilary, Jeremy. AB, Swarthmore Coll., 1962; JD, Harvard U., 1965; LLD (hon.), Northeastern U., 1980, Swarthmore Coll., 1991. Bar: N.Y. 1966. Law clk. to Hon. Bailey Aldrich U.S. Ct. Appeals (1st cir.), Boston, 1965-66; atty. NAACP Legal Def. Fund, Jackson, Miss., 1966-68; law clk. Justice John Harlan, U.S. Supreme Ct., 1968-69; prof. law Stanford U., 1969—, Kenneth and Harle Montgomery prof. pub. interest law, Richard E. Lang prof. and dean, 1987-99; pres. William and Flora Hewlett Found., Menlo Park, Calif., 1999—. Author: Processes of Constitutional Decisionmaking, 1992. Mem. Am. Acad. Arts and Scis. Home: 814 Tolman Dr Palo Alto CA 94305-1026 Office: William and Flora Hewlett Found 2121 Sand Hill Rd Menlo Park CA 94025 Business E-Mail: pbrest@hewlett.org.

BRETT, STEPHEN M., lawyer, retired entertainment company executive; BS, U. Pa., 1962, JD, 1966. Bar: N.Y. 1966, Colo. 1971. Assoc. Dewey, Ballantine, Bushby, Palmer & Wood, 1966-71; ptnr. Sherman & Howard, 1971-88; exec. v.p. legal, gen. counsel, sec. United Artists Entertainment Co., Denver, 1988-91; gen. counsel, v.p., sec. Tele-Comm., Inc., Englewood, Colo., 1991—, exec. v.p., gen. counsel, 1991-2000. Office: 183 Inverness DR W Englewood CO 80112-5203

BREUER, MELVIN ALLEN, electrical engineering educator; b. LA, Feb. 1, 1938; s. Arthur and Bertha Helen (Friedman) B.; m. Sandra Joyce Scalir, Apr. 7, 1967; children: Teri Lynn, Jeffrey Steven. BS in Engring., UCLA, 1959, MS in Engring., 1961; PhD in Elec. Engring., U. Calif., Berkeley, 1965. Asst. prof. U. So. Calif., LA, 1965-71, assoc. prof., 1971-80, prof., 1980—, chmn. elec. engring. systems dept., 1991—94, 2000—03, chair engring. faculty coun., 1997-98, Charles Lee Powell prof., 1995—. Co-author: Diagnosis and Reliable Design, 1976, Digital Systems Testing and Testable Design, 1990; editor, co-author: Design Automation, 1972; editor: Digital Systems Design Automation, 1975; editor-in-chief Jour. Design Automation, 1980-82; co-editor: Knowledge Based Systems for Test and Diagnosis, 1990; contbr. articles to profl. jours. Recipient Assocs. award U. So. Calif., 1991, Okawa Rsch. award, 2003; Fulbright-Hays scholar, 1972. Life fellow IEEE (Taylor Booth award for edn. 1993); mem. Sigma Xi, Tau Beta Pi, Eta Kappa Nu. Democrat. Office: U So Calif University Park Los Angeles CA 90089-2562

BREUER, STEPHEN ERNEST, religious organization administrator, consultant; b. July 14, 1936; came to U.S., 1938, naturalized, 1945; s. John Hans Howard and Olga Marion (Haar) B.; m. Gail Fern Breitbart, Sept. 4, 1960 (div. 1986); children: Jared Noah, Rachel Elise; m. Nadine Bendit, Sept. 25, 1988. BA cum laude, UCLA, 1959; gen. secondary credential, 1960. Tchr. L.A. City Schs., 1960-62; dir. Wilshire Blvd. Temple Camps, LA, 1962—84; instr. Hebrew Union Coll., LA, 1965-76, 1992—, field instr., 1977-81; dir. Edgar F. Magnin Religious Sch., LA, 1970-80; field instr. San Francisco State U., 1970-80; exec. dir. Wilshire Blvd. Temple, LA, 1980—2004; instr. U. Judaism, 1991; field instr. Calif. State U., San Diego; prin. Steve Breuer Assocs., LA, 2005—. Exec. dir. Progressive Assn. of Reform Day Schs., 2005—08; instr. Acad. Jewish Religion, Calif., 2008—. V.p. L.A. Youth Programs Inc., 1967-77; youth advisor L.A. County Commn. Human Rels., 1969-72, bd. dirs. Cmty. Rels. Conf. So. Calif., 1965-85; bd. dirs. Alzheimer's Disease and Related Disorders Assn., 1984-95, v.p. L.A. County chpt., 1984-86, pres., 1986-88, nat. exec. com., 1987-95, nat. devel. chair, 1992-95, Calif. state coun. pres. 1987-92, chmn. of Calif. gov.'s adv. com. on Alzheimer's disease, 1988-97; mem. goals program City of Beverly Hills, Calif., 1985-91; bd. dirs. Pacific S.W. regional Union Am. Hebrew Congregations, 1985-88, nat. bd., exec. com., 1993-97; bd. dirs. Echo Found., 1986-88, Mazon-Jewish Response to Hunger, 1993-97, 2003-, Wilshire Stakeholders exec. com., 1987-94, Internat. Rescue Com. West Coast Bd., 1999-2005; treas. Wilshire Cmty. Prayer Alliance, 1986-88; active United Way; founded Steve Breuer Consulting for Non Profits, 2005—; v.p. Century City Homeowner's Alliance, 2007—. Recipient Svc. award L.A. County Bd. Suprs., 1982, 87, Ventura County Bd. Suprs., 1982, 87, L.A. City Coun., 2005, Weinberg Chai Lifetime Achievement award Jewish Fed. Coun. L.A., 1986, Nat. Philanthropy Day L.A. medallion, 1993, Recognition award L.A. County Redevel. Agy., 1994, award L.A. Bus. Coun., 1997, award L.A. City Coun., 2005, Sherut L'am Svc. to People award Hebrew Union Coll., 2005; Steve Breuer Conference Ctr. named in his honor at Wilshire Blvd. Temple Camps, Malibu, 1990. Mem.: ASCD, NATA, Nata Breuer Leadership Fund, Progressive Assn. Reform Day Schs. (exec. dir. 2005—), Jewish Profl. Network, So. Calif. Conf. Jewish Communal Workers, Am. Mgmt. Assn., Jewish Communal Profls. So. Calif., Profl. Assn. Temple Adminstrs. (pres. 1985—88), L.A. Assn. Jewish Edn. (bd. dirs.), Nat. Assn. Temple Educators (Kaminker curriculum award 1973), Nat. Assn. Temple Adminstrs. (nat. bd. dirs. 1987—, v.p. 1991—93, pres. 1993—97, Svc. to Judaism award 1989, Svc. to the Cmty. award 1990, Svc. award 1994, Steve Breuer Leadership Fund established 2004), So. Calif. Camping Assn. (bd. dirs. 1964—82), Century City Homeowners' Alliance (v.p. 2006—), Assn. Reform Zionists Am. (bd. dirs. 1993—98), People for the Am. Way, Los Angeles County Mus. Contemporary Art, Maple Mental Health Ctr. of Beverly Hills, Living Desert, Wildlife Fedn., Ctr. for Environ. Edn., Wilderness Soc., UCLA Alumni Assn, World Union for Progressive Judaism, Jewish Resident Camping Assn., Amnesty Internat. Office: 3663 Wilshire Blvd Los Angeles CA 90010-2798 Home Phone: 310-556-3386; Office Phone: 213-388-2401. Personal E-mail: sebwbt@aol.com. Business E-Mail: seb@wbtla.org.

BREUNIG, ROBERT GLASS, museum director; b. Indpls., Nov. 16, 1945; s. Henry Latham and Nancy (Tyree) B.; m. Karen Enyedy Breunig, Feb. 16, 1979; 1 child, Lydia Ann. BA, Ind. U., 1968; PhD, U. Kans., 1973. Asst. prof. anthropology No. Ariz. U., Flagstaff, 1972-74; educator Mus. Northern Ariz., Flagstaff, 1975-77, curator, 1977-81, curator, head dept. anthropology, 1981-82, dir., 2004—; chief curator, dep. dir. Heard Mus., Phoenix, 1982-85; exec. dir. Desert Botanical Garden, Phoenix, 1985-94, Santa Barbara Mus. Natural History, Calif., 1994-97, Lady Bird Johnson Wildflower Ctr., Austin, 1997—2003. Vis. asst. prof. anthropology U. Conn., 1974, Denison U., Granville, 1975; trustee Ctr. for Plant Conservation, St. Louis, 1991-94, 99—; mem. bd. dirs. (presdl. appointment) Nat. Mus. Svcs. Bd., Washington, 1992-02. Mem. Am. Assn. Mus. Office: Museum of Northern Arizona 3101 N Ft Valley Rd Flagstaff AZ 86001 Office Phone: 928-774-5213. Office Fax: 928-779-1527.

BREVIG, ERIC, special effects expert, executive; BFA, UCLA, 1979, MFA, 1982. With Walt Disney Prodns., Dream Quest Images, 1984-90; visual effects dir. Indsl. Light & Magic, San Rafael, Calif., 1991—. Graphics projects include (films) D.A.R.Y.L., 1985, Buckeroo Bonzai, Magic Journeys, Captain EO, 1986, The Seventh Sign, 1988, The Lost Boys, Big Business, 1988, Scrooged, 1988, The Abyss, 1989 (Oscar award), Total Recall, 1990, Hook, 1991, The Nutcracker, 1993, Wolf, 1994, Disclosure, 1994, The Indian in the Cupboard, 1995, Men in Black, 1995, Snake Eyes, 1998, Wild Wild West, 1999, Pearl Harbor, 2001, K-19: The Widowmaker, 2002, Signs, 2002, The Hunted, 2003, Peter Pan, 2003, Twisted, 2004, The Day After Tomorrow, 2004, The Village, 2004, The Island, 2005; (TV Series) Amazing Stories; (comml.) Diet Pepsi "Two Michaels"; dir.

(TV series) Xena: Warrior Princess, 1995, (films) Journey to the Center of the Earth, 2008 Office: Industrial Light Magic PO Box 29909 San Francisco CA 94129-0909

BREWER, CAROL A., biology professor; BA in Biology, Calif. State U., Fullerton, 1981; BS in Sci. Edn., U. Wyo., 1985, MS in Zoology and Physiology, 1986, PhD in Botany, 1993. Cert. sr. ecologist Ecol. Soc. Am., 2000. Prof. divsn. biol. scis. U. Mont., Missoula, assoc. dean Coll. Arts and Scis. Bd. dirs. Mont. Natural Hist. Ctr., 1995—2000, Ecol. Soc. Am., 2000—06, Biomimicry Inst., 2007—; mem. sr. mgmt. team Nat. Ecol. Obs. Network, 2005—; mem. exec. adv. bd. Earth and Sky Radio Series, 2006—; mem. nat. adv. bd. Long Term Ecol. Rsch. Network, 2006—. Contbr. articles to sci. jours.; assoc. editor: Conservation Biology, 2001—, mem. editl. bd.: Frontiers in Ecology and the Environment, 2005—. Recipient Fulbright Sr. Scholar award, Argentina, 1998; Inst. Internat. Edn. fellowship, 1986—87. Mem.: Soc. Conservation Biology, Brit. Ecol. Soc., Am. Inst. Biol. Scis. (Edn. award 2007), Ecol. Soc. Am. (life; v.p. edn. and human resources 2000—06), Phi Delta Kappa. Office: U Mont Coll Arts and Sci LA 136 Missoula MT 59812 Office Phone: 406-243-6013. Office Fax: 406-243-4184. Business E-Mail: carol.brewer@umontana.edu.

BREWER, DAVID L., III, school system administrator, retired military officer; b. Farmville, Va., May 19, 1946; m. Richardene Brewer; 1 child, Stacey. BS in Biology, Prairie View A&M U.; MA in Nat. Security & Strategic Studies, Naval War Coll. Enlisted USN, 1970, advanced through grades to vice adm., 2002, ret., 2006; elec. warfare officer USS Little Rock; minority recruiting officer Naval Recruiting Dist., Memphis, 1972—75; combat info. ctr. officer USS Calif., 1975; weapons officer USS William H. Standley, 1978—80; engrng. officer USS Okinawa, 1981—83; exec. officer USS Fresno, 1983—84; enlisted cmty. mgr. combat sys. ratings Office of Chief of Naval Ops., Washington, 1985—86; comdr. USS Bristol County, 1986—88; spl. asst. equal opportunity Chief Naval Ops., 1988; comdr. USS Mount Whitney, 1991—92, US Naval Forces Marianas, 1994—96, Amphibious Group THREE, 1997—99; vice chief naval edn. and tng. Pensacola, Fla., 1999—2001; comdr. Military Sealift Command (MSC), 2001—06; supt. LA Unified Sch. Dist., 2006—. Head David and Mildred Brewer Found. Decorated Def. Superior Svc. medal, Legion of Merit with gold star, Meritorious Svc. medal with gold star, Navy Achievement medal; recipient Disting. Grad. Leadership award, Naval War Coll., Navy League of US Vincent T. Hirsch Maritime award Office: LA Unified Sch Dist Office of Supt PO Box 3307 Los Angeles CA 90051 Office Phone: 213-241-7000. Office Fax: 213-241-8442. E-mail: superintendent@lausd.net.

BREWER, ERIC A., computer science educator; BS in Computer Sci., U. Calif., Berkeley; D in Computer Sci., MIT. Rsch. asst. MIT, 1989-94; prof. computer sci. divsn. U. Calif., Berkeley; dir. Inktomi, 1996, interim pres., CEO, 1996, chief tech. officer, 1996-97, chief scientist, 1997. Contbr. articles to profl. jours. Founder Fed. Search Found., 2000. Named Most Influential Person on the Architecture of the Internet, Industry Std.; named a Global Leader for Tomorrow, World Econ. Forum; named one of Top 10 Innovators, InfoWorld, Top 100 Young Innovators Under 35, Tech. Rev., 1999, Top 100 Most Influential People for the 21st Century, 12 e-Mavericks, Forbes mag. Mem.: NAE. Office: Computer Sci Divsn U Calif Berkeley 623 Soda Hall Berkeley CA 94720-1776 Office Phone: 510-642-8143. Office Fax: 510-642-5775. E-mail: brewer@cs.berkeley.edu.

BREWER, JAN (JANICE KAY BREWER), Governor of Arizona; b. Hollywood, Calif., Sept. 26, 1944; d. Perry Wilford and Edna Clarice (Bakken) Drinkwine; m. John Leon Brewer, Jan. 1, 1963; children: Ronald Richard, John Samuel, Michael Wilford. HHD (hon.), LA Chiropractic Coll., 1970. Cert med. asst. Valley Coll., Burbank, Calif., 1963, practical radiol. techician cert. Valley Coll., Burbank, Calif., 1963. Pres. Brewer Property & Investments, Glendale, Ariz., 1970—; mem. Ariz. Ho. Representatives from Dist. 19, Phoenix, 1983—86, Ariz. State Senate from Dist. 19, Phoenix, 1987—96, majority whip, 1993—96; mem. Maricopa County Bd. Supr., 1997—2002; sec. state State of Ariz., Phoenix, 2003—09, gov., 2009—. State com. woman Rep. Party, Phoenix, 1970, Phoenix, 83; legis. liaison Arrowhead Republic Women; treas. Nat. Assn. Lt. Gov., 2004; bd. dir. Motion Picture & TV Commn. Recipient Freedom award, Vets. of Ariz., 1994; named Woman of Yr., Chiropractic Assn. Ariz., 1983, Legislator of Yr., Behaviour Health Assn. Ariz., 1991, NRA, 1992. Mem.: Am. Legis. Exch. Coun., Nat. Fedn. Rep. Women, NOW. Republican. Lutheran. Office: Office of Governor 1700 W Washington Phoenix AZ 85007 Office Phone: 602-542-4331. Office Fax: 602-542-7601.*

BREWER, JOHN CHARLES, journalist; b. Cin., Oct. 24, 1947; s. Harry Marion and Barbara Ann (Burrier) B.; m. Adeline Laude, Dec. 22, 1973 (div. 1994); children: Andrew John, Jeffrey Joseph; m. Ann Hagen Kellett, 1997 (dec. Mar. 2005). BS, Calif. State Poly. U., Pomona, 1970. Newsman, photographer Daily Report, Ontario, Calif., 1967-69; newsman AP, LA, 1969-74, news editor, 1974-75, asst. chief bur. Seattle, 1975-76, chief of bur., 1976-82, LA, 1982-86, gen. exec. membership dept. NYC, 1986-88; exec. editor news svc. The N.Y. Times, 1988-90, editor in chief news svc., 1990-97; pres. N.Y. Times Syndication Sales Corp., 1990-97; publisher, editor Peninsula Daily News, Port Angeles, Wash., 1998—. Bd. dirs. Port Angeles C. of C., Olympic Meml. Hosp. Found., Port Angeles Downtown Assn. Mem. Fedn. of Fly Fishers, Northwest Steelheaders-Trout Unlimited, Nat. Steelhead Trout Assn., Rotary Internat., Kiwanis. Republican. Roman Catholic. Office: Peninsula Daily News 305 W 1st St Port Angeles WA 98362-2205 Home Phone: 360-452-4639; Office Phone: 360-417-3500. Business E-Mail: john.brewer@peninsuladailynews.com.

BREWER, PETER GEORGE, ocean geochemist; b. Ulverston, Eng., Dec. 30, 1940; came to U.S., 1967, naturalized, 1982; s. Frederick and Irene (Clarkson) B.; m. Hilary Williams, Mar. 29, 1966; children: Jillian Anne, Alastair Michael, Erica Christine. BSc, Liverpool U., Eng., 1962, PhD, 1967. From asst. scientist to sr. scientist Woods Hole Oceanog. Inst., Mass., 1967—78, sr. scientist, 1978—91; program dir. marine chemistry NSF, 1981—83; exec. dir. Monterey Bay Aquarium Rsch. Inst., Pacific Grove, Calif., 1991—96, sr. scientist, 1996—. Leader of ocean sci. expeditions; mem. Environ. Task Force, 1992-93, NAS Ocean Studies Bd., 1986-94, Com. on Climate Change and the Ocean, 1987-90; convenor NATO A.R.I. on Chem. Dynamics of Upper Ocean, Jouy en Jossas, France, 1983; mem. NAS panel on policy implications of greenhouse gas warming: mitigation, 1989-91; mem. NAS carbon dioxide adv. com., 1982-83; vis. prof. U. Wash., 1979; mem. GEOSECS sci. adv. com., 1972-78. Assoc. editor: Geophys. Rsch. Letters, 1977-79, Jour. Marine Rsch., 1974-81, Deep-Sea Rsch., 1984-87, Jour. of Oceanography, 1994—; contbr. over 140 articles to sci. publs. Chmn. Gordon Rsch. Conf. on Chem. Oceanography, 1980; vice-chmn. Joint Global Ocean Fluxes Com., SCOR, 1987-90; mem. adv. bd. Applied Physics Lab., U. Wash., 1991-96. Grantee NSF, NASA, Office Naval Rsch., Dept. Energy. Fellow AAAS, Am. Geophys. Union. Office: Monterey Bay Aquarium Rsch Inst 7700 Sandholdt Rd Moss Landing CA 95039-0628 Business E-Mail: brpe@mbari.org.

BREWER, RICHARD B., biotechnology company executive; m. Debbie Brewer (div.). BS in Biology, Va. Poly. Inst. and State U.; MBA, Northwestern U. With Genentech, Inc., 1984—95; sr. v.p. U.S. sales and mktg. Genentech Europe Ltd. and Genentech Can., Inc.; exec. v.p. ops. Heartport, Inc., 1996—98, COO; pres., CEO, dir. Scios Inc. ($2.4 billion merger with Johnson & Johnson), Sunnyvale, Calif., 1998—2004; mng. ptnr. Crest Asset Mgmt. Mem. adv. bd. Kellogg Grad. Sch. Mgmt., Ctr. for Biotech., Northwestern U., 2001—; mem. corp. roundtable Am. Heart Assn., 1993—94, chmn. pharm. roundtable, 1994—95; bd. dirs. Dendreon Corp., Agensys, Inc., Corus Pharma, Corgentech Inc., Faster Cures, SRI Internat., 2006—. Office: Corgentech 650 Gateway Blvd South San Francisco CA 94080

BREWER, ROY EDWARD, lawyer; b. Atlanta, Dec. 22, 1949; s. Roy Mullins and Martha JoAnn (Still) Brewer; m. Catherine Elizabeth Schindler, May 5, 1979; children: Garrett Edward, Alex Winston. BA in Polit. Sci., U. Fla., 1971, MA in Polit. Sci., 1973; JD, U. Pacific, 1982. Bar: Calif. 1984, U.S. Dist. Ct. (ea. dist.) Calif. 1984, U.S. Supreme Ct. 1990. Regional planner North Cen. Fla. Regional Planning Council, Gainesville, Fla., 1975-78; dir. met. affairs Sacramento Met. C. of C., 1978-79; dir. land planning Raymond Vail and Assocs., Sacramento, 1979-84; pvt. practice Sacramento, 1984-89; ptnr. Hunter McCray Richey & Brewer, Sacramento, 1989-95, Hunter, Richey, DiBenedetto & Brewer, Sacramento, 1995—2000, mng. ptnr., 1993—2000; ptnr. Brewer Law Firm, 2000—06, Brewer Lofgren LLP, 2006—. Bd. dirs. Am. River Natural History Assn., 1986—90, pres., 1988—89; bd. dirs. No. Calif. Rugby Football Union, 1985—88, pres., 1985—88; chmn. Sacramento Ad-hoc Charter Comm., 1988—90; bd. dirs. Healthcare, 1987—90, chmn., 1988—89; bd. dirs. Sacramento Met. C. of C., 1985—91, 2007—, pres., 1990; trustee ARC, 1989—90; chmn. Local Govt. Reorgn. Com., 1988; chair Leadership Sacramento, 2000, co-chair, 2001—03; sr. fellow Am. Leadership Forum, Mt. Valley Chpt., 2005—, bd. dirs., 2007—, Sacramento Symphony Assn., 1987—95, Am. Lung Assn., 1988—92, Sacramento Downtown Partnership, 1997—99; chmn. Los Rios CC Dist. Capital Campaign, 2005—. Recipient Sacramento Regional Pride award for cmty. devel., 1991, Exceptional Performers award, Air Force Assn., 1991, Sacramentan of the Yr. award, 1991; named among Best and Brightest, Sacramento Mag., 1985. Mem.: Am. Inst. Cert. Planners. Avocations: rugby, karate, scuba diving, snowboarding. Office Phone: 916-944-8896.

BREWSTER, RUDI MILTON, judge; b. Sioux Falls, SD, May 18, 1932; s. Charles Edwin and Wilhemina Therese (Rud) B.; m. Gloria Jane Nanson, June 27, 1954; children: Scot Alan, Lauri Diane (Alan Lee), Julie Lynn Yahnke. AB in Pub. Affairs, Princeton U., 1954; JD, Stanford U., 1960. Bar: Calif. 1960. From assoc. to ptnr. Gray, Cary, Ames & Frye, San Diego, 1960-84; judge U.S. Dist. Ct. (so. dist.) Calif., San Diego, 1984—98, sr. judge, 1998—. Capt. USNR, 1954-82 Ret. Fellow Am. Coll. Trial Lawyers; mem. Am. Bd. Trial Advs., Internat. Assn. Ins. Counsel, Am. Inns of Ct. Republican. Lutheran. Avocations: skiing, hunting, gardening. Office: US Dist Ct Ste 4165 940 Front St San Diego CA 92101-8902 Office Phone: 619-557-6190. Business E-Mail: Rudi_Brewster@casd.uscourts.gov.

BREYER, CHARLES ROBERTS, judge, lawyer; b. San Francisco, Nov. 3, 1941; s. Irving Gerald and Anne Adele (Roberts) B.; m. Sydney Rachel Goldstein, Jan. 17, 1976; children: Kate, Joseph. AB, Harvard U., 1963; JD, U. Calif., Berkeley, 1966. Bar: U.S. Dist. Ct. (no. dist.) Calif. 1976, U.S. Ct. Appeals (9th cir.) 1976. Law clk. U.S. Dist. Ct. (no. dist.) Calif., San Francisco, 1966, asst. dist. atty., 1967-72; mem. task force Watergate Spl. Pros., Washington, 1972-74, chief asst dist. atty. San Francisco, 1979; ptnr. Coblentz, Cahan, McCabe & Breyer, San Francisco, 1974-79, 80-97; judge U.S. Dist. Ct. (no Calif.), San Francisco, 1997—. Dir. Lawyers Com. in Human Rights, N.Y., 1990—. Capt. U.S. Army, 1966-72. Office: Phillip Burton Fed Bldg US Courthouse PO Box 36060 San Francisco CA 94102

BREYER, JIM (JAMES WILLIAM BREYER), venture capitalist; b. New Haven, July 26, 1961; s. John Paul and Eva Breyer; m. Susan Zaroff, June 20, 1987. BS, Stanford U., 1983; MBA, Harvard U., 1987. Sr. bus. analyst McKinsey & Co., NYC, 1983-85; assoc. Accel Ptnrs., San Francisco, 1987-90, gen. ptnr., 1990-95, mng. gen. ptnr., 1995—. Bd dirs. RealNetworks, Inc., 1995-, Wal-Mart Stores, Inc., 2001-, Marvel Entertainment, Inc., 2006-, Facebook, Inc.; chmn., Stanford Engring Venture Fund, honorary prof., Yuela Acad., Hunan U., 2005- Bd. associates Harvars Bus. Sch., Pacific Cmty. Ventures, Stanford Tech. Ventures Program, Technet; bd. trustees San Francisco Mus. Modern Art, Menlo Sch. Baker scholar Harvard U., 1987. Mem. Nat. Assn. Venture Capitalists (bd. dirs.), Western Assn. Venture Capitalists (bd. dirs.), Harvard Bus. Sch. Club of No. Calif. Avocations: art, films. Office: Accel Partners 428 University Ave Palo Alto CA 94301-1812*

BREYNE, MATTHEW M., finance company executive; m. Cathy Breyne. B Fin., No. Ill. U., 1979. With Heller Fin., Chgo., 1987—; pres., COO Finova Group Inc., Scottsdale, Ariz., pres., CEO; also bd. dirs. Office: Finova Group Inc 4800 N Scottsdale Rd Scottsdale AZ 85251-7623

BRIAN, BRAD D., lawyer; b. Merced, Calif., Apr. 19, 1952; BA, U. Calif., Berkeley, 1974; JD magna cum laude, Harvard U., 1977. Bar: Calif. 1977, U.S. Ct. Appeals (3d cir.) 1978, U.S. Dist. Ct. (ctrl. dist.) Calif. 1978, U.S. Ct. Appeals (9th cir.) 1980. Law clk. to Hon. John J. Gibbons U.S. Ct. Appeals (3d cir.), 1977-78; asst. U.S. atty. Office U.S. Atty. (ctrl. dist.) Calif., 1978-81; hearing examiner L.A. City Police Commn., 1982; atty., ptnr. Munger, Tolles & Olson, LA, 1981—. Lectr. in law U. So. Calif. Law Ctr., 1983; instr. Nat. Inst. Trial Advocacy, 1986; guest instr. Harvard Law Sch. Trial Advocacy Program, 1983; past pres. & mem. bd. dir. Legal Aid Found. Los Angeles; mem. bd. dir. Western Justice Ctr; mem. Indigent Def. Panel & chmn. Pro Se panel, U.S Dist Ct. Los Angeles. Co-editor, Internal Corporate Investigations, 2d ed. 2002; bd. editors Harvard Law Rev., 1975-77, mng. editor and treas., 1976-77. Mem. bd. dir. Los Angeles County Music Ctr.; vice chmn. bd. dir. Joffrey Ballet, 1990—91. Named one of Top 50 Trial Lawyers in Los Angeles, Los Angeles Bus. Jour., 1999, 100 Most Influential Lawyers in Calif., Los Angeles Daily Jour., 1998—2002. Fellow, Am. Coll. Trial Lawyers; mem. ABA (chmn. pre-trial practice and discovery, litigation sect. 1987-89, liaison with fed. jud. confs. 1989-91, chair task force on civil justice reform act of 1990), Fed. Bar Assn. (past pres. L.A. chptr.), State Bar Calif., L.A. County Bar Assn. (mem. fed. practice standards com. 1980-82). Office: Munger Tolles & Olson LLP 355 S Grand Ave Fl 35 Los Angeles CA 90071-1560 Office Phone: 213-683-9280. Business E-Mail: brianbd@mto.com.

BRICKER, NEAL S., physician, educator; b. Denver, Apr. 18, 1927; s. Eli D. and Rose (Quiat) B.; m. Miriam Thalenberg, June 24, 1951 (dec. 1974); children: Dusty, Cary, Susan, Daniel Baker; m. Ruth T. Baker, Dec. 28, 1980. BA, U. Colo., 1946, MD, 1949. Diplomate Am. Bd. Internal Medicine (bd. govs. 1972-79, chmn. nephrology test com. 1973-76). Intern, resident Bellevue Hosp., NYC, 1949-52; sr. asst. resident Peter Bent Brigham Hosp., Boston, 1954-55, asso. dir. cardio-renal lab., 1955-56; instr. Harvard, 1955-56; fellow Howard Hughes Med. Inst., 1955-56; from asst. prof. to prof. Washington U., 1956-72, dir. renal div., 1956-72; Mem. sci. adv. bd. Nat. Kidney Found., 1962-69, chmn. research and fellowship grants com., 1964-65, mem. exec. com., 1968-71; prof. medicine, chmn. dept. Albert Einstein Coll. Medicine, 1972-76; prof. medicine U. Miami, Fla., 1976-78, vice chmn. dept., 1976-78; Disting. prof. medicine UCLA, 1978-86; disting. prof. medicine, dir. sci. and tech. planning Loma Linda (Calif.) U., 1986-92; exec. v.p. Naturon Pharm., Riverside, Calif., 1992; clin. prof. medicine UCR/UCLA Program in Biomed. Scis., UCR, 1996—. Cons. NIH, 1964-68, chmn. gen. medicine study sect., 1966-68, chmn. renal disease and urology tng. grants com., 1969-71; vis. investigator Inst. Biol. Chemistry, Copenhagen, 1960-61; investigator Mt. Desert Island Biol. Labs.; advisor on behalf Inst. Medicine to Sen. Lowell Weicker. Assoc. editor: Jour. Lab. and Clin. Medicine, 1961-67, Kidney Internat, 1972; editorial com.: Jour. Clin. Investigation, 1964-68, Physiol. Revs, 1970-76, Am. Heart Assn. Pubis. Com., 1974-79, Calcified Tissue Internat., 1978-86, Proc. Soc. Exptl. Biology and Medicine, 1978-86; editor: Supplements, Circulation and Circulation Research, 1974-79; contbr. articles to profl. jours., chpts. to books. Served with USNR, 1944-45; Served with U.S. Army, 1952-54. Recipient Gold-Headed Cane award U. Colo., 1949, Silver and Gold Alumni award, 1975; USPHS Research Career award, 1964-72; Skylab Achievement award NASA, 1974; Pub. Service award, 1975; George Norlin Silver medal award U. Colo. 1982, citation Kidney Found. So. Calif., 1984; honoree 50th Ann. Wash. U. Med. Sch. Renal Divsn., 2004. Fellow A.C.P.; mem. Am. Fedn. for Clin. Research, Central Soc. Clin. Research (council 1970-73), Assn. Am. Physicians, Am. Soc. for Clin. Investigation (pres. 1972-73, chmn. com. nat. med. policy 1973-77, Disting. Service award 1969), Internat. Soc. Nephrology (exec. com. 1966-81, v.p. 1966-69, treas. 1969-81, history honoree, video legacy honoree 2004), Internat. Congress Nephrology (pres. 1981-84), Am. Soc. Nephrology (1st pres., John Peters medal 1991), Am. Physiol. Soc., Soc. for Exptl. Biology and Medicine, Western Soc. Clin. Research, So. Soc. Clin. Investigation, Nat. Acad. Scis. (com. on space biology and medicine, ad hoc panel on renal and metabolic effects space flight 1971-72, mem. drug efficacy com. 1966-68, com. space biology, chmn. medicine in space sci. bd. 1972-81, com. chmn. 1978-81, chmn. com. renal and metabloic effects space flight 1972-74, chmn. study com. on life scis. 1976-81, mem. space sci. bd. 1977-81), Internat. Soc. nephrology, (hon.), Inst. Medicine of NAS, Internat. Soc. Nephrology, Sigma Xi, Alpha Omega Alpha. Home: 4240 Piedmont Mesa Claremont CA 91711-2332 Office: UCR/UCLA Riverside CA 92521-0121

BRICKNER, DAVID, religious organization administrator, consultant; b. Beverly, Mass., Sept. 29, 1958; s. Avi Stanley and Leah Esther (Kendal) B.; m. Patrice Anne Vasataro, Dec. 29, 1979; children: Isaac, Ilana. Diploma in Jewish Studies, Moody Bible Inst., 1981; BA in Jewish Studies, Northeastern Ill. U., 1986; MA in Jewish Studies, Fuller Sem., 1994. Ordained min. Bapt. Gen. Conf., 1993. Mobile team leader Jews for Jesus, USA, 1981-84, chief of station Chgo., 1985-89, min.-at-large San Francisco, 1989-95, chief of station NYC, 1995-96, exec. dir. San Francisco, 1996—. Portfolio holder Jews for Jesus South Africa, 1988-96, bd. dirs., 1989—; pres. bd. dirs. Jews for Jesus USA, San Francisco, 1996—; bd. dirs. Jews for Jesus Europe, London, 1996—. Author: Mishpochah Matters, 1996, Future Hope, 1999. Mem. Lausaunne Consultation on Jewish Evangelism, Evangelical Theol. soc., Evangelical Missiological Soc. Office: Jews for Jesus 60 Haight St San Francisco CA 94102-5895 Office Phone: 415-864-2600.

BRIDGE, BOBBE JEAN, former state supreme court justice; b. 1944; m. Jonathan J. Bridge; children: Rebecca, Don. BA magna cum laude, U. Wash; MA, U. Mich., PhD in Polit. Sci.; JD, U. Wash., 1976. Superior Ct. judge King County, Wash., 1990-1999; chief judge King County Juvenile Ct., Wash., 1994-97, asst. presiding judge Wash., 1997-98, presiding judge Wash., 1998-99; justice Wash. State Supreme Ct., 1999—2007. Chmn. Judicial Info. Sys. Comm, Legislative Comm.; co-chmn. Unified Family Ct. Bench-Bar Task Force. Bd. dirs. YWCA, Becca Task Force, State Commr. on Children in Foster Care, Seattle Children's Home, Catalyst for Kids Youth Care, Tech. Adv. Com. Female Juvenile Offenders, Adv. Com. Adolescent Life Skills Program, Street Youth Law Program, Northwest Mediation Svc., Woodland Pk. Zoological Soc., Wash. Coun. Crime and Delinquency, Women's Funding Alliance, Alki Found., Privacy Fund, Seattle Arts Commn., U. Wash. Arts and Sci. Devel., Greater Seattle C. of C., Metrocenter YMCA, Juvenile Ct. Conf. Com.; mem. King County Task Force on Children and Families, Wash. State's Dept. Social and Health Svcs. Children., Youth, Family Svcs. Adv. Com., Child Protection Roundtable, Govs. Juvenile Justice Adv. Com.; chmn. State Task Force on Juvenile Issues, Coun. Youth Crisis Work Group, Families-at-Risk sub-com., Bd. Dirs. Ctr. Career Alternatives, Candidate Evaluation Com. Seattle-King Mcpl. League, Law and justice Com. League Women Voters; co-chmn. Govs. Coun. on Families, Youth, and Justice; pres. Seattle Women's Commn., Seattle Chpt. Am. Jewish Com.,bd. dirs., asst. sec.-treas. Jewish Fedn. Greater Seattle, chmn., vice chmn. Cmty. Rels. Coun. Named Judge of Yr. Wash. Women Lawyers, 1996; recipient Hannah G. Solomon award Nat. Coun. Jewish Women, 1996, Cmty. Catalyst award Mother's Against Violence in Am., 1997, Women Making a Difference award Youthcare, 1998, Annual Family Advocate award, 2002; honored "woman helping women" Soroptimist Internat. of Kent, 1999. Mem. Nat. Kidney Found., Ctr. Women and Democracy, Phi Beta Kappa.

BRIDGE, HERBERT MARVIN, retail executive; b. Seattle, Mar. 14, 1925; s. Ben and Sally (Silverman) B.; m. Shirley Selesnick, Jan. 25, 1948 (dec. June 02, 2008); children: Jonathan J., Daniel E. BA in Polit. Sci., U. Wash., Seattle, 1947. Pres. Ben Bridge Jeweler Inc., Seattle, 1955—76, chmn., 1977—. Pres. Downtown Seattle Assn., 1980-81; past pres., Am. Jewish Com.; bd. dirs. Naval Acad. Found., Naval Undersea Mus., Alliance for Edn.; past chmn. Puget Sound

USO; chmn. sr. adv. bd. Goodwill Games of 1990; co-chmn. King County chpt. United Way, 2000-01. Rear adm. USNR, 1942-85. Decorated Legion of Merit with Gold Star in lieu of 2d award; recipient Israel Bonds Masada award, 1974, Am. Jewish Com. Human Rels. award, 1978, Navy League scroll hon., 1980, 96, Alumni Legend award U. Wash., 1987, Vol. of Yr. award Jewish Fedn., 1991, Humanitarian award Privacy Fund, 1991, Heritage award Mus. History and Industry, 1993, A.K. Guy Cmty. Svc. award YMCA, 1995, Cmty. Svc. award Sea 1st, 1998, Citizen of Yr. award Seattle-King County, 2001, Achievement medal Fred Hutchinson Cancer Ctr., 2003, Lifetime Achievement award Jewelry Info. Ctr., 2005, Outstanding Jeweler, Calif. 24K Club, 2008; named to Nat. Jewelers Hall of Fame, 1998, Puget Sound Bus. Hall of Fame, 1999, Maritime Supporter of Yr., Navy League and Seattle Yacht Club, 2007. Mem.: Greater Seattle C. of C. (past pres.), Pacific N.W. Jewelers (past pres.), Am. Gem. Soc. (head trustee 1993—2000, Cert. Gemologist, Triple Zero award 2001, Shipley award 2003), Rotary, City Club (founder), Wash. Athletic Club (past pres.), Naval Res. Assn. (past pres.), Shriners. Democrat. Office: PO Box 1908 Seattle WA 98111-1908 Home Phone: 206-441-4444; Office Phone: 206-239-6868. Personal E-mail: hmbridge1@aol.com.

BRIDGE, JONATHAN JOSEPH, lawyer, retail executive; b. Seattle, Mar. 19, 1950; s. Herbert Marvin and Shirley Geraldine (Selesnick) B.; m. Bobbe Jean Chaback, May 20, 1978; children: Donald, Rebecca. BA with honors, U. Wash., 1972, JD, 1976. Bar: Wash. 1976, U.S. Dist. Ct. (we. dist.) Wash. 1976, U.S. Ct. Mil. Appeals 1977, U.S. Ct. Appeals (9th cir.) 1979, U.S. Supreme Ct. 1980. Legal service officer USN, Oak Harbor, Wash., 1976-79, staff judge adv. Bremerton, Wash., 1979-81; exec. v.p. Ben Bridge Jeweler, Inc., Seattle, 1981-90, gen. counsel, co-chief exec. officer, 1990—. Bd. dirs. Ben Bridge Corp., Seattle, Jewelers Am., N.Y.C., Jewelers Vigilance Com., N.Y., Wis., Assn. Wash. Bus., Seattle, Assn. Wash. Bus., Wash. Cts. Hist. Soc.; v.p. Evergreen Children Assoc. 2008. Bd. dirs. King County Mental Health Bd., Seattle, 1984, Wash. Retail Assn., 1985-94, Evergreen Children's Assn., 1998—, Seattle Police Found., 2001-04; vice chmn. Seattle Urban League, 1986-88, chmn., 1988-89; pres. Am. Jewish Com., Seattle, 1986-88; counsel Pacific Northwest Jewelers Assn., 1988-2000, treas., 1990, pres., 1995-97; bd. dirs. Alliance for Edn., 1990—, chair, 2007-; mem. bd. Ctr. for Career Alternatives, 1981—; precinct committeeman, 1990-96; bd. dirs. U. Wash. Law Sch. Found., 1994-, pres., 2003-05; v.p. Ctr. for Children and Youth Justice, 2006-2007, sec., 2006-2007. Served to lt. comdr. USN, 1972-81, Vietnam, to capt. Res., 1981-2003. Mem. ABA, Wash. State Bar Assn. (vice chair legal svcs. to the armed forces sect. 2006—), Seattle/King County Bar Assn., Judge Advocates Assn., Greater Seattle C. of C., U. Wash. Alumni Assn. (bd. dirs. 1986-93), U. Wash. Law Sch. Alumni Assn. (pres. 1989-91), Wash. Athletic Club, Columbia Tower Club, City Club. Democrat. Jewish. Office: Ben Bridge Jeweler Inc PO Box 1908 Seattle WA 98111-1908 Home Phone: 206-283-4860. E-mail: jbridge@benbridge.com.

BRIDGES, B. RIED, lawyer; b. Kansas City, Mo., Oct. 20, 1927; s. Brady R. and Mary H. (Nieuwenhuis) B.; 1 son, Ried George. BA, U. So. Calif., 1951, LLB, 1954. Bar: Calif. 1954. Ptnr. Bonne, Bridges, Mueller & O'Keefe, L.A. and Las Vegas, 1958—. Fellow Am. Coll. Trial Lawyers, Internat. Acad. Trial Lawyers; mem. Calif. Bar Assn., Am. Bd. Trial Advs. (diplomate), Balboa of Mazatlan (Sinaloa, Mex.). Republican. Avocation: sportfishing. Home: 1001 Kensington Ct Carson City NV 89703-5431 Office: Bonne Bridges Mueller O'Keefe & Nichols 3441 S Eastern Ave Ste 402 Las Vegas NV 89109-3314 Office Phone: 775-841-0118. Personal E-mail: b.ried.bridges@charter.net.

BRIDGES, EDWIN MAXWELL, education educator; b. Hannibal, Mo., Jan. 1, 1934; s. Edwin Otto and Radha (Maxwell) B.; m. Marjorie Anne Pollock, July 31, 1954; children: Richard, Rebecca, Brian, Bruce. BS, U. Mo., 1954; MA, U. Chgo., 1956, PhD, 1964. English tchr. Bremen Community High Sch., Midlothian, Ill., 1954-56; asst. prin. Griffith (Ind.) High Sch., 1956-60, prin., 1960-62; staff assoc. U. Chgo., 1962-64, assoc. prof., 1967-72; assoc. dir. Univ. Coun. for Edn. Adminstrn., Columbus, Ohio, 1964-65; asst. prof. Washington U., St. Louis, 1965-67; assoc. prof. U. Chgo., 1967-72; prof. U. Calif., Santa Barbara, 1972-74; prof. edn. Stanford (Calif.) U., 1974—. Mem. nat. adv. panel Ctr. for Rsch. on Ednl. Accountability and Tchr. Evaluation, 1990-95; external examiner U. Hong Kong, 1990-92; vis. prof. Chinese U., Hong Kong, 1976, 96; disting. vis. prof. Beijing U., 2002; cons. World Bank, China, 1986, 89; dir. Midwest Adminstrn. Ctr., Chgo., 1967-72. Author: Managing the Incompetent Teacher, 1984, 2d edit., 1990, The Incompetent Teacher, 1986, 2d edit., 1991, Problem Based Learning for Administrators, 1992; co-author: Introduction to Educational Adminstration, 1977, Implementing Problem-based Leadership Development, 1995. Recipient of the R.F. Campbell Lifetime Achievement award, 1996; named Outstanding Young Man of Ind., C. of C., 1960; named hon. prof. and cert. of honor So. China Normal U., 1989, Citation of Merit for Outstanding Achievement and Meritorious Svc. in Edn., U. Mo. Coll. Edn., 1999. Mem. Am. Ednl. Rsch. Assn. (v.p. 1974-75). Office: Stanford U Sch Edn Stanford CA 94305 E-mail: bridges@stanford.edu.

BRIDGES, GEORGE S., academic administrator, sociology educator; m. Kari Tupper; children: Anna, James, Lauren, Seth. BA cum laude, U. Wash., 1972; MA in Criminology, U. Pa., 1973, PhD in Sociology, 1979. Social scientist Office of Policy and Planning Office of Atty. Gen., US Dept. Justice, 1976, asst. adminstr. Fed. Justice Rsch. Program, 1977—81; adj. prof. Inst. Criminal Justice and Criminology, U. Md., 1980—81; asst. prof. Dept. Sociology and Legal Studies Program Case Western Reserve U., 1981—82; asst. prof. Dept. Sociology U. Wash., Seattle, 1982—88, assoc. prof., 1989—97, prof., 1998—2005, acting dir. Soc. and Justice Program, 1988—89, 1992, dir., 1996—98, assoc. dean, assoc. vice provost Office of Undergraduate Edn., 1998—2001, acting dean, 2001—02, vice provost, 2001—05, dean, 2002—05; pres., prof. Whitman Coll., Walla Walla, Wash., 2005—. Dep. editor Criminology, 1984—87; author: Inequality, Crime, and Social Control, 1994; co-author: Crime and Society: Criminal Justice, 1996, Crime and Society: Crime, 1996, Crime and Society: Juvenile Delinquency, 1996, Teaching and Learning in Large Classes, 2000; contbr. articles to profl. jours. Recipient J. Francis Finnegan Meml. Prize in Criminology, U. Pa., 1974, Award for Outstanding Achievement by Scholar, Wash. Coun. on Crime and Delinquency, 1995. Mem.: Soc. Study of Social Problems, Law and Soc. Assn., Am. Soc. Criminology, Am. Sociological Assn., Am. Assn. Higher Edn., Alpha Kappa Delta, Phi Eta Sigma. Avocations: hiking, skiing. Office: Whitman Coll Memorial Bldg 303,304 345 Boyer Ave Walla Walla WA 99362 Office Phone: 509-527-5132. Business E-Mail: bridges@whitman.edu.

BRIDGES, JEFF, actor; b. Los Angeles, Dec. 4, 1949; s. Lloyd Vernet & Dorothy (Simpson) B.; m. Susan Bridges, June 5, 1977; 3 children Actor: (films) Halls of Anger, 1970, The Last Picture Show, 1971, Fat City, 1972, Bad Company, 1972, The Iceman Cometh, 1973, Lolly-Madonna XXX, 1973 The Last American Hero, 1973, Thunderbolt and Lightfoot, 1974, Hearts of the West, 1975, Rancho Deluxe, 1975, King Kong, 1976, Stay Hungry, 1976, Somebody Killed Her Husband, 1978, Winter Kills, 1979, The American Success Company, 1979, Heaven's Gate, 1980, Cutter's Way, 1981, Tron, 1982, (voice only) The Last Unicorn, 1982, Kiss Me Goodbye, 1982, Starman, 1984, Against All Odds, 1984, Jagged Edge, 1985, The Morning After, 1986, 8 Million Ways To Die, 1986, Nadine, 1987, Tucker, 1988, See You In The Morning, 1989, The Fabulous Baker Boys, 1989, Texasville, 1990, The Fisher King, 1991, American Heart, 1992, The Vanishing, 1993, Fearless, 1993, Blown Away, 1994, Wild Bill, 1995, White Squall, 1996, The Mirror Has Two Faces, 1996, The Big Lebowski, 1998, Arlington Road, 1999, Forever Hollywood, 1999, The Muse, 1999, Simpatico, 1999, The Contender, 2000, Scenes of the Crime, 2001, K-Pax, 2001, Masked and Anonymous, 2003, Seabiscuit, 2003, The Moguls, 2005, Stick It, 2006, Iron Man, 2008; (TV appearances) Sea Hunt (2 episodes), 1958, The Lloyd Bridges Show (3 episodes), 1962-63, The Loner, 1965, The F.B.I., 1969, The Most Deadly Game, 1970; (TV movies) Silent Night, Lonely Night, 1969, In Search of America, 1971, The Girls in Their Summer Dresses and Other Stories by Irwin Shaw, 1981, Hidden in America, 2002; narrator: (TV specials) Raising the Mammoth, 2000, Lewis & Clark: Great Journey West, 2002.

BRIDGES, WILLIAM BRUCE, electrical engineer, educator, researcher; b. Inglewood, Calif., Nov. 29, 1934; s. Newman K. and Doris L. (Brown) Bridges; m. Carol Ann French, Aug. 24, 1957 (div. 1986); children: Ann Marjorie, Bruce Kendall, Michael Alan; m. Linda Josephine McManus, Nov. 15, 1986. BEE, U. Calif., Berkeley, 1956, MEE (GE Rice fellow), 1957, PhD in Elec. Engring. (NSF fellow), 1962. Assoc. elec. engring. U. Calif., Berkeley, 1957-59, grad. rsch. engr., 1959-61; mem. tech. staff Hughes Rsch. Labs. divsn. Hughes Aircraft Co., Malibu, Calif., 1960-77, sr. scientist, 1968-77, mgr. laser dept., 1969-70; prof. elec. engring. and applied physics Calif. Inst. Tech., Pasadena, 1977—2002, Carl F Braun prof. engring., 1983—2002, Carl F Braun prof. engring. emeritus, 2002—, exec. officer elec. engring., 1978-81. Lectr. U. So. Calif., LA, 1962—64; Sherman Fairchild Disting. scholar Calif. Inst. Tech., 1974—75; bd. dirs. Access Laser Corp. Author (with C. K. Birdsall): (book) Electron Dynamics of Diode Regions, 1966; contbr. articles to profl. jours.; assoc. editor: IEEE Jour. Quantum Electronics, 1977—82, Jour. Optical Soc. Am., 1978—83. Mem. sci. adv. bd. USAF, 1985—89. Recipient L. A. Hyland Patent award, 1969, Lifetime Achievement award for excellence in tchg., Assoc. Students of Calif. Inst. Tech., 2003; named Disting. Engring. Alumnus, U. Calif., Berkeley, 1995, Hon. Alumnus, Calif. Inst. Tech., 2003. Fellow: IEEE (Quantum Electronics award 1988), Laser Inst. Am. (Arthur L. Schawlow award 1986), Optical Soc. Am. (objectives and policies com. 1981—86, 1989—91, bd. dirs. 1982—84, v.p. 1986, pres.-elect 1987, pres. 1988, past pres. 1989); mem.: Am. Acad. Arts and Scis., Am. Radio Relay League (life), Nat. Acad. Scis., Nat. Acad. Engring., Tau Beta Pi, Sigma Xi, Phi Beta Kappa, Eta Kappa Nu (One of Outstanding Young Elec. Engrs. 1966). Achievements include invention of noble gas ion laser; patents in field. Avocation: amateur radio. Office: Calif Inst Tech Moore Bldg 136-93 Pasadena CA 91125-9300 Office Phone: 626-395-4809. Business E-Mail: w6fa@caltech.edu.

BRIDGMAN, GEOFF, lawyer; b. Seattle, July 2, 1967; BA magna cum laude, Ctrl. Wash. Univ., 1988; JD summa cum laude, Seattle Univ., 1995. Bar: Wash. 1995. Gen. litig. atty. Ogden Murphy Wallace P.L.L.C., Seattle. Contbr. articles to numerous profl. jours. Named Seattle Rising Star, SuperLawyer Mag., 2006. Mem.: ABA, Wash. State Trial Lawyers Assn., Wash. State Bar Assn. Office: Ogden Murphy Wallace Ste 2100 1601 Fifth Ave Seattle WA 98101-1686

BRIERLEY, JAMES ALAN, biohydrometallurgy consultant; b. Denver, Dec. 22, 1938; s. Everette and Carrie (Berg) B.; m. Corale Louise Beer, Dec. 21, 1965 BS in Bacteriology, Colo. State U., 1961; MS in Microbiology, Mont. State U., 1963, PhD, 1966. Research scientist Martin Marietta Corp., Denver, 1968-69; asst. prof. biology N.Mex. Inst. Mining and Tech., Socorro, 1966-68, from asst. prof. to prof. biology, chmn. dept. biology, 1969-83; research dir. Advanced Mineral Techs., Golden, Colo., 1983-88; chief microbiologist Newmont Metall. Svcs., Englewood, Colo., 1988-2000; chief rsch. scientist biohydrometallurgy Newmont Mining Corp., 2000-01; cons. Brierley Consultancy, LLC, Highlands Ranch, Colo., 2001—. Vis. fellow U. Warwick, Coventry, Eng., 1976, vis. prof. Catholic U., Santiago, Chile, 1983; adj. prof. dept. metallurgy U. Utah, 1994-96; cons. Mountain State Mineral Enterprises, Tucson, 1980, Sandia Nat. Lab., Albuquerque, 1976, Bechtel Civil and Minerals, Scottsdale, Ariz., 1984, Newmont Gold Co., 1988, Newmont Mining Corp., 2001-06, Smith-Pachter Attys. at Law, 2002-03, Barrick Gold Corp., 2005. Contbr. numerous articles to profl. jours.; patentee in field. Served to staff sgt. Air N.G., 1956-61. Recipient Wadsorth Extractive Metall. award, Soc. Mining, Metall. & Exploration, 2000, Honor Alumnus award, Colo. State U., 2001; grantee 32 rsch. grants. Fellow: AAAS; mem.: Nat. Acad. Engring., Mining and Metall. Soc. Am. Avocations: travel, gardening, hiking, exercise. Home: 2074 East Terrace Dr Highlands Ranch CO 80126-2692 Office: Brierley Consultancy PO Box 260012 Highlands Ranch CO 80163-0012 E-mail: j.brierley@worldnet.att.net.

BRIGDEN, JOHN, lawyer; b. 1964; BS in Elec. Engring. with honors, Purdue U.; JD with honors, Georgetown U. Lic.: Va., Wash., DC, US Paten and Trademark Office. Dir. intellectual property Silicon Graphics, Inc., 1997—2000; v.p. bus. devel., gen. counsel Shutterfly, Inc., 2000—01; v.p., gen. counsel, sec. VERITAS Software Corp., Mountain View, Calif., 2001—03, sr. v.p., gen. counsel, sec., 2003—. Mem.: Calif. Bar Assn.

BRIGGS, BURTON A., medical educator; b. Orange, NJ, July 24, 1939; s. Carolyn Sue Briggs; 2 children. BS, Walla Walla Coll., 1961; MD, Loma Linda U., 1966; MA in Mgmt., Claremont Grad. Sch., 1990. Diplomate Am. Bd. Med. Examiners, Am. Bd. Anesthesiology; lic. physician, Calif., Mass. Intern Loma Linda (Calif.) U. Hosp., 1966-67; asst. resident in anesthesia Mass. Gen. Hosp., Boston, 1967-68, 69-70, clin. and rsch. fellow, 1968-69, chief resident, 1969, asst. in anesthesia, co-dir. recovery room/acute care unit, 1972-75; instr. anesthesia Harvard Med. Sch., Boston, 1972-75; asst. prof. anesthesia and surgery Loma Linda U., 1975-83, asst. prof. pediatrics, 1982-87, assoc. prof. anesthesiology and surgery, 1983-87, prof. anesthesiology, prof. surgery, 1987—. Dir. surg. intensive care Loma Linda U. Med. Ctr., 1975-92, chief sect. critical care, 1983-92, med. dir. transport svcs., 1986—, med. dir. operating room svcs., 1991—, bd. trustees, 1986-90; dir. surg. intensive care J.L. Pettis Meml. VA Hosp., 1977-78; sec.-treas. Loma Linda Anesthesiology Med. Group, Inc., 1981-95, sec., 1995—, chmn. billing and reimbursement com., 1995—; chief anesthesiology svcs. Riverside Gen. Hosp., 1985-86;vis. prof. Socieda de Brasileira de Anestesiologia, 1980, Peking (China) Union Med. Coll., 1986; oral examiner Med. Bd. of Calif., 1990—; interviewer regional area Harvard/Radcliffe Colls., 1994—; bd. dirs. faculty physicians and surgeons Loma Linda U. Sch. Medicine, 1995—. Author: Principles of Critical Care, 1987; contbr. articles and abstracts to profl. jours., chpts. to books; article reviewer New Eng. Jour. Medicine, 1973-75, Jour. Critical Care Medicine, 1975-91; examiner Am. Bd. Anesthesiology, 1983-90. With U.S. Army, 1970-71. Fellow Am. Coll. Anesthesiology, Am. Coll. Critical Care Medicine; mem. Am. Soc. Anesthesiologists, Soc. Critical Care Medicine, San Bernardino County Med. Soc., Calif. Soc. Anesthesiology (alt. del. dist. 2 1983-86), Calif. Med. Assn., Loma Linda U. Sch. Medicine Alumni Assn. (bd. dirs. 1994—, CFO 1995—), Assn. Anesthesia Clin. Dirs. (bd. dirs. 1994—), Alpha Omega Alpha.

BRIGGS, STEVE CLEMENT, lawyer; b. Vernon, Tex., Jan. 26, 1947; s. Galen Pierce and Virginia Irene (Sebert) B. BA, U. Mich., 1970; postgrad., U. Calif., Berkeley, 1970; JD, U. Colo., 1975. Bar: Colo. 1975, U.S. Dist. Ct. Colo. 1975, U.S. Ct. Appeals (10th cir.) 1976, U.S. Ct. Claims 1984. Law clk. to chief judge U.S. Dist. Ct. Colo., Denver, 1975-76; asst. atty. gen. anti-trust sect. State of Colo., Denver, 1976-78; ptnr. Hutchinson, Black, Hill & Cook, Boulder, Colo., 1978—92; judge Colo. Ct. Appeals, 1992—2000; mediator, arbitrator Jud. Arbiter Group, Inc., 2000—. Chair dean's club U. Colo. Law Sch., Boulder, 1985; bd. dirs. Vol. and Info. Ctr., Boulder, 1979-80, United Way, Boulder, 1980, Boulder Philharm., 1990—; v.p. bd. dirs. Counseling Ctr., Boulder, 1983-86. Recipient Outstanding Vol. Legal Svcs. award Eco-Cycle, 1984, Disting. Alumni award U. Colo Sch. Law, 2003. Mem. Colo. Bar Assn. (bd. govs. 1988—, exec. coun. 1990—, pres. 2004-05), Boulder County Bar Assn. (pres. 1986-87). Avocations: golf, travel, movies, reading. Office: Judicial Arbiter Group 1601 Blake St #400 Denver CO 80202 Office Phone: 303-572-1919. Fax: 303-571-1115. Business E-Mail: sbriggs@jaginc.com.

BRIGGS, WINSLOW RUSSELL, plant biologist, educator; b. St. Paul, Apr. 29, 1928; s. John DeQuedville and Marjorie (Winslow) B.; m. Ann Morrill, June 30, 1955; children: Caroline, Lucia, Marion. BA, Harvard U., 1951, MA, 1952, PhD, 1956; D in Natural Sci. (hon.), U. Freiburg, Germany, 2002, D (hon.) in Plant Biology, 2002. Instr. biol. scis. Stanford (Calif.) U., 1955-57, asst. prof., 1957-62, assoc. prof., 1962-66, prof., 1966-67; prof. biology Harvard U., 1967-73, Stanford U., 1973—; dir. dept. plant biology Carnegie Instn. of Washington, Stanford, 1973-93. Hon. editor molecular plant New Chinese Jour. Author: (with others) Life on Earth, 1973; mem. editl. bd. Ann. Rev. Plant Physiology, 1961-72; contbr. articles on plant growth and devel. and photobiology to profl. jours. Vol. Calif. State Pk. sys. Recipient Alexander von Humboldt U.S. Sr. Scientist award, 1984-85, Sterling Hendricks award USDA Agrl. Rsch. Svc., 1995, DeWitt award for partnership Calif. State Pks., 2000, Finsen medal Assn. Internat. Photobiology, 2000; John Simon Guggenheim fellow, 1973-74, Deutsche Akademie der Naturforscher Leopoldina, 1986. Fellow AAAS, Am. Soc. Plant Physiologists (pres. 1975-76, Stephen Hales award 1994, Adolph Gude award, 2007); mem. NAS, Calif. Bot. Soc. (pres. 1976-77), Am. Acad. Arts and Scis., Am. Inst. Biol. Scis. (pres. 1980-81), Am. Soc. Photobiology, Bot. Soc. Am., Nature Conservancy, Sigma Xi. Avocation: Chinese cooking. Home: 480 Hale St Palo Alto CA 94301-2207 Office: Carnegie Inst Washington Dept Plant Biology 260 Panama St Stanford CA 94305-4101

BRIGHAM, SAMUEL TOWNSEND JACK, III, lawyer; b. Honolulu, Oct. 8, 1939; s. Samuel Townsend Jack, Jr. and Betty Elizabeth (McNeil) B.; m. Judith Catherine Johnson, Sept. 3, 1960; children: Robert Jack, Bradley Lund, Lori Ann, Lisa Katherine. BS in Bus. magna cum laude, Menlo Coll., 1963; JD, U. Utah, 1966. Bar: Calif. 1967. Asso. firm Petty, Andrews, Olsen & Tufts, San Francisco, 1966-67; accounting mgr. Western sales region Hewlett-Packard Co., North Hollywood, Calif., 1967-68; atty. Hewlett-Packard Co., Palo Alto, Calif., 1968-70, asst. gen. counsel, 1971-73, gen. atty., asst. sec., 1974-75, sec., gen. counsel, 1975-82, v.p., gen. counsel, 1982-85, v.p. corp. affairs, gen. counsel, mgr./dir. law dept., 1985—, sr. v.p. corp. affairs, gen. counsel, mgr./dir. law dept., 1994—. Lectr. law Menlo Coll.; speaker profl. assn. seminars. Bd. dirs. Palo Alto Area YMCA, 1974-81, pres., 1978; bd. govs. Santa Clara County region NCCJ; trustee Menlo Sch. and Coll.; bd. dirs. Just Say No. Served with USMC, 1957-59. Mem. ABA, Calif. Bar Assn., Peninsula Assn. Gen. Counsel, MAPI Law Council, Am. Corp. Counsel Assn. (chmn. 1985, bd. dirs. 1983—), Am. Soc. Corp. Secs. (pres. No. Calif. Chpt. 1983—), Assn. Gen. Counsel (sec.-treas. 1991—). Office: Hewlett-Packard Co 3000 Hanover St Palo Alto CA 94304-1181 Home: 1945 Knollwood Ln Los Altos CA 94024-6721

BRILEY, JOHN RICHARD, writer; b. Kalamazoo, June 25, 1925; s. William Treve and Mary Stella (Daly) B.; m. Dorothy Louise Reichart, Aug. 23, 1950; children: Dennis Patrick, Paul Christian, Mary Sydney, Shaun William. BA, U. Mich., 1951, MA, 1952; PhD, U. Birmingham, Eng., 1961. Lectr. Gen. Motors, Detroit, 1947-50; dir. orientation USAF, London, 1955-60; writer MGM, Elstree, Eng., 1960-64; freelance writer Trevone Prodns. Inc., L.A. and Amersham, Eng., 1970—; Bob Shaye artist is residence U. Mich., 1995. Vis. lectr. Univ. Mich., 1969; vis. prof. U. Mich., 1998. Author: (criticism) Shakespeare Survey, 1964, (novels) The Traitors, 1968, The Last Dance, 1978, Cry Freedom, 1988, The first Stone, 1997, (plays) Seven Bob a Buck, 1964, So Who Needs Men!, 1976; screenwriter: (films) (with Jack Trevor Story) Invasion Quartet, 1961, (with Story) Postman's Knock, 1962, Children of the Damned, 1964, Pope Joan, 1972, That Lucky Touch, 1975, The Medusa Touch, 1978, Eagle's Wing, 1979, Gandhi, 1982 (Academy award best original screenplay 1982), Enigma, 1983, Marie, 1985, (with Stanley Mann) Tai-Pan, 1986, Cry Freedom, 1987, (with Cary Bates and Mario Puzo) Christopher Columbus: The Discovery, 1992,, Molokai--The Story of Father Damien, 1999, (TV series) Hits & Misses, 1962, The Airbase, 1965. Served to capt. USAF, 1943-46. Recipient Golden Globe award Fgn. Press Assn., Los Angeles, 1983, Acad. award Acad. Motion Picture Arts and Scis., Los Angeles, 1983, Christopher award St. Christopher Soc., N.Y., 1983, 85, 88. Mem. Writers Guild Great Britain (exec. com. 1975-85), Writers Guild Am., Authors Guild, Dramatists Guild. Avocations: swimming, tennis, skiing. Home: PO Box 2365 Sun Valley ID 83353-2365

BRILLIANT, ASHLEIGH ELLWOOD, cartoonist, writer; b. London, Dec. 9, 1933; came to the U.S., 1956, naturalized, 1969; s. Victor and Amelia (Adler) B.; m. Dorothy Low Tucker, June 28, 1968. BA with honors, Univ. Coll., London, 1955; MA in Edn., Claremont Grad. Sch., 1957; PhD in Am. History, U. Calif., Berkeley, 1964. Tchr. English Hollywood H.S., LA, 1956-57; tchg. asst., reader in history U. Calif., Berkeley, 1960-63; asst. prof. history Ctrl. Oreg. Coll., Bend, 1964-65, Floating Campus divsn. Chapman Coll., Orange, Calif., 1965-67; entertainer in coffeehouses, outdoor spkr. San Francisco, 1967-68; syndicated cartoonist, dir. Brilliant Enterprises, pub. and licensing, San Francisco, Santa Barbara, Calif., 1967—. Creator Pot-Shots postcards, T-shirts, cocktail napkins, tote-bags, other items; mem. faculty Sonoma State U., Santa Barbara City Coll.; vis. scholar Ctrl. Oregon Cmty. Coll., 2002. Author: I May Not Be Totally Perfect, But Parts of Me Are Excellent, And Other Brilliant Thoughts, 1979, I Have Abandoned My Search for Truth and Am Now Looking for a Good Fantasy, 1980, Appreciate Me Now and Avoid the Rush, 1981, I Feel Much Better Now That I've Given Up Hope, 1984, All I Want Is A Warm Bed and A Kind Word, and Unlimited Power, 1985, I Try to Take One Day At A Time, But Sometimes Several Days Attack Me At Once, 1987, The Great Car Craze: How Southern California Collided With The Automobile in the 1920's, 1989, We've Been Through So Much Together and Most of It Was Your Fault, 1990, Be A Good Neighbor and Leave Me Alone, 1992, I Want to Reach Your Mind...Where is it Currently Located, 1994, I'm Just Moving Clouds Today-Tomorrow I'll Try Mountains, 1999; illustrator: The Illuminated Life, 1995, Adult Development and Aging, 1995, Give Yourself the Unfair Advantage!, 1995, Designing Effective Organizations, 1995, The Baby Boomers' Guide to Living Forever, 2000, Multiple Streams of Internet Income, 2001, Breaking Free From Boomerang Love, 2004; founder, leader Ban Leafblowers and Save Our Town, 1996. Recipient Raymond B. Bragg award, 1987, Disting. Alumnus of Yr. award Claremont Grad. U., 2000; Claremont Grad. Sch. scholar, 1956; Haynes fellow, 1962, Panama-Pacific fellow, 1963; nominated Poet Laureate, City Santa Barbara, Calif., 2007. Mem. Newspaper Comics Coun., No. Calif. Cartoonists Assn., Mensa. Home and Office: 117 W Valerio St Santa Barbara CA 93101-2927 E-mail: ashleigh@west.net.

BRILLIANT, LARRY (LAWRENCE BRENT BRILLIANT), preventive medicine physician, entrepreneur; b. May 5, 1944; m. Girija Brilliant; children: Joe, Jon, Iris. Student, U. Mich.; MD, Wayne State U., 1969; MPH, U. Mich., 1977; DSc (hon.), Knox Coll., 2004. Cert. Preventive Medicine and Pub. Health. Med. officer, smallpox eradication and epidemiol. adv. Inter Country Team WHO (regional office-South East Asia, New Delhi), 1973—77; asst. prof., Internat. Health and Epidemiology, Sch. Pub. Health U. Mich., 1977—80, assoc. prof., dept. epidemiology, Sch. Pub. Health, 1981—88; co-founder, CEO The WELL (Whole Earth 'Lectronic Link), 1985—; co-founder, chair Seva Found., Berkeley, 1979, bd. dir., 1979—; mem. GBN network; exec. dir. Google.org, 2006—09; chief philanthropy evangelist Google Inc., 2009—. Co-founder, CEO of a series of tech.-based companies Network Technologies Inc. and SoftNet Systems; co-founder, CEO Cometa Networks (joint venture with AT&T, IBM and Intel), 2004; epidemiologist, survey mgr. WHO Prevention of Blindness Prog., Katmandu, Nepal, 1980—81; staff mem. WHO Global Commn. to certify smallpox eradicated in Burma, India, Nepal and Iran; last UN WHO med. officer to visit Iran in search of hidden smallpox; vol. first responder for smallpox bioterrorism response effort Ctrs. for Disease Control; spkr. in field. Contbr. articles to profl. jours.; co-author: The Management of Smallpox Eradication in India, 1985; co-author: (with R.P. Pokhrel, N. Grasset, G. Brilliant) The Epidemiology of Blindness in Nepal, 1988; author: Boffa Newsletters. Bd. dir. Wavy Gravy Camp Winnarainbow; volunteered in Sri Lanka for tsunami relief, 2005; worked in India with WHO polio eradication program; established Pandefense; mem. Dean's adv. bd. Berkeley Sch. Pub. Health; mem. adv. bd. Grateful Dead-created Rex Found., Presidio World Coll. MBA program in sustainable bus., Future in Review (FiRe). Recipient Best Online Pub. award for WELL, Computer Press Assn., 1990, several awards from WHO and Govt. India for work in smallpox eradication, Peacemaker prize, Ctr. for Peace and Conflict Resolution, Wayne State U., Detroit, 2005, Ted prize (awards-a wish to change the world), 2006; named Internat. Pub. Health Hero, U. Calif., Berkeley Sch. Pub. Health; named one of the 100 Most Influential People in the World, TIME mag., 2008. Achievements include helping manage the WHO smallpox eradication program in South Asia; served as physician to members of the Grateful Dead. Mailing: Google Inc 1600 Amphitheatre Pky Mountain View CA 94043*

BRIMMER, CLARENCE ADDISON, federal judge; b. Rawlins, Wyo., July 11, 1922; s. Clarence Addison and Geraldine (Zingsheim) B.; m. Emily O. Docken, Aug. 2, 1953; children: Geraldine Ann, Philip Andrew, Andrew Howard, Elizabeth Ann. BA, U. Mich., 1944, JD, 1947. Bar: Wyo. 1948. Pvt. practice law, Rawlins, 1948-71; mcpl. judge, 1948-54; U.S. commr., magistrate, 1963-71; atty. gen. Wyo. Cheyenne, 1971-74; U.S. atty., 1975; chief judge U.S. Dist. Ct. Wyo., Cheyenne, 1975-92, dist. judge, 1975—. Mem. panel multi-dist. litigation, 1992-2000; mem. Jud. Conf. U.S., 1994-97, exec., 1995-97. Sec. Rawlins Bd. Pub. Utilities, 1954-66; Rep. gubernatorial candidate, 1974; trustee Rocky Mountain Mineral Law Found., 1963-75. With USAAF, 1945-46. Mem. ABA, Wyo. Bar Assn., Laramie County Bar Assn., Carbon County Bar Assn., Am. Judicature Soc., Masons, Shriners, Rotary. Episcopalian. Office: US Dist Ct 2120 Capitol Ave Rm 2603 Cheyenne WY 82001

BRIMMER, PHILIP A., federal judge; b. Rawlins, Wyo., 1959; AB, Harvard Coll., Cambridge, Mass., 1981; JD, Yale Law Sch., New Haven, 1985. Bar: Colo. 1985. Law clk. to Hon. Zita L. Weinshienk US Dist. Ct. Colo., 1985—87; assoc. Kirkland & Ellis, Colo., 1987—94; dep. dist. atty Denver Dist. Atty.'s Office, 1994—2001, chief dep. dist. atty, 2001; asst US atty. US Atty.'s Office Dist. Colo., 2001—06, chief major crimes sect, 2006, chief spl. prosecutions sect., 2006—08; judge US Dist. Ct. Colo., 2008—. Office: Alfred A Arraj US Courthouse A641 Rm A601 901 19th St Denver CO 80294 Office Phone: 303-335-2794.*

BRIN, SERGEY MIHAILOVICH, information technology executive; b. Moscow, Aug. 21, 1973; s. Michael and Genia Brin; m. Anne Wojcicki, May 2007. BS in Math. & Computer Sci., with honors, U. Md., College Park, 1993; MS, Stanford U., 1995; MBA (hon.), Instituto de Empresa. Co-founder Google, Inc., Mountain View, Calif., 1998, pres., 1998—2001, pres. tech., 2001—. Bd. dirs. Google, Inc., 1998—; spkr. World Econ. Forum and the Technol., Entertainment and Design Conf.; spkr. in the field. Author: (Articles) Extracting Patterns and Relations from the World Wide Web; Scalable Techniques for Mining Casual Structures; Beyond Market Baskets: Generalizing Association Rules to Correlations; co-author (with Larry Page): Dynamic Data Mining: A New Architecture for Data with High Dimensionality; guest appearence on Charlie Rose Show, CNBC, CNNfn. Co-recipient (with Larry Page) Marconi prize, 2004; named Bus. Leader of Yr. for Google, Inc., Scientific Am. 50, 2005; named one of Persons of Week (with Larry Page), ABC World News Tonight, 2004, The 100 Most Influential People in the World, TIME mag., 2005, Forbes Richest Americans, Forbes mag., 2006—, World's Richest People, 2007—08, The 50 Who Matter Now, CNNMoney-.com Bus. 2.0, 2006, 2007, The 50 Most Important People on the Web, PC World, 2007, The 25 Most Powerful People in Bus., Fortune Mag., 2007; fellow NSF. Jewish. Office: Google Inc 1600 Amphitheatre Pkwy Mountain View CA 94043 Office Fax: 650-618-1499.

BRINGARDNER, JOHN MICHAEL, lawyer, clergyman; b. Columbus, Ohio, Nov. 7, 1957; s. John Krepps and Elizabeth (Evans) B.; m. Emily Presley, June 19, 1982; children: John Taylor, Michael Steven, Malee Elizabeth. BA, U. Central Fla., Orlando, 1979; post-grad., Mercer U., 1979; JD, Fla. State U., 1981. Bar: Fla. 1982, Calif. 1994, U.S. Dist. Ct. (mid. dist.) Fla., U.S. Dist. Ct. (no. dist.) Fla., U.S. Ct. Appeals (11th cir.). Assoc. McFarlain, Bobo, Sternstein, Wiley & Cassidy, Tallahassee, Fla., 1982-87, Finley, Kumble Wagner, Tallahassee, 1987; minister Boston Ch. of Christ, 1987-90; evangelist Bankok Christian Ch., 1990-92, Metro Manila Christian Ch., 1992-93; gen. counsel Internat. Chs. of Christ, LA, 1993—. Bd. dirs. Eye Care Corp., Orlando, Fla., Quality Coffee Corp., Tallahassee. Mem. ABA, Fla. Bar Assn. Avocations: football, baseball, triathlons, hiking, music. Office: La International Church of Christ 3731 Wilshire Blvd Ste 810 Los Angeles CA 90010-2850

BRINKER, CHARLES JEFFREY, chemistry and chemical engineering educator; b. Easton, Pa., Nov. 28, 1950; BS in Ceramic Sci. with honors, Rutgers U., 1972, MS in Ceramic Sci., 1975, PhD in Ceramic Sci., 1978. Mem. tech. staff inorganic materials chemistry Sandia Nat. Labs., Albuquerque, 1979—; disting. mem. technical staff to sr. scientist Sandia Nat. Labs, Albuquerque, 1991—; prof. chemistry and chem. engring. U. N.Mex., Albuquerque, Disting. Nat. Lab. Prof. Chemistry and Chem. Engring., 1991—, co-dir. ctr. micro-engineered materials. Co-editor: Better Ceramics Through Chemistry, 1984, 6th edit., 1994; assoc. editor Jour. Am. Ceramic Soc.; mem. editl. bd. Chemistry of Materials, Jour. Sol-Gel Sci. and Tech., Jour. Porous Materials, Current Opinion in Solid State and Materials Sci.; author: Sol-Gel Science, 1990; contbr. articles to profl. jours. Recipient Basic Energy Scis. award Dept. Energy, 1986, 92, 94, 95, Zachariasen award, 1988 Jour. Non-Crystalline Solids, 1985-87, Ralph K. Iler award in chemistry of colloidal materials Am. Chem. Soc., 1996, NOVA award Lockheed Martin, 1996, R&D 100 award, 1996, E.O. Lawrence award, 2002. Fellow Am. Ceramic Soc.; mem. Materials Rsch. Soc. (founder, co-organizer), Keramos, Nat. Academy Engring. Office: Advanced Materials Lab 1001 University Blvd SE Albuquerque NM 87106-4325

BRISCOE, JOHN, lawyer; b. Stockton, Calif., July 1, 1948; s. John Lloyd and Doris (Olsen) B.; m. Carol E. Sayers; children: John Paul, Katherine JD, U. San Francisco, 1972. Bar: Calif. 1972, U.S. Dist. Ct. (no., ea. and ctrl. dists.) Calif. 1972, U.S. Supreme Ct. 1978, U.S. Ct. Appeals (9th cir.) 1981, Permanent Ct. Arbitration (The Hague) 2005. Dep. atty. gen. State of Calif., San Francisco, 1972—80; ptnr. Washburn and Kemp, San Francisco, 1980—88, Washburn, Briscoe & McCarthy, San Francisco, 1988—2002, Stoel Rives LLP, San Francisco, 2002—05, Briscoe Ivester and Bazel LLP, San Francisco, 2005—. Author: Surveying the Courtroom, 1984, rev. edit., 1999, Falsework, 1997, Tadich Grill, 2002; editor: Reports of Special Masters, 1991; contbr. articles to profl. and lit. jours Mem.: ABA, Am. Soc. Internat. Law, San Francisco Bar Assn. Roman Catholic. Office: Briscoe Ivester & Bazel LLP 155 Sansome St 7th Fl San Francisco CA 94104 Home Phone: 415-994-5701; Office Phone: 415-402-2700. Business E-Mail: jbriscoe@briscoelaw.net.

BRISCOE, MARY BECK, federal judge; b. Council Grove, Kans., Apr. 4, 1947; m. Charles Arthur Briscoe. BA, U. Kans., 1969, JD, 1973; LLM, U. Va., 1990. Rsch. asst. Harold L. Haun, Esq., 1973; atty.-examiner fin. divsn. ICC, 1973—74; asst. U.S. atty. for Wichita and Topeka, Kans. Dept. Justice, 1974—84; judge Kans. Ct. Appeals, 1984—95, chief judge, 1990—95; judge US Ct. Appeals (10th cir.), Topeka, 1995—. Recipient Univ. Kans. Law Soc. Disting. Alumnus award, 2000; named to Women's Hall of Fame, Univ. Kans., 2001. Fellow: Kans. Bar Found., Am. Bar Found.; mem.: ABA, Women Attys. Assn. Topeka, Kans. Bar Assn. (Outstanding Svc. award 1992), Topeka Bar Assn., Nat. Assn. Women Judges, Am. Judicature Soc., U. Kans. Law Soc., Kans. Hist. Soc., Washburn Law Sch. Assn. (hon.). Office: US Ct Appeals 10th Cir 645 Massachusetts Ste 400 Lawrence KS 66044-2235 also: US Ct Appeals 10th Cir Byron White US Courthouse 1823 Stout St Denver CO 80257

BRITTEN, ROY JOHN, biophysicist; b. Washington, Oct. 1, 1919; s. Rollo Herbert and Marion Hale B.; m. Jacqueline Reid, 1986 (dec. Sept. 2001); children: Gregory, Kenneth. BS, U. Va., 1941; PhD, Princeton U., 1951. Staff mem. dept. terrestrial magnetism Carnegie Instn., Washington, 1951-89; sr. research assoc. Calif. Inst. Tech., Corona del Mar, 1973-81, disting. Carnegie sr. rsch. assoc. biology, 1981-99, emeritus, 1999—. Adj. prof., dept. ecology and evolution, U. Calif., Irvine, 1991—; discoverer repeated DNA sequences in genomes of higher organisms. Inventor in field. Named Disting. Carnegie Sr. Research Assoc. in Biology, 1981-99. Fellow Am. Acad. Arts and Scis., AAAS; mem. Nat. Acad. Scis. Office: Calif Inst Tech Kerchkhoff Marine Lab 101 Dahlia Ave Corona Del Mar CA 92625-2814 Business E-Mail: rbritten@caltech.edu.

BRITTON, DENNIS A., former newspaper editor, executive; b. Santa Barbara, Calif., 1940; m. Theresa Romero Britton; children: Robert, Patrick, Anne. Attended, San Jose State U. Joined L.A. Times, 1966, copy editor, reporter, news editor, asst. nat. editor, nat. editor, 1977-83, dep. mng. editor; editor Chgo. Sun-Times, 1989-96, exec. v.p., until 1996; editor-in-chief Denver Post, 1996-99. Mem. Nat. Assn. Hispanic Journalists. Office: Denver Post 1560 Broadway Denver CO 80202-5177

BRITTON, M(ELVIN) C(REED), JR., rheumatologist; b. San Francisco, Apr. 11, 1935; s. Melvin Creed and Mathilda Carolyn (Epeneter) B.; m. Mary Elizabeth Phillips, Nov. 2, 1957; children: Elizabeth Carolynne, Lisa Marie. AB, Dartmouth Coll., 1957, MS, 1958; MD, Harvard U., 1960. Diplomate Am. Bd. Internal Medicine, Am. Bd. Rheumatology, Am. Bd. Quality Assurance. Resident Dartmouth Coll. Sch. Medicine, Hanover, NH, 1964-67; fellow Harvard U. Sch. Medicine, Boston, 1967-69; ptnr. Palo Alto (Calif.) Med. Clinic, 1969—, chmn. dept. medicine, 1990-97. Pres. med. staff Stanford (Calif.) U. Med. Ctr., 1985-87, mem. med. staff bd., 1969-87; bd. dirs. Hosp. Conf. No. Calif., 1988-92, Inst. for Med. Quality, 1998—, treas., 1999-2003, chmn. bd., 2003—; mem. Relative Value Update Commn., 1996— Contbr. articles to med. jours. Pres. Found. for Med. care Santa Clara county, Campbell, 1983-89; mem. Bay Area Lupus Found., 1978—, chmn., 1987-88, 94-95; v.p. Calif. Founds. for Med. Care, 1996, pres., CEO, 1999-2001. Fellow ACP, Am. Coll. Rheumatology (bd. dirs. 1986-89, Paulding Phelps medal 1994, mastership 2000, Disting. Svc. award 2004), Calif. Acad. Medicine (exec. com. 1996-2000, pres. 2001-03); mem. AMA (alt. del. 1988-2003, del. 2003——, chair governing coun., splty. and svcs. soc. 2004-05), Calif. Med. Assn., Santa Clara County Med. Soc. (pres. 1980-81, Bd. Svc. award 1988), Arthritis Found. No. Calif. (chmn. bd. dirs. 1984-87, Disting Svc. award 1985), Vintners Club (San Francisco, v.p. 1975-78), Cosmos Club (Washington). Republican. Episcopalian. Avocations: skiing, travel, enology. Office: Palo Alto Med Clinic 795 El Camino Real Palo Alto CA 94301-2726 Home Phone: 650-326-0856; Office Phone: 650-853-6056. Personal E-mail: rheumdc@aol.com.

BRITTON, THOMAS WARREN, JR., retired management consultant; b. Pawhuska, Okla., June 16, 1944; s. Thomas Warren and Helen Viola (Haynes) Britton; m. Jerlyn Kay Davis, 1964 (div. 1970); 1 child, Natalie Dawn; m. Deborah Ann Mansour, Oct. 20, 1973; 1 child, Kimberly Ann. BSME, Okla. State U., 1966, MS in Indsl. Engring. and Mgmt., 1968. Cons. Arthur Young & Co., LA, 1968—72, mgr., 1972—76, prin., 1976—79, ptnr., 1979—88, office dir. mgmt. svcs. dept. Orange County, Calif., 1979—88; ptnr. Price Waterhouse, LA, 1988—95, ptnr.-in-charge West Coast Nat. Aerospace and Def. Industry practice, 1988—95, west coast mfg. and logistics practice, 1988—95; ptnr., chmn. US MCS Tech. Industry Practice PricewaterhouseCoopers, LA, 1995—2000, chmn. Global MCS Tech. Industry Practice, 1995—2000, COO MCS west bus. unit, chmn. global MCS tech. industry practice, 2000—02; ret., 2002. Lectr. in field. Mem. creative growth bd. City of San Dimas, Calif., 1976—77, chmn. Planning Commn., 1977—83; trustee World Affairs Coun. Orange County, 1980; v.p. ann. fund, pres., chmn. long range planning, bd. pres. South Coast Repertory Theater, 1982—92; trustee Providence Speech and Hearing Ctr., 1985—90, Spl. Olympics So. Calif., 1995—97; mem. devel. com. U. Calif.-Irvine Med. Sch.; chmn. Costa Mesa Arts Coun., 1984. Capt. USAR, 1971—86. Mem. LA Inst. CPAs, Mgmt. Adv. Svcs. Com., Am. Prodn. and Inventory Control Soc., Am. Inst. Indsl. Engrs., Greater Irvine Indsl. League, Okla. State U. Alumni Assn., Jonathan Club, Ridgeline Country Club, Santa Ana Country Club, Kappa Sigma. Home: 9881 Orchard Ln Villa Park CA 92861-3105 Personal E-mail: tom_britton@msn.com.

BROAD, ELI, foundation administrator, art collector; b. NYC, June 6, 1933; s. Leon and Rebecca (Jacobson) B.; m. Edythe Lois Lawson, Dec. 19, 1954; children: Jeffrey Alan, Gary Stephen. BA in Acctg. cum laude, Mich. State U., 1954; LLD (hon.), Southwestern U., 2000; HHD (hon.), Mich. State U., 2002. CPA Mich., 1956. Cert. public acct., 1954-56; asst. prof. Detroit Inst. Tech., 1956; co-founder, chmn., pres., CEO SunAmerica Inc. (formerly Kaufman & Broad, Inc.), LA, 1957-2001; chmn. SunAmerica Inc. (formerly Kaufman & Broad, Inc., now AIG Retirement Svcs. Inc.), 2001—05, Kaufman and Broad Home Corp., LA, 1989-93, chmn. exec. com., 1993-95; founder, chmn. Kaufman and Broad Home Corp. (now KB Home), LA, 1993—. Mem. exec. com. adv. bd. Fed. Nat. Mortgage Assn., 1972-73; active Calif. Bus. Roundtable, 1986-2000; co-owner Sacramento Kings and Arco Arena, 1992-99; trustee Com. for Econ. Devel., 1993-95; mem. real estate adv. bd. Citibank, N.Y.C., 1976-81; bd. dirs. Sacramento Kings and ARCO Arena; co-owner Sacramento Kings & Arco Arena, 1992-99. Mem. bd. dirs. LA World Affairs Coun., 1988-2003, chmn., 1994-97, DARE Am., 1989-95, hon. mem. bd. dirs. 1995—; founding trustee Windward Sch., Santa Monica, Calif., 1972-77; bd. trustees Pitzer Coll., Claremont, Calif., 1970-82, chmn. bd. trustees, 1973-79, life trustee, 1982—, Haifa U., Israel, 1972-80, Calif. State U., 1978-82, vice chmn. bd. trustees, 1979-80, trustee emeritus, 1982—, Mus. Contemporary Art, LA, 1980-93, founding chmn., 1980, Archives Am. Art, Smithsonian Instn., Washington, 1985-98, Am. Fedn. Arts, 1988-91, Leland Stanford Mansion Found., 1992-2000, Calif. Inst. Tech., 1993—, Armand Hammer Mus. Art and Cultural Ctr. UCLA, 1994-99; pres. Calif. Non-Partisan Vote Registration Found., 1971-72; chancellor's assoc. UCLA, 1971—, mem. vis. com. Grad. Sch. Mgmt., 1972-90, trustee UCLA Found., 1986-96, exec. com. bd. visitors Sch. of the Arts & Architecture, 1997—; assoc. chmn. United Crusade, LA, 1973-76; chmn. Mayor's Housing Policy Com., LA, 1974-75; del., spkr. Fed. Econ. Summit Conf., 1974, State Econ. Summit Conf., 1974; mem. contemporary coun. LA County Mus. Art, 1973-79, bd. trustees acquisitions com., 1978-81, trustee, 1995—; bd. fellows, mem. exec. com. The Claremont (Calif.) Colls., 1974-79; nat. trustee Balt. Mus. Art, 1985-91; mem. adv. bd. Boy Scouts Am., 1982-85, LA Bus. Jour., 1986-88; mem. adv. coun. Town Hall of Calif., 1985-87; trustee Dem. Nat. Com. Victory Fund, 1988, 92, 96; mem. painting and sculpture com. Whitney Mus., NYC, 1987-89; chmn. adv. bd. ART/LA, 1989; bd. overseers The Music Ctr. of LA County, 1991-92, mem. bd. govs., 1996-98, hon. gov. 1998—; mem. contemporary art com. Harvard U. Art Mus., Cambridge, Mass., 1992-2004; mem. internat. dirs. coun. Guggenheim Mus., NYC, 1993-98; trustee Mus. Modern Art, NYC, 2004—; active Nat. Indsl. Pollution Control Coun., 1970-73, Maeght Found., St. Paul de Vence, France, 1975-80, Mayor's Spl. Adv. Com. on Fiscal Adminstrn., LA, 1993-94; bd. dirs. UCLA/Armand Hammer Mus. Art And Cultural Ctr., 1994-1999; co-founder Broad Found., 1999—; bd. regents Smithsonian Inst., 2004—. Recipient Man of Yr. award, City of Hope, 1965, Golden Plate award, Am. Acad. Achievement, 1971, Housing Man of Yr. award, Nat. Housing Coun., 1979, Humanitarian award, NCCJ, 1977, Am. Heritage award, Anti Defamation League, 1984, Pub. Affairs award Coro Found., 1987, Honors award, visual arts, L.A. Arts Coun., 1989, Lifetime Achievement award, LA C. of C., 1999, Visionary award, Harvard Bus. Sch. Assn. So. Calif., 1999, Visionary award, KCET, 1999, Julius award, U. So. Calif. Sch. Policy, Planning and Devel., 2001, Chmn.'s award, Asia Soc. So. Calif., 2000, Teach for Am. Ednl. Leadership award, 2001, Exemplary Leadership in Mgmt. award, UCLA, The Anderson Sch., 2002, Alexis de Tocqueville award, United Way, 2002, Brass Ring award United Friends the Children, 2003, Civic Medal Hon. LA C. of C., 2004, Earl Warren Outstanding Pub. Svc. award Am. Soc. Pub. Adminstrn. LA Metro. Chpt., 2004, Frederick R. Weisman award Ams. for the Arts, 2005, Svc. to Cmty. award Am. Inst. to Architects LA Chpt., 2005, Louise T. Blouin Found. award, 2006; named one of Top 200 Collectors, ARTnews Mag., 2004-08, World's Richest People, Forbes Mag., 1999—, Forbes Richest Americans, 1999—; Eli Broad Coll. Bus. and Eli Broad Grad. Sch. Bus. named in his honor, Mich. State U., 1991; Edythe and Eli Broad Art Ctr. named in his honor, UCLA; knighted Chevalier in Nat. Order Legion of Honor, France, 1994. Fellow: AAAS; mem.: Calif. Club, Hillcrest Country Club (LA),

Regency Club, Beta Alpha Psi. Avocation: Collecting contemporary art. Office: Broad Found Ste 1200 10900 Wilshire Blvd Los Angeles CA 90024 Office Fax: 310-954-5051.

BROADBENT, AMALIA SAYO CASTILLO, graphic arts designer; b. Manila, May 28, 1956; came to U.S., 1980, naturalized, 1985; d. Conrado Camilo and Eugenia de Guzman (Sayo) Castillo; m. Barrie Noel Broadbent, Mar. 14, 1981 (div. Apr. 1999); children: Charles Noel Castillo, Chandra Noel Castillo. BFA, U. Santo Tomas, 1978; postgrad., Acad. Art Coll., San Francisco, Alliance Francaise, Manila, Karilagan Finishing Sch., Manila Computer Ctr.; BA, Maryknoll Coll., 1972. Designer market rsch. Unicorp Export Inc., Makati, Manila, 1975-77; asst. advt. mgr. Dale Trading Corp., Makati, 1977-78; artist, designer, pub. rels. Resort Hotels Corp., Makati, 1978-81; prodn. artist CYB/Young & Rubicam, San Francisco, 1981-82; freelance art dir Ogilvy & Mather Direct, San Francisco, 1986; artist, designer, owner A.C. Broadbent Graphics, San Francisco, 1982—. Faculty graphic design and advt. depts. Acad. Art U., San Francisco. Works include: Daing na Isda, 1975, (Christmas coloring) Pepsi-Cola, 1964 (Distinctive Merit cert.), (children's books) UNESCO, 1973 (cert.). Pres. Pax Romana, Coll. of Architecture and Fine Arts, U. Santo Tomas, 1976-78, chmn. cultural sect., 1975; v.p. Atelier Cultural Soc., U. Santo Tomas, 1975-76; mem. Makati Dance Troupe, 1973-74; vol. spl. events San Francisco Mus. of Modern Art. Recipient Merit cert. Inst. Religion, 1977. Mem. Alliance Francaise de San Francisco. Roman Catholic. Office: 4380A Eagle Peak Rd Concord CA 94521-3427 Personal E-mail: amybroadbent@comcast.net.

BROADFOOT, ALBERT LYLE, physicist; b. Milestone, Sask., Can., Jan. 8, 1930; came to U.S., 1963; s. Morris Alexander and Lydia Georgina (Jacklin) B.; m. Katherine Eileen Deacon, Sept. 26, 1964; children: Alexander Lyle, Marilyn Louise. BE in Engring., Physics, U. Sask., Saskatoon, 1956, M.Sc. in Physics, 1960, PhD in Physics, 1963. Engr. Def. Rsch. Bd., Ottawa, Ont., Canada, 1956-58; jr. physicist space div. Kitt Peak Nat. Obs., Tucson, 1963-64, asst. physicist, 1964-68, assoc. physicist, 1968-70, physicist, 1971-79; rsch. scientist, assoc. physicist Earth and Space Scis. Inst., U. So. Calif., 1979-82; sr. rsch. scientist Lunar and Planetary Lab., U Ariz., Tucson, 1982—. Office: U Ariz Lunar and Planetary Lab 162 Sonett Space Scis Bldg Tucson AZ 85721-0001 Home: 202 N Cactus Loop Green Valley AZ 85614-3106 E-mail: alb@vega.lpl.arizona.edu.

BROADWATER, BRUCE A., mayor; b. Columbus, Ohio, Sept. 1, 1938; m. Peggy Broadwater; children: Josh, Jeremy AA, East L.A. Coll.; BA in Human Rels., U. San Francisco. Owner ins. agy., Garden Grove, Calif.; consumer complaint analyst Calif. Dept. Ins.; elected Garden Grove City Coun., 1992-94; elected mayor City of Garden Grove, 1994—, dep. labor commr., 2003—. Bd. dirs. Am. Host Found.; active scouting programs, Boy Scouts Am. With U.S. Army, 1957-59, Germany. Mem. Garden Grove C. of C. (past pres.).

BROCCHINI, RONALD GENE, architect; b. Oakland, Calif., Nov. 6, 1929; s. Gino Mario and Yoli Louise (Lucchesi) B.; m. Myra Mossman, Feb. 3, 1957; 1 child, Christopher Ronald BA in Architecture with honors, U. Calif., Berkeley, 1953, MA in Architecture with honors, 1957. Registered architect, Calif., Nev. Architect, designer SMP, Inc., San Francisco, 1948-53, designer, assoc., 1956-60; assoc. architect Campbell & Wong, San Francisco, 1961-63; prin. architect Ronald G. Brocchini, Berkeley, Calif., 1964-67, Worley K Wong & Ronald G Brocchini Assocs., San Francisco, 1968-87, Brocchini Architects, Berkeley, 1987—. Lectr. Calif. Coll. Arts and Crafts, Oakland, 1981-83; commr. Calif. Bd. Archtl. Examiners, 1961-89; mem. exam. com. Nat. Coun. Archtl. Registration Bds., 1983-85. Author: Long Range Master Plan for Bodega Marine Biology, U. Calif., 1982; prin. works include San Simeon Visitor Ctr., Hearst Castle, Calif., Mare Island Med.-Dental Facillity, IBM Ednl. and Data Processing Hdqrs., San Jose, Calif., Simpson Fine Arts Gallery, Calif. Coll. Arts, Ceramics and Metal Crafts, Emery Bay Pub. Market Complex, Analytical Measurement Facility, U. Calif., Berkeley, Bodega Marine Biology Campus, U. Calif., Berkeley, Fromm & Sichell (Christian Bros.) Hdqrs., The Nature Co., Corp. Offices, Berkeley, Merrill Coll., Athletic Facilities, U. Calif., Santa Cruz, Coll. III Housing, U. Calif., San Diego, Ctr. Pacific Rim Studies, U. San Francisco, married student housing Escondido II, III, IV, Stanford (Calif.) U. With U.S. Army, 1953-55. Recipient Bear of Yr. award U. Calif., Berkeley, 1987, Alumni Citation, 1988; recipient 22 Design Honor awards for architecture, Design award State of Calif. Dept. Rehab., 1995. Fellow AIA (bd. dirs. Calif. coun., pres. San Francisco chpt. 1982); mem. Bear Backers Club (bd. dirs. U. Calif.-Berkeley athletic coun.), Berkeley Breakfast Club (bd. govs.), Order of the Golden Bear, Chi Alpha Kappa. Republican. Roman Catholic. Avocations: auto restoration, photography, sports, art. Office: Brocchini Architects Inc 1600 Shattuck Ave Ste 224 Berkeley CA 94709

BROCK, ISAAC, musician; b. Issaquah, Wash., July 9, 1975; Guitarist & lead singer Modest Mouse, 1993—, Ugly Casanova. Singer: (albums) (with Modest Mouse) This is a Long Drive for Someone with Nothing to Think About, 1996, Lonesome Crowded West, 1997, The Fruit That Ate Itself, 1997, The Moon & Antarctica, 2000, Sad Sappy Sucker, 2001, Good News for People Who Love Bad News, 2004, We Were Dead Before the Ship Even Sank, 2007, (with Ugly Casanova) Sharpen Your Teeth, 2002; prodr. (for Wolf Parade) Apologies to the Queen Mary, 2005, Wolf Parade, 2005; actor: (films) Christmas on Mars, 2005. Named to Rock & Roll Hall of Fame (with Metallica), 2009. Office: c/o Up Records Box 21328 Seattle WA 98111 also: c/o Epic Records 550 Madison Ave New York NY 10022 Office Phone: 206-320-9004. Office Fax: 206-320-9075.

BROCKLEY, JOHN P., airport terminal executive; Dir. aviation Port of Portland, Oreg. Home: 2077 Bay Meadows Drive West Linn OR 97068-2288

BROCKOVICH-ELLIS, ERIN, legal researcher; b. Lawrence, Kans., June 22, 1960; d. Frank and Betty Jo Pattee; m. Shawn Brown, 1982 (div. 1987); children: Matthew, Katie; m. Steven Brockovich, 1989 (div. 1990); 1 child, Elizabeth; m. Eric A. Ellis, Mar. 1999. Student, Kans. State U.; MA (hon.), Jones Internat. U.; LLD (hon.), Lewis A. Clark Law Sch., 2005; LHD, Loyola Marymount U., 2007. Management trainee K-Mart, Calif.; electrical engineer trainee Fluor Engineers and Constructors; sec. E.F. Hutton, Reno; former file clerk Masry & Vititoe, Westlake Village, Calif., dir. rsch., exec. cons.; pres. Brockovich Rsch. and Cons., 2006—. Cons. Girardi & Keese, Weitz & Luxenberg, 2008—; lectr. in field. Co-author (with Marc Eliot): Take It From Me: Life's a Struggle, But You Can Win, 2001; actor: (films) Erin Brockovich, 2000; (TV series) Challenge America, 2001, Final Justice, 2003. Recipient Scales of Justice award, Ct. TV, Spl. Citizen award, The Children's Health Environmental Coalition, Mothers & Shakers award, Redbook mag., Lifesaver award, Lymphoma Rsch. Found. Am., World Social Nominations award, 2004, 2005, Julius B. Richmond award, Harvard Sch. Pub. Health, 2005, Profiles in Courage award, Santa Clara Trial Lawyers Assn.; named Ms. Pacific Coast, 1981. Achievements include spearheaded largest toxic tort injury settlement in US history, 1996; settled second case for $335 million, 2006; subject of hit movie "Erin Brockovich", 2000. Office: c/o William Morris Agy 151 El Camino Dr Beverly Hills CA 90212 Office Phone: 818-991-8900. Personal E-mail: erin@bokovich.com.

BROD, FRANK H., computer software company executive, accountant; B in Industrial Mgmt., Ill. Inst. Tech. Corp. v.p., controller The Dow Chemical Co.; corp. v.p. fin. and adminstrn., chief accounting officer Microsoft Corp., Redmond, Wash., 2006—. Mem. Emerging Issues Task Force, Fin. Accounting Standards Bd.; immediate past chair Tech. Com. on Corp. Reporting, Fin. Execs. Internat.; mem. Standards Adv. Group, Pub. Co. Accounting Oversight Bd. (PCAOB), Standards Adv. Coun., Internat. Accounting Standard Bd. Recipient Sells Award, Am. Inst. of CPAs, Allred Award, Tex. Soc. of CPAs for Profl. Excellence. Office: Microsoft Corp One Microsoft Way Redmond WA 98052-6399

BRODERSEN, ROBERT W., engineering educator; BSEE, BS in Math., Calif. State Polytechnic U., 1966; MS in Engring., MIT, 1968, PhD in Engring., 1972. Mem. technical staff Ctrl. Rsch. Lab. Texas Instruments, 1972-76; prof. dept. elec. engring. and computer scis. U. Calif., Berkeley, 1976—, John R. Whinnery chair, 1995—. Nat. chair Info. Sci. and Tech. Study Group, 1992-94. Contbr. articles to profl. jours., chpts. to books including Anatomy of a Silicon Compiler, 1992, Low Power Digital CMOS Design, 1995; patentee in field. Recipient Best Paper award Eascon, 1973, Internat. Solid States Circuits Conf., 1975, European Solid-States Circuits Conf., 1978. Fellow IEEE (editl. bd. various jours., Morris Libermann award 1983, Solid-States Circuits award 1997); mem. Nat. Acad. Engring. Achievements include research in application of integrated circuits as applied to personal communication systems. Office: U Calif Dept EECS 402 Cory Hl # 1770 Berkeley CA 94720-0001

BRODSKY, STANLEY JEROME, physics educator, consultant; b. St. Paul, Jan. 9, 1940; s. Sidney Charles and Esther (Levitt) Brodsky; children: Stephen Andrew, David Jonathan; m. Judith Ellen Preis, June 29, 1986. BS in Physics, U. Minn., 1961, PhD in Physics, 1964. Rsch. assoc. Columbia U., NYC, 1964-66, Stanford Linear Accelerator Ctr., Stanford U., Menlo Park, Calif., 1966-68, mem. permanent staff theoretical physics, 1968-75, assoc. prof., 1975-76, prof., 1976—, head theoretical physics grp., 1996—2002. Vis. AVCO assoc. prof. physics dept. Cornell U., 1970; vis. prof. natural scis. Inst. Advanced Study, Princeton, 1982; mem. sci. and ednl. adv. com. Lawrence Berkeley Lab., U. Calif., 1986-92; vis. prof. Max Planck Inst. Nuc. Physics, Heidelberg, Germany, 1987-88, Coll. William and Mary, 2003; lectr., disting. spkr. colloquium series U. Minn., 1989, Duke U., 1997; mem. prog. adv. com. Gesellschaft für Schwerionenforschung mbH, Darmstadt, Germany, 2004-, Brookhaven Nat. Lab., 2003-06; Disting. fellow Thomas Jefferson Lab., 2003; mem. sci. adv. bd. Hadron Physics Integrated Infrastructure Initiative of European Commn., 2006-. Co-author: Lectures on Lepton Nucleon Scattering and Quantum Chromodynamics, 1982, Quarks and Nuc. Forces, 1982, Nuclear Chromodynamics, 1989; mem. bd. referees, editl. bd. Phys. Rev., Jour. Am. Physics, 1987—; assoc. editor Particle Physics, Nuc. Physics, 1993—. Mem. com. on fundamental cons. NRC, NAS, 1972-75; mem. exec. bd. Weizmann Inst. of Sci. Forum, 1977—; chmn. rev. panel for theoretical physics NSF, 1980-81. US/Israel Binational Found. grantee Weizmann Inst., 1986-90; recipient Sr. Disting. US Scientist award Alexander von Humboldt Found., 1987—. Fellow Am. Phys. Soc. (particles and fields divsn., vice-chair Hadronic Physics to Print Gr., 2008), J.J. Sakurai prize for Theoretical Particle Physics, 2007, Max Planck Inst. Nuc. Physics (external sci. mem.). Achievements include theoretical developments in elementary particles physics, especially exclusive processes in quantum chromodynamics, two photon processes and nuclear chromodynamics. Office: Stanford Linear Accelerator Ctr 2575 Sand Hill Rd Menlo Park CA 94025-7015 Business E-Mail: sjbth@slac.stanford.edu.

BRODY, ADAM JARED, actor; b. San Diego, Dec. 15, 1979; s. Mark Brody and Valerie Seifman. Attended, MiraCosta Coll., Oceanside, Calif. Actor: (TV films) Now What, 1995, The Sausage Factory, 2000, Growing Up Brady, 2000; (TV series) The Amanda Show, 1999, Undressed, 1999, Once and Again, 2000—01, Gilmore Girls, 2002—03, The O.C., 2003—07 (Teen Choice award for Choice TV Actor - Drama/Action Adventure, 2004, 2005, 2006); (films) Never Land, 2000, The Silencing, 2000, Roadside Assistance, 2001, American Pie 2, 2001, According to Spencer, 2001, The Ring, 2002, Home Security, 2003, Grind, 2003, Missing Brendan, 2003, Mr. & Mrs. Smith, 2005, Thank You for Smoking, 2005, In the Land of Women, 2007, The Ten, 2007, Smiley Face, 2007, Death in Love, 2008. Avocations: surfing, basketball. Office: c/o Endeavor Agy 9601 Wilshire Blvd 3rd Fl Beverly Hills CA 90212

BRODY, WILLIAM RALPH, academic administrator, radiologist, educator; b. Stockton, Calif., Jan. 4, 1944; m. Wendy Brody; 2 children. BSEE, MIT, 1965, MSEE, 1966; MD, Stanford U., 1970, PhD in Elec. Engring., 1975. Intern to resident and fellow dept. cardiovasc. surgery Stanford U. Sch. Medicine, Calif., 1970—73, tng. med. fellow cardiovasc. surgery, resident diagnostic radiology, 1975—77, assoc. prof. to prof. dept. radiology, dir. rsch. labs., 1977—86; with USPHS Nat. Heart, Lung, and Blood Inst., Balt., 1973—75; prof. Stanford U., 1982—84; founder, pres., CEO Resonex, Inc., 1984—87, chmn. bd. dirs., 1987—89; radiologist-in-chief Johns Hopkins Hosp., Balt., 1987—94; mem. staff depts. elec., computer engring., biomedical engring. Johns Hopkins U. Sch. Medicine, 1987—94, Martin Donner prof., dir. dept. radiology, 1987—94; prof. radiology, provost U. Minn. Acad. Health Ctr., 1994—96, spl. asst. to pres., 1996; pres. Johns Hopkins U., 1996—2008, Salk Inst. for Biological Studies, La Jolla, 2009—. Bd. dir. Medtronic Inc., Merc. Bankshares; mem. Pres.'s Fgn. Intelligence adv. bd. Contbr. articles to profl. jours. Mem. sci. adv. com. Whitaker Found., 1992—97, governing com., 1997—; fellow coun. cardiovasc. radiology Am. Heart Assn.; mem. internat. adv. bd. Nat. U. Singapore Inst. Sys. Sci., 1994—97; trustee Goldseker Found., 1996; mem. internat. acad. adv. panel, 1997; bd. dirs. Greater Balt. Com., 1997; trustee Balt. Mus. Art, 1997. Recipient Established Investigator award, Am. Heart Assn., 1980—84. Fellow: NAS (Inst. Medicine), IEEE, Am. Acad. Arts & Scis., Am. Inst. Med. and Biomedical Engring., Am. Coll. Cardiology, Am. Coll. Radiology; mem.: NAE, Internat. Soc. Magnetic Resonance in Medicine. Achievements include patents in field. Office: Salk Inst for Biological Studies Office of Pres PO Box 85800 San Diego CA 92186-5800 Office Phone: 858-453-4100 1261. E-mail: wrbrody@salk.edu.*

BROGDEN, STEPHEN RICHARD, library director; b. Des Moines, Sept. 26, 1948; s. Paul M. and Marjorie (Kueck) B.; m. Melinda L. Raine, Jan. 1, 1983; 1 child, Nathan. BA, U. Iowa, 1970, MA, 1972. Caretaker Eya Fechin Branham Ranch, Taos, N.Mex., 1970-72; dir. Harwood Found. U. N.Mex., Taos, 1972-75; vis. lectr. U. Ariz., Tucson, 1975-76; rd. mgr. Bill and Bonnie Hearne, Austin, Tex., 1976-79; head fine arts Pub. Libr. Des Moines, 1980-90; dep. dir. Thousand Oaks (Calif.) Libr., 1990-99, dir., 1999—; bd. mem. Folk Alliance Region West, 2008—. Chair Met. Coop. Libr. Sys., 2001; bd. mem. Pacific Pioneer Broadcasters, 2005—. Author book revs., Annals of Iowa, 1980; columnist Taos News, 1973. V.p. Hospice of the Conejo, 2004—05; bd. dirs. Thousand Oaks Libr. Found., 1999—; bd. mem. Pacific Pioneer Broadcasters, 2005—. Mem. ALA, Calif. Libr. Assn., Films for Iowa Librs. (pres. 1983-86), Metro Des Moines Libr. Assn. (pres. 1980). Office: Thousand Oaks Libr 1401 E Janss Rd Thousand Oaks CA 91362-2199 Office Phone: 805-449-2660 ext. 215. Business E-Mail: sbrogden@mx.tol.lib.ca.us.

BROGLIATTI, BARBARA SPENCER, retired television and motion picture executive, consultant; b. LA, Jan. 8, 1946; d. Robert and Lottie Spencer; m. Raymond Haley Brogliatti, Sept. 19, 1970. BA in Social Scis. and English, UCLA, 1968. Asst. press. info. dept. CBS TV, LA, 1968-69, sr. publicist, 1969-74; dir. publicity Tandem Prodns. and T.A.T. Comm. (Embassy Comm.), LA, 1974-77, corp. v.p., 1977-82; sr. v.p. worldwide publicity, promotion and advt. Embassy Comm., LA, 1982-85; sr. v.p. worldwide corp. comm. Lorimar Telepictures Corp., Culver City, Calif., 1985-89; pres., chmn. Brogliatti Co., Burbank, Calif., 1989-90; sr. v.p. worldwide TV publicity, promotion and advt. Lorimar TV, 1991-92; sr. v.p. worldwide TV publicity, promotion and pub. rels. Warner Bros., Burbank, 1992-97; sr. v.p. corp. comm. Warner Bros., Inc., 1997-2000; sr. v.p., chief corp. comm. officer Warner Bros. Entertainment Inc., 2000—04; exec. v.p., chief corp. comm. officer Warner Bros., 2004—05; ret., 2008. Pub. rels. cons. Alliance of Motion Picture and Television Prodr., 1980—; advisor com. acad. advanced program UCLA, 2002—; bd. govs. UCLA Found., 2003—; adj. prof. comm. Bradley U., Peoria, Ill., 2006—; cons. pub. rels. Alliance of Motion Picture and TV Prodrs., 1980—; bd. mem. MEND Poverty, 2009—. Mem. bd. govs. TV Acad., LA, 1984-86, UCLA Found., 2003—; bd. dir. Nat. Acad. Cable Programming, 1992-94; mem. Hollywood Women's Polit. Com., 1992-93; mem. steering com. LA Free Clinic, 1997-98. Recipient Gold medal Broadcast Promotion and Mktg. Execs., 1984. Mem. Am. Diabetes Assn. (bd. dir. LA chpt. 1992-93), Am. Cinema Found. (bd. dir. 1994-98), Dir. Guild Am., Publicists Guild, Acad. TV Arts and Scis. (vice chmn. awards com.); adv. com. UCLA Acad. Advancement Prog.

BROKAW, MEREDITH A., women's health care company director; BA, English and Comm., U. SD; LLD (hon.), St. John's U. Founder Penny Whistle Toys, Inc., 1978-97; dir. Women First HealthCare, Inc., San Diego, 1998—. Dir. Gannett Co., Inc. Author 8 books on parenting and children's activities. Trustee Bank Street Coll. Edn., Ednl. Broadcasting Corp., Conservation Internat.

BROKAW, NORMAN ROBERT, talent agency executive; b. NYC, Apr. 21, 1927; s. Isadore David and Marie (Hyde) B.; children: David M., Sanford Jay, Joel S., Barbara M., Wendy E., Lauren Quincy. Student pvt. schs., Los Angeles. With William Morris Agy., Inc., Beverly Hills, Calif., 1943—, sr. agt. and co. exec., 1951-74, v.p. world-wide ops., 1974-80, exec. v.p., dir., 1980—, co-chmn. bd., 1986-91, pres., CEO, 1989-91, chmn. bd., CEO, 1991-97, chmn. bd. worldide, 1997—2007; chmn. emeritus, 2008—. Pres. Betty Ford Cancer Ctr., Cedars-Sinai Med. Ctr., L.A., 1978—; bd. dirs. Cedars-Sinai Med. Ctr.; industry chmn. United Jewish Welfare Fund, 1975. With U.S. Army, World War II. Mem. Acad. Motion Picture Arts and Scis., Hillcrest Country Club (L.A.). Clients, past and present, include former Pres. and Mrs. Gerald R. Ford, Bill Cosby, Gen. Alexander Haig Jr., Gen. Claudia Kennedy, Tony Randall, Donald Regan, Senator John Edwards, Senator James Jeffords, Attorney David Boies, C. Everett Koop, Kim Novak, Priscilla Presley, Andy Griffith, Senator Fred Thompson, Juliette Lewis, Marcia Clark, Christopher Darden; former clients included Marilyn Monroe, Barbara Stanwyck, Susan Hayward. Office: William Morris Agy 1 William Morris Pl Beverly Hills CA 90212-2775 also: William Morris Agy Inc 1325 Avenue Of The Americas New York NY 10019-6026

BROM, ROBERT HENRY, bishop; b. Arcadia, Wis., Sept. 18, 1938; Student, St. Mary's Coll., Winona, Minn., Gregorian U., Rome. Ordained priest Diocese of Winona, Minn., 1963; bishop Diocese of Duluth, Minn., 1983—89, ordained bishop, 1983; coadjutor bishop Diocese of San Diego, 1989—90, bishop, 1990—. Roman Catholic. Office: Diocese of San Diego Pastoral Ctr PO Box 85728 San Diego CA 92186-5728 Office Phone: 858-490-8200. Office Fax: 858-490-8272.

BROMSTAD, ANGELA, broadcast executive; married; 2 children. B, U. So. Calif. Asst. Telepictures Productions; dir. creative affairs Freyda Rothstein Productions, 1988—91, v.p. creative affairs, 1991—94; dir. miniseries & motion pictures for television NBC Entertainment, 1994—96, v.p. miniseries & television, 1996; v.p. miniseries & motion pictures for television NBC Studios, 1997—99, v.p. primetime series, 1999—2000, v.p. drama devel., 2000, sr. v.p. drama devel., 2000—03, exec. v.p., 2003—04; co-pres. NBC Universal TV Studio (name changed to Universal Media Studios, 2007), 2004—05, pres., 2005—07; pres. primetime entertainment NBC & Universal Studios, 2008—. Named one of The 100 Most Powerful Women in Entertainment, The Hollywood Reporter, 2006. Office: NBC Universal Studios 100 Universal City Plz Universal City CA 91608 Office Phone: 818-777-1000.*

BRONESKY, JOSEPH J., lawyer; b. Milw., Aug. 6, 1947; m. Jacquelin A. Medina, Mar. 15, 1985; children: Jessica, Amanda, Antoinette. BA, Marquette U., 1969; JD, U. Chicago, 1972. Bar: Wis. 1972, U.S. Ct. Mil. Appeals 1974, U.S. Supreme Ct. 1975, Colo. 1977, U.S. Dist. Ct. Colo. 1977. Law clk. to judge Latham Castle U.S. Ct. Appeals 7th cir., Chgo., 1972-73; assoc. Sherman & Howard, Denver, 1976-80, ptnr., 1980—. Asst. editor U. Chgo. Law Review, 1971-72. Bd. dirs. Camp Fire Denver area coun. 1983-86, Montessori Sch. Denver, 1992-94, Mile Hi coun. Girl Scouts U.S., Denver, 1992—, fin. com. 1989—. Lt. JAGC USN, 1973-76. Mem. ABA, Colo. Bar Assn., Colo. Trial Lawyers Assn. Roman Catholic. Avocations: skiing, bicycling, hiking. Office: Sherman & Howard 633 17th St Ste 3000 Denver CO 80202-3665

BRONSON, JOSEPH R., manufacturing company executive; BS in Acctg., Fairfield U.; MBA, U. Conn. CPA. With Schlumberger Ltd., 1979—84, group controller, 1983—84; v.p., CFO, Kubota Pacific Computer, Stardent Computer Inc., 1989—90; corp. controller Applied Materials Inc., Santa Clara, Calif., 1984, v.p., gen. mgr. implant divsn., 1990, group v.p. worldwide mfg. ops., 1994, group v.p., 1996, CFO, 1998—2000, exec. v.p., CFO, 2000—04; bd. dir. Form Factor Inc., Livermore, Calif., 2002—, pres., mem. office of chief exec., 2004—. Bd. dir. Jacob Engring. Group, Advanced Energy Industries. Chmn. adv. bd. Leavey Sch. Bus., Santa Clara, Calif. Office: Form Factor Inc 7005 S Front Rd Livermore CA 94551

BRONSTEIN, ARTHUR J., linguistics educator; b. Balt., Mar. 15, 1914; s. Gershon and Bessie B.; m. Elsa Meltzer, May 15, 1941; children: Nancy Ellen, Abbot Alan. BA, CCNY, 1934; MA, Columbia U., 1936; PhD, NYU, 1949. Vis. scholar and rsch. assoc. in linguistics U. Calif., Berkeley, 1987—; prof. Queens Coll., NYC, 1938-67; Fulbright prof. U. Tel Aviv, (Israel), 1967-68, U. Trondheim, (Norway), 1979; prof. linguistics Lehman Coll. and Grad. Sch., CUNY, 1968-83, prof. emeritus, 1983—; exec. officer PhD program in speech and hearing scis. CUNY, 1969-72; exec. officer Ph.D. program in linguistics Grad. Sch., CUNY, 1981-83; cons. in field; with dept. linguistics U. Calif., Berkeley. Author: Pronunciation of American English, 1960, Essays in Honor of C.M. Wise, 1970, Biographical Dictionary of the Phonetic Sciences, 1977; project dir.: Dictionary of American English Pronunciation Served with Signal Corps and AGD USAAF, 1942-46. Fellow Am. Speech and Hearing Assn., Internat. Soc. Phonetic Scis., Dictionary Soc. N.Am., N.Y. Acad. Sci.; mem. MLA, Linguistics Soc. Am., Am. Dialect Soc., Internat. Phonetic Assn., Am. Assn. Phonetic Scis., Phi Beta Kappa. Office: U Calif Dept Linguistics Berkeley CA 94720-0001 E-mail: arthurb@socrates.berkeley.edu.

BRONSTEIN, PHIL, publishing executive; b. 1950; s. Roan Joseph Bronstein; m. Sharon Stone, Feb. 14, 1998 (div. Jan. 29, 2004); 1 adopted child, Roan Joseph. Reporter Sta. KQED-TV, San Francisco; reporter, fgn. corr. San Francisco Examiner, 1980-90, mng. editor-news, 1990—91, exec. editor, 1991—2000; sr. v.p., exec. editor San Francisco Chron., 2000—03, editor, 2003—08, exec. v.p., 2003—, editor-at-large, 2008—, Hearst Newspapers, 2008—. Mem.: Am. Soc. Newspaper Editors (chmn. Internat. com. 2003—04). Office: San Francisco Chronicle 901 Mission St San Francisco CA 94103 also: Hearst Newspapers 959 8th Ave New York NY 10019 E-mail: pbronstein@sfchronicle.com.

BRONSTER, MARGERY S., retired state attorney general, lawyer; b. NY, Dec. 12, 1957; married; 1 child. BA in Chinese Lang., Lit. and History, Brown U., 1979; JD, Columbia U., 1982. Bar: N.Y. 1983, Hawaii 1988, U.S. Dist Ct. (So. & Ea. N.Y. & Hawaii dist.), U.S. Tax Ct., U.S. Ct. Appeals (Ninth & Eleventh cir.). Assoc. Sherman & Sterling, NY, 1982—87; ptnr. Carlsmith, Ball, Wichman, Murray, Case & Ichiki, Honolulu, 1988—94; atty. gen. State of Hawaii, 1994—99; ptnr. Bronster Crabtree & Hoshibata, Honolulu, 1999—. Co-chair planning com. Citizens Conf. Jud. Selection, 1993; chair State of Hawaii Tobacco Prevention & Control Adv. Bd. Author: Litigating a Class Action Suit in Hawaii, 2001. Mem. nat. gov. bd. Common Cause. Recipient Fellow of the Pacific award, Hawaii Pacific Univ., 2000, Profiles in Courage award, SW Bell Conf. We. Atty. Gen., 2000, Advocate of the Year, Hawaii Cancer Soc., 1999, Kelley-Wyman Atty. Gen. of Yr. award, Nat. Assn. Atty. Gen., 1999, Top Cop award, State of Hawaii Law Enforcement Coalition, 1999, Hawaii Woman Lawyer of the Year, Hawaii Women Lawyers, 1998, Tommy Holmes award, Sex Abuse Treatment Ctr., 1998; scholar Harlan Fisk Stone. Office: Bronster Crabtree Hoshibata Suite 2300 Pauahi Tower 1001 Bishop St Honolulu HI 96813 Home Phone: 808-739-2513; Office Phone: 808-524-5644. Business E-Mail: mbronster@bchlaw.net.

BROOK, ROBERT HENRY, public health service officer, internist, educator; b. NYC, July 3, 1943; s. Benjamin and Elizabeth (Berg) Brook; m. Susan Jean Weiss, June 26, 1966 (div. 1980); children: Rebecca, Daniel; m. Jacqueline Barbara Kosecoff Plaut, Jan. 17, 1982; children: Rachel, Davida. BS, U. Ariz., 1964; MD, Johns Hopkins U., 1968, ScD, 1972. Diplomate Am. Bd. Internal Medicine. Intern Balt. City Hosp., 1968—69, resident in medicine, 1969—72; project officer Nat. Ctr. Health Svcs. Rsch., HEW, Washington, 1972—74; vice-chmn. medicine UCLA, 1990—92, dir. clin. scholar program, 1974—, prof. of medicine and pub. health, Ctr, for Health Svcs., 1974—; dir. health program RAND Corp., Santa Monica, Calif., 1990—, v.p., 1998—, corp. fellow. Mem. editl. bd.: Health Adminstrn. Press, 1986—92, Jour. Gen. Internal Medicine, 1987—89, Health Policy, 1986—; published (article) Defining and Measuring Quality Care: A Perspective from US Researchers (Peter Reizenstein prize, 2000); contbr. articles to profl. jours. Dir. Robert Wood Johnson Clin. Scholars Program; chair of panel to advise Statewide Health Planning and Develop., Calif. office, 2002. Asst. surgeon USPHS, 1972—76. Recipient Rsch. prize, Baxter Found. Health Svcs., 1988, Robert J. Glaser award, Soc. Gen. Internal Medicine, Gustav O. Lienhard award for the advancement of personal health services, Inst. Medicine, 2005; named one of one of 75 pub. health heroes of Johns Hopkins U., 1991; fellow Lita Annenberg Biomed. fellow, Inst. Humanistic Studies, 1981. Fellow: ACP (Richard and Hinda Rosenthal Found. award); mem.: Western Assn. Physicians, Johns Hopkins Soc. Scholars, Assn. Am. Physicians, Assn. Health Svcs. Rsch. (bd. dirs. 1982—89, Disting. Health Svc. Rschr. award), Am. Soc. Clin. Investigation, Inst. Medicine NAS. Democrat. Jewish. Home: 1474 Bienveneda Ave Pacific Palisades CA 90272-2346 Office: Rand Corp 1700 Main St Santa Monica CA 90401-3297 Office Phone: 310-393-0411 ext. 7368. Business E-Mail: robert-brook@rand.org.

BROOKS, ALBERT (ALBERT EINSTEIN), actor, writer, film director; b. Los Angeles, July 22, 1947; s. Harry and Thelma (Leeds) Einstein. Appeared in films Taxi Driver, 1976, Private Benjamin, 1980, Twilight Zone-The Movie, 1983, Unfaithfully Yours, 1983, Terms of Endearment, 1983, Broadcast News, 1987 (Acad. award nominee Best Supporting Actor), I'll Do Anything, 1994, The Scout, 1994, Critical Care, 1997, Out of Sight, 1998, Dr. Dolittle (voice), 1998, The In-Laws, 2003, Finding Nemo (voice), 2003; dir., writer, actor films Real Life, 1979, Modern Romance, 1982, Lost in America, 1985, Defending Your Life, 1991, Mother, 1996, Out of Sight, 1998, The Muse, 1999, My First Mister, 2001; writer, actor The Scout, 1994, Critical Care, 1997; TV appearances include The Tonight Show, Merv Griffin Show, Steven Allen Show, Gold Diggers, The Simpsons (voice only) 1993; dir., writer short films Saturday Night Live, 1975-76; recs. include Comedy Minus One, A Star is Bought (Grammy nomination). Office: c/o William Morris Agy One William Pl Beverly Hills CA 90212

BROOKS, BRAD, computer software company executive; M in Internat. Mgmt., Thunderbird Sch. Global Mgmt. Mktg. exec. Enron, Lucent Technologies, AT&T; joined Microsoft Corp., Redmond, Wash., 2002, gen. mgr. product mktg. Windows Bus. Group, corp. v.p. Windows Consumer Product Mktg., 2008—. Office: Microspft Corp One Microsoft Way Redmond WA 98052-6399

BROOKS, CHARLES LEE, III, computational biophysicist, educator; b. Detroit, May 14, 1956; married; 2 children. BS in Chemistry and Physics, Alma Coll., Mich., 1978; PhD in Physical Chemistry, Purdue U., 1982. Postdoc. fellow Harvard U., Boston, 1982-85, NIH, 1983-85; from asst. prof. to prof. Carnegie Mellon U., 1985—94, prof., 1994—; prof. molecular biology Scripps Rsch. Inst., 1994—. Mem. spl. rev. panels, site visit coms., mem. reviewers reserve Cell Biology & Biophysics Divsn. A study section, NIH; reviewer, mem. cellular and molecular biophysics panel, NSF; mem. adv. bd. Nat. Biomed. Computation Resource Inst., San Diego Supercomputing Ctr., sr. fellow, 1997; presenter in field. Mem. editl. bd. Proteins, 1995—, Biochimica et Biophysica Acta, 2000—, Physical Chemistry Chemical Physics, 2000—; editor: Jour. Computational Chemistry, 2004; contbr. over 200 articles to profl. jours.; author 1 book, several book chpts. A.P. Sloan fellow, 1990-93, AAAS, 2000; grantee Swedish Rsch. Coun., 1992. Office: Scripps Rsch Inst Dept Molecular Biology TPC6 10550 N Torrey Pines Rd La Jolla CA 92037-1000 Business E-Mail: brooks@scripps.edu.

BROOKS, JOHN WHITE, lawyer; b. Long Beach, Calif., Sept. 3, 1936; s. John White and Florence Belle (O'Grady) B.; m. Elizabeth Ann Bellmore, June 21, 1958; children: Stephen Sanford, John Tinley. AB, Stanford U., 1958, LLB, 1966. Assoc. Luce, Forward, Hamilton and Scripps, San Diego, 1966-71, ptnr., 1971-81, sr. ptnr., 1981—2004, sr. internat. counsel, 2004—; founding chmn. Internat. Svcs. Group, 1989—. Mem. Internat. Coun. Inst. Ams., Pacific Coun. Internat. Policy. 1996-98; panelist Ctr. for Internat. Comml. Arbitration, 1987—; bd. dirs. Union of Pan-Asian Communities,, 1989-98, Ctr. for Dispute Resolution, 1986—; chmn. Pacific Rim Adv. Coun., 1984-91. Author: Passport Pal, The Pacific Rim, 1996-2000, The Heads Up Report, International Corporate Compliance & Due Diligence Primer, 2008; contbr. articles to profl. jours. Mem. Commn. of the Californias, 1977—79; chmn. San Diego Regional Yr. 2000 Working Group, 1998—2000; dir. Corp. Fin. Coun. of San Diego, 1977—82, chmn., 1980—81; bd. visitors Stanford Law Sch., 1978—80. Lt. USN, 1958—63. Alfred P. Sloan scholar, Stanford U., 1958, Rocky Mountain Mineral Law Found. Research scholar, 1966. Mem. ABA (bus. law sect., com. on internat. commercial transactions, subcom. on Asia-Pacific law and internat. bus. structures and agreements, com. on negotiated transactions, internat. law sect., subcom. on multinat. corps., com. on internat. comml. Transactions, com. on corp. compliance, subcom. on compliance set-up and structure, subcom. on developing codes of conduct and compliance policies), Calif. Bar Assn. (bus. law sect. com. on corps. 1977, vice chmn. com. on internat. practice 1986-87, exec. com. internat. law sect. 1987), San Diego County Bar Assn., Internat. Bar Assn. (com. on issues and trading in securities 1980-89, com. on procedures for settling disputes 1980—, com. on bus. orgns. 1989—), Inter-Pacific Bar Assn. (com. on internat. trade), Am. Arbitration Assn. (panel of arbitrators 1975-96), State Bar Calif. Avocations: greenhouse gardening, horse competitions, helicopters, wine, food. Office: Luce Forward Hamilton & Scripps 600 W Broadway Ste 2600 San Diego CA 92101-3372 Office Phone: 619-699-2410. Business E-Mail: jwbrooks@luce.com.

BROOKS, MEL, film producer and director, actor, scriptwriter; b. June 28, 1926; Author: sketch Of Fathers and Sons in New Faces of 1952, 1957, sketch Shinbone Alley; co-author: sketch All American, 1962; writer (TV series) Your Show of Shows, also Caesar's Hour, The Sid Caesar, Imogene Coca, Carl Reiner, Howard Morris Special, 1967 (Emmy award for outstanding writing achievement in a comedy-variety), co-creator Get Smart, recordings include 2000 Years, 2000 and One Years, 2000 and Thirteen Years, 2000 Year Old Man in the Year 2000, 1997 (Grammy award for Best Spoken Word Album Comedy, 1998), writer, dir. (films) The Producers, 1968 (Acad. award for Best Original Screenplay), writer, dir., actor The Twelve Chairs, 1970, co-writer, dir., actor Blazing Saddles, 1974, Young Frankenstein, 1974, The Silent Movie, 1976, co-writer, dir., prodr., star Robin Hood: Men In Tights, 1993, Dracula: Dead and Loving It, 1995, prodr., dir., co-writer and star High Anxiety, 1977, Spaceballs, 1987, Life Stinks!, 1991, writer, dir., prodr., star History of the World-Part I, 1981, writer, narrator The Critic, 1964 (Acad. award for best animated short subject); actor(voice only): (films) Robots, 2005; actor, prodr. (films) To Be or Not To Be, 1983; prodr.: (films) 84 Charing Cross Road, 1987; prodr.: (films) The Elephant Man, 1980, Frances, 1982, My Favorite Year, 1982, Fly I, 1986, Fly II, 1989; guest actor (TV series) Mad About You (Emmy award for outstanding guest actor in a comedy series, 1997, 1998, 1999), co-writer, composer, prodr. (Broadway musical) The Producers, 2001 (3 Tony awards, Grammy nomination for best song written for motion picture, 2005), Young Frankenstein, 2007. Office: c/o The Culver Studios 9336 Washington Blvd Culver City CA 90232-2628

BROOKS, ROBERT EUGENE, decision support software designer; b. Chgo., June 13, 1946; s. Robert Eugene and Shirley Mae (Kunkel) B.; m. Tonya Thompson, Aug. 19, 1969; children: Shannon, Gabriel, Cyrus, Aleisha, Aaron, Ethan, David. AB in Arts and Scis., U. Calif., Berkeley, 1968; MA in Physics, U. Tex., 1972; PhD in Mgmt., MIT, 1975. Asst. prof. bus. U. So. Calif., LA, 1975—76; prin. Robert Brooks & Assocs., Norwalk, Calif., 1976-79; v.p. Transportation and Econ. Research Assocs., Washington, 1979-82; pres. RBAC, Inc., LA, 1982—84; v.p. software devel. Profit Mgmt. Devel. Inc., LA, 1984—87; ind. cons., 1987—. Cons. Arthur D. Little, Inc., Cambridge, Mass., 1972-75, Chase Econometrics, Bala Cynwyd, Pa., 1976, Mathematica, Inc., Princeton, N.J., 1977-78, 82, McDonnell-Douglas Corp., 1987-97, fed. and state govts., Washington, Sacramento, Austin, Tex., 1976-83, Logistic Solutions, 1990-95, Ventana Systems, 1987-97. Author: (computer models) GASNET, 1976, GASNET2, 1977, NETS, 1981, CMOTSIM, 1982; Profit Maker, 1986, GPCM, 1987. Mem. Inst. Mgmt. Scis. Mem. Ch. Scientology. Avocations: sports, music, new mathematics. Home: 20336 Howard Ct Woodland Hills CA 91364-5668

BROOKS, RUBEN B., judge; b. El Paso, Tex. BA, UCLA, 1971; JD, Yale U., 1974. Assoc. Page, Polin, Busch and Boatwright, 1983-93; magistrate judge U.S. Dist. Ct. (so. dist.) Calif., San Diego, 1993—. Mem. ABA, Calif. State Bar Assn., San Diego County Bar Assn., La Raza Lawyers Assn.

BROOMFIELD, ROBERT CAMERON, federal judge; b. Detroit, June 18, 1933; s. David Campbell and Mabel Margaret (Van Deventer) B.; m. Cuma Lorena Cecil, Aug. 3, 1958; children: Robert Cameron Jr., Alyson Paige, Scott McKinley. BS, Pa. State U., 1955; LLB, U. Ariz., 1961. Bar: Ariz. 1961, US Dist. Ct. Ariz. 1961. Assoc. Carson, Messinger, Elliot, Laughlin & Ragan, Phoenix, 1962-65, ptnr., 1966-71; judge Ariz. Superior Ct., Phoenix, 1971-85, presiding judge, 1974-85; judge US Dist. Ct. Ariz., Phoenix, 1985—, chief judge, 1994-99; judge Fgn. Intelligence Surveillance Ct. (FISC), 2002—. Faculty Nat. Jud. Coll., Reno, 1975-82. Contbr. articles to profl. jours. Adv. bd. Boy Scouts Am., Phoenix, 1968-75; tng. com. Ariz. Acad., Phoenix, 1980—; pres. Paradise Valley Sch. Bd., Phoenix, 1969-70; bd. dirs. Phoenix Together, 1982—, Crisis Nursery, Phoenix, 1976-81; chmn. 9th Cir. Task Force on Ct. Reporting, 1988—; space and facilities com. U.S. Jud. Conf., 1987-93, chmn., 1989-93, chmn. security, space and facilities com., 1993-95, budget com., 1997—, chmn. economy subcom., 2003—; founding mem. Sandra Day O'Connor Inn of Ct., 1988-94. Recipient Faculty award Nat. Jud. Coll., 1979, Disting. Jurist award Miss. State U., 1986, Disting. Citizen award U. Ariz. Alumni Assn., 2006. Mem. ABA (chmn. Nat. Conf. State Trial Judges 1983-84, pres. Nat. Conf. Met. Cts. 1978-79, chmn. bd. dirs. 1980-82, Justice Tom Clark award 1980, bd. dirs. Nat. Ctr. for State Cts. 1980-85, Disting. Svc. award 1986), Ariz. Bar Assn., Maricopa County Bar Assn. (Disting. Pub. Svc. award 1980), Ariz. Judges Assn. (pres. 1981-82), Am. Judicature Soc. (spl. citation 1985), Maricopa County Med. Soc. (Disting. Svc. medal 1979), Rotary. Office: US Dist Ct Sandra Day O'Connor Cthse 401 West Washington St #626 SPC 61 Phoenix AZ 85003-2158 Home Phone: 602-265-2068; Office Phone: 602-322-7540. Business E-Mail: robert_broomfield@azd.uscourts.gov.*

BROPHY, DENNIS RICHARD, psychology and philosophy professor, academic administrator, minister; b. Milw., Aug. 6, 1945; s. Floyd Herbert and Phyllis Marie (Ingram) B. BA, Washington U., 1967, MA, 1968; MDiv, Pacific Sch. Religion, 1971; PhD in Indsl. & Orgnl. Psychology, Tex. A&M U., 1995. Cert. coll. tchr., Calif. Ednl. rschr. IBM Corp., White Plains, NY, 1968—71; edn. minister Cmty. Congl. Ch., Port Huron, Mich., 1971—72, Bethlehem United Ch. Christ, Ann Arbor, Mich., 1972—73, Cmty. Congl. Ch., Chula Vista, Calif., 1974; philosophy instr. Southwestern Coll., Chula Vista, 1975; assoc. prof. psychology & philosophy Northwest Coll., Powell, Wyo., 1975—96, prof., 1996—, assessment testing coord., 1999—2007. Chmn. social sci. divsn., 1992-95; religious edn. cons. Mont.-No. Wyo. Conf. United Ch. of Christ. Mem. APA (Daniel Berlyne award 1996), Wyo. Coun. Humanities, Soc. Indsl. Orgnl. Psychology, Soc. Tchg. of Psychology, Yellowstone Assn. United Ch. Christ, Phi Beta Kappa, Phi Kappa Phi, Sigma Xi, Omicron Delta Kappa, Theta Xi, Golden Key Nat. Honor Soc. Faculty Outstanding Svc. award, 2003. Home: 533 Avenue C Powell WY 82435-2401 Office: Northwest Coll 231 W 6th St Powell WY 82435-1898 Office Phone: 307-754-6133. Business E-Mail: dennis.brophy@northwestcollege.edu.

BROPHY, GREG, state legislator; b. Sept. 6, 1966; m. Angela Brophy; children: Megan, Jordan, David. BS in Animal Scis., Colo. State U., Ft. Collins. Farmer; aide, Senator Wayne Allard US Senate; mem. Dist. 63 Colo. House of Reps., Denver, 2002—05; mem. Dist. 1 Colo. State Senate, Denver, 2005—, asst. minority leader. Mem. County & State Farm Bur., Colo. Republican. Office: Colo State Capitol 200 E Colfax Rm 271 Denver CO 80203 Office Phone: 303-866-6360. Business E-Mail: greg@gregbrophy.net.*

BRORBY, WADE, federal judge; b. Omaha, 1934; BS, U. Wyo., 1956, JD with honor, 1958. Bar: Wyo. County and prosecuting atty. Campbell County, Wyo., 1963—70; ptnr. Morgan Brorby Price and Arp, Gillette, Wyo., 1961—88; judge US Ct. Appeals (10th cir.), Cheyenne, Wyo., 1988—2001, sr. judge, 2001—. With USAF, 1958—61. Mem.: Wyo. Bar Assn. (commr. 1968—70), Campbell County Bar Assn. Office: US Ct Appeals 10th Cir PO Box 1028 Cheyenne WY 82003-1028 also: Byron White US Courthouse 1823 Stout St Denver CO 80257

BROSNAHAN, JAMES JEROME, lawyer; b. Boston, Jan. 12, 1934; s. James Jerome and Alice B. (Larkin) B.; m. Carol Simon, Nov. 8, 1958; children: Amy Rebecca, James Jerome III, Lisa Katherine. BBA, Boston Coll., 1956; LLB, Harvard U., 1959. Bar: Ariz. 1960, U.S. Ct. Appeals (9th cir.) 1961, Calif. 1963 (chmn. fed. courts commn. 1974-75), U.S. Dist. Ct. (no. dist.) Calif. 1964, U.S. Supreme Ct. 1970, U.S. Dist. Ct. (cen. dist.) Calif. 1974. Asst. U.S. atty. U.S. Dist. Ct. Ariz., Phoenix, 1961-63, U.S. Dist. Ct. (no. dist.) Calif., San Francisco, 1963-66; assoc. to ptnr. Cooper, White & Cooper, San Francisco, 1966-75; ptnr. Morrison & Foerster, San Francisco, 1975—. Spl. counsel Calif. Legislature Join Sub-Com. Crude Oil Pricing, 1973-74; chmn. Fed. Ctrs. com. State Bar Calif., 1974; chmn. del. U.S. Ct. Appeals (9th cir.) Jud. Conf., 1977-78, lawyer rep., 1977-79; mem. jud. coun. Calif. Adv. Com. on Gender Bias in the Cts., 1987-90; frequent lectr., panelist continuing legal edn. programs, various orgns., schs., and pub. interest groups. Author: Trial Handbook for California Trial Lawyers, 1974; contbr. articles to profl. jours. Treas. Mexican-Am. Legal Def. Fund, San Francisco, 1981-83, nat. bd. dirs. 1980-84; bd. dirs. ACLU, keynote speaker 1987; bd. dirs. Sierra Club Legal Def. Fund, 1974-77; bd. dirs. Legal Svcs. for Children, Inc., 1984—; civil adv. bd. Racketeer-Influenced and Corrupt Orgns., 1985—. With USAF, 1960. Named one of Five Best Attys. in San Francisco, San Francisco Examiner, 1980, one of 7200 Best Attys. in Am., 1987, one of 100 Powerful Lawyers, Nat. Law Jour., 1988, 1998, Legend of Law, Lawyers Club, San Francisco, 2002, one of the Top Ten Lawyers in Bay Area, San Francisco Chronicle, 1998, Best Lawyers in America, 2006, Top 10 Criminal Def. Lawyers, U.S. Lawyer Rankings, 2006, Top 100 Most Influential Lawyers in America, Nat. Law Jour., 2006, 500 Leading Litigators in America, The Law Dragon, 2006; recipient Am. Legal Def. and Edn. Legal Svcs award, 1985, MALDEF Legal Svcs. award, 1985, Polit. Parties and Dem. award, Meiklejohn award, 1986, Father Moriarty Cen. Am. Refugee Recognition award, 1987, Wm. O. Douglas award, 1988, Faculty award Nat. Inst. Trial Advocacy, Tree of Life award Jewish Nat. Fund, William J. Brennan Jr. award, U. Va., 2003, Champion of Justice award Loyola Law Sch. Marymount U., 2005. Fellow Am. Coll. Trial Lawyers (Samuel E. Gates Award, 2000), Internat. Acad. Trial Lawyers, Internat. Soc. Barristers, ABA Found.; mem. ABA (adv. com. to pres.-elect program on competency and contg. legal edn. 1979, active numerous panels, programs, convs., Pro Bono Publico award, 1987, sect. on individual rights and responsibilities), Calif. Bar Assn. (chmn. panel on cross-exam 1981), Am. Law Inst., Am. Bd. Trial Advs. (named Trial Lawyer of Yr., 2001), Nat. Inst. for Trial Advocacy (bd. trustees 1992), Bar Assn. San Francisco (past pres. 1977), Practicing Law Inst. (bd. dirs. 1975-77, chmn. com. on employment of minority 1988), Am. Judicature Soc. (bd. dirs.),

Calif. Attys. for Criminal Justice (bd. dirs. 1981-83, San Francisco bail projects 1987—), Am. Bd. Criminal Lawyers, Com. on Minority Employment, Am. Lawyers Newspapers Group, Inc. (nat. bd. of contbrs. 1988—), Harvard Law Sch. Alumni Assn., U.S. Supreme Ct. Hist. Soc. Nat. Products Unit Lawyers Coop. (Am. jurists editorial adv. bd.). Clubs: Barristers (San Francisco) (pres. 1968). Office: Morrison & Foerster LLP 425 Market St San Francisco CA 94105-2482 Office Phone: 415-268-7000. Business E-Mail: jbrosnahan@mofo.com.

BROSNAN, PETER LAWRENCE, documentary filmmaker; b. Bklyn., July 6, 1952; s. John Joseph and Audrey Barbara (Holran) B. BFA, NYU, NYC, 1974; MA, U. So. Calif., 1979, Pepperdine U., 1995. Documentary filmmaker, writer, LA, 1980—. Dir. DeMille Project, Hollywood Heritage, L.A., 1988—. Author: (screenplays) Heart of Darkness, 1992, The Ark, 1994, Perfect Target, 1996; co-author: (book) PML Report, 1989; writer: (documentary film) Ghosts of Cape Horn, 1980 (World Ship Trust award); prodr., dir.: (TV documentary) The Lost City, 1992; writer, segment prodr.: (PBS series) Faces of Culture, 1983-84 (Emmy award 1984), Writer Marketing, 1984 (Emmy award 1985); dir.: (documentary) Sand Castles, 1995, In Pro Per (comm. award 2005). Democrat. Personal E-mail: thxpete@mac.com.

BROTHERS, LYNDA LEE, lawyer; b. Palo Alto, Calif., Nov. 21, 1945; BS in genetics, U. Calif., Berkeley, 1968; MS in biochemical genetics, U. Va., 1971; JD, Golden Gate U., 1976. Bar: Calif. 1976, Wash. 1986. Counsel com. sci. and tech. subcom. environment and atmosphere US Ho. of Reps., Washington, 1977-79; dep. asst. sec. for environment US Dept. Energy, Washington, 1979-81; asst. dir. solid, hazardous and radioactive waste and air pollution Wash. Dept. Ecology, Olympia, 1984-86; with Heller, Ehrman, White & McAuliffe, Seattle, 1986-90; ptnr. Davis, Wright & Tremaine, Seattle, 1990—2000, Sonnenschein Nath & Rosenthal LLP, San Francisco, 2000—. Mem. Bd. on Radioactive Waste Mgmt. NRC, 1989—96. Mem. editorial bd. Golden Gate U. Law Rev., 1976; contbr. articles to sci. and legal jours. Mem. N.W. Citizens' Forum on High Level Nuclear Waste at Hanford, 1986-88; pres. Washington Environ. Found., 1983-90. Office Phone: 415-882-0344. Office Fax: 415-543-5472. Business E-Mail: lbrothers@sonnenschein.com.

BROTMAN, DAVID JOEL, architectural firm executive, consultant; b. Balt., Jan. 21, 1945; BS in Architecture, U. Cin., 1968. Registered arch. Ariz., Calif., Colo., D.C., Fla., Ga., Hawaii, La., Md., N.J., N.Y., Nev., Ohio, Oreg., Tex., Utah. Arch. Locke & Jackson, Balt., 1968, The Archtl. Affiliation, Towson, Md., 1968-75; joined RTKL, Balt., 1975-79, arch. Dallas, 1979-90, v.p., 1984—2000, exec. v.p., mng. dir. LA, 1990-2000, vice chmn., 1994-2000; prin. Sunset Consultants, Malibu, Calif., 2000—. Tchr. U. Tex. Sch. Architecture, Arlington, Catonsville (Md.) C.C.; arbitrator Am. Stock Exch., N.Y. Stock Exch., Nat. Assn. Security Dealers. Prin. works include Galleria at South Bay, Redondo Beach, Calif., Eton Sq. (Design Tex. Soc. Archs., 1986), Computer Sci. Corp., Fairfax County, Va., AT&T Customer Tech. Ctr., Dallas (Honor award Dallas chpt. AIA 1988), Tysons Corner Ctr., McLean Va. (Design award Monitor Ctrs. and Stores of Excellence 1989, Design award Internat. Shopping Ctrs. 1989, Exceptional Design award Fairfax County, Va. 1990, Modernization Excellence award Bldgs., 1990, Excellence award Urban Land Inst. 1992), St. Andrews (Scotland) Old Course Hotel, Tower City Ctr., Cleve., Eastland Shopping Ctr., Melbourne, Australia, Morley City Shopping Ctr., Perth, Australia, Dong An Market, Beijing, Desert Passage at Alladin, Las Vegas, Sci. and Tech. Mus., Shanghi, $25 Market St., San Francisco, many others; contbr. articles to profl. jours. Mem.: AIA (pres. Calif. coun. 2004, Calif. regional dir.), Urban Land Inst., Nat. Coun. Archtl. Registration Bds., Internat. Coun. Shopping Ctrs. Home Phone: 310-457-0931; Office Phone: 310-457-6048. Personal E-mail: sunset100@verizon.net.

BROTMAN, JEFFREY H., wholesale distribution executive; b. 1942; married; 2 children. BA in polit. sci., U. Wash., JD, 1967. Ptnr. Lasher-Brotman & Sweet, 1967-74; with ENI Exploration Co., 1975-83; co-founder Costco Wholesale Corp., 1983, chmn. bd., chief exec. officer, 1983-88, chmn. bd., 1988—93, vice chmn., 1993—94, chmn., 1994—. Dir. Starbucks, 1988—99, Garden Botanika, 1989—98, Seattle-First Nat. Bank, 1990—99, The Sweet Factory, Inc., 1992—98. Trustee Seattle Art Mus., 1990—, Seattle Found., 1991—, U. Wash. Med. Ctr. Bd., 1991—, King County United Way Bd., 1996—; co-chair King County United Way Campaign Bd., 1997—, chair, 1997; regent U. Wash., 1998—2004, v.p. bd. regents, 2002—03, chair bd. regents, fin. and audit com., 2000—. Office: Costco Wholesale 999 Lake Dr Issaquah WA 98027*

BROTMAN, MARTIN, gastroenterologist; b. Winnipeg, MB, Canada, June 26, 1939; MD, U. Manitoba, 1962. Diplomate Am. Bd. Internal Medicine, Gastroenterology Am. Bd. Internal Medicine. Intern Winnipeg Gen. Hosp., 1962—63; resident internal medicine Mayo Grad. Med. Sch., Rochester, Minn., 1963—65, fellow gastroenterology, 1965—67; med. adminstr. San Francisco; pvt. practice; chmn. med. dept. Calif. Pacific Med. Ctr., San Francisco, 1992—95, pres., CEO, 1995—, interim CEO St. Luke's Hosp., 2005. Clin. prof. med. U. Calif. San Francisco, 1982—. Mem.: AMA, ASGE, AASLD, Am. Soc. Internal Medicine, Am. Coll. Physicians, Am. Gastroentrol. Assn. (pres.-elect 2001—02, pres. 2002—03). Home: 2333 Buchanan P-1200 San Francisco CA 94115 Office: California Pacific Med Ctr PO Box 7999 San Francisco CA 94120 Address: Pacific Internal Med Ctr 2100 Webster St #423 San Francisco CA 94115-2380

BROWDER, JOHN GLEN, former congressman, educator; b. Sumter, SC, Jan. 15, 1943; s. Archie Calvin and Ila (Frierson); m. Sara Rebecca Moore; 1 child, Jenny Rebecca. BA in History, Presbyn. Coll., 1965; MA in Polit. Sci., PhD in Polit. Sci., Emory U., 1971. Asst. in pub. relations Presbyn. Coll., Clinton, S.C., 1965; sportswriter The Atlanta Jour., 1966; investigator U.S. Civil Service Commn., Atlanta, 1966-68; prof. polit. sci. Jacksonville (Ala.) State U., 1971-87; mem. Ala. Ho. of Reps., Montgomery, 1982-86; sec. of state State of Ala., Montgomery, 1987-89; mem. 101st-104th Congresses from 3d Ala. dist., Washington, 1989-96; disting. vis. prof. nat. security affairs Naval Postgrad. Sch., Monterey, Calif., 1997—; eminent scholar in Am. democracy Jacksonville State Univ., Ala., 1999—. Contbr. articles to newspapers, profl. jours.; author: Study Guide for The Future of American Democracy, 2004. Mem. Am. Polit. Sci. Assn., So. Polit. Sci. Assn. Democrat. Methodist. Office: Naval Postgrad Sch NS/BG Nat Security Affairs Dept Monterey CA 93943 E-mail: igbrowder@nps.navy.mil.

BROWER, GREGORY A., prosecutor, lawyer; b. South Milwaukee, Wis., Feb. 8, 1964; m. Loren Brower; children: Hayley, Kaitlin. AB, U. Calif. Berkeley, 1986; JD, George Washington U., 1992. Litig. assoc. Ropers, Majeski, Kohn & Bentley, San Francisco, 1992—94, Laxalt & Nomura, 1994—99; ptnr. Jones Vargas, 1999—2003; mem. Nevada State Assembly from Dist. 37, 1999—2001, minority whip, 2001; legis. counsel Exec. Office US Attorneys US Dept. Justice, 2003—04; inspector gen. US Govt. Printing Office, 2004—06, gen. counsel, 2006—07; US atty. Dist. Nev. US Dept. Justice, 2007—. Svc. warfare officer USN, 1987—89. Republican. Office: US Atty's Office 333 Las Vegas Blvd S Ste 5000 Las Vegas NV 89101

BROWN, ALAN J., electrical engineer; b. San Diego, Nov. 8, 1963; s. Vance E. and Doris C. B. BSEE, Calif. State U., Sacramento, 1987; MBA, U. San Diego, 1992. Registered profl. engr., Calif., Nev., Ariz. From engr. to pres. BSE Engring. (formerly Brown and Zammit Engring.), San Diego, 1987—. Mem. IEEE, Inst. Mgmt. Accts., Illuminating Engring. Soc. (pres. San Diego chpt. 1991-92), Soc. Mil. Engrs. (pres. San Diego post 1996-97), Internat. Assn. Electrical Inspectors. Office: Bse Engineering 9665 Chesapeake Dr Ste 365 San Diego CA 92123-1352

BROWN, AMOS CLEOPHILUS, minister; b. Jackson, Miss., Feb. 20, 1941; s. Louetta Robinson Brown; m. Jane Evangeline Smith, June 25, 1966; children: Amos Cleophilus, David Josephus, Kizzie Maria. BA, Morehouse Coll., Atlanta, 1964; MDiv, Crozer Sem., Chester, Pa., 1968; DMin, United Sem., Dayton, Ohio, 1990; DDiv, Va. Sem., Lynchburg, 1984. Ordained to ministry, Am. Bapt. Chs. and Nat. Bapt. USA, Inc., 1965. Pastor St. Paul's Bapt. Ch., West Chester, Pa., 1966-70, Pilgrim Bapt. Ch., St. Paul, 1970-76, Third Bapt. Ch., San Francisco, 1976—; mem. City and County of San Francisco Bd. Suprs., 1996—. Instr. philosophy Cheyney (Pa.) State Coll., 1968-70; nat. chmn. Nat. Bapt. Commn. on Civil Rights and Human Svcs., 1982—; chmn. Bay Area Ecumenical Pastors Conf., 1980—. Vice pres. governing bd. San Francisco Community Coll., 1987-89. Recipient Martin Luther King Ministerial award, Colgate Rochester Div. Sch., 1984, Man of the Yr., San Francisco Bus. and Profl. Women's Clubs, 1985. Mem. NAACP, Rotary, Masons, Alpha Phi Alpha. Democrat. Office: Third Bapt Ch 13499 McAllister St San Francisco CA 94117 also: Board of Suprs City Hall 1 Dr Carlton B Goodlett Pl San Francisco CA 94102-4603

BROWN, BARBARA BLACK, publishing company executive; b. Eureka, Calif., Dec. 11, 1928; d. William Marion and Letitia (Brunia) Black; m. Vinson Brown, June 18, 1950 (dec. Dec. 1991); children: Tamara Pinn, Roxana Hodges, Keven. BA, Western State Coll., Gunnison, Colo. Owner, mgr. Naturegraph Pubs., Inc., Los Altos, Calif., 1950-53, San Martin, Calif., 1953-60, Healdsburg, Calif., 1960-76, Happy Camp, Calif., 1976—. Author: Barns of Yesteryear, and others; co-author: Sierra Nevadan Wildlife Region, The Californian Wildlife Region, 1999; contbr., pub. over 100 books on natural history and Native Ams. Mem. Am. Booksellers Assn., Ind. Book Pub. Assn., Baha'i World Faith. Office: Naturegraph Pubs Inc 3543 Indian Creek Rd Happy Camp CA 96039-9706 Office Phone: 530-493-5353.

BROWN, BARBARA JUNE, hospital and nursing administrator; b. Milw., Aug. 17, 1933; d. Carl W. and Nora Anne (Damrow) Rydberg; children: Deborah, Robert, Andrea, Michael, Steven, Jeffrey. BSN, Marquette U., Milw., 1955, MSN, 1960, EdD, 1970. RN, Wis.; cert. nurse adminstr. advanced. Adminstr. patient care Family Hosp., Milw., 1973-78; assoc. clin. prof. U. Wash., Seattle, 1980-87; assoc. adminstr. nursing Virginia Mason Hosp., Seattle, 1980-87; assoc. exec. dir. King Faisal Specialist Hosp., Riyadh, Saudi Arabia, 1987-91; adj. prof. Univ. Ariz., 2001—. Project dir. NIH, Sexual Assault Treatment Ctr., Milw., 1975-78; lectr., cons., 1974—. Founder, editor-in-chief: Nursing Adminstrn. Quar., 1976—; editor-in-chief, regional v.p. Nurse Week, Mountain West, 2000—04; editor-in-chief: Modern Nurse, 2005—06. Vol. ski instr. for disabled, Winter Park, Colo. Fellow: Nat. Acad. Practice, Am. Acad. Nursing (governing coun.); mem.: ANA, Grand County Pub. Health and Emergency Svcs. (chmn. health adv. com. 1994—96), Nat. League Nursing (bd. govs. 2002—05, bd. dirs.), Am. Orgn. Nurse Execs., Sigma Theta Tau. Office Phone: 520-825-5629. Personal E-mail: naqbb@aol.com.

BROWN, BENJAMIN ANDREW, retired journalist; b. Red House, W.Va., Apr. 30, 1933; s. Albert Miller and Mary Agnes (Donegan) B.; m. Joanne Gretchen Harder, May 22, 1956; children: Benjamin Andrew, Gretchen, Mark, Betsy Brown Larson. BA in Journalism, Fla. State U., 1955. Sportswriter Charleston (W.Va.) Daily Mail, 1955-57; with AP, 1957-93, gen. exec. NYC, 1976-78, 82-93, chief bur. Los Angeles, 1978-82; assoc. Am. Newspapers Cons., Ltd., Milw., 1993-95. Bd. dirs. Last Chance Press Club, Helena, Mont., 1969; v.p. Minn. Press Club, 1975. Office: PO Box 3012 Paso Robles CA 93447-3012 Personal E-mail: babrown@charter.net.

BROWN, BIRCHEL S., steel products company executive; b. 1940; BS in Indsl. Mgmt., Purdue U.; MBA, U. Chgo. Sr. v.p. steel and wire ops. Northwestern Steel and Wire; sr. v.p. ops. Geneva Steel Holdings Corp., Vineyard, Utah, 1999—. Office: Geneva Steel Holdings Corp 10 S Geneva Rd Vineyard UT 84058 Office Fax: 801-227-9090.

BROWN, BOB (ROBERT JOSEPH BROWN), former state official; b. Missoula, Mont., Dec. 11, 1947; s. Clifford Andrew and Jeanne M (Knox) Brown; m. Susan Kay Stoeckig, Sept. 20, 1975; children: Robin Sue, Kelly Charlynn. BS in History, Mont. State U, 1970, BS in Polit. Sci., 1974; MEd, U. Mont., 1988. Cert. secondary tchr. State rep. Mont. Ho. Reps., Helena, 1971—74; senator 2d dist. Mont. State Sen., Helena, 1974—96; tchr. history Whitefish H.S., 1990—91; Tchr. govt., history Big Fork (Mont.) High Sch., 1979—86; tchr. history, econs. Flathead High Sch., Kalispell, Mont., 1986—89; instr. Flathead Valley C.C., 1990, 1994, dir. U. Mont. Ext., 1991—98; dir. govt. & pub. relations Columbia Falls Aluminum Co., 1998—2000; sec. state State of Mont., 2001—04; sr. fellow O'Connor Ctr. Rocky Mt. West U. Mont. With USN, 1972—73. Mem.: Mont. Edn. Assn. (Golden Gavel award 1979), Packyderm, Rotary, Am. Legion, Kiwanis, Moose, Phi Delta Kappa. Republican. Avocation: fishing. Office: Montant Univ Ctr Rocky Mt West 32 Campus Dr MS 3096 Missoula MT 59812 Office Phone: 406-243-7717.

BROWN, BRENDA, library director; m. Mark Brown; 4 children. MLS, U. Ariz., 1989. Libr. clk. U. Ariz., 1986; reference and youth svcs. libr. Scottsdale Librs., Ariz.; with Peoria Pub. Libr., Ariz., 1996—98, dir., 1998—2004; mgr. Chandler Pub. Libr., Ariz., 2004—. Past pres. Ariz. Libr. Assn., co-chair legis. com. Office: Chandler Pub Libr 22 S Delaware St Chandler AZ 85225 Office Phone: 480-782-2817. Office Fax: 480-782-2823. E-mail: brenda.brown@chandleraz.gov.

BROWN, BRYAN, actor; b. Australia, June 23, 1947; m. Rachel Ward. Mem. Nat. Theatre Gt. Britain, Theatre Australia. Actor: (feature films) Newsfront, 1979, Breaker Morant, 1979, The Chant of Jimmie Blacksmith, 1980, Winter of Our Dreams, 1981, Far East, 1982, F/X, 1986, Cocktail, 1988, Gorillas in the Mist, 1988, The Irishman, Weekend of Shadows, Third Person Plural, Money Movers, Palm Beach, Cathy's Child, The Odd Angry Shot, Blood Money, Stir, Taipan, The Good Wife, (TV mini-series) A Town Like Alice, 1981, Against the Wind, The Thorn Birds.

BROWN, CAROLYN SMITH, communications educator, consultant; b. Salt Lake City, Aug. 12, 1946; d. Andrew Delbert and Olive (Crane) Smith; m. David Scott Brown, Sept. 10, 1982. BA magna cum laude, U. Utah, 1968, MA, 1972, PhD, 1974. Instr. Salt Lake Ctr., Brigham Young U., Salt Lake City, 1976-78, vis. asst. prof. Provo, 1978; asst. prof. Am. Inst. Banking, Salt Lake City, 1977—; prof., chmn. English, communication and gen. edn. depts. Latter Day Saints Bus. Coll., Salt Lake City, 1973—, dean acad. affairs, 1986-96, v.p. for acad. affairs, 1996—, acting v.p. for student affairs, 1999-2000. Founder Career Devel. Tng., Salt Lake City, 1979—, pres., 1979; cons. in-house seminars 1st Security REalty Svcs., USDA Natural Resource Conservation Svc., Utah Power & Light, Utah Soc. Svcs., Adminstrv. Office of Cts., HUD, Intermountain Health Care, Fidelity Investments, Am. Inst. Banking; mem. N.W. Assn. Schs. and Colls. Liaison, 1980—, Utah Bus. Coll. Dean's Com., 1990—. Author: (book) Writing Letters & Reports That Communicate, 8th edit., 1994, (poem) In Memory of the Baby Deers, 1996, Waiting (Editor's Choice award for Outstanding Achievement in Poetry), 1998. Demi-soloist Utah Civic Ballet (now Ballet West), Salt Lake City, 1964-68; active Mormon Ch.; C. of C. Bus. Edn. com., 1991-92. Named Tchr. of Month, Salt Lake City Kiwanis, 1981; NDEA fellow, U. Utah, 1972. Mem. Am. Bus. Communications Assn. (lectr. West/N.W. regional chpt. 1987), Delta Kappa Gamma (2d v.p. 1977-79), Lambda Delta Sigma (Outstanding Woman of Yr. 1983), Kappa Kappa Gamma (Outstanding Alumnus in Lit. 1974). Clubs: Alice Louise Reynolds Literary (Salt Lake City) (v.p. 1978-79, sec. 1985-86). Republican. Avocations: walking, hiking, slide lectures on Israel and literary topics. Office: Lds Business College 95 N 300 W Salt Lake City UT 84101-3503 Office Phone: 801-524-8160.

BROWN, CATHIE, city official; b. Seattle, Mar. 23, 1944; d. G. Warren and Dorothy (Patterson) Cryer; m. Tom Brown, July 1, 1967; children: Amy, James W. BA in Criminology, U. Calif., Berkeley, 1966; MPA, Calif. State U., Hayward, 1985. Juvenile probation officer Santa Clara (Calif.) County, 1967-72; founder, dir. Tri-Valley Haven for Women, Livermore, Calif., 1976-79; planning commr. City of Livermore, 1980-82, city coun. mem., 1982-89, mayor, 1989—; exec. dir. Alameda County Project Intercept, Hayward, 1986-92. Dir. Svcs. for Families of Inmates, Pleasanton, Calif., 1981-82; active County Justice System Adv. Group, Oakland, Calif., 1990—; co-founder Tri-Valley Community Fund, Pleasanton. Active Alameda County Mayors' Conf., 1989—; del. Assn. Bay Area Govts., 1982-89; founder Youth For Action, Livermore, 1984-86, Youth Task Force, Livermore, 1989-90. Named Woman of Yr. Calif. State Legislature, 1990. Mem. League Calif. Cities (pres. East Bay div. 1982-89), MPA Alumni Assn. (pres. Calif. State U. chpt. 1989—). Democrat. Avocations: music, racquetball, reading. Home: 1098 Angelica Way Livermore CA 94550-5701

BROWN, CHADWICK EVERETT, professional football player; b. Pasadena, Calif., July 12, 1970; Degree in mktg., U. Colo., 1992. Linebacker Pitt. Steelers, 1993-97; owner Pro Exotics, Boulder, Colo.; linebacker Seattle Seahawks, 1997—. Named to Pro Bowl, 1996. Office: care Seattle Seahawks 11220 NE 53d St Kirkland WA 98033

BROWN, CHARLES GAILEY, lawyer, retired state attorney general; b. Mansfield, Ohio, June 6, 1950; s. Charles Gailey and Emily (Campbell) B.; divorced; 1 child, Tara Jeanne; m. Melissa Burkholder, Apr. 29, 1989. BA, Denison U., 1971; JD, Yale U., 1975. Bar: Ohio 1975, D.C. 1975, W.Va. 1978. Staff atty. FTC, Washington, 1975-78; dep. atty. gen. State of W.Va., Charleston, 1978-82, atty. gen., 1985-89; pvt. practice law Charleston, 1982-85; of counsel Law Offices of Shawn Khorrami. Named Democrat of Yr. W.Va. Young Dems., 1985 Mem. ABA (antitrust sect.), Assn. Trial Lawyers Am. (State Pub. Ofcls. award 1987), W.Va. State Bar Assn., Phi Beta Kappa. Lutheran. Avocations: jogging, baseball, reading. Office: Law Office Shawn Khorrami 14550 Haynes St 3rd fl Van Nuys CA 91411

BROWN, CHARLES R., lawyer; b. Twin Falls, Idaho, Aug. 25, 1945; Bar: Utah 1971, U.S. Tax Ct. 1972, U.S. Ct. Claims 1972, U.S. Ct. Appeals (D.C. cir.) 1972, U.S. Dist. Ct. Utah 1976, U.S. Ct. Appeals (10th cir.) 1976, U.S. supreme Ct. 1977. Trial atty. Office Chief Counsel IRS, 1971-76; ptnr. Hunter & Brown, Salt Lake City, 1976—. Mem. ABA (tax. sect., real property, probate and trust law), Utah State Bar Assn. (chmn. tax. sect. 1981-82, Tax Practitioner of Yr. 1995-96, bar commr. 1992-93 94—, chmn. standing com. on solo and small firm practice 1993-94), Salt Lake County Bar Assn. Office: Hunter & Brown One Utah Ctr 201 S Main St Ste 1300 Salt Lake City UT 84111-2216

BROWN, DAVID RICHARD, school system administrator, minister; b. Manhattan, Kans., Oct. 22, 1929; s. Marion Arthur and Dorothy (Bailey) B.; m. Jeanette Christine Phoenix, July 28, 1962; children: David M., Mark, Thomas. BA, U. So. Calif., 1951; MDiv, U. Chgo., 1955; postgrad., U. So. Calif., 1956-57. Ordained minister, Presbyn. Ch. Assoc. pastor Federated Community Ch., Flagstaff, Ariz., 1957-59; minister of edn. Lakeside Presbyn. Ch., San Francisco, 1959-62; pastor of edn. 1st Presbyn. Ch., Medford, Oreg., 1962-69, pastor Newark, Calif., 1969-75; founder, pastor Community Presbyn. Ch., Union City, Calif., 1975-89; founder, supt. Christian Heritage Acad., Fremont, Calif., 1984—2000; organizing pastor New Life Presbyn. Ch., Fremont, 1989—99; asst. prof. Chabot Coll., Hayward, Calif., 1975-80; pastor New Life Presbyn. Ch., Castro Valley, Calif., 1999—. Moderator Presbytery of No. Ariz., 1959, Presbytery of No. Calif., 2001—02; religion editor The Valley Citizen, Danville, Calif., 2000—06. Dir.: various Shakespearian theatrical prodns., 1982—84 (Thesbian award, 1984); author: Shakespeare for Everyone to Enjoy, 2007. Pres. Boys Christian League, L.A., 1953-54, Coconino Assn. for Mental Health, Flagstaff, 1958-59; chaplain Mozumdar YMCA Camp, Crestline, Calif., 1952-56; chmn. Tri-City Citizens Action Com., 1986-90. Recipient plaque, KC, 1989. Mem. Rotary (chpt. pres. 1988-89, Paul Harris fellow 1989). Avocations: skiing, stamps, choir, drama. E-mail: revdavidbrown@sbcglobal.net.

BROWN, DAVID W., lawyer; b. Seattle, Jan. 29, 1955; Student, Albion Coll.; BS, U. Oreg., 1977, JD, 1980. Bar: Oreg. 1980. Ptnr. Miller, Nash, Wiener, Hager & Carlsen, Portland, Oreg. Mem. Oreg. State Bar. Office: Miller Nash Wiener Hager & Carlsen 111 SW 5th Ave Ste 3500 Portland OR 97204-3699

BROWN, DONALD MALCOLM, plastic surgeon; b. Nelson, N.Z., May 28, 1945; came to U.S., 1947; s. Donald Roland and Edna M. (McPherson) B.; m. Susan E. Boeing, Sept. 3, 1989. MD, U. B.C., 1970. Diplomate Am. Bd. Otolaryngology and Plastic Surgery. Resident in otolarngology Manhattan Eye and Ear Hosp., NYC, 1976; resident in plastic surgery Columbia U., NYC, 1980; pvt. practice San Francisco, 1981—. Vis. prof. plastic surgery U. Liberia, Africa, 1980-81. Mem. AMA, Calif. Med. Assn., San Francisco Med. Assn., Am. Soc. Plastic and Reconstructive Surgery, Am. Soc. Aesthetic Surgery, Pacific Union Club, St. Francis Yacht Club. Avocations: flying, skiing, windsurfing. Office: 2100 Webster St Ste 429 San Francisco CA 94115-2380

BROWN, DONALD WESLEY, lawyer; b. Cleve., Jan. 2, 1953; s. Lloyd Elton Brown and Nancy Jeanne Hudson. AB summa cum laude, Ohio U., 1975; JD, Yale U., 1978. Bar: Calif. 1978, U.S. Dist. Ct. (no. dist.) Calif. 1978, U.S. Dist. Ct. (cen. dist.) Calif. 1990. Assoc. Brobeck, Phleger & Harrison, San Francisco, 1978-85, ptnr., 1985—2003, Covington & Burling, San Francisco, 2003—. Democrat. Home: 2419 Vallejo St San Francisco CA 94123-4638 Office: Covington & Burling One Front St San Francisco CA 94111 Home Phone: 415-776-8841; Office Phone: 415-591-7063. Business E-Mail: dwbrown@cov.com.

BROWN, DUSTIN, professional hockey player; b. Ithaca, NY, Nov. 4, 1984; m. Nicole Brown; 1 child, Jake Austin. Right wing LA Kings, 2003—, capt., 2008—; right wing Manchester Monarchs (AHL), 2004—05. Mem. Team USA, World Jr. Championships, Czech Republic, 2002, Canada, 03, Team USA, IIHF World Championship, Czech Republic, 2004, Riga, Latvia, 06, Canada, 08. Recipient Ace Bailey Meml. Award, 2008; named to NHL All-Star Game, 2009. Office: LA Kings Hockey Club 1111 S Figueroa St, Ste 3100 Los Angeles CA 90015*

BROWN, EDEN ROSE, lawyer; 1 child, Natalie. BA in History, Psychology, U. Calif., Berkeley, 1984; JD, Northwestern Sch. Law. Bar: Oreg., Hawaii, US Ct. Mil. Rev., US Ct. Mil. Appeals, US Dist. Ct. (we. dist. Wash.), US Supreme Ct. Spl. asst. US atty., 1989—93; prin. Law Office of Eden Rose Brown, Salem, Oreg. Appt. to JAG Air Nat. Guard Coun., 1999; lectr. in field. Co-author, editor: Giving - Philanthropy For Everyone, 2003; contbr. articles to profl. pubs. Spanish translator various mil. humanitarian missions; bd. dirs. Oreg. Jewish Cmty. Found., Marion-Polk County Med. Found., Cedar Sinai Pk., Portland, Oreg., Willamette Humane Soc., Salem's Riverfront Carousel. JAG USAF, 1989—93, state judge adv. Oreg. Air Nat. Guard, 1993—2001, lt. col. JAG USAFR. Recipient Meritorious Svc. medal, Pres. George H.W. Bush; named one of Top 100 US Attys., Worth Mag., 2006—08, Oreg. Super Lawyer, 2006—08. Mem.: Air Nat. Guard Assn. US, Mid-Valley Tax Coun., Willamette Valley Estate Planning Coun., Wealth Counsel (founding mem., mem. Nat. Study Group), Nat. Acad. Elder Law Attys., Nat. Network Estate Planning Attys. (charter mem.), Judge Adv. Assn., ABA (probate and trusts sect.), Hawaii Bar Assn., Oreg. Bar Assn. (probate and trusts sect.). Avocations: flying, kayaking, skiing, scuba diving, travel. Office: 1011 Liberty St S Salem OR 97302 Office Phone: 503-581-1800. Office Fax: 503-581-1818. Business E-Mail: eden@edenrosebrown.com.

BROWN, FREDERICK LEE, health facility administrator; b. Clarksburg, W.Va., Oct. 22, 1940; s. Claude Raymond and Anne Elizabeth (Kiddy) B.; m. Shirley Fiille Brown; children: Gregory Lee, Michael Owen-Price, Kyle Stephen, Kathryn Alexis. BA in Psychology, Northwestern U., Evanston, Ill., 1962; MBA in Health Care Adminstrn., George Washington U., Washington, 1966; LHD (hon.), U. Mo., 1995. Vocat. counselor Cook County Dept. Pub. Aid, Chgo., 1962-64; from adminstrv. resident to v.p. ops. Meth. Hosp. Ind., Inc., Indpls., 1965—72, v.p. ops., 1972-74; exec. v.p., COO Meml. Hosp. DuPage County, Elmhurst, Ill., 1974-82, Meml. Health Svcs., Elmhurst, 1980-82; pres., CEO CH Health Techs., Inc., St. Louis, 1983-93, Christian Health Svcs., St. Louis, 1986-93, CH Allied Svcs., Inc., St. Louis, 1988-93, BJC Health Sys., St. Louis, 1993—98, vice-chmn., 1999—2000; pres., CEO Christian Hosp. NE-NW, 1982—88, No. Ariz. Healthcare, Flagstaff, 2003—04. Adj. instr. Washington U. Sch. Medicine, St. Louis, 1982—2001; mem. chancellor's coun. U. Mo., 1990—94; mem. exec. com. HealthLink, Inc., 1986—92; pres., CEO Village North, Inc., 1986—93; chmn. shareholder comm. com. Am. Healthcare Systems, Inc., 1985—86, vice chmn., 1992; bd. dirs. Commerce Bank St. Louis, Am. Excess Inc. Ltd.; mem. corp. assembly Blue Cross Blue Shield Mo., 1991—95; vis. scholar, exec. in residence The George Washington U., 2001—02. Contbr. articles to profl. jours. Co-chmn. hosp. divsn. United Way Greater St. Louis, 1983, chmn., 1984, chmn. health svcs. divsn., 1985—86, vice chmn. region, 1988, bd. dirs., 1986—2001, exec. com., 1991—, chmn. audit com., 1992—2001; active Kammergild Chamber Orch., 1984—88, v.p., 1985—88, bd. dirs., 1987—91; active Mo. Heart Inst., 1988—92, Alton Meml. Hosp., 1987—91, bd. dirs., 1987—91; mem. exec. bd. St. Louis Area coun. Boy Scouts Am., 1989—2000, activities coun. chmn., 1993—95; chmn. Friends of Scouting Campaign, 1991—92; mem. medicaid budget task force Mo. Dept. Social Svcs., 1990; mem. emergency rm. svcs. task force St. Louis Regional Med. Ctr., 1985; mem. corp. assembly Blue Cross Blue Shield of Mo., 1991; bd. dirs. Sold on St. Louis, 1991—93, St. Louis Reg. Commerce & Growth Assn., 1993—98; bd. trustees Webster Hills Math. Ch., 1990—92, communion steward, 1987. Fellow Am. Coll. Healthcare Execs. (chmn. credentials com. 1978, chmn. task force governance and constituencies 1986-88; mem. Gold Medal award com. 1985, com. on ethics 1989-91, chmn. awards and testimonials com., 1992-93, bd. regents 1991-93, gov. dist. V, 1993-98); mem. Am. Acad. Med. Adminstrs. (life, state dir. 1988—, Health Care Exec. of Yr. 1990, Statesman in Healthcare, 1992), Hosp. Pres.'s Assn., Advt. Club Greater St. Louis, Am. Hosp. Assn. (coun. on mgmt. 1987, alt. del. for healthcare systems 1988-90, del. to ho. of dels. for health care systems 1991, fin. com. chair 1995, chair-elect 1998, chmn. 1999), APHA, George Washington U. Alumni Assn. for Health Svcs. Adminstrn. (preceptor 1975-93, Alumnus of Yr. award 1981, Frederick Gibbs award, 1993), Hosp. Assn. Met. St. Louis (bd. dirs. 1984-94, chmn. bd. 1988-89, sec. 1985-86, treas. 1987, chmn. coun. on pub. affairs and comm. 1985, vice chmn. 1987, various coms.), Greater St. Louis Health Care Alliance (co-chair 1992-96), Mo. Hosp. Assn. (mem. coun. on rsch. and policy devel. 1983-88, chmn. coun. on multi-instnl. hosps. 1986-88, mem. dist. coun. pres.'s 1986-89, bd. dirs. 1988-92, chmn. bd. trustees 1990), Ctrl. Ea. Profl. Rev. Orgn. (bd. dirs. 1982-85, various coms.), St. Louis Met. Med. Soc. (lay advisor 1990-92), Healthcare Execs. Study Soc., Internat. Health Policy and Mgmt. Inst. (bd. dirs. 1988—), Am. Protestant Health Assn. (bd. dirs. 1988-93, chmn. 1992-93), Pinnacle Peak Country Club, Forest Highlands Country Club. Republican. Home: 8409 E La Junta Rd Scottsdale AZ 85255-2859 Office Phone: 928-607-3069. Personal E-mail: fredlbrown@cox.net.

BROWN, GEOFFREY FRANCIS, public defender, lawyer; b. San Francisco, May 20, 1943; m. Wai Yung, 1973; children: Miranda, Simone, Olivia. BA in Polit. Sci., U. Calif., Berkeley, 1964; JD, San Francisco Law Sch., 1970. Bar: Calif. 1971, U.S. Dist. Ct. (no. dist.) Calif. 1971, U.S. Ct. of Appeals (9th cir.) 1971. Dep. pub. defender City of San Francisco, 1971-77, elected pub. defender, 1978—. Adj. prof. law New Coll. Calif. Sch. of Law; legal expert KRON-TV and Bay TV, 1995-97; cons. US AID in Italy, 1985, Bolivia, 1991, Argentina, 1995; bd. dirs. San Francisco Law Sch., 1998—; mem. human rsch. com. U. Calif., San Francisco, 1998—. Contbr. numerous articles to profl. jours. and newspapers, presented papers at legal symposia. Mem. Mayor's Task Force on Jail Overcrowding, 1979-95, Mayor's Coun. on Criminal Justice, 1979—; bd. dirs. San Francisco Neighborhood Legal Assistance Found., 1988-96. Mem. Calif Pub. Defenders Assn. (bd. dirs. 1979—, pres. 1984), Nat. Legal Aid and Defenders Assn. (defender com. 1981-82). Office: California Public Utilites Commn 505 Van Ness Ave San Francisco CA 94102

BROWN, GERALD G., operations research specialist, educator; BS, MBA, Calif. State U., Fullerton, 1969; PhD, U. Calif., LA, 1974. Asst. prof. ops. rsch. Naval Postgraduate Sch., Monterey, 1973, assoc. prof. ops. rsch., 1975—76, assoc. prof. ops. rsch. and computer sci., 1976—80, prof. ops. rsch., 1980—, assoc. chmn. for rsch., disting. prof. ops. rsch. Bd. mem. Inst. Ops. Rsch. and Mgmt. Sci. Mil. Ops. Rsch. Soc. Recipient Outstanding Tchg. award, Naval Postgraduate Sch., 1973, Sigma Xi Rsch. award, 1976, Barchi prize, Mil. Ops. Rsch. Soc., 2007; INFORMS fellow, 2005. Mem.: NAE. Achievements include research in large-scale optimization theory and its military and industrial applications; large-scale mathematical programming. Office: Grad Sch Operational Info Scis Naval Postgrad Sch Dept Ops Rsch Monterey CA 93943 Office Phone: 831-656-2140. Business E-Mail: gbrown@nps.edu.

BROWN, HANK, former academic administrator, former senator; b. Denver, Feb. 12, 1940; s. Harry W. and Anna M. (Hanks) B.; m. Nana Morrison, Aug. 27, 1967; children: Harry, Christy, Lori. BS, U. Colo., 1961, JD, 1969; LLM, George Washington U., 1986. Bar: Colo. 1969; CPA, 1988. Asst. pres. Monfort of Colo., Inc., Greeley, 1969—70, corp. counsel, 1970—71; v.p. Monfort Food Distbg., 1971—72, v.p. corp. devel., 1973—75, v.p. internat. ops., 1975—78, v.p. lamb div., 1978—80; mem. Colo. State Senate, 1972—76, asst. majority leader, 1974—76; mem. 97th-101st Congresses from Colo. 4th dist., 1981—90; US senator from Colo. Washington, 1991—96; pres. U. No. Colo., Greeley, 1998—2002, Daniels Fund, 2002—05; interim pres. U. Colo., 2005—06, pres. Denver, 2006—08. Chmn. Fgn. Rel. subcom. Near Ea. and South Asian affairs, Judicorp subcom. on constl. law. Co-author: Lessons and Legacies. With USN, 1962—66. Decorated Air medal, Vietnam Svc. medal, Nat. Defense medal, Naval Unit citation. Republican. Congregationalist. Office Phone: 303-860-5601. Office Fax: 303-860-5660, 303-860-5610. Business E-Mail: OfficeOfThePresident@cu.edu.

BROWN, J. MARTIN, oncologist, educator; b. Doncaster, Eng., Oct. 15, 1941; married; 2 children. BSc, U. Birmingham, 1963; MSc, U. London, 1965; DPhil in Radiation Biology, Oxford U., 1968. NIH fellow radiation biology Stanford U. Med. Ctr., Calif., 1968-70, rsch. assoc. Calif., 1970-71, from asst. prof. to assoc. prof. Calif., 1971-84, prof., dir. divsn. radiation biology Calif., 1984—, dir. Cancer Biology Rsch. Lab. Calif., 1985—. Sr. fellow Am. Cancer Soc. Dernham, 1971-74; mem. adv. com. biol. effects of ionizing radiations NAS, 1971—. Recipient Bruce F. Cain Meml. award, Am. Assn. Cancer Rsch., 1999. Mem. AAAS, Am. Assn. Cancer Rsch., Am. Soc. Therapeutical Radiology & Oncology, Brit. Inst. Radiology, Brit. Assn. Cancer Rsch., Radiation Rsch. Soc. (9th Rsch. award 1980). Achievements include research in mammalian cellular radiobiology, tumor radiobiology, experimental chemotherapy, bioreductive cytotoxic agents, radiation carcinogenesis. Office: Stanford U Med Sch Cancer Biology Rsch Lab Dept of Radiation & Oncology GK103 Stanford CA 94305-5468

BROWN, JACK A., state legislator, rancher, real estate broker; b. St. Johns, Ariz., May 2, 1929; m. Beverly Van Camp; children: David, Norman, Cynthia, Douglas, Carol, Michael, Jonna, Heidi. BA in Agriculture and Econs., Brigham Young U., Provo, Utah, 1953. Mem. Dist. 5 Ariz. House of Reps., 1963-74, 87-96, 2004—, dem. leader, 1969-72, asst. minority leader, 1989-92, 2007—09; mem. Ariz. State Senate, 1999—2004. Chmn. Apache County Fair & Racing Com., 1975—. Vol. Boy Scouts of America. Named one of Modern Ariz. Legislature's Shining Stars, The Arizona Republic, 2008. Mem.: Apache County Cattle Growers (pres.), Apache County Bd. Realtors, Apache County Farm Bureau (pres.), Ariz. Cattle Growers' Assn., Ariz. C. of C., Ariz. Farm Bureau, Kiwanis Club. Democrat. Office: Ariz House Reps Capitol Complex 1700 W Washington Rm 316 Phoenix AZ 85007-2844 Office Phone: 602-926-4129. Office Fax: 602-417-3010. Business E-Mail: jbrown@azleg.gov.*

BROWN, JACK H., supermarket company executive; b. LA, June 14, 1939; Student, San Jose State U, UCLA. V.p. Sages Complete Marktes, San Bernardino, Calif., 1960-67, Marsh Supermarkets, Yorktown, Ind., 1971-77; pres. Pantry Supermarkets, Pasadena, Calif., 1977-79; pres. mid-west divsn. Cullum Cos., Dallas, 1979-81; pres., CEO Stater Bros. Markets, Colton, Calif., 1981—; also chmn. Trustee U. Redlands, Calif.; bd. dirs. Goodwill Industries of inland Empire, San Bernardino; bd. councillors Calif. State U., San Bernardion. With USNR, 1956-62. Recipient Horatio Alger award Disting. Ams., 1992, Bus. Exec. of Yr. award U. so. Calif., 1993; Calif. State U., San Berardino Sch. Bus. named in his honor, 1992. Mem. Western Assn. Food Chains (v.p., bd. dirs., pres. 1987-88), Calif. Retailers Assn. (bd. dirs.), Food Mktg. Inst. (vice chmn.), So. Calif. Grocers Assn., Food Employers Coun. (bd. govs.), Life Savs. and Loan Assn. (dir.), Elks. Republican. Presbyterian. Office: Stater Bros Markets PO Box 150 San Bernardino CA 92402-0150

BROWN, JAMES W., gastroenterologist; b. Detroit, May 20, 1938; BS, U. Nebr., 1960; MD, Northwestern U., Chgo., 1964. Diplomate Am. Bd. Internal Medicine, Am. Bd. Internal Medicine in Gastroenterology. Gastroenterologist Wenatchee (Wash.) Valley Clinic, 1970—; chief gastroenterology U.S. Naval Hosp., San Diego. Vice-chmn., bd. dirs. Wenatchee Valley Clinic, 1992-95, chmn., CEO, 1996-2001; bd. dirs. NCW Cmty. Bank, Wenatchee. Contbr. articles to profl. jours. Chmn. bd. dirs. Mustard Seed Neighbor Ctr., Wenatchee, 1990-92, bd. dirs. 1989-95, 2004-. Lt. comdr. USN, 1968-70. Fellow Am. Coll. Gastroenterology; mem. Alpha Omega Alpha. Methodist. Avocations: cooking, hiking, reading, physical fitness, travel, golf.

BROWN, JERRY, JR., (EDMUND GERALD BROWN JR.), state attorney general, former mayor, governor; b. San Francisco, Apr. 7, 1938; s. Edmund Gerald and Bernice (Layne) Brown; m. Anne B. Gust, June 18, 2005 BA in Latin/Greek, U. Calif., Berkeley, 1961; JD, Yale U., New Haven, 1964. Bar: Calif. 1965. Rsch. atty. Calif. Supreme Ct., 1964-65; atty. Tuttle & Taylor, LA, 1966-69; sec. state State of Calif., Sacramento, 1970-74, gov., 1975-83; chmn. Calif. Dem. Party, 1989-90; Dem. candidate for Pres. of US, 1992; mayor City of Oakland, Calif., 1999—2007; atty. gen. State of Calif., Sacramento, 2007—. Practiced law, LA. Author: (book) Dialogues, 1988. Trustee LA Cmty. Colls., 1969. Democrat. Office: Office of Atty Gen Calif Dept Justice PO Box 944255 Sacramento CA 94244-2550*

BROWN, JOSEPH E., landscape architecture executive; b. 1947; BA, Cath. U., 1970; M in Landscape Architecture and Urban Design, Harvard U., 1972. With Edaw, Inc., San Francisco, 1973—, now pres. Office: Edaw Inc 150 Chestnut St San Francisco CA 94111-1004

BROWN, KATE, state official, former state legislator; b. Torrejon de Ardoth, Spain, 1960; m. Dan Brown; stepchildren: Dylan, Jessie. BA, U. Colo.; JD, Lewis and Clark Coll. Atty. Tennyson, Winemiller & Lavalle, 1991—94; mem. Oreg. House Representatives from Dist. 13, 1991-96; adj. prof. adminstrn. justice Portland State U., 1994; mem. Oreg. State Senate from Dist. 21, 1997—2009, majority leader, 2004—09; sec. state State of Oreg., Salem, 2009—. Recipient Outstanding Young Oregonian award, Oreg. Jaycees, 1993, Nat. Pub. & Cmty. Svc. award, Am. Mental Health Counselors Assn., 2004. Mem.: Women's Legislators' Lobby, Multnomah Bar Assn., Oreg. Women's Polit. Caucus, Oreg. Trial Lawyers Assn. Democrat. Office: Office Sec of State 141 State Capitol Bldg Salem OR 97310-0722 Office Phone: 503-986-1523. Office Fax: 503-986-1616. Business E-Mail: oregon.sos@state.or.us.*

BROWN, KATHLEEN, diversified financial services company executive; b. 1946; d. Edmund G. and Bernice Brown; m. George Rice (div. 1979); children: Hilary, Alexandra, Zebediah; m. Van Gordon Sauter, 1980; 2 stepsons. BA in History, Stanford U., 1969; JD, Fordham U., 1985. Mem. L.A. Bd. Edn., 1975-80; atty. O'Melveny & Myers, NYC, LA; commr. L.A. Bd. Pub. Works, 1987-89; treas. State of Calif., 1990-94; exec. v.p. Bank of Am., LA, 1994-99, pres. Pvt. Bank for Investment Mgmt. Group, 1999—2001; sr. pvt. wealth adv. investment mgmt. divsn. Goldman, Sachs & Co., LA, 2001—03, sr. adv., head of pub. fin. We. region, 2003—. Co-chmn. Capital Budget Commn., Washington, 1997—. Mem. Pacific Coun. on Internat. Policy, Stanford Inst. for Internat. Studies; dir. Children's Hosp. L.A., San Francisco Ballet, Calif. Endowment, LA C. of C. Democrat. Office: Goldman Sachs & Co Fox Plz Ste 2600 2121 Ave Stars Los Angeles CA 90067

BROWN, KEITH E., lawyer; b. 1943; BS, Oreg. State Univ.; JD, Stanford Univ. Bar: Alaska 1969. Atty Brown Waller & Gibbs, Anchorage. Mem.: ABA (bd. gov. 2004—). Office: Brown Waller & Gibbs Suite 202 821 North St Anchorage AK 99501 Office Phone: 907-276-2050. Office Fax: 907-276-2051.

BROWN, KEITH LAPHAM, retired ambassador; b. Sterling, Ill., June 18, 1925; s. Lloyd Heman and Marguerite (Briggs) B.; m. Carol Louise Liebmann, Oct. 1, 1949; children: Susan, Briggs (dec.), Linda, Benjamin. Student, U. Ill., 1943-44, Northwestern U., 1946-47; LLB, U. Tex., 1949. Bar: Tex., Okla., Colo. Assoc. Lang, Byrd, Cross & Ladon, San Antonio, 1949-55; v.p., gen. counsel Caulkins Oil Co., Oklahoma City, 1955-70, Denver, 1955-70; founder, developer Vail Assocs., Colo., 1962; pres. Brown Investment Corp., Denver, 1970-87; developer Colo. State Bank Bldg., Denver, 1971; amb. to Lesotho Dept. State, 1982-84, amb. to Denmark Copenhagen, 1988-92; ret., 1992; chmn. Brown Investment Corp., Denver, 1993—. Mem. adv. bd. Ctr. for Strategic and Internat. Studies. Chmn. Rep. Nat. Fin. Com., 1985-88; hon. trustee, past pres. bd. Colo. Acad.; mem. Am. Acad. Diplomacy. Ensign USN, 1943-46. Mem. Coun. Am. Ambs. (pres.), San Antonio Country Club, Bohemian Club. Republican. Presbyterian. also: 11 Auburn Pl San Antonio TX 78209-4739 Office: 1490 Colo State Bank Bldg 1600 Broadway Denver CO 80202-4927 Home Phone: 210-804-0556; Office Phone: 303-830-7379.

BROWN, LAWRENCE GEORGE, prosecutor; b. San Francisco, Feb. 17, 1964; s. Roger Garnier and Dona Beverly Brown; m. April Garlyn Brown, Jan. 6, 1996; 1 child, Harrison. AA, Santa Rosa Jr. Coll., 1984; B in Polit. Sci., U. Calif., Davis, 1986, JD, 1989. Bar: Calif. 1989. Dep. dist. atty. Ventura County Dist. Atty.'s Office, Calif., 1989-94; dep. exec. dir. Calif. Dist. Atty.'s Assn., Sacramento, 1994-96, exec. dir., 1996—2003; fist asst. US atty. (ea. dist.) Calif. US Dept. Justice, Sacramento, 2003—09, acting US atty., 2009—. Vis. prof. U. Calif. Davis Sch. Law, 1998-2000. Mem. Nat. Assn. Prosecutor Coords. (pres. 2000—), Nat. Dist. Attys. Assn. (bd. dirs. 2000—), Anthony M. Kennedy Inn of Ct. Home: 1360 51st St Sacramento CA 95819-4115 Office: US Atty's Office 501 I St, Ste 10-100 Sacramento CA 95814 Office Phone: 916-554-2700. Office Fax: 916-554-2900.*

BROWN, LILLIAN ERIKSEN, retired nursing administrator, consultant; b. Seattle, Feb. 7, 1921; d. Peter Louis and Lena (Lien) Eriksen; m. Jan. 21, 1942 (div. Nov. 1963); children: Patricia Lee, Michael Gregory, Kevin William. Student, U. Calif., Berkeley, 1939-40; diploma, St. Luke's Hosp. Sch. Nursing, San Francisco, 1943; AB, Calif. State U., San Francisco, 1952; MPA, U. So. Calif., 1975. RN, Calif. Pub. health nurse San Francisco Dept. Health, 1946-50; asst. dir. nursing San Francisco Gen. Hosp., 1950-56; dir. nursing Weimar (Calif.) Med. Ctr., 1956-62, Orange County Med. Ctr., Orange, Calif., 1962-76; assoc. dir. hosp. and clins., dir. nursing, lectr. U. Calif. Med. Ctr., Irvine, 1976-82; assoc. hosp. adminstr. King Khalid Eye Specialist Hosp., Riyadh, Saudi Arabia, 1982-86; cons. AMI-Saudi Arabia Ltd., Jeddah, 1986-90. Chmn. Western Teaching Hosp. Coun. Dirs. Nursing, 1972-75, 80-81; mem. planning project com. Calif. Dept. Rehab., 1967-69, mem. adv. com., 1970-73; mem. ad hoc president's com. on hosp. governance U. Calif., 1981-82; pres. dirs. nursing coun. Hosp. Coun. So. Calif., 1972-74, mem. pers. practices com., 1976-78, 80-83, area rep., 1975-82; mem. dept. nursing adv. com. to establish baccalaureate program U. So. Calif., 1980-82; mem. adv. bd. various coll. nursing programs. Contbr. articles to profl. jours. Sec. Olive (Calif.) Little League, 1967-72; mem. com. on emergency med. svcs. Orange County Health Planning Coun., 1977-78, mem. health promotion task force, 1978-79. 2d lt. Nurse Corps, U.S. Army, 1944-45. Recipient Lauds and Laurels award U. Calif., Irvine, 1981 Fellow Am. Acad. Nurses; mem. ANA (cert. nurse adminstr. advanced), Nat. League for Nursing, APHA, Am. Orgn. Nurse Execs., Nat. Critical Care Inst. Edn., Calif. Nurses Assn. (Lillian E. Brown award named in her honor 1989), Calif. Orgn. for Nurse Execs. (hon.), Calif. Soc. for Nursing Svc. Adminstr., NOW. Democrat. Avocations: travel, stamp collecting/philately. Home: 1806 N Nordic Pl Orange CA 92865-4637

BROWN, LISA J., state legislator; b. Robinson, Ill., Oct. 9, 1956; 1 child, Lucas. Assoc. prof. econs. Eastern Wash. U.; assoc. prof., orgnl. leadership program Gonzaga U., Spokane, Wash.; mem. Dist. 3 Wash. House of Reps., Olympia, 1992—96, Wash. State Senate, Olympia, 1996—, majority leader, 2005—. Recipient Achievement award Woman's Club Spokane, 1988, Women Achievement Govt. award YWCA, 1997, Hunger Fighter award Anti-Hunger & Nutrition Coalition, 1997, Annual award for Saving Women's Lives, Wash. State Pub. Health Assn., 1998, Sizzle award Fuse, 2008; named Ofcl. of Yr. Citizen's League Greater Spokane, 1997. Mem.: Spokane Aids Network. Democrat. Office: Dist Office 25 W Main Ste 239 Spokane WA 99201 also: 307 Legislative Bldg PO Box 40403 Olympia WA 98504-0403 Office Phone: 509-456-2760. Office Fax: 360-786-7604. Business E-Mail: Brown.Lisa@leg.wa.gov.*

BROWN, LOWELL C., lawyer; b. Salt Lake City, Oct. 21, 1954; BA magna cum laude, U. Ut., 1980, JD, 1982. Bar: Calif. 1983. Ptnr. Foley & Lardner LLP, LA, chmn. health provider ops. practice group. Asst. adj. prof. U. Southern Calif. Author: Et Tu, Counselor: May In-House Atty. File Qui Tam Action Against Atty.'s Employer?, 1999. Mem.: Healthcare Fin. Mgmt. Assn., Healthcare Assn. Southern Calif. (profl. svc. com. 1991—), Calif. Soc. Healthcare Atty. (pres. 2000—01), Am. Health Lawyers Assn. (credentialing & peer rev. com., regulation, accreditation & payment com.), ABA (health law sect.), L.A. Bar Assn. (health law sect., exec. com. 1990—91, chmn. 1993—94, accreditation, licensure & certification interest group, chmn. 1998—99). Fluent in spanish. Office: Foley & Lardner LLP 2029 Century Park E Ste 3500 Los Angeles CA 90067-3021 Office Fax: 310-975-7842. Business E-Mail: lcbrown@foley.com.

BROWN, LOWELL SEVERT, physicist, researcher; b. Visalia, Calif., Feb. 15, 1934; s. Volney Clifford and Anna Marie Evelyn (Jacobson) B.; m. Shirley Isabel Mitchell, June 23, 1956; 1 son, Stephen Clifford. AB, U. Calif., Berkeley, 1956; PhD (NSF predoctoral fellow 1956-61), Harvard U., 1961; postgrad., U. Rome, 1961-62, Imperial Coll., London, 1962-63. From rsch. assoc. to assoc. prof. physics Yale U., 1963-68; mem. faculty U. Wash., Seattle, 1968—, prof. physics, 1970-2001, prof. emeritus, 2001—; mem. staff Los Alamos Nat. Lab., N.Mex., 2001—. Vis. prof. Imperial Coll., London, 1971-72, Columbia U., N.Y.C., 1990; vis. scientist Brookhaven Nat. Lab., summer, 1965-68, Lawrence Berkeley Lab., summer 1966, Stanford Accelerator Ctr., summer, 1967, CERN, Geneva, summer, 1979, Inst. for Theoretical Physics, U. Calif., Santa Barbara, winter 1999; mem. Inst. Advanced Study, Princeton, N.J., 1979-80; cons. Los Alamos Nat. Lab., spring 1999, vis. scientist, 1991; vis. physicist Deutches Elektronen-Synchrontron, Hamburg, 1986 Author: Quantum Field Theory, 1992; mem. editl. bd. Phys. Rev., 1978-81; editor Phys. Rev. D, 1987-95; contbr. articles to profl. publs. Trustee Seattle Youth Symphony Orch., 1986—95. Postdoctoral fellow NSF, 1961-63; sr. post-doctoral fellow, 1971-72; Guggenheim fellow, 1979-80 Mem. Ferrari Club of Am. (dir. Northwest region 1999-2003). Office: X-3 MS F644 PO Box 1668 Los Alamos NM 87545 Personal E-mail: gt330@comcast.net.

BROWN, MICHAEL R., former defense industry executive; b. Kans. BEd, Ottawa U. Mktg. mgr. Singer; mktg. mgr. Amecom divsn. Litton Industries, Inc., College Park, Md., 1968-77, v.p. bus. devel. electronic warfare comm. sys., 1977-87, v.p. bus. devel. electronic warfare sys. group, 1987-89, corp. v.p., group exec. electronic warfare sys., 1989-92, corp. sr. v.p., 1992-95, exec. commd., control, comm. sys. group, 1995, pres., 1995—, CEO, 1998—, chmn., 1999—2001. Mem. L.A. World Affairs Coun. Inducted into U. Ottawa Sports Hall of Fame. Mem. Navy League U.S., Assn. U.S. Army, Air Force Assn., Armed Forces Comm. Electronics Assn., Nat. Def. Indl. Assn., Aerospace Industries Assn., Assn. Old Crows. Office: Litton Industries Inc 21240 Burbank Blvd Woodland Hills CA 91367-6675

BROWN, PAMELA S., former attorney general; BA in Cultural Anthropology, U. Wash., 1982, JD with honors, 1988. Tech. dir, news dir., news ed. KOMO TV, ABC, Seattle, 1981—85; Rule 9 atty., King County prosecutors and Wash. State, atty. gen., consumer protection div., 1986—87; criminial def. atty. Seattle, 1987—89; criminal prosecutor, off. of atty. gen. No. Mariana Islands, 1989—90, chief sen. legal counsel, 1990—94; ptnr. Long & Brown, attys. at law, 1994—98; pvt. practice, 1998—99; fed. ombudsman, off. of ombudsman, off. of insular affairs US Dept. Interior, Saipan, 1999—2001; of counsel Teker Civille Torres and Tang attys. at law and MP mng. atty. for Saipan Off., Labor, Immigration and Civil Litig., Saipan, 2001—02; legal counsel to gov. No. Mariana Islands, Saipan, 2002—03, atty. gen., 2003—06. Mem. Am. Bar Assn., Commonwealth Bar Assn.

BROWN, PAT CRAWFORD, actress; b. NYC, June 29, 1929; d. Thomas J. and Charlotte (Huber) Crawford; m. Calvin B. Brown, Jan. 3, 1961 (dec. Dec. 1976); 1 child, Charlotte Brown Swanson. BA in Speech and Lit., Coll. of New Rochelle, 1951; MFA in Theatre, Fordham U., 1958. Cert. secondary tchr., Calif. Tchr. L.A. City Schs., Carson, Calif., 1964-84. Entertainment dir. U.S. Army Spl. Svcs., Kaiserslautern, Fed. Republic Germany, 1959-61; bd. dirs. Theatre West, Hollywood, Calif., 1988-90; producer, bd. dirs. Torrance (Calif.) Community Theatre, 1980-84. Actor: (films) Elvira, Mistress of the Dark, 1988, 18 Again, 1988, Upworld, 1990, The Rocketeer, 1991, Sister Act, 1992, Sister Act 2: Back in the Habit, 1993, Reality Bites, 1994, Romy and Michele's Hight School Reunion, 1997, Johnny Skidmarks, 1998, The Godson, 1998, Jack Frost, 1998, Forces of Nature, 1999, Playing Mona Lisa, 2000, The Woman Every Man Wants, 2001, The Medicine Show, 2001, Daredevil, 2003, Stuck on You, 2003, Crazylove, 2005, You, Me and Dupree, 2006, Norbit, 2007, others, (TV series) Desperate Housewives, 2004-; guest appearances (TV series) Moonlighting, Chicken Soup, Mama's Family, Teddy Z, Knots Landing, Dear John, Who's the Boss?, Coach, Designing Women, Murphy Brown, L.A. Law, Carol Burnett Show, ER, Home Improvement, Murder She Wrote, Ellen, Fresh Prince, Profiler, Pretender, Dark Skies, Beverly Hills, 90210, Coach, Caroline in the City, Two Guys, a Girl and a Pizza Place, The Norm Show, Malcom & Eddie, The Drew Carey Show, Suddenly Susan, 3rd Rock from the Sun, NYPD Blue, State of Grace, The Steve Harvey Show, Lizzie McGuire, Buffy the Vampire Slayer, Judging Amy, The Bernie Mac Show, Life with Bonnie, Monk, Jack & Bobby, Arrested Development, Gilmore Girls, CSI: Las Vegas, Raines Short Whisperer; also numerous other theatrical prodns. Chair recycling com. Burchett Gardens Home Owners Assn., Glendale, Calif., 1990. Recipient Best Actress award Dramalogue Mag., 1988. Mem. Actors Equity Assn., AFTRA, SAG, Theatre West (St. Seema award 1989) Avocations: piano, tennis, swimming, guitar, marionettes. Office: Don Carroll 2126 N Gower St Los Angeles CA 90068 Office Phone: 323-462-7100. Personal E-mail: patcbrown@aol.com.

BROWN, PATRICK O., molecular biologist, educator; b. Washington, Sept. 23, 1954; m. Sue Klapholz; children: Zach, Ariel, Isaac. BA with honors, U. Chgo., 1976, PhD, 1980, MD, 1982. Pediat. resident Children's Meml. Hosp., Chgo., 1982—85; post-doctoral fellowship U. Calif., San Francisco, 1985—88; asst. prof. biochemistry and pediatrics Stanford U. Sch. Medicine, Calif., 1988—95, assoc. prof. biochemistry Calif., 1995—2000, prof. biochemistry Calif., 2000—. Investigator Howard Hughes Med. Inst., 1988—; bd. dir., co-founder Pub. Libr. Sci. (PLoS), 2003—. Contbr. scientific papers articles to profl. jours. Recipient Millennium Pharma. award for Genomics Rsch. in Clin. Immunology, 2001, BioTech Helsinki Prize, 2003; named one of America's Best in Science and Medicine, Time mag. Fellow: World Tech. Network (World Tech. Network award (Media and Journalism) 2005), AAAS; mem.: NAS (NAS award in molecular biology 2000). Office: Stanford Sch Medicine B439 300 Pasteur Dr Stanford CA 94305 Address: Pub Libr Sci 185 Berry Street Ste 3100 San Francisco CA 94107 Business E-Mail: pbrown@cmgm.stanford.edu.

BROWN, PERRY JOE, dean; Student, Foothill Coll., Los Altos, Calif., 1962-63; BS in Forestry, Utah State U., 1967, MS in Forest Recreation, 1968, PhD in Outdoor Recreation & Social Psych, 1971; postgrad., U. Mich., 1968, 69-70. Lectr. forest sci. Utah State U., Logan, 1968-71, asst. prof. forest sci., 1971-73; asst. prof. and assoc. prof. recreation resources Colo. State U., 1973—79; assoc. dean instrn., continuing edn. and internat. programs Oreg. State U., 1988-94; dean Coll. Forestry and Conservation U. Mont., Missoula, 1994—, prof. forest resources, 1994—, dir. Mont. Forest and Conservation Expt. Sta., 1994—. Social sci. project leader Oreg. State U.-Nat. Park Svc. Coop. Park Studies Unit, 1990-93; interim dir. Oreg. Tourism Inst., Oreg. State Sys. Higher Edn., 1987-89; mem. adv. bd. Va. Poly. Inst. and State U. Coll. Forestry and Wildlife; mem. numerous panels and task forces NAS, regional planning commns., fed. and state agys. and domestic and internat. profl. orgns.; profl. cons. to numerous fed., state and internat. land mgmt. agys., univs., cos. and the Forest Ecosystem Mgmt. Assessment Team social sci. team; leader Rocky Mountain Coop. Ecosys. Studies Unit; mem. nat. adv. bd. Nat. Forest Found., 2002—. Editor Utah Tourism and Recreation Rev., 1972-73; assoc. editor Jour. Leisure Rsch., 1977-79, Jour. Leisure Scis., 1982-85; mem. editl. bd. Jour. Forest and Landscape Rsch., 1993-99, Internat. Demand of Wilderness, 2002-; author over 110 books, articles, papers and reports including 3 books and 21 book chpts. Recipient Cert. of Appreciation, USDA Forest Svc., 1988. Fellow Acad. Leisure Scis., Soc. Am. Foresters, Human Dimensions in Wildlife Study Group, Internat. Union Forestry Rsch. Orgns. (leader forest recreation, landscape planning and nature conservation sect. 1986-96, dep. coord. divsn. 6 1996-), Nat. Assn. Profl. Forestry Schs. and Colls. (western region chair, exec. bd. 1996-97, pres.-elect 1998-00, pres. 2000-02, past pres. 2002-04). Office: U Mont Coll Forestry and Conservation Missoula MT 59812-0001

BROWN, RALPH BROWNING, sociologist, educator; b. Twin Falls, Utah, Jan. 25, 1960; s. Boyd Hayes and Charilla Browning Brown; m. Jerilyn M. Muhlestein, June 5, 1984; children: Nicole M., Aisha M., Jessica M. BA, Utah State U., 1986, MS, 1988; PhD, U. Mo., 1992. Asst. prof. sociology Miss. State U., Starkville, Miss., 1992—97, assoc. prof. sociology, 1997—98, Brigham Young U., Provo, Utah, 1998—2005, prof. sociology, 2005—. Grad. coord. Miss. State U., 1997—98; grad. coord. sociology Brigham Young U., 1999—2005, faculty dir. southeast Asian internship, 2003—, assoc. dept. chair sociology, 2005, coord. internat. devel. minor, 2007—; mem. scientific com., minerals mgmt. US Dept. Interior Outer Continental Self, 2006—. Translator: Examining Islam in the West: Addressing Accusations, Correcting Misunderstandings; contbr. chapters to books, articles to profl. jours. Adv. Charles Redd Ctr. for Western Studies, Provo, 2004. Alcuin Tchg. fellowship, Brigham Young U. Gen. Edn., 2005. Mem.: Rural Sociol. Soc. (mem. coun., chmn. program, chmn. devel. com., Excellence in Instrn. award 2004). Democrat. Lds Ch. Office: Brigham Young University 2034 JFSB Provo UT 84602 Office Fax: 801-422-0625. Business E-Mail: ralph_brown@byu.edu.

BROWN, ROBERT ALAN, geophysicist, educator; b. LA, June 11, 1934; s. Carl Clayton and Olive (Hirst) B.; m. Marcia Louise Jobe, Dec. 12, 1957; children: Vanessa, Morgan, Tristin. BS, U. Calif., Berkeley, 1957, MS, 1963; PhD, U. Wash., 1969. Fellow U. Wash., Seattle, 1969-70, Nat. Ctr. Atmospheric Sci., Boulder, Colo., 1970-71; rsch. prin. investigator U. Wash. Polar Sci. Ctr., Seattle, 1971—83; prof. atmospheric sci. U. Wash., Seattle, 1983—. Adj. prof.: Naval Postgrad. Sch., 1983, Fraunhofer Inst., Garmish, Germany, 1991, U. Concepcion, Chile, 1996, 2003, Ecole Poly., Paris, 1997. Author: Analytic Methods in Planetary Boundary Layer Models, 1973, Fluid Mechanics of the Atmosphere, 1991, The Tree or the Panzaic Plea, 2005; co-author: The Panzaic Principle, 1971, Microwave Remote Sensing for Ocean and Marine Weather Forecast Models, Ency. of Earth System Science, Surface Waves and Fluxes: Current Theory, Polar Oceanography, 1990; editor Pacific Ocean Remote Sensing Congress book series, 1992—, Remote Sensing of the Pacific Ocean with Satellites, 1998; contbr. over 80 articles to profl. jours. 1st lt. U.S. Army, 1957-59. Recipient Disting. Sci. award, Pan Ocean Remote Sensing Confs., 2000. Fellow Am. Meteorol. Soc.; mem. Am. Geophys. Union, Am. Oceanographic Soc., Sigma Xi, Phi Kappa Psi. Democrat. Office: U Wash Dept Atmospheric Sci PO Box 351640 Seattle WA 98195-0001 Office Phone: 206-543-8438. Business E-Mail: rabrown@atmos.washington.edu.

BROWN, ROBERT MUNRO, museum director; b. Riverside, NJ, Mar. 4, 1952; s. James Wendell and Janet Elizabeth (Munro) B.; m. Mary Ann Noel, June, 1973 (div. 1977); m. Claudia Leslie Haskell, Jan. 14, 1978. BA in Polit. Sci. cum laude, Ursinus Coll., 1973; MA in Social Scis., Rivier Coll., 1978; PhD in Early Am. History, U. N.H., 1983. Grad. asst. dept. history U. N.H., Durham, 1979-83, instr., 1983-84; site curator T.C. Steele State Hist. Site Ind. State Mus. System, Nashville, Ind., 1984-91; exec. dir. Hist. Mus. at Ft. Missoula, Mont., 1991—. Hist. interpreter Strawberry Banke, Portsmouth, N.H., 1980-83; instr. Rivier Coll., Nashua, N.H., 1986-91, N.H. Coll., Nashua and Salem, 1986-91; supr. pub. programs Mus. Am. Textile History, North Andover, Mass., 1985-91; sec.-treas. Western Mont. Heritage Ctr./No. Rockies Heritage Ctr., 1992-93; mem. grad. com. U. Mont., 1993; mem. steering com. Ft. Missoula, 1993; reviewer Inst. Mus. and Libr. Svcs., 1993--; reviewer Am. Assn. Mus.-Mus. Asessment Programs, 1997—; mem. Mont. Com. of the Humanities Spkrs. Bur., 1995—; lectr., presenter, chair panels in field. Contbr. articles to profl. jours. Trustee Historic Harrisville, N.H., 1989-91; bd. dirs. United Peoples Found., 1991-93, v.p., 1993; mem. planning com. Western Mont. Heritage Ctr., 1991, U. Mont. Centennial Celebration, 1992, Leadership Missoula, 1992; active open space, parks and resource planning and mgmt. project team City of Missoula, 1993; mem. blue ribbon task force Five Valleys Luth. Retirement Cmty. Planning Com., 1994, Western Mont. Vol. Ctr. Coun., 2004-05. Grantee, Mass. Coun. on Arts and Humanities, 1986—88, Int. Mus. Svcs., 1988—91, 1993, 1995, 1997, 1999, AT&T, 1988, Am. Wool Coun., 1988, BayBank, 1989, Am. Yarn Assn., 1989, Insured Titles, 1990—2005, North Andover Arts Lottery Coun., 1989—90, Mass. Cultural Coun., 1990, Greater Lawrence Cmty. Found., 1991, Mass. Arts Lottery Coun., 1991, Gallery Assn. for Greater Art, 1991, 1992, 1994—98, Mont. Comm. for Humanities, 1991—2005, Sinclair Oil Co., 1991, Mont. Rail Link, 1992, 1998, 1999, 2001—03, U. Mont. Found., 1992, Pepsi-Cola Co., 1992—97, 2001—07, Coca-Cola Bottling Co., 1998, Cmty. Med. Ctr., 1999, St. Patrick Hosp., 1999, U.S. WEST Found., 1992, 1995, The Missoulian, 1992, 1995, 2005, 2006, Champion Internat., 1992, Mont. Cultural Trust, 1993, 1995, 1997, Missoula Rotary, 1993, Tex. Mus. Austin, 1993, Inst. Mus. Svcs., 1993, 1995, 1997, 1999, 2002, Zip Beverage Co., 1994, 2000—07, Bitterroot Motors, 1994—2007, Grizzly Hackle, 1994, University Motors, 1995, 1996, Earl's Distbg., 1996, Norwest Bank, 1996—98, ALPS, 2001, 2002, Southgate Mall, 1997—2007, NEH, 2003; fellow, Kellogg Found., 1987; scholar, U. N.H., 1979—83; rsch. grantee, 1982. Mem.: Greater Boston Mus. Educator's Roundtable (steering com. 1988—90), Mtn. Plains Mus. Assn. (Mont. state rep. 1995—97, ann. meeting local arrangements chair 1997, chmn. scholarship com. 1998, sec. 1998—2000, chmn. scholarship com. 1999—2004, ann. meeting program co-chair 2000, treas. 2001—04), Western Mont. Fundraisers Assn. (charter 1991, v.p. 1993—95, pres. 1995—97), Mus. Assn. Mont. (panelist 1994, conf. host 2007), Mont. Hist. Soc., Assn. Records Mgrs. and Adminstrs. (charter Big Sky chpt. 1992—94), Am. Assn. State and Local History (state membership rep. 1996—98, state awards chair 2001—, program com. 2003, mem. coun. 2005—, Leadership History award 2007), Am. Assn. Mus. (peer-reviewer 2000—03), Kiwanis (Sentinel chpt.), Masons (Missoula chpt.), Phi Alpha Theta. Democrat. Avocations: canoeing, cross country skiing, snowshoeing. Home: 216 Woodworth Ave Missoula MT 59801-6050 Office: Hist Mus at Ft Missoula Ft Missoula Bldg 322 Missoula MT 59804 Office Phone: 406-728-3476. Business E-Mail: ftmslamuseum@montana.com.

BROWN, RONALD G., automotive company executive; b. 1937; Pres. North Star Plating Co., 1968; chmn. bd. dirs. Keystone Automotive Industries, Inc., Pomona, Calif., 1997—. Mem. Bumper Recycling Assn. N.Am. (bd. dirs., v.p.). Office: 700 E Bonita Ave Pomona CA 91767 Office Fax: 909-624-9136.

BROWN, SHONA L., Internet company executive; b. 1966; BS in Computer Systems Engring., Carleton U.; MA in Economics & Philosophy, Oxford U.; PhD in Indsl. Engring. & Engring. Mgmt., post-doctorate in Indsl. Engring. & Engring. Mgmt., Stanford U. Prof. indsl. engring. Stanford U.; with McKinsey & Co., 1995—2000, ptnr. Global Strategy Practice, 2000—03; v.p. bus. ops. Google Inc., 2003—06, sr. v.p. bus. ops., 2006—. Bd. dirs. PepsiCo, Inc., 2009—. Co-author (with Kathleen Eisenhardt): Competing on the Edge: Strategy as Structured Chaos, 1998. Bd. dirs. San Francisco Jazz Organization, The Bridgespan Group, The Exploratorium. Office: Google Inc 1600 Amphitheatre Pky Mountain View CA 94043 Office Phone: 650-623-4000. Office Fax: 650-618-1499.*

BROWN, STEPHEN LAWRENCE, environmental consultant; b. San Francisco, Feb. 16, 1937; s. Bonnar and Martha (Clendenin) B.; m. Ann Goldsberry, Aug. 13, 1961; children: Lisa, Travis, Meredith. BS in Engring. Sci., Stanford U., 1958, MS in Physics, 1961; PhD in Physics, Purdue U., 1963. Ops. analyst Stanford Rsch. Inst., Menlo Park, Calif., 1963-74, program mgr., 1974-77, dir. Ctr. Resource and Environ. Systems Studies, 1977-80, dir. Ctr. Health and Environ. Rsch., 1980-83; assoc. dir. Commn. on Life Scis. NAS, Washington, 1983-86; prin. Environ Corp., Arlington, Va., 1986-91; mgr. risk assessment ENSR Cons. and Engring., Alameda, Calif., 1992-93; dir. Risks of Radiation and Chem. Compounds (R2C2), Oakland, Calif., 1993—. Mem. sci. adv. bd. EPA, Washington, 1991—; mem. coms. SAB, NAS, 1980-87. Contbr. over 20 articles to profl. jours., chpts. to books; author over 100 reports in field. Mem. Internat. Soc. Exposure Assessment, Soc. for Risk Analysis, Phi Beta Kappa, Sigma Xi, Sigma Pi Sigma, Tau Beta Pi. Home: 117 Ironwood Rd Alameda CA 94502-6668

BROWN, STEVEN HARRY, engineering executive; b. Phila., Sept. 16, 1948; ABS, Temple U., 1970, BS, 1971; MA, West Chester U., Pa., 1974. Diplomate Am. Acad. Health Physics (panel examiner 1988-91, appeals com. 1999-2001). Health physicist Temple U., Phila., 1969-71; tchr. phys. sci. Phila. Sch. Dist., 1971-76; mgr. radiation protection Westinghouse Electric Corp., Lakewood, Colo., 1976-80; mgr. western regional office Radiation Mgmt. Corp., Phila., 1980-82; prin. safety analysis engr. Rockwell Internat., Golden, Colo., 1982-83, program mgr. waste isolation pilot project, 1983-85; sr. project mgr. West Valley Demonstration Project Dames and Moore, West Valley, NY, 1985-87; dir. Radiol. Svcs., 1987-92; v.p. govt. svcs. Internat. Tech. Corp., Englewood, Colo., 1992—2006; v.p. radiol. ops. Shaw Group, Centennial, Colo., 2003—07; pres. SHB, Inc., Centennial, 2007—. U.S. rep. Internat. Conf. on Radiation Hazards in Mining, Beijing, 1986. Mem. Nat. Health Physics Soc. (pres. Rocky Mountain chpt. 1982-83, 2008-09, chmn. uranium com., Colo. Mining Assn. Office Phone: 303-941-1506. Personal E-mail: shb12@msn.com.

BROWN, STUART I., ophthalmologist, educator; b. Chgo., Mar. 1, 1933; s. Leonard and Ann (Gladin) B.; m. Isabel Bodor; children: Sarah, Emily BMS, U. Ill., Chgo., 1955, MD, 1957. Intern Jackson Meml. Hosp., Miami, Fla., 1957-58; resident in opthalmology, Eye, Ear, Nose and Throat Hosp., Tulane Med.Sch., New Orleans, 1961; fellow in cornea Mass. Eye and Ear Infirmary, Boston, 1962-66; clin. asst. prof. dept. opthalmology N.Y. Hosp.-Cornell Med. Ctr., NYC, 1966, dir. cornea svcs. cornea rsch. lab., 1966-69, clin. assoc. prof., 1970-73; chmn., prof. dept. opthalmology U. Pitts. Sch. Medicine, 1974-82, U. Calif. Sch. Medicine, San Diego, 1983—. Bd. dirs. nat. adv. commn. Nat. Eye Bank, Inc. Recipient Heed Ophthalmic Found. award, 1976 Mem. Am. Acad. Ophthalmology, AMA, Assn. Rsch. in

Vision and Ophthalmology, Assn. U. Profs. Ophthalmology, Internat. Soc. Eye Rsch. Office: U Calif San Diego Shiley Eye Ctr - Ophthalmol 9415 Campus Dr La Jolla CA 92093-0946 E-mail: sbrown@eyecenter.ucsd.edu.

BROWN, TOD DAVID, bishop; b. San Francisco, Nov. 15, 1936; s. George Wilson and Edna Anne (Dunn) Brown. BA, St. John's Coll., 1958; STB, Gregorian U., Rome, 1960; MA in Theology, U. San Francisco, 1970, MAT in Edn., 1976. Ordained priest Diocese of Monterey, Calif., 1963, dir. edn., 1980—82, chancellor, 1982—89, vicar gen., chancellor, 1983—89; pastor St. Francis Xavier, Seaside, Calif., 1977—82; ordained bishop Diocese of Boise City, Idaho, 1989, bishop Idaho, 1988—98, Diocese of Orange, Calif., 1998—. Past mem. 3rd millennium com. US Conf. Cath. Bishops, past chmn. com. ecumenical and inter religious affairs, past mem. com. mission, pastoral practices, past chair laity com., chmn. subcom. inter religious affairs; mem. Episcopal bd. govs. N.Am. Coll. Named Papal Chaplain Pope Paul VI, 1975. Mem.: Sovereign Mil. Hospitaller Order of St. John of Jerusalem of Rhodes and of Malta, Equestrian Order of the Holy Sepulchre of Jerusalem, Canon Law Soc. America (past mem. bishop's com. on liturgy, econ. concerns of the Holy See), Cath. Biblical Assn., Cath. Theol. Soc. America. Roman Catholic. Avocations: films, travel, reading, exercise. Office: Diocese of Orange Marywood Ctr 2811 E Villa Real Dr Orange CA 92867-1932 Office Phone: 714-282-3000. Office Fax: 714-282-3029.

BROWN, WALTER FRANCIS, JR., lawyer; AB, U. Calif., Berkeley, 1982; JD, U. Notre Dame, 1985. Bar: Ariz. 1986, Calif. 1987, US Ct. Appeals (9th cir.), US Dist. Ct. (no., ea. and ctrl. dists. Calif.), US Dist. Ct. (ea. dist. Wis.), US Dist. Ct. (dist. Ariz.). Asst. US atty. (ctrl. dist. Calif.) US Dept. Justice, LA, 1989—94; with Thelen Reid & Priest; ptnr. Gray Cary, San Francisco, Orrick, Herrington & Sutcliffe LLP, 2003—. Named one of Top 10 Trial Lawyers in Am., Nat. Law Jour., 2006, Am.'s Leading Lawyers, Chambers USA, 2006. Mem.: ABA, State Bar Calif., State Bar Ariz. Office: Orrick Herrington & Sutcliffe LLP The Orrick Bldg 405 Howard St San Francisco CA 94105 Office Phone: 415-773-5995. Office Fax: 415-773-5759. E-mail: wbrown@orrick.com.

BROWN, WAYNE J., former mayor; b. 1936; BS, Ariz. State U. Staff acct. Arthur Andersen & Co. CPA's, 1960-63; mng. ptnr. Wayne Brown & Co. CPA's, 1964-79; dir. acctg. Ariz. State Dept. Adminstrn., 1979-80; chmn. & CEO Brown Evans Distbg. Co., Mesa, Ariz., 1980—; mayor City of Mesa, 1996—2000. Office: 306 S Country Club Dr Mesa AZ 85211

BROWN, WILLIAM E., retail executive; With McCormick, Inc., McKesson Corp., 1972-77; sr. v.p. Vivitar Corp., 1977-80; chmn., CEO Central Garden & Pet, Walnut Creek, Calif., 1980—2003, chmn., 2003—07, chmn., CEO, 2007—. Office: Ctrl Garden & Pet 1340 Treat Blvd Walnut Creek CA 94597

BROWN, WILLIE LEWIS, JR., former mayor, state legislator, lawyer; b. Mineola, Tex., Mar. 20, 1934; s. Willie Lewis and Minnie (Boyd) B.; children: Susan, Robin, Michael. BA, San Francisco State Coll., 1955; LL.D., Hastings Coll. Law, 1958; postgrad. fellow, Crown Coll., 1970, U. Calif.-Santa Cruz, 1970. Bar: Calif. 1959. Mem. Calif. State Assembly, Sacramento, 1964-95, speaker, 1980-95, chmn. Ways and Means Com., 1971-74; chmn. revenue and taxation com., 1976-79; Democratic Whip Calif. State Assembly, 1969-70, majority floor leader, 1979-80, chmn. legis. black caucus, 1980, chmn. govtl. efficiency and economy com., 1968-84; mayor San Francisco, 1995—2004. Mem. U. Calif. bd. regents, 1972, Dem. Nat. Com., 1989-90; co-chmn. Calif. del. to Nat. Black Polit. Conv., 1972, Calif. del. to Nat. Dem. Conv., 1980; nat. campaign chmn. Jesse Jackson for Pres., 1988. Mem. State Legis. Leaders Found. (dir.), Nat. Conf. State Legislatures, NAACP, Black Am. Polit. Assn. Calif. (co-founder, past chmn.), Calif. Bar Assn., Alpha Phi Alpha, Phi Alpha Delta Democrat. Methodist.

BROWNE, JOHN CHARLES, physicist, researcher, lab administrator; b. Pottstown, Pa., July 29, 1942; s. Charles Ignatius and Mary Agnes (Titzer) B.; m. Susan Mary Mazzarella, Dec. 30, 1972 (div. Dec. 1984); children— Christopher Ryan, Adam Charles; m. Marti Moore, May 4, 1985; 1 child, Courtney Keese. BS, Drexel U., 1965; PhD, Duke U., 1969; DSc (hon.), Drexel U., 1998. Instr. Duke U., Durham, NC, 1969-70; staff scientist Lawrence Livermore Lab., Calif., 1970-79; group leader Los Alamos Nat. Lab., 1979-81, div. leader, 1981-84, assoc. dir., 1984-93; dir. Los Alamos Neutron Sci. Ctr., Los Alamos, 1993—97; lab. dir. Los Alamos Nat. Lab., 1997—2003, sr. scientist, 2003, ret, 2003; owner JCB Sci. Cons., LLC, 2005—. Contbr. articles to profl. jours. Bd. mem. Hertz Found., 2000—, Nev. Test Site Historical Found., 2004—. NASA fellow, 1965-67 Fellow AAAS, Am. Phys. Soc. Avocations: golf, hiking, skiing, tennis. Office Phone: 435-668-7265. E-mail: jcbrowne729@msn.com.

BROWNING, JAMES ROBERT, federal judge; b. Great Falls, Mont., Oct. 1, 1918; s. Nicholas Henry and Minnie Sally (Foley) Browning; m. Marie Rose Chapell. BA, Mont. State U., Missoula, 1938; LLB with honors, U. Mont., 1941, LLD (hon.), 1978, Santa Clara U., 1989. Bar: Mont. 1941, D.C. 1953, U.S. Supreme Ct. 1952. Spl. atty. antitrust divsn. US Dept. Justice, 1941—43, spl. atty. gen. litigation sect. antitrust divsn., 1946—48, chief antitrust dept. N.W. regional office, 1948—49, asst. chief gen. litigation sect. antitrust divsn., 1949—51, 1st asst. civil divsn., 1951—52, exec. asst. to atty. gen., 1952—53, chief, Exec. Office for US Attys., 1953; pvt. practice Washington, 1953—58; lectr. NYU Sch. Law, 1953, Georgetown U. Law Center, 1957—58; law clk. US Supreme Ct., Washington, 1958—61; judge US Ct. Appeals (9th cir.), 1961—76, 1988—2000, chief judge, 1976—88, sr. judge, 2000—. Reed justice com. on continuing edn., tng. and adminstrn. Jud. Conf. of US, 1967—68, com. on ct. adminstrn., 1969—71, chmn. subcom. on jud. stats., 1969—71, com. to study the illustrative rules of jud. misconduct, 1969, com. on the budget, 1971—77, adminstrn. office, subcom. on budget, 1974—76, mem., 1976—88, exec. com. of conf., 1978—87, com. to study the illustrative rules of jud. misconduct, 1985—87, com. to study U.S. jud. conf., 1986—88, com. on internat. conf. of appellate judges, 1987—90; David T. Lewis disting. judge-in-residence U. Utah, 1987; Blankenbaker lectr. U. Mont., 1987; Sibley lectr. U. Ga., 1987; lectr. Human Rights Inst., Santa Clara U. Sch. Law, Strasbourg. Editor-in-chief: Mont. Law Rev. Dir. Western Justice Found.; chmn. 9th Cir. Hist. Soc. 1st lt. US Army, 1943—46. Decorated Bronze Star; recipient Devitt Disting. Svc. to Justice award, 1990; named to, Order of the Grizzly, U. Mont., 1973; scholar in residence, Santa Clara U., 1989, U. Mont., 1991. Mem.: FBA (bd. dirs. 1945—61, nat. coun. 1958—62), ABA (judge adv. com. to standing com. on Ethics and Profl. Responsibility 1973—75), Am. Soc. Legal History (adv. bd. jour.), Am. Judicature Soc. (chmn. com. on fed. judiciary 1973—74, bd. dirs. 1972—75, Herbert Harley award 1984), Inst. Jud. Adminstrn., Am. Law Inst., Mont. Bar Assn. (Jameson award 2001), D.C. Bar Assn., Nat. Lawyers Club (bd. govs. 1959—63). Office: US Ct Appeals 9th Cir 95 7th St San Francisco CA 94103

BROWNING, RODERICK HANSON, banker; b. Salt Lake City, Oct. 9, 1925; s. Frank M. and Eugenia H. B.; m. Mary Wadsworth, Mar. 7, 1956; children— Patricia Ann, Jonathan Wadsworth, Frank Wadsworth, Anthony Stuart, Carolyn Rae. AB, Stanford U., 1948. Vice pres. Bank of Utah, Ogden, 1954-59, chmn., 1959—; chmn. bd., pres. Bank of Brigham City, Utah, 1973—; chmn. bd. Bank No. Utah, Clearfield, 1971—; dir. Salt Lake City br. Fed. Res. Bank San Francisco, 1969-74. Bd. dirs., treas. Ogden Indsl. Devel. Corp., Weber County (Utah) Indsl. Devel. Bur.; adv. bd. St. Benedicts Hosp.; bd. dirs. Weber State Coll., Ogden; former pres. United Fund No. Utah. Served with U.S. Army, 1948-53. Mem. Am. Bankers Assn., Utah Bankers Assn. (former mem. exec. com.), Am. Legion. Clubs: Rotary (Ogden); Weber, Alta, Ogden Golf and Country. Office: Bank of Utah 2605 Washington Blvd Ogden UT 84401-3626

BROWNLEE, DONALD EUGENE, II, astronomer, educator; b. Las Vegas, Nev., Dec. 21, 1943; s. Donald Eugene and Geraldine Florence (Stephen) B.; m. Paula Szkody. BS in Elec. Engring, U. Calif., Berkeley, 1965; PhD in Astronomy, U. Wash., 1970. Research assoc. U. Wash., 1970-77, asso. prof. astronomy, 1977-89; asso. geochemistry Calif. Inst. Tech., Pasadena, 1977-82; prof. astronomy U. Wash., 1989—. Cons. NASA, 1976— Author papers in field, chpts. in books. Grantee NASA, 1975; recipient J. Lawrence Smith medal Nat. Acad. of Sciences, 1994. Fellow Am. Acad. Arts & Scis.; mem. Internat. Astron. Union, Am. Astron. Assn., Meteoritical Soc. (Leonard medal 1996), Com. Space Rsch. Dust, NAS (NASA PI stardust mission). Office: U Wash Dept Astronomy Seattle WA 98195-0001

BROWNLEY, JULIA, state legislator; b. Aiken, SC, Aug. 28, 0952; children: Hannah, Fred. BA in Polit. Sci., George Washington U., 1975; MBA, Am. U., 1979. Member then president, Santa Monica-Malibu School Bd, formerly; California State Assemblyman, District 41, 2006-; chair, Subcommittee No 2 on Education Fin, currently. YWCA Woman of the Year, 2005. Democrat. Office: Dist 41 6355 Topanga Canyon Blvd Suite 205 Woodland Hills CA 91367 Office Phone: 818-596-4141, 310-395-3414. Fax: 818-596-4150. Business E-Mail: assemblymember.brownley@assembly.ca.gov.

BROWNLIE, ROBERT WILLIAM, lawyer; b. Sasebo, Japan, Mar. 5, 1962; s. Robert Philip and Sachiko (Sugita) B.; m. Perla Esteban, Jan. 7, 1989. BA in Economics, U. Calif. San Diego, 1985; JD, U. Calif. Davis, 1988. Bar: Calif. 1988, U.S. Dist. Ct. (so., ea. ctrl. & no. dist. Calif.), U.S. Ct. Appeals (5th, 9th cir.), US Ct. Fed. Claims, US Supreme Ct. Rsch. asst. U. Calif. Davis Sch. of Law, 1986-87, teaching asst., 1987-88; summer assoc. Gray, Cary, Ames & Frye, San Diego, 1987, assoc., 1988-90, Milberg, Weiss, Bershad, Specthrie & Lerach, San Diego, 1990-92, Gray, Cary, Ware & Freidenrich, San Diego, 1992-95, mem., 1995—2004; ptnr., co-chmn. Securities Litigation practice group DLA Piper Rudnick Gray Cary, San Diego, 2005—. Contbr. articles to profl. jours. Pres., v.p., bd. dirs. Asian Bus. Assn., San Diego, 1994-98; bd. dirs. San Diego Mediation Ctr., 1994-95; fin. com. mem. San Diego Automotive Mus., 1993-95. Mem. ABA (mem. class action and derivative litigation com.), Nat. Asian Pacific Am. Bar Assn. (bd. dirs. 1997-99), Calif. Bar Assn., San Diego County Bar Assn. (legis. com. mem. 1988-95), Pan Asian Lawyers Assn. of San Diego (v.p., pres., bd. dirs. 1995-99), Order of Coif, Phi Kappa Phi. Democrat. Avocations: automobile enthusiast, golf, travel, sailing, boating. Home: 1450 Woodglen Ter Bonita CA 91902-4283 Office: DLA Piper US LLP 401 B St Ste 1700 San Diego CA 92101-4297 Office Phone: 619-699-3665. Office Fax: 858-699-2701. Business E-Mail: robert.brownlie@dlapiper.com.

BROWNSON, JACQUES CALMON, architect; b. Aurora, Ill., Aug. 3, 1923; s. Clyde Arthur and Iva Kline (Felter) B.; m. Doris L. Curry, 1946; children: Joel C., Lorre J., Daniel J. (dec. Jan 2005). BS in Architecture, Ill. Inst. Tech., 1948, MS, 1954. Instr., asst. prof. architecture Ill. Inst. Tech., 1949-59; prof. architecture, chmn. dept. U. Mich., 1966-68; chief design C.F. Murphy Assocs., Chgo., 1959—61; project arch., chief designer Chgo. Civic Ctr. Archs., 1961—68; dir. state bldg. divsn. State of Colo., Denver, 1986—88; pvt. practice Denver, 1988—. Former mng. arch. Chgo. Pub. Bldg. Commn.; past dir. planning and devel. Auraria Ctr. for Higher Edn., Denver; bd. dirs. Capital Constrn., Denver; guest lectr. architecture in U.S. and Europe. Prin. works include Chgo. Civic Ctr., Lake Denver, Colo., 1985, Chgo. Tribune/Cabrini Green Housing, 1993; author: History of Chicago Architects, 1996, Oral History of Jacuqes Calmon Brownson, 1996. Recipient award for Geneva House Archtl. Record mag., 1956; Design award for steel framed factory Progressive Architecture mag., 1957. Home and Office: 659 Josephine St Denver CO 80206-3722 Office Phone: 303-321-8505.

BROWNSTEIN, BARBARA LAVIN, geneticist, educator, director; b. Phila., Sept. 8, 1931; d. Edward A. and Rose (Silverstein) Lavin; m. Melvin Brownstein, June 1949 (div. 1955); children: Judith Brownstein Kaufmann, Dena. Asst. editor Biol. Abstracts, Phila., 1957-58; research fellow dept. microbial genetics Karolinska Inst., Stockholm, 1962-64; assoc. Wistar Inst., Phila., 1964-68; assoc. prof. molecular biology, dept. biology Temple U., Phila., 1968-74, prof., 1974-96, prof. emeritus, 1996—, chmn. dept., 1978-81, provost, 1983-90; sr. assoc. Ctr. Ednl. Rsch. U. Wash., Seattle, 1994—. Vis. scientist dept. tumor cell biology Imperial Cancer Rsch. Fund Labs., London, 1973-74; bd. dirs. Univ. City Sci. Ctr., Greater Phila. Econ. Devel. Coun., Forum Exec. Women; program officer NSF, 1992-93; sr. assoc. Inst. Ednl. Inquiry, Seattle, 1994—. Bd. dirs. Lopez Island Sch., 2001—. Recipient Liberal Arts Alumni award for excellence in teaching Temple U., 1980; recipient Outstanding Faculty Woman award Temple U., 1980 Fellow AAAS; mem. Am. Soc. Cell Biology, N.Y. Acad. Sci., Assn. Women in Sci., NSF (program officer 1992-93). Home: PO Box 835 Lopez Island WA 98261 Personal E-mail: bbrownst@msn.com.

BRUBAKER, CRAWFORD FRANCIS, JR., federal agency administrator, aerospace scientist, consultant; b. Fruitland, Idaho, Apr. 23, 1924; s. Crawford Francis and Cora Susan (Flora) B.; m. Lucile May Christensen, May 5, 1945; children: Eric Stephen, Alan Kenneth, Craig Martin, Paul David. BA, Pomona Coll., 1946; MBA, U. Pa., 1948. Office mgr. Lockheed Calif. Co., Burbank, 1948-54, sales adminstr., 1954-57, with fighter contracts divsn., field office rep., 1959-65, asst. dir. fighter sales, 1965-69, dep. mgr. bid and proposals, 1969-74, mgr. govt. sales, 1974-76; dir. internat. mktg. devel. and policy Lockheed Corp., Burbank, 1976-83; dep. asst. sec. for aerospace U.S. Dept. Commerce, Washington, 1983-87; internat. aerospace cons., 1987—. Vice chmn. Industry Sector Adv. Com., Washington, 1979-83; mem. Aero. Policy Rev. Com., Washington, 1983-87. Vice chmn. So. Calif. Dist. Export Coun., L.A., 1980-83, 88-91, chmn., 1992-93. Lt. (j.g.) USN, 1943-45, PTO. Mem. AIAA, Am. Def. Preparedness Assn., Sigma Alpha Epsilon. Republican. Presbyterian. Avocations: coin collecting/numismatics, golf, fishing, photography. E-mail: bru102@royaloaksmail.com.

BRUCE, JAMES EDMUND, retired utilities executive; b. Boise, Idaho, June 23, 1920; s. James E. and Bessie (Barcus) B.; m. Lois I. Stevens, Aug. 24, 1946; children: James E., IV, Steven, Robert, David. Student, Coll. Idaho, 1937-39; BA, Portland U., 1941; postgrad., Georgetown U., 1941-42; LLB, U. Idaho, 1949. Bar: Idaho 1948. Asst. atty. gen. State of Idaho, 1948-49; dep. pros. atty. Ada County, Idaho, 1949-51; with Idaho Power Co., Boise, 1951-87, v.p., 1968-74, pres., chief operating officer, 1974-76, pres., chief exec. officer, 1976-85, chmn., 1985-87, ret., 1987. Dir. Albertson's Inc., First Security Corp., 1981-93; chmn. Blue Cross of Idaho, 1988-90. Bd. dirs. Mountain States Legal Found., 1977-88; mem. St. Alphonsus Found., Boise State U. Found., Bishop Kelly Found., Boise Park Bd., 1958-78; chmn. Idaho State Lottery; Idaho chmn. U.S. Savs. Bonds, 1976-85; chmn. bd. trustees St. Alphonsus, 1985-2002; trustee Coll. Idaho, YMCA, Idaho Nature Conservancy; pres. Ada County Hwy. Dist. Commn. With U.S. Army, 1942-46. Mem. ABA, Boise Execs. Assn., Edison Electric Assn. (dir. 1978-85), N.W. Electric Light and Power Assn. (pres. 1982), Boise C. of C., Arid Club, Crane Creek Country Club, Rotary, Elks, K.C. Roman Catholic.

BRUCE, WILLIAM A., airport executive; BS in Polit. Sci., UCLA, 1967; MPA, Calif. State U., LA, 1971. Budget analyst, chief negotiator employee rels. City of L.A., 1969-80, various other positions, 1980-99; dir. airports adminstrn. L.A. World Airports, 1999—. Office: Los Angeles Dept Airports 1 World Way Los Angeles CA 90045-5803

BRUCH, CAROL SOPHIE, law educator; b. Rockford, Ill., June 11, 1941; d. Ernest and Margarete (Willstätter) B.; m. Jack E. Myers, 1960 (div. 1973); children: Margarete Louise Myers Feinstein, Kurt Randall Myers. AB, Shimer Coll., 1960; JD, U. Calif.-Berkeley, 1972; Dr. honoris causa, U. Basel, 2000. Bar: Calif. 1973, U.S. Supreme Ct. 1980. Law clk. to Justice William O. Douglas U.S. Supreme Ct., 1972-73; acting prof. law U. Calif., Davis, 1973—78, prof., 1978—2001, rsch. prof., prof. emeritus, 2001—05, chair doctoral program in human devel., 1996—2001, disting. rsch. prof., disting. prof. emeritus, 2005—. Acad. vis. law dept. U. Munich, 1978-79, 92, U. Cologne, 1990, U. Cambridge, 1990, London Sch. Econs. and Polit. Sci., 1991, Kings Coll., London, 1991; vis. prof. U. Calif., Berkeley, 1983, Columbia U., 1986, U. Basel, 1994, vis. Fulbright prof. Hebrew U., Jerusalem, 1996-97; vis. fellow Fitzwilliam Coll., Cambridge, Eng., 1990, U. Calif. Humanities Rsch. Inst., Irvine, 1999, vis. scholar Inst. for Advanced Legal Studies (Univ. London), 1991, UCLA Ctr. Study of Women, 2004-05; cons. to Ctr. for Family in Transition, 1981, Calif. Law Revision Commn., 1979-82, NOW Legal Def. and Edn. Fund, 1980-81; lectr., legis. drafting and testimony, 1976—; mem. U.S. del. 4th Inter-Am. Specialized Conf. on Pvt. Internat. Law, OAS, 1989. Contbr. articles to legal jours. Editor Calif. Law Rev., 1971; editorial Bd. Family Law Quar., 1980-87; Representing Children, 1995—, Am. Jour. of Comparative Law, 2001—; lectr. in field. Mem. adv. com. child support and child custody Calif. Commn. on Status of Women, 1981-83, child support adv. com. Calif. Jud. Coun., 1991-94, adv. com. on private internat. law U.S. Dept. State, 1989—, internat. child abduction steering com. Internat. Ctr. for Missing and Exploited Children (London), 1999-2001; host parent Am. Field Service, Davis, 1977-78. Max Rheinstein sr. rsch. fellow Alexander von Humboldt Found., Fed. Republic Germany, 1978-79, 92, Fulbright fellow, Western Europe, 1990, Fulbright Sr. Scholar, Israel, 1997, Disting. Pub. Svc. award U. Calif. Davis Acad. Senate, 1990. Mem. ABA, Calif. State Bar Assn., Am. Law Inst., Internat. Soc. Family Law (exec. coun. 1994-2000, 2002—), Internat. Acad. Comparative Law, Order of Coif. Democrat. Jewish. Office: U Calif Sch Law 400 Mrak Hall Dr Davis CA 95616-5201

BRUCKHEIMER, JERRY LEON, producer; b. Detroit, Sept. 21, 1945; m. Linda Bruckheimer. Grad., U. Ariz., DFA (hon.), 2006. Former prodr., art dir. advt. agy.; co-founder Don Simpson/Jerry Bruckheimer Films, 1983. Assoc. prodr. (films) Culpepper Cattle Company, 1972, Rafferty and the Gold Dust Twins, 1975; prodr. (films) American Gigolo, 1980, Young Doctors in Love, 1982,(with George Pappas) Farewell My Lovely, 1975, (with Dick Richards) March or Die, 1977, (with William S. Gillmore) Defiance, 1980, (with Ronnie Caan) Thief, 1981, Cat People, 1982, (with Don Simpson) Flashdance, 1983, Beverly Hills Cop, 1984, Thief of Hearts, 1984, Top Gun, 1986, Beverly Hills Cop II, 1987, Days of Thunder, 1990, Bad Boys, 1995, Crimson Tide, 1995, Dangerous Minds, 1995, The Rock, 1996, Con Air, 1997, Enemy of the State, 1998, Armageddon, 1998, Gone in 60 Seconds, 2000, Coyote Ugly, 2000, Remember the Titans, 2000, Pearl Harbor, 2001, Black Hawk Down, 2001, Bad Company, 2002, Kangaroo Jack, 2003, Pirates of the Caribbean: The Curse of the Black Pearl, 2003, Bad Boys II, 2003, Veronica Guerin, 2003, King Arthur, 2004, National Treasure, 2004, Glory Road, 2006, Pirates of the Caribbean: Dead Man's Chest, 2006, Deja Vu, 2006, Pirates of the Caribbean: At World's End, 2007, National Treasure: Book of Secrets, 2007; exec. prodr. (films): (with Don Simpson) The Ref, 1994, Soldier of Fortune, 1997, Dangerous Minds, 1995, (TV films) Max Q, 1998, Swing Vote, 1999; exec. prodr. (TV series): CSI: Crime Scene Investigation, 2000, The Amazing Race, 2001— (Primetime Emmy for Outstanding Reality-Competition Program, Acad. TV Arts and Scis., 2003-08), CSI: Miami, 2002, Without a Trace, 2002-06, Profiles From the Front Line, 2003, Skin, 2003, Cold Case, 2004-06, Close to Home, 2005, CSI: NY, 2006. Recipient ShoWest award Prodr. of Yr., 1999, David O. Selznick Lifetime Achievement award Prodrs. Guild of Am., 2000, Salute to Excellence award Mus. TV and Radio, 2006, Norman Lear Achievement award in TV, 2007; named Variety Showman of Yr., 2006; named one of The 50 Most Powerful People in Hollywood Premiere mag., 2003-05, The 100 Most Powerful Celebrities, Forbes.com, 2006, 2007, 2008, The 50 Smartest People in Hollywood, Entertainment Weekly, 2007; named to LA Times Power Issue, 2006, Premiere Mag. Power Players List, 2006. Office: Jerry Bruckheimer Films 1631 10th St Santa Monica CA 90404-3705

BRUEN, JAMES A., lawyer; b. South Hampton, NY, Nov. 29, 1943; s. John Francis and Kathryn Jewell (Arthur) B.; m. Carol Lynn Heller, June 13, 1968; children: Jennifer Lynn, Garrett John. BA cum laude, Claremont Men's Coll., 1965; JD, Stanford U., 1968. Bar: Calif. 1968, US Dist. Ct. (no., ea., so. and ctrl. dists.) Calif. 1970, US Ct. Claims

1972, US Tax Ct. 1972, US Ct. Appeals (9th cir.) 1972, US Ct. Appeals (10th cir.) 2006, US Supreme Ct. 1973, US Dist. Ct. Ariz. 1993, N.Mex. 1999. Atty. FCC, Washington, 1968—70; asst. U.S. atty. criminal div. Office of U.S. Atty., San Francisco, 1970—73, asst. U.S. atty. civil divsn., 1973—75, chief of civil divsn., 1975—77; ptnr. Landels, Ripley & Diamond, San Francisco, 1977—2000, Farella Braun & Martel LLP, San Francisco, 2000—. Faculty Practising Law Inst. Def. Rsch. Inst., ABA/Am. Law Inst. Co-author: Pharmaceutical Products Liability, 1989; contbg. editor: Hazardous Waste and Toxic Torts Law and Strategy, 1987-92; contbr. numerous articles to profl. jours. Fellow Am. Bar Found., Am. Coll. Environ. Lawyers; mem. ABA (vice chmn. environ. quality com. nat. resources sect. 1989-93, co-chmn. enforment litig. subcom. environ. litig. com. litig. sect. 1990-92), Am. Inn Ct. (master-at-large), Internat., Soc. for Environ. Epidemiology. Avocations: scuba diving, travel. Office: Farella Braun & Martel Russ Bldg 17th Fl 235 Montgomery St San Francisco CA 94104 Office Phone: 415-954-4430. Business E-Mail: jbruen@fbm.com.

BRUENING, GEORGE E., virologist; b. Chgo., Aug. 10, 1938; Diploma, Carroll Coll., 1960; MS, U. Wis., 1963, PhD in Biochemistry, 1965. Prof. biochemistry U. Calif., Davis, 1967—83, prof. plant pathology, 1984—; Guggenheim Meml. Found. fellow, 1974-75. Vis. scientist plant path., Cornell U., Ithaca, N.Y., 1974-75, vis. scientist biochemistry, U. Adelaide, Australia, 1981; vis. scientist plant indsl. CSIRO, Canberra, Australia, 1989. Fellow Am. Phytopath Soc.; mem. Nat. Acad. Sci., Soc. Microbiol. UK, AAAS. Office: Dept Plant Pathology U Calif Davis Davis CA 95616

BRUFF, HAROLD HASTINGS, law educator, former dean; b. 1944; BA in Am. History and Lit., Williams Coll.; JD magna cum laude, Harvard U. Law faculty Ariz. State U., Tempe, 1971-79; sr. atty.-advisor Office of Legal Counsel, U.S. Dept. Justice, 1979-81; cons. to chmn. Pres.'s Commn. on the Accident at Three Mile Island, 1981; law faculty U. Tex., Austin, 1983-85, John S. Redditt prof. law, 1985-92; Donald Rothschild rsch. prof. George Washington U. Law Sch., Washington, 1992-96; dean U. Colo. Sch. Law, Boulder, 1996—2003, Charles Inglis Thomson prof. law, 2003—. Contbr. articles to profl. jours. Mem. ABA, Phi Beta Kappa. Office: U Colo Boulder Sch Law 208 Fleming Law Bldg Campus Box 401 Boulder CO 80309-0001 E-mail: Harold.Bruff@colorado.edu.

BRUICE, THOMAS C., chemist, educator; b. LA, 1925; BS, U. So. Calif., 1950, PhD, 1954. Postdoctoral fellowship UCLA; asst. prof. biochemistry Yale Med. Sch., 1955—58; assoc. prof. biochemistry Johns Hopkins Med. School, 1958—60; prof. chemistry Cornell U., 1960—64, U. Calif., Santa Barbara, 1964—95, rsch. prof. chemistry and biochemistry, 1995—. Contbr. articles to profl. journals. Served USN, 1943—46. Recipient Richard C. Tolman Medal of So. Calif. Sect., Am. Chem. Soc., 1979, Repligen Medal, 1987, Arthur C. Cope Scholar Award, 1987, Alfred Bader Medal, 1988, Renaud Award of Mich. State Sect., 1988, James Flack Norris Award, 1996, Career Devel. Award, NIH, 1956, Lifetime Investigator Award, 1962, MERIT Award, 1990, 1997; Guggenheim Fellow, 1979—80. Fellow AAAS, Royal Soc. Chemistry; mem. NAS (Award in Chem. Sciences, 2005), Am. Acad. Arts and Sciences. Office: U Calif Santa Barbara Dept Chemistry and Biochemistry 9510 Santa Barbara CA 93106-9510 Office Phone: 805-893-2044. Office Fax: 805-893-4120. Business E-Mail: tcbruice@chem.ucsb.edu.

BRULTE, JAMES L., state legislator; b. Glen Cove, NY, Apr. 13, 1956; BA, Calif. State Poly. U. Mem. staff U.S. Senator S.I. Hayakawa, Rep. Nat. Com., 1981; asst. to asst. sec. for res. affairs Dept. Def., from 1984; later White House advance rep. for Vice Pres. of U.S.; mem. Calif. State Assembly, 1990-96, Calif. State Senate, 1996—, vice chair budget and fiscal rev. com., mem. fin., investment and internat. trade com., vice chair energy, utilities and comms. com. Served with Calif. Air N.G., 1974. Republican. Office: State Capitol Rm 5087 Sacramento CA 95814 also: 10861 Foothill Blvd Ste 325 Rancho Cucamonga CA 91730-3859

BRUMMEL, LISA E., computer software company executive; b. Conn., Nov. 7, 1959; BA in Sociology, Yale U., 1981; MBA, UCLA. Sales mgmt. Prentice Hall Inc.; from mgr. to corp. v.p. home products divsn. Microsoft Corp., Redmond, Wash., 1989, corp. v.p. home & retail divsn., 1995—2005, corp. v.p. human resources, 2005, sr. v.p. human resources, 2005—; co-owner Seattle Storm, WNBA, 2008—. Active Hopelink cmty.svc. programs; vol. U. Wash. Med. Ctr.; bd. dir. Wash. Acad. Performing Arts. Office: Microsoft Corp One Microsoft Way Redmond WA 98052-6399

BRUNELLO-MCCAY, ROSANNE, sales executive; b. Cleve., Aug. 26, 1960; d. Carl Carmello and Vivan Lucille (Caranna) B.; m. Walter B. McCay, Feb. 26, 1994; children: Angela Breanna, Mikala Bell. Student, U. Cin., 1978—81, Cleve. State U., 1981—82. Indsl. sales engr. Alta Machine Tool, Denver, 1982; mem. sales./purchases Ford Tool & Machine, Denver, 1982-84; sales/ptnr. Mountain Rep. Enterprises, Denver, 1984-86; pres., owner Mountain Rep. Ariz., Phoenix, 1986—; pres. Mountain Rep. Oreg., Portland, 1990—, Mountain Rep. Wash., 1991—, Mountain Rep. Calif., Sunnyvale, 1997—, San Clemente, 1998—, Port Clinton, Ohio, 1999—; we. regional sales mgr. Offshore Internat., Inc., Tucson, 2002—. Sec. Computer & Automated Systems Assoc., 1987, vice chmn., 88, chmn., 89. Active mem. Rep. Party, 1985—; mem. Phoenix Art Mus., Grand Canyon Minority Coun., 1994; vol. fundraiser Make-A-Wish Found., 1995—, Leukemia Soc., 2006; founder Ariz. Sonora Corridor Network. Named Mrs. Chandler Internat., Mrs. Ariz. Internat. Orgn., 1996, Mrs. East Valley U.S., 1997; finalist Mrs. Ariz. Internat., 1996, Ms. Ariz. 2000, Ms. U.S. Continental Pageant; nominated The 19th Ann. Athena award Greater Phoenix C. of C., 2006. Mem. NAFE, Soc. Mfg. Engrs. (pres. award 1988), Computer Automated Assn. (sec. 1987, vice chmn. 1988 chmn. 1989), Manufacturers and Agents Nat. Assn. (chair-elect 2002), Nat. Hist. Soc., Italian Cultural Soc., Tempe C. of C., Vocat. Ednl. Club Am. (mem. exec. bd., pres. 1987—). Roman Catholic. Avocations: sports, aerobics, dance, skiing, golf, tennis. Office: Mountain Rep 254 S Lakeview Blvd Chandler AZ 85225-5792 Office Phone: 480-899-1900. Business E-Mail: rosanne@mtnrep.com.

BRUNER, NANCY J., publishing executive; B, N.Mex. State U.; MFA, U. So. Calif. With US West Media Group, Denver; cons. dir. bus. devel. Spring Multimedia, Kansas City; dir. new media Seattle Times, now v.p. new media. Office: Seattle Times PO Box 70 Seattle WA 98111-0070

BRUNETT, ALEXANDER JOSEPH, archbishop; b. Detroit, Jan. 17, 1934; s. Raymond and Cecilia Gill Brunett. BA, Sacred Heart Seminary; STL in Sacred Theology, Pontifical Gregorian U., STB. Ordained priest Archdiocese of Detroit, 1958; assoc. pastor St. Rose of Lima Parish, Detroit, 1959—61, St. Alphonsus Parish, Dearborn, 1961—62; chaplain Univ. Mich., Ann Arbor, 1962—64, Ea. Mich. Univ., Ypsilanti, 1968; academic dean St. John's Provincial Sem., Plymouth, 1969—73; dir. Div. of Ecumenical and Interreligious Affairs Archdiocese of Detroit, 1973—91; pastor St. Aidan Parish, Livonia, Mich., Shrine of Little Flower Parish, Royal Oak, Mich., 1991—94; ordained bishop, 1994; bishop Diocese of Helena, Mont., 1994—97; archbishop Archdiocese of Seattle, Wash., 1997—. Mem. Internat. Roman Cath.-World Meth. Dialogue; co-chair Anglican-Roman Cath. Internat. Commn.; chmn. Archdiocesan Theol. Commn.; vicar N.W. Wayne Vicariate, Archdiocese of Detroit; nat. chmn. Third Jewish-Christian Dialogue, Detroit. Editl. writer Mich. Cath. newspaper. Bd. trustees Cath. Near East Welfare Assn.; mem. bd. dirs. St. Patrick Seminary, Menlo Park, Calif., Mundelein Seminary, Ill. Recipient DOVE Award, Ecumenical Inst. for Jewish-Christian Studies, 1996. Mem.: Nat. Assn. of Diocesan Ecumenical Officers (pres. 1974—81), US Conf. of Cath. Bishops Com. on Ecumenical and Interreligious Affairs (chmn. 1996). Roman Catholic. Office: Archdiocese Of Seattle 710 9th Ave Seattle WA 98104-2017

BRUNETTI, MELVIN T., federal judge; b. Reno, 1933; m. Gail Dian Buchanan; children: Nancy, Bradley, Melvin Jr. Attended, U. Nev., 1951-53, 1956-57, 1960; JD, U. Calif., San Francisco, 1964. Mem. firm Vargas, Bartlett & Dixon, 1964-69, Laxalt, Bell, Allison & Lebaron, 1970-78, Allison, Brunetti, MacKenzie, Hartman, Soumbeniotis & Russell, 1978-85; judge US Ct. Appeals (9th cir.), Reno, 1985-99, sr. judge, 1999—. Mem. Council of Legal Advisors, Rep. Nat. Com., 1982-85. Served with US Army N.G., 1954-56. Mem. State Bar of Nev. (pres. 1984-85, bd. govs. 1975-84). Office: US Ct Appeals Ste 506 US Courthouse 400 S Virginia St Reno NV 89501-2194

BRUNGER, AXEL THOMAS, biophysicist, researcher, educator; b. Leipzig, Germany, Nov. 25, 1956; came to U.S., 1982; s. Hans and Hildegard (Müller) B. Diploma, Hamburg U., Germany, 1980; PhD, Tech. U. Munich, 1982. Postdoctoral fellow Max-Planck Inst., Martinsried, Germany, 1984; rsch. assoc. Harvard U., Cambridge, Mass., 1982-83, 85-87; asst. investigator Howard Hughes Med. Inst., New Haven, 1987-92, assoc. investigator, 1992-95, investigator, 1995—; asst. prof. Yale U., New Haven, 1987-91, assoc. prof., 1991-93, prof., 1993-2000, Stanford U., Calif., 2000—. Recipient Röntgen prize for biosci. Würzburg U., 1995, Gregori Aminoff prize Royal Swedish Acad. Scis., 2003, Nat. Acad. of Sci., 2005; NATO postdoctoral fellow Deutscher Akademischer Austauschdienst, Bonn, Germany, 1982-83 Mem. AAAS, NAS, Am. Crystallographic Assn., Am. Chem. Soc., Protein Soc. Achievements include studies of protein structure and function, developments in macromolecular x-ray crystallography and solution NMR spectroscopy. Office: Stanford U J H Clark Ctr Rm E300-C 318 Campus Dr Stanford CA 94305-5432

BRUNNER, HOWARD WILLIAM, professional land surveyor; b. Mobile, Ala., July 24, 1946; s. Joseph Edward and Beaulah (Howard) B.; m. Linda Marie Parker, Dec. 20, 1963 (div. June 1978); children: Leah Marie, Anne Marie; m. Catherine Cecilia Byrnes, June 27, 1981; 1 child, Jordan Thomas Howard. Grad. high sch., Santa Rosa, Calif. Lic. profl. land surveyor, Calif., Wash., Nev. Survey technician Roemer & Estes, Mill Valley, Calif., 1964-65, Ken Frost & Assocs., Mill Valley, 1965-66; engring. aide County of Marin, San Rafael, Calif., 1966-75; pres. Engring. Field Svcs., San Rafael, 1975-77, Brunner, Phelps & Assocs., Inc., Cotati, Calif., 1977-80; v.p. Ray Carlson & Assocs., Inc., Santa Rosa, Calif., 1980-92; ptnr. Bedford Brunner, Santa Rosa, 1993-96; prin. Howard W. Brunner, Profl. Land Surveyor, Santa Rosa, 1996—. Expert examiner, profl. land surveyor, cons., registrar, tech. adv. com. mem., expert witness, chmn. item writing com. Bd. Registration for Profl. Engrs. and Land Surveyors, Sacramento, 1985-2006. Mem. Geysers Geothermal Assn. (bd. dirs. 1985-92), Calif. Land Surveyors Assn. (treas. 1987-88, sec. 1988-89, pres. 1990), Am. Consulting Engrs. Coun. (chmn. coun. profl. land surveyors 1995-96). Roman Catholic. Avocations: boating, skiing, skin diving, antique automobiles. Home: 420 Mcdonough Heights Rd Healdsburg CA 95448-4659 Office: 250 Healdsburg Ave Ste 201 Healdsburg CA 95448 Office Phone: 707-433-9760.

BRUNS, GEORGE H., electronics executive; Founder, pres. Systron-Donner Corp.; founder, dir. Giga-tronics Inc., San Ramon, Calif., 1980, chmn., 1980, CEO, 1995—. Gen. ptnr. The Bruns Co.; bd. dirs. Testronics, Inc., McKinney, Tex., Peninsula Wireless Comm., Inc., Sunnyvale, Calif., ASCOR, Inc., Fremont, Calif. Mem. exec. com. Calif. Found. for the Retarded; chmn. bd. Calif. Shakespeare Festival. Office: 4650 Norris Canyong Rd San Ramon CA 94583-1320 Fax: 925-328-4700.

BRUSCA, RICHARD CHARLES, biologist, researcher, educator; b. LA, Jan. 25, 1945; s. Finny John and Ellenora C. (McDonald) B.; m. Caren Irene Spencer, 1964 (div. 1971); children: Alec Matthew, Carlene Anne; m. Anna Mary Mackey, 1980 (div. 1987); m. Wendy Moore, 1998. BS, Calif. Poly. State U., 1967; MSc, Calif. State U., LA, 1970; PhD, U. Ariz., 1975. Curator, rsch. Aquatic Insects Lab., Calif. State U., LA, 1969—70; resident dir. U. Ariz. and U. Sonora (Mex.) Coop. Marine Lab., Sonora, 1970—71; prof. biology U. So. Calif., LA, 1975—86; head Invertebrate Zoology sect. Los Angeles County Mus. Natural Hist., 1984—87; Joshua L. Baily curator, chmn. dept. invertebrate zoology San Diego Natural History Mus., 1987—93; prof., dir. grad. program in marine biology U. Charleston, SC, 1993—98, assoc. dir. Grice Marine Lab. SC, 1993—98; sr. rsch. scientist Columbia U., 1998—2001; rsch. scientist, dept. ecology and evolutionary biology U. Ariz., 1998—; exec. program dir. Ariz.-Sonora Desert Mus., Tucson, 2003—. Dir. acad. programs Catalina Marine Sci. Ctr., U. Southern Calif., 1980—83; adj. prof. Centro de Investigación en Alimentación y Desarrollo, 1999—; field rschr. No., Ctrl. and So. Ams., Galapagos Island, Polynesia, Australia, New Zealand, Antarctica, Saharan and Sub-Saharan Africa, Europe, Caribbean; bd. dirs. Orgn. for Tropical Studies, Slocum-Lunz Found., Intercultural Ctr. for the Study of Deserts and Oceans, Sonoran Sea Aquarium, Tucson, Discover Life in Am.; mem. panels NAS/NSF; chairperson adv. com. Smithsonian Instn.; adv. com. Systematics Agenda 2000; chairperson adv. com., inland waters crustacea specialist Internat. Union for Conservation of Nature Species Survival Commn.; mem. adv. bd. All Species Found., 2001; mem. adv. bd. Sch. Natural Resources U. Ariz., 2003—; mem. sci. and tech. adv. team Sonoran Desert Conservation Plan, Pima County, Ariz. Author: Common Intertidal Invertebrates of the Gulf of California, 1980; co-author: A Naturalist's Seashore Guide, 1978, Invertebrates, 1990, 2d edit., 2003, English, Spanish, Portuguese, Italian transls., Isopod Systematics and Evolution, 2001, Seashore Guide to Northern Gulf of California, 2004, Conserving Migratory Pollinators and Nectar Corridors in Western North America, 2004, Distributional Checklist of the Macrofauna of the Gulf of California, 2005; contbr. over 150 articles to sci. jours. Recipient U.S. Antarctic Svc. medal, 1965, numerous rsch. awards; granteee NSF, Nat. Geog. Soc., Charles Lindberg Found, David & Lucile Packard Found., NOAA, Nat. Park Svc., Dept. Def., Am. Philos. Assn., others. Fellow: AAAS, Linnean Soc. London; mem.: Soc. for Systematic Biology, Assn. Sea Cortez Rschrs. (hon.; life), Crustacean Soc. (pres.), Sigma Xi. Avocations: Mexican and Mesoamerican indigenous art and culture, Latin American politics. Office: Ariz-Sonora Desert Mus 2021 N Kinney Rd Tucson AZ 85743 Office Phone: 520-883-3007. Business E-Mail: rbrusca@desertmuseum.org.

BRUSIC, KEN, editor-in-chief; m. Pam Brusic; 1 child, Mike. BA in English, U. Denver; MA, U. Colo., 1972. With Boulder Daily Camera; journalism fellow U. Mich.; city editor Wichita Eagle and Wichita Beacon, 1978—79; assoc. prof. U. Mont., Missoula; spl. projects editor The Patriot Ledger, Quincy, Mass.; mng. editor The Sun of San Bernardino, Balt. News Am.; projects editor Orange County Register, Santa Ana, Calif., 1989—90, asst. mng. editor, 1990—92, mng. editor, 1992—97, exec. editor, 1997—2002, editor, 2002—; sr. v.p. Freedom Comm., Inc. Head of content Freedom Orange County Info., 2002; mem. adv. bd. Asian Am. Journalists Assn., LA. Avocations: motorcycling, reading, running. Office: Orange County Register PO Box 11626 625 N Grand Ave Santa Ana CA 92701 Office Phone: 714-796-2226. Office Fax: 714-565-3681. E-mail: kbrusic@ocregister.com.

BRUST, DAVID, physicist; b. Chgo., Aug. 24, 1935; s. Clifford and Ruth (Klapman) B. BS, Calif. Inst. Tech., 1957; MS, U. Chgo., 1958, PhD, 1964. Rsch. assoc. Purdue U., Lafayette, Ind., 1963—64, Northwestern U., Evanston, Ill., 1964—65, asst. prof. physics, 1965—68; theoretical rsch. physicist U. Calif. Lawrence Radiation Lab., Livermore, 1968—73. Cons. Bell Telephone Lab., Murray Hill, N.J., 1966. Campaign coord. No. Calif. Scientists and Engrs. for McGovern, 1972. NSF travel grantee, 1964; NSF rsch. grantee, 1966-68. Mem. Am. Phys. Soc., Am. Assn. Coll. Profs., Internat. Solar Energy Soc., Astron. Soc. of Pacific, Nature Conservancy, Calif. Acad. Sci., Commonwealth Club. of Calif., World Affairs Coun. No. Calif., Commonwealth Club Anza Borrego Desert, Natural History Assn., Planetary Soc., Sierra Club, Sigma Xi. Office: PO Box 13130 Oakland CA 94661-0130

BRYAN, BOB CHARLES, professional tennis player; b. Camarillo, Calif., Apr. 29, 1978; s. Wayne and Kathy. Attended, Stanford U., 1996—98. Profl. tennis player ATP, 1998—. Mem. Bryan Bros. Band. Mem. WECAAN, Andrea Jaeger's Silver Lining Found., Elton John's AIDS Found., Tennis For Africa. Named Doubles Team of Yr. (with brother Mike Bryan), 2006 ATP Awards, ATPTennis.com Fans' Favorite Doubles Team; named to ATP Player Coun., 2006. Mem.: Sigma Alpha Epsilon. Achievements include winning over 100 jr. doubles titles with brother Mike; winning 51 career doubles titles, ATP; winning Davis Cup, 2007, US Open, 2005, 2008, Australian Open, 2009; mem. US Men's Olympic Team, Athens, 2004, Beijing, 2008. Avocations: music, keyboards, basketball. Office: Bryan Brothers 1774 Ramona Dr Camarillo CA 93010

BRYAN, GREYSON, lawyer; b. LA, 1949; BA with distinction and honors, Stanford U., 1971; JD cum laude, Harvard U., 1976. Bar: Calif. 1976, NY 1978, DC 1985, Japan (Gaikokuho-Jimu-Bengoshi, withdrew in 1990) 1987. Dir. tng. Harvard Law Sch. Internat. Tax Program, 1979—81, rsch. assoc., 1981—82; adj. prof. law, regulation internat. bus. UCLA Sch. Law, 1994—97; adj. prof. internat. bus. law UCLA Anderson Grad. Sch. Mgmt., 1995—98; established, partner-in-charge O'Melveny & Myers LLP, Tokyo, 1987—90, co-chair global practice group, 1990—94, ptnr. litig. Los Angeles, Calif., coordinates internat. practice, head litig. dept. internat. practice group. Cons., Office of Tax Analysis US Dept. Treasury; mem. litig. dept. of yr. American Lawyer; founding mem. Pacific Coun. on Internat. Policy. Articles editor Harvard Internat. Law Jour.; contbr. articles to profl. jours. Assoc. and acting dir. Volunteers in Asia, Inc., 1971—73; mem. bd. student advisors Harvard U.; chmn. Asia Soc. So. Calif. Ctr., 1992—2001; bd. visitors Stanford U. Inst. Internat. Studies, 1995—2004. Sheldon Traveling Fellow, 1976—77, sr. fellow, UCLA Sch. Pub. Policy and Social Rsch., 1998—99. Mem.: Am. Law Inst. (mem. tax advisory group, fed. income tax project 1982—84), DC Bar. Office: O'Melveny & Myers LLP 1999 Avenue of the Stars 7th Fl Los Angeles CA 90067-6035 Office Phone: 310-246-8444. Office Fax: 310-246-6779. Business E-Mail: gbryan@omm.com.

BRYAN, JAMES D., career officer; b. Birmingham, Ala. BS in Edn., Jacksonville State U.; grad., U.S. Army War Coll. Commd. 2d lt. U.S. Army, advanced through grades to brig. gen., 1997; early assignments include bn. signal officer 82d airborne divsn., 3d bn.; signal ops. officer, instr. U.S. Army JFK Spl. Warfare Ctr., 1971-72; bn. maintenance officer, S-3 122d signal bn., Korea, 1972-73; S-4, S-3 and commdg. officer support bn. 7th Spl. Forces Group, Ft. Bragg, N.C., 1973-77; bn. signal officer, 1st bn. 52d mechanized infantry 1st Armored Divsn., Bamberg, Germany, 1977-79; S-3 93d signal brigade, 1979-80; tng. and mgr. systems dir. U.S. Army Recruiting Command, 1980-83; asst. chief of staff comms.-electronics 1st Spl. Ops. Command, 1985-86; then comdr. 112th Spl. Ops. Signal Bn., 1986-88; mem. jt. staff for J-6, CINC C4 systems support officer USSOCOM, USCENTCOM, FORSCOM, 1988-91; chief J-6 architecture integration and interoperability divsn., 1991-93; comdr. 35th signal brigade XVIII Airborne Corps, 1993-95; exec. officer to dir. of info. systems for Command, Control Comm. and Computers, Hdqrs., U.S. Dept. Army, 1995-97. Dep. DISC4, Dept. of Army, Washington, 1997-99, dir. command, control, comm. and computer sys., U.S. Pacific Command, Camp H.M. Smith, Hawaii, 1999—.

BRYAN, KAREN SMITH, lawyer; BA in Psychology, Bryn Mawr Coll., 1972; MA, UCLA, 1973; JD, U. So. Calif., 1979. Bar: Calif. 1979. With Latham & Watkins LLP, LA, 1979—, ptnr., 1987—. Mem. planning com. U. So. Calif. Tax Inst. Named So. Calif. Super Lawyer, 2003—08; named one of Am.'s Leading Bus. Lawyers, Chambers & Ptnrs., 2003—08. Mem.: ABA (corp. tax com. and ind. income tax com.). Office: Latham & Watkins LLP 355 S Grand Ave Los Angeles CA 90071-1560 Office Phone: 213-485-1234. Business E-Mail: karen.bryan@lw.com.

BRYAN, RICHARD H., lawyer, educator, former senator, Former United States Senator, Nevada; b. Washington, July 16, 1937; m. Bonnie Fairchild; 3 children. BA, U. Nev., 1959; LLB, U. Calif., San Francisco, 1963. Bar: Nev. 1963, DC 2002. Dep. dist. atty., Clark County, Nev., 1964—66; pub. defender, 1966—68; counsel Clark County Juvenile Ct., 1968—69; mem. Nev. Assembly, 1969—73,

Nev. Senate, 1973—79; atty. gen. State Nev., 1979—83, gov., 1983—89; senator from Nev. U.S. Senate, 1989—2001; ptnr., mem. exec. com. Lionel, Sawyer & Collins, 2001—. Former mem. U.S. Senate coms. on commerce, sci. and transp., Dem. Policy Com., Fin. Com., Banking, Housing and Urban Affairs Com., Senate Nominating Steering and Coord. Com., Select Com. on Intelligence; adj. prof. polit. sci. U. Nev., Las Vegas, 2001—. Former pres. Clark County Legal Aid Soc.; bd. dirs. Las Vegas C. of C.; bd. trustees Nev. Devel. Authority, 2001—. 2d lt. US Army, 1959—60. Recipient Disting. Svc. award, Vegas Valley Jaycees. Mem.: ABA, Coun. of State Govts. (past pres.), Am. Judicature Soc., Clark County Bar Assn., Elks, Masons, Lions, Phi Alpha Theta, Phi Alpha Delta. Democrat. Office: Lionel Sawyer & Collins 1700 Bank Am Plaza 300 S 4th St Las Vegas NV 89101

BRYAN, ROBERT J., federal judge; b. Bremerton, Wash., Oct. 29, 1934; s. James W. and Vena Gladys (Jensen) B.; m. Cathy Ann Welander, June 14, 1958; children: Robert James, Ted Lorin, Ronald Terence. BA, U. Wash., 1956, JD, 1958. Bar: Wash. 1959, U.S. Dist. Ct. (we. dist.) Wash. 1959, U.S. Tax Ct. 1965, U.S. Ct. Appeals (9th cir.) 1985. Assoc., then ptnr. Bryan & Bryan, Bremerton, 1959-67; judge Superior Ct., Port Orchard, Wash., 1967-84; ptnr. Riddell, Williams, Bullitt & Walkinshaw, Seattle, 1984-86; judge U.S. Dist. Ct. (we. dist.) Wash., Tacoma, 1986—. Mem. State Jail Comm., Olympia, Wash., 1974-76, Criminal Justice Tng. Com., Olympia, 1978-81, State Bd. on Continuing Legal Edn., Seattle, 1984-86; mem., sec. Jud. Qualifications Commn., Olympia, 1982-83; chair Wash. Fed.-State Jud. Coun., 1997-98; mem. 9th Cir. Jud. Coun., 2001-03. Author: (with others) Washington Pattern Jury Instructions (civil and criminal vols. and supplements), 1970-85, Manual of Model Criminal Jury Instructions for the Ninth Circuit, 1992, Manual of Model Civil Jury Instruction for the Ninth Circuit, 1993. Chmn. 9th Ct. Jury Com., 1991-92; bd. dirs. Fed. Jud. Ctr., 2000-04. Served to maj. USAR. Mem.: 9th Cir. Dist. Judges Assn. (sec.-treas. 1997—99, v.p. 1999—2001, pres. 2001—03). Office: US Dist Ct 1717 Pacific Ave Rm 4427 Tacoma WA 98402-3234

BRYANT, ANDY D., computer company executive; BA in Econs., U. Mo.; MBA in Fin., U. Kans. With Chrysler Corp., Ford Motor Co.; contr. comml. memory sys. operation Intel Corp., Santa Clara, Calif., 1981-83, sys. group contr., 1983-87, dir. fin. for corp., 1987-90, v.p., dir. fin. Intel products group, 1990-94, corp. v.p., CFO, 1994—99, sr. v.p., CFO, chief enterprise services officer, 1999—2001, exec. v.p., CFO, chief enterprise services officer, 2001—07, exec. v.p., CAO, 2007—. Bd. dir. Columbia Sportswear Co., Kryptiq Inc., McKesson Corp., 2008—. Office: Intel 2200 Mission College Blvd Santa Clara CA 95054-1537

BRYANT, ARTHUR H., lawyer; b. Harrisburg, Pa., Aug. 11, 1954; s. Albert Irwin and Marjorie (Weinrib) B.; m. Nancy Kaye Johnson, Aug. 17, 1991; stepchildren, Vinnie and Mango Johnson; 1 child, Wallace Johnson Bryant. AB with hons., Swarthmore Coll., 1976; JD, Harvard U., 1979; D (hon.), Ripon Coll., 1998. Bar: Pa. 1981, U.S. Dist. Ct. (ea. dist.) Pa. 1981, U.S. Ct. Appeals (3d cir.) Pa. 1981, U.S. Ct. Appeals (11th cir.) Ga. 1985, U.S. Ct. Appeals (6th cir.) Ohio 1986, U.S. Ct. appeals (D.C. cir.) 1986, U.S. Ct. Appeals (9th cir.) Calif. 1987, U.S. Ct. Appeals (7th cir.) Ill. 1988, U.S. Ct. Appeals (5th cir.) Tex. 1988, D.C., 1989, U.S. Supreme Ct. 1989, U.S. Ct. Appeals (1st cir.) 1996. Intern Rosenman, Colin & Freund, NYC, 1978, N.Y. Civil Liberties Union, NYC, 1978, Cambridge & Somerville Legal Svcs., Cambridge, Pa., 1979; law clk. U.S. Dist. Ct. (so. dist.), Tex., 1979-80; atty. Kohn, Savett, Marion & Graf., Phila., 1980-84; staff atty. Trial Lawyers for Pub. Justice, Washington, 1984-87; exec. cir. Pub. Justice, Washington, 1987—. Recipient George Moscone Meml. award Consumer Atty. Assn. L.A., 2003; named one of 20 young lawyers making a difference in the world ABA Barrister mag., 1991, one of 50 most influential people in coll. sports Coll. Sports Mag., 1994, one of 45 lawyers whose vision and commitment are changing lives The Am. Lawyer, 1997, one of 100 most influential lawyers in Am. Nat. Law Jour., 2000, 2006; recipient Wasserstein Pub. Interest law fellowship, 1996; Honored by Oreg. Trial Lawyers Asn., renamed pub. svc. award to Arthur H. Bryant Pub. Justice Award, 2003. Mem. ABA (Pursuit of Justice award 2003), Am. Assn. for Justice. Office: Pub Justice 555 Twelfth St Ste 1620 Oakland CA 94607 Office Phone: 510-622-8150. Business E-Mail: abryant@publicjustice.net.

BRYANT, DIANE M., information technology executive; B in Elec. Engring., U. Calif., Davis, 1985. Joined Intel Corp., 1985, dir. engring. mobile products grp., gen. mgr. enterprise processor divsn., 1998, dir. corp. platform office, v.p. digital enterprise grp., gen. mgr. server platforms grp., 2004—08, v.p., chief info. officer, 2008—. Achievements include patents in field. Office: Intel Corp 2200 Mission Coll Blvd Santa Clara CA 95054 Office Phone: 408-765-8080.

BRYANT, KOBE, professional basketball player; b. Phila., Aug. 23, 1978; s. Joe "Jellybean" and Pam Bryant; m. Vanessa Laine, Apr. 18, 2001; children: Natalia Diamante, Gianna Maria-Onore. Guard L.A. Lakers, 1996—. Mem. US Men's Sr. Nat. Basketball Team, 2006, Beijing, 08. Recipient ESPY award, Undeniable Performance, ESPN, 2006, ESPY award, Best NBA Player, 2008, Gold medal, men's basketball, Beijing Olympic Games, 2008; named Nat. HS Player of Yr. (Lower Merion HS), 1996, NBA All-Star Slam Dunk Champion, 1997, NBA All-Star Game MVP, 2002, 2007, NBA All-Star Game co-MVP, 2009, NBA MVP, 2008; named one of The Most Influential People in the World of Sports, Bus. Week, 2007, 2008, The 100 Most Powerful Celebrities, Forbes.com, 2008; named to All-NBA 1st Team, 2002—04, 2006—09, NBA All-Defensive 1st Team, 2000, 2003—04, 2006—08, Western Conf. All-Star Team, NBA, 1998, 2000—09. Achievements include being the youngest player ever (19 yrs. of age) to appear in an NBA All-Star game, 1998; member of the NBA Championship winning LA Lakers, 2000, 2001, 2002; leading the NBA in: field goals, 2003, 2006, 2007; scoring, 2003, 2006-08; points per game, 2006, 2007; field goal attempts, 2006-08; scoring a career high 81 points in a single game (second-highest total in NBA history), 2006. Office: LA Lakers 555 N Nash St El Segundo CA 90245-2818*

BRYANT, LELAND MARSHAL, business and nonprofit executive; b. Gainesville, Ga., Apr. 28, 1950; s. William Marcus and Pierre Lou (Milner) B.; children: Shauna, Natalie, Marcus, Jacob. Student, Vanderbilt U., 1968-70; BBA with hons., U. Tex., 1972; MBA, U. Pa., 1978. CPA, Tex. Acct. Arthur Andersen and Co., Dallas, 1978-81; exec. v.p. Walter Bennet Comms., Dallas, 1981-89; pres. Grand Canyon Railway, Flagstaff, Ariz., 1989-97; v.p., CFO, Grand Canyon (Ariz.) Assn., 1997—. Pres. Fray Marcos Hotel, Flagstaff, 1995-97. Bd. dirs. Grand Canyon Nat. Park Found., 1995—; nat. adv. bd. No. Ariz. U., Flagstaff, 1994-97. Mem. AICPA, Grand Canyon Assn. (bd. dirs. 1995-97), Nat. Parks Conservation Assn. (nat. adv. coun. 1995-98). Republican. Office: Grand Canyon Assn PO Box 399 Grand Canyon AZ 86023-0399

BRYANT, NEIL, state legislator, lawyer; b. Spokane, Wash., July 8, 1948; m. Mary Bryant. BA, Paficic Luth. U.; JD, Willamette U. Mem. Oreg. Legislature, Salem, 1992—, chair jud. com., mem. rules and elections com., mem. subcom. on human resources, mem. ways and means com., majority whip. Chair Bend Urban Renewal Dist., Deschutes County Children and Youth Svcs. Commn.; mem. Your Cmty. 2000. Republican. Home: PO Box 1151 Bend OR 97709-1151 Office: S-206 State Capitol Salem OR 97310-0001 E-mail: nmbryant@empnet.com.

BRYANT, PETER JAMES, biologist, educator; b. Bristol, Eng., Mar. 2, 1944; came to U.S., 1967; s. Sydney Arthur and Marjorie Violet (Virgurs) B.; m. Toni Boettger, 1980; children: Katherine Emily, Sarah Grace. B.Sc. (Special) in Zoology with 1st class honors, Kings Coll., London, Eng., 1964; M.Sc. in Biochemistry, Univ. Coll., London, Eng., 1965; D.Phil. in Genetics, U. Sussex, Falmer, Eng., 1967. Postdoctoral research fellow Devel. Biology Ctr., Case Western Res. U., Cleve., 1967-70; postdoctoral research fellow Devel. Biology Lab., U. Calif.-Irvine, 1967-70, lectr. dept. devel. and cell biology, 1970-71, asst. prof., 1971-74, assoc. prof., 1974-77, prof. dept. devel. and cell biology, 1977—, vice chmn. dept. devel. and cell biology, 1978-79, dir. Devel. Biology Ctr., 1979—. Nat. and internat. lectr.; reviewer NSF, NIH. Contbr. numerous articles, book revs., abstracts to Cell, Proc. Nat. Acad. Sci., Jour. Cell Sci., Devel., Nature Sci., Jour. Insect Physiology, Developmental Biology, other profl. publs.; reviewer Cell, Devel. Biology, Genetics, Sci., Can. Jour. zoology, numerous other profl. jours.; assoc. editor: Developmental Biology, 1976-85, editor-in-chief, 1985-95. Bd. dirs. Orange County Natural History Mus., 1987-92. Recipient numerous grants NIH, NSF, 1974—, Am. Cetacean Soc. grantee, 1980-81, Nat. Marine Fisheries Svc. grantee, 1981; recipient Disneyland Community Svc. award (on behalf of Am. Cetacean Soc., Orange County chpt.), 1980. Mem. Soc. Devel. Biology, Genetics Soc. Am., Internat. Soc. Devel. Biologists, Soc. Exptl. Biology, Am. Cetacean Soc. (pres. 1982, founding pres. Orange County chpt. 1977-80). Avocations: photography, sailing, hiking, model building.

BRYANT, ROBERT LEAMON, mathematics educator; b. Harnett County, NC, Aug. 30, 1953; s. James Ray and Josephine (Strickland) B. BS, NC State U., Raleigh, 1974; PhD in Math., U. NC, Chapel Hill, 1979. Asst. prof., math. Rice U., Houston, 1979-81, assoc. prof., math., 1981-82, prof., math., 1982-85, Noah Harding prof., math., 1986—88; prof. Duke U., Durham, ND, 1984, arts and scis. prof., math., 1987-88, Juanita M. Kreps prof. math., 1988—; prof., math. U. Calif., Berkeley, 2007—. Assoc. prof. Harvard U., 1982; mem. Max Planck Inst., 1985, Institue des Hautes Etudes Scientifiques, 1985, Instituto Nacional de Matematica Pura e Applicada, 1986, 90, visitor, 96; W.R. Reynolds prof. U. NC, Chapel Hill, 1987; visitor U. Adelaide, 1993, Nankai Inst. Math., 1995; director's visitor Inst. for Advanced Study, 1993; Andre Aisenstadt prof. Centre de Recherches Mathematique, 1984; prof. Inst. Elie Cartan, 1998; Samuel Eilenberg prof. Columbia U., 2004; Nachdiplom lectr. Eidgenössische Technische Hochschule Zürich, 2006; mem. Math. Sciences Rsch. Inst., Berkeley, Calif., 1983, Berkeley, 94, trustee, 1999—2001, chmn. bd. trustees, 2001—04, sr. visitor, 2001, Clay rsch. prof., 2001—02, Simons Rsch. prof., 2003, co-organizer, rsch. program in differential geometry, 03, dir.-elect, 07, dir., 2007—; dir. undergrad. program Inst. for Advanced Study (IAS)/Park City Math. Inst. (PCMI), 1993—2000, mem. steering com., 2006—07, dir., 2007—; invited lectr. in field. Mem. editl. bd. Duke Mathematical Journal, 1997, Differential Geometry and Its Applications, 1999, Communications in Analysis and Geometry, 2002; contbr. articles to profl. jours. Academic mem. bd. dir. Vietnam Edn. Found., 2002—05; bd. visitor Harvard U., 2001—04. Mem., NSF Postdoctoral Fellow, Inst. for Advanced Study, 1979-80, Alfred P. Sloan fellow, 1982-84; recipient Presdl. Young Investigator award NSF, 1984-89, Trinity Coll. Disting. Tchg., 1992, Disting. Alumni award, Coll. Phys. and Math. Sciences, NC State U. Alumni Assn., 2005 Fellow: NAS, Am. Acad. Arts & Sciences; mem.: Math. Assn. Am. (southeastern sect. lectr. 2001—03, Southeastern Region Disting. Tchg. 1993), Am. Math. Soc. (past chair, com. on publications 1998—2004, exec. coun. 2000—04, assoc. editor 2005—08, mem. editl. bd. com. 2006—, v.p. 2007, mem. editl. bd. com. and on von Neumann Symposium Com., coun. mem.-at-large, Coun. Am. Math. Soc., mem. task force on membership 1998—2000, editor, Transactions 1992—97), Chamber Arts Soc. Durham, NC (dir., dir. emeritus), Phi Beta Kappa. Democrat. Office: Duke U PO Box 90320 111 Physics Building Science Dr Durham NC 27706-0320 also: Math Scis Rsch Inst Office 119 17 Gauss Way Berkeley CA 94720-5070 Home: 1420 Grizzly Peak Blvd Berkeley CA 94708-2202 Office Phone: 919-660-2805, 510-642-0143. Office Fax: 919-660-2821, 510-642-8609. Business E-Mail: bryant@math.duke.edu.

BRYANT, THOMAS LEE, retired magazine editor; b. Daytona Beach, Fla., June 15, 1943; s. Stanley Elson and G. Bernice (Burgess) Bryant; m. Patricia Jean Bryant, June 30, 1979. BA in Polit. Sci., U. Calif., Santa Barbara, 1965, MA in Polit. Sci., 1966. Fgn. svc. officer U.S. Dept. State, Washington, Buenos Aires, 1967-69; radio broadcaster KDB Sta., Santa Barbara, Calif., 1969-72; editor to editor-in-chief Road & Track Hachette Filipacchi Media Inc., Newport Beach, Calif., 1972—2008; ret., 2008. Mem.: Sports Car Club America, Motor Press Guild, Internat. Motor Press Assn. Avocations: golf, skeet shooting. Office Phone: 212-767-6000.

BRYANT, WARREN F., retail executive; BA, Calif. State U., LA; MBA, Azusa Pacific U. Sr. v.p. supermarket divsn. Dillon Co. Inc., pres., CEO, 1995—99; sr. v.p. Kroger Co., 1999—2002; CEO, pres. Long Drug Stores Corp., 2002—, chmn., 2003—, acting COO, 2003, 2005—. Bd. dirs. Pathmark Stores Inc., Boise Cascade Corp. Office: 141 N Civic Dr Walnut Creek CA 94596

BRYANT, WOODROW WESLEY, architect; b. San Jose, Calif., June 5, 1949; s. Foy Eldean and Loraine (McKee) B.; m. Becky Ann Hoffmaster, June 27, 1981; 1 stepson: Jeremy Saul Martin. Student, Am. River Coll., Sacramento, Calif., 1968; BArch, Calif. State Polytechnic U., 1973. Registered architect, Calif., Nev., Utah, Idaho, Ariz. Designer, project mgr. Angello & Vitiello Assoc., Sacramento, 1971-75; draftsman Caywood, Nopp & Ward, Sacramento, 1975; architect W. Bryant Enterprises, Sacramento, 1975-76, Wright, Bryant & Johnson, Ketchum, Idaho, 1976—. Bd. dirs. Elkhorn Archtl. Design Commn., Uniform Bldg. Code Bd. Appeals, Ketchum, Uniform Fire Code Bd. Appeals, Ketchum, Blaine County, Idaho. Recipient Best Archtl. Interior Detailing award, Custom Builder mag., 1993. Mem. AIA. Avocations: photography, painting, computer graphics, skiing, sailing. Office: Wright Bryant & Johnson PO Box 21 Sun Valley ID 83353-0021

BRYK, ANTHONY S., educational association administrator; BS Summa Cum Laude, in chem., Boston Coll., 1970; EdD, Harvard Grad. Sch Edn., 1977. Instr. to asst. to assoc. prof. Harvard Grad. Sch. Edn., 1973—85; vis. assoc. prof. U. Chgo., Edn. and Sociology Dept., 1984—85; assoc. prof. to prof. U. Chgo, Dept. Edn. and Coll., 1985—2000; Marshall Field IV prof. U. Chgo., Dept Sociology, 1997—2004; fellow Stanford U., Ctr. for Advanced Studies in Behavioral Sci., 2002—03; Spencer prof. edn. Sch. Edn. and of Orgnl. Behavior Stanford U., 2004—08; pres. The Carnegie Found. for Advancement of Tchg., 2008—. Founding dir. Consortium on Chgo. Sch. Rsch.; prin. investigator Ctr. for Rsch. Edn of Students at Risk, Johns-Hopkins U., Howard U. Recipient Sch. Reform Achievement award, Chgo. Assn. Local Sch. Coun., 1998, Philomethia Club Boston Coll. award, 1970, The Palmer A. Johnson award, Am. Ednl. Rsch. Assn., 1991, Willard Waller award, Am. Sociol. Assn., 1991—93, Disting. Contbns. to Edn. & Scholarship prize, Thomas B. Fordham Found., 2003. Mem.: Nat. Acad. Edn., Am. Statis. Assn., Am. Ednl. Rsch. Assn. (Disting. Career Contbns. award 2003), Am. Sociol. Assn., Sigma Xi, Alpha Sima Nu. Office: Carnegie Found for Advancement Tchg 51 Vista Lane Stanford CA 94305 Office Phone: 650-566-5100. Office Fax: 650-326-0278.*

BRYNER, ALEXANDER O., former state supreme court justice; b. Tientsin, China, 1943; m. Carol Crump; 2 children. BA, Stanford U., 1966, JD, 1969. Law clk. to Chief Justice George Boney Alaska Supreme Ct., 1969-71; legal editor Bancroft Whitney Co., San Francisco, 1971; with Pub. Defender Agy., Anchorage, 1972-74; ptnr. Bookman, Bryner & Shortell, 1974; Alaska dist. ct. judge Anchorage, 1975-77; U.S. atty. Alaska, 1977-80; chief judge Alaska Ct. Appeals, 1980-97; state supreme ct. justice Alaska Supreme Ct., Anchorage, 1997—2007, state supreme ct. chief justice, 2003—06.

BRYSON, JOHN E., retired utilities executive; b. NYC, July 24, 1943; m. Louise Henry BA with distinction, Stanford U., 1965; student, Freie U. Berlin, Federal Republic Germany, 1965-66; JD, Yale U., 1969. Bar: Calif., Oreg., D.C. Asst. in instrn. Law Sch., Yale U., New Haven, 1968-69; law clk. U.S. Dist. Ct., San Francisco, 1969-70; co-founder, atty. Natural Resources Def. Council, 1970-74; vice chmn. Oreg. Energy Facility Siting Council, 1975-76; assoc. Davies, Biggs, Strayer, Stoel & Boley, Portland, Oreg., 1975-76; chmn. Calif. State Water Resources Control Bd., 1976-79; vis. faculty Stanford U. Law Sch., Calif., 1977-79; pres. Calif. Pub. Utilities Commn., 1979-82; ptnr. Morrison & Foerster, San Francisco, 1983-84; sr. v.p. law and fin. So. Calif. Edison Co., Rosemead, 1984; exec. v.p., chief fin. officer Edison Internat. and So. Calif. Edison Co., 1985-90, chmn. of bd., CEO Rosemead, 1990-99; chmn., pres., CEO Edison Internat., 2000—08. Lectr. on pub. utility, energy, communications law.; former mem. exec. com. Nat. Assn. Regulatory Utility Commrs., Calif. Water Rights Law Rev. Commn., Calif. Pollution Control Financing Authority; former mem. adv. bd. Solar Energy Research Inst., Electric Power Research Inst., Stanford Law Sch.; bd. dirs. Pacific Am. Income Shares Inc., The Boeing Co., Walt Disney Co. Mem. bd. editors, assoc. editor: Yale U. Law Jour. Past bd. dirs. World Resources Inst., Washington, Calif. Environ. Trust, Claremont U. Ctr., Grad. Sch., Stanford U. Alumni Assn.; bd. dirs. The Keck Found., Calif. Endowment, 2003-; former trustee Stanford U., 1991. Woodrow Wilson fellow Mem. Calif. Bar Assn., Oreg. Bar Assn., D.C. Bar Assn., Nat. Assn. Regulatory Utility Commrs. (exec. com. 1980-82), Stanford U. Alumni Assn. (bd. dirs. 1983-86), Phi Beta Kappa.

BRYSON, LOUISE HENRY, retired broadcast executive; b. 1944; m. John E. Bryson; 4 children. BA, U. Wash.; M in Arts & Teaching, Stanford U., 1969, MBA, 1979. V.p. Viacom Cablevision; gen. mgr. Westinghouse Group W's; sr. cons. Showtime Events Television; v.p. NBC, 1990—93; sr. v.p. affiliate sales & mktg. FX Networks, Inc., 1994—99; exec. v.p., distbn. & bus. devel. Lifetime Entertainment Television, 1999—2005, pres. distbn. & bus. develop., 2005—08; exec. v.p. gen. mgr. Lifetime Movie Network, 2005—08. Past dir. & chmn. KCET TV, LA; past dir. So. Calif. Public Radio; dir. Investment Co. of Am.; past. mem. PBS Nat. Bd. Mem. bd. councilors Annenberg Sch. for Comm., U. So. Calif.; mem. advisory coun. Stanford U. Grad. Sch. Bus.; trustee J. Paul Getty Trust, 1998—, vice chmn., 2004—06, chmn., 2006—. Recipient Excellence in Pub. TV Leadership award, PBS Nat. Bd., 1998. Office: J Paul Getty Trust 1200 Getty Ctr Dr Los Angeles CA 90049

BUBAR, JOSEPH BEDELL, JR., pastor; b. Rochester, NH, June 7, 1947; BA in History, Gordon Coll., 1968; MDiv, Trinity Evang. Divinity Sch., 1972. Sr. pastor Bethany Evan. Free Ch., La Crosse, Wis., 1980-97, Grace Bible Ch., ArroyoGrande, Calif., 1997—. Bd. dirs. Bethany-St. Joe Care Ctr., La Crosse; vice chmn. Christian Svc. Brigade, Wheaton, Ill., 1980-89. Bd. dirs. Forest Lakes dist. Evan. Free Ch. of Am., 1989-91; bd. dirs., bd. chmn. Mission USA, 1989-91, vice-moderator, 1991-93, moderator, 1993-95.

BUBE, RICHARD HOWARD, retired materials scientist, educator; b. Providence, Aug. 10, 1927; s. Edward Neser and Ella Elvira (Baltteim) B.; m. Betty Jane Meeker, Oct. 9, 1948 (dec. Apr. 2, 1997); children: Mark Timothy, Kenneth Paul, Sharon Elizabeth, Meryl Lee; m. Mary Anne Harman, Sept. 9, 2000. Sc.B., Brown U., 1946; MA, Princeton U., 1948, PhD, 1950. Mem. sr. research staff RCA Labs., Princeton, N.J., 1948-62; prof. materials sci. and elec. engring. Stanford U., 1962-92, chmn. dept., 1975-86, assoc. chmn. dept., 1990-91, ret., 1997, prof. emeritus, 1992—. Cons. to industry and govt. Author: A Textbook of Christian Doctrine, 1955, Photoconductivity of Solids, 1960, The Encounter between Christianity and Science, 1968, The Human Quest: A New Look at Science and Christian Faith, 1971, Electronic Properties of Crystalline Solids, 1974, Electrons in Solids, 1981, 3d edit., 1992, Fundamentals of Solar Cells, 1983, Science and the Whole Person, 1985, Photoelectronic Properties of Semiconductors, 1992, Putting It All Together: Seven Patterns for Relating Science and Christian Faith, 1995, One Whole Life: Personal Memoirs of Richard H. Bube, 1995, Photoinduced Defects in Semiconductors, 1996, Photovoltaic Materials, 1998; also articles; editor Jour. Am. Sci. Affiliation, 1969-83; mem. editl. bd. Solid State Electronics, 1975-94, Christians in Sci.; assoc. editor Ann. Rev. Materials Sci., 1969-83. Fellow Am. Phys. Soc., AAAS, Am. Sci. Affiliation; mem. Am. Soc. Engring. Edn. (life), Internat. Solar Energy Soc., Sigma Xi. Evangelical. Home: 753 Mayfield Ave Stanford CA 94305-1043 Personal E-mail: richardhbube@comcast.net.

BUBLÉ, MICHAEL, singer; b. 1975; Signed to 143 Records (Reprise), 2001. Singer: (albums) Michael Bublé, 2003 (double platinum, #1 in Canada), Down With Love Soundtrack, 2003, Let It Snow, 2003, Spider-Man 2 Original Motion Picture Soundtrack, 2004, It's Time, 2005, Caught in the Act, 2005, Chistmas, 2006, Call Me Irresponsible, 2007 (Grammy award, Best Traditional Pop Vocal Album, 2008), (CD/DVD) Come Fly With Me, 2004; guest appearance Dancing with the Stars, 2006. Office: Reprise Records Warner Brothers Records Inc 3300 Warner Blvd Burbank CA 91505

BUCALO, LOUIS RANDALL, biotechnology executive; b. NYC, Oct. 10, 1958; s. Louis and Anne (Aragona) B. Degree magna cum laude, Harvard Coll., 1980; degree, Stanford U. Med. Sch., 1980. Cons. Bain and Co., San Francisco, 1985-86; v.p. United Biomed. Inc., Lake Success, N.Y., 1987-88; assoc. dir. Titon Biosceis. Inc., Alameda, Calif., 1989—; CEO Titan Pharmaceuticals, Inc., S. San Francisco, CA. Mem. AMA, Assn. Clin. Pharmacology.

BUCCIERI, SHIRLEY H., lawyer; b. Terre Haute, Ind., Sept. 23, 1951; d. Mike and Dorothy Louise Hanna; m. Alexander C. Buccieri, Aug. 11, 1973; 1 child. BS in Maths., Purdue U., 1973; JD, U. Akron, 1982. Various positions GM Corp., Warren, Ohio, 1973-81, supt. indsl. engring., 1981-83; assoc. Gibson, Dunn & Crutcher, San Francisco, 1983-91, ptnr., 1991-95; sr. v.p., gen. counsel, sec. Transamerica Corp., San Francisco, 1995—. Mem. dean's adv. coun. Sch. Sci. Purdue U., 1999, West Lafayette, Ind., 1998—; mem. affil. leadership team Stanford U., Palo Alto, Calif., 1998—; old master Purdue U., 1999. Recipient Women in Leadership award San Francisco Bus. Times, 1997, 98, 99. Mem. Phi Beta Kappa. Roman Catholic.

BUCHANAN, JOAN, state legislator; 5 children. Dir. Comml. Ops. Delta Dental; pres. San Ramon Co. Sch. Bd.; mem. Dist. 15 Calif. State Assembly, 2008—. Democrat. Office: PO Box 942849 Rm 4167 Sacramento CA 94249-0015 also: 2694 Bishop Dr Ste 275 San Ramon CA 94583 Office Phone: 916-319-2015, 925-328-1515. Office Fax: 916-319-2115, 925-328-1514.*

BUCHANAN, JOHN EDWARD, JR., museum director; b. Nashville, July 24, 1953; m. Lucy Buchanan. BA in English Lit. with honors, U. of the South, 1975; MA in Art History, Vanderbilt U., 1979. Exec. dir. Lakeview Mus. of Arts and Scis., Peoria, Ill., 1982-86; dir. The Dixon Gallery and Gardens, Memphis, 1986—94; exec. dir. Portland Art Mus., Portland, Oreg., 1994—2006; dir. mus. Fine Arts Mus. San Francisco, 2006—. Presdl. appointee nat. mus. svcs. bd. Inst. Mus. & Libr. Svcs. Recipient Chevalier dans l'Ordre des Arts et des Lettres, French Govt., Chevalier, Legion of Honor. Mem.: Am. Ceramics Cir., Assn. Art Mus. Dirs. Office: de Young Mus Golden Gate Park 50 Hagiwara Tea Garden Dr San Francisco CA 94118

BUCHANAN, TOM, academic administrator; m. Jacque Buchanan; 1 child, Eric. BS, SUNY; MS, Univ. Wyo.; PhD, Univ. Ill., Urbana-Champaign. Instr. Pa. State Univ., Univ. Ill.; asst. prof. Univ. Wyo., Laramie, 1979—85, assoc. prof., 1988—91, prof. geog., 1991, assoc dean, Coll. Arts & Sci., 1991—97, assoc. provost, 1997—98, v.p. acad. affairs, 1998—2005, pres., 2005—. Past. pres. NW Acad. Forum. Office: Univ of Wyoming Dept 3434 1000 E University Ave Laramie WY 82071

BUCHHEIT, PAUL, computer programmer, entrepreneur; married. BS in Computer Sci., Case Western Reserve U., 1998. With Intel, Google, Inc.; co-founder FriendFeed, Inc., Mountain View, Calif. Investor Xobni, ScanScout, Meraki; advisor imo.im. Achievements include being the creator and lead developer of Gmail; being the 23rd employee at Google; suggested Google's now famous motto "Don't be evil" at a 2001 company meeting; created the first AdSense prototype. Office: FriendFeed Inc 333 W Evelyn Ave Mountain View CA 94041

BUCHHOLZ, DEBBY, lawyer; B, U. Calif, San Diego; JD, Harvard Law Sch. Gen. counsel John F. Kennedy Ctr. Performing Arts, Washington; gen mgr La Jolla Playhouse, La Jolla, Calif., 2003—. Office: La Jolla Playhouse 2910 La Jolla Village Dr PO Box 12039 La Jolla CA 92039

BUCHI, MARK KEITH, lawyer; b. Salt Lake City; m. Denise Kimball, June 4, 1973; 7 children. BS, MBA, U. Utah, 1974, JD, 1978. Bar: Utah 1978. Divsn. chief tax and bus. Utah Atty. Gen. Office, Salt Lake City, 1980-83, asst. atty. gen., 1978-83; chmn. Utah Tax Commn., Salt Lake City, 1983-86; atty. Holme Roberts & Owen, Salt Lake City, 1986-88, ptnr., 1988-89, mng. ptnr., 1989-95, chmn. firmwide exec. com., 2000—01. Mem. tax recodification commn. Utah State Tax Commn., Salt Lake City, 1984-91; mem. Utah Govs. Tax Rev. Commn., Salt Lake City, 1991—; mem. exec. com. Multistate Tax Commn., Boulder, Colo., 1985-86. Mem. tax platform com. Utah Rep. Party, 1986. Mem. ABA, Utah Taxpayers Assn. (chmn. 1992, bd. dirs. 1990—). Mem. Lds Ch. Avocations: golf, water-skiing, fishing, gardening, carpentry. Office: Holme Roberts & Owen LLP 299 S Main St #1800 Salt Lake City UT 84111-2219 E-mail: buchim@hro.com.

BUCHWALD, JED ZACHARY, environmental health researcher, science history educator; b. NYC, June 25, 1949; BA, Princeton U., 1971; MA, Harvard, 1973, PhD, 1974. Instr., dir. Inst. History Philosophy Sci. and Tech. U. Toronto, 1974—92; prof., dir. Dibner Inst. for History of Sci. and Tech. MIT, 1992—2001; Doris & Henry Dreyfuss prof. of history Calif. Inst. Tech., Pasadena, 2001—. Author: (book) The Creation of Scientific Effects, 1994; co-editor: Isaac Newton's Natural Philosophy, 2000, Histories of the Electron, 2001; contbr. articles to profl. jours. Recipient award for excellence in environ. health rsch., Lovelance Inst., Albuquerque, 1995; named MacArthur fellow, John D. and Katherine T. MacArthur Found., 1995. Office: Calif Inst tech Div Humanities & Soc Sci MC 101-40 Pasadena CA 91125

BUCK, LINDA B., medical educator; b. Seattle, Jan. 29, 1947; BS in Psychology, U. Wash., Seattle, 1975, BS in Microbiology, 1975; PhD in Immunology, U. Texas Southwestern Med. Ctr., Dallas, 1980. Postdoctoral fellow Columbia U., 1980—84; assoc. Howard Hughes Medical Inst., Columbia U., NY, 1984—91; asst. investigator Howard Hughes Medical Inst., 1994—97, assoc. investigator, 1997—2000, full investigator, 2001—; asst. prof. neurobiology Harvard U., Boston, 1991—96, assoc. prof. neurobiology, 1996—2001, prof. neurobiology, 2001—02; full mem., divsn. basic sciences, dir. Buck Lab Fred Hutchinson Cancer Rsch. Ctr., Seattle, 2002—; affiliate prof. physiology & biophysics U. Wash. Sch. of Medicine, Seattle, 2003—. Director's Lecture NIH, 1999; Ulf von Euler Lecture Karolinska Inst., Sweden, 1999; bd. dirs. Internat. Flavors & Fragrances Inc., 2007—. Contbr. articles to profl. jours. Recipient McKnight Scholar award, McKnight Endowment Fund for Neuroscience, 1992, Takasago award for Rsch. in Olfaction, Takasago Corp., 1992, Disting. Alumnus, Grad. Sch., U. Tex. Southwestern Med. Ctr., 1995, Louis Vuitton-Moet Hennessy Sci. for Art prize, R. H. Wright award in Olfactory Rsch, 1996, Unilever Sci. award, 1996, Lewis S. Rosenstiel award for Disting. Work in Basic Med. Rsch., 1997, Kenji Nakanishi award for Rsch. in Olfaction, Gairdner Found. Internat. award, 2003, Perl/U. NC Neuroscience Prize, 2003, Golden Plate award, Acad. Achievement, 2005; co-recipient of Nobel Prize in Medicine, 2004; named one of Leading Women and Minority Scientists, NY Acad. Sciences, 2005. Fellow: AAAS, Am. Acad. Arts and Scis.; mem.: Inst. of Medicine, NAS. Achievements include discovery of odorant receptors and the organization of the olfactory system. Office: Basic Scis Divsn Fred Hutchinson Cancer Rsch Ctr A3-020 1100 Fairview Ave N PO Box 19024 Seattle WA 98109-1024 Office Phone: 206-667-6316. Office Fax: 206-667-1031. E-mail: lbuck@fhcrc.org.*

BUCKLAND, MICHAEL KEEBLE, librarian, educator; b. Wantage, Eng., Nov. 23, 1941; came to U.S., 1972; s. Walter Basil and Norah Elaine (Rudd) B.; m. Waltraud Leeb, July 11, 1964; children: Anne Margaret, Anthony Francis. BA, Oxford U., 1963; postgrad. diploma in librarianship, Sheffield U., 1965, PhD, 1972. Grad. trainee Bodleian Library, Oxford, Eng., 1963-64; asst. librarian U. Lancaster (Eng.) Library, 1965-72; asst. dir. for tech. svcs. Purdue U. Libraries, West Lafayette, Ind., 1972-75; assoc. prof. Sch. of Info. U. Calif., Berkeley, 1976-79, dean, 1976-84, prof., 1979—2003, prof. emeritus Sch. Info., 2004—, asst. v.p. library plans and policies, 1983-87; v.p. Ind. Coop. Library Svcs. Auth., 1974-75. Co-dir. Electronic Cultural Atlas Initiative, 2000—; vis. scholar Western Mich. U., 1979; vis. prof. U. Klagenfurt, Austria, 1980, U. New South Wales, Australia, 1988, NORSLIS vis. prof., Tromsø & Uppsala, 2008. Author: Book Availability and the Library User, 1975, (with others) The Use of Gaming in Education for Library Management, 1976, Reader in Operations Research for Libraries, 1976, Library Services in Theory and Context, 1983, 2d edit., 1988, Information and Information Systems, 1991, Redesigning Library Services, 1992, Emanuel Goldberg and his Knowledge Machine, 2006; editor: Historical Studies in Information Science, 1998, Robert Gitler and the Japan Library School, 1999. Fulbright Rsch. scholar U. Tech., Graz, Austria, 1989. Mem. ALA, Am. Soc. Info. Sci. (pres. 1998), Calif. Libr. Assn. Office: U Calif Sch Info Berkeley CA 94720-4600

BUCKLEY, DANIEL P., lawyer; b. Washington, Sept. 5, 1968; BS, Mont. State U.; JD summa cum laude, Gonzaga U., 1994. Bar: 1994. Assoc. Berg, Lilly & Tollefsen, P.C., 1994—99, ptnr., Foust Buckley, P.C., Bozeman, Mont. Mem. Gonzaga Law Review, 1992—94. Mem.: Nat. Assn. Criminal Def. Lawyers, Mont. Criminal Def. Lawyers Assn., Am. Trial Lawyers Assn., Mont. Trial Lawyers Assn. Office: Foust Buckley PC 2040 N 22nd Ave Ste 2 Bozeman MT 59718-2741 Office Phone: 406-587-3346.

BUCKLEY, MIKE CLIFFORD, lawyer; b. Atlanta, Sept. 1, 1944; s. Clifford Robert Buckley and Winifred Davis (Clayton) Coleman; m. Elizabeth Trimble, June 17, 1967. AB, U. Calif., Berkeley, 1966; JD, U. Calif., 1969. Bar: Calif. 1969. Assoc. Lawler, Felix & Hall, LA, 1969-72; asst. West Coast counsel ITT, LA, 1972-74; ptnr. Crosby, Heafey, Roach & May, Oakland, Calif., 1974—2002, Reed Smith LLP, Oakland, 2003—. Pres. TeleNetwork, Inc., Oakland, 1984-92; treas. Salem Luth. Home of the East Bay Inc., 1992-98; lectr. Calif. Continuing Edn. of Bar, Berkeley, 1978-2002; workshop leader Hastings Coll. Advocacy, San Francisco, 1981-85; adv. com. U.S. Bankruptcy Ct., San Francisco, 1984-89. Mem. Calif. Bar Assn., Alameda Bar Assn., San Francisco Bar Assn. Democrat. Home: 246 Pershing Dr Oakland CA 94611-3235 Office: Reed Smith Crosby Heafey LLP PO Box 2084 Oakland CA 94604-2084 Office Phone: 510-466-6704. Business E-Mail: mbuckley@reedsmith.com. E-mail: mbuckley@chrm.com.

BUCKLIN, CHRISTINE B., information technology executive; b. 1963; m. Randolph Bucklin; 3 children. AB in Math., suma cum laude, Dartmouth Coll., Hanover, NH, 1984; MBA, Stanford Grad. Sch. Bus., Calif. Rsch. assoc. Booz, Allen & Hamilton, NYC, 1984—86; mgmt. cons., ptnr. McKinsey & Co., LA, 1988—99; entrepreneur-in-residence idealab!, Pasadena, Calif., 1999; COO Internet Brands Inc. (originally founded as CarsDirect.com), Culver City, Calif., 2000—08; sr. v.p. corp. strategic planning Sun Microsystems, Inc., Santa Clara, Calif., 2008—. Named one of The Top 100 Women in N.Am. Automotive Industry, Automotive News, 2000. Office: Sun Microsystems Inc Worldwide Hdqs 4150 Network Circle Santa Clara CA 95054 Office Phone: 650-960-1300.*

BUCKMASTER, JIM, online community bulletin board company executive; B in BioChemistry summa cum laude, Va. Tech; studied medicine and classics, U. Mich. Lead web developer Inter-University Consortium for Polit. and Soc. Rsch., U. Mich.; dir. web develop. dotcom Creditland, Quantum Corp.; chief tech. officer, CFO, lead programmer Craigslist, San Francisco, pres., CEO, 2000—. Bd. transportation, San Francisco. Built the world's first multi-teraybte database-driven public website at the University Michigan; Craigslist is a network of local community bulletion boards, where millions of people research subjects such as: jobs, housing, goods & services, events, friendships, and advice. Office: Craigslist 1319 9th Ave San Francisco CA 94122-2308 Office Phone: 415-566-6394. Office Fax: 415-504-6394. Business E-Mail: jim@craigslist.org.

BUCKNER, JOHN KNOWLES, investor; b. Springfield, Mo., Sept. 8, 1936; s. Ernest Godfrey and Mary Helen (Knowles) B.; m. Lorraine Catherine Anderson, Sept. 22, 1962; children: John Knowles, Allison. BA, Williams Coll., 1958; MS, Mass. Inst. Tech., 1960; PhD, nuclear engring., Stanford U., 1965; grad., Advanced Mgmt. Program, Harvard, 1974. Mgr. analysis dept. EG&G Inc., Bedford, Mass., 1966-70; dir. electronic data processing, controller, v.p. financial ops. Eastern Gas & Fuel Assos., Boston, 1970-77; exec. v.p., chief operating officer, dir. Waters Assos., Inc., Milford, Mass., 1977-80; v.p., chief fin. officer Prime Computer, Inc., Natick, Mass., 1980-83; sr. v.p., chief fin. officer EG & G, Inc., Wellesley, Mass., 1983-86; vice chmn., chief fin. officer Control Data Corp., Mpls., 1986-89; chmn. Pensco Pension Svcs. Inc., San Francisco, 1989-98, Bohdan Automation, Inc., Mundelein, Ill., 1994-98. Contbr. articles on engring., data analysis and systems to profl. jours. AEC spl. fellow nuclear sci. and engring., 1959, 62-65 Mem.: Assn. Univs. for Rsch. in Astronomy (bd.d ir. 2003—), Sigma Xi, Phi Beta Kappa, Chi Psi. Office: Pensco Pension Svcs Inc 450 Sansome St 14th Fl San Francisco CA 94111-3306

BUCKNER, PHILIP FRANKLIN, newspaper publisher; b. Worcester, Mass., Aug. 25, 1930; s. Orello Simmons and Emily Virginia (Siler) B.; m. Ann Haswell Smith, Dec. 21, 1956 (div. Nov. 1993); children: John C., Frederick S., Catherine A.; m. Mary Emily Aird, Dec. 15, 1995 (div. Sept. 1997). AB, Harvard U., 1952; MA, Columbia U., 1954. With Bay State Abrasive Products Co., 1954-59; Reporter Lowell (Mass.) Sun, 1959-60; pub. East Providence (R.I.) Post, 1960-62; asst. to treas. Scripps League Newspapers, Seattle, 1964-66, divsn. mgr., 1966-71; pres. Buckner News Alliance, Seattle, 1971—. Pub. daily newspaper group including Carlsbad (N.Mex.) Current-Argus, 1971-90, Pecos (Tex.) Enterprise, 1971—, Fontana (Calif.) Herald-News, 1971-89, Banning and Beaumont (Calif.) Gazette, 1971-74, Lewistown (Pa.) Sentinel, 1971-93, Tiffin (Ohio) Advertiser-Tribune, 1973-93, York (Pa.) Daily Record, 1978-2004, Winsted (Conn.) Citizen, 1978, Excelsior Springs (Mo.) Standard, 1978, Oroville (Calif.) Mercury-Register, 1983-89, Corona (Calif.) Independent, 1984-89, Minot (N.D.) News, 1989-93, York (Pa.) Dispatch, 2004—. Avocation: mountain climbing. Office: Buckner News Alliance 2101 4th Ave Ste 1870 Seattle WA 98121-2345

BUCY, RICHARD SNOWDEN, aerospace engineering and mathematics educator, consultant; b. Washington DC, July 20, 1935; s. Edmond Howard and Marie (Glinke) B.; m. Ofelia Teresa Rivva, Aug. 25, 1961; children: Phillip Gustav, Richard Erwin. BS in Math., MIT, 1957; PhD in Math. Stats., U. Calif.-Berkeley, 1963. Researcher in math. Rsch. Inst. Advanced Studies, Towson, Md., 1960-61, 63-64; rsch. asst. U. Calif., Berkeley, 1961-63; asst. prof. math. U. Md., College Park, 1964-65; assoc. prof. aerospace engring. U. Colo., Boulder, 1965-66; prof. aerospace engring. and math. U. So. Calif., Los Angeles, 1966—; professeur associe French Govt., Toulouse, 1973-74, Nice, 1983-84, 90-91. Vis. prof. Technische Universität Berlin, 1975-76; co-dir. NATO Advanced Study Inst. on Non-linear Scholastic Problems, Algarve, Portugal; cons. to industry Author: Filtering for Stochastic Processes, 1968, 2d edit., 1987, Nonlinear Stochastic Problems, 1984, Lectures on Discrete Filtering Theory, 1994; editor Jour. Info. Scis., Jour. Math. Modelling and Sci. Computing; founding editor (jour.) Stochastics, 1971-77; contbr. numerous articles to profl. publs. Recipient Humboldt prize Govt. W. Germany, Berlin, 1975-76; Air Force Office Sci. Sch. grantee, 1965-81, NATO Rsch. grantee, 1979—. Fellow IEEE (del. to Soviet Acad. of Scis. Info. Theory Workshop); mem. Am. Math. Soc. Republican. Home: 420 S Juanita Ave Redondo Beach CA 90277-3824 Office: U So Calif Dept Aerospace Engring Los Angeles CA 90089-0001

BUDINGER, THOMAS FRANCIS, radiologist, educator; b. Evanston, Ill., Oct. 25, 1932; married, 1965; 3 children. BS in Chemistry magna cum laude, Regis Coll., 1954; MS in Phys. Oceanography, U. Wash., Seattle, 1957; MD, U. Colo., Denver, 1964; PhD in Med. Physics, U. Calif. Berkeley, 1971. Cert. in nuc. medicine 1973, lic. Calif., Pa. Asst. chemist Regis Coll., Colo., 1953—54; analytical chemist Indsl. Labs., 1954; sr. oceanographer U. Wash., 1961—66; physicist Lawrence Livermore Lab., U. Calif., 1966—67; resident physician Donner Lab. and Lawrence Berkeley Lab., 1967—76; H. Miller Prof. med. rsch. and group leader rsch. medicine Donner lab., prof. elec. engring. and computer sci. Donner Lab., U. Calif. Berkeley, 1976—. With Peter Bent Brigham Hosp., Boston, 1964; dir. med. svc. Lawrence Berkeley Lab., 1968—76, sr. staff scientist, 1980—; chmn. study sect. NIH, 1981—84; prof. radiology U. Calif. San Francisco, 1984—. Contbr. scientific papers to profl. publs. Recipient NASA Group Achievement award, 1976, Spl. Achievement award in nuc. tech. for med. diagnostics, Am. Nuc. Soc., 1984, Alumni Achievement award, Regis Coll., 1987, Merit award for Alzheimer's rsch., NIH, 1990; named Eugene P. Pendergrass New Horizons lectr., Radiol. Soc. North America, 1993. Fellow: Soc. Magnetic Resonance, Am. Inst. Med. and Biol. Engring.; mem.: NAE (councillor 2006—08, home sec. 2008—), AAAS, Soc. Magnetic Resonance in Medicine (pres. 1984—85, Disting. Svc. medal 1989), Soc. Nuc. Medicine (Hermann L. Blumgart Cardiovascular lectureship 1987, Paul C. Aebersold award for basic sci. 1989, Disting. Sci. award 1991), NY Acad. Scis., Am. Geophys. Union. Achievements include research in imaging body functions, electrical, magnetic, sound and photon radiation fields, electron microscopy, polar oceanography; nuclear magnetic resonance, reconstruction tomography and instrument development, and cardiology. Avocation: crew. Office: Lawrence Berkeley Nat Lab Ctr for Functional Imaging 1 Cyclotron Rd Mail Stop 55-121 Berkeley CA 94720-0001 Office Phone: 510-486-5435. Office Fax: 510-486-4768. Business E-Mail: tfbudinger@lbl.gov.

BUDOFF, MATTHEW JAY, cardiologist; m. Victoria Billit, Oct. 3, 1998; children: Daniel Oliver, Garrett Clark. BS in Biochemistry, U. Calif., Riverside, 1986; MD, George Wash. U., DC, 1990. Lic. physician DC, 1990, bd. cert. Internal Medicine 1994, bd. cert. Cardiology 1997. Internal medicine internship and residency Harbor UCLA Med. Ctr., Torrance, Calif., 1990—93, cardiology fellow, 1994—97; rschr. physician LA Biomedical Rsch., Torrance, 1997—; asst. prof. UCLA Sch. Medicine, 1997—2003, assoc. prof., 2003—. Editor (author): Enhancing Heart Health, 2003, Cardiac CT Imaging, 2006, Atlas of Cardiac CT, 2007; contbr. articles to profl. jours., chapters to books. Named one of Am. Top Doctors for Men, 2007; named to LA Superdoctors, 2007. Fellow: Am. Coll. Cardiology, Am. Heart Assn., Am. Heart Assn. (life; bd. dirs. 2000—06); mem.: Soc. Atherosclerosis and Prevention (founder, pres. 2006—), Soc. Cardiovascular CT (founding mem., exec. bd. mem. 2004—). Achievements include patents for imaging. Office: Los Angeles Biomedical Research Institut 1124 West Carson Street Torrance CA 90502 Business E-Mail: mbudoff@labiomed.org.

BUDZINSKI, JAMES EDWARD, interior designer; b. Jan. 4, 1953; s. Edward Michael and Virginia (Caliman) B. Student, U. Cin., 1971-76. Mem. design staff Perkins & Wills Archs., Inc., Chgo., 1973-75, Med. Architectonics, Inc., Chgo., 1975-76; v.p. interior design Interior Environs., Inc., Chgo., 1976-78; pres. Jim Budzinski Design, Inc., Chgo., 1978-80; dir. interior design Robinson, Mills & Williams, San Francisco, 1980-87; dir. design, interior arch. Whisler Patri, San Francisco, 1987-90; v.p. design sales and mktg. Deepa Textiles, 1990-95; v.p. Workplace Studio One Workplace L. Ferrari, San Jose, Calif., 1997-2000; strategic envisioner OneWorkplace, 2000—04; ind. design cons. Jim Budzinski Design, Residential Design and Devel., 2004—. Instr. design Harrington Inst. Design, Chgo.; cons. Chgo. Art Inst., Storwal Internat., Inc.; spkr. profl. confs. Designs include 1st Chgo. Corp. Pvt. Banking Ctr., 1st Nat. Bank Chgo. Monroe and Wabash Banking Ctr., 1978, IBM Corp., San Jose, Deutsche Bank, Frankfort, Crowley Maritime Corp., San Francisco, office for Brobeck, Phleger and Harrison, offices for chmn. bd. Fireman's Fund Ins. Cos., Nob Hill Club, Fairmont Hotel, San Francisco, offices for Cooley, Goodword, Castro, Huddleson, and

Tatum, Palo Alto, Calif., offices for Pacific Bell Acctg. divsn., San Francisco, showroom for Knoll Internat., San Francisco, lobby, lounge TransAm. Corp. Hdqs., San Francisco, offices for EDAW, San Francisco, showroom for Steelcase, Inc., Bally of Switzerland, N.Am. Flagship store, San Francisco; corp. Hdqs. Next Inc., Redwood City, Calif., Schafer Furniture Design, Lobby Renovation 601 California, San Francisco, Bennedetti Furniture Inc. Furniture Design; interiors Minnis Residence, Seattle and Napa, Calif., Cortesi Residence, Cobb, Wolz/Polldine Residence, O'Brien Residence, Cobb, Calif. Pres. No. Calif. chpt. Design Industries Found. for AIDS. Home: PO Box 1181 Cobb CA 95426-1181 E-mail: jbudzinski@oneworkplace.com.

BUECHNER, JOHN C., academic administrator; Dir. govtl. rels., then dir. pub. affairs U. Colo. System Office, Denver, until 1989; chancellor U. Colo., Denver, 1988-96, pres., 1996—2000, pres. emeritus, 2000—. Office: U Colo-Denver Office of Pres Campus Box 35 Boulder CO 80309-0035

BUESCHER, BERNARD A. (BERNIE BUESCHER), state official, air transportation executive; b. 1949; m. Mary Elizabeth Buescher, 1972; children: Michael, Elizabeth, Marcia, Susan. BBA, U. Notre Dame, South Bend, 1971; JD, U. Colo., Boulder, 1974. Law clk. to Justice Paul V. Hodges, Colo. Supreme Ct., 1974—75; ptnr., shareholder, officer Williams, Turner & Holmes P.C., Grand Junction, Colo., 1975—89; pres. West Star Engine Corp., Grand Junction, 1987-92, West Star Aviation, Grand Junction, 1987—96, West Star Capital Leasing, Inc., West Star Conversions, Inc., 1987—96; mgr. Connections at work, LLC, 1996—; interim mgr. Colo. State Fair, 1996—97; exec. dir. Colo. Dept. Health Care Policy and Financing, 1997—98; atty. pvt. practice, Grand Junction, 1998—2000; COO Mesa Systems, Inc., 2000—02; mem. Colo. House of Reps., 2005—08; sec. state State of Colo., Denver, 2009—. Mem. bd. dirs. Home Loan Indsl. Bank, 1983—97, Home Loan and Investment Co., 1983—97; mem. bd. dirs. co-founder Heritage Trust Co., 1993—96; COO Grand Valley Cath. Edn., Inc., 1999—2004; project mgr. Grand Valley Catch Outreach, 2003—. Mem. Colo. Econ. Devel. Commn., 1991—94; mem. bd. dirs. Am. Cancer Soc.; mem. Mesa County Bd. Adjustment, 1979—87, chmn., 1981—87; mem. bd. dirs. Family Health West Found., 1989—92, Mesa County Econ. Devel. Coun., 1989—96, bd. chmn., 1992—93; pres. Mesa County Bus. Edn. Foundations, Inc., 1992—94, bd. mem., 1999—2001; mem. Colo. Transp. Commn., 1994—97; mem. bd. dirs. Ara Parseghian Med. Rsch. Found., 1994—, Colo. Pub. Radio, Western Colo. Ctr. for Arts, St. Mary's Hosp., 1999—2004, vice chair, 2001—02, chairperson, 2002—04. Named Co-Citizen of Yr. (with wife Mary Beth), Grand Junction C. of C., 2004, Legislator of Yr., Colo. Women's Bar Assn., 2005, Colo. Assn. Conservation Districts, 2006, Home Care Assn. Colo., 2006, U. Colo., 2006, United Veteran's Com., 2006, Colo. Econ. Devel. Coun., 2006, 2008, Colo. Assn. Social Workers, 2008, Colo. Non Profit Assn., 2008. Mem.: Colo. Hosp. Assn. (mem. bd. dirs. 2002—04). Democrat. Avocations: golf, reading. Office: Office Sec State Dept State 1700 Broadway Denver CO 80290 Office Phone: 303-894-2200 ext. 7900. Office Fax: 303-869-4860. Business E-Mail: secretary@sos.state.co.us.*

BUFANO, RALPH A., retired museum executive; BS in Fine Arts, U. Minn. Dir. Exptl. Aircraft Aviation Found., Oshkosh, Wis.; pres. Kansas City (Mo.) Mus.; exec. dir. Ward Found. Mus., Salisbury, Md.; pres., CEO The Mus. of Flight, Seattle, 1991—2005. Fellow: Fedn. Aeronautica Internat. (Paul Tissadier award for svcs. to aeros. and airsports), Royal Aero. Soc. Office: The Mus of Flight 9404 E Marginal Way S Seattle WA 98108-4097 Personal E-mail: ralph.bufano@comcast.net.

BUFFETT, JIMMY (JAMES WILLIAM BUFFETT), vocalist, songwriter, writer; b. Pascagoula, Miss., Dec. 25, 1946; s. James Delaney and Lorraine (Peets) B.; m. Margie Washichek, 1969 (div.), m. Jane Slagsvol, Aug. 27, 1977; children: Savannah Jane, Sarah Delaney and Cameron Marley. BS in History and Journalism, U. So. Miss., 1969. Free-lance journalist Inside Sports, Outside mag. Singer: (albums) Down to Earth, 1970, High Cumberland Jubilee, 1971, White Sport Coat and a Pink Crustacean, 1973, Living and Dying in 3/4 Time, 1974, A1A, 1974, Rancho Deluxe (film soundtrack), 1975, Havana Daydreamin', 1976, Changes in Latitudes, 1977, Son of a Son of a Sailor, 1978, You Had To Be There, 1978, Volcano, 1979, Coconut Telegraph, 1981, Somewhere Over China, 1981, One Particular Harbor, 1983, Riddles in the Sand, 1984, Last Mango in Paris, 1985, Songs You Know By Heart, 1985, Floridays, 1986, Hot Water, 1988, Off To See The Lizard, 1989, Feeding Frenzy, 1990, Boats, Beaches, Bars & Ballads, 1992, Before the Beach, 1993, Fruit Cakes, 1994, Barometer Soup, 1995, Banana Wind, 1996, Christmas Island, 1996, Don't Stop the Carnival, 1998, Beach House on the Moon, 1999, Buffett Live-Tuesdays, Thursdays, Saturdays, 1999, Captain America, 2002, Far Side of the World, 2002, License to Chill, 2004, Take the Weather With You, 2006, Live at Texas Stadium, 2007, Live in Anguilla, 2007; (songs) Margaritaville; author: (novels) Tales from Margaritaville, 1988, Where is Joe Merchant?, 1992, A Novel Tale, 1992, Daybreak on the Equator, 1997, A Pirate Looks at Fifty, 1998, Sea Level: Adventures of a Saltwater Angler, 2002, A Salty Piece of Land, 2004 (Publishers Weekly bestseller), Swine Not?, 2008; (memoirs) A Pirate Looks at Fifty, 1998; co-author:(with Savannah Jane Buffett) The Jolly Mon, 1988, Trouble Dolls, 1990; actor: (films) Rancho Deluxe, 1975, FM, 1978, Repo Man, 1984, Dr Duck's Super Secret All-Purpose Sauce, 1985, Hook, 1991, Cobb, 1994, Congo, 1995; actor, prodr.: Hoot, 2006; actor: (TV series) CCTV Network 90, 1981, From the Earth to the Moon, 1998. Chmn. Save the Manatee Commn., Fla.; hon. dir. Greenpeace Found. Mem. Cousteau Soc. Democrat. Roman Catholic. Office: c/o Rand Holston Creative Arts Agy 2000 Ave of the Americas Los Angeles CA 90067 also: c/o Howard Kaufman HK Mgmt 9200 Sunset Blvd Los Angeles CA 90069

BUFFINGTON, JOHN DOUGLAS, ecologist; b. Jersey City, Nov. 26, 1941; s. John Franklin and Rosemary Eileen (Snowdy) B.; m. Mary Elizabeth Coughlin, Jan. 23, 1965; children: Jill Anne, John Matthew. BS cum laude, St. Peter's Coll., Jersey City, 1963; MS, U. Ill., 1965, PhD, 1967. Asst. prof. Ill. State U., Normal, 1969-72; scientist, asst. divsn. dir. Argonne (Ill.) Nat. Lab., 1972-77; sr. staff scientist Pres.'s Coun. Environ. Quality, Washington, 1977-80; chief office biol. svcs. U.S. Fish & Wildlife Svc., Washington, 1980-83, dep. reg. dir., 1983-89, regional dir., 1989-93; acting regional dir. Nat. Biol. Survey, Washington, 1993-95; dir. Alaska Sci. Ctr., 1995-97; regional chief biologist U.S. Geol. Survey, Seattle, 1997-99, regional dir., 2000—. Mem. U.S. negotiating delegation Conv. Biol. Diversity, 1990-93. Capt. U.S. Army, 1967-69. Recipient Meritorious Svc. award U.S. Dept. Interior, 1994. Mem. Ecol. Soc. Am. (applied sect. chmn. 1981, Washington chpt. chmn. 1981). Office: US Geol Survey 900 1st Ave Ste 800 Seattle WA 98104

BUFFORD, SAMUEL LAWRENCE, federal judge; b. Phoenix, Nov. 19, 1943; s. John Samuel and Evelyn Amelia (Rude) B.; m. Julia Marie Metzger, May 13, 1978. BA in Philosophy, Wheaton Coll., 1964; PhD, U. Tex., 1969; JD magna cum laude, U. Mich., 1973. Bar: Calif., N.Y., Ohio. Instr. philosophy La. State U., Baton Rouge, 1967-68; asst. prof. Ea. Mich. U., Ypsilanti, 1968-74; asst. prof. law Ohio State U., Columbus, 1975-77; assoc. Gendel, Raskoff, Shapiro & Quittner, LA, 1982-85; atty. Paul, Weiss, Rifkind, Wharton & Garrison, NYC, 1974-75, Sullivan Jones & Archer, San Francisco, 1977-79, Musick, Peeler & Garrett, LA, 1979-81, Rifkind & Sterling, Beverly Hills, Calif., 1981-82, Gendel, Raskoff, Shapiro & Quittner, LA, 1982-85; U.S. bankruptcy judge Ctrl. Dist. Calif., 1985—. Cons. in field; lectr. in field. Sr. author: International Insolvency, 2001, editor-in-chief: Am. Bankruptcy Law Jour., 1990—94; contbr. articles to profl. jours. Younger Humanist fellowship NEH. Mem. ABA, L.A. County Bar Assn. (mem. profl. responsibility and ethics com. 1979—, chair profl. responsibility and ethics com. 1985-86, chair ethics 2000 liaison com. 1997-2002), Order of Coif. Office: US Bankruptcy Ct 255 E Temple St Ste 1582 Los Angeles CA 90012-3332

BUGBEE-JACKSON, JOAN, sculptor, educator; b. Oakland, Calif., Dec. 17, 1941; d. Henry Greenwood and Jeanie Lawler (Abbot) B.; m. John Michael Jackson, June 21, 1973; 1 child, Brook Bond. BA in Art, U. Calif., San Jose, 1964, MA in Art and Ceramics, 1966; student, Nat. Acad. Sch. Fine Arts, NYC, 1968-72. Instr. pottery Greenwich House Pottery, NYC, 1969-71, Craft Inst. Am., NYC, 1970-72, Cordova Ext. Ctr., U. AK, 1972-79, Prince William Sound Cmty. Coll., 1979—. One-woman exhbn. in Maine, NYC, Alaska, Calif.; group exhbns. include Allied Artists Am., 1970-72, Nat. Acad. Design, 1971, 74, Nat. Sculpture Soc. Ann., 1971, 72, 73, Alaska Woman Art Show, 1987, 88, Cordova Visual Artists, 1991-96, Alaska Artists Guild Show, 1994, Am. Medallic Sculpture Nat. Travelling Exhbn., 1994-95, pres. Cordova Arts and Pageants Ltd., 1975-76; commns. include Merle K. Smith Commemorative plaque, 1973, Eyak Native Monument, 1978, Anchorage Pioneer's Home Ceramic Mural, 1979, Alaska Wildlife Series Bronze Medal, 1980, Armin F. Koernig Hatchery Plaque, 1985, Cordova Fishermen's Meml. Sculpture, 1985, Alaska's Five Gov., bronze relief, Anchorage, 1986, Reluctant Fishermen's Mermaid, bronze, 1987, Charles E. Bunnell, bronze portrait statue, Fairbanks, 1988, Alexander Baranof Monument, Sitka, Alaska, 1989, Wally Noerenberg Hatchery Plaque, Prince William Sound, Alaska, 1989, Russian-Alaskan Friendship Plaque (edit. of 4), Kayak Island, Cordova, Alaska and Vladivostok & Petropavlovsk-Kamchatskiy, Russia, 1991, Sophie-Last Among Eyak Native People, 1992, Alaska Airlines Medal Commn., 1993, Hosp. Aux. plaque, 1995, La Cirena, Mex., 1998, Alaska Vets. Monument lifesize bronze, Anchorage, 2001, Alaska R.R.: Sheffield Plaque, 2002, Joe Redington Sr., Father of the Iditarod, statue, Wasilla, Alaska, 2003, Pioneer Aviator Monument, Anchorage, 2005; also other portraits. Bd. dir. Alaska State Coun. Arts, 1991-95. Scholar, Nat. Acad. Sch. Fine Arts, 1969-72; recipient J.A. Suydam Bronze medal, 1969, Dr. Ralph Weiler prize, 1971, Helen Foster Barnet award, 1971, Daniel Chester French award, 1972, Frishmuth award, 1971, Allied Artists Am. award, 1972, C. Percival Dietsch prize, 1973, citation Alaska Legis., 1981, 82; named Alaskan Artist of Yr., 1991; Alaska Gov. Award, 2002. Fellow Nat. Sculpture Soc. Address: PO Box 374 Cordova AK 99574-0374 E-mail: artworks@ctcak.net.

BUGLI, DAVID, conductor, arranger, composer; b. NYC, Apr. 2, 1950; BMus, Ithaca Coll., 1972; MMus, U. Mass., 1978. Founder, musical dir., condr. Carson City Symphony (formerly Carson City Chamber Orch.), Nev., 1984—. Tchr. music Pub. Sch., 1972—77; computer programmer/analyst, 1979—; 1st pres. Carson Access TV Found., 1991. Office: Carson City Symphony PO Box 2001 Carson City NV 89702-2001 E-mail: dbugli@aol.com.

BUGLIOSI, VINCENT T., lawyer, writer; b. Hibbing, Minn., Aug. 18, 1934; s. Vincent and Ida (Valerie) B.; m. Gail Margaret Talluto, July 21, 1956; children: Wendy Suzanna, Vincent John. BBA, U. Miami, Fla., 1956; LLB, UCLA, 1964. Bar: Calif. 1964. Dep. dist. atty., Los Angeles County, 1964-72; pvt. practice law Beverly Hills, Calif., 1972—. Prof. criminal law Beverly Sch. Law, Los Angeles, 1968-74 Author: Outrage: The Five Reasons Why O.J. Simpson Got Away with Murder, 1996, The Phoenix Solution: Gettin Serious About Winning America's Drug War, 1996, No Island of Sanity: Paula Jones v. Bill Clinton- The Supreme Court on Trial, 1998, The Betrayal of America: How the Supreme Court Undermined the Constitution and Chose Our President, 2001, Reclaiming History: The Assassination of President John F. Kennedy, 2007 (Edgar award for best fact crime book 2008), The Prosecution of George W. Bush for Murder, 2008; co-author: (with Curt Gentry) Helter-Skelter: The True Story of the Manson Murders, 1974 (Edgar award for best fact crime book 1975), (with Ken Hurwitz) Till Death Us Do Part: A True Murder Mystery, 1978 (Edgar award for best fact crime book 1979), (with Bruce B. Henderson) And the Sea Will Tell, 1991. Candidate for dist. atty., Los Angeles County, 1972, Dem. candidate Calif. atty. gen., 1974. Served to capt. AUS, 1957. Office: 3699 Wilshire Blvd #850 Los Angeles CA 90010

BUHLER, JILL LORIE, editor, writer; b. Seattle, Dec. 7, 1945; d. Oscar John and Marcella Jane (Hearing) Younce; 1 child, Lori Jill Moody; m. John Buhler, 1990; stepchildren: Christie Reynolds, Cathie Zatarian, Mike. AA in Gen. Edn., Am. River Coll., Sacramento, 1969; BA in Journalism with honors, Sacramento State U., Calif., 1973. Reporter Carmichael (Calif.) Courier, 1968-70; mng. editor Quarter Horse of the Pacific Coast, Sacramento, 1970-75, editor, 1975-84, Golden State Program Jour., 1978, Nat. Reined Cow Horse Assn. News, Sacramento, 1983-88, Pacific Coast Jour., Sacramento, 1984-88, Nat. Snaffle Bit Assn. News, Sacramento, 1988; pres., CEO Comm. Plus, Port Townsend, Wash., 1988—; bd. sec. N.W. Maritime Ctr., 2001—; editor-in-chief Peninsula Lifestyle mag., 2006—. Mag. cons., 1975—; profl. photographer, owner Studio J. Photography, Port Townsend, Wash., 2009-. Interviewer Pres. Ronald Regan, Washington, 1983; mng. editor Wash. Thoroughbred, 1989-90; editor-in-chief Peninsula Lifestyle Mag., 2005-. Mem. 1st profl. communicators mission to USSR, 1988; bd. dirs. Carmichael Winding Way, Pasadena Homeowners Assn., 1985-87; mem. scholarship com. Thoroughbred Horse Racing's United Scholarship Trust; mem. governing bd. Wash. State Hosp. Assn., 1996-2000, mem. legis. policy com., 1999—, hosp. commr. Jefferson Healthcare, 1995—, chair bd. dirs. 1997-2000, 2006-, sec., 2004; mem. Jefferson County Bd. Health, 1997—, vice chmn., 1998, chmn. 2001; mem. Wash. State Health Care Leadership Com., 2003-. Recipient 1st pl. feature award, 1970, 1st pl. editl. award Jour. Assn. Jr. Colls., 1971, 1st pl. design award WCHB Yuba-Sutter Counties, Marysville, Calif., 1985, Photography awards, 1994, 95, 96, Kiwanis Hixon award, 2008. Mem. Am. River Jaycees (Speaking award 1982), Am. Horse Publs. (1st Pl. Editl. award 1983, 86), Port Townsend C. of C. (trustee, v.p. 1993, pres. 1994, officer 1996, 97, 98), Mensa (bd. dirs., asst. local sec., activities dir. 1987-88, membership chair 1988-90), Kiwanis Internat. (chair maj. emphasis program com., treas. 1992—), 5th Wheel Touring Soc. (v.p. 1970). Republican. Roman Catholic. Avocations: sailing, photography. Home Phone: 360-385-1375; Office Phone: 360-301-6099. Personal E-mail: jillb@olypen.com.

BUIST, NEIL ROBERTSON MACKENZIE, pediatric educator, medical association administrator; b. Karachi, India, July 11, 1932; m. Sonia Chapman; children: Catriona, Alison, Diana. Degree with commendation, U. St. Andrews, Scotland, MB, ChB, 1956; Diploma of Child Health, London U., England, 1960. Diplomate Am. Bd. Med. Genetics, Am. Bd. Clinical Genetics. House physician internal medicine Arbroath Infirmary, 1956-57; house physician externe cardiopulmonary dept. Hosp. Marie Lannelongue, Paris, 1957; house surgeon Royal Hosp. Sick Children, Edinburgh, Scotland, 1957; commd. far east med. officer Regimental Military Svc., 1957-60; house physician Royal Infirmary, Dundee, Scotland, 1960; registrar internal medicine Maryfield Hosp., Dundee, Scotland, 1960-62; lectr. child health U. St. Andrews, Dundee, Scotland, 1962-64; rsch. fellow pediatric microchemistry, Sch. Health Sci. U. Colo., Denver, 1964-66; asst. prof. pediatrics, Sch. Medicine U. Oreg., Portland, 1966-70; dir. Pediatrics Metabolic Lab, Oreg. Health Sci. U., Portland, 1966-93, Metabolic Birth Defects Ctr., Oreg. Health Sci. U., Portland, 1966-98; assoc. prof. pediat. and med. genetics Oreg. Health Sci. U., Portland, 1970—76, prof. pediat. and med. genetics, 1976—98, prof. emeritus. Med. cons. Northwest Regional Newborn Screening Program, Portland, 1970—; vis. prof. WHO, China, 1988, U. Colo., 1990, Wesley Med. Ctr., Kans., 1991, Phoenix Children's Hosp., Ariz., 1991, Tucson Med. Ctr., Ariz., 1991, U. Ill., Chgo., 1991, Kapoiolani Med. Ctr., Hawaii, 1992, Shriners Hosp. for Crippled Children., Hawaii, 1992, Ark. Children's Hosp., 1993, Australasian Soc. for Human Genetics, New Zealand, 1994, LBJ Med. Ctr., Americas Samoa, 1994, Mahidol U., Bangkok, 1996, U. P.R., 1996, U. Auckland (New Zealand), 1997, Ctrl. Valley Children's Hosp., 1996-, U. Rochester, 2004, emergency disaster response physician, N.W. Med. Teams Internat., Afghanistan, 2002, Ethiopia, 2004, Sri Lanka, 2005. Author: (with others) Textbook of Pediatrics, 1973, Inherited Disorders of Amino Acid Metabolism, 1974, 1985, Clinics in Endocrinolog and Metabolism: Aspects of Neonatal Metabolism, 1976, Textbook of Pediatrics, 1978, Practice of Pediatrics, 1980, Management of High-Risk Pregnancy, 1980, Current Occular Therapy, 1980, Practice of Pediatrics, 1981, Clinics in Endocrinology and Metabolism: Aspects of Neonatal Metabolism, 1981, Textbook of Pediatrics, 1984, Disorders of Fatty Acid Metabolism in the Pediatric Practice, 1990, Birth Defects Encyclopedia, 1990, 1991, Treatment of Genetic Disease, 1991, Pediatric Clinics of North Americs Medical Genetics II, 1992, Forfar & Arneil's Textbook of Paediatrics, 1992, 97, Galactosemia New Frontiers in Research, 1993, New Horizons in Neonatal Screening, 1994, New Trends in Neonatal Screening, 1994, Alpha-1-Antitrypsin Deficiency, 1994, Diseases of the Fetus and Newborn, 1995, Inborn Metabolic Diseases: Diagnosis and Treatment, 1995; cons. editor: Inborn Metabolic Disease Text, 1995; editorial bd. mem.: Jour. of Inherited Metabolic Diseases, 1977—, Kelley Practice of Pediatrics, 1980-87, Screening, 1991-96; jour. reviewer: Am. Jour. of Human Genetics, Jour. of Pediatrics, Pediatric Rsch., Screening. Adv. com. Tri County March of Dimes, Portland, 1977—; physician Diabetic Children's Camp, 1967—, Muscle Biopsy Clinic Shriners Hosp., 1989—; bd. dirs. Mize Info. Enterprises, Dallas, 1987—. Fellow Royal Coll. Physicians Edinburgh, Fogarty Internat. Vis. Scientist, Royal Coll. Physicians Edinburgh; mem. Brit. Med. Assn., Western Soc. Pediatric Rsch. (coun. mem. 1966—), Pacific North West Pediatric Soc., Am. Pediatric Soc., Soc. for the Study of Inborn Errors of Metabolism, Soc. for Inherited Metabolic Disorders (treas. 1977-2000, pres. 2000-02), Oreg. Pediatric Soc., Oreg. Diabetes Assn., Portland Acad. Pediatrics, Internat. Newborn Screening Soc. Coun. (founding mem. 1988—). Avocations: fishing, gardening, travel.

BUKATY, RAYMOND M., lawyer; b. NYC, Aug. 19, 1957; BA, Stanford U., 1979; MBA, JD, U. Southern Calif., 1983. Bar: Calif. 1983. Atty. Riordan & McKinzie, Los Angeles, Calif.; asst. gen. counsel Fluor Corp., Aliso Viejo, Calif., 1995—97, sr. counsel, 1998; v.p. corp. law Western Digital, Lake Forest, Calif., 1999—2002, v.p., gen. counsel, sec., 2002—04, sr. v.p., gen. counsel, sec., 2004—. Bd. mem. Mercy House, Orange County, Calif., Orange County ARC. Mem.: ABA, Orange County Bar Assn., Calif. State Bar Assn. Office: Western Digital 20511 Lake Forest Dr Lake Forest CA 92630-7741

BUKRY, JOHN DAVID, geologist; b. Balt., May 17, 1941; s. Howard Leroy and Irene Evelyn (Davis) Snyder. Student, Colo. Sch. Mines, 1959—60; BA, Johns Hopkins U., 1963; MA, Princeton U., 1965, PhD, 1967; postgrad., U. Ill., 1965—66, De Anza Coll., 1995—96. Geologist U.S. Army Corps Engrs., Balt., 1963; rsch. asst. Mobil Oil Co., Dallas, 1965; geologist U.S. Geol. Survey, La Jolla, Calif., 1967-84, scientist emeritus, 1996-98; geologist U.S. Minerals Mgmt. Svc., La Jolla, 1984-86, U.S. Geol. Survey, Menlo Park, Calif., 1986-96, scientist emeritus, 1998—; rsch. assoc. Geol. Rsch. Divsn. Scripps Instn. Oceanography-U. Calif., San Diego, 1970—2003. Cons. Deep Sea Drilling Project, La Jolla, 1967-87; lectr. Vetlesen Symposium, Columbia U., NYC, 1968, 3d Internat. Planktonic Conf., Kiel, Germany, 1974, Brit. Petroleum Exploration Seminar on nannoplankton biostratigraphy, Houston, 1989; shipboard micropaleontologist on D/V Glomar Challenger, 5 Deep Sea Drilling Project cruises, 1968-78; mem. stratigraphic correlations bd. NSF/Joint Oceanog. Instns. for Deep Earth Sampling, 1976-79; vis. scholar U. Calif., 2003-. Author: Leg I of the Cruises of the Drilling Vessel Glomar Challenger, 1969, Coccoliths from Texas and Europe, 1969, Leg LXIII of the Cruises of the Drilling Vessel Glomar Challenger, 1981; editor: Marine Micropaleontology, 1976-83, mem. editl. bd. Micropaleontology, 1985-90. Mobil Oil, Princeton U. fellow, 1965-67; Am. Chem. Soc., Princeton U. fellow, 1966-67. Fellow AAAS, Geol. Soc. Am., Explorers Club; mem. NSTA, Hawaiian Malacological Soc., Paleontol. Rsch. Inst., Am. Assn. Petroleum Geologists, Mars Soc., Planetary Soc., Soc. Econ. Paleontologists and Mineralogists, Internat. Nannoplankton Assn., Ecol. Soc. Am., European Union Geoscis., Oceanography Soc., Mus. Contemporary Art San Diego, San Diego Mus. Art, San Diego Natural History Mus., U. Calif.-San Diego Ida and Cecil Green Faculty Club, San Diego Shell Club, Princeton Club No. Calif., Sigma Xi. Achievements include research in stratigraphy, paleoecology and taxonomy for 300 new species of marine nannoplankton used in ocean history studies; new study of Holocene global climate change showing Medieval Warm and Little

Ice Age in nannoplankton cored in the Gulf of California, Santa Barbara basin and Gulf of Alaska. Avocations: basketball, photography, shell and mineral collecting. Office: US Geol Survey MS-910 345 Middlefield Rd Menlo Park CA 94025-3591 Business E-Mail: dbukry@usgs.gov.

BULL, BRIAN STANLEY, pathologist, educator; b. Watford, Hertfordshire, Sept. 14, 1937; arrived in U.S., 1954, naturalized, 1960; s. Stanley and Agnes Mary (Murdoch) B.; m. Maureen Hannah Huse, June 3, 1963; children: Beverly Velda, Beryl Heather. BS in Zoology, Walla Walla Coll., 1957; MD, Loma Linda U., Calif., 1961. Diplomate Am. Bd. Pathology. Intern Yale U., 1961-62, resident in anat. pathology New Haven, 1962-63; resident in clin. pathology NIH, Bethesda, Md., 1963-65, fellow in hematology and electron microscopy, 1965-66, staff hematologist, 1966-67; rsch. asst. dept. anatomy Loma Linda U., 1958, dept. microbiology, 1959, asst. prof. pathology, 1968-71, assoc. prof., 1971-73, prof., 1973—, chmn. dept. pathology, 1973—, chmn. dept. pathology and human anatomy, 1993—, assoc. dean for acad. affairs Sch. Medicine, 1993-94, dean Sch. Medicine, 1994—2003. Cons. mfrs. of med. testing devices; mem. Internat. Commn. Standardization in Hematology, pres., 1997-99, inaugural lectr. Houwen Meml. Lectures, Internat. Soc. Lab. Hematology, 2005; founding dir. Centrify Health, bd. dirs. Mem. bd. editors Blood Cells, Molecules and Diseases, 1995-, editor-in-chief, 1995-95; contbr. chpts. to books, articles to med. jours.; patentee in field; editor-in-chief Blood Cells NY Heidelberg, 1985-94. Editor Understanding Genesis: Contemporary Adventist Perspectives, 2006. Served with USPHS, 1963-67. Nat. Inst. Arthritis and Metabolic Diseases fellow, 1967-68; recipient Merck Manual award, 1961, Mosby Scholarship Book award, 1961; Ernest B. Cotlove Meml. lectr. Acad. Clin. Lab. Physicians and Scientists, 1972; named Alumnus of Yr., Walla Walla Coll., 1984, Loma Linda U. Sch. Medicine Alumni Assn., Honored Alumnus, Loma Linda U. Sch. Medicine, 1987, Humanitarian award, 1991; named Citizen of Yr., Loma Linda C. of C., 1997, President's award, Loma Linda U. Adventist Health Scis. Ctr., 2003, Disting. U. Svc. award Sch. Medicine Loma Linda U., 2003, Inaugural lectr. Houwen Meml. lectr. Internat. Soc. for Lab. Hematology, 2005. Fellow Am. Soc. Clin. Pathologists, Am. Soc. Hematology, Coll. Am. Pathologists, FDA Panel on Hematology and Pathology Devices, Nat. Com. on Clin. Lab. Stds., NY Acad. Scis.; mem. AMA, Calif. Soc. Pathologists, San Bernadino County Med. Soc. (William C. Cover Outstanding Contbn. to Medicine award 1994), Acad. Clin. Lab. Physicians and Scientists, Am. Assn. Pathologists, Sigma Xi, Alpha Omega Alpha. Adventist. Achievements include patents in field of blood analysis instrumentation; development of quality control algorithms for blood analyzer calibration; origination of techniques and instrumentation for the measurement of thrombosis risk and for regulation of anti-coagulation during cardiopulmonary bypass and solid organ transplantation. Office: LLUMC Rm 2516 11234 Anderson St Loma Linda CA 92354-2871 Office Phone: 909-558-4094. Business E-Mail: bbull@llu.edu.

BULL, GEORGE E., III, finance company executive; BA in Econ., U. Calif., Davis. Pres. GB Capital, 1983—97; chmn., CEO, founder Redwood Trust, Inc., 1994—. Bd. dirs. Marin Cmty. Found. Office: Redwood Trust Inc One Belvedere Place Ste 300 Mill Valley CA 94941

BULL, HENRIK HELKAND, architect; b. NYC, July 13, 1929; s. Johan and Sonja (Geelmuyden) B.; m. Barbara Alpaugh, June 9, 1956; children: Peter, Nina. BArch, MIT, 1952. With Mario Corbett, San Francisco, 1954-55; pvt. practice, 1956-68; ptnr. Bull, Field, Volkmann, Stockwell, Calif., 1968-82, Bull, Volkmann, Stockwell, Calif., 1982-90, Bull Stockwell and Allen, Calif., 1990-93, Bull, Stockwell, Allen & Ripley, San Francisco, 1993-96, BSA Archs., San Francisco, 1996—. Vis. lectr. Syracuse U., 1963; mem. adv. com. San Francisco Urban Design Study, 1970-71. Works include Sunset mag. Discovery House, Tahoe Tavern Condominiums, Lake Tahoe, Calif., Snowmass Villas Condominiums, Aspen, Colo., Northstar Master Plan Village and Condominiums, Moraga Valley Presbyn. Ch., Calif., Spruce Saddle Restaurant and Poste-Montane Hotel, Beaver Creek, Colo., Bear Valley visitor ctr., Point Reyes, Calif., The Inn at Spanish Bay, Pebble Beach, Calif., Taluswood Cmty., Whistler, B.C., Jackson Gore Inn, Okemo, Vt. 1st lt. USAF, 1952—54. Fellow AIA (pres. N. Calif. chpt. 1968, Firm award Calif. chpt. 1989). Democrat. Office: BSA Architects 501 Folsom St 4th Fl San Francisco CA 94105 Office Phone: 415-281-4720. Business E-Mail: hbull@bsaarchitects.com.

BULL, JAMES ROBERT, publishing executive; b. Evanston, Ill., Jan. 9, 1956; s. David C. and Mary Louise (Stowers) B.; m. Erin M. Mulligan, Nov. 30, 1991. BA, Colby Coll., 1978. Sponsoring editor Mayfield Pub. Co., Mount View, Calif., 1984-96; pres., pub. Bull Pub. Co., Palo Alto, Calif., 1994—. Office: Bull Publishing Co PO Box 1377 Boulder CO 80306-1377

BULLERDICK, KIM H., lawyer, petroleum executive; b. Richmond, Ind., 1953; BA, Wittenberg U., 1975; JD, U. Va., 1978. Legal dept. dir. Giant Industries, Inc., Scottsdale, Ariz., 1998—2000, v.p., corp. sec., subs. officer, 1998—, gen. counsel, 2000—.

BULLOCK, STEVE, state attorney general; b. Missoula, Mont. m. Lisa Bullock; children: Caroline, Alexandria, Cameron. Grad., Claremont McKenna Coll.; JD with honors, Columbia U. Chief legal counsel sec. of state State of Mont., 1996, exec. asst. atty. gen. Mont. Dept. Justice, acting chief dep., 1997—2001, atty. gen., 2009—; atty. Steptoe & Johnson, Washington, 2001—04; pvt. practice Helena, Mont., 2004—08. Adj. prof. George Washington U. Sch. Law, 2001—04. Office: Office of Atty Gen Dept Justice PO Box 201401 Helena MT 59620-1401 Office Phone: 406-444-2026. Office Fax: 406-444-3549.

BULLOUGH, ROBERT VERNON, JR., educational studies professor; b. Salt Lake City, Feb. 12, 1949; s. Robert Vernon and Dolores Elaine (Clarke) B.; m. Dawn Ann Mortensen, June 18, 1976; children: Joshua Benjamin, Seth Thomas, Adam Neve, Rachel Elizabeth. BS in History, U. Utah, 1971, MEd, 1973; PhD, Ohio State U., 1976. Tchr. East High Sch., Salt Lake City, 1971-73; teaching assoc., then fellow Ohio State U., Columbus, 1973-76; asst. prof., then assoc. prof. U. Utah, Salt Lake City, 1976-89, prof. ednl. studies, 1989—99, emeritus prof., 1999—; dir. rsch. Ctr. Improvement Tchr. Edn. and Schooling and prof. tchr. edn. Brigham Young U., 1999—. Mem. Holmes Group Writing Com., 1984-86. Author: Democracy in Education: Boyd H. Bode, 1981, Human Interests in the Curriculum: Teaching and Learning in a Technological Society, 1984, The Forgotten Dream of American Education, 1988, First Year Teacher: A Case Study, 1989, Emerging as a Teacher, 1992, First Year Teacher--Eight Years Later, 1997, Becoming a Student of Teaching, 1995, 2d edit., 2001, Uncertain Lives: Children of Promise, Teachers of Hope, 2001, Stories of the Eight Year Study and Reexamining Secondary Education in America, 2007, Counternarratives: Studies of Tchr. Edn. and Becoming and Being a Tchr., 2008; mem. editl. bds.; contbr. articles to profl. jours. Recipient Outstanding Writing award, AACTE, 1997. Mem. Am. Ednl. Rsch. Assn. (Outstanding Book award divsn. B 2003, Karl G. Maeser Rsch. and Creative Arts award, 2007), Profs. of Curriculum, Phi Beta Kappa, Phi Kappa Phi, Phi Delta Kappa. Mem. Lds Ch. Avocations: book collecting, house restoration, furniture restoration. Office: Brigham Young U 149 McKay Bldg Provo UT 84602 Business E-Mail: bob_bullough@byu.edu.

BULOW, JEREMY ISRAEL, economist; b. NYC, Jan. 30, 1954; s. Norman W. and Tova H. Bulow; m. Rhona Mahony; children: Talia, Maya, Zoe. BA, MA, Yale U., 1975; PhD, MIT, 1979. Prof. econs. Stanford (Calif.) Bus. Sch., 1979—; dir. Bur. Econs, Fed. Trade Commn., Washington, 1998—. Fellow Econometric Soc., Am. Acad. Arts & Scis. 2004; mem. ABA (vice chair antitrust sect. 1999—). Office: Stanford Bus Sch 450 Memorial Dr Stanford CA 94305-5015

BUNCHMAN, HERBERT HARRY, II, plastic surgeon; b. Washington, Feb. 23, 1942; s. Herbert H. and Mary (Halleran) B.; m. Marguerite Frassioli, Mar. 21, 1963 (div. Jan. 1987); children: Herbert H. III., Angela K., Christopher; m. Janet C. Quinlan, Oct. 4, 1998. BA, Vanderbilt U., 1964; MD, U. Tenn., 1967. Diplomate Am. Bd. Surgery, Am. bd. Plastic Surgery. Resident in surgery U. Tex., Galveston, 1967-72, resident in plastic surgery, 1972-75; practice medicine specializing in plastic surgery Mesa, Ariz., 1975—; chief surgery Desert Samaritan Hosp., 1978-80. Contbr. articles to profl. jours. Eaton Clin. fellow, 1975. Mem. AMA, Am. Soc. Plastic Surgery, Am. Soc. Aesthetic Plastic Surgery, Singleton Surgical Soc., Tex. Med. Assn., So. Med. Assn. (grantee 1974), Ariz. Med. Assn. Office: Plastic Surgery Cons PC 1520 S Dobson Rd Ste 314 Mesa AZ 85202-4727 Office Phone: 480-833-5200. Office Fax: 480-833-2967. Business E-Mail: office@bunchman.com.

BUNCKE, GREGORY M., plastic surgeon; b. NYC, Jan. 16, 1956; MD, Georgetown U., 1981. Cert. Am. Bd. Plastic Surgery, 1989, added qualification in Surgery of the Hand, 1992. Intern in gen. surgery and plastic surgery Stanford U. Hosp., 1981—82, resident in plastic surgery, 1982—87; fellow in hand and microsurgery Davies Med. Ctr., San Francisco, 1985—86, dir. Buncke Clinic; asst. clin. prof. surgery U. Calif. San Francisco. Fellow: Am. Coll. Surgeons; mem.: Am. Soc. Surgery of the Hand, Am. Soc. Reconstructive Microsurgery, Am. Soc. Plastic Surgeons. Office: Davies Med Ctr MOB Annex 45 45 Castro St Ste 140 San Francisco CA 94114 Office Phone: 415-565-6136. E-mail: gbuncke@buncke.org.

BUNCKE, HARRY J., retired plastic surgeon, educator; Grad., Lehigh U.; MD, NY Med. Coll., 1951. With Met. Hosp., Flower and Fifth Ave. Hosp., NY Med. Coll., 1952—55; residency in plastic surgery Bronx Veterans Admin. Hosp. and NY Hosp., Cornell Med. Sch., 1954—56; Marks Fellow in plastic and maxollofacial surgery Queen Victoria Hosp., Sussex, England, 1956; sr. registrar plastic surgical and burn unit Glasgow Royal Infirmary, Scotland, 1957; mem. plastic surgery staff Mills Mem. Hosp., San Mateo, 1959—; dir. div. microsurgical replantation Ralph K. Davies Med. Ctr., San Francisco, 1975—; dir. emeritus The Buncke Clinic; ret. Prof. surgery U. Calif., San Francisco; assoc. clin. prof. surgery Stanford U.; vis. prof. and delivered disting. lectureships at more then 50 instns. Author: 15 movies and television tapes, four books and over 400 publs. Recipient Hon. Award, Am. Assn. Plastic Surgery, 1979, Markowitz Award, Acad. Surgical Rsch., Jacobson Innovation Award, Am. Coll. Surgeons, 2004; named Prof. Honoris Causae, French Ministry Edn. Mem.: Japanese Soc. for Hand Surgery, Spanish Soc. Microsurgery, French Soc. Plastic and Reconstructive Surgeons, Internat. Soc. Reconstructive Microsurgery (chmn. 1977), Am. Soc. Surgery of Hand (pres. 1980), Italian Soc. Microsurgery. Achievements include first to perform toe-to-hand transplant in a rhesus monkey, 1966; the first microvascular transplant in world, 1969; the first great toe-to-thumb transplant in US, 1972; the first successful scalp replant in the US, 1976; the first four-finger replant in the US, 1976; the first latissimus seratus transplant, 1979; with Dr. Rudolf Bantic, the first successful tongue replant in the world, 1997.

BUNDE, CON, state legislator; b. Mankato, Minn., Aug. 4, 1938; m to Angelene; children: Joylene & Kurt. BS in Speech Pathology, Ctrl. Wash. U., 1962—66, MS in Speech and Hearing Pathology, 1967—70. Member, Alaska Bd Fish & Game Southcentral Citizens Advisor Committee, currently; Alaska State Representative, District 18, 1993-2002, vice chairman, Finance & Legislature Budget & Audit Committees, formerly, Alaska House Representative; vice president, Education Comn of States, 98-99; Alaska State Senator, District P, 2003-.Commercial air taxi pilot, currently; professor speech communications, Univ Alaska, formerly; ret. Specialist 4th class US Army. UAA Outstanding Educator of Year, 91; Legislator of Year, Advisor Bd Alcoholism & Drug Abuse, 97. Nat Rifle Association; Aircraft Owners & Pilots' Association; Alaska Outdoor Coun; Alaskan Bowhunters Association; Alaska Airmen's Association; Bowhunters of America; Alaska Water Fowl Association, Sports Fishing Association; Izaak Walton League; Ducks Unlimited. Republican. Avocations: aviation, hunting, fishing. Office: Dist P 716 W Fourth Ste 400 Anchorage AK 99501-2133 also: State Capitol Rm 504 Juneau AK 99801 Office Phone: 907-465-4843, 907-269-0181. Office Fax: 907-465-3871, 907-269-0184. Business E-Mail: representative_con_bunde@legis.state.ak.us.*

BUNDERSON, HAROLD R., state legislator; b. Stone, Idaho; m. Mary Bunderson; 3 children. B. CPA. Acct., ptnr. Arthur Andersen & Co.; ret.; residential real estate developer; mem. Idaho Senate, Dist. 14, Boise, 1992—. Vice-chair transp. com.; mem. judiciary and rules, health and welfare, fin., and local govt. and tax. coms. Author: Idaho Entrepreneurs, Profiles in Business. Bd. mem., past pres., Ore-Ida Coun.; sch. bond election co-chair, Meridian/Eagle Sch. Dist., 1990; bd. mem., past pres., Boy Scouts Am., we. region; past pres., past gen. campaign chair, United Way of Ada County, Inc. Republican. Office: State Capitol PO Box 83720 Boise ID 83720-3720

BUNDGAARD, SCOTT, state legislator; b. Oklahoma City, Jan. 11, 1968; BS in Bus. Adminstrn., Grand Canyon U., 1990; postgrad., Wharton Sch. Bus., 1992, Ariz. State U., 1992. Prodr. Y95 Morning Zoo, 1989; asst. mgr. GAP, Inc., 1990-91; dir. tng. svcs. IBM and Manpower, 1991-94; stock broker Dean Witter Reynolds Inc.; mem. Ariz. Ho. of Reps., 1994-96, Ariz. Senate, Dist. 19, Phoenix, 1996—; mem. banking and ins. com., vice-chmn. econ. devel. com.; chmn. fin. com., mem. fin. instns. and retirement com.; mem. commerce agr. and natural resources com. Basketball coach Peoria Boys and Girls Club, Glendale Pks. and Recreation, Ariz. Youth Sports; bd. mem. Leadership West; exec. mem. Maricopa County Sheriff's Posse; H.S. youth group leader Calvary Cmty. Ch.; founding dir. Rotaract, 1989. Named Coach of the Yr., Kids Basketball Assn., 1994. Mem. Am. Legis. Exch. Coun. (banking and labor task force, banking, ins. and real estate task force), Coun. State Govts. Western Legis. Conf. (econ. devel./NAFTA com.). Republican.

BUNDRANT, CHARLES H., food products executive; Pres., CEO Trident Seafoods Corp., Seattle, 1973—. Office: Trident Seafoods Corp 5303 Shilshole Ave NW Seattle WA 98107-4000

BUNDY, ROBERT CHARLES, former prosecutor; b. Long Beach, Calif., June 26, 1946; s. James Kenneth and Kathleen Ilene (Klosterman) B.; m. Virginia Bonnie Lembo, Feb. 3, 1974; 2 children. BA cum laude, U. So. Calif., LA, 1968; JD, U. Calif., Berkeley, 1971. Bar: Alaska 1972, Calif. 1972. Supervising atty. Alaska Legal Svcs. Corp., Nome, Alaska, 1972-75; dist. atty. Second Jud. Dist., Nome, 1975-78; asst. dist. atty. Alaska Dept. Law, 1978-80, asst. atty. gen. antitrust sect., 1980-82; chief asst. dist. atty. Alaskan Dept. Law, Anchorage, 1982-84; ptnr. Bogle & Gates, Anchorage, 1984-94; U.S. atty. for Alaska dist. U.S. Dept. Justice, Anchorage, 1994—2001. Mem. Trout Unlimited, Alaska Flyfishers.

BUNKER, JOHN BIRKBECK, cattle rancher, retired sugar company executive; b. Yonkers, NY, Mar. 28, 1926; s. Ellsworth and Harriet (Butler) B.; m. Emma Cadwalader, Feb. 27, 1954. BA, Yale U., 1950. With Nat. Sugar Refining Co., 1953-62; pres. Gt. Western Sugar Co., Denver, 1966; pres., CEO Holly Sugar Co., Colorado Springs, Colo., 1967-81, chmn., CEO, 1971-81; pres., CEO Calif. and Hawaiian Sugar Co., San Francisco, 1981-88, vice chmn., 1988-89, ret., 1989; gen. ptnr. Bunker Ranch Co., 1989—; chmn. Wheatland Bankshares and First State Bank of Wheatland, 1992-99, dir. emeritus. Trustee Colo. Coll., 1973-94; trustee emeritus Asia Found., 1985-94. Mem. Wyo. Nature Conservancy, Wyo. Stockgrowers Assn., Wyo. Heritage Found. Home: 1451 Cottonwood Ave Wheatland WY 82201-3412

BUNN, PAUL A., JR., oncologist, educator; b. NYC, Mar. 16, 1945; s. Paul A. Bunn; m. Camille Ruoff, Aug. 17, 1968; children: Rebecca, Kristen, Paul H. BA cum laude, Amherst Coll., 1967; MD, Cornell U., 1971. Diplomate Nat. Bd. Med. Examiners, Am. Bd. Internal Medicine, Am. Bd. Med. Oncology. Intern U. Calif., H.C. Moffitt Hosp., San Francisco, 1971-72, resident, 1972-73; clin. assoc. medicine br. Nat. Cancer Inst., NIH, Bethesda, Md., 1973-76; sr. investigator med. oncology br. Nat. Cancer Inst., Washington VA Hosp., 1976-81; asst. prof. medicine med. sch. Georgetown U., 1978-81; head cell kinetic sect., Navy med. oncology br. Nat. Cancer Inst., Bethesda, 1981-84; assoc. prof. medicine uniformed svcs. Univ. Health Scis., Bethesda, 1981-84; prof. medicine health scis. ctr. U. Colo., Denver, 1984—, head divsn. med. oncology, 1984-94, dir. cancer ctr., 1987—. Instl. rev. bd. NIH, Nat. Cancer Inst., 1982-84; intramural support contract rev. com. Nat. Cancer Inst., 1982-84; cancer com. U. Colo., 1984—, faculty senate health scis. ctr., 1985—, exec. com. sch. medicine, 1987—; med. bd. Univ. Hosp., 1987—; external sci. advisor cancer ctr. U. Miami, 1988-92, U. Ark., 1989-94, U. Va., 1991-94, others; oncology drug adv. com. FDA, 1992-96; sci. secretariat 7th World Conf. Lung Cancer, 1994; bd. dirs. Univ. Hosp. Resource Coun.; oncology drug adv. com. FDA, 1992-96. Author: Carboplatin (JM-8) Current Perspectives and Future Directions, 1990, Clinical Experiences With Platinum and Etoposide Therapy in Lung Cancer, 1992, (with M.E. Wood) Hematology/Oncology Secrets, 1994; assoc. editor Med. and Pediatric Oncology, 1984—, Jour. Clin. Oncology, 1991—, Cancer Rsch., 1992—, others; contbr. chpts. to books and articles to profl. jours. Bd. dirs. Colo. divsn. Am. Cancer Soc., 1989—, Leukemia Soc. Am., 1991—; bd. dirs. The Cancer Venture, 1993-94, Fair Share Colo., 1993-94; chmn. Solid Tumor Oncology Edn. Found., 1996—. With USPHS, 1973-84. Decorated Medal of Commendation; recipient Sci. of Yr. award Denver chpt. ARCS, 1992; named one of 400 Best Drs. in Am., Good Housekeeping Mag., 1991, 92; grantee Schering Plough, 1988-89, Burroughs Wellcome, 1991—, Bristol-Myers Squibb, 1993—, others. Fellow ACP; mem. AAAS, Am. Soc. Hematology (mem. sci. subcom. neoplasia 1989-92), Am. Assn. Cancer Rsch., Am. Soc. Clin. Oncology (chair program subcom. 1985-86, 90, pres.-elect 2001—), Am. Fedn. Clin. Rsch., Am. Assn. Cancer Insts. (bd. dirs. 1992—), Internat. Assn. Study Lung Cancer (bd. dirs. 1988—, pres. 1994-97, exec. dir.), Western Assn. Physicians, S.W. Oncology Group, Lung Cancer Study Group, Alpha Omega Alpha. Office: U Colo Cancer Ctr PO Box 6511 MS 8111 Aurora CO 80045 E-mail: paul.bunn@uchsc.edu.

BUNNETT, JOSEPH FREDERICK, chemist, educator; b. Portland, Oreg., Nov. 26, 1921; s. Joseph and Louise Helen (Boulan) B.; m. Sara Anne Telfer, Aug. 22, 1942 (dec. Oct. 2006); children: Alfred Boulan, David Telfer, Peter Sylvester (dec. Sept. 1972). BA, Reed Coll., 1942; PhD, U. Rochester, 1945. Mem. faculty Reed Coll., 1946-52, U. N.C., 1952-58; mem. faculty Brown U., 1958-66, prof. chemistry, 1959-66, chmn. dept., 1961-64; prof. chemistry U. Calif., Santa Cruz, 1966-91, prof. emeritus, 1991—. Erskine vis. fellow U. Canterbury, N.Z., 1967; vis. prof. U. Wash., 1956, U. Wurzburg, Germany, 1974, U. Bologna, Italy, 1988; rsch. fellow Japan Soc. for Promotion of Sci., 1979; Lady Davis vis. prof. Hebrew U., Jerusalem, Israel, 1981; mem. adv. coun. dept. chemistry Princeton (N.J.) U., 1985-89; mem. NRC com. on alternative chem. demilitarization techs., 1992-93; mem. Dept. Def. panel on Gulf War Health Effects, 1993-94; co-chmn. peer rev. com. Russian-Am. Joint Evaluation Program, 1995-96; co-chmn. NATO Advanced Rsch. Workshop on Chem. Problems Associated with Old Arsenical and Mustard Munitions, Lodz, Poland, 1996; working group chem. weapons destruction, scientific adv. bd. Orgn. Prohibition Chem. Weapons, 1999—. Co-editor: Arsenic and Old Mustard: Chemical Problems in the Destruction of Old Arsenical and Mustard Munitions, 1998; contbr. articles to profl. jours. Trustee Reed Coll., 1970-97, trustee emeritus, 1997—. Fulbright scholar, U. Coll., London, 1949—50, U. Munich, 1960—61, Guggenheim fellow, 1960—61. Fellow AAAS, Internat. Union Pure and Applied Chemistry (chmn. commn. phys. organic chemistry 1978-83, sec. organic chemistry divsn. 1981-83, v.p. 1983-85, pres. 1985-87, chmn. task force on sci. aspects of destruction of chem. warfare agts. 1991-95, chmn. com. on chem. weapon destruction 1995-2001, fellow, 2002)); mem. Am. Acad. Arts. and Scis., Am. Chem. Soc. (editor jour. Accounts of Chem. Rsch. 1966-86, James Flack Norris award 1992), Royal Soc. Chemistry, Pharm. Soc. Japan (hon.), Acad. Gioenia (U. Catania, hon.), Soc. Argentina de Investigaciones en Quimica Organica (hon.), Soc. Chimica Italiana (hon.). Home: 608 Arroyo Seco Santa Cruz CA 95060-3148 Office: U Calif

Dept Chemistry Santa Cruz CA 95064 Office Phone: 831-459-2261. Office Fax: 831-459-2935. Personal E-mail: bunnett@cruzio.com. Business E-Mail: bunnett@chemistry.ucsc.edu.

BUNTING, KENNETH FREEMAN, newspaper editor; b. Houston, Dec. 9, 1948; s. Willie Freeman and Sarah Lee (Peterson) B.; m. Juliana Amy Jafvert, July 13, 1989; 1 child, Maxwell Freeman. Student, U. Mo., 1966-67; AA in Journalism, Lee Coll., 1968; BA in Journalism and History, Tex. Christian U., 1970; advanced exec. program, Northwestern U., 1996. Mgmt. trainee, reporter Harte-Hanks Newspapers Inc., Corpus Christi, Tex., 1970-71; reporter, then copy editor San Antonio Express-News, 1971-73; exec. asst. to Hon. G.J. Sutton Tex. Ho. of Reps., San Antonio, 1973-74; reporter Cin. Post, 1974-78, Sacramento Bee, 1978; reporter, asst. city editor, state capitol corr. L.A. Times, 1978-87; capitol bur. chief, city editor, dep. mng. editor, sr. editor Ft. Worth Star-Telegram, 1987-93; mng. editor Seattle Post-Intelligencer, 1993-99; exec. editor Seattle Post-Intelligence, 2000—. Journalism instr. Orange Coast Coll., Costa Mesa, Calif., 1981-82; mem. adv. bd. Maynard Inst., Oakland, Calif., 1994—. Bd. dirs. Seattle Symphony, 1995-97; mem. commn. Woodland Park Zoo, Seattle, 1995-96, 98; mem. Leadership Ft. Worth; former mem. journalism adv. bd. Tex. Christian U.; former mem. minorities task force Assn. for Edn. in Journalism and Mass Comms.; past pres. Press Club, Orange County, Calif.; past bd. dirs. Covington (Ky.) Cmty. Ctr.; past 1st v.p. Young Dems. of Tex.; past treas., mem. exec. bd. Freedom of Info. Found. of Tex.; leadership coun. ARC; bd. dirs. Alfred Friendly Press Fellowships. Mem. Nat. Assn. Black Journalists, AP Mng. Editors Assn. (mem. ethics com. 1995-96, bd. dirs. 1996-99), Am. Soc. Newspaper Editors (mem. diversity, leadership coms., chair edn. com., bd. dirs. 1999—), Soc. Profl. Journalists (bd. dirs. western Wash. chpt. 1995-96), Seattle C. of C. (mem. cmty. devel. roundtable 1994—), Alliance for Edn. (bd. dirs.), Tex. Christian U. Alumni Assn. (bd. dirs.), Freedom of Info. Found. Tex., Rainier Club, Washington Athletic Club. Unitarian Universalist. Avocations: tennis, bridge, reading. Office: Seattle-Post Intelligencer PO Box 1909 101 Elliott Ave W Seattle WA 98111

BUNZA, LINDA HATHAWAY, editor, writer, composer, director; b. Hartford, Conn., Feb. 23, 1946; m. Geoffrey J. Bunza; children: Stephen, Matthew. BA, Bates Coll., 1968; MA, The Hartford Sem. Found., 1971; PhD, Syracuse U., 1974. Editl. asst. The Harvard Ednl. Rev., Cambridge, Mass., 1974—76; mng. editor The Andover Rev., Andover, Mass., 1976—79; dir. Columbia Rsch. Inst. Arts and Humanities, Portland, Oreg., 1998—2002. Editor Renaissance Mag., Hartford, 1963—64; editl. asst. Symposium Mag., Syracuse, NY, 1973—74; editor Soc. Arts, Religion, and Contemporary Culture, NYC, 1974—78; lectr. in field. Composer: (Classical Music Composition) There is Something Still Floating, 1999, Report From A Spiral, 1998, Snow Mountain, 2000, RiverMusic, 1995, Mythology of Clouds, 1993, Sphere, 1992, Cascadia, 1989, Widmanstatten Lines, 1987, View from a Mobius Strip, 1986, Sounds from the Olympic Peninsula, 1998, Electric Night, 1984, Odalisque, 1982, Awakening Night, 1981; editor: (Book) Adventures and Misadventures of Dr. Sonjee by Dr. Prasanna Pati, Snehalata Press, 2001, (Novel) Against Parched Winds by Kanta Luthra, (Book) Art of Literary Criticism, 2000; author: Theories of Modern Art-I, 1972, Theories of Modern Art-II, 1973, Theories of Modern Art-III, 1973; author: (catalog) Blue Note: The Art of Bruce Warner, 2000, Air, 2001, Where Art Reveals Itself in Symbols, Words are Hard to Find, 2001; mem. editl. bd. Anima Mag., 1973—95. Bd. dirs. Fear No Music 20th Century Ensemble, 2000—02, Third Angle New Music Ensemble, Portland, 2000—04, Contemporary Art Coun., Portland Art Mus., 2001—04, Portland Baroque Orch., 2000—04; arts and culture com. City Club of Portland, 2000—04, arch. com., 1999—2002. Recipient Pres.'s award, Beaverton Arts Commn., 2000. Mem.: Portland Inst. Contemporary Art, European and Am. Art Coun., Portland Art Mus., Northwest Bookfest (program com.), Ancient Egypt Studies Assn., The Coll. Music Soc., Soc. Composers Internat., Friends William Stafford Assn. (life). Office: Columbia Rsch Inst Arts and Humanities PO Box 25316 Portland OR 97298 Personal E-mail: bunza@teleport.com. Business E-Mail: columbiaarts@aol.com.

BUNZEL, JOHN HARVEY, political science professor; b. NYC, Apr. 15, 1924; s. Ernest Everett and Harriett (Harvey) B.; m. Barbara Bovyer, May 11, 1963; children: Cameron, Reed. AB, Princeton U., 1948; MA, Columbia U., 1949; PhD, U. Calif.-Berkeley, 1954; LL.D., U. Santa Clara, 1976. Mem. faculty San Francisco State U., 1953-56, 63-70, vis. scholar Ctr. Advanced Study in Behavioral Scis., 1969-70; mem. faculty Mich. State U., East Lansing, 1956-57, Stanford U., Calif., 1957-63; pres. San Jose State U., Calif., 1970-78; sr. research fellow Hoover Inst. Stanford U., Calif., 1978—. Mem. U.S. Commn. on Civil Rights, 1983-86. Author: The American Small Businessman, 1962; Anti-Politics in America, 1967; Issues of American Public Policy, 1968; New Force on the Left, 1983, Challenge to American Schools: The Case For Standards and Values, 1985, Political Passages: Journeys of Change Through Two Decades 1968-1988, 1988, Race Relations on Campus: Stanford Students Speak, 1992; contbr. articles to profl. jours., popular mags., newspapers. Weekly columnist San Jose Mercury-News. Bd. dirs. No. Calif. Citizenship Clearing House, 1959-61; mem. Calif. Atty. Gen.'s Adv. Com., 1960-61; del. Calif. Democratic Conv., 1968; del. Dem. Nat. Conv., 1968 Recipient Presdl. award No. Calif. Polit. Sci. Assn., 1969, cert. of Honor San Francisco Bd. Suprs., 1974, Hubert Humprey Pub. Policy award Policy Studies Orgn., 1990; grantee Ford Found., Rockefeller Found., Rabinowitz Found. Mem. Am. Polit. Sci. Assn. Home: 1519 Escondido Way Belmont CA 94002-3634 Office: Stanford U Hoover Inst Stanford CA 94305

BURATTI, BONNIE J., aerospace scientist; b. Bethlehem, Pa., Mar. 24, 1953; d. Ralph J. and Hildegard M. (Singles) B.; children: Nathan, Reuben, Aaron. MS, MIT, 1976, Cornell U., 1980, PhD, 1983. Summer intern Maria Mitchell Observatory, Nantucket, Mass., 1973; assoc. scientist Am. Sci. and Engring., Cambridge, Mass., 1974-76; rsch. asst. MIT, Cambridge, 1977-83; rsch. and teaching asst. Cornell U., Ithaca, N.Y., 1977-83; post-doctoral Jet Propulsion Lab. Calif. Inst. Tech., Pasadena, 1983-85, rsch. scientist Jet Propulsion Lab., 1985—. Cons. NASA, Washington, 1989—. Contbr. articles to profl. jours. Mem. MIT Ednl. Coun., Internat. Astro. Union, Am. Astro. Soc., Am. Women in Sci., Am. Geophys. Union. Office: Calif Inst Tech Jet Propulsion Lab 4800 Oak Grove Dr # 501 Pasadena CA 91109-8001

BURATTO, STEVEN K., chemistry educator; b. Clarkston, Wash., Dec. 3, 1964; s. Steven A. and Beth B. (Anderson) B.; m. Lauro Oliver, July 21, 1990; 1 child, William R. BS magna cum laude, U. Puget Sound, 1987; PhD, Calif. Inst. Tech., 1992. Mem. tech. staff AT&T Bell Labs., Murray Hill, N.J., 1992-94; asst. prof. chemistry U. Calif., Santa Barbara, 1994—. Contbr. articles to sci. jours. Recipient Henry and Camille Dreyfus New Faculty award Henry and Camille Dreyfus Found., 1994; trustee scholar U. Puget Sound, 1983-87, Wyatt meml. scholar, 1986-87; scholar AT&T Bell Labs., 1989-92. Mem. AAAS, Am. Phys. Soc., Phi Beta Kappa. Office: U Calif Dept Chemistry Santa Barbara CA 93106

BURBIDGE, E. MARGARET, astronomer, educator; b. Davenport, Eng. d. Stanley John and Marjorie (Stott) Peachey; m. Geoffrey Burbidge, Apr. 2, 1948; 1 child, Sarah. BS, PhD, U. London; Sc.D. hon., Smith Coll., 1963, U. Sussex, 1970, U. Bristol, 1972, U. Leicester, 1972, City U., 1973, U. Mich., 1978, U. Mass., 1978, Williams Coll., 1979, SUNY, Stony Brook, 1985, Rensselaer Poly. Inst., 1986, U. Notre Dame, 1986, U. Chgo., 1991. Mem. staff U. London Obs., 1948-51; rsch. fellow Yerkes Obs. U. Chgo., 1951-53, Shirley Farr fellow Yerkes obs., 1957-59, assoc. prof. Yerkes Obs., 1959-62; rsch. fellow Calif. Inst. Tech., Pasadena, 1955-57; mem. Enrico Fermi Inst. for Nuclear Studies, 1957-62; prof. astronomy dept. physics U. Calif. San Diego, 1964—89; dir. Royal Greenwich Obs. (Herstmonceux Castle), Hailsham, Eng., 1971-73; univ. prof. U. Calif., San Diego, 1984-91, prof. emeritus, 1991—, rsch. prof. dept. physics, 1990—. Lindsay Meml. lectr. Goddard Space Flight Ctr., NASA; Abby Rockefeller Mauze prof. MIT, 1968; David Elder lectr. U. Strathclyde, 1972; V. Gildersleeve lectr. Barnard Coll., 1974; Jansky lectr. Nat. Radio Astronomy Observatory, 1977; Brode lectr. Whitman Coll., 1986; Hitchcock lectr. U. Calif., Berkeley, 2001. Author (with G. Burbidge): Quasi-Stellar Objects, 1967; editor: Observatory mag., 1948—51; mem. editl. bd.: Astronomy and Astrophysics, 1969—85. Recipient Bruce Gold medal, Astronomy Soc. Pacific, 1982, U.S. Nat. medal of Sci., 1984, Sesquicentennial medal, Mt. Holyoke Coll., 1987, Einstein medal, World Cultural Coun., 1988; co-recipient Warner prize in Astronomy, 1959; fellow hon. fellow, Univ. Coll., London, Girton Coll., Lucy Cavendish Coll., Cambridge. Fellow: Royal Astron. Soc. (Gold medal 2005), Am. Acad. Arts and Scis., Nat. Acad. Scis. (chmn. sect.12 astronomy 1986), Royal Soc.; mem.: Internat. Astron. Union (pres. commn. 28 1970—73), Am. Astron. Soc. (v.p. 1972—74, pres. 1976—78, Henry Norris Russell lectr. 1984), Grad. Women Sci. (hon.). Office: U Calif-San Diego Ctr Astrophysics Space Scis Mail Code # 0424 La Jolla CA 92093 Home Phone: 858-459-4968; Office Phone: 858-534-4477. Business E-Mail: mburbidge@ucsd.edu.

BURBIDGE, GEOFFREY, astrophysicist, educator; b. Chipping Norton, Oxon, Eng., Sept. 24, 1925; s. Leslie and Eveline Burbidge; m. Margaret Peachey, 1948; 1 dau. B.Sc. with spl. honors in Physics, Bristol U., 1946; PhD, U. Coll., London, 1951. Asst. lectr. U. Coll., London, 1950-51; Agassiz fellow Harvard, 1951-52; research fellow U. Chgo., 1952-53, Cavendish Lab., Cambridge, Eng., 1953-55; Carnegie fellow Mt. Wilson and Palomar Obs., Calif. Inst. Tech., 1955-57; asst. prof. dept. astronomy U. Chgo., 1957-58, assoc. prof., 1958-62, U. Calif. San Diego, La Jolla, 1962-63, prof. physics, 1963-83, 88—; dir. Kitt Peak Nat. Obs., Tucson, 1978-84. Phillips vis. prof. Harvard U., 1968; bd. dirs. Associated Univs. Research in Astronomy, 1971-74; trustee Associated Univs., Inc., 1973-82 Author: (with Margaret Burbidge) Quasi-Stellar Objects, 1967, (with F. Hoyle and J. Narlikar) A Different Approach to Cosmology, 2000; editor Ann. Rev. Astronomy and Astrophysics, 1973-2004; sci. editor Astrophys. Jour., 1996-02; contbr. articles to sci. jours. Recipient Jansky prize, Nat. Radio Astronomy Observatory, 1985, Vainu Bappu Meml award, Indian Nat. Acad. Sci., 1989, NAS award for Scientific Reviewing, 2007. Fellow Royal Soc. London, Am. Acad. Arts and Scis., Royal Astron. Soc. (recipient Gold medal 2005), Am. Phys. Soc., AAAS; mem. Am. Astron. Soc.(recipient Helen Warner prize, 1959), Internat. Astron. Union, Astron. Soc. Pacific (pres. 1974-76, Bruce medal 1999). Office: U Calif-San Diego 0424 Ctr Astrophysics Space Scis La Jolla CA 92093 Office Phone: 858-534-6626. Business E-Mail: gburbidge@ucsd.edu.

BURCH, ROBERT DALE, lawyer; b. Washington, Jan. 30, 1928; s. Dallas Stockwell and Hepsy (Berry) B.; m. Joann D. Hansen, Dec. 9, 1966; children: Berkeley, Robert Brett, Barrett Bradley. Student, Va. Mil. Inst., 1945—46; BS, U. Calif. Berkeley, 1950, JD, 1953. Bar: Calif. bar 1954. Since practiced in, L.A. and Beverly Hills; ptnr. Gibson, Dunn & Crutcher, 1961—93. Lectr. U. So. Calif. Inst. Fed. Taxation, 1960, 62, 65, 75; guest lectr. U. Calif.-L.A. Law Sch., 1959; lectr. C.E.B. seminars U. Calif.; founder Robert D. Burch Ctr. for Tax Policy and Pub. Fin., U. Calif., Berkeley. Author: Federal Tax Procedures for General Practitioners; Contbr. profl. jours., textbooks. Bd. dirs. charitable founds. With AUS, 1945-47. Mem. Beverly Hills Bar Assn. (bd. govs., chmn. probate and trust com.), Law Trust, Tax and Ins. Council (past czar), Los Angeles World Affairs Council. Home: 1301 Delresto Dr Beverly Hills CA 90210-2100 also: 333 S Grand Ave Los Angeles CA 90071-1504 Office: Gibson Dunn & Crutcher 1043 Roscomare Rd Los Angeles CA 90077-2227

BURCHARD, JOHN KENNETH, retired chemical engineer; b. St. Louis, May 12, 1936; s. Kenneth Reginald and Vernora Emma (Angell) B.; m. Elizabeth Lee Suesserott, Aug. 23, 1958; children—John Christopher, Gregory Charles. BS, Carnegie Mellon U., 1957, MS, 1959, PhD, 1962. Head systems analysis group United Tech. Ctr., Sunnyvale, Calif., 1961-68; chief scientist Combustion Power Co., Menlo Park, Calif., 1968-70; lab. dir. EPA, Research Triangle Park, N.C., 1970-80; dir. chem. engring. div. Research Triangle Inst., Research Triangle Park, 1980-83; pres. Search Assocs., Inc., Chapel Hill, N.C., 1983-85; dir. Office of Research Adminstrn. U. Cen. Ark., Conway, 1985-87; asst. dir. Office Research Devel. Ariz. State U., Tempe, 1987-90; mgr. spl. projects Ariz. Dept. Environ. Quality, Phoenix, 1990-98, sr. sci. advisor, 1998-2001; vol. Tempe (Ariz.) Police Dept., 2001—. Mem. bd. sci. advisors N.C. Energy Inst. Contbr. articles to profl. jours. Served with AUS, 1963-64. Shell Oil fellow, 1958-59; NSF fellow, 1960-61 Mem. Am. Inst. Chem. Engrs., Soc. Rsch. Adminstrs., Sigma Xi, Tau Beta Pi.

BURCH-PESSES, THOMAS MICHAEL, music educator; b. Oxnard, Calif., Jan. 31, 1945; s. Albert J. and Doris V. Pesses (Stepmother); m. R. Jane Burch-Pesses, Nov. 16, 1988. BS, SUNY, Albany, 1989; MusM, Cath. U. Am., Washington, 1992, D in Musical Arts, 1995. Cert. adjudicator Oreg., 1995. Enlisted musician USN, Washington, 1962—71, bandmaster, 1971—95; prof. music Pacific U., Forest Grove, Oreg., 1995—; condr. Oreg. Symphonic Band, Portland, Oreg. Asst. leader U.S. Naval Acad. Band, Annapolis, Md., 1974—77, U.S. Navy Band, Washington, 1984—86; musical dir. Midshipmen Drum and Bugle Corps, Annapolis, Md., 1989—93; leader U.S. Naval Acad. Band, Annapolis, 1989—93; head USN Music Program, Washington, 1993—95. Editor: Overture in C by Simon Catel, 1995; contbr. articles to profl. jours.; arranger: Mary Lou's Mass, 2004; author: Canadian Band Music: A Qualitative Guide to Canadian Composers and Their Music for Band, 2008. Recipient George S. Howard citation of Musical Excellence, John Philip Sousa Found., 1992, Excellence in Tchg. award, S.S. Johnson Found., 2006; Wye fellow, Aspen Inst., 1999. Mem.: Am. Bandmasters Assn., Oreg. Music Educators Assn. (coll. chair 1989—2002, 2d v.p. 2002—), Nat. Band Assn. (mil. liaison 1992—95, Oreg. state chair 1997—2005, Citation of Excellence 2006), Oreg. Band Dirs. Assn., Coll. Band Dirs. Nat. Assn., Music Educators Nat. Conf., Phi Beta Mu. Avocations: running, travel, comic book collecting. Home: 5598 SE Sierra St Hillsboro OR 97123 Office: Pacific U 2043 College Way Forest Grove OR 97116 Personal E-mail: burchpem@aol.com. Business E-Mail: burchpem@pacificu.edu.

BURD, STEVEN A., food service executive; b. 1949; m. Chris Burd; 2 children. BS, Carroll Coll., 1971; MA in Econs., U. Wis., 1973. With fin. and mktg. So. Pacific Transp. Co., San Francisco; with Arthur D. Little, NYC, 1982-87; mgmt. cons., Safeway Stores Kohlberg Kravis Roberts & Co., 1986—91; cons. Stop & Shop Cos., Boston, 1988-89; cons., interim CEO Fred Meyer Inc., Portland, Oreg., 1991—92; pres. Safeway Inc., 1992—, CEO, 1993—, chmn., 1998—. Dir. Kohl's Corp. Office: Safeway Inc 5918 Stoneridge Mall Rd Pleasanton CA 94588-3229

BURDEKIN, RICHARD CHARLES KEIGHLEY, economics professor; b. Poole, Dorset, Eng., Dec. 16, 1958; arrived in US, 1982; s. Charles Walter and Dorothy Agnes Burdekin; m. Yanjie Feng, Mar. 24, 1991; children: Eileen Frances, Emma Dorothy, Josephine Ellen. BA, U. Warwick, Coventry, Eng., 1981; MSc, U. Bristol, Eng., 1982; PhD, U. Houston, 1985. Vis. scholar Fed. Res. Bank Dallas, 1985—86; asst. prof. econs. U. Miami, Coral Gables, Fla., 1986—89; Jonathan B. Lovelace prof. econs. Claremont McKenna Coll., Calif., 1989—. Vis. sr. fellow East-West Ctr., Honolulu, 2005; edit. bd. mem. Economics Sys, 2008—, Open Economics Jours., 2008—. Author: (books) Budget Deficits and Economic Performance, 1992, Establishing Monetary Stability in Emerging Market Economies, 1995, Confidence, Credibility and Macroeconomic Policy: Past, Present, Future, 1995, Distributional Conflict and Inflation: Theoretical and Historical Perspectives, 1996, Deflation: Current and Historical Perspectives, 2004, China's Monetary Challenges: Past Experiences and Future Prospects, 2008; contbr. articles to profl. jours. Chiang Ching-kuo Scholar grantee, 2004—05. Mem.: Am. Econ. Assn., Western Econ. Assn., Chinese Economist Soc. Avocations: travel, swimming, water sports. Office: Claremont McKenna College 500 E Ninth St Claremont CA 91711 Office Fax: 909-621-8249. Business E-Mail: richard.burdekin@claremontmckenna.edu.

BURDEN, JAMES EWERS, lawyer; b. Sacramento, Oct. 24, 1939; s. Herbert Spencer and Ida Elizabeth (Brosemer) B.; m. Kathryn Lee Gardner, Aug. 21, 1965; children: Kara Elizabeth Crabtree, Justin Gardner. BS, U. Calif., Berkeley, 1961; JD, U. Calif., Hastings, 1964; postgrad., U. So. Calif., 1964-65. Bar: Calif. 1965, Tax Ct. U.S. 1969, U.S. Supreme Ct. 1970. Assoc. Elliott and Aune, Santa Ana, Calif., 1965, White, Harbor, Fort & Schei, Sacramento, 1965-67, Miller, Starr & Regalia, Oakland, Calif., 1967-69, ptnr., 1969-73, Burden, Aiken, Mansuy & Stein, San Francisco, 1973-82, James E. Burden, Inc., San Francisco, 1982—; co-founder, COO, sec. KineMed, Inc., Emeryville, Calif., 2001—05, also bd. dirs.; co-founder, dir., CBO Emiliem, Inc., Emeryville, 2006—. Co-founder Gloucestershire Innovation Centre, Gloucester, Eng., EuroGen Pharmas. Ltd., Gloucester, Info4cars, Inc., Asheville, NC; underwriting mem. Lloyds of London, 1986-93; instr. U. Calif., Berkeley, Merritt Coll. 1968-74; pres., prin. Dorset Capital LLC. Contbr. articles to profl. jours. Mem.: Inst. of Dirs. (London), St. Andrews Golf Club (Fife, Scotland), Faculty Club U. Calif. Berkeley, Univ. Club, Commonwealth Club of Calif., Claremont Country Club. Office: One Maritime Plz 4th Fl San Francisco CA 94111-3407 Office Phone: 415-421-0404. Personal E-mail: jimburden@dorsetcapllc.com.

BURDGE, RABEL JAMES, sociology educator; b. Columbus, Ohio, Dec. 14, 1937; s. Alonzo Marshall and Mariam Francis (Prentice) B.; m. Sharon Sue Payne, June 30, 1962 (dec. June 1975); children: Stephanie, Amy, Jill; m. Joyce Loretta Piggush, Aug. 2, 1977. BS, Ohio State U., 1959, MS, 1961; PhD, Pa. State U., 1965. Asst. prof. sociology U.S. Air Force Acad., Colo., 1966-68; lectr. U. Colo., Colorado Springs, 1966-68; asst. prof. sociology U. Ky., Lexington, 1968-72, assoc. prof., 1972-76; assoc. prof. environ. sociology, rural sociology, urban and regional planning and leisure studies; dept. agrl. econs. and leisure studies U. Ill. Inst. Environ. Studies, Urbana, 1976-80, prof., 1980—96; prof. emeritus U. Ill., 1996—; prof. sociology and environ. studies Western Wash. U., Bellingham, 1996—. Vis. scholar Sch. of Australian Environ. Studies, Griffith U., Brisbane, 1982, 86, hon. prof., 1991—; vis. prof. Sch. Planning and Landscape, U. Manchester, Eng., 2002. Author: (with N. Cheek and D. Field) Leisure and Recreation Places, 1976, (with Paul Opryszek) Coping with Change: An Interdisciplinary Assessment of the Lake Shelbyville Reservoir, 1981, (with E.M. Rogers) Social Change in Rural Societies, A Rural Sociology Textbook, 3d edit., 1988, A Community Guide to Social Impact Assessment, 1998, 3d edit., 2004, A Conceptual Approach to Social Impact Assessment, 1994, 2d edit., 1998, The Concepts, Process and Methods of Social Impact Assessment, 2004; editor Jour. Leisure Rsch., 1971-74; co-editor, founder: Leisure Scis., an Interdisciplinary Jour., 1977-82, Society and Nat. Resources: An Internat. Jour., 1988-98; co-editor Longman-Cheshire Internat. Environ. Studies Series, 1990—; contbr. articles to profl. publs. Mem. Whatcan County Planning Commn., 2003—. Capt. arty. Army USMC, 1965—68. Recipient George B. Hartzog Jr. award for environ. rsch. Clemson U., 1995. Lifetime Achievement award Internat. Assn. Society and Natural Resources, 2004. Mem. AAAS, Am. Sociol. Assn., Rural Sociol. Soc. (v.p. 1982-83, treas. 1994-2000, editor The Rural Sociologist, 1994-2000, named Disting. Rural Sociologist, 1996), Nat. Recreation and Park Assn. (Theodore/Franklin D. Roosevelt award for outstanding rsch. 1982), Internat. Assn. for Impact Assessment (pres. 1990-91, treas. 1993-96, Rose-Hulman Inst. Tech. award for contbns. to impact assessment), Acad. Leisure Scis., Sigma Xi, Phi Kappa Phi, Gamma Sigma Delta, Alpha Kappa Delta. Democrat. Methodist. Home: PO Box 4056 Bellingham WA 98227-4056 Home Phone: 360-676-9892. Personal E-mail: burdge@comcast.net.

BURDGE, RICHARD JAMES, JR., lawyer; b. Long Beach, Calif., Dec. 4, 1949; children: Kristin Alexis, Lindsay Michelle, Margaret Lynn, Kelly Anne. BS, Yale U., 1972; JD, UCLA, 1979. Bar: Calif. 1979, U.S. Dist. Ct. (cen. dist.) Calif. 1979, U.S. Ct. Appeals (9th cir.) 1980, U.S. Dist. Ct. (no. dist.) Calif. 1984, U.S. Supreme Ct. 1984, U.S. Dist. Ct. (ea. dist.) Calif. 1987, U.S. Dist. Ct. (so. dist.) Calif. 1990. Assoc., then ptnr. Lillick, McHose & Charles, LA, 1979-86; ptnr. Dewey Ballantine and predecessor firms, LA, 1986—. Del. L.A.

County Bar Del. to Calif. State Bar Conf. of Dels., 1988—. Mng. editor UCLA Law Rev., 1978-79, mem. editl. staff, 1977-78. Chmn. UCLA Law Ann. Fund, 1989-91; co-chair UCLA Law Libr. Alumni Campaign, 1994-97. Lt. USN, 1972-76. Mem. Assn. Bus. Trial Lawyers (gov. 1989-91, 93-95, ann. seminar chair 1992, jud. coll. chair 1995, treas. 1995-96, sec. 1996-97, v.p. 1997-98, pres. 1998-99), L.A. County Bar Assn. (trustee 1999—), Chancery Club.

BURDICK, GINNY MARIE, state legislator; b. Portland, Oreg., Dec. 3, 1947; children: Kate, Shannon. BA in Psychol., U. Puget Sound, 1969; MA in Journalism, Oreg. U., 1973. Reporter Port Angeles Daily News, Wash., 1969—71; reporter, editor Daily News, Eugene, Oreg., Register-Guard, 1972—73, AP, 1973—75, Bur. Nat. Affairs, 1976—78, Legal Times of Washington, 1978—79; environ. issues mgr. Atlantic Richfield Co., 1981—84; self-employed crisis mgmt. specialist, 1989—2004; v.p., sr. counsel Gard & Gerber Advt. and Pub. Rels., 2004—06; comm. cons. in crises comm.; mem. Dist. 18 Oreg. State Senate, 1996—. Mem., chair senate judiciary comm. Oreg. State Senate, 1999—, mem., chair fin. and revenue comm. Democrat. Office: Oreg State Senate 900 Court St NE S-213 Salem OR 97301 Home: 6227 SW 18th Dr Portland OR 97239-1912 Office Phone: 503-986-1718. E-mail: sen.ginnyburdick@state.or.us.*

BURDICK, ROGER S., state supreme court justice; BS, U. Colorado; JD, U. Idaho Sch. of Law, 1974. Bank examiner Dept. Finance, Boise, Idaho, 1970—71; atty. Webb, Pike, Burton & Carlson, Twin Falls, 1974—80; dep. prosecuting atty. Ada County; ptnr. Hart and Burdick, Jerome, 1976—80; prosecuting atty. Jerome County, 1980—81, magistrate judge, 1981—93; dist. judge Twin Falls County, 1993—2001; administrative judge Fifth Jud. Dist., 2001—03; justice Idaho Supreme Ct., 2003—. Former chmn. Juvenile Rules Com.; mem. Idaho Jud. Coun., 1990—2001; dist. judge Snake River Basin Water Adjudication, 2001—03. Mem.: Magistrate Judges Assn. (pres. 1989—91), Idaho State Bar Assn., Dist. Judges Assn. (pres. 2001—03). Office: Idaho Supreme Ct PO Box 83720 Boise ID 83720-0101

BURGEE, JOHN HENRY, architect; b. Chgo., Aug. 28, 1933; s. Joseph Zeno and Helen (Dooley) B.; m. Gwendolyn Mary Henson, June 30, 1956; 1 son, John Gerard. BArch, U. Notre Dame, 1956, DEngr (hon.), 1983. Supt. constrn. Holabird & Root & Burgee, Chgo., 1955-56; project mgr. Naess & Murphy, Chgo., 1958-61; adminstr. design, project architect C. F. Murphy Assos., Chgo., 1961-65; assoc. ptnr. C. F. Murphy Assocs., 1965-67, ptnr., 1967; assoc. Philip Johnson (Architects), NYC, 1967-68; ptnr. Johnson/Burgee, NYC, 1968-82, John Burgee Architects, NYC, 1982-98, Santa Barbara, Calif., 1998—. Chmn. Archtl. Rev. Bd., Bronxville, N.Y., 1974-75; chmn. Bronxville Planning Commn., 1975-77 Works include, I.D.S. Center, Mpls., Niagara Falls Conv. Center, Pennzoil Place, Houston, Crystal Cathedral, Los Angeles, AT&T Hdqrs., N.Y.C., PPG Hdqrs., Pitts., Transco Tower, Houston, Republic Bank, Houston, Nat. Center for Performing Arts, Bombay, 101 California Street, San Francisco, International Place, Boston, 190 South LaSalle Street, Chicago, IBM Headquarters, Atlanta, Mus. of Broadcasting, New York Canadian Broadcast Ctr., Toronto, Takashamya Dept. Store, N.Y., Capital Holding Ctr., Louisville, Puerto de Europa, Madrid, One Detroit Ctr., Marina Hotel and Shopping Ctr., Singapore, Ch. St. Mary, Lakeville, Conn., Hahn, Montecito, Calif. Pres. German-Am. Club, Bad Kreuznach, Germany, 1957-58; chmn. bldg. material sect. Met. Crusade of Mercy, Chgo., 1966-67; pres. Chgo. Br. North Montessori Sch. Bd., 1962-63, Lawrence Park Hilltop Assn., 1974-75; chmn. architecture com. Statue of Liberty/Ellis Island Centennial Commn.; mem. adv. coun. Coll. Engring. U. Notre Dame, 1982-88; bd. dirs. Lenox Hill Hosp., 1982-91, Parsons Sch. of Design, 1985-92, U. Notre Dame, 1988—, Chgo. Athenaeum, 1989-92, Music Acad. of the West, 2002-, 1st vice chmn., 2003, chmn., 2005. With US Army, 1956—58. Recipient Reynolds Aluminum prize, 1978, honor award U. Notre Dame, 1981, Chgo. Architecture award. Fellow AIA, Urban Design Inst.; mem. Archtl. League N.Y. (dir.), Inst. Architecture and Urban Studies (dir. 1983, chmn., pres. 1984) Clubs: Saddle Cycle (Chgo.), Arts (Chgo.), University (Chgo.), Shenarock Shore (Rye, N.Y.), Am. Yacht, Century Assn. Home: 639 Hot Springs Rd Santa Barbara CA 93108-2030 E-mail: burgeearchitect@cox.net.

BURGER, EDMUND GANES, architect; b. Yerington, Nev., Mar. 28, 1930; s. Edmund Ganes and Rose Catherine (Kobe) B.; m. Shirley May Pratini, Jan. 21, 1968; 1 dau., Jane Lee. B.M.E., U. Santa Clara, 1951; B.Arch., U. Pa., 1959. Engr. Gen. Electric Co., 1951-52; design engr. U. Calif. Radiation Lab., 1952-57; John Stewardson fellow in architecture, 1959; architect Wurster, Bernardi & Emmons, San Francisco, 1960-63; founder Burger & Coplans, Inc. (Architects), San Francisco, 1964, pres., 1964-79; owner Edmund Burger (Architect), 1979—. Guest lectr. U. Calif., Berkeley. Important works include Acorn Housing Project, Oakland, Calif., Crescent Village Housing Project, Suisun City, Calif., Coplans residence, San Francisco, Betel Housing Project, San Francisco, Grand View Housing Project, San Francisco, Albany (Calif.) Oaks Housing, Grow Homes, San Pablo, Calif., Mariposa Housing, Dunleavy Plaza Housing, Potrero Ct. Housing, San Francisco, Lee residence, Kentfield, Calif., Burger residences, Lafayette, Calif., Oceanside, Oreg., and El Cerrito, Calif., Yamhill Valley Vineyards Winery, McMinneville, Oreg., Portico De Mar, shop and restaurant complex, Barcelona, Spain, Hendrickson residence, Newport Beach, Calif., Hamilton residence, Winters, Calif., Sanders residence, Yuba City, Calif., Strack/Villars residence, Kentfield, Calif., Breton residence, Oakland, Visitors Facilities Yosemite Nat. Park, Calif., Rogers Residence, El Cerrito, Calif, Stern Grove Outdoor Theater, San Francisco, Petersen Residence, El Cerrito, Blum Residence, Beverly Hills, Calif., Pride and Joy Presch.-Day Care Ctr., Moncrief residence, St. Thomas, US Virgin Islands; author: Geomorphic Architecture, 1986. Recipient citation for excellence in community architecture AIA, 1969, award of merit AIA, award of merit Homes for Better Living, 1970, 79, 1st Honor award, 1973, 81, Holiday award for a beautiful Am., 1970, Honor award 4th Biennial HUD awards for design excellence, 1970, Bay Area awards for design excellence, 1969, 74, 78, Apts. of Year award Archtl. Record, 1972, Houses of Year award, 1973, Calif. Affordable Housing Competition award, 1981, HUD Building Value into Housing award, 1981, Community Design award Calif. Council AIA, 1986; design grant Nat. Endowment for Arts, 1980, HUD, 1980; constrn. grant HUD, 1981. Office: 8445 Wildcat Dr El Cerrito CA 94530 Office Phone: 510-237-8336.

BURGER, EUGENE J., property manager; Pres., CEO Eugene Burger Mgmt. Corp., Greenbrae, Calif., 1979—. Office: Eugene Burger Management Corp 6600 Hunter Dr Rohnert Park CA 94928-2418

BURGES, JUDY M., state legislator; b. La Junta, Colo., July 21, 1943; married; 3 children. AA, Yavapai Coll., Prescott, Ariz., 1984; BA in Mgmt., U. Phoenix, 1993, MBA, 1996. Budget coord. Cyprus Begdad Copper Co., 1976—81; acct. clk. Yavapai County Govt., 1984—96; mem. Dist. 4 Ariz. House of Reps., 2004—, vice-chair pub. employees, retirement & entitlement reform com., mem. transp. & infrastructure com. Vice-chair Ariz. Rep. Assembly. Bd. dirs. Habitat for Humanity, 2003. Mem.: Skull Valley Hist. Soc. (bd. dirs.). Republican. Lutheran. Mailing: Ariz House Reps 1700 W Washington Rm 342 Phoenix AZ 85007 Office Phone: 602-926-5861. Office Fax: 602-417-3104 602-417-3104. Business E-Mail: jburges@azleg.gov.*

BURGESS, CHARLES ORVILLE, history professor; b. Portland, Oreg., Jan. 18, 1932; s. Rex Orville and Glendora Almanda (Sundrud) B.; m. Cora Cloepfil, June 22, 1952; children: Donna Claire Majer, Jo Dell Nicholls, Robert Charles; m. Patricia Stewart Anderson, Apr. 22, 1976; children: Marc Richard Anderson, Brian Stewart Anderson, Tricia Louise Crozier, Kristen Anne Klein. BA, U. Oreg., 1957; MS (Danforth fellow), U. Wis., 1958, PhD, 1962; Nat. Postdoctoral fellow, Harvard U., 1967-68. Asst. prof. U. Calif., Riverside, 1962-64; asst. prof. history edn. U. Wash., Seattle, 1964-66, assoc. prof., 1966-70, prof., 1970—, chmn. area ednl. policy studies, 1970-92; prof. emeritus, 1992. V.p. divsn. F Am. Ednl. Rsch. Assn., 1977-79; fgn. expert Peoples Republic of China, 1984-85. Author: The Origins of American Thought (published in China as Meiguo Sixiang Yuanyuan); 1988. (with M.L. Borrowman) What Doctrines to Embrace, 1969, Profile of an American Philanthropist (Nettie Fowler McCormick), 1962; co-editor: (with Charles Strickland) G. Stanley Hall on Natural Education, 1965; co-author: (with Y. Yang and G. Zhu) Cultivating the World of Selfhood (published in China as Kaituo Zi Wode Shijie), 1997. Wash. com. civil rights ACLU, 1965-67; bd. dirs. Seattle Folklore Soc., 1966—. With USAF, 1950-54. Mem.: History of Edn. Soc. (pres. 1971—72), Phi Beta Kappa. Home: 14350 22nd Ave SW Burien WA 98166

BURGESS, LARRY EUGENE, library director, historian, educator; b. Montrose, Colorado, July 18, 1945; s. Eugene Floyd and Edyth Eleanor (Faussone) B.; m. Charlotte Reid (Gaylord), Oct. 7, 1973. BA, U. Redlands, Calif., 1967; MA, Claremont Grad. Sch., 1969, PhD, 1972. Archivist A.K. Smiley Pub. Libr., Redlands, Calif., 1972-85, libr. dir., 1986—. Adj. prof. history, U. Redlands, 1972—, U. Calif., Riverside, 1979—; book reviewer Lincoln Herald, 1988—. Author: Mohonk: Its People and Spirit, 1980; (with others) A Day with Mr. Lincoln, (with others), 1994; co-author: The Hunt for Willie Boy, 1994. Vice-chmn. Calif. Heritage Preservation Commn., 1977-84; Hist. Soc. So. Calif., L.A., pres., 2003—06; bd. dirs. U. Redlands, 1987—. Recipient Archival Award of Excellence Calif. Heritage Preservation Commn., 1991; Preservation Merit Award Calif. Hist. Soc., 1992, Cmty. Enrichment Award Hist. Soc. So. Calif., 1994. Mem. Soc. Am. Archivists, So. Calif. Archivists (past pres.), Zamorano Club (bd. dir. 1994—, pres. 1999-2002), Rotary Club Relands (pres. 1999-2000). Avocations: travel, gardening, book collecting. Home: 923 W Fern Ave Redlands CA 92373-5877 Office: A K Smiley Pub Libr 125 W Vine St Redlands CA 92373-4728 Home Phone: 909-793-1529; Office Phone: 909-798-7565. E-mail: admin@aksmiley.org, admin@akspl.org.

BURGESS, MARY ALICE (MARY ALICE WICKIZER), publisher; b. San Bernardino, Calif., June 21, 1938; d. Russell Alger and Wilma Evelyn (Swisher) Wickizer; m. Michael Roy Burgess, Oct. 15, 1976; children from previous marriage: Richard Albert Rogers, Mary Louise Rogers Reynnells. AA, Valley Coll., San Bernardino, 1967; BA, Calif. State U., San Bernardino, 1975, postgrad., 1976-79, U. Calif., Riverside, 1976-79. Lic. real estate salesman, Calif.; real estate broker, Calif. Sec.-treas. Lynwyck Realty & Investment, San Bernardino, 1963-75; libr. asst. Calif. State U., San Bernardino, 1974-76, purchasing agt., 1976-81; co-pub. The Borgo Press, San Bernardino, 1975-99; owner MilleFleurs Info. Svcs., 2000—. Co-pub: (with Robert Reginald) Science Fiction and Fantasy Book Review, 1979-80; co-author (with M.R. Burgess) The Wickizer Annals: The Descendents of Conrad Wickizer of Luzerne County, Pennsylvania, 1983, (with Douglas Menville and Robert Reginald) Futurevisions: The New Golden Age of the Science Fiction Film, 1985, (with Jeffrey M. Elliot and Robert Reginald) The Arms Control, Disarmament and Military Science Dictionary, 1989, (with Michael Burgess) The House of the Burgesses, 2d edit., 1994; author: The Campbell Chronicles: A Genealogical History of the Descendants of Samuel Campbell of Chester County, Pennsylvania, 1989, (with Boden Clarke) The Work of Katherine Kurtz, 1992-93, (with Michael Burgess and Daryl F. Mallett) State and Province Vital Records Guide; editor: Cranberry Tea Room Cookbook, Still The Frame Holds, Defying the Holocaust, Risen from the Ashes: A Story of the Jewish Displaced Persons in the Aftermath of World War II, Being a Sequel to Survivors (Jacob Biber), 1989, Ray Bradbury: Dramatist (Ben P. Indick), 1989, Across the Wide Missouri: The Diary of a Journey from Virginia to Missouri in 1819 and Back Again in 1821, with a Description of the City of Cincinnati, (James Brown Campbell), Italian Theatre in San Francisco, Into the Flames: The Life Story of a Righteous Gentile, Jerzy Kosinski: The Literature of Violation, The Little Kitchen Cookbook, Victorian Criticism of American Writers, 1990, The Magic That Works: John W. Campbell and The American Response to Technology, 1993, Libido into Literature: The "Primèra Època" of Benito Pérez Galdós, 1993, A Triumph of the Spirit: Stories of Holocaust Survivors, 1994, A Way Farer in a World in Upheaval, 1993, William Eastlake: High Desert Interlocutor, 1993, The Price of Paradise: The Magazine Career of F. Scott Fitgerald, 1993, The Little Kitchen Cookbook, rev. edit., 1994, An Irony of Fate: William March, 1994, Hard-Boiled Heretic: Ross Macdonald, 1994, We The People!, 1994, The Chinese Economy, 1995, Voices of the River Plate, 1995, Chaos Burning on My Brow, 1995; co-editor and pub. (with Robert Reginald) of all Borgo Press publs.; also reviewer, indexer, researcher and editor of scholarly manuscripts. Chmn. new citizens Rep. Women, San Bernardino, 1967; libr. San Bernardino Geneal. Soc., 1965-67; vol. Boy Scout Am., Girl Scouts U.S., Camp Fire Girls, 1960s. Recipient Real Estate Proficiency award Calif. Dept. Real Estate, San Bernardino, 1966. Mem. City of San Bernardino Hist. and Pioneer Soc., Calif. State U. Alumni Assn., Cecil County (Md.) Hist. Soc., Gallia County (Ohio) Hist. and Geneal. Soc., DAR (membership and geneal. records chmn. 1964-66, registrar and vice regent San Bernardino chpt. 1965-67). Avocations: genealogy, films, travel. Office: MilleFleurs PO Box 2845 Box 2845 San Bernardino CA 92406-2845

BURGESS, MICHAEL (ROBERT REGINALD), librarian, writer; b. Fukuoka, Kyushu, Japan, Feb. 11, 1948; came to U.S., 1949; s. Roy Walter and Betty Jane (Kapel) B.; m. Mary Alice Wickizer, Oct. 15, 1976; stepchildren: Richard Albert Rogers, Mary Louise Reynnells AB with honors, Gonzaga U., 1969; MLS, U. So. Calif., 1970. Periodicals librarian Calif. State U., San Bernardino, 1970-81, chief cataloger, 1981-94, prof., 1984—2005, head tech. svcs. and collection devel., 1994—2005, emeritus, 2005—. Editor Newcastle Pub. Co., North Hollywood, Calif., 1971—92; pub. Borgo Press, San Bernardino, 1975—99, Brownstone Books, San Bernardino, 1991—99, Sidewinder Press, San Bernardino, 1991—99, Unicorn & Son, San Bernardino, 1991—99, Burgess & Wickizer, San Bernardino, 1991—99, Emeritus Enterprises, 1993—99, Starmont House, 1993—99; assoc. editor SFRA Rev., 1993—94, Millefleurs Info. Svcs., San Bernardino, 2000—; editor Wildside Press/Borgo Press Imprint, 2005—. Author 113 books under pen names Michael Burgess, R(obert) Reginald, Boden Clarke, and others, with occasional co-authors, including: Stella Nova, 1970, Cumulative Paperback Index, 1939-1959, 1973, Contemporary Science Fiction Authors, 1975, The Attempted Assassination of John F. Kennedy, 1976, Things to Come, 1977, Up Your Asteroid!, 1977, Science Fiction and Fantasy Literature, a Checklist, 1700-1974, 1979, The Paperback Price Guide, 1980, 2nd edit., 1983, Science Fiction & Fantasy Awards, 1981, If J.F.K. Had Lived, 1982, The House of Burgesses, 1983, 2nd edit., 1994, The Wickizer Annals, 1983, Tempest in a Teapot, 1983, A Guide to Science Fiction & Fantasy in the Library of Congress Classification Scheme, 1984, 2nd edit., 1988, The Work of Jeffrey M. Elliot, 1984, Futurevisions, 1985, Lords Temperal & Lords Spiritual, 1985, 2nd edit., 1995, The Work of Julian May, 1985, The Work of R. Reginald, 1985, The Work of George Zebrowski, 1986, 2nd edit., 1990, 3rd edit., 1996, Mystery and Detective Fiction in the Library of Congress Classification Scheme, 1988, The Work of William F. Nolan, 1988, 2nd edit., 1998, The Arms Control, Disarmament, and Military Security Dictionary, 1989, Hancer's Price Guide to Paperback Books, 3d edit., 1990, Reginald's Science Fiction and Fantasy Awards, 2nd edit., 1991, 3d edit., 1993, Reference Guide to Science Fiction, Fantasy, and Horror, 1992, Science Fiction and Fantasy Literature, 1975-1991, 1992, The Work of Robert Reginald, 2nd edit., 1992, The State and Province Vital Records Guide, 1993, The Work of Katherine Kurtz, 1993, St. James Guide to Science Fiction Writers, 1996, CSUSB Faculty Authors, Composers and Playwrights, 1996, 2d. edit., 2006, BP 250, 1996, Xenograffiti, 1996, 2nd edit., 2005, Codex Derynianus, 1998, Katydid and other Critters, 2001, The Dark-Haired Man, 2004, The Exiled Prince, 2004, Quaestiones, 2004, Murder in Retrospect, 2005, Codex Derynianus II, 2005, Classics of Fantastic Literature, 2005, The Eastern Orthodox Churches, 2005, Quaestiones, 2005, Trilobite Dreams, 2006, BP 300, 2007, The Phantom's Phantom, 2007, Invasion! Or, Earth vs. the Aliens, 2007, The Nasty Gnomes, 2008; editor: Ancestral Voices, 1975, Alistair MacLean, 1976, Ancient Hauntings, 1976, Phantasmagoria, 1976, R.I.P., 1976, The Spectre Bridegroom and Other Horrors, 1976, John D. MacDonald and the Colorful World of Travis McGee, 1977, Dreamers of Dreams, 1978, King Solomon's Children, 1978, They, 1978, Worlds of Never, 1978, Science Fiction & Fantasy Book Review, 1980, 2d edit., 2007, Candle for Poland, 1982, The Holy Grail Revealed, 1982, The Work of Bruce McAllister, 1985, rev. edit., 1986, George Orwell's Guide Through Hell, 1986, 2nd edit., 1994, The Work of Charles Beaumont, 1986, 2nd edit., 1990, California Ranchos, 1988, 2d edit., 2007, The Work of Chad Oliver, 1989, The Work of Colin Wilson, 1989, The Work of Ian Watson, The Work of Reginald Bretnor, 1989, The Work of Ross Rocklynne, 1989, To Kill or Not To Kill, 1990, The Work of Dean Ing, 1990, The Work of Jack Dann, 1990, The Work of Pamela Sargent, 1990, 2nd edit., 1996, The Trilemma of World Oil Politics, 1991, The Work of Louis L'Amour, 1991, The Work of Brian W. Aldiss, 1992, Geo. Alec Effinger, 1993, Polemical Pulps, 1993, Sermons in Science Fiction, 1994, The Work of Elizabeth Chater, 1994, The Work of Jack Vance, 1994, The Work of William Eastlake, 1994, The Work of William F. Temple, 1994, The Work of Gary Brandner, 1995, The Work of Stephen King, 1996, Running From The Hunter, 1996, San Quentin, 2005, Cal State Cooks, 1965-2006, Viva California!, 2007, Across the Wide Missouri, 2007, First-century Palestinian Judaism, 2007; author of 13,000 essays, 30 short stories; editor 1,500 books for Wildside Press and others. Recipient MPPP award, 1987, Lifetime Collectors award for Contbn. to Bibliography, 1993, Pilgrim award, 1993; named title II fellow U. So. Calif., 1969-70. Mem. NEA, ACLU, Sci. Fiction and Fantasy Writers Am., Mystery Writers Am., Calif. Tchrs. Assn., Calif. Faculty Assn. (statewide librs. task force 1986-89, 93-2005, editor newsletter 1987-89), Internat. PEN, U.S.A. Ctr. West, Sci. Fiction Rsch. Assn., Horror Writers Am. Democrat. Avocations: genealogical and historical research, films. Office: Millefleurs PO Box 2845 San Bernardino CA 92406-2845 also: Calif State U Libr 5500 University Pkwy San Bernardino CA 92407-2318 E-mail: robert@millefleurs.tv.

BURGESS, TIMOTHY M., federal judge, former prosecutor; b. San Francisco, 1956; BA, U. Alaska, 1978, MBA, 1982; JD, Northeastern U., 1987. Legis. asst. to Frank H. Murkowski US Senate; assoc. Gilmore and Feldman, Anchorage, 1987—89; asst. US atty. Dist. AK US Dept. Justice, Anchorage, 1989—2001, US atty., 2001—06; judge US Dist. Ct. AK, Anchorage, 2006—. Mem.: AK Bar Assn. Office: US Dist Ct 222 W 7th St #33 Anchorage AK 99513

BURGIN, GEORGE HANS, computer scientist, educator; b. Liestal, Switzerland, Feb. 13, 1930; s. Jakob and Fanny B.; m. Ulrike Franziska, July 8, 1960; children: Bernard, Claudia, Paul. Diploma in engring., Swiss Fed. Inst. Tech., Zurich, 1953, PhD, 1961. Cert. profl. engr., Calif. Design specialist Gen. Dynamics Corp., San Diego, 1962-64; sr. scientist Decision Sci., 1964-82; chief scientist Titan Systems, 1982-94; prin. staff engr. Titan Info. Systems, 1994-96, chief engr., 1996-98; staff engr. CommQuest Techs., 1998-99, IBM/Encinitas, 1999-2000, Triton Newtork Systems, 2000—01; sr. staff scientist Natural Selection, Inc., La Jolla, Calif., 2002—. Lectr. San Diego State U., 1979—89. Contbg. author: book Simulation, 2d edit., 1989; author: (program) Adaptive Maneuvering Logic; contbr. articles profl. jours. 1st lt. Swiss Army. Mem.: IEEE (sr. life). Achievements include invention of adaptive maneuvering logic air combat simulation program; patents for algorithm for a quadrature modulator precompensation. Home: 6284 Avenida Cresta La Jolla CA 92037-6505 Office: Natural Selection Inc 9330 Scranton Rd San Diego CA 92121 Business E-Mail: gburgin@natural-selection.com.

BURGUM, DOUG, software company executive; b. Arthur, ND; 3 children. BA, N.D. State Univ.; MBA, Stanford Univ. Grad. Sch. of Bus., 1980; PhD (hon.), N.D. State Univ. Cons. McKinsey & Co., Chgo., 1980—83; pres., chmn., CEO Great Plains, 1984—2001; sr. v.p. Microsoft, 2001—. Bd. mem. Stanford Grad. Sch. Bus.; founder Doug Burgum Family Fund. Office: Microsoft Corp One Microsoft Way Redmond WA 98052-6399

BURKE, CAMERON S., legal association administrator; b. Nov. 23, 1953; m. Barbara; 3 children. BA in History, U. Oreg., 1976; MS in Judicial Adminstrn., U. Denver, 1980. Calendar & courtroom clk. U.S.

Dist. Ct., Idaho, 1976-79; trial court adminstr. Lincoln County Cir. & Dist. Cts., 1981-85; chief deputy clk. U.S. Dist. Ct., Ariz., 1985-89; court exec. U.S. Dist. & Bankruptcy Cts., Idaho, 1989—. Contbr. articles to profl. jours. Chi Psi Ednl. scholar. Mem. Am. Judicature Soc., Nat. Ctr. State Cts., Nat. Assn. Ct. Mgmt., Oreg. Assn. Ct. Adminstrn. (past pres.), Fed. Ct. Clks. Assn. (past pres., Bob Christ award 1996, Angie award 2000), Ariz. Cts. Assn. (past pres.). Office: US Dist & Bankruptcy Cts Fed Bldg & US Courthouse 550 W Fort St # 39 Boise ID 83724-0101

BURKE, CHERYL, dancer; b. Calif., May 1984; Ballroom dancer, 1995—; winner San Francisco Open Latin Championship, 2005, Ohio Star Ball Rising Star Championship, 2005; profl. dancer Dancing with the Stars, ABC, 2006—, season 2 winner, with partner Drew Lachey, 2006, season 3 winner, with partner Emmitt Smith, 2006. Office: c/o Terry Lindholm 1611A N El Centro Ave Hollywood CA 90028 also: c/o Susan Madore Guttman Assocs 118 S Beverly Dr Ste 201 Beverly Hills CA 90212

BURKE, E. JAMES, state supreme court justice, lawyer; b. Wilmington, Del., June 26, 1949; s. Earl J. Burke and Elizabeth M. (Glenn) Jones; m. Michele C. Haney, Aug. 16, 1975 (div. May 1981); 1 child, Erick; m. Linda G. Matthew, Apr. 15, 1982; children: Matthew, Leanna. BS in Psychology, St. Joseph's U., Phila., 1971; JD, U. Wyo., 1977. Bar: Wyo. 1977, U.S. Dist. Ct. Wyo. 1977, U.S. Ct. Appeals (10th cir.) 1981. Ptnr. Burke, Woodard and O'Donnell, Hanes & Burke P.C., Cheyenne, Wyo., 1977—2001; judge Dist. Ct. Laramie County, 2001—04; justice Wyo. Supreme Ct., 2005—. Mem. Cheyenne-Laramie County Economic Joint Powers Bd.; founder, dean People's Law School prog. Served to 1st lt. USAF, 1971-74. Mem. Wyo. Bar Assn., Laramie County Bar Assn., Assn. Trial Lawyers Am. (state del. 1985—), Wyo. Trial Lawyers Assn. (bd. dirs. 1977—, pres. 1980), Western Trial Lawyers Assn. (bd. dirs. 1979—, pres. 1986—), Cheyenne C. of C. (leadership award 1986). Office: Wyo Supreme Ct 2301 Capitol Ave Cheyenne WY 82001

BURKE, EDMOND WAYNE, retired judge, lawyer; b. Ukiah, Calif., Sept. 7, 1935; s. Wayne P. and Opal K. B.; children from previous marriage: Kathleen R., Jennifer E.; m. Anna M. Hubbard, Dec. 29, 1990. AB, Humboldt State Coll., 1957, MA, 1958; JD, U. Calif., 1964. Bar: Calif., Alaska, Mont. Individual practice law, Calif. and Alaska, 1965-67; asst. atty. gen. State of Alaska, 1967; asst. dist. atty. Anchorage, Alaska, 1968-69; judge Superior Ct., Alaska, 1970-75; justice Supreme Ct. State of Alaska, Anchorage, 1975-93, chief justice, 1981-84; of coun. Bogle & Gates, 1994-95; mem. Burke Bauermeister, Anchorage, 1996—. Republican. Presbyterian.

BURKE, JAN HELENE, writer; b. Houston, Aug. 1, 1953; d. John Francis and Velda Marie Fischer; m. Timothy Edward Burke, May 28, 1988. BA, Calif. State U., Long Beach, 1978. Author: (novels) Goodnight, Irene, 1993, Hocus, 1997, Harm, 1999, Bloodlines: An Irene Kelly Novel, 2005. Recipient readers award and Macavity award for short story Ellery Queen Mystery Mag., 1994, Ellery Queen Mystery Mag. award, Agatha award. Mem. Mystery Writers Am., Am. Crime Writers League, Internat. Crime Writers Assn., Sisters in Crime. Fax: 562-429-1811. E-mail: jan@janburke.com.

BURKE, KATHLEEN J., foundation administrator; Exec. v.p., pers. rels. officer BankAmerica Corp., San Francisco, now vice chmn., pers. rel. officer; exec. dir. Stupski Family Found., Mill Valley, Calif., 2000—. Office: # 110 2 Belvedere Dr Mill Valley CA 94941-2418 E-mail: kathleen@stupski.com.

BURKE, KENNETH JOHN, lawyer; b. Washington, Aug. 23, 1939; s. John Lawrence and Edna Catherine B.; m. Judith Ann Blass (div. July 1979); children: Jill Shannon, Corey Edmund, Erin Elisabeth; m. Gay Ann Crosier, June 4, 1983; 1 child, John Tynan. BS in Physics, Coll. Holy Cross, 1961; JD, U. Denver, 1969. Bar: Colo. 1969, U.S. Dist. Ct. Colo. 1969, U.S. Ct. Appeals (10th cir.) 1969, U.S. Supreme Ct. 1977. Assoc. Fuller & Evans, Denver, 1969-71; trial atty. U.S. Dept. Justice, Denver, 1971-74; ptnr. Bermingham, White, Burke & Ipsen, Denver, 1974-77, Holme, Roberts & Owen, Denver, 1977-86, Burke & Burke, 1986-88, Massey, Burke & Showalter, 1988-90, Baker & Hostetler, Denver, 1990-99, Bennington Johnson & Reeve, Denver, 1999—. Contbr. numerous articles to legal jours. 1st lt. USAF, 1962-66. Mem. ABA (vice chmn. water resources com. 1987-92, energy and natural resources litigation com. 1986-87), Colo. Bar Assn. Republican. Avocations: astronomy, fly fishing. Office: Ste 3500 370 17th St Denver CO 80202-5690

BURKE, MARIANNE KING, state agency administrator, finance executive, consultant; b. Douglasville, Ga., May 30, 1938; d. William Horace and Evora (Morris) King; divorced; 1 child, Kelly Page. Student, Ga. Inst. Tech., 1956-59, Anchorage C.C., 1964-66, Portland State U., 1968-69; BBA, U. Alaska, 1976. CPA, Alaska. Sr. audit mgr. Price Waterhouse, 1982-90; v.p. fin., asst. sec. NANA Regional Corp., Inc., Anchorage, 1990-95; v.p. fin. NANA Devel. Corp., Inc., Anchorage, 1990-95; sec.-treas. Vanguard Industries, J.V., Anchorage, 1990-95, Alaska United Drilling, Inc., Anchorage, 1990-95; treas. NANA/Marriott Joint Venture, Anchorage, 1990-95; v.p. fin. Arctic Utilities, Inc., Anchorage, 1990-95, Tour Arctic, Inc., Anchorage, 1990-95, Purcell Svcs., Ltd., Anchorage, 1990-95, Arctic Caribou Inn, Anchorage, 1990-95, NANA Oilfield Svcs., Inc., Anchorage, 1990-95, NANA Corp. Svcs., Inc., Anchorage, 1992-95; dir. divsn. ins. State of Alaska, 1995-99; pres. Marianne K. Burke Cons., 1999—. Cons. Ins. Regulatory and Devel. Authority of India, 2002—, Superintendencia de Banca y Seguros de Peru, 2004, Ins. Supervisory Commn. Republic of Albania, 2004, Saudi Arabian Monetary Authority, 2006—; cons. Bosnia and Herzegovina ins. sector Fin. Svcs. Vol. Corps, 2003, cons. assessment mission in Kosovo, 05, cons. assessment of ins. cos. supervision, Croatia, 05; mem. State of Alaska Medicaid Rate Commn., 1985—88, State of Alaska Bd. Accountancy, 1984—87; bd. dirs. Nat. Assn. Ins. Commrs. Edn. and Rsch. Found.; chair Bd. Equalization Municipality of Anchorage, 2004—; instr. IAIS Core Ins. Principles, Croatia, 2006; corp. governance devel. Mid. Eastern and North African Countries and Hawkamah, 2008. Bd. dirs. Alaska Treatment Ctr., Anchorage, 1978, Alaska Hwy. Cruises; treas. Alaska Feminist Credit Union, Anchorage, 1979-80; mem. fund raising com. Anchorage Symphony, 1981. Mem. AICPA, Internat. Assn. Ins. Suprs. (funded mem.), Alaska Soc. CPAs, Govtl. Fin. Officers U.S. and Can., Fin. Execs. Inst. (bd. dirs.), Nat. Assn. Ins. Commrs. (bd. dirs.). Avocations: travel, reading. Home: 3818 Helvetia Dr Anchorage AK 99508-5016 Office Phone: 907-563-9790. Personal E-mail: mkburke@gci.net.

BURKE, ROBERT BERTRAM, lawyer, political scientist, lobbyist; b. Cleve., July 9, 1942; s. Max and Eve (Miller) B.; m. Helen Choate Hall, May 5, 1979 (div. Oct. 1983). BA, UCLA, 1963, JD, 1966; LLM, London Sch. Econs., 1967. Bar: D.C. 1972, U.S. Supreme Ct. 1977, Calif. 1978. Exec. dir. Lawyer's Com. Civil Rights Under Law, Washington, 1968-69; ptnr. Fisk, Wolfe & Burke, Paris, 1969-71; assoc. O'Connor & Hannan, Washington, 1972-74; pvt. practice Washington, 1974-79, LA, 1978-93; contract lobbyist GCG Rose & Kindel, L.A., Sacramento, Washington, 1993—2007; mng. ptnr. Bob Burke & Co. Ltd., 2007—. Cons. Commonwealth Pa., Harrisburg, 1973. Chmn. So. Calif. Hollings for Pres., 1984; pres. Bldg. and Appeals Bd. City of L.A.; bd. dirs. Vols. of Am.; mem. exec. com. State Bar of Calif. pub. law sect. Mem. ABA UCLA Law Alumni Assn. (pres.). Jewish. Home: 277 S Irving Blvd Los Angeles CA 90004-3809 Office Phone: 213-896-8920. Personal E-mail: bob@bobburkela.com.

BURKE, TIMOTHY JOHN, lawyer; b. Syracuse, NY, June 5, 1946; s. Francis Joseph and Alice Marie Burke; m. Denise Kay Blied, Mar. 18, 1978; 1 child, Aimee Noel; 1 child from a previous marriage, Ryan Alexander. BA with distinction, Ariz. State U., 1967, JD cum laude, 1970. Bar: Ariz. 1970, U.S. Dist. Ct. Ariz. 1970, U.S. Ct. Appeals (9th cir.) 1974. Trial atty. Antitrust divsn. U.S. Dept. Justice, Washington, 1970-72, asst. to dir. ops., 1972-74; assoc. Fennemore Craig, Phoenix, 1974—, dir., 1978—. Part-time instr. legal writing Ariz. State U., 1974-75, adj. faculty assoc. profl. responsibility Coll. of Law, 2001-03. Mem. panel rev. bd. Phoenix United Way, 1975-76; bd. dirs. Florence Crittenton Svcs., Phoenix, 1980-88, pres., 1985-87; bd. dirs. Law Soc. Ariz. State U. Coll. Law, 1991-97, 99—, pres., 2000-05; bd. dirs. Valley of Sun Cmtys. in Schs., 1995-2001. Recipient spl. commendation U.s. Dept. Justice, 1973 Fellow Am. Bar Found., Ariz. Bar Found.; mem. ABA (antitrust and litigation sects., vice chmn. bus. torts and unfair competition com. 1996-98, chair 1998-2001, vice chmn. state enforcement com., 2001-04, editor Bus. Torts and Unfair Competition Newsletter 1996-98), FBA, Assn. Profl. Responsibility Lawyers (bd. dirs. 1993-98, pres. 1996-97), State Bar Ariz. (coun. antitrust sect., chmn. 1985-88, chmn. advt. com. 1992-94, ethics com. 1994-2001, chmn. 1995-2001, mem. task force on future of profession 2000, mem. case conflicts com. 2001-, mem. unauthorized practice of law adv. com., 2003-, chmn. 2006—), Maricopa County Bar Assn. Office: Fennemore Craig 3003 N Central Ave Ste 2600 Phoenix AZ 85012-2913 Home Phone: 602-266-2217; Office Phone: 602-916-5334. Business E-Mail: tburke@fclaw.com.

BURKE, WILLIAM THOMAS, lawyer, educator; b. Brazil, Ind., Aug. 17, 1926; JD, U. Ind., 1953; JSD, Yale U., New Haven, Conn., 1959. Bar: Ind. 1953. Rsch. assoc. and lectr. Yale U., 1956-62; assoc. prof. Ohio State U., 1962-64, prof., 1964-68, U. Wash. Sch. Law, Seattle, 1968-99, prof. emeritus, 1999—. Mem. adv. com. Law of Sea Task Force, Dept. State; mem. A217 Ocean Policy Com., NAS. Author: (with M. S. McDougal) The Public Order of the Oceans, 1962, Contemporary Legal Problems in Ocean Development, 1969, (with Legatski and Woodhead) National and International Law Enforcement in the Ocean, 1975, The New International Law of Fisheries, 1994, International Law of the Sea-Documents and Notes, 1997, 99. Personal E-mail: sealaw1@comcast.net. Business E-Mail: burke@u.washington.edu.

BURKE, YVONNE WATSON BRATHWAITE (MRS. WILLIAM A. BURKE), lawyer; b. LA, Oct. 5, 1932; d. James A. and Lola (Moore) Watson; m. William A. Burke, June 14, 1972; 1 child, Autumn Roxanne; 1 stepchild, Christine. AA, U. Calif., 1951; BA, UCLA, 1953; JD, U. So. Calif., 1956; Doctorate (hon.), Pepperdine U. Bar: Calif. 1956. Mem. Calif. Assembly, 1966-72, chmn. urban devel. and housing com., 1971, 72; mem. 93d-95th Congresses, 1973—79, House Appropriations Com.; chmn. Congl. Black Caucus, 1976; Los Angeles county supervisor 4th dist., 1979—80; ptnr. Jones, Day, Reagis & Pogue, 1987—92. Dep. corp. commr., hearing officer Police Commn., 1964-66; atty., staff McCone Commn. (investigation Watts riot), 1965; past chmn. L.A. Fed. Res. Bank; U.S. adv. bd. Nestle. Vice chmn. 1984 U.S. Olympics Organizing Com.; bd. dirs. or bd. advisers numerous orgns.; former regent U. Calif., Bd. Ednl. Testing Svc.; Amateur Athletic Found.; former bd. dirs. Ford Found., Brookings Inst.; mem. bd. supr's. 2d Dist., L.A. County Bd. of Supr's., 1992—, chair, 1993-94, 97-98, 2002-03; bd. govs. L.A. Met. Transp. Authority; pres. So. Calif. Assn. Govts., 2006, LA Coliseum Commn., 2006. Recipient Profl. Achievement award UCLA, 1974, 84; named one of 200 Future Leaders Time mag., 1974, Alumni of Yr., UCLA, 1996; recipient Achievement awards C.M.E. Chs.; numerous other awards, citations.; fellow Inst. Politics John F. Kennedy Sch. Govt. Harvard, 1971-72; Chubb fellow Yale, 1972 Office: 500 W Temple St Rm 866 Los Angeles CA 90012 Office Phone: 213-972-2222. Business E-Mail: yburke@bos.lacounty.gov.

BURKET, JOHN MCVEY, retired dermatologist; b. Des Moines, Oct. 4, 1935; s. George Austin and Elma (McVey) B.; m. Janice Lee Feilmeyer, Dec. 29, 1956; children: Denise, Bradley, Brent, Diana, Dawn, Brian. BA, U. Iowa, 1957, MD, 1960. Diplomate Am. Bd. Dermatology, Am. Bd. Dermopathology. Resident in dermatology U. Iowa Hosp., Iowa City, 1964; chief dermatology USAF, March AFB, 1964-66; pvt. practice dermatology Medford, Oreg., 1966—. Contbr. articles to profl. jours., chpts. to books. Avocations: hunting, fishing.

BURKETT, MARVIN D., electronics executive; b. 1943; BS, MBA, U. Ariz. With semicondr. divsn. Raytheon Co., to 1972; v.p., contr., chief planning officer Advanced Micro Devices, Inc., 1972-88, sr. v.p., chief adminstrv. officer, CFO, 1989-98; exec. v.p. worldwide fin., CFO, Packard Bell NEC Inc., Sacramento, 1998—; CFO, chief adminstrv. officer Arcot Sys., Inc., Santa Clara, Calif., 2000—. Office: Arcot Systems Inc 455 W Maude Ave # 210 Sunnyvale CA 94085-3517

BURKEY, MARCIA B., corporate financial executive; Degree, Macalester Coll.; M, Columbia U. Various sr. fin. positions SBC Warburg (now UBS Warburg); various exec. fin. positions including regional mgr. Bechtel Enterprises Holdings Inc., San Francisco, 1996-2000, mng. dir., CFO, 2000—.

BURKHART, WILLIAM HENRY, lawyer; b. Chgo., Jan. 3, 1931; s. Claude Albert and Mary Vern (Hall) B.; m. Rosemary Purcell, Apr. 28, 1973; 1 child, Aaron. BS Bus., Northwestern U., 1953; JD, U. Mich., 1958, MBA, 1959; LLM Taxation, NYU, 1963. Bar: Mich. 1958, N.Y. 1964, Washington 1975; CPA, Mich. Tax supr. Coopers & Lybrand, Detroit, 1960-62; assoc. atty. Cahill Gordon & Reindel, NYC, 1963-72; tax ptnr. Preston, Gates & Ellis, Seattle, 1974—. Chmn. Seattle Tax Group, 1986, Seattle Internat. Tax Roundtable, 1983-85; bd. dirs. Atty. CPA Tax Clinic, Seattle. Lt. (j.g.) USN, 1953-55. Mem. Washington Athletic Club. Home: 10554 Riviera Pl NE Seattle WA 98125-6937 Office: 925 4th Ave Ste 2900 Seattle WA 98104-1158 E-mail: billb@prestongates.com.

BURLINGAME, ALMA LYMAN, chemist, educator; b. Cranston, RI, Apr. 29, 1937; s. Herman Follett Jr. and Rose Irene (Kohler) B.; children: Mark, Walter; m. Marilyn F. Schwartz, Feb. 14, 1993 (dec. Aug. 24, 2004); 1 stepchild, Corey Schwartz. BS, U. R.I., 1959; PhD, MIT, 1962. Asst. prof. U. Calif., Berkeley, 1963-68, assoc. chemist, 1968-72, rsch. chemist, 1972-78, prof. San Francisco, 1978—, Univ. Coll., London, 1996—2002. Vis. prof. Ludwig Inst. for Cancer Rsch., London, 1993-94. Editor: Topics in Organic Mass Spectrometry, 1970, Mass Spectrometry in Health and Life Science, 1985, Biological Mass Spectrometry, 1990, Mass Spectrometry in the Biological Sciences, 1995, Mass Spectrometry in Biology and Medicine, 2000, Biological Mass Spectrometry, Methods in Enzymology, 2005, Mass Spectrometry: Modified Proteins and Glycoconjugates, Methods in Enzymology, 2005; co-editor: Molecular and Cellular Proteomics, 2006—; dep. editor Molecular and Cellular Proteomics, 2002—06; contbr. articles to profl. jours. With USAR, 1954-62. Guggenheim Found. fellow, 1970. Fellow AAAS. Office: U Calif Dept Pharm Chemistry San Francisco CA 94143-0446 Office Phone: 415-476-5641. Business E-Mail: alb@cgl.ucsf.edu.

BURNETT, CHARLES, film director, screenwriter, producer; b. Vicksburg, Miss., Apr. 13, 1944; m. Gaye Shannon-Burnett; children: Johnathan, Steven. BA, UCLA, 1971, MFA, 1977. Dir., co-writer: (documentaries) America Becoming, 1991; dir.: Dr. Endesha Ida Mae Holland, 1998; (TV films) Nightjohn, 1996, Oprah Winfrey Presents: The Wedding, 1998, Selma, Lord, Selma, 1999, Finding Buck McHenry, 2000; dir., co-writer: Nat Turner: A Troublesome Property, 2003; dir.: (films) Several Friends, 1969, The Horse, 1973, The Final Insult, 1997, The Annihilation of Fish, 2000; dir., writer, prodr., cinematographer, editor: Killer of Sheep, 1977 (US Film Festival Spl. Jury prize, 1981, Berlin Film Festival Critics' prize, 1981, NY Film Critics Cir. Spl. Critics' award, 2007); dir., writer, prodr., cinematographer My Brother's Wedding, 1983; writer, cinematographer Bless Their Little Hearts, 1984; dir., writer To Sleep with Anger, 1990 (Sundance Film Festival Spl. Jury prize, 1990, Nat. Soc. Film Critics award for screenplay, 1990, Ind. Spirit award for dir. and screenplay, 1990); The Glass Shield, 1995; When It Rains, 1995; Namibia: The Struggle for Liberation, 2007; dir., editor Olivia's Story, 2000. MacArthur Found. grantee, 1988-93, Nat. Endowment for the Arts grantee, 1985, Rockefeller Found. Fellowship, 1988, Spl. Achievement Honor, African Am. Film Critics Assn., 2007. Office: Broder Kurland Webb Uffner 10250 Constellation Blvd Los Angeles CA 90067-6200

BURNETT, JERRY, state treasurer; MBA, U. Alaska Southeast, 1987, MPA, 1989. Adminstrv. services dir. Alaska Dept. Corrections; adminstrv. services dir., legis. liaison Alaska Dept. Revenue, Juneau, 2004—08, acting dep. commr. treasury divsn., 2008, dep. commr. treasury divsn., 2009—. Adj. prof. bus. U. Alaska Southeast, 1983—2002. Office: Juneau Commrs Office PO Box 110400 Juneau AK 99811-0400 Office Phone: 907-465-2300, 907-465-3669. Fax: 907-465-2389. E-mail: jerry.burnett@alaska.gov.*

BURNETT, T-BONE (HENRY JOHN BURNETT), music producer, musician; b. St. Louis, Jan. 14, 1948; m. Sam Phillips, 1989 (div.); 1 child, Simone. Rec. artist: (with Alpha Band) The Alpha Band, 1976, Spark in the Dark, 1977, The Statue Makers of Hollywood, 1978, (with Elvis Costello as the Coward Brothers) The People's Limousine, 1985, (solo recs. as J. Henry Burnett) The B-52 Band & the Fabulous Skylarks, 1972, (solo recs.) Truth Decay, 1980, Trap Door, 1983, Proof Through the Night, 1983, Behind the Trap Door, 1984, T Bone Burnett, 1986, The Talking Animals, 1988, The Criminal Under My Own Hat, 1992, The True False Identity, 2006, Twenty Twenty, 2006, Tooth of Crime, 2008; prodr.: Sunday Kind of Love for The Van Dykes, 1966, Paralyzed for The Legendary Stardust Cowboy, 1968, Delbert and Glen for Delbert and Glen, 1971, Live at the New Bluebird Nightclub for Robert Ealey and His Five Careless Lovers, 1972, There Is a Love for Maria Muldaur, 1982, Time Step for Leo Kottke, 1983, ...And a Time to Dance for Los Lobos, 1985, Downtown for Marshall Crenshaw, 1985, Peter Case for Peter Case, 1986, King of America for Elvis Costello, 1986, Love and Hope and Sex and Dreams for BoDeans, 1986, The Turning for Leslie (Sam) Phillips, 1987, By the Light of the Moon for Los Lobos, 1987, In Dreams: His Greatest Hits for Roy Orbison, 1987, Spike for Elvis Costello, 1988, Shuffletown for Joe Henry, 1990, Cruel Inventions for Sam Phillips, 1991, Nothing but a Burning Light for Bruce Cockburn, 1991, Go Slow Down for BoDeans, 1993, August and Everything After for Counting Crows, 1993, Martinis and Bikinis for Sam Philips, 1994, Dart to the Hart for Bruce Cockburn, 1994, Bringing Down the Horse for The Wallflowers, 1996, Electro-Shok Blues for Eels, 1998, Five Easy Pieces, 1998, Hell Among the Yearlings for Gillian Welch, 1998, Evan & Jaron, 2000, Down from the Mountain, 2001 (Grammy award for Best Traditional Folk Album), A Wonderful World, 2003 (Grammy award for Best Traditional Pop Album), They Ain't Making Jews Like Jesus Anymore for Kinky Friedman, 2005, Raising Sand for Robert Plant and Alison Krauss, 2007 (Grammy award for Album of Yr., 2009), Story for Brandi Carlile, 2007, Life Death Love and Freedom for John Mellencamp, 2008, One Kind Favor for B.B. King, 2008; prodr. (film & TV soundtracks) Stealing Beauty, 1996, The Big Lebowski, 1998, Clay Pigeons, 1998, Hope Floats, 1998, The Horse Whisperer, 1998, Down to You, 2000, Keeping the Faith, 2000, O Brother, Where Art Thou?, 2000 (2 Grammy awards for Album of Yr. and Best Soundtrack Album), Jay & Silent Bob Strike Back, 2001, Divine Secrets of the Ya-Ya Sisterhood, 2002, Our Little Corner of the World, 2002, Cold Mountain, 2003 (Anthony Asquith award for Film Music, BAFTA, 2004), Crossing Jordan, 2003, A Mighty Wind, 2003, The L Word, 2004, The Ladykillers, 2004, Walk the Line, 2005 (Grammy award for Best Compilation Soundtrack Album, 2007), Happy Feet, 2006, Across the Universe, 2007. Named Songwriter of Yr., Rolling Stone Critics Poll, 1983; recipient Grammy award for Best Non-Classical Prodr. of Yr., 2001. Office: Addis Wechsler 955 Carrillo Dr Fl 3 Los Angeles CA 90048-5400

BURNHAM, CLIFFORD WAYNE, geology educator, director; b. Murietta, Calif., Oct. 24, 1922; AB magna cum laude, Pomona Coll., 1951; MS in Geology, Calif. Inst. Tech., 1953, PhD in Geochem., 1955. Geologist Riverside Cement co., 1951; asst. prof. econ. geology Pa. State U., 1955-59, assoc. prof. geochem., 1959-65, prof. geochem., 1965-86, prof. emeritus, 1986—, head dept. geoscis., 1974-85. Adj. prof. U. Ind., 1987—. Ariz. State U., 1992—. Contbr.

articles to profl. jours. Lt. USN, 1942-46. Fellow Am. Geophys. Union, Geol. Soc. Am. (Roebling medal 1998), Mineralogical Soc. Am.; mem. AAAS, Geochem. Soc. (pres. 1974), Soc. Econ. Geologists, Phi Beta Kappa, Sigma Xi.

BURNHAM, JOHN LUDWIG, agent; b. LA, Mar. 1, 1953; s. Jerome Ludwig and Linda (Benjamin) B.; m. Andrea Buckland Feldstein, Aug. 12, 1989; 1 child, Daisy. BA, UCLA, 1976, JD, 1980. Agt. Kohnner Levy, LA, 1979-81, ICM, LA, 1981-84, William Morris Agy., Beverly Hills, Calif., 1984—, co-head, sr. v.p. movie dept., 1991—. Office: William Morris Agy Inc 1 William Morris Pl Beverly Hills CA 90212 Office Phone: 310-859-4000. Office Fax: 310-859-4462.

BURNINGHAM, KIM RICHARD, educational association administrator, former state legislator; b. Salt Lake City, Sept. 14, 1936; s. Rulon and Margie (Stringham) Burningham; m. Susan Ball Clarke, Dec. 19, 1968; children: Christian, Tyler David. BS, U. Utah, 1960; MA, U. Ariz., 1967; MFA, U. So. Calif., 1977. Cert. secondary tchr., Utah. Tchr. Bountiful (Utah) High Sch., 1960-88; mem. Utah Ho. of Reps., Salt Lake City, 1979-94; cons. Shipley Assocs., Bountiful, 1989-94, Franklin Covey, 1994—. Gubernatorial appointee as exec. dir. Utah Statehood Centennial Commn., 1994—96; mem. Utah State Bd. Edn., 1999—, vice chmn., 2000—01, chmn., 2001—07; bd. dirs. Nat. Assn. State Bds. Edn., 2000—01, pres.-elect, 2004, pres., 2005—06, past pres., 2006, bd. dir., 2009—. Author dramas for stage and film, also articles; columnist, Davis County Clipper, 2000—. Mem. state strategic planning com. Utah Tomorrow, 1989—2003. Recipient Carl Perkins Humanitarian of Yr. award, ACTE, 2002, Hero of Edn. award, Utah Sch. Bds. Assn., 2008, Friends of Children award, Utah PTA, 2008. Mem. NEA, PTA (life), Utah Edn. Assn., Davis Edn. Assn., Nat. Forensic League. Mem. Lds Ch. Avocations: gardening, history. Home: 932 Canyon Crest Dr Bountiful UT 84010-2002 E-mail: krb84010@aol.com.

BURNISON, BOYD EDWARD, lawyer; b. Arnolds Park, Iowa, Dec. 12, 1934; s. Boyd WIlliam and Lucile (Harnden) B.; m. Mari Amaral; children: Erica Lafore, Alison Katherine. BS, Iowa State U., 1957; JD, U. Calif., Berkeley, 1961. Bar: Calif. 1962, U.S. Supreme Ct. 1971, U.S. Dist. Ct. (no. dist.) Calif. 1962, U.S. Ct. Appeals (9th cir.) 1962, U.S. Dist. Ct. (ea. dist.) Calif. 1970, U.S. Dist. Ct. (ctrl. dist.) Calif. 1992. Dep. counsel Yolo County, Calif., 1962-65; assoc. Steel & Arostegui, Marysville, Calif., 1965-66, St. Sure, Moore & Hoyt, Oakland, Calif., 1966-70; ptnr. St. Sure, Moore, Hoyt & Sizoo, Oakland and San Francisco, 1970-75; v.p. Crosby, Heafey, Roach & May, P.C., Oakland, 1975-2000, also bd. dirs.; pres. Boyd E Burnison A Profl. Law Corp., Walnut Creek, Calif., 2001—05, Diablo, 2005—. Advisor Berkeley YMCA, 1971—, Yolo County YMCA, 1962—65, bd. dir., 1965; trustee, sec., legal counsel Easter Seal Found., Alameda County, 1974—79, hon. trustee, 1979—; trustee Alameda County Law Libr., 2001—, v.p., 2003—05, pres., 2005—07; mem. Diablo Mcpl. advisory coun., 2007—; bd. dir. Easter Seal Soc. Crippled Children and Adults of Alameda County Calif., 1972—75, Moot Ct. Bd., U. Calif., 1960—61, East Bay Conservation Corps, 1997—2000, treas., 2000. Named Vol. of Yr., Berkeley YMCA, 1999. Fellow: ABA Found. (life); mem.: ABA (equal employment law com., labor rels., employment law sect. 1972—2004), Sproul Assoc. Boalt Hall Law Sch. U. Calif. Berkeley, Indsl. Rels. Rsch. Assn., Contra Costa County Bar Assn. (labor law sect.), Bar Assn. San Francisco (labor law sect.), Yuba Sutter Bar Assn., Yolo County Bar Assn. (sec. 1965), Alameda County Bar Found. (bd. dirs. 1993—95), Alameda County Bar Assn. (chmn. memberships and directory com. 1973—74, chmn. law office econs. com. 1975—77, chmn. memberships and directory com. 1980, assn. dir. 1981—85, vice chmn. bench bar liaison com. 1983, pres. 1984, chmn. 1984, Disting. Svc. award 1987), State Bar Calif. (spl. labor counsel 1981—84, labor and employment law sect. 1982—), Nat. Conf. Bar Pres.'s, Rotary (Paul Harris fellow), Round Hill Country Club, Iowa State Alumni Assn., Order Knoll, Phi Delta Phi, Pi Kappa Alpha. Democrat. Home: PO Box 743 2704 Caballo Ranchero Dr Diablo CA 94528-0743 Office: Boyd E Burnison A Profl Law Corp PO Box 743 Diablo CA 94528 Home Phone: 925-820-3019; Office Phone: 925-855-9032. Office Fax: 925-855-9332. Personal E-mail: bburnison@sbcglobal.net.

BURNS, BRENDA, state senator; b. LaGrange, Ga., Nov. 22, 1950; 3 children. Mem. Ariz. Senate, Dist. 17, Phoenix, 1994—; pres. Ariz. Senate, 1996—2000. Nat. chair Am. Leg. Exch. Coun., 1999; exec. bd. Am. Legis. Exch. Coun. Republican.

BURNS, BRIAN PATRICK, lawyer; b. Cambridge, Mass., July 12, 1936; s. John Joseph and Alice (Blake) B.; m. Sheila Ann O'Connor, June 23, 1962; children: Sheila Ann, Brian Patrick, Sean Richard, Roderick O'Connor. BA, Holy Cross Coll., 1957; LLB, Harvard U., 1960. Bar: Mass. 1960, N.Y. 1961, Calif. 1965. Law clk., spl. asst. to regional adminstr. New York Regional Office, SEC, 1958-59; assoc. Webster, Sheffield, Fleischmann, Hitchcock & Brookfield, NYC, 1960-64; ptnr. Cullinan, Hancock, Rothert & Burns, San Francisco, 1965-74; sr. ptnr. Cullinan, Burns & Helmer, San Francisco, 1975-78; firm Burns & Whitehead, San Francisco, 1978-86; chmn., chief exec. officer, chmn. exec. com. Boothe Fin. Corp., San Francisco, 1981-87, also bd. dirs.; chmn. Robert Half Internat. Inc., 1987-88; chmn., CEO BF Enterprises Inc., 1987—. Dir. U.S. Banknote Corp., N.Y.C., from 1967, chmn. exec. and fin. coms., 1973-76; dir. Coca Cola Bottling Co., N.Y., 1974-86, chmn. exec. com., 1979-86; dir. Kellogg Co., 1979-89, chmn. fin. com. 1984-89; dir. Calif. Jockey, 1980-89; dir., chmn. audit com. Flexi-Van Corp., N.Y.C., 1984-85; dir., chmn. exec. com. Pinnacle Petroleum Corp., The Woodlands, Tex., 1983-85; dir., chmn. ops. review com. Brink's Inc., Chgo., 1976-78; dir., chmn. acquisition com. Pacific Holding Corp., Los Angeles, 1972-78; dir., mem. exec. com. Beverly Wilshire Hotel, Beverly Hills, Calif., Calif., 1967-86; dir., chmn. exec. com. USR Industries, The Woodlands, 1980-83; dir., chmn. audit com. ROCOR Internat., Palo Alto, Calif., 1976-82; underwriting mem. Lloyds of London, 1978-89; lectr. continuing edn. of bar U. Calif., 1969, 74, 76, advanced bus. seminar, 1971; seminar on investment opportunities in wine industry McGraw Hill Coll., N.Y., 1973, Legal Edn. Inst., 1976. Bd. dirs. Boys Club of San Francisco, 1971-80, Am. Irish Found., 1978-87, Am. Ireland Fund, 1987—; trustee Holy Cross Coll., 1978-89. Mem. ABA (mem. small bus. com. corp. bus. and banking sect. 1972-76), State Bar Cal. (vice chmn. com. on corps. 1971-75), Bar Assn. San Francisco (chmn. com. on corp. banking and bus. law 1968-69), Calif. Jockey Club (dir. San Mateo, Calif. 1988-89). Clubs: Royal Dublin Soc.; Bohemian, Burlingame Country, Family, Olympic, Sky, N.Y. Athletic, Les Ambassadeurs, Mil. and Hospitaller Order St. Lazarus of Jerusalem (comdr. companion). Roman Catholic. Office: BF Enterprises Inc 100 Bush St Ste 1250 San Francisco CA 94104-3914

BURNS, EDWARD J., JR., actor, film director; b. Valley Stream, NY, Jan. 29, 1968; s. Edward Sr. and Molly Burns; m. Christy Turlington, June 7, 2003; children: Grace, Finn. BA, Hunter Coll. Entrepreneur Irish Twin Prodn. Co. Co-owner Irish Twins Prodn. Co.; owner Marlboro Road Gang Films. Actor, dir., writer (films) The Brothers McMullen, 1995 (Jury Spl. prize Deauville Film Festival, 1995, Ind. Spirit award, 1995, Nova award, 1995, Grand Jury prize Sundance Film Festival, 1995), She's the One, 1996, No Looking Back, 1998, Sidewalks of New York, 2001; actor: (films) Saving Private Ryan, 1998, Any Given Sunday, 1999, 15 Minutes, 2001, Life or Something Like It, 2002, Confidence, 2003, The River King, 2005, A Sound of Thunder, 2005, The Holiday, 2006, One Missed Call, 2008; actor, dir. (films) Looking for Kitty, 2004, writer, actor, prodr., dir. Ash Wednesday, 2002, writer, prodr. (TV series) The Fighting Fitzgeralds, 2001, writer (films) Flight of the Phoenix, 2004. Recipient ShoWest award for Screenwriter of Yr., 1996.

BURNS, MARCELLINE, retired psychologist, researcher; BA in Psychology, San Diego State U., 1955; MA, Calif. State U., LA, 1969; PhD, U. Calif., Irvine, 1972. Co-founder So. Calif. Rsch. Inst., LA, 1973—2003, ret., 2003. Cons., expert witness alcohol and drug effects on performance, FSTs, HGN, and drug recognition; lectr. in field. Contbr. articles to profl. jours. Recipient Public Svc. award U.S. Dept. Trans., 1993. Achievements include research on alcohol and drug effects, field sobriety tests and drug recognition. Office Phone: 805-382-4696. Personal E-mail: mburns4430@roadrunner.com.

BURNS, MARVIN GERALD, lawyer; b. LA, July 3, 1930; s. Milton and Belle (Cytron) B.; m. Barbara Irene Fisher, Aug. 23, 1953; children: Scott Douglas, Jody Lynn, Bradley Frederick. BA, U. Ariz., 1951; JD, Harvard U., 1954. Bar: Calif. 1955. With US Army, 1955—56. Mem.: Beverly Hills Tennis, Sycamore Park Tennis. Home: 10350 Wilshire Blvd Ph 4 Los Angeles CA 90024-4734 Office: 9107 Wilshire Blvd Ste 800 Beverly Hills CA 90210-5533 Home Phone: 310-275-4045; Office Phone: 310-278-6500. Business E-Mail: mburns@lurie-zepeda.com. E-mail: burns5401@aol.com.

BURNS, MICHAEL JOSEPH, operations and sales-marketing executive; b. Passaic, NJ, Feb. 18, 1943; s. Michael Joseph and Ellen Kathryn B.; m. Emma Anne, Dec. 19, 1964; children: Michael, Jeffrey, Tricia, Stephen. BA in English, William Paterson Univ., Wayne, NJ, 1964; JD, Seton Hall U., Newark, 1975. Bar: NJ 1975. Purchasing analyst Am. Brands Co., 1972-75; div. purchasing mgr. Dutch Boy Paints, NL Industries, 1975-76; v.p. purchasing Dutch Boy, Inc., 1977-78; pres., gen. mgr. Dutch Boy, Inc. (Dutch Boy coatings div.), 1978-80; pres., CEO Kroehler Mfg. Co., Naperville, Ill., 1980-88; pres., COO Rymer Co., Rolling Meadows, Ill., 1983-88; pres. Emerald Group, Lake Forest, Ill., 1989-90; pres., CEO Designer Foods, Inc., Wilmington, Del., 1990-91; chmn., pres., CEO SeaWatch Internat., Ltd., Easton, Md., 1991-99; pres., CEO Pioneer Human Svcs., Seattle, 1999—2007; ret. Bd. dirs. Second Chance, 1999-07, Eastside Acad., 2001-07. Served to capt. USMCR, 1964-67, Vietnam. NJ State scholar; recipient Disting. Alumni award Wm. Paterson Univ. Mem. ABA, Am. Arbitration Assn. Presbyterian. Office Phone: 206-768-1990. Personal E-mail: mike.burns@p-h-s.com.

BURNS, RICHARD DEAN, historian, educator, writer; b. Des Moines, June 16, 1929; s. Richard B. and Luella (Everling) B.; m. Frances R. Sullivan, Jan. 14, 1950 (dec. July 1993); 1 son, Richard Dean; m. Glenda F. Burns, Sept. 21, 1996; stepchildren: Scott E. Burns, Kent C. Burns, Dana Burns Mayadag. BS with honors, U. Ill., 1957, MA, 1958, PhD, 1960. Prof. emeritus Calif. State U., LA, 1960-92, prof., 1970-92, chmn. dept., 1969-72, 86-92. Pubr./pres. Regina Books, 1980—; vis. lectr. L.A. City Coll., Whittier Coll., U. Minn., Mpls., 1964-65, UCLA, U. So. Calif.; program cons., lectr. Western Ctr., NEH, 1973-75. Author: (with W. Fisher) Armament and Disarmament, 1964, (with D. Urquidi) Disarmament in Historical Perspective, 4 vols, 1969, (with E. Bennett) Diplomats in Crisis, 1975; (with L. Brune) The Quest for Missile Defenses: 1944-2003, 2004, (with Joseph M. Siracusa) Historical Dictionary of the Kennedy: Johnson Era, 2007, (with N.A. Graebner, & J. Siracusa) Revisiting the End of the Cold War, 2008, The Evolution of Arms Control: From Antiquity to the Nuclear Age, 2009; editor: An Arms Control and Disarmament Bibliography, 1977, Guide to American Foreign Relations Since 1770, 1982, (with M. Leitenberg) The Wars in Vietnam, Cambodia, and Laos, 1945-82, 1984, Harry S. Truman: A Bibliography of His Times and Presidency, 1984, Herbert Hoover: A Bibliography of His Times and Presidency, 1991, Encyclopedia of Arms Control and Disarmament, 3 vols., 1993, (with A. DeConde, F. Logevall) Encyclopedia of American Foreign Policy, 3 vols., 2002, (with Lester Brune) Chronological History of U.S. Foreign Relations, 3 vols., 2002, Chronology of the Cold War, 2005; bibliographer, series editor: War/Peace Bibliographies, 1973—; contbr. articles to profl. jours. Served with USAF, 1947-56. Named Univ. Outstanding Prof., 1978-79; Social Sci. Rsch. Coun. fellow, 1959-60; grantee NEH, 1978-79, U.S. Inst. Peace, 1991-92. Mem. Conf. on Peace Rsch. (nat. coun. 1970-72), Soc. Historians Am. Fgn. Rels. (nat. coun. 1986-89), Phi Kappa Phi, Phi Alpha Theta. Office: Regina Books PO Box 280 Claremont CA 91711-0280 Office Phone: 909-624-8466.

BURNS, ROBERT, state legislator; b. Rolfe, Iowa, May 26, 1938; m. Gayle Burns, 1960; children: Mark, Michael. Student, Glendale Cmty. Coll. Aviation electronics technician USN, 1958—62; programming analyst Honeywell, 1962—78; pres. BGM Investments Inc., 1971—; mem. Ariz. House of Reps., 1989—2000; mem. Dist. 9 Ariz. State Senate, 2003—, pres. Bd. dirs. Ctrl. Ariz. Water Conservation Dist., 2001—02; mem. West Glendale Cmty. Coalition. Bd. dirs. Friends of West Valley Recreation Corridor. Mem.: Ariz. State C. of C., Glendale Catlin Ct. Merchants Assn., Glendale C. of C., Nat. Fedn. Ind. Businesses, Phoenix C. of C., Glendale Kachina Rotary Club, Sun City Rep. Club. Republican. Roman Catholic. Office: Ariz State Senate Capitol Complex 1700 W Washington Rm 204 Phoenix AZ 85007-2890 Office Phone: 602-926-5993. Office Fax: 602-417-3255. Business E-Mail: rburns@azleg.gov.*

BURNS, SCOTT, columnist; b. Cambridge, Mass., Nov. 9, 1940; s. Robert Milton Clark Burns and Joanne (Mahoney) Blasius; m. Allegra Wendy Eames, Dec. 11, 1965 (div. Sept. 1990); children: Jasper Bayard (dec.), Oliver Byron; m. Carolyn Jo Schroeder, Jan. 2, 1995. BS, MIT, 1962. Columnist, editor Boston (Mass.) Herald Am., 1977-83; columnist Dallas (Tex.) Morning News, 1985—2006; syndicated columnist, 1980—. Author: Squeeze It Til The Eagle Grins, 1972, Home, Inc., 1975; co-author: The Coming Generational Storm, 2004. Home: 50 Calle Sin Sonte Santa Fe NM 87507 Personal E-mail: sburnscolumn@yahoo.com.

BURNSIDE, MARY BETH, biology professor, researcher; b. San Antonio, Apr. 23, 1943; d. Neil Delmont and Luella Nixon (Kenley) B. BA, U. Tex., 1965, MA, 1967, PhD in Zoology, 1968. Instr. med. sch. Harvard U., Boston, 1970-73; asst. prof. U. Pa., Phila., 1973-76, U. Calif., Berkeley, 1976-77, assoc. prof., 1977-82, prof., 1982—, dean biol. scis., 1984-90, chancellor prof., 1996-99, vice chancellor rsch., 2000—. Mem. nat. adv. eye coun. NIH, 1990-94; mem. sci. adv. bd. Lawrence Hall of Sci., Berkeley, 1983—, Whitney Labs., St. Augustine, Fla., 1993-97; mem. bd. sci. councillors Nat. Eye Inst., 1994—. Mem. editl. bd. Invest. Ophthalmol. Vis. Sci., 1992-94; contbr. numerous articles to profl. jours. Mem. sci. adv. bd. Mills Coll., Oakland, Calif., 1986-90; trustee Bermuda Biol. Sta., St. George's, 1978-83; dir. Miller Inst., Berkeley, Calif., 1995-98. Recipient Merit award NIH, 1989-99, Outstanding Alumna award U. Tex., 1999; rsch. grantee, NIH, 1972—, NSF. Fellow AAAS; mem. Am. Soc. Cell Biology (coun. 1980-84). Avocation: hiking. Office: U Calif MC # 3200 335 Life Scis Addn # 3200 Berkeley CA 94720-0001

BURR, ROBERT LYNDON, information services specialist; b. Boonville, NY, May 9, 1944; s. James Isaac and Virginia Ellen (Davidson) B.; m. Angela Delores Tucci, June 26, 1965; 1 son, Robert Anthony. Student, U. Rochester, 1962-65; AB, Canisius Coll., 1972; MS in L.S, Case-Western Res. U., 1973; Ed.D., Gonzaga U., 1981. Asst. prodn. mgr., purchasing mgr. Carleton Controls Corp., Buffalo, 1966-71; asst. to pres. Audn Corp., Buffalo, 1971-72; circulation services librarian Coll. William and Mary, Williamsburg, Va., 1973-77; dean libr. svcs. Gonzaga U., Spokane, 1977—, adj. asso. prof. edn., 1979—, assoc. acad. v.p., 1996—. Library cons. Contbr. articles to profl. jours. Trustee Mus. Native Am. Cultures, 1979—. Served with AUS, 1967-69. Mem. ALA (nat. research award 1974), Nat. Libraries Assn., Wash. Library Assn., Pacific N.W. Library Assn., AAUP, Mensa, Moses Lake Golf and Country Club. Office: Gonzaga U Foley Ctr 502 E Boone Ave Spokane WA 99258-0001

BURRELL, GARLAND E., JR., federal judge; b. LA, July 4, 1947; BA in Sociology, Calif. State U., 1972; MSW, Washington U., Mo., 1976; JD, Calif. Wes. Sch. Law, 1976. Bar: Calif. 1976, U.S. Dist. Ct. (ea. dist.) Calif. 1976, U.S. Ct. Appeals (9th cir.) 1981. Dep. dist. atty. Sacramento County, Calif., 1976-78; dep city atty. Sacramento, 1978-79; asst. U.S. atty., dep. chief civil divsn. Office of U.S. Atty. for Ea. Dist. Calif., 1979-85, asst. U.S. atty., chief civil divsn., 1990-92; litigation atty. Stockman Law Corp., Sacramento, Calif., 1985-86; sr. dep. city atty. Office of City Atty., Sacramento, 1986-90; judge U.S. Dist. Ct. (ea. dist.) Calif., Sacramento, 1992—. With USMC, 1966-68. Office: Dist Ct 501 I St Sacramento CA 95814-7300

BURROUGHS, GARY L., city official; b. Independence, Kans., Apr. 9, 1943; Auditor City of Long Beach, 1992—. Office: Office of City Auditor Civic Center Plz 333 W Ocean Blvd Fl 8 Long Beach CA 90802-4604

BURROWS, JAMES, television and motion picture director, producer; b. LA, Dec. 30, 1940; s. Abe Burrows. BA, Oberlin Coll.; MFA, Yale U. Co-founder Charles Burrows Charles Productions. Off-Broadway prodns.: dir. (motion picture) Partners, 1982, (TV films) Butterflies, 1978, More Than Friends, 1978, Every Stray Dog and Kid, 1981, Dexter Prep Pilot, 2002, (TV pilots) Lou Grant, Dear John, Night Court, Wings, Roc, Stark Raving Mad, The Weber Show/ Cursed, The Boys Are Bak, 1994, Veronica's Closet, 1997, Good Morning, Miami, 2002, Bram and Alice, 2002, Two and a Half Men, 2003,(TV series episodes) The Mary Tyler Moore Show, The Bob Newhart Show, Frasier, Friends, Newsradio, Third Rock from the Sun, (TV series) Rhoda, 1974-78, Laverne & Shirley, 1976-83, Busting Loose, 1977, The Betty White Show, 1977-78, Husbands, Wives & Lovers, 1978, Taxi, 1978-82, A New Kind of Family, 1979, The Associates, 1979-80, Good Time Harry, 1980, Night Court, 1984-92, Valerie, 1986-88, The Tortellis, 1987, Wings, 1990-97, The Fanelli Boys, 1990-91, Flying Blind, 1992-93, Cafe American, 1993-94, The Preston Episodes, 1995, Partners, 1995-96, Hudson Street, 1995, Caroline in the City, 1995-99, Men Behaving Badly, 1996-97, George & Leo, 1997-98, Dharma & Greg, 1997-2002, Union Square, 1997-98, Conrad Boom, 1998, Jessie, 1998-2000, Stark Raving Mad, 1999-2000, Ladies Man, 1999-2001, Madigan Men, 2000, Cursed, 2000-01, The Stones, 2004, Beverly Hills S.U.V., 2006, Four Kings, 2006, Courting Alex, 2006, Teachers, 2006, Back to You, 2007-; co-creator, co-exec. producer, dir. Cheers, 1982-93, exec. producer, dir. The Secret Lives of Men, 1998, All is Forgiven, 1986, Will & Grace, 1998-2006. Recipient Dirs. Guild Am. award for comedy direction, 1984, 91, 94, 99, Emmy awards NATAS for dir. in comedy series Taxi, 1979-80, 81-82 seasons, Cheers, 1982-83, 90-91 seasons; Emmy award as co-producer Cheers, 1982-83, 83-84, 89-90, 90-91 seasons; Emmy award as director of a Comedy Series for Fraiser, 1994, American Comedy award for Lifetime Achievement, 1996, US Comedy Festival Career Tribute award, 2006; named to Acad. TV Arts & Sciences Hall of Fame, 2006 Office: Broder Webb Chervin Silbermann 10250 Constellation Blvd Ste P Los Angeles CA 90067-6213

BURSLEY, KATHLEEN A., lawyer; b. Washington, Mar. 20, 1954; d. G.H. Patrick and Claire (Mulvany) B. BA, Pomona Coll., 1976; JD, Cornell U., 1979. Bar: N.Y. 1980, U.S. Dist. Ct. (ea. and so. dists.) N.Y. 1980, U.S. Ct. Appeals (5th and 11th cirs.) 1981, Fla. 1984, U.S. Dist. Ct. (mid. dist.) Fla. 1984, Tex. 1985, Mass. 1995. Assoc. Haight, Gardner, Poor & Havens, NYC, 1979-81; counsel Harcourt Brace Jovanovich, Inc., NYC and Orlando, Fla., 1981-85, v.p. and counsel San Antonio and Orlando, 1985-92; assoc. gen. counsel pub. Harcourt Gen., Inc., Chestnut Hill, Mass., 1992—; gen. counsel Harcourt, Inc., Chestnut Hill, Mass., 1992—; v.p. Harcourt Gen., Inc., 1998—. Mem. Maritime Law Assn. (proctor). Home: 3839 Chestnut Ave Long Beach CA 90807-3203 E-mail: kbursley@harcourtgeneral.com.

BURT, RICHARD, lawyer; V.p. fin. and devel. Sandoz Corp., 1978—89, v.p., gen. counsel, sec., 1978—89; v.p. legal affairs ABB subs. Asea Brown Boveri Ltd., NY, 1989; sr. v.p., gen. counsel, sec. ABB Inc. N.Am. subs. ABB Group, Zurich, Switzerland; sr. v.p., gen. counsel Bechtel, San Francisco, 2002—. Mem.: Am. Corp. Counsel Assn. (Westchester/So. Conn. chpt.).

BURT, THOMAS WILLIAM, computer software company executive, lawyer; b. Spokane, Wash., Jan. 24, 1955; s. Jack Wallace and Peggy (Windes) Burt; m. Ann Darling, Apr. 2, 1989; children: Trevor D., Griffin D., Caroline D. AB in Human Biology, Stanford U., 1976; JD, U. Wash., 1979. Bar: Wash. 1979, U.S. Ct. Appeals (9th cir.) 1979, U.S. Dist. Ct. (we. dist.) Wash. 1980. Law clk. to judge Ozell Trask U.S. Ct. Appeals (9th cir.), Phoenix, 1979-80; ptnr., atty. Riddell, Williams, Bullitt & Walkinshaw, Seattle, 1980-95; corp. v.p., dep. gen. counsel litig. Microsoft Corp., Redmond, Wash., 2003—. Bd. dirs.

Bainbridge Island Land Trust, Wash. 1990-91. Mem. ABA, Wash. Bar Assn., Seattle-King County Bar. Avocations: sports car racing, skiing, sailing. Office: Microsoft Corp One Microsoft Way Redmond WA 98052 Office Phone: 425-703-6323. Business E-Mail: tburt@microsoft.com.

BURTENSHAW, DON M., state senator; b. Shelton, Idaho, Aug. 14, 1933; m. Beverly Burtenshaw; children: Michel, Steven, Lynn, Van, Sharon, Annette, David, Lee. Diploma, Ucon (Idaho) H.S., 1951. Carpenter, 1953-63; farmer, rancher, 1955-98; agri-businessman, 1963-98; Rep. senator dist. 26 Idaho State Senate, 1996—. Mem. commerce and human resources, edn., resources and environ. coms. Idaho State Senate, vice chair agrl. affairs. Mem. sch. bd.; scout leader; dir. Owsley Canal Co.; pres. Cattle Coop. Named Farmer of Yr. Mem. Lds Ch. Office: 1603 N 1000 E Terreton ID 83450 also: Idaho State Senate State Capitol PO Box 83720 Boise ID 83720-0081 Fax: 208 663-4499. E-mail: infocntr@lso.state.id.us.

BURTON, BRIAN JOSEPH (DANGER MOUSE), sound recording engineer, musician; b. White Plains, NY; Mem. Danger Mouse (DM) & Jemini, Dangerdoom, Gnarls Barkley, 2004—. Prodr.: (albums) The Chilling Effect, as Pelican City, 1999, Rhode Island, as Pelican City, 2000, Ghetto Pop Life, for DM & Jemini, 2003, Lexoleum, 2003, Genocide in Sudan, 2004, Slickness, for Prince Po, 2004, Twenty Six Inch EP, for Danger Mouse & Jemini, 2004, The Grey Album, 2004 (Best Record of Yr., Entertainment Weekly, 2004), Demon Days, for Gorillaz, 2005, Fear of a Black Tangent, for Busdriver, 2005, Healthy Distrust, for Sage Francis, 2005, The Mouse and the Mask, for DangerDoom, 2005, Pieces of the People We Love, for The Rapture, 2006, St. Elsewhere, for Gnarls Barkley, 2006 (Grammy award for Best Alternative Music Album, 2007), Dramt for Light Years in the Belly of a Mountain, for Sparklehorse, 2006, The Good, the Bad, & the Queen, 2007, The Odd Couple, for Gnarls Barkley, 2008; prodr.: (songs) Crazy, 2006 (2 MTV Video Music awards for Best Direction & Best Editing, MTV Europe Music award for Best Song, 2006, Grammy award for Best Alternative Performance, 2007, Soul Train award for Best Soul Single, 2007), Smiley Faces, 2006 (Best Editing, MTV Video Music Awards, 2007), Run, 2008 (Best Art Direction, Best Choreography, MTV Video Music Awards, 2008). Recipient Rave award, Wired mag., 2005, Left Field Woodie award, mtvU, 2006, Best Group award (as Gnarls Barkley), Black Entertainment TV (BET) Awards, 2007; named one of Men of Yr., GQ mag., 2004. Office: Waxploitation Inc 11601 Wilshire Blvd Los Angeles CA 90025

BURTON, JOHN L., political organization administrator, retired state legislator; b. Cin., Dec. 15, 1932; 1 child, Kimiko. AB, San Francisco State Coll., 1954; LLB, U. San Francisco Law Sch., 1960. Bar: Calif. 1961. Pvt. practice atty.; mem. Calif. House of Reps., Sacramento, 1964-74, 88-96, US House of Reps., Washington, 1974-82; mem. Dist. 3 Calif. State Senate, Sacramento, 1997—2004, pres. pro tempore, 1998—2004; ret., 2004; founder John Burton Found., San Francisco, 2004—; chmn. Calif. Dem. Party, Sacramento, 2009—. Founder Point Reyes Wilderness Area, Farallon Marine Sanctuary. Served with US Army, 1954—56. Named Legislator of Yr. Calif. Abortion Rights Action League, Animal Rights Legislator of Yr.; recipient Cmty. United Against Violence award, Sean Mcbride award, award Ancient Order of Hibernians. Democrat. Office: Calif Dem Party 1401 21st St Ste 200 San Francisco CA 95811 also: John Burton Found 235 Montgomery St Ste 1142 San Francisco CA 94104*

BURTON, JOHN PAUL (JACK BURTON), lawyer; b. New Orleans, Feb. 26, 1943; s. John Paul and Nancy (Key) Burton; m. Anne Ward; children: Jennifer, Michele Kfouri, Marcos Maiken, Susanna, Derek, Catherine. BBA magna cum laude, La. Tech. U., 1965; LLB, Harvard U., 1968. Bar: N.Mex. 1968, U.S. Dist. Ct. N.Mex. 1968, U.S. Ct. Appeals (10th cir.) 1973, U.S. Supreme Ct. 1979. Assoc. Rodey, Dickason, Sloan, Akin & Robb, Albuquerque, 1968-74, dir., 1974—, chmn. comml. dept., 1980-81, mng. dir. Santa Fe, 1986-90. Settlement facilitator N.Mex. 1st Jud. Dist., 1997—. Co-author: Boundary Disputes in New Mexico, 1992, Unofficial Update on the Uniform Ltd. Liability Co. Act, 1994, Effective Boundary Dispute Resolution in New Mexico, 2004. Pres. Brunn Sch., 1987—89, divsn. chmn., 1993—95, 1999—2001, exec. com., 1997—99; chmn. drafting com. on uniform durable powers of atty. Nat. Coun. Commrs. on Uniform State Laws, 2003—06; vice chair St. Simeon's Found., 1986—87. Named one of Best Lawyers in Am., 1986—, Southwest Super Lawyers, 2007—. Fellow: Am. Coll. Real Estate Lawyers; mem.: ABA, Chartered Inst. Arbitrators, N.Mex. State Bar Assn. (chmn. comml. litig. sect. 1985—86, Bus. Lawyer of Yr. 2004), Am. Arbitration Assn. (comml. panel arbitrators, large, complex case panel arbitrators, panel mediators), Am. Coll. Mortgage Attys., Am. Law Inst. Office: Rodey Dickason Sloan Akin & Robb PA PO Box 1357 Santa Fe NM 87504-1357 Office Phone: 505-954-3900. Business E-Mail: jburton@rodey.com.

BURTON, LAWRENCE DEVERE, agriculturist, educator; b. Afton, Wyo., May 27, 1943; s. Lawrence VanOrden and Maybell (Hoopes) B.; m. Arva Merrill, Nov. 20, 1967; children: LauraLee, Paul, Shawn, Renee, Kaylyn, Kelly, Brett. BS, Utah State U., 1968; MS, Brigham Young U., 1972; PhD, Iowa State U., 1987. Tchr. agr. Box Elder County Sch. Dist., Brigham City, Utah, 1967—68, Morgan County Sch. Dist., Morgan, Utah, 1968—70, Minidoka County Sch. Dist., Rupert, Idaho, 1972—79, Cassia County Sch. Dist., Declo, Idaho, 1979—84; instr. Iowa State U., Ames, 1984—87; coord. area vocat. edn. Idaho State Divsn. Vocat. Edn., Pocatello, 1987—88, state supr. agrl. sci. and tech. Boise, 1988—97, dir. rsch., 1997—99; mem. telecomm. coun. Idaho State Bd. Edn., 1997—98, mem. coun. acad. affairs and programs, 1997—; instrnl. dean Coll. So. Idaho, Twin Falls, 2000—05. Biochem. cons. rep. Ctr. for Occupational Rsch. and Devel., Waco, Tex., 1989-94; chmn. Nat. Task Force, Agrl. Edn. Ind. Study Honors program, 1993, mem. tech. commn.; mem. Nat. Task Force, Environ. Edn., 1996. Author: Agriscience and Technology, 1991, 97, Fish and Wildlife Science, 1995, 2d edit., 2003, Introduction to Forestry Science, 2d edit., 2008, Agriscience, Fundamentals and Applications, 2000, 4th edit., 2007; Environ. Sci. Fundamentals and Applications, 2008; contbr. articles to profl. jours. Vice-chmn. Minidoka County Fair Bd., Rupert, Idaho, 1977-80. Mem. Am. Vocat. Assn., Am. Vocat. Info. Assn., Nat. Vocat. Agrl. Tchrs. Assn., Idaho Vocat. Agrl. Tchrs. Assn. (pres. 1981-82, Adminstr. of Yr. 1989), Nat. Assn. Suprs. Agrl. Edn. (we. v.p. 1990-91, nat. pres. 1993-94), Gamma Sigma Delta, Alpha Zeta. Mem. Lds Ch. Home Phone: 208-732-8123; Office Phone: 208-420-9423. Business E-Mail: ldevereb@yahoo.com.

BURTON, MICHAEL LADD, anthropology educator; b. Long Beach, Calif., June 6, 1942; s. Warren Nathan Burton and Dorothy Brent (Braden) Asquith; children: Melissa, Christopher; m. Ellen Greenberger, Aug. 26, 1979. BS in Econs., MIT, 1964; PhD in Anthropology, Stanford U., 1968. Rsch. fellow Harvard U., 1968-69; asst. prof. U. Calif., Irvine, 1969-76; rsch. fellow U. Nairobi, Kenya, 1973-74; assoc. prof. U. Calif., Irvine, 1976-83, prof., 1983—, chmn., dept. anthropology, 1986-91, 2003—05. Contbr. articles to profl. jours. NSF grantee, 1981-89, 91-93. Mem. Am. Anthropol. Assn., Soc. for Cross-Cultural Rsch., Soc. Econ. Anthropology, Soc. Applied Anthropology, Assn. Social Anthropology of Oceania. Home: 10 Morning Sun Irvine CA 92603-3715 Office: U Calif Dept Anthropology Irvine CA 92697-5100 Office Phone: 949-824-7208. Business E-Mail: mlburton@uci.edu.

BURTON, PAUL FLOYD, retired social worker; b. Seattle, May 24, 1939; s. Floyd James and Mary Teresa (Chovanak) B.; m. Roxanne Maude Johnson, July 21, 1961; children: Russell Floyd, Joan Teresa. BA, U. Wash., 1961, MSW, 1967. Juvenile parole counselor Divsn. Juvenile Rehab. State of Wash., 1961-66; social worker VA, Seattle, 1967-72; social worker, cons. Work Release Program, King County, Wash., 1967-72; supr., chief psychiatry sect. Social Work Svc. VA, Topeka, 1972-73; pvt. practice Topeka and L.A., 1972—; chief social work svc. VA, Sepulveda, Calif., 1973-98; assoc. dir. Cmty. Care Svcs., VA Greater L.A. Healthcare System, 1998—2001, dir. cmty. residential care, 2001—08. EEO coord. Med. ctr., 1974-77; social worker, consultant & educator. Recipient Va. Social Work Pioneer award, 2004; named VA Social Worker of Yr., U.S. Dept. VA Social Work Leadership Coun., 2002. Mem. NASW (newsletter edito Puget Sound chpt. 1970-71), Acad. Cert. Social Workers, Ctr. for Studies in Social Functioning, Soc. Social Svc. Leaders Healthcare, Assn. Va. Social Workers (founder 1979, charter mem. and pres. 1980-81, newsletter editor 1982-83, 89-91, pres. elect 1993-95, pres. 1995-97, newsletter editor 2000-2002, treas. 2003-06). Home: 9451 Petit Ave North Hills CA 91343

BURTON, RANDALL JAMES, lawyer; b. Sacramento, Feb. 4, 1950; s. Edward J. and Bernice Mae (Overton) B.; m. Kimberly D. Rogers, Apr. 29, 1989; children: Kelly Jacquelyn, Andrew Jameson. BA, Rutgers U., 1972; JD, Southwestern U., 1975. Bar: Calif. 1976, U.S. Dist. Ct. (ea. dist.) Calif. 1976, U.S. Dist. Ct. (no. dist.) Calif. 1990, Supreme Ct. 1991. Assoc. Brekke & Mathews, Citrus Heights, Calif., 1976; pvt. practice Sacramento, 1976—93; ptnr. Burton & White, Sacramento, 1993—; judge pro tem Sacramento Small Claims Ct., 1982—, Sacramento Traffic Ct., 2004—. Bd. dirs. North Highlands Recreation and Park Dist., 1978—86, Family Svc. Agy. Sacramento, 1991—96; active local bd. 22 Selective Svc., 1982—2001; active 20-30 Club Sacramento, 1979—90, pres., 1987. Recipient Disting. Citizen award Golden Empire Coun., Boy Scouts Am. Mem.: Sacramento Young Lawyers Assn., Sacramento Bar Assn., Rotary (pres. Foothill-Highlands club 1980—81). Presbyterian. Office: 1325 Howe Ave Ste 214 Sacramento CA 95825

BURTON, ROBERT LYLE, accounting firm executive; m. Lee Sanders; 2 children. Diploma, Kinman Bus. U. CPA. With LeMaster & Daniels, Spokane, Wash., 1963-86, mng. ptnr., 1986-97, sr. advisor, 1997—. Adv. bd. acctg. dept. U. Wash.; chmn. The Am. Group of CPA Firms. Trustee Econ. Devel. Coun.; past chmn. Samaritan Hosp. Found., Moses Lake, Wash. Mem. AICPA (agri-bus. com., adv. group B), Washington Soc. CPAs (former dir., v.p., com. chmn., legis. com.), Spokane Club, Inland Empire Fly Fishermen, Moses Lake Golf and Country Club, Rotary. Office: LeMaster and Daniels PLLC 601 W Riverside Ave Ste 700 Spokane WA 99201-0622

BURTON CAHILL, MEG, state legislator; b. Salem, NJ, Mar. 8, 1954; m. Dennis Cahill; children: Jim, Maret, Lyn, Brendan. BFA, Ariz. State U., 1976, MPA, 1998. Ceramic artist O'Bair Studio, 1976—82, Tir Na Nog Studio, 1982—; mem. Dist. 27 Ariz. House of Reps., 2001—02, mem. Dist. 17, 2003—07, Ariz. State Senate, 2007—, mem. judiciary com., vets. & mil. affairs. com. Ceramics instr., Tempe/Scottsdale, Ariz., 1975—82; founding mem. Ariz. Bi-Partisan Bi-Cameral Children's Caucus; commr. Phoenix Mayor's Commn. Disability Issues, 2002—. Mem. gov. bd. Ariz. Emergency Med. Svcs., 2004—. Democrat. Office: Ariz State Senate Capitol Complex 1700 W Washington Rm 313 Phoenix AZ 85007 Office Phone: 602-926-4124. Office Fax: 602-417-3245. Business E-Mail: mburtoncahill@azleg.gov.*

BURTT, BEN, sound designer, director, editor; b. Syracuse, NY, July 12, 1948; m. Margaret L. Darragh; 3 children. BA in Physics, Allegheny Coll., 1970; MA in Motion Picture Prodn., U. Southern Calif., 1975. Still photographer, mem. camera crew Indsl. Light & Magic, San Rafael, Calif., 1975; successively supervising sound editor/sound designer, picture editor, writer, dir. Sprocket Systems divsn. of Lucasfilm Ltd. (now Skywalker Sound), San Rafael, Calif., 1975—. Lectr. Stanford U., Soc. Motion Picture and TV Engrs., Allegheny Coll., Syracuse U., Mus. Film and Photography, UK; cons. NASA. Creator, photographer spl. effect sequence (TV movie) Killdozer; sound editor, sound designer (film) The Big Fight, Deathrace 2000; stuntman (film) Attack on Precinct 13; supervising sound editor, sound designer (films) Star Wars (Oscar award), More American Graffiti, 1979, The Empire Strikes Back, 1980 (Oscar award, Brit. Acad. award), Raiders of the Lost Ark, 1981 (Oscar award, Golden Reel award), Return of the Jedi, 1983 (Oscar nomination), Indiana Jones and the Temple of Doom, 1984, Willow, 1988 (Oscar nomination), Nutcracker The Movie, Indiana Jones and the Last Crusade, 1989 (Oscar award), Always, 1989 (short subjects) The Dream is Alive, Niagara: Miracles, Myths and Magic, 1986, Alamo, The Price of Freedom, The Living Seas, Star Wars: Episode I - The Phantom Menace, 1999, Star Wars: Episode II - Attack of the Clones, 2002, Star Wars: Episode III - Revenge of the Sith, 2005, Munich, 2005, Indiana Jones and the Kingdom of the Crystal Skull, 2008; designer spl. sound effects (films) Invasion of the Body Snatchers, 1978, Alien, Dark Crystal, 1982, ET: The Extraterrestrial, 1982 (Oscar award), Howard the Duck, 1986, The Great Heep, 1986, Wellington's Victory, Ryan vs. Dorkman 2, 2007, WALL-E, 2008; sound editor Sprocket Systems 10 Year Retrospective, The Sound of the Alamo, Wind Turbine Falls, Volume Six, In The Footsteps of Fremont, The True Story of GLORY Continues; writer (films, TV series) The Adventures of Mungo Baobab, WOW!, SOUNDTRACK!; dir. Blue Planet, 1990, To The Stars, In The Footsteps of Fremont, The True Story of GLORY Continues; producer, dir. 15 TV commls. various advt. agys., NY Recipient TEC award, 1985, Gold Record The Story of Star Wars. Office: LucasArts PO Box 29908 San Francisco CA 94129-0908

BUSCEMI, STEVE, actor; b. Bklyn., Dec. 13, 1957; m. Jo Andres, 1987; 1 child, Lucian. Student, Lee Strasberg Inst., NYC. Fireman; stand-up comedian NYC. Appeared in films Parting Glances, 1986, Sleepwalk, 1986, Kiss Daddy Good Night, 1987, Vibes, 1988, Heart of Midnight, 1989, Slaves of New York, 1989, Mystery Train, 1989, The Grifters, 1990, Miller's Crossing, 1990, King of New York, 1990, Zandalee, 1991, Barton Fink, 1991, Billy Bathgate, 1991, Criscross, 1992, In the Soup, 1992, Reservoir Dogs, 1992, Me and the Mob, 1992, Twenty Bucks, 1993, The Hudsucker Proxy, 1994, Airheads, 1994, Pulp Fiction, 1994, Floundering, 1994, Desperado, 1995, Things to Do in Denver When You're Dead, 1995, Fargo, 1996, Black Kites, 1996, Kansas City, 1996, Search for One-Eye Kimmy, 1996, Escape from L.A., 1996, The Real Blonde, 1997, Divine Trash, 1997, Con Air, 1997, The Big Lebowski, 1998, The Wedding Singer, 1998, Louis et Frank, 1998, Armageddon, 1998, The Impostors, 1998, Big Daddy, 1999, 28 Days, 2000, Ghost World, 2000, Monsters Inc. (voice), 2001, Domestic Distrubance, 2001, The Laramie Project, 2002, Mr. Deeds, 2002, Spy Kids 2: Island of Lost Dreams, 2002, Deadrockstar, 2002, Spy Kids 3-D: Game Over, 2003, Big Fish, 2003, Home on the Range (voice), 2000-2004, Who's the Top?, 2005, The Island, 2005, Romance and Cigarettes, 2005, Art School Confidential, 2006, Paris, je t'aime, 2006, Monster House (voice), 2006, Delirious, 2006, Charlotte's Web (voice), 2006, I Think I Love My Wife, 2007, Interview, 2007, (voice) Igor, 2008; (TV films) Borders, 1989, The Last Outlaw, 1994; prodr., dir. (films) What Happened to Pete?, 1993; dir. (films) Trees Lounge, 1996; actor, dir. writer Interview, 2007; TV appearances include Tales from the Crypt, 1993, Miami Vice, L.A. Law, The Sopranos, others. Office: c/o Endeavor Agy 9601 Wilshire Blvd Beverly Hills CA 90212

BUSCH, JOYCE IDA, small business owner; b. Madera, Calif., Jan. 24, 1934; d. Bruno Harry and Ella Fae (Absher) Toschi; m. Fred O. Busch, Dec. 14, 1956; children: Karen, Kathryn, Kurt. BA in Indsl. Arts and Interior Design, Calif. State U., Fresno, 1991. Cert. interior designer, Calif. Stewardess United Air Lines, San Francisco, 1955-57; prin. Art Coordinates, Fresno, 1982—, Busch Interior Design, Fresno, 1982—. Art cons. Fresno Cmty. Hosp., 1981-83; docent Fresno Met. Mus., 1981-84. Treas. Valley Children's Hosp. Guidance Clinic, 1975-79, Lone Star PTA, 1965-84,; mem. Mothers Guild San Joaquin Mem. H.S., 1984-88. Mem. Am. Soc. Interior Designers. Republican. Roman Catholic. Avocations: gardening, art history. Office Phone: 559-260-3202.

BUSH, BILLY, television personality; s. Jonathan and Jodi Bush; m. Sydney Bush; children: Josephine, Mary Bradley. B in internat. studies and govt., Colby Coll., 1994. Host afternoon show WLKZ-FM, NH; host midday show WARW-FM, Washington; host "Billy Busy and the Bush League Morning Show" WWZZ-FM, Washington, 1997—2001; East coast corr. Access Hollywood, 2001—04, co-anchor, 2004—; host Let's Make a Deal, NBC, 2003. Contbr. The Today Show, NBC; co-host Miss USA, 2003, 04, Miss Universe, 2003. Office: Access Hollywood NBC Studios 3000 W Alamea Ave Burbank CA 91523 Office Phone: 818-526-7000.

BUSH, SARAH LILLIAN, retired historian; b. Kansas City, Mo., Sept. 17, 1920; d. William Adam and Lettie Evelyn (Burrill) Lewis; m. Walter Nelson Bush, June 7, 1946 (dec.); children: William Read, Robert Nelson. AB, U. Kans., Lawrence, 1941; BS, U. Ill., Champaign-Urbana, 1943. Clk. circulation dept. Kansas City Pub. Library, 1941-42, asst. librarian Paseo br., 1943-44; librarian Kansas City Jr. Coll., 1944-46; substitute librarian San Mateo County Library, Woodside amd Portola Valley, Calif., 1975-77; various temporary positions, 1979-87; owner Metriguide, Palo Alto, Calif., 1975-78. Author: Atherton Lands, 1979, rev. edition 1987. Editor: Atherton Recollections, 1973. Pres., v.p. Jr. Librarians, Kansas City, 1944-46; courtesy, yearbook & historian AAUW, Menlo- Atherton branch (Calif.) Br.; asst. Sunday sch. tchr., vol. Holy Trinity Ch., Menlo Park, 1955-78; v.p., membership com., libr. chairperson, English reading program, parent edn. chairperson Menlo Atherton High Sch. PTA, 1964-73; founder, bd. dirs. Friends of Atherton Community Library, 1967-2002, oral historian, 1968-2002, chair Bicentennial event, 1976; bd. dirs. Menlo Park Hist. Assn., 1979-82, oral historian, 1973-2002; bd. dirs. Civic Interest League, Atherton, 1978-81; mem. hist. county commn. Town of Atherton, 1980-87; vol. Palo Alto Auxiliary serving Lucile Packard Children's Hosp. at Stanford, 1967—, oral historian, 1978—, historian, 1980—; vol. United Crusade, Garfield Sch., Redwood City, 1957-61, 74-88, Encinal Sch., Menlo Park, Calif., 1961-73, program dir., chmn. summer recreation, historian, sec.; vol. Stanford Mothers Club, 1977-81, others; historian, awards chairperson Cub Scouts Boy Scouts Am.; founder Atherton Heritage Assn. 1989, bd. dirs., 1989-2004, dir., 1989-94; mem. Guild Gourmet, 1971—, Mid Peninsula History Consortium, 1993-95; oral historian St. Andrew's Ch., Saratoga, Calif., 2003-06; vol. Los Gatos Meadows, 2004, Calif. Recipient Good Neighbor award Atherton Civic Interest League, 1992. Mem. PTA (life). Episcopalian. Avocations: gourmet cooking, entertaining, reading.

BUSH, WESLEY G., aerospace transportation executive; B in Elect. Engring., MIT, MSEE; grad., UCLA. With engring. staff Aerospace Corp.; corp. v.p., pres. space tech. Comsat Labs; from. sys. engr. to v.p., gen. mgr. telecomm. programs divsn. TRW Aero. Sys., 1987—99, pres., CEO, 2001—03; v.p., gen. mgr. TRW Ventures, 2000—01; pres., CEO, global aeronautical sys. TRW-United Kingdom, 2001—03; corp. v.p., pres. space tech. Northrop Grumman Corp. (acquired TRW), LA, 2003—05; corp. v.p., CFO Northrop Grumman Corp., LA, 2005—06, pres., CFO, 2006—07, pres., COO, 2007—. Office: Northrop Grumman Corp 1840 Century Park E Los Angeles CA 90067-2199

BUSH, WILLIAM MERRITT, retired lawyer; b. Long Beach, Calif., June 23, 1941; s. Lloyd Merritt and Barbara Ann (Bufkin) B.; m. Dorothy Irene Vasvary, June 25, 1966; children: Steven Merritt, Amy Elizabeth. BA, Stanford U., 1963; JD, U. Calif., Hastings, 1966. Bar: Calif. 1967, U.S. Dist. Ct. (ctrl. dist.) Calif. 1967, U.S. Dist. Ct. (so. dist.) Calif. 1976. Assoc. Dannemeyer & Tuohey, Fullerton, Calif., 1967, Miller, Bush & Minnott, Fullerton, Calif., 1967-69, ptnr., 1970-88; pvt. practice Fullerton, Calif., 1989—2008. Human rels. commr., City of Fullerton, 1971-77; mem. site coun., Fullerton H.S., 1986-88. Fellow Am. Acad. Matrimonial Lawyers 1981-2008; mem. Orange County Bar Assn. 1970-2008 (dir. 1982-85), Calif. State Bar 1967-2009 (mem. family law cons. group, family law sect. 1979, mem. family law adv. commn. 1979-85, chmn. commn. 1982-85, bd. legal specialization 1982-89, chmn. 1987-88). Republican. Methodist. Avocations: computers, walking.

BUSHEE, WARD, III, editor; b. Redding, Calif., 1949; m. Claudia Bushee; children: Ward Gardiner, Mary Standish. BS in History, San Diego State U., 1971. Sports editor Gilroy Dispatch, Calif., 1973—75; asst. city editor/sports editor/reporter/copy editor The Californian, Salinas, Calif., 1975—79; sports editor Marin County Ind. Jour., Calif., 1979—82; asst. content editor sports USA Today, Arlington, Va., 1982—85; asst. mng. editor sports Westchester Suburban Newspapers, 1985—86; exec. editor Argus Leader, Sioux Falls, SD, 1986—90; editor Reno Gazette-Jour., Nev., 1990—99, Cin. Enquirer, 1999—2002; v.p. news Ariz. Republic, 2002—08, editor, 2002—08; exec. v.p., editor The San Francisco Chronicle, 2008—. Bd. trustees Walter Cronkite Sch. Journalism Endowment, Ariz. State U. Named Editor of Yr., 1992, 97, 2005, Gannett Co., Inc., Pres.'s Ring winner 1992-97, 99-2001, 04, 05. Mem. Nev. Press Assn. (pres. 1993, 94, API discussion leader 1996). Office: The San Francisco Chronicle 901 Mission St San Francisco CA 94103

BUSHEY, RICHARD KENNETH, utility executive; b. Alhambra, Calif., May 1, 1940; s. Kenneth H. and Dale E. (Wheeler) B.; m. Janeil Deane Anderson, Feb. 23, 1963; 1 child, Michael. BS, UCLA, 1963; postgrad., U. So. Calif., 1965; grad. Pub. Utility Execs. program, U. Mich., 1973; grad. fin. program, Stanford U., 1976. Acct., supr., mgr. So. Calif. Edison Co., Rosemead, 1963-74, asst. treas., 1974-75, asst. contr., 1975-84, v.p., contr., 1984—, Edison Internat., Rosemead, 1988—, supplemental employee. Lst lt. U.S. Air N.G., 1963-70. Mem. L.A. C. of C., UCLA Alumni Assn., Phi Kappa Psi.

BUSHNELL, RODERICK PAUL, lawyer; b. Buffalo, Mar. 6, 1944; s. Paul Hazen and Martha Atlee Bushnell; m. Suzann Yvonne Kaiser, Aug. 27, 1966; 1 child, Arlo Phillip. BA, Rutgers U., 1966; JD, Georgetown U., 1969. Bar: Calif. 1970, U.S. Supreme Ct. 1980.; cert. Civil Trial Advocate, Nat. Bd. Trial Advocates. Atty. dept. water resources, Sacramento, 1969-71; ptnr. Bushnell, Caplan Fielding, San Francisco, 1971—. Adv. bd. dirs. Bread & Roses, Inc., Mill Valley, Calif. Named a No. Calif. Super Lawyer, Law and Politics, 2006—09. Mem. ATLA, ABA (labor and employment sects.), San Francisco Bar Assn. (labor and employment sects.; arbitrator), San Francisco Superior Ct. (arbitrator), Fed. Ct. Early Neutral Evaluator, Calif. Bar Assn. (labor and employement sects.), Consumer Attys. Calif. (labor and employement sects.), San Francisco Trial Lawyers Assn., Nat. Employment Lawyers Assn., Calif. Employment Lawyers Assn. Office: Bushnell Caplan Fielding 900 Kearny St Ste 299 San Francisco CA 94133 Office Phone: 415-217-3800. Business E-Mail: rbushnell@sprynet.com.

BUSS, JERRY (GERALD HATTEN BUSS), professional sports team owner; b. Salt Lake City, 1934; children: John, Jim, Jeanie, Jane. BS in Chemistry, U. Wyo.; MS, PhD in Chemistry, U. So. Calif., 1957. Chemist Bur. Mines; mem. faculty dept. chemistry U. So. Calif.; mem. missile divsn. McDonnell Douglas, LA; ptnr. Mariani-Buss Assocs.; former owner LA Strings; chmn. bd., owner NBA LA Lakers, 1979—; owner NHL LA Kings, 1979—88. Office: LA Lakers 555 N Nash St El Segundo CA 90245

BUSTAMANTE, CARLOS J., biophysicist, educator; b. Lima, Peru, May 8, 1951; BS in Biology, Cayetano Heredia U., Lima, Peru, 1973; MSc in Biochemistry, San Carlos U., Lima, 1978; DSc in Biophysics, U. Calif, Berkeley, 1981. Asst. prof. Dept. Chemistry U. N.Mex, 1982—86, assoc. prof., 1986—89, presidential lectr. in chemistry, 1986, prof., 1989—90, U. Oregon, 1991—98, Howard Hughes Med. Inst. Investigator, 1994—98, U. Calif., Berkeley, 2000—, prof. of Molecular and Cell Biology, Physics, and Chemistry, 1998—. Mem. Sci. Adv. Bd. Searle Scholars Prog., 1997—2000; Head advanced microscopics dept. Lawrence Berkeley Nat. Lab. Phys. Bioscis. Divsn.; served on Interfaces Adv. Com. Burroughs Wellcome Fund, 2001—03, bd. dir., 2004—. Contbr. articles to profl. jours. Fellow Alfred P. Sloan, 1985; scholar Fulbright, 1975—80, Searle, 1984, (eminent) New Mexico, 1989. Fellow: Am. Phys. Soc.; mem.: NAS (Alexander Hollaender award in Biophysics 2004). Office: Univ Calif Berkeley Dept Physics 231 Birge Hall Berkeley CA 94720 E-mail: carlos@alice.berkeley.edu.

BUSTAMANTE, CRUZ M., former lieutenant governor; b. Dinuba, Calif., Jan. 4, 1953; s. Cruz and Dominga Bustamante Jr.; m. Arcelia De La Pena; children: Leticia, Sonia, Marisa. BA, Fresno State U. Past intern for Congressman B.F. Sisk, Washington; formerly with Fresno employment and tng. commn. City of Fresno, past program dir. summer youth employment tng. program, 1977—83; past dist. rep. Congressman Rick Lehman and Assemblyman Bruce Bronzan State of Calif.; mem. Calif. State Assembly, 1993, spkr. of assembly, 1996-98; lt. gov. State of Calif., 1998—2007. Mem. US Census Monitoring Bd. Trustee Calif. State U.; regent U. Calif.; chair State Lands Commn.; vice chair Aerospace States Assn. Named Legislator of Yr. Assn. Mexican Am. Educators, U. Calif. Alumni Assn.; recipient True Am. Role Model award Mexican Am. Polit. Assn., Calif. Coastal Hero award, Pres.'s award NAACP, Friend of Labor award Mexican Am. Polit. Assn. Democrat. also: 300 S Spring St Ste 12702 Los Angeles CA 90013 Address: 2550 Mariposa Mall Rm 5006 Fresno CA 93721 Office: Office Of Lt Governor Cruz Bustamont 1303 10TH St Sacramento CA 95814-4905

BUSTAMANTE, TOMMY A., protective services official; married; 3 children. B of Criminal Justice, N.Mex. State U., 1984. U.S. marshal U.S. Marshal Svc., Dept. of Justice, Brownsville, Tex., 1986-91, supervisory dep. U.S. marshal Albuquerque, 1991-98, chief dep. U.S. marshal for Dist. of N.Mex., 1998—.

BUTCHER, DOROTHY B., state legislator; single; children: three, one grandchild. Colorado State Representative, District 46, 2002-; member Bus Affairs & Labor, Appropriations and Legislature Coun, currently, Colorado House Representative; majority whip, currently, Colorado House Representative.ret financial analyst. Democrat. Mailing: State Capitol 200 E Colfax Rm 271 Denver CO 80203 Office Phone: 303-866-2968. E-mail: dorothy.butcher.house@state.co.us.

BUTCHER, EDWARD B., state legislator; b. July 20, 1943; m to Pam; 1963; children: Trevis, Ross, Rebecca, and nine grandchildren. Montana State Representative, District 29, 2005-, Montana House Representative; Ch Fergus Co Govt Review Commerce 1994-; State senate District 47, 2001-05; Ch Senate Highway & Transportation Commerce 2003-05; ch House Argentina com 2005-07.High Sch Governor teacher 1967-68; Assistant Prof Valley City State Univ ND, 1968-71; Lectucer university of Great Falls, MT, 1974-80; Ranch owner 1971-present; Evans Bron Nat Sales Director, 1986-88; Aftco Assoc, Senior Consultant, 1988-present; Aftco Senior Regional Manager, 2000-present. Republican. Lutheran. Mailing: PO Box 89 Winifred MT 59489-0089 E-mail: senatorbutcher@3riverdbs.net.*

BUTCHER, EUGENE CORNING, pathologist, science educator; b. St. Louis, Jan. 6, 1950; BS in Chemistry, MIT, 1972; MD, Washington U., St. Louis, 1976. Lic. Calif. State Bd. Med. Examiners. Pathology residency Stanford U., Calif., 1976—77, 1979—80, NIH postdoctoral fellowship, dept. pathology, 1977—79, sr. fellow, Am. Cancer Soc., 1980—82; asst. prof., dept. pathology Stanford U. Med. Ctr., 1982—89, assoc. prof., dept. pathology, 1989—99, prof., dept. pathology, 1999—. Cons. Genentech, Tularik, Protein Design Labs., BioCarb, Inc., SAB, MedImmune, Inc., SAB, Thios pharms, Schering AG; staff physician VA Palo Alto Health Care Sys., 1982—, dir., serology and immunology sect., 1982—; mem. exec. com. Stanford Digestive Disease Ctr., 1983—; co-dir., surg. pathology Immunohistologic Diagnosis Svc., Stanford, 1983—93; adj. prof. Mont. State U., Billings, 1992—; sci. cofounder, vice chair LeukoSite, Inc., Cambridge, Mass., 1993—99; mem. Western VA Network VISN Com. on Rsch. Redesign, 1996—97; SAB Millennium Pharms., Cambridge, Mass., 1999—; co-founder BioSeek, Inc., Burlingame, Calif., 2000—; group mem. Immune Disorders Med. Rsch. Adv. Group, 2000—04. Recipient Eloranta award, 1971, Warner-Lambert/Parke-Davis award, Am. Assn. Pathologists, 1989, AAI-Huang Found. Meritorious Career award, 1999, Crafoord prize, Swedish Acad. Scis., 2004; scholar, Leukemia Soc. Am., 1982—87. Mem.: Am. Assn. Physicians, Am. Heart Assn. (coun. mem. 1989—93, Established Investigator 1987—92), Phi Beta Kappa. Achievements include elucidating the cellular and molecular mechanisms of white blood cell migration and trafficking; research in immunology; vascular biology. Office: Stanford U Med Ctr MC5324 Dept Pathology 300 Pasteur Dr Rm L-235 Stanford CA 94305

BUTENHOFF, SUSAN GRACE, public relations executive; b. NYC, Jan. 13, 1960; BA in Internat. Rels. with hons., Sussex U., 1982; MPhil, Wolfson Coll. Cambridge U., 1985. Account exec. Ellen Farmer Prodns., 1984-85, Ketchum Pub. Rels., NYC, 1988-90, v.p., account supr., 1990-91; prin., CEO Access Pub. Rels., San Francisco, 1991—, pres., CEO. Mem. Pub. Rels. Soc. Am. Office: Access Comm 101 Howard St Fl 2D San Francisco CA 94105-1629

BUTER, IRWIN, lawyer; Ptnr. Buter, Buzzard & Dunaetz, LLP, LA. Lectr. LA County Family Law Symposium, 1979—93, Calif. Continuing Edn. of Bar, 1980—95. Mem.: LA County Bar Assn. (chmn. family law sect. 1986—87, mem. exec. com. family law sect. 1977—91). Office: Buter Buzzard & Dunaetz LLP Ste 820 11611 San Vicente Blvd Los Angeles CA 90049 Office Phone: 310-820-6700. Office Fax: 310-207-4612. E-mail: buter@bbdflaw.com.

BUTERA, BARCLAY, interior designer; BA, Brigham Young Univ. Pres., CEO Barclay Butera Home, Newport Beach, LA, NYC, Park City, 1993—; creative dir. Hotel L'Auberge del Mar, Del Mar, Calif., Grupo Lomo Del Lago project, Mexico. Author: Barclay Butera, 2008. Named one of Top 125 Designers, House Beautiful mag., Top 50 Designers, Elements of Living. Office: Barclay Butera Home 1745 Westcliff Dr Newport Beach CA 92660 Office Phone: 949-650-8570.

BUTLER, DASCHEL E., protective services official; Chief of police, Berkeley, Calif. Office: 2100 Martin Luther King Jr Way Berkeley CA 94704-1109

BUTLER, DAVID, lawyer; b. St. Paul, June 11, 1930; s. Francis David and Alida (Bigelow) B.; m. Diana Dodge Duffy, Aug. 29, 1952 (div. 1957); children: Anne, Lawrence David; m. Barbara Williams Clark, July 12, 1958; children: Molly Elizabeth, Peter, Katherine BA, Princeton U., 1952; LLB, Harvard U., 1957. Bar. Colo. 1958, U.S. Dist. Ct. Colo. 1958. Assoc. Holland & Hart, Denver, 1957-63, ptnr., 1963-95, chmn. mgmt. com., 1990-95; of counsel, 1996—. Gen. counsel 1st Interstate Bank Denver, 1984-86; bd. dirs. UMB Bank Colo., Denver. Mem. bd. editors Harvard Law Rev., 1955-57. Chmn. lawyers adv. com. United Way, Denver, 1989—94; trustee Graland Country Day Sch., Denver, 1971—79, Legal Aid Found., Colo., 1991—97, chmn., 1993—97, Colo. Planning Group for Legal Svcs. to the Poor, 1995—2002; bd. dirs. Met. Denver Legal Aid Soc., 1971—74; trustee Colo. Lawyers Trust Account Found., 2000—05, pres., 2005; chmn. Colo. Access to Justice Commn., 2003—04, sec., 2005—07; bd. dirs. Colo. Ctr. Law and Policy. 1st lt. US Army, 1952—54. Mem. ABA, Colo. Bar Assn. (chmn. tax sect. 1970, Jacob V. Schaetzel pro bono award 2002), Denver Bar Assn. Office: Holland & Hart 555 17th St Ste 3200 Denver CO 80202-3979

BUTLER, DAVID J., newspaper editor; b. Taylorville, Ill., June 19, 1950; s. Donald and Jeanie B.; m. Kathryn Lee, Nov. 2, 1991. BS in Journalism and Photography, Southern Ill. U., 1972. Metro editor, reporter The Southern Illinoisan, Carbondale, Ill., 1972-78; asst. city editor The Sun-Sentinel, Fort Lauderdale, Fla., 1978; mng. editor The Messenger-Inquirer, Owensboro, Ky., 1978-81, Jacksonville Jour., Fla., 1981-83; asst. mng. editor Rocky Mountain News, Denver, 1983-88; editor New Haven Register, New Haven, 1988-96, LA Daily News, 1997—2005; v.p. LA Newspaper Group; editor, pub. The Detroit News, 2005—07; v.p. for news MediaNews Group, Inc., Denver, 2007—; v.p., exec. editor San Jose Mercury News, Calif., 2008—. Office: San Jose Mercury News 750 Ridder Park Dr San Jose CA 95190

BUTLER, JACK FAIRCHILD, electric power industry executive; b. El Centro, Calif., July 18, 1933; s. Jack Orval and Dorothy (Marsh) B.; m. Colette Alice Guerard, Sept. 6, 1959; children— Alice, Jack, Michael, Patricia. Student, San Jose State Coll., 1951-54; BS, U. Calif., Berkeley, 1959, MS, 1960, PhD, 1962. Research staff mem. Mass. Inst. Tech., Lincoln Lab., Lexington, Mass., 1962-68; staff scientist Gen. Dynamics Corp., Pomona, Calif., 1968-71; sr. staff mem. Arthur D. Little, Inc., Cambridge, Mass., 1971-74; co-founder, co-owner, dir., pres. Laser Analytics, Inc., Lexington, 1974-81; founder, owner, dir., pres. Butler Research and Engring., Inc., 1981-85; co-founder, co-owner, dir., pres. San Diego Semicondrs., Inc., 1985-91, Aurora Techs. Corp., 1991-95; co-founder, co-owner, pres. Digirad (formerly Aurora Techs. Corp.), 1995-98; ret., 1998. Contbr. articles to sci. jours. Served with USMC, 1954-57. Mem. IEEE (life), AAAS, Am. Inst. Physics (life), Gen. Soc. Mayflower Descs. (life).

BUTLER, JAMES ROBERTSON, JR., lawyer; b. Cleve., May 29, 1946; s. James Robertson and Iris Davis (Welborn) B. AB magna cum laude, U. Calif., Berkeley, 1966, JD, 1969. Bar: Calif. 1970, U.S. Tax Ct. 1977, U.S. Supreme Ct. 1980, Nev. 1997. Chmn. real estate dept. and Global Hospitality Group Jeffer, Mangels, Butler & Marmaro, LLP, LA, Calif., 1982—. Founder, chmn. JMBM Global Hospitality Group Briefing Series, 1991—, ULI Los Angeles Hospitality Product Coun., 2000—; expert panelist on hospitality industry topics NYU Hospitality Industry Investment Conf., UCLA Hospitality Investment Conf., Calif. Soc. CPAs ann. hospitality confs., 1992, 93, 94, 95; spkr., panelist Robert Morris Assocs. Nat. Conf., Chgo., 1989, nat. ann. conf. Ind. Bankers Assn. Am., 1992; frequent guest expert securities, real estate and banking various TV programs, 1985—; participant comml. real estate workouts workshop FDIC & RTC Nat. Tng. Conf., San Antonio, 1989, San Diego, 1990; adv. bd. Bur. Nat. Affairs, Washington. Author: Arbitration in Banking, A Robert Morris Associates State of the Art Book, 1988, Lender Liability: A Practical Guide, A BNA Special Report, 1987; editor Global Hospitality Advisor 1991—, Banking Law Report Capital Adequacy series, 1985, Global Hospitality Advisor, 1991—, Calif. Law Rev.; co-chmn. adv. council Money and Real Estate: The Jour. of Lending, Syndication, Joint Ventures, and the Third Market; contbr. chpt., Mapping the Minefield--Lender's Liability, The Workout Game, Solutions to Problem Real Estate Loans, 1987; contbr. more than 100 articles to profl. jours, chaps. to books. Mem. Am. Arbitration Assn., Comml. Arbitration Panel; founding dir. Liberty Nat. Bank; Charter Adv. bd. dirs., Adv. Council of the Banking Law Inst. Recipient Kraft Prize U. Calif., 1966; Bartley Cavenaugh Crum scholar U. Calif. Sch. Law, 1969. Mem. ABA (corp., banking and bus. law sect., taxation sect.), Urban Land Inst. (chmn. hospitality product coun., exec. com. L.A. Dist. coun. 2000—), Internat. Soc. Hospitality Cons., L.A. County Bar Assn., Century City Bar Assn. (chmn. fin. instn. sect. 1990-91), Beverly Hills Bar Assn., Calif. League of Savs. Instns. (chmn. arbitration com. 1987, 88), Young Pres.' Orgn. (internat. hospitality conference, Milan, 2001), L.A County Bar Assn. Avocation: computers. Office: Jeffer Mangels Butler & Marmaro LLP 1900 Ave Stars 7th Fl Los Angeles CA 90067 Office Fax: 310-712-8526. E-mail: jbutler@jmbm.com.

BUTLER, JON TERRY, computer engineering educator, researcher; b. Balt., Dec. 26, 1943; s. Herbert Harriss and Vera Esse (Buck) B.; m. Susan Beth Wood, Feb. 24, 1968 (div. Aug. 1996); 1 child, Anne Elizabeth; m. Fujiko Sakaguchi, Jan. 31, 1998. BEE, Rensselaer Poly. Inst., 1966, M in Engring., 1967; PhD, Ohio State U., 1973. Registered profl. engr., Ohio. NRC postdoctoral assoc. Air Force Avionics Lab., Wright-Patterson AFB, Ohio, 1973-74; sr. postdoctoral assoc. Naval Postgrad. Sch., Wright-Patterson AFB, Ohio, 1980-81; assoc. prof. Northwestern U., Evanston, Ill., 1974-87; prof. Naval Postgrad. Sch., Monterey, Calif., 1987—, Navalex Chair prof., 1985-87. Editor: Multi-Valued Logic in VLSI, 1991; contbr. articles to profl. jours. Capt. USAF, 1967—70. Recipient Faculty Performance award Naval Postgrad. Sch., 1990-93. Fellow IEEE; mem. IEEE Computer Soc. (chmn. multiple-valued logic com. 1980-81, Disting. vis. 1982-86, press editor 1986-90, editor-in-chief Computer mag. 1991-92, editor-in-chief Computer Soc. Press 1993-97, chmn. Computer Soc. fellows evaluation com. 1999, chmn. Computer Soc. transactions ops. com. 1998-99, chmn. Computer Soc. Press ops. com. 2000—, Meritorious Svc. award 1988, 92, TAB Pioneer award 1989, cert. appreciation 1982, 89, 91, 95, 96, 99, 2000, Disting. Svc. award 1995, Third Centennial medal 2000, bd. govs. 1991-97). Presbyterian. Office: Naval Postgrad Sch Dept Elec Computer Engring Code EC-BU Monterey CA 93943-5121 E-mail: Jon_Butler2@redshift.com.

BUTLER, LESLIE ANN, artist, writer, editor; b. Salem, Oreg., Nov. 19, 1945; d. Marlow Dole and Lala Ann (Erlandson) Butler. Student, Lewis and Clark Coll., 1963-64; BS, U. Oreg., 1969; postgrad., Portland State U., 1972-73, Lewis and Clark Coll., 1991. Creative trainee Ketchum Advt., San Francisco, 1970-71; asst. advt. dir. Mktg. Systems, Inc., Portland, Oreg., 1971-74; prodn. mgr., art dir., copywriter Finzer-Smith, Portland, 1974-76; copywriter Gerber Advt., Portland, 1976-78; freelance copywriter Portland, 1983-84, 83-85; copywriter McCann-Erickson, Portland, 1980-81; copy chief Brookstone Co., Peterborough, NH, 1981-83; creative dir. Whitman Advt., Portland, 1984-87; prin. L.A. Advt., 1987—; portrait artist. Author: The Dream Road and Other Tales From Hidden Hills, 1997; editor (arts and antiques): Living mag.; designer of fence featured in Better Homes & Gardens, 2000; one-woman shows include Ocean Lodge, Cannon Beach Oreg., 2004, Fifth Ave. Stes., Porland, 2004, Lawrence Gallery, Portland, 2004, City Hall, 2005, Fifth Avenue Suites, 2006, exhibitions include Sikta Art Invitational, Portland, 2003, 2004, Rhodes Stingfellow Gallery, Cannon Beach, Oreg., 2004—06, Brodrick Gallery, Portland, 2004, Goitlieb Gallery, Portland, Oreg., 2005—, Associated Arts Regional Juried Fine Arts Show, Ocean Shores, Wash., 2005, Coos Art Mus., Richland, Wash., 2005, Oregon Art Beat, 2006, exhibitions include many others, exhibited in group shows at Grants Pass Mus. Art, 2006, Represented in permanent collections George and Barbara Bush, Houston, Rue McClanahan, Beverly Hills, Michael Jackson, Hollywood, Gary Maffei and Marc Linter, Portland. Spokeswoman Nat. Alopecia Areata Found., San Rafeal, Calif., 2004; Co-founder, v.p., newsletter editor Animal Rescue and Care Fund, 1972—81; mem. Friends of the Performing Arts Ctr., Portland Art Mus., Oreg. Humane Soc.; pres. OMSI; bd. dirs. Portland Opera Assn., 2000—02, Oreg. Humane Soc., 2002—. Recipient Internat. Film and TV Festival N.Y. Finalist award, 1985, 86, 87, 88, Internat. Radio Festival of N.Y. award, 1984, 85, 88, Hollywood Radio and TV Soc. Internat. Broadcasting award, 1981, TV Comml. Festival Silver Telly award, 1985, TV Comml. Festival Bronze Telly, 1986, AVC Silver Cindy, 1986, Los Angeles Advt. Women LULU, 1986, 87, 88, 89 Ad Week What's New Portfolio, 1986, N.W. Addy award Seattle Advt. Fedn., 1984, Best in the West award, 1985, Portland Advt. Fedn. Rosey Finalist award, 1986, Nat. winner Silver Microphone award, 1987, 88, 89. Mem.: Portland Art Mus., Portland Inst, Contemporary Art, Nat. Oil and Acrylic Painters Soc., People for Ethical Treatment of Animals. E-mail: labartist@aol.com.

BUTLER, R THOMAS (TOM), state legislator; b. Ontario, Oreg., Apr. 25, 1946; m to Darlene; children: five. Malheur Co commissioner, formerly; chairman, Co Budget Bd & Ambulance Serv District, formerly; member, Malheur Co Bd Equalization & Ratio Rev, 90-97, Idaho-Ore Planning & Develop Finance Committee & Association Oregon Counties Community Develop Committee, formerly; commissioner, Housing Authority Malheur Co, formerly; treasurer, Republican Cent Committee, formerly, precinct committeeman, currently; Oregon State Representative, District 60, 99-.Owner & manager, Truck Stop & Travel Plaza, currently; real estate development & tax instructor, currently. America Inst & Oregon Soc CPAs; Boy Scouts America; Rotary. Republican. Latter-Day Saints. Mailing: 900 Court St NE, H-286 Salem OR 97301 E-mail: butler.rep@state.or.us.

BUTOW, ROBERT JOSEPH CHARLES, historian, educator; b. San Mateo, Calif., Mar. 19, 1924; s. Frederick W.C. and Louise Marie B.; m. Irene Elkeles; 1 child, Stephanie Cecile. BA magna cum laude, Stanford U., 1947, MA, 1948, PhD, 1953. Instr. history Princeton U., 1954—59, asst. prof., 1959—60, rsch. assoc. Ctr. of Internat. Studies, 1954—60; assoc. prof. East Asian history and internat. studies U.

Wash., Seattle, 1960—66, prof., 1966—90, prof. emeritus, 1990—. Mem. Inst. for Advanced Study, 1962-63. Author: Japan's Decision to Surrender, 1954, 67, Tojo and the Coming of the War, 1961, 69, The John Doe Associates: Backdoor Diplomacy for Peace, 1941, 1974. 2d lt. U.S. Army, 1943-46. Grantee Social Sci. Rsch. Coun., 1956-57, Rockefeller Found., 1956-57, Eleanor Roosevelt Inst., 1977-78; Guggenheim fellow, 1965-66, 78-79, fellow Woodrow Wilson Ctr., 1987-88, Japan Found., 1987-88. Mem. Assn. of Mems. of Inst. for Advanced Study, Soc. Historians of Am. Fgn. Rels., World War Two Studies Assn. Office: U Wash Box 353650 Seattle WA 98195-3650 Home Phone: 206-323-8592; Office Phone: 206-543-4370. E-mail: rbutow@u.washington.edu.

BUTTERFIELD, ALEXANDER PORTER, air transportation executive, former federal official; b. Pensacola, Fla., Apr. 6, 1926; s. Horace Bushnell and Susan A. (Alexander) B.; m. Charlotte Mary Maguire, Sept. 9, 1949 (div. Jan. 1985); children: Leslie Carter (dec.), Alexander Porter Jr., Susan Carter Holcomb, Elisabeth Gordon Buchholz. BS, U. Md., 1956; MS, George Washington U., 1967; MA, U. Calif., 2005; PhD (hon.), Embry-Riddle U., 1973. Commd. 2d lt. USAF, 1949, advanced through grades to col., 1966, ret., pilot, fighter-gunnery instr., parachutist, weapons officer, mem. Skyblazers (U.S. jet aerobatic team Europe), 1949-53; aide to comdr. 4th Allied Tactical Air Force (NATO), 1954-55; ops. officer interceptor squadron, 1955-56; asst. prof. USAF Acad., 1957-59; sr. aide to comdr.-in-chief US Pacific Air Forces, 1959-62; comdr. fighter squadron Okinawa, 1962-63; comdr. tactical reconnaissance task forces S.E. Asia, 1963-64; tactical air warfare policy planner USAF, 1964-65; mil. asst. to spl. asst. to sec. US Dept. Def., 1965-66; student Nat. War Coll., 1966-67; sr. U.S. mil. rep. and comdr. in chief Pacific rep. US Dept. Def., Australia, 1967-69; retired, 1969; dep. asst. to Pres. The White House, 1969-73; adminstr. FAA, 1973-75; lectr. Ethics in Govt. Am. Program Bur., 1975-76; exec. v.p., COO Internat. Air Svc. Co. Ltd., 1977—79; pres., COO Calif. Life Corp., 1979—80. Chmn. GMA Corp., Global Network Inc., 1981—82; chmn., CEO Armistead & Alexander, Inc., 1983—94. Contbr. articles to profl. jours. and nat. mags.; mem. editl. bd. LA County Mus. Natural History mag. Terra, 1983-86. Presidentially apptd. mem. Nat. Armed Forces Mus. adv. bd. Smithsonian Instn., 1970—76; mem. mil.-sci. expdn. to South Pole, 1968; leader of US govt. and industry del. to Moscow for ministerial level talks on tech. and trade, 1973; key witness select com.'s hearings on Watergate US Senate, 1973; key witness during deliberations of impeachment of Pres. Richard Nixon US Ho. of Reps. Jud. Com., 1974; chmn. Chancellor's Assocs. U. Calif., San Diego, 2005—06; bd. dirs. Internat. Flight Safety Found., 1976—81, LA County Mus. Natural History, 1981—85. Decorated Legion of Merit, DFC, Air medal with 3 bronze oak leaf clusters, Bronze Star. Mem.: SAG, Air Force Assn., Tailhook Assn., Coun. for Excellence in Govt., Am. Film Inst., Thunderbird Alumni Assn., Bel-Air Country Club (L.A.), Univ. Club (San Diego). Home: 5340 Toscana Way # 416 San Diego CA 92122

BUTTERFIELD, DEBORAH KAY, sculptor; b. San Diego, May 7, 1949; m. John Buck; 2 children. BA, U. Calif., Davis, 1971, MFA, 1973; DFA (hon.), Mont. State U., 1998, Rocky Mountain Coll., Billings, Mont., 1997, Whitman Coll., Walla Walla, Wash., 2004. Asst. prof. sculpture U. Wis., Madison, 1975-76, Mont. State U., Bozeman, 1979-81, adj. prof., 1981-84. One-man shows include Lowe Mus. Art U. Miami, Coral Gables, Fla., 1992, San Diego Mus. Art, 1996, Yellowstone Art Mus., Billings, Mont., 2003-04, The Contemporary Mus. Art, Honolulu, 2004, Appleton Mus. Art, Ocala, Fla., 2004, U. Art Mus., U. La., Lafayette, 2005, Neuberger Art Mus., Purchase N.Y., 2005, Norton Mus. Art, West Palm Beach, Fla., 2005; exhibited in groups shows U. Mus. Berkeley, Calif., 1974, Whitney Mus. Am. Art, N.Y., 1979, Albright-Knox Gallery, Buffalo, 1979, Israel Mus., Jerusalem, 1980, Arco Ctr. Visual Art, 1981, Walker Art Ctr., Mpls., 1982, Dallas Mus. Fine Arts, 1982, Oakland, 1983, Chgo., 1985, Contemporary Art Ctr., Honolulu, 1986, Whitney Mus., 1988, Contemporary Art Mus., Honolulu, 1993, Seattle Mus. Art, 1994, The White House, Washington, Yale U., New Haven, 1997; represented in permanent collections Whitney Mus. Am. Art, N.Y., San Francisco Mus. Contemporary Art, Israel Mus., Jerusalem, Walker Art Ctr., Mpls., Met. Mus. Art, N.Y., Hirshhorn Mus., Washington, Seattle Art Mus., UCLA Sculpture Garden, L.A. Mus. Contemporary Art; commd. Copley Square, Boston, Portland (Oreg.) Airport, Denver Art Mus., Kansas City (Mo.) Zoo, White House, Washington, 2000, Monte Carlo, Monaco, 2000, Smithsonian Instn., Washington, San Francisco Internat. Airport. Nat. Endowment Arts grantee, 1977, 80, Guggenheim grantee, 1980; Commission Portland Internat. Airport.

BUTTERFIELD, STEWART, Internet company executive; m. Caterina Fake; 1 child, Sonnet Beatrice. BA with honors, U. Victoria; MPhil, Cambridge U. Dir. Communicate.com; co-founder, CEO Ludicorp, Vancouver, 2002—05; co-founder Flickr.com, 2004; dir. product mgmt. Yahoo!, San Francisco, 2005—. Cons. Telus, CBC, The Economist; founder 5K competition. Speaker in field. Co-recipient with Caterina Fake, Webby Breakout of Yr. award, 2005; named one of 100 Most Influential People, Time mag., 2006, 50 Who Matter Now, CNNMoney.com Bus. 2.0, 2006. Mem.: Internat. Acad. Digital Arts & Scis. Office: Yahoo 701 First Ave Sunnyvale CA 94089 E-mail: stewart@ludicorp.com.

BUURSMA, WILLIAM F., architect; BArch, U. Mich., 1964; MArch, U. Pa., 1965. Lic. arch. With various archtl. design firms; joined John Graham Assocs/DLR Group, Seattle, 1976—, prin. Tchg. fellow U. Tenn., also assoc. prof. France program. Prin. works include Madigan Army Med. Ctr., Ft. Lewis, Wash., Clackamas Town Ctr., Portland, Oreg., Kauai Hilton Resort and Condominium Complex, Hawaii, high-rise office bldgs., retail shopping malls, and numerous other complexes. Mem. AIA. Office: John Graham Assoc 900 4th Ave Ste 700 Seattle WA 98164-1003

BUXBAUM, RICHARD M., lawyer, educator; b. 1930; AB, Cornell U., 1950, LLB, 1952; LLM, U. Calif., Berkeley, 1953; D (hon.), U. Osnabrück, 1992, Eötvös Lorand U., Budapest, Hungary, 1993, U. Cologne, 2006. Bar: Calif. 1953, NY 1953. Pvt. practice, Rochester, NY, 1957—61; prof. U. Calif., Berkeley, 1961—, dean internat. and area studies, 1993-99. Hon. prof. U. Peking, 1998. Editor-in-chief Am. Jour. Comparative Law, 1987-2004. Property commn. mem. Found. for Responsibility, Remembrance, and the Future, Germany, 2001—06. Recipient Humboldt prize, 1991, German Order of Merit, 1992, Officier Arts et Lettres, France, 1997, Order of Rio Branco, Brazil, 1998. Mem. AAAS, Am. Law Inst., Internat. Acad. Comparative Law, German Soc. Comparative Law (corr.), Coun. on Fgn. Rels. Office: U Calif Sch Law 888 Simon Hall Berkeley CA 94720-0001 Office Phone: 510-642-1771. Business E-Mail: bux@berkeley.edu.

BUZUNIS, CONSTANTINE DINO, lawyer; b. Winnipeg, Man., Can., Feb. 3, 1958; came to U.S., 1982; s. Peter and Anastasia (Ginakes) B. BA, U. Man., 1980; JD, Thomas M. Cooley Law Sch., 1985. Bar: Mich. 1986, U.S. Dist. Ct. (ea. and we. dists.) Mich. 1986, Calif. 1986, U.S. Dist. Ct. (so. dist.) Calif. 1987, U.S. Supreme Ct. 1993. Assoc. Church, Kritselis, Wyble & Robinson, Lansing, Mich., 1986, Neil, Dymott, Frank, McFall & Trexler, San Diego, 1987-94, ptnr., 1994—. Arbitrator San Diego County Mcpl. and Superior Cts.; judge pro tem San Diego Mcpl. Ct. Sec., treas. Sixty Plus Law Ctr., Lansing, 1985; active Vols. in Parole, San Diego, 1988—; bd. dirs. Hellenic Cultural Soc., 1993-98. Mem. Mich. Bar Assn., Calif. Bar Assn., San Diego County Bar Assn., Desert Bar Assn., So. Calif. Def. Coun., State Bar Calif. (gov. 9th dist. young lawyers divsn. 1991-94, 1st v.p. 1993-94, pres. 1994-95, bd. govs. 1995-96) San Diego Barristers Soc. (bd. dirs. 1991-92), San Diego Def. Lawyers Assn. (bd. dirs. 2003-05, sec. 2003-04), Risk Ins. Mgmt. Soc. (assoc.), San Diego Ins. Adjusters Assn. (assoc.), Pan Arcadian Fedn., Order of Ahepa (chpt. bd. dirs., v.p. 1995-98, chpt. pres. 2001-04, chair bd. govs. 2004-05), Hellenic Cultural Soc., Phi Alpha Delta. Office: 3419 Overpark Rd San Diego CA 92130-1865 also: Neil Dymott Frank McFall & Trexler 1010 2nd Ave Ste 2500 San Diego CA 92101-4959 Fax: 619-238-1562. E-mail: cbuzunis@neildymott.com.

BYBEE, JAY SCOTT, federal judge, former federal agency administrator; b. Oakland, Calif., Oct. 27, 1953; s. Rowan Scott and Joan (Hickman) B.; m. Dianna Jean Greer, Feb. 15, 1986; children: Scott, David, Alyssa, Ryan. BA, Brigham Young U., 1977, JD, 1980. Bar: DC 1981, US Ct. Appeals (4th cir.) 1983, US Supreme Ct. 1985, US Ct. Appeals (5th cir.) 1986, US Ct. Appeals (2d, 9th, 10th and DC cirs.) 1987. Law clk. to Hon. Donald Russell US Ct. Appeals (4th cir.), 1980-81; assoc. Sidley & Austin, Washington, 1981-84; atty., Office Legal Policy US Dept. Justice, Washington, 1984—86, atty. civil divsn., 1986—89; assoc. counsel to Pres. The White House, Washington, 1989-91; prof. law La. State U., Baton Rouge, 1991-98, U. Nev., Las Vegas, 1999—2001; asst. atty. gen. Office Legal Counsel US Dept. Justice, Washington, 2001—02; judge US Ct. Appeals (9th cir.), San Francisco, 2003—. Contbr. articles to profl. jours. Missionary Mormon Ch., Santiago, Chile, 1973-75. Edwin S. Hinckley scholar, Brigham Young U., 1976-77. Mem. Phi Kappa Phi. Avocations: piano, all sports, reading. Office: US Ct Appeals Lloyd B George US Courthouse Ste 3099 333 Las Vegas Blvd Las Vegas NV 89101*

BYBEE, RODGER WAYNE, science administrator; b. San Francisco, Feb. 21, 1942; s. Wayne and Mary Genevieve (Mungon) B.; m. Patricia Ann Brovsky, May 28, 1966. BA, Colo. State Coll., 1966; MA, U. No. Colo., 1969; PhD, NYU, 1975. Tchr. sci. Greeley (Colo.) Pub. Schs., 1965-66; instr. sci. U. No. Colo., Greeley, 1966-70; teaching fellow NYU, NYC, 1970-72; instr. edn. Carleton Coll., Northfield, Minn., 1972-75, asst. prof., 1975-81, assoc. prof., chmn. dept., 1981-85; assoc. dir. Biol. Scis. Curriculum Study, Colorado Springs, 1986-95, acting dir., 1992-93; exec. dir. Ctr. Sci., Math. and Engring. Edn. NRC, Washington, 1995-99; exec. dir. BSCS, Colorado Springs, Colo., 1999—. Mem. adv. bd. for sci. assessment Nat. Assessment Ednl. Progress, Princeton, N.J., 1987-89, 92-93, 95-96; mem. adv. bd. Social Sci. Edn. Consortium, Boulder, Colo., 1987-90; chairperson working group on curriculum NRC project on Nat. Sci. Ednl. Stds., 1993-95; chmn. Sci. Framework 2006, Orgn. Econ. Coop. and Devel., Paris, France. Author: numerous books; contbr. numerous articles to profl. jours. NSF grantee, 1986—. Fellow AAAS (mem.-at-large 1987-90, chair sect. Q 1993-94, coun. del.), Nat. Assn. Rsch. Sci. Teaching (rsch. coord. 1986-89). Home: PO Box 563 Frisco CO 80443-0563 Office: BSCS 5415 Mark Dabling Blvd Colorado Springs CO 80918-3842 E-mail: rbybee@bscs.org.

BYCZYNSKI, EDWARD FRANK, lawyer, corporate financial executive; b. Chgo., Mar. 17, 1946; s. Edward James and Ann (Ruskey) B.; children: Stefan, Suzanne. BA, U. Wis., 1968; JD, U. Ill., 1972; Cert. de Droit, U. Caen, France, 1971. Bar: Ill. 1972, U.S.Dist. Ct. (no. dist.) Ill. 1972, U.S. Supreme Ct. 1976. Title officer Chgo. Title Inst. Co., 1972-73; ptnr. Haley, Pirok, Byczynski, Chgo., 1973-76; pres. Alderstreet Investments, Portland, Oreg., 1976-82, Nat. Tenant Network, Portland, 1981—. Asst. regional counsel SBA, Chgo., 1973-76; pres. Bay Venture Corp., Portland, 1984—. Contbr. articles to profl. jours. Mem. ABA, Ill. Bar Assn. Independent. Home: PO Box 2377 Lake Oswego OR 97035-0614 Office: 525 1st St Ste 105 Lake Oswego OR 97034-3100 Business E-Mail: efb@ntnonline.com.

BYER, ROBERT LOUIS, applied physics educator, university dean; b. Pasadena, Calif., May 9, 1942; s. Herbert Louis and Wilfrie (Schulz) B.; m. Eva Maria Guzsella, Aug. 15, 1964; children: Scott, Douglas, Mark, Evi-Lynn. BA in Physics, U. Calif., Berkeley, 1964; MS in Applied Physics, Stanford U., 1967, PhD in Applied Physics, 1969. Scientist Spectra Physics, Mountain View, Calif., 1964-65; asst. prof. Stanford (Calif.) U., 1969-74, assoc. prof., 1974-79, prof., 1979—, chair dept. applied physics, 1980-83, assoc. dean humanities and sci., 1984-86, dean rsch., 1987-92, chair dept. applies physics, 2000—. Bd. dirs. Lightwave Electronics Corp., Mountain View, Polystor, Gen. Lasertronics Corp. Contbr. 350 articles to profl. jours.; holder over 30 patents. Recipient Arthur L. Schawlow Awd. 1998, NAS award 2000. Fellow IEEE (millennium medal 2000), AAAS, Am. Phys. Soc., Optical Soc. Am. (Adolph Lomb medal 1972, bd. dirs. 1986-89, v.p. 1992, pres.-elect 1993, pres. 1994); mem. NAE, Lasers and Electro-Optic Soc. (pres. 1984), Calif. Coun. on Sci. and Tech. (vice chmn.). Office: Stanford University Dept of Applies Physics Stanford CA 94305 E-mail: Byer@Stanford.edu.

BYERS, BROOK, venture capitalist, investor; b. 1946; BSEE, Ga. Inst. Tech., 1968; MBA, Stanford Grad. Sch. Bus., Calif.; degree (hon.), U. Calif., San Francisco, 2007. Co-founder, ptnr. Kleiner, Perkins, Caufield & Byers, 1972—. Bd. mem. Stanford Eye Coun., Stanford Bio-X Adv. Coun., U. Calif San Francisco Med. Found.; bd. dirs. CardioDX, Genomic Health Inc., Five Prime Therapeutics, OptiMedica, Pacific Bioscis., Inc., Tethys Biosci., XDx, Inc.; past chmn. Idec Pharms., Vision Rsch. Found., Athena Neuroscis., Hybritech; past bd. dirs. Signal Pharms., Arris Pharms., Pharmacopeia, Gen-Probe, Calif. Healthcare Inst. Bd. mem. New Shcools Found.; co-chair U. Calif. San Francisco Capital Campaign; past. bd. dirs. Entrepreneurs Found., Asian Art Mus., San Francisco; past adv. bd. mem. Ga. Inst. Tech.; past bus. adv. coun. mem. Stanford U. Grad. Sch. Fellow: Am. Acad. Arts & Scis.; mem.: Western Assn. Venture Capitalists (past pres.), Nat. Venture Capital Assn. Democrat. Office: Kleiner Perkins Caufield & Byers 2750 Sand Hill Rd Menlo Park CA 94025 Office Phone: 650-233-2750. Office Fax: 650-233-0300. Business E-Mail: brookb@kpcb.com.

BYERS, PETER H., geneticist; b. NYC, May 31, 1943; MD, Case Western Reserve U., 1969. Diplomate Am. Bd. Internal Medicine, Am. Bd. Molecular Genetics, clin. geneticist. Intern U. Calif., San Francisco, 1969, resident, 1969-70; fellow U. Wash., Seattle, 1974-77, asst. prof. pathology and medicine, 1979-82, assoc. prof., 1982-86, prof., 1986—. Editor Am. Jour. Human Genetics, 1994-99. Fellow AAAS, Am. Soc. Human Genetics, Am. Soc. for Clin. Investigation; mem. Am. Bd. Med. Genetics (pres. 1997). Office: U Wash Dept Pathology PO Box 357470 Seattle WA 98195-7470

BYERS, TOM H., management science and engineering educator; BS in Indsl. Engring. and Ops. Rsch. (highest honors), U. Calif., Berkeley, 1975; MBA, Haas Sch. Bus., U. Calif., Berkeley, 1980, PhD in Bus. Adminstrn. (mgmt. sci.), 1982. Mgmt. cons. Accenture (Anderson Consulting), 1975—77; group product mgr. Digital Rsch., 1982—85; exec. v.p., gen. mgr. Symantec, 1985—90; pres., co-founder Slate (sold to Compaq), 1990—93; lectr., rsch. asst., tchg. asst., Haas Sch. Bus. U. Calif., Berkeley, 1979—82, lectr., indsl. engring. and ops. rsch., 1980—82, lectr., Haas Sch. Bus., 1994—95; adj. lectr., dept. mgmt. sci. and engring. Stanford U., Calif., 1994—95, adj. cons. assoc. prof., dept. mgmt. sci. and engring. Calif., 1995—98, assoc. prof., dept. mgmt. sci. and engring. Calif., 1998—2002, prof., dept. mgmt. sci. and engring. Calif., 2002—; acad. dir. Am. Electronics Assn./Stanford Exec. Inst., 1995—; founder, co-dir. Stanford Technology Ventures Program (STVP), Calif., 1995—. Sr. bus. advisor Interval Rsch. Corp., 1994—98; bd. dirs. MyThings, 1995—, BioFuelBox, 1995—, Flywheel Ventures, 1995—; previously served on the following bd. dirs. Visio (now part Microsoft Corp.), AlphaBlox (now part IBM) and Reactivity (now part of Cisco); several svc. positions Stanford U., 2001—; vis. prof. London Bus. Sch. and U. Coll. London, 2004—06; mem. adv. coun. World Econ. Forum's Global Agenda Coun. on Entrepreneurship, Am. Soc. for Engring. Edn. Entrepreneurship Divsn., Nat. Found. for Tchg. Entrepreneurship for inner-city youth; invited presenter in field. Contbr. several articles to profl. jours.; co-author: Technology Ventures: From Idea to Enterprise, 2nd edit., 2007. Recipient Innovation in Pedagogy award, Acad. Mgmt. Mayfield Fellows Program, 1998, No. Calif. Entrepreneur of Yr. award in the supporter category, Ernst & Young, 1998, Edwin M. Appel prize for Bringing entrepreneurial vitality to academia, Price-Babson Symposium for Entrepreneurship Edn., 1999, Stanford Technology Ventures Program awarded Nat. Specialty Program award, US Assn. for Small Bus. and Entrepreneurship, 2002, Outstanding Entrepreneurship Educator of Yr. award, 2005, Entrepreneurial Svc. award, Nat. Found. for Tchg. Entrepreneurship, 2002, Nat. Leavey award for Excellence in Private Enterprise Edn., Freedoms Found., 2003, Stanford Technology Ventures Program was given the NASDAQ Ctr. for Entrepreneurial Excellence award, Nat. Consortium Entrepreneurship Ctrs., 2004, Kauffman award for excellence in engring. and technology entrepreneurship edn., Am. Soc. Engring. Edn., 2005, Gores award, Stanford U., 2005; co-recipient with Tina Seelig, Nat. Olympus Innovation award, Nat. Collegiate Inventors and Innovators Alliance, 2008; Regents Scholar, U. Calif., Berkeley, 1980—82, Buzz & Barbara McCoy U. Fellow in Undergraduate Edn., Stanford U., 2002, 2007. Mem.: NAE (co-recipient, Bernard M. Gordon prize 2009), Tau Beta Pi (award for excellence in undergraduate tchg., Stanford Sch. Engring. 2002), Phi Beta Kappa. Office: Stanford U Management Sci and Engring Terman Engineering Ctr 3rd Fl Rm 417 380 Panama Way Stanford CA 94305-4026 Office Phone: 650-725-8271. Office Fax: 650-723-1614. Business E-Mail: tbyers@stanford.edu.*

BYERS, WILLIAM D., engineering executive; BS in Chem. Engring., Oreg. State U., 1973; MBA, U. Oreg., 1981. Registered profl. engr., Oreg., 1982, Am. Acad. Environmental Engrs., 1982. Mem. staff CH2M Hill, 1981—94, v.p., 1994—, dir. tech. devel., 1994—. Mem.: AIChE (pres. 2004). Office: vp Technol Devel 2300 NW Walnut Blvd Corvallis OR 97330 Office Phone: 541-768-3510. Business E-Mail: bill.byers@ch2m.com.

BYNAGLE, HANS EDWARD, library director, philosophy educator; b. Ruurlo, The Netherlands, Feb. 24, 1946; came to U.S., 1956; s. Cornelius Adrian and Maria (Kalfsbeek) B.; m. Janet Mae Monsma, June 27, 1969; children: Maria Elizabeth, Derek Johannes. BA, Calvin Coll., 1968; PhD, Columbia U., 1973; MLS, Kent State U., 1976. Asst. prof. philosophy Union Coll., Schenectady, N.Y., 1972-73, Coll. Wooster, Ohio, 1974-75; dir. learning resources Friends U., Wichita, Kans., 1976-82; dir. library Eckerd Coll., St. Petersburg, Fla., 1982-83; dir. library, prof. Whitworth Coll./U., Spokane, Wash., 1983—. Author: Philosophy: A Guide to the Reference Literature, 1986, 3d edit., 2006; mem. editl. bd. Christian Scholar's Rev., 1992—; numerous rev. to profl. jours. Named one of Outstanding Young Men of Am., 1982. Mem. ALA, Assn. Coll. and Rsch. Librs. (chmn. Kans. chpt. 1980-81). Presbyterian. Avocation: music. Home: 1122 W Bellwood Dr Spokane WA 99218-2907 E-mail: hbynagle@whitworth.edu.

BYNUM, ANDREW, professional basketball player; b. Plainsboro, NJ, Oct. 27, 1987; Grad., St. Joseph HS, Metuchen, NJ. Ctr. LA Lakers, 2005—. Named McDonald's HS All-Am., 2005. Achievements include being the youngest player ever drafted in the NBA (17 years, 8 months, 2 days), 2005; being the youngest player ever to play in an NBA regular season game (18 years, 6 days), 2005. Avocations: reading, music, computers. Office: LA Lakers 555 N Nash St El Segundo CA 90245

BYRD, CHRISTINE WATERMAN SWENT, lawyer; b. Oakland, Calif., Apr. 11, 1951; d. Langan Waterman and Eleanor (Herz) Swent; m. Gary Lee Byrd, June 20, 1981; children: Amy, George. BA, Stanford U., 1972; JD, U. Va., 1975. Bar: Calif. 1976, U.S. Dist. Ct. (ctrl., so. no., ea. dists.) Calif., U.S. Ct. Appeals (9th cir.). Law clk. to Hon. William P. Gray U.S. Dist. Ct., LA, 1975—76; assoc. Jones, Day, Reavis & Pogue, LA, 1976—82, ptnr., 1987—96; asst. U.S. atty. criminal divsn. U.S. Atty.'s Office, Ctrl. Dist. Calif., LA, 1982—87; ptnr. Irell & Manella, LA, 1996—. Mem. Calif. Law Revision Commn., 1992-97. Author: The Future of the U.S. Multinational Corporation, 1975; contbr. articles to profl. jours. Named Best Lawyers in World, Best Lawyers in America. Fellow: Coll. Comml. Arbitrators, Am. Coll. Trial Lawyers; mem.: ABA (vice chmn. ADR Advocacy in Litig. 2003—05), Assn. Bus. Trial Lawyers (bd. govs. 1996—99), 9th Jud. Cir. Hist. Soc. (pres. 1997—2002, bd. dirs. 1986—), Century City Bar Assn. (bd. govs. 2001—05), Stanford Profl. Women L.A. County, Am. Arbitration Assn. (large and complex case panel 1992—, nat. energy panel 1998—, class action panel 2004—, bd. dirs. 1999—), Women Lawyers Assn. L.A. County, L.A. County Bar Assn., Calif. State Bar (com. fed. cts. 1985—88), Stanford U. Alumni Assn. Republican. Office: Irell & Manella LLP 1800 Ave Of Stars Ste 900 Los Angeles CA 90067-4276 Office Phone: 310-277-1010. Business E-Mail: cbyrd@irell.com.

BYRD, MILTON BRUCE, academic administrator; b. Boston, Jan. 29, 1922; s. Max Joseph and Rebecca (Malkiel) B.; m. Susanne J. Schwerin, Aug. 30, 1953; children: Deborah, Leslie, David. AB cum laude, Boston U., 1948, MA, 1949; PhD, U. Wis., 1953; postgrad. (fellow), U. Mich., 1961-62. Teaching asst. English U. Wis., 1949-53; instr., asst. prof. English Ind. U., 1953-58; asst. prof., assoc. prof. humanities So. Ill. U., 1958-62, head div. humanities, 1958-60, supr. acad. advisement, 1959-60, asso. dean, 1960- 62; v.p. acad. affairs No. Mich. U., 1962-66; pres. Chgo. State U., 1966-74; provost Fla. Internat. U., 1974-78; pres. Adams State Coll., Alamosa, Colo., 1978—80; v.p. corp. devel. Frontier Cos., Anchorage, 1981-85; pres. Charter Coll., 1985—2005, pres. emeritus, 2005—. Bd. dirs Chgo. Council for Urban Edn., Union for Experimenting Colls. and Univs., Am. Assn. State Colls. and Univs., Resource Devel. Council Alaska, Alaska Commn. Econ. Edn.; v.p. Common Sense for Alaska, Inc.; former pres. Alaska Support Industry Alliance; pres. Alaska World Affairs Coun. Author: (with Arnold L. Goldsmith) Publication Guide for Literary and Linguistic Scholars, 1958; contbr. to profl. jours. Vice chmn. Alaska Commn. on Postsecondary Edn. With USAAF, 1943—46. Mem. MLA, Nat. Council Tchrs. English, Coll. English Assn., Am. Studies Assn., AAUP, Fla. Assn. Univ. Adminstrs. (former pres.), Rocky Mountain Athletic Conf. (former pres.), Assn. for Higher Edn., Pub. Relations Soc. Am., NEA, Alaska Press Club, Mich. Edn. Assn., Phi Beta Kappa, Phi Delta Kappa. Clubs: Rotary. Office: # 120 2221 E Northern Lights Blvd Anchorage AK 99508-4143 Business E-Mail: mbyrd@chartercollege.edu, mbb@eci.net.

BYRNE, JOHN VINCENT, educational consultant; b. Hempstead, NY, May 9, 1928; s. Frank E. and Kathleen (Barry) B.; m. Shirley O'Connor, Nov. 26, 1954; children: Donna, Lisa, Karen, Steven. AB, Hamilton Coll., 1951, JD (hon.), 1994; MA, Columbia U., 1953; PhD, U. So. Calif., 1957. Research geologist Humble Oil & Refinery Co., Houston, 1957-60; assoc. prof. Oreg. State U., Corvallis, 1960-66, prof. oceanography, 1966—, chmn. dept., 1968-72, dean Sch. Oceanography, 1972-76, acting dean research, 1976-77, dean research, 1977-80, v.p. for research and grad. studies, 1980-81, pres., 1984-95; adminstr. NOAA, Washington, 1981-84; U.S. commr. Internat. Whaling Commn., 1982—85; pres. Oreg. State U., 1984-95; higher edn. cons. Corvallis, 1996—. Program dir. oceanography NSF, 1966-67; exec. dir. Kellogg Commn. on Future of State and Land Grant Univs., 1996-2000; dir. Harbor Br. Ocean Inst., Oregon Coast Aquarium. Recipient Carter teaching award Oreg. State U., 1964. Fellow AAAS, Geol. Soc. Am.; mem. Geol. Soc. Am., Am. Geophys. Union, Sigma Xi, Chi Psi. Home: 3190 NW Deer Run St Corvallis OR 97330-3107 Office: Autzen House 811 SW Jefferson Ave Corvallis OR 97333-4506 Office Phone: 541-737-3542. Business E-Mail: john.byrne@oregonstate.edu.

BYRNES, ERIC JAMES, professional baseball player, radio, television personality; b. Redwood City, Calif., Feb. 16, 1976; m. Tarah Byrnes. Attended, UCLA, 1995—98. Outfielder Oakland Athletics, 2000—05, Colo. Rockies, 2005, Balt. Orioles, 2005, Ariz. Diamondbacks, 2006—. Analyst, Baseball Tonight ESPN; analyst FOX Sports; fill-in host Sta. KNBR, San Francisco; host, The Eric Byrnes Show FSN, Ariz.; host, Hustle with Eric Byrnes XM Satellite Radio, 2007—. Office: Ariz Diamondbacks Chase Field 401 E Jefferson St Phoenix AZ 85001*

BYRNES, JAMES BERNARD, museum director, consultant; b. NYC, Feb. 19, 1917; s. Patrick J.A. and Janet E. (Geiger) B.; m. Barbara A. Cecil, June 10, 1946; 1 son, Ronald L. Student, N.A.D., 1936-38, Am. Artist Sch., 1938-40, Art Students League, 1940-42, U. Perugia, Italy, 1951, Inst. Meschini, Rome, 1952. Art tchr. mus. activity program NYC Bd. Edn., 1936-40; indsl. designer Michael Saphier Assos., NYC, 1940-42; audio visual specialist USNR, 1944—45; with LA County Mus., 1946-47, assoc. curator modern contemporary art, 1947-48, curator, asst. to dir., 1948-53; dir. Colorado Springs Fine Arts Center, 1954-55; from assoc. dir. to dir. NC Mus. Art, 1956-60; dir. New Orleans Mus. Art, 1961-71, dir. emeritus, 1989—; dir. Newport Harbor Art Mus., Newport Beach, Calif., 1972-75. Vis. lectr. U. Fla., 1961, Newcomb Coll., Tulane U., 1963; art cons. Author: Masterpieces of Art, W.R. Valentiner Memorial, 1959, Tobacco and Smoking in Art, 1960, Fetes de la Palette, 1963, Edgar Degas, His Family and Friends in New Orleans, 1965, Odyssey of an Art Collector, 1966, Art of Ancient and Modern Latin America, 1968, The Artist as Collector of Primitive Art, 1975, also numerous mus. catalogs. Decorated knight Order Leopold II (Belgium); recipient Isaac Delgado Meml. award, New Orleans Mus. of Art, 1998. Mem. Am. Soc. Interior Design (hon. life), Am. Soc. Appraisers (sr.), Retired Appraisers Assn. Am. Office: James B Byrnes and Assocs 7820 Mulholland Dr Los Angeles CA 90046-1223

BYRNES, LAWRENCE WILLIAM, dean; b. Windsor, Ont., Can., June 17, 1940; s. Carl Wilfred and Alice Hendrie (Thomson) B.; m. Margaret Amelia Snavely, June 26, 1965; children: Andrew Carl, Mary Margaret. BA in Social Sci., Mich. State U., 1963, MA in History, 1967, PhD in Edn., 1970. Tchr. social studies Grosse Pointe (mich.) Schs., 1963-66; prof. Calif. State U., Northridge, 1969-78; dean edn. Southeastern La. U., Hammond, 1978-83, Moorhead (Minn.) State U., 1983-88, Edinboro (Pa.) U., 1988-91; dir. Ctr. for Teaching and Learning U. So. Colo., 1991-95; dean Coll. Edn. and Tech. Eastern N.Mex. U., Portales, 1995—. Ptnr., cons. ML Byrnes and Assocs., Erie, Pa. Author: Religion and Republic Education, 1975; co-author: Total Quality Management in Higher Education, 1991, The Quality Teacher: Implementing TQM in the Classroom, 1992. Mem. Gov.'s Steering Com. on Strengthening Quality in Schs., N. Mex. Mem. Am. Assn. Colls. Tchr. Edn. (chmn. global and internat. tchrs. edn. com.), N. Mex. Assn. Colls. Tchr. Edn. (pres.), Phi Delta Kappa (pres. Moorhead chpt. 1987-88, historian Erie chpt. 1991—, hist. South Colo. chpt. 1994—) Democrat. Episcopalian. Avocations: running, drums, music. Home: 416 E 17th Ln Portales NM 88130-9266 Office: ENMU Coll Edn & Tech Portales NM 88130

BYYNY, RICHARD LEE, former academic administrator, physician, educator; b. South Gate, Calif., Jan. 6, 1939; s. Oswald and Essa Burnetta (McGinnis) B.; m. Jo Ellen Garverick, Aug. 25, 1962; children: Kristen, Jan, Richard. BA in History, U. So. Calif., 1960, MD, 1964. Intern and resident in internal medicine Columbia Presbyn. Med. Ctr., NYC, 1964-66, chief resident, 1968-69; fellow in endocrinology Vanderbilt U., Nashville, 1969-71; asst. prof. medicine U. Chgo., 1971-74, head div. internal medicine, 1972-77, assoc. prof., 1975-77; prof. internal medicine U. Colo., Denver, 1977—, head divsn. internal medicine, 1977-94, vice-chmn. dept. medicine Health Scis. Ctr., 1977-85, exec. vice chancellor, 1994-95, v.p. acad. affairs, 1995-97, chancellor Boulder, 1997—2005; exec. dir. Ctr. for Health Policy U. Colo. Hosp., 2005—06. Med. dir. ambulatory care, 1990-92; mem. Coun. on Econ. Devel., Boulder, Colo., bd. dirs. Rocky Mtn. region Inst. Internal Edn., 2004—. Author: A Clinical Guide in the Care of Older Women, 1990, 2d edit., 1995; contbr. articles to profl. jours., chapters to books. Pres. Ill. Council Continuing Med. Edn., Ill., 1976-77; bd. dirs. Denver affiliate Am. Heart Assn., 1987-98 (pres. 1994-95), Boulder Com. Hosp., 1997-2007, Bank of Boulder, Boulder Econ. Coun., arm of Boulder C. of C., US Coun. on Competitiveness Big 12 Conf. Capt. USAF, 1966-68. Recipient Merck award U. So. Calif., 1964; Am. Coun. Edn. fellow, 1992-93. Fellow ACP; mem. AAAS, Soc. for Gen. Internal Medicine (pres. 1979-80), Am. Soc. Hypertension, Western Soc. Clin. Investigation, Endocrine Soc., Am. Fedn. for Clin. Rsch., Am. Coun. Edn. (commn. leadership instl. effectiveness), Boulder Country Club, Alpha Omega Alpha (bd. dirs. 1996—). Avocations: tennis, skiing, running, surfing, sailing. Home: 2900 Park Lake Dr Boulder CO 80301-5139 Office: 4200 E 9th Ave Box C299 Denver CO 80262 Home Phone: 303-665-3854. Business E-Mail: richard.byyny@uchsc.edu.

CABELLERO, ANNA M., state legislator; m. Juan Uranga. BA in Sociology, U. Calif., San Diego; JD, U. Calif., Los Angeles. Atty. Calif. Rural Legal Assistance; founder, ptnr. Caballero, Matcham & McCarthy, 1982; exec. dir. Partners for Peace; mem. Salinas Planning Comm., Salinas City Coun., 1991—98; mayor City of Salinas, 1998—2006; mem. Dist. 28 Calif. State Assembly, Calif., 2006—. Democrat. Office: 100 W Alisal St Ste 134 Salinas CA 93901 also: PO Box 942849 Rm 5119 Sacramento CA 94249-0028 Office Phone: 831-759-8676, 916-319-2028. Office Fax: 831-759-2961. E-mail: Assemblymember.Caballero@assembly.ca.gov.*

CABLE, JOHN FRANKLIN, lawyer; b. Hannibal, Mo., Dec. 22, 1941; s. John William and Dorothy (Stanley) C.; m. Leslie Gibbs, Apr. 5, 1965; children: Coventry, Tory, John. AB, Stanford U., 1964; LLB, Harvard U., 1967. Bar: Oreg. 1967. Assoc. Miller, Nash, Wiener, Hager & Carlsen, Portland, Oreg., 1967-73, ptnr., 1973—2007; mng. dir. Obsidian Fin. Group, Portland, 2007—. Office: Obsidian Fin Group 10260 SW Greenburg Rd Ste 1150 Portland OR 97223 Business E-Mail: fcable@obsidianfinance.com.

CABLE, THOMAS LEE (TOM CABLE), professional football coach; b. Merced, Calif., Nov. 26, 1964; children: Amanda, Alexander, Zachery. Attended, U. Idaho, Moscow. Player Indpls. Colts, 1987; grad. asst. U. Idaho Vandals, 1987—88, head coach, 2001—03; grad. asst. San Diego State U. Aztecs, 1989; defensive line coach Calif. State U. Fullerton Titans, 1990; offensive line coach U. Nev. Las Vegas Runnin' Rebels, 1991, U. Calif. Golden Bears, 1992—97, U. Colo. Buffaloes, 1998, offensive coord., 1999; offensive coord., offensive line coach UCLA Bruins, 2004—05; offensive line coach Atlanta Falcons, 2006, Oakland Raiders, 2007—08, interim head coach, 2008, head football coach, 2009—. Office: Oakland Raiders 1220 Harbor Bay Pky Alameda CA 94502*

CABRASER, ELIZABETH JOAN, lawyer; b. Oakland, Calif., June 23, 1952; AB, U. Calif., Berkeley, 1975; JD, U. Calif., 1978. Bar: Calif. 1978, U.S. Dist. Ct. (no., ea., cen. and so. dists.) Calif. 1979, U.S. Ct. Appeals (2d, 3rd, 5th, 6th, 9th, 10th, and 11th cirs.) 1979, U.S. Tax Ct. 1979, U.S. Dist. Ct. Hawaii 1986, U.S. Dist. Ct. Ariz. 1990, U.S. Supreme Ct. 1996. Ptnr. Lieff, Cabraser, Heimann & Bernstein LLP, San Francisco, 1978—. Contbr., editor California Causes of Action, 1998, Moore's Federal Practice, 1999, editor-in-chief California Class Actions Practice and Procedures, 2003; contbr. articles to law jours. Recipient Presdl. Award of Merit, Consumer Attys. Calif., 1998, Matthew O. Tobriner Pub. Svc. award, Legal Aid Soc., 2000, Disting. Jurisprudence award, Anti-Defamation League, 2002, U. Calif., Berkeley Sch. Law Citation award, 2003; named one of The 100 Most Influential Lawyers in America, Nat. Law Jour., 1997, 2000, 2006, The Top 50 Women Lawyers, 1998, The 50 Most Influential Women Lawyers in America, 2007, The Top Ten Lawyers in Bay Area, San Francisco Chronicle, 2003. Mem. ABA (tort and ins. practice sect., sect. litig. com. on class action and derivative skills, chair subcom. on mass torts), ATLA, Coun. Am. Law Inst., Calif. Constn. Rev. Commn., Nat. Ctr. for State Cts. (mass tort conf. planning com.), Women Trial Lawyer Caucus, Consumer Attys. Calif., Calif. Women Lawyers, Assn. Bus. Trial Lawyers, Nat. Assn. Securities and Comml. Attys., Bay Area Lawyers for Individual Freedom, Bar Assn. San Francisco (v.p. securities litig., bd. dirs.). Office: Lieff Cabraser Heimann & Bernstein LLP Embarcadero Ctr W 30th Fl 275 Battery St San Francisco CA 94111-3305 E-mail: ecabraser@lchb.com.

CABRERA, ANGEL, dean, finance educator; b. Madrid, Aug. 5, 1967; came to U.S., 1991; s. Angel and Virtudes (Izquierdo) C.; m. Elizabeth Jean Frazer, Mar. 19, 1994. Degree in telecommunication engring., Univ. Politecnica, Madrid, 1990; MS in Psychology, Ga. Inst Tech, 1993, PhD in Psychology, 1995. Rsch. engr. Univ. Politecnica, Madrid, 1990-91, asst. prof., 1990-91; mgr. Accenture, 1995-96; vis. prof. Carlos III U., 1997-98; prof. Instituto de Empresa, Madrid, 1998—2004, dir. human resource dept., 1999-2000, dean, 2001—04; pres. Thunderbird, Garvin Sch. of Internat. Mgmt., Glendale, Ariz., 2004—. Contbr. articles to profl. jours. Goethe Inst. scholar DAAD, 1989, Fulbright scholar, 1991-95. Mem. APA, European Soc. Cognitive Psychology, Cognitive Sci. Soc.

CABRERA, ORLANDO LUIS, professional baseball player; b. Cartagena, Colombia, Nov. 2, 1974; s. Jolbert and Josefina Cabrera; m. Eliana Cabrera. Shortstop Montreal Expos, 1997—2004, Boston Red Sox, 2004, LA Angels of Anaheim, 2005—07, Chgo. White Sox, 2008, Oakland Athletics, 2009—. Recipient Gold Glove award, 2001, 2007. Achievements include being a member of the World Series Champion Boston Red Sox, 2004; leading the American League in: fielding percentage (.938), 2007. Office: Oakland Athletics McAfee Coliseum 7000 Coliseum Way Oakland CA 94621 Office Phone: 714-940-2000.*

CACHOLA, ROMY MUNOZ, state legislator; b. Vigan, Ilocos Sur, Philippines, Mar. 8, 1938; m. Erlinda M. Cachola; children: Lyla, Earl. LLB, M.L. Quezon U., The Philippines, 1961. Mem. State Ho. of Reps., 1984—2000. Chair com. on water and land use Ho. of Reps., past chair house tourism com., 1987-98, chair exec. matters com., 2001, chair zoning com., 2001. Bd. govs. Kalihi YMCA; bd. dirs. Susannah Wesley Cmty. Ctr.; hon. chmn. Statewide Sakada Com.; pres. St. Anthony's Sch. Bd. Recipient Pub. Servant of Yr. Community Advocate Mag., 1990, Disting. Legislator award Dem. State Legis. Leaders Assn., 1990. Mem. Filipino C. of C., Ilocos Surian Assn. of Hawaii, St. Anthony's Filipino Cath. Club, Waipahu Bus. Assn. (past. pres.), Kalakaua Lions Club, Kalihi Bus. Assn. (bd. dirs.). Office: Honolulu Hale 530 South King St Honolulu HI 96813

CADMAN, BILL LEE, state legislator; b. Hollywood, Md., Oct. 4, 1960; m. Lisa Cadman; children: Austin, Alex. BA, Calif. State U., 1989. Mktg. dir., 1990—92; devel. dir. Lifeskills Colo. Springs, 1992—94; office mgr., Rep. Joel Hefley US House of Reps., 1994—2000; owner Advantage Mktg.; mem. Dist. 15 Colo. House of Reps., Denver, 2000—07; mem. Dist. 10 Colo. State Senate, Denver, 2007—. Mem. Joint Com. on Legis. Coun., Info. and Tech. Com., Local Govt. and Energy; vice-chair State, Vets. and Mil. Affairs; bd. mem. Colorado Rep. Party, 1996—98. Bd. dirs. Chins Up Youth and Family Svcs.; chmn. Colorado Springs Nat. Day of Prayer, 1992—93; bd. dirs. Ptnrs. Youth Mentoring, 1995—97. Republican. Office: State Capitol 200 E Colfax Rm 300 Denver CO 80203 Office Phone: 303-866-5525. E-mail: bill.cadman.house@state.co.us.*

CADMAN, EDWIN CLARENCE, health facility administrator, retired educator; b. Bandon, Oreg., May 14, 1945; s. Edwin Herbert Cadman and Gloria (Ranellie) Wilson; children: Tim, Kevin, Brian. AB, Stanford U., 1967; MD, U. Oreg., 1971. Intern in internal medicine Stanford U. Hosp., Calif., 1971-74; fellow in oncology Yale U., New Haven, 1974-76, asst. prof. medicine, 1976-79, assoc. prof. medicine, 1979-83, prof., chmn. medicine, 1987-94, prof., 1994—99; prof. medicine, dir. Cancer Rsch. Inst. U. Calif., San Francisco, 1983-87, vice chmn. dept. medicine, 1985-87; chief of staff, sr. v.p. med. affairs Yale New Haven Hosp., 1994—99; dean, prof. John A. Burns Sch. of Med. Univ. of Hawaii, 1999—2005. Prof. Am. Cancer Soc., 1985-87. Contbr. over 300 articles to profl. jours. Basketball coach Novato (Calif.) Park and Recreation, 1985. Capt. USNG, 1972-78. Recipient Gold Headed Cane award U. Oreg. Med. Sch., 1971. Fellow AAAS, ACP; mem. AFCR (pres. 1984-86), ASCI, AAP, ASCO/AACR, AOA. Avocations: running, fishing, reading. Office: John A Burns Sch Med 1960 E West Rd Honolulu HI 96822 Office Phone: 808-692-0891. Business E-Mail: cadman@hawaii.edu.

CAFFERATA, PATRICIA DILLON, state official; b. Albany, NY, Nov. 24, 1940; d. Kenneth P. and Barbara Vucanovich (Farrell) Dillon; m. H. Treat Cafferata, June 17, 1961; children: Elisa, Reynolds, Farrell. Student, Mills Coll., 1958—61; BA, Lewis and Clark Coll., 1963; JD, Southwestern Sch. Law, 1989—. Mem. Nev. Assembly, 1980—82; treas. State of Nev., Carson City, Nev., 1982—86; nominee Gov. of Nev., 1986; dist. atty. Lincoln County, Nev., 1992, Lander County, Nev., 1995—96, Esmeralda County, Nev., 2000—03; of counsel Jenkins Law Office, Reno, 2005—. Named Outstanding Freshman Legislator, Nev. State Med. Assn., 1981. Roman Catholic. Office: Jenkins Law Office 423 W Plumb Ln Reno NV 89509 Office Phone: 775-324-9970.

CAGE, NICOLAS (NICOLAS COPPOLA), actor; b. Long Beach, Calif., Jan. 7, 1964; s. August Coppola and Joy Vogelsang; m. Patricia Arquette, Apr. 8, 1995 (div. May 18, 2001); m. Lisa Marie Presley, Aug. 10, 2002 (div. May 16, 2004); m. Alice Kim, July 30, 2004; 1 child, Kal-el Coppola; 1 child, Weston. Grad., UCLA; DFA (hon.), Calif. State Fullerton, 2001. Actor: (feature films) Fast Times At Ridgemont High, 1982, Valley Girl, 1983, Rumble Fish, 1983, Racing with the Moon, 1984, Birdy, 1984, The Boy in Blue, 1986, The Cotton Club, 1984, Peggy Sue Got Married, 1986, Raising Arizona, 1986, Moonstruck, 1988, Vampire's Kiss, 1989, Never on a Tuesday, 1989, Tempo di Uccidere, 1989, Fire Birds, 1990, Wild at Heart, 1990, Zandalee, 1991, Honeymoon in Vegas, 1992, Time to Kill, 1992, Amos & Andrew, 1993, Red Rock West, 1993, Deadfall, 1993, Guarding Tess, 1994, It Could Happen to You, 1994, Trapped in Paradise, 1994, Kiss of Death, 1995, Leaving Las Vegas, 1995 (Best Actor award LA Film Critics 1995, Best Actor award NY Film Critics 1995, Golden Globe award for best actor 1996, Acad. award for best actor 1996), The Rock, 1996, The Funeral, 1996, Con Air, 1997, Face Off, 1997, Welcome to Hollywood, 1998, Snake Eyes, 1998, City of Angels, 1998, 8MM, 1999, Bringing Out the Dead, 1999, Gone in 60 Seconds, 2000, Family Man, 2000, Captain Corelli's Mandolin, 2001, Windtalkers, 2002, Adaptation, 2002, Matchstick Men, 2003, National Treasure, 2004, The Weather Man, 2005, (voice) The Ant Bully, 2006, World Trade Center, 2006, Ghost Rider, 2007, Grindhouse, 2007, National Treasure: Book of Secrets, 2007, Bangkok Dangerous, 2008, Knowing, 2009; actor, prodr.: (films) Sonny (also dir.), 2002, Lord of War, 2005, The Wicker Man, 2006, Next, 2007; prodr.: (films) Shadow of the Vampire, 2000, The Life of David Gale, 2003. Named one of The 100 Most Powerful Celebrities, Forbes.com, 2008. Office: Saturn Films 9000 W Sunset Blvd Ste 911 West Hollywood CA 90069-5809

CAHILL, THOMAS ANDREW, physicist, researcher; b. Paterson, NJ, Mar. 4, 1937; s. Thomas Vincent and Margery (Groesbeck) C.; m. Virginia Ann Arnoldy, June 26, 1965; children: Catherine Frances, Thomas Michael. BA, Holy Cross Coll., Worcester, Mass., 1959; PhD in Physics; NDEA fellow, UCLA, 1965. Asst. prof. in residence UCLA, 1965-66; NATO fellow, rsch. physicist Centre d'Etudes Nucleaires de Saclay, France, 1966-67; prof. physics U. Calif., Davis, 1967-94; acting dir. Crocker Nuc. Lab., 1972, dir., 1980—89. Dir. Inst. Ecology, 1972-75; cons. NRC of Can., Louvre Mus. UN Global Atmospheric Watch, 1990—; mem. Internat. Com. on PIXE and Its Application, Calif. Atty. Gen., Nat. Audubon Soc., Mono Lake Com. Author: (with J. McCray) Electronic Circuit Analysis for Scientists, 1973; editor Internat. Jour. Pixe, 1989—; contbr. articles to profl. jours. on physics, applied physics, hist. analyses and air pollution. Prin. investigator IMPROVE Nat. Air Pollution Network., 1987-97; co-dir. Crocker Hist. and Archeol. Projects; head U. Calif. Delta Group, Davis, 1997-. OAS fellow, 1968, Japanese Nat. Rsch. fellow, Kyoto, 1992. Mem. Am. Phys. Soc., Air Pollution Control Assn., Am. Assn. Aerosol Rsch., Sigma Xi Democrat. Roman Catholic. Home: 1813 Amador Ave Davis CA 95616-3104 Office: U Calif Dept Physics One Shields Ave Davis CA 95616 Office Phone: 530-752-4674. Business E-Mail: tacahill@ucdavis.edu.

CAHN, DAVID STEPHEN, cement company executive; b. LA, Jan. 12, 1940; s. Edward Lincoln and Monya C.; m. Mary Constance Maschio, June 18, 1960 (div. 1972); children: Elizabeth Suzanne, Deborah Michelle; m. Sharon Ann Marting, Sept. 8, 1972; 1 child, Melissa Jacquiline. BS with honors, U. Calif.-Berkeley, 1962, MS, 1964, DEng, 1966. Engr. Bethlehem Steel Corp., 1966-68; research engr. Amcord, Inc., Riverside, Calif., 1968-71, dir. environ. matters Newport Beach, Calif., 1971-77, v.p., 1977-80; dir. environ. affairs Calif. Portland Cement Co., Los Angeles, 1980-82, v.p. regulatory matters, 1982-84, CalMat Co., 1984-90; sr. v.p. corp. svcs. Calif. Portland Cement Co., Glendora, 1990—. Recipient Rossiter W. Raymond award Soc. Mining Engrs., 1972 Mem.: AIChE, ASTM, AIME, Calif. Mfrs. and Tech. Assn. (past chmn. bd.), Calif. Mining Assn. (past pres.), Air and Waste Mgmt. Assn. Republican. Office: Calif Portland Cement Co 2025 E Financial Way Glendora CA 91741-4692

CAHN, JOHN WERNER, metallurgist, educator; b. Germany, Jan. 9, 1928; arrived in U.S., 1939, naturalized, 1945; s. Felix H. and Lucie (Schwarz) C.; m. Anne Hessing, Aug. 20, 1950; children: Martin Charles, Andrew, Lorie Selma. BS, U. Mich., 1949; PhD, U. Calif., Berkeley, 1953; DSc (hon.), Northwestern U., 1990, U. d'Evry, France, 1996. Instr. U. Chgo., 1952-54; with rsch. lab. GE, 1954-64; prof. metallurgy MIT, 1964-78; ctr. scientist Nat. Inst. Stds. and Tech. (formerly Nat. Bur. Stds.), 1978—84, sr. fellow, 1984—2006, emeritus, 2006. Vis. prof. Isreli Inst. Tech., Haifa, 1971—72, 1980; cons. in field, 1986—; chmn. Gordon Conf. Phys. Metallurgy, 1964; affil. prof. physics and astronomy U. Wash., Seattle, 1984—; rsch. fellow Japan Soc. Promotion of Sci., 1981—82. Research and articles on surfaces and interfaces, thermodynamics, phase changes, quasicrystals. Recipient Dickson prize, Carnegie Mellon U., 1981, Gold medal, U.S. Dept. Commerce, 1982, Von Hippel award, Materials Rsch. Soc., 1985, Stratton award, Nat. Bur. Stds., 1986, Michelson-Morley prize, Case Western Res. U., 1991, William Hume-Rothery award, Minerals, Metals and Materials Soc., 1993, Harvey prize, Israel Inst. Tech., 1995, Nat. Medal of Sci., 1998, Bakhuis-Roozeboom medal, Netherlands Acad. Sci., 1999, Heyn medal, German Materials Soc., 2001, Bower award in Sci., Franklin Inst., 2002; fellow Guggenheim Found., 1960. Fellow: Am. Soc. Metals Internat. (Saveur award 1989), Am. Inst. Metallurg. Engrs., Am. Acad. Arts and Scis.; mem.: Japan Inst. Metals (gold medal 1994), Am. Ceramics Soc. (hon.), Indian Materials Rsch. Soc. (hon.), French Soc. for Metals and Materials (hon. medal 2005), NAE, NAS. Office: Univ Wash Dept Physics and Astronomy Seattle WA 98195-1580

CAHN, ROBERT NATHAN, physicist; b. NYC, Dec. 20, 1944; s. Alan L. and Beatrice (Geballe) C.; m. Frances C. Miller, Aug. 22, 1965; children: Deborah, Sarah. BA, Harvard U., 1966; PhD, U. Calif., Berkeley, 1972. Rsch. assoc. Stanford (Calif.) Linear Accelerator Ctr., 1972-73; rsch. asst. prof. U. Wash., Seattle, 1973-76; asst. prof. U. Mich., Ann Arbor, 1976-78; assoc. rsch. prof. U. Calif., Davis, 1978-79; sr. staff physicist Lawrence Berkeley Nat. Lab, 1979-91; div. dir. Lawrence Berkeley Lab., 1991-96, sr. scientist, 1996—, dep. dir. physics divsn. Author: Semi Simple Lie Algebras and Their Representations, 1984; co-author: Experimental Foundations of Particle Physics, 1989. Fellow Am. Phys. Soc. (sec.-treas. divsn. particles and fields 1992-94).

CAIN, BRUCE EDWARD, political science professor, consultant; b. Boston, Nov. 28, 1948; s. Arthur James and Ruth Elizabeth (Osterberg) Cain; children: Timothy, Andrew. BA, Bowdoin Coll., 1970; BPhil, Oxford U., 1972; PhD in Polit. Sci., Harvard U., 1976. Asst. prof. Calif. Inst. Tech., Pasadena, 1976—82, assoc. prof., 1983—86, prof. polit. sci., 1986—89, U. Calif., Berkeley, 1989—, acting dir. Inst. Govtl. Studies, 1997—99, dir. Inst. Govtl. Studies, 1999—, dir. Washington Ctr. Washington, 2005—. Cons. Calif. State Assembly, 1981-82, L.A. City Coun., 1986, Fairbank and Assocs., L.A., 1985-86, L.A. Times, 1986-89, Ariz. State Legis. Redistricting, 2002; polit. analyst KTVU, 1998—; expert witness N.Y. State Bd. Elections, 2004. Author: The Reapportionment Puzzle, 1984, The Personal Vote, 1987, Congressional Redistricting, 1990; co-author (with Elizabeth R. Gerber): Voting at the Political Fault Line: California's Experiment with the Blanket Primary, 2002; contbr. articles to profl. jours. Rhodes scholar Oxford U., 1970-72. Mem.: Am. Polit. Sci. Assn., Am. Acad. Arts and Scis. Office: U Calif Washington Ctr 1608 Rhode Island Ave NW Washington DC 20036 Home Phone: 415-336-0570; Office Phone: 510-642-1474. E-mail: bruce.cain@ucdc.edu.

CAIN, DOUGLAS MYLCHREEST, lawyer; b. Chgo., Sept. 8, 1938; s. Douglas M. Jr. and Louise C. (Coleman) C.; m. Constance Alexis Adams Moffit, Apr. 18, 1970; children: Victoria Elizabeth Moffit, Alexandra Catherine Moffit. AB, Harvard U., 1960; JD with distinction, U. Mich., 1966; LL.M., N.Y. U., 1970. Bar: Colo. 1966, U.S. Ct. Appeals (10th cir.) 1972, U.S. Supreme Ct. 1972. Assoc. Sherman & Howard, L.L.C., Denver, 1966-72, ptnr., 1972-93; equity mem., 1993—; chmn. policy council Sherman & Howard, Denver, 1984-87; adj. prof. law U. Denver, 1972-78. Mem. Rocky Mountain Estate Planning Council, pres., 1976-77 Assoc. editor: Mich. Law Rev, 1964-66; contbr. articles to profl. jours. Bd. dirs. Craig Hosp. Found., 1980-86, v.p., 1984-85, pres., 1986-87, 88-89; bd. dirs. Colo. Jud. Inst., 1990-96, chmn., 1992-93; bd. dirs. Colo. chpt. Am. Diabetes Assn., 1993, Breathe Better Found., 1993-2007, Colo. Coun. Econ. Edn., 1996-98, Fortune Found., 1998—; mem. Estate Planning Seminar Group. With USN, 1960—63. Named one of Best Lawyers in America & Super Lawyer. Fellow Am. Coll. Tax Coun., Am. Coll. Trust and Estate Counsel; mem. ABA, Colo. Bar Assn. (gov. 1980-82), Greater Denver Tax Coun. Assn. (v.p. 1987, pres. 1988), Assn. Harvard Alumni (regional dir. 1978-81), Rocky Mountain Harvard Club (pres. 1977-78, 92-93), Denver Country Club, Mile High Club, Rotary. Home: 1960 Hudson St Denver CO 80220-1459 Office: Sherman & Howard LLC 633 17th St Ste 3000 Denver CO 80202-3665 Home Phone: 303-322-8161; Office Phone: 303-299-8122. Business E-Mail: dcain@sah.com.

CAIN, WILLIAM STANLEY, experimental psychologist, educator, researcher; b. NYC, Sept. 7, 1941; s. William Henry and June Rose (Stanley) Cain; m. Claire Murphy, Oct. 30, 1993; children: Justin, Alison stepchildren: Michael, Jennifer, Courtney. BS, Fordham U., 1963; MSc, Brown U., 1966, PhD, 1968. From asst. fellow to fellow John B. Pierce Lab., New Haven, 1967—94; from instr. to assoc. prof. dept. epidemiology, pub. health, and psychology Yale U., New Haven, 1967—84, prof., 1984—94; prof. otolaryngology U. Calif., San Diego, 1994—. Mem. sensory disorders study sect. NIH, Bethesda, Md., 1991—95; mem. sci. adv. bd. Ctr. Indoor Air Rsch., Linthicum, Md., 1991—99, exec. editor Chemosensory Perception, 2007—. Mem. editl. bd. Chem. Senses, 1985—94, mem. editl. adv. bd. Indoor Air, 1990—2000, 2005—, Physiology and Behavior, 1995—96; editor: 5 books, 1971—; contbr. articles to profl. jours. Recipient Jacob Javits/Claude Pepper award, NIH, 1984, Sense of Smell Rsch. award, Fragrance Rsch. Fund, 1986. Fellow: ASHRAE (Crosby Field award 1984), APA, Acad. Indoor Air Rsch.; mem.: N.Y. Acad. Scis. (pres. 1986), Assn. Chemoreception Scis. (exec. chmn. 1983—84, Max Mozell award 2006). Home: 4459 Nabal Dr La Mesa CA 91941-7168 Office: U Calif Dept Surgery 9500 Gilman Dr MC957 La Jolla CA 92093-0957 Office Phone: 858-622-5831. Business E-Mail: wcain@ucsd.edu.

CAINE, STEPHEN HOWARD, data processing executive; b. Washington, Feb. 11, 1941; s. Walter E. and Jeanette (Wenborne) C. Student, Calif. Inst. Tech., 1958-62. Sr. programmer Calif. Inst. Tech., Pasadena, 1962-65, mgr. sys. programming, 1965-69, mgr. programming, 1969-70; pres. Caine, Farber & Gordon, Inc., Pasadena, 1970—; gen. mgr. Gatekeeper Systems, Pasadena, 1995—. Lectr. applied sci. Calif. Inst. Tech., Pasadena, 1965-71, vis. assoc. elec. engring., 1976, vis. assoc. computer sci., 1976-84; dir. San Gabriel Valley Learning Ctrs., 1992-95; game mgr. tech. Rose Bowl Game, 2007-. Mem. AAAS, IEEE, Nat. Assn. Corrosion Engrs., Am. Ordnance Assn., Assn. Computing Machinery, Pasadena Tournament of Roses Assn. (vice-chmn. com. 1996-2000, chmn. com. 2000-07, bd. dirs. 2004-07, hon. dir. 2007—), Athanaeum Club (Pasadena), Houston Club. Home: 77 Patrician Way Pasadena CA 91105-1039

CAIRNS, ELTON JAMES, chemical engineering professor, consultant; s. James Edward and Claire Angele (Larzelere) C.; m. Miriam Esther Citron, Dec. 26, 1974; 1 dau., Valerie Helen; stepchildren: Benjamin David, Joshua Aaron. BS in Chemistry, Mich. Tech. U., Houghton, 1955, BSChemE, 1955; PhD in Chem. Engring., U. Calif., Berkeley, 1959. Phys. chemist GE Rsch. Lab., Schenectady, NY, 1959-66; group leader, then sect. head chem. engring. divsn. Argonne (Ill.) Nat. Lab., 1966-73; asst. head electrochemistry dept. GM Rsch. Labs., 1973-78; assoc. lab. dir., dir. energy and environment divsn. Lawrence Berkeley (Calif.) Nat. Lab., 1978-96, head Energy Conversion and Storage Program, 1982—98, head Berkeley Electrochemical Rsch. Coun., 1982—, C.D. Hollowell meml. lectr., 1996; prof. chem. engring. U. Calif., 1978—. Cons. in field; mem. numerous govt. panels. Author: (with H.A. Liebhafsky) Fuel Cells and Fuel Batteries, 1968; mem. editl. bd. Advances in Electrochemistry and Electrochem. Engring., 1974—, Internat. Jour. Electrochemical Sci., 2006-; divsn. editor Jour. Electrochem. Soc., 1968-91; regional editor Electrochimica Acta, 1984-99, editor, 2000-04; contbr. articles to profl. jours. Recipient IR-100 award, 1968, Centennial medal Case Western Res. U., 1980, R & D 100 award, 1992, Melvin Calvin medal of distinction Mich. Technol. U., 1998; named Croft lectr. U. Mo., 1979, McCabe lectr. U. NC, 1993; grantee DuPont Co., 1956; Dow Chem. Co. fellow, univ. fellow, NSF fellow, Std. Oil Co. Calif. grantee, U. Calif., Berkeley. Fellow Am. Insts. Chemists, Electrochem. Soc. (chmn. phys. electrochem. divsn. 1981-84, v.p. 1986-89, pres. 1989-90, Francis Mills Turner award 1963); mem. AIChE (chmn. energy conversion com. 1970-94), AAAS, Am. Chem. Soc., Internat. Soc. Electrochemistry (hon.; chmn. electrochem. energy conversion divsn. 1977-85, U.S. nat. sec. 1983-89, v.p. 1984-88, pres. 1999-2000), Intersoc. Energy Conversion Engring. Conf. (steering com. 1970-2003, gen. chmn. 1976, 90, 97, program chmn. 1983, co-chair internat. meeting on lithium batteries 2002), Sigma Xi (pres. Berkeley chpt. 2002-03). Achievements include patents in field. Home: 239 Langlie Ct Walnut Creek CA 94598-3615 Office: Lawrence Berkeley Nat Lab MS 70RO108B 1 Cyclotron Rd Berkeley CA 94720-0001 Office Phone: 510-486-5028. Personal E-mail: ejcairns@cal.berkeley.edu. Business E-Mail: ejcairns@lbl.gov, cairns@cchem.berkeley.edu.

CALABRETTA, MARTI ANN, state senator; b. Sandusky, Ohio, Dec. 14, 1940; d. Wilfred and Ida (Gerding) Beutler; m. Joseph Miller, Feb. 2, 1963 (div. Mar. 1976); m. Bennie G. Calabretta, Dec. 18, 1976; children: Joseph, Patrick, Rebecca, Debora, John, Ben, Lisa. Student, Case Western Res. U., 1961-63; BA, U. Utah, 1963, MSW, 1966; cert. mental health mgmt., U. Wash., 1981. Mental health specialist 4 Corners Mental Health Services, Moab, Utah, 1972-75, Idaho Mental Health Services, Coeur d'Alene, Idaho, 1975-81; sch. social worker Wallace (Idaho) Sch. Dist., 1981-85; state senator Boise, Idaho, 1984—. Pres. Valley Coordinating Corp., Kellogg, Idaho, 1982-86; mem. Pvt. Industry Council, Coeur d'Alene, 1984—, Idaho State Council on Developmental Disabilities, 1986—; vice chmn. Silver Valley Human Resources task force, Kellogg, 1982—. Mem. Idaho Edn. Assn. (del. 1983-84), Nat. Conf. State Legis. (health and welfare com.). Democrat. Episcopalian. Avocation: quilting. Home: Nuchols Gulch PO Box 784 Osburn ID 83849-0784

CALDERA, LOUIS EDWARD, law educator, former federal official; b. El Paso, Tex., Apr. 1, 1956; s. Benjamin Luis Caldera and Soledad (Siqueiros); m. Eva Orlebeke Caldera. BS, U.S. Mil. Acad., 1978; JD, MBA, Harvard U., 1987. Bar: Calif. 1987. Commd. 2nd lt. US Army, 1978, advanced through ranks to capt., 1982, resigned commn., 1983; assoc. O'Melveny & Myers LLP, LA, 1987-89, Buchalter, Nemer, Fields & Younger, LA, 1990-91; dep. county counsel County of LA, 1991-92; mem. Calif. State Assembly from 46th Dist., LA, 1992-97, chmn. banking and fin. com.; mng. dir., COO Corp. for Nat. Svc., Washington, 1997-98; sec. Dept. Army, US Dept. Def., Washington, 1998—2001; vice chancellor for univ. advancement Calif. State U., 2001—03; pres. U. N.Mex, Albuquerque, 2003—06; prof. law U. N.Mex Law Sch., 2006—; dir. Military Office The White House, Washington, 2009. Democrat. Roman Catholic.*

CALDERONI, FRANK A., computer company executive; B in acctg. & fin., Fordham Univ.; MBA, Pace Univ. Fin. mgmt. positions through v.p. & div. CFO IBM, 1980—2000; sr. v.p. fin. & adminstrn., CFO SanDisk Corp., 2000—02; v.p., CFO QLogic Corp., 2002—04; v.p. worldwide sales fin. Cisco Systems Inc., San Jose, Calif., 2004—07, sr. v.p. customer solutions fin., 2007—08, exec. v.p., CFO, 2008—. Office: Cisco Systems Inc 170 W Tasman Dr San Jose CA 95134-1706

CALDERONI, ROBERT M., software company executive; BS in Acctg. and Fin., Fordham U. CPA, Calif. Various fin. mgmt. positions IBM, Apple Computers, 1996-97; sr. v.p. fin., CFO Avery Dennison, Pasadena, Calif., 1997—2001; CFO Ariba, Inc., Sunnyvale, Calif., 2000—01, exec. v.p., CFO, 2001, pres., 2001—04, CEO, 2001—, chmn., 2003—. Bd. dirs. Ariba, Inc.; bd. dir. Juniper Networks, Inc. Office: Ariba Inc 807 11th Ave Sunnyvale CA 94089 Office Phone: 650-390-1000.

CALDWELL, DALTON, Internet company executive, application developer; b. El Paso, Tex. BA in Psychology, Stanford U., BS in Symbolic Sys. Software developer VA Software; founder, CEO, v.p. engring. imeem, Inc., San Francisco, 2003—. Spkr. in field. Office: imeem, Inc 139 Townsend St, Ste 400 San Francisco CA 94107 Office Phone: 415-762-0135.

CALDWELL, DAVID ORVILLE, physics professor; b. LA, Jan. 5, 1925; s. Orville Robert and Audrey Norton (Anderson) C.; m. Miriam Ann Planck, Nov. 4, 1950 (div. Apr. 1978); children: Bruce David, Diana Miriam; m. Edith Helen Anderson, Dec. 29, 1984. BS in Physics, Calif. Inst. Tech., 1947; postgrad., Stanford U., 1947-48; MA in Physics, UCLA, 1949, PhD in Physics, 1953. From instr. to assoc. prof. physics MIT, Cambridge, 1954-63; vis. assoc. prof. physics Princeton U., NJ, 1963-64; lectr. physics dept. U. Calif., Berkeley, 1964-65, prof. physics Santa Barbara, 1965—94, prof. emeritus and rsch. prof., 1995—. Cons. U. Calif. Radiation Lab., Berkeley, 1957-58, 64-67, Am. Sci. and Engring., Boston, 1959-60, Inst. Def. Analyses, Washington, 1960-67; exec. dir. U. Calif. Intercampus Inst. for Rsch. at Particle Accelerators, 1984-95, dir. U. Calif. Inst. for Nuc. and Particle Astrophysics and Cosmology, 1995-2000. Contbr. numerous articles to profl. jours. Served to 2d lt. USAAF, 1943-46. Recipient von Humboldt Sr. Disting. Sci. award, 1987; rsch. grantee Dept. Energy, 1966-2002; Ford Found. fellow, 1961-62, NSF fellow 1953-54, 1960-61, Guggenheim fellow, 1971-72. Fellow Am. Phys. Soc.; mem. Phys. Soc. (exec. com. 1976-78). Democrat. Avocations: tennis, skiing. Office: U Calif Physics Dept Santa Barbara CA 93106 also: Stanford U Varian Physics Bldg Stanford CA 94305-4060 Business E-Mail: caldwell@slac.stanford.edu.

CALDWELL, KIM A., company executive; Exec. v.p. global tech. and new bus. devel. Avery Dennison Corp., Pasadena, Calif., 1998—. Office: Avery Dennison Corp 150 N Orange Grove Blvd Pasadena CA 91103-3534

CALDWELL, NANCI, former computer software company executive; b. Brockville, Can., Mar. 26, 1958; BA in Psychology, Queen's U.; diploma in Exec. Mktg. Mgmt. Program, U. We. Ont. With Xerox Corp.; from mem. staff to v.p. mktg. Hewlett Packard Co., 1982—2001, v.p. mktg. HP Svcs., 2001; sr. v.p., chief mktg. officer PeopleSoft Inc., Pleasonton, Calif., 2001—02, exec. v.p., 2002—04, chief mktg. officer, 2002—04. Bd. dirs. Citrix Systems Inc., 2008—, Deltek Systems, Inc., LiveOps, Inc., Sophos Plc.

CALDWELL, NIKKI, women's college basketball coach; b. Oak Ridge, Tenn., 1972; BS in Pub. Rels., U. Tenn., 1994. Analyst FOX Sports Net South, 1994—97; cable TV sports host Shop at Home, 1997—98; grad. asst. U. Tenn. Lady Volunteers, 1998—99, asst. coach, 2002—08, U. Va. Cavaliers, 1999—2002; head coach UCLA Bruins, 2008—. Recipient Gloria Ray Leadership award. Avocations: golf, movies. Office: UCLA Athletic Dept JD Morgan Ctr PO Box 24044 Los Angeles CA 90024 Office Phone: 310-825-8699.

CALDWELL, WALTER EDWARD, editor, small business owner; b. LA, Dec. 29, 1941; s. Harold Elmer and Esther Ann (Fuller) Caldwell; m. Donna Edith Davis, June 27, 1964; 1 child, Arnie-Jo. AA, Riverside City Coll., Calif., 1968. Sales and stock profl. Sears Roebuck & Co., Riverside, 1963-65; dispatcher Rohr Corp., Riverside, 1965-67; trainee Aetna Fin., Riverside, 1967-68, mgr. San Bruno, Cal., 1968-70, Amfac Thrift & Loan, Oakland, Calif., 1970-74; free lance writer San Jose, Calif., 1974-76; news dir. Sta. KAVA Radio, Burney, Calif., 1977-79; editor-pub. Mountain Echo, Fall River Mills, Calif., 1979-81. Co-author: (book) Yearbook of Modern Poetry, 1976. Participant Am. Leadership Conf., San Diego, 1989; pres. United Way, Burney, 1979, co-chmn., 1977, chmn., 1979; disaster relief worker ARC, Redding, Calif., 1988—91, disaster action team leader, 1991—95; bd. dirs. Shasta County Women's Refuge, Redding, 1988—91, Shasta County Econ. Devel. Task Force, 1985—86, exec. bd. dirs., 1988; leader Girl Scouts U.S., San Jose, 1973—76; announcer various local parades; trustee Mosquito Abatement Dist., Burney, 1978—87, 1989—, chmn., 1990—; commr. Burney Fire Protection Dist., 1987—91, v.p., 1990, pres., 1991; chmn. Burney Basin Days Com., Calif., 1983—95, Hay Days Com., 1995—96; alt. commr. Local Agy. Formation Commn. Shasta County, 1995—; mem. Intermountain Hospice, 1998—2006; del. Farmers and Ranchers Congress, St. Louis, 1985; candidate Shasta County Bd. Suprs., 1992; bd. dirs. Shasta County Econ. Devel. Corp., 1986—90, Crossroads, 1985; pres. Intermountain Devel. Corp., 1989. With USMC, 1959—63. Mem.: Calif. Newspaper Pubs. Assn., Fall River Valley C. of C. (bd. dirs. 1991, pres. 1995), Burney Basin C. of C. (advt. com. 1982, Cmty. Action award 1990—93), Shriners (sec.-treas. 1992—94), Masons (master 1995), Moose, Lions (student spkr. chmn. Fall River 1983—97, co-chmn. disaster com., newsletter chmn. dist. 4-C1 1989—91, 1st v.p. 1991, pres. 1992), Rotary (pres. 1977—78, chmn. bike race 1981—85), Am. Legion (2d vice comdr. 2000—02, post boys state chmn. 2001—02, citation of recognition 1987, Cmty. Action award 1989, 1993). Republican. Avocations: photography, painting, archaeology. Office: Mountain Echo Main St Fall River Mills CA 96028 also: PO Box 224 Fall River Mills CA 96028-0224 Business E-Mail: mtecho@frontiernet.net. E-mail: mtecho@shasta.com.

CALE, CHARLES GRIFFIN, lawyer, real estate and corporate financial company executive; b. St. Louis, Aug. 19, 1940; s. Julian Dutro and Judith Hadley (Griffin) C.; m. Jessie Leete Rawn, Dec. 30, 1978; children: Whitney Rawn, Walter Griffin, Elizabeth Judith. BA, Principia Coll., Elsah, Ill., 1961; LLB, Stanford U., 1964; LLM, U. So. Calif., 1966. Bar: Calif. 1965. Pvt. practice, LA, 1965—81, 1985—90; ptnr. Adams, Duque & Hazeltine, LA, 1970—81, Morgan, Lewis & Bockius, LA, 1985—90. Bd. dirs., co-chmn., CEO World Cup USA 1994, Inc., L.A., 1991. Group v.p. sports L.A. Olympic Organizing Com., 1982-84; assoc. counselor U.S. Olympic Com., 1985, spl. asst. to pres., 1985-89, asst. to pres, dir. olympic del., 1989-92; bd. dirs. Century 21 Real Estate-Can. Ltd., 1995-97, NIke Inc., 72-78, Rapattoni Corp., 2001—, Foresters Equity Svcs. Corp., 2001—. Trustee St. John's Hosp. and Med. Ctr., Santa Monica, Marymount H.S., 1996-2004; asst. chief de mission U.S. Olympic Team, 1988; bd. dirs. Hallum Prevention of Child Abuse Fund, 1976-96. Recipient Gold medal of Youth and Sports, France, 1984. Mem.: State Bar Calif., Ind. Order Foresters (bd. dirs. 1993—2001), Birnam Wood Golf Club, The Beach Club, L.A. Country Club, Calif. Club. Office: PO Box 688 Pacific Palisades CA 90272-0688

CALENDAR, RICHARD LANE, biochemistry educator; b. Hackensack, NJ, Aug. 2, 1940; s. Howard L. and Jean (Wappler) C.; m. Gunilla Viola Jansen, Jan. 6, 1969 (div. Sept. 1983); children: Hugo Raphael, Johanna Magdalena. BS in Chemistry, Duke U., 1962; PhD in Biochemistry, Stanford U., 1967. Helen Hay Whitney fellow Karolinska Inst., Stockholm, 1966-68; mem. faculty dept. cell and molecular biology U. Calif., Berkeley, 1968—, asst. prof. to prof., 1968—76. Alexander von Humboldt fellow, Munich, 1973, Guggenheim fellow, Stockholm, 1979-80. Mem.: Am. Acad. Microbiology. Home: 940 Euclid Ave Berkeley CA 94708-1436 Office: U Calif 401 Barker Hall Berkeley CA 94720-3208 E-mail: richard@socrates.berkeley.edu.

CALFEE, ROBERT CHILTON, psychologist, educator; b. Lexington, Ky., Jan. 26, 1933; s. Robert Klair and Nancy Bernice (Stipp) C. BA, UCLA, 1959, MA, 1960, PhD, 1963. Asst. prof. psychology U. Wis., 1964-66, assoc. prof., 1966-69; assoc. prof. edn. Stanford U., 1969-71, prof., 1971-98, prof. emeritus, 1998—; assoc. dean research and devel., dir. Ctr. for Ednl. Rsch., 1976-80; with Sch. Edn. U. Calif., Riverside, 1998—2005. Cons. and speaker in field; vice-chmn. State of Calif. Commn. for Establishment of Acad. Content and Performance Stds., 1996-2002; mem. com. on equivalancy and linkage of ednl. tests NRC/NAS, 1998-2000, Energy and Edn. Task Force, 2005-; mem. ednl. adv. bd., Leapfrog Edn., 1997-. Author: Human

Experimental Psychology, 1975, Cognitive Psychology and Educational Practice, 1982, Experimental Methods in Psychology, 1985, Handbook of Educational Psychology, Teach Our Children Well, 1995, (with Marilyn J. Chambliss) Textbooks for Learning, 1999; editor: Jour. Ednl. Psychology, 1984-90, Ednl. Assessment, 1992-2002. Trustee Palo Alto (Calif.) Sch. Dist., 1984-88; vice chair Calif. Commn. for Ednl. Stds.; chair ednl. adv. bd. Leapfrog Enterprises. Served with USAF, 1953—57. Guggenheim Meml. fellow, 1972; fellow Center for Advanced Study in Behavioral Scis., 1981-82 Fellow AAAS, APA; mem. Am. Ednl. Rsch. Assn., Internat. Reading Assn. (named to Hall of Fame), Nat. Conf. Rsch. in English, Psychonomic Soc., Nat. Coun. Tchrs. English, Nat. Soc. Study of Edn. (bd. trustees), Sigma Xi. Office: U Calif Sch Edn 1207 Sproul Hall Riverside CA 92521-0001 Home: 995 Wing Pl Stanford CA 94305 Office Phone: 951-827-2774. Business E-Mail: robert.calfee@ucr.edu.

CALHOUN, JOHN JOSEPH (JACK), retail executive; b. Lafayette, Ind., May 27, 1964; s. Robert James and Elizabeth (Callaghan) C. BS, Purdue U., West Lafayette, Ind., 1987; MBA, Harvard U., 1992. Asst. brand mgr. Procter & Gamble, Cin., 1987-90, Hunt Valley, Md., 1992-93; cons. Corp. Decision, Boston, 1991; mktg. mgr. Levi Strauss & Co., San Francisco, 1993-94; account supr. Foote, Cone & Belding, San Francisco, 1994-95; v.p. dir. account mgmt. Citron Haligman Bedecarre, San Francisco, 1995-98; sr. v.p. group dir. Young & Rubicam, San Francisco, 1998, gen. mgr. San Francisco office; exec. v.p. brand mgmt. and advt. Charles Schwab & Co.; exec. v.p. merchandising and mktg. Banana Republic Gap, Inc., San Francisco, 2003, interim pres. Banana Republic. Office: Banana Republic Gap Inc 2 Folsom St San Francisco CA 94105 Office Phone: 650-952-4400.

CALISE, NICHOLAS JAMES, lawyer; b. NYC, Sept. 15, 1941; s. William J. and Adeline (Rota) C.; m. Mary G. Flannery, Nov. 10, 1965; children: James R., Lori K. AB, Middlebury Coll., 1962; MBA, JD, Columbia U., 1965. Bar: N.Y. 1965, Conn., 1974, Ohio, 1986, Colo. 2000. Assoc., ptnr. Olvany, Eisner & Donnelly, NYC, 1969-76; corp. staff atty. Richardson-Vicks Inc., Wilton, Conn., 1976-82, div. counsel, dir. planning and bus. devel. home care products div. Memphis, 1982-84; staff v.p., sec., asst. gen. counsel The B.F. Goodrich Co., Akron, Ohio, 1984-89, v.p., sec., assoc. gen. counsel, 1989-99. Mem. Flood and Erosion Control Bd., Darien, Conn., 1976, Rep. Town Meeting, Darien, 1977-78; chmn. Zoning Bd. Appeals, Darien, 1978-82; Justice of the Peace, Darien, 1982; bd. dirs. Cordillera Property Owners Assn., 2002-05, pres. 2005-06; bd. dirs. Mirabel Cmty. Assn., 2006-, pres., 2007-. Served to lt. USN, 1965—68, capt. JAGC USNR, 1984—96, ret. USNR, 1996. Mem.: ABA, Ohio Bar Assn., Colo. Bar Assn., N.Y. State Bar Assn., Am. Corp. Counsel Assn., Am. Soc. Corp. Secs. (bd. dirs. 1990—93, pres. Ohio chpt. 1991—92, chmn. nat. conf. com. 1997, mem. various coms.), U.S. Naval Inst., Naval Res. Assn. (life), Navy League (life), Res. Officers' Assn. (life), Judge Advs. Assn. (life), Mirabel Golf Club, Club Cordillera (bd. dirs. 2003—06, pres. 2003—05), Country Club of Hudson (bd. trustees 1996—99, sec. 1997—99, Bracebridge H. Young Disting. Svc. award 2001), Am. Legion. Roman Catholic. Home: 36745 N Tilt St Scottsdale AZ 85262 Home Phone: 480-659-0724; Office Phone: 480-659-0725. Personal E-mail: caliselaw@yahoo.com.

CALKINS, LOREN GENE, religious organization administrator, pastor; b. Walla Walla, Wash., Feb. 6, 1942; s. Albert T. and Verna M. (Smith) C.; m. Lorena L. Tittle, Apr. 19, 1962; children: Lance E., Lonny G., LaRae L. BS, George Fox Coll., Newburg, Oreg., 1967; MDiv, We. Evangel. Sem., Portland, Oreg., 1970; DMin, San Francisco Theol. Sem., 1980. Ordained to ministry Free Methodist Ch., 1970. Sr. pastor Free Meth. Ch., Carlton, Oreg., 1965-68, West Linn, Oreg., 1968-69, Eugene, Oreg., 1970-72, Christian and Missionary Alliance, Bainbridge Island, Wash., 1972-74, Memphis, 1975-79, Spokane, 1979-84, Dallas (Oreg.) Alliance Ch., 1995—; dist. dir. ext. Christian and Missionary Alliance, Canby, Oreg., 1984-89, dist. supt. Ft. Worth, 1989-95. Ch. growth cons. Christian and Missionary Alliance, 1984—, stewardship cons., 1985—. Trustee Crown Coll., St. Bonifacius, Minn., 1989—, LeTourneau U., Longview, Tex., 1991—. Mem. Nat. Assn. Evangelicals (local pres. 1970-72, 80-84), Kiwanis. Republican. Office: Dallas Alliance Ch 775 E Ellendale Ave Dallas OR 97338-3007

CALL, JOHN G., corporate financial executive; With Ernst & Young LLP, San Francisco, 1987—93; sr. v.p., CFO, sec.-treas. Friedman's, Inc., 1993—97; sr. v.p., CFO, corp. sec. Ross Stores, Newark, Calif., 1997—. Sch. accountancy and info. sys. adv. bd. Marriott Sch. Brigham Young U. Office: Ross Stores 4440 Rosewood Dr Pleasanton CA 94588-3433 Office Phone: 925-965-4315.

CALLAHAN, CONSUELO MARIA, federal judge; b. Palo Alto, Calif., June 9, 1950; married; 2 children. BA, Leland Stanford Jr. Univ., 1972; JD, McGeorge Sch. Law, Univ. Pacific, 1975; LLM, Univ. Va., 2004—. Bar: Calif. 1975. Dep. city atty. City of Stockton, Stockton, Calif., 1975—76; dep. dist. atty. Dist. Atty. Office, San Joaquin County, Calif., 1976—82, sup. dist. atty., 1982—86; ct. comm. Mcpl. Ct. of Stockton, Stockton, Calif., 1986—92; judge San Joaquin County Superior Ct., San Joaquin, Calif., 1992—96; assoc. judge Ct. Appeal, State of Calif., Calif., 1996—2003; judge US Ct. Appeals (9th cir.), 2003—. Recipient Award for Criminal Justice Programs, Gov., Susan B. Anthony Award for Women of Achievement, Stockton Peacemaker of the Yr., 1997, Mexican-Am. Hall of Fame, San Joaquin County, 1999. Achievements include first hispanic, first woman named to San Joaquin Co. Superior Ct. Office: US Ct Appeals 501 I St Sacramento CA 95814 Office Phone: 916-930-4160.

CALLAHAN, DANIEL J., lawyer; b. Chgo., Sept. 13, 1949; children: Caitlin, Michael. BA magna cum laude, Western Ill. U., 1976; JD with honors, U. Calif., Davis, 1979. Bar: Calif. 1980, Hawaii 1980, US Tax Ct. 1981, US Ct. Appeals (9th cir.) 1981, US Dist. Ct. (dist. Hawaii) 1981, US Dist. Ct. (all dist. Calif.) 1983, US Supreme Ct. 1997. Editor U. Calif. at Davis Law Rev., 1978; founder, mng. ptnr. Callahan & Blaine, Santa Ana, Calif., 1984—. Sponsor Elizabeth Glaser Pediatric Aids Found., YMCA, Orange County, Braille Inst., CHOC found. Children & Good Sheppard Luth. Charities. Recipient Pres. Pro Bono award, Calif. State Bar, 1994; named Trial Lawyer of Yr., OCTLA, 2000, Orange County, 2004, Calif. Bus. Litig. Trial Lawyer of Yr., Calif. Lawyer Mag., 2003; named one of Hot 25, OC Metro Mag., 2000, Top 10 Trial Lawyers in Am., Nat. Law Jour., 2004. Mem.: Pi Sigma Alpha, Am. Inns of Ct., Assn. Bus. Trial Lawyers, Assn. Trial Lawyers of Am., Consumer Attys. Calif., Orange County Trial Lawyers Assn., ABA, Fed. Bar Assn., Hawaii State Bar Assn., LA County Bar Assn., Orange County Bar Assn. (chair Law Practice Mgmt. Sect. 1993—95, chair Bus. Litig. Sect. 1996, voted Top Gun 2000, 2004), Phi Kappa Phi. Office: Callahan & Blaine Ste 900 3 Hutton Centre Dr Santa Ana CA 92707 Office Phone: 714-241-4444.

CALLAHAN, MICHAEL JOHN, lawyer; m. Dana Weintraub; 2 children. BS in Internat. Affairs and Arab Studies, Georgetown U., 1990; JD with honors, U. Conn., 1995. Bar: Calif. Atty. Skadden, Arps, Slate, Meagher & Flom, LLP, 1995—99; mgr. bus. devel., corp. counsel electronics Electronics for Imaging Inc., 1999; corp. counsel Yahoo!, Inc., Sunnyvale, Calif., 1999—2000, sr. corp. counsel, 2000, assoc. gen. counsel, 2000—01, dep. gen. counsel, asst. sec., 2001—03, gen. counsel, sec., 2003—, also sr. v.p., 2003—. Office: Yahoo Inc 701 First Ave Sunnyvale CA 94089 Office Phone: 408-349-3300. Office Fax: 408-349-3301.

CALLAHAN, PATRICIA R., bank executive; BSME, MIT, M in Mgmt. and Fin. Various mgmt. positions Crocker Nat. Bank, 1977—84, sr. v.p., mgr. corp. svcs., 1984—93; dir. human resources Wells Fargo & Co., 1993—97, exec. v.p. wholesale banking sys. fin. and ops., 1997—98, exec. v.p., dir. human resources, 1998—2005, exec. v.p. compliance & risk mgmt., 2005—. Bd. dirs. United Way Bay Area; bd. trustees Dominican U. Calif. Office: Wells Fargo & Co 420 Montgomery St San Francisco CA 94163

CALLAN, JOSI IRENE, museum director; b. Yorkshire, Eng., Jan. 30, 1946; came to U.S., 1953; d. Roger Bradshaw and Irene (Newbury) Winstanley; children: James, Heather, Brett Jack; m. Patrick Marc Callan, June 26, 1984. BA in Art History summa cum laude, Calif. State U., Dominguez Hills, 1978, MA in Behavioral Scis., 1981. Dir. community rels./alumni affairs Calif. State U., Dominguez Hills, adminstrv. fellow office chancellor Long Beach, assoc. dir. univ. svcs. office chancellor, 1979-85; dir. capital campaign, assoc. dir. devel. Sta. KVIE-TV, Sacramento, 1985-86; dir. project devel. Pacific Mountain Network, Denver, 1986-87; dir. mktg. and devel. Denver Symphony Orch., 1988-89; assoc. dir. San Jose (Calif.) Mus. Art, 1989-91, dir., 1991-99, Mus. of Glass, Tacoma, 1999—2006; interim CEO Experience Music Project & Sci. Fiction Mus., Seattle, 2006—. Asst. prof. sch. social and behavioral scis. Calif. State U., Dominguez Hills, 1981—; mem. adv. com. Issues Facing Mus. in 1990s JKF U., 1990-91. Mem. com. arts policy Santa Clara Arts Coun., 1990-92; chair San Jose Arts Roundtable, 1992-93; active ArtTable, 1992—, Community Leadership San Jose, 1992-93, Am. Leadership Forum, 1994, bd. dirs., 2000—; mem. adv. bd. Bay Area Rsch. Project, 1992—; mem. Calif. Arts Coun., Visual Arts Panel, 1993-95, Santa Clara Arts Coun. Visual Arts Panel, 1993; bd. dirs. YWCA, 1993—. Recipient Leadership award Knight Found., 1995; Women of Vision honoree Career Action Ctr., 1998; fellow Calif. State U., 1982-83. Mem. AAUW, Am. Assn. Mus., Nat. Soc. Fund Raising Execs. (bd. dirs. 1991), Colo. Assn. Fund Raisers, Art Mus. Devel. Assn., Assn. Art Mus. Dirs., We. Mus. Assn., Calif. State U. Alumni Coun. (pres. 1981-83), Rotary Internat. Office: EMP/SFM Ste 200 300 6th Ave N Seattle WA 98109 E-mail: CEO@empsfm.org.

CALLÉ, CRAIG R.L., finance company executive; b. Greenwich, Conn., Dec. 17, 1959; s. Hans Martin Erich and Mary Ann (Sadtler) C.; m. Catherine Maechling, June 18, 1993. BA, BS in Econ., U. Pa., 1981; MBA, Harvard U., 1985. Fin. analyst Salomon Bros. Inc., NYC, 1981-83, assoc., 1985-88, v.p., 1988-91; treas. Crown Cork & Seal Co., Inc., 1991, v.p. & treas., 1991-95, sr. v.p. fin., treas., 1995—2004; exec. v.p., CFO IPWireless, Inc.; founder, CEO common.net, 2001—06; v.p., treas., v.p. fin. prof. and direct segments Gateway, Inc., Irvine, Calif., 2006—. Mem. Harvard Club NYC, Phila. Cricket Club. Republican. Office: Gateway Inc 7565 Irvine Center Dr Irvine CA 92618 Business E-Mail: craig.calle@gteway.com.

CALLETON, THEODORE EDWARD, lawyer, educator; b. Newark, Dec. 13, 1934; s. Edward James and Dorothy (Dewey) C.; m. Elizabeth Bennett Brown, Feb. 4, 1961; children: Susan Bennett, Pamela Barritt, Christopher Dewey.; m. Kathy E'Beth Conkle, Feb. 22, 1983; 1 child, James Frederick. BA, Yale U., 1956; LLB, Columbia U., 1962. Bar: Calif. 1963, U.S. Dist. Ct. (so. dist.) Calif. 1963, U.S. Tax Ct. 1977. Assoc. O'Melveny & Myers, LA, 1962-69, Agnew, Miller & Carlson, LA, 1969, ptnr., 1970-79; pvt. practice LA, 1979-83; ptnr. Kindel & Anderson, LA, 1983-92, Calleton & Merritt, Pasadena, Calif., 1992-99, Calleton & Trytten, Pasadena, 1999—2002; pvt. practice Pasadena, 2002—06; ptnr. Calleton, Merritt, DeFrancisco & Real-Salas, Pasadena, 2006—. Academician Internat. Acad. Estate and Trust Law, 1974—; lectr. Calif. Continuing Edn. Bar, 1970—96, U. So. Calif. Tax Inst., 1972, 76, 91, Calif. State U., LA, 1974—93, Practicing Law Inst., 1976—86, Am. Law Inst., 1985; bd. dirs. UCLA/Continuing Edn. of Bar Estate Planning Inst., 1979—; adj. prof. Golden Gate U. Law Sch., 1997—2000, Loyola U. Sch. Law, 2002—07. Author: The Short Term Trust, 1977, A Life Insurance Primer, 1978, Calleton's Wills and Trusts, 1992—2003; co-author: California Will Drafting Practice, 1982, Tax Planning for Professionals, 1985, California Estate Planning, 2002, California Revocable Trusts, 2003; contbr. articles to profl. jours. Chmn. Arroyo Seco Master Planning Comm., Pasadena, Calif., 1970-71; bd. dirs. Montessori Sch., Inc., 1964-68, chmn., 1966-68, Am. Montessori Soc., N.Y.C., 1967-72, chmn., 1969-72; trustee Walden Sch. of Calif., 1970-86, 90-94, chmn., 1980-86; trustee Episc. Children's Home of L.A., 1971-75; bd. dirs. L.A. Master Chorale Assn., 1989-94, San Gabriel Valley Coun., Boy Scouts of Am., 2002-05. Lt. USMC, 1956-59. Fellow Am. Coll. Trust and Estate Counsel; mem. L.A. County Bar Assn. (chmn. taxation sect. 1980-81, chmn. probate and trust law sect. 1981-82, Dana Latham Meml. award 1996), Aurelian Honor Soc., Elihu, Beta Theta Pi, Phi Delta Phi. Home: 301 Churchill Rd Sierra Madre CA 91024-1354 Office: 131 N El Molino Ave Ste 300 Pasadena CA 91101 Office Phone: 626-395-0860. Business E-Mail: ted@cmdrlaw.com.

CALLEY, JOHN, former motion picture company executive, film producer; b. NJ, 1930; m. Olinka Schoberova, 1972 (div.); m. Meg Tilly, 1995 (div.); 1 child, Sabrina; stepchildren: Emily, David, Will. Dir. nighttime programming, dir. programming sales NBC, 1951-57; prodn. exec. and TV producer Henry Jaffe Enterprises, 1957; v.p. radio and TV Ted Bates Advt. Agy., 1958; exec. v.p., film producer Filmways, Inc., 1960-69; with Warner Bros., Inc., Burbank, Calif., 1969-87, exec. v.p. world-wide prodn., 1969-75, pres., 1975-80, vice chmn. bd., 1977-80, cons., 1980-87; independent film prodr., 1987—93; pres., COO, United Artists Pictures, 1993-96; pres., CEO, Sony Pictures Entertainment, Inc., Culver City, Calif., 1996—98, chmn., CEO, 1998—2003. Prodr. (films): Face in the Rain, 1963, The Loved One, 1965, Eye of the Devil, 1967, Don't Make Waves, 1967, Ice Station Zebra, 1968, Castle Keep, 1969, Catch-22, 1970, Fat Man and Little Boy, 1989, Postcards from the Edge, 1990, The Remains of the Day, 1993, Closer, 2004, The Da Vinci Code, 2006, The Jane Austen Book Club, 2007. Recipient Career Achievement award, LA Film Critics Assn., 2009.*

CALLIES, DAVID LEE, lawyer, educator; b. Chgo., Apr. 21, 1943; s. Gustav E. and Ann D. Callies; m. Laurie Breeden, Dec. 28, 1996; 1 child, Sarah Wayne Callies. AB, DePauw U., 1965; JD, U. Mich., 1968; LLM, U. Nottingham, England, 1969. Bar: Ill. 1969, Hawaii 1978, U.S. Supreme Ct. 1974. Spl. asst. states atty., McHenry County, Ill., 1969; assoc. firm Ross, Hardies, O'Keefe, Babcock & Parsons, Chgo., 1969-75, ptnr., 1975-78; prof. law Richardson Sch. Law, U. Hawaii, Honolulu, 1978—; Benjamin A. Kudo prof. law U. Hawaii, Honolulu, 1995—. Mem. adv. com. on planning and growth mgmt. City and County of Honolulu Coun., 1978-88, mem. citizens adv. com. on State Functional Plan for Conservation Lands, 1979-93. Author: (with Fred P. Bosselman) the Quiet Revolution in Land Use Control, 1971 (with Fred P. Bosselman and John S. Banta) The Taking Issue, 1973, Regulating Paradise: Land Use Controls in Hawaii, 1984, (with Robert Freilich and Tom Roberts) Cases and Materials on Land Use, 1986, 5th edit., 2008, Preserving Paradise: Why Regulation Won't Work, 1994 (in Japanese 1994, in Chinese 1999), Land Use Law in the United States, 1994; editor: After Lucas: Land Use Regulation and the Taking of Property Without Compensation, 1993, Takings: Land Development Conditions and Regulatory Takings After Dolan and Lucas, 1995, (with Hylton, Mandelker and Franzese) Property Law and the Public Interest, 1998, 3rd edit., 2003, 3rd edit., 2008, (with Kotaka) Taking Land, 2002, (with Curtin and Tappendorf) Bargaining For Development: A Handbook, 2003, (with Bosselman, et al) Customary Law & Sustainable Development, 2005; co-editor Environ. and Land Use Law Rev., 2000—. Named Best Prof., U. Hawaii Law Sch., 1990-91, 91-92, 2007-08; Mich. Ford Found. fellow U. Nottingham (Eng.), 1969, life mem. Clare Hall, Cambridge U., 1999. Fellow: Am. Coll. Real Estate Lawyers, Am. Inst. Cert. Planners; mem.: ABA (chmn. com. on land use, planning and zoning 1980—82, coun. sect. on state and local govt. 1981—85, sec. 1986—87, exec. com. 1986—90, chmn. 1989—90, coun. sect. on state and local govt. 1995—, Lifetime Achievement award 2006), Internat. Bar Assn. (coun. Asia Pacific Forum 1993—96, co-chair Acads. Forum 1994—96, chair 1996—98), Ill. Bar Assn., Am. Bar Found., Am. Assn. Law Schs. (chair, state & local gov. sect. 2004), Hawaii State Bar Assn. (chair, real property and fin. svc. sect. 1997), Am. Planning Assn., Am. Law Inst., Lambda Alpha Internat. (pres. Aloha chpt. 1989—90, internat. v.p. Asia-Pacific region 2001—, Internat. Mem. of Yr. 1994). Home: 4620 Sierra Dr Honolulu HI 96816 Office: U Hawaii Richardson Sch Law 2515 Dole St Honolulu HI 96822-2328 Office Phone: 808-956-6550. Business E-Mail: dcallies@hawaii.edu.

CALLISON, NANCY FOWLER, nurse administrator; b. Milw., July 16, 1931; d. George Fenwick and Irma Esther (Wenzel) Fowler; m. B.G. Callison, Sept. 25, 1954 (dec. Feb. 1964); children: Robert, Leslie, Linda. Diploma, Evanston Hosp. Sch. Nursing, 1952; BS, Northwestern U., 1954. RN, Calif.; cert. case mgr. Staff nurse, psychiat. dept. Downey VA Hosp., 1954-55; staff nurse Camp Lejeune Naval Hosp., 1955, 59-61; obstet. supr. Tri-City Hosp., Oceanside, Calif., 1961-62; pub. health nurse San Diego County, 1962-66; sch. nurse Rich-Mar Union Sch. Dist., San Marcos, Calif., 1966-68; head nurse San Diego County Community Mental Health, 1968-73; dir. patient care services Southwood Mental Health Ctr., Chula Vista, Calif., 1973-75; program cons. Comprehensive Care Corp., Newport Beach, Calif., 1975-79; dir. Manpower Health Care, Culver City, Calif., 1979-80; dir. nursing services Peninsula Rehab. Ctr., Lomita, Calif., 1980-81; clinic supr., coordinator utilization and authorizations, acting dir. provider relations Hawthorne (Calif.) Community Med. Group, 1981-86; mgr. Health Care Delivery Physicians of Greater Long Beach, Calif., 1986-87; cons. Quality Rev. Assocs., West L.A., 1988-93; case mgr. Mercy Physicians Med. Group, 1992-93; med. mgmt. specialist The Zenith Ins., 1993—99, Zurich Ins., 2001—04. Clin. coord., translator Flying Samaritans, 1965-, mem. internat. bd. dirs., 1975-77, 79-86, 89-95, 2005—, dir. San Quentin project, 1991-93, dir. univ. program, 1996-2000, pres. South Bay chpt., 1975-81, v.p., 1982-85, bd. dirs. San Diego chpt., 1987-90, pres. San Diego chpt. 1991-92, adminstr. Clinica Esperanza de Infantil Rosario Beach 1990-93; dir. Playas Rosario Clinic, 2004—; dir. Playas Rsch. Clinic. Mem. Rehab. Nurse Coord. Network (bd. dirs., treas. 1997-98), U.S.-Mex. Border Health Assn., Cruz Roja Mexicana (Delegacion Rosario 1986-92). Personal E-mail: callnawc@hotmail.com.

CALLOWAY, LARRY, writer; b. Lovell, Wyo., Nov. 21, 1937; s. Joseph Charles and Frances (Linda) C.; children: Lara, Maia. BA, U. Colo., 1962; MA, St. John's Coll., 2001. Staff writer United Press Internat., 1963-69; gov. and polit. writer The Associated Press, Santa Fe, 1969-79; bureau chief, zoned-edition editor The Albuquerque Jour., 1980-88, featured columnist, 1988—2001; freelance writer Crestone, Colo., 2001—. Stanford U. fellow, 1979-80. Home: POB 903 Crestone CO 81131

CALMAN, CRAIG DAVID, actor, writer; b. Riverside, Calif., June 11, 1953; Student, Pacific U., Forest Grove, Oreg., 1971-72, U. de Querétaro, Mex., 1972-73; BA in Motion Picture/TV, UCLA, 1975. Sr. admitting worker UCLA Med. Ctr., 1974-76; actor/playwright Old Globe Theatre, San Diego, 1977-78, Off Broadway and regional, NYC and East Coast, 1979-86; exec. asst. various film/TV studios and law firms, LA, 1986-89, Orion Pictures Corp., LA, 1989-90; dir. staged readings LA, 1991—, The Transcription Co., 1998—2008. Actor with starring roles (TV and film) ADP Industrial, Teamwork, Macbeth, Flesteron in Amazonia, co-starring roles in Commercial Break, Sullivan's Travels; actor with co-starring/lead roles (theatre) in Book of the Dead, Dark Lady of the Sonnets, Hamlet, Rosencrantz and Guildenstern are Dead, Much Ado About Nothing, Too True to be Good, Henry V, Richard III, The Rivals, Merchant of Venice, A Day for Surprises, The Tavern, The Earrings of Madame De..., The Firebugs, Christophe: For the Love of Freedom Part III, Madness in Valencia, and others; columnist FilmZone, 1995-97. Author play/screenplays: The Turn of the Century, Strangled Nocturne, Skidoo Ruins, Life Without Father, Patterns Woven In A Park; author: The Turn of the Century; author one-act plays, screenplays, full-length plays, poetry; writer asst. Hal Roach, Bel Air, Calif., 1987-88; writer, dir., prodr. The Calista Zipper Story, 2008 (Purple Heart award 2009). Vol. book reader Recording for the Blind, L.A., 1991—. Recipient Old Globe Theatre Atlas award for best actor in a comedy role for Too True to be Good, 1977-78; Helene Wurlitzer Found. of N.Mex. Writers Residency grantee, 1988; finalist Walt Disney fellowship program, 1992, Chesterfield Film Writers Project, 1997. Mem. SAG,

Actors Equity Assn., Actors Studio West (playwright/dir. unit 2000-2005, Mark Rydell's Director's Unit, 2003-04). Office Phone: 323-906-8886. Personal E-mail: craigcalman@earthlink.net.

CALTABIANO, ANNE, library director; Mgr. Glendale Pub. Libr., Ariz. Office: Glendale Pub Libr 5959 W Brown St Glendale AZ 85302 Office Phone: 623-930-3569. E-mail: ACaltabiano@glendaleaz.com.

CALVERT, KEN, United States Representative from California; b. Corona, Calif., June 8, 1953; AA, Chaffey Coll., 1973; BA Econs., San Diego State U., 1975. Congl. aide to Rep. Vitor Veysey, Calif., 1975-79; gen. mgr. Jolly Fox Restaurant, Corona, Calif., 1975-79, Marcus W. Meairs Co., Corona, Calif., 1979-81; pres., gen. mgr. Ken Calvert Real Properties, Corona, Calif., 1980—91; mem. US Congress from 43rd Calif. dist., 1992—2003, US Congress from 44th Calif. dist., 2003—, mem. armed svcs. com., resources com., appropriations com. Corona/Norco youth chmn. for Nixon, 1968; Reagan-Bush campaign worker, 80; co chmn. Wilson for Senate Campaign, 1982, George Deukmejian election, 1978, 82, 86, George Bush election, 1988, Pete Wilson senate elections, 1982, 88, Pete Wilson for Gov. election, 1990; chmn. Riverside Rep. Party, 1984—88; mem. Corona/Norco Rep. Assembly, Baltic Caucus, Coalition Autism Rsch. & Edn., Coastal Caucus, Diabetes Caucus, Fire Caucus, Def. Study Grp., Hellenic Caucus, Human Rights Caucus, India Caucus, Intellectual Property Caucus, Internat. Anti-Piracy Caucus, Law Enforcement Caucus, Med. Tech. Caucus, Missing & Exploited Children's Caucus, Moroccan Caucus, Nat. Guard & Reserve Caucus, Native Am. Caucus, Navy/Marine Corps Caucus, Real Estate Caucus, Sportsman's Caucus, Test & Evaluation Caucus, Travel & Tourism Caucus, Western Caucus, Wine Caucus, Zero Capital Gains Tax Caucus, Rep. Steering Com.; co-chair Generic Drug Equity Caucus, Manufactured Housing Caucus, Congl. Caucus Fight & Control Methamphetamine. Mem. exec, bd. Corona Cmty. Hosp.; mem. adv. com. Corona Airport, Temescal/El Cerrito Cmty. Plan. Mem.: Corona C. of C. (pres. 1990), Monday Morning Group, Elks, Riverside County Lincoln Club (founder, chair), Corona Rotary Club (pres. 1991). Republican. Office: US Ho Reps 2201 Rayburn Ho Office Bldg Washington DC 20515-0544 also: Office of Ken Calvert Ste 200 3400 Central Avenue Riverside CA 92506

CALVIN, ALLEN DAVID, psychologist, educator; b. St. Paul, Feb. 17, 1928; s. Carl and Zelda (Engelson) C.; m. Dorothy VerStrate, Oct. 5, 1953; children: Jamie, Kris, David, Scott. BA in Psychology cum laude, U. Minn., 1950; MA in Psychology, U. Tex., 1951, PhD in Exptl. Psychology, 1953. Instr. Mich. State U., East Lansing, 1953-55; asst. prof. Hollins Coll., 1955-59, assoc. prof., 1959-61. Dir. Britannica Ctr. for Studies in Learning and Motivation, Menlo Park, Calif., 1961; prin. investigator grant for automated tchg. fgn. langs. Carnegie Found., 1960; USPHS grantee, 1960; pres. Behavioral Rsch. Labs., 1962-74; prof., dean Sch. Edn., U. San Francisco, 1974-78; Henry Clay Hall prof. orgn. and leadership, 1978—; prof. Pacific Grad. Sch. Psychology, 1984-2001, pres., 1984-. Author textbooks. Served with USNR, 1946-47. Mem. Am. Psychol. Assn., AAAS, Sigma Xi, Psi Chi. Home: 1645 15th Ave San Francisco CA 94122-3523 Office: 405 Broadway St Redwood City CA 94063 also: Pacific Grad School Of Psychology 405 Broadway St Redwood City CA 94063-3133 Home Phone: 415-516-1338; Office Phone: 650-843-3402, 650-421-4802. Business E-Mail: a.calvin@pgsp.edu.

CAMACHO, CHARLOTTE DLG, principal, elementary school educator; m. Mike Camacho; 3 children. BA in Early Childhood Edn., San Diego State Univ. Kindergarten, first grade tchr., Saipan, No. Marianas; prin. Gregorio T. Camacho Elem. Sch., Saipan, No. Marianas. Named No. Marianas Islands Tchr. of Yr., 2006. Office: Gregorio T Camacho Elem Sch PO Box 501370 Saipan MP 96950

CAMACHO, FELIX PEREZ, Governor of Guam; b. Camp Zama, Japan, Oct. 30, 1957; s. Carlos G. and Lourdes Perez Camacho; m. Joann Gumataotao Garcia Camacho; children: Jessica Lourdes, Felix James, Maria Amparo. BBA in Fin., Marquette U., 1980. Ins. mgr. property casualty divsn. Pacific Fin. Corp.; account adminstr. IBM; dep. dir. Pub. Utility Agy., Guam, 1988—92; senator Commonwealth of Guam, 1992—2002, majority whip, chmn. com. on tourism, 2000—02, gov., 2002—. Mem.: Nat. Coun. State Legislators, Asian Pacific Parliamentarian Union, Knights of Columbus. Republican. Roman Catholic. Office: Office of the Governor PO Box 2950 Hagatna GU 96932

CAMBRE, RONALD C., mining executive; m. Gail Cambre. BSCE, La. State U.; postgrad., Harvard U. Chmn. bd. Rio Tinto Minera SA; various positions, including pres., CEO Freeport-McMoRan Resource Ptnrs. subs. Freeport-McMoRAn Inc., 1964-93; v.p., sr. technical adviser to chmn. Freeport-McMoRan Inc., 1988-93; vice chmn., CEO, bd. dirs. Newmont Mining Corp., Denver, 1993—, pres., 1994—, chmn. bd. dirs., 1995—. Vice chmn., CEO, chmn. bd. dirs. Newmont Gold Co. subs. Newmont Mining Corp. Office: Newmont Mining 1700 Lincoln St Denver CO 80203

CAMBY, MARCUS D., professional basketball player; b. Hartford, Conn., Mar. 22, 1974; Attended, U. Mass., 1993—96. Ctr. Toronto Raptors, 1996—98, NY Knicks, 1998—2002, Denver Nuggets, 2002—08, LA Clippers, 2008—. Founder Cambyland Found. Recipient John R. Wooden award, 1996, Naismith award, 1996, Chopper Travaglini award, 2004; named Coll. Player of Yr., The Sporting News, 1996, Athlete of Yr., NY mag., 1999, Defensive Player of Yr., NBA, 2007; named to All-Rookie First Team, 1997, All-Defensive First Team, 2007, 2008. Achievements include leading the NBA in blocked shots, 1998, 2006, 2007, 2008. Office: LA Clippers 1111 S Figueroa St Ste 1100 Los Angeles CA 90015

CAMERON, ALEX BRIAN, accountant, educator; b. Fresno, Calif., Nov. 20, 1943; s. Alexander Archer and Francette (Maize) C.; m. Judy Lea Helphrey, June 7, 1969; children: Michelle, Michael. BA, Eastern Wash. U., 1969, MBA, 1970; PhD, U. Utah, 1982. Cert. in mgmt. acctg. Mgr. prodn. planning Bunker Hill Mining Co., Kellog, Idaho, 1970-77; asst. prof. Wash. State U., Pullman, 1978-79; assoc. prof. Eastern Wash. U., Cheney, 1981-87, prof., 1987—, chmn. dept. acctg., 1988-89, assoc. dean, 1990-97, interimm v.p. bus. and fin., 1998-99, interim dean Coll. Bus. and Pub. Adminstrn., 1999-2001. Contbr. articles to profl. jours. Avocations: sailing, golf, volleyball. Home: 15212 Pinnacle Ln Veradale WA 99037-9163 Office: 668 N Riverpoint Blvd Spokane WA 99202-1677 Home Phone: 509-921-5815. Personal E-mail: jcameron55@comcast.net. Business E-Mail: acameron@ewu.edu.

CAMERON, HEATHER ANNE, publishing executive; b. Montreal, Quebec, Can., Mar. 12, 1951; came to U.S., 1981; d. Douglas George and Jeanne Sutherland (Thompson) C.; m. Ward Eric Shaw, Dec. 20, 1980; 1 child, Geoffrey Cameron. BA, Queen's U., Kingston, Ont., Can., 1973; MLS, McGill U., Montreal, 1977. Head reference and bibliography sect. Nat. Libr. Can., Ottawa, 1977-80; head editl. dept. Librs. Unltd., Inc., Denver, 1981-86; v.p. acquisitions and editl. devel. ABC-CLIO, Inc., Santa Barbara, Calif., 1986-92, pres., pub. Santa Barbara, Denver and, Eng., 1992-97; v.p., gen. mgr. Westgroup, San Francisco, 1997—. Bd. dirs. Friends of Librs. U.S.A., v.p., 1996, pres., 1997—. Mem. ALA (com. chair 1993—), Friends of Librs., USA (dir. 1994—, pres. 1997-2000), Amnesty Internat., Phi Beta Mu. Office: Thomson-West 425 Market St San Francisco CA 94105 Office Phone: 415-344-5010. Business E-Mail: heather.cameron@thomson.com.

CAMERON, JAMES, film director, screenwriter, producer; b. Kapuskasing, Ont., Can., Aug. 16, 1954; s. Philip and Shirley Cameron; m. Sharon Williams, 1974 (div. 1985); m. Gale Ann Hurd, 1985 (div. 1989); m. Katheryn Bigelow, 1989 (div. 1991); m. Linda Hamilton, 1997 (div. 1999), 1 child, Josephine Archer Cameron; m. Suzy Amis, 2000; children, Clair and Elizabeth Rose. Grad. in Physics, Calif. State U., Fullerton. Head Lightstorm Entertainment, Burbank, Calif., 1992—; CEO Digital Domain, 1993—. Art dir. Battle Beyond the Stars, 1980, prodn. designer Galaxy of Terror, 1981, creator spl. effects Escape from New York, 1981; dir.: (films) Piranha II: The Spawning, 1981, Terminator 2 3-D, 1996; (TV films) Earthship, 2001; screenwriter Rambo: First Blood Part II, 1985, Strange Days, 1995, exec. prodr. Point Break, 1991, dir., screenwriter Xenogenesis, 1978, The Terminator, 1984, Aliens, 1986, The Abyss, 1989, dir., prodr., editor (films) Titanic, 1997 (Academy award for Best Picture and Best Dir., 9 others, 1997), dir., prodr. Ghosts of the Abyss, 2002, (TV) Expedition Bismarck, 2002, dir., prodr., screenwriter Terminator II: Judgement Day, 1991 (6 Academy award nominations, Ray Bradbury award for dramatic screenwriting, 5 Saturn awards Acad. Sci. Fiction, 5 MTV Movie awards, People's Choice award), True Lies, 1994, writer, exec. prodr. (TV series) Dark Angel, 2000—; author: (films) Terminator 3: Rise of the Machines, 2003; prodr.: (films) Volcanos of the Deep Sea, 2003, Aliens of the Deep, 2005; (TV films) Titanic Adventure, 2005, Last Mysteries of the Titanic, 2005; (documentaries) The Lost Tomb of Jesus, 2007. Mem. adv. bd. Science Fiction Mus. and Hall of Fame. Named one of 50 Smartest People in Hollywood, Entertainment Weekly, 2007. Mem.: Am. Cinema Editors. Office: Lightstorm Entertainment 919 Santa Monica Blvd Santa Monica CA 90401-2704

CAMERON, JUDITH LYNNE, secondary school educator; b. Oakland, Calif., Apr. 29, 1945; d. Alfred Joseph and June Estelle (Faul) Moe; m. Richard Irwin Cameron, Dec. 17, 1967; 1 child, Kevin Dale. AA in Psychol., Sacramento City Coll., 1965; BA in Psychol., German, Calif. State U., 1967; MA in Reading Specialization, San Francisco State U., 1972; postgrad., Chapman Coll.; PhD, Am. Inst. Hypnotherapy, 1987; PhD in Parapsychology, St. John's U., 2005. Cert. tchr., Calif. Tchr. St. Vincent's Cath. Sch., San Jose, Calif., 1969-70, Fremont (Calif.) Elem. Sch., 1970-72, LeRoy Boys Home, LaVerne, Calif., 1972-73, Grace Miller Elem. Sch., LaVerne, Calif., 1973-80, resource specialist, 1980-84; owner, mgr. Pioneer Take-out Franchises, Alhambra and San Gabriel, Calif., 1979-85; resource specialist, dept. chmn. Bonita H.S., LaVerne, Calif., 1984—2008; mentor tchr. in space sci. Bonita Unified Sch. Dist., 1988-99, rep. LVTV; owner, therapist So. Calif. Clin. Hypnotherapy, Claremont, Calif., 1988—2007, Earth Angel Hypnotherapy & Healing, 2007—. Bd. dirs., recommending tchr., asst. dir. Project Turnabout, Claremont, Calif.; Teacher-in-Space cons. Bonita Unified Sch. Dist., LaVerne, 1987-99; advisor Peer Counseling Program, Bonita High Sch., 1987—; advisor Air Explorers/Edwards Test Pilot Sch., LaVerne, 1987—; mem. Civil Air Patrol, Squadron 68, Aerospace Office, 1988-92; selected amb. U.S. Space Acad.-U.S. Space Camp Acad., Huntsville, Ala., 1990; named to national (now internat.) tchg.faculty challenger Ctr. for Space Edn., Alexandria, Va., 1990; regional coord. East San Gabiel Valley Future Scientists and Engrs. of Am.; amb. to U.S. Space Camp, 1990; mem. adj. faculty Challenger Learning Ctr. Calif. State U., Dominguez Hills, 1994, state sch. accreditation team, 2000, 03, 05, negotiating team, 1998-2003; rep. ceremony to honor astronauts Apollo 11, White House, 1994; exec. bd. Bonita Unfied tchrs. assoc., 1995—, negotiating team, 1998-2003; flight dir. mission control, Challenger Learning Ctr., Long Beach, Ca., 2002—; mem. WASC accrediting team, Calif. Vol. advisor Children's Home Soc., Santa Ana, 1980-81; dist. rep. LVTV Channel 29, 1991; regional coord. East San Gabriel Valley chpt. Future Scientists and Engrs. of Am., 1992; mem. internat. invesigation Commn. UFOs, 1991; field mem. Ctr. for Search for Extraterrestrial Intelligence, 1996; tchr., leader Ctr. for the Study Extraterrestrial Intelligence, 1997—. Recipient Tchr. of Yr., Bonita H.S., 1989, continuing svc. award, 1992; named Toyolaa Tchr. of Yr., 1994. Mem. NEA, AAUW, Internat. Investigations Com. on UFOs, Coun. Exceptional Children, Am. Psychol. Assn., Calif. Assn. Resource Specialists, Calif. Elem. Edn. Assn., Calif. Tchrs. Assn., Calif. Assn. Marriage and Family Therapists, Planetary Soc., Mutual UFO Network, Com. Sci. Investigation L5 Soc., Challenger Ctr. Space Edn., Calif. Challenger Ctr. Crew for Space Edn., Orange County Astronomers, Chinese Shar-Pei Am., Concord Club, Rare Breed Dog Club (L.A.), gardening club of Am., ctr. for the extraterrestrial intelligence, diplomat, 1997. Republican. Avocations: skiing, banjo, guitar, flying, astrophotography. Home: 3257 La Travesia Dr Fullerton CA 92835-1455 Office: Bonita High Sch 115 W Allen Ave San Dimas CA 91773-1437 Office Phone: 714-992-0360.

CAMERON, PAUL DRUMMOND, health facility administrator; b. Pitts., Nov. 9, 1939; s. Nelson Drummond and Veronica (Witco) C.; m. Virginia May Rusthoi; 3 children. BA, L.A. Pacific Coll., 1961; MA, Calif. State U., LA, 1962; PhD, U. Colo., 1966. Asst. prof. psychology Stout State U., Menomonie, Wis., 1966-67, Wayne State U., Detroit, 1967-69; assoc. prof. psychology U. Louisville, 1970-73, Fuller Grad. Sch. Psychology, Pasadena, Calif., 1976-79; assoc. prof. marriage and family U. Nebr., Lincoln, 1979-80; pvt. practice psychologist Lincoln, 1980-83; chmn. Family Rsch. Inst., Washington, 1982-95, Colo. Springs, 1995—. Reviewer Am. Psychologist, Jour. Gerontology, Psychol. Reports, Brit. Med. Jour., Can. Med. Assn. Jour.; presenter, expert witness, cons. in field. Author: Exposing the AIDS Scandal, 1988, The Gay 90's, 1993; contbr. articles to profl. jours. Mem. Ea. Psychol. Assn. Republican. Lutheran. Achievements include pioneer investigation of health effects of second-hand tobacco smoke; investigator of first comprehensive national random sample of sexuality. Office: Family Rsch Inst PO Box 62640 Colorado Springs CO 80962-2640 Home Phone: 303-681-3124; Office Phone: 303-681-3113. E-mail: pdcameron@juno.com.

CAMP, JOSEPH SHELTON, JR., film producer, director, writer; b. St. Louis, Apr. 20, 1939; s. Joseph Shelton and Ruth Wilhelmena (McLaulin) C.; m. Andrea Carolyn Hopkins, Aug. 7, 1960; children: Joseph Shelton III, Brandon Andrew. BBA, U. Miss., 1961. Jr. account exec. McCann-Erickson Advt., Houston, 1961-62; owner Joe Camp Real Estate, Houston, 1962-64; account exec. Norsworthy-Mercer, Dallas, 1964-69; dir. TV commls. Jamieson Film Co., Dallas, 1969-71; founder, pres., writer, producer, dir. feature films Mulberry Square Prodns., Inc., Dallas, 1971-90, Gulfport, Miss., 1991-94, Chapel Hill, N.C., 1994—. Producer, dir., writer films including Benji, 1974, Hawmps, 1976, For the Love of Benji, 1977, The Double McGuffin, 1979, Oh Heavenly Dog, 1980, Benji The Hunted, 1987; TV spls. The Phenomenon of Benji, 1978, Benji's Very Own Christmas Story, 1978, Benji at Work, 1980, Benji (Takes a Dive) at Marineland, 1981; TV series Benji, Zax and the Alien Prince, 1983; author: Underdog, 1993. Bd. trustees Piney Woods Country Life Sch., Warren Wilson Coll.; adv. bd. N.C. Sch. of Arts, Sch. of Film Making. Mem. Dir.'s Guild Am., Writer's Guild Am. Office: 29067 Aerie Rd Valley Center CA 92082-5728

CAMPANA, MICHAEL EMERSON, hydrogeology and hydrology educator, researcher; b. May 13, 1948; BS in Geology, Coll. William and Mary, 1970; MS in Hydrology, U. Ariz., 1973, PhD in Hydrology, 1975. Cert. profl. geologist, Ind.; profl. hydrogeologist Am. Inst. Hydrology. Assoc. faculty Pima C.C., Tucson, 1973-75; asst. prof. hydrogeology dept. geol. scis. Mackay Sch. Mines U. Nev., Reno, 1976-79, assoc. prof., 1979-83, 84-89; asst. rsch. prof. Water Resources Ctr. Desert Rsch. Inst., Reno, 1976-79, assoc. rsch. prof. Water Resources Ctr., 1979-83, 84-89; assoc. prof. dept. geology Ga. State U., Atlanta, 1983-84; assoc. prof. dept. earth and planetary scis. U. N.Mex., Albuquerque, 1989-97, prof. dept. earth and planetary scis., 1997—, dir. water resources program, 1997—. Vis. assoc. prof. earth scis. bd. U. Calif., Santa Cruz, 1988-89; bd. dirs. Ground Water Pub. Co.; mem. nat. rsch. coun. com. U.S. Geol. Survey Water Resources Rsch. Assoc. editor: Environ. and Engring. Geosci., 1995—, Ground Water, 1999—; guest co-editor: Hydrogeology Jour. E.S. Simpson meml. issue. Active Vols. in Tech. Assistance, 1984—, Vols. in Overseas Coop. Asstistance, 1995—, Lifewater Internat., 1997—. Fulbright scholar Univ. Coll. Belize, 1995-96. Mem. Am. Geophys. Union, Am. Inst. Hydrology, Internat. Assn. Hydrogeologist, Internat. Assn. Hydrol. Scis., Internat. Water Resources Assn., N.Am. Benthol. Soc., Geol. Soc. Am., European Geophys. Soc., Assn. Ground Water Scientists and Engrs. (bd. dirs. 1997—). Achievements include research to investigate and quantify the interactions between hydrologic systems and stream ecosystems in forested montane catchments; research in watershed hydrology, in regional subsurface flow system delineation and ground-water resource assessment; delineation of flow systems using hydraulic, environmental isotopic and geochemical data, environmental fluid mechanics. Office: U NMex Dept Earth & Planetary Scis Albuquerque NM 87131-0001 Home: 3359 NW Poppy Dr Corvallis OR 97330-3476

CAMPANELLA, YVETTE LYNN, cosmetics executive; b. Rockland County, NY, May 31, 1952; d. John Alfred and Marie Christine (Hill) Johnson; m. John Deloach Campanella, Sept. 22, 1978; 1 child, Jon Thomas. BA in Psychology, Vassar Coll., 1974. Operational analyses and controls sr. analyst Met. Life Ins. Co., NYC, 1975—78; indsl. engr. Security Pacific Bank, LA, 1979; dir. mktg. rsch. and adminstrn. Max Factor & Co., Hollywood, Calif., 1979—. Mem.: Am. Mgmt. Assn., Am. Inst. Indsl. Engrs., Nat. Assn. Female Execs. Conglist. Office: 2049 Century Park E Ste 1400 Los Angeles CA 90067-3116

CAMPBELL, ALLAN MCCULLOCH, bacteriology educator; b. Berkeley, Calif., Apr. 27, 1929; s. Lindsay and Virginia Margaret (Henning) C.; m. Alice Del Campillo, Sept. 5, 1958; children—Wendy, Joseph. BS in Chemistry, U. Calif., Berkeley, 1950; MS in Bacteriology, U. Ill., 1951; PhD, 1953; PhD (hon.), U. Chgo., 1978, U. Rochester, 1981. Instr. bacteriology U. Mich., 1953-57; research asso. Carnegie Inst., Cold Spring Harbor, NY, 1957-58; asst. prof. biology U. Rochester, NY, 1958-61, assoc. prof. NY, 1961-63, prof. NY, 1963-68; prof. biol. sci. Stanford U., Calif., 1968—, Barbara Kimball Browning prof. humanities and sciences Calif., 1992—. Author: Episomes, 1969; co-author: General Virology, 1978; editor Gene, 1980-90, mem. editl. bd., 1990—; assoc. editor Virology, 1963-69; assoc. editor Ann. Rev. Genetics, 1969-84, editor, 1984—; spl. editor Evolution, 1985-88; editl. bd. Jour. Bacteriology, 1966-72, Jour. Virology, 1967-75, New Biologist, 1989-92. Served with AUS, 1953-55. Recipient Research Career award USPHS, 1962-68 Mem. NAS, Am. Soc. Microbiology (Abbott-ASM Lifetime Achievement award 2004), Soc. Am. Naturalists, Genetics Soc. Am.; fellow AAAS, Am. Acad. Microbiology, Am. Acad. Arts and Scis. Democrat. Home: 947 Mears Ct Stanford CA 94305-1041 Office: Stanford U Herrin Labs RM 339A Mail Code 5020 Dept Biol Stanford CA 94305-5020 Home Phone: 650-493-6153. Business E-Mail: AMC@stanford.edu.

CAMPBELL, BRUCE ALAN, corporate coach; b. Washington, Jan. 19, 1944; s. Albert Angus and Jean Lorraine (Winter) C.; m. Jennifer Lee Drew, May 3, 1968 (div. Dec. 1986); children: Kirsten, Robert; m. Lorna Marion Wise Ekholm, Aug. 21, 1993. BA, Oberlin Coll., 1966; MA, U. Mich., 1968, PhD, 1971. Asst. prof. to assoc. prof. U. Ga., Athens, 1971-83, dir. survey rsch. ctr., 1981-83; v.p. Marktrend Mkt. Rsch., Vancouver, B.C., Canada, 1983-84; pres., CEO Campbell Goodell Traynor Consul, Vancouver, B.C., Canada, 1984—2000; sr. cons. CGT Rsch. Internat. (formerly named Campbell Goodell Traynor Consul), Vancouver, B.C., Canada, 2000—02; v.p. Corp. Insights, Inc., Vancouver, 1992-96; pres. Argus Strategies, Ltd., Vancouver, B.C., 1988—. Dir. Downtown Vancouver Assn., 1989-96, pres., 1994-96, mem. adv. bd., 1996—; dir. Parking Corp. of Vancouver, 1992-2000, v.p., 1994-96, chmn. bd., 1996-98; bd. dir s. Downtown Vancouver Bus. Improvement Assn., 1994-96; mem. Vancouver Econ. Devel. Commn., 1996. Author: The American Electorate, 1979, profl. jours. Avocations: musical theatre, minor hockey officiating. Office: Argus Strategies Ltd 2224 W 15th Ave Vancouver BC Canada V6K 2Y7 Office Phone: 604-732-8865.

CAMPBELL, CHAD, state legislator; b. Phoenix, Mar. 5, 1973; BS in Environ. Sci., Northern Ariz. U., 2006. Mem. Dist. 14 Ariz. House of Reps., 2007—, minority whip, mem. commerce com., govt. com. Mem. Phoenix Environ. Quality Commn., 2006—. Bd. dirs. Ctr. Progressive Leadership, 2007—, Communities in Sch.'s of Ariz., 2007—; mem. adv. bd. Ariz. Latino Leadership Inst., 2007—. Recipient Eagle for Enterprise award, Ariz. Small Bus. Assn.; named one of Tech Ten Legislators of 2008, Ariz. Tech. Coun. Democrat. Office: Ariz House Reps Capitol Complex 1700 W Washington Rm

333 Phoenix AZ 85007 Office Phone: 602-576-7414, 602-926-3026. Office Fax: 602-417-3037. Business E-Mail: chcampbell@azleg.gov. E-mail: chad@chadcampbell.org.*

CAMPBELL, CHARLES TAYLOR, chemistry educator; b. Beaumont, Tex., Apr. 30, 1953; married; 1 child. BS, U. Tex., Austin, 1975, PhD, 1979. Summer grad. student Sandia Nat. Labs, N.Mex., 1977; postdoctoral rsch. assoc. U. Munich, 1979-81; staff mem. Los Alamos Nat. Lab., N.Mex., 1981-86; assoc. prof. Ind. U., Bloomington, 1986-89, U. Wash., Seattle, 1989-92, prof. chemistry, 1992—, adj. prof. physics, 1994—, co-dir., Ctr. for Nanotechnology, 1997—2003, dir., Ctr. for Nanotechnology, 2003—04, Lloyd E. and Florence M. West Endowed Professorship in Chemistry, 2004—; co-dir. Pacific Northwest Nat. Lab., 2001—, U. Wash. Joint Inst. for Nanoscience, 2001—. Mem. Dept. Energy Labs Tech. Rsch. Program Review, Catalysis/Chem. Conversion, 1996, Dept. Energy/Oak Ridge Nat. Lab Chem. Sciences Program Review, 1997, Lawrence Berkeley Nat. Lab, Materials Sci. Review, 1998; mem. scientific adv. com., Pacific Northwest Nat. Labs EMSL, 2003-; mem. internat. scientific adv. bd., Fritz Haber Inst., Max Planck Soc., Berlin, Germany, 2005-; scientific adv. bd. Prolinx, Inc., Bothell, Wash., 2001-2003, Lumera, Inc., Bothell, Wash., 2004-, Asemblon, Inc., Seattle, Wash., 2005-; bd. dir., Wash. Tech. Ctr., 1997-2000, Internat. Workshop on Oxide Surfaces, 2006-; presenter in field. Mem. editl. bd. Jour. of Catalysis, 1991-93, Jour. Chem. Physics, 2002-2004, Current Topics in Catalysts, 2004-; chief editor Surface Sci., 2002-; patentee in field; contbr. articles to profl. jours. Recipient DuPont Young Faculty award, 1988-89, Camille and Henry Dreyfus Found. Tchr./Scholar award, 1988-92, John Yarwood Meml. award Brit. Vacuum Coun., 1989, Alexander von Humboldt Rsch. award, 2001; NSF NATO postdoctoral fellow U. Munich, 1979-80, Alexander von Humboldt fellow U. Munich, 1980-81, Alfred P. Sloan rsch. fellow, 1986-88; Lubrizol Found. scholar U. Tex., 1973-74, Alcoa and Dean's Office scholar U. Tex., 1974-75. Mem. Am. Chem. Soc. (treas. colloid & surface divsn. 1984-89, vice-chmn. 1991, chmn.-elect 1992, chmn. 1993, co-chmn. continuing symposium on surface and colloid chemistry of advanced materials 1988-91, Am. Chem. Soc. Colloid and Surface Chemistry award, 2001, Arthur W. Adamson award for Disting. Svc. in the Advancement of Surface Chemistry, 2007), N.Am. Catalysis Soc. (Pacific Coast Catalysis Soc. Repr., 2006-), Am. Vacuum Soc. (exec. com. N.Mex. chpt. 1983-84), Phi Eta Sigma (pres. Lamar U. chpt. 1971), Phi Lambda Upsilon (nat. v.p., 1999-2002, nat pres., 2002-2005). Office: Dept Chemistry U Wash Bagley 36 Box 351700 Seattle WA 98195-1700 Office Phone: 206-616-6085, 206-616-4270, 206-616-2969, 206-616-2967. Office Fax: 206-616-6250. Business E-Mail: campbell@chem.washington.edu.

CAMPBELL, CLOVES C., JR., state legislator; b. Phoenix; m. Lanette Campbell; children: Daivon, Chanette, Cloves III. Degree in Polit. Sci., Pitzer Coll., Claremont, Calif. Pub., chmn. Ariz. Informant Newspaper; mem. Dist. 16 Ariz. House of Reps., 2007—, mem. appropriations, com., banking & ins. com. Founding mem. Ariz. African-Am. Legis. Days Coalition. Bd. dirs. Tanner Chapel African Meth. Episcopal Ch., Mountain Park Health Assn., Black Theatre Troupe, 100 Black Men of Phoenix; mem. cmty. adv. bd. Salvation Army. Democrat. Office: Ariz House Reps Capitol Complex 1700 W Washington Rm 124 Phoenix AZ 85007 Office Phone: 602-399-8034, 602-926-3042. Office Fax: 602-417-3117. Business E-Mail: clcampbell@azleg.gov. E-mail: ccampbell@voteforcloves.com.

CAMPBELL, DAVID NEIL, physician, educator; b. Peoria, Ill., Dec. 1, 1944; s. William Neil and Lillian May (Hunter) C.; m. Charlyn Harris, Nov. 16, 1968; children: Scott, Chris, Brad. BA, Northwestern U., 1966; MD, Rush Med. Sch., 1974. Resident in gen. and cardiothoracic surgery U. Colo. Health Sci. Ctr., Denver, from asst. prof. to prof. surgery, 1988-95, prof. surgery, 1995—. Cons., Denver, Colo., 1986—. Lt. U.S. Army, 1966-67, Korea. Office: U Colo Health Sci Ctr 4200 E 9th Ave # C310 Denver CO 80220-3706 Office Phone: 720-777-6624. Business E-Mail: campbell.david@tchden.org.

CAMPBELL, DEMAREST LINDSAY, artist, writer, interior designer; d. Peter Stephen III and Mary Elizabeth (Edwards) C.; m. Dale Gordon Haugo, 1978. BFA in Art History, MFA in Asian Art History, MFA in Theatre Design. Designer interiors, historic renovation, mural art Demarest Campbell Art and Interiors, San Francisco, 1975—; chargeman scenic artist Am. Conservatory Theatre, 1976—. Designed, painted and sculpted over 300 prodns. for Broadway, internat. opera, motion pictures. Mem. NOW, Asian Art Mus. Soc., San Francisco. Mem. Internat. Alliance of Theatrical Stage Employees, Art Dirs. Guild and Scenic, Title and Graphic Artists (Local 800), Sherlock Holmes Soc. London, Amnesty Internat., Nat. Trust for Hist. Preservation (Gt. Britian and U.S.A. chpt.), Shavian Malthus Soc. (charter Gt. Britian chpt.), Humane Soc. of U.S. (millennium mem.), The Drones Club. Avocations: medical history, pre-twentieth century military history.

CAMPBELL, FINLEY ALEXANDER, geologist, consultant; b. Kenora, Ont., Can., Jan. 5, 1927; s. Finley McLeod and Vivian (Delve) C.; m. Barbara Elizabeth Cromarty, Oct. 17, 1953; children—Robert Finley, Glen David, Cheryl Ann. B.Sc., Brandon Coll., U. Man., Can., 1950; MA, Queen's U., Kingston, Ont., 1956; PhD, Princeton U., 1958. Exploration and mining geologist Prospectors Airways, Toronto, 1950-58; asst. and asso. prof. geology U. Alta., Can., Edmonton, 1958-65; prof., head dept. geology U. Calgary, Alta., 1965-69, v.p. capital resources, 1969-71, v.p. acad., 1971-76, prof. geology, 1976-84, v.p. priorities and planning, 1984-88, prof. emeritus, 1988—; geol. cons., 1988—. Bd. dirs., vice chmn. Can Energy Research Inst. Contbr. articles on geol. topics to profl. jours. Bd. dirs. Calgary Olympic Devel. Assn.; mem. minister's adv. bd. Tyrrell Mus. Palaeontology. Decorated Queen's Jubilee medal Can.; recipient Commemorative medal for 125th Anniversary of Can., Geology medal Brandon U. Honor Soc.; Sir James Dunne fellow, 1955-56; Princeton Alumni fellow, 1957-58. Fellow Royal Soc. Can.; mem. Assn. The Univ. of Calgary (pres. emeritus), Geol. Assn. Can., Mineral Assn. Can., Soc. Econ. Geologists, Assn. Profl. Geologists Alta., Am. Mineral Soc. Royal Soc. Can., Can. Inst. Mining and Metallurgy, Brandon Univ. Alumni Assn. (reg. dir., Disting. Svc. award Hockey Hall of Fame 1994), Glenmore Yacht Club, Silver Springs Golf and Country Club, Clearwater Bay Yacht Club. Home: 3408 Benton Dr NW Calgary AB Canada T2L 1W8 Office: U Calgary Dept Geology and Geophysics Calgary AB Canada T2N 1N4 Business E-Mail: campbelf@ucalgary.ca.

CAMPBELL, IAN DAVID, opera company director; b. Brisbane, Australia, Dec. 21, 1945; came to U.S., 1982; m. Ann Spira; children: Benjamin, David. BA, U. Sydney, Australia, 1967. Prin. tenor singer The Australian Opera, Sydney, 1967-74; sr. music officer The Australia Council, Sydney, 1974-76; gen. mgr., stage dir. The State Opera of South Australia, Adelaide, 1976-82; asst. artistic adminstr. Met. Opera, NYC, 1982-83; gen. dir., artistic dir. San Diego Opera, 1983—. Guest lectr. U. Adelaide, 1978; guest prof. San Diego State U., 1986—; cons. Lyric Opera Queensland, Australia, 1980-81; bd. dirs. Opera Am., Washington, 1986-95, 1997-01, chmn., 2001-04; chmn. judges Met. Opera Auditions, Sydney, 1989, Masterclasses, Music Acad. of the West, 1993-96. Prodr., host San Diego Opera Radio Program, 1984-01, At the Opera with Ian Campbell, 2001-05; stage director La Bohème, 1981, 05 (San Diego opera), The Tales of Hoffmann, 1982 (both in South Australia), Falstaff (San Diego opera), 1999, Cavalleria Rusticana/Pagliacci (Santa Barbara Grand opera), 1999, Il Trovatore (San Diego opera), 2000, Tosca (San Diego opera), 2002, Katya Kabanova and La Traviata (San Diego opera), 2004, La Bohème (San Diego opera), 2005. Mem., bd. dirs. San Diego Conv. and Visitors Bur., 1997-2002. Recipient Peri award Opera Guild So. Calif., 1984; named Headliner of Yr., San Diego Press Club, 1991, Father of Yr., San Diego, 1997. Fellow: Australian Inst. Mgmt.; mem.: Rotary, San Diego Press Club. Avocation: golf. Office: San Diego Opera 1200 3rd Ave Fl 18 San Diego CA 92101-4112 Office Phone: 619-232-7636. Business E-Mail: ian.campbell@sdopera.com.

CAMPBELL, JEFFREY C., health products executive; b. July 16, 1960; m. Susan Campbell; children: Grace, Eric, Patrick. BA in Econs., Stanford U., 1985; MBA, Harvard U., 1990. CPA Deloitte, Haskins & Sells, 1986—88; sr. analyst fin. Am. Airlines, 1990—92, mgr. fin. planning, 1992—93, mng. dir. internat. planning, 1993—95, mng. dir. corp. fin. and banking, 1995—98, v.p. corp. devel., treas., 1998—2000, v.p. Europe, 2000—02, sr. v.p. fin., CFO, 2002—03; sr. v.p., CFO McKesson Corp., San Francisco, 2003, exec. v.p., CFO, 2004—. Office: McKesson Corp One Post St San Francisco CA 94104*

CAMPBELL, JOHN RICHARD, pediatric surgeon; b. Pratt, Kans., Jan. 16, 1932; s. John Ross and Laura (Harkrader) C.; m. Susan Charlotte Baker, June 9, 1962; children: Kathryn, John Richard, George Ridgway. BA, U. Kans., 1954, MD, 1958. Diplomate Am. Bd. Surgery with cert. of spl. qualifications in pediatric surgery. Rotating intern Hosp. U. Pa., 1958-59; resident in gen. surgery U. Kans. Hosp., 1959-63; resident in pediatric surgery Children's Hosp. of Phila., 1965-67; asst. instr. U. Pa. Med. Sch., 1965-67; mem. faculty U. Oreg. Health Scis. Ctr., Portland, 1967—, prof. surgery emeritus, 2000, prof. surgery and pediatrics emeritus, 2000—, chief pediatric surgery, prof. emeritus surgery and pediats., 2000—; surgeon-in-chief Doernbecher Children's Hosp., Portland, 1967-99. Cons. VA, Shriners Crippled Children's hosps., Alaska Native Med. Ctr., Anchorage. Served to lt. comdr. M.C. USNR, 1963-65. Mem. A.C.S., Soc. Acad. Surgeons, Am. Acad. Pediatrics, Am. Pediatric Surg. Assn., Pacific Assn. Pediatric Surgeons, North Pacific Pediatric Soc., North Pacific Surg. Assn., Pacific Coast Surg. Assn., Portland Acad. Pediatrics, Portland Surg. Soc. Presbyterian. Office: Oreg Health Scis Univ 745 SW Gaines St # Cdw7 Portland OR 97239-2901 Office Phone: 503-494-7764. Business E-Mail: campbell@ohsu.edu.

CAMPBELL, KENNETH EUGENE, JR., vertebrate paleontologist, ornithologist; b. Jackson, Mich., Nov. 4, 1943; s. Kenneth Eugene and Betty Louise (Duffey) C. BS, U. Mich., 1966, MS, 1967; PhD, U. Fla., 1973. Research asso. Fla. State Mus., Gainesville, 1972-74; asst. prof. zoology U. Fla., Gainesville, 1974-77, asst. prof. geology, 1975-77; curator vertebrate paleontology/ornithology Natural History Mus. Los Angeles County, LA, 1977—. Acting dir. George C. Page Mus., 1995-96. Contbr. articles to sci. publs. Mem. AAAS, Am. Ornithologists' Union, Assn. Tropical Biology, Cooper Ornithol. Soc., Soc. Vertebrate Paleontology, Wilson Ornithol. Soc., Asian Paleontology and Evolution Soc. (pres. 2000-), Sigma Xi. Office: Natural History Mus 900 Exposition Blvd Los Angeles CA 90007-4057 E-mail: kecampbe@bcf.usc.edu.

CAMPBELL, MARY KATHRYN, chemistry professor; b. Phila., Jan. 20, 1939; d. Henry Charles and Mary Kathryn (Horan) C. AB in Chemistry, Rosemont Coll., 1960; PhD, Ind. U., 1965. Instr. Johns Hopkins U., 1965-68; asst. prof. chemistry Mt. Holyoke Coll., South Hadley, Mass., 1968-74, assoc. prof., 1974-81, prof., 1981, prof. emeritus chemistry, 2004; vis. scholar U. Paris VII, 1974-75; vis. prof. U. Ariz., 1981-82, 88-89. Mem. panel on grad. fellowships NSF, 1979-81 Author: Biochemistry, 1991, 6th edit., 2005; co-author: Understand! Biochemistry, 1999, Introduction to General, Organic and Biochemistry, 9th edit., 2009; contbr. articles to profl. jours. Fellow Woodrow Wilson Found., 1960, NSF, 1960-64, NIH, 1964-65; grantee in field Mem. Am. Chem. Soc., AAAS, Sigma Xi Office: 4516 E La Estoncia Tucson AZ 85718

CAMPBELL, MARY STINECIPHER, retired chemist; b. Chattanooga, Feb. 26, 1940; d. Jesse Franklin and Florence Gladys (Marshall) S.; m. John David Fowler Jr. (div. Mar. 1979); children: John Christopher, Jesse David; m. Billy M. Campbell (dec. 2006), Jan. 1995. BA, Earlham Coll., 1962; PhD, U. N.C., 1967. Cert. organic fruit grower. Postdoctoral researcher Research Triangle Inst., Research Triangle Park, NC, 1966-68, 74-76; staff Los Alamos (N.Mex.) Nat. Lab., 1976—2004; ret., 2004. Adj. prof. organic, inorganic and phys. chemistry U. N.Mex. Grad. Ctr., Los Alamos, 1989—, instr. chemistry lab., 1989; vis. scientist AFOSR (AFATL), Eglin AFB, Fla., 1980-81. Contbr. articles to profl. jours.; inventor ammonium nitrate explosive systems and other explosive salts. Commr. Acequia Sancochada Cmty. ditch; mem. Habitat for Humanity. Mem. Am. Chem. Soc., N.Mex. Network Women in Sci. and Engring. (v.p. 1985-86, pres. 1986-87, No. chpt. pres. 1999), Bio-Integral Rsch. Ctr., N.Mex. Apple Coun. Democrat. Unitarian Universalist. Avocations: skiing, dog training, hiking, singing, gardening. Personal E-mail: bmcampbell@newmexico.com.

CAMPBELL, ROBERT CHARLES, minister, theology studies educator; b. Chandler, Ariz., Mar. 9, 1924; s. Alexander Joshua and Florence (Betzner) C.; m. Lotus Idamae Graham, July 12, 1945; children: Robin Carl, Cherry Colleen. AB, Westmont Coll., 1944; BD, Eastern Baptist Theol. Sem., 1947, ThM, 1949, ThD, 1951, DD (hon.), 1974; MA, U. So. Calif., 1959; postgrad., Dropsie U., 1949-51, U. Pa., 1951-52, NYU, 1960-62, U. Cambridge, Eng., 1969; DLitt (hon.), Am. Bapt. Sem. of West, 1972; HHD (hon.), Alderson-Broaddus Coll., 1979; LHD (hon.), Linfield Coll., 1982; LLD (hon.), Franklin Coll., 1986. Ordained to ministry Am. Bapt. Ch., 1947; pastor 34th St. Bapt. Ch., Phila., 1945-49; instr. Eastern Bapt. Theol. Sem., Phila., 1949-51; asst. prof. Eastern Coll., St. Davids, Pa., 1951-53; assoc. prof. N.T. Am. Bapt. Sem. of West, Covina, Calif., 1953-54, dean, prof., 1954-72; gen. sec. Am. Bapt. Chs. in U.S.A., Valley Forge, Pa., 1972-87; pres. Eastern Bapt. Theol. Sem., Phila., 1987-89, ret. Vis. lectr. Sch. Theology at Claremont, Calif., 1961-63, U. Redlands, Calif., 1959-60, 66-67, Fuller Theology Seminary, Calif., 1992-97; Bd. mgrs. Am. Bapt. Bd. of Edn. and Publ., 1956-59, 65-69; v.p. So. Calif. Bapt. Conv., 1967-68; pres. Am. Bapt. Chs. of Pacific S.W., 1970-71; Pres. N.Am. Bapt. Fellowship, 1974-76; mem. exec. com. Bapt. World Alliance, 1972-90, v.p., 1975-80; mem. exec. com., gov. bd. Nat. Council Chs. of Christ in U.S.A., 1972-87; del. to World Council of Chs., 1975, 83, mem. central com., 1975-90. Author: Great Words of the Faith, 1965, The Gospel of Paul, 1973, Evangelistic Emphases in Ephesians, Jesus Still Has Something To Say, 1987. Baptist. Home: 1763 Royal Oaks Dr No Apt D20 Bradbury CA 91010

CAMPBELL, ROBERT HEDGCOCK, investment banker, lawyer; b. Ann Arbor, Mich., Jan. 16, 1948; s. Robert Miller and Ruth Adele (Hedgcock) C.; m. Katherine Kettering, June 17, 1972; children: Mollie DuPlan, Katherine Elizabeth, Anne Kettering. BA, U. Wash., 1970, JD, 1973. Bar: Wash. 1973, Wash. State Supreme Ct. 1973, Fed. 1973, U.S. Dist. Ct. (we. dist.) Wash. 1973, Ct. Appeals (9th cir.) 1981. Assoc. Roberts & Shefelman, Seattle, 1973-78, ptnr., 1978-85; sr. v.p. Lehman Bros., Inc., Seattle, 1985-87, mng. dir., 1987—. Bd. dirs. Pogo Producing Co., 1999-2007; dir., treas. Nat. Assn. Bd. Lawyers, Hinsdale, Ill., 1982-85; pres., trustee Wash. State Soc. Hosp. Attys., Seattle, 1982-85; mem. econs. dept. vis. com. U. Wash., 1995-97; mem. Law Sch. dean's adv. bd. U. Wash., 1999—. Contbr. articles to profl. jours. Trustee Bellevue (Wash.) Schs. Found., 1988-91, pres., 1989-90; nation chief Bellevue Eastside YMCA Indian Princess Program, 1983-88; trustee Wash. Phikeia Found., 1983-91, Sandy Hook Yacht Club Estates, Inc., 1993-98; mem. Wash. Gov.'s Food Processing Coun., 1990-91. Mem. U. Wash. Varsity Swimming Alumni Bd. Republican. Avocations: skiing, wind surfing, bike riding, physical fitness, golf. Home: 8604 NE 10th St Medina WA 98039-3915 Office: Lehman Bros Bank of America Tower 701 5th Ave Ste 7101 Seattle WA 98104-7016 Home Phone: 425-454-0228; Office Phone: 206-344-5888. Personal E-mail: ibe2ski@msn.com. Business E-Mail: rhcampbe@lehman.com.

CAMPBELL, SCOTT ROBERT, lawyer, former food products executive; b. Burbank, Calif., June 7, 1946; s. Robert Clyde and Jenevieve Anne (Olsen) C.; Patricia Marie Bovan, Dec 30, 2003; 1 son, Donald Steven. BA, Claremont Men's Coll., 1970; JD, Cornell U., 1973. Bar: Ohio 1973, U.S. Dist. Ct. (so. dist.) Ohio 1974, Minn. 1976, Calif. 1989, U.S. Dist. Ct. (no. dist.) Calif. 1989, U.S. Ct. Appeals (9th cir.) 1989, U.S. Dist. Ct. (cen. and so. dists.) Calif. 1990, U.S. Ct. Appeals (5th cir.) 1991, U.S. Tax Ct. 1991, U.S. Ct. Appeals (fed. cir.) 2001, U.S. Ct. Appeals (11th cir.) 2004, U.S. Dist. Ct. (ea. dist.) Calif. 2005. Assoc. Taft, Stettinius & Hollister, Cin., 1973—76; atty. Mpls. Star & Tribune, 1976—77; sr. v.p., gen. counsel, sec. Kellogg Co., Battle Creek, Mich., 1977—89; ptnr. Furth Fahrner Mason, San Francisco, 1988—2000, Zelle, Hofmann, Voelbel, Mason & Gette, LLP, San Francisco, 2000—. U.S. del. ILO Food and Beverage Conf., Geneva, 1984; participant, presenter first U.S.-USSR Legal Seminar, Moscow, 1988; speaker other legal seminars. Mem. ABA, Ohio Bar Assn., Minn. Bar Assn., Calif. Bar. Assn. Office: Zelle Hofmann Voelbel Mason & Gette LLP 44 Montgomery St Ste 3400 San Francisco CA 94104 Office Phone: 415-633-1903. Personal E-mail: srclaw@ix.netcom.com. Business E-Mail: scampbell@zelle.com.

CAMPBELL, THOMAS J., state legislator, chiropractor; b. Bklyn., Oct. 27, 1954; s. Charles Marvin and Edna Mary (Sacer) C.; m. C. Lynn Hearn, July 2, 1983. AA in Social Scis., Fla. Tech. U., 1974; BA in Police Sci. and Adminstrn., Seattle U., 1977; DC, Life Chiropractic Coll., 1983; postgrad. in orthopedics, L.A. Chiropractic Coll., 1984-90. Diplomate Am. Acad. Pain Mgmt.; cert. chiropractic rehab. dr. Nat. Bd. Chiropractic Examiners-Physiotherapy; lic. chiropractor, Wash., Fla. Pvt. practice Chiropractic Spinal Care, Inc., 1984—; mem. Dist. 2 Wash. House Reps., 1992—96, 1998—. Served to capt. Spl. Forces US Army, 1977—85. Recipient Appreciation for Svc. award Chiropractic Disciplinary Bd., 1989-93, Gov. Appreciation Certificate Wash. State Disciplinary Bd., Legislator of Yr. award Wash. State Labor Coun., 1999, Wash. State Trial Attys., 1999, Wash. State Vet. Assn., 1994, Wash. State Nurses Assn., 2000, others. Fellow Internat. Coll. Chiropractors; mem. Am. Chiropractic Assn. (alt. del. House of Dels. 1988-92), Wash. State Chiropractic Assn. (chmn. mem. com. 1984-85, dist. 4A 1985-86, dir. exec. bd. 1985-88, vice-chmn. disciplinary bd. 1990-93, legislative affairs com. 1986, Pres. award 1985, Dist. of the Yr. award 1985-86, Chiropractor of Yr. 1987, 89-91, 2001, Appreciation award 1994, Exceptional Svc. award 1994), Wash. State Chiropractic Assn., Pierce County Chiropractic Assn., Chiropractic Rehab. Assn. (bd. dirs.). Republican. Avocations: scuba diving, boating, fishing. Home: PO Box 443 Spanaway WA 98387-0443 Business E-Mail: campbell.tom@leg.wa.gov.*

CAMPBELL, TOM, state agency administrator, dean, former congressman; b. Chgo., Aug. 14, 1952; s. William J. and Marie Campbell; m. Susanne (Martin) Campbell. BA, MA in Econs. with highest honors, U. Chgo., 1973, PhD in Econs. with highest dept. fellowship, 1980; JD magna cum laude, Harvard U., 1976. Law clk. to Judge George E. MacKinnon U.S. Ct. Appeals (D.C. cir.), 1976-77; law clk. to Justice Byron R. White U.S. Supreme Ct., Washington, 1977-78; assoc. Winston & Strawn, Chgo., 1978-80; White Ho. fellow Office Chief of Staff, Washington, 1980-81; exec. asst. to dep. atty. gen. Dept. Justice, Washington, 1981; dir. Bur. Competition FTC, Washington, 1981-83; mem. 101st, 102nd, 104th, 105th, 106th Congresses from Calif. 12th Dist., 1989—93; mem. com. on sci., space and tech., com. on judiciary, banking, fin. and urban affairs; mem. Calif. State Senate, 1993-95, 104th-106th Congresses from Calif. 15th Dist., 1995-2001; mem. com. internat. rels., com. on banking, joint econ. com.; dean Haas Sch. Bus. U. Calif., Berkeley, 2002—; dir. dept. fin. State of Calif., 2004—. Prof. Stanford Law Sch., 1983-2002; bd. dirs., DEMOS. Referee Jour. Polit. Economy, Internat. Rev. Law and Econs. Nat. adv. bd. Haas Ctr. Pub. Svc., Stanford U. Mem. ABA (antitrust sect., coun. 1985-88, program chmn. 1983-84), Coun. on Fgn. Rels., World Affairs Coun. No. Calif. (chair 2003-). Republican. Office: State of Calif Dept Fin 915 L St Sacramento CA 95814 Office Phone: 914-445-4141.

CAMPBELL, WILLIAM V., computer company executive; b. Pitts. married; 1 son. BS in Econs., MS in Econs., Columbia U. V.p. J. Walter Thompson, NYC; dir. mktg. film divsn. Eastman Kodak Co.; v.p. mktg. Apple Computer Inc., 1983, v.p. sales, 1984, v.p. distgn. svc. and support, exec. v.p., 1984, group exec. of U.S.; founder, pres., CEO Claris Corp. (purchased by Apple Computer), 1990; pres., CEO GO Corp., 1990-94, Intuit, 1994-98, 1999—2000, chmn. bd., 1998—.

Bd. dirs. Great Plains Software, SanDisk, Apple Computer Inc. Dir. Nat. Football Found. and Hall of Fame. Named to InfoWorld's Top 25 CTOs, 2004. Office: Intuit Inc 2535 Garcia Ave Mountain View CA 94043-1111

CAMPION, EDMUND JOSEPH, composer, educator; b. Dallas, Tex., July 9, 1957; s. James Timothy Campion and Mary Louise Kucera; m. Danielle De Gruttola. BA, U. Tex., 1984; MA, Columbia U., 1987, DMA, 1993. Prof. music U. Calif., Berkeley, 1996—, Jerry and Evelyn Hemmings Chambers Chair Music, 2005—. Co-dir. Ctr. New Music and Audio Technologies, Berkeley, 1996—; interviewee Computer Music Jour., 2004. Composer: Losing Touch, 1994, Domus Aurea, 2000, L'Autre (The Other), 2000. Recipient Lili Boulonger Composition award, U. Mass., 1993, Rome prize, Am. Acad. in Rome, 1995, Hinrichsen award, Am. Acad. of Arts and Letters, 1999, Commande d'Etat, French Min. Culture, 2005. Achievements include works published by Billaudot Editions and Henry Lemoine, Paris, Peters Editions, N.Y. Avocations: computers, music. Office: U Calif Dept Music #1200 104 Morrison Hall Berkeley CA 94720-1200 Fax: 510-642-7918. E-mail: campion@cnmat.berkeley.edu.

CAMPOS, DAVID, city supervisor, lawyer; b. Puerto Barrios, Guatemala, 1970; BA, Stanford U., Calif., 1993; JD, Harvard U., Cambridge, Mass., 1996. With San Francisco City Atty.'s Office, 1999—2004; lead counsel San Francisco Unified Sch. Dist., 2004—07; supr., Dist. 9 San Francisco Bd. Supervisors, 2008—, chair pub. safety com., mem. rules com., budget & fin. com. Co-chair Bay Area Lawyers for Individual Freedom; elected mem. San Francisco Dem. Ctrl. Com.; commr. San Francisco Police. Mem.: San Francisco La Raza Lawyers Assn. (bd. dirs.). Democrat. Office: City Hall 1 Dr Carlton B Goodlett Pl Rm 24 San Francisco CA 94102 Office Phone: 415-554-5144. Office Fax: 415-554-6255.*

CAMPOS, NORA, Councilwoman; d Eloy & Rosa C; BA, San Francisco State U. Acct. coord. Lancaster Group Usa; cmty. rels. coord. San José City Coun., chief of staff, councilwoman, Dist. 5, 2001—. Chair Adelante Mujer Hispana Conf., 1997—. Mem. HOPE PAC-Hispana for Polit Equality, Am. GI Forum, 2001—; bd. mem. Latino caucus League of Calif. Cities, bd. mem. housing policy com.; adv. bd. mem. downtown/East Valley policy Santa Clara Valley Transportation Authority, adv. bd. mem. Tasman East Capitol light rail; com. mem. Am. Cancer Soc. Latino Outreach, 1997—98; bd. mem. East San Jose Youth Found., 1998—, Pacific Neighbors, Inc.-Sister Cities, 2000—, Camp Fire Boys and Girls, 2000—. Mem.: Police Athletic League, Assn. Bay Area Govts. (coun. liaison), Commonwealth Club. Office: San Jose City Coun 200 E Santa Clara St San Jose CA 95113 Office Phone: 408-535-4905. Office Fax: 408-292-6462. Business E-Mail: District5@sanjoseca.gov.*

CANADY, RICHARD WARREN, lawyer; b. Boone, Iowa, Dec. 7, 1934; s. Cecil M. and Myra N. (Shurtz) Canady; m. Carol Jean Canady, Feb. 1, 1960; children: Michael Warren, Kelly Lynn. BS, Iowa U., 1956, JD with distinction, 1959; LLM, Georgetown U., 1962. Bar: Iowa 1959, Calif. 1962. With Navy JAG, 1960—62; law clk. to judge US Ct. Appeals 9th Cir., 1962—63; assoc. White, Froelich & Peterson, San Diego, 1963—64; ptnr. Howard, Rice, Nemerovski, Canady, Falk & Rabkin, San Francisco, 1968—, mng. ptnr., 1968—74, 1986—90. Trustee, pres. Iowa Law Sch. Found., 1991—2001. Named a No. Calif. Super Lawyer, 2005—06, 2007, 2008; named one of Best Lawyers America, 2007, 2008, Top 10 Mergers and Acquisitions Lawyers, US Lawyer Rankings, 2006, 2007, 2008. Mem.: ABA, San Francisco Bar Assn., Iowa Bar Assn., State Bar Calif., Mission Hills Country Club, Olympic Club, San Francisco Golf Club, Pacific Union Club, Order of Coif. Presbyterian. Office: Howard Rice Nemerovski Canady Falk & Rabkin 3 Embarcadero Ctr Fl 7 San Francisco CA 94111-4024 E-mail: rcanady@howardrice.com.

CANALES, JAMES EARL, JR., foundation president; b. San Francisco, Nov. 6, 1966; s. James Earl Canales Sr. and Maritsa M. (Solorzano) Espinoza. BA, Stanford U., 1988, MA, 1989. English tchr., class dean San Francisco Univ. H.S., 1989-91, dir. admissions, 1991-93; program assoc. The James Irvine Found., San Francisco, 1993-95, program officer, spl. asst. to pres., 1995-97, chief adminstrv. officer, corp. sec., 1997-99, v.p., corp. sec., 1999—2003, pres. and CEO, 2003—. Bd. dirs. Nat. Ctr. Nonprofit Bds., Washington, 1996—2003, Stanford U., Calif., 2006—; chair bd. dirs. Coll. Access Found. Calif. Chair bd. dir. Larkin St. Youth Ctr., San Francisco, 1992—99; bd. dirs. Nat. Assn. Cmty. Leadership, Indpls., 1994—97, KQED, Inc., San Francisco, 1999—2005, Monterey Bay Aquarium, San Francisco; trustee San Francisco Day Sch., 1996—99; bd. regents St. Ignatius Coll. Preparatory, 2001—03. Andrew W. Mellon Edn. Found. fellow, 1988-89. Mem. Stanford Alumni Assn. (bd. dir. 1997-05, vice chmn. 2001-03, chmn. 2003-05). Democrat. Roman Catholic. Home: 21 Carmel St San Francisco CA 94117-4332 Office: 575 Market St Ste 3400 San Francisco CA 94105 E-mail: jcanales@irvine.org.

CANBY, WILLIAM CAMERON, JR., federal judge; b. St. Paul, May 22, 1931; s. William Cameron and Margaret Leah (Lewis) Canby; m. Jane Adams, June 18, 1954; children: William Nathan, John Adams, Margaret Lewis. AB, Yale U., 1953; LLB, U. Minn., 1956. Bar: Minn. 1956, Ariz. 1972. Law clk. US Supreme Ct. Justice Charles E. Whittaker, 1958—59; assoc. firm Oppenheimer, Hodgson, Brown, Baer & Wolff, St. Paul, 1959—62; assoc., then dep. dir. Peace Corps, Ethiopia, 1962—64, dir. Uganda, 1964—66; asst. to US Senator Walter Mondale, 1966; asst. to pres. SUNY, 1967; prof. law Ariz. State U., 1967—80; judge US Ct. Appeals (9th cir.), Phoenix, 1980—96, sr. judge, 1996—; chief justice High Ct. of the Trust Ter. of the Pacific Islands, 1993—94. Bd. dirs. Ariz. Ctr. Law in Pub. Interest, 1974—80, Maricopa County Legal Aid Soc., 1972—78, D.N.A.-People's Legal Svcs., 1978—80; Fulbright prof. Makerere U. Faculty Law, Kampala, Uganda, 1970—71. Author: American Indian Law, 2004; note editor: Minn. Law Rev., 1955—56; contbr. articles to profl. jours. Precinct and state committeeman Dem. Party Ariz., 1972—80; bd. dirs. Ctrl. Ariz. Coalition for Right to Choose, 1976—80. 1st lt. USAF, 1956—58. Mem.: Maricopa County Bar Assn., State Bar Ariz., Order of Coif, Phi Beta Kappa. Office: Sandra Day O'Connor US Courthouse 401 W Washington St SPC 55 Phoenix AZ 85003-2156 Office Phone: 602-322-7300.

CANCIAMILLA, JOSEPH, state legislator; b. Pittsburg, Calif., Apr. 19, 1955; m. Laura Canciamilla. BA, St. Mary's Coll., 1978; JD, John F. Kennedy Sch. Law, 1986. Mem. sch. bd. Pittsburg Sch. Dist., 1973—87; lawyer, 1986—; mayor, councilman City of Pittsburg, 1987—96; county supr. Contra Costa County, 1996—2000; mem., dist. 11 Calif. State Assembly, 2000—. Co-owner Pittsburg Funeral Chapel, 1992—; mem. Aging and Long-Term Care Com., Revenue and Taxation Com., Vet. Affairs Com., Jobs Econ. Devel. and the Economy Com. Mem.: State Bar Calif., NAACP (life), Young Mens Inst., Italian Am. Club. Democrat. Mailing: PO Box 942849 Rm 2141 Sacramento CA 94249-0011 Office: 815 Estudillo St Martinez CA 94553 Office Phone: 916-319-2011.

CANFIELD, JACK, writer, speaker, trainer; b. Ft. Worth, Aug. 19, 1944; s. Elmer Elwyn and Ellen Waterhouse (Taylor) C.; m. Judy Ohlbaum, 1971 (div. Nov. 1976); children: Oran, Kyle; m. Georgia Lee Noble, Sept. 9, 1978 (div. dec. 1999); 1 child, Christopher. BA, Harvard U., 1966; MEd, U. Mass., 1973; PhD, U. Santa Monica, 1981. Educator Clinton (Iowa) Job Corps Ctr., 1968-69; dir. edn. W.C. Stone Found., Chgo., 1969-70; co-dir. New Eng. Ctr., Leverett, Mass., 1971-77; instr. U. Mass., Amherst, 1978-80; dir. ednl. svcs. Insight of Tng. Seminars, Santa Monica, Calif., 1981-83; pres. Self-Esteem Seminars, Culver City, Calif., 1983—, Santa Barbara, Calif., 1983—; CEO Chicken Soup for the Soul Ent., Santa Barbara, 1998—. Pres. Inst. Holistic Edn., Amherst, 1975-81; mem. adv. bd. The Wyland Found., Laguna, Calif., 1997—. Author: Personalized Learning: Confluent Processes in the Classroom, 1976, Self-Esteem and Peak Performance: A Transcript, 1991, Los Angeles Dodgers Team Esteem Program: A Self-Esteem Curriculum Guide, 1992; co-author: (with H.C. Wells) About Me: A Curriculum for a Developing Self, 1971, Japanese edit., 1977, 100 Ways to Enhance Self-Concept in the Classroom: A Handbook for Teachers and Parents, 1976, rev. edit., 1993, (with others) Self-Esteem in the Classroom: A Curriculum Guide, 1986, (with A. Mecca, et al) Toward A State of Esteem: The Final Report of the California Task Force to Promote Self-Esteem and Personal and Social Responsibility, 1990, (with. F. Siccone) 101 Ways to Develop Student Self-Esteem and Responsibility in the Classroom, Vol. II: The Power to Succeed in School and Beyond, 1992, vol. I, 1994, (with M.V. Hansen) Chicken Soup for the Soul: 101 Stories to Open the Heart and Rekindle the Spirit, 1993, large print edit., 1996, various translations (Abby award Am. Booksellers Assn. 1995, other awards, #1 N.Y. Times Best Seller List over 2 years, #1 Pubs. Weekly Best Seller List over 2 years, others), Dare to Win, 1994, various translations, 1996—, (with K. Goldberg) Follow Your Dreams: A Goals Setting Workbook, 1994, (with M.V. Hansen) A 2nd Helping of Chicken Soup for the Soul: 101 More Stories to Open the Heart and Rekindle the Spirit, 1995, large print edit., 1996, various translations (various awards), The Aladdin Factor: How to Ask for and Get Everything You Want in Life, 1995, various translations, (with M.V. Hansen and D. Von Welanetz Wentworth) Chicken Soup for the Soul Cookbook: Stories and Recipes from the Heart, 1995, (with M.V. Hansen) A 3rd Serving of Chicken Soup for the Soul: 101 More Stories to Open the Heart and Rekindle the Spirit, 1996, (with J. Miller) Heart at Work: Stories and Strategies for Building Self-Esteem and Reawakening the Soul at Work, 1996, various translations, (with M.V. Hansen) The Chicken Soup for the Soul Journal, 1996, (with M.V. Hansen, P. Aubery, and N. Mitchell) Chicken Soup for the Surviving Soul: 101 Stories of Courage and Inspiration from Those Who Have Survived Cancer, 1996, various translations, (with M.V. Hansen and B. Spilchuk) A Cup of Chicken Soup for the Soul, 1996, (with M.V. Hansen and P. Hansen) Condensed Chicken Soup for the Soul, 1996, Chicken Soup for the Kid's Soul, 1998, (with M.V. Hansen, M. Shimoff, and J. Hawthorne) Chicken Soup for the Woman's Soul: 101 Stories to Open the Heart and Rekindle the Spirits of Women, 1996, various translations, Chicken Soup for the Mother's Soul: 101 Stories to Open the Hearts and Rekindle the Spirits of Women, 1997, (with M.V. Hansen, M. Rutte, M. Rogerson, and T. Clauss) Chicken Soup for the Soul at Work: 101 Stories of Courage Compassion and Creativity in the Workplace, 1996, (with M.V. Hansen, H. McCarty, and M. McCarty) A Fourth Course of Chicken Soup for the Soul: 101 Stories to Open the Heart and Rekindle the Spirit, 1997, (with M.V. Hansen and K. Kirberger) Chicken Soup for the Teenage Soul: 101 Stories About Life, Love and Learning, 1997, (with M.V. Hansen and P. Aubery) Chicken Soup for the Christian Soul: 101 Stories to Open the Hearts and Rekindle the Spirits of Christians, 1997, (with M.V. Hansen) A Little Sip of Chicken Soup for the Soul: Inspiring Stories of Self-Affirmation, 1997, Another Sip of Chicken Soup for the Soul: Heartwarming Stories of the Love Between Parents and Children, 1997, A Fifth Portion of Chicken Soup for the Soul: 101 Stories to Open the Heart and Rekindle the Spirit, 1998, (with M.V. Hansen, M. Becker, DVM, and C. Kline) Chicken Soup for the Pet Lover's Soul: 101 Stories to Open the Hearts and Rekindle the Spirits of Pet Lovers, 1998, (with M.V. Hansen and R. Camacho) Chicken Soup for the Country Soul: 101 Stories Served up Country Style and Straight from the Heart, 1998, (with M.V. Hansen, P. Hansen and I. Dunlap) Chicken Soup for the Kid's Soul, 1998, (with M.V. Hansen, M. Shimoffand J. Hawthorne) A 2nd Chicken Soup for the Woman's Soul, 1998, (with M.V. Hansen and K. Kirberger) Chicken Soup for the Teenage Soul II, 1998, Chicken Soup for the Teenage Soul Journal, 1998, (with M.V. Hansen, M.& C. Donnelly and B. DeAngelis) Chicken Soup for the Couple's Soul, 1999 (with M.V. Hansen, J. Aubery and M.& C. Donnelly) Chicken Soup for the Golfer's Soul, 1999, (with M.V. Hansen, Ki. Kirberger and D. Clark) Chicken Soup for the College Soul, 1999 (with M.V. Hansen and H. McNamara) Chicken Soup for the Unskinkable Soul, 1999, (with M.V. Hansen, M. Shimoff and J. Hawthorne) Chicken Soup for the Single Soul, 1999, (with M.V. Hansen, M. Becker and Carol Kline) Chicken Soup for the Cat and Dog Lover's Soul, 1999 (with M.V. Hansen and Don Dible) Chicken Soup for the Dental Soul, 1999, (with P. Meyer, B. Chesser, M.V. Hansen and A. Seeger) Chicken Soup for the Golden Soul, 2000, (with Janet Switzer) The Success Principles: How to Get From Where You Are to Where You Want to Be, 2005, (with M.V. Hansen, P. Aubery and N. Autio) Chicken Soup for the Christian Family Soul, 2000. Named Outstanding Young Man of Am., US Jaycees, 1978; recipient So. Calif. Book Publicist of the Yr. award, L.A., 1995, Body Mind Spirit Book award Body Mind Spirit Mag., 1996, Chancellor's Medal, U. Mass., 1998, Promise to the Earth award Nat. Arbor Day Found., 1998, Oprah's Angel Network award, 1999, Golden Plate award, Acad. Achievement, 2004. Mem. Nat. Coun. for Self-Esteem (founder, bd. dirs. 1986-98, adv. bd. 1986—, Nat. Leadership award 1993), Nat. Spkrs. Assn. (Cert. Speaking Profl. award 1989). Democrat. Avocations: tennis, travel, guitar. Office: The Jack Canfield Cos PO Box 30880 Santa Barbara CA 93130 Office Phone: 805-563-2935. Office Fax: 805-563-2945.

CANIPAROLI, VAL WILLIAM, choreographer, dancer; b. Renton, Wash., Sept. 12, 1951; s. Francisco and Leonora (Marconi) C. Student, Wash. State U., Pullman, 1969—71, San Francisco Ballet Sch., 1971—72. Dancer San Francisco Opera, 1973, San Francisco Ballet, 1973—; co-dir. OMO, San Francisco, 1985; resident choreographer San Francisco Ballet, 1983—, Ballet West, 1993—97, Tulsa Ballet, 2001—. Choreographer (ballets) Street Song, 1980, Pacific Northwest Ballet, Seattle, 1980, 91, The Bridge, 1998, Love-lies-Bleeding, 1982, Aria, 1998, Slow, 1998, Ciao Marcello, 1997, Hamlet and Ophelia, 1985, In Perpetuum, 1990, Aubade, 1985 (Isadora Duncan award 1986), Narcisse, 1987, Ririe Woodbury Dance Co., 1988, Ritual, 1990, A Door is Ajar, 1990, Jacob's Pillow Dance festival, 1990, Pulcinella, 1991, Concerto Grosso, 1992, Seeing Stars, 1993, Lady of the Camellias, 1993, Ballet West, 1994, Lambarena, 1995, Capriccio, Chgo. Lyric Opera, 1994, Bow Out, 1995, San Francisco Symphony Pops, 1995-96, Prawn Watching, 1996, Djangology, 1997, Open Veins, 1998, Book of Alleged Dances, 1998, Going for Baroque, 1999, Attention Please, 1999, The Nutcracker, 2001, Torque, 2001, Jaybird Lounge, 2001, Death of a Moth, 2001, Unspoken, 2002, No Other, 2002, boink!, 2002, Gustav's Rooster, 2003, Vivace, 2003, Sonata for Two Pianos and Percussion, Boston Ballet, 2004, A Doll's House, San Francisco, 2004, A Christmas Carol, ACT, 2005, Songs, 2005, Violin, 2006, Richmond Ballet, Suite, 2007, others. Recipient Isadora Duncan award, 1987, 97, 2001, Choo-San Goh and H. Robert Magee Found. award for choreography, 1994, 97; Nat. Endowment Arts fellow, 1981-88. Fellow Calif. Arts Coun. Choreographers. Avocations: music, theater, dance. Office: San Francisco Ballet 455 Franklin St San Francisco CA 94102-4471

CANNELL, CYNDY MICHELLE, elementary school principal; b. Salt Lake City, July 27, 1948; d. Nick M. and Eugenie E. (Pfanmuller) Fasselin; m. Peter Anthony Cannell, Oct. 13, 1973; children: Peter John, David. BA, U. Utah, 1970, MA, 1973. Cert. adminstr., supr. severly handicapped, spl. edn., emotionally handicapped, gifted and talented. Tchr. Hab Ctr., 1973-74, Hill View Elem Sch., 1974-78; coord. spl. needs. Granite Sch. Dist., Salt Lake City, 1978-79, tchr. leader youth in custody, 1979-80, coord. spl. edn., 1980-84; asst. prin. Western Hills Elem. Sch., Salt Lake City, 1984-85; prin. Webster Elem. Sch., Salt Lake City, 1985-90, Plymouth Elem. Sch., Salt Lake City, 1990-95, Twin Peaks Elem. Sch., Salt Lake City, 1995—2000; field asst. Utah State Office Edn., 2000—01; coord. spl. edn. unit Cottonwood Heights Elem., 2002. Mem. state strategic planning com. for edn., 1990-91, elem. prin. adv. com., 1990-96, spl. edn. strategic planning com., 1990-91, exec. class size steering com., 1990, ptnrs. in edn. com., 1985—, sch. lunch com., 1989-91, emer. preparedness com., 1989-90; mem. Women's State Legis. Coun., Utah, 1991-92; co-coord. Corp. Games, 1988—. Contbr. articles to profl. mags. Prin. rep. to state PTA Community Involvement Commn., 1989-90, Oquirrh South PTA Coun., 1989; mem. Utah Youth Village Scholarship Com., 1996—. Named Outstanding Educator of Yr. Nat. PTA Phoebe Apperson Hearst, 1990, Outstanding Adminstr. Utah Congress of Parents and Tchrs., 1989-90, Region V PTA, 1988-90. Mem. Granite Assn. Elem. Sch. Prins. (sec. 1998—, Innovator of Yr. 1997-98), Granite Assn. Sch. Adminstrs. (sec., treas. 1990-91) Utah Assn. Sch. Adminstrs., Nat Assn. Elem. Adminstrs., Granite Assn. Sch. Adminstrs. Avocations: skiing, reading, tennis, golf, travel. Home: 10331 S 2375 E Sandy UT 84092-4422 Office: Cottonwood Heights Elem 9361 S 300 E Sandy UT 84070-2902

CANNON, CHRISTOPHER BLACK, former United States Representative from Utah, lawyer; b. Salt Lake City, Oct. 20, 1950; m. Claudia Fox, 1978; 8 children. BS, Brigham Young U., 1974; attended, Harvard Bus. Sch., 1975—76; JD, Brigham Young U., 1980. Bar: Utah 1980. Atty., Provo; asst. assoc. solicitor US Dept. Interior, 1983—84, assoc. solicitor, 1984—86; cons. to asst. sec. for productivity, tech. & innovation US Dept. Commerce, 1986—87; co-owner Geneva Steel, Orem, Utah, 1987—90; owner Cannon Industries, Inc., 1990—95; fin. chmn. Utah Rep. Party, 1991—92; mem. nat. fin. com. Lamar Alexander for Pres., 1995—96; mem. US Congress from 3rd Utah Dist., 1997—2009, mem. judiciary com., chmn. comml. and adminstrv. law subcommittee, mem. govt. reform com., mem. resources com., chmn. Western Caucus, 2003—09. Del. Rep. Nat. Conv., 1992, 1996. Republican. Lds Ch.*

CANNON, JOSEPH A., steel products company executive, political party official; b. Salt Lake City, July 31, 1941; BA in Polit. Sci., Brigham Young U., 1974, JD cum laude, 1977. Asst. adminstr. EPA, 1981-85; assoc. Pillsbury, Madison & Sutro, Washington, 1985-87; dir. Geneva Steel Holdings Corp., Vineyard, Utah, 1987—, chmn. bd. dirs., 1987—, pres., 1987-91, CEO, 1991—. Chmn. Utah Rep. Party, 2001—. Mem. Am. Iron and Steel Inst. (dir., mem. policy and planning com.), N.Am. Steel Coun. Republican. Mem. Lds Ch. Office: Geneva Steel Holdings Corp 10 S Geneva Rd Vineyard UT 84058 also: Utah Rep Party 117 E South Temple Salt Lake City UT 84111

CANNON, REUBEN, casting company executive, film producer; b. Chgo., Feb. 11, 1946; m. Linda Elsenhout, 1978; 4 children. Attended, Southeast City Coll. With Universal Studios, 1970—78, casting dir.; head TV casting Warner Bros., 1977—78; founder Reuben Cannon & Assocs., 1978—. Prodr.: (TV films) The Women of Brewster Place, 1989; (films) Get on the Bus, 1996, Down on the Delta, 1998, Dancing in September, 2000, Bui Doi, 2001, Love Don't Cost a Thing, 2003, Woman Thou Art Loosed, 2004, Diary of a Mad Black Woman, 2005, Madea's Family Reunion, 2006, Daddy's Little Girls, 2007, House of Payne, 2007, Why Did I Get Married?, 2007, Meet the Browns, 2008; exec. prodr.: (TV series) The Good News, 1997. Named to Power 150, Ebony mag., 2008. Office: Reuben Cannon & Assocs 5225 Wilshire Blvd Ste 526 Los Angeles CA 90036 Office Phone: 323-939-3190. Office Fax: 323-939-7793.

CANNON, ROBERT HAMILTON, JR., aerospace engineering educator; b. Cleve., Oct. 6, 1923; s. Robert Hamilton and Catharine (Putnam) C.; m. Dorothea Alta Collins, Jan. 4, 1945 (dec. Apr. 1988); children: Philip Gregory, Douglas Charles, Beverly Jo, Frederick Scott, David John, Joseph Collins, James Robert; m. Vera Berlin Crie, May 27, 1989. BS, U. Rochester, 1944; Sc.D. (du Pont fellow), MIT, 1950. Rsch. engr. Baker Mfg. Co., Evansville, Wis., 1946-50; instr. MIT, 1949-50; research engr. Bendix Aviation Research Labs., Detroit, 1950-51; with Autonetics div. N.Am. Aviation Inc., Downey, Calif., 1951-57, supr. automatic flight control systems, 1951-54, systems engr. inertial nav. instruments and systems, 1954-57; assoc. prof. mech. engring. MIT, 1957-59; mem. faculty Stanford U., 1959-74, prof. aeros. and astronautics, 1962-74, founder Guidance and Control Lab., 1960—69; chief scientist USAF, 1966-68; asst. sec. U.S. Dept. Transp. Washington, 1970-74; chmn. div. engring. and applied sci. Calif. Inst. Tech., Pasadena, 1974-79; Charles Lee Powell prof. aeronautics and astronautics Stanford U., 1979—, chmn. dept., 1979-90, founder aerospace robotics lab., 1980—97, dir. emeritus, 1997—; chmn. sci. adv. com. to CEO GM, 1979-84. Mem. Draper Corp., 1975—; vice chmn. sci. adv. bd. USAF, 1968-70; chmn. assembly engring. NRC, 1974-75, chmn. energy engring. bd., 1975-81, mem. com. on nuc. and alt. energy sources, 1975-78, aeros. and space engring. bd., 1975-79, 1985-92, governing bd., 1976-78, commn. underwater vehicles, ocean studies bd., 1991-94; chmn. Gen. Electric Space Sta. Adv. Bd., 1985-87; chmn. Pres.'s Com. on Nat.

Medal of Sci., 1984-88; chmn. NASA Flight Telerobotic Servicer Commn., 1987-91; tech. adv. coun. Boeing Corp., 1984-94. R.R. Donnelley, 1984-89, Comsat, 1985-87, United Techs. Corp., 1989-92. Author: Dynamics of Physical Systems, 1967; also articles. Served to lt. (j.g.) USNR, 1944-46. Fellow AIAA (dir. 1968-70), Am. Acad. Arts and Scis., Internat. Acad. Astronautics; mem. Nat. Acad. Engring. (councillor 1975-81), Sigma Xi, Theta Chi (chpt. pres. 1943-44), Tau Beta Pi. Achievements include development of hydrofoil boats, automatic flight control, inertial guidance instruments and systems, space vehicle control, drag-free satellite; co-founder of Einstein experiment gravity probe b gyro test of gen. relativity in orbiting satellite; technical assessment of climatic impact of stratospheric flight; research in wave-actuated upwelling pump, flexible-robot and space-robot control systems, autonomous underwater robots and automonous task-commanded helicopters. Office: Stanford U Dept Aeronautics & Astronautics Durand Bldg Rm 356 Stanford CA 94305-8468

CANTOR, ALAN BRUCE, management consultant, application developer; b. Mt. Vernon, NY, Apr. 30, 1948; s. Howard and Muriel Anita C.; 1 child, Alec Brandon. BS in Social Scis., Cornell U., 1970; MBA, U. Pa., 1973. Mgmt. cons. M & M Risks Mgmt. Svcs., NYC, 1974-78; nat. svcs. officer spl. projects divsn. Marsh & McLennan Risk Mgmt. Svcs., LA, 1980-81; sr. v.p. sr. cons. prin. Warren, Mc Veigh & Griffin, Inc., 1981-82; founder, pres. Cantor & Co., 1982—; ptnr. BDE Entertainment, 2006—; ptnr., prodr. DeBrino/Cantor Entertainment, 2007—; mng. dir. Strategic Partnerships & Mktg., webconference.com, 2007—. Co-mgr. Air Travel Rsch. Group, NYC, 1977-79; instr. risk mgmt. program Am. Mgmt. Assn.,; lectr. Risk and Inst. Mgmt. Soc. Conf., 1975-87, Med. Edn. Spkrs. Bur. So. Calif., 1990—; seminars How to Use Spreadsheets in Risk Mgmt., 1986-89, How to Use Computers in Risk Mgmt., 1989-93. Contbr. articles to profl. jours. Cons., vol. Urban Cons. Group, N.Y.C.; elder Beverly Hills Presbyn. Ch., 1991—; co-project dir. East European Orphans Toy Ministry, 1999—2000. Mem. Cornell Alumni Assn. N.Y.C. (bd. govs., program chmn.), Cornell Alumni Assn. So. Calif., Wharton Bus. Sch. Club (N.Y.C., chmn., mem. adv. com. L.A.), L.A. Athletic. Achievements include design of airline industry model; development of Riskmap risk mgmt. software products; Riskmap Windows version, Exposure Base Mgmt. Sys., patient care monitoring sys., Med. Quality Mgmt. Sys. Plus, Med. Quality Mgmt. Sys. Plus Windows version, MQMS Plus; Qualworx; patents for risk financing simulation model. Personal E-mail: alanbcantor@yahoo.com. Business E-Mail: acantor@webconference.com.

CANTOR, CHARLES ROBERT, biochemistry professor; b. Bklyn., Aug. 26, 1942; s. Louis and Ida Dianne (Banks) C. AB summa cum laude, Columbia U., 1963; PhD, U. Calif., Berkeley, 1966. Asst. prof. chemistry Columbia U., NYC, 1966-69, assoc. prof. chemistry and biol. scis., 1969-72, prof., 1972-81, prof., chmn. genetics and devel., dep. dir. Comprehensive Cancer Ctr. Coll. Physicians and Surgeons, 1981-89; dir. Human Genome Ctr. Lawrence Berkeley Lab, 1988-90; prof. molecular biology U. Calif., Berkeley, 1989-92; prof. biomed. engring. Boston U., 1992—, chmn., 1994-98, dir. Ctr. for Advanced Biotech., 1992—, prof. pharmacology, 1995—; prin. scientist human genome project Dept. Energy, 1990-92; chief sci. officer Sequenom, Inc., 1998—; also bd. dirs., 2000—. Sherman Fairchild vis. scholar Calif. Inst. Tech., 1975-76; mem. biophysics and biophys. chemistry study sect. NIH, 1971-75; mem. cell and molecular basis of disease rev. com. Nat. Inst. Gen. Med. Scis., 1977-81, coun. mem., 1986-89; mem. ozone update com. NRC, 1983, mem. rsch. opportunities in biology com., 1985-89, com. on the human genome, 1986-89, com. on bits of power, 1995-96; trustee Cold Spring Harbor Lab., 1977-83; mem. proposal rev. panel Stanford Sychrotron Radiation Lab., 1976-88; mem. U.S. Nat. Commn., Internat. Union Pure & Applied Biophysics, 1986-94, vice chmn., 1988-91, chmn., 1991-94; sci. adv. bd. Hereditary Disease Found., 1987-89; mem. coun. Human Genome Orgn., 1989-92, v.p. 1990-92, pres. America's, 1991-98; chmn. Department of Energy Human Genome Coordinating com., 1989-92; adv. com. Searle Scholars program, 1987-93, chair, 1993-94, mem. adv. com. program in parasite biology MacArthur Found., 1990-93; mem. sci. adv. coun. Roswell Park Cancer Inst. 1992-98; sci. adv. com. European Molecular Biology Lab., 1989-94; bd. sci. counselors Nat. Ctr. for Biotechnology Info., Nat. Libr. Medicine, 1990-95; cons. Incyte Pharm. Inc., 1992-98, Genelabs, Inc., 1988-, Samsung Advanced Inst. Tech., 2000-04; mem. coun. Internat. Union Pure and Applied Biophysics, 1993-99; vis. com. biology Brookhaven Nat. Lab., 1986-89; bd. dirs. and chair sci. adv. com. Avitech Diagnostics, Inc. (formerly ATGC Inc.), 1992-1997; mem. nomenclature com. IUBMB, 1989-; chair adv. com. European Bioinformatics Inst., 1993-94; mem. USDA Genome Adv. Com., 1992-98; co-chair biotech. adv. coun. Fisher Sci., 1994—; mem. biology adv. com. Lawrence Livermore Nat. Lab., 1995-07, chair 2000-04; chair sci. adv. com. Sequenom, Inc., Sequenom Instruments GmbH, 1995-, mem. sci. adv. com., Aclara, Inc., 1996-2003, Caliper, Inc., 1996-; bd. dirs. ExSar, Inc. (formerly Carta, Inc., formerly Thermaphore, Inc.), 1999-2004, SIGA Inc. (formerly Plexus Inc.), The Molecular Scis. Inst., 2004-07, Select pharm., 2003-2004 (chair sci adv. bd., 2003-); mem. sci. adv. com., Odyssey Inc., 2002-; pres. Biochemist, Inc., 2001-2002; mem. FASEB consensus conf. on fed. funding, 1995-2000; quest scholar Quest Diagnostics, Inc., 1997-99; mem. biotech. coun. Dept. of Energy, 1996-99; mem. unconventional pathogen countermeasures adv. com. DARPA (Def. Advanced Projects Rsch. Agy., 1996-2000; mem. adv. com. Uppsala Bio-X, 2004-06; adj. prof. biomed. engring., U. Calif., San Diego, 2002-, mem. bd. dirs., Dithera, Inc., Retrotope, Inc., 2008-, secs. Author: (with Paul R. Schimmel) Biophysical Chemistry, I, II, III, (with Cassandra L. Smith) Genomics; assoc. editor Ann. Rev. Biophysics, 1983-93. Trustee Assoc. Univs. Inc., 1999-2000; bd. dirs. Keystone Confs., 1999-2006. Recipient Fresenius award Phi Lambda Upsilon, 1972; Eli Lilly award in biol. chemistry Am. Chem. Soc., 1978; Alfred P. Sloan fellow, 1969-71; Guggenheim fellow, 1973-74; Nat. Cancer Inst. outstanding investigator grantee, 1985, Analytica prize, 1988; ISCO prize, 1989, Sober prize ASBMB, 1990. Fellow AAAS, Biophys. Soc. (mem. coun. 1977-81, Emily Gray prize 2000, fellow 2000); mem. Am. Acad. Arts and Scis., NAS, Am. Soc. Biol. Chemists, Am. Chem. Soc., Soc. Analytical Cytology, Harvey Soc., Am. Soc. Human Genetics, Biomed. Engring. Soc., Japanese Biochem. Soc. (hon.). Home: 526 Stratford Ct Apt E Del Mar CA 92014-2767 Office: Sequenom Inc 3595 John Hopkins Ct San Diego CA 92121 Office Phone: 858-202-9012. E-mail: ccantor@sequenom.com.

CANTOR, JAMES ELLIOT, lawyer; b. Detroit, Mar. 14, 1958; s. Bernard J. and Judith (Levin) C.; m. Susan Elaine Finger, Dec. 26, 1983; children: Tilly Samantha, Brian Alexander. BS in Natural Resources, U. Mich., 1980; JD, Cornell U., 1986. Bar: Alaska 1986. Assoc. Perkins Coie, Anchorage, 1986-91; asst. atty. gen. environ. sect. Alaska, Atty. Gen.'s Office, Anchorage, 1991-98, supervising atty. transp. sect., 1998—, chief asst. atty. gen., 2003—. Mem. Eagle River (Alaska) Pk. and Recreation Bd. of Suprs., 1989-95, chmn., 1991-92; dir. Anchorage (Alaska) Trails and Greenways Coalition, 1994-97; commr. Municipality of Anchorage, The Municipality of Anchorage Heritage Land Bank Adv. Commn., 1999—2005, chmn., 2002-03; trustee Congregation Beth Sholom, 2004-08. Avocation: dog sled racing. Office: Atty Gen Office 1031 W 4th Ave Ste 200 Anchorage AK 99501-5903

CANTWELL, MARIA E., United States Senator from Washington; b. Indpls., Oct. 13, 1958; d. Rose and Paul Cantwell. BA in Public Adminstrn., Miami U., Ohio, 1981. Public relations cons. Cantwell and Associates, 1981—87; state repr. Dist. 44 Wash., 1987—92; mem. 103rd Congress from 1st Wash. dist., Washington, 1993—95; v.p. mktg. Progressive Networks, Seattle, 1995—97; sr. v.p. consumer and e-commerce Real Networks (formerly Progressive Networks), Seattle, 1997—2000; US Senator from Wash., 2001—. Mem. com. commerce, sci. and transp. US Senate, com. energy and natural resources, com. Indian affairs, com. small bus. and entrepreneurship. Bd. dirs. Wash. Econ. Develop. Fin. Authority. Recipient Cyber Champion award, Bus. Software Alliance, 2003, Friend of Blues, Experience Music Project-Vulcan, Inc., 2003; named Woman of Yr., KING-TV Evening Mag., 2001. Democrat. Roman Catholic. Office: US Senate 717 Hart Senate Bldg Washington DC 20510 also: District Office Ste 3206 915 Second Ave Seattle WA 98174-1011 Office Phone: 202-224-3441, 206-220-6400. Office Fax: 202-228-0514, 206-220-6404.*

CANUP, ROBIN M., astrophysicist, science administrator; BS magna cum laude in Physics, Duke U., NC; MS in Astrophysy., Planetary and Atmospheric Scis., PhD in Astrophysy., Planetary and Atmospheric Scis., U. Colo., Boulder. Rsch. assoc. lab. atmospheric and space physics U. Colo., 1995—98; sr. rsch. scientist S.W. Rsch. Inst. Dept. Space Studies, 1998—99, asst. dir., 1999—2005, dir., 2005—07, exec. dir., 2007—. Vis. prof. divsn. geol. and planetary scis. Calif. Inst. Tech., 2005; mem. planetary sci. subcommittee NASA Adv. Coun., 2006—. Contbr. articles to sci. jours.; mem. editl. bd.: Icarus, 2003—06. Recipient Harold C. Urey prize, Am. Astron. Soc. (Divsn. Planetary Scis.); named an Brilliant 10, Popular Sci. mag., 2004. Fellow: Am. Geophys. Union (Macelwane medal 2004); mem.: Phi Beta Kappa. Avocation: ballet. Office: Dept Space Studies SW Rsch Inst 1050 Walnut St Ste 300 Boulder CO 80302 E-mail: robin@boulder.swri.edu.

CAOUETTE, DAVID PAUL, public relations executive; b. Sanford, Maine, Aug. 6, 1960; s. Paul Henry and Barbara (Stackpole) C. BA with distinction, U. Maine, Orono, 1983. Editor employee communications Union Mutual Life Ins. Co., Portland, Maine, 1981-84, pub. rels. acct. exec., 1984-85; mgr. employee communications UNUM Life Ins. Co., Portland, 1985-87; v.p., mgr. communications Integrated Resources, Inc., NYC, 1987-89; asst. dir. corp. communications Fin. Guaranty Ins. Co., NYC, 1989—; a.v.p. corp. comms. GE Capital/FGIC, NYC, 1989-94; corp. comms. dir. AT&T Capital, Morristown, N.J., 1994-98; fin. comm. dir. AT&T Corp., Basking Ridge, NJ, 1998—2001; v.p. corp. media rels. and fin. comms. AT&T Wireless Svcs. Corp., Redmond, Wash., 2001—05; v.p. corp. commn. The Walt Disney Co., Burbank, Calif., 2005—06; pvt. practice, 2007; exec. dir. and head media relations Merck & Co., Whitehouse Sta., NJ, 2008—. Ptnr., co-founder Interactive Communications, Inc., Merrick, N.Y., 1989—. Recipient Grand award ARC awards, 2002, Best of Show NIRI, Seattle, 2002, 2003, Nicholson Annual Report award, 2004 Mem. Internat. Assn. Bus. Communicators, Pub. Rels. Soc. Am., Nat. Investor Rels. Inst. Democrat. Roman Catholic. Office: The Walt Disney Co 500 S Buena Vista St Burbank CA 91521 Home: 1450 N Genesee Ave Los Angeles CA 90046-3930 Business E-Mail: david.caouette@merck.com.

CAPDEVILLE, ALEX, academic administrator; b. Opheim, Mont. A, B, M, Mont. State U. - Northern; PhD, Colo. State U. CEO Helena Coll. Tech., 1978—2000; chancellor Mont. State Univ., Northern, Havre, 2000—. Mem.: Northwest Assn. Schools and Colleges. Mailing: Montana State Univ Northern PO Box 7751 Havre MT 59501

CAPECCHI, MARIO RENATO, genetics educator; b. Verona, Italy, Oct. 6, 1937; BS in Chemistry and Physics, Antioch Coll., Yellow Springs, Ohio, 1961; PhD in Biophysics, Harvard U., Cambridge, Mass., 1967. Jr. fellow biophysics Soc. Fellows Harvard U., 1967—69, asst. prof. dept. biochemistry Sch. Medicine, 1969—71, assoc. prof., 1971—73; prof. biology U. Utah, Salt Lake City, 1973—89, prof. human genetics Sch. Medicine, 1989—, disting. prof. human genetics and biology, 1993—; investigator Howard Hughes Med. Inst., Salt Lake City, 1988—. Mem. bd. sci. counselors Nat. Cancer Inst. Recipient Biochemistry award, Am. Chem. Soc., 1969, Bristol-Myers Squibb award, Disting. Achievement in Neuroscience Rsch., 1992, Inernat. award, Achievements in Med. Scis., Gairdner Found., Can., 1993, Alfred P. Sloan Jr. prize, Outstanding Basic Sci. Contbns. to Cancer Rsch., GM, 1994, Molecular Bioanalytics prize, 1996, Kyoto Prize in Basic Scis., 1996, Franklin medal for Advancing Our Knowledge of Phys. Scis., Franklin Inst., 1997, Rosenblatt prize for Excellence, 1998, Baxter award, Disting. Rsch. in Biomedical Scis., Assn. Am. Med. Colls., 1998, Horace Mann Disting. Alumni award, Antioch Coll., 2000, Premio Phoenix-Anni Verdi for Genetics Rsch. award, Associazione Anni Verdi, Italy, 2000, Jiménez-Diáz prize, Fundacion Concita Rabago de Jiminez-Diaz, 2001, Albert Lasker award, Basic Med. Rsch., 2001, Nat. Medal of Sci., 2001, John Scott Medal award, 2002, Utah Gov.'s Medal of Sci. and Tech. award, 2002, Massry prize, 2002, Wolf prize in Medicine, 2002—03, Pezcollar Found. Internat. Cancer Rsch. award, Am. Assn. Cancer Rsch., 2003, March of Dimes prize in devel. biology, 2005; co-recipient Nobel Prize in Physiology or Medicine, 2007. Mem. NAS, Am. Biochem. Soc., Am. Soc. Biol. Chemistry, Am. Soc. Microbiology, Molecular Med. Soc., NY Acad. Scis., Soc. Devel. Biology, Internat. Genome Soc., Genetics Soc. Am., Am. Acad. Microbiology, European Acad. Scis. Achievements include research in gaining an understanding of how the information encoded in the gene is translated by the cell, elucidating the mechanism of genetic recombination in mouse embryo-derived stem (ES) cells, developing gene targeting in the mouse, gaining an understanding of embryonic and neuronal mammalian development through the use of gene targeting. Office: Howard Hughes Med Inst Univ Utah 15 N 2030 E Rm 5440 Salt Lake City UT 84112-5331 Office Phone: 801-581-7096. Office Fax: 801-585-3425. E-mail: mario.capecchi@genetics.utah.edu.

CAPELLAS, MICHAEL D., information technology executive; b. Aug. 19, 1954; m. Marie Capellas; 2 children. BBA Kent St. U., 1976. With Republic Steel Corp., 1976—81; corp. dir. for info. systems, contr. and treas. of Asia Pacific ops. Schlumberger Ltd., 1981—96; founder, mng. ptnr. Benchmarking Partners, Cambridge, Mass., 1996; dir. supply chain mgmt. SAP Am., 1996—97; sr. v.p., gen. mgr. for global energy bus. Oracle Corp., 1997—98; chief info. officer Compaq Computer Corp., Houston, 1998-99, acting COO, 1999, pres., CEO, 1999—2000, chmn., CEO, 2000—02; pres. Hewlett-Packard Co., 2002; chmn., CEO WorldCom Inc. (now MCI), 2002—04; pres., CEO MCI, Inc., Ashburn, Va., 2004—06; acting pres & CEO Serena Software, Inc., 2006—07; sr. adv. Silver Lake Partners, 2007—; chmn., CEO First Data Corp., Greenwood Village, Colo., 2007—. Bd. dirs. Cisco Systems, 2006—. Bd. govs. Boys & Girls Clubs Am.; bd. trustees Am. U., Washington. Recipient Hope Technology Award, ctr. for Missing and Exploited Children. Mem.: bd. of Trustees of American University in Wash. DC. Avocations: travel, golf, running, music. Office: First Data Corp 6200 S Quebec St Greenwood Village CO 80111 Office Phone: 703-886-5600. Office Fax: 212-885-0570.

CAPEZZA, JOSEPH C., health insurance company executive; Gen. practice mgr., ins. industry specialist Coopers & Lybrand LLP, 1976—83; v.p., contr. Skandia Am. Reinsurance Co., 1983—85; v.p., CFO Willcox Inc. Reinsurance Intermediaries, 1985—90; sr. v.p., CFO Reliance Reinsurance Corp., 1990—2000, Group Health Inc., 2000—01; CFO Harvard Pilgrim Health Care, Wellesley, Mass., 2002—07; exec. v.p., CFO Health Net, Inc., Woodland Hills, Calif., 2007—. Mem.: Soc. Ins. Fin. Mgmt. (pres. 2000—01, 2001—02, exec. com.). Office: Health Net Inc 21650 Oxnard St Woodland Hills CA 91367

CAPIZZI, MICHAEL ROBERT, lawyer, former prosecutor; b. Detroit, Oct. 19, 1939; s. I.A. and Adelaide E. (Jennelle) C.; m. Sandra Jo Jones, June 22, 1963; children: Cori Anne, Pamela Jo. BSBA, Ea. Mich. U., 1961; JD, U. Mich., 1964. Bar: Calif. 1965, U.S. Dist. Ct. (so. dist., cent. dist.) Calif. 1965, U.S. Ct. Appeals (9th cir.) 1970, U.S. Supreme Ct. 1971, U.S. Ct. Fed. Claims 2001, U.S. Dist. Ct. (east. dist.) Calif. 2004, U.S. Dist. Ct. (No. Dist.) CA, 2007. Dep. dist. atty., Orange County, Calif., 1965-68; head writs, appeals and spl. assignments sect., 1968-71; asst. dist. atty., dir. spl. ops., 1971-86; legal counsel, mem. exec. bd. Interstate Organized Crime Index, 1971-79, Law Enforcement Intelligence Unit, 1971-95, chief asst. dist. atty., 1986-90, dist. atty., 1990-99; pvt. practice, 1999—. Instr. criminal justice Santa Ana Coll., 1967-76, Calif. State U., 1976-87. Commr. City Planning Commn., Fountain Valley, Calif., 1971-80, vice chmn. 1972-73, chmn. 1973-75, 79-80; candidate for Rep. nomination Calif. Atty. Gen., 1998. Fellow Am. Coll. Trial Lawyers; mem. Nat. Dist. Attys. Assn. (bd. dirs. 1995-96, v.p. 1996-99), Calif. Dist. Attys. Assn. (outstanding prosecutor award 1980, v.p. 1995, pres. 1996), Calif. Bar Assn., Orange County Bar Assn. (chmn. cts. com. 1977, chmn. coll. of trial advocacy com. 1978-81, bd. dirs. 1977-81, sec.-treas. 1982, pres. 1984). Republican. Office: PO Box 1938 Santa Ana CA 92702-1938 Office Phone: 714-283-1878. Business E-Mail: mrclaw@socal.rr.com.

CAPLAN, KAREN B., food products executive; CEO, pres. Frieda's, Los Alamitos, Calif. Recipient awards in innovation and gen. excellence Working Woman mag. Office: Frieda's 4465 Corporate Center Dr Los Alamitos CA 90720-2561

CAPOSSELA, CHRIS, computer software company executive; married; 1 child. B in Computer Sci. and Econs., Harvard U. Product mgr. Visual FoxPro and Access Microsoft Corp., Redmond, Wash., speech asst. to chmn. Bill Gates, chief staff for pres. Microsoft's Europe, Middle East and Africa (EMEA) region, gen. mgr. project bus. unit, sr. v.p. Info. Worker Product Mgmt. Group, 2008—. Avocations: tennis, travel. Office: Microsoft Corp One Microsoft Way Redmond WA 98052

CAPOZZI, ANGELO, surgeon; b. Solvay, NY, Apr. 20, 1933; s. Angelo and Daminana (Pirro) C.; m. Louise Armanetti, June 18, 1960; children: Angelo III, Leonard, Jeanne. BS, U. Notre Dame, 1956; MD, Loyola U., Chgo., 1960. Diplomate Am. Bd. Plastic Surgery. Intern St. Francis Hosp., Evanston, Ill., 1960-61, resident in gen. surgery, 1962-64; resident in plastic surgery U. Wis., Madison, 1964-66; chief plastic surgery USAF, Travis AFB, Calif., 1966-68; chief dept. plastic surgery St. Marys Hosp., San Francisco, 1974-77; assoc. clin. prof. dept. surgery U. Calif., San Francisco; chmn. dept. plastic and reconstructive surgery St. Francis Meml. Hosp., San Francisco, 1987-98, dir. plastic surgery residency program, 1987-98. Mem. tchg. staff St. Francis Meml. Hosp., Bothin Burn Ctr., San Francisco, 1968-98; chief plastic surgery Shriners Hosp., San Francisco, 1999—, pres. Calif. Soc. of Plastic Surgeons, 1998-99. Author: Change of Face, 1984; contbr. articles to profl. jours. Mem. parks and recreation com. City of Tiburon, Calif., 1973. Capt. USAF, 1966-68. Recipient Alumni citation Loyola U., 1983, Bru Brunnier fellow award San Francisco Rotary Found., 1996; named Man of Yr., U. Notre Dame Alumni, 1983. Mem. San Francisco Olympic Club, San Francisco Rotary (Outstanding Svc. award 1993, Svc. Above Self award 1995), Rotoplast, Inc. (founding mem.). Avocations: running, biking. Office: 1199 Bush St Ste 640 San Francisco CA 94109-5977

CAPPELLO, A. BARRY, lawyer; b. Bklyn., Feb. 21, 1942; s. Gus and Ann (Klukoff) C.; children: Eric Rheinschild, Blythe, Brent, Dominic, Vincent. AB, UCLA, 1962, JD, 1965. Bar: Calif. 1966, U.S. Dist. Ct. (cen. dist.) Calif. 1966, U.S. Ct. Appeals (9th cir.) 1974, U.S. Dist. Ct. (no. dist.) Calif. 1981, U.S. Ct. Appeals (7th cir.) 1983, U.S. Supreme Ct. 1983, U.S. Dist. Ct. (ea. dist.) Calif. 1986, U.S. Ct. Appeals (10th cir.) 1986, U.S. Dist. Ct. (so. dist.) Calif. 1988. Dep. atty. gen. State of Calif., LA, 1965—68; chief trial dep., asst. dist. atty. Santa Barbara County, 1968—70, city atty., 1971—77; mng. ptnr. Cappello & Noel, Santa Barbara, 1977—. Lectr. complex bus. litigation, lender liability, adv. trial techniques. Author: Lender Liability, 4th edit., 2009, Lender Liability: A Practical Guide, 1987, AmJur Model Trials and Proofs of Facts; contbr. more than 200 articles to profl. legal and bus. jours. Named Best Lawyer in Am. Woodard/White, Inc., 1992-, Super Lawyer, 2007-09; named one of Top 100 Trial Lawyers Calif., Am. Trial Lawyers Assn., 2007-. Mem. ABA, ATLA, Consumer Attys. Calif. Avocation: triathalons. Office: Cappello & Noël 831 State St Santa Barbara CA 93101-3227 Office Phone: 805-564-2444. Business E-Mail: abc@cappellonoel.com.

CAPPS, LOIS RAGNHILD GRIMSRUD, United States Representative from California, former school nurse; b. Ladysmith, Wis., Jan. 10, 1938; d. Jurgen Milton and Solveig Magdalene (Gullixson) Grimsrud; m. Walter Holden Capps, Aug. 21, 1960 (dec.); children: Lisa Margaret, Todd Holden, Laura Karolina. BSN with honors, Pacific Luth. U., 1959; MA in Religion, Yale U., 1964; MA in Edn., U. Calif., Santa Barbara, 1990. RN Calif., cert. sch. nurse, Calif. Asst. instr. Emanuel Hosp. Sch. Nursing, Portland, Oreg., 1959-60; surgery fl. nurse Yale/New Haven Hosp., 1960-62, head nurse, out patient, 1962-63; staff nurse Vis. Nurse Assn., Hamden, Ct., 1963-64; sch.

nurse Santa Barbara Sch. Dists., Calif., 1968-70, 77-98; dir. teenage pregnancy and parenting project Santa Barbara, 1985-86; mem. US Congress from 23rd Calif. dist., Washington, 1998—, mem. budget com., energy & commerce com., natural resources com. Mem. Addiction, Treatment, & Recovery Caucus, Bi-Partisan Pro-Choice Caucus, Aerospace Caucus, Art Caucus, Coalition Autism Rsch. & Edn., Bike Caucus, Congl. Brain Injury Task Force, Climate Change Caucus, Cmty. Coll. Caucus, Diabetes Caucus, Global Health Caucus, Goods Movement Caucus, Hearing Health Caucus, Congl. Heart & Stroke Coalition, Human Rights Caucus, Intelligent Transp. Sys. Caucus, Nat. Parks Caucus, Native Am. Caucus, Oceans Caucus, Organics Caucus, Passenger Rail Caucus, Port Security Caucus, Recycling Caucus, Renewable Energy & Energy Efficiency Caucus, Specialty Crop Caucus, Congl. Task Force Alzheimers Disease, Congl. Task Force Internat. HIV/AIDS, Tourism & Travel Caucus, Vision Caucus, Wine Caucus, Zoo & Aquarium Caucus, Congl. Working Grp. Parkinson's Disease, Dem. Homeland Security Task Force, Out of Iraq Caucus, Prescription Drug Task Force, New Dem. Coalition; co-chair Nat. Marine Sanctuary Caucus, Ho. Cancer Caucus, Coastal Caucus, Congl. Caucus Women's Issues, Biomed. Rsch. Caucus; founder, co-chair Nursing Caucus; founder Sch. Health & Safety Caucus; bd. dirs. Santa Barbara Women's Polit. Com. Active Grace Luth. Ch.; bd. dirs. Am. Red Cross, Am. Heart Assn., Santa Barbara, 1989—, Adoption Ctr., Santa Barbara, 1986—90, Family Svc. Agy., Santa Barbara, 1994—. Mem.: Goleta Valley C. of C., Santa Barbara C. of C., Am. Assn. Univ. Women. Democrat. Lutheran. Office: US House of Reps 1707 Longworth Ho Office Bldg Washington DC 20515-0523 Home: 1216 State Street Suite 403 Santa Barbara CA 93101 Fax: 202-225-5632. E-mail: lois.capps@mail.house.gov.

CAPRIOLI, JOSEPH, ophthalmologist; b. Deer Park, NY, May 15, 1954; m. Tracey Caprioli, June 1993; 1 child, Isabella; children from previous marriage: Peter, Joseph, Jessica, Marie. BS, SUNY, Stony Brook, 1975; MD, SUNY, Buffalo, 1979; MA Privatum, Yale U., 1993. Diplomate Nat. Bd. Med. Exmainers, Am. Bd. Ophthalmology; lic. physician, N.Y., Pa., Conn. Dir. Glaucoma Sect., 1984—; intern Yale U. Sch. Medicine, New Haven, 1979-80, resident ophthalmology, 1984-88, asst. prof. ophthalmology, dir. glaucoma svc., 1984-97, assoc. prof. ophthalmology, 1988-93, prof. ophthalmology, 1993-97; fellow glaucoma Wills Eye Hosp., Phila., 1983-84; acting chmn. Yale U. Sch. Medicine, New Haven, 1993-95; prof. ophthalmology, dir. glaucoma sect. UCLA/Jules Stein Eye Inst., LA, 1997—. Lectr. Ill. Soc. for Preservation of Blindness, 1992; mem. basic sci. and clin. glaucoma panels, planning subcom. Nat. Adv. Eye Coun., NIH, 1990, visual scis. A study sect. NIH/Nat. Eye Inst., 1992-94, chmn., 1994—; steering com. Advanced Glaucoma Intervention Study, NIH, 1988-91; lectr. in field. Book rev. editor Ophthalmic Surgery, 1984-89; mem. editl. bd. Ophthalmic Surgery, 1989—, Am. Jour Ophthalmology, 1991—, Investigative Ophthalmology and Visual Sci., 1992—, Jour. Glaucoma, 1991-94; editor: Ophthalmology Clinics of North America: Contemporary Issues in Glaucoma, 1991; contbr. articles to profl. jours., chpts. to books. Recipient Jules Francois prize, 1989, Alcon Rsch. Inst. award, 1992, Rudin prize for glaucoma rsch., 1996; grantee Hoechst-Roussel Pharms., Inc., 1985-86, NIH/Nat. Eye Inst., 1987-89, 93—, New Haven Found., 1988-89, Merck Sharp & Dohme, 1989-90, 92-93, Alcon Pharms., 1989-90, Robert Leet and Clara Guthrie Patterson Trust, 1989-92, Alcon Rsch. Inst., 1992, Lewis Rudin Glaucoma prize, 1997. Fellow ACS, Am. Acad. Ophthalmology (mem. quality of care com. glaucoma panel 1988—, chmn. 1991—); mem. Am. Ophthalmological Soc., Assn. for Rsch. in Vision and Ophthalmology, Internat. Soc. Eye Rsch., Am. Glaucoma Soc., Soc. Neurosci., Glaucoma Soc. of Internat. Gongress Ophahtlmology, New Eng. Ophthalmol. Soc. Avocations: piano, cabinetmaking, exercise. Office: Jules Stein Eye Inst Dept Opthalmology 100 Stein Plz # 2-118 Los Angeles CA 90095-7065

CAPRON, ALEXANDER MORGAN, lawyer, educator, bioethicist; b. Hartford, Conn., Aug. 16, 1944; s. Willaim Mosher and Margaret (Morgan) Capron; m. Barbara A. Brown, Nov. 9, 1969 (div. Dec. 1985); 1 child, Jared Capron-Brown; m. Kathleen West, Mar. 4, 1989; children: Charles Spencer West Capron, Christopher Gordon West Capron, Andrew Morgan West Capron. BA, Swarthmore Coll., 1966; LLB, Yale U., 1969; MA (hon.), U. Pa., 1975. Bar: D.C. 1970, Pa. 1978. Law clk. to presiding judge U.S. Ct. Appeals, Washington, 1969—70; lectr., rsch. assoc. Yale U., 1970—72; asst. prof. law U. Pa., 1972—75, assoc. prof., 1975—78, vice dean, 1976, prof. law and human genetics, 1978—82; exec. dir. Pres.'s Commn. for Study of Ethical Problems in Med. and Biomedical and Behavioral Rsch., Washington, 1980—83; prof. law, ethics and pub. policy Law Ctr. Georgetown U., Washington, 1983—84, inst. fellow Kennedy Inst. Ethics, 1983—84; Topping prof. law, medicine and pub. policy U. So. Calif., LA, 1985—89, univ. prof., 1989—, prof. medicine and law, 1991—, Henry W. Bruce prof. equity, 1991—2006, Scott H. Bice chair in healthcare law, policy and ethics, 2006—; co-dir. Pacific Ctr. for Health Policy and Ethics, LA, 1990—; dir. ethics and health WHO, 2002—03, dir. ethics, trade, human rights and health law, 2003—06. Mem. bd. advisors Am. Bd. Internal Medicine, 1985—95, chmn., 1991—95; cons. NIH, mem. subcom. on human gene therapy, 1984—92, mem. recombinant DNA adv. com., 1990—95; chmn. Congrl. Biomedical Ethics Adv. Commn., 1987—91; mem. Joint Commn. on Accreditation of Healthcare Orgns., 1994—, mem. ethics adv. com., 1984—85; mem. Nat. Bioethics Adv. Commn., 1996—2001. Author (with Katz): Catastrophic Diseases: Who Decides What?, 1976; author: (with others) Genetic Counseling: Facts, Values and Norms, 1979, Law, Science and Medicine, 1984, supplements, 1987, 1989, 2d edit., Treatise on Health Care Law, 1991; contbr. articles to profl. jours. Bd. mgrs. Swarthmore Coll., 1982—85; bd. trustees The Century Found. Fellow: AAAS, Hastings Ctr. (bd. dirs. 1975—98, Inst. Soc., Ethics and Life Scis.), Am. Coll. Legal Medicine (hon.); mem.: AAUP (exec. com. Pa. chpt.), Internat. Assn. Bioethics (mem. bd. 1992—96, 2001—, v.p. 2003—05, pres. 2005—), Am. Soc. Law, Medicine and Ethics (pres. 1988—89), Inst. Medicine of NAS (bd. dirs. 1985—90), Swarthmore Coll. Alumni Soc. (v.p. 1974—77). Office: U So Calif Gould Sch Law Los Angeles CA 90089-0071 Home Phone: 310-450-1815; Office Phone: 213-740-2557. Business E-Mail: acapron@law.usc.edu.

CARATAN, ANTON G., food products executive; b. 1955; With Anton Caratan & Son, Delano, Calif., 1976—, ptnr., 1984—. Office: Anton Caratan & Son 1625 Road 160 Delano CA 93215-9436

CARD, STUART KENT, psychologist, researcher; b. Detroit, Dec. 21, 1943; s. Stuart Llewellyn and Kathleen Marie (Wolfe) C.; m. Josefina Bulatao Jayme, Jan. 26, 1972; children: Gwyneth Megan, Tiffany Heather. AB in Physics, Oberlin Coll., Ohio, 1966; MS, Carnegie Mellon U., 1970, PhD in Psych., 1978; doctorate in Sci. (hon.), Oberlin Coll., 2008. Acting dir. Oberlin Coll. Computer Ctr., 1967; mem. rsch. staff Xerox Palo Alto Rsch. Ctr., Calif., 1974-86, prin. scientist, 1986-90, mgr. user interface rsch., 1988—2007, rsch. fellow, 1990, sr. rsch. fellow. Cons. Psychol. Svc. Pitts., 1968-73; adh. assoc. prof. dept. psych. Stanford U., 1983; chmn. human factors summer study on automation in combat aircraft for the 1990s Air Force/NRC, Woods Hole, Mass., 1980; charter mem. Bd. on Army Sci. and Tech., NRC, Washington, 1982-85; group leader NATO Advanced Workshop on Man-Machine Sys., Loughborough, Eng., 1983; blue ribbon com. on Army aviation aircrew integration NASA/Army, Moffitt Field, Calif., 1983. Editl. bd. Behavioral and Info. Tech., London, 1984, Human-Computer Interaction, 1984, ACM Transactions on Office Info. Sys., 1988-90, Cambridge U. Press, 1991; assoc. editor ACM Transactions on Human-Computer Interaction, 1992; co-author: The Psych. of Human-Computer Interaction, 1983; co-editor: Human Performance Models for Computer-Aided Engring., 1990; co-designer computer sys.: Rooms, 1986, Info. Visualizer, 1991; author: Readings in Information Visualization, 1999. Troop leader Girl Scouts US, Palo Alto, Calif., 1985-86; coach Odyssey of the Mind, Palo Alto, 1993-94; chair cognition models NAS Panel on Pilot Performance Models for Computer-Aided Engring., Washington, 1987-89. Recipient Bower award and prize for Achievement in Sci., Franklin Inst., 2007. Fellow Assn. Computing Machinery (prog. chair conf. on human factors in software 1991, program com., 1983-94, faculty doctoral consortium 1985, 88, Computer-Human Interaction Lifetime Achievement award, 2000), World Tech. Network; mem. IEEE, Cognitive Sci. Soc., Human Factors Soc., Computer-Human Interaction Acad., Sigma Xi, NAE. Achievements include patents in field. Office: Palo Alto Rsch Ctr 3333 Coyote Hill Rd Palo Alto CA 94304-1314 Office Phone: 650-812-4362. E-mail: stuart.card@parc.com.

CARDENAS, TONY, councilman; b. San Fernando Valley, Calif. m to Norma; children: Cristian, Andres & Vanessa (stepdaughter). BEE, U. Calif., Santa Barbara. Eng. specialist Hewlett Packard; assemblyman, Dist. 39 Calif. State Assembly, 1997—2002; owner, pres. Our Cmty. Real Estate Co.; councilman, Dist. 6 LA City Coun., 2004—. Mem. Coalition Against the Pipeline; commr. El Pueblo de LA Hist. Monument; mem. LA Bus. Advisor Com. San Fernando Valley Assn. Realtors. Democrat. Address: Re/Max Metro Realty 1075 N Maclay Ave San Fernando CA 91340 Office: 200 N Spring St Rm 455 Los Angeles CA 90012 also: Dist Office 14410 Sylvan St Ste 215 Van Nuys CA 91401 Office Phone: 213-473-7006, 818-778-4999. Office Fax: 213-847-0549, 818-778-4998. E-mail: councilmember.cardenas@lacity.org.

CARDIFF, ROBERT DARRELL, pathology educator; b. San Francisco, Dec. 5, 1935; s. George Darrell and Helen (Kohfield) C.; m. Sally Joan Bounds, June 23, 1962; children: Darrell, Todd, Shelley. BS, U. Calif., Berkeley, 1958, PhD, 1968; MD, U. Calif., San Francisco, 1962. Intern King's County Hosp., Bklyn., 1962-63; resident in pathology U. Oreg., Portland, 1963-66; NIH fellow U. Calif., Berkeley, 1966-68, mem. faculty med. sch. Davis, 1971—, prof. pathology Med. Sch., 1977—2005, disting. prof., 2005—, chair dept. pathology, 1990-96; dir. Ctr. for Med. Informatics U. Calif. Davis Healthcare Sys., 1996-98, faculty Ctr. for Comparative Medicine; chair Med. Informatics Grad. Group, 2002—04; dir. Ctr. Genomic Pathology, 2007—. Mem. sci. adv. bd. Contra Costa Cancer Fund, Walnut Creek, Calif., 1985-99; mem. Univ.-Wide AIDS Task Force, Berkeley, 1984-87; vis. prof. Sun-Yat Sen U. Med. Sci., Peoples Republic of China, 1985, 93, Harvard Med. Sch., 1990, U. Calif. San Diego, 1998-99. Mem. editl. bd. Human Pathology, 1992-2004, Tumor Markers, 1992—, Internat. Jour. Oncology, 1992—, Jour. Mamgland Biol. and Neoplasia, 1998—; contbr. articles to profl. jours Lt. col. US Army, 1968—71. Recipient Triton Rsch. award, Triton Bioscis., Inc., 1985, Sadusk award, Peralta Cancer Inst., 1986, Dist. Prof. award, 2005. Master: AAUP (exec. com. 1983—85); fellow: AAAS; mem.: Ctr. for Genomic Pathology (dir.), No. Calif. Pathology Soc. (pres. 1990—96), Sacramento Pathology Soc. (bd. dirs. 1985—96), Internat. Assn. Breast Cancer Rsch. (bd. dirs. 1984—96, pres. 2003—06, chair 2006—, chair, bd. govs. 2006—), Internat. Acad. Pathology, Pluto Soc., Sigma Xi. Avocations: basketball, skiing, jogging. Office: U Calif-Davis Ctr for Comparative Medicine 98 County Rd & Hutchison Dr Davis CA 95616 Office Phone: 530-752-2726. Business E-Mail: rdcardiff@ucdavis.edu.

CARDILLO, JAMES G., automotive executive; Grad. in Bus. Adminstrn., Cleve. State U. Mgmt. positions Rockwell Corp.; with Peterbilt Motors Co., 1990—99, sr. exec.; chmn., pres. DAF Trucks N.V. PACCAR, England, 1999—2004, sr. v.p. Bellevue, Wash., 2004—06, exec. v.p., 2006—08, pres., 2008—. Office: PACCAR PO Box 1518 Bellevue WA 98009 Office Phone: 425-468-7400. Office Fax: 425-468-8216.

CARDONE, BONNIE JEAN, freelance/self-employed photojournalist; b. Chgo., Feb. 21, 1942; d. Frederick Paul and Beverly Jean Rittschof; m. David Frederick Cardone, June 9, 1963 (div. 1978); children: Pamela Susan, Michael David. BA, Mich. State U., 1963. Editorial asst. Mich. State Dental Assn. Jour., Lansing, 1963-64; asst. editor Nursing Home Adminstr. mag., Chgo., 1964-65, Skin Diver Mag., LA, 1976-77, sr. editor, 1977-81, photographer, 1981—, exec. editor, 1981-97, editor, 1997-99; mystery novelist, 1999—. Author: Fireside Diver, 1993; co-author: Shipwrecks of Southern California, 1989. Named Woman Diver of Yr. Women's Scuba Assn., 1999; recipient Calif. Scuba Svc. award St. Brendan Corp., 1999; named to Women Diver's Hall of Fame, 2000, Women's Scuba Assn. Mem. Calif. Wreck Divers Club (Wreck Divers Hall of Fame, 2003), Hist. Diving Soc. (bd. dirs. 1997-2001). E-mail: bjcardone@hotmail.com.

CARDOZA, DENNIS A., United States Representative from California; b. Merced, Calif., Mar. 31, 1959; m. Kathleen McLoughlin; children: Joey, Brittany, Elaina. BA, U. Md., 1982. Intern to Rep. Martin Frost, Washington; mem. Atwater City Coun., 1984—87, Merced City Coun., 1994—95, Calif. State Assembly, 1996—2002, US Congress from 18th Calif. dist., 2003—, sr. whip, mem. agr. com., resources com., rules com. Co-chair Blue Dog Coalition; mem. Calif. Gov.'s Commn. Vet.'s Homes, Dem. Steering & Policy Com. Named Legis. of Yr., U. Calif., 2001, Small Bus. Roundtable, 2001, Small Bus. Assn., 2001, Calif. Sheriff's Assn., 2001, 2002. Democrat. Roman Catholic. Office: US Ho Reps 435 Cannon Ho Office Bldg Washington DC 20515-0518

CARDWELL, KENNETH HARVEY, architect, educator; b. LA, Feb. 15, 1920; s. Stephen William and Beatrice Viola (Duperrault) C.; m. Mary Elinor Sullivan, Dec. 30, 1946; children: Kenneth William, Mary Elizabeth, Ann Margaret, Catherine Buckley, Robert Stephen. AA, Occidental Coll.; AB, U. Calif.-Berkeley; postgrad., Stanford U. Lic. architect, Calif. Draftsman Thompsen & Wilson Architects, San Francisco, 1946-48, Michael Goodman, Architect, Berkeley, Calif., 1949; architect W.S. Wellington, Architect, Berkeley, 1950-59; prin. Kolbeck, Cardwell, Christopherson, Berkeley, 1960-66; prof. dept. arch. U. Calif.-Berkeley, 1950-82; prin. Kenneth H. Cardwell Architect, Berkeley, 1982—. Author: Bernard Maybeck, 1977. Pres. Civic Art Commn., Berkeley, 1963-65; mem. Bd. Adjustments, 1967-69, Alameda County Art Commn., 1969-72. Served to 1st lt. USAAF, 1941-45. Decorated D.F.C.; decorated Air medal with 3 oak leaf clusters; Rehman fellow, 1957; Graham fellow, 1961; recipient Berkeley citation U. Calif., 1982. Fellow: AIA; mem.: Berkeley Hist. Soc. (pres. 1997—2000), Alpha Rho Chi. Home and Office: 1210 Shattuck Ave Berkeley CA 94709-1413 Office Phone: 510-845-6475. Business E-Mail: cardwell@berkeley.edu.

CAREN, ROBERT POSTON, aerospace scientist; b. Columbus, Ohio, Dec. 25, 1932; s. Robert James and Charlene (Poston) C.; m. Linda Ann Davis, Mar. 27, 1963; children: Christopher Davis, Michael Poston. BS, Ohio State U., 1953, MS, 1954, PhD, 1961. Sr. physicist N.Am. Aviation, Columbus, 1959-60; assoc. research scientist research and devel. div. Lockheed Missiles and Space Co., Inc., Palo Alto, Calif., 1962-63, research scientist, 1963-66, sr. mem. research lab., 1966-69, mgr. def. systems space systems div., 1969-70, mgr. infared tech. R & D div., 1970-71, research dir., 1972-76, chief engr., 1976-86, v.p. gen. mgr. R & D div., 1986—, corp. v.p. sci. and engring., 1987-98; chmn. LITEX Inc., 1998—2000. Bd. dirs. LITEX Corp.; mem. U.S./Israel Sci. and Tech. Commn., 1997—. Contbr. articles to profl. jours.; patentee in field. Fellow AIAA, AAAS, AAS, Soc. Automotive Engrs.; mem. NAE, IEEE (sr.), Am. Def. Preparedness Assn. (past chmn. rsch. divsn.), Am. Phys. Soc., Aerospace Industries Assn. (past chmn. tech. and ops. coun.), Calif. Coun. on Sci. and Tech., Sigma Pi Sigma, Pi Mu Epsilon. Home: 6039 Gleneagles Cir San Jose CA 95138-2372 Office: 1220 Ventura Blvd Ste 2250 Sherman Oaks CA 91403-5338 Personal E-mail: rcaren@comcast.net.

CAREW, THOMAS JAMES, neuroscientist, educator; b. Calif. m. Mary Jo Carew. BS in Psychology, Loyola U., Los Angeles; MS, Calif. State U., Los Angeles; PhD, U. Calif., Riverside, 1970. Prof. psychiatry Columbia U. Coll. of Physicians & Surgeons, 1970—76, NYU Sch. of Medicine, 1976—83; prof. Yale U., 1983—90, John M. Musser prof., chair dept. psychology, 1990—99; prof. neurobiology & behavior U. Calif., Irvine, Calif., 1999—2001, Donald Bren prof. & chair Ctr. for Neurobiology of Learning & Memory, 2001—. Author several articles published in various journals; co-author: (books) Perspectives in Neural Systems and Behavior, 1989, Mechanistic Relationships Between Development and Learning, 1998; author: Behavioral Neorobiology, 2000. Recipient Merit award, NIH, 1990, Dylan Hixon prize, 1990. Fellow: AAAS, Am. Acad. Arts & Sciences; mem.: Soc. Neuroscience (pres. 2007), Soc. Exptl. Psychology. Achievements include research in neural basis of behavior and animal behavior. Office: U Calif 2205 McGaugh Hall 301 Qureshey Research Lab Mail Code 4550 Irvine CA 92697-4550 Office Phone: 949-824-6114. Office Fax: 949-824-2447. Business E-Mail: tcarew@uci.edu.

CAREY, CHASE (CHARLES G.), broadcast executive; BA, Colgate U., Hamilton, NY, 1976; MBA, Harvard U., 1981. Sr. v.p. Columbia Pictures, 1981—88; exec. v.p., CFO Fox Inc., 1988—92, COO, 1992—94; chmn., CEO Fox TV Group, 1994—2000; co-COO News Corp., 1997—2002; dir., pres., CEO Sky Global Networks, Inc., 2001—02; pres., CEO DirecTV Group, El Segundo, Calif., 2003—, bd. dirs., 2005—. Bd. dirs. Fox Entertainment Group, Inc., 1992—2002, News Corp., 1996—, NDS Group, Inc., 1996—2002, News Am. Inc., 1998—2002, Gemstar-TV Guide Internat., Inc., 2000—02, Brit. Sky Broadcasting plc, 2003—, Gateway, Inc., Yell Fin. B.V. Bd. trustees Colgate U. Named one of The Most Influential People in the World of Sports, Bus. Week, 2007, 2008. Office: DirecTV Group 2230 E Imperial Hwy El Segundo CA 90245 Office Phone: 310-964-5000.

CAREY, JOHN CLAYTON, pediatrician, educator, medical geneticist; b. Balt., 1946; MD, Georgetown U., 1972; MPH, U. Calif., Berkeley, 1976. Diplomate Am. Bd. Med. Genetics, Am. Bd. Pediatrics. Prof. pediat. U. Utah Med. Ctr., Salt Lake City, vice chmn. Dept. Pediat. Co-author: Medical Genetics, 3d edit., 2003, Care of the Child with Trisomy 18/13, 1996, rev. edit. 2000. Softly Written, Softly Spoken, 2002; editor-in-chief Am. Jour. Med. Genetics; contbr. over 200 articles to profl. jours. Med. advisor Support Orgn. Trisomy 18, 13 and Related Disorders, Utah Birth Defects Network, Pregnancy Risk Line. Office: U Utah Med Ctr Pediatrics 2C412 SOM 50 N Medical Dr Salt Lake City UT 84132-0001 Office Phone: 801-581-8943.

CAREY, MATT, Internet company executive; Sr. v.p., Chief Technology Officer Wal-Mart, 1985—2006; Chief Tech. Officer eBay marketplaces; sr. v.p., Chief Tech. Officer eBay. Mem. adv. bd. Hewlett-Packard, Dell Computers, IBM. Office: eBay 2145 Hamilton Ave San Jose CA 95125

CAREY, PETER KEVIN, reporter; b. San Francisco, Apr. 2, 1940; s. Paul Twohig and Stanleigh M. (White) C.; m. Joanne Dayl Barker, Jan. 7, 1978; children: Brendan Patrick, Nadia Marguerite. BS in Econs., U. Calif., Berkeley, 1964. Reporter San Francisco Examiner, 1964, Livermore Ind., Calif., 1965-67, editor, 1967; aerospace writer, spl. projects, bus. tech. and investigative reporter San Jose Mercury, Calif., 1967—2007, bus. economy writer, 2007—. Pulitzer prize juror, 2002—03. Recipient Pulitzer prize for internat. reporting Columbia U., 1986, George Polk award L.I. U., 1986, Investigative Reporters and Editors award, 1986, staff Pulitzer prize for gen. reporting, Columbia U., 1990, Thomas L. Stokes award Washington Journalism Ctr., 1991, Malcolm Forbes award Overseas Press Club of Am., 1993, Gerald Loeb award UCLA Grad. Sch. Mgmt., 1993, Pulitzer Writer & Editors award Soc. Am. Bus. Editors and Writers, 2008; NEH profl. journalism fellow, Stanford U., 1983-84. Mem. Internat. Consortium of Investigative Journalists, Soc. Profl. Journalists, Investigative Reporters and Editors. Avocation: piano. Office: San Jose Mercury-News 750 Ridder Park Dr San Jose CA 95190 Business E-Mail: pcarey@mercurynews.com.

CAREY, W. DAVID P., hotel executive; m. Kathy Carey; 4 children. BSEE, Stanford U.; MBA with distinction, Santa Clara U., JD cum laude. Assoc. Carlsmith Tichman Case Mukai and Ichiki; exec. v.p., gen. counsel Outrigger Hotels, Inc., Honolulu, 1986-88, pres., 1988—, CEO, 1994—. Mem. Hawaii Tourism Authority. Mem. ABA, Hawaii Hotel Assn., Urban Land Inst., Hawaii State Bar Assn., Young Pres.' Orgn., Hawaii Bus. Roundtable, Beta Gamma Sigma. Avocations: soccer, golf. Office: Outrigger Hotels and Resorts 2375 Kuhio Ave Honolulu HI 96815-2992

CARGO, DAVID FRANCIS, former Governor of New Mexico; b. Dowagiac, Mich., Jan. 13, 1929; s. Francis Clair and Mary E. (Harton) C.; m. Ida Jo Anaya, 1960; c. Veronica Ann, David Joseph, Patrick Michael, Maria Elena Christina, Eamon Francis. AB, U. Mich., 1951, M of Pub. Adminstrn., 1953, JD, 1957. Bar: Mich. 1957, N.Mex. 1957, Oreg. 1974. Pvt. practice, Albuquerque, 1957; asst. dist. atty., 1958-59; mem. N.Mex. House of Reps., Santa Fe, 1962; gov. State of N.Mex., Santa Fe, 1967-71; practice law Santa Fe, 1970-73, Portland, Oreg., 1973-83. Bd. dirs. N.Mex. State Lottery Authority; mem. Interstate Compact; bd. mem. Fort Stanton Found. Chmn. Four Corners Regional Commn., 1967-71, Oil and Gas Conservation Commn., N.Mex. Lottery Authority, Cumbres & Toltec RR Commn.; chmn. N.Mex. Young Reps., 1959-61, Clackamas County Rep. Ctrl. Com.; mem. Israel Bond Com.; former mem. bd. govs. St. John Coll.; bd. dirs. Albuquerque Tech. Vocat. Sch.; chmn. governing bd. Albuquerque Tv.I. C.C.; mem. Albuquerque City Pers. Bd., N.Mex. State Lottery Authority; adv. bd. mem. N.Mex. State Fair; exec. bd. Found. for Open Govt.; bd. dirs. N.Mex. State Libr. Found.; elected state chair libr. bond chmn., 2002; bd. dirs. N.Mex. State Lottery, Cumbres and Toltec R.R.; chmn. bd. commrs. Cumbres and Toltec Scenic Rlwy.; founder David F. Cargo Cmty. Libr., Mora, N.Mex.; mem. Alburque City Labor Bd. With U.S. Army, 1953-55. Named Man of Yr. Albuquerque Jr. C. of C., 1964, Congregation Albert Brotherhood Man of Yr., 2001, 2002; recipient Outstanding Conservationist award N.Mex. Wildlife Assn., 1969, 70, Human Rights award, Office African Affairs & NAACP, 2008; David F. Cargo Libr., Mora, N.Mex., named in his honor. Mem. NAACP (life), KC, Mich. Bar Assn., Oreg. Bar Assn., N.Mex. Bar Assn., Albuquerque Bar Assn., Isaac Walton League (past v.p. N.Mex.), World Affairs Coun. Oreg. (pres.), Interstate Oil and Gas Compact, Isaak Walton League Oreg., Hispano C. of C., Am. Leadership Conf. (bd. dirs.), Nat. Fedn. Blind, Oreg. State Film Commn. Republican. Home: 6422 Concordia Rd NE Albuquerque NM 87111-1228

CARLETTI, CHRISTOPHER M., lawyer; b. Denver, Nov. 27, 1955; BA cum laude, U. Puget Sound, 1977; JD, U. Calif., 1980. Bar: Wash. 1980. Ptnr., chair Transactions Dept. Preston Gates & Ellis LLP, Seattle. Mem.: Seattle-King County Bar Assn. (mem. professionalism com. 1990—93), Wash. State Bar Assn. (mem. Legis. Com. 1989—91, mem. Interprofessional Com. 1993—95). Office: Preston Gates & Ellis LLP Ste 2900 925 Fourth Avenue Seattle WA 98104-1158 Office Phone: 206-370-8314. Office Fax: 206-307-6024. E-mail: chrisc@prestongates.com.

CARLSMITH, JAMES MERRILL, psychologist, educator; b. New Orleans, Apr. 12, 1936; s. Leonard Eldon and Hope (Snedden) C.; m. Lyn Kuckenberg, July 27, 1963; children— Christopher, Kimberly, Kevin. AB, Stanford U., 1958; PhD, Harvard U., 1963. Asst. prof. Yale U., 1962-64; from asst. prof. to prof. psychology Stanford U., 1964—, asso. dean grad. studies, 1972-75; fellow (Center for Advanced Study in Behavioral Scis.), 1975. Author: Social Psychology, 1970, Methods of Research In Social Psychology, 1976. Dir. Boys Town Center, 1980—. Office: Stanford U Dept Psychology Stanford CA 94305

CARLSON, ARTHUR W., lawyer; b. Chgo., Oct. 3, 1945; s. Arthur W. Sr. and Florence (Maul) C.; m. Jeri S. Waite, June 28, 1986; children: Mackenzie Waite Carlson, Sara Elizabeth Carlson. AB, Pomona Coll., 1967; JD, Duke U., 1971. Bar: Calif. 1972. Prin. Angle, Carlson & Goldrick, Santa Barbara, Calif., 1994—. Pres., bd. trustees Santa Barbara Mus. Natural History, 1990-93, 94-95. Office: Arthur Carlson A Professional Corporatio 8 E Figueroa St Ste 210 Santa Barbara CA 93101-2745

CARLSON, CURTIS R., electronics research industry executive; b. 1945; BS in Physics, Worcester Polytechnic Inst., 1967; MS, Rutgers U., PhD, 1973; DSc (hon.), Worcester Polytechnic Inst., 2006. Mem. tech. staff RCA Lab. (became Sarnoff Corp. and part of SRI, 1987), Princeton, NJ, 1973-1981; founder, leader high definition TV program SRI Internat., Sarnoff Corp., Princton, NJ, 1981-84, exec. v.p., 1995-98, head ventures and licensing, pres., CEO Menlo Park, Calif., 1998—; dir. Info. Systems Lab, 1984-90; vp, info. systems Sarnoff Corp., 1990-95. Co-founder, exec. dir. Nat. Info. Display Lab., 1990; past mem. adv. bd. USAF; past mem. rsch. lab. tech. assessment bd. U.S. Army; active Joint Civilian Ops. Conf., 1996; vis. disting. scientist, U. Wash., 1998; served on several govt. task forces; cons. and presenter in field. Author 15 U.S. patents in the fields of image quality, image coding and computer vision; co-author (with William Wilmot) Innovation: The Five Disciplines for Creating What Customers Want, 2006 Recipient Dr. Robert H. Goddard award for profl. achievements, Worcester Polytechnic Inst., 2002; co-recipient Otto Schade prize for display performance and image quality, Soc. for Info. Display, 2006. Mem. IEEE, Soc. Motion Picture and TV Engrs., Highlands Group (charter mem.), Sigma Xi, Tau Beta Pi. Avocation: violin. Address: SRI Internat 333 Ravenswood Ave Menlo Park CA 94025 E-mail: inquiry.line@sri.com.

CARLSON, DALE ARVID, retired dean; b. Aberdeen, Wash., Jan. 10, 1925; s. Edwin C.G. and Anna A. (Anderson) C.; m. Jean M. Stanton, Nov. 11, 1948; children: Dale Ronald, Gail L. Carlson Manahan, Joan M. Carlson Lee, Gwen D. Carlson Lundgren. AA, Grays Harbor Coll., 1947; BSCE, U. Wash., 1950, MSCE, 1951; PhD, U. Wis., 1960. Registered profl. engr., Wash., 1955. Water engr. City of Aberdeen, 1951-55; asst. prof., assoc. prof., prof., chmn. dept. civil engring. U. Wash., Seattle, 1955-76, dean Coll Engring., 1976-80, dean emeritus, 1980—, dir. Valle Scandinavian Exch., 1980—2002; chmn. dept. civil engring. Seattle U., 1983-88, acting dean sci. and engring., 1990, dean sci. and engring., 1990-92. Vis. prof. Tech. U. Denmark, Copenhagen, 1970, Royal Coll. Agr., Uppsala, Sweden, 1976, Uppsala, 78; adv. com., dept. Scandinavian studies U. Wash., 2003—, adv. com. dept. civil and environ. engring., 2006—, adv. com. Valle Scandinavian exch. program, 2006—. Contbr. articles to profl. jours. Exec. bd. Pacific N.W. Synod Luth. Ch. in Am., chmn. fin. com., 1980-84, treas., 1986-87, bd. edn., fin. com. Evang. Luth. Ch. in Am., 1987-91; v.p. Nat. Luth. Campus Ministry, 1988-91; treas. N.W. Washington synod Evang. Luth. Ch. in Am., 1996-2000, mem. synod candidacy com., 2001-07; exec. bd. Nordic Heritage Mus., 1981-86; bd. dirs. Hearthstone Retirement Ctrs., 1984-93, Evergreen Safety Coun., 1980-86. With AUS, 1943-45. Named Outstanding Grad. Weatherwax H.S., Aberdeen, 1972, Outstanding Grad. Grays Harbor Coll., 1947; guest of honor Soppeldagene, Trondheim, 1978. Mem. ASCE, Internat. Water Acad., Am. Soc. Engring. Educators, Am. Acad. Environ. Engring., Am. Water Works Assn., Am. Scandinavian Found., Swedish Am. C. of C. (bd. dirs. 1994-99), Norwegian Am. C. of C., Rainier Club, Rotary, Phi Beta Kappa, Sigma Xi, Chi Epsilon. Home: 9235 41st Ave NE Seattle WA 98115-3801 Business E-Mail: dcarlson@engr.washington.edu.

CARLSON, DON M., state senator; b. Wash. m. Jan Carlson; children: Rusty, Doug. BA, Western Wash. U., MA in Edn.; postgrad., U. Wash. Tchr., coach Hudson's Bay H.S., Columbia River H.S.; Rep. rep. dist. 49 Wash. Ho. of Reps., 1993-2000; Rep. senator dist. 49 Wash. State Senate, 2000—. Mem. edn., higher edn., human svcs. and corrections coms. Wash. State Senate, Rep. asst. floor leader; commr. Western Interstate Commn. on Higher Edn.; mem. Joint Com. on Pension Policy, Oral History Review Bd. Precinct committeeman Clark County Bd. Adjustment, 1970—; bd. dirs. Mainstream Reps. Wash.; coach baseball, softball; former coach volleyball Columbia River H.S., Clark Coll.; mem. First Christian Ch.; mem. adv. bd. Ft. Vancouver Seafarers Ctr. Recipient Medal of Honor award DAR, VIP award Coll. Women's Programs Coun., award Clark Coll. Hall of Fame, Cornerstone award Assn. Wash. Bus., Guardian of Small Bus. award Nat. Fedn. Ind. Bus., Legis. Excellence award Wash. State Ret. Tchr. Assn., Legis. Extraordinaire award Wash. Pub. Employees Assn., Outstanding Legislator award Wash. Paralyzed Vet. Am. Mem. Vancouver C. of C. Office: PO Box 40449 106B Irv Newhouse Bldg Olympia WA 98504-0449 Fax: 360 786-7819. E-mail: carlson_do@leg.wa.gov.

CARLSON, ERIK B., lawyer; b. 1947; BA, Dartmouth College; JD, George Washington U. Law Sch. Sr. atty. Western Crude Oil Inc.; asst. gen. counsel Davis Oil Co.; sr. v.p., gen. counsel, sec. Duke Energy Field Svcs. (formerly Associated Natural Gas Corp.), 1983—98, TransMontaigne Inc., Denver, 1998—. Office: TransMontaigne Inc 370 17th St Ste 2750 PO Box 5660 Denver CO 80217 Office Phone: 303-626-8265. Office Fax: 303-626-8228. Business E-Mail: ecarlson@transmontaigne.com.

CARLSON, GARY R., publishing executive; b. Ishpeming, Mich. s. James H. and Vivian M. (Maki) C.; m. Mardee G. Parkinson, Aug. 21, 1963 (div.Apr. 21, 1991); children: Bruce S., Robyn L.; m. Maryanne Koschier, June 25, 1994. BA Far Eastern Langs. and Lit., U. Mich., 1969. Sales rep. John Wiley and Sons, Ann Arbor, Mich., 1970-72, editor NYC, 1972-80, pub., 1980-84; pres. SoftPress, Inc., Monroe, N.Y., 1984-86; v.p., dir. acquisitions W.H. Freeman and Co./Scientific Am. Books, NYC, 1986-92; v.p., editor-in-chief Macmillan Coll. Pub., Inc., NYC, 1992-94; v.p., editorial dir., publisher Wadsworth Pub. Co., Belmont, Calif., 1994-97; pub., exec. editor Brooks Cole Pub., 1998—2000; exec. editor Prentice-Hall, 2001—. Editor: (textbooks and trade books) General Chemistry by James B. Brady, 1975, Organic Chemistry by T.W.G. Solomons, 1976, Fundamentals of General, Organic and Biological Chemistry by John R. Holom, 1978, Basic Inorganic Chemistry by A. Cotton and G. Wilkinson, 1977; contbg. author: The Videodisc Book, 1984. With USAF, 1963-67, Taiwan. Mem. Am. Assn. Pubs.

CARLSON, JAMES ROY, animal science educator; b. Windsor, Colo., Mar. 9, 1939; married; two children. BS, Colo. State U., 1961; MS, U. Wis., 1964, PhD in Biochemistry, 1966. From asst. prof. animal sci. Wash. State U., 1966-70, assoc. prof. animal sci., 1971-75, chmn. grad. program nutrition, 1973-83, prof. animal sci., 1976-96, assoc. dean of rsch., 1996-2000, assoc. dean emeritus. Chmn. dept. animal sci. Wash. State U., 1982-93, assoc. dir. agr. rsch. ctr., 1993-94, assoc. dean agr. rsch. ctr., 1994—. Mem. Am. Inst. Nutrition, Am. Soc. Animal Sci., Soc. Exptl. Biol. Medicine. Home: 99 Moosewood Ln Sagle ID 83860-8811

CARLSON, JOHN EARL, lawyer; b. Seattle, May 18, 1952; s. William Richard and H. Joan (Fitzpatrick) C.; m. Audrey Fucilla, Aug. 31, 1984; children: William Grant, Andrew Ivan. AA, Wenatchee Valley Coll., 1972; BA, U. Wash., 1975; JD, U. Puget Sound, 1978. Bar: Wash. 1975, Ill. 1980, Calif. 1980. Asst. to pres. ABA, Chgo., 1978-80; assoc. Lawler, Felix & Hall, LA, 1980-84, Brobeck, Phleger & Harrison, San Francisco, 1984-86, ptnr., 1986—. Bd. visitors Sch. Law, U. Puget Sound, Tacoma, 1982—. Mem. ABA (nat. v.p. law student divsn. 1977-78), Wash. State Bar Assn., Bar Assn. of San Francisco (chmn. bridge the gap com. 1985-87), State Bar of Calif., Ill. State Bar Assn. Roman Catholic. Avocations: basketball, skiing, running, art. Office: Brobeck Phleger & Harrison Spear St Tower 1 Market Plz Fl 31 San Francisco CA 94105-1100

CARLSON, LAWRENCE EVAN, mechanical engineering educator; b. Milw., Dec. 22, 1944; s. John Walfred and Louise Marie (Altseimer) C.; m. Elizabeth M. Studley, Jan. 28, 1967 (div. 1979); 1 child, Jeremy L.; m. Poppy Carlson Copeland, June 15, 1985. BS, U. Wis., 1967; MS, U. Calif., Berkeley, 1968, DEng, 1971. Asst. prof. mech. engring. U. Ill., Chgo., 1971-74; asst. prof., dept. engring. design and econ. evaluation U. Colo., Boulder, 1974-78, assoc. prof., dept. mech. engring., 1978-94, prof., dept. mech. engring., 1994—2007. Cons. Ponderosa Assn., Lafayette, Colo., 1982-93; co-founder, co-dir. Integrated Tchg. and Learning (ITL) Program, U. Colo., Boulder, 1992-; presenter in field. Contbr. many articles to profl. jours. Mary E. Switzer Disting. rsch. fellow Nat. Inst. on Disability and Rehab. Rsch., 1990-91, IDEO Fellow, IDEO Product Design and Develop., Palo Alto, Calif., 2001; recipient Bronze award Lincoln Arc Welding, 1981, Ralph R. Teetor award Soc. Automotive Engrs., 1976; co-recipient Bernard M. Gordon prize, NAE, 2008. Mem. ASME, Am. Soc. for Engring. Edn., Internat. Soc. Prosthetics/Orthotics. Achievements include patents in Rotary Thumb Prosthesis and Locking Mechanism for Voluntary Closing Prosthetic Prehensor. Office: Coll Engring and Applied Sci Univ Colo 427 UCB Boulder CO 80309-9762 Office Phone: 303-492-7222. Office Fax: 303-492-3498. E-mail: lawrence.carlson@colorado.edu.

CARLSON, ROBERT CODNER, industrial engineering educator; b. Granite Falls, Minn., Jan. 17, 1939; s. Robert Ledin and Ada Louise (Codner) C.; children: Brian William, Andrew Robert, Christina Louise. BSME, Cornell U., 1962; MS, Johns Hopkins U., 1963, PhD, 1976. Mem. tech. staff Bell Tel. Labs., Holmdel, NJ, 1962-70; asst. prof. Stanford (Calif.) U., Stanford, 1970-77, assoc. prof., 1977-82, prof. indsl. engring., 1982-2000, prof. mgmt. sci. & engring., 2000—. Program dir., lectr., cons. various spl. programs U.S., Japan, France, 1971—; cons. Japan Mgmt. Assn., Tokyo, 1990—, Boeing, L.A., 1998—, GKN Automotive, London, 1989—, Rockwell Internat., L.A., 1988—; vis. prof. U. Calif., Berkeley, 1987-88, Dartmouth Coll., Hanover, N.J., 1978-79; vis. faculty Internat. Mgmt. Inst., Geneva, 1984, 88. Contbr. articles to profl. jours. Recipient Maxwell Upson award in Mech. Engring. Cornell U., 1962; Bell Labs. Systems Engring. fellow, 1962-63, Bell Labs. Doctoral Support fellow, 1966-67. Mem. INFORMS (chmn. membership com. 1981-83), Inst. Indsl. Engrs., Am. Soc. Engring. Edn., Am. Prodn. and Inventory Control Soc. (bd. dirs. 1975-81), Confrerie des Chevaliers du Tastevin, Tau Beta Pi, Phi Kappa Phi, Pi Tau Sigma. Avocations: wine tasting, travel. Home Phone: 650-327-9179; Office Phone: 650-723-9110. Business E-Mail: r.c.carlson@stanford.edu.

CARLSON, ROBERT EDWIN, lawyer; b. Bklyn., Oct. 11, 1930; s. Harry Victor and Lenore Marie (Hanrahan) C.; m. Maureen Eleanor Donnelly, Aug. 24, 1963; children: John T., Katherine L., Elizabeth A., Robert E. Jr. BS, U. Oreg., 1953; JD, U. Calif., San Francisco, 1958; LLM, Harvard U., 1963. Bar: Calif. 1959, U.S. Dist. Ct. (ctrl. dist.) Calif. 1959, U.S. Ct. Appeals (9th cir.) 1959. Assoc. Kindel & Anderson, LA, 1958-63, ptnr., 1963-67, Agnew, Miller & Carlson, LA, 1967-80, Hufstedler, Miller, Carlson & Beardsley, LA, 1980-88, Paul, Hastings, Janofsky & Walker LLP, LA, 1988—, chmn. corp. practice group investment mgmt., 1988—2001. Pres. Constl. Rights Found., LA, 1978-80, LA County Bar Found., 1988-89; exec. com. bus. sect. LA Bar Assn., 1982-89; bd. dirs. Legal Aid Found., LA. Bd. dirs. Westridge Sch. for Girls, Pasadena, Calif., 1985-91, Trust for Pub. Land, San Francisco, 1987—; chair bd. Skid Row Housing Trust, LA, 1989-2000; mem. Pasadena Cmty. Found., 2001—; bd. visitors Santa Clara Law Sch., 1986-92. With U.S. Army, 1953-55. Recipient Griffin Bell award Dispute Resolution Svcs., Inc., 1992, Katherine Krause award Inner City Law Ctr., 1996. Mem. ABA (securities com., co-chair com. devel. investment svcs., task force to prepare guidebook for dirs. mut. funds 1995, chair youth edn. for citizenship, Chgo. 1982-85), Calif. State Bar (corp. com. 1990-94), Valley Hunt Club, Chancery Club, Calif. Club. Democrat. Avocations: hiking, tennis, reading, skiing. Office: Paul Hastings Janofsky & Walker LLP 515 S Flower St Fl 23 Los Angeles CA 90071-2300 Office Phone: 213-683-6299. Office Fax: 213-627-0705. Business E-Mail: robertcarlson@paulhastings.com.

CARLSON, ROBERT MICHAEL, artist; b. Bklyn., Nov. 19, 1952; s. Sidney Carlson and Vickey (Mihaloff) Woodward; m. Linda Schneider; m. Mary Elizabeth Fontaine, Feb. 24, 1984; 1 child, Nora. Student, CCNY, 1970-73; studied with Flora Mace and Joey Kirkpatrick, Pilchuck Glass Sch., 1981, studied with Dan Dailey, 1982. Teaching asst. Pilchuck Sch., Stanwood, Wash., 1986, 88, mem. faculty, 1989-90, 92, 95, Pratt Fine Arts Ctr., Seattle, 1988-90, Penland (N.C.) Sch. Crafts, 1994, Bild-Werk Sch., Germany, 1996-2000. Mem. artists adv. com. Pilchuck Sch., 1989, 90; vis. artist Calif. Coll. Arts and Crafts, Oakland, 1989, Calif. State U., Fullerton, 1991, blossom summer program Kent State U., Ohio, 1991, U. Ill., Urbana-Champaign, 1993, Toledo Mus. of Art Sch., 1994; visual-artist-in-residence Centrum Found., Port Townsend, Wash., 1992; prof. artist-in-residence Pilchuck Sch., Wash.; faculty The Glass Furnace, Riva, Turkey, 2005 One-man shows include Foster White Gallery, Seattle, 1987, 90, 92, The Glass Gallery, Bethesda, Md., 1988, Heller Gallery, N.Y.C., 1989, 95, Betsy Rosenfield Gallery, Chgo., 1991, 92, MIA Gallery, Seattle, 1994, Habitat Gallery, Florida, 1998, 2001, 06, William Traver Gallery, Seattle, 2000, 04, others; exhibited in group shows at Traver Gallery, Seattle, 1984, 89, Mindscape Gallery, Evanston, Ill., 1984, 86, Tucson Mus. Art., 1984 (Purchase award), 86 (Award of Merit), Hand and Spirit Gallery, Scottsdale, Ariz., 1985, 86, Craftsman Gallery, Scarsdale, N.Y., 1985, Robert Kidd Gallery, Birmingham, Mich., 1985, 88, Gazebo Gallery, Gatlinburg, Tenn., 1985, The Glass Gallery, Bethesda, Md., 1986 (Jurors award), 91, 92, 94, Artists Soc. Internat., San Francisco, 1987 (Critics Choice award), William Traver Gallery, Seattle, 1987, 90, 91, 92, Japan Glass Artcrafts Assn., Tokyo, 1987, Heller Gallery, 1988, 89, 90, 91, 93, 94, 95, 96, 97, Washington Sq. Ptnrs., 1988, Foster White Gallery, 1988, 90, Bellvue Art Mus., Wash., 1988, 91, 94, Am. Arts and Crafts Inc., San Francisco, 1989, Mus. Craft and Folk Art, San Francisco, 1989, Great Am. Gallery, Atlanta, 1989, Dorothy Weiss Gallery, San Francisco, 1989, Habitat Gallery, Farmington Hills, Mich., 1990, 93, Philabaum Gallery, Tucson, 1990, Greg Kucera Gallery, Seattle, 1990, Connell Gallery, Atlanta, 1990, Net Contents Gallery, Bainbridge Island, Wash., 1991, Seattle Tacoma Internat. Airport Installation, 1991, 95, Pratt Fine Arts Ctr., Seattle, 1991, Crystalex, Novy Bor, Czechoslovakia, 1991, Whatcom County Mus., Bellingham, Wash., 1992, Art Gallery West Australia, 1992, 1004 Gallery, Port Townsend, 1992, Bainbridge Island Arts Coun., 1992, MIA Gallery, 1993, Betsy Rosenfield Gallery, Chgo., 1993, Blue Spiral Gallery, Asheville, N.C., 1995, Huntington Mus., 1996, Salem Art Assn., 1996, Judy Yovens Gallery, Houston, 1997, Internat. Glass Art Exchange, Tucson, 1997, Habitat Gallery, Boca Raton, Fla., 1998, 2000, 06, Habitat Gallery, Farmington Hills, Mich., 1998, Tampa (Fla.) Mus. Art, 1998, 2005, Traver Gallery, 2001, Glass Gallery, 2001, Glasmus., 2000, Kentucky Art & Luak Gall., 2000, Fine Arts Mus. San Francisco, 2004, Soc. Arts and Crafts, Boston, 2005, Chantagua Ctr. Visual Arts, N.Y., 2005, L.A. County Mus. Art, 2006, Soc. Contemporary Craft, Pitts., 2007; represented in permanent collections Corning (N.Y.) Mus. Glass, Tucson Mus. Art, Toledo Mus. Art, Mus. Glass, Tacoma, Wash., Tampa Mus. Art, Glasmuseum Frauenau, Germany, Glasmuseum Ebeltoft, Denmark, Valley Nat. Bank, Phoenix, Fountain Assocs., Portland, Oreg., Iceland Air Co., Reykjavik, Iceland, Crocker Banks, L.A., Davis Wright Tremain, Seattle, Meiwa Trading Co., Tokyo, Safeco Ins. Corp., Seattle, Crystalex Corp., L.A. County Mus. Art, Indpls. Mus. Art. Bd. dirs. Am. Craft Coun., 1997-99. Fellow Tucson Pima Arts Coun., 1987, NEA, 1990; John Hauberg fellow, 2000. Mem. Glass Art Soc. (conf. lectr. 1991, bd. dirs. 1992-97, v.p. 1994-95, pres. 1995-97, Lifetime Mem. award 2004). Office: PO Box 11590 Bainbridge Island WA 98110 Home Phone: 206-892-3206; Office Phone: 206-842-3206. E-mail: bobway@robertcarlson.net.

CARLSON, ROBERT WELLS, internist, educator; b. Concord, Calif., Apr. 14, 1952; s. Robert L. Carlson and Mae E. Fox. BS in Biol. Sci., Stanford U., 1974, MD, 1978. Diplomate Am. Bd. Internal Medicine, Am. Bd. Med. Oncology. Intern Barnes Hosp., St. Louis, 1978-79, resident, 1979-80, Stanford (Calif.) Univ. Hosp., 1980-81; fellow Stanford U., 1981-83, clin. asst. prof., 1983-85, asst. prof., 1985-92, assoc. prof., 1992-97, prof., 1997—, assoc. chief for clin. affairs divsn. oncology, 1994-96. Exec. officer No. Calif. Oncology Group, Palo Alto, 1984-87, group chmn., 1987-91. Bd. dirs. Theatreworks, Palo Alto, 1994-99. Recipient Career Devel. award Am. Cancer Soc., 1987-90. Fellow ACP; mem. Am. Soc. Clin. Oncology, Am. Assn. Cancer Rsch. Office: Stanford Cancer Ctr 875 Blake Wilbur Dr MC 5826 Stanford CA 94305 Home Phone: 650-854-9495; Office Phone: 650-725-6457. Business E-Mail: rcarlson@stanford.edu.

CARLSON, ROGER DAVID, psychologist, educator, minister; b. Berkeley, Calif., Nov. 19, 1946; s. George Clarence and Elizabeth (Norris) C.; m. Ema T. Paviolo, June 11, 1977 (div. 1994); children: Erik Andreas Paviolo, Lucas Sven Paviolo, Justin Nikolaus Paviolo. AB, Calif. State U., Sacramento, 1968, MA, 1969; PhD, U. Oreg., Eugene, 1972; cert. theol. studies, Pacific Sch. of Religion, Berkeley, Calif., 1994; MDiv, Pacific Sch. Religion, Berkeley, Calif., 1996. Ordained deacon, 1996, elder, 1998 United Meth. Ch.; lic. psychologist Pa., 1977, Calif., 2001, Oreg., 2002, Washington, 2009. Assoc. prof. psychology Lebanon Valley Coll., Annville, Pa., 1972-85; rsch. assoc. Eugene Pub. Schs., 1985-87; assoc. prof. edn. Williamette U., Salem, Oreg., 1987-88; vis. assoc. prof. psychology Whitman Coll.,

Walla Walla, 1988—89, 1990—91; assoc. prof. psychology Ea. Wash. U., 1991-92; adj. prof. Linfield Coll., 1993—; pastor Coburg (Oreg.) United Meth. Ch., 1992-94, Florence (Oreg.) United Meth. Ch., 1994—2001, Covenant United Meth. Ch., Reedsport, Oreg., 1995—99, 1st United Meth. Ch. of Stayton, Oreg., 2001—03, Bennett Chapel United Meth. Ch., Portland, Oreg., 2003—; assoc. prof. psychology Pacific U., Forest Grove, 2005—07. Vis. scholar dept. history and philosophy of sci., life mem. Cambridge (Eng.) U., 1979-80; life mem. Wolfson Coll., Cambridge U.; psychologist, pvt. practice, 1977-1985, 2001—, pastoral counselor, 2009-. Author books, contbr. rsch. papers, jour. articles and book chpts. on numerous subjects in field. Mem. Friends Radio Sta. KPFA, v.p. 1969, pres. 1970; Wolfeboro Pioneer, Boy Scouts Am., 1959; co-founder, Pathways of Faith, Florence, Oreg., 1998; bd. dirs., Ecumenical Ministries Oreg., 2003-04; pres. Oreg. Soc. of Clin. Hypnosis, 2006-07. Recipient Presdl. Sports award. Fellow Am. Coll. Heraldry; mem. APA, Oreg. Psychol. Assn., Oreg. Soc. Clin. Hypnosis (v.p. 2005-06, pres. 2006-07), Am. Psychol. Soc., Soc. for Clin. and Exptl. Hypnosis, Am. Coll. Psychology, Soc. for Philosophy and Psychology (mem. exec. com. 1975-76), Am. Assn. Sexuality Educators, Counselors, Therapists, SAR, Airplane Owners and Pilots Assn., Sons Union Vets. Civil War, Am. Radio Relay League, Vasa Lodge, Order of St. Luke, Psi Chi. Methodist. Office Phone: 503-245-2929. Business E-Mail: r.d.carlson.80@cantab.net.

CARLSON, STACY C., former motion picture association executive; b. Burbank, Calif., Sept. 6, 1960; BA in Econ., Calif. State U., 1982; MBA, Stanford U., 1988. Legis. asst. to Rep. Bill Thomas, 1982-84; chief of staff Kern County Bd. Suprs., 1984-86; various positions including sr. v.p. strategic planning and spl. projects Silicon Valley Bank, Santa Clara, Calif., 1989-93; minority staff dir. Com. House Adminstrn., 1993-94; staff dir. Com. House Oversight, 1995—97; mng. dir. emerging growth divsn. Imperial Bank (now Comerica), 1997—99; sr. advisor for pub. law & policy Akin, Gump, Strauss, Hauer & Feld, LLP, 1999—2004; dir. Washington DC office Office Gov. Calif., 2004; exec. v.p. govt. affairs Motion Picture Assn. Am., Encino, Calif., 2005.

CARLSON, TERRANCE L., lawyer, aerospace transportation executive; b. Superior, Wis., Jan. 21, 1953; s. Einar August and Carol (McAuley) C.; m. Jeanette Michele Leehr, Mar. 13, 1987; children: Aurora Brita Leehr, Henry Einar, Stephen Michael. BS in Bus. with high distinction, U. Minn., 1975; JD cum laude, U. Mich., 1978. Bar: Calif. 1978, U.S. Dist. Ct. (cen. dist.) Calif. 1978. With Gibson, Dunn & Crutcher, 1978-94, London, 1981-87, ptnr.-in-charge Hong Kong, 1987-89; v.p., gen counsel AlliedSignal Aerospace, Torrance, CA, 1994; dep. gen. counsel AlliedSignal (now Honeywell Internat.); sr. v.p. bus. devel., gen. counsel, sec. PerkinElmer Inc., 1999—2001; sr. v.p., gen. counsel, corp. sec. Medtronic Inc., Mpls., 2001—. Adj. prof. London Law Ctr. U. Notre Dame, 1983-87, Pepperdine U., London, 1984; exec. dir. Annual Multi-Species Invitational (Since 1973). Contbr. articles to legal publs. Mem. Soc. English and Am. Lawyers (com. 1985-87), Royal Auto. Club, Am. Club. Avocations: fishing, guitar. Office: Allied Signal Aerospace 2525 W 190th St Torrance CA 90504-6002 also: Medtronic Inc 710 Medtronic Pky NE Minneapolis MN 55432-5604

CARLSON, THOMAS EDWARD, judge; b. 1947; m. Cynthia Hustad. BA, Beloit Coll., 1969; JD, Harvard U., 1975; LLM, NYU, 1985. Bar: Calif. 1976; U.S. Dist. Ct. (no. dist.) Calif. 1977, U.S. Dist. Ct. (cen. dist.) Calif. 1984, U.S. Ct. Appeals (9th cir.) 1978. Law clk. to Hon. Thomas Roberts Supreme Ct. R.I., 1975-76; law clk. to Hon. Donald Wright Supreme Ct. Calif., 1976-77; assoc. atty. Cooper, White & Cooper, San Francisco, 1977-78; dep. staff dir. Ninth Cir. Ct. Appeals, San Francisco, 1978-84; judge U.S. Bankruptcy Ct. No. Dist. Calif., San Francisco, 1985—. Mem. Nat. Conf. Bankruptcy Judges. Office: US Bankruptcy Ct Calif PO Box 7341 235 Pine St Fl 19 San Francisco CA 94120

CARLTON, JOHN L., lawyer; AB summa cum laude, UCLA, 1973, JD, 1979. Bar: Calif. 1979, US Dist. Ct. (ctrl. dist. Calif.) 1980, US Ct. Appeals (9th cir.) 1981, US Ct. Appeals (5th cir.) 2006, US Supreme Ct. 2007. Atty. Kadison, Pfaelzer, Woodard, Quinn & Rossi, LA; asst. US atty. Ctrl. Dist. Calif., LA, 1987—98; ptnr. Arnold & Porter LLP, LA. Named a So. Calif. Super Lawyer, Law & Politics and LA Mag., 2005, 2006. Office: Arnold & Porter LLP 44th Fl 777 S Figueroa St Los Angeles CA 90017-5844 Office Phone: 213-243-4101. Office Fax: 213-243-4199. E-mail: John.Carlton@aporter.com.

CARLYLE, RANDY, professional hockey coach, retired professional hockey player; b. Sudbury, Ont., Can., Apr. 19, 1956; m. Corey Carlyle; children: Craig, Derek, Alexis. Defenseman Toronto Maple Leafs, 1976—78, Pitts. Penguins, 1978—84, Winnipeg Jets, 1984—93, asst. coach, 1995—96, Manitoba Moose, 1996—97, head coach, 1997—2001, 2004—05; asst. coach Washington Capitals, 2002—04; head coach Anaheim Ducks (formerly Mighty Ducks of Anaheim), 2005—. Achievements include being the head coach of Stanley Cup Champion, Anaheim Ducks, 2007. Office: Anaheim Ducks 2695 E Katella Ave Anaheim CA 92806

CARMAN, MICHAEL DENNIS, museum director; b. Monahans, Tex., Nov. 6, 1938; s. Herbert Charles and Marie Noelie (Watkins) C.; m. Malica Jean Brunet, Jan. 27, 1967 (div. June 1984); m. Sharon Ruth Morrisson, Nov. 29, 1985. BA in History, San Diego State U., 1970, MA in History, 1973. Commd. USN, 1956, advanced through grades to petty officer I, resigned, 1966; curator San Diego Hist. Soc., 1973-77, Pioneers Mus., Colorado Springs, Colo., 1978-82; chief curator Network Curatorial Services, Colorado Springs, 1982-84; dir. Ariz. State Capitol Mus., Phoenix, 1984—. Author: United States Customs and the Madero Revolution, 1975; contbr. articles to profl. jours. Mem. Am. Assn. Mus. (MAP evaluator 1980-86, curator com., sec. 1982-83), Am. Assn. State and Local History (rep. 1974-77, cons. 1975—), Mus. Assn. Ariz., Cen. Ariz. Mus. Assn. (v.p. 1987-89). Clubs: Phoenix City. Avocations: woodworking, hiking, photography. Office: Ariz State Capitol Mus 1700 W Washington St Phoenix AZ 85007-2812

CARMICHAEL, DAVID RICHARD, lawyer, retired insurance company executive; b. Sept. 4, 1942; BS, UCLA, 1964, JD, 1967. Bar: Calif. 1968. Assoc. Adams, Duque & Hazeltine, LA, 1967-72; gen. counsel The Housing Group, Irvine, Calif., 1972-77; assoc. counsel Pacific Mut. Life Ins. Co., 1977-81, v.p., assoc. gen. counsel, 1981-89, corp. sec., 1981—83, 2nd v.p., assoc. gen. counsel, 1983—92, v.p., investment counsel, 1989-92, sr. v.p., gen. counsel, 1992—2007. Dir. & chmn. Ca. Life & Health Ins. Guarantee Assn.; dir. Assn. Ca. Life Ins. Companies, Assn. Life Ins. Counsel.

CARMICHAEL, GARY ALAN ALAN, social studies educator; b. Missoula, Mont., May 7, 1964; s. Glen Alan Carmichael and Jerri Ruth (Haines) Maclay. BA, U. Mont., 1989. Cert. tchr., Mont. Telecommunication specialist, social studies chmn., libr. media specialist Saco Pub. Schs., 1990-93; libr. media specialist Great Falls Pub. Schs., 1993—97; now social studies tchr. White Fish (Mont.) H.S., 1997—. Mem. adv. com. No. Mont. Curriculum Consortium, 1990-93; coach speech, debate, drama team, Saco, 1990-93; trainer, online resource, Discovery Channel Sch. Pres. Circle K Internat., U. Mont., 1986, gov. Mont. dist., 1984. Named Mont. Tchr. of Yr., 2007. Mem. Mont. Libr. Assn., Mont. Coun. for Social Studies, Theta Chi (pres.), U. Mont. Alumni Assn.; Whitefish Edn. Assn. (past v.p.). Office: Whitefish HS 600 East 2nd St Whitefish MT 59937

CARMICHAEL, IAN STUART EDWARD, geologist, educator; b. London, Mar. 29, 1930; came to U.S., 1964; s. Edward Arnold and Jeanette (Montgomerie) C.; children by previous marriages: Deborah, Graham, Alistair, Anthea. BA, Cambridge U., Eng., 1954; PhD, Imperial Coll. Sci., London U., 1958. Lectr. geology Imperial Coll. Sci. and Tech., 1958-63; NSF sr. fgn. sci. fellow U. Chgo., 1964; mem. faculty U. Calif.-Berkeley, 1964—, prof. geology, 1967—, chmn. dept., 1972-76, 80-82, assoc. dean, 1976-78, 85-00, assoc. provost, 1986-2000, dir. Lawrence Hall of Sci., 1996—2003, acting dir. bot. garden, 1997—98; adj. prof. U. of Mich., 2002—. Author: Igneous Petrology, 1974; editor-in-chief Contbns. to Mineralogy and Petrology, 1973-90; contbr. numerous papers to profl. jours. Guggenheim fellow, 1992; recipient Arthur L. Day medal Geol. Soc. Am., 1991. Fellow Royal Soc. London, Mineral Soc. Am. (Roebling medal 1997), Mineral Soc. Gt. Britain (Schlumberger medal 1992), Am. Geophys. Union (Bowen award 1986), Geol. Soc. of London (Murchison medal 1995). Office: U Calif Berkeley Dept Earth/Planetary Sci Berkeley CA 94720-4767

CARMONA, RICHARD HENRY, former Surgeon General of the United States; b. NYC, Nov. 22, 1949; m. Diana Sanchez; 4 children. AA, Bronx Cmty. Coll., CUNY; BS in biology and chemistry, U. Calif., San Francisco, 1977, MD, 1979; MPH, U. Ariz., 1998. Surgical resident U. Calif., San Francisco; prof. surgery, pub. health and family and cmty. medicine U. Ariz., 1985—2002; dir., trauma services Tucson Med. Ctr., 1985—93; surgeon, dep. sheriff Pima County Sheriff's Dept., 1986—2002; CEO Kino County Cmty. Hosp., 1995—96, Pima Health Care System, 1997—99; chmn. State of Ariz. So. Regional Emergency Med. Sys., 1990—2002; surgeon gen. US Dept. Health & Human Services, Washington, 2002—06; vice chmn. Canyon Ranch, Tucson, 2006—, CEO health divsn., 2006—; pres. Canyon Ranch Inst., Tucson, 2006—; prof. pub. health, Mel & Enid Zuckerman Coll. Pub. Health U. Ariz., Tucson, 2006—. With US Army, 1967—70. Named one of Top 10 Latinos in Healthcare, LatinoLeaders mag., 2004. Fellow: Am. Coll. Surgeons.

CARNAHAN, ORVILLE DARRELL, state legislator, academic administrator; b. Elba, Idaho, Dec. 25, 1929; s. Marion Carlos and Leola Pearl (Putnam) C.; m. Colleen Arrott, Dec. 14, 1951; children: Karen, Jeanie, Orville Darrell, Carla. BS, Utah State U., 1958; MEd, U. Idaho, 1962, EdD, 1964. Vocat. dir., v.p. Yakima (Wash.) Valley Coll., 1964; chancellor Eastern Iowa C.C. Dist., Davenport, 1969—71; pres. Highline Coll., Midway, Wash., 1971—76; assoc. Utah Commn. for Higher Edn., Salt Lake City, 1976—78; pres. So. Utah U., Cedar City, 1978—81, Salt Lake C.C., Salt Lake City, 1981—90, pres. emeritus, 1990—; mem. Utah Ho. of Reps., 1993—99; ret., 1999. Cons. in field. Active Boy Scouts Am. Served with U.S. Army, 1952-54, Korea. Mem. Am. Vocat. Assn., NEA, Idaho Hist. Soc., Utah Hist. Soc., Alpha Tau Alpha, Phi Delta Kappa, Rotary Internat. Mem. LDS Ch. Home: 1653 Cornerstone Dr South Jordan UT 84095-5501 Office: Salt Lake CC 4600 S Redwood Rd Salt Lake City UT 84123-3197 Personal E-mail: odcarn@comcast.net.

CARNASE, THOMAS PAUL, graphics designer, consultant; b. Bronx, NY, Sept. 15, 1939; BFA, NYC CC, 1959. Assoc. designer Sudler & Hennessey, Inc., NYC, 1959-64; pres., designer Bonder & Carnase Studio, Inc., NYC, 1964-68; v.p., ptnr. Lubalin, Smith, Carnase, Inc., NYC, 1969-79; pres. Carnase, Inc., NYC, 1979—, Carnase Computer Typography, NYC, 1979—, World Typeface Ctr., Inc., NYC, 1981—. Adv. com. NYC CC, 1977—; guest lectr., juror in field. Exhibited in group show Whitney Mus. Am. Art, NYC; editor Ligature jour., 1981—; designer numerous typefaces; represented in permanent collection at Cooper Hewitt Nat. Design Mus. Recipient award of Excellence, Communication Arts mag.; cert. of Distinction Creativity mag.; archived drawings and records gifted to The Cary Graphic Arts Collection at Rochester Inst. Tech., 2004. Mem. NY Art Dirs. Club, NY Type Dirs. Club, Soc. Publ. Designers, Am. Inst. Graphic Arts Home: 300 E Molino Rd Palm Springs CA 92262 Office: Carnase Inc 300 East Molino Rd Palm Springs CA 92262

CARNESALE, ALBERT, engineering educator, former academic administrator; b. Bronx, NY, July 2, 1936; m. Robin Gerber, Apr. 6, 2002; children: Keith, Kimberly. BME, Cooper Union, 1957; MS, Drexel U., 1961, LLD (hon.), 1993; PhD, NC State U., 1966, LLD (hon.), 1997; AM (hon.), Harvard U., 1979; ScD (hon.), NJ Inst. Tech., 1984. Prof. NC State U., Raleigh, 1962—69, 1972—74, John F. Kennedy Sch. Govt., Harvard U., Cambridge, Mass., 1974—97, acad. dean, 1981—91, dean, 1991—95; provost, Lucius N. Littauer prof. pub. policy and adminstrn. Harvard U., 1994—97; chief def. weapons sys. US Arms Control and Disarmament Agy., Washington, 1969—72; chancellor UCLA, 1997—2006, prof. pub. policy, mechanical and aerospace engring., 2006—. Author: Nuclear Power Issues and Choices: Report of the Nuclear Energy Policy Study Group, 1977, Living with Nuclear Weapons, 1983, Hawks, Doves and Owls: An Agenda for Avoiding Nuclear War, 1985, Superpower Arms Control: Setting the Record Straight, 1987, Fateful Visions: Avoiding Nuclear Catastrophe, 1988; co-author: New Nuclear Nations: Consequences for US Policy, 1993. Recipient Gano Dunn award Outstanding Profl. Achievement, Cooper Union, NYC. Fellow: Am. Acad. Arts and Scis.; mem.: LA World Affairs Coun., Internat. Inst. for Strategic Studies, Coun. on Fgn. Rels. Business E-Mail: acarnesale@ucla.edu.

CARNEY, JANE W., lawyer; BA, U. Calif., Riverside; JD, U. Calif., Davis. Founding ptnr. Carney & Delany LLP, 1994—. Gov. bd. mem. S. Coast Air Quality Mgmt. Dist.; chair Citizens U. Com.; trustee Riverside Cmty. Coll.; vice chair Econ. Devel.; chair Mayor's Strategic Action Team for Good Jobs; bd. mem. James Irvine Found. Recipient Citizen of the Yr., Greater Riverside Chamber of Commerce, Woman of Achievement award, Black Voice News, Woman of the Yr. award, Calif. State Senate. Mem.: Riverside County Bar Assn. (former pres., former chair ad-hoc courts com., Krieger Meritorious Svc. award). Office: Carney Delany Llp 3850 Vine St Ste 240 Riverside CA 92507-4225

CARNEY, KEVIN, principal; b. 1969; Prin. Desert Sky Middle Sch., Vail Sch. Dist., Tucson. Mem. Boy Scouts and Girl Scouts of Am., sch. partnerships with Rita Ranch, YMCA and Southwest Youth Sports, Citizen Sch. Prog., Oasis Ch. Named one of 40 Under 40, Tucson Bus. Edge, 2006. Mem.: Homeowners Assn. Office: Desert Sky Middle School 9850 E Rankin Loop Tucson AZ 85747 Office Phone: 520-762-2704.

CARNOCHAN, WALTER BLISS, retired humanities educator; b. NYC, Dec. 20, 1930; s. Gouverneur Morris and Sibyll Baldwin (Bliss) C.; m. Nancy Powers Carter, June 25, 1955 (div. 1978); children—Lisa Powers, Sarah Bliss, Gouverneur Morris, Sibyll Carter; m. Brigitte Hoy Fields, Sept. 16, 1979. AB, Harvard, 1953, A.M., 1957, PhD, 1960. Asst. dean freshmen Harvard U., 1954-56; successively instr., asst. prof., assoc. prof., prof. English, Stanford (Calif.) U., 1960-94, prof. emeritus, 1994—, chmn. dept. English, 1971-73, dean grad. studies, 1975-80, vice provost, 1976-80, dir. Stanford Humanities Ctr., 1985-91, Anthony P. Meier Family prof. humanities, 1988-91, Richard W. Lyman prof. humanities, 1993-94, Richard W. Lyman prof. emeritus, 1994—, acting dir. Stanford Humanities Ctr., 1999. Mem. overseers com. to visit Harvard Coll, 1979-85, mem. bd. advisors Ehrenpreis Ctr. for Swift Studies, 1984—. Author: Lemuel Gulliver's Mirror for Man, 1968, Confinement and Flight: An Essay on English Literature of the 18th Century, 1977, Gibbon's Solitude: The Inward World of the Historian, 1987, The Battleground of the Curriculum: Liberal Education and American Experience, 1993, Momentary Bliss: An American Memoir, 1999, The Sad Story of Burton, Speke and the Nile; or was John Hanning Speke a Cad: Looking at the Evidence, 2006, Golden Legends: Images of Abyssinia, Samuel Johnson to Bob Marley, 2008. Trustee Mills Coll., 1978-85, Athenian Sch., 1975-88, Berkeley (Calif.) Art Mus., 1983-96, 98-2001. Home: 138 Cervantes Rd Portola Valley CA 94028-7725

CAROLLA, ADAM, actor, radio personality, film producer, scriptwriter; b. Phila., May 27, 1964; m. Lynette Helen Paradise, Sept. 28, 2002; children: Santino, Natalia. Carpenter; boxing trainer; co-founder Jackhole Industries. Appearances on (radio) Kevin and Bean Show, co-host Loveline, 1995—2005, Adam Carolla Show; actor: (films) Art House, 1998, Hairshirt, 1998, Splendor, 1999, Jay and Silent Bob Strike Back, 2001, (voice) Save Virgil, 2004, Farewell Bender, 2006, Head, Heart and Balls...or Why I Gave Up Smoking Pot, 2007; actor, exec. prodr., writer (films) The Hammer, 2007, co-host (TV series) Loveline, 1996—2000, writer The Man Show, 1999—2001, Jimmy Kimmel Live!, 2003; actor(voice): (TV series) Buzz Lightyear of Star Command, 2000, Family Guy, 2000—06, Drawn Together, 2004—08; writer, exec. prodr. (TV series) Crank Yankers, 2002; exec. prodr.: (TV series) Gerhard Reinke's Wanderlust, 2003, The Adam Carolla Project, 2005, The Andy Milonakis Show, 2005—06; performer: (TV series) Dancing with the Stars, 2008; exec. prodr.: (TV films) Windy City Heat, 2003; co-author: The Dr. Drew and Adam Book: A Survival Guide to Life and Love. Office: c/o The Adam Carolla Show CBS Radio 5670 Wilshire Blvd Ste 200 Los Angeles CA 90036

CARON, DAVID DENNIS, lawyer, educator; b. Hartford, Conn., June 28, 1952; s. Laurier Dennis and Rita Gertrude (Lafond) C.; m. R'Sue Popowich Caron, May 24, 1975; children: Peter, Marina. BS, USCG Acad., 1974; MSc, U. Wales, 1980; JD, U. Calif., Berkeley, 1983; diploma, Hague Acad. Internat. Law, 1984; Doctorandus, Leiden U., 1985, Dr. jur., 1990. Bar: Calif. 1983. Legal asst. Iran-U.S. Claims Tribunal, The Hague, The Netherlands, 1983-86; sr. rsch. fellow Max Planck Inst. Comparative Public & Internat. Law, 1985—86; assoc. Pillsbury, Madison & Sutro, San Francisco, 1986-87; C. William Maxeiner disting. prof. law U. Calif., Berkeley, Calif., 1987—; co-dir. Law of the Sea Inst., Earl Warren Legal Inst., Univ. Calif., Berkeley. Dir. studies, Hague Acad. Internat. Law, The Hague, The Netherlands, 1987; vis. prof. law Cornell U., 1990; mem. precedent panel, U.N. Compensation Commn.; mem. U.S. Dept. State adv. com. Public Internat. Law. Editor: Perspectives on U.S. Policy Toward the Law of the Sea, 1985, Law of the Sea: U.S. Policy Dilemma, 1983, Soclogocial and Social Dimensions of Global Change, 1994; editor-in-chief Ecology Law Quar., 1982-83; bd. editors Am. Jour. Internat. Law, 1991—; contbr. numerous articles to profl. jours. Lt. USCG, 1974-79. Fulbright scholar in U.K., 1979-80, Environ. Conservation fellow Nat. Wildlife Fedn., Washington, 1980-81; recipient Thelen Marrin prize for writing U. Calif., Berkeley, 1983, Deak prize for writing Am. Soc. Internat. Law, 1991. Mem. UN Assn., Internat. Studies Assn., Am. Soc. Internat. Law (exec. coun. 1990—), San Francisco Commn. on Fgn. Rels., Coun. on Fgn. Rels., Order of the Coif. Avocation: classical choral works. Home: 2750 Elmwood Ave Berkeley CA 94705-2312 Office: U Calif Sch Law Boalt Hall Berkeley CA 94720

CAROOMPAS, CAROLE JEAN, artist, educator; b. Oregon City, Nov. 14, 1946; d. John Thomas and Dorothy Lietta (Dirks) Caroompas. BA, Calif. State U., Fullerton, 1968; MFA in Painting, U. So. Calif., 1971. Instr. El Camino Coll., Torrance, Calif., 1971—72; vis. artist Calif. State U., Northridge, 1972—75; instr. Immaculate Heart Coll., LA, 1973—76; vis. artist Calif. State U., Fullerton, 1976—78; instr. U. Calif., Irvine, 1976—80, Claremont Grad. Sch., Calif., 1976—79, Art Ctr. Coll. Design, Pasadena, Calif., 1978—86, UCLA Ext., 1984—93; prof. fine arts Otis Coll. Art and Design, LA, 1981—. Vis. artist Anderson Ranch Art Ctr., Aspen, Colo., 1996, Aspen, 98, Aspen, 2005. One-woman shows include Jan Baum Art Gallery, LA, 1978—82, Karl Bornstein Gallery, 1985, LA Contemporary Exhbns., 1989, U. Calif., Irvine, 1990, Sue Spaid Fine Art, LA, 1992, 1994, P.P.O.W., NYC, 1994, Otis Coll. Art and Design Art Gallery, 1997—98, Mark Moore Gallery, Santa Monica, 1997, 1999, 2000, Western Project, Culver City, Calif., 2004, 2007, exhibited in group shows at Pasadena Mus. Art, 1972, Whitney Mus. Art, 1978, Mus. Modern Art1976, NYC, LA County Mus., 1982, Corcoran Gallery Art, Washington, 1993, Under Constrn. Armory Ctr. Arts, Pasadena, 1995, UCLA Hammer Mus. Art, 1996, 2000, LA County Mus. Art, 1996, Beaver Coll., 1996, LA Mcpl. Art Gallery, 1997, Calif. State U., Fullerton, 2001, San Jose Mus., 2002, Rosamund Felson Gallery, Santa Monica, 2003, Lewis and Clark Coll., Portland, Oreg., 2003, San Luis Obispo Art Ctr., 2003, Western Project, Culver City, 2006, 2006, The Lab., San Francisco, 2006, LA Mcpl. Art Gallery, 2007, Riverside Mus., Calif., 2007, Track 16, Santa Monica, 2007—08, Claremont Grad. U., 2008; singer: 2 individual albums, (albums) The Record: 13 Vocal Artists; contbr. articles to profl. jours. Grantee, NEA, 1987, 1993, Visual Arts Funding Initiative, Calif. Cmty. Found., 2005, Peter S. Reed Found., 2006; Faculty Devel. grantee, New Sch. Social Rsch., 1989, Support grantee, Esther and Adolph Gottlieb Found., 1993, Guggenheim Meml. fellow, 1995, Individual Artist's fellow, City of L.A. Cultural Affairs Dept., 2000, Peter S. Reed Found. grantee, 2006. Office: Otis Coll Art and Design 9045 Lincoln Blvd Los Angeles CA 90045-3505 Office Phone: 310-838-0609.

CARPENETI, WALTER L., state supreme court justice; b. San Francisco, Dec. 01; m. Anne Dose, 1969; children: Christian, Marianna, Lia, Bianca. AB in History with distinction, Stanford U., 1967; JD, U. Calif., Berkeley, 1970. Law clk. Justice John H. Dimond Alaska Supreme Ct., 1970-71; partner Carpeneti & Carpeneti, San Francisco, 1972-74; supervisor Alaska Public Defender Agency, Juneau, Alaska, 1974-78; partner Carpeneti & Council, Juneau, 1978-81; judge Alaska Superior Ct., Juneau, 1981-98; justice Alaska State Supreme Ct., Juneau, 1998—. Mem. Alaska Judicial Council, 1980—81, Alaska Commn. on Judicial Conduct, 1992—95. Office: Alaska Supreme Ct PO Box 114100 Juneau AK 99811-4100 Office Phone: 907-463-4771.

CARPENTER, FRANK CHARLES, JR., electronics engineer; b. LA, June 1, 1917; s. Frank Charles and Isobel (Crump) Carpenter; m. Beatrice Josephine Jolly, Nov. 3, 1951; children: Robert Douglas, Gail Susan, Carol Ann. BSEE cum laude, Calif. State U., Long Beach, 1975, MSEE, 1981. Self-employed design and mfr. aircraft test equipment, LA, 1946—51; engr. Hoffman Electronics Corp., LA, 1951—56, sr. engr., 1956—59, project mgr., 1959—62; engr.-scientist McDonnell-Douglas Astronautics Corp., Huntington Beach, Calif., 1963—69, spacecraft telemetry, 1963—67, biomed. electronics, 1967—69, flight test instrumentation, 1969—76; lab. test engr. Northrop Corp., Hawthorne, Calif., 1976—82, spl. engr., 1982—83, mgr. transducer calibration lab. Pico-Rivera, Calif., 1983—86. Contbr. articles to profl. jours. With USNR, 1941—47. Mem.: IEEE (life), Amateur Radio Relay League. Achievements include patents for transistor squelch circuit; helicaland whip antenna. Home: 2037 Balearic Dr Costa Mesa CA 92626-3514

CARPENTER, JOHN HOWARD, director, screenwriter; b. Carthage, NY, Jan. 16, 1948; s. Howard Ralph and Milton Jean (Carter) C; m. Adrienne Barbeau, Jan. 1, 1979 (div. 1984); m. Sandra Ann King, Dec. 1, 1990; 1 child, John Cody. Student, U. So. Calif., 1972. Co-writer, editor, composer: (short film) The Resurrection of Bronco Billy, 1970 (Academy award best live action short subject 1970); writer, prodr., dir., composer: (films) Dark Star, 1974; writer, dir., composer: (films) Assault on Precinct 13, 1976, Halloween, 1978, The Fog, 1980, Escape from New York, 1981, Prince of Darkness, 1987, They Live, 1988, Escape from L.A., 1996, Ghosts of Mars, 2001; writer, prodr., composer: (films) Halloween II, 1981; prodr., composer: (films) Halloween III: Season of the Witch, 1982; writer, prodr.: (films) The Fog, 2005; dir.: (films) The Thing, 1982, Starman, 1984, Memoirs of an Invisible Man, 1992, In the Mouth of Madness, 1994, Escape from L.A., 1996, Vampires, 1998, Halloween H2O, 1998; (TV movies) Elvis, 1979; dir., composer: (films) Christine, 1983, Big Trouble in Little China, 1986; exec. prodr.: (films) The Philadelphia Experiment, 1984, (TV movies) John Carpenter Presents Body Bags, 1993; writer: (films) The Eyes of Laura Mars, 1978, Black Moon Rising, 1986, (TV movies) Zuma Beach, 1978, Better Late Than Never, 1979, El Diablo, 1990, Blood River, 1991; writer, dir.: (TV movies) Someone's Watching Me!, 1978; composer: (films) Halloween V: The Revenge of Michael Myers, 1989. Mem. ASCAP, Dirs. Guild Am. West, Writers Guild Am. West. Avocations: music, helicopter piloting. Office: ICM 8942 Wilshire Blvd Beverly Hills CA 90211-1934

CARPENTER, KENNETH JOHN, retired nutrition educator; b. London, May 17, 1923; came to U.S., 1977; s. James Frederick and Dorothy (George) C.; m. Daphne Holmes, June 22, 1944 (dec. 1974); 1 child, Roger Hugh; m. Antonina Pecoraro, June 18, 1977. BA, U. Cambridge, Eng., 1944, PhD, 1948, ScD, 1974. Mem. sci. staff Rowett Inst., Aberdeen, Scotland, 1948-56; lectr., then reader in nutrition U. Cambridge, 1956-77; prof. nutrition U. Calif., Berkeley, 1977-91; ret. Author: History of Scurvy and Vitamin C, 1986, Protein and Energy, 1994, Beriberi, White Rice and Vitamin B, 2000; editor: Pellagra, 1982. Kellogg fellow Harvard U., 1955-56, Commonwealth fellow Cen. Food Tech. Rsch. Inst., Mysore, India, 1961, fellow Sidney Sussex Coll., Cambridge, U.K., 1961-77. Fellow Am. Inst. Nutritional Sci.(Atwater medal 1993, Hatch medal 1993); mem. History of Sci. Soc. Avocations: art history, gardening. Home: 6201 Rockwell St Oakland CA 94618-1350

CARPENTER, RAY WARREN, engineering educator, materials engineer; b. Berkeley, Calif., 1934; s. Fritz Josh and Ethel Thordis (Davisson) C.; m. Ann Louise Leavitt, July 10, 1955; children: Shannon R., Sheila A., Matthew L. BS in Engring., U. Calif., Berkeley, 1958, MS in Metallurgy, 1959, PhD in Metallurgy, 1966. Registered profl. engr., Calif. Sr. engr. Aerojet-Gen. Nucleonics, San Ramon, Calif., 1959-64; sr. metallurgist Stanford Rsch Inst., Menlo Park, Calif., 1966-67; mem. sr. rsch. staff Oak Ridge (Tenn.) Nat. Lab., 1967-80; prof. Solid State Sci. & Engring. Ariz. State U., Tempe, 1980—, prof. chem. and materials engring., 2003—, prof. sch. materials, 2007—, dir. Facility for High Resolution Electron Microscopy, 1980-83, dir. Ctr. for Solid State Sci., 1985-91, also bd. dirs. Ctr. for Solid State Sci. Chmn. doctoral program on sci. and engring. of materials, 1987-90, 94-98; vis. prof. U. Tenn., 1976-78; adj. prof. Vanderbilt U., Nashville, 1979-81. Contbg. author books; contbr. articles to profl. rsch. jour. and symposia; editor Phys. and Material Scis., Jour. of the Microscopy Soc. of Am., 1994-97; editor Microscopy and Microanalysis, 1995-2000; dep. editor Acta Materialia, 2001-2006. Recipient awards, Internat. Metallographic Soc. and Am. Soc. for Metals competition, 1976, 77, 79; Faculty Disting. Achievement award Ariz. State U. Alumni Assn., 1990. Mem. ASM Internat. (chpt. officer, vice chair 2005-06), Electron Microscopy Soc. Am. (pres. 1989, dir. phys. sci. 1980-83), Metall. Soc. of AIME, Materials Rsch. Soc., Am. Phys. Soc., Am. Ceramic Soc., Sigma Xi. Office: Ariz State U Ctr Solid State Sci Tempe AZ 85287-1704 Home Phone: 480-354-5299; Office Phone: 480-965-4549. Business E-Mail: carpenter@asu.edu.

CARPENTER, STEVEN A., Internet company executive; Studied at, London Sch. Econs., 1992; BA cum laude, Tufts U., 1994; MBA, Harvard U., 2004. Sr. mgr. bus. devel. Snapfish.com Corp., 2000—01; dir. bus. devel. myCFO, 2000—02; sr. products mgr. RealNetworks, Inc., 2004—05, sr. dir. strategy and bus. ops. Digital Music Divsn., 2005—06; founder, CEO Cake Fin. Corp., San Francisco, 2001—. Lectr. Harvard U. Office: Cake Fin 500 Third St, Ste 260 San Francisco CA 94107

CARR, DAVID TURNER, physician; b. Richmond, Va., Mar. 12, 1914; s. John Ernest and Mary Lela (King) Carr; m. Rosemary Rudow, June 18, 1948 (div. 1953); 1 child, Jennifer Anne Carr Oderkirk; m. Christine Nadeau, Dec. 27, 1979. Student, U. Richmond, 1931-33; MD, Med. Coll. Va., 1937; MS in Medicine, Mayo Grad. Sch. Medicine, 1947. Intern, then asst. resident Grady Hosp., Atlanta, 1937-39; resident chest diseases Bellevue Hosp., NYC, 1940-41; fellow medicine Mayo Clinic, 1943-47, cons. medicine, 1947-79, chmn. dept. oncology, 1975; dir. Mayo Comprehensive Cancer Ctr., 1975; assoc. dir. Ctr. Cancer Control, 1976-79; prof. medicine Mayo Med. Sch., 1964-79, M.D. Anderson Hosp. and Tumor Inst., Tex. Med. Ctr., Houston, 1979-92; med.-legal cons., 1992—. Mem.-at-large bd. dirs. Am. Lung Assn., 1959—74, v.p., 1971—72; bd. dirs. Rochester Civic Theatre, 1951—70, pres., 1965—67; bd. dirs. at large Am. Cancer Soc., 1967—74, pres. Minn. divsn., 1974—75, mem. am. joint com. cancer, 1971—79, chmn. am. joint com. cancer, 1979—82. Fellow: AAAS, ACP; mem.: Am. Thoracic Soc. (v.p. 1963—64), Internat. Assn. Study Lung Cancer (v.p. 1974—76, pres. 1976, treas. 1976—82), Ctrl. Soc. Clin. Rsch., Peruvian Atni-Tb Assn. (hon.), Rochester C. of C. (pres. 1959—60). Achievements include research in pulmonary diseases. Home and Office: PO Box 9300 Rancho Santa Fe CA 92067 Office Phone: 858-759-1798.

CARR, GERALD FRANCIS, language educator; b. Pitts., Dec. 29, 1930; s. James Patrick and Hannah (Sweeney) C.; m. Irmengard Rauch, June 12, 1965; children: Christopher, Gregory. EdB, Duquesne U., 1958; MA, U. Wis., 1960, PhD, 1968. Instr. in German Duquesne U., Pitts., 1960-62, asst. prof. German, 1964-68; tchg. asst. U. Wis., Madison, 1962-64; asst. prof. German Ea. Ill. U., Charleston, 1968-70, assoc. prof. German, 1970-75, prof. German, 1975-87, Calif. State U., Sacramento, 1987—. Co-editor: Linguistic Method: Essays in Honor of Herbert Penzl, 1979, The Signifying Animal: The Grammar of Language and Experience, 1980, Language Change, 1983, The Semiotic Bridge, 1989, On Germanic Linguistics, 1992, Insights in Germanic Linguistics I, 1995, Insights in Germanic Linguistics II, 1996, Semiotics Around the World, 1996, Essays for Irmengard Rauch, 1998, New Insights in Germanic Linguistics I, 1999, New Insights in Germanic Linguistics II, 2000, New Insights in Germanic Linguistics III, 2002; series editor: Studies in Old Germanic Languages and Literatures, assoc. editor: Interdisciplinary Jour. for Germanic Linguistics and Semiotic Analysis. Cpl. USMC, 1951—54. Dist. tchg. fellow, U. Wis., 1966. Mem. MLA, Internat. Assn. for Semiotic Studies (co-dir. 5th congress 1994), Am. Coun. Tchrs. Fgn. Lang., Semiotic Soc. Am., Am. Assn. Tchrs. of German, Soc. German Philology, Calif. Fgn. Lang. Tchr. Assn., Semiotic Circle Calif., Kappa Phi Kappa, Delta Phi Alpha. Avocations: books, antiques. Office: Calif State U 6000 J St Sacramento CA 95819-2605 Home Phone: 707-746-7480; Office Phone: 916-278-6379.

CARR, JAMES FRANCIS, lawyer; b. Buffalo, May 7, 1946; s. Maurice Kilner and Cecelia Francis (Harmon) C.; children: James Robert, Marguerite Louise. BS, USAF Acad., 1968; JD, George Washington U., 1971. Bar: D.C. 1972, Mich. 1972, Pa. 1972, U.S. Dist. Ct. D.C. 1972, U.S. Ct. Appeals (D.C. cir.) 1972, U.S. Supreme Ct. 1975, Colo. 1979, U.S. Dist. Ct. Colo. 1979, U.S. Ct. Appeals (10th cir.) 1979. Atty. Unity Ctr., Meadville, Pa., 1971-73; asst. pros. atty. Genesee County, Flint, Mich., 1973-79; 1st asst. atty. gen. State of Colo., Denver, 1979-82, 85—; assoc. Sumners, Miller & Clark, Denver, 1982-83, Miles & McManus, Denver, 1983-85. Mem. Colo. Bd. Law Examiners, 1992-02; spkr. in field. Contbr. articles to profl. jours. Mem. Mich. Pub. Consultation Panel of Internat. Joint Commn., 1976-78; treas. Denver South High Sch. PTSA, 1988-91, pres., 1991-93; athletic dir. Most Precious Blood Sch., 1988-90; bd. dirs. Pioneer Jr. Hockey Assn., 1988-90. Mem.: ATLA, ABA (tort and ins. practice sect., chmn. environ. law com. 1978—81, editor-in-chief The Brief 1981—87, liaison jud. adminstrn. divsn. 1987—90, chmn. govt. liability com. 1988—89, mem. coun. govt. and pub. sector lawyers divsn. 1991—97, chmn. govt. liability com. 1992—93, commn. on mental and phys. disability law 1995—2001, chmn. emerging issues com. 1996—97, sect. sec. 1997—99, ho. of dels. 1997—2002, chmn. commn. on mental and phys. disability law 1998—2001, TIPS coun. 1999—2002, standing com. pub. edn. 2001—04, ho. of dels. 2004—), Colo. Bar Assn. (chmn. profl. discipline com. 1992—93, chmn. health law sect. 1993—94, program chmn. ann. meeting 1993—94, chmn. law edn. com. 1993—96, chair publs. com. 1995—97, chmn. profl. discipline com. 1998—99, bd. govs. 2003—05, chair ADR sect. 2004—05, coun. licensure enforcement and regulation), Denver Bar Assn. (chmn. pub. legal ednl. com. 1989—91, ABA del. 1997—2002, chmn. pub. legal ednl. com. 1999—2004, trustee 2002—05). Democrat. Roman Catholic. Home: 10406 W Glasgow Ave Littleton CO 80127-3468 Office: Atty Gen Office 1525 Sherman St Fl 5 Denver CO 80203-1760 Home Phone: 303-978-1776; Office Phone: 303-866-5283. Business E-Mail: jim.carr@state.co.us.

CARR, MICHAEL HAROLD, geologist; b. Leeds, Eng., May 26, 1935; came to U.S., 1956, naturalized, 1965; s. Harry and Monica Mary (Burn) C.; m. Rachel F. Harvey, Apr. 14, 1961; son, Ian M. B.Sc., London U., 1956; MS, Yale U., 1957, PhD, 1960. Rsch. assoc. U. Western Ont., 1960-62; with U.S. Geol. Survey, 1962—; chief astrogeologic studies br. U. Geol. Survey, Menlo Park, Calif., 1973-79; mem. Mariner Mars Imaging Team, 1969-73; leader Viking Mars Orbiter Imaging Team, 1969-80; mem. Voyager and Galileo Jupiter Imaging Teams, 1978—. Interdisciplinary scientist, Mars Global Surveyor. Author: The Surface of Mars, The Geology of the Terrestrial Planets, Water on Mars. Recipient Exceptional Sci. Achievement medal NASA, 1977, Disting. Svc. award Dept. of Interior, 1988, Lifetime Achievement award in space sci. and tech. Nat. Air and Space Mus., 1994. Fellow Geol. Soc. Am., Am. Geophys. Union. Home: 1389 Canada Rd Redwood City CA 94062-2452 Office: US Geol Survey 345 Middlefield Rd Menlo Park CA 94025-3591

CARR, RUTH MARGARET, plastic surgeon; b. Waco, Tex., July 2, 1951; MD, U. Okla., 1977. Intern U. Okla. Med. Sch., Oklahoma City, 1977-78; resident U. Okla. Health Sci. Ctr., Oklahoma City, 1978-81, UCLA, 1981-83; plastic surgeon St. John's Hosp., 1989—. Clin. asst. prof. UCLA, 1983—, U. So. Calif., 1984-. Mem.: Bay Surgical Soc. (pres. 2004), Calif. Soc. Plastic Surgeons (parliamentarian 2004—05), Am. Soc. Plastic Surgeons. Office: 1301 20th St Ste 470 Santa Monica CA 90404-2082 Home Phone: 310-284-8321; Office Phone: 310-315-0222. Business E-Mail: rcarr@ucla.edu.

CARR, THOMAS A., lawyer; BA in Sociology, St. John's U., NY, 1979; JD with highest honors, NY Law Sch., 1984. Former asst. US atty., NY; former partner Barrett, Gilman & Ziker; city atty. Seattle, 2001—. Mem. King County Bd. Developmentally Disabled, Wash., 1995—97, Metro S.W. Sounding Bd., Wash., 1997—98, Elevated Transp. Co. Coun., Seattle, 1998—, chmn., 1998—2001; mem. King County Metro Transit Adv. Com., 1999—. Mem.: King County Bar Assn. Office: 600 4th Ave 4th Fl PO Box 94769 Seattle WA 98124-4769 E-mail: thomas.carr@seattle.gov.

CARR, WILLARD ZELLER, JR., retired lawyer; b. Richmond, Ind., Dec. 18, 1927; s. Willard Zeller and Susan (Brownell) C.; m. Margaret Paterson, Feb. 15, 1952; child: Jeffrey Westcott. BS, Purdue U., 1948; JD, Ind. U., 1951. Bar: Calif. 1951, U.S. Supreme Ct. 1963. Ptnr. Gibson, Dunn & Crutcher, Los Angeles, 1952—. Mem. nat. panel arbitrators Am. Arbitration Assn.; former labor relations cons. State of Alaska; lectr. bd. visitors Southwestern U. Law Sch.; mem. adv. council Southwestern Legal Found., Internat. and Comparative Law Ctr. Trustee Calif. Adminstrv. Law Coll.; bd. dirs. Employers' Group, Calif. State Pks. Found., L.A. coun. Boy Scouts Am.; mem. Mayor's Econ. Devel. Policies Com.; past chmn. Pacific Legal Found.; past chmn. men's adv. com. Los Angeles County-U. So. Calif. Med. Ctr. Aux. for Recruitment, Edn. and Service; past chmn. bd. Wilshire Republican Club; past mem. Rep. State Ctrl. Com.; past mem. pres.'s coun. Calif. Mus. Sci. and Industry; mem. Nat. Def. Exec. Res., L.A. World Affairs Coun.; chmn. bd. councilors Andrus Sch. Gerontology, U. So. Calif.; bd. dirs., sec. L.A. Police Meml. Found.; past chmn. L.A. sect. United Way; mem. adv. com. Los Angeles County Human Rels. Commn., past commr., Calif. State World Trade Commn.; former chmn. L.A. chpt. ARC. Fellow Am. Bar Found.; mem. Internat. Bar. Assn. (past chmn. labor law com. of bus. law sect., past chmn. labor employment practice group), The Federalist Soc., Calif. Bar Assn., L.A. County Bar Assn., L.A. C. of C. (past chmn. 1980), Calif. C. of C. (past chmn., 1991) Office: Gibson Dunn & Crutcher 333 S Grand Ave 49th Fl Los Angeles CA 90071-3197 Office Phone: 213-229-7238. Business E-Mail: wcarr@gibsondunn.com.

CARRARO, JOSEPH J., state legislator; b. Queens, NY; son of Joseph G Carraro & Katherine C; married 1976 to Linda Foster, division; children: Kitty, Mia, Joey & Lisa. New Mexico State Senator, District 23, 1985-88 & 1993-, chairman, Joint Legislature Investment Committee, formerly, vice chairman, Senate Education Committee, Senate Corp Committee & Legislature Education Study, formerly, Nat Conf of State Legislature Committee on Governor Oper, formerly, member, Education & Judiciary Committees, formerly, Finance & Ways & Means Committees, currently, New Mexico State Senate.Stock broker, Merrill Lynch, New York, 1970-74; owner, restaurant, 1980-95; consultant, Carraro and Assoc Int Bus Consult, 1987-; professor, Univ Phoenix, 1996-2001. Auth, Manuscript, The Convenience Ethic. Small Businessman of Year, Chamber of Commerce. Kiwanis Club; Optimists Club; Exec Management Association. Republican. Roman Catholic. Address: 10216 Carraro PL NW Albuquerque NM 87114 Mailing: State Capitol Rm 110 Santa Fe NM 87503 Office Phone: 505-986-4387. E-mail: jcarraro@state.nm.us; joecarraro@aol.com.

CARREL, ANNETTE FELDER, writer; b. San Francisco, Dec. 11, 1929; m. Robert E. Carrel (dec. 1989); 3 children. AA, Notre Dame Coll.; BA, Lone Mountain Coll.; MA in Spl. Edn., U. Calif., San Francisco. Home: 501 Via Casitas Apt 1107 Greenbrae CA 94904-1939

CARRERE, TIA (ALTHEA RAE DUHINIO JANAIRO), actress; b. Honolulu, Jan. 2, 1967; d. Alexander and Audrey Janairo; m. Elie Samaha Nov. 22, 1992 (div. Feb., 2000); m: Simon Wakelin Dec. 31, 2002; 1 child Bianca. Profl. model. Actress (films): Zombie Nightmare, 1987, Aloha Summer, 1988, The Road Raiders, 1989, Fatal Mission, 1990, Instant Karma, 1990, Showdown in Little Tokyo, 1991, Harley Davidson and the Marlboro Man, 1991, Shutdown in Little Tokyo, 1991, Little Sister, 1992, Wayne's World, 1992, Rising Sun, 1993, Quick, 1993, Wayne's World 2, 1993, Treacherous, 1994, Hostile Intentions, 1994, True Lies, 1994, My Teacher's Wife, 1995, The Immortals, 1995 (also assoc. prodr.), Learning Curves, Hollow Point, Bad with Numbers, Jury Duty, 1995, Hollow Point, 1996, High School High, 1996, Top of the World, 1997, Kull the Conqueror, 1997, Scar City, 1998, 20 Dates, 1998 (also exec. prodr.), Merlin: The Return, 1999, Meet Prince Charming, 1999, Five Aces, 1999, Torn Apart, 2004, Back in the Day, 2005; (TV movies) Intimate Stranger, 1992, Nothing But the Truth, 1995, Natural Enemy, 1997, Dogboys, 1998; (TV guest appearances) The A-Team, 1986, MacGyver, 1986, 1988, Tour of Duty, 1987, Anything But Love, 1989, Quantum Leap, 1990, Married With Children, 1990, Tales for the Crypt, 1992, The New Hollywood Squares, Murphy's Law, General Hospital, 1985-87, The Road Raiders, 1989, Fine Gold, 1990, Murder One, 1995-96, Veronica's Closet, 1998, Relic Hunter, 1999-2002; (TV spl.) Circus of the Stars; (TV miniseries) Noble House, 1988, Supernova, 2005; performer (TV series) Dancing with the Stars, 2006; co-exec. prodr. If...Dog...Rabbit..., 1999; (voice actress) Happily Ever After: Fairy Tales for Every Child, 1995, Hercules, 1998, The Night of the Headless Horseman, 1999, Lilo & Stitch, 2002, Stitch! The Movie, 2003, Aloha, Scooby-Doo, 2005, Duck Dodgers, 2004-05, Megas XLR, 2004, Lilo & Stitch 2: Stitch Has a Glitch, 2005, American Dragon:Jake Long, 2005, Lilo & Stitch: The Series, 2003, Leroy & Stitch, 2006; presenter The MTV Movie Awards, 1992; singer (albums) Dream, 1993, Hawaiiana, 2007, (with Daniel Ho) 'Ikena, 2008 (Grammy award for Best Hawaiian Music Album, 2009). Recipient Female Star 1994 award NATO/Sho West; named one of 50 Most Beautiful People in the World, People Mag., 1992. Office: United Talent Agy 9560 Wilshire Blvd Fl 5 Beverly Hills CA 90212-2400

CARREY, JIM, actor; b. Newmarket, Ont., Can., Jan. 17, 1962; s. Percy and Kathleen Carrey; m. Melissa Womer, Mar. 28, 1987 (div. Dec. 11, 1995); 1 child, Jane; m. Lauren Holly Sept. 23, 1996 (div. July 29, 1997). Actor: (films) Finders Keepers, 1984, Once Bitten, 1985, Peggy Sue Got Married, 1986, The Dead Pool, 1988, Earth Girls Are Easy, 1989, Pink Cadillac, 1989, High Strung, 1991, Ace Ventura: Pet Detective, 1993 (also screenwriter), The Mask, 1994, Dumb and Dumber, 1994, Batman Forever, 1995, Ace Ventura: When Nature Calls, 1995, The Mask's Revenge, 1996, Liar, Liar, 1996, The Cable Guy, 1996, The Truman Show, 1997 (Golden Globe award for best performance by an actor in a motion picture 2000), Simon Birch, 1998, Man on the Moon, 1999 (Golden Globe for best performance by an actor in a motion picture 2000), Me, Myself and Irene, 2000, How the Grinch Stole Christmas, 2000, The Majestic, 2001, Bruce Almighty, 2003, Eternal Sunshine of the Spotless Mind, 2004, Lemony Snicket's A Series of Unfortunate Events, 2004, The Number 23, 2007, (voice) Horton Hears a Who!, 2008, Yes Man, 2008; actor, prodr. (films) Fun with Dick and Jane, 2005; actor (TV series) The Duck Factory, 1984, In Living Color, 1990-94; (TV movies) Mike Hammer: Murder Takes All, 1989, Doing Time on Maple Drive, 1992 Star on the Hollywood Walk of Fame, 2000, Muhammad Ali Celebrity Entertainer award, 2006; named one of 50 Most Powerful People in Hollywood, 2004-06. Office: Creative Artists Agency 2000 Avenue Of The Stars Los Angeles CA 90067-4700

CARREY, NEIL, lawyer, educator; b. Bronx, NY, Nov. 19, 1942; s. David L. and Betty (Kurtzburg) Carrey; m. Karen Krysher, Apr. 9, 1980; children: Jana, Crhistopher;children from previous marriage: Scott, Douglas, Dana. BS in Econs., U. Pa., 1964; JD, Stanford U., 1967. Bar: Calif. 1968. Mem. firm, v.p. corp. DeCastro, West, Chodorow, Inc., LA, 1967-97; of counsel Jenkens & Gilchrist, LA, 1998—2007, Baker & Hostetler LLP, LA, 2007—. Instr. program legal paraprofls. U. So. Calif., 1977—89, lectr. Dental Sch., 1987—; lectr. Employee Benefits Inst., Kansas City, Mo., 1996. Author: Nonqualified Defered Compensation Plans-The Wave of the Future, 1985. Treas. Nat. Little League, Santa Monica, 1984—85, pres., 1985—86, coach, 1990—95; referee, coach Am. Soccer Youth Orgn., 1989—95; officer Vista Del Mar Child Care Ctr., LA, 1968—84; coach Bobby Sox Softball Team, Santa Monica, Calif., 1986—88, bd. dirs., 1988, umpire in chief, 1988; pres. Gail Dorin Music Found., 1994—; bd. dirs. Santa Monica Youth Athletic Found., 1995—2004, Santa Monica Police Activities League, 1995—, pres., 1999—2001; dir. Small Bus. Coun. Am., 1995—, Santa Monica HS Booster Club, 1995—97; v.p. Sneaker Sisters, 1996—2001; pres. Santa Monica Jr. Rowing, 1997—2002; legal cons. 33d Dist. Calif. PTA, 1997—99; sec. Santa Monica Leaders Club, 1999—2000; women's sports adv. bd. U. Pa., 1998—2003; pres. Chris Carrey Charitable Found., 2000—; v.p. bd. Ivan and Sam Found., 2002—05; active Cir. of Care Children's Hosp., 2003—; chair coms. Santa Monica-Malibu Sch. Dist., 1983—2004, prop 39 bond oversight com., 2007—, vice chmn.; recreation and parks commr. City of Santa Monica, 1999—; bd. dirs. Padres Contra el Cancer, 2001—03, v.p., 2002—03, pres., 2003—05, pres. emeritus, 2005—06. Mem.: LWV (dir. 1997—2003), Santa Monica Pier (steering com. mem.), Stop Cancer (ways & means com. mem.), Acad. Country Music, Country Music Assn., U. Pa. Alumni Soc. (pres. 1971—79, dir. 1979—87), Children's Hosp. L.A. (adv. coun. 2001—, new hosp. com. 2007), Mountaingate Tennis Club, Alpha Kappa Psi (life). Jewish. Home: 616 23d St Santa Monica CA 90402-3130 Office: 12100 Wilshire Blvd Fl 15 Los Angeles CA 90025-7120 Office Phone: 310-442-8835. Business E-Mail: ncarrey@bakerlaw.com.

CARRICA, JEAN LEON, business educator; b. Albuquerque, June 1, 1931; s. Jean and Marie (Louissena) C.; m. Margaret Kiser, Jan. 24, 1938; children: Annette, Brigitte, Michelle, Loren, John, JD, Creighton U., 1961; MBA, Ind. U., 1963; PhD, U. Nebr., 1967. Asst. prof. Rockhurst Coll., Kansas City, Mo., 1965-67; assoc. prof. Creighton U., Omaha, 1967-73, dean Sch. Bus., 1973-82, Loyola Coll., Balt., 1982-84; prof. Gonzaga U., Spokane, Wash., 1984—. Pro bono cons. on small bus. Co-author: (book) Present Value Applications for Accountants, 1990; contbr. numerous articles to profl. jours. Mem. Greater Balt. Com., 1982-84; pres. Legion of Mary Curia, Spokane, 1988-94. Staff sgt. USAF, 1951-54. Mem. Beta Gamma Sigma (pres. 1993—). Home: 14766 Boyd St Omaha NE 68116-6654

CARRICO, STEPHEN J., construction company executive; b. 1954; Grad., Ctrl. Mich. U., 1977. CPA. With Straka, Jarackas & Co., Detroit, 1977-84; various positions Hensel Phelps Constrn. Co., Greeley, Colo., 1984—, now v.p. fin. Office: Hensel Phelps Construction 420 Sixth Ave Greeley CO 80632

CARRIGAN, JIM R., arbitrator, mediator, retired judge; b. Mobridge, SD, Aug. 24, 1929; s. Leo Michael and Mildred Ione (Jaycox) C.; m. Beverly Jean Halpin, June 2, 1956. PhB, JD, U. N.D., 1953; LLM in Taxation, NYU, 1956; LLD (hon.), U. Colo., 1989, Suffolk U., 1991, U. N.D., 1997. Bar: N.D. 1953, Colo. 1956. Asst. prof. law U. Denver, 1956—59; vis. assoc. prof. NYU Law Sch., 1958, U. Wash. Law Sch., 1959—60; Colo. jud. adminstr., 1960—61; prof. law U. Colo., 1961—67; ptnr. Carrigan & Bragg (and predecessors), 1967—76; bd. regents U. Colo., 1975—76; justice Colo. Supreme Ct., 1976—79; judge U.S. Dist. Ct. Colo., 1979—95. Mem. Colo. Bd. Bar Examiners, 1969-71; lectr. Nat. Coll. State Judiciary, 1964-77, 95; bd. dirs. Nat. Inst. Trial Advocacy, 1971-2006, chmn. bd. 1986-88, also mem. faculty, 1972—; adj. prof. law U. Colo, 1984, 1991—; bd. dirs. Denver Broncos Stadium Dist., 1996—; mem. steering com. new U. Colo. Law Bldg., 2005-. Editor-in-chief: N.D. Law Rev., 1952-53, Internat. Soc. Barristers Quar., 1972-79; editor: DICTA, 1957-59; contbr. articles to profl. jours. Bd. visitors U. N.D. Coll. Law, 1983-85. Recipient Disting. Svc. award Nat. Coll. State Judiciary, 1969, Outstanding Alumnus award U. N.D., 1973, Regent Emeritus award U. Colo., 1977, B'nai Brith Civil Rights award, 1986, Thomas More Outstanding Lawyer award Cath. Lawyers Guild, 1988, Oliphant Disting. Svc. award Nat. Inst. Trial Advocacy, 1993, Constl. Rights award Nat. Assn. Blacks in Criminal Justice (Colo. chpt.), 1992, Disting. Svc. award Colo. Bar Assn., 1994, Amicus Curiae award ATLA, 1994, Colo. Trial Lawyers Assn. Lifetime Achievement award, 2000. Fellow Colo. Bar Found., Boulder County Bar Found.; mem. ABA (action com. on tort system improvement 1985-87, TIPS sect. long range planning com., 1986-97; coun. 1987-91, task force on initiatives and referenda 1990-92, size of civil juries task force 1988-90, class actions task force 1995-97), Colo. Bar Assn., Boulder County Bar Assn., Denver Bar Assn., Cath. Lawyers Guild, Inns. of Ct., Internat. Soc. Barristers, Internat. Acad. Trial Lawyers (bd. dirs. 1995—), Fed. Judges Assn. (bd. dirs. 1985-89), Am. Judicature Soc. (bd. dirs. 1985-89), Tenth Circuit Dist. Judges Assn. (sec. 1991-92, v.p. 1992-93, pres. 1994-95), Order of Coif, Phi Beta Kappa, Arrupe Jesuit HS (bd. trustees 2008-). Roman Catholic. Office: Judicial Arbiter Group 1601 Blake St Ste 400 Denver CO 80202-1328 Office Phone: 303-572-1919, 303-494-1444. Personal E-mail: carrigan2350@earthlink.net. Business E-Mail: info@jaginc.com.

CARRIKER, ROBERT CHARLES, history professor; b. St. Louis, Aug. 18, 1940; s. Thomas B. and Vivian Ida (Spaunhorst) C.; m. Eleanor R. Gualdoni, Aug. 24, 1963; children: Thomas A., Robert M., Andrew J. BS, St. Louis U., 1962, AM, 1963; PhD, U. Okla., 1967. Asst. prof. Gonzaga U., Spokane, Wash., 1967-71, assoc. prof., 1972-76, prof. history, 1976—2002, disting. prof. Coll. Arts and Scis., 2003—. Author: Fort Supply, Indian Territory, 1970, 90, The Kalispel People, 1973, Father Peter De Smet, 1995, 1998, (with Harry Fritz) America Looks West, 2002, Ocian in View!, 2005; editor: (with Eleanor R. Carriker) Army Wife on the Frontier, 1975, (with William L. Lang) Great River of the West, 1999; book rev. editor Columbia mag., 1987—. Mem. Wash. Lewis and Clark Trail Com., 1978-99; commr. Wash. Maritime Bicentennial, Olympia, 1989-92; bd. dirs. Wash. Commn. for Humanities, Seattle, 1988-94. Burlington No. Found. scholar, 1985, 96; recipient Disting. Svc. award Lewis and Clark Trail Heritage Found., 1989. Mem. Wash. State Hist. Soc. (trustee 1981-90, v.p. 1993-2000), Western Hist. Assn., Phi Alpha Theta (councilor 1985-87), exec. coun., Phi Alpha Theta (History Honor Soc.) Roman Catholic. Avocations: travel, photography, cartography. Office: Gonzaga U 502 E Boone Ave Spokane WA 99258-0001 Business E-Mail: carriker@gonzaga.edu.

CARRIL, PETE (PETER J. CARRIL), professional basketball consultant; b. Bethlehem, Pa., July 10, 1930; m. Dolores L. Halteman; children: Lisa, Peter. B, Lafayette Coll., 1952; MA in Ednl. Adminstrn., Lehigh U., Pa. Basketball coach Easton HS, Pa., Reading HS, Pa.; head coach Lehigh U. Mountain Hawks, 1966—67, Princeton U. Tigers, NJ, 1967—96; asst. coach Sacramento Kings, 1996—2006, cons., 2009—. Co-author: The Smart Take from the Strong: The Basketball Philosophy of Pete Carril, 1997. Named to Naismith Basketball Hall of Fame, 1997. Achievements include head coach of the National Invitational Tournament winning Princeton Tigers, 1975; being the winningest coach in Ivy League history (525-273). Office: Sacramento Kings Arco Arena One Sports Pky Sacramento CA 95834*

CARRINGTON, JAMES C., botanist, educator; BS, U. Calif., Riverside, 1982; PhD, U. Calif., Berkeley, 1986. Prof., fellow Inst. Biol. Chemistry Wash. State U., Pullman. Recipient Ruth Allen award Am. Phytopathol. Soc., 2000. Office: Inst Biol Chemistry Wash State U PO Box 646340 Pullman WA 99164-6340

CARROLL, EARL HAMBLIN, federal judge; b. Tucson, Mar. 26, 1925; s. John Vernon and Ruby (Wood) C.; m. Louise Rowlands, Nov. 1, 1952; children: Katherine Carroll Pearson, Margaret Anne BSBA, U. Ariz., 1948, LLB, 1951. Bar: Ariz., US Ct. Appeals (9th and 10th cirs.), US Ct. of Claims, US Supreme Ct. Law clk. Ariz. Supreme Ct., Phoenix, 1951-52; assoc. Evans, Kitchel & Jenckes, Phoenix, 1952-56, ptnr., 1956-80; judge US Dist. Ct. Ariz., Phoenix, 1980—, sr. judge, 1994—. Spl. counsel City of Tombstone, Ariz., 1962-65, Maricopa County, Phoenix, 1968-75, City of Tucson, 1974, City of Phoenix, 1979; designated mem. US Fgn. Intelligence Surveillance Court by Chief Justice US Supreme Ct., 1993-99; chief judge Alien Terrorist Removal Ct., 1996-01, 2001—06. Mem. City of Phoenix Bd. of Adjustment, 1955-58; trustee Phoenix Elem. Sch. Bd., 1961-72; mem. Gov.'s Council on Intergovtl. Relations, Phoenix, 1970-73; mem. Ariz. Bd. Regents, 1978-80. Served with USNR, 1943-46; PTO Recipient Nat. Service awards Campfire, 1973, 75, Alumni Service award U. Ariz., 1980, Disting. Citizen award No. Ariz. U., Flagstaff, 1983, Bicentenial award Georgetown U., 1988, Disting. Citizen award U. Ariz., 1990, Sidney S. Woods Alumni Svc. award, 2000, Disting. Alumnus award, 2007. Fellow Am. Coll. Trial Lawyers, Am. Bar Found.; mem. ABA, Ariz. Bar Assn., U. Ariz. Law Coll. Assn. (pres. 1975), Sigma Chi (Significant Sig award 1991, Hall of Fame award 2007), Phi Delta Phi. Democrat. Office: US Dist Ct US Courthouse Ste 521 401 W Washington SPC 48 Phoenix AZ 85003-2151 Office Phone: 602-322-7530.

CARROLL, ELLEN A., judge, lawyer; b. San Francisco, Feb. 6, 1947; BA, Mundelein Coll., 1970; JD with honors, U. San Francisco, 1980. Bar: Calif. 1980. Law clk. to Hon. Lloyd King No. Dist. Calif., 1981; partner Bronson, Bronson & McKinnon, San Francisco, 1988-93; counsel Murphy, Weir & Butler, San Francisco, 1993-98; judge U.S. Bankruptcy Ct., LA, 1998—. Com. lawyer reps. of U.S. Bankruptcy Ct. No. Dist. Calif., 1988-90. Mem. ABA (bus. bankruptcy com., uniform comml. code com., bus. law sect. 1990—), State Bar Calif. (mem. uniform comml. code com. 1985-88), Bar Assn. San Francisco (bd. dirs. 1992—, chair 1989, comml. law and bankruptcy sect.), Bay Area Bankruptcy Forum (bd. dirs. 1991-92). Address: US Bankruptcy Ct Cent Calif 1634 Roybal Fed Bldg & US Ct House 255 E Temple St Los Angeles CA 90012-3332

CARROLL, KAREN COLLEEN, pathologist, infectious diseases specialist; b. Balt., Nov. 7, 1953; d. Charles Edward and Ida May (Simms) C.; m. Bruce Cameron Marshall, Feb. 13, 1982; children: Kevin Charles Marshall, Brian Thomas Marshall. BA, Coll. Notre Dame of Md., 1975; MD, U. Md., 1979. Diplomate Am. Bd. Internal Medicine, Am. Bd. Infectious Diseases, Am. Bd. Pathology. Intern U. Md., 1979-80, U. Rochester, AHP, 1980-82, chief med. resident in internal medicine, 1982-83; fellow infectious diseases U. Mass., 1984-86; fellow med. microbiology Health Scis. Ctr. U. Utah, 1989-90; asst. prof. pathology U. Utah Med. Ctr., Salt Lake City, 1990-97, adj. asst. prof. infectious diseases, 1990-97, assoc. prof. pathology, adj. assoc. prof. infectious disease, 1997—2002; dir. microbiology lab. Associated Regional and Univ. Pathologists, Inc., Salt Lake City, 1990—; prof. pathology and medicine John Hopkins Med. Instns., 2002—, dir. med. microbiology divsn., 2002—. Contbr. articles to profl. jours. Fellow Am. Acad. Microbiology, Coll. Am. Pathologists, Infectious Diseases Soc. Am.; mem. Am. Soc. for Microbiology. Avocations: skiing, hiking, reading. Office Phone: 410-955-5077. Personal E-mail: kcmicro@hotmail.com.

CARROLL, MORGAN, state legislator; b. Denver, Nov. 24, 1971; BA, U. Colo., 1996, JD, 2000. Ptnr. Bradley & Carroll, PC; mem. Dist. 36 Colo. House of Reps., Denver, 2005—08; mem. Dist. 29 Colo. State Senate, Denver, 2009. Co-founder Internat. Ethics Soc. Democrat. Jewish. Office: Colo State Capitol 200 E Colfax Denver CO 80203 Office Phone: 303-866-4879. Business E-Mail: morgan.carroll.senate@state.co.us.*

CARROLL, PETE, college football coach; b. San Francisco, Sept. 15, 1951; m. Glena Carroll; children: Brennan, Nathan, Jaime. BS in Bus. Adminstrn., Univ. Pacific, 1973, MS in Physical Edn., 1976. Grad. asst., wide receivers coach Univ. Pacific Tigers, 1974—75, grad. asst., secondary coach, 1975—77; grad. asst., secondary Univ. Ark. Razorbacks, 1977—78; secondary coach Iowa St. Univ. Cyclones, 1978, Ohio St. Univ. Buckeyes, 1979; def. coord., secondary coach North Carolina St. Wolfpack, 1980—82; asst. head coach, offensive coord. Univ. Pacific Tigers, 1983; def. backs coach Buffalo Bills, 1984—85, Minn. Vikings, 1985—90; def. coord. N.Y. Jets, 1990—94, head coach, 1994; defensive coord. San Francisco 49ers, 1995—97; head coach New England Patriots, 1997-99; head coach, defensive coord. U. So. Calif. Trojans, LA, 2001—. Recipient Coach of Yr. award, Am. Football Coaches Assn., 2003. Achievements include coaching U. So. Calif. to the 2003 & 2004 BCS Nat. Championship. Office: U So Calif 203 Heritage Hall Los Angeles CA 90089*

CARROLL, TERRANCE D., state legislator, lawyer; BA in Polit. Sci. with honors, Morehouse Coll., Atlanta, 1992; MDiv, Iliff Sch. Theology, Denver, 1999; JD, U. Denver Coll. Law, 1999; grad. summer leadership inst., Harvard U. Divinity Sch., Harvard U. John F. Kennedy Sch. Govt. Ordained min. Atty. Greenberg Traurig, LLP; mem. Dist. 7 Colo. House of Reps., Denver, 2003—, asst. majority leader, 2008, spkr. of the house, 2009—. Mem. Colo. Sec. State's Blue Ribbon Election Panel; mem. election law task force Colo. Lawyers Com. Named an African Am. Who Makes a Difference, Urban Spectrum Mag., 1999, Up and Coming African Am. Leader, Rocky Mountain News, 1999; Marshall Meml. fellow, German Marshall Fund, 2006. Mem.: Minoru Yasui Inns of Ct. (mem. exec. coun.), Am. Constn. Soc. (mem. steering com., Denver lawyer chpt.). Democrat. Office: Colo State Capitol 200 E Colfax Rm 246 Denver CO 80203 Office Phone: 303-866-2346. Business E-Mail: terrance.carroll.house@state.co.us.*

CARROLL, WILLIAM, publishing company executive; Mgr., dir. Auto Book Press, Coda Publs.; dir., N.Mex. Books Coda Publs., Raton, N.Mex. Office: New Mex Books Coda Publs PO Box 71 Raton NM 87740-0071

CARROLL, WILLIAM JEROME, civil engineer; b. LA, Nov. 23, 1923; s. William Jerome and Adeline Marie (Verden) C.; m. Louise May Judson, June 6, 1944; children: Charisse Jean, Charles Gary, Christine Louise, Pamela Ann. BS, Calif. Inst. Tech., 1948, MS, 1949. Indsl. waste engr. Los Angeles County Engr., 1949-51; engr. James M. Montgomery (Cons. Engr., Inc.), Pasadena, Calif., 1951-56, v.p., 1956-69, pres., 1969-85, chmn. bd., 1985-90; vice chmn. bd. Montgomery Watson, 1991-98. Served with USAAF, 1943-46. Named So. Calif. Engr. of Yr., 1983; recipient Disting. Alumni award Calif. Inst. Tech., 1996. Mem. NAE, ASCE (nat. bd. dirs. 1976—, nat. v.p. 1986-87, pres. elect 1988, pres. 1988-89, Pres.'s medal 1997), Acad. Engrs. Russian Fedn., World Fedn. Engring. Orgns. (pres. 1991-95), Am. Acad. Environ. Engrs. (diplomate, pres. 1980—, Hoover medal 1994, Gordon Maskew Fair award 1992), Am. Water Works Assn., Water Pollution Control Fedn., Cons. Engrs. Assn. Calif. (pres. 1972), Alumni Assn. Calif. Inst. Tech. (pres. 1976), Pasadena C. of C., Am. Assn. Engring. Socs. (Kenneth Roe award 1992). Republican. Home: 2315 Rue des Chateaux Carlsbad CA 92008-2250 Office: Montgomery Watson Harza 618 Michillinda Ave Ste 200 Arcadia CA 91007-1625 E-mail: william.carroll@mw.com.

CARRUTHERS, GARREY EDWARD, former governor of New Mexico, academic administrator; b. Alamosa, Colo., Aug. 29, 1939; s. William Core and Frankie Jane (Shoults) C.; m. Katherine Thomas, May 13, 1961; children: Deborah Ann Carruthers Joyce, Carol Lynn, Stephen Edward. BS in Agr., N.Mex. State U., 1964, MS in Agrl. Econs., 1965; PhD in Econs., Iowa State U., 1968. Asst. prof. dept. agrl. economics and agrl. bus. N.Mex. State U., Las Cruces, 1968—72, assoc. prof. dept. economics and agrl. bus., 1972—79, prof. agrl. economics and agrl. bus., 1979—81, 1984—87, dean, vice provost, 2003—; spl. asst. US Sec. of Agr., Washington, 1974-75; acting dir. N.Mex. Water Resources Research Inst., 1976-78; pres. Garrey Carruthers Assocs. Inc., 1979; chmn. N.Mex. Rep. Party, 1977—79; asst. sec. interior for land and water resources Dept. Interior, Washington, 1981-83, asst. sec. interior for land and minerals mgmt., 1983-84; Gov. State of N.Mex., 1987-90; pres., CEO Cimarron Ins. Svc. Corp., Albuquerque, 1990—. Coord. N. Mex.'s 2nd Congl. Dist. Ford presdl. campaign, 1976, co-chmn. Dona Ana County; Dallas panel commn. White House Fellowships, 1976; mem. Rep. Nat. com., 1977-79, state ctrl. com., 1977-81, exec. com., 1979-81; chmn. John Connally Presdl. Campaign, N.Mex., 1980 Contbr. articles to profl. jours. Recipient Nat. Acad. Found. Fellow award 1990. Mem. America for Change, Am. Agrl. Econs. Assn., Western Agrl. Econs. Assn., Am. Acad. Polit. and Social Services, Univ. Golf Assn. (former v.p., pres.), Rodeo Club (former adv.), Breakfast Optimist Club (former pres, v.p.), Agr. Econ. Club (former adv.), Sigma Xi, Omicron Delta Kappa. Lodges: Optimist of Las Cruces (former v.p., pres.). Republican. Avocations: golf, flying, jogging, driving 1967 mustang. Office: 7801 Academy NE Bldg 1 Ste 203 Albuquerque NM 87109

CARSON, DENNIS A., immunologist, researcher, cancer biologist; married. BA, Haverford Coll.; MD, Columbia U., 1970; postgraduate rsch. tng., Salk Inst. Former divsn. head immunology Scripps Clinic and Rsch. Found.; resident U. Calif., San Diego, postdoctoral fellow, 1974—77, prof. medicine, 1995—, dir. Sam and Rose Stein Inst. Rsch. Aging; dir. Rebecca and John Moores U. Calif. Cancer Ctr., 2003—. Founder, bd. dirs. Dynavax Tech. Corp., San Diego, Salmedix Inc., San Diego; founder Vical Inc., San Diego, Triangle Pharm. Inc., San Diego. Recipient Bruce F. Cain Meml. award, Am. Assn. Cancer Rsch., 2004, Lee C. Howley Sr. prize for arthritis rsch., Arthritis Found. Mem.: Inst. Medicine, NAS. Achievements include development of new agent called 2-chlorodeoxyadenosine (2-CdA), now marketed as the drug Leustatin, for the treatment of hairy cell leukemia, other lymphoid cancers, multiple sclerosis, and psoriasis. Avocations: reading, walking.

CARSON, ELLEN GODBEY, lawyer; b. Kingsport, Tenn., Apr. 30, 1955; d. Lewis Anderson and Doris Louise (Dempsey) C.; m. Robert Carson Godbey, June 2, 1979. BA summa cum laude, U. Tenn., Knoxville, 1976; JD cum laude, Harvard U., 1980. Consumer complaint specialist FTC, Boston, 1980; atty. civil rights divsn. HHS, Washington, 1980-81; assoc. Landis, Cohen, Rauh & Zelenko, Washington, 1981-87, Paul Johnson Alston & Hunt, Honolulu, 1987-91; ptnr., dir. Alston Hunt Floyd & Ing, Honolulu, 1991—. Mem. disciplinary bd. Hawaii Supreme Ct., 1990-95. Former pres., dir. D.C. Rape Crisis Ctr., Washington, Sex Abuse Treatment Ctr., Honolulu, Hale Kipa Youth Svcs., Honolulu; pres., trustee Ctrl. Union Ch., 1998-2002; past dir. Aloha United Way, Hawaii Women's Legal Found. Named Outstanding Woman Profl., YWCA, 1990; recipient Outstanding Svc. award Hawaii Women Lawyers, 1991, ABA Margaret Brent Women Lawyers of Achievement award, 2006; named one of Best Lawyers in Am., 2005—. Mem. Hawaii State Bar Assn. (pres., dir. 1995-1996, Pro Bono award 1989), Hawaii Women Lawyers (pres., dir. 1989-90, Women Lawyer of Yr. 1992, Disting. Svc. award 2000), Hawaii Justice Found. (v.p., dir. 1996-2002), Inst. Human Svcs. (pres., dir. 1996-2002). Avocations: scuba, quilting. Office: Alston Hunt Floyd & Ing 18th Fl ASB Tower 1001 Bishop St Ste 1800 Honolulu HI 96813-3689 Office Phone: 808-524-1800. E-mail: ecarson@ahfi.com.

CARSON, JAY WILMER, pathologist, educator; b. Ki-Jang, Korea, Oct. 6, 1933; came to U.S., 1960; s. Han Kyu and Jin Chan (Son) Cha; m. Jennifer C. White, June 28, 1968 (dec. Aug. 1990); m. Teresa M. Alberda, July 14, 1995. MD, Seoul Nat. U., 1958. Diplomate Am. Bd. Pathology. Intern Bellevue Hosp. Ctr., NYC, 1961-62; resident in pathology Albert Einstein Coll. Medicine, NYC, 1963-66; fellow U. Montreal, Que., Canada, 1967-68; chief anatomic pathology VA Hosp., Martinez, Calif., 1969-91; dir. cytopathology VA Med. Ctr., San Francisco, 1992-96; assoc. clin. prof. U. Calif. Med. Sch., San Francisco, 1992—. Aviation med. examiner FAA, Oklahoma City, 1987-96; assoc. clin. prof. U. Calif., Davis, 1985—; hosp. comdr. 347th Gen. Hosp., Sunnyvale, Calif., 1992-1993, 6253d Army Hosp., Santa Rosa, Calif., 1994-96. Patentee needle aspiration device. Mem. chmn.'s adv. bd. Nat. Rep. Com., Washington, 1995-96. Col. USAR, 1971-96. Decorated Order of Military Med. Merit, Meritorious Svc.

Medal with one oakleaf cluster, Sr. Flight Surgeon Badge. Fellow Coll. Am. Pathologists; mem. Internat. Acad. Pathology, Assn. Mil. Surgeons U.S. (life), Res. Officers Assn. (life), U.S. Army War Coll. Alumni Assn. (life), Soc. U.S. Army Flight Surgeons (life). Avocations: skiing, sailing, music. Home: 1550 Sorrel Ct Walnut Creek CA 94598-4800 Personal E-mail: jntcarson@astound.net

CARSON, SCOTT E., aerospace transportation executive; b. Aug. 8, 1946; BBA, MBA, Wash. State U. Fin. analyst B-1 Bomber Avionics Program The Boeing Co., 1973, mgmt., 1976, exec. v.p. bus. resources Boeing Info., Space & Defense Sys., 1997, head Connexion by Boeing, 2000, mem. exec. coun., 2000—, sr. exec. Pacific N.W., exec. v.p., 2006—; v.p., CFO Boeing Comml. Airplanes, 1998, v.p. sales, 2004—06, pres., CEO, 2006—. Boeing exec. focal Wash. State U., chair nat. bd. advisors Coll. Bus. and Econs., advisory bd. Coll. Engring. and Architecture; bd. govs. Wash. State U. Found. Recipient Bus. Leadership award, U. Wash. Exec. MBA Program, 2002. Fellow: Royal Aeronautical Soc. Office: Boeing Comml Airplanes PO Box 3707 Seattle WA 98124 Office Phone: 206-655-2121, 312-544-2000.

CARSON, WALLACE PRESTON, JR., retired state supreme court justice; b. Salem, Oreg., June 10, 1934; s. Wallace Preston and Edith (Bragg) C.; m. Gloria Stolk, June 24, 1956; children: Scott, Carol, Steven (dec. 1981). BA in Politics, Stanford U., 1956; JD, Willamette U., 1962. Bar: Oreg. 1962, U.S. Dist. Ct. Oreg. 1963, U.S. Ct. Appeals (9th cir.) 1968, U.S. Supreme Ct. 1971, U.S. Ct. Mil. Appeals 1977; lic. comml. pilot FAA. Pvt. practice law, Salem, Oreg., 1962-77; mem. Oreg. House of Reps., 1967—71, majority leader, 1969—71; mem. Oreg. State Senate, 1971—77, minority floor leader, 1971—77; judge Marion County Cir. Ct., Salem, 1977-82; assoc. justice Oreg. Supreme Ct., Salem, 1982—2006, chief justice, 1992—2005. Dir. Salem Area Community Council, 1967-70, pres., 1969-70; mem. Salem Planning Commn., 1966-72, pres., 1970-71; co-chmn. Marion County Mental Health Planning Com., 1965-69; mem. Salem Community Goals Com., 1965; Republican precinct commiteeman, 1963-66; mem. Marion County Rep. Central Exec. Com., 1963-66; com. predinct edn. Oreg. Rep. Central Com., 1965; vestryman, acolyte, Sunday Sch. tchr., youth coach St. Paul's Episcopal Ch., 1935—; task force on cts. Oreg. Council Crime and Delinquency, 1968-69; trustee Willamette U., 1970—; adv. bd. Cath. Ctr. Community Services, 1976-77; mem. comporehensive planning com. Mid-Willamette Valley Council of Govts., 1970-71; adv. com. Oreg. Coll. Edn. Tchr. Edn., 1971-75; pres. Willamette regional Oreg. Lung Assn., 1974-75, state dir., exec. com., 1975-77; pub. relations com. Williamette council Campfire Girls, 1976-77; criminal justice adv. bd. Chemeketa Community Coll., 1977-79; mem. Oreg. Mental Health Com., 1979-80; mem. subcom. Gov's Task Force Mental Health, 1980; You and Govt. Adv. Com. Oreg. YMCA, 1981—. Served to col. USAFR, 1956—59. Recipient Salem Disting. Svc. award, 1968; recipient Good Fellow award Marion County Fire Svc., 1974, Minuteman award Oreg. N.G. Assn., 1980; fellow Eagleton Inst. Politics, Rutgers U., 1971 Mem. Marion County Bar Assn. (sec.-treas. 1965-67, dir. 1968-70), Oreg. Bar Assn., ABA, Willamette U. Coll. Law Alumni Assn. (v.p. 1968-70), Salem Art Assn., Oreg. Hist. Soc., Marion County Hist. Soc., Stanford U. Club (pres. Salem chpt. 1963-64), Delta Theta Phi.

CARSTEN, JACK CRAIG, venture capitalist; b. Cin., Aug. 24, 1941; s. John A. and Edith L. C.; m. Mary Ellis Jones, June 22, 1963; children: Scott, Elizabeth, Amy. BS in Physics, Duke U., 1963. Mktg. mgr. Tex. Instruments, Dallas, Houston, 1965-71, integrated circuits gen. mgr. Houston, 1971-75; v.p. sales and mktg. Intel Corp., Santa Clara, Calif., 1975-79, v.p., microcomputer gen. mgr., 1979-82, sr. v.p., components gen. mgr., 1982-87; gen. ptnr. U.S. Venture Ptnrs., Menlo Park, Calif., 1988-90; venture capitalist Tech. Investments, Los Altos, Calif., 1990-99, Horizon Ventures LLC, Los Altos, 2000—. Bd. dirs. several privately held firms. Contbr. articles to profl.jours. Office: Horizon Ventures LLC 4 Main St Los Altos CA 94022-2998 E-mail: jack@carsten.com.

CARSTENSEN, LAURA LEE, psychology professor; b. Phila., Nov. 2, 1953; d. Edwin Lorenz Carstensen and Pam. McDonald; m. Ian H. Gotlib, Aug. 27, 1995; 1 child, David Joseph Pagano. BS, U. Rochester, 1978; MA, W.Va. U., 1980, PhD, 1983. Asst. prof. Ind. U., Bloomington, 1983-87, Stanford U., Calif., 1987-94, assoc. prof., 1995, prof. psychology, Barbara D. Finberg dir. Inst. Rsch. on Women and Gender, 1997—2001, dir. Life-span Devel. Lab. Sci. cons. Max Planck Inst. Human Devel. & Edn., Berlin, 1992—; assoc. dir. Terman gifted project Stanford U., 1994—. Author book chpt.; co-author Psychology: The Study of Human Experience, 1991; co-editor: Handbook of Clinical Gerontology, 1987; contrib. articles to profl. jours. Recipient First Investigator award, Nat. Inst. Aging, 1987; Guggenheim Fellow, 2003—04. Fellow APA, Gerontol. Soc. Am. (mem.-at-large 1994—, Kalish Innovative Publication award 1993), Am. Psychol. Soc. Office: Stanford U Dept Psychology Bldg 420 Jordan Hall Stanford CA 94305-2130 E-mail: LLC@psych.stanford.edu.

CARTER, BRUCE L.A., biotechnologist, director; BSc in Botany with honors, U. Nottingham, Eng.; PhD in Microbiology, Queen Elizabeth Coll., U. London. Lectr. Trinity Coll., U. Dublin, Ireland, 1975—82; head molecular genetics G.D. Searle & Co., Ltd., 1982—86; v.p. R&D ZymoGenetics, Seattle, 1986—88, pres., 1988—94, chmn. bd., 1994—98, pres., CEO, 1998—, chmn., 2005—, dir., 1987—; corp. exec. v.p., chief sci. officer Novo Nordisk A/S, 1994—2000.

CARTER, C. MICHAEL, lawyer; b. Apr. 18, 1945; BS in Acctg., U. Calif., Berkeley, 1967; JD, George Washington U., 1973. Atty. Winthrop, Stimson, Putnam & Roberts; divsn. counsel Singer Co., 1981—83; sr. corp. counsel, asst. sec. R.J. Reynolds Inc., 1983—87; sr. v.p., opers., bd. mem. Concurrent Computer Corp., 1987—94; exec. v.p., gen. counsel, corp. sec. Pinkerton's, Inc., 1994—2000; sr. v.p., gen. counsel, corp. sec. Dole Food Co., Westlake Village, Calif., 2000—. Bd. dirs. Dole Food Co., Inc., Westlake Village, Calif. Bd. trustees George Washington U. Office: Dole Food Co One Dole Dr Westlake Village CA 91362 Office Phone: 818-879-6600, 818-879-6810. Office Fax: 818-874-4893. E-mail: michael_carter@na.dole.com.

CARTER, DAVID O., judge; b. Providence, Mar. 28, 1944; m. Mary Ellen Carter. BA cum laude, UCLA, 1967, JD, 1972. Bar: Calif. 1972, U.S. Dist. Ct. (ctrl. dist.) Calif. 1972. Asst. dist. atty. Dist. Atty.'s Office, Santa Ana, Calif., 1972-81; judge Orange County Mcpl. Ct., Westminster, 1981-82, Laguna Niguel, 1982, Orange County Superior Ct., Santa Ana, 1982-98, U.S. Dist. Ct. for Ctrl. Dist. Calif., Santa Ana, 1998—. Spkr. Supreme Ct. Rio de Janeiro and Brazilan Fed. Prosecutors, 1993; civilian participant Nat. Security Forum, Air War Coll., Montgomery, Ala., 1992; mem. faculty Calif. Judges Coll., 1983-89, 91-97, Jud. Criminal Law Inst., 1989, 90, 93, 97, Contributing Edn. Bar, 1994-95. Bd. dirs. Brandy's Friends, 1995—, Orange County on Track, 1996—, Children's Bur., 1996—, Kindercamrarina, 1997—. Decorated Bronze Star, Purple Heart; recipient vol. award City of Santa Ana, 1990, Patriot of Yr. award Patriots Day Parade, Laguna Beach, 1991, Exceptional Support award Police Res. Officers, Santa Ana, 1995, Disting. Vis. Prof.'s award U. Calif., Irvine, 1996-2002, Exceptional Citizen's award Mayor of Santa Ana, 1998, Franklin West award 2003; Athletic scholar UCLA. Mem. Orange County Bar Assn. (bd. dirs. 1978), Orange County Bar Assn. (bd. dirs. 1994), Calif. Dist. Attys. Assn. (charter), DAV, VFW, Am. Legion, Mil. Order Purple Heart, 1st Bn. 9th Marine Network, Survivors of Khe Sanh. Office: US Dist Ct Ctrl Dist Calif Ronald Reagan Fed Bldg 411 W 4th St Santa Ana CA 92701-4500

CARTER, DENNIS LEE, marketing professional; b. Louisville, Oct. 23, 1951; s. Bernard Lee and Opal Delores (Jaggers) C.; m. Janice Lea Herbert, Dec. 31, 1976; children: Serra Kimberly, Scott Winston. BSEE, BS in Physics, Rose Hulman Inst., Terre Haute, Ind., 1973; MSEE, Purdue U., 1974, DSc (hon.), 1996; MBA, Harvard U., 1981. Instr. elec. engring. tech. Purdue U., West Lafayette, Ind., 1975; collateral engr. Rockwell-Collins, Cedar Rapids, Iowa, 1975-76, design engr., 1976-79; product mktg. engr. Intel Corp., Santa Clara, Calif., 1981-83, software products mktg. mgr., 1983-85, tech. asst. to pres., 1985-89, end-user mktg. mgr., 1989-90, gen. mgr. end-user components divsn., 1990-91, dir. corp. mktg., 1991-92, v.p., dir. corp. mktg., 1992-98, v.p., dir. strategic mktg., 1998—. Inventor radio reception path monitor for a diversity sys., 1985. Episcopalian. Avocation: baseball.

CARTER, HAROLD O., agricultural economics educator; b. Eaton Rapids, Mich., Dec. 13, 1932; s. Ola Gay and Lillian Darlene (Fox) C.; m. Janet M. Edger, June 21, 1952; children: Teresa, Lisa, Brian, Michael, Alison. BS, Mich. State U., 1954, MS, 1955; PhD, Iowa State U., 1958. From asst. prof. to assoc. prof. agrl. econs. U. Calif., Davis, 1958-66, prof. to prof. emeritus, 1966-93, 93—, chmn. dept. Davis, 1970-76, 87-89, dir. Agrl. Issues Ctr., 1985-96. Vis. prof. Agrl. Coll. Sweden, Uppsala, 1967, Ctr. Agrl. Econs. U. Naples, Italy, 1972, dept. agrl. econs U. Sydney, Australia, 1984; economist Giannini Found. Agrl. Econs. Fellow Am. Agrl. Econs. Assn. (Outstanding Rsch. awards 1963, 67, 71, 75, 89, Best Jour. Article award 1968), Western Agrl. Econs. Assn. (Outstanding Extension award 1975, Outstanding Rsch. award 1962, 69, 71). Republican. Office: U Calif Dept Agrl Econs Davis CA 95616 Home: 5116 Independence Dr Fairfield CA 94533-9743

CARTER, JAMES C., lawyer, apparel executive; b. Pendleton, Oreg., Aug. 7, 1948; m. Julie Carter; children: Emily, Tyler. AB in Econs., Stanford U., 1971; JD, U. Oreg., 1976. Bar: Oreg. 1976, US Fed. Ct. 1978. With Schulte, Anderson, Downes & Carter, Portland, Oreg.; gen. counsel US and Ams. Nike, Inc., Beaverton, Oreg., 1998—2003, v.p., gen. counsel, 2003—, chief legal officer, 2003—. Chair Classroom Law Project; mem. dean's adv. coun. U. Oreg. Law Sch. Mem.: Oreg. Assn. Def. Counsel. Avocations: travel, golf, running, bicycling. Office: Nike Inc 1 Bowerman Dr Beaverton OR 97005-6453

CARTER, JOHN D., metal products executive; Ptnr. law firm, San Francisco; various sr. mgmt. positions including exec. v.p., dir. and pres. Bechtel Enterprises, Inc. Bechtel Group, Inc., 1982—2002; cons., 2002—05; pres., CEO Schnitzer Steel Industries, Inc., Portland, Oreg., 2005—08, chmn., 2008—. Dir. NW Natural Gas Co., FLIR Systems, Inc.; chmn. bd. Kuni Automotive. Mailing: Schnitzer Steel Industries Inc PO Box 10047 Portland OR 97296-0047 Office: Schnitzer Steel Industries Inc 3200 NW Yeon Ave Portland OR 97210 Office Phone: 503-224-9900.

CARTER, LARRY R., computer company executive; BS in Bus. Adminstrn. and Acctg., Ariz. State U. Various positions including v.p., contr. MOS group Motorola, Inc.; CFO, v.p. fin. and adminstrn. SGS Thompson Microelectronics, Inc.; v.p. fin., CFO VLSI Tech., Inc.; v.p., corp. contr. Advanced Micro Devices; CFO Cisco Sys., 1995—2003, bd. dir., 2000—, sr. v.p., office of pres., 2003—. Bd. dir. QLogic Corp. Trustee Loyola Marymount Univ. Recipient Disting. Achievement award, Ariz. State Univ. Coll. Bus., 2000. Office: Cisco Systems Inc 170 W Tasman Dr San Jose CA 95134-1706

CARTER, ROBERTA ECCLESTON, counseling administrator; b. Pitts. d. Robert E. and Emily B. (Bucar) Carter; divorced; children: David Michael Kiewlich, Daniel Michael Kiewlich. Student, Edinboro State U., 1962-63; BS, California State U. Pa., 1966; MEd, U. Pitts., 1969; MA, Rosebridge Grad. Sch., 1987. Tchr. Bethel Park Sch. Dist., Pa., 1966-69; writer, media asst. Field Edni. Pub., San Francisco, 1969-70; educator, counselor, specialist Alameda Unified Sch. Dist., Calif., 1970—. Master trainer Calif. State Dept. Edn., Sacramento, 1984—; personal growth cons., Alameda, 1983—. Author: People, Places and Products, 1970, Teaching/Learning Units, 1969; co-author: Teacher's Manual Let's Read, 1968. Mem. AAUW, NEA, Internat. Assn. Marriage and Family Counselors, Calif. Fedn. Bus. and Profl. Women (legis. chair Alameda br. 1984-85, membership chair 1985), Calif. Edn. Assn., Alameda Edn. Assn., Charter Planetary Soc., Oakland Mus., Big Bros of East Bay, Alameda C. of C. (svc. award 1985). Avocations: gardening, travel. Home: 1516 Eastshore Dr Alameda CA 94501-3118 Office Phone: 510-522-7981.

CARTER, RONALD MARTIN, SR., pharmaceutical executive; b. Chgo., Nov. 18, 1925; s. Jack Edward and Anna (Press) C.; m. Joy Wolf, Nov. 14, 1946; children: Ronald M. Jr., Craig Alan. Student, U. Ill., 1942-43, 45-46. Sales mgr. Preston Labs., Inc., Chgo., 1948-52; v.p. Myers-Carter Labs., Inc., Phoenix, 1952-69, pres., 1969-75, Carter-Glogau Labs., Inc., Glendale, Ariz., 1975-86, Steris Labs., Inc., Phoenix, 1987—, The Pharmikon Co., 1987—. Cons. Internat. Exec. Service Corp., Stamford, Conn., 1985—. Served as cpl. U.S. Army, 1943-45. Mem. Drug, Chem. Allied Trades, Generic Pharm. Industry Assn., Nat. Assn. Pharm. Mfrs., Nat. Pharm. Alliance (pres. 1983-84). Clubs: Arizona, Plaza (Phoenix). Democrat. Jewish. Avocations: hunting, fishing. Home: 5707 N 40th St Phoenix AZ 85018-1108 Personal E-mail: roncar@cox.net.

CARTER, SCOTT, television producer; m. Bebe Johnsen; children: Calla, Colette. Writer (TV series) MTV's Mouth to Mouth, 1988, prodr., writer Night After Night with Allen Havey, 1989—92, co-creator, exec. prodr., writer SportsMonster, 1990—91, exec. prodr. The Olympiacs, 1992, exec. prodr., writer Exhale with Candice Bergen, 2000—02, Politically Incorrect, 1993—2000, cons. prodr., co-head writer Earth to America, 2005, exec. prodr., writer Real Time with Bill Maher, 2006—, co-exec. prodr. Ain't It Cool News, 2001, exec. prodr. The Conspiracy Zone, 2002, author & performer (one-man shows) Heavy Breathing, Suspension Bridge. Recipient CableACE award for Talk Show Series for Politically Incorrect, 1995, 1996, 1997, Johnny Carson Prodr. of Yr. award for Real Time with Bill Maher, Prodrs. Guild Am., 2007; named one of 50 Creatives to Watch, Variety, 1997.

CARTER, WILLIAM G., lawyer; b. Oct. 1940; m. Barbara Carter; children: Elizabeth, Andrew. BS, U. Oreg., 1962, LLB, 1965. Bar: Oreg. 1965. Prosecutor Douglas County, Oreg.; gen. trial practice Medford, Oreg.; mcpl. judge; pro tem circuit judge Jackson County, Oreg.; prin. William G. Carter Mediation & Arbitration, Medford, Oreg. Mem. State Professional Responsibility Bd., 1993—95, chmn., 1995; mem. Minimum Continuing Legal Edn. Bd., 1995—97, chmn., 1997. Mem.: Jackson County Bar Assn. (pres.), Oreg. State Bar Assn. (mem. disciplinary bd. 1998—2000, regional chmn. disciplinary bd. 2000, bd. gov. 2001—04, pres. 2004). Office: William G Carter Arbitration and Mediation 10 Crater Lake Ave PO Box 70 Medford OR 97501 Office Phone: 541-773-8471. Office Fax: 541-245-6674. Business E-Mail: wilcar@aol.com.

CARTER, WILLIAM GEORGE, III, career officer; b. Buffalo, June 18, 1944; s. William George Jr. and Elaine Ruth (Weber) C.; m. Linda Fay Yener, Oct. 2, 1965; children: Kris Ann, William George. BS, U. Tampa, 1972; MA, U. Shippensberg, 1982; MPE, U. Pitts., 1984. Commd. 2d. lt. U.S. Army, 1965, advanced through grades to lt. gen., 1995; various command and staff positions, 1964-77; exec. officer 3d Brigade, 1st Armored Div., Bamberg, Fed. Republic Germany, 1977-79; comdr. 1st Bn., 52d Inf., Bamberg, 1979-81, G3 1st Armored Div., VII U.S. Corps, Ansbach, Fed. Republic Germany, 1981-83; chief Plans and Integration Office, Hdqrs. U.S. Army, Washington, 1983-86; comdr. 1st Brigade, 4th Inf. Div., Ft. Carson, Colo., 1986-88; exec. asst. Office Chief of Staff Army, Washington, 1988-89; asst. div. comdr. 1st Inf. Div., Ft. Riley, Kans., 1989-91; comdr. Nat. Tng. Ctr., Ft. Irwin, Calif., 1991-93, 1st Armored Divsn., 1993-95; chief of staff Allied Forces So. Europe, 1995-97; exec. v.p. SY Technologies, Washington, 1993—. Decorated DDSM with oak leaf cluster, DSM with oak leaf cluster, Legion of Merit with six oak leaf clusters, Bronze Star with V device and two oak leaf clusters, Purple Heart with oak leaf cluster. Mem. Soc. of the Big Red One, Alpha Chi. Avocations: golf, hunting.

CARTER, WILMER AMINA, state legislator; m Ratibu Jacocks; children: three. BA in English, Calif. State U., San Bernadino, MA in Edn. Elected then re-elected, Rialto Unified School District Bd Education, 1983 then 1987, 1991, and 1995; California State Assemblyman, District 62, 2006-.Staff member then district director to Congressman George Brown, 73-99. Wilmer Amina Carter High School is the first high school in the Inland Empire named after a living African American woman. Democrat. Office: Dist 62 335 North Riverside Ave Rialto CA 92376 Office Phone: 909-820-5008. Office Fax: 909-820-5098. Business E-Mail: Assemblymember.Carter@assembly.ca.gov.

CARTMELL, NATHANIEL MADISON, III, lawyer; b. NYC, Oct. 22, 1951; s. Nathaniel Madison Jr. and Ruth Kincer (Davies) C.; m. Suzanne Cameron Pettus, Jan. 3, 1981; children: Nathaniel Madison IV, Edmund Winston, Samuel Chapman Davies. BA, Yale U., 1973; JD, Vanderbilt U., 1978. Bar: Calif. State 1983, D.C. 1980, Va. State 1978. Mem. faculty Williston Northampton Sch., Easthampton, Mass., 1973-75; assoc. Hunton & Williams, Richmond, Va., 1978-80, Washington, 1980-81; atty. U.S. Synthetic Fuels Corp., Washington, 1981; assoc. Pillsbury Madison & Sutro LLP, Washington, 1982-83, San Francisco, 1983-86; ptnr. Pillsbury Winthrop Shaw Pittman, LLP, San Francisco, 1987—, mgr. corp. and securities group, 1994-96, chmn. mergers and acquisitions specialty team, 1999—, mem. mng. bd., 2008—. Alumni bd. dirs. Vanderbilt Law Sch., 1998-2001; alumni coun. Phillips Acad., 1997-2000; bd. govs. Phelps Assn., 2004—; bd. dirs. YMCA, San Francisco, 2004—. Mem. ABA (mem. fed. regulation of securities com., bus. law sect. 1990—), Calif. State Bar (mem. corps. com., bus. law sect. 1989-91). Episcopalian. Office: Pillsbury Winthrop Shaw Pittman LLP 50 Fremont St San Francisco CA 94105 Home Phone: 510-848-2999; Office Phone: 415-983-1570. Office Fax: 415-983-1200. Business E-Mail: nathaniel.cartmell@pillsburylaw.com.

CARTWRIGHT, CHAS, national monument administrator; married. BA in Anthropology, Mich. State U., 1972. Seasonal fire fighter, fire lookout, river ranger U.S. Forestry Svc., Calif. and Idaho, 1972-75; seasonal archaeologist B.L.M., Idaho, Ariz. and Utah, 1979-87, archaeologist Great Basin and Colorado Plateau, Utah, 1979-87; archaeololgist Arches and Canyonlands Nat. Parks, Natural Bridges Nat. Monument Nat. Pk. Svc., 1987-89, supt. Hovenweep Nat. Monument Utah and Colo., 1989-98, supt. Knife River Indian Villages Nat. Hist. Site N.D., 1989-98, supt., dir. Devils Tower (Wy.) Nat. Monument, 1998—. Office: care Devils Tower Monument PO Box 10 Devils Tower WY 82714-0010

CARTWRIGHT, DERRICK, museum director; BA, U. Calif., Berkeley; MA, UCLA, 1988; PhD in Art Hist., U. Mich., 1994. Prof. art hist. U. San Diego, 1993—98; dir. Musée d'Art Américain, Giverny, France, 1998—2000, Hood Mus. Art, Dartmouth Coll., 2001—04, San Diego Mus. Art, 2004—, Founders gallery. Dir.: Domains of Wonder: Selected Masterworks of Indian Painting, Personal Views: Regarding Private Art Collections in San Diego, Rhythms of India: The Art of Nandalal Bose. Office: San Diego Mus Art PO Box 122107 San Diego CA 92112-2107

CARUANA, PATRICK PETER, retired military officer; b. St. Louis, Nov. 11, 1939; BSEE, USAF Acad., 1963; Grad., Squadron Officer Sch., Maxwell AFB, Ala. 1968; MS in Math., Tex. A&M U., 1972; Grad., Air Command & Staff Coll., Maxwell AFB, Ala., 1977, Indsl. Coll. Armed Forces, Ft. Lesley J. McNair, 1984. Commd. 2d lt. USAF, 1963, advanced through grades to lt. gen., 1994; C-119 crew chief USAF Reserve, Scott AFB, Ill., 1957—59; K-135 co-pilot, then aircraft comdr. 916th Air Refueling Squadron, Travis AFB, Calif., 1965—69; pilot, sr. command post contr. 315th Tactical Airlift Wing, Phang Ranf AFB, South Vietnam, 1970; asst. prof. math. USAF Acad., Colorado Springs, Colo., 1972—76; aircraft comdr. then squadron ops. officer 920th Air Refueling Squadron, Wurtsmith AFB, Mich., 1977—80; comdr. 11th Air Refueling Squadron, Altus AFB, Okla., 1980-82; chief applications divsn. tanker directorate, dep. chief of staff for ops. Strategic Air Command (SAC), Offutt AFB, Nebr., 1982-83; vice comdr 376th Strategic Wing, Kadena Air Base, Japan, 1984—85, comdr., 1985—86, 384th Air Refueling Wing, McConnell AFB, Kans., 1986-87; dep. dir. strategic, spl. operational forces &

airlift programs USAF, Washington, 1987-89; comdr. 42d Air Divsn., Grand Forks AFB, ND, 1989—90, 1991; dir. strategic forces, US Ctrl. Air Forces, comdr. 17th Air Divsn. (Provisional) Operation Desert Storm, Riyadh, Saudi Arabia, 1990-91; dep. chief of staff for ops. Strategic Air Command (SAC), Offutt AFB, Nebr., 1991—92; dir. long range power projections USAF, Washington, 1993-94, dir. special ops. forces airlift & tng. programs, 1993-94; comdr. 14th Air Force, Vandenberg AFB, Calif., 1994; vice comdr. Air Force Space Command, Peterson AFB, Colo., 1994—97; v.p., program mgr. TRW Space & Electronics, 1999—2002; v.p. Northrop Grumman Space Technology, 2002—05; vice chmn. Focus on the Family, 2006—09, chmn., 2009—. Bd. dirs. Focus on the Family, 1996—, Liquidmetal Technologies, Inc., 2006—. Co-author: Logistics Supportability for the Advanced Tactical Fighter, 1984 (Air Force Assn. award 1984). Exec. dir. C. of C., Wichita, 1986, Grand Forks, 1990. Decorated D.F.C., Legion of Merit with two oak leaf clusters, Meritorious Svc. medal, Air medal with four oak leaf clusters, USAF Commendation Medal, Presdl Unit Citation, Air Force Outstanding Unit award with oak leaf cluster, Nat. Def. Svc. medal with oak leaf cluster, Vietnam Svc. medal with seven oak leaf cluster Southwest Asia Svc. medal, Republic of Vietnam Gallantry Cross with Palm, Republic of Vietnam Campaign medal, Kuwait Liberation medal; named Italian-Am. Man of Yr., UNICO, 1991. Mem. Air Force Assn., Aircraft Owners and Pilots Assn., Air Force Sgts. Assn., Assn. of Grads. USAF Acad., Phi Mu Epsilon. Avocations: golf, flying, researching bible topics, reading. Office: Focus on the Family 8605 Explorer Dr Colorado Springs CO 80920*

CARUSO, MARK JOHN, lawyer; b. LA, Apr. 27, 1957; s. John Mondella and Joyce Dorothy C.; m. Judy F. Velarde, Aug. 15, 1987. BS cum laude, Pepperdine U., 1979, JD cum laude, 1982. Bar: Calif. 1982, N.Mex. 1987, U.S. Dist. Ct. (ctrl. dist.) Calif. 1982, U.S. Dist. Ct. N.Mex. 1987, U.S. Dist. Ct. (no. and so. dists.) Calif. 1995, U.S. Ct. Appeals (9th cir.) 1983, U.S. Ct. Appeals (10th cir.) 1987. Law clk. Fed. Trade Commn., LA, 1980—82; pvt. practice, Burbank, Calif., 1982—, Albuquerque, 1987—. Mem. N.Mex. Ho. of Reps., 1990-95, labor com., consumer and pub. affairs com., workers compensation oversight interim com., ct. correction and justice interim com., jud. com., labor com.; lobbyist Nat. Right to Work Com., 1984-86, Employee Rights Campaign Com., 1984-86; exec. dir. N.Mex. Citizens Right to Work, 1984-86, Okla. Freedom to Work Com., 1985-86; lectr. breast implant and diet drug litig.; expert witness drug litig. malpractice actions. Col., aide de camp to gov. State N. Mex., 1987; chmn. N. Mex. Mcpl. Boundary Commn., 1988—; del. Rep. Nat. Conv., 1988, 92; Sandoval county chmn. George Bush for Pres., 1988; campaign mgr. Boulter US Congress, Tex., 1975-82, Coll. Rep., 1975-82; staff mem. Ronald Reagan for Pres., 1979,80; mem. Young Am. for Freedom LA chpt., 1979-82, Legacy Ch., Albuquerque. Recipient Am. Jurisprudence award, 1981, Platinum award, N.Mex. Free Enterprise Adv., 1986. Mem. ATLA, Breast Implant Litigation Group, Consumer Attys. Calif., Assn. Trial Lawyers Am., Albuquerque Hispano C. of C., Greater Albuquerque C. of C. Office: 4302 Carlisle Blvd NE Albuquerque NM 87107-4811 Office Phone: 505-883-5000. Office Fax: 505-883-5012.

CARVALHO, WAYNE G., protective services official; Chief of police, Hilo, Hawaii. Office: City of Hilo Police Dept 349 Kapiolani St Hilo HI 96720-3912

CARVER, CRAIG R., lawyer; b. Aug. 5, 1948; AB with distinction, Stanford U., 1970; JD, U. Mich., U. Denver, 1974. Bar: Colo. 1974. Ptnr. Gibson, Dunn & Crutcher, Denver, 1982-96, Carver & Kinchoff, 2003—04, Carver Kinchhoff Schwarg NcNab & Bailey, LLC, 2004—; mem., mgr. Alfers & Carver, L.L.C., Denver, 1996—2003. Bd. trustees Rocky Mountain Mineral Law Found., 1982-84, 92-94, 99-2003, treas., 2002-03. Mem. ABA, Colo. Bar Assn., Denver Bar Assn. Office: Ste 1700 1600 Stout St Denver CO 80202-3164 Office Phone: 303-592-7674. Business E-Mail: ccarver@cksmb.com.

CASAMENTO, CHARLES JOSEPH, pharmaceutical industry executive; b. Hoboken, NJ, June 8, 1945; s. Charles Vincent and Mary (Brignola) C.; m. Evelyn Ann Kenez, June 8, 1968 (div. 1983); children: Christopher Charles, Suzanne Marie; m. Doris Ann Mason, May 25, 1985. BS in Pharmacy, Fordham U., 1968; MBA in Mktg., Iona Coll., 1971. Registered pharmacist, N.J., N.Y. Mgr. Sandoz Pharm. Div., East Hanover, N.J., 1970-71, fin. planner, 1972-73, product coordinator, 1973-74, mgr. new product planning, 1974-75, mgr. new product planning and licensing, 1975-77; mgr. product devel. Hoffmann-La Roche, Nutley, N.J., 1977-79; dir. new products and acquisitions Johnson & Johnson, New Brunswick, N.J., 1979-83; v.p. bus. devel. Am. Critical Care div. Am. Hosp. Supply, Waukegan, Ill., 1983-86; sr. v.p., gen. mgr. Genzyme Corp., Boston, 1986-89; pres. and CEO Interneuron Pharmaceuticals Inc., 1989-93; chmn., pres and CEO RiboGene Inc., Hayward, CA, 1993—. Lectr. in field. Campaign mgr. Rep. Com., Veron, N.J., 1976; coach Little League, Upper Saddle River, 1978-79, Little League, Basking Ridge, 1980-82, local Soccer League, Upper SAddle River, 1978-79; pres. Ch. Parrish Council, 1979. Mem. Licensing Exec. Soc., Am. Pharm. Assn., Comml. Devel. Assn., Assn. Corp. Growth, Cambridge Racquet Club. Episcopalian. Avocations: photography, golf.

CASANOVA, ALDO JOHN, sculptor; b. San Francisco, Feb. 8, 1929; s. Felice and Teresa (Papini) C.; children: Aviva, Liana, Anabelle. BA, San Francisco State U., 1950, MA, 1951; PhD, Ohio State U., 1957. Asst. prof. art San Francisco State U., 1951-53; asst. prof. Antioch (Ohio) Coll., 1956-58; asst. prof. art Tyler Sch. Art, Temple U., Phila., 1961-64, Tyler Sch. Art, Temple U. (Italy campus), Rome, 1968-70; prof. art Scripps Coll., Claremont, Calif., 1966—, chmn. art dept., 1971-73; vis. prof. SUNY, 1981; faculty mem. Skowhegan Sch. Painting and Sculpture, Maine, summers 1973-74. One-man shows include Esther Robles Gallery, L.A., 1967, Santa Barbara (Calif.) Mus., 1967, Calif. Inst. Tech., 1972, Carl Schlosberg Fine Arts, L.A., 1977, SUNY, 1981, Casanova Retrospective Williamson Galleries, Claremont Colls., Calif. 2002; represented in permanent collections Whitney Mus., San Francisco Mus. Art, San Diego Mus. Sculpture Garden, Hirshhorn Collection, Cornell U., Columbus (Ohio) Mus., UCLA Sculpture Garden, Calif. Inst. Tech., Pasadena, Univ. Judaism, L.A., Air and Space Mus., Washington, Collection of Nat. Acad. of Design, N.Y.C., 1993, Robert Feldmuth Meml. Commn., W.M. Keck Sci. Ctr., Claremont, Calif., 1995, Orange County Mus., Calif., 1996, Rancho Santa Ana Botanic Gardens, Claremont, Calif., Palm Springs Mus., Calif., Brookgreen Gardens, Pawley's Island, SC. Recipient Prix-de-Rome Am. Acad. in Rome, 1958-61; Louis Comfort Tiffany award, 1970 Fellow: Am. Acad. in Rome; mem.: NAD, Nat. Sculpture Soc. Democrat. Roman Catholic. Office Phone: 909-621-3424.

CASE, CHARLES G., II, federal judge; b. Phoenix, Jan. 17, 1948; BA cum laude, Harvard U., 1969; JD magna cum laude, Ariz. State U., 1975. Bar: Ariz. 1975. With Lewis and Roca, Phoenix, 1975-88, Meyer, Hendricks, Victor, Osborn & Maledon P.C., Phoenix, 1988-93; judge U.S. Bankruptcy Ct., Phoenix, 1994—. Judge pro tempore Ariz. Ct. Appeals; adj. prof. law Ariz. State U., 1988-91, 97—. Contbg. author Comml. Law and Practice Guides, 1991. Mem. ABA. Office: 2929 N Central Ave Fl 9 Phoenix AZ 85012-2752

CASE, EDWARD ESPENETT, former United States Representative from Hawaii, lawyer; b. Hilo, Hawaii, Sept. 27, 1952; m. Audrey Nakamura, 2001; children from previous marriage: James, David stepchildren: David, Megan. BA, Williams Coll., 1975; JD, U. Calif., 1981. Aide to US Rep. Spark Matsunaga US Congress, Washington, 1975—78; clk. to Hon. William S. Richardson Hawaii Supreme Ct., 1981—82; clk. Hawaii Dept. Labor; from assoc. to mng. ptnr. Carlsmith Ball, Honolulu, 1983—; mem. Hawaii House of Reps., 1994—2002, majority leader, 1999—2000; mem. US Congress from 2nd Hawaii Dist., Washington, 2002—06, mem. edn. and workforce com., agr. com., small bus. com. Mem. Manoa Neighborhood Bd., Honolulu, 1985—89. Named Legislator of Yr., Honolulu Weekly, 1995, Small Bus. Hawaii, 2000, New Economy Legislator of Yr., Hawaii Tech. and Trade Assn., 2000. Democrat.*

CASE, JAMES HEBARD, lawyer; b. Lihue, Hawaii, Apr. 10, 1920; s. Adrial Hebard and Elizabeth (McConnell) C.; m. Suzanne Catherine Espenett, Sept. 18, 1948; children: Edward E., John H. (dec.), Suzanne D., Russell L., Elisabeth, Bradford. AB, Williams Coll., 1941; JD, Harvard U., 1949. Bar: Hawaii 1949, U.S. Supreme Ct. 1985. Assoc. Pratt, Tavares & Cassidy, Honolulu, 1949-51, Carlsmith & Carlsmith, Hilo, Hawaii, 1951-59; ptnr. Carlsmith Ball, Honolulu, 1959—2002, of counsel, 2002—. Bd. dirs. ML Resources, Hilo, 1986-2006. Trustee Hanahauoli Sch., Honolulu, 1970-82, Ctrl. Union Ch., Honolulu, 1984-88, Arcadia Retirement Residence, Honolulu, 1985-91. Lt. comdr. USNR, 1943-46, PTO. Mem. ABA, Hawaii Bar Assn., Hawaii Yacht Racing Assn. (bd. dirs. 1994-2000), Pacific Club (bd. dirs. 1978-82), Kaneohe Yacht Club (Honolulu). Republican. Congregationalist. Avocations: sailing, tennis. Home: 3757 Round Top Dr Honolulu HI 96822-5043 Office: Carlsmith Ball PO Box 656 Honolulu HI 96809-0656 Home Phone: 808-949-8272; Office Phone: 808-523-2501. Business E-Mail: jcase@carlsmith.com.

CASE, STEVE (STEPHEN M.), healthcare investment company executive, former media and entertainment company executive; b. Honolulu, Aug. 21, 1958; m. Joanne Case (div.); 3 children; m. Jean Case. BA in Polit. Sci., Williams Coll., 1980. With mktg. dept. Procter & Gamble, 1980—82; mng. new pizza devel. Pizza Hut divsn. PepsiCo, 1982—83; with Control Video, 1983—85, Quantum Computer Svcs., 1985—92; co-founder, CEO America Online, 1992—2001, chmn., 1995—2001, AOL Time Warner, NYC, 2001—03, Exclusive Resorts LLC, Denver, 2004—; chmn., CEO Revolution Health Group, 2005—. Bd. dirs. America Online, 1992—2001, Time Warner Inc. (previously AOL Time Warner), 2001—05; launched Revolution Health.com, 2007—; investor RediClinic, 2006—. Named Named Entrepreneur of Yr., Inc. Mag., 1994. Avocation: reading political science and social history. Office: Exclusive Resorts LLC 1515 Arapahoe St Denver CO 80202-3150

CASE, TED JOSEPH, biologist, educator; b. Sioux City, Iowa, July 19, 1947; BS with honors, U. Redlands, Calif., 1969; PhD, U. Calif., Irvine, 1974. Postgrad. rsch. entomologist U. Calif., Davis, 1973-75; asst. prof. dept. biol. scis. Purdue U., West Lafayette, Ind., 1975-78; asst. prof. dept. biology U. Calif., San Diego, 1978-82, assoc. prof., 1982-86, prof., 1986—, chair dept. biology, 1992-94. Assoc. editor Oecologia, 1986-92, U. Calif. Publs. in Entomology, 1980-92, Evolution, 1984-88, Ecology, 1994—; contbr. numerous articles to profl. jours. Named Outstanding Alumnus, U. Redlands, 1979; Woodrow Wilson fellow, 1969; grantee NSF, 1984-87, 88-91, 90-91, 91-92, 93—, Apple Computer Co., 1987, Nat. Geog. Soc., 1988-91, 92-93, Calif. Dept. Fish and Game, 1995-96, Calif. Met. Water Dist., 1995—, others. Fellow Am. Acad. Arts & Sci.; mem. Am. Soc. Naturalists, Ecol. Soc. Am.

CASE, THOMAS R., career officer; BS in Geography, U.S. Air Force Acad., 1969; Grad., Squadron Officer Sch., 1973; MS in Systems Mgmt., U. So. Calif., LA, 1975; Diploma, U.S. Army Command/Gen. Staff, Coll., 1979, Nat. War Coll., 1987. Commd. 2d lt. USAF, 1969, lt. gen., 1998; various assignments to dir. opers. U.S. Cen. Command, MacDill AFB, Fla., 1997, dep. comdr.-in-chief, chief of staff, 1997-98; comdr. Alaskan Command, 11th Air Force/N.Am. Aerospace Def. Command, Elmendorf AFB, Alaska, 1998—. Decorated Def. Disting. Svc. medal, Legion of Merit with oak leaf cluster, Disting. Flying Cross with oak leaf cluster, Def. Meritorious Svc. medal, Meritorious Svc. medal with two oak leaf clusters, Air medal with 10 oak leaf clusters. Office: 11 AF/CC 9480 Pease Ave Ste 101 Elmendorf AFB AK 99506-2100

CASELLI, VIRGIL P., real estate executive; b. San Francisco, May 29, 1940; s. Americo P. and Cressida N. C.; m. Mary T. McKeon, July 18, 1970; children— Monica, Megan, Virgil Paul. BS, U. Calif., Berkeley, 1963; MBA, U. San Francisco, 1973. Security analyst Wells Fargo Bank, San Francisco, 1963-65; purchasing agt. Raychem Corp., Menlo Park, Calif., 1965-70; founding dir., v.p. 1st Montgomery Corp., San Francisco, 1970-72; div. mgr. Kaiser-Aetna Co., Oakland, Calif., 1972-75; chief exec. officer, exec. v.p., gen. mgr. Ghiradelli Sq., San Francisco, 1975-82; pres. Comml. Property Ventures, Inc., San Francisco, 1982—; CEO C.P. Ventures (named changed Comml. Property Ventures, Inc.), San Francisco, 1990—. Bd. dirs. San Francisco Conv. and Visitors Bur., 1975-83, Cable Car Friends, San Francisco, 1975—, The Guardsmen, Francisco, 1977-79; pres. Fisherman's Wharf Mchts. Assos., 1976-77, San Francisco Parking and Garage Owners Assocs., 1977, dir. Market St. Railway, San Francisco, 2005-. Founder, pres., C.O.B., Com. to Save Cable Cars, 1979-87; trustee U. Calif.-Berkeley Found., 1981-89; bd. dirs. Golden Gate Nat. Parks Assocs., 1983-95, chmn., 1983-87; mem. adv. com. U. San Francisco; mem. adv. coun. Bologna Ctr., Johns Hopkins U. Sch. Advanced Internat. Studies, 1985-92. Comdr. USCG Res., ret. Mem. Soc. Real Property Adminstrs., Bldg. Owners and Mgrs. Inst. Internat. Republican. Roman Catholic. Office: CP Ventures PO Box 1116 Belvedere Tiburon CA 94920-4116 E-mail: vpcaselli@cpventures.us.

CASEY, BARBARA A. PEREA, state legislator, school superintendent; b. Las Vegas, N.Mex., Dec. 21, 1951; d. Joe D. and Julia A. (Armijo) Perea; m. Frank J. Casey, Aug. 5, 1978. BA, N.Mex. U., 1972; MA, Highland U., Las Vegas, N.Mex., 1973. Instr. N.Mex. Highlands U., Las Vegas, 1972-74; tchr. Roswell Ind. Schs., Roswell, N.Mex., 1974-96; supt. Hondo Valley Pub. Schs., N.Mex.; mem. N.Mex. Ho. of Reps., 1984—; supt. Hondo (N.Mex.) Valley Pub. Schs., 1996—2000, West Las Vegas (N.Mex.) Schs., Las Vegas, 2000—. Instr. N.Mex. Mil. Inst., Roswell, 1977-82, Roswell Police Acad., 1984. N.Mex. advisor Nat. Trust for Hist. Preservation. Mem. NEA (Adv. of of Yr.), AAUW, Am. Bus. Women's Assn., N.Mex. Endowment for Humanities. Democrat. Roman Catholic. Avocations: hunting, reading, writing, poetry. Home: 509 Raynolds Ave Las Vegas NM 87701-4323

CASEY, DANIEL E., psychiatrist, educator; b. West Springfield, Mass., Jan. 24, 1947; s. Arthur and Gloria Casey. BA in Psychology, U. Va., 1969, MD, 1972. Diplomate Am. Bd. Psychiatry and Neurology. Resident in psychiatry U. Oreg., Portland, 1973-74, Brown U., Providence, 1974-76; staff psychiatrist VA Med. Ctr., Portland, 1976—2003, chief psychiatry rsch., psychopharmacology, 1980—2003; affiliate sci. Oreg. Regional Primate Rsch. Ctr., Portland, 1980—; prof. psychiatry Oreg. Health and Sci. U., Portland, 1985—, prof. neurology, 1992—. Pres., bd. dirs. Danicas Found., Portland. Author books; Contbr. over 200 articles to profl. jours. Office: Oreg Health and Sci U GH249 Psychiatry Rsch 3181 SW Jackson Park Rd Portland OR 97239 Office Phone: 503-418-1291. E-mail: caseyd@ohsu.edu.

CASEY, M. MICHAEL, food products executive; BS in Econ., Harvard Coll., MBA. V.p. W.R. Grace & Co.; dir. Family Restaurants, 1986—88; pres., CEO El Torito Restaurants, Inc., 1988—93; exec. v.p., CFO Family Restaurants, Inc., 1993—95; sr. v.p., CFO Starbucks, Seattle, 1995—97, exec. v.p., CFO, chief adminstrv. officer, 1997—. Office: Starbucks PO Box 34067 Seattle WA 98124-1067

CASEY, MARY A., telecommunications company executive; Dir. operator svcs. Call Am., 1988-91; dir. customer svc. WCT, 1991-93; co-founder, sec. STAR Telcom., Inc., Santa Barbara, Calif., 1993—; pres. STAR Telecom., Inc., Santa Barbara, Calif., 1996—. Office: Star Telecommunications 2544 Joshua Ct Oxnard CA 93036-6204

CASEY, NANCY J., women's healthcare company executive; BA in English, San Diego State U. Owner, mgr. Nancy Casey Pub. Rels., 1985-97; dir. pub. rels. WestCom Group, 1987-90; sales asst. Dale Fitzmorris, 1990-92; co-founder, co-CEO, As We Change, LLC, 1995-98; v.p. catalog ops. Women First HealthCare, Inc., San Diego, 1998-99, v.p. pub. rels., 1999—.

CASEY, SUE (SUZANNE MARGUERITE PHILIPS), actress, real estate broker; b. LA, Apr. 8, 1926; d. Burke Dewey and Mildred Louise (Hansen) Philips; children: Colleen O'Shaughnessy, John Joseph Durant III, Christopher Kent Durant, Diane Durant; m. Jack Hoffmann (div.); stepchildren: Joy Hoffmann, Kristen Hoffmann Blutman. Student, UCLA Extension, 1972-75. Lic. real estate broker and saleswoman, Calif. With Coldwell Banker, Beverly Hills, Calif. Appeared in numerous movies, including swimming in 5 Esther Williams films, singing and dancing in over 20 films, Goldwyn Girl, 1945-47; (with Judy Garland) Star Is Born, Surf Terror, 1965, Catalina Caper, 1967, Happy Ending, Secrets of Monte Carlo, The Family Jewels, Marriage Young Stockbroker, The Big Circus, The Errand Boy, Two Weeks in Another Town, Paint Your Wagon, Camelot, Evil Speak, 1981, Swamp Country, Ladies Man, Lucky Lady, Annie Get Your Gun, Show Boat, Carpetbaggers, Rear Window, Breakfast at Tiffany's, The Scarf, Main Event, Brady Bunch Sequel, 1996, American Beauty, 1999; appeared in TV shows, including Hunter, Hotel, Hart to Hart, White Shadow, Sunny Valley, Lucy, Gunsmoke, Arnie, Marcus Welby, Sky Terror, Dallas, Days of Our Lives, Unsolved Mysteries, Rosie O'Neill, Haggerty, Emergency, California Fever, I Love Lucy, Farmer's Daughter, Beverly Hillbillies, Delta House, Bodies of Evidence, The Faculty, Divorce Court, Colgate Comedy Shows, Carol Burnett Shows, Red Skelton Show, Roy Bolger Show, All Star Revues, Bob Hope Specials, Ann Southern Show, Family Medical Center, Red Shoe Diaries, What Love Sees, Boy Meets World, 1997, Diagnosis Murder, 1999; has appeared in over 200 TV commls.; stage appearances include Picnic, Goodnight Ladies. Ball chmn. The Footlighters, Inc., 1971-73, 93-94, press chmn., 1972-73, pres., 1982-83, 98-99, parliamentarian, 1983-94, 99-00,02-03, hospitality chmn., 1992-93. Named Ms. Sr. Am. of L.A., 1993. Mem.: AFTRA, SAG, Actors Equity Assn. Office: Coldwell Banker 301 N Canon Dr Beverly Hills CA 90210-4722 Office Phone: 310-777-6344. E-mail: suecaseyla@yahoo.com.

CASEY, THOMAS W., former bank executive; BS in Acctg., Kings Coll., Wilkes-Barre, Pa. Audit supr. Coopers & Lybrand, 1984—90; with Citicorp, 1990—92; from advisor/contr., to analyst GE Capital Corp., 1992—99, sr. v.p., CFO GE Fin., 1999—2002; exec. v.p., CFO Washington Mut., Inc., Seattle, 2002—08. Mem. Pres.'s Coun. Washington Mut., Inc.*

CASH, ROY DON, retired gas and petroleum company executive; b. Shamrock, Tex., June 27, 1942; s. Bill R. and Billie Mae (Lisle) C.; m. Sondra Kay Burleson, Feb. 20, 1966; 1 child, Clay Collin. BS in Indsl. Engring., Tex. Tech U., 1966. Former engr. Amoco Prodn. Co.; v.p. Mountain Fuel Supply, Salt Lake City, 1976-79; pres. Wexpro Co., Salt Lake City, 1979-80; pres., CEO Mountain Fuel Supply Co., Salt Lake City, 1980-84, Questar Corp., Salt Lake City, 1984-85, pres., chmn., CEO, 1985—2003, now bd. dirs. Bd. dirs. Zions Bancorp., Aegis Ins. Svcs., Inc., Nat. Fuel Gas, TODCO. Trustee Holy Cross Hosp., 1987-90, Salt Lake Organizing Com. of 2002 Olympic Winter Games, 1991—2002, So. Utah U., 1992-97; bd. dirs. Utah Symphony Orch., Salt Lake City, 1983-86, 93—2004, Gas Rsch. Inst., 1991-93, Lubbock Symphony Orch., 2003—, Tex. Tech Found., 2002—. Mem. Soc. Petroleum Engrs., Rocky Mountain Oil and Gas Assn. (bd. dirs., pres. 1982-84), Utah Mfrs. Assn. (bd. dirs. 1983-89, chmn. 1986), Pacific Coast Gas Assn. (bd. dirs. 1981-85, 87-97, chmn. 1993-94), Am. Gas Assn. (bd. dirs. 1989-95), Am. Petroleum Inst. (bd. dirs. 1986-91), Nat. Petroleum Coun., Ind. Petroleum Assn. of Am., Salt Lake Area C. of C. (bd. dirs. 1981-84, 89-92, chmn. 1991-92), Alta Club, Jeremy Ranch Golf and Country Club. Avocations: boating, skiing, tennis, fishing, hunting. Office: Questar Corp PO Box 45433 Salt Lake City UT 84145-0433

CASHELL, ROBERT A. (BOB CASHELL), Mayor, Reno, Nevada, former lieutenant governor, business executive; b. Longview, Tex., Apr. 22, 1938; m. Nancy Parker; children: Robert, Patrick, Catherine, Jane. BSBA, Stephen F. Austin State U., 1961. Prin., owner Boomtown, 1967—88; mgmt. trainee Exxon Corp., Houston, sales rep. Oakland, Calif.; mem. bd. regents U. Nev. Sys., 1979—82; lt. gov. State of Nev., Carson City, 1982—86; mayor City of Reno, 2002—; prin., owner Alamo Travel Ctr., Topaz Lodge and Casino; chmn. bd. Cashell Enterprises. Mem. Reno (Nev.) Sparks Conv. and Vis. Authority, Truckee Meadows Water Authority, Truckee Meadows

Tourism Facility; liaison Redevelopment Agy. Citizen's Adv. Com.; chmn. Nev. Econ. Devel. and Tourism Commn., 1983—. Chmn. White House Fellowship Selection Com., Nev. Comprehensive Health Planning Bd., Nev. Higher Edn. Commn., Sierra Nev. Mus. Art; founder YMCA Youth Soccer; mem. adv. bd. Nev. Youth Ctr.; chmn. Nev. Tourism Adv. Coun.; bd. dirs. Sierra Arts Found.; former mem. bd. dirs. U. Nev.-Reno Wolf Pack Boosters; former bd. dirs. City of Reno C. of C. Mem.: Nat. Assn. Truck Stop Operators (bd. dirs.), North Nev. Petroleum Retailers. Office: City of Reno PO Box 1900 Reno NV 89505 also: Cashell Enterprises Inc 1950 E Greg St Sparks NV 89431-6558 Office Phone: 775-334-2001. E-mail: cashellr@cityofreno.com.*

CASIDA, JOHN EDWARD, toxicology and entomology professor; b. Phoenix, Dec. 22, 1929; s. Lester Earl and Ruth (Barnes) Casida; m. Katherine Faustine Monson, June 16, 1956; children: Mark Earl, Eric Gerhard. BS, U. Wis., 1951, MS, 1952, PhD, 1954; D (hon.), U. Buenos Aires, 1997. Research asst. U. Wis., 1951-53, mem. faculty, 1954-63, prof. toxicology & entomology, 1959-63, U. Calif.-Berkeley, 1964—; scholar-in-residence Bellagio Study and Conf. Center, Rockefeller Found., Lake Como, Italy, 1978. Messenger lectr. Cornell U., 1985; Sterling B. Hendricks lectr. USDA and Am. Chem. Soc., 1992; dir. Environ. Chemistry and Toxicology Lab., U. Calif., Berkeley, 1964—; William Muriece Hoskins chair in chem. and molecular entomology U. Calif., Berkeley, 1996—, faculty rsch. lectr., 1998; lectr. in sci. Third World Acad. Scis., Buenos Aires, 1997. Author: rsch. publs. With USAF, 1953. Recipient medal, 7th Internat. Congress Plant Protection, Paris, 1970, Disting. Svc. award, USDA, 1988, Wolf prize in agr., Wolf Found., Isreal, 1993, Koro-Sho prize, Pesticide Sci. Soc. Japan, 1995; named Jeffery lectr., U. New South Wales, Australia, 1983; fellow Haight traveling fellow, 1958—59, Guggenheim fellow, 1970—71. Fellow: Entomol. Soc. (Bussart Meml. award 1989); mem.: NAS, European Acad. Scis., Soc. Environ. Toxicology and Chemistry (Founder's award 1994), Pesticide Sci. Soc. Japan (hon.), Soc. Toxicology (hon.), Am. Chem. Soc. (Internat. award rsch. pesticide chemistry 1970, Spencer award in agrl. and food chemistry 1978), Royal Soc. UK (fgn.). Home: 1570 La Vereda Rd Berkeley CA 94708-2036

CASILLAS, JACQUELINE NIETO, hematologist, oncologist, educator; b. Long Beach, Calif., June 25, 1966; MD, UCLA, 1995. Cert. Pediat., 1998, Pediat. Hematology-Oncology, 2002. Intern pediat. UCLA Med. Ctr., 1995—96, resident, 1996—98, fellowship pediat.-hematology-oncology, 1998—2001; physician pediat. hematology/oncology, Jonsson Comprehensive Cancer Ctr. (JCCC), UCLA, mem. Endocrine Surgery Program, mem. JCCC Patients and Survivors Program Area. Clin. instr. David Geffen Sch. Medicine, UCLA, 1998—2001, asst. prof. Dept. Pediat., 2001—. Office: Jonsson Comprehensive Cancer Ctr 10833 Le Conte Ave Los Angeles CA 90095 Office Phone: 310-825-6185, 310-206-8089. E-mail: jcasillas@mednet.ucla.edu.

CASNOCHA, BENEDICT T., entrepreneur; b. Mar. 1, 1988; Grad., Univ. HS, San Francisco, 2006. Founder & chmn. Comcate, Inc., San Francisco, 2000—. Former mem. adv. bd. BizWorld Found. Author: Ben Casnocha: The Blog, 2004— (named one of Top 25 Blogs in Silicon Valley, San Jose Bus. Jour., 2005), My Start-Up Life: What a (Very) Young CEO Learned on His Journey Through Silicon Valley. Named one of 25 Who are Changing the World of Internet & Politics, PoliticsOnline, 2003, Best Entrepreneurs Under 25, Bus. Week, 2006. Office: Comcate Inc Ste 4200 44 Montgomery St San Francisco CA 94104 Office Phone: 415-517-1547. Office Fax: 415-249-4901. E-mail: ben@comcate.com.

CASPER, GERHARD, law educator, retired academic administrator; b. Hamburg, Germany, Dec. 25, 1937; s. Heinrich and Hertha Casper; m. Regina Koschel, Dec. 26, 1964; 1 child, Hanna. Legal state exam, U. Freiburg, U. Hamburg, 1961; Dr.iur.utr., U. Freiburg, Germany, 1964; LLM, Yale U., 1962, LLD (hon.), 2000, John Marshall Law Sch., 1982, Chgo.-Kent Coll. Law, 1987; PhD (hon.), Uppsala U., 2000. Asst. prof. polit. sci. U. Calif., Berkeley, 1964—66; assoc. prof. law and polit. sci. U. Chgo., 1966—69, prof., 1969—76, Max Pam prof. Am. and fgn. law, 1976—80, William B. Graham prof. law, 1980—87, William B. Graham disting. svc. prof. law, 1987—92, dean law sch., 1979—87, provost, 1989—92; prof. law Stanford U., 1992—, pres., 1992—2000, pres. emeritus, 2000—, Peter and Helen Bing prof. undergraduate edn., 2000—, sr. fellow Inst. Internat. Studies. Vis. prof. law Cath. U., Louvain, Belgium, 1970, U. Munich, 1988, 91. Author: Realism and Political Theory in American Legal Thought, 1967, Separating Power, 1997; co-author: (with Richard A. Posner) The Workload of the Supreme Court, 1976; co-editor: The Supreme Ct. Rev., 1977-91, Successor trustee Yale U., 2000—; bd. dirs. Am. Acad. in Berlin, 2000—; bd. trustees Ctrl. European U., Budapest. Fellow Am. Acad. Arts and Sciences; mem. Internat. Acad. Comparative Law, Am. Bar Found. (bd. dirs. 1979-87), Coun. Fgn. Rels., Am. Law Inst. (coun. 1980—), Am. Philos. Soc., The Trilateral Commn., 1996—, Order pour la mérite für Wissenschaften und Kunste. Office: Stanford U Stanford Inst for Internat Studies E114 Encina Hall Stanford CA 94305-6055 Office Phone: 650-723-2482. E-mail: gcasper@stanford.edu.

CASPER, WAYNE ARTHUR, city official, educator; b. Detroit, June 10, 1949; s. Arthur Eugene and Arlene (Burke) C.; m. Catherine Adelle Lyons, Jan. 22, 1972; children: Catherine, Jeff. BS, U. Ariz., 1971, MS, 1979. Buyer City of Tucson, 1971-74, adminstrv. asst., 1974-75, asst. purchasing agt., 1975-81; procurement dir. State of Ariz., Phoenix, 1981-90; dir. procurement City of Tucson, 1990—. Advisor, City of Mesa Risk Mgmt. Adv. Coun., 1983-88. Mem. Nat. Assn. State Purchasing Inst. (pres. 1991), Nat. Inst. Govtl. Purchasing (Ariz. chpt. treas. 1983, sec. 1984, v.p. 1985, pres. 1986). Roman Catholic. Office: City of Tucson PO Box 27210 Tucson AZ 85726-7210

CASSARD, CHRISTOPHER D., lumber company executive; CFO and treas. North Pacific Group, Portland, Oreg. Office: North Pacific Group PO Box 3915 Portland OR 97208-3915 Office Fax: (503) 238-2646.

CASSELL, PAUL GEORGE, law educator, former federal judge; b. Orange, Calif., June 5, 1959; s. William and Jeanne (Taylor) C.; m. Patricia Smith, Aug. 6, 1988; children: Anna Christine, Emily Elizabeth, Sarah Rose. BA, Stanford U., 1981, JD, 1984. Bar: Utah 1992. Law clk. to Hon. Antonin Scalia US Ct. Appeals (DC Cir.), Washington, 1984-85; law clk. to Chief Justice Warren Burger US Supreme Ct., Washington, 1985-86; assoc. dep. atty. gen. US Dept. Justice, Washington, 1986-88, asst. U.S. atty. (ea. dist.) Va. Alexandria, 1988-91; assoc. prof. U. Utah Coll. Law, Salt Lake City, 1992—97, prof. law, 1997—2000, 2002—08, Farr prof. law, 2000—02, Ronald M. Boyce presdl. prof. law, 2008—; judge US Dist. Ct. Utah, Salt Lake City, 2002—07. Mem. Utah Coun. on Victims, Salt Lake City, 1993—; chair, Judicial Conf. Com. on Criminal Law, 2005 Co-author (with Hugo Bedau): Debating the Death Penalty: The Experts From Both Sides Make Their Case, 2004; co-author: (with Douglas Beloof & Steve Twist) Victims in Criminal Procedure, 2006. Mem. Nat. Victims Constl. Amendment Network, 1994—. Recipient Faculty Achievement award for Teaching Excellence, S.J. Quinney Coll. Law, 1997, Paul M. Bator Award, The Federalist Soc., 1998. Republican. Office: U Utah Coll Law 332 S 1400 E Salt Lake City UT 84112 Office Fax: 801-858-6897. E-mail: cassellp@law.utah.edu.*

CASSIDY, SAMUEL H., lawyer, humanities educator; children: Rachael, Sarah, Samuel H. IV. BA, U. Okla., 1972; JD, U. Tulsa, 1975; postgrad., Harvard U., 1991. Bar: Okla., 1975, U.S. Supreme Ct. 1977, U.S. Ct. Appeals (10th cir.), 1977, Colo. 1982. Pvt. practice law, 1975—; mem. Colo. State Senate, 1991-94; lt. gov. State of Colo., 1994-95; pres. Jefferson Econ. Coun., 1995-97; pres., CEO Colo. Assn. Commerce and Industry, 1997-2000; chair dept. bus. ethics and legal studies U. Denver, 2001—. Bd. dirs. Capital Reporter; instr. U. Tulsa, 1978-81, Tulsa Jr. Coll., 1979; owner High Country Title Co.; developer of residential and commercial real estate, pres. Sam Cassidy, Inc. oil and gas exploration and production co., mem. agriculture and natural resources com., 1991-92, state, mil. and vet. affairs com., 1991-92, local govt. com. 1991, legal svcs. com. 1991-92, hwy. legis. review com. 1991-93, nat. hazards mitigation coun., 1992-93, appropriations com., 1993, judiciary com., 1993; pres. Econ. Devel. Coun. of Colo., 1997-98; exec. com. legis coun., 1993-94, senate svcs. com. 1993; elected Senate Minority Leader, 1993-94, exec. com. Colo. Gen. Assembly; sr. fellow U. Denver, 1997—. Bd. dirs. Colo. DLC, 1993-95, Leadership Jefferson County, Rocky Flats Local Impacts Initiative, dir.; chmn. bd. Arts Comm., Inc. Named Outstanding Legislator for 1991 Colo. Bankers Assn., ACLU Outstanding Legis. 1994; recipient Outsatnding Legis. Efforts award Colo. Counties, Guardian of Small Bus. award, NFIB, 1992, 94; fellow Gates Found., 1991, U. Denver sr. fellow. Mem. Colo. Bar Assn. (bd. gov. 1993-94), S.W. Colo. Bar Assn., Nat. Conf. State Legis. (Colo. rep., task force on state-tribe rels.), Rotary (hon. mem., sustainging Paul Harris fellow), Club 20 (bd. dirs.), San Juan Forum (chmn., bd. dirs.). Avocations: photography, skiing, fishing. Home: # 128 2800 S University Blvd Denver CO 80210 E-mail: scassidy@du.edu.

CASSMAN, MARVIN, biochemist; b. Chgo., Apr. 4, 1936; s. Harry and Anna (Singer) C.; m. Alice M. Baker, June 24, 1972. BA, U. Chgo., 1954, BS, 1957, MS, 1959; PhD, Albert Einstein Coll. Medicine, 1965. Postdoctoral fellow U. Calif., Berkeley, 1965-67, asst. prof. Santa Barbara, 1967-75; adminstr. Nat. Inst. Gen. Med. Sci. NIH, Bethesda, Md., 1975-78, sect. chief, 1978-84, program dir., 1984-89, dep. dir., 1989-93, acting dir., 1993-96, dir., 1996—2001; exec. dir. Inst. for Quantitative Biomedical Rsch., U. Calif., San Francisco, 2001—. Mem. staff subcom. in sci., rsch. and tech. U.S Ho. of Reps., Washington, 1982-83; sr. policy analyst Office Sci. and Tech. Policy The White House, Washington, 1985-86. Recipient Sr. Exec. Svc. award USPHS, 1987, Pres. Meritorious award, 1991. Jewish. Avocations: music, racquetball. Office: U Calif 513 Parnassus Ave Rm 5115 San Francisco CA 94143-0400 Home: 875 Haight St San Francisco CA 94117-3216

CASSO, EDWARD E., state legislator; b. Thornton, Colo., 1975; m. Selena Casso; children: Cecelia, Aristotle. BA, U. Colo., Boulder, 1997. Intern, Rep. David Skaggs, US House of Reps.; precinct committeeman Boulder County Dem. Party; mem. Dist. 32 Colo. House of Reps., Denver, 2007—. Past chmn. State Dem. Party Outreach Comm.; former at-large capt. Adams County Dem. Party; former vice-chmn. Adams County Young Dems. Democrat. Office: Colo State Capitol 200 E Colfax Denver CO 80203 Office Phone: 303-866-2964.*

CASTELLINO, RONALD AUGUSTUS DIETRICH, radiologist, educator; b. NYC, Feb. 18, 1938; s. Leonard Vincent and Henrietta Wilhelmina (Geffken) C.; m. Joyce Cuneo, Jan. 26, 1963; children: Jeffrey Charles, Robin Leonard, Anthony James. Student, Creighton U., Omaha, 1955-58, MD, 1962. Diplomate: Am. Bd. Radiology. Rotating intern Highland Alameda County Hosp., Oakland, Calif., 1962-63; USPHS/Peace Corps physician Brazil, 1963-65; resident in diagnostic radiology Stanford U. Hosp., 1965-68, chief resident, 1967-68; asst. prof. radiology Stanford U. Med. Sch., 1968-74, assoc. prof., 1974-81, prof., 1981-93, chief diagnostic oncologic radiology, 1970-89, chief CT body scanning, 1979-89, dir. div. diagnostic radiology and assoc. chmn. dept. radiology, 1981-86, acting chmn. dept. diagnostic radiology and nuclear medicine, 1986-89, prof. emeritus NYC, 1993—; chair dept. radiology, Carroll and Milton Petrie chair Meml. Sloan Kettering Cancer Ctr., NYC, 1990-98; prof. radiology Cornell Med. Sch., 1994-98, chief med. officer R-2 tech., 1998—2007, chief med. officer hologic, 2007—. Mem. U.S. Cancer del., People's Republic China, 1977 Co-editor: Pediatric Oncologic Radiology, 1977; assoc. editor; Lymphology, 1973-97, Investigative Radiology, 1985-94, Academic Radiology, 1994-97, Radiology, 1986-94, Postgrad. Radiology, 1986-98; contbr. numerous rsch. papers to profl. jours., chpts. to books. Recipient T.F. Eckstrom Fund award, 1978; Guggenheim fellow, 1974-75 Mem.: N.Y. Acad. Medicine, N.Y. Roentgen Soc., Calif. Acad. Medicine, N.Am. Soc. Lymphology (charter), Soc. Cancer Imaging (charter), Soc. Thoracic Radiology (charter), Calif. Radiol. Soc., Calif. Med. Assn. (adv. panel sect. radiology 1972—89), Western Angiography Soc. (charter), Internat. Cancer Imaging Soc. (charter), Am. Roentgen Ray Soc., Soc. Cardiovascular and Interventional Radiology (charter), Radiol. Soc. N.Am., Assn. Univ. Radiologists (exec. com. 1981—85), Am. Coll. Radiology, Internat. Soc. Lymphology (exec. com. 1975—85), Am. Soc. Therapeutic Radiation Oncologists (hon.), Alpha Omega Alpha. Personal E-mail: rcastellino@sbcglobal.net.

CASTELLO, JOHN L., pharmaceutical executive; Chmn. bd., CEO, pres. Xoma Corp., Berkeley, Calif. Office: Xoma Corp 2910 7th St Ste 100 Berkeley CA 94710-2743

CASTILLO, SUSAN, school system administrator; b. LA, Aug. 14, 1951; m. Paul Machu. BA in Comm., Oreg. State U., 1981. Mem. staff Oreg. Pub. Broadcasting Radio, 1979-82; journalist, reporter legis. sessions Sta. KVAL-TV, Salem, 1991, 93, 95, journalist, reporter Eugene, 1982-97; mem., Dist. 20 Oreg. State Senate, Salem, 1997—2002, vice chair edn. com., mem. health and human svcs. com., mem. transp. com., asst. Dem. leader legis. sessions, 1999, 2001; supt. pub. instrn. State of Oreg., Salem, 2003—. Leader Oreg. Women's Health & Wellness Alliance. Mem. Gov.'s Task Force on DUII, 1997, Gov.'s Task Force on Cmty. Right to Know; bd. dirs. Oreg. Commn. on Hispanic Affairs, 1997, Birth to Three, Oreg. Environ. Coun.; mem. adv. com. Oreg. Passenger Rail Adv. Coun.; mem. Labor Comm.'s Adv. Com. on Agrl. Labor; vice-chair Farm Worker Housing Task Force. Democrat. Achievements include being the first Hispanic woman to serve in Oregon legislature. Office: Oregon Dept Education 255 Capitol St NE Salem OR 97310-0203 Office Phone: 503-947-5740. E-mail: superintendent.castillo@state.or.us.

CASTLE, EMERY NEAL, economist, educator; b. Eureka, Kans., Apr. 13, 1923; s. Sidney James and Josie May (Tucker) C.; m. Merab Eunice Weber (dec.), Jan. 20, 1946; 1 child, Cheryl Diana Delozier; m. Betty Thompson, Mar. 18, 2000. BS, Kans. State U., 1948, MS, 1950; PhD, Iowa State U., 1952, LHD (hon.), 1997, Oreg. State U., 2006. Economist Fed. Res. Bank of Kansas City, 1952—54; from asst. prof. to prof. dept. agrl. econs. Oreg. State U., Corvallis, 1954—65, dean faculty, 1965—66, prof., head dept. agrl. econs., 1966—72, dean Grad. Sch., 1972—76, Alumni disting. prof., 1970, prof. grad. faculty econs., 1986—93; v.p., sr. fellow Resources for the Future, Washington, 1976—79, pres., 1979—86. Vice-chmn. Environ. Quality Commn. Oreg., 1988-95. Editor: The Changing American Countryside: Rural People and Places, 1995. Recipient Alumni Disting. Service award Kans. State U., 1976; Disting. Service award Oreg. State U., 1984. Fellow AAAS, Am. Assn. Agrl. Economists (pres. 1972-73), mem. Am. Acad. Arts and Scis. Home: 4649 SW Hollyhock Cir Corvallis OR 97333 Home Phone: 541-752-3755. Personal E-mail: emerycastle@comcast.net.

CASTLEBERRY, ARLINE ALRICK, architect; b. Mpls., Sept. 19, 1919; d. Bannona Gerhardt and Meta Emily (Veit) Alrick; m. Donald Montgomery Castleberry, Dec. 25, 1941; children: Karen, Marvin. B in Interior Architecture, U. Minn., 1941; postgrad., U. Tex., 1947-48. Designer, draftsman Elizabeth & Winston Close, Architects, Mpls., 1940-41, Northwest Airlines, Mpls., 1942-43, Cerny & Assocs., Mpls., 1944-46; archtl. draftsman Dominick and Van Benscotten, Washington, 1946-47; ptnr. Castleberry & Davis Bldg. Designers, Burlingame, Calif., 1960-65; prin. Burlingame, 1965-90; ret. Recipient Smith Coll. scholarship. Mem. AIA, Am. Inst. Bldg. Designers (chpt. pres. 1971-72), Commaisini, Alpha Alpha Gamma, Chi Omega. Democrat. Lutheran. Home and Office: 1311 Parrott Dr San Mateo CA 94402-3630 E-mail: dcac6@juno.com.

CASTLEBERRY, W. THOMAS, financial company executive; b. Tuscon, Aug. 3, 1937; s. Wayne Texas and Dorothy (Roby) C.; m. Jean Ann Mrocek, Oct. 24, 1972; children: Melanie, Mark, Kelly, Cheryl, Nicole, Matthew. BS, U. Calif., Davis, 1960. Cons. Touche Ross, San Francisco, 1967-69; sr. v.p. Crocker Nat. Bank, 1969-72; sr. v.p. $D Ramada Inns, Phoenix, 1972-78; v.p. EDS, Phoenix, 1978-80; chmn. CEO Anasazi, Phoenix, 1980-83, 87-93; sr. v.p. VISA, Phoenix, 1983-87, FDC, Phoenix, 1993-95; vice chmn., CEO Rezsolutions, Phoenix, 1996—99; chmn. bd. & CEO Eldorado Computing, Inc., Phoenix, 2000—. Capt. U.S. Army, 1960-61, with USNG, 1961-72. Mem. Phoenix Boys and Girls Clubs. Office: Eldorado Computing Inc 5353 N 16th St Ste 400 Phoenix AZ 85016

CASTOR, WILBUR (WEBB) WRIGHT, futurist, writer, consultant, playwright, actor; b. Harrison Twp., Pa., Feb. 3, 1932; s. Wilbur Wright and Margaret (Grubbs) C.; m. Donna Ruth Schwartz, Feb. 9, 1963; children: Amy, Julia, Marnie. BA, St. Vincent Studies, 1959; PhD, Calif. U. Advanced Studies, 1990. Sales rep. IBM, Pitts. and Cleve., 1959-62; v.p. data processing ops. Honeywell, Waltham, Mass., 1962-80; pres., chief exec. officer Aviation Simulation Tech., Lexington, Mass., 1980-82; sr. v.p. Xerox Corp., El Segundo, Calif., 1982-89; freelance cons., 1989—. Author: (play) Un Certaine Soirire, 1958, (mus. comedy) Breaking Up, 1960, (stage play) This is Your Wife, 1997, (book) The Information Age and the New Productivity, 1990, (ballet) Animal Crackers, 2003; contbg. author: How To Manage Change Effectively, 1985; contbr. articles to profl. jours. Mem. Presdl. Rep. Task Force; pres., bd. dirs. Internat. Acad., Santa Barbara, Olendorf Found., Ryan Bldg. Group, 2003-, SAVE; chmn. bd. dirs. Marymount Coll., 1999—; bd. dir. USC Rossier Sch., LA Bio Med. Capt. USN, 1953—58, with USAFR, 1958—76. Named Disting. Alumnus of Yr., St. Vincent Coll., 1990. Mem. The Strategy Bd., U. Denver "Netthink", World Future Soc., Aircraft Owners and Pilots Assn., U.S. Senators Club. Avocations: flying, scuba diving, music, reading, writing. Home: 19 Georgeff Rd Rolling Hills Estates CA 90274-5272

CASTRO, JOSEPH ARMAND, music director, pianist, composer, orchestrator; b. Miami, Ariz., Aug. 15, 1927; s. John Loya and Lucy (Sanchez) C.; m. Loretta Faith Haddad, Oct. 21, 1966; children: John Joseph, James Ernest. Student, San Jose State Coll., 1944-47. Mus. dir. Herb Jeffries, Hollywood, Calif., 1952, June Christy, Hollywood, 1959-63, Tony Martin, Hollywood, 1962-64, Anita O'Day, Hollywood, 1963-65, Folies Bergere, 1980-89, Tropicana Hotel, Las Vegas, Nev., 1980-97, Desert Inn, Las Vegas, 1992-93; orch. leader Mocambo Night Club, Hollywood, 1952-54; soloist Joe Castro Trio, LA, NYC, Honolulu, 1952-65, Sands Hotel, Desert Inn, Las Vegas, 1975-80; with Joe Castro Trio and Loretta Castro, 1995—. Co-founder JoDo Inc., 1964, Clover Records, 1964. Recs. include (in 1950s) Zoot Sims, Oscar Pettiford, Lucky Thompson, Ron Jefferson, Sonny Truitt, Doris Duke's Farms, Falcon Lair Beverly Hills, LA, Cool School with June Christy, 1960, Anita O'Day Sings Rodgers and Hart, 1961, Lush Life, 1966, Groove-Funk-Soul, Mood Jazz, Atlantic Records, Ballads for Night People with June Christy, Road Show with Stan Kenton Orch., Best of June Christy Jazz Series, Spotlight on June Christy, Anita O'Day, Verve Records, Billy May Swing Rodgers & Hart, also albums with Teddy Edwards, Stan Kenton, Jimmy Borges with Joe Castro Trio, 1990, Loretta Castro with Joe Castro Trio, 1990; command performance, Queen Elizabeth II, London Palladium, 1989, Concerts with Jimmy Borges and Honolulu Symphony Pops Concerts, 1991; jazz concert (with Nigel Kennedy) Honolulu Symphony, 1990; jazz-fest, Kailua-Kona, Hawaii, 1990. With US Army, 1946-47. Roman Catholic. Home and Office: 2812 Colanthe Ave Las Vegas NV 89102-2026 Office Phone: 702-878-2898. Fax: 702-878-9588. E-mail: jolo1@earthlink.net.

CASTRO, LEONARD EDWARD, lawyer; b. LA, Mar. 18, 1934; s. Emil Galvez and Lily (Meyerholtz) Castro; 1 child, Stephen Paul. AB, UCLA, 1959, JD, 1962. Bar: Calif. 1963, US Supreme Ct. 1970. Assoc. Musick, Peeler & Garrett, LA, 1962—68, ptnr., 1968—. Mem. bd. editors, note and comment editor UCLA Law Rev., 1961—62; panelist, spkr. legal edn. programs. Contbr. chapters to books. Mem.: ABA, LA County Bar Assn. Office: Musick Peeler & Garrett 1 Wilshire Blvd Ste 2000 Los Angeles CA 90017-3876

CASTRO, MARIA GRACIELA, medical educator, geneticist, researcher; b. Buenos Aires, Mar. 2, 1955; d. Nestor Antonio Castro and Maria Esther Rodriquez; m. Pedro Ricardo Lowenstein, Jan. 12, 1988; 1 child, Elijah David Lowenstein. BSc 1st class in Chemistry, Nat. U. La Plata, Argentina, 1979, MSc in Biochemistry, 1981, PhD in Biochemistry, 1986. Fogarty postdoctoral fellow Lab. Neurochemistry and Neuroimmunology Nat. Inst. Child Health and Human DEvel., NIH, Bethesda, Md., 1986—88; sr. rsch. fellow Lab. Molecular Endocrinology, dept. biochemistry and physiology U. Reading, England, 1988—90; lectr. neurosci., dept. physiology U. Wales Coll., Cardiff, 1991—95; sr. lectr. medicine Sch. Medicine U. Manchester, England, 1995—98, prof. molecular medicine, 1998—2001; prof. medicine UCLA, 2002—, prof. molecular pharmacology, 2004—. Lectr. dept. molecular and life scis. U. Abertay, Dundee, Scotland, 1991—92; dir. molecular medicine and gene therapy U. Manchester, England, 1996—; expert Women in Sci. Tech., Sheffield, 1996—; mem. neurosci. panel Wellcome Trust, 1999—; co-dir. dept. molecular medicine Cedars-Sinai Med. Ctr., 2001—, co-dir. bd. govs. Gene Therapeutics Rsch. Inst., 2001—; bd. govs. The Linda Tallen and David Paul Kane Found., 2003—; mem. Jonsson Comprehensive Cancer Ctr. UCLA, 2004—, mem. Brain Rsch. Inst., 2005—; chair in gene therapeutics Medallions Group, 2006—. Mem. editl. bd.: Jour. Endocrinology, Jour. Molecular Endocrinology, Current Gene Therapy, Gene Therapy, Pituitary, 2000, Neuro Molecular Medicine, 2001—; contbr. articles to profl. jours. Rsch. grantee, Brit. Heart Found., 1997, Med. Rsch. Coun., 1998, Biotech. and Biol. Rsch. Coun., 1999—2000, Wellcome Trust, 1999, NIH, Nat. Inst. Neurol. Disorders and Stroke, 2003—. Mem.: Am. Soc. Microbiology, Soc. Neuro-oncology, Am. Assn. Immunologists, Am. Assn. Cancer Rsch., Nat. Inst. Neurol. Disorders and Stroke, Internat. Soc. Nerovirology (founding mem.), Soc. Neurosci., Endocrine Soc., Am. Gene Therapy Assn. Achievements include patents in field; research in program in development of gene therapy for chronic neurological diseases and brain cancer; application to FDA to start a Phase I clinical trial for glioma in human patients. Business E-Mail: castromg@cshs.org.

CASTRO, RAUL HECTOR, lawyer, Former Governor, Arizona, ambassador; b. Cananea, Mexico, June 12, 1916; arrived in US, 1926, naturalized, 1939; s. Francisco D. and Rosario (Acosta) C.; m. Patricia M. Norris, Nov. 13, 1954; children: Mary Pat, Beth. BA, Ariz. State Coll., 1939; JD, U. Ariz., 1949; LL.D. (hon.), No. Ariz. U., 1966, Ariz. State U., 1972, U. Autonoma de Guadalajara, Mex. Bar: Ariz. 1949. Fgn. service clk. Dept. State, Agua Prieta, Mexico, 1941-46; instr. Spanish U. Ariz., 1946-49; sr. ptnr. Castro & Wolfe, Tucson, 1949-51; dep. county atty. Pima County, Ariz., 1951-54; county atty., 1954-58; judge Pima County Superior Ct., Tucson, 1958-64, Juvenile Ct., Tucson, 1961-64; US ambassador to El Salvador, 1964—68, Bolivia, 1968—69; practice internat. law Tucson, 1969-74, Phoenix, 1980—; gov. State of Ariz., 1975-77; US ambassador to Argentina, 1977-80; sr. ptnr. Castro, Zipf & Rogers, 1982—92, Castro & Zipf, 1992—. Operator Castro Pony Farm, 1954—64. Pres. Pima County Tb and Health Assn., Tucson Youth Bd., Ariz. Horseman's Assn.; Bd. dirs. Tucson chpt. A.R.C., Tucson council Boy Scouts Am., Tucson YMCA, Nat. Council Christians and Jews, YWCA Camp; Bd. Mem. Ariz. N.G., 1935-39. Recipient Outstanding Naturalized Citizen award Pima County Bar Assn., 1964, Outstanding Am. Citizen award DAR, 1964, Pub. Service award U. Ariz., 1966, John F. Kennedy medal Kennedy U., Buenos Aires, Disting. Citizens award, 1977, Matias Delgado award, Govt. El Salvador. Mem. Am. Fgn. Service Assn., Am. Judicature Soc., Inter-Am. Bar Assn., Ariz. Bar Assn., Pima County Bar Assn., Nat. Council Crime and Deliquency (bd. dirs.), Assn. Trial Lawyers Am., Council Am. Ambassadors, Nat. Assn. Trial Judges, Nat. Council Juvenile Ct. Judges, Fed. Bar Assn., Nat. Lawyers Club, Phi Alpha Delta, Phi Sigma Delta. Clubs: Rotarian. Democrat. Roman Catholic. Office Phone: 520-287-3132.

CASTRUITA, RUDY, school system administrator; BA in Social Sci., Utah State U., 1966, MS in Sch. Adminstrn., 1967; EdD, U. So. Calif., 1983. Cert. adminstrv. svcs., std. secondary, pupil svcs. Dir. econ. opportunity program City of El Monte, Calif., 1966-67; secondary tchr., counselor, program coord. El Monte Union High Sch. Dist., 1967-75, asst. prin. Mountain View High Sch., 1975-80; prin. Los Alamitos (Calif.) High Sch. Los Alamitos Unified Sch. Dist., 1980-85; asst. supt. secondary divsn. Santa Ana (Calif.) Unified Sch. Dist., 1985-87, assoc. supt. secondary divsn., 1987-88, supt., 1988-94; supt. schs. San Diego County, 1994—. Adj. prof. Calif. State U., Long Beach, 1981-88, mem. adv. com. dept. ednl. adminstrn., 1983-86; adj. prof. U. San Francisco, 1984-88; mem. State Tchr. of Yr. Selection Com., 1988, Student Tchr. Edn. Project Coun., SB 620 Healthy Start Com., SB 1274 Restructuring Com., Joint Task Force Articulation, State High Sch. Task Force; mem. Latino eligibility study U. Calif., mem. ednl. leadership inst.; mem. state adv. coun. Supt. Pub. Instrn.; Delta Epsilon lectr. U. So. Calif.; rep. Edn. Summit; mem. selection com. Calif. Ednl. Initiatives Fund; co-chair subcom. at risk youth Calif. Edn. Com., 1989; mentor supt. Harvard Urban Supt.'s Program, 1993—. Chair Orange County Hist. Adv. Coun., South El Monte Coordinating Coun.; mem. exec. coun. Santa Ana 2000; mem. articulation coun. Rancho Santiago C.C. Dist.; active Hacienda Heights Recreation and Pks. Commn., Santa Ana City Coun. Stadium Blue Ribbon Com.; exec. dir. Orange County coun. Boy Scouts Am.; mem. adv. com. Bowers Mus.; mem. exec. bd. El Monte Boys Club; hon. lifetime mem. Calif. PTA; bd. dirs. Santa Ana Boys and Girls Club, Orange County Philharm. Soc., Santa Ana Pvt. Industry Coun., El Monte-South El Monte Consortium, Drug Use is Life Abuse, EDUCARE sch. edn. U. So. Calif. Named Supt. of Yr. League United Latin Am. Citizens, 1989; state finalist Nat. Supt. Yr. award, 1992. Mem. ASCD, Assn. Calif. Sch. Adminstrs. (rep. region XVII secondary prins. com. 1981-85, presenter region XVII 1984, Calif. Supt. of Year award 1991, Marcus Foster award 1991), Calif. Sch. Bds. Assn. (mem. policy and analysis com.), Assn. Calif. Urban Sch. Dists. (pres. 1992—), Orange County Supts. (pres.), Santa Ana C. of C. (bd. dirs.), Delta Epsilon (pres. 1990-91), Phi Delta Kappa. Office: San Diego County Supt Office 6401 Linda Vista Rd San Diego CA 92111-7319

CASWELL, PAULETTE REVA WATSTEIN, educational consultant, researcher; d. Ben and Lillian (Cohen) Watstein; m. Charles Frank Caswell III, Jan. 8, 1983 (dec. 1996); 1 child, David Allan Philip. AA, West L.A. C.C., 1971; BA, Calif. State U., 1975; JD, Whittier Coll., 1982; DD (hon.), St. Alban's Ch. of the Way, 1974; MS, U. So. Calif., 1997; AS, Excelsior Coll., 1998, BS, 1999; PhD, U. So. Calif., 2003. Diplomate Am. Bd. Profl. Disability Analysts, lic. pvt. pilot, pvt. investigator. Dir. Mensa of L.A., 1977—83; CEO, founder Amicus, Inc., 1985—; internat. 2d v.p. WRAD, Inc., 1985—2005. Editor: Consumer Rights, 1982; contbr. articles to pamphlets, booklets, chapters to books. Mem.: ABA, TASA Network, Mensa (life), Phi Delta Kappa, Phi Beta Delta. Avocation: languages. Office Phone: 323-653-9140.

CATE, JAN HARRIS, lawyer; b. NYC, Jan. 9, 1964; BA with honors, Univ. Calif., San Diego, 1986; JD, Boston Univ., 1989. Bar: Calif. 1989. Ptnr., leader Bank Fin. practice Pillsbury Winthrop Shaw Pittman, LA. Contbr. articles to profl. jours. Mem.: LA County Bar Assn. Office: Pillsbury Winthrop Shaw Pittman Suite 2800 725 S Figueroa St Los Angeles CA 90017 Office Phone: 213-488-7539. Office Fax: 213-629-1033. Business E-Mail: jan.cate@pillsburylaw.com.

CATE, RODNEY MICHAEL, academic administrator; b. Sudan, Tex., May 9, 1942; s. Tommy A. and Elsie P. (Cherry) C.; m. Patricia Cate, June 11, 1941; children: Brandi, Shani. BS in Pharmacy, U. Tex., 1965; MS in Family Studies, Tex. Tech. U., 1975; PhD in Human Devel. and Family Studies, Pa. State U., 1979. Asst. prof. Tex. Tech. U., Lubbock, 1978-79, Oreg. State U., Corvallis, 1979-83, assoc. prof., 1983-85; prof., dept. chmn. Washington State U., Pullman, 1985-90; assoc. dean Iowa State U., Ames, 1990-94; dir Sch. Family and Consumer Resources U. Ariz., Tucson, 1994-99, prof., 1999—. Co-author: Courtship, 1992; editor: Family and Cons. Rsch. Jour., 1992; contbr. articles to profl. jours. Lt. USN, 1966-69. Mem. Am. Assn. Family and Cons. Scis. Assn. (James D. Moran Meml. Rsch. award 1991), Am. Psychol. Assn., Nat. Coun. on Family Rels., Internat. Soc. for the Study Personal Relationships. Democrat. Office: U Ariz Sch Family and Consumer Resources Bldg 33 Tucson AZ 85721-0033

CATER, JACK ERNEST, acoustical engineer, researcher; b. NYC, Apr. 28, 1950; s. Ernest Everett Cater, Jr. and June Mary Cater; m. Judy Jerstad, Nov. 24, 1973; children: Joanne, Jennifer. SBEE, MIT, 1972, SM in Ocean Engring., 1974. Cons. Lincoln Lab., Lexington, Mass., 1972—73; rsch. employee MIT, 1972—74; sr. engr. BBN Sys. and Techs. Corp., San Diego, 1977—. Asst. scoutmaster Boy Scouts Am., 1976—. Lt. USNR, 1974—77. Recipient Silver Beaver award, St. George's medal; named Eagle Scout, Boy Scouts Am. Mem.: IEEE, N.Y. Acad. Scis., Acoustical Soc. Am., Sigma Xi. Office: BBN Labs Inc 4015 Hancock St Ste 101 San Diego CA 92110-5153

CATES, GILBERT, television and film producer, theater director; b. NYC, June 6, 1934; s. Nathan and Nina (Peltzman) Katz; m. Jane Betty Dubin, Feb. 9, 1957 (div.); children: Melissa Beth, Jonathan Michael, David Sawyer, Gilbert Lewis; m. Judith Reichman, Jan. 25, 1987; stepchildren: Ronit Reichman, Anat Reichman. BS, Syracuse U., 1955, MA, 1965. Prof. theatre, film and TV UCLA, 1990—, dean, 1990-99; with Cates-Doty Prodns., Inc.; prodr. dir. Geffen Playhouse, LA, 1995—. Com. mem. 1 drama dept. Syracuse U., 1969-73. TV prodr., dir. Haggis Baggis, 1959, Camouflage, 1961-62, Internat. Showtime, 1962-64, Hootenanny, 1962, To All My Friends on Shore, 1972, The Affair, 1974, After the Fall, 1974, Johnny, We Hardly Knew Ye, 1977, The Kid From Nowhere, 1982, Country Gold, 1982, Faerie Tale Theatre, 1982, Hobson's Choice, 1983, Consenting Adult, 1984, Child's Cry?, 1986, Fatal Judgement, 1988, One More Time, 1988, Muffin Man, 1989, Call Me Anna, 1990, Absolute Strangers, 1991, Overruled, 1992, Confessions-Two Faces of Evil, 1994, Innocent Victims, 1995, A Death in the Family - Masterpice Theatre, 2001, Collected Stories-PBS, 2002; film prodr., dir.: The Painting, 1962, Rings Aroung the World, 1967, I Never Sang for My Father, 1970, Summer Wishes, Winter Dreams, 1973, Dragonfly, 1976, The Promise, 1978, The Last Married Couple in America, 1979, O God, Book II, 1980, Backfire, 1986; theatrical prodr.: You Know I Can't Hear You When the Water's Running, 1967, I Never Sang for My Father, 1968, The Chinese and Doctor Fish, 1970, Solitaire-Double Solitaire, 1971; dir.: Voices, 1972, Tricks of the Trade, 1980, Collected Stories, 1999, Under the Blue Sky, 2002, Paint Your Wagon, 2004, Cat on a Hot Tin Roof, 2005, A Picasso, 2007; prodr.: Ann. Acad. Awards, 1990-1995, 97-99, 2001, 03-06, 08, To Life, America Celebrates Israel's 50th (CBS-TV), 1998, America Celebrates Ford's Theater (ABC-TV), 1999, 2000, 02, 03, 04, 05, 06, 07, CBS at 75, 2003. Bd. dirs. Israeli Cancer Rsch. Fund, 1992-94. Recipient Best Short Film award Internat. Film Importers and Distbrs., 1962, Chancellor's medal Syracuse U., 1974, Emmy award, 1991, Star on Hollywood Walk of Fame, 1994, Jimmy Doolittle award L.A. Theater, 1998, Best Prodn. Ovation award, 1999, Lifetime Dirs. Achievement award Caucus of Prodrs., Writers and Dirs., 1998, Arents award Syracuse U., 2003, Career Achievement award Am. Soc. Cinematographers, 2004, Cinema Audio Soc., 2007. Mem. Dirs. Guild Am. (hon. life award 1990, v.p. Ea. region 1965, Western region 1980—, pres. 1983-87, Robert B. Aldrich award 1989, nat. sec.-tras. 1997—, Pres.'s award 2005), Acad. Motion Picture Arts and Scis. (bd. govs., chmn. bd. dirs. 1985-94, 2003—), Women in Film (bd. dirs. 1993-94. v.p. 2003), League N.Y. Theatres. Office: 10920 Wilshire Blvd Ste 1840 Los Angeles CA 90024-6510 E-mail: gil@geffenplayhouse.com.

CATHEY, WADE THOMAS, electrical engineering educator; b. Greer, SC, Nov. 26, 1937; s. Wade Thomas Sr. and Ruby Evelyn (Waters) C.; children: Susan Elaine, Cheryl Ann. BS, U. S.C., 1959, MS, 1961; PhD, Yale U., 1963. Group scientist Rockwell Internat., Anaheim, Calif., 1962-68; from assoc. prof. to prof. elec. engring. U. Colo., Denver, 1968-85, chmn. dept. elec. engring. and computer sci., 1984-85, chmn. faculty senate, 1982-83, prof. Boulder, 1985-97, rsch. prof., 1997—2003, prof. emeritus elec. engring., 2003—; chief tech. officer CDM Optics, 2005—06. Pres. CDM Optics, 1996-2005; dir. NSF Ctr. Optoelectronic Computing Sys., Boulder, 1987-93; cons. in field, 1968—. Author: Optical Information Processing and Holography, 1978; contbr. articles to profl. jours.; inventor in field. Croft fellow, U. Colo., 1982, Faculty fellow, U. Colo., 1972-73. Fellow IEEE, Optical Soc. Am. (topical editor 1977-79, 87-90), Soc. Photo-Optic Instrumentation Engrs. Achievements include extend focal depth and passive ranging in imaging systems, research on matching image acquisiton and signal processing systems.

CATMULL, EDWIN EARL, film company executive, computer graphics engineer; b. Parkersburg, W.Va., Mar. 31, 1945; married; 5 children. BS in Computer Sci. and Physics, U. Utah, PhD in Computer Sci., 1974. V.p. computer divsn. Lucasfilm, Ltd., 1979—86; co-founder, pres. Pixar Animation Studios, Emeryville, Calif., 1986, pres., 1986—88, chmn., chief tech. officer, 1988—91, pres., 1991—, Walt Disney Animation Studios, 2007—. Recipient Coons award, 1993, Academy award of Merit, 2001, John von Neumann medal, IEEE, 2006, Gordon E. Sawyer award, Acad. Motion Pictures Arts & Sciences, 2009; named to High-Tech Hall of Fame, Utah Info. Tech. Assn., 2001. Mem. NAE, Acad. Motion Picture Arts and Scis. (Sci. and Tech. engring. award, sci. and tech. awards com.). Achievements include research in computer graphics, video editing, video games, digital video, digital computer graphics and animation. Office: Pixar Animation Studios 1200 Park Ave Emeryville CA 94608*

CATTERALL, WILLIAM A., pharmacology, neurobiology educator; b. Providence, Oct. 12, 1946; s. William V. and Alice C.; children: W. Douglas, Elizabeth R.; m. Christine E. BA in Chemistry, Brown U., 1968; PhD in Physiol. Chemistry, Johns Hopkins U., 1972. Postdoctoral research fellow Lab. of Biochem. Genetics NIH, Bethesda, Md., 1972-76, staff scientist, 1976-77; assoc. prof. dept. pharmacology U. Wash., Seattle, 1977-82, prof., 1982—, chmn. dept. pharmacology, 1984—, chmn. interdisciplinary com. on neurobiology, 1986—. Editor: Molecular Pharmacology, 1986—90; contbr. chapters to books, articles to profl. jours. Recipient Young Scientist award Passano Found., 1981, Jacob Javits Neurosci award, NIH, 1984, 91, Basic Sci. prize Am. Heart Assn., 1992, Bristol Myers Squibb award, 2003; numerous grants. Mem. Nat. Acad. Sci., Inst. of Medicine, Am. Acad. Arts and Sci., Am. Soc. Pharmacology and Exptl. Therapeutics, Soc. for Neurosci., Am. Soc. Biol. Chemists. Avocations: sailing, skiing. Office: Univ Wash Dept Pharmacology PO Box 357280 Seattle WA 98195-7280 E-mail: wcatt@u.washington.edu.

CATTERTON, MARIANNE ROSE, occupational therapist; b. St. Paul, Feb. 3, 1922; d. Melvin Joseph and Katherine Marion (Bole) Maas; m. Elmer John Wood, Jan. 16, 1943 (dec.); m. Robert Lee Catterton, Nov. 20, 1951 (div. 1981); children: Jenifer Ann Dawson, Cynthia Lea Uthus. Student, Carleton Coll., 1939—41, U. Md., 1941—42; BA in English, U. Wis., 1944; MA in Counseling Psychology, Bowie State Coll., 1980; postgrad., No. Ariz. U., 1987—91. Registered occupl. therapist, Occupl. Therapy Cert. Bd. Occupl. therapist VA, NYC, 1946—50; cons. occupl. therapist Fondo del Seguro del Estado, PR, 1950—51; dir. rehab. therapies Spring Grove State Hosp., Catonsville, Md., 1953—56; occupl. therapist Anne Arundel County Health Dept., Annapolis, Md., 1967—78; dir. occupl. therapy Ea. Shore Hosp. Ctr., Cambridge, Md., 1979—85; cons. occupl. therapist Kachina Point Health Ctr., Sedona, Ariz., 1986. Regional chmn. Conf. on revising Psychiat. Occupl. Therapy Edn., 1958-59; instr. report writing Anne Arundel C.C., Annapolis, 1974-78. Editor: Am. Jour. Occupl. Therapy, 1962—67. Active Md. Mental Health Assn., 1959—60; mem. task force on occupl. therapy edn. Md. Dept. Health, 1971—72; chmn. Anne Arundel Gov. Com. on Employment of Handicapped, 1959—63; gov.'s com. to study vocat. rehab. Md., 1960; com. mem. Annapolis Youth Ctr., 1976—78; curator Dorchester County Heritage Mus., Cambridge, 1982—83; citizen interviewer Sedona Acad. Forum, 1993, 1994; vol. Respite Care, 1994—98, Verde Valley Caregivers, 1993—; ministerial search com. Unitarian Ch. Anne Arundel County, 1962; v.p., officer Unitarian-Universalist Fellowship Flagstaff, 1988—93, v.p., 1993—97; co-moderator, founder Unitarian-Universalist Fellowship Sedona, 1994—96, pres., 1997—98, co-pres., 2001—03. Mem.: Dorchester County Mental Health Assn. (pres. 1981—84), Md. Occupl. Therapy Assn. (del. 1953—59), Am. Occupl. Therapy Assn. (chmn. history com. 1958—61), PR Occupl. Therapy Assn. (co-founder 1950), Sedona Muses, Population Connection, Ret. Officers Assn., Pathfinder Internat., Air Force Assn. (sec. Barry Goldwater chpt. 1991—92, 1994—2006), Toastmasters, Internat. Club (chmn. publicity Annapolis chpt. 1966), Severn Town Club (treas. 1965, sec. 1971—72, 1994—95), Delta Delta Delta. Republican. Home: 415 Windsong Dr Sedona AZ 86336-3745 Home Phone: 928-282-6707.

CATTRALL, KIM, actress; b. Liverpool, Eng., Aug. 21, 1956; d. Dennis and Shane Cattrall; m. Larry Davis, 1975 (div.); m. Andre J. Lyson, 1982 (div. 1989); m. Mark Levinson, Sept. 4, 1998. Student, London Acad. Music and Dramatic Art, Banff Sch. Fine Arts, Alta., Can.; grad., Am. Acad. Dramatic Arts, NYC. Actor: (films) Rosebud, 1975, Tribute, 1980, Ticket to Heaven, 1981, Porky's, 1982, Police Academy, 1984, Turk 182!, 1985, City Limits, 1985, Hold-Up, 1985, Big Trouble in Little China, 1986, Mannequin, 1987, Masquerade, 1988, Palais Royale, 1988, Midnight Crossing, 1988, The Return of the Musketeers, 1989, La Famiglia Buonanotte, 1989, Honeymoon Academy, 1990, Bonfire of the Vanities, 1990, Star Trek VI: The Undiscovered Country, 1991, Split Second, 1992, Breaking Point, 1993, Live Nude Girls, 1995, Above Suspicion, 1995, Where Truth Lies, 1996, Unforgettable, 1996, Exception to the Rule, 1997, Modern Vampires, 1998, Baby Geniuses, 1999, The Devil and Daniel Webster, 2001, 15 Minutes, 2001, Crossroads, 2002, Ice Princess, 2005, Sex and the City: The Movie, 2008; (TV films) Sins of the Past, 1984, Miracle in the Wilderness, 1992, Double Vision, 1992, Two Golden Balls, 1994, Running Delilah, 1994, OP Center, 1995, The Heidi Chronicles, 1995, Every Woman's Dream, 1996, Invasion, 1997, Creature, 1998, 36 Hours to Die, 1999, Sex and the Matrix, 2000, My Boy Jack, 2008; (TV series) Angel Falls, 1993, Sex and the City, 1998—2004 (SAG award, 2001, Golden Globe award, 2002, Women in Film Lucy award, 1999), Him and Us, 2006—; (TV miniseries) Wild Palms, 1993, (various TV guest appearances); (plays) Whose Life Is It Anyway?, 2005; co-author (with Mark Levinson): Satisfaction, 2002; author: Sexual Intelligence, 2005.

CATZ, SAFRA A., computer software company executive; b. Israel, 1961; married; 2 children. BA, U. Pa., Phila., 1983, JD, 1986. Various investment banking positions Donaldson, Lufkin & Jenrette, 1986—94, sr. v.p., 1994—97, mng. dir., 1997—99; sr. v.p. Oracle Corp., Redwood City, Calif., 1999, exec. v.p., 1999—2004, co-pres., 2004—, interim CFO, 2005—08. Bd. dirs. Oracle Corp., 2001—. Named one of The 100 Most Powerful Women, Forbes mag., 2005—08, 50 Women to Watch, Wall St. Jour., 2005, 50 Most Powerful Women in Bus., Fortune mag., 2008, Most Influential Women in Technology, Fast Company, 2009. Office: Oracle Corp 500 Oracle Pky Redwood Shores CA 94085 Office Phone: 650-506-7000. Office Fax: 650-506-7200.

CAUBLE, ROBERT C., research scientist; BS in Physics, U. Ariz.; PhD in Nuc. Engring., U. Mich., 1980. Staff Berkeley Rsch. Assocs. Naval Rsch. Lab., Washington; rsch. scientist Lawrence Livermore (Calif.) Nat. Lab., 1985—. Recipient Am. Physical Soc. award for Excellence in Plasma Physics Rsch. 1998. Office: Lawrence Livermore Nat Lab PO Box 808 Livermore CA 94551-0808

CAVANAUGH, KENNETH CLINTON, retired real estate consultant; b. Fremont, Mich., Apr. 30, 1916; s. Frank Michael and Buryll Marie (Preston) C.; m. Barbara Blythe Boling, Feb. 24, 1979; children from previous marriage: Patricia Ann, James Lee, John Thomas. BS in Forestry, Mich. State U., 1939. County supr. Farm Security Adminstrn., USDA, Kalamazoo, 1939-43; community mgr. PHA, Willow Run, Mich., 1946-49, dir. fiscal mgmt. Washington, 1949-55, dir. elderly housing Housing & Home Fin. Agy., 1955-57, reg. dir. San Juan, 1957-58; dir. housing programs HUD, Washington, 1958-73; controller/dep. dir. San Francisco Housing Authority, 1973-78; pres. Ken C. Cavanaugh & Assocs., pvt. internat. housing and community devel. cons., Vista, Calif., 1978—; fin. finder Merrill Lynch-Huntoon Paige Co., San Francisco, 1979-81, Western Pacific Fin. Co., Newport

Beach, Calif., 1981-83; gen. ptnr. The Knolls, Rogers, Ark., 1980-89. Exec. dir. Arlington (Va.) Youth Found., 1950-58; advisor Salvation Army adv. bd., Honolulu, 1985-88. Served to capt. USN, 1943-46, USNR, 1946-73. Recipient Superior Svc. award, Pub. Housing Adminstrn., 1956. Mem. Nat. Assn. Housing & Redevel. Ofcls., Ret. Officers Assn., Res. Officers Assn., Naval Res. Assn., Shadowridge Golf Club (Vista), Masons. Avocations: golf, travel. Home and Office: PO Box 749 Vista CA 92085-0749 Home Phone: 760-727-5581. Personal E-mail: blythecav@aol.com.

CAVANAUGH, MICHAEL EVERETT, lawyer, arbitrator, mediator; b. Seattle, Dec. 23, 1946; s. Wilbur R. Cavanaugh and Gladys E. (Herring) Barber; m. Susan P. Heckman, Sept. 7, 1968. AB, U. Calif., Berkeley, 1973; JD, U. Wash., 1976. Bar: Wash. 1976, U.S. Dist. Ct. (we. dist.) Wash. 1977, U.S. Ct. Appeals (9th cir.) 1977, U.S. Dist. Ct. (ea. dist.) Wash. 1978. Staff atty. U.S. Ct. of Appeals (9th crct.) Calif., San Francisco, 1976-77; from assoc. to ptnr. Preston & Thorgrimson, Seattle, 1981-85; ptnr. Bogle & Gates, Seattle, 1985-97, assoc., 1977-81, ptnr., 1985-97; propr. Michael E. Cavanaugh, J.D., Arbitration and Mediation, Seattle, 1997—. Contbg. author: Employment Discrimination Law, 3d edit., 1995. Mem.: Nat. Acad. Arbitrators. Avocations: sailing, creative writing, music. Office: 1004 Commercial Ave #369 Anacortes WA 98221 E-mail: mec@cavanaugh-adr.com.

CAVENEE, WEBSTER K., director; b. Sept. 12, 1951; BS in Biology, Kansas State U., 1973. Vis. rsch. scientist Ctr. Cancer Rsch. MIT, 1979—81; assoc. Howard Hughes Med. Inst., U. Utah, 1981—83; assist. then assoc. prof. microbiology & molecular genetics U. Cincinnati, 1983—86; vis. prof. Karolinska Inst., Stockholm, 1985; dir. Ludwig Inst. Cancer Rsch., prof. medicine, neurology, pathology, & human genetics McGill U., 1986—91; Sokolow vis. prof. U. Calif., San Francisco, 1988, dir., prof. Ludwig Inst. for Cancer Rsch. LaJolla, 1991—. Mem. GM Adv. Council, Cancer Rsch. Found.; chair exec. com. World Alliance Cancer Rsch. Organizations, 2002; fellow Nat. Found. Cancer Rsch., 2003. Fellow: Am. Acad. Microbiology, Internat. Union Against Cancer, Am. Assn. Cancer Rsch.; mem.: NAS, Inst. Medicine, Am. Soc. Clinical Investigation (hon.), Am. Soc. Microbiology, Am. Assn. for Advancement of Sci., Am. Soc. Human Genetics. Office: Ludwig Inst 9500 Gilman Dr La Jolla CA 92093-0660 E-mail: wcavenee@ucsd.edu.*

CAWOOD, ELIZABETH JEAN, public relations executive; b. Santa Maria, Calif., Jan. 6, 1947; d. John Stephen and Gertrude Margaret (Shelton) Dille; m. Neil F. Cawood, Jan. 4, 1975; 1 child, Nathan Patrick. BA, Whitworth Coll., 1964-68. Dir. pub. info. Inland Empire Goodwill, Spokane, Wash., 1967-72; adminstrv. asst. N.W. Assn. Rehab. Industries, Seattle, 1973-74; pres., counselor Cawood, Eugene, Oreg., 1974—. Pres. Women in Comm., Inc., 1981-83; stragegy bd. Benton Lane Lincoln Linn Region, 1993-99, chair, 1993-94; bd. dirs. AAA Oreg./Idaho, 1999—. Editor: Dictionary of Rehabilitation Acronyms, (newsletters) INTERCOM, Family Communicator, Oreg. Focus, (dictionary) Work-Oriented Rehabilitation Dictionary and Synonyms, 1st and 2nd edits. Bd. dirs. Laurel Hill Ctr., 1993-2008, v.p., 2001, pres. 2002-2004; bd. dirs. Lane County Boy Scouts Am., 1986-2001, Eugene Action Forum, 1981-86, Birth-to-Three, 1982-85, Lane County chpt. ARC, 1982-83, 84-89, Lane County chpt. Am. Cancer Soc., 1984-87, Eugene Opera, 1985-88, Joint Com. Econ. Diversification, 1985-89, 91-93, Lane County United Way, 1987-93, campaign cabinet, 2002-04, chair leadership, 2001-2003, Lane Econ. Com., vice chmn., 1990-95, chair, 1996-2001; bd. dirs. So. Willamette Pvt. Industry Coun., 1985-88, pres., 1988; chmn. Eugene Pvt. Industries Coun., 1981-83, vice chmn., 1983-84; chmn. Bus. Owners Network, Eugene, 1980-81; advisor Eugene Jr. League; trustee Nature Conservancy, Oreg., 1999—, exec. com., 2005—; advisor Sustainable Advantage Conf., U. Oreg., 2004-08; mem. educator quality task force Chalkboard Project, 2005-06. Recipient Hunger Buster award, Oreg. Food Bank, 2006. Mem. LWV (bd. dirs. 1979), Pub Rels. Soc. Am. (bd. dirs. Columbia River chpt. 1987-88, advisor U. Oreg. chpt. 1987-91, pres. Greater Oreg. chpt. 1991-92, bd. dirs. 1991-93), Oreg. Nat. Rehab. Assn. (pres. 1980-81), Profl. Women's Network (bd. dirs. Oreg. chpt. 1982), Eugene C. of C. (bd. dirs. 1980-87, 92-97, local govt. affairs coun. 1999-2002, econs. devel. coun. 2002-2004, chmn. econ. devel. 1982-83, bd. dirs. exec. com. 1984-87, v.p. 1987, 93, chmn. edn. com., pres.-elect 1994, pres. 1995), Mid-Oreg. Advt. Club (bd. dirs. 1985-87), Oreg. Sales and Mktg. Execs. (bd. dirs. 1985-87), Eugene/Springfield Assn. Quality and Performance (chmn. 1991-93, bd. dirs. 1991-94), Internat. Assn. Sports and Human Performance (bd. dirs. 1993), Rotary (Eugene pub. rels. chair 2000-2004, bd. mem. 2008-), Eugene City Club (bd. dirs. 1992-98, pres.-elect 1995, pres. 1996), Oreg. Rsch. Inst. (bd. mem. 2008-). Office: Cawood 1200 High St Ste 200 Eugene OR 97401-3266 Home Phone: 541-746-4894; Office Phone: 541-484-7052. Business E-Mail: liz@cawood.com.

CAYETANO, BENJAMIN JEROME, former governor, former state senator and representative; b. Honolulu, Nov. 14, 1939; s. Bonifacio Marcos and Eleanor (Infante) C.; m. Vicky Tiu, 1997; children: Brandon, Janeen, Samantha, Cayetano, Marissa, William Liu. BA, UCLA, 1968; JD, Loyola U., 1971; LLD (hon.), U. Philippines, 1995; D in Pub. Svc. (hon.), Loyola Marymount U., 1998. Bar: Hawaii 1971. Pvt. practice, Honolulu, 1971—83; commr. Hawaii Housing Authority, 1972—74; mem. Hawaii Ho. of Reps., 1975-78; bar examiner Hawaii Supreme Ct., 1976—78; mem. Hawaii Senate from 6th dist., 1979-86; lt. gov. State of Hawaii, 1986-94, gov., 1994—2002. Adv. U. Hawaii Law Rev., 1982-84, adv. coun., U. Hawaii Coll. Bus. Adminstrn., 1982-93. Author: Ben: A Memoir, From Street Kid to Governor, 2007. Mem. bd. regents Chaminade U., 1980-83; chmn. Western Gov.'s Assn., 1999. Named one of 10 Most Effective Legislators, Honolulu Star-Bulletin, 1975-78; recipient Excellence in Leadership medallion, Ascia-Pacific Academic Consortium for Pub. Health, 1991, UCLA Alumni award for excellence in pub. svc., 1993, UCLA Medal, 1995, Disting. Leadership award, UCLA John E. Anderson Sch. of Mgmt., 1995,, Award for Ethics in Govt., Am. Soc. Pub. Adminstrn., Hawaii chap., 1995, Leadership award Harvard Found., 1996, Disting. Citizens award, Aloha Coun. Boy Scouts Am., 1997, Edward A. Dickson Alumnus of Yr. award UCLA, 1998, Disting. Alumnus of Yr., Loyola Law Sch., 2002. Mem.: Nat. Gov. Assn., Nat. Conf. Lt. Gov., Nat. Assn. Sec. of State, Legal Aid Soc. Hawaii (bd. dirs.). Democrat. Home: 95-110 Leolani St Mililani HI 96789-3608 E-mail: gov@gov.state.hi.us.

CAZIER, BARRY JAMES, electrical engineer, software developer; b. Phoenix, May 10, 1943; s. James Henry and Dorothy Marie (Lynton) C.; m. Susan Arline Shewey, June 13, 1964 (dec. July 1979); children: Suzanne, Bryan; m. Illene D. Miller, Dec. 19, 1994. Student, Colo. Sch. Mines, 1961-62; BSEE, U. Colo., 1965; student advanced bus. adminstrn., Ariz. State U., 1974-77. Mfg. mgmt. Gen. Electric, Richland, Wash., 1965-66, Warren, Ohio, 1966-67, system engr. Schenectady, N.Y., 1967-69; project mgr. Honeywell, Phoenix, 1970-80, dir. field ops., 1980-85, program mgr., 1985-99. Prin. Cazier Software Designs, Scottsdale, Ariz., 1985—. Adv. Jr. Achievement, Phoenix, 1972. Mem.: IBM PC Users (Phoenix). Avocations: music, jogging, camping, fishing, reading. Home: 8508 E Via Montoya Scottsdale AZ 85255-4936 Personal E-mail: bjcarrier@cox.net.

CAZIMERO, ROBERT, musician; Studied hula with Aunty Ma'iki Aiu Lake. Former band mem. Monarch Room, Royal Hawaiian Hotel, Waikiki; founder, dir. hula dance troupe Halau Na Kamalei, 1975—; bassist The Brothers Cazimero; world-renowned hula teacher. Musician: (albums) The Brothers Cazimero, Vol. 1, 1975, The Brothers Cazimero, Vol. 2, 1976, The Brothers Cazimero in Concert, 1977, Ho'ala, 1978, Waikiki, My Castle by the Sea, 1979, Hawaii, in the Middle of the Sea, 1980, Captured Magic, 1981, Hawaiian Hula Eyes, 1982, Proud Family, 1983, Island in Your Eyes, 1984, The Brothers Cazimero Christmas Collection, 1985, In This Time Past (Songs from Mama's Songbook), 1986, Sound of the Sea Surrounds Me, 1986, Hawaiian Paradise, 1989, The Brothers Cazimero Christmas Collection, Vol. 2, 1991, Follow Me, 1992, The Caz Live, 1993, Hokule'a, 1995, Christmas, 1996, Destination Paradise, 1998, Proud to Be, 2002, Some Call It Aloha...Don't Tell, 2004, Caz Christmas, 2006, Destiny, 2008, (solo) Robert Cazimero, 1978, Rnc, 2002, RCHNK, 2003. Fellow US Artists, 2008. Office: c/o Mountain Apple Co 1330 Ala Moana Blvd Ste 001 Honolulu HI 96814*

CECERE, DOMENICO, homebuilding company executive; b. June 10, 1949; BA in Fin. and Acctg., U. Okla. V.p. fin. indsl. controls Honeywell, Inc., v.p. fin. home and bldg. controlling bus., v.p. fin. European bus. Brussels; v.p., contr. Owens Corning, Toledo, 1993-95, pres. roofing sys. bus., 1995-98, sr. v.p., CFO, 1998-2000, exec. v.p., COO, 2000-01; cons. Gryphon Investors; sr. v.p., CFO KB Home, LA, 2002—. Office: 7th Fl 10990 Wilshire Blvd Los Angeles CA 90024

CEE-LO, (THOMAS DECARLO CALLAWAY), singer; b. Atlanta, May 30, 1974; m. Christina Johnson, 2000 (div. 2005); 1 child, Kingston. Mem. Goodie Mob, 1995—, Gnarls Barkley, 2004—. Singer: (albums) Cee-Lo Green & His Perfect Imperfections, 2002, Cee-Lo Green...Is the Soul Machine, 2004, Art of Noise: The Best of Cee-Lo, 2006, Closet Freak: The Best of Cee-Lo Green the Soul Machine, 2006, (with Goodie Mob) Soul Food, 1995, Still Standing, 1998, World Party, 1999, (with Gnarls Barkley) St. Elsewhere, 2006 (Grammy award for Best Alternative Music Album, 2007), The Odd Couple, 2008, (songs) Crazy, 2006 (2 MTV Video Music awards for Best Direction & Best Editing, MTV Europe Music award for Best Song, 2006, Grammy award for Best Alternative Performance, 2007, Soul Train award for Soul Single, 2007), Smiley Faces, 2006 (Best Editing, MTV Video Music Awards, 2007), Run, 2008 (Best Art Direction, Best Choreography, MTV Video Music Awards, 2008); actor: (films) Mystery Men, 1999. Recipient Left Field Woodie award, mtvU, 2006, Best Group award (as Gnarls Barkley), Black Entertainment TV (BET) Awards, 2007. Office: Waxploitation Inc 11601 Wilshire Blvd Los Angeles CA 90025

CELESTE, RICHARD F., academic administrator, retired ambassador, Former Governor, Ohio; b. Cleve., Nov. 11, 1937; s. Frank P. & Margaret L. Celeste; m. Dagmar Braun, 1962 (div.); children: Eric, Christopher, Gabriella, Noelle, Natalie, Stephen; m. Jacqueline Lundquist, 1994; 1 child, Sam; 6 stepchildren. BA in History magna cum laude, Yale U., 1959; PhB in Politics, Oxford U., 1962; LHD (hon.), Capital U., 1984; LLD (hon.), Miami U., 1984; Doctorate in Pub. Svc. (hon.), Rio Grande Coll., 1984. Staff liaison officer Peace Corps, 1963, dir., 1979-81; spl. asst. to Amb. Chester Bowles, New Delhi, 1963-67; mem. Ohio Ho. of Reps., Columbus, 1970-74, majority whip, 1972-74; lt. gov. State of Ohio, Columbus, 1974-79, gov., 1983-91; mng. ptnr. Celeste & Sabety, Ltd., Columbus, Ohio, 1991—97; chmn. Nat. Health Care Campaign, 1993—94; US amb. to India US Dept. State, New Delhi, 1997—2001; co-chair, Homeland Security Proj. The Century Found., 2002—; pres. Colorado Coll., 2002—. Bd. dirs. HealthSouth Rehabilitation Corp., Birmingham, Ala., 1992—97, Navistar Internat., Chgo., 1993—97, Republic Engrd. Steels, Massilon, Ohio, 1993—97; N.Am. adv. bd. BP Oil, Cleve., 1994—97; chmn. adv. bd. Pacific NW Nat. Lab., 1994—97; chair bd. trustees Health Effects Inst., 2001; Northern Command bd. mem. Ind. Strategic Assessment Group, 2003—; chmn. critical infrastructure roundtable Nat. Rsch. Coun., 2004—06. Author: It's Not Just Politics America, 1976, Pioneering a Hunger Free World, 1977. Mem. Ohio Dem. Exec. Com., Coun. Fgn. Rels; co-chair Imagine Downtown, 2005-06; mem. adv. bd. Colo. Festival World Theatre, 2003-, Colo. Springs Downtown Partnership, 2003-, Inst. Internat. Edn., 2003-; bd. mem. United Bd. Christian Higher Edn. in Asia, 2004-06. Rhodes scholar Oxford U., 1960, Eng.; fellow Case Western Reserve U., 1995-97. Mem. AAAS (chmn. adv. bd. 1996-97), Am. Soc. Pub. Adminstrn. Nat. Assn. Ind. Colleges & Universities (bd. mem. 2006-08), Am. Coun. Edn. (bd. mem. 2004-), Nat. Academies (lifetime assoc. mem.) Italian Sons & Daughters of Am., Morys New Haven, Elizabethan Club, New Haven, Phi Beta Kappa (Speaker of Yr. award, 2006). Democrat. Methodist. Office: Office Pres Colorado Coll 14 E Cache La Poudre St Colorado Springs CO 80903 E-mail: dkceleste@aol.com.

CELLA, JOHN J., freight company executive; b. 1940; married. BBA, Temple U., 1965. Regional mgr. Japan ops. Airborne Freight Corp., Seattle, 1965-71, v.p. Far Ea. ops., 1971-72, sr. v.p. internat. div., from 1982, now exec. v.p. internat. div. Office: Airborne Freight Corp 3101 Western Ave Seattle WA 98121-1043

CELLIERS, PETER H., physicist; Physics rschr. Lawrence Livermore (Calif.) Nat. Lab. Recipient Plasma Physics Rsch. Excellence award, 1998. Mem. Am. Phys. Soc. Office: Lawrence Livermore Nat Lab U Calif 7000 East Ave Livermore CA 94550-9516

CENARRUSA, PETE T., retired state official; b. Carey, Idaho, Dec. 16, 1917; s. Joseph and Ramona (Gardoqui) C.; m. Freda B. Coates, Oct. 25, 1947; 1 son, Joe Earl (dec.). BS in Agr., U. Idaho, 1940. Tchr. high sch., Cambridge, Idaho, 1940-41, Carey and Gleans Ferry, Idaho, 1946; tchr. vocat. agr. VA, Blaine County, Idaho, 1946-51; farmer, woolgrower, nr. Carey, 1946-95; mem. Idaho Ho. of Reps., 1951-67, speaker, 1963-67; sec. state of Idaho, 1967—90, 1991—2002. Mem. Idaho Bd. Land Commrs., Idaho Bd. Examiners; pres. Idaho Flying Legislators, 1953-63; chmn. Idaho Legis. Council, 1964—, Idaho Govt. Reorgn. Com.; Idaho del. Council State Govts., 1963— Elected ofcl., mem. BLM Adv. Coun., Boise Dist.; Rep. adminstr. Hall of Fame, 1978; sr. mem. State Bd. Land Commrs., 1967-96; dean Nations Secs. of State, 1967—. Maj. USMCR, 1942-46, 52-58. Named Hon. Farmer Future Farmers Am., 1955; inductee Agrl. Hall of Fame, 1973, Idaho Athletic Hall of Fame, 1976, Basque Hall of Fame, 1983, Idaho Hall of Fame, 1998; recipient Am. Century award for Idaho Washington Times Found. Mem. Blaine County Livestock Mktg. Assn., Idaho Wool Growers Assn. (chmn. 1954), Carey C. of C. (pres. 1952), U. Idaho Alumni Assn., Gamma Sigma Delta, Tau Kappa Epsilon. Republican. Achievements include serving longer than any constitutional official elected in Idaho concluding with 50 years on 12/1/00.

CEPPOS, JERRY (JEROME MERLE CEPPOS), dean, former newspaper editor; b. Wash., Oct. 14, 1946; s. Harry and Florence (Epstein) C.; m. Karen E. Feingold, Mar. 7, 1982; children: Matthew, Robin. BS in Journalism, U. Md., 1969; postgrad., Knight-Ridder Exec. Leadership Program, 1989-90. Reporter, asst. city editor, night city editor Rochester Democrat & Chronicle, NY, 1969-72; from asst. city editor, to nat. editor, to asst. mng. editor The Miami Herald, Fla., 1972-81; various editl. positions, including assoc. editor San Jose Mercury News, Calif., 1981—83, mng. editor, 1983—85, exec. editor, sr. v.p., 1995-99; v.p. news Knight Ridder, 1999—2005; tchr. media diversity San Jose U.; fellow media ethics Markkula Ctr. Applied Ethics, Santa Clara U., 2007; dean Donald W. Reynolds Sch. Journalism, U. Nev., Reno, 2008—. Bd. visitors Coll. Journalism, U. Md., 1999-; pres. Accrediting Coun. on Edn. in Journalism and Mass Comm. 1998-04. Recipient Journalism award, Soc. Profl. Journalists' Nat Ethics, 1997, Disting. Journalism Alumnus award, U. Md., 2001. Mem. AP Mng. Editors (past pres.), Am. Soc. Newspaper Editors, Calif. Soc. Newspaper Editors (former mem. bd. dirs., past pres.), Soc. Profl. Journalists, Assn. for Edn. in Journalism and Mass Comm. Office: Donald W Reynolds Sch Journalism U Nev Mail Stop 310 Reno NV 89557-0310 Office Phone: 775-784-6531.

CERA, MICHAEL, actor; b. Brampton, Canada, June 7, 1988; s. Luigi and Linda Cera. Actor: (TV series) Rolie Polie Olie, 1998, I Was a Sixth Grade Alien, 1999, Braceface, 2001, The Grubbs, 2002, Arrested Development, 2003—06 (Future Classic award, TV Land Awards, 2004), (voice) Howard Stern: The High School Years, 2006,: (TV films) What Katy Did, 1999, Switching Goals, 1999, Custody of the Heart, 2000, The Familiar Stranger, 2001, My Louisiana Sky, 2001, Walter and Henry, 2001, Stolen Miracle, 2001, Exit 9, 2003, Wayside School, 2005; (films) Ultimate G's, 2000, Steal This Movie, 2000, Frequency, 2000, Confessions of a Dangerous Mind, 2002, Darling Darling, 2005, Superbad, 2007, Juno, 2007 (Most Promising Performer, Chgo. Film Critics Assn. Awards, 2007), Extreme Movie, 2008, Nick & Norah's Infinite Playlist, 2008; (TV miniseries) I Was a Rat, 2001; dir., prodr., editor, writer, actor (films) Clark and Michael, 2006. Office: c/o Paradigm Talent Agy 360 N Crescent Dr North Bldg Beverly Hills CA 90210

CERAN, JENNIFER ELLEN, treasurer; b. NYC, July 30, 1963; BA in Comm. and French, Vanderbilt U., 1985; MBA in Fin. and Acctg., U. Chgo., 1989. Fin. asst. Merrill Lynch, NYC, 1985-86, mktg. assoc., 1986-87; sr. bus. analyst corp. devel. Sara Lee Corp., Chgo., 1989-90, mgr. internat. treas., 1992-94, sr. mgr. internat. treas., 1994-96, asst. treas. Utrecht, Netherlands, 1996—2003; head treasury ops. Cisco Systems Inc., Dublin, 2000—01, head global treasury ops. San Jose, Calif., 2001—02, asst. treas., 2002—03; v.p., treas. eBay Inc., 2003—. Treas. Elmhurst Hist. Soc., 1991—96. Mem.: Dutch Assn. Corp. Treas. Office: eBay Inc 2145 Hamilton Ave San Jose CA 95125

CERBO, MICHAEL P., state legislator; b. Phila., Oct. 17, 1953; Colorado State Representative, District 2, 2003-. Democrat. Roman Catholic. Mailing: Colo State Capitol 200 E Colfax Denver CO 80203 Office Phone: 303-866-2911. E-mail: michael.cerbo.house@state.co.us.

CERF, VINTON GRAY, information technology executive; b. New Haven, June 23, 1943; s. Vinton Thruston and Muriel (Gray) C.; m. Sigrid L. Thorstenberg, Sept. 10, 1966; children: David, Bennett. BS, Stanford U., 1965; MS in Computer Sci., UCLA, 1970, PhD in Computer Sci., 1972; PhD (hon.), Capitol Coll., Gettysburg Coll., U. Balearic Islands, U. Lulea, Swiss Fed. Inst. Tech.; PhD (hon.), George Mason U., U. Twente, U. Rovira and Virgili, U. Pisa, Tschingua U., U. Beijing, U. Poets and Telecomm., Rensselaer Polytech. Inst. Sys. engr. IBM Corp., 1965-67; prin. programmer UCLA, 1967-72; asst. prof. elec. engring. and computer sci. Stanford U., Calif., 1972-76; sr. programmer Jacobi Sys. Corp., Santa Monica, Calif., 1968-70; program mgr. info. processing techniques office Def. Advanced Rsch. Projects Agy., U.S. Dept. Def., Arlington, Va., 1976-81, prin. scientist, 1981-82; dir. sys. devel. MCI Comm. Corp., 1982-83; v.p. engring. MCI Digital Info. Svcs. Co., Washington, 1983-86; v.p. Corp. for Nat. Rsch. Initiatives, Reston, Va., 1986-94; sr. v.p. technology strategy MCI, Ashburn, Va., 1994—2005; v.p., chief internet evangelist Google Inc., Mountain View, Calif., 2005—. Author: A Practical View of Communication Protocols, 1979. Named to Datamation Hall of Fame, 1989, Nat. Inventors Hall of Fame, 2006; recipient Kilby award, 1995, Silver medal Internat. Telecomms. Union, 1995, Industry Legend award Computer and Comms. Industries Assn., 1996, NEC Computer and Comm. prize, 1996, Computer Networks and Smithsonian Leadership award, 1996, Nat. Medal of Tech., 1997, Fellow award, Computer History Mus., 2000, Prince of Asturias award, 2002, Presdl. Medal of Freedom, The White House, 2005; named one of the 50 Most Important People on the Web, PC World, 2007; Marconi fellow, 1998. Fellow IEEE (Kobayashi award 1992, Alexander Graham Bell award 1997), AAAS, Assn. Computing Machinery (chmn. SIG Comm. 1987-91, coun. 1990-92, Software award), Internat. Fedn. Info. Processing, Internet Activities Bd. (chmn. 1979-82, 89-91), Internet Soc. (pioneer mem., trustee 1992-2002, pres. 1992-95, v.p. chpts. 1996-97, chmn. 1998-99); mem. NAE (Charles Stark Draper award, 2001), Sigma Xi. Office: Google Inc 1600 Amphitheatre Pkwy Mountain View CA 94043 Home Phone: 703-448-0965; Office Phone: 703-234-1823. E-mail: vint@google.com.

CERNY, CHARLENE ANN, director; b. Jamaica, NY, Jan. 12, 1947; d. Albert Joseph and Charlotte Ann (Novy) Cerny; children: Elizabeth Brett Cerny-Chipman, Kathryn Rose Cerny-Chipman. BA, SUNY, Binghamton, 1969. Cert. Fundraising Exec. Curator Latin-Am. folk art Mus. Internat. Folk Art, Santa Fe, 1972-84, mus. dir., 1984-99; dir. advancement Santa Fe Prep. Sch., 1999—2007; founder Santa Fe Internat. Folk Art Market, exec. dir., 2007—. Adv. bd. C.G. Jung Inst., Santa Fe, 1990-98. Mem. Mayor's Commn. on Children and Youth, Santa Fe, 1990-93, adv. bd. Recipient Exemplary Performance award State of N.Mex., 1982, Internat. Ptnr. Among Mus. award, Mayor's Recognition award, 1999, Mus. N.Mex. Regents award, 1999; Smithsonian Instn. travel grantee, 1976; Florence Dibell Bartlett Meml. scholar, 1979, 91; Kellogg fellow, 1983. Mem. Am. Assn. Mus. Internat. Coun. Mus. (bd. dirs. 1991—, exec. bd. 1991-

95), Am. Folklore Soc., Mountain-Plains Mus. Assn., N.Mex. Assn. Mus. (chair membership com. 1975-77). Office: PO Box 2087 Santa Fe NM 87505 Office Phone: 505-476-1190.

CERNY, JOSEPH, III, chemistry professor, retired dean, director; b. Montgomery, Ala., Apr. 24, 1936; s. Joseph and Olaette Genette (Jury) C.; m. Barbara Ann Nedelka, June 13, 1959 (div. Nov. 1982); children: Keith Joseph, Mark Evan; m. 2d Susan Dinkelspiel Stern, Nov. 12, 1983. BS in Chem. Engring., U. Miss.-Oxford, 1957; postgrad. Fulbright scholar, U. Manchester, Eng., 1957-58; PhD in Nuclear Chemistry, U. Calif.-Berkeley, 1961; PhD in Physics (hon.), U. Jyväskylä, Finland, 1990. Asst. prof. chemistry U. Calif., Berkeley, 1961-67, assoc. prof., 1967-71, prof., 1971—, chmn. dept. chemistry, 1975-79, head nuclear sci. div., 1979-84, assoc. dir. Lawrence Berkeley Lab., 1979-84, dean grad. div., 1985-2000, provost for research, 1986-94, vice chancellor for rsch., 1994-2000. Mem. Nat. Acad. Scis. Physics Commn., chair nuclear physics panel, 1983-86; mem. NASA Adv. Coun., Univ. Rels. Task Force, 1991-93, NRC Study of Rsch. Doctorates, 1992-95, chmn. nuc. sci. adv. subcom. edn., 2003-04. Editor: Nuclear Reactions and Spectroscopy, 4 vols., 1974; contbr. numerous articles to field to profl. jours. Served with U.S. Army, 1962-63. Recipient E.O. Lawrence award AEC, 1974, A. von Humboldt sr. scientist award, 1985; named to U. Miss. Alumni Hall of Fame, 1988. Fellow AAAS, Am. Phys. Soc.; mem. Am. Chem. Soc. (Nuclear Chemistry award 1984), Assn. Grad. Schs. (v.p., pres. 1992-94). Democrat. Home: 860 Keeler Ave Berkeley CA 94708-1324 Office: Lawrence Berkeley Nat Lab Univ Calif Bldg 88 Berkeley CA 94720 Office Phone: 510-486-7852. E-mail: jcerny@berkeley.edu.

CERRELL, JOSEPH ROBERT, political scientist, public relations consultant; b. NYC, June 19, 1935; BA, U. of So. Calif., 1957. Exec. dir. Dem. Party of Calif., 1959-66; disting. vis. prof. Pepperdine U., Malibu, Calif., 1994—; exec. v.p. Palumbo & Cerrell, Washington, 1989—; CEO Cerrell Assocs. Inc., pub. affairs cons. co., LA. Adj. prof. U. So. Calif., 1978-94. Pres. Calif. Mus. Found.; bd. dirs. Long Beach (Calif.) Aquarium. Mem. PRSA, Am. Assn. of Polit. Cons., Internat. Assn. of Polit. Cons., Nat. Italian Am. Fedn. (chair). Office: Cerrell Assocs Inc 320 N Larchmont Blvd Fl 2D Los Angeles CA 90004-3012 E-mail: joe@cerrell.com.

CERVANTES, JOSEPH, state legislator; b. Las Cruces, NM, Jan. 19, 1961; m Jennifer Cervantes; children: Alexandra, Isabella & Juliana. Co commissioner, Doña Ana Co, 1999-2001; New Mexico State Representative, District 52, 2003-.Architect, Nagel & Assoc, 1985-87; Cervantes & Assoc, 1987-89; attorney, Modrall Sperling Roehl & Sisk Law, 1991-98, Cervantes Moberly PC Law, 1998-2004. America Bar Association; America Inn of Courts; Leadership New Mexico (board director 2001-2002; New Mexico First (board director 2001-2002. Democrat. Roman Catholic. Office: Capitol Add NM State Capitol Rm 205B Santa Fe NM 87503 Office Phone: 505-986-4242. E-mail: cervanteslaw@zianet.com.

CESARIO, THOMAS CHARLES, dean; b. Kenosha, Wis., June 19, 1940; BS, U. Wis., 1961, MD, 1965. Resident in internal medicine Harvard U., 1965-67; fellow Harvard and U. Calif., Irvine, 1969-72; dean med. sch. U. Calif., Irvine, 1994—. Office: U Calif Coll Medicine 252 Irvine Hall Irvine CA 92697-3950 Home Phone: 949-640-6416; Office Phone: 949-824-5747. E-mail: tccesari@uci.edu.

CHABIN, TOM, state legislator; m. Delia Fernandez Chabin (dec.); 1 child, Rodrigo Santiago. BS in Am. Studies, Northern Ariz. U., 1976. Dir. Northern Ariz. U. Activity Ctr., 1976—78; pub. info. officer Native Americans for Cmty. Action, 1978; asst. to vice chmn. Hopi Tribe, 1979; mgr. & planner Seckuku Enterprises, 1979—80; self employed State Ariz. & Oil Venders, 1981; asst. mgr. Babbitt's Kykostsmovi Trading Post, 1981—82; adv. Hopi Tribal Ct., 1982—84; pres. & gen. mgr. Chabin-Fernandez Corp.-Reservation Bus. Svcs., 1984—99; dist. 4 supr. Coconino County Bd. Suprs., 1992—2000; pub. policy consultant, 2001—03; dir. bus. devel. Tuba City Regional Health Care Corp., 2003—04; obudsman Northern Ariz. Coun. Govts. Area Agy. on Aging, 2006—07; mem. Dist. 2 Ariz. House of Reps., 2007—. Mem. Bennett Freeze Task Force, 1995, Coconino County Planning & Zoning Commn., Tuba City Pub. Sch. Bd.; founding bd. KNAU Radio Activities, 2004—06; bd. dirs. & coach Tuba City/Moenkopi Little League Inc., 2004—05; bd. dirs. Flagstaff Football & Yell League Inc., 2005. Democrat. Office: Capitol Complex 1700 W Washington Rm 318 Phoenix AZ 85007-2890 Office Phone: 602-926-5160. Office Fax: 602-417-3002. Business E-Mail: tchabin@azleg.gov.*

CHABRA, ANAND, public health physician, epidemiologist; b. Bukit Mertajam, Malaysia, May 16, 1966; s. Harbans L. and Lilly Chabra; m. Michelle E.D. Chabra, Mar. 25, 1995; children: Isaac, David. BA, Stanford U., 1988; MD, U. Wash., 1993; MPH, U. Calif., Berkeley, 1995. Diplomate Am. Bd. Pub. Health and Gen. Preventive Medicine, 1998, 2008. Pediatric intern U. Calif., San Francisco, 1993-94, resident preventive medicine Berkeley, 1994-96; med. epidemiologist Calif. Maternal and Child Health, Berkeley, 1996-99; maternal, child and adolescent health dir. San Mateo County, Calif., 1999—, med. dir., calif. children's svcs., 2008—. Mem. preventive medicine resident adv. com. U. Calif. Berkeley, U. Calif. San Francisco, 1994-96, resident mem., 1998-; mem. exec. com., Calif. Perinatal Quality Care Collaborative, 1997-99; mem. Adolescent Health Collaborative, 1999-; treas. exec. com. MCAH Action, 2000-03, chair, integrated child health program com., 2002-03, pres. exec. com., 2003-04, past pres. exec. com., 2004-06; mem. communicable disease control and environ. health com., Calif. Conf. Local Health Officers, 1999-2003; mem. teen pregnancy prevention program work group Calif. Dept. Health Svcs., 2001, mem. CDC, Health Resources Svcs. Adminstrn. joint adv. com. bioterrorism preparedness, 2003-04, mem. caring for Calif.'s children adv. workgroup, 2005; maternal and child health bur. Title V grant reviewer, Health Resources and Svcs. Adminstrn., Dept. HHS, 2002, mem. oral health initiative adv. com., San Francisco Found., 2006-09, mem. cmty. adv. com. Lucile Packard Children's Hosp., Stanford, 2007-; mem. aadv. com. Preteer Alliance, Starford,2003-. Mem. editl. bd., Wellness Newsletter, U. Calif., Berkeley, 1994-95; contbr. articles to profl. jours. Program svcs. com. mem., No. Calif. chpt. March of Dimes, San Francisco, 1999—2004, co-chmn. firearm safety com., 2000—03; chmn. Bay Area Regional Immunization Registry, 2005—08. Recipient Outstanding Resident, Student Presentation award, Prevention 96, 1996, Celebrating Excellence in Pub. Health award, March of Dimes, 2004, SAFE KIDS Coalition award, Most Innovative award, CityMatCH, 2004; named a Super Star, Maternal, Child and Adolescent Health Action, 2004; fellowship, James S. Westra Meml. Endowment, 1993, scholarship, King County Med. Soc. Aux., 1990. Fellow: Am. Coll. Preventive Medicine (mem. adolescent health com. 2002—, cons. preventative practice com. 2002—); mem.: APHA, San Mateo County Med. Assn., Calif. Pub. Health Assn., Calif. Med. Assn., Am. Assn. Pub. Health Physicians (mem. adv.com. 2005—08), Christian Med. Assn., Calif. Acad. Preventive Medicine (bd. dirs. 1997—2000), CityMatch, Stanford Alumni Assn. Office: San Mateo County Health Family Health Svcs 2000 Alameda De Las Pulgas Ste 200 San Mateo CA 94403 E-mail: achabra@co.sanmateo.ca.us.

CHACE, WILLIAM MURDOUGH, former university administrator, literature educator; b. Newport News, Va., Sept. 3, 1938; s. William Emerson and Grace Elizabeth (Murdough) Chace; m. JoAn Elizabeth Johnstone, Sept. 5, 1964; children: William Johnstone, Katherine Elizabeth. BA in English, Haverford Coll., 1961; MA in English, U. Calif., Berkeley, 1963; PhD in English, U. Calif., 1968; LLD (hon.), Amherst Coll., 1990, William Coll., 1992. Instr. Stillman Coll., Tuscaloosa, Ala., 1963—64; teaching asst. U. Calif., Berkeley, 1964—66, acting instr., 1967—68; asst. prof. English Stanford U., 1968—74, assoc. prof., 1974—80, prof., 1980, assoc. dean Sch. Humanities and Scis., 1981—85, vice provost for acad. planning and devel., 1985—88; pres. Wesleyan U., Middletown, Conn., 1988—94, Emory U., Atlanta, 1994—2003. Dir. Sun Trust Banks; cons. Hewlett-Packard, Hallmark Cards, Inc., Hawaiian Ednl. Fund, Midwestern Mgmt. Assn.; vis. prof. The Coll. Aboard the Delta Queen, 1979, 80, 82, The Coll. in Western Europe and Brit. Isles, 1985; lectr. to libr. assocs. Stanford U., 1976; lectr. 6th Internat. James Joyce Symposium, Dublin, 1977, MLAL Ann. Conv., 1977, 78, Tufts Symposium, 1978, English Conf. U. Calif., Berkeley, 1979, Eighth Internat. James Joyce Symposium, Dublin, 1982, IBM Internat. Bus. and Acad. Conf., Monte Carlo, 1984, Ezra Pound Centennial Colloquium, San Jose State U., 1985, Ann. Meeting of Assn. of Grad. Liberal Studies Programs, St. Louis, 1986, Chico State U., La. State U., 1987, U. Utah Sch. Medicine Pub. Lecture series, 1987, No. Calif. Sci. Meeting Am. Coll. Physicians, Monterey, Calif., 1987, 13th Internat. James Joyce Symposium, 1992; presenter Joyce and History conf. Yale U., 1990; spkr. Fleur Cowles Flair Symposium, U. Tex., Austin, 2000. Author: James Joyce: A Collection of Critical Essays, 1973, The Political Identities of Ezra Pound and T.S. Eliot, 1973, Lionel Trilling: Criticism and Politics, 1980, 100 Semesters: My Adventures as Student, Professor and University President and What I Learned along the Way, 2006; co-author: Graham Greene: A Revaluation, 1990; co-editor: Justice Denied: The Black Man in White America, 1970, An Introduction to Literature, 1985; co-editor: (with JoAn E. Chace) Making It New, 1972; contbr. articles to profl. jours. Home: 227 Navarra Dr Scotts Valley CA 95066-3739 Office Phone: 650-329-1962. Personal E-mail: billchace@yahoo.com.

CHADDERDON, MARGE, state legislator; b. Poplar, Mont., Dec. 1, 1937; BA, Coll. Great Falls, 1957. Co-owner chain of floorcovering stores; mem. Dist. 4 Idaho House of Reps., Boise. Republican. Roman Catholic. Office: Dist Office 109 Lakeview Dr Coeur D' Alene ID 83814 also: Legis Services Office PO Box 83720 Boise ID 83720-0054 Office Phone: 208-769-9309. Office Fax: 208-667-7920.*

CHAFE, WALLACE LESEUR, linguist, educator; b. Cambridge, Mass., Sept. 3, 1927; s. Albert J. and Nathalie (Amback) C.; m. Mary Elizabeth Butterworth, June 23, 1951 (div. 1980); children— Christopher, Douglas, Stephen; m. Marianne Mithun, Jan. 25, 1985 BA, Yale U., 1950, MA, 1956, PhD, 1958. Asst. prof. U. Buffalo, 1958-59; linguist Bur. Am. Ethnology, Smithsonian Instn., 1959-62; mem. faculty U. Calif.-Berkeley, 1962-86, prof. linguistics, 1967-86, U. Calif., Santa Barbara, 1986-91, prof. emeritus, 1991—, rsch. prof., 2003—. Author: Seneca Thanksgiving Rituals, 1961, Seneca Morphology and Dictionary, 1967, Meaning and the Structure of Language, 1970, The Pear Stories, 1980, Evidentiality, 1986, Discourse, Consciousness, and Time, 1994, The Importance of Not Being Earnest, 2007. Served with USNR, 1945-46. Mem. Linguistic Soc. Am., Am. Psychol. Assn., Am. Psychol. Soc. Office: Univ Calif Dept Linguistics Santa Barbara CA 93106 Home Phone: 805-563-1152.

CHAFFETZ, JASON, United States Representative from Utah, former corporate communications executive; b. Los Gatos, Calif., Mar. 26, 1967; m. Julie Marie Johnson, Feb. 1991; children: Max, Ellis, Kate. BA in Comm., Brigham Young U., 1989. Campaign mgr. Jon Huntsman, Jr. for Gov.; chief of staff Gov. Jon Huntsman, Jr.; owner Maxtera Utah, Inc.; mem. US Congress from 3rd Utah Dist., 2009—. Commr. Highland City Planning Commn.; chmn. Utah Nat. Guard Adjutant Gen. Review. Trustee Utah Valley State Coll. Mem.: BYU Utah County Cougar Club (pres.), Cougar Club (mem. bd. dirs.). Republican. Office: US Congress 1032 Longworth House Office Bldg Washington DC 20515-4403 also: Dist Office 51 S University Ave Ste 319 Provo UT 84601 Office Phone: 202-225-7751, 801-851-2500. Office Fax: 202-225-5629, 801-851-2509.*

CHAHINE, MOUSTAFA TOUFIC, atmospheric scientist; b. Beirut, Jan. 1, 1935; s. Toufic M. and Hind S. (Tabbara) C.; m. Marina Bandak, Dec. 9, 1960; children: Tony T., Steve S. BS, U. Wash., 1956, MS, 1957; PhD, U. Calif., Berkeley, 1960. With Jet Propulsion Lab., Calif. Inst. Tech., Pasadena, 1960—, mgr. planetary atmospheres sect., 1975—, sr. research scientist, mgr. earth and space scis. div., 1978-84, chief scientist, 1984—2001. Vis. scientist MIT, 1969-70; vis. prof. Am. U., Beirut, 1971-72; regent's lectr. UCLA, 1989-90; mem. NASA Space and Earth Sci. Adv. Com., 1982-85; mem. climate rsch. com. Nat. Acad. Scis., 1985-88, bd. dirs. atmospheric scis. and climate, 1988—; chmn. sci. steering group Global Energy and Water Cycle Experiment World Meteorol. Orgn., 1988-99; cons. U.S. Navy, 1972-76 Contbr. articles to profl. jours. Recipient medal for exceptional sci. achievements NASA, 1969, NASA Outstanding Leadership medal, 1984, William T. Pecora award, 1989, Jule G. Charney award, 1991, Losey Atmospheric Scis. award AIAA, 1993, NASA Exceptional Achievement medal, 2000, William Nordberg medal Com. on Space Rsch., 2002, NASA Exceptional Achievement medal, 2007. Fellow AAAS, Am. Geophys. Union, Am. Phys. Soc., Royal Soc., Am. Meteorol. Soc.; mem. Internat. Acad. Astronautics, US Nat. Acad. Engring., Sigma Xi. Office: 4800 Oak Grove Dr Pasadena CA 91109-8001 Office Phone: 818-354-6057. Business E-Mail: chahine@jpl.nasa.gov.

CHAI, WINBERG, political science professor, foundation administrator; b. Shanghai, Oct. 16, 1932; came to U.S., 1951, naturalized, 1973; s. Ch'u and Mei-en (Tsao) C.; m. Carolyn Everett, Mar. 17, 1966 (dec. 1996); children: Maria May-lee, Jeffrey Tien-yu. Student, Hartwick Coll., 1951-53, LittD, 2002; BA, Wittenberg U., 1955; MA, New Sch. Social Rsch., 1958; PhD, NYU, 1968; DHL, Wittenberg U., 1997; DL, Hartwick Coll., 2002. Lectr. New Sch. Social Rsch., 1957-61; vis. asst. prof. Drew U., 1961-62; asst. prof. Fairleigh Dickinson U., 1962-65, U. Redlands, 1965-68, assoc. prof., 1969-73, chmn. dept., 1970-73; prof., chmn. Asian studies CCNY, 1973-79; disting. prof. polit. sci., v.p. acad. affairs, spl. asst. to pres. U. S.D., Vermillion, 1979-82; prof. polit. sci., dir. internat. programs U. Wyo., Laramie, 1988—. Chmn. Third World Conf. Found., Inc., Chgo., 1982—; pres. Wang Yu-fa Found., Taiwan, 1989—; exec. editor Asian Affairs, 1997-. Author: (with Ch'u Chai) The Story of Chinese Philosophy, 1961, The Changing Society of China, 1962, rev. edit., 1969, The New Politics of Communist China, 1972, The Search for a New China, 1975; editor: Essential Works of Chinese Communism, 1969; (with James C. Hsiung) Asia in the U.S. Foreign Policy, 1981; (with James C. Hsiung) U.S. Asian Relations: The National Security Paradox, 1983; (with Carolyn Chai) Beyond China's Crisis, 1989, In Search of Peace in the Middle East, 1991; (with Cal Clark) Political Stability and Economic Growth, 1994, China Mainland and Taiwan, 1994, rev. edit. 1996, Hong Kong Under China, 1998; editor: Saudi Arabia: A Modern Reader, 2005; co-editor: (with May-lee Cai) China = A to Z, 2007; co-translator: (with Ch'u Chai) A Treasury of Chinese Literature, 1965; co-author (with May-Lee-Chai) The Girl from Purple Mountain, 2001, China A to Z, 2007; assoc. editor: Berkshire Encyclopedia of China, 2009. Haynes Found. fellow, 1967, 68; Ford Found. humanities grantee, 1968, 69, Pacific Cultural Found. grantee, 1978, 86, NSF grantee, 1970, Hubert Eaton Meml. Fund grantee, 1972-73, Field Found. grantee, 1973, 75, Henry Luce Found. grantee, 1978, 80, S.D. Humanities Com. grantee, 1980, Pacific Culture Fund grantee, 1987, 90-91. Mem. AAAS, AAUP, NAACP, Am. Polit. Sci. Assn., Am. Assn. Chinese Studies (pres.1978-80), N.Y. Acad. Scis., Internat. Studies Assn. Democrat. Home: 1071 Granito Dr Laramie WY 82072-5045 Office: Univ Wyoming Dept 3197 1000 E University Ave Laramie WY 82071-4098 Office Phone: 307-766-6771, 307-766-7484.

CHAIRSELL, CHRISTINE, academic administrator; children: T., Tyler. EdD, U. Nev. Las Vegas, MA in polit. sci., BA in polit. sci., U. Nev. Las Vegas. Acting pres. Nev. State Coll., 2002; assoc. vice chancellor U. & CC Sys. Nev.; assoc. vice pres. Computing Svc.; dean spl. programs CC So. Nev.; dir. environ. edn. U. Nev. Las Vegas, faculty polit. sci. dept. Pres. Aqua Vision, 1992—94; mem. Leadership Las Vegas Class, 1993. Recipient women of achievement edn., Las Vegas Chamber Commerce, 1993.

CHAKRIN, LEWIS M., consumer products company executive; Degree in Engring., NYU, 1969, MBA in Fin., 1976, PhD in Fin., 1978; M in Ops. Rsch., Columbia U., 1971. V.p. product mgmt. and consumer svcs. AT&T, 1998—2000; sr. v.p., chief strategy officer AT&T Wireless Svc., Inc., Redmond, Wash., 2000—01, exec. v.p. corp. strategy and bus. devel., 2001—.

CHAMBERLAIN, ADRIAN RAMOND, transportation engineer; b. Detroit, Nov. 11, 1929; s. Adrian and Leila (Swisher) C.; m. Melanie F. Stevens, May 19, 1979; children: Curtis (dec.), Tracy, Thomas (dec.). BS, Mich. State U., 1951, D Engring., 1971; MS, Wash. State U., 1952; PhD, Colo. State U., 1955; LittD, Denver U., 1974. Registered profl. engr., Colo. lic. real estate broker, Colo., 1981-91. Rsch. engr. Phillips Petroleum Co., 1955; rsch. coord., civil engr. Colo. State U., 1956-57, chief civil engr. sect., 1957-61, acting dean engring., 1959-61, v.p., 1960-66, exec. v.p., treas., governing bd., 1966-69, pres., 1969-80; chmn. bd. dirs. Univ. Nat. Bank, 1964-69, dir., 1964-74; pres., dir. Mitchell & Co., Inc., 1981-85; exec. v.p. Simons, Li & Assocs., Inc., 1985-87; pres., CEO, Chemagnetics, Inc., Ft. Collins, Colo., 1987-89; exec. dir. Colo. Dept. Hwys., Denver, 1987-91, Colo. Dept. Transp., 1991-94; v.p. engring. cons. firm Parsons Brinckerhoff, Denver, 1998—. Chmn. NSF Commn. Weather Modification, 1964-66; mem. Nat. Air Quality Criteria Adv. Com., 1967-70; vice chmn. rsch. and tech. coord. com. Fed. Hwy Admiinstrn. of Transp. Rsch. Bd., NRC, 1991-94. Colo. commr. Western Interstate Commn. on Higher Edn., 1974-78; pres. State Bd. Agr. Sys., 1978-80; trustee Cystic Fibrosis Found., 1971-84; bd. trustees Univ. Corp. for Atmospheric Rsch., 1967-72, 74-81, chmn. bd. trustees, 1977-79; pres. Black Mountain Ranch, Inc., 1969-85; bd. dirs. Nat. Ctr. for Higher Edn. Mgmt. Sys., 1975-80, chmn. bd. dirs., 1977-78; bd. visitors Air U., USAF, 1973-76, chmn., 1975-76; exec. com. Nat. Assn. State Univs. and Land Grant Colls., 1976-80, pres.-elect, 1978-79, chmn., 1979-80; mem. adv. coun. to dir. NSF, 1978-81; chmn. Ft. Collins-Loveland Airport Authority, 1983-86; bd. dirs. Synergetics Internat. Inc., 1987-90; mem. exec. com. strategic hwy. rsch. commn. Transp. Rsch. Bd. NRC, 1989-93, chmn. strategic transp. rsch. study hwy. safety, 1989-90, exec. com., 1991-96, vice-chmn., 1992, chmn., 1993; mem. Gov.'s Cabinet, State of Colo., 1987-94; mem. Info. Mgmt. Commn., 1988-93. Fulbright student U. Grenoble, 1955-56 Mem. ASCE, NAE, Am. Assn. State Hwy. and Transp. Ofcls. (policy com. 1987-92, v.p. 1990-91, pres. 1991-92, bd. dirs. 1992-94, chmn. standing com. on adminstrn. 1993-94), Am. Trucking Assn. (v.p. for freight policy 1994-98, mng. dir. found. 1998), Order of Aztec Eagle, Mex., Nat. Assoc. Nat. Acads., Western Stock Show Assn., Sigma Xi, Tau Beta Pi, Phi Kappa Phi, Chi Epsilon. Office: Parsons Brinckerhoff 555 17th St Ste 500 Denver CO 80202-3937 Office Phone: 303-832-9091. Business E-Mail: chamberlain@pbworld.com.

CHAMBERLAIN, BARBARA KAYE, communications executive; b. Lewiston, Idaho, Nov. 6, 1962; d. William Arthur and Gladys Marie (Humphrey) Greene; m. Dean Andrew Chamberlain, Sept. 13, 1986 (div.); children: Kathleen Marie, Laura Kaye; m. Daniel Eric Pocklington, Apr. 11, 1998 (div.); m. Eric Lee Abbott, July 7, 2007. BA in English cum laude, BA in Linguistics cum laude, Wash. State U., 1984; MPA, Ea. Wash. U., 2002. Temp. sec. various svcs., Spokane, Wash., 1984-86; office mgr. Futurepast, Spokane, 1986-87; dir. mktg. and prodn. Futurepast: The History Co., Melior Publs., Spokane, 1987-88, v.p., 1988-89; founder, owner PageWorksInk, 1989—2006; mem. dist. 2 Idaho State Ho. of Reps., 1990-92; mem. Idaho State Senate, 1992-94; dir. comm. and pub. affairs Wash. State U., Spokane, 1998—. Adj. faculty North Idaho Coll., 1995, trustee, 1996-2001, bd. chair, 1999-2001. Author North Idaho's Centennial, 1990; editor Washington Songs and Lore, 1988. Bd. dirs. Mus. North Idaho Coeur d'Alene, 1990-91, Ct. Apptd. Spl. advocates, 1993-96; bd. dirs. Spokane Pub. Rels. Coun., 1999-2004, pres., 2002-03; bd. dirs. Friends of the Falls, 2005—, pres., 2007-08; co-chair Citizens for Spokane Schs., 2005-; bd. dirs. Deaconess/Valley Healthcare Found., 2007-; chair, Bike to Work Spokane, 2007-. Named Child Advocate Legislator of Yr., Idaho Alliance for Children, Youth and Families, 1993. Democrat. Office: Academic Ctr PO Box 1495 Spokane WA 99210-1495

CHAMBERLAIN, WILLIAM EDWIN, JR., management consultant; b. St. Louis, June 8, 1951; s. William Edwin Sr. and Grace (Salisbury) C. AA in Bus. Mgmt., Mesa C.C., Arz., 1983; BBA, U.

Phoenix, 1988; MBA, Almeda U., 2005. Tng. and human resources devel. specialist Motorola, Inc., Phoenix, 1979-87; pres., seminar spkr. Chamberlain Cons. Svcs., Reno, 1987—. Curator, dir. ops. U.S. Wolf Refuge. Mem. Network for Profl. Devel. Avocations: wildlife preservation and management, hiking, backpacking, tennis, basketball, racquetball. Office Phone: 775-475-0510. Business E-Mail: bill@uswolfrefuge.org.

CHAMBERLIN, DONALD DEAN, computer engineer; b. San Jose, Calif., Dec. 21, 1944; BS, Harvey Mudd Coll., 1966; PhD in Elec. Engring., Stanford U., 1971. Rsch. staff mem. IBM, San Jose, Calif., 1971—. Adj. prof. Santa Clara U., 1992-95. Author: Using the New DB2: IBM's Object-Relational Database System, 1996, A Complete Guide to DB2 Universal Database, 1998; contbr. articles to profl. jours. Fellow Assn. Computing Machinery; mem. Nat. Acad. Engring., Inst. Elec. & Electronics Engrs. Office: Almaden Research Ctr IBM 650 Harry Rd San Jose CA 95120-6001 Fax: 408-927-3215. E-mail: chamberlin@almaden.ibm.com.

CHAMBERLIN, MICHAEL JOHN, retired biochemistry professor; b. Chgo., June 7, 1937; s. John Windsor and Marian (McMichael) C.; m. Caroline Marie Kane, Jan. 31, 1981. AB, Harvard U., 1959; PhD, Stanford U., 1963. Asst. prof. virology U. Calif., Berkeley, 1963—67, assoc. prof. molecular biology, 1967—71, assoc. prof. biochemistry, 1971—73; prof., 1973—99, U. Calif., Berkeley, 1973, vice chmn. dept. biochemistry, 1983—88, prof. biochemistry and molecular biology, 1989; emeritus prof., 1999. Mem. physiol. chemistry study sect. NIH, 1970-74, molecular biology study sect., 1980-84; mem. study sect. Am. Heart Assn., 1983-86. Mem. editorial bd. Jour. Biol. Chemistry, 1975-78, Biochemistry, 1993—; contbr. articles to profl. jours. Recipient Charles Pfizer award Am. Chem. Soc., 1974. Mem. NAS, AAAS, Am. Acad. Arts and Scis., Am. Soc. Biochemistry and Molecular Biology, Am. Soc. Microbiology, Am. Acad. Microbiology, Phi Beta Kappa, Sigma Xi. Personal E-mail: profmjc@berkeley.edu.

CHAMBERS, CAROLYN SILVA, communications company executive; b. Portland, Oreg., Sept. 15, 1931; d. Julio and Elizabeth (McDonnell) Silva; widowed; children: William, Scott, Elizabeth, Silva, Clark. BBA, U. Oreg. V.p., treas. Liberty Comm., Inc., Eugene, Oreg., 1960-83; pres. Chambers Comm. Corp., Eugene, 1983-95, chmn., 1996—; chmn., CEO, bd. dirs. Chambers Constrn. Co., 1986—. Bd. dirs., dep. chair bd. Fed. Res. Bank, San Francisco, 1982-92; bd. dirs. Portland Gen. Corp.; bd. dirs. U.S. Bancorp. Mem. Sacred Heart Med. Found., 1980—, Sacred Heart Gov. Bd., 1987-92, Sacred Heart Health Svcs. Bd., 1993-95, PeaceHealth Bd., 1995—; mem. U. Oreg. Found., 1980—, pres., 1992-93; chair U. Oreg. Found., The Campaign for Oreg., 1988-89; pres., bd. dirs. Eugene Arts Found.; bd. dirs., treas., dir. search com. Eugene Symphony; mem. adv. bd. Eugene Hearing and Speech Ctr., Alton Baker Park Commn., Pleasant Hill Sch. Bd.; chmn., pres., treas. Civic Theatre, Very Little Theatre; negotiator, treas., bd. dirs., mem. thrift shop Jr. League of Oreg. Recipient Webfoot award U. Oreg., 1986, U. Oreg. Pres.'s medal, 1991, Disting. Svc. award, 1992, Pioneer award, 1983, Woman Who Made a Difference award Internat. Women's Forum, 1989, U. Oreg. Found. Disting. Alumni award, 1995, Tom McCall awrd Oreg. Assn. Broadcasters, 1995, Disting. Alumni award U. Oreg., 1995, Outstanding Philanthropist award Oreg. chpt. Nat. Soc. Fund Raising Execs., 1994. Mem. Nat. Cable TV Assn. (mem. fin. com., chmn. election and by-laws com., chmn. awards com., bd. dirs. 1987-89, Vanguard award for Leadership 1982), Pacific Northwest Cable Comm. Assn. (conv. chmn., pres.), Oreg. Cable TV Assn. (v.p., pres., chmn. edn. com., conv. chmn., Pres.'s award 1986), Calif. Cable TV Assn. (bd. dirs., conv. chmn., conv. panelist), Women in Cable (charter mem., treas., v.p., pres., recipient star of cable recognition), Wash. State Cable Comm. Assn., Idaho Cable TV Assn., Community Antenna TV Assn., Cable TV Pioneers, Eugene C. of C. (first citizen award, 1985). Home: PO Box 640 Pleasant Hill OR 97455-0640 Office: Chambers Comm Corp PO Box 7009 Eugene OR 97401-0009

CHAMBERS, JOAN LOUISE, retired librarian, dean; b. Denver, Mar. 22, 1937; d. Joseph Harvey and Clara Elizabeth (Carleton) Baker; m. Donald Ray Chambers, Aug. 17, 1958 BA in English Lit., U. No. Colo., Greeley, 1958; MS in L.S., U. Calif.-Berkeley, 1970; MS in Systems Mgmt., U. So. Calif., 1985; cert., Coll. for Fin. Planning, 1989. Libr. U. Nev., Reno, 1970-79; asst. univ. libr. U. Calif., San Diego, 1979-81, univ. libr. Riverside, 1981—85; dean librs., prof. Colo. State U., Ft. Collins, 1985-97, emeritus dean and prof., 1997—. Mgmt. intern Duke U. Libr., Durham, N.C., 1978-79; sr. fellow UCLA Summer, 1982; cons. tng. program Assn. of Rsch. Libraries, Washington, 1981; libr. cons. Calif. State U., Sacramento, 1982-83, U. Wyo., 1985-86, 94-95, U. Nebr., 1991-92, Calif. State U. System, 1993-94, Univ. No. Ariz., 1994-95. Contbr. articles to profl. jours., chpts. to books. Bd. dir. Consumers Union, 1996-2006. U. Calif. instl. improvement grantee, 1980-81; State of Nev. grantee, 1976, ARL grantee, 1983-84. Mem.: PEO, Colo. Mountain Club, Phi Kappa Phi, Kappa Delta Phi, Phi Lambda Theta, Beta Phi Mu. Avocations: hiking, snow shoeing, skiing, bicycling, tennis. Home and Office: PO Box 1477 Edwards CO 81632-1477 E-mail: chambers@vail.net.

CHAMBERS, JOHN THOMAS, computer systems network executive; b. Cleve., Aug. 23, 1949; s. June and John Chambers; m. Elaine Prater, 1974; 2 children. BS, BA, W.Va. U., 1971, JD, 1974; MBA, Ind. U., 1975. Mktg. mgr. IBM, 1976—82; v.p. central U.S. ops. Wang Laboratories, 1983—87, sr. v.p., Americas/Asia/Pacific ops., 1987—89, sr. v.p., U.S. ops., 1989—90; sr. v.p. worldwide ops. Cisco Systems, Inc., San Jose, Calif., 1991-94, exec. v.p., 1994-95, pres., CEO, 1995—2006, chmn., CEO, 2006—. Vice chmn. Nat. Infrastructure adv. coun., 2002—; Served on Bill Clinton Trade Policy com.; bd. dirs. Cisco Sys. Inc., 1993—, Clarify, Inc., San Jose, 1995—96, Arbor Software, Sunnyvale, Calif., 1995—96, Wal-Mart Stores, Inc. Bentonville, Ark., 2000—06. Recipient Woodrow Wilson Award for Corp. Citizenship, Woodrow Wilson Center for internat. ctr. for Scholars of the Smithsonian Inst., Lifetime Achievement award, Smithsonian Inst., Presdl. award, Ron Brown award for Corp. Leadership, Bus. Coun., Frederick D. Patterson Award, United Negro Coll. Fund; named one of 50 Who Matter Now, Business 2.0, 2007, 25 Most Powerful People in Bus., Fortune Mag., 2007, The 100 Most Influential People in the World, TIME mag., 2008. Office: Cisco Sys Inc 170 W Tasman Dr Bldg 10 San Jose CA 95134-1706 E-mail: jochambe@cisco.com.

CHAMBERS, KENTON LEE, botany educator; b. LA, Sept. 27, 1929; s. Maynard Macy and Edna Georgia (Miller) C.; m. Henrietta Laing, June 21, 1958; children: Elaine Patricia, David Macy. AB with highest honors, Whittier Coll., 1950; PhD (NSF fellow), Stanford U., 1955. Instr. biol. scis. Stanford (Calif.) U., 1954-55; instr. botany, asst. prof. Yale U., New Haven, Conn., 1956-60; assoc. prof., prof. botany Oreg. State U., Corvallis, 1960-90, prof. emeritus, 1991—. Curator Herbarium, 1960-90; program dir. systematic biology NSF, Washington, 1967-68. Contbr. articles in field to profl. jours. Fellow AAAS; mem. Bot. Soc. Am. (Merit award 1990, Centennial award, 2006), Am. Soc. Plant Taxonomists, Am. Inst. Biol. Scis., Calif. Bot. Soc. Home: 4761 SW Hollyhock Cir Corvallis OR 97333-1385 Office: Oreg State U Herbarium Botany Dept Corvallis OR 97331-2902 E-mail: chamberk@science.oregonstate.edu.

CHAMBERS, THOMAS JEFFERSON, state supreme court justice; b. Yakima, Wash., Oct. 11, 1943; s. Thomas J. and Doris May (Ellyson) C.; m. Judy Larene Cable, June 11, 1967; children: Jolie, Jana, Tommy. BA in Polit. Sci., Wash. State U., 1966; JD, U. Wash., 1969. Bar: Wash., U.S. Dist. Ct. (we. and ea. dists.) Wash. 1969. Assoc. Lycette, Diamond & Sylvester, Seattle, 1969-71, Barokas & Martin, Seattle, 1972; sole practice Seattle, 1972—2001; justice Wash. Supreme Ct., 2001—. Mem. Internat. Smile Power Found.; hon. bd. mem. Rise n' Shine Found. Recipient Outstanding Judge of Yr., King County Wash. Women Lawyer, 2006, Good Neighbor of Yr., Seattle Housing Authority, 1999, Disting. Alumni award, Yakima CC, 1998. Mem. Wash. State Trial Lawyers Assn. (pres. 1985-86, Trial Lawyers of Yr., 1989), Am. Bd. Trial Advs. (pres. Wash. chpt. 1993, Trial Lawyers of Yr., 1996), Am. Trial Lawyers Assn. (past mem. bd. govs.1987-90), Wash. State Bar Assn. (pres. 1996-97). Avocations: flying, scuba diving. Office: PO Box 40929 Olympia WA 98504-0929

CHAMBLISS, LINDA R., obstetrician, consultant; b. Summit, NJ, Feb. 13, 1951; d. Robert E. and Alice (Dunne) C.; children: Alice, Kevin, Christopher, Daniel Patrick. BSN, Duke U., Durham, NC, 1973; MD, Mich. State U., East Lansing, 1980; MPH, Johns Hopkins U., Balt., 2004. Diplomate with spl. certification in maternal-fetal medicine Am. Bd. Ob-Gyn. Pediat. intern U. Chgo., 1980—81; resident in ob-gyn. Cook County Hosp., Chgo., 1981—85; fellow in maternal-fetal medicine U. So. Calif.-LA County Hosp., LA, 1988—90; chief obstetrics Indian Health Svcs., Tuba City, Ariz., 1985-88; clin. prof. ob-gyn. U. Ariz., 2001—06; prof. ob-gyn. St. Louis U., 2006—, med. dir. labor and delivery, 2006—; dir., maternal fetal medicine Dept. Ob-Gyn. St. Joseph Hosp. Med. Ctr., Ariz. Comdr. USPHS, 1985—. Recipient Nat. Edn. award, Coun. on Resident Edn. in Ob-Gyn., 1995, 2007, Nat. Faculty Excellence award, 1995, Alumna Excellence award, Mich. State U., 1996, Alumni award, 2001; named Tchr. of Yr., Dept. Ob-Gyn., Maricopa Med. Ctr., 1991, Alumni of Yr., Mich. State U., Coll. Human Medicine, 2000. Fellow ACOG; mem. AMA (cons.), AAUW, Soc. Maternal Fetal Medicine, Am. Women's Med. Assn., Am. Inst. Ultrasound Medicine. Democrat. Office: 500 W Thomas Rd Ste 800 Phoenix AZ 85013 Home Phone: 602-710-1712; Office Phone: 602-470-7013, 608-406-2865. Personal E-mail: lrchambliss@yahoo.com.

CHAMEAU, JEAN-LOU, academic administrator; b. 1953; m. Carol Carmichael. M in Civil Engring., Stanford U., 1977, PhD in Civil Engring., 1981. Joined Purdue U., 1980, prof. civil engring., head geotechnical engring. program; dir. Sch. Civil and Environ. Engring. Ga. Inst. Tech., 1991, dean Coll. Engring., provost, v.p. academic affairs, 2001—06, Ga. Rsch. Alliance Eminent Scholar; pres. Calif. Inst. Tech., 2006—. Pres. Golder Assocs., Inc., 1994—95; bd. dirs. MTS Sys. Corp. Recipient Presdl. Young Investigator Award, NSF, Casagrande Award, ASCE, Rodney D. Chipp Meml. Award, Soc. of Women Engrs., 2004. Office: Calif Inst Tech Office of Pres 1200 E California Blvd Pasadena CA 91125 Office Phone: 626-395-6301. Business E-Mail: chameau@caltech.edu.

CHAMPAGNE, DUANE WILLARD, sociology educator; b. Belcourt, ND, May 18, 1951; m. Carole Goldberg; children: Talya, Gabe, Demelza. BA in Math., N.D. State U., 1973, MA in Sociology, 1975; PhD in Sociology, Harvard U., 1982. Teaching fellow Harvard U., Cambridge, Mass., 1981-82, rsch. fellow, 1982-83; asst. prof. U. Wis., Milw., 1983-84, UCLA, 1984-91, assoc. prof., 1991-97, prof., 1997—. Publs. dir. Am. Indian Studies Ctr., UCLA, 1986-87, assoc. dir., 1990, acting dir., 1991, dir., 1991-02, affiliate faculty UCLA Native Nations Law and Policy Ctr., 2003-, acting dir. Tribal Learning Cmty. and Edn. Exch., 2004-05; adminstrv. co-head interdepartmental program for Am. Indian studies UCLA, 1992-93; vis. prof. Harvard U., 2006—. Author: American Indian Societies, 1989, Social Order and Political Change, 1992, Service Delivery for Native American Children in Los Angeles County, 1996, The ACCIP Community Service Report: A Second Century of Dishonor-Federal Inequities and California Indians, 2002, Social Change and Cultural Continuity Among Native Nations, 2007; editor: Native Am. Studies Assn. Newsletter, 1991—92, Native North American Almanac, 1994, 2d edit., 2001, Chronology of Native North American, 1994, Native America: Portrait of the Peoples, 1994, Native American Activism: Alcatraz to the Longest Walk, 1997, Contemporary Native American Issues, 1999, Contemporary Native American Cultural Issues, 1999, Special Issue on Indigenous Issues: Hagar, International Social Science Review, 2001, Native American Studies in Higher Education: Models for Collaboration Between Indigenous Nations, 2002, The Future of Indigenous Peoples' Strategies for Survival and Development, 2003, Education, Equity and Empowerment Among Indigenous Peoples: The Case of the Palestinians, 2005, Indigenous and Minority Education: International Perspectives on Empowerment, 2005, Indigenous Peoples and the Modern State, 2005, Indigenous Education and Empowerment: International Perspectives, 2006, American Indian Nations: Yesterday, Today and Tomorrow, 2007; book rev. editor: Am. Indian Culture and Rsch. Jour., 1984—86; editor, 1986—2002; series editor: Contemporary American Indian Issues, 1998—, sr. editor: Indian Country Today, 2006—08; contbr. articles to profl. jours. Mem. City of L.A. Cmty. Action Bd., 1993, L.A. County/City Am. Indian Commn., 1992—, chair, 1993, 1995—97, 2000—02, 2004, 2005—, sec., 2002, vice chair, 1997—2000; mem. subcom. for cultural and econ. devel. L.A. City/County Native Am. Commn., 1992—93, 2004; bd. dirs. Ctr. for Improvement of Child Caring, 1993—, Greater L.A. Am. Indian Culture Ctr., Inc., 1993, incorporator, 1993; trustee Southwest Mus., 1994—97, Nat. Mus. Am. Indian, 1998—2003; master Coll. Humanities and Social Sci., N.D. State U., 1996. Recipient LA Sr. Health Peer Counseling Cmty. Vol. Cert. of Recognition, 1996; Writer of Yr. award Cir. Native Writers and Storytellers, 1999; honoree Nat. Ctr. Am. Indian Enterprise, 1999; grantee Rockefeller Found., 1982-83, U. Wis. Grad Sch. Rsch. Com., 1984-85, Wis. Dept. Edn., 1984-85, 87-88, 88-89, NSF, 1985-88, 88-89, Nat. Endowment for Arts, 1987-88, 91-92, NRC, 1988-89, Nat. Sci. Coun., 1989-90, John D. and Catherine T. MacArthur Found., 1990-91, Hayes Found., 1990-93, Calif. Coun. for Humanities, 1991-92, Ford Found., 1990-92, Gale Rsch. Inc., 1991-93, 93-95, Rockwell Corp., 1991-93, GTE, 1992-93, Kellog Found., 1997-2000, Pequot Mus. and Rsch. Ctr., 1997-2002, So. Calif. Indian Ctr., 1998; Fund for the Improvement of Post Secondary Edn., 1998-2003, NEH, 2002—, Dept. Justice, 2001-05, NEH, 2003-05, San Manuel Band of Serrano Indians Endowment, 2004—, Dept. Justice, 2006—; Am. Indian scholar, 1973-75, 80-82, Minority fellow Am. Sociol. Assn., 1975-78, RIAS Seminar fellow, 1976-77; Rockefeller Postdoctoral fellow, 1982-83, NSF fellow, 1985-88, Postdoctoral fellow Ford Found., 1988-89. Avocations: chess, jogging. Home: 2152 Balsam Ave Los Angeles CA 90025 Office: UCLA Native Nations Law and Policy Ctr Dept Sociology 264 Haines Hall Los Angeles CA 90095-1551 Office Phone: 310-475-6475. Business E-Mail: champagn@ucla.edu.

CHAMPION, WILL, musician; b. Hampshire, England, July 31, 1978; Student in Anthropology, U. Coll. London. Drummer Coldplay, 1998—. Musician: (albums) Parachutes, 2000 (Grammy award for Best Alternative Music Album, 2001), A Rush of Blood to the Head, 2002 (Grammy award for Best Alternative Music Album, 2002), Live 2003, 2003, X&Y, 2005 (Juno award for Best Internat. Album, 2006), Love, Actually, 2006, Viva La Vida, 2008 (Grammy award for Rock Album of Yr., 2009), (songs) In My Place, 2002 (Grammy award for Best Rock Performance By A Duo Or Group With Vocal, 2002), Clocks, 2002 (Grammy award for Record of Yr., 2003), Speed of Sound, 2005 (MTV Europe award for Best Song, 2005), Viva La Vida, 2009 (Song of Yr. and Best Group Pop Vocal Performance, Grammy Awards, 2009). Recipient Favorite Alternative Artist (Coldplay), Am. Music Awards, 2005; named World's Best Rock Act, World's Best-Selling Rock Act, and Best-Selling Brit. Artist, World Music Awards, 2008. Office: Capital Records 1750 North Vine Street 10th Floor Hollywood CA 90028

CHAN, FRED S.L., electronics company executive; BSEE, MSC, U. Hawaii. Co-founder, pres., CEO CADCAM Tech., Inc.; founder, pres., CEO AC Design, Inc.; pres., dir. Niche Tech., Inc., 1991-93; pres. ESS Tech., Fremont, Calif., 1985—, dir., 1986—, CEO, 1994—. Chmn. bd. dirs. ESS Tech. Office: ESS Technology,Inc 48401 Fremont Blvd Fremont CA 94538

CHAN, JACKIE, actor, film director; b. Hong Kong, Apr. 7, 1954; s. Chi-Ping and Lee-Lee Chan; m. Lin Fong Chiao; 1 child: J.C. Trained, Peking Opera Sch. Films include: Little Tiger of Guangdong, Little Tiger from Canton, Hand of Death, 1975, New Fist of Fury, 1976, Shaolin Wooden Men, 1976, To Kill with Intrigue, 1977, Snake in the Eagle's Shadow, Snake and Crane Arts of Shaolin, Magnificent Bodyguards, 1978, Drunken Master, 1978, Spiritual Kung Fu, 1978, The Fearless Hyena, Dragon Fist, 1979, The Young Master, 1980, Half a Loaf of King Fu, Battle Creek Brawl, 1980, The Cannonball Run, 1981, The Dragon Lord, 1982, Marvelous Fists, 1982, Winners and Sinners, 1983, The Fearless Hyena Part 2, Project A, 1983, Cannonball Run II, 1984, Wheels on Meals, 1984, My Lucky Stars, 1985, The Protector, 1985, Twinkle Twinkle Lucky Stars, 1985, Heart of the Dragon, 1985, Police Story, 1986, Armour of God, 1987, Project A Part 2, 1987, Dragons Forever, 1987, Police Story II, 1987, Mr. Canton and Lady Rose, 1989, Amour of God II: Operation Condor, 1991, Island of Fire, 1991, Twin Dragons, 1992, Police Story III: Super Cop, 1992, City Hunter, 1993, Crime Story, 1993, Drunken Master II, 1994, Rumble in the Bronx, 1994, Thunderbolt, 1994, Police Story IV: First Strike, 1996, Mr. Nice Guy, 1997, Rush Hour, 1998, Who Am I?, 1998, Gorgeous, 1999, The King of Comedy, 1999, Gen-X Cops, 1999, Shanghai Noon, 2000, The Accidental Spy, 2001, Rush Hour 2, 2001, The Tuxedo, 2002, Shanghai Knights, 2003, The Medallion, 2003, Around the World in 80 Days, 2004, Fa dou daai jin, 2004, San gin chaat goo si, 2004, San Wa, 2005, Rush Hour 3, 2007, The Forbidden Kingdom, 2008, (voice) Kung Fu Panda, 2008, actor, exec. prodr. The Shinjuku Incident, 2009. Recipient Lifetime Achievement award MTV, 1995, Best Picture award Hong Kong Film, 1989, Best Action Choreography Hong Kong Film, 1996, 99, 2002, Maverick Tribute award Cinequest San Jose Film Festival, 1998, PETA Humanitarian award, 1999, Internat. Lifetime Achievement award, Internat. Leadership Found., 2000, Taurus Hon. award, Outstanding Achievement for Acting in Actions Film, World Stunt awards, 2002. Named Goodwill Amb., 2004. Office: c/o William Morris Agy One William Morris Pl Beverly Hills CA 90212

CHAN, PHILIP J., medical educator; married; 3 children. BA cum laude in biology, Kalamazoo Coll., 0979; MS in Physiology, Mich. State U., 1981, PhD in Physiology, 1983. Diplomate Am. Bd. Bioanalysis. Dir. sperm processing & IVF and embryo transfer lab. Kennedy Meml. Hosps./U. Med. Ctr., Cherry Hill, NJ, 1983—87; dir. labs. Hillcrest Fertility Ctr., Tulsa, 1987—89; dir. andrology/male reproduction and molecular biology labs. Loma Linda U. Obstetrics Med. Group, Calif., 1989—. Mgr. info. sys. lab. computers and network Loma Linda U. Ob-Gyn. Med. Group, Inc., 1991—; from instr. to asst. prof. U. Medicine and Dentistry of N.J. Sch. Osteopathic Medicine, 1983-87; assoc. prof. Oral Roberts U. Sch. Medicine, 1987-89; from assoc. prof. to prof. Loma Linda U. Sch. Medicine, 1989—; mem. comparative medicine study sect. NIH, 1994-98, chmn. site visit Nat. Ctr. for Rsch. Resources, 1999; insp. Coll. Am. Pathologists, 1993—. Contbr. articles to profl. jours. Recipient Walter-MacPherson First Pl. Rsch. award The Walter E. Macpherson Soc., 1997, Outstanding Attending Staff Physician award WYETH, 2003, Nat. Faculty award Coun. on Resident Edn. in Ob-Gyn., 2006. Mem. Am. Soc. Reproductive Medicine, Soc. Assisted Reproductive Tech., Am. Assn. Bioanalysts. Avocations: computers, stamp collecting/philately, coin collecting/numismatics, piano. Office: Loma Linda U Fac Med Office Dept Ob-Gyn Ste 3950 11370 Anderson St Loma Linda CA 92354-3450 Personal E-mail: pchann@yahoo.com.

CHAN, SHU-PARK, electrical engineering educator; b. Canton, China, Oct. 10, 1929; came to U.S., 1951, naturalized, 1965; s. Chi-Tong and Shui-Ying (Mok) C.; m. Stella Yok-Sing Lam, Dec. 28, 1956; children: Charlene Li-Hsiang, Yau-Gene. BEE, Va. Mil. Inst., Lexington, 1955; MEE, U. Ill., 1957, PhD, 1963. Instr. elec. engring. and math. Va. Mil. Inst., 1957-59; instr. elec. engring. U. Ill., 1960-61, rsch. assoc., 1961-62, asst. prof. math., 1962-63; assoc. prof. elec. engring. U. Santa Clara, 1963-68, prof., 1968-92, chmn. elec. engring. and computer sci. dept., 1969-84; Nicholson Family Chair prof. Santa Clara U., 1987-92, prof. emeritus, 1992—, acting dean Sch. Engring., 1987-88; founder, pres. Internat. Technol. U., Santa Clara, 1994—; pres. Chu Hai Coll., Hong Kong, 1995-96. Prin. investigator NSF, NASA; Univ. fellow U. Ill., 1959-60; vis. spl. chair prof. elec. engring. dept. Nat. Taiwan U., 1973-74; spl. lectr. Acad. Sci., Peking, China, summer 1980; hon. prof. elec. engring. dept. U. Hong Kong, 1980-81; hon. prof. Anhuei U., China, 1982; spl. chair Tamkang U., Taipei, Taiwan, 1981; apptd. mem. J. William Fulbright Fgn. Scholarship Bd., 1991-93; founder, pres. Internat. Tech. U. Found., 1994—. Author: introductory Topological Analysis of Electrical Networks, 1969, (with others) Analysis of Linear Networks and Systems—A

Matrix-Oriented Approach with Computer Applications, 1972, (with E. Moustakas) Introduction to the Applications of the Operational Amplifier, 1974; editor: Network Topology and Its Engineering Applications, 1975, Graph Theory and Applications, 1982. Chmn. bd., pres. Acad. Cultural Co., Santa Clara; founder, pres. China Exptl. U. Found., 1985—; chmn. Santa Clara County Bicentennial Chinese Festival Com.; pres. Chinese Arts and Culture Inst., 1976—; trustee Inst. Sino-Am. Studies, San Jose, Calif., 1971-76, West Valley-Mission C.C. Dist., Calif., 1988. Recipient Disting. Elec. Engring. Alumnus award U. Ill., 1983, 1991 Rschr. of Yr. award Sch. Engring., Santa Clara U., 1992, Courvoisier Leadership award in Edn., 1994; named Engr. of Yr. in Engring. Edn. San Francisco session AIAA, 1994, Chinese Am. Pioneer award Orgn. Chinese Ams., San Francisco, 1996; Hon. Prof. award S. China Normal U., Guangzhou, China, 1997—, Educator of Yr. award Chinese Consol. Benevolent Assn. and Chinese Consol. Women's Assn., 1999, Mayor's award City of San Francisco, 1999. Fellow IEEE (past chmn. circuit theory group San Francisco sect., chmn. asilomar conf. circuits and sys. 1970); mem. Am. Soc. Engring. Edn., Chineses Alumni Assn. U. Santa Clara (pres.), U. Santa Clara Faculty Club (pres. 1971-72), Sigma Xi, Tau Beta Pi, Eta Kappa Nu, Pi Mu Epsilon, Phi Kappa Phi. Home: 2085 Denise Dr Santa Clara CA 95050-4557 Office Phone: 408-331-1014. Business E-Mail: spchan@itu.edu.

CHAN, SUNNEY IGNATIUS, retired chemistry educator; b. San Francisco, Oct. 5, 1936; s. Sun and Hip-For (Lai) C.; m. Irene Yuk-Hing Tam, July 11, 1964; 1 son, Michael Kenneth. BSChemE, U. Calif., Berkeley, 1957, PhD in Chemistry, 1960; DSc honoris causa, Hong Kong Bapt. U., 2003. Asst. prof. chemistry U. Calif., Riverside, 1961—63; mem. faculty Calif. Inst. Tech., Pasadena, 1963—, prof. chem. physics, 1968—92, prof. biophys. chemistry, 1976—92, George Grant Hoag prof. biophys. chemistry, 1992—2001, exec. officer for chemistry, 1977—80, 1989—94, master student houses, 1980—83, chmn. faculty, 1987—89, George Grant Hoag prof. biophys. chemistry emeritus, 2002—; dir. Inst. of Chemistry Academia Sinica, Taipei, Taiwan, 1997—99; disting. rsch. fellow Academia Sinica, Taipei, 1997—2006, v.p., 1999—2003, chair disting. rsch. fellow, 2006—; chair prof Nat. taiwan U., 2006—; hon. chair prof. Nat. Cheng Kung U., 2006—, Chinese U. Hong Kong, 1996—. Trustee, Croucher Found., Hong Kong, 1999-2006, R. T. Major lectr. U. Conn., 1998; Wilson T.S. Wang Disting. Internat. prof. Chinese U. Hong Kong, 1993; Reilly lectr. U. Notre Dame, 1973-74; Chan Meml. lectr. U. Calif., Berkeley, 1984; Lee Wee Nam vis. prof. Nanyang Tech. U., Singapore, 2006; K.T. Li prof. Sci. Tech., Nat. Cheng-Kung U., Taiwan, 2007; Felicia Wu Meml. lectr., Taiwan Biophys. Soc., 2009; cons. in field. Author numerous articles in field. Recipient CB Net award in biophysics, 2005; Guggenheim fellow, 1968-69; Sloan fellow, 1965-67; NSF Postdoctoral fellow, 1960-61; Fogarty fellow NIH, 1986, K.T. Li. Sci. & Tech. award, Taiwan, 2007, Academic award, Chinese Chemical Soc. Taipei, 2007. Fellow AAAS, Biophys. Soc., Am. Phys. Soc.; mem. Academia Sinica, Am. Chem. Soc., Chinese Am. Chem. Soc. (chmn. bd. 1988-97), Chinese Chem. Soc. Taipei (Acad. award 2007), Am. Soc. Biochemistry and Molecular Biology (William C. Rose award 2004), Biophys. Soc. Taiwan (pres. 1998-2001), So. Calif. Chinese Engrs. and Scientists Assn. (Progress award 1971), Chinese Collegiate Colleagues So. Calif. (v.p. 1970-71, pres. 1971-72), Chinese Am. Faculty Assn. (pres. 1988, Achievement award 1991, Disting. Svc. award 2000), Third World Acad. Scis., Phi Beta Kappa, Sigma Xi, Tau Beta Pi, Alpha Chi Sigma, Phi Tau Phi (pres. 1981-83, nat. pres. 2004-) Home: 327 Camino Del Sol South Pasadena CA 91030-4107 Office: Calif Inst Tech Chem Dept Pasadena CA 91125-0001 Office Phone: 626-395-6508. Personal E-mail: sunneychan@yahoo.com. Business E-Mail: chans@its.caltech.edu.

CHANCELLOR, WILLIAM JOSEPH, agricultural engineering educator; b. Alexandria, Va., Aug. 25, 1931; s. John Miller and Caroline (Sedlacek) C.; m. Nongkarn Bodhiprasart, Dec. 13, 1960; 1 child, Marisa Kuakul BS in Agr., BSME, U. Wis., 1954; MS in Agrl. Engring., Cornell U., 1956, PhD, 1957. Registered profl. agrl. engr., Calif. Prof. agrl. engring. U. California.-Davis, 1957-94; prof. emeritus. Vis. prof. agrl. engring. U. Malaya, Kuala Lumpur, Malaysia, 1962-63; UNESCO cons. Punjab Agrl. U., 1976 Contbr. articles to profl. jours.; patentee transmission, planters, dryer, 1961-73 East/West Ctr. sr. Fellow, Honolulu, 1976 Fellow Am. Soc. Agrl. Engrs. (Kishida Internat. award 1984, John Deere Gold Medal award 2004); mem. NAE, Soc. Automotive Engrs., Sigma Xi: found. mem. Asian Assoc. Agrl. Engrs. Office: Univ of California Dept Biol & Agrl Engineering Davis CA 95616 Business E-Mail: wjchancellor@ucdavis.edu.

CHANDLER, CARROL H. (HOWIE CHANDLER), career military officer; b. Mar. 16, 1952; BS, USAF Acad., 1974; MA in Mgmt., Webster U., 1978; Grad., Squadron Office Sch., Maxwell AFB, Ala., 1978, Air Command & Staff Coll., 1982, Nat. War Coll., Ft. Lesley J. McNair, Washington, DC, 1992, Exec. Program Gen. Officers Russian Fedn. & US, JFK Kennedy Sch. Govt., Harvard U., 1997, Navy Sr.Leader Bus. Course, Kenan Flagler Bus. Sch., U. NC, 2003. Commd. 2d. lt. USAF, 1974, advanced through grades to gen., 2007; student undergraduate pilot training Laughlin AFB, 1974—75; T-38 instr. pilot, flight examiner, 1975-78; instr. pilot, asst. ops. officer 560th Flying Training Squadron, Randolph AFB, Tex., 1978-81; squadron standardization officer, flight comdr. & wing flight examiner 67th Tactical Fighter Squadron, Kadena AFB, Japan, 1981—83; chief air-to-air tactics branch, directorate standardization & evaluation Pacific Air Forces (PACAF), Hickam AFB, Hawaii, 1983—85; aide-de-camp to comdr. in chief US Pacific Command, Camp H.M. Smith, Hawaii, 1985; air force aide to chmn. Joint Chiefs of Staff US Dept. Def., Washington, 1985-87; asst. ops. officer, chief standardizations & evaluation divsn. 18th Wing 44th Tactical Fighter Squadron, Kadena AFB, Japan, 1987; ops. officer 67th Tactical Fighter Squadron, Kadena AFB, Japan, 1987—88; comdr. 44th Fighter Squadron, Kadena AFB, 1988—90; chief ops. inspection divsn., Office Insp. Gen. Pacific Air Forces (PACAF), Hickam AFB, Hawaii, 1990—92; chief air force divsn., sr. USAF adv. to Royal Saudi Air Force US Mil. Training Mission, Riyadh, Saudi Arabia, 1992-94; comdr. 554th Support Group, Nellis AFB, Nev., 1994-95, 33rd Fighter Wing, Eglin AFB, Fla., 1995-96, 56th Fighter Wing, Luke AFB, Ariz., 1996-98; chief of staff Hdqs. Allied Air Forces So. Europe, Naples, Italy, 1998—99, asst. chief of staff for ops. A-3 Divsn., 1999—2000; dir. expeditionary aerospace force implementation Office Dep. Chief of Staff Air & Space Ops., USAF, Washington, 2000, dir. operational plans, 2000—01; dir. Aerospace Ops. Air Combat Command, Langley AFB, 2001—02; comdr. Alaskan Command Alaskan N.Am. Aerospace Def. Command Region, 11th Air Force & Task Force, Elmendorf AFB, Alaska, 2002—05; dep. chief of staff for ops. USAF, Washington, 2005—08; comdr. Pacific Air Forces (PACAF) & Air Component Command, Hickam AFB, Hawaii, 2008—; exec. dir. Pacific Air Combat Ops. Staff, Hickam AFB, Hawaii, 2008—. Decorated Def. Disting. Svc. medal, Disting. Svc. medal, Def. Superior Svc. medal, Legion of Merit, Def. Meritorious Svc. medal with oak leaf cluster, Meritorious Svc. medal with silver oak leaf cluster, Air Force Commendation medal, Combat Readiness medal with oak leaf cluster, S.W. Asia Svc. medal with bronze star, NATO medal (Fed. Rep. of Yugoslavia).

CHANDLER, EDWIN RUSSELL, clergyman, writer; b. LA, Sept. 9, 1932; s. Edwin Russell Sr. and Mary Elizabeth (Smith) C.; m. Sandra Lynn Swisher, Aug. 24, 1957 (div. 1977); children— Heather, Holly, Timothy John; m. Marjorie Lee Moore, Dec. 21, 1978; 3 stepchildren Student, Stanford U., 1950-52; BS in Bus. Adminstrn., UCLA, 1952-55; postgrad., U. So. Calif. Grad. Sch. Religion, 1955, New Coll., Edinburgh, Scotland, 1955-56; M.Div., Princeton Theol. Sem., 1958; grad., Washington Journalism Ctr., 1967. Ordained to ministry Presbyterian Ch., 1958. Asst. pastor 1st Presbyn. Ch., Concord, Calif., 1958-61; pastor Escalon Presbyn. Ch., Calif., 1961-66; reporter Modesto Bee, Calif., 1966-67; religion editor Washington Star, 1968-69; news editor Christianity Today, Washington, 1969-72; reporter Sonora Daily Union Dem., Calif., 1972-73; religion writer L.A. Times, 1974-92; interim pastor 1st Presbyn. Ch., Columbia, Calif., 1995-96. Author: The Kennedy Explosion, 1972, Budgets, Bedrooms and Boredom, 1976; co-author: Your Family--Frenzy or Fun?, 1977, The Overcomers, 1978, Understanding the New Age, 1988 (Silver Angel award 1989, Wilbur award 1989), Racing Toward 2001, 1992, Doomsday, 1993, Feeding the Flock, 1998; contbr. articles to profl. jours. Recipient Arthur West award United Methodist Communications Council, 1978, Faith and Freedom award Religious Heritage of Am., 1993; co-recipient Silver Angel award, Religion in Media, 1985 Mem. Religion Newswriters Assn. (pres. 1982-84, co-founder ann. Chandler award 2003, James O. Supple Meml. award, 1976, 1984, 86, John M. Templeton Reporter of Yr. award 1984, 87, 89), Religion Newswriters Assn. (Lifetime Achievement award, 2007), Phi Delta Theta Republican. Avocations: travel, beekeeping, birdwatching, theater. Home and Office: 14493 Kebra Ln Sonora CA 95370-9477 Personal E-mail: erchandler@aol.com.

CHANDLER, MARK D., computer systems network executive, lawyer; b. 1956; m. Chris Kenrick; 3 children. AB, Harvard U., 1978; JD, Stanford U., 1981. Bar: Calif. 1982. Law clk. to Spl. Master J. Keith Mann, 1981—83; atty. Law Office of James E. Baer, Palo Alto, Calif., 1983—85; fellow Robert Bosch Found., 1985—86; with mktg. dept. Sienna Capital Corp., 1986—88; v.p., corp. devel., gen. counsel Maxtor Corp., 1988—94; gen. counsel Stratacom, Inc., 1994—96; mng. atty., Europe, the Middle East, Africa Cisco Systems, Inc., 1996—2001, v.p., worldwide legal services, 2001, gen. counsel San Jose, Calif., 2001—, v.p. legal services, 2001—06, sec., 2003—, sr. v.p. legal services, gen. counsel, 2006—. Office: Cisco Sys Inc 255 W Tasman Dr San Jose CA 95134-1705 Office Phone: 408-527-0238. E-mail: mark.chandler@cisco.com.

CHANDOR, STEBBINS BRYANT, pathologist; b. Boston, Dec. 18, 1933; s. Kendall Stebbins Bryant and Dorothy (Burrage) C.; m. Mary Carolyn White, May 30, 1959; children: Stebbins Bryant Jr., Charlotte White. BA, Princeton U., 1955; MD, Cornell U., 1960. Diplomate Am. Bd. Pathology. Intern Bellevue Hosp., NYC, 1960-61, resident, 1965-66, Stanford U. Med. Ctr., Palo Alto, Calif., 1962-65; pathologist Tripler Army Med Ctr, Honolulu, 1966—69; instr. Cornell U., Ithaca, NY, 1966; asst. prof. U. So. Calif. Med. Ctr., LA, 1969-73, assoc. prof., 1974-76, SUNY, Stony Brook, 1976-80; dir. clin. lab. Univ. Hosp., Stony Brook, 1978-80; dir. JMMS Labs., Huntington, 1981-91; prof., chmn. dept. pathology Marshall U. Sch. Medicine, Huntington, W.Va., 1981—91, assoc. dean for clin. affairs, 1990-91; prof., vice chmn. Sch. Medicine U. So. Calif., 1991—2004, dir. labs. U. Hosp., 1991—2004, prof. emeritus, 2004—. Bd. dirs. Immunopathology Med. Ctr., 1969—76; mem. provosts oversight com. U. So. Calif., 2005—; pres. Ret. Faculty Assn., U. So. Calif., 2007—08. Contbr. articles to profl. jours. Pres. San Marino Tennis Found., 1975; governing bd. U. Path. Consortium, 1999-2004. Served to maj. USAR, 1966-69. Decorated Army Commendation medal; recipient Physicians Recognition award AMA, 1983, 86, 89, 93, 99, 04. Fellow Am. Assn. Med. Colls., Am. Soc. Clin. Pathologists (dep. commn. 1993-98, continuing edn. bd. dirs. 1990-96, chair by-law com., 1993-96, chmn. pathology group, 1993-98, v.p. 1997-98, pres. 1999-2000, awards com. 2001-), Coll. Am. Pathologists (state commr. I&A program 1987-91, dist. commr. 1991-99); mem. Calif. Soc. Pathologists (sec.-treas. 1974-75, pres.-elect 1975-76), Assn. Am. Pathologists, W.Va. Assn. Pathologists (pres. 1985-86), Assoc. Path. Chmn. Acad. Clin. Lab. Physicians and Scientists (rep. CAS 1991-2003, adminstrv. bd. 1997-2003), Am. Assn. Med. Colls. (exec. coun. 1998-2000), LA Acad. Medicine, Rt. Faculty Assn. (bd. dirs. 2005—), U. So. Calif. Ret. Faculty Assn. (bd. dirs. 2005—, v.p. 2006-07, pres.-elect 2006-07, pres. 2007—), Princeton Club, Valley Club (v.p. 1975, bd. dirs. 1993), City Club (v.p. 1988-89, pres. 1989-90), San Gabriel Country Club, Valley Hunt Club, The Valley Club of Montecito. Republican. Episcopalian. Home: 2170 East Valley Dr Santa Barbara CA 93108 Office: 2011 Zonal Ave Los Angeles CA 90033-1034 Office Phone: 323-442-9615. Personal E-mail: sbchandor@verizon.net. Business E-Mail: chandor@usc.edu.

CHANDY, K. MANI, computer science educator; B Tech. in Elec. Engring., Indian Inst. Technology, Madras, 1965; MSEE, Polytechnic Inst. of Bklyn., 1966; PhD in Elec. Engring., MIT, 1969. Engr. Honeywell Electronic Data processing, Waltham, Mass., 1966-67; staff IBM Cambridge Scientific Ctr., 1969-70; asst. prof. computer scis. U. Tex., Austin, 1970-73, assoc. prof., 1973-78, prof., 1978-89; prof. computer scis. Calif. Inst. Technology, Pasadena, 1989—; Simon Ramo prof., exec. officer dept. computer scis Calif. Inst. Tech.; acting site dir. Ctr. for Rsch. in Parallel Computing, Caltech Site, 1994. Acting chmn. dep. computer scis., 1978-79, chmn. 1983-85, Regent's chair, 1988-89; scientific adv. panel Advanced Systems Inst., B.C., Can., 1986-89; mem. NSF panels; lectr. in field. Assoc. editor: Jour. of Capacity Mgmt., 1983-88, Info. Executive, 1983-88, Jour. of Info. Econs., 1983-88. Recipient John Sherman Fairchild scholarship John Sherman Fairchild Found., 1987-88, A.A. Michelson award, Computer Measurement Group, Dallas, 1985. Fellow IEEE (Koji Kobayashi Computers and Comms. award 1995, assoc. editor: IEEE Transactions on Software Engring. 1985-87); mem. NAE, Assn. Computing Machinery, Soc. for Computer Simulation Office: Calif Inst Technology Computer Sci 256 80 Pasadena CA 91125-0001

CHANG, BARBARA KAREN, medical educator, director; b. Milltown, Ind., Jan. 6, 1946; m. M.F. Joseph Chang-Wai-Ling, Oct. 6, 1967; children: Carla Marie Yvonnette, Nolanne Arlette. BA, Ind. U., 1968; MA, Brandeis U., 1970; MD, Albert Einstein Coll. Medicine, 1973. Diplomate Am. Bd. Internal Medicine, Am. Bd. Med. Oncology, Am. Bd. Hematology. Resident in internal medicine Montefiore Med. Ctr., Bronx, NY, 1973-75; fellow in hematology/oncology Duke U. Med. Ctr., Durham, NC, 1975-78; staff physician VA Med. Ctr., Augusta, Ga., 1978-95, chief hematology/oncology, 1980-89, assoc. chief of staff edn., 1990-95, chief of staff, chief med. officer Albuquerque, 1995—2002; prof. medicine Med. Coll. Ga., Augusta, 1978-95; assoc. dean U. N.Mex. Sch. Medicine, Albuquerque, 1995—2002; cons. Capital Assets Realignment for Enhanced Svcs. Program VA Ctrl. Office, Washington, 2002—03, dir. program evaluation Office Academic Affiliations, 2003—07, acting dir. grad. med. edn., 2006—07; dir., Med. and Dental Edn., 2007—. Mem. Sci. Adv. Bd., Washington, 1983-88; mem. expert panels computer applications Dept. Vets. Affairs, Washington, 1988-95; Va. liasion to steering com. group on resident affairs Assn. Am. Med. Colls., 2000-06; Va. rep. Coun. Grad. Med. Edn., 2006-, Accreditation Coun. Grad. Med. Edn., 2006-; presenter in field. Contbr. numerous articles on cancer rsch. to profl. jours. Youth coord. Am. Hemerocallis Soc., Augusta, 1993-95, pres. local chpt. 1997, Albuquerque, garden judge 1997-03, region 6 youth liaison, 2000-01, exhbn. judge, 2001—, nat. youth liaison com., 2003-. Grantee Nat. Cancer Inst., Am. Cancer Soc., 1978-93; David M. Worthen award Acad. Excellence Dept. Vet. Affairs, 2000. Fellow ACP, Am. Soc. Clin. Oncology, Bioelectromagnetic Soc. (bd. dirs. 1983-86). Office: Dept Vets Affairs Med Ctr 1501 San Pedro Dr SE Albuquerque NM 87108-5153 Business E-Mail: barbara.chang@va.gov.

CHANG, CARMEN, lawyer; b. Nanjing, China, 1948; BA, Sarah Lawrence Coll., 1970; MA, Stanford U., 1973, JD with distinction, 1993. Bar: Calif. 1994, U.S. Ct. Appeals (9th cir.) 1994. Ptnr. Shearman & Sterling, LLP, Menlo Park, Calif., 2003—05; ptnr., leader China practice Wilson Sonsini Goodrich Rosati, Palo Alto, Calif., 2005—. Spkr. in field; mem. adv. bd. Stanford Project Regions of Innovation and Entrepreneurship Asia-Pacific Rsch. Ctr. Stanford U., Stanford, Calif. Contbr. articles to profl. jours. Fluent in English, Mandarin, Cantonese, Japanese. Office: Wilson Sonsini Goodrich & Rosati 650 Page Mill Rd Palo Alto CA 94304 Business E-Mail: cchang@wsgr.com.

CHANG, DANIEL HAIMING, engineering executive; b. Guangzhou, Guang Dong, China, Apr. 16, 1953; came to U.S., 1981; s. Qizhong and Puqiong (Ye) C.; m. Caili Li; 1 child, Miao Miao. BE of Ceramic Engring., South China U. of Tech., Guangzhou, 1976, ME of Ceramic Engring., 1981; MS in Materials Sci., U. So. Calif., LA, 1984. Foreman Guangzhou Cement Plant, 1970-72, asst. to chief engr., 1976-78; materials scientist Philips Components, LA, 1984-85; mem. mgmt. team, sr. rsch. engr. Kyocera, San Diego, 1985-88; pres., CEO AEM, Inc., San Diego, 1988—. Holder 1 patent and 3 patents pending. Mem. IEEE (assoc.), Am. Ceramic Soc., U.S.-China Entrepreneur Assn. (pres. 1993-97), San Diego Chinese Assn. (v.p. 1993-97). Avocations: reading books and magazines, walking and running along the beach, competitive sports, driving fast cars. Office: AEM Holding Inc 11525 Sorrento Valley Rd San Diego CA 92121-1307 E-mail: dchang@aem-usa.com.

CHANG, HENRY C., library administrator; b. Canton, China, Sept. 15, 1941; came to U.S., 1964, naturalized, 1973; s. Ih-ming and Lily (Lin) C.; m. Marjorie Li, Oct. 29, 1966; 1 dau., Michelle. LLB, Nat. Chengchi U., 1962; MA, U. Mo., 1966; MA in Libr. Sci., U. Minn., 1968, PhD, 1974. Reader advisor Braille Inst. Am., LA, 1965-67, dir. libr. svcs., 1990—; reference libr. U. Minn., Mpls., 1968-70, instr., libr., 1970-72, asst. head govt. document divsn., 1972-74; libr. dir., lectr. in social scis. U. of the V.I., St. Croix, 1974-75, dir. divsn. librs., museums and archeol. svcs., 1975-88; dir. V.I. Libr. Tng. Inst., 1975-76; coord., chmn. V.I. State Hist. Records Adv. Bd., 1976-88, pres., libr. cons., 1988-89; project dir. Calif. Telephone Reader Program, 2000—. Chmn. microfilm com. ACURIL, 1977-88; mem. V.I. Bicentennial Commn., 1975-77, Ft. Frederik Commn., 1975-76; adv. com. on rsch. tng. Caribbean Rsch. Inst., 1974-75; coord. Libr. Conf., 1977-87; project dir. cultural heritage project NEH, 1979-83; chmn. nat. collection devel. com. nat. libr. svcs. Libr. of Congress, 1998, chmn. western conf. group, 2001-04; commr. Accreditation Commn. for Acupuncture and Oriental Medicine, 2004-, chair stds. and criteria com., 2006-. Author: A Bibliography of Presidential Commissions, Committees, Councils, Panels and Task Forces, 1961-72, 1973, Taiwan Democraphy, 1964-71: A Selected Annotated Bibliography of Government Documents, 1973, A Selected Annotated Bibliography of Caribbean Bibliographies in English, 1975, A Survey of the Use of Microfilms in the Caribbean, 1978, Long-Range Program for Library Development, 1978, Institute for Training in Library Management and Communications Skill, 1979; contbr. numerous articles and book revs. on libr. sci. to profl. jours. Chmn. bd. dirs. Eden Found. for People with Disabilities, 1995—96; mem. adv. com. Nat. Std. and Guideline Svcs., Libr. Congress Network Librs., 2002—05. 2d lt. Taiwan Army, 1962—63. Recipient Libr. Adminstrs. Devel. Program fellowship award, 1972, Cert. of Appreciation, Govt. V.I., 1985, Eden Found., 1999, L.A. Internat. Lions Club award, 1992, 1995, Driver Safety award, 1993, Cert. of Achievement, Braille Inst., 2001, Network Libr. of Yr. award, Libr. of Congress, 2004—05, 2005, Libr. Award, Am. Libr. Assn., 2007, Libr. award, Assn. Specialized and Coop. Libr. Agys., 2007; named Mem. Staff of Yr., Coll. V.I., 1974—75; grantee, Nat. Commn. on Librs. and Info. Sci. Mem. ALA (counselor 1980-84), AAUP, Asian Pacific ALA (chmn. fin. com. 1993-96), Population Assn. Am., Am. Sociol. Assn., Chinese Am. Profl. Soc. Home: 3713 Lowry Rd Los Angeles CA 90027-1437 Office: Braille Inst Am 741 N Vermont Ave Los Angeles CA 90029-3594 Office Phone: 323-906-3185, 323-660-3880. Business E-Mail: dls@braillelibrary.org.

CHANG, I-SHIH, aerospace engineer; b. Taipei, Taiwan, Dec. 2, 1945; came to U.S., 1968; s. I.H. and T.C. Chang; m. O.J. Chang, May 25, 1974; children: Anna, Brandon Degree in mech. engring., Taipei Inst. of Tech., 1965; MS, U. Kans., 1969; PhD, U. Ill., 1973. Scientist assoc.-rsch. Lockheed Missiles & Space, Huntsville, Ala., 1973-76; mem. tech. staff Rockwell Internat., Anaheim, Calif., 1976-77, The Aerospace Corp., El Segundo, Calif., 1977-80, engring. specialist, 1980-90, sr. engring. specialist, 1990-91, disting. engr., 1991—. Contbr. articles to profl. jours. Fellow AIAA (chair 2005-07, solid rockets tech. com., dep. dir. propulsion and energy group, 2008-); mem. Phi Kappa phi. Democrat. Office: The Aerospace Corp M4-967 2350 E El Segundo Blvd El Segundo CA 90245-4691 Office Phone: 310-336-5917. E-mail: i-shih.chang@aero.org.

CHANG, JANE P., chemical engineering educator; BS, Nat. Taiwan U., 1993; MS, MIT, 1995, PhD, 1998. Engring. intern Merck and Co., Inc., Lansdale, Pa., 1994, Dow Chem. Co., Midland, Mich., 1994; postdoctoral mem. tech. staff Bell Labs, Lucent Technologies, Murray Hill, NJ, 1998—99; asst. prof. chem. engring. UCLA, 1999—2003, assoc. prof. chem. engring., 2003—05, prof. chem. engring. 2005—, dept. vice chair, 2007—. Chair com. undergrad. admission and rels.

with schs. UCLA, 2005—06. Contbr. articles to profl. jours. Recipient Chancellor's Career Devel. award, UCLA, 2000—02, Career award, Nat. Sci. Found., 2002, Excellence in Tchg. award, TRW, 2002, Young Investigator award, Office of Naval Rsch., 2003, Hugo Schuck Best Paper award, Am. Automatic Control Coun., 2004; named Prof. of Yr., UCLA, 2003—04. Mem.: Material Rsch. Soc., Am. Vacuum Soc. (Coburn and Winters award 1996, Peter Mark award 2005), Am. Inst. Chem. Engrs., Am. Physics Soc., Electrochem. Soc., Am. Chem. Soc., Phi Tau Phi. Office: UCLA Chem and Biomolecular Engring Dept BH 5532-D 420 Westwood Plz Los Angeles CA 90095

CHANG, JERRY LESLIE, state legislator; b. Hilo, Hawaii, Sept. 15, 1947; children: Jensen, Ren, Jade, Jaycie. AA, Mauna Coll.; BA in Sociology, U. Hawaii, Hilo. Sec., treas., mgr. Puueo Poi Factory Inc., Hilo; v.p. Seawind Realty Inc., Hilo, 1975—; mem. Dist. 2 Hawaii House of Reps., 1983—, legis. aide, 1988, chair higher edn. com. Bd. dirs. Hawaii County Econ. Devel. Coun., Steadfast Housing Devel. Corp.; mem. Big Island Substance Abuse Coun. Bd. dirs. Ctr. Sustainable Future. Sgt. 7th Spl. Forces US Army, 1967—70. Mem.: Japenese C. of C., Hawaii Isle C. of C., Hawaii Island Portuguese C. of C., Big Island Amateur Boxing Assn., Exchange Club Hilo, Big Island Road Runners. Democrat. Mailing: Hawaii State Capitol 415 S Beretania St Rm 435 Hilo HI 96813 Office Phone: 808-586-6120. Office Fax: 808-586-6121. Business E-Mail: repchang@Capitol.hawaii.gov.*

CHANG, MEI-CHU, mathematics professor; PhD, U. Calif., Berkeley. Prof. U. Calif., Riverside, 1987—.

CHANG, SUSAN MARINA, neuroscientist; d. Charmaine Zelia and Kenneth Winston Chang; m. Douglas George Wilkinson, June 11, 1983; children: Marina Margaret Wilkinson, Sean Robert Wilkinson. MD, U. BC, Can., 1985. Attending physician U. Calif., San Francisco, 1993—, prof., 2004—, dir. divsn. neuro-oncology, 2005—. Achievements include research in neuro-oncology.

CHANG, WILLIAM SHEN CHIE, electrical engineering educator; b. Nantung, Jiangsu, China, Apr. 4, 1931; s. Tung Wu and Phoebe Y.S. (Chow) C.; m. Margaret Huachen Kwei, Nov. 26, 1955; children: Helen Nai-yee, Hugh Nai-hun, Hedy Nai-lin. BSE, U. Mich., 1952, MSE, 1953; PhD, Brown U., 1957. Lectr., rsch. assoc. in elec. engring. Stanford (Calif.) U., 1957-59; asst. prof. elec. engring. Ohio State U., 1959-62, assoc. prof., 1962-65; prof. dept. elec. engring. Washington U., St. Louis, 1965—79, chmn. dept., 1965-71, dir. Applied Electronic Scis. Lab., 1971-79, Samuel Sachs prof. elec. engring., 1976-79; prof. dept. elec. and computer engring. U. Calif., San Diego, 1979—, chmn. dept., 1993-96. Author: Principles of Quantum Electronics, 1969, RF Photonic Technology in Optical Fiber Links, 2002, Principles of Lasers and Optics, 2005; Contbr. articles to profl. jours. Recipient Disting. Prof. Achievement award, U. Mich., Ann Arbor; named Samuel Sachs Prof., Washington U., St. Louis. Fellow: IEEE, Am. Optical Soc.; mem.: Am. Phys. Soc. Achievements include research in quantum electronics and guided wave optics. Home: 12676 Caminito Radiante San Diego CA 92130 Office: U Calif San Diego MS-0407 Dept Elec/Computer Engring La Jolla CA 92093-0407 Office Phone: 858-534-2737. Business E-Mail: wchang@ucsd.edu.

CHANG, WILLIAM ZHI-MING, research scientist; b. Shanghai, June 6, 1955; s. Yinfang Chang and Shanlin Chen; m. Sandra Schlachter, Aug., 1987; 1 child, Caroline Dagmar. BS, U. So. Calif., 1984, MS, 1985, PhD, 1992. Rsch. assoc. U. So. Calif., LA, 1992-93; rsch. scientist Max Planck Soc. x-ray optics group Friedrich-Schiller U., Jena, Germany, 1993-96; sr. scientist advanced rsch. and applications corp. Aracor, Sunnyvale, Calif., 1996—. Contbr. articles to profl. jours. and books. Disting. scholar Microbeam Analysis Soc., San Jose, Calif., 1991, Boston, 1992. Mem. Optical Soc. Am. Achievements include patents in field. Avocations: opera, calligraphy. Home: 8592 Peachtree Ave Newark CA 94560-3342 Office: Rapiscan Labs Inc 520 Almanor Ave Sunnyvale CA 94085-3533 Office Phone: 408-961-9722. Personal E-mail: wchang@rapiscansystems.com.

CHANOS, GEORGE J., former state attorney general; b. Wauwatosa, Wis., Aug. 1958; m. Adriana Escobar Chanos; 1 child, Alexandra. BA in Psychology, UNLV, 1981; JD, U. San Diego, 1985. Assoc. Finley, Kumble, Wagner, Heine, Underberg, Manley, Myerson and Casey, San Diego; ptnr. Chanos, Escobar, Chanos, Las Vegas, 1995—2005; atty. gen. State of Nev., Carson City, 2005—07. Chmn. Nev. Policy Rsch. Inst., 1998. Chmn. bd. dirs. Jr. Achievement of So. Nev., 1997. Republican.

CHAO, ALLEN Y., pharmaceutical executive; m. Lee Hwa-Chao. PhD in Indsl., Physical Pharmacy, Purdue Univ., 1973, DSc (hon.), 2000. Founder Watson Pharm., Inc., Corona, Calif., 1984, CEO, 1985—2007, chmn., 1996—2008.

CHAO, CEDRIC C., lawyer; b. Cambridge, Mass., Apr. 9, 1950; BA, Stanford U., 1972; JD, Harvard U., 1977. Bar: Calif. 1977, U.S. Dist. Ct. (no. dist.) Calif. 1977, U.S. Ct. Appeals (9th cir.) 1979, U.S. Supreme Ct. 1988. Law clk.to Hon. William H. Orrick U.S. Dist. Ct. (no. dist.) Calif., San Francisco, 1977-78; asst. U.S. atty. U.S. Atty.'s Office, San Francisco, 1978-81; assoc. Morrison & Foerster, San Francisco, 1981-83, ptnr., 1983—. Lawyer del. 9th cir. judicial conf., 1990-92; chair magistrate judge selection com. No. Dist. Calif., 1996. Author: Creating Your Discovery Plan, 1999. Named One of Calif.'s Top 25 Lawyers Under Age 45, Calif. Law Bus., 1994. Fellow Am. Bar Found.; mem. ABA (standing com. fed. judiciary, 1991-94), State Bar Calif. (com. profl. responsibility and conduct 1980-84, exec. com. litigation sect. 1986-91, vice chair 1989-90, chair 1990-91), San Francisco Bar Assn. (bd. dirs. 1988-90), Am. Law Inst., Asian Am. Bar Assn. Greater Bay Area (bd. dirs. 1977-82, pres. 1982), 9th Judicial Cir. Hist. Soc. (trustee 2000—), San Francisco C. of C. (bd. dirs. 1996-99), Singapore Am. Bus. Assn. (bd. dirs. 1999—, pres. 2001), World Affairs Coun. No. Calif. (trustee 1994-99), Commonwealth Club Calif. (quar. chair 1989). Office: Morrison & Foerster 425 Market St San Francisco CA 94105-2482 E-mail: cchao@mofo.com.

CHAO, HOWARD H., lawyer; b. Taipei, Republic of China, June 13, 1954; came to U.S., 1958; s. Kuang-Chu and Jun-Jing (Su) C. BS in Math. with highest distinction, Purdue U., 1976; JD, U. Calif. Boalt Hall Sch. Law, Berkeley, 1980. Bar: Calif. 1980, U.S. Dist. Ct. (No. Dist. Calif.) 1980, Hong Kong, 1997. Assoc. O'Melveny & Myers LLP, Los Angeles, 1980—, ptnr. Menlo Park, Calif., partner-in-charge, Shanghai, chair, internat. practice group. Exec. sec. Los Angeles Com. Fgn. Relations, 1984-85; vis. prof. Fudan U., Shanghai, Republic of China, 1985, Beijing (Republic of China) U. of Internat. Bus., 1985. Assoc. editor Calif. Law Review, 1977—80. Rotary Internat. fellow, Geneva, 1979-80. Mem. Law Soc. Hong Kong, Phi Beta Kappa, Order of Coif. Office: O'Melveny & Myers LLP 2765 Sand Hill Rd Menlo Park CA 94025-7019 Address: O'Melveny & Myers LLP Kerry Centre 20F 1515 Nanjing Rd West Shanghai 200040 China also: O'Melveny & Myers LLP Suite 1905 Tower Two Lippo Ctr 89 Queensway Central Hong Kong Office Phone: 650-473-2628. Fax: 8621 5298 5500, 852 2522 1760; Office Fax: 650-473-2601. Business E-Mail: hchao@omm.com.

CHAPELA, IGNACIO H., biologist, researcher; b. Mex. City, Mex., Sept. 12, 1959; s. Gonzalo Chapela Montañéz and Maria De La Luz Mendoza; m. Laura García-Moreno, July 23, 1987; 1 child: Inés. Biologo, Nat. U. Mex., Mex. City, 1984; PhD, U. Wales, Cardiff, 1987. Scientist Sandoz, Ltd, Basel, Switzerland, 1989-91. Vis. prof. Cornell U., Ithaca, N.Y., 1987-88, 92-93; founder, scientific dir. Mycological Facility: Oaxaca (Mex.), 1994—; cons. World Bank Group, Washington, 1994, Pan-Am. Health Orgn., Washington, 1994; adv. bd. Andes Pharmaceuticals, Washington, 1995—; asst. prof. U. Calif., Berkeley. Contbr. articles to profl. jours. Fellow Instituto Nacional de Cardiologia, Mex. City, Mex., 1981-84; grantee Am. Philos. Soc., Phila., 1988, MacArthur Fdn., 1993, Vice Chancellors & Prins. of Brit. U., Wales, 1985-87. Mem. Brit. Mycological Soc. Ecology Com., 1985—, Mycological Soc. of Am., 1995—. Achievements include elucidation of symbiotic relationships of fungi and other organisms conservation through revaluation of biodiversity in Latin Am. Home: 3144 O St NW Washington DC 20007-3116 Office: U Calif Environ Sci Policy & Mgmt Berkeley CA 94720-0001

CHAPIN, CHARLES E., geologist, mineralogist; b. Porterville, Calif., Oct. 25, 1932; m. Carol R. Giles, 1958; children: Giles M., John E., Laura A. Geol. Engr., Colo. Sch. Mines, 1954, DSc in Geochemistry, 1965. Asst. prof. geology U. Tulsa, 1964-65; asst. prof. N.Mex. Inst. Mining and Tech., 1965-68, assoc. prof., head dept. geosci., 1968-70; geologist N.Mex. Bur. Mines and Mineral Resources, 1970-76, sr. geologist, 1976-91, dir., 1991-99, dir. emeritus. Recipient Van Diest Gold medal Colo. Sch. Mines, 1980. Mem. Geol. Soc. Am., Soc. Econ. Paleontologists and Mineralogists, Am. Geophys. Union, Am. Assn. Petroleum Geologists, Soc. Econ. Geologists, Sigma Xi. Office: NM Bur Mines & Mineral Resources Inst Mining and Mineral Tech Campus Station Socorro NM 87801

CHAPIN, DWIGHT ALLAN, columnist, writer; b. Lewiston, Idaho, June 16, 1938; s. Don Merle and Lucille Verna (Walker) C.; m. Susan Enid Fisk, Feb. 14, 1963 (div. 1973); children— Carla, Adam; m. Ellen Gonzalez, Aug. 10, 1983 BA, U. Idaho, 1960; MS in Journalism, Columbia U., 1961. Reporter Lewiston Morning Tribune, Idaho, 1956-62; reporter, editor Vancouver Columbian, Wash., 1962-65; sportswriter Seattle Post-Intelligencer, 1965-67, Los Angeles Times, 1967-77; columnist San Francisco Examiner, 1977-2000, San Francisco Chronicle, 2000—. Co-author: Wizard of Westwood, 1973; contbr. numerous articles to popular mags. Served with USNG, 1962-68 Recipient Sports Writing award AP, Calif./Nev., 1968-69; Baseball Writing award Am. Assn. Coll. Baseball Coaches Mem. Sigma Delta Chi (sports writing award Wash. state 1964, 65, 66) Democrat. Avocation: trading card and sports memorabilia collecting. Office: San Francisco Chronicle 901 Mission St San Francisco CA 94103-2988 Office Phone: 415-777-7201. E-mail: dchapin@sfchronicle.com.

CHAPIN, F. STUART, III, ecologist; BA in biology, Swarthmore Coll., 1966; PhD in bio. scis., Stanford U., 1973. Asst. and assoc. prof. U. Alaska, Fairbanks, 1973—84, prof. ecology, 1984—86, 1996—; asst. dir. Inst. Arctic Biology, 1981—83; prof. biology U. Calif., Berkeley, 1989—98. Vis. instr. biology Peace Corps U. Javeriana, Colombia, 1966—68. Co-author: Principles of Terrestrial Ecosystem Ecology, 2002; editl. bd. mem. Physiological Ecology Series, Ecology and Soc. Recipient Kempe award, 1996; fellow, Guggenheim, 1979. Mem.: Ecol. Soc. Am., Ecology Inst., Swedish Royal Acad. Agriculture and Forestry, Am. Acad. Arts and Scis., NAS. Office: U Alaska Inst Arctic Biology Dept Biology and Wildlife Fairbanks AK 99775 Business E-Mail: terry.chapin@uaf.edu.

CHAPMAN, BRUCE KERRY, institute executive; b. Evanston, Dec. 1, 1940; s. Landon Lincoln Chapman and Darroll Jesamine (Carlson Swanson) Shinn; m. Sarah Gilmore Williams, Aug. 22, 1976; children: Adam Winthrop, Andrew Howard. BA cum laude, Harvard U., 1962; Doctorate (hon.), Monmouth Coll., Ill., 1983. Pub. Advance Mag., Washington, Cambridge, Mass., 1960-64; editorial writer N.Y. Herald Tribune, NYC, 1965-66; cons., speech writer Wash. State Commn. on Civil Disorders, Seattle, 1966-71; mem. city coun. City of Seattle, 1971-75; sec. of state State of Wash., Olympia, 1975-81; dir. U.S. Census Bur., Washington, 1981-83; dep. asst. to Pres. The White House, Washington, 1983-85; U.S. amb. State Dept. (UN Offices), Vienna, 1985-88; sr. fellow Hudson Inst., Indpls., 1988-91; pres. Discovery Inst., Seattle, 1991—. Author: The Wrong Man in Uniform, 1967, (with G. Gilder) The Party that Lost Its Head, 1966; author (documentary film) A Memory for the Future, 1975-76; author, dir. (documentary film) The Market, 1976. V.p. Harvard Young Reps., Cambridge, 1962; candidate for gov. State of Wash., 1980. Episcopalian. Avocations: travel, gardening, films. Home: 208 Columbia St Seattle WA 98104-1508

CHAPMAN, DUANE LEE (DOG CHAPMAN), bail enforcement agent, television personality; b. Denver, Feb. 1, 1953; s. Wesley and Barbara Chapman; m. Beth Smith, May 20, 2006; children: Duane Lee, Leland, Lyssa, Tucker, Christopher, Barbara(dec.), Wesley, Cecily, Bonnie Jo, Gary. Owner Da Kine Bail Bonds, Honolulu. Actor: (films) Aussie Park Boyz, 2004; (TV series) Dog the Bounty Hunter, 2005—, (TV appearances) The Osbournes, 2005, George Lopez, 2005; co-author (with Kent Black): You Can Run But You Can't Hide: The Life and Times of Dog the Bounty Hunter, 2007. Achievements include the apprehension of over 6,000 fugitives, including most notably Andrew Luster in Mexico, June 18, 2003. Office: Da Kine Bail Bonds 1383 Queen Emma St Honolulu HI 96813

CHAPMAN, FAY L., lawyer, bank executive; b. San Jose, Calif., Dec. 17, 1946; BA, UCLA, 1968; JD, NYU, 1972. Bar: NY 1973, Wash. 1975. Atty. Foster Pepper & Shefelman, Seattle, 1979—97; exec. v.p., gen. counsel Washington Mutual, Inc., Seattle, 1997—99; sr. exec. v.p., gen. counsel Washington Mutual, Inc, Seattle, 1999—2007; cons. Washington Mutual, Inc., Seattle, 2008—. Mem. ABA, Wash. Bankers Assn., Wash. Savs. League. Office: Washington Mutual Inc 1301 2nd Ave Ste 3301 Seattle WA 98101

CHAPMAN, GARY T., aeronautical engineer, educator; b. Elmwood, Wis., Apr. 28, 1934; married, 1954; 4 children. BA, U. Minn., 1957; MS, Stanford U, 1963, PhD in Aeronautics and Astronautics, 1970. Rsch. scientist fluid mechanics, 1957-71; rsch. scientist aerodynamics, 1971-73; chief Aerodynamics Rsch. Br., 1974-78; staff scientist fluid mechanics Ames Rsch. Ctr. NASA, 1978-89; vis. rsch. engr. U. Calif., Berkeley, 1989—, now adj. prof. Vis. prof. aerodynamics Iowa State U., 1973-74, U. Fla., 1981-82, project scientist, 1979-81 Recipient Ground Testing award AIAA, 1997. Mem. AAAS (assoc. fellow), Am. Soc. Engring. Edn., Soc. Indsl. and Applied Mechanics, Sigma Xi. Achievements include research in basic fluid mechanics; viscous flows including separation; vortices and turbulence; bodies and winged bodies at high angles of attack and flow modeling.

CHAPMAN, JOHN, computer scientist; BS in Elec. Engring., Univ. Alberta. Telephony interface designer ROLM, IBM, Siemens; now chief arch., disting. engr. Cisco Sys. Achievements include developing leading technologies, such as: DOCSIS Set-top Gateway specifications; Modular Cable Modem Termination Sys.; Wideband DOCSIS; Multimedia Traffic Engring. Office: Cisco Sys 170 W Tasman Dr San Jose CA 95134-1706

CHAPMAN, MICHAEL WILLIAM, orthopedist, educator; b. Newberry, Mich., Nov. 29, 1937; m. Elizabeth Casady; adopted sons: Mark, Craig. AA, Am. River Coll., Sacramento, Calif., 1957; BA, U. Calif., Davis, 1958; BS, U. Calif., San Francisco, 1959, MD, 1962. Diplomate Am. Bd. Orthopaedic Surgery (ad hoc appeal com. 1986, site visitor 1986, certification renewal com. 1985-88, certification renewal com. chmn. 1986-88). Intern San Francisco Gen. Hosp., 1962-63, asst. chief orthopaedic surgery svc., 1971-79, acting chief orthopaedic surgery svc., 1972-73; resident in orthopaedic surgery U. Calif., San Francisco, 1963-67, asst. prof. dept. orthopaedic surgery, Sch. Medicine, 1971-76, assoc. prof. dept. orthopaedic surgery, Sch. Medicine, 1976-79; resident in orthopaedic surgery U. Calif. Hosps., San Francisco, 1963-64, Samuel Merritt Hosp., Oakland, Calif., 1964, Highland-Alameda County Hosp., Oakland, 1965, Children's Hosp. of the East Bay, Oakland, 1966, Shriners Hosp., Honolulu, 1966-67; fellow Nat. Orthopaedic Hosp., London, 1967-68; chmn. dept. orthopaedic surgery U. Calif., Davis, Sacramento, 1979-99, prof. dept. orthopaedic surgery, 1981-2000, David Linn chair orthopaedic surgery, 1998-2001, prof. emeritus, 2000—. Panelist Calif. Crippled Children Svcs. Panel in Orthopaedic Surgery; cons. VA Hospital, Martinez, Calif.; co-chmn. Zimmer Trauma Panel, 1983-84; vis. prof. Fresno Valley Med. Ctr., 1975, Dept. Orthopaedics, U. Calif., Davis, 1976, U. Hawaii, Honolulu, 1977; vis. prof., cons. to Surgeon Gen. U.S. Army, Europe, 1978; vis. prof. U. Basel, Switzerland, 1979, Phoenix Orthopaedic Residency Program, 1979, Stanford U., 1981, U. Hawaii, 1982, U. So. Calif., L.A., 1984, SUNY, Buffalo, 1985, U. Utah, 1985, U. Iowa Coll. Medicine, 1987, Duke U. Sch. Medicine, 1988, U. Calif. Irvine, Div. Orthopaedics, 1990, U. S.C., 1990, Mass. Gen. Hosp., Harvard U., 1990, Boston U., 1994, Stanford U., 1995, Med. Coll. Pa., 1996, numerous others; also guest lectr. numerous instns.; insp. for residency rev. com. ad hoc appeal com. Accreditation coun. for Grad. Med. Specialist Site, 1983-86. Editor: (with M. Madison) Operative Orthopaedics, 1988 (Best New Book in Clin. Medicine Assn. Am. Pubs.); contbr. numerous articles and numerous abstracts to profl. jours.; presenter exhibits, audiovisual programs, some 500 other presentations; cons. editor Skiing Mag., 1973-77; mem. bd. assoc. editors Clin. Orthopaedics and Related Rsch., 1982-85, Internat. Med. Soc. Paraplegia, 1972-80; reviewer Jour. Bone and Joint Surgery, 1980-85, trustee, 1995-03, sec. to bd. trustees, 1999, chmn. bd. trustees, 2000; past reviewer New Eng. Jour. Medicine; patentee in field. With U.S. Army, 1968-70. Decorated Army Commendation medal; recipient Outstanding Tchg. award U. Calif., San Francisco, 1972, Outstanding Tchr. award U. Calif., Davis, 1984, 93; named One of Best 100 Doctors Am., Good Housekeeping Mag.; Fogarty Sr. Internat. fellow NIH, 1978-79, 80-81; grantee Johnson & Johnson, 1983-84, Zimmer Inc., 1983-85, 85-86, 87-90, Interpore Internat., 1985-86, 89-90, Collagen Inc., 1985-86, 88-89, Upjohn Inc., 1985-86, Orthopaedic Rsch. and Edn. Found., 1988-89. Mem. AMA (Physicians Recognition award 1989-96), ACS, Am. Acad. Orthopaedic Surgeons (bd. dirs. 1982-83, numerous coms., Zimmer award for Disting. Contbn. to Orthop. Surgery, 2002), Am. Orthopaedic Assn. (bd. dirs. 1985-86, pres. 1990-91, various coms.), Internat. Orthopaedic Assn., Assn. for Study of Internal Fixation (N.Am. chpt.), Internat. Soc. Orthopaedic Surgery and Traumatology, Internat. Soc. for Fracture Repair, Brit. Orthopaedic Assn., South African Orthopaedic Assn. (hon.), Am. Acad. Orthopaedic Surgeons, Am. Assn. for Surgery of Trauma, Am. Bd. Med. Spltys., Assn. Am. Med. Colls., Leroy C. Abbott Orthopaedic Soc., Austrian Trauma Assn., Paul R. Lipscomb Soc., Northwestern Med. Assn., Orthopaedic Rsch. Soc., Orthopaedic Trauma Assn., Sierra Club, U. Calif. San Francisco Alumni Assn., Western Orthopaedic Assn., Houston Orthopaedic Assn. (hon.), Calif. Med. Assn., Calif. Orthopaedic Assn., Sacramento-El Dorado Med. Soc., Wilson Interurban Orthopaedic Soc., Alpha Omega Alpha. Avocations: skiing, mountain climbing, backpacking, tennis, bicycling. Office: U Calif-Davis Sch Med Dept Orthopedics 4860 Y St Ste 3800 Sacramento CA 95817-2307

CHAPMAN, ORVILLE LAMAR, chemist, educator; b. New London, Conn., June 26, 1932; s. Orville Carmen and Mabel Elnora (Tyree) C.; m. Faye Newton Morrow, Aug. 20, 1955 (div. 1980); children: Kenneth, Kevin; m. Susan Elizabeth Parker, June 15, 1981. BS, Va. Poly. Inst., 1954; PhD, Cornell U., 1957. Instr. chemistry Iowa State U., 1957-59, asst. prof., 1959-62, assoc. prof., 1962-65, Prof. chemistry, 1965-74; prof. chemistry UCLA, 1974—. Cons. Mobil Chem. Co., 1964—98. Recipient NYAS award, 1974, Founders prize, Tex. Instruments, George and Freda Halpern award in phothchemstry, N.Y. Acad. Scis., 1978, Outstanding Patent of Yr. award, Mobil Corp., 1992, Best Use of Info. Tech. in Edn. and Academia award, Computer World/Smithsonian Instn. Mem. Am. Chem. Soc. (award in pure chemistry 1968, Arthur C. Cope award 1978, Midwest award 1978, Havinga medal 1982, McCoy award UCLA, 1985). Home: 1213 Roscomare Rd Los Angeles CA 90077-2202 Office: UCLA Dept of Chemistry 607 Charles E Young Dr E Los Angeles CA 90095 Office Phone: 310-825-4883. Office Fax: 310-267-2288. E-mail: olc@chem.ucla.edu.

CHAPMAN, REX, professional sports team executive, retired professional basketball player; b. Bowling Green, Ky., Oct. 5, 1967; s. Wayne Chapman; m. Bridget Chapman; children: Caley Michelle, Zeke Everett. Student, U. Ky., 1986—88. Player Charlotte Hornets, 1988—91, Washington Bullets, 1992—95, Miami Heat, 1995—96, Phoenix Suns, 1996—2000, basketball ops. position, 2002—05; scout Minn. Timberwolves, 2005—06; v.p. player pers. Denver Nuggets, 2006—. Named to NBA All-Rookie Second Team, 1989. Avocations: golf, swimming, music. Office: Denver Nuggets 1000 Chopper Cir Denver CO 80204

CHAPMAN, RONALD WILLIAM, physician, county official; b. Sept. 17, 1961; MPH in Health Behavior and Health Edn., U. Mich.; MD, U. So. Calif., 1989. Cert. Family Medicine. Cmty. health educator; resident North Colorado Med. Ctr.; fellow Univ. Calif., San Francisco Dept. Family Practice; health adminstrn. fellow Mercy Healthcare, Sacramento; pub. health officer, dept. dir. Solano County Health and Social Svcs., Calif., 1999—; part-time practice Sacramento. Trains family practice residents on the in-patient medicine svc. Mercy Gen. Hosp., Sacramento. Recipient Nathan Davis award for Outstanding Govt. Svc. (career pub. servant at the county level), AMA, 2008. Mem.: Solano County Med. Soc. Office: 275 Beck Ave MS 5-240 Fairfield CA 94533-6804 Office Phone: 707-784-8600. Office Fax: 707-421-6618. Business E-Mail: rwchapman@solanocounty.com.

CHAPMAN, ROSALYN M., federal judge; b. Chgo., May 16, 1943; BA cum laude, U. Mich., 1964; JD, Boalt Hall, 1967. Adminstrv. law judge Office of Adminstrv. Hearings State of Calif., 1977-95; apptd. magistrate judge cen. dist. U.S. Dist. Ct. Calif., 1995. Arbitrator Fed. Mediation and Conciliation Svc. and Am. Arbitration Assn.; assoc. dir. Western Ctr. on Law and Poverty; lectr. UCLA Sch. Law. Office: US Courthouse 312 N Spring St Los Angeles CA 90012-4701 Fax: 213-894-4949.

CHAPMAN, SAMUEL GREELEY, political science professor, criminologist; b. Atlanta, Sept. 29, 1929; s. Calvin C. and Jane (Greeley) C.; m. Patricia Hepfer, June 19, 1949 (dec. Dec. 1978); children: Lynn Randall, Deborah Jane; m. Carolyn Hughes, June 1, 1991. AB, U. Calif.-Berkeley, 1951, MA, 1959. Officer Police Dept., Berkeley, 1951-56; police cons. Pub. Adminstrn. Service, Chgo., 1956-59; asst. prof. Sch. Police Adminstrn., Mich. State U., East Lansing, 1959-63; police chief Multnomah County, Portland, Oreg., 1963-66; asst. dir. Pres.'s Commn. on Law Enforcement and Adminstrn. of Justice, Nat. Crime Commn., Washington, 1966-67; prof. dept. polit. sci. U. Okla., Norman, 1967-91; prof. emeritus, 1991—; chmn. athletic council U. Okla., 1971-72, 79-80. Adj. prof. criminal justice U. Nev., Reno, 1995—; assoc.'s disting. lectr., 1985-86. Author: Dogs in Police Work, 1960, The Police Heritage in England and America, 1962, Police Patrol Readings, 1964, rev. edit., 1970, Perspectives on Police Assaults in the South Central United States, 1974, Short of Merger, 1976, Police Murders and Effective Countermeasures, 1976, Police Dogs in North America, 1979, 2d. edit., 1990, Cops, Killers and Staying Alive: The Murder of Police Officers in America, 1986; Murdered On Duty: The Killing of Police Officers in America, 1998; contbr. chpts. to books, articles to profl. jours. Mem. Norman City Council, 1972-83, mayor pro-tem, 1975-76, 79-80, 81-83. Recipient Amoco Found. award, 1986. Mem. Nev. Hist. Soc. (docent, Docent of Yr, 2006), Alpha Delta Phi. Republican. Congregationalist. Home and Office: 680 Kane Ct Reno NV 89512-1354 Office Phone: 775-786-9011.

CHAPMAN HOLLEY, SHAWN SNIDER, lawyer; b. LA, Apr. 11, 1962; d. Henry Stewart and Freddi (Snider) King; m. Michael J. Chapman, Sept. 12, 1992; m. Dorian Holley; 1 child, Olivia Rose BA in English, UCLA, 1984; JD, Southwestern U., 1988. Bar: Calif. 1988, U.S. Dist. Ct. (ctrl. dist.) Calif. 1989. Deputy pub. defender L.A. County Pub. Defenders Office, 1988-94; mng. ptnr. The Cochran Firm (formerly Law Offices of Johnnie L. Cochran Jr.), LA, 1994—2006; ptnr. Kinsella Weitzman Iser Kump & Aldisert LLP, Santa Monica, Calif., 2006—. Chief legal corr. E! Network. Commr. of community affairs Southwestern U. Sch. Law, L.A., 1987. Mem. Black Pub. Defenders Assn., Black Women Lawyers, Langston Bar Assn. Democrat. Office: Kinsella Weitzman Iser Kump & Aldisert LLP 808 Wilshire Blvd 3rd Fl Santa Monica CA 90401

CHAPPELL, CHARLES FRANKLIN, meteorologist, consultant; b. St. Louis, Dec. 7, 1927; s. Hubert Guy and Wilma Halle (Lindsey) C.; m. Doris Mae Kennedy, Aug. 4, 1951; children— Christa Ann, Susan Lynne, Deborah Louise BS, Washington U., St. Louis, 1949; postgrad., St. Louis U., 1952-54; MS, Colo. State U., 1967, PhD, 1971. Flight data engr. McDonnell Aircraft Co., St. Louis, 1950-55; weather forecaster U.S. Weather Bur., Kansas City, Mo., 1956-67; research assoc. Colo. State U., Ft. Collins, 1967-70; assoc. prof. Utah State U., Logan, 1970-72; research meteorologist NOAA, Boulder, Colo., 1972-79, research dir., 1979-87; head applied sci. group Nat. Ctr. for Atmospheric Research, Boulder, 1988-89, sr. scientist coop. program for operational meteorology edn. and tng., 1989-94; meteorologist cons., Boulder, 1995—. Cons. meteorologist Midwest Weather Service, Kansas City, Mo., 1958-60 Assoc. editor Jour. Atmospheric Sci., 1984-87; contbr. articles to prof. jours. (Best Sci. Paper award in NOAA-Environ. Research Labs. 1981). Served as seaman 1st class USN, 1945-46 Recipient silver medal Dept. Commerce, 1957 Fellow Am. Meteorol. Soc.; mem. Nat. Weather Assn., Weather Modification Assn., Am. Geophys. Union, Phi Kappa Phi. Avocations: hiking, painting, gardening, piano. Home and Office: 3110 Heidelberg Dr Boulder CO 80305-7010

CHAPPELL, WILLARD RAY, physics educator, environmental scientist; b. Boulder, Colo., Feb. 27, 1938; s. Willard Bruce and Mildred Mary (Weaver) C.; m. Juanita June Benetin, Mar. 5, 1981; children: Ginger Ferguson, Robert Ferguson. BA in Math., U. Colo., 1962, PhD in Physics, 1965; A.M. in Physics, Harvard U., 1963. Postdoctoral research assoc. Smithsonian Astrophys. Obs., Cambridge, Mass., 1965-66; postdoctoral research assoc. Lawrence Livermore Lab., Calif., 1966-67; asst. prof. physics U. Colo., Boulder, 1967-70, assoc. prof., 1970-73, prof., 1973-76, prof. physics, dir. Ctr. for Environ. Scis. Denver, 1976—. Chmn. Dept. Energy Oil Shale Task Force, 1978-83; mem. adv. com. to dir. on health scis. Los Alamos Nat. Lab.; mem. Colo. Gov.'s Sci. Adv. Com., 1974-76, chmn., 1975-76 Author: Transport and Biological Effects of Molybdenum in the Environment, 1975 Served with U.S. Army, 1956-58 NSF fellow, 1962-65; grantee Fleishman Found., 1969-71, NSF, 1971-76, EPA, 1975-79, Dept. Energy, 1976-83, U.S. Bur. Mines, 1979-81 Mem. Am. Phys. Soc., AAAS, Soc. Environ. Geochemistry and Health (exec. com. 1981-83, 86-88, sec./treas. 1988—), Phi Beta Kappa Democrat.

CHAPUT, CHARLES J., archbishop; b. Concordia, Kans., Sept. 26, 1944; s. Joseph and Marian (DeMarais) Chaput. BA, St. Fidelis Coll. Sem., 1967; attended, Catholic U., 1969; MA, Capuchin Coll., Washington, 1970, U. San Francisco, 1971. Professed Order of Friars Minor Capuchin, 1968, ordained priest, 1970; instr. in theology, spiritual dir. St. Fidelis Coll., Herman, Pa., 1971—74; exec. sec., dir. communications Capuchin Province of St. Augustine, Pitts., 1974—77; pastor Holy Cross parish, Thornton, Colo., 1977; vicar provincial Capuchin Province of Mid-Am., 1977—80, sec., treas., 1980—83, chief exec., provincial minister, 1983—88; ordained bishop, 1988; bishop Diocese of Rapid City, SD, 1988—97; archbishop Archdiocese of Denver, 1997—. Author: Living the Catholic Faith: Rediscovering the Basics, 2000. Roman Catholic. Office: Cath Pastoral Ctr 1300 S Steele St Denver CO 80210-2526 Office Phone: 303-715-3129. Business E-Mail: shepherd@archden.org.

CHAR, PATRICIA HELEN, lawyer; b. Honolulu, Mar. 23, 1952; d. Lincoln S. and Daisy Char; m. Thomas W. Bingham, Mar. 20, 1982; children: Matthew Thomas Bingham, James Nathan Bingham. BA, Northwestern U., 1974; JD, Georgetown U., 1977. Bar: Wash. 1977, U.S. Dist. Ct. (we. dist.) Wash. 1977, U.S. Dist. Ct. (ea. dist.) Wash. 1982, U.S. Ct. Appeals (9th cir.) 1981, U.S. Supreme Ct. 1984. Assoc. Bogle & Gates, Seattle, 1977-84; ptnr., mem. Bogle & Gates PLLC, Seattle, 1984-99; of counsel Garvey, Schubert & Barer, Seattle, 1999-2000; ptnr. Kirk Preston Gates Ellis LLP, Seattle, 2000—06, Kirkpatrick & Lockhart Preston Gates Ellis LLP, Seattle, 2007—. Author: Ownership By a Fiduciary, 1997. Trustee YWCA, Seattle-King County-Snohomish County, 1997-2006, United Way King County, 2004-06, Childrens Hosp. and Regional Med. Ctr., Seattle, 2006—; vol. King County Big Sisters, United Way of King County, Seattle, 1987-90, Guardian Ad Litem Program, Seattle, 1987-93 Fellow Am. Coll. Trust and Estate Counsel; mem. ABA, Wash. State Bar Assn. (co-author chpts. 3 and 4 Wash. Civil Procedure Deskbook 1992). Office: Kirkpatrick & Lockhart Preston Gates Ellis LLP 925 4th Ave #2900 Seattle WA 98104-1158 Office Phone: 206-623-7580. Business E-Mail: pat.char@klgates.com.

CHAR, VERNON FOOK LEONG, lawyer; b. Honolulu, Dec. 15, 1934; s. Charles A. and Annie (Ching) C.; m. Evelyn Lau, June 14, 1958; children: Richard, Daniel, Douglas, Charles, Elizabeth. BA, U. Hawaii, 1956; LLB, Harvard U., 1959. Bar: Hawaii 1959. Dep. atty. gen. Office of Atty. Gen., Honolulu, 1959-60, 62-65; ptnr. Damon Key Char & Bocken, Honolulu, 1965-89, Char, Sakamoto, Ishii, Lum & Ching, Honolulu, 1989—. Chmn. Hawaii Ethics Commn., Honolulu, 1968-75, Hawaii Bicentennial US Constitution, 1986-91; mem. Hawaii Tourism Authority, 2003—. Mem. ABA (bd. govs. 1991-94), Hawaii Bar Assn. (pres. 1985), U. Hawaii Alumni Assn. (pres. 1989-90). Home: 351 Anonia St Honolulu HI 96821-2052 Office: Char Sakamoto Ishii Lum & Ching Davies Pacific Ctr 841 Bishop St Ste 850 Honolulu HI 96813-3957 Office Phone: 808-522-5133. Business E-Mail: vflchar@lawcsilc.com.

CHAREN, MONA, columnist; b. NYC, Feb. 25, 1957; d. George and Claire (Rosenfeld) C.; m. Robert P. Parker. BA, Columbia U., 1979; JD, George Wash. U., 1984. Editorial assoc. Nat. Review Mag., NYC, 1979-81; speechwriter White House, Washington, 1984, assoc. dir., office of pub. liaison, 1985-86; speechwriter Jack Kemp for Pres., Washington, 1986; syndicated columnist Creators Syndicate, LA, 1987—. Panelist The Capital Gang CNN, Washington. Contbr. articles profl. mags. and publs.; author: Useful Idiots, 2003, Do-Gooders, 2005. Republican. Jewish. Office: Creators Syndicate 5777 W Century Blvd Ste 700 Los Angeles CA 90045-5675 Home Phone: 703-759-5919. Personal E-mail: charenmail@cox.net.

CHARLES, RAY, musician, composer, lyricist, arranger, conductor; b. Chgo., Sept. 13, 1918; s. Isador and Gertrude (Gendon) Offenberg; m. Bernice Rosengarden, Oct. 16, 1940; children: Michael, Jonathan, Wendy. Grad. high sch., Chgo. Mem., choral arranger radio choirs, Chgo.; choral dir., vocal arranger Perry Como; dir. Ray Charles Singers; choral arranger, dir. Your Hit Parade. Cons. Muppet Show. Recorded albums (6 Grammy nominees); composer, lyricist TV spls. including The 1st Nine Months are the Hardest, 1971 (Emmy award 1971), The Funny Side of Marriage, 1971 (Emmy award 1972); TV spls. with John Denver, Frank Sinatra, Bing Crosby, Julie Andrews, Mac Davis, The Carpenters, Acad. Awards, Kennedy Ctr. Honors, Salute to Billy Wilder; co-dir. music (TV series) Sha-Na-Na; conductor Broadway play Finian's Rainbow; choral work (films) Funny Lady, Racing With Moon; singer (TV series theme song) Three's Company. With USN, 1944-46. Mem. AFTRA, NARAS, SAG, Am. Fedn. Musicians, Acad. TV Arts and Scis. Office: Ray Charles Enterprises Inc 2107 W Washington Blvd Ste 200 Los Angeles CA 90018-1597

CHARLSON, MICHAEL LLOYD, lawyer; b. Pitts., Sept. 1, 1958; s. Benjamin Charlson and Sheila (Ostrow) Flodberg; m. Elizabeth Stone, Aug. 31, 1986 (div. June 2006); children: Doria, Meredith. BS, MS in Biol. Sci., Stanford U., 1981; JD, U. Calif., Berkeley, 1985. Bar: Calif. 1985, D.C. 2002, N.Y. 2003, U.S. Dist. Ct. (no. and ea. dists.) Calif. 1987, U.S. Ct. Appeals (9th cir.) 1990, U.S. Dist Ct. (cen. dist.) Calif., U.S. Dist. Ct. (so. dist.) Calif. 1992, U.S. Supreme Ct. 1994. Law clk. to Judge William C. Canby U.S. Ct. Appeals (9th cir.), Phoenix, 1985-86; ptnr. Heller Ehrman LLP, Menlo Park, Calif., 1986—. Dir. Legal Aid Soc., San Mateo, Calif., 2000—03, ODC/San Francisco, Calif., 2000—. Mem. atty. div. Jewish Fedn. San Francisco, 1987—. Mem. ABA (editl. bd. Litigation mag. 1989—92), Santa Clara (Calif.) Bar Assn., Order of Coif. Democrat. Office: Heller Ehrman LLP 275 Middlefield Rd Menlo Park CA 94025-3506 Home: 1421 Dolores St San Francisco CA 94110-4320 Office Phone: 650-324-7083. Fax: 650-324-6020. E-mail: michael.charlson@hellerehrman.com.

CHARLSON, ROBERT JAY, atmospheric sciences educator; b. San Jose, Calif., Sept. 30, 1936; s. Rolland Walter and Harriet Adele (Stucky) C.; m. Patricia Elaine Allison, Mar. 16, 1964; children: Daniel Owen, Amanda Marcella. BS in Chemistry, Stanford U., 1958, MS in Chemistry, 1959; PhD in Atmospheric Scis., U. Wash., 1964; postgrad. (Fulbright scholar), London U., 1964-65; PhD (hon.), Stockholm U., 1993. Rsch. engr. Boeing Co., Seattle, 1959-62; rsch. asst. prof. dept. civil engring. U. Wash., Seattle, 1965-69, assoc. prof. atmospheric chemistry, 1969-71, assoc. prof. civil engring. and geophysics, 1971-74, prof. atmospheric chemistry in civil engring. geophysics and environ. studies, 1974-94, prof. atmospheric scis., 1985-98, adj. prof. chemistry, 1985-96, prof., 1996-98, prof. emeritus, 1998—; King Carl XVI Gustaf prof. environ. sci. Sweden, 1999-2000. Author: (with S.S. Butcher) An Introduction to Air Chemistry, 1972; assoc. editor: Jour. Applied Meteorology, 1971-73; co-editor: Global Biogeochemical Cycles, 1992; Earth System Science: From Biogeochemical Cycles to Global Change, 2000; mem. editorial bd. Jour. Boundary Layer Meteorology, 1971-86, Water, Air and Soil Pollution, 1971-85; contbr. articles on atmosphere chemistry to profl. jours.; patentee in field. Co-recipient Gerbier/Mumm award World Meteorol. Orgn., 1988; grantee USPHS, EPA, NSF, NASA, NOAA. Fellow Am. Meteorol. Soc., Am. Geophys. Union; mem. AAAS, Am. Chem. Soc., Sigma Xi, Phi Lambda Upson (hon.). Office: U Wash Dept Atmospheric Scis PO Box 351640 Seattle WA 98195-0001

CHARLTON, JOHN KIPP, pediatrician; b. Omaha, Jan. 26, 1937; s. George Paul and Mildred (Kipp) C.; m. Susan S. Young, Aug. 15, 1959 (dec. June, 2003); children: Paul, Cynthia, Daphne, Gregory. AB, Amherst Coll., 1958; MD, Cornell U., 1962. Intern Ohio State U. Hosp., Columbus, 1962-63; resident in pediatrics Children's Hosp., Dallas, 1966-68, chief resident in pediatrics, 1968-69; fellow in nephrology U. Tex. Southwestern Med. Sch., Dallas, 1969-70; pvt. practice medicine specializing in pediatrics, Phoenix, from 1970; chmn. dept. pediatrics Maricopa Med. Ctr., Phoenix, 1971-78, 84-93, pres. med. staff, 1991; med. dir., bd. dirs. Crisis Nursery, Inc., 1977—. Clin. assoc. prof. pediat. U. Ariz. Coll Medicine, asst. dean for student affairs, 2000-2007; dir. student coun, 2007-. Author articles and book revs. in field. Pres. Maricopa County Child Abuse Coun., 1977-81; bd. dirs. Florence Crittenton Svcs., 1980-83, Ariz. Children's Found., 1987-91; mem. Gov.'s Coun. on Children, Youth and Families, 1984-86. Officer M.C., USAF, 1963-65. Recipient Hon. Kachina award for volunteerism, 1980, Jefferson award for volunteerism, 1980, Horace Steel Child Advocacy award, 1993, Cmty. Quarterback award, 2003; named Clin. Sci. Educator of Yr., U. Ariz., 1997, 99, 2000, 2001, Best Doctor in Am., 1996-2006, MISS Found. Phoenix award, 2006; named a Health Care Hero Phoenix Review Jour., 2007. Mem. Am. Acad. Pediatrics, Ariz. Pediatric Soc., Maricopa County Pediatric Soc. (past pres.). Office: Maricopa Med Ctr 2601 E Roosevelt St Phoenix AZ 85008-4973 Home: 4040 N 58th St Phoenix AZ 85018 Business E-Mail: kipp_charlton@medprodoctors.com.

CHARLTON, PAUL K., former prosecutor, lawyer; b. 1960; m. Susan Charlton; 2 children. BA in Spanish, U. Ariz., 1983; JD, Ariz. State U., 1988. Law clk. to Thomas Kleinschmidt Ariz. Ct. Appeals; law clk. to Atty. Gen. Bob Corbin State of Ariz., Phoenix, asst. atty. gen.; asst. US atty. Dist. Ariz. US Dept. Justice, Phoenix, 1991—2001, US atty., 2001—07. Recipient Prosecutor of Yr., Fed. law Enforcement Officer's Assn., 1997.

CHARNAS, CHARLES N., lawyer, computer company executive; BA, Stanford U.; JD, U. Calif., Berkeley. Joined Hewlett-Packard Co., Palo Alto, Calif., 1989, asst. sec., 1999, head corp., securities and mergers and acquisitions sect., 1999, v.p., dep. gen. counsel, 2002—, acting gen. counsel, 2006—07. Office: Hewlett-Packard Co 3000 Hanover St Palo Alto CA 94304 E-mail: charles.charnas@hp.com.

CHARNEY, DOV, apparel executive; b. Montreal, Jan. 31, 1969; s. Morris and Sylvia (Safdie) Charney. Attended, Tufts U. Founder, chmn., pres., CEO Am. Apparel Inc., 1997—. Recipient Ernst & Young Entrepreneur of Yr. Award, 2004, Man of Yr., Counselor award, Advertising Specialty Inst.; named Man of Yr., GQ, 2003, Man of Yr., Grand All-Star Award, Apparel Mag., 2004, Man of Yr., LA Apparel Industry, Fashion Industries Guild, 2004, Most Beautiful People, Paper Mag.; named one of 100 Most Powerful People of So. Calif., LA Times Mag., 2006; named to The Power 50, Details mag., 2006. Office: Am Apparel Inc 747 Warehouse St Los Angeles CA 90021 Office Phone: 213-448-0226. Office Fax: 213-448-0334.

CHARNEY, SCOTT, computer software company executive, lawyer; BA in History and English, SUNY, Binghamton; JD, Syracuse U. Asst. dist. atty. Bronx County Dist. Atty's. Office, dep. chief investigations bur.; chief computer crime and intellectual property sect. Criminal Divsn., US Dept. Justice; prin., head Cybercrime Prevention and Response Practice PricewaterhouseCoopers; joined Microsoft Corp., 2002, chief security strategist, 2002, now corp. v.p. trustworthy computing, Core Oper. Sys. Divsn. Former chair Group of Eight Nations (G8) Subgroup on High-Tech Crime; vice chair, head US delegation to an ad hoc group of experts on global cryptography policy Organ. Econ. Cooperation and Devel.; mem. adv. bd. Software Engring. Inst., Carnegie-Mellon U. Recipient Marshall Award for Outstanding Legal Achievement, 1995, Atty. Gen.'s Award for Disting. Svc., 1998. Mem.: ABA, Am. Health Lawyers Assn., Armed Forces Comm. and Electronics Assn. (Award for Excellence, Washington Chap. 2000). Office: Microsoft Corp One Microsoft Way Redmond WA 98052-6399

CHARWAT, ANDREW FRANCISZEK, engineering educator; b. Poland, Feb. 10, 1925; came to U.S., 1945; s. Franciszek and Wanda (Niec) C.; m. Halina M. Stieglitz, Aug. 18, 1948 (dec.); 1 child, Danuta K. Charwat McCall. M Engring., Stevens Inst. Tech., 1948; PhD, U. Calif., Berkeley, 1952. Aerodynamicist Propulsion Research Corp., Los Angeles, 1952-53; designer Northrup Aircraft Corp., Los Angeles, 1953-55; prof., dept. mech. and aerospace engring. UCLA, 1955-92, prof. emeritus, 1992—. Cons. to numerous industry and govt. agys., 1955—; expert witness various legal cases; dir. Univ. Study Ctr., Lyon and Grenoble, France, 1986-88. Contbr. over 80 articles and research papers. Guggenheim fellow, 1962. E-mail: acharwat@ucla.edu.

CHASE, DAVID (DAVID DECAESARE), scriptwriter, television director and producer; b. Mt. Vernon, NY, Aug. 22, 1945; Student in Filmmaking, Sch. Visual Arts, NY; degree, NYU; MA in Film, Stanford U., Calif. Dir.: (TV series) Alfred Hitchcock Presents, 1985; writer, dir. (TV series) Almost Grown, 1988, writer Kolchak: The Night Stalker, 1974, (TV films) Grave of the Vampire, 1972, Moonlight, 1982, writer, prodr. (TV series) The Rockford Files, 1976—80 (Emmy award, 1977), writer, exec. prodr. I'll Fly Away, 1991 (Norman Felton award Prodrs. Guild Am., 1993), Northern Exposure, 1990, writer, prodr. (TV films) Off the Minnesota Strip, 1980 (Writers Guild Am. award, 1980, Emmy award, 1979), writer, prodr., dir. (TV series) The Sopranos, 1999—2007 (Emmy award for College episode, 1998, Golden Globe award, 1999, Norman Felton award Prodrs. Guild Am., 2000, Outstanding Directorial Achievement award Dirs. Guild Am., 1999, Peabody award, 2000, Drama Series of Yr. award Am. Film Inst., 2001, Primetime Emmy for Outstanding Writing for a Drama Series (Made in America) & Outstanding Drama Series, Acad. TV Arts and Scis., 2007, Best Episodic TV-Drama, Producers Guild Am., 2008), prodr. (TV films) The Rockford Files: A Blessing in Disguise, 1995, writer, prodr., dir. The Rockford Files: The Punishment and Crime, 1996. Recipient Paddy Chayefsky Laurel award for TV, Writers Guild America West, 2008, Norman Lear Achievement award in TV, Prodrs. Guild America, 2009. Office: David Harbert United Talent Agency 9560 Wilshire Blvd Ste 500 Beverly Hills CA 90212

CHASE, DEBRA MARTIN, film producer; b. Great Lakes, Ill., Oct. 11, 1956; d. Robert Douglas and Beverly M. (Barber) Martin. BA magna cum laude, Mt. Holyoke Coll., Mass., 1977; JD, Harvard Law Sch., 1981. Assoc. Butler & Binion, Houston, 1981—82, Mayor, Day & Caldwell, Houston, 1982—83; atty. Tenneco, Inc., 1984—85; atty. motion picture dept. Columbia Pictures, 1989—90, exec. asst., 1990—91, dir. creative affairs, 1991; sr. v.p., prodr. Mundy Lane

Entertainment, 1992—95; exec. v.p., prodn. ptnr. BrownHouse Prodns., 1995—99; founder, prodr. Martin Chase Prodns., 2000—. Bd. dirs. Film Forum, NYC; prodn. mentor U. So. Calif. Exec. prodr.: (TV films) Hank Aaron: Chasing the Dream, 1995, Rodgers & Hammerstein's Cinderella, 1997; (films) Courage Under Fire, 1996; co-prodr.: The Preacher's Wife, 1996; prodr.: (films) The Pelican Brief, 1993, The Princess Diaries, 2001, The Cheetah Girls, 2003, The Princess Diaries 2: Royal Engagement, 2004, The Sisterhood of the Traveling Pants, 2005, The Sisterhood of the Traveling Pants 2, 2008. Founding mem., vol. Contemporary Friends of Studio Mus., Harlem; vol. Heartland Film Festival; del. Dem. Nat. Conv., 1988; cmty. resource adv. com. LA County Mus. Art; bd. dirs. Columbia Coll., Chgo. Named an Outstanding Woman in Mktg. & Comm., Ebony mag., 2007; named one of 50 African Am. women shaping the world, 2003, 100 Most Influential African Americans in US, Savoy mag., 2003, Top 50 Powerbrokers in Hollywood, Black Enterprise mag., 2007; named to Power 150, Ebony mag., 2008. Office: Martin Chase Prodns 500 S Buena Vista St Burbank CA 91521

CHASE, MARILYN, journalist; b. LA; AB in English, Stanford U., 1971; MA in Journalism, U. Calif., Berkeley, 1973. Reporter Wall St. Jour., San Francisco, 1978—94, health columnist, 1994—99, sr. spl. writer health and medicine, 1999—. Author: (book) The Barbary Plague: The Black Death in Victorian San Francisco, 2003. Office: Wall St Jour 201 California St Ste 1350 San Francisco CA 94111-5022

CHASE, ROBERT ARTHUR, surgeon, educator; b. Keene, NH, Jan. 6, 1923; s. Albert Henry and Georgia Beulah (Bump) Chase; m. Ann Crosby Parker, Feb. 3, 1946; children: Deborah Lee, Nancy Jo, Robert N. BS cum laude, U. N.H., 1945, DSc (hon.), 1993; MD, Yale, 1947. Diplomate Am. Bd. Surgery, Am. Bd. Plastic Surgery. Intern New Haven Hosp., 1947—48, asst. resident, 1949—50, sr. resident surgery, 1952—53, chief resident surgeon, 1953—54; mem. faculty Yale Sch. Medicine, 1948—54, 1959—62, asst. prof. surgery, 1959—62; mem. faculty U. Pitts., 1957—59, resident plastic surgeon, also teaching fellow, 1957—59; attending surgeon VA Hosp., W. Haven, Conn., 1959—62, Grace New Haven Community Hosp., 1959—63; prof., chmn. dept. surgery Stanford Sch. Medicine, 1963—74, Emile Holman prof. surgery, 1972—; prof. surgery U. Pa., 1974—77; attending surgeon Pa. Hosp., Hosp. U. Pa., Grad. Hosp., Phila., 1974—77; pres., dir. Nat. Bd. Med. Examiners, Phila., 1974—77; prof. anatomy Stanford (Calif.) U., 1977—. Cons. plastic surgery Christian Med. Coll. and Hosp., Vellore, India, 1962; cons. to surgeon gen. USAF, 1970—; Benjamin K. Rank prof. Australasian Coll. Surgeons, 1974. Author: Atlas of Hand Surgey; editor: Video-surgery, 1974—; mem. editl. bd.: Med. Alert Communication, —; contbr. articles to profl. jours. Mem. bd. overseers Dartmouth Med. Sch., 1998-; mem. found. bd. U. N.H., 1998-. Maj. M.C. AUS, 1949—57. Recipient Francis Gilman Blake award, Yale Sch. Medicine, 1962, Henry J. Kaiser award, Stanford U. Sch. Medicine, 1978, 1979, 1984, 1986, 1990, 1993, Calif. Golden Apple award, 1991, Albion William Hewlett award, 1992, Pettee award, U. N.H., 1998; named an Hand Ctr. in his name, Stanford U., 2004. Fellow: ACS, Australasian Coll. Surgeons (hon.); mem.: AMA, NAS, Halsted Soc., Am. Soc. Most Venerable Order Hosp., St. John of Jerusalem, Inst. Medicine (exec. com. 1976, coun. 1986—), Soc. Univ. Surgeons, Found. Am. Soc. Plastic and Reconstructive Surgery (dir.), Am. Cancer Soc. (clin. fellowship com.), James IV Assn. Surgeons, Pacific Coast Surg. Soc., Western Surg. Assn., Soc. Clin. Surgery, Plastic Surgery Rsch. Coun., Am. Assn. Surgery Trauma, Am. Soc. Cleft Palate Rehab., Am. Soc. Surgery Hand (pres.), Conn. Med. Soc., Santa Clara County Med. Soc., Am. Surg. Assn., San Francisco Surg. Soc., Calif. Acad. Medicine (pres.), Am. Soc. Clin. Anatomists (hon.; pres.), South African Soc. Plastic and Reconstructive Surgery (hon.), South African Soc. Surgery Hand (hon.), Am. Assn. Plastic Surgery (hon.), Am. Assn. Clin. Anatomists (hon.; pres.), Am. Assn. Plastic Surgeons (hon.), Sigma Xi, Phi Beta Kappa. Home: 69 Pearce Mitchell Pl Stanford CA 94305 Office: Stanford U Div Anatomy 269 Campus Dr Stanford CA 94305-5102 Home Phone: 650-473-9049; Office Phone: 650-725-6618. E-mail: rchase6880@aol.com.

CHASE, SHARI, real estate company executive, broker; Pres., CEO Chase Internat. Distinctive Properties, Lake Tahoe, Nev., 1986—. Co-founder Nev. Rock Art Found.; bd. mem. Barton Hosp. Found. Named one of 35 Most Influential People in Luxury Real Estate, 2006, 100 Most Influential Real Estate Leaders, Inman News, 2007. Mem.: Arisan Group. Avocations: travel, art, architecture, archaeology. Office: Chase Internat Distinctive Properties PO Box 10470 190 Hwy 50 Lake Tahoe NV 89448 Office Phone: 775-588-6132. Office Fax: 775-588-1206. Business E-Mail: sharichase@chaseinternational.com.

CHASSMAN, LEONARD FREDRIC, retired labor union administrator; b. Detroit, Sept. 30, 1935; s. Joachim and Lillian (Abrams) C.; m. Phyllis Perlman, Aug. 25, 1957; children: Mark, Cheryl, Gregory. BA, UCLA, 1957. Rep. AFTRA, LA, 1959-63, SAG, LA, 1963-65; staff exec. Writers Guild Am., West, Inc., LA, 1965-77, exec. dir., 1978-82; nat. exec. sec. Screen Extras Guild Inc., 1982-84; Hollywood exec. dir. SAG Inc., 1984—2001, trustee SAG prodrs. pension and health funds; bd. dirs. Entertainment Industry Found. Pres. Hollywood Entertainment Labor Coun. Bd. dirs. L.A. Pvt. Industry Coun.

CHATARD, PETER RALPH NOEL, JR., aesthetic plastic surgeon; b. New Orleans, June 25, 1936; s. Peter Ralph Sr. and Alberta Chatard; m. Patricia Myrl White, Jan. 31, 1963; children: Andrea Michelle, Faedra Noelle, Tahra Deonne. BS in Biology, Morehouse Coll., 1956; MD, U. Rochester, 1960. Diplomate Am. Bd. Plastic Surgery, Am. Bd. Otolaryngology. Intern Colo. Gen. Hosp., 1960-61; asst. resident in gen. surgery Highland Gen. Hosp., Rochester, NY, 1963-64; resident in otolaryngology Strong Meml. Hosp., Rochester, 1964-67; resident in plastic and reconstructive surgery U. Fla., 1980-82; staff otolaryngologist Group Health Corp. of Puget Sound, Seattle, 1967-68; practice medicine specializing in otolaryngology Seattle, 1968-80; practice medicine specializing in plastic surgery, 1982—; clin. asst. prof. otolaryngology, head and neck surgery U. Wash., Seattle, 1975—. Plastic surgery cons. western sec. Maxillofacial Rev. Bd. State of Wash., 1982-90, cons. Conservation of Hearing Program, 1968-80; trustee Physicians and Dentist Credit Bur., 1974-80, 84-87, pres. 1976-77, 84-85; active staff mem. Northwest Hosp., Seattle; courtesy staff Swedish Hosp., Overlake Hosp., Bellevue, Stevens Meml. Hosp., Edmond, Wash., Seattle, others. Capt. USAF, 1961-63. Fellow ACS, Am. Rhinologic Soc., Seattle Surg. Soc., Am. Acad. Facial Plastic and Reconstructive Surgery, Am. Acad. Otolaryngology-Head and Neck Surgery, Northwest Acad. Otolaryngology and Head and Neck Surgery, Soc. for Ear, Nose and Throat Advances in Children, Pacific Oto-Ophthalmological Soc.; mem. Am. Soc. Plastic Surgery, Am. Soc. for Aesthetic Plastic Surgery, Inc., Lipoplasty Soc. N. Am., Wash. Soc. Plastic Surgeons, Nat. Med. Assn., King County Med. Soc., Wash. State Med. Assn., N.W. Soc. of Plastic Surgeons. Avocations: photography, cynology, microcomputing, architecture. Home: 13211 Frazier Pl NW Seattle WA 98177-4132 Office: Peter Chatard PO Box 75297 Seattle WA 98175-0297 Office Phone: 206-522-0200. Business E-Mail: aesteempsc@aol.com. E-mail: chatard@aol.com.

CHATER, SHIRLEY, health educator; m. Norman Chater, Dec. 5, 1959 (dec. Dec. 1993); children: Cris, Geoffrey. BS, U. Pa., 1956; MS, U. Calif., San Francisco, 1960; PhD, U. Calif., Berkeley, 1964; DHL (hon.), Univ. Pa., 1997. Asst., assoc., prof. dept. social and behavioral scis. Sch. Nursing U. Calif.-San Francisco, Sch. Edn.-Berkeley, 1964—86; asst. vice chancellor acad. affairs U. Calif., San Francisco, 1974—77, vice chancellor acad. affairs, 1977—82; council assoc. Am. Council Edn., Washington, 1982—84; sr. assoc. Presdl. Search Consultation Svc. Assn. Governing Bds., Washington, 1984—86; pres. Tex. Woman's U., Denton, 1986—93; chair Gov's health policy task force State of Texas, 1992; commr. U.S. Social Security Adminstrn., Washington, 1993—97; Regent's prof. Inst. for Health and Aging U. Calif., San Francisco, 1997—98. Vis. prof. Inst. Health & Aging U. Calif., San Francisco, 1998—. Mem. commn. on women Am. Coun. on Edn.; bd. dirs. Carnegie Found. for Advancement of Tchg., United Educators Ins. Risk Retention Group, Denton United Way, 1986—93. Mem.: Nat. Acad. Nursing, Nat. Acad. Social Ins., Nat. Acad. Pub. Adminstrn., Internat. Alliance, San Francisco Women's Forum West, Inst. Medicine NAS. Office: 20 Sheridan Ct Mill Valley CA 94941-1227

CHATFIELD, ROBERT EVANS, finance professor, college administrator; b. Brockton, Mass., Apr. 17, 1953; s. Ellie Mae and William Chatfield; m. Hyun Kyung Park, Jan. 1, 2003; 1 child, Jay Takeoka. BA in Bus. Adminstrn., Ea. Nazarene Coll., Quincy, Mass., 1975; MS in Econ., Purdue U., West Lafayette, Ind., 1977, PhD in Fin. Econ., 1979. Asst. prof. fin. U. N.Mex, Albuquerque, 1979—81, Tex. Tech U., Lubbock, 1981—88; chair, dept. of fin. U. Nev., Las Vegas, 1991—98, dir., mba programs, 2003—, prof. of fin., 1988—. Contbr. fin. jour. article. Recipient President's Excellence Tchg. award, Tex. Tech U., 1983, Outstanding Tchr. award, Krannert Sch. of Mgmt., Purdue U., 1977; Ayres Fellowship, Stonier Grad. Sch. Banking, 1986. Independent. Avocations: travel, tennis, white-water rafting. Office: Univ Nevada Las Vegas 4505 Maryland Pkwy Las Vegas NV 89154-6008 E-mail: robert.chatfield@unlv.edu.

CHATHAM, RUSSELL, artist; b. San Francisco, Oct. 27, 1939; m. Mary Fanning (div.); m. Doris Meyer (div.); m. Suzanne Porter; children: Georgina, Lea, Rebecca, Paul. Student, San Francisco. Painter, writer, Calif.; landscape artist, lithographer, Mont., 1972—. Address: PO Box 659 Livingston MT 59047-0659 Also: c/o Angler Art & Gifts Cherry Creek North 201 Fillmore St Unit D Denver CO 80206-5015

CHATTERJEE, KANU, cardiologist, educator; b. Calcutta, India, Mar. 1, 1934; s. Gopal Lal and Basanti Chatterjee; m. Docey Edwards, May 9, 1975. MD, R.G. Kar Med. Coll., Calcutta, India, 1956. Cert. Internal Medicine Am. Bd. Internal Medicine, 1973, diplomate Cardiovascular Disease Am. Bd. Cardiology, 1975. Resident, internal medicine Royal Coll. Physicians, Edinburgh, 1965, fellow, cardiovascular disease London, 1965; Lucie Stern Prof. Medicine U. Calif., San Francisco, 1989—2002, Ernest Gallo Disting. Prof. Medicine, 2002—. Contbr. several articles to profl. jours.; editl. bd. mem. Circulation, American Journal of Cardiology, and Journal of Critical Care. Recipient Gifted Teacher award, Am. Coll. Cardiology, 1990. Achievements include discovery of First to discover: post pacing t-wave changes; First to discover vasodilators in mitral regurgitation; First to discover relationship between endocardial potentials and ventricular volume. Office: Univ Calif San Francisco 505 Parnassus Ave Ste M-1182 San Francisco CA 94143-0124 Office Fax: 415-502-8627.

CHATTERJEE, SHARMILA, marketing educator; arrived in US, 1986, naturalized; d. Sunil N. and Pronoti Chatterjee; m. Arup K. Chakraborty, July 8, 1992; 1 child, Meenakshi. PhD in Mktg., U. Pa., 1994. Asst. prof. Fairfield U., Conn., 1995—98, Golden Gate U., San Francisco, 1998—2000, assoc. prof., chair dept. mktg., 2000—, Nagel T. Miner prof. bus., 2004—, prof., 2005—. Vis. prof. MIT Sloan Sch. Mgmt., 2006—, sr. lectr., 2009—. Contbr. articles to profl. jours. Mem.: Informs, Am. Mktg. Assn. (mgr. collegiate activities San Francisco chpt. 1998—). Avocations: reading, music. Office: 1 Amherst St E40-166 A Cambridge MA 02142 Office Phone: 617-253-8214. Business E-Mail: schatterjee@mit.edu.

CHAUDHRI, JAVADE, lawyer, utilities executive; b. Nairobi, Kenya, Apr. 30, 1952; BS, Yale U., 1975, MS, 1977; JD, Georgetown U., 1980. Bar: DC 1980, Calif. 2000. Atty. Surrey & Morse, Washington, 1980—86; ptnr. Jones, Day, Reavis & Pogue (merger with Surrey & Morse), Washington, 1986—93; sr. ptnr. Winston & Strawn, Washington, 1993—99; v.p. law, dep. gen. counsel Gateway, Poway, Calif., 1999—2001, sr. v.p., gen. counsel, 2001—03; exec. v.p., gen. counsel Sempra Energy, San Diego, 2003—. Vis. faculty mem. Internat. Devel. Law Inst., Rome, Internat. Law Inst., Washington. Mem.: ABA, Calif. Bar. Office: Sempra Energy 101 Ash St San Diego CA 92101-3017

CHAVEZ, ALBERT BLAS, financial executive; b. LA, Jan. 1, 1952; s. Albert Blas and Yolanda (Garcia) Chavez; m. Irma Laura Cavazos, Dec. 21, 1996. BA, U. Tex., El Paso, 1979; MBA, Stanford U., 1985. CPA Calif. Mem. profl. staff Deloitte Haskins and Sells, LA, 1980—83; planning analyst corp. fin. planning Boise Cascade Co., Idaho, 1984; treasury analyst corp. treasury RCA Corp., NYC, 1985; asst. contr. RCA/Ariola Records, Mexico City, 1986; fin. analyst corp. exec. office GE Co., Fairfield, Conn., 1987—90; cons. corp. fin. Entertainment Industry and Litig. Support Svcs., LA, 1990—91; co-founder, sr. v.p., CFO El Dorado Comm., Inc., LA, 1991—98; fin. cons. entertainment and tech. industries, 1999—2003; sr. v.p., CFO SiTV, Inc., LA, 2003—06; COO, mng. dir. Lombardia Capital Ptnrs., Inc., Pasadena, Calif., 2006—08. Bd. dirs., vice chmn., treas. L.A. Conservation Corp., 1990—; bd. dirs. Wave Cmty. Newspapers, 1999—2000. Recipient Jerry I. Porras award, Stanford Bus. Sch., 2006; named one of 100 Influentials, Hispanic Bus. Mag.'s, 2006. Mem.: AICPA, Calif. Soc. CPA. Democrat. Home: 4820 Carmel Rd La Canada Flintridge CA 91011

CHÁVEZ, DENISE ELIA, performance writer, actress; b. Las Cruces, N.Mex., Aug. 15, 1948; d. Ernesto E. and Delfina (Rede) C.; m. Daniel Zolinsky, Dec. 29, 1984. BA in Theatre, N.Mex. State U., 1971; MFA in Theatre, Trinity U., 1974; MA in Creative Writing, U. N.Mex., 1984, PhD (hon.), 2005. Prof. English and theatre Northern N.Mex. C.C., Española, 1977-80; artist-in-the-schs. N.Mex. Arts Divn., Santa Fe, 1977-83; prof. theatre U. Houston, 1988-91; asst. prof. creative writing, playwriting, and Chicano lit. N.Mex. State U., Las Cruces, 1996-99. Prof. creative writing Munson Sr. Ctr., Las Cruces; tchr. theatre and creative writing N.Mex. Sch. Visually Handicapped; vis. prof. creative writing N.Mex. State U., 1992-93, 95-96; artistic dir. Border Book Festival, 1994—; del. forum U.S.-Soviet Dialogue, Moscow and Russia; mem. N.Mex. Street Theatre; presenter reading workshops; lectr. in field. Author: The Last of Menu Girls, 1986 (Puerto del Sol Fiction award 1986), Face of an Angel, 1994 (Am. Book award 1995, Premio Aztlán award 1995, Mesilla Valley Author of Yr. 1995), (plays) Plaza, 1989, The Flying Tortilla Man, 1987, The Woman Who Knew the Language of the Animals, 1993; one woman shows include Women in the State of Grace, U.S. Recipient Human Svcs. award citizen advocacy Doña Ana County, Creative Artist award Cultural Arts Coun., Houston, 1990, Rockefeller Playwriting award Rockefeller Found., N.Mex., 1984, Writers of Pass award El Paso Herald Post, 1995, Gov.'s award achievement in arts in lit., 1995, Luminaria award N.Mex. Cmty. Found., 1996, Woman Distinction award Soroptimist Internat. Ams. Club, 1996, Papen Family Arts award, 1998, Lit. award Hispanic Heritage Found., 2003, Hispanic Heritage award, 2003, The Don Luis Leal award 2005; grantee NEA, 1982, U. Houston, 1989; scholar U. Houston, 1988; fellow Rockefeller Found., 1984, Lila Wallace-Readers Digest fellow, 2000-03. Democrat. Roman Catholic. Avocations: swimming, bowling, movies. Office Phone: 575-523-3988. Office Fax: 575-525-8741. Business E-Mail: bbf@zianet.com.

CHAVEZ, EDWARD, Mayor, Stockton, California, protective services official; b. Stockton, Calif., Mar. 22, 1943; m. Nancy Ruhr; children: Eric, Jill. AA, San Joaquin Delta Coll., 1971; BA, Calif. State U., 1972; MS, Calif. Polytechnic Pomona, 1990; grad., POST Command Coll., Delinquency Control Inst., Leadership Stockton Program, FBI Nat. Acad. With USAF, 1962-70; officer Stockton Police Dept., 1973, sgt., 1980, lt., 1986, capt., 1990, dep. chief of police, 1990, acting chief of police, 1993, chief of police, 1993—2004; mayor Stockton, Calif., 2004—. Bd. dirs. St. Joseph's Med. Ctr., San Joaquin United Way, Lilliput Childrens Svcs., Greater Stockton C. of C.; active Hispanics for Polit. Action; adv. com. Leadership, Stockton. With USAF, 1962-70. Mem. Calif. Peace Officers Assn., Hispanic Am. Police Command Officer's Assn., Mexican Am. C. of C., Stockton E. Rotary, Coun. for Spanish Speaking (past bd. dirs.), Leadership Stockton Alumni Assn. Office: 425 N El Dorado St Stockton CA 95202

CHAVEZ, EDWARD L., councilman, mayor; b. LA, Dec. 9, 1963; s. Abenicio Pacheco and Magdalena (Peralta) C. BA, UCLA, 1989; AA, Rio Hondo Coll., Whittier, Calif., 1985; postgrad., Claremont Grad. U., Calif. Tchr. Whittier Union High Sch. Dist., 1990-91; adminstrv. asst. to state assemblywoman Sally Tanner Calif. Legislature, 1991-92; councilman City of La Puente, Calif., 1990—2000, mayor Calif., 1997—2000; mem. Calif. Ho. of Reps., 2000—. Councilman City of La Puente, Calif., 1990—; pres. bd. edn. Bassett Unified Sch. Dist., La Puente, 1987-91. Democrat. Roman Catholic. Avocations: golf, tennis, racquetball, baseball. Office: PO Box 942849 Sacramento CA 94249

CHAVEZ, EDWARD L., state supreme court chief justice; b. Santa Fe, Oct. 15, 1957; BA in Pers. Mgmt. with honors, Eastern New Mexico U., 1978; JD, New Mexico Sch. of Law, 1981. Bar: N.Mex 1981. Ptnr. Carpenter & Chavez, Ltd.; assoc. justice N. Mex. Supreme Ct., Santa Fe, 2003—07, chief justice, 2007—. Spl. counsel N.Mex Disciplinary Bd., 1987—95; lectr. Nat. Inst. Trial Advocacy, 1998—99; adj. prof. U. N.Mex; chmn. disciplinary bd. Supreme Ct. N.Mex. Mem. Ctr. Civic Values; trustee U. N.Mex Mental Health Ctr., 1989; mem. Task Force Regulation Lawyer Advt., 1990. Fellow: Internat. Acad. Trial Lawyers, Am. Coll. Trial Lawyers; mem.: ATLA (minority del.), Hispanic Nat. Bar Assn., N.Mex. Hispanic Bar Assn., Am. Inns Ct., Trial Lawyers Pub. Justice, State Bar N.Mex, N.Mex Trial Lawyers Assn. (feature editor newsletter 1987—90, bd. dirs. 1990—, pres. 1997—98), Nat. Spinal Cord Injury Assn. Office: NMex Supreme Ct Box 848 Santa Fe NM 87504

CHAVEZ, ERIC, professional baseball player; b. LA, Dec. 7, 1977; Third base Oakland Athletics, 1998—. Recipient Am. League Gold Glove Award, 2001—05. Office: Oakland Athletics Net Assoc Coliseum 7000 Coliseum Way Oakland CA 94621

CHAVEZ, GILBERT ESPINOZA, bishop emeritus; b. Ontario, Calif., May 9, 1932; Attended, St. Francis Sem., El Cajon, Calif., Immaculate Heart Sem., San Diego, U. Calif. Ordained priest Diocese of San Diego, Calif., 1960, aux. bishop Calif., 1974—2007, aux. bishop emeritus Calif., 2007—; ordained bishop, 1974. Roman Catholic. Office: St Joseph Cathedral 1535 3rd Ave San Diego CA 92101-3101 also: Diocese of San Diego 3888 Paducah Dr PO Box 85728 San Diego CA 92186 Office Phone: 619-239-0229. Office Fax: 619-239-3788.

CHAVEZ, JEANETTE, editor; BS in Journalism, U. Colo., 1973. Mem. staff Office of U.S. Rep. Spark Matsunaga, Washington; reporter Colorado Springs (Colo.) Sun, 1973—74; reporter, copy desk chief, city editor, news editor Ft. Collins (Colo.) Coloradoan, 1974—81; copy editor Daily Herald, Arlington Heights, Ill., 1981—82; copy editor, then news editor bus. sect. Chgo. Sun Times, 1982—84; dep. news editor Denver Post, 1984—86, news editor, 1987—88, asst. mng. editor, 1988—91, assoc. editor features, 1991—97, mng. editor, 1997—. Office: Denver Post 101 W Colfax Ave Denver CO 80202

CHAVEZ, MARTIN JOSEPH, Mayor, Albuquerque, lawyer; b. Albuquerque, Mar. 2, 1952; s. Lorenzo Armijo and Sara (Baca) C.; m. Margaret Aragon de Chavez, July 29, 1988; children: Martinique, Ezequiel Lorenzo. BS, U. N.Mex., 1975; JD, Georgetown U., 1978. Staff asst. US Senate, Washington, 1976-77; dep. dir. LULAC Nat. Scholarship Fund, Washington, 1977-78; law clk. N.Mex. Atty. Gen., 1978-79; pvt. practice, 1979-86, 87-93, 98—; first and founding dir. N.Mex. Workers Compensation Adminstrn., 1986-87; mem. N.Mex. Senate, 1988-93; mayor City of Albuquerque, 1993-97, 2001—. Mem. Med. Rev. Commn., 1990—; bd. dirs. Senior Arts Project, 1987—, Tree New Mex., 1991-92. Mem. Citizens Rev. Bd., 1988—; bd. dirs. N.Mex. First, Sr. Arts; founding mem., bd. dirs. Tree N.Mex.; mem. Citizens Adv. Bd., N.Mex. Med. Rev. Commn., U.S. Conf. Mayors (adv. coun., urban water coun., homeland security comm.), Nat. Conf. Dem. Mayors (vice chair fin., 2003), Albuquerque/Bernalillo Water Utility Authority (chmn. 2003); Dem. candidate for Gov., 1998. Recipient Outstanding Young Men of Am. award, 1984, Appreciation award Friends of Albuquerque Petroglyphs, 1989, Cert. Appreciation, Am. Merchant Marines, 1989, Disting. Svc. award N.Mex. Dietetic Assn., 1989, Appreciation award West Mesa Little League, 1989, Excellence in Edn. award Friend of Edn., 1990, Appreciation award FHP N.Mex., Inc., 1990, Devoted and Invaluable Svc. award Indian Pueblo Cultural Ctr., 1990, Recognition award Ind. Ins. Agts. N.Mex., 1991, Accomplishment, Dedication and Performance award West Mesa High Sch., 1991, N.Mex. State Meml. award, 1991, Exemplary Dedication and Svc. award Sec. of State, 1991, Cert. Spl. Appreciation, MADD, 1991, Disting. Svc. award Hispanic Bar Assn., 1992, Legis. Recognition award Dem. Party N.Mex., 1992, Commitment to Edn. award Alamosa Elem. Sch., 1992, Recognition and Appreciation award N.Mex. First, 1992, Dedication award Albuquerque Hispano C. of C., 1993, Pride of N.Mex. award Hispanic Round Table, 1993; named Outstanding Youth Advocate, Youth Devel., Inc., 1993. Mem. N.Mex. State Bar Assn. (Pub. Svc. Recognition award 1989). Avocation: fly fishing. Office: Office of the Mayor PO Box 1293 Albuquerque NM 87103 Office Phone: 505-768-3000. Office Fax: 505-768-3019. E-mail: mayor@cabq.gov.*

CHAVEZ, MICHAEL ROBINSON, photojournalist; Photographer AP, Ctrl. America/Mexico, 1994—95; staff photographer The Washington Post, 1999—2007, LA Times, 2007—. Photographer Metro Collective, 2006—. Exhibitions include Peru, Havana, Cuba, Washington, NYC, Calif., Visa Pour l'Image Photojournalism Festival, France, Brooks Inst. Photography, Santa Barbara, Ojo Ajeno, Lima. Recipient Nat. Journalism award for Photojournalism, Scripps Howard Found., 2008; named Photographer of Yr., White House News Photographers' Assn., 2004, 2007. Office: LA Times 202 W 1st St Los Angeles CA 90012 E-mail: michael@robinsonchavez.com.*

CHAVEZ, NELBA R., state and former federal agency administrator; b. Mar. 9, 1940; BA in Sociology and Psychology, U. Ariz.; MSW, UCLA; PhD in Philosophy, U. Denver; student sr. exec. program in state and local govt., Harvard U. From therapist to exec. dir., CEO, COO La Frontera Ctr., Tuscon, 1971-89; prin. Chavez and Assocs., 1989-91; dir. juvenile probation svcs. City and County of San Francisco, 1991-94; adminstr. Substance Abuse and Mental Health Svcs. Adminstrn., U.S. Dept. Health and Human Svcs., Washington, 1994-2000; dep. dir. Ariz. Rehab. Svcs. Dept. Econ. Security, Phoenix, 2003—. Bd. dirs. nat. coalition of Hispanic Health and Human Svc. Organs,; mem. U.S. Senate Hispanic Adv. Com., Pres. Nat. Coun. on Handicapped, White House Prevention Com. on Drug-Free Am. Mem. Tucson Mayor's Task Force on Children. Recipient Outstanding Leadership award Ariz. State U., 1985, Dedication and Commitment award Tenth Ann. Chicano Conf., 1989, Disting. Svc. award Nat. Assn. Profl. Asian Am. Women, 1995, Mujer 95 award League United L.Am. Citizens, 1995, Rafael Tavares, MD, Meml. award Assn. Hispanic Mental Health Profls., 1995, Nat. Health Leadership award Nat. Coalition Hispanic Health and Human Svcs., 1997, Leadership award Fedn. Families for Children's Mental Health, 1997, Nat. Coun. on Aging award for Leadership in Health Promotion, 2000; named to Honor Roll Latino Behavioral Health Inst., 1998. Office: Ariz Rehab Svcs Dept Econ Security 1789 W Jefferson 2NW PO Box 6123 Phoenix AZ 85007

CHAVEZ, VICTOR EDWIN, judge; b. LA, Aug. 28, 1930; s. Raymond C. and Sarah (Baca) C.; m. Marlene Schell Chavez; children: Victoria, Catherine, Stephanie, Christopher, Robert, Elizabeth. BS, Loyola U., LA, 1953, JD, 1959. Bar: Calif. 1960. Mem. firm Early, Maslach, Foran and Williams, LA, 1960-69, Pomerantz and Chavez, LA, 1969-90; judge L.A. Superior Ct., 1990—, asst. presiding judge, 1997, 98, presiding judge, 1999—2000. Mem. exec. com. L.A. Superior Ct., 1996, 2003—04. Mem. com. State Bar Examiners, 1972-76; del. to State Bar, 1971-75; bd. regents Loyola Marymount U., 1973-78. 1st lt. USAF, 1953-55. Mem. ABA (standing com. on fed. judiciary 1979-86), L.A. County Bar Assn., Mex.-Am. Bar Assn. of L.A.(pres. 1971), Am. Bd. Trial Advocates (pres. L.A. chpt. 1979), Law Soc., Internat. Acad. Trial Judges, Nat. Conf. Met. Cts. (bd. dirs. 2000—, exec. com. 2000—). Office: Dept 96 111 N Hill St Los Angeles CA 90012-3117 Office Phone: 213-893-1021.

CHAVEZ-HOUCK, REBECCA, state legislator; b. May 17; m. Martin Chavez-Houck. BA, MPA, U. Utah. Pub. rels.; mem. Dist. 24 Utah House of Reps., 2009—. Democrat. Office: W030 State Capitol Complex Salt Lake City UT 84114 Mailing: 643 16th Ave Salt Lake City UT 84103 Office Phone: 801-538-1029, 801-608-4467. Office Fax: 801-538-1908. Business E-Mail: rchouck@utah.gov.

CHAVIRA-SLIVA, CLARICE F. See SILVA, CLARICE F.

CHAYKIN, ROBERT LEROY, manufacturing and marketing executive; b. Miami, Fla., May 2, 1944; s. Allan Leroy and Ruth Chaykin; m. Patty Jean Patton, Feb. 1971 (div. May 1975); children: Stephanie Lee, Michele Alee; m. Evalyn Marcy Slodzina, Sept. 3, 1989; children: Catrina Celia, Ally Sue. BA in Polit. Sci., U. Miami, Fla., 1965, LLB, 1969. Owner, operator Serrating Svcs. Miami, 1969-71, Serrating Svcs. Las Vegas, Nev., 1971-84; pres. Ser-Sharp Mfg., Inc., Las Vegas, 1984—; nat. mktg. dir. Coserco Corp., Las Vegas, 1987—2006; owner, agt. AAABA Bail Bonds, Las Vegas, Nev., 2006—. Patentee in mfg. field. With US Army, 1962. Recipient 2d degree black belt Tae Kwon Do, Profl. Karate Assn., 1954—61. Avocations: travel, camping. Office Phone: 702-643-3333. Personal E-mail: sersharp1@hotmail.com.

CHAZEN, STEPHEN I., oil industry executive; b. Buffalo, Aug. 26, 1946; s. Michael M. and Marcia Chazen; m. Patricia L. Orr, Dec. 18, 1971. AB, Rutgers U., 1968; PhD, Mich. State U., 1973; MS, U. Houston, 1977. Lab. mgr. Northrop Svcs., Inc., Houston, 1973-77; dir. project evaluation Columbia Gas Devel. Corp., Houston, 1977-81; v.p. Merrill Lynch, Houston, 1982-86, mng. dir. NYC, 1987-93; exec. v.p. Occidental Petroleum Corp., LA, 1994—2004, sr. exec. v.p, 2004—07, CFO, 1999—, pres., 2007—. Bd. dirs. Washington Mutual, Inc., 2008. Office: Occidental Petroleum Corp 10889 Wilshire Blvd Los Angeles CA 90024-4201

CHEADLE, DONALD FRANK, actor; b. Kansas City, Mo., Nov. 29, 1964; 2 children. Actor: (films) 3 Days, 1984, Moving Violations, 1985, Punk, 1986, Hamburger Hill, 1987, Colors, 1988, Roadside Prophets, 1992, The Meteor Man, 1993, Things to Do in Denver When You're Dead, 1995, Devil in a Blue Dress, 1995, Rosewood, 1997, Volcano, 1997, Boogie Nights, 1997, Bulworth, 1998, Out of Sight, 1998, Mission to Mars, 2000, The Family Man, 2000, Traffic, 2000, Things Behind the Sun, 2000, Manic, 2001, Swordfish, 2001, Rush Hour 2, 2001, Ocean's Eleven, 2001, The Hire: Ticker, 2002, The United States of Leland, 2003, The Assassination of Richard Nixon, 2004, Hotel Rwanda, 2004, Ocean's Twelve, 2004, The Other Side of Simple, 2006, The Dog Problem, 2006, Reign Over Me, 2007, Ocean's Thirteen, 2007, Talk To Me, 2007 (Best Actor, African Am. Film Critics Assn., 2007), Traitor, 2008, Hotel for Dogs, 2009; actor, prodr. (films) Crash, 2004 (winner, Outstanding Performance by a Cast in Motion Picture, SAG awards, 2006, Best First Feature, Independent Spirit award, 2006); actor: (TV films) Lush Life, 1993, Rebound: The Legend of Earl The Goat Manigault, 1996, The Rat Pack, 1998 (Golden Globe award for Best Performance in a Supporting Role, 1999), A Lesson Before Dying, 1999, Fail Safe, 2000, (TV appearances) Hill Street Blues, 1981, Fame, 1982, L.A. Law, 1986, The Bronx Zoo, 1987, Hooperman, 1988, Night Court, 1984, Booker, 1989, China Beach, 1988, The Simpsons, 1989, The Fresh Prince of Bel-Air, 1990, Picket Fences, 1992, The Golden Palace, 1992, Hangin' with Mr. Cooper, 1992, The Bernie Mac Show, 2001, ER, 2002; co-author (with John Prendergast): Not on Our Watch: The Mission to End Genocide in Darfur and Beyond, 2007 (NAACP Image award for Outstanding Literary Work-Non-Fiction, 2008); prodr.: (TV series) Crash, 2008. Named to Power 150, Ebony mag., 2008. Office: c/o Liberman-Zerman Mgmt 252 North Larchmont Blvd Los Angeles CA 90004

CHEATHAM, ROBERT WILLIAM, retired lawyer; b. St. Paul, June 4, 1938; s. Robert William and Hildegard Frances Cheatham; m. Kay C. Sarnecki, Mar. 20, 1964; children: Ann Marie, Lynn Marie, Paul William. BCE, U. Minn., 1961, JD, 1966. Bar: Calif. 1967, U.S. Dist. Ct. (no. dist.) Calif. 1967. Assoc. Brobeck, Phleger & Harrison, San Francisco, 1967-74, ptnr., 1974-88, Cheatham & Skovronski, San Francisco, 1988-96, Cheatham & Tomlinson, San Francisco, 1996-97, Cassidy, Cheatham, Shimko & Dawson, San Francisco, 1997-2000, Foley & Lardner, San Francisco, 2000—04; ret., 2004. Speaker on continuing legal edn., San Francisco. Co-author: Calif. Attorneys Guide to Real Estate Syndicates, 1970, Cheatham and Merritt California Real Estate Forms and Commentaries, 1984-90. Mem. ABA, Calif. Bar Assn. Business E-Mail: rwcheatham@sbcglobal.net.

CHEDID, JOHN GEORGE, bishop emeritus; b. Eddid, Lebanon, July 4, 1923; Educated, Sems. in Lebanon and Pontifical Urban Coll., Rome. Ordained priest Faithful of the Oriental Rite, 1951; priest Eparchy of St. Maron of Bklyn., 1977, aux. bishop, 1980—94; ordained bishop, 1981; bishop Eparchy of Our Lady of Lebanon of LA, 1994—2000, bishop emeritus, 2000—. Roman Catholic. Office: Our Lady of Lebanon Ch 333 S San Vicente Blvd Los Angeles CA 90048-3313 also: PO Box 16397 Beverly Hills CA 90209 Office Phone: 310-247-8322. Office Fax: 310-858-0856.

CHEESEMAN, DOUGLAS TAYLOR, JR., wildlife tour executive, photographer, educator; b. Honolulu, July 16, 1937; s. Douglas Taylor Cheeseman and Myra Bettencourt; m. Gail Macomber, Apr. 7, 1963; children: Rosie M., Ted F. BA, San Jose State U., Calif., 1959, MA, 1964. Cert. secondary tchr., Calif. Naturalist Crater Lake (Oreg.) Nat. Park, summers 1959-60; tchr. biology Woodside High Sch., Redwood City, Calif., 1961-65; teaching asst. U. Colo., Boulder, 1966-67; prof. biology De Anza Coll., Cupertino, Calif., 1967—, dir. environ. study area, 1970—, dir. Student Ecology Rsch. Lab., 1990—; pres. Cheeseman's Ecology Safaris, Saratoga, Calif., 1981-98; expedition leader Ioffe, Antarctic, 1998—. Instr. wildlife and natural history photography, Saratoga, 1984—; rsch. cooperator Fish and Wilflife Svc., 1972—; spkr. Calif. Acad. Antarctic Ecology, Am. Acad. African Birds, 1996; expdn. leader Sengey Vavilov, Antarctic, 1994; active in saving flora and fauna in third world; expdn. leader, Antarctica, 1996, ship Alla Tarasova, 1996; expdn. leader in Antarctic, 1998, 2000, Polar Star Antartic, 2002, 04, 06, 07, 08; lectr., spkr. in field. Photographs represented in books and on calendars. Recipient Outstanding Svc. and Tchr. award, Pres.'s award De Anza Coll., 1988, Nat. Leadership award U. Tex., Austin, 1989; NSF fellow, 1969, 71; NEDA Title III grantee, 1970. Mem. Ecol. Soc. Am., Am. Ornithologists Union, Am. Soc. Mammalogists, Brit. Trust Ornitology, Brit. Ornithologists Union, AfricanWildlife Soc., Marine Mammal Soc. (founding), Calif. Native Plants Soc., Bay Area Bird Photographers (co-founder), Santa Clara Valley Audubon Soc. (bd. dirs., v.p., program chmn. 1983—), Cooper Soc. Avocations: wildlife research and photography, rainforest conservation. Home: 20800 Kittridge Rd Saratoga CA 95070-6322 Office: De Anza Coll Dept Biology Cupertino CA 95014 Office Phone: 408-741-5330. Personal E-mail: info@cheeseman.com, doug@cheesemans.com.

CHEETHAM, ALAN HERBERT, paleontologist; b. El Paso, Tex., Jan. 30, 1928; s. Herbert and Hildegard Marguerite (Moreton) C.; m. Marjorie Rogers, Apr. 20, 1951; children: Alan Christopher, Jan Alison, Susan Hilarie, Hilary Taber. BS, N.Mex. Inst. Mining & Tech., 1950; MS, La. State U., 1952; PhD, Columbia U., 1959. Instr. paleontology La. State U., Baton Rouge, 1954-60, asst. prof., 1960-63, assoc. prof., 1963-66, cons. prof., 1966-72; assoc. curator Smithsonian Instn., Washington, 1966-69, curator, 1969-87, sr. invertebrate paleontologist, 1987-2001, sr. scientist emeritus, 2001—. Guest prof. U. Stockholm, 1964—65; adj. prof. U. N.Mex., 1994—97. Author: Geological Society of America, Memoir 91, 1963; editor: Animal Colonies, 1973, Fossil Invertebrates, 1987; contbr. articles to profl. jours. Recipient Raymond C. Moore medal for paleontol., 1997, Disting. Achievement Alumni award, N.Mex. Inst. Mining and Tech., 1990; fellow Humble Oil Co., 1951, NSF, 1952, 1961. Fellow: Paleontol. Soc. (medal 2001), AAAS; mem.: Paleontol. Rsch. Instn., Soc. Sedimentary Geology, Internat. Bryozoology Assn. Home and Office: 3101 Old Pecos Trail 647 Santa Fe NM 87505 Office Phone: 505-955-1840. Business E-Mail: cheethamam@msn.com.

CHEEVER, SHARON ANN, insurance company executive, lawyer; b. LA, Calif., May 5, 1955; BA, BS in Psychology & Sociology, San Diego St. U., 1982; JD magna cum laude, U. San Diego, 1982. Bar: Calif. 1983. Assoc. O'Melveny & Myers LLP, 1982—86; asst. v.p. Pacific Life Ins. Co., Newport Beach, Calif., 1986—92, v.p., investment coun., 1992—2008, sr. v.p., gen. coun., 2008—. Exec. editor San Diego Law Rev., 1981—82; bd. dir. Pacific Life Ins. Co., 2008—. Recipient Am. Jurisprudence Awards in Torts, Civil and Criminal Procedure. Mem.: Calif. Bar Assn., Assn. Life Ins. Coun., Am. Coll. Investment Coun. Office: Pacific Life Ins Co Legal Dept 700 Newport Center Dr Newport Beach CA 92660 E-mail: sharon.cheever@pacific.com.

CHEIFETZ, LORNA GALE, psychologist; b. Phoenix, Mar. 22, 1953; d. Walter and Ruth Cheifetz. BS, Chapman Coll., Orange, Calif., 1975; D of Psychology, Ill. Sch. Profl. Psychology, 1981. Psychology intern Cook County Hosp., Chgo., 1979-80; clin. psychologist City of Chgo., 1980-84, Phoenix Inst. for Psychotherapy, 1984-87; pvt. practice Phoenix, 1987—. Cons. to judges, attys., cts., 1984—; adj. faculty Met. U., Phoenix, 1984-88, Ill. Sch. Profl. Psychology, 1982-86. Contbr. chpt. to book Listening and Interpreting, 1984; contbg. editor Internat. Jour. Communicative Psychoanalysis and Psychotherapy, 1991-93. Cons., vol. Ariz. Bar Assn. Vol. Lawyer Program, 1985—; co-coord. Psychology Info. Referral Svc., Maricopa County, Ariz., 1984-96. Named Psychologist of Yr. Ariz. Bar Assn., 1987, 95, 99. Mem. APA (activist 1989—), Nat. Register Health Svc. Providers in Psychology. Home: 2633 E Indian School Rd Ste 365 Phoenix AZ 85016-6777

CHEIT, EARL FRANK, economist, educator; b. Mpls., Aug. 5, 1926; s. Morris and Etta (Warshausky) C.; m. June Doris Andrews, Aug. 28, 1950; children: Wendy, David, Ross, Julie. BS, U. Minn., 1947, LLB, 1949, PhD, 1954. Rsch. economist, prof. Sch. Bus. Adminstrn. U. Calif., Berkeley, 1960—, exec. vice chancellor, 1965-69, dean Sch. Bus. Adminstrn., 1976-82, 90-91, dean emeritus Sch. Bus. Adminstrn., 1995; dir. Inst. Indsl. Rels. Program officer in charge higher edn. and rsch. Ford Found., 1972-73; assoc. dir., sr. rsch. fellow Carnegie Coun. on Policy Studies in Higher Edn., 1973-75; sr. adv. con. Asian-Pacific econ. affairs Asia Found.; dir. CNF Transp., Inc., Shaklee Corp., 1976-2001, Simpson Mfg. Corp. Author: The Useful Arts and the Liberal Tradition, 1975, The New Depression in Higher Education, 1971, Foundations and Higher Education, 1979; editor: The Business Establishment, 1964. Trustee Richmond (Calif.) Unified Sch. Dist., 1961-65, Russell Sage Found., NYC, 1979-89, Mills Coll., 1991-; chmn. State of Calif. Wage Bd. for Agrl. Occupations, 1980-81. Office: U Calif Haas Sch Bus Berkeley CA 94720-1900 Office Phone: 510-642-2448. Business E-Mail: cheit@haas.berkeley.edu.

CHELAPATI, CHUNDURI VENKATA, civil engineering educator; b. Eluru, India, Mar. 11, 1933; came to U.S., 1957, naturalized, 1971; s. Lakshminarayana and Anjamma (Kanumuri) Chunduri. B.E. with honors, Andhra U., India, 1954; diploma in civil and hydraulics, Indian Inst. Sci., Bangalore, India, 1956; MS, U. Ill., 1959, PhD, 1962. Jr. engr. Office of Chief Engr., State of Andhra, India, 1954-55; asst. prof. structural engring. Birla Coll. Engring., Pilani, India, 1956-57; research asst. dept. civil engring. U. Ill., 1957-62; asst. prof. engring. Calif. State U., Los Angeles, 1962-65, assoc. prof. Long Beach, 1965-70, prof. civil engring., 1970—96, vice chmn. dept., 1971-73, chmn. dept., 1973-79, coordinator profl. engring. rev. programs, 1972-81, dir. continuing engring. edn., 1982—96, dir. CADDS Research Ctr., 1986—96; pres. C.V. Chelapati & Assos., Inc., Huntington Beach, Calif., 1979—2001. Cons. USN Civil Engring. Lab., 1962—68, 1975—94, Holmes & Narver, Inc., Anaheim, Calif., 1968—73; pres. Profl. Engring. Devel. Publs., 1988—, Continuing Profl. Edn. Inst., 2000—, Irvine Institute of Technology, 2002—. Contbr. articles to profl. jours. Mem. ASCE, Am. Soc. Engring. Edn., Structural Engrs. Assn. So. Calif., Earthquake Engring. Research Inst., Seismol. Soc. Am., Am. Concrete Inst., Am. Inst. Steel Constrn., Sigma Xi, Chi Epsilon, Tau Beta Pi, Phi Kappa Phi. Office: 8659 Research Dr Ste 200 Irvine CA 92618 Home: 21 Shadowcast Newport Coast CA 92657-1647 Home Phone: 949-715-0536; Office Phone: 949-585-9137. Business E-Mail: cvc@irvine-institute.org.

CHELLAM, KRIS, data processing executive; Cert. in Edn., Cambridge U., 1968; Degree in Acctg., U. London, 1975. Chartered acct., Inst. Chartered Accts. Eng., 1975, Inst. Chartered Accts. Wales, 1975. Fin. mgr. Intel Corp., 1979—91; v.p. fin. & adminstrn., CFO Atmel Corp., 1991—98; sr. v.p. fin., CFO Xilinx, Inc., San Jose, Calif., 1998—. Office: Xilinx Inc 2100 Logic Drive San Jose CA 95124-3400

CHEMERINSKY, ERWIN, dean, law educator; b. Chgo., May 14, 1953; s. Arthur and Raeda Chemerinsky; m. Catherine Fisk, 1993; 4 children. BS, Northwestern U., 1975; JD cum laude, Harvard U., 1978. Bar: Ill. 1978, D.C. 1979. Atty. civil divsn. US Dept. Justice, Washington, 1978—79; assoc. Dobrovir, Oates & Gebhardt, Washington, 1979—80; asst.prof.law De Paul U., Chgo., 1980—83, assoc. prof., 1983—84, U. So. Calif., LA, 1984—87, prof., 1987—2004; Alston & Bird prof. law Duke U., Durham, NC, 2004—; founding dean Donald Bren Sch. Law U. Calif., Irvine, 2008—. Vis. assoc. prof. U. So. Calif., 1983—84; mem. task force Diversity State Govt. Gov., 1999—2000; lectr. in field. Author: Interpreting the Constitution, 1987, 1990 Supplement to Federal Jurisdiction, 1990, 1992 Supplement to Federal Jurisdiction, 1992, Federal Jurisdiction, 1989, Constitutional Law: Principles and Policies, 1997, Constitutional Law, 2001, Supreme Ct. Rev.: October 2000 Term, 2001, 17th Annual Section 1983 Civil Rights Litigation, 2001, Fourth Annual Supreme Court Review: October 2001 Term, 2003, Enhancing Government: Federalism for the 21st Century, 2008; mem. editl. adv. bd.: Calif. Lawyer, 1994, Aspen (Colo.) Law & Bus., 2001—. Bd. dirs. Progressive Jewish Alliance, 2000—; bd. dirs., regional coun. Am. Jewish Congress, 1993—98; chmn. LA (Calif.) Charter Reform Commn., 1997—99. Recipient Clarence Darrow award, People's Coll. Law, 2001, Community Svc. award, Anti-Defamation League, 2001, We. Ctr. on Law & Poverty, 2001, President's award, Criminal Courts Bar Assn., 2003, Freedom of Info. award, Soc. Profl. Journalists, 2003; named one of The Most Influential Lawyers in Calif., Daily Jour., 1998—2003, The Top 20 Legal Thinkers in America, Legal Affairs, 2005. Mem.: AAUP (litigation com. 1991—95), ABA (tech. asst. constn. drafting), ACLU (bd. dirs. 1987—98, exec. com. 1991—98), Am. Assn. Law Schs. (planning com. mini workshop 1989, steering com. profl. responsibility 1987—90, task force profl. responsibility 1987). Office: Donald Bren Sch Law U Calif Irvine Irvine CA 92697

CHEMLA, DANIEL S., physics educator; Grad., l'Ecole Nat. Super Telecomms., Paris; DSc, U. Paris, 1972. Mem. tech. staff, group leader, dept. head Ctr. Nat. d'Etudes des Telecomms., Berkeley; with AT&T Bell Labs., Holmdel, NJ, 1981-83, head of quantum physics and electonic rsch. dept., 1983-91; prof. physics, dir. materials scis. divsn. Lawrence Berkeley Nat. Lab., U. Calif., Berkeley, 1991—; dir. Advanced Light Source U. Calif., Berkeley, 1998—. Contbr. articles to profl. jours. Fellow IEEE (Quantum Electronics award 1995, Humboldt Rsch. award 1995), Optical Soc. Am. (R. W. Wood prize 1988), Am. Phys. Soc.; mem. NAS. Achievements include research in manybody interactions and quantum size effects in semiconductor nanostructures and detection and spectroscopy of single molecules and single molecular paris. Fax: 510-486-7769. E-mail: dschemla@lbl.gov.

CHEN, ARTHUR, physician, hospital administrator; BS in Zoology, U. Calif., Davis, MD. Resident in social medicine Montefiore Hosp./Albert Einstein Coll. of Medicine, Bronx; clin. and family physician Asian Health Svcs., Oakland, 1983—; former emergency room physician/instructor, assoc. med. dir. Inst. of Emergency Medicine, Albert Einstein Coll. of Medicine, Bronx; former exec. dir. Chinatown Health Clinic, NYC; health officer Alameda County, 1996—2001; med. dir. Alameda Alliance for Health, 2001—. Mem. planning com. Nat. Assn. of County & City Health Officials Mobilization for Action Through Planning and Partnerships; bd. chair Asian and Pacific Islander Am. Health Forum; mem. Kellogg Nat. Fellowship Program, 1989—92; fellow Public Health Leadership Inst., 1996—97; exec. com. mem. Calif. Conference of Local Health Officers, 1997—2001; mem. CDC/Agy. for Toxic Substances & Disease Registry Task Force on Public Health Workforce Develop., 1999, Task Force on Culturally and Linguistically Competent Physicians and Dentists, Calif. Dept. Consumer Affairs, 2001—. Bd. dirs. Calif. Endowment, 2003—, vice chair, bd. dirs., 2004—. Mem.: Alameda Contra Costa County Med. Assn. (exec. councilmember 1999—2000). Office: Alameda Alliance for Health 1240 S Loop Rd Alameda CA 94502

CHEN, IRVIN SHAO YU, microbiologist, educator; b. Toms River, NJ, Sept. 29, 1955; s. Tseh-An and Cheh-Chen (Chang) C.; m. Diven Sun, June 21, 1981; children: Katrina Nai Ching, Kevin Nai Hong. BA, Cornell U., 1977; PhD, U. Wis., 1981. Asst. prof. UCLA Sch. Medicine, 1984-86, assoc. prof., 1986-90, prof., 1990—. Dir. AIDS Inst. UCLA, 1991—, Core BSL3 SCID-hu Mouse Lab., 1989—, Core Human REtrovirus Lab., 1989—, AIDS Ctr. Virology Lab., 1986, UCLA Sch. of Medicine Core Human Retrovirus Facility, 1989; Wellcome vis. prof. microbiology East Carolina U., 1993; bd. dirs. Arthur Ashe Found. for the Defeat of AIDS. Mem. editl. adv. bd. Oncogene, 1986, Cancer Cells, 1989; mem. editl. bd. AIDS Rsch. and Human Retrovirus, 1990, Jour. of Virology, 1991; contbr. articles to Sci., Nature, Cell; contbr. chpt.: HTLV-I and HTLV-II in Virology, 1990. Grantee NIH, 1982—, U. Calif. U. Task Force on AIDS, 1986—; recipient Jr. Faculty award Am. Cancer Soc., 1984, Scholar award Leukemia Soc. Am., 1989, Stohlman Scholar award, 1992, Jr. Faculty award Am. Cancer Soc., 1984, Richard F. Dwyer-Eleanor W. Dwyer Award for Exellence Jonsson Comprehensive Cancer Ctr., 1984, Merit award Nat. Cancer Inst. Mem. AAAS, Am. Soc. Microbiology, Jonsson Comprehensive Cancer Ctr. Achievements include patent for retroviral polypeptides associated with human transformation; first to achieve molecular cloning of human T-cell leukemia virus type II, discovery of trans-activation gene as essential gene for HTLV-II, molecular basis for HIV-1 tropism for macrophages. Office: UCLA Sch Medicine Dept Medicine and Immunology 11-934 Factor Los Angeles CA 90024-1678

CHEN, JOHN S., computer company executive; b. Hong Kong, July 1, 1955; came to U.S., 1974; s. Peter and Harmie (Lee) C.; m. Sherry Hai, Nov. 5, 1980; children: Jacqueline, Stephanie. BSEE, Brown U., 1978; MSEE, Calif. Inst. Tech., 1979. V.p. pres., gen. mgr. Unisys, Blue Bell, Pa., 1979-91; exec. v.p. Pyramid Tech., San Jose, Calif., 1991—92, COO, 1992—95, pres., 1993—95, CEO, 1995—97; pres. Sybase, Inc., Dublin, Calif., 1997—, chmn., CEO, 1998—. Mem., bd. dirs., Sybase, Inc., 1997-, Walt Disney Co., 2003- Republican. Roman Catholic. Office: Sybase Inc One Sybase Dr Dublin CA 94568

CHEN, LU, neurobiologist, biology professor; BS, U. Sci. and Tech., China, 1993; PhD, U. So. Calif., 1998. Postdoctoral fellow U. So. Calif., 1998—99, U. Calif., San Francisco, 1999—2002, asst. prof. neurobiology Berkeley, 2003—, mem., Helen Wills Neuroscience Inst. Author: (articles) published in journals such as Nature, Jour. of Neuroscience, and Proceedings of the Nat. Acad. of Sciences USA. Named an Disting. Young Scholars in Med. Rsch., W.M. Keck Found., 2005; MacArthur Fellow, John D. and Catherine T. MacArthur Found., 2005. Office: Univ Calif Berkeley Dept Molecular & Cell Biology 124 Life Sciences Addition # 3200 Berkeley CA 94720-3200 Office Phone: 510-643-8163. Office Fax: 510-643-6791. E-mail: luchen@berkeley.edu.

CHEN, SHOEI-SHENG, retired mechanical engineer; b. Taiwan, Jan. 26, 1940; s. Yung-cheng and A-shu Chen; m. Ruth C. Lee, June 28, 1969; children: Lyrice, Lisa, Steve. BS, Nat. Taiwan U., 1963; MS, Princeton U., 1966, MA, 1967, PhD, 1968. Rsch. asst. Princeton U., 1965—68; asst. mech. engr. Argonne Nat. Lab., Ill., 1968—71, mech. engr., 1971—80, sr. mech. engr., 1980—2001; ret., 2001. Cons. to Internat. Atomic Energy Agy. to assist developing countries in R & D of nuc. reator sys. components, 1977, 79, 80, 94; cons. NASA, NRC, Rockwell Internat., others. Author: Flow-Induced Vibration of Circular Cylinderical Structures, 1987; mem. internat. adv. editl. bd. Acta Mechanica Solida; adv. bd. JSME Internat. Jour.; assoc. editor Applied Mechs. Rev., Jour. of Pressure Vessels Tech.; contbr. articles to profl. jours. Recipient Disting. Performance award U. Chgo., 1986, ASME pressure vessel and piping medal, 2001. Fellow ASME (chmn. tech. subcom. on fluid and structure interactions pressure vessels and piping divsn. 1987-90, honors chmn. 1990-94, exec. com. 1990-96, organizer symposia, tech. program chmn. 1994, conf. chair ASME/JSME pressure vessels and piping conf. 1995, pressure vessels and piping divsn., chmn. 1995-96, senate pres. 1997-98, honors and awards chair of materials and structures tech. group 1996-99), Instn. Diagnostic Engrs.; mem. Am. Acad. Mechanics, Acoustical Soc. Am., Sigma Xi. Personal E-mail: ss@sschen.com. E-mail: sschen88@gmail.com.

CHEN, STEPHEN SHI-HUA, pathologist, biochemist; b. Taipei, Taiwan, Republic of China, Dec. 25, 1939; came to U.S., 1965; s. Ah-wen and Shun (Pan) C.; m. Hsin-Hsin Yii, July 5, 1969; children: Peter T., Margaret T. MD, Nat. Taiwan U., 1964; PhD, U. Pitts, 1972. Diplomate Am. Bd. of Pathology. Asst. prof. pathology U. Pitts., 1972-76; staff pathologist Presbyn. Hosp., Pitts., 1973-76; asst. prof. pathology dept. Stanford U., Palo Alto, Calif., 1976-80, clin. assoc. prof. pathology dept., 1980-96, clin. prof., 1996—; staff pathologist Veterans Affairs Med. Ctr., Palo Alto, 1976—. Contbr. articles to Jour. Cellular Physiology, Jour. Chromatography, Clinica Chimca Acta. Fellow Coll. Am. Pathologists; mem. Am. Soc. Investigative Pathology, U.S. and Can. Acad. Pathology Inc., Am. Soc. Clin. Pathologists, Am. Soc. Cytopathology. Achievements include chromatography of phospholipids. Office: Vets Affairs Med Ctr 113 3801 Miranda Ave Palo Alto CA 94304-1207

CHEN, STEVE SHIH, Internet company executive; b. Aug. 1978; Student in Computer Sci., U. Ill., Urbana-Champaign. With PayPal, 1999—2005, Facebook; co-founder, chief tech. adv. YouTube Inc. (sold to Google in 2006), San Mateo, Calif., 2005—. Recipient Vanguard award, Prodrs. Guild of America, 2008; named (with Chad Hurley) Webby Person of Yr., 2007; named one of 50 Who Matter Now, CNNMoney.com Bus. 2.0, 2006, The World's Most Influential People, TIME mag., 2007, The 25 Most Influential People in Web Music, Powergeek 25, 2007, 50 Most Important People on the Web, PC World, 2007. Fellow: World Tech. Network (with Chad Hurley) World Tech. award-Entertainment 2006). Office: Youtube INC 1000 Cherry Ave FL 2 San Bruno CA 94066-2315

CHEN, TONY F., mathematics professor, dean; BS in Engring., Calif. Inst. Tech., 1973, MS in Aeronautics, 1973; PhD in Computer Sci., Stanford U., 1978. Rsch. fellow, applied math dept. Calif. Inst. Tech., 1978—79; asst. prof., computer sci. dept. Yale U., 1979—84, assoc. prof., computer sci. dept., 1984—86; prof., dept. math. UCLA, 1986—, grad. vice chair, math. dept., 1996—97, chair, math dept., 1997—2000, dean, phys. sciences, 2001—08; asst. dir. math. and phys. sciences NSF, 2008—. Prin. investigator, bd. trustee Inst. for Pure and Applied Math., UCLA, 1999—, dir., 2000—01; mem., Nat. Com. on Math. Nat. Acad.; mem. adv. com. Lawrence Livermore Nat. Lab. Computation Directorate, 2000—04; mem. U. Space Rsch. Assn. Sci. Coun. for Applied Math. and Computer Sci.; one of five delegates representing the US at the Gen. Assembly at the Internat. Math. union, Santiago de Compostela, Spain, 2006; co-dir. UCLA, NIH Ctr. for Computational Biology. Mem. editl. bd. Soc. Indsl. and Applied Math. Jour. Scientific Computing, Asian Jour. Math.; contbr. articles to rsch. publs. Mem.: Assn. for Computing Machinery, IEEE (won two best paper award), NSF (mem. adv. com., math. and phys. sci. 1999—2002, chair, search com. for dir. NSF divsn. math. sciences 2002, mem. com. visitors, divsn. math. sci., asst. dir., math and phys. sciences 2006—), Am. Math. Soc. (chair., com. on committees 1999—, mem. editl. bd.), Soc. Indsl. and Applied Math. (chair, com. on sci. policy, bd. trustee 2000—, former mem. com. human rights). Office: UCLA Math Dept MS 7519E Box 951555 Los Angeles CA 90095-1555 Address: UCLA Math Dept 520 Portola Plz Math Sciences Bldg 6363 Mailcode 155505 Los Angeles CA 90095 also: Dept Math UCLA Inst Pure and Applied Math 1158A IPAM Bldg Box 957121 Los Angeles CA 90095-7121 Office Phone: 310-825-2601. Office Fax: 310-206-6673. Business E-Mail: chan@math.ucla.edu.

CHEN, WAI-FAH, civil engineering educator; b. Chekiang, China, Dec. 23, 1936; m. Lily Chen; children: Eric, Arnold, Brian. BS, Cheng-Kung U., 1959; MS, Lehigh U., 1963; PhD, Brown U., 1966. From asst. prof. to prof. civil engring. Lehigh U., 1966-76; prof. civil engring. Purdue U., Lafayette, Ind., 1976-92, head structural engring., 1980-99, George E. Goodwin disting. prof., 1992-99; dean engring. U. Hawaii, Honolulu, 1999—2006. Cons. Exxon Products, 1979, Karagozian & Case Structural Engrs., 1985, Ga. Tech., 1987, Skidmore, Owings & Merrill, 1987, World Bank, 1988—. Editor-in-chief The Handbook of Structural Engineering, 1997, Bridge Engineering Handbook, 1999, Earthquake Engineering Handbook, 2002, The Civil Engring. Handbook, 2d edit., 2002. Mem.: ASCE (hon.), Academia Sinica, Nat. Acad. Engring., Am. Inst. Steel Constrn., Am. Concrete Inst., Am. Acad. Mech., Structural Stability Rsch. Coun., Internat. Assn. Bridge & Structural Engring. Office: U Hawaii Dept Civil and Environ Engring 2540 Dole St Holmes Hall 383 Honolulu HI 96822-2303 Office Phone: 808-956-9618. Personal E-mail: chenwilfred@hotmail.com. Business E-Mail: chenwf@eng.hawaii.edu.

CHEN, WAI-KAI, electrical engineering and computer science educator, consultant; arrived in US, 1959, naturalized, 1966; s. You-Chao and Shui-Tan (Shen) C.; m. Shirley Shiao-Ling, Jan. 13, 1939; children— Jerome, Melissa BS in Elec. Engring., Ohio U., 1960, MS in Elec. Engring., 1961; PhD in Elec. Engring., U. Ill., Urbana, 1964. Asst. prof. Ohio U., 1964-67, assoc. prof., 1967-71, prof., 1971-78, disting. prof., 1978-81; prof., head dept. elec. engring. and computer sci. U. Ill., Chgo., 1981-2001, prof. emeritus, 2001—; vis. assoc. prof. Purdue U., 1970-71; v.p. internat. tech. U. Santa Clara, Calif., 1999—2005. Hon. prof. Tianjing U., Peoples Republic of China, 1990, Beijing U. of Posts and Telecomms., Beijing U. of Aeronautics and Astronautics, 1992. Author: Applied Graph Theory, 1970, Theory and Design of Broadband Matching Networks, 1976, Applied Graph Theory: Graphs and Electrical Networks, 1976, Active Network and Feedback Amplifier Theory, 1980, Linear Networks and Systems, 1983, Passive and Active Filters: Theory and Implementations, 1986, The Collected Papers of Professor Wai-Kai Chen, 1987, Broadband Matching: Theory and Implementations, 1988, Theory of Nets, 1990, Linear Networks and Systems: Computer-Aided Solutions and Implementations, 1990, Active Network Analysis, 1991, Modern Network Analysis, 1992, Computer-Aided Design of Comm. Networks World Scientific, 2000, Circuit Analysis and Feedback Amplifier Theory, 2005, Nonlinear and Distribution Circuits, 2005, Passive, Active and Digital Filters, 2005, Feedback Networks: Theory and Circuit Applications, 2007; editor: Brooks/Cole Series in Electrical Engineering, 1982-84; editor in chief Advanced Series in Elec. and Computer Engring., 1986—, Jour. Circuits, Sys. and Computers, 1989—, The Circuits and Filters Handbook, 1995, 2nd edit., 2003, 3rd edit., 2009, The VLSI Handbook, 2000, 2nd edit., 2006, Design Automation, Languages and Simulations, 2003, VLSI Technology, 2003, Memory, Microprocessor and ASIC, 2003, Analog Circuits and Devices, 2003, Logic Design, 2003, VLSI Technology, 2003, The Electrical Engineering Handbook, 2004, Passive, Active and Digital Filters, 2005, Circuit Analysis and Feedback Amplifier Theory, 2005, Nonlinear and Distributed Circuits, 2005, Feedback Networks: Theory and Circuit Applications, 2007; editor: The VLSI Series, 2000—; assoc. editor Jour. Circuits, Systems and Signal Processing, 1981-04; editor in charge Advanced Series in Circuits and Systems, World Scientific Publ. Co., 1991—; sect. editor Encyclopedia of Physical Science & Technology, 1998-2001. Recipient Lester R. Ford award Math. Assn. Am., 1967, Baker Fund award Ohio U., 1974, 78, Disting. Accomplishment award Chinese Acad. & Profl. Assn. in Mid-Am., 1985, Disting. Guest Prof. award Chuo U., Tokyo, 1987, Outstanding Svc. award Chinese Acad. & Profl. Assn. in Mid-Am., 1988, Outstanding Achievement award Mid-Am. Chinese Sci. & Tech. Assn, 1988, Disting. Alumnus award Elec. and Computer Engring. Dept. Alumni Assn. U. Ill. Urbana-Champaign, 1988, Alexander von Humboldt award Alexander von Humboldt Stiftung, Fed. Republic of Germany, 1985, Rsch. award U. Ill. Chgo. Coll. Engring., 2000, hon. prof. award Nanjing Inst. of Technology and Zhejing U., Peoples Republic of China, 1985, The Northeast U. Tech., East China Inst. Tech., Nanjing Inst. of Posts & Telecommunications, AnHui U., Chengdu Inst. Radio Engring., Wuhan Univ.; Rsch. Inst. fellow Ohio U., 1972, Japan Soc. for Promotion of Sci., 1986, Sr. U. Scholar award U. Ill., 1986, Ohio U. Alumni Medal Merit for Disting. Achievement in Engring. Edn., 1987, Hon. Prof. award Hangzhan U. of Electronic Tech., China, 1990, Disting. Prof. award Internat. Technol. U., 1995, Hon. Prof. award Taichung U. Healthcare and Mgmt., Taiwan, 2002, Disting. Alumnus award Taipei U. Sci. and Tech., Taiwan, 2002, Certificate of Spl. Congl. Recognition, 2004. Fellow IEEE (Circuits and Sys. Soc. Meritorious Svc. award 1997, Edn. award 1998, Golden Jubilee medal 2000, Third Millennium medal 2000), AAAS; mem. NSPE, IEEE Cirs. and Sys. Soc. (adminstrv. com. 1985-87, exec. v.p. 1987, assoc. editor Trans. on Cirs. and Sys. 1977-79, editor 1991-93, pres.-elect 1993, pres. 1994), Md.-Am. Chinese Sci. and Tech. Assn. (bd. dirs. 1984-86, 89-93, pres. 1991-92), Chinese Acad. and Profl. Assn. Mid-Am. (advisor to bd. dirs. 1984-89, pres. 1986-87), Soc. Indsl. and Applied Math., Assn. Computing Machinery, Tensor Soc. Gt. Britain, Sigma Xi (sec.-treas. Ohio U. chpt. 1981), Phi Kappa Phi, Eta Kappa Nu. Office: Internat Technol U 3802 Belmont Ter Fremont CA 94539-8358 Office Phone: 408-556-9031. Business E-Mail: wkchen@ece.uic.edu.

CHENAULT, CHARLES (MIKE CHENAULT), state legislator; b. Hobbs, N.Mex., Feb. 25, 1957; m. Tanna Chenault; children: Brandon, Elisha, Shanda, Miranda. V.p. construction co.; mem. Dist. 34 Alaska House of Reps., Juneau, 2000—, house spkr. Mem. sch. bd. Kenai (Alaska) Peninsula Borough, 1999—2000; mem. Kenai Fire Svc. Bd., 1999—2000. Mem.: North Peninsula C. of C. (past pres., bd. dirs.), Moose, Elks. Republican. Avocations: golf, fishing, snow machines, bowling, computers. Office: State Capitol Rm 505 Juneau AK 99801-1182 also: Dist 34 145 Main St Lp Ste 223 Kenai AK 99611 Office Phone: 907-465-3779. Fax: 907-465-7184; Office Fax: 907-465-2833. Business E-Mail: representative_mike_chenault@legis.state.ak.us.*

CHENEY, JAMES ADDISON, civil engineering educator; b. LA, Feb. 2, 1927; s. Burton Howard and Esther Jesse (Dumaresq) C.; m. Frankyee Jane Jackson, June, 23, 1951 (dec. Oct. 1966); children: John Addison, Linanne Dando, Matthew Jackson, Sarah Allan, Sharla Ryan, Jennifer Dumaresq; m. Barbara Louise Chadwick, June 1967 (div. Feb. 1987); children: Michael Chadwick, David Grant; m. Elaine Disbrow Barratt, Apr. 1988. BS, UCLA, 1951, MS, 1953; PhD, Stanford U., 1963. Registered profl. civil engr., Calif. Assoc. engr. L.T. Evans, Foundation Engrs., Los Angeles, 1953-55; staff engr. Lockheed Missile and Space Co., Sunnyvale, Calif., 1955-65; prof. civil engring. U. Calif., Davis, 1962-91, prof. emeritus civil engring., 1991—. Contbr. over 50 articles to scientific jours. Served with USN, 1944-45. Recipient Silver Beaver award, Golden Empire coun. Boy Scouts Am., 2002. Fellow ASCE; mem. Alpha Sigma Phi. Republican. Episcopalian. Home: 418 Anza Ave Davis CA 95616-0404 Office: U Calif Dept Civil Engring Davis CA 95616 E-mail: jacheney@ucdavis.edu.

CHENG, ALBERT, communications executive; b. Hawaii, 1971; married. BS, Mass. Inst. Tech.; MBA, Harvard U. Grad. Sch. Bus. Adminstrn. Bus. strategy cons. Boston Consulting Grp.; dir., Bus. Devel. Fox/Liberty Networks; dir., Distbn. Strategy Fox Cable Networks Grp.; v.p., Nat. Accounts and Distbn. Strategy ABC Cable Networks, 2000, sr. v.p., Distbn. Strategy and Ops., 2002—04; sr. v.p., Bus. Strategy and Devel. Disney and ESPN Networks Affiliate Sales and Mktg.; exec. v.p., Digital Media Disney-ABC TV Grp., Burbank, Calif., 2005—. Named one of 40 Executives Under 40, Multichannel News, 2006. Mem.: Nat. Assn. for Multi-Ethnicity in Comm. (treasurer). Office: Disney ABC Television Group 500 S Buena Vista St Burbank CA 91521

CHENG, TSEN-CHUNG, electrical engineering educator; b. Shanghai, Dec. 24, 1944; s. Yik Yu and Shun Lan (Tsui) C.; m. Doris Tin Gen Lee, Aug. 25, 1974; 1 child, Jason. BS, MIT, 1969, MSEE, 1970, ScD, 1974. Asst. prof. U. So. Calif., Los Angeles, 1974-80, assoc. prof., 1980-84, Lloyd F. Hunt prof., dir. electric power program, 1984—. Pres. T.C. Cheng ScD Inc., San Marino, Calif., 1981—; cons. Los Angeles Dept. Water and Power, 1984—, So. Calif. Edison Co., 1982—, Pacific Gas & Electric Co., San Francisco, 1982—, and numerous other pub. utilities and elec. and electronic mfrs. worldwide. Patentee in field; author over 120 publs. Recipient Outstanding Elec. Engring. faculty award U. So. Calif., 1976, Engring. Service award U. So. Calif., 1981. Fellow IEEE (relay com. award 1986, Best Paper award 1988), Sigma Xi, Eta Kappa Nu, Tau Beta Pi. Office: Univ of So Calif Phe 634 Dept Ee Ep # 634 Los Angeles CA 90089-0001 Office Phone: 213-740-4712. Personal E-mail: tccheng@socal.rr.com. Business E-Mail: tcheng@usc.edu.

CHENG, WAN-LEE, mechanical engineer, educator; b. Yi-Hsin, Chiang-Su, China, Dec. 28, 1945; arrived in U.S., 1971; s. Teh-Chih and Mei-Nung (Shih) Cheng; m. Viki Shu-Whei Lu, Dec. 16, 1972; children: Julie Wheichung, Paul Yichung, Lisa Yenchung. BS, Chung Yuan U., Taiwan, 1969; MEd, Sul Ross State U., 1972; PhD, Iowa State U., 1976. Mech. engr. Taiwan Power Co., Taipei, 1970-71; instr. Iowa State U., Ames, 1974-76; asst. prof., then prof. U. N.D., Grand Forks, 1976-85; prof., chmn. dept. design and industry San Francisco State U., 1985-2000, assoc. dean Coll. Creative Arts, 2000—05, acting dean Coll. Creative Arts, 2005—06; dean Coll. Creative Arts, 2006; pres. Chung Yuan Christian U., 2006—. Cons. High-Tech Mobile Lab., N.D. Vocat. Edn. Dept., Bismarck, 1984—85; vis. prof. Nat. Sci. Coun. and Chung Yuan U., Taiwan, 1990—91; dean Coll. Design Chung Yuan Christian U., Taiwan, 1994—95. Author: computer software; mem. rev. bd. Jour. Indsl. Tech., 1986—89, Jour. Tech. Studies, 2002—, mem. editl. bd. Jour. Design Sci., 2001—; contbr. articles to profl. jours. Session elder 1st Presbyn. Ch., Grand Forks, 1984—85, Lakeside Presbyn. Ch., 1989—91. Recipient Indsl. Arts Profl. Devel. award, N.D. Indsl. Arts Assn., 1985, Outstanding Tchg. and Faculty Devel. award, Burlington No. Found., 1985, Outstanding Profl. Indsl Tech. award, Nat. Assn. Indsl. Tech., 1992; 10 grants, U. N.D., 1979—85. Mem.: Chinese Am. Econ. and Tech. Devel. Assn. (pres. 1997—99), Chinese Inst. Engrs. (v.p. 1993), Soc. Mfg. Engrs. (sr.), Joint Alumni Assn. Chinese Univs. and Colls. No. Calif. (pres. San Francisco 1988—89), Chung Yuan Alumni Assn. No. Calif. (pres. San Francisco 1987—88), Epsilon Pi Tau (trustee Gamma Gamma chpt. Grand Forks 1984—85, Laureate award Beta Beta chpt. San Francisco 1991, Disting. Svc. award 2000), Phi Kappa Phi.

CHER, (CHERILYN SARKISIAN), singer, actress; b. El Centro, Calif., May 20, 1946; d. Gilbert and Georgia LaPiere; m. Sonny Bono, Oct. 27, 1964 (div. June 26, 1975); 1 child, Chastity; m. Gregg Allman, June 30, 1975 (div. Jan. 16, 1979); 1 child, Elijah Blue. Student drama coach, Jeff Corey. Singer with husband as team, Sonny and Cher, 1964-74; star TV shows: Cher, 1975-76, The Sonny and Cher Show, 1976-77; concert appearances with husband, 1977, numerous recs., TV, concert and benefit appearances with Sonny Bono; TV appearances, ABC-TV, 1978, appearance with Sonny Bono in motion pictures, Good Times, 1966, Chastity, 1969; TV spl. appearances, Cher: The Farewell Tour, 2003 (Emmy award for Outstanding Variety, Music or Comedy Special, 2003); film appearances include Come Back to the Five and Dime, Jimmy Dean, Jimmy Dean, 1982, Silkwood, 1983, Mask, 1985 (Best Actress, Cannes Internat. Film Festival), The Witches of Eastwick, 1987, Suspect, 1987, Moonstruck (Golden Globe award 1988, Acad. award for best actress, 1988), 1987, Mermaids, 1990, The Player, 1992, Pret-a-Porter, 1994, Faithful, 1996, Tea With Mussolini, 1999, Stuck on You, 2003; TV movies Club Rhino, 1990, If These Walls Could Talk, 1996, Happy Birthday Elizabeth: A Celebration of Life, 1997, AFI's 100 Years...100 Movies, 1998; helped form rock band, Black Rose, 1979; recorded albums include Black Rose, 1980, Cher, 1988, Heart of

Stone, 1989 (Double Platinum and 3 Gold Singles), Love Hurts, 1991, It's A Man's World, 1996, The Casablanca Years, 1996, Believe, 1998 (Grammy award best dance recording 1999), Not Commercial, 2000, Living Proof, 2002; exec. prodr. Sonny & Me: Cher Remembers, 1998. Recipient People's Choice award for Favorite All-Around Female Star, 1989, Vanguard award, GLAAD, 1998, Star on Walk of Fame, 1998, Lucy award for Women in Film, 2000, TV Land award, 2007.

CHERNIN, PETER F., multimedia company executive; b. Harrison, NY, May 29, 1951; m. Megan Chernin; 3 children. BA in English Lit., U. Calif. Berkeley, 1974. Pres. Lorimar Film Entertainment, 1988—89; pres. entertainment group Fox Broadcasting Co., LA, 1989—92; chmn., CEO Fox Entertainment Group, Beverly Hills, Calif., 1992—96; pres., COO News Corp., 1996—. Bd. dirs. News Corp., 1996—, E*TRADE Group, Inc., 1999—2003, DIRECTV Group, Inc., 2003—08, Am. Express Co., 2006—. Bd. dirs. Friends of the Global Fight Against AIDS, Tuberculosis and Malaria; chmn. Malaria No More. Democrat. Office: News Corp Rm 5080 10201 W Pico Blvd Bldg 100 Los Angeles CA 90064-2606*

CHERNO, MELVIN, humanities educator; b. El Paso, Feb. 24, 1929; s. Sol and Deborah (Andes) C.; m. Dolores Ellen Himelstein, Dec. 25, 1950; children— Steven Philip, Paige Elise, Julie Rosanne AB, Stanford U., 1950; AM, U. Chgo., 1952; PhD, Stanford U., 1955. Instr. Bakersfield Coll., Calif., 1955-60; successively asst. prof., assoc. prof., prof. Oakland U., Rochester, Mich., 1960-80; Vaughan prof. tech., culture and comm. U. Va., Charlottesville, 1980-2000, Vaughan prof. emeritus humanities, 2001—, prin. second residential coll., 1991-95, 2000-01, co-prin., 1995-96. Co-editor: (4-vol. anthology) Western Society..., 1967; editor, translator: (essay) Feuerbach on Luther, 1968; contbr. articles on historical topics to profl. jours. Former mem. Am. Hist. Assn., Am. Soc. Engring. Edn., So. Hist. Assn., Soc. for History of Tech., Soc. Lit. & Sci., Soc. for 19th Century Studies. Fellow Ford Found., 1953-55, Deutscher Akademische Austauschdienst, 1966, Inst. für Europäische Geschichte, 1966 Mem. Phi Beta Kappa. Home: 2850 Classic Dr Apt 2419 Highlands Ranch CO 80126

CHERNY, ROBERT WALLACE, historian, educator; b. Marysville, Kans., Apr. 4, 1943; s. Clarence L. and Lena M. (Hobbs) C.; m. Rebecca Ellen Marshall, June 11, 1967; 1 child, Sarah Catherine. BA with distinction, U. Nebr., 1965; MA, Columbia U., 1967, PhD, 1972. From instr. history to prof. San Francisco (Calif.) State U., 1971—81, prof., 1981—, assoc. dean behavioral and social scis., 1984, acting dean behavioral and social scis., 1985, chmn. history dept., 1987-92; interim dean undergrad. studies San Francisco State U., 2005—08. Disting. Fulbright lectr. Moscow State U., 1996; vis. rsch. scholar U. Melbourne, 1997; mem. academic senate San Francisco (Calif.) State U., 1981-84, 95-2005, chmn. academic senate, 2002-04; cons. in field. Author: A Righteous Cause: The Life of William Jennings Bryan, 1985, rev. edit., 1994, Populism, Progressivism and the Transformation of Nebraska Politics, 1981, American Politics in the Gilded Age, 1869-1868, 1997; co-author (with William Issel): San Francisco, 1865-1932, 1986; co-author: San Francisco: Presidio, Port and Pacific Metropolis, 1981; co-author: (with Carol Berkin, Christopher L. Miller, James L. Gormly) Making America: A History of the United States, 1995, 5th edit., 2008; co-author: (with R. Griswold del Castillo and G. Lemke-Santangelo) Competing Visions: A History of California, 2005; co-editor (with William Issel and Keiran Taylor): American Labor and the Cold War: Unions, Politics and Postware Political Culture, 2004. Mem. San Francisco Landmarks Preservation Adv. Bd., 2003—, v.p., 2006—. Woodrow Wilson fellow, 1965-66, Woodrow Wilson dissertation fellow, 1969, NEH fellow, 1992-93. Mem. Am. Hist. Assn., Orgn. Am. Historians (treas. 2003-08), S.W. Labor Studies Assn. (pres. 1982-86), Calif. Hist. Soc., Soc. Historians of Gilded Age and Progressive Era (pres. 1995), Nebr. State Hist. Soc., HNet--Humanities and Social Studies Online (pres. 2003, v.p. tchg. 2005-06). Democrat. Office: San Francisco State U Dept of History 1600 Holloway Ave San Francisco CA 94132-4155

CHEROUTES, MICHAEL LOUIS, lawyer; b. Chgo., Apr. 27, 1940; s. Louis Samuel Cheroutes and Maria Jane (Zimmerman) Dodd; m. Trisha Flynn, Oct. 30, 1965; children: Michael Louis Jr., Trisha Francesca, Matthew Dodd. BA, Harvard U., 1962; LLB, Stanford U., 1965. Bar: Colo. 1965. Assoc., then ptnr. Sherman & Howard, Denver, 1965-85; chief of staff to Rep. Patricia A. Shroeder U.S. Ho. of Reps., Washington, 1972-74; ptnr. Davis, Graham & Stubbs, Denver, 1985-93, Hogan & Hartson LLP, London, Moscow, Denver, 1993—2005, of counsel Denver, 2005—, dir. pub. fin. practice group. Contbr. articles to profl. jours. Mem. Colo. Commn. on Higher Edn., 1988-91, chmn., 1989-91; mem. state bd. Gt. Outdoors Colo. Trust Fund, 1996-97. Mem. ABA, Colo. Bar Assn., Nat. Assn. Bond Lawyers. Avocation: sailing. Office: Hogan & Hartson LLP One Tabor Ctr 1200 17th St Ste 1500 Denver CO 80202-5840 Home Phone: 303-871-9730; Office Phone: 303-899-7310. Business E-Mail: mlcheroutes@hhlaw.com.

CHERRY, JAMES DONALD, pediatrician; b. Summit, NJ, June 10, 1930; s. Robert Newton and Beatrice (Wheeler) C.; m. Jeanne M. Fischer, June 19, 1954; children: James S., Jeffrey D., Susan J., Kenneth C. BS, Springfield Coll., Mass., 1953; MD, U. Vt., 1957; MSc in Epidemiology, London Sch. Hygiene and Tropical Medicine, 1983. Diplomate Am. Bd. Pediat., Am. Bd. Pediat. Infectious Diseases. Intern, then resident in pediat. Boston City Hosp., 1957-59; resident in pediat. Kings County Hosp., Bklyn., 1959-60; rsch. fellow in medicine Harvard U. Med. Sch.-Thorndike Meml. Lab., Boston City Hosp., 1961-62; instr. pediatrics U. Vt. Coll. Medicine, also asst. attending physician Mary Fletcher DeGoesbriand Meml. hosps., Burlington, Vt., 1960-61; asst. prof., then assoc. prof. pediat. U. Wis. Med. Sch., Madison, 1963-66; assoc. attending physician Madison Gen., U. Wis. hosps., 1963-66; dir. John A. Hartford Rsch. Lab., Madison Gen. Hosp., 1963-66. Mem. faculty St. Louis U. Med. Sch., 1966-73, prof. pediatrics, 1969-73, vice chmn. dept., 1970-73; mem. staff Cardinal Glennon Meml. Hosp. Children, St. Louis U. Hosp., 1966-73; chief divsn. infectious diseases UCLA Med. Ctr. UCLA Sch. Medicine, 1973-2000, prof. pediat., 1973--; acting chmn. dept. pediatrics UCLA Med. Ctr., 1977-79; attending physician, chmn. infection control com. UCLA Med. Ctr., 1975-93; cons. Project Head Start; vis. worker dept. cmty. medicine Middlesex Hosp. and Med. Sch., London, 1982-83; vis. worker Common Cold Rsch. Unit, 1969-70; acad. visitor U. Cambridge, Eng., 2000-01. Co-editor: (Textbook) Pediatric Infectious Diseases, 1981, 6th edit., 2009; assoc. editor Clin. Infectious Diseases, 1990—99, Am. regional editor Vaccine, 1991—2000, cons. editor Pediatric Research, 2004—; contbr. scientific papers numerous in field; edtl. reviewer (profl. jours). Bd. govs. Alexander Graham Bell Internat. Parents Orgn., 1967-69. With USAR, 1958-64. Recipient Disting. Academic Achievement award, U. Vt., 1984, Med. Sci. award, Med. Alumni UCLA, 2005; John and Mary R. Markle scholar acad. medicine, 1964. Mem. AAAS, APHA, Am. Acad. Pediat. (mem. exec. com. Calif. chpt. 2 1975-77, mem. com. infectious diseases 1977-83, assoc. editor 19th Red Book 1982), Am. Soc. Microbiology,Soc. Pediat. Rsch., Infectious Diseases Soc. Am., Am. Epidemiol. Soc., Am. Pediat. Soc., L.A. Pediat. Soc., Internat. Orgn. Mycoplasmologists, Am. Soc. Virology, Soc. Hosp. Epidemiologists Am., Pediat. Infectious Diseases Soc. (pres. 1989-91, Disting. Physician award 2003), Alpha Omega Alpha. Office: UCLA David Geffen Sch Medicine and Mattel Children's Hosp Dept Pediatrics Rm 22-442 10833 Le Conte Ave Los Angeles CA 90095-1752 Home Phone: 310-395-3915; Office Phone: 310-825-5226. Business E-Mail: jcherry@mednet.ucla.edu.

CHERRY, MICHAEL A., state supreme court justice; b. St. Louis; 2 children. BA, U. Mo., 1966; JD, Washington U. Sch. Law, 1969. Ptnr. Manos & Cherry, Cherry, Bailus & Kelesis; dep. pub. defender Clark County, Nev., justice of the peace pro tem & small claims referee Nev.; alt. mcpl. judge Cities of Las Vegas and Henderson, Nev.; chief Clark County Spl. Pub. Defender's Office, 1997—98; judge 8th Jud. Dist. Ct., Dept. 17, 1998—2006; assoc. justice Nev. Supreme Ct., 2006—. Spl. master MGM Grand Hotel Fire Litig., Nev., 1981, Las Vegas Hilton Fire Litig., 1983; instr. U. Phoenix, 1994. Office: Nev Supreme Ct 201 S Carson St Carson City NV 89701-4702

CHESBRO, WESLEY, state legislator; b. Glendale, Calif., Aug. 20, 1952; m. Cindy Chesbro; children: Collin, Alan. Student, Humboldt State U.; BA in Orgnl. Behavior, U. San Francisco. Founder, exec. dir. Northcoast Environ. Ctr., 1971—74; mem. Dist. 2 Calif. State Senate, 1998—2006, chair standing com. on revenue and taxation, chair select com. on Calif.'s wine industry, chair select com. on devel. disabilities and mental health, mem. budget and fiscal rev. com., edn. com., mem. environ. quality com., govtl. orgn. com., VA com.; mem. Dist. 1 Calif. State Assembly, 2008—. Founding mem. Calif. Integrated Waste Mgmt. Bd., 1990-98, 2006-08; mem. Humboldt County Bd. Suprs., 1980-90; mem. Arcata City Coun., 1974-80; bd. mem. Calif. Mental Health Oversight and Accountability Commn., Open Door Cmty. Health Centers, Humboldt Bay Housing and Devel. Corp. Democrat. Office: State Capitol PO Box 942849 Sacramento CA 94249-0001 Office Phone: 916-319-2001. Office Fax: 916-319-2101. Personal E-mail: wesleychesbro@gmail.com.*

CHESNE, EDWARD LEONARD, physician; b. Chgo., June 11, 1931; m. Carol Chesne; children: Lauren, Christopher, Greig. BA, U. Chgo., 1950; MD, Northwestern U. Med. Sch., Chgo., 1955. Lic. phys., Ill., Hawaii. Capt. U.S. Army, 1957. Fellow Am. Coll. Physicians, Am. Coll. Cardiology, Coun. Clin. Cardiology, Am. Heart Assn. Office: 1380 Lusitana St Ste 1002 Honolulu HI 96813-2461 Home Phone: 805-524-2575; Office Phone: 808-521-7402.

CHESNEY, MARGARET A., medical educator, researcher; BA in Psychology and Sociology, Whitman Coll., Walla Walla, Wash., 1971; MA in Psychology, Colo. State U., 1973, PhD in Psychology, 1975. Postdoctoral fellow dept. psychiatry Temple U., Phila., 1975—76; dir. and sr. health psychologist dept. behavioral medicine SRI Internat., 1976—87; assoc. prof. prevention scis. group, dept. epidemiology U. Calif., San Francisco, 1987—89, prof. prevention scis. group, 1989—, co-dir. Ctr. for AIDS Prevention Studies, 1994—; dir. behavioral core AIDS Clin. Trials Group San Francisco Gen. Hosp., 1994—. Sci. cons. behavioral medicine Stanford U. Med. Ctr., 1978—; chair working group on psychosocial factors in AIDS clin. trials and vaccine trials NIMH, 1993—; chair working group for women's health initiative clin. trial NIH, 1993—; co-chair recruitment, adherence, retention com. AIDS Clin. Trials Group, 1995—; mem. HIV vaccine working group NIAID, 1994—95; mem. data safety and monitoring bd. Women's Health Initiative NIH, 1993—; mem. panel on AIDS interventions and rsch. NAS, 1988—90; mem. AIDS adv. com. Nat. Heart, Lung and Blood Inst., 1987—93. Contbr. numerous articles to profl. jours.; co-author (with Ray Rosenman): Anger and Hostility in Cardiovascular and Behavioral Disorders. Mem.: APA (pres. health psychology divsn. 1990—91, Ann. Award for Outstanding Contbn. to Health Psychology 1982), Am. Psychosomatic Soc. (pres.-elect 1996, Ann. Award for Outstanding Contbn. to Health Psychology 1985), Inst. Medicine of NAS, Phi Beta Kappa, Sigma Xi.

CHESNEY, MAXINE M., judge; b. 1942; BA, U. Calif., Berkeley, 1964, JD, 1967. Trial atty. Office Dist. Atty., San Francisco, 1968-69, sr. trial atty., 1969-71, prin. trial atty., 1971-76, head atty., 1976, asst. chief dep., 1976-79; judge San Francisco Mcpl. Ct., 1979-83, San Francisco Superior Ct., 1983-95, U.S. Dist. Ct. (no. dist.) Calif., San Francisco, 1995—. Bd. dirs. San Francisco Child Abuse Coun., 1976-79, Hosp. Audiences, 1978-81. Mem. Fed. Judges Assn., Nat. Assn. Women Judges, Edward J. McFetridge Am. Inn of Ct., U.S. Assn. Constl. Law, Queen's Bench, Ninth Jud. Cir. Hist. Soc. Office: US Dist Ct No Dist Calif PO Box 36060 450 Golden Gate Ave San Francisco CA 94102-3661

CHESNOFF, DAVID ZELTNER, lawyer; b. Paterson, NJ, May 13, 1955; BA cum laude, Alfred U., 1976; JD, Suffolk U., 1979. Bar: Tex. 1979, US Dist. Ct. (so. dist. Tex.) 1979, Nev. 1981, US Dist. Ct. (dist. Nev.) 1981, US Dist. Ct. (ea. dist. Mich.) 1988, US Dist. Ct. (dist. Mont.) 1989, US Dist. Ct. (dist. Ariz.) 1997, US Dist Ct. (so., ctrl. and no. dists. Calif.), US Dist. Ct. (dist. Ala.), US Dist. Ct. (dist. Mass.), US Dist. Ct. (dist. NJ), US Dist. Ct. (dist. N.Mex.), US Dist. Ct. (dist. Utah), US Dist. Ct. (dist. Vt.), US Ct. Appeals (1st, 2nd, 3rd, 5th, 6th, 8th, 9th, 10th & 11th cirs.), US Supreme Ct. 1988. Ptnr. Goodman & Chesnoff, Las Vegas, Nev., Chesnoff & Schonfeld, Las Vegas. Legal cons. ABC; prof. Mercer Law Sch., Macon, Ga.; spkr. in field. Guest appearances American Justice, City Confidential, CNBC TV, Charlie Rose Show. Mem.: Am. Inns of Ct., Am. Bd. Criminal Lawyers, Assn. Trial Lawyers Am., Nat. Assn. Criminal Def. Lawyers (vice chmn. continuing legal edn. com. 1991—92, mem. lawyers assistance strike force 1993, bd. dirs.), Nev. Trial Lawyers Assn., State Bar Tex., State Bar Nev., Clark County Bar Assn. Office: Chesnoff & Schonfeld PC 520 S Fourth St Las Vegas NV 89101-6593 Office Phone: 702-384-5563. Office Fax: 702-598-1425.

CHESTER, MARVIN, physics educator; b. NYC, Dec. 29, 1930; s. Herman and Sadye C.; m. Ruth Chester (div. 1960); 1 child, Karen; m. Sandra Chester (div. 1963); 1 child, Lisa; m. Elfi Bollert, July 30, 1977; children: Chaim Peter, Sadye Vera. BS, CCNY, 1952; PhD, Calif. Inst. Tech., 1961. Prof. physics U. Calif., LA, 1961-92, prof. emeritus, 1992—. Sr. rsch. fellow U. Sussex, Eng., 1973. Author: Primer of Quantum Mechanics, 1987; contbr. articles to profl. jours. Recipient Alexander von Humboldt award, Von Humboldt Stifftung, 1974-75. Mem. Am. Phys. Soc. Office: UCLA Dept Physics Los Angeles CA 90024

CHEUNG, JOHN B., research and development executive; b. 1943; COO Quest Integrated, Inc., Kent, Wash.; pres. Flow Dril Corp., Kent. Office: Flow Dril Corp 21411 72nd Ave S Kent WA 98032-2416

CHEUNG, SHERI T., lawyer; b. Gardena, Calif., Jan. 28, 1973; BA, Smith Coll., 1994; JD, Univ. So. Calif., 1997. Bar: Calif. 1997, US Dist. Ct. Ctrl. Calif., US Dist. Ct. So. Calif., US Ct. Appeals Ninth Cir. Assoc., intellectual property, labor & employment litigation Hogan & Hartson LLP, LA. Named a Rising Star, So. Calif. Super Lawyers, 2005—06. Office: Hogan & Hartson LLP Ste 1400 1199 Ave of the Stars Los Angeles CA 90067 Office Phone: 310-785-4600. Office Fax: 310-785-4601. Business E-Mail: stcheung@hhlaw.com.

CHEUNG, YIN-WONG, economics professor; b. Macao, June 11, 1957; s. Kai-Ming Cheung and Oi Chan; m. TikLing D. Wong, Oct. 31, 1956; children: Ivy N., Vincent W. B of Social Scis., U. Hong Kong, 1980; MA in Econs. with distinction, U. Essex, Eng., 1984; PhD, U. Pa., Phila., 1990. Fgn. exch. dealer Bank Tokyo, Hong Kong, 1980—83; prof. econs. U. Calif., Santa Cruz, 1990—. Guest prof. Shandong U., Jinan, China, 2004—. Co-author (with Y.H. Liu and W.C. Lo): An Introduction to Financial Options (in Chinese); co-author: (with M.D. Chinn, E. Fujii) The Economic Integration of Greater China, 2007; editor: Multinational Fin. Jour., 2001—, Pacific Econ. Rev., 2003—, Internat. Jour. Applied Econs., 2004—; assoc. editor: Applied Fin. Econs., 1999—, Internat. Econ. Jour., 2005—, Economie Internat., 2006—; Jour. Econs. and Mgmt., 2006—, Pacific Basin Fin. Jour., 2006—; assoc. editor Economics e-Journal, 2007—; contbr. articles to profl. jours. Recipient Lawrence Robbin's Econs. prize, U. Pa., 1986; fellow, 1985—86, 1986—87, 1988—89; Hiram C. Haney fellow, 1989. Mem.: Chinese Econ. Assn. N.Am. (life; v.p. 2001—02, pres. 2007). Office: Economics Dept University of California 1156 High Street Santa Cruz CA 95064 Business E-Mail: cheung@ucsc.edu.

CHEUVRONT, KENNETH DAVID, state legislator; b. Phoenix, May 11, 1961; s. Jerry Fredric and Lois Jean (Christensen) Cheuvront. Student, Institut Études Européenes, Nante, France; BA in Polit. Sci., Claremont McKenna Coll., Calif., 1983; M in Internat. Fin., Am. Grad. Sch. Internat. Mgmt., Glendale, Ariz., 1986. Fl. trader Commodities Exchange Ctr., NYC, 1986—89; pres. Cheuvront Construction, Phoenix, 1989—; mem. Dist. 25 Ariz. House of Reps., 1995—2002, Dem. leader, 2001—02; owner Cheuvront Wine & Cheese, Phoenix, 2003—; mem. Dist. 15 Ariz. State Senate, 2003—, mem. commerce & govt. com., fin. com. Chmn. Ariz. Dem. Legis. Campaign Com., 1997—. Del. Dem. Nat. Conv., 1996, 2000; bd. dirs. Combined Met. Phoenix Arts & Sci. (COMPAS), 1990—, Phoenix Parks & Recreation, 1992—94. Recipient Ariz. AIDS Policy Alliance award, 1998, Barry Goldwater Human Rights award, 1999; named Man of Yr., Echo Mag., 1997. Democrat. Office: Ariz State Senate Capitol Complex 1700 W Washington Rm 315 Phoenix AZ 85007 Office Phone: 602-926-5325. Office Fax: 602-417-3149. Business E-Mail: kcheuvro@azleg.gov.*

CHEVALIER, PAUL EDWARD, retired retail executive, lawyer; b. NYC, Jan. 30, 1939; s. Arthur and Grace (Eaton) C.; 1 child, Marc. BA, Columbia U., 1960, LLB, MBA, Columbia U., 1966; AMP, Harvard U., 1979. Bar: Ill. 1968, U.S. Supreme Ct. 1974. Dir. labor rels. Carter Hawley Hale Stores, Inc., LA, 1972-74, v.p. employee rels., 1974-86, sr. v.p. employee rels., 1986-93; pres. Chevalier Cons. Group, 1993-98. Vice chmn. We. Fed. Credit Union, 1989-93; bd. dirs., exec. com. Sedona Cultural Park, 2000—04; chmn. emeritus Jonathan Art Found. Past pres., bd. dirs. Calif. Employment Law Coun.; chmn. Art and Culture Commn., City of Sedona, 1999-2003; bd. dirs. Ariz. Humanities Coun., 2002-04; mem. Harvard Bus. Sch. Alumni Coun., 1989-92; mem. adv. coun. Verde Valley United Way, 2006—, Seduna Cmty Found. Bd., 2008-. Lt. USN, 1960-66. Mem. Nat. Retail Fedn. (chmn. employee rels. com. 1979-82), Calif. Retail Assn., Harvard Bus. Sch. Assn. (bd. dirs. 1980-90, pres. 1984-85). Personal E-mail: westwinds3@aol.com.

CHEW, GEOFFREY FOUCAR, physicist; b. Wash., June 5, 1924; s. Arthur Percy and Pauline Lisette (Foucar) C.; m. Ruth Wright, June 10, 1945 (dec. Apr. 1971); children— Berkeley, Beverly; m. Denyse Odette Mettel, Dec. 30, 1971; children— Pierre-Yves, Jean-Francois, Pauline BS in Physics, George Washington U., 1944; PhD in Physics, U. Chgo., 1948. Research physicist Los Alamos Sci. Lab., N.Mex., 1944-46; research physicist Lawrence Berkeley Lab., Calif., 1948-49; asst. prof. physics U. Calif., Berkeley, 1949-50; asst. prof., assoc. prof. physics U. Ill., Urbana, 1950-56; prof. physics U. Calif., Berkeley, 1957—, chmn. dept. physics, 1974-78, Miller prof., 1981-82, dean physical scis., 1986-92. Group leader theoretical physics Lawrence Berkeley Lab., Calif., 1964-83; vis. prof. Princeton U., N.J., 1970-71; sci. assoc. CERN, Geneva, 1978-79; vis. prof. U. Paris, 1983. Author: S-Matrix Theory of Strong Interactions, 1961; Analytic S Matrix, 1966; contbr. articles to profl. jours. Chmn. passport com. Fedn. Am. Scientists, Washington, 1951-56 Recipient E.O. Lawrence award AEC, 1969, Disting. Alumni award George Washington U., 1974, Berkeley citation U. Calif., 1991; Churchill Coll. overseas fellow, 1962 Fellow Am. Phys. Soc. (Hughes prize 1962); mem. Nat. Acad. Scis., Am. Acad. Arts and Scis. Home: 10 Maybeck Twin Dr Berkeley CA 94708-2037 Business E-Mail: gfchew@sbcglobal.net.

CHEW, RON ALPHA, museum director; b. Seattle, May 17, 1953; s. Soo Hong and Gam Har (Wee) C.; m. Loan Thi Nguyen. Attended, U. Wash., 1971—75, degree, 2002. Editor Internat. Examiner, Seattle, 1977-80, 81-88; exec. dir. McKenzie River Gathering Found., Seattle, 1980-81; multicultural program coord. Seattle Cen. C.C., 1988-89; confidential sec. Commn. in Asian Am. Affairs, Seattle, 1989-91; exec. dir. Wing Luke Asian Mus., Seattle, 1991—. Coord. Chinese Oral History Project, Seattle, 1990; pres. Nat Coun. on Humanities, 2001. Bd. dirs. Chinese Info. and Svc. Ctr., Seattle, 1991, Inter-Im Cmty. Devel. Assn., Seattle, 1979; adv. bd. Northwest Nikkei Newspaper, 1989; pub. com. Kin On Chinese Nursing Home, 1987; publ. bd. Seattle Cen. C.C., 1990; cmty. media adv. coun. Amerasia Jour., 1988-89; publ. adv. com. Neighborhood House, Seattle, 1988. David Douglas fellow Wash. Hist. Soc., 1993; named to Hall of Fame, Dept. Communication, U. Wash.; recipient Leadership for a Changing World award, Ford Found., 2004. Mem. Internat. Dist. Econ. Assn. (cmty. svc. award 1988), Western Mus. Assn. (Dirs. Chair award 2004), Wash. Mus. Assn. (instnl. excellence award 1993), Assn. King County Hist. Orgns. (outstanding exhibit award 1993), Asian Am. Journalist Assn. (co-founder Seattle chpt., treas. 1985-89), Northwest

Minority Publishers Assn. (co-founder, sec. 1987-88). Avocations: research of chinese american history, seattle's chinatown. Office: Wing Luke Asian Museum 719 S King St Seattle WA 98104-3035

CHIATE, KENNETH REED, lawyer; b. Phoenix, June 24, 1941; s. Mac Arthur and Lillian (Lavin) C.; m. Jeannette Jensen, Aug. 21, 1965; children: Gregory Jensen, Carley MaKay. BA with honors, Claremont Men's Coll., 1963; JD, Columbia U., 1966; postgrad., U. So. Calif. Law Sch., 1967. Bar: Calif. 1967, U.S. Dist. Ct. (cen. dist.) Calif. 1967, Ariz. 1971, U.S. Dist. Ct. Ariz. 1971, U.S. Dist. Ct. (no. Dist.) Calif. 1982. Law clk. presiding justice U.S. Dist. Ariz., 1971; ptnr. Lillick McHose & Charles, LA, 1971-91, Pillsbury Winthrop, LLP (formerly Pillsbury Madison), LA, 1991—. Arbitrator Los Angeles Superior Ct. Arbitration Panel, 1979-82; mcpl. ct. judge protem Los Angeles, 1979-81; vice chmn. Los Angeles Open Com., 1969-71. Named among Calif. Lawyers of Yr. 2000, Calif. Mag.; named one of So. Calif. Superlawyers, L.A. Mag., 2004. Mem. ABA, L.A. County Bar Assn., Calif. State Bar Assn., Ariz. State Bar Assn., Maricopa County Bar Assn., Am. Trial Lawyers Assn., L.A. Bus. Trial Lawyers Assn. Office: Quinn Emanuel Urquhart Oliver & Hedges LLP 865 Figueroa St 10th Fl Los Angeles CA 90017 Office Phone: 213-443-3000. E-mail: kenchiate@quinnemanuel.com.

CHIAVERINI, JOHN EDWARD, construction company executive; b. Providence, Feb. 6, 1924; s. John and Sadie (Ginsberg) C.; m. Cecile Corey, Mar. 31, 1951; children: Caryl Marie, John Michael. Cert. in advanced san. engring., U. Ill., 1945; BS in Civil Engring., U. RI, Kingston, 1947. Registered profl. engr., Mass., RI. Project engr. Perini Corp., Hartford, Conn., 1950-51, project mgr., 1951-55, asst. project mgr. Pitts. and Que., 1955-61, v.p. Framingham, Mass., 1965-84, sr. v.p. San Francisco, 1984—; pres., dir. Compania Perini S.A., Colombia, 1961—; v.p., exec. mgr. Perini Yuba Assocs., Marysville, Calif., 1966-70, v.p. Western ops., 1970-78, 79-84, group v.p., 1978-79; sr. v.p. spl. projects Perini Corp., 1984-90, dir., asst. to chmn., 1991—. Engring and constrn. cons., 1990—. Mem. U.S. com. Internat. Commn. on Large Dams; bd. dirs. Bldg. Futures Coun., 1990—, vice chmn., 1993, chmn., 1994—; active Civil Engring. Rsch. Found., 1990—, mem. corp. adv. bd., 1992—; mem. Cons. Constructors Coun. Am. Served to 2d lt. USAAF, 1944-46. Recipient Golden Beaver Supervision award, 1989, San Francisco Bay Area Coun. Boy Scouts Am., 1989, Good Scout award, 1989; named to RI Engring. Hall of Fame, 1997. Fellow ASCE (mem. exec. com. constrn. divsn., vice chmn. 1994-95, chmn. 1995—), Soc. Am. Mil. Engrs. (Acad. of Fellows 1997, pres. San Francisco post 1991-92, bd. dirs.); mem. NSPE (life), Am. Arbitration Assn., Calif. Soc. Profl. Engrs., Dispute Resolution Bd. Found., Beavers (bd. dirs.), Moles, Commonwealth Club of Calif., KC, Rotary (mem. dispute resolution bd. found.), Consulting Constructor's Coun. Am. Republican. Roman Catholic. Home and Office: 37 Dutch Valley Ln San Anselmo CA 94960-1045 Office Phone: 415-454-8251. Personal E-mail: ceejayiii@aol.com.

CHICK, LAURA NEWMAN, state official, former city official; b. Long Island, NY, 1944; children: Katherine, Care. BA in History, UCLA; MSW, U. So. Calif. City councilwoman from Dist. 3 City of L.A., 1993—2002, contr., 2001—09; insp. gen. State of Calif., Sacramento, 2009—. Vice chair Pub. Works Commn. Named Pub. Elected Official of the Yr., Nat. Assn. Social Workers, 2008. Mem.: California State Bar (bd. govs. 2006—, chair audit com.). Democrat. Office: Office of the Inspector General PO Box 348780 Sacramento CA 95834 Office Phone: 916-830-3600. Office Fax: 916-928-5974.*

CHICOINE, NICOLE MOONEY, lawyer; b. Portland, Ore., Mar. 7, 1972; BS cum laude, Univ. Ore., 1996; JD, Univ. Wash., 1999. Bar: Wash. 1999. Tax controversy and white collar criminal defense atty. Chicoine & Hallett, P.S., Seattle, 1999—. Contbr. articles to numerous profl. jours. Named Seattle Rising Star, SuperLawyer Mag., 2006. Mem.: ABA, Legis. Com. Tax Coun. (chmn. 2005—), Wash. State Bar Assn. Office: Chicoine and Hallett 719 2nd Ave ste 425 Millenium Tower Seattle WA 98104

CHIEN, DAVID YING, biotechnologist, epidemiologist; s. James Ching Chien and Josephine Wong; m. Chia-Chia Hsu, Aug. 31, 1974; children: Amy Jo, Yvonne Shiao. PhD, U. Calif., Berkeley, 1978. Sr. dir. rsch. Chiron Corp., Emeryville, Calif., 2000—06, Novartis Vaccine, Diagnostics Inc., Emeryville, 2006—. Sponsor Culture to Culture Found., Alamo, Calif., 2003—08. Grant, NIAID, 2003—07. Mem.: ASM, ASCO. Achievements include development of HBV vaccine, HBsAg, anti- HBc, HBe/anti- HBe diagnosis; research in HCV vaccine and therapeutic drug development; HGV, SARS, hanta virus, pandemic flu viral. Home: 1121 Douglas Ct Alamo CA 94507 Office: Novartis Vaccine & Diagnostics Inc 4560 Horton St Emeryville CA 94608 Office Fax: 510-923-2586; Home Fax: 925-932-3492. Personal E-mail: yingdavid@aol.com. Business E-Mail: david.chien@novartis.com.

CHIEN, SHU, physiology and bioengineering educator; b. Beijing, June 23, 1931; arrived in US, 1954, naturalized, 1971; s. Shih-liang and Wan-tu (Chang) Chien; m. Kuang-Chung Hu, Apr. 7, 1957; children: May Chien Busch, Ann Chien Guidera. MD, Nat. Taiwan U., Taipei, 1953; PhD in Physiology, Columbia U., 1957. Instr. physiology Columbia U. Coll. Physicians & Surgeons, NYC, 1956-58, asst. prof., 1958-64, assoc. prof., 1964-69, prof., 1969-88, dir. divsn. circulatory physiology and biophysics, 1974-88; dir. Inst. Biomedical Scis. Academia Sinica, Taipei, 1987-88; prof. bioengineering and medicine U. Calif. San Diego, La Jolla, 1988—, bioengineering group coord., 1989-94, dir. Whitaker Inst. Biomedical Engring., 1991—, chmn. dept. bioengineering, 1994-99, 2002—05, univ. prof., 2002—, Y.C. Fung prof., 2006—. Chmn. adv. com. Am. Bur. Med. Advancement in China, NYC, 1991-03, Inst. Biomedical Scis., Academia Sinica, Taipei, 1991-2004, Nat. Health Rsch. Inst., Taipei, 1991-2004. Editor: Vascular Endothelium in Health and Disease, 1988, Molecular Biology in Physiology, 1989, Molecular Biology of Cardiovascular System, 1990; co-editor: Nuclear Magnetic Resonance in Biology and Medicine, 1986, Handbook of Bioengineering, 1986, Clinical Hemorheology, Applications in Cardiovascular and Hematological Disease, Diabetes, Surgery and Gynecology, 1987, Fibrinogen, Thrombosis, Coagulation and Fibrinolysis, 1990, Biochemical and Structural Dynamics of the Cell Nucleus, 1990, others; contbr. more than 400 sci. articles on physiology, bioengineering and related biomedical rsch. to profl. jours. Recipient Fahraeus award European Soc. Clin. Haemorheology, London, 1981, Melville award ASME, 1990, 96, Zweifach award World Congress of Microcirculation, Louisville, 1991, Spl. Creativity Grant award NSF, 1985-88, Merit Grant award NIH, 1989-99, Nat. Health medal, Taiwan, 1998, Poiseuille Gold Medal Internat. Congress Biorheology, 2002, Asian Am. Engr. of Yr. for Disting. Life Time Achievement Chinese Inst. Learning, 2005, Lifetime Achievement award Soc. Chinese Bioscientists in Am. Fellow Biomedical Engring. Soc. (pres. 2006-, ALZA award 1993, Disting. Svc. award 2001), Am. Acad. Arts and Scis. (Founders award 2006); mem. NAE (Founders award 2006), Academia Sinica, Taipei, Am. Physiol. Soc. (pres. 1990-91, Ray Daggs award 1999, Walter B. Cannon Lecture award, 2003), Internat. Soc. Biorheology (v.p. 1983-89, pres. 2005-), Microcirculatory Soc. (pres. 1980-81, Landis award 1983), N.Am. Soc. Biorheology (chmn. steering com. 1985-86), Fedn. Am. Socs. for Exptl. Biology (pres. 1992-93), Am. Inst. Med. and Biol. Engring. (pres. 2000-01, Pierre Galletti award 2004), Inst. Medicine, NAS Internat. Union Physiol. Sci. (treas. 1997-01, chair Internat. Congress 2005), Chinese Acad. Scis. (fgn.). Achievements include elucidation of the mechanism of red cell aggregation in terms of energy balance at cell surface; demonstration of the role of endothelial cell turnover in the transport of protein molecules into the artery wall; research on the molecular basis and physiological implications of blood cell deformability; studies on the effects of mechanical forces on endothelial cell gene expression, signal transduction, and remodeling. Office: U Calif San Diego Dept Bio Engring 9500 Gilman Dr La Jolla CA 92093-0412 Home Phone: 858-622-0888; Office Phone: 858-534-5195. Business E-Mail: shuchien@ucsd.edu.

CHIHARA, CHARLES SEIYO, philosophy educator; b. July 19, 1932; s. George I. and Mary N. (Fushiki) C.; m. Carol J. Rosen, June 14, 1964; 1 child, Michelle N. BS, Seattle U., 1954; MS, Purdue U., 1956; PhD, U. Wash., 1960. Instr. U. Wash., Seattle, 1961-62; asst. prof. U. Ill., Urbana, 1962-63, U. Calif., Berkeley, 1963-68, assoc. prof., 1968-74, prof. philosophy dept., 1974—2000, emeritus prof., 2000—. Author: Ontology and the Vicious-Circle Principle, 1973, Constructibility and Mathematical Existence, 1990, The Worlds of Possibility, 1998, A Structural Account of Mathematics, 2004. NEH fellow for ind. rsch., Paris, 1985-86, U. Calif., 1994-95; postdoctoral fellow Mellon Found., 1964-65, Humanities Rsch. fellow U. Calif., 1967-68; U. Calif. Pres.'s rsch. fellow in humanities, 1996-97. Office: Univ Calif Dept Philosophy Berkeley CA 94720-0001 Office Phone: 510-642-2722. Business E-Mail: charles1@socrates.berkeley.edu.

CHIHULY, DALE PATRICK, artist; b. Tacoma, Wash., Sept. 20, 1941; s. George and Viola C.; m. Silvia Peto (div.); 1 son with Leslie Jackson. BA in Interior Design, U. Wash., 1965; MS in Sculpture, U. Wis., 1967; MFA in Ceramics, RISD, 1968; Doctorate (hon.), Brandeis U., 2000. Apprentice Venini Glass Factory, Murano, Venice, Italy, 1968; instr., head glass program RISD; instr. Haystack Mtn. Sch., Maine; founder, Pilchuk Sch., 1971. Mem. various juries and panels Nat. Endowment for Arts One-man exhbns. include U. Minn., 1976, Handler Galleries, Houston, 1977, Crocker Art Mus., Sacamento, Calif., 1984, Bellevue (Wash.) Art Mus., 1984-87, Israel Museum, Jerusalem 1990, Hudson River Museum, Yonkers 1990, Contemporary Museum Honolulu 1990, Azabu Museum, Tokyo Japan 1990, Museum of Arts and Crafts, Hamburg 1992, Marlborough Gallery, NY, 2006, Franklin Park Conservatory, Columbus, Ohio, 2006, and others; group shows include Charles Cowles Gallery, N.Y. 1981-83, "World glass Now" Hokkaido Museum of Modern Art, Sapporo, Japan, 1982, Columbus Coll. Art and Design, Ohio, 1983; installation exhbns.: Chihuly Over Venice, 1995-96, Chihuly in the Light of Jerusalem 2000, Tower of David Mus. of the History of Jerusalem, 2000, Crystal Tree of Light, White House Millennium Celebation, 2000 (permanently installed at the Clinton Presdl. Ctr., Little Rock 2004), Chihuly in the Park: A Garden of Glass, Garfield Park Conservatory, Chgo., 2001-02, Chihuly at the Victoria & Albert, London, 2001, Chihuly Bridge of Glass, Tacoma, 2002, Salt Lake Art Ctr., Olympics, 2002, Mille Fiori, Tacoma Art Mus., 2003, A Transparent Legacy, Seattle Art Mus., Washington, 2006, Niijima Float Installation, Tacoma Art Mus., Washington, 2006, Material Matters, LA County Mus. Art, Calif., 2006; represented in permanent collections including Seattle Art Mus., Met. Mus. Art, N.Y.C., Wadsworth Atheneum, Hartford, Conn., Phila. Mus. Art, Corning Mus. Glass, N.Y., Lannan Found., Palm Beach, Fla., Mus. Art of RISD, Providence, Victoria and Albert Mus., London, Mus. Contemporary Crafts of Am., Crafts Council, N.Y.C.; dir. Pilchuk Glass Ctr., Stanwood, Wash.; author: Chihuly: Glass, 1982, Chihuly: Color Glass and Form, 1986. Recipient Louis F. Tiffany Found. award, 1967; named First Nat. Living Treasure, Inst. for Human Potential, U. N.C., Wilmington, 1992; Nat. Endowment for Arts grantee, 1975, 77, Governor's Art Award (Washington State) 1984, 85; Fulbright fellow, Murano, Italy, 1968 Mem.: Providence Art.

CHIKALLA, THOMAS DAVID, retired science facility administrator; b. Milw., Sept. 9, 1935; s. Paul Joseph and Margaret Ann (Dittrich) C.; m. Ruth Janet Laun, June 20, 1960; children: Paul, Mark, Karyn. BS in Metallurgy, U. Wis., 1957, PhD in Metallurgy, 1966; MS in Metallurgy, U. Idaho, 1960. Research scientist Gen. Electric Co., Richland, Wash., 1957-62; sr. research scientist Battelle Pacific N.W. Labs., Richland, 1964-72, sect. mgr., 1972-80, programs mgr., 1980-83, dept. mgr., 1983-86, assoc. dir., 1986-95; ret., 1995. Tchr. U. Wis., Madison, 1962-64. Contbr. articles to profl. jours. Fellow AEC. Fellow Am. Ceramic Soc. (counselor 1974-80); mem. AAAS, Am. Nuclear Soc., Sigma Xi. Clubs: Desert Ski (pres. 1958-59), Alpine. Republican. Roman Catholic. Avocations: skiing, golf, woodworking, mountain climbing. Home: 2108 Harris Ave Richland WA 99352-2021 E-mail: healey1828@aol.com.

CHILDEARS, LINDA, foundation administrator; b. Council Bluffs, Iowa, Jan. 25, 1950; d. Nolan Glen and Mary Lucile (Dunken) Jackson. Grad., U. Wis., Am. Inst. Banking; student, U. Colo., U. Denver. Various positions First Nat. Bank Bear Valley (formerly Norwest Bank Bear Valley), Colo., 1969-79; v.p. adminstrn. First Nat. Bancorp., 1979-83; pres., CEO, Equitable Bank of Littleton, 1983—87; founder The Fin. Consortium; pres., CEO, Young Ams. Bank, Denver, 1987—2005; pres., CEO Daniels Fund, 2005—. Bd. dirs., First State Bancorporation, 2007- Contbr. articles to Time and Newsweek. Bd. dirs. Cherry Creek Art Festival, Denver, 1989-96, Jr. Achievement, Mile High United Way, Cherry Creek Bus. Improvement Dist., U. Denver Bridge Project; mem. adv. bd., nat. past pres. Camp Fire Coun. Colo., Daniels Coll. of Bus.; bd. mem. Cableland Home Found. Named hon. life mem. Nat. CampFire, past chmn., numerous other awards Camp Fire Inc. Mem. Am. Bankers Assn. (past chmn. Edn. Found.), Found. Tchg. Econs. (trustee), Colo. Bankers Assn., Metro C. of C. Republican. Office: Daniels Fund 101 Monroe St Denver CO 80206

CHILDERS, CHARLES EUGENE, mining company executive; b. West Frankfort, Ill., Oct. 29, 1932; s. Joel Marion and Cora E. (Choate) C.; m. Norma A. Casper, June 8, 1952; children: Joel M., Katrina K. BS, U. Ill., 1955; LLD (hon.), U. Saskatchewan, 1994. With Duval Corp., Carlsbad, N.Mex., 1955-62, Internat. Minerals Corp. (IMC), 1963-77; v.p. Esterhazy oper. IMC, 1977-79; pres. IMC Coal, Lexington, 1979-81; v.p. potash oper. IMC, 1981-82, v.p. expansion and devel., 1982-87; pres., chief exec. officer Potash Corp. of Sask., Inc., Saskatoon, Can., 1987-90, chmn., pres., chief exec. officer, 1990-98, chmn., chief exec. officer, 1998-99, chmn., 1999—. Bd. dirs., past chmn. bd. Canpotex Ltd., Sask., Found. for Agronomic Rsch.; past chmn. bd. The Fertilizer Inst.; bd. dirs. Conf. Bd. Can., Battle Mountain Gold Corp.; past chmn. Potash and Phosphate Inst.; mem. fertilizer industry adv. com. to FAO. Dir. at large Jr. Achievement of Can. 1st lt. U.S. Army, 1955-57. Mem. AIME, Can. Inst. Mining and Metallurgy, Sask. Potash Producers Assn. (past. chmn.), Internat. Fertilizer Industry Assn. (past pres.). Republican. Baptist.

CHILDS, DONALD RICHARD, pediatric endocrinologist; b. Chgo., Sept. 14, 1945; s. Robert Henry Edward and Dorothy Jane (Mills) C.; m. Diane E. Martin, Apr. 26, 1972 (div. 1981); 1 child, Elena M.; m. Jacquelynne Celeste Bostrom, Aug. 26, 1989; stepchildren: Brandon R. Alexander, Eric T. Alexander. MD, U. Mich., 1970. Diplomate Am. Bd. Pediatrics. Intern Children's Hosp., LA, 1970-71; resident William Beaumont Hosp., Royal Oak, Mich., 1973-75; fellow U. Calif., Davis, 1975-77; pvt. practice Riverside, Calif., 1977—. Capt. U.S. Army, 1971-73. Fellow Am. Acad. Pediatrics; mem. Am. Diabetes Assn., Calif. Perinatal Assn., Calif. Med. Assn., Endocrine Soc., Juvenile Diabetes Found. Avocations: music, water-skiing. Office: 7160 Brockton Ave Riverside CA 92506-2614

CHILLINGWORTH, LORI, bank executive; 1 child. Grad., Pacific Coast Banking Sch., U. Wash. Sr. v.p., mgr. women's fin. group Zions Bank (subsidiary of Zions Bancorp.), Salt Lake City, 1997—. Bd. mem. Family Counseling Ctr., Pete Sauzo Bus. Ctr., Salt Lake Community Coll. Found., Utah Micro-Enterprise Loan Fund; mem., credit com. Salt Lake County Revolving Loan Fund. Named one of 25 Women to Watch, US Banker, 2005, 2006, 2007. Office: Zions Bank One S Main St Salt Lake City UT 84111

CHILTON, LANCE ALIX, pediatrician; b. Akron, Ohio, Nov. 2, 1944; BA in Human Scis., Johns Hopkins U., 1966, MD, 1969. Diplomate American Board of Pediatrics. Intern U. Wash., Seattle, 1969—70; resident pediat. U. Pitts., 1972—74; faculty mem., dept. pediatrics U. N.Mex., 1975—82, prof. pediatrics, 2005—; former pediatrician Gallup Indian Med. Ctr.; pediatrician U. N.Mex. Hosp., N.Mex., 1975—82; former pediatrician Lovelace Pediat., Albuquerque, 1982—2005; pediatrician Lovelace Med. Ctr., N.Mex., 1982—2005, St. Vincent Regional Med. Ctr., Santa Fe, 1995—, Holy Cross Hosp., Taos, 2005—, U. N.Mex. Hosp., 2005—. Prof. pediatrics U. N.Mex., 1975—81, 2005—. Columnist: Albuquerque Jour. Mem., Advosory Com. Immunazation Practices Ctr. Disease Control. Recipient Cmty. Svc. award, N.Mex. Med. Soc., 2006. Mem.: N.Mex. Med. Soc., N.Mex. Pub. Health Assn., N.Mex. Pediat. Soc., Am. Acad. Pediat. (mem. first Indian child project adv. com., former chmn. com. on Native Am. child health, vice chair Dist. VIII, Native Am. Child Health Adv. award 2002). Office: 306A San Pablo SE Albuquerque NM 87108 Office Phone: 505-272-9242.

CHILVERS, ROBERT MERRITT, lawyer; b. Long Beach, Calif., Oct. 23, 1942; s. James Merritt and Elizabeth Louise (Blackburn) C.; m. Sandra Lee Rigg, Sept. 5, 1969; children: Jeremy Merritt, Jessica Rigg. AB, U. Calif., Berkeley, 1972; JD, Harvard U., 1975. Bar: Calif. 1975, U.S. Dist. Ct. (no. dist.) Calif. 1975, U.S. Ct. Appeals (9th cir.) 1980, U.S. Supreme Ct. 1980, U.S. Dist. Ct. (ctrl. dist.) Calif. 1981, U.S. Ct. Fed. Claims, 1984, U.S. Dist. Ct. (ea. dist.) Calif. 1987, U.S. Ct. Appeals (fed. cir.) 1987. Assoc. Brobeck, Phleger & Harrison, San Francisco, 1975-82, ptnr., 1982-93; spl. master U.S. Dist. Ct. (no. dist.) Calif., 1994-99; pres. Chilvers & Taylor, San Rafael, Calif., 1996—. Neutral evaluator and mediator U.S. Dist. Ct. (no. dist.) Calif., 2001—; faculty U. Calif. Hastings Sch. Law, San Francisco, 1983-89, Emory U., Atlanta, 1984-90, fed. practice program U.S. Dist. Ct. (no. dist.) Calif., 1984-86, Nat. Inst. for Trial Advocacy, 1986—, Cardozo Law Sch., Yeshiva U., N.Y.C., 1993-99, Stanford U. Law Sch., 1994—, Widener U. Sch. Law, Wilmington, 1994-96, U. San Francisco Sch. Law, 1994—. Mem. Calif. Sch. Bds. Assn., 1985—89; trustee Mill Valley Sch. Dist., Calif., 1985—89, chmn. Calif., 1987—89; bd. dirs. Marin County Sch. Bds. Assn., Calif., 1985—86, Artisans, Mill Valley, Calif., 1999—2001. With USMC, 1964—71. Mem. Calif. Bar Assn. (commendation for Outstanding Contbns. to the delivery of vol. legal svcs. 1984), Marin County Bar Assn., Tau Beta Pi, Sigma Tau. Office: Chilvers & Taylor 83 Vista Marin San Rafael CA 94903-5228 Office Phone: 415-444-0875.

CHIN, MING W., state supreme court justice; b. Klamath Falls, Oreg., Aug. 31, 1942; m. Carol Lynn Joe, Dec. 19, 1971; children: Jennifer, Jason. BA in Polit. Sci., U. San Francisco, 1964, JD, 1967; LLD (hon.), Southwestern U. Sch. of Law, 1996, Golden Gate Un. Sch. of Law, 1997, U. San Diego Sch. of Law, 1998, Western State U. Sch. of Law, 1998. Bar: Calif. 1970, U.S. Fed. Ct., U.S. Tax Ct. Assoc., head trial dept. Aiken, Kramer & Cummings, Oakland, Calif., 1973—76, prin., 1976—88; dep. dist. atty. Alameda County, Calif., 1970—72; judge Alameda County Superior Ct., 1988—90; assoc. justice divsn. 3 Ct. Appeal 1st Dist., 1990—94; presiding justice 1st Dist. Ct. Appeal Divsn. 3, San Francisco, 1994—96; state supreme ct. assoc. justice Calif. Supreme Ct., San Francisco, 1996—. Author: California Practice Guide: Employment Litigation, 2005. Capt. US Army, 1967—69, Vietnam, Capt. USAR, 1969—71. Decorated US Army Commendation medal, Bronze Star; recipient Learned Hand award, Am. Jewish Com., 1997, Legal Impact award, Asian Pacific Am. Legal Ctr. of So. Calif., 1997, Citizen of the Yr. award, Chinese Americans United for Self Empowerment, 1998, Public Service & Govt. Leadership award, Asian Bus. Assn., 1998, Trailblazer award, Nat. Asian Pacific Am. Bar Assn., 1999; named Outstanding Judge of the Yr., So. Alameda County Bar Assn., 1989, Honoree for Service in Field of Law, Chinese Consolidated Benevolent Assn. & Chinese Women's Assn. of Am., 1997. Mem.: ABA, Asian Am. Bar Assn., San Francisco Dist. Atty.'s Commn. Hate Crimes, Alameda County Bar Assn., State Bar Calif., Calif. Judges Assn., Commonwealth Club of Calif. (pres. 1998), Alpha Sigma Nu. Office: Supreme Court Calif 350 McAllister St Fl 1 San Francisco CA 94102-4783 Office Phone: 415-865-7050. E-mail: ming.chin@jud.ca.gov.

CHIN, SUE SOONE MARIAN (SUCHIN CHIN), artist, photojournalist; b. San Francisco; d. William W. and Soo-Up (Swebe) C. Grad., Calif. Coll. Art, Mpls. Arts Inst.; scholar, Schaeffer Design Ctr.; student, Yasuo Kuniyoshi, Louis Hamon, Rico LeBrun. Photojournalist All Together Now Show, 1973, East-West News, Third World Newscasting, 1975-78, Sta. KNBC Sunday Show, LA, 1975, 76, Live on 4, 1981, Bay Area Scene, 1981. Chmn. Full Moon Products; pres., bd. dirs. Aumni Oracle Inc. Graphics printer, exhbns. include: Kaiser Ctr., Zellerbach Pla., Chinese Culture Ctr. Galleries, Capricorn Asunder Art Commn. Gallery (all San Francisco), Newspace Galleries,

New Coll. of Calif., L.A. County Mus. Art, Peace Pla. Japan Ctr., Congress Arts Comm., Washington, 1989; SFWA Galleries, Inner Focus Show, 1989—, Calif. Mus. Sci. and Industry, Lucien Labaudt Gallery, Salon de Medici, Madrid, Salon Renacimento, Madrid, 1995, Life is a Circus, SFWA Gallery, 1991, 94, UN/50 Exhibit, Bayfront Galleries, 1995, Somar Galleries, 1997, 2003 (Merit award 2003), Sacramento State Fair, 2000, Star Child, Women thru the Ages - Somarts Gallery, 2000, Kings Gallery, San Francisco, 2004, AFL-CIO Labor Studies Ctr., Washington, Asian Women Artists (1st prize for conceptual painting, 1st prize photography), 1978, Yerba Buena Arts Ctr. for the Arts Festival, 1994; represented in permanent collections L.A. County Fedn. Labor, Calif. Mus. Sci. and Industry, AFL-CIO Labor Studies Ctr., Australian Trades Coun., Hazeland and Co., also pvt. collections; author: (poetry) Yuri and Malcolm, The Desert Sun, 1994 (Editors Choice award 1993-94). Del. nat., state convs. Nat. Women's Polit. Caucus, 1977-83, San Francisco chpt. affirmative action chairperson, 1978-82, nat. conv. del., 1978-81, Calif. del., 1976-81. Recipient Honorarium AFL-CIO Labor Studies Ctr., Washington, 1975-76, Bicentennial award 1976; award Centro Studi Ricerche delle Nazioni, Italy, 1985; bd. advisors Psycho Neurology Found. Bicentennial award LA County Mus. Art, 1976, 77, 78, Mandalay Merit award Som Arts Gallery, 2003. Mem. Asian Women Artists (founding v.p., award 1978-79, 1st award in photography of Orient 1978-79, Merit award 2003), Calif. Chinese Artists (sec.-treas. 1978-81), Japanese Am. Art Coun. (chairperson 1978-84, dir.), San Francisco Women Artists, San Francisco Graphics Guild, Pacific/Asian Women Coalition Bay Area, Chinatown Coun. Performing and Visual Arts. Address: PO Box 421415 San Francisco CA 94142-1415

CHING, CHAUNCEY TAI KIN, agricultural studies educator, economist; b. Honolulu, July 25, 1940; m. Theodora Lam, July 7, 1962; children: Donna, Cory. AB in Econs., U. Calif., Berkeley, 1962; MS in Agrl. Econs., U. Calif., Davis, 1965, PhD in Agrl. Econ., 1967. Asst. prof. U. N.H., Durham, 1968-72; assoc. prof. U. Nev., Reno, 1972-77, prof., head div. agrl. and resource econs., 1977-80; prof., chmn. dept. agrl. and resource econs. U. Hawaii, Honolulu, 1980-84, prof. agrl. econs., 1992—, dir. Hawaii Inst. Tropical Agr. and Human Resources, 1984-92. Recipient Charles H. Seurferle award, U. Nev., Reno, 1977. Office: Hawaii Inst Tropical Agr 3050 Maile Way # 202 Honolulu HI 96822-2231 Office Phone: 202-262-6619. E-mail: cc@cching.com.

CHING, DAVID T., food products executive; BSEE magna cum laude, U. Wis.; MS in Computer Scis., U. Calif., Berkeley; MS in Mgmt. Sci., Stanford U. Formerly with Bell Canada and Control Data Canada, Ltd., Toronto; sr. v.p. info. systems Lucky Stores, Inc., 1989-93; gen. mgr. in N. Am. Brit.-Am. Cons. Group, 1993-94; sr. v.p., chief info. officer Safeway, Inc., Pleasanton, Calif., 1994—. Bd. dir. Petco, 2005—, TJX Companies. Office: Safeway Inc PO Box 99 Pleasanton CA 94566-0009

CHINNIS, C. CABELL, JR., lawyer; b. Washington, May 28, 1958; BA in Pub. Affairs, Princeton Univ.; Kennedy fellow, Harvard Univ., 1980—81; JD, Yale Univ., 1984. Bar: Pa. 1986, DC 1988, Calif. 2002, US Tax Ct. 1988. Law clk. Hon. John Minor Wisdom, US Ct. of Appeals (fifth cir.), 1984—85, Hon. Lewis F. Powell Jr., US Supreme Ct., 1985—86; atty. Latham & Watkins, Washington, 1986—93; pvt. practice, 1993—94; assoc. Mayer, Brown, Rowe & Maw LLP, Washington, 1994—97, ptnr., 1997—2001, Palo Alto, Calif., 2001—, now ptnr.-in-charge, Palo Alto office, 2003—. Mng. editor Yale Law Jour., 1984. Mem.: Phi Beta Kappa. Office: Mayer Brown Rowe & Maw LLP Ste 300 3000 El Camino Palo Alto CA 94306-2112 Office Phone: 650-331-2020. Office Fax: 650-331-2067. Business E-Mail: cchinnis@mayerbrownrowe.com.

CHIORAZZI, MICHAEL GERARD, law librarian, educator; b. Jersey City, Dec. 3, 1954; s. John Dominic and Dolores (Bonn) Chiorazzi; m. Vickie Bletso, May 30, 1982; 3 children. BA, U. Miami, 1976; JD, Gonzaga U., 1980; MLL, U. Wash., 1981. Legal rsch. instr., dep. dir. Law Libr. Boston Coll. Sch. Law, Newton, Mass., 1989—96; reference libr., sr. instr. legal rsch. Duke U. Sch. Law, 1981—89; faculty mem. James E. Rogers Coll. Law, U. Ariz., Tucson, 1996—, prof. law & info. resources and libr. sci., dir. Law Libr. Editor: Legal Reference Svcs. Quarterly, 1999—; contbr. articles to profl. jours. Democrat. Office: U Arizona Coll Law Law Libr 1201 E Speedway Blvd Tucson AZ 85721 Home: 3854 E Marble Peak Pl Tucson AZ 85718 Office Phone: 520-621-5477. Office Fax: 520-621-3138. Business E-Mail: michael.chiorazzi@law.arizona.edu.

CHIPLIN, JOHN, medical company executive; b. 1958; BS in Pharmacy, U. Nottingham, Eng.; PhD in Biochemistry, U. Nottingham. CEO Superscape plc; with Molecular Design Ltd., Biosym Technologies, Inc.; co-founder, CEO, pres. GeneFormatics, Inc., San Diego. Mem.: Inst. of Dirs., Royal Soc. of Arts, The Pharm. Soc.

CHIRCO, JUDY, Councilwoman; m. Ed Chirco; children: Steve, Matt. BS, San José State U., 1994. Property mgr., San José; councilwoman, Dist. 9 San José City Coun., 2002—, vice mayor. Vol. Home and Sch. Club; mem. Cambrian Sch. Bd.; bd. mem. People Acting in Cmty. Together. Office: San Jose City Coun 200 E Santa Clara St San Jose CA 95113 Office Phone: 408-277-5275. Office Fax: 408-292-6471. Business E-Mail: District9@sanjoseca.gov.*

CHIROT, DANIEL, sociology and international studies educator; b. Bélâbre, France, Nov. 27, 1942; arrived in U.S.A., 1949. s. Michel and Hélène C.; m. Cynthia (Kenyon), July 19, 1974; children: Claire, Laura. BA in Social Studies, Harvard U., 1964; PhD in Sociology, Columbia U., 1973. Job and Gertrud Tamaki prof. internat. studies U. Wash., Seattle, 1975—, chair internat. studies program, 2001—04. Author: Social Change in a Peripheral Soc., 1976, Social Change in the Twentieth Century, 1977, Social Change in the Modern Era, 1986, Modern Tyrants: The Power and Prevalence of Evil in Our Age, 1994, How Societies Change, 1994; author (with Clark McCauley) Why Not Kill Them All?, 2006; editor: The Origins of Backwardness in Ea. Europe, 1989, The Crisis of Leninism and the Decline of the Left, 1991, (with Anthony Reid) Essential Outsiders, 1997, (with Martin Seligman) Ethnopolitical Warfare, 2001; CARE cons John Simon Guggenheim fellow 1991-92, Sr. fellow US Inst. of Peace, 2004-2005 Avocations: skiing, hiking. Office: U Wash Jackson Sch Intl Studies PO Box 353650 Seattle WA 98195-3650

CHISUM, EMMETT DEWAIN, historian, researcher, archaeologist; b. Monroe, La., Mar. 19, 1922; BA in Social Sci., Northwestern State U., 1942; MA in Social Sci., La. State U., 1946; MA in History, U. Wyo., 1952, MA in Polit. Sci. an dAnthropology, 1961. Tchr. sci. Cameron (La.) Parish Sch. System, 1947-51; tchr. English Welsh (La.) High Sch., 1946-47; social sci. librarian U. Wyo., Laramie, 1954-77, prof. rsch. history, archeology, 1977—. Mem. faculty senate U. Wyo., 1986—. Author: (books) Guide to Library Research, 1969, Guide to Research in Political Science, 1970, Guide to Research in Education, 1974, Memories: University of Wyoming 1886-1986, 1987; contbr. articles to Ency. of Lir. and Info. Sci. (45 vols.), 1986—, profl. jours. Mem. AAAS, ALA, Am. Archeol. Soc., Western Pol. Sci. Assn., Am. Assn. for State and Local History for Wyo. Publs. (Agnes Milstead award for Outstanding Librarianship 1995). Home: 2032 Holliday Dr Laramie WY 82070-4803

CHIU, ARTHUR NANG LICK, engineering educator, consultant; b. Singapore, Mar. 9, 1929; came to U.S., 1948; s. S.J. and Y.N. (Wong) C.; m. Katherine N. Chang, June 12, 1952; children: Vicky, Gregory. BSCE, BA, Oreg. State U., 1952; MSCE, MIT, 1953; PhD in Structural Engring., U. Fla., 1961. Lic. profl. engr., Hawaii. Instr. U. Hawaii, Honolulu, 1953-54, asst. prof., 1954-59, assoc. prof., 1959-64, chmn. dept. civil engring., 1963-66; prof. structural engring. Colo. State U. (on assignment to Asian Inst. Tech., Bangkok, Thailand), 1966-68; acting assoc. dean research, tng. and fellowships grad. div. U. Hawaii, Monoa, 1968, assoc. dean rsch., tng. and fellowships grad. div. Manoa, 1972-76, prof. civil engring., 1964-95, emeritus prof. civil engring., 1995—. Rsch. specialist Space and Info. Sys. divsn. N.Am. Aviation, Inc. (now Rockwell Internat.), Downey, Calif., 1962; vis. scholar UCLA and vis. assoc. Calif. Inst. Tech., Pasadena, 1970; vis. rsch. scientist Naval Civil Engring. Lab., Port Hueneme, Calif., 1976-77; mem. several univ. coms., U. Hawaii; co-chmn. Indo-US Workshop on Wind Disaster Mitigation, 1985, U.S.-Asia Conf. on Engring. for Mitigating Natural Hazards Damage, 1987, 92, U.S.-Japan seminar Wind Effects on Structures, 1970, 74; spkr. in field. Contbr. articles, papers to profl. jours. Recipient Lifetime Achievement award Hawaii Coun. Engring. Socs., 1998, Engr. of Yr. award Hawaii Soc. of Profl. Engrs., 1989, Harold T. Larsen award Chi Epsilon, 1982; NSF sci. faculty fellow, 1959, 60, Phi Kappa Phi fellow, 1952; NSF research grantee 1970—. Hon. mem. ASCE (chmn. wind effects com. 1994-00, Kaoiki earthquake damage assessment team 1983, past pres. Hawaii sect., vice-chmn. coun. disaster reduction 1997—, control mem. 1994-97, mem. aerodynamics com. 1996-00), NSPE, NRC (past chmn., leader Hurricane Iwa damage assessment team, 1982, com. on natural disasters 1985-93, co-chmn. wind engring. panel), Am. Concrete Inst., Structural Engrs. Assn. Hawaii (past. pres., leader Hurricane Iniki damage assessment team 1992), Applied Technology Coun. (bd. dirs. 1996—, v.p. 1999, pres. 2000), Am. Soc. Engring. Edn., Earthquake Engring. Rsch. Inst., Pan-Pacific Tall Bldgs. Conf. (chmn.), Blue Key, Sigma Xi, Chi Epsilon (nat. pres. 1986-88, 88-90, Pacific Dist. councillor 1982-2000, councillor emeritus 2000—, trustee emeritus U. Hawaii chap. 1999—), Pi Mu Epsilon, Phi Eta Sigma, Tau Beta Pi, Phi Beta Delta, Phi Kappa Phi. Home: 1654 Paula Dr Honolulu HI 96816-4316 Office: U Hawaii Manoa Dept Civil Engring 2540 Dole St Honolulu HI 96822-2303 Fax: 808-956-5014. E-mail: achiu@hawaii.edu.

CHIU, DAVID, city supervisor, lawyer; b. Cleve., Apr. 2, 1970; AB in Govt., Harvard Coll.; JD, Harvard Law Sch.; M in Pub. Policy, Harvard John F. Kennedy Sch. Govt. Bar: 1997. Law clk. to Hon. James Browning US Ct. Appeals (9th cir.); staff atty. Lawyers' Com. Civil Rights, San Francisco; criminal prosecutor Dist. Atty's Office, San Francisco; Dem. counsel US Senate Constn. Subcom.; aide to senator Paul Simon Senate; co-founder, COO Grassroots Enterprise Inc.; supr., Dist. 3 San Francisco Bd. Supervisors, 2008—, pres., 2009—, mem. land use & econ. devel. com., Transp. Authority. Judge-arbitrator Polk St. Cmty. Ct., San Francisco; pres. bd. dirs. Youth Leadership Inst.; chmn. bd. dirs. Chinatown Cmty. Devel. Ctr. Named one of Best Lawyers Under 40, Nat. Asian Pacific Am. Bar Assn., 2004. Mem.: Asian Am. Bar Assn. Greater Bay Area (past pres.). Democrat. Office: City Hall 1 Dr Carlton B Goodlett Pl Rm 244 San Francisco CA 94102 Office Phone: 415-554-7450. Office Fax: 415-554-7454. Business E-Mail: David.Chiu@sfgov.org.

CHIU, DOROTHY, retired pediatrician; b. Hong Kong, Aug. 8, 1917; came to U.S., 1946; d. Yan Tse Chiu and Connie Kwai-Ching Wan; m. Kitman Au; children: Katherine, Margo, Doris, James, Richard. BS, Lingnan U., 1939; MD, Nat. Shanghai Med. Coll., 1945. Diplomate Am. Bd. Pediats. Sch. physician L.A. Sch. Dist., 1954-55; pvt. practice Burbank, Calif., 1955—56, San Fernando, Calif., 1956—2000. Staff pediatrician Holy Cross Med. Ctr., Mission Hills, Calif., 1961-2000. Bd. dirs. Burbank Cmty. Concert, 1970-80. Fellow Am. Acad. Pediats.; mem. Calif. Med. Assn., L.A. County Med. Assn. Republican. Avocations: handicrafts, music, travel, reading, photography.

CHIU, JOHN TANG, physician; b. Macao, Jan. 8, 1938; s. Lan Cheong and Yau Hoon C.; m. Bonnie Doolan, Aug. 28, 1965 (div. Apr. 1986); children: Lisa, Mark, Heather; m. Karin Adams, Jan. 3, 2000. Student, U. Vt., BA, 1960, MD, 1964. Diplomate Am. Bd. Allergy & Immunology. Pres. Allergy Med. Group, Inc., Newport Beach, Calif., 1969-72, 1972—. Clin. prof. medicine U. Calif., Irvine, 1975—. Contbr. articles to profl. jours. Active Santa Ana Heights Adv. Commn., 1982-83; life mem. Orange County Sheriff's Adv. coun., 1987—, Recipient Freshman Chem. Achievement award Am. Chem. Soc., 1958. Fellow Am. Acad. Allergy Asthma and Immunology, Am. Coll. Allergy and Immunology, Am. Coll. Chest Physicians (sec. steering com. allergy 1977-81), Orange County Med. Assn. (chmn. comm. com. 1985-88, comm. com., mem. bull. editl. bd. 1995-2001). Avocations: skiing, golf, aerobics, travels. Office: Allergy Med Group Inc 400 Newport Center Dr Newport Beach CA 92660-7601 Office Phone: 949-644-1422. Personal E-mail: allergymed@yahoo.com.

CHIU, PETER YEE-CHEW, physician; came to U.S., 1965; naturalized, 1973; s. Man Chee and Yiu Ying Chiu; m. Elisa; children: Emma, Clara. BS, U. Calif., Berkeley, 1969, MPH, 1970, DrPH, 1975; MD, Stanford U., 1983. Diplomate Am. Bd. Family Practice, Am. Bd. Preventive Medicine; registered profl. engr., Calif.; registered environ. health specialist, Calif. Asst. civil engr. City of Oakland, Calif., 1970-72; assoc. water quality engr. Bay Area Sewage Services Agy., Berkeley, 1974-76; prin. environ. engr. Assn. Bay Area Govts., Berkeley, 1976-79; intern San Jose (Calif.) Hosp., 1983-84, resident physician, 1984-86; ptnr. Chiu and Crawford, San Jose, 1986-89, Good Samaritan Med. Group, San Jose, 1989-90, The Permanente Med. Group, 1991—. Adj. prof. U. San Francisco, 1979-83; adj. clin. assoc. prof. Stanford U. Med. Sch., 1987—. Contbr. articles to profl. publs.; composer, pub. various popular songs Asia, US. Bd. mem. Calif. Regional Water Quality Control Bd.,Oakland, 1979-84, Bay Area Comprehensive Health Planning Coun., San Francisco, 1972-76; mem. Santa Clara County Ctrl. Dem. Com., 1987—; mem. exec. bd. Calif. State Dem. Ctrl. Com.; commr. U.S. Presdl. Commn. on Risk Assessment and Risk Mgmt., Washington, 1993-97; mem. U.S. Presdl. Rank Rev. Bd., Washington, 2000; hearing bd. mem. alt. Bay Area Air Quality Mgmt. Dist., San Francisco, 2002—. Recipient Resident Tchr. award Soc. Tchrs. Family Medicine, 1986, Resolution of Appreciation award Calif. Regional Water Quality Control Bd., 1985, Norman Mineta Lifetime Achievement award Silicon Valley Asian Pacific Am. Dem. Club, 2006. Fellow Am. Acad. Family Physicians; mem. Chi Epsilon, Tau Beta Pi. Democrat. Achievements include co-authored one of the first comprehensive regional environmental management plans in US; pioneered a comprehensive framework for enviromental health risk management. Avocations: songwriting, recording. Office: The Permanente Med Group 770 E Calaveras Blvd Milpitas CA 95035-5491

CHIZECK, HOWARD JAY, engineering educator; BS, Case Western Res. U., 1974, MS, 1976; DSc, MIT, 1982. From asst. prof. to prof. sys. engring. Case Western Res. U., Cleve., 1981-95, prof., chair, 1995-98; prof., chair elec. engring. U. Wash., Seattle, 1998—2003, prof. elec. engring., 2003—. Office Phone: 206-221-3591. E-mail: chizeck@ee.washington.edu.

CHIZEN, BRUCE R., computer software company executive; b. 1955; BS, CUNY Bklyn Coll., 1978. Mgr. merchandising Mattel Electronics, 1980—83; dir. sales Ea. Region Microsoft Corp., 1983—87; founding sr. mgr. to v.p. sales and worldwide mktg. to v.p., gen. mgr. Claris Clear Choice Claris Corp., 1987—94; v.p., gen. mgr. profl. graphics divsn. and consumer divsn. Adobe Systems, Inc., San Jose, Calif., exec. v.p. worldwide products and mktg., 1994—99, pres., 1999—2005, CEO, 2000—07, strategic adv., 2007—. Bd. dirs. Adobe Systems, Inc., 2000—. Synopsys, Inc., 2001—, PBS Found., 2005—. Bd. dirs. Children's Discovery Mus., San Jose. Named one of 50 Who Matter Now, Business 2.0, 2007. Office: Adobe Systems Inc 345 Park Ave San Jose CA 95110-2704

CHMELKA, BRADLEY FLOYD, chemical engineering educator; b. Phoenix, Feb. 23, 1960; BSChemE, Ariz. State U., 1982; PhD in Chem. Engring., U. Calif., Berkeley, 1990. Retort startup engr. Unocal Oil Shale Ops., Parachute, Colo., 1982-84; NSF-chemistry postdoctoral fellow dept. chemistry U. Calif., 1990; NSF-NATO postdoctoral fellow Max-Planck-Institut für Polymerforschung, Mainz, Germany, 1991; asst. prof. dept. chem. engring. U. Calif., Santa Barbara, 1992-95, assoc. prof., 1995-99, prof., 1999—. Recipient Young Investigator award NSF, 1992, Tchr.-Scholar award Camille & Henry Dreyfus Found., 1992; Sci. and Engring. Packard fellow David & Lucile Packard Found., 1993, Rsch. fellow Alfred P. Sloan Found., 1996. Mem. AIChE, Am. Chem. Soc., Am. Phys. Soc., Materials Rsch. Soc. Achievements include devel. and application of nuclear magnetic resonance spectroscopy methods to the characterization of optical, mechanical, absorption and transport properties of new solid-state materials; correlation of macroscopic material properties and function with molecular structure and dynamics, particularly in heterogeneous macromolecular solids. Office: U Calif Dept Chem Engring Santa Barbara CA 93106

CHO, EUNG-RAE (BRIAN), bank executive; b. 1961; BS, Hong-Ik U., 1983; MS, Calif. State U., 1989. CPA. Sr. v.p., CFO Wilshire State Bank, LA, 1995—, Wilshire Bancorp, LA, 2004, exec. v.p., CFO, 2005—. Recipient Elijah Watt Sells Award Gold Medal, 1988. Office: Wilshire Bancorp Inc 3200 Wilshire Blvd Los Angeles CA 90010 Office Phone: 213-387-3200. Office Fax: 213-427-6562.

CHO, HYUN JU, retired veterinary research scientist; b. Chinju, Korea, June 12, 1939; s. Gil Rae and Sun Gae (Park) C.; m. Kim Bok Mee, June 13, 1967; children— Jae Shin, Elisa, Jane. D.V.M., Gyeongsang Nat. U., 1963; M.Sc., Seoul Nat. U., 1966; PhD, U. Guelph, 1973. Vet. rsch. scientist Inst. Vet. Rsch., Anyang, Republic of Korea, 1965—70; vis. scientist Wallaceville Animal Rsch. Ctr., New Zealand, 1968; rsch. scientist Animal Diseases Rsch. Inst. Can. Food Inspection Agy., Lethbridge, Alta., Canada, 1973—2000. Contbr. articles to profl. jours. Achievements include discovering virus of Aleutian disease of mink and developed practical diagnostic test for it. Home: 14 Coachwood Rd W Lethbridge AB Canada T1K 6B6 E-mail: chojdvm@shaw.ca.

CHO, JOHN, actor; b. Seoul, Republic of Korea, June 16, 1972; m. Kerri Higuchi, 2006. Degree in English and lit., U. Calif., Berkeley. Actor: (films) Shopping for Fangs, 1997, Wag the Dog, 1997, Exchange Value, 1998, Yellow, 1998, American Pie, 1999, Bowfinger, 1999, American Beauty, 1999, The Flinstones in Viva Rock Vegas, 2000, Among Others, 2000, Delivering Milo, 2001, Down to Earth, 2001, Pavilion of Women, 2001, Evolution, 2001, American Pie 2, 2001, Better Luck Tomorrow, 2002, Big Fat Liar, 2002, Solaris, 2002, American Wedding, 2003, Western Avenue, 2003, See This Movie, 2004, Harold & Kumar Go to White Castle, 2004, In Good Company, 2004, Bam Bam and Celeste, 2005, American Dreamz, 2006, Bickford Shmeckler's Cool Ideas, 2006, Smiley Face, 2007, The Air I Breathe, 2007, West 32nd, 2007, Harold & Kumar Escape from Guantanamo Bay, 2008, Star Trek, 2009; (TV films) The Tiger Woods Story, 1998, Earth vs. the Spider, 2001, Untitled David Diamond/David Weissman Project, 2005, Up All Night, 2007; (TV series) Off Centre, 2001—02, The Men's Room, 2004, Kitchen Confidential, 2005—06, Ugly Betty, 2007; singer: (band) Left of Zed. Office: c/o Principato Young Mgmt 9465 Wilshire Blvd Ste 880 Beverly Hills CA 90212*

CHO, LEE-JAY, social scientist, demographer; b. Kyoto, July 5, 1936; came to U.S., 1959; s. Sam-Soo and Kyung-Doo (Park) C.; m. Eun-Ja Chun, May 20, 1973; children: Kaia Nuy, Sang-Mun Ray, Han-Jae Jeremy. BA, Kookmin Coll., Seoul, Korea, 1959; MA in Govt., George Washington U., 1962; MA in Sociology, U. Chgo., 1964, PhD in Sociology, 1965; D in Econs. (hon.), Dong-A U., 1982; DSc in Demography, Tokyo U., 1983; D in Econs., Keio U., Tokyo, 1989; D in Econs. (hon.), Russian Acad. Scis., 2000. Statistician Korean Census Coun., 1958-61; research assoc., asst. prof. sociology Population Rsch. and Tng. Ctr., U. Chgo., 1965-66; assoc. dir. Cmty. and Family Study Ctr., 1969-70; sr. demographic adv. to Malaysian Govt., 1967-69; assoc. prof. U. Hawaii, 1969-73, prof., 1973-78; asst. dir. East-West Population Inst., East-West Ctr., Honolulu, 1971-74, dir., 1974-92; pres. pro tem East-West Ctr., 1980-81, v.p., 1987-98, sr. advisor, 1988—2006. Cons. in field; mem. NAS Com. on Population and Demography; mem. U.S. 1980 Census Adv. Com., Dept. Commerce. Author: (with others) Differential Current Fertility in the United States, 1970; editor: (with others) Introduction to Censuses of Asia and the Pacific: 1970-74, 1976, (with Kazumasa Kobayashi) Fertility Transition in East Asian Populations, 1979, (with Suharto, McNicoll and Mamas) Population Growth of Indonesia, 1980, The Own-Children Method of Fertility Estimation, 1986, (with R. Retherford and M. Choe) Economic Development of Republic of Korea: A Policy Perspective, 1989, (with Y.H. Kim) Korea's Political

Economy: An Institutional Perspective, 1994, (with Yada) Tradition and Change in the Asian Family, 1994, (with Y.H. Kim) Hedging Bets on Growth in a Globalizing Industrial Order, 1997, (with Y.H. Kim) Korea's Choices in Emerging Global Competition and Cooperation, 1998, (with Y.H. Kim) Ten Paradigms of Market Economies and Land Systems, 1998, (with Y.H. Kim) The Multi-Lateral Trading System in a Globalizing World, 2000, Restructuring the National Economy, 2001, Restructuring the Korean Financial Market in a Global Economy, 2002, (with C.N. Kim and C.S. Ahn) A Changing Korea in Regional and Global Contexts, 2004; contbr. numerous articles on population and econ. devel. to profl. jours. Bd. dirs. Planned Parenthood Assn., Hawaii, 1976-77. Population Coun. fellow U. Chgo., 1963-64; Ford Found. grantee, 1977-79; Population Coun. grantee, 1973-75; Dept. Commerce grantee, 1974-78; recipient Award of Mugunghwa-Jang, govt. Republic of Korea, 1992, 4th N.E. Asia Niigata prize, 1996. Mem. Internat. Statis. Inst. (tech. adv. com. World Fertility Survey), Internat. Union Sci. Study Population, Population Assn. Am., Am. Statis. Assn., Am. Sociol. Assn., N.E. Asia Econ. Forum (founding chmn.). Home: 1718 Halekoa Dr Honolulu HI 96821-1027 Office: 1601 E West Rd Honolulu HI 96848-1601 Office Phone: 808-591-8688. Personal E-mail: leejaycho@gmail.com.

CHO, ZANG HEE, physics professor; b. Seoul, Korea, July 15, 1936; came to U.S., 1972; m. Jung Sook. BSc, Seoul Nat. U., 1960, MSc, 1962; PhD, Uppsala U., Sweden, 1966. Assoc. prof. Stockholm U., 1971-76, UCLA, 1972-78; prof. Columbia U., NYC, 1979-85; prof. radiological sci. U. Calif., Irvine, 1985—; hon. chair prof. Korea Acad. Indsl. Tech., 1990—. Assoc. dir. Imaging Rsch. Ctr., Columbia U., 1979-84; dir. Nuclear Magnetic Resonance rsch. U. Calif., Irvine, 1985—; organizer tech. programs, symposia and workshops; mem. U.S. nat. adv. coun. complementary and alt. medicine NIH. Author: Foundations of Medical Imaging, 1993; editor-in-chief Internat. Jour. Imaging Sys. and Tech., 1994—; guest editor IEEE Nuclear Sci., 1974, Computers Medicine and Biology, 1976, Image Sci. and Tech., 1989; mem. editorial bd. Physics in Medicine and Biology, Inst. Physics, U.K., 1993, Magnetic Resonance in Medicine, 1984, Computerized Med. Imaging and Graphics, 1989; author/co-author more than 200 original sci. papers in internat. tech. and sci. jours. Named Disting. Scientist, Asilomar, 1982; recipient Grand Sci. prize Seoul, 1984, Jacob Javits Neurosci. award, NIH, 1984, Sylvia Sorkin Greenfield award Am. Assn. Med. Physicists, 1989, Nat. Applied Sci. prize (presdl. award) Korea Sci. Found., 1995, Nat. Acad. Sci. prize Nat. Acad. Scis., Republic of Korea, 1997. Fellow IEEE, Instn. Elec. Engrs. (U.K.), Third World Acad. Sci., Korea Acad. Sci. and Tech. (life); mem. Inst. Medicine of NAS, Nat. Acad. Scis. Republic of Korea. Home: 29 Harbor Pointe Dr Corona Del Mar CA 92625-1333 Office: Univ Calif Dept Radiological Sci Irvine CA 92697-0001

CHONG, ALBERT VALENTINE, artist, educator; b. Kingston, Jamaica, W.I., Nov. 20, 1958; came to U.S., 1977; s. Albert George and Gloria Agnes (Chin) C.; m. Frances Irene Ann Charteris, Nov. 23, 1982; children: Ayinde Jordan, Chinwe Amelia. BFA, Sch. of Visual Arts, NYC, 1981; MFA, U. Calif., San Diego, 1991. Instr. Sch. of Visual Arts, NYC, 1986-88; adjunct faculty Mira Costa Coll., Oceanside, Calif., 1989-90, vis. scholar, 1990-91; asst. prof. art U. Colo., Boulder, 1991—. Program auditor, cons. N.Y. State Coun. on the Arts, N.Y.C., 1984-88. Author: (book) Ancestral Dialogues, 1993; one-man shows include Allen Meml. Art Mus., Oberlin (Ohio) Coll., 1998, William Benton Mus. Art, U. Conn., Storrs, 1998, William King Regional Arts Ctr., Abingdon, Va., 1999, Kiang Gallery, Atlanta, 1999, U. Art Gallery Atrium, U. Mass., Dartmouth, 1999, Carl Keller Gallery, Denver, 1999, Waterloo (Iowa) Mus. Art, 2000, Robert B. Menschel Photography Gallery, Schine Student Ctr., Syracuse (N.Y.) U., 2000; group exhbns. include MEIAC, Spain, 1998, XXIV Biennial, São Paulo, Brazil, 1998, Emmanuel Gallery, Denver, 1999, CUNY, Harlem, 1999, City Gallery East, Atlanta, 1999, Yale U. Art Gallery, New Haven, 2000, Anacostia Mus. and Ctr. for African Am. History and Culture, Washington, 2000. Recipient Regional fellowship NEA, Santa Fe, N. Mex., 1991, Artist's fellowship, Washington, 1992. Office: Univ Colo Boulder PO Box 318 Boulder CO 80309-0318 Home: 140 Cherokee Way Boulder CO 80303-4202

CHONG, ARTHUR, lawyer; B, U. Calif., Berkeley; grad., Harvard Law Sch., 1978. Bar: Calif. 1978. Assoc. McCutchen, Doyle, Brown & Enersen, San Francisco; with McKesson Corp., 1981—2005, dep. gen. counsel, 1999—2005; exec. v.p., gen. counsel Safeco Corp., Seattle, 2005—. Office: Safeco Corp Safeco Plz 4333 Brooklyn Ave NE Seattle WA 98185 Office Phone: 206-545-5000. Office Fax: 206-545-5559.

CHONG, RICHARD DAVID, architect; b. LA, June 1, 1946; s. George and Mabel Dorothy (Chan) C.; m. Roze Gutierrez, July 5, 1969; children: David Gregory, Michelle Elizabeth. BArch, U. So. Calif., 1969; MArch, UCLA, 1974. Registered architect, Utah, Calif., Wyo., Wash. Assoc. Pulliam, Matthews & Assocs., Los Angeles, 1969-76; dir. Asst. Community Design Ctr., Salt Lake City, 1976-77; prin. Richard D. Chong & Assocs., Salt Lake City and L.A., 1977—. Planning cons. Los Angeles Harbor Dept., 1974-76; asst. instr. So. Calif. Inst. Architecture, Santa Monica, 1973-74; vis. design critic Calif. State Poly. U., Pamona, 1975, U. Utah, Salt Lake City, 1976-78; design instr. Calif. State Poly. U., 1975-76; adj. asst. prof. urban design, U. Utah, 1980-84; bd. dirs. Utah Housing Coalition, Salt Lake City; Salt Lake City Housing Adv. and Appeals Bd., 1976-80; presenter Rail-Volution Conf., Washington, 1996. Author: Design of Flexible Housing, 1974; prin. works include Airmen's Dining Hall, 1985 (1st Pl. Mil. Facility Air Force Logistics Command, 1986), Oddfellows Hall, 1984 (Heritage Found. award, 1986), Light Rail Sys. for Salt Lake City. Mem. Task Force for the Aged Housing Com. Salt Lake County, Salt Lake City, 1976-77; Salt Lake City Mortgage Loan Instns. Rev. Com., 1978; bd. dirs. Neighborhood Housing Svcs. of Fed. Home Loan Bank Bd., Salt Lake City, 1979-81, devel. com.; vice-chmn. Water Quality Adv. Coun., Salt Lake City, 1981-83; vice-chmn. Salt Lake City Pub. Utilities Bd., 1985-87; mem. adv. bd. Pub. Utilities Commn., Salt Lake City, 1985—; bd. dirs. Kier Mgmt. Corp.; bd. mem. Camp Kostopulos, Altro Nat. Risk Mgmt. Adv. Bd., 1996—, Ft. Douglas Social Adv. Bd., 1996—, Altro Nat. Safety Bd., 1996-01. Mem. AIA (jury mem. Am. Soc. Interior Designs Ann. awards 1981-82, treas. Salt Lake chpt. 1988-89, treas. Utah Soc. 1991, sec. 1992, pres.-elect AIA Utah 1993, pres. 1994-95), Am. Inst. Planning (juror Ann. Planning award 1984-85), Am. Planning Assn., Am. Arbitration Assn., Nat. Panel Arbitrators, Cottonwood Country Club. Democrat. Avocations: tennis, sailing, travel. Office: Richard D Chong & Assocs 244 Edison St Salt Lake City UT 84111-2307 also: 714 W Olympic Blvd Ste 732 Los Angeles CA 90015-1439

CHONG, VERNON, retired surgeon, military officer; b. Fresno, Calif., Nov. 13, 1933; s. Seu Ling and Ruth (Lee) C.; m. Ann Sumiko Kawana, Sept. 7, 1957; children: Christopher Lee, Gerald Scott, Douglas James. BA, Stanford U., 1955, MD, 1958. Diplomate Am. Bd. Surgery. Intern Gen. Hosp. of Fresno (Calif.) County, 1958-59, resident in gen. surgery, 1959-63; commd. capt. USAF, 1963, advanced through ranks to maj. gen., 1987; chief gen. surgery svc. USAF Hosp., Scott AFB, Ill., 1963-65, staff surgeon, dir. edn. Tachikawa AFB, Japan, 1965-68; staff surgeon, instr. surgery David Grant USAF Med. Ctr., Travis AFB, Calif., 1968-70, dep. comdr., dir. hosp. svcs., 1976—78, comdr., 1978—81; surgeon, chief surgery, dir. hosp. svcs. USAF Acad. Hosp., Colorado Springs, Colo., 1970-74; dep. comdr. USAF Regional Hosp., March AFB, Calif., 1974—76; comdr. Malcolm Grow USAF Med. Ctr., Andrews AFB, Md., 1981-85; command surgeon Hdqrs., Mil. Airlift Command, Scott AFB, 1985-87; comdr. Wilford Hall USAF Med. Ctr., Lackland AFB, Tex., 1987-90, Joint Mil. Med. Command, San Antonio; command surgeon Hdqrs. Air Tng. Command, Randolph AFB, Tex., 1990-91, Hdqrs. U.S. European Command, 1991-94; ret., 1994; network dir. Vets. Integrated Svc. Network VA, Grand Prairie, Tex., 1995-2000; spl. asst. to network dir. Vets. Integrated Svc. Network-21, McClellan Clinic, Sacramento, 2000—03, ret., 2003. Bd. dirs. Alamo chpt. ARC, San Antonio, 1987-88, No. Calif. Retired Officers Cmty. Law, 2004; trustee Air Force Village Found., 1987-90; bd. dirs. San Antonio chpt. ARC, 1995—, No. Calif. Ret. Officers Cmty., 2004—, Calif. Vets. Bd., 2004—. Decorated D.S.M., Legion of Merit with bronze oak leaf cluster; recipient Order of Sword award USAF, 1989. Fellow ACS (gov. 1985-90); mem. Assn. Mil. Surgeons U.S. (bd. mgrs. 1997—, chmn. 2002-04), Soc. Air Force Clin. Surgeons (bd. govs. 1971-73), Am. Coll. Physician Execs., Calif. Vets Bd. Methodist. Avocation: physical fitness. Home: 1820 Starview Ln Lincoln CA 95648

CHOPER, JESSE HERBERT, law educator, dean; b. Wilkes-Barre, Pa., Sept. 19, 1935; s. Edward and Dorothy (Resnick) C.; m. Mari Smith; children: Marc Steven, Edward Nathaniel. BS, Wilkes U., 1957, DHL, 1967; LLB, U. Pa., 1960. Bar: D.C. 1961. Instr. Wharton Sch. U. Pa., 1957-60; law clk. to Chief Justice Earl Warren U.S. Supreme Ct., 1960-61; asst. prof. U. Minn. Law Sch., 1961-62, assoc. prof., 1962-65; prof. Law Sch. U. Calif., Berkeley, 1965—, dean, 1982-92, Earl Warren prof. Pub. Law, 1991—. Vis. prof. Harvard U., 1970—71, Milan U., 1992, Autonoma U., Barcelona, 1996, Vrije U., Amsterdam, 1999, Fordham U., 1999, New South Wales U., 2002. Author: Constitutional Law: Cases-Comments-Questions, 10th edit., 2006, The American Constitution, Cases and Materials, 9th edit., 2001, Constitutional Rights and Liberties, Cases and Materials, 9th edit., 2001, Corporations, Cases and Materials, 7th edit., 2008, The Supreme Court and Its Justices, 2d edit., 2001, Judicial Review and the National Political Process, 1980, Securing Religious Liberty, 1995; contbr. articles to profl. jours. Mem. AAUP, Am. Law Inst., Am. Acad. Arts and Scis., Order of Coif, Calif. Horse Racing Bd. Jewish. Office: U Calif Sch Law Berkeley CA 94720-0001 Office Phone: 510-642-0339. Business E-Mail: choperj@law.berkeley.edu.

CHOPP, FRANK V., state legislator; b. Bremerton, Wash., May 13, 1953; m. Nancy Long; children: Nate, Ellie. BA magna cum laude, U. Wash, Seattle, 1975. Dir. Cascade Cmty. Ctr., 1975—76; mgr. North Cmty. Svc. Ctr. Seattle Dept. Human Resources, 1976—79, 1981—83; adminstrv. dir. Pike Market Sr. Ctr., 1980—81; exec. dir. Fremont Pub. Assn., 1983—2000; part-time lectr. U. Wash. Grad. Sch. Pub. Affairs, 1992-95; mem. Dist. 43 Wash. House of Reps., Olympia, 1994—, spkr. of the house, 1999—; pres. Solid Ground (formerly Fremont Pub. Assn.), 2000—06, sr. adv., 2006—. Democrat. Office: Dist Office 444 NE Ravenna Blvd Ste 106 Seattle WA 98115 also: 339C Legislative Bldg PO Box 40600 Olympia WA 98504-0600 Office Phone: 360-786-7920, 206-729-3223. Business E-Mail: chopp.frank@leg.wa.gov.*

CHOPRA, ANIL KUMAR, civil engineering educator; b. Peshawar, India, Feb. 18, 1941; came to U.S., 1961, naturalized, 1977; s. Kasturi Lal and Sushila (Malhotra) C.; m. Hamida Banu, Dec. 7, 1976. BSc in Engring., Banaras Hindu U., Varanasi, India, 1960; MS, U. Calif., Berkeley, 1963, PhD, 1966. Design engr. Standard Vacuum Oil Co., New Delhi, 1960-61, Kaiser Engrs. Overseas Corps, India, 1961; asst. prof. civil engr. U. Minn., Mpls., 1966-67; mem. faculty U. Calif., Berkeley, 1967—, prof. civil engring., 1976-92, Johnson prof. engring., 1992—. Dir. Applied Tech. Coun., Palo Alto, 1972-74; mem. com. natural disasters NRC, 1980-85, chmn., 1982-83; adv. com. on structural safety of VA facility Dept. Vet. Affairs, Washington, 1995-2000; consulting bd. for earthquake analysis Calif. Divn. Safety of Dams, 1996-; cons. earthquake engring. to govt. and industry. Author: Dynamics of Structures, A Primer, 1981, Dynamics of Structures: Theory and Applications to Earthquake Engineering, 1995, 3d edit., 2007, Earthquake Dynamics of Structures, A Primer, 2006—; gen. editor: Earthquake Engring. & Structural Dynamics Jour., 1996—; contbr. articles to more than 300 profl. pubs. Recipient Gold medal Banaras Hindu U., 1960, Disting. Alumnus award, 1980, certificate of merit for paper Indian Soc. Earthquake Tech., 1974, honor award Assn. Indians in Am., 1985, AT&T Found. award Am. Soc. Engring. Edn., 1987, Disting. Tchg. award Berkeley Campus, 1999, Nat. award Ministry Sci. and Tech., Govt. Venezuela, 2003. Fellow: Structural Engrs. Assn. Calif.; mem.: NAE (elected in 1984), ASCE (EMD exec. com. 1981—87, chmn. 1985—86, mem. STD exec. com. 1988—92, chmn. 1990—91, Walter L. Huber prize 1975, Norman medal 1979, Reese rsch. prize 1989, Norman medal 1991, Newmark medal 1993, Howard award 1998, Norman medal 2001), U.S. Com. on Large Dams, Earthquake Engring. Rsch. Inst. (bd. dirs. 1990—93, George W. Housner medal 2002), Internat. Assn. Earthquake Engring. (hon.), Structural Engrs. Assn. No. Calif. (bd. dirs. 1987—89), Seismol. Soc. Am. (bd. dirs. 1982—83). Home: 635 Cross Ter Orinda CA 94563 Office: Univ Calif Dept Civil Engring Berkeley CA 94720-0001

CHOPRA, DEEPAK, preventive medicine physician, writer; b. Oct. 22, 1946; s. Krishna Chopra; m. Rita Chopra; children: Mallika, Gotham. Grad., All India Inst. Med. Sci. Founder, CEO, medical dir. edn. prog. The Chopra Center, La Costa Resort and Spa, 1995—. Author: Return of the Rishi, 1989, Quantum Healing, 1990, Perfect Health, 1990, Unconditional Life, 1991, Creating Health, 1991, Creating Affluence, 1993, Ageless Body, Timeless Mind, 1993, Restful Sleep, 1994, Perfect Weight, 1994, Journey Into Healing, 1994, The Seven Spiritual Laws of Success, 1995, Return of Merlin, 1995, Como Crear Abundancia/How to Create Wealth, 1999, Everyday Immorality: A Concise Course in Spiritual Transformation, 1999, How to Know God: The Soul's Journey into the Mystery of Mysteries, 2000, The Daughters of Joy: An Adventure of the Heart, 2002, Book of Secrets: Unlocking the Hidden Dimensions of Your Life, 2004, Peace Is the Way: Bringing War and Violence to an End in Our Time, 2005 (Quills award-religion/spirituality, 2005), Ask The Kabala: Oracle Cards/Kabala Guidebook, 2006, Power Freedom and Grace: Living from the Source of Lasting Happiness, 2006, Life After Death: The Burden of Proof, 2006, Kama Sutra: Including the Seven Spiritual Laws of Love, 2006, Buddha: A Story of Enlightenment, 2007, The Third Jesus: The Christ We Cannot Ignore, 2008; (with David Simons, Vicki Abrams) Magical Beginnings, Enchanted Lives, 2005; albums include A Gift of Love, 2001, Grow Younger, Live Longer, 2001, The Soul of Healing Meditations, 2001, The New Physics of Healing, 2002, Chakra Balancing, 2004, Body, Mind & Soul, vol. 2, 2007, Whispers of Spirit & Happiness, 2008, Rasa Living Wellness, vol. 1, 2008. Office: Chopra Ctr for Well Being 2100 Costa del Mar Rd Carlsbad CA 92009

CHOPRA, INDER JIT, endocrinologist; b. Gujranwala, India, Dec. 15, 1939; came to U.S., 1967; s. Kundan Lal and Labhwati (Bagga) C.; m. Usha Prakash, Oct. 16, 1966; children: Sangeeta, Rajesh, Madhu. B of Medicine and BS, All India Inst. Med. Scis., New Delhi, India, 1961, MD, 1965. Intern All India Inst. Med. Scis., New Delhi, 1961-62, clin. resident, 1962-65, registrar in medicine, 1966-67; resident Queens Med. Ctr., Honolulu, 1967-68; fellow in endocrinology Harbor Gen. Campus UCLA Sch. Medicine, 1968-71; asst. prof. of medicine UCLA, 1971-74, assoc. prof., 1974-78, prof., 1978—. Mem. VA Merit Rev. Bd. in Endocrinology, 1988-91. Contbr. more than 280 rsch. articles, revs. and book chpts. to profl. lit. Recipient Rsch. Career Devel. award, NIH, 1972. Master Am. Coll. Physicians; mem. Endocrine Soc. (Ernst Oppenheimer award 1980), Am. Thyroid Assn. (Van Meter-Armour award 1977, Parke-Davis award 1988, Disting. Svc. award 1995), Am. Soc. Clin. Investigation, Assn. of Am. Physicians, Western Assn. Physicians, Am. Fed. for Clin. Rsch. Achievements include patent for radioimmunoassay for measurement of thyroxine and triiodothyonine. Office: UCLA Sch Medicine Ctr for Health Scis 24-130 Warren Hall 900 Veteran Ave Los Angeles CA 90024-2703 Home Phone: 818-222-5683; Office Phone: 310-825-2346. Business E-Mail: ichopra@mednet.ucla.edu.

CHORIN, ALEXANDRE JOEL, mathematician, educator; b. Warsaw, June 25, 1938; came to U.S., 1962, naturalized, 1971; s. Joseph and Hannah (Judowicz) C.; m. Alice Louise Jones, Aug. 11, 1965 (div. June 2006); 1 son, Ethan Daniel; m. Esther Brass, Mar. 23, 2007. Diploma in engring., Swiss Fed. Inst. Tech., Lausanne, 1961; MSc, NYU, 1964, PhD, 1966; DSc (hon.), Israel Inst. Tech., 2003, Swiss Fed. Inst. Tech., 2005. Rsch. scientist NYU, 1966-69, asst. prof. math., 1969-71; assoc. prof. U. Calif., Berkeley, 1972-73, prof., 1973—, Miller rsch. prof., 1971-72, 82-83, Chancellor's prof., 1997-2000, Univ. prof., 2002—; sr. staff scientist Lawrence Berkeley Lab., 1980—; dir. Ctr. Pure and Applied Math. U. Calif., Berkeley, 1980—82, 1995—2004. Disting. vis. prof. Inst. for Advanced Study, Princeton, N.J., 1991-92; faculty rsch. lectr. U. Calif., Berkeley, 1999-00; vis. prof. Coll. France, 1992. Author: (with J. Marsden) A Mathematical Introduction to Fluid Dynamics, 1979, Computational Fluid Mechanics, selected papers, 1989, Vorticity and Turbulence, 1994, (with O.H. Hald) Stochastic Tools for Mathematics and Science, 2005; contbr. articles to profl. jours. Recipient Nat. Acad. Scis. award, 1989, Norbert Wiener prize Am. Math. Soc., Soc. Indsl. Applied Math., 2000, Sarlo award, Berkeley, 2008; fellow Sloan Found., 1972-74, Guggenheim Found., 1987-88. Fellow Am. Acad. Arts and Scis.; mem. NAS. Office: U Calif Dept Math Berkeley CA 94720-0001 Home: 522 Colusa Ave Berkeley CA 94707 Business E-Mail: chorin@math.berkeley.edu.

CHOU, KUO-CHEN, biophysical chemist; b. Guangdong, China, Aug. 14, 1938; came to U.S., 1980; s. Hsiu-Chi Chou and Bi-Kun Luo; m. Wei-Zhu Zhong, Apr. 12, 1968; 1 child, James Jeiwen Chou. BS, Nanking U., China, 1960, MS, 1962; PhD, Shanghai (Peoples Republic China) Inst. Biochemistry, 1976; DSc, Kyoto U., Japan, 1983. Jr. scientist Shanghai Inst. Biochemistry, Chinese Acad. Sci., 1976-78, assoc. prof., 1978-79; vis. assoc., prof. Chem. Ctr. Lund (Sweden) U., 1979-80; vis. assoc. prof. Max-Planck Inst. Biophys. Chemistry, Göttingen, Fed. Republic Germany, 1979-80; vis. assoc. prof. chemistry Cornell U., Ithaca, NY, 1980-83, sr. scientist Baker Lab., 1984-85; prof. biophysics U. Rochester, 1985—86; sr. scientist Eastman Kodak Co., Rochester, 1986-87, Upjohn Labs., Kalamazoo, 1987—92, sr. prin. scientist, 1993—99, rsch. advisor, 1999—2002; sr. rsch. adviser Pharmacia & Upjohn, Kalamazoo, 1995—, Pfizer, 2002—; founding pres. and chief scientist Gordon Inst. Life Sci., 2003—; hon. pres., chmn. scientific com. Tianjin Inst. Bioinformatics and Drug Discovery, China, 2003—07; adv. prof. Shanghai Jiao Tong U., 2004—, Tonghai U., 2004—, Northwestern Poly. U., 2007—, Guangx U., 2007—. Editor Jour. Molecular Sci., 1983-86, Progress in Physics, 1981-85, bioinformatics sect. Amino Acids, 2004-07; assoc. editor: Medicinal Chemistry, 2004—, Jour. Theoretical Biology, 2005—; regional editor: Western Am., Protein and Peptide Letters, 2006-; mem. editl. bd. Current Peptide and Protein Sci., 2000—, Cancer Therapy, 2003-, Current Proteomics, 2007-, Jour. Biophysics, 2008-; editor-in-chief Jour. Biomed. Sci. and Engring., 2008-; editl. bd. mem. Intedisciplinary Sci., 2007-; editor-in-chief Open Bioinformatics Jour., 2008-; contbr. more than 360 rsch. articles and rev. papers to profl. jours. Recipient Sci. and Tech. award Shanghai Com. of Sci. and Tech., 1977, Nat. medal of Sci., Nat. Acad. of Sci., China, 1978, Disting. Leadership award Am. Biog. Inst., N.C., 1989, Commemorative medal of Honor, Am. Biog. Inst., 1991; named for Leadership and Achievement, Internat. Biog. Ctr., Cambridge, U.K., 1990. Fellow Am. Inst. Chemistry; mem. AAAS, N.Y. Acad. Scis., Biophysical Soc., Am. Chem. Soc., Sigma Xi. Achievements include rsch. in bioinformatics, protein conformation and folding; graph theory in chem. reaction systems; enzyme kinetics; DNA codon usage analysis; prediction of enzyme functional class; prediction of protein subcellular localization; prediction membrane protein type, prediction of signal pettides, prediction of protease type, prediction of enzyme functional class, prediction protien-protien interaction, sys. biology; structure and function of antifreeze protein; prediction of HIV protease cleavage site; low-frequency collective motions of biomacromolecules and their biol. functions; structures of growth hormone and membrane proteins, proton-pumping mechanism of membrane proteins, inhibition kinetics of HIV reverse transcriptase, structure and binding site of adhesion proteins, apoptosis, human GFAT, G-protein couple receptors; GABA and GPCR receptors, cyclin-dependent kinases, molecular mechanism of Alzheimer's Disease; BACE1/BACE2, Alpha-7 nicotinic acetylcholine receptor, Ions channels, binding mechanism of coronavirus main proteinase with ligands; drug design for SARS therapy; prediction signal peptides and their cleavage sites. Office: 13784 Torrey Del Mar Dr San Diego CA 92130

CHRAPATY, DEBRA J., computer software company executive; BA in Econs., Temple U.; MBA, NYU. With Bertelsmann AG, EMI Records Group Inc., Fed. Reserve Bank of NY; chief tech. officer

NBA; pres., COO E*TRADE Technologies, AllBusiness Inc.; v.p. tech. Organic Inc.; corp. v.p. MSN ops. Microsoft Corp., Redmond, Wash., 2003, now corp. v.p. global found. svcs. Recipient Chief of Yr. Award, Info. Week, 1998; named one of Top 100 Leaders for the Next Millennium, CIO Mag. Office: Microsoft Corp One Microsoft Way Redmond WA 98052-6399

CHRISPEELS, MAARTEN JAN, biology professor; b. Kortenberg, Belgium, Feb. 10, 1938; married, 1966; 2 children. PhD in Agronomy, U. Ill., 1964. Rsch. asst. agronomy U. Ill., La Jolla, 1963-64; rsch. assoc. plant biochemistry Rsch. Inst. Advanced Studies, 1964-65, AEC, 1965-67; rsch. assoc. microbiology Perdue U., 1967, from asst. prof. to assoc. prof., 1967-79; prof. biology U. Calif., San Diego, 1979—. Program mgr. competitive rsch. grant office USDA, 1979. John. S. Guggenheim Found. fellow, 1973-74. Mem. AAAS, NAS, Am. Soc. Plant Physiologists (Stephen Hales prize 1996), Am. Soc. Cell Biologists. Office: U Calif at San Diego Div Biological Sci 9500 Gilman Dr La Jolla CA 92093-0116

CHRISTEN, MORGAN, state supreme court justice; m. Jim Torgerson; 2 children. BA, Univ. Wash., 1983; JD, Golden Gate Univ., 1986. Bar: Alaska 1987. Law clk. Judge Brian Shortell; assoc. Preston, Gates & Ellis, 1987—92, ptnr., 1992—2001; judge Alaska Superior Ct., Anchorage, 2001—09; presiding judge Alaska 3d Jud. Dist., 2005—09; assoc. justice Alaska Supreme Ct., 2009—. Bd. dir. Rasmuson Found., Alaska Cmty. Found. Recipient Light of Hope award, 2004, Athena Soc. award, Anchorage C. of C., 2004, Cmty. Outreach award, Alaska Supreme Ct., 2008; co-recipient Philanthropist of the Yr., 2006. Mem.: Anchorage Assn. Women lawyers (pres.). Mailing: Alaska Supreme Ct PO Box 114100 Juneau AK 99811-4100*

CHRISTENSEN, BECKY VANDERHOOF, lawyer; m. Raymond T. Sheehan, Jr., July 15, 2000; children: Todd Sheehan, Casey Sheehan, Tiffany Sheehan. BS in Econs., Va. Tech., Blacksburg, 1980; JD, U. Va., Charlottesville, 1983. Bar: Calif. 1990, Wash. 1983. Assoc. atty. Ferguson & Burdell, Seattle, 1983, Munns Kofford, Pasadena, Calif., 1983; ptnr. Chan & Christensen, LA, 1994—96; mng. atty. Law Offices Becky Christensen, Malibu, Calif., 1996—2004; ptnr. O'Connor Christensen & McLaughlin, Irvine, Calif., 2004—06, Eclipse Group LLP, Irvine, 2006—. Editl. review bd. Jour. Law, Ethics and Intellectual Property. Nat. adv. bd. Yes I Can, Canoga Park, Calif., 2002—. Mem.: Am. Intellectual Property Law Assn. (anti counselor subcom.), Nat. Assn. Women Bus. Owners (legal counsel 2006—). Office: Eclipse Group LLP 1920 Main St # 150 Irvine CA 92614

CHRISTENSEN, BRUCE LEROY, former academic administrator, commercial broadcasting executive; b. Ogden, Utah, Apr. 26, 1943; s. LeRoy and Wilma (Olsen) C.; m. Barbara Lucelle Decker, June 17, 1965; children— Jennifer, Heather, Holly, Jesse BA cum laude, U. Utah, 1968; MS, Northwestern U., 1969. Radio and TV news reporter KSL, Inc., Salt Lake City, 1965-68, state house corr., 1969-70; weekend sports writer WGN Radio and TV News, 1968-69; instr. U. Utah, 1969-70, adj. assoc. prof. broadcast regulation, 1980-81, gen. mgr. Sta. KUED-TV and KUER-FM, 1979-82, dir. media svcs., 1981-82; asst. to dir. univ. rels. Brigham Young U., 1970-72, asst. prof., 1971-79, dir. dept. broadcast svcs., 1972-79; pres. Nat. Assn. Pub. TV Stas., Washington, 1982-84; pres., chief exec. officer PBS, Washington, 1984-93; dean Coll. Fine Arts and Comm., prof. comm. Brigham Young Univ., Provo, 1993-2000; sr. v.p. New Media Bonneville Internat., Salt Lake City, 2000—. Bd. govs. Pacific Mt. Network, 1979-82, chmn., 1978-80; vice chmn. (USA) Internat. Coun. Nat. Acad. Arts and Scis., 1990-91, pres. Internat. Coun. NATAS, 1992-93; pres. Prix Italia, 1993; producer, writer Channel 5 Eye-Witness News, 1967-68; bd. dirs. Bonneville Internat. Corp., Fund for Ancient and Mormon Studies, Lance Armstrong Found. for Cancer Rsch. Exec. producer numerous TV documentaries including The Great Dinosaur Discovery, 1973, A Time to Dance, 1976, Navajo, 1976, Christmas Snows, Christmas Winds, 1978 (Emmy award 1978). Bd. dirs. Utah Lung Assn., 1976-82, pres., 1978-80 Recipient Disting. Alumnus award U. Utah, 1989; Allen-Heath fellow Medill Sch. Journalism Northwestern U., 1969; recipient Ralph Lowell medal Corp. for Pub. Broadcasting, 1994. Fellow Internat. Coun. NATAS; mem. Rocky Mountain Corp. for Pub. Broadcasting (bd. dirs.), Sigma Delta Chi (pres. U. Utah chpt. 1967-68), Kappa Tau, Phi Kappa Phi. Avocation: photography. Office: Bonnieville Internat PO Box 1160 Salt Lake City UT 84110-1160

CHRISTENSEN, HAROLD GRAHAM, lawyer; b. Springville, Utah, June 25, 1926; s. Harold and Ruby (Graham) C.; m. Gayle Sutton, June 17, 1950; children: Steven H., David S., Susan; m. Jacquita W. Corry, Dec. 13, 1988. AB, U. Utah, 1949; JD, U. Mich., 1951. Bar: Utah 1952. Ptnr. firm Skeen, Worsley, Snow & Christensen (and successor firms), Salt Lake City; dep. atty. gen. of the U.S., 1988-89; of counsel Snow Christensen & Martineau, P.C., Salt Lake City, 1992—. Practitioner-in-residence, U. Utah, 1989; vis. prof. Coll. Law, U. Calif., San Francisco, 1990; disting. vis. prof. Bond U., Queensland, Australia, 1991. Served with USNR, 1944-46. Fellow Am. Coll. Trial Lawyers, Am. Bar Found.; mem. Utah State Bar (pres. 1975-76), Utah Bar Found. (trustee 1978), Salt Lake County Bar (pres. 1972-73), Am. Inns of Ct. Found. (trustee 1983-89). Home: 2269 Pheasant Way Salt Lake City UT 84121-1312 Office: 10 Exchange Pl 11th Floor Salt Lake City UT 84111 Office Phone: 801-521-9000. Business E-Mail: hchristensen@scmlaw.com.

CHRISTENSEN, HAYDEN, actor; b. Vancouver, BC, Canada, Apr. 19, 1981; s. David and Alie Christensen. Actor: (TV series) Family Passions, 1993; (films) Street Law, 1995, In the Mouth of Madness, 1995, Strike!, 1998, The Virgin Suicides, 1999, Life as a House, 2001, Star Wars: Episode II Attack of the Clones, 2002, Shattered Glass, 2003, Star Wars: Episode III Revenge of the Sith, 2005 (Best Villain, MTV Movie awards, 2006), Factory Girl, 2006, Virgin Territory, 2007, Awake, 2007, Jumper, 2008; (TV films) Love and Betrayal: The Mia Farrow Story, 1995, Harrison Bergeron, 1995, No Greater Love, 1996, Freefall, 1999, Trapped in a Purple Haze, 2000, R2-D2: Beneath the Dome, 2001, numerous TV guest appearances. Office: c/o The Gersh Agy 232 N Canon Dr Beverly Hills CA 90210

CHRISTENSEN, RAY RICHARDS, lawyer; b. Salt Lake City, July 7, 1922; s. E.R. and Carrie (Richards) C.; m. Carolyn Crawford, July 9, 1954 (dec. 1986); children: Carlie, Paul Ray, Joan, Eric.; m. Jeanne F. Pyke, June 24, 1989. LL.B., U. Utah, 1944. Bar: Utah 1944. Enforcement atty. OPA, 1946; law clk. to Utah Supreme Ct. Justice Wolfe, 1947-48; practice in Salt Lake City, 1949—; ptnr. Christensen & Jensen, P.C. (and predecessors), 1949—. Mem. Utah Bar Commn., 1963-66. Bd. dirs. Salt Lake City Jr. C. of C., 1949-53, v.p., 1950-52. Served with AUS, 1943-46. Recipient award, Fed. Bar Assn., 2005. Fellow Internat. Acad. Trial Lawyers (bd. dirs. 1982-88), Am. Coll. Trial Lawyers (state chmn. 1984-85); mem. ABA (mem. council jr. bar conf. 1952-56, ho. of dels. 1966-68, 73-79, mem. council bar activities sect. 1967-70), Utah State Bar (pres. 1965-66, Utah Lawyer of Yr. 1981, Utah Trial Lawyer of Yr. 1993, Lifetime Svc. to Bar award 2006), Salt Lake County Bar Assn., Western States Bar Conf. (pres. 1969-70), Phi Eta Sigma, Phi Kappa Phi. Home: 992 Oak Hills Way Salt Lake City UT 84108-2022 Office: Christensen & Jensen PC 15 W South Temple Ste 800 Salt Lake City UT 84101 Office Phone: 801-323-5000. Business E-Mail: ray.christensen@chrisjen.com.

CHRISTENSEN, RICHARD MONSON, mechanical and materials engineer; b. Idaho Falls, July 3, 1932; married, 1958; 2 children. BSc, U. Utah, 1955; ME, Yale U., 1956, DEng, 1961. Structural engr. Convair Divsn., Gen. Dynamics, 1956-58; with technical staff TRW Systems, 1961-64; asst. prof. mech. engring. U. Calif. Berkeley, 1964-67; staff rsch. engr. Shell Devel. Co., 1967-74; prof. mech. engring. Washington U., 1974-76; sr. scientist technical staff Lawrence Livermore (Calif.) Nat. Lab., 1976—. Lectr. U. So. Calif., 1962-64, U. Calif. Berkeley, 1969-70, 78, 80, U. Houston, 1973; mem. U.S. Nat. Com. Theoretical and Applied Mechanics, 1980-82, 85-94; mem. Dept. Energy Panel, 1985-87; cons. prof. Stanford U., 1994—, rsch. prof., 1996—; Sir Geoffrey Taylor Meml. lectr. U. Fla., 1991. Assoc. editor Jour. Applied Mechanics, 1984-90. Fellow ASME (chmn. applied mechanics divsn. 1980-81, hon. mem. 1992, William Prager medal); mem. Nat. Acad. Engring. (Worcester Reed Warner Gold medal), Am. Chem. Soc., Soc. Rheology. Achievements include research in properties of polymers, in wave propagation, in failure theories, in crack kinetics, in composite materials. Office: Lawrence Livermore Nat Lab PO Box 808 Livermore CA 94551-0808

CHRISTENSEN, RONALD E., physician; b. Seattle, Oct. 22, 1948; MD, U. Tenn., Coll. Medicine, 1975. Intern Riverside Gen. Co. Hosp., 1974—75; resident in family practice San Bernardino Co. Hosp., 1975—77; asst. assoc. clinical prof. U. Alaska, Coll. Nursing and Health Sci.; preceptor U. Wash.; physician, family practice Arrowhead Reg. Med. Ctr. Trustee Am. Bd. Family Practice, 1999—2004, treas., 2002—03, pres., 2003—04. Mem.: Am. Acad. Family Physicians (bd. dirs. 1995—98). Avocations: fishing, skiing. Office: Independence Park Med Svc 9500 Independence Dr #900 Anchorage AK 99507-4600 Office Fax: 907-522-1343.

CHRISTIAENS, CHRIS (BERNARD FRANCIS), financial analyst, state legislator; b. Conrad, Mont., Mar. 7, 1940; s. Marcel Jules and Virgie Jeanette (Van Spyk) C. BA in Chemistry, Coll. Gt. Falls, 1962, M in human svcs., 1994. Fin. and ins. mgr. Rice Motors, Gt. Falls, Mont., 1978-84; mem. Mont. Senate, Dist. 23, Helena, 1983-87, 1991—; majority whip 49th legis., 1985-86; fin. planner Jack Stevens CPA, Gt. Falls, 1984-85; adminstr., fin. analyst Gt. Falls Pre-Release, 1986-92; mem. Reforming States Group Health Care Reform, 1994—; ops. dir. Mont. Farmers Union, 2004—. Owner Oak Oak Inn-Bed and Breakfast, 1989-95; faculty U. Gt. Falls, part-time 1995—; bd. dirs. World Wide Press Inc., svc. rep., 1994—; gen. mgr. Gt. Falls Transit Dist.; adj. faculty U. Great Falls, 1994—; steering com. Reforming States Group; lobbyist Mont. Landlord Assn., 2002—, Mont. Farmers Union, 2002—, Mont. State Legislature, 2003—. Chmn. Balance of State Pvt. Industry Coun., Mont., 1984-2002; mem. Mont. Human Rights Commn., 1981-84; bd. dirs. St. Thomas Child and Family Ctr., Gt. Falls, 1983—, Coll. of Gt. Falls, 1984—, Cascade County Mental Health Assn., 1986—, Salvation Army, Habitat for Humanity, 1992-95; adv. bd. State Drug and Alcohol Coun., State Mental Health Coun., Cambridge Court Sr. Citizen Apt. Complex, 1986; bd. dirs. treas. Gt. Falls Cmty. Food Bank, 1984-86; Dem. committeeman Cascade County, 1976-82; Mont. del. to Nat. Rules Conv., 1980; pub. chmn. Cascade County chpt. ARC, 1986; treas. Cascade County Mental Health Ctr.; vice chmn. Gov.'s Task Force on Prison Overcrowding, regional jail com.; mem. Re-Leaf Gt. Falls Com., 1989—, steering com.; active Gt. Falls and Cascade County Housing Task Force, 1995—; sec. Montanan's for the Coal Trust, 2003—; mem. steering com. Mont. Vets. Meml., 2002—. Recipient Outstanding Young Alumni award Coll. of Gt. Falls, 1979, Hon. Alumni Achievement award, 1994; Disting. Svc. award Rocky Mountain Coun. Mental Health Ctrs., 1995. Mem. Gt. Falls Ski Club, Toastmasters, Optimists, Big Sky Cum Christo. Roman Catholic. Avocations: skiing, tennis, fishing, reading, hiking. Address: 600 36th St S Great Falls MT 59405-3508

CHRISTIAN, GARY D., chemistry professor; b. Eugene, Oreg., Nov. 25, 1937; s. Roy C. and Edna Alberta (Trout) Gonier; m. Suanne Byrd Coulbourne, June 17, 1961; children: Dale Brian, Fred, Tanya Danielle, Tabitha Star. BS, U. Oreg., 1959; MS, U. Md., 1962, PhD, 1964; PhD (hon.), Chiang Mai U., 2005. Rsch. analytical chemist Walter Reed Army Inst. Rsch., Washington, 1961-67; asst. prof. U. Md., College Park, 1965-66, U. Ky., Lexington, 1967-70, assoc. prof., 1970-72; prof. chemistry U. Wash., Seattle, 1972—2006, acting chmn. dept., 1990, assoc. chmn., 1991—92, divisional dean sci., 1993—2001, prof. emeritus, 2006—. Vis. prof. Free U. Brussels, 1978-79; invited prof. U. Geneva, 1979; cons. Ames Co., 1968-72, Beckman Instruments, Inc., 1972-84, 88, Westinghouse Hanford Co., 1977-83, Tech. Dynamics, 1983-85, Porton Diagnostics, 1990-91, Bend Rsch., 1992-93, E.I. DuPont de Nemours, Inc., 1993; examiner Grad. Record Exam., 1985-90. Author: Analytical Chemistry, 6th edit., 2003, Instrumental Analysis, 1978, 2d edit., 1986, Atomic Absorption Spectroscopy, 1970, Trace Analysis, 1986, Problem Solving in Analytical Chemistry, 1988, Calculations in Pharmaceutical Sciences, 1993; editl. bd. Analytical Letters, 1971-2004, Can. Jour. Spectroscopy, 1974-96, Analytical Instrumentation, 1974-93, Talanta, 1980-88 (spl. editor USA honor issue, 1989), Analytical Chemistry, 1985-89, Critical Revs. in Analytical Chemistry, 1985—, The Analyst, 1986-90, Jour. Saudi Chem. Soc., 1995—; editor in chief Talanta, 1989—, Electroanalysis, 1988— (65th Birthday Spl. Issue, 2002), Jour. Pharm. and Biochem. Analysis, 1990-97, Fresenius' Z. Analytical Chem., 1991-93, Laborator Automation, 1992—, Quimica Analitica, 1993-2001, Sensors, 2001-, Jordanian Jour. Chemistry, 2005-, Inetrnat. Jour. Electro Sci., 2006-; contbr. articles to profl. jours. Recipient Medal of Honor, U. Libre, Brussels, 1978, Talanta medal, Elsevier Sci., 1995, Commemorative medal, Charles U., 1999, Geoff Wilson medal, Deakin U., 2003, Sr. Scholar Silver award, Thailand Rsch. Fund, 2004; Fulbright Hays scholar, 1978—79. Mem. Am. Chem. Soc. (sect. chmn. 1982-83, chmn. elect divsn. analytic chemistry 1988-89, chmn. 1989-90, divsn. Analytical Chemistry award for Excellence in Tchg. 1988, Fisher award in analytical chemistry 1996), Soc. Applied Spectroscopy (sect. chmn. 1982), Spectroscopy Soc. Can., Am. Inst. Chemists (cert.), Soc. Electroanalytical Chemistry (bd. dirs. 1993-98), Chem. Soc. Thailand, Soc. Western Analytical Profs., Japan Soc. Analytical Chemistry (Sci. Honor medal 2003, Honorary mem., 2006), U. Md. (cir. of discovery inductee, 2007). Republican. Home: PO Box 26 Medina WA 98039-0026 Office: Univ Wash Dept Chemistry Box 351700 Seattle WA 98195-1700 Home Phone: 425-454-9361; Office Phone: 206-543-1635. Office Fax: 206-685-3478. Business E-Mail: christian@chem.washington.edu.

CHRISTIAN, RALPH GORDON, veterinary pathologist, agriculturalist, consultant, researcher; b. Lethbridge, Alta., Can., Apr. 17, 1942; s. Wesley Peel and Mary (Patterson) C.; m. Brenda Esther Kheong, 1976. DVM, U. Guelph, Ont., Can., 1966; Diploma in Vet. Pathology, U. Sask., Saskatoon, 1971. Cert. in vet. pathology Am. Coll. Vet. Pathologists. Instr. Vet. Sch. U. Melbourne, Australia, 1977; dir. animal health divsn. Alta. Dept. Agr., Edmonton, 1982-87; acting asst. dep. min. Alta. Agrl. Prodn. Sector, Edmonton, 1987; exec. dir. Alta. Agrl. Rsch. Inst., Edmonton, 1987—2000; exec. dir. rsch. divsn. Alta. Dept. Agr., Food and Rural Devel., Edmonton, 1987-2000; pres. Ralph Christian Cons., Inc., 2001—. Br. head pathology br. Alta. Agr. Vet. Lab., Edmonton, 1972-79, 79-82; lab. head Vet. Lab., Fairview, Alta., 1970-72; instr., resident pathology dept. Western Coll. Vet. Medicine, Saskatoon, 1969-70. Mem. Am. Coll. Vet. Pathologists, Can. Vet. Med. Assn. (chmn. specialization com. 1986-88), Alta. Vet. Med. Assn. (pres. 1981-82). Avocations: skiing, equine driving. Home and Office: RR 1 Edmonton AB Canada T6H 5T6 Personal E-mail: rbchristi@shaw.ca.

CHRISTIANSEN, DAVID K., health facility administrator; b. Logan, Utah, Sept. 10, 1952; s. John R. and Lucele (Kartchner) C.; m. Cynthia Ann Kutsko, July 28, 1982. BS, Brigham Young U., 1977; M in Health Care Adminstrn., U. Ala., 1979. Purchasing asst. McDonald Health Clinic, Provo, Utah, 1975—77; adminstrv. resident Bapt.-Montclair Hosp., Birmingham, Ala., 1978—79, adminstrv. asst., 1979—80; asst. adminstr. Lakeview Cmty. Hosp., Bountiful, Utah, 1980—83; adminstr. Shasta Gen. Hosp., Redding, Calif., 1983—84; CEO Knoxville (Iowa) Cmty. Hosp., 1984—89; COO Med. Ctr. Independence, Kansas City, Mo., 1989—92; CEO Newman Regional Hosp., Emporia, Kans., 1992—96; exec. v.p. MED/MAX Health Mgmt., San Diego, 1996—99; exec. dir. Salt Lake Sr. Clinic, 1999—2001; area adminstr. CHD-Meridan Healthcare Mgmt., 2001—03; CEO Mount Ogden Eye Ctr., 2003—. Cons. Ctr. Health Studies, Nashville, 1981—83; mem. faculty Ctr. Health Studies/Hosp. Cor. Am., Nashville, 1981—83. Explorer advisor Boy Scouts Am., Birmingham, 1977-80; campaign coord. United Way, Bountiful, 1983; exec. bd. dir. Boy Scouts Am., Topeka, 1994-96. Named Outstanding Young Man of Am., U.S. Jaycees, 1982. Fellow Am. Coll. Healthcare Execs.; mem. Knoxville C. of C. (chmn. commerce com. 1986-87), Emporia Kans. C. of C. (bd. dir. 1994-96), Rotary (membership chmn. Redding 1984, Knoxville bd. dir. 1987-89).

CHRISTIANSEN, LARRY K., college president; AA, North Iowa Area C.C.; BA in Bus. Edn., U. Northern Iowa; MS in Ednl. Adminstrn., Drake U.; DEd, U. N.D. Distributive edn. coord., chmn. bus. dept. Perry (Iowa) Cmty. H.S., 1967-74; assoc. prof., chmn. bus. divsn. U. Minn. Tech. Coll., Crookston, 1974-82; dean adminstrv. svc., acting dean of instrn., assoc. dean Glendale C.C.; pres. Mesa C.C. Chair acad. internat. exec. adv. bd. Nat. C.C.; mem. Megacorp Bd.; adv. bd. Nat. Campus Compact Cmty.; spkr. in field. Author: (with others) A Case Approach, 1980; co-author: To the Future and Counselor's Guide to the Future. Pres. East Valley Partnership Bd.; cabinet chair Mesa United Way, 1996; campaign chair Maricopa C.C. Dist. Mem. Mesa C. of C. (nat. campus compact cmty. adv. bd.), Mesa Baseline Rotary, Nat. Assn. of Distributive Edn. Tchrs. Office: 1833 W Southern Ave Mesa AZ 85202-4822

CHRISTIANSEN, WALTER HENRY, aerospace scientist, educator; b. McKees Rocks, Pa., Dec. 14, 1934; s. Walter Henry and Elizabeth (Miller) C.; m. Joan Marilyn Swisler, Aug. 5, 1960; children: Walter, Audrey. BS in Mech. Engring., Carnegie Inst. Tech., 1956; MS in Aero. Engring., Calif. Inst. Tech., 1957, PhD, 1961. Sr. scientist Jet Propulsion Lab., Pasadena, Calif., 1961-62, 1963-67; rsch. assoc. prof. aero. and aeronautics U. Wash., Seattle, 1967-70, assoc. prof., 1970-74, prof., 1974—2001, dept. chmn., 1992-98, prof. emeritus, 2001—. Cons. Boeing Sci. Rsch. Lab., 1967-69, Math. Scis. N.W., 1970-85, Spectra Tech., 1985-88, 91. Contbr. articles to profl. jours.; patentee in field. Com. mem. Directions for 70's Bellevue (Wash.) Sch. Dist., 1970. Served to capt. U.S. Army, 1961-63. Dept. Def. grantee, 1970-91, NSF grantee, 1977, 80, NASA grantee, 1980-89; Mesta Machine fellow, 1952-56, Convair fellow, 1958, Boeing fellow, 1960. Fellow AIAA (Pacific N.W. chpt. Sect. award 1972); mem. Am. Phys. Soc., Sigma Xi, Tau Beta Pi, Pi Tau Sigma, Theta Xi. Home: 9633 NE 28th St Bellevue WA 98004-1846 Office: Dept Aero & Astro Box 352400 Univ Wash Seattle WA 98195-0001 Business E-Mail: walt@aa.washington.edu.

CHRISTIE, DOUG (DOUGLAS DALE CHRISTIE), entrepreneur, former professional basketball player; b. Seattle, May 9, 1970; s. John and Norma Malone; m. Jackie Christie; children: Chantell, Ta'kari, Douglas Jr. B in Sociology, Pepperdine U., Malibu, Calif., 1992. Guard, forward LA Lakers, 1992—94, NY Knicks, 1994-96, Toronto Raptors, 1996—2000, Sacramento Kings, 2000—05, Orlando Magic, 2005, Dallas Mavericks, 2005, LA Clippers, 2007; co-founder Jackie Christie, Inc., Infinite Love Prodns., Infinite Love Pub., Jean Rah Fya Records, 2007—. Actor: (reality show) The Christies Committed, 2006; co-author (with Jackie Christie): No Ordinary Love, 2007. Founder Infinite Love Found. Named MVP, West Coast Conf., 1992, 1st Team All Conf., 1992; named to NBA All-Defensive 2d Team, 2001, 2002, 2004, NBA All-Defensive 1st Team, 2003, West Coast Conf. Hall of Honor, 2009. Achievements include leading the NBA in: steals (183), 2001. Avocations: fishing, golf, rhythm and blues, reggae and rap music. Office: Jackie Christie Inc 15127 NE 24th St # 350 Redmond WA 98052

CHRISTIE, HANS FREDERICK, retired utilities executive; b. Alhambra, Calif., July 10, 1933; s. Andreas B. and Sigrid (Falk-Jorgensen) C.; m. Susan Earley, June 14, 1957; children: Brenda Lynn, Laura Jean BS in Fin., U. So. Calif., 1957, MBA, 1964. Treas. So. Calif. Edison Co., Rosemead, 1970-75, v.p., 1975-76, sr. v.p., 1976-80, exec. v.p., 1980-84, pres., dir., 1984-87; pres., chief exec. officer The Mission Group (non-utility subs. SCE Corp.)., Seal Beach, Calif., 1987-89, ret., 1989, cons., 1989—. Bd. dirs. L.A. Ducommun Inc., L.A., A.E. Com., L.A., Am. Mut. Fund, Inc., AMCAP, Am. Variable Ins., I.H.O.P. Corp., AECom Tech., L.A., Internat. House of Pancakes, Inc., Southwest Water Co., L.A., Smallcap World Fund, L.A., Bond Fund Am., Inc., L.A., Tax-Exempt Bond Fund Am., L.A., Ltd. Term Tax-Exempt Bond Fund Am., Am. High Income Mcpl. Bond Fund, Capital Income Builder, L.A., Capital World Bond Fund, L.A., Capital World Growth Fund, Capital World Growth and Income Fund, Intermediate Bond Fund Am., L.A., Intermediate Tax-Exempt

Bond Fund Am., Capital World Growth 2d Income Fund, L.A.; trustee Cash Mgmt. Trust Am., New Economy Fund, L.A., Am. Funds Income Series, L.A., The Am. Funds Tax-Exempt Series II, Am. High Income Trust, L.A., Am. High-Inc Mun. Board Fund, Am. Variable Ins. Trust, U.S. Treasury Fund Am., L.A Bd. councillor sch. policy, planning and devel. U. So. Calif., 1981—2001; trustee Occidental Coll., 1984—96, Idlwild Sch. Arts, 1998—2002, Chadwick Sch., Natural History Mus. Los Angeles County, 1984—2002. With US Army, 1953—55. Named Outstanding mem. Arthritis Found., L.A., 1975, Outstanding Trustee, Multiple Sclerosis Soc. So. Calif., 1979 Mem. Pacific Coast Elec. Assn. (bd. dirs. 1981-87, treas. 1975-87), L.A. C. of C. (bd. dirs. 1983-87), Calif. Club. Republican. Avocations: swimming, horseback riding, bicycling. Home: 548 Paseo Del Mar Palos Verdes Estates CA 90274-1260 Office: PO Box 144 Palos Verdes Peninsula CA 90274-0144 Personal E-mail: hfc548@aol.com.

CHRISTMAN, ALBERT BERNARD, historian; b. Colorado Springs, Colo., May 18, 1923; s. James S. and Olga C.; m. Kate Gresham, July 1945 (div. July 1952); 1 child, Lloyd James; m. Jean Stewart, Apr. 4, 1954 (dec. Sept. 1984); children: Neil Stewart, Laura Elizabeth; m. Janet Kunert, April 26, 2005. BA, U. Mo., Columbia, 1949, BJ, 1950; MA, Calif. State U., Dominguez Hills, 1982. Reporter Comml. Leader, North Little Rock, 1950-51; tech. editor, writer Naval Ordnance Test Sta., China Lake, Calif., 1951-55, head presentation divsn., 1956-63; historian, info. specialist Naval Weapons Ctr., China Lake, Calif., 1963-72, head pubs., 1973-79; historian Navy Labs., San Diego, 1979-82; freelance historian, writer San Marcos, Calif., 1982—. Author: Sailors, Scientists and Rockets, 1971, Naval Innovators, 1776-1900, 1989, Target Hiroshima, Deak Parsons and the Creation of the Atomic Bomb, 1998; co-author: Grand Experiment at Inyokern, 1979; contbr. articles to profl. jours. Founding mem. Red Rock Canyon State Park Adv. Com., Tehachapi, Calif., 1969-74. Pvt. U.S. Army, 1942-45; maj. USAFR, ret. Recipient Robert H. Goddard Meml. award Nat. Space, 1972, Superior Civilian Svc. award Dept. of The Navy, 1982, Helen Hawkins Meml. Rsch. grants, 1994, 2000. Mem. Maturango Mus. (trustee-sec. 1973-76), USN Inst., OX-5 Aviation Pioneers, San Diego Aerospace Mus., Authors Guild, Writers Studio. Democrat. Unitarian Universalist. Avocations: photography, hiking. Home: 2855 Carlsbad Blvd Apt S-236 Carlsbad CA 92008

CHRISTMAN, ARTHUR CASTNER, JR., science advisor, consultant; b. North Wales, Pa., May 11, 1922; s. Arthur Castner and Hazel Ivy (Schirmer) C.; m. Marina Ilia Dieterichs, Apr. 17, 1945; children: Candace Lee Canto, Tatiana Marina Harvey, Deborah Ann Clark, Arthur C. III, Keith Ilia, Cynthia Ellen Buckwalter. BS in Physics, Pa. State U., 1944, MS, 1950. Teaching asst. dept. physics Pa. State U., State College, 1943-44, grad. asst., 1946-48; instr. dept. physics George Washington U., Washington, 1948-51; cons. U.S. Navy, 1950-51; physicist ops. research office Johns Hopkins U., Chevy Chase, Md., 1951-58; sr. physicist SRI Internat., Menlo Park, Calif., 1958-62, head ops. research group, 1962-64, dept. mgr., 1965-67, dir. dept., 1968-71, dir. tactical weapons systems, 1971-75; sci. advisor to comdg. gen. and dep. chief staff combat devel. U.S. Army tng. and doctrine command Ft. Monroe, Va., 1975-87; cons. in field, 1988—. Author numerous publs. Pres. Valle Verde Continuing Care Retirement Cmty. Coun., 1991—93, 1994—95, Am. Bapt. Homes of West Assn. of CCRC Resident Presidents, 1991—92; bd. mgrs. fin. com. Valle Verde, 1988—97; mem. Valle Verde Adv. Bd., 1997—2006, fin. com., 1988—2006, chair environ. svcs. com., 1999—2006, exec. com., 2002—06, sec., 2002—06; continuing care contracts statutes rev. task force State of Calif., 1999—2000; umpire Palo Alto Little League, Calif., 1962—72; bd. dirs. Am. Bapt. Homes of the West, 1997—, fin. and investment com., 1998—2006, audit com., 1999, 2001—03, 2006—07, chair investment com., 2002—06, compensation com., 2007—, Cornerstone bd. dirs., 2001—, fin. com., 2004—; bd. dirs. Ctrl. Coast Commn. for Sr. Citizens Area Agy. on Aging, 1993. Lt. USNR, 1944—46, PTO. Decorated Meritorious Civilian Service award Dept. Army, 1983, Exceptional Civilian Service award Dept. Army, 1987; recipient Presdl. Rank, 1985, Governance award Am. Bapt. Homes of the West, 2002, Trustee of Yr. award Calif. Assn. Homes and Svcs. for the Aging, 2004. Fellow AAAS; mem. Am. Phys. Soc., Inst. for Ops. Rsch. and the Mgmt. Scis. (U.S. del. internat. confs. Operational Rsch., France 1960, Norway 1963, U.S. 1966, Ireland 1972), Santa Barbara Lawn Bowls Club (bd. dirs. 1990-93), MacKenzie Park Lawn Bowls Club, Sigma Xi, Sigma Pi Sigma, Delta Chi (chpt. pres.). Republican. Baptist (deacon, trustee). Avocations: lawn bowling, photography. Home and Office: 1028 B Senda Verde Santa Barbara CA 93105-4407 Personal E-mail: achristman@abhow.com.

CHRISTOFFERSEN, RALPH EARL, chemist, researcher, director; b. Elgin, Ill., Dec. 4, 1937; s. Arthur Henry and Mary C.; m. Barbara Hibbard, June 10, 1961; children: Kirk Alan, Rachel Anne. BS, Cornell Coll., 1959, LLD (hon.), 1983; PhD, Ind. U., 1963. Asst. prof. chemistry U. Kans., Lawrence, 1966-69, assoc. prof., 1969—72, prof., 1972-81, asst. vice chancellor for acad. affairs, 1974-75, assoc. vice chancellor for acad. affairs, 1976-79, vice chancellor for acad. affairs, 1979-81; pres. Colo. State U., Ft. Collins, 1981-83; exec. dir. Upjohn Co., 1983-85, v.p. biotech. and basic rsch. support, 1985-87, v.p. discovery rsch., 1987-89; v.p. rsch. SmithKline Beecham, King of Prussia, Pa., 1989-90, sr. v.p. rsch., 1990-92; CEO, pres. Ribozyme Pharms., Inc., Boulder, Colo., 1992-2001, chmn. bd., 2001; gen. ptnr. Morgenthaler Ventures, 2001—. Bd. dirs. GlobeImmune Corp., Ethos Corp., Catalyst Bioscis., Galleon Pharm., Stemgent Corp., Siena Neuropharm. Inc., Tragara Pharm. Contbr. articles to profl. jours. NIH fellow, 1962-63, 64-66. Fellow Sigma Xi, Phi Lambda Upsilon; mem. Colo. BioSci. Assn.

CHRISTOFFERSON, CARLA JEAN, lawyer, professional sports team executive; b. ND, 1967; d. Edna Ellison. Attended, Williston State Coll., ND; BA summa cum laude, U. ND, Grand Forks, 1989; JD, Yale U., New Haven, 1992. Bar: Calif. 1992. Law clerk, the Hon. W. Matthew Byrne, Jr. US Dist. Ct. (ctrl. dist. Calif.); ptnr., head LA office O'Melveny & Myers LLP, LA, 2001—; co-owner LA Sparks, 2006—. Mem., Office of the Chair O'Melveny & Myers LLP, nat. hiring ptnr., talent. devel. ptnr., 2004—06, values award com. Notes editor: Yale Law Jour. Bd. dirs. Women's Care Cottage, LA Libr. Found. Named Miss Teen ND, 1985, First Runner-Up, Miss Teen USA, 1985, Miss ND, 1989; named a Southern Calif. Super Lawyer, 2005, 2006, 2007, 2008. Mem.: Nat. Assn. Female Execs., LA County Bar Assn. Office: O'Melveny & Meyers LLP 400 S Hope St Los Angeles CA 90071-2899 also: LA Sparks 1111 S Figueroa St Ste 3100 Los Angeles CA 90001 Office Phone: 213-430-8359. Office Fax: 213-430-6407. Business E-Mail: cchristofferson@omm.com.

CHRISTOL, CARL QUIMBY, lawyer, political science professor; b. Gallup, SD, June 28, 1913; s. Carl and Winifred (Quimby) C.; m. Jeannette Stearns, Dec. 18, 1949 (dec.); children: Susan Quimby Christol-Deacon, Richard Stearns (dec.). AB, U. S.D., 1934, LLD (hon.), 1977; AM, Fletcher Sch. Law and Diplomacy, 1936; postgrad., Institut Universitaire des Hautes Etudes Internationales, Geneva, 1937-38, U. Geneva, 1937-38; PhD, U. Chgo., 1941; LLB, Yale U., 1947; postgrad., Acad. Internat. Law, The Hague, 1950. Bar: S.D. 1948, Calif. 1949. Assoc. firm Guthrie, Darling and Shattuck, Los Angeles, 1948-49; of counsel Fizzolio, Fizzolio & McLeod, Sherman Oaks, Calif., 1949-94; assoc. prof. polit. sci. U. So. Calif., 1949-59, prof., 1959-87, prof. emeritus, 1987—, chmn. dept. polit. sci., 1960-64, 75-77. Stockton chair internat. law U.S. Naval War Coll., 1962-63, cons., 1963-70; cons. World Law Fund; mem. L.A. Mayor's Adv. Com. Human Rels., Commn. to Study Orgn. of Peace; mem. adv. panel on internat. law Dept. State, 1970-76; v.p. Ct. of Man Found., 1971-77; scholar-in-residence Rockefeller Found. Bellagio Conf. and Study Ctr., Italy, 1980. Author: Transit by Air in International Law, 1941, Introduction to Political Science, 1957, 4th edit., 1982, Readings in International Law, 1959, The International Law of Outer Space, 1966, The International Legal and Institutional Aspects of the Stratosphere Ozone Problem, 1975, The Modern International Law of Outer Space, 1982, Space Law: Past, Present and Future, 1991, International Law and U.S. Foreign Policy, 2004, 2d edit., 2006; bd. editors: Western Polit. Quar, 1970-75, Internat. Lawyer, 1975-84, Space Policy, 1985—, Internat. Legal Materials, 1985—, Australian Internat. Law Jour., 1998—2002; contbr. articles to profl. jours. Bd. dirs. Los Angeles County Heart Assn., 1956—61, Santa Barbara County chpt. UNA-UNESCO, 2006—. Served to lt. col. AUS, 1941—46, col. Res. ret. Decorated Bronze Star medal; recipient Dart award U. So. Calif., 1970, Assos. award for excellence in teaching, 1977, Raubenheimer award, 1982, Disting. Emeritus award, 1990, Rockefeller Found. fellow, 1958-59; Borchard Found. lectr., 2002. Mem. ABA, AIAA, Am. Soc. Internat. Law (exec. coun. 1973-76), Internat. Studies Assn. (chmn. internat. law sect. 1977-78), Internat. Acad. Astronautics, State Bar Calif., UN Assn. LA (pres. 1961-63), Am. Polit. Sci. Assn., Internat. Inst. Space Law (pres. Am. br. 1973-75, Lifetime Achievement award 1998), Internat. Law Assn., UN Assn. U.S. (dir. 1967-69), Masons, Blue Key, Skull and Dagger, Phi Beta Kappa, Phi Kappa Phi (award 1987), Alpha Tau Omega. Presbyterian. Office: U So Calif Polit Sci Dept Los Angeles CA 90089-0044 Home: 5500 Calle Real C124 Santa Barbara CA 93111 Personal E-mail: carlqc@cox.net.

CHRISTOPHER, JAMES WALKER, architect, educator; b. Phila., Nov. 5, 1930; s. Arthur Bailey and Cornelia (Slater) C.; m. Carolyn Kennard, July 9, 1955; children: William W., Kathryn A., Kimberley, James S., Pamela W. BA, Rice U., 1953, BS in Architecture, 1953; M.Arch., MIT, 1956. Registered architect, Utah, Colo., Nev., Idaho, Wyo. Asst. prof. architecture U. Utah, Salt Lake City, 1956-60, adj. prof. architecture, 1983; archtl. designer various firms, Salt Lake City, 1960-63; founding prin. Brixen & Christopher Architects, Salt Lake City, 1963—. Architect, Phase I, Snowbird, Alta Canyon, Utah (AIA Western Mountain Region award 1971), Nunemaker Place Chapel, Salt Lake City (AIA Western Mountain Region award 1977), Congregation Kol Ami, Salt Lake City (AIA Western Mountain Region award 1977), Block 53 Master Plan, Salt Lake City (Utah chpt. AIA award 1979). Mem. Utah Environ. Transp. Coun., Salt Lake City, 1970-77, vice chmn., 1970-75; mem. Big Cottonwood Citizens Planning Com., Salt Lake County, Utah, 1975, Salt Lake City Downtown Planning Com., 1981, Utah Transit Authority Transplan, Salt Lake City, 1982; trustee Utah Heritage Found., 2004-08, v.p., 2006. Served to lt. (j.g.) USNR, 1953-55. Fellow AIA (pres. Utah Soc. 1970 12 Utah Soc. Design awards, 12 Western Mountain Region Design awards 1968-83, 8 nat. Design awards 1975-83, Presdl. citation 1982, nat. design and planning com. 1976-2005, chmn. R/UDAT task group 1987-91, 98-2002, we. mountain region Firm of the Yr. award 1987, Silver medal 1991, Utah Soc. Bronze medal 1999). Clubs: Alta (pres. 2007). Episcopalian. Home: 2954 Millcreek Rd Salt Lake City UT 84109-3108 Office: Brixen & Christopher Architects 252 S 2nd E Salt Lake City UT 84111-2487

CHRISTOPHER, WARREN MINOR, lawyer, former United States Secretary of State; b. Scranton, ND, Oct. 27, 1925; s. Ernest W. and Catharine Anna (Lemen) Christopher; m. Marie Josephine Wyllis, Dec. 21, 1956; children: Lynn, Scott, Thomas, Kristen. Student, U. Redlands, 1942—43; BS magna cum laude, U. So. Calif., 1945; LLB, Stanford U., 1949; LLD (hon.), Occidental U., 1977, Bates Coll., 1981, Brown U., 1981, Claremont Coll., 1981. Bar: Calif. 1949, US Supreme Ct. 1953, DC 1972, NY 1984. Law clk. to Justice William O. Douglas US Supreme Ct., Washington, 1949—50; dep. atty. gen. US Dept. Justice, Washington, 1967—69; dep. sec. US Dept. State, Washington, 1977—81, sec., 1993—97; mem. firm O'Melveny & Myers, LLP, 1950—67, 1969, ptnr., 1958—67, 1969—76, 1981—93, chmn., 1982—92, sr. ptnr., 1997—. Spl. counsel to Gov. State of Calif., Sacramento, 1959; cons. Office Under Sec. State, 1961—65; mem. bd. bar examiners State Bar Calif., 1966—67; bd. dirs. So. Calif. Edison Co., First Interstate Bancorp, Lockheed Corp.; chmn. bd. trustee Carnegie Corp. NY; mem. Calif. Coordinating Coun. for Higher Edn., 1960—67, pres., 1963—65; vice chmn. Gov.'s Commn. on LA Riots, 1965—66; chmn. US dels. to US-Japan Cotton Textile Negotiations, 1961, Geneva Conf. on Cotton Textiles, 1961; spl. rep. sec. state for Wool Textile Meetings, London, Rome, Tokyo, 1964—64; mem. Trilateral Commn., 1975—77, 1981—88; mem. internat. adv. coun. Inst. Internat. Studies; chmn. Ind. Commn. on L.A. Police Dept., 1991; co-chmn. Pacific Coun. on Internat. Policy; headed search for Gov. Clinton's running mate (Sen. Al Gore); served as dir. presdl. transition process. Author: In the Stream of History: Shaping Foreign Policy for a New Era, 1998, Chances of a Lifetime, 2001; co-author: American Hostages in Iran: The Conduct of a Crisis, 1985; pres. Stanford Law Review, 1947—48. Dir., vice chmn. Coun. on Fgn. Rels., 1982—91; mem. US-Korea Wisemen Coun., 1991—93; trustee Stanford U., 1971—77, 1981—93, pres. bd. trustees, 1985—88; dir. LA World Affairs Coun.; mem. exec. com. Am. Agenda, 1988. Lt. (j.g.) USNR, 1943—46. Decorated Presdl. Medal of Freedom; recipient Harold Weill award, NYU, 1981, Louis Stein award, Fordham U., 1981, Jefferson award, Am. Inst. for Pub. Svc., UCLA medal, U. Va., Thomas Jefferson award in law, First Civic Medal of Honor, LA C. of C., 2003, Lifetime Achievement award, The Am. Lawyer mag., 2006. Fellow: AAAS, Am. Coll. Trial Lawyers, Am. Bar Found.; mem.: ABA (ho. dels. 1975—77, chmn. standing com. fed. judiciary 1975—77), Am. Law Inst., LA County Bar Assn. (pres. 1974—75), Calif. Bar Assn. (gov. 1975—77), Chancery Club, Calif. Club, Order of Coif, Phi Kappa Phi. Achievements include negotiating the release of 52 American hostages in Iran, 1981. Office: O'Melveny & Meyers LLP 1999 Avenue of Stars 7th Fl Los Angeles CA 90067-6035 Address: O'Melveny & Meyers LLP 400 South Hope St Los Angeles CA 90071-2899 Office Phone: 310-246-6750. Office Fax: 310-246-6779. Business E-Mail: wchristopher@omm.com.

CHRONLEY, JAMES ANDREW, real estate executive; b. Springfield, Mass., July 31, 1930; s. Robert Emmett and Eleanor Andrus (Sullivan) C.; m. Monique Mary Delpech, July 29, 1955; children: Mary Elizabeth, James Michael, Jean Louise, Patricia, Joseph Patrick, John Peter, Robert Emmett. AB, Brown U., 1952; diploma in real estate, U. R.I., 1963; MBA, Pepperdine U., 1991. With Arco Co., 1954-74, Ea. area mgr., until 1972; nat. real estate dir. Atlantic Richfield Co., LA, 1972-74; v.p. restaurant real estate Marriott Corp., Washington, 1974-78; exec. v.p. Burger Chef Systems, Inc., Indpls., 1978—83, pres., 1983; sr. v.p. devel. Taco Bell, Irvine, 1983-94. Served with AUS, 1952-54. Mem. KC, Nat. Assn. Corp. Real Estate Execs. (chpt. pres. 1979, chmn. bd. 1985-87, elected trustee 1987-92), Am. Arbitration Assn., Internat. Exec. Svc. Corps, Orange County Assn. Investment Mgrs. Roman Catholic. Office: Taco Bell 14602 Bel Aire St Irvine CA 92604-2201 Personal E-mail: moniqueusa@cox.net.

CHU, CARMEN, city supervisor; b. LA, 1978; BA in Pub. Policy, Occidental Coll., LA, 2000; MA in Pub. Policy, U. Calif., Berkeley, 2003. Acct. coord./strategic planning asst. IW Group, Inc.; legis. analyst intern San Francisco Bd. Supervisors; cons. Pub. Fin. Mgmt., Inc.; budget analyst, then dir. pub. policy & fin. Office Mayor Gavin Newsom, San Francisco, 2004—07; interim supr., Dist. 4 San Francisco Bd. Supervisors, 2007, supr., 2008—, chair city ops. & neighborhood svcs. com., vice chair rules com., mem. budget & fin. com., Transp. Authority. Mem. California State Assn. Counties, Urban Counties Caucus. Democrat. Office: Ciyt Hall 1 Dr Carlton B Goodlett Pl Rm 24 San Francisco CA 94102 Office Phone: 714-554-7460. Office Fax: 714-554-7432. Business E-Mail: Carmen.Chu@sfgov.org.*

CHU, JAMES, electronics executive; b. Taiwan; m. Lily Chu; children: Tina, Kevin. Various sales positions, Taiwan; pres. Taiwanese keyboard mfg. co., U.S., 1986; founder Keypoint Tech. Corp., 1987-90; reorganized Keypoint Tech. Corp. (now ViewSonic Corp.), 1990; chmn., CEO ViewSonic Corp., Walnut, Calif., 1990—. Avocations: reading, tennis, exploring internet.

CHU, JUDY MAY, assemblywoman; b. LA, July 7, 1955; d. Judson and May C.; m. Michael Eng, Aug. 8, 1978. BA in Math., UCLA, 1974; MA in Clin. Psychology, Calif. Sch. Profl. Psychology, 1977, PhD, 1979. Lectr. UCLA, 1980-86; assoc. prof. L.A. City Coll., 1981-88; prof. East L.A. Coll., Monterey Park, 1988—2001; mem. Monterey Park City Council, 1988—2001, Calif. State Assembly, 2001—. Chair, select com. on hate crimes Calif. State Assembly, mem. select com. on language access, mem. rules, labor and employment com., environ. safety and toxic materials com., human svcs. com. & transportation com. Author, editor: Linking Our Lives: Chinese American Women in Los Angeles, 1984; contbr. articles profl. jours. Mem. city coun. City of Monterey Park, 1988—, mayor, 1990-91, 94-95; bd. dirs. Garvey Sch. Dist., 1985-88; chair Commn. for Sex Equity, L.A. Unified Sch. Dist., 1984-85; bd. dirs. Rebuild L.A.; mem. adv. com. U.S. Census Bur., 1994—; Bd. dirs. Gabriel Valley chpt. ARC; bd. dirs. Asian Youth Ctr., San Gabriel Valley United Way, West San Gabriel Valley Juvenile Diversion Project. Named One of 88 Leaders for 1988, L.A. Times, 1988, Dem. of Yr., 59th Assembly Dist. Dem. Com., 1989, Vol. of Yr. San Gabriel Valley chpt. United Way, 1989, L.A. Outstanding Founder, 1995; recipient Achievement award Asian Pacific Family Ctr., 1980, Pub. Svc. award Asian Pacific Legal Ctr., 1989, award for Excellence in Pub. Svc., UCLA Alumni, 1991, Leadership award West San Gabriel Valley chpt. ARC. Mem. Soroptimists. Office: Calif State Assembly PO Box 942849 Sacramento CA 94249 Business E-Mail: assemblymember.chu@asm.ca.gov.

CHU, KANSEN, councilman; b. Taiwan; arrived in US, 1976; m. Daisy Chu; children: Ann, Walt. BEE, Nat. Taipei U. Tech., 1975; MEE, Cal State Northridge, 1981. Microdiagnostics microprogrammer IBM, 1978—96; pres., owner Ocean Harbor Chinese Restaurant, 1989—; dist. rep. to Senator Elaine Alquist, 2004—06; dist. dir. to Assemblymember Rebecca Cohn, 2006; councilman, Dist. 4 San José City Coun., 2007—. Bd. trustee Berryessa Union Sch. Dist., 2002—07; mem. Pvt. Industry Coun., 1995—97, Santa Clara County Mental Health Bd., 1997—2005; bd. mem. KNTV Channel 11 Cmty. Bd., 1997—99, Santa Clara Valley Metro YMCA, 1998—, Vietnamese Voluntary Found., 1998—, Shin Shin Edn. Found., 2003—, Neighborhood Accountability Bd. of Berryessa, 2003—04; mem. adv. bd. Vision New America, 2002—, Californians for Justice, 2005—; mem. Asian Law Alliance. Recipient US Congl. award, Congressman Norm Mineta, US Congl. Resolution for Cmty. Svc., Congresswoman Anna Eshoo, Commanding Gen.'s award, US Marine Corps Res., Cmty. Leadership Father award, Bldg. Peaceful Families, Excellent Cmty. Svc. award, Santa Clara County Sheriff, Partnership in Cmty. award, Asian Law Alliance, Restorative Justice and Cmty. Svc. award, Santa Clara County Probation Dept. Office: San Jose City Coun 200 E Santa Clara St San Jose CA 95113 Office Phone: 408-535-4904. Office Fax: 408-292-6459. Business E-Mail: district4@sanjoseca.gov.*

CHU, MORGAN, lawyer; b. NYC, Dec. 27, 1950; s. Ju Chin and Ching (Chen) Chu; m. Helen M. Wong, Dec. 29, 1970. BA, UCLA, 1971, MA, 1972, PhD, 1973; MSL, Yale U., 1974; JD magna cum laude, Harvard U., 1976. Bar: Calif. 1976, US Dist. Ct. (ctrl. dist. Calif.) 1977, US Dist. Ct. (no. dist. Calif.) 1980, US Ct. Appeals (9th cir.) 1980, US Dist. Ct. (so. dist. Calif.) 1984, US Dist. Ct. (ea. dist. Calif.) 1986, US Ct. Appeals (fed. cir.) 1989, US Supreme Ct. 1991. Law clk. to Hon. Charles M. Merrill U.S. Ct. Appeals 9th Cir., San Francisco, 1976—77; assoc. Irell & Manella LLP, LA, 1977-82, ptnr., 1982—, co-mng. ptnr., 1997—2003, exec. com., 1984—. Adj. prof. UCLA Sch. Law, 1979—82; judge pro tem LA Mcpl. Ct., 1980. Mem. editl. bd. Litig. News, 1981—84. Recipient Significant Achievement Excellence and Innovation Alternative Dispute Resolution award, Ctr. Pub. Resources, 1987, Dream Team award, Calif. Law Bus., 1992, UCLA medal, 2007; named One Top IP Lawyer, Calif. Lawyer, 1992, Exec. Yr. Law, La. Bus. Jour., 1994, Best IP Lawyer Nation, Corp. Bd. Mem., 2001, 12 Superstars, 2001, Number One IP Lawyer Calif., Chambers Global, 2003—04, Top Super Lawyer So. Calif., LA Mag., 2004, Top IP Lawyer US First Chambers Excellence award, 2006; named one of 10 New Superstars, Legal Times Wash., 1983, 100 Most Influential Lawyers Am., Nat. Law Jour., 1994, Top 20 Lawyers La. Firms, Calif. Law Bus., 1994, 10 Top Trial Lawyers Am., 1995, Top 45 Lawyers Under 45, Am. Lawyer, 1995, 10 Most Influential Lawyers Calif., Calif. Law Bus., 1999, 100 Most Influential Lawyers

Am., 2000, 100 Most Influential Lawyers Calif., LA Daily Jour.; fellow, Am. Coll. Trial Lawyers. Fellow: Am. Coll. Trial Lawyers; mem.: ABA (chmn. high tech. intellectual property and patent trials subcommittee 1986—90, trial practice com., litig. sect.), LA Intellectual Property Law Assn. (bd. dirs. 1991—93, bd. dirs. pub. counsel 1993—, exec. com. bd. dirs. pub. counsel 1995—), LA County Bar Assn. (judiciary com. 1983—2001), Calif. Bar Assn. Office: Irell & Manella LLP Ste 900 1800 Ave of the Stars Los Angeles CA 90067-4276 Office Phone: 310-203-7000. Office Fax: 310-203-7199. Business E-Mail: mchu@irell.com.

CHU, RODERICK GONG-WAH, educational association administrator; b. NYC, Jan. 17, 1949; s. Norton Yuen and Frances (Liang) C. BS in Math. and Physics, U. Mich., 1969; MBA with honors, Cornell U., 1971; D in Pub. Svc. (hon.), U. Rio Grande, 1999; LHD (hon.), Youngstown State U., 1999; ArtsD (hon.), Cin. State Tech. and CC, 2001; AS (hon.), Edison CC, 2001; D in Pub. Svc. (hon.), Otterbein U., 2003; HHD (hon.), Capital U., 2003; LHD (hon.), Shawnee State U., 2004; LLD (hon.), Marietta Coll., 2006. Staff analyst Arthur Andersen and Co., NYC, 1971—75, mgr., 1975—81, ptnr., 1981—83; commr. Taxation and Fin., pres. State Tax Commn. State of NY, Albany, 1983—88; ptnr. Andersen Cons., NYC, 1988—95, worldwide mng. ptnr. state and local govt. practice, 1989—91, worldwide mng. ptnr. govt. practice, 1991—92; chancellor Ohio Bd. Regents, Columbus, Ohio, 1998—2006, chancellor emeritus, 2006—; interim pres. Edn. Commn. of the States, Denver, 2006—. Bd. dir. Housing Fin. Agy., Med. Care Facilities Fin. Agy.; adv. bd. Coun. Excellence in Govt., 1991-93, trustee, 1993-95, NYC real property tax reform commn., 1993; mem. Ohio Workforce Devel. Bd., 1998-1999, Ohio Commn. on African Am. Males, 1998-2006. Bd. dir., bd. overseers Jacob's Pillow Dance Festival, Becket, Mass., 1984-97; mem. Cornell U. Coun., 1988-92, 94-98, 2001-05, dean's alumni exec. coun. Johnson Sch. Grad. Mgmt., 1988-90, adv. coun., 1991-98, outdoor edn. adv. coun., 1992-98, strategic planning adv. bd., 1992-96; trustee SUNY, 1990-98, chmn. exec. compensation com., 1993-98; pres.'s adv. coun. China Inst. Am., 1990-94; co-chair pres. circle The Asia Soc., 1994-97; adv. bd. Barnard-Columbia Ctr. Leadership in Urban Pub. Policy, 1994-98; mem. State Higher Edn. Exec. Officers, 1998-, treas., 2002, pres., 2003, Gov.'s Workforce Policy Bd., 1999-2006, MidWest Higher Edn. Commn., 2000-06, Edn. Commn. of States, 2001-06, exec. com., 2003-06, steering com., 2004-06, Nat. Commn. on Arts in Edn., 2004-05, Nat. Ctr. Learning and Citizenship, 2005-06, Ohio Third Frontier Commn., 2003-06, Gov.'s Commn. on Higher Edn. and the Econ., 2003-04, Educators Stds. Bd., 2004-06, SchoolNet Commn., 2004-05, eTech Ohio Commn., 2005-06; trustee The Coll. Bd., 2004-, chmn. audit com., 2005—, Ohio Hist. Soc., 1998-2006. Recipient Man of Yr. award Chinese-Am. Planning Coun., 1984, NYC Police Dept., Asian Jade Soc., 1984, Disting. Achievement award United Chinese Am. League, 1985, Spl. Recognition award Asian Ams. for Affirmative Action, 1986, Champion of Excellence award Orgn. Chinese Am., 1986, Outstanding Chinese Entrepreneur award Chinese Mgmt. Assn., 1991, Disting. Friend award, So. State CC, 2002; Paul Harris fellow Rotary Internat., 1988, 92. Mem. Am. Soc. Pub. Adminstrn. (hon.), Cornell Club (NYC), Capital Club (Columbus), New Albany Country Club, Met. Opera Club, Cornell Asian Alumni Assn., Phi Kappa Phi. Republican. Lutheran. Avocations: skiing, photography, golf, fly fishing. Office: Education Comm Of The States 700 Broadway Ste 810 Denver CO 80203-3442 Office Fax: 303-296-8332. Personal E-mail: rgwchu@gmail.com.

CHUA, LEON O., electrical engineering and computer science educator; b. June 28, 1936; m. Diana Chua; children: Amy Lynn, Michelle Ann, Katrin Faye, Cynthia Mae. BSEE, Mapua Inst. Tech., 1959; MS, MIT, 1961; PhD, U. Ill., Urbana-Champaign, 1964; doctorate (hon.), Ecole Poly. Lausanne, Switzerland, 1983, U. Tokushima, Japan, 1984, Tech. U. Dresden, Germany, 1992, Tech. U. Budapest, Hungary, 1994, U. Santiago de Compostela, Spain, 1995, U. Frankfurt, Germany, 1996, Tech. U. Iasa, Romanua, 1997, U. Catania, Italy, 2000, AGH U. Sci. Tech., Krakow, Poland, 2003. Asst. prof. Purdue U., Lafayette, Ind., 1964-67, assoc. prof., 1967-70; prof. U. Calif., Berkeley, 1970—. Cons. various electronic industries; Miller Rsch. prof. Miller Inst., 1976. Author: Introduction to Nonlinear Network Theory, 1969; CNN: A Paradigm for Complexity, 1998, A Nonlinear Dynamics Perspective on Wolfram's New Kind of Science, 2007; co-author: Computer Aided Analysis of Electronic Circuits: Algorithms and Computational Techniques, 1975, Linear and Nonlinear Circuits, 1987, Practical Numerical Algorithms for Chaotic Systems, 1991, Methoddds of Qualitative Theory in Nonlinear Dynamics Part 1, 1998, Part 2, 2002; dep. editor Internat. Jour. Circuit Theory and Applications; editor Internat. Jour. Bifurcation and Chaos; contbr. numerous articles to profl. jours. Patentee in field. Recipient Frederick Emmons Terman award, 1974, Alexander von Humboldt Sr. US Scientist award Tech. U. Munich, 1982-83, Vis. US Scientist award Japan Soc. for Promotion Sci., 1983-84, Myril B. Reed Best Paper prize, 1985, Prof. Invite Internat. award French Ministry Edn., 1986, M.E. Van Valkenhurg award, 1995, 1998, Top 15 Cited Authors in Engring. award, Current Contents ISI Database, 2002; Cambridge U. sr. vis. fellow, Eng., 1982. Fellow IEEE (Browder J. Thompson Meml. Prize award 1967, W.R.G. Baker Prize award 1973, Centennial medal 1985, Guillemin-Cauer prize 1985, Neural Networks Pioneer award 2000, Gustav Kirchhoff award 2005); mem. European Acad. Scis. (elected fgn. mem. 1997), Soc. Circuits and Systems IEEE (editor Trans. on Cirs. and Systems 1973-75, pres. 1976). Achievements include the prediction and description of the memristor, the fourth basic type of passive circuit element, in 1971 which was a hypothetical device until a team of researchers at HP Labs were able to fabricate and phsically implement one in 2008; invention of Chua's circuit, a simple electronic circuit that exhibits classic chaos theory behavior. Office: Univ Calif Dept Elec Engring & Computer Sci 253 Cory Hall #1770 Office 564 Cory Hall Berkeley CA 94720-1770 Office Phone: 510-642-3209. Office Fax: 510-845-4267. Business E-Mail: chua@eecs.berkeley.edu.

CHUANG, ALFRED SZE, information technology executive; b. Hong Kong, 1961; BS in Computer Sci., U. San Francisco, 1982; MS in Computer Sci., U. Calif. Davis, 1986. Mgmt. positions in software product devel., network infrastructure, systems architecture & operations mgmt. Sun Microsystems, Inc., 1986—94; founder Sun Intercontinental Ops.; corp. dir., chief scientist SunIntegration Svcs.; co-founder (with Bill Coleman and Ed Scott) BEA Sys., Inc., San Jose, Calif., 1995—, pres., 2001—, CEO, 2001—, chmn., 2002—. Bd. dirs. Tealeaf Tech., Inc. Trustee U. San Francisco. Office: BEA Systems Inc 2315 N First St San Jose CA 95131 Office Phone: 408-570-8000. Office Fax: 408-570-8901. E-mail: alfred.chuang@bea.com.

CHUANG, KEVIN, electronics manufacturing executive; CFO Synnex, Fremont, Calif. Office: Synnex Corporation 44201 Nobel Dr Fremont CA 94538-3178 Office Fax: (510) 668-3777.

CHUANG, TSU-YI, dermatologist, epidemiologist, educator; b. Amoy, China, May 21, 1946; arrived in U.S., 1976, naturalized, 1988; s. Hsi and Kia-Ling (Huang) C.; m. Lydia Ling-Chuan Lee, Dec. 22, 1973; children: Chester, Nancy. BM, Nat. Taiwan U., Taipei, 1971; MPH in Epidemiology, U. Wash., 1978. Diplomate Am. Bd. Dermatology, Am. Bd. Preventive Medicine. From asst. prof. to assoc. prof. dermatology U. Wis., Madison, 1984-92; chief dermatology svc. Middleton VA Med. Ctr., Madison, 1984-90; assoc. prof. dermatology Wright State U., Dayton, Ohio, 1990-95, dir. immunopathology lab., 1994-95; dir. dermatology clinic Frederick A. White Health Ctr., Dayton, 1995; prof. dermatology Ind. U., Indpls., 1995—2003, med. dir. melanoma program, 1996—2003, Arthur L. Norins prof., dir. dermatology clinic, 1999—2001; clin. prof. dermatology U. South Fla. Coll. Medicine, Tampa, 2004—06, U. So. Calif., LA, 2007—. Vis. prof. Wright State U., Dayton, 1990, Nat. Taiwan U., Taipei, 1991-97; vis. scientist Mayo Clinic, Rochester, 1986-92, Moss lectr. Meriter Found., 2002; mem. guidelines/outcomes com., 1996-2001, melanoma guidelines task force, 1997-2001, melanoma/skin cancer com., 2004-2008, adv. editor Dermalogica Sinica 2008-. Co-author: Conn's Current Therapy, 1992, The Challenge of Dermato-Epidemiology, 1997, Sleisenger & Fordtran's Gastrointestinal and Liver Disease, 2002; ad hoc reviewer Arch Dermatol., Chgo., 1990-99, Jour. Am. Acad. Dermatology, 1986-2004, Internat. Jour. Dermatology, 2001-08; editor Dermatologica Sinica, Taipei, 1994-96; contbr. over 100 articles to profl. jours. Pres. Rochester (Minn.) Chinese Culture Assn., 1980-82; v.p. Orgn. of Chinese Ams., Madison, 1986-90; pres. Midwest Chinese Christian Assn., Dayton, 1993-94, Indpls., 1996-97, Indiana Chinese-Am. Profls. Assn., Indlps. 1998. Rsch. grantee U. Wis., 1985-89, Schering, Glaxo, Genentech, Amgen 1986-2004; VA merit rev. bd. grantee Dept. Vets. Affairs, 1986-88, 90-94; recipient Burdette-Kunkel award Mary Margaret Walther Program for Cancer Care Rsch., 1996-97, 21st Century Research & Technology Fund award, 2000-02, Fellow Am. Acad. Dermatology (editl. cons. Am. Acad. Dermatology jour. 1986-2004), Am. Soc. for Dermatol. Surgery; mem. Ind. Chinese Profls. Assn. (pres. 1998). Achievements include first historical cohort study of human papilloma virus infection in U.S. in a defined population, first historical cohort study of genital herpes virus infection in U.S. in a defined population, first incidence study of polymyalgia rheumatica in the U.S. in a defined population, first population-based incidence study of skin cancer in U.S. in two well-defined populations. Office: Desert Oasis Health Care 69-844 Hwy 111 Ste A Rancho Mirage CA 92270 Office Phone: 760-318-4869. Business E-Mail: chuang007@yahoo.com.

CHUI, CHARLES K., mathematics professor; b. Macau, May 7, 1940; m. Margaret K. Lee, Aug. 22, 1964; children: Herman, Carie. BS, U. Wis., 1962, MS, 1963, PhD, 1967. Asts. prof. math. SUNY, Buffalo, 1967-70; assoc. prof. math. Tex. A&M U., College Station, 1970-74, prof. math., 1974-89, disting. prof. math., 1989—, dir. Ctr. for Approximation Theory, 1988-99, joint appointment in stats., computer sci. and electrical engring.; cons. prof. statistics Stanford U., 1997—; chief tech. officer TeraLogic, Inc., Mountain View, Calif., 1996-2000. Author: Multivariate Splines, 1988 (translated into Japanese and Chinese), An Introduction to Wavelets, 1992 (translated into Japanese and Chinese), Wavelets, A Mathematical Tool for Signal Analysis, 1997 (translated into Japanese); co-author: Elements of Calculus, 1983, 2nd edit., 1988, Kalman Filtering with Real-Time Applications, 1987, 2nd edit., 1991, 3d edit., 1997, Linear Systems and Optimal Control, 1988, Signal Processing and Systems Theory, Selected Topics, 1992, Hx Control, 1998; editor: Approximation Theory and Functional Analysis, 1991, Wavelets: A Tutorial in Theory and Applications, 1992 (translated into Japanese), (series) Wavelet Analysis and Its Applications, Approximations and Decompositions; co-editor: Approximation Theory II, 1976, Approximation Theory IV, 1983, Approximaition Theory V, 1986, Topics in Multivariate Approximation, 1987, Approximation Theory VI, vols. 1 and II, 1989, Multivariate Approximation Theory IV, 1989, Approximation Theory VII, 1992, Approximation Theory VIII, 1995; editor-in-chief Applied and Computational Harmonic Analysis: Wavelets, Signal Processing and Applications; editor: Wavelets: Theory, Algorithms, and Applications, Approximation Theory and Its Applications, Jour. Approximation Theory, Advances in Computational Math., Annals Numerical Math., Electronic Jour. Differential Equations, Advances in Computational Math., Neurocomputing; assoc. editor Jour. Math. Rsch. and Exposition, Revista de Matemáticas Aplicadas; patentee spline-wavelet signal analyses and methods for processing signals; patent pending method and apparatus for video image compression and decompression using boundary-spline-wavelets. Named. Hon. Prof., Ningxia U., China, 1987; Erskine fellow U. Canterbury, New Zealand, 1987; fellow Houston Advanced Rsch. Ctr., 1994. Fellow IEEE; mem. Am. Math. Soc., Math. Assn. Am., Soc. for Indsl. and Applied Math., Assn. Former Students Tex. A&M U. (Disting. Rsch. Achievement award 1981, 94). Roman Catholic. Avocations: music, fishing.

CHUI, CHI ON, electrical engineer, educator; b. New Territories, Hong Kong, Jan. 23, 1977; s. Yu Chi Chui and Hau Ming Cheung; m. Hoi Yan Yiu, June 3, 2004. BEng in Elec. Engring., Hong Kong U. Sci. and Tech., 1999; MS in Elec. Engring., Stanford U., 2001, PhD in Elec. Engring., 2004. Doctoral rsch. asst. Stanford U., Calif., 2000—04, grad. tchg. asst., 2001—03; rschr.-in-residence Intel Corp., Santa Clara, Calif., 2004—06; asst. prof. elec. engring. U. Calif., LA, 2007—. Cons. asst. prof. Stanford U., 2005—06. Reviewer Jour. of the Electrochem. Soc., 2002., Intel Corp. fellow, 2003, Microsoft Corp. grantee, 2003, Hong Kong Soc. Accts. scholar, 1996, Hong Kong Telecom Inst. of Info. Tech. scholar, 1998, Chiap Hua Cheng's Found. scholar, 1999, Hong Kong & Kowloon Elec. Appliances Mchts. Assn. scholar, 1999. Mem.: IEEE (sr.; reviewer, IEEE Electron Device Letters 2003—), Materials Rsch. Soc. Achievements include patents pending for High-k dielectric for thermodynamically-stable substrate-type materials; MOS interface with reactive metal overlayers; Germanium substrate-type materials and approach therefor; first to Seminal contribution to incorporate high-permittivity gate dielectrics for germanium MOS field-effect device application; invention of Two low-noise photodetector architectures in Group IV semiconductor; A novel self-aligned MOS field-effect transistor fabrication process; development of Various germanium MOS technologies including three generations of gate dielectric, two generations of dopant incorporation, and three generations of MOS field-effect transistors. Office: Elec Engring Dept Box 951594 6730B Boelter Hall Los Angeles CA 90095-1594 Home: 5781 Hesperia Ave Encino CA 91316

CHUMBLEY, AVERY B., state legislator; b. Champaign, Ill., Mar. 19, 1955; m. Mary Jay Chumbley. Student, Parkland C.C., Champaign, Ill.; grad., Ford Mktg. Inst., Dearborn, Mich. Pres. Wailuku Agribus. Co., Inc.; gen. mgr. Maui Tropical Plantation; mem. Hawaii Ho. of Reps., Honolulu, 1992-94, Hawaii Senate, Honolulu, 1994—, co-chair jud. com., mem. edn. and tech. com., mem. labor and environ. com. Apptd. Maui rep. Hawaii State Bd. Agr.; Maui Hist. Commn.; mem. steering com. Edn. Commn. of the States; dir. pub. policies World Sustainable Agr. Assn.; bd. dirs. Fmaily Lit. Adv. Bd., Maui Vis. Bur., Maui Econ. Devel. Bd., Maui Cmty. Arts and Cultural Ctr.; mem. Am. Cancer Assn.; pres. Maui County Fair Assn. Named Ofcl. of Yr. Maui Cmty. Choice, 1993, Cert. Appreciation and Recognition award Hawaii State Adult and Cmty. Edn. Adv. Coun., 1995, Mahalo award Friends of the Libr. of Hawaii, 1996, Ohana award Jr. League of Honolulu, 1997, Cert. of Appreciation Keiki Injury Prevention Coalition, 1998. Mem. Nat. Congress Parents and Tchrs. (hon. life mem.). Democrat. Office: State Capitol 415 S Capitol Rm 230 Honolulu HI 96813

CHUN, JENNIFER, communications executive; b. 1971; Law degree, Berkeley Sch. Law, U. Calif. Assoc. Pillsbury Madison & Sutro; v.p. bus. and legal affairs Fox Cable Networks, 2000, sr. v.p. bus. and legal affairs. Named one of 40 Executives Under 40, Multichannel News, 2006.

CHUN, JONATHAN J., state legislator; b. Hilo, Hawaii, Jan. 26, 1957; m. Sandra Chun; children: Lauren, Jason. BA, U. Hawaii; JD cum laude, Gonzaga U. Assoc. White & Thom; dep. corp. counsel City of County of Honolulu; 1st dep. county atty. Office of the County Atty., County of Kauai; of counsel Belles, Graham, Proudfoot & Wilson, Honolulu; mem. Hawaii Senate, Dist. 7, Honolulu, 1998—; mem. ways and means com. Hawaii Senate, Honolulu, mem. water, land, and Hawaiian affairs com., mem. govt. ops. and housing com. Mem. Gonzaga Law Rev., 1980, tech. editor, 1981. Asst. coach Lihue T-Ball League; mem. King Kaumuali'i Elem. Sch. PTA; bd. dirs. 'Ae Kamali'i Presch. Bd., Lihue Christian Ch., Ho'ike Pub. Access TV; bd. dirs., bd. elders, youth ministry team Lihue Missionary Ch. Mem. Kauai Bar Assn. Democrat. Office: State Capitol 415 S Beretania St Honolulu HI 96813-2407 E-mail: senchun@capitol.hawaii.gov.

CHUNG, KYUNG CHO, Korean history specialist, writer, educator; b. Seoul, Korea, Nov. 13, 1921; s. Yang Sun and Kyung Ok (Peng) C.; m. Yosi S. Chung, Oct. 10, 1958; children: In Kyung, In Ja. Student, Waseda U., Tokyo, 1941-43; BA, Seoul Nat. U., 1947; postgrad., Columbia U., 1948-49; MA, N.Y. U., 1951; LL.D., Pusan Nat. U., 1965; Litt.D., Sungkyunkwan U., 1968; MA, Monterey Inst. Fgn. Studies, 1974. Mem. faculty U.S. Def. Lang. Inst., Monterey, Calif., 1951-92, Monterey Inst. Fgn. Studies, 1973-74, Hartnell Coll., Salinas, Calif., 1974-93. Pres. Korean Rsch. Coun.; adviser Korean Assn., Monterey, 1974—, Am.-Korean Found., Crossroads, Inc., 1992, Asia Devel. Inc.; treas. Korean Rsch. Bull.; hon. prof. Kunkuk U.; pres. South Carmel Hills Assn., 1962-99; hon. chmn. Inst. Far Eastern Studies Joint Rsch. Program U.S.-Russia-Korea-Japan-China, 1993—; chmn. Korea-Am. Assn. Author: Korea Tomorrow, 1957, New Korea, 1962, Seoul (Ency. Americana), 1965, Naeil Hankuk, 1965, Sae Hankuk, 1968, Korea: The Third Republic, 1972, Korean Unification, 1973, Korea Reunion and Reunification, 1974, Kankuk Gaido, 1988, The Korea Guidebook: North and South Korea, 6th edit., 2002, Korea edit., 2002, Hankuk-chongran, 1999, East and West 1000 Munsun, 1995, Japanese Kangoku Gaizobuk, 2002. Recipient Superior Performance award, U.S. Govt., 1964, Recognition award of 40 Yrs. Svc., 1991, Excellency medal, 1992, Korean Prime Min. citation, 1965, cert. of achievement, U.S. Def. Lang. Inst., 1976, Outstanding Performance award, 1980, Commendation award, 1991, Olympic-Svc. Gold medal, Korean Pres., 1989, Spl. Commendation award, 1990, Fifa World Cup Svc. award, 2002, Spl. award medal, Korean Govt., 2002, Excellency Svc. award medal, Overseas Korean Found., 2003, Spl. Commendation plaque award, Mayor of Korea, 2006, Cmty. Svc. award, Pres. Korean Assn., 2007. Mem. AAUP, Am. Assn. Asian Studies, Am. Assn. Modern Langs., Am.-Korean Polit. Assn., Carmel Found., Korean Rsch. Coun. (pres. 2008-). Democrat. Mem. Korean Ch. Home and Office: 25845 S Carmel Hills Dr Carmel CA 93923-8310 Office Phone: 831-624-4929.

CHUNG, TONG SOO, lawyer; BA magna cum laude, Harvard U., 1977; MA in Public Affairs, Princeton U., 1980; JD, UCLA Sch. of Law, 1984. Financial analyst Exxon Corp., 1980—81; assoc. Whitman & Ransom, Los Angeles, Calif., 1984—86; co-founder, of counsel Lim, Ruger & Kim, LLP (formerly Kim, Chung & Lim), Los Angeles, Calif., 1986—; dir. export promotion & coord. Internat. Trade Administration, US Dept. Commerce, 1994, former dir. advocacy ctr., 1995—2000, former acting dep. asst. secy. for svc. industries & fin., 2000—01. Sr. advisor Sewon Telecom. Commr. Los Angeles County Private Industry Council, 1988—92; mem. Calif. Economic Develop. Advisory Com. on Asia, 1989—91; commr. Los Angeles Fire and Police Pension System, 1991—93, Calif. Postsecondary Ed. Commn., 1992—93; bd. dirs. Constitutional Rights Found.; founding mem. The Ethnic Coalition; founding pres. Korean Am. Coalition. Office: Lim, Ruger & Kim, LLP 1055 W Seventh St Ste 2800 Los Angeles CA 90017

CHURCH, STEVE, electronics executive; BS, Calif. State Poly. U., Pomona. Gen. mgr. So. Calif. divsn. Schweber Electronics; Western area mgr. and dir. distbn. Signetics (now Philips Semiconductor); v.p., SW area dir. then v.p. corp. mktg. Hamilton Hallmark Avnet, Inc., 1991—2001, pres. Electronics Mktg./Ams., co-pres. Electronics Mktg./Global, 2001—03, sr. v.p. and dir. svcs. and strategic bus. devel., 2003—, sr. v.p., chief human resources devel. officer. Exec. in residence Tex. A&M U., College Station, 2000—. Bd. advisors Ctr. Svcs. Leadership Coll. Bus. Ariz. State U. Avocations: skiing, running, tennis, golf, reading. Office: Avnet Inc 2211 S 47th St Phoenix AZ 85034-6403 Office Phone: 480-643-2000.

CHURCH-GAULTIER, LORENE KEMMERER, retired government official; b. Jordan, Mont., Oct. 18, 1929; d. Harry F. and Laura (Stoller) Kemmerer; m. Scott Johnston, Sept. 8, 1948 (div. 1953); children: Linda M., Theodore O.; m. Fred C. Church, May 9, 1956 (dec. 1967); children: Ned B., Nia J.; m. Charles F. Gaultier, Oct. 1996 (dec. Jan. 2000); m. Harry J. Michael, June 19, 2004. Student, Portland CC, 1973—76, Portland State U., 1978—79. Sec. intelligence div. IRS, Portland, Oreg., 1973-75; trade asst. Internat. Trade Adminstrn., U.S. Dept. Commerce, Portland, 1975-84, internat. trade specialist, 1984-94; ret., 1995. Mem. NAFE, World Affairs Coun., N.W. China Coun., Portland C. of C. (Europe 1992 com. 1988-89, internat. trade adv. bd. 1988-89, treas. dist. export coun. 1996—),

Western Internat. Trade Coun. Democrat. Roman Catholic. Avocations: music, growing roses. Home: 19725 SW Pike St Beaverton OR 97007-1446 Office: US Dept Commerce US&FCS 121 SW Salmon St Portland OR 97204-2901

CHURCHILL, BRUCE B., broadcast executive; b. Riverside, Calif., Aug. 30, 1957; s. James G. and Nancy (Wilkers) C. BA, Stanford U., Calif., 1979; MBA, Harvard U., 1984. Corp. lending officer Crocker Bank, San Francisco, 1979-82; assoc. McKinsey & Co. Inc., LA, 1984-88; v.p. fin. planning Paramount Pictures, LA, 1989; sr. v.p. fin. Fox TV; dep. CEO STAR Group Ltd., 1996—2000, pres., COO, 2000—03; CFO DIRECTV Group, El Segundo, Calif., 2004—05, exec. v.p., pres. DIRECTV L.Am., LLC and New Ventures, 2005—. Office: DIRECTV Group 2230 E Imperial Hwy El Segundo CA 90245 Office Phone: 310-964-5000.

CHURCHILL, JAMES ALLEN, lawyer; b. Kingsport, Tenn., Sept. 13, 1935; s. Robert Lang and Jamie Louise (Hill) C.; m. Jackeen Kelleher, Aug. 9, 1958; children: James Allen Jr., Courtney Bartlett. AB, Princeton U., 1957; LLB, Harvard U., 1960; M in Civil Law, Tulane U., 1963. Bar: La. 1961, U.S. Dist. Ct. (ea. dist.) La. 1962, U.S. Ct. Appeals (5th cir.) 1965, Calif. 1989. Ptnr. Lemle, Kelleher, Kohlmeyer & Matthews, New Orleans, 1960-79; dir. Barham & Churchill, New Orleans, 1979-88; ptnr. Pillsbury Madison & Sutro, L.A. and Tokyo, 1988-95; sr. v.p., gen. counsel., corp. sec. Ventura Foods, LLC, City of Industry, Calif., 1995—. Mem. ABA, Am. Law Inst., Calif. Bar Assn., La. Bar Assn., Calif. Club (L.A.), Boston Club (New Orleans), Annandale Golf Club. Office: Ventura Foods 40 Pointe Dr Brea CA 92821-3698

CHURCHILL, MAIR ELISA ANNABELLE, medical educator; b. Liverpool, Eng., Nov. 28, 1959; BA in Chemistry, Swathmore Coll., Pa., 1981; PhD in Chemistry, Johns Hopkins U., 1987. Lab. asst. Swarthmore Coll., 1979-81; teaching asst. Johns Hopkins U., Balt., 1981-83; non-clin. sci. staff grade I MRC Lab. Molecular Biology, Cambridge, Eng., 1987-93; asst. prof. biophysics U. Ill., Urbana, 1993-98; assoc. prof. biophysics U. Colo., Denver, 1998—. Contbr. numerous articles to profl. jours. Am. Cancer Soc. fellow, 1987-89, Cambridge U. fellow, 1988-91. Mem. Am. Chem. Soc., Sigma Xi (assoc.). Office: U Colo Health Scis Dept Pharm PO Box 6511 MS8303 Aurora CO 80045

CHURCHILL, WARD LEROY, social sciences educator, advocate; b. Urbana, Ill., Oct. 2, 1947; s. Jack Churchill and Maralyn L. (Allen) Debo; m. Leah R. Kelly, Aug. 8, 1995 (div.); 1 child, Jasmine Ann; m. Natsu Saito AA, Ill. Ctrl. Coll., 1972; BA, Sangamon State U., 1974, MA, 1975; LHD (hon.), Alfred U., 1992. Program dir. Boulder Valley Sch. Dist., Boulder, 1977-78, U. Colo., Boulder, 1978-90, assoc. prof., 1991-97, prof., 1997—2007, chmn., Dept. Ethnic Studies, 1997—2005. Vis. prof. Alfred U., N.Y., 1990-91. Author: Pacifism as Pathology: Reflections on the Role of Armed Struggle, 1986, Struggle for the Land: Indigenous Resistance to Genocide, Ecocide and Expropriation in Contemporary North America, 1993, Indians Are Us?: Culture and Genocide in Native North America, 1994, Since Predator Came: Notes on the Struggle for American Indian Liberation, 1995, From a Native Son: Selected Essays in Indigenism, 1985-1995, 1996, A Little Matter of Genocide: Holocaust and Denial in the Americas 1492 to the Present, 1997, Fantasies of the Master Race: Literature, Cinema and the Colonization of American Indians, 1998, Struggle for the Land: North American Resistance to Genocide, Ecocide, and Colonization, 2002, Acts of Rebellion: The Ward Churchill Reader, 2002, Life in Occupied America, 2003, On the Justice of Roosting Chickens: Reflections on the Consequences on U.S. Imperial Arrogance and Criminality, 2003, Kill the Indian, Save the Man: The Genocidal Impact of American Indian Residential Schools, 2004; co-author (with Jim VanderWall) Agents of Repression: The FBI's Secret Wars Against the Black Panther Party and the American Indian Movement, 1988, The COINTELPRO Papers: Documents from the FBI's Secret War Against Domestic Dissent, 1991; editor: New Studies on the Left, 1987-94; contbg. editor: Z Magazine, 1987—, Issues in Radical Therapy, 1982-87, Dark Night Field Notes, 1992—. Mem. governing coun. Colo. AIM, Denver, 1993—, co-dir., 1982-93; comms. dir. Am. Indian Anti-Defamation Coun., Denver, 1992-94; mem. steering com. Yellow Thunder Camp, Rapid City, S.D., 1981-85. Recipient Gustavus Myers award in writing Gustavus Myers Ctr., 1984. Avocation: films.*

CHURGIN, AMY, former publishing executive; Grad., Lehigh U., Bethlehem, Pa., 1977; MA in Art Hist., Hunter Coll., NYC. Assoc. pub. Seventeen Mag., 1992—94; Pub. K III Mag. Corp. (now Primedia Corp.-NY Mag.), NYC, 1994—99; group pub., NY, Chgo. Automobile Mag., 1999; v.p., pub. Archtl. Digest, Condé Nast, LA, 1999—2006; pub. Gourmet Mag., 2006—07; sr. v.p. corp. sales Condé Nast Media Grp., 2007—08. Organizer Architecture Days.

CICCIARELLI, JAMES CARL, immunology educator; b. Toluca, Ill., May 26, 1947; s. Maurice and Helen (Ippolito) Cicciarelli; m. Mary Jane Manning, June 2000; 1 child from previous marriage, Nicola. BS, Tulane U., 1969; PhD, So. Ill. U., 1977. Lic. clin. lab. dir., Calif. Fellow dept. surgery UCLA, 1977-79, asst. prof. immunology, 1980-87, assoc. prof., 1987-91; prof. urology, surgery and microbiology U. So. Calif., LA, 1992—. Lab. dir. Metic Transplant Lab., Inc., L.A., 1984—; bd. dirs. So. Calif. Organ Procurement Agy.; clin. lab. dir. Am. Bd. Bioanalysis, 1991—; mem. histocompatibility com. United Network Organ Sharing, 1991-94; mem. sci. adv. com. United Network for Organ Sharing, 1997—; lab. dir. Sharp Hosp. and Clinic, San Diego; mem. sci. adv. bd. BioArray Solutions, 2001—. Contbr. articles to profl. jours., chpts. to books. Rsch. grant NIH, 1985-88. Mem. Am. Soc. Histocompatibility and Immunogenetics, Internat. Transplant Soc., Am. Soc. Transplant Physicians, Internat. Soc. Heart Lung Transplantation. Libertarian. Roman Catholic. Avocations: boating, biking, skiing, tennis, running. Home: 5 Ringbit Rd W Rolling Hills CA 90274-5241 Office: USC Dept Urology Metic Transplant Lab 2100 W 3rd St Ste 280 Los Angeles CA 90057-1922

CICCONE, AMY NAVRATIL, art librarian; b. Detroit, Sept. 19, 1950; d. Gerald R. and Ruth C. (Kauer) Navratil. BA, Wayne State U., 1972; AM in Library Sci., U. Mich., 1973. Rsch. libr. Norton Simon Mus., Pasadena, Calif., 1974-81; chief libr. Chrysler Mus., Norfolk, Va., 1981-88; head libr. Architecture and Fine Arts Libr. U. So. Calif., LA, 1988-97, acting asst. univ. libr. pub. svcs., 1993-95, ref. libr., 1997—2004, assoc. coord. collection devel., 2004—. Contbr. articles to profl. jours. and chpts to books; cons. editor Art Reference Svcs., 1990-98. Mem. Art Libraries Soc. N.Am. (moderator Decorative Arts Roundtable, 1991-93, facilities standards com. 1986-91, chmn. strategic planning task force 1994-96, vice-chmn. So. Calif. chpt. 1989, chmn. 1990, chmn. 2001 conf.), Rsch. Librs. Group, Art & Architecture Group (steering com. 1992-94). Office: U So Calif Libr Los Angeles CA 90089-0187 Office Phone: 213-740-1958. Business E-Mail: aciccone@usc.edu.

CICCONE, MADONNA LOUISE VERONICA **See MADONNA**

CIMINO, JAY, automotive company executive; BA, U of Denver. CEO Phil Long Dealerships, Colorado Springs, Colo. Office: Phil Long Mitsubishi 1114 Motor City Dr Colorado Springs CO 80906-1313

CIRILLO, EDWARD J., state legislator, retired financial planner; b. Troy, NY, Feb. 2, 1934; m. Regina Cirillo; three children. BBA in Acctg., Siena Coll.; MA in Bus. Enterprise, SUNY, Binghamton. Mem. fin. mgmt. staff IBM Corp.; ret.; mem. Ariz. Senate, Dist. 15, Phoenix, 1996—; vice chmn. appropriations subcom.; mem. fin., transp. and rules com.; chmn. fin. instns. and retirement com.; vice-chmn. appropriations com. Village trustee Tarrytown, N.Y.; chair Tarrytown GOP; pres. Property Owners and Residents Assn.; trustee Sun City Mus. Art; v.p. Rep. Club. Mem. Rotary Club (pres.), Elks Lodge (exalted ruler).

CISNEROS, CARLOS R., state legislator; b. Questa, NM, 1951; New Mexico State Senator, District 6, 1985-, chairman, Education Committee, formerly, Ways & Means, currently, member, Judiciary Committee, formerly, Indian & Cult Affairs & Committees' Committees, currently, New Mexico State Senate.Employee, Union Oil of California Ins, currently. Democrat. Address: PO Box 1129 Questa NM 87556 Mailing: State Capitol Rm 328B Santa Fe NM 87503 Office Phone: 505-986-4861. E-mail: carlos.cisneros@nmlegis.gov.

CISSNA, SHARON, state legislator; b. Seattle, Apr. 5, 1942; c Robin Naughton. BA, U. Alaska, Anchorage, 1972; MS, Alaska Pacific U., 1992. Alaska State legislation aide, 71, 73 & 95; co-chairwoman, Alaska Voters for Open Primary, formerly; chairwoman, Chugach State Park Ad Hoc Committee, formerly; president, Chugach State Park Citizen Advisor Bd, formerly; Alaska State Representative, District 21, 1999-2002, member, Labor & Commerce Committee & Special Committees on Econ Develop & Tourism, Mil & Vet Affairs, 99-, Alaska House Representative; Alaska State Representative, District 22, 2003-. Owner, publisher serv businesses, 72-; counr/consult, Solutions, 94-; board member, World Wide Design, Inc, currently. Alaska Press Women; Alyeska Toastmasters; Univ Alaska & Alaska Pacific Univ Alumni Asns; Women League of Voters; PTA (board member, formerly). Democrat. Avocations: Long Distance Bicycling, gardening, Sketching. Mailing: 716 West Fourth Ave Ste 360 Anchorage AK 99501-2133 Office: State Capitol Rm 420 Juneau AK 99801-1182 Office Phone: 907-465-3875, 907-269-0190. Office Fax: 907-465-4588, 907-269-0193. Business E-Mail: representative_sharon_cissna@legis.state.ak.us.*

CIURCZAK, ALEXIS, librarian; b. Long Island, NY, Feb. 13, 1950; d. Alexander Daniel and Catherine Ann (Frangipane) C. BA Art History magna cum laude, U. Calif., LA, 1971; MA Libr. Sci., San Jose State U., 1975; cert. tchr. ESL, U. Calif., Irvine, 1985. Intern IBM Rsch. Libr., San Jose, Calif., 1974-75; tech. asst. San Bernardino Valley Coll. Libr., Calif., 1975; tech. svcs. librarian Palomar Coll., San Marcos, Calif., 1975-78, pub. svcs. librarian, 1978-81, libr. dir., 1981-86, pub. svcs. librarian, 1987—, instr. Libr. Technology Cert. Program, 1975—; exchange librarian Fulham Pub. Libr., London, 1986-87; coord. San Diego C.C. Consortium Semester-in-London Am. Inst. Fgn. Study, 1988-89. Fulbright fellow, 2d Air Divsn. Meml. Libr., Norwich, Eng., 2004—05. Mem. ALA, San Diego Libr. Svcs. com., Calif. Libr. Media Educators Assn., Patronato por Niños, Kosciuszko Found., So. Calif. Tech. Processes Group, Pacific Coast Coun. Latin Am. Studies, Libros, Reforma, Libr. Assn. (British), Calif. Libr. Assn., Calif. Tchrs. Assn., Phi Beta Kappa, Beta Phi Mu. Office: Palomar CC 1140 W Mission Rd San Marcos CA 92069-1415 also: Meml Libr Forum Millennium Plain Norwich NR2 1AW Norfolk England Home Phone: 949-493-7165; Office Phone: 760-744-1150. E-mail: alexis.ciurczak@palomar.edu.

CLABBY, MICHAEL, computer graphics designer, educator; m. Cindy Clabby; 1 child, Casey. Computer graphics, multimedia tchr. Lake City H.S., Coeur d' Alene, Idaho. Named Idaho Tchr. of Yr., 2007. Office: Lake City High Sch. 3101 Ramsey Rd Coeur D' Alene ID 83815 Business E-Mail: mclabby@sd271.k12.id.us.

CLAES, DANIEL JOHN, physician; s. John and Claribel Claes; m. Gayla Christine Claes, Jan. 19, 1974. AB magna cum laude, Harvard U., 1953, MD cum laude, 1957. Intern UCLA, 1957-58; Bowyer Found. fellow rsch. in medicine LA, 1958-61; pvt. practice specializing in diabetes, 1962—. V.p. Am. Eye Bank Found., 1978—83, dir. rsch., 1980—, pres., 1983—, chmn., CEO, 1995—; pres. Heuristic Group of Orgns., 1981—, Cavendish Assocs., 2002—, CTO, 2007—, CEO, 2008—; biotech. cons. SIRA Techs., 1995—. Contbr. articles to profl. jours. Mem. LA Mus. Art, 1960—. Mem.: AAAS, AMA, Cell Transplantation Soc., Diabetes Tech. Soc., Am. Math. Soc., Internat. Pancreas and Islet Transplant Assn., Internat. Diabetes Fedn, Am. Diabetes Assn. (profl. coun. on immunology, immunogenetics and transplantation), LA County Med. Assn., Calif. Med. Assn., Royal Commonwealth Club (London), Harvard and Harvard Med. Sch. So. Calif. Club. Achievements include research in supercomputer bioinformatics in medicine, computational chemistry, molecular modeling, quantum chemistry, genomics, proteomics and preventive care; ongoing research in epigenetics and cardiovascular disease. Office: Am Eyebank Found 15237 W Sunset Blvd Ste 108 Pacific Palisades CA 90272-3690

CLAFLIN, ARTHUR CARY, lawyer; b. Bowling Green, Ohio, July 7, 1950; s. Edward Scott and Mona Sophia (Cretney) C.; m. Gretchen Elaine Anders, May 31, 1975; children: Rachel Anders, Emily Anders. BA magna cum laude, Wesleyan U., 1972; JD, Yale U., 1975. Bar: Wash. 1975, U.S. Dist. Ct. (we. dist.) Wash. 1975, U.S. Dist. Ct. (ea. dist.) Wash. 1981, U.S. Ct. Appeals (9th cir.) 1979, U.S. Ct. Appeals (5th cir.) 1982. Assoc. Bogle & Gates, Seattle, 1975-81, ptnr., 1981-99, Claflin & Christensen, Seattle, 1999-2000; mem. Hall, Zanzig, Claflin, McEachern, Seattle, 2000—. Mem. Phi Beta Kappa. Presbyterian. Office: Hall Zanzig Claflin McEachern 1200 5th Ave Ste 1414 Seattle WA 98101-3106 Office Phone: 206-292-5900. Business E-Mail: aclaflin@hallzan.com.

CLAFLIN, BRUCE L., software company executive; BA in Polit. Sci., Pa. State U. Formerly with IBM Corp.; gen. mgr. IBM PC Co., 1989-93; pres. PC Co. Americas, 1993-94, gen. mgr. products and brand mgmt., 1994-97; former sr. v.p. and gen. mgr. sales and mktg. Digital Equipment Corp., 1997-98; pres., COO 3Com Corp., Santa Clara, Calif., 1998—2001, pres., CEO, 2001—06, sr. advisor to CEO, 2006—. Bd. dirs. Advanced Micro Devices, 2003—, Time Warner Telecom, 3Com Corp., 2001—. Mass. Bus. Roundtable. Alumni fellow Pa. State U., 1998.

CLAGUE, DAVID A., geologist; b. Phila., Aug. 3, 1948; married; 1 child. PhD in Earth Sci., Scripps Inst. Oceanography, 1974. With nat. rsch. coun. U.S. Geol. Survey, 1974-75, rsch. geologist, 1979-96; asst. prof. geology Middlebury Coll., 1975—79; scientist-in-charge Hawaiian Volcano Obs., 1991-96; dir. rsch. an devel. Monetary Bay Aquarium Rsch. Inst., 1996-99, sr. scientist, 1999—. Fellow Geol. Soc. Am., Am. Geophys. Union, Calif. Acad. Sci. Office: Monterey Bay Aquarium Rsch Inst 7700 Sandholdt Rd Moss Landing CA 95039-9644 E-mail: clague@mbari.org.

CLAMAN, MATTHEW W., lawyer, acting Mayor, Anchorage; b. Boston, May 26, 1959; m. Lisa Rieger Claman, 1990; children: Maia, Benjamin. BA in History, Colo. Coll., 1981; JD with honors, U. Tex., Austin, 1987. Bar: Alaska 1988, US Dist. Ct. (Dist. Alaska) 1989, US Supreme Ct. 1992, US Ct. Appeals (9th Cir.) 1992; cert. EMT Alaska. Atty. Mendel & Associates, Anchorage; rep. Anchorage Assembly, 2007—08, chmn., 2008—09; acting mayor City of Anchorage, Alaska, 2009—. Chmn. Heritage Land Bank Adv. Commn., 2006—07. Bd. mem. Anchorage Unitarian Universalist Fellowship, Trailside Discovery, Alaska Ctr. for Environment, Planned Parenthood of Alaska. Mem.: Maritime Law Assn., Assn. Trial Lawyers Am. (admiralty sect.), ABA (litig. sect.), Alaska Bar Assn. (pres.-elect 2006—07, pres. 2007—08, admiralty sect., bd. governors 2002). Avocations: hiking, bicycling, skiing. Mailing: Mayors Office PO Box 196650 Anchorage AK 99519-6650 Office Fax: 907-343-7180.*

CLAPP, LAURI, state representative; b. Denver, Dec. 1, 1962; m. Rolley Clapp; 3 children. State rep. dist. 37 Colo. Ho. of Reps., Denver, 1998—, vice chair joint com. on health, edn., welfare and instns. and HECF, chair health, environment, welfare and instns. com., mem. judiciary com. Mem.: VFW Women's Aux., Englewood Hist. Soc., Arapahoe County Rep. Men's Club, Englewood Women's Rep. Club, Cherry Creek Rep. Women's Club. Republican. Avocation: canning james, jellies and syrups. Office: State Capitol # 320 200 E Colfax Ave Denver CO 80203

CLAPTON, ERIC, musician, singer; b. Ripley, Surrey, Eng., Mar. 30, 1945; s. Edward Fryer and Patricia Molly Clapton; m. Patricia Anne Boyd, March 27, 1979 (div. 1988); m. Melia McEnery, Jan. 1, 2002; children: Julie Rose, Ella May, Sophie 1 child (with Yvonne Kelly), Ruth; 1 child (with Lory Del Santo), Conor (dec. 1991) Student, Kingston Art Sch. Guitarist The Roosters, 1963, Casey Jones & the Engineers, 1963, The Yardbirds, 1963—65; guitarist, singer John Mayall's Bluesbreakers, 1965—66; guitarist Powerhouse, 1966; guitarist, singer Cream, 1966—68, Blind Faith, 1969; guitarist Delaney and Bonnie & Friends, 1969—70; guitarist, singer Derek and the Dominos, 1970—71; solo artist, 1970—. Guitarist (albums with The Yardbirds) Five Live Yardbirds, 1964, For Your Love, 1965, Having A Rave Up, 1965, guitarist, singer (albums with John Mayall's Bluesbreakers) Bluesbreakers with Eric Clapton, 1966, (albums with Cream) Fresh Cream, 1966, Disraeli Gears, 1967, Wheels of Fire, 1968, Goodbye, 1969, Live Cream, 1970, Live Cream Volume II, 1972, Strange Brew: The Very Best of Cream, 1983, Those Were the Days, 1997, BBC Sessions, 2003, Cream Gold, 2005, Royal Albert Hall London 2-6 May 2005, 2005, guitarist (albums with Blind Faith) Blind Faith, 1969; guitarist (albums with Delaney and Bonnie & Friends) On Tour with Eric Clapton, 1970; singer, guitarist (albums with Derek and the Dominos) Layla And Other Assorted Love Songs, 1970, In Concert, 1973, The Layla Sessions: The 20th Anniversary Edition, 1990, Live at the Fillmore, 1994, (solo albums) Eric Clapton, 1970, 461 Ocean Boulevard, 1974, There's One in Every Crowd, 1975, E.C. Was Here, 1975, No Reason to Cry, 1976, Slowhand, 1977, Backless, 1978, Just One Night, 1980, Another Ticket, 1981, Time Pieces: Best of Eric Clapton, 1982, Money and Cigarettes, 1983, Behind the Sun, 1985, Time Pieces Vol. II 'Live' in the 70's, 1985, August, 1987, Crossroads, 1988, One Moment in Time, 1988, Journeyman, 1989, 24 Nights, 1991, Unplugged, 1992 (Winner of 6 Grammy awards including Album of Yr., Record of Yr.), From the Cradle, 1994 (Grammy award Best Traditional Blues Album), The Cream of Clapton, 1995, Crossroads II: Live in the Seventies, 1996, Retail Therapy, 1997, Pilgrim, 1998, Clapton Chronicles: The Best of Eric Clapton 1981-1999, 1999, The Blues, 1999, Reptile, 2001 (Grammy award Best Pop Instrumental Perf.), One More Car, One More Rider, 2002, Me and Mr. Johnson, 2004, Sessions for Robert J., 2004, Back Home, 2005, Complete Clapton, 2007, (soundtrack) Rush, 1992, (albums with others) A Concert for Bangladesh, 1972 (Grammy award Album of Yr.), (soundtrack with The Band & others) The Last Waltz, 1976, (albums with others) Rainbow Concert, 1973, singer, guitarist Bob Dylan 30th Anniversary Concert Celebration, 1993, singer, guitarist (albums with B.B. King) Riding with the King, 2000 (Grammy award Best Trad. Blues Album), (albums with J.J. Cale) The Road to Escondido, 2006; prodr. (with Rod Stewart): (albums) Beginnings, 2004; composer: (songs) BBC miniseries Edge of Darkness, 1986, (film score) Lethal Weapon, 1986, Homeboy, 1988, Lethal Weapon 2, 1989, The Van, 1996, Nil by Mouth, 1997; co-composer (film score) Lethal Weapon 3, 1992; performer: (films) The Concert for Bangladesh, 1972, The Last Waltz, 1978, Bob Dylan 30th Anniversary Concert Celebration, 1993, The Rolling Stones Rock 'N' Roll Circus, 1996; author: Clapton: The Autobiography, 2007. Founder Crossroads Centre, 1997—. Recipient Silver Clef Award Outstanding Achievement in World of British Music, presented by Princess Michael of Kent, 1983, Lifetime Achievement Award, British Phonographic Inst., 1987, presented with silver model of a Fender Stratocaster by Prince Charles to commemorate 25th yr. in music industry, 1988, Best Guitarist Award, Internat. Rock Awards, 1989, Living Legend Award, 1990, W.C. Handy Award For Blues, 16th Annual Ceremony, 1995, Man of Yr. Award music: solo artist, GQ Mag., 1999, Stevie Ray Vaughan, Music Assistance Program, 1999, Commander of the British Empire, 2003; named one of The 100 Greatest Guitarists of All-Time, Rolling Stone mag.; named to the Rock & Roll Hall of Fame, (as mem. of The Yardbirds, 1992, as mem. of Cream, 1993, as solo artist, 2000). Achievements include minor planet named "(4305) Clapton" in his honor, 1990; first triple inductee into Rock & Roll Hall of Fame. Office: c/o Warner Bros Records 3300 Warner Blvd Burbank CA 91505-4632

CLAREY, PATRICIA T., health insurance company executive, former state official; BS, Union Coll., Schenectady, NY, 1975; MPA, Harvard U. John F. Kennedy Sch. of Govt., Cambridge, Mass., 1983. Govt. affairs rep. Chevron Corp., San Francisco; govt. rels. position

Ashland Oil, Inc.; dep. dir. legis. affairs Nat. Park Svc., Washington; congl. liaison US Dept. Interior, Washington, 1986—89; dep. chief of staff to Gov. State of Calif., Sacramento; v.p. public affairs Transamerica Corp., San Francisco, 1999—2001; pres. Transamerica Found., San Francisco, 1998; v.p. govt. rels. Health Net, Inc. (formerly known as Foundation Health Sys., Inc.), LA, 2001—03; ran primary campaign for Gov.-elect Arnold Schwarzenegger; chief of staff to Gov. State of Calif., Sacramento, 2003—06; COO Health Net of Calif., Inc., Woodland Hills, Calif., 2006—08; sr. v.p., chief regulatory officer Health Net, Woodland, Calif., 2008—. Former bd. dir. Calif. Found. on the Environ. and the Economy; mem. joint pub. adv. com. Commn. for Environ. Cooperation of N.Am., 2003—. Office: Health Net of Calif Inc 21281 Burbank Blvd Woodland Hills CA 91367

CLARK, ALAN FRED, physicist; b. Milw., June 29, 1936; BS in Physics, U. Wis., Madison, 1958, MS in Nuclear Engring., 1959; PhD in Nuclear Sci., U. Mich., Ann Arbor, 1964. NAS-NRC postdoctoral assoc. Nat. Bur. Standards, Boulder, Colo., 1964-66, physicist, 1966-78, chief cryogenic properties of solids, 1978-80, group leader supercondr. and magnetic measurements, 1981-87; liaison scientist Office Naval Rsch., London and Europe, 1987-89; group leader fundamental elec. measurements Nat. Inst. Stds., Gaithersburg, Md., 1989-92, 95-98, sr. scientist electricity divsn., 1992-94, dep. chief optoelectronics divsn. Boulder, Colo., 1998-2001, chief magnetic tech. divsn., 2001—. Chmn., founder Internat. Cryogenic Materials Conf. Bd., Boulder, Colo., 1975—; mem. Internat. Cryogenic Engring. Conf. Bd., 1982—. Contbr. over 150 articles to profl. jours.; editor Cryogenics Jour., 1982-94, IEEE Trans. Applied Superconductivity, 1994-98, 8 conf. proceedings, 4 books. Recipient Superior Rsch. Nat. Bur. Standards, 1967, 74, 82, 83, 84, 85, 86, 93-97. Fellow IEEE, Am. Phys. Soc.; mem. ASTM (chmn. superconductor com. 1980-89), IEEE Superconductivity Com. (chmn. 1989-94), Internat. Acad. Electrotech. Scis. Office: Nat Inst Standards & Tech MS 816 00 325 Broadway Boulder CO 80305 E-mail: aclark@boulder.nist.gov.

CLARK, BRUCE ROBERT, geologist, consultant; b. Pitts., June 17, 1941; s. Harold Thomas and Florence (Miller) Clark; m. Karen Pelton Heath, Dec. 30, 1967; children: Adam, Andrea. BS, Yale U., 1963; PhD, Stanford U., 1967. Asst. prof. U. Mich., Ann Arbor, 1968-73, assoc. prof., 1973-77; v.p. Leighton and Assocs., Inc., Irvine, Calif., 1977-85, pres., 1986—2002, CEO, 1988—2002, sr. cons., 2002—. Contbr. articles to profl. jours. Commr. Calif. Seismic Safety Commn., 2000—07, chmn., 2001—03; chmn. bd. dirs. YMCA Orange County, Calif., 1999—2002. Fellow: Geol. Soc. Am.; mem.: Seismol. Soc. Am., Assn. Engring. Geologists, Am. Geophys. Union, Earthquake Engring. Rsch. Inst. (bd. dirs. 2002—06). Office: Leighton Group Inc 17781 Cowan Irvine CA 92614-6009 Home Phone: 949-644-2052. Personal E-mail: bruce-clark@cox.net.

CLARK, BURTON ROBERT, sociologist, educator; b. Pleasantville, NJ, Sept. 6, 1921; s. Burton H. and Cornelia (Amole) C.; m. Adele Halitsky, Aug. 31, 1949; children: Philip Neil (dec.), Adrienne. BA, UCLA, 1949, PhD, 1954; Doctorate (hon.), U. Strathclyde, 1998, U. Turku, Finland, 2000. Asst. prof. sociology Stanford (Calif.) U., 1953-56; rsch. assoc., asst. prof. edn. Harvard U., 1956-58; assoc. prof., then prof. edn. and assoc. rsch. sociologist, then rsch. sociologist U. Calif., Berkeley, 1958-66; prof. sociology Yale U., 1966-80, chmn. dept., 1969-72, chmn. higher edn. rsch. group, 1973-80; Allan M. Cartter prof. higher edn. UCLA, 1980-91, prof. emeritus, 1991—. Author: Adult Education in Transition, 1956, The Open Door College, 1960, Educating the Expert Society, 1962, The Distinctive College, 1970, The Problems of American Education, 1975, Academic Power in Italy, 1977, The Higher Education System, 1983, The Academic Life, 1987, Places of Inquiry, 1995, Creating Entrepreneurial Universities, 1998, Sustaining Change in Universities, 2004, On Higher Education: Selected Writings, 1956-2006, 2008; co-author: Students and Colleges, 1972, Youth: Transition to Adulthood, 1973, Academic Power in the United States, 1976, Academic Power: Patterns of Authority in Seven National Systems of Higher Education, 1978; editor: Perspectives on Higher Education, 1984, The School and The University, 1985, The Academic Profession, 1987, The Research Foundations of Graduate education, 1993; co-senior editor: Encyclopedia of Higher Education, 1992. Served with AUS, 1942-46. Recipient Comenius medal UNESCO, 1998. Fellow Brit. Soc. for Rsch. in Higher Edn., AAAS, Am. Ednl. Rsch. Assn. (Am. Coll. Testing award 1979, Divsn. J. Disting. Rsch. award 1988, Outstanding Book award 1989); mem. Am. Sociol. Assn., Assn. Study Higher Edn. (pres. 1979-80, Rsch. Achievement award 1985, Howard Bowen Disting. Svc. award 1997), Nat. Acad. Edn. (v.p. 1989-93), Consortium Higher Edn. Rschrs., European Assn. for Instnl. Rsch. (disting. mem.) Home: 201 Ocean Ave 1710B Santa Monica CA 90402 Office: UCLA Grad Sch Edn and Info Studies Los Angeles CA 90095-1521 Office Phone: 310-458-1640. Business E-Mail: clark@gseis.ucla.edu.

CLARK, CHARLES SUTTER, interior designer; b. Venice, Calif., Dec. 21, 1927; s. William Sutter and Lodema Ersell (Fleeman) Clark. Student, Chouinard Art Inst., LA, 1950—51. Interior designer LM.H. Co., Great Falls, Mont., 1956—62, Andreason's Interiors, Oakland, Calif., 1962—66, Western Contact Furnishers Internat., Oakland, 1966—70, Design Five Assocs., Lafayette, Calif., 1972—73; owner, interior designer Charles Sutter Clark Interiors, Greenbrae, Calif., 1973—91, San Rafael, Calif., 1991—. With USAF, 1951—55. Recipient award, Mont. State Fair, 1953—55. Mem.: Am. Soc. Interior Designers. Home: 429 El Faisan Dr San Rafael CA 94903-4517 Personal E-mail: csutterclark@global.net. E-mail: csutterclark@sbc.net.

CLARK, COLIN WHITCOMB, mathematics professor; b. Vancouver, BC, Can., June 18, 1931; s. George Savage and Irene (Stewart) C.; m. Janet Arlene Davidson, Sept. 17, 1955; children: Jennifer Kathleen, Karen Elizabeth, Graeme David. BA, U. B.C., 1953; PhD, U. Wash., 1958; DSc (hon.), U. Victoria, 2000. Instr. math. U. Calif., Berkeley, 1958-60; asst. prof. math. U. B.C., 1960-65, assoc. prof., 1965-68, prof., 1968-94, acting dir. Inst. Applied Math., 1983-86, prof. emeritus, 1994—. Vis. prof. math. N.Mex. State U., 1970-71; vis. scientist Fisheries and Oceanography div. C.S.I.R.O., Cronulla, Australia, 1975-76, Ecology and Evolutionary Biology, U. Ariz., 1992; Regents lectr. U. Calif., Davis, 1986; vis. prof. Biol. Scis. Cornell U., 1987; vis. prof. Princeton U., 1997. Author: The Theoretical Side of Calculus, 1972, Mathematical Bioeconomics, 1976, 2d edit., 1990, Elementary Mathematical Analysis, 1982, Bioeconomic Modelling and Fisheries Management, 1985; (with J. Conrad) Resource Economics: Notes and Problems, 1987; (with J. Yoshimura, eds.) Adaption in Stochastic Environments, 1993; (with M. Mangel) Dynamic Modeling in Behavorial Ecology, 1988, Dynamic State Variable Models in Ecology, 2000, The Worldwide Crisis in Fisheries, 2007; contbr. articles to profl. jours. Fellow Royal Soc. Can., Royal Soc. (U.K.); mem. Can. Applied Math. Soc. (pres. 1981-83), Resource Modeling Assn. (pres. 1988-90). Office: Univ BC Dept Math Vancouver BC Canada V6T 1Z2 Personal E-mail: colin_clark@shaw.ca.

CLARK, DAVID SCOTT, law educator, consultant; b. San Diego, Nov. 24, 1944; s. Homer Granville and Edna Susan (Maunus) C.; m. Marilee Oakes Wilson, Mar. 29, 1970; children: Richard, Susanna, Eliina, Liisa, David Scott II. AB, Stanford U., 1966, JD, 1969, JSM, 1972. Bar: Calif. 1972. Vis. prof. law U. Costa Rica, San Jose, 1969-71; asst. dir. studies in law and devel. Stanford Law Sch., Calif., 1973-75; asst. prof. law La. State U., Baton Rouge, 1976-78; assoc. prof. law U. Tulsa, 1978-81, prof., 1981—2002, dir. comparative and internat. law ctr., 1993—2001; Wilson prof. law Willamette U., Salem, Oreg., 2002—. Vis. scholar Max Planck Inst., Hamburg, Germany, 1984-85, 92; disting. vis. prof. So. Ill. U., Carbondale, 1987; vis. prof. law U. Colo., 1989; disting. vis. prof. Loyola U., Chgo., 1996; Fulbright sr. chair in comparative law, U. Trento, Italy, 1999; vis. prof. law U. Houston, 1999; vis. scholar, Inst. Advanced Legal Studies, London, 2000-01; disting. vis. prof. law, Bucerius Law Sch., Hamburg, Germany, 2002, 07. Author: Comparative Law, 1978, Law and Social Change, 1979, The Civil Law Tradition, 1994, Oklahoma Civil Pretrial Procedure, 1995, The Organization of Lawyers and Judges, 2003; editor: Comparative and Pvt. Internat. Law, 1990, Introduction to the Law of the United States, 1992, 2d edit., 2002, Oxford Companion to American Law, 2002, American Law in the 21st Century, 2006, Encyclopedia of Law and Society: American and Global Perspectives, 2007, (jours.) Am. Jour. Comparative Law; contbr. articles to profl. jours. NEH grantee, 1981; von Humboldt Stiftung sr. research fellow, 1984-87. Mem.: ABA (internat. law and practice sect.), Am. Coun. Learned Socs. (exec. com. 1996—99, chair 1997—99, bd. dirs. 1997—99), Law and Soc. Assn., Internat. Acad. Comparative Law, Inns of Ct. (Inner Temple, London) (rsch. fellow 2000), Am. Soc. Comparative Law (exec. com. 1986—88, treas. 1989—95, v.p. 1998—2002, pres. 2002—06, hon. pres. 2006—08). Democrat. Unitarian Universalist. Avocations: running, bicycling. Office: Willamette U Coll Law 245 Winter St SE Salem OR 97301 Home Phone: 503-373-3703; Office Phone: 503-370-6403. Office Fax: 503-370-6375. Business E-Mail: dsclark@willamette.edu.

CLARK, DICK, performer, producer; b. Mt. Vernon, NY, Nov. 30, 1929; m. Kari Wigton; children— Richard, Duane, Cindy. Grad., Syracuse U., 1951. Founder Dick Clark Corp. Prodns., Dick Clark Film Group, Dick Clark Communications, Inc., a group of casual dining restaurants, Dick Clark's American Bandstand Grill, Dick Clark's AB Grill, Dick Clark's Bandstand — Food, Spirits & Fun, and Dick Clark's AB Diner. Announcer, Sta. WRUN, summer 1950; then staff announcer, Sta. WOLF; rejoined, Sta. WRUN, then joined, Sta. WKTV, announcer, Sta. WFIL, Phila., 1952; host Am. Bandstand, 1956-89 (Outstanding Popular Music Program, Popular Music Mag. 1958, Daytime Emmy award 1981-82, 82-83), 32d Ann. Emmy Awards, 1981, Daytime Emmy Awards; formed, Dick Clark Prodns., 1956. Leading ind. T.V. producer with over 8500 hours of programming to credit, including The Savage Seven, 1968, Psych-Out, 1968, Killers Three, 1968, The Man in the Santa Claus Suit, 1979, The Birth of the Beatles, 1979, Elvis, 1979, The Dark, 1979, Murder in Texas, 1981, Demon Murder Case, 1983, Woman Who Willed a Miracle, 1983 (5 Emmmy awards, Peabody award), Remo Williams: The Adventure Begins, 1985, Copacabana, 1985, Liberace, 1988, Town Bully, 1988, Promised a Miracle, 1988, Death Dreams, 1991, Elvis and the Colonel: The Untold Story, 1993, Secret Sins of the Father, 1994, The Good Doctor: The Paul Fleiss Story, 1996, Deep Family Secrets, 1997; producer/host TV series: American Bandstand, The Dick Clark Show, Where the Action Is, The Rock'n Roll Years, others; host Dick Clark's Rock 'n Roll Revue, $ 20,000 Pyramid (Emmy award 1978-79), $25,000 Pyramid (Emmy award 1984-85, 85-86), $100,000 Pyramid, Miss USA, Miss Teen USA, Miss Universe; host/exec. producer Super Bloopers and New Practical Jokes, New Years Rockin' Eve, 1972-, 40th Anniversary of American Bandstand; exec. producer Acad. of Country Music Awards, Am. Music awards, Golden Globe Awards, Soap Opera Awards, Daytime Emmy Awards, Cable Ace Awards; author: Your Happiest Years, 1959, To Goof or Not To Goof, 1963, Rock, Roll and Remember, 1976, Dick Clark & Richard Robinson, Looking Great, Staying Young, 1981, Dick Clark's The First 25 Years of Rock 'N Roll, 1981, The History of American Bandstand, 1985, Dick Clark's Guide to Good Grooming, 1985; producer VH1's Best fo American Bandstand, 1996, 97, Primetime Country, 1996, 97, Beyond Belief: Factor Fiction, 1997, The Weird Al Show, 1997, Dick Clarks's American Bandstand Collectors Edition, 1997; Donny & Marie, 1998-2000, Your Big Break, 1999, 2000, Greed, 1999, 2000; founder Dick Clark Media Archives. Recipient 6 Emmy awards as both prodr. and host, Grammy Nat. Trustees award, 1990, Am. Classic award ASCAP, 1990, Billboard Radio award Countdown Am., 1991, Disting. Svc. award Nat. Assn. Broadcasting, 1993, Daytime Emmys Lifetime Achievement award, 1994, Lifetime Achievement award Am. D.J. Assn., 1994, Lifetime Achievement award Syracuse U., 1994; named to Emerson Radio Hall of Fame, 1990, Broadcasting Mag. Hall of Fame, 1992, Rock 'N' Roll Hall of Fame, 1993, Internat. Person of Yr., NAPTE, 1990, Person of Yr., Phila. Advt. Club, 1995; inducted TV Hall of Fame, 1993. Achievements include honored with tribute at 2006 Emmy awards. Office: Dick Clark Prodns Inc 9200 Sunset Blvd Los Angeles CA 90069*

CLARK, EARNEST HUBERT, JR., tool company executive; b. Birmingham, Ala., Sept. 8, 1926; s. Earnest Hubert and Grace May (Smith) C.; m. Patricia Margaret Hamilton, June 22, 1947; children: Stephen D., Kenneth A., Timothy R., Daniel S., Scott H., Rebecca G. BS in Mech. Engring, Calif. Inst. Tech., 1946, MS, 1947. Chmn., chief exec. officer Friendship Group, Baker Hughes, Inc. (formerly Baker Oil Tools, Inc.), LA, 1947-89, v.p., asst. gen. mgr., 1958-62, pres., chief exec. officer, 1962-69, 75-79, chmn. bd., 1969-75, 79-87, 87-89, ret., 1989; chmn. The Friendship Group, Newport Beach, Calif., 1989—. Bd. dirs. Regenesis Inc. Past chmn., bd. dirs. YMCA of U.S.A.; past chmn. bd. YMCA for Met. L.A.; mem. nat. coun. YMCA; trustee Harvey Mudd Coll. With USNR, 1944-46, 51-52. Mem. AIME, Am. Petroleum Inst., Petroleum Equipment Suppliers Assn. (bd. dirs.), Tau Beta Pi. Office: Friendship Group 3822 Calle Ariana San Clemente CA 92672-4502 Home Phone: 949-498-0866. Personal E-mail: ehclarkjr@cox.net.

CLARK, EDWARD, bishop; b. Milw., Nov. 30, 1946; MA, St. John's, Camarillo, Calif., 1972; MS, Mt. St. Mary's Coll., 1983; STL, Pontifical Gregorian Univ., Rome, 1986, STD, 1988. Ordained priest Archdiocese of LA, 1972; rector St. John's Sem., 1994—2001; ordained bishop, 2001; aux. bishop Archdiocese of LA, 2001—. Roman Catholic. Office: Archdiocese of LA 3424 Wilshire Blvd Los Angeles CA 90010 Office Phone: 213-637-7288. Office Fax: 213-637-6510.

CLARK, EVE VIVIENNE, linguist, educator; b. Camberley, U.K., July 26, 1942; arrived in U.S., 1967; d. Desmond Charles and Nancy (Aitken) Curme; m. Herbert H. Clark, July 21, 1967; 1 child, Damon Alistair. MA with honors, U. Edinburgh, Scotland, 1965, PhD, 1969. Rsch. assoc. Stanford (Calif.) U., 1969-71, from asst. prof. to assoc. prof., 1971-83, prof., 1983—, prof. humanities, 2007—. Author: Ontogenesis of Meaning, 1979, Acquisition of Romance, 1985, The Lexicon in Acquisition, 1993, First Language Acquisition, 2003; co-author: Psychology and Language, 1977. Fellow Ctr. for Advanced Study in the Behavioral Scis., 1979-80, Guggenheim Found., 1983-84. Mem. Dutch Acad. Scis. (fgn.). Business E-Mail: eclark@psych.stanford.edu.

CLARK, GARY R., newspaper editor; b. Cleve., June 27, 1946; s. Dale Francis and Mary Louise (Rozeski) C.; m. Caryn Elaine Helm, Dec. 18, 1976; children: Jessica Lynn, Brian Michael. BA, Ohio State U., 1973, MA, 1978. Reporter Chronicle-Telegram, Elyria, Ohio, 1973-77, The Plain Dealer, Cleve., 1978-88, state editor, 1988-89, nat. editor, 1989, city editor, 1989-90, mng. editor, 1990—2000; city editor The Columbus Dispatch, 2000—02; mng. editor for news The Denver Post, 2003—. Tchg. assoc. Ohio State U., Columbus, 1977-78; juror, Pulitzer Prize, 1996. Sgt. USMC, 1966-69, Vietnam. Recipient Best of Show award, Ohio Soc. Profl. Journalists, 1999. Mem. AP Mng. Editors, Am. Soc. Newspaper Editors, Investigative Reporters and Editors, Cleve. City Club. Office: Mng Ed Denver Post 1560 Broadway Denver CO 80202

CLARK, GLEN EDWARD, judge; b. Cedar Rapids, Iowa, Nov. 23, 1943; s. Robert M. and Georgia L. (Welch) C.; m. Deanna D. Thomas, July 16, 1966; children: Andrew Curtis, Carissa Jane. BA, U. Iowa, 1966; JD, U. Utah, 1971. Bar: Utah 1971, U.S. Dist. Ct. Utah 1971, U.S. Ct. Appeals (10th cir.) 1972. Assoc. Fabian & Clendenin, 1971-74, ptnr., 1975-81, dir., chmn. banking and comml. law sect., 1981-82; judge U.S. Bankruptcy Ct. Dist. Utah, Salt Lake City, 1982-86, chief judge, 1986—. Bd. govs. nat. Conf. Bankruptcy Judges, 1988-94; mem. com. on bankruptcy edn. Fed. Jud. Ctr., 1989-92; vis. prof. U. Utah, Salt Lake City, 1977-79, 83; pres. Nat. Conf. Bankruptcy Judges, 1992-93; chair bd. trustees Nat. Conf. Bankruptcy Judges Endowment for Edn., 1990-92; vis. assoc. prof. law Univ. Utah; instr. adv. bus. law Univ. Utah. Articles editor: Utah Law Review. With U.S. Army, 1966-68. Finkbine fellow U. Iowa. Fellow Am. Coll. Bankruptcy (charter, mem. bd. regents 1995-2000, dir. found. 2002-03); mem. Jud. Conf. U.S. (mem. com. jud. br. 1992-99, 10th cir. bankruptcy appellate panel 1996—), Utah Bar Assn., Order of Coif. Presbyterian. Office: 365 US Courthouse 350 S Main St Salt Lake City UT 84101-2106

CLARK, JAMES HENRY, publishing company executive; b. Chgo., Aug. 30, 1931; s. James Henry and Mildred Beth (Rutledge) C.; children: Garrette Elizabeth, James Henry. AB, U. Calif.-Berkeley, 1959. With personnel dept. Fireman's Fund, San Francisco, 1959-60; coll. textbook salesman Prentice-Hall Inc., Berkeley, 1960-63, regional editor, 1963-64, editor Englewood Cliffs, N.J., 1964-67; dir. Western editorial office, Belmont, Calif., 1967-68; assoc. pub. Aldine Pub. Co., Chgo., 1969; editor-in-chief coll. div. Harper & Row Pubs., Inc., NYC, 1969-70, pub., v.p., 1970-77; dir. Univ. Press U. Calif., Berkeley, 1977—. Served with USAF, 1949-53. Mem. Am. Assn. Univ. Presses (pres. 1986.) Office: U Calif Univ Press 2120 Berkeley Way Berkeley CA 94720-5804

CLARK, JAMES W., state legislator; b. Braddock, Pa., Feb. 22, 1944; m. Vickie Parker-Clark; children: Phyllis, Sean, Julie. BSBA, U. Tampa, 1973; MS in Internat. Rels., Troy State U., Germany, 1979; MBA, U. Idaho, 1989. Owner A to Z Consultants, 1989—2000; adj. prof. Ea. Wash. U., 1989—, Lewis Clark State Coll., 1990—; mem. Dist. 3 Idaho House of Reps., Boise, 1996—. Lt. col. US Army, 1967—87, Germany, South America, Vietnam. Mem.: C. of C., Mil. Order World Wars, Ret. Officers Assn., Am. Legion (Northwest Leadership Conf.). Republican. Roman Catholic. Office: Legis Services Office PO Box 83720 Boise ID 83720*

CLARK, JIM, communications executive; b. Plainview, Tex., 1945; BS in Physics, La. State U., MS in Physics, 1971; PhD in Computer Sci., U. Utah, 1974. Asst. prof. U. Calif., Santa Cruz, 1974-78; assoc. prof. Stanford (Calif.) U., 1979-82; founder, chmn. Silicon Graphics, 1982-94, myCFO; co-founder, chmn. Netscape Comms. Corp., Mountain View, Calif., 1994—; co-founder, bd. dir. Healtheon/WebMD, 1996—. Author: (book) Netscape Time: the Making of the Billion-Dollar Start-Up that Took Microsoft.

CLARK, JOHN M., III, lawyer; b. Memphis, Feb. 27, 1950; BA, Rice U., 1972; JD, Stanford U., 1975. Bar: Calif. 1975. Law clk. U.S. Dist. Ct., LA, 1975-77; European counsel Nat. Semiconductor Corp., Santa Clara, Calif., 1979-82, corporate counsel, 1982-85, assoc. gen. counsel, 1985-86, v.p., assoc. gen. counsel, 1986-92, sr. v.p., gen. counsel, sec., 1992—. Office: Nat Semiconductor Corp 2900 Semiconductor Dr Santa Clara CA 95051-0606 Office Phone: 408-721-6529. Office Fax: 408-739-9803. E-mail: john.clark@nsc.com.

CLARK, KAREN HEATH, lawyer; b. Pasadena, Calif., Dec. 17, 1944; d. Wesley Pelton and Lois (Ellenberger) Heath; m. Bruce Robert Clark, Dec. 30, 1967; children: Adam Heath, Andrea Pelton. Student, Pomona Coll., Claremont, Calif., 1962—64; BA, Stanford U., 1966; MA in History, U. Wash., 1968; JD, U. Mich., 1977. Bar: Calif. 1978. Instr. Henry Ford C.C., Dearborn, Mich., 1968-72; assoc. Gibson, Dunn & Crutcher LLP, Irvine, Calif., 1977-86, ptnr., 1986—2003, adv. counsel, 2004—. Bd. dirs. Dem. Found. Orange County, 1989-91, 94—, Planned Parenthood Orange County, Santa Ana, Calif., 1979-82, New Directions for Women, Newport Beach, 1986-91, Human Options, 2001-03, Freedom Writers Found., 2004—, Women in Leadership, chair, 1995-99; trustee Newport Beach Pub. Libr., 2001—, vice chair, 2006-; mem. deans adv. coun. Sch. Humanities, U. Calif., Irvine, 2000—. Recipient Choice award Planned Parenthood of Orange & San Bernardino Counties, 1996. Mem. Women in Leadership (founder 1993). Personal E-mail: karen-clark@cox.net.

CLARK, KIM BRYCE, academic administrator; b. Salt Lake City, Mar. 20, 1949; s. Merlin and Helen Mar (Hickman) C.; m. Sue Lorraine Hunt, June 14, 1971; children: Bryce, Erin, Jonathan, Andrew, Michael, Julia, Jennifer. BA in economics, Harvard U., 1974, MA in economics, 1977, PhD in economics, 1978. From asst. prof. to prof. Harvard Bus. Sch., Boston, 1978-89, Harry E. Figgie prof. bus. adminstrn., 1989-95, dean, 1995—2005, also George F. Baker prof. adminstrn.; pres. Brigham Young U.-Idaho, Rexburg, 2005—. Bd. dirs. Ceramics Process System Corp., Milford, Mass., Analysis Group, Belmont, Mass., Automotive Industries, Inc. Co-author: Industrial Renaissance, 1983, Dynamic Manufacturing, 1988, Product Development Performance, 1991, Revolutionizing Product Development, 1992, Leading Product Development, 1995, Design Rules: The Power of Modularity, 2000; editor: The Uneasy Alliance, 1985; co-editor: The Perpetual Enterprise Machine, 1994; contbr. articles to profl. jours. Coord. Belmont Youth Basketball, 1983—. Mem. IEEE (assoc. mem.), Am. Econ. Assn., Inst. Mgmt. Sci. Avocations: golf, jogging. Office: Brigham Young U 525 S Ctr St Rexburg ID 83460 Office Phone: 208-496-1111. Business E-Mail: clarkk@byui.edu.

CLARK, MELVIN EUGENE, chemical company executive; b. Ord, Nebr., Oct. 2, 1916; s. Ansel B. and Ruth Joy (Bullock) C.; m. Virginia May Hiller, Sept. 16, 1938; children: John Robert, Walter Clayton, Dale Eugene, Merry Sue. BSChemE cum laude, U. Colo., 1937; grad. exec. program, Columbia U., 1952; grad. advanced mgmt. program, Harvard U., 1961. Asst. editor Chem. Engring., McGraw-Hill, NYC, 1937-41; mktg. staff Wyandotte Chem. Corp., Mich., 1941-53; chief program br. War Prodn. Bd., Washington, 1942-44; v.p. mktg. Frontier Chem. Co., Wichita, 1953-69; exec. v.p. chems. div. Vulcan Materials Co., Birmingham, Ala., 1969-81, v.p. planning, chems. and metals group, 1981-82; cons., 1982—. Pres. Chlorine Inst., 1977-80 Contbr. numerous articles to profl. jours. Recipient U. Colo. Alumni Recognition award, 1972; named Chem. Market Rsch. Assn. Man of Year, 1963, Disting. Engring. Alumnus, U. Colo., 1985, Centennial medalist Coll. of Engring., U. Colo., 1994, Geroge Norlin award U. Colo., 2005 Mem. AIChE, Comml. Devel. and Mktg. Assn., Am. Chem. Soc., Boulder Country Club, Tau Beta Pi, Pi Mu Epsilon. Republican. Mem. Christian Ch. Home and Office: 7145 Cedarwood Cir Boulder CO 80301-3716 E-mail: meclark1@aol.com.

CLARK, MICHAEL PHILLIP, English educator; b. Marlin, Tex., May 27, 1950; s. Burton Francis and Nelda (Blount) C.; m. Kathleen Mack, 1971 (div. 1973); m. Katherine Weber, May 26, 1977. BA magna cum laude, Rice U., 1972; MA, U. Calif., Irvine, 1973, PhD, 1977. Asst. prof. U. Mich., Ann Arbor, 1977-83; prof. in English and comparative lit. U. Calif., Irvine, 1983—. Author: Michael Foucault, 1983, Jacques Lacan, 1989; contbr. articles to profl. publs. Mem. MLA, Soc. Early Americanists. Office: U Calif Dept English Irvine CA 92697-0001

CLARK, NOEL A., physics professor; BS, John Carroll U., University Heights, Ohio, 1963, MS, 1965; PhD in Physics, MIT, Cambridge, 1970. Rsch. fellow to asst. prof. applied physics Harvard U.; faculty mem. to prof. physics dept., dir. Liquid Crystal Materials Rsch. Ctr. U. Colo., Boulder, 1977—. Co-founder Displaytech Inc., Longmont, Colo., 1984. Contbr. articles to sci. jours. Recipient IR100, Soc. Info. Display, Lab. Apparatus Competition First prize, Am. Assn. Physics Tchrs.; grantee Guggenheim Found. fellowship, 1985—86. Fellow: AAAS, Am. Phys. Soc. (Oliver E. Buckley Condensed Matter prize 2006); mem.: NAS. Office: Liquid Crystal Group U Colo Dept Physics 390 UCB Boulder CO 80309-0390 Office Phone: 303-492-6420. E-mail: clarkn@colorado.edu.

CLARK, PETER BRUCE, retired publishing executive; b. Detroit, Oct. 23, 1928; s. Rex Scripps and Marian (Peters) C.; m. Lianne Schroeder, Dec. 21, 1952 (dec. Jan. 1996); children: Ellen Clark Brown, James. BA, Pomona Coll., 1952, LL.D. (hon.), 1972; M.P.A., Syracuse U., 1953; PhD, U. Chgo., 1959; H.H.D., Mich. State U., 1973, Lawrence Inst. Tech., 1982; LL.D. (hon.), U. Mich., 1977. Research assoc., then instr. polit. sci. U. Chgo., 1957-59; asst. prof. polit. sci. Yale U., 1959-61; with Evening News Assn., Detroit, 1960-86, corp. sec., 1960-61, v.p., 1961-63, pres., 1963-86, chmn. bd., chief exec. officer, dir., 1969-86; pub. Detroit News, 1963-81, also dir.; dir. Gannett Co., Inc., 1986-99. Regent's prof. UCLA Grad. Sch. Mgmt., 1987; chmn. Fed. Res. Bank Chgo., 1975-77, former chmn. br. Fed. Res. Bank Detroit. Served with AUS, 1953-55. Mem.: Am. Soc. Newspaper Editors, Am. Newspaper Pub. Assn. (dir. 1966—74), Ironwood Country Club.

CLARK, PHILLIP R., lawyer; b. Indpls., Oct. 6, 1948; AB magna cum laude, Wabash Coll., 1970; JD cum laude, Harvard U., 1976. Bar: Colo. 1976. Ptnr. Holme, Roberts & Owen, LLP, Denver, 1976—. Exec. com. Rocky Mountain Mineral Law Found.; mem. IPAMS Royalties Com., Ind. Petroleum Assn. Mountain States. Recipient Best Lawyers in Am. Mem. Colo. Bar Assn., Denver Bar Assn., Phi Beta Kappa 1976, bd. dir. sec. & bd. coun Colo. Oil & Gas Assn. legal, Legis. & Regulatory Com. Office: Holme Roberts & Owen LLP 1700 Lincoln St Ste 4100 Denver CO 80203-4541 Office Phone: 303-861-7000. Office Fax: 303-866-0200. Business E-Mail: phillip.clark@hro.com.

CLARK, RAYMOND OAKES, banker; b. Ft. Bragg, NC, Nov. 9, 1944; s. Raymond Shelton and Nancy Lee (McCormick) C.; m. Patricia Taylor; children: Matthew Patrick, Geoffry Charles. BBA, U. Ariz., 1966; postgrad., U. Wash., 1984-86. Mgmt. trainee First Interstate Bank, Phoenix, 1966, credit analyst, 1968-69, asst. br. mgr. Scottsdale, Ariz., 1969-72, asst. v.p., br. mgr. Tempe, 1972-90, v.p. br. mgr. Scottsdale, 1990-92, v.p. mgr. main office Phoenix, 1992—. Mem. Bd. Fairhope (Ala.) Bd. Adjustments Appeals, 2003—, State Ala., Baldwin County Bd. Equalization Appeals, 2004—. Bd. tax equalization Baldwin County, Ala., 2003—; bd. zoning adjustments City Fairhope, Ala., 2003—.

CLARK, RICHARD WARD, management consultant; b. NYC, Oct. 23, 1938; s. Richard Leal and Dorothy Jane (Whittaker) C. BA with distinction, U. Rochester, NY, 1960; MBA in Fin., U. Pa., 1962. Corp. planning analyst Campbell Soup Co., Camden, NJ, 1965-67; asst. product mgr. Gen. Mills, Inc., Mpls., 1967-70; sr. fin. analyst McKesson Corp., San Francisco, 1970-71, asst. divsn. controller, 1971-72, divsn. controller, 1972-78, gen. mgr. grocery products devel., 1978-79; v.p., controller McKesson Foods Group/McKesson Corp., 1979—82, v.p. fin., 1982—85, dir. strategic planning, 1985-87; v.p. fin., CFO, Provigo Corp., San Rafael, Calif., 1987-90; cons. on hotel devel., Napa Valley Assocs., S.A., San Francisco, 1990-92, health care cons., 1993-97; mgmt. cons. securities and ins. litig., 1998—. Author: Some Factors Affecting Dividend Payout Ratios, 1962; musician (albums) Dick Clark at the Keyboard, I Love a Piano, 1990, I Play the Songs, 1993, On My Way to You, 1997, Christmas Piano with Violin, 1999. Mem. adv. bd. Salvation Army, San Francisco, 1984—, chmn., 1993-2000; serving brother Order St. John, 2005—. Lt. (j.g.) USNR, 1962-64, PTO. Fellow, St. Andrew's Soc.; Sherman fellow, U. Rochester, 1960. Mem. Bohemian Club, Beta Gamma Sigma, St. Francis Yacht Club. Republican. Presbyterian. Avocations: piano, skiing, singing, fitness training. Home: 2201 Sacramento St Apt 401 San Francisco CA 94115-2314 Home Phone: 415-567-7574; Office Phone: 415-733-6575. Personal E-mail: rwclark8@earthlink.net.

CLARK, ROGER EARL, lawyer; b. New Orleans, Oct. 23, 1946; s. Earl B. and Erma Le (Chambers) Clark; m. Barbara Jo Columbus, Oct. 23, 1946; 1 child, Kelly Elizabeth. BA, Rice U., 1968; JD, Harvard U., 1971. Bar: Ill. 1971, Colo. 1973. Assoc. Pope, Ballard, Shepard and Fowle, Chgo., 1971—73, Hammond and Chilson, Loveland, Ohio, 1973—76, Lynn A. Hammond Law Offices, 1976—80; ptnr. Hammond, Clark and White, 1980—97, Hammond and Clark, 1997; now ptnr. Clark Williams and Matsunaka LLC. Bd. dirs. Loveland Econ. Devel. Coun., 1992—94, Hospice of Larimer County, 1994—, pres., 1997—98; bd. dirs. Rocky Mountain Pub. Broadcasting Sys., Inc., 1999—2005, Northern Colo. Econ. Devel. Corp., 2001—05. Mem.: ABA, Loveland C. of C. (bd. dirs. 1983—89, pres. 1988), Colo. Trial Lawyers Assn., Larimer County Bar Assn. (pres. 1984—85), Colo. Bar Assn. (exec. coun. young lawyers sect. 1977—83, chmn. 1982—83, bd. govs. 1985—87, chmn. gen. practice sect. 1985—87, v.p. 1986—87, bd. govs. 1996—98, pres.-elect 2004, pres. 2005—06), Loveland Sertoma (pres. 1980—81). Democrat. Methodist. Home: 1220 W 6th St Loveland CO 80537-5347 Office: Clark Williams and Matsunaka LLC Suite 1-2881 N Monroe Ave Loveland CO 80538

CLARK, R(UFUS) BRADBURY, lawyer, director; b. Des Moines, May 11, 1924; s. Rufus Bradbury and Gertrude Martha (Burns) C.; m. Polly Ann King, Sept. 6, 1949; children: Cynthia Clark Maxwell, Rufus Bradbury, John Atherton. BA, Harvard U., 1948, JD, 1951; diploma in law, Oxford U., Eng., 1952; D.H.L., Ch. Div. Sch. Pacific, San Francisco, 1983. Bar: Calif. 1952. Assoc. O'Melveny & Myers, LA, 1952-62, sr. ptnr., 1961-93; mem. mgmt. com., 1983-90; of counsel O'Melveny & Myers LLP, LA, 1993—. Bd. dirs. Econ. Resources Corp., BIC Covina Corp., BCS Winter Haven Corp., Avoco Internat. Corp., John Tracy Clinic, also pres. 1982-88, Ch. Charitable Found. Episcopal Diocese L.A., 2000—. Editor: California Corporation Laws, 7 vols, 1976-2009. Chancellor Protestant Episcopal Ch. in the Diocese of L.A., 1967-2005, chancellor emeritus, 2006-, hon. canon, 1983—. Capt. U.S. Army, 1943-46. Decorated Bronze Star with oak leaf cluster, Purple Heart with oak leaf cluster; Fulbright grantee, 1952. Mem.: ABA (task force on audit letters 1976—93, com. on opinions 1988—92, com. law and acctg., com. on opinions 2000—), L.A. County Bar Assn., State Bar Calif. (chmn. drafting com. on gen. corp. law 1973—81, exec. com. bus. law sect. 1977—78, drafting com. on nonprofit corp. law 1980—84, exec. com. bus. law sect. 1984—87, sec. 1986—87, com. nonprofit orgns. 1991—, task force and standing com. on opinions 1999—), Alamitos Bay Yacht Club (Long Beach, Calif.), Chancery Club, Harvard Club. Republican. Office: O'Melveny & Myers LLP 400 S Hope St Los Angeles CA 90071-2899 Office Phone: 213-430-6123. Business E-Mail: bclark@omm.com.

CLARK, SCOTT H., lawyer; b. Logan, Utah, Jan. 7, 1946; BA with honors, U. Utah, 1970; JD, U. Chgo., 1973. Bar: Utah 1973. Ptnr. Ray, Quinney & Nebeker P.C., Salt Lake City, 1980—. Mem. ABA, Utah State Bar, Salt Lake County Bar Assn., Phi Beta Kappa, Phi Kappa Phi, Pi Sigma Alpha. Office: Ray Quinney & Nebek PC PO Box 45385 Salt Lake City UT 84145-0385 E-mail: SClark@RQN.com.

CLARK, THOMAS P., JR., lawyer; b. NYC, Sept. 16, 1943; AB, U. Notre Dame, 1965; JD, U. Mo., Kansas City, 1973. Bar: Calif. 1973. Shareholder Stradling, Yocca, Carlson & Rauth P.C., Newport Beach, Calif., 1978—. Editor-in-chief The Urban Lawyer, 1972-73; contbr. articles to profl. jours. Capt. USMC, 1966-70. Mem. State Bar Calif., Orange County Bar Assn., Phi Kappa Phi. Office: Stradling Yocca Carlson & Rauth PC 660 Newport Center Dr Ste 1600 Newport Beach CA 92660-6458 Business E-Mail: tclark@sycr.com.

CLARK, TRENT L., government public affairs manager; b. Jackson Hole, Wyo., July 12, 1961; s. Richard L. and Carolyn T. Clark; m. Rebecca L. Lee, May 23, 1986; children: Brittany, Kathleen, Christin, Alexander. AS, Ricks Coll., 1980; BA, Brigham Young U., 1984; cert. pub. health, Harvard U., 1995. Legis. staff U.S. Senate, Washington, 1983-90; chief environ. economist Joint Econ. Com. Congress, Washington, 1990-91; state dir. Idaho Farm Svcs. Adminstrn., Boise, 1991-93; sr. comms. specialist Monsanto Co., Soda Springs, Idaho, 1993-98; fed. affairs mgr. Solutia, Inc., Soda Springs, Idaho, 1998-99; dir. govt. and pub. affairs Monsanto Co., Soda Springs, Idaho, 1999—. Dir. Get the Waste Out, Soda Springs, 1996; vice chmn. Idaho Rep. Orgn., Region 6, Pocatello, 1998; chmn. Idaho Rural Devel. Coun., Boise, 1997, 2003—; former chmn. Idaho Rep. Party, 1999-2002. Recipient Merit award USDA, 1992, Gov.'s Safety Conf. award Gov. Idaho, 1998. Mem. Idaho Assn. Commerce and Industry (vice chmn., dir. 1993—), Idaho Coun. on Industry and the Environment (dir. 1998—), Soda Springs C. of C. (pres. 1998-99). Mem. Lds Ch. Avocations: fencing, backcountry horsepacking. Office: Monsanto 1853 Highway 34 Soda Springs ID 83276-5227 Office Phone: 208-547-1348. Business E-Mail: Trent.L.Clark@monsanto.com.

CLARK, WILL (WILLIAM NUSCHLER CLARK JR.), professional sports team administrator, retired professional baseball player; b. New Orleans, Mar. 13, 1964; Student, Miss. State U. Infielder San Francisco Giants, 1986-93, spl. asst., 2009—; infielder Texas Rangers, 1994-99, Balt. Orioles, 1999, St. Louis Cardinals, 2000; ret., 2000; spring tng. advisor Ariz. Diamondbacks, 2005—08. Mem. US Olympic Baseball Team, 1984. Recipient Golden Spikes award USA Baseball, 1985, Silver Slugger award, 1989, 91, Nat. League Gold Glove award, 1991; named Nat. League Championship Series MVP, 1989; named to Coll. All-Am. Team The Sporting News, 1984-85, Nat. League All-Star team, 1988-93, Am. League All-Star team, 1994, Coll. Baseball Hall of Fame, 2006, Bay Area Sports Hall of Fame, 2007, Miss. Sports Hall of Fame, 2008. Achievements include leading the National League in: walks, runs batted in, 1988; runs, 1989. Office: San Francisco Giants 24 Willie Mays Plz San Francisco CA 94107*

CLARK, WILLIAM PATRICK, JR., lawyer, former United States Secretary of the Interior; b. Oxnard, Calif., Oct. 23, 1931; s. William Pettit and Bernice (Gregory) Clark; m. Joan Brauner, May 5, 1955; children: Monica, Peter, Nina, Colin, Paul. Ed., Stanford U., 1949—51; JD, Loyola U. Law Sch., LA, 1955. Bar: Calif. 1958. Sr. ptnr. Clark, Cole & Fairfield, Oxnard, Calif., 1958—66; chief of staff Gov. Ronald Reagan, Sacramento, 1966—69; judge Superior Ct. San Luis Obispo County, Calif., 1969—71; justice Ct. Appeals, LA, 1971—73, Supreme Ct. Calif., San Francisco, 1973—81; dep. sec. US Dept. State, Washington, 1981—82; asst. to Pres. for nat. security affairs NSC, 1982—83; sec. US Dept. Interior, 1983—85; of counsel Rogers & Wells, Washington, 1985—. Pres. Clark Co., Paso Robles, Calif.; acting chmn. bd. Morrison-Knudsen Corp., Boise, Idaho; presdl. emissary to chmn. Navajo and Hopi Indian Tribes; chmn. Pres.' Task Force on Nuc. Weapons Program Mgmt., 1985; mem. Pres.' Task Force on Def. Mgmt., 1985—86; treas. Ronald Reagan Presdl. Found. Served wtih US Army, 1951—53. Roman Catholic.

CLARKE, JAMES WESTON, emeritus political science professor, writer; b. Elizabeth, Pa., Feb. 16, 1937; s. Alonzo Peterson and Beatrice (Weston) C.; m. Jeanne Nienaber; children: Julianne, Michael BA, Washington and Jefferson Coll., 1962; MA, Pa. State U., 1964, PhD, 1968. Asst. prof. Fla. State U., 1967-71; assoc. prof. U. Ariz., Tucson, 1971-76, prof. polit. sci., 1976—, chmn. dept., 1973-78, univ. disting. prof., 2000. Author: American Assassins: The Darker Side of Politics, 1982, Last Rampage: The Escape of Gary Tison, 1988, On Being Mad or Merely Angry: John W. Hinckley Jr. and Other Dangerous People, 1990, The Lineaments of Wrath: Race, Violent Crime, and American Culture, 1998, Defining Danger: American Assassins and the New Domestic Terrorists, 2006. Served with USMC, 1955-58 Recipient James Gillespie Blaine prize Washington and Jefferson Coll., 1962, Matthew Brown Ringland prize, 1962, Burlington Northern Found. award for excellence in tchg., 1987, Golden Key Nat. Honor Soc. award for tchg., 1989, Social and Behavioral Scis. award for outstanding tchg., 1991, 96;named to the Elizabeth Forward HS Hall of Fame, 2005; Udall fellow, 1993; Fulbright scholar, Ireland, 1999 Mem. Am. Polit. Sci. Assn. (Outstanding Tchg. in Polit. Sci. 2000). Home: 855 E Placita Leslie Tucson AZ 85718-1960 Office: U Ariz 315 Social Sci Bldg Tucson AZ 85721-0001 Office Phone: 520-621-7600. Business E-Mail: jclarke@email.arizona.edu.

CLARKE, JOHN, physics professor; b. Cambridge, Eng., Feb. 10, 1942; arrived in U.S., 1968; s. Victor Patrick and Ethel May (Blowers) C.; m. Grethe Fog Pedersen, Sept. 15, 1979; 1 child, Elizabeth Jane. BA, Cambridge U., 1964, MA, PhD, Cambridge U., 1968, ScD (hon.), 2003. Postdoctoral scholar U. Calif.-Berkeley, 1968-69, asst. prof. physics, 1969-71, assoc. prof., 1971-73, prof., 1973—, faculty rsch. lectr., 2005; chair exptl. physics Luis W. Alvarez Meml., 1994—. Contbr. numerous articles to profl. jours. Guggenheim fellow, 1977-78, Sloan Found. fellow, 1970-72, Miller Inst. Basic Rsch. fellow, 1975-76, 94-95; recipient Charles Vernon Boys prize Brit. Inst. Physics, 1977, award Soc. Exploration Geophysics, 1979, Outstanding Tchg. award U. Calif., 1983, Fritz London award for low temperature physics, 1987, Fed. Lab. Consortium award for excellence in technology transfer, 1992, divsn. materials scis. award in solid state physics Dept. Energy, 1986, 92, IEEE U.S. Activities Bd. Electrotechnology Transfer award, 1995, Comstock prize Physics NAS, 1999, Coun. on Superconductivity award IEEE, 2002, Olli V. Lounasmaa prize Finnish Acad. Sci. and Letters, 2004; named Calif. Scientist of Yr., 1987, One of 50, Scientific Am., 2002. Fellow AAAS, Royal Soc. London (Hughes medal 2004), Am. Phys. Soc. (Joseph F. Keithley Advances in Measurement Sci. award 1998), Brit. Inst. Physics, Christ's Coll. (hon.), Royal Soc. Arts and Scis. (Gothenburg, Sweden) (fgn. mem. 2007). Office: U Calif Dept Physics 366 LeConte Hall #7300 Berkeley CA 94720-7300

CLARKE, JULIA L., library director; Student, Millsaps Coll., Jackson, Miss.; MS in Libr. Sci., U. NC, Chapel Hill. Reference libr. U. Memphis, Main Libr., Knoxville, Tenn.; head reference and circulation functions U. of the South Jesse Ball du Pont Libr., Sewanee, Tenn.; head circulation dept. Green Hills br. Nashville Pub. Libr., mgr. Thompson Ln. and Donelson brs.; with Carnegie Libr., Clarksdale, Miss., Albuquerque/Bernalillo County Libr. Sys., 1985—, children's libr. Esperanza Libr., mgr. Lomas-Tramway Libr., mgr. Taylor Ranch Libr., mgr. Wyo. Libr., asst. dir., 2000—06, acting dir., 2006—07, dir., 2007—. Office: Albuquerque Bernalillo County Libr Sys 501 Copper Ave NW Albuquerque NM 87102 Office Phone: 505-768-5122. E-mail: jclarke@cabq.gov.

CLARKE, PAULA KATHERINE, anthropologist, researcher, social studies educator; b. Berkeley, Gloucestershire, Eng., July 27, 1946; d. Percy George and Grace Anne C.; m. Warren Ted Hamilton. BA, U. Calif., Berkeley, 1982; PhD, U. Calif., San Francisco, 1991. Prof. anthropology and sociology Columbia Coll., Sonora, Calif., 1997—. Participant Oxford Round Table Diversity in Soc., 2006; spkr. in field. Contbr.: Men and Masculinities: A Social, Cultural, and Historical Encyclopedia, 2003; contbr. articles to ednl. jours. (Nominated-Kathleen Gregory Klein Award by Women's Caucus/Popular and Am. Culture Assn. for best unpublished article on feminism and popular culture, 1999). Creator Future Promise Award scholarship Columbia Coll., Sonora, 2001. Recipient Excellence in Tchg. award, Tuolumne County Bd. Edn., 2002, Oxford U. Press award, Am. Anthrop. Assn., 2008. Office: Columbia Coll 11600 Columbia College Dr Sonora CA 95370 Office Phone: 209-588-5356. Business E-Mail: clarkep@yosemite.edu.

CLARKE, PETER, communications and health educator; b. Evanston, Ill., Sept. 19, 1936; s. Clarence Leon and Dorothy (Whitcomb) C.; m. Karen Storey, June 4, 1962 (div. 1984); 1 child, Christopher Michael. BA, U. Wash., 1959; MA, U. Minn., 1961, PhD, 1963. Dir., asst. prof. Comm. Rsch. Ctr. U. Wash., Seattle, 1965-68, assoc. prof. Sch. Comm., 1967-72, dir. Sch. Comm., 1971-72; prof. dept. journalism U. Mich., Ann Arbor, 1973-74, chmn., prof. dept. journalism, 1975-78, chmn., prof. dept. comm., 1979-80; dean, prof. Annenberg Sch. Comm., U. So. Calif., LA, 1981-92, prof., 1993—; prof. preventive medicine U. So. Calif. Keck Sch. Medicine, LA, 1985—. Co-dir. From the Wholesaler to the Hungry, 1991—; dir. Ctr. for Health and Med. Comm., 1997—; cons. for various fed. and state govt. commns. on mass media and social problems. Co-author: (with Susan H. Evans) Covering Campaigns: Journalism in Congressional Elections, 1983, Surviving Modern Medicine: How to Get the Best from Doctors, Family and Friends, 1998; editor: New Models for Communication Research, 1973; co-editor: (with Susan H. Evans) The Computer Culture, 1985; contbr. articles to profl. jours. Numerous Fed., corp., pvt. founds. grants. Office: U So Calif Annenberg Sch Comm 3502 Watt Way Los Angeles CA 90089-0054 Home Phone: 310-395-8598; Office Phone: 213-740-0940. E-mail: chmc@usc.edu.

CLARKE, PETER J., physicist, technology executive; b. NYC; m. Carole; 5 children. BS in Physics, Iona Coll., 1959; postgrad., Union Coll. With Rsch. Lab. GE, Schenectady, N.Y., with Vacuum Products divsn.; with product devel. labs. Veeco Instruments, Plainview, N.Y.; founder, pres. Sputtered Films, Inc., Santa Barbara, Calif. Contbr. articles to profl. jours. With USAF. Scholarship established in honor of Peter J. and Carole Clarke. Mem. Am. Vacuum Soc. (Albert Nerken award 1998), Soc. Vacuum Coaters (Nathaniel Sugerman Meml. award 1998). Achievements include patents for S-Gun, the first magnetron sputtering device, C-to-C Coater Cassette to Cassette wafer metallizer, the first automated system for vacuum coating wafers using physical vapor deposition (PVD), Endeavor, a PVD cluster tool used in semiconductor industry to manufacture system interconnects and in under-bump metallization, Shamrock tm MR/GMR orbital planetary PVD system with produces magneto-resistive and gian magneto-resistive thin films for the magnetic storage industry, numerous other patents. Office: Sputtered Films 700 Becknell Rd Ste C Goleta CA 93117-3290 E-mail: pjclarke@sputtered-films.com.

CLARKE, STEVEN GERARD, chemistry professor; b. LA, Nov. 19, 1949; BA in Chemistry/Zoology magna cum laude, Pomona Coll., 1970; PhD in Biochemistry & Molecular Biology, Harvard U., 1976. NIH undergrad. fellow Glynn Rsch. Labs., Bodmin, England, summer 1969; NSF predoctoral fellow Harvard U., 1970-73, biochemistry and molecular biology instr., 1973-74; Miller Inst. fellow U. Calif., Berkeley, 1976-78; asst. prof. chemistry and molecular biology UCLA, 1978-83, assoc. prof. chemistry and biochemistry, 1983-87, prof. chemistry and biochemistry, 1987—, dir. Molecular Biology Inst., 2001—. Vis. fellow molecular biology Princeton (N.J.) U., 1986-87, U. Wash., 2004-05; mem. sci. com. 1st Internat. Symposium on Post-Translational Modifications of Proteins and Aging, Lacco Ameno d'Ischia, Naples, Italy, 1987; chair, symposium organizer ann. meeting Am. Soc. for Biochemistry and Molecular Biology, Atlanta, 1991; mem. adv. bd. nutrition and metabolism sect. biol. aging Nat. Inst. Aging, NIH, 1993; co-chair Fedn. Am. Socs. for Exptl. Biology summer rsch. conf., Vt., 1995; dir. Molecular Biology Inst., U. Calif., L.A., Calif., 2001— Assoc. editor Protein Sci., 1995-98, mem. editl. adv. bd., 1994-95; mem. editl. bd. Jour. Biol. Chemistry, 1994-98; contbr. more than 200 articles to profl. jours. Woodrow Wilson fellow, 1970; grantee Am. Heart Assn., 1984-85, 85-86, 87-88, 89, NSF, 1989, 90, 91, NIH, 1995. Mem. Am. Chem. Soc. (Ralph F. Hirschmann award 1996), Am. Soc. Biochemistry and Molecular Biology, The Protein Soc., Assn. Med. and Grad. Depts. Biochemistry, Phi Beta Kappa, Alpha Chi Sigma. Office: UCLA Dept Chemistry & Biochem 607 Charles E Young Dr East Los Angeles CA 90095-1569 Home Phone: 310-820-1106; Office Phone: 310-825-8754. Business E-Mail: clarke@mbi.ucla.edu.

CLARKE, THOMAS E., apparel executive; b. Binghamton, NY, Aug. 8, 1951; married. MS, U. Fla., Gainesville, 1977; D in Biomechanics, Pa. State U., 1980. With Nike, Inc., 1980—, rschr. Sports and Rsch. Lab Exeter, NH, various positions, 1983-94, divisional v.p. mktg., 1987—89, corp. v.p., 1989—90, gen. mgr., 1990, pres., COO Beaverton, Oreg., 1994-2000, bd. dirs., 1994—2004, co-CFO Beaverton, Oreg., 2000, pres. new bus. develop. Avocation: running (competitive marathon runner). Office: Nike Inc One Bowerman Dr Beaverton OR 97005-6453 Office Phone: 503-671-6453.

CLARK-LANGAGER, SARAH ANN, curator, academic administrator; b. Lynchburg, Va., May 14, 1943; m. Craig T. Langager, 1979. BA in Art History, Randolph-Macon Woman's Coll., 1965; postgrad., U. Md., 1968; MA in Art History, U. Wash., 1970; PhD in Art History, CUNY, 1988. Assoc. edn. dept., lectr. Yale U. Art Gallery, New Haven, 1965-67, Albright-Knox Art Gallery, Buffalo, 1967-68; asst. to dir. Richard White Gallery, Seattle, 1969-70; curatorial asst. to curators painting and sculpture San Francisco Mus. Modern Art, 1970; assoc. edn. dept., lectr. Seattle Art Mus., 1971-73, 74-75; asst. curator, and then assoc. curator modern art, lectr. Seatle Art Mus., 1975-79; curator 20th century art, lectr. Munson-Williams-Proctor Inst., Utica, NY, 1981-86; asst. prof. art history, dir. Univ. Art Gallery, U. North Tex., Denton, 1986-88; dir. Western Gallery, curator outdoor sculpture collection Western Wash. U., Bellingham, 1988—, mem. adj. faculty, 1988—. Lectr., cons. in edn. NY Cultural Ctr., NYC, 1973-74; editl. asst. October, MIT Press, NYC, 1980; lectr. art history South Seattle C.C., 1975; lectr. 20th century art Cornish Inst. Fine Arts, Seattle, 1977-78; sole rep. for N.Y. State, Art Mus. Assn. Am., 1984-86; bd. dirs. Wash. Art Consortium; cons. State of Wash. Save Outdoor Sculpture, 1994-2000, others. Contbr. articles to profl. jours.; curator exhbns., 1970—, including Rodney Ripps traveling exhbn., 1983, Sculpture Space: Recent Trends, 1984, Order and Enigma: American Art Between the Two Wars, 1984, Stars over Texas: Top of the Triangle, 1988, Public Art/Private Visions, 1989, Drawing Power, 1990, Focus on Figure, 1992, Chairs: Embodied Objects, 1993, Northwest Native American and First Nations People's Art, 1993, New Acquisitions, 1995, Stars and Stripes: American Prints and Drawings, 1995, Photographs from America, 1996, NW Artists' Books, 1999, Decades of Giving: Virginia Wright and Sculpture at Western, 1999, Surface Tension, 2003, A Sofa and..., 2003, Noguchi & Dance, 2005, The Al Vera Lesse Collection, West Wash., 2006, Fabric of Identity, WWU, 2007, others; author: Master Works of American Art from the Munson-Williams-Proctor Institute, 1989, Audiophone Tour for Sculpture Collection-20 Interviews, 1991, The Outdoor Sculpture Collection: The Development of Public Art at Western, 2000, The Italian Period in Susan Bennerstoom, 2000, Sculpture in Place: A Campus as Site, 2002, Isamu Noguchi: Beyond Red Square, 2004, (jurors statement, essays) Appalachian State U. Recipient Woman of Merit in Arts award Mohawk Valley C.C. and YWCA, Utica, 1985; Kress Found. fellow U. Wash., 1970; Helena Rubenstein Found. scholar CUNY Grad. Ctr., 1980. Office: Western Wash U Western Gallery Fine Arts Complex Bellingham WA 98225-9068 Office Phone: 360-650-3963. Business E-Mail: sarah.clarklangager@wwu.edu.

CLARKSON, KELLY BRIANNE, singer; b. Burleson, Tex., Apr. 24, 1982; d. Steve Clarkson, Jeanne and Jimmy Taylor (Stepfather). Winner inaugural Am. Idol contest, 2002; 2d place World Idol contest, 2004. Singer: (albums) Thankful, 2003 (Reached #1 on the Billboard Charts, 2004), Breakaway, 2004, My December, 2007, All I Ever Wanted, 2009, (songs) Before Your Love/A Moment Like This, 2002 (Billboard best selling single of yr.), Because of You, 2004 (MTV Video Music award for Best Female Video, 2006); actor: (films) Issues 101, 2002, From Justin to Kelly, 2003; singer: (films) Love Actually, 2003, Ella Enchanted, 2004, The Princess Diaries 2: Royal Engagement, 2004. Recipient Best Female Video and Best Pop Video for Since U Been Gone, MTV Video Music Awards, 2005, Favorite Adult Contemporary Artist, Am. Music Awards, 2005, Favorite Female Performer, People's Choice Awards, 2006, Best Pop Vocal Album, Grammy awards, 2006, Best Female Pop Vocal Performance, 2006, Choice Music: Female Artist, Teen Choice Awards, 2006, Favorite Female Artist, Am. Music Awards, 2006, Favorite Artist Adult Contemporary, 2006; co-recipient Song Writer award for Miss Independent (with Rhett Lawrence), ASCAP, 2004.

CLARKSON, PATRICIA, actress; b. New Orleans, Dec. 29, 1959; d. Buzz and Jackie Clarkson. Student, La. State U.; B in Theatre Arts, Fordham U., 1982; MFA, Yale U. Actor: (films) The Untouchables, 1987, The Dead Pool, 1988, Rocket Gibraltar, 1988, Everybody's All-American, 1988, Tune in Tomorrow, 1990, Jumanji, 1995, Pharaoh's Army, 1995, High Art, 1998, Playing by Heart, 1998, Simply Irresistable, 1999, Wayward Son, 1999, The Green Mile, 1999, Joe Gould's Secret, 2000, Falling Like This, 2000, The Pledge, 2001, Wendigo, 2001, The Safety of Objects, 2001, Welcome to Collinwood, 2002, Far from Heaven, 2002, Heartbreak Hospital, 2002, The Baroness and the Pig, 2002, Pieces of April, 2003 (Acad. award nomination for best supporting actress, 2004), All the Real Girls, 2003, The Station Agent, 2003, Dogville, 2003, Miracle, 2004, The Woods, 2005, The Dying Gaul, 2005, Good Night, and Good Luck, 2005, The Woods, 2006, All the King's Men, 2006, No Reservations, 2007, Lars and the Real Girl, 2007, Married Life, 2007, Blind Date, 2008, Phoebe in Wonderland, 2008, Elegy, 2008, Vicky Cristina Barcelona, 2008; (TV films) The Old Man and the Sea, 1990, Legacy of Lies, 1992, An American Story, 1992, Four Eyes and Six-Guns, 1992, Blind Man's Bluff, 1992, Caught in the Act, 1993, She Led Two Lives, 1994, London Suite, 1996, Wonderland, 2002, Carrie, 2002; (TV series) Davis Rules, 1991, Murder One, 1995—96; (TV miniseries) Queen, 1993, (TV guest appearance) Six Feet Under, 2001—05 (Emmy for outstanding guest actress in a drama series, 2002), Frasier, 2001, (stage appearances) A Cheever Evening, 1993, Raised in Captivity, 1995, Three Days of Rain, 1997, The Maiden's Prayer, 1998, Streetcar Named Desire, 2004. Office: c/o Scott Bankston Jeff Morrone Mgmt 9350 Wilshire Blvd #224 Beverly Hills CA 90212

CLAWSON, BYDE W., lawyer; b. Tucson; BA summa cum laude, Claremont McKenna Coll., 1974; JD, UCLA, 1977; attended, London Sch. Econ. & Polit. Sci., London. Bar: Calif. 1977. Ptnr. Bingham McCutchen LLP, E Palo Alto, co-chmn. comml. tech. practice group. Named a No. Calif. Super Lawyer, Law & Politics & SF Mag., 2004. Mem.: State Bar Calif. Office: Bingham McCutchen LLP 1900 University Ave East Palo Alto CA 94303 Office Phone: 650-849-4830. Office Fax: 650-849-4800. Business E-Mail: byde.clawson@bingham.com.

CLAY, BRYAN EZRA, Olympic track and field athlete; b. Austin, Tex., Jan. 3, 1980; m. Sarah Smith; 2 children. BA in Social Work, Azusa Pacific U., 2003. Olympic decathlete USA Track & Field, Inc., Athens, Greece, 2004, Beijing, 2008. Recipient Silver medal, heptathlon, World Indoor Championships, 2004, 2006, Gold medal, heptathlon, 2008, Gold medal, decathlon, World Outdoor Championships, 2005, Silver medal, decathlon, Athens Olympic Games, 2004, Gold medal, decathlon, Beijing Olympic Games, 2008; named Decathlon Champion, Nat. Assn. Intercollegiate Athletics, 2000, USA Outdoor Champion, 2004, 2005, 2008. Office: c/o USOC One Olympic Plz Colorado Springs CO 80909

CLAYTON, MACK LOUIS, surgeon, educator; b. Round Mountain, Ala., Nov. 25, 1921; s. James Euclid and Alma (Longshore) C.; m. Sara Elizabeth Lee, June 3, 1948; children: James Lee, Lee Alison. BS, U. Ariz., 1942; MD, Columbia U., 1945. Diplomate Am. Bd. Orthopedic Surgery. Founder Denver Orthopedic Clinic, 1952-90; physician Denver Broncos, 1969-73, U.S. Ski Team, 1971; clin. prof. orthopedic surgery U. Colo., 1985-95, disting. clin. prof., 2000—. Author, editor: Surgery for Rheumatoid Arthritis, 1992; contbr. numerous articles to profl. jours. Elder Presbyn. Ch., Denver, 1958; with armed forces, 1946-48. Recipient Best Clinical Rsch. award U. Colo Med. Sch., 1958, 25 yrs. svc. award Arthritis Found., 1982. Mem. Am. Orthop. Assn., Am. Soc. for Surg. of Hand, Clin. Orthop. Soc. (pres. 1978). Avocations: skiing, golf, fishing, hunting. Home: 2552 E Alameda Ave Unit 18 Denver CO 80209-3324

CLAYTON, PAUL DOUGLAS, health care administrator; b. Salt Lake City, Mar. 9, 1943; PhD in Physics, U. Ariz. Dir. Ctr. for Advanced Tech., Columbia Presbyn. Med. Ctr., 1994-98, dir. clin. info. svc., 1992-98; chmn., prof. med. info. Columbia U., 1987-98; info. sys. dir., dir. clin. info. sys. Intermountain Health Care, 1998—; prof. med. info. U. Utah, 2001—. Mem. Inst. Medicine of Nat. Acad. Sci., Am. Med. Info. Assn. (pres. 1998-99).

CLAYTON, RAYMOND EDWARD, municipal official; b. Saskatoon, Sask., Can., Nov. 6, 1942; m. Alanet Gayle Johnson; children: Grant, Sheila, Matthew, Daniel. B. of Commerce, U. Sask., 1964; MA in Econs., 1965. Dir. rsch. Dept. Mcpl. Affairs, Govt. Sask., Regina, 1965-67, Dept. Edn., Govt. Sask., Regina, 1967-69, dir. ednl. adminstrn., 1969-77, dep. minister, 1979-84; dir. taxation and fiscal policy Dept. Fin., Govt. Sask., Regina, 1977-78; dep. minister Dept. Urban Affairs, Govt. Sask., Regina, 1978-79; chmn. Govt. Fin. Commn., Regina, 1984-86; asst. dep. minister Dept. Energy & Mines, Govt. Sask., Regina, 1986-94, dep. minister, 1994—2002; pres. Sask. Property Mgmt. Corp., Regina, 2002—04; pres., CEO Sask. Transp. Co., Regina, 2004—. Office Phone: 306-787-2116. E-mail: rclayton@stcbus.ca.

CLAYTON, WAYNE CHARLES, protective services official, educator; b. Topeka, Dec. 16, 1932; s. Alford Henry and Anna Ellen (Lynch) C.; m. Donna Marie Corrigan, March 3, 1962; Mark Wayne, Leslie Marie. AA in Liberal Arts, Mt. San Antonio Coll., 1959; BS, Calif. State U., LA, 1968. cert. tchr., Calif. From reserve police officer to dep. chief El Monte Police Dept., 1957-1978, chief, 1978—. Mem. session FBINA, 1980. With U.S. Navy, 1952-56. Recipient Golden Apple award West San Gabriel Valley Adminstrs. Assn., 1982, Spl. Medallion award Boys Club Am., 1982, Disting. Svc. award Dept. Youth Authority, 1983, Outstanding Svc. award C. of C., 1983, Spl. Appreciation award El Monte Police Officers Assn., 1985, Calif. Police Chief Officer of the Yr. award Internat. Union Police Assns. AFL-CIO, 1986, Exec. of Yr. award Exec. Mag., 1986, Dr. Byron E. Thompson Disting. Scouter award El Monte Explorer Post # 522, 1988, Appreciation award, 1992, Outstanding Svc. award Internat. Footprint Assn., 1991, award for continuing concern and dedication to the well being of Officers of El Monte Police Dept. Calif. Orgn. of Police and Sheriffs, 1991, Police Chief of the Yr. Perpetual award First Annual Shriners Club, 1994, C. of C. Citizen of Yr., 1994, Coord. Coun. Lifetime Achievement award, 1995. Mem. FBI Nat. Acad. Assocs., L.A. County Police Chiefs Assn., San Gabriel Valley Police Chiefs Assn., San Gabriel Valley Peace Officers Assn. (past pres.), Boys and Girls Club of San Gabriel Valley (v.p.), Civitan of El Monte (internat., charter pres. 1973). Democrat. Roman Catholic. Avocations: fishing, water-skiing, reading. Office: Police Dept Box 6008 11333 Valley Blvd El Monte CA 91731-3210

CLEARY, THOMAS CHARLES, technology company executive; b. Chgo., Nov. 15, 1921; s. Thomas Harold and Mary Margaret (Russell) C.; m. Barbara Winnifred Johnson, Dec. 18, 1948; children: Thomas Robert, Margaret Mary Cleary Nurmia, Mary Ann Cleary Robitaille. BS in Mech. Engring., UCLA, 1949. Pres., gen. mgr. Whittaker Corp., Denver, 1950-63; dir. program mgmt. Litton Industries, Woodland Hills, Calif., 1963-65; asst. gen. mgr. Teledyne Sys., Inc., 1965-66; v.p., CEO Viking Industries, Chatsworth, Calif., 1966-67; v.p. Power Conversion, Inc., Long Beach, Calif., 1967-68; chmn. bd. dirs., mng. dir. TRW Electronic Comp. Co., Taiwan, Republic of China, 1968-69; pres., CEO Deutsch Relays, Inc., East Northport, NY, 1969-89, Struthers Dunn-Hi G, Pitman, NJ, 1989-91; chmn., CEO G&H Tech., Inc., Camarillo, Calif., 1992—. Author: Dynamic Management System, 1990, Management By Intent, 1991. Fundraiser Meml. Sloan-Kettering Cancer Ctr., N.Y., 1989—; mem. chancellor's assocs. UCLA, 1992—, mem. exec. com., dean's coun., sch. engring., 1992—; mem. bd. councillors UCLA Found., 1997. Capt. inf. U.S. Army, 1942-50, PTO. Named Entrepreneur of Yr. in mfg. Greater L.A. Area, 1997. Republican. Roman Catholic. Achievements include patents in the gyroscope and relay areas. Office: G&H Tech Inc 750 W Ventura Blvd Camarillo CA 93010-8382

CLEAVER, JAMES EDWARD, radiologist, educator; b. Portsmouth, England, May 17, 1938; came to the U.S., 1964; s. Edward Alfred and Kathleen Florence (Cleveley) C.; m. Christine J. Cleaver, Aug. 8, 1964; children: Jonathan, Alison. BA, St. Catharine's Coll., 1961; PhD, U. Cambridge, 1964. Rsch. fellow Mass. Gen. Hosp., Boston, 1964-66; asst. rsch. biophysicist lab. radiobiology environ. health U. Calif., San Francisco, 1966-68, asst. prof. radiology, 1968-70, assoc. prof. radiology, 1970-74, prof. radiology, 1974—; vis. prof. Imperial Cancer Rsch. Fund, London, 1973-74, prof. radiology, 1975-96, prof. dermatology, 1996—. Contbr. over 350 articles to profl. jours. Recipient Lila Gruber award Am. Acad. Dermatology, 1976, Sr. Investigator award Am. Soc. Photobiology, 1995, Luigi Provasoli award Phycol. Soc. Am., 1992, J. Little award for radiation rsch. Harvard U., 2003. Mem. NAS, Nat. Coun. on Radiation Protection, Radiation Rsch. Soc. (councillor 1982-84, Rsch. award 1973).

CLEGG, JAMES STANDISH, physiologist, biochemist, educator; b. Aspinwall, Pa., July 27, 1933; divorced; 3 children; m. Eileen Clegg; 1 stepchild. AA in Biology, Coffeyville Coll., 1953; BS in Zoology, Pa. State U., 1958; PhD in Biology, Johns Hopkins U., 1961. Rsch. assoc. biologist Johns Hopkins U., 1961-62; asst. prof. zoology U. Miami, 1962-64, from assoc. prof. biology to prof., 1964-70; prof. sect. molecular and cellular biology U. Calif., Davis, 1986—, dir. Bodega Marine Lab., 1986-98. With CNRS Thias France, 1983; pres. Nat. Assn. Marine Labs., 1992-94. With US Army, 1953—55. Recipient Fulbright Sr. Rsch. award U. London, 1978, U. Ghent, 1999; Wilson fellow, 1958-59. Fellow AAAS; mem. Am. Soc. Zoologists, Am. Soc. Cell Biology, Biophys. Soc., Soc. Cryobiology, Sigma Xi. Independent. Achievements include research in comparative biochemistry and biophysics; mechanisms of cryptobiosis; properties and role of water in cellular metabolism; cytoplasmic organization. Office: U Calif Bodega Marine Lab PO Box 247 Bodega Bay CA 94923-0247 Home Phone: 707-875-2215; Office Phone: 707-875-2010. Business E-Mail: jsclegg@ucdavis.edu.

CLEGG, MICHAEL TRAN, genetics educator, researcher; b. Pasadena, Calif., Aug. 1, 1941; AA, Sacramento City Coll., 1967; BS, U. Calif., Davis, 1969, PhD, 1972. Asst. prof. Brown U., Providence, 1972—76; assoc. prof. U. Ga., Athens, 1976—82, prof., 1982—84; prof. genetics U. Calif., Riverside, 1984—2004, acting dean Coll. Natural and Agrl. Scis., 1994—97, dean Coll. Natural and Agrl. Scis., 1997—2000, Donald Bren prof. biol. scis., ecology and evolutionary biology Irvine, 2004—. Chmn. biology bd., NRC, mem. commn. on life scis., 1990-96, chmn., 1998-2000. Co-author: Principles of Genetics, 1988; co-editor: Plant Population Genetics, 1989, Molecular Evolution, 1990; contbr. articles to sci. jours. Sgt. US Army, 1960—63. Guggenheim Found. fellow, 1981-82; recipient Darwin prize Edinburgh U., 1995. Fellow Am. Acad. Arts & Scis., Third World Acad. Scis. (assoc.); mem. NAS (fgn. sec. 2002-), Am. Soc. Naturalists (v.p. 1986), Am. Genetics Assn. (pres. 1987), Soc. for the Study of Evolution (v.p. 1986), Genetics Soc. Am., Soc. Molecular Biology and Evolution (pres.-elect 2001, pres. 2002). Avocations: skiing, flying. Office: Ecology & Evolutionary Biology U Calif 321 Steinhaus Hall Irvine CA 92697-2525 Office Phone: 949-824-4490. Office Fax: 949-824-2181. E-mail: mclegg@uci.edu.

CLEMENT, DOUGLAS BRUCE, medical educator; b. Montreal, Que., Can., July 15, 1933; BSc, U. Oreg., 1955; MD, U. B.C., Vancouver, Can., 1959. Intern St. Mary's Hosp., San Francisco, 1960; adj. assoc. prof. Simon Fraser U., 1976-79; from asst. to assoc. prof. U. B.C., Vancouver, 1979-90, prof., 1990-99, prof. emeritus, 1999—. Vis. assoc. prof. Simon Fraser U., 1979-88; coach track and field team U. B.C., 1981-87, mem. family practice promotion and tenure com., 1987-98, mem. search com. dept. family practice, 1988-89, co-founder clin. fellowship sports medicine Allan McGavin Sports Medicine Ctr.; cons. in sports medicine; radio, TV presenter, speaker in field. Regional editor Sports Tng., Medicine and Rehab., 1987-88; mem. editorial bd. Clin. Sports Medicine, 1989-90, Clin. Jour. Sports Medicine, 1991-2000, The Physician and Sports Medicine, 1999-2000; sect. editor Can. Jour. Sport Scis., 1990-93; contbr. articles to profl. jours. and chpts. to books. Named to Can. Olympic Hall Fame, 2006; recipient Vanier award, 1965, Centennial medal, 1967, Op. Lifestyle medal, 1980, Longines/Wittnauer Coaching Excellence award, 1989, Order of Can. medal, 1991, Can. 125 medal, 1992, Lifetime Achievement award Sports Medicine Coun. Can., 1992, Wallace Wilson award, 1995, R.T. McKenzie medallion, 1999; named to U. B.C. Sports Hall of Fame, 1995, B.C. Sports Hall of Fame, 2000; named Coach of Yr., Sport B.C., 1988. Daryl Thompson award, Sport B.C., 2000, Geoff Gowan award, Coaching Assn. Can., 2001, Silver Medal award of Merit, B.C. Med. Assn., 2002, Queen's medal, 2002; grantee Sport Can., 1984, 86, Beecham Labs., 1984, Ciba Geigy, 1985, Sport Medicine Coun. Can., 1985-86, CFLRI, 1990; Town Club scholar U. Oreg., 1954. Fellow Am. Coll. Sports Med., Can. Acad. Sport Medicine (travelling. past pres., mem. accreditation com. 1987-97); mem. Can. Med. Assn., Can. Assn. Sport Sci. (past sec.), Can. Ctr. Drug Free Sport (mem. sci. adv. com. 1992), Can. Olympic Assn. (gen. mgr. Can. team Pan Am. Games 1975, mem. com. doping control, com. accreditation sports sci. facilities, bd. dirs. 1985-93), Athletics Can. (chmn. med. com. 1981-87, mem. sports sci. com. 1983-87, nat. coach various games), B.C. Athletics (master coach 1988—, Coach of Yr. 1987-92), B.C. Med. Assn. (mem. com. athletics and recreation health planning coun. 1971-96, bd. dirs. 1999-2000), Sports Medicine Coun. B.C. (chmn. high performance sports sci. unit 1985-89, com. anti-doping 1989-92), Achilles Internat. Athletics Soc.

(chmn. 1964-72, 86—), Kajak Track and Field Club (co-founder, coach 1962-99). Achievements include research on effect of exercise on the human body, stressor effects of running on local tissue as well as central effects. Home Phone: 604-261-6220. Fax: 604-264-0749. Personal E-mail: dclement007@mac.com.

CLEMENTE, CARMINE DOMENIC, anatomist, educator; b. Penns Grove, NJ, Apr. 29, 1928; s. Ermanno and Caroline (Friozzi) Clemente; m. Juliette Vance, Sept. 19, 1968. AB, U. Pa., 1948, MS, 1950, PhD, 1952; postdoctoral fellow, U. London, 1953—54. Asst. instr. anatomy U. Pa., 1950—52; mem. faculty UCLA, 1952—, prof., 1963—95, chmn. dept. anatomy, 1963—73, dir. brain rsch. inst., 1976—87, prof. pathology, neurobiology and anatomy, 1995—, Disting. prof. neurobiology and anatomy, 2004—; prof. surg. anatomy Charles R. Drew U. Medicine and Sci., LA, 1974—. Hon. rsch. assoc. Univ. Coll., U. London, 1953—54; vis. scientist Nat. Inst. Med. Rsch., Mill Hill, London, 1988—89, London, 1991; cons. VA Hosp., Sepulveda, Calif., 1956—96, NIH; mem. med. adv. panel Bank Am.-Giannini Found., 1963—98; chmn. sci. adv. com., bd. dirs. Nat. Paraplegia Found.; bd. dirs. Charles R. Drew U., 1985—94. Author: Aggression and Defense: Neurol Mechanisms and Social Patterns, 1967, Physiological Correlates of Dreaming, 1967, Sleep and the Maturing Nervous System, 1972, Anatomy: An Atlas of the Human Body, 1975, 5th edit., 2006, Clemente's Anatomy Dissector, 2001, 2d edit., 2006; editor: Gray's Anatomy, 1973, 30th Am. edit., 1985; editor-in-chief: Exptl. Neurology, 1973—86, assoc. editor: Neurol. Rsch., Jour. Clin. Anatomy; contbr. articles to sci. jours. Recipient award for merit in sci., Nat. Paraplegia Found., 1973, 23rd Ann. Rehfuss Lectr. and medal, Jefferson Coll., 1986, award for excellence in med. edn., UCLA, 1996, Award of Extraordinary merit, UCLA Med. Alumni Assn., 1997, Significant Early Contributor award, Sleep rsch. Soc., 2003, Disting. Tchr. award, Alpha Omega Alpha, 2006; fellow John Simon Guggenheim Meml. Found., 1988—89. Fellow: Am. Assn. Anatomists (v.p. 1972, pres. 1976—77, Henry Gray award 1993); mem.: NAS (mem. com. on neuropathology, mem. BEAR coms.), Soc. for Neurosci., Japan Soc. Promotion of Sci. (Rsch. award 1978), NY Acad. Scis., Med. Rsch. Assn. Calif. (bd. dirs. 1976—87), AMA-Assn. Am. Med. Colls. (mem. liason com. on med. edn. 1981—87, AOA Robert Glaser Tchg. award 2006), Internat. Brain Rsch. Orgn., Biol. Stain Commn., Assn. Anatomy Chairmen (pres. 1972), Nat. Bd. Med. Examiners (bd. dirs. 1978—84, mem. anatomy test com. 1980—84), Coun. Acad. Socs. (mem. adminstrv. bd. 1973—81, chmn. 1979—80), Assn. Am. Med. Colls. (mem. exec. com. 1978—81, disting. svc. mem. 1982), Am. Neurol. Assn., Am. Assn. Clin. Anatomists (Honored Mem. of Yr. 1993), Am. Acad. Neurology, Am. Physiol. Soc., Brain Rsch. Inst. (dir. 1976—87), Pavlovian Soc. N.Am. (pres. 1972, Ann. award 1968), Am. Acad. Cerebral Palsy (hon.), Inst. Medicine of NAS (mem. sci. adv. bd.), Alpha Omega Alpha, Sigma Xi. Democrat. Home: 11737 Bellagio Rd Los Angeles CA 90049-2158 Office: UCLA Sch Medicine Dept Neurobiology Los Angeles CA 90095-0001 Office Phone: 310-825-9566. Business E-Mail: cdclem@ucla.edu.

CLEMENTS, JOHN ALLEN, physiologist; b. Auburn, NY, Mar. 16, 1923; s. Harry Vernon and May (Porter) C.; m. Margot Sloan Power, Nov. 19, 1949; children: Christine, Carolyn. MD, Cornell U., 1947; MD (honoris causa), U. Berne, Switzerland, 1990, Philipps U., Marburg, Germany, 1992; ScD (honoris causa), U. Manitoba, 1993. Rsch. asst. dept. physiology Med. Coll. N.Y., Cornell U., Ithaca, 1947-49; commd. 1st lt. U.S. Army, 1949, advanced through grades to capt., 1951; asst. chief clin. investigation br. Army Chem. Ctr., 1951-61; assoc. rsch. physiologist U. Calif., San Francisco, 1961-64, prof. pediat., 1964—2004, Julius H. Comroe Jr. prof. pulmonary biology, 1987—2004; mem. staff Cardiovascular Research Inst. Cardiovasc. Rsch. Inst., San Francisco, 1961—2004, mem. grad. group in biophysics, 1987—2004. Career investigator Am. Heart Assn., 1964-93; mem. group in biophysics and med. physics U. Calif., Berkeley, 1969-87; cons. Surgeon Gen. USPHS, 1964-68, Surgeon Gen. U.S. Army, 1972-79; sci. counselor Nat. Heart and Lung Inst., 1972-75; Bowditch lectr. Am. Physiol. Soc., 1961; 2d ann. lectr. Neonatal Soc., London, 1965; Distinguished lectr. Can. Soc. Clin. Investigation, 1973; mem. Nat. Heart Lung and Blood Adv. Coun., 1990-93; Ulf von Euler Meml. lectr. Karolinska Inst., 1996. Mem. editorial bd.: Jour. Applied Physiology, 1961-65, Am. Jour. Physiology, 1965-72, Physiol. Reviews, 1965-72, Jour. Developmental Physiology, 1979-85; assoc. editor: Am. Rev. Respiratory Diseases, 1973-79; chmn. publs. policy com.: Am. Thoracic Soc., 1982-86; assoc. editor: Ann. Rev. Physiology, 1988-93, Am. Jour. Physiology: Lung Cellular and Molecular Physiology, 1988-94. Recipient Dept. Army R & D Achievement award, 1961, Modern Medicine Disting. Achievement award, 1973, Howard Taylor Ricketts medal and award U. Chgo., 1975, Mellon award U. Pitts., 1976, Calif. medal Am. Lung Assn. Calif., 1981, Trudeau medal Am. Lung Assn., 1982, Internat. award Gairdner Found., 1983, J. Burns Amberson lecture award Am. Thoracic Soc. and Am. Lung Assn., 1991, Christopher Columbus Discovery award NIH, 1992, Albert Lasker Clin. Med. award, 1994, Virginia Apgar award Am. Acad. Pediat., 1994, Warren Alpert Found. award, 1995, Discover award Pharm. Rsch. and Mfrs. of Am.; named Mayo Clinic Disting. Lectr. in Med. Sci., 1993, Am. Physiol. Soc. Julius H. Conroe Disting. Lectr., 2000. Fellow AAAS, Am. Acad. Arts and Scis., Am. Coll. Chest Physicians (hon.), Royal Coll. Physicians (London); mem. NAS, Western Assn. Physicians, Western Soc. Clin. Rsch., Perinatal Rsch. Soc. (councillor 1973-75), Am. Lung Assn. (hon., life) Office: U Calif Sch Medicine Cardiovascular Rsch Inst 3333 California St Ste 150 San Francisco CA 94118-1944 Business E-Mail: john.clements@ucsf.edu.

CLEMINS, ARCHIE RAY, career officer; b. Mt. Vernon, Ill., Nov. 18, 1943; s. Archie Cornell and Earline (Pepple) C.; m. Marilyn Paddick, June 30, 1967; children: Becky, Travis. BSEE, U. Ill., 1966, MSEE, 1972. Commd. ensign USN, 1966, advanced through grades to rear adm., 1991; engr. officer USS Tunny, Charleston, S.C., 1972-75; staff engr. Comdr. in Chief, U.S. Pacific Fleet, Pearl Harbor, Hawaii, 1975-78; exec. officer USS Parche, Mare Islands, Calif., 1978-81; comdg. officer USS Pogy, Mare Islands, 1982-85; exec. asst. Dep. Chief of Naval Ops., Washington, 1985-86; comdr. Submarine Group 7, Yokosuka, Japan, 1986-88; chief of staff, comdr. U.S. Seventh Fleet, Yokosuka, 1988-90; comdr. Tng. Command, U.S. Pacific Fleet, San Diego, 1990-2000; pres. Caribou Technologies, Inc., Boise, Idaho, 2000—. Mem.: NAE. Republican. Office: Caribou Technologies, Inc 2041 White Pine Ln Boise ID 83706-4048

CLEVELAND, CHARLES SIDNEY, secondary school educator; b. Portland, Oreg., Apr. 8, 1951; s. Sidney Charles and Virginia May (Seitzinger) C.; m. Joyce Kristine Nofziger, Nov. 5, 1972; children: Justin Charles, Christpher Joseph Sidney. BS, Portland State U., 1974; MAT, Lewis and Clark Coll., 1980. Geography tchr. Hillsboro (Oreg.) Union High Dist., 1976-98, Hillsborough (Oreg.) H.S., 1998—. Pres. Hillsboro (Oreg.) Active 20-30 Club, 1989, Oreg. Soccer Coaches Assn., 1983-84; asst. scoutmaster Boy Scouts Am., Hillsboro, 1991—; bd. dirs. Oreg. Geog. Alliance, 1987-93, Hillsboro Edn. Assn., 1983-86, 92—. Recipient Instructional Leadership Inst. award Nat. Geog. Soc., 1989; named Oreg. and Region IV Soccer Coach of Yr. by Nat. High Sch. Athletic Coaches Assn., 1984, Outstanding Young Man by Hillsboro C. of C., 1976. Mem. Assn. Am. Geographers, Nat. Coun. Geog. Edn. (Disting. Teaching Achievement award 1992), Nat. Coun. Social Studies, Oreg. Coun. Social Studies (bd. dirs.), Active 20-30 Internat. (life), Elks. Avocations: photography, soccer, scout leader. Office: Hillsborough HS 3285 SE Roodridge Rd Hillsboro OR 97123

CLEVENGER, JEFFREY GRISWOLD, mining company executive; b. Boston, Sept. 1, 1949; s. Galen William and Cynthia (Jones) C. BS in Mining Engring., N.Mex. Inst. Mining and Tech., Socorro, 1973; grad. advanced mgmt. program, Harvard U., 1996. Engr. Phelps Dodge, Tyrone, N.Mex., 1973-78, gen. mine foreman, 1979-81, mine supt., 1981-86, Morenci, Ariz., 1986, gen. supt., 1987; asst. gen. mgr. Chino Mines Co., Hurley, N.Mex., 1987-88, Phelps Dodge, Morenci, 1988-89, gen. mgr., 1989-92; pres. Phelps Dodge Morenci, Inc., 1989-92, Morenci Water & Electric Co., 1989-92; sr. v.p. Cyprus Copper Co., Tempe, 1992-93; pres. Cyprus Climax Metals Co., Tempe, 1993—; sr. v.p. Cyprus Amax Minerals Co., Littleton, Colo., 1993-97, exec. v.p., 1998—. Contbr. articles to profl. jours. Bd. dirs. Valley of the Sun YMCA, Mining Hall of Fame; chmn. Copper Devel. Assn. Recipient Disting. Achievement award N.Mex. Inst. Mining & Tech., 1988. Mem. AIME (chmn. S.W. N.Mex. chpt. 1982), Soc. Mining Engrs. (Robert Peele award 1984), Mining and Metall. Soc. Am., Coppr Devel. Assn. (chmn.), Elks.

CLEVER, LINDA HAWES, physician; b. Seattle; d. Nathan Harrison and Evelyn Lorraine (Johnson) Hawes; m. James Alexander Clever, Aug. 20, 1960; 1 child, Sarah Lou. AB with distinction, Stanford U., 1962, MD, 1965. Diplomate Am. Bd. Internal Medicine, Am. Bd. Preventive Medicine in Occupl. Medicine. Intern Stanford U. Hosp., Palo Alto, Calif., 1965—66, resident, 1966—67, fellow in infectious disease, 1967—68; fellow in cmty. medicine U. Calif., San Francisco, 1968—69, resident, 1969—70; med. dir. Sister Mary Philippa Diagonostic and Treatment Ctr. St. Mary's Hosp., San Francisco, 1970—77; chmn. dept. occupl. health Calif. Pacific Med. Ctr., San Francisco, 1977—. Clin. prof. medicine U. Calif. Med. Sch., San Francisco; NIIH rsch. fellow Sch. Medicine, Stanford U., 1967—68; mem. nat. adv. panel Inst. Rsch. on Women and Gender, 1990—, chair panel, 1998—2000; mem. San Francisco Comprehensive Health Planning Coun., 1971—76; bd. dirs., mem. Calif.-OSHA Adv. Com. on Hazard Evaluation Sys. and Info. Svc., 1979—85, Calif. Statewide Profl. Stds. Rev. Coun., 1977—81, San Francisco Regional Commn. on White House Fellows, 1979—81, 1983—89, 1992, 95, chmn., 1977—81, 2001—02; bd. sci. counselors Nat. Inst. Occupl. Safety and Health, 1995—2001. Editor We. Jour. Medicine, 1990—98; contbr. articles to profl. jours. Trustee Stanford U., 1972—76, 1981—91, v.p., 1985—91; pres. RENEW, 2000—; bd. dirs. Sta. KQED, 1976—83, chmn., 1979—81; bd. dirs. Ind. Sector, 1980—86, vice chmn., 1985—86; bd. dirs. San Francisco U. H.S., 1983—90, chmn., 1987—88; active Womens Forum West, 1980—, bd. dirs., 1992—93; mem. Lucile Packard Children's Hosp. Bd., 1993—97, Lucile Packard Found. Children, 1997—99; mem. policy adv. com. U. Calif. Berkeley Sch. Pub. Health, 1995—, chair, 1995—2000; bd. dirs. The Redwoods Retirement Cmty., 1996—2001, Buck Inst. for Rsch. in Aging, 2000—; bd. govs. Stanford Med. Alumni Assn., 1997—2002, 2003—, pres., 2003—05; bd. dirs. No. Calif. Presbyn. Homes and Svcs., 2000—, No. Calif. Presbyn. Homes and Svcs. Found., 2004—, chair, 2008—. Master: ACP (gov. No. Calif. region 1984—89, chmn. bd. govs. 1989—90, regent 1990—96, vice chair bd. regents 1994—95); fellow: Am. Coll. Occupl. and Environ. Medicine; mem.: APHA, We. Assn. Physicians (pres. 2003), We. Occupl. Medicine Assn., Calif. Acad. Medicine, Calif. Med. Assn., Inst. Medicine NAS, Stanford U. Women's Club (bd. dirs. 1971—80), Chi Omega. Office: 2300 California St Ste 304 San Francisco CA 94115-1931 Office Phone: 415-600-3321. Business E-Mail: linda.clever@ucsf.edu.

CLICK, CARRIE, public relations executive; b. 1970; Degree in Humanities, Pepperdine U., degree in Spanish, M in Pub. Policy. Cert. Internat. Bus. Protocol Cons. Protocol Sch. of Washington, DC, profl. certification Susan Peterson Productions, Inc., Comm. Ctr. Intern rsch. Heritage Found., Washington; dep. assoc. dir. for Outreach Office of Faith-Based Cmty. Initiatives, The White House; dir., founder Click on...Etiquette. Mem. Southern Ariz. Ctr. Against Sexual Assault, New Parents Network, South of 45; bd. dirs. El Rio Found. Named one of 40 Under 40, Tucson Bus. Edge, 2006. Office: Click on Etiquette 6719 E Camino Principal Tucson AZ 85715 Office Phone: 800-377-3132. Office Fax: 800-377-3135.

CLICK, JAMES H., automotive executive; Co-CEO Tuttle-Click Automotive Group. Office: 14 Auto Center Dr Irvine CA 92618-2802

CLIFFORD, GERALDINE JONCICH, retired education educator; b. San Pedro, Calif., Apr. 17, 1931; d. Marion and Geraldine Joncich; m. William F. Clifford, July 12, 1969 (dec. 1993). AB, UCLA, 1954, MEd, 1957; EdD, Columbia U., 1961. Tchr., San Lorenzo, Calif., 1954-56, Maracaibo, Venezuela, 1957-58; researcher Inst. Lang. Arts, Tchrs. Coll., Columbia, 1958-61; asst. prof. edn. U. Calif., Berkeley, 1962-67, asso. prof., 1967-74, prof., 1974-94, assoc. dean, 1976-78, chmn. dept. edn., 1978-81, acting dean Sch. Edn., 1980-81, 82-83, dir. edn. abroad program, 1988, 89, prof. grad. sch. Berkeley, 1994—97, prof. emerita, 1994. Author: The Sane Positivist: A Biography of Edward L. Thorndike, 1968, The Shape of American Education, 1975, Ed Sch: A Brief for Professional Education, 1988, Lone Voyagers: Academic Women in Coeducational Universities, 1870-1937, 1989, Equally in View: The University of California, Its Women, and The Schools, 1995. Macmillan fellow, 1958-59, Guggenheim fellow, 1965-66, Rockefeller fellow, 1977-78; recipient Willystine Goodsell award. Mem. History Edn. Soc., Am. Ednl. Rsch. Assn., Phi Beta Kappa, Pi Lambda Theta. Home: Apt 733 1661 Pine St San Francisco CA 94109-0420 Business E-Mail: gcliffor@berkeley.edu.

CLIFT, WILLIAM BROOKS, III, photographer; b. Boston, Jan. 5, 1944; s. William Brooks C. and Anne (Pearmain) Thomson; m. Vida Regina Chesnulis, Aug. 8, 1970; children: Charis, Carola, William. Free lance comml. photographer in partnership with Steve Gersh under name Helios, 1963-71; pres. William Clift Ltd., Santa Fe, 1980-85. Cons. Polaroid Corp., 1965-67 Photographer one-man shows, Carl Siembab Gallery, Boston, 1969, Mus. Art, U. Oreg., Eugene, 1969, New Boston City Hall Gallery, 1970, U. Mass., Berkshire Mus., Pittsfield, Mass., William Coll., Addison Gallery of Am. Art, Wheaton Coll., Mass., Worcester Art Mus., 1971, Creative Photography Gallery, MIT, 1972, St. John's Coll. Art Gallery, Santa Fe, 1973, Wiggin Gallery, Boston Pub. Library, 1974, Australian Ctr. for Photography, Sydney, 1978, Susan Spiritus Gallery, Newport Beach, Calif., 1979, MIT Creative Photography Gallery, 1980, William Lyons Gallery, Coconut Grove, Fla., 1980, Eclipse Gallery, Boulder, Colo., 1980, Atlanta Gallery of Photography, 1980, Phoenix Art Mus., 1981, Jeb Gallery, Providence, 1981, Portfolio Gallery, 1981, Images Gallery, Cin., 1982, Boston Atheneum, 1983, Bank of Santa Fe, 1984, Susan Harder Gallery, N.Y.C., 1984, Cleve. Art Mus., 1985, Art Inst. Chgo., 1987, Amon Carter Mus., Ft. Worth, 1987, Clarence Kennedy Gallery, Cambridge, Mass., 1988, Equitable Gallery, N.Y.C., 1993, Vassar Coll. Art Mus., N.Y., 1994, Vassar Coll. Art Gallery, N.Y., 1995; exhibited in group shows Gallery 216, N.Y., N.Y. Grover Cronin Gallery, Waltham, Mass., 1964, Carl Seimbab Gallery, Boston, 1966, Lassall Jr. Coll., 1967, Hill's Gallery, Santa Fe, Tyler Mus. Art, Austin, Tex., Dupree Gallery, Dallas, 1974, Quindacqua Gallery, Washington, 1978, Zabriskie Gallery, Paris, 1978, Am. Cultural Ctr., Paris, 1978; photographer AT&T Project-Am. Images, 1978, Seagram's Bicentennial Project, Courthouse, 1975-77, Readers Digest Assn. Project, 1984, Hudson River Project, 1985-92; author: Photography Portfolios, Old Boston City Hall, 1971, Photography Portfolios, Courthouse, 1979, Photography Portfolios, New Mexico, 1975, Certain Places, Photographs, 1987, A Hudson Landscape, Photographs, 1993. Nat. Endowment for Arts photography fellow, 1972, 79; Guggenheim fellow, 1974, 80, N.Mex. Gov.'s Excellence in The Arts award, 1987 Home and Office: PO Box 6035 Santa Fe NM 87502-6035

CLIFTON, RICHARD RANDALL, federal judge; b. Framingham, Mass., Nov. 13, 1950; s. Arthur Calvin and Vivian Juanita (Himes) C.; m. Teresa Morano Aleshire, Oct. 15, 1988; children: David Madison, Katherine Kaleilani. AB, Princeton U., 1972; JD, Yale U., 1975. Bar: Ill. 1975, Hawaii 1976, US Dist. Ct. Hawaii 1976, US Ct. Appeals (9th cir.) 1976, US Ct. Appeals (2d cir.) 1979, US Supreme Ct. 1982. Law clk. to judge US Ct. Appeals (9th cir.), Honolulu, 1975-76, judge, 2002—; from assoc. to ptnr. Cades, Schutte, Fleming & Wright, Honolulu, 1977—2002. Adj. prof. law U. Hawaii, Honolulu, 1979-89. Co-author: The Shreveport Plan: An Experiment in the Delivery of Legal Services, 1974. Mem. dist. com. Nancy J. Stivers Meml. Fund, Honolulu, 1984—; bd. dirs. Hawaii Pub. Radio, Honolulu, 1991—, chmn., 1995-2000; mem. Hawaii State Jud. Conf., 1987-90; 1st vice chmn. Hawaii Rep. Party, 1989-93, chmn. rules com., 1987-90, gen. counsel, 1993-2001; bd. dirs. Hawaii Women's Legal Found., 1987—, Ninth Jud. Cir. Hist. Soc., 1996—; mem. Hawaii State Reapportionment Com., 1991-92. Mem. ABA, Hawaii Bar Assn., Am. Law Inst. Office: US Court of Appeals 999 Bishop St #2010 Honolulu HI 96813

CLIMAN, RICHARD ELLIOT, lawyer; b. NYC, July 19, 1953; s. David Arthur and Mary (Vitale) C. AB cum laude, Harvard U., 1974, JD cum laude, 1977. Bar: Calif. 1977. Assoc. Pettit & Martin, San Francisco, 1977-83, ptnr., 1984-94; ptnr., head mergers and acquisitions group Cooley Godward Kronish LLP, Palo Alto, San Francisco, Calif., 1994—. Co-chair Doing Deals Practising Law Inst., 1997-2002, Tech. Mergers and Acquisitions Inst. Glasser LegalWorks, 1999-2001, West Coast Forum on Tech. M&A, 2007; adv. bd. BNA Mergers & Acquisitions Law Report; exec. com. Securities Reg. Inst., Corp. Counsel Ctr., Sch. Law Northwestern U., mem., adj. faculty UCLA Sch. Law, 2009; lectr. and panelist in field. Contbr. articles to profl. jours. Named one of 500 Leading Lawyers in America, Lawdragon, 2005—08, 100 Most Influential Lawyers in America, Nat. Law Jour., 2006. Mem. ABA (sect. bus. law, chair com. on negotiated acquisitions 2002-06, co-chair Nat. Inst. on Negotiating Bus. Acquisitions 2003—). Home: 1 Tulip Ln San Carlos CA 94070-1551 Office: Cooley Godward Kronish LLP 5 Palo Alto Sq 3000 El Camino Real Palo Alto CA 94306-2120 Home Phone: 650-594-1641; Office Phone: 650-843-5174. E-mail: rcliman@cooley.com.

CLINE, THOMAS WARREN, geneticist, educator; b. Oakland, Calif., May 6, 1946; married, 1986. AB, U. Calif. Berkeley, 1968; PhD in Biochemistry, Harvard U., 1973. Fellow devel. genetics Helen Hay Whitney Found., U. Calif. Irvine, 1973-76; from asst. to prof. biology Princeton U., 1976-90; prof. genetics and devel. U. Calif. Berkeley, 1990—. Recipient Molecular Biology award NAS, 1992. Fellow AAAS, Am. Acad. Arts and Scis.; mem. U.S. Nat. Acad. Scis., Genetics Soc. Am. Achievements include research in development regulation of gene expression in Drosophila melanogaster with emphasis on oogenesis, sex determination, and X-chromosome dosage compensation. Office: U Calif 16 Barker Hall MC 3204 Berkeley CA 94720-3204 Office Phone: 510-643-5632.

CLINTON, JACK W., dean; DMD, Oreg. Health and Sci. U. Sch. Dentistry, 1964. Assoc. dean clin. affairs Oreg. Health and Sci. U. Sch. Dentistry, interim dean, 2003—04, dean, 2004—. Pres. Sch. of Dentistry Alumni Assn., 1979—80. Mem.: ADA, Internat. Coll. Dentists (vice regent), Am. Assn. Dental Schools, Am. Assn. Dental Examiners. Office: Oreg Health and Sci U Sch Dentistry 611 SW Campus Dr Portland OR 97239

CLINTON, RICHARD M., lawyer; b. Milw., June 25, 1941; s. William J. and Idella (Loftis) C.; m. Barbara Lynch, June 14, 1969; children: Amanda, Camille, Rebecca. BS, U. Wis., 1963, JD, 1967; LLM, George Washington U., 1971. Bar: Wis. 1967, Wash. 1971, U.S. Ct. Appeals (9th cir.) 1972, U.S. Dist. Ct. (ea. dist.) Wash. 1975. Instr. legal writing U. Wis. Law Sch., Madison, 1966-67; trial atty. antitrust div. U.S. Dept. Justice, Washington, 1967-71; assoc. Bogle & Gates, Seattle, 1971-75, mem., 1975-99; ptnr., sr. trial atty., litig., and co-chmn., anti-trust practice Dorsey & Whitney LLP, Seattle, 1999—. Fellow Am. Coll. Trial Lawyers; mem. ABA, Wash. Bar Assn. (pres. antitrust sect. 1982-83), Fed. Bar Assn. (pres. 1986-87), Wash. Athletic Club, Columbia Tower Club. Roman Catholic. Avocations: sailing, skiing, fishing, hiking, travel. Office: Dorsey & Whitney LLP Ste 3400 US Bank Centre 1420 5th Ave Seattle WA 98101-4010 Office Phone: 206-903-8851. Office Fax: 206-903-8820. E-mail: clinton.richard@dorsey.com.

CLOPTON, KAREN VALENTIA, lawyer, president civil services commission; BA with honors, Vassar Coll., 1980; JD, Antioch U., 1983. Bar: Calif. Maguire fellow internat. and comparative labor studies, London, 1984; trial atty NLRB, Washington, San Francisco; counsel Leland, Parachini, Steinberg, Matzger & Melnick LLP, San Francisco, 1998—. Lectr. mgmt. tng. programs emphasizing preventive labor rels.; mem. faculty San Francisco State U. Coll. Extended Learning. Past mem. L.A. Dist. Atty.'s Office Youth Adv. Bd; pres. San Francisco City and County Civil Service Commn. Mem. Lawyers

Club of San Francisco (bd. govs.), Calif. Young Lawyers Assn. (Jack Berman Individual award of achievement 1994). Office: Leland Parachini et al 333 Market St Ste 2700 San Francisco CA 94105-2128

CLOSE, BETSY L., state representative; b. Shelton, Wash., May 4, 1950; m. Chris Close; 4 children. BA, Wash. State U., 1972, Ctrl. Wash. U., 1974; MS, Oreg. State U., 1978. Tchr. Wash. State Pub. Schs., 1974—76; grad. tchg. asst. Oreg. State U., Corvallis, 1976—78; instr., job devel. Benton County, 1978—79; tchr. Albany Pub. Schs., 1979—81; mem. Oreg. Ho. of Reps., 1998—. Chair Benton County Rep. Party, 1996—98; bd. dirs. Palestine Rural Fire, 1997—. Republican.

CLOSE, GLENN, actress; b. Greenwich, Conn., Mar. 19, 1947; d. William and Bettine Close; m. Cabot Wade 1969 (div. 1971); m. James Marlas, 1984 (div. 1987); 1 child, Annie Maude Starke; m. David Shaw, Feb. 3, 2006. BA in drama and anthropology, Coll. William and Mary, 1974. Joined New Phoenix Repertory Co., 1974. Co-owner The Leaf and Bean Coffee House, Bozeman, Montana, 1993-94. Actor: (Broadway debut) Love for Love, 1974; (Broadway plays) The Rules of the Game, 1974, The Member of the Wedding, 1975, Rex, 1976, Barnum, 1980—81 (Tony award nomination for best featured actress in a musical, 1980), The Real Thing, 1984—85 (Tony award for best actress in a play, 1984), Benefactors, 1985—86, Death and the Maiden, 1992 (Tony award for best actress in a play, 1992), Sunset Boulevard, 1994—95 (Tony award for best actress in a musical, 1995), (other theatre appearances include) Uncommon Women and Others, The Singular Life of Albert Nobbs, 1982, Childhood, 1985, Joan of Arc at the Stake, 1985, Sunset Boulevard (LA), 1993—94, The Vagina Monologues, 1998; (films) The World According to Garp, 1982, The Big Chill, 1983, Greystoke: The Legend of Tarzan, Lord of the Apes (voice), The Natural, 1984, The Stone Boy, 1984, Jagged Edge, 1985, Maxie, 1985, Fatal Attraction, 1987, (voice) Gandahar, 1988, Dangerous Liaisons, 1988, Immediate Family, 1989, Reversal of Fortune, 1990, Hamlet, 1990, Meeting Venus, 1991, Hook, 1991, The House of the Spirits, 1993, The Paper, 1994, Mary Reilly, 1996, 101 Dalmations, 1996, Mars Attacks!, 1996, Paradise Road, 1997, Air Force One, 1997, Cookie's Fortune, 1999, (voice) Tarzan, 1999, Things You Can't Tell Just by Looking at Her, 2000, 102 Dalmations, 2000, The Safety of Objects, 2001, (voice) Pinocchio, 2002, Le Divorce, 2003, The Stepford Wives, 2004, Nine Lives, 2005, Heights, 2005, The Chumscrubber, 2005, (voice) Hoodwinked, 2005, Tarzan II, 2005, Evening, 2007; (TV films) The Rules of the Game, 1975, Too Far to Go, 1979, Orphan Train, 1979, The Elephant Man, 1982, Something About Amelia, 1984, Stones for Ibarra, 1988, She'll Take Romance, 1990, In the Gloaming, 1997, The Lion in Winter, 2003 (Golden Globe Award for best actress in a mini-series or TV movie, 2005, Screen Actors Guild Award for best actress in a TV movie or miniseries, 2005), Strip Search, 2004; (TV series) The Shield, 2005, Damages, 2007— (Best Performance by an Actress in a Television Series - Drama, Golden Globe award, Hollywood Fgn. Press Assn., 2008, Primetime Emmy for Outstanding Lead Actress in a Drama Series, Acad. TV Arts and Scis., 2008); actor, exec. prodr. (TV films) Sarah, Plain and Tall, 1991, Skylark, 1993, Serving in Silence: The Margarethe Cammermeyer Story, 1995 (Emmy award for best actress in a miniseries or special, 1995), Sarah, Plain and Tall: Winter's End, 1999, Baby, 2000, The Ballad of Lucy Whipple, 2001, South Pacific, 2001; exec. prodr.: (TV films) Journey, 1995. Recipient Woman of Yr. Award Hasty Pudding Theatricals, Harvard U., 1990, Dartmouth Film Award, 1990, Sherry Lansing Leadership award Sherry Lansing Found., 2008; named one of Top 25 Entertainers or Yr., Entertainment Weekly, 2007 Mem. Phi Beta Kappa.

CLOSE, SANDY, journalist; b. NYC, Jan. 25, 1943; BA, U. Calif., Berkeley, 1964. Exec. dir., editor Pacific News Svc., San Francisco. MacArthur fellow, 1995. Office: Pacific News Service 275 9th St 3rd Fl San Francisco CA 94103-3825

CLOSE, TIMOTHY (JOHN TIMOTHY CLOSE), museum director; BFA, Ariz. State U.; MFA, Calif. Inst. Arts. Cert. Mus. Mgmt. Inst., J. Paul Getty Trust, Berkeley, Calif. Exec. dir. Arlington Arts Ctr., Va., Albany Mus. Art, Ga., 1994—2000, Boise Art Museum, Boise, Idaho, 2000—06; dir. Mus. Glass, Tacoma, 2006—. Represented in permanent collections Houston Art Mus., MoMA, NYC. Mem.: Assn. Art Mus. Dirs., Inst. Mus. & Libr. Services (panel reviewer), Am. Assn. Museums (accreditation com. peer reviewer). Office: Mus Glass 1801 Dock St Tacoma WA 98402-3217 Office Phone: 253-284-4750. E-mail: info@museumofglass.org.

CLOW, LEE, advertising agency executive; b. LA, 1943; Degree, Santa Monica City Coll., Calif. Formerly with N. W. Ayer & Son; art dir. Chiat/Day, LA, 1973—77, assoc. creative dir., 1977—82, creative dir., 1982—84; pres., chief creative officer, sr. art dir. Chiat/Day/Mojo, LA, 1984; various positions TBWA/Chiat/Day, LA; chmn., chief creative officer TBWA»orldwide, 1995—. Bd. dir. Oakley Inc., 2002—. Served in US Army. Recipient Lifetime Achievement award, Clio Awards Festival, 2004; named Creative Exec. of Yr., USA Today, 1997; named to Hall of Fame, NY Art Dirs. Club, 1990, Creative Hall of Fame, The One Club for Art & Copy, 1997, Advt. Hall of Fame, Mus. Modern Art. Office: TBWA Chiat/Day 5353 Grosvenor Blvd Los Angeles CA 90066 Office Phone: 310-305-5000.*

CLOWES, ALEXANDER WHITEHILL, surgeon, educator; b. Boston, Oct. 9, 1946; s. George H.A. Jr. and Margaret Gracey (Jackson) Clowes; m. Monika Meyer (dec.); m. Susan E. Detweiler. AB, Harvard U., 1968, MD, 1972. Resident in surgery Case Western Reserve, Cleve., 1972-74, 76-79; rsch. fellow in pathology Harvard Med. Sch., Boston, 1974-76; fellow in vascular surgery Brigham and Womens Hosp. Harvard Med. Sch., 1979-80; asst. prof. surgery U. Wash., Seattle, 1980-85, assoc. prof., 1985-90, prof., 1990—, assoc. chmn. dept., 1989-91, acting chmn. dept., 1992-93, adj. prof. pathology, 1992, chief divsn. vascular surgery, 1995—2007, dept. vice chmn., 1995—, V. Paul Gavora and Helen S. and John A. Schilling prof. surgery, 2005—. Contbr.:, author (numerous sci. papers). Trustee Marine Biol. Labs, Woods Hole, Mass., 1989—2000, Seattle Symphony, 1994—2006, v.p., 1998—2006, 2008—; bd. dirs. Seattle Chamber Music Festival, 1990. Recipient Rsch. Career Devel. award, NIH, 1982—87; Tng. fellow, 1974—77, Loyal Davis Traveling Surg. scholar, ACS, 1987. Mem.: N.Am. Vascular Biology Orgn. (pres. 2001-02), Soc. Vascular Surgery, Seattle Surg. Soc., Internat. Soc. Applied Cardiovasc. Biology, Am. Soc. Cell Biology, Am. Heart Assn. (coun. on arteriosclerosis), Am. Assn. Pathologists, Am. Surg. Assn., Quisset Yacht Club, Cruising Club Am., Sigma Xi. Episcopalian. Home: 3425 Perkins Ln W Seattle WA 98199-1858 Office: U Wash Dept Surgery PO Box 356410 Seattle WA 98195-6410

CLOWES, JOHN HOWARD, lawyer; BA, U. Calif., Santa Barbara, 1976; JD, U. Calif., Berkeley, 1982. Bar: Calif. 1982. Ptnr., co-chmn. Emerging Growth & Venture Capital practice grp. DLA Piper Rudnick Gray Cary, San Francisco. Named a No. Calif. Super Lawyer, San Francisco mag., 2004. Mem.: ABA. Office: DLA Piper US LLP Suite 800 555 Mission St San Francisco CA 94105-2933 Office Phone: 415-836-2510. Office Fax: 415-836-2501. Business E-Mail: howard.clowes@dlapiper.com.

CLUFF, LLOYD STERLING, earthquake geologist; b. Provo, Utah, Sept. 29, 1933; s. Colvin Sterling and Melba Cluff; m. Janet L. Peterson, Dec. 21, 1976; children: Tanya, Sasha, Branden. BS in Geology, U. Utah, 1960. Registered profl. geologist, Calif.; cert. engring. geologist, Calif. Jr. geologist El Paso Natural Gas Co., Salt Lake City, 1957-59; tchg. asst. dept. geology U. Utah, Salt Lake City, 1958-60; geologist Lottridge Thomas & Assocs., Salt Lake City, 1960; v.p., prin. geologist Woodward-Clyde Cons., San Francisco, 1960—85; assoc. prof. geology and geophysics U. Nev., Reno, 1967-73; dir. dept. geoscis. Pacific Gas and Electric Co., San Francisco, 1985—. Cons. Trans-Alaska Pipeline Siting Study, 1972-74; Aswan High Dam seismic safety evaluation, Govt. of Egypt, 1982-86; mem. com. Nat. Earthquake Hazards Reduction Program, Washington, 1987, Decade for Natural Disaster Reduction, Washington, 1989; advisor Venezuela Pres.'s Earthquake Safety Com., 1967-72; advisor Joint Legis. Com. on Seismic Safety, State of Calif., 1970-74; chmn. seismic rev. panel Calif. Pub. Utilities Commn., San Francisco, 1980-81; mem. Calif. Seismic Safety Commn., 1985-99, chmn., 1988-90, 95-97; adv. bd. So. Calif. Earthquake Ctr., 1996-2001, 04—; chmn. Tech. Adv. Bd. on Earthquake Risk, Israel, 1996-2004; adv. panel on earth scis. NSF, 1992-95; chmn. com. on practical lessons from the Loma Prieta Earthquake NAS, 1994; organizing com. for Pub. Policy Partnership 2000-White House Confs. on Natural Disaster Loss Reduction, 1997-98; com. on assessing costs of natural disasters NAS, 1998-99, bd. natural disasters NAS, 1997-2000, Natural Disaster Roundtable, 2000—; nat. pre-disaster mitigation program adv. panel FEMA, 1998-99; external adv. panel for Pacific Earthquake Engring. Rsch. Ctr., 1998-99, implementation adv. bd., 1999—; natural disaster panel Heinz Ctr. Inst. for Natural Disasters, 2000-02; chmn. sci. earthquake studies adv. com. USGS Nat. Earthquake Hazards Reduction Program, 2002-2007, seismic adv. bd. Design and Constrn. Panama Canal, 2003- Recipient Hogentagler award ASTM, 1968, Alfred E. Alquist medal, Calif. Earthquake Safety Found., 1998, John Wesley Powell award, USGS, 2000, William Joyner Meml. Lecture award Seismol. Soc. Am. and Earthquake Engring. Rsch. Inst., 2003, Lifetime Achievement award Western States Seismic Policy Coun., 2006, George W. Housner medal Earthquake Engring. Rsch. Inst.,2009; named Woodward lectr., San Francisco, 1979, Sinotech Dist. lectr., Taiwan, 2002. Fellow Calif. Acad. Scis.; mem. NAE, Seismol. Soc. Am. (pres. 1982-83), Assn. Engring. Geologists (pres. 1968-69), Earthquake Engring. Rsch. Inst. (hon., pres. 1993-95, chmn. Internat. Conf. on Seismic Zonation, Nice, France 1995), Geol. Soc. Am., Structural Engrs. Assn. No. Calif. (H.J. Degenkolb award 1992), Nat. Acad. Delegation Islamic Rep. of Iran, 2000. Independent. Avocations: photography, skiing, mountain climbing, hiking, bicycling. Office: Pacific Gas & Elec Co 245 Market St San Francisco CA 94105-1797 Office Phone: 415-973-2791. E-mail: lsc2@pge.com.

CLYDE, CALVIN GEARY, civil engineer, educator; b. Springville, Utah, Sept. 5, 1924; s. Edward and Hannah (Mendenhall) C.; m. Brigitta Straumer, Nov. 24, 1948; children: Rixa, Eric S., DeAnn, Carla, Andrea, Loretta, Mark E., Tania. Student, Utah State U., 1942-43, No. State Tchrs. Coll., 1943-44, Brigham Young U., 1946; BS, U. Utah, 1951; degrees in civil engring., U. Calif., Berkeley, MS, 1952, PhD, 1961. Registered engr. and land surveyor, Utah; consecrated bishop Mormon Ch., 1976. Assoc. prof. civil engring. U. Utah, Salt Lake City, 1953-63; prof. Utah State U., Logan, 1963-89, prof. emeritus, 1989—, assoc. dir. Utah Water Research Lab., 1965-77, acting dir. Utah Water Research Lab., 1975-76. Cons. in ground water, fluid mechanics, hydraulics, hydropower, hydrology and water resources planning, 1953—. Contbr. articles to profl. jours. Served with U.S. Army, 1943-46, ETO. Science faculty fellow NSF, Berkeley, 1959-60. Fellow ASCE (pres. Utah sect. 1969-70, Utah Civil Engr. of Yr. 1979); mem. Am. Soc. Engring. Edn. (chmn. Rocky Mountain sect. 1962-63), AIAA, Nat. Water Well Assn., Internat. Assn. Hydraulic Research. Republican. Avocations: skiing, hiking, camping, fishing. Home: 839 N 1400 E Logan UT 84321-3629 Office: Utah State U Water Research Lab # 82 Logan UT 84322-0001

CLYDE, ROBERT ALLAN, computer software engineer; b. Salt Lake City, June 9, 1959; s. Allan Roy and Janet (Wright) C.; m. Lisa Marie DeFranco, July 14, 1981; children: Elizabeth, Julie. BS in Computer Sci., Brigham Young U., 1984. V.p. engring./mktg. Clyde Digital Systems, Orem, Utah, 1981-91; v.p., gen. mgr. Security Products divsn. Raxco, Orem, 1991-94; v.p. security svcs. Axent Techs., Orem, 1994-96; v.p., gen. mgr. Security Mgmt. Bus. unit Axent, Orem, 1996—2000; v.p., chief tech. officer Symantec Corp., Cupertino, Calif., 2001—. Author: (software product) Contrl, Audit, KBlock; inventor systems for parallel monitoring. Mem. IEEE, Info. Security Assn., EDP Auditors Assn., Assn. for Computing Machinery. Avocations: fishing, camping. Office: Symantec Corp 20330 Stevens Creek Blvd Cupertino CA 95014

COALE, KENNETH HAMILTON, biogeochemist, educator; b. NYC, Jan. 24, 1955; s. Franklin Steele Coale and Mary Louise (Price) Moses; m. Susan Elizabeth Lange, June 23, 1979; children: Megan Elizabeth Coale, Tyler Hamilton Coale. BA in biology, U. Calif., 1977, PhD in biology, 1988. Marine tech. Moss Landing (Calif.) Marine Labs., 1976-77; asst. specialist U. Calif., Santa Cruz, 1978-83, assoc. specialist, 1983, rsch. asst., 1983-88; postdoctoral researcher Moss Landing (Calif.) Labs., 1988, sr. rsch. assoc., 1991-92, adj. prof., 1992—; acting dir. Moss Landing Marine Labs., 1998—2001, dir., 2001—. Vis. scientist KFA Juelich Germany, NIOZ, The Netherlands, 1982; guest editor Deep Sea Rsch., Oxford, Sidney, London, 1994—. Co-author: Dynamic Processing in the Chemistry of the Upper Oceans, 1986; contbr. articles to profl. jours. Sec., bd. dirs. Land Trust of Santa Cruz Co., 1991-2000; bd. dirs. Friends of MLML, 1998—. Recipient rsch. grants in field. Fellow Calif. Acad. Sci.; mem. AAAS, Am. Geophysical Union, Am. Soc. Limnology & Oceanography, Oceanography Soc., Am. Chemical Soc. Achievements include development of 234th; 238 U disequilibria as a tracer for chemical biological removal process; development of DPASV to determine copper complexation in the North Pacific Ocean, COPi and chief scientist of the Iron Ex and SOFex experiments. Office: Moss Landing Marine Labs 8272 Moss Landing Rd Moss Landing CA 95039-9647 E-mail: coale@mlml.calstate.edu.

COAN, PATRICIA A., retired judge; b. NYC, July 21, 1945; 2 children. BSN, Georgetown U., 1967; JD, U. Denver, 1981. Bar: Colo. 1982; RN N.Y., Conn., Mont. Pvt. practice, Denver, 1982-96; magistrate judge U.S. Dist. Ct. for Dist. Colo., Denver, 1996—2006. Bd. dirs. Colo. Lawyers Health Program. Mem. Women's Bar Assn., Colo. Bar Assn., Denver Bar Assn., Sigma Theta Tau, Alpha Sigma Nu.

COATES, THOMAS DUANE, pediatrician, hematologist, educator; b. Bay City, Mich., 1945; MD, U. Mich., 1975. Cert. Pediat., 1980, Pediatric Hematology-Oncology, 1982. Intern pediat. Riley Children's Hosp., Ind., 1975—76, resident pediat. hematology Ind., 1976—78, fellowship Ind., 1978—81; assoc. prof. pediat. and pathology Keck Sch. Medicine, U. So. Calif.; head hematology Children's Ctr. for Cancer and Blood Diseases Children's Hosp. LA. Contbr. articles to med. jours. Office: Childrens Hosp LA 4650 Sunset Blvd, MS #54 Los Angeles CA 90027 Office Phone: 323-361-2352. Office Fax: 323-660-9321. E-mail: tcoates@usc.edu.

COATES, THOMAS J., medical association administrator; BA in Philosophy, San Luis Rey Coll., 1968; MA in Psychology, San Jose State U., 1971; PhD in Counseling Psychology, Stanford U., 1977. Mem. faculty Stanford Heart Disease Prevention Program; with Johns Hopkins U.; dir. behavioral medicine unit div. gen. internal medicine U. Calif., San Francisco, 1984—, mem. med. attending staff, 1984—, prof. div. gen. internal medicine dept. medicine, 1990—, dir. Ctr. AIDS Prevention Studies, 1991—. Spl. advisor family health internat.'s AIDS prevention project USAIDS; chair global programme on AIDS steering com. social and behavioral studies unit WHO. Contbr. articles to profl. jours. Mem.: NAS (mem. Inst. Medicine). Office: UCLA Dept Med Divsn Infectious Dis Prevention & Policy Rsch 10940 Wilshire Blvd Ste 1220 Los Angeles CA 90024-7320

COATS, NATHAN B., state supreme court justice; m. Mary Ricketson; 1 child, Johanna. BA in Econs., U. Colo., 1971, JD, 1977. Assoc. Hough, Grant, McCarren and Bernard, 1977-78; asst. atty. gen. Appellate Sect., Colo., 1978-83, dep. atty. gen. Colo., 1983-86; adj. prof. U. Colo., Colo., 1990; chief appellate dep. dist. atty. 2d Jud. Dist., Denver, 1986-2000; justice Colo. Supreme Ct., 2000—. Chief reporter Erickson Commn. on Officer-Involved Shootings, 1996-97; lectr. Denver Police Acad., 1986-97; reporter Govs. Columbine Commn., 1999-2000; mem. Colo. Supreme Ct. Criminal Rules Com., 1983-2000, chmn., 1997-2000, Colo. Bd. Law Examiners, 1984-94, Colo. Supreme Ct. Appellate Rules Com., 1985-2000, Colo. Supreme Ct. Civil Rules Com., Colo. Supreme Ct. Criminal Pattern Jury Instructions Com., 1987-2000, Colo. Supreme Ct. Jury Reform Pilot Project Com., 1998-2000, Colo. Dist. Attys. Coun. Legis. Com., 1990-2000. Office: Colo State Supreme Ct Judicial Bldg 2 E 14th Ave Denver CO 80203-2115

COBB, JOHN, state legislator; b. Mont., Jan. 22, 1954; m to Cheryl Lux; children: two. Montana State Representative, District 42, 1985-94, District 50, 1995-01; Montana State Senator, District 9, 2001-, Montana State Senate.Atty & rancher, currently. Republican. Address: PO Box 388 Augusta MT 59410 Mailing: State Capitol Helena MT 59620-1701

COBB, JOHN CANDLER, medical educator; b. Boston, July 8, 1919; s. Stanley and Elizabeth Mason (Almy) C.; m. Helen Imlay-Franchot, July 27, 1946; children: Loren, Nathaniel, Bethany, Julianne. BS in Astronomy cum laude, Harvard U., 1941, MD, 1948; MPH, Johns Hopkins U., 1954. Diplomate Nat. Bd. Med. Examiners, Am. Bd. Preventive Medicine and Pub. Health; lic. physician, Conn., Md., N.Mex. Intern Yale New Haven Hosp., 1948-49, fellow in pediatrics, 1949-50; jr. asst. resident Yale Psychiatric Clinic, 1950-51; instr. pediatrics and psychiatry Johns Hopkins U., 1951-56, asst. prof. material and child health, 1954-56; cons. Indian Health divsn. USPHS, Albuquerque, 1956-60; prof. preventive medicine U. Colo., Denver, 1965-85, emeritus prof., 1985—, chmn. dept., 1966-73. Dir. med. social rsch. project on population Govt. of Pakistan, 1960-64; cons. Am. Friends Svc. Com., Algeria, 1964; short term cons. WHO, Indonesia and Western Pacific Region, 1969, 70-73, USAID, Togo and Niger, 1979; exch. prof. Guangxi Med. Coll., Nanning, China, 1985-86; coord. ethics seminars U. Health Scis. Ctr., 1980-85; pres. World Hand Assocs., 1985--; cons. in field. Contbr. numerous articles to profl. jours. Bd. dirs., pres. Am. Assn. Planned Parenthood Physicians, 1966-67; bd. dirs., Planned Parenthood Fedn. Am., 1972-73, chmn. Task Force for Preparing 314(b) Agy. Grant Application, 1969; mem., chmn. health com. of Gov. Lamm and U.S. Congressman Wirth's Task Force on Rocky Flats Nuc. Weapons Plant, Denver, 1974-75; mem. Gov.'s Task Force on Health Effects of Air Pollution, 1978-79; commr. Air Pollution Control Commn. of Colo., 1976-79; mem. air quality policy com. Denver Regional Coun. of Govts., 1978-80, environ. council, U. Colo., 1970-75, Gov.'s Sci. adv. Counc., Colo., 1973-80, Gov.'s Blue Ribbon Task Force on Transp., Colo., 1977; bd. dirs. ROMCOE Ctr. for Environ. Problem Solving, 1978-81, Colo. Coalition for Full Employment, 1978-80; mem. Am. Friends Svc. Com. Adv. Group on Rocky Flats/Nuclear Weapons Project, 1979-85; mem. sci. adv. bd., Three Miles Inland Pub. Health Fund, 1982-86, owning mem. Chaordic Commons. Recipient Florence Sabin award Colo. Pub. Health Assn., 1979, Jack Gore Meml. Peace award Am. Friends Svc. Com., 1980; U.S. EPA grantee, 1975-82. Mem. AAAS, WHO, Internat. Solar Energy Soc., Am. Solar Energy Soc., bd. dir., N.Mex Solar Energy Assn., 1990-96, Internat. Physicians for Prevention of Nuclear War (del. to Congresses in Moscow and Montreal), Appropriate Rural Tech. Assn. (bd. dirs. 1987-2002, v.p. 1991-92), Nat. Resources Def. Coun. (bd. advisors 1991-92), N.Mex. Solar Energy Assn. (bd. dirs. 1995-98), Physicians for Human Rights, Physicians for Social Reponsibility.

COBB, MILES ALAN, retired lawyer; b. Salt Lake City, May 8, 1930; s. Miles Cobb and June (Ray) Cobb Wilson; children: Jennifer, Melissa, Mary. BS, U. Calif.-Berkeley, 1953, LL.B., 1958. Bar: Calif. 1958. Assoc. Bronson, Bronson & McKinnon, San Francisco, 1958-65, ptnr., 1965-76, 78-84; gen. counsel FDIC, Washington, 1976-78; pres. Bell Savs & Loan Assn., San Mateo, Calif., 1984-85. Author: Federal Regulation of Depository Institutions, 1984. Served to 1st lt. U.S. Army, 1953-55; Korea Democrat. Avocations: photography, golf, gardening. E-mail: macobb@sbcglobal.net.

COBB, ROY LAMPKIN, JR., retired computer sciences corporation executive; b. Oklahoma City, Sept. 23, 1934; s. Roy Lampkin and Alice Maxine Cobb; m. Shirley Ann Dodson, June 21, 1958; children: Kendra Leigh, Cary William, Paul Alan. BA, U. Okla., 1972; postgrad., U. Calif., Northridge, 1976-77. Naval aviation cadet USN, 1955, advanced through grades to comdr., 1970, ret., 1978; mktg./project staff engr. Gen. Dynamics, Pomona, Calif., 1978-80; mgr. dept. support svcs. Computer Scis. Corp., Point Mugu, Calif.,

1980-97; ret. Decorated Navy Commendation medal, Air medal (13). Mem. Assn. Naval Aviators, Soc. Logistic Engrs. (editor Launchings 1990-98), Navy League, Las Posas Country Club, Spanish Hills Country Club. Republican. Home: 2481 Brookhill Dr Camarillo CA 93010-2112 E-mail: cobbweb@aol.com.

COBB, TY, lawyer; b. Great Bend, Kans., Aug. 25, 1950; s. Grover Cowling and Elizabeth Anne (McCleary) C.; m. Leigh Elliott Stevenson, Aug. 21, 1976; children: Chance Wyatt, Chelsea Leigh, Brady Elliott, Chloe Elizabeth. AB, Harvard U., 1972; JD, Georgetown U., 1978. Bar: DC 1979, US Dist. Ct. DC 1979, US Dist. Ct. Md. 1979, US Ct. Appeals (4th and DC cirs.) 1979, US Ct. Internat. Trade 1980, US Ct. Appeals (3d cir.) 1987, US Supreme Ct. 1986, Md. 1987, Colo. 1998, US Ct. Appeals (10th cir.) 1999. Legis. adminstrv. asst. US Ho. of Reps., Washington, 1974-75; law clk. to fed. judge US Dist. Ct., Balt., 1978-79; assoc. Collier, Shannon, Rill & Scott, Washington, 1979-81; asst. U.S. atty. Office of US Atty., Balt., 1981-86, chief criminal cases, 1984-86; mid-Atlantic regional coord. Organized Crime Drug Enforcement Task Force US Dept. Justice, Balt., 1985—86; ptnr. Hogan & Hartson LLP, Washington and Balt., 1988-98, mng. ptnr. Denver, 1998—, dir. litig. practice group. Spl. trial counsel Office of Ind. Counsel HUD, 1994-95; instr. US Atty. Gen.'s Adv. Inst., US Dept. Justice, 1983-86; mem. Jud. Conf. of US Ct. Appeals (4th cir.); trustee Grand Canyon Trust, 2004—. Contbr. articles to profl. jours. Chmn. Md. lawyers Dole for Pres., 1986-87; counsel Forest Glen Park Civic Assn., Montgomery County, Md., 1981-84, Colo. Fed. Jud. Selection Com., 2001—; bd. trustees Grand Canyon Trust, 2004—. Fellow Am. Coll. Trial Lawyers (com. on fed. criminal procedure); mem. ABA, Internat. Bar Assn., Harvard Alumni Assn. (bd. dirs. 1990-92), Congress of Fellows Ctr. for Internat. Legal Studies. Republican. Office: Hogan & Hartson LLP 555 13th St NW Ste 800 E Washington DC 20004-1161 also: Hogan & Hartson LLP One Tabor Ctr 1200 17th St Ste 1500 Denver CO 80202-5835 Office Phone: 202-637-6437, 303-899-7300. Office Fax: 202-637-5910. Business E-Mail: tcobb@hhlaw.com.

COBB, VIRGINIA HORTON, artist, educator; b. Oklahoma City, Nov. 23, 1933; d. Wayne and Ruth (Goodale) Horton; m. Bruce L. Cobb, Dec. 30, 1951 (div. 1985); children: Bruce Wayne, Julianna, William Stuart, M. Jerrold Friedman, 1988. Student, U. Colo., 1966-67, Community Coll., Denver, 1967; student of, William Schimmel, Ariz., 1965-66, Edgar Whitney, NYC, 1966, Chen Chi, 1974. Comml. artist and designer Ruth Horton Studios, Oklahoma City, 1954-63; instr. seminars, 1974—, N.Mex. Watercolor Soc., Albuquerque, 1976, Okla. Mus. Art, Oklahoma City, 1976, Upstairs Gallery Workshops, Arlington, Tex., 1977, 78, 79, 80, St. Louis Art Guild, 1980, Alaska Water Color Soc., Anchorage, 1981, Needham (Mass.) Art Center, 1981, N.C. Watercolor Soc., Charlotte, 1981, San Diego Watercolor Soc., 1981, S.C. Water Color Soc., Florence, 1981, Hawaii Water Color Soc., 1989, Trillium Workshops, Toronto, 1989, 90, Baffin Island, 1992, Maui, Hawaii, 1993, Vancouver Island, 1990, 91. Guest instr. Crafton Hills Coll. Master Seminars, Yucaipa, Calif., 1979, 80, 81, U. Alaska, Anchorage, 1981, Master Class/Santa Fe Painting Workshops/Friedman Cobb Studios, 1989—, Palos Verdes Art Ctr., 2007; guest lectr. Watermedia 2000, Houston; lectr. Sta. KRDO-TV, 1977, Francis Marion Coll., Florence, 1981, Sta. KAKM, Anchorage, 1981, Nat. Watercolor Soc., 2007, Studio Workshops, 2005, 2006, 2007; guest spkr. Watermedia, Houston, 2003. Author: Discovering The Inner Eye, 1988; author (with Jerrold Friedman) Alice...on bristol, 1996, (with Polly Hammett) Designsense, 2003; contbr. articles to art publs.; one-woman shows include Jack Meier Galleries, Houston, 1979-81, 83-85, San Juan Coll., 1995, Art Resources, St. Paul, 1988, Sturh Mus., Grand Island, Nebr., 1982; exhibited in group shows at Nat. Acad., 1982, 1985, NAD, NYC, 1978-81, San Bernardino (Calif.) County Mus., 1978, Nat. Watercolor Invitational, Rochester, NY, 1981, Rocky Mountain Nat. Watermedia Exhbt., Golden, Colo., 1978-79, 81, Albuquerque Mus. Art, 1985, Am. Watercolor Soc., 1985, Internat. Waters: A Touring Exhibit, Canada, 1991, USA, 1992, Great Britain, 1992, Scotland, 1993; represented in permanent collections, NAD, Jefferson County (Colo.) Public Libr., Foothills Art Ctr., Golden, Colo., St. Lawrence U., Canton, NY, N.Mex. Watercolor Soc., Albuquerque, Santa Fe Mus. Fine Arts. Recipient Foothills Art Ctr. award, 1976, Edgar Fox award Watercolor U.S.A., 1973, Denver award Rocky Mountain Nat. Exhbn., 1981, Am. Artist Achievement award, 1994. Mem. NAD (Walter Biggs Meml. award 1978, 81), Nat. Watercolor Soc. (Strathmore Paper Co. award 1975), Am. Watercolor Soc. (Paul B. Remmey Meml. award 1974, Arches Paper Co. award 1977, Edgar Whitney award 1978, Mary Pleishner Meml. award 1980, High Winds medal 1981, Silver medal of Honor 1983, guest demonstrator 1980, nat. juror 1981, Dolphin fellow 1982, juror Watercolor West 1990, Juror award 1999), N.Mex. Watercolor Soc. (hon.), Rocky Mountain Watermedia Soc. Personal E-mail: veacobb@yahoo.com.

COBBAN, WILLIAM AUBREY, paleontologist; b. Anaconda, Mont., Dec. 31, 1916; s. Ray Aubrey and Anastacia (McNulty) C.; m. Ruth Georgina Loucks, Apr. 15, 1942; children: Georgina, William, Robert. BA, U. Mont., 1940; PhD, Johns Hopkins U., 1949. Geologist Carter Oil Co., Tulsa, 1940—46; paleontologist U.S. Geol. Survey, Washington, 1948—92, emeritus scientist, 1992—. Contbr. numerous articles to profl. jours. Recipient Meritorious Svc. award Dept. Interior, 1974, Disting. Svc. award US Dept. Interior, 1986; honoree 6th Internat. Symposium, Cephalopods--Recent and Past, 2004, Dallas Peck Outstanding Sci. Emeritus award, US Geol. Survey, Denver, 2006. Fellow AAAS, Geol. Soc. Am.; mem. Soc. Econ. Paleontologists and Mineralogists (hon.; Disting. Pioneer Geologist award 1985, Raymond C. Moore Paleontology medal 1990), Rocky Mountain Assn. Geologists (hon.), Mont. Geol. Soc. (hon.), Wyo. Geol Assn. (hon.), Paleontol. Soc. Am. (Paleontol. medal 1985), Assn. Petroleum Geologists, Paleontol. Rsch. Inst. (Gilbert Harris award 1996), Rocky Mountain Assn. Geologists (Outstanding award 2001), Phi Beta Kappa, Sigma Xi. Republican. Mem. United Ch. of Christ. Office: US Geol Survey Federal Ctr PO Box 25046 # 980 Denver CO 80225 Office Phone: 303-236-5670.

COBBLE, JAMES WIKLE, chemistry professor; b. Kansas City, Mo., Mar. 15, 1926; s. Ray and Crystal Edith (Wikle) C.; m. Margaret Ann Zumwalt, June 9, 1949 (dec.); children—Catherine Ann, Richard James. Student, San Diego State Coll., 1942-44; BA, No. Ariz. U., 1946; MS, U. So. Calif., 1949; PhD, U. Tenn., 1952. Chemist Oak Ridge Nat. Lab., 1949-52; postdoctoral research asso. U. Calif., Berkeley, 1952-55, instr. dept. chemistry, 1954; asst. prof. dept. chemistry Purdue U., Lafayette, Ind., 1955-58, asso. prof., 1958-61, prof., 1961-73; prof., dean Grad. div. San Diego State U., 1973—; v.p. rsch., dean Grad. divsn. San Diego State U., 1997—. Cons. in field. Contbr. articles to sci. publs. Mem. bd. visitors USAF Air Univ., 1984—92, chmn., 1988—90; vpres. San Diego State Univ. Found., 1975—; trustee Calif. Western Law Sch., 1987—93; mem. Joint Grad. Bd., 1973—78; Lt. (j.g.) USNR, 1945—46. Recipient E.O. Lawrence award U.S. AEC, 1970, Disting. Svc. award USAF, 1992; Guggenheim fellow, 1966; Robert A. Welch Found. lectr., 1971. Fellow Am. Inst. Chemists, Am. Phys. Soc.; mem. Am. Chem. Soc., Sigma Xi, Phi Kappa Phi, Alpha Chi Sigma, Phi Lambda Upsilon. Home: 1380 Park Row La Jolla CA 92037-3709

COBBS, PRICE MASHAW, social psychiatrist; b. LA, Nov. 2, 1928; s. Peter Price and Rosa (Mashaw) C.; m. Evadne Priester, May 30, 1957 (dec. Oct. 1973); children: Price Priester, Marion Renata; m. Frederica Maxwell, May 26, 1985 AB, U. Calif.-Berkeley, 1953; MD, Meharry Med. Coll., 1958. Intern San Francisco Gen. Hosp., 1958-59; psychiat. resident Mendocino State Hosp., Talmage, Calif., 1959-61, Langley Porter Neuro-Psychiat. Inst., San Francisco, 1961-62; pres., CEO Pacific Mgmt. Systems, San Francisco, 1967—; CEO Cobbs, Inc. Mgmt. cons. in workforce diversity numerous cos., govt. agys. and community projects; conducted seminars UN, Dept. State; guest lectr. leading colls. and univs.; chair 1st Ann. Nat. Diversity Conf., San Francisco, 1991; speaker 1st Internat. Diversity Conf., Johannesburg, South Africa, 1991; vis. cons., lectr. workforce diversity, South Africa, 1993; co-founder, pres. Renaissance Books, Inc.; adv. bd. Black Scholar. Author: My American Life: From Rage to Entitlement, 2005, (with William H. Grier) Black Rage, 1968, The Jesus Bag, 1971, (with Judith L. Turnock) Cracking the Corporate Code: From Survival to Mastery, 2000; contbr. State of Black America 1988, 89. Bd. dirs. Shared Interest; founding mem. Diversity Collegium. Served to cpl. U.S. Army, 1951-53 Recipient Pathfinder award Assn. Humanistic Psychology, 1993, Al Martins Heritage award, The Exec. Leadership Coun., Harvey Russell award, PepsiCo, 2003. Fellow Am. Psychiat. Assn.; mem. Nat. Med. Assn., NAACP (life), Nat. Acad. Scis.; charter mem. Nat. Urban League. Achievements include pioneering in discipline of ethnotherapy to understand differences in race, culture and ethnicity. Office: Pacific Mgmt System 3528 Sacramento St San Francisco CA 94118-1850 Personal E-mail: cozycobbs@aol.com.

COBLENTZ, CASSANDRA, curator; BA in Art History and English, Cornell U., Ithaca, NY, 1996; MA, Bard Coll., Annandale-on-Hudson, NY, 2002. Asst. gallery dir. Kohn Turner Gallery, LA, 1997—98, Gallery Contemporary Photography, Santa Monica, Calif., 1998—99; project coord., sch. and tchr. divsn. J. Paul Getty Mus., LA, 1999—2000; visitors svcs., edn. asst. Dia Ctr. for Arts, NYC, 2001—02; curatorial fellow Fabric Workshop and Mus., Phila., 2002—03; head, acad. initiatives UCLA Hammer Mus., 2003—05; asst. curator Scottsdale Mus. Contemporary Art, Ariz., 2005—07, assoc. curator, 2007—. Gallery tchr. J. Paul Getty Mus., 1997—2000. Contbr. articles to profl. publs. Office: Scottsdale Mus Contemporary Art 7380 E Second St Scottsdale AZ 85251 Office Phone: 480-874-4637. Business E-Mail: cassandrac@sccarts.org.

COBURN, LAWRENCE, Internet company executive; BA, Georgetown U., 1991; MBA, Emory U., 1995. Dir. human resources Nortel, Brazil; mgr. network solutions Nortel Networks; dir. human resources Larscom, 2002; founder, pres. RateItAll, Inc., San Francisco, 1999—. Office: RateItAll, Inc 3338 17th St, Ste 206 San Francisco CA 94110 Office Phone: 415-626-6645. E-mail: lawrence@rateitall.com.

COBURN, ROBERT CRAIG, philosopher, educator; b. Mpls., Jan. 25, 1930; s. William Carl and Esther Therice C.; m. Martha Louise Means, July 12, 1974. BA, Yale U., 1951; BD, U. Chgo., 1954; MA, PhD, Harvard U., 1958. Asst. prof. philosophy U. Chgo., 1960-65, assoc. prof., 1965-68, prof., 1968-71; prof. philosophy U. Wash., Seattle, 1971—2005, emeritus prof. philosophy, 2005—. Vis. assoc. prof. philosophy Cornell U., 1966, U. Bergen, Norway, spring 1986; condr. NEH summer seminar, 1983; cons. ERDA. Author: The Strangeness of the Ordinary: Issues and Problems in Contemporary Metaphysics, 1989; contbr. articles to philos. jours., chpts. to books. Ordained elder Rocky Mountain Conf. United Methodist Ch. Andrew Mellon postdoctoral fellow in philosophy U. Pitts., 1961-62; NSF grantee, 1968-69 Mem. Am. Philos. Assn. (exec. com. Pacific div. 1973-74), AAUP, Soc. Values in Higher Edn., Phi Beta Kappa. Home: 6852 28th Ave NE Seattle WA 98115-7145

COCCHIARELLA, VICKI MARSHALL, state legislator; b. Livingston, Mont., Dec. 19, 1949; d James Marshall & Ruth E Officer M; married to 1973 to Larry Ray Cocchiarella; children: Cara Jo & Michael James. Montana State Representative, District 59, 1989-94, District 64, 1995-99, Minority Leader, formerly, Montana House Representative; Montana State Senator, District 47, 1999-, Montana State Senate.Property manager, 1975-; teaching asst, Univ Montana, 1979-80, administration clerk, 1981-93; claims adjuster, Worker's Compensation, 1993-. Democrat. Address: 535 Livingston Missoula MT 59801 Mailing: State Capitol Helena MT 59620 Home Phone: 406-728-7723; 406-543-1296; Office Phone: 406-444-4800.

COCHRAN, JAMES ALAN, emeritus mathematics professor, department chairman, dean; b. San Francisco, May 12, 1936; s. Commodore Shelton and Gwendolyn Audrey (Rosenau) C.; m. Katherine Koehler Kern, Sept. 6, 1958; children: Cynthia Royal, Sarah Lynn. BS in Physics, Stanford U., 1956, MS in Physics, 1957, PhD in Math., 1962. Mem. tech. staff, supr. applied math. Bell Telephone Labs. Inc, Whippany, NJ, 1962-72; prof. math. Va. Poly. Inst. and State U., Blacksburg, 1972-78; prof., chmn. dept. math. Wash. State U., Pullman, 1978-84, prof., 1978-89, prof. math. Richland, Wash., 1999—2003, prof. emeritus, 2003—, campus exec. officer and founding dean tri-cities, 1989-98; staff assoc. First Presbyn. Ch., Kennewick, Wash., 2001—. Vis. prof. math. Stanford U., 1968-69, Wash. State U., 1977, U. NSW, Sydney, Australia, 1985, Southeast U., Nanjing, China, 1994; fgn. scholar math. and mechanics Nanjing Inst. Tech., 1984; vis. fellow Deakin U., Victoria, Australia, 1985, 87. Author: Analysis of Linear Integral Equations, 1972, Applied Mathematics: Principles, Techniques, and Applications, 1982, Advanced Engineering Mathematics, 1987; also articles. Mem. nat. coun. Boy Scout Am., 1973-76, 99-2001, mem. local coun., 1974-77, 82-84, 93—, coun. pres., 1999-2001, mem. western region, 1996-02; chmn. bd. commrs. Morris County (N.J.) Area Libr. Sys., 1971-72; mem. bd. dirs. Tri-Cities Sci. and Tech. Park Assn., 1990-2003, chmn., 1990-93; bd. dirs. Wash. Environ. Industry Assn., 1990-95, TRIDEC, 1996-2001; dir. state bd. Math. Engring. Sci. Achievement, 1992-2001; mem. Am. Pub. TV Stas. Bd., 1992-96; exec. com. Tri-Cities Commercialization Partnership, 1993-97; mem. Hanford Adv. Bd., 1994-2003; sr. advisor Tri-Cities Corp. Coun. for the Arts, 1991-2000; bd. trustees Tri-Cities Prep Found., 2003—. Recipient Silver Beaver award Boy Scouts Am., 1997, Disting. Eagle Scout award, 1997, Founders award Wash. State U., Tri Cities, 2003, God and Svc. award Presbyn. Ch. U.S.A., 2004; fellow: Paul Harris fellow, Rotary Internat., 2008; Gordon vis. fellow, Deakin U., Victoria, Australia, 1985. Mem. Am. Math. Soc., Math. Assn. Am., Soc. Indsl. Applied Math., Nat. Eagle Scout Assn. (young man pres. 1957-58, adviser 1958-71, Disting. Service award 1976), Phi Beta Kappa, Sigma Xi, Golden Key, Alpha Phi Omega. Republican. Presbyterian. Home: 1927 Cypress Pl Richland WA 99354-2414 Office: First Presbyn Ch 2001 W Kennewick Ave Kennewick WA 99336 Personal E-mail: cochran.ja@gmail.com.

COCHRAN, JOHN HOWARD, plastic and reconstructive surgeon; b. Muncie, Ind., Sept. 6, 1946; s. John H. and Lois M. (Woolridge) C.; m. Elizabeth M. Cochran; 1 child, Ryan K. BS cum laude, Colo. State U., 1968; MD, U. Colo. Sch. Medicine, 1973. Intern surgery U. Calif., San Diego, 1973-74; resident head and neck surgery Stanford U., Palo Alto, Calif., 1974-77; resident plastic surgery U. Wis., Madison, 1979-81; pvt. practice plastic surgery Denver, 1981-90; chief plastic surgery St. Joseph Hosp., Denver, 1987-93, Colo. Med. Group, Denver, 1990-95; chmn. dept. surgery St. Joseph Hosp., 1993-99; exec. med. dir. Med. Group, Denver. Pres. bd. trustees Kilimanjaro Children's Hosp. Tanzania, E. Africa, 1989—. Fellow Am. Soc. Plastic and Reconstructive Surgery, Am. Coll. SUrgeons, Acad. Otolaryngology, Head and Neck Surgery; mem. Am. Assn. Plastic Surgeons. Avocations: fly fishing, skiing. Office: 10350 E Dakota Ave Denver CO 80231-1314

COCHRAN, STEVE, lawyer; b. LA, Mar. 18, 1957; BA, U. Calif., Santa Cruz, 1979; JD, U. Calif., Berkeley, 1982. Bar: Calif. 1982, US Dist Ct. 1983, Ctrl. Dist. Calif., US Ct. Appeals, Ninth Cir. 1986, US Dist. Ct., Ea. Dist. Calif. 1991. Law clk. Hon. William P. Gray Ctrl. Dist. of Calif.; extern clk. Hon. Cecil F. Poole U.S. Ct. Appeals, 9th Cir.; ptnr. Katten Muchin Rosenman, LA, 1991—. Mem. adv. bd. Nat. Circuit Judicial Conf. Mem. adv. bd. 9th Cir. Jud. Conf., 2004—. Mem.: LA Criminal Cts. Bar Assn., Calif. Attys. Criminal Justice, State Bar of Calif. Office: Katten Muchin Rosenman Ste 2600 2029 Century Park E Los Angeles CA 90067-3012 Office Phone: 310-788-4455. Office Fax: 310-712-8455. Business E-Mail: steve.cochran@kattenlaw.com.

COCHRAN, SUSAN MILLS, research librarian; b. Grinnell, Iowa, Nov. 21, 1949; d. Lawrence Omen and Louise Jane (Morgan) Mills; m. Stephen E. Cochran, July 1, 1972; children: Bryan, Jeremy. Libr. Iowa Geneal. Soc., Des Moines, 1987-96; rsch. libr. Royal Gorge Regional Mus. & History Ctr. (formerly Local History Ctr., Canon City Pub. Libr.), Colo., 1997—. Editor: Mingo, Iowa 1884-1984, 1984; contbr. articles to profl. jours. Past mem. Jasper County Cemetery Commn., Newton; mem. Jasper County His. Soc.; past bd. dirs. Jasper County Libr., Newton, Iowa. Mem. Iowa Geneal. Soc., Jasper County Geneal. Soc. Avocations: genealogy, history, birding. Office: Royal Gorge Regional Mus & History Ctr 612 Royal Gorge Blvd Canon City CO 81212 Address: PO Box 1460 Canon City CO 81215 Office Phone: 719-269-9036. E-mail: historycenter@canoncity.org.

COCHRAN, WENDELL ALBERT, science editor; b. Carthage, Mo., Nov. 29, 1929; s. Wendell Albert and Lillian Gladys (Largent) C.; m. Agnes Elizabeth Groves, Nov. 9, 1963; remarried Corinne Frances Des Jardins, Aug. 25, 1980. AB, U. Mo., Columbia, 1953, A.M. in Geology, 1956, B.J., 1960. Geologist ground-water br. U.S. Geol. Survey, 1956-58; reporter, copyeditor Kansas City Star, Mo., 1960-63; editor Geotimes and Earth Sci. mags., Geospectrum newsletter, Alexandria, Va., 1963-84; v.p. Geol. Survey Inc., Bethesda, Md., 1984-86; tech. editor Okla. Geol. Survey, 1998—2006; freelance editor, cons., 2006—. Co-author: Into Print: A Practical Guide to Writing, Illustrating, and Publishing, 1977; sr. editor: Geowriting: A Guide to Writing, Editing and Printing in Earth Science, 1973; contbr. articles to profl. jours. and encys. Mem. Earth Sci. Editors (Outstanding Contbns. award 1982), Dog in the Night-time. Home: 4351 SW Willow St Seattle WA 98136-1769 Office Phone: 206-932-8227. Personal E-mail: atrypa@eskimo.com.

COCHRAN, WILLIAM MICHAEL, librarian; b. Nevada, Iowa, May 6, 1952; s. Joseph Charles and Inez (Larson) Cochran; m. Diane Marie Ohm, July 24, 1971. BLS, U. Iowa, Iowa City, 1979, MA with distinction in Libr. Sci., 1983; MA in Pub. Adminstrn., Drake U., Des Moines, Iowa, 1989. Dir. Red Oak Pub. Libr., Iowa, 1984; patron svcs. libr. Pub. Libr. of Des Moines, 1984-87; LSCA program coord. State Libr. of Iowa, Des Moines, 1987-88, dir. libr. devel., 1988-89, asst. state libr., 1989-90; dir. Parmly Billings Libr., 1990—. Mem. White House Conf. on Libr. and Info. Svcs. Mem. mayor's com. on homelessness, 2006—. Mem.: Mont. Ctr. for Book Adv. Com., Libr. Adminstrn. and Mgmt. Assn., Pub. Libr. Assn., Mont. Gov.'s Blue Ribbon Telecommunications Task Force, Mont. Libr. Assn. (pres. 1998—99, named Libr. of Yr. 1998), ALA, Beta Phi Mu. Office: Parmly Billings Libr 510 N Broadway Billings MT 59101-1156

COCKRUM, WILLIAM MONROE, III, investment banker, educator; b. Indpls., July 18, 1937; s. William Monroe C. II and Katherine J. (Jaqua) Moore; children: Catherine Anne Cockrum Dean, William Monroe IV AB with distinction, DePauw U., 1959; MBA with distinction, Harvard U., 1961. With A.G. Becker Paribas Inc., LA, 1961-84, mgr. nat. corp. fin. div., 1968-71, mgr. pvt. investments, 1971-74, fin. and adminstrv. officer, 1974-80, sr. v.p., 1975-78, vice chmn., 1978-84; prin. William M. Cockrum & Assocs., LA, 1984—; faculty Northwestern U., 1961—63. Vis. lectr. Anderson Grad. Sch. Mgmt. UCLA, 1984—88, adj. prof., 1988—; vis. prof. Warwick U., England, 2004—, Cranfield U., England, 2006—. Mem. Deke Club (NYC), UCLA Faculty Club, Alisal Golf Club (Solvang, Calif.), Bel-Air Country Club (LA), Delta Kappa Epsilon. E-mail: bcockrum@anderson.ucla.edu.

CODON, DENNIS P., lawyer; V.p., gen. counsel, corp. sec. Unocal Corp., LA, 1999—.

COE, ROBERT CAMPBELL, retired surgeon; b. Seattle, Nov. 14, 1918; s. Herbert Everett and Lucy Jane (Campbell) C.; m. Josephine Austin Weiner, Mar. 24, 1942; children: Bruce Everett, Virginia Austin, Matthew Daniel. BS, U. Wash., 1940; MD, Harvard U., 1950. Diplomate: Am. Bd. Thoracic Surgery, Am. Bd. Surgery. Intern Mass. Gen. Hosp., Boston, 1950-51, asst. resident, 1951-54, chief surg. resident, 1955, chief surg. clinics, 1956; instr. surgery Med. Sch. Harvard U., 1956; pvt. practice medicine specializing in thoracic and vascular surgery Seattle, 1957-84. Hon. mem. staff Children's Hosp.; attending surgeon Swedish Hosp.; cons. thoracic surgeon Firland Sanitarium, Seattle, 1957-68, Children's Hosp. Tumor Clinic, 1968-84; mng. ptnr. Invex & Inpark med. offices, Seattle, 1970-88; clin. prof. U. Wash., 1973-2000; mem. Wash. State Med. Disciplinary Bd., 1981-86; chmn. med. adv. bd. Physio-control. div. Eli Lilly, 1979-85;

pres. 1st Mercer (Wash.) Corp., 1969-73, 80-91, treas., 1973-80; owner, operator Hidden Valley Guest Ranch Cle Elum, Wash., 1969-93; developer Kula Estate, Maui, Hawaii; treas. 13th Internat. Cancer Congress. Editor: King County Med. Soc. Bull, 1964-70; mem. adv. bd. Pacific N.W. Mag. 1968-85; contbr. articles to profl. jours. Mem. Mayor's Harbor Adv. Com., 1958-61; chmn. bd. N.W. Seaport, Inc., hist. mus. Seattle, 1974-75; mem. Mercer Island City Coun., 1988-92. With USNR, 1941-46. Decorated Bronze Star, Presdl. Unit citation. Fellow ACS; mem. North Pacific Surg. Assn. (sr. mem.), Pacific Coast Surg. Assn. (sr. mem.), King County Med. Soc. (jud. coun. 1972-78, chmn. 1976-78), Seattle Surg. Soc. (pres. 1969), Psi Upsilon, Seattle Yacht Club, Cruising of Am. Club (bd. govs. 1992-95). Episcopalian. Home: 12600 SE 38th St Ste 240 Bellevue WA 98006-6112

COEN, ETHAN, film director, writer; b. Saint Louis Park, Minn., Sept. 21, 1957; married. Student in Philosophy, Princeton U. Former statis. typist Macy's, NYC. Screenwriter (with Joel Coen) Crime Wave (formerly XYZ Murders); prodr.: (films) Blood Simple, 1984, Raising Arizona, 1987, Miller's Crossing, 1990, Barton Fink, 1991 (Palme D'Or award, Best Dir. award, Cannes Internat. Film Festival, 1996), The Hudsucker Proxy, 1994, Fargo, 1996 (Best Dir. award, Cannes Internat. Film Festival, 1996, Acad. award for Best Screenplay, 1997, CFCA award for Best Screenplay, 1997, Golden Satellite award for Best Motion Picture, 1997, Ind. Spirit award for Best Feature, 1997, WGA Screen award for Best Screenplay, 1997), The Big Lebowski, 1998, The Naked Man, 1998; writer, dir., prodr. (films) O Brother, Where Art Thou?, 2000, The Man Who Wasn't There, 2001, Intolerable Cruelty, 2003, The Ladykillers, 2004, No Country for Old Men, 2007 (Best Adapted Screenplay award, Nat. Bd. Review, 2007, Best Screenplay, Best Director & Best Picture awards, NY Film Critics Circle, 2007, Best Picture, Boston Soc. Film Critics, 2007, Critics Choice award, Broadcast Film Critics Assn., 2008, Golden Globe award for Best Screenplay/Motion Picture, 2008, Outstanding Directorial Achievement in Feature Film, Directors Guild of America, 2008, Best Feature Film, Producers Guild of America, 2008, Best Dir., Brit. Acad. Film and TV Arts, 2008, Best Adapted Screenplay, Writers Guild of America, 2008, Acad. awards for Best Adapted Screenplay, Best Directing, Best Picture, 2008), Burn After Reading, 2008, writer, dir. Paris, I Love You, 2006; exec. prodr.: (films) Down From the Mountain, 2000; writer (films) A Fever in the Blood, 2002, Bad Santa, 2003, Romance & Cigarettes, 2005. Named one of The 100 Most Influential People in the World, TIME mag., 2008. Fellow: Am. Acad. Arts & Scis. Office: care UTA c/o Jim Berkus 9560 Wilshire Blvd Beverly Hills CA 90212-2427

COEN, JOEL, film director, writer; b. Saint Louis Park, Minn., Nov. 29, 1954; s. Ed and Rena Coen. Student, Simon's Rock Coll.; student in film, NYU. Screenwriter (with Ethan Coen) Crime Wave (formerly XYZ Murders), Writer, dir. (films) The Man Who Wasn't There, 2001, Intolerable Cruelty, 2003, Paris, I Love You, 2006, dir., screenwriter Blood Simple, 1984, Raising Arizona, 1987, Miller's Crossing, 1990, Barton Fink, 1991 (Palme D'Or award, Best Dir. award, Cannes Internat. Film Festival, 1991), The Hudsucker Proxy, 1994 (Ind. Spirit award for Best Feature, 1997), Fargo, 1996 (Best Dir. award, Cannes Internat. Film Festival, 1996, CFCA award for Best Screenplay, 1997, Golden Satellite award for Best Motion Picture, 1997, WGA Screen award for Best Screenplay, 1997, Acad. award for Best Screenplay, 1997), The Big Lebowski, 1998, O Brother, Where Art Thou?, 2000; exec. prodr.: (films) Down From the Mountain, 2000, Bad Santa, 2003, Romance & Cigarettes, 2005; writer, prodr., dir. (films) The Ladykillers, 2004, No Country for Old Men, 2007 (Best Adapted Screenplay award, Nat. Bd. Review, 2007, Best Screenplay, Best Director & Best Picture awards, NY Film Critics Circle, 2007, Best Picture, Boston Soc. Film Critics, 2007, Critics Choice award, Broadcast Film Critics Assn., 2008, Golden Globe award for Best Screenplay/Motion Picture, 2008, Outstanding Directorial Achievement in Feature Film, Directors Guild of America, 2008, Best Feature Film, Producers Guild of America, 2008, Best Dir., Brit. Acad. Film and TV Arts, 2008, Best Adapted Screenplay, Writers Guild of America, 2008, Acad. awards for Best Adapted Screenplay, Best Directing, Best Picture, 2008), Burn After Reading, 2008. Named one of The 100 Most Influential People in the World, TIME mag., 2008. Fellow: Am. Acad. Arts & Scis. Office: United Talent Agy c/o Jim Berkus 9560 Wilshire Blvd Fl 5 Beverly Hills CA 90212-2400

COERPER, GIL, Councilman, Huntington Beach, California; b. Kennosha, Wis. m. Louann Coerper; children: Michael, Scott. Officer Huntington Beach Police Dept., 1963—2002; admissions coord. LA & Orange counties US Mil. Acad., West Point; adv. Boy Scouts Am. Mil. Explorer Post 558, Calif.; exec. bd. adv. Huntington Beach Search & Rescue Explorer Post; mayor City of Huntington Beach, 2006—08, councilman, 2002—. Chmn. Third Battalion First Marine Regiment Com.; mem. Downtown Econ. Devel., Neighborhood Watch, Oakview Task Force, Intergovernmental Rels., Santa Ana Blue Ribbon, Competitive Svcs., Animal Care Svcs., Beautification, Landscape, & Tree coms. Rep. Southern Calif. Assn. Govts. Cmty., Econ. & Human Devel. com., Calif. League Cities Public Safety, Housing, Cmty. & Econ. Devel. Policy coms., League Cities, Orange County Div., Public Safety, Housing, Cmty. & Econ. Devel. Policy coms., Orange County Transp. Authority I-405 Project & Citizen's Adv. coms., Orange County Vet. Adv. Commn. With USN, Korea (1950-1952), ret. lt. col. Calif. Mil. Res. Recipient Merit award, Boy Scouts of America Exploring Div., 2004, Silver Beaver award, 2004. Mem.: Huntington Beach Police Officers Assn. (former pres.), Calif. Police Officers Rsch. Assn. (former dir.), Calif. Peace Officers Meml. Found. (adv.). Office: City Hall 200 Main St Huntington Beach CA 92648 Office Phone: 714-536-5553. Fax: 714-536-5233. E-mail: glcoerp1@gte.net.*

COFFIN, BOB, state legislator; b. Anaheim, Calif., Oct. 7, 1942; m. Mary Coffin; children: James, Walter, Anna Maria. BS in Bus. Adminstr. & Acctg., UNLV. Antiquarian book dealer; ins. broker; mem. Nev. State Assembly, 1982—85, Nat. Conf. of State Legislatures' Del. to Costa Rica, 1985; internat. observer Nicaraguan Elections, 1990; owner Bob Coffin Ins., 1969—, Bob Coffin Books, 1989—; mem. Clark County Dist. 5 Nev. State Senate, 1986—. With USAR, 1962. Democrat. Office: 401 South Carson St Room 2128 Carson City NV 89701 also: 1139 5th Pl Las Vegas NV 89104-1413 Office Phone: 775-684-1427, 702-384-9501. Business E-Mail: bcoffin@sen.state.nv.us.

COFFIN, JAMES ROBERT, state legislator, small business owner; b. Anaheim, Calif., Oct. 7, 1942; m. Mary Hausch; children: James, Walter, Anna Marie. BS in Acctg. and Bus. Adminstrn., U. Nev., Las Vegas, 1969. Owner Bob Coffin Ins., Las Vegas, 1969—, Bob Coffin Books, Las Vegas, 1989—; mem. Nev. Assembly, 1983-86, Nev. Senate, Dist. 3 Clark County, 1986—; mem. fin. com., taxation com., natural resources com. Nev. State Senate. Chair Western Legis. Conf. Annual Meeting, 1993. With USAR, 1962. Named Man of Yr. Nev. Women's Polit. Caucus, 1995. Mem. Nat. Fedn. Ind. Bus., Nat. Conf. State Legislatures (invitational com. Am. Leadership Conf.), U. Nev. Las Vegas Alumni Assn., Latin C. of C. Nev. (bd. dirs.), Las Vegas C. of C., Sigma Alpha Epsilon. Democrat. Home: 1139 5th Pl Las Vegas NV 89104-1413 Office: Nev State Legis Bldg 401 S Carson St Rm 203 Las Vegas NV 89104-1413 E-mail: bcoffin@sen.state.nv.us.

COFFIN, JUDY SUE, lawyer; b. Beaumont, Tex., Aug. 17, 1953; d. Richard Wilson and Genie (Mouton) C.; m. Gary P. Scholick, Nov. 10, 1983; children: Jennie Sue, Kate Frances. BA, U. Tex., 1974; JD, So. Meth. U., 1976. Bar: Tex. 1977, Calif. 1982. Atty. NLRB, Tex., 1977-80; shareholder Littler Mendelson, San Francisco, 1980-99, also bd. dirs.; sr. counsel, employment and labor law Cath. Healthcare West, San Francisco, Calif., 2000—. Office: Catholic Healthcare West CHW 185 Berry St Ste 300 San Francisco CA 94107-1773 E-mail: jcoffin@chw.edu.

COFFIN, THOMAS M., federal magistrate judge; b. St. Louis, May 30, 1945; s. Kenneth C. and Agnes M. (Ryan) C.; m. Penelope Teaff, Aug. 25, 1973; children: Kimberly, Laura, Colleen, Corey, Mary, Brendan, T.J. BA, St. Benedict's Coll., 1967; JD, Harvard, 1970. Bar: Mo. 1970, Calif. 1972, Oreg. 1982, U.S. Dist. Ct. (so. dist.) Calif. 1971, U.S. Dist. Ct. Oreg. 1980, U.S. Ct. Appeals (9th cir.) 1971. Asst. U.S. atty., chief criminal divsn. U.S. Attys. Office, San Diego, 1971-80, asst. U.S. atty., supr. asst. U.S. atty. Eugene, Oreg., 1980-92; U.S. Magistrate judge U.S. Dist. Ct., Eugene, Oreg., 1992—. Sr. litigation counsel U.S. Dept. Justice, 1984. Mem. Oreg. Bar Assn. Avocations: soccer, jogging. Office: US Dist Ct 211 E 7th Ave Eugene OR 97401-2774

COFFINGER, MARALIN KATHARYNE, retired career officer, consultant; b. Ogden, Iowa, July 5, 1935; d. Cleo Russell and Katharyne Frances (McGovern) Morse. BA, Ariz. State U., 1957, MA, 1962; diploma, Armed Forces Staff Coll., 1972, Nat. War Coll., 1977; postgrad., Inst. for Higher Def. Studies, 1985. Commd. 2nd lt. USAF, 1963, advanced through grades to brig. gen., 1985; base comdr., dep. base comdr. Elmendorf AFB, Anchorage, Alaska, 1977-79; base comdr. Norton AFB, San Bernardino, Calif., 1979-82; chmn. spl. and incentive pays Office of Sec. Def., Pentagon, Washington, 1982-83; dep. dir. pers. programs USAF Hdqrs., Pentagon, Washington, 1983-85; command dir. NORAD, Combat Ops., Cheyenne Mountain Complex, Colo., 1985-86; dir. pers. plans USAF Hdqrs., Pentagon, Washington, 1986-89; ret. USAF, 1989; dir. software products ops. Walsh America, 1992-94. Mem. Phoenix Symphony Orch., 1954—63; prin. flutist Sonoran Wind Quartet, Scottsdale Cmty. Orch. Band, Scottsdale Concert Band, Ariz.; keynote spkr., mem. dedication ceremonies Vietnam Meml. Com., Phoenix, 1990. Decorated Air Force D.S.M., Def. Superior Svc. medal, Legion of Merit, Bronze Star.; recipient Nat. Medal of Merit. Mem. NAFE, Air Force Assn. (vet./retiree coun., pres. Sky Harbor chpt. 1990), Mil. Officers' Assn. Am., Maricopa County Sheriff's Exec. Posse, Ariz. State U. Alumni Assn. (Profl. Excellence award 1981), Nat. Assn. Uniformed Svcs., Recording for the Blind and Dyslexic, Joe Foss Inst. (advisory bd.). Roman Catholic. Home: 8059 E Maria Dr Scottsdale AZ 85255-5418 E-mail: mkcoffinger@cox.net.

COFFMAN, DENNY, state legislator; m. Bonnie Coffman; children: Amy, Katie. BA in Bus. Adminstrn. Mem. Dist. 6 Hawaii House of Reps., 2008—. Founding dir. Cmty. Enterprises; mem. La'aloa Connector Rd. Adv. Group. Democrat. Office: State Capitol 415 S Beretania St Rm 317 Honolulu HI 96813 Office Phone: 808-586-9605. Office Fax: 808-586-9608. Business E-Mail: repcoffman@capitol.hawaii.gov.

COFFMAN, MIKE (MICHAEL H. COFFMAN), United States Representative from Colorado, former state official; b. Ft. Leonard Wood, Mo., Mar. 19, 1955; s. Harold and Dorothy Coffman; m. Cynthia Coffman. B, U. Colo., 1979; student, Vaishnav Coll., India, U. Veracruz, Mexico; grad. Sr. Exec. Prog. State/Local Govt., Harvard U. John F. Kennedy Sch. Govt., 1995. Founder, pres. Colo. Property Mgmt. Grp., Inc., Aurora, 1983; mem. Colo. State Ho. of Reps., 1988—94, Colo. State Senate, 1994—98, chmn. fin. com.; treas. State of Colo., Denver, 1998—2006, sec. state, 2007—08; mem. US Congress from 6th Colo. Dist., 2009—. Mem. Univ. Park United Meth. Ch. Served in US Army, 1972—74 USAR, 1975—78, major USMC, 1979—82, served in USMCR, 1983—94, major USMC, 1994, civil officer USMC, 2005—06. Mem.: South Metro C. of C., Aurora C. of C., Am. Legion, Vets. of Fgn. Wars. Republican. Office: US Congress 1508 Longworth House Office Bldg Washington DC 20515-0606 also: Dist Office 9220 Kimmer Dr Ste 220 Lone Tree CO 80124 Office Phone: 202-225-7882, 720-283-9772. Office Fax: 202-226-4623, 720-283-9776.*

COFONI, PAUL MICHAEL, information technology executive; b. Westerly, RI, Oct. 14, 1948; s. Sylvester James and Sarah Eleanor (Castagna) Cofoni; m. Karen Sue Tapley, May 31, 1970; 2 children. BS in Math., U. R.I., 1970; student in Sr. Exec. Program, MIT, 1989. With Gen. Dynamics, 1974—91; from v.p. Tech. Mgmt. Group Ea. Region to pres. Tech. Mgmt. Group Computer Scis. Corp., El Segundo, Calif., 1991—2001, with, 2001—05, pres. Fed. Sector, 2001—05; pres. U.S. ops. CACI Internat. Inc., Arlington, Va., 2005—07, pres., CEO, 2007—. With US Army, 1970—74. Mem.: AIAA, Info. Tech. Assn. Am. (bd. dirs.), Armed Forces Comms. and Electronics Assn. (bd. dirs.), Nat. Def. Indsl. Assn. (bd. dirs.), The Bus. Roundtable. Office: CACI Internat Inc Three BallStrom Plz 1100 N Glebe Road Arlington VA 22201

COGDILL, DAVID, state legislator; b. Long Beach, Calif., Dec. 31, 1950; m Stephanie; children: David Jr & Meghan; two grandchildren. California State Assemblyman, District 25, formerly, vice chairman, Committee on Rules, formerly, member Comt: Budget, Agri & Joint Legislative Audit Committee, formerly, Minority Floor Leader, formerly, California State Assembly; board director, Bridgeport Fire Protection District, Mono Co; member, Modesto City Coun, 91-96; California State Senator, District 14, 2006-, California State Senate-.Real estate appriaser, chief appraiser, Mono Co, California Assessor's Off, 71-79; partner, Cogdill & Gioma, 81-; president, Bridgeport Sch PTA; board director, Stanislaus Co YMCA. Friend of Year Award, Hispanic Chamber of Commerce, 95; President Award, Stanislaus Co YMCA, 98; Legislative Leadership Award, California Bldg Industry Association, E Award for Excellence, Leadership Modesto, an affiliate of the Modesto Chamber of Commerce, Champion of the California Merit Shop Movement, Associated Builders and Contractors, Patti Mattingly Distinguished Legislative Award, Regional Council of Rural Counties, Assembly Member of the Year, California State Sheriffs™ Association, Legislator of the Year for 2004, California Forestry Association, Legislator of the Year, California Mobilehome Parkowners Alliance, Legislative Special Recognition Award, VFW, Legislator of the Year, California Women in Timber Association, Modesto Man of the Year, VFW. Republican. Office: State Capitol PO Box 942849 Rm 305 Sacramento CA 94249-0025 also: Dist 14 1308 West Main St Ste C Ripon CA 95366 Office Phone: 209-599-8540. Office Fax: 209-599-8547. Business E-Mail: Senator.Cogdill@senate.ca.gov.

COGGIN, CHARLOTTE JOAN, cardiologist, educator; b. Takoma Park, Md., Aug. 6, 1928; d. Benjamin and Nanette (McDonald) C. BA, Columbia Union Coll., 1948; MD, Loma Linda U., 1952, MPH, 1987; DSc (hon.), Andrews U., 1994. Diplomate Am. Bd. Pediatrics. Intern L.A. County Gen. Hosp., 1952-53, resident in medicine, 1953-55; fellow in cardiology Children's Hosp., LA, 1955-56, White Meml. Hosp., LA, 1955-56; rsch. assoc. in cardiology, house physician Hammersmith Hosp., London, 1956-57; resident in pediatrics and pediatric cardiology Hosp. for Sick Children, Toronto, Ont., Canada, 1965-67; cardiologist, asst. prof. medicine, co-dir. heart surgery team Loma Linda (Calif.) U., 1961-73, assoc. prof., 1973-91, prof. medicine, 1991—. Asst. dean. Sch. Medicine Internat. Program, 1973—75; v.p. for global outreach Loma Linda U. Health Scis. Ctr., 1998—; assoc. dean. Sch. Medicine Internat. Program, 1975—, spl. asst. to univ. pres. for interat. affairs, 1991; co-dir., cardiologist heart surgery team missions to, Pakistan and Asia, 63, Greece, 67, Greece, 69, Saigon, Vietnam, 1974—75, Saudi Arabia, 1976—87, China, 1984, China, 1989—91, Hong Kong, 1985, Zimbabwe, 88, Zimbabwe, 93, Kenya, 88, Nepal, 92, China, 92, Myanmar, 95, North Korea, 96. Author: Atrial Septal Defects, motion picture (Golden Eagle Cine award and 1st prize Venice Film Festival 1964); contbr. articles to med. jours. Recipient award for service to people of Pakistan City of Karachi, 1963, Medallion award Evangelismos Hosp., Athens, Greece, 1967, Gold medal of health South Vietnam Ministry of Health, 1974, Charles Elliott Weinger award for excellence, 1976, Wall Street Jour. Achievement award, 1987, Disting. Univ. Svc. award Loma Linda U., 1990; named Honored Alumnus Loma Linda U. Sch. Medicine, 1973, Outstanding Women in Gen. Conf. Seventh-day Adventists, 1975, Alumnus of Yr., Columbia Union Coll., 1984, Outstanding Achievement in Edn., Adventist Alumni Achievement award, 1999. Mem. AAUP, AAUW, Am. Coll. Cardiology, AMA (physicians adv. com. 1969—), Calif. Med. Assn. (com. on med. schs., com. on member svcs.), San Bernardino County Med. Soc. (chmn. comm. com. 1975-77, mem. comm. com, 1987-88, editor bull., 1975-76, William L. Cover, M.D. Outstanding Contbn. to Medicine award 1995), Am. Heart Assn., Med. Rsch. Assn. Calif., Calif. Heart Assn., Am. Acad. Pediatrics, World Affairs Coun., Internat. Platform Assn., Calif. Museum Sci. and Industry MUSES (Outstanding Woman of Yr. in Sci. 1969), Am. Med. Women's Assn., Loma Linda Sch. Medicine Alumni Assn. (pres. 1978), Alpha Omega Alpha, Delta Omega. Democrat. Home: 25052 Crestview Dr Loma Linda CA 92354-3415 Personal E-mail: jcoggin@verizon.net.

COGHILL, JOHN B., state legislator; b. Fairbanks, Alaska, Aug. 15, 1950; m. Luann Coghill; children: Shaun (John), Joshua, Jayme. Deleg, Republican Nat Conv, 96; Alaska State Representative, District 32, 1999-2002, co-chmn, Health, Education & Social Serv Committee, 99-, vice chairman, Special Committee on Mil & Vet Affairs, 99-, member, State Affairs Committee, 99-, Alaska House Representative; Alaska State Representative, District 11, 2003-, majority leader, 2003-06, Alaska House Representative. Concrete cutter, formerly; pastor's asst, currently; private sch history teacher, currently. Staff sgt. USAF. Republican. Avocations: carpentry, history. Mailing: 3340 Badger Rd Ste 290 North Pole AK 99705 Office: State Capitol Rm 214 Juneau AK 99801-1182 Office Phone: 907-465-3719, 907-488-5725. Office Fax: 907-465-3258, 907-488-4271. Business E-Mail: representative_john_coghill@legis.state.ak.us.*

COGHLAN, JOHN PHILIP, corporate financial executive; b. San Francisco; life ptnr. Tina Vindum; children: Kearney, Callan. BA in Psychology, with honors in social thought, Stanford U.; MA in Economics and Public Policy, Princeton U.; MBA, Harvard U. Founder, COO San Francisco Grocery Express. Ltd.; joined Charles Schwab & Co., 1986, gen. mgr. Schwab Instl., 1992—97, exec. v.p., 1992—2005, enterprise pres. retirement plan services, 1997—2001, enterprise pres. services for investment managers, 1998—2001, enterprise pres. Schwab Instl., 2001—02, vice chmn., 1999—2005, enterprise pres. individual investor's bus., 2002—05; pres. CEO Visa USA, 2005—. Bd. dirs. Success Metrics, San Francisco, CollectAmerica, Denver. Pres. bd. dirs. San Francisco Lighthouse for the Blind; bd. dirs. Glide Meml. Ch. Mem.: Internat. Bd. of Practices and Standards for Certified Financial Planners (Nat. Advisory Coun.). Office: Visa USA 900 Metro Center Blvd Foster City CA 94404

COGMAN, DON V., public relations executive; Grad. with honors, U. Okla. Chief of staff to US Senator Dewey Bartlett, 1972-76; v.p. govt. affairs MAPCO Inc., 1980-89; founder RCF Group, Washington, 1988—92; pres., CEO Washington region Burson-Marsteller, 1991-94; pres., CEO The Americas, 1995; vice-chmn., COO Burson-Marsteller Worldwide; pres., COO Burson-Marsteller, 1998—2000; exec. v.p. corp. affairs Young & Rubicam Inc., NYC, 2000; chmn. CC Investments LLC, Scottsdale, Ariz.; sr. counselor Feldman & Ptnrs., LA, 2007—. Bd. dir. Am. Coun. Young Polit. Leaders, White House Adv. Bd. on Pvt. Sector Iniatives; former pres. Vote Am. Found.; chmn. Nat. Fed. of Ind. Bus. Edn. Found.; mem., Nat. Coun. on the Arts Nat. Endowment for the Arts; bd. dir. Fund for am. Studies, Washington, Acting Co., NYC. Fellow: Hudson Inst.; mem.: Juilliard Ovation Soc. Office: Nat Endowment for the Arts 1100 Pennsylvania Ave NW Washington DC 20506-0001 also: Feldman & Ptnrs Ste 2000 8491 Sunset Blvd Los Angeles CA 90069 Office Phone: 310-360-0211. E-mail: don@feldmanandpartners.com.

COHAN, CHRISTOPHER J., professional sports team owner; b. Salinas, Calif., 1951; s. Helen; m. Angela Cohan; 3 children. BA, Ariz. State U., 1973. With Feather River Cable TV Corp., Orinda, Calif., 1973-77; founder, owner Sonic Comm., 1977—98; owner, CEO NBA Golden State Warriors, Calif., 1995—. Mem. adv./fin. com. NBA Bd. Govs. Founder Warriors Found., 1997—; established Ann. Angela and Christopher Cohan Cmty. Svc. Award, 2000. Office: Golden State Warriors 1011 Broadway Oakland CA 94607

COHEE, ROY G., state legislator; b. Billings, Mont., Sept. 16, 1949; m. Barbara Cohee; children: Sean, Shelly. Attended, Casper Coll., 1969. With City Transp. Co. Inc., 1966—, pres., 1986—; precinct committeeman, 1996—; mem. Dist. 35 Wyo. House of Reps., 1999—, Majority Fl. Leader, 2005—06, Spkr. of the House, 2007—08. Rotary;

Wyo. Trucking Assn.; Casper C of C; Casper Petroleum Club; Am. Trucking Assn.; Cowboy Joe Club; Casper Country Club. Republican. Catholic. Mailing: 2046 Rustic Drive Casper WY 82609 Office: 213 State Capitol Bldg Cheyenne WY 82002 also: PO Box 50098 Casper WY 82605 Home Phone: 307-237-7885; Office Phone: 307-777-7881, 307-266-1667. Office Fax: 307-777-5466, 307-473-8119. Business E-Mail: royc@alluretech.net. E-mail: royc@trib.com.*

COHEN, ALBERT, musician, educator; b. NYC, Nov. 16, 1929; s. Sol A. and Dora Cohen; m. Betty Joan (Berg), Aug. 28, 1952; children: Eva Denise, Stefan Berg. BS, Juilliard Sch. Music, 1951; MA, NYU, 1953, PhD, 1959; postgrad., U. Paris, 1956-57. Mem. faculty U. Mich., Ann Arbor, 1960-70, assoc. prof. music, 1964-67, prof., 1967-70; prof. music, chmn. dept. SUNY, Buffalo, 1970-73, Stanford U., 1973-87, William H. Bonsall prof. music, 1974—, prof. emeritus, 2000—. Editor: Broude Bros. Ltd., N.Y.C., Info. Coordinators, Detroit. Author: Treatise on the Composition of Music, 1962, Elements or Principles of Music, 1965; (with J.D. White) Anthology of Music for Analysis, 1965; (with L.E. Miller) Music in the Paris Academy of Sciences, 1666-1793, An Index, 1979, Music in the French Royal Academy of Sciences, 1981, Music in the Royal Society of London 1660-1806, 1987; editor: J.B. Lully, Ballet de Flore, 2001; contbr. articles to profl. jours. Guggenheim fellow, 1968-69; NEH fellow, 1975-76, 82-83, 85-89, Fulbright fellow, 1956-1957. Mem. Internat. Musicol Soc., Am. Musicol Soc., French Musicol Soc., Music Libr. Assn. Office: Stanford U Dept Music Stanford CA 94305

COHEN, ANDREW, news analyst, lawyer; b. Montreal; BA, Boston U., 1988, JD, 1991. Assoc. Gorsuch Kirgis, Boston, 1991; legal analyst, commentator CBS News Radio, 1997—, CBS News, CBS 4, Denver. Author: (law column) Gavel to Gavel, Bench Conference. Recipient S.P.J. Award for Best Spot News coverage. Office: CBS 4 1044 Lincoln St Denver CO 80203

COHEN, ARNOLD NORMAN, gastroenterologist; b. NYC, Nov. 5, 1949; s. Norman and Edna Clara (Arnold) C.; m. Colleen Ruth Carey; children: Eric Arnold, Leslie Carey. BA summa cum laude, Hobart Coll., 1971; MD, Harvard U., 1975. Diplomate Am. Bd. Internal Medicine, Am. Bd. Gastroenterology. Resident internal medicine U. Pa., Phila., 1975-78, asst. instr. medicine, 1977-78; fellow gastroenterology, instr. medicine Northwestern U., Chgo., 1978-80; asst. clin. prof. medicine U. Wash. Med. Sch., Seattle, 1980—2007; mem. faculty Spokane (Wash.) Family Medicine Residency, 1980—; pvt. practice gastroenterology Spokane, 1980—. Mem. various coms. St. Lukes-Deaconess Hosp., Spokane, 1980—; pres. med. staff St. Lukes Hosp., 1985-86; clin. assoc. prof., medicine U. Washington Sch. Medicine, 2007-. Contbr. articles to profl. jours. and textbooks. Fellow ACP, Am. Coll. Gastroenterology; mem. Am. Soc. Gastrointestinal Endoscopy, Am. Gastroent. Soc., Wash. Med. Soc., Spokane Internal Med. Soc., Phi Beta Kappa, Alpha Omega Alpha. Avocations: shooting sports, martial arts, swimming. Home: 3514 S Jefferson St Spokane WA 99203-1441 Office: Spokane Digestive Disease Ctr 801 W 5th Ave Spokane WA 99204-2823 Office Phone: 509-747-5145.

COHEN, CYNTHIA MARYLYN, lawyer; b. Bklyn., Sept. 5, 1945; AB, Cornell U., 1967; JD cum laude, NYU, 1970. Bar: NY 1971, US Ct. Appeals (2nd cir.) 1972, US Dist. Ct. (so. and ea. dists.) NY 1972, US Supreme Ct. 1975, US Dist. Ct. (ctrl. and no. dists.) Calif. 1980, US Ct. Appeals (9th cir.) 1980, US Dist. Ct. (so. dist.) Calif. 1981, US Dist. Ct. (ea. dist.) Calif. 1986. With Paul, Hastings, Janofsky & Walker LLP, LA, NYC. Bd. dirs. NY chpt. Am. Cancer Soc., 1977-80; active Pres.'s Coun. Cornell Women; lawyer rep. Ninth Cir. Jud. Conf. Recipient Am. Jurisprudence award for evidence, torts and legal instns., 1968-69; John Norton Pomeroy scholar NYU, 1968-70, Founders Day Cert., 1969. Mem. ABA, Assn. Bar City NY (trade regulation com. 1976-79), Assn. Bus. Trial Lawyers, Fin. Lawyers Conf., NY State Bar Assn. (chmn. class-action com. 1979), State Bar Calif., LA County Bar Assn., Order of Coif, Delta Gamma. Avocations: tennis, bridge, rare books, wines. Home: 4531 Dundee Dr Los Angeles CA 90027-1213 Office: Paul Hastings Janofsky & Walker LLP 515 S Flower St 25th Fl Los Angeles CA 90071 Home Phone: 323-663-1869; Office Phone: 213-683-6000. Business E-Mail: cynthiacohen@paulhastings.com.

COHEN, DANIEL MORRIS, museum administrator, marine biologist, researcher; b. Chgo., July 6, 1930; s. Leonard U. and Myrtle (Gertz) C.; m. Anne Carolyn Constant, Nov. 4, 1955; children—Carolyn A. Leech, Cynthia S. BA, Stanford U., 1952, MA, 1953, PhD, 1958. Asst. prof., curator fishes U. Fla., Gainesville, 1957-58; systematic zoologist Bur. Comml. Fisheries, Washington, 1958-60; dir. systematics lab. Nat. Marine Fisheries Service, Washington, 1960-81, sr. scientist Seattle, 1981-82; chief curator life scis. Los Angeles County Mus. of Natural History, 1982-93, dep. dir. rsch. and collections, 1993-95; emeritus, 1995—. Adj. prof. biology U. So. Calif., 1982-98. Contbr. numerous articles to profl. jours. Mem. adv. coun. Cordell Bank Nat. Marine Sanctuary. Fellow AAAS, Calif. Acad. Sci. (rsch. assoc.); mem. Am. Soc. Ichthyologists and Herpetologists (v.p. 1969, 70, pres. 1985, Gibbs award 1997), Biol. Soc. Washington (pres. 1971-72), Soc. Systematic Biology (mem. coun. 1976-78). Avocations: gardening, cooking, reading, hiking. Home: PO Box 192 Bodega Bay CA 94923-0192 Home Phone: 707-875-9285. Business E-Mail: dmco@monitor.net.

COHEN, ELAINE HELENA, pediatrician, cardiologist, educator; b. Boston, Oct. 14, 1941; d. Samuel Clive and Lillian (Stocklan) C.; m. Marvin Leon Gale, May 7, 1972; 1 child, Pamela Beth Gale. AB, Conn. Coll., 1963; postgrad., Tufts U., 1963—64; MD, Woman's Med. Coll. Pa., 1969. Diplomate Am. Bd. Pediat. Pediat. intern Children's Hosp. of L.A., 1969-70, resident in pediat., 1970-71; fellow in pediat. cardiology UCLA Ctr. Health Scis., 1971-72, L.A. County/U. So. Calif. Med. Ctr., LA, 1972-74; pediatrician Children's Med. Group of South Bay, Chula Vista, Calif., 1974—. Clin. instr. dept. pediat. UCLA Sch. Medicine, 1971-72, U. So. Calif., L.A., 1972-74; asst. clin. prof. dept. pediat. U. Calif., Calif. Sch. Medicine, San Diego, 1974-98, preceptor dept. pediat., 1992—, assoc. clin. prof. dept. pediat., 1998—. Fellow Am. Acad. Pediat.; mem. Calif. Med. Assn., San Diego County Med. Soc. Avocations: sketching, design. Office: Children's Med Group South Bay 280 E St Chula Vista CA 91910-2945 Office Phone: 619-425-3951. Personal E-mail: leongalemarvin@msn.com.

COHEN, FRED EHRENKRANZ, biophysics professor; b. Miami Beach, Fla., Sept. 10, 1956; s. James Cohen and Ruth Belle (Ehrenkranz) Levkoff; m. Carolyn Beth Klebanoff, July 19, 1981; 1 child, Alison. BS, Yale U., 1978; MD, Stanford U., 1984; PhD, Oxford U., Eng., 1980. Asst. prof. U. Calif., San Francisco, 1985-91, assoc. prof., 1991—94, prof. Medicine, Cellular & Molecular Pharmacology, Pharm. Chemistry, and Biochemistry & Biophysics, 1994—, chief, Div. of Endocrinology and Metabolism, 1995—96. Mem. sci. and med. adv. bd. Chrion Corp., Emeryville, Calif., 1988—, sci. adv. bd. Procept, Inc., Cambridge, Mass., 1988—. Assoc. editor Jour. Molecular Biology, London, 1990—; mem. editorial bd. Protein Engring., 1992—, Perspectives in Drug Discovery & Design, 1993—. Recipient Silver Knight in Math. award The Miami Herald, 1974, Robert C. Bates fellowship Yale U., 1977, Merriman prize Yale U., 1978; Rhodes scholar, 1978, Searle scholar, 1988. Fellow ACP, Am. Acad. Arts and Sciences; mem. Am. Soc. Clin. Investigation, Endocrine Soc. (Weitzman Young Investigator award 1992). Western Assn. of Physicians, Biophys. Soc., Inst. Medicine (2004). Office: U Calif San Francisco 600 16th St N472J Box 2240 San Francisco CA 94143-2240 E-mail: cohen@cmpharm.ucsf.edu.

COHEN, GARY J., lawyer; b. Tucson, 1968; Grad., Northwestern U. Atty. Mesch, Clark & Rothschild, P.C., Tucson, 1993—, ptnr., litig. section. Bd. mem. Tucson Jewish Cmty. Ctr.; mem. Tucson Fiesta Bowl com., Tucson City Magistrate Merit Selection Com., City of Tucson Anti-Hate Crime Task Force, Pima County Teen Ct., Lawyers for Literacy. Mem.: Southwest Section of US Tennis Assn. Office: Mesch, Clark & Rothschild PC 259 N Meyer Ave Tucson AZ 85701-1090 Office Phone: 520-624-8886. Office Fax: 520-798-1037.

COHEN, HARVEY JOEL, pediatric hematology and oncology educator; b. NYC, July 4, 1943; s. Phillip and Ida (Teitel) C.; m. Ilene Verne Bookseger, Aug. 15, 1965; children: Philip Jason, Jonathan Todd. BS, Bklyn. Coll., 1964; MD, PhD, Duke U., 1970. Intern Children's Hosp., Boston, 1970-71, resident, 1973-74; instr. pediatrics Harvard U. Med. Sch., Boston, 1974-76, asst. prof., 1976-79, assoc. prof., 1979-81; assoc. prof. pediatrics U. Rochester (N.Y.) Med. Ctr., 1981-84, prof., 1984-93, assoc. chmn. dept., 1987-93, chief pediatric hematology and oncology, 1981-93; chmn. dept. pediatrics Stanford (Calif.) U. Sch. Medicine, 1993—2006, prof., 1993—; chief staff Lucile Salter Packard Children's Hosp. at Stanford, 1993—2006. Med. advisor Montgomery Med. Ventures, San Francisco, 1984—97; sci. advisor St. Jude Children's Rsch. Hosp., Memphis, 1985—90, 2001—; chmn. hematology study sect. NIH, Washington, 1986—88. Editor: Hematology: Basic Principles and Practice, 1991, 94, 99, 2005. Med. dir. Camp Good Days and Spl. Times, Rochester, 1981—93, Monroe County chpt. Am.Cancer Soc., Rochester, 1983—93; med. dir. Rochester br. Cooley's Anemia Found., 1984—93; bd. dirs. Lucile Pakcard Children's Hosp., 1993—97, Lucile Packard Found. for Children's Health, 1997—2000, Lucile Pakcard Children's Hosp., 2000—06, Ronald McDonald House of Palo Alto, Calif., 1995—2005, Children's Health Coun., 1996—2005. Tng. grantee Nat. Inst. Gen. Med. Scis., 1983-90, Nat. Inst. Child Health and Human Devel., 1990-94. Mem. Soc. for Pediatric Rsch. (pres. 1988-89), Am. Soc. for Clin. Investigation, Am. Pediatric Soc. Democrat. Jewish. Achievements include research in on continuous assay for superoxide production, effect of selenium on synthesis of glutathione peroxidase; relationship of in vitro and in vivo killing of leukemic cells by asparaganse clinical trials in childhood leukemia; comparative proteomics in pediatric diseases. Office: Stanford U Sch Medicine Dept Pediatrics Rm H-310 Stanford CA 94305 Office Phone: 650-723-5104 can't process batch details. Business E-Mail: punko@stanford.edu.

COHEN, JON STEPHAN, lawyer; b. Omaha, Nov. 9, 1943; s. Louis H. and Bertha N. (Goldstein) C.; children: Carolyn, Sherri, Barbara, Shayna, Jordan; m. Cheryl A. Jiroux, Oct. 7, 1994. Student, London Sch. Econs., 1963-64; BA, Claremont Men's Coll. (now Claremont McKenna Coll.), 1965; JD, Harvard U., 1968. Bar: Ariz. 1968. Assoc. Snell & Wilmer, Phoenix, 1968-73, ptnr., 1973—. Bd. dirs. Vika Corp., Phoenix, Ariz. Tech. Coun., Phoenix, Ariz. Sci. Ctr., Phoenix, Ariz. Bus. Leadership, Phoenix. Bd. dirs. Kronos Rsch. Inst., Phoenix. Fellow Ariz. Bar Found.; mem. ABA, Ariz. Bar Assn., Maricopa County Bar Assn., Village Athletic Club. Avocations: record collecting, skiing, racquetball. Home: 6901 E Northern Ave Paradise Valley AZ 85253 Office: Snell & Wilmer One Arizona Ctr Phoenix AZ 85004-0001 Office Phone: 602-382-6247. Business E-Mail: jcohen@swlaw.com.

COHEN, KARL PALEY, nuclear energy consultant; b. NYC, Feb. 5, 1913; s. Joseph M. and Ray (Paley) C.; m. Marthe H. Malartre, Sept. 20, 1938; children: Martine-Claude Leboue, Elisabeth M. Brown, Beatrix Josephine Cashmore. AB, Columbia U., 1933, MA, 1934, PhD in Phys. Chemistry, 1937; postgrad., U. Paris, 1936—37. Rsch. asst. to Prof. H. C. Urey Columbia U., 1937-40; dir. theoretical divsn. SAM Manhattan Project, 1940—44; physicist Std. Oil Devel. Co., 1944-48; tech. dir. H.K. Ferguson Co., 1948-52; v.p. Walter Kidde Nuc. Lab., 1952-55; cons. AEC, sr. sci. Columbia U., 1955; mgr. advance engring. atomic power equipment dept. GE, 1955-65, gen. mgr. breeder reactor devel. dept., 1965-71, mgr. strategic planning, nuc. energy divsn., 1971-73, chief scientist, nuc. energy group, 1973-78; cons. prof. Stanford U., 1978-81. Author: The Theory of Isotope Separation as Applied to Large Scale Production of U-235, 1951; contbr. articles to profl. jours. Recipient Energy Rsch. prize, Alfried Krupp Found., 1977. Fellow AAAS, Am. Nuc. Soc. (pres. 1968-69, bd. dirs.), Am. Inst. Chemists (Chem. Pioneer award 1979); mem. NAE, IEEE, Am. Phys. Soc., Phi Beta Kappa, Sigma Xi, Phi Lambda Upsilon. Home and Office: 928 N California Ave Palo Alto CA 94303-3405 Personal E-mail: karlpc@comcast.net.

COHEN, LARRY, computer software company executive; Product mktg. dir. Collabra Software; product line mgr. software divsn. Apple Computer; joined Microsoft Corp., Redmond, Wash., 1995, mgr. mktg. and bus. devel. efforts Microsoft Network, 1995, dir. consumer online svcs. group, founder, gen. mgr. Silicon Valley bus. rels. group, corp. v.p. corp. comm., 2008—. Office: Microsoft Corp One Microsoft Way Redmond WA 98052-6399 E-mail: larryco@microsoft.com.

COHEN, LAWRENCE EDWARD, sociologist, educator, criminologist; b. LA, July 20, 1945; s. Louis and Florence (White) C. BA, U. Calif., Berkeley, 1969; MA, Calif. State U., 1971; PhD, U. Wash., 1974; postdoctorate study, SUNY, Albany, 1973-75. Rsch. assoc. Sch. of Criminal Justice, SUNY, Albany, 1973-76; asst. prof. U. Ill., Urbana, 1976-80; assoc. prof. U. Tex., Austin, 1980-85; prof. Ind. U., Bloomington, 1985-88, U. Calif., Davis, 1988—. Cons. editor Social Forces, 1981-84, Jour. Criminal Law and Criminology, 1982-2000, Am. Sociol. Rev., 1982-84, Am. Jour. Sociology, 1990-98, Criminology, 1996-98; contbr. numerous articles to profl. jours. Sgt. USMC, 1963-66, Vietnam. Grantee NIMH, 1978-80, NSF, 1983-89. Mem. Am. Sociol. Assn., Am. Soc. Criminology, Acad. Criminal Justice Scis., Soc. for Study Social Problems. Office: U Calif Dept Sociology Davis CA 95616 Business E-Mail: lecohen@ucdavis.edu.

COHEN, LEONARD (NORMAN COHEN), poet, writer, musician; b. Montreal, Que., Can., Sept. 21, 1934; s. Nathan B. and Masha (Kline) C.; children: Adam, Lorca. BA, McGill U., 1955; postgrad., Columbia.; LLB (hon.), Dalhousie U., 1971; LLD (hon.), McGill U., 1992. Author: (poetry) Let Us Compare Mythologies, 1956, The Spice Box of Earth, 1961, Flowers for Hitler, 1964, Parasites of Heaven, 1966, Selected Poems, 1956-68, 1968, The Energy of Slaves, 1972, Death of a Lady's Man, 1979, Book of Mercy, 1984, Stranger Music: Selected Music and Songs, 1993, Dance Me to the End of Love, 1995, Book of Longing, 2006, (novels) The Favorite Game, 1963, Beautiful Losers, 1966; albums include: The Songs of Leonard Cohen, 1968, Songs from a Room, 1969, Songs of Love & Hate, 1971, Live Songs, 1973, New Skin for the Old Ceremony, 1974, Death of a Ladies' Man, 1977, Recent Songs, 1979, Various Positions, 1985, I'm Your Man, 1988, The Future, 1992, Cohen Live, 1993, More Best Of, 1997, Songs from Love & Hate, 1999, Field Commander Cohen: Tour of 1979, 2001, Ten New Songs, 2001, Koln 1988, 2001, Dear Heather, 2004, Blue Alert, 2006, Book of Longing, 2007. Decorated Officer, Order of Can., 1991, Companion, 2002; named to Rock & Roll Hall of Fame, 2008; recipient McGill Lit. award, 1956, Que. Lit. award, 1964, Gov. Gen.'s Performing Arts award, Can., 1993, Hall of Fame award, Can. Songwriters, 2006. Office: c/o Macklam Feldman Mgmt 200-1505 W 2nd Ave Vancouver BC Canada V6H 3Y4 E-mail: leonardinfo@mfmgt.com.

COHEN, MALCOLM MARTIN, psychologist, researcher; s. Nathan and Esther Cohen; m. Marilyn Jerrow, Jan. 2, 1959 (dec. 1967); m. Eleanor Johnson, June 30, 1969 (div. 1988); m. Suzana Gal, Feb. 14, 1988. BA, Brandeis U., Waltham, Mass., 1959; MA, U. Pa., Phila., 1961, PhD, 1965. Lic. psychologist, Pa. Asst. instr. U. Pa., Phila., 1961-63; rsch. psychologist Naval Air Engring. Ctr., Phila., 1963-67; supervisory rsch. psychologist Naval Air Devel. Ctr., Warminster, Pa., 1967-82; asst. chief biomed. rsch. divsn. NASA-Ames Rsch Ctr., Moffett Field, Calif., 1982-85, chief neurosci. br., 1985-88, rsch. scientist, 1988—2005, chief human info. processing rsch., 2000—05, Ames assoc., 2005—07; pvt. practice, 2006—. Lectr. dept. aeros. and astronautics Stanford U., 1983—92, lectr., cons. prof. human biology program, 1994—2005; cons. in field. Assoc. editor Habitation Jour., 2004-2007; contbr. articles to profl. jours. Founding mem. Common Cause of Phila., 1973. Recipient Exceptional Sci. Achievement medal NASA 1994. Fellow AIAA (assoc., Jeffries Aerospace Medicine & Life Scis. Rsch. award, 2008), Aerospace Med. Assn. (editl. bd. Aviation Space and Environ. Medicine 1985-93, assoc. editor 2001-03, Environ. Sci. award 1985, William F. Longacre award 1989), Aerospace Human Factors Assn. (pres. 1992, Henry L. Taylor Founder award 2009); mem. AAAS, NY Acad. Scis., Nat. Space Biomed. Rsch. Inst. (external adv. coun. 2009), Sigma Xi. Jewish. Achievements include patents for light bar to monitor human acceleration tolerance. Avocations: scuba diving, photography, chess. Personal E-mail: malcohen@aol.com.

COHEN, MARSHALL HARRIS, astronomer, educator; b. Manchester, NH, July 5, 1926; s. Solomon and Mollie Lee (Epstein) C.; m. Shirley Kekst, Sept. 19, 1948; children: Thelma, Linda, Sara. BEE, Ohio State U., 1948, MS, 1949, PhD, 1952. Rsch. assoc. Ohio State U., Columbus, 1950-54; asst. prof. elec. engring. Cornell U., Ithaca, N.Y., 1954-58, assoc. prof., 1958-63, assoc. prof. astronomy, 1963-66; prof. applied electro-physics U. Calif., San Diego, 1966-68; prof. radio astronomy Calif. Inst. Tech., Pasadena, 1968-90, prof. astronomy, 1990-96, exec. officer for astronomy, 1981-84, prof. emeritus, 1996. Prof. associé U. Paris VI, 1989; mem. numerous coms. NSF, NRC, vis. coms. various obs. in U.S., Fed. Republic Germany. Contbr. articles, book revs. to profl. jours.; patentee radio astronomy. With U.S. Army, 1943-46. Co-recipient Rumford medal Am. Acad. Arts and Scis., 1971; Guggenheim Found. fellow Paris Obs., 1960-61, MIT/Inst. Astronomy, Cambridge, Eng., 1980-81; Morrison fellow Lick Obs., 1988. Fellow AAAS; mem. NAS (chmn. sect. astronomy 1989-92), Am. Astron. Soc. (publ. bd. 1980-83), Astron. Soc. Pacific (bd. dirs. 1969-72), Am. Acad. Arts and Scis., Internat. Union for Sci. Radio (chmn. commn. V of U.S. nat. com. 1970-73), Internat. Astron. Union (U.S. nat. com. 1989-92). Avocation: hiking. Office: Calif Inst Tech Dept Astronomy Pasadena CA 91125-0001

COHEN, MARVIN LOU, physics professor; b. Montreal, Que., Can., Mar. 3, 1935; came to U.S., 1947, naturalized, 1953; s. Elmo and Molly (Zaritsky) C.; m. Merrill L. Gardner, Aug. 31, 1958 (dec. Apr. 1994); children: Mark, Susan; m. Suzy R. Locke, Sept. 8, 1996. AB, U. Calif., 1957; MS, U. Chgo., 1958, PhD, 1964. Mem. tech. staff Bell Telephone Labs., Murray Hill, N.J., 1963-64; asst. prof. physics U. Calif., Berkeley, 1964-66, assoc. prof., 1966-69, prof. physics, 1969-95, univ. prof., 1995—, prof. Miller Inst. Basic Resch. in Sci., 1969-70, 76-77, 88, chmn., 1977-81, U. Calif. Faculty Rsch. lectr., 1997—. Chmn. Gordon Rsch. Conf. Chemistry and Physics of Solids, 1972; U.S. rep. to Semicondr. Commn., Internat. Union Pure and Applied Physics, 1975-81; Alfred P. Sloan fellow Cambridge U., Eng., 1965-67; vis. prof. Cambridge U., Eng., 1966, U. Paris, France, 1972-73, summers 68, 75, 87, 88, U. Hawaii, Honolulu, 1978-79, Technion, Haifa, Israel, 1987-88; chmn. planning com. Pure and Applied Sci. Inst. U. Hawaii, 1980—; mem. selection com. Presdl. Young Investigator Awards, 1983; mem. Com. on Nat. Synchrotron Radiation Facilities, 1983-84; chmn. 17th Internat. Conf. on Physics of Semicondrs., 1984; mem. exec. com. Govt.-Univ.-Industry Research Roundtable, 1984—; vice chmn. Govt.-U. Industry Research Roundtable Working Group on Sci. and Engring. Talent, 1984—; mem. rev. bd. for Ctr. for Advanced Materials Lawrence Berkeley Lab., 1986-87; mem. panel on Implications for Mechanisms of Support and Panel on High Temperature Superconductivity, NAS, NSF, 1987; mem. adv. bd. Tex. Ctr. for Superconductivity, 1988-90, vice chair, 1991—; mem. U.S. del. to Bilateral Dialog R&D in the U.S. and Japan, NRC, 1989; mem. sci. policy bd. Stanford Synchrotron Rad. Lab., 1990-92; dist. lectr. Hong Kong U. Sci. and Tech., 2001; Loeb lectr. Harvard U., 2004. Editorial bd. Perspectives in Condensed Matter Physics, 1987—; adv. bd. Internat. Jour. Modern Physics B., 1987—, Modern Physics Letters B, 1987—; assoc. editor Materials Sci. and Engring., 1987—; contbr. more than 600 articles to tech. jours. Mem. vis. com. Ginzton Lab., Stanford U., 1991; mem. sci. policy com. Stanford Linear Accelerator, 1993-95. Recipient Outstanding Accomplishment in Solid State Physics award U.S. Dept. Energy, 1981, Sustained Outstanding Rsch. in Solid State Physics award U.S. Dept. Energy, 1990, Cert.of Merit, Lawrence Berkeley Lab., 1991, Nat. Medal of Sci., 2001, Presdl. award, 2002, Foresight Inst. Richard P. Feynman prize in Nanotechology, 2003; A.P. Sloan fellow, 1965-67, Guggenheim fellow, 1978-79, 90-91. Fellow AAAS, Am. Phys. Soc. (exec. coun. divsn. solid state physics 1975-79, chmn. 1977-78, Buckley prize com. 1980-81, chmn. 1981, Lilienfeld prize com. 1994—, Isakson Prize com. 1995-98, chmn. 1999, exec. bd., coun. panel pub. affairs, investment com., budget com. 2003, v.p.

2003, pres.-elect 2004, pres. 2005, past-pres. 2006, Oliver E. Buckley prize for solid state physics 1979, Julius Edgar Lilienfeld prize 1994); mem. NAS (chmn. condensed matter physics search/screening com. 1981-82, 1988—, chmn. Comstock prize com. 1988, nominating com. for selection of pres., v.p., councilors 1992-93), Am. Acad. Arts and Scis. (com. award initiatices in rsch. 2004, Nat. Medal Sci. 2001), Nat. Acad. Scis., Am. Philos. Soc., Am. Inst. Physics (mem. governing bd. 2003-07, mem. nominating com. 2003-06). Home: 201 Estates Dr Piedmont CA 94611-3315 Office: U Calif Dept Physics #7300 Berkeley CA 94720-0001

COHEN, POLLY, film company executive; Degree in Chinese Studies, U. Calif. San Diego; MFA, U. Southern Calif. With Jersey Films; creative exec. Warner Bros. Pictures, 1997—98, prodn. exec., 1998—99, v.p. prodn., 1999—2003, sr. v.p. prodn., 2003—06, exec. v.p. prodn., 2006; pres. Warner Ind. Pictures, 2006—. Named one of The 100 Most Powerful Women in Entertainment, Hollywood Reporter, 2006, 2007. Achievements include fluency in Chinese language. Office: Warner Independent Pictures 4000 Warner Blvd Burbank CA 91522 Office Phone: 818-954-6000. Office Fax: 212-954-7667.

COHEN, SASHA (ALEXANDRA PAULINE COHEN), ice skater; b. Westwood, Calif., Oct. 26, 1984; d. Roger and Galina Cohen. Appeared in films: Blades of Glory, 2007; author: (book) Sasha Cohen: Autobiography of a Champion Figure Skater, 2005. Achievements include Recipient Gardena Winter Trophy, 1999; winner, Junior Grand Prix, Stockholm, Sweden, 1999; 2nd place, U.S. Championships, 2000; winner, Pacific Coast Sectional, 2000; Finlandia Trophy, 2001; 3rd place, Trophee Lalique, 2001; Silver medalist, U.S. Nats. Championship, 2001-2002; 2nd place, U.S. Championships, 2002; 4th place, World Championships, 2002; 4th place, Olympic Winter Games, 2002; 2nd place, Hersheys Kisses Challenge, 2002; 4th place, Campbells Classic, 2002; 1st place, Skate Can., 2002; 1st place, Trophee Lalique, 2002; 2nd place, Cup of Russia, 2002; 1st place, Crest White Strips Challenge, 2002; bronze medalist, U.S. Nats., 2003; 4th place, Worlds, 2003; champion, Grand Prix Finals, 2003; 1st place, Trophee Lalique, 2004; 1st place, Skate Can., 2004; 1st place, Skate Am., 2004; 1st place, Campbells Soup, 2004; silver medallist, World Championships, 2004-2005; 1st Place, U.S. Nats., 2006; silver medallist, Torino Olympics, Italy, 2006. Avocations: art, jewelry making, reading, designing costumes. Office: 9 Journey c/o Ice Palace Aliso Viejo CA 92656

COHEN, STANLEY NORMAN, geneticist, educator; b. Perth Amboy, NJ, Feb. 17, 1935; s. Bernard and Ida (Stolz) Cohen; m. Joanna Lucy Wolter, June 27, 1961; children: Anne, Geoffrey. BA, Rutgers U., 1956, ScD (hon.), 1994; MD, U. Pa., 1960, ScD (hon.), 1995. Intern Mt. Sinai Hosp., NYC, 1960-61; resident Univ. Hosp., Ann Arbor, Mich., 1961-62; clin. assoc. arthritis and rheumatism br. Nat. Inst. Arthritis and Metabolic Diseases, Bethesda, Md., 1962-64; sr. resident in medicine Duke U. Hosp., Durham, NC, 1964-65; Am. Cancer Soc. postdoctoral rsch. fellow Albert Einstein Coll. Medicine, Bronx, 1965-67, asst. prof. devel. biology and cancer, 1967-68; mem. faculty Stanford (Calif.) U., 1968—, prof. medicine, 1975—, prof. genetics, 1977—, chmn. dept. genetics, 1978-86, K.-T Li Prof., 1993—. Mem. com. recombinant DNA molecules NAS-NRC, 1974; mem. com. on genetic experimentation Internat. Coun. Sci. Unions, 1977—96. Mem. editl. bd. Jour. Bacteriology, 1973—79, Molecular Microbiology, 1986—2005, Procs. Nat. Acad. Sci., 1996—, Current Opinion in Microbiology, 1997—. Trustee U. Pa., 1997—2002. With USPHS, 1962—64. Recipient Burroughs Wellcome Scholar award, 1970, Mattia award, Roche Inst. Molecular Biology, 1977, Albert Lasker basic med. rsch. award, 1980, Wolf prize, 1981, Marvin J. Johnson award, 1981, Disting. Grad. award, U. Pa. Sch. Medicine, 1986, Disting. Svc. award, Miami Winter Symposium, 1986, Nat. Biotech award, 1989, de la Vie prize, LVMH Inst., 1988, Nat. Medal Sci., 1988, City of Medicine award, 1988, Nat. Medal of Tech., 1989, Spl. award, Am. Chem. Soc., 1999, Lemelson MIT Prize, MIT, 1996, Albany Med. Ctr. prize in medicine and biomedical rsch., 2004, The Shaw prize in Life Sci. and Medicine, 2004, Innovation Biosci. award, The Economist, 2005, John Stearns Medicine Lifetime Achievement award, NY Acad. Medicine, 2007; named to Nat. Inventors Hall of Fame, 2001; Guggenheim fellow, 1973, faculty scholar, Josiah Macy, Jr., 1975—76. Fellow: AAAS, Am. Acad. Microbiology; mem.: NAS (chmn. genetics sect. 1988—91), Am. Philos. Soc., Inst. Medicine, Assn. Am. Physicians, Am. Soc. Clin. Investigation, Am. Soc. Pharmacology and Exptl. Therapeutics, Am. Soc. Microbiology (Cetus award 1988), Genetics Soc. Am., Am. Soc. Biol. Chemists, Am. Philos. Soc., Alpha Omega Alpha, Phi Beta Kappa, Sigma Xi. Achievements include obtaining, with Herbert Boyer, first patent in the field of recombinant deoxyribonucleic acid (DNA), 1980. Office: Stanford U Sch Med Dept Genetics Rm M-322 Stanford CA 94305

COHEN, S(TEPHEN) MARSHALL, philosophy educator; b. NYC, Sept. 27, 1929; s. Harry and Fanny (Marshall) C.; m. Margaret Dennes, Feb. 15, 1964; children: Matthew, Megan. BA, Dartmouth Coll., Hanover, NH, 1951; MA, Harvard U., 1953, Oxford U., 1977. Jr. fellow, Soc. of Fellows Harvard U., Cambridge, Mass., 1955-58, asst. prof. philosophy and gen. edn., 1958-62; asst. prof. U. Chgo., 1962-64, assoc. prof., 1964-67, acting chair Coll. Philosophy, 1965-66; assoc. prof. Rockefeller U., NYC, 1967-70; prof. philosophy Richmond Coll. (now Coll. of S.I.), 1970-83; exec. officer program in philosophy Grad. Ctr. CUNY, 1975-83; prof. philosophy and law U. So. Calif., LA, 1983—97, dean divsn. humanities, 1983-94, interim dean Coll. Letters, Arts and Sci., 1993-94, Univ. prof. philosophy and law emeritus, 1998—, dean emeritus Coll. Letters, Arts and Sci., 1998—. Lectr. Lowell Inst., Boston, 1957-58; vis. fellow All Souls Coll., Oxford, Eng., 1976-77; mem. Inst. for Advanced Study, Princeton, N.J., 1981-82. Editor: The Philosophy of John Stuart Mill, 1961, Philosophy and Public Affairs, 1970-99, Philosophy and Society series, 1977-83, Ethical, Legal and Political Philosophy series, 1983-99; co-editor: Film Theory and Criticism, 1974, 79, 85, 92, 98, 2009, War and Moral Responsibility, 1974, The Rights and Wrongs of Abortion, 1974, Equality and Preferential Treatment, 1977, Marx, Justice and History, 1980, Medicine and Moral Philosophy, 1982, What Is Dance?, 1983, International Ethics, 1985, Punishment, 1995. Rockefeller Found. humanities fellow, 1977, Guggenheim fellow, 1976-77. Mem. Am. Philos. Assn., Am. Coun. Learned Socs. (bd. dirs. 1987-91, 93-2004), Coun. on Internat. Ednl. Exch. (bd. dirs. 1991-94). Democrat. Jewish. Office: U Southern Calif Dould Sch Law Los Angeles CA 90089-0071 Home Phone: 310-276-4399; Office Phone: 213-740-4794. Business E-Mail: mcohen@law.usc.edu.

COHEN, STUART F., investment company executive; BS in Quantitative Bus. Analysis, Ariz. State U. Sr. positions in US sales and mktg. divsn., IBM Personal Computer Co. and Networking Divsn. IBM; v.p. worldwide mktg., corp. officer InFocus Corp.; v.p. mktg. and bus. devel. RadiSys Corp.; CEO Open Source Devel. Labs, Beaverton, Oreg., 2003—06; with OVP Venture Partners, 2006—. Office: OVP Venture Partners 5550 SW Macadam Ave Ste 300 Portland OR 97239 Office Phone: 503-626-2455. Office Fax: 503-626-2436. Business E-Mail: stuartcohen@osdl.org.

COHEN, VALERIE A., entertainment company executive; b. 1956; BA, Middlebury Coll.; JD, Harvard U. Law clerk NJ Supreme Court; ptnr. Leisure Newton & Irvine, Dewey Ballentine; sr. v.p. bus. devel. Walt Disney Co., Burbank, Calif., assistant general counsel, corp. sr. v.p., 1995—. Office: Walt Disney Co 500 S Buena Vista St Burbank CA 91521-0006

COHEN, WILLIAM, law educator; b. Scranton, Pa., June 1, 1933; s. Maurice M. and Nellie (Rubin) C.; m. Betty C. Stein, Sept. 13, 1952 (div. 1976, dec. 2000); children: Barbara Jean, David Alan (dec. 1995), Rebecca Anne; m. Nancy M. Mahoney, Aug. 8, 1976; 1 dau., Margaret Emily. BA, UCLA, 1953, LLB, 1956. Bar: Calif. 1961. Law clk. to U.S. Supreme Ct. Justice William O. Douglas, 1956-57; from asst. prof. to assoc. prof. U. Minn. Law Sch., 1957-60; vis. asso. prof. UCLA Law Sch., 1959-60, mem. faculty, 1960-70, prof., 1962-70, Stanford (Calif.) Law Sch., 1970—, C. Wendell and Edith M. Carlsmith prof. law, 1983-99, Carlsmith prof. emeritus, 1999—. Vis. prof. law European U. Inst., Florence, Italy, fall 1977; Merriam vis. prof. Ariz. State U. Law Sch., Spring 1981 Author: Constitutional Protection of Expression and Conscience: The First Amendment, 2003; co-author: The Bill of Rights, a Source Book, 1968, Comparative Constitutional Law, 1978, Constitutional Law Cases and Materials, 1981, 7th edit., 2005, Constitutional Law: The Structure of Government, 1981, Constitutional Law: Civil Liberty and Individual Rights, 1982, 5th edit., 2007. Home: 698 Maybell Ave Palo Alto CA 94306-3819 Office: Stanford Law Sch Nathan Abbott Way Stanford CA 94305 Business E-Mail: wcohen@stanford.edu.

COHEN, WILLIAM ALAN, finance educator, management consultant, writer; b. Balt., June 25, 1937; s. Sidney Oliver and Theresa (Bachman) C.; m. Janice Dawn Stults, Jan. 3, 1963 (div. Jan. 1966); 1 child, William Alan II; m. Nurit Kovnator, May 28, 1967; children—Barak, Nimrod. BS, U.S. Mil. Acad., 1959; MBA, U. Chgo., 1967; MA, Claremont Grad. Sch., 1978; PhD, Indsl. Coll. of the Armed Forces, 1989. Registered profl. engr., Israel. Project mgr. Israel Aircraft Industries, 1970-73; mgr. rsch. and devel. Sierra Engring. Co., Sierra Madre, Calif., 1973-76; pres. Global Assocs., 1973—2003; mgr. advanced tech. mktg. McDonnell-Douglas Co., Huntington Beach, Calif., 1976-78; prof. mktg. Calif. State U., LA, 1979—2002, dir. bur. bus. and econ. rsch., 1979-83, chmn. mktg. dept., 1986—89; pres. Calif. Am. U., LA, 2002—03, Inst. of Leader Arts, LA, 2003—; prof. bus. adminstrn. Touro Univ. Internat., 2003—06; pres. US Grad. U., 2006—. Bd. dir. Inst. Bus. Devel.; cons. Fortune 500 cos. Author: The Executives Guide to Finding a Superior Job, 1978, 83, Principles of Technical Management, 1980, Successful Marketing for Small Business, 1981, How to Sell to Government, 1981, The Entrepreneur and Small Business Problem Solver, 1983, 89, Direct Response Marketing, 1984, Building a Mail Order Business, 1982, 85, 91, 96, Making It Big as a Consultant, 1985, 90, 2001, Winning on the Marketing Front, 1986, High Tech Management, 1986, Developing a Winning Marketing Plan, 1987, The Students Guide to Finding a Superior Job, 1987, 93, The Practice of Marketing Management, 1988, 91, The Entrepreneur and Small Business Financial Problem Solver, 1983, 2006, The Art of Leader, 1990, The Entrepreneur and Small Business Marketing Problem Solver, 1991, Get a Great Job Fast, 1993, The Paranoid Corporation and Eight Other Ways Your Company Can Be Crazy, 1993, The Marketing Plan, 1994, 98, 2001, Making It!, 1994, Model Business Plans for Service Businesses, 1995, Model Business Plans for Product Businesses, 1995, The Stuff of Heroes: The 8 Universal Laws of Leadership, 1998, The New Art of the Leader, 2000, Marketing Your Small Business Made E-Z, 2000, The Wisdom of the Generals, 2001, Break the Rules, 2001, The Art of the Strategist, 2004, Special Ops Leadership, 2006; contbr. numerous articles to profl. jours. Maj. USAF, 1959-70, maj.-gen. USAFR, ret. Decorated Disting. Svc. Medal, Legion of Merit, D.F.C. with 3 oak leaf clusters, Meritorious Svc. medal with 2 oak leaf clusters, Air medal with 11 oak leaf clusters, numerous other U.S. and fgn. awards; named Disting. Grad. Indsl. Coll. Armed Forces, 1989; recipient Ministry Def. award State of Israel, 1976, Outstanding Svc. award Nat. Mgmt. Assn., 1979, Pres.'s award West Point Soc., 1982, Outstanding Prof. award, 1983, Chgo. Tribune Gold medal, George Washington medal Freedoms Found. at Valley Forge, 1986, CSULA Statewide Outstanding Prof., 1996, Great Tchr. in Mktg. award Acad. of Mktg. Sci., 1999. Fellow Acad. Mktg. Sci.; mem. Direct Mktg. Assn. (fellow 1980, 83), World Mktg. Congress (del. N.S. 1983), Direct Mktg. Club So. Calif. (bd. dirs., grantee 1981), Am. Mktg. Assn. (award 1982), West Point Soc. (pres., bd. dirs. 1981-82), Beta Gamma Sigma, Phi Sigma Phi. Republican. Jewish.

COHEN-VADER, CHERYL DENISE, municipal official; b. Ft. Bragg, NC, Mar. 23, 1955; BA, Princeton U., 1977; MBA, Columbia U., 1983. Treas. internat. divsn. commodity import-export financing Bank of N.Y., NYC, 1977-81; v.p. Citicorp Securities Markets, Inc. Citicorp, NYC, 1983-90; v.p. Weldon, Sullivan, Carmichael & Co., 1990-92; asst. v.p. Kirkpatrick Pattis, 1993-95; mgr. revenue dept. City of Denver, 1996—, dep. mayor, 2003—04. Mem. Mcpl. Securities Rulemaking Bd., 1998-2001. Bd. dirs. Mile High chpt. ARC, Colo. Episcopal Found., 1998-2001; bd. dirs. Black Ch. Intitiatives, 1998—. Recipient Consortium of Grad. Mgmt. Edn. fellowship, 1981-83, Recognition of Achievement award Five Points Bus. Assn., Inc., 1995, Leadership Denver award Denver C. of C., 1994; honored in Living Portraits of African-Am. Women Nat. Coun. Negro Women, 1997. Mem. Govt. Finance Officers Assn. Office: City Denver Revenue Dept McNichols Bldg Rm 300 144 W Colfax Ave Denver CO 80202-5391

COHN, CARL A., school system administrator; BA in Philosophy, St. John's Coll.; MA in Counseling, Chapman U.; EdD in Urban Edn. Policy, UCLA. Teacher pub. schools, counselor, cent. office admin.; supt. Long Beach Unified Sch. District; clinical prof. Rossier Sch. Edn., USC, 2002—05; apptd. by Federal Ct. as ind. monitor of spl. edn. consent decree LA sch. sys., 2003; supt. San Diego Unified Sch. Dist., 2005—. Appointee Nat. Asessment Gov. Bd.; fac. adv. Broad Supt. Academy; consul. GKK; exec. search consul. Calif. Sch. Bd. Assn.; mem. bd. Re-Inventing Schools Coalition, Wallace Foundation Education Leadership Adv. Com., Nat. Heritage Acad.; pres. Urban Sch. Imagineers. Recipient Harold W. McGraw Jr prize in Edn, 2001. Office: San Diego Schools Office of the Superintendent 4100 Normal St San Diego CA 92103 Office Phone: 619-725-8000.

COHN, DANIEL HOWARD, laboratory director; b. Santa Monica, Calif., Aug. 24, 1955; s. Sidney Lorber and Mynda Ellen (Zimmerman) C.; m. Ludmila Bojman, May 16, 1982; children: Zachary, Marissa, Rachel. BA, U. Calif., Santa Barbara, 1977; PhD, Scripps Inst. Oceanography, 1983. Postdoctoral fellow U. Wash., Seattle, 1983-88; 0sch. scientist, asst. prof. Cedars-Sinai Med. Ctr./UCLA, 1988-93, assoc. prof., 1993-97, prof., 1997—. Mem. genetics tng. program UCLA, 1988—; reviewer various jours. and granting agys. Editorial bd. various jours.; contbr. articles to profl. jours. and books. Grants com. chair, bd. dirs. Concern Found. for Cancer Rsch., L.A., 1988—. Recipient Martin Kamen award U. Calif., San Diego, 1983, Eckhart prize Scripps Inst. Oceanography, 1983; postdoctoral award NIH, 1985-88, grantee, 1988—. Mem. AAAS, Phi Beta Kappa. Democrat. Jewish. Avocations: gardening, golf, volleyball, water-skiing, skiing. Office: Cedars-Sinai Med Ctr 8700 Beverly Blvd Los Angeles CA 90048-1865

COHN, MARJORIE F., law educator, legal association administrator; b. Pomona, Calif., Nov. 1, 1948; d. Leonard L. and Florence Cohn; m. Pedro López children: Victor, Nicolas; m. Jerome P. Wallingford. BA, Stanford U., 1970; JD, Santa Clara U., 1975. Bar: Calif. 1975, U.S. Dist. Ct. (so. dist.) Calif. 1982, U.S. Dist. Ct. (no. dist.) Calif. 1983. Staff atty. Nat. Lawyers Guild, San Francisco, 1975-76, Agrl. Labor Rels. Bd., Sacramento, 1976-78, Appellate Defenders, Inc., San Diego, 1987-91; dep. pub. defender Fresno County Pub. Defender's Office, Fresno, Calif., 1978-80; pvt. practice Monterey and San Diego Counties, San Diego, 1981-87; prof. law Thomas Jefferson Sch. Law, San Diego, 1991—. Legal analyst on TV, radio and in print media. Co-author: Cameras in the Courtroom: Television and the Pursuit of Justice, 1998, Cowboy Republic: Six Ways the Bush Gang Has Defied the Law; editor-in-chief Guild Practitioner, 1994-2003. Recipient Golden Apple award, Student Bar Assn., Thomas Jefferson Sch. Law, 1995—98, Svc. to Legal Edn. award, San Diego County Bar Assn., 2005, Top Attys. award, San Diego, 2006, Witkin award, 2007. Mem. Nat. Lawyers Guild (nat. exec. com. 1996-2006, exec. v.p. 2003-06, pres. 2006-), Calif. Attys. for Criminal Justice. Office: Thomas Jefferson Sch Law 2121 San Diego Ave San Diego CA 92110-2986 Office Phone: 619-374-6923. Business E-Mail: marjorie@tjsl.edu.

COKELET, GILES ROY, biomedical engineering educator; b. NYC, Jan. 7, 1932; s. Roy S. and Anna M. (Trippel) C.; m. Sarah Drew, June 15, 1963; children: Becky, Bradford BS, Calif. Inst. Tech., 1957, MS, 1958; ScD, MIT, 1963. Rsch. engr. Dow Chem. Co., Williamsburg, Va., 1958-60; asst. prof. Calif. Inst. Tech., Pasadena, 1964-68; assoc. prof. Mont. State U., Bozeman, 1969-76, prof., 1976-78, U. Rochester, NY, 1978-98; rsch. prof. Mont. State U., Bozeman, 1998—. Contbr. articles to profl. jours. With U.S. Army, 1954-55, Japan. Recipient Sr. U.S. Scientist award Humboldt-Stiftung, Bonn, Fed. Republic Germany, 1981-82, 88. Fellow AAAS; mem. Biomed. Engring. Soc., Microcirculatory Soc., No. Am. Soc. Biorheology, Internat. Soc. Biorheology (past pres., Poiseuille medal 1999). Avocations: stamp collecting/philately, hiking. Office: Mont State U Dept Chem and Biol Engring Bozeman MT 59717-0001 Office Phone: 406-994-5928. Business E-Mail: giles_c@coe.montana.edu.

COKER, MICH, lawyer; b. Gulfport, Miss., 1975; BS in Spanish, Millsaps Coll., 1997; postgraduate diploma in Sci., U. Queensland, Brisbane, Australia, 1998; studied Internat. Law & Comparative Constl. Law, U. Nairobi, Kenya, 2000; JD, James E. Rogers Coll. of Law, U. Ariz., 2002; LLM in Taxation, U. Washington Sch. of Law, 2003. Legal cons. Wash. Environ. Coun., Seattle; atty. Snell & Wilmer LLP, Tucson. Author: (publications) Saving the Sierra: Alternative Mechanisms for Conserving Northern Mexico's Last Wild Places, 2003, Avoiding Employee Lawsuits 101: Top Ten Employee Mistakes, 2006. Bd. dir. Tucson Audubon Soc., Tucson Hispanic Chamber of Commerce, chair, Pub. Policy Com. Named one of 40 Under 40, Tucson Bus. Edge, 2006. Mem.: Pima County Bar Assn., FBA, ABA, State Bar of Ariz. Avocation: hiking. Office: Snell & Wilmer LLP One S Church Ave Ste 1500 Tucson AZ 85701 Office Phone: 520-882-1209.

COLANGELO, JERRY JOHN, professional sports team executive; b. Chicago Heights, Ill., Nov. 20, 1939; s. Larry and Sue (Drancek) C.; m. Joan E. Helmich, Jan. 20, 1961; children: Kathy, Kristen, Bryan, Mandie. BA, U. Ill., 1962. Ptnr. House of Charles, Inc., 1962—63; assoc. D.O. Klein & Assocs., 1964—65; dir. merchandising Chgo. Bulls, 1966—68; gen. mgr. Phoenix Suns, 1968—87, exec. v.p., 1987, pres., 1987—99, CEO, 1987—2007, chmn., 1999—; CEO Arizona Diamondbacks, Phoenix, 1998—2004, exec. emeritus, 2004—. Mng. dir. USA Basketball Men's Sr. Nat. Team prog., 2005—. Named Most Influential Sports Figure in Ariz. for Twentieth Cent., Ariz. Republic, Top Businessperson, Phoenix Bus. Jour., NBA Exec. of Yr., 1976, 1981, 1989, 1993; named one of Most Influential People in the World of Sports, Bus. Week, 2008; named to Naismith Meml. Basketball Hall of Fame, 2004, Suns' Ring of Honor, 2007. Mem. Basketball Congress Am. (former exec. v.p., dir.), Phi Kappa Psi. Clubs: Univ., Phoenix Execs. Republican. Baptist. Office: USA Basketball 5465 Mark Dabling Blvd Colorado Springs CO 80918-3842

COLBERG, TALIS JAMES, former state attorney general; b. Alaska, 1958; m. Krystyna Colberg; 2 children. BA in Oriental Hist., Pacific Lutheran U., 1979; JD, Pepperdine U., 1983; PhD in No. Studies, U. Alaska, 2008. Bar: Alaska 1984. Assoc. atty. Kopperud and Hefferan, Wasilla, Alaska, 1984—85; staff counsel Travelers Ins. Companies, 1985—92; pvt. practice atty., 1992—2006; atty. gen. State of Alaska, 2006—09. Adj. hist. instr. ea. and western civilization Matanuska-Susitna Coll., 1992—. Mem. Greater Palmer C. of C., 1992—, Matanuska-Susitna Valleys State Pk. Adv. Bd., 1998—2001; dir. bd., sec., pres. Alaska State Fair, Inc., 1995—2001; bd. dirs. Alaska Humanities Forum, 2002—06, chmn., 2004—05. Mem.: Rotary (past pres.). Republican.*

COLBURN, DONALD D., lawyer; b. Seward, Nebr., May 20, 1948; BA, U. Nebr., Lincoln, 1970, JD with distinction, 1974. Bar: Ariz. 1974, Tex. 1994. Law clk. for Chief Justice Nebr. Supreme Ct., 1973-74; sr. ptnr. Snell & Wilmer, Phoenix, 1974-99; ptnr. Colburn Law Offices, Phoenix, 1999—. Office: Colburn Law Offices 7501 N 16th St Ste 200 Phoenix AZ 85020-4677

COLBURN, KEITH W., electronics executive; Chmn. bd., CEO Consolidated Electrical Distributors, Thousand Oaks, Calif., 1999—. Office: Consolidated Electrical Distributors Inc 31356 Via Colinas Ste 107 Westlake Village CA 91362

COLDEWEY, JOHN CHRISTOPHER, English literature educator; b. Beloit, Wis., June 13, 1944; s. George Henry and Frances Mary (McLoughlin) C.; m. Carolyn Culver (div.); children: Christopher, Devin; m. Christine May Rose, Sept. 9, 1989. BA, Lewis U., 1966; student, U. London, Eng., 1966; MA, No. Ill. U., 1967; PhD, U. Colo., 1972. Acting asst. prof. English U. Wash., Seattle, 1972-73, asst. prof. English, 1973-79, assoc. prof. English, 1979-91, prof. English, 1991—, dir. grad. studies, 1995-99; postdoctoral rsch. fellow Nottingham (Eng.) U., 1979-80; Fulbright exchange prof. U. East Anglia, Norwich, Eng., 1986-87. Lectr., speaker and reader in field. Author: Pseudomagia: A 17th Century Neo-Latin Tragicomedy by William Mewe, 1979, Renaissance Latin Drama in England, Vol. IV, 1987, Vol. 14, 1991, Contexts for Early English Drama, 1989, Early English Drama: An Anthology, 1993, Drama: Classical Through Contemporary, 1998, rev., 2001, Medieval Drama: Critical and Cultural Studies (4 Vols.), 2007; editor: Modern Lang. Quar., 1983-93; contbr. chpts. to books, articles to profl. jours. Bd. dirs. Friends U. Wash. Libr., 1991-99 (pres. 1995-97); hon. advisor Brit. Univs. Summers Schs. Program, 1977-94. Fellow Medieval Acad. Am., 1974-75; grantee Am. Coun. Learned Socs., 1974-75, 1976-77, 86-87, 89-90, grantee NEH, 1979-80, 82-83, 92-93, fellow, 1999-2000. Mem. Coun. Editors Learned Jours. (pres. 1992-94, v.p. 1990-92, sec.-treas. 1989-90), Medieval and Renaissance Drama Soc. (exec. coun. 1997-98, v.p. 1998-00), Medieval European Drama Coun. (Am. rep. 1997-99). Avocations: skiing, bicycling, mountain travel, running. Home: 333 35th Ave E Seattle WA 98112-4923 Office: U Wash Dept English Box 354330 Seattle WA 98195-0001 Office Phone: 206-543-2183. Business E-Mail: jcjc@u.washington.edu.

COLDREN, LARRY ALLEN, electrical engineering educator, consultant; b. Lewistown, Pa., Jan. 1, 1946; s. Roscoe Calvin and Mary (Hutchinson) C.; m. Donna Kauffman, Sept. 4, 1966; children: Christopher William, Bret Allen. BS, AB, Bucknell U., 1968; MS, Stanford U., 1969, PhD, 1972. Registered profl. engr., N.J. Mem. tech. staff Bell Labs., NJ, 1968-84, supr. NJ, 1984; prof. U. Calif., Santa Barbara, 1984—, Fred Kavli prof. optoelectronics and sensors Dept. Engring.; chmn., chief tech. officer Agility Commns., 1998—. Contbr. over 500 papers to tech. jours.; patentee in field. Recipient John Tyndall award, 2004. Fellow IEEE (mem. ad com. 1988-94), Optical Soc. Am., IEE; mem. NAE, Phi Beta Kappa, Tau Beta Pi, Pi Mu Epsilon, Sigma Pi Sigma. Presbyterian. Avocation: flying. Home: 4665 Via Vistosa Santa Barbara CA 93110-2333 Business E-Mail: coldren@ece.ucsb.edu.

COLE, CHARLES EDWARD, lawyer, state attorney general; b. Yakima, Wash., Oct. 10, 1927; married; 3 children. BA, Stanford U., 1950, LLB, 1953. Law clk. Vets. Affairs Commn. Territory of Alaska, Juneau, 1954, Territorial Atty. Gen.'s Office, Fairbanks, Alaska, 1955-56, U.S. Dist. Ct. Alaska, Fairbanks, 1955-56; city magistrate City of Fairbanks, 1957-58; pvt. practice law, 1957-90; atty. gen. State of Alaska, 1990-94; pvt. law comml. litigation, 1995—. Profl. baseball player, Stockton, Calif. and Twin Falls, Idaho, summers of 1950, 51, 53. With U.S. Army, 1946-47. Mem. Calif. State Bar, Washington State Bar Assn., Alaska Bar Assn. Office: Law Dept State of AK Office of Atty Gen PO Box 110300 Juneau AK 99811-0300 also: Law Offices of Charles E Cole 406 Cushman St Fairbanks AK 99701-4632

COLE, CRAIG W., grocery chain executive; b. 1950; s. Jack Cole; m. Sue Cole. Saxophonist, singer rock band; mgr. human rels. dept. Foss Launch and Tug; asst. to exec. dir. Wash. Human Rights Commn.; legis. aide; pres., CEO Brown & Cole Stores Inc., Bellingham, Wash., 1986—. Chmn. bd. Assoc. Grocers. Former councilman Whatcom County, Wash.; former mem. Wash. Gov.'s Com. on Employment of Handicapped, Gov.'s Com. on Affirmative Action; former trustee Western Wash. U.; mem. Wash. Gov.'s Commn. on Early Learning. Mem. Food Mktg. Inst. (bd. dirs.). Office: Brown & Cole Stores Inc PO Box 9797 Bellingham WA 98227-9797

COLE, DAVID MACAULAY, journalist, consultant; b. Richmond, Calif., Feb. 17, 1954; s. Frederick George and Norma Ann C. Student, San Francisco State U., 1972-77. Mng. editor Feed/Back Mag., San Francisco, 1974-78, exec. editor, 1978-83; asst. music editor Rolling Stone Mag., San Francisco, 1976-77; from copy editor to asst. mng. editor The San Francisco Examiner, 1979-87, asst. mng. editor, 1987-89; prin., owner The Cole Group, Pacifica, Calif., 1989—. Editor, publisher The Cole Papers, 1989—, NewsInc., 1997—; author: Cole's Notes--Profiles in Pagination, 1996, Cole's Guide to Publishing Systems, 1994, 95, 96, 97; contbg. editor Presstime Magazine, 1994-2005, TechNews Mag., 1994-2003; columnist, Publish Mag., 1997. Trustee Jr. Statesman Found, San Mateo, Calif., 1997—, exec. com., 2001-05. Mem. Nat. Press Photographers Assn., Soc. News Design, Soc. Profl. Journalists (v.p. local chpt. 1979). Avocation: steam train preservation. Office: The Cole Group PO Box 719 Pacifica CA 94044-0719 Fax: 650-475-8479. E-mail: dmc@colegroup.com.

COLE, GARY MICHAEL, actor; b. Park Ridge, Ill., Sept. 20, 1956; m. Teddi Siddall, Mar. 8, 1992; 1 child, Mary. Attended, Ill. State U. Actor: (TV films) Heart of Steel, 1983, Fatal Vision, 1984, A Matter of Principle, 1984, First Steps, 1985, Vital Signs, 1986, Echoes in the Darkness, 1987, Those She Left Behind, 1989, The Old Man and the Sea, 1990, Son of the Morning Star, 1991, The Switch, 1993, When Love Kills: The Seduction of John Hearn, 1993, A Time to Heal, 1994, Fall from Grace, 1994, For My Daughter's Honor, 1996, Lies He Told, 1997, American Adventure, 2000, Neurotic Tendencies, 2001, Cadet Kelly, 2002, The Brady Bunch in the White House, 2002, Criminology 101, 2003, (voice) Kim Possible: A Sitch in Time, 2003, Pop Rocks, 2004, (voice) Kim Possible: So the Drama, 2005, Wanted, 2005, That Guy, 2006, (voice) The Dukes of Hazzard: The Beginning, 2007,; (films) Lucas, 1986, In the Line of Fire, 1993, The Brady Bunch Movie, 1995, A Very Brady Sequel, 1996, Cyclops, Baby, 1997, Santa Fe, 1997, Gang Related, 1997, A Simple Plan, 1998, I'll Be Home for Christmas, 1998, Office Space, 1999, Kiss the Sky, 1999, The Gift, 2000, The Rising Place, 2001, One Hour Photo, 2002, I Spy, 2002, Win a Date with Tad Hamilton!, 2004, Dodgeball: A True Underdog Story, 2004, The Ring Two, 2005, Mozart and the Whale, 2005, Talladega Nights: The Ballad of Ricky Bobby, 2006, My Wife Is Retarded, 2007, Breach, 2007, American Pastime, 2007, Goodnight Vagina, 2007, Conspiracy, 2008, Pineapple Express, 2008; (TV series) Midnight Caller, 1988—91, American Gothic, 1995—96, Crusade, 1999, Family Affair, 2002—03, Wanted, 2005, The West Wing, 2003—06, (voice) Family Guy, 2000—07, Harvey Birdman, Attorney at Law, 2000—07, Kim Possible, 2002—07, 12 Miles of Bad Road, 2008, Desperate Housewives, 2008; (TV miniseries) From the Earth to the Moon, 1998. Office: c/o Envoy Entertainment 2637 Centinela Ave Ste 8 Santa Monica CA 90405

COLE, GEORGE THOMAS, lawyer; b. Orlando, Fla., Mar. 14, 1946; s. Robert Bates and Frances (Arnold) C.; m. Peggy Ellen Stimson, May 23, 1981; children: Leslie Elizabeth, Ashley Ellen, Robert Warren. AB, Yale U., 1968; JD, U. Mich., 1975. Bar: Ariz. 1975. With Fennemore, Craig, von Ammon, Udall & Powers, Phoenix, 1975-81; ptnr. Fennemore Craig, P.C., Phoenix, 1981—. Mem. Ariz. State U. Coun. for Design Excellence. Served to lt. (j.g.) USN, 1968-71. Named one of, Best Lawyers in Am. Real Estate, 2007, S.W. Super Lawyers Real Estate, 2007. Fellow: Ariz. Bar Found. (founding); mem.: Maricopa Bar Assn., Ariz. Bar Assn. (coun. real property sect. 1985—88, chmn. 1987—88), Cmty. Assns. Inst., Nat. Golf Found. (assoc.), ULI (cmty. devel. coun. 1995—2001, 2003—), Ariz. Assn. Home Bldrs., Nat. Assn. Home Bldrs., Phoenix Cmty. Alliance (bd. mem.), White Mountain Country Club (Pinetop, Ariz.), Paradise Valley Country Club (Phoenix), Yale Club (pres. 1984). Republican. Methodist. Home: 5102 E Desert Park Ln Paradise Valley AZ 85253-3054 Office: Fennemore Craig 3003 N Central Ave Ste 2600 Phoenix AZ 85012-2913 Office Phone: 602-916-5308. E-mail: gcole@fclaw.com.

COLE, JAMES W., dean; BS, Northeast Mo. State U., Kirksville, 1963; DO, Kans. City Coll. Osteo. Medicine, Mo., 1967. Intern Tucson Gen. Hosp., 1967—68; resident in pathology and lab. medicine Cherry Hill Med. Ctr., NJ, 1976—79; fellow in fed. health care policy Ohio U. Coll. Osteo. Medicine, Athens, 1994—95; dean Midwestern U. Ariz. Coll. Osteo. Medicine, Glendale, 1996—. Office: Ariz Coll Osteo Medicine 19555 N 59th Ave Glendale AZ 85308

COLE, K.C., journalist, writer; BA, Barnard Coll. Writer, editor Saturday Rev., San Francisco; editor Newsday; sci. commentator Pasadena Pub. Radio (KPCC); sci. writer L.A. Times, 1994—. Adj. prof. UCLA; tchr. sci. writing Yale U., Wesleyan U.; mem. Jour. Women Symposium; dir. PEN West; vis. prof. U. So. Calif. Annenberg, 2006—. Author: (book) The Hole in the Universe: How Scientists Peered Over the Edge of Emptiness and Found Everything, The Universe and the Teacup: The Mathematics of Truth and Beauty, First You Build a Cloud: Reflections on Phyics as a Way of Life, Mind Over Matter: Conversations with the Cosmos, 2003; contbg. writer: The New Yorker, The New York Times, Washington Post, Newsday, Esquire, Newsweek, others. Recipient Writing prize, Am. Inst. Physics, 1995, Edward R. Murrow award, Skeptics Soc., 1998, Elizabeth A. Wood Sci. Writing award, Am. Crystallographic Assn., 2001; fellow Math. Sci. Rsch. Inst., Exploratorium. Office: LA Times 202 W First St Los Angeles CA 90012 Office Phone: 213-237-7354. Office Fax: 213-237-4712. Business E-Mail: kc.cole@latimes.com.

COLE, MACK, state legislator, rancher; b. Forsyth, Mont., June 4, 1936; m. Judy Cole; 3 children. BS, Mont. State U., 1958; MS, Thunderbird Grad Sch. Mgmt., 1962. Rancher; with Bur. Indian Affairs; mem. Mont. Senate, Dist. 4, Helena, 1995—; chair state adminstrn. com. Mont. State Senate, mem. hwys./transp. com., conf. com., natural resources com. With Bur. Indian Affairs. Republican. Roman Catholic. Office: PO Box 286 Hysham MT 59038-0286

COLE, NATALIE MARIA, singer; b. LA, Feb. 6, 1950; d. Nathaniel Adam and Maria (Harkins) Cole; m. Marvin J. Yancy, July 31, 1976 (div. 1980); 1 child, Robert Adam; m. Andre Fischer, Sept. 16, 1989 (div. 1995); m. Rev. Kenneth Dupress, Oct. 12, 2001 (div. 2004). BA in Child Psychology, U. Mass., 1972. Rec. singles and albums, 1975—; albums include Dangerous, 1985, Everlasting, 1987, The Natalie Cole Collection, 1987, Inseparable, Thankful, Good To Be Back, 1989, Unforgettable, 1991 (4 grammys, 3 grammys 1992), Too Much Weekend, 1992, I'm Ready, 1992, I've Got Love On My Mind, 1992, Take A Look, 1993 (Grammy award nominee best jazz vocal 1994), Holly and Ivy, 1994, Stardust (2 Grammy awards), Magic of Christmas, 1999, Snowfall on the Sahara, 1999, Greatest Hits, 2000, Ask a Woman Who Knows, 2002, Leavin', 2006, Still Unforgettable, 2008 (Grammy award for Best Traditional Pop Vocal Album, 2009), Caroling, Caroling Christmas, 2008; television appearances include Big Break (host), 1990, Lily in Winter, 1994; appeared in TV movies The Wizard of Oz in Concert (as Glinda), 1995, Always Outnumbered, 1998, Freak City, 1999; co-author: Angel on My Shoulder, 2000; composer Easter Egg Escapade, 2005. Recipient Grammy award for best new artist, 1975, best Rhythm and Blues female vocalist 1976; recipient 1 gold single, 3 gold albums; recipient 2 Image awards NAACP 1976, 1977; Am. Music award 1978, other awards. Mem.: Nat. Assn. Rec. Arts & Scis., AFTRA, Delta Sigma Delta. Baptist. Home: 700 N San Vicente Blvd Ste G910 West Hollywood CA 90069-5061*

COLE, RICHARD CHARLES, lawyer; b. Albany, NY, Apr. 23, 1950; s. Charles Stanley and Doris Jean (Hatch) Cole; children: Jack Patrick, Charles Michael, Will. BA magna cum laude, Cornell U., 1972; JD, Harvard U., 1975. Bar: N.Y. 1976, Calif. 1989, U.S. Dist. Ct. (so. and ea. dists.) N.Y. 1977, U.S. Ct. Apeals (D.C. cir.) 1980, U.S. Ct. Appeals (2d and 5th cirs.) 1981, U.S. Dist. Ct. (no, ea., so. and ctrl. dists.) 1989, U.S. Supreme Ct. 1995. Assoc. LeBoeuf, Lamb, Leiby & MacRae, NYC, 1975-83, ptnr., 1984-89, LeBoeuf, Lamb, Greene & MacRae, San Francisco, 1989-95; pvt. practice Mill Valley, 1996—. Mem.: ABA. Avocations: woodwind instruments, school volunteering, jazz. Home: 255 Sycamore Ave Mill Valley CA 94941-2931 Office Phone: 415-383-2558. Personal E-mail: dickcc@pacbell.net.

COLE, ROBERT K., diversified financial services company executive; MBA, Wayne State U. Pres. NBD Bancorp and Pub. Storage, Triple Five Inc., real estate devel., 1990—94; pres., COO-fin. Plaza Home Mortgage Corp., 1994—95; co-founder New Century Fin. Corp., Irvine, Calif., 1995, chmn., CEO, 1995—2006, chmn., 2006—. Bd. dirs. Option One Mortgage Corp. (subs. Plaza Home Mortgage), 1994—95, New Century Mortgage, 1995—. Office: New Century Fin Corp Ste 1000 18400 Von Karman Ave Irvine CA 92612 Office Phone: 949-440-7032.

COLE, STEPHEN E., magistrate judge; b. Powell, Wyo., Apr. 18, 1947; BA, U. Wyo., 1969, JD, 1974. Pvt. law practice, Worland, Wyo.; judge Worland Mcpl. Ct., 1975-81, Ten Sleep Mcpl. Ct., 1977-81; justice of the peace Washakie County Justice Ct., 1977-81; magistrate judge U.S. Dist. Ct. Wyo., 1975—. Office: PO Box 387 Yellowstone National Park WY 82190-0387 E-mail: stephen_cole@wyd.uscourts.gov.

COLE, TERRI LYNN, organization administrator; b. Tucson, Dec. 28, 1951; m. James R. Cole II. Student, U. N.Mex., 1975-80; cert., Inst. Orgn. Mgmt., 1985. Cert. chamber exec. With SunWest Bank, Albuquerque, 1971-74, employment adminstr., 1974-76, communications dir., 1976-78; pub. info. dir. Albuquerque C. of C., 1978-81, gen. mgr., 1981-83, pres., 1983—. Pres. N.Mex. C. of C. Execs. Assn., 1986-87, bd. dirs., 1980—; bd. regents Inst. for Orgn. Mgmt., Stanford U., 1988—, vice chmn., 1990-91, chmn., 1991; bd. dirs. Hosp. Home Health, Inc. Recipient Bus. Devel. award Expn. Mgmt. Inc., 1985, Women on Move award YWCA, 1986; named one of Outstanding Women of Am., 1984. Mem. Am. C. of C. Execs. Assn. (chmn. elect bd. 1992—). Republican. Avocations: skiing, bicycling, gardening. Office: Greater Albuquerque C of C PO Box 25100 Albuquerque NM 87125-0100

COLE, WILLIAM LOUIS, lawyer; b. LA, May 13, 1952; AB magna cum laude, U. Calif., Irvine, 1974; JD, Stanford U., 1977. Bar: Calif. 1977. Atty. Mitchell, Silberberg & Knupp, LA, mng. ptnr., 1991—97, mem. exec. com., 1997—. Mem. ABA (co-chair sports and entertainment com. 2003-05), State Bar Calif., Los Angeles County Bar Assn. (mem. exec. com. labor law sect. 1989-90), Order of Coif, Phi Beta Kappa. Office: Mitchell Silberberg & Knupp 11377 W Olympic Blvd Los Angeles CA 90064-1625 Office Phone: 310-312-2000. Business E-Mail: wlc@msk.com.

COLELLA, PHILIP, mathematician; BS, MS, PhD, U. Calif. Head applied numerical algorithms group Lawrence Berkeley Nat. Lab. Recipient Sidney Fernbach award, IEEE, 1998, SIAM/ACM prize for computational sci. and engring., 2003. Mem.: NAS (mem. bd. math. scis. and their applications). Office: Lawrence Berkeley Nat Lab 1 Cyclotron Rd MS 50A-1148 Berkeley CA 94720 Office Phone: 510-486-5412. Office Fax: 510-495-2505. E-mail: PColella@lbl.gov.

COLEMAN, CHARLES CLYDE, physicist, educator; b. York, Eng., July 31, 1937; arrived in U.S., 1941; s. Jesse C. and Geraldine (Doherty) C.; m. Sharon R. Slutsky, Aug. 12, 1976; children: Jeffrey Andrew, Matthew Casey. BA, UCLA, 1959, MA, 1961, PhD, 1968. Asst. prof. physics Calif. State U., LA, 1968-71, assoc. prof. 1971-76, prof., 1976—2002, prof. emeritus, 2002—. Cons. Gen. Dynamics Corp., 1975-77, China Lake Naval Rsch. Labs., 1981; dir. Csula Accelerator Facility; exec. dir. Csula Applied Physics Inst., 1978-83; sr. rsch. fellow Darwin Coll., Cambridge (Eng.) U., 1975-76; project specialist Chinese Provincial Univs. Devel. Project of World Bank, 1987-90; vis. prof. physics U. Istanbul, Turkey, 1969, 72, U. Sydney, Australia, 1977, Arya Mar U., Iran, 1976, U. Natal, South Africa, 1977, UCLA, 1990-91, U. Leicester, U.K., 1995-2001, Hubei U., Wuhan, China, 2002; mem. NASA rev. panel, 1992. Author: Modern Physics for Semiconductor Science, 2007; contbr. articles to sci. publs.; referee Solid State Electronics, Phys. Rev., Phys. Rev. Letters, Jour. Phys. Chem. Solids, Jour. Solid State Chem., Jour. Optical Materials. Trustee Calif. State U. LA Found., 1981-85. Grantee NSF, 1975-2002, Rsch. Corp., 1987-91; NATO Collaborative Rsch. grantee, 1991—2002; NATO Sr. Rsch. fellow Cavendish Lab. (U.K.), 1983-84, Am. Chem. Soc. Rsch. Faculty fellow, 1990. Fellow Brit. Interplanetary Soc., Royal Philatelic Soc. (London); mem. Am. Phys. Soc., Am. Radio Relay League, Sigma Xi, Phi Kappa Phi, Phi Beta Delta, Sigma Pi Sigma. Office: Calif State U Dept Physics Los Angeles CA 90032 Office Phone: 323-343-2100. E-mail: ccolema@calstatela.edu.

COLEMAN, COURTNEY STAFFORD, mathematician, educator; b. Ventura, Calif., July 19, 1930; s. Courtney Clemon and Una (Stafford) C.; m. Julia Wellnitz, June 26, 1954; children: David, Margaret, Diane. BA, U. Calif., Berkeley, 1951; PhD, Princeton U., 1955. Asst. prof. Wesleyan U., Middletown, Conn., 1955-58; from asst. prof. to full prof. Harvey Mudd Coll., Claremont, Calif., 1959-98. Lectr. Princeton (N.J.) U., 1954-55; rsch. in field. Author, editor: Differential Equations Models, 1983; editor, translator: Local Methods in Nonlinear Differential Equations, 1988; author: (with others) Differential Equations, 1987, Differential Equations Laboratory Workbook, 1992 (EDUCOM award for best math./computer course materials), Ordinary Differential Equations: A Modeling Perspective, 1998, 2d edit., 2004, ODE Architect, 1999 (award of excellence and Gold medal for best CD-ROM in edn.); mem. editl. bd. Jour. of Differential Equations, 1964—, UMAP Jour., 1980—. Mem. Am. Math. Soc., Math. Assn. Am., Soc. Indsl. Applied Math. Office: Harvey Mudd Coll Math Dept 1250 N Dartmouth Ave Claremont CA 91711 Personal E-mail: colemancourtney@hotmail.com. E-mail: coleman@hmc.edu.

COLEMAN, DEBI (DEBORAH ANN), investment and former computer company executive; b. Central Falls, RI, Jan. 22, 1953; d. John Austin and Joan Mary Coleman. BA, Brown U., 1974; MBA, Stanford U., 1978; PhD in Engring. (hon.), Worcester Poly., Mass., 1987. With fin. mgmt. tng. program Gen. Electric, Providence, 1975-76; with fin. mgmt. Hewlett-Packard Co., Cupertino, Calif., 1978-81; contr. Macintosh/Apple 32 group Apple Computer Inc., Cupertino, Calif., 1981-84, dir. ops., 1984-85, v.p. worldwide mfg., 1985-87, CFO, 1987-89, chief info. officer, 1990-92, CIO, 1990-92; v.p. materials ops. Tektronix Inc., Wilsonville, OR, 1992-94; pres., CEO Merix Corp., Forest Grove, Ill., 1994—2001, chmn., 1999—2001; mng. ptnr. SmartForest Ventures, Portland, Oreg., 2001—. Mem. U.S. Dept. Def. Mfg. Sci. Tech. Bd., 1988-91; bd. dirs. VMX, Inc., Software Pub Corp., Octel, Reply! Inc., 2006- Mem. adv. coun. Stanford Inst. Mfg. Automation, 1985-87; mem. Harvard U. Bus. Sch. Vis. Com., 1987—, Com. of 200, 1987—; trustee San Jose/Cleve. Ballet, 1989-92, Brown U., 1994—. Named a Henry Crown Fellow, Aspen Inst., 1997. Mem. Internat. Women's Forum. Democrat. Roman Catholic. Office: SmartForest Ventures 319 SW Washington St Ste 720 Portland OR 97204

COLEMAN, FRAN NATIVIDAD, state representative; b. Denver, July 5, 1945; m. Ben H. Coleman; stepchildren: Pam DiMarco, Steve, Craig, Wayne; children: Matt Lopez, Mitch Lopez. BA in Bus. Adminstrn., Loretto Heights Coll., 1987; MS in Telecomm., Denver U., 1992; cert. govt. contracting, U. Phoenix, Denver, 1995. State rep., dist. 1 Colo. House Rep., Denver, 1998—, mem. joint com. on legis. audit, mem. bus. affairs and labor, and local govt. coms. Mem. Bus. Affairs and Labor Com., Joint Com. on Legis. Audit, Local Govt. Com. Adv. bd. LARASA, Ft. Logan Citizens; apptd. Denver Corrections Bd., 1992—97. Mem.: Nat. Alliance for Mentally Ill, Women in Govt. Democrat. Roman Catholic. Avocations: reading, golf, gardening, exercise. Office: State Capitol #357 200 E Colfax Ave Denver CO 80203

COLEMAN, PAUL JEROME, JR., physicist, researcher; b. Evanston, Ill., Mar. 7, 1932; s. Paul Jerome and Eunice Cecile (Weissenberg) C.; m. Doris Ann Fields, Oct. 3, 1964; children: Derrick, Craig. BS in Engring. Math., U. Mich., 1954, BS in Engring. Physics, 1954, MS in Physics, 1958; PhD in Space Physics, UCLA, 1966. Rsch. scientist Ramo-Wooldridge Corp. (name now Northrop Grumman), El Segundo, Calif., 1958-61; instr. math. U. So. Calif., LA, 1958-61; mgr. interplanetary scis. program NASA, Washington, 1961-62; rsch.

scientist UCLA, 1962-66, prof. geophysics, space physics, 1966—; asst. lab. dir., mgr. Earth and Space Scis. divsn., chmn. Inst. Geophysics and Planetary Physics Nat. Lab., Los Alamos, N.Mex., 1981-86; dir. Inst. Geophysics and Planetary Physics UCLA, 1989-92; dir. Nat. Inst. for Global Environ. Change, 1994-96; pres. Univs. Space Rsch. Assn., Columbia, Md., 1981-2000, Girvan Inst. Tech., 2002—. Bd. dirs. Axcess Inc., Dallas, Knowledge Vector, Inc., Durham, N.C., others; mem. adv. bd. San Diego Supercomputer Ctr., 1986-90, chmn., 1987-88, others; trustee Univs. Space Rsch. Assn., Columbia, Md., 1981-2000, Am. Tech. Alliances, 1990-2002, Internat. Small Satellite Orgn., 1992-96; vis. scholar U. Paris, 1975-76; vis. scientist Lab. for Aeronomy Ctr. Nat. Rsch. Sci., Verrieres le Buisson, France, 1975-76; com. mem. numerous sci. and ednl. orgns., cons. numerous fin. and indsl. cos. Co-editor: Solar Wind, 1972; co-author: Pioneering the Space Frontier, 1986; mem. editorial bd. Geophysics and Astrophysics Monographs, 1970—; assoc. editor Cosmic Electrodynamics, 1968-72; contbr. revs. to numerous profl. jours. Apptd. to Nat. Commn. on Space, Pres. of U.S., 1985, apptd. to Space Policy Adv. Bd., Nat. Space Coun., v.p. of U.S., 1991; bd. dirs. St. Matthew's Sch., Pacific Palisades, Calif., 1979-82, v.p., 1981-82. 1st lt. USAF, 1954-56, Korea. Recipient Exceptional Sci. Achievement Medal NASA, 1970, 1972, spl. recognition for contributions to the Apollo Program, 1979; Guggenheim fellow 1975-76, Fulbright scholar, 1975-76, Rsch. grantee NASA, NSF, Office Naval Research, Calif. Space Inst., Air Force Office Sci. Research, U.S. Geol. Survey. Mem. Internat. Acad. Astronautics, Bel Air Bay Club (L.A.), Birnam Wood Golf Club (Monteceito, Calif.), Cosmos Club (Washington), Valley Club (Montecito, Calif.), Eldorado Country Club (Indian Wells, Calif.), Tau Beta Pi, Phi Eta Sigma. Avocations: flying, skiing, racquetball, tennis, golf. Home: 1323 Monaco Dr Pacific Palisades CA 90272-4007 Office: UCLA Inst Geophysics & Planetary Physics 405 Hilgard Ave Los Angeles CA 90095-9000 Home Phone: 310-474-8702; Office Phone: 310-825-1776. Business E-Mail: pcoleman@igpp.ucla.edu.

COLEMAN, ROBERT GRIFFIN, geology educator; b. Twin Falls, Idaho, Jan. 5, 1923; s. Lloyd Wilbur and Frances (Brown) C.; m. Cathryn J. Hirschberger, Aug. 7, 1948; children: Robert Griffin Jr., Derrick Job, Mark Dana. BS, Oreg. State U., 1948, MS, 1950; PhD, Stanford U., 1957. Mineralogist AEC, NYC, 1952-54; geologist U.S. Geol. Survey, Washington, 1954-57, Menlo Park, Calif., 1958-80; prof. geology Stanford U., Calif., 1981-93, prof. emeritus Calif., 1993—. Vis. petrographer New Zealand Geol. Survey, 1962-63; br. chief isotope geology U.S. Geol. Survey, Menlo Park, 1964-68, regional geologist, Saudi Arabia, 1970-71, br. chief field geochemistry and petrology, Menlo Park, 1977-79; vis. scholar Woods Hole Oceanographic Inst., Mass., 1975; vis. prof. geology Sultan Qaboos U., Oman, 1987, 89; cons. geologist, 1993—; instr. geobotany field sch. Siskiyou Inst., Oreg., 1998-99. Author: Ophiolites, 1977, Geologic Evolution of the Red Sea, 1993, Ultrahigh Pressure Metamorphism, 1995; contbr. articles to profl. jours. Named Outstanding Scientist, Oreg. Acad. Sci., 1977; Fairchild scholar Calif. Inst. Tech., Pasadena, 1980; recipient Meritorious award U.S. Dept. Interior, 1981 Fellow AAAS, Geol. Soc. Am. (coun.), Am. Mineral Soc. (coun., editor), Am. Geophys. Union; mem. Nat. Acad. Scis., Russian Acad. Sci. (fgn. assoc.). Republican. Avocations: wood carving, art. Home: 2025 Camino Al Lago Atherton CA 94027-5938 Business E-Mail: rcoleman@stanford.edu.

COLEMAN, THOMAS YOUNG, lawyer; b. Richmond, Va., Jan. 6, 1949; s. Emmet Macadium and Mary Katherine (Gay) C.; m. Janet Clare Norris, Aug. 30, 1980; children: Dana Alicia (dec.), Amanda Gay, Blair Norris. BA, U. Va., 1971, JD, 1975. Bar: Va. 1975, U.S. Dist. Ct. (we. dist.) Va. 1975, U.S. Ct. Appeals (4th cir.) 1976, Calif. 1977, U.S. Dist Ct. (no. dist.) Calif. 1977. Law clk. to Hon. James C. Turk, chief judge U.S. Dist. Ct. (we. dist.) Va., Charlottesville, 1975-76; assoc. Morrison & Foerster LLP, San Francisco, 1976-79; v.p., counsel Calif. 1st Bank (now Union Bank of Calif.), San Francisco, 1979-85; of counsel Orrick, Herrington & Sutcliffe LLP, San Francisco, 1985-86, chmn. profl. devel. com., ptnr., 1987—, gen. counsel, ptnr. in charge profl. devel. Speaker in field; vis. atty. Clifford-Turner Solicitors (now Clifford Chance), London, 1984. Mem. bus. gifts com. San Francisco Symphony. Mem. Internat. Bankers Assn. in Calif. (co-counsel). Office: Orrick Herrington & Sutcliffe LLP 405 Howard St San Francisco CA 94105-2669 Office Phone: 415-773-5870. Office Fax: 415-773-5759. Business E-Mail: tycoleman@orrick.com.

COLEMAN SMITH, SALAAM, communications executive; b. 1970; m. Christopher Smith; 1 child, Asa. BS in Indsl. Engring., Stanford U. Mgmt. cons.; v.p., Programming Nickelodeaon/Nick at Nite; programming and creative exec. MTV Networks; sr. v.p., Programming E! Networks, 2003—06; sr. v.p. Style Network, E! Entertainment, Inc., 2006, exec. v.p., 2006—. Prin. mem. strategic planning team, Nickelodeon Networks. Named one of Top 35 Executives Under 35, Hollywood Reporter, 2003, 40 Executives Under 40, Multichannel News, 2006; Walter Kaitz Found. Cable TV Industry fellowship. Office: E! Entertainment Television Inc 5750 Wilshire Blvd Los Angeles CA 90036

COLES, MARTIN, beverage service company executive; b. Cardiff, Wales, July 24, 1955; BS biochemistry, U. of Wales, 1977. Mgr. prodn. Proctor & Gamble; v.p. manufacturing, logistics, customer service, and franchised bottling ops. PepsiCo, 1987—92; dir. Logistics for Europe NIKE Inc., 1992—94; v.p., gen. mgr. Nike Europe, 1994—97; exec. v.p., global sales Nike Inc., 1997—2000; pres., CEO Letsbuyit.com, 2000—01; sr. v.p. Internat Ops. Gateway, Inc., 2001; exec. v.p. of Global Operating Units Reebok Internat., Ltd., 2001—02, exec. v.p., 2001—04, pres., CEO, 2002—04; pres. Starbucks Coffee Internat., 2004—07; COO Starbucks Corp., 2007—. Office: Starbucks Corp 2401 Utah Ave S Seattle WA 98134 Office Phone: 206-447-1575. Office Fax: 206-682-7570.

COLLAS, JUAN GARDUÑO, JR., lawyer; b. Manila, Apr. 25, 1932; s. Juan D. and Soledad (Garduño) C.; m. Maria L. Moreira, Aug. 1, 1959; children: Juan Jose, Elias Lopes, Cristina Maria, Daniel Benjamin. LLB, U. of Philippines, Quezon City, 1955; LLM, Yale U., 1958, JSD, 1959. Bar: Philippines 1956, Ill. 1960, Calif. 1971, U.S. Supreme Ct. 1967. Assoc., Sy Cip, Salazar & Assocs., Manila, 1956-57; atty. N.Y., N.H. & H. R.R., New Haven, 1959-60; assoc. Baker & McKenzie, Chgo., 1960-63, ptnr., Manila, 1963-70, San Francisco, 1970-95, Manila, 1995—. Contbr. articles to profl. jours. Trustee, sec. Friends of U. of Philippines Found. in Am., San Francisco, 1982—; co-chmn. San Francisco Lawyers for Better Govt., 1982—; chmn. San Francisco-Manila Sister City Com., 1986-92. Recipient Outstanding Filipino Overseas in Law award, Philippine Ministry Tourism Philippines Jaycees, 1979. Mem. ABA, Am. Arbitration Assn. (panelist), Ill. State Bar Assn., State Bar Calif., Integrated Bar of Philippines, Filipino-Am. C. of C. (bd. dirs. 1974-91, 94-96, pres. 1985-87, chmn. bd. dirs. 1987-89, 95-96). Republican. Roman Catholic. Clubs: Green Hills Country Club, Villa Taverna (San Francisco). Office: Baker & McKenzie 2 Embarcadero Ctr Ste 2400 San Francisco CA 94111-3909

COLLEN, MORRIS FRANK, retired medical administrator, physician, consultant, researcher; b. St. Paul, Nov. 12, 1913; s. Frank Morris and Rose Collen; m. Frances B. Diner, Sept. 24, 1937; children: Arnold Roy, Barry Joel, Roberta Joy, Randal Harry. BEE, U. Minn., 1934, MB with distinction, 1938, MD, 1939; DSc (hon.), U. Victoria, BC, Can., 2004. Diplomate Am. Bd. Internal Medicine. Intern Michael Reese Hosp., Chgo., 1939—40; resident LA County Hosp., 1940—42; chief med. service Kaiser Found. Hosp., Oakland, Calif., 1942—52, chief of staff, 1952—53; physician in chief San Francisco Med. Ctr.; med. dir. West Bay divsn. Permanente Med. Group, 1953—62, dir. med. methods rsch., 1962—79, dir. tech. assessment, 1979—83, cons. divsn. rsch., 1983—. Chmn. exec. com. Permanente Med. Group, Oakland, 1953—73; dir. Permanente Svcs., Inc., Oakland, 1958—73; adj. asst. prof. biomed. informatics Uniformed Svcs. U. Health Scis., 2000—05; chmn. health care sys. study sect. USPHS, 1968—72, mem. adv. com. demonstration grants, 1967, advisor VA, 68; mem. adv. com. Automated Multiphasic Health Testing, 1971; discussant Nat. Conf. Preventive Medicine, Bethesda, Md., 1975; mem. com. on tech. in health care NAS, 1976; mem. adv. group Nat. Commn. on Digestive Diseases, U.S. Congress, 1978; mem. adv. panel to U.S. Congress Office of Tech. Assessment, 1980—85; mem. peer rev. adv. group TRIMIS program Dept. Def., 1978—90; program chmn. 3rd Internat. Conf. Med. Informatics, Tokyo, 1980; chmn. bd. sci. counselors Nat. Libr. Medicine, 1985—87, mem. lit. selection tech. rev. com., 1997—2002, chmn., 2000—02; chmn. tech. evaluation group Application of Advanced Network Infrastructure in Health and Disaster Mgmt., 2002, chmn. tech. group, 02; program chmn. Internat. Conf. Health Promotion, Atlanta, 2003. Author: Treatment of Pneumococcic Pneumonia, 1948, Hospital Computer Systems, 1974, Multiphasic Health Testing Services, 1978, History of Medical Informatics, 1995; editor: Permanente Med. Bull., 1943—53; mem. editl. bd.: Preventive Medicine, 1970—80, Jour. Med. Sys., Methods Info. Medicine, 1980—97, Diagnostic Medicine, 1980—84, Computers in Biomed. Rsch., 1987—94; contbr. more than 200 articles to profl. jours., chpts. to books. Fellow Ctr. Advanced Studies in Behavioral Scis., Stanford U., 1985—86; scholar Johns Hopkins Centennial scholar, 1976, scholar-in-residence, Nat. Libr. Medicine, 1987—2002. Fellow: ACP, Am. Coll. Med. Informatics (pres. 1987—88, Morris F. Collen medal named in his honor 1993), Am. Inst. Med. and Biol. Engring., Am. Coll. Chest Physicians, Am. Coll. Cardiology; mem.: NAS, AMA, Salutis Unitas (v.p. 1972), Internat. Health Evaluation Assn. (pres. 1995—96, Lifetime Achievement award 1992, Computers in Health Care Pioneer award 1992, David E. Morgan award for achievement in health care info. 1998, Japan Shigeaki Hinohara award for preventive medicine 2001, Cummings Psyche award for behavioral medical rsch. 2001, Morris F. Collen Permanente Rsch. award named in his honor 2003, 2009), Am. Med. Informatics Assn. (bd. dirs. 1985—96), Nat. Acad. Practice in Medicine (chmn. 1982—88, co-chmn. 1989—91), Soc. Adv. Med. Sys. (pres. 1973), Am. Fedn. Clin. Rsch., Inst. Medicine (chmn. tech. subcom. for improving patient records 1990, chmn. workshop on informatics in clin. preventive medicine 1991), Internat. Med. Informatics Assn. Sr. Officers Club, Tau Beta Pi, Alpha Omega Alpha. Achievements include named a library after his name at Kaiser Permanente, Oakland, California. Office: 2175 Ygnacio Valley Rd #228 Walnut Creek CA 94598 also: 2000 Broadway Oakland CA 94612 Personal E-mail: mfcollen@aol.com.

COLLETT, ROBERT LEE, financial company executive; b. Ardmore, Okla., July 1, 1940; s. Pat (Dowell) Conway; m. Sue Walker Healy; 1 child, Catherine April. BA in Math., Rice U., 1962; MA in Econs., Duke U., 1963. Actuary Milliman & Robertson, Inc., Phila., 1966-70, prin. Houston, 1970-89, pres., 1990, pres., CEO Houston and Seattle, 1991-92, Seattle, 1992—2002. Bd. dirs. Seattle Symphony, 1992—2002; chmn. Millenium Global, 2000—. Fellow Soc. Actuaries (chmn. internat. sect. 1992—); mem. Rainier Club. Episcopalian. Avocations: travel, music. Office: Milliman & USA Inc 1301 5th Ave Ste 3800 Seattle WA 98101-2646

COLLETTI, NED LOUIS, JR., professional sports team executive; b. 1954; m. Gayle Colletti; children: Lou, Jenna. BA in Journalism, No. Ill. U. With media rels., baseball ops. dept. Chgo. Cubs, 1982—94; v.p., asst. gen. mgr. San Francisco Giants, 1995—2005; gen. mgr. LA Dodgers, 2005—. Spkr. in field. Author: Golden Glory: Notre Dame vs. Purdue, 1983, You Gotta Have Heart: Dallas Green's Rebuilding of the Cubs, 1985. Vol. Salesian Boys and Girls Club, San Francisco; Charlie Wedemeyer Family Outreach Program. Recipient Robert O. Fishel award for Pub. Excellence; named to Triton Coll. Sports Hall of Fame, 1993. Office: LA Dodgers 1000 Elysian Park Ave Los Angeles CA 90012

COLLIER, CHARLES ARTHUR, JR., lawyer; b. Columbus, Ohio, Apr. 18, 1930; s. Charles Arthur and Gertrude Clara (Roe) C.; m. Linda Louise Biggs, Aug. 5, 1961; children: Sheila Collier Rogers, Laura Collier Prescott. AB magna cum laude, Harvard U., 1952, LLB, 1955. Law clk. U.S. Dist. Ct. (cen. dist.) Calif., LA, 1959-60; assoc. Freston & Files, LA, 1960-66; assoc., ptnr. Mitchell, Silberberg & Knupp, LA, 1967-82; ptnr. Irell & Manella, LA, 1982-95, of counsel, 1995—2003; ret., 2003. Lectr. Calif. Continuing Edn. of Bar, 1976-89; advisor Restatement of Property, Donative Transfers, 1990—; speaker numerous local bar assns. Contbr. articles to profl. jours Recipient Arthur K. Marshall award Probate and Trust sect. L.A. County Bar Assn. Fellow Am. Coll. Trust and Estate Counsel (chmn. state laws com. 1986-89, regent 1989-98, joint editl. bd. uniform trust and estate acts 1988-2006, chmn. expanded practice com. 1989-92, chmn. nominating com. 1998-99, spkr. 1988, exec. com. 1989-98, treas. 1992-93, sec. 1993-94, v.p. 1994-95, pres.-elect 1995-96, pres. 1996-97, immediate past pres. 1997-98), ABA Found.; mem. ABA (mem. real property, trust and probate law sect. spkr. 1985, 89, moderator teleconf. 1998, coun. 1989-93, chmn. com. trust adminstrn. 1982-85, chmn. task force on fiduciary litigation 1986-89, sr. lawyers divsn., vice chair wills, probate and trusts com. 1999-2000, chair 2000-01, 08-, vice chair book pub. com. 2000-06, chair editl. bd. 2001—06, sec. 2005-07, vice chmn. 2007—, others), Estate Planning, Trust and Probate Law Sect. of State Bar Calif. (chmn. 1980-81, vice chmn. 1979-80, mem. exec. com. 1977-82, advisor 1982-85, chmn. probate com. 1977-78, mem. legislation com. 1977-80, sect. liaison to Calif. Law Revision Commn. 1982-88), Harvard Alumni Assn. (dir. 1975-77, v.p. 1979-82), Harvard Club So. Calif. (pres. 1970-72). Office: Irell & Manella LLP 1800 Ave Of Stars Ste 900 Los Angeles CA 90067-4276 Home Phone: 626-792-5914. Business E-Mail: ccollier@irell.com.

COLLIER, DAVID, political science professor; b. Chgo., Feb. 17, 1942; s. Donald and Malcolm (Carr) C.; m. Ruth Berins, Mar. 10, 1968; children: Stephen, Jennifer. BA, Harvard U., 1965; MA, U. Chgo., 1967, PhD, 1971. From instr. to assoc. prof. Ind. U., Bloomington, 1970—78; from assoc. prof. to Robson prof. polit. sci. U. Calif., Berkeley, 1978—, chmn. dept. polit. sci., 1990—93, 2003. Faculty fellow U. Notre Dame, 1986, 87; vis. prof. U. Chgo., 1989; chmn. Ctr. for Latin Am. Studies U. Calif., Berkeley, 1980-83; co-dir., co-founder Stanford-Berkeley Joint Ctr. for Latin Am. Studies, 1981-83. Author: Squatters and Oligarchs: Authoritarian Rule and Policy Change in Peru, 1976; co-author: Shaping the Political Arena, 1991 (Prize, Best Book on Comparative Politics, Am. Polit. Scis. Assn. 1993—), Rethinking Social Inquiry, 2004 (Best Book award Am. Polit. Sci. Assn.); co-author, editor: The New Authoritariansim in Latin America, 1979; co-editor: Oxford Handbook of Polit. Methodology, Method in the Social Sciences, 2008; contbr. articles to profl. jours. Disting. Faculty Mem. award U. Calif., 2005; fellow Social Sci. Rsch. Coun. and Am. Coun. Learned Socs., 1974-75, 79-80, 88-89, Guggenheim Found., 1988-89, Ctr. for Advanced Studies in Behavioral Scis., Stanford, 1994-95; grantee NSF 1975-77, 80-83 Fellow: Am. Acad. Arts and Sci.; mem.: Latin Am. Studies Assn., Am. Polit. Sci. Assn. (pres. comparative politics sect. 1997, founding pres. qualitative methods sect. 2002—03). Office: Univ Calif Dept Polit Sci 210 Barrows Hall Berkeley CA 94720-1950

COLLIGAN, EDWARD T., computer company and communications executive; B, U. Oreg. V.p., strategic and product marketing Radius Corp.; v.p. marketing Palm Inc.; former pres., COO Handspring, Inc. (acquired by palmOne, Inc. in 2003), 1998—2003; sr. v.p., gen. mgr., Wireless Bus. Unit Palm Inc., Sunnyvale, Calif., 2003—04, pres., 2004—, interim CEO, 2005, CEO, 2005—. Office: Palm Inc 950 W Maude Ave Sunnyvale CA 94085 Office Phone: 408-503-7000.

COLLIGAN, JOHN C. (BUD COLLIGAN), multimedia company executive; married; 3 children. BS in Internat. Econs., Georgetown U., 1976; MBA, Stanford U., 1983. With Macintosh divsn. Apple Computer Corp., 1983-85, head higher edn. mktg. and sales, 1985-89; pres., CEO Authorware, Inc., 1989-92; chmn. Macromedia, Inc., San Francisco, 1992-98; ptnr. Accel Ptnrs., Palo Alto, Calif., 1998—. Bd. dirs. S3 Corp., c/net Inc. Mem. Interactive Multimedia Assn. (bd. dirs.). Office: Accel Ptnrs 428 University Ave Palo Alto CA 94301-1812

COLLINS, AUDREY B., judge; b. 1945; BA, Howard U., 1967; MA, Am. U., 1969; JD, UCLA, 1977. Asst. atty. Legal Aid Found. LA, 1977-78; with Office LA County Dist. Atty., 1978-94, dept. dist. atty., 1978-94, asst. dir. burs. ctrl. ops. and spl. ops., 1988-92, asst. dir. atty., 1992-94; judge. US Dist. Ct. (Ctrl. Dist.) Calif., 1994—. Dep. gen. counsel Office Spl. Acad. scholar Howard U.; named Lawyer of Yr., Langston Bar Assn., 1988; honoree Howard U. Alumni Club So. Calif., 1989; recipient Profl. Achievement award UCLA Alumni Assn., 1997, Ernestine Stahlhut award Women Lawyers Assn., 1999, Bernard S. Jefferson Justice of Yr. award John M. and Langston Bar Assn., 2006. Mem. FBA, Nat. Assn. Women Judges, Nat. Bar Assn. (life), Assn. Bus. Trial Lawyers (bd. dirs. 2004—), State Bar Calif. (com. bar examiners, chmn. subcom. on moral character 1992-93, co-chmn. 1993-94), LA County Bar Assn. (exec. com. litig. sect. 1999-2002, task force on criminal justice sys. 2002-03), Assn. LA County Dist. Attys. (pres. 1983), Black Women Lawyers LA County, Women Lawyers LA (life, bd. dirs. 2005-, bd. govs. 2005-06), Calif. Women Lawyers (life), Order of Coif, Phi Beta Kappa. Office: US Dist Ct Edward R Roybal Fed Bldg 255 E Temple St Ste 670 Los Angeles CA 90012-3334

COLLINS, CLARENCE, musician; b. Bklyn., Mar. 17, 1941; Co-founding mem. the Imperials (formerly the Duponts and the Chesters), 1956—. Singer: (songs) Tears on My Pillow, 1958, Goin' Out of My Head, 1964, Hurt So Bad, 1965, others, (albums) We are the Imperials, 1959, Shades of the '40s, 1961, I'm on the Outside (Looking In), 1964, Payin' Our Dues, 1967, Reflections, 1967, Movie Grabbers, 1968, Out of Sight, Out of Mind, 1969, Little Anthony & the Imperials, 1970, On a New Street, 1973, You'll Never Know, 2008. Recipient Pioneer award, Rhythm & Blues Found., 1993; named to Vocal Group Hall of Fame, 1999, Long Island Music Hall of Fame, 2006, Rock & Roll Hall of Fame, 2009. Office: Imperials Plus Inc 3567 Fair Bluff St Las Vegas NV 89135 Office Phone: 702-360-5596. Office Fax: 702-243-5502. E-mail: wahoocollins@aol.com.

COLLINS, CURTIS ALLAN, oceanographer; b. Sept. 16, 1940; s. Ralph Charlie and Noma Lovella (Buckley) C.; m. Judith Ann Petersen, Dec. 22, 1962; children: Nathaniel Christopher and Hillary Victoria. BS, U.S. Mcht. Marine Acad., 1962; MS, Oreg. State U., 1964, PhD, 1967. Instr. Chapman Coll. (Calif.) in Barcelona, Spain, 1964; 3d mate on ship Reynolds Metals, Corpus Christi, Tex., 1967-68; rsch. scientist Govt. of Can., Nanaimo, B.C., 1968-70; ocean engr. Cities Svc. Oil, Tulsa, 1970-72; program dir. NSF, Washington, 1972-87; prof. dept. oceanography Naval Postgrad. Sch., Monterey, 1987—, chmn., 1987-94, faculty chmn., 2002. Guest investigator Woods Hole Oceanographic Instn., Mass., 1983; commr. Moss Landing Harbor Dist., 1993-94, pres. 1994. vis. prof. U. Calif., Santa Cruz, 1998; Oceanography editor Geophys. Rsch. Letters, 1996-98; vis. scholar Scripps Instn. Oceanography U. Calif. San Diego, 2005. Capt. USNR, ret. Decorated Armed Forces Res. Def. medal; recipient Admiral E.S. Land award Dept. Commerce, 1962, Meritorious Svc. award NSF, 1987, grad. fellow NSF, 1963-64, Fulbright fellow Instituto Investigaciones Oceanológicas U. Autonomia de Baja, Calif., 1994-95. Mem. Am. Geophys. Union (Oceans Scis. award 1985, pres. ocean scis. sect. 1993-94, chmn. editl. bd. 2002-04, chmn. publ. com. 2004-06), Ocean Soc. Japan. Home: 1400 Fredericks San Luis Obispo CA 93405 Office: Naval Postgrad Sch Code OcCo-833 Dyer Rd Rm 331 Monterey CA 93943 Office Phone: 831-656-3271. Business E-Mail: collins@nps.edu.

COLLINS, DENNIS ARTHUR, retired foundation administrator; b. Yakima, Wash., June 9, 1940; s. Martin Douglas and Louise Constance (Caccia) C.; m. Mary Veronica Paul, June 11, 1966; children: Jenifer Ann, Lindsey Kathleen. BA, Stanford U., 1962, MA, 1963; LHD, Mills Coll., 1994, U. San Diego, 2002. Assoc. dean admissions Occidental Coll., Los Angeles, 1964-66, dean admissions, 1966-68, dean of students, 1968-70; headmaster Emma Willard Sch., Troy, N.Y., 1970-74; founding headmaster San Francisco U. High Sch., 1974-86; pres. James Irvine Found., San Francisco, 1986—2002; ret.

Trustee Coll. Bd., N.Y.C., 1981-85, Ind. Ednl. Svcs., Princeton, N.J., 1981-85, Calif. Assn. Ind. Schs., L.A., 1982-86, Branson Sch., 1987-89, Aspen Inst. Nonprofit Sector rsch. Fund, 1992—; chmn. bd. So. Calif. Assn. Philanthropy, L.A., 1989-91, No. Calif. Grantmakers, 1987-90; dir. Rebuild L.A., 1992-93. Trustee Cathedral Sch. for Boys, San Francisco, 1976-82, Marin Country Day Sch., Corte Madera, Calif., 1978-84, San Francisco Exploratorium, 1984-86, Ind. Sector, Washington, 1987-95, Am. Farmland Trust, Washington, 1992—, Occidental Coll, Nat. Ctr. for Pub. Policy and Higher Edn., Ctr. for Philanthropy and Pub. Policy; bd. dirs., vice chmn. Children's Hosp. Found., San Francisco, 1984-86; chmn. bd. dirs. Coun. for Cmty. Based Devel., Washington, 1989-92. Mem. Council on Founds., World Trade Club, Univ. Club, Calif. Club (LA). Democrat. Episcopalian. Home: 19170 Old Winery Rd Sonoma CA 95476-4842

COLLINS, FRANK EDWIN, lawyer; b. Jackson, Mo., Apr. 10, 1954; s. Arthur Black and Margaret Collins; m. Barbara Jo Justice, Oct. 26, 1974; children: Justin, Eric, Keith, Garrett. BA, U. Mo., Kansas City, 1976, JD, 1979. Bar: Mo. 1979. Counsel Mo. Divsn. Ins., Jefferson City, 1979-81; assoc. gen. counsel Blue Cross/Blue Shield, Kansas City, Mo., 1981—86; gen. counsel, sec. Prime Health, Inc., 1986—97; exec. v.p., gen. counsel, sec. Sierra Health Svcs., Las Vegas, Nev., 1997—. Pres. Sierra Health Holdings, Inc.; sec. S.W. Realty, Inc., Sierra Acquisition Corp., Prime Holdings, Inc., others; bd. dirs. numerous subsidiaries of Sierra Health Svc. Bd. dirs. United Way, Las Vegas. Mem. Mo. Bar Assn. Office: Sierra Health Svcs 2724 N Tenaya St PO Box 15645 Las Vegas NV 89128 Office Phone: 702-242-7189. Office Fax: 702-242-1532. E-mail: fcg104@sierrahealth.com.

COLLINS, GILBERT WILSON, physicist; b. Livermore, Calif., Sept. 13, 1961; s. Gilbert Wilson and Betty Jean (Buchagen) C.; m. Rebecca Marie Carrozza, June 18, 1983; children: Gilbert Wilson, Natasha Marie, Alexander Brian. BSBA, U. Cin., 1983; MS, Ohio State U., 1986, PhD in Physics, 1989. Physicist Lawrence Livermore (Calif.) Nat. Lab., 1989—. Contbr. articles to profl. jours. including Phys. Rev. B., Phys. Rev. Letters. Mem. Am. Phys. Soc., Sigma Pi Sigma. Achievements include research on determination and characterization of storage and disposal mechanisms for energetic impurities in solid molecular hydrogen, of solid hydrogen containing energetic impurities and how may be used as the next generation of rocket propellents, of solid heavy hydrogen with no rotationally excited molecules and possibility of fuel with 50 percent higher cross section for nuclear fusion than unpolarized heavy hydrogen; determination of effect of unpaired atoms and electrons on molecular rotations and thermal transport in solid hydrogen. Home: 10655 Morgan Territory Rd Livermore CA 94550-9448 Office: Lawrence Livermore Lab PO Box 808 Mail Code L-482 7000 East Ave Livermore CA 94550-9516

COLLINS, JAMES FRANCIS, toxicologist; b. Balt., Jan. 26, 1942; s. James Murphy and Mary M. (Dolan) C.; m. Barbara Joan Betka, June 21, 1969; children: Chris, Cavan. BS, Loyola Coll., Balt., 1963; PhD, U.N.C., 1968. Diplomate Am. Bd. Toxicology. Fellow NIH, Bethesda, Md., 1968-75; faculty mem., rsch. chemist U. Tex. Health Sci. Ctr. and VA Med. Ctr., San Antonio, 1975-86; staff toxicologist Calif. EPA and Dept. Health Svcs., Oakland, Calif., 1986—. Instr. U. Calif. Berkeley/Extension, 1987-95; instr. U. San Francisco, 1995—. Contbr. numerous articles to profl. jours., publs. Mem. Am. Soc. Biochemistry and Molecular Biology. Democrat. Roman Catholic. Avocation: reading. Home: 822 Rogers Way Pinole CA 94564-2409 Office: Calif EPA 1515 Clay St Fl 16 Oakland CA 94612-1499 E-mail: jcollins@oehha.ca.gov, collins113@juno.com.

COLLINS, JIM, management researcher, author; b. Boulder, Colo., Jan. 25, 1958; BS, Stanford U., 1980, MBA, 1983. Mem. faculty Stanford Grad. Sch. Bus.; founder & dir. mgmt. rsch. lab. Boulder, Colo., 1995—. Co-author (with William C. Lazier): Beyond Entrepreneurship: Turning Your Business into an Enduring Great Company, 1992, Managing the Small to Mid-Sized Company: Concepts & Cases, 1994; co-author: (with Jerry I. Porras) Built to Last: Successful Habits of Visionary Companies, 1994; author: Good to Great: Why Some Companies Make the Leap...And Others Don't, 2001, Good to Great & the Social Sectors: A Monograph to Accompany Good to Great, 2005; frequent contbr. to business magazines. Recipient Disting. Teaching award, Stanford U. Grad. Sch. Bus., 1992. Avocation: rock climbing. Office: c/o Laura Schuchat PO Box 1699 Boulder CO 80306 Office Phone: 720-565-4045. Office Fax: 303-447-1392. E-mail: laura@jimcollins.com.

COLLINS, MARIBETH WILSON, retired foundation administrator; b. Portland, Oreg., Oct. 27, 1918; d. Clarence True and Maude (Akin) Wilson; m. Truman Wesley Collins, Mar. 12, 1943; children: Timothy Wilson and Terry Stanton (twins), Cherida Smith, Truman Wesley Jr. BA, U. Oreg., 1940. Pres. Collins Found., Portland, 1964—2006; ret. Trustee Collins Pine Co., Collins Found. Life trustee Willamette U., Salem, Oreg., also mem. campus religious life. Mem. Univ. Club, Gamma Phi Beta. Republican. Methodist. Home: 2275 SW Mayfield Ave Portland OR 97225-4400 Office: Collins Found 1618 SW 1st Ave Ste 505 Portland OR 97201-5708 Personal E-mail: maribeth@teleport.com.

COLLINS, MARY ANN, lawyer; b. Aurora, Colo., May 12, 1953; d. Harold Ernest and Gertrude Elizabeth (Shannon) C.; m. Ronald Jay Sklar, Jan. 20, 1984; 1 child, Jacob Michael. BA, Western Ill. U., 1974; MA in Polit. Sci., U. Ill., 1976; JD, Loyola U., 1980. Bar: Ill. 1980, Calif. 1984. Assoc. Chapman and Cutler, Chgo., 1980-83, Orrick, Herrington & Sutcliffe, San Francisco, 1983-88, ptnr., 1988—. Chair transp. fin. group. Orrick, Herrington & Sutcliffe, San Francisco, co-chair health care, higher edn., and 501(c) revenue transactions group. Contbr. articles to profl. jours. Mem. ABA, Calif. Bar Assn., San Francisco Mcpl. Forum. Office: Orrick Herrington & Sutcliffe 405 Howard St San Francisco CA 94105 Office Phone: 415-773-5998. E-mail: marycollins@orrick.com.

COLLINS, MICHAEL K., lawyer; b. Sikeston, Mo., Feb. 13, 1943; AB, Washington U., St. Louis, 1965, JD, 1969. Bar: Calif. 1970, U.S. Dist. Ct. (cen., so. and no. dists.) Calif. 1970, U.S. Ct. Appeals (9th cir.) 1970. With Greenberg, Glusker, Fields, Claman & Machtinger, LA, 1969—. Editor-in-Chief Washington U. Law Quar., 1968-69. Mem. Assn. Bus. Trial Lawyers, State Bar Calif., L.A. County Bar Assn. (exec. com. real property sect. 1981-83), Century City Bar Assn., Order of Coif, Wilshire Hunting Club. Office: Greenberg Glusker Fields Claman & Machtinger Ste 2100 1900 Avenue Of The Stars Los Angeles CA 90067-4502

COLLINS, PATRICIA A., lawyer, judge; b. Camp Lejeune, NC, Mar. 12, 1954; d. Thomas and Margaret (Parrish) C. BA, U. Va., 1976; JD, Gonzaga U., 1982. Bar: Alaska 1982, U.S. Dist. Ct. Alaska, U.S. Ct. Appeals (9th cir.) 1982. Assoc. Guess & Rudd, Anchorage and Juneau, 1982-84, 85-87; asst. pub. defender Alaska Pub. Defender's Office, Ketchikan, 1984-85; prin. Collins Law Office, Juneau, 1987-95; judge Alaska Dist. Ct., Ketchikan, 1995-1999, Juno Superior Ct., Alaska, 1999—. Part time fed. magistrate judge U.S. Cts., Juneau, 1988-95, Kitchikan, 1996—; adj. prof. U. Alaska, Juneau, 1991-95. Mem. Alaska Bar Assn., Ketchikan Sailing Club. Office: Alaska Superior Ct 114100 Juneau AK 99811-4100

COLLINS, RICHARD FRANCIS, microbiologist, educator; b. St. Paul, Minn., Jan. 22, 1938; s. Francis Bernard and Maude Roegene (Night) C.; m. Deanne Margaret Scafati, Dec. 28, 1960 (div. 1970); children: Lisa, Mark, Michael; m. Judy A. Wright, Feb. 15, 1978; children: Kristyn, Todd. AB, Shepherd Coll., 1962; MA, Wake Forest U., 1968; PhD, U. Okla., 1973. Tchr. Alexandria (Va.) Schs., 1962-66; instr. U. Okla., Oklahoma City, 1972-73; lab. dir. Infectious Disease Svc. U. Ill./Rockford Sch. of Medicine, 1974-80; asst. prof. U. Ill., Rockford, 1973-80; assoc. prof. U. Osteo. Medicine and Health Scis., Des Moines, 1980-85, faculty pres., 1990-91, pres.-elect, 1997-98, prof., dept. head, 1985-95; prof., divsn. head Midwestern U., Glendale, 1997—. Cons. U.S. EPA, Washington, 1975-81; mem. Nat. Bd. Podiatry Examiners, Princeton, N.J., 1983-96, Nat. Bd. Osteo. Med. Examiners, Des Plaines, Ill., 1994-97; participant mission project Christian Med. Soc., Dominican Republic, 1977. Mem. editorial bd. African Jour. Clin. Exptl. Immunology, 1979-83; contbr. articles to profl. jours. Vol. Blank Guild, Iowa Meth. Hosp., Des Moines, 1988-91. Recipient awards NSF, 1962-67, fellowship NIH, 1969-70, Gov.'s Vol. awards State of Iowa, 1988, 89. Mem. Am. Soc. for Microbiology, Am. Soc. Tropical Medicine and Hygiene, Sigma Xi (pres. 1987-90, 96-97, treas. 1990-91). Avocations: photography, auto restoration. Home: 4131 W Tierra Buena Ln Phoenix AZ 85053-3717 Office: Midwestern U Ariz Coll Osteo Medicine 19555 N 59th Ave Glendale AZ 85308-6813 Office Phone: 623-572-3258. Business E-Mail: rcolli@midwestern.edu.

COLLMAN, JAMES PADDOCK, chemistry professor; b. Beatrice, Nebr., Oct. 31, 1932; married. B.Sc., U. Nebr., 1954, MS, 1956; PhD (NSF fellow), U. Ill., 1958; Docteur Honoris Causa, U. Dijon, France, 1988, U. Borgogne, 1988; D (hon.), U. Nebr., 1988. Instr. chemistry U. N.C., Chapel Hill, 1958-59, asst. prof., 1959-62, asso. prof., 1962-67; prof. chemistry Stanford U., 1967—; George A. and Hilda M. Daubert prof. chemistry Stanford U., 1980—. Frontiers in Chemistry lectr., 1964, Nebr. lectureship, 1968; Venable lectr. U. N.C., 1971; Edward Clark Lee lectr. U. Chgo., 1972; vis. Erskine fellow U. Canterbury, 1972; Plenary lectr. French Chem. Soc., 1974; Dreyfus lectr. U. Kans., 1974; Disting. inorganic lectr. U. Rochester, 1974; Reilley lectr. U. Notre Dame, 1975; William Pyle Philips lectr. Haverford Coll., 1975; Merck lectr. Rutgers U., 1976; FMC lectr. Princeton, 1977; Julius Steiglitz lectr. Chgo. sect. Am. Chem. Soc., 1977; Pres.'s Seminar Series lectr. U. Ariz., 1980; Frank C. Whitmore lectr. Pa. State U., 1980; Plenary lectr. 3d IUPAC Symposium on Organic Synthesis, 1980, 2d Internat. Kyoto Conf. on New Aspects Inorganic Chemistry, 1982, Internat. Symposium on Models of Enzyme Action, Brighton, Eng., 1983, Internat. Symposium, Italy, 1984; Brockman lectr. U. Ga., 1981; Samuel C. Lind lectr. U. Tenn., 1981, Syntex Disting. lectr. Colo. State U., 1983; Disting. vis. lectr. U. Fla., 1983; vis. prof. U. Auckland, New Zealand, 1985; Nelson J. Leonard lectr. U. Ill., 1987; plenary lectr. Internat. Symposium on Activation of Dioxygen and Homogeneous Catalytic Oxygenations, Tsukuba, Japan, 1987; plenary lectr. 12th Internat. Symposium on Macrocyclic Chem., Hiroshima, Japan, 1987; lectr. Texas A&M, 1988; J. Clarence Karcher lectr. U. Okla., 1989; Musselman lectr. Gettysburg Coll., 1990; Davis lectr. U. New Orleans, 1991; PLU lectr. Okla. State U., 1991; lectr. 5th Internat. Fischer Symposium, Karlsruhe, Ger., 1991; lectr. Enchem Conf., 1991; Pratt lectr. U. Va., 1992, others; lectr. series Harvard/MIT, 1992, Yale U., 1993; invited speaker symposia, univs., confs. Recipient Disting. Teaching award Stanford U., 1981, Calif. Scientist of Year award, 1983, Allan V. Cox medal for excellence in fostering undergrad. rsch., 1988, LAS Alumni Achievement award Coll. Liberal Arts and Scis. U. Ill., 1994, John C. Bailar Jr. medal, 1995, Joseph Chatt medal Royal Soc., 1998 Hans Fischer award in polyphrin chemistry Internat. Conf. Porphyrins and Phthalocyanines, 2002; named George A. and Hilda M. Daubert Prof. Chemistry (endowed chair, Stanford U.), 1980; Guggenheim fellow, 1977-78, 85-86, Churchill fellow, Cambridge, 1977—, Bing fellow, 1996. Fellow AAAS, Calif. Acad. Sci. (hon.); mem. Am. Chem. Soc. (Calif. sect. award 1972, Soc. award in inorganic chemistry 1975, Arthur C. Cope scholar 1986, Pauling award Puget Sound and Oreg. sect. 1990, Disting. Svc. award in inorganic chemistry 1991, Alfred Bader award 1997, Joseph Chatt lectr. 1998, Marker lectr. medal 1999), NY Acad. Sci. (Basolo medal 2000, Hans Fischer Porphyrin Chemistry award 2002), Chem. Soc. (London), Nat. Acad. Sci., Am. Acad. Arts and Scis., Phi Beta Kappa, Sigma Xi, Phi Lambda Upsilon, Alpha Chi Epsilon (Hans Fischer award 2002, Oesper award 2007). Office: Stanford U Dept Chemistry Stanford CA 94305 Office Phone: 650-725-0283. Business E-Mail: jpc@stanford.edu.

COLÓN, BRIAN S., lawyer, political organization administrator; BBA, N.Mex State U., 1998; JD, U. N.Mex., 2001. Atty. Aguilar Law Offices, PC, 2001—07; ptnr. Robles Rael & Anaya, PC, 2007—. Mem. State Bar of N.Mex Com. on Diversity, 2003—; bd. mem. N.Mex Coll. Success Network; commr. Judicial Selection Com. Chmn. Dem. Party of N.Mex.; bd. trustees Albuquerque Cmty. Found.; chair bd. dirs. Popejoy Hall. Named an Outstanding Young Lawyer of Yr., N.Mex State Bar Assn.; named one of Forty Under 40 Power Brokers, N.Mex Bus. Weekly. Mem.: Am. Inns of Ct., N.Mex Hispanic Bar Assn. (bd. dirs. 2001—). Democrat. Office: Robles, Rael & Anaya, PC Suite 700 500 Marquette Ave, NW Albuquerque NM 87102 also: Dem Party of NMex 1301 San Pedro NE Albuquerque NM 87110 Office Phone: 505-242-2228. Office Fax: 505-242-1106. E-mail: brian@nmdemocrats.org.

COLSON, ELIZABETH FLORENCE, anthropologist; b. Hewitt, Minn., June 15, 1917; d. Louis H. and Metta (Damon) C. BA, U. Minn., 1938, MA, 1940, Radcliffe Coll., 1941, PhD, 1945; D of Sociology, Brown U., 1979; DSc, U. Rochester, 1985, U. Zambia, 1992. Asst. social sci. analyst War Relocation Authority, 1942-43; research asst. Harvard, 1944-45; research officer Rhodes-Livingstone Inst., 1946-47, dir., 1948-51; sr. lectr. Manchester U., 1951-53; assoc. prof. Goucher Coll., 1954-55; research assoc., assoc. prof. African Research Program, Boston U., 1955-59, part-time, 1959-63; prof. anthropology Brandeis U., 1959-63, U. Calif.-Berkeley, 1964-84, prof. emeritus, 1984—; vis. prof. U. Zambia, 1987. Lewis Henry Morgan lectr. U. Rochester, 1973; vis. rsch. assoc. Refugee Studies Program Queen Elizabeth House, Oxford, 1988-89. Author: The Makah, 1953, Marriage and the Family Among The Plateau Tonga, 1958, Social Organization of the Gwembe Tonga, 1960, The Plateau Tonga, 1962, The Social Consequences of Resettlement, 1971, Tradition and Contract, 1974, A History of Nampeyo, 1992; jr. author Secondary Education and the Formation of an Elite, 1980, Voluntary Efforts in Decentralized Management, 1983, sr. author For Prayer and Profit, 1988, The History of Nampeyo, 1991; sr. editor: Seven Tribes of British Central Africa, 1951; jr. editor People in Upheaval, 1987. AAUW travelling fellow, 1941-42, fellow Ctr. Advanced Study Behavioral Scis., 1967-68, Fairchild fellow Calif. Inst. Tech., 1975-76. Fellow Am. Anthrop. Assn., Assn. Social Anthropologists of the Commonwealth, Royal Anthrop. Inst. (hon.); mem. Nat. Acad. Sci., Am. Acad. Arts and Scis., Am. Assn. African Studies (Disting. Africanist award 1988), Soc. Applied Anthropology, Soc. Woman Geographers, Phi Beta Kappa. Avocations: walking, opera, reading. Office: Univ Calif Dept Anthropology Berkeley CA 94720-0001 Personal E-mail: gwembe@uclink.berkeley.ed.

COLSON, WILLIAM E., management company executive; Founder Holiday Mgmt. Co. (Holiday Retirement Corp.), 1970—; pres., mng. gen. ptnr. Colson & Colson Construction Co.; pres. Colson & Colson Gen. Contractor, Inc. Bd. dirs. mem Emeritus Corp.; exec. bd. mem. Am. Srs. Housing Assn. Office: Holiday Retirement Corp PO Box 1411 Salem OR 97309

COLTON, ROY CHARLES, management consultant; b. Phila., Feb. 26, 1941; s. Nathan Hale and Ruth Janis (Baylinson) C. BA, Knox Coll., 1962; MEd, Temple U., 1963. With Sch. Dist. of Phila., 1963-64; sys. analyst Wilmington Trust Co., 1967-69; exec. recruiter Atwood Consultants Inc., Phila., 1969-71; pres. Colton Bernard Inc., San Francisco, 1971—. Occasional lectr. Fashion Inst. Tech., Phila. Coll. Textiles and Scis. Served with AUS, 1964-66. Mem. San Francisco Fashion Industries, San Francisco C. of C., Calif. Exec. Recruiter Assn., Nat. Assn. Exec. Recruiters, Am. Apparel Mfrs. Assn., Am. Arbitration Assn. (panel arbitrators). Office: Colton Bernard Inc 1900 Market St Philadelphia PA 19103-3527 Office Fax: 415-399-0750. Business E-Mail: rcolton@coltonbernard.com.

COLTON, STERLING DAVID (DAVID COLTON), lawyer; b. 1955; s. Sterling Don and Ellie Colton. BA in economics, Brigham Young U., 1979, JD, 1982. Bar: Utah 1982. Ptnr. VanCott, Bagley, Cornwall & McCarthy, Salt Lake City; sr. counsel for exploration and devel. group Phelps Dodge Mining Co., 1988-95; v.p., counsel Phelps Dodge Exploration Corp., 1995-98; v.p., gen. counsel Phelps Dodge Corp., Phoenix, 1998-99, sr. v.p., gen. counsel, 1999—. Mem. ABA, Utah Bar Assn. Office: Phelps Dodge Corp 1 N Ctrl Ave Phoenix AZ 85004-2306

COLUMBUS, CHRIS J., film director, screenwriter; b. Spangler, Pa., Sept. 10, 1958; s. Alex Michael and Mary Irene (Puskar) C., m. Monica Devereux, 1983; 4 children. BFA, NYU, 1980. Writer: (films) Reckless, 1983, Gremlins, 1984, Goonies, 1985, Young Sherlock Holmes, 1985, Little Nemo, 1992; dir.: (films) Adventures in Babysitting, 1987, Home Alone, 1990, Home Alone 2: Lost in New York, 1992, Mrs. Doubtfire, 1993; dir., writer: Heartbreak Hotel, 1988, Only the Lonely, 1991; prodr., writer: Christmas with the Kranks, 2004; dir., writer, prodr.: Nine Months, 1995; dir., prodr.: Stepmom, 1998, Bicentennial Man, 1999, Rent, 2005; dir. exec. prodr: Harry Potter and the Sorcerer's Stone, 2001 (Las Vegas Film Critics award, 2001, Broadcast Film Critics Award, 2001), Harry Potter and the Chamber of Secrets, 2002; exec. prodr.: Fantastic Four, 2005; prodr.: Jingle All the Way, 1996, Harry Potter and the Prisoner of Azkaban, 2004, 3-D Rocks, 2005. Recipient Golden Plate award, Acad. Achievement, 2006. Democrat.

COLVIN, HARRY WALTER, JR., physiology educator; b. Schellsburg, Pa., Dec. 5, 1921; s. Harry Walter and Maude Elizabeth (Girven) C.; m. Marie Catherine McNinch, Apr. 8, 1950; children: Sarah Lee, William McNinch. BS, Pa. State U., 0950; PhD, U. Calif., Davis, 1957. Instr. Okla. State U., Stillwater, 1955-57; assoc. prof. physiology U. Ark., Fayetteville, 1957-65; prof. U. Calif., Davis, 1965—. Cons. Pel-Freez Biologicals, Inc., Rogers, Ark., 1960-65. Assoc. editor Hilgardia, 1981-92; contbr. articles to profl. jours. Served with U.S. Army, 1942-45, ETO. Decorated Bronze Star, Purple Heart; recipient Outstanding Advisor award, 1982—83, 1984—85, 1987—88, Magnar Ronning award for Outstanding Tchg.; grantee Fulbright award, Yugoslavia, 1972, Argentina, 1986. Mem. Am. Dairy Sci. Assn., Am. Soc. Animal Sci., Sigma Xi, Phi Kappa Phi, Alpha Zeta, Gamma Sigma Delta, Phi Sigma, Phi Eta Sigma. Avocations: golf, flying. Home: 1515 Shasta Dr Apt 3326 Davis CA 95616 Office: U Calif Davis Dept Neurobiology Physiol & Behavior Davis CA 95616 E-mail: hwcolvin@ucdavis.edu.

COMANOR, WILLIAM S., economist, educator; b. Phila., May 11, 1937; s. Leroy and Sylvia (Bershad) C.; children: Christine, Katherine, Lauren, Gregory. Student, Williams Coll., 1955—57; BA, Haverford Coll., 1959; MA, PhD, Harvard U., 1964; postgrad., London Sch. Econs., 1963—64. Spl. econ. asst. to asst. atty. gen. Antitrust divsn. U.S. Dept. Justice, Washington, 1965-66; asst. prof. econs. Harvard U., Cambridge, Mass., 1966-68; assoc. prof. Stanford (Calif.) U., 1968-73; dir. bur. econs. FTC, Washington, 1978-80; prof. econs. U. Calif., Santa Barbara, 1975—, dept. chmn., 1984-87; prof. Sch. Pub. Health UCLA, 1990—. Author: National Health Insurance in Ontario, 1980, Advertising and Market Power, 1974, Competition Policy in Europe and North America, 1990, Competition Policy in the Global Economy, 1997, Law and Economics of Child Support Payments, 2004; contbr. articles to profl. jours. Recipient Dist. fellow award, Indsl. Orgn. Soc., 2003. Mem.: Indsl. Orgn. Soc. (pres. 1991, Disting. Fellow award 2003), Am. Econ. Assn. Office: U Calif Dept Econs Santa Barbara CA 93106 Home: 14701 Valley Vista Blvd Sherman Oaks CA 91403 Office Phone: 310-206-1694. Business E-Mail: comanor@ucla.edu.

COMEAU, CAROL SMITH, school system administrator; b. Berkeley, Calif., Sept. 4, 1941; d. Floyd Franklin and Bessie Caroline (Campbell) Smith; m. Dennis Rene Comeau, Dec. 27, 1962; children: Christopher, Michael, Karen. BS in Edn., U. Oreg., 1963; M in Pub. Sch. Adminstrn., U. Atlanta, 1985. Third grade tchr., Springfield, Oreg., 1963—64; elem. sch. tchr. Ocean View Elem. Sch., Anchorage, 1975—84, 2d-6th grade tchr.; 6th grade tchr. Spring Hill Elem. Sch., 1985—86; adminstrv. intern Tudor Elem. Sch., Anchorage, 1986—87; prin. Orion Elem. Sch., 1987—89; prin. dir. elem. edn. Anchorage Sch. Dist., 1990—93, asst. supr. instr., 1993—2000, supt., 2000—. Mem. exec. com. Coun. Great City Schools, 2003—. Chair Anchorage United Way, 2004; bd. dirs. KAKM pub., 1990—92, Alaska Ctr. Performing Arts. Recipient Alaska Supt. of Yr., 2003, ATHENA award, Anchorage C. of C., 2004; named Tchr. of Yr., Anchorage Sch. Dist. PTA Coun., 1976; named one of Top 25 Most Powerful Alaskans, 2002. Mem.: NEA, Kappa Delta Pi, Phi Delta Kappa. Democrat. Home: 13632 Jarvi Dr Anchorage AK 99515-3934 Office: Anchorage School District 5530 E Northern Lights Blvd Anchorage AK 99504-3135 Home Phone: 907-345-4916; Office Phone: 907-742-4312. Business E-Mail: comeau_carol@asdk12.org.

COMES, ROBERT GEORGE, research scientist; b. Bangor, Pa., July 7, 1931; s. Victor Francis and Mabel Elizabeth (Mack) Comes; m. Carol Lee Turinetti, Nov. 28, 1952; children: Pamela Jo, Robert George II, Shawni Lee, Sheryl Lynn, Michelle Ann. Student, U. Detroit, 1957—58, Oreg. State Coll., 1959—60, U. Nev., 1960, Regis Coll., 1961—62. Liaison engr. Burroughs Corp., Detroit, 1955—60; sr. engr. Martin Marietta Corp., Denver, 1960—62; mgr. reliability and maintainability engring. Burroughs Corp., Paoli, Pa., 1962—63, Colorado Springs, Colo., 1963—67; program mgr., rsch. scientist Kaman Scis. Corp., Colorado Springs, 1967—75; dir. engring. Sci. Applications, Inc., Colorado Springs, 1975—80; mgr. space def. programs Burroughs Corp., Colorado Springs, 1980—82; tech. staff mem. Mitre Corp., Colorado Springs, 1982—85; dir. Colorado Springs ops. Beers Assoc., Inc., 1985; dir. space programs Electro Magnetic Applicaitons, Inc., Colorado Springs, 1985—87; dir. Space Sys. Profl. Mgmt. Assocs., Inc., 1987—88; mgr. Computer Svcs., Inc., Colorado Springs, 1989—; dir. mktg. RGC Assocs, Colorado Springs, 1990—. Chmn. Reliability and Maintainability Data Bank Improvement Program Govt.-Industry Data Exch. Program, 1978—80; cons. in field. Author: Maintainability Engineering Principles and Standards, 1962. Youth dir. Indian Guides program YMCA, 1963—64; scoutmaster Boy Scouts Am., 1972—73; chmn. bd. dirs. Pikes Peak Regional Sci. Fair, 1972—84. With USAF, 1951—55. Mem.: AAAS, Am. Soc. Quality Control, Soc. Logistics Engrs., Inst. Environ. Scis., Colorado Springs Racquet Club. Presbyterian. Achievements include invention of Phase Shifting aircraft power supply. Home and Office: RGC Associates 4309 Tipton Ct Colorado Springs CO 80915-1034 Home Phone: 719-596-4764; Office Phone: 719-596-4764.

COMFORT, ROBERT DENNIS, lawyer; b. Camden, NJ, Nov. 22, 1950; s. Joseph Albert Sr. and Elizabeth (Rogers) C.; m. Loretta Masullo, Aug. 24, 1974; 1 child, Adam. AB summa cum laude, Princeton U., 1973; JD magna cum laude, Harvard U., 1976. Bar: Pa. 1976, N.J. 1977, U.S. Dist. Ct. N.J. 1977, U.S. Dist. Ct. (ea. dist.) Pa. 1977, U.S. Ct. Appeals (3d cir.) 1977, U.S. Tax Ct. 1978, U.S. Claims Ct. 1983. Law clk. to Hon. James Hunter III U.S. Ct. Appeals 3d Cir., Phila., 1976-77; law clk. to Lewis F. Powell Jr. U.S. Supreme Ct., Washington, 1977-78; assoc. Morgan, Lewis & Bockius, Phila., 1978-82, ptnr., 1982-2000; v.p. tax and tax policy Amazon.com, Seattle, 2000—. Adj. prof. U. Pa. Law Sch., Rutgers-Camden Law Sch. Mem. ABA, Phila. Bar Assn. (vice chair tax sect. 1990-92, chair 1993-94). Avocations: golf, camping, music, history, fishing. Office: Amazon com PO Box 81226 Seattle WA 98108-1300

COMFORT, STEPHANIE GEORGES, telecommunications industry executive; b. Mar. 12, 1963; m. Christopher C. Comfort; 3 children. BA in Econs., Wellesley Coll., Mass., 1985; MBA, U. Pa. Wharton Sch. With Wertheim Schroder & Co., Inc., Salomon Brothers, Inc.; portfolio mgr., strategist Morgan Stanley, sr. telecomm. svcs. analyst; head investor rels. program Qwest Comm. Internat., Inc., Denver, exec. v.p. corp. strategy, 2008—. Former bd. mem. The Kempe Found.; bd. mem. Christopher J. Georges Journalism Found. Harvard U.; class treas. Wellesley Coll. Named a Top Analyst, Wall St. Jour.; named to All Star Survey, Instl. Investor. Office: Qwest Comm Internat Inc 1801 California St Denver CO 80202 Office Phone: 303-992-1400. E-mail: stephanie.comfort@qwest.com.

COMINGS, DAVID EDWARD, medical geneticist; b. Beacon, NY, Mar. 8, 1935; s. Edward Walter and Jean (Rice) C.; m. Shirley Nelson, Aug. 9, 1958; children: Mark David, Scott Edward, Karen Jean; m. Brenda Gursey, Mar. 20, 1982. Student, U. Ill., 1951—54; BS, Northwestern U., 1955, MD, 1958. Intern Cook County Hosp., Chgo., 1958-59, resident in internal medicine, 1959-62; fellow in med. genetics U. Wash., Seattle, 1964-66; dir. dept. med. genetics City of Hope Med. Ctr., Duarte, Calif., 1966—2003, dir. emeritus, 2003—; dir. Carlsbad Sci. Found., Monrovia, Calif., 2004—. Mem. genetics study sect. NIH, 1974-78; mem. sci. adv. bd. Hereditary Disease Found., 1975-, Nat. Found. March of Dimes, 1978-92. Author: Tourette Syndrome and Human Behavior, 1990, Search for the Tourette Syndrome and Human Behavior Genes, 1996, The Gene Bomb, 1996; editor: (with others) Molecular Human Cytogenetics, 1977; mem. editl. bd.: (with others) Cytogenetics and Cell genetics, 1979—; editor-in-chief Am. Jour. Human Genetics, 1978-86. Served with U.S. Army, 1962-64. NIH grantee, 1967-. Mem. Assn. Am. Physicians, Am. Soc. Clin. Investigation, AAAS, Am. Soc. Human Genetics (dir. 1974-78, pres. 1988), Am. Soc. Cell Biology, Am. Fedn. Clin. Rsch., Western Soc. Clin. Rsch., Coun. Biology Editors. Office: Carlsbad Sci Found 110 Mill Rd Monrovia CA 91016

COMMANDER, EUGENE R., lawyer; b. Sioux City, Iowa, Jan. 10, 1953; BA in Architecture, Iowa State U., 1975; JD with distinction, U. Iowa, 1977. Bar: Iowa 1977, Colo. 1981. Mem. Hall & Evans, LLC, Denver, 1981—. Mem. ABA (forum com. on constrn. industry, subcoms. on bonds, liens, ins. and contract documents, tort and ins. practice sect. coms. on fidelity, surety law, property ins.), AIA (profl. affiliate, Colo. chpt.), Am. Arbitration Assn. (panel constrn. industry arbitrators 1983—), Am. Law Firm Assn. (constrn. industry practice group), Def. Rsch. Inst. (constrn. law and fidelity and surety law coms.), Profl. Liability Underwriting Soc.

COMMONS, GEORGE W., plastic surgeon; b. Johnstown, Pa., 1942; BS, Allegheny Coll., Meadville, Pa.; MD, U. Pa. Sch. Medicine, 1968. Cert. Am. Bd. Plastic Surgery. Intern, plastic surgery Stanford U. Med. Ctr., Calif., 1968—69, fellow plastic surgery, rehabilitation, resident gen., plastic surgery, 1969—74, chief resident plastic, reconstructive surgery; med. dir. Plastic Surgery Ctr., Calif., 1990—2008, Palo Alto Ctr. for Plastic Surgery, Calif., 2008—; staff appointments Menlo Park Surgical Hosp., 1994—2008, Sequoia Hosp., 1976—2008, El Camino Hosp., 1976—2008. Adjunct clinical asst. prof. plastic surgery dept. Stanford U. Hosp.; cons. in field; cons., plastic and reconstructive surgery US Army, USAF, and USN in the Far East, Ctrl. Luzon Gen. Hosp., San Fernando, Republic Philippines, Philippine Air Force; cons., lectr. U. Far East, Manila, Republic Philippines; surgeon-in-charge, plastic and reconstructive Surgery, rehabilitation program for underprivileged children USAF, Philippine Air Force. Contbr. articles to profl. jours. Maj. USAF, chief, plastic and reconstructive surgery USAF Hosp., Clark AFB, Republic Philippines, med. civic action program dir., Clark AFB. Decorated USAF Accommodation medal. Fellow: ACS; mem.: Internat. Soc. Plastic Surgery, AMA, Calif. Soc. Plastic Surgeons, Calif. Med. Assn., Am. Soc. Aesthetic Plastic Surgery, Am. Soc. Plastic Surgery, Military Plastic Surgical Assn., Santa Clara County Med. Soc. Assn., Philippines Plastic Surgical Assn. (hon.), Alpha Omega Alpha. Office: Palo Alto Ctr Plastic Surgery 1515 El Camino Real Ste C Palo Alto CA 94306 Office Phone: 650-328-4570. Office Fax: 650-322-8481. Business E-Mail: gcommons@pacfps.com.

COMPTON, ALLEN T., retired state supreme court justice; b. Kansas City, Mo., Feb. 25, 1938; 3 children. BA, U. Kans., 1960; LL.B., U. Colo., 1963. Pvt. practice, Colorado Springs, 1963-68; staff atty. Legal Svcs. Office, Colorado Springs, 1968-69, dir., 1969-71; supervising atty. Alaska Legal Svcs., Juneau, Alaska, 1971-73; pvt. practice Juneau, 1973-76; judge Superior Ct., Alaska, 1976-80; justice Alaska Supreme Ct., Anchorage, 1980-98, state supreme ct. chief justice, 1995-97, ret., 1998. Office Phone: 907-783-3189. E-mail: atcgwd@aol.com.

COMPTON, CHARLES (KIP), communications executive; b. 1972; BS in Computer Sci., Mass. Inst. Tech., MEE in EE and Computer Sci. Dir., Tech. Strategy Cisco Systems, Inc., 1998—2001, dir., Entertainment Solutions, 1998—2001, sr. dir., Video & IPTV Devel., 2006—; v.p., Vide and Media Engring. Comcast Cable Comm., 2003—06. Named one of 40 Executives Under 40, Multichannel News, 2006. Office: Cisco Systems Inc 170 W Tasman Dr Bldg 10 San Jose CA 95134-1706 Office Phone: 408-526-4000. Office Fax: 408-526-4100.

COMPTON, CHARLES (CHRIS) T., lawyer; BS with honors, USAF Acad., 1965; JD, NYU, 1968. Bar: Calif., DC, US Ct. Appeals, ninth cir., US Ct. Mil. Appeals, US Supreme Ct. With Wilson Sonsini Goodrich & Rosati, Palo Alto, Calif., 1980, ptnr., chmn. antitrust dept. Lectr. U. Calif. Berkeley, Boalt Hall; adj. lectr. Santa Clara U. Sch. Law. Contbr. articles to profl. jour. Bd. mem. Silicon Valley Law Found. Mil. judge USAF. Named a No. Calif. Super Lawyer, Law & Politics mag., 2004, San Francisco mag., 2004; named one of Best Lawyers in Am., 2006. Office: Wilson Sonsini Goodrich & Rosati 650 Page Mill Rd Palo Alto CA 94304-1050 Office Phone: 650-493-9300. Office Fax: 650-493-6811. E-mail: ccompton@wsgr.com.

COMPTON, KEVIN R., venture capitalist, professional sports team executive; married; 2 children. V.p., gen. mgr. network sys. team Businessland (now Siemens); joined Kleiner Perkins Caufield & Byers, Menlo Park, Calif., 1990, gen. ptnr. Co-owner San Jose Sharks, 2002—, Cleveland Barons (Am. Hockey League), San Jose Earthquakes. Named one of Top 20 Venture Capitalists in the World. Office: Kleiner Perkins Caufield & Byers 2750 Sand Hill Rd Menlo Park CA 94025 also: San Jose Sharks HP Pavilion 525 W Santa Clara St San Jose CA 95113

COMRIE, SANDRA MELTON, human resource executive; b. Plant City, Fla., Sept. 15, 1940; d. Finis and Estelle (Black) Melton; m. Allan Crecelius; children: Shannon Melissa, Colleen Megan. BA, UCLA, 1962, grad. exec. program, 1984. Div. mgr. City of L.A., 1973-77, asst. pers. dir., 1977-84; v.p. Transam. Life Cos., LA, 1984-89; chief operating officer Treacy & Rhodes Consultants, Solana Beach, Calif., 1989-92; exec. dir. Reward Strategy Group, Inc., Del Mar, Calif., 1992-98. Bd. dirs. Found. for Employment and Disability, Sacramento, Clif.; mem. Asian Pacific Employment Task Force, Los Angeles, 1986-89. Bd. dirs. L.A. Urban League, 1985-92, Vols. of Am.-L.A., 1985-89; active United Way Downtown Bus. Consortium, Child Care Task Force, L.A., 1985-86; mem. adv. bd. L.A. City Child Care, 1987-89. Recipient Young Woman of Achievement award Soroptimists of Los Angeles, 1979. Mem. Internat. Pers. Mgmt. Assn (mem. assessment coun., co-chair program com. for 1982 nat. conf., chair human rights com. 1983, pres. 1985), So. Calif. Pers. Mgmt. Assn., Planning Forum, Human Resource Planning Soc., Soc. for Human Resource Mgmt., Am. Compensation Assn., Am. Mgmt. Assn., L.A. C. of C. (human resources com. 1986-89). Democrat. Avocation: travel. Office: Reward Strategy Group Inc 9276 Scranton Rd Ste 120 San Diego CA 92121

COMUS, LOUIS FRANCIS, JR., lawyer; b. St. Marys, Ohio, Feb. 26, 1942; BA, Antioch Coll., 1965; JD, Vanderbilt U., 1968. Bar: N.Y. 1969, Ariz. 1973. Dir. Fennemore Craig P.C., Phoenix, 1975—. Notes editor Vanderbilt Law Rev., 1967-68. Fellow Am. Coll. Trust and Estate Counsel; mem. ABA, State Bar Ariz., Maricopa County Bar Assn. Office: Fennemore Craig PC 3003 N Central Ave Ste 2600 Phoenix AZ 85012-2913 Home Phone: 602-996-9391; Office Phone: 602-916-5314. E-mail: lcomus@fclaw.com.

CONDIE, CAROL JOY, anthropologist, science administrator; b. Provo, Utah, Dec. 28, 1931; d. LeRoy and Thelma (Graff) Condie; children: Carla Ann, Erik Roy, Paula Jane. BA in Anthropology, U. Utah, 1953; MEd in Elem. Edn., Cornell U., 1954; PhD in Anthropology, U. N.Mex., 1973. Edn. coord. Maxwell Mus. Anthropology, U. N.Mex., Albuquerque, 1973, interpretation dir., 1974-77; asst. prof. anthropology U. N.Mex., 1975-77; cons. anthropologist, 1977-78; pres. Quivira Rsch. Ctr., Albuquerque, 1978—. Cons. anthropologist U.S. Congl. Office Tech. Assessment, chair Archeol. Resources Planning Adv. Com., Albuquerque, 1985-86; leader field seminars Crow Canyon Archeol. Ctr., 1986-97; appointee Albuquerque dist. adv. coun., bur. land mgmt. U.S. Dept. Interior, 1989; study leader Smithsonian Instn. Tours, 1991; mem. Albuquerque Heritage Conservation Adv. Com., 1992. Author: The Nighthawk Site: A Pithouse Site on Sandia Pueblo Land, Bernalillo County, New Mexico, 1982, Five Sites on the Pecos River Road, 1985, Data Recovery at Eight Archeological Sites on the Rio Nutritas, 1992, Data Recovery at Eight Archeological Sites on Cabresto Road Near Questa, 1992, Archeological Survey in the Rough and Ready Hills/Picacho Mountain Area, Dona Ana County, New Mexico, 1993, Archeological Survey on the Canadian River, Quay County, New Mexico, 1994, Archeological Testing at LA 103387, Nizhoni Extension, Gallup, McKinley County, New Mexico, 1995, Two Archeological Sites on San Felipe Pueblo Land, New Mexico, 1996, Four Archeological Sites at La Cienega, Santa Fe County, New Mexico, 1996, A Brief History of Berino, Berino Siding, and Early Mesilla Valley Agriculture, Dona Ana County, New Mexico, 1997, Main Street Project, Aztec, New Mexico, 2004, Testing and Data Recovery at Seven Sites Cabezon Subdivision Sandoval Co., 2005, Archeological Survey of 355 Acres...on the San Clemente Grant, Valencia County, N.Mex., 2006; author: (with M. Kent Stout) Historical and Architectural Study of the Old Peralta Elementary School, Valencia County, New Mexico, 1997, Archeological Survey of 720 Acres on Ball Ranch, Sandoval County, New Mexico, 1998; author: (with H.H. Franklin and P.J. McKenna) Results of Testing at Three Sites on Tesuque Pueblo Land, Santa Fe County, New Mexico, 1999, Cultural Resources Investigations at the Old Roswell Airport for the Proposed Cielo Grande Recreation Area, Chaves County, New Mexico, 2000, Archeological Survey in Las Lomas de la Bolsa, Santa Fe County, New Mexico, 2001, A Plethora of Walls...the Vigil Properties, Old Town Albuquerque, 2002; author: (with P.W. Bauer, R.P. Lozinsky and L.G. Price) Albuquerque: A Guide to Its Geology and Culture, 2003; author: (with Carol Raish) Indigenous and Traditional Use of Fire in Southwestern Grassland, Woodland, and Forest Ecosystems, 2003; author: (with Susan Dewitt) Doves Along the Ditchbank: La Orilla de la Acequia Historic District, 2003; author: Archeological Survey of Acres in the Cabezon Subdivision, Sandoval Co., 2004, Archeological Survey at the Cerrito Pelado Scoria Mine, Santa Fe Co., 2005, Archeological Survey in Rio del Oro Subdivision, Valencia Co., 2006, The Old First Church of the Nazarene: An Unusual Richardsonian Romanesque Building in Roswell, 2007, Main Street Improvement Project, Eunice, Lea Co., 2008; co-editor: Anthropology in the Desert West, 1986. Mem. Downtown Core Area Schs. Com., Albuquerque, 1982. Ford Found. fellow, 1953-54; recipient Am. Planning Assn. award, 1985-86, Gov.'s award, 1986. Fellow: Am. Anthrop. Assn.; mem.: Albuquerque Archaeol. Soc. (pres. 1992), N.Mex. Archaeol. Coun. (pres. 1982—83, Hist. Preservation award 1988), Archaeol. Soc. N.Mex. (trustee 2001—08), Soc. Am. Archaeology (chmn. Native Am. rels. com. 1983—85), Hist. Albuquerque Inc., The Archaeol. Conservancy (bd. dirs. 2003—), N.Mex. Heritage Preservation Alliance, Maxwell Mus. Assn. (bd. dirs. 1980—83), Las Arañas Spinners and Weavers Guild (pres. 1972). Democrat. Avocations: spinning, weaving, gardening. Home and Office: Quivira Research Ctr 1809 Notre Dame Dr NE Albuquerque NM 87106-1011 Office Phone: 505-255-9264. E-mail: cjc1540@qwest.net.

CONDON, BRODY KIEL, computer graphics designer; b. Nayarit, Mex., 1974; BFA in Sculpture, U. Fla., 1997; MFA in Visual Arts, U. Calif. San Diego, 2002; attended, Skowhegan Sch. Painting & Sculpture, 2001. Visiting prof. Central Nationalities U., Beijing, 2002, ICAM, U. Calif. San Diego, 2003; adj. prof. studio arts U. Calif. Irvine, 2004—. One-man shows include Staring Contest, Sushi Visual Art, San Diego, 2000, Half Life, Marcuse Gallery, San Diego, 2001, Chinatown, C-Level, LA, 2002, Adam Killer, Electronic Orphanage, LA, 2002, EndGames, The Kitchen, NY, 2003, Untitled War, Machine, LA, 2004, exhibited in group shows at Flauma: Series for Non-Architecture, Space Untitled, NY, 2001, Glitch, Oslo Art Acad., Norway, 2001, New Fangle, Herbst Exhbn. Hall, San Francisco, 2002, Provocations, Next Art Festival, Orlando, Fla., 2003, While You Were Playing, Flux Factory, NY, 2003, Digital Media, Am. Mus. Moving Image, NY, 2003, Electrofringe, New Castle, New South Wales, 2003, Whitney Biennial, Whitney Mus. Am. Art, 2004. Geraldine R. Dodge Found. Fellowship, Coll. Art Assn., 2001, Future of the Present Grant, Franklin Furnace, 2002.

CONDON, ROBERT EDWARD, surgeon, educator, consultant; b. Albany, NY, Aug. 13, 1929; s. Edward A. and Catherine (Kilmartin) C.; m. Marcia Jane Pagano, June 16, 1951; children: Sean Edward, Brian Robert. AB, U. Rochester, 1951, MD, 1957; MS, U. Wash., 1965. Diplomate Am. Bd. Surgery, Nat. Bd. Med. Examiners. N.Y. Bd. Regents scholar U. Rochester, 1957; intern King County Hosp., Seattle, 1957-58; resident dept. surgery U. Wash. Sch. Medicine (and affiliated hosps.), 1958-65; postdoctoral rsch. fellow Nat. Heart Inst., 1961-63; asst. prof. surgery Baylor Coll. Medicine, Houston, 1965-67; assoc. prof. surgery U. Ill. Coll. Medicine, Chgo., 1967-69, prof., 1969-70; prof., head dept. surgery U. Iowa Coll. Medicine, Iowa City, 1971-72; prof. surgery Med. Coll. Wis., Milw., 1972—98, prof. emeritus, 1998, chmn. dept. surgery, 1979-95; chief surg. svcs. Wood VA Hosp., Milw., 1972-81. Attending surgeon Froedtert Meml. Luth. Hosp., 1982-98; cons. Columbia Hosp., Milw., St. Joseph Hosp., Milw.; clin. prof. surgery U. Wash., 2000-08, clin. prof. emeritus, 2008. Author: (with others) Abdominal Pain: A Guide to Rapid Diagnosis, 2d edit., 1995, Manual of Surgical Therapeutics, 9th edit., 1996, Hernia, 4th edit., 1995, Surgical Care, 1980. Recipient sr. class award as Outstanding Faculty Mem. Baylor U. Coll. Medicine, 1966, Excellence in Tchg. award Phi Chi, 1967, Cert. Appreciation U. Iowa Coll. Medicine, 1971, Tchr. of Yr. award U. Iowa Coll. Medicine, 1972, Tchr. of Yr. award Med. Coll. Wis., 1983, 95, Disting. Svc. award Med. Coll. Wis., 1993, Disting. Alumnus award U. Wash., 1998; rsch. fellow Guggenheim Found., 1963-64. Mem. ACS (bd. govs.), Am. Surg. Assn. (v.p.), Surg. Infection Soc. (pres.), Am. Assn. Surgery of Trauma, Internat. Soc. Surgery, Collegium Internationale Chirurgiae Digestivae (pres.), Assn. for Acad. Surgery, Ctrl. Surg. Assn. (pres.), So. Surg. Assn., We. Surg. Assn., Wis. Surg. Soc. (pres.), Milw. Surg. Soc. (pres.), Chgo. Surg. Soc., Soc. Univ. Surgeons, Soc. Clin. Surgery, Milw. Acad. Medicine, Soc. Surgery Alimentary Tract (v.p.), Milw. Acad. Surgery (pres.). Home and Office: 2722 86th Ave NE Clyde Hill WA 98004-1653 Office Phone: 425-453-7860. E-mail: recrecmd@comcast.net.

CONDON, TOM (THOMAS JOSEPH CONDON), sports agent, retired professional football player; b. Derby, Conn., Oct. 26, 1952; married; 1 child. Tom. BA in Philosophy & Sociology, Boston Coll., 1974; JD, U. Balt., 1981. Profl. football player Kans. City Chiefs, 1974—84, New England Patriots, 1985; sports agent IMG Talent Agy., Cleve., 1991—2006, Creative Artists Agy., Beverly Hills, 2006—. Pres. NFL Players Union, 1984—86. Named The Most Powerful Agent in Football, The Sporting News, 2006; named one of The Most Influential People in the World of Sports, Bus. Week, 2007, 2008; named to Boston Coll. Varsity Club Athletic Hall of Fame, 1984. Achievements include acting as an agent for over 24 first-round NFL Draft picks.

CONE, LAWRENCE ARTHUR, medical educator; b. NYC, Mar. 23, 1928; s. Max N. and Ruth (Weber) C.; m. Julia Haldy, June 6, 1947 (dec. 1956); m. Mary Elisabeth Osborne, Aug. 20, 1960; children: Lionel Alfred. AB, NYU, 1948; MD, U. Berne, Switzerland, 1954; DSc (hon.), Rocky Mountain Coll., 1993. Diplomate Am. Bd. Internal Medicine, Am. Bd. Infectious Diseases, Am. Bd. Allergy and Immunology, Am. Bd. Med. Oncology. Intern Dallas Meth. Hosp., 1954-55, resident internal medicine, 1955; resident Flower 5th Hosp., NYC, 1957-59, Met. Hosp., NYC, 1959-60; rsch. fellow infectious diseases and immunology NYU Med. Sch., NYC, 1960-62; from asst. prof. to assoc. prof. NY Med. Coll., NYC, 1962-72, chief sect immunology and infectious diseases, 1962-72; assoc. clin. prof. medicine Harbor UCLA Med. Sch., 1984—2004; clin. prof. internal medicine U. Calif., Riverside, 1998—; clin. prof. medicine UCLA, 2004—07. Career scientist Health Rsch. Coun. N.Y.C., 1962-68; chief sect. immunology and infectious diseases Eisenhower Med. Ctr., Rancho Mirage, Calif., 1973-2002, chmn. dept. medicine, 1976-78, pres. elect, pres., past pres. med. staff, 1984-90; cons. infectious disease Desert Hosp., Palm Springs, Calif., 1980-85; lectr. basic sci. U. Calif., Riverside Biomed. Scis.; mem. mycosis study group NIAID, 1993—, co-investigator

Coccidiodomycosis study group, 1993—, eastern coop. oncology group affil. Stanford U., 1994, 2003-. Contbr. articles to profl. jours. Bd. dirs., trustee Desert Bighorn Rsch. Inst., Palm Desert, Calif., pres., bd. dirs., 1995-99; nat. adv. coun., trustee Rocky Mountain Coll., Billings, Mont., 2001—; mem. med. adv. staff Coll. of Desert, Palm Desert; Pres. Cir. Desert Mus., Palm Springs, Calif., Idaho Conservation League, Gilcrease Mus., Tulsa, Sun Valley Ctr. for Arts and Humanities. L.A. County Mus., Smithsonian Inst., Buffalo Bill Historic Mus., Cody, Wyo.; mem. Nat. Mus. Wildlife Art, Yellowstone Art Mus., Billings, Mont.; life mem. The Living Desert, Palm Desert, L.A. County Mus.; mem. cmty. adv. coun. Jr. League; CEO Genetic Rsch. Inst. of Desert; sustaining mem. Rep. Nat. Com. Recipient Outstanding Contbn. to Medicine award Riverside County Med. Assn., 1998, Disting. Achievement award AMC Cancer Rsch. Ctr., 1998, Steven Chase award, 2000, Eisenhower Med. Ctr. award. Fellow ACP, Royal Soc. Medicine, Interam. Soc. Chemotherapy, Am. Coll. Allergy, Am. Acad. Allergy and Immunology, Infectious Diseases Soc. Am., Am. Geriatric Soc. (founding fellow we. divsn.); mem. AAAS, Internat. AIDS Soc., Am. Fedn. Clin. Rsch., Am. Soc. Microbiology, Reticulocudothelial Soc., Am. Fedn. for Clin. Rsch., Faculty Soc. UCLA, Surg. Soc. N.Y. Med. Coll. (hon.), Woodstock Artists Assn., Harvey Soc., N.Y. Acad. Scis., European Soc. Clinical Microbiology and Infectious Disease, Internat. Soc. Infectious Disease, NYU Alumni Assn., Berne Alumni Assn., Hoover Found., Yellowstone Art Mus., Autry Mus. Western Heritage, Nat. Mus. Am. Indian, Palm Springs Art Mus., Lotos Club, Tamarisk Country Club, Faculty Soc. UCLA Harbor Med. Ctr., O'Donnell Golf Club, Sigma Xi. Republican. Avocations: golf, fishing, hunting, skiing. Home: 765 Via Vadera Palm Springs CA 92262-4170 Office: Probst Profl Bldg #308 39000 Bob Hope Dr Rancho Mirage CA 92270-3221 also: Larkspur Condominiums PO Box 1503 Sun Valley ID 83353-1503 also: 5004 Rt 213 Olivebridge NY 12461 Office Phone: 760-346-5688. Personal E-mail: lacmedicine@aol.com.

CONGDON, ROGER DOUGLASS, theology studies educator, minister; b. Ft. Collins, Colo., Apr. 6, 1918; s. John Solon and Ellen Avery (Kellogg); m. Rhoda Gwendolyn Britt, Jan. 2, 1948; children: Rachel Congdon Lidbeck, James R., R. Steven, Jon B., Philip F., Robert N., Bradford B., Ruth A. Mahner, Rebecca York Brooks, Rhoda J. Miller, Marianne C. Potter, Mark Alexander. BA, Wheaton Coll., 1940; postgrad, Eastern Bapt. Sem., 1940-41; ThM, Dallas Theol. Sem., 1945; ThD, Dallas Theology Sem., 1949. Ordained to ministry Bapt. Ch., 1945. Exec. sec., dean Altanta Bible Inst., 1945-49; prof. theology Carver Bible Inst., Atlanta, 1945-49; prof. Multnomah Bible Coll., Portland, Oreg., 1950-87; pastor Emmanuel Bapt. Ch., Vancouver, Wash., 1985—. Past dean of faculty, dean of edn., v.p., chmn. libr. com., chmn. achievement-award com., chmn. lectureship com., advisor grad. div. and mem. pres.'s cabinet Multnomah Bible Co.; chmn. Chil Evang. Fellowship of Greater Portland, 1978-97; founder, pres. Preaching Print Inc., Portland, 1953—. Founder, speaker semi-weekly radio broadcast Bible Truth Forum, KPDQ, Portland, Oreg., 1989—, DZAM, Manila, Philippines, 1996—, Radio Africa 2, 1998—, Radio E. Africa, 2003—; author: The Doctrine of Conscience, 1945. Chmn. Citizen's Com. Info. on Communism, Portland, 1968-75. Recipient Outstanding Educators of Am. award, 1972, Loraine Chafer award in Systematic Theology, Dallas Theol. Sem., 1949. Mem. Am. Assn. Bible Colls. (chmn. testing com. 1953-78), N.Am. Assn. Bible Colls. (N.W. rep. 1960-63), Near East Archaeol. Soc., Evang. Theol. Soc. Republican. Home: 16539 NE Halsey St Portland OR 97230-5607 Office: Emmanuel Bapt Ch 14810 NE 28th St Vancouver WA 98682-8357 Office Phone: 360-254-8510. Personal E-mail: gwen.congden@gmail.com.

CONGER, HARRY MILTON, mining company executive; b. Seattle, July 22, 1930; s. Harry Milton Jr. and Caroline (Gunnell) C.; m. Phyllis Nadine Shepherd, Aug. 14, 1949 (dec.); children: Harry Milton IV, Preston George; m. Rosemary L. Scholz, Feb. 22, 1991. Degree in Bus. Adminstrn. (hon.), SD Sch. Mines Tech., 1983; degree in Engring. (hon.), Colo. Sch. Mines, 1988, degree (hon.). Registered profl. engr., Ariz., Colo. Shift foreman Asarco, Inc., Silver Bell, Ariz., 1955-64; mgr. Kaiser Steel Corp. Eagle Mountain Mine, 1964-70; v.p., gen. mgr. Kaiser Resources, Ltd., Fernie, B.C., Canada, 1970-73, Consolidation Coal Co. (Midwestern div.), Carbondale, Ill., 1973-75; v.p. Homestake Mining Co., San Francisco, 1975-77, pres., 1977-78, pres., chief exec. officer, 1978-82, chmn., pres., chief exec. officer, 1982-86, chmn., chief exec. officer, 1986-96, chmn., 1996-98, chmn., CEO emeritus, also bd. dirs., 1998, ret., 1998, PG& E Corp., 1982—2001, Baker Hughes Inc., 1987—97, Calmat Inc., 1986—97. Bd. dir., ASA Ltd., Apex Silver Mines; chmn. Am. Mining Congress, 1986—89, World Gold Coun., 1995—97. Trustee Calif. Inst. Tech. With C.E. US Army, 1956. Recipient Disting. Achievement medal Colo. Sch. Mines, 1978, Am. Mining Hall of Fame, 1990, Disting. Svc. award Am. Mining Congress, 1995. Mem. NAE, Nat. Mining Assn. (hon. bd. dirs.), Am. Inst. Mining Engrs. (disting., Charles F. Rand gold medal 1990), Mining and Metallurgy Soc. Am., Mining Club, Bohemian Club, Pacific Union Club. Republican. Episcopalian. Personal E-mail: hmcongerIII@sbcglobal.net.

CONLEY, MARK A., lawyer; b. Phila., Nov. 22, 1951; BA magna cum laude, U. Pa., 1973; JD, Columbia U., 1977. Bar: NY 1978, Calif. 1989. With Debevoise & Plimpton, Will and Emery; ptnr. corp. law Katten Muchin Zavis Rosenman, LA. Mem.: U. So. Calif. Inst. for Corp. Counsel, LA Venture Assn., LA County Bar Assn., Calif. State Bar Assn. Office: Ste 2600 2029 Century Park E Los Angeles CA 90067 Office Phone: 310-788-4690. Office Fax: 310-712-8225. E-mail: mark.conley@kmzr.com.

CONLISK, RAIMON L., high technology management consulting executive; Pres. Conlisk Assocs., Fremont, Calif.; chmn. Exar Corp. Chmn. bd. dirs. SBE, Inc., San Ramon, Calif.; bd. dirs. Xetel, Inc. Office: 48720 Kato Rd Fremont CA 94538

CONLY, JOHN FRANKLIN, retired engineering educator; b. Ridley Park, Pa., Sept. 11, 1933; s. Harlan and Mary Jane (Roberts) Conly; m. Jeannine Therese McDonough, Apr. 14, 1967; children: J. Paul, Mary Ann. BS, U. Pa., 1956, MS, 1958; PhD, Columbia U., 1962. Instr. U. Pa., Phila., 1956-58; rsch. asst. Columbia U., NYC, 1959-62; asst. prof. engring. San Diego State U., 1962-65, assoc. prof., 1965-69, prof., 1969—2003, prof. emeritus, 2003—, chmn. dept., 1971-74, 77-85, wind tunnel dir., 1978—2001. D. and F. Guggenheim fellow, 1958. Fellow: AIAA (assoc.; sect. chmn. 1970, best U.S. sect.). Independent. Episcopalian. Office: San Diego State U Dept Aerospace Engring San Diego CA 92182

CONN, ERIC EDWARD, plant biochemist; b. Berthoud, Colo., Jan. 6, 1923; s. William Elmer and Mary Anna (Smith) C.; m. Louise Carolyn Kachel, Oct. 17, 1959; children: Michael E., Kevin E. BA in Chemistry cum laude, U. Colo., Boulder, 1944; PhD in Biochemistry, U. Chgo., 1950. Instr. biochemistry U. Chgo., 1950-52; instr. U. Calif., Berkeley, 1952-53, asst. prof., 1953-58, assoc. prof. Davis, 1958-63, prof., 1964—. Author: (with P.K. Stumpf) Outlines of Biochemistry, 1963, 5th edit., 1987; editor: (with P.K. Stumpf) (book series) Biochemistry of Plants, 1980-90. With U.S. Army, 1945-46. Recipient Pergamon Phytochemistry prize and cert., 1994;, USPHS fellow, 1960, Fulbright Rsch. grantee, 1965, Australian acacia "Acacia conniana" named in his honor, 1984. Mem. NAS, Phytochem. Soc. N.Am. (hon. life mem., pres. 1971-72, editor in chief 1984-89), Am. Soc. Plant Biology (pres. 1986-87, Charles Reid Barnes life mem.), Am. Soc. Biol. Chemistry, Am. Chem. Soc. Democrat. Avocations: gardening, stamp collecting/philately. Office: Univ Calif Sect Molecular & Cellular Biol Davis CA 95616 Home Phone: 530-753-4174; Office Phone: 530-752-3611. Business E-Mail: eeconn@ucdavis.edu.

CONN, ROBERT WILLIAM, venture capital investor; b. NYC, Dec. 1, 1942; s. William Conrad and Rose Marie (Albanese) C.; children: Carole, William. BChemE, Pratt Inst., 1964; MS in Mech. Engring., Calif. Inst. Tech., 1965, PhD in Engring. Sci., 1968. NSF postdoctoral fellow Euratom Cmty. Rsch. Center, Ispra, Italy, 1968-69; rsch. assoc. Brookhaven Nat. Lab., Upton, N.Y., 1969-70; vis. assoc. prof. U. Wis., Madison, 1970-72, assoc. prof., 1972-75, prof., 1975-80, dir. fusion tech. program, 1974-79, Romnes faculty prof., 1977-80; prof. engring. and applied sci. UCLA, 1980-93, dir. Inst. Plasma and Fusion Rsch., 1987-93; dean Sch. Engring., Zable prof. engring. U. Calif., San Diego, 1994—2002; founder, chmn. bd. Trikon Tech., Inc. (formerly Plasma & Materials Techs., Inc., LA, 1986-93; mng. dir. Enterprise Ptnrs. Venture Capital, 2002—. Chair, sec. Energy's Fusion Energy Adv. Com., 1991-96; cons. to govt. and industry. Author papers, chpts. in books. Recipient Curtis McGraw Rsch. award Am. Assn. Engring. Edn., 1982, U.S. Dept. Energy E.O. Lawrence Meml. award, 1984, Fusion Power Assocs. Leadership award, 1992, Disting. Assoc.'s award Sec. of Energy, Dept. of Energy, 1996, Calif. Inst. Tech. Disting. Alumni Yr. award, 1998; named San Diego Outstanding Educator of Yr., 1997. Fellow Am. Nuclear Soc. (Outstanding Achievement award for excellence in research fusion div. 1979), Am. Phys. Soc.; mem. NAE. Office: Enterprise Ptnrs VC 2223 Avenida de la Playa Ste 300 La Jolla CA 92037 Business E-Mail: rwconn@epvc.com.

CONNELLY, JAMES P., prosecutor; b. Hartford, Conn., Apr. 15, 1947; BA, Marquette U., 1969; JD, Georgetown U., 1972. Bar: Wis. 1972. Spl. asst. to Sec. of Treasury, 1975-76; ptnr. Foley & Lardner, Milw.; U.S. atty. U.S. Dist. Ct. (ea. dist.) Wash., Spokane, 1994—. Editor-in-chief Georgetown Law Jour., 1971-72. Mem. State Bar Wis., Phi Alpha Delta. Office: US Atty Office US Courthouse PO Box 1494 920 W Riverside Ave Spokane WA 99210-1494

CONNER, LINDSAY ANDREW, lawyer; b. NYC, Feb. 19, 1956; s. Michael and Miriam Conner. BA summa cum laude, UCLA, 1976; MA, Occidental Coll., 1978; JD magna cum laude, Harvard U., 1980. Bar: Calif. 1980, U.S. Dist. Ct. (cen. dist.) Calif. 1983. Assoc. Kaplan, Livingston, Goodwin, Berkowitz & Selvin, Beverly Hills, Calif., 1980—81, Fulop & Hardee, Beverly Hills, 1982—83, Wyman, Bautzer, Kuchel & Silbert, LA, 1983—86; ptnr., entertainment dept. head Hill Wynne Troop & Meisinger, LA, 1986—93; screenwriter and prodr. 54 St. Prodns., LA, 1994—99; COO, I-Drop, Inc., LA, 1999—2005; ptnr. Dickstein Shapiro, LA, 2006—, head Dept. Entertainment, 2006—. Author: (with others) The Courts and Education, 1977; editor: Harvard Law Rev., 1978-80. Trustee L.A. Community Coll., 1981-97, bd. pres., 1989-90; pres. Calif. Community Coll. Trustees, 1992-93. Mem. ABA, UCLA Alumni Assn. (life), Harvard-Radcliffe Club, Phi Beta Kappa.

CONNERY, SIR SEAN (THOMAS SEAN CONNERY), actor; b. Edinburgh, Aug. 25, 1930; s. Joseph and Euphamia C.; m. Diane Cilento, Dec. 6, 1962 (div. Sept. 6, 1973); 1 son, Jason; m. Micheline Roquebrune, 1975; 1 stepdaughter. DLitt (hon.), Heriot-Watt U., 1981, St. Andrews U., 1988. Founder Fountainbridge Films, Los Angeles, 1992—2002. First theater appearance in road show co. of South Pacific, Eng., 1953, also in Macbeth, Judith; Actor (films)Let's Make Up, 1955, No Road Back, 1956, Action of the Tiger, 1957, Hell Drivers, 1957, Time Lock, 1957, Another Time, Another Place, 1958, Tarzan's Greatest Adventure, 1959, Darby O'Gill and the Little People, 1959, The Frightened City, 1961, Operation Snafu, 1961, The Longest Day, 1962, Dr. No., 1962, From Russia With Love, 1963, Marnie, 1964, Woman of Straw, 1964, Goldfinger, 1964, The Hill, 1965, Thunderball, 1965, A Fine Madness, 1966, You Only Live Twice, 1967, Shalako, 1968, The Molly Maguires, 1970, The Red Tent, 1971, The Anderson Tapes, 1971, Diamonds are Forever, 1971, The Offence, 1973, Zardoz, 1974, The Terrorists, 1974, Murder on the Orient Express, 1974, The Wind and the Lion, 1975, The Man Who Would be King, 1975, Robin and Marian, 1976, The Next Man, 1976, A Bridge Too Far, 1977, The Great Train Robbery, 1979, Cuba, 1979, Meteor, 1979, Outland, 1981, Time Bandits, 1981, Sword of the Valiant, 1982, Wrong is Right, 1982, Five Days One Summer, 1982, Never Say Never Again, 1983, Highlander, 1986, The Name of the Rose, 1986, The Untouchables, 1987 (Acad. award for Best Supporting Actor), The Presidio, 1988, Indiana Jones and the Last Crusade, 1989, Family Business, 1989, The Hunt for Red October, 1990, The Russia House, 1990, Highlander 2: The Quickening, 1991, Robin Hood: Prince of Thieves, 1991, Rising Sun, 1993, A Good Man in Africa, 1994, Just Cause, 1995, First Knight, 1995, The Rock, 1996, (voice only) Dragon Heart, 1996, Playing By Heart, 1998; actor, prodr., Entrapment, 1999, Finding Forrester, 2000; actor, exec. prodr. The Avengers, 1998, The League of Extraordinary Gentlemen, 2003; actor, co-exec. prodr.: Medicine Man, 1992; (TV movies) Requiem For a Heavyweight, 1957, Women in Love, 1957, The Square Ring, 1959, The Crucible, 1959, Colombe, 1960, Without the Grail, 1961, MacBeth, 1961, Anna Karenina, 1961, Male of the Species, 1969, Blitz, 2006; prodr., dir.: The Bowler and the Bonnet (film documentary), I've Seen You Cut Lemons (London stage); prodr.: Something Like the Truth, Playing by Heart, 1998, (narrator) Macbeth, 1999; actor (video games) James Bond 007: From Russia with Love (voice only), 2005; author (autobiography) Being a Scot, 2008. With Brit. Royal Navy. Named Star of the Yr., Nat. Assn. Theater Owners, 1987, Commander of Arts, France; recipient Tribute award Brit. Acad. Film and Television Arts, 1990, Career Achievement award Nat. Bd. Rev., 1993, Cecil B. DeMille Golden Globe award Hollywood Fgn. Press Assn., 1996, Lifetime Achievement award ShoWest Conv., 1999, Order Brit. Empire (OBE), 2000, Life Achievement award Am. Film Inst., 2005, Campidoglia prize, 2006

CONNOLLY, JOHN EARLE, surgeon, educator; b. Omaha, May 21, 1923; s. Earl A. and Gertrude (Eckerman) C.; m. Virginia Hartman, Aug. 12, 1967; children: Peter Hart, John Earle, Sarah. AB, Harvard U., 1945, MD, 1948. Diplomate: Am. Bd. Surgery (bd. dirs. 1976-82), Am. Bd. Thoracic and Cardiovascular Surgery, Am. Bd. Vascular Surgery. Intern. in surgery Stanford U. Hosps., San Francisco, 1948-49, surg. research fellow, 1949-50, asst. resident surgeon, 1950-52, chief resident surgeon, 1953-54, surg. pathology fellow, 1954-55, 1957-60, John and Mary Markle Scholar in med. scis., 1957-62; surg. registrar professional unit St. Bartholomew's Hosp., London, 1952-53; resident in thoracic surgery Bellevue Hosp., NYC, 1955; resident in thoracic and cardiovascular surgery Columbia-Presbyn. Med. Ctr., NYC, 1956; from instr. to assoc. prof. surgery Stanford U., 1957-65; prof. U. Calif., Irvine, 1965—, chmn. dept. surgery, 1965-78; attending surgeon Stanford Med. Ctr., Palo Alto, Calif., 1959-65; chmn. cardiovascular and thoracic surgery Irvine Med. Ctr. U. Calif., 1968—; attending surgeon Children's Hosp., Orange, Calif., 1968—, Anaheim (Calif.) Meml. Hosp., 1970—. Vis. prof. Beijing Heart, Lung, Blood Vessel Inst., 1990, A.H. Duncan vis. prof. U. Edinburgh, 1984; Hunterian prof. Royal Coll. Surgeons Eng., 1985-86, Kinmonth lectr., 1987, Hume Lectr. Soc. for Clin. Vascular Surgery, 1998; King James IV lectr. Royal Coll. Surgeons Edinburgh, 2003; Dist. Prof. Lectr. Uniformed Svcs. U. Health Scis., Bethesda, 1998; adv. coun. Nat. Heart, Lung, and Blood Inst.-NIH, 1981-85; Emile F. Holman lectr. Stanford U. Sch. Medicine, 2005; cons. Long Beach VA Hosp., Calif., 1965—. Contbr. articles to profl. jours.; mem. editl. bd.: Jour. Cardiovascular Surgery, 1974-03, chief editor, 1985-96; mem. editl. bd. Western Jour. Medicine, 1975—, Jour. Stroke, 1979—, Jour. Vascular Surgery, 1983-95. Bd. dirs. Audio-Digest Found., 1974—, Franklin Martin Found., 1975-80; regent Uniformed Svcs. U. Health Scis., Bethesda, 1992-03. Served with AUS, 1943-44. Recipient Cert. of Merit, Japanese Surg. Soc., 1979, 90. Fellow ACS (gov. 1964-70, regent 1973-82, vice chmn. bd. regents 1980-82, v.p. 1984-85), Royal Coll. Surgeons Eng., 1982 (hon.), Royal Coll. Surgeons Ireland, 1988 (hon.), Royal Coll. Surgeons Edinburgh, 1983 (hon.); mem. Japanese Surg. Soc. (hon.), Vascular Soc. of Great Britian & Ireland (hon.), Bd. of Regents, Nat. Library Medicine NIH, Bethesda, Md., Am. Surg. Assn., Soc. U. Surgeons, Am. Assn. Thoracic Surgery (coun. 1974-78), Pacific Coast Surg. Assn. (pres. 1985-86), San Francisco Surg. Soc., L.A. Surg. Soc., Soc. Vascular Surgery, Western Surg. Assn., Internat. Cardiovascular Soc. (pres. 1977), Soc. Internat. Chirurgie, Soc. Thoracic Surgeons, Western Thoracic Surg. Soc. (pres. 1978), Orange County Surg. Soc. (pres. 1984-85), James IV Assn. Surgeons (councillor 1983—), San Francisco Golf Club, Pacific Union Club, Bohemian Club (San Francisco), Harvard Club (N.Y.C.), Big Canyon Club (Newport Beach, Calif.), Cypress Point Club (Pebble Beach). Home: 7 Deerwood Ln Newport Beach CA 92660-5108 Office Phone: 714-456-5756. E-mail: jeconnol@uci.edu.

CONNOLLY, THOMAS JOSEPH, bishop emeritus; b. Tonopah, Nev., July 18, 1922; s. John and Katherine (Hammel) C. Attended, St. Joseph Coll. and St. Patrick Sem., Menlo Park, Calif., Catholic U. America, 1949—51; JCD, Lateran Pontifical U., Rome, 1952; DHL (hon.), U. Portland, 1972. Ordained priest Diocese of Reno, 1947; asst. St. Thomas Cathedral, Reno, 1947, asst., rector, 1953-55; asst. Little Flower Parish, Reno, 1947-48; sec. to bishop, 1949; asst. St. Albert the Gt., Reno, 1952-53, pastor, 1960-68, St. Joseph Ch., Elko, 1955-60, St. Theresa's Ch., Carson City, Nev., 1968-71; ordained bishop, 1971; bishop Diocese of Baker, Bend, Oreg., 1971-2000, bishop emeritus, 2000—. Tchr. Manogue High Sch., Reno, 1948-49; chaplain Serra Club, 1948-49; officialis Diocese of Reno; chmn. bldg. com., dir. Cursillo Movement; moderator Italian Cath. Fedn.; dean, mem. personnel bd. Senate of Priests; mem. Nat. Bishops Liturgy Com., 1973-76; region XII rep. to adminstrv. bd. Nat. Conf. Cath. Bishops, 1973-76, 86-89, mem. adv. com., 1974-76; bd. dirs. Cath. Communications Northwest, 1977-82. Mem.: K.C. (state chaplain Nev. 1970-71). Roman Catholic. Office: Diocese of Baker PO Box 5999 911 SE Armour Dr Bend OR 97702-1489 Office Phone: 541-388-4004. Office Fax: 541-388-2566.

CONNOR, ROBERT W., JR., federal judge; b. 1942; Magistrate judge U.S. Dist. Ct. Wyo., Sheridan, 1977—; ptnr. Conner and Smith, Sheridan. Office: PO Box 607 Sheridan WY 82801-0607

CONNOR, WILLIAM ELLIOTT, internist, educator; b. Pitts., Sept. 14, 1921; s. Frank E. and Edna S. (Felt) C.; m. Sonja Lee Newcomer, Sept. 19, 1969; children: Rodney William, Catherine Susan, James Elliott, Christopher French, Peter Malcolm. BA, U. Iowa, 1942, MD, 1950. Diplomate Am. Bd. Internal Medicine, Am. Bd. Nutrition, Am. Bd. Clin. Lipidology. Intern USPHS Hosp., San Francisco, 1950-51; resident in internal medicine San Joaquin Gen. Hosp., Stockton, Calif., 1951-52; practice medicine specializing in internal medicine Chico, Calif., 1952-54; resident in internal medicine VA Hosp., Iowa City, 1954-56; cons., 1967-75; mem. faculty U. Iowa Coll. Medicine, 1956-75, prof. internal medicine, 1967-75; acting dir., then dir. Clin. Research Center, 1967-75, dir. lipid-atherosclerosis sect., cardiovascular div., 1974-75. Vis. prof. Basic Sci. Med. Inst., Karachi, Pakistan, Ind. U., 1961-62, Baker Med. Rsch. Inst., Melbourne, Australia, 1982; vis. fellow clin. sci. Australian Nat. U., Canberra, 1970; prof. cardiology and metabolism-nutrition, dept. medicine, 1975-79, head sect. clin. nutrition, 1979-90, acting head, head div. endocrinology, metabolism and nutrition, 1984-90, prof. sect. clin. nutrition, 1990—, dir. lipid-atherosclerosis lab., assoc. dir. Clin. Rsch. Ctr., Oreg. Health Scis. U. Portland, 1975-94; chmn. heart and lung program project com. Contbr. numerous articles to med. jours.; editor Jour. Lab. and Clin. Medicine, 1970-73; mem. editorial bds., reviewer profl. jours. Mem. Johnson County (Iowa) Cen. Dem. Com., 1965-69; mem. nat. council Fellowship Reconciliation; nat., North Central and Pacific Northwest bds. Am. Friends Service Com. Served with AUS, 1943-46. Research fellow Am. Heart Assn., 1956-58; ACP traveling fellow Sir William Dunn Sch. Pathology, Oxford, Eng., 1960; recipient Career Devel. Research award Nat. Heart Inst., 1962-73, Discovery award Med. Research Found. Oreg. Mem. AAAS, ACP, AMA, AAUP (pres. U. Iowa chpt. 1968-69, pres. Oreg. Health Sci. U. chpt. 1978-79), Am. Diabetes Assn. (vice chmn. food and nutrition com. 1972-74), Am. Dietitic Assn. (hon.), Am. Fedn. Clin. Rsch., Am. Heart Assn. (chmn. coun. arteriosclerosis 1975-78, exec. com. coun. epidemiology 1967-70, exec. com. coun. cerebral vascular disease 1966-68, C. Lyman Duff meml. lectrue 1989), Am. Soc. Clin. Nutrition (pres. 1978), Nat. Acad. Sci. (food and nutrition bd. 1986-89), Am. Inst. Nutrition, Am. Oil Chemists Soc., Am. Physiol. Soc., Am. Soc. Clin. Investigation, Am. Soc. Study Arteriosclerosis, Assn. Am. Physicians, Ctrl. Soc. Clin. Rsch., Nutrition Soc., Soc. Exptl. Biology and Medicine (coun. 1971-72, pres. Iowa sect. 1971-72), Western Assn. Physicians, Western Soc. Clin. Rsch., Phi Beta Kappa, Sigma Xi, Alpha Omega Alpha. Achievements include research in nutrition, lipid metabolism, blood vessel diseases. Home: 2600 SW Sherwood Pl Portland OR 97201-2285 Office: Oreg Health Scis U L465 Portland OR 97201 Office Phone: 503-494-2001. Business E-Mail: connorw@ohsu.edu.

CONNORS, JOHN G., venture capitalist, former computer software company executive; b. 1959; m. Kathy Connors. BS in Acctg., U. Mont., 1984. CPA. Corp. contr. PIP Printing, Inc.; with fin. dept. Safeco Corp., Deloitte, Haskins and Sells; mgmt. Microsoft Corp., 1989, gen. mgr. worldwide fin. ops., corp. contr., 1994-96, chief info officer, 1996—99, v.p. worldwide enterprise group, 1999, sr. v.p. fin., CFO, 1999—2005; ptnr. Ignition Partners LLC, Bellevue, Wash., 2005—. Bd. dirs. Certus Software, Inc, 2005—, Nike, Inc., 2005—, Jobster, Inc., 2005—, BioPassword, Inc., 2005—, Rim-Tec, 2006—. Bd. trustees Swedish Medical Ctr. Recipient Disting. Alumni award, U. Mont., 1997. Office: Ignition Partners LLC 11400 SE 6th St Ste 100 Bellevue WA 98004

CONOVER, RICHARD CORRILL, lawyer; b. Jan. 12, 1942; s. John Cedric and Mildred (Dunn) C.; m. Cathy Harlan, Dec. 19, 1970; children: William Cedric, Theodore Cyril. BS, U. Nebr., Lincoln, 1965, MS, 1966; JD, Cornell U., 1969. Bar: N.Y. 1970, Mont. 1982, U.S. Dist. Ct. (so. and ea. dists.) N.Y. 1971, U.S. Supreme Ct. 1977, U.S. Ct. Customs and Patent Appeals 1979, U.S. Dist. Ct. Mont. 1984, U.S. Tax Ct. 1986. Assoc. Brumbaugh, Graves, Donohue & Raymond, NYC, 1969—73, Townley, Updike, Carter & Rodgers, NYC, 1974—75; assoc. gen. counsel legal office Automatic Data Processing, Inc., Clifton, NJ, 1975—77; assoc. Nims, Howes, Collison & Isner, NYC, 1977—81; pvt. practice Mont., 1981—. Lectr. indsl. and mech. engring. dept. Mont. State U., 1981—97. Mem.: ABA, Am. Patent Law Assn., Mont. Bar Assn. Home: PO Box 1329 Bozeman MT 59771-1329 Office: Ste 404 104 E Main St Bozeman MT 59715-4787 Home Phone: 406-586-1249; Office Phone: 406-587-4240. Personal E-mail: richard.conover1@gmail.com.

CONQUEST, ROBERT (GEORGE ROBERT ACWORTH CONQUEST), writer, historian, poet; b. Malvern, Worcestershire, Eng., July 15, 1917; s. Robert Folger Westcott and Rosamund Alys (Acworth) C.; m. Joan Watkins, 1942 (dis. 1948); children: John, Richard; m. Tatiana Mihailova, 1948 (dis. 1963); m. Caroleen Macfarlane, 1964 (dis. 1978); m. Elizabeth Neece, Dec. 1, 1979. Student, Winchester Coll., Eng., 1931-35, U. Grenoble, France, 1935-36, U. Oxford, 1936-39; MA, U. Oxford, Eng., 1972; DLitt, U. Oxford, 1975. First sec. H.M. Fgn. Svc., Sofia, Bulgaria, U.N., London, 1946-56; rsch. fellow London Sch. Econs., 1956-58; vis. poet U. Buffalo, NY, 1959-60; lit. editor The Spectator, London, 1962-63; sr. fellow Russian Inst. Columbia U., NYC, 1964-65; fellow Woodrow Wilson Internat. Ctr., Washington, 1976-77; sr. rsch. fellow Hoover Inst., Stanford (Calif.) U., 1977-79, 81—. Disting. vis. scholar Heritage Found., Washington, 1980-81; adv. bd. Freedom House, N.Y.C., 1980—; rsch. assoc. Ukrainian Rsch. Inst. Harvard U., Cambridge, Mass., 1983—; adj. fellow Washington Ctr. Strategic Studies., 1984—. Author: Poems, 1955, A World of Difference, 1955, Common Sense About Russia, 1960, Power and Policy in the USSR, 1961, The Pasternak Affair, 1962, Between Mars and Venus, 1962, (with Kingsley Amis) The Egyptologists, 1965, Russia after Khrushchev, 1965, The Great Terror, 1968, Arias from a Love Opera, 1969, The Nation Killers, 1970, Where Marx Went Wrong, 1970, V I Lenin, 1972, Kolyma: The Arctic Death Camps, 1978, Coming Across, 1978, The Abomination of Moab, 1979, Forays, 1979, Present Danger: Towards a Foreign Policy, 1979, We and They: Civic and Despotic Cultures, 1980, (with Jon M. White) What to do When the Russians Come, 1984, Inside Stalin's Secret Police: NKVD Politics 1936-39, 1985, The Harvest of Sorrow: Soviet Collectivization and the Terror-Famine, 1986, New and Collected Poems, 1988, Stalin and the Kirov Murder, 1988, Tyrants and Typewriters, 1989, The Great Terror: A Reassessment, 1990, Stalin: Breaker of Nations, 1991, Demons Don't, 1999, Reflections on a Ravaged Century, 1999, The Dragons of Expectation, 2005. Capt. inf. Brit. Army, 1939-46, ETO. Decorated officer Order Brit. Empire, companion Order St. Michael and St. George; recipient Alexis de Tocqueville award, 1992, Light Verse award Acad. Arts and Letters, 1997, Presdl. Medal of Freedom, The White House, 2005; Jefferson Lecture Humanities, Washington, 1993, Richard M. Weaver prize for scholarly letters, 1999; Royal Soc. Lit. fellow, 1972. Fellow Brit. Acad., Brit. Interplanetary Soc., AAAL-Michael Braude Award Light Verse, Royal Soc. Lit., Am. Acad. Arts & Sci., Soc. Promotion Roman Studies; Mem. Literary Soc.; Clubs: Travellers (London). Home: 52 Peter Coutts Cir Stanford CA 94305-2506 Office: Stanford U Hoover Inst Stanford CA 94305-6010

CONRAD, LAUREN KATHERINE, television personality, apparel designer; b. Laguna Beach, Calif., Feb. 1, 1986; d. Jim and Katherine Conrad. Student, Fashion Inst. Design and Merchandising, LA, 2005—. Intern 3 Dots clothing line, LA, Teen Vogue, LA, 2005—08; designer Lauren Conrad collection, 2007—; guest handbag designer Linea Pelle. Promoter Designer's World video game, 2006; spokesperson Mark Cosmetics, 2007—; dress designer for trophy presenters Emmy Awards, 2008. Star (TV reality series) Laguna Beach: The Real Orange County, 2004—05, The Hills, 2006—09 (Choice TV Female Reality Star, Teen Choice Awards, 2006, 2007, Choice TV Female Reality/Variety Star, Teen Choice Awards, 2008), appearances include (TV specials) VH1 Big in 05, 2005, MTV Video Music Awards, 2006, 2007, 2008, Teen Choice Awards, 2007, MTV VMA Pre Show Royale, 2007, guest appearances include (TV series) Jimmy Kimmel Live!, 2007, Live with Regis and Kelly, 2007, 2008, Ellen, 2008, Rachel Ray, actress (films) Epic Movie, 2007, co-host (TV films) Legally Blonde: The Musical, 2007, appearances in Teen Vogue Mag., 2006, Seventeen Mag., 2006, CosmoGIRL Mag., 2007, People Mag., 2008, Teen People. Named one of The 100 Most Powerful Celebrities, Forbes.com, 2008. Office: c/o Max Stubblefield United Talent Agy 9560 Wilshire Blvd Ste 500 Beverly Hills CA 90212-2401

CONRAD, PAUL FRANCIS, cartoonist; b. Cedar Rapids, Iowa, June 27, 1924; s. Robert H. and Florence G. (Lawler) C.; m. Barbara Kay King, Feb. 27, 1954; children: James, David, Carol, Elizabeth. BA, U. Iowa, 1950. Editorial cartoonist Denver Post, 1950-64, L.A. Times, 1964-93; cartoonist L.A. Times Syndicate, 1973-2000, Tribune Media Svcs., 2000—. Richard M. Nixon chair Whittier Coll., 1977-78 Exhibited sculpture and cartoons LA County Mus. Art, 1979, Libr. of Congress, 1999; permanent collection Am. Treasures Libr. of Congress; author: The King and Us, 1974, Pro and Conrad, 1979, Drawn and Quartered, 1985, CONArtist: Thirty Years With The Los Angeles Times, 1993, Drawing The Line, 1999. Served with C.E. AUS, 1942-46, PTO. Recipient Editl. Cartoon award, Sigma Delta Chi, 1963, 1969, 1971, 1981—82, 1988, 1997, Pulitzer prize editl. cartooning, 1964, 1971, 1984, Overseas Press Club award, 1970, 1981, Journalism award, U. So. Calif., 1972, Robert F. Kennedy Journalism award 1st prize, 1985, 1990, 1992, 1993, Hugh M. Hefner 1st Amendment award, 1990, Lifetime Achievement award, Am. Assn. Editl. Cartoonists, 1998, Lifetime Pub. Svc. award, Edmund G. Brown Inst. Pub. Affairs, 2000; fellow sr. fellow, Sch. Pub. Policy and Social Rsch., UCLA, 2001—03. Fellow Soc. Profl. Journalists; mem. Phi Delta Theta. Democrat. Roman Catholic. Office: 904 Silver Spur Rd 358 Rolling Hills Estates CA 90274 Home Phone: 310-377-1806; Office Phone: 310-544-0497.

CONRAN, JAMES MICHAEL, consumer advocate, public policy consultant; b. NYC, Mar. 15, 1952; s. James Adrian and Mary Ellen (McGarry) C.; m. Phyllis Jean Thompson, Aug. 1, 1984; children: Michael O., Thomas O. BA, Calif. State U., Northridge, 1975; MA in Urban Studies, Occidental Coll., 1978. Mgr. regulatory rels. Pacific Bell, San Francisco, 1985-88, mgr. pub. affairs & pub. issues, 1988-91; dir. State of Calif. Dept. Consumer Affairs, Sacramento, 1991-94; founder, pres. Consumers First, 1994—; adj. prof. Agneo Sch. Bus., Golden Gate U. B. dirs. Consumer Competative Choice, Consumer Fedn. Calif., Consumer Action, World Instn. Disabilities, Calif. Small Bus. Assoc., Calif. Small Bus. Roundtable, Consumer for Competitive Choice, Consumer Interest Rsch. Inst., Nat. Consumers League, Elec. Consumers Alliance, TRW Consumer Adv. Coun., Great Western Fin. Corp., Consumer Adv. Panel, Electric Inst. Consumer Adv. Panel; mem. Coun. Licensing Enforcement and Regulation; nat. bd. certification occupl. therapy World Inst. on Disabilities; mem. consumer adv. panel So. Calif Edison; mem. telecomms. consumer adv. panel SBC; consumer adv. coun. FCC. Contbr. articles to profl. jours. Bd. dirs. Fight Back! Found., L.A., 1991—, Disabled Children's Computer Group, Orinda, Calif., Telecomm. Edn. Trust Fund-Calif. Pub. Utilities Commn., San Francisco, 1990-91; chair adminstrv. sect. United Calif. State Employees Campaign, Sacramento; mem. Stream Preservation Commn., Orinda, 1988-91. Fellow Coro Found., 1977, Levere Meml. Found., 1976. Mem. Coro Assocs., Calif. Agenda for Consumer Edn., FCC Consumer Adv. Coun., Sigma Alpha Epsilon, AT&T (consumer adv. panel). Roman Catholic. Avocations: camping, skiing, scuba diving, hiking. Office Phone: 925-253-1937. E-mail: consumersfirst@pacbell.net.

CONROY, THOMAS FRANCIS, insurance company consultant; b. Chgo., Sept. 26, 1938; s. Thomas Francis and Eleanor Althea (Heatherly) C.; m. Mary Elizabeth Schaeffer, June 19, 1965; children: Alexandra B., Margaret E. BSc, De Paul U., 1959; MBA, U. Chgo., 1969. CPA, CDP. Mgr. Ernst & Whinney, Chgo., 1959-74; exec. v.p. fin., treas., contr. Security Life of Denver, 1974-93; prin. Ea. Hemisphere Trading Corp., Denver, 1990—2003; pres. Security Life Reins., 1993-99, ING Re Internat., 2000-01; mng. prin. Strategic Reins. Cons. Internat., Englewood, Colo., 2001—; mng. ptnr. Mann Conroy Eisenberg & Assoc., LLC, Greensboro, 2002—. Bd. dirs. Teton Petroleum Co., Auspice Corp. Trustee Denver Chamber Orch., 1988-93; bd. dirs. Buffalo Mountain Met. Dist., 1984-95, Denver affiliate Susan G. Komen Found., 2002-06. Capt. U.S. Army, 1960-62. Fellow Life Mgmt. Inst. Roman Catholic. Home Phone: 303-761-6238; Office Phone: 303-762-8812. Business E-Mail: tom-conroy@strategicre.com.

CONROY, WILLIAM B., retired university administrator; b. Malone, NY; m. Patricia Conroy; children: Kathryn, William Michael, David, Carol, Kevin. B in History magna cum laude, U. Notre Dame, 1953; MEd, Syracuse U., 1959, PhD in Social Sci., 1963. Tchr. U. Tex., U. Wash., Tex. Tech. U.; exec. v.p. N.Mex. State U., Las Cruces, 1985-97, interim pres., 1994-95, pres., 1997—2001, now pres. emeritus. Mem. Nat. Coun. Geog. Edn., Assn. Am. Geographers, Southwestern Social Sci. Assn. (past pres.), N.Mex. Coun. Univ. Presidents, Las Cruces C. of C. (bd. trustees town-gown com.). Office: NMex State U MSC 388 PO Box 30001 Las Cruces NM 88003-8001 Fax: 505-646-6344. E-mail: wconroy@nmsu.edu.

CONSEY, KEVIN EDWARD, museum administrator; b. NYC, Jan. 15, 1952; s. Edward and Dorothy (Kemmann) C.; m. Susan Mary Kirsch, Aug. 26, 1972. BA, Hofstra U., 1974; M in Mus. Practice, MA, U. Mich., 1977; MBA, Northwestern U., 1999. Dir. Emily Lowe Gallery, Hofstra U., Hempstead, N.Y., 1977-80, San Antonio Mus. Art., 1980-83; dir., chief exec. officer Newport Harbor Art Mus., Newport Beach, Calif., 1983-89, Mus. Contemporary Art, Chgo., 1989-2000; dir. art mus. and pacific film archive U. Calif., Berkeley, 2000—07. Panelist profl. devel. Nat. Endowment for Arts, Washington, 1987-88, John D. and Catherine T. MacArthur Found., Nat. Arts Journalism Fellowship program, 45th Venice Biennale Sch. of Curators, Mus. Studies Program at the Art Inst. of Chgo., Ill. Arts Alliance, Calif. Arts Coun., Tex. Commn. on the Arts, NY State Coun. on the Arts, panelist challenge grant, 1988, panelist mus. program, 1989-90, panelist F.A.C.I.E., 1991-94; bd. dir. Com. Internat. Mus. Modern Art. Bd. dir. Nat. Audubon Soc., Chgo. Latin Sch., Golden Gate Chpt., Berkeley Cmty. Found.; advisory com. Girls Inc., Oakland, Calif. Hofstra U. scholar, 1970-74, Guggenheim Mus. intern, 1976; grantee Nat. Mus. Act, 1976-77; teaching fellowships U. Va., Toledo Mus. Art, Ohio, U. Mich. Mus. Art, Nat. Gallery Art, Wash., DC, Solomon R. Guggenheim Mus., NYC. Mem. Assn. Art Mus. Dirs., Coll. Art Assn., Internat. Assn. Art Critics

CONSIDINE, TERRY, real estate company executive; m. Betsy Considine. BA, Harvard College, 1968; JD, Harvard Law Sch., 1971. Founder, CEO Considine Co., Denver, 1975—87; state senator Colo., 1987—92; CEO Property Asset Mgmt., Denver, 1987—94; chmn., pres., CEO AIMCO, Denver, 1994—. Rep. candidate for U.S. Senate, 1992. Office: AIMCO Ste 1100 4582 S Ulster St Pkwy Denver CO 80237 Office Phone: 303-757-9101.

CONSTANT, PETE, councilman; b. Dearborn, Mich., Oct. 22, 1963; m to Julie; children: Amanda, Alexander, Pete Jr, Samantha, Sydney. V.p. Germain Photography, Inc., 1979—87, Constant Color, Inc., 1985—87; reserve police officer San José Police Dept., 1986—89, police officer, 1989—2000; pres., CEO Image Concepts, Inc./Sharper Image Photography, 1992—2004; mng. ptnr. Collins & Constant Investments, LLC, 1999—2002; profl. photographer, owner Constant Image Photography, 2003—; pub., CEO VOX Publs. Corp., 2004—; councilman, Dist. 1 San José City Coun., 2007—. Mem. bd. dirs. Young Audiences of Northern Calif., Silicon Valley Crime Stoppers, Salvation Army of Santa Clara County, Rotary Club of San José North. Recipient Day-to-Day Excellence award, San José Police Dept., City Mgr.'s award of Excellence, Employee Suggestion award, Legion of Honor award, Am. Police Hall of Fame, William Poelle Lifesaving award; named Project Crackdown Officer of Yr., San José Police Dept. Mem.: Lynhaven Neighborhood Assn. (pres.), San José Police Officers Assn. (dir.). Office: San Jose City Coun 200 E Santa Clara St San Jose CA 95113 Office Phone: 408-535-4901. Business E-Mail: district1@sanjoseca.gov.*

CONSTANTINI, LOUIS O., financial consultant, stockbroker; b. Columbus, Ga., Jan. 12, 1948; s. Louis T. and Edna G. (Spears) C.; m. Mary Ann Jennings, Feb. 9, 1974; children: Rachel J., Emily J. BA, U. Fla., 1972. Cert. fin. mgr. Intelligence officer CIA, Washington and overseas, 1972-76; fin. cons. Merrill Lynch & Co., El Paso, Tex., 1976—2007, Morgan Stanley & Co., Las Cruces, N.Mex., 2007—, sr. pres. Chmn. El Paso Estate Planning Coun., 1982. Decorated Bronze Star, Combat Infantryman Badge, Cross of Gallantry with Gold Star (Republic of Vietnam). Mem. Sigma Phi Epsilon (Disting. Alumnus award 1999), Frederick A. Cook Soc. (bd. dirs.). Avocation: Arctic exploration. Home: 5155 Hunters Chase Rd Las Cruces NM 88011-2553 Office: Morgan Stanley & Co 3050 Roadrunner Pkwy B Las Cruces NM 88011 Office Phone: 575-522-8500. Personal E-mail: newmex@comcast.net.

CONSUL, VINCENT A., lawyer; b. Alameda, Calif., June 7, 1953; BA, Univ. Calif., Berkeley, 1975; JD, Univ. Pacific, 1980. Bar: Calif. 1980, Nev. 1981, US Dist. Ct. (Dist. Nev.) 1981, US Ct. Appeals (9th Cir.) 1984, US Supreme Ct. 2003. Dep. dist. atty. Clark County, Nev., 1980—83; asst. US atty. Dist. of Nev., 1983—85; ptnr. Dickerson, Dickerson, Consul & Pocker, Boies Schiller & Flexner, Las Vegas. Bd. dirs. 8th Judicial Dist. Pro Bono Found., 1997—2005. Recipient Am. Jurisprudence award for family law. Mem.: ABA, Eighth Judicial Dist. Pro Bono Found. (mem. bd. dir. 1997—2004), State Bar of Calif., State Bar of Nev. (bd. gov. 1997—2007, pres. 2005—06). Office: Boies Schiller & Flexner Ste 800 300 S 4th St Las Vegas NV 89101 Office Phone: 702-382-7300. Office Fax: 702-382-2755. Business E-Mail: vconsul@bsfllp.com.

CONTE, MARIO G., JR., lawyer; BA in English, St. Michael's Coll., Vt., 1965; MS in Pharmacology and Physiology, N.Y. Med. Coll., 1968; JD cum laude, U. Conn., 1978. Bar: Conn. 1978, U.S. Dist. Ct. Conn., Calif. 1979, U.S. Dist. Ct. (so. dist.) Calif., U.S. Ct. Appeals (9th cir.), U.S. Supreme Ct. Law clk. to sr. judge Robert C. Zampano U.S. Dist. Ct. for Dist. Ct., 1978-79; ptnr. Jamison, Conte and McFadden, 1983; trial atty. Fed. Defenders San Diego, Inc., 1979-82, chief trial atty., 1984-91, exec. dir., 1991—, also mem. Fed. Defender's Newsletter. Adj. prof. law U. San Diego Sch. Law, Calif. Western Sch. Law; mem. faculty Nat. Criminal Def. Coll. Contbg. author: Defending a Federal Criminal Case. Bd. dirs. Nat. Clearinghouse for Battered Women, San Diego, San Diego chpt. Arthritis Found. Recipient President's Accommodation award. Mem. Inst. for Criminal Def. Advocacy (bd. dirs.), San Diego Criminal Def. Bar Assn. (bd. dirs.).

CONTI, PETER SELBY, astronomy educator; b. NYC, Sept. 5, 1934; s. Attilio Carlo and Marie (Selby) C.; m. Carolyn Safford, Aug. 26, 1961; children: Michael, Karen, Kathe BS, Rensselaer Poly. Inst., 1956; PhD, U. Calif-Berkeley, 1963; Honoris Causa degree, U. Utrecht, 1993. Rsch. fellow Calif. Inst. Tech., Pasadena, 1963-66; asst. prof. astronomy U. Calif./Santa Cruz, 1966-71; astronomer Lick Obs., Santa Cruz, 1966-71; prof., fellow Joint Inst. Lab. Astrophysics U. Colo., Boulder, 1971-99, chmn., 1989-90, chmn. dept. astrophys., planetary scis., 1980-86, prof. emeritus, 1999—. Chmn. bd. dirs. Assoc. Univs. for Rsch. in Astronomy Inc., Tuscon, 1983-86; vis. prof. U. Utrecht, Netherlands, 1969-70, Minnaert prof., 1995. Editor: Mass Loss and Evolution of O-type Stars, 1979, O Stars and Wolf Rayet Stars, 1988; receiving editor: New Astronomy, 1996-, New Astronomy Reviews, 1998-; contbr. over 200 articles to profl. jours. Served to lt. (j.g.) USNR, 1956-59 Recipient Gold medal U. Liege, Belgium, 1975; Fulbright fellow, 1969-70 Fellow AAAS (chmn. sect. D in astronomy 1980); mem. Am. Astron. Soc. (councillor 1983-86), Astron. Soc. of Pacific, Internat. Astron. Union (organizing com. 1983-85, v.p. 1985-88, pres. 1988-91, commn. 29 stellar spectra). Home: 3225 Mariner Ln Longmont CO 80503 Office: U Colo-Boulder Joint Inst Lab Astrophysics Campus Box 440 Boulder CO 80309-0440

CONTI, SAMUEL, federal judge; b. LA, July 16, 1922; s. Fred and Katie C.; m. Dolores Crosby, July 12, 1952; children: Richard, Robert, Cynthia. BS, U. Santa Clara, 1945; LLB, Stanford U., 1948, JD. Bar: Calif. 1948. Pvt. practice, San Francisco and Contra Costa County, 1948-60; city atty. City of Concord, Calif., 1960-69; judge Superior Ct. Contra Costa County, 1968-70, U.S. Dist. Ct. (no. dist.) Calif., San Francisco, 1970-88, sr. judge, 1988—. Mem. Ctrl. Contra Costa Bar Assn. (pres.), Concord C. of C. (pres.), Alpha Sigma Nu. Office: US Dist Ct 450 Golden Gate Ave Ste 36052 San Francisco CA 94102-3482

CONTINETTI, ROBERT E., chemistry professor; Prof. dept. chemistry and biochemistry U. Calif. San Diego, La Jolla, 1992—, Kurt Schuler scholar, chmn. dept. Recipient Packard Found. fellow, 1994. Fellow: Am. Phys. Soc. Office: U Calif San Diego Dept Chem & Biochem MC-0340 9500 Gilman Dr La Jolla CA 92093-0340 Office Phone: 858-534-5559. E-mail: rcontinetti@ucsd.edu.

CONTOS, PAUL ANTHONY, engineer, investment consultant; b. Chgo., Mar. 18, 1926; s. Anthony Dimitrios and Panagiota (Kostopoulos) C.; m. Lilian Katie Kalkines, June 19, 1955 (dec. Apr. 1985); children: Leslie, Claudia, Paula, Anthony. Student, Am. TV Inst., Chgo., 1946-48, U. Ill., 1949-52, 53-56, Ill. Inst. Tech., 1952-53, U. So. Calif., 1956-57. Engr. J.C. Deagan Co., Inc., Chgo., 1951-53, Lockheed Missile and Space Co., Inc., Sunnyvale, Calif., 1956-62, engring. supr., 1962-65, staff engr., 1965-88; genealogy rsch. San Jose, Calif., 1970—; pres. PAC Investments, Saratoga, Calif., 1984-88, San Jose, Calif., 1988—, also advisor, cons., 1984—. Author memoirs & short stories. Mem. Pres. Coun. U. Ill., 1994—. With U.S. Army, 1944-46, ETO. Decorated Purple Heart, Bronze Star medal, Combat Infantryman badge, African Mid. Ea. Campaign medal with 2 bronze stars, WWII Victory medal, Army of Occupation medal with Germany clasp, Good Conduct medal, Honorable Svc. Lapel Button WWII, Meritorious Unit citation, Sharp Shooter Badge with Rifle Bar. Mem. DAV (life, comdr. Chgo. unit 1948-51), VFW (life), Pi Sigma Phi (pres. 1951-53). Republican. Greek Orthodox. Avocations: genealogy, reading, writing. Home and Office: Paseo Villas No 407 130 E San Fernando Street San Jose CA 95112-7414 Personal E-mail: pcontos_2000@yahoo.com. Business E-Mail: paulacontos@illinoisalumni.org.

CONTRERAS, THOMAS J., JR., career officer; b. Morenci, Ariz. m. Gloria Rachel Gutierrez, Sept. 4, 1965; children: Naomi, Thomas. BS in Chemistry and Secondary Edn., No. Ariz. U., 1967; MS in Phys. Organic Chemistry, U. Utah, 1969; PhD in Physiology, Uniformed Svcs. U. Health Sci., 1983. Commd. lt. (j.g.) USN, 1971, advanced through grades to capt.; prin. investigator Naval Blood Rsch. Lab., Boston, 1972-76, Armed Forces Radiobiology Rsch. Inst., Bethesda, Md., 1976-79, Naval Med. Rsch. Inst., Bethesda, 1982-85; rsch. area mgr. combat casualty care Naval Med. R&D Command, Bethesda, 1985-87; tech. area mgr. biomed. and chem./biol. warfare def. program Office of Naval Tech., Office of Chief of Naval Rsch., Arlington, Va., 1987-91, dep. dir. support technologies directorate, 1989-91; exec. officer Naval Health Rsch. Ctr., San Diego, 1991-95; comdg. officer Naval Med. Rsch. Inst., Bethesda, 1995-98, Naval Med. Rsch. Ctr., Forest Glen, Md., 1998-99, Naval Health Rsch. Ctr., San Diego, 1999-2001. Contbr. articles to profl. jours. Decorated Joint Svc. Commendation medal, Meritorious Svc. medal with 2 gold stars, Legion of Merit with gold star; recipient Hispanic Engring. Nat. Achievement award for profl. achievement in govt., 1991, Hispanic Mag. Role Model of the Yr. award, 1992, Nat. Image Inc. Meritorious Svc. award, 1993, No. Ariz. U. Disting. Citizen award, 1995, Outstanding Alumnus award of Dept. Chemistry, 1995. Mem. Soc. Armed Forces Med. Lab. Scientists, Soc. for Advancement of Chicanos and Native Americans in Sci., Assn. Naval Svc. Officers. Office: Commanding Officer Naval Health Rsch Ctr PO Box 85122 San Diego CA 92186-5122 E-mail: co@nhrc.navy.mil.

CONWAY, CONNIE, state legislator; b. Bakersfield, Calif., Sept. 25, 1950; d. John R. and Clara Conway; children: Anthony, Timothy. Attended, Fresno State U. Former dist. mgr. CorVel Corp., 1991—94; Wellness Coordinator Kaveah Delta, 1988—91; dir. Tulare Redevelopment Agy.; supr. Dist. 2 Tulare County, chair bd. supervisors, 2005, 2008; mem. Dist. 34 Calif. State Assembly, Calif., 2008—. Republican. Catholic. Office: PO Box 942849 Rm 2174 Sacramento CA 94249-0034 Address: 113 N Church St Ste 504 & 505 Visalia CA 93291 Office Phone: 916-319-2034.*

CONWAY, CRAIG A., retired computer company executive; b. Ft. Wayne, Ind., Oct. 17, 1954; m. Tina Conway; 2 children. BS in Math. & Computer Sci., SUNY, Brockport, 1976. Applications cons. Tymeshare, 1976—79; with Atari, 1979—83; dir. worldwide distbn. Digital Research, 1983—85; exec. v.p. mktg., sales & ops. Oracle Corp., 1985—93; pres., CEO TGV Software, Inc., 1993—96, OneTouch Systems., 1996—99, PeopleSoft Inc., Pleasanton, Calif., 1999, 1999—2004. Bd. dirs. Aspect Telecomm. Corp., SalesLogix Corp., Salesforce.com Inc., 2005-. Recipient Cap Gemini Ernst & Young Leadership award for Global Integration, 2002. Address: Salesforce-.com Inc One Market Ste 300 San Francisco CA 94105

CONWAY, JOHN E., federal judge; b. 1934; BS, U.S. Naval Acad., 1956; LLB magna cum laude, Washburn U., 1963. Assoc. Matias A Zamora, Santa Fe, 1963-64; ptnr. Wilkinson, Durrett & Conway, Alamogordo, N.Mex., 1964-67, Durrett, Conway & Jordon, Alamogordo, 1967-80, Montgomery & Andrews, P.A., Albuquerque, 1980-86; city atty. Alamogordo, 1966-72; mem. N.Mex. State Senate, 1970-80, minority leader, 1972-80; chief fed. judge U.S. Dist. Ct. N.Mex., Albuquerque, 1994—2000, sr. fed. judge, 2000—. Mem. Jud. Resources Com., 1995—98. 1st lt. USAF, 1956-60. Mem. 10th Cir. Dist. Judges Assn. (pres. 1995-98), Fed. Judges Assn. (bd. dirs. 1996-2001), Nat. Commrs. on Uniform State Laws, N.Mex. Bar Assn., N.Mex. Jud. Coun. (vice chmn. 1973, chmn. 1973-75, disciplinary bd. of Supreme Ct. of N.Mex. vice chmn. 1980, chmn. 1981-84.). Office: US Dist Ct Chambers #740 333 Lomas Blvd NW Albuquerque NM 87102-2272 Office Phone: 505-348-2200. Business E-Mail: jconway@nmcourt.fed.us.

CONWAY, JOHN S., history professor; b. London, Dec. 31, 1929; s. Geoffrey S. and Elsie (Philips) C.; m. Ann P. Jefferies, Aug. 10, 1957; children— David, Jane, Alison BA, Cambridge U., Eng., 1952; MA, Cambridge U., 1955, PhD, 1956. Asst. prof. U. Man., Can., 1955-57; asst. prof., assoc. prof., then prof. history U. B.C., Vancouver, 1957-94, prof. emeritus, 1995—. Mem. editl. bd. dirs. Holocaust and Genocide Studies, Kirchliche Zeitgeschichte; Smallman Disting. vis. prof. history U. Western On., 1998. Author: The Nazi Persecution of the Churches, 1968, 2d edit., 1997. Contbr. numerous articles on churches and the holocaust to topical publs. Pres. Tibetan Refugee Aid Soc., Can., 1971-81; chmn. Vancouver Coalition with World Refugees, 1982-84. Recipient Queen's Silver Jubilee medal, 1977. Mem. Can. Inst. Internat. Affairs, German Studies Assn., Can. Hist. Assn. Anglican. Home: 4345 Locarno Crescent Vancouver BC Canada V6R 1G2 Office: U BC Dept History East Mall Vancouver BC Canada V6T 1Z1 E-mail: jconway@interchange.ubc.ca.

CONWAY, NANCY ANN, newspaper editor; b. Foxboro, Mass., Oct. 15, 1941; d. Leo T. and Alma (Goodwin) C.; children: Ana Lucia DaSilva, Kara Ann Martin. Cert. in med. tech., Carnegie Inst., 1962; BA in English, U. Mass., 1976, cert. in secondary edn., 1978. Tchr. Brazil-Am. Inst., Rio de Janeiro, 1963-68; freelance writer, editor Amherst, Mass., 1972-76; staff writer Daily Hampshire Gazette, North Hampton, Mass., 1976-77; editor Amherst Bull., 1977-80, Amherst Record, 1980-83; features editor Holyoke (Mass.) Transcript/Telegram, 1983-84; gen. mgr. Monday-Thursday Newspapers, Boca Raton, Fla., 1984-87; dir. editorial South Fla. Newspaper Network, Deerfield Beach, 1987-90; pub., editor York (Pa.) Newspapers, Inc., 1990-95; metro editor Denver Post, 1995-96; exec. editor, v.p. Alameda Newspaper Group Oakland (Calif.) Tribune, 1996—2003; editor The Salt Lake (Utah) Tribune, 2003—. Bd. dirs. Math.: Opportunities in Engring., Sci. and Tech.-Pa. State, York, 1991-95. Recipient writing awards, state newspaper assns. Mem. Am. Soc. Newspaper Editors, Soc. Profl. Journalists. Avocations: literature, photography, gardening. Office: The Salt Lake Tribune 90 S 400 W Ste 700 Salt Lake City UT 84101-1431 Business E-Mail: nconway@angnewspapers.com.

CONWAY, ROBERT EDWARD, corporate executive; b. Waynesboro, Pa., Feb. 6, 1954; s. Gerald R. and Laura C. (Davis) C.; m. Carolyn Jean Hurd, Aug. 24, 1991. BA, Marquette U., 1976; MBA, U. Cin., 1980. CPA, Wis. Internal auditor Allis Chalmers Corp., Milw., 1977, supr. cost acctg. Cin., 1977-79; plant acct. Hazleton Systems, Inc., Cin., 1979-80, fin. analyst Aberdeen, Md., 1980-81; acct. mgr. Hazleton Labs. Washington, Vienna, Va., 1981-82; contr. fin. Hazleton Wis., Inc., Madison, 1982-83, contr. fin. and adminstrn., 1983-85, dir. life scis. div. and adminstrn., 1985-88, gen. mgr., 1988-89, corp. v.p., gen. mgr., 1989-96. Mem. bd. visitors Sch. Pharmacy, U. Wis., Madison. Mem. Madison C. of C. (1st vice chmn. 1992—). Roman Catholic. Home: 1167 Pintail Ct Boulder CO 80303-1466 Office: Array BioPharma Inc 3200 Walnut St Boulder CO 80301

CONWAY, TIM, comedian; b. Willoughby, Ohio, Dec. 15, 1933; m. Mary Anne Dalton, 1961; children: Kelly Ann, Timothy, Patrick, Jaimie, Corey, Seann. Student, Bowling Green State U., Ohio. Writer, dir., occasional performer, Sta. KYW-TV, Cleve.; regular TV series The Steve Allen Show, 1961, McHale's Navy, 1962-66, The John Gary Show, 1966, Rango, 1967, (host) Turn-On, 1965, The Tim Conway Show, 1970, The Carol Burnett Show, 1975-79, The Tim Conway Comedy Hour, 1980-81, Tim Conway's Funny America, 1990, (voice) Disney's Hercules, 1998; other TV appearances include: Hollywood Palace, Steve Allen Show, Garry Moore Show, That's Life; film appearances include McHale's Navy, 1964, McHale's Navy Joins the Air Force, 1965, The World's Greatest Athlete, 1973, The Apple Dumpling Gang, 1975, Gus, 1976, The Shaggy D.A., 1976, Cannonball Run II, 1984, Cyclone, 1987, Dear God, 1996, Speed 2: Cruise Control, 1997, Air Bud 2, 1998, View from the Swing, 2000; actor, writer Billion Dollar Hobo, 1978, They Went That-a-Way and That-a-Way, 1978, The Prizefighter, 1979, The Private Eyes, 1981, The Longshot, 1986; also numerous nightclub appearances, TV commls.; TV movie Roll, Freddy, Roll, 1974; appeared on episodes TV series Married...with Children, The Larry Sanders Show, Coach, Diagnosis Murder, The Simpsons (voice), Touched by an Angel, Suddenly Susan, The Drew Carey Show, The Wild Thornberrys (voice), Ellen, The Roseanne Show, Clueless, Mad About You, SpongeBob SquarePants (voice), Hermie: A Common Caterpillar (voice), Hermie & Friends (voice); videos include Dorf's Golf Bible, 1987, Dorf on Golf, 1987, Dorf and the First Games of Mount Olympus, 1988, Dorf Goes Auto Racing, 1990, Dorf Goes Fishing, 1993, Dorf on the Diamond, 1996, Tim and Harvey in the Great Outdoors, 1998. Served in U.S. Army. Recipient Emmy awards, 1973, 77, 78. Mem. AFTRA. Office: Conway Enterprises PO Box 17047 Encino CA 91416-7047

COOK, BRIAN R., corporate professional; BA in Acctg., We. Wash. U. CPA. Various fin. and managerial positions Sea Galley Stores, Inc.; chmn. bd., pres. & CEO Direct Focus, Inc., Vancouver, Wash., 1986—.

COOK, DEBBIE, lawyer, councilwoman; b. Corpus Christi, Tex., Jan. 22, 1954; m. John Fisher; 1 child. BS in Earth Scis., Calif. State U., Long Beach, 1976; JD, Western State U. Coll. Law, Fullerton, 1995; grad. Nat. Preparedness Leadership Initiative, Harvard U. Kennedy Sch. Govt.; degree (hon.), Orange Coast Coll., Costa Mesa. Bar: Calif. 1994. Owner office equipment bus., Westminster, Calif., 1978—92; atty. Bolsa Chica Land Trust, Huntington Beach, Calif.; mayor City of Huntington Beach, Calif., 2007—. Mem. Huntington Beach City Coun., 2000—; regional coun. mem. So. Calif. Assn. Govt.'s, chair energy & environ. com.; pres. Orange County divsn. League Calif. Cities, chair adminstrv. policies com.; chair Orange County Parks Commn.; mem. borders com. San Diego Assn. Govt.'s; bd. dirs. Assn. Study of Peak Oil & Gas, Post Carbon Inst. Past pres. Vista View School, Fountain Valley, Calif.; former coach girl's volleyball team Dwyer Jr. HS, Huntington Beach. Democrat. Office: City Coun 2000 Main St Huntington Beach CA 92648 Mailing: Campaign Address 412 Olive Ave #313 Huntington Beach CA 92648 E-mail: hbdac@hotmail.com.

COOK, DONALD EVAN, pediatrician, educator; b. Pitts., Mar. 24, 1928; s. Merriam E. and Bertha (Gwin) C.; m. Elsie Walden, Sept. 2, 1951; children: Catherine, Christopher, Brian, Jeffrey. BS, Colo. Coll., 1952; MD, U. Colo., 1955. Diplomate Am. Bd. Pediat., 1961. Intern Fresno County Gen. Hosp., Calif., 1955-56; resident in gen. practice Tulare (Calif.) County Gen. Hosp., 1956-57; resident in pediatrics U. Colo., 1957-59; practice medicine specializing in pediatrics Aurora, Colo., 1959—64, Greeley (Colo). Med. Clinic, 1964—86, Greeley Sports Medicine Clinic, 1988—93; med. adv. Centenninal Develop. Svcs., Inc., 1993-95; clin. faculty U. Colo., clin. prof., 1977—; pres. Am. Acad. Pediatrics, Elk Grove Village, Ill., 1999-2000; ret. from practice, 2004. Organizer, dir. Sports Medicine Px Exam. Clinic for Indigent Weld Co. athletes, 1990—96; mem. adv. bd. Nat. Ctr. Health Edn., San Francisco, 1978—80; mem. adv. com. inmaternal and child health programs Colo. State Health Dept., 1981—84, chmn., 1981—84; preceptor Sch. Nurse Practitioner program U. Colo., 1978—88; affiliate prof. nursing U. No. Colo., 1996; vol. physician Monfort Children's Clinic, 2002—05. Mem. Weld County Dist. 6 Sch. Bd., 1973—83, pres., 1973—74, 1976—77, chmn. dist. 6 accountability com., 1972—73, mem. adv. com. dist. 6 teen pregnancy program, 1983—85; mem. Weld County Task Force on Teen-aged Pregnancy, 1986—89, Dream Team Weld County Task Force on Sch. Dropouts, 1986—92; mem.Weld County Interagy. Screening Bd., Weld County Cmty. Ctr. Found., 1984—89; mem. Weld County Task Force Spkrs. Bur. on AIDS, 1987—94, Weld County Task Force Adolescent Health Clinic, Task Force Child Abuse, C. of C.; bd. dirs. No. Colo. Med. Ctr., 1993—98, No. Colo. Med. Ctr. Found., 1994—; med. advisor Weld County Sch. Dist. VI-Nurses, 1987—2004; mem. Sch. Dist. 6 Health Coalition, Task Force on Access to Health Care; group leader neonatal group Colo. Action for Healthy People Colo. Dept. Pub. Health, 1985—86; co-founder Coloradians for Seatbelts on Sch. Buses, 1985—90; co-founder, v.p. Coalition of Primary Care Physicians Colo., 1986; mem. adv. com. Greeley Ctrl. Drug and Alcohol Abuse, 1984—86; bd. dirs. Rocky Mtn. Ctr. for Health Promotion and Edn., 1984—2006, v.p., 1992—93, pres., 1994—95; med. cons. Sch. Dist. 6, 1989—2004; mem. bd. dirs. United Way Weld County, 1993—98; founder, med. dir. Monfort Children's Clinic, 1994—98, vol. physician, 1998—2004. With USN, 1946—48. Recipient Disting. Svc. award, Jr. C. of C., 1962, Svc. to Mankind award, Sertoma Club, 1972, Disting. Citizenship award, Elks, 1975—76, 2000—01, Spark Plug award, U. No. Colo., 1981, Mildred Doster award, Colo. Sch. Health Coun. for Sch. Health Contbns., 1992, Svc. award, Eta Sigma Gamma, 1996, Citizen of Yr. award, No. Colo. Med. Ctr. Found., 1996, Humanitarian of Yr. award, Weld County United Way, 1996, Alfred Winchester Humanitarian award, Greeley/Weld Sr. Found., Inc., 1996, Silver and Gold award, U. Colo. Med. Alumni Assn., 1997, Franklin Geggenbach award, 1997, Denver Children's Hosp. Pediatric Alumni award, 1997, Benezet award, Colo. Coll., 2000, Edn. Ptnr. of the Yr. award, Greeler-Weld C. of C., 2004, 2006, Leeann Anderson Cmty. Care award, Greeley C. of C., 2006. Mem.: AMA (chmn. sch. and coll. health com. 1980—82, James E. Strain Cmty. Svc. award 1987, 1994), Centennial Pediatric Soc. (pres. 1982—86), Colo. Med. Soc. (com. in sports medicine 1980—90, com. chmn. 1986—90, chmn. com. sch. health 1988—91, A.H. Robbins Cmty. Svc. award 1974), Weld County Med. Soc. (pres. 1968—69), Adams Aurora Med. Soc. (pres. 1964—65), Am. Acad. Pediat. (chmn. sch. health com. 1975—80, mem. task force on new age of pediatrics 1982—85, chmn. Colo. chpt. 1982—87, media spokesperson Speak Up for Children 1983—, Ross edn. and award com. 1985—86, alt. dist. VIII chmn. 1987—93, mem. coun. sects. mgmt. 1991—92, chmn. alt. dist. chmn. com. 1991—93, dist. chmn. dist. VIII 1993—98, mem. search com., exec. dir. candidate for pres. 1998, pres. elect 1998—99, v.p. AAP 1998—99, pres. 1999—2000, 1999—2000, immediate past pres. 2000—01, dist. VIII catch facilitator 2000—06, tomorrows children's task force 2001—04, reimbursement task force 2002—04), Colo. Med. Soc. Sch. Health Com. (chmn. 1967—78), Colo. Coll. Alumni Assn. (bd. dirs. 2003—, co-chmn. class 52 50th reunion com.), Rotary (bd. dirs. Greely chpt. 1988—91, chmn. immunization campaign Weld County 1994, mem. immunization com. 1994—, mem. adv. bd. Greeley Promises for Children 2001—, bd. dirs. Greely chpt. 2003—05, mem. task force on indigent care 2004—, mem. sch. readiness task force 2004—, William D. Farr award 2007, Cmty. Svc. award 2007). Republican. Methodist. Office: Monfort Children's Clinic 100 N 11th Ave Greeley CO 80631 Office Phone: 970-352-0072. Personal E-mail: ecook4130@msn.com. Business E-Mail: dcook@aap.org.

COOK, MELANIE K., lawyer; b. Salt Lake City, June 3, 1953; BS, UCLA, 1974, JD, 1978. Bar: Calif. Ptnr. Bloom Hergott Cook Diemer & Klein, Beverly Hills, Calif., 1987—2002, Bloom Hergott Diemer & Cook, Beverly Hills, Calif., 1992—2002, Ziffren, Brittenham, Branca, Fischer, Gilbert-Lurie, Stiffelman & Cook, LLP, LA, 2004—. Named one of The 100 Most Powerful Women in Entertainment, Hollywood Reporter, 2006, 2007, 100 Power Lawyers, 2007. Office: 1801 Century Park W Los Angeles CA 90067-6406 Office Phone: 310-552-6535.

COOK, MERRILL A., former congressman, explosives industry executive; b. Phila., May 6, 1946; s. Melvin A. and Wanda (Garfield) C.; m. Camille Sanders, Oct. 24, 1969; children: Brian, Alison, Barbara Ann, David, Michelle. BA magna cum laude, U. Utah, 1969; MBA, Harvard U., 1971. Profl. staff cons. Arthur D. Little, Inc., Cambridge, Mass., 1971-73; mng. dir. Cook Assocs., Inc., Salt Lake City, 1973-78; pres. Cook Slurry Co., Salt Lake City, 1978—; mem. U.S. Congress from 2d Utah dist., 1997-2001. Patentee in field. Del. Rep. Nat. Conv., Kansas City, Mo., 1976, San Diego, 1996, Phila., 2000. Mem. Salt Lake City C. of C., Phi Kappa Phi. Republican. Mem. Lds Ch.

COOK, NENA, lawyer; b. Salt Lake City, Jan. 25, 1966; BA, Gonzaga U., 1988; JD, Willamette U., 1991. Bar: Oreg. 1991, Wash., US Supreme Ct., US Ct. Appeals (9th Cir.), US Dist. Ct. (Dist. Oreg.) 1992, US Dist. Ct. (Ea. Dist. Wash.) 2000, US Dist. Ct. (We. Dist. Wash.) 2000. Ptnr. Sussman Shank LLP, Portland, Oreg. Chair employment law group Sussman Shank LLP; spkr. in field. Prodn. editor: Willamette Law Rev., 1990—91; contbr. articles to profl. jours. Chair Leadership Coll. Adv. Bd., 2006. Named one of Forty under 40 Outstanding Leadership in Bus. and Civic Affairs, Portland Bus. Jour., 2002. Mem.: ABA, Soc. Human Resource Mgmt., Portland Human Resource Mgmt. Assn., Fed. Bar Assn., Oreg. Women Lawyers, Oreg. State Bar Assn. (mem. fed. practice procedure com. 1997—99, chmn. 1998—99, ninth cir. jud. conf. rep. 2000—03, mem. bd. govs. 2002—05, pres.-elect 2004, pres. 2005, mem. jud. screening com.), Wash. State Bar Assn. Office: Sussman Shank LLP 1000 SW Broadway Ste 1400 Portland OR 97205 Office Phone: 503-227-1111, 503-243-1626. Office Fax: 503-248-0130. E-mail: nena@sussmanshank.com.

COOK, PAUL J., state legislator; m Jeanne. BS in Tchg., Southern Conn. State U.; MA, U. Calif., Riverside; MPA, Calif. State U., San Bernadino. Councilman and Mayor, Yucca Valley, formerly; California State Assemblyman, District 65, 2006-. Bronze Star and two Purple Hearts. Leadership posts, United Way and Red Cross local chapters, formerly; former exec director, Yucca Valley Chamber of Commerce; member, Disabled American Veterans, Veterans of Foreign Wars, and American Legion. Republican. Office: Dist 65 34932 Yucaipa Blvd Yucaipa CA 92399 Office Phone: 909-790-4196. Office Fax: 909-790-0479. Business E-Mail: Assemblymember.Cook@assembly.ca.gov.

COOK, PAUL MAXWELL, technology company executive; b. Ridgewood, NJ; BSChemE, MIT, 1947. With Stanford Rsch. Inst., Menlo Park, Calif., 1948-53, Sequoia Process Corp., 1953-56, Raychem Corp., Menlo Park, Calif., 1957-95, founder, former pres., CEO, until 1990, chmn., bd. dirs., until 1995; chmn., CEO CellNet Data Sys., San Carlos, Calif., 1990-94; chmn., bd. dirs. SRI Internat., 1993-98; chmn. DIVA Sys. Corp., Menlo Park, Calif., 1995—, CEO, 1995-99; founder, CEO, Agile TV Corp., 2000—. Mem. exec. com. San Francisco Bay Area Coun., 1988-94, chmn., 1990-91. Recipient Nat. Medal Tech., 1988; named to San Francisco Bay Area Bus. Hall of Fame, 1999. Mem. NAE, Am. Acad. Sci., Environ. Careers Orgn. (past chmn., bd. trustees), MIT Corp. (life, emeritus). Office: Diva Sys Corp 15233 Ventura Blvd 9th Fl Sherman Oaks CA 91403-2201 E-mail: pcook@agile.tv.

COOK, RICHARD A., aerospace engineer; BS in Engring. Physics, U. Colo.; MS in Aerospace U., U. Tex., 1989. With Jet Propulsion Lab., Pasadena, Calif., 1989—, flight ops. mgr. Mars Pathfinder project. Office: Jet Propulsion Lab 4600 Oak Grove Dr Pasadena CA 91109

COOK, RICHARD W. (DICK COOK), film company executive; b. Bakersfield, Calif., Aug. 20, 1950; BA in Polit. Sci., U. So. Calif., 1972. Ride operator Disneyland, Anaheim, Calif., sales rep., 1971-74, sales mgr., 1974-77; mgr. pay TV and non-theatrical releases Disney Studios, 1977-80; asst. domestic sales mgr. Buena Vista, 1980-81, v.p., asst. gen. sales mgr., 1981-84, v.p., gen. sales mgr., 1985-88, sr. v.p. domestic distbn., 1988-94; pres. Buena Vista Pictures Distbn., 1994; pres. worldwide mktg. Buena Vista Pictures Mktg., 1994-97; chmn. Walt Disney Motion Pictures Group, Burbank, Calif., 1997—2002, Walt Disney Studios, 2002—. Bd. dirs. Found. Motion Picture Pioneers, Verdugo Hills Hosp., Will Rogers Found.; pres. The Chandler Sch.; pres. bd. trustees Flintridge Prep. Sch.; trustee U. So. Calif., 1998—. Recipient George Washington Medal of Freedom, Freedoms Found. Valley Forge; named one of 50 Most Powerful People in Hollywood, Premiere mag., 2004—06, 50 Smartest People in Hollywood, Entertainment Weekly, 2007. Mem.: Acad. Motion Picture Arts and Scis. Office: Walt Disney Studios 500 S Buena Vista St Burbank CA 91521-0006

COOK, ROBERT CROSSLAND, chemist, researcher; b. New Haven, June 5, 1947; s. Russell C. and Tensia (Veazey) C. BS in Chemistry, Lafayette Coll., 1969; MPh in Phys. Chemistry, Yale U., 1971, PhD in Theoretical Chemistry, 1973. Mem. faculty Lafayette Coll., Easton, Pa., 1973-81; staff scientist Lawrence Livermore (Calif.) Nat. Lab., 1981—. Instr. Calif. State U., Hayward, 1985-86, 94, Chabot Coll., 1986-90, Las Positas Coll., 1990-92; mem. vis. faculty Dartmouth Coll., Hanover, N.H., 1977, 78, 79, Colo. State U., Ft. Collins, 1980. Contbr. articles to profl. jours. Grantee in field. Mem. Am. Chem. Soc., Am. Phys. Soc., Sigma Xi. Office: Lawrence Livermore Nat Lab L-479 PO Box 808 Livermore CA 94551-0808 Business E-Mail: bobcook@llnl.gov.

COOK, SCOTT DAVID, computer software company executive; b. Glendale, Calif., July 26, 1952; m. Signe Ostby; children: David, Karl, Annie. BA in Economics and Math., U. So. Calif.; MBA, Harvard U.

Various mktg. positions to brand mgr. Procter & Gamble; cons. Bain Co.; co-founder Intuit Inc., Menlo Park, Calif., 1983, pres., CEO, 1984-94, chmn. bd., 1993—98, chmn. exec. com., 1998—. Bd. dirs. Intuit Inc., 1984—, eBay, 1998—, The Procter & Gamble Co., 2000—. Bd. trustees Asia Found.; bd. visitors Harvard Bus. Sch., Ctr. Brand and Product Mgmt., Intuit Scholarship Found. Recipient Lifetime Achievement award, Software Publishers Assn., 1994, PC mag., 2003; named one of Forbes' Richest Americans, 2006. Mem.: Phi Beta Kappa. Office: Intuit Inc 2632 Marine Way Mountain View CA 94043 Office Phone: 650-944-6000.

COOK, STEPHEN CHAMPLIN, retired shipping company executive; b. Portland, Oreg., Sept. 20, 1915; s. Frederick Stephen and Mary Louise (Boardman) C.; m. Dorothy White, Oct. 27, 1945 (dec. Sept. 1998); children: Mary H. Cook Goodson, John B., Samuel D., Robert B. (dec.). Student, U. Oreg., Eugene, 1935-36. Surveyor U.S. Engrs. Corp., Portland, Oreg., 1934-35; dispatcher Pacific Motor Trucking Co., Oakland, Calif., 1937-38; manifest clk. Pacific Truck Express, Portland, 1939; exec. asst. Coastwise Line, San Francisco, 1940-41, mgr. K-Line svc., 1945-56; chartering mgr. Ocean Svc. Inc. subs. Marcona Corp., San Francisco, 1956-75, 1975—. Author 1 Charter Party, 1957. Steering com. Dogwood Festival, Lewiston, Idaho, 1985-92; sec. Asotin County Reps., Clarkston, Wash., 1986-88; adv. bd. Clarkston Pt. Commrs., 1989-92. Lt. USN, 1941-45, PTO; grand marshall Asotin Christmas Parade, 2006. Recipient Pres.'s award Marin (Calif.) coun. Boy Scouts Am., 1977, Order of Merit, 1971, 84, Skillern award Lewis Clark coun., 1982, Silver Beaver award 1987; Lewis-Clark Valley Vol. award, 1987, Youth Corps award Nat. Assn. Svc. and Conservation Corps, 1990, Pres.'s Spl. award Clarkston C. of C., 1983, Asotin Citizen of Yr. award, 1999. Mem. VFW, Asotin County Hist. Soc. (hon. life pres. 1982-83, bd. dirs.), Asotin C. of C. (v.p. 1994-95). Republican. Mem. Stand for United Ch. of Christ. Avocations: hiking, camping, stamp collecting/philately.

COOK, TIMOTHY D., computer company executive; b. Ala., 1960; BS in Indsl. Engring., Auburn U., 1982; MBA, Duke U. With IBM Corp., Research Triangle Park, NC, 1982—94; sr. v.p. fulfillment Intelligent Electronics Inc., 1994—96, COO, Reseller divsn., 1996—97; v.p. corp. materials Compaq Computer Corp., 1997—98; sr. v.p. worldwide ops. Apple Computer Inc., Cupertino, Calif., 1998—2000, sr. v.p. worldwide ops. sales & support, 2000—02, exec. v.p. worldwide sales & ops., 2002—05, interim CEO, 2004; COO Apple Inc. (formerly Apple Computer Inc.), Cupertino, Calif., 2005—. Bd. dirs. Nike Inc., 2005—. Fuqua scholar Duke U. Avocations: bicycling, football. Office: Apple Inc 1 Infinite Loop Cupertino CA 95014-2083*

COOK, TONY MICHAEL, church administrator, legislative staff member; m. Joy Cook; children: Michael, Libby. BA, Wash. State U., 1970; JD, Stanford U., 1973. Bar: Wash. 1973. With Senate Rsch. Ctr., 1973, U. Wash.; mem. staff Utilities and Transp. Commn., 1977; counsel Wash. State Senate, 1991, sec., 1999—; counsel Legis. Ethics Bd., 1997; sec. U.S. Senate, 1999—2002; mgr. property Dept. Gen. Adminstrn., 2003—05; gen. presbyter Presbytery Olympia, 2005. Business E-Mail: tnjcook@gocougs.wsu.edu.

COOK, WILLIAM HOWARD, architect; b. Evanston, Ill., Dec. 19, 1924; s. Clare Cyril and Matilda Hermine (Schuldt) C.; m. Nancy Ann Dean, Feb. 1, 1949; children: Robert, Cynthia, James. BA, UCLA, 1947; BArch, U. Mich., 1952. Chief designer Fabrica de Muebles Camacho-Roldan, Bogota, Colombia, S.Am., 1949-52; assoc. architect Orus Eash, Traverse City, Mich., Ft. Wayne, Ind., 1952-60; ptnr. Cook & Swaim (architects), Tucson, 1961-68; project specialist in urban devel. Banco Interamericano de Desarrollo, Buenos Aires, Argentina, 1968-69; pres. Cain, Nelson, Wares, Cook and Assocs., architects, Tucson, 1969-82. Vis. lectr. architecture U. Ariz., 1980-89; coord. archtl. exch. with U. LaSalle, Mexico City, 1983, 85, 87, 89, 93. Served to lt. (j.g.) USNR, 1943-46. Fellow AIA (pres. So. Ariz. 1967); mem. Ariz. Soc. Architects (pres. 1970). Home and Office: 3365 E 2nd St Tucson AZ 85716

COOKE, JACKIE (JACQUELINE MARIE COOKE), elementary school educator; BS, Portland State U., Oreg., 1981, MA, 1992. Tchr. Portland Metro area, 1981—; first grade tchr. West Gresham Elem. Sch., Gresham. Co-editor (and webmaster): Oreg. Coun. Tchrs. of Math. profl. jour. Named Oreg. Tchr. of Yr., 2007. Office: West Gresham Elem Sch 330 W Powell Blvd Gresham OR 97080 Business E-Mail: jackie_cooke@gbsd.gresham.k12.or.us.

COOKE, JOHN F., entertainment company executive; Exec. v.p. corp. affairs Walt Disney Co., Burbank, Calif.; exec. v.p. external affairs J. Paul Getty Trust, LA, 2000—.

COOKE, JOHN P., cardiologist, educator, researcher; BA in Biology, Cornell U., 1976; MD, Wayne State U., 1980; PhD in Physiology, Mayo Grad. Sch. of Medicine, 1985. Diplomate Am. Bd. Internal Medicine, Am. Bd. Cardiovascular Disease; cert. instr. advanced cardiac life support Am. Heart Assn. Assoc. physician Brigham and Women's Hosp., Boston, 1987-90; asst. prof. medicine Harvard Med. Sch., Boston, 1987-90, Stanford (Calif.) U. Sch. of Medicine, 1990-95, dir. sect. vascular medicine, 1991—, assoc. prof. medicine, 1995—, dir. sect. cardiovascular medicine, 1995—. Mem. editl. bd. Jour. Vascular Medicine and Biology, 1990—; contbr. articles to profl. jours. Rsch. fellow Mayo Grad. Sch. of Medicine, 1980-87; Merck fellow Am. Coll. Cardiology, 1985-86; recipient Henry Christian award Am. Fedn. Clin. Rsch., 1990, Vascular Acad. award NIH, 1991. Mem. Soc. Vascular Medicine and Biology (fouder). Office: Stanford U Divsn Cardiovascular Medicine 300 Pasteur Dr Palo Alto CA 94304-2203

COOLEDGE, RICHARD CALVIN, lawyer; b. Charleston, SC, Apr. 20, 1943; s. Russell Clarence and Lorena Ann (Weymuth) C.; m. Nancy Jean Western, June 15, 1965 (div. Dec. 1986); children: Dean Richard, Mark Alan, Jocelyn Joy; m. Jeanine Diana Smith, Apr. 12, 1989 (div. Nov. 1993). BA in Econs. with honors, U. Mo., Columbia, 1965; JD, U. Mich., 1968. Bar: Ariz. 1969, U.S. Dist. Ct. Ariz. 1969, U.S. Ct. Appeals (9th cir.) 1973, U.S. Supreme Ct. 1973. Mem. Brown & Bain P.A., Phoenix, 1968—2004, Perkins Coie Brown & Bain, Phoenix, 2004—. Contbg. editor: Banking and Lending Institutions Forms, Business Workouts Manual; contbr. articles to profl. jours. Fellow Ariz. Bar Found.; mem. Motorcycle Safety Found. (instr. 1994-2003), BMW Owners Assn. Avocations: motorcycling, golf, music, aviculture. Office: Perkins Coie Brown & Bain PA 2901 N Central Ave Fl 20 Phoenix AZ 85012-2700 Home Phone: 602-791-9996; Office Phone: 602-351-8425. Business E-Mail: rcooledge@perkinscoie.com.

COOLEY, STEVE, prosecutor; b. L.A., May 1, 1947; m. Jana Cooley; 2 children. BA, Calif. State U., LA, 1970; JD, U. So. Calif., 1973. Joined Dist. Attys. Office, 1973; dist. atty. L.A. County, 2000—. Recipient Leaders in Pub. Svc. award, Encino C. of C., Cmty. Justice award, Calif. NAACP; named Alumnus of Yr., Calif. State U., L.A., 1998, Pros. of the Yr., Century City Bar Assn., 2001, L.A. County Bar Assn., 2005, Champion of the People, Nat. Black Pros. Assn., Crime Victims Star of the Yr., Justice for Homicide Victims. Mem.: Phi Kappa Phi. Office: County of Los Angeles Foltz Justice Ctr 210 W Temple St Ste 18000 Los Angeles CA 90012-3210 Business E-Mail: scooley@lacountyda.org.*

COOLEY, VERNON JACKMAN, orthopedic surgeon; b. Salt Lake City, Mar. 28, 1963; B, U. Utah, 1986; MD, Harvard Med. Sch., 1991. Cert. Nat. Bd. Med. Examiners, 1991, in sports medicine Accreditation Coun. for Grad. Med. Edn., 1997, Am. Bd. Orthopaedic Surgery, 1999. Orthopedic surgery internship U. Wash., Seattle, 1991—92, orthopedic surgery residency, 1992—96; sports medicine/arthroscopy fellowship Orthopedic Specialty Hosp., Salt Lake City, 1996—99, chief surgery, 1997—2007; knee specialist Rosenberg Cooley Metcalf Clinic, Park City, Utah. Team physician Olympus HS, 2000—; physician Park City Olympic Venue, 2000—02, US Ski Team, US Snowboard Team, US Speedskating Team. Mem. sports medicine adv. com. Utah HS Activities Assn., 1997—. Mem.: Western Orthopaedic Assn., Utah State Orthopaedic Soc. (pres. 2005—07), Utah Med. Assn., Salt Lake County Med. Soc., Nat. Orthopedic Edn. Soc., Am. Orthopaedic Soc. Sports Medicine, Am. Acad. Orthopaedic Surgeons. Office: Rosenberg Cooley Metcalf Clinic 1820 Sidewinder Dr Park City UT 84060 Office Phone: 435-655-6600. Office Fax: 435-655-2388.

COOLEY, WES, former congressman; b. LA, Calif., Mar. 28, 1932; married; 4 children. AA, El Camino C. C.; BS in Bus., U. So. Calif., 1958. Asst. to pres. Hyland Labs. divsn. Baxter Labs. Allergan Pharmaceuticals; asst. to chmn. bd. ICN, divsn. mgr., dir. drug regulatory affairs; v.p. Virateck divsn.; founder, co-owner Rose Labs., Inc., 1981—; mem. Oregon State Senate, 1992-94; congressman 104 Congress from 2nd Oreg. dist., 1994-96. Mem. House Com. Agriculture, House Com. Resources, House Com. Veteran Affairs, Subcommittee Gen. Farm Commodities, Subcommittee on Livestock, Dairy and Poultry, Subcommittee on Nat. Pks., Forests and Lands, Subcom. Water and Power Resources. With U.S. Army Spl. Forces, 1952-54. Address: 25550 Walker Rd Bend OR 97701-9323 E-mail: honwescooley@cs.com.

COOLIDGE, MATTHEW, curator; B in Environ. Studies, Boston U., 1991. Founder, dir. Ctr. Land Use Interpretation, Culver City, Calif., 1994—. Adj. prof. Calif. Coll. Arts, San Francisco, 2003—. Exhibitions include Hinterland: A Voyage into Exurban Southern California, LA Contemporary Exhibitions, 1997, Commonwealth of Technology, Mass. Inst. Technology Cambridge, 1999, The Nellis Range Complex: Landscape of Conjecture, Ctr. Land Use Interpretation LA, 1999, Emergency State: First Responder and Law Enforcement Training Architecture, 2004; author: (book) Commonwealth of Technology: Extrapolations on the Contemporary Landscape in Massachusetts, 1999, Overlook: Exploring the Internal Fringes of America with the Center for Land Use Interpretation, 2006. Recipient Lucelia Artist award, Smithsonian Am. Art Mus., 2006; Guggenheim fellow, 2004, media arts fellowship, Rockefeller Found., 2005, Nat. Video Resources, 2005. Office: Ctr Land Use Interpretation 9331 Venice Blvd Culver City CA 90232 Office Phone: 310-839-5722. Office Fax: 310-839-6678.

COOMBE, BOB (ROBERT D.), academic administrator; BA in Chemistry, Williams Coll., 1970; PhD in Phys. Chemistry, U. Calif., Berkeley, 1973. Postdoctoral rsch. assoc. U. Toronto, Canada, 1973—74; tech. staff Rockwell Internat. Sci. Ctr., 1974—81; asst. prof. U. Denver, 1981—85, assoc. prof., 1985—89, prof., 1989—, dean grad. studies, 1985—87, chair dept. chemistry and biochemistry, 1988—95, dean natural scis., math. and engring., 1995—2001, provost, 2001—06, chancellor, 2006—. Office: U Denver Office of Chancellor 2199 S University Blvd Denver CO 80208 Office Phone: 303-871-2111. E-mail: tcoe@du.edu, chancelr@du.edu.

COOMBE, GEORGE WILLIAM, JR., lawyer, retired bank executive; b. Kearny, NJ, Oct. 1, 1925; s. George William and Laura (Montgomery) Coombe; m. Marilyn V. Ross, June 4, 1949; children: Susan, Donald William, Nancy. BA, Rutgers U., 1946; LLB, Harvard U., 1949; MLA, Stanford U., 2005. Bar: NY 1950, Mich. 1953, Calif. 1976. Practice US Supreme Ct., NYC, 1949—53, Detroit, 1953—69; atty., mem. legal staff Gen. Motors Corp., Detroit, 1953—69, asst. gen. counsel, sec., 1969—75; exec. v.p., gen. counsel Bank of Am., San Francisco, 1975—90; ptnr. Graham and James, San Francisco, 1991—95; sr. fellow Stanford Law Sch., 1995—. Lt. USNR, 1942—46. Mem.: NYC Bar Assn., Los Angeles Bar Assn., San Francisco Bar Assn., Calif. Bar Assn., Mich. Bar Assn., Am. Bar Assn., Phi Gamma Delta, Phi Beta Kappa. Presbyterian. Home: 2190 Broadway St Apt 2E San Francisco CA 94115-1312 Personal E-mail: gwcoombe@sbcglobal.net.

COONEY, JOHN P., judge; b. Sedalia, Mo., Jan. 21, 1932; Student, Westminster Coll., 1949-51, So. Oreg. Coll., 1957-59; JD, Willamette U., 1962. Bar: Oreg. 1962. Pvt. practice, Oreg., 1962-94; part-time U.S. magistrate judge Medford, 1990-94; full-time U.S. magistrate judge, 1994—. Mem. Oreg. Bar Assn. Office: US Dist Ct James Redden US Courthouse 310 W 6th St Rm 302 Medford OR 97501-2766

COONEY, MICHAEL RODMAN, state legislator; b. Washington, Sept. 3, 1954; son of Gage Rodman Cooney & Ruth Brodie C; married 1979 to Dee Ann Marie Gribble; children: Ryan Patrick, Adan Cecelia & Colin Thomas. Mont. State Rep., 1976-79; exec asst to US Senator Max Baucus, Montana, 1979-89; sec. of State, Mont., 1988-2001; member, Proj Democracy Comn, currently; member, Federal Elec Commission's Clearinghouse Advisor Panel, currently; Mont. State Senator, Dist 26, 2003-04, Dist 40, 2005-, chairman, Finance and Claims Committee, currently, Mont. State Senate. Member board director, Cooney Brokerage, 1973-75, vice president, 1975-76.mem. Dist 40, Mont. House of Reps.2002-06; mem. Dist 40, Mont. State Senate 2007- Musician's Union; Young Democratic (v.p, 1971-72); Democratic Association Secretaries State (chmn., currently); nat. assn. Secretaries of State (pres., 1996-97). Democrat. Roman Catholic. Home: 713 Pyrite Ct Helena MT 59601-5877 Mailing: State Capitol PO Box 201706 Helena MT 59620 Home Phone: 406-443-0144. E-mail: cooneyemail@aol.com.*

COONING, CRAIG R., career officer; BSc in Engring., Auburn U., 1973; grad. student, U. Ala., 1976—77, MBA, 1977; student, Squadron Officer Sch., 1979, Air Command and Staff Coll., 1982, Armed Forces Staff Coll., 1986; course, Nat. Security Mgmt. course, 1986; student, Indsl. Coll. Armed Forces, 1993—94; sr. acquisition course, Nat. Def. U., 1994. Vice comdr. Space and Missile Sys. Ctr., L.A. Air Force Base, 1973; sys. program officer dir., warranted contract officer, plant rep. office comdr., comd. ROTC program Auburn U., 1973—; procurement contracting officer San Antonio Air Logistics Ctr., Kelly AFB, Tex., 1973—76; contracting and mfg. career mgmt. assignment officer Air Force Mil. Personnel Ctr., Randolph AFB, Tex., 1982—86; dep. comdr. Detachment 48 Air Force Contract Mgmt. divsn. Air Force Plant Rep. Office Hughes Missile Sys. Group, Tucson, 1986—88; comdr. Detachment 43 Air Force Contrac Mgmt. divsn. Air Force Plant Rep. Office Morton Thiokol Inc., Brigham City, Utah, 1988—90; chief Commodities Contracting divsn. Contracting Directorate, Hill AFB, Utah, 1990—91; dir. Directorate Specialized Mgmt., Hill AFB, Utah, 1991—93, Space Acquisition, Office Undersec. Air Force, Wash., 1993—. Decorated Legion of Merit, Meritorious Svc. medal with five oak leaf clusters.

COONTS, STEPHEN PAUL, writer; b. Morgantown, W.Va., July 19, 1946; s. Gilbert Gray and Violet (Gadd) C.; m. Nancy Quereau, Feb. 19, 1971 (div. 1985); children: Rachael Diane Quereau, Lara Danielle Quereau, David Paul; m. Deborah Buell, Apr. 12, 1995. AB in Polit. Sci., W.Va. U., 1968; JD, U. Colo., 1979. Commd. ensign USN, 1968, with attack squadron 196 Whidbey Island, Wash., flight instr., asst. catapult-arresting gear officer USS Nimitz; pvt. practice Hymes & Coonts Attys., Buckhannon, W.Va., 1980-81; in-house counsel Petro-Lewis Corp., Denver, 1981-86; freelance novelist, 1986—. Author: Flight of the Intruder, 1986 (Author of Yr. award U.S. Naval Inst. 1986), Final Flight, 1988, The Minotaur, 1989, Under Siege, 1990, The Cannibal Queen: An Aerial Odyssey Across America, 1992, The Red Horseman, 1993, The Intruders, 1994, War In the Air, 1996, Fortunes of War, 1998, Cuba, 1999. Trustee W.Va. Wesleyan Coll., 1990-98. Inductee Acad. of Dist. Alumni W.Va. U., 1992.

COONTZ, STEPHANIE JEAN, history professor, writer; b. Seattle, Aug. 31, 1944; d. Sidney Coontz and Patricia (McIntosh) Waddington; 1 child, Kristopher. BA with honors, U. Calif., Berkeley, 1966; MA, U. Wash., Seattle, 1970. Mem. faculty Evergreen State Coll., Olympia, Wash., 1975—. Dir. rsch. and pub. edn. Coun. Contemporary Families, 1993—. Author: The Way We Never Were: American Families and the Nostalgia Trap, 1992, The Social Origins of Private Life: A History of American Families, 1988, The Way We Really Are: Coming to Terms With America's Changing Families, 1997, Marriage, A History: From Obedience to Intimacy, or How Love Conquered Marriage, 2005; (with others) Women's Work, Men's Property: On the Origins of Gender and Class, 1986, History and Family Theory, vol. II, 1989; contbr. numerous articles to profl. jours. Woodrow Wilson Found. fellow, 1968-69; recipient Washington Gov's. Writer's award, 1989, Dale Richmond award Am. Acad. Pediatrics, 1995, Visionary Leadership award Coun. Contemporary Families, 2004. Mem. Am. Studies Assn., Am. Hist. Assn., Orgn. Am. Historians. Office: Evergreen State Coll 2700 Evergreen Pwy NW Olympia WA 98505-0001 Address: c/o Viking Publicity 375 Hudson St New York NY 10014 Home: 12419 Tilley Rd S Olympia WA 98512-9168 Office Phone: 360-867-6703. Business E-Mail: coontz@evergreen.edu.

COOP, FREDERICK ROBERT, retired city manager; b. San Diego, Mar. 1, 1914; s. Ernest Frederick and Hazel (Angier) C.; m. Jean Haven, Feb. 11, 1939; children: Susan, Robert, Thomas, Elizabeth. AB, U. Calif., Berkeley, 1935; MS in Pub. Adminstrn, U. So. Calif., 1937. Pers. technician Calif. State Pers. Bd., 1937-41; pers. dir. Pasadena, Calif., 1941-49; pers. cons. UN, 1947; city mgr. Inglewood, Calif., 1949-56, Fremont, Calif., 1956-58; chief pub. svcs. divsn. U.S. Ops. Mission to Yugoslavia, 1958-61; city mgr. Newport Beach, Calif., 1961-64, Phoenix, 1964-69; regional dir. HEW, San Francisco, 1969-71; dir. pub. adminstrn. svcs. Arthur D. Little, Inc., San Francisco, 1972-78; pres. Coop Mgmt. Svcs. Inc., 1978—91. Pres., bd. dirs. Pub. Svc. Skills Inc. Served to lt. comdr. USNR, WW II. Named Young Man of Yr. Pasadena Jr. C. of C., 1947. Mem. Internat. City Mgmt. Assn. (regional v.p. 1965-67, Disting. Svc. award 2000), Am. Soc. Pub. Adminstrn. (bd. dirs.), Nat. Acad. Pub. Adminstrn., League Calif. Cities (hon. life, city mgrs. dept.).

COOPER, ALLEN DAVID, medical researcher, educator; b. NYC, Sept. 18, 1942; s. Samuel and Fay (Sussman) C.; m. Kristina Speer, 1997; children: Ian, Todd. BA, NYU, 1963; MD, SUNY Downstate Med. Ctr., NYC, 1967. Intern then resident Boston City Hosp., 1967-69; resident fellow in gastroenterology U. Calif., San Francisco, 1969-72; clin. asst. prof. medicine U. Tex. Med. Sch., San Antonio, 1972-74; asst. prof. medicine Stanford (Calif.) U., 1974-80, assoc. prof. medicine, 1980-89, courtesy assoc. prof. physiology, 1987-90, prof. medicine, 1990—, chief divsn. gastroenterology & hepathology, 2003—; dir. Palo Alto (Calif.) Med. Found. Rsch. Inst., 1986—2003. Sci. adv. bd. ChemTrak. Recipient Scholastic Achievement award Am Inst. Chem., 1963; Univ. fellow Stanford U., 1981-83, Andrew W. Mellon Found. fellow, 1977-79. Fellow ACP, Molecular Medicine Soc.; mem. Am. Soc. Clin. Investigation, Am. Soc. Biochemistry and Molecular Biology, Western Soc. Clin. Investigation (sec.-treas. 1988, pres. 1992), Am. Fedn. Clin. Rsch. (pres. 1974), South Beach Yacht Club, Single Handed Sailing Soc., Pi Lambda Xi, Alpha Omega Alpha. Avocation: sailing. Home: 88 King St Apt 325 San Francisco CA 94107-4026 E-mail: adc@stanford.edu.

COOPER, BILLY J., lawyer; b. Great Lakes, Ill., July 21, 1956; BA with high honors, Ohio No. Univ., 1978; JD, Univ. Okla., 1981. Bar: Okla. 1981, Va. 1989, Colo. 1992. Gen. counsel & mem. exec. com. Foster Wheeler Environ. Corp.; ptnr., Public Policy, Bus. Transactions practices, mem. mgmt. com., mng. ptnr. Denver office Patton Boggs LLP, Denver. Chmn. & legal liaison Product Stewardship Code Legal Adv. Group, 1992. Served to lt. comdr. JAGC USN, 1981—88. Decorated Commendation medal USN, Achievement medal (2), Sea Svc. Deployment medal, Meritorious Unit medal. Mem.: Colo. Bar Assn., ABA (vice chmn. Law of the Sea com. 1991). Office: Patton Boggs LLP Suite 1900 1660 Lincoln St Denver CO 80264-1901 Office Phone: 303-894-6326. Office Fax: 303-894-9239. Business E-Mail: bcooper@pattonboggs.com.

COOPER, BRADLEY, actor; b. Phila., Jan. 5, 1975; m. Jennifer Esposito, Dec. 21, 2006. Degree in English, Georgetown U., 1997; MFA, Actors Studio Dramam Sch., NYC. Host (TV series) Treks in a Wild World, 2000; actor: (TV series) The Street, 2000—01, Alias, 2001—06, Touching Evil, 2004, Jack & Bobby, 2004—05, Kitchen

Confidential, 2005—06, Nip/Tuck, 2007—08; (films) Wet Hot American Summer, 2001, My Little Eye, 2002, Carnival Knowledge, 2002, Stella Shorts 1998-2002, 2002, Wedding Crashers, 2005, Failure to Launch, 2006, The Comebacks, 2007, Older Than America, 2008, The Rocker, 2008, The Midnight Meat Train, 2008, New York, I Love You, 2008, Yes Man, 2008, He's Just Not That Into You, 2009; (TV films) The Last Cowboy, 2003, I Want to Marry Ryan Banks, 2004. Office: c/o Thruline Entertainment 9250 Wilshire Blvd Beverly Hills CA 90212

COOPER, CORINNE, communications consultant, lawyer; b. Albuquerque, July 12, 1952; d. David D. and Martha Lucille (Rosenblum) Cooper. BA magna cum laude, U. Ariz., 1975, JD summa cum laude, 1978. Bar: Ariz. 1978, US Dist. Ct. Ariz. 1978, Mo. 1985. Assoc. Streich, Lang, Weeks & Cardon, Phoenix, 1978—82; asst. prof. U. Mo., Kansas City, 1982—86, assoc. prof., 1986—94, prof., 1994—2000, prof. emerita, 2000—; pres. Profl. Presence, Comm. Cons., Tucson, 2001—. Vis. prof. U. Wis., Madison, 1985, Madison, 91, U. Pa., Phila., 1988, U. Ariz., 1993, U. Colo., 1994. Author (with Bruce Meyerson): A Drafter's Guide to Alternative Dispute Resolution, 1991; author: How to Build a Law Firm Brand, 2005; editor: The Portable UCC, 1993, 3d edit., 2001, 4th edit., 2004, Getting Graphic I, 1993, II, 1994, The New Article 9, 1999, 2d edit., 2000; editor in chief: Bus. Law Today, 1995—97; mem. editl. bd. ABA Jour., 1999—2005; author, editor: Attorney Liability in Bankruptcy, 2006; contbr. articles to profl. jours., chapters to books. Legal counsel Mo. for Hart campaign, 1984; dir. issues Goddard for Gov. campaign, 1990. Mem.: ABA (mem. editl. bd. Bus. Law Today 1991—97, mem. unifrom comml. code com., chmn. bus. sect. membership com. 1992—94, mem. coun. bus. sect. 1992—96, sect. bus. law pubs. 1998—2002, mem. standing com. strategic comm. 2001—03, coun. gen. practice sect. 2003—05), Mo. Bar Assn. (mem. comml. law com.), Ariz. Bar Assn., Am. Assn. Law Schs. (mem. comml. law 1982—2000), Am. Law Inst., Phi Beta Kappa, Order of Coif, Phi Kappa Phi. Democrat. Jewish. Office: Profl Presence 4558 N 1st Ave Tucson AZ 85718 Office Phone: 520-795-0522. Business E-Mail: c2@professionalpresence.com.

COOPER, EDWIN LOWELL, anatomy educator; b. Oakland, Tex., Dec. 23, 1936; s. Edwin Ellis and Ruthesther (Porché) C.; m. Helene Marie Antoinette Tournaire, Sept. 13, 1969; children— Astrid Madeleine, Amaury Tournaire. BS, Tex. So. U., 1957; MS, Atlanta, 1959; PhD, Brown U., 1963. UHPHS postdoctoral fellow UCLA, 1962-64, asst. prof. anatomy, 1964-69, assoc. prof., 1969-73, prof., 1973—. Vis. prof. Instituto Politecnico Nacional, Mexico City, 1966; Mem. adv. com. Office Sci. Personnel, NRC, 1972-73; mem. bd. sci. counselors Nat. Inst. Dental Research, 1973— Author: Comparative Immunology; Editor: Phylogeny of Transplantation Reactions, 1970, Invertebrate Immunology, 1974; founding editor: Internat. Jour. Developmental and Comparative Immunology, 1977—. Guggenheim fellow, 1970; Fulbright scholar, 1970; Eleanor Roosevelt fellow Internat. Union Against Cancer, 1977-78 Fellow AAAS (council 1971, chmn. sect. 1976); mem. Soc. Invertebrate Pathology (founding), Pan Am. Congress Anatomy (founding), Am. Assn. Anatomy, Transplantation Soc., Am. Assn. Immunologists, Am. Soc. Zoologists (program officer 1974—, founder div. comparative immunology 1975, pres.), Brit. Soc. Immunology, Societe d'Immunologie Francaise, Sigma Xi. Office: UCLA Sch Medicine Dept Neurobiology 10833 Le Conte Ave Los Angeles CA 90095-3075

COOPER, GREGORY M., protective services official; Chief of police, Provo, Utah. Office: 48 S 300 W Provo UT 84601-4362

COOPER, JAY LESLIE, lawyer; b. Chgo., Jan. 15, 1929; s. Julius Jerome and Grayce (Wolkenheim) Cooper; m. Darice Richman, July 30, 1970; children: Todd, Leslie, Keith. JD, De Paul U., 1951. Bar: Ill. 1951, Calif. 1953, U.S. Supreme Ct. 1965, N.Y. 1987. Ptnr. Cooper, Epstein & Hurewitz (and predecessors), Beverly Hills, Calif., 1955-93, Manatt, Phelps & Phillips, LA, 1993—2001; shareholder Greenberg Traurig, LLP, 2002—. Guest lectr. Advanced Profl. Program Legal Aspects of Music and Rec. Industry, U. So. Calif., 1968, 70, 75, Entertainment Industry Conf., 1971, Harvard Law Sch., 1985, Calif. Copyright Conf., 1967, 71, 73, 75, 77, 97, v.p., 1975, pres., 1976-77; co-chmn. annual program The Rec. Contract, UCLA, 1977—; lectr. Midem, 1977-95, 96-97; adj. prof. entertainment law Loyola U. Law Sch., LA, 1978-80; moderator UCLA Seminar, 1994. Profl. musician with, Les Brown, Charlie Barnet, Frank Sinatra, Los Angeles Philharm. others, 1945-55; editor: (with Irwin O. Spiegel) Record and Music Publishing Forms of Agreement in Current Use, 1971, Annual Program on Legal Aspects of Entertainment Industry, Syllabus, 1966-70; co-author: Talent in the New Millennium, 2001, The Work Made For Hire Conundrum, 2001. Recipient Tex. Star award for outstanding contbn. and achievement in entertainment law Tex. Bar, 2006; named Entertainment Lawyer of Yr. Billboard mag., 1975, Best of the Best, 2000, Entertainment Atty of Yr., Beverly Hills Bar Assn., 2003, So. Calif. Super Lawyers, L.A. Mag., 2004-05, Leading Business Lawyer, Chambers and Partners US Guide, Entertainment Lawyer of Yr., Century City Bar Assn., 2005; named to Best Lawyers in Am., 1987—, Svc. award Crammy Fdn.-ELI, 2009. Mem.: NARAS (chpt. pres. 1973—75, nat. pres. 1975—77), ABA (chmn. forum on entertainment and sports industries 1983—86), Internat. Assn. Entertainment Lawyers (exec. com.), LA Copyright Soc., Ill. Bar Assn., Calif. Bar Assn., LA County Bar Assn., Calif. Copyright Soc. (pres. 1976). Office: Greenberg Traurig LLP 2450 Colorado Ave #400 E Santa Monica CA 90404 Office Phone: 310-586-7888. Business E-Mail: cooper@gtlaw.com.

COOPER, MARTIN, electronics company executive; b. Chgo., Dec. 26, 1928; s. Arthur and Mary C.; children from previous marriage: Scott David, Lisa Ellen; m. Arlene Harris, Jan. 26, 1991. BSEE, Ill. Inst. Tech., 1950, MSEE, 1957. Rsch. engr. Teletype Corp., Chgo., 1953-54; with Motorola, Inc., Schaumburg, Ill., 1954-83, ops. dir., 1967-76, divsn. mgr., 1977-78, v.p., corp. dir. R & D, 1978-83; chmn., CEO Cellular Bus. Systems, Inc., 1983-86, Cellular Pay Phone Inc., Chgo. and Del Mar, Calif., 1986-92, Arraycomm, Inc., San Jose, Calif., 1992—. Mem. computer-telecommunications bd. NRC, 1979-83; mem. indsl. adv. bd. U. Ill.-Chgo., 1980-90. Patentee in field. Trustee, mem. pres.'s counsel Ill. Inst. Tech. Served with USNR, 1950-54. Fellow IEEE (pres. vehicular tech. soc. 1973-74, telecomms. policy bd. 1976—, award for contbns. to radiotelephony, Centennial medal awardee), Internat. Electronics Consortium (disting. lectr., adv. bd.), Radio Club of Am. (Fred Link award). Office: Arraycomm Inc 100 Via De La Valle Del Mar CA 92014-2031 Business E-Mail: marty@arraycomm.com.

COOPER, MICHAEL JEROME, professional basketball coach, former professional basketball player; b. LA, Apr. 15, 1956; Grad., U. N.Mex., 1978. Player LA Lakers, 1978—90, spl. asst. to gen. mgr. Jerry West, 1991—93, asst. coach, 1994—97, LA Sparks, 1999, head coach, 1999—2004, 2007—, NBA Devel. League Albuquerque Thunderbirds; asst. coach Denver Nuggets, 2004, interim head coach, 2004—05. Named to NBA All-Def. First Team, 1982, 84, 85, 87, 88; named NBA Defensive Player of Yr., 1987; co-recipient NBA Walter Kennedy Citizenship award, 1986., WNBA Coach of Yr. award, 2000. Achievements include being a member of five NBA Championship teams, 1980, 82, 85, 87, 88; led the Sparks to two WNBA Championships as head coach, 2001, 02. Office: LA Sparks 888 S Figueroa St Ste 2010 Los Angeles CA 90017

COOPER, MILTON E., computer science company professional; V.p. program devel. Computer Scis. Corp., El Segundo, Calif., 1984-92, v.p., pres. federal sector, 1992—. Chmn. bd. dirs. AFCEA Internat. Recipient 21st Century Commerce Leadership award for Industry, Assn. for Enterprise Integration, 1999, Leadership award AFCEA, 1997. Office: Computer Scis Corp 2100 E Grand Ave El Segundo CA 90245-5024

COOPER, PAUL DOUGLAS, lawyer; b. Kansas City, Mo., July 22, 1941; s. W.W. and Emma Marie (Ringo) C.; m. Elsa B. Shaw, June 15, 1963 (div. 1991); children: Richard, Dean; m. Kay J. Rice, Aug. 30, 1992 (div. 2004); 1 child, Natanya BA in English, U. Mich., 1963; LLB, U. Calif., 1966. Bar: Colo. 1966, U.S. Dist. Ct. Colo. 1966, U.S. Ct. Appeals (10th cir.) 1967, U.S. Supreme Ct. 1979. Dep. dist. atty., Denver, 1969-71; asst. U.S. atty. Dist. of Colo., 1971-73; ptnr. Yegge, Hall & Evans, Denver, 1973-80; pres., dir. Cooper & Kelley PC, Denver, 1980-94, Cooper & Clough PC, Denver, 1994—. Faculty trial practice seminar Denver U. Law Sch., 1982; spl. asst. U.S. atty. Dist. of Colo., 1973-75; spl. prosecutor Mar. 1977 term, Garfield County Grand Jury; pres. Bow Mar Owners, Inc., 1976-77; mem. English adv. bd. U. Mich., 2000—. Mem. English adv. bd. Univ. Mich., 2000—. Recipient Spl. Commendation award for outstanding svc., 1972. Mem. ABA, Am. Bd. Trial Advocates, Colo. Bar Assn. (interprofl. com., bd. govs.), Denver Bar Assn. (trustee, 1st v.p. 1982-83), Colo. Med. Soc. (chmn. interprofl. com., Denver bar liaison com), Internat. Assn. Def. Counsel (exec. com. 1989-92). Republican. Office: 1512 Larimer St Ste 600 Denver CO 80202-1610 Home: 777 Niwot Ridge Ln Lafayette CO 80026 Home Phone: 720-887-8066; Office Phone: 303-607-0077. Business E-Mail: pcooper@cooper-clough.com.

COOPER, ROBERT E., lawyer; b. Sept. 6, 1939; AB, Northwestern U., 1961; LLB, Yale U., 1964. Bar: Calif. 1965. Joined Gibson Dunn & Crutcher LLP, 1964—, now ptnr. litig. dept. LA. Bd. dir. Nat. Inst. of Transplantation Found., 1989; sec. Citizens Rsch. Found., 1980—90; mem. Calif. Law Revision Commn., 1996—99. Mem. Yale Law Jour., 1963—64, contbg. author Antitrust Advisor, 1971. Fellow: Am. Coll. Trial Lawyers; mem.: ABA, Los Angeles County Bar Assn. (vice-chmn., criminal practice and procedure com., antitrust law sect. 1984—86), US Courts for Ninth Cir., Phi Beta Kappa, Order of Coif. Office: Gibson Dunn & Crutcher LLP 333 S Grand Ave Los Angeles CA 90071-3197 Office Phone: 213-229-7179. Office Fax: 213-229-6179. Business E-Mail: rcooper@gibsondunn.com.

COOPER, ROBERTA, former mayor; b. Mar. 18, 1937; m. Jerrel Cooper. BA, MA. Ret. secondary sch. tchr.; mem. Hayward (Calif.) City Coun., 1988-92; mayor City of Hayward, 1994—2006. Former mem. Gen. Plan Revision Task Force, dir. League of Calif. Cities. Active Eden (Calif.) Youth Ctr., Literacy Plus, Hayward Edn. Assn. Democrat. Avocations: reading mysteries, gardening.

COOPER, SARAH JEAN, nursing educator; b. Wallace, Idaho, Oct. 3, 1940; d. Kenneth Albert and Jean Saxsonia (Horton) Merryweather; m. George Harlan Cooper, Aug. 5, 1961; children: John, Matthew, Thomas. Diploma, Sacred Heart Sch. Nursing, 1961; BSN, Pacific Luth. U., 1974; MN, U. Wash., Seattle, 1979. Assoc. dir. nursing St. Alphonsus Hosp., Boise, Idaho; asst. dir. nursing and staffing St. Luke's Regional Med. Ctr., Boise, mgr. patient care support svcs.; nursing dept. Walla Walla Cmty. Coll., Wash. Instr. nursing Walla Walla C.C. Kellogg Found. fellow; Pew grantee. Mem. Sigma Theta Tau. Office: Nursing Dept Walla Walla Cmty Coll 500 Tausick Way Walla Walla WA 99362 E-mail: sargeo@bmi.net.

COOPER, WILLIAM SECORD, information science educator; b. Winnipeg, Man., Can., Nov. 7, 1935; m. Helen Clare Dunlap, July 22, 1964. BA, Principia Coll., 1956; MSc, MIT, 1959; PhD, U. Calif., Berkeley, 1964. Alexander von Humboldt scholar U. Erlangen, Germany, 1964-65; asst. prof. info. sci. U. Chgo., 1966-70; assoc. prof. info. sci. U. Calif., Berkeley, 1971-76, prof., 1976-94, prof. Grad. Sch., 1994-96, prof. emeritus, 1996—. Miller prof. Miller Inst., Berkeley, 1975-76. Hon. rsch. fellow Univ. Coll., London, 1977-78; ACM/SIGIR Triennial Rsch. award, 1994. Office: Univ Calif Sch Info Mgmt & Sys Berkeley CA 94720-0001 Office Phone: 510-642-4690. Business E-Mail: wcooper@calmail.berkeley.edu.

COOPERMAN, DANIEL, computer company executive, lawyer; b. Perth Amboy, NJ, Nov. 27, 1950; s. Eli Louis and Dorothy (Salinger) C.; m. Linda Louise Schmidt, June 10, 1979; children: Jeffrey Eli, Justin Andrew. AB summa cum laude, Dartmouth Coll., Hanover, NH, 1972; JD, MBA, Stanford U., Calif., 1976. Bar: Calif. 1976. Cons. McKinsey & Co., San Francisco, 1976-77; atty. McCutchen, Doyle, Brown & Enersen, San Francisco, 1977-83, ptnr., 1983-97, mng. ptnr. San Jose, Calif., 1989—95; sr. v.p., gen. counsel, sec. Oracle Corp., Redwood Shores, Calif., 1997—2007; sr. v.p., gen. counsel PeopleSoft Corp., Walnut Creek, Calif., 2004—05; sr. v.p., gen. counsel, sec. Apple Inc., Cupertino, Calif., 2007—. Chmn. Software & Info. Ind. Assn. Sec., bd. dirs. Children's Discovery Mus., San Jose, Calif., 1993—; bd. advs. Cmty. Found. Santa Clara County, San Jose, 1994—. Mem. Santa Clara County Bar Assn. (chair bus. law sect. 1992-93), NASDAQ's Listing and Hearing Rev. Coun., ABA's Com. Corp. Gen. Counsel, Adv. Coun. Law, Sci. & Tech. Program Stanford Law Sch. Avocation: squash. Office: Apple Inc 1 Infinite Loop Cupertino CA 95014

COOPER-SMITH, JEFFREY PAUL, botanic garden administrator; b. New Haven, July 12, 1951; s. Robert Ernest and Marilyn (Blake) C.-S.; m. Maria de los Angeles Gonzalez Alvarado, 1981 (div. 1995); 1 child, Brandon Andrés. BA in Botany and Biology summa cum laude, Pomona Coll., 1974; MA in Botany, Duke U., 1978; postgrad. Duke U./Cornell U., 1974-78; MBA in Fin. and Mktg., U. Chgo., 1985. Sci. instr. Costa Rica Acad., San Antonio de Belén, 1978-80; prof. Sch. Biol. Scis. Universidad Nacional, Heredia, Costa Rica, 1980-82; analyzer promotional programs Citibank, U.S.A., Chgo., 1984; bus. devel. assoc. ICI Ams., Inc., Wilmington, Del., 1985-87; mgr. capital planning S.E. Bank, N.A., Miami, Fla., 1987-89; comml. svcs. mgr. Nat. Starch & Chem. (Unilever), Bridgewater, N.J., 1990-91; exec. dir. U.S. Botanic Garden, Washington, 1992, Coyote Point Museum for Environmental Education, San Mateo, Calif. Cons. reforestation project Ministry Environ., Maracaibo, Venezuela, 1979. Vol. Red Cross, Costa Rica, 1978-82. Mem. Internat. Coun. of Mus., Am. Assn. Mus., Bat Conservation Internat., Orgn. Tropical Studies, Nature Conservancy. Avocations: music, gardening, swimming, natural history, foreign cultures. Address: Coyote Point Museum for Environmental Education 1651 Coyote Point Dr San Mateo CA 94401

COOR, LATTIE FINCH, university president; b. Phoenix, Sept. 26, 1936; s. Lattie F. and Elnora (Witten) C.; m. Ina Fitzhenry, Jan. 18, 1964 (div. 1988); children: William Kendall, Colin Fitzhenry, Farryl MacKenna Witten; m. Elva Wingfield, Dec. 27, 1994. AB with high honors (Phelps Dodge scholar), No. Ariz. U., 1958; MA with honors (Univ. scholar, Universal Match Found. fellow, Carnegie Corp. fellow), Washington U., St. Louis, 1960, PhD, 1964; LLD (hon.), Marlboro Coll., 1977, Am. Coll. Greece, 1982, U. Vt., 1991, No. Ariz. U., 2002. Adminstrv. asst. to Gov. Mich., 1961-62; asst. to chancellor Washington U., St. Louis, 1963-67, asst. dean Grad. Sch. Arts and Scis., 1967-69, dir. internat. studies, 1967-69, asst. prof. polit. sci., 1967-76, vice chancellor, 1969-74, univ. vice chancellor, 1974-76; pres. U. Vt., Burlington, 1976-89, Ariz. State U., Tempe, Ariz., 1990—2002, prof. pub. affairs, Ernest W. McFarland Ariz. Heritage chair in leadership and pub. policy, pres. emeritus, 2002—, chmn. leadership and pub. policy. Cons. HEW; spl. cons. to commr. U.S. Commn. on Edn., 1971-74; chmn. Commn. on Govtl. Rels., Am. Coun. on Edn., 1976-80; dir. New Eng. Bd. Higher Edn., 1976-89; co-chmn. joint com. on health policy Assn. Am. Univs. and Nat. Assn. State Univs. and Land Grant Colls., 1976-89; mem. pres. commn. NCAA, 1984-90, chmn. div. I, 1989; mem. Ariz. State Bd. Edn., 1993-98; chmn. Pacific 10 Conf., 1995-96; chmn., CEO Ctr. Future Ariz., 2002—. Trustee emeritus Am. Coll. Greece. Mem. Nat. Assn. State Univs. and Land Grant Colls. (chmn. bd. dirs. 1991-92), New Eng. Assn. Schs. and Colls. (pres. 1981-82), Am. Coun. on Edn. (bd. dirs. 1991-93, 2000-02), Kellogg Commn. on Future of State and Land-Grant Univs. Office: Ctr for Future of Ariz 541 E Van Buren Ave Ste B-5 Phoenix AZ 85004 Office Phone: 480-727-5005. Business E-Mail: Lattie.Coor@asu.edu.

COORS, JEFFREY H., technology manufacturing executive; b. Denver, Feb. 10, 1945; s. Joseph. B.Chem. Engring., Cornell U., 1967, M.Chem. Engring., 1968. With Coors Porcelain Co., 1968-70; with Adolph Coors Co., Golden, Colo., 1970-92, pres., 1985-89; chmn., chief exec. officer Coors Techs. Cos., Golden, 1989-92; pres. ACX Techs., Golden, 1992—2000; chmn., pres., CEO Graphic Packaging Corp., 2000—03; exec. chmn. bd. Graphic Packaging Internat., Inc., Golden, Colo., 2003—06.

COORS, PETER HANSON, brewery company executive; b. Denver, Sept. 20, 1946; s. Joseph and Holly (Hanson) C.; m. Marilyn Gross, Aug. 23, 1969; children: Melissa, Christien, Carrie Ann, Ashley, Peter, David. BS in Idsl. Engring., Cornell U., 1969; MBA, U. Denver, 1970; PhD (hon.), Regis U., 1991; PhD, Wilberforce U., 1991, Johnson & Wales U., 1997. Prodn. trainee, specialist Adolph Coors Co., Golden, Colo., 1970-71, dir. fin. planning, 1971-75, asst. sec.-treas., 1974-76, dir. market research, 1975-76, v.p. self distbn., 1976-77, v.p. sales and mktg., 1977-78, sr. v.p. sales and mktg., 1978-82, div. pres. sales, mktg. and adminstrn., 1982-85, exec. v.p., 1991—93; pres. Coors Brewing Co. (formerly brewing div.), Golden, Colo., 1985—92; vice-chmn., CEO Coors Brewing Co., Golden, Colo., 1993—2002, chmn., 2002—05; vice chmn. Molson Coors Brewing Co., Golden, Colo., 2005—. Bd. dirs. U.S. Bancorp, Inc., H. J. Heinz Co., Energy Corp. of Am. Bd. dirs. Nat. Wildlife Fedn., 1978-81, Wildlife Legis. Fund, 1987—, Colo. Hosp., 2004-; hon. bd. dirs. Colo. Spl. Olympics Inc., 1978—; trustee Colo. Outward Bound Sch., 1978—, Adolph Coors Found., Pres.'s Leadership Com., U. Colo., 1978—; chmn. Nat. Commn. on the Future of Regis Coll., 1981-82, chmn. devel. com., 1983—, now trustee. Mem. Nat. Indls. Adv. Council, Opportunities Ctrs. of Am., Young Pres.' Orgn., Ducks Unlimited (nat. trustee 1979, sr. v.p., mem. mgmt. com., exec. com. 1982—, dir. Can. 1982—, pres. 1984-85, chmn. bd. 1986—) Clubs: Met. Denver Exec. (dir 1979, pres. 1981—). Office: Molson Coors Brewing Co PO Box 4030 Golden CO 80401

COORS, WILLIAM K., retired brewery company executive; b. Golden, Colo., Aug. 11, 1916; BSChemE, Princeton U., 1938, grad. degree in chem. engring., 1939. Pres. Adolph Coors Co., Golden, Colo., 1955—2000, chmn. bd., 1961—2002, ACX Techs., Inc., 1992—2000. Recipient Daniel L. Ritchie award, 1991.

COOTS, LAURIE, advertising executive; 1 child, Christopher. Student, Colorado State U. Joined Chiat/Day as sec. on Apple Computer bus., 1984; named new bus. coord., 1986; dir. new bus. and adminstrn., 1989; COO LA office, 1993—97; (Chiat/Day merges with TBWA, 1995); chief mktg. officer N. Am. TBWA/Chiat/Day, LA, 1997—2001, chief mktg. officer worldwide, 2001—. Office: TBWA Chiat/Day LA 5353 Grosvenor Blvd Los Angeles CA 90066

COPE, THOMAS FIELD, lawyer; b. Oak Park, Ill., Feb. 29, 1948; s. Benjamin Thomas and Myra Norma (Lees) C.; m. Ann Wattis, Mar. 21, 1970; children: Elizabeth Ann, Philip Thomas. BA, U. Denver, 1970, JD, 1974, MA, 1976; PhD, U. Chgo., 2001. Bar: Colo. 1974, Ill. 1978, Wyo. 1996, D.C. 2001. Assoc. Holme Roberts & Owen, Denver, 1974-78, 81-83, ptnr., 1984—2003, of counsel, 2003—. Instr. IIT Chgo.-Kent Coll. Law, 1980—81, Loyola U. Sch. Law, Chgo., 1980—81; chief of party ABA Ctrl. European and Eurasian Law Initiative, Moldova, 2002—03; adj. prof. U. Denver Coll. Law, 2003—04. Co-editor: Colorado Environmental Law Handbook, 1989, 4th rev. edit., 1996, Colorado Environmental Compliance Update, 1993-96; contbg. editor Oil & Gas Law and Taxation Rev., Oxford, Eng., 1987-93; mng. editor Shepard's Environ. Liability in Comml. Transactions Reporter, 1990-92; mem. bd. editors Denver Law Jour., 1972-74; contbr. articles to profl. jours. Bd. dirs. Colo. Fourteeners Initiative, 1996-2002, Colo. Mountain Club Found. (bd. dirs. 2006—). Mem. Am. Law Inst., Am. Soc. Legal History, Irish Legal History Soc., Selden Soc. (state corr. Colo. 1997—), Rocky Mountain Mineral Law Found. (mem. grants com. 1983-95, chmn. 1995-2002), Order St. Ives, Am. Alpine Club, Colo. Mountain Club (chair high altitude mountaineering sect. 2001-02). Democrat. Mem. Orthodox Ch. in Am. Avocations: mountain climbing, history, paleontology. Home: 2800 S University Blvd #108 Denver CO 80210-6072 Office: Holme Roberts & Owen LLP 1700 Lincoln St Ste 4100 Denver CO 80203-4541 Office Phone: 303-866-0295. E-mail: thomas.cope@hro.com.

COPELAND, ROBERT GLENN, lawyer; b. San Diego, Mar. 15, 1941; s. Glenn Howard and Luella Louise (Schmid) C.; m. Harriet S. Smith, June 27, 1964 (div. Jan. 1977); children: Katherine Louise, Matthew Robert; m. Lynne Newman, Oct. 10, 1993; 1 child, Zachary Newman. AB, Occidental Coll., 1963; JD, U. So. Calif., 1966. Bar: Calif. 1966, U.S. Dist. Ct. Calif. (so. dist.), 1967. Ptnr. Gray, Cary, Ware & Freidenrich, San Diego, 1966-95, Luce, Forward Hamilton & Scripps, LLP, 1995—2004, Duane Morris LLP, 2004—08, Shappard Mullin Richty & Hampton LLP, 2008—. Mem. ABA, Calif. Bar Assn. Avocations: shooting, fly fishing, hiking, racquetball. Office Phone: 619-744-2228. Business E-Mail: rcopeland@sheppardmullin.com.

COPES, PARZIVAL, economist, researcher; b. Nakusp, BC, Can., Jan. 22, 1924; s. Jan Coops and Elisabeth Catharina Coops-van Olst; m. Dina Gussekloo, May 1, 1946; children: Raymond Alden, Michael Ian, Terence Franklin. BA in Econs. & Polit. Sci., U. B.C., 1949, MA in Econs., 1950; PhD in Econs., London Sch. Econs., 1956; D in Mil. Sci. (hon.), Royal Roads Mil. Coll., 1991; D in Philosophy (hon.), U. Tromsö, 1993; DLitt (hon.), Meml. U. Newfoundland, 2004. Economist, statistician Dominion Bur. of Stats., Ottawa, Canada, 1953—57; from assoc. prof. to prof., head econs. dept. Meml. U. Nfld., St. John's, Canada, 1957—64; founding dir. econ. rsch. Inst. Social and Econ. Rsch. Meml. U. Nfld., St. John's, 1961-64; prof. Simon Fraser U., Burnaby, B.C., Canada, 1964—91, founding head dept. econs. and commerce, 1964-69, chmn. dept. econs. and commerce, 1972—75, founding dir. Ctr. for Can. Studies, 1978—85, founding dir. Inst. of Fisheries Analysis, 1980—94, prof. emeritus, 1991—. Gov. Inst. Can. Bankers, Montreal, Que., 1967-71; dir. Can.-Fgn. Arrangements Project, Can. Govt. Dept. Environment, 1976; pres., chmn. Pacific Regional Sci. Conf. Orgn., 1977-85; spl. advisor to Minister of Fisheries, B.C., 1998; initiator, dir. collaborative rsch. and tng. agreement with Asian Fisheries Social Sci. Rsch. Network, 1989-94. Author: The Statistical Measurement of Morbidity Frequency, 1957, St. John's and Newfoundland: An Economic Survey, 1961, The Backward-Bending Supply Curve of the Fishing Industry, 1970, The Resettlement of Fishing Communities in Newfoundland, 1972, Factor Rents, Sole Ownership and the Optimum Level of Fisheries Exploitation, 1972, A Critical Review of the Individual Quota as a Device in Fisheries Management, 1986, The Extended Economics of an Innate Common Use Resource: The Fishery, 1998, Equity and the Rights Basis of Fishing in Iceland and Canada: Reflections on the Icelandic Supreme Court Decision, 1999, Sharing the Fishery Resources of the North Pacific for Mutual Advantage: Toward an International Management Regime, 1999, Aboriginal Fishing Rights and Salmon Management in British Columbia: Matching Historical Justice with the Public Interest, 2000, (with G Palsson) Challenging ITQs: Legal and Political Action in Iceland, Canada and Latin America, 2001, Fisheries Management Options: The Case for Limited Entry over ITQs, 2001, An Exploration of Fishery Access Rights and Community-Based Fishery Management for the Central and North Coast of British Columbia, 2003, A Vision for Community-Based Development of the Fisheries Sector on the Central and North Coast of British Columbia, 2003.(with A. Charles) Socio-Economics of Individual Transferable Quotas and Community-Based Fishery Management, 2004. With Netherlands Resistance Army, 1942—45, attached Can. Army, 1945—46, attached British Mil., with Can. Officers Tng. Corps, 1946—50, lt. Can. Army, 1950—51, lt. Cameron Highlanders Ottawa Can. Army, 1953—55, capt. 113 Manning Depot Can. Army Militia, 1955—57, capt. to maj. CO112 Manning Depot Can. Army Militia, 1957—63, attached, Govt. Germany. Decorated officer Order of Can.; recipient Can. Forces Decoration, Can. Army, 1963. Fellow Acad. Natural Scis. of Russian Fedn. (fgn.); mem. Internat. Inst. Fisheries Econs. and Trade (exec. com. 1982-86, Disting. Svc. award 1996), Internat. Assn. for Study of Common Property, Can. Regional Sci. Assn. (pres. 1983-85), Can. Econs. Assn. (v.p. 1972-73), Assn. for Can. Studies, Western Regional Sci. Assn. (pres. 1977-78), Social Sci. Fedn. Can. (dir., v.p. 1979-83), Can. Assn. Univ. Tchrs., Internat. Arctic Sci. Com., Simon Fraser U. Faculty Assn. (life). Achievements include some of earliest research contributions to establish sub-discipline of fisheries economics; writing, speaking, research and international consulting in fisheries policy and resource management. Home and Office: 4661 Amblewood Dr Victoria BC VBY1C1 Canada Business E-Mail: copes@sfu.ca.

COPLEY, DAVID C., publishing executive; s. Helen K. and James S. Copley (Stepfather). BSBA, Menlo Coll., 1975. Pres., CEO, chmn. Copley Press, Inc., La Jolla, Calif., 1988—; chair, exec. com., chmn. sr. mgmt. bd. and bd. dir. The Copley Press, Inc., La Jolla, Calif.; pub. The San Diego Union-Tribune, 2001—, The Borrego Sun. Chair, pres. Copley N.W., Inc., Puller Paper Co.; pres. Copley News Svc.; trustee Copley Ohio Newspapers, The Peoria Jour. Star, Inc., The Gales. Print. and Publ. Co.; pres. Copley Northwest, Inc. and puller paper Co., others. Mem. editl. bd. San Diego Union-Tribune. Pres., trustee & pres. James S. Copley Found.; trustee Canterbury Sch., San Diego Crew Classic Found.; trustee emeritus La Jolla Playhouse, Am. Craft Coun., Mus. Photog. Arts; pres. assoc., pres. adv. com., exhibits com. Zool. Soc. San Diego; adv. bd. San Diego Automotive Mus.; pres. coun. Scripps Clinic and Rsch. Found., San Diego Kind Corp.; active Pres. Club U. San Diego, San Diego Aerospace Mus., San Diego Hall Sci., San Diego Maritime Mus., San Diego Coun. on Literacy. Named one of 400 Richest Americans, Forbes, 2005, 2006. Mem. Nat. Newspaper Assn., U.S. Humane Soc., San Diego Hist. Soc., San Diego Humane Soc., Bachelor Club San Diego. Office: The Copley Press Inc PO Box 1530 La Jolla CA 92038-1530 Office Phone: 858-454-0411.

COPMAN, LOUIS, radiologist; b. Phila., Jan. 17, 1934; s. Jacob and Eve (Snyder) C.; m. Avera Schuster, June 8, 1958; children: Mark, Linda. BA, U. Pa., 1955, MD, 1959. Diplomate Am. Bd. Radiology; Nat. Bd. Med. Examiners. Commd. ensign Med. Corps USN, 1958; advanced through grades to capt. M.C. USN, 1975; ret., 1975; asst. chief radiology dept. Naval Hosp., Pensacola, Fla., 1966—69; chief radiology dept. Doctors Hosp., Phila., 1969—73; radiologist Mercer Hosp. Ctr., Trenton, NJ, 1973—75; chmn. radiology dept. Naval Hosp., Phila., 1975—84; chief. radiology dept. Naval Med. Clinic, Pearl Harbor, Hawaii, 1984—89; pvt. practice radiologist Honolulu, 1989—92. Cons. Radiology Svcs., Wilmington, Del., 1978-84, Yardley (Pa.) Radiology, 1979-84. Author: The Cuckold, 1974. Capt. med. corps USN, 1958—89, ret., 1989. Recipient Albert Einstein award in Medicine, U. Pa., 1959. Mem. AMA, Assn. Mil. Surgeons U.S., Royal Soc. Medicine, Radiol. Soc. N.Am., Am. Coll. Radiology, Photographic Soc. Am., Sherlock Holmes Soc., Phi Beta Kappa, Alpha Omega Alpha. Avocations: photography, hang-gliding, scuba diving. Home: PO Box 384767 Waikoloa HI 96738-4767 Office: 68-1771 Makanahele Pl Waikoloa HI 96738-5128 Office Phone: 808-883-0059. Personal E-mail: louiscopman@earthlink.net.

COPPERSMITH, SAM, lawyer, former congressman; b. Johnstown, Pa., May 22, 1955; m. Beth Schermer, Aug. 28, 1983; children: Sarah, Benjamin, Louis. AB in Econs. magna cum laude, Harvard U., 1976; JD, Yale Law Sch., 1982. Bar: Calif. 1982, Ariz. 1983. Fgn. svc. officer U.S. Dept. State, Port of Spain, Trinidad and Tobago, 1977—79; law clk. to Judge William C. Canby Jr. U.S. Ct. Appeals (9th cir.), Phoenix, 1982—83; atty. Sacks, Tierney & Kasen, P.A., Phoenix, 1983—86; asst. to Mayor Terry Goddard City of Phoenix, 1984; atty. Jones, Jury, Short & Mast P.C., Phoenix, 1986—88, Bonnett, Fairbourn & Friedman P.C., Phoenix, 1988—92; mem. 103d Congress from 1st Ariz. Dist., 1993—95; atty. Coppersmith Gordon Schermer Owens & Nelson PLC, 1995—. Former dir., pres. Planned Parenthood Ctrl. and No. Ariz.; former chair City of Phoenix Bd. Adjustment; former dir. Ariz. Cmty. Svc. Legal Assistance Found., 1986—89; trustee Devereux Found., 1997—; chair Ariz. Dem. Party, 1995—97. Mem. ABA, Maricopa County Bar Assn. Democrat. Office: Coppersmith Gordon Schermer Owens & Nelson PLC 2800 N Central Ave Ste 1000 Phoenix AZ 85004-1007 E-mail: sam@cgson.com.

COPPOLA, NICOLAS See CAGE, NICOLAS

COPPOLILLO, HENRY PETER, psychiatrist; b. Cervicati, Cosenza, Italy, July 27, 1926; s. Vincent Louis and Maria Giovanna (Chidichimo) C.; m. Ruthann Butler, June 6, 1962 (dec. Apr. 1993); children: Catherine, Peter, Robert. Student, U. Ill., 1943-44; MD, U. Rome, 1955. Lic. physician, Ill., Mich., Tenn., Colo.; diplomate Am. Bd. Psychiatry and Neurology. Intern Cook County Hosp., Chgo., 1955-56; resident U. Chgo. Clinics, Chgo., 1956-59; assoc. attending physician Michael Reese Hosp., Chgo., 1959-66; asst. prof. to prof. U. Mich., Ann Arbor, 1966-70; prof. psychiatry Vanderbilt U., Nashville, 1970-76, U. Colo. Med. Sch., Denver, 1976-85; pvt. practice specializing in psychiatry Englewood, Colo., 1985—; clin. prof. psychiatry U. Colo. Sch. Medicine, 1997—. Clin. instr. dept. psychology U. Colo., Boulder, 1985—, Denver U., 1985—. Author: Psychodynamic Psychotherapy of Children, 1987; contbr. articles to profl. jours. Mem. Nat. Assn. Christians & Jews. Named Tchr. of the Yr., Residents & Fellows Psychiatry U. Mich., 1971, Disting. Tchr., Child. Psychiatriy Fellows, U. Colo., 1985. Fellow Am. Psychiatric Assn., Am. Acad. Child and Adolescent Psychiatry. Avocations: fishing, skiing, woodworking. E-mail: papacop@qwest.net.

CORAM, DAVID JAMES, gaming industry professional; b. San Diego, Oct. 17, 1962; s. Thomas Harry and Joan Catherine (Reuter) C.; m. Irma Elizabeth Aquino, Jan. 14, 1989 (dec. July 1991); children: Catherine May, Corinna Briann, Carston James, Caitlin Kay; m. Corinna Kay Ward, May 6, 1995. AS with honors, Miramar Coll., 1989; grad. with honors, Southwestern Coll., 1986; BA in Bus. Adminstrn. summa cum laude, Am. Intercontinental U., BA in Human Resource Mgmt. summa cum laude. Computer oper. Cubic Data Sys., San Diego, 1981-83, Electronic Data Sys., San Diego, 1983-84; ct. svc. officer San Diego County Marshal, 1985-86, dep. marshal, 1986-2000, sheriff, 2000-01; regulatory compliance adminstr. Harrah's Rincon Casino, 2001—04; pres., CFO Eagle Country Gaming Cons. Nev. Corp., 2002—07, pres./CEO, 2004—07; regulatory compliance mgr. Pala Casino, 2004. Pres., CEO Coram Cons. Group, 1994—; owner franchise Fantastic Sams Hair Salon, 1998-2007; gen. mgr. Kla-Mo-Ya Casino Chiloqin, Oreg., 2006-07, Cahuilla Casino, 2007-08. Coach Temecula Valley Soccer Assn., 1987-2002; mediator San Diego Cmty. Mediation Ctr., 1990-2001; dir. planning devel., 1999-2000; coach S.W. Soccer Club, Temecula, Calif., 2002; mem. nominating com. Outstanding Young Women Am. Awarded Gold medal soccer Ariz. Police Olympics, 1990, 91, Silver medal, 1993, Marksmanship award San Diego Marshal, Outstanding Young Men Am. award, 1989; 2d pl. Mid. Weight San Diego Gold's Gym Classic, 1993, Bronze medal Bodybuilding Calif. Police Olympics, 1994. Mem. Calif. State Marshal's Assn. (dir. state bd. 1994), San Diego County Marshal's Assn. (parliamentarian 1988, dir. 1989-91, 93-94), San Diego County Marshal's Athletic Fedn. (dir. 1993-95), Nat. Physique Com. (contest judge). Republican. Avocations: golf, baseball, camping, computers, weightlifting. Office: Coram Cons Group 45620 Corte Montril Temecula CA 92592-1206 Business E-Mail: eaglecountrygamingconsultants@msn.com.

CORASH, MICHÈLE B., lawyer; b. May 6, 1945; BA, Mt. Holyoke Coll., 1967; JD cum laude, NYU, 1970. Legal advisor to chmn. FTC, 1970-72; dep. gen. counsel U.S. Dept. Energy, 1979; gen. counsel EPA, 1979-81; ptnr. Morrison & Foerster, San Francisco and L.A. Bd. editors Toxics Law Reporter; bd. advisors Jour. Environ. Law and Corporate Practice, Ecology Law Quarterly; mem. nat. editl. adv. bd. Prop 65 Clearingho. Bd. dirs. Calif. Counsel on Environ. and Econ. Balance, 1991—; mem. blue ribbon commn. Calif. Environ. Protection Agy. Unified Environ. Statute; mem. V.P. Bush Regulatory Task Force, 1981, mem. adv. council Environ. Curriculum Stanford Law Sch., bd. adv. Hastings West-Northwest Jour. Environmental Law & Practice. Named one of Best Lawyers in Am., Environ. Law, Corp. Counsel, Am. Lawyer, 2003, Top 50 Women Litigators in Calif., Daily Journal Extra, 2003, 100 Most Influential Lawyers in Calif., Daily Journal, 2002, 2005, Top 30 Women Litigators in Calif., 2002—05. Mem. ABA (mem. standing com. on environ. 1988-91, chair com. environ. crimes 1990), Inter-Pacific Bar Assn. (chair environ. law com.). Office: Morrison & Foerster 425 Market St San Francisco CA 94105-2482 Business E-Mail: mcorash@mofo.com.

CORBETT, ELLEN M., state legislator; b. Oakland, Calif., Dec. 31, 1954; c Ryan. Attended, Calif. State U., Hayward, 1971; BS in Polit. Sci., U. Calif., Davis, 1977; JD, McGeorge Sch. of Law, 1981. City councilwoman, 1991-1995 & mayor, 1995-1998, San Leandro, California; California State Assemblywoman, District 18, 1998-2004, member, Rules, Health, Housing Community Develop, Judiciary & Local Govt Committees, Select Committees on Aerospace Indust, Rural Econ Develop, Calif-Mex Affairs, Education & Technology, Sch Facilities Finance & Joint Committee on Rules, formerly, chair, Committee Revenue and Taxation, Committee on Judiciary, formerly, chair, Select Committees on Biotechnology and Earthquake Safety and Preparedness, formerly, California State Assembly; California State Senator, District 10, 2006-.Atty, formerly; fundraiser, board member San Leanardo Girls Inc; board member San Leanardo Cof C, California Conservatory Theater; advisor board member, United States Conf Mayors and the Nat League of Cities' Public Safety and Crime Prevention Steering Committee, formerly. Legislator of the Year, California Mobile home Residents; Chiropractors; California State Univ Program for Education and Rsch in Biotechnology; Alameda County Democratic Cent Committee; 2004 Friend of Public Education, Association California Sch Administrator. Democrat. Office: State Capitol Rm 5108 Sacramento CA 94248 also: Corbett Properties 220 Juana Ave San Leandro CA 94577 also: Dist 10 39155 Liberty St #F610 Fremont CA 94537 Office Phone: 510-794-3900. Office Fax: 510-794-3940. Business E-Mail: Senator.Corbett@senate.ca.gov.*

CORBETT, LUKE ROBINSON, lawyer; b. Pinehurst, NC, May 21, 1930; s. Paschal Butler and Delia Jane (McKenzie) C.; m. Joan Cole (div.); children: Steven, Rebecca, Laurie, Charles, Carolyn. AB in Polit. Sci., U. N.C., 1956, JD, 1959. Bar: Calif. 1959, U.S. Dist. Ct. (so. dist.) Calif. 1960. Assoc. Lindley, Scales & Patton, San Diego; ptnr. Scales, Patton, Ellsworth & Corbett, San Diego; shareholder, dir., pres. Lindley, Scales & Corbett and predecessor firm, San Diego; sr. counsel Butz, Dunn, DeSantis & Bingham, 2006—. 1st lt. USAF, 1951-55. Mem. ABA, San Diego County Bar Assn. (bd. dirs., treas., v.p. 1971-74), Am. Bar Found., San Diego County Bar Found. (bd. dirs.), State Bar Calif. (del., chmn. exec. com. conf. of dels. 1975-78), Am. Inns. of Ct. (master Louis F. Welch chpt. 1984), Assn. of Bus. Trial Lawyers (bd. dirs.). Office: Butz Dunn & DeSantis 101 W Broadway Ste 1700 San Diego CA 92101 Home: 3966 Pringle St San Diego CA 92103 Office Phone: 619-233-4777. Business E-Mail: lrcorbett@butzdunn.com.

CORBIN, ROSEMARY MACGOWAN, former mayor; b. Santa Cruz, Calif., Apr. 3, 1940; d. Frederick Patrick and Lorena Maude (Parr) MacGowan; m. Douglas Tenny Corbin, Apr. 6, 1968; children: Jeffrey, Diana. BA, San Francisco State U., 1961; MLS, U. Calif., Berkeley, 1966. Libr. Stanford (Calif.) U., 1966-68, Richmond (Calif.) Pub. Libr., 1968-69, Kaiser Found. Health Plan, Oakland, Calif., 1976-81, San Francisco Pub. Libr., 1981-82, U. Calif., Berkeley, 1982-83; mem. coun. City of Richmond, 1985-93, vice mayor, 1986-87, mayor, 1993—2001. Mem. Solid Waste Mgmt. Authority, 1985-2001, Contra Costa Hazardous Materials Commn., Martinez, Calif., 1987-2001, San Francisco Bay Conservation and Devel. Commn., 1994-2001; mem. League of Calif. Cities Environ. Affairs Com., 1994-2001; mem. energy and environ. com. U.S. Conf. Mayors and Nat. League of Cities, 1993-2001. Contbr. articles to profl. publs. Pres. Ujima Family Svcs.; chair Richmond Historic Preservation Com.; mem. Rosie the Riveter Trust Bd., San Francisco Bay Trail Bd.; bd. mem. Inst. for Local Govt. Mem. LWV, NOW, Nat. Women's Polit. Caucus, Calif. Libr. Assn., Sierra Club. Democrat. Avocations: reading, hiking, golf, gardening, quilting. Home: 114 Crest Ave Richmond CA 94801-4031

CORBIN, WILLIAM R., wood products executive; BS in Forest Products, U. Wash., 1964; MS in Forestry, Yale U., 1956. Cons. forest products, Seattle, 1970's; v.p. ops. Vancouver Plywood Co., Inc.; v.p. So. timber and wood products Zellerbach Corp., 1974; sr. v.p. timber and wood products, group pres.; exec. v.p. wood products Weyerhaeuser Co., 1992-95, 98—, exec. v.p. timberlands and distbn., 1995-98. Bd. dirs. Weyerhaeuser Can. Ltd.; mem. mgmt. bd. World TimerFund. Trustee, mem. exec. com. Weyerhaeuser Co. Found., mem. policy com.; mem. adv. bd. U. Wash. Sch. Bus. Adminstrn. and Coll. Forest Resources, charter mem. internat. adv. bd. Inst. Environment and Natural Resroce Rsch. and Policy; v.p., mem. exec. com. The Mountains to Sound Greenway Trust. Office: Weyerhaeuser PO Box 9777 Federal Way WA 98063-9777

CORBRIDGE, JAMES NOEL, JR., law educator; b. Mineola, NY, May 27, 1934; s. James Noel Sr. and Edna (Springer) C.; children: Loren, Stuart. AB, Brown U., 1955; LLB, Yale U., 1963. Assoc. Lord, Day & Lord, NYC, 1963-65; asst. prof. law U. Colo., Boulder, 1965-67, assoc. prof., 1967-73, prof., 1973—, v.p. student affairs, 1970-72, v.p. student and minority affairs, 1972-74, vice chancellor acad. affairs, 1974-77, interim vice chancellor acad. services, 1979-81, acting vice chancellor acad. affairs, 1986, chancellor, 1986—. Vis. scholar Inst. for Advanced Legal Studies U. London, 1977, 85, Univ. Linkoping, Sweden, 1985, 1997. Contbr. articles to profl. jours. Served to lt. (j.g.) USNR, 1957-60. Mem. Colo. Bar Assn., Boulder County Bar Assn., Internat. Assn. Water Lawyers, Internat. Water Resources Assn. Clubs: Boulder Country. Episcopalian. Avocations: golf, woodcarving, birdwatching. Home: 1635 Dilar Dr Grove OK 74344-5500 Office: U Colo PO Box 401 Boulder CO 80309-0401

CORCORAN, ANTHONY AUSTIN, union organizer, state senator; b. Bessboro, County Cork, Ireland, May 17, 1949; came to U.S., 1952; s. Patrick Joseph and Thelma Elizabeth (Gonda) C.; m. Jeannie Marie Merrick, Mar. 14, 1976; 1 child, Simon. Student, Goddard Coll., 1975-76, U. San Francisco, 1967-70. Mental health counselor State of Vt., Waterbury, 1973-76; dep. sheriff Lane County, Eugene, Oreg., 1980-84; welfare worker State of Oreg., Eugene, 1984-88; union organizer Oreg. Pub. Employees Union, Eugene, 1988—; mem. Oreg. Ho. of Reps., Salem, 1995-98, Oreg. Senate, Salem, 1998—. Bd. dirs. Coast Fork Learning Ctr., Cottage Grove, Oreg., 1985-87, Lane County Corrections Adv. Com., Eugene, 1983-94; coach, referee Kidsports and Cottage Grove Recreation, 1984-86; chair Lane Co. Dem. Platform Conv., 1991-93. Avocations: tennis, golf. Home: 34475 Kizer Creek Rd Cottage Grove OR 97424-9411 Office: Oreg Senate S-314 State Capitol Salem OR 97310-0001

CORCORAN, MAUREEN ELIZABETH, lawyer, director; b. Iowa City, Feb. 4, 1944; d. Joseph and Velma (Tobin) C. BA in English with honors, U. Iowa, 1966, MA in English, 1967; JD, Hastings Coll. of Law, San Francisco, 1979. Bar: Calif. 1979, D.C. 1988, U.S. Ct. Appeals (9th cir.), 1979, U.S. Dist. Ct. (no. dist.) Calif., 1979, U.S. Dist. Ct. (cen. dist.) Calif., 1979, US. Ct. Appeals (D.C. cir.) 1983. Assoc. Hassard Bonnington Rogers & Huber, San Francisco, 1979-81; spl. asst. to gen. counsel HHS, Washington, 1981-83; assoc. Weissburg & Aronson, San Francisco, 1983-84; gen. counsel U.S. Dept. Edn., Washington, 1984-86; ptnr. Pillsbury Winthrop LLP (and predecessor firms), San Francisco, 1987—; bd. dirs. Hastings Coll. Law U. Calif., San Francisco, 1993—2005, chmn., 1998-2000. Chmn. Managed Health Care Conf., 1989; mem. AIDS adv. com. Ctrs. for Disease Control, 1989-91; spkr. health law mtgs. Author: (book) Managed Care Contracting: Advising the Managed Care Organization, 1996; contbr. articles on health law to profl. jours. Mem. U.S. delegation to 1985 World Conf. to Review and Appraise Achievements of UN Decade for Women, Nairobi, Kenya, 1985; mem. Adminstrv. Conf. U.S., Washington, 1985. Mem. ABA (sect. health law), Calif. State Bar Assn., Am. Health Lawyers Assn. Office: Pillsbury Winthrop LLP Ste 1004 50 Fremont St San Francisco CA 94105

CORDILEONE, SALVATORE JOSEPH, bishop; b. San Diego, June 5, 1956; BA, Univ. San Diego, 1978; STB, Pontifical Gregorian Univ., Rome, 1981, JCL, 1987, JCD, 1989. Ordained priest Diocese of San Diego, 1982; parochial vicar La Mesa, Calif., 1982—85; sec. to bishop Diocese of San Diego, 1989—91; pastor Our Lady of

Guadeloupe parish, Calexio, Calif., 1991—95; official Supreme Tribunal of the Apostolic Signatura, Rome, 1995—2002; ordained bishop, 2002; aux. bishop Diocese of San Diego, 2002—09; bishop Diocese of Oakland, 2009—. Roman Catholic. Office: Diocese of Oakland 2900 Lakeshore Ave Oakland CA 94610-3697 Office Phone: 510-893-4711. Office Fax: 510-893-0945.*

CORDOVA, RICHARD D., hospital administrator; b. Montebello, Calif. married; 3 children. BBA, Calif. State U., LA, 1972; MBA, Pepperdine U., 1984. With Dept. Health Svcs., County of LA, 1973—91, assoc. hosp. adminstr. of ops. Olive View Med. Ctr., 1978—86, adminstr. Gen. Hosp. LA County (LAC/USC Med. Ctr.), 1986—91; with Dept. of Pub. Health, City and County of San Francisco, 1991—98, CEO San Francisco Gen. Hosp., 1991—97, exec. adminstr. Cmty. Health Network, 1997—98; chief ops. officer Kaiser Permanente Health Plan, So. Calif., 1999—2002, pres. So. Calif. Region, 2002—04; pres., COO Childrens Hosp. LA, 2005—. Founding mem. San Francisco Pub. Health Authority, 1996—98; mem. Coun. on Grad. Med. Edn., 1996—98; bd. dirs. Inst. Diversity in Health Mgmt. Recipient Top 10 Latinos in Healthcare, LatinoLeaders mag., 2004; named one of Top 100 Hispanic Leaders, Hispanic Bus. Mag., 2003. Mem.: Am. Coll. of Health Care Execs. (diplomat 1980—). Office: Childrens Hosp LA 4650 Sunset Blvd Los Angeles CA 90027

COREY, LAWRENCE, medical educator; b. Detroit, Feb. 14, 1947; s. Aaron Corey; m. Amy Helaine Glasser, June 22, 1969; children: Leslie, Jordon, Daniel. AB with high distinction, U. Mich., 1967, MD, 1971. Diplomate Am. Bd. Internal Medicine. Intern U. Mich. Med. Ctr. Hosps., Ann Arbor, 1971-72, jr. asst. resident, 1972-73; epidemic intelligence svc. officer Ctr. for Disease Control, Atlanta, 1973-75; sr. fellow in medicine dept. internal medicine U. Wash., Seattle, 1975-77; attending physician internal medicine U. Washington Children's Hosp. and Med. Ctr., Seattle, 1977—; asst. prof. depts. lab. medicine, microbiology, immunology U. Wash., Seattle, 1977-81, assoc. prof. depts. lab. medicine and microbiology, 1981-84, prof. depts. lab. medicine and microbiology, 1984—, head diagnostic virology div., dept. lab. medicine; head, clin. rsch. divsn. program in infectious diseases Fred Hutchinson Cancer Rsch. Ctr., Seattle. Co-dir. Vaccine and Infection Disease Inst., sr. v.p. Fred Hutchinson Rsch. Ctr., chair in med. virology, dept. laboratory med. U. Wash., prin. investigator HIV Vacccine Trials Network; cons. physician infectious diseases U. Wash. afiliated hosps., 1977—; chmn., co-chmn. course com. U. Wash., Seattle, 1986—; trustee-at-large U. Physicians, U. Wash., Seattle, 1992; acting dir. U. Wash. Ctr. for AIDS Rsch., 1989-90, head retrovirology core, 1989—; chmn. exec. com. clin. trials group NIAID AIDS, 1988-92; mem. program com. for 29th and 30th ICAAC, 1990-91; mem. subcom. IDSA/FDA guidlines for new anti-infective drugs, 1988-92; moderator panel on devel. of AIDS vaccines Inst. Medicine NAS, 1990, surrogate markers for licensing HIV compounds, 1989; mem. infectious diseases subspecialty com. Am. Coll. Physicians, 1988; mem. exec. com. Am. Venereal Disease Assn., 1988—; chmn. sci. adv. bd. Herpes Resource Ctr. Am. Social Health Assn., 1985—; mem. internat. bd. dirs. Internat. Soc. for Sexually Transmitted Disease Rsch., 1986-91; mem. bd. dirs. Am. Social Health Assn., 1986-90; cons. WHO, 1982. Author: (with others) Medical Microbiology: An Introduction to Infectious Diseases, 1984, Second Edition, 1990; editor: (with others) Medicine in a Changing Soc., Vol. I, 1972, Vol. II, 1977, Antiviral Chemotherapy: New Directions for Clinical Applications and Research, 1986, Second Edition, 1989, Third Edition, 1993, AIDS Dx/Rx, 1990; assoc. editor: Jour. Infectious Diseases, 1989—; editorial bd. numerous jours.; contbr. chpts. to books and articles to profl. jours. Recipient Spl. Svc. award Nat. Reyes Syndrome Found., 1983, Spl. Svc. award Nat. Insts. Allergy and Infectious Diseases, 1992, Pan Am. Soc. Clin. Virology award, Parran award, Am. Soc. for STD Rsch., U. Mich. Med. Sch. Disting. Alumnus award. Fellow Infectious Disease Soc. Am., Am. Coll. Physicians; mem. Internat. Immunocompromised Host Soc., Assn. Am. Physicians, Am. Soc. Clin. Investigation, Western Assn. Physicians, Western Soc. Clin. Investigation, Am. Fedn. Clin. Rsch. (councilor Western sect. 1978-81, nat. councilor 1982-83, nat. sec.-treas. 1983-86), Am. Venereal Diseases Assn. (exec. com. 1989—, Achievement award 1984), Acad. Clin. Lab. Physicians and Scientists, Am. Epidemiological Soc., Washington State Pediatric Soc. Office: Fred Hutchinson Cancer Rsch Ctr 1100 Fairview Ave N Campus Box 358080 PO Box 19024 Seattle WA 98109 Office Phone: 206-667-6770. Office Fax: 206-667-4411. Business E-Mail: lcorey@u.washington.edu.

CORK, LINDA KATHERINE, veterinary pathologist, educator; b. Texarkana, Tex., Dec. 14, 1936; d. Albert James and Martine Sessions (Buntyn) Collins; m. P.S. Cork Jr., Mar. 1955 (div. 1965); children: Robin E., Jerald W. BS, Tex. A&M U., 1969, DVM, 1970; PhD, Wash. State U., 1974. Diplomate Am. Coll. Vet. Pathologists. Fellow Wash. State U., Pullman, 1970-74; asst. prof. U. Ga., Athens, 1974-76, Johns Hopkins U., Balt., 1976-82, assoc. prof., 1982-88, assoc. dir. rsch. Alzheimer's Disease Rsch. Ctr., 1985-93, prof., 1988-93; prof., chmn. Dept. Comparative Medicine Stanford U., 1994—. Coun. mem. NIH div. Rsch. Resources, Bethesda, Md., 1985-89; adv. bd. Registry Comparative Pathology, Bethesda. Grantee Nat. Inst. on Aging, 1985-89, Nat. Inst. Health, 1986-91, 86-93, 87-92. Mem. Inst. Medicine, Am. Assn. Neuropathologists (chmn. June 1988), Am. Assn. Pathology, U.S.-Can. Acad. Pathology. Methodist. Avocation: music. Office: Stanford Univ Dept Comparative Medicine MSOB Bldg Stanford CA 94305-5415

CORMAN, EUGENE HAROLD (GENE CORMAN), motion picture producer; b. Detroit, Sept. 24, 1927; s. William and Anne (High) C.; m. Nan Chandler Morris, Sept. 4, 1955; children: Todd William, Craig Allan. BA, Stanford U., 1948. Vice-pres. Music Corp. Am., Beverly Hills, Calif., 1950-57; owner, operator Corman Co., Beverly Hills, 1957—; pres. Penelope Prodn. Inc., Los Angeles, 1965—, Chateau Prodn. Inc., Los Angeles, 1972—; v.p. 20th Century Fox TV, Beverly Hills; exec. v.p. 21st Century Film Corp. of Worldwide Prodn. Producer: The Big Red One, 1978-79, F.I.S.T, 1977-78. Bd. dirs. Fine Arts Commn. Beverly Hills. Recipient Emmy award for A Woman Called Golda, Cath. Christopher award for A Woman Called Golda Mem. Acad. Motion Picture Arts and Scis. (chmn. screening com. 2008-), LA County Mus. Art (patron), MOMA, Theta Delta Chi. Roman Catholic.

CORN, WANDA MARIE, fine arts educator; b. New Haven, Nov. 13, 1940; d. Keith M. and Lydia M. (Fox) Jones; m. Joseph J. Corn, July 27, 1963. BA, NYU, 1963, MA, 1965, PhD, 1974. Instr. art history Washington Sq. Coll., NYU, 1965—66; lectr. Mills Coll., Oakland, Calif., 1970, vis. asst. prof., 1971, asst. prof., 1972—77, assoc. prof., 1977—80, Stanford U., Calif., 1980—89, prof., 1989—. Lectr. U. Calif., Berkeley, 1970, vis. asst. prof., 76; vis. curator Fine Arts Mus., San Francisco, 1972, 73, 76, Mpls. Inst. Arts, 1983—84, Grant Wood travelling exhbn. to Whitney Mus. Am. Art, NYC, Art Inst. Chgo.; rsch. assoc. Smithsonian Instn., 1983—; chair dept. art Stanford U., 1989—91; acting dir. Stanford Mus., 1989—91; dir. Stanford Humanities Ctr., 1992—95; Clark prof. Williams Coll., 2004; Kress prof. Ctr. for Advanced Study in the Visual Arts, Nat. Gallery Art, 2006—07. Author: The Color of Mood, American Tonalism, 1880-1910, 1972, The Art of Andrew Wyeth, 1973, Grant Wood: The Regionalist Vision, 1983, The Great American Thing: Modern Art and National Identity, 1915-1935, 2000; exhibitions include Figge Art Mus., Davenport, Iowa, 2005, Tacoma Art Mus., 2006; contbr. articles to profl. jours. Commr. Smithsonian Am. Art Mus., 1988—95; bd. dirs. Terra Found. Am. Art, 1999—, Found. for Am. Art, 2002—. Recipient Graves award, 1974—75, Fleischman award for scholar excellence, 2006, CAA Disting. Tchg. of Art History award, 2007, Women's Caucus for Art Life Time Achievement award, 2007; grantee, Am. Coun. Learned Socs., 1982, 1986; Ford Found. fellow, 1966—70, Radcliffe Inst., 2003—04, Smithsonian fellow, 1978—79, Woodrow Wilson fellow, 1979—80, Stanford Humanities Ctr. fellow, 1982—83, Regents fellow, Smithsonian Instn., 1987, Phi Beta Kappa scholar, 1984—85. Mem.: Assn. Historians of Am. Art, Am. Studies Assn. (nat. coun. 1986—89), Women's Caucus for Art, Coll. Art Assn. (bd. dirs. 1970—73, 1980—84, program chmn. ann. meeting 1981, mem. numerous coms.). Office: Stanford U Dept Art and Art History Stanford CA 94305-2018 Business E-Mail: wcorn@stanford.edu.

CORNABY, KAY STERLING, lawyer, retired state senator; b. Spanish Fork, Utah, Jan. 14, 1936; s. Sterling A. and Hilda G. Cornaby; m. Linda Rasmussen, July 23, 1965; children: Alyse, Derek, Tara, Heather, Brandon. AB, Brigham Young U., 1960; postgrad. law, Heidelberg, Germany, 1961-63; JD, Harvard U., 1966. Bar: NY 1967, Utah 1969, U.S. Patent and Trademark Office 1967. Assoc. Brumbaugh, Graves, Donahue & Raymond, NYC, 1966-69; ptnr. Mallinckrodt & Cornaby, Salt Lake City, 1969-72; sole practice Salt Lake City, 1972-85; mem. Utah State Senate, 1977-91, majority leader, 1983-84; shareholder Jones, Waldo, Holbrook & McDonough, Salt Lake City, 1985—. Mem. Nat. Commn. on Uniform State Laws, 1988-93; mem. adv. bd. U. Mich. Ctr. for Study of Youth Policy, 1990-93; mem. Utah State Jud. Conduct Commn., 1983-91, chmn., 1984-85, Utah State Sentencing Commn., 2002-; bd. dirs. KUED-KUER Pub. TV and Radio, 1982-88, adv. bd., 1990, bd. dirs. Salt Lake Conv. and Visitors Bur., 1985—2006. Mem. N.Y. Bar Assn., Utah Bar Assn., Utah Harvard Alumni Assn. (pres. 1977-79), Harvard U. Law Sch. Alumni Assn. (pres. 1995—). Office: Jones Waldo Holbrook & McDonough Ste 1500 170 S Main St Salt Lake City UT 84101-1644

CORNELL, CHRIS (CHRISTOPHER JOHN CORNELL), singer, musician; b. Seattle, Wash., July 20, 1964; s. Ed and Karen (Cornell) Boyle; m. Susan Silver, Sept. 1990 (div. 2002); 1 child, Lillian Jean; m. Vicky Karayiannis, Mar. 2004; children: Toni, Christopher Nicholas. Musician Jones St. Band, Shemps, 1982-84; singer Soundgarden, 1984—97, Temple of the Dog, 1990, Audioslave, 2001—07. Singer: (albums with Soundgarden) Ultramega OK, 1988, Louder Than Love, 1989, Screaming Life/Fopp, 1990, Badmotorfinger, 1991, Superunknown, 1994, Down on the Upside, 1996, (albums with Temple of the Dog) Temple of the Dog, 1990, (albums with Audioslave) Audioslave, 2002, Out of Exile, 2005, Revelations, 2006, (solo albums) Euphoria Morning, 1999, Carry On, 2007, Scream, 2008; prodr.: (albums with Screaming Trees) Uncle Anesthesia, 1991; actor: (films) Singles, 1992. Recipient ASCAP Film & TV Music award, 2007. Office: c/o Suretone Records 2220 Colorado Ave Santa Monica CA 90404

CORNELL, ERIC ALLIN, physics professor; b. Palo Alto, Calif., 1961; s. Allin and Elizabeth (Greenberg) Cornell; children: Elixa, Sophia. BS in Physics with honors, Stanford U., 1985; PhD in Physics, MIT, 1990. Tchr. English as Fgn. Lang. Taichung YMCA, Taiwan, 1982; rsch. asst. Stanford (Calif.) U., 1982—85; tchg. fellow Harvard Ext. Sch., 1989; postdoctoral Rowland Inst., Cambridge, Mass., 1990; postdoctorate Joint Inst. Lab. Astrophysics, Boulder, Colo., 1990—92; asst. prof. adj. dept. physics U. Colo., Boulder, 1992—95; staff scientist Nat. Inst. Stds. and Tech., Boulder, 1992—; fellow JILA U. Colo and Nat. Inst. Stds. and Tech., Boulder, 1994—; prof. adj. dept. physics U. Colo., Boulder, 1995—. Contbr. over 30 articles to profl. jours.; patentee in field. Recipient Grad. fellowship, NSF, 1985—88, Undergrad. Rsch. award for Excellence, Firestone, 1985, Samuel Wesley Stratton award, 1995, Newcomb-Cleveland prize, 1995—96, Carl Zeiss award, 1996, Fritz London prize in low temperature physics, 1996, Gold medal, Dept. Commerce, 1996, Presdl. Early Career award in sci. and engring., 1996, I.I. Rabi prize in atomic, molecular and optical physics, Am. Phys. Soc., 1997, King Faisal Internat. prize in sci., 1997, Alan T. Waterman award, NSF, 1997, Benjamin Franklin Medal in Physics, 1999, The Nobel Prize in Physics, 2001. Fellow: Am. Phys. Soc., 1997, Optical Soc. of Am., 2000 (R.W. Wood Prize 1999), Am. Acad. Arts & Scis., 2005; mem.: Royal Netherlands Acad. of Arts & Sci. (Lorentz Medal, 1998), NAS, 2000. Office: Univ Colo JILA Campus Box 440 Boulder CO 80309-0440

CORNWALL, JOHN MICHAEL, physics professor, consultant; b. Denver, Aug. 19, 1934; s. Paul Bakewell and Dorothy (Zitkowski) Cornwall; m. Ingrid Linderos, Oct. 16, 1965. AB, Harvard U., 1956; MS, U. Denver, 1959; PhD, U. Calif., 1962. NSF postdoctoral fellow Calif. Inst. Tech., Pasadena, 1962-63; mem. Inst. Advanced Study, Princeton, NJ, 1963-65; prof. physics UCLA, 1965—. Vis. prof. Niels Bohr Inst., Copenhagen, 1968—69, Inst. Physique Nucléaire, Paris, 1973—74, MIT, 1974, 87, Rockefeller U., NYC, 1988; cons. Inst. Theoretical Physics, Santa Barbara, Calif., 1979—80; assoc. Ctr. Internat./Strategic Affairs UCLA, 1987—; dir.'s adv. com. Lawrence Livermore Labs., 1991—, chmn., 2002—07; mem. Def. Sci. Bd., 1992—93, mem. task force, 1996; chmn. external rev. com. accelerator oper. and technol. divsn. Los Alamos Nat. Labs., 1995—97, rev. com. advanced hydrodynamics facility, 2001—; adv. bd. Los Alamos Neutron Scattering Ctr., 2000—01; chmn. external rev. com. Ctr. Internat. Security and Arms Control Stanford U., 1996; adv. commn. Accelerator Prodn. Tritium Project, 1997—2000; prof. sci. and policy analysis RAND Grad. Sch., 1998—; sci. and tech. panel Def. Threat Reduction Agy., 2000—02; rev. com. Advanced Accelerator Applications, 2001—02; mem. Missile Def. Agy. Countermeasures White Team, 2001—; tech. adv. group Integrative Grad. Edn. Rsch. and Tng. program in pub. policy and nuc. threat U. Calif., 2003—; chmn. predictive sci. panel Nat. Nuc. Security Adminstrn., Dept. Energy, 2004—; program rev. panel Nat. Ignition Facility Lawrence Livermore Labs., 2005; mem. study group quantification of margins and uncertainties NAS, 2007—; chmn. Weapons Complex and Integration Directorate Review Com. Lawrence Livermore Nat. Lab., 2008—; cons. in field; chmn. Nuclear Weapon 21st Century US Nat. Security. Author: (with others) Academic Press Ency. of Science and Technology, Union of Concerned Scientists Report on Nat. Missile Def., other encys. and books; contbr. numerous articles to profl. jours. With US Army, 1956—58. Grantee Dept. Energy, NSF, NASA, Dept. Edn.; pre and postdoctoral fellow NSF, 1960-63, A.P. Sloan fellow, 1967-71. Fellow: AAAS, Am. Phys. Soc.; mem.: NY Acad. Sci., Am. Geophys. Union. Avocations: jogging, bicycling, golf, bridge. Office: UCLA Dept Physics & Astronomy Los Angeles CA 90095-0001 Business E-Mail: cornwall@physics.ucla.edu.

CORONITI, FERDINAND VINCENT, physics and astronomy professor; b. Boston, June 14, 1943; s. Samuel Charles and Ethel Marie (Havlik) C.; m. Patricia Ann Smith, Aug. 30, 1969; children: Evelyn Marie, Samuel Thomas. AB, Harvard U., 1965; PhD, U. Calif.-Berkeley, 1969. Rsch. physicist UCLA, 1967-70, asst. prof. physics, 1970-74, assoc. prof., 1974-78, prof. physics and astronomy, 1978—. Cons. TRW Systems Contbr. articles to sci. jours. NASA grantee, 1974, NSF grantee, 1974—. Fellow Am. Geophys. Union, Am. Phys. Soc.; mem. Am. Astron. Soc., Internat. Union Radiol. Sci. Home: 10475 Almayo Ave Los Angeles CA 90064-2301 Office: UCLA Dept Physics & Astronomy 405 Hilgard Ave Los Angeles CA 90095-1547 Office Phone: 310-825-3923. E-mail: coroniti@astro.ucla.edu.

COROTIS, ROSS BARRY, civil engineer, educator, academic administrator; b. Woodbury, NJ, Jan. 15, 1945; s. A. Charles and Hazel Laura (McCloskey) C.; m. Stephanie Michal Fuchs, Mar. 19, 1972; children: Benjamin Randall, Lindsay Sarah. SB, MIT, Cambridge, 1967, SM, 1968, PhD, 1971. Lic. profl. engr., Ill., Md., Colo., structural engr., Ill. Asst. prof. dept. civil engring. Northwestern U., Evanston, Ill., 1971-74, assoc. prof. dept. civil engring., 1975-79, prof. dept. civil engring., 1979-81, Johns Hopkins U., Balt., 1981-82, Hackerman prof., 1982-83, Hackerman prof., chmn. dept. civil engring., 1983-90, Hackerman prof., assoc. dean engring., 1990-94; dean Coll. Engring. and Applied Sci. U. Colo., Boulder, 1994-2001, Denver Bus. Challenge prof., 2001—. Mem. bldg. rsch. bd. Nat. Rsch. Coun., Washington, 1985-88; lectr. profl. confs. Editor in chief Internat. Jour. Structural Safety, 1991-2000; contbr. articles to profl. jours. Mem. Mayor's task force City of Balt. Constrn. Mgmt., 1985. Recipient Engring. Tchg. award Northwestern U., 1977, Disting. Engring. Alumnus award U. Colo. Coll. Engring. and Applied Scis., 2000, U. Colo. Boulder Faculty Assembly award, 2006; named Md. Engr. of Yr., Balt. Engrs. Week Coun., 1989; Rsch. grantee NSF, Nat. Bur. Stds., US Dept. Energy, 1973-96. Fellow: ASCE (chmn. safety bldgs. com. 1985—89, v.p. Md. chpt. 1987—88, pres. 1988—89, chmn. tech. adminstrv. com. structural safety and reliability 1988—92, chmn. probabilistic methods com. 1996—98, editor Jour. Engring. Mechanics 2004—, Walter L. Huber rsch. prize 1984, Civil Engr. of Yr. award Md. chpt. 1987, Outstanding Educator award Md. chpt 1992); mem.: NAE (natural disasters roundtable steering com. 2002—05, fin. and budget com. 2003—06, civil engring. sect. sec. 2003—06, nominating com. 2004, vice chair 2007—08, chmn. 2008—), Nat. Inst. Bldg. Scis. (mem. multihazard mitigation coun. 2002—, affiliate), Nat. Inst. Stds. and Tech. (bd. on assessment 1999, chair panel on bldg. and fire rsch. lab. 2002—07, chair 2008—), Am. Nat. Stds. Inst. (chmn. live loads com. 1978—84, Jefferson Sci. fellow 2007—08), Am. Concrete Inst. (chmn. structural safety com. 1986—88), Am. Soc. Engring. Edn. (mem. pub. policy com. 1998—2001, mem. deans exec. bd. 1998—2001), Internat. Assn. Structural Safety and Reliability (chair exec. bd. 1998—2001, Sr. Rsch. prize 2005). Office: U Colo Coll Engring & Applied Sci PO Box 428 Boulder CO 80309-0428 Home Phone: 303-449-1235; Office Phone: 303-735-0539.

CORRAO, LAUREN, broadcast executive; BA in Semiotics, Brown U. V.p., exec. prodr. MTV; v.p. comedy devel. Fox Broadcasting Co., v.p. alternative and late night devel.; exec. prodr. Touchstone TV; sr. v.p. original programming and devel. Comedy Central, 2002—05, exec. v.p. original programming and devel., 2005, pres. original programming and devel. Named one of The 100 Most Powerful Women in Entertainment, Hollywood Reporter, 2007. Office: Comedy Central 2049 Century Park E Ste 4000 Los Angeles CA 90067

CORREA, LOU, state legislator; m to Esther; children: Alex, Andres, Adan & Emilia. BA in Economics, Calif. State U., Fullerton; MBA, JD, UCLA. Bd member, Orange Co Community Develop Coun, currently; Orange Cty Bd Supervisors, District 1, formerly; California State Assemblyman, District 69, 1998-2004, chair, Committee Business and Professions, Public Employees, Retirement & Soc Security, Select Committees on Mobilehomes, formerly; member Appropriations, Banking & Fin, Insurance, Education, Consumer Protection, Governmental Efficiency & Econ Develop, Local Govt, Transportation, Veteran's Affairs, & Budget Committee., formerly; appointed member, California Small Bus Bd, formerly, California State Assembly; California State Senator, District 34, 2006-.Investment banker & real estate brocker, formerly; Taught, Rancho Santiago Cmty Col District, formerly; Bd member, Orange Cty Community Develop Council, California Small Bus, Orange Cty Boy Scouts. High Tech Legislator of the Year, America Electronics Association, Legislator of the Year, Peace Officers Research Association California, Golden State Mobile Home Owners League, California Coalition of Nurse Practitioners, California Sexual Assault Investigators Association, Crime Victims United of California, California Optometric Association, California Hispanic C of C & Boys and Girls Clubs of America, Orange County Area Council, Hunger Fighter Award, California Hunger Coalition, Superintendent's Bravo! Award, Santa Ana Unified Sch District. California State Bar; California Real Estate Bd. Democrat. Catholic. Office: Dist 34 2323 North Broadway Ste 245 Santa Ana CA 92706 Office Phone: 714-558-4400. Business E-Mail: Senator.Correa@senate.ca.gov.

CORRIGAN, CAROL A., state supreme court justice; b. Stockton, Calif., Aug. 16, 1948; d. Arthur Joseph and Genevieve Catherine (Green) C. BA, Holy Names Coll., 1970; postgrad., St. Louis U., 1970-72; JD, U. Calif., San Francisco, 1975. BAr: Calif. 1975, U.S. Dist. Ct. Calif. 1975. Dep. dist. atty. Office Dist. Atty. Alameda County, Oakland, Calif., 1975—85; adj. prof. law U. Calif. Hastings Coll. Law, San Francisco, 1981-87, 89, U. Calif., Berkeley, 1984-87, U. San Francisco, 1987—89; sr. dep. dist. atty. Office Dist. Atty. Alameda County, Oakland, 1985-87; mcpl. ct. judge Oakland, Piedmont and Emeryville Jud. Dist., Oakland, 1987-91; judge Alameda County Superior Ct, 1991-94; assoc. justice Calif. Ct. Appeals, 1994—2006, Calif. Supreme Ct., San Francisco, 2006—. Adj. prof. sociology and polit. sci. Holy Names Coll., Oakland, 1976-80; vis. prof. law U. Puget Sound Sch. Law, Tacoma, 1981; spl. cons. Pres.'s

Task Force on Victims of Crime, Washington, 1982, White House Conf. on Drug Free Am., 1988; mem. Pres.'s Commn. on Organized Crime, Washington, 1983-86; mem. faculty, cons. Nat. Inst. Trial Advocacy, South Bend, Ind., 1982—, Alaska Dept. Law, Fairbanks, 1983, Hawaii Dist. Atty. and Pub. Def.'s Office, Honolulu, 1981-83, Nat. Coll. Dist. Attys., Houston, 1984-87; trustee Holy Names Coll., 1987—. Author: Report Task Force on Victims of Crime, 1982, book chpts.; contbr. articles to profl. jours.; editor Point of View, 1981-84. Bd. dirs. Goodwill Industries of East Bay, Oakland, 1984-87, St. Vincent's Day Home, Oakland, 1984—; mem. adv. bd. St. Mary's Community Ctr. for Elderly, Oakland, 1985-87; trustee Holy Names Univ., Oakland, 1988—, chair, 1990-95. Mem. ABA, Calif. State Bar Assn., Alameda County Bar Assn., Asia Found. (advisor 1987), Calif. Dist. Attys. Assn. (bd. dirs.). Roman Catholic. Office: Calif Supreme Ct 350 McAllister St San Francisco CA 94102

CORRIGAN, JAMES JOHN, JR., pediatrician, dean, educator; b. Pitts., Aug. 28, 1935; BS, Juniata Coll., Huntingdon, Pa., 1957; MD, U. Pitts., 1961. Diplomate Am. Bd. Pediats. (hematology-oncology). Intern, then resident in pediat. U. Colo. Med. Ctr., 1961-64; trainee in pediat. hematology-oncology U. Ill. Med. Center, 1964-66; assoc. in pediat. Emory U. Med. Sch., 1966-67, asst. prof. Atlanta, 1967-71; mem. faculty U. Ariz. Coll. Medicine, Tucson, 1971-90, prof. pediat., 1974-90; chief sect. pediat. hematology-ongology, also dir. Mountain States Regional Hemophilia Ctr., U. Ariz., Tucson, 1978-90; chief of staff U. Med. Ctr. U. Ariz., Tucson, 1984-86; prof. pediat., vice dean for acad. affairs Tulane U. Sch. Medicine, New Orleans, 1990-93, interim dean, 1993-94, dean, 1994-2000, v.p., 2000—02, prof. emeritus pediat., 2002—; clin. prof. pediat. U. Ariz. Coll. Medicine, Ariz., 2003—. Assoc. editor Am. Jour. Diseases of Children, 1981-89, 90-93, interim editor, 1993; contbr. numerous papers to med. jours. Grantee NIH, Mountain States Regional Hemophilia Ctr., Ga. Heart Assn., GE, Am. Cancer Soc. Mem. Am. Acad. Pediatrics, Am. Soc. Hematology, Soc. Pediatric Rsch., Western Soc. Pediatric Rsch., Am. Heart Assn. (coun. thrombosis), Internat. Soc. Thrombosis and Haemostasis, Am. Pediatric Soc., World Fedn. Hemophilia, Pima County Med. Soc. (v.p., 1986—, pres. 1988—), Alpha Omega Alpha. Republican. Roman Catholic. Office: Univ Ariz Health Scis Ctr Dept Pediatrics 1501 N Campbell Ave Tucson AZ 85724 Business E-Mail: jcorrig@tulane.edu.

CORRIGAN, ROBERT ANTHONY, academic administrator; b. New London, Conn., Apr. 21, 1935; s. Anthony John and Rose Mary (Jengo) C.; m. Joyce D. Mobley, Jan. 12, 1975; children by previous marriage: Kathleen Marie, Anthony John, Robert Anthony; 1 stepdau., Erika Mobley. AB, Brown U., 1957; MA, U. Pa., 1959, PhD, 1967; LHD (hon.), Golden Gate U., 1995; DFA (hon.), Chung Yuan U., Taiwan, 2007; LLD (hon.), Obirin U., Japan, 2009; LHD, San Francisco U., 2009. Rschr. Phila. Hist. Commn., 1957—59; lectr. Am. civilization U. Gothenburg, Sweden, 1959-62, Bryn Mawr Coll., 1962-63, U. Pa., 1963-64; prof. U. Iowa, 1964-73; dean U. Mo., Kansas City, 1973-74; provost U. Md., 1974-79; chancellor U. Mass., Boston, 1979-88; pres. San Francisco State U., 1988—. Author: American Fiction and Verse, 1962, 2d edit., 1970, also articles, revs.; editor: Uncle Tom's Cabin, 1968. Vice chmn. Iowa City Human Rels. Commn., 1970-72, Gov.'s Commn. on Water Quality, 1983-84; chmn. Md. Com. Humanities, 1976-78, Assn. Urban Univs., 1988-92; mem. Howard County Commn. Arts, Md., 1976-79; bd. dir. John F. Kennedy Libr.; trustee San Francisco Econ. Devel. Corp., 1989-92, Adv. Coun. Calif. Acad. Scis., Calif. Hist. Soc., 1989-92; chmn., bd. dir. Calif. Compact, 1990—; mem. exec. com. Campus Compact, 1991—; chmn. Pres. Clinton's Steering Com. Coll. Pres. for Am. Reads and Am. Counts, 1996-2000. Smith-Mundt prof., 1959-60; Fulbright lectr., 1960-62; grantee Std. Oil Co. Found., 1968, NEH, 1969-74, Ford Found., 1969, Rockefeller Found., 72-75, Dept. State, 1977; recipient Clarkson Able Collins Jr. Maritime History award, 1956, Pa. Colonial Soc. Essay award, 1958, 59, William Lloyd Garrison award Mass. Ednl. Opportunity Assn., 1987, Cmty. Svc. award Anti-Defamation League, 2007; Disting. Urban Fellow Assn. Urban U., 1992. Mem. Am. Assn. Colls. and Univs. (chmn. 2006-07), San Francisco C. of C. (bd. dirs., chmn. 2006-08), San Francisco World Affairs Coun. (bd. dirs.), Pvt. Industry Coun. (bd. dirs.), Boston World Affairs Coun. (1983-88), Greater Boston C. of C. (v.p. 1987-89), Fulbright Alumni Assn. (bd. dirs. 1978-80), Univ. Club, St. Francis Yacht Club, Bankers Club, Commonwealth Club (bd. dirs. 1995-99), Phi Beta Kappa. Democrat. Office: San Francisco State U 1600 Holloway Ave San Francisco CA 94132-1722 Office Phone: 415-338-1381. Business E-Mail: corrigan@sfsu.edu.

CORRIGAN, WILFRED J., computer company executive; b. 1938; Divsn. dir. Motorola, Phoenix, 1962-68; pres. Fairchild Camera & Instrument, Sunnyvale, Calif., 1968-80; CEO LSI Logic Corp., Milpitas, Calif., 1980—2005, chmn., 1980—2005, non-exec chmn., 2005—. Bd. dir. Silicon Power Corp., FEI Co., Lucas Film Entertainment Co. Recipient Robert N. Noyce award, Semiconductor Industry Am., 1998. Fellow: London's City and Guild Inst., Imperial Coll., Royal Acad. Engring. Office: LSI Logic Corp 1621 Barber Ln Milpitas CA 95035

CORRY, DALILA BOUDJELLAL, internist, educator; b. El-Arrouch, Algeria, July 7, 1943; came to U.S., 1981; MD, U. Algiers, 1974. Diplomate in internal medicine and nephrology Am. Bd. Internal Medicine. Intern Hosp. Mustapha Algiers, 1972-73; resident Hosp. Tenon, Paris, 1975-79; fellow in nephrology UCLA, 1981-83; chief renal divsn. Olive View-UCLA Med. Ctr., Sylmar, Calif., 1983—; from asst. prof. to prof. clin. medicine UCLA, 1993, prof. clin. medicine, 2001—. Fellow Am. Heart Assn. Office: Olive View-UCLA Med Ctr Dept Medicine 2B182 14445 Olive View Dr Sylmar CA 91342-1437 Office Phone: 818-364-3205. Business E-Mail: dbcorry@ucla.edu.

CORTNER, HANNA JOAN, retired political scientist, researcher; b. Tacoma, Wash., May 9, 1945; d. Val and E. Irene Otteson; m. Richard Carroll Cortner, Nov. 14, 1970. BA in Polit. Sci. magna cum laude with distinction, U. Wash., 1967; MA in Govt., U. Ariz., 1969, PhD in Govt., 1973. Grad. tchg. and rsch. asst. dept. govt. U. Ariz., Tucson, 1967-70, rsch. assoc. Inst. Govt. Rsch., 1974-76, rsch. assoc. forest-watershed and landscape resources divsns. Sch. Renewable Natural Resources, 1975-82, adj. assoc. prof. Sch. Renewable Natural Resources, 1983-89; exec. asst. Pima County Bd. Suprs., 1985-86; adj. assoc. prof. renewable natural resources, assoc. rsch. scientist Water Resources Rsch. Ctr. U. Ariz., Tucson, 1988-89, prof., rsch. scientist Water Resources Rsch. Ctr., 1989-90, prof., rsch. scientist, dir. Water Resources Rsch. Ctr., 1990-96, prof., rsch. scientist Sch. Renewable Resources, 1997-2000; rsch. prof., assoc. dir. Ecol. Restoration Inst. No. Ariz. U., Flagstaff, 2001—04; ret. Program analyst USDA Forest Svc., Washington, 1979-80; vis. scholar Inst. Water Resources, Corps of Engrs., Ft. Belvoir, Va., 1986-87; com. arid lands AAAS, 1986-89; com. natural disasters NAS/NRC, 1988-91, com. on planning and remediation of irrigation-induced water quality impacts, 1994-95; rev. com. nat. forest planning Conservation Found., Washington, 1987-90; chair adv. com. renewable resources planning techs. for pub. lands Office of Tech. Assessment U.S. Congress, 1989-91; policy coun. Pinchot Inst. Conservation Studies, 1991-93, bd. dirs. 2005-; co-chair working party on evaluation of forest policies Internat. Union Forestry Rsch. Orgns., 1990-95, chair working party on forest instns. and forestry adminstrn., 1996; vice-chair Man and the Biosphere Program, Temperate Directorate, US Dept. State, 1991-96; cmtys. com. steering com., Am. Forest Congress, 1996-2004, rsch. com., 1996-97; sci. adv. com. Consortium for Environ. Risk Evaluation, 1996-97; cons. Greeley and Hansen, Cons. Engrs., US Army Corps Engrs., Ft. Belvoir, US Forest Svc., Washington, Portland, Oreg., Ogden, Utah. Assoc. editor Society and Natural Resources, 1992-94; book reviewer We. Polit. Sci. Quar., Am. Polit. Quar., Perspectives, Natural Resources Jour., Climatic Change, Society and Natural Resources, Jour. of Forestry, Environment; mem. editl. bd. Jour. Forest Planning, 1995—, Forest Policy and Econs., 1999-2002; co-author: The Politics of Ecosystem Management, 1999, George W. Bush's Healthy Forests, 2005; co-editor: The State and Nature, 2002; contbr. articles to profl. jours. Bd. dirs. Planned Parenthood So. Ariz., 1992-94, planning com., 1992, bd. devel. and evaluation com., 1994; bd. dirs. N.W. Homeowners Assn., 1982-83, v.p., 1983-84, pres., 1984; vice chmn., chmn. Pima County Bd. Adjustment Dist. 3, 1984; active Tucson Tomorrow, 1984-88; water quality subcom. Pima Assn. Govts., 1983-84, environ. planning adv. com., 1989-90, chmn., 1984, mem. Avra Valley task force, 1988-90; bd. dirs. So. Ariz. Water Resources Assn., 1984-86, 87-95, sec., 1987-89, mem. com. alignment and terminal storage, 1990-94, CAP com., 1988-92, chair, 1989-90, basinwide mgmt. com., 1983-86, chair, 1992-93; active Ariz. Interagy. Task Force on Fire and the Urban/Wildland Interface, 1990-92; wastewater mgmt. adv. com. Pima County, 1988-92, subcom. on effluent reuse Joint CWAC-WWAC, 1989-91, citizens water adv. com. Water Resources Plan Update Subcom., 1990-91; bd. dirs. Ctrl. Ariz. Water Conservation Dist., 1985-90, fin. com., 1987-88, spl. studies com., 1987-88, nominating com., 1987; mem. Colo. River Salinity Control, 1989-90; chair adv. com. Tucson Long Range Master Water Plan, 1988-89; water adv. com. City of Tucson, 1984. Travel grantee NSF/Soc. Am. Foresters; Rsch. grantee US Geol. Survey, US Army Corps of Engrs., USDA Forest Svc., Soil Conservation Svc., Utah State U., Four Corners Regional Commn., Office of Water Rsch. & Tech.; Sci. & Engring. fellow AAAS, 1986-87; recipient Copper Letter Appreciation cert. City of Tucson, 1985, 89, SAWARA award, 1989. Mem. Am. Water Resources Assn. (nat. award com. 1987-90, statues and bylaws com. 1989-90, tech. co-chair ann. meeting 1993), Am. Forests Assn. (forest policy ctr. adv. coun. 1991-95), Soc. Am. Foresters (task force on sustaining long-term forest health and productivity 1991-92, com. on forest policy 1994-96, sci. and tech. bd. 2001-04), Am. Polit. Sci. Assn., Western Polit. Sci. Assn. (com. on constrn. and bylaws 1976-80, chair 1977-79, exec. coun. 1980-83, com. on profl. devel. 1984-85, com. on status of women 1984-85), Nat. Fire Protection Assn. (tech. com. on forest and rural fire protection 1990-94), Phi Beta Kappa, AAUW (Flagstaff br. treas. 2008-). Democrat. Achievements include research in political and socioeconomic aspects of natural resources policy, administration, and planning, water resources management, ecosystem management, wildland fire policy and management. Home: 6064 E Mountain Oaks Flagstaff AZ 86004-7222 Personal E-mail: hannacortner@aol.com.

CORWIN, STANLEY JOEL, book publisher; b. NYC, Nov. 6, 1938; s. Seymour and Faye (Agress) C.; m. Donna Gelgur; children: Alexandra, Donna, Ellen. AB, Syracuse U., 1960. Dir. subsidiary rights, v.p. mktg. Prentice-Hall, Inc., Englewood Cliffs, NJ, 1960-68; v.p. internat. Grosset & Dunlap, Inc., NYC, 1968-75; founder, pres. Corwin Books, NYC, 1975; pres., pub. Pinnacle Books, Inc., LA, 1976-79; pres. Stan Corwin Prodns. Ltd., 1980—; pres., CEO Tudor Pub. Co., NYC and L.A., 1987-90. Lectr. Conf. World Affairs U. Colo., 1976, U. Denver, 1978, Calif. State U., Northridge, 1980, Learning Annex; participant Pubmart Seminar, NYC, 1977, UCLA, 1985, 93, 98; guest lectr. U. So. Calif., 1987—, iVillage Internet Chat Room, Bestseller Seminars, 1999—; columnist Buddhascape Internet Network; expert witness nat. media trials. Author: Where Words Were Born, 1977, How to Become a Best Selling Author, 1984, 3rd edit., 1999, The Creative Writer's Companion, 2001; contbr. articles L.A. Times, N.Y. Times, short stories to Signature mag. and Silent Voices Lit. mag.; prodr.: (films) Remo Williams-The Adventure Begins, 1986, (video) How to Golf with Jan Stephenson, 1987; exec. prodr.: The Elvis Files TV Show, 1991, The Marilyn Files, 1993; pub.: The Movie Script Libr., 1994. Mem. Pres. Carter's U.S. Com. on the UN, 1977. Served with AUS, 1960. Nat. prize winner short story contest Writers' Digest, 1966 Mem. Assn. Am. Pubs., PEN. Home and Office: 9309 Burton Way Beverly Hills CA 90210

CORY, WALLACE NEWELL, retired civil engineer; b. Olympia, Wash., Mar. 10, 1937; s. Henry Newell and Gladys Evelyn (Nixon) C.; m. Roberta Ruth Matthews, July 4, 1959; children: Steven Newell, Susan Evelyn Cory Carbon. BS in Forestry, Oreg. State U., 1958, BSCE, 1964; MSCE, Stanford U., 1965. Registered profl. engr., Idaho, Oreg. Asst. projects mgr. CH2 M/Hill, Boise, Idaho, 1965-70; environ. mgr. Boise Cascade Corp., 1970-78, dir. state govt. affairs, 1978-82; dir. indsl. group JUB Engrs., Boise, 1982-84; chief engr. Anchorage Water & Wastewater, 1984-90; dir. pub. works City of Caldwell, Idaho, 1990-92; prin. engr. Montgomery Watson, Pasadena, Calif., 1992-95; adminstr. Idaho Divsn. Environ. Quality, Boise, 1995-98; planning and assessment leader Alexandria Wastewater Project Chemonics Interntа., 1998-99. Precinct committeeman Idaho Rep. Com., Boise, 1968-72, region chmn., 1973-77. Capt. USAF, 1958-62. Fellow ASCE; mem. NSPE, Idaho Soc. Profl. Engrs. (pres. 1976-77, Young Engr. of Yr. award 1971), Air Pollution Control Assn. (chmn. Pacific N.W. sect. 1977-78), Idaho Assn. Commerce and Industry (chmn. environ. com. 1974-75). Avocations: hunting, fishing, shooting. Home: 7247 Cascade Dr Boise ID 83704-8635

COSBY, BILL, actor, television producer; b. Phila., July 12, 1937; s. William Henry and Anna C.; m. Camille Hanks, Jan. 25, 1964; children: Erika Ranee, Erinn Chalene, Ennis William (dec.), Ensa Camille, Evin Harrah. Student, Temple U.; MA, U. Mass., 1972, EdD, 1976; MusD (hon.), Berklee Coll. Music, 2004. Pres. Rhythm and Blues Hall of Fame, 1968—. Appeared in numerous night clubs, including The Gaslight, N.Y.C., Hungry I, San Francisco, Shoreham Hotel, Washington, Basin St. East, N.Y.C., Hilton, Las Vegas, Nev., Harrah's Lake Tahoe; guest appearances on numerous TV shows, including The Electric Co., 1971-72, Capt. Kangaroo, Touched by an Angel, 1997, 99, King of Queens, 1999, Everybody Loves Raymond, 1999, Becker, 1999, Tonight Show with Jay Leno, 2005, ABC News Nightline, 2005, Dr. Phil, 2005; co-star: TV show I Spy, 1965-68;star (TV show) The Team That Changed the World, 2005, Hey Hey Hey: Behind the Scenes of 'Fat Albert', 2004; star (TV series) The Bill Cosby Show, 1969-71, The New Bill Cosby Show, 1972-73, (host, voices) Fat Albert and the Cosby Kids, 1972-79, Cos, 1976, (host, voices) The New Fat Albert Show, 1979-82, The Cosby Show, 1984-92, The Cosby Mysteries, 1994-95, Cosby, 1996-2000; host, TV game show You Bet Your Life, 1992-93, Kids Say the Darndest Things, 1998-2000, Jack Paar "As I Was Saying...", 1997; interviewee 4 Little Girls (TV), 1997; exec. prodr. TV show A Different World, 1987-93, Here and Now, 1992-93; TV movies include I Spy Returns, 1994, The Bill Cosby Mystery Movies, 1994; recs. include: Revenge (Grammy award Nat. Acad. Performing Arts and Scis. 1967), To Russell, My Brother, With Whom I Slept, 1968 (Grammy award), Why Is There Air, 1965 (Grammy award), Wonderfulness, 1966 (Grammy award), It's True, It's True, Bill Cosby is a Very Funny Fellow...Right, 1963, I Started Out as a Child, 1964 (Grammy award), Reunion, 1982, Bill Cosby...Himself, 1983 (dir., prodr.), Those of You With or Without Children, You'll Understand, (jazz albums) Where You Lay Your Head, 1990, My Appreciation, 1991, Hello Friend: To Ennis With Love, 1997; films include Hickey and Boggs, 1972, Man and Boy, 1972, Uptown Saturday Night, 1974, Let's Do It Again, 1975, Mother, Jugs and Speed, 1976, A Piece of the Action, 1977, California Suite, 1978, (voice) Aesop's Fable, 1978, Devil and Max Devlin, 1979, Bill Cosby...Himself, 1985, Leonard: Part VI, 1987, Ghost Dad, 1990, The Meteor Man, 1993, Jack, 1996; exec. prodr., writer Fat Alber, 2004; co-exec. prodr., writer (TV series) Fatherhood, 2004; recipient 4 Emmy awards 1966, 67, 68, 69, 8 Grammy awards, named number 1 in comedy field Top Artists on Campus Poll (album sales) 1968; author: The Wit and Wisdom of Fat Albert, 1973, Bill Cosby's Personal Guide to Power Tennis, Fatherhood, 1986, Time Flies, 1988, Love and Marriage, 1989, Childhood, 1991. Served with USNR, 1956-60. Recipient Bob Hope Humanitarian award, Academy of Television Arts & Sciences, 2003; named to Hall of Fame, Acad. TV Arts and Scis., 1994, NAACP Image Awards Hall of Fame, 2007, Power 150, Ebony mag., 2008. Achievements include setting concert attendance record Radio City Music Hall, 1986.

COSMEZ, MARK H., II, electronics executive; BA in Chemistry, Calif. State U., Hayward, 1973, MB in Acctg., 1976. CPA Calif. Corp. contr. ShareBase Corp., 1988-94, The Software Toolworks, 1994-95; v.p. fin., CFO Internat. Microcomputer Software, Inc.; CFO Pacific Bell Pub. Comm.; v.p. fin., CFO Giga-tronics, 1997—. Office: Giga-tronics Inc 4650 Norris Canyon Rd San Ramon CA 94583-1320 Fax: 925-328-4700.

COSMIDES, LEDA, cognitive psychologist, educator; b. Phila., May 7, 1957; d. George James and Nasia (Murlas) Cosmides; m. John Tooby, May 16, 1979. AB in Biology, Harvard U., 1979, PhD in Psychology, 1985. Postdoctoral scholar Dept. of Psychology, Stanford (Calif.) U., 1985-89; fellow Ctr. for advanced Study in Behavioral Scis., Stanford, 1989-90; asst. prof. psychology U. Calif., Santa Barbara, 1991-94, assoc. prof. psychology, 1994, prof., co-dir. Ctr. for Evolutionary Psychology, 1994—. Editorial bd. Cognition, Paris, 1992—; editor: The Adapted Mind, 1992; contbr. articles to profl. jours. Recipient Prize for Behavioral Sci. Rsch. AAAS, 1988, Early Career award APA, 1993; Zentrum fur interdisziplinaire Forschung, U. Bielefeld, Germany fellow, 1991; Dir.'s Pioneer Award, NIH, 2005. Mem. Am. Psychol. Soc., Psychonomics Soc., Human Behavior and Evolution Soc. (governing bd. 1990-92). Achievements include establishing foundations of evolutionary psychology; cognitive adaptions for social exchange. Office: Univ of Calif Dept Psychology Rm 2213 Santa Barbara CA 93106-9660 Office Phone: 805-893-7107. E-mail: cosmides@psych.ucsb.edu.

COSS, DAVID, mayor; s. Ron and Millie Coss; m. Carol Rose Coss; children: Celedina, Dylan, Molly. BS, N.Mex. State U.; MS, So. Ill. U., 1981. Surface water scientist City of Santa Fe, mgr. environ. protection divsn., dir. pub. works dept., 1995—96, city mgr., 1996, environ. protection mgr. state land office, mem. city coun., 2002—06, mayor Santa Fe, 2006—. Mem. Regional Planning Authority, Buckman Direct (Water) Diversion Bd.; chmn. Water Conservation Com. Office: 200 Lincoln Santa Fe NM 87501 Office Phone: 505-955-6590. Office Fax: 505-955-6695. E-mail: mayor@santafenm.gov.

COSSINS, EDWIN ALBERT, biology professor, academic administrator; b. Havering, Eng., Feb. 28, 1937; came to Can., 1962; s. Albert Joseph and Elizabeth H. (Brown) C.; m. Lucille Jeannette Salt, Sept. 1, 1962; children: Diane Elizabeth (dec. 1995), Carolyn Jane. BSc, U. London, 1958, PhD, 1961, DSc, 1981. Rsch. assoc. Purdue U., Lafayette, Ind., 1961-62; from asst. prof. to prof. U. Alta., Edmonton, Can., 1962-96, acting head dept. botany, 1965-66, assoc. dean of sci., 1983-88, prof. biol. scis. emeritus, 1996—. Mem. grant selection panel Natural Scis. and Engring. Research Council, Ottawa, Ont., Can., 1974-77, 78-81 Author: (with others) Plant Biochemistry; 1980, 1988, Folates and Pterins, 1984. Assoc. editor Can. Jour. Botany, 1969-78. Contbr. numerous articles to profl. jours. Recipient Centennial medal Govt. of Can., 1967 Fellow Royal Soc. Can. (life); mem. Can. Soc. Plant Physiologists (western dir. 1968-70, pres. 1976-77, Gold medal 1998), Faculty Club (U. Alta.), Derrick Golf and Winter Club. Avocations: gardening, golf, curling, cross country skiing. Home: 99 Fairway Dr Edmonton AB Canada T6J 2C2 Business E-Mail: ecossins@ualberta.ca.

COSTA, GUSTAVO, Italian studies scholar; b. Rome, Mar. 21, 1930; came to U.S., 1961; s. Paolo and Ida (Antonangelo) C.; m. Natalia Zalessow, June 8, 1963; 1 child, Dora L. Maturità Classica, Liceo Virgilio, Rome, 1948; PhD cum laude, U. Rome, 1954. Asst. Istituto di Filosofia, Rome, 1957-60; instr. Italian Univ. de Lyon, Lyons, France, 1960-61, U. Calif., Berkeley, 1961-63, asst. prof., 1963-68, assoc. prof., 1968-72, prof., 1972-91, prof. emeritus, 1991—, chmn. dept. Italian, 1973-76, 88-91. Vis. prof. Scuola di Studi Superiori, Naples, 1984, Inst. Philosophy, U. Rome La Sapienza, 1992, Scuola Europea di Studi Avanzati, Naples, 2003, Inst. Italiano per Gli Studi Filosofici, Naples, 2004; reviewer RAI Corp., Rome, 1982-89 Author: La leggenda dei secoli d'oro nella lett. ital., 1972, Le antichità germaniche nella cultura italiana, 1977, Il sublime e la magia da Dante a Tasso, 1994, Vico e l'Europa: Contro la boria delle nazioni, 1996, Malebranche y Vico, 1998, Vico e l' Inquisizione, 1999, Malebranche e Roma, 2003, La Santa Sede di fronte a Locke, 2003, La Congregazione dell'Indice e Jonathan Swift, 2004, Thomas Burnet e la censura pontificia, 2006, Alle Origini Del Pensiero Economico-Sociale Moderno: La Congregazione Dell' Indice E Bernard Handeville, 2008; mem. editl. bd. Nouvelles de la République des Lettres, New Vico Studies, Cuadernos sobre Vico. Inst. Italiano Studi Storici fellow, Naples, Italy, 1954-57, Guggenheim Meml. Found. fellow, N.Y.C., 1977; grantee French Govt., Paris, 1956, Belgian Govt., Brussels, 1956, Targa d'oro Apulia, Italy, 1990. Mem. Am. Assn.

Tchrs. Italian, Am. Soc. for Eighteenth-Century Studies, Renaissance Soc. Am., Dante Soc. Am. Avocations: gardening, stamp collecting/philately. Office: U Calif Dept Italian Studies Berkeley CA 94720-2620 Office Phone: 510-642-5055.

COSTA, JIM, United States Representative from California; b. Fresno, Calif., Apr. 13, 1952; BA Polit. Sci., Calif. State U., Fresno, 1974. Spl. asst. to rep. John Krebs US Ho. of Reps., 1975-76; adminstrv. asst. assembly mem. Richard Lehman, 1976-78; mem. Calif. State Assembly, 1978-94; US senator from Calif., 1994—2002, chmn. agr. & water resources com., mem. housing & land use com., fin., investment and internat. trade com., transp. com.; CEO Costa Group, 2002—04; mem. US Congress from 20th Calif. dist., 2005—; mem. agriculture com., resources com., fgn. affairs com., internat. rels. com. Mem. Blue Dog Coalition; co-founder Congl. Water Caucus; co-founder, co-chair Congl. Victims' Rights Caucus; senate rep. Calif. World Trade Commn., 1995—2004; pres. Nat. Conf. State Legislatures, 2000—01. Bd. mem. Fresno-Madera Agy. on Aging. Mem.: Fresno Historical Soc. (bd. dirs.), Fresno County Farm Bur. (mem. steering com.), Fresno Cabrillo Club. Democrat. Roman Catholic. Office: US Ho Reps 1004 Longworth Ho Office Bldg Washington DC 20515-0520 Office Phone: 202-225-3341.

COSTA, WALTER HENRY, architect; b. Oakland, Calif., July 2, 1924; s. Walter H.F. and Mamie R. (Dunkle) C.; m. Jane Elisabeth Ledwich, Aug. 28, 1948; 1 dau., Laura. BA, U. Calif., Berkeley, 1948, MA, 1949. Designer Mario Corbett (architect), San Francisco, 1947-48, Ernst Born (architect), San Francisco, 1949; draftsman Milton Pflueger, San Francisco, 1950-51; designer Skidmore, Owings & Merrill, San Francisco, 1951-57, participating assoc., then assoc. prtnr., 1957-69, gen. prtnr., 1969-89, ret., 1990. Bd. dirs. East Bay Regional Park Dist., 1977-87, pres., 1984-85; mem. city council, Lafayette, Calif., 1972-76, mayor, 1973. Served with USSNR, 1943-46. Mem.: AIA. Home: 2130 Cactus Ct #2 Walnut Creek CA 94595

COSTANZO, PATRICK M., construction executive; Sr. v.p. for heavy constrn. Granite Constrn. Inc., Watsonville, Calif. Office: Granite Construction Company PO Box 50085 Watsonville CA 95077-5085

COSTA-ZALESSOW, NATALIA, foreign language educator; b. Kumanovo, Republic of Macedonia, Dec. 5, 1936; arrived in US, 1951; d. Alexander P. and Katarina (Duric) Z.; m. Gustavo Costa, June 8, 1963; 1 child, Dora. BA in Italian, U. Calif., Berkeley, 1959, MA in Italian, 1961, PhD in Romance Langs. and Lits., 1967. Tchg. asst. U. Calif., Berkeley, 1959—63; instr. Mills Coll., Oakland, Calif., 1963; asst. prof. San Francisco State U., 1968—74, assoc. prof., 1974—79, prof., 1979—98, coord. Italian program, 1992—98, prof. emerita, 1998—. Author: Scrittrici italiane dal XIII al XX secolo, Testi e critica, 1982; editor: Anima, 1997; transl.: Her Soul, 1996; contbr. articles to profl. jours. Sidney M. Ehrman scholar U. Calif., Berkeley, 1957-58, Gamma Phi Beta scholar U. Calif., Berkeley, 1958, Herbert H. Vaughan scholar U. Calif., Berkeley, 1959-60, Advanced Grad. Traveling fellow in romance lang. and lit. U. Calif., Berkeley, 1964-65. Mem. MLA, Am. Assn. Tchrs. Italian, Renaissance Soc. Am., Dante Soc. Am., Croatian Acad. Am. Roman Catholic. Avocations: swimming, hiking, opera. Office: San Francisco State U Dept Fgn Lang and Lit San Francisco CA 94132

COSTELLO, DONALD FREDRIC, lawyer; b. Tacoma, Nov. 8, 1948; s. Bernard Peter and Ada Harriet (Morrill) Costello; 1 child, Don Eric costello. BA, Calif. State U., San Francisco, 1970; JD, U. Calif., 1974. Bar: Calif. 1974, US Supreme Ct. 1980. Assoc. Frolik-Filley & Schey, San Francisco, 1974—78; mem. Salomon & Costello, 1978—80, Law Offices Donald F. Costello, Palo Alto, Calif., 1980—84, Santa Cruz, 1984—. Lectr. U. Santa Clara, 1980, Stanford U., 1983; faculty Hastings Coll. Trial Adv., 1988—; expert witness on med. malpractice law Calif. Senate Jud. Com., 1987. Mem. planning commn. City of Belmont, Calif., 1976. Mem.: ABA, Million Dollar Advocates Forum (pres.), Am. Soc. Law and Medicine, Calif. Trial Lawyers Assn. (contbr. articles to Forum), Assn. Trial Lawyers Am. Home: PO Box 2684 Del Mar CA 92014-5684 Office Phone: 831-425-5770. Office Fax: 831-430-9868.

COSTELLO, FRANCIS WILLIAM, lawyer; b. Cambridge, Mass., Apr. 16, 1946; s. Frank George and Anna M. (Sinnott) C. BA, Columbia U., 1968, JD, 1973. Bar: NY 1974, Calif. 1977. Assoc. Whitman & Ransom, NYC, 1973-74, Anderson, Mori & Rabinowitz, Tokyo, 1974—76, Whitman & Ransom, LA, 1976-82, ptnr., 1982-93, Whitman, Breed, Abbott & Morgan, LA, 1993-2000, Holland & Knight, LLP, LA, 2000—. Bd. dirs. Hattori Found., LA, Hamazawa Investment Co., LA, Japan Travel Bur. Internat., LA; dir. com. Holland & Knight, LLP., LA, Calif., 2001-04. Served with US Army, 1968-70, Vietnam. Mem. ABA, State Bar Calif., State Bar NY, LA County Bar Assn., Pumpkin Ridge Golf Club (Oreg.), Wilshire Country Club (LA), Calif. Club (LA). Home: 415 Knight Way La Canada Flintridge CA 91011-2725 Office Phone: 213-896-2452. Business E-Mail: fcostell@hklaw.com.

COSTELLO, JOHN H., III, business and marketing executive; b. Akron, Ohio, June 2, 1947; s. John H. Jr. and Lia Costello; children from previous marriage, Michael, Jeffrey, Matthew. BS in Indsl. Mgmt., Akron U., 1968; MBA, Mich. State U., 1970. Mktg. dir. Procter & Gamble Co., Cin., 1971—84; sr. v.p. Pepsi-Cola USA, Purchase, NY, 1984—86; exec. v.p. Wells, Rich, Greene, Inc., NYC, 1986—88; pres., chief oper. officer Nielsen Mktg. Rsch. U.S.A., Chgo., 1988—93; sr. exec. v.p. Sears, Roebuck & Co., Hoffman Estates, Ill., 1993—98; pres. Auto Nation, Inc., Ft. Lauderdale, Fla., 1999—; CEO MVP.com, 1999—2001; chief global mktg. officer Yahoo!, 2001—02; exec. v.p. mdse. and mktg. Home Depot, 2002—05; pres., consumer & retail Pay By Touch, 2006—07; pres., CEO Zounds, 2007—08. Sr. mktg. execs. panel Conf. Bd., NYC, 1985-87; industry speaker on bus. trends and issues, 1985—; bd. dirs. The Quaker Oats Co, Sears Can., Bombay Co. Mem. exec. bd. NE Ill. coun. Boy Scouts Am., 1993-97; trustee Multiple Sclerosis Soc., Chgo., 1990-2003, vice chmn., 1995—; bd. dirs. Nat. Multiple Sclerosis Soc., 1989—, chair fundraising, 1990-94, mem. exec. com., 1990-94, chair nominating com., 1996—; trustee Ga. Acquarium, 2006-. Named one of 30 Most Influential People in Mktg., Advt. Age, Top 10 Merchants, DSN Retailing Today; named to, Retail Mktg. Hall of Fame, 1997. Mem. Am. Film Inst. (trustee 2005—), Assn. Nat. Advertisers (bd. dirs. 1995—, vice chmn. 1998, chmn. 1999), Direct Ad Coun. (bd. dirs. 1996—, vice chmn. 1998, chmn. 2000), Direct Retail Advt. and Mktg. Assn. (bd. dirs. 1995—, Retail Mktg. Hall of Fame 1997), Econ. Club Chgo., Conway Farms Golf Club, Congl. Country Club. Episcopalian. Avocations: skiing, golf, travel, fly fishing. Home: 4716 Northside Dr NW Atlanta GA 30327-4552 Home Phone: 404-497-0628; Office Phone: 404-414-4414. Office Fax: 480-633-1165. Personal E-mail: jhc860@yahoo.com.

COSTELLO, RICHARD NEUMANN, advertising agency executive; b. Phila., Sept. 2, 1943; s. Joseph Neumann and Katherine Cash (Birkhead) C.; m. Ann M. Dodds, Oct. 24, 1970; children: Brian Stuart, Gregory Scott. BA in English, U. Pa., 1965, MBA in Mktg., 1967. Account mgr. Ogilvy & Mather, Inc., NYC, 1967-71; v.p. Rosenfeld, Sirowitz & Lawson, Inc., NYC, 1971-73; pres. Baron, Costello & Fine, Inc., NYC, 1973-77, TBWA Advt., Inc., NYC, 1977-95, internat. bd. dirs., 1984-96, COO, 1987-94; pres., CEO TBWA Chiat/Day-East, 1995-96; pres. universal strategic mktg. group Universal Studios Inc., Universal City, Calif., 1996-98; pres. New Bus. Initiatives Univ. Studios, Inc., 1998—. Mem. Young Pres.'s Orgn. Office: Universal Studios Inc 100 Universal City Plz Universal City CA 91608-1002

COSTERTON, JOHN WILLIAM FISHER, microbiologist; b. Vernon, BC, Can., July 21, 1934; married, 1955; 4 children. BA in Bacteriology and Immunology, U. BC, 1955, MS in Bacteriology and Immunology, 1956; PhD in Microbiology, U. Western Ont., Can., 1960. Prof. biology Baring Union Christian Coll., Punjab, India, 1960-62, dean sci., 1963-64; fellow bot. Cambridge (Eng.) U., 1965; prof. assoc. microbiology McGill U., 1966-67, asst. prof., 1968-70; assoc. prof. U. Calgary, Alta., Can., 1970-75, prof. microbiology Alta., 1975-93, indsl. rsch. chair biofilm microbiology Alta., 1985-93; dir. Ctr. Biofilm Engring. Mont. State U., Bozeman, 1993—. Author 2 books on biofilms; contbr. more than 750 articles to profl. jours. Recipient Sir Frederick Haultain prize, 1985, Isaac Walton Killam prize, 1990. Mem. Can. Soc. Microbiology, Am. Soc. Microbiology (Proter & Gamble award in Applied and Environ. Microbiology, 2005). Achievements include research in architecture of bacterial cell walls and including extracellular carbohydrate coats; originator of universal biofilm theory in microbiology; thought of as leader in the biofilm concept in engring., medicine, dentistry, and environ. sci. Office: Montana State Univ Ctr Biofilm Engineering 366 EPS Bldg PO Boc 173980 Bozeman MT 59717-3980

COSTIGAN, RICHARD, III, lawyer; BA, U. Ga., 1988; JD, Cumberland U., 1991. Prin. cons. budget com., appropriations com. Calif. State Assembly, chief of staff, office of minority leader, chief of staff Assembly Rep. Caucus; sr. advisor Manatt, Phelps & Phillips, LLP; v.p. govt. rels. and chief policy advocate Calif. C. of C.; dep. chief of staff, legis. affairs sec. to Gov. Arnold Schwarzenegger State of Calif., 2003—06; co-mng. dir. McKenna Long & Aldridge LLP, Sacramento, 2006; sr. dir., state govt. and affairs Manatt, Phelps & Phillips LLP, Sacramento, 2007—. Office: Manatt Phelps & Phillips LLP 1215 K St Ste 1900 Sacramento CA 95814 Office Phone: 916-552-2370. Office Fax: 916-552-2323. E-mail: rcostigan@manatt.com.

COTCHETT, JOSEPH WINTERS, lawyer, writer; b. Chgo., Jan. 6, 1939; s. Joseph Winters and Jean (Renaud) C.; children— Leslie F., Charles P., Rachael E., Quinn Carlyle, Camilla E. BS in Engring., Calif. Poly. Coll., 1960; LLB, U. Calif. Hastings Coll. Law, 1964. Bar: Calif. 1965, DC 1980. Ptnr. Cotchett, Pitre & McCarthy, Burlingame, Calif., 1965—. Mem. Calif. Jud. Coun., 1975-77, Calif. Commn. on Jud. Performance, 1985-89, Commn. 2020 Jud. Coun., 1991-94; select com. on jud. retirement, 1992—. Author: (with R. Cartwright) California Products Liability Actions, 1970, (with F. Haight) California Courtroom Evidence, 1972, (with A. Elkind) Federal Courtroom Evidence, 1976, (with Frank Rothman) Persuasive Opening Statements and Closing Arguments, 1988, (with Stephen Pizzo) The Ethics Gap, 1991, (with Gerald Uelmen) California Courtroom Evidence Foundations, 1993; contbr. articles to profl. jours. Chmn. San Mateo County Heart Assn., 1967; pres. San Mateo Boys and Girls Club, 1971; bd. dirs. U. Calif. Hastings Law Sch., 1981-93. With Intelligence Corps, U.S. Army, 1960-61; col. JAGC, USAR, ret. Named one of Top Ten Lawyers in Bay Area, San Francisco Chronicle, 2003. Fellow Am. Bar Found., Am. Bd. Trial Advs., Am. Coll. Trial Lawyers, Internat. Acad. Trial Lawyers, Internat. Soc. of Barristers, Nat. Bd. Trial Advs. (diplomate civil trial adv.), State Bar Calif. (gov. 1972-75). Clubs: Commonwealth, Press (San Francisco). Office: 840 Malcolm Rd Burlingame CA 94010-1401 also: 9454 Wilshire Blvd Ste 907 Beverly Hills CA 90202

COTE, BRIAN E., financial executive; b. Hartford, Conn. m. Mary E. Cote, May 3, 1981; children: Mary E., David A., Rebecca L. BA in Psychology, Calif. State U., Northridge; postgrad., UCLA. Mgr. strategic planning Am. Express Internat. Bank, Frankfurt, Fed. Republic Germany, 1981-84; 1st v.p., divsn. mgr. Security Pacific Nat. Bank, LA, 1985-90; CFO, v.p. fin. and adminstrn. CATS, Ontario, Calif., 1990-94; fin. exec. WesCorp FCU, San Dimas, Calif., 1994; v.p., CFO DiTech Funding, 1998—99; CFO Kinecta Federal Credit Union, 1999—2004; exec. v.p., CFO Chinatrust Bank, 2004—06; exec. v.p., pres., CFO Downey Saving and Loan Assn. FA, 2006—. Republican. Avocation: competitive bicycle racing. Office: Downey Savings and Loan 3501 Jamboree Rd Newport Beach CA 92660

COTSAKOS, CHRISTOS MICHAEL, retired internet financial services company executive; b. Paterson, NJ, July 29, 1948; s. Michael John and Lillian (Scoulikas) C.; m. Hannah Batami Fogel, July 1, 1973; 1 child, Suzanne Renee. BA in Communications and Polit. Sci., William Paterson Coll., 1972; MBA, Pepperdine U., 1984. Tour guide Universal Studios, Burbank, Calif., 1973; courier Fed. Express Corp., Burbank, 1973-74, sales rep. Long Beach, Calif., 1974, sta. mgr. San Jose, Calif., 1974, we. dist. mgr., 1974, region engring. mgr. Denver, 1975, mng. dir. Chgo., 1975-80, v.p. Sacramento, 1980-92; pres., COO Nielsen, Europe, Middle East, Africa, 1992-93; pres., CEO Nielsen Internat., 1993-95; pres., co-CEO, COO, dir. A.C. Nielsen, Inc., 1995-96; CEO, chmn. E*TRADE Group, Inc., Palo Alto, Calif., 1996—2003. Instr. Consumers River Coll., Placerville, Calif., 1985-86; bd. dirs. Airlifeline, Sacramento, Nat. Processing, Inc., Louisville, Forté Software, Inc., Oakland, 4th Comms. Network, San Jose, Datacard, Mpls. Author: (book) It's Your Money: The E*Trade Step by Step Guide to Online Investing, 2000. Served as sgt. U.S. Army, 1967-70, Vietnam. Decorated Bronze Star, 1967, Purple Heart, 1967. Mem. World Econ Forum (Davos, Switzerland), Sutter Club, Comstock Club.

COTSEN, LLOYD E., retired consumer products company executive; b. Feb. 25, 1929; m. Margit Cotsen. Grad., Princeton U., 1950; MBA, Harvard U., 1957. With Neutrogena Corp. (formerly Natone), 1957—95; pres. Neutrogena Corp., 1967—95, CEO, 1982—95, chmn., 1991—95; pres. Cotsen Mgmt. Corp., LA, 1994—. Mem. bd. trustees J. Paul Getty Trust, 2002—. Avocation: Collector of world-wide folk art.

COTTAM, KEITH M., librarian, educator, administrator; b. St. George, Utah, Feb. 13, 1941; s. Von Bunker and Adrene (McArthur) Cottam; m. Laurel Springer, June 16, 1961 (div. Feb. 4, 2000); children: Mark Patrick, Lisa Diane, Andrea Jill, Brian Lowell, Heather Dawn; m. Mary Bultena Albertson, Oct. 5, 2001. BS, Utah State U., 1963; MLS, Pratt Inst., 1965. Trainee Bklyn. Pub. Libr., 1963—65, asst. instr. reading improvement program, 1964—65, adult services libr., 1965; asst. social scis. libr., instr. So. Ill. U., Edwardsville, 1965—67; head, social sci. libr., instr. asst. prof. Social Scis. Libr., Brigham Young U., Provo, Utah, 1967—72; supr., inst. Libr. Technician Program Brigham Young U., Provo, Utah, 1969—72; head undergrad. libr., assoc. prof. U. Tenn., Knoxville, 1972—75, asst. dir. librs., assoc. prof., 1975—77; asst. dir. for pub. svcs. and employee rels. Vanderbilt U. Libr. (formerly Joint Univ. Librs.), Nashville, 1977—80, assoc. dir., 1980—82, acting dir., 1982—83; dir. libraries, prof. U. Wyo., Laramie, 1983—2000, dean univ. librs., 2001; assoc. dean outreach sch., dir. U. Wyo./Casper Coll. Ctr., Casper, 2001—05, emeritus prof., 2005—; interim dir. Casper Coll. Goodstein Libr., 2008—. Cons. tng. program Assn. Rsch. Librs., 1979—80; mem. Leadership Wyo. Tng. Program, 2002—03; bd. dirs. Casper Area C. of C., 2004—, pres., 2009—; bd. dirs. ServeWyo. (formerly Wyo. Commn. Nat. and Cmty. Svc.), 2003—09, Platte River Pkwy. Trust, 2004—, pres., 2008—. Author: Writer's Research handbook, 1977, 2d edit., 1978; editor Utah Libraries jour., 1971-72; mem. editl. bd. RQ jour., 1980-84; contbr. articles to profl. jours. Fellow Coun. Libr. Resources, 1975-76; sr. fellow UCLA Grad. Sch. Libr. Info. Sci., 1985-86. Mem.: ALA, Wyo. Libr. Assn. (pres. 1998—99), Phi Kappa Phi, Beta Phi Mu. Republican. Mem. Ch. of Jesus Christ of Latter-day Saints. Avocations: bicycling, racing and touring, free-lance writer, gardening. Business E-Mail: kcottam@uwyo.edu, kcottam@caspercollege.edu.

COTTER, JOHN BURLEY, ophthalmologist; b. Zanesville, Ohio, Sept. 14, 1946; s. John Burley and Evelyn Virginia (Ross) C.; m. Perrine Abauzit, Aug. 17, 1977; children: Neils John, Jeremy Pierre. BA, U. Kans., 1968; med. degree, U. Kans., Kansas City, 1968-72. Ophthalmology resident U. Mo., Kansas City, 1976-79; family practice Ashland Hosp., Kans., 1973-74; emergency room physician Providence-St. Margaret Hosp., Kansas City, Kans., 1974-75; family orthopedic practice Mountain Med. Assocs., Vail, Colo., 1975-76; ophthalmologist, pvt. practice Duluth, Minn., 1979-82; surgeon-chief out-patient clinic King Khaled Eye Specialist Hosp., Riyadh, Saudi Arabia, 1983-90, mem. exec. com., 1985-90; asst. clin. prof. King Saud U., Riyadh, Saudi Arabia, 1985-90; corneal splst., refractive surgeon in assn. Greensboro, NC, 1990—2006; corneal sugeon San Luis Obispo, Calif., 2006—. Seminar chmn. Status of Refractive Surgery, Riyadh, 1986; active Nat. Survey Eye Disease and Ea. Province Survey Coun., Saudi Arabia, 1984, 90; assoc. med. dir. NC Eye Bank, 2004—, adj. asst. prof. Dept. Family Med. U. NC Sch. Med., 2005—. Author: (booklet) Radial Keratotomy, 1986; contbr. articles to profl. jours. Rsch. grantee Contact Lens Assn. of Ophthalmology, 1981, Lasers Steering Com. King Khalid Eye Hosp. at Hosp. Hotel Dieu, Paris, 1988; ORBIS fellow Baylor U., Houston, 1982. Fellow Am. Acad. Ophthalmology; mem. AMA, Internat. Assn. Ocular Surgeons, Internat. Soc. Refractive Keratoplasty, Societe Francaise D'Ophthalmologie, Saudi Ophthalmologisl Soc., Am. Soc. Cataract and Refractive Surgery. Avocations: wind surfing, scuba diving, running, math games. Office: 1270 Peach St San Luis Obispo CA 93401 Office Phone: 805-541-1342. Personal E-mail: cotterjbc@yahoo.com.

COTTER, PATRICIA O'BRIEN, state supreme court justice; b. South Bend, Ind., 1950; m. Michael W. Cotter, 1979; 2 children. BS in Polit. Sci. and History with honors, We. Mich. U, 1972; JD, Notre Dame, 1977. Pvt. practice, South Bend, 1977—83, Great Falls, Mont., 1984; ptnr. Cotter & Cotter, Great Falls, 1985—2000; justice Mont. Supreme Ct., 2001—. Chair lawyer representatives Ninth Circuit Judicial Conf., 1996—98, exec. com., 1998; mem. commn. on judicial conduct Mont. Supreme Ct. Mem.: Mont. Trial Lawyers Assn. (chair amicus com. 1993—99, Public Service award 1992, 1998). Office: Rm 323 PO Box 203003 Helena MT 59620

COTTLE, GAIL ANN, retail executive; b. Yakima, Wash. Student, U. Wash. With Nordstrom, Inc., 1969—, corp. mdse. mgr. Brass Plum Jr. Women's Apparel, 1982-92, v.p., officer Jr. Women's Apparel divsn., 1985-92, exec. v.p. product devel. Seattle, 1992-2000; pres. Nordstrom Product Group, Seattle, 2000—. Trustee P.N. Ballet. Ford Found. grantee. Mem. Columbia Tower Club, Fashion Group Internat., Broadmoor Golf Club, Thunderbird Golf Club. Office: Nordstrom Inc 1617 6th Ave Seattle WA 98101-1742

COTTRELL-ADKINS, LEONE, opera company director; Artistic dir., founder Kitsap Peninsula Opera, Bremerton, Wash., 1992—. Office: Kitsap Peninsula Opera PO Box 1071 Bremerton WA 98337-0223 Office Phone: 360-377-8119.

COUGHENOUR, JOHN CLARE, federal judge; b. Pittsburg, Kans., July 27, 1941; s. Owren M. and Margaret E. (Widner) C.; m. Gwendolyn A. Kieffaber, June 1, 1963; children: Jeffrey, Douglas, Marta. BS, Kans. State Coll., 1963; JD, U. Iowa, 1966. Bar: Iowa 1963, D.C. 1963, U.S. Dist. Ct. (we. dist.) Wash. 1966. Ptnr. Bogle & Gates, Seattle, 1966-81; vis. asst. prof. law U. Washington, Seattle, 1970-73; judge U.S. Dist. Ct. (we. dist.) Wash., Seattle, 1981—2006, chief judge, 1997—2004, sr. judge, 2006—. Recipient William L. Dwyer Outstanding Jurist award, King County Bar Assn. Mem. Iowa State Bar Assn., Wash. State Bar Assn., Ninth Cir. Dist. Judges' Assn. (past pres.). Office: Dist Judge Ste 16229 700 Stewart St Seattle WA 98101-1271

COUGHLIN, NATALIE, Olympic swimmer; b. Vallejo, Calif., Aug. 23, 1982; d. Jim and Zennie Coughlin. Grad., U. Calif., Berkeley, 2004. Club swimmer Calif. Aquatics; mem. US Olympic Swim Team Olympic Games, Athens, Greece, 2004, Beijing, 2008. Co-author (with Michael Silver): Golden Girl: How Natalie Coughlin Fought Back, Challenged Conventional Wisdom, and Became America's Swimming Champion, 2006. Recipient James Sullivan award, AAU, 2001—02, 2005, Gold medal, 100m backstroke, World Championships, 2001, Gold medal, 400m freestyle relay, 2003, Gold medal, 800m freestyle relay, 2005, Gold medal, 100m freestyle, 100m backstroke, 100m butterfly, 800m freestyle relay, Pan Pacific Championships, 2002, Gold medal, 100m freestyle, all three relays, 2006, Gold medal, 100m backstroke, 800m freestyle relay; Silver medal,

400m freestyle, medley relay; Bronze medal 100m freestyle, Athens Olympic Games, 2004, Gold medal, 100m backstroke; Silver medal, 400m freestyle relay; Bronze medal, 200m individual medley, Beijing Olympic Games, 2008; named Nat. HS Swimmer of Yr., 1998, NCAA Swimmer of Yr., 2001—03, Female Swimmer of Yr., Swimming World Mag., 2002, Sportswoman of Yr., Women's Sports Found., 2003, Female Athlete of Yr., Sports Illus. on Campus, 2004; grantee Gold medal, 100m backstroke, 800m freestyle relay, World Championships, 2007. Achievements include winning 13 National Titles, 1998-2006; winning 11 NCAA Titles, University of California-Berkeley, 2001-04; holding the world record for the 100m backstroke, 2008. Office: c/o USA Swimming One Olympic Plz Colorado Springs CO 80909

COUGHLIN, SHAUN R., research scientist; BS, MS, MIT, 1976, PhD, 1981; MD, Harvard Med. Sch., 1982. Intern, resident Mass. Gen. Hosp., 1982—84; postdoctoral asst. rsch. cardiologist, clin. fellow Cardiovascular Rsch. Inst., U. Calif., San Francisco, 1984—86, dir., 1997—; asst. prof. U. Calif., San Francisco, 1986—91, assoc. prof., 1991—96, prof. medicine, 1996—, prof. cellular and molecular pharmacology, 1997—. Dir. Millennium Pharm., Inc. Recipient Jeffrey M. Hoeg award, Am. Heart Assn., 2000, Freedom to Discover award for Disting. Achievement in Cardiovascular Rsch., Bristol-Myers Squibb, 2004. Mem.: Inst. Medicine, NAS. Office Phone: 415-476-6174. Office Fax: 415-476-8173. Business E-Mail: coughlin@cvrimail.ucsf.edu.

COUGHRAN, WILLIAM M., JR., information technology executive, researcher; s. William M. Coughran, Sr. and Marianne Coughran; m. Bridget A. McGuire, Sept. 2, 1972; children: Megan J., Brendan W. BS, MS, Calif. Inst. Tech., 1975, Stanford U., 1977, PhD, 1980. V.p. Computing Scis. Rsch. Ctr., Bell Labs, Murray Hill, NJ, 1996—99; sr. v.p. Bell Labs Rsch. Silicon Valley, Palo Alto, Calif., 1998—2000; CEO, founder Entrisphere, Inc., Santa Clara, Calif., 2000—02; prin. Coughran Consulting, Palo Alto, 2003; v.p. engring. Google, Mountain View, Calif., 2003—. Bd. dirs. nSolutions, Inc., Santa Clara, Calif., Clearwell Sys. Inc. Office: Google Inc 1600 Amphitheatre Pkwy Mountain View CA 94043-1351 Personal E-mail: bill@coughran.net.

COUILLAUD, BERNARD J., executive; M in Physics & PhD, U. Bordeaux, France, 1968. Asst. prof. U. Bordeaux, France, 1968-72, assoc. prof., 1972-74, 80-82, prof., 1982-83; pres., CEO Coherent, Inc., Santa Clara, (Calif.) U., 1983—. Vis. prof. Stanford (Calif.) U., 1982-83. CNRS fellow, 1975-76, 79-80, vis. scholar Stanford U., 1980-82. Office: Coherent Inc PO Box 54980 Santa Clara CA 95056-0980 also: MS P41 PO Box 54980 Santa Clara CA 95056-0980

COUNTS, STANLEY THOMAS, retired military officer, retired electronics executive; b. Okfuskee County, Okla., July 3, 1926; s. Claud Curtley and Thelma (Thomas) C.; m. Bettejan Heft, Nov. 18, 1949; children:Ashlie Heft Jenkins. BS, U.S. Naval Acad., 1949; BS in Elec. Engring, U.S. Naval Postgrad. Sch., 1954, MS in Elec. Engring, 1955. Commd. ensign U.S. Navy, 1949, advanced through grades to rear adm., 1972; comdg. officer USS Bronstein, 1963-64; comdg. officer USS Towers, 1966-68; project mgr. NATO Seasparrow Surface Missile System, 1968-70; comdg. officer USS Chgo., 1970-71; dir. ships, weapons, electronics and asso. systems Office Asst. Sec. Def. for Installations and Logistics Washington, 1971-73; dep. comdr. Naval Ordnance Systems Command, 1973-74; designated Naval ordnance engr., 1974; comdr. (Naval Ordnance Systems Command), 1974; vice comdr. Naval Sea Systems Command, 1974-76; comdr. Cruiser-Destroyer Group 5 San Diego, 1976-78; ret., 1978; exec. Hughes Aircraft Co., Fullerton, Calif., 1979-89; ret., 1989; aerospace cons., chief exec. officer Bjan Enterprises, La Jolla, Calif., 1989-99. Chmn. Seasparrow steering com. NATO, 1973-76. Bd. dirs. San Diego chpt. Freedoms Found. at Valley Forge, 1992-94, 97-98; bd. dirs. Greater La Jolla Meals on Wheels, Inc., 1998—, pres., 2000-04 Decorated Legion of Merit with three oak leaf clusters, Bronze Star with combat distinguishing device. Mem. VFW, Surface Navy Assn. (life, bd. dirs. 1985-93), U.S. Naval Inst. (life), DAV (life), Ret. Officers Assn. (life), Navy League, USNA Alumni Assn. (life), Am. Legion, Rest and Aspiration Club San Diego. Home: 856 La Jolla Rancho Rd La Jolla CA 92037-7408 Personal E-mail: radmstc1949@aol.com.

COUPE, JAMES WARNICK, lawyer; b. Utica, NY, Mar. 3, 1949; s. J. Leo and Helen Carbery (Brennan) C.; m. Andrea Jean Schaaf, Nov. 26, 1983; children: Helen Shriver, Benjamin Warnick, Charlotte Fitzgerald. AB, Hamilton Coll., 1971; JD, Vanderbilt U., 1974. Bar: N.Y. 1975, Calif. 1981, Tenn. 1995, U.S. Dist. Ct. (so. and ea. dists.) N.Y. 1975, U.S. Ct. Appeals (2d cir.) 1975. Law clk. to judge U.S. Dist. Ct. (so. dist.) N.Y., NYC, 1974-75; assoc. Donovan, Leisure, Newton & Irvine, NYC, 1975-79, Phillips, Nizer, Benjamin, Krim & Ballon, NYC, 1979-81; sr. atty. Atlantic Richfield Co., LA, 1981-86; chief counsel Beverly Enterprises, Inc., Pasadena, Calif., 1986-88; gen. counsel Completion Bond Co., Inc., Century City, Calif., 1988-93; exec. Sullivan Curtis Monroe Ins. Brokers, Pasadena, Calif., 1993-95; v.p. bus. & legal affairs Cinema Completions Internat. Inc., LA, 1995-97; sr. v.p. bus. and legal affairs Cinema Completions Internat., 1997—2002; atty. pvt. practice, 2002—. Mem. L.A. County Bar Assn., State Bar Calif. Republican. Roman Catholic. Office: Law Offices of James W Coupe 777 S Figueroa St Ste 4700 47th Fl Los Angeles CA 90017 Office Phone: 213-406-1171. Business E-Mail: barrister74@msn.com.

COURT, LOIS, state legislator; m. Patrick Reynolds; children: Nathan, Brendan. BA in English, U. Colo., 1975; MA in Pub. Adminstrn., U. Colo. Grad. Sch. Pub. Affairs, 1996. Legis. aide & campaign mgr. State Rep. Andy Kerr; legis. aide State Rep. Dan Gibbs; campaign mgr. Doug Linkart, councilwoman Cathy Reynolds; dir. adminstrn., volunteerism & neighborhood response Office of Mayor Wellington Webb; mem. Dist. 6 Colo. House of Reps., Denver, 2008—. Instr. polit. sci. & Am. govt. Denver Cmty. Coll., Red Rocks Cmty. Coll. Co-founder & exec. dir. Balance Colo.; campaign mgr. Citizens Against 12. Mem.: City Club Denver (exec. dir.). Democrat. Office: State House 200 E Colfax Denver CO 80203 Office Phone: 303-866-2967. Business E-Mail: lois.court.house@state.co.us.*

COURT, STEVE, state legislator; b. July 21, 1950; m. Susan Court; 4 children. BS in Bus. Adminstrn., U. Mass, Lowell. Mem. From Dist. 18 Ariz. House of Reps., 2008—. Republican. Office: Capitol Complex 1700 W Washington Rm 118 Phoenix AZ 85007-2890 Office Phone: 602-926-4467. Office Fax: 602-417-3018. Business E-Mail: scourt@azleg.gov.

COURTNEY, PETER C., state legislator; b. Philadelphia, Pa., June 18, 1943; m to Margie Brenden; children: Peter, Sean & Adam. BA, U. RI, 1965, MPA, 1966; JD, Boston U., 1969. City councilman, Salem, Oreg., 1974-80; mem., Salem Mass. Transit Bd, 1979-80; mem. Dist. 33, Oreg. House of Reps., 1981-84 & 1989, former vice chmn. Legis. Rules & Reapportionment Com., former mem. Rules & Elec & Judiciary Committees, former Dem. Leader; mem. Dist. 17, Oreg. State Senate, 1999-2002, Asst. Minority Leader, 1999, chmn. Ways & Means Com., 1995, former vice chmn. Info Management & Technology & Judiciary Committees, former mem. Ed. Com., mem. Dist. 11, 2003-, Senate Pres., 2003-. Atty; asst to pres. & acting dir., Western Oreg. State Col; former polit. commentator, KPTV, Portland & KSLM Radio, Salem. YMCA (bd. dir., currently); United Way (past bd. dir.); Salem Boys & Girls Club. Democrat. Roman Catholic. Office: 900 Court St NE S-201 Salem OR 97301 Office Phone: 503-986-1600. Business E-Mail: sen.petercourtney@state.or.us.

COURTOIS, JEAN-PHILIPPE, computer software company executive; DECS, The Ecole Superieure de Commerce, Nice, France. Product mgr. Memsoft; channel sales rep. Microsoft France, 1984—86, So. Europe sales mgr., head mktg. dept., 1986—89, dep. gen. mgr., 1989—91, gen. mgr. sales and mktg., 1991—94, gen. mgr., 1994—98; v.p. Worldwide Customer Mktg., Microsoft Corp., Redmond, Wash., 1998—2000, sr. v.p., 2000—, pres., Europe, Mid. East & Africa, 2000—03, CEO, Microsoft Europe, Mid. East & Africa, 2003—05, sr. v.p., 2005—; pres. Microsoft Internat., 2005—. Office: Coeur Defense Tour B La Defense 4 100 Esplanade du Gen de Gau 92932 Paris France also: Microsoft Corp One Microsoft Way Redmond WA 98052-6399 Office Phone: 00 33 17099 10 00.

COURVILLE, ARTHUR F., lawyer; b. Jan. 5, 1959; BA, Stanford U., 1981; MBA, JD, U. Calif., 1987. Bar: Calif. 1987. Atty. Gibson, Dunn & Crutcher, 1987—92; with Symantec Corp., Cupertino, Calif., 1993—, dir. legal dept., 1994—97, dir. product mgmt. Internet tools bus. unit, 1997, dir. legal dept., 1998, v.p., gen. counsel, 1999—. Bd. dirs. Bus. Software Alliance; trustee Software Patent Inst. Office: Symantic Corp 20330 Stevens Creek Blvd Cupertino CA 95014-2132 Office Phone: 408-517-8000. Office Fax: 408-517-8186. E-mail: artcourv@symantec.com.

COUSER, WILLIAM GRIFFITH, nephrologist, academic administrator, educator; b. Lebanon, NH, July 11, 1939; s. Thomas Clifford and Winifred Priscilla (Ham) C. BA, Harvard U., 1961, MD, 1965; BMS, Dartmouth Med. Sch., 1963. Diplomate Am. Bd. Internal Medicine. Intern Moffitt Hosp./U. Calif. Med. Ctr., San Francisco, 1965-66, 66-67; resident Boston City Hosp., 1969-70; asst. prof. medicine U. Chgo., 1972-73; asst. prof. Boston U., 1972-77, assoc. prof., 1977-82; prof., head divsn. nephrology U. Wash., Seattle, 1982—2002, Belding Scribner prof. medicine, 1995—2004, affiliate prof. medicine, 2004—. Mem. sci. adv. bd. Kidney Found. Mass., Boston, 1974—82; mem. rsch. grant com. Nat. Kidney Found., NYC, 1981—86; mem. rev. bd. for nephrology VA, Washington, 1981—84; mem. exec. com. Coun. on Kidney in Cardiovasc. Disease, Am. Heart Assn., Dallas, 1982—85; mem. pathology A study sect. NIH, chmn., 1988—89; subsplty. bd. in nephrology Am. Bd. Internal Medicine, 1988—92; dir. George M. O'Brien Kidney Rsch. Ctr. U. Wash., 1993—2003. Co-editor: Immunologic Renal Diseases, 1997, 2d edit. 2001; contbr. numerous articles, chpts., abstracts to profl. publs.; mem. editl. bd. Kidney Internat., 1982-96, Am. Jour. Kidney Diseases, Am. Jour. Nephrology, Jour. Am. Soc. Nephrology, editor-in-chief, 2001-07. Served to capt. U.S. Army, 1967-69, Vietnam. Recipient Purple Heart, Bronze Star award, Rsch. Career Devel. award NIH, 1975-80, Method to Extend Rsch. in Time award, 1991-97; fellow Nat. Kidney Found., 1971, David Hume award, 2007, NIH, 1973; grantee, 1974-2004. Fellow: ACP, AAAS, Am. Heart Assn., Royal Coll. Physicians, Western Assn. Physicians (cons.), Am. Assn. Exptl. Pathology, Am. Soc. Nephrology (coun. 1991—98, pres. 1996), Am. Soc. Clin. Investigation (v.p. 1983—84), Am. Assn. Physicians, Internat. Soc. Nephrology (coun. 1999, v.p. 2001—03, pres.-elect 2003—05, pres. 2005—07, exec. com. mem. 2001—); mem.: Commn. Global Advancement Nephrology (head 2007—), Am. Soc. Nephrology. Mailing: 16050 169th Ave NE Woodinville WA 98072 Business E-Mail: wgc@u.washington.edu.

COUSINEAU, MICHAEL R., healthcare educator, researcher; m. Nancy Briare; children: Rebecca J., Patrick R. DPH, UCLA, 1987. Prof. U. South Calif., Ctr. Cmty. Health Studies, LA, 1995—, dir., 1995. Office: Univ South California Unit 80 1000 Fremont Dr Alhambra CA 91803 Business E-Mail: cousinea@usc.edu.

COVELL, RUTH MARIE, medical educator, academic administrator; b. San Francisco, Aug. 12, 1936; d. John Joseph and Mary Carolyn (Coles) Collins; m. James Wachob Covell, 1963 (div. 1972); 1 child, Stephen; m. Harold Joachim Simon, Jan. 4, 1973; 1 child, David. Student, U. Vienna, Austria, 1955-56; BA, Stanford U., 1958; MD, U. Chgo., 1962. Clin. prof. and assoc. dean sch. medicine U. Calif. San Diego, La Jolla, 1969—; dir. Acad. Geriatric Resource Ctr. Bd. dirs. Calif. Coun. Geriatrics and Gerontology, Beverly Found., Pasadena, Alzheimer's Family Ctr., San Diego, San Diego Epilepsy Soc., Devel. Svcs. Inc., San Ysidro Health Ctr., NIH SBIR Stude Sect. Geriatrics; cons. Agy. Health Care Po licy and Rsch.; chair Calif. Ctr. Access to Care Adv. Bd. Contbr. articles on health planning and quality of med. care to profl. jours. Mem. AMA (sect. on med. schs. governing coun.), Am. Health Svcs. Rsch., Assn. Tchrs. Preventive Medicine, Am. Pub. Health Assn., Assn. Am. Med. Colls. Group on Instl. Planning (chair 1973-74, sec. 1983-84), Phi Beta Kappa, Alpha Omega Alpha. Home: 1604 El Camino Del Teatro La Jolla CA 92037-6338 Office: U Calif San Diego Sch Medicine La Jolla CA 92093-0602

COVERT, MICHAEL HENRI, healthcare facility administrator; b. Chgo., Apr. 7, 1949; s. Leonard and Shirley Gladys (Jeffe) C.; m. Janie Sibley; children: Madison, J. Ben, Brienn. BS in Bus., Washington U., St. Louis, 1970, M in Health Adminstrn., 1972. Adminstrv. asst. St. Agnes Hosp., White Plains, N.Y., 1969; adminstrv. resident Hillcrest Med. Ctr., Tulsa, 1971-72, asst. adminstr., 1972-73, adminstr., 1973-80; exec. v.p., chief operating officer St. Francis Regional Med. Ctr., Wichita, Kans., 1980-85; CEO Ohio State Univ. Hosps., Columbus, 1985-88; sr. v.p. Physician Corp. of Am., Wichita, Kans., 1988-89; ind. mgmt. cons. Wichita, 1989-91; acting dir. community health Wichita/Sedgwick County, Wichita, Kans., 1991-92; pres., CEO Sarasota (Fla.) Meml. Hosp., 1992—2000; pres. Washington Hosp. Ctr., Washington, 2000—02; CEO, pres. Palomar Pomerado Health Sys., 2003—. Pres.-elect Franklin County Hosp. Coun., Columbus, 1987-88; adj. faculty Ohio State U., 1985—, Washington U., St. Louis, 1992—; bd. dirs. Voluntary Hosp. Am., Fla., 1998-00, exec. com., 1999-00. Bd. dirs. United Way Sarasota, 1993—2000, campaign chair, 1996—97, chair, 1998—99; bd. visitors Georgetown Sch. Nursing and Health Adminstrn., 2001—02; del. Am. Hosp. Assn., State of Fla., 1996. Fellow: Am. Coll. Healthcare Execs. (accreditation commn. grad. edn. in health care adminstrn. 1988—94, chair commn. 1991—94, regent west ctrl. Fla. ACHE 1997—2000); mem.: Healthcare Alumni Assn. (chair Washington U. 1994—95), D.C. Hosp. Assn. (treas. 2001—02), Assn. Cmty. Hosps. and Health Sys. Fla. (bd. dirs. 1995—97, chair 1998—99), Sarasota C. of C. (chair 1995—96), Univ. Club (v.p. 1996, chair-elect 1997—99, chair 1998—99). Office: Palomar Pomerado Health Sys 15255 Innovation Dr Ste 204 San Diego CA 92128

COVEY, MICHAEL J., forest products and real estate executive; b. Mont. B in Forestry, Univ. Mont.; MBA, Univ. Oreg. Various positions to exec. v.p. Plum Creek Timber Co., Atlanta, 1982—2005; pres., CEO Potlatch Corp., Spokane, Wash., 2006—07, chmn., pres., CEO, 2007—. Chmn. bd. Potlatch Corp., 2007—. Office: Potlatch Corp 601 W Riverside Ave Ste 1100 Spokane WA 99201 Office Phone: 509-835-1516. Office Fax: 509-835-1559.

COVEY, STEPHEN MERRILL RICHARDS, business consultant, speaker, author; b. Provo, Utah, Apr. 25, 1962; s. Stephen Richards and Sandra Renee (Merrill) C.; m. Jerolyn Shae Hutchings, Apr. 26, 1985; children: Stephen Hutchings, McKinlee Louise. BA magna cum laude, Brigham Young U., Provo, Utah, 1985; MBA, Harvard U., 1989. Leasing agt. Trammell Crow Co., Dallas, 1985-87; summer assoc. First Boston Corp., NYC, 1988; pres., CEO Covey Leadership Ctr. (now FranklinCovey Co.), Provo, 1989, also bd. dirs.; now co-chairman FranklinCovey Co. Author: Seven Habits of Highly Effective People, 1990, Principle-Centered Leadership, 1991, First Things First, 1994, Seven Habits of Highly Effective Families, 1997, Living the Seven Habits, 1999, Seven Habits of Highly Effective Teens, 1998, Beyond the Seven Habits, 2003, The Eighth Habit, 2004, translations into multiple languages, numerous audio books. Recipient Mc-Feely award for significant contributions to mgmt. and edn., Internat. Mgmt. Coun., Thomas More Coll. Medallion for svc. to humanity. Mem. Lds Ch. Avocations: travel, reading, sports. Office: FranklinCovey Co 2200 W Parkway Blvd Salt Lake City UT 84119 Office Phone: 801-975-1776. Office Fax: 801-817-8313.

COVIN, DAVID L., retired political science professor; b. Chgo., Oct. 3, 1940; s. Odell Jerry and Lela Jane (Clements) Johnson; m. Judy Bentinck Smith, May 7, 1965; children: Wendy, Holly. BA, U. Ill., 1962; MA, Colo. U., 1966; PhD, Wash. State U., 1970. From asst. prof. to assoc. prof. govt. and Pan African studies Calif. State U., Sacramento, 1970—79, prof., 1979—, assoc. dean gen. studies, 1972-74, acting dir. Pan African studies, 1979-81, dir. Pan African studies, 1986—2004, ret., 2006. Commr. Edn. Mgmt. and Evaluation Commn., 1977—81; trustee Congl. Black Caucus, Washington, 1977—92; adj. prof. Union Grad. Sch., 1979—82; mem. Criminal Justice Brain Trust; co-dir. Race and Democracy in Ams. Project, 1999—. Author: (novel) Brown Sky, 1987 (Best New Novel 1987 Calif. Black Faculty and Staff Assn. News), Axe: The Unified Black Movement in Brazil, 1978-2000, 2006, short stories; contbr. articles to profl. jours.; mem. bd. editors Jour. Pan African Studies. Active Sacramento Black Area Caucus, 1972—, Com. Fair Adminstrn. Justice, Sacramento, 1985—; edn. co-chmn. Sacramento Black Cmty. Activist Com., 1985—90; founder, bd. dirs. Black Sci. Resource Ctr.; bd. dirs. Women's Civic Improvement Ctr.; founder Sacramento Congress of African Peoples, 2002; founder, facilitator The Black Group, 2005—; co-chmn. Nat. Black Ind. Polit. Party, Sacramento, 1981—85. Recipient Cmty. Svc. award, Sacramento Area Black Caucus, 1976, Omega Psi Phi, 1982, All African People's Revolutionary Party, 1986, John L. Livingston Disting. Faculty Lecture award, 1992, medal of honor, Cooper Woodson Coll., 1998, Walter R. Bremond Cmty. Svc. award, Sacramento Black United Fund, 1998, Sacramento Observer medallion for edn., 2003, Cmty. Svc. award, Coll. Social Scis. and Interdisciplinary Studies, 2004; David Covin Cmty. Libr. Established, 2004. Mem.: Assn. Caribbean Studies, Western Polit. Sci. Assn. (mem. com. status blacks), Nat. Conf. Black Polit. Scientists (pres. 2003—05), Nat. Coun. Black Studies. Avocations: fishing, skiing, reading. Home: 4131 44th St Sacramento CA 95820-2829 Office: Calif State U 6000 J St Sacramento CA 95819-2605 Home Phone: 916-456-4981. Business E-Mail: covindl@csus.edu.

COVINGTON, GERMAINE WARD, municipal agency administrator; BS in Social Work, Ind. State U., 1966; MA in Urban Studies, Occidental Coll., 1972; postgrad., Harvard U., 1998. Budget analyst City of Seattle, Office Mgmt. and Budget, 1978-87; cmty. affairs mgr. City of Seattle, Engring. Dept., 1987-90, property and ct. svcs. mgr., 1990-91, dir. exec. mgmt., 1993-94, acting dir. drainage and wastewater utility, 1993-94; dep. chief staff City of Seattle, Mayor's Office, 1991-93; dir. office for civil rights City of Seattle, 1994—. Office: Seattle Office for Civil Rights 700 3rd Ave Ste 250 Seattle WA 98104-1827 Office Phone: 206-684-4500. E-mail: germaine.covington@seattle.gov.

COVITZ, CARL D., investment company executive, federal and state official; b. Boston, Mar. 31, 1939; s. Edward E. and Barbara (Matthews) C.; m. Aviva Habert, May 15, 1970; children: Philip, Marc. BS, Wharton Sch., U. Pa., 1960; MBA, Columbia U., 1962. Product mgr. Bristol-Myers Co., NYC, 1962-66; dir. mktg. Rheingold Breweries, NYC, 1966-68; nat. mktg. mgr. Can. Dry Corp., NYC, 1968-70; v.p. mktg., dir. corp. devel. ITT/Levitt & Sons, Lake Success, NY, 1970-73; owner, pres. Landmark Communities, Inc., Beverly Hills, Calif., 1973-87, pres., 1989-91; dep. sec. HUD, Washington, 1987-89; sec. bus., transp. and housing State of Calif., Sacramento, 1991-93; pres. Landmark Capital, Inc. (formerly Landmark Communities, Inc.), 1993—; chmn. bd. Century Housing Corp., 1995-2000. Bd. dirs. Arden Realty Group, chmn. acquisition com., Molina Healthcare, Inc., 2002-03; chmn. bd. Fed. Home Loan Bank, San Francisco, 1989-91; trustee SunAmerica Annuities Funds, 2000—, Phoenix Kane Anderson Mut. Funds, 2000-05 Exec. com. Presl. Commn. Cost Control and Efficiency (Grace Commn.); co-chmn. Dept. Def. Task Force; past chmn. ops. com. Mus. Contemporary Art LA; chmn. LA County Delinquency and Crime Commn.; dir. Columbia U. Grad. Bus. Sch. Alumni Assn. Mem. Young Pres. Orgn.; chmn. LA Housing Authority Commn., 1989-91. Mem.: Road Corporate Ctr. Global Risk and Security (bd. advisors 2007—), Washington Inst. Near East Policy (trustee 2007—). Office: 9595 Wilshire Blvd Beverly Hills CA 90212-2512 Office Phone: 310-273-7320. Business E-Mail: cdc@landmarkcapital.com.

COWAN, GEORGE ARTHUR, chemist, bank executive, director; b. Worcester, Mass., Feb. 15, 1920; s. Louis Abraham and Anna (Listic) C.; m. Helen Dunham, Sept. 7, 1946. BS, Worcester Poly.

Inst., 1941, DSc (hon.), 2002; DSc, Carnegie-Mellon U., Pitts., 1950, DSc and Tech. (hon.), 2002; DHL (hon.), Coll. Santa Fe, N.Mex., 2003. Rsch. asst. Princeton U., 1941-42, U. Chgo., 1942-45; mem. staff Columbia U., NYC, 1945; mem. staff, dir. rsch., sr. fellow Los Alamos Sci. Lab., N.Mex., 1945-46, 49-88, sr. fellow emeritus, 1988—; tchg. fellow Carnegie Mellon U., Pitts., 1946-49. Chmn. bd. dirs. Trinity Capital Corp., Los Alamos, 1974-95; pres. Santa Fe Inst., 1984-91; mem. The White House Sci. Coun., Washington, 1982-85, cons., 1985-90, Air Force Tech. Applications Ctr., 1952-88; chmn. Los Alamos Nat. Bank, 1965-94, dir., 1995-2006, dir. emeritus, 2006—. Contbr. sci. articles to profl. jours. Bd. dirs. Santa Fe Opera, 1964-79; treas. Santa Fe Opera Found., 1970-79; regent N.Mex. Inst. Tech. Socorro, 1972-75; pres. The Delle Found.; bd. dirs. Adv. Bd. Ctr. Neural Basis Cognition, Carnegie-Mellon U. Recipient E.O. Lawrence award, 1965, Disting. Scientist award N.Mex. Acad. Sci., 1975, Robert H. Goddard award Worcester Poly. Inst., 1984, Enrico Fermi award, Presdl. Citation, Dept. Energy, 1990; disting. fellow Santa Fe Inst., Los Alamos Nat. Lab. medal, 2003. Fellow AAAS, Am. Phys. Soc., Am. Acad. Arts and Scis.; mem. Am. Chem. Soc., N.Mex. Acad. Sci., Sigma Xi. Avocations: skiing, fly fishing. Home: 721 42nd St Los Alamos NM 87544-1804 Office: Santa Fe Inst 1399 Hyde Park Rd Santa Fe NM 87501-8943 Business E-Mail: gac@santafe.edu.

COWAN, STEPHEN A., lawyer; b. Balt., May 11, 1943; Student, U. Mich., 1961—62; AB with distinction, U. Calif., Berkeley, 1965, MBA cum laude, 1966; JD cum laude, Harvard U., 1969. Bar: Calif. 1970, D.C. 1970. Mng. ptnr. O'Melveny & Meyers, San Francisco; ptnr. Piper Rudnick LLP, 2004—. Co-author: Attorney's Guide of California Professional Corporations, 2d edit., 1973; contbr. articles to profl. jours. Angell scholar U. Mich. Mem. ABA (chmn. real estate specialization com. 1974-80, real property legal practice methods 1974-80, coun. mem. real property probate and trust sect. 1979-86, mem. standing com. lawyers title guaranty funds 1979-84, fin. officer 1986-92, divsn. dir. 1992-94, chair elect 1994-95, chair, 1995-96), Am. Coll. Real Estate Lawyers (bd. govs. 1983-85, 90-92), Anglo-Am. Real Property Inst., State Bar Calif. (chmn. real property law sect. 1979-81), Bar Assn. San Francisco (chair corps. com. 1974, bd. dirs. 1975-76, Barristers Club), Phi Beta Kappa, Beta Gamma Sigma. Office: Piper Rudnick LLP 333 Market St San Francisco CA 94105-2150 E-mail: stephen.cowan@piperrudnick.com.

COWAN, STUART MARSHALL, lawyer; b. Irvington, NJ, Mar. 20, 1932; s. Bernard Howard and Blanche (Hertz) C.; m. Marilyn R.C. Toepfer, Apr., 1961 (div. 1968); m. Eleanor Schmerel, June, 1953 (dec.); m. Jane Alison Averill, Feb. 24, 1974 (div. 1989); children: Fran Lori, Robin L., Michael L., Catherine R.L., Erika R.L., Bronwen P.; m. Victoria Yi, Nov. 11, 1989. BS in Econs., U. Pa., 1952; LLB, Rutgers U., 1955. Bar: N.J. 1957, Hawaii 1962, U.S. Supreme Ct. 1966. Atty. Greenstein & Cowan, Honolulu, 1961—70; counsel Cowan & Frey, Honolulu, 1970—89; pvt. practice, 1989—; of counsel Price Okamoto Himeno & Lum, 1993—. Arbitrator Fed. Mediation & Conciliation Svc., Honolulu, 1972—, Am. Arbitration Assn., Honolulu, 1968—, Hawaii Pub. Employee Rels. Bd., 1972—. Pres. Hawaii Epilepsy Soc., 1984-86, 2004—; acquisition chair Hawaii Family Support Ctr., 1995-97; bd. dirs. Hawaii Epilepsy Found. Lt. USN, 1955-61. Mem. ABA, ATLA (state committeeman for Hawaii 1965-69, bd. gov. 1972-78), Hawaii Bar Assn., Am. Judicature Soc., Consumer Lawyers Hawaii, Hawaii Trial Lawyers Assn. (v.p. 1972-78), Japan-Hawaii Lawyers Assn., Soc. Profls. in Dispute Resolution, Inter Pacific Bar Assn., Honolulu Symphony Soc. (bd. dirs. 1989-99), Royal Order of Kamehameha, Order of St. Stanislas, Sovereign Order of St. John of Jerusalem Knights Hospitallers, Mil. Order of Temple at Jerusalem, Queen's Club, Mil. Order of World Wars, Waikiki Yacht Club, St. Francis Yacht Club, Royal Hawaiian Ocean Racing Club, Hawaii Scottish Assn. (chieftain 1983-88), St. Andrews Soc., Caledonian Soc. (vice chieftain 1983-85), Honolulu Pipes and Drums (sec. treas. 1985-90), Celtic Pipes and Drums Honolulu, New Zealand Police Pipe Band, Masons (York Rite, Scottish Rite No. and So. jurisdictions), 33d deg., Aloha Shrine, Salaam Shrine, Grand Lodge Hawaii (grand orator 1992, 2007, sr. grand steward 1993, jr. grand warden 1994, sr. Grand Warden 1995 grand Master 1997), Red Cross of Constantine, Royal Order Scotland, Pearl Harbor (master 1971, 2001-04), Lodge Progres de l'Oceanie, Masonic Kilties NJ, Azure-Masada (#51 NJ), USS Missouri Meml. Assn., Nat. Sojourners (pres. 2005—06), Chinese Acacia Club, Royal Hawaiian Ocean Racing Club. US Coast Guard Aux., Navy League of U.S. (nat. dir. 2004-09). Jewish. Home: 47-339 Mapumapu Rd Kaneohe HI 96744-4922 Office: Ste 728 Ocean View Ctr 707 Richards St Honolulu HI 96813-4616 also: 47-653 Kamehameha Hwy # 202 Kaneohe HI 96744-4965 Office Phone: 808-538-1113. Personal E-mail: stuartgm@juno.com.

COWDERY, JOHN J., state legislator; b. Adrian, Mo., Feb. 11, 1930; son of George Edwin Cowdery & Opal Ashbaugh C; married 1951 to Juanita Neva Kinslow; children: Pamela, Ann, Thomas & Bill McHenry (stepsons). Legislator, Anchorage Caucus, formerly; chairman, Oil & Gas, Labor & Commerce Comns, Alaska House Representative, 83-85; spec project manager, Munic Alaska, formerly; Alaska State Representative, District 17, 97-01, chairman, Rules Committee, currently, vice chairman, Utility Restructuring, World Trade & State/Fed Relations Special Committees, formerly, member, Legislature Coun, Transportation Committee & Committee on Committees, formerly, Alaska House Representative; Alaska State Senator, District I, 2001-02; Alaska State Senator, District O, 2003-.Businessman, formerly; ret. Republican. Office: 716 W Fourth Ave Anchorage AK 99501-2133 Mailing: PO Box 230251 Anchorage AK 99523 Fax: 907-465-2069. E-mail: representative_john_cowdery@legis.state.ak.us.

COWELL, FULLER A., newspaper publisher; m. Christmas Cowell; 1 child, Alexis. BBA, U. Alaska Fairbanks. With McClatchy Newspapers, 1981-93; pub. Gavilan Newspapers, Calif., 1987-91, Anchorage Daily News, 1993—. Former pub. Cordova Times. Office: Anchorage Daily News PO Box 149001 Anchorage AK 99514-9001

COWENS, DAVID WILLIAM (DAVE COWENS), professional basketball coach and retired player, insurance executive; b. Newport, Ky., Oct. 25, 1948; m. Deborah Cmaylo; children: Meghan, Samantha. BS, Fla. State U., 1970. Basketball player Boston Celtics, 1970-80, head coach (68 games), 1978-79; player Milw. Bucks, 1983; owner, pres., dir. David W. Cowens Basketball Sch., Inc., Needham, Mass., 1972—; pres. Survivors Income Option, Inc. (life ins.), 1987—; head coach Charlotte Hornets, 1996-98; assist. coach Denver Nuggets, 1998-99, head coach, 1999-2000, Golden State Warriors, 2000—. Athletic dir. Regis Coll., Weston, Mass., 1981-82; coach Bay State, Continental Basketball Assn., 1984-85; chmn. bd. New Eng. Sport Mus. Named Rookie of Yr. 1970-71, NBA Most Valuable Player, 1972-73; mem. NBA All Star teams, yearly 1971-77, NBA Championship team, 1974, 76; honored by having his number retired; inducted into Naismith Meml. Basketball Hall of Fame, 1990. Office: Golden State Warriors 1011 Broadway Oakland CA 94607-4027 Home: 26 E Main St Norton MA 02766-2311

COWGILL, URSULA MOSER, biologist, educator, environmental consultant; b. Bern, Switzerland, Nov. 9, 1927; came to U.S., 1943, naturalized, 1945; d. John W. and Mara (Siegrist) Moser. AB, Hunter Coll., 1948; MS, Kans. State U., 1952; PhD, Iowa State U., 1956. Staff MIT, Lincoln Lab., Lexington, Mass., 1957-58; field work Doherty Found., Guatemala, 1958-60; research assoc. dept. biology Yale U., New Haven, 1960-68; prof. biology and anthropology U. Pitts., 1968-81; environ. scientist Dow Chem. Co., Midland, Mich., 1981-84, assoc. environ. cons., 1984-91; environ. cons., 1991—. Environ. measurements adv. com. Sci. Adv. Bd. EPA, 1976-80; Internat. Joint Commn., 1984-89. Contbr. articles to profl. jours. Trustee Carnegie Mus., Pitts., 1971-75. Grantee NSF 1960-78, Wenner Gren Found., 1965-66, Penrose fund Am. Philos. Soc., 1978; Sigma Xi grant-in-aid, 1965-66 Mem. AAAS, Am. Soc. Limnology and Oceanography, Internat. Soc. Theoretical and Applied Limnology. Achievements include research in ecology, biology and minerology. Home and Office: PO Box 1329 Carbondale CO 81623-1329 Office Phone: 970-963-2488. Personal E-mail: ucowgill@hughes.net. Business E-Mail: ucowgill@direcway.com.

COWLES, WILLIAM STACEY, newspaper publisher; b. Spokane, Wash., Aug. 31, 1960; s. William Hutchinson 3rd and Allison Stacey C.; m. Anne Cannon, June 24, 1989. BA in Econs., Yale Coll., 1982; MBA in Fin., Columbia U., 1986. With The Spokesman Rev., Spokane, Wash., 1989—, pres., pub., 1992—. Office: Cowles Publishing Co PO Box 2160 Spokane WA 99210-2160 Office Phone: 509-459-5217. Business E-Mail: staceyc@spokesman.com.

COWLEY, SAMUEL C., lawyer, transportation services executive; BA in Econs., Brigham Young U., Provo, Utah; JD, Cornell Law Sch. Bar: NY, Ariz. Atty. Reid & Priest, NYC, Snell & Wilmer LLP, Phoenix, 1990—2005; exec. v.p., gen. counsel Swift Transp. Co., Inc., Phoenix, 2005—, also dir., 2005—. Office: Swift Transp Co Inc 2200 S 75th Ave Phoenix AZ 85043 Office Phone: 602-269-9700.

COX, CHARLES SHIPLEY, oceanography researcher, educator; b. Paia, Hawaii, Sept. 11, 1922; s. Joel Bean and Helen Clifford (Horton) C.; m. Maryruth Louise Melander, Dec. 23, 1951; children: Susan (dec.), Caroline, Valerie, Ginger, Joel. BS, Calif. Inst. Tech., 1944; PhD, U. Calif., San Diego, 1955. From asst. rschr. to prof. U. Calif., San Diego, 1955—. Rschr. in field. Fellow AAAS, NAS (Alexander Agassiz medal 2001), Am. Geophys. Union (Maurice Ewing medal 1992), Royal Astron. Soc. Democrat. Office: U Calif San Diego Scripps Inst Oceanography La Jolla CA 92093-0213 E-mail: cscox@ucsd.edu.

COX, CHERYL, Mayor, Chula Vista, California; d. John Willett; m. Greg Cox; children: Elizabeth, Emmie. MA in Polit. Sci., San Diego State U.; PhD in Edn., U. So. Calif. Former tchr., prin., & adminstr. Chula Vista Elem. Sch.; former pres. bd. dirs. Sharp Chula Vista Med. Ctr.; former asst. prof. Nat. Univ., La Jolla, Calif.; mayor City of Chula Vista, Calif., 2006—. Mem. Charter Review Commn., 2002, Urban Devel. Com., 2003—05, Ad Hoc Com. for Campaign Finance Reform; bd. trustees Chula Vista Elem. Sch. Dist., Nature Ctr. Recipient Kate Sessions Environ. award, San Diego Urban Corps., 2007, Leadership and Involvement award, Chula Vista C. of C., 2007, Trailblazer award, Calif. Women's Leadership Assn., 2008. Republican. Office: 276 Fourth Ave Chula Vista CA 91910 E-mail: cherylcox@chulavistaca.gov.*

COX, DAVID JACKSON, biochemistry professor; b. NYC, Dec. 22, 1934; s. Reavis and Rachel (Dunaway) C.; m. Joan M. Narbeth, Sept. 6, 1958 (dec. Oct. 8, 1982); children: Andrew Reavis, Matthew Bruce, Thomas Jackson; m. Tamara L. Compton, Nov. 26, 1983. BA, Wesleyan U., 1956; PhD, U. Pa., 1960. Instr. biochemistry U. Wash., 1960-63; asst. prof. chemistry U. Tex., 1963-67, assoc. prof., 1967-73; prof., head dept. biochemistry Kans. State U., 1973-89; prof. chemistry Ind. U./Purdue U., Ft. Wayne, 1989-2000, prof. emeritus, 2000—. Vis. prof. U. Va., 1970-71; dean arts scis. Ind. U./Purdue U., Ft. Wayne, 1989-96. NSF predoctoral fellow, 1956-59; NSF sr. postdoctoral fellow, 1970-71 Mem. Am. Soc. Biochemistry, Molecular Biology Soc., Am. Chem. Soc., Phi Beta Kappa, Sigma Xi. Democrat. Presbyterian. Home: 309 Crown Ln Bellingham WA 98229-5929 Personal E-mail: comcox@yahoo.com.

COX, DAVID R., geneticist, educator; BS Brown U.; MD, PhD Genetics, U. Washington; Res. Fell., U. Calif - San Francisco. Cert. Am. Bd. Pediatrics, Am. Bd. Med. Genetics. Mem. faculty U. Calif. San Francisco, 1980—93; prof. genetics, pediatrics sch. of medicine Stanford U., 1993—2000; co-dir. Stanford Human Genome Center, 1993—2000; co-founder, chief sci. officer Perlegen Sciences, Inc., Mountain View, Calif., 2000—. Mem.: Inst. Medicine (mem. Health Sciences Policy bd.). Office: Perlegen Sciences Inc 2021 Stierlin Ct Mountain View CA 94043 Office Phone: 650-625-4500. Office Fax: 650-625-4510.

COX, DONALD CLYDE, electrical engineering educator; b. Lincoln, Nebr., Nov. 22, 1937; s. Elvin Clyde and C. Gertrude (Thomas) C.; m. Mary Dale Alexander, Aug. 27, 1961; children: Bruce Dale, Earl Clyde. BS, U. Nebr., 1959, MS, 1960, DSc (hon.), 1983; PhD, Stanford U., 1968. Registered profl. engr., Ohio, Nebr. With Bell Tel. Labs., Holmdel, NJ, 1968-84, head radio and satellite systems rsch. dept., 1983-84; mgr. radio and satellite systems rsch. divsn. Bell Comm. Rsch., Red Bank, NJ, 1984-91, exec. dir. radio rsch. dept., 1991-93; prof. elec. engring. Stanford (Calif.) U., 1993—, Harald Trap Friis Prof. Engring., 1994—2008, dir. telecomms., 1993-99. Em. commns. U.S. nat. com. Internat. Union of Radio Sci.; participant enbanc hearing on Personal Comm. Sys., FCC, 1991; mem. rsch. visionary bd. Motorola Labs., 2002-03. Contbr. articles to profl. jours.; patentee in field. 1st lt. USAF, 1960-63. Recipient Guglielmo Marconi prize in Electromagnetic Waves Propagation, Inst. Internat. Comm., 1983, Alumni Achievement award U. Nebr., 2002; Johnson fellow, 1959-60. Fellow IEEE (Morris E. Leeds award 1985, Alexander Graham Bell medal 1993, Millenium medal 2000), AAAS, Bellcore 1991, Radio Club Am.; mem. NAE, Comm. Soc. of IEEE (Leonard G. Abraham Prize Paper award 1992, Comms. Mag. Prize Paper award 1990), Vehicular Tech. Soc. of IEEE (Paper of Yr. award 1983), Antennas and Propagation Soc. of IEEE (elected mem. adminstrn. com. 1986-88), Sigma Xi. Achievements include rsch. in wireless communication systems, cellular radio systems, radio propagation. Home: 924 Mears Ct Stanford CA 94305-1029 Office: Stanford U Dept Elec Engring Packard 361 Stanford CA 94305-9515 Home Phone: 650-813-1716; Office Phone: 650-723-5443. Business E-Mail: dcox@spark.stanford.edu.

COX, FRED B., software company executive; b. 1934; Founder Emulex, pres., CEO, 1988-90, chmn. bd. Founder, mgr. various cos. including Microdata (acquired by McDonnell Douglas Corp.); mktg. exec. IBM Corp. Office: 3535 Harbor Blvd Costa Mesa CA 92626

COX, JOSEPH WILLIAM, former academic administrator, education educator; b. Hagerstown, Md., May 26, 1937; s. Joseph F. and Ruth E. C.; m. Regina M. Bollinger, Aug. 17, 1963; children: Andrew, Matthew, Abigail. BA, U. Md., 1959, PhD, 1967; Doctor (hon.), Towson State U., 1990. Prof. dept. engring. & tech. mgmt. Portland State U.; successively instr., asst. prof., assoc. prof., prof. history Towson (Md.) State U., 1964-81, dean evening and summer programs, 1972-75, acting pres., 1978-79, v.p. acad. affairs and dean of univ., 1979-81; prof. history, v.p. acad. affairs. No. Ariz. U., Flagstaff, 1981-87; pres. So. Oregon U., Ashland, 1987-94; chancellor Oreg. Univ. Sys., Eugene, 1994—2002, Disting. Pub. Svc. prof. Author: Champion of Southern Federalism: Robert Goodloe Harper of South Carolina, 1972, The Early National Experience: The Army Corps of Engineers, 1783-1812, 1979; mem. bd. editors Md. Hist. Mag., 1979-89; columnist So. Oreg. Hist. Mag., 1989-94; contbr. articles to profl. jours. Bd. dirs. Oreg. Hist. Soc., Oreg. Shakespearean Festival, 1989-95, So. Oreg. Econ. Devel. Bd., 1988-94, Jackson/Josephine Co., Western Bank, 1993-97, Portland Ctr. Stage, 1999. Mem. AAUP, Am. Assn. Higher Edn., Am. Assn. State Colls. and Univs., Phi Kappa Phi, Omicron Delta Kappa. Episcopalian. Home: 3845 Spring Blvd Eugene OR 97405

COX, PAT, artist; b. Pasadena, Calif., Mar. 6, 1921; d. Walter Melville and Mary Elizabeth (Frost) Boadway; m. Dale William Cox Jr., Feb. 19, 1946; children: Brian Philip, Dale William III, Gary Walter. BA, Mills Coll., 1943, MA, 1944. Graphic artist Pacific Manifolding Book Co., Emeryville, Calif., 1944-45; tchr. art to adults China Lake, Calif., 1957-63; tchr. art to children Peninsula Enrichment Program, Rancho Palos Verdes, Calif., 1965-67; graphic artist Western Magnum Corp., Hermosa Beach, Calif., 1970-80; tchr. art workshop Art at Your Fingertips, Rancho Palos Verdes, 1994-95. One-woman shows include Palos Verdes Art Ctr., Rancho Palos Verdes, Calif., 1977, 79, 83, 92, Thinking Eye Gallery, LA, 1988, Ventura Coll. Art Galleries, Calif., 1994, Mendenhall Gallery, Whittier Coll., Calif., 1995, The Gallery at Stevenson Union, So. Oreg. U., Ashland, 1996, Fresno Art Museum, Fresno, Calif., 1999; two person exhibits Laguna Art Mus., Laguna Beach, Calif., 1971, Creative Arts Gallery, Burbank, Calif., 1993; group exhibits include Long Beach Mus. Art, Art Rental Gallery, 1979, LA County Mus. Art, Art Rental Gallery, 1979, Palm Springs Mus. Art, 1980, Laguna Art Mus., 1981, N.Mex. Fine Arts Gallery, 1981, Pacific Grove Art Ctr., 1983, Phoenix Art Mus., 1983, Riverside Art Mus., 1985, Laguna Art Mus., 1986, Zanesville Art Ctr., Ohio, 1987, The Thinking Eye Gallery, LA, 1987, 89, Hippodrome Gallery, Long Beach, 1988, N.Mex. State Fine Arts Gallery, 1988, Newport Harbor Art Mus., 1988, Downey Mus. Art, 1990, 92, Internat. Contemporary Art Fair LA, 1986, 87, 88, 92, U. Tex. Health Sci. Ctr., 1992, Long Beach Arts, 1991, 92, 93, Young Aggressive Art Mus., Santa Ana, 1993, U. Ark. Fine Arts Gallery, Fayetteville, 1994, Laura Knott Art Gallery, Bradford Coll., Mass., 1994, Bridge Street Gallery, Big Fork, Mont., 1994, St. John's Coll. Art Gallery, Santa Fe, 1995, LA Harbor Coll., Calif., 1995, Walker Art Collection, Garnett, Kans., 1995, San Francisco State U., 1996, Coleman Gallery, Albuquerque, 1996, Loyola Law Sch., LA, 1996, San Bernardino County Mus., 1996, Prieto Gallery, Mills Coll., Oakland, Calif., 1996, U. So. Calif. Hillel Gallery, LA, 1997, The Stage Gall. Merrick, NY, 1999, Nabisco Gall., E. Hanover, NJ, 2000, California State U., LA, 2001, Pasadena Historical Mus. Gallery, Calif., 2002, Schneider Mus. Art So. Oreg. U., Ashland, Oreg., 2003, Bioloa U., La Miranda, Calif., 2006, Albuquerque Mus Art., 2007, Sidney and Berne Davis Art Ctr., Ft. Myers, Fla., 2008. Trustee LA Art Assn., 1972-79, Somarts Bay Gallery, San Francisco, 2004, LA World Airports Exhbm., 2005; bd. dirs. Palos Verdes Art Ctr., 1966-70, 87-89, chair exhbn. com., 1982-85, co-chair Art for Fun(d)s Sake, 1966; judge Tournament of Roses Assn., Pasadena, 1975; mem. strategic planning Palos Verdes Art Ctr., 1988; mem. Pacific Pl. Planning Commn. Percent for Art, San Pedro, Calif., 1989; juror Pasadena Soc. Artists, 1973, 81, Women Painters West, 1984-85; bd. dirs. Calif. State U. 2005; office term R.E. Holding Co., 2005-. Recipient Silver Pin award Palos Verdes Art Ctr., 1988, Calif. Gold Discovery award V.I.P. Jury Panel, LA, 1994. Mem. Nat. Watercolor Soc. (juror 1981, 1st v.p. 1980, 4th v.p. 1984), Nat. Mus. Women in the Arts, Oakland Mus. Art, Mus. Contemporary Art, LA County Mus. Art, Palos Verdes Cmty. Art Assn. (cert. appreciation 1981). Avocations: gardening, reading.

COX, PAUL ALAN, ethnobotanist, educator; b. Salt Lake City, Oct. 10, 1953; s. Leo A. and Rae (Gabbitas) C.; m. Barbara Ann Wilson, May 21, 1975; children: Emily Ann, Paul Matthew, Mary Elisabeth, Hillary Christine, Jane Margaret. BS, Brigham Young U., 1976; MSc, U. Wales, 1978; AM, Harvard U., 1978, PhD, 1981; DSc (hon.), U. Guelph, Can., 2000. Teaching fellow Harvard U., Cambridge, Mass., 1977-81; Miller research fellow Miller Inst. Basic Research in Sci., Berkeley, Calif., 1981-83; asst. prof. Brigham Young U., Provo, Utah, 1983-86, assoc. prof., 1986-91, prof., 1991—98, dean gen. edn. and honors, 1993-97; King Gustav XVI prof. environ. sci. Swedish Biodiversity Ctr., 1997—98; dir. Nat. Tropical Botanical Garden, Kalaheo, Hawaii, 1998—2004, Inst. for Ethnomedicine, Provo, 2004—. Disting. prof. Brigham Young U., Hawaii, 2000—; ecologist Utah Environ. Coun., Salt Lake City, 1976; project ecologist Utah MX Coordination Office, Salt Lake City, 1981. Mem. editl. bd. Pacific Studies. Recipient Bowdoin prize, The Goldman Environ. prize, 1997; Danforth Found. fellow, 1976-81, Fulbright fellow, 1976-77, NSF fellow, 1977-81, Linnean Soc. fellow, named NSF Presdl. Young Investigator, 1985-90, Hero of Medicine, Time Mag., 1997, Rachel Carson award, 1999. Mem. AAAS, Brit. Ecol. Soc., Internat. Soc. Ethnopharmacology (former pres.), Am. Soc. Naturalists, Assn. Tropical Biology, Soc. Econ. Botany (former pres.), Seacology Found. (founder and chmn.), AIDS Rsch. Alliance (bd.), Ctr. for Plant Conservation (bd.). Mem. Lds Ch. Office: Inst for Ethnomedicine PO Box 3464 Jackson WY 83001 Office Phone: 801-375-6214.

COX, RICHARD HORTON, civil engineering executive; b. Paia, Hawaii, Oct. 10, 1920; s. Joel B. and Helen Cliford (Horton) C.; m. Hester Virginia Smith, Dec. 12, 1942 (dec. Aug. 12, 1995); children: Millicent, Janet, Lydia, Evelyn, David, Samuel (dec.). BS, Calif. Inst. Tech., Pasadena, 1942, MS, 1946. Registered profl. engr., surveyor, Hawaii. Supr. rocket range Calif. Inst. Tech., Pasadena, 1942—46;

civil engr. McBryde Sugar Co., Eleele, Hawaii, 1946—56; land mgr. Alexander & Baldwin, Honolulu, 1956—71, v.p., 1971—86; engring. cons. Honolulu, 1986—. Mem. State Commn. on Water Resource Mgmt., 1987-94, 95-99. Fellow: ASCE; mem.: NSPE, AAAS, Am. Geophys. Union. Mem. Soc. Of Friends. Home and Office: 1951 Kakela Dr Honolulu HI 96822-2156

COYLE, MARIE BRIDGET, retired microbiologist, lab administrator; b. Chgo., May 13, 1935; d. John and Bridget Veronica (Fitzpatrick) Coyle; m. Zheng Chen, Oct. 30, 1995 (div. Aug. 2000). BA, Mundelein Coll. (now part of Loyola U.), Chgo., 1957; MS, St. Louis U., 1963; PhD, Kans. State U., Manhattan, 1965. Diplomate Am. Bd. Med. Microbiology. Sci. instr. Sch. Nursing Columbus Hosp., Chgo., 1957-59; research assoc. U. Chgo., 1967-70; instr. U. Ill., Chgo., 1970-71; asst. prof. microbiology U. Wash., Seattle, 1973-80, assoc. prof., 1980-94, prof., 1994-2000; ret., 2000. Assoc. dir. Univ. Hosp., Seattle, 1973—76; dir. microbiology labs Harborview Med. Ctr. U. Wash., Seattle, 1976—, co-dir. postdoctoral tng. clinic microbiology, 1978—96, dir. postdoctoral tng. clinic microbiology, 1996—2000. Contbr. articles to profl. jours. Recipient Pasteur award, Ill. Soc. Microbiology, 1997, Profl. Recognition awards, Am. Bd. Med. Microbiology, Am. Bd. Med. Lab. Immunology, 2000. Fellow: Am. Acad. Microbiology; mem.: Am. Soc. Microbiology (chmn. clin. microbiology divsn. 1984—85, mem. coun. policy com. 1996—99, bd. govs. 2000—, bioMerieux Vitek Sonnenwirth Meml. award 1994), Acad. Clin. Lab. Physicians and Scientists (sec.-treas. 1980—83, mem. exec. com. 1985—90), Kappa Gamma Pi. Avocation: hiking. Business E-Mail: mbcoyle@u.washington.edu.

COYLE, ROBERT EVERETT, federal judge; b. Fresno, Calif., May 6, 1930; s. Everett LaJoya and Virginia Chandler C.; m. Faye Turnbaugh, June 11, 1953; children— Robert Allen, Richard Lee, Barbara Jean BA, Fresno State Coll., 1953; JD, U. Calif., 1956. Bar: Calif. Ptnr. McCormick, Barstow, Sheppard, Coyle & Wayte, 1958-82; chief judge U.S. Dist. Ct. (ea. dist.) Calif., 1990-96, sr. judge, 1996—. Former chair 9th Cir. Conf. of Chief Dist. Judges, chair 9th Cir. space and security com., mem. com. on state and fed. cts. Mem. Calif. Bar Assn. (exec. com. 1974-79, bd. govs. 1979-82, v.p. 1981), Fresno County Bar Assn. (pres. 1972). Office: US Dist Ct 5116 US Courthouse 1130 O St Fresno CA 93721-2201 Office Phone: 559-498-7318.

COYNE, JOHN F., computer company executive; B Mech. Engring., Univ. Coll., Dublin, 1971. Mgmt. positions Western Digital Corp., Ireland, 1983—97, Malaysia, 1997—2000, sr. v.p. worldwide ops. Lake Forest, Calif., 2000—05, exec. v.p., COO, 2005—06, pres., COO, 2006—07, pres., CEO, 2007—. Office: Western Digital Corp 20511 Lake Forest Dr Lake Forest CA 92630-7741

COYNE, JOSEPH FRANCIS, JR., lawyer; b. Springfield, Mass., Feb. 26, 1955; s. Joseph Francis Sr. and Carolyn Coyne; m. Melinda Ward, Aug. 30, 1980; 1 child, Caitlin Siobhan. BA, U. Notre Dame, 1977; JD, Stanford U., 1980. Bar: Calif. 1980. Assoc. Sheppard, Mullin, Richter & Hampton LLP, LA, 1980, ptnr., mem. exec. com.; corp. v.p., sec. and deputy general counsel Northrop Grumann, 2009—. Mem.: ABA, Calif. State Bar Assn., LA County Bar Assn. Office: Northrop Grumann 1840 Century Park E Los Angeles CA 90067-2199 Office Fax: 213-620-1398. E-mail: jcoyne@sheppardmullin.com.*

CRABBS, ROGER ALAN, publishing executive, director, small business owner, military officer, educator; b. Cedar Rapids, Iowa, May 9, 1928; s. Winfred Wesley and Faye (Woodard) C.; m. Marilyn Lee Westcott, June 30, 1951; children: William Douglas, Janet Lee Crabbs Turner, Ann Lee Crabbs Menke. BA in Sci., State U. Iowa, 1954; MBA, George Washington U., 1965, DBA, 1973; M Christian Leadership, We. Sem., 1978. Commd. 2nd lt. USAF, 1950, advanced through grades to lt. col., 1968, Ret., 1972; assoc. prof. mgmt. U. Portland, Oreg., 1972-79; prof. bus. George Fox Coll., Newberg, Oreg., 1979-83; pres. Judson Bapt. Coll., The Dalles, Oreg., 1983-85. Pres. Host Pubs. Inc., pres., chmn. various corps., 1974-96; past chmn. nat. adv. bd. Travelhost, Inc.; pres. Crabbs and Co., 2005-; cons. in field. Author: Employee Motivation in the Panama Canal Company, 1973, The Infallible Foundation for Management-The Bible, 1978, The Secret of Success in Small Business Management-Is in the Short Range, 1983; co-author: The Storybook Primer on Managing, 1976. Past pres. English Speaking Union, 1994-96, bd. dir., 1994-97; Dir., Conv. and Vis. Bur. of Washington County, v.p., 1986-2001, Oakhills Townhouse Assn., v.p., 1991-95. Decorated Air Force Commendation medal with oak leaf cluster, Meritorious Service medal Dept. Def.; proclaimed Am. for Peace, Rep. of Korea, 2007; rated Command Air Force Missileman; recipient Jack Rosenberg Cmty. Svcs. award, 2000, regional, dist. and nat. awards SBA, Bonnie Hays Tourism award, 2001. Mem.: Mil. Officers Assn. America, Am. Legion, Korean War Vets. Assn., Svc. Corps Ret. Execs., Acad. Mgmt., Assn. Atomic Vets., 51st Fighter Interceptor Wing Assn., Air Force Assn., Lang Syne Soc. of Portland, Rotary (past pres.), Masons, Phi Mu Alpha, Delta Epsilon Sigma, Alpha Kappa Psi. Republican. Business E-Mail: host2@verizon.net.

CRABTREE-IRELAND, DUNCAN, lawyer; b. 1972; m. John Crabtree-Ireland; 1 child, Watson. BS in Fgn. Svc., Georgetown U., 1994; JD, U. Calif., Davis, 1998. Dep. dist. atty. LA County; counsel SAG, LA, 2000—02, asst. gen. counsel, 2002—05, dep. gen. counsel, 2005—06, interim gen. counsel, 2006, dep. nat. exec. dir., gen. counsel, 2006—. Lectr. law U. So. Calif.; judge pro tem, ct. apptd. arbitrator LA Superior Ct. Mem.: Lesbian and Gay Lawyers Assn. LA (treas.), LA County Bar Assn. (bd. trustees exec. com. labor & employee law sect.). Avocations: sailing, reading, movies, travel. Office: Screen Actors Guild 5757 Wilshire Blvd Los Angeles CA 90036-3600 Office Phone: 323-549-6043. Office Fax: 323-395-5997. E-mail: dci@sag.org.

CRAFORD, M. GEORGE, physicist, research administrator; b. Sioux City, Iowa, Dec. 29, 1938; BA, U. Iowa, 1961; MS, U. Ill., 1963, PhD in Physics, 1967. Mem. staff Monsanto, St. Louis, 1967-74, Palo Alto, Calif., 1974-79; mgr. R&D optoelec. divsn. Hewlett Packard, San Jose, Calif., 1979—2001; chief tech. officer Lumileds Lighting, San Jose, Calif., 2001—. Recipient Nat. Medal Technology, US Dept. Commerce, 2002. Fellow IEEE; mem. Nat. Acad. Engring. Achievements include development of visible light emitting diodes; nitrogen-doped GaAsP technology; first to develop AlInGaP LED's, AlGaAs and GaN products. Office: Lumileds Lighting LLC 370 W Trimble Rd San Jose CA 95131

CRAFT, CHERYL MAE, neurobiologist, anatomist, researcher; b. Lynch, Ky., Apr. 15, 1947; d. Cecil Berton and Lillian Lovelle C.; m. Laney K. Cormney, Oct. 14, 1967 (div. Sept. 1980); children: Tyler Craft Cormney, Ryan Berton Cormney (dec.); m. Richard N. Lolley (dec.). BS in Biology, Chemistry and Math., Valdosta State Coll., 1969; cert. in Tchg. Biology and Math., Ea. Ky. U., 1971; PhD in Human Anatomy and Neurosci., U. Tex., San Antonio, 1984. Undergrad. rsch. asst. Ea. Ky. U., Richmond, 1965-67; tchg. asst. dept. cell-structural biology U. Tex. Health Sci. Ctr., San Antonio, 1979-84; postdoctoral fellowship lab. devel. neurobiology NICHD and LMDB/NEI, Bethesda, Md., 1984-86; instr. dept. psychiatry U. Tex. Southwestern Med. Ctr., Dallas, 1986-87, asst. prof., 1987-91; dir. lab. Molecular Neurogenetics Schizophrenia Rsch. Ctr., VA Med. Ctr., Dallas, 1988-94; dir. Lab. Molecular Neurogenetics Mental Health Clinic Rsch. Ctr., U. Tex. Southwestern Med. Ctr., 1990-94; assoc. prof. U. Tex. Southwestern Med. Ctr., 1991-94; Mary D. Allen chair Doheny Eye Inst. U. So. Calif. Keck Sch. Medicine, LA, Calif., 1994—, founding chmn. dept. cell and neurobiology, 1994—2004. Ad hoc reviewer NEI/NIH, Bethesda, 1993—; reviewer Molecular Biology, NSPB Fight for Sight Grants, 1991-94; STAR-sci. adv. bd. U. So. Calif./Bravo Magnet H.S., L.A., 1995—. Contbr. author: Melatonin: Biosynthesis, Physiological Effects, 1993; exec. editor Exptl. Eye Rsch. jour., 1993—; editor Molecular Vision. Recipient Merit award for rsch. VA Med. Ctr., 1992, 93, 94, nomination for Women in Sci. and Engring. award Dallas VA, 1992, 93; NEI fellow, 1986, NICHD/NIH fellow, 1986. Mem. AAAS, AAUW, Assn. for Rsch. in Vision and Ophthalmology (chair program planning com. 1991-94), Am. Soc. for Neurochemistry (Jordi Folch Pi Outstanding Young Investigator 1992), Sigma Xi (sec./treas. 1986-93, pres. 1993-94). Avocations: reading, travel. Office: U So Calif Keck Sch Medicine 1355 San Pablo St Rm 405 DVRC Los Angeles CA 90033 Office Phone: 323-442-6694. Personal E-mail: eyesightresearch@hotmail.com. Business E-Mail: ccraft@usc.edu.

CRAIG, DANIEL, actor; b. Chester, Eng., Mar. 2, 1968; s. Tim and Carol Olivia Craig; m. Fiona Loudon, 1992 (div. 1994); 1 child. Grad., Guildhall Sch. Music and Drama. Actor: (films) The Power of One, 1992, A Kid in King Arthur's Court, 1995, Saint-Ex, 1996, Obsession, 1997, Love and Rage, 1998, Elizabeth, 1998, The Trench, 1999, I Dreamed of Africa, 2000, Some Voices, 2000, Lara Croft: Tomb Raider, 2001, Road to Perdition, 2002, Occasional, Strong, 2002, The Mother, 2003, Sylvia, 2003, Enduring Love, 2004, Layer Cake, 2004, The Jacket, 2005, Fateless, 2005, Munich, 2005, (voice) Renaissance, 2006, Infamous, 2006, Casino Royale, 2006, The Invasion, 2007, The Golden Compass, 2007, Quantum of Solace, 2008, Defiance, 2008; (TV films) Genghis Cohn, 1993, Sharpe's Eagle, 1993, Kiss and Tell, 1996, The Fortunes and Misfortunes of Moll Flanders, 1996, The Ice House, 1997, Shockers: The Visitor, 1999, Copenhagen, 2002, Archangel, 2005. Office: c/o Rick Kurtzman Creative Artists Agy LCC 2000 Ave Of The Stars Los Angeles CA 90067

CRAIG, LARRY EDWIN, former United States Senator from Idaho, congressman; b. Council, Idaho, July 20, 1945; m. Suzanne Thompson; 3 children. BA in Polit. Sci. and Agrl. Economics, U. Idaho, 1969; postgrad, George Washington U., 1970; PhD (hon.), N.W. Nazarene U. V.p. Craig Ranches Inc., Midvale, Idaho, 1974—; mem. Idaho State Senate, 1974-80, US Congress from 1st Idaho dist., 1981—91; US Senator from Idaho, 1991—2009; chmn. Rep. Policy Com., 1997—2003, Vet. Affairs Com., 2003—07; mem. Appropriations, Energy & Natural Resources Coms. Chmn. Idaho Rep. State Senate Races, 1976-78; mem. Nat. Congressional Coun., Nat. Found. Defense Analysis; mem. com. appropriations US Senate, com. energy and natural resources, com. veterans affairs, spl. com. aging. Pres. Young Rep. League Idaho, 1976-77; mem. Idaho Rep. Exec. Com., 1976-78; chmn. Rep. Ctrl. Com. Washington County, 1971-72; advisor vocat. edn. in pub. schs. US Dept. Health, Edn. & Welfare, 1971-73; mem. Idaho Farm Bur., 1965-79. Served with US Army, 1970—72. Recipient Disting. Svc. award, Am. Legion, 2000; named to The Idaho Hall of Fame, 2007. Mem. NRA (bd. dirs. 1983—), Future Farmers of Am. (v.p. 1966-67). Republican. Methodist.*

CRAIG, SIDNEY RICHARD, theatrical agent; b. Cleve. s. Norman Benjiman and Rose Craig. BA in Bus. and Social Psychology, U. So. Calif., 1967. Adv. bd. D.E.F. Found., L.A., 1991—. Judge Tops and Blue USAF World Talent Competition, 1973—. With USN, 1966-68. Mem. Acad. Motion Picture Arts and Scis., Assn. Talent Agts. (v.p., bd. dirs. 1982—), D.E.F. Found. Office: Craig Agy 8485 Melrose Pl # E Los Angeles CA 90069-5311

CRAIG, STUART N., film production designer; b. Norwich, Norfolk, Eng., Apr. 14, 1942; s. Norman and Kate C.; m. Patricia Stangroom, Dec. 29, 1965; children: Laura, Rebecca. Assoc., Royal Coll. Art, London, 1966. Prodn. designer: (films) The Elephant Man, 1980 (Academy award nomination best art direction 1980), Gandhi, 1981 (Academy award best art direction 1982), Greystoke: The Legend of Tarzan, Lord of the Apes, 1983, The Mission, 1986 (Academy award nomination best art direction 1986), Cry Freedom, 1987, Dangerous Liaisons, 1988 (Academy award best art direction 1988), Chaplin, 1992 (Academy award nomination best art direction 1992), Shadowlands, 1993, The Secret Garden, 1993, Mary Reilly, 1996, The English Patient, 1996 (Academy award for best art direction 1996), In Love and War, 1996, The Avengers, 1998, Notting Hill, 1999, The Legend of Bagger Vance, 2000, Harry Potter and the Sorcerer's Stone, 2001, Harry Potter and the Chamber of Secrets, 2002, Harry Potter and the Prisoner of Azkaban, 2004, Harry Potter and the Goblet of Fire, 2005 (British Acad. Film and TV Arts award for prodn. design, 2006), Harry Potter and the Order of the Phoenix, 2007; co-prodr., prodn. designer: (films) Cal, 1984. Recipient Lifetime Achievement award, Art Dirs. Guild, 2008; named Officer of British Empire, 2002. Office: c/o The Skouras Agy 1149 3rd St Santa Monica CA 90403 Office Phone: 310-395-9550.

CRAIGHEAD, JOHN JOHNSON, wildlife biologist; b. Wash., Aug. 14, 1916; married; 3 children. BA, Pa. State U., 1939; MS, U. Mich., 1940, PhD, 1950. Biologist NY Zool. Soc., 1947-49; dir. survival tng. for armed forces US Dept. Def., 1950-52; wildlife biologist, leader Mont. coop. rsch. unit Bur. Sport Fisheries and Wildlife, 1952-77; prof. zoology and forestry U. Mont., 1952-77; bd. dirs., founder Craighead Wildlife-Wildlands Inst., Missoula, Mont., 1978—. Recipient Conservation award Am. Motors, 1978, John Oliver LaGorce Gold medal Nat. Geog. Soc., 1979, Centennial award, 1988, Lud Browman award Scientific and Tech. Writing, U. Mont., 1990; grantee NSF, AEC, NASA, U.S. Forest Svc., Mont. Fish and Game Dept. Mem. AAAS, Wildlife Soc., Wilderness Alliance. Office: Craighead Wildlife-Wildlands Inst 5200 Miller Creek Rd Missoula MT 59803-1904

CRAM, BRIAN MANNING, school system administrator; AA, Dixie Jr. Coll., 1959; BA (hon.), U. Utah, 1961; MA, Ariz. State U., 1962, EdS, 1964, EdD (hon.), 1967. Asst. prin. Clark (Nev.) H.S., 1965-69, prin., 1969-73; asst. supt. Clark County (Nev.) Sch. Dist., 1973-78; supt. schs. Clark County (Nev.) Sch. Dist., 1989—; prin. Western H.S., 1978-89. Cons. Glendale Unified Sch. Dist., Whittier Sch. Dist., South Bay Union H.S. Dist., Elk Grove Unified Sch. Dist., No. Ill. U., State of Hawaii; co-chmn. Supt.'s Coun. Ednl. Tech., Coll. Prep Feasibility sub-com.; mem. Spkrs. Bur. Pay as You Go Bond Plan, Disting. Scholar's com., Extended Day com., In-Svc. com., State Attendence Audit, Spl. Assistance Team, Computer Mgmt. Project, Prin. Attendance adv. com., Prin.'s Math Curriculum com; spkr. in field. Contbr. articles to profl. jours. Bd. dirs. Boulder Dam Area Coun. Boy Scouts Am., Las Vegas Coun. PTA, United Way, Clark County Sch. Dist. Articulation Com., Nev. Assn. Handicapped, Nev. Devel. Authority, Nev. Inst. Contemporary Art, Animal Found., Las Vegas Mus. Nat. History, Southwest Regional Ednl. Lab., Nat. Coun. Christians and Jews; adv. bd. U. Nev. Las Vegas Spl. Svcs., U. Nev. Sch. Medicine, Clark County C.C. Mem. Nev. Assn. Secondary Sch. Prins. (past sec.), Nev. Educator Awards Selection Com., Clark County Assn. Sch. Administrs. (chmn. negotiations, past exec. coun., past sec., past pres.), Ariz. State U. Alumni Assn. (past pres. So. Nev. chpt.), Greater Las Vegas C. of C., Latin C. of C., Nev. Black C. of C., Rotary, Phi Delta Kappa. Office: Clark County School District 2832 E Flamingo Rd Las Vegas NV 89121-5295 Home: 2155 Lipari Ct Las Vegas NV 89123-3920

CRAMER, CHUCKIE, legislative staff member; b. Havre, Mont., Nov. 7, 1941; Sgt.-at-arms Mont. Ho. of Reps., Helena, 1985-88, Mont. State Senate, Helena, 1995—.

CRAMER, JAMES DALE, physicist, scientific company executive; b. Canton, Ohio, Aug. 4, 1937; s. Dale and Vera Arlene (Lindower) C.; m. Geraldine M. Bendoski, July 20, 1957; children: Karen Lynn, Eric James. BS, Calif. State U., Fresno, 1960; MS, U. Oreg., 1962; PhD, U. N.Mex., 1969. Mem. tech. staff U. Calif., Los Alamos, 1962-70; v.p. Davis-Smith Corp., San Diego, 1970-73; mem. tech. staff Sci. Applications, Inc., LaJolla, Calif., 1970-73, group v.p. Albuquerque, 1973-80, dir., 1974-80; pres. Sci. & Engring. Assocs., Inc., Albuquerque, 1980—. Cons. in field; pres. Albuquerque Mus. Found., 1981-83. Contbr. articles to profl. publs. Mem. Am. Phys. Soc., IEEE.

CRAMER, JOHN GLEASON, JR., experimental physicist, educator; b. Houston, Oct. 24, 1934; s. John Gleason and Frances Ann (Sakwitz) C.; m. Pauline Ruth Bond, June 2, 1961; children: Kathryn Elizabeth, John Gleason III, Karen Melissa. BA, Rice U., 1957, MA, 1959, PhD in Physics, 1961. Postdoctoral fellow Ind. U., Bloomington, 1961-63, asst. prof., 1963-64; asst. prof. physics U. Wash., Seattle, 1964-68, assoc. prof., 1968-74, prof., 1974—, dir. nuclear physics lab., 1983-90. Guest prof. W. Ger. Bundesministerium and U. Munich, 1971-72; mem. program adv. com. Los Alamos Meson Physics Facility, Los Alamos Nat. Lab., 1976-78, Nat. Superconducting Cyclotron Lab., 1983-87, TRIUMF (U. B.C.), 1985-88; program adviser-cons. Lawrence Berkeley Lab., Calif., 1979-82; mem. exec. coun. STAR Collaboration, 1991—, CERN Experiments NA 35 and NA 49, 1991—; guest prof. Hahn-Meitner Inst., West Berlin, 1982-83, Max-Planck-Inst. für Physik, Munich, Germany, 1994-95. Author: Twistor, 1989, Einstein's Bridge, 1997; columnist Analog Mag., 1983—; contbr. articles to physics and popular publs. Fellow: AAAS, Am. Phys. Soc. (panel on pub. affairs 1998—2001). Home: 7002 51st Ave NE Seattle WA 98115-6132 Office: U Wash Dept Physics PO Box 351560 Seattle WA 98195-1560

CRAMER, OWEN CARVER, classics educator, department chairman; b. Tampa, Fla., Dec. 1, 1941; s. Maurice Browning and Alice (Carver) C.; m. Rebecca Jane Lowrey, June 23, 1962; children: Alfred, Thomas, Ethan, Benjamin AB, Oberlin Coll., 1962; PhD, U. Tex., 1973. Spl. instr. U. Tex., Austin, 1964-65; instr. in classics Colo. Coll., Colorado Springs, 1965-69, asst. prof. classics, 1969-75, assoc. prof. classics, 1975-84, M.C. Gile prof. classics, 1984—, dir. comparative lit., 1993—2002, Bemis humanities chair, 2006—. Cons. humanist Colo. Humanities Program, Denver, 1982-83; vis. prof. U. Chgo., 1987-88; reader Advanced Placement Latin Exam., 1995-99; summer faculty Wyo. Humanities Coun. program, 2004. Editorial asst. Arion, 1964-65; contbr. papers, articles on Greek lang. and lit. to profl. publs., 1974—; contbr. classical music revs. to Colorado Springs Sun, 1984-86. Chorus tenor Colo. Opera Festival, Colorado Springs, 1976-82; mem. El Paso County Dem. Ctrl. Com., Colo., 1968-88; ordained elder Presbyn. Ch., 1992; mem. alumni coun. Oberlin Coll., 1992-02, 2006-. Recipient Boettcher Faculty Excellence award Colo. Coll., 2005; Hon. Woodrow Wilson fellow, 1962, fellow U. Tex., Austin, 1962-64. Mem. Am. Philol. Assn. (campus adv. svc. 1989, chmn. com. on smaller depts. 1979-80), Am. Comparative Lit. Assn., Classical Assn. Middle West and South, Modern Greek Studies Assn., Colo. Classics Assn., Round Table (Colorado Springs) Club, Phi Beta Kappa. Home: 747 E Uintah St Colorado Springs CO 80903-2546 Office: Colo Coll Dept Classics Colorado Springs CO 80903 Home Phone: 719-634-3392; Office Phone: 719-389-6443. Business E-Mail: ocramer@coloradocollege.edu.

CRANDALL, KEITH C., dean; Assoc. dean U. Calif., Berkeley. Recipient Peurifoy Constrn. Rsch. award, 1998. Mem. ASCE. Office: U Calif Civil Environ Engring Dept 215 Mclaughlin Hall Berkeley CA 94720-1712

CRANDALL, RICH, state legislator; m. Patrice Crandall; children: Melissa, Kathryn, Camille, Allyson, Brianne, Rhett, Savanna. BS, MS in Acctg., Brigham Young U., Provo, Utah, 1993; MBA, U. Notre Dame, Ind., 1997. CPA Ariz. Ptnr., CFO Crandall Corp. Dietitians; founder, pres. CN Resource; mem. Dist. 19 Ariz. House of Reps., 2007—, chair edn. com., mem. commerce com., appropriations com. Bd. dirs. Mesa Sch. Bd., Mesa Bank, Bringing Hope to Single Moms Found. Mem.: Mesa C. of C., Mesa Baseline Rotary. Republican. Office: Ariz House Reps Capitol Complex 1700 W Washington Rm 113 Phoenix AZ 85007 Home Phone: 928-772-1332; Office Phone: 602-926-3020. Office Fax: 602-417-3119. Business E-Mail: rcrandall@azleg.gov.*

CRANE, LANSING E., paper company executive; b. Dalton, Mass., Oct. 12, 1945; m. Katie Crane, Dec. 7, 2002; 2 children. Grad., Yale U., New Haven; JD, Boston U., 1970. Former lawyer, New Haven; bd. dirs. Crane & Co., Inc., Dalton, Mass., 1985, pres., CEO, 1995—. Former faculty mem. psychiatry and law Yale U., New Haven. Bd. dirs. Colonial Theatre, Pittsfield, Mass.; bd. trustees Austen Riggs Ctr., Stockbridge, Mass.; bd. mem. Norman Rockwell Mus., Stockbridge, Mass. Named one of VIP 23, Berkshire Eagle, 2003. Achievements include running the company that has been supplying almost all of the paper used for US currency since 1879. Avocations: swimming, golf, hiking, skiing, reading. Home: 445 Pine St Boulder CO 80302-4735

CRANE, ROBERT MEREDITH, health facility administrator; b. 1947; m. Susan Crane, May 5, 1973; 1 child, Alexis Meredith. BA, Coll. of Wooster, 1969; M Pub. Adminstrn., Cornell U., Ithaca, NY, 1971. Health planning specialist U.S. Dept. Health, Edn. and Welfare, Rockville, Md., 1971-73, tech. assistance bur. chief, 1973-76, regulatory methods bur. chief, 1976-77; sr. staff assoc. U.S. Ho. of Reps., Washington, 1977-79; dep. commr. N.Y. State Health Dept., Albany, 1979-82; dir. N.Y. State Office Health Sys. Mgmt., Albany, 1982-83; v.p. govt. rels. Kaiser Found. Health Plan, Oakland, Calif., 1983-88, sr. v.p. nat. accts. and pub. rels., 1988-92, sr. v.p. quality mgmt., 1992-94, sr. v.p., chief adminstrv. officer, 1994-99, sr. v.p., rsch. and policy devel., dir. Inst. for Health Policy, 1999—2007; pres. Kaiser Permanente Internat., Oakland, 2004—. Bd. dirs. Acad. Health Svcs. Rsch. and Health Policy, 2000—; mem. Nat. Acad. Social Ins., 2000-03. Campaign cabinet United Way Bay area, 1989-90; steering com. Bay Area Econ. Forum, 1988-94, Bay Area Coun., 1991—; selection judge, preceptor Coro Found., San Francisco, 1985-86; chmn. bd. Alpha Ctr., 1992-98; co-chair conf. bd. Coun. of Shared Bus. Svcs. Execs., 1996—; trustee Employee Benefits Rsch. Inst. Sr. exec. fellow Harvard U., 1981. Mem. APHA (chmn. cmty. health planning sect. 1983-84, bd. govs. 1979-81), Am. Health Planning Assn. (bd. dirs. 1986-92). Presbyterian. Avocations: tennis, golf. Office: Kaiser Found Health Plan 1 Kaiser Plz Oakland CA 94612-3610

CRANE, RON G., state treasurer; b. Nampa, Idaho; m. Cheryl Crane; 6 children. Founder Crane Alarm Svc., 1980—; state legislator Idaho, 1982—98, state treas., 1998—. Mem. Idaho Nat. Guard, 1971—77. Named Soldier of the Year, Idaho, 1975. Mem.: Nat. Assn. State Auditors, Controllers and Treas. (exec. com.), Nat. Assn. State Treas. (exec. com.). Republican. Office: Idaho State Treas 700 W Jefferson Rm 102 PO Box 83720 Boise ID 83720-0091 Office Phone: 208-334-3200. Office Fax: 208-332-2960. Business E-Mail: rgcrane77@cableone.net.

CRANK, PATRICK J., lawyer, former state attorney general; b. Pueblo, Colo., Dec. 30, 1959; m. Anna Crank; children: Abbigail, Jerry, Zachary, Noah. BA, U. Wyo., 1982, JD, 1985. With Wyo. Atty. Gen. Office, 1985—86, Natrona County Dist. Atty. Office, 1987—90, US Atty. Office for Dist. Wyo., 1990—2002; atty. gen. State of Wyo., Cheyenne, 2003—07; shareholder Speight, McCue & Crank, PC, Cheyenne, 2007—. Democrat. Avocations: hunting, fishing, camping. Office: Speight, McCue & Crank, PC 2515 Warren Ave, Ste 505 PO Box 1709 Cheyenne WY 82001 Office Phone: 307-634-2994. Office Fax: 307-635-7155.

CRANSTON, MARY BAILEY, lawyer; b. Palo Alto, Calif., Dec. 29, 1947; d. James Alfred and Bettye (Luhnow) Bailey; m. Harold David Cranston, Aug. 15, 1970; children: Susan Anne, John David. AB in polit. sci., Stanford U., 1969, JD, 1975; MA in psychology, UCLA, 1970. Bar: Calif. 1975. Assoc. atty. Pillsbury, Madison & Sutro, San Francisco, 1975-82, ptnr., 1983—2001, firm chair, 1999—2001; (Pillsbury, Madison & Sutro merged with Winthrop, Stimson, Putnam & Roberts, 2001); ptnr. Pillsbury Winthrop LLP, San Francisco, 2001—, firm chair, 2001—04; (Pillsbury Winthrop LLP merged with Shaw Pittman LLP, 2005); firm chair Pillsbury Winthrop Shaw Pittman LLP, San Francisco, 2005—06, chair emeritus, 2007—, sr. ptnr., 2007—. Faculty The Rutter Group, 1984—, Calif. Continuing Edn. of the Bar, 1985—, Nat. Inst. Trial Advocacy, San Francisco, 1986—; bd. dirs. GrafTech Internat. Ltd., 1999—, Bay Area Coun., 1999—, Visa Inc., 2007—, Juniper Networks Inc., 2007—, Internat. Rectifier Corp., 2008—. Contbr. articles to profl. journals; mem. editl. bd. Nat. Law Jour., 2004—. Trustee San Francisco Ballet, 1996, Stanford U., 2000—; mem. The Yosemite Fund; mem. nat. centennial com. Girl Scouts USA, 2001; bd. dirs. Legal Services for Children, San Francisco, 1983—87, San Francisco C. of C., 1999—2001; bd. dirs. hist. soc. US Dist. Ct. No. Dist. Calif., 2001—; bd. mem. Episcopal Charities, 2003—; exec. com. bd. visitors Stanford Law Sch., 1977—80, 1996—, chair bd. visitors, 2001; chair bd. advisors we. region Catalyst, 2004—; bd. governors Commonwealth Club of Calif. Recipient Stanford Associates Award for disting. svc., Stanford U., 1999, Disting. Jurisprudence Award, Anti-Defamation League, 2000, Award of Merit, Bar Assn. San Francisco, 2002, Athena Award, 2004; named one of The 100 Most Influential Lawyers in Calif., LA Daily Jour., 1999—2002, The 50 Most Influential Bus. Women in the Bay Area, San Francisco Bus. Times, 1999—2003, The 100 Most Influential Lawyers in Am., Nat. Law Jour., 2000, The 2 Best Law Firm Leaders in the US, Of Counsel, 2002. Fellow: Am. Coll. Trial Lawyers; mem.: Assn. Bus. Trial Lawyers (bd. dirs. 1993—97), Calif. State Bar (mem. com. on women 1986—89, chair sect. of antitrust and trade regulation 1998—99), ABA (mem. commn. on women 1993—2000, coun. mem. antitrust sect. 1994—97, officer antitrust sect. 1997—2000, Margaret Brent award 2005), Am. Law Inst., Stanford Alumni Assn. (bd. dirs. 1986—93, 2001—, pres. 1990), Cap & Gown (Stanford) (treas. 1974—75). Avocations: reading, sports. Office: Pillsbury Winthrop Shaw Pittman 50 Fremont St Ste 1474 San Francisco CA 94105 Office Phone: 415-983-1621. Office Fax: 415-983-1200. Business E-Mail: mary.cranston@pillsburylaw.com.

CRAPO, MICHAEL DEAN, United States Senator from Idaho, former congressman, lawyer; b. Idaho Falls, May 20, 1951; s. George Lavelle and Melba (Olsen) C.; m. Susan Diane Hasleton, June 22, 1974; children: Michelle, Brian, Stephanie, Lara, Paul. BA in Polit. Sci., summa cum laude, Brigham Young U., 1973; postgrad., U. Utah, 1973-74; JD cum laude, Harvard U., 1977. Bar: Calif. 1977, Idaho 1979. Law clk. to Hon. James M. Carter US Ct. Appeals (9th cir.), San Diego, 1977-78; assoc. atty. Gibson, Dunn & Crutcher, LA, 1978-79; atty. Holden, Kidwell, Hahn & Crapo, Idaho Falls, 1979-92, ptnr., 1983-92; mem. Idaho State Senate from 32A Dist., 1985—93, asst. majority leader, 1987—89; pres. Pro Tempore, 1989-92; congressman U.S. House of Reps., 2d Idaho dist., Washington, 1993—99; mem. commerce com., new mem. leader 103rd Congress, sophomore class leader 104th Congress, co-chair Congl. Beef Caucus, dep. whip western region U.S. House of Reps., Washington, vice chair energy and power subcom., strategic planning leader House Leadership 105th Congress, mem. house resources com., mem. commerce com., mem. resources com.; US Senator from Idaho, 1999—; dep. whip 108th congress US Senate. Precinct committeeman Dist. 29, 1980-85; vice chmn. Legislative Dist. 29, 1984-85; Mem. Health and Welfare Com., 1985-89, Resources and Environ. Com., 1985-90, State Affairs Com., 1987-92; Rep. Pres. Task Force, 1989; mem. com. agr., nutrition and forestry US Senate, com. banking, housing and urban affairs, com. budget, com. fin., com. Indian affairs. Leader Boy Scouts Am., Calif., Idaho, 1977-92; mem. Bar Exam Preparation, Bar Exam Grading; chmn. Law Day.; Bonneville County chmn. Phil Batt gubernatorial campaign, 1982. Named one of Outstanding Young Men of Am., 1985; recipient Cert. of Merit Rep. Nat. Com., 1990, Guardian of Small Bus. award Nat. Fedn. of Ind. Bus., 1990, 94, Cert. of Recognition Am. Cancer Soc., 1990, Idaho Housing Agy., 1990, Idaho Lung Assn., 1985, 86, 89, Friend of Agr. award Idaho Farm Bur., 1989-90, medal of merit Rep. Presdl. Task Force, 1989, Nat. Legislator of Yr. award Nat. Rep. Legislators Assn., 1991, Golden Bulldog award Watchdogs of the Treas., 1996, Thomas Jefferson award Nat. Am. Wholesale Grocers Assn.-Ind. Food Distbrs. Assn., 1996, Spirit of Enterprise award US C. of C., 1993, 94, 95, 96, Watchdogs of Treasury Golden Bulldog award Am. Frozen Food Inst., 2000, Ground Water Protector award Nat. Ground Water Assn., 2002, Best and Brightest award Am. Conservative Union, 2003. Mem. ABA (antitrust law sect.), Idaho Bar Assn., Rotary. Republican. Mem. Lds Ch. Avocations: sports, backpacking, hunting, skiing. Office: US Senate 239 Dirksen Senate Ofc Bldg Washington DC 20510-0001 also: District Office Ste 205 251 East Front St Boise ID 83702-7312 Office Phone: 202-224-6142, 208-334-1776. Office Fax: 202-228-1375, 208-334-9044.*

CRASEMANN, BERND, physicist, researcher; b. Hamburg, Germany, Jan. 23, 1922; came to U.S., 1946, naturalized, 1955; s. Pablo Joaquin and Hildegard Carlota (Verwerk) C. AB, UCLA, 1948; PhD, U. Calif.-Berkeley, 1953. With Lavadora de Lanas S.A., Viña del Mar, Chile, 1941-46; asst. prof. physics U. Oreg., Eugene, 1953-58, assoc. prof., 1958-63, prof., 1963-89, prof. emeritus, 1989—, chmn. dept., 1976-84, dir. Chem. Physics Inst., 1984-87. Guest assoc. physicist Brookhaven Nat. Lab., Upton, N.Y., 1961-62; vis. prof. U. Calif., Berkeley, 1968-69, Université Pierre et Marie Curie, Paris, 1977; vis. scholar Stanford U., 1983; cons. Lawrence Radiation Lab., 1954-68, physicist, 1968-69; mem. com. on atomic and molecular sci. NRC/Nat. Acad. Scis., 1976-82; vis. scientist NASA Ames Rsch. Ctr., 1975-76; mem. panel on radiation rsch. NRC, 1985-87, chair bd. on assessment of NIST programs panel on atomic molecular and optical physics, 1989-90; chair exec. com. Advanced Light Source Users, 1984-88, sci. policy bd., 1989-92; chair adv. bd. Basic Energy Scis. Synchrotron Radiation Ctr. Argonne Nat. Lab, 1991-93; mem. U. Chgo. Review Com. for Argonne Nat. Lab. Physics Divsn., 1993-98; U.S. advisor in physics U.S.-Mex. Found. for Sci., 1994-97. Author (with J.L. Powell): Quantum Mechanics, 1961; editor: Atomic Inner-Shell Processes, 1975, Atomic Inner-Shell Physics, 1985, Phys. Rev. A, 1992—2006; mem. editl. bd.: Phys. Rev. C, 1978, Atomic Data and Nuc. Data Tables, 1982—2000, mem. publs. bd.: Am. Inst. Physics, 1992—2000; contbr. articles to sci. jours. Mem. region XIV selection com. Woodrow Wilson Nat. Fellowship Found., 1959-61, 62-68. Recipient Ersted award for distinguished teaching U. Oreg., 1959; NSF research grantee, 1954-64; U.S. AEC grantee, 1964-72; NASA grantee, 1972-79; AFOSR grantee, 1979-86; NSF grantee, 1986-95. Fellow AAAS, Am. Phys. Soc. (chmn. div. electron and atomic physics 1981-82, councillor 1983-86, mem. com. on internat. sci. affairs 1997-2000, chmn. 2000); mem. ACLU, Am. Assn. Physics Tchrs. (pres. Oreg. sect. 1956-57), Croatian Acad. Scis. and Arts (corr. mem.), Sierra Club, Phi Beta Kappa. Office: Univ Oreg 26 W 30th Ave Apt 3724 Eugene OR 97405 Business E-Mail: berndc@uoregon.edu.

CRASWELL, RICHARD, law educator; b. 1954; BA in Econs. with high honors, Mich. State U., 1974; JD cum laude, U. Chgo., 1977. Atty. office policy planning FTC, 1977—81, atty. bur. competition and bur. economics, 1982, atty.-advisor to commr. David A. Clanton, 1982—83; asst. prof. U. So. Calif. Law Ctr., 1983—85, assoc. prof., 1985—88, prof. law, 1988—94, Carolyn Craig Franklin prof., 1991—94, assoc. dean, 1988—90; prof. law U. Chgo. Law Sch., 1994—98, Stanford Law Sch., 1998—, William F. Baxter - Visa Internat. prof. law, 2002—, assoc. dean, 1999—2001. Adj. prof. Georgetown U. Law Ctr., 1983; vis. prof. U. Chgo. Law Sch., 1987—88, Stanford Law Sch., 1993. Victor H. Kramer Fellow, Yale Law Sch. and Yale Instn. for Social & Policy Studies, 1981—82. Office: Stanford Law Sch Crown Quadrangle 559 Nathan Abbott Way Stanford CA 94305-8610 Office Phone: 650-725-8542. Office Fax: 650-723-8230. Business E-Mail: rcraswel@stanford.edu.

CRAVER, THEODORE F., JR., utilities and energy executive; BA, MBA, Univ. So. Calif. Various capital markets trading, underwriting and mktg. positions Security Pacific Nat. Bank, 1973, Bankers Trust Co. of NY, 1980—84; various fin. mgmt. positions including exec. v.p. and corp. treas. First Interstate Bancorp, 1984—96; various fin. and exec. mgmt. positions Edison Internat., 1996—2000, exec. v.p., CFO, treas. Rosemead, Calif., 2000—05; chmn., CEO Edison Mission Energy, 2005—08; CEO Edison Capital, 2005—08; chmn., pres., CEO Edison Internat., Rosemead, Calif., 2008—. Bd. dir. HealthNet, Inc., 2004—. Office: Edison Internat 2244 Walnut Grove Ave Rosemead CA 91770-3714

CRAWFORD, AARON JAMAL (JAMAL CRAWFORD), professional basketball player; b. Seattle, Mar. 20, 1980; Attended, U. Mich., Ann Arbor, 1999—2000. Guard Chgo. Bulls, 2000—04, NY Knicks, 2004—08, Golden State Warriors, 2008—. Office: Golden State Warriors 1011 Broadway Oakland CA 94607

CRAWFORD, CAROL ANNE, marketing professional; b. San Francisco, Jan. 17, 1945; d. Kenneth H. and Marcella (Schloesser) Crawford. BA, San Jose State U., Calif., 1967; MBA in Mktg., Golden Gate U., 1985. Food publicist J. Walter Thompson, San Francisco, 1967—70; asst. mktg. and sales promotion dir. Eastridge Shopping Ctr., San Jose, 1970—72; consumer info. specialist Carl Byoir & Assocs., San Francisco, 1972—78; account supr. Ketchum Pub. Rels., San Francisco, 1978—80; v.p. dir. pub. rels. Grey Advt., San Francisco, 1980—82; dir. corp. comms. S&O Cons., San Francisco, 1982—84; mgr. mktg. and pub. rels. GTE Sprint, 1984—86; dir. pub. rels. U.S. Sprint, 1986; prin. Crawford Comms., San Francisco, 1986—. Instr. pub. rels. Golden Gate U., 1987—94; instr. pub. rels. U. Extension U. Calif., Berkeley, 1994—97; cons. in field; lectr. in field. Adv. bd. Hospice by the Bay; bd. mgrs. YMCA, Embarcadero, Calif., 1980—82. Mem.: San Francisco Publicity Club, San Francisco PR Roundtable, Home Economists in Bus. (past chpt. chmn., past chmn. nat. pub. rels.), San Francisco (Calif.) Profl. Food Soc. (recording sec. 1992—94, com. svcs. chmn. 1995), Pub. Rels. Soc. Am. (past chpt. pres. San Francisco chpt.), Commonwealth Club. Office: Crawford Comms 423 Lansdale Ave San Francisco CA 94127-1616

CRAWFORD, CHACE, actor; b. Lubbock, Tex., July 18, 1985; s. Chris and Dana (Plott) Crawford. Attended, Pepperdine U. Actor: (TV films) Long Lost Son, 2006; (films) The Covenant, 2006, Loaded, 2008, The Haunting of Molly Hartley, 2008; (TV series) Gossip Girl, 2007— (Choice TV Breakout Star Male, Teen Choice Awards, 2008), (guest appearance) Family Guy, 2008. Office: ICM LA 10250 Constellation Blvd Los Angeles CA 90067

CRAWFORD, DAVID L., astronomer; b. Tarentom, Pa., Mar. 2, 1931; s. William Letham and A. Blanche (Livingstone) C.; m. Mary Louise Mueller, Aug. 16, 1940; children: Christine, Deborah, Lisa. PhD, U. Chgo., 1958. Rsch. asst. Yerkes Obs., Chgo., 1953-57; asst. prof. Vanderbilt U., Nashville, 1957-59; staff astronomer Kitt Peak Nat. Obs., Tucson, 1960-96, emeritus astronomer, 1997—. Rsch. asst. McDonald Obs., 1955-57; project mgr. Kitt Peak Nat. Obs., 1963-73, assoc. dir. rsch., 1970-73, head office univ. rels., 1984-85, head office of tech. transfer, 1993-95; exec. dir. Internat. Dark-Sky Assn., 1987—, pres. bd. dirs. GNAT, Inc., 1993—. Recipient outstanding svc. award Astron. League, 1992. Fellow AAAS (coun. 1986-89, com. on coun. affairs 1986-88), Illuminating Engring. Soc. N.Am. (roadway lighting com., outdoor environ. lighting impact com., sports lighting com.); mem. Am. Astron. Soc. (coun. 1972-75, Van Briesbrock award 1997), Astron. Soc. Pacific (bd. dirs. 1970-76, nominating com., publs. com.), Internat. Astron. Union (active numerous commns., exec. coms., past chmn. working group on amateur/profl. rels.). Avocations: travel, reading, teaching, trout fishing, photography. Office: IDA 3225 N First Ave Tucson AZ 85719 Office Phone: 520-293-3198. E-mail: crawford@darksky.org, ida@darksky.org.

CRAWFORD, DEBRA P., women's healthcare company executive; BSBA in Acctg., San Diego State U. CPA, Calif. Dir. fin., mfg. contr. Advanced Cardiovasc. Sys., Inc., 1992-94; v.p. fin. and adminstrn., treas., asst. sec. IVAC Corp., 1994; CFO, v.p., CFO, treas., sec. IVAC Med. Sys., Inc., 1995-96; CFO, treas. IVAC Holdings, Inc., 1996; ind. fin. cons., acting CFO or corp. devel. fin. cons., 1997-98; v.p., CFO, treas. Women First HealthCare, Inc., San Diego, 1998—, asst. sec., 1998-99, sec., 1999—.

CRAWFORD, DENISE F., lawyer; BS, Calif. Polytechnic Univ., 1999; JD, Univ. San Diego, 2002. Bar: Calif. 2002. Assoc., criminal defense Law Offices of Jennifer L. Keller, Irvine, Calif. Named a Rising Star, So. Calif. Super Lawyers, 2006. Office: Law Offices of Jennifer L Keller Ste 560 18500 Von Karman Ave Irvine CA 92612-1043 Office Phone: 949-476-8700. Office Fax: 949-476-0900.

CRAWFORD, DONALD WESLEY, philosophy educator, university official; b. Berkeley, Calif., July 30, 1938; s. Arthur Loyd and Josephine (Gareffa) C.; m. Sharon Dee Messenger, Nov. 5, 1960; children: Kathryn, Alison. BA, U. Calif., Berkeley, 1960; PhD, U. Wis., 1965. From tchg. asst. to dean U. Wis., Madison, 1962—89, dean Coll. Letters and Sci., 1989-92; asst. prof. U. Sask., Saskatchewan, Canada, 1965-68; vice chancellor acad. affairs U. Calif., Santa Barbara, 1992-93, exec. vice chancellor, 1993-98, prof., 1992—2004, prof. emeritus, 2004—, dir. London Ctr. for Edn. Abroad program, 1998-2000, dep. assoc. provost, 2001—. Author: Kant's Aesthetic Theory, 1974; editor Jour. Aesthetics and Art Criticism, 1989-93. Bd. dirs. Meriter Hosp., Madison, 1989-92, Santa Barbara Bot. Garden, 1993-98, U. Calif. Santa Barbara Found., 1992-98, U. Calif. Trust (U.K.), 2000—. NEH fellow, 1974. Mem. Am. Soc. for Aesthetic, Brit. Soc. for Aesthetic. Office: U Calif Dept Philosophy South Hall Santa Barbara CA 93106 E-mail: crawford@philosophy.ucsb.edu.

CRAWFORD, E. DAVID, urologist, surgeon, researcher; b. Cin., June 6, 1947; s. Elward G. and Gertrude E. (Wagner) C.; m. Barbara Schoborg, June 28, 1969; children: Michael, Marc, Ryan. BS, U. Cin., 1969, MD, 1973. Intern Good Samaritan Hosp., Cin., 1973-74, resident, 1974-77; asst. and assoc. prof. urology U. N.Mex. Sch. Medicine, Albuquerque, 1978-83; assoc. prof. to prof. surgery/urology U. Miss. Med. Ctr., Jackson, 1983-86; prof., chmn. div. urology U. Colo. Denver, Sch. Medicine, Denver, 1986—. Chmn. genitourinary com. S.W. Oncology Group, 1979—. Editor: (textbook) Genitourinary Cancer Surgery; contbr. numerous articles to profl. publs. Chmn. Prostate Cancer Edn. Coun., N.Y.C., 1989. Fellow ACS; mem. Am. Soc. Clin. Oncology. Office: U Colo Denver Mail Stop F710 PO Box 6510 Aurora CO 80045 Office Phone: 720-848-0195. Business E-Mail: david.crawford@uchsc.edu.

CRAWFORD, HARRY, state legislator; b. Shreveport, La., Apr. 17, 1952; m to Gwen Perry; children: Beau, Clarissa, Andrew, Trevor. Attended, La. State U. Alaska State Representative, District 22, 2000-02; Alaska State Representative, District 21, 2003-. Member, Exec Bd, Iron Workers Local #751, currently. Scenic Foothills Community Coun (president & secy-treas, formerly). Democrat. Mailing: 716 W Fourth Ave Ste 540 A Anchorage AK 99501-2133 Office: State Capitol Rm 400 Juneau AK 99801-1182 Office Phone: 907-465-3438, 907-269-0100. Office Fax: 907-465-4565, 907-269-0105. Business E-Mail: Representative_Harry_Crawford@legis.state.ak.us.*

CRAWFORD, MARC, former professional hockey coach; b. Belleville, Ont., Can., Feb. 13, 1961; Left wing Vancouver Canucks, 1981—87; head coach Quebec Nordiques, 1994—95, Colo. Avalanche, 1995—97, Vancouver Canucks, 1998—2006, LA Kings, 2006—08. Head coach Team Can. Nagano Olympic Games, 1998. Recipient Louis A.R. Pieri Meml. award, 1993, Jack Adams Award, 1995; named NHL Coach of Yr., The Sporting News, 1995. Achievements include being the coach of Stanley Cup Champion Colorado Avalanche, 1996.

CRAWFORD, MICHAEL HOWARD, cardiologist, educator, researcher; b. Madison, Wis., July 10, 1943; s. William Henry and A. Kay (Keller) C.; m. Janis Raye Kirschner, June 23, 1968; children: Chelsea Susan, Dinah Jaye, Stuart Michael. AB, U. Calif., Berkeley, 1965; MD, U. Calif., San Francisco, 1969. Diplomate in internal medicine and cardiovasc. disease Am. Bd. Internal Medicine. Med. resident, internal medicine U. Calif. Hosps., San Francisco, 1969-71; sr. med. resident, internal medicine Beth Israel Deaconess Med. Ctr., Boston, 1971-72; tchg. fellow Harvard Med. Sch., Boston, 1971-72; cardiology fellow U. Calif. Hosps., San Diego, 1972-74; asst. prof. medicine U. Calif. Sch. Medicine, San Diego, 1974-76, U. Tex. Health Sci. Ctr., San Antonio, 1976-78, assoc. prof. medicine, 1978-82, prof. medicine, 1982-89; Robert S. Flinn prof. cardiology U. N.Mex. Sch. Medicine, Albuquerque, 1989—2001; prof. medicine Mayo Med. Sch., Minn., 2001—03, U. Calif., San Francisco, 2003—, Lucie Stern chair cardiology, 2005—. Asst. dir. Ischemic Heart Disease Specialized Ctr. Rsch., San Diego, 1975—76; adj. scientist S.W. Found. Biomedical Rsch., San Antonio, 1980—89; co-dir. div. cardiology U. Tex. Health Sci. Ctr., San Antonio, 1983—89; chief div. cardiology U. N.Mex. Sch. Medicine, Albuquerque, 1989—2001; cons. cardiovasc. diseases Mayo Clinic, Scottsdale, Ariz., 2001—03; chief clin. cardiology U. Calif. San Francisco Med. Ctr., 2003—07; chief divsn. cardiology U. Calif., San Francisco, 2007—. Editor: Current Diagnosis and Treatment in Cardiology, 1995, 2d edit., 2004, Cardiology, 2001, 2d edit., 2003; editor Clin. Cardiology Alert newsletter, 1990—; cons. editor (periodical) Cardiology Clinics, 1989-; mem. editl. bd. Circulation Jour., 1990-99, Jour. Am. Coll. Cardiology, 1992-95, 2003-; contbr. several articles to profl. jours. Pres. Am. Heart Assn., San Antonio, 1981, Austin, Tex., 1987, chmn. coun. clin. cardiology, Dallas, 1989, pres., Albuquerque, 1995-96. Recipient Paul Dudley White award, Assn. Mil. Surgeons of U.S., 1981; Merit Review grantee, Dept. VA, 1985—91, Rsch. Tng. grantee, Nat. Heart Lung Blood Inst., 1993—2004. Fellow: ACP, Am. Heart Assn. (chmn., coun. on clin. cardiology), Am. Coll. Cardiology (bd. trustees 1998—2003); mem.: Western Assn. Physicians (pres. 2008—), Assn. Univ. Cardiologists (pres. 2005—06), So. Soc. Clin. Investigation, Am. Soc. Echocardiography (bd. dirs. 1980—83). Avocation: skiing. Office: U Calif Divsn Cardiology 505 Parnassus Ave Box 0124 San Francisco CA 94143-0124 Home: 5 Cecilia Ct Belvedere Tiburon CA 94920-2190 Office Phone: 415-502-8584. Business E-Mail: crawfordm@medicine.ucsf.edu.

CRAWFORD, RANDI, health facility administrator; d. Edward F. Calesa. BA in Liberal Arts, Villanova U. Cons. on creation and prodn. children's programming Fox TV, Lifetime TV, DIC Entertainment, Saban Entertainment, 1991-95; rsch. analyst Calesa Assocs., 1995-97; co-founder, v.p. mktg. rsch., sec. Women First HealthCare, Inc., San Diego, 1997-98, v.p. ednl. program devel., 1998—.

CRAWFORD, RONALD MERRITT, history and geography educator; b. San Diego, Apr. 21, 1949; s. Leslie Merritt and Annie Louise (Briden) C. BA in History and Geography, UCLA, 1971, MA in History, 1972. Cert. standard secondary tchr. Tchr. social scis. divsn. Anchorage C.C., 1972-87; prof. Coll. Arts and Scis. U. Alaska Anchorage, 1987—, chmn. history/geography dept., 1988—. V.p. Anchorage C.C. Campus Assembly, 1985-87; 1st v.p. Faculty Senate U. Alaska Anchorage, 1987-89, 2d v.p., 1990-91; mem. Univ. Assembly, 1988-89; mem. Bartlett lectr. com. U. Alaska Anchorage, 1987-90, audio-visual adv. bd., 1989—, promotion and tenure appeals com., 1989-90; mem. exec. bd. Alaska C.Cs. Fedn. Tchrs., 1984—, Harry S. Truman scholarship com. Anchorage C.C., 1978-82; advisor Golden Key Honor Soc., 1993—, Campus Cinema Film Series, 1972—, Anchorage C.C. Student Assn., 1983-85; coord. history/geography discipline Anchorage C.C., 1979-87; columnist Anchorage Daily News, 1984-87; host Alaska Home and Gardens Program Sta. KAKM-TV, 1990. Host fund drives Sta. KAKM-TV, 1983—; guest speaker Anchorage Sch. Dist. Community Resource Ctr., 1972—, McLaughlin Youth Ctr., 1975—; advisor Friends of Libr. Film Program Loussac Libr., 1985—; presenter geography awareness programs Alaska Staff Devel. Network Summer Acad., 1990, 91, Alaska Geog. Alliance Inst., 1992, 93. Recipient Disting. Teaching Achievement award Alaska State Legislature, 1992, Disting. Teaching Achievement award Nat. Coun. Geog. Edn., 1992. Mem. Am. Fedn. Tchrs., Am. Film Inst., Nat. Coun. Geographic Edn., Alaska Geography Alliance, Assn. Pacific Coast Geographers, Univ. Film and Video Assn., Phi Alpha Theta. Avocations: travel, movies, hiking, photography, videography. Home: PO Box 670572 Chugiak AK 99567-0572 Office: U Alaska Dept History & Geography 3211 Providence Dr Anchorage AK 99508-4614

CRAWFORD, ROY EDGINGTON, III, lawyer; b. Topeka, Dec. 23, 1938; s. Roy E. and Ethel Trula (Senne) C.; children: Michael, Jennifer. BS, U. Pa., 1960; LL.B., Stanford U., 1963. Bar: Calif. 1964, U.S. Ct. Mil. Appeals 1964, U.S. Tax Ct. 1969, U.S. Dist. Ct. (no. dist.) Calif. 1971, U.S. Ct. Claims 1974, U.S. Supreme Ct. 1979. Assoc. Brobeck Phleger & Harison, San Francisco, 1967-73, ptnr., 1973—2003; spl. counsel Heller Ehrman LLP, San Francisco, 2003—07; counsel McDermott Will & Emery LLP, 2008—. Contbr. chpts. to books; bd. editors: Stanford U. Law Rev., 1962-63. Served to capt. AUS, 1964-67. Recipient award of merit U.S. Ski Assn., 1980. Mem. ABA (chmn. com. on state and local taxes 1979-81), Calif. State Bar Assn., San Francisco Bar Assn., Calif. Trout (bd. dirs. 1970-1992, v.p. 1975-94, sec.-treas. 1994-2001), The Nature Conservancy of Idaho (bd. dirs. 1994-2003), Yosemite Inst. (bd. dirs. 1997-2007), Beta Gamma Sigma. Office: McDermott Will & Emery LLP 3150 Porter Dr Palo Alto CA 94304 Business E-Mail: rcrawford@mwe.com.

CREAGER, JOE SCOTT, geology and oceanography educator; b. Vernon, Tex., Aug. 30, 1929; s. Earl Litton and Irene Eugenia (Keller) C.; m. Barbara Clark, Aug. 30, 1951 (dec.); children: Kenneth Clark, Vanessa Irene; m. B. J. Wren, Sept. 5, 1987 (dec.); m. Eva R. Milligan, Mar. 18, 2001 (div.); m. Joanne L. Thronson, Aug. 7, 2004. BS, Colo. Coll., 1951; postgrad., Columbia, 1952-53; MS, Tex. A&M U., 1953, PhD, 1958. Asst. prof. dept. oceanography U. Wash., Seattle, 1958-61, assoc. prof., 1962-66, prof. oceanography, 1966-91, prof. geol. scis., 1981-91, prof. emeritus, 1991—, asst. chmn. dept. oceanography, 1964-65, assoc. dean arts and scis. for earth and planetary scis., 1966-95, assoc. dean for rsch., 1966-91, divisional dean emeritus, 1995—; program dir. for oceanography NSF, 1965-66; chief scientist numerous oceanographic expdns. to Arctic and Sub-arctic including Leg XIX of Deep Sea Drilling project, 1959-91. Vis. geol. scientist Am. Geol. Inst., 1962, 63, 65; U.S. Nat. coord. Internat. Indian Ocean Expedition, 1965-66; vis. scientist program lectr. Am. Geophys. Union, 1965-72; Battelle cons., advanced waste mgmt., 1974; cons. to U.S. Army C.E., 1976, U.S. Depts. Interior and Commerce, 1975; exec. sec., exec. com., chmn. planning com. Joint Oceanographic Insts. Deep Earth Sampling, 1970-72, 76-78; mem. evaluation com. Northwest Assn. Schs. and Colls., 1989-99. Mem. editorial bd. Internat. Jour. Marine Geology, 1964-91; assoc. editor Jour. Sedimentary Petrology, 1963-76; asst. editor Quaternary Research, 1970-79; contbr. articles to profl. jours. Skipper Sea Scout Ship, Boy Scouts Am., Bryan, Tex., 1957; coach Little League Baseball, Seattle, 1964-71, sec., 1971; cons. sci. curriculum Northshore Sch. Dist., 1970; mem. Seattle Citizens Shoreline Com., 1973-74, King County Shoreline Com., 1980. Served with U.S. Army, 1953-55. Colo. Coll. scholar, 1949-51; NSF grantee, 1962-82; ERDA grantee, 1962-64; U.S. Army C.E. grantee, 1975-82; Office of Naval Research grantee; U.S. Dept. Commerce grantee; U.S. Geol. Survey grantee. Fellow Geol. Soc. Am., AAAS; mem. Internat. Assn. Quaternary Research, Am. Geophys. Union, Internat. Assn. Sedimentology, Internat. Assn. Math. Geologists, Soc. Econ. Paleontologists and Mineralists, Marine Tech. Soc. (sec.-treas. 1972-75), Sigma Xi, Beta Theta Pi, Delta Epsilon. Home: 7449 NE 118th Pl Kirkland WA 98034 Office: U Wash PO Box 353765 Seattle WA 98195-3765 Personal E-mail: bjnjoe@att.net.

CREGAN, NORA C., lawyer; b. Phila. BA magna cum laude, Middlebury Coll., 1984; JD with honors, U. Chgo., 1991. Bar: Calif. 1991, U.S. Dist. Ct., Ctrl. & No. Dist. Calif. 1992, U.S. Ct. Appeals, ninth cir. 1992, Wash. 1995, U.S. Dist. Ct., We. Dist. Wash. 1995. With Morgan Stanley, NYC; law clk. to Hon. Eugene A. Wright U.S. Ct. Appeals, ninth cir., Seattle; ptnr. Bingham McCutchen LLP, San Francisco, co-chairperson pro bono com. Mem.: San Francisco Lawyers Com., Nat. Lawyers Com. Civil Rights Under Law (bd. dirs.). Office: Bingham & McCutchen LLP 3 Enbarcader Ctr San Francisco CA 94111 Office Phone: 415-393-2060. Office Fax: 415-393-2286. Business E-Mail: nora.cregan@bingham.com.

CREGG, HUGH ANTHONY See LEWIS, HUEY

CREIGHTON, NORMAN P., bank executive; B in Banking and Fin. with honors, U. Mont. With Ariz. Bank, Gt. Western Bank and Trust; pres., CEO Imperial Bank, Inglewood, Calif., 1985-97, CEO, vice chmn., 1997—. Bd. dirs. Imperial Bancorp. Bd. dirs. Ind. Colls. So. Calif., U. Mont. Found. Mem. Assn. Res. City Bankers, Def. Orientation Conf. Assn.

CREMIN, ROBERT W., manufacturing executive; b. 1940; BS in Metallurgical Engring., Polytech. Inst. Brooklyn; MBA, Harvard U. Grad. Sch. Bus. Mktg. mgmt. Omark Inds., Portland, Oreg.; exec. mgmt. Esterlin Techs., Bellevue, Wash., 1989-97, pres., COO, 1997-01, pres., COO, chmn. bd. dirs., 2001—. Office: #1500 500 108TH Ave NE Bellevue WA 98004-5500

CREWS, FREDERICK CAMPBELL, humanities educator, writer; b. Phila., Feb. 20, 1933; s. Maurice Augustus and Robina (Gaudet) C.; m. Betty Claire Peterson, Sept. 9, 1959; children: Gretchen Detre, Ingrid Márquez. AB, Yale U., 1955; PhD, Princeton U., 1958. Faculty U. Calif., Berkeley, 1958—, instr. in English, 1958-60, asst. prof., 1960-62, assoc. prof., 1962-66, prof., 1986-94, vice-chair for grad. studies, 1988-92, chair dept., 1992-94; prof. emeritus, 1994—. Mem. study fellowship selection com. Am. Coun. Learned Socs., 1971-73; mem. selection com. summer seminars Nat. Endowment for Humanities, 1976-77; Ward-Phillips lectr. U. Notre Dame, 1974-75, Dorothy T. Burstein lectr. UCLA, 1984; Frederick Ives Carpenter vis. prof. U. Chgo., 1985; Lansdowne visitor U. Victoria, 1987-88; John Dewey lectr., 1988, Nina Mae Kellogg lectr. Portland (Oreg.) State U., 1989; mem. exec. com. bd. dirs. Mark Twain Project, 1984-; faculty rsch. lectr. U. Calif., Berkeley, 1991-92; David L. Kubal Meml. lectr. Calif. State U., L.A., 1994; mem. sci. and profl. adv. bd. False Memory Syndrome Found., 1994—; mem. exec. coun. Com. for Sci. Skeptical Inquiry, 2000-. Author: The Tragedy of Manners, 1957, E.M. Forster: The Perils of Humanism, 1962, The Pooh Perplex, 1963, The Sins of the Fathers, 1966, The Patch Commission, 1968, The Random House Handbook, 1974, 6th edit., 1992, Out of My System, 1975, Skeptical Engagements, 1986, 2000, The Critics Bear it Away, 1992, Postmodern Pooh, 2001, Follies of the Wise, 2006; co-author: The Borzoi Handbook for Writers, 1985, 3d edit., 1993; prin. author: The Memory Wars, 1995; editor: The Red Badge of Courage (Crane), 1964, Great Short Works of Nathaniel Hawthorne, 1967, Starting Over, 1970, Psychoanalysis and Literary Process, 1970, The Random House Reader, 1981, Unauthorized Freud, 1998; mem. contbg. bd. editors The Common Review, 2000—. Recipient Essay prize Nat. Endowment Arts, 1968, Disting. Tchg. award U. Calif., Berkeley, 1985, Spielvogel Diamonstein PEN prize, 1992; named Fulbright lectr. Turin, Italy, 1961-62; fellow Am. Coun. Learned Socs., 1965-66, Ctr. for Advanced Study in Behavioral Scis., 1965-66, Guggenheim Found., 1970-71, Am. Acad. Arts and Scis., 1992. Fellow: Coun. for Sci. Medicine and Mental Health (mem. exec. coun., mem. com. skeptical inquiry). Home: 636 Vincente Ave Berkeley CA 94707-1524 Personal E-mail: fredc@berkeley.edu.

CREWS, JAMES CECIL, hospital administrator; b. Marshalltown, Iowa, July 29, 1937; married. BA, U. Wis., 1959; MA, U. Iowa, 1964. Asst. adminstr. Meth. Asbury Hosps., Mpls., 1964, adminstrv. resident, 1963-64, adminstr., 1964-66, Illini Hosp., Silvis, Ill., 1966-69, Charleston Gen. Hosp., W.Va., 1969-72; exec. v.p. Charleston Area Med. Ctr., Charleston, W.Va., 1972-81, pres., 1981-88; exec. v.p., COO VHA Enterprises Inc., Irving, Tex., 1988-89, acting pres., CEO, 1989-90; pres., CEO Samaritan Health Svcs., Phoenix, 1990, Samaritan Health System, Phoenix, 1991—. Mem. W.Va. Hosp. Assn. (bd. dirs., pres 1979—). Office: Samaritan Health System 1441 N 12th St Phoenix AZ 85006-2837

CREWS, WILLIAM ODELL, JR., religious organization administrator; b. Houston, Feb. 8, 1936; s. William O. Sr. and Juanita (Pearson) C.; m. Wanda Jo Ann Cunningham; 1 child, Ronald Wayne. BA, Hardin Simmons U., 1957, HHD, 1987; BDiv, Southwestern Bapt. Theol. Sem., 1964; DD, Calif. Bapt. Coll., 1987; DMin, Golden Gate Bapt. Theol. Sem., 2000. Ordained to ministry Bapt. Ch., 1953. Pastor Grape Creek Bapt. Ch., San Angelo, Tex., 1952-54, Plainview Bapt. Ch., Stamford, Tex., 1955-57, 1st Bapt. Ch., Sterling City, Tex., 1957-60, 7th St. Bapt. Ch., Ballinger, Tex., 1960-65, Woodland Heights Bapt. Ch., Brownwood, Tex., 1965-67, Victory Bapt. Ch., Seattle, 1967-72, Met. Bapt. Ch., Portland, Oreg., 1972-77; dir. comm. N.W. Bapt. Conv., Portland, 1977-78; pastor Magnolia Ave Bapt. Ch., Riverside, Calif., 1978-86; pres. Golden Gate Bapt. Theol. Sem., Mill Valley, Calif., 1986—2003, chancellor, 2003—. Pres. N.W. Bapt. Conv., Portland, 1974-76, So. Bapt. Gen. Conv. Calif., Fresno, 1982-84. Trustee Fgn. Mission Bd., Richmond, Va., 1973-78, Golden Gate Bapt. Theol. Sem., 1980-85, Marin Cmty. Hosp. Found., 1992-95; bd. dirs. Midway Seatac Boys Club, Des Moines, 1969-72, Marin Gen. Hosp., 1998-2004, North Bay Coun., 1998—. Mem. Marin County C. of C. (bd. dirs. 1987-95), Midway C. of C. (bd. dirs. 1968-72), Rotary (bd. dirs. San Rafael chpt. 1992—, pres. Portland club 1975-76, pres.-elect Riverside club 1984-85). Baptist. Home: 3505 NW 9th Ave Camas WA 98607 Office: Golden Gate Bapt Theol Sem 3200 NE 109th Vancouver WA 98632 Business E-Mail: billcrews@ggbts.edu.

CRIMINALE, WILLIAM OLIVER, JR., applied mathematics professor; b. Mobile, Ala., Nov. 29, 1933; s. William Oliver and Vivian Gertrude (Sketoe) C.; m. Ulrike Irmgard Wegner, June 7, 1962; children: Martin Oliver, Lucca. BS, U. Ala., 1955; PhD, Johns Hopkins U., 1960. Asst. prof. Princeton (N.J.) U., 1962-68; asso. prof. U. Wash., Seattle, 1968-73, prof. oceanography, geophysics, applied math., 1973—, chmn. dept. applied math., 1976-84. Cons. Aerospace Corp., 1963—65, Boeing Corp., 1968—72, AGARD, 1967—68, Lenox Hill Hosp., 1967—68, ICASE, NASA Langley, 1990—2003; guest prof., Canada, 1965, 2001, France, 1967—68, Germany, 1973—74, Sweden, 1973—74, Scotland, 1985, 89, 91, England, 90, 91, Stanford U., 1990, Brazil, 92, 2001, Italy, 1999, Crete, 2005; Nat. Acad. exch. scientist USSR, 1969, 72. Author: Stability of Parallel Flows, 1967, Theory and Computation in Hydrodynamic Stability, 2003; contbr. articles to profl. jours. Served with U.S. Army, 1961-62. Boris A. Bakmeteff Meml. fellow, 1957-58, NATO postdoctoral fellow, 1960-61, Alexander von Humboldt Sr. fellow, 1973-74, Royal Soc. fellow, 1990-91. Fellow Am. Phys. Soc.; mem. Am. Acad. Mechanics, Am. Geophys. Union, Fedn. Am. Scientists. Home: 1635 Peach Ct E Seattle WA 98112-3428 Office: U Wash Dept Applied Math Box 352420 Seattle WA 98195-2420 Office Phone: 206-543-9506. Business E-Mail: lascala@amath.washington.edu.

CRIPPEN, BRUCE D., former state legislator, real estate manager; b. Billings, Mont., June 13, 1932; m. Mary Crippen; 4 children. BS, U. Mont., 1956, grad. Sch. Law, NYU. Mem. Mont. Ho. of Reps., Billings, 1981-99, minority whip, 1985-86, minority leader, 1991-92, 93-94; pres. pro tempore Mont. Senate, Billings, 1997-98, pres., 1999, mem. ethics com., jud. com., legis. adminstrn. com., rules com. Served USN, 1952-54. Lutheran.

CRISCI, MATHEW G., financial consultant and author; b. NYC; s. Mathew Anthony and Frances (Coscia) C.; m. Mary Ann, Nov. 14, 1968; children: Mathew Joseph, Mark David, Mitchell Justin. BS, Iona Coll., New Rochelle, NY. Sr. v.p. Young & Rubicam, Inc., NYC and Sydney, Australia, 1968—82; exec. v.p., COO, bd. dirs. Integrated Barter Internat., NYC and LA, 1982—85; sr. v.p., gen. mgr., bd. dirs. Chiat/Day Advt. Inc., San Francisco, 1986—90; exec. v.p., mng. dir. Lowe Lintas Worldwide, NYC, 1991—97; exec. v.p., chief mktg. officer Alton Entertainment Co., LA, 1997—2001, also bd. dirs.; chief mktg. officer, sr. v.p., ptnr. Asset Mktg. Sys., San Diego, 2001—06, bd. dirs.; pres. MGC Cos., LLC, 2007—, CEO. Author: Observations of a Kind, 1998, Little Fanny Cuscia, 2003, Michael & Sandra, 2004, Alexandria Plummet & Friends, 2006, Mary Jackson-Peale, 2007, Lilia, 2008, Papa Cado, 2009. Office Phone: 760-390-2055, 760-804-7360. Business E-Mail: mattcrisci@gmail.com.

CRISP, DAVID, atmospheric physicist, research scientist; b. Las Vegas, Nev., May 10, 1956; s. Carroll and Louise (Martin) C.; m. Joy Anne Miller, June 13, 1981. BS in Edn. Curriculum and Instrn., Tex. A&M U., 1977; MA in Geophys. Fluid Dynamics, Princeton U., 1981, PhD in Geophys. Fluid Dynamics, 1983. Cert. secondary sch. tchr., Tex. Rsch. asst. Geophys. Fluid Dynamics Program, Princeton, N.J., 1979-83; postdoctoral fellow planetary sci. dept. Calif. Inst. Tech., Pasadena, 1984-86, rsch. scientist Jet Propulsion Lab., 1986—. Mem. planetary sci. data steering group NASA, Washington, 1975—. Contbr. articles to profl. publs. Grad. student fellow NASA, 1981-83; recipient Group Achievement award NASA, 1986, 94, Cert. of Appreciation NASA, 1991, 93, 94. Mem. Am. Astron. Soc., Am. Geophys. Union, Am. Meteorol. Soc. Achievements include patent for high performance miniature hygrometer and method thereof. Office: Calif Inst Tech Jet Propulsion Lab 241-105 4800 Oak Grove Dr Pasadena CA 91109

CRISP, MICHAEL GRAVES, publishing executive; b. Heath, Ky., July 4, 1937; s. Dwight Dean and Marie (Graves) C.; m. Jean Leslie Millspaugh, June 12, 1965; children: Michael Dwight, Jennifer Leslie, Meredith Brooke. AB, Colgate U., 1959; SEP, Stanford U., 1973. Editor-in-chief McGraw-Hill, NYC, 1962-70; v.p., pub. Sci. Rsch. Assn., Chgo., 1970-85; chmn., CEO Crisp Publs. Inc., Menlo Park, Calif., 1985—. Bd. dirs. Mayfield Pub., Mountain View, Calif., Journeyware Multimedia, San Francisco, No. Calif. Employers Group, San Francisco, Crisp Publs., Inc., Menlo Park; adj. faculty U. Calif. Extension, Berkeley, 1990-94. Author: The Book Publishing Industry, 1984; editor: Rate Your Skills as a Manager, 1991, Twelve Steps to Self-Improvement, 1991, Achieving Job Satisfaction, 1994. Bd. dirs. Ladera (Calif.) Community Assn., 1972-74. Lt. j.g. USCG, 1959-62. Named Top Ten Bay Area Employers, Career Community Edn. Ctr., San Mateo, Calif., 1993, 100 Fastest Growing Bay Area Cos., San Francisco Business Times, 1993. Mem. Instrnl. Systems Assn., Tng. Media Assn., Am. Soc. Assn. Execs., U.S. C. of C., Internat. Soc. Retirement Planners, Nat. Soc. for Performance and Instruction. Republican. Avocations: winemaking, golf, travel, cooking. Office: PO Box 7443 Menlo Park CA 94026-7443

CRISTIANO, MARILYN JEAN, speech communication educator; b. New Haven, Jan. 10, 1954; d. Michael William and Mary Rose (Porto) C. BA, Marquette U., 1975, MA, 1977; postgrad., Ariz. State U., 1977; EdD, Nova Southeastern U., 1991. Speech comm. instr. Phoenix Coll., 1977-87, Paradise Valley C.C., Phoenix, 1987—. Presenter at profl. confs., workshops and seminars, comm. and humanities divsn. chair, Paradise Valley Cmty. Coll. Author tng. manual on pub. speaking, 1991, 92, 95, 97, 99, 2002,2004. Named Technology Tchr. of Yr. for Ariz. Cmty. Colls., CCS Presentation Systems and Proxima Corp., 2000. Mem. Nat. Comm. Assn., Western States Comm. Assn., Ariz. Comm. Assn. Avocation: video and digital photography. Office: Paradise Valley CC 18401 N 32nd St Phoenix AZ 85032-1210 Business E-Mail: marilyn.cristiano@pvmail.maricopa.edu.

CRISWELL, ELEANOR CAMP, psychologist; b. Norfolk, Va., May 12, 1938; d. Norman Harold Camp and Eleanor (Talman) David; m. Thomas L. Hanna (dec. 1990). BA, U. Ky., 1961, MA, 1962; EdD, U. Fla., 1969. Asst. prof. edn. Calif. State Coll., Hayward, 1969; prof. psychology, former chair Calif. State U., Sonoma, 1969—2008; emeritus prof. Sonoma State U., 2008. Faculty adviser Humanistic Psychology Inst., San Francisco, 1970-77; dir. Novato Inst. Somatic Rsch. and Tng.; editor Somatics jour.; cons. Venturi, Inc., Autogenic Sys., Inc.; clin. dir. Biotherapeutics, Kentfield Med. Hosp., 1985-90; founder Humanistic Psychology Inst. (now Saybrook Grad. Sch.), 1970. Author: How Yoga Works, 1987, Biofeedback and Somatics, 1995; co-editor: Biofeedback and Family Practice Medicine, 1983; patentee optokinetic perceptual learning device. Mem. APA (past pres. divsn. 32), Biofeedback Soc. Calif. (past pres.), Assn. for Humanistic Psychology (past pres.), Somatic Soc. (pres.), Equine Hanna Somatics (founder), Internat. Assn. Yoga Therapists (v.p.). Office: Novato Inst 1516 Grant Ave #212 Novato CA 94945 Home Phone: 415-897-6044; Office Phone: 415-897-0336. Business E-Mail: ecriswel@ix.netcom.com.

CRISWELL, STEPHEN, astronomer; Program mgr. Fred Lawrence Whipple Obs., Amada, Ariz. Project mgr. Very Energetic Radiation Imaging Telescope Array Sys. (VERITAS), a collaboration which pioneered the Imaging Atmospheric Cherenkov Technique for the detection of very high energy (VHE) gamma rays. Mailing: Fred Lawrence Whipple Obs PO Box 6369 Amado AZ 85645-6369 Office: Fred Lawrence Whipple Observatory 670 Mt Hopkins Rd Amado AZ 85645 Office Phone: 520-670-5702. Office Fax: 520-670-5714. E-mail: scriswell@cfa.harvard.edu.

CROCKER, MYRON DONOVAN, federal judge; b. Pasadena, Calif., Sept. 4, 1915; s. Myron William and Ethel (Shoemaker) C.; m. Elaine Jensen, Apr. 26, 1941; children— Glenn, Holly. AB, Fresno State Coll., 1937; LL.B., U. Calif., Berkeley, 1940. Bar: Calif. bar 1940. Spl. agt. FBI, 1940-46; practiced law Chowchilla, Calif., 1946-58; asst. dist. atty. Madera County, Calif., 1946-51; judge Chowchilla Justice Ct., 1952-58, Superior Ct. Madera County, 1958-59; U.S. judge Ea. Dist. Calif., Sacramento, 1959—; now sr. judge Eastern Dist. Calif., Sacramento. Mem. Madera County Rep. Ctrl. Com., 1950—. Named Outstanding Citizen Chowchilla, 1960 Mem. Chowchilla C. of C. (sec.) Clubs: Lion. Lutheran. Office: US Dist Courthouse 1130 O St Rm 5007 Fresno CA 93721-2201

CROCKER, THOMAS DUNSTAN, economics professor; b. Bangor, Maine, July 22, 1936; s. Floyd M. and Gloria F. (Thomas) C.; m. Sylvia Fleming, Dec. 31, 1961 (div. Sept. 1986); children: Sarah Lydia, Trena Elizabeth; m. Judith Powell, Sept. 9, 1989. AB, Bowdoin Coll., 1959; PhD, U. Mo., 1967. Asst. prof. econs. U. Wis., Milw., 1963-70; assoc. prof. U. Calif., Riverside, 1970-75; prof. U. Wyo., Laramie, 1975-2001, chairperson dept. econs. and fin., 1991-93, dir. Sch. Environment and Natural Resources, 1993-98, J.E. Warren disting. prof of Energy and Environment, 1997—, disting. prof. emeritus, 2001—. Sr. rsch. assoc. U. Calif., Berkeley, 1973, Pa. State U., 1974; mem. sci. adv. bd. EPA, Washington, 1973—76, mem. panel, 1974, 75, 78, 81, 95, 97, 2001—02, 2004—06, NSF, 1977—80, 2002—03; cons. Asarco, Inc., 1985—89, Mathtech, Inc., Princeton, NJ, 1987—88, Shea and Gardner, Washington, 1989, Arco, Inc., 1992, A. Coors Co., 1992, Eastern Rsch. Group, 1997, Indsl. Econs., Inc., Cambridge, Mass., 1998—99; mem. panel on long range transport issues U.S. Congress, Washington, 1981; mem. Gov.'s Competition Rev. Com., State of Wyo. Co-author: Environmental Economics, 1971; author, editor: Economic Perspectives on Acid Deposition Control, 1984; editorial coun. Jour. Environ. Econs. and Mgmt., 1973-88, 95-99; contbr. articles to profl. jours. Mem. com. impacts pollution on agriculture Orgn. for Econ. Cooperation and Devel., Paris, 1987-88. Grantee, NSF, 1968, 1973, 1981, EPA, 1971, 1976—85, 1997—2005; scholar, Fulbright Found., 2001—06. Mem.: European Assn. Environ. Resource Econs., Assn. Environ. Resource Econs. (contributed papers com. 1989, fellow 2008, Rsch. of Enduring Quality award 2002), Am. Econ. Assn. (mem. awards structure com. 1981—83), The Nature Conservancy. Republican. Avocations: skiing, bicycling, travel, trekking, rafting. Office: Univ Wyo Dept Econs Laramie WY 82071 Home Phone: 307-742-5169; Office Phone: 307-766-6423. Business E-Mail: tcrocker@uwyo.edu.

CROCKETT, CLYLL WEBB, lawyer; b. Preston, Idaho, Feb. 16, 1934; s. Frank Lee and Alta (Webb) C.; m. Nan Marie Mattice, June 27, 1958; children: Jeffrey Webb, Nicole, Karen, Cynthia. BS, Brigham Young U., 1958; MBA Northwestern U, 1959; LL.B., U. Ariz., 1962. Bar: Ariz. 1962, U.S. Supreme Ct. 1970. Clk. Ariz. Supreme Ct., 1962-63; ptnr. Fennemore Craig, Phoenix, 1968—. Instr. eve. div. Mesa (Ariz.) C.C.; bd. dirs. S.W. Airlines Co. Mem. editorial bd. Ariz. Law Rev, 1961. Mem. charter rev. com., Scottsdale, Ariz., 1966-67; mem. bd. adjustment, Scottsdale, 1968-73, chmn., 1971-73; bd. dirs. Maricopa Mental Health Assn., 1976-78, Phoenix Cmty. Alliance, Valley Forward Assn.; mem. Mesa Crime Commn., 1980-82; mem. social scis. adv. bd. LDS Ch.; mem. State of Ariz. Gov.'s Regulatory Rev. Coun; mem. bd. of adjustment City of Mesa, 1996—. Mem. ABA, State Bar Ariz., Maricopa County Bar Assn., Am. Judicature Soc., Phoenix C. of C., Ariz. Acad. Republican. Home: 1510 N Gentry Cir Mesa AZ 85213-4001 Office: Fennemore Craig Ste 2600 3003 North Central Ave Phoenix AZ 85012-2913

CROCKETT, DONALD HAROLD, composer, music educator; b. Pasadena, Calif., Feb. 18, 1951; s. Harold Brown and Martha Amy C.; m. Karen Anne Gallagher Crockett, Nov. 11, 1972 (div. 1986); 1 child: Katherine Jane Crockett; m. Vicki Lyn Ray, June 6, 1988 (div. 2002) MusB, U. So. Calif., 1974, MusM, 1976; PhD, U. Calif., Santa Barbara, 1981. Composer-in-residence Pasadena Chamber Orch., 1984-86, L.A. Chamber Orch., 1991-97. Asst. prof. U. So. Calif., L.A. 1981-84, assoc. prof., 1984-94, prof. 1994—; music dir., condr. U. So. Calif. Contemporary Music Ensemble, L.A., 1984—, Xtet, 1992-; sr. composer-in-residence Chamber Music Conf. and Composers Forum of the East, 2002—. Composer: Celestial Mechanics oboe and string quartet, 1990, Array string quartet number 1, 1987, Roethke Preludes for Orchestra, 1994, Concerto for Piano and Wind Ensemble, 1988, Scree for cello, piano and percussion, 1997, Island for concert band, 1998, The Falcon's Eye for solo guitar, 2000, Cascade for orchestra, 2001, Blue Earth for orchestra, 2002, The Ceiling of Heaven for piano quartet, 2004, Fanfares and Laments for orchestra, 2005, Winter Variations Solo Guiter, 2006. Recipient Friedheim award Kennedy Ctr., Washington, 1991, Aaron Copland award Copland House, 1998, Sylvia Goldstein award Copland House, 2003; Goddard Lieberson fellow Am. Acad. Arts and Letters, N.Y.C., 1994; Nat. Endowment for the Arts grantee, Washington, 1993; artists' fellow Calif. Arts Coun., 1999; Guggenheim fellow, 2006; Bogliasco fellow, 2006. Mem. BMI, Am. Music Ctr., Am. Composers Forum, Phi Kappa Phi. Avocations: reading, backpacking, skiing. Office: Univ Southern Calif Thornton School Of Music Los Angeles CA 90089-0851 E-mail: dcrocket@usc.edu.

CROFTS, RICHARD A., academic administrator; PhD in Reformation History, Duke U. Mem. faculty U. Toledo; assoc. v.p. rsch., dean Grad. Sch. E. Tenn. State U.; dep. commr. acad. affairs Mo. Univ. Sys., Helena, 1994-96, commr. higher edn., 1996—. Office: Montana University System 46 N Last Chance Gulch Helena MT 59601-4122

CROLL, TONY, cinematographer, television director; Cinematographer: (films) The Journey Of Jared Price, 2000, Down and Out with the Dolls, 2001, Kid Bang, 2002; (TV series) Survivor: Marquesas, 2002, Ultimate Albums, 2002, Survivor: Thailand, 2002, My Life Is a Sitcom, 2004, Next Action Star, 2004; cinematographer, dir.: (TV series) The Surreal Life, 2003, Average Joe: Hawaii, 2004, Average Joe: Adam Returns, 2004; dir., dir.: (TV series) Outback Jack, 2003, Three Wishes, 2005— (DGA Award for Outstanding Directorial Achievement in Reality Programs, 2005), America's Next Top Model, 2008 (Outstanding Directorial Achievement in Reality Programs, Dirs. Guild America, 2009); prodr., prodr.: (TV series) Outback Jack, 2003, Hell's Kitchen, 2005; camera operator (TV series) Fear Factor, Ultimate Albums, 2002, The Bachelor, 2002, Meet My Folks, 2002, Operation Junkyard, 2002, The Bachelorette, 2003, Survivor: The Amazon, 2003, The Family, 2003, The Apprentice, 2004. Office: c/o caa 9830 Wilshire Blvd Beverly Hills CA 90212

CROMBIE, DOUGLASS DARNILL, aerospace communications system engineer; b. Alexandra, New Zealand, Sept. 14, 1924; arrived in U.S., 1962, naturalized, 1967; s. Colin Lindsay and Ruth (Darnill) C.; m. Pauline L.A. Morrison, Mar. 2, 1951. BSc, Otago U., Dunedin, New Zealand, 1947, MSc, 1949. New Zealand nat. rsch. fellow Cavendish Lab., Cambridge, England, 1958-59; head radio physics divsn. New Zealand Dept. Sci. and Indsl. Rsch., 1961-62; chief spectrum utilization divsn., chief low frequency group Inst. Telecom. Scis., Dept. Commerce, Boulder, Colo., 1962-71, dir. inst., 1971-76; dir. Inst. Telecom. Scis., Nat. Telecom. and Info. Adminstrn., Boulder, 1976-80; chief scientist Nat. Telecom. and Info. Agy., 1980-85; sr. engring. specialist Aerospace Corp., LA, 1985—. Served with New Zealand Air Force, 1943-44. Recipient Gold medal Dept. Commerce, 1970, citation, 1972. Fellow IEEE; mem. NAE. Office: The Aerospace Corp PO Box 92957 Los Angeles CA 90009-2957 Home: 5471 Torrance Blvd Apt 207 Torrance CA 90503

CROMLEY, BRENT REED, lawyer, state senator; b. Great Falls, Mont., June 12, 1941; s. Arthur and Louise Lilian (Hiebert) C.; m. Dorothea Mae Zamborini, Sept. 9, 1967; children: Brent Reed Jr., Giano Lorenzo, Taya Rose. AB in Math., Dartmouth Coll., 1963; JD with honors, U. Mont., 1968. Bar: Mont. 1968, U.S. Dist. Ct. Mont. 1968, U.S. Ct. Appeals (9th cir.) 1968, U.S. Supreme Ct. 1978, U.S. Ct. Claims 1988, U.S. Ct. Appeals (D.C. cir.) 1988. Law clk. to presiding justice U.S. Dist. Ct. Mont., Billings, 1968-69; assoc. Hutton & Sheehy and predecessor firms, Billings, 1969-77, ptnr., 1977-78, Moulton, Bellingham, Longo & Mather, P.C., Billings, 1979—, also bd. dirs.; mem. Mont. Ho. of Reps., 1991-92, Mont. Senate, 2003—; pres. State Bar Mont., 1998-99. Contbr. articles to profl. jours. Mem. Yellowstone Bd. Health, Billings, 1972—; chmn. Mont. Bd. Pers. Appeals, 1974-80. Mem. ABA (appellate practice com.), ACLU, Internat. Assn. Def. Counsel, State Bar Mont. (chmn. bd. trustees 1995-97, trustee 1991—, pres. 1998-99), Yellowstone County Bar Assn. (various offices), Internat. Assn. Def. Counsel, Christian Legal Soc., Internat. Brotherhood of Magicians, Kiwanis. Avocations: running, magic. Home: 235 Parkhill Dr Billings MT 59101-0660 Office: Moulton Bellingham Longo & Mather PC 27 N 27th St Ste 1900 Billings MT 59101-2399 E-mail: Cromley@moultonlawfirm.com.

CROMWELL, JAMES, actor; b. LA, Jan. 27, 1940; s. John Cromwell and Kay Johnson; m. Anne Ulvestad, Nov. 27, 1976 (div. 1986); 3 children; m. Julie Cobb, May 29, 1986. Attended, Carnegie Inst. Tech. Actor (films) Murder by Death, 1976, The Cheap Detective, 1978, The Man with Two Brains, 1983, Tank, 1984, Revenge of the Nerds, 1984, Oh, God! You Devil, 1984, The House of God, 1984, Explorers, 1985, Revenge of the Nerds II: Nerds in Paradise, 1987, The Rescue, 1988, The Runnin' Kind, 1989, Pink Cadillac, 1989, The Babe, 1992, Romeo is Bleeding, 1993, Babe, 1995 (Oscar award nominee for best supporting actor), Star Trek: First Contact, 1996, Eraser, 1996, Owd Bob, 1997, The People vs. Larry Flynt, 1996, The Education of Little Tree, 1997, L.A. Confidential, 1997, Snow Falling on Cedars, 1998, Deep Impact, 1998, Species II, 1998, Babe: Pig in the City, 1998, Winter, 1998, The General's Daughter, 1999, The Green Mile, 1999, Space Cowboys, 2000, Spirit: Stallion of the Cimarron (voice), 2002, Sum of All Fears, 2002, The Nazi, 2002, Blackball, 2003, The Snow Walker, 2003, I, Robot, 2004, The Longest Yard, 2005, Dante's Inferno, 2006, The Queen, 2006, Becoming Jane, 2007, Spider-Man 3, 2007, Tortured, 2008, W., 2008; (TV series) All in the Family, 1971, Hot L. Baltimore, 1975, The Nancy Walker Show, 1976, The Last Precinct, 1986, Easy Street, 1986, Mama's Boy, 1988, Walking After Midnight, 1999, Citizen Baines, 2001, Six Feet Under, 2004-05; (TV miniseries) Once an Eagle, 1976, Dream West, 1986, Fail Safe, 2000, The Magnificent Ambersons, 2002, RFK, 2002, A Death in the Family, 2002, Angels in America, 2003, 24, 2007; (TV films) The Girl in the Empty Grave, 1977, Deadly Game, 1977, A Christmas Without Snow, 1980, The Rainmaker, 1982, Spraggue, 1984, Alison's Demise, 1987, China Beach, 1988, Christine Cromwell: Things That Go Bump in the Night, 1989, Miracle Landing, 1990, In a Child's Name, 1991, Revenge of the Nerds III: The Next Generation, 1992, The Shaggy Dog, 1994, Revenge of the Nerds IV: Nerds in Love, 1994, RKO 281, 1999, Fail Safe, 2000, The Magnificent Ambersons, 2002, Salem's Lot, 2004, Pope John Paul II, 2005, Avenger, 2006, Hit Factor, 2008; (TV guest appearances) The Rockford Files, 1974, All in the Family, 1974, Barney Miller, 1977, 1979, 1981, M*A*S*H, 1977, Three's Company, 1977, Eight is Enough, 1979, Little House on the Prairie, 1980, Dallas, 1984, 1985, Hardcastle and McCormick, 1985, Scarecrow and Mrs. King, 1986, Star Trek: the Next Generation, 1990, 1993, Home Improvement, 1994, Picket Fences, 1995, The Client, 1996, ER, 2001, Enterprise, 2001, 05, The West Wing, 2004.

CRON, STEVEN MICHAEL, lawyer; b. LA, Feb. 17, 1948; BA, UCLA, 1970; JD, U. Calif., Hastings Coll. Law, 1973. Bar: Calif. 1974. Dep. pub. defender LA County Pub. Defender's Office, 1974—80; ptnr. Cron, Israels & Stark, Santa Monica, Calif. Adj. prof. Pepperdine U. Sch. Law; legal commentator Fox News, CNN, MSNBC. Named Super Lawyer, L.A. Mag., 2004, 2005. Mem.: Nat. Assn. Criminal Defense Lawyers, Calif. Attys. for Criminal Justice, Nat. Conf. Bar Pres., State Bar Calif. (mem. Com. Profl. Responsibility and Conduct), LA County Bar Assn., Santa Monica Bar Assn. (mem. bd. trustees 1987—94, pres. 1992—93), Zeta Beta Tau. Office: Cron, Israels & Stark 1541 Ocean Ave Ste 200 Santa Monica CA 90401 Office Phone: 310-421-9888. Personal E-mail: smcron@aol.com.

CRONIN, BRIAN, state legislator; b. New York, NY; m. Veronica Cronin; children: Kyra, Alana. BA in Hist., Haverford Coll.; MA in Edn., Harvard U.; grad., Leadership Boise. Tchr. Boston Pub. Schs., Scarsdale High Sch.; press sec. Jerry Brady, Mayor Dave Bieter; writer & editor Scholastic Inc.; comm. specialist & mag. editor Jr. Chamber Internat.; founder & owner Cronin & Assocs., 2003—; co-founder Garabatos Spanish Preschool, 2006—; mem. Dist. 19 Idaho House of Reps., 2008—. Chmn. Ada County Democrats, 2005—07; del. Dem. Nat. Convention, 2008. Vol. WorldTeach-Universidad Technica de Manabi, Ecuador, 1993, Agy. for New Americans, Am. Red Cross, Direct Impact Response Team, United Way Cmty. Impact Rev. Team; former mem. Ada County Hwy. Dist. Neighborhood Adv. Com.; bd. dirs. Boise State Radio, Idaho Human Rights Edn.; mem. Boise C. of C. Small Bus. Success Ctr. Mem.: Boise Young Profl., Idaho Hispanic C. of C., Boise Met. C. of C. Democrat. Office: Capitol Annex PO Box 83720 Boise ID 83720-0054 also: 825 E Jefferson St Boise ID 83712 Home Phone: 208-334-8849; Office Phone: 208-334-2475, 208-429-8493. Office Fax: 208-334-2125. Business E-Mail: bcronin@house.idaho.gov.*

CROOK, ANNA MARIE, state legislator; b. Crossroads, N.Mex., Dec. 6, 1934; d. Joe H. and Esther Jane (McClure) Barnes; m. Jerry W. Crook; m. Keigm, Kevin. BA, Ea. N.Mex. U., 1956. Clk. Len Co. Electric; with Midwest Rsch., Kansas City, Mo., 1955—56; legal dept. Skelly Oil Co., Kansas City, 1957-58; property mgr., bus. mgr. Jerry Crook, 1958—; mem. Dist. 64 N.Mex. House of Reps., 1994—. Fashion cons. Doncaster, 1983-99. Republican. Baptist. Avocation: golf. Home: 1041 Fairway Ter Clovis NM 88101-2806 Office: 1041 Fairway Ter Clovis NM 88101 also: State Capitol N Office of the Clerk Rm 203J Santa Fe NM 87503 Office Phone: 574-986-4454, 505-986-4454. E-mail: anna.crook@nmlegis.gov.*

CROOK, SEAN PAUL, aerospace systems division director; b. Pawtucket, RI, July 6, 1953; s. Ralph Frederick and Rosemary Rita (Dolan) C.; m. Mary Wickman, June 10, 1978; children: Kimberly Anne, Kelly Dolan, Erin Webster, Mary Katherine. BSME, U.S. Naval Acad., 1975; MBA, U. So. Calif., 1991. Commd. ensign USN, 1975, advanced through grades to lt., 1979, resigned, 1981; sr. systems engr. space divsn. GE, Springfield, Va., 1982-84; sr. aerospace systems engr. Martin Marietta Aero. Def. Systems, Long Beach, Calif., 1984-87; sr. aerospace system engring. mgr. Martin Marietta Aero Def. Systems, Long Beach, Calif., 1987-93; chief engr. GDE Sys. Inc., A Tracer Co., San Diego, 1993-96, program mgr., 1996-99; program dir. BAE Sys., San Diego, 1999-2001; divsn. dir. BAE Sys. Network Sys., San Diego, 2001—. Sec., bd. dirs. Guardian Minerals Inc. Comdr. USNR, 1992-97. Mem. Am. Mgmt. Assn., U. So. Calif. Exec. MBA Alumni Assn. (bd. dirs.), U.S. Naval Acad. Alumni Assn. Home: 23565 Via Calzada Mission Viejo CA 92691-3625 Office: BAE Sys PO Box 509008 San Diego CA 92150-9008 Office Phone: 858-592-5395. Personal E-mail: scrook9344@aol.com. Business E-Mail: sean.crook@baesystems.com.

CROOKE, STANLEY THOMAS, pharmaceutical executive; b. Indpls., Mar. 28, 1945; m. Nancy Alder (dec.); 1 child, Evan; m. Rosanne M. Snyder. BS in Pharmacy, Butler U., 1966; PhD, Baylor Coll., 1971, MD, 1974. Asst. dir. med. rsch. Bristol Labs., NYC, 1975-76, assoc. dir. med. rsch., 1976-77, assoc. dir. R&D, 1977-79, v.p. R&D, 1979-80, Smith Kline & French Labs., Phila., 1980-82; pres. R&D Smith Kline French, Phila., 1982-88; chmn. bd., CEO ISIS Pharms., Inc., Carlsbad, Calif., 1989. Chmn. bd. dirs. GES Pharms., Inc., Houston, 1989-91; adj. prof. Baylor Coll. Medicine, Houston, 1982, U. Pa., Phila., 1982-98; chmn. bd. dirs. GeneMedicine, Houston, 1996-98; bd. dirs. Calif. Healthcare Inst., 1993-2003, Indsl. Biotech. Assn., Washington, Idun Pharms., San Diego 1997-2002, Epix Med., Cambridge, Mass., 1996-2005, BIO, Washington, 1993-94; mem. sci. adv. bd. SIBIA, La Jolla, Calif. 1992-99; adj. prof. pharmacology UCLA, 1991, U. Calif. San Diego, 1994; bd. dirs. Synsorb Biotech Inc., Calgary, Can., 1999-2002; bd. dirs. Axon Instruments, Inc., Foster City, Calif. 1999-2004, Valentis, Inc., Burlingame, Calif., 1999-2002, Antisense Therapeutics Ltd., Toorak, Victoria, Australia, 2002-06, Applied Molecular Evolutions, Inc., San Diego, Calif., 2001-02, Biocom/San Diego, Calif., 2003—; mem. arts and scis. adv. coun. No. Ariz. U., 2002- Mem. editl. adv. bd. Molecular Pharmacology, 1986-91, Jour. Drug Targeting, 1992; editl. bd. Antisense Rsch. and Devel., 1994; sect. editl. bd. for biologicals and immunologicals Expert Opinion on Investigational Drugs, 1995. Trustee Franklin Inst., Phila., 1987-89; bd. dirs. Mann Music Ctr., Phila., 1987-89; children's com. Children's Svcs., Inc., Phila., 1983-84; adv. com. World Affairs Coun., Phila. Recipient Julius Stermer award, Phila. Coll. Pharmacy and Sci., 1981, Outstanding Lectr. award, Baylor Coll. Medicine, 1984, Disting. Prof. award, U. Ky., 1986. Mem. AAAS, Am. Assn. for Cancer Rsch. (state legis. com.), Am. Soc. for Microbiology, Am. Soc. Pharmacology and Exptl. Therapeutics, Am. Soc. Clin. Pharmacology and Therapeutics, Am. Soc. Clin. Oncology, Indsl. Biotech. Assn. (bd. dirs. 1992-93). Achievements include numerous patents in field. Office: ISIS Pharms Inc 1896 Rutherford Rd Carlsbad CA 92008-7208 E-mail: scrooke@isisph.com.

CROOKSTON, R. KENT, agronomy educator; b. Magrath, Alta., Can., Mar. 8, 1943; s. Bryan Grant and Lisadore (Brown) C.; m. Gayle Loraine Jones, June 22, 1966; children: Rebecca, Casey, Polly, Daniel, Elizabeth, Emily, Sadie. BS, Brigham Young U., 1968; MS, U. Minn., 1970, PhD, 1972. Postdoctoral fellow Agr. Can., Lethbridge, Alta., 1972; rsch. assoc. Cornell U., Ithaca, NY, 1972-74; from asst. prof. to prof. U. Minn., St. Paul, 1974—82, dir. sustainable agr. program Coll. Agr., 1988-92, head dept. agronomy, 1990-98. Adj. prof. Inst. Agronomique Et Veterinaire Hassan II, Rabat, Morocco, 1984—; dean Coll. Biology and Agr., Brigham Young U., Provo, Utah, 1998-2005, assoc. dir. faculty ctr., 2007-. Author rsch. manuscripts. With Can. armed forces, 1962. Fellow Am. Soc. Agronomy, Crop Sci. Soc. Am. Avocations: painting, woodworking, writing, photography. Home: 1055 N 1100 E Orem UT 84097-4390 Office: Faculty Ctr 4450 WSC Bringham Young Univ Provo UT 84602-5250 Office Phone: 801-422-9142. Business E-Mail: kent_crookston@byu.edu.

CROSBY, FAYE JACQUELINE, psychology professor, writer; b. Bethesda, Md., July 12, 1947; d. Robert A. and Andrée (Cohen) Newman; children: Matthew, Timothy. BA, Wheaton Coll., Mass., 1969; postgrad., London Sch. Econs., 1973-74; PhD, Boston U., 1976. Lectr. R.I. Coll., Providence, 1976-77; asst. prof. psychology Yale U., New Haven, 1977-82, assoc. prof., 1982-85; prof. psychology Smith Coll., Northampton, Mass., 1985-98, U. Calif., Santa Cruz, 1997—, vice provost acad. affairs, 2000, chair academic senate, 2005—07. Prof. J.L. Kellogg Grad. Sch. Mgmt. Northwestern U., Evanston, Ill., 1992-93. Author: Relative Deprivation and Working Women, 1982, Juggling: The Unexpected Advantage of Balancing Careers and Home for Women and Their Families, 1991, Affirmative Action is Dead; Long Live Affirmative Action, 2004; co-author: Justice, Gender and Affirmative Action, 1992, Affirmative Action, Pros and Cons of Policy and Practice, 1996; editor: Spouse, Parent, Worker, 1987; co-editor: Affirmative Action in Perspective, 1989, Women's Ethnicities, 1996, Mentoring Dilemmas, 1999, Sex, Race and Merit, 2000, The Psychology and Management of Workplace Diversity, 2005, Sex Discrimination in the Workplace, 2007; contbr. articles to profl. jours. Office: U Calif Santa Cruz Psych Dept Santa Cruz CA 95064 Office Phone: 831-459-3568. Business E-Mail: fjcrosby@uscs.edu. E-mail: fjcrosby@cats.ucsc.edu.

CROSBY, GLENN ARTHUR, chemistry professor; b. Youngwood, Pa., July 30, 1928; s. Edwin Glenn and Bertha May (Ritchey) C.; m. Jane Lichtenfels, May 29, 1950; children: Brian, Alan, Karen. BS, Waynesburg Coll., 1950; PhD, U. Wash., 1954. Rsch. assoc. Fla. State U., Tallahassee, 1955-57, vis. asst. prof. physics, 1957; asst. prof. chemistry U. N. Mex., Albuquerque, 1957-62, assoc. prof. chemistry, 1962-67; prof. chemistry and materials sci. Wash. State U., Pullman, 1967—2001, chmn. chem. physics program, 1977-84, prof. emeritus, 2001—. Mem. adv. com. Rsch. Corp., Tucson, 1981—88, 1990—92; vis. prof. phys. chemistry U. Tubingen, Germany, 1964; vis. prof. physics U. Canterbury, Christchurch, New Zealand, 1974; Humboldt sr. scientist, vis. prof. phys. chemistry U. Hohenheim, Germany,

1978—79; mem. commn. on life scis. NRC, 1991—96, com. on programs for advanced study math and sci. in U.S. h.s., 1999—2001. Author: Chemistry: Matter and Chemical change, 1962; also numerous sci. and sci.-related articles Recipient U.S. Sr. Scientist award Humboldt Found., Fed. Republic Germany, 1978-79, Catalyst award Chem. Mfrs. Assn., 1979, Disting. Alumnus award Waynesburg Coll., 1982, Wash. State U.Faculty Excellence award in instrn., 1984, Wash. State U. Faculty Excellence award for pub. svc., 1989, Disting. Prof. award Wash. State U. Mortar Bd., 1990, Wash State U. Legacy of Excellence award, 2006, Pres.'s medallion Waynesburg Coll. for disting. lifetime sci. and ednl. achievement, 1998; named Prof. of Yr., U. N.Mex., 1967; NSF fellow U. Wash., Seattle, 1953-54; Rsch. Corp. Venture grantee, 1960; Fulbright fellow, 1964. Fellow: AAAS, Inter-Am. Photochem. Soc.; mem.: Nat. Sci. Tchrs. Assn., Am. Phys. Soc., Am. Chem. Soc. (numerous activities including chmn. divsn. chem. edn. 1982, chmn. com. on edn. 1990—91, bd. dirs. 1994—2002, Western Conn. sect. Vis. Scientist award 1981, Nat. award in chem. edn. 1985, Harry and Carol Mosher award Santa Clara Valley sect. 1998, Divsn. Chem. Edn. Outstanding Svc. award 2003, Western Region award 2007, Charles Parsons award 2009), Sigma Xi, Sigma Pi Sigma, Phi Kappa Phi. Home: 1208 E Excelsior Rd Spokane WA 99224-9257 E-mail: gac@wsunix.wsu.edu.

CROSBY, MICHAEL P., science administrator; BS, Old Dominion U., MS with honors; PhD in Marine-Estuarine-Environ. Sci., U. Md. Various sci. positions Nat. Marine Fisheries Svc., U.S. Army Corps Engrs., Nat. Cancer Inst., NIH; numerous faculty positions U. S.C., Coastal Carolina U., U. Charleston, Salisbury State U.; exec. dir. nat. sci. bd. Nat. Oceanic and Atmospheric Adminstrn., nat. rsch. coord. ocean and coastal resource mgmt., chief scientist sanctuaries and reserves, sr. adv. internat. sci. policy under sec. office internat. affairs; sr. sci. adv. marine and coastal ecosystems U.S. Agency Internal Devel.; exec. officer, office dir. Nat. Sci. Bd., 2003—. Mem. numerous nat. and internat. sci. panels and adv. coms. Panelist, reviewe: numerous sci. jours.; editor: numerous books and manuals on marine protected areas and coral reefs. Grantee NSF, Nat. Oceanic and Atmospheric Adminstrn., EPA, DOD, USAID, others. Fellow: Royal Linnean Soc. London; mem.: AAAS, Pacific Congress Marine Sci. and Tech., Sci. Rsch. Soc., Estuarine Rsch. Fedn., Nat. Shellfisheries Assn., Coastal Soc., Nat. Areas Assn., Sigma Xi. Office: Univ Hawaii Hilo 200 W Kawili Street Hilo HI 96720 Office Phone: 703-292-7000. E-mail: mcrosby@nsf.gov.

CROSBY, NORMAN LAWRENCE, comedian; b. Boston, Sept. 15, 1927; s. John and Ann (Lansky) C.; m. Joan Crane Foley, Nov. 1, 1966; children: Daniel Joseph, Andrew Crane. Student, Mass. Sch. Art, Boston. Ind. comedian, entertainer, 1947—. Nat. spokesman Anheuser-Busch Natural Light Beer. Began work as comedian in New Eng. clubs, frat. and polit. dinners, numerous civic and charity functions; N.Y.C. debut Latin Quarter; several appearances London Palladium, regular appearances at all major hotels in Las Vegas, numerous other night clubs, concert halls, theaters, TV variety and panel shows; host: (syndicated TV series) Norm Crosby's Comedy Shop; nat. co-host on Jerry Lewis Muscular Dystrophy Assn. Telethon. Nat. hon. chmn. better Hearing Inst., Washington; trustee Hope for Hearing Found., UCLA; sponsor Norm Crosby Ann. Celebrity Golf Tournament benefitting City of Hope. With USCG, 1945-46. Recipient Jack Benny Comedy award Authors and Celebrities, 1981, Star on Hollywood (Calif.) Walk of Fame, Hollywood C. of C., 1982, Lifetime Achievement award in Entertainment, Touchdown Club, Washington, 1988, Victory award, Kennedy Ctr. Pres. George Bush, 1991; honored by USO and given privilege of laying wreath at tomb of Unknown Soldiers, Washington, 2001; named Internat. Variety Clubs Man of Yr., 1986; recipient Lifetime Achievement award in Comedy, Emerson Coll., Boston Comedy Festival. Mem. Friars Club (N.Y.C., L.A.; 20th term Internat. Amb. of Good Will for City of Hope), Masons, Shriners. Jewish. Personal E-mail: jonoprod@webtv.net.

CROSBY, PETER ALAN, management consultant; b. Santa Barbara, Calif., Oct. 20, 1945; s. Harold Bartley and Margaret Maida (Peterson) C.; m. Stephanie Jay Ellis, Dec. 20, 1969; children: Kelly Michelle, Michael Ellis. BS in Engring., U. Calif., Berkeley, 1967; MS in Ops. Rsch., Stanford U., 1969; ED, Stanford Bus. Sch., 1971. Cert. mgmt. cons. Logistics inventory analyst Ford Motor Co., Palo Alto, Calif., 1967-71; corp. ops. planning analyst FMC Corp., San Jose, Calif., 1972; assoc. mgmt. cons. A.T. Kearney, Inc., San Francisco, 1972-75; mgr. materials mgmt. cons. svcs. Coopers & Lybrand, Los Angeles, 1976-78; ptnr. gen. cons. unit (Case & Co.) Towers Perrin Forster & Crosby, LA, 1978-81; prin. Crosby, Gustin, Rice & Co. (CGR Mgmt. Cons.), 1981—. Dir. Carbide Products Internat. Co. Mem. adv. bd. dirs. Stanton Chase. Mem. Coun. Logistic Mgmt., Inst. Mgmt. Cons. (past pres.), Food Cons. Group, Assn. for Corp. Growth, Phi Gamma Delta. Office: CGR Mgmt Consultants Ste 1900 1901 Avenue Of The Stars Los Angeles CA 90067-6020 Office Phone: 310-553-6837. Personal E-mail: crosbycgr@cs.com. Business E-Mail: petecrosby@cgrmc.com.

CROSHERE, AUSTIN, professional basketball player; b. LA, May 1, 1975; Grad., Providence Coll., 1997. Power forward Ind. Pacers, 1997—2006, Dallas Mavericks, 2006—07, Golden State Warriors, 2007—. Office: Golden State Warriors 1011 Broadway Oakland CA 94607

CROSLEY, DAVID RISDON, chemical physicist; b. Webster City, Iowa, Mar. 4, 1941; s. Carlton Whitley and Helen Elizabeth (Mingle) C.; m. Barbara DeVries, Sept. 7, 1963 (div. 1985); 1 child, Stephen Risdon. BS, Iowa State U., 1962; MA, Columbia U., 1963, PhD, 1966. Postdoctoral fellow Joint Inst. Lab. Astrophysics, Boulder, Colo., 1966-68; prof. U. Wis., Madison, 1968-75; rsch. chemist Ballistic Rsch. Lab., Aberdeen, Md., 1975-79; program mgr. SRI Internat., Menlo Park, Calif., 1979-88, assoc. lab. dir., 1988-95, lab. dir., 1995—2001, sr. staff scientist, 2001—. Cons. Battelle, Columbus, Ohio, 1975-81, Sci. Applications Internat. Corp., La Jolla, Calif., 1982-86, NASA, Washington, 1984-89; vis. prof. Ruhr U., Bochum, Fed. Republic of Germany, 1988, U. Paris, Orsay, France, 1989, U. Bielefeld, Germany, 1997, U. Leeds, Eng., 2004. Editor: Laser Probes of Combustion Chemistry, 1980; contbr. over 190 articles to sci. jours. NSF grad. fellow, 1964-66. Fellow Am. Phys. Soc., AAAS; mem. Am. Chem. Soc., Combustion Inst., Am. Geophysical Union, Pi Mu Epsilon, Phi Lambda Upsilon, Sigma Chi. Democrat. Achievements include research in laser-induced fluorescence spectroscopy, quantum state specific collisional energy transfer, gas-phase reaction kinetics and laser-based diagnostic techniques, environmental monitoring and applications to small molecules important in the chemistry of combustion, the atmosphere and materials processing. Office: SRI Internat Molecular Physics Lab Menlo Park CA 94025 Home Phone: 650-494-8727; Office Phone: 650-859-2395. Business E-Mail: david.crosley@sri.com.

CROSS, BRUCE MICHAEL, lawyer; b. Wash., Jan. 30, 1942; AB magna cum laude, Dartmouth Coll., 1964; JD magna cum laude, Harvard U., 1967. Bar: Wash. 1967. Law clk. to Hon. Frank P. Weaver Supreme Ct. Wash., 1967-68; mem. Perkins Coie LLP, Seattle, 1969—. Office: Perkins Coie LLP 1201 3rd Ave Fl 40 Seattle WA 98101-3099 Home Phone: 206-270-9215; Office Phone: 206-359-8453. Business E-Mail: bcross@perkinscoie.com.

CROSS, KATHRYN PATRICIA, education educator; b. Normal, Ill., Mar. 17, 1926; d. Clarence L. and Katherine (Dague) C. BS, Ill. State U., Normal, 1948; MA, U. Ill., Urbana, 1951, PhD, 1958; LLD (hon.), Ill. State U., 1970; DS (hon.), Northeastern U., Boston, 1975; HHD (hon.), Grand Valley State Colls., Mich., 1975; D in Pedagogy (hon.), Our Lady of Lake U., Tex., 1977; LHD (hon.), Hood Coll., Md., 1979; DS (hon.), Loyola U., Chgo., 1980; LHD (hon.), Marymount Manhattan Coll., NY, 1982, Coll. St. Mary, 1985, De Paul U., Chgo., 1986, Thomas Jefferson U., Pa., 1987; LittD (hon.), SUNY, 1988; DHL (hon.), Open U., The Netherlands, 1989; LHD (hon.), Rider Coll., NJ, 1992, U. Mass., Lowell, 1995, Coll. Lifelong Learning, NH, 1999. Math. tchr. Harvard (Ill.) Community High Sch., 1948-49; rsch. asst. dept. psychology U. Ill., Urbana, 1949-53, asst. dean of women, 1953-59; dean of women then dean of students Cornell U., Ithaca, N.Y., 1959-63; dir. coll. and univ. programs Ednl. Testing Svc., Princeton, N.J., 1963-66; rsch. educator Ctr. R&D in Higher Edn. U. Calif., Berkeley, 1966-77; rsch. scientist, sr. rsch. psychologist, dir. univ. programs Ednl. Testing Svc., Berkeley, 1966-80; prof. edn., chair dept. adminstrn., planning & social policy Harvard U., Cambridge, Mass., 1980-88; Elizabeth and Edward Conner prof. edn. U. Calif., Berkeley, 1988-94, David Pierpont Gardner prof. higher edn., 1994-96. Mem. sec. adv. com. on automated personal data sys. Dept. HEW, 1972-73; del. to Soviet Union, Seminar on Problems in Higher Edn., 1975; vis. prof. U. Nebr., 1975-76; vis. scholar Miami-Dade CC, 1987; trustee Berkeley Pub. Libr., 1998-2002; spkr., cons. in field; bd. dirs. Elderhostel, 1999-; nat. adv. bd. Ctr. for First-Year Experience, 2000-. Author: Beyond the Open Door: New Students to Higher Education, 1971 (Sch. and Soc. Outstanding Books in Edn. award, 1971); author: (with S. B. Gould) Explorations in Non-Traditional Study, 1972; author: (with J. R. Valley and Assocs.) Planning Non-Traditional Programs: An Analysis of the Issues for Postsecondary Education, 1974; author: Accent on Learning, 1976 (Am. Coun. Edn. Borden medal, 1976), Adults as Learners, 1981; author: (with Thomas A. Angelo) Classroom Assessment Techniques, 1993; author: (with Mimi Harris Steadman) Classroom Research, 1996; author: (with Elizabeth Barkley and Claire Major) Collaborative Learning Techniques: A Handbook for College Faculty, 2005; contbr. articles, monographs to profl. publs., chapters to books; mem. editl. bd. several ednl. jours., cons. editor (ednl. mag.) Change, 1980—. Active Nat. Acad. Edn., 1975—, Coun. for Advancement of Exptl. Learning, 1982-85; trustee Bradford Coll., Mass., 1986-88, Antioch Coll., Yellow Springs, Ohio, 1976-78; nat. adv. bd. Nat. Ctr. of Study of Adult Learning, Empire State Coll., Okla. Bd. Regents; higher edn. rsch. program Pew Charitable Trusts; vis. com. Harvard Grad. Sch. Edn., 1998—; bd. dirs. Elderhostel, 1999—; trustee Berkeley Pub. Libr., 1999—, Carnegie Found., 1999—. Recipient Leadership award, Assn. Continuing Higher Edn., 2000, Lifetime Contbns. to Learning Assistance and Devel. Edn. award, Am. Coun. Devel. Edn., 2000, Morris Keeton award, Coun. For Adult Exptl. Learning, 2005, Tchrs. Coll. medal, Columbia U., 2006; named to Hall of Fame, Internat. Adult and Continuing Edn., 1997. Fellow League for Innovation in CC (nat. adv. bd. Learning Coll. Project 2000-); mem. Am. Assn. Higher Edn. (bd. dirs. 1987—, pres. 1975, chair 1989-90), Am. Assn. Comty. and Jr. Colls. (vice chair commn. of future comty. colls.), Carnegie Found. Advancement of Tchg. (adv. com. on classification of colls. and univs., trustee 1998-), Nat. Ctr. for Devel. Edn. (adv. bd.), New Eng. Assn. Schs. and Colls. (commn. on instns. higher edn. 1982-86), Am. Coun. Edn. (commn. on higher edn. and adult learner 1986-88). Business E-Mail: patcross@berkeley.edu.

CROSSON, JOHN ALBERT, advertising executive; b. LA, Oct. 5, 1961; s. Albert J. and Virginia (Kienzle) C.; m. Carolyn Stevens, Oct. 3, 1992. BA, Loyola Marymount U., 1983; MBA, U. So. Calif., 1984. Exec. v.p. Dailey & Assocs. Advt., LA, 1984-98; exec. v.p., mng. dir. L.A., Grey Advt., 1998—. Lectr. Loyola Marymount U., L.A., 1986-89. Avocations: tennis, golf.

CROUCH, PAUL FRANKLIN, minister, religious organization administrator; b. St. Joseph, Mo., Mar. 30, 1934; s. Andrew Franklin and Sarah Matilda (Swingle) C.; m. Janice Wendell Bethany, Aug. 25, 1957; children: Paul F., Matthew W. BTh, Central Bible Coll. and Sem., Springfield, Mo., 1955. Ordained to ministry, 1955; dir. fgn. missions film and audio visual dept. Assemblies of God, 1955-58; assoc. pastor 1st Assembly of God, Rapid City, S.D., 1958-60, Central Assembly of God, Muskegon, Mich., 1960-62; gen. mgr. TV and film prodn. center Assemblies of God, Burbank, Calif., 1962-65; gen. mgr. Sta. KREL, Cornona, Calif., 1965-71, Sta. KHOF, KHOF-TV, Glendale, Calif., 1971-73; founder, pres. Sta. KTBN-TV, Trinity Broadcasting Network, Los Angeles, 1973—. Recipient Best Religious film award Winona Lake Film Festival, 1956 Mem. Nat. Assn. Religious Broadcasters, Western Religious Broadcasters Assn., Assn. Christian TV Stas. (founder) Office: Trinity Broadcasting Network 2442 Michelle Dr Tustin CA 92780-7015

CROUCH, PETER E., engineering educator; b. Newcastle upon Tyne, Eng. BSc in Engring. Sci., U. Warwick, Eng., 1973, MSc in Control Theory, 1974; PhD in Applied Scis., Harvard U., 1977. Lectr. in control theory dept. elec. engring. U. Warwick, England, 1977—85, acting dir. Control Theory Ctr., 1983—84; rsch. assoc. divsn. applied sciences Harvard U., 1982; vis. assoc. prof. dept. math. Ariz. State U., 1984—85, assoc. prof. dept. elec. and computer engring., 1985—88, prof. dept. elec. engring., 1988—, acting chair dept. elec. and computer engring., 1988—89, dir. Ctr. for Systems Sci. and Engring., 1989—95, chair dept. elec. engring., 1992—95, dean, Ira A. Fulton Sch. Engring., 1995—2006. Assoc. editor Jour. of Math. Control and Info., 1984—, Systems and Control Letters, 1988—93, Math. of Control, Signals and Systems, 1989—, Jour. of Dynamical and Control Systems, 1994—; mem. bd. Internat. Performance Conf. on Computers and Comm., 1995—; mem. bd. advisors Inst. Systems & Robotics, Portugal, 1995—. Author: numerous papers and jour. articles. Recipient Hartree Premium Award, Instn. Elec. Engineers, 1982; Frank Knox Meml. Fellowship, 1974—76. Fellow: IEEE (assoc. editor Transactions on Automatic Control 1986—88, assoc. editor at large 1995—); mem.: Ariz. Soc. Profl. Engineers, Am. Soc. Engring. Edn., Soc. Indsl. and Applied Math., Am. Math. Soc.

CROW, GORDON F., state legislator; b. LA, Dec. 15, 1950; m. Sandy Crow; 1 child, Andrew. Media cons.; owner, pub. rels. agy.; senator, dist. 3 Idaho State Senate, Boise, 1994—. Chair commerce and human resources com.; mem. health and welfare, and resources and environment coms. With U.S. Army. Mem. Coeur d'Alene (Idaho) C. of C., Rotary. Republican. Office: State Capitol PO Box 83720 Boise ID 83720-3720

CROW, MICHAEL M., academic administrator; m. Sybil Francis; 3 children. BA in Polit. Sci. and Environ. Studies, Iowa State U., 1977; D in Pub. Adminstrn., Syracuse U. Exec. vice provost Columbia U., prof. sci., tech. policy; prof. tech. mgmt. Iowa State U., dir., inst. phys. rsch. & tech; pres. Ariz. State U., Tempe, 2002—. Co-author: Limited by Design, 1998, Synthetic Fuel Technology Development in the United States, 1998; contbr. articles to profl. jours.;, editor numerous books. Fellow: Nat. Acad. Pub. Adminstrn. Avocations: hiking, mountain biking. Office: Ariz State Univ 300 E Univ ASU Fulton Ctr 4th Fl PO Box 877705 Tempe AZ 82587-7705 Office Phone: 480-965-8972. Office Fax: 480-965-0865.

CROWE, CLAYTON T., engineering educator; Prof. Sch. Mech. and Materials Engring. Wash. State U., Pullman. Recipient Fluids Engring. award ASME, 1995. Office: Wash State U Sch Mech & Materials Engring Pullman WA 99164-0001

CROWE, JAMES QUELL (JIM), communications executive; b. Camp Pendleton, Calif., July 2, 1949; s. Henry Pierson and Mona (Quell) C.; m. Pamela L. Powell, June 20, 1986; children: Sterling, Angela, James Michael. BS in Mech. Engring., Rensselaer Poly. Inst., 1972; MBA, Pepperdine U., 1982. Project engr. Cozzolino Constrn. Co., Port of Albany, NY, 1971-73; ind., cons. engr. Albany, 1973-74; engr. Morrison-Knudsen, Saratoga, NY, 1974-75, project engr. Washington, 1975-76, project mgr. various cities, 1976-80, v.p. ops. Boise, 1980-83, group v.p. power, 1983-86; pres. Kiewit Indsl. Co., Omaha, 1986—91; pres., CEO MFS Communications, 1993—97, Level 3 Communications, Broomfield, Colo., 1997—2000, CEO, 2000—08, pres., CEO, 2008—. Chmn., CEO MFS Comms. Co., Inc., Omaha, 1988-97; chmn. WorldCom, Inc., 1997; bd. dir. Level 3 Comms., Inc., 1993—; dir. RCN Corp., Commonwealth Tel. Mem. NAE, Am. Nuclear Soc. Office: Level 3 Comm Inc 1025 Eldorado Blvd Broomfield CO 80021

CROWELL, JOHN B., JR., lawyer, former government official; b. Elizabeth, NJ, Mar. 18, 1930; s. John B. and Anna B. (Trull) C.; m. Rebecca Margaret McCue, Feb. 13, 1954; children: John P., Patrick E., Ann M. AB, Dartmouth Coll., 1952; LL.B., Harvard U., 1957. Bar: NJ bar 1958, Oreg. bar 1959. Law clk. to Judge Gerald McLaughlin U.S. Ct. Appeals, Newark, 1957-59; atty. Ga.-Pacific Corp., Portland, Oreg., 1959-72; gen. counsel La.-Pacific Corp., Portland, 1972-81; asst. sec. for natural resources and environment Dept. Agr., Washington, 1981-85; ptnr. Lane Powell Spears Lubersky, Portland, 1986-98, of counsel, 1998—. Served with USN, 1952-54. Mem. Am. Ornithologists Union, Wilson Ornithol. Soc., Cooper Ornithol. Soc., Soc. Am. Foresters, Soil Conservation Soc. Am. Clubs: Univ. (Portland). Republican. Presbyterian. Home: 1185 Hallinan Cir Lake Oswego OR 97034-4970 Office: Lane Powell 601 SW 2nd Ave Ste 2100 Portland OR 97204-3154 Office Phone: 503-778-2172. Business E-Mail: crowellj@lanepowell.com.

CROWELL, JOHN C(HAMBERS), geology educator, researcher; b. State College, Pa., May 12, 1917; s. James White and Helen Hunt (Chambers) C.; m. Betty Marie Bruner, Nov. 22, 1946; 1 child, Martha Lynn Crowell Bobroskie. BS in Geology, U. Tex., 1939; MA in Oceanographic meteorology, Scripps Inst. Oceanography UCLA, 1946; PhD in Geology, UCLA, 1947; DSc (hon.), U. Louvain, Belgium, 1966. Geologist Shell Oil Co., Inc., Ventura, Calif., 1941-42; from instr. to prof. geology UCLA, 1947-67, chmn. dept., 1957-60, 63-66; prof. geology U. Calif., Santa Barbara, 1967-87, prof. emeritus, 1987, rsch. geologist Inst. for Crustal Studies, 1987—. Chmn. Office of Earth Scis., NRC, Nat. Acad. Scis., 1979-82. Served to capt. U.S. Army USAAF, 1942-46. Fellow AAAS, Geol. Soc. Am. (Penrose medal 1995), Am. Acad. Arts and Scis.; mem. Am. Assn. Petroleum Geologists, Am. Geophys. Union, Nat. Acad. Scis. Achievements include special research in structural geology, tectonics, interpretation sedimentary rocks, studies of San Andreas fault system, California tectonics, ancient glaciation, continental drift. Office: 300 Hot Springs Rd Apt 211 Santa Barbara CA 93108 E-mail: crowell@geol.ucsb.edu.

CROWLEY, JOSEPH MICHAEL, electrical engineer, educator; b. Phila., Sept. 9, 1940; s. Joseph Edward and Mary Veronica (McCall) C.; m. Barbara Ann Sauerwald, June 22, 1963; children: Joseph W., Kevin, James, Michael, Daniel. BS, MIT, 1962, MS, 1963, PhD, 1965. Vis. scientist Max Planck Inst., Goettingen, W.Ger, 1965-66; asst. prof. elec. engring. U. Ill., Urbana, 1966-69, assoc. prof., 1969-78, prof., dir. applied electrostats. research lab., 1978-88; pres. JMC Inc., 1981-91, Electrostatic Applications, 1986—; Piercey Disting. prof. chem. engring. U. Minn., 1993. Adj. prof. U. Ill., 1988-94; cons. to several corps. Contbr. articles to profl. jours.; patentee ink jet printers. Pres. Champaign-Urbana Bd. Cath. Edn., 1978-80. Recipient Gen. Motors scholarship, 1958-62; AEC fellow, 1962-65; NATO fellow, 1965-66 Fellow IEEE, Electrostats. Soc. Am. (pres. 1992-95), Am. Phys. Soc., Soc. Inf. Display, Mensa. Roman Catholic.

CROWLEY, JOSEPH NEIL, political science professor, former academic administrator; b. Oelwein, Iowa, July 9, 1933; James Bernard and Nina Mary (Neil) C.; m. Johanna Lois Reitz, Sept. 9, 1961; children: Theresa, Neil, Margaret, Timothy. BA, U. Iowa, 1959; MA, Calif. State U., Fresno, 1963; PhD (Univ. fellow), U. Wash., 1967. Reporter Fresno Bee, 1961-62; asst. prof. polit. sci. U. Nev., Reno, 1966-71, asso. prof., 1971-79, prof., 1979—, chmn. dept. polit. sci., 1976-78, pres., 1978-2000, pres. emeritus, regents prof., 2001—, interim pres., 2005—06, San Jose State U., 2003—04. Bd. dirs. Citibank Nev., 1985-2006; policy formulation officer EPA, Washington, 1973-74; dir. instl. studies Nat. Commn. on Water Quality, Washington, 1974-75. Author: Democrats, Delegates and Politics in Nevada: A Grassroots Chronicle of 1972, 1976, Notes From the President's Chair, 1988, No Equal in the World; An Interpretation of the Academic Presidency, 1994, The Constant Conversation: A Chronicle of Campus Life, 2000, In the Arena: The NCAA's First Century, 2006; editor: (with R. Roelofs and D. Hardesty) Environment and Society, 1973. Chair Nev. Rhodes Scholar Comm., 1988—2000, mem., 2002—04; mem. coun. NCAA, 1987—92, mem. pres.'

commn., 1991—92, pres., 1993—95; bd. dirs. Nat. Consortium for Acads. and Sports., 1992—; bd. dirs. campaign chmn. No. Nev. United Way, 1985; bd. dirs. campaing chmn., 1997—2002; bd. dir. Collegiate Women Sports Awards, 1994—; mem. Commn. on Colls., 1980—87; mem. adv. commn. on mining and minerals rsch. U.S. Dept. Interior, 1985—91; mem. Nev. Humanities Commn., 2004—. Recipient Thornton Peace Prize U. Nev., 1971, Humanitarian of Yr. award NCCJ, 1986, Alumnus of Yr. award Calif. State U., Fresno, 1989, ADL Champion of Liberty award, 1993, Disting. Alumni award U. Iowa, 1994, Giant Step award Ctr. for Study of Sport in Soc., 1994, William Anderson award AAHPERD, 1998, Lifetime Achievement award Nat. Consortium for Acads. and Sports, 2001, Nev Arts and Humanities award for pub. svc., 2000, Nev. Edn. Hall of Fame, 2003; Nat. Assn. Schs. Pub. Affairs and Adminstrn. fellow, 1973-74. Mem.: Nat. Assn. State Univs. and Land Grant Colls. (bd. dirs. 1998—2000). Office: U Nev Mail Stop 310 Reno NV 89557 Home Phone: 775-747-3605; Office Phone: 775-784-1500. Business E-Mail: crowley@unr.edu.

CROWN, ERIC J., information systems executive; BSc in Bus. Computer Info. Sys., Ariz. State U., 1984. Chmn., CEO, founder Insight Enterprises, Tempe, Ariz., 1988—. Office: Insight Enterprises 6820 S Harl Ave Tempe AZ 85283-4318 E-mail: ecrown@insight.com.

CROWN, TIMOTHY A., information technology executive; BS in Bus. and Computer Sci., U. Kans., 1986. Adminstrv. analyst NCR Corp., 1986-87; various positions to pres. Insight Enterprises, Tempe, Ariz., 1988-89, co-CEO, co-chmn., 1994—2004, chmn., 2004—. Ind. computer bus. cons., 1987-88. Office: Insight Enterprises 6820 S Harl Ave Tempe AZ 85283

CROZIER, ALAIN, computer software company executive; b. Montreal, Can. married; children: Arthur, Alice. B in Math. and Econs., U. Claude Bernard; B in Mgmt., Institut Suprieur de Gestion. Mng. cons. Peat Marwick, Paris; joined Microsoft Corp., 1994, bus. controller Microsoft France, fin. and op. dir. France, controller South Pacific and Americas region, worldwide controller, CFO Sales, Mktg. and Svcs. Group (SMSG), 2002—05, corp. v.p., CFO SMSG, 2005—. Avocations: art, travel, skiing. Office: Microsoft Corp One Microsoft Way Redmond WA 98052-6399

CROZIER, SCOTT A., lawyer; b. 1950; BA, Ariz. State U., 1975, JD, 1978. Bar: Ariz. 1978. Asst. counsel Talley Industries, Inc., 1980-87; sr. counsel, dir. environ. svcs. dept. Phelps Dodge Corp., 1987-90, assoc. gen. counsel, dir., 1990-91, v.p., gen. counsel, 1991—99; sr. v.p., gen. counsel PetSmart, Inc., 1999—, corp. sec., 2000—, chief compliance officer, 2005—. Former enforcement atty. securities div. Ariz. Corp. Commn.; former special asst. atty. gen. Ariz. Atty. General's Office. Office: PetSmart Inc 19601 N 27th Ave Phoenix AZ 85027

CRUDUP, BILLY, actor; b. Manhasset, NY, July 8, 1968; 1 child, William Atticus Parker. Grad., U. NC, Chapel Hill; MFA, NYU, 1994. Actor: (Broadway plays) Arcadia, 1995 (Theater World award, 1995), Bus Stop, 1996, The Three Sisters, 1997, The Elephant Man, 2002, The Pillowman, 2005, The Coast of Utopia, 2006—07 (Tony award for Best Featured Actor in a Play, 2007); (films) Sleepers, 1996, Everyone Says I Love You, 1996, Inventing the Abbotts, 1997, Grind, 1997, Snitch, 1998, Without Limits, 1998, The Hi-Lo Country, 1998, Princess Mononoke (voice only), 1999, Jesus' Son, 1999, Waking the Dead, 2000, Almost Famous, 2000, World Traveler, 2001, Charlotte Gray, 2001, Big Fish, 2003, Stage Beauty, 2004, Trust the Man, 2005, Mission: Impossible III, 2006, The Good Shepherd, 2006, Dedication, 2007, Pretty Bird, 2008, Watchmen, 2009. Office: c/o Creative Artists Agency 9830 Wilshire Blvd Beverly Hills CA 90212

CRUMB, R. (ROBERT DENNIS CRUMB), cartoonist; b. Phila., Aug. 30, 1943; s. Charles Sr. C.; m. Dana Morgan (div. 1977); m. Aline Kominski, 1978. Colorist Am. Greetings Corp., 1963-67; cartoonist Fantagraphics Books, Seattle, 1967—; founder, pub., editor Zap Comix, 1968—, Weirdo mag., 1981—89; band mem. R. Crumb & His Cheap Suit Seranaders, 1972—. Editor and pub.: Zap Comix #0-14, 1968-2004, Weirdo #1-28, 1981-93; author and illustrator: Bijou Funnies, 1968-71, Head Comix, 1968, Snatch Comics, 1968-69, R. Crumb's Comics & Stories, 1969, Motor City Comics, 1969-70, Yellow Dog Comics, 1969, R. Crumb's Fritz the Cat, 1969, Mr. Natural, 1970-71, San Francisco Comic Book, 1970, Uneeda Comix, 1970, Despair, 1970, Hytone Comix, 1971, Home Grown Funnies, 1971, The People's Comics, 1972, XYZ Comics, 1972, Funny Aminals, 1972, Black & White Comics, 1973, El Perfecto Comics, 1973, Artistic Comics, 1973, Zam Zap, 1974, Dirty Laundry Comics, 1974, 1978, Arcade Comics Revue, 1975-76, Snarf #6, 1976, (with Harvey Pekar) American Splendor, 1976-77, 1979-80, 1982-83, R. Crumb's Carload o' Comics, 1976, Best Buy Comics, 1979, Snoid Comics, 1979, Hup, 1987, 1989, 1992, ID, 1990-91, (with Aline Kominski) My Troubles with Women, 1991, Weirdo Art of R. Crumb, 1992, Complete Dirty Laundry Comics, 1993, Self Loathing Comics, 1995, 1997, Art & Beauty, 1996, 2003, Mystic Funnies, 1997, 1999, 2002, and many others; illustrator: The Monkey Wrench Gang by Edward Abbey, 1985; frequent contbr. to comic mags.; subject of documentaries: The Confessions fo Robert Crumb, 1987, Crumb, 1994; creator cartoon character Fritz the Cat. Recipient Harvey Spl. award for Humor, 1990, Grand prix de la ville d'Angoulême, 1999. Office: Fantagraphics Books 7563 Lake City Way NE Seattle WA 98115-4218 E-mail: fbicomix@fantagraphics.com.

CRUMLEY, ROGER LEE, surgeon, educator, otolaryngologist; b. Perry, Iowa, Oct. 8, 1941; s. Dwight Moody and Helen Ethelwyn (Anderson) C.; m. Janet Lynn Conant, Nov. 13, 1987; children: Erin Kelly Helen, Danielle Nicole. BA, Simpson Coll., 1964; MS, U. Iowa, 1975, MD, 1967; MBA, U. Phoenix, 1999. Diplomate Am. Bd. Otolaryngology (dir. 1992—2004). Intern L.A. County Gen. Hosp., 1967-68; resident in surgery Highland-Alameda Hosp., Oakland, Calif., 1968-69; bn. surgeon 1st Marine Div., Vietnam, 1968-69; resident in otolaryngology U. Iowa, Iowa City, 1971-75; chief otolarygology San Francisco Gen. Hosp., 1975-81; assoc. prof., then prof. U. Calif., San Francisco, 1981-87, prof., chief otolaryngology-head and neck surgery Irvine, 1987—2007. Guest prof. Humboldt U., East Berlin, 1982, M.S. McLeod vis. prof. S. Australian Postgrad. Edn. Ctr., Adelaide, 1988; treas., pres. Am. Acad. Facial Plastic Surgeons, 1994-95, Triological Soc., 2002-03; McBride lectr. U. Edinburgh, 1998. Contbr. articles and book chpts. to profl. pubs. With USN, 1969-71, Vietnam. Recipient Alumni Achievement award Simpson Coll., 1984. Fellow ACS, Am. Acad. Otolaryngology (bd. dirs. 1988—, award 1989); mem. Soc. Univ. Otolaryngologists, Triological Soc. (pres. 2002-), Bohemian Club (San Francisco), Center Club (Costa Mesa, Calif.). Republican. Methodist. Avocations: music, piano, jazz flügelhorn, running, skiing. Office: U Calif-Irvine Med Ctr Dept Otolaryngology Head & Neck 101 The City Dr S Orange CA 92868-3201 Home Phone: 714-289-0253; Office Phone: 714-456-7017. Business E-Mail: scrumley@uci.edu.

CRUMP, SAM, state legislator; m. Colleen Crump; 4 children. BA in Govt., U. San Francisco, 1986, MA in Pub. Adminstrn., 2002; JD, Santa Clara U., Calif., 1989. Prosecutor, judge advocate gen. US Army; legis. counsel Calif. Judges Assn.; founding ptnr. Boates & Crump, Anthem, Ariz.; mem. Dist. 6 Ariz. House of Reps., 2007—, chair govt. com., mem. mil. affairs & pub. safety com., transp.& infrastructure com. Active St. Rose Cath. Ch., Anthem. Mem.: Rotary Club. Republican. Catholic. Office: Ariz House Reps Capitol Complex 1700 W Washington Rm 302 Phoenix AZ 85007 Home Phone: 623-551-3502; Office Phone: 602-926-3014. Office Fax: 602-417-3048. Business E-Mail: scrump@azleg.gov. E-mail: samcrump@qwest.net.*

CRUSE, ALLAN BAIRD, mathematician, computer scientist, educator; b. Aug. 28, 1941; s. J. Clyde and Irma R. Cruse. Postgrad. (Woodrow Wilson fellow), U. Calif., Berkeley, 1962-63; MA, 1965. Fellow Dartmouth Coll., 1963-64; instr. U. San Francisco, 1966-73; asst. prof. math., 1973-76; assoc. prof., 1976-79; prof., 1979—. Chmn. math. dept. 1988-91; vis. instr. Stilman Coll., summer 1967; vis. assoc. prof. Emory U., spring 1978; prof. computer sci. Sonoma State U., 1983-85; cons. math edn. NSF fellow, 1972-73. Author: (with Millianne Granberg) Lectures on Freshman Calculus, 1971; rsch. publs. in field. Mem. Am. Math. Soc., Math. Am. Math. Soc., Math. Assn. Am. (chmn. No. Calif. sedt. 1995-96), Assn. Computing Machinery, U. San Francisco Faculty Assn., Sigma Xi (dissertation award 1974). Office: U San Francisco Harney Sci Ctr San Francisco CA 94117

CRUTZEN, PAUL JOSEF, research meteorologist, chemist; b. Amsterdam, The Netherlands, Dec. 3, 1933; married; 2 children. PhD in Meteorology, Stockholm U., 1973; DSc (hon.), York U., Can., 1986, U. Catholique de Louvain, Belgium, 1992, U. East Anglia, Norwich, Eng., 1994, Aristotle U., Thessaloniki, Greece, 1996, U. Liège, Belgium, 1997, U. San José, Costa Rica, 1997, Tel Aviv U., 1997, Oreg. State U., 1997, U. Chile, Santiago, 1997, U. Bourgogne, Dijon, France, 1997, U. Athens, Greece, 1998, Democritus U. Thrace, Xanthi, 2001, Nova Gorica Polytech., Slovenia, 2002, U. Hull, 2002. Sr. scientist, dir. Air Quality Div., Nat. Ctr. Atmospheric Rsch., Boulder, Colo., 1977—80; adj. prof. Atmospheric Scis. Dept., Colo. State U., 1976—81; prof. Max-Planck-Inst. fur Chemie, Mainz, Germany, 1980—2000; exec. dir. Max-Planck-Inst. for Chemistry, Mainz, Germany, 1983—85; prof. dept. geophys. scis. U. Chgo., 1987—91; prof. Scripps Inst. Oceanography, U. Calif., La Jolla, 1992—, Utrecht U., Inst. Marine and Atmospheric Scis., Netherlands, 1997—2000, prof. emeritus, 2000—. With Bridge Constrn. Bur., City of Amsterdam, 1954—58, House Constrn. Bur, Gaevle, Sweden, 1958—59; vis. fellow St. Cross Coll., Oxford, England, 1969—71; mem. adv. coun. Volvo Environment Prize, 1993—; mem. Sci. and Tech. Adv. Panel UN Environment Programme, 1993—98; mem. Prix Lemaitre Com., Belgium, 1994—; mem. European Sci. and Tech. Assembly European Union, Brissles, 1997—99; mem. Sci. Adv. Group Sch. Environ. Scis., U. East Anglia, 1995—; mem. Global Change Com. German Rsch. Coun. and Fed. Min. Rsch. and Tech., 1998—99; vice chmn., sci. com. Internat. Geosphere-Biosphere Project, 1998—; co-chief scientist, Indian Ocean Expt. Scripps Instn. Oceanography, 1999; mem. Steering Com. Ctr. for Atmospheric Scis., U. Calif., Berkeley, 2000—; mem. Framework Prog. Expert Adv. Group European Commn., 2001—; mem. adv. com. Inst.: Urbanization, Emissions and Global Carbon Cycle, START, Washington, DC, 2002—. Editor: Jour. Atmospheric Chemistry; mem. editl. bd. Jour. Atmospheric Chemistry. Mil. service the Netherlands, 1956—58. Recipient Discover Scientist of Yr., Rolex, 1984, Leo Szilard Award, Am. Physical Soc., 1985, Tyler Prize for Environment, 1989, Volvo Entertainment Prize, 1991, German Environ. Prize, Fed. Found. for Environment, 1994, Global Ozone Award, UN Environment Prog., 1995, Max-Planck Rsch. Prize, 1994, Nobel prize in Chemistry, 1995, Minnie Rosen Award, Ross U., 1996, Louis J. Battan Author's Award, Am. Meteorological Soc., Award for outstanding contributions to Sci. and Soc., Karamanlis Inst. for Democracy Athens, Greece, 2001; named Commandeur in de Orde van de Nederlandse Leeuw, Queen of Netherlands, 1996. Mem.: German Soc. Natural Scientists and Physicians (mem. exec. bd. 1995—2000), Coun. Pontifical Acad. Scis., Acad. Nat. dei Lincei, Rome, The Vatican, Pontifical Academy, Academia Europea, Royal Swedish Acad. Engring., Royal Swedish Acad. Scis., World Innovation Found. (WIF) (hon.), Commn. on Atmospheric Chemistry and Global Pollution (hon.), Internat. Ozone Commn. (hon.), Internat. Polar Found. (hon.), Swedish Meteorol. Soc. (hon.), European Geophys. Soc. (hon.), Am. Meteorol. Soc. (hon.), Russian Acad. Scis. (assoc.), NAS (assoc.). Office: Scripps Inst Oceanography UCSD 9500 Gilman Dr La Jolla CA 92093-0221 Business E-Mail: air@mpch-mainz.mpg.de, pcrutzen@ucsd.edu.

CRUZ, DENIS J., elementary school educator; b. Waterloo, Iowa; Tchg. cert. Calif. State Univ.-Long Beach. Lang. arts. tchr. Whittier (Calif.) Elem. Sch. Named Calif. Tchr. of Yr., 2006. Mem.: Whittier Elem.Tchr. Assn. Office: Katherine Edwards Mid Sch 6812 S Norwalk Blvd Whittier CA 90606 E-mail: cruzin5@mylifeline.net.

CRUZ, MICHAEL W., Lieutenant Governor of Guam, surgeon; s. Miguel de Gracia and Rosalinda Quinata Cruz; m. Jennifer Rosario Cruz; children: Shaunn, Mika'ele, Christine, Christian Payumo. BS in Biology, Walla Walla Coll.; MD, Loma Linda U. Sch. Med., 1984. Surgeon, Guam; med. dir. Guam Meml. Hosp.; senator Territory of Guam, 2004—07, chmn. Com. on Health and Human Svcs., vice chmn. Com. on Natural Resources, Utilities and Micronesian Affairs, Com. on Aviation, Immigration, Labor and Housing, lt. gov., 2007—. Contbr. articles to profl. jours. Pres. Ayuda Found. Col. Guam Army Nat. Guard. Decorated Bronze Star Medal; recipient Nat. Govs. Award, 2004. Fellow: Am. Coll. Surgeons; mem.: Guam Med. Soc. Office: Office of Lt Gov PO Box 2950 Hagatna GU 96932 Office Phone: 671-475-9380. Office Fax: 671-477-2007. E-mail: ltgov@mail.gov.gu.

CRUZ, PENÉLOPE, actress; b. Madrid, Apr. 28, 1974; d. Eduardo and Encarna Cruz. Studied classical ballet, Nat. Conservatory, Madrid. Actor: (films) El Laberinto griego, 1991, Belle époque, 1992, Jamón, jamón, 1992, La Ribelle, 1993, La Celestina, 1996, Más que amor, frenesí, 1996, Et Hjørne af paradis, 1997, Carne trémula, 1997, Abre los ojos, 1997, Don Juan, 1998, The Man with Rain in His Shoes, 1998, Talk of Angels, 1998, La Niña de tus ojos, 1998, The Hi-Lo Country, 1998, Todo sobre mi madre, 1999, Volavérunt, 1999, Woman on Top, 2000, All the Pretty Horses, 2000, Blow, 2001, Captain Corelli's Mandolin, 2001, Sin noticias de Dios, 2001, Vanilla Sky, 2001, Waking Up in Reno, 2002, Masked and Anonymous, 2003, Fanfan la tulipe, 2003, Gothika, 2003, Noel, 2004, Head in the Clouds, 2004, Sahara, 2005, Chromophobia, 2005, Bandidas, 2006, Volver, 2006 (Hollywood Actress of the Yr. award, Hollywood Awards, 2006, Best Actress, European Film Awards, 2006, Runner-up, Best Actress award, LA Film Critics Assn., 2006), The Good Night, 2007, Elegy, 2008, Vicky Cristina Barcelona, 2008 (Best Supporting Actress Nat. Bd. Review, 2008, Best Supporting Actress NY Film Critics Cir., 2008, Best Supporting Actress Boston Soc. Film Critics, 2008, Best Supporting Actress, LA Film Critics Assn., 2009, Best Supporting Actress, Brit. Acad. Film and TV Arts, 2009, Acad. award for Best Actress in a Supporting Role, 2009, Ind. Spirit award for Best Supporting Female, Film Ind., 2009); (TV films) Framed, 1992. Founder Sabera Found. Recipient Best Film award, Elle Mag., 2007; named a Knight in Order of Arts and Letters, France, 2006; named one of The World's Most Influential People, TIME mag., 2009. Office: Creative Artists Agency 2000 Avenue Of The Stars Los Angeles CA 90067-4700*

CRYSTAL, DARREN, Internet company executive, application developer; Studied at, U. Tex., Austin. With IBM Global Svcs., Maxserv, Eaton Semiconductors; network engr. Dell Corp.; software architect Level 3 Comm.; co-founder, chief tech. officer Photobucket, Denver, 2003—. Spkr. in field. Office: Photobucket PO Box 13003 Denver CO 80201

CSIKSZENTMIHALYI, MIHALY, psychology professor; b. Fiume, Italy, Sept. 29, 1934; came to U.S., 1956; s. Alfred and Edith (Jankovich) C.; m. Isabella Selega, Dec. 30, 1961; children: Mark, Christopher. BA, U. Chgo., 1960, PhD, 1965. Reporter European News Service, Rome, 1952-56; free-lance artist Rome, 1954-56; translator U.S.A. Pubs., Chgo., 1958-64; prof. sociology Lake Forest (Ill.) Coll., 1965-70; prof. psychology human devel., edn. U. Chgo., 1971—90; prof. psychology Claremont Grad. U., 1990—. Adv. bd. Ency. Britannica, Chgo., 1985—, J.P. Getty Mus., Malibu, Calif., 1985—. Author: Beyond Boredom and Anxiety, 1975, Flow: The Psychology of Optimal Experience, 1990, The Evolving Self, 1993, Creativity, 1996, Finding Flow in Everyday Life, 1997, Good Business, 2003; (with others) The Creative Vision, 1976, The Meaning of Things, 1981, Being Adolescent, 1984, Optimal Experience, 1988, Television and the Quality of Life, 1990, The Art of Seeing, 1990, Talented Teenagers, 1993, Creating Worlds, 1994, Becoming Adult, 2000, Good Work, 2001, A Life Worth Living, 2006, Experience Sampling, 2006. Fulbright Sr. scholar, 1984, 1990, Fellow Ctr. for Advanced Studies in the Behavioral Sci., 1994-95. Fellow Am. Acad. Arts and Scis., Am. Acad. Edn., Am. Acad. Leisure Scis., Am. Acad. Polit. and Social Scis.; mem. Quadrangle Club. Avocations: mountain climbing, reading, art, chess. Home: 700 Alamosa Dr Claremont CA 91711 Office: 1021 N Dartmouth Ave Claremont CA 91711 Home Phone: 909-621-7345. Business E-Mail: miska@cgu.edu.

CUADRA, CARLOS ALBERT, library and information scientist, consultant; b. San Francisco, Dec. 21, 1925; s. Gregorio and Amanda (Mendoza) C.; m. Gloria Nathalie Adams, May 3, 1947; children: Mary Susan Cuadra Nielsen, Neil Gregory, Dean Arthur. AB in Psychology with highest honors, U. Calif., Berkeley, 1949, PhD in Psychology, 1953. Staff psychologist VA, Downey, Ill., 1953-56; with Sys. Devel. Corp., Santa Monica, Calif., 1957-78, mgr. libr. and documentation sys. dept., 1968-70, mgr. edn. and libr. sys. dept., 1971-74; gen. mgr. SDC Search Svc., 1974-78; founder Cuadra Assocs., LA, 1978—. Founder, editor: Ann. Rev. of Info. Sci. and Tech., 1964—75; contbr. articles to profl. jours. Mem. Nat. Commn. Librs. and Info. Sci., 1971-84. Served with USN, 1944-46. Recipient Merit award Am. Soc. Info. Sci., 1968, Best Info. Sci. Book award Am. Soc. Info. Sci., 1969, Miles Conrad award Nat. Fedn. Abstracting and Info. Svcs., 1980, Roger Summit award Assn. Ind. Info. Profls., 2001; named Disting. Lectr. of Yr., Am. Soc. Info. Sci., 1970, hon. fellow Nat. Fedn. Abstracting and Info. Svcs., 1997. Mem. Info. Industry Assn. (bd. dirs., Hall of Fame award 1980), Chem. Abstracts Soc. (governing bd. 1991-96), Am. Chem. Soc. (governing bd. pub. 1997-2000), Phi Beta Kappa. Home: 13213 Warren Ave Los Angeles CA 90066-1750 Office: Cuadra Associates 3415 S Sepulveda Blvd Ste 210 Los Angeles CA 90034-6060 Office Phone: 310-591-2490.

CUBBISON, CHRISTOPHER ALLEN, newspaper editor; b. Honolulu, Dec. 22, 1948; s. Donald Cameron and Mary (Pritchett) C.; m. Linda Cicero, Jan. 3, 1976; children: Genevieve, Cameron. BJ, U. Mo., 1971. Reporter N.Y. Daily News, NYC, 1971-72, St. Petersburg (Fla.) Times, 1972-76, asst. city editor, 1976-78; editor various locations including The Miami Herald, 1978-89; asst. mng. editor Rocky Mountain News, Denver, 1989-90, mng. editor projects, 1990—. Avocations: golf, skiing. Home: 10603 Oliver St Fairfax VA 22030-3913 Office: Rocky Mountain News 101 W Colfax Ave # 500 Denver CO 80202-5315

CUBIN, BARBARA LYNN, former United States Representative from Wyoming; b. Salinas, Calif., Nov. 30, 1946; d. Russell G. and Barbara Lee (Howard) Sage; m. Frederick William Cubin, Aug. 1; children: William Russell, Frederick William III. BS in Chemistry, Creighton U., 1969. Chemist Wyo. Machinery Co., Casper, Wyo., 1973-75; social worker State of Wyo.; mem. Wyo. House Reps., 1987-92, Wyo. State Senate from Dist 29, 1993-94; pres. Spectrum Promotions and Mgmt., Casper, 1993-94; mem.-at-large US Congress from Wyo., Washington, 1995—2009, mem. resources com., energy and commerce com. Mem. steering com. Exptl. Program to Stimulate Competitive Rsch. (EPSCOR); mem. Coun. of State Govts.; active Gov.'s Com. on Preventive Medicine, 1992; vice chmn. Cleer Bd. Energy Coun., Irving, Tex., 1993—; chmn. Wyo. Senate Rep. Conf., Casper, 1993—; mem. Wyo. Rep. Party Exec. Com., 1993; pres. Southridge Elem. Sch. PTO, Casper, Wyo. Toll fellow Coun. State Govts., 1990, Wyo. Legislator of Yr. award for energy and environ. issues Edison Electric Inst., 1994. Mem. Am. Legis. Exch. Coun., Rep. Women. Republican. Avocations: bridge, golf, singing, reading, hunting.*

CUDDY, DANIEL HON, bank executive; b. Valdez, Alaska, Feb. 8, 1921; s. Warren N. and Lucy H.; m. Betty Puckett, Oct. 6, 1947; children: Roxanna, David, Gretchen, Jane, Lucy, Laurel. BA, Stanford U., 1946; LLD (hon.), U. Alaska, 2000. Bar: Alaska 1948. Pvt. practice, Anchorage, 1948-53; pres. First Nat. Bank Anchorage, 1951—, chmn. bd.; consul for the Netherlands, 1975—85. With U.S. Army, World War II, ETO. Named Alaskan of Yr., 2002; named a William A. Egan Outstanding Alaskan, Alaska State C. of C., 2006. Office: First Nat Bank 101 W 36th Ave Anchorage AK 99503-5904

CUFFEY, KURT M., geophysicist, geochemist, educator; PhD, U. Wash., 1999. Asst. prof. to prof. depts. geography and earth and planetary scis. U. Calif., Berkeley. Contbr. articles to sci. jours. Recipient Macelwane medal, Am. Geophys. Union, 2003; named one of Brilliant 10, Popular Sci. mag., 2004. Office: Dept Geography U Calif Berkeley 507 McCone Hall Berkeley CA 94720-4740 Office Phone: 510-643-1641. Office Fax: 510-642-3370. E-mail: kcuffey@berkeley.edu.

CULBERTSON, LESLIE S., computer company executive; B, Lewis and Clark U., 1971. Cost mgr. British Petroleum/Standard Oil Ohio; acctg. mgr., controller Intel, Santa Clara, Calif., 1979—98, dir. corp. fin., 1997—, v.p., co-dir. materials orgn., 1998—2000, v.p., gen. mgr. sys. mfg., 2000—. Office: Intel 2200 Mission Coll Blvd Santa Clara CA 95052

CULICK, FRED ELLSWORTH CLOW, engineering and physics professor; b. Wolfeboro, NH, Oct. 25, 1933; s. Joseph Frank and Mildred Beliss (Clow) C.; m. Frederica Mills, June 11, 1960; children: Liza Hall, Alexander Joseph, Mariette Huxham. Student, U. Glasgow, Scotland, 1957-58; SB, MIT, 1957, PhD, 1961. Rsch. fellow Calif. Inst. Tech., Pasadena, 1961-63, asst. prof., 1963-66, assoc. prof., 1966-70, prof. mech. engring. and jet propulsion, 1970-97, Richard L. and Dorothy M. Hayman prof. mech. engring., 1997—, prof. jet propulsion, 1997—. Cons. to govt. agys. and indsl. orgns. Fellow AIAA, Internat. Acad. Astronautics; mem. Internat. Fedn. Astronautics, Am. Phys. Soc. Home: 1375 Hull Ln Altadena CA 91001-2620 Office: Calif Inst Tech Caltech 205-45 207 Guggenheim Pasadena CA 91125 Office Phone: 626-395-4783. Business E-Mail: fecfly@caltech.edu.

CULLEN, BRUCE F., anesthesiologist; b. Iowa City, May 6, 1940; MD, UCLA, 1966. Intern Blodgett Meml. Hosp., Grand Rapids, Mich., 1966-67; resident in anesthesiology U. Calif., San Francisco, 1967-70; chief anesthesiologist Harborview Med. Ctr., Seattle. Prof. U. Wash. Office: U Wash HMC Anesthesiology 325 9th Ave Seattle WA 98104-2420

CULLEN, JACK JOSEPH, lawyer; b. Sept. 20, 1951; s. Helen Cullen; children: Cameron, Katherine. BA, Western Wash. State Coll., 1973; JD, U. Puget Sound, 1976. Bar: Wash. 1977, U.S. Dist. Ct. (we. dist.) Wash. 1977, U.S. Dist. Ct. (ea. dist.) Wash. 1977, U.S. Tax Ct. 1984, U.S. Ct. Appeals (9th cir.) 1980. Staff atty. Wash. State Bar Assn., Seattle, 1977-79; assoc. Hatch & Leslie, Seattle, 1979-85, mng. ptnr., 1985-91; ptnr. Foster Pepper & Shefelman, Seattle, 1991-96, mng. ptnr., 1996—2002, mng. chair, 1991—. Spkr. in field. Co-author: Prejudgment Attachment, 1986. Active Frank Lloyd Wright Bldg. Conservancy, 1989—; trustee Seattle Repertory Theater, 1999-2002. Mem. ABA (bus. law sect.), Am. Bankruptcy Inst., Wash. State Bar Assn. (creditor-debtor sect., chair exec. 1982-90, spl. dist. counsel 1988—, hearing officer 1990), Seattle-King County Bar Assn. (bankruptcy rules subcom. 1988-90), Vancouver-Seattle Involvency Group (charter mem. 1990—), U.S. Sport Parachuting Team (nat. and world champions 1976, instrument rated pilot). Office: Foster Pepper & Shefelman PLLC 1111 3rd Ave Ste 3400 Seattle WA 98101-3299 E-mail: jc@foster.com.

CULLEN, JAMES G., telecommunications industry executive; b. 1942; Married. BA, Rutgers U., 1964; Postgrad., M.I.T. With NJ Bell Tel. Co., Newark, 1964, pres., CEO, 1989—93; pres. Bell Atlantic Corp., 1993—95, vice chmn., 1995—98, pres., COO, 1998—2000. Bd. dir. Nuestar Inc., Johnson & Johnson Inc., Prudential Life Ins. Co.; dir., non-exec. chmn. Agilent Technologies Inc.

CULLINAN, MARY PATRICIA, academic administrator, literature and language professor; BA, U. Pa., 1972; MA, U. Wis., 1973, PhD in English Lit., 1978. Writing cons. MBA Program U. Calif., Berkeley, 1980—81; lectr. Dept. Mktg. Calif. State U., Hayward, 1981—87, assoc. prof., dir. Composition Program, 1987—91, prof. Dept. English, 1992, interim dean Sch. Arts, Letters and Social Scis., 1992—93, dir. Office of Faculty Devel. and Faculty Ctr. for Excellence in Tchg., 1994—96, dean Coll. Arts, Letters and Scis. Stanislaus, 1996—2003; provost, v.p. Academic Affairs, prof. English Stephen F. Austin State U., 2003—06; pres. So. Oreg. U., Ashland, 2006—. Author: Susan Ferrier, Business Communication: Principles and Processes, Business English for Industry and the Professions; co-editor: American Women Writers: Diverse Voices in Prose Since 1845. Office: So Oreg U Office of Pres 1250 Siskiyou Blvd Ashland OR 97520-5032 E-mail: cullinanm@sou.edu.

CULLUM, JOHN, actor, singer; b. Knoxville, Tenn., Mar. 2, 1930; m. Emily Frankel; 1 child, John David. BA, U. Tenn. Former tennis player and real estate salesman. NY debut with Shakespearewrights, 1957; joined NY Shakespeare Festival, 1960; Broadway debut in Camelot, 1962; played Laertes in Hamlet, 1964; other Broadway appearances include On A Clear Day You Can See Forever, 1965 (Theatre World award 1965), Man of La Mancha, 1966, 1776, 1969, Vivat! Vivat Regina, 1972, Shenendoah, 1975 (Tony award as best actor 1975), The Trip Back Down, 1977, On the Twentieth Century, 1978 (Tony award as best actor in musical 1978), Deathtrap, 1979, Whistler, 1981 (Drama Desk award), Private Lives (with Richard Burton and Elizabeth Taylor), 1983, Doubles, 1985, The Boys in Autumn (with George C. Scott), 1986, Urinetown, 2002, Purlie, 2005, The Other Side, 2005, 110 in the Shade, 2007, Cymbeline, 2007; other leading roles include plays Hamlet, Cyrano de Bergerac, The Conscientious Objector, 2008; film appearances include: All the Way Home, 1963, Hawaii, 1966, 1776, 1972, The Prodigal, 1982, Sweet Country, 1985, Marie, 1985, The Boys in Autumn (with George C. Scott), 1986, Ricochet River, 1998, Held Up, 1999, Blackwater Elegy, 2003, The Notorious Bettie Page, 2005, The Night Listener, 2006; concert readings include The Golden Apple, 2005; appeared in TV films A Man Without a Country, 1973, The Day After, 1984, Shootdown, 1988, With a Vengeance, 1992, Inherit the Wind, 1999; TV films include Summer, 1980, Carl Sandburg, 1981; TV series include Buck James, 1987-88, Northern Exposure, 1990-95 (Emmy nomination, Supporting Actor, Comedy, 1993), ER, 1997-2000, To Have & To Hold, 1998, Law & Order: Special Victims Unit, 2003-07; TV appearance in All My Children, 1997; spokesman for arts and entertainment cable TV, Victorian Days. Served with U.S. Army.

CULP, GORDON LOUIS, consulting engineer, management consultant; b. Topeka, Dec. 30, 1939; s. Russell Louis and Dorothy Marion (Wilson) C.; m. Rosemary Anne Smith, Apr. 7, 1990. BS in Civil Engring., U. Kans., 1961, MS in Environ. Health Engring., 1962; MA in Applied Psychology, U. Santa Monica, 1991. Registered profl. engr., Calif., Nev., Wash., Oreg.; cert. Myers Briggs practitioner MBTI Cert. Program, Gainsville, Fla. San. engr. USPHS, Cin., 1962-64, CH2M/Hill Engrs., Corvallis, Oreg., 1964-66; rsch. engr. Neptune Microfloc, Corvallis, 1966-70; rsch. mgr. Battelle N.W., Richland, Wash., 1970-71; regional mgr. CH2M/Hill Engrs., Reston, Va., 1971-73; pres. Culp, Wesner Culp (acquired by HDR Engring. 1986), Cameron Park, Calif., 1973-93, Smith Culp Consulting, Las Vegas, Nev., 1993—. Author: New Concepts in Water Purification, 1974, Handbook of Advanced Wastewater Treatment, 1978, 2d edit., 2001, Managing People (including Yourself) for Project Success, 1991,The Lead Dog Has the Best View: Leading Your Project Team to Success, 2005, others. Named one of four Outstanding Graduates in Hist. of Civil Engrg. Program, U. Kans. Mem. ASCE, Am. Water Works Assn., Water Environment Fedn., Am. Acad. Environ. Engrs., Assn. Psychol. Type, Rotary (pres. 1977-78). Office: Smith Culp Consulting 653 Ravel Ct Las Vegas NV 89145-8628 Office Phone: 702-360-1120. Business E-Mail: gordon@smithculp.com.

CULPEPPER, DAVID CHARLES, lawyer; b. Quantico, Va., Mar. 15, 1946; s. Carlton Milburn and Eleanor Louise (Hart) C.; m. Marie T. Francher, June 21, 1969; children: Larissa, Danielle. BA, Santa Clara U., Calif., 1968; JD, U. Oreg., 1974. Bar: Oreg. 1974, U.S. Dist. Ct. Oreg. 1974, U.S. Tax Ct. 1974, U.S. Ct. Appeals (9th cir.) 1974. Ptnr. Miller, Nash, Wiener, Hager & Carlsen, Portland, Oreg., 1974—. Contbg. author: Advising Oregon Businesses, 1986, 89; contbr. articles to profl. jours. Mem. ABA (partnership com. taxation sect. 1983), Oreg. Bar Assn. (chair exec. com. tax sect. 1992-93), Portland Tax Forum (bd. dirs., co-chair tax force on ltd. liability co. legis.). Office: Miller Nash Wiener Hager & Carlsen 111 SW 5th Ave Ste 3500 Portland OR 97204-3699

CULTON, PAUL MELVIN, retired counselor, educational administrator, professor, interpreter; b. Council Bluffs, Iowa, Feb. 12, 1932; s. Paul Roland and Hallie Ethel Emma (Paschal) C. AB, Crossroads Coll., 1955; BS, U. Nebr., Omaha, 1965; MA, Calif. State U., Northridge, 1970; EdD, Brigham Young U., 1981. Cert. tchr., Iowa. Tchr. Iowa Sch. for Deaf, Council Bluffs, 1956-70; ednl. specialist Golden West Coll., Huntington Beach, Calif., 1970-71, dir. disabled students, 1971-82, instr., 1982-88; counselor El Camino Coll., Via Torrance, Calif., 1990-93, acting assoc. dean, 1993-94, counselor, 1994-97, lectr., 1997—2006; prof. First Global C.C., Nong Khai, Thailand, 2006. Interpreter various state and fed. cts., Iowa, Calif., 1960-90; asst. prof. Calif. State U., Northridge, Fresno, Dominguez Hills, 1973, 76, 80, 87-91, L.A., 1999—; vis. prof. U. Guam, Agana, 1977; prof. First Global C.C., NongKhai, Thailand, 2006; mem. allocations task force, task force on deafness, trainer handicapped students Calif. C.C.s, 1971-81 Editor: Region IX Conf. for Coordinating Rehab. and Edn. Svcs. for Deaf proceedings, 1970, Toward Rehab. Involvement by Parents of Deaf conf. proceedings, 1971; composer Carry the Light, 1986. Bd. dirs. Gay and Lesbian Cmty. Svcs. Ctr., Orange County, Calif., 1975-77; founding sec. Dayle McIntosh Ctr. for Disabled, Anaheim and Garden Grove, Calif., 1974-80; active Dem. Cent. Com. Pottawattamie County, Council Bluffs, 1960-70; del. People to People N.Am. Educators Deaf Vis. Russian Schs. & Programs for Deaf, 1993. League for Innovation in Community Coll. fellow, 1974. Mem. Calif. Assn. Postsecondary Edn. and Disability (founding v.p.), Registry of Interpreters for Deaf, Am. Sign Lang. Tchrs. Assn., Nat. Assn. Deaf. Mem. Am. Humanist Assn. Avocations: vocal music, languages, community activism, travel, politics. Personal E-mail: pmculton@socal.rr.com.

CUMALAT, JOHN, physics professor; BA in Physics, U. Calif., Santa Barbara, 1970, MA in Physics, 1971, PhD in Physics, 1977. Rsch. assoc. Fermi Nat. Accelerator Lab., 1977—79, Robert R. Wilson fellow, 1979—81; asst. prof. U. Colo., Boulder, 1981—85, assoc. prof., 1985—91, prof., 1991—, chair, dept. physics. Rschr. in field; spkr. in field. Contbr. articles to numerous profl. jours. Recipient Outstanding Jr. Investigator award, Dept. Energy, 1982. Fellow: Am. Phys. Soc. Office: Univ Colo Boulder Dept Physics 390 UCB Boulder CO 80309-0390 Office Phone: 303-492-0297. Office Fax: 303-492-3352. Business E-Mail: john.p.cumalat@colorado.edu.

CUMMING, GEORGE ANDERSON, JR., lawyer; b. Washington, Apr. 16, 1942; s. George Anderson and Gene (Chapman) C.; m. Linda Lucille Harder, Aug. 25, 1963; children: Mary Elizabeth, Andrew Gordon. AA, Coll. San Mateo, 1962; AB magna cum laude, San Francisco State U., 1963; JD, U. Calif., Berkeley, 1967. Bar: Calif. 1967, U.S. Dist. Ct. (no. dist.) Calif. 1967, U.S. Ct. Appeals (9th cir.) 1967, U.S. Supreme Ct. 1974. Assoc. Brobeck, Phleger & Harrison, San Francisco, 1967-75, ptnr., 1975-98; spl. trial counsel antitrust divsn. U.S. Dept. Justice, Washington, 1996-97; with Brobeck Phleger & Harrison, San Francisco, 1998—. Fellow Am. Coll. Trial Lawyers; mem. ABA, San Francisco Bar Assn., Order of Coif. Avocation: model building. Office: Brobeck Phleger & Harrison Antitrust Divsn One Market Spear St Tower San Francisco CA 94105

CUMMING, THOMAS ALEXANDER, brokerage house executive; b. Toronto, Ont., Can., Oct. 14, 1937; s. Alison A. and Anne B. (Berry) C.; m. E. Mary Stevens, Mar. 12, 1965; children: Jennifer, Allison, Katy. BAS, U. Toronto, 1960. Registered profl. engr., Can. With Bank of Nova Scotia, 1965-88; spl. rep. Toronto, 1965-68; br. mgr. Dublin, 1969-71, London, 1971-75; v.p. Calgary, Alta., Canada, 1975-80; sr. v.p. Calgery, Alta., Canada, 1980-85, Toronto, 1986-88; pres., CEO Alta. Stock Exchange, Calgary, 1988-99. Bd. dirs. Pengrowth Energy Trust; chair Canadian Investor Protection Fund, Balancing Pool. Mem. Assn. Profl. Engrs., Calgary C. of C. (pres. 1991), Calgary Golf and Country Club, Calgary Petroleum Club. Home and Office: 2906 10th St SW Calgary AB Canada T2T 3H2

CUMMINGS, BARTON, musician; b. Newport, NH, July 10, 1946; s. C. Barton and Ruth (Ricard) C.; m. Florecita L. Lim, July 23, 1983 BS in Music Edn., U. N.H., 1968; MusM, Ball State U., Muncie, Ind., 1973. Dir. music Alton (N.H.) Pub. Sch., 1971-72; lectr. San Diego State U., 1974-79; instr. music Point Loma Coll., San Diego, 1976-79; instr. San Diego Community Coll. Dist., 1977-79, Delta State U., Cleveland, Miss., 1979-82; supr. Clarksdale Separate Sch. Dist., 1982-84; dir. music Walnut (Calif.) Creek Concert Band, 1985—98, Richmond Unified Sch. Dist., 1988—94, Golden Hills Concert Band, 1990—98; condr. Devil Mountain Symphony, 1991—93. Tuba player Vallejo Symphony Orch., 1988-92, Concord Pavilion Pops Orch., 1985-92, Brassworks of San Francisco, 1985-93, Solano Dixie Jubilee. Author: The Contemporary Tuba, 1984, The Tuba Guide, 1989, Teaching Techniques for Brass Instruments, 1989; composer over 100 pub. compositions; recorded on Capra, Coronet and Crystal, Channel Classics, Mark labels. Mem. ASCAP, T.U.B.A., Phi Mu Alpha Sinfonia. Avocations: travel, cooking, writing, composing, reading. Home: 550 Cambridge Dr Benicia CA 94510-1316 Personal E-mail: cbc_21@yahoo.com.

CUMMINGS, NANCY, library director; b. Reno; BA, U. Nev., Las Vegas; MLS, San Jose State Coll., Calif. Sys. adminstr. Clark County Libr. Sys., Las Vegas; dir. Yuma County Libr. Dist., Ariz., Washoe County Libr. Sys., Reno, 1995—. Mem. Peace Corps, Philippines. Recipient Disting. Svc. award, Ariz. Libr. Assn., 1994; named Libr. of Yr., 1988. Office: Washoe County Libr Sys 301 S Center St Reno NV 89501-2102 Office Phone: 775-327-8340. Office Fax: 775-327-8393. E-mail: ncummings@washoecounty.us.

CUMMINS, JOHN STEPHEN, bishop emeritus; b. Oakland, Calif., Mar. 3, 1928; s. Michael and Mary (Connolly) Cummins. AB, St. Patrick's Coll., 1949. Ordained priest Archdiocese of San Francisco, 1953; asst. pastor Mission Dolores Ch., San Francisco, 1953-57; mem. faculty Bishop O'Dowd H.S., Oakland, 1957-62; chancellor Diocese of Oakland, 1962-71; rev. monsignor, 1962; domestic prelate, 1967; exec. dir. Calif. Cath. Conf., Sacramento, 1971-77; ordained bishop, 1974; aux. bishop Diocese of Sacramento, Sacramento, 1974—77; bishop Diocese of Oakland, Oakland, 1977—2003, bishop emeritus, 2003—. Campus min. San Francisco State Coll., 1953—57, Mills Coll., Oakland, 1957—71; trustee St. Mary's Coll., 1968—79. Roman Catholic.

CUMMISKEY, CHRIS, state legislator; b. Point Pleasant, NJ, Aug. 15, 1964; Student, Brophy Coll., 1983; BA in Comm., Ariz. State U., 1987. Mem. Ariz. Ho. Reps., 1990-94, Ariz. Senate, Dist. 25, Phoenix, 1994—; asst. minority leader Ariz. State Senate, mem. banking com., mem. ins. and elections com., mem. commerce and econ. devel. com., mem. fin. com., others, asst. floor leader. Active Dem. Leadership Coun. Nat. Adv., Valley Citizen League, Fiesta Bowl, Boys Club Phoenix and Scottsdale; bd. dirs. Valley Leadership; sponsor Ariz. Town Hall, Ariz. Acad.; precinct committeeman. Mem. Nat. Conf. State Legislatures, Ariz. Policy Forum, Nucleus Club, Ariz. State U. Alumni Assn. Democrat.

CUNNINGHAM, ANDREA LEE, public relations executive; b. Oak Park, Ill., Dec. 15, 1956; d. Ralph Edward and Barbara Ann C.; m. Rand Wyatt Siegfried, Sept. 24, 1983. BA, Northwestern U., 1979. Feature writer Irving-Cloud Pub. Co., Lincolnwood, Ill., 1979-81; account exec. Burson-Marsteller Inc., Chgo., 1981-83; group account mgr. Regis McKenna Inc., Palo Alto, Calif., 1983-85; founder, owner, pres. Cunningham Communication Inc., Santa Clara, Calif., 1985—. Mem. Am. Electronics Assn., U.S. C. of C., Young Pres.' Orgn., Software Pubs. Assn., Boston Computer Soc., Leadership Calif., U.S. Cambridge C. of C. Republican. Avocations: running, roller skating, aerobics, racquetball.

CUNNINGHAM, BRIAN C., lawyer, corporate executive; b. Sparta Ill., Oct. 17, 1943; s. Robert C. and Gail L. (McDill) C.; m. Martha Elizabeth Kerr; children: Laura, Scott, Colby. BSEE, Washington U., St. Louis, 1965, JD, 1970. Bar: NY 1971, Mo. 1980, Calif. 1983, US Dist. Ct. (so. dist.) NY 1974, US Dist. Ct. (no. dist.) Calif. 1983. Vol., US Peace Corps, Washington, 1965-67; assoc. Winthrop, Stimpson Putnam & Roberts, NYC, 1970-79; assoc. corp. counsel Monsanto, St. Louis, 1979-82; v.p., sec., gen. counsel Genentech, South San Francisco, 1982—1989; ptnr., life sci., health care groups, Cooley Godward LLP, 1989-98, of counsel, 2003-, Palo Alto; pres., COO, Rigel Pharmaceuticals, Inc., 1998-2003; also CEO Dao-Gen Inc., San Francisco. Office: Cooley Godward et al 5 Palo Alto Sq Ste 400 Palo Alto CA 94306-2122 Home: 1919 Octavia St Apt 1 San Francisco CA 94109-3341 E-mail: bcunningham@scu.edu.

CUNNINGHAM, JANIS ANN, lawyer; b. Seattle, May 13, 1952; d. Luvern Victor and Anna Jane Rieke; m. D. John Cunningham, June 10, 1972; children: Emily Jane, Laura Christine. BS with honors, U. Wis., Milw., 1973; JD, U. Wash., 1976. Bar: Wash. 1976, U.S. Dist. Ct. (we. dist.) Wash. 1976, U.S. Ct. Appeals (9th cir.) 1976. Law clk. to Hon. Eugene A. Wright U.S. Ct. Appeals (9th cir.), Seattle, 1976-77; assoc. Karr, Tuttle, & Campbell, Seattle, 1977-84; ptnr. Karr, Tuttle, Koch, Campbell, Mawer & Sax, Seattle, 1984-89; ptnr., Personal Planning Area Perkins Coie LLP, Seattle, 1989—. Lectr. community property law U. Wash., Seattle, 1984, mem. estate planning coun. adv. bd., 1984-85. Co-author: Washington Practical Probate, 1982, 5th rev. edit., 1988; editor in chief U. Wash. Law Rev., 1975-76. Mem. estate plnning com. Am. Heart Assn., Seattle, 1978; bd. dirs. Community Services for the Blind, Seattle, 1977-79. Fellow Am. Coll. Trust and Estate Counsel; mem. Wash. State Bar Assn. (Real Property, Probate & Trust Section, exec. com. 1988-95, chmn. 1993-94), Seattle Estate Planning Coun., King County Bar Assn. (Real Property, Probate & Trust Section, pres 1986-87), Order of Coif. Avocations: hiking, canoeing. Office: Perkins Coie LLP 1201 3rd Ave 48th Fl Seattle WA 98101-3029 Office Phone: 206-359-8607. Office Fax: 206-359-9607. Business E-Mail: jcunningham@perkinscoie.com.

CUNNINGHAM, JOEL DEAN, lawyer; b. Seattle, Feb. 19, 1948; s. Edgar Norwood and Florence (Burgunder) C.; m. Amy Jean Radewan, Oct. 1, 1970; children: Erin Jane, Rad Norwood. BA in Econs., U. Wash., 1971, JD with high honors, 1974. Lawyer, ptnr. Williams, Kastner & Gibbs, Seattle, 1974-95; ptnr. Luvera, Barnett, Brindley, Beninger & Cunningham, Seattle, 1995—. Fellow Am. Coll. Trial Lawyers, Internat. Soc. Barristers; mem. Am. Bd. Trial Attys. (pres. Washington chpt. 1994), Damage Attys. Round Table, Order of Coif. Avocations: fishing, bicycling, boating. Office: Luvera Barnett Brindley Beninger & Cunningham 6700 Columbia Ctr 701 5th Ave Seattle WA 98104-7097

CUNNINGHAM, ROBERT D., lawyer; BA, Occidental Coll., Calif., 1971; JD, UCLA, 1975. Bar: Calif. 1975. Assoc. Lawler, Felix & Hall, LA, 1975-78; atty. Buena Vista Pictures Distbn., Inc., Burbank, Calif., 1978-84, v.p., sec., gen. counsel, 1984-96; sr. v.p., sec., gen. counsel Buena Vista Pictures Distbn., Inc. (now Walt Disney Pictures & TV), Burbank, Calif., 1996—. Office: Walt Disney Pictures & TV 500 S Buena Vista St Burbank CA 91521-0006

CUNNINGHAM, RON, choreographer, artistic director; b. Chgo., Sept. 15, 1939; m. Carrine Binda, June 12, 1982; children: Christopher, Alexandra. Student, Allegro Ballet, 1961-65, Am. Ballet Theatre, 1968-70; studies with Merce Cunningham, NYC, 1968-70; BS in Mktg., Roosevelt U., 1966. Dancer Allegro Am. Ballet Co., Chgo., 1962-66; artistic dir. Ron Cunningham Contemporary Dance Co., Chgo., 1966-68; dancer Lucas Hoving Dance Co., 1968-72, Lotte Goslar Pantomime Circus, 1968-72, Daniel Nagrin Dance Co., 1968-72; prin. dancer, resident choreographer Boston Ballet, 1972-85; artistic dir. Balt. Ballet, 1985-86; artistic assoc. Washington Ballet, 1986-87; ind. choreographer, 1987-88; artistic dir. Sacramento Ballet, 1988—. Panelist various regional and state art councils, 1979—; dir. Craft of Choreography, 1985; adjudicator, master tchr. Nat. Assn.

Regional Ballet, 1985—, Am. Coll. Dance Assn., 1986. Dancer, choreographer 40 original internat. ballets, 1972—, 4 ballets Nat. Choreography Plan, 1978—, Cinderella, Peoples Republic of China, 1980. Nat. Endowment Arts fellow, 1977, 86, Mass. Art Coun. fellow, 1984, Md. Arts Coun. fellow, 1988. Mem. Nat. Assn. Regional Ballet, Dance/U.S.A. Avocation: archeology--bronze age cultures.

CURB, JESS DAVID, medical educator, researcher; b. Raton, N.Mex., Dec. 29, 1945; s. Leslie Calvin and Evelyn Lula (Lindley) C.; m. Beatriz Lorenza Rodriquez; children: Jess Calvin, William Noa, Maria Lorenza, Isabel Alani. BA, U. Colo., 1967; MD, U. N.Mex., Albuquerque, 1971; MPH, U. Tex., Houston, 1974. Diplomate, cert. geriatric medicine Am. Bd. Internal Medicine. Intern Harlem Hosp., Columbia U., NYC, 1971-72; rsch. assoc. U. Tex. Sch. Pub. Health and Medicine, Houston, 1973-76, asst. prof., 1978-80; resident internal medicine Northwestern U. Sch. Medicine, Chgo., 1976-78; asst. prof. Baylor Coll. Medicine, Houston, 1980-83; assoc. prof. U. Hawaii, Honolulu, 1983-85, prof., 1985-87; assoc. dir. Nat. Inst. on Aging, Bethesda, Md., 1986-89; prof. geriatric medicine, chief Divsn. Clin. Epidemiology U. Hawaii, Sch. Medicine, Honolulu, 1989—, Dir. Transitional Rsch., 2007—; CEO, med. dir. Pacific Health Rsch. Inst., 1995—2003, pres., 2003—07. Contbr. articles to profl. jours. Grantee Honolulu Heart Program, Nat. Heart, Lung and Blood Inst., Honolulu, 1989-2003, Hawaii Asia Aging Study, Nat. Inst. on Aging, Honolulu, 1994-2002, Women's Health Initiative, NIH, Honolulu, 1994—, Family Blood Pressure Program, 1995—. Fellow ACP, Am. Heart Assn. (coun. on epidemiology); mem. Am. Geriatric Soc. Office: U Hawaii 651 Ilalo St MEB 223 Honolulu HI 98613 Business E-Mail: curb@hawaii.edu.

CURD, JOHN GARY, physician, scientist; b. Grand Junction, Colo., July 2, 1945; s. H. Ronald and Edna (Hegsted) C.; m. Karen Wendel, June 12, 1971; children: Alison, Jonathan, Edward, Bethany. BA, Princeton U., 1967; MD, Harvard U., 1971. Diplomate Am. Bd. Internal Medicine, Am. Bd. Rheumatology, Am. Bd. Allergy and Immunology. Rsch. assoc. NIH, Bethesda, Md., 1973-75; fellow in rheumatology U. Calif., San Diego, 1975-77; fellow in allergy-immunology Scripps Clinic, La Jolla, Calif., 1977-78, fellow in allergy-immunology Stanford Exec. Program, 2000, asst. mem. rsch. inst., 1978-81, mem. div. rheumatology, 1981-91, head div. rheumatology, vice chmn. dept. medicine, 1989-91; pres. med. staff Green Hosp., La Jolla, 1988-90; clin. dir. Genentech Inc., South San Francisco, Calif., 1991-96, sr. dir., head clin. sci., 1996-97, v.p. clin. devel., 1997—99; sr. v.p. pres. Vaxgen, 1999—2001; pres. chief med. officer Novacea, 2001—. Author numerous. sci. papers in field. Med. dir. San Diego Scleroderma Found., 1983-91; sec. San Diego Arthritis Found., 1986-87. Lt. comdr. USPHS, 1973-75. Mem. Princeton Club No. Calif. Republican. Home: 128 Reservoir Rd Hillsborough CA 94010-6957 Office Phone: 650-228-1810. Business E-Mail: curd@novacea.com.

CURRAN, DARRYL JOSEPH, photographer, educator; b. Santa Barbara, Calif., Oct. 19, 1935; s. Joseph Harold and Irma Marie (Schlagel) C.; m. Doris Jean Smith, July 12, 1968. AA, Ventura Coll., 1958; BA, UCLA, 1960, MA, 1964. Designer, installer UCLA Art Galleries, 1963-65; mem. faculty Los Angeles Harbor Coll., 1968-69, UCLA Ext., 1972-79, Sch. Art Inst. Chgo., 1975; prof. art Calif. State U., Fullerton, 1967-2001, chmn. art dept., 1989-99; curator various shows, 1971—. Bd. dirs. Los Angeles Center Photog. Studies, 1973-77, pres., 1980-83; juror Los Angeles Olympics Photog. Comms. Project, 1983. One-man shows include U. Chgo., 1975, U. R.I., 1975, Art Space, L.A., 1978, Photoworks Gallery, Richmond, Va., 1979, Alan Hancock Coll., Santa Maria, Calif., 1979, G. Ray Hawkins Gallery, L.A., 1981, Portland (Maine) Sch. Art, 1983, Grossmont Coll., San Diego, 1982, (retrospective) Chaffey Coll., Alta Loma, Calif., L.A. Ctr. for Photog. Studies, 1984, U. Calif. Ext. Ctr., San Francisco, 1986, Cuesta Coll., San Luis Obispo, Calif., 1992, Cypress Coll., 1993, Tex. Woman's U., Denton, 1997, Irvine Valley Coll., 1997, Ellen Kim Murphy Gallery, Santa Monica, 2000, William Marten Gallery, Rochester, N.Y., 2001, No. Ky. U., 2002, Carnegie Art Mus., Oxnard, Calif., 2003; two-person show No. Ky. U., 1995; group exhbns. include Laguna Mus. Art, San Francisco, 1992, Friends of Photography, San Francisco, 1993, U.S. Info. Agy. Empowered Images, 1994—, USIA, Jan Abrams Gallery, L.A., 1995; group exhbns. include Mt. St. Mary's Coll., 1997, Ranch Santiago Coll., 1997, Norton Simon Mus., Pasadena, 2006, Pasadena Mus. California Art, 2006, U. Ky., 2006; represented in permanent collections Mus. Modern Art, Royal Photog. Soc., London, Nat. Gallery Can., Ottawa, Mpls. Inst. Art, Oakland Mus., U. N.Mex., UCLA, Seagram's Collection, N.Y.C., Mus. Photog. Arts, San Diego, Phila. Mus. Art, J. Paul Getty Mus., Phila. Mus. Art, San Francisco Mus. Art. Bd. dirs. Cheviot Hills Home Owners Assn., 1973. Served with U.S. Army, 1954-56. Recipient Career Achievement award Calif. Mus. Photography, 1986; NEA Photographers fellow, 1980; Honored Educatior award Soc. Photographic Edn., 1996. Mem. Soc. Photog. Edn. (dir. 1975-79, honored educator 1996). Home: 10537 Dunleer Dr Los Angeles CA 90064-4317 Personal E-mail: localdj@mindspring.com.

CURRAN, MARY, lawyer; b. NYC, Aug. 29, 1947; d. Philip Joseph and Catherine Mary (Galvin) C.; m. John Michael Quigley, Feb. 4, 1978; children: Oliver, Jane-Claire. AB, Fordham U., 1969; JD, Yale U., 1981; PhD, Columbia U., 1992. Bar: Calif. 1981, U.S. Dist. Ct. (no. and ctrl. dists.) Calif. 1981, 90. Asst. prof. Yale U., New Haven, 1975-79; assoc. McCutchen, Doyle, Brown & Enersen, San Francisco, 1981-84; sr. atty. Dean Witter Reynolds, Inc., San Francisco, 1984-85, v.p., 1985-87, asst. gen. counsel, 1987-92, sr. v.p., assoc. gen. counsel, 1992-97; gen. counsel, sr. v.p. Morgan Stanley, San Francisco, 1997—2002; mng. dir., gen. counsel Sutton Place Mgmt., LLC, San Francisco, 2002—. Mem. ABA, State Bar Calif., Bar Assn. San Francisco (cert. of commendation 1990-91). Office: Sutton Place Mgmt LLC 433 California St 11th Fl San Francisco CA 94104 Business E-Mail: mcurran@forwardmgmt.com.

CURRIE, JANET M., economics professor; b. Kingston, Ont., Can., Mar. 29, 1960; came to U.S., 1983; d. Kenneth Lyell and Edrith Delores Currie; m. William Bentley MacLeod, May 18, 1996; children: Joana Marion, Daniel Bentley. BA, U. Toronto, 1982, MA, 1983; PhD in Econs., Princeton U., 1988. Asst. prof. econs. UCLA, 1988-91, MIT, Cambridge, Mass., 1992, assoc. prof. econs., 1993, UCLA, 1994-95, prof. econs., 1995—, Charles E. Davidson prof. econs., 2005—; prof. econs. Columbia U., NYC, 2005—. Panel mem. NAS, Washington, 1998-99, 2000-01, NSF, Washington, 1998-2001; rsch. assoc. Nat. Bur. Econ. Rsch., 1995—; mem. Brookings Roundtable on Children and Families, 1998—; affiliate Joint Ctr. Poverty Rsch., 1998—; cons. RAND, 1993—. Author: Welfare and the Well Being of Children, 1994; contbr. chpts. to books, articles to profl. jours.; co-editor Jour. Labor Econs., 1994-2000; mem. edit. bd. Quar. Jour. Econs., 1995—; assoc. editor Jour. Health Econs., 2000—02. Alfred P. Sloan Found. fellow, 1993-95, Olin fellow Nat. Bur. Econ. Rsch., 1993, Can. Inst. Advanced Rsch. fellow, 1998-2000. Avocation: gardening. Office: UCLA Dept Econs 405 Hilgard Ave Los Angeles CA 90095-1477 also: Columbia U Econs Dept Internat Affairs Bldg, MC 3323 420 W 118th St New York NY 10027 Office Phone: 212-854-4520. E-mail: jc2663@columbia.edu.

CURRIE, PHILIP JOHN, research paleontologist, educator, museum curator; b. Toronto, Ont., Can., Mar. 13, 1949; children: Tarl, Devin, Brett. BSc, U. Toronto, 1972; MSc, McGill U., 1975, PhD in Biology (with distinction), 1981. Curator paleontology Provincial Mus. Alta., Edmonton, Canada, 1976-81; mus. curator Palaeontology Mus. and Rsch. Inst., Drumheller, Alta., Canada, 1981-82; asst. dir. rsch. Tyrrell Mus. Palaeontology, Drumheller, Alta., Canada, 1982-89, head dinosaur rsch., 1989—2005; head dinosaur rsch., prof. biol. sciences dept. U. Alberta, Canada, 2005—. Sec. Alta. Paleontology Adv. Com., 1977-89; treas. Palaeontology Can., 1981-84; adj. prof. U. Saskatchewan.; bd. dir. scientific com., Palaeontological Rsch. Inst., Calgary; mem. President's internat. alumni coun., U. Toronto. Author: Flying Dinosaurs, 1991, Dinosaur Renaissance, 1994; co-author: The Great Dinosaurs, 1994, 101 Questions About Dinosaurs, 1996, Troodon, 1997, Albertosaurus, 1998, Centrosaurus, 1998, Sinosauropteryx, 1999; co-editor: Dinosaur Systematics, 1990, Dinosaur Encyclopedia, 1997, Newest and Coolest Dinosaurs, 1998, Flying Dragons-Studies on the Transitions from Dinosaurs to Birds, 2003, Dinosaur Provincial Park, A Spectacular Ancient Ecosystem Revealed, 2005; bd. advisor, Science Fiction and Fantasy Writers of Am.; contbr. articles to profl. publs.; featured in numerous articles and programs. Recipient Commendation medal 125th Anniversary of Govt. of Can., 1993, Sir Frederick Haultain award Govt. of Alta., 1988, Michel Halbouty award Am. Assn. Petroleum Geologists, 1999. Fellow Royal Soc. Can.; mem. Soc. Vertebrate Paleontology (program officer 1985-87, conf. chmn. 1988, conf. chmn. Mesozoic Terrestrial Ecosystems 1987), Paleontol. Soc., Can. Soc. Petroleum Geologists, Am. Soc. Zoologists, Sigma Xi. Achievements include research in fossil reptiles including Permian Sphenacodonts from Europe and United States; Permian eosuchians from Africa and Madagascar; Jurassic and Cretaceous dinosaurs from Canada, Argentina and Asia and their footprints; co-leader in the excavations of Mapusaurus raseae species from Patagonia, Argentina.

CURRIE, ROBERT EMIL, retired lawyer; b. Jackson, Tenn., Oct. 10, 1937; s. Forrest Edward Currie and Mary Elizabeth (Nuckolls) Empson; m. Brenda Ray Eddings, July 2, 1960; children: Cheryl Lynn, Forrest Clayton, Kristin Emil. BS with distinction, U.S. Naval Acad., 1959; LLB cum laude, Harvard U., 1967. Bar: Calif. 1967, U.S. Ct. Appeals (9th cir.) 1970, U.S. Supreme Ct. 1979. Assoc. Latham & Watkins, LA, 1967-75, ptnr. Costa Mesa, Calif., 1975—2003, mng. ptnr., 1993—96; ret., 2003. Dir. Constl. Rights Found., Orange County, Calif., 1986-91; lawyer rep. 9th Cir. Jud. Conf., 1991-93. Mem. exec. com. Orange County coun. Boy Scouts Am., Costa Mesa, 1982-95. Capt. USNR, 1955-83. Recipient Silver Beaver award Boy Scouts Am., Orange County coun., 1991. Fellow Am. Coll. Trial Lawyers; mem. Orange County Bar Assn. (dir. 1984-91), U.S. Supreme Ct. Hist. Soc. (chmn. So. Calif. 1992-93), Orange County Bar Found. (dir. 1999—). Home: 24 Pinehurst Ln Newport Beach CA 92660 Business E-Mail: robert.currie@lw.com.

CURRY, CYNTHIA J. R., geneticist; b. Cleve., July 20, 1941; MD, Yale U., 1957. Diplomate Am. Bd. Med. Genetics; Am. Bd. Pediatrics. Intern U. Wash., Seattle, 1967-68, resident, 1968-69, U. Minn., Mpls., 1969-70; fellow med. genetics U. Calif., San Francisco, 1975-76; med. faculty UCSF, Fresno, Calif.; med. dir. genetics Valley Children's Hosp., Madera, Calif., 1976—. Contbr. 15 chpt. to books, numerous articles to profl. jours. Office: Valley Childrens Hosp Genetic Med FC21 9300 Valley Childrens Pl Madera CA 93638-8762

CURRY, DANIEL ARTHUR, judge; b. Phoenix, Mar. 28, 1937; s. John Joseph and Eva May (Wills) C.; m. Joy M. Shallenberger, Sept. 5, 1959. BS, Loyola U., Los Angeles, 1957, LL.B., 1960. Bar: Calif. 1961, Hawaii 1972, N.Y. 1978. Pvt. practice, L.A. County, Calif., 1964—67; counsel Technicolor, Inc., Hollywood, Calif., 1967-70; sr. v.p., gen. counsel Amfac, Inc., Honolulu and San Francisco, 1970—87; v.p., gen. counsel Times Mirror, LA, 1987-92; judge Superior Ct. of State of Calif., 1992-98; assoc. justice Calif. Ct. Appeal 2d dist., LA, 1998—. Capt. USAF, 1961—64. Office: Calif Ct Appeal 2d Dist 4th Fl North Tower 300 S Spring St Los Angeles CA 90013-1230 Office Phone: 213-830-7440. Personal E-mail: danlcurry@aol.com.

CURRY, KATHLEEN E., state legislator; b. Denver, July 11, 1960; m. Greg Peterson; 2 children. BA in Agrl. and Resource Econs., U. Mass., Amherst, 1982; MS in Water Resources Planning and Mgmt., Colo. State U., Ft. Collins, 1994. Phys. scientist State of Colo. Water Conservation Bd.; mgr. Upper Gunnison River Water Conservancy Dist., 1998—2004; mem. Dist. 61 Colo. House of Reps., Denver, 2004—, spkr. pro tempore. Democrat. Unitarian. Office: Colo State Capitol 200 E Colfax Denver CO 80203 Office Phone: 303-866-2945. Business E-Mail: kathleen.curry.house@state.co.us.*

CURRY, THOMAS JOHN, bishop; b. Drumgoon, Ireland, Jan. 17, 1943; BA, U. Coll., Dublin, 1963; MA, Loyola Marymount U., 1973; PhD, Claremont U., 1983. Ordained priest Archdiocese of LA, Calif., 1967; ordained bishop, 1994; aux. bishop Archdiocese of LA, 1994—. Roman Catholic. Office: Santa Barbara Pastoral Region 3240 Calle Pinon Santa Barbara CA 93105-2760 also: Archdiocese of LA 3424 Wilshire Blvd Los Angeles CA 90010-2241 Office Phone: 805-682-0442. Office Fax: 805-682-7509.

CURTIN, DAVID STEPHEN, newswriter; b. Kansas City, Mo., Dec. 18, 1955; s. Gerald and Nadine (Pemberton) C. BS in Journalism, U. Colo., 1978. Newswriter Littleton (Colo.) Independent, 1976-77, Boulder (Colo.) Daily Camera, 1978-79, Greeley (Colo.) Daily Tribune, 1979-84, Durango (Colo.) Herald, 1984-87, Colorado Springs (Colo.) Gazette Telegraph, 1987-97, Denver Post, 1997—. Pulitzer Prize juror, 1991-92. Recipient Pulitzer Prize for feature writing, 1990. Democrat. Methodist. Avocations: skiing, hiking, mountain climbing.

CURTIN, THOMAS LEE, ophthalmologist; b. Columbus, Ohio, Sept. 9, 1932; s. Leo Anthony and Mary Elizabeth (Burns) C.; m. Constance L. Sallman; children: Michael, Gregory, Thomas, Christopher, Kenton. BS, Loyola U., LA, 1954; MD, U. So. Calif., 1957; cert. navy flight surgeon, US Naval Sch. Aerospace Med., 1959. Diplomate Am. Bd. Ophthalmology. Intern Ohio State U. Hosp., 1957-58; resident in ophthalmology U.S. Naval Hosp, San Diego, 1961-64; pvt. practice medicine specializing in ophthalmology Oceanside, Calif., 1967—. Mem. staff Tri City, hosps.; sci. adv. bd. So. Calif. Soc. Prevention Blindness, 1973-76; bd. dirs. North Coast Surgery Ctr., Oceanside, 1987-96; cons. in field. Trustee Carlsbad Unified Sch. Dist., 1975—83, pres., 1979, 1982, 1983; trustee Carlsbad Libr., 1990—99, pres., 1993, 1998; bd. dirs. Mission San Luis Rey, Oceanside, Calif., 2006—08. Officer MC USN, 1958—67. Mem. AMA, Calif. Med. Assn., San Diego County Med. Soc., Am. Acad. Ophthalmology, Aerospace Med. Assn., San Diego Acad. Ophthalmology (pres. 1979), Carlsbad Rotary, El Camino Country Club. Repubican. Roman Catholic. Office: 3231 Waring Ct Ste S Oceanside CA 92056-4510 Personal E-mail: curtintl@hotmnail.com.

CURTIS, D. JAY, lawyer; b. Stillwater, Okla., Dec. 9, 1942; s. Dale R. and Muriel (Morris) Curtis; m. Kathryn Hoops, Aug. 6, 1965; children: Dale, Jonathan, Tyler, Bryan, Andrew. BS in Acctg., U. Utah, 1968, JD, 1971. Bar: Utah 1971, US Dist. Ct. (dist. Utah) 1971, US Tax Ct. 1984. Ptnr. Kesler, Gordon & Curtis, Salt Lake City, 1971—76, Nielsen & Sr. and predecessor, Salt Lake City, 1977—89; shareholder Ray, Quinney & Nebeker, P.C., Salt Lake City. Served USAR, 1961—68. Named one of Top 100 Attys., Worth mag., 2006—08, Best Lawyers in Am., 2007—08. Mem.: Estate Planning Coun. Salt Lake City, Salt Lake County Bar Assn., Utah Bar State Assn. (chmn. lawyer benefits com. 1980—83), ABA, Mountain State Pension Conf. (mem. 1974, pres. 1979), Holy Cross Found. (planned giving com. 1985), Primary Children's Med. Ctr. (deferred gifts com. 1980—81). Republican. Mem. Lds Ch. Office: Ray Quinney & Nebeker PO Box 45385 36 S State St Ste 1400 Salt Lake City UT 84111-0385 Office Phone: 801-323-3314. E-mail: jcurtis@rqn.com.

CURTIS, JOHN JOSEPH, lawyer, writer; b. Fairmont, W.Va., Nov. 23, 1942; s. John Joseph and Marie Francis (Christopher) C.; m. Shirley Ann Slater, Oct. 15, 1971 (div. June 1993); children: Christopher, Kevin. AB, U. W.Va., 1964, JD, 1967. Bar: W.Va. 1967, Ill. 1972, Calif. 1979. Pvt. practice law, South Charleston, W.Va., 1967-68; chief counsel, asst. dir. W.Va. Tax Dept., Charleston, 1968-71; tax atty. Sears, Roebuck & Co., Chgo., 1971-73; chief tax counsel, dir. taxes Pacific Lighting, LA, 1973-87; ptnr. Baker & Hostetler, LA, 1987-93, Law Offices of John Curtis, LA, 1994—. Author: The Code, 2004. Com. mem. Pasadena Tournament Roses, 1978-93. Lt. comdr. USNR, 1968-80. Mem. ABA, L.A. County Bar Assn. (chmn. com. 1989), Calif. Bar Assn., Inst. Property Tax, So. Calif.Tax Found. (pres. 1990-96), L.A. Taxpayers Assn. (pres. 1990-95), Calif. Taxpayers Assn. (pres. 1987-88). Avocations: skiing, scuba, fishing. Office Phone: 909-803-8166. Personal E-mail: jcurtis595@aol.com.

CURTIS, LEGRAND R., JR., lawyer; b. Ogden, Utah, Aug. 1, 1952; BA summa cum laude, Brigham Young U., 1975; JD cum laude, U. Mich., 1978. Bar: Utah 1978, U.S. Ct. Appeals (10th cir.) 1985, U.S. Ct. Claims 1986, U.S. Supreme Ct. 1987. Ptnr. Manning, Curtis Bradshaw & Bednar, LLC, Salt Lake City, 1997—. Mem. Utah State Bar, Salt Lake County Bar Assn. Office: Manning Curtis Bradshaw & Bednar LLC 10 Exchange Pl Ste 300 Salt Lake City UT 84111-5104

CURTIS, MICHAEL, lawyer; b. Albuquerque, Aug. 11, 1949; BA, Columbia U., 1971; JD, Willamette U., 1977. Bar: Oreg. 1977, U.S. Dist. Ct. Oreg. 1977. Ptnr. Curis & Correll, Portland, Oreg. Mem.: ABA, Am. Acad. Forensic Scis., Nat. Legal Aid and Defender Assn., Oreg. Criminal Def. Lawyers Assn. (life), Nat. Assn. Criminal Def. Lawyers (life). Office: Curtis & Correll 4300 NE Fremont St Ste 230 Portland OR 97213 Office Phone: 503-284-0763. E-mail: curtismichael@qwest.net.

CURTISS, ROY, III, life sciences professor; b. May 27, 1934; m. Josephine Clark, Dec. 28, 1976; children: Brian, Wayne, Roy IV, Lynn, Gregory Clark, Eric Garth, Megan Kimberly. BS in Agr., Cornell U., 1956; PhD in Microbiology, U. Chgo., 1962; DSc (hon.), So. Ill. U., Edwardsville, 2003. Instr., rsch. asst. Cornell U., 1955-56; jr. tech. specialist Brookhaven Nat. Lab., 1956-58; fellow microbiology U. Chgo., 1958-60, USPHS fellow, 1960-62; biologist Oak Ridge Nat. Lab., 1963-72; lectr. microbiology U. Tenn., Knoxville, 1965-72, lectr. Grad. Sch. Biomed. Scis. Oak Ridge, 1967-69, prof., 1969-72, assoc. dir., 1970-71, interim dir., 1971-72; Charles H. McCauley prof. microbiology U. Ala., Birmingham, 1972-83; sr. scientist Inst. Dental Rsch., 1972-83, Comprehensive Cancer Ctr., 1972-83, dir. molecular cell biology grad. program, 1973-82; dir., sr. scientist Cystic Fibrosis Rsch. Ctr., 1981-83; prof. cellular and molecular biology Sch. Dental Medicine Washington U., St. Louis, 1983-91, George William and Irene Koechig Freiberg prof. biology, 1984—2005, chmn. dept. biology, 1983-93, dir. Ctr. Plant Sci. and Biotech., 1991-94, George William and Irene Koechig Freiburg prof. emeritus, 2005—; prof. life scis. Ariz. State U., Tempe, 2004—, co-dir. Ctr. Infectious Diseases and Vaccinology, Biodesign Inst., 2004—06, dir. Ctr. Infectious Diseases and Vaccinology, Biodesign Inst., 2007—, directorate mem. Biodesign Inst., 2007—. Mem. Ctr. Infectious Disease, Washington U., St. Louis; vis. prof. Inst. Venezolana de Investigaciones Científicas, 1969, U. P.R., 1972, U. Católica de Chile, 1973, U. Okla., 1982; recombinant DNA molecule program adv. com. NIH, 1974-77, genetic basis disease rev. com., 1979-83, chmn., 1981-83, vaccine study panel, 2001-04, chmn. bacterial biodefence rev. com., 2003-2004, Immune Def. Mechanisms, Mucosa Rev. Com., 2009-; genetic biology com. NSF, 1975-78; mem. diseases rsch. adv. bd. Midwest Regional Ctr. Excellence in Biodefense and Emerging Infections, 2003-05; mem. exec. com. Sch. Life Sci. Ariz. State U., 2005-07. Editor: Jour. Bacteriology, 1970-76, Infection and Immunity, 1985-92, Escherichia coli and Salmonella: Cellular and Molecular Biology, 1993-96, 2006-, exec. editor-in-chief, 2000-05, exec. editor, 2006—. Active Oak Ridge City Coun., 1969-72, Cystic Fibrosis Found., rsch. devel. program rev. com. 1984-89, Conf. Rsch. Workers on Animal Diseases, Heiser Found. Sci. Adv. Bd., 1996-2004; bd. dirs. Am. Type Culture Collection, 1989-99, presdl. adv., 2003—; bd. dirs. Whitfield Sch., 1997-2005, exec. com., 2002-2005; founder, dir. and sci. adv. MEGAN Health, Inc., 1992-2000, v.p. rsch., 1998-99; bd. govs. Ariz. Arts Sci. Tech. Acad., 2006-; mem. Mo. Seed Capital Investment Bd., 2000-03. Recipient Sardinia Sci. award, 2003; named Mo. Inventor of Yr., 1997, Ariz. Biosci. Rschr. of Yr., 2007; Global Health grant, Bill & Melinda Gates Found., 2005-. Fellow: AAAS, Acad. Sci. St. Louis, Am. Acad. Microbiology; mem.: NAS, Ariz. Arts, Sci. and Tech. Acad., Internat. Soc. Vaccines, World Health Orgn. (steering com. immunology of TB 1982—85), Coun. Advancement Sci. Writing (dir. 1976—82, v.p. 1978—82), N.Y. Acad. Scis., Am. Soc. Microbiology (parliamentarian 1970—75, dir. 1977—80, editl. bd. ASM News 1987—99, dir. 1989—94, 1999—2004), Soc. Gen. Microbiology, Internat. Soc. Mucosal Immunology, Am. Assn. Avian Pathologists, Genetics Soc. Am. (chmn. genetics stock ctrs. com. 1987—89),

Gateway Strikers Soccer Club (pres. 1995—2001, chmn. bd. dirs. 2001—05, founder), Sigma Xi. Home: 6732 N Joshua Tree Ln Paradise Valley AZ 85253-3245 Office: CIDV The Biodesign Inst Ariz State U Tempe AZ 85287-5401

CURZON, SUSAN CAROL, academic administrator; b. Poole, Eng., Dec. 11, 1947; came to U.S., 1952. d. Kenneth Nigel and Terry Marguerite (Morris) C. AB, U. Calif., Riverside, 1970; MLS, U. Wash., 1972; PhD, U. So. Calif., 1983. Spl. libr. Kennecott Exploration, San Diego, 1972-73; various positions LA County Pub. Libr., 1973-89; dir. libr. Glendale Pub. Libr., Calif., 1989-92; dean libr. Calif. State U., Northridge, 1992—. Cons. Grantsmanship Ctr., L.A., 1981-83; vis. lectr. Grad. Sch. Libr. and Info. Sci. UCLA, 1986-92. Author: Managing Change, Managing the Interview. Libr. of Year Libr. Jour., 1993. Mem. ALA, Calif. Libr. Assn. Democrat. Avocation: history. Office: Calif State U Libr Office of the Dean 18111 Nordhoff St Northridge CA 91330-8326 Office Phone: 818-677-2271.

CUSACK, JOAN, actress; b. NYC, Oct. 11, 1962; d. Richard and Nancy C.; m. Richard Burke 1993; 2 children. BA, U. Wis., 1985. Stage appearances include Road, 1988, Brilliant Traces, 1989, Cymbeline, 1989; TV appearances include Saturday Night Live (regular 1985-86 season), The Mother, 1994, What About Joan, 2001-02, A Very Merry Muppet Christmas, 2002; film appearances include Cutting Loose, 1980, My Bodyguard, 1980, Class, 1983, Grandview USA, 1984, Sixteen Candles, 1984, The Allnighter, 1987, Broadcast News, 1987, Stars and Bars (aka An Englishman in New York), 1988, Married to the Mob, 1988, Working Girl, 1988 (Acad. award nominee best supporting actress 1989), Say Anything, 1989, Men Don't Leave, 1989, My Blue Heaven, 1990, The Cabinet of Dr. Ramirez, 1991, Hero, 1992, Toys, 1992 (also musician), Addams Family Values, 1993, Corrina, Corrina, 1994, Nine Months, 1995, Two Much, 1996, Mr. Wrong, 1996, A Smile Like Yours, 1997, In and Out, 1997, Grosse Pointe Blank, 1997, Arlington Road, 1999, Runaway Bride, 1999, (voice) Toy Story 2, 1999, Arlington Road, 1999, Cradle Will Rock, 1999, High Fidelity, 2000, Where the Heart Is, 2000, School of Rock, 2003, Looney Toons-Back in Action, 2003, Raising Helen, 2004, The Last Shot, 2004, Ice Princess, 2005, (voice) Chicken Little, 2005, Friends With Money, 2006, Martian Child, 2007, War, Inc., 2008, Kit Kittredge: An American Girl, 2008, Confessions of a Shopaholic, 2009. Office: United Talent Agy Inc 9560 Wilshire Blvd Fl 5 Beverly Hills CA 90212

CUSAMANO, GARY M., real estate executive; BS Agrl. Econ., U. Calif., Davis. COO, Newhall Land & Farming Co., Valencia, Calif., 1987—, pres., 1989—, also bd. dirs. Bd. dirs. Watkins-Johnson. Chmn. bd. dirs. Calif. C. of C.; bd. dirs. Henry Mayo Newhall Meml. Hosp. Office: The Newhall Land & Farming Co 23823 Valencia Blvd Valencia CA 91355-2103

CUSHMAN, KAREN LIPSKI, writer; b. Chgo. married; 1 child, Leah. BA in English/Greek, Stanford U., 1963; MA in Human Behavior, USIU, 1977; MA in Mus. Studies, JFK U., 1987. Faculty mus. studies dept. John F. Kennedy U., San Francisco. Author: Catherine, Called Birdy, 1994, The Midwife's Apprentice, 1995 (John Newberry award 1996), The Ballad of Lucy Whipple, 1996, Matilda Bone, 2000, Rodzina, 2003. Office: 17804 Thorsen Road Sw Vashon WA 98070

CUSSLER, CLIVE ERIC, author; b. Aurora, Ill., July 15, 1931; s. Eric E. and Amy (Hunnewell) C.; m. Barbara Knight, Aug. 28, 1955; children: Teri, Dirk, Dayna. Student, Pasadena City Coll., 1949-51; PhD in Maritime History, N.Y. State Maritime Coll., 1997. Owner Bestgen & Cussler Advt., Newport Beach, Calif., 1961-65; creative dir. Darcy Advt., Hollywood, Calif., 1965-67; chmn. Nat. Underwater and Marine Agy. Author: (novels) The Mediterranean Caper, 1973, Iceberg, 1975, Raise the Titanic!, 1976, Vixen 03, 1978, Night Probe, 1981, Pacific Vortex, 1982, Deep Six, 1984, Cyclops, 1986, Treasure, 1988, Dragon, 1990, Sahara, 1992, Inca Gold, 1994, Shock Wave, 1995, Sea Hunters, 1996, Flood Tide, 1997, Clive Cussler & Dirk Pitt Revealed, 1998, Atlantis Found, 1999, Valhalla Rising, 2001, Serpent, 1999, Blue Gold, 2000, Fire Ice, 2002, Sea Hunters II, 2002, White Death, 2003, Golden Buddha, 2003, Trojan Odyssey, 2003, Sacred Stone, 2004, (with Dirk Cussler) Black Wind, 2004, (with Paul Kemprecos) Lost City, 2004, Polar Shift, 2005, (with Jack DuBrul) Dark Watch, 2005, (with Paul Kemprecos) The Navigator, 2007, (with Jack Dubrul) Skeleton Coast, 2006, The Adventures of Vin Fiz, 2006, (with Dirk Cussler) Treasure of Khan, 2007, The Chase, 2007, (with Jack De Brul) Plague Ship, 2008. Served in USAF, 1950-54. Recipient Disting. Svc. award, Nat. Maritime Hist. Soc., Navy Meml. Heritage award, Nat. Trust for Hist. Preservation award, numerous advt. awards, Thriller Master Lifetime Achievement award, Internat. Thriller Writers. Fellow Nat. Soc. Oceanographers, N.Y. Explorers Club (Lowell Thomas Underwater Explorers award), Royal Geog. Soc. London, Classic Car Club Am. Achievements include discovery of over 60 historic shipwrecks.

CUSTEN, BARBARA S., library director; m. Tim Klug. Dir. South State Coop. Libr. Sys., Calif., Santiago Libr. Sys., Met. Coop. Libr. Sys., Pasadena, Calif., Riverside Pub. Libr., Calif., 2005—08; asst. dir. LA Pub. Libr., 2008—. Bd. dirs. Califa. Office: LA Pub Libr Ctrl Branch 630 W 5th St Los Angeles CA 90071 Office Phone: 213-228-7000.

CUTLER, DAVID NEIL, SR., software engineer; b. Lansing, Mich., Mar. 13, 1942; BS, Olivet Coll., Mich., 1965. Programmer E.I. duPont Nemours and Co.; software engr. Digital Equipment Corp., Microsoft Corp., Redmond, Wash., 1988—, sr. disting. engr., tech. fellow, 2000—. Affiliate prof., computer sci. dept. U. Washington. Recipient 2007 Nat. Medal Technology and Innovation. Mem.: NAE. Achievements include patents in field; designer and developer of several operating systems including VAX/VMS, RSX-11M and VAXELN (Digital Equipment Corporation) and Windows NT (Microsoft Corp.). Avocation: auto racing. Office: Microsoft Corp 1 Microsoft Way Redmond WA 98052-6399

CUTLER, JAY, professional football player; b. Santa Claus, Ind., Apr. 29, 1983; s. Jack and Sandy Cutler. BA in Human & Orgnl. Devel., Vanderbilt U., Nashville, 2005. Quarterback Denver Broncos, 2006—09, Chgo. Bears, 2009—. Founder Jay Cutler Found., 2007—. Named Offensive Player of Yr., Southeastern Conf., 2005; named to Am. Football Conf. Pro Bowl Team, NFL, 2008. Office: Chicago Bears 1000 Football Dr Lake Forest IL 60045 also: Jay Cutler Found PO Box 631934 Highlands Ranch CO 80163

CUTONE, KATHALEEN KELLY, athletic representative, figure skater and former judge; Athletic rep. U.S. Figure Skating Assn., Colo. Springs, Colo., 1998—. Placed 16th Nat. Sr. competition, 1997, 2nd place Ea. Sr., 1997, New England Sr., 1997, 12th place Nat. Sr., 1996, 4th place Ea. Sr., 1996, 1st place New England Sr., 1996, 6th place World Univ. Games, 1995, 11th place Nat. Sr. competition, 1995, tie for 5th place Nat. Sr., 1995, 2d place Ea. Sr., 1995, 3rd place Ea. Sr., 1995, 1st place Nat. Collegiates, 1994, 12th place U.S. Olympic Festival, 1990, others. Mem. U.S. Figure Skating Assn. Office: USFSA 20 1st St Colorado Springs CO 80906-3624

CUTRI, ROC MICHAEL, research scientist; Dep. exec. dir., Infrared Processing and Analysis Ctr. (IPAC) Calif. Inst. Tech., Pasadena. Co-recipient James Craig Watson medal, NAS, 2007. Achievements include being one of the project scientists& task lead for the Two Micron All Sky Survey (2MASS) project. Office: Infrared Processing and Analysis Ctr Calif Inst Tech MS 100-22 770 S Wilson Ave Pasadena CA 91125 Office Phone: 626-395-1828. Office Fax: 626-397-7018. Business E-Mail: roc@ipac.caltech.edu.

CUTTER, GARY RAYMOND, biostatistician; b. St. Louis, Feb. 18, 1948; s. Daniel and Mildred (Mandel) C.; m. Sharon R. Gornek, Aug. 24, 1969; children: Corey N., Scott J., Todd J. BA in Math., U. Mo., 1970; MS in Biometry, U. Tex., Houston, 1971, PhD in Biometry, 1974. Asst. prof. biometry U. Tex. Sch. Pub. Health, Houston, 1974-78; expert, cons. Nat. Cancer Inst., Bethesda, Md., 1978-79; assoc. prof. biostats. U. Ala., Birmingham, 1979-89; prof. pub. health St. Jude Children's Rsch. Hosp., Memphis, 1979-89, chair biostats and info. sys., 1989-91; pres. Pythagoras, Inc., Birmingham, 1991—; chmn. Ctr. for Rsch. Methodology and Biometrics AMC Cancer Rsch. Ctr., Denver, 1994—. Adj. prof. U. Colo. Health Sci. Ctr., Denver, 1994—, U. Denver, 1996—, U. Nev., Reno, 1999—. Author: A Module of Math., 1972, (with others) Evaluation of Health Education and Promotion Programs: Principles, Guidelines and Methods for the Practitioner, 1984, 2d edit., 1994; contbr. numerous articles to profl. jours. Bd. dirs. Legal Environ. Assistance Found., Birmingham, 1986-89, Temple Emanu El, Birmingham, 1987-89, Jewish Cmty. Ctr., Birmingham, 1984-88, Fair Share for Health, Denver, 1994-96. Grantee NIH, NHLBI, NIDDK, NCI, Multiple Sclerosis Soc., others. Mem. APHA, Am. Statis. Assn., Am. Biometric Soc., Soc. Clin. Trials, Am. Optometric Assn., Mountain Brook Soccer Club (bd. dirs. 1983-94), Mountain Brook Athletic Assn. (bd. dirs. 1986-88). Office: AMC Cancer Rsch Ctr 1600 Pierce St Denver CO 80214-1897

CYNADER, MAX SIGMUND, psychology and physiology professor, researcher; b. Berlin, Feb. 24, 1947; arrived in Can., 1951; s. Samuel and Maria (Kraushar) C.; m. Ann Lynn Langford, Sept. 26, 2004; children: Madeleine Maria, Rebecca Kay, Alexandra Josephine. BSc, Mc Gill U., Montreal, Que., Can., 1967; PhD, MIT, 1972. Fellow neuroanatomy Max-Planck Inst. Psychiatry, Munich, 1972-73; asst. prof. psychology Dalhousie U., 1973-77, assoc. prof., 1977-81, assoc. prof. physiology, 1979-84, prof. psychology, 1981-84, Killam rsch. prof., 1984-88, prof. physiology, 1984-88; prof. psychology U. B.C., 1988—, prof. physiology, 1988—, prof. dept. ophthalmology, 1988—, dir., 1997—; dir. Brain Rsch. Ctr., U. B.C. and Vancouver Coastal Health, 1997. Mem. pres.'s workshop on five yr. plan strengthening sci. support in Can. Natural Scis. and Engring. Rsch. Coun. Can., 1984, workshop for Steacie fellows, 1988; mem. task force on curriculum devel. in Can. neurosci., 1984; mem. spl. adv. panel on rsch. preparedness USAF, 1985; rep. Internat. Human Frontiers Sci. program Med. Rsch. Coun. Can., 1988; mem. grants com. behavioural scis. Med. Rsch. Coun. Can., program grants com. 1989—; referee senate rev. grad. program in neurosci. U. Western Ont., 1989; mem. math., computational and theoretical spl. rev. com. NIMH, 1989—; external reviewer Med. Rsch. Coun. Can., Alta. Heritage Fund Med. Rsch., NIH, NSF, USAF Office Sci. Rsch., Multiple Sclerosis Soc. Can., Vancouver Found., March of Dimes, Fight for Sight; CRC chair in brain devel., 2001-08. Mem. editorial bd. jours. Behavioral Brain Rsch., Clin. Vision Scis., Concepts in Neurosci., Devel. Brain Rsch., Exptl. Brain Rsch., Neural Networks, Visual Neurosci.; mem. adv. bd. series Rsch. Notes in Neural Computing; contbr. articles to profl. jours. Recipient Killam Rsch. prize U. B.C., 1989—; E.W.R. Steacie fellow Natural Sci. and Engring. Rsch. Coun. Can., 1979, Can. Inst. Advanced Rsch. fellow, 1986—, Bank of Montreal fellow Can. Inst. for Advanced Rsch., 1998, BC Biotech award, 2007; grantee Med. Rsch. Coun. Can., 1973—, Natural Sci. and Engring. Rsch. Coun. Can., 1975—, NIH, 1978-81, Killam Rsch. Prof., 1984, B.C. Sci. & Tech. Champion, 2004. Fellow Can. Inst. Advanced Rsch., Royal Soc. Can.; mem. Soc. Neurosci. (Halifax chpt., pres. 1985, edn. com. 1986-89), Can. Assn. Neurosci. (pres. 1986), Assn. Rsch. Otolaryngology, Assn. Rsch. in Vision and Opthalmology, Can. Physiol. Soc., Internat. Brain Rsch. Orgn., Internat. Soc. Devel. Neurosci., Internat. Strabismol. Assn., World Fedn. Neuroscientists, Can. Acad. health Svc.(elect-mem., 2006) Achievements include being named semifinalist Can. Astronaut program, 1983. Office: U BC Vancouver Hosp Brain Rsch Ctr 2211 Wesbrook Mall Vancouver BC Canada V6T 2B5 Home Phone: 604-921-2418; Office Phone: 604-822-1388. Business E-Mail: cynader@brain.ubc.ca.

CZACHOR, BRUCE, lawyer, consultant; b. Bklyn., May 7, 1961; BA in Polit. sci., SUNY, Binghampton, 1983; JD magna cum laude, NY Law Sch., 1987. Bar: NY 1988, NJ 1988, DC 1989, Calif. 2004. Letter of credit analyst Chase Manhattan Bank, NYC, 1983-84; law clk. to Hon. George Gallagher US Ct. Appeals (DC cir.), Washington, 1987-88; law clk. to Hon. Judge John Reilly; ptnr. Shearman & Sterling LLP, NYC & Toronto, 1988—94, mng. ptnr. Menlo Park, Calif., co-mng. ptnr. San Francisco. Mem. ABA, NY Bar Assn., NJ Bar Assn. Republican. Office: Shearman & Sterling LLP 525 Market St San Francisco CA 94105 Office Phone: 650-838-3632. Office Fax: 650-743-6630. Business E-Mail: bczachor@shearman.com.

CZOPEK, VANESSA, library director; b. Berkeley, Calif. m. Paul Czopek; 4 children. Grad., Calif. State U.; MLS, U. Ariz. Branch coord. Stanislaus County Libr., 1996, county libr. Modesto, Calif., 2001—. Contbr. articles to profl. publs. Past pres. Modesto Kiwanis Club; bd. dirs. Haven Women's Ctr. Mem.: Calif. County Librarians Assn. (pres.), Public Library Assn., Calif. Library Assn. Office: Stanislaus County Libr 1500 I St Modesto CA 95354 Office Phone: 209-558-7801. Office Fax: 209-529-4779. E-mail: czopkv@mail.co.stanislaus.ca.us.

D'ACCONE, FRANK ANTHONY, music educator; b. Somerville, Mass., June 13, 1931; s. Salvatore and Maria (DiChiappari) D'A. MusB, Boston U., 1952, MusM, 1953; AM, Harvard U., Cambridge, Mass., 1955, PhD, 1960. Asst. prof. music SUNY at Buffalo, 1960-63, assoc. prof., 1964-68; prof. music UCLA, 1968-94, chmn. dept., 1973-76; chmn. faculty UCLA Coll. Fine Arts, 1976-79; chmn. dept. musicology UCLA, 1989-93. Vis. prof. music Yale U., 1972-73 Author: The History of a Baroque Opera, 1985, The Civic Muse, 1997, Music in Renaissance Florence, 2006, Music and Musicians in 16th Century Florence, 2007; editor: Music of the Florentine Renaissance, vols. 1-12, 1967-94; gen. editor Corpus Mensurabilis Musicae, 1986-2001; co-editor Musica Disciplina, 1990-2001; contbr. articles to profl. jours. Fellow Am. Acad. Rome, 1963-64, Fulbright Found., 1963-64, NEH, 1975; recipient G.K. Delmas Venetian Studies award, 1977, J.S. Guggenheim Found. award, 1980, Internat. Galilei prize, Pisa, 1997. Fellow Am. Acad. Arts and Scis.; mem. Am. Musicol. Soc. (hon., dir. 1973-74), Internat. Musicol. Soc. Home: 725 Fontana Way Laguna Beach CA 92651-4010 Office: U Calif Dept Music Los Angeles CA 90024 Personal E-mail: fondac@cox.net.

DACHS, ALAN MARK, investment company executive; b. NYC, Dec. 7, 1947; s. Sidney and Martha (Selz) D.; m. Lauren B. Dachs, June 23, 1973. BA, Wesleyan U., Middletown, Conn., 1970; MBA, NYU, 1978. Account officer Chem. Bank, NYC, 1971-74; various positions Bechtel Group, Inc., San Francisco, 1974-81; v.p., CFO Dual Drilling Co., Wichita Falls, Tex., 1981-82; sr. v.p., mng. dir. Bechtel Investments, Inc., San Francisco, 1982-89; pres., dir., mem. exec. com. and CEO Fremont Group, LLC, San Francisco, 1989—. Bd. dirs. Bechtel Group, Bechtel Enterprises, Inc. Charter trustee, chair bd. trustees Wesleyan U.; trustee The Brooking Instn., The Conf. Bd. Fellow: Am. Acad. Arts & Scis. Office: Fremont Group LLC 199 Fremont St Ste 2500 San Francisco CA 94105-2261

DACHS, LAUREN BECHTEL, non-profit organization executive; Undergraduate degree in psychology, Stanford U., 1971. Founder, chair Lake Sch., Oakland, Calif.; pres. S.D. Bechtel Jr. Found., Calif., Calif. Mem. adv. coun. Ctr. for Underrepresented Engring. Students (CUES), U. Calif.-Berkeley Coll. Engring.; bd. dirs. Nature Conservancy Calif., Laural Found., Lend Trust Alliance; mem. Think Again Steering Com. Stanford U., 2002—, mem. parents' program adv. bd., 2004—06; bd. visitors Freeman Spogli Inst. for Internat. Studies, Stanford U., 2001—06; bd. trustee Stanford U., 2006—; mem. Woods Inst. Environ., Stanford Adv. Coun. Fellow: Am. Acad. Arts & Scis. Office: SD Bechtel Jr Found Stephen Bechtel Fund PO Box 193809 San Francisco CA 94119-3809 Office Phone: 415-284-8675. Office Fax: 415-284-8571.

DACKAWICH, S. JOHN, sociology educator, academic administrator; b. Loch Gelley, W.Va., Jan. 31, 1926; s. Samuel and Estelle (Jablonski) D.; m. Shirley Jean McVay, May 20, 1950; children: Robert John, Nancy Joan. BA, U. Md., 1955; PhD, U. Colo., 1958. Instr. U. Colo., 1955-57, Colo. State U., 1957-59; prof., chmn. sociology Calif. State U., Long Beach, 1959-70, prof. sociology Fresno, 1970-94, chmn. dept., 1970-75, prof. sociology emeritus, 1994—. Pvt. practice survey rsch., 1962-. Author: Sociology, 1970, The Fiery Furnace Effect, 2000; contbr. articles and rsch. papers to profl. publs. Mem. Calif. Dem. Ctrl. Com., 1960-62; co-dir. Long Beach Ctrl. Area Study, 1962-64, Citizen Participation Study, Fresno. With USMCR, 1943-46, U.S. Army, 1950-53. Mem. Am. Sociol. Assn., Pacific Sociol. Assn. Home: 5841 W Judy Ct Visalia CA 93277-8601 Office: Calif State U Dept Sociology 5340 N Campus Dr Fresno CA 93740-8019

DACKOW, OREST TARAS, insurance company executive; b. Wynyard, Sask., Can., Sept. 17, 1936; s. Luke Dackow and Irene Stacheruk; m. Florence Dorothy Waples, Sept. 20, 1958; children: Trevor Wade, Heather Lynn, Donna Louise B in Commerce with honors, U. Man., Winnipeg, Can., 1958; grad. advanced mgmt. program, Harvard U., 1976. Enrolled actuary. V.p. individual ops. Great-West Life Ins. Co., Winnipeg, Man., Can., 1976-78, sr. v.p. individual ops., 1978-79, sr. v.p. U.S., 1979-83; exec. v.p., COO U.S. Great-West Life Assurance Co., Denver, 1983-88, exec. v.p. corp. fin. and control Winnipeg, 1988-90, pres., 1990-94, dir., 1992—; pres., CEO, dir. Great-West Lifeco Inc., Inglewood, Colo., 1992—. Bd. dirs. London Life. Bd. dirs. Met. YMCA, Winnipeg, 1971-80, pres., 1979-80; bd. dirs. Met. YMCA, Denver, 1981-84, Colo. Alliance of Bus., 1986-87, Nat. Jewish Ctr. for Immunology and Respiratory Medicine, 1985-2001, Health Scis. Centre Rsch. Found., 1990-94, Instrumental Diagnostics Devel. Office, 1992-94. Fellow Soc. Actuaries, Can. Inst. Actuaries; mem. Am. Acad. Actuaries. Avocation: sailing.

DAFFORN, GEOFFREY ALAN, biochemist; b. Cunningham, Kans., Feb. 4, 1944; s. Francis Elston and Anna Elizabeth Dafforn; m. Gail McLaughlin, July 14, 1973; 1 child, Christine Elizabeth. BA cum laude, Harvard U., 1966; PhD, U. Calif., Berkeley, 1970. Postdoctoral fellow U. Calif., Berkeley, 1973; asst. prof. U. Tex., Austin, 1974; from asst. prof. to assoc. prof. Bowling Green (Ohio) State U., 1974-81; sr. chemist Syva Co., Palo Alto, Calif., 1982-87, rsch. fellow, 1987—, group mgr., 1999—2000; prin. scientist Nugen Techs., San Carlos, Calif., 2001—04; lectr. dept. chemistry Santa Clara U., Calif., 2005—. Author articles and abstracts; patentee in field. Grantee Army Rsch. Office, 1979-82, Am. Chem. Soc., 1975-80. Mem. AAAS, Am. Chem. Soc., Sierra Club. Office: Santa Clara U Dept Chemistry 500 El Camino Real Santa Clara CA 95053 E-mail: gdafforn@scu.edu.

DAFOE, DONALD CAMERON, surgeon, educator; b. Appleton, Wis., Nov. 22, 1949; BS in Zoology, U. Wis., 1971, MD, 1975. Diplomate Am. Bd. Surgery. Intern Hosp. of U. of Pa., Phila., 1975-76, resident, 1976-80, Measey rsch. fellow, 1978-80, chief resident, 1980-81, clin. fellow, Culpeper Found. fellow, 1981-82; asst. prof. surgery U. Mich., Ann Arbor, 1982-87; dir. clin. pancreas transplantation program u. Mich., Ann. Arbor, 1984-87; assoc. prof. surgery U. Mich., Ann Arbor, 1987; assoc. prof. surgery, chief divsn. transplantation Hosp. of U. of Pa., Phila., 1987-91, Stanford (Calif.) U. Med. Ctr., 1991-99, dir. kidney/kidney pancreas program, 1999-2000; Chief ofSurgery Thomas Jefferson Sch. of Med., 2000—. Reviewer various publs.; mem. editorial bd. Transplantation Sci., 1992, The Chimera, 1993; contbr. over 100 articles to profl. jours; also numerous book chpts. Mem. ACS, Am. Surg. Assn., Am. Diabetes Assn., Am. Soc. Transplant Surgeons, Assn. for Acad. Surgery, Soc. Internat. de Chirurgie, The Transplantation Soc., Pacific Coast Surg. Assn., Ctrl. Surg. Assn., Frederick A. Coller Surg. Soc., Soc. Univ. Surgeons, Surg. Biology Club II, Ravdin-Rhoads Surg. Soc., United Network for Organ Sharing, Calif. Transplant Donor Network, Western Assn. Transplant Surgeons. Office: 750 Welch Rd Ste 200 Palo Alto CA 94304-1509

DAGNON, JAMES BERNARD, human resources executive; b. St. Paul, Jan. 31, 1940; s. James Lavern and Margaret Elizabeth D.; m. Sandra Ann McGinley, June 4, 1960; children: Sheri T. Dagnon Tice, Terry J., Laurie M. Zinn, Diana L. Felner. BS in Bus. with distinction, U. Minn., St. Paul, 1979, cert. in Indsl. Rels., 1978. Various clerical positions No. Pacific Ry. Co., St. Paul, 1957-70; supr., then mgr. pers. rsch. and stats. Burlington No. R.R. Co., St. Paul, 1970, mgr.

manpower planning, 1970-78, dir. compensation and orgnl. planning, 1978-81; asst. v.p. compensation and benefits Burlington No. Inc., Seattle, 1981-84, from v.p. labor rels. to exec. v.p. employee rels. Ft. Worth, 1984-95; sr. v.p. employee rels. Burlington No. Santa Fe Rlwy. Co., Ft. Worth, 1995-97; sr. v.p. people The Boeing Co., Seattle, 1997—2002; pres. Christian Living Inst., 2004. Bd. dirs. Inroads Inc., Seattle Inroads Inc.; chmn. Corp. Champions, Ft. Worth, 1994—96; trustee Cook-Ft. Worth Children's Med. Ctr., 1995—97; bd. dirs. United Way Met. Tarrant County, 1995—97, Wash. State Gov.'s Commn. on Higher Edn. in 2020; trustee Bellevue C.C., 1999—2006; bd. dirs., trustee Wash. Early Learning Found., 1999—2003; pres. Cath. Evang. Outreach, Seattle, 1981—84, Christian Living Inst., 2004—; bd. dirs. Western Wash. Cath. Charismatic Renewal, 2004—. Capt. USAR, 1957—70. Fellow Nat. Acad. Human Resources; mem. Beta Gamma Sigma. Republican. Avocations: scuba diving, photography. Home: PO Box 605 Medina WA 98039-0605

DAHLBERG, KENNETH C., engineering executive; b. Camden, NJ, Oct. 19, 1944; BSEE, Drexel U., 1967; MSEE, U. So. Calif., 1969; student, UCLA bus. sch.for advanced edn. for execs. Various engring., program mgmt., leadership positions Hughes Electronics Corp., 1967, corp. v.p.; sr. v.p. Hughes Aircraft Co.; pres., COO Raytheon Sys. Raytheon Co., Washington, 1997—2000, exec. v.p. bus. devel., 2000—03; exec. v.p. Gen. Dynamics; pres., CEO Sci. Applications Internat. Corp., San Diego, 2003—04, chmn., pres., CEO, 2004—06, chmn., CEO, 2006—. Mem. IEEE, Am. Soc. Naval Engrs., Nat. Def. Indsl. Assn. (bd. dirs.), Surface Navy Assn., U.S. Navy League (life), Assn. U.S. Army. Office: Sci Applications Internat Corp 10260 Campus Point Dr San Diego CA 92121

DAHLGREN, DOROTHY, museum director; b. Coeur d'Alene, Idaho; BS in Museology and History, U. Idaho, 1982; M in Orgnl. Leadership, Gonzaga U., 1998. Dir. Mus. North Idaho, Coeur d'Alene, 1982—. Author: (with Simone Carbonneau Kincaid) In All the West No Place Like This: A Pictorial History of the Coeur d'Alene Region, 1996, Roads Less Traveled Through the Coeur D' Alene Historical Driving Tours of Benewah, Kootenai and Shoshone Counties. Mem. no. region com. Idaho Heritage Trust. Office: Museum North Idaho PO Box 812 Coeur D' Alene ID 83816 Office Phone: 208-664-3448. E-mail: dd@museumni.org.

DAHLSTROM, NANCY, state legislator; b. Baltimore, Aug. 13, 1957; m to Kit Dahlstrom; children: Colby, Shayna, Misty & Matthew. AS in Human Svcs., Wayland Bapt. U., 1992, BS in Human Svcs./Bus., 1994; M in Org. Mgmt./Human Resources, U. LaVerne, 1997. Alaska State Representative, District 18, 2003-.Support specialist, sales rep and accounting exec, Alascom; Marketing manager, partnership development, AT&T Alascom; Sr sales manager, GCI; Manager key accounting, Chugach Electric Association; Vocat Counselor, Work-force Prog, UAA. Young Republicans; America Marketing Association; NRA; Eagle River Chamber of Commerce; Alaska Outdoor Coun; Children's Miracle Network; 2000 Winter Special Olympics (volunteer); Relief-Soc (president, formerly). Republican. Avocations: reading, travel, needlepoint. Office: State Capitol Rm 409 Juneau AK 99801-1182 Office Phone: 907-465-3783. Office Fax: 907-465-2293. Business E-Mail: representative_nancy_dahlstrom@legis.state.ak.us.*

DAIE, JALEH, investment company executive; Exec. ptnr. Aurora Equity; head sci. & tech. The David and Lucile Packard Found.; prof., dept. chair Rutgers U., New Brunswick, NJ, dir. plant biology grad. program, dept. chmn., founder, dir. Interdisciplinary Ctr.; sr. sci. advisor U. Wis. System, Madison; prof. U. Wis. Sci. liaison to pres.'s nat. sci. and tech. coun.; spl. asst. office of chief scientist NOAA, U.S. Dept. Commerce, Commn. Biotech. and Global Food Security, Ctr. Internat. Strat. Studies; dir. Leadership Found., US Civilian Rsch. Devel. Found., bd. dirs.; treas., exec. com. U.S. Space Found.; treas. Legacy Found.; trustee World Affairs Coun. No. Calif.; spkr. in field; mem. White House Fellow selection panel; mem. adv. bd. Nokia/Innavent, Investigen, Teksia, U. Calif., Davis, Common Wealth Club, Lightfull Foods. Inducted into Hall of Fame Women in Tech. Internat.; named to 25 Smartest, Madison mag., Internat. Women Forum; featured Leaders of Sci., The Scientist; Henry Rutgers Rsch. fellow, Tchg. Acad. fellow U. Wis.; recipient lifetime achievement award Teksia. Fellow: AAAS; mem.: Coun. of Sci. Soc. Presidents (chmn.), Assn. Women in Sci. (pres.), Band of Angels, Phi Kappa Phi, Sigma Xi (bd. dirs.).

DAILEY, DIANNE K., lawyer; b. Great Falls, Mont., Oct. 10, 1950; d. Gilmore and Patricia Marie (Linnane) Halverson. BS, Portland State U., 1977; JD, Lewis & Clark Coll., 1982. Assoc. Bullivant, Houser, Bailey PC, Portland, Oreg., 1982-88, ptnr., 1988—, pres., 2002—06. Contbr. articles to profl. jours. Fellow: Am. Bar Found.; mem.: ABA (chair task force on involvement of women 1990—93, governing coun. 1992—99, liaison to commn. on women 1993—97, vice chair tort and ins. practice sect. 1995—96, chair-elect tort and ins. practice sect. 1996—97, standing com. environ. law 1996—99, chair tort and ins. practice sect. 1997—98, chair sect. officers conf. 1998—2001, governing coun. 2003, del. 2003, ins. coverage litigation com., chair task force CERCLA reauthorization, law practice mgmt. sect., comm. com.), Fedn. Ins. and Corp. Counsel, Def. Rsch. Inst., Multnomah Bar Assn. (bd. dirs. 1994—95), Oreg. State Bar, Wash. Bar Assn.

DAILY, GRETCHEN CARA, ecologist, environmental services administrator; b. Wash., Oct. 19, 1964; d. Charles Dennis and Suzanne Rachel (Schubert) D. BS, Stanford U., 1986, MS, 1987, PhD, 1992. Ctr. for Conservation Biology/Nature Conservancy fellow Stanford (Calif.) U., 1988-92; Winslow/Heinz postdoctoral fellow U. Calif., Berkeley, 1992—; assoc. prof. biology Stanford (Calif.) U., dir., Tropical Rsch. Program, Ctr. for Conservation. Sci. advisor IPAT Prodns. (film), Stanford, 1995. Author (with PR Ehrlich & AH Ehrlich) The Stork and the Plow: The Equity Solution to the Human Dilemma, 1995, Nature's Services: Societal Dependence on Natural Ecosystems, 1997, (with Katherine Ellison) The New Economy of Nature: The Quest to Make Conservatoin Profitable, 2002; Contbr. over 150 articles to profl. jours. Recipient Frances Lou Kallman award Stanford U., 1992, 21st Century Scientist award, 2000; Named Pew scholar in conservation and environ., Pew Found., 1994, Fellow, Aldo Leopard Leadership Program, 1999, Smith Sr. Scholar, The Nature Conservancy, 2003. Mem. Rocky Mtn. Biol. Lab; Fellow, Am. Acad. Arts & Sciences, NAS. Office: Stanford U Ctr Conservation Biology 385 Serra Mall Stanford CA 94305 Office Phone: 650-723-9452. Office Fax: 650-725-1992. E-mail: gdaily@stanford.edu.

DAINES, N. GEORGE, lawyer; b. 1949; m. Mindy Daines; 6 children. BA, Utah State U.; JD, Yale U. Bar: Utah 1976. Chief judge U.S. Ct. Appeals (10th Cir.); ptnr. Barrett & Daines, Logan, Utah, Daines, Wyatt & Allen, LLP, Cache County, 2003—. Tchr. bus. and real estate law Utah State U.; founder, prin. owner Cache Valley Bank; bd. dirs. Utah Prosecution Coun. Mem. bd. editors: Yale Law Jour. Active in the historical renovation of prime historic sites in Cache Valley. Mem.: Utah State Bar (mem. exec. com., jud. evaluation com., pres.-elect 2003—04, pres. 2004—). Office: Daines Wyatt & Allen LLP 101 N Main Logan UT 84321 Office Phone: 435-716-8361. Office Fax: 435-716-8381. E-mail: george@legal.state.ut.us.

DALE, DAVID C., physician, educator; b. Knoxville, Tenn., Sept. 19, 1940; s. John Irvin and Cecil (Chandler) D.; m. Rose Marie Wilson, June 22, 1963 BS magna cum laude, Carson-Newman Coll., 1962; MD cum laude, Harvard U., 1966. Intern and resident Mass. Gen. Hosp., 1966-68; resident U. Wash. Hosp., Seattle, 1971-72; clin. assoc. NIH, 1968-71; prof., assoc. chmn. dept. medicine U. Wash., Seattle, 1976-82, dean Sch. of Medicine, 1982-86. Contbr. numerous articles to profl. jours. Served to comdr. USPHS, 1968-70, 72-74 Mem. Am. Soc. Hematology, Assn. Am. Physicians, Am. Soc. for Clin. Investigation, ACP Avocations: woodworking, gardening, backpacking, sports. Office: U Wash Sch Medicine PO Box 356422 Seattle WA 98195-6422 Business E-Mail: dcdale@u.washington.edu.

DALE, DEBORAH, foundation executive; b. 1967; Chief devel. officer Primavera Found., Tucson. Involved with Voices for Edn., Ariz. Women's Conf., Southern Ariz. Ctr. Against Sexual Assault; Taste of Nation founding com. mem. Share Our Strength; com. mem. Mayor's Costume Ball for Arts; former bd. mem. Cmty. Shares; former bd. chair Mus. Contemporary Art; co-chair Tucson Suffragettes Virgin Voter Ball. Named one of 40 Under 40, Tucson Bus. Edge, 2006. Mem.: Assn. Fundraising Professionals (govt. rels. chair).

DALE, JIM, actor; b. Rothwell, Northamptonshire, Eng., Aug. 15, 1935; s. William and Miriam Smith; m. Julie Schafler; children by previous marriage: Belinda, Murray, Adam, Toby. Actor Nat. Theatre Co., Old Vic, Eng.; plays The Card, Taming of the Shrew, Scapino, NYC, Scapino, 1974, Barnum, 1980 (Tony award 1980), Joe Egg, 1985, Me and My Girl 1986-89, Privates on Parade, 1989, Travels with My Aunt, Long Wharf Theatre, 1994, UK Radio "The Music Man", 1994, Oliver, 1995, Candide, 1997, Three Penny Opera, 2005 (Outer Critics' Cir. award, outstanding featured actor in a musical, 2006, Drama Desk award, outstanding featured actor in a musical, 2006); films: Raising the Wind, Carry On Spying, Carry On Cleo, Carry On Cowboy, Lock Up Your Daughter, The National Health, Digby, Joseph Andrews, Pete's Dragon, Scandalous, 1985, Adventures of Huckleberry Finn (TV), 1985, Carry On Columbus, 1992, (voice) Lincoln, 1992, The American Clock, 1993, The Hunchback, 1997; comedian (debut) solo, Savoy, London, 1951; songwriter Georgy Girl; host TV spl. Ringling Bros. Barnum and Bailey Circus, 1985; guest appearances on The Equalizer, 1985, The Ellen Burstyn Show, 1986, TV guest appearances, 1987-90; narrator (audiobooks) Harry Potter and the Sorcerer's Stone, 1999, Harry Potter and the Chamber of Secrets, 1999, Harry Potter and the Prisoner of Azkaban, 2000, Harry Potter and the Goblet of Fire, 2000, King of Shadows, 2000, Harry Potter and the Order of the Phoenix, 2003, A Christmas Carol, 2003 (Audie award, Best Classical Audio Book, 2005, Audiofile Earphone award, 2005), Peter and the Starcatchers, 2004 (Audie award, Best Children's Audio Book, Best Male Narrator, 2005), Harry Potter and the Half-Blood Prince, 2005, Around the World in 80 Days, 2005 (Audie award, Best Classical Audio Book for Children, 2006), Peter Pan, 2006, Peter and the Shadow Thieves, 2006 (Audiofile Earphone award, 2006, Audie award, Best Male Narrator, 2007), Escape from the Carnivale, 2006, Arthur and the Invisibles, 2006, Peter and the Secret of Rundoon, 2007, Harry Potter and the Deathly Hallows, 2007 (Grammy award, Best Spoken Word Album for Children, 2008), Cave of the Dark Wind, 2007 Recipient Mem. Brit. Empire, 2003, Thespian award for Excellence in the Theatre, Friars Club Am., 2006, Children's Narrator of Yr. award, Publishers Weekly, 2006; named to Hall of Fame, Audio Publishers Assn., 2006. Achievements include Guinness World Record for creating and recording 146 different character voices for the audiobook of Harry Potter and the Deathly Hallows, 2007.

DALE, MARCIA LYN, nursing educator; b. Ft. Dodge, Iowa, Mar. 4, 1938; d. William R. and Erma (Umland) Bradley; m. William G. Dale, Jr., June 30, 1967; children: Dori Lyn, Devin Glenn. BS, U. Wyo., 1960; M. Nursing, U. Wash., 1961; EdD, U. No. Colo., 1981. Prof. U. Wyo., Laramie, 1971—, dean sch. nursing, assoc. dean coll. health scis., 1991—. Recipient Disting. Alumni award Sch. Nursing U. Wyo., 1985. Fellow Am. Acad. Nursing; mem. Wyo. Nurses Assn. (Wyo.'s Search for Excellence Leadership award 1989), Wyo. League for Nursing, Sigma Theta Tau. Home: 827 Evergreen St Cheyenne WY 82009-3218

DALEN, JAMES EUGENE, cardiologist, educator; b. Seattle, Apr. 1, 1932; s. Charles A. and Muriel E. (Jeanise) Robinson. BS, Wash. State U., 1955; MA, U. Mich., 1956; MD, U. Wash., 1961; MPH, Harvard U., 1972. Intern and asst. med. resident Boston City Hosp., 1961—63; sr. resident New Eng. Med. Ctr., Boston, 1963—64; rsch. fellow in cardiology Harvard Med. Sch., Peter Bent Brigham Hosp., Boston, 1964—67, assoc. dir. cardiovasc. lab., 1967—75; instr., asst. prof., assoc. prof. medicine Harvard Med. Sch., 1967—75; chmn. dept. cardiovasc. medicine U. Mass. Med. Sch., 1975—77, prof., chmn. dept. medicine, 1977—88; physician-in-chief U. Mass. Hosp., 1977—88; acting chancellor U. Mass., Worcester, 1986—87; editor Archives Internal Medicine, 1987—2004; dean, vice provost med. affairs U. Ariz. Coll. Medicine, Tucson, 1988—95, dean, v.p. health scis., 1995—2001. Mem. edit. bd. Jour. AMA, 1987—2004; contbr. articles to profl. jours. With USN, 1951—53. Mem.: ACP, Am. Coll. Chest Physicians (pres. 1985—86), Am. Coll. Cardiology, Assn. Univ. Cardiologists. Home: 5305 N Via Velazquez Tucson AZ 85750-5989 Office: 1840 E River Rd Ste 120 Tucson AZ 85718 Office Phone: 520-577-8180. Personal E-mail: jamesdalen@yahoo.com.

DALESIO, WESLEY CHARLES, former aerospace educator; b. Paterson, NJ, Mar. 26, 1930; s. William James and Sarah (Sheets) Delison; m. Dorothy May Zellers, Nov. 17, 1951 (dec.); children: Michael Kerry, Debra Kaye Dalesio Weber. Student, Tex. Christian U., 1950, U. Tex., Arlington, 1957. Enlisted USAF, 1948, advanced through grades to sr. master sgt., 1968, aircraft engine mech., mgmt. analyst worldwide, 1948-70; ins. agt. John Hancock Ins., Denver, 1970-71; office mgr. Comml. Builder, Denver, 1972-73; aerospace educator Sch. Dist. 50, Westminster, Colo., 1973-93. Dir. aerospace edn. CAP, Denver, 1982—86, Denver, 1994—2000. Active Crimestoppers, Westminster, 1988-91, Police and Citizens Teamed Against Crime, Westminster, 1992-93. Lt. col. ret. CAP, 1981-2004. Mem. Nat. Assn. Ret. Mil. Instrs. (charter mem.), Westminster Edn. Assn., 7th Bomb Wing B-36 Assn. (life), Internat. Platform Assn., Nat. Aeronautic Assn., Acad. Model Aeronautics, Arvada Associated Modelers (life). Episcopalian. Avocations: antiques, leatherwork, flying miniature aircraft, model car collecting. Home: 2537 W 104th Cir Westminster CO 80234-3507

DALESSIO, DONALD JOHN, internist, neurologist, educator; b. Jersey City, Mar. 2, 1931; s. John Andrea and Susan Dorothy (Minotta) Dalessio; m. Jane Catherine Schneider, Sept. 4, 1954 (dec. Mar. 1998); children: Catherine Leah, James John, Susan Jane. BA, Wesleyan U., 1952; MD, Yale U., 1956. Diplomate Am. Bd. Internal Medicine. Intern N.Y.C. Hosp., 1956—57, asst. resident in medicine and neurology, 1959—61; resident in medicine Yale Med. Ctr., 1961—62; pres. med. staff Scripps Clinic, La Jolla, Calif., 1974—78; chmn. dept. medicine Scripps Clin., La Jolla, 1974—89, chmn. emeritus, 1989—, cons., 1982—, pres. med. group, 1980—81; clin. prof. neurology U. Calif., San Diego, 1973—. Physician in chief Green Hosp., La Jolla, 1974—89; pres. Am. Assn. Study Headache, Chgo., 1974—76; chmn. Fedn. We. Soc. Neurology, Santa Barbara, Calif., 1976—77; Musser-Burch lectr. Tulane U., 1979; Kash lectr. U. Ky., 1979. Author: (book) Wolff's Headache, 7th edit., 2001, Approach to Headache, 1973, Approach to Headache, 6th edit., 1999; editor: Headache jour., 1965—75, 1979—84, Scripps Clinic Personal Health Letter; mem. editl. bd. Jour. AMA, 1977—87; columnist: San Diego Tribune. Pres. Nat. Migraine Found., Chgo., 1977—79. Capt. US Army, 1957—59. Recipient Disting. Alumnus award, Wesleyan U., 1982. Fellow: ACP; mem.: World Fedn. Neurology (Am. sec. 1980—90, rsch. group migraine), Am. Acad. Neurology (assoc.), La Jolla Beach/Tennis Club, La Jolla Country Club. Avocations: tennis, squash, piano. Home: 8891 Nottingham Pl La Jolla CA 92037-2131 Office: Scripps Clinic & Rsch Found 10666 N Torrey Pines Rd La Jolla CA 92037-1092

DALEY, DORIAN ESTELLE, lawyer, computer software company executive; b. Stockton, Calif., Apr. 20, 1959; BA, Stanford U., 1981; JD, Santa Clara U., 1986. Bar: Calif. 1987. Atty. comml. litig. Landels, Ripley & Diamond, San Francisco; joined Oracle Corp., 1992, v.p., assoc. gen. counsel, sr. v.p., gen. counsel, sec., 2007—. Mem.: State Bar Calif. Office: Oracle Corp 500 Oracle Parkway Redwood City CA 94065 Office Phone: 415-506-5500.

DALEY, RICHARD HALBERT, museum director; b. Centralia, Ill., Oct. 8, 1948; s. Richard Glen D.; m. Lucy W. Costen, Nov. 27, 1976. Student, Lake Forest Coll., Ill., 1966-67; BS, Colo. State U., 1970, MS, 1972. Instr. Colo. State U., Ft. Collins, 1972; from dir. biol. svcs. to dir. programs Mo. Bot. Garden, St. Louis, 1973-84; exec. dir. Mass. Hort. Soc., Boston, 1984-91, Denver Botanic Gardens, 1991-94; instr. Environ. Ethics Denver U., 1992-94; exec. dir. Sonara Desert Museum, Tucson, Ariz., 1994—. Mem. editorial com. Am. Mus. Natural History, N.Y.C., 1983-92. Bd. trustees Ctr. for Plant Conservation, 1994—. Mem. Am. Assn. Bot. Gardens (bd. trustees), Hort. Club Boston, Rotary Club Denver. Office: Ariz Sonara Desert Museum 2021 N Kinney Rd Tucson AZ 85743-9719

DALEY-LAURSEN, STEVEN B., academic administrator, dean, environmental scientist, educator; BS in Conservation and Resource Devel., U. Md.; MS in Forest Resources Mgmt., U. Idaho, 1979, PhD in Forest Sci., 1984. Rsch. assoc. U. Idaho, 1979, dean, prof. Coll. Natural Resources, 2002—, interim pres., 2008—; asst. prof., natural resources extension specialist Mont. State U., U. Mont., 1984; extension prof., dir., co-founder Interdisciplinary Ctr. for Environ. Learning and Leadership U. Minn., 1988—2002. Nat. pub. policy chair Nat. Assn. Univ. Forest Resources Programs. Recipient Sec.'s Nat. Honor Award, US Dept. Agrl.; fellow Mondale Emerging Leaders Pub. Policy Program, U. Minn., Kellogg Found. Nat. Leadership Program, U. Wis. Mem.: Nat. Assn. State Univs. and Land Grant Colls., Soc. Am. Foresters. Office: U Idaho Coll Natural Resources PO Box 441142 Moscow ID 83844-1142 also: Office of Pres Adminstrn Bldg, Rm 105 PO Box 443151 Moscow ID 83844-3151 Office Phone: 208-885-6442. E-mail: stevendl@uidaho.edu.

DALIS, IRENE, mezzo soprano, performing arts association administrator; b. San Jose, Calif., Oct. 8, 1925; d. Peter Nicholas and Mamie Rose (Boitano) D.; m. George Loinaz, July 16, 1957; 1 child, Alida Mercedes. AB, San Jose State Coll., 1946; MA in Teaching, Columbia U., 1947; MMus (hon.), San Jose State U., 1957; studied voice with, Edyth Walker, NYC, 1947-50, Paul Althouse, 1950-51, Dr. Otto Mueller, Milan, Italy, 1952-72; MusD (hon.), Santa Clara U., 1987; DFA (hon.), Calif. State U., 1999. Prin. artist Berlin Opera, 1955-65, Met. Opera, NYC, 1957-77, San Francisco Opera, 1958-73, Hamburg (Fed. Republic Germany) Staatsoper, 1966-71; prof. music San Jose State U., Calif., 1977—2004; founder, gen. dir. Opera San Jose, 1984—. Dir. Met. Opera Nat. Auditions, San Jose dist., 1980-88. Operatic debut as dramatic mezzo-soprano Oldenburgisches Staatstheater, 1953, Berlin Staedtische Opera, 1955; debut Met. Opera, N.Y.C., 1957, 1st Am.-born singer, Kundry Bayreuth Festival, 1961, opened, Bayreuth Festival, Parsifal, 1963; commemorative Wagner 150th Birth Anniversary; opened 1963 Met. Opera Season in Aida; premiered: Dello Joio's Blood Moon, 1961, Henderson's Medea, 1972; rec. artist Parsifal, 1964 (Grand Prix du Disque award); contbg. editor Opera Quar., 1983. Recipient Fulbright award for study in Italy, 1951, Woman of Achievement award Commn. on Status of Women, 1983, Pres.'s award Nat. Italian Am. Found., 1985, award of merit People of San Francisco, 1985, San Jose Renaissance award for sustained and outstanding artistic contbn., 1987, Medal of Achievement Acad. Vocal Arts, 1988; named Honored Citizen City of San Jose, 1986; inducted into Calif. Pub. Edn. Hall of Fame, 1985, others. Mem. Beethoven Soc. (mem. adv. bd. 1985—), San Jose Arts Round Table, San Jose Opera Guild, Am. Soc. Univ. Women, Arts Edn. Week Consortium, Phi Kappa Phi, Mu Phi Epsilon. Office: Opera San Jose 2149 Paragon Dr San Jose CA 95131 Office Phone: 408-437-4450. Business E-Mail: dalis@operasj.org.

DALIS, PETER T., athletic director; BS in Phys. Edn., UCLA, 1959, MS in Edn., 1963. Dir. Cultural & Recreational Affairs Dept. UCLA, 1963-83, athletic dir., 1983—. Capital project cons. U. Conn., U. New South Wales, Australia; spl. events com. Pacific-10 Conf., chair TV com. Mem. L.A.-Athens Sister City Com., L.A. Sports Coun., Rose Bowl Mgmt. Com.; bd. dirs. So. Calif. Com. Olympic Games. Named Axios Sportsman of Yr., 1987-88. Office: UCLA Dept Athletics PO Box 24044 Los Angeles CA 90024-0044

DALLAS, SANDRA, writer; b. Wash., June 11, 1939; d. Forrest Everett and Harriett (Mavity) Dallas; m. Robert Thomas Atchison, Apr. 20, 1963; children: Dana Dallas, Povy Kendal Dallas. BA, U.

Denver, 1960. Asst. editor U. Denver Mag., 1965-66; editl. asst. Bus. Week, Denver, 1961-63, 67-69, bur. chief, 1969-85, 90-91, sr. corr., 1985-90; freelance editor, 1990—2001. Book reviewer Denver Post, 1961—, regional book columnist, 1980—. Author: Gaslights and Gingerbread, 1965, rev. edit., 1984, Gold and Gothic, 1967, No More Than 5 in a Bed, 1967, Vail, 1969, Cherry Creek Gothic, 1971, Yesterday's Denver, 1974, Sacred Paint, 1980, Colorado Ghost Towns and Mining Camps, 1985, Colorado Homes, 1986, Buster Midnight's Cafe, 1990, reissued, 1998, The Persian Pickle Club, 1995, The Diary of Mattie Spenser, 1997, Alice's Tulips, 2000, The Chili Queen, 2002, The Quilt that Walked to Golden, 2004, New Mercies, 2005, Tallgrass, 2007; editor: The Colorado Book, 1993; contbr. articles to popular mags. Bd. dirs. Vis. Nurse Assn., Denver, 1983—85, Hist. Denver, Inc., 1979—82, 1984—87, Rocky Mountain Quilt Mus., 2001—04, Historic Georgetown, Inc., 2002—05. Recipient Wrangler award Nat. Cowboy Hall of Fame, 1980, Lifetime Achievement award Denver Posse of Westerners, 1996, disting. svc. award U. Colo., 1997; named Colo. Exceptional Chronicler of Western History by Women's Library Assn. and Denver Pub. Library Friends Found., 1986; finalist Spur award We. Writers of Am., 1998, Women Writing the West Willa award, 2001, 03, 05, recipient, 2003, Benjamin Franklin award Ind. Book Pub. Assn., 2005 Mem. Women's Forum Colo., Denver Woman's Press Club, Western Writers Am. (Spur award 2003), Women Writing the West. Democrat. Presbyterian. Home and Office: 750 Marion St Denver CO 80218-3434

DALLAS, SATERIOS (SAM DALLAS), aerospace engineer, researcher, consultant; b. Detroit, May 9, 1938; s. Peter and Pauline (Alex) D.; m. Athena Ethel Spartos, July 12, 1964; children: Gregory Dean, Paula Marie. BS in Aero. Engrng., U. Mich., 1959, BS in Engrng. Math., 1960; MS in Astrodynamics, UCLA, 1963, PhD in Engrng., 1968. Rsch. engr. astrodynamics dept. Jet Propulsion Lab., Pasadena, Calif., 1965-78, supr. tech. group mission design, 1978-82, flight engrng. office mgr. Voyager Project, 1982-84, sci. and mission design mgr. Magellan Project, 1984-89, tech. mgr. spacecraft analysis, 1989-90, mission mgr. Mars Observer Project, 1990-93, mission mgr. Mars Global Surveyor Project, 1994-97, mission mgr. space interferometry mission, 1997-99, flight project mentor, 2002—04, cons., 2004—. Instr. Pepperdine U., Malibu, Calif., 1973-75; lectr. on space missions Kennedy Space Ctr., Cape Canaveral, Fla., 1988, Australian Dept. Industry, Tech. and Commerce, Canberra, 1988, USAF-CAP-PLR Ctr. Aerospace Edn., Las Vegas, Neb., 1991. Author: Progress in Astronautics and Aeronautics, 1964, Natural and Artificial Satellite Motion, 1979; contbr. articles to sci. jours. Coach Glendale (Calif.) Little League, 1979-82; com. mem. troop 125 Boy Scouts Am., Glendale, 1980. Recipient Apollo achievement award NASA, 1969, cert. of recognition, 1974, Laurels award Aviation Week, 1989, 94, Exceptional Achievement award NASA, 1998. Mem. AIAA, Am. Astron. Soc. (astrodynamics tech. com. 1970-80). Republican. Greek Orthodox. Avocations: skiing, hiking, woodworking, tennis, computer applications development. Home: 3860 Karen Lynn Dr Glendale CA 91206-1218 E-mail: ssd1938@hotmail.com.

DALRYMPLE, GARY BRENT, research geologist; b. Alhambra, Calif., May 9, 1937; s. Donald Inlow and Wynona Edith (Pierce) D.; m. Sharon Ann Tramel, June 28, 1959; children: Stacie Ann, Robynne Ann Sisco, Melinda Ann Dalrymple McGurer. AB in Geology, Occidental Coll., 1959; PhD in Geology, U. Calif., Berkeley, 1963; DSc (hon.), Occidental Coll., Los Angeles, 1993. Rsch. geologist U.S. Geol. Survey, Menlo Park, Calif., 1963-81, 84-94, asst. chief geologist we. region, 1981-84; dean, prof. Coll. Oceanic and Atmospheric Sci., Oreg. State U., Corvallis, 1994-2001, dean and prof. emeritus, 2001—. Vis. prof. sch. earth scis. Stanford U., 1969-72, cons. prof., 1983-85, 90-94; disting. alumni centennial spkr. Occidental Coll., 1986-87. Author: Potassium-Argon Dating, 1969, Age of Earth, 1991, Ancient Earth, Ancient Skies, 2004; contbr. chpts. to books and articles to profl. jours. Fellow NSF, 1961-63; recipient Meritorius Svc. award U.S. Dept. Interior, 1984, Public Svc. award Geological Soc. Am., 2001, Nat. medal Sci., 2003. Fellow Am. Geophys. Union (pres.-elect 1988-90, pres. 1990-92), Am. Acad. Arts and Scis.; mem. NAS (chair geology sect. 1997-2000), Am. Inst. Physics (bd. govs. 1991-97), Consortium for Oceanographic Rsch. and Edn. (bd. govs. 1994-2001), Joint Oceanographic Inst. (bd. govs. 1994-2001, chair 1996-98). Achievements include discovery that the earth's magnetic field reverses polarity and determination of time scale of these reversals for the past 3.5 million years; development of ultra-fast high-sensitivity thermoluminescence analyzer for studying lunar surface processes; development and refinement of K-Ar and 40 Ar/39 Ar dating methods and instrumentation, continuous laser probe for determining ages of microgram-sized mineral samples; research on volcanoes in the Hawaiian-Emperor volcanic chain, chronology of lunar basin formation, development and improvement of isotopic dating techniques and instrumentation, geomagnetic field behavior, plate tectonics of the Pacific Ocean basin, evolution of volcanoes, various aspects of Pleistocene history of the western U.S. Home: 1847 NW Hillcrest Dr Corvallis OR 97330-1859 Personal E-mail: brentandsharon@comcast.net.

DALTO, BILLY, state representative; b. NYC, Oct. 21, 1976; BA, Willamette U., 1998. Legis. aide State Rep. Jackie Winters, 2000—01; pres. Dalto and Assocs. Inc., 2001—; mem. Oreg. Ho. of Reps., 2002—. Republican. Office: 900 Court St North East H-291 Salem OR 97301

DALTON, BONNIE, life science administrator; MBA in Mgmt. Dep. chief life sci. divsn. Ames Rsch. Ctr., Moffett Field, Calif. Recipient NIH Pub. Health fellowship. Avocations: flying, gardening, playing piano. Office: NASA Ames Rsch Ctr Life Sciences Divsn Moffett Field CA 94035

DALTON, WILLIAM J., Mayor, Garden Grove, California; b. San Francisco, Calif. m. Sandra Dalton; children: Pamela, William Jr., Paula, Bob, Brian. BA in Adminstrn. of Justice, Calif. State U., Fullerton. Ret. lt. Garden Grove Police Dept.; councilman City of Garden Grove, 1998—2004, mayor, 2004—. Chmn. Orange County Sanitary Dist. Ops. Com.; bd. dirs. Orange County Transp. Authority. Mem.: Garden Grove Lions Club, Garden Grove Elks Club. Avocation: police & fire badge collecting. Office: 11222 Acacia Pkwy Garden Grove CA 92840 Office Phone: 714-741-5104.*

DALY, CHRIS, city supervisor; b. Silver Spring, Md., 1972; m. Sarah Low Daly; children: Jack, Grace. Student, Duke U., Durham, NC. Nat. coord. non-profit orgn. Empty the Shelters, San Francisco, 1993; co-founder Mission Agenda, 1995; supr., Dist. 6 San Francisco Bd. Supervisors, 2000—, chair rules com., past chair budget & fin. com., health & human svcs. com. Co-founder Mission Anti-Displacement Coalition; mem. joint policy com., regional planning com. Assn. Bay Area Govt.'s; adj. faculty New Coll. Calif.; mem. San Francisco County Transp. Authority, chair, 2003. Mem. steering com. San Francisco Tenants Union. Recipient Young Ams.' Medal for Svc., US Congress, 1989. Democrat. Office: 1 Dr Carlton B Goodlett Pl Rm 244 San Francisco CA 94102-4689 Office Phone: 415-554-7970. Fax: 415-554-7974. E-mail: chris_daly@ci.sf.ca.us.*

DALY, DONALD F., retired engineering company executive; b. Morristown, NJ, Jan. 10, 1933; s. John F. and Sophie E. (Podeski) D.; m. Bennie L. London, Nov. 2, 1963; children: Stephen, David, Eric. ME, Stevens Inst. Tech., 1955. Equipment engr. Corning (N.Y.) Glass Works, 1955-56; sales engr. Mundet Cork, 1958-60; process engr. Thiokol Chem. Corp., 1961-65; dir. engrng. Syntex Corp., 1966-78; v.p., project mgr. Indsl. Design Corp., 1978-2000; dir. Tech. Design & Constrn. Co., Portland, Oreg., 1992-94; ret., 2000. Republican. Avocations: golf, skiing.

DALY, ROBERT ANTHONY, international relief organization, former professional sports team and film company executive; b. Bklyn., Dec. 8, 1936; s. James and Eleanor Daly; m. Carole Bayer; 1 stepchild, Cristopher Bacharach; children: Linda Marie, Robert Anthony, Brian James. Student, Bklyn. Coll.; PhD in Fine Arts (hon.), Am. Film Inst.; DHL (hon.), Trinity Coll. From dir. bus. affairs to v.p. bus. affairs, to exec. v.p. CBS TV Network, 1955—80; pres. CBS Entertainment Co., 1977—80; chmn., CEO Warner Bros., Burbank, Calif., 1982—94; chmn., co-CEO Warner Music Group, 1995—99; chmn., CEO, mng. ptnr. L.A. Dodgers, 1999—2004; chmn. Save the Children Fedn., Inc., Westport, 2005—. Bd. dirs. Am. Film Inst. Trustee Am. Film Inst. Mem.: NATAS, Hollywood Radio and TV Soc., Motion Picture Pioneers, Acad. Motion Picture Arts and Scis. Roman Catholic. Office: 10877 Wilshire Blvd #610 Los Angeles CA 90024 also: Save the Children 2000 M St NW Ste 500 Washington DC 20036

DALY, TIMOTHY, actor; b. NYC, Mar. 1, 1956; s. James Daly and Hope Newell; m. Any Van Nostrand, Sept. 18, 1982; children: Sam, Emelyn. BA, Bennington Coll. Theatre appearances include Fables For Friends, 1984, Oliver, Oliver, 1985 (Boradway debut), Coastal Disturbances, 1987 (Theatre World award 1987); films include Diner, 1982, Just the Way You Are, 1984, Made In Heaven, 1987, Spellbinder, 1988, Love or Money, 1989, Year of the Comet, 1992, Caroline at Midnight, 1994, Dr. Jekyll and Ms. Hyde, 1995, Denise Calls Up, 1995, The Associate, 1996, The Object of My Affection, 1998, Seven Girlfriends, 1999, Basic, 2003, Against the Ropes, 2004, Return to Sender, 2004, The Good Student, 2008; TV appearances include (series) Ryan's Four, 1983, Almost Grown, 1988, Wings, 1990-97, Superman, 1996-1999, The Fugitive, 2000-01, Eyes, 2005-07, The Nine, 2006-07, Private Practice, 2007-; (movies) I Married A Centerfold, 1984, Mirrors, 1985, Red Earth, White Earth, 1989, In The Line of Duty: Ambush in Waco, 1993, Dangerous Heart, 1994, Witness to the Execution, 1994, Execution of Justice, 1999, A House Divided, 2000, The Outsider, 2002, Wilder Days, 2003, Edge of America, 2003, Bereft, 2004, (TV mini series) Alex Haley's Queen, 1993; (guest appearances) The Sopranos, 2004-07, Law & Order: Special Victims Unit, 2007, Grey's Anatomy, 2007. Office: c/o McClure and Assoc Pub Rels 5225 Wilshire Blvd, Ste 909 Los Angeles CA 90036

DALZELL, RICK, information technology executive; BS in Engrng., US Mil. Acad. Bus. devel. mgr. E-Sys., Inc., 1987—90; with info. sys. divsn. Wal-Mart Stores, Inc., 1990—94, v.p. info. sys., 1994—97; v.p., chief info. officer Amazon.com, Seattle, 1997—2000, sr. v.p., chief info. officer, 2000—01, sr. v.p. worldwide arch. and platform software, chief info. officer, 2001—. With US Army, 1983—90.

DAMASIO, ANTONIO R., psychology and neurology professor, researcher; b. Lisbon, Portugal, Feb. 25, 1944; arrived in US, 1975, naturalized; m. Hanna Damasio. MD, U. Lisbon, 1969, DMS, 1974. Intern U. Hosp., Lisbon, 1969-72; chief Language Rsch. Lab., Ctr. de Estudos Egas Moniz, 1971—75; prof. auxiliar in neurology U. Lisbon Med. Sch., 1974—75; vis. asst. prof. U. Iowa, Iowa City, 1975—76, assoc. prof. dept. neurology, 1976-80, chief Divsn. of Behavioral Neurology & Cognitive Neuroscience, 1977—2005, prof. neurology, 1980—2005, dir. Alzheimer's Disease Rsch. Ctr., 1985—2005, head Dept. Neurology, 1986—2005, M.W. Van Allen Disting. prof., 1989—2005, dist. adj. prof. neurology, 2005—; prof. psychology, neuroscience and neurology U. So. Calif., LA, 2005—, dir. Brain and Creativity Inst., 2005—, David Dornsife prof. neuroscience Coll. of Letters, Arts and Scis., 2006—. Adj. prof. Salk Inst., San Diego, 1989—; mem. planning subcom. Nat. Adv. Neurol. Disorders Stroke Coun. Author: Lesion Analysis in Neuropsychgology, 1989 (award Assn. Am. Pubs. 1990); mem. editorial bd. Trends in Neuroscis., 1986-91, Behavioral Brain Rsch., 1988—, Cerebral Cortex, 1990—, Jour. Neurosci., 1990, Cognitive Brain Rsch., Learning and Memory, spl. brain issue Sci. Am, 1992, Descartes' Error: Emotion, Reason, and the Human Brain, 1994, The Feeling of What Happens: Body and Emotion in the Making of Consciousness, 1999. Recipient Disting. prof. award U. So. Calif., Prix Plasticite' Neuronale, Ispen Found., 1997, Golden Brain award, 1995, The Reenpää prize, Finland, 2000, Arnold Pfeffer Prize, 2002, Dr. William Beaumont award AMA, 1990, Pessoa prize Portuguese govt., 1992, Prince of Asturias Award for Sci. and Tech. Rsch., 2005, Presdl. Medal of the Am. Psychoanalytic Assn., 2006. Fellow Am. Acad. Neurology, Am. Neurol. Asns.; mem. NAS Inst. Medicine, Soc. for Neurosci., Acad. Aphasia (pres. 1983), Behavioral Neurology Soc., (pres. 1985), Royal Soc. Medicine Belgium (elected), European Acad. Arts and Scis. (elected), Am. Acad. Arts and Scis, Acad. Scis., Lisbon. Office: Brain and Creativity Inst U So Calif 3641 Watt Way Ste 126 Los Angeles CA 90089-2520 Office Phone: 213-821-2377. Office Fax: 213-821-3099. E-mail: damasio@usc.edu.

DAMASIO, HANNA, psychology and neuroscience professor, researcher; b. Portugal; naturalized; m. Antonio R. Damasio. MD, U. Lisbon, 1969, PhD (hon.), 2001, U. Aachen, 2002. Med. internship Univ. Hosp., Lisbon, Portugal, 1970—72, residency neurology, 1972—74; fellow-assoc. Dept. Neurology, U. Iowa, 1975—76, instr., 1976—77, dir. The Migraine Clinic, 1977—88, asst. prof., 1977—81, assoc. prof., 1981—85, dir. Lab. for Neuroimaging and Human Neuroanatomy, 1982—2005, co-dir. Divsn. Cognitive Neuroscience, 1985—2005, prof., 1985—2005, disting. prof., 1998—2005, disting. adj. prof., 2005—; prof. psychology, neuroscience and neurology U. So. Calif., LA, 2005—, dir. Dana and David Dornsife Cognitive Neuroscience Imaging Ctr., 2005—, Dana Dornsife prof. neuroscience Coll. Letters, Arts and Scis., 2006—. Rsch. fellow Aphasia Rsch. Ctr., Boston, 1967; sr. registrar Princess Margaret Migraine Clinic, London, 1975; adj. prof. Salk Inst. for Biological Studies, La Jolla, Calif., 1994—. Bd. editor Human Brain Mapping, 1992—, NeuroImage, 2002—; contbr. articles to profl. jours. Recipient Pessoa Prize, 1992, Order of Santiago da Espada, 1995, Jean-Louis Signoret Prize in Cognitive Neuroscience, 2004. Mem.: Internat. Neuropsychological Soc., Am. Acad. Neurology, Memory Disorders Rsch. Soc., Am. Soc. Neuroimaging, Am. Acad. Arts and Scis., Am. Neurological Assn. Office: Brain and Creativity Inst U So Calif 3641 Watt Way Ste 126 Los Angeles CA 90089-2520 Office Phone: 213-821-0731. E-mail: hdamasio@college.usc.edu.

D'AMICO, MICHAEL, architect, urban planner; b. Bklyn., Sept. 11, 1936; s. Michael and Rosalie (Vinciguerra) D'Amico; m. Joan Hand, Nov. 26, 1955; children: Michael III, Dion Charles. BArch, U. Okla., 1961; postgrad., So. Meth. U. Sch. Law, 1962—63, Coll. Marin, 1988—89, San Francisco Law Sch., 1994—. Supr. advanced planning sect. Dallas Dept. City Planning, 1961—63; designer, planner in charge Leo A. Daly Co., San Francisco, 1963—66; project planner Whisler, Patri Assocs., San Francisco, 1966—67; arch., urban planner D'Amico & Assocs., San Francisco, NY, Guam, 1967—73; pres. D'Amico & Assocs., Inc., Mill Valley and San Francisco, Calif., and Guam, 1973—, Jericho Alpha Inc., 1979—82, Alpha Internet Sys., Inc., 1996—; chief ops. officer Patri Merker, 2006—09. Cons. arch., planner City of Seaside, Calif., 1967—72, 1979—81, 1989—; cons. urban devel., Eureka, Calif., 1967—82; cons. planner, Lakewood, Calif.; redevel. cons., Daly City, Calif., 1975—77; redevel. advisor Tamalpais Valley Bus. Assn., 1975—77; archtl. and hist. analyst Calif. Dept. Transp., 1975—77; agt. Eureka, Calif., Coastal Commn., 1977—79; devel. cons. City of Scotts Valley, 1977—95, City of Suisun, 1988—89, City of Union City, 1989—91. Mem. steering com. San Francisco Joint Com. Urban Design, 1967—72. Recipient 1st prize, Port Aransas (Tex.) Master Plan Competition, 1964, Design award, Karachi Mcpl. Authority, 1987, Merit award, St. Vincent's/Silveira. Mem.: AIA (inactive, Cmty. Design award 1970), Solar Energy Soc. Am., World Future Soc., Calif. Assn. Planning Cons. (sec.-treas. 1970—72), Am. Planning Assn., Am. Inst. Cons. Planners. Office: 525 Midvale Way Mill Valley CA 94941-3705 Business E-Mail: alphais@alphais.com.

DAMON, WILLIAM VAN BUREN, developmental psychologist, educator, writer; b. Brockton, Mass., Nov. 10, 1944; s. Philip Arthur and Helen (Meyers) D.; m. Wendy Obernauer (div. 1982); children: Jesse Louis, Maria; m. Anne Colby, Sept. 24, 1983, 1 child, Caroline. BA, Harvard U., 1967; PhD, U. Calif., Berkeley, 1973. Social worker N.Y.C. Dept. Social Svcs., 1968-70; prof. psychology Clark U., Worcester, Mass., 1973-89, dean Grad Sch., 1983-87, chmn. dept. edn., 1988-89; Disting. vis. prof. U. P.R., 1988; prof., chair edn. dept. Brown U., Providence, 1989-92, prof., Mittlemann Family dir. Ctr. for Study of Human Devel., 1993-98, univ. prof., 1997-98; fellow Ctr. for Advanced Study in the Behavioral Scis., 1994-95; prof., dir. Ctr. on Adolescence Stanford (Calif.) U., 1997—. Sr. fellow Hoover Instn., 1999—; mem. study sect. NIMH, Bethesda, Md., 1981-84; cons. State of Mass., 1976, State of Calif., 1978, Allegheny County, Pa., 1979, Pinellas County, Fla., 1990, Com. of Va., 1993, Hawaii, 1995, Children's TV Workshop, 1991-09, Annenberg Adv. Coun. on Excellence in Children's TV, 1996-99, Project for Excellence in Journalism, 2000-; mem. nat. adv. bd. Fox Family TV Network, 1998-2001. Author: Social World of the Child, 1977, Social and Personality Development, 1983, Self-Understanding in Childhood and Adolescence, 1988, The Moral Child, 1988, Child Development Today and Tomorrow, 1989, Some Do Care, 1992, Greater Expectations, 1995 (Parent's Choice Book award, 1995), The Youth Charter, 1997, Handbook of Child Psychology, 2006;: Good Work, 2001, Bringing in a New Era in Character Education, 2002, Noble Purpose, 2003, The Moral Advantage, 2004, Taking Philanthropy Seriously, 2006; editor: The Path to Purpose, 2008, New Directions for Child Devel., 1978—2005. Trustee Bancroft Sch., Worcester, Mass., 1982-84; mem. adv. bd. Ednl. Alliance, 1991—; mem. bd. advisors John Templeto Found., 2005—. Grantee Carnegie Corp., N.Y.C., 1975-79, 97—, Spencer Found., 1980, 92-96, 98-2001, N.Y. comty. Trust, 1984-88, Inst. Noetic Scis., 1988-90, MacArthur Found., 1990-95, Pew Charitable Trusts, 1990-95, 98-2000, Ross Inst., 1996—, Hewlett Found., 1997—, The Templeton Found., 1998—, Atlantic Philanthropies, 2003-. Mem. APA, Jean Piaget Soc. (bd. dirs. 1983-87), Am. Ednl. Rsch. Assn., Soc. for Rsch. in Child Devel., Nat. Acad. Edn., Harvard Clubs of N.Y. and Boston. Republican. Episcopalian. Office: Stanford U Ctr on Adolescence Cypress Bldg C Stanford CA 94305-4145 Office Phone: 650-725-8205. Business E-Mail: wdamon@stanford.edu.

DAMOOSE, GEORGE LYNN, lawyer; b. Grand Rapids, Mich., Feb. 2, 1938; s. George G. and Geneva J. (Joseph) D.; m. Carol Sweeney, Dec. 7, 1968; children: Alison Dana, George Christopher. AB cum laude, Harvard U., 1959, JD cum laude, 1965. Bar: Calif. 1966, U.S. Tax Ct., 1973. Assoc. O'Melveny and Myers, LA, 1965-72; ptnr. Jennings, Engstrand, Henrikson, P.C., San Diego, 1972-76, Procopio, Cory, Hargreaves, and Savitch, San Diego, 1976—. Bd. dirs. San Diego Civic Light Opera Assn., 1984-90, 92; trustee The Bishops Sch., La Jolla, 1987-90, La Jolla Chamber Music Soc., 1988-89; commr. San Diego Crime Commn., 1987-90. Served to lt. (j.g.) USN, 1959-62. Mem. Am. Bar Found., San Diego County Bar Assn. (chmn. tax sect. 1974-75, 86-87), Calif. Bar Assn. (ind. inquiry and rev. panel, program for certifying legal specialists 1986-87), State Bar Calif. (exec. com., taxation sect. 1990-95, chair 1994-95, chair CEB joint adv. com. taxation 1996-98), San Diego C. of C. (bd. dirs. 1994-96), La Jolla Country Club, La Jolla Beach and Tennis Club. Republican. Episcopalian. Avocations: music, reading, golf, travel. Home: 208 Avenida Cortez La Jolla CA 92037-6502 Office: Procopio Cory et al 530 B St Ste 2100 San Diego CA 92101-4496 Office Phone: 619-515-3218.

DAMRELL, FRANK C., JR., judge; BA, U. Calif., Berkeley, 1961; JD, Yale U., 1964. Judge U.S. Dist. Ct. (ea. dist.) Calif., 1997—. Office: 501 I St Sacramento CA 95814-7300

DANCE, FRANCIS ESBURN XAVIER, communication educator; b. Bklyn., Nov. 9, 1929; s. Clifton Louis and Catherine (Tester) D.; m. Nora Alice Rush, May 1, 1954 (div. 1974); children: Clifton Louis III, Charles Daniel, Alison Catherine, Andrea Frances, Frances Sue, Brendan Rush; m. Carol Camille Zak, July 4, 1974; children: Zachary Esburn, Gabriel Joseph, Caleb Michael, Catherine Emily BS, Fordham U., 1951; MS, Northwestern U., 1953, PhD, 1959. Instr. speech Bklyn. Adult Labor Schs., 1951; instr. humanities, coord. radio and TV U. Ill. at Chgo., 1953—54; instr. Univ. Coll. U. Chgo., 1958; asst. prof. St. Joseph's (Ind.) Coll., Ind., 1958—60; asst. prof., then assoc. prof. U. Kans., 1960—63; mem. faculty U. Wis., Milw., 1963—71, prof. comm., 1965—71, dir. Speech Comm. Ctr., 1963—70; prof. U. Denver, 1971—, John Evans prof., 1995—; prof.

homiletics St. John Vianney Theol. Sem., 2002—05, John Evans prof. emeritus, 2006—. Content expert and mem. faculty adv. bd. to Internat. U. on Knowledge Channel, 1993-95; cons. in field. Author: The Citizen Speaks, 1962, (with Harold P. Zelko) Business and Professional Speech Communication, 1965, 2d edit., 1978, Human Communication Theory, 1967, (with Carl E. Larson) Perspectives on Communication, 1970, Speech Communication: Concepts and Behavior, 1972, The Functions of Speech Communication: A Theoretical Approach, 1976, Human Communication Theory, 1982, (with Carol C. Zak-Dance) Public Speaking, 1986, Speaking Your Mind, 1994, 2d edit., 1996, Public Speaking: Finding Your Voice and Speaking your Mind, 2007; editor Jour. Comm., 1962-64, Speech Tchr., 1970-72; adv. bd. Jour. Black Studies; editl. bd. Jour. Psycholinguistic Rsch; contbr. articles to profl. jours. Bd. dirs. Milw. Mental Health Assn., 1966-67. 2d lt. AUS, 1954-56. Knapp Univ. scholar in comm., 1967-68; recipient Outstanding Prof. award Std. Oil Found., 1967; Master Tchr. award U. Denver, 1985, Univ. Lectr. award U. Denver, 1986. Fellow Internat. Comm. Assn. (pres. 1967); mem. Nat. Comm. Assn. (pres. 1982), Psi Upsilon. Office: U Denver Dept Human Comm Studies Denver CO 80208-0001 Business E-Mail: fdance@du.edu.

DANDO, PAT, city official; City coun., San Jose, Calif. Office: 801 N 1st St Rm 600 San Jose CA 95110-1704

DANE, ERIC, actor; b. San Francisco, Nov. 9, 1972; m. Rebecca Gayheart, Oct. 29, 2004. Actor: (TV films) Serving in Silence: The Margarethe Cammermeyer Story, 1995, Seduced by Madness: The Diane Borchardt Story, 1996, Ball & Chain, 2001, Helter Skelter, 2004, Painkiller Jane, 2005, Wedding Wars, 2006; (films) The Basket, 1999, Sol Goode, 2001, Feast, 2005, X-Men: The Last Stand, 2006, Open Water 2: Adrift, 2006, Marley & Me, 2008; (TV series) Gideon's Crossing, 2000—01, The American Embassy, 2002, Charmed, 2003—04, Las Vegas, 2004, Grey's Anatomy, 2006— (Outstanding Performance by an Ensemble in a Drama Series, SAG, 2007), (voice): (video game) X-Men: The Official Game, 2006. Office: c/o Grey's Anatomy Los Feliz Tower 4th Fl 4151 Prospect Ave Los Angeles CA 90027

D'ANGELO, ROBERT WILLIAM, lawyer; b. Buffalo, Nov. 10, 1932; s. Samuel and Margaret Theresa Guercio D'A.; m. Ellen Frances Neary, Sept. 17, 1959; children: Christopher Robert, Gregory Andrew. BBA, Loyola U., LA, 1954; JD, UCLA, 1960. Bar: Calif. 1960; cert. specialist taxation law. Practiced in, LA, 1960-89; mem. firm. Myers & D'Angelo, Pasadena, Calif., 1967—. Adj. prof. law, taxation Whittier Coll. Sch. of Law., 1981. Served to capt. USAF, 1954—57. Mem. ABA, AICPA, State Bar Calif., L.A. County Bar Assn., Wilshire Bar Assn., Pasadena Bar Assn., Calif. Soc. CPAs, Am. Assn. Atty. CPAs, Calif. Assn. Atty. CPAs (pres. 1980), Phi Delta Phi, Alpha Sigma Nu. Home: 1706 Highland Ave Glendale CA 91202-1265 Office: 301 N Lake Ave Ste 800 Pasadena CA 91101-4108 Office Phone: 626-792-0007. Personal E-mail: m-dlaw@pacbell.net.

D'ANGELO MELBY, DONNA MARIE, lawyer; BA, U. Calif., 1972; JD, Calif. Western Sch. Law, 1978. Bar: Calif. 1979. Ptnr. Sonnenschein, Nath & Rosenthal LLP, LA. Apptd. Jud. Sect. Adv. Panel; spkr. in field. Contbr. articles to profl. jours. Bd. dirs. Wellness Cmty. Foothills. Named one of Top 30 Women Litigators, L.A. and San Francisco Daily Jour., 2002, 2003, 2004, 100 Most Influential Attys. in Calif., L.A. Daily Jour., San Francisco Recorder, 2004, Top 5% So. Calif. Super Lawyers, Los Angeles Mag. & Law and Politics, 2004, 2005. Fellow: Internat. Soc. Barristers, Am. Coll. Trial Lawyers; mem.: ABA (mem. litigation sect., labor sect., employment sect), Fedn. Def. and Corp. Counsel, Internat. Assn. Def. Counsel, Def. Rsch. Inst., State Bar Calif. (trustee legal svcs. trust fund commn. 1985—86, 1997), L.A. Bar Assn. (mem. labor and employment law sect.), Fed. Bar Assn., Women Lawyers Assn. L.A., Calif. Women Lawyers, Am. Bd. Trial Advocates (exec. com. L.A. chpt. 1995—, mem. pres.'s coun. 1997, co-chair civil justice and nat. office com. 2001, nat. bd. dirs., nat. pres. 2005, pres. L.A. chpt. 2004). Home: 601 S FIGUEROA ST STE 2500 Los Angeles CA 90017-5709 Office Phone: 213-892-5027. Business E-Mail: dmelby@sonnenschein.com.

DANIEL, JAMES RICHARD, accountant, corporate financial executive; b. Chgo., June 26, 1947; s. Elmer Alexander and June B. (Bush) D.; m. Marsha Ruth Stone, Nov. 8, 1969; children: Jennifer Rae, Michael James. BS in Acctg., U. Ill., 1970; MBA, Loyola U., 1974. CPA, Ill., La. Dir. fin. Baxter Travenol Labs., Chgo., 1974-79; corp. contr. Bio-Rad Labs. Inc., Richmond, Calif., 1979-81; v.p., treas., contr. Lykes Bros. Steamship Co. Inc., New Orleans, 1981-84; CFO SCI Systems Inc., Huntsville, Ala., 1984-91; sr. v.p., CFO Dell Computer Corp., Austin, Tex., 1991-93; exec. v.p., CFO, pres. hdqrs. support, treas. MicroAge, Inc., Tempe, 1993-2000; cons., 2000-01; sr. v.p., CFO PetsMart Inc., Phoenix, 2001. Mem. issuer affairs com. NASDAQ, 1995-2001. With U.S. Army, 1970-73. Recipient Outstanding Alumnus award Loyola U. Grad. Sch. Bus., 1995. Mem. AICPA. Republican. Home: 1695 Cherokee Ln Wickenburg AZ 85390 Office Phone: 928-684-6189. E-mail: jdanieletal@aol.com.

DANIEL, PATRICK D., energy executive; m. Dora Daniel; 2 children. BS chem. engring., Univ. Alta.; MS chem. engring., Univ. BC. Pres. IPL Energy U.S.; CEO Interprovincial Pipe Line Inc.; exec. v.p., COO energy transp. svc. Enbridge Energy, pres., COO, pres., CEO, 2001—. Office: Enbridge Energy 3000 Fifth Ave Pl 425 First St SW Calgary AB T2P 3L8 Canada

DANIEL, ROLLIN KIMBALL, plastic surgeon; b. Montgomery, Ala., Aug. 14, 1943; BA cum laude, Vanderbilt U., Nashville, 1965; MD, Columbia U. Coll. Physicians & Surgeons, NYC, 1969; MSc in Experimental Surgery, McGill U., Montreal, Quebec, Canada, 1974. Cert. Am. Bd. Plastic Surgery. Intern, gen. surgery Barnes Hosp., St. Louis, 1969—70; resident, plastic surgery McGill U., Montreal, Canada, 1971—73, resident, hand surgery, 1973—75; resident, craniofacial surgery U. Louisville, Ky., 1975—76; fellow U. Toronto, Canada, 1984; pvt. practice rhinoplasty Newport Beach, Calif. Chief plastic surgery Hoag Meml. Hosp. Presbyterian, Newport Beach, 1998—2000, Royal Victoria Hosp.; prof. surgery McGill U.; clinical prof. plastic surgery U. Calif, Irvine. Contbr. articles to profl. jours., chapters to books;, author med. textbooks. Fellow: ACS, Quebec Coll. Physicians & Surgeons, Royal Coll. Surgeons Canada; mem.: Am. Soc. Aesthetic Plastic Surgery, Am. Soc. Plastic Surgeons, Am. Bd. Plastic Surgery. Office: 1441 Avocado Ste 308 Newport Beach CA 92660 Office Phone: 949-721-0494. Office Fax: 949-721-4138.

DANIEL, THOMAS L., zoology educator; b. NYC, Aug. 21, 1954; BS in Anthropology and Engring., U. Wis., 1976, MS in Zoology and Engring., 1978; PhD in Zoology, Duke U., 1982; postgrad., Calif. Inst. Tech. Myron A. Bantrell postdoctoral fellow in sci. and engring. Calif. Inst. Tech., 1982-84; asst. prof. dept. zoology U. Wash., Seattle, 1984-88, assoc. prof. dept. zoology, 1988-92, prof. dept. zoology, 1992—, Joan and Richard Komen Chair of Biol. External grad. faculty Oreg. State U., 1987—; mem. various coms. at U. Wash. including chair grad. admissions dept. zoology, 1989-91, chair grad. program dept. zoology, 1991-94, dir. math. biology tng. program, 1993—; panel mem. physiol. processes NSF, 1991—; presenter in field. Mem. editl. bd. Jour. Exptl. Biology, Cambridge U., 1988-90, 93—; contbr. articles to profl. jours. Grantee NSF, 1984-87, 88-91, 91-93, 93, U. Wash., 1987-88, J. Fluke Co., 1988, Reticon, Inc., 1988, Am. Soc. Zoologists Symposium on Efficiency in Organisms, 1988-89, Whitaker Found. for Biomed. Rsch., 1988-91, Howard Hughes Found., 1989-94, M.J. Murdock Meml. Trust, 1989-94, Apple Computer, 1991; MacArthur fellow, 1996. Office: U Wash Dept Biology 106 Kincaid Hall PO Box 351800 Seattle WA 98195-1800

DANIEL, WILEY YOUNG, federal judge; b. Louisville, Sept. 10, 1946; s. Wiley Daniel & Lavinia Y.; m. Ida S. Daniel; children: Jennifer, Stephanie, Nicole. BA in History, Howard U., 1968, JD, 1971. Assoc. Wright McKean & Cudlip, 1971—77; ptnr. Gorsuch, Kirgis, Campbell, Walker & Grover, Denver, 1977-88; shareholder Popham, Haik, Schnobrich & Kaufman Ltd., Denver, 1988-95, mng. ptnr., 1993-95; judge US Dist. Ct. Colo., Denver, 1995—, chief judge, 2008—. Dir. Wayne County Neighborhood Legal Services, 1974—76; adj. prof. law Detroit Coll. Law, 1974—77, U. Colo. Sch. Law, 1977—80, 2000—; dir. Pers. Svc. Bd., 1979—83; dir., vice chmn. Iliff Sch. Theology, 1983—. Trustee Am. Inns of Ct. Found.; bd. dirs., mentor Bridge Project; mem. Just Beginning Found.; chair, Colo. State Bd. Agrl., 1989-95 Recipient Disting. Svc. award, Kappa Alpha Psi Fraternity, 1999. Mem. ABA, Nat. Bar Assn., Colo. Bar Assn. (pres. elect, 1991-92, pres. 1992-93), Denver Bar Assn. (trustee, 1990-93), Sam Cary Bar Assn. (Disting. Svc. award, 1986), State Bd. Architecture. Democrat. Office: Alfred A Araj US Courthouse 901 19th St Denver CO 80294

DANIELOVITCH, ISSUR See **DOUGLAS, KIRK**

DANIELS, CAROLINE, publishing executive; b. San Francisco, Dec. 11, 1948; d. William L. and Gladys Daniels; m. Jack Wernick, Nov. 30, 1985 (div.); children: Martin Wernick, Katherine Wernick. Student, U. Dijon, France, 1965; BA in Psychology, U. Colo., 1970; postgrad., Harvard U., 1983-85. Export agt. Air Oceanic Shippers, San Francisco, 1972-73; library supr. Aircraft Tech. Pubs., San Francisco, 1973-75, ops. mgr., 1975-80, v.p., 1980-82, exec. v.p. Brisbane, Calif., 1982-84, pres., 1984—86, CEO, chmn. bd. dirs., 1984—. Pres. adv. bd. Embry Riddle Aero. U.; bd. dirs. Acad. Art U., San Francisco; past bd. dirs. Jr. Achievement of Bay Area. Mem.: Gen. Aviation Mfg. Assn. (bd. dirs., former exec. com., former chmn. pub. affairs com., chmn. safety affairs com.), San Francisco Opera Guild (bd. dirs.). Office: Aircraft Tech Pubs 101 S Hill Dr Brisbane CA 94005-1251 Office Phone: 415-330-9500.

DANIELS, GREGORY MARTIN, screenwriter; b. NYC, June 13, 1963; m. Susan Daniels, Sept. 1991. BA, Harvard U., 1985. Staff writer cable TV show Not Necessarily the News, Hollywood, Calif., 1985-87; staff writer TV show The Wilton-North Report, Hollywood, 1987; freelance co-writer TV pilots The Rich Hall Show, Goodnight America, 1987; staff writer TV show Saturday Night Live, NYC, 1988—90; co-exec. prodr. The Simpsons; exec. prodr. King of The Hill, 1997—; prodr., writer, dir. The Office, 2005—. Recipient Emmy award for Outstanding Animated Series, 1999, Danny Thomas Prodr. of Yr. award in Episodic TV - Comedy, Producers Guild of Am., 2007, Primetime Emmy for Outstanding Writing for a Comedy Series (The Office), Acad. TV Arts and Scis., 2007. Mem. Writers Guild Am. West, AFTRA, ASCAP. Address: 846 1/4 N Formosa Ave Los Angeles CA 90046-7648

DANIELS, JAMES WALTER, lawyer; b. Chgo., Oct. 13, 1945; s. Ben George and Delores L. (Wolanin) D.; m. Gail Anne Rihacek, June 14, 1969; children: Morgan, Abigail, Rachel. AB, Brown U., 1967; JD, U. Chgo., 1970. Bar: Calif. 1970, US Dist. Ct. (ctrl. dist.) Calif. 1970, US Tax Ct., 1972, US Supreme Ct. 1979. Assoc. firm Latham & Watkins, L.A. and Newport Beach, Calif., 1970-77, ptnr., 1977—2005. Arbitrator Orange County Superior Ct., Santa Ana, Calif., 1978—88, judge pro tem, 1979—87. Fin. dir. St. Elizabeth Ann Seton Parish, Irvine, Calif., 1975-82; sec. Turtlerock Tennis Com., Irvine, 1981-83, 86—, pres., 1985-86; bd. dirs. Turtlerock Terr. Homeowners Assn., 1983-85, 87-89. Mem. Irvine Racquet Club, Indian Ridge Country Club. Democrat. Roman Catholic. Home: 19241 Beckwith Ter Irvine CA 92603 Office: 3315 Fairview Rd Costa Mesa CA 92626

DANIELS, JOHN PETER, lawyer; b. NYC, Feb. 5, 1937; s. Jack Brainard and Isabelle (McConachie) D.; m. Lynn Eldridge, Aug. 28, 1978 (div. Jan. 1980); m. Susan Gurley, Apr. 1, 1983. AB, Dartmouth Coll., 1959; JD, U. So. Calif., 1963. Bar: Calif. 1964; diplomate Am. Bd. Trial Advocates. Assoc. Bolton, Groff and Dunne, LA, 1964-67, Jones and Daniels, LA, 1967-70, Acret and Perrochet, LA, 1971-81; ptnr. Daniels, Baratta and Fine, LA, 1982-99, Daniels, Fine, Israel & Schonbuch, LA, 1999—. Mem. Assn. So. Calif. Def. Counsel (bd. dirs. 1975-80), Fedn. Ins and Corp. Counsel. Clubs: Wilshire Country (Los Angeles). Avocations: scuba diving, golf, hunting. Office: Daniels Fine Israel & Schonbuch 1801 Century Park E Fl 9 Los Angeles CA 90067-2302 Office Phone: 310-556-7900. Business E-Mail: daniels@dfis-law.com.

DANIELS, JOHN R., oncologist, educator; b. Detroit, May 9, 1938; BA, Stanford U., 1959, MD, 1964. Diplomate Am. Bd. Internal Medicine. Postdoctoral fellow dept. cell biology Albert Einstein Coll. Medicine, 1964; intern in medicine Stanford U. Sch. Medicine, 1964-65; rsch. assoc. Nat. Inst. Dental Rsch., NIH, 1966-69; sr. resident in medicine Stanford U. Sch. Medicine, 1969-70, instr. div. oncology, 1970-71, asst. prof. div. oncology, 1971-78, clin. assoc. prof. div. oncology, 1978-79; v.p. for sci. and tech. affairs Collagen Corp., 1978-79; CEO, dir. Target Therapeutics, 1985-89; assoc. prof. medicine div. oncology U. So. Calif. Sch. Medicine, LA, 1979—, assoc. prof. radiology, 1990—. Bd. dirs. Collagen Corp. Contbr. over 85 articles to profl. jours.; 9 patents in field. Mem. Am. Assn. for Cancer Rsch., Am. Soc. Clin. Oncology. Home: 842 N Las Casas Ave Pacific Palisades CA 90272-2340

DANIELS, LORI S., state legislator, insurance agent; b. Burlingame, Calif., Nov. 5, 1955; d. Robert William and Sue Ann (McCowen) McCroskey; m. Stephen L. Daniels, June 19, 1976 (div. June 1980). Student, Ariz. State U., 1973-76; BA in Mgmt., U. Phoenix, 1994. CLU. Trainer Campus Crusade for Christ, San Bernadino, Calif., 1977-79; with instalment loans dept. Ariz. Bank, Mesa, 1979-80; ins. agt. State Farm Ins., Chandler, Ariz., 1980—; mem. Ariz. Ho. Reps., 1992-00; majority leader Ariz. Ho. Reps., Dist. 6, 1997-00; mem. Ariz. Senate, Dist. 6, Phoenix, 2001—. Bus. cons. Jr. Achievement, Mesu, 1987-92; mem. various com. including ways and means, rules, 1997—. V.p. Valley of Sun United Way, Phoenix, 1991-93, chmn. Chandler Area Reg. Coun., 1991-92. Recipient Small Bus. Person of Yr. award Gilbert C. of C., 1989. Mem. Chandler C. of C. (v.p. cmty. devel. 1991-92, v.p. membership svc., 1992-93, Pres.'s award 1990, Chamber cup 1992). Republican. Office: 1700 W Washington St Ste 110 Phoenix AZ 85007-2812 Home: 1690 W Grand Canyon Dr Chandler AZ 85248-4817

DANIELS, RICHARD MARTIN, public relations executive; b. Delano, Calif., Feb. 24, 1942; s. Edward Martin and Philida Rose (Peterson) D.; m. Kathryn Ellen Knight, Feb. 28, 1976; children: Robert Martin, Michael Edward. AA, Foothill Coll., 1965; BA, San Jose State U., 1967; MA, U. Mo., 1971. News reporter Imperial Valley Press, El Centro, Calif., summers 1963-66, San Diego Evening Tribune, 1967-68, Columbia (Mo.) Daily Tribune, 1969-70; nat. news copy editor Los Angeles Times, 1966-67; staff writer San Diego Union, 1971-74, real estate editor, 1974-77; v.p. pub. rels. Hubbert Advt. & Pub. Rels., Costa Mesa, Calif., 1977-78; ptnr. Berkman & Daniels, San Diego, 1979-91; prin. Nuffer, Smith, Tucker, Inc., 1991-94, RMD Comms., 1994-97, 99—; exec. dir. comms. San Diego City Schs., 1997-99; prin. RMD Comms., 1999—. Lectr. various bus. groups and colls. Chmn. bd. dirs. March of Dimes San Diego County, 1984-87; bd. dirs. Nat. Coun. Vols., 1983-91 2005—; past pres. Escondido Rotary Club, 1995—, past. chmn. Escondido C. of C.; coun. mem. Escondido City Coun., 2006—; mayor Pro Team, 2008-. Served with USN, 1959-62. Mem. Pub. Rels. Soc. Am. (accredited), Counselors Acad. Republican. Office Phone: 760-738-1890. E-mail: dick@rmdcomm.com.

DANIELS, RONALD DALE, conductor; b. San Mateo, Calif., Aug. 19, 1943; s. Worth W. and Margurite Pearl (Chandler) D.; 1 child, Ryan Stark. BMus, San Francisco Conservatory, 1968. Condr., music dir. Musical Arts of Contra Costa (Calif.) County, 1968-75, U. Calif., Berkeley, 1973-75, Contra Costa Symphony, 1976-79, Reno (Nev.) Philharm., 1979-98, conductor Laureate, 1998—. Guest conductor various orchs.; grants rev. cons. in field. With USMC, 1966. Recipient Lucien Wulsin award Baldwin Piano Co., Tanglewood Festival, 1968, Gov.'s Art award State of Nev., 1981. Avocations: ice skating, skiing, sailing, hiking, astronomy. Office: Reno Philharm Assn Ste 3 925 Riverside Dr Reno NV 89503 Home: 19430 SE 30th St Camas WA 98607-9437

DANIELSON, JUDITH A., state legislator; b. Boise, Dec. 30, 1951; m. John Danielson; children: Jason, Jaymee. Student, Boise State U., U. Idaho, Long Beach City Coll. Nurse/LPN, 1971-81; dep. sheriff for juvenile offenders; mem. Idaho Ho. of Reps., Boise, 1989-94, Idaho Senate, Dist. 8, 1994—. Past Boise County Commr.; past City Coun. pres.; vice chair resources and environment com.; mem. fin., health and welfare, and transp. coms. Active bicycle safety program for Boy Scouts. Mem. Ida-Ore Planning Devel. Assn. (v.p.), PTA, Idaho Assn. Pvt. Industry Couns. (past chair), Adams County Devel. Corp. Republican. Office: State Capitol PO Box 83720 Boise ID 83720-3720

DANIHER, JOHN M., retired engineer; b. LaJunta, Colo., Aug. 2, 1926; s. Gerald and Mary Isabelle (Manly) Daniher; m. Edna Erle Hoshall, Sept. 4, 1948; children: Lyn Mari, Suzanne Laurie, Patricia Gail, Jerome Matthew, Michael Kevin. AB, Western State Coll., Gunnison, Colo., 1948; postgrad., Idaho State U., 1957—74, U. Idaho, 1974—76. H.S. tchr., Grand Junction, Colo., 1948—52; salesman Century Metalcraft, Denver, 1952—53; chem. plant supr. U.S. Chem. Corps., Denver, 1953—56; sr. engr. instrument and controls Phillips Petroleum Co., Idaho Falls, 1956—76; project engr. E G & G Idaho, Idaho Falls, 1976—85, engring. specialist, 1985—91. Adv. Ea. Idaho Vocat. Tech. Sch., 1975—80. Cubmaster Boy Scouts Am., 1970—75, asst. scoutmaster, 1975—80; v.p. Bonneville Unit Am. Cancer Soc., 1994, pres., v.p., 1995—. Recipient Cub Man of Yr. award, Bo Scouts Am., 1973. Mem.: Am. Nuc. Soc., KC (state dep. 1979—81, Supreme coun. 1979—84, 1994). Roman Catholic. Home: 250 12th St Idaho Falls ID 83404-5370 Home Phone: 208-522-8472.

DANIS, MARK WILMOT, lawyer; AB in Philosophy, U. Calif., Berkeley, 1982; JD magna cum laude, U. Calif., 1989. Bar: Calif. 1990. Software programmer Automatic Data Processing; law clk. to Hon. Lawrence W. Pierce U.S. Ct. Appeals, second cir., 1989—90; ptnr. Morrison & Foerster LLP, San Diego, co-mng. ptnr. ops. Guest speaker joint meeting San Diego & Orange County Intellectual Property Law Assns., 2000. Mem.: San Diego County Bar Assn., Assn. Bus. Trial Lawyers, San Diego Intellectual Property Law Assn., Calif. State Bar. Office: Morrison Foerster Llp 12531 High Bluff Dr San Diego CA 92130-3014 Office Phone: 858-720-5108. Office Fax: 858-720-5125. Business E-Mail: mdanis@mofo.com.

DANN, FRANCIS JOSEPH, dermatologist, educator; b. NYC, Aug. 26, 1946; s. Richard William and Helen (Brennan) D. BA, Columbia U., 1968, MD, 1972. Bd. cert. dermatologist Am. Bd. Dermatology. Pvt. practice specializing in dermatology, 1976-99; asst. clin. prof. dermatology UCLA, 1993—. Recognized expert med. reviewer State of Calif., 1995; specialized tng. in leprosy USPHS Hosp., Carville, La., 1972, 95. Contbr. articles to profl. and med. jours. Recipient Cert. of Appreciation for charitable med. missions to The Philippines, 1986, 88, 92. Mem. AMA, Am. Acad. Dermatology, Philippine Med. Assn. Hawaii, L.A.-Metro Dermatology Soc., Pacific Dermatology Soc., L.A. Acad. Medicine (bd. dirs. 1995-99), Aloha Med. Mission. Roman Catholic. Avocations: sports, photography.

DANNER, BRYANT CRAIG, lawyer; b. Boston, Nov. 18, 1937; s. Nevin Earle and Marjorie (Harms) D.; m. Judith I. Baker, Aug. 23, 1958; 1 child Debra Irene. BA, Harvard U., 1960, LLB, 1963. Bar: Calif. 1963, U.S. Dist. Ct. (cen. dist.) Calif. 1963. Assoc. Latham & Watkins, LA, 1963-70, ptnr., 1970-92; sr. v.p., gen. counsel So. Calif. Edison Co., Rosemead, Calif., 1992-95, exec. v.p., gen. counsel, 1995—2005, Edison Internat., Rosemead, 2000—05. Mem. L.A. County Bar Assn. (chmn. environ. sect. 1988-89). Avocations: fly fishing, astronomy.

DANOFF, ERIC MICHAEL, lawyer; b. Waukegan, Ill., June 30, 1949; m. Barbara Madsen, May 27, 1979; children: Nicholas Madsen Danoff, Alexander Madsen Danoff. AB, Dartmouth Coll., 1971; JD, U. Calif., Berkeley, 1974. Bar: Calif. 1974, U.S. Dist. Ct. (no., cen., ea. and so. dists.) Calif., U.S. Ct. Appeals (9th cir.), U.S. Supreme Ct. Assoc. Graham & James, San Francisco, 1974-80, ptnr., 1981-97, Kaye, Rose & Ptnrs., San Francisco, 1998-2001, Emard Danoff

PortTamulski & Paetzold LLP, San Francisco, 2001—. Contbr. articles to profl. publs. Mem. Maritime Law Assn. Office: Emard Danoff Port Tamulski & Paetzold LLP Ste 400 49 Stevenson St San Francisco CA 94105 Office Phone: 415-227-9455. E-mail: edanoff@edptlaw.com.

DANOPOULOS, CONSTANTINE P., political science professor; b. Agios Vassilis, Arcadia, Greece, Feb. 22, 1948; arrived in USA, 1966, naturalized; s. Panos Constantine and Athanasia Panos Danopoulos; m. Vickie Sachs, Jan. 25, 1975; children: Peter Constantine, Andrew Constantine. PhD in Polit. Sci., U. Mo., Columbia, 1980. Prof. polit. sci. Southwest Mo. State U., 1978—80, Ball State U., Ind., 1980—82, San Jose State U., Calif., 1983—. Contbr. articles to profl. jours. Pres., chair Rsch. Com. Armed Forces & Soc., San Jose, 1994—2000. Fulbright Scholar, Greece, Fulbright Commn., 2008. Mem.: Internat. Polit. Sci. Assn. (life; mem. exec. bd., rsch. com. on armed forces 2000—07). Independent. Greek Orthodox. Avocations: travel, writing, cooking. Office: San Jose State Univ One Washington Sq San Jose CA 95192-0119 Office Fax: 408-924-5556. Personal E-mail: danopoulos@comcast.net. Business E-Mail: cdanopou@email.sjsu.edu.

DANZIGER, BRUCE EDWARD, structural engineer; b. NYC, Feb. 14, 1964; s. Frederick Benjamin Danziger and Elise Lee (Saranow) Gold. BS in Archtl. Engring., Calif. Poly. U., 1988. Lic. structural engr. Calif. Assoc. prin. Ove Arup & Ptnrs., London, 1988-90, assoc. Sevilla, Spain, 1990-92, LA, 1992-93, 2002—, NYC, 1993-97, San Francisco, 1997—2002, project engr., 2002—. Mem. faculty So. Calif. Inst. Architecture; Bedford vis. prof. RPI, 2006—. Recipient 1st prize MakMax Membrane Design Competition, 1993, Hon. Mention award, 1995, 96, Bamboo Bridge Honor award Am. Inst. Architects, 2006. Office: ARUP 12777 W Jefferson Blvd Ste 200 Los Angeles CA 90066 Office Phone: 310-578-4182. Business E-Mail: bruce.danziger@arup.com.

DANZIGER, JAMES NORRIS, political science professor; b. LA, May 28, 1945; s. Edward and Beverly Jane Danziger; m. Lesley Robson, June 12, 1971; children: Nicholas James, Vanessa Margaret. BA, Occidental Coll., LA, 1966; MA, Sussex U., Brighton, Eng., 1968; MA, PhD, Stanford U., 1974. Prof. polit. sci. U. Calif., Irvine, 1972—, chmn. dept. polit. sci., 1974-76, 81-83, 88-92, assoc. dean Sch. Social Scis., 1978-81, chmn. acad. senate, 1994-95, dean of undergrad. edn., 1995-99; rsch. assoc. Ctr. Rsch. Info. Tech. and Orgns., Irvine, 1974—, dir., 2000-01, assoc. dir., 2001—; scholar-in-residence LaVerne (Calif.) U., 1983-84. Vis. prof. U. Pitts., 1996, Aarhus (Denmark) U., 1985, U. Va., 2008. Author: Making Budgets, 1978, Understanding the Political World, 1991, 9th edit.; co-author: Computers and Politics, 1982, People and Computers, 1986; mem. editl. bd. Local Govt. Studies, 1981—2003; assoc. editor Social Sci. Computer Rev., 1987-92; mem. editl. bd. Internat. Jour. Electronic Govt. Rsch. Bd. dirs. South Laguna Civic Assn., 1983-86, chair South Laguna Annexation Task Force, 1986, bd. dirs. Irvine Campus Housing Authority, 1996-2004. Recipient Disting. Teaching award U. Calif., 1979, Daniel Aldrich disting. svc. award, 1997; Marshall scholar Govt. of U.K., 1966-68; named Disting. Faculty Lectr. U. Calif. Acad. Senate, 1987, IBM Faculty fellow, 2003—; NSF grantee, 1973-79, 80-83, 1996-98, 99—. Mem. Am. Polit. Sci. Assn. (Leonard White award 1974), ASPA (Marshall Dimock award 1977), Phi Beta Kappa (pres. local chpt. 1988-89, sec.-treas. local chpt. 1996-99, Pi Sigma Alpha (pres. local chpt. 1987—). Avocations: travel, basketball, literature. Office: U Calif Sch Social Scis Irvine CA 92697-5100 Office Phone: 949-824-5533. E-mail: danziger@uci.edu.

DANZIGER, LOUIS, graphic designer, educator; b. NYC, 1923; m. Dorothy Patricia Smith, 1954. Student, Art Ctr. Sch., Los Angeles, 1946-47, New Sch., NYC, 1947-48. Asst. art dir. War Assets Adminstrn., Los Angeles, 1946-47; designer Esquire mag., NYC, 1948; freelance designer, cons. Los Angeles, 1949—; instr. graphic design Art Ctr. Coll. Design, Los Angeles, 1952-60, 86—, Chouinard Art Inst., Los Angeles, 1960-72; instr. Calif. Inst. Arts, 1972-88, head graphic design program, 1972-82; vis. prof. Harvard U., Cambridge, Mass., summers 1978-80, 83, 84, 86-88; instr. Art Ctr. Coll. Design. Mem. graphic evaluation panel Fed. Design Program, Nat. Endowment Arts, 1975—; design cons. Los Angeles County Mus. Art, 1957— Served with cav. U.S. Army, 1943-45; PTO Recipient Disting. Achievement award Contemporary Art Coun., L.A. County Mus. Art, 1982, Disting. Designer award NEA, 1985, "Stars of Design" Lifetime Achievement award Pacific Design Ctr., 1997, numerous awards and medals in art design. Mem. Alliance Graphique Internationale, Am. Inst. Graphic Arts (medal 1998), Am. Ctr. for Design (hon.). Home: PO Box 660189 Arcadia CA 91066-0189

DARABONT, FRANK, screenwriter, director; b. Montebeliard, France, Jan. 28, 1959; Screenwriter: (films) (with Wes Craven, Chuck Russell, and Bruce Wagner) A Nightmare on Elm Street 3: Dream Warriors, 1987, (with Russell) The Blob, 1988, (with Mick Garris, Jim Wheat, and Ken Wheat) The Fly II, 1989, (with Steph Lady) Mary Shelley's Frankenstein, 1994; dir.: (TV movies) Till Death Do Us Part, 1990, Buried Alive, 1990, (TV series) The Young Indiana Jones Chronicles, 1992-; screenwriter, dir.: (films) The Shawshank Redemption, 1994 (Academy award nomination best adapted screenplay 1994, Humanitas prize for best screenplay), The Green Mile, 1999, The Majestic (also prodr.), 2001, The Mist (also prodr.), 2007, exec. prodr., writer: (TV movies) Black Cat Run

DARBEE, PETER A., utilities executive; b. 1954; BA in Econ., MBA, Darmouth Coll.; Nuclear Reactor Technology Program, MIT. Mgmt. Salomon Brothers, AT&T; investment banker, v.p. Goldman Sachs; v.p., CFO, controller Pacific Bell; v.p., CFO Advance Fibre Commns., Inc.; sr. v.p., CFO, treas. PG&E Corp., 1999—2005, pres., CEO, 2005, chmn., CEO, 2006—. Mem. San Francisco Com. on Jobs. Office: PG&E 1 Market Spear Tower San Francisco CA 94105

DARBY, G(EORGE) HARRISON, lawyer; b. NYC, Jan. 24, 1942; s. Stephen John and Madge B. (Leh) D. BA, Muhlenberg Coll., 1963; LLB, Bklyn. Law Sch., 1967. Bar: N.Y. 1967. Of counsel Jackson Lewis LLP, L.A. and other offices, 1967—. Mem. child adv. group Internat. Inst. of L.A., 1989-96. Office: Jackson Lewis LLP 725 South Figueroa St Los Angeles CA 90017-5408

DARBY, MICHAEL RUCKER, economist, educator; b. Dallas, Nov. 24, 1945; s. Joseph Jasper and Frances Adah (Rucker) D.; children: Margaret Loutrel, David Michael; Lynne Ann Zucker-Darby, 1992; stepchildren: Joshua R. Zucker, Danielle T. Zucker. AB summa cum laude, Dartmouth Coll., 1967; MA, U. Chgo., 1968, PhD, 1970. Asst. prof. econ. Ohio State U., 1970-73; vis. asst. prof. econ. UCLA, 1972-73, assoc. prof., 1973-78, prof., 1978-87, 96—, prof. Anderson Grad. Sch. Mgmt., 1987-94, Warren C. Cordner prof. money and fin. mkts., 1995—, vice-chmn., 1992-93; dir. John M. Olin Ctr. for Policy, 1993—; assoc. dir. orgnl. rsch. program UCLA Inst. for Social Sci. Rsch., 1995—2000; assoc. dir. Ctr. Internat. Sci., Tech., Cultural Policy Sch. Pub. Affairs, UCLA, 1996—; rsch. assoc. Nat. Bur. Econ. Rsch., 1976-86, 92—; asst. sec. for econ. policy U.S. Dept. Treasury, Washington, 1986-89; mem. Nat. Commn. on Superconductivity, 1988-89; under sec. for econ. affairs U.S. Dept. Commerce, Washington, 1989-92; adminstr. Econs. and Stats. Adminstrn., 1990-92. V.p., dir. Paragon Industries, Inc., Dallas, 1964—83; mem. exec. com. Western Econ. Assn., 1987—90, v.p., 1998—99, pres.-elect, 1999—2000, pres., 2000—01; chmn. The Dumbarton Group, 1992—; adj. scholar Am. Ent. Inst. for Pub. Policy Rsch., 1992—; economist stats. income divsn. IRS, 1992—94; mem. regulatory coord. adv. com. Commodity Futures Trading Commn., 1992—96. Author: Macroeconomics, 1976, Have Controls Ever Worked: The Post-War Record, 1976, Intermediate Macroeconomics, 1979, 2d edit., 1986, The Effects of Social Security on Income and the Capital Stock, 1979, The International Transmission of Inflation, 1981, Labor Force, Employment, and Productivity in Historical Perspective, 1984, Reducing Poverty in America: Views and Approaches, 1996; editor Jour. Internat. Money and Fin., 1981-86, mem. editl. bd., 1986—; mem. editl. bd. Am. Econ. Rev., 1983-86, Contemporary Policy Issues, 1990-93, Contemporary Econ. Policy, 1994—, Internat. Reports, 1992—. Bd. dirs. The Opera Assoc., 1992—; mem. acad. adv. bd. Ctr. Regulation and Econ. Growth of the Alexis de Tocqueville Instn., 1993-96. Recipient Alexander Hamilton award U.S. Treasury Dept., 1989; sr. fellow Dartmouth Coll., 1966-67, Woodrow Wilson fellow, 1967-68, NSF grad. fellow, 1967-69, FDIC grad. fellow, 1969-70, Harry Scherman rsch. fellow Nat. Bur. Econ. Rsch., 1974-75, vis. fellow Hoover Instn., Stanford U., 1977-78. Mem. AAAS, Am. Econ. Assn., Am. Fin. Assn., Am. Statis. Assn., Am. Law & Econs. Assn., Nat. Assn. Bus. Economists, Royal Econ. Soc., So. Econ. Assn., Western Econ. Assn., N.Y. Acad. Scis., Capitol Hill Club (D.C.), Nat. Econ. Club. Episcopalian. Office: UCLA Anderson Grad Sch Mgmt Los Angeles CA 90095-0001 Home: 7044 Judi St Dallas TX 75252-6120

DARDEN, CHRISTOPHER ALLEN, lawyer, writer; b. Martinez, Calif., Apr. 7, 1956; m. Marcia Carter, Aug. 31, 1997. BA in Criminal Justice, Calif. State U., San Jose; JD, U. Calif., San Francisco, 1980. Bar: Calif. 1980. Former atty. Nat. Labor Rels. Bd.; former asst. head dep. in spl. investigations divsn. L.A. County Dist. Attys. Office, former dep. dist. atty. in maj. crimes divsn.; actor, writer, 1996—; faculty Calif. State Univ., Los Angeles, 1995; assoc. prof. law Sch. Law Southwestern U., LA, 1996—99; atty. Darden & Assoc., Los Angeles, 1999—. Former legal commentator NBC, CNBC and CNN. Author: (with Jess Walter) In Contempt, 1996; author (with Dick Lochte) The Trials of Nikki Hill, 1999, L.A. Justice, 2000, The Last Defense, 2002, Lawless, 2004. Recipient Crystal Heart award, Loved Ones of Homicide Victims, 1998, Humanitarian of the Year, Eli Home, 2000. Mem.: Am. Trial Lawyers Assn., Nat. Bar Assn. (life). Office: Darden & Associates 5757 W Century Blvd Los Angeles CA 90045 Office Phone: 310-568-1804. Business E-Mail: dardenatty@aol.com.

DARDEN, EDWIN SPEIGHT, SR., architect; b. Stantonsburg, NC, Oct. 14, 1920; s. Edwin Speight and Sallie (Jordan) D.; m. s. Pauline K. Bartlett, Feb. 26, 1944; children: Edwin Speight III, Judith Ann, Diane Russell. BS in Archtl. Engring., Kans. State U., 1947. Registered architect, Calif. Assoc., Fred L. Swartz and William G. Hyberg, Fresno, Calif., 1949-59; ptnr. Nargis and Darden (Architects), Fresno, 1959-69; pres. Edwin S. Darden Assocs., Inc., Fresno, 1969-85, cons., 1985—2005. Bd. dirs. Murphy Bank; mem. state adv. bd. Office of Architecture and Constrn., 1970-78; cons. ednl. facilities, 1975—. Prin. works include Clovis (Calif.) High Sch., 1969, Clovis W. High Sch., 1976, Ahwahnee Jr. High Sch., Fresno, 1966, Tehipite Jr. High Sch., Fresno, 1973, Fresno County Dept. Health, 1978, Floyd B. Buchanan Edn. Ctr., Clovis, 1990. Served to 1st lt. C.E., AUS, 1942-46. Fellow AIA; mem. Sigma Phi Epsilon, Alpha Kappa Psi. Clubs: Fresno Rotary. Presbyterian. Office: Edwin S Darden Associates Inc 6790 N West Ave #104 Fresno CA 93711-1393 E-mail: esda@pacbell.net.

DARLING, JUANITA MARIE, correspondent; b. Columbus, Ohio, Apr. 7, 1954; d. Robert Lewis and Joanne Mae (Oiler) D. BA in L.Am. Studies, BA in Comms., Calif. State U., Fullerton, 1976; MA in Internat. Journalism, U. So. Calif., LA, 1989; bur. chief, L.A. Times, Ctrl. America. Reporter Daily News Tribune, Fullerton; bus. editor The News, Mexico City; reporter Orange County Register, Santa Ana, Calif.; corr. L.A. Times, Mexico City, El Salvador, Cen. Am. bur. chief. Office: LA Times Times Mirror Sq Los Angeles CA 90053

DARLING-HAMMOND, LINDA, education professor; b. Cleve., Dec. 21, 1951; BA magna cum laude, Yale U., 1973; EdD in Urban Edn., Temple U., 1978. Dir., sr. social scientist Edn. & Human Resources Program RAND Corp., 1985—89; William F. Russell prof. edn. Columbia U. Teacher's Coll., 1989—98, co-dir. Nat. Ctr. for Restructuring Edn., Schools and Teaching, 1989—98; Charles Ducommon prof. teaching & teaching edn. Stanford U., 1998—, prin. investigator, co-dir., Sch. Redesign Network (SRN) & Stanford Leadership Inst., 2000—. Chair stds. drafting panel Coun. Chief State Sch. Officers, Interstate New Tchr. Assessment and Support Consortium, 1991—; mem. Nat. Adv. Commn., The Coll. Bd., Equity 2000, 1993—, Carnegie Corp. Task Force on Learing in the Primary Grades, 1994—; exec. dir. Nat. Commn. on Tchg. and America's Future, 1994—2001, bd. mem., 2001—; mem. adv. bd. Ctr. for Policy Rsch. in Edn., 1996—; mem. tech. rev. panel for the schools an staffing survey US Dept. Edn., 1997—; mem. Internat. Adv. Coun., San Francisco Exploratorium, 1998—; faculty sponsor Stan Stanford Teaching Edn. Program, 1998—2004; co-chair Calif. Profl. Devel. Task Force, 2000; mem. advisory bd. George Lucas Edn. Found., 2000—, Ctr. for Teaching Quality, 2001—; bd. mem. Alliance for Excellent Edn., 2005—; prin. investigator, co-dir. Stanford Ctr. for Opportunity Policy in Edn. (SCOPE), 2008—; mem. advisory bd. Nat. Coun. for Educating Black Children, 2007; mem. advisory panel Nat. Staff Devel. Coun., 2007—; mem. Coun. Chief State School Officers Formative Assessment Advisory Group, 2007—. Co-author (with Jacqueline Ancess and Beverly Falk): Authentic Assessment in Action: Studies of Schools and Students at Work, 1995; author: The Right to Learn: A Blueprint for Creating Schools that Work, 1997 (Am. Ednl. Rsch. Assn. Outstanding Book award, 1998), Instructional Leadership for Systemic Change: The Story of San Diego's Reform, 2005, Powerful Teacher Education, 2006; editor: Professional Development Schools: Schools for Developing a Profession, 1994; co-editor (with Gary Sykes): Teaching as the Learning Profession: A Handbook of Policy and Practice, 1999 (Nat. Staff Devel. Coun. Outstanding Book award, 2000); co-editor: (with John Bransford) Preparing Teachers for a Changing World: What Teachers Should Learn and Be Able to Do, 2005; contbr. articles to profl. jours. Mem.: Nat. Acad. Edn. (chair com. on tchr. edn. 2000—). Office: Stanford Univ Sch Edn 485 Lasuen Mall Stanford CA 94305-3096 E-mail: ldh@stanford.edu.

DARMSTANDLER, HARRY MAX, retired military officer; b. Indpls., Aug. 9, 1922; s. Max M. and Nonna (Holden) D.; m. Donna L. Bender, Mar. 10, 1957; children: Paul William, Thomas Alan. BS, U. Omaha, 1964; MS, George Washington U., 1965; grad., Nat. War Coll., 1965. Commd. 2d lt. USAAF, 1943; advanced through grades to maj. gen. USAF, 1973; served with 15th Air Force, 1943, 5th Air Force, Republic of Korea, 1952; comdr.-in-chief Pacific, 1960—63; served with joint chiefs of staff, 1965—68; supreme comdr. Allied Powers Europe, 1969—71; comdr. 12th Air Divsn. SAC, 1972, dep. chief of staff for plans, 1973; spl. asst. to chief of staff USAF, 1974—75; chmn. bd., CEO Rancho Bernardo Savs. Bank, San Diego, 1983—90; ptnr. Allied Assocs., Colorado Springs, Colo., 1968—, D & H Inc., Woodland Park, Colo., 1979—; founding ptnr. Assocs. Group, San Diego, 1995—2005. Cons. Mid East matters and bd. dirs. Palomar Pomerado Health Found, San Diego; bd. dirs. Clean Found., San Diego. Author numerous articles on nat. def. requirements. Elder, Rancho Bernardo Community Presbyn. Ch., San Diego. Decorated D.S.M. with oak leaf cluster, Legion of Merit with oak leaf cluster, D.F.C., Air medal with 2 oak leaf clusters; research fellow UCLA, 1969. Mem. AIAA, Order Daedalians, Soc. Strategic Air Command, Eagle Scout Alumni Assn., Bernardo Heights Country Club (San Diego, past pres.), Phi Tau Alpha. Home: La Jolla Village Towers 8515 Costa Verde Blvd #1958 San Diego CA 92122 Personal E-mail: dhank32@sbcglobal.net.

DARNELL, RAY D., city official; Dir. Rio Grande Zool. Park, Albuquerque; dir. cultural svcs. dept. City of Albuquerque, 2000—; dir. Albuquerque Biological Park, Albuquerque, N.M. Office: City of Albuquerque PO Box 1293 Albuquerque NM 87103-1293

DARRINGTON, DENTON C., state legislator; b. Burley, Idaho, Apr. 30, 1940; son of Clifford H Darrington & Ila Crossley D; married 1963 to Virgene Kay Lind; children: Lyn, Dee, Kim, Kae & Matt. BS, Utah State, 1963. Committeeman, Declo Precinct, 76-78; chairman, Cassia Co Republican Committee, Idaho, currently; finance chairman, Declo Hist Committee, currently; Idaho State Senator, District 24 & 25, 1982-2002, chairman, judiciary & rules comt, currently, member, health & welfare, state affairs comts, currently, Idaho State Senate; Idaho State Senator, District 27, 2003-. Farmer & teacher, currently. Co-ed, Declo, My Town, My People, Declo Hist Comt, 74; Forgotten Trails, Cora Lind, 79. Idaho's Outstanding Republican Co Chairman, Republican Hall of Fame, 80; Outstanding Republican Legislator, Republican Hall of Fame, 86; Friend of Agriculture Award, Farm Bureau, 87-88 & 91-92; Outstanding Citizen, Farmer, Businessman, Burley Chamber of Commerce. Cassia Co Farm Bureau; Declo Sch Alumni Association; Cassia Co Hist Soc. Republican. Mem Lds Church. Address: 302 S Hwy 77 Declo ID 83323 Office: State Capitol Bldg PO Box 83720 Boise ID 83720-0081 Home Phone: 208-654-2712; Office Phone: 208-332-1000. Fax: 208-334-5397. E-mail: infocntr@lso.state.id.us.

DASENBROCK, REED WAY, state official, former academic administrator, literature educator; b. Sept. 18, 1953; Degree, McGill U., Oxford U.; PhD, Johns Hopkins U., 1982. Asst. prof. N.Mex. State U., Las Cruces, 1982—86, assoc. prof., 1986—91, prof. Eng., 1991—2001, dept. head, 1994; prof. English & dean Coll. Arts & Sci. U. N. Mex., Albuquerque, 2001—05, interim provost & v.p. acad. affairs, 2005—06, provost & v.p. acad. affairs, 2006—07; cabinet sec. higher end. N.Mex. Higher Edn. Dept., Santa Fe, 2007—. Jerome S. Cardin vis. chair humanities Loyola Coll., Md., 1992—93. Author (or editor): of 8 books & over 100 scholarly papers. Office: NMex Higher Edn Dept NMex Sch for Deaf campus 1068 Cerrillos Rd Santa Fe NM 87505-1650 Office Phone: 505-476-6500. Office Fax: 505-476-6511.

DASHIELL, G. RONALD, protective services official; US marshal US Dist. Ct. (ea. dist.) Wash., Spokane. Office: US Courthouse 920 W Riverside Ave Ste 888 Spokane WA 99201-1008

DATE, ELAINE SATOMI, physiatrist, educator; b. San Jose, Calif., Feb. 19, 1957; BS, Stanford U., 1978; MD, Med. Coll. Pa., 1982. Diplomate of Nat. Bd. Med. Examiners. Diplomate Am. Bd. Phys. Medicine and Rehab. Dir. phys. medicine and rehab. Stanford U. Sch. Medicine, Calif., 1985—, rehab. medicine sect. chief, 1988-90, head phys. medicine and rehab. div., 1990—, assoc. prof. dept. functional rehab., 1995—; rehab. medicine chief Palo Alto VA Med. Ctr., Calif., 1988—. Fellow Am. Acad. Phys. Medicine and Rehab., Am. Assn. Electromyography and Electrodiagnosis. Avocations: reading, jogging.

DATTA, SUBHENDU K., mechanical engineer, educator; b. Howrah, India, Jan. 15, 1936; s. Srish Chandra and Prabhabati Datta; m. Bishakha Roy; 1 child, Kinshuk. BSc with honors, Presidency Coll., Kolkata, 1954; MSc, Calcutta U., 1956; PhD, Jadavpur U., 1962. Lectr. Math. Rsch. Ctr., Madison, Wis., 1962—63; postdoctoral fellow Rensselaer Poly. Inst., Troy, NY, 1963—64; asst. prof. Indian Inst. Tech., Kanpur, 1965—67, U. Manitoba, Winnipeg, Canada, 1967—68; from asst. prof. to prof. U. Colo., Boulder, 1968—2007, prof. emeritus, 2007—. Vis. asst. prof. U. Colo., Boulder, 1964—65; cons. Nat. Inst. Stds. and Tech., Boulder, Colo., 1985—2004. Contbr. articles to profl. jours.; author: Elastic Waves in Composite Media and Structures. Recipient Fulbright award, 1962, 1996; grantee, NSF, 1970—88, Office of Naval Rsch., 1985—92, Dept. Energy, 1995—2003. Fellow: ASME, Am. Acad. Mechanics (bd. dir. 1995—98). Home: 4670 Holiday Dr Unit 301 Boulder CO 80304 Office: Univ Colo Ucb 427 Boulder CO 80309-0427 Business E-Mail: subhendu.datta@colorado.edu.

DATYE, ABHAYA KRISHNA, chemical and nuclear engineer, educator; B in Tech., Indian Inst. Tech., 1975; MS, U. Cin., 1980; PhD, U. Mich., 1984. Asst. prof., assoc. prof. engring. U. N.Mex., Albuquerque, 1984-93, prof. chem. and nuclear engring., 1993—. Dir. Ctr. for Microengineered Ceramics, U. N.Mex., 1994—; tchg. asst. U. Cin., 1978-80; rsch. asst. U. Mich., Ann Arbor, 1980-84; presenter in field; cons. Integrated Circuit Engring. Corp., Scottsdale, Ariz., 1986-88, PDA Engring., Albuquerque, 1986-89, Allied-Signal, Des Plaines, Ill., 1990—, W.R. Grace & Co., Columbia, Md., 1992—, Chevron Rsch., Richmond, Calif., 1992—. Contbr. numerous articles to profl. jours.; reviewer jours. in field. Grantee Sandia Nat. Labs., 1985-87, 87-88, 88-89, 89-91, 91-92, 92-93, 93-94, Engring. Found., 1985-86, NSF, 1987-89, 89-90, 90-93, 92-95, 93-97, Am. Chem. Soc., 1989-90, 91-92, 93-95, Allied Signal, Mobil R&D, Waste Edn. Rsch.

Consortium, 1993-94, 94-95. Mem. AIChE, Am. Chem. Soc., Am. Vacuum Soc. (N.Mex. chpt. chair 1995, Symposium organizer 1994), N.Am. Catalysis Soc. (Symposium organizer Albuquerque 1992, program com. co-chair Snowbird, Utah, 1995), Electron Microscopy Soc. Am. (session co-chmn. 1986, 88). Office: Univ NM NSF Ctr Micro-Engineered Ceramic Farris 203 Albuquerque NM 87131-0001 E-mail: datye@unm.edu.

DAUCHER, DONALD ALFRED, lawyer; b. Buffalo, Apr. 2, 1945; BS, U. Rochester, 1967; JD, Duke U., 1971. Bar: Calif. 1972. Mng. ptnr. Paul, Hastings, Janofsky & Walker, San Diego, 1971—. Mem. Order Coif, Beta Gamma Sigma. Office: Paul Hastings Janofsky & Walker LLP 695 Town Ctr Dr Costa Mesa CA 92626 Office Phone: 714-668-6257. Office Fax: 714-668-6357. Business E-Mail: dondaucher@paulhastings.com.

DAUCHY, CRAIG EDWARD, lawyer; b. San Diego, Mar. 3, 1949; s. Walter E. and Philippa (Robbins) D.; m. Ellen Dauchy, July 12, 1971 (div.); 1 child, Philip A.; m. Lola Sue Crawford, Jan. 25, 1992; children: Winston Scott Crawford, Kendra Crawford. BA, Yale U., 1971; MBA, JD, Stanford U., 1975. Bar: Calif. 1975. Assoc. Cooley Godward LLP, San Francisco, 1975-81, ptnr., 1981—. Bd. dirs. TechLaw Group, Pitts., Arterial Vascular Engring., Santa Rosa, Calif. Co-author: The Entrepreneur's Guide to Business Law, 1997; contbr. articles to mags. Trustee Nueva Sch., Hillsborough, Calif., 1993—; mem. bd. visitors Stanford Law Sch. Mem. ABA, Calif. Bar Assn., San Francisco Bar Assn., Palo Alto Hills Golf and Country Club. Office: Cooley Godward LLP Bldg 5 3000 El Camino Real Palo Alto CA 94306-2197 Office Phone: 650-843-5033. Fax: 650-849-7400. E-mail: cdauchy@cooley.com.

DAUER, DONALD DEAN, investment company executive; b. Fresno, Calif., June 1, 1936; s. Andrew and Erma Mae (Zigenman) D.; m. LaVerne DiBuduo, Jan. 23, 1971; children: Gina, Sarah. BS in Bus. Adminstrn., Calif. State U. Fresno; postgrad., U. Wash., 1964. Loan officer First Savs. and Loan, Fresno, 1961-66, v.p., 1966-71, sr. v.p., 1971-81, exec. v.p., 1978-81; pres. Uniservice Corp., Fresno, 1976-81, Don Dauer Investments, Fresno, 1981—; pres., chief oper. officer Riverbend Internat. Corp., Sanger, Calif., 1985-89. Chmn. bd. dirs. Univ. Savs. and Loan, 1991-92, acting pres., CEO, 1992; loan officer Norwest Mortgage, 1993-95; mgr. CMB Fin., 1995-96. Chmn. bd. dirs. City of Fresno Gen. Svcs. Retirement Bd., 1973-83, West Fresno Econ. and Bus. Devel. Program Bd., 1980-83; pres. bd. dirs. Cen. Calif. United Cerebral Palsy Assn., 1979-82; bd. dirs. Valley Children's Hosp. Found., Fresno, 1984-93; trustee, chmn. Valley Children's Hosp., 1987-93; bd. dirs. Youth for Christ USA, 1988-94, Twilight Haven Inc., 2000—; vice chmn. Riverbend Internat., 1975-91. Mem. Soc. Real Estate Appraisers (past pres.). Office: 2733 W Palo Alto Ave Fresno CA 93711-1110 Office Phone: 559-431-2764. Personal E-mail: dddauer@yahoo.com.

DAUER, EDWARD ARNOLD, law educator; b. Providence, Sept. 28, 1944; s. Marshall and Shirley (Moverman) Dauer; m. Carol Jean Egglestone, June 16, 1966; children: E. Craig, Rachel P. AB, Brown U., 1966; LLB cum laude, Yale U., 1969; MPH, Harvard U., 2001. Bar: Conn. 1978, Colo. 1986. Asst. prof. law sch. U. Toledo, 1969-72; assoc. prof. law U. So. Calif., LA, 1972-74; assoc. prof. Yale U., New Haven, 1975-85, assoc. dean, 1978-83, dep. dean Law Sch., 1983-85; dean, prof. U. Denver, 1985-90, dean emeritus, prof., 1991—2007. Of counsel Popham, Haik, Schnobrich and Kaufman, 1990—97; vis. scholar Harvard U. Sch. Pub. Health, 1996—2004; pres. CEJAD Aviation Corp. Author: (book) Materials on a Nonadversarial Legal Process, 1978, Conflict Resolution Strategies in Health Care, 1993, Manual of Dispute Resolution: ADR Law and Practice, 1994 (CPR Book award, 1994), Health Care Dispute Resolution, 2000; contbr. articles to profl. jours. Founder, pres. Nat. Ctr. Preventive Law; bd. dirs. New Haven Cmty. Action Agy., 1978—81; mem. Colo. Commn. Higher Edn., 1987—91; bd. dirs. Cerebral Palsy Found., Denver, 1989—, pres., 1992—95; commr. Colo. Advanced Tech. Inst., 1989—91; pres. Legacy Found. Cerebral Palsy, 2007—, Common Good Colo., 2007—; exec. dir. Colo. Coalition Patient Safety, 2007—. Recipient W. Quinn Jordan award, Nat. Blood Found., 1994, Paella award, Harvard Sch. Pub. Health, 1996, Sanbar award, Am. Coll. Legal Medicine, 1999. Mem.: Am. Law Inst. (life), Univ. Club, Cherry Creek Athletic Club, Order of Coif. Republican. Home: 127 S Garfield St Denver CO 80209 Office: U Denver Coll Law 2255 E Evans Ave Denver CO 90208 Office Phone: 303-871-6278. Business E-Mail: edauer@law.du.edu.

DAUGHENBAUGH, RANDALL JAY, retired chemical company executive, consultant; b. Rapid City, SD, Feb. 10, 1948; s. Horace Allan and Helen Imogene (Reder) Daughenbaugh; m. Mary R. Wynja, Aug. 25, 1973; children: Jason Allan, Jill Christen. BS, S.D. Tech., 1970; PhD, U. Colo., 1975. Rsch. chemist Air Prod. and Chem., Allentown, Pa., 1975-80; rsch. dir. Chem. Exch. Industries, Boulder, Colo., 1980-83; pres. Hauser Chem. Rsch., Inc., Boulder, 1983-93, chief tech. officer, exec. v.p., 1993-99; ret. Contbr. articles to profl. jours. Recipient IR-100 award, R&D Mag., 1993; named Engrepreneur of the Yr., Inc. Mag., 1992. Mem.: Am. Chem. Soc. Achievements include patents in field. Home: 10755 Sheridan Lake Rd Rapid City SD 57702-6506 Office Phone: 605-343-1126. Personal E-mail: rjdaugh@rapidnet.com.

DAUGHERTY, LEO, literature and language educator; b. Louisville, May 16, 1939; s. F.S. and Mollie Repass (Brown) D.; m. Virginia Upton; 1 child, Mollie Virginia; m. Lee Graham. AB in Fine Arts and Lit., Western Ky. U., 1961; MA in English, U. Ark., 1963; PhD in Am. Lit., Tex. A&M U., 1970; postgrad., Harvard U., 1970-71. Cert. fine arts tchr. Asst. prof. lit. U. Wis., Superior, 1962-63; teaching fellow East Tex. State U., Commerce, 1963-65; asst. prof. lit. Frederick Coll., Portsmouth, Va., 1965-66, Va. State U., Norfolk, 1966-68; prof. lit. and linguistics Evergreen State Coll., Olympia, Wash., 1972—96, prof. emeritus, 1996—; lectr. interdisciplinary studies U. Va., Charlottesville, 2000—. Acad. dean Evergreen State Coll., Olympia, 1975-76, founding dir. Ctr. Study of Sci. and Human Values, 1990—; past grant evaluator NEH. Author: The Teaching of Writing at Evergreen, 1984; contbr. short stories, articles to profl. and literary jours. Active Friends of Bodleian Libr., Oxford, Eng., 1983—; assocs. Alderman Libr., U. Va., 1996—. Recipient NEH award, 1973. Mem.: MLA (life), Soc. Lit. and Sci., Shakespeare Assn. Am., Active Malone Soc. Avocations: painting, aerobics, travel, piano. Office: Univ Va Zehmer Hall Charlottesville VA 22903 Business E-Mail: ld8t@virginia.edu.

DAUGHTON, DONALD, lawyer; b. Grand River, Iowa, Mar. 11, 1932; s. F.J. and Ethel (Edwards) D.; m. Sally Daughton; children by previous marriage: Erin, Thomas, Andrew, J.P. BSc, U. Iowa, 1953, JD, 1956. Bar: Iowa, 1956, Ariz., 1958. Asst. county atty. Polk County, Des Moines, Iowa, 1956, 1958-59; atty. Snell & Wilmer, Phoenix, 1959-64, Browder and Daughton, Phoenix, 1964-65; judge Superior Ct. of Ariz., Phoenix, 1965-67, 97—; atty. Browder Gillenwater and Daughton, Phoenix, 1967-72, Daughton Feinstein and Wilson, Phoenix, 1972-86, Daughton Hawkins and Bacon, Phoenix, 1986-88; resident mng. ptnr. Brian Cave, Phoenix, 1988-92; atty. Daughton Hawkins Brockelman Guinnan and Patterson, Phoenix, 1992-97. Asst. county atty. Polk County, 1958-59 chmn. Phoenix Employees Relations Bd., 1976. Pres. Maricopa County Legal Aid Soc., 1971-73. 1st lt. JAG, USAF, 1956-58. Fellow Am. Bar Found., Ariz. Bar Found. (founder); mem. ABA (bd. govs. 1989-92, exec. com. 1991-92), State Bar Ariz. (chmn. pub. rels. com. 1980-84, jud. evaluation poll com. 1984-94), Iowa State Bar, Maricopa County Bar Assn. (bd. dirs. 1962-64), 9th Cir. Jud. Conf. (lawyer rep. 1981-84, 88), Nat. Acad. Arbitrators, Chartered Inst. Arbitrators, Univ. Club.

DAUM, JOHN F., lawyer; b. Washington, May 9, 1943; BA summa cum laude, Harvard U., 1965; LLB, Yale U., 1969. Bar: D.C. 1971, Calif. 1972. Ptnr. O'Melveny & Myers LLP, LA, mem. policy com. Lectr., fed. cts. and fed. jurisdiction U So. Calif. Law Sch. Mem. Yale Law Jour., 1967—69. Mem. ABA, LA County Bar Assn.(mem. com. of fed. procedure), Order of the Coif, Phi Beta Kappa. Office: O'Melveny & Myers LLP 400 S Hope St Los Angeles CA 90071-2899 Office Phone: 213-430-6111. Office Fax: 213-430-6407. Business E-Mail: jdaum@omm.com.

DAVENPORT, DAVID, lawyer, educator, academic administrator; b. Sheboygan, Wis., Oct. 24, 1950; s. E. Guy and Beverly J. (Snoddy) D.; m. Sally Nelson, Aug. 13, 1977; children— Katherine, Charles, Scott. BA, Stanford U., 1972; JD, U. Kans., 1977. Bar: Calif. 1977, U.S. Dist. Ct. (so. dist.) Calif., 1977. Assoc. Gray, Cary, Ames & Frye, San Diego, 1977—78; min. Ch. of Christ, San Diego, 1979; law prof. Pepperdine U., Malibu, Calif., 1980—99, gen. counsel, 1981—83, exec. v.p., 1983—86, pres., 1985—2000, dist. prof. pub. policy, 2003—. Rsch. fellow Hoover Instn., 2001—. Co-author: Shepherd Leadership; contbr. Fed. Antitrust Law, 1985, articles to profl. jourls. Mem. Adminstrv. Conf. of U.S., Washington, 1984-86; bd. overseers Hoover Inst., Stanford U.; bd. dirs. Am. Internat., Salem Cmty., Forest Lawn Meml. Parks Assn.; bd. dirs. Common Sense Calif., co-chair. Mem. Order of Coif. Republican. Office: Pepperdine U 24255 Pacific Coast Hwy Malibu CA 90263-0002 Business E-Mail: david.davenport@pepperdine.edu.

DAVENPORT, ROGER LEE, research engineer; b. Sacramento, Oct. 27, 1955; s. Lee Edwin and Ada Fern (Henderson) D.; m. Cynthia Ann Carle, June 20, 1998. AB Physics, U. Calif., Berkeley, 1977; MSME, U. Ariz., 1979. Assoc. engr. Solar Energy Rsch. Inst., Golden, Colo., 1979-82; cons. Darmstadt, Fed. Republic Germany, 1982-84; missionary Eastern European Sem., Vienna, Austria, 1984-87; staff researcher Sci. Applications Internat. Corp., San Diego, 1987—. Mem. Am. Solar Energy Soc. (life), Phi Beta Kappa. Office: SAIC 10210 Campus Point Dr M/S A-1 San Diego CA 92121 Home: 541 Crouch St Oceanside CA 92054 Office Phone: 858-826-5079. Business E-Mail: solarguy@cal.berkeley.edu.

DAVENPORT, TERRY DEAN, beverage service company executive, marketing executive; b. Petoskey, Mich., Feb. 8, 1958; s. Dean Davenport; m. Valerie Ann Thomson; 1 child, Kasey Lauren. AA in Comml. Art, Ferris State U., 1978, BS in Mktg., 1980; MA in Advt., Northwestern U., 1982. Pub. designer Ferris State U., Big Rapids, Mich., 1980-81; designer Northwestern U., Evanston, Ill., 1982; asst. account exec. Tracy Wlve, Inc., Dallas, 1982—83, account exec., 1983—84, acct. supr., 1984—85, v.p. group supr., 1985-86; v.p. mgmt. rep. BBDO, Inc., NYC, 1986; v.p. mktg. Taco Bell Corp., Irvine, Calif., 1991—94; sr. v.p. Arby's, Ft. Lauderdale, Fla., 1994—97; chief mktg. officer Einstein Bagels, Golden, Colo., 1997, KFC Corp., 1997—98, chief concept & mktg. officer, 1998—2001, sr. v.p. new concepts, 2001, sr. v.p. for concept design & multibranding; v.p. global brand strategy & mktg. Starbucks Corp., Seattle, 2006—08, sr. v.p. mktg., 2008—. Account mgr.: (TV commls.) Dragnet, Tostitos, 1985 (Clio award). Recipinet Andy award. Avocations: golf, baseball, sailing. Office: Starbucks Corp 2401 Utah Ave S Seattle WA 98134 Office Phone: 206-447-1575. Office Fax: 206-682-7570.

DAVID, CLIVE, events executive; b. Manchester, Eng., June 6, 1934; came to U.S., 1957, naturalized, 1962; s. Marcus Wiener and Claire Rose (Levy) Wiener Kattenburg. Student, Blackpool Tech. Coll., 1951-52, Royal Coll. Art, 1955-57. Designer Chippendale's, London, 1955-57; asst. to pres. pub. relations Maybruck Assocs., NYC, 1959; Ea. regional dir. City of Hope, Phila., 1960-62; pres. Clive David Assocs., NYC, Clive David Enterprises div. Party Enterprises Ltd., Beverly Hills, Calif., Party Enterprises, Ltd., Beverly Hills, 1962—. Lectr. Party Planning par excellence, 1966—. Arranger major parties including Miss Universe Coronation Ball, Miami Beach, 1965, State visit of Queen Elizabeth and Prince Philip, Duke of Edinburgh, Bahamas, 1966, An Evening at the Ritz-Carlton, Boston, 1967, 69, Un Ballo in Maschera, Venice, 1967, An Evening over Boston, 1968, M.G.M. Cavalcade of Style, L.A., 1970, Symposium on Fund Raising through Parties, L.A., 1970, Great Midwest Limestone Cave Party, Kansas City, 1972, Une Soiree de Gala, Phila., 1972, 11th Anniv. of the Mike Douglas Show, Phila., 1972, The Mayor's Salue to Volunteers, Los Angeles, 1972, Twenty Fifth Anniv. Salute to Israel, Jerusalem, 1973, The Bicentenary, 1976, The World Affairs Council Silver Ball, Boston, 1977, The Ohio Theatre Jubilee, Columbus, 1978, Mayor's Salute to Vols., 1978, Dedication and Gala Performance, Northwestern U. Performing Arts Ctr., 1980, Metromedia Gala, Los Angeles Bicentennial, 1981, The Albemarle Weekend, Charlottesville, 1985, The La Costa Weekend, Carlsbad, 1987, The Embassy Ball, N.Y.C., 1987, The Lagoon Cycle Premiere, Los Angeles, 1987, State Visit Gala for Her Majesty Queen Elizabeth, Miami, 1991, The Grand Brazilian Clambake, Southampton, 1995, The Democratic Senatorial Campaign Committee Gala, Charlottesville, 1996, DSCC reception for Hillary Rodham Clinton, 1996, Rep. Nat. Conv. Team 100 Reception, San Diego, 1996; mem. Pres.' Summit for Am.'s Future Leadership Roundtable, Phila., 1997, Rep. Govs. Conf. Opening Banquet, 1999; contbr. articles to profl. jours. Served with Royal Arty. Brit. Army, 1953-55. Recipient Freedom Found. award Valley Forge, Pa., 1961, City of Hope award Phila., 1962, Mayor's medal for vol. services Los Angeles, 1972, Shalom award State of Israel, 1974, Mayor's medal City of Columbus; named hon. citizen City of Columbus. Mem. AFTRA Jewish.

DAVID, LARRY, television scriptwriter and producer, actor; b. Bklyn., July 2, 1947; m. Laurie Lennard, Mar. 31, 1993 (separated 2007); 2 children. BA in History, U. Md., College Park. Staff writer: Fridays, 1980-82, Saturday Night Live, 1984-85; creator, writer: Norman's Corner, 1989; exec. prodr., co-creator: (TV series) The Seinfeld Chronicles, 1989, Seinfeld, 1990-98 (Emmy award outstanding comedy series 1993, Emmy award outstanding writing comedy series 1993); writer/dir. Sour Grapes, 1998; exec. prodr., writer, actor HBO comedy special Larry David: Curb Your Enthusiasm, (TV series) Curb Your Enthusiasm, 2000- (AFI award best comedy series, 2001, Emmy nomination best lead actor & best comedy series, 2002, 2003); actor: (films) Second Thoughts, 1983, Can She Bank a Cherry Pie?, 1983, Radio Days, 1987, New York Stories, 1989.

DAVIDOW, JEFFREY, think-tank executive, former ambassador; b. Boston, Jan. 26, 1944; m. Joan Labuzoski; 2 children. BA, U. Mass., 1965; MA, U. Minn., 1967; postgrad., Osmania U., Hyderabad, India, 1968-69. Joined Fgn. Svc., Dept. State, 1969; polit. officer Santiago, Chile, 1974-76, US Embassy, Capetown/Pretoria, 1976-78; desk officer Office So. African Affairs US Dept. State, 1978-79; Congl. fellow, 1979-82; head U.S. Liaison Office US Embassy, Harare, Zimbabwe, 1982-83; fellow Ctr. for Internat. Affairs, Harvard U., 1983-85; dir. Office Regional Affairs and Office So. African Affairs, Dept. State, 1985-86; dep. chief of mission US Embassy, Caracas, Venezuela, 1986-88; US amb. to Republic of Zambia, US Dept. State, Lusaka, 1988-90, dep. asst. sec. for African affairs Washington, 1990-93, US amb. to Venezuela Caracas, 1993-96, asst. sec. for inter-Am. affairs Washington, 1996-98, US amb. to Mex. Mexico City, 1998—2002; pres. Inst. of the Americas, La Jolla, Calif., 2003—. Vis. fellow John F. Kennedy Sch. Govt. & David Rockefeller Ctr. for Latin Am. Studies, Harvard U., 2002—03. Author: The US and Mexico: The Bear and the Porcupine, 2004. Fellow Ctr. Internat. Affairs, Harvard U., 1982. Fellow Am. Polit. Sci. Assn. (congrl. staff aide). Office: Institute of the Americas 10111 N Torrey Pines Rd La Jolla CA 92037 Office Phone: 858-453-5560 107. Office Fax: 858-453-2165.*

DAVIDSON, ERIC HARRIS, molecular and developmental biologist, educator; b. NYC, Apr. 13, 1937; s. Morris and Anne D. Davidson. BA, U. Pa., 1958; PhD, Rockefeller U., 1963. Research asso. Rockefeller U., 1963-65, asst. prof., 1965-71; asso. prof. devel. molecular biology Calif. Inst. Tech., Pasadena, Calif., 1971-74, prof., 1974—, Norman Chandler prof. cell biology, 1981—. Author: Gene Activity in Early Development, 3d edit., 1986, Genomic Regulatory Systems, 2001, Regulatory Genome, 2006; contbr. scientific papers. Grantee, NIH, 1965—, NSF, 1972—. Mem.: NAS. Achievements include research in DNA sequence organization; gene expression during embryonic development; gene regulation; evolutionary mechanisms; gene networks. Office: Calif Inst Tech Div Biology Mail Code 156 29 Pasadena CA 91125-0001 Office Phone: 626-395-4937. Business E-Mail: davidson@caltech.edu.

DAVIDSON, ERNEST ROY, chemist, educator; b. Terre Haute, Ind., Oct. 12, 1936; s. Roy Emmette and Opal Ruth (Hugunin) D.; m. Reba Faye Minnich, Jan. 27, 1956; children: Michael Collins, John Philip, Mark Ernest, Martha Ruth. BSc, Rose-Hulman Inst. Tech., 1958, DEng (hon.), 1998; PhD, Ind. U., 1961; PhD (hon.), Uppsala U., 2000. NSF Postdoctoral fellow U. Wis.-Madison, 1961-62; asst. prof. chemistry U. Wash., 1962-65, assoc. prof., 1965-68, prof., 1968-84, Ind. U., Bloomington, 1984-86, disting. prof., 1986—2002, chmn. dept. chemistry, 1999—2002; prof. U. Wash., Seattle, 2002—. Disting. vis. prof. Ohio State U., 1974-75; vis. prof. IMS, Japan, 1984, Technion, Israel, 1985; vis. scholar U. N.C., 2002—; Boys-Rahman lectr. Royal Soc. Chemistry, 2002; adj. prof. U. N.C., Chapel Hill, 2005—. Editor: Jour. Computational Physics, 1975-98, Internat. Jour. Quantum Chemistry, 1975—, Jour. Chem. Physics, 1976-78, 98—, Chem. Physics Letters, 1977-84, Jour. Am. Chem. Soc., 1978-83, Jour. Phys. Chemistry, 1982-90, Accounts of Chem. Rsch., 1984-92, Theoretica Chimica Acta, 1985-98, Chem. Revs., 1986—; contbr. numerous articles on density matrices and quantum theory of molecular structure to profl. jours. Union Carbide fellow Rose-Hulman Inst. Tech., 1958; NSF fellow Ind. U., 1961; recipient Hirschfelder prize in theoretical chemistry, 1997-98, Schrodinger medal, 2001, Nat. medal of sci., 2002; Sloan fellow, 1967-68; Guggenheim fellow, 1974-75; laureate l'Academie Internationale des Sciences Moleculaires Quantiques, 1971. Fellow Am. Phys. Soc., Sigma Xi; mem. NAS, Am. Chem. Soc. (Computers in Chemistry award 1992, Theoretical Chemistry award 2000), Am. Acad. Arts and Scis., Ind. Acad. Sci. (Chemist of Yr. award 1999), Phi Lambda Upsilon, Tau Beta Pi. Office: U Wash Dept Chemistry Bagley 303A Seattle WA 98195-1700

DAVIDSON, EZRA C., JR., obstetrician, gynecologist, academic administrator, educator; b. Water Valley, Miss., Oct. 21, 1933; s. Ezra Cap and Theresa Hattie (Woods) Davidson; children: Pamela, Gwendolyn, Marc, Ezra K. BS cum laude, Morehouse Coll., 1954; MD, Meharry Med. Coll., 1958. Diplomate Am. Bd. Ob-Gyn. (examiner 1973-). Intern San Diego County Gen. Hosp., 1958—59; resident in ob-gyn. Harlem Hosp., NYC, 1963—66, asst. attending ob-gyn, obstet. coordinator maternal and infant care clinics, 1967—68; dir. departmental research, assoc. attending, acting chmn. ob-gyn, co-dir. coagulation research lab. Roosevelt Hosp., NYC, 1968—70; fellow blood coagulation, asst. ob-gyn Columbia U. Coll. Physicians and Surgeons, NYC, 1966—67, instr. dept. ob-gyn, 1967—69, asst. clin. prof., 1970; cons. ob-gyn Office Health Affairs, OEO, Washington, 1970—72; prof. Charles R. Drew U. of Medicine and Sci., LA, 1971—, acad. v.p., 1982—87, chmn. dept. ob.-gyn., 1971—96, assoc. dean primary care, 1997—; prof. U. So. Calif., Los Angeles, 1971—80, UCLA, 1980—. Chief svc. dept. ob-gyn. King/Drew Med. Ctr., LA, 1971—96; attending physician dept. ob-gyn. L.A. County-U. So. Calif. Med. Ctr., 1971—80; mem. nat. med. adv. com. nat. found. March of Dimes, 1972—76; bd. cons. Internat. Childbirth Edn. Assn., 1973—81; mem. sec.'s adv. com. population affairs HEW, 1974—77, chmn. svcs. task force, 1975—77; chmn. bd. dirs. L.A. Regional Family Planning Coun., 1975—77; bd. dirs. Nat. Alliance Sch. Age Parents, 1975—79; mem. corp. bd. Blue Shield, Calif., 1989—; chair DHHS Sec.'s Adv. Com. on Infant Mortality, 1990—93; active FDA, 1990—96, chmn. fertility and maternal health drugs adv. com., 1992—96; mem. adv. com. to the dir. NIH, 1995—98, mem. dirs. adv. panel on clin. rsch., 1995—98; mem. roundtable on health care quality Inst. on Medicine, 1995—98; mem. coun. grad. med. edn. HHS, 1997—2000; bd. dirs., chair med. policy com. Blue Shield of Calif., 1998—2002. Bd. dirs. The Calif. Wellness Found., 1995—, chmn., 1996—98; bd. dirs. Children's Bur. So. Calif., 1999—, v.p., 1995—99, pres., 1999—2002; bd. dirs. Jacobs Inst. of Womens Health, 1999—; chmn. bd. trustees Blue Shield Calif. Found., 2004—. With USAF, 1959—63. Fellow Johnson Found. Health Policy, Inst. Medicine, NAS, 1979—80. Fellow: ACS, L.A. Ob-Gyn. Soc. (pres. 1982—83), Royal Coll. Ob-Gyn., Am. Coll. Ob-Gyn. (nat. sec. 1983—89, pres.-elect 1989—90, pres. 1990—91); mem.: Calif. Tech. Assessment Forum (chair 2002—), Assn. of Acad. Minority Physicians (pres. 2002—03), Golden State Med. Assn. (pres.

1989—90), Assn. Profs. Ob-Gyn. (pres. 1989—90), Nat. Med. Assn. (chmn. nat. sect. ob-gyn. 1975—77, mem. sci. coun. 1979—88, bd. trustee 1989—95, chmn. bd. trustees 1992—95), Ob-Gyn. Assembly So. Calif. (chmn. 1989—90), Pacific Coast Ob-Gyn. Soc., N.Am. Soc. Pediatric and Adolescent Gynecology (pres.-elect 1993—94, pres. 1994—95), Am. Ob-Gyn. Soc. Office: 12021 Wilmington Ave Los Angeles CA 90059-3019

DAVIDSON, GILBERT, city manager; b. 1975; Dep. town mgr., Marana, Ariz. Adv. coun., Student Affairs U. Ariz.; undergraduate adv. bd. Eller Coll. Mgmt. Bd. mem. Ariz. Town Hall. Named one of 40 Under 40, Tucson Bus. Edge, 2006. Mem.: Rotary Club, Elks Lodge, Masonic Lodge. Avocation: U. Ariz. sporting events. Office: Town Manager 11555 W Civic Ctr Dr Marana AZ 85653 Office Phone: 520-382-1999.

DAVIDSON, GORDON, theater producer and director; b. Bklyn., May 7, 1933; s. Joseph H. and Alice (Gordon) D.; m. Judith Swiller, Sept. 21, 1958; children: Adam, Rachel. BA, Cornell U.; MA, Case Western Res. U.; LHD (hon.), Bklyn. Coll.; D. Performing Arts (hon.), Calif. Inst. Arts; DFA (hon.), Claremont U. Ctr. Stage mgr. Phoenix Theatre Co., 1958-60, Am. Shakespeare Festival Theatre, 1958-60, Dallas Civic Opera, 1960-61, Martha Graham Dance Co., 1962; mng. dir. Theatre Group at UCLA, 1965-67; founding dir./prodr. Center Theatre Group Mark Taper Forum, Ahmanson Theatre, Kirk Douglas Theatre, 1967—2005; co-founder New Theatre For Now, Mark Taper Forum, 1970. Past mem. theatre panel Nat. Endowment for Arts; past pres. Theatre Communications Group; mem. adv. council Internat. Theatre Inst.; mem. adv. com. Cornell Ctr. for Performing Arts; cons. Denver Center for the Performing Arts; bd. dirs. several arts orgns. including Am. Arts Alliance. Producer, dir. over 150 major theatrical prodns. including The Deputy, 1965, Candide, 1966, The Devils, 1967, Who's Happy Now, 1967, In the Matter of J. Robert Oppenheimer, 1968 (N.Y. Drama Desk award), Murderous Angels, 1970, Rosebloom, 1970, The Trial of the Catonsville Nine, 1971 (Obie award, Tony award nomination), Henry IV, Part I, 1972, Mass, 1973, Hamlet, 1974, Savages, 1974 (Obie award), Too Much Johnson, 1975, The Shadow Box, 1975 (Tony award, Outer Critics Circle Best Dir. award), And Where She Stops Nobody Knows, 1976, Getting Out, 1977, Black Angel, 1978, Terra Nova, 1979, Children of a Lesser God, 1979, The Lady and the Clarinet, 1980, Chekhov in Yalta, 1981, Tales from Hollywood, 1982, The American Clock, 1984, The Hands of Its Enemy, 1984, Traveler in the Dark, 1985, The Real Thing, 1986, Ghetto, 1986, A Lie of the Mind, 1988; dir. operas including Cosi Fan Tutte, Otello, Beatrice and Benedick, Carmen, La Boheme, Il Trovatore, Harriet, A Woman Called Moses, A Midsummer Night's Dream, 1988; TV film The Trial of the Catonsville Nine, 1971; exec. producer Zoot Suit, 1981; producer for TV It's the Willingness, PBS Visions Series, 1979, Who's Happy Now?, NET Theatre in Am. Series; dir. A Little Night Music, 1990. Trustee Ctr. for Music, Drama and Art; past pres. League Resident Theatres; past v.p. Am. Nat. Theatre Acad; advisor Fund for New Am. Plays; mem. adv. bd. Nat. Found. for Jewish Culture. Recipient N.Y. Drama Desk award for direction, 1969; recipient Los Angeles Drama Critics Circle awards for direction, 1971, 74, 75, Margo Jones award New Theatre for Now, 1970, 76, Obie award, 1971, 77, Outer Critics Circle award, 1977, Tony award for direction, 1977, award John Harvard, award Nat. Acad. TV Arts and Scis., award Nosotros Golden Eagle, award N.Y. League for Hard of Hearing, award N.Y. Speech and Hearing Assn., award Am. Theatre Assn., award Los Angeles Human Relations Commn.; Guggenheim fellow, 1983, Pulitzer Prize in Drama for the Kentucky Cycle and Angels in America (Part One- Millennium Approaches). Mem. League Resident Theatres (past pres.), ANTA (v.p. 1975), Nat. Endowment for the Arts. Office: Mabery Road Prods INC 4211 Jackson Ave Culver City CA 90232 Office Phone: 213-972-7353, 310-842-8886.

DAVIDSON, GORDON KIRBY, lawyer; b. Port Chester, NY, July 30, 1948; BSEE with great distinction, Stanford U., 1970, MS in Elec. Engring. and Computer Systems, 1971, JD, 1974. Bar: Calif. 1974. Law clk. to Judge Ben C. Duniway U.S. Ct. Appeals (9th cir.), 1974-75; ptnr. Fenwick & West LLP, Mountain View, Calif., 1980—, chmn., 1995—. Named a Nathan Abbott scholar, Stanford U. Law Sch., 1974; named one of 100 Most Influential Lawyers, Nat. Law Jour., 2000, 2006, 50 Most Powerful Venture Capital Dealmakers, Forbes Mag., 2001, 100 People Who Changed Our World, Upside Mag., 2001, ten best corp. lawyers in Calif., Calif. Lawyer Mag., 2004, ten best lawyers in Northern Calif., San Francisco Mag., 2004, top 100 venture capital deal makers, Forbes Mag.'s Midas List, 2004, 2005. Mem. ABA, State Bar Calif., Order Coif, Phi Beta Kappa. Office: Fenwick & West LLP Silicon Valley Center 801 California St Mountain View CA 94041

DAVIDSON, HERBERT ALAN, Near Eastern languages and cultures educator; b. Boston, May 25, 1932; s. Louis Nathan and Ettabelle (Baker) D.; m. Kinneret Bernstein; children: Rachel and Jessica. BA, Harvard U., 1953, MA, 1955, PhD, 1959. Lectr. Harvard U., Cambridge, Mass., 1960-61; asst. prof. UCLA, 1961-66, assoc. prof., 1966-72, prof., 1972-94, prof. emeritus, 1994—, chmn. dept. near eastern langs. and cultures, 1984-91. Author: The Philosophy of Abraham Shalom, 1964, medieval Hebrew transls. of Averroes' Middle Commentary on the Isagoge and Categories, 1969, English transl., 1969, Proofs for Eternity, Creation, and the Existence of God in Medieval Islamic and Jewish Philosophy, 1987, Alfarabi, Avicenna, and Averroes on Intellect, 1992, Moses Maimonides, The Man and His Works, 2004; contbr. articles and book revs. to profl. jours. Office: UCLA Dept Near Ea Langs and Cultures 405 Hilgard Ave Los Angeles CA 90095-9000

DAVIDSON, KEAY, newswriter; Sci. writer Sentinel Star, Orlando, Fla., 1979—81, L.A. Times San Diego Bur., 1981—85, San Francisco Examiner, 1986—2000, San Francisco Chronicle, 2000—. Author (with George Smoot): Wrinkles in Time, 1993; author: Twister: The Science of Tornadoes and the Making of a Natural Disaster Movie, 1996, Carl Sagan: A Life, 1999; contbg. writer: Scientific American, New Scientist, National Geographic, Sky and Telescope, NY Times, Washington Post, Best Am. Sci. Writing, 2004. Recipient Westinghouse Sci. Journalism award, 1986, Sci. in Soc. award, Nat. Assn. Sci. Writers. Office: San Francisco Chronicle 901 Mission St San Francisco CA 94103-2988 Office Fax: 415-896-1107. Business E-Mail: kdavidson@sfchronicle.com.

DAVIDSON, MAYER B., endocrinologist, educator, researcher; b. Balt., Apr. 11, 1935; s. David and Esther (Crockin) D.; m. Naomi Berger, Nov. 25, 1961 (div. 1977); children: Elke W., Seth J.; m. Roseann Herman, Aug. 31, 1980. AB, Swarthmore Coll., 1957; MD, Harvard U., 1961. Diplomate Am. Bd. Internal Medicine, Am. Bd. Endocrinology and Metabolism. Intern Bellevue Hosp., NYC, 1961-62, jr. asst. resident, 1962-63; sr. asst. resident U. Wash. Affiliated Hosps., Seattle, 1963-64; rsch. fellow dept. endocrinology and metabolism King County Hosp., U. Wash., Seattle, 1964-66; asst. prof. medicine UCLA Sch. Medicine, 1969-74, acting chief div. endocrinology and metabolism, 1973-74, from assoc. prof. to prof., 1974-95, clin. prof., 1996—2006; with Drew U., 2006—. Dir. diabetes program Cedars-Sinai Med. Ctr., L.A., 1979-95; assoc. dir. clin. diabetes City of Hope Nat. Med. Ctr., 1995-98; dir. clin. trials unit Charles R. Drew U.; nat. advisor Diabetes Ctr. Humana Hosp., Phoenix, 1985-91; attending physician diabetic clinic Boston City Hosp., 1966-68; clin. asst. Harvard Med. Sch., 1968-69; cons. AMA Dept. Drugs. Author: Diabetus Mellitus: Diagnosis and Treatment, 4th edit., 1998, The Complete Idiot's Guide to Type 2 Diabetes, 2nd edit., 2009; founding editor: Current Diabetes Reports, 2000—02, editor-in-chief: Diabetes Care, 2002—06; contbr. chapters to books. Co-founder, bd. dirs. free med. facility Venice (Calif.) Family Clinic, 1970. Maj. Med. Svc. Corps U.S. Army, 1966-69. USPHS rsch. fellow Nat. Inst. Arthritis and Metabolic Diseases, 1965-66; recipient Upjohn award for Outstanding Diabetes Educator, 1990, Robert H. Williams/Rachmiel Levine award for sci. contbns. and humanism in tng. young rschrs., 1995, Banting medal for Disting. Svc., 1998; named to Best Doctors in Am., 1992-93, 95-96, 96-97. Fellow ACP; mem. AAAS, Am. Diabetes Assn. (rsch. prizes 1965, 66, R&D award 1974-75, rsch. 1978-81, bd. dirs. 1986-89, 93-99, v.p. 1995-96, pres.-elect 1996-97, pres. 1997-98), Am. Fedn. Clin. Rsch., Western Soc. Clin. Rsch., Endocrine Soc., Am. Soc. Clin. Investigation, Western Assn. Physicians, Am. Assn. Diabetes Educators (editl. bd. jour. 1980-83), Boylston Med. Soc., Am. Diabetes Assn. (pres. 1997-98), Sigma Xi. Democrat. Jewish.

DAVIDSON, ROBERT C., JR., manufacturing executive; b. Memphis, Oct. 3, 1945; s. Robert C. Sr. and Thelma (Culp) D.; m. Alice Faye Berkley, Jan. 5, 1978; children: Robert III, John Roderick, Julian. BA, Morehouse Coll., 1967; MBA, U. Chgo., 1969. V.p. Urban Nat. Corp., Boston, 1972-74, Avant Garde Enterprises, Los Angeles, 1974-76; pres. Surface Protection, Industries, Los Angeles, 1976—, now CEO. Bd. dirs. Pasadena Art Workshop, 1986—; planning commr. City of Pasadena, 1986—. Mem. Young Pres. Orgn. Clubs: 100 Black Men (Los Angeles). Avocations: tennis, skiing. Office: Robert C Davidson Jr 1750 Lombardy Rd Pasadena CA 91106-4127

DAVIDSON, ROBERT WILLIAM, not-for-profit executive; b. Colfax, Wash., Sept. 18, 1949; s. William Martin and Lena (Soli) D.; m. Molly Evoy, Apr. 16, 1977; children: Ford Patrick, Matthew Harpur, Marshall Andrew. AB, Harvard U., 1971; MBA, U. Wash., 2000. Exec. dir. Sabre Found., Cambridge, Mass., 1971-72; adminstrv. asst. Congressman Joel Pritchard, Washington, 1973-79; asst. sec. state State of Wash., Olympia, 1979-80; pres. Frayn Fin. Printing, Seattle, 1982-87, Frayn Printing Co., Seattle, 1985-87; exec. dir. Woodland Park Zool. Soc., Seattle, 1987—94, pres., 1986—87; prin. Alistar Capital Group, Bellevue, Wash., 1994—2001; CEO Seattle Aquarium Soc., Seattle, 2002—. Chmn. pub. funding com. Mayor's Zoo Commn., Seattle, 1984-85; bd. dirs. Discovery Inst., 1992-2004, Internat. Snow Leopard Trust, 1994-96; sch. bd. Cath. Archdiocese Seattle, 1995-98; active King County Bond Oversight Com., 1986-93 Mem. N.W. Devel. Officers Assn. (pres. 1994), Downtown Rotary Club (v.p. found. 1997-98, bd. dirs. 2005-), Wash. Athletic Club. Republican. Roman Catholic. Avocation: photography. Office: 1415 Western Ave # 505 Seattle WA 98101 Home Phone: 425-455-5760; Office Phone: 206-838-3910. Business E-Mail: bob@aquariumsociety.org.

DAVIDSON, ROGER H(ARRY), political science professor; b. Washington, July 31, 1936; s. Ross Wallace and Mildred (Younger) D.; m. Nancy Elizabeth Dixon, Sept. 29, 1961; children: Douglas Ross, Christopher Reed. AB magna cum laude, U. Colo., 1958; PhD, Columbia U., 1963. Asst. prof. govt. Dartmouth Coll., Hanover, NH, 1962-68; assoc. prof. polit. sci. U. Calif., Santa Barbara, 1968-71, prof., 1971-83, assoc. dean letters and sci., 1978-80, vis. prof., 1994, 1999—; sr. specialist Congl. Rsch. Svc., Washington, 1980-88; prof. govt., politics U. Md., College Pk., 1981-99. Profl. staff mem. U.S. Ho. of Reps., Washington, 1973—74; rsch. dir. U.S. Senate, Washington, 1976—77; cons. White House, 1970—71, U.S. Com. on Violence, Washington, 1968—69, Ctr. for Civic Edn., 2002—; Leon Sachs vis. scholar Johns Hopkins U., Balt., 1997; John Marshall Disting. Fulbright prof. Debrecen U., Hungary, 2002. Author: The Role of the Congressman, 1969; co-author: A More Perfect Union, 4th edit., 1989, Congress and Its Members, 12th edit., 2009; editor: The Postreform Congress, 1992; co-editor: Masters of the House, 1998, Workways of Governance, 2004, Understanding the Presidency, 5th edit., 2008; contbr. articles to profl. jours. Co-chmn. Upper Valley Human Rights Coun., Hanover, N.H., 1966-68; chmn. Goleta Valley Citizens Planning Group, Santa Barbara, 1974-76; rsch. com. of legis. specialists Internat. Polit. Sci. Assn.; adv. commn. on records of Congress Nat. Archives and Records Adminstrn., 1995-99; bd. dirs. Governance Inst., 1986—, Archtl. Found. of Santa Barbara, 2003—, U. Calif. Santa Barbara Affiliates, 2006—. Woodrow Wilson Nat. Found. fellow, 1958, Gilder fellow Columbia U., 1960, Faculty fellow Dartmouth Coll., 1965-66, Disting. Polit. Scientist Santa Barbara City Coll., 2005-06. Fellow Nat. Acad. Pub. Adminstrn.; mem. Nat. Capital Area Polit. Sci. Assn. (pres. 1985-86), Legis. Studies Group (charter, nat. chmn. 1980-81), Am. Polit. Sci. Assn. (joint com. project 87-Am. Hist. Assn./Am. Polit. Sci. Assn., chmn. congl. fellowship com. 1990, 93, endowed programs com. 1994-95, chmn. 1995-96, co-chmn. exec. com. centennial campaign 1997-2003, bd. dirs. centennial ctr. 2006—), Western Polit. Sci. Assn. (bd. editors 1977-78). Baptist. Avocations: music, history. Home: Villa L 400 E Pedregosa St Santa Barbara CA 93103-1970 Office: Dept Polit Sci U Calif Santa Barbara CA 93106

DAVIDSON, SUZANNE MOURON, lawyer; b. Oxford, Miss., Aug. 5, 1963; d. Bertrand D. Jr. and Barbara Jean (Baca) Mouron; m. Garrison H. Davidson III, Dec. 12, 1987; children: Jane Harrington, Catherine Stender. AB in English Lit., U. Calif., 1985, JD, 1988. Assoc. Peterson, Ross, LA, 1988-89; asst. litigation counsel Ticor Title Ins., Rosemead, Calif., 1989-91; corp. counsel Forest Lawn, Glendale, Calif., 1991—. Deacon San Marino Cmty. Ch., 1995-98, elder, 2000-2003; bd. dirs. San Marino Cmty. Ch. Nursery Sch., 1995-2000; mem. Jr. League, Pasadena, Calif., 1989—, Nat. Charity League Jrs. (San Marino), 2002—, bd. dirs, 2003—. Mem. Calif. State Bar Assn., L.A. County Bar Assn., Pasadena Athletic Club, Salt Air Club, Chi Omega (chmn. nat. area rush info. 1988-95). Presbyterian. Office: Forest Lawn Co Legal Dept 1712 S Glendale Ave Glendale CA 91205-3320

DAVIE, EARL WARREN, biochemistry educator; b. Tacoma, Wash., Oct. 25, 1927; s. Charles William and Teckla E. Davie; m. Anita Thalia Roe, July 15, 1952; children: James, John, Karen, Marilyn. BS in Chemistry, U. Wash., 1950, PhD in Biochemistry, 1954; MD (hon.), Lund U., Sweden, 1995. Asst. prof. biochemistry Western Res. U., Cleve., 1956-62, assoc. prof. Biochemistry, 1962, U. Wash., Seattle, 1962-66, chmn. biochemistry dept., 1975-84, prof. biochemistry, 1966—. Mem. Nat. Heart, Lung, Blood Adv. Coun., NIH, Bethesda, Md., 1985-90. Mem. editorial bd. Jour. Biol. Chemistry, 1968-73, 75-80; assoc. editor Biochemistry, 1980—, Fibrinolysis, 1986-93; contbr. over 180 articles on basic rsch. in hematology to profl. jours. Sec. Am. Soc. Biol. Chemistry, Bethesda, 1975-78; mem. exec. com. coun. on thrombosis Am. Heart Assn., Dallas, 1972-74; bd. trustees Wash. State Heart Assn., 19743-76. Recipient Internat. prize French Assn. for Hemophilia, Paris, 1983, Waterford Bio-Med. Rsch. prize Scripps Clinic & Rsch. Found., 1985, Robert P. Grant medal Internat. Soc. on Thrombosis & Hemostasis, Tokyo, 1989, Stratton medal Am. Soc. Hematology, 1993, Disting. Achievement award Am. Heart Assn., 1995, Bristol-Myers Squibb award for cardiovasc./metabolic rsch., 1999; fellow Nat. Found. for Infantile Paralysis, Mass. Gen. Hosp., 1954, Commonwealth Fund, U. Geneva, 1966. Mem. NAS, Am. Acad. Arts and Scis., Royal Danish Acad. Scis. and Letters (fgn.), Japanese Biochem. Soc. (fgn.). Achievements include establishment of mechanisms for blood coagulation, isolation and characterization of various proteins involved; determination of the structure of their genes. Office: U Wash Dept Biochemistry Sj 70 Seattle WA 98195-0001

DAVIES, CAROL B., computer programmer, researcher; married, 1968; 2 children. Contractor NASA Ames Rsch. Ctr., Moffett Field, Calif., 1968, with Pioneer Space Project, contractor with Sterling Software, 1980, rsch. specialist; tchr. statistics, cons. to computer sci. dept. U. Singapore, 1976-80. Vol. Stanford Health Libr.; tutor for local mid. sch. Office: NASA Ames Rsch Ctr Moffett Field CA 94035

DAVIES, COLLEEN T., lawyer; b. Sacramento, Oct. 22, 1958; married; children: Katie, Patrick. BA with honors in English lit., U. Calif., Davis, 1980; JD, Santa Clara U., 1983. Bar: Calif. 1983. With Crosby, Heafey, Roach & May (combined with Reed Smith LLP, 2003), 1983—2003; ptnr., mem. exec. com. Reed Smith LLP, Oakland, Calif., 2003—. Comments editor Santa Clara Law Rev., 1982—83; mem. Product Liability Adv. Coun. Mem.: ABA, Def. Rsch. Inst. (pharm. & med. device sect.), Alameda County Bar Assn., Calif. State Bar, Phi Beta Kappa. Office: Reed Smith LLP 1999 Harrison St Ste 2400 Oakland CA 94612 Office Phone: 510-763-2000. Office Fax: 510-273-8832. Business E-Mail: cdavies@reedsmith.com.

DAVIES, DAVID GEORGE, lawyer, educator; b. Waukesha, Wis., July 19, 1928; s. David Evan and Ella Hilda (Degler) D.; m. Elaine Kowalchik, May 12, 1962; children: Thea Kay, Bryn Ann, Degler Evan. BS, U. Wis., 1950, JD, 1953. Bar: Wis. 1953, Ariz. 1959. Trust rep. First Nat. Bank of Ariz., Phoenix, 1957-58, asst. trust officer, 1958-62, trust officer, head bus. devel. in trust dept., 1962-66, v.p., trust officer, 1966; practice in Phoenix, 1967—; assoc. Wales & Collins, 1967-68; ptnr. Wales, Collins & Davies, 1968-75, Collins, Davies & Cronkhite, Ltd., 1975-85, David G. Davies, Ltd., 1986—. Instr. bus. law local chpt. C.L.U.s, 1965; instr. estate and gift taxation, 1973—; instr. estate planning Phoenix Coll., 1968—; past instr. Maricopa County Jr. Coll. Pres. Central Ariz. Estate Planning Council; pres., bd. dirs. Vis. Nurse Service, United Fund Agy.; chmn. bd. Beatitudes Campus of Care; bd. dirs. Phoenix chpt. Nat. Hemophilia Found.; bd. dirs., treas. trusteeship St. Luke's Hosp. Med. Ctr., Phoenix, 1982—; mem. adv. bd. planned giving com. Salvation Army, 1997—. Served to capt. JAGC, AUS, 1953-57. Mem. Central Assn. Life Underwriters (asso.), ABA, Wis. Bar Assn., State Bar Ariz., Am. Assn. Homes for Aged (legal affairs com., future com.) Congregationalist (chmn. bd. trustees, moderator). Office: 5110 N 40th St Ste 236 Phoenix AZ 85018-2151 Office Phone: 602-956-1521.

DAVIES, HUGH MARLAIS, museum director; b. Grahamstown, South Africa, Feb. 12, 1948; came to U.S., 1956; s. Horton Marlais and Brenda M. (Deakin) D.; children: Alexandra, Dorian; m. Lynda Forsha; 1 stepdaughter, Mackenzie Forsha Fuller. AB summa cum laude, Princeton U., 1970, MFA, 1972, PhD, 1976. Dir. Univ. Gallery, U. Mass., Amherst, 1975-83; David C. Copley dir. Mus. Contemporary Art (formerly La Jolla Mus. Contemporary Art), San Diego, 1983—. Vis. prof. fine arts Amherst Coll., 1980-83; mem. adv. coun. dept. art and archeology Princeton U., 1989—, panel mem. fed. adv. com. internat. exhbns., 1990-94; co-curator Whitney Mus. Am. Art Biennial, 2000. Author: (book) Francis Bacon: The Papal Portraits of 1953, 2001, Francis Bacon: The Early and Middle Years, 1928-1958; co-author: Sacred Art in a Secular Century: 20th Century Religious Art, 1978, Francis Bacon (Abbeville), 1986. Nat. Endowment Arts fellow, 1982, 95. Mem. Am. Assn. Mus., Coll. Art Assn., Assn. Art Mus. Dirs. (trustee 1994-2001, pres. 1997-98). Office: Mus Contemporary Art San Diego 700 Prospect St La Jolla CA 92037-4228 Office Phone: 858-454-3541.

DAVIES, PAUL LEWIS, JR., retired lawyer; b. San Jose, Calif., July 21, 1930; s. Paul Lewis and Faith (Crummey) D.; m. Barbara Bechtel, Dec. 22, 1955 (dec. June 2001); children: Laura (Mrs. Segundo Mateo), Paul Lewis III. AB, Stanford U., 1952; JD, Harvard U., 1957. Bar: Calif. 1957. Assoc. Pillsbury, Madison & Sutro, San Francisco, 1957—63, ptnr., 1963—89; gen. counsel Chevron Corp., 1984—89. Hon. trustee Calif. Acad. Scis., trustee, 1970-83, chmn., 1973-80; pres. Herbert Hoover Found.; bd. overseers Hoover Instn., chmn., 1976-82, 91-93; hon. regent U. of Pacific, regent, 1959-90. Lt. U.S. Army, 1952-54. Mem. Bohemian Club, Pacific-Union Club, Villa Taverna, Claremont Country Club, Cypress Point Club, Sainte Claire Club, Collectors Club, Explorers Club, St. Francis Yacht Club, Palo Alto (Calif.) Club, Phi Beta Kappa, Pi Sigma Alpha Republican. Office: 3697 Mt Diablo Blvd Ste 205 Lafayette CA 94549 Office Phone: 925-284-8180. E-mail: pauldaviesjr@yahoo.com.

DAVIES, THOMAS MOCKETT, JR., history professor; b. Lincoln, Nebr., May 25, 1940; s. Thomas Mockett and Faith Elizabeth (Arnold) D.; m. Eloisa Carmela Monzón Abate, June 10, 1968 (dec. Jan. 1994); 1 dau., Jennifer Elena; m. Rosemarie Adele Lindsay, Jan. 7, 1995. BA, U. Nebr., 1962, MA, 1964; student, Universidad Nacional Autónoma de México, 1961; PhD, U. N.Mex., 1970; postdoctoral fellow, U. Tex., Austin, 1969-70. Lectr. U. N.Mex. Peace Corps Tng. Center, 1964-66; asst. prof. Latin Am. history San Diego State U., 1968-72, assoc. prof., 1972-75, prof. Latin Am. history, 1975—2001, dir. Ctr. for Latin Am. Studies, 1979—2001, chmn. Latin Am. studies, 1979—2001, prof. dir. emeritus ctr. Latin Am. studies. Author: (with others) Historia, problema y promesa. Homenaje a Jorge Basadre, 1978, Research Guide to Andean History: Bolivia, Chile, Ecuador and Peru, 1981, The

Spanish Civil War: American Hemisphere Perspectives, 1982, EL APRA de la Ideología a la Praxis, 1989, Latin American Military History: An Annotated Bibliography, 1992; author: Indian Integration in Peru: A Half Century of Experience, 1900-48, 1974 (co-winner Hubert Herring Meml. award Pacific Coast Coun. on Latin Am. Studies 1973), (with Victor Villaneuva) 300 Documentos Para la Historia del APRA; Conspiraciones Apristas de 1935 a 1939, 1979, Secretos Electorales del APRA: Correspondencia y Documentos de 1939, 1982; (with Brian Loveman) The Politics of Anti-Politics: The Military in Latin America, 1978, 3d rev. edit., 1997, Che Guevara: Guerrilla Warfare, 1985 (Hubert Herring Meml. award 1985, 3d rev. edit., 1997); mem. editorial bd. Hispanic Am. Hist. Rev., 1985-1990; Contbr. (with Brian Loveman) articles to profl. jours. Recipient Outstanding Faculty award San Diego State U. Alumni Assn., 1981, 97, 1st ann. Internat. Scholar award Phi Beta Delta, 1992, Wiley W. Manuel award Calif. State Bar Assn., 1995, 98; grantee Dept. Edn. for Nat. Resource Ctr. for L.Am. Studies, 1979-2001, San Diego State U. Found., 1971-73, 75, 76, 79, 80, San Diego State U., 1988, 89, 90, William and Flora Hewlett Found., 1997-2001; fellow Henry L. and Grace Doherty Charitable Found., 1966-68 Mem. Latin Am. Studies Assn., Conf. Latin Am. History (exec. sec. 1979-84), Pacific Coast Council Latin Am. (bd. govs. 1989-91, pres. 1996-97), Rocky Mountain Council on Latin Am. Studies (exec. com. 1980—2001, pres. 1996-97), Am. Hist. Assn., Consortium L.Am. Studies Programs (exec. sec.-treas. 1994-2001). Home: 7524 Maplewood Dr NW Albuquerque NM 87120-3923

DAVIES, WILLIAM RALPH, service executive; b. Santa Barbara, Calif., Aug. 17, 1955; s. Ralph Emmett and Georgann Marie (Cordingly) D.; m. Karen L. Blake, May 12, 1984 (div. 1999), Sidney Manheim AA in Real Estate, Am. River Coll., 1978; BS in Fin., Ins. and Real Estate, Calif. State U., Sacramento, 1980; postgrad. in Internat. Bus., Golden Gate U., 1982-84. Real estate assoc. Kiernan Realtors, Sacramento, 1975-77; co-owner real estate firm Sacramento, 1977; pvt. practice real estate cons., property mgr., 1978-80; broker assoc. MBA Bus. Svcs., Sacramento, 1980-85, pres., 1985—, El Dorado Hills, 1984—. Bd. dirs. WRD, Inc., El Dorado Hills, Vista Sr. Living, Inc., El Dorado Hills, v.p., 1999—2001. Republican. Avocations: history, bridge, golf. Office: 895 Embarcadero Dr Ste 203 El Dorado Hills CA 95762 E-mail: wdavies@mbabiz.com.

DAVIS, AL (ALLEN DAVIS), professional football team executive; b. Brockton, Mass., July 4, 1929; s. Louis and Rose Davis; m. Carol Segall, July 11, 1954; 1 child, Mark. Student, Wittenberg Coll., 1947; AB in English, Syracuse U., NY, 1950. Asst. football coach Adelphi Coll., 1950—51; head football coach US Army, Ft. Belvoir, Va., 1952—53; player, pers. scout Balt. Colts, 1954; line coach The Citadel, 1955—56, U. So. Calif., 1957—59; offensive end coach LA Chargers, 1960—62; gen. mgr., head coach Oakland Raiders, 1963—66, owner, mng. gen. ptnr., 1966—82; commr. Am. Football League, 1966; owner, mng. gen. ptnr. LA Raiders, 1982—95; pres., gen. ptnr. Oakland Raiders, 1995—. Former mem. mgmt. council and competition com. NFL. With AUS, 1952—53. Recipient Retired Players Award of Excellence, NFL Players Assn., 1991; named Profl. Coach of Year, AP, UPI, Sporting News, Pro-Football Illus., 1963, Young Man of Yr., Oakland C. of C., 1963; named to Pro Football Hall of Fame, 1992. Mem.: Am. Football Coaches Assn. Office: Oakland Raiders 1220 Harbor Bay Pkwy Alameda CA 94502-6570*

DAVIS, ARTHUR DAVID, psychology educator, musician; m. Gladys Lesley Joyce, Dec. 29, 1965 (dec.); children: Kimali, Mureithi. Student, Manhattan Sch. Music, 1953-56, Juilliard Sch. Music, 1953-56; BA summa cum laude, CUNY, 1973; MA, City Coll., NYC, 1976, NYU, 1976, PhD with distinction, 1982. Lic. sch. psychologist. Musician various worldwide tours, 1962—, NBC-TV Staff Orch., NYC, 1962-63, Westinghouse TV Staff Orch., NYC, 1964-68, CBS-TV Staff Orch., NYC, 1969-71; prof. Manhattan Community Coll., NYC, 1971-86, U. Bridgeport, Conn., 1978-82; psychologist Lincoln Med. and Mental Health Ctr., Bronx, 1982-85; sch. psychologist, cons. Lakeside Union Free Sch. Dist., Spring Valley, NY, 1985—86; psychologist, tchr. N.Y. Med. Coll., Valhalla, 1982-87; prof. Orange Coast Coll., Costa Mesa, Calif., 1987—, Calif. State U., Fullerton, 1988-90, U. Calif., Irvine, 1993—94; CEO, pres. Arkimu Inc., 1993—; psychologist Cross Cultural Ctr., San Diego, 1986-91; mem. faculty U. Calif., Irvine, 1999—2001. Cons. Head Start, Bklyn., 1981-82, Orange County Minority AIDS, Santa Ana, Calif., 1987-88, Orange County Fair Housing, Costa Mesa, 1988, Sickle Cell Anemia Assn., Santa Ana, Calif., 1987-88, Human Rels. Orange County City, Costa Mesa, 1988-89, William Grant Still Mus., L.A., 1988-90; musician various symphonies Radio City Music Hall Orch. Nat. Symphony, Symphony of the Air N.Y. Philharmonic, Met. Opera Orch., L.A. Philharmonic, 1995; John Coltrane, others, 1960-. Author: The Arthur Davis System for Double Bass, 1976, A Brief History of Jazz, 1995; record composer Interplay, 1980, Art Davis LIFE, 1986, Reemergance, ARKIMU, 1985, Dr. Art Davis, Live, Soulnote, 1987, Art Davis, A Time Remembered, 1995; composer (CD) Puttin on the Ritz, 2002. Composer, condr., mem. coun. Dialogue, Costa Mesa, 1988, Art's Boogie, 1979; mgr. Little League of Cortlandt, N.Y., 1979-82; pack master Cub Scouts Am., Cortlandt and Croton, N.Y., 1979-80, dist. chmn., 1980-81; bd. dirs. Local 47 Musicians' Union, Hollywood, Calif., 1993-97, Orange County Urban League, Inc., 1992-95; chmn. Better Advantages for Students and Soc., Corona del Mar, Calif., 1993; adv. bd. dirs. John W. Cultrane Cultural Soc., Inc. Recipient Lion award, Black MBA Assn., 1985, Chancellor's Disting. Lectr.'s award, U. Calif., Irvine, 1991—92, Exemplary Stds. in Music Edn. award, Orange County Urban League, 1993, Congl. award, 2002, Congl. Lifetime Achievement as a jazz legend, Ann. Dr. Art Davis Scholarships established in his honor, Dr. Art Davis Fan Club, Gladys David Scholarship established in honor of his late wife, 1995, Better Advantages for Students and Soc.; named World's Foremost Double Bassist, IBA, 1969—; grantee, NIMH, 1976—77. Mem. APA, ASCAP, SAG, Am. Soc. Music Arrangers & Composers, Chamber Music Am., N.Y. Acad. Scis., Astron. Soc. of the Pacific (charter), Orange County Psychol. Assn., Assn. of Black Psychologists, Planetary Soc. (charter), Am. Hort. Soc., Nat Trust for Hist. Preservation Soc., Rec. Musicians Assn., Stanford U. Alumni Assn., NYU Alumni Assn., CCNY Alumni Assn., Sierra Club. Avocations: astronomy, gourmet cooking, gardening, photography, dxing. Office: ARKIMU 3535 E Coast Hwy # 50 Corona Del Mar CA 92625-2404 E-mail: drart@artdavis.com.

DAVIS, BARON, professional basketball player; b. LA, Apr. 13, 1979; Attended, UCLA, 1997—99. Point guard Charlotte Hornets (renamed New Orleans Hornets), 1999—2005, Golden State Warriors, 2005—08, LA Clippers, 2008—. Prodr.: (documentaries) Made in America, 2008. Named to NBA All-Star Team, 2002, 2004. Achievements include winning the NBA All-Star Skills Challenge, 2004. Office: LA Clippers 1111 S Figueroa St Ste 1100 Los Angeles CA 90015

DAVIS, BART M., state legislator; b. Rapid City, SD, Mar. 7, 1955; m. Marion Davis; 6 children. BA, BYU, 1978; JD, U. Idaho, 1980. Bar: Idaho 1981. Bd. mem. & officer Idaho State Bar Bankruptcy Law Section, 1983—88, chmn., 1986—87; lawyer rep. 9th Circuit Jud. Conf. Ct. Appeals, 1993—95, 1995—98; mem. Dist. 33 Idaho State Senate, 1998—, majority leader, 2002—; vice chmn. & sec. Elec. Wholesale Supply Co., 2004—. Republican. Mem. Lds Ch. Office: State Capitol Bldg PO Box 83720 Boise ID 83720-0081 Office Phone: 208-332-1000, 208-529-4993, 208-552-8100. Office Fax: 208-334-2125. Business E-Mail: bmdavis@senate.idaho.gov.*

DAVIS, BETTYE JEAN, state legislator; b. Homer, La., May 17, 1938; d. Dan and Rosylind (Daniel) Ivory; m. Troy J. Davis, Jan. 21, 1959; children: Anthony Benard, Sonja Davis Wade. Cert. nursing, St. Anthony's, 1961; BSW, Grambling State U., 1971; postgrad., U. Alaska, 1972. Psychiat. nurse Alaska Psychiat. Inst., 1967-70; asst. dir. San Bernardino (Calif.) YWCA, 1971-72; child care specialist DFYS Anchorage, 1975-80, soc. worker, 1980-82, foster care coordinator, 1982-87; dir. Alaska Black Leadership Edn. Program, 1979-82; exec. dir. Anchorage Sch. Bd., 1982-89; mem. Alaska Legislature, 1990—2000, Alaska Senate, 2000—. Chair Children's Caucus Alaska Legis., 1992—. Pres. Anchorage Sch. Bd., 1986-87; bd. dirs. Blacks in Govt., 1980-82, March of Dimes, 1983-85, Anchorage chpt. YWCA, 1989-90, Winning with Stronger Edn. Com., 1991, Alaska 2000, Anchorage Ctr. for Families, 1992—, active Anchorage chpt. NAACP, bd. dirs., 1978-82; mem. State Bd. Edn., 1997-2000. Toll fellow Henry Toll Fellowship Program, 1992; named Woman of Yr., Alaska Colored Women's Club, 1981, Child Care Worker of Yr., Alaska Foster Parent Assn., 1983, Social Worker of Yr., Nat. Foster Parents Assn., 1983, Outstanding Bd. Mem., Assn. Alaska Sch. Bds., 1990,; recipient Outstanding Achievement in Edn. award Alaska Colored Women's Club, 1985, Outstanding Women in Edn. award Zeta Phi Beta, 1985, Boardsmanship award Assn. Alaska Sch. Bds., 1989, Woman of Achievement award YWCA, 1991, Outstanding Leadership award Calif. Assembly, 1992. Mem. LWV, Nat. Sch. Bd. Assn., Nat. Caucus of Black Sch. Bd. Mems. (bd. dirs. 1986-87), Alaska Black Caucus (chair 1984—), Alaska Women's Polit. Caucus, Alaska Black Leadership Conf. (pres. 1976-80), Alaska Women Lobby (treas.), Nat. Caucus of Black State Legis. (chair region 12, 1994—), Women Legislators Lobby, Women's Action for New Directions, North to Future Bus. and Prof. Women (pres. 1978-79, 83), Delta Sigma Theta (Alaska chpt. pres. 1978-80). Clubs: North to Future Bus. and Profl. Women (past pres.). Democrat. Baptist. Avocations: cooking, Scrabble, stamp collecting/philately, coin collecting/numismatics, reading. Home: 2240 Foxhall Dr Anchorage AK 99504-3350 Office: State Capitol Rm 30 Juneau AK 99801-1182 also: Dist K 716 W 4th Ave Ste 450 Anchorage AK 99501 Office Phone: 907-265-3822, 907-269-0144. Office Fax: 907-465-3756, 907-269-0148. Business E-Mail: Senator_Bettye_Davis@legis.state.ak.us. E-mail: bdavis@ak.net.*

DAVIS, CRAIG ALPHIN, lawyer, manufacturing company executive; b. Oakland, Calif., July 28, 1940; s. Alphin Craig and Joyce Ida (Nevers) D.; m. Betty Rankin, July 13, 1963; children: Chelsea Alyson, Channing MacLaren. AB in Polit. Sci, U. Calif., Berkeley, 1964, JD, 1967. Bar: Calif. 1968. Assoc. Heller, Ehrman, White & McAuliffe, San Francisco, 1968-71; counsel Aluminum div. AMAX Inc., San Mateo, Calif., 1971-74; dir. law Alumax Inc., San Mateo, 1974, gen. counsel, sec., 1974-84, v.p., 1978-82, group v.p., gen. counsel, 1982-84, sr. v.p., 1984-86, exec. v.p., 1986-89; internat. bus. transaction advisor, of counsel Hughes, Hubbard & Reed, NYC, 1990—; chmn. Ravenswood Aluminum Corp., NYC, 1992—; chmn. & CEO Century Aluminum Co., Monterey, Calif. Mem. editorial bd., research editor: Hastings Law Jour, 1966-67. Mem. ABA, State Bar Calif. Office: Century Aluminum Co 2511 Garden Rd Monterey CA 93940

DAVIS, DONALD ALAN, news correspondent, author; b. Savannah, Ga., Oct. 5, 1939; s. Oden Harry and Irma Artice (Gay) Davis; m. Robin Murphy, Mar. 17, 1983 (dec. May 11, 2005); children from previous marriage: Russell Glenn, Randall Scott. BA in Journalism, U. Ga., 1962. Reporter Athens (Ga.) Banner-Herald, 1961-62, Savannah Morning News, 1962; with UPI, 1963-65, 1967-83, Vietnam corr., 1971-73, New Eng. editor, 1977-80, White House corr., 1981-83; reporter, editor St. Petersburg (Fla.) Times, 1965-66; polit. reporter, columnist San Diego Union, 1983-91; pub. Pacific Rim Report newsletter, 1985-88. Instr. journalism Boston U., 1979; instr. writing U. Colo., 1998-99; lectr. U.S. Naval War Coll., 1983, Queen Elizabeth 2, 1991. Author: The Milwaukee Murders, 1991, The Nanny Murder Trial, 1992, Bad Blood, 1994, Death of an Angel, 1994, Fallen Hero, 1994, Appointment with the Squire, 1995, Death Cruise, 1996, A Father's Rage, 1996, The Gris-Gris Man, 1997, Hush, Little Babies, 1997, The Last Man on the Moon, 1999, JonBenet, 2000, Dark Waters, 2002, Lightning Strike, 2005, Shooter, 2005, Kill Zone, 2006, Stonewall Jackson, 2006, Dead Shot, 2008, Clean Kill, 2009. Fellow Keizai Koho Ctr., Tokyo, 1985, Overseas Press Club, 2000. Unitarian. E-mail: tedsalad@mesanetworks.net.

DAVIS, EARL JAMES, chemical engineering professor emeritus; b. St. Paul, July 22, 1934; s. Leo Ernest and Mary (Steiner) D.; children: Molly Kathleen, David Leo. BS cum laude, Gonzaga U., 1956; PhD, U. Wash., 1960. Design engr. Union Carbide Chems. Co., South Charleston, W.Va., 1956; from asst. prof. chem. engring. to assoc. prof. Gonzaga U., Spokane, Wash., 1960-68, dir. computing ctr., 1967-68; rsch. fellow Imperial Coll., London U., 1964-65; assoc. prof. chem. engring. Clarkson U., 1968-73, head socio-environ. program, 1972-74, prof., 1973-78, chmn. chem. engring. dept., 1973-74, assoc. dir. Inst. Colloid and Surface Sci., 1974-78; prof., chmn. chem. and nuclear engring. dept. U. N.Mex., 1978-80; dir. engring. divsn., prof. Inst. Paper Chemistry, Appleton, Wis., 1980-83; rsch. fellow in chem. engring. U. Wash., Seattle, 1957-60, prof. chem. engring., 1983—, assoc. vice provost for rsch., 2001—03. Guest prof. Tech. U. of Vienna, Austria, 2000; sr. scientist, cons. Unilever Rsch. Lab., Port Sunlight, Eng., 1974-75; vis. scholar NAS/Chinese Acad. Scis., China, 1989; adj. prof. Sichuan U., Chengdu, China, 2001—. Assoc. editor Aerosol Sci. and Tech., 1993-97; mem. editl. bd. Jour. Colloid and Interface Sci., 1984-86; mem. editl. bd. Jour. Aerosol Sci., 1992-98, editor-in-chief, 1999—; mem. adv. bd. Surface and Colloid Sci., 2000—; regional editor (N.Am. and S.Am.) Colloid and Polymer Sci., 1994-99; contbr. articles to sci. publs. NSF fellow, 1964-65, grantee, 1963-89, 92—2003; recipient Burlington No. award for rsch., 1988; Leeds and Northrup fellow U. Wash., 1960. Fellow AAAS, mem. Am. Chem. Soc., Am. Assn. Aerosol Rsch. (treas. 1990-92, David Sinclair award 1991, v.p. 1996-97, pres. 1997-98), Soc. Applied Spectroscopy, Gesellschaft für Aerosolforschung, Sigma Xi. Achievements include research in air pollution control, aerosol physics and chemistry and colloid science. Office: U Wash Dept Chem Engring PO Box 351750 Seattle WA 98195-1750 Business E-Mail: davis@cheme.washington.edu.

DAVIS, EDMOND RAY, lawyer; b. Glendale, Calif., Sept. 4, 1928; s. Archie Allen and Eve Mae (Hoover) D.; m. Ruby Evelyn Davis, Oct. 17, 1954; children: Phillip A., Sandra A. Student, Pepperdine Coll.; JD, U. Calif., San Francisco, 1952. Bar: Calif. 1952, U.S. Dist. Ct. (cen. dist.) Calif. 1952. Assoc. Bailie, Turner & Sprague, 1955-60; trust counsel Security Pacific Nat. Bank, 1960-67; ptnr. Overton, Lyman & Prince, LA, 1967-87, Brobeck, Phleger & Harrison, LA, 1987-99, Davis & Whalen, North Hollywood, Calif., 1999—. Chmn., pub. adminstr. Pub. Guardian Adv. Commns., Los County Bd. Suprs., 1974-76; bd. dirs. Braille Inst. Am., Inc., Children's Bur. So. Calif., Children's Bur. Found., Fifield Manors, Inc.; pres. LA Jaycees, 1962; mem. legal com. Music Ctr. Found., Performing Arts Council, LA county, 1980-85. With U.S. Army, 1952-54. Recipient Alumni award Pepperdine Coll., 1962. Fellow Am. Coll. Trust and Estate Counsel (chmn. Calif. chpt. 1981-86); mem. Internat. Acad. Estate and Trust Law (academician), State Bar of Calif. (chmn. estate planning, trust and probate law sect. 1977-78), L.A. County Bar Assn. (exec. com., probate and trust law sect. 1986-89, Arthur K. Marshall award Probate and Trust Law sect. 1991), Order of Coif, Calif. Club, Chancery Club. Office: 5200 Lankershim Blvd Ste 380 North Hollywood CA 91601-3155 Home Phone: 626-799-7234; Office Phone: 818-752-2880. Office Fax: 818-752-2990. Business E-Mail: edavis@daviswhalen.com.

DAVIS, GENE, state legislator; b. Salt Lake City, July 2, 1945; s. John and Glenna; m. Penny Lou Davis; 2 children. Cert. in electronic engring., Radio Operational Engring., Burbank, Calif., 1963; LLB, LaSalle Ext. U., Chgo., 1974. Announcer Radio Sta. KNAK, Salt Lake City, 1965-75; prodn. continuity dir. Radio Sta. KALL AM/FM, Salt Lake City, 1976-86; owner G. Davis Advt. & Pub. Rels., Salt Lake City, 1986-91; pub. rels. profl. Valley Mental Health, Salt Lake City, 1990—; mem. Dist. 3 Utah House of Reps., 1986—98; asst. minority whip Utah State Senate, 1998—2004, mem. Dist. 3, 1999—, minority whip. Treas. Comm. Fed. Credit Union, Salt Lake City, 1981-86. Vice-chair East County Recreation Bd., Salt Lake City, 1991—2000. Mem. Sugar House Rotary Club (pres. 2003-04), Sugar House Cmty. Coun. (chmn. 1984-85). Democrat. Mem. Lds Ch. Avocations: golf, gardening, politics. Mailing: 865 Parkway Ave Salt Lake City UT 84106-1704 Office: W115 Capitol Complex Salt Lake City UT 84114 Office Phone: 801-273-6394, 801-538-1035. Office Fax: 801-326-1475. Business E-Mail: gdavis@utahsenate.org.*

DAVIS, GEORGE DONALD, executive land use policy consultant; b. Oneida, NY, Nov. 19, 1942; s. Pearl Floyd and Kathrine Virginia (Connolly) D.; m. Anita Face Riner, June 26, 1976; children: Maria Lisa, Brett Hollis, Sarah Bessie, Lara Emily; stepchildren: Andrea G. Riner, Joel S. Riner. BS in Forestry, SUNY, 1964; postgrad., Cornell U., 1971. Forester, pub. land adminstr. U.S. Forest Svc. Dept. Agr., Colo., 1964-68; ecologist Gov. Rockefeller's N.Y. State Temp. Study Commn. on Future of Adirondacks, 1969—71; pvt. land use and natural resources cons. Ithaca, NY, 1971; dir. planning Adirondack Park Agy., Ray Brook, NY, 1971-76; exec. dir. Wilderness Soc., Washington, 1976-77; spl. asst. U.S. Forest Svc., Washington, 1977-79; dep. forest supr. Idaho Panhandle Nat. Forests, Coeur d'Alene, 1979-82; land use, natural resource cons. Wadhams, NY, 1982-94; program dir. Adirondack Coun., 1983-88; exec. dir. Adirondack Land Trust, 1984-88; prin. Davis Assocs., 1988—. Pres. Ecol. Sustainable Devel., Inc., 1994—97; coord. Global Assocs. in Sustainable Devel., 1997—2002; project dir. Land Use Policy and Allocation Program for Lake Baikal Watershed in Russia, 1991—93, Lake Hovsgol/Selenge River Wateshed in Mongolia, 1992—94, Ussuri River Watershed in Russian Far East and China, 1993—97, Altai Rep., Russia, 1994—97; exec. dir. Gov. Cuomo's Commn. on Adirondacks in the 21st Century, 1989—90; mem. environ. task force Rockefeller Bros. Fund; mem. Hudson Basin project task force Rockefeller Found. Co-author: The Unfinished Agenda, 1977, Developing a Land Conservation Strategy, 1987; author: Ecosystem Representative as a Criterion for World Wilderness Designation, 1987, 2020 Vision: Fulfilling the Promise of the Adirondack Park, 1988, Completing the Adirondack Wilderness System, 1990, The Lake Baikal Region in the Twenty-First Century: A Model of Sustainable Development or Continued Degradation?, 1993, A Comprehensive National Program of Sustainable Land Use Policies for the Lake Hovsgol-Selenge River Watershed, 1994, A Sustainable Land Use and Allocation Program for the Ussuri/Wusuli River Watershed and Adjacent Territories, 1996; contbr. to profl. publs. Active Gov. N.Y. State Forest Industry Task Force, 1987-89, N.Y.-New Eng. Gov. Task Force on No. Forest Lands, 1988-90. MacArthur fellow, 1989—. Roman Catholic. Home and Office: 2482 N 32d St Springfield OR 97477-7900 E-mail: davisassoc1@aol.com.

DAVIS, GEORGE S., manufacturing executive; Grad. in Econs. and Polit. Sci., Claremont McKenna Coll., Calif.; MBA, UCLA. Sr. pres. fin. Europe, Mid. East and Africa Atlantic Richfield Co.; corp. treas. Applied Materials, Inc., 1999—2005, head corp. bus. devel. group, 2005—06, sr. v.p., CFO, 2006—. Chmn. North Am. adv. bd. Semiconductor Equipment and Materials Internat. Bd. trustees San Jose Repertory Theatre. Office: Applied Materials Inc PO Box 58039 Santa Clara CA 95052-8039 Office Phone: 408-727-5555.

DAVIS, GRAY (JOSEPH GRAHAM DAVIS), lawyer, former governor; b. NYC, Dec. 26, 1942; m. Sharon Ryer, Feb. 20, 1983. BA cum laude, Stanford U., 1964; JD, Columbia U., 1967. Chief of staff to Gov. Jerry Brown State of Calif., Sacramento, 1975—81, mem. Calif. State Assembly, 1983—87, state contr., 1987—95, lt. gov., 1995-99, gov., 1999—2003; of counsel Loeb & Loeb, LA, 2004—. Chmn. Housing and Community Devel. Com., Calif. Coun. on Criminal Justice, Franchise Tax Bd., State Lands Commn.; mem. Bd. Equalization, State Tchrs. Retirement System, Pub. Employees Retirement System, Nat. Coun. Institutional Investors; U. Calif. Regent, Calif. State U. trustee; mem. intergovtl. policy adv. com. on trade Office of U.S. Trade Rep. Founder Calif. Found. for the Protection of Children. Capt. US Army. Democrat. Office: Loeb & Loeb 1010 Santa Monica Blvd Ste 2200 Los Angeles CA 90067

DAVIS, HARLEY CLEO, retired military officer; b. Van Buren, Ark., May 7, 1941; s. Aleta (Johnson) Davis; m. Patricia Ann White, Mar. 9, 1985. BS, Ark. Tech. U., 1963; MA, Ea. Ky. U., 1972; exec. devel. program, U. N.H., 1987. Commd. 2d lt. U.S. Army, 1963, advanced through grades to maj. gen., 1993; platoon leader 1st Bn.,

50th inf., 2d Armored Div., 1963; various assignments, 1963-80; comdr. 3d Bn., 5th Spl. Forces Group, Ft. Bragg, NC, 1980-82; chief leadership br. Hdqrs. Dept. of the Army, Washington, 1982-84; chief of staff JFK Spl. Warfare Ctr. and Sch., Ft. Bragg, 1985-86; comdr. 5th Spl. Forces Group, Ft. Campbell, Ky., 1987-89; asst. comdt. JFK Spl. Warfare Ctr. and Sch., Ft. Bragg, 1989-91; dep. comdg. gen. U.S. Army Sp. Ops. Command, Ft. Bragg, 1991-92; comdg. gen. U.S. Army Spl. Forces Command (Airborne), Ft. Bragg, 1992-95; dep. comdg. gen. Fifth U.S. Army (west), Ft. Lewis, Wash., 1995-97. Sr. mentor Jt. Spl. Ops. U., 2007—. Decorated DSM with oak leaf cluster, Legion of Merit, Soldier's medal, Bronze Star with two oak leaf clusters, Air medal with oak leaf cluster. Home Phone: 301-570-6253.

DAVIS, J. ALAN, writer, film and television producer; Student, Marlborough Coll., Eng., 1979; BA with distinction, So. Meth. U., 1983; JD with honors, U. Tex., 1987. Bar: Calif. 1988. Assoc. O'Melveny & Myers, LA, 1987-89, Rosenfeld, Meyer & Susman, Beverly Hills, Calif., 1989-90; pvt. practice LA, 1990-94; ptnr. Davis & Benjamin, LA, 1995-98, Garvin, Davis & Benjamin, LLP, LA, 1998-99; head legal and bus. affairs Warner Bros. Internat. TV Prodn., Burbank, Calif., 2000—02; pres. Periscope Ltd., LA, 2002—. Mem. Calif. Bar Assn., Beverly Hills Bar Assn., Brit. Acad. Film and TV Arts, L.A. (mng. dir. 1998, bd. dirs., chmn. Britannia awards 2004). Avocations: skiing, scuba diving, tennis.

DAVIS, J. STEVE, advertising agency executive; b. Alliance, Nebr., Feb. 26, 1945; s. John P. and Ruth M. (Annen) D.; m. Courtney Boyd Crowder, June 28, 1973 (div. Oct. 2000); children: Cullen Boyd, J. Scott, Robert Charles. BA, U. Nebr., 1967. Asst. account exec. Benton & Bowles Inc., NYC, 1972-73, account exec., 1973-76, v.p., account supr., 1976-79, sr. v.p., mgmt. supr., 1978-79, 81-85, sr. v.p., account dir. Brussels, 1979-81, NYC, 1985-90; pres. Altschiller Reitzfeld Davis Tracy-Locke, Inc., NYC; exec. v.p., gen. mgr. J. Walter Thompson, Chgo., 1990-96, dir. worldwide bd., 1991; pres., CEO, dir. Young & Rubicam, NYC, 1996-97; chmn., CEO Wells BDDP, New York, NY, 1998; pres., COO Qorvis Media Group, Inc., San Francisco, 1997-98; pres. Qorvis Media Group, San Francisco, 1998-99. Bd. dirs. Qorvis Media Group, San Francisco; pres., CEO Giraffe Inc., San Carlos. Founders Coun. Our Lady of Missippi Valley; bd. dirs. Steppenwolf Theatre Co., Chgo., 1993, Off The Street Club, 1993, pres., 1995. Named Exec. of Yr. Midwest Advt. Agy., 1992. Mem. Chgo. Econs. Club (chmn. advt. & mass media membership com. 1995), Westmoreland Club, Sigma Chi (publs. bd. 1998—, Significant Sig 1996). Home: 17 Thundercloud Rd Santa Fe NM 87506-0121 E-mail: giraffa@mindspring.com.

DAVIS, JAMES ALLAN, gerontologist, educator; b. Portland, Oreg., May 20, 1953; m. Louis Carol Lindsay. BS, U. Oreg., 1975, MS, 1976, EdD, 1980. State mental health gerontologist Oreg. Mental Health Div., Salem, 1978-80; project dir. Oreg. Long Term Care Tng. Project, Salem, 1979-80; tng. specialist Nat. Assn. Area Agys. on Aging., Washington, 1981; asst. dir. for internships and vol. svc. exptl. learning programs U. Md., 1981-86, mem. rsch. and instructional faculty, 1982-86; com. adminstr. Oreg. State Human Resources Com., Salem, 1987; exec. dir., legis. dir. Oreg. State Coun. Sr. Citizens, Salem, 1987—; program coord. for sr. mental health care Oreg. Sr. and Disabled Svc. Div., Salem, 1989—2001; pres. James A. Davis and Assocs. Inc., Portland, 1991—; state project dir. Oreg. Assn. RSVPs, 1995—2007; assoc. prof. dept. human scis. Marylhurst U., Oreg., 2005—. Vis. asst. prof. Ctr. for Gerontology, U. Oreg., 1990-92; co-chair Audio-Visual Program, Internat. Congress Gerontology, 1985; nat. gerontology acad. adv. panel, Nat. Hosp. Satellite Network, 1983-85; lobbyist United Srs. Oreg., Oreg. State Coun. Sr. Citizens, Oreg. State Denturist Assn., Oreg. State Pharmacist Assn., Oreg. Soc. Physician Assts., Oreg. Legal Techs. Assn., Oreg. Dental Lab. Assn., Wash. Denturist Assn., Nat. Denturist Assn.; adj. asst. prof. Urban Studies Inst. on Aging, Portland State U., 2003-04; assoc. prof. human scis. dept. Marylhurst U., 2001—, co-chair diversity com. and faculty devel. com.; chair Nat. Coalition Consumer Orgn., 2008-, Nat. Leadership Coun. on Aging, 2008-; presenter in field. Co-author: TV's Image of the Elderly, 1985; contbg. editor Retirement Life News, 1988-92; sr. issues editor Sr. News, 1989-96; contbr. articles to profl. jours.; producer, host approximately 400 TV and radio programs. Founding pres. Oreg. Alliance for Progressive Policy, 1988-89; co-chair mental health com., vice chair legis. com., Gov.'s Commn. on Sr. Svcs., 1988-89; exec. coun., media chair Human Svcs. Coalition Oreg., 1988-89; bd. dirs. Oreg. Health Action Campaign, 1988-92; 2d v.p., bd. dirs. Oreg. Medicaid Com., 1996—2002; co-chair Oreg. Medicare/Medicaid Coalition, 1995—2001, Oreg. Long Term Care Campaign, 1996-98; mem. Gov's. Task Force for Volunteerism, State of Md., 1983-84, State Legis. Income Tax Task Force, 1990; vice chair Oreg. State Bd. Denture Technology, 1991-96; mem. com. for assessment on needs for volunteerism, Gov.'s Vol. Coun., State of Md., 1984-86; mem. exec. bd. dirs. Oreg. Advocacy Coalition of Srs. and People with Disabilities, 1997—, co-chair 1999-2007; chmn., bd. dirs. Oreg. Campaign for Patient Rights, 1997-2003. Recipient Disting. Svc. award City of Salem, 1980, Spl. Human Rights award, 1981, Svc. award U. Md., 1984, Hometown U.S.A. award Community Cable TV Producers, 1988, Disting. Svc. award Oreg. State Coun. Sr. Citizens, 1991. Mem.: Oreg. State Coun. of Sr. Citizens (Disting. Svc. of Sr. award 2000), Alzheimers Assn. of Oreg. (Pub. Policy award 2000), Nat. Denturist Assn. (exec. dir. 1982—89), Gerontol. Soc. Am. (mental health task force 1982—84, co-chmn. 1983—84), Nat. Assn. State Mental Health Dir. (nat. exec. com. 1978—80, vice chmn. 1979—80, spl. cons.81 1981—82, mem. aging div., co-chmn. nat. program com. 1984—87, nat. media chair 1985—92), Nat. Gray Panthers (nat. exec. com. 1984—87, nat. bd. dirs. 1984—92, program co-chmn. nat. biennial conv. 1986, nat. health task force 1981—, co-chmn. 1983—84, chmn. mental health subcom. 1981—86, editor Health Watch 1982—84, state program developer Oreg. chpt. 1979—80, 1989, lobbyist 1987—, gov.'s patient protection work group 2000—01). Democrat. E-mail: davisjasr@aol.com.

DAVIS, JOHN MACDOUGALL, lawyer; b. Seattle, Feb. 20, 1914; s. David Lyle and Georgina (MacDougall) D.; m. Ruth Anne Van Arsdale, July 1, 1939; children: Jean, John, Bruce, Ann, Margaret, Elizabeth. BA, U. Wash., 1936, LLB, JD, 1940. Bar: Wash. 1940. Assoc. Poe, Falknor, Emory & Howe, Seattle, 1940-45; pvt. practice Seattle, 1945-46; ptnr. Davis & Riese, Seattle, 1946-48, Emory, Howe, Davis & Riese, Seattle, 1948-50, Howe, Davis & Riese, Seattle, 1951-53, Howe, Davis, Riese & Aiken, Seattle, 1953-58, Howe, Davis, Riese & Jones, Seattle, 1958-68, Davis, Wright, Todd, Riese & Jones, Seattle, 1969-85; of counsel Davis, Wright & Jones, Seattle, 1985-89, Davis Wright Tremaine, Seattle, 1990—. Lectr. U. Wash. Law Sch., 1947-52; pres. Seattle Bar Assn., 1960. Bd. dirs. Virginia Mason Hosp., Seattle, 1952-79, pres., 1970-72; bd. dirs. Pacific Sci. Ctr., 1971-90, dir. emeritus, 1990—, past pres., past chmn.; trustee Whitman Coll., 1971-86, chmn., 1983-86; bd. dirs. Blue Cross Wash. and Alaska, 1982-89, Diabetic Trust Fund, 1954—, Wash. Student Loan Guaranty Assn., 1978-83; mem. adv. bd. Chief Seattle council Boy Scouts Am.; mem. Mercer Island Sch. Bd., 1956-66. With USNG, 1931—34. Recipient Disting. Eagle Scout award, 1982 Mem. ABA, Wash. State Bar Assn. (merit award 1965), Seattle-King County Bar Assn. (pres. 1960-61), Order of Coif, Rainier Club (Seattle), The Mountaineers Club (Svc. award, 1974), Phi Delta Phi, Alpha Delta Phi. Clubs: Rainier (Seattle). Presbyterian. Avocation: mountain climbing. Home: 9104 Fortuna Dr #6223 Mercer Island WA 98040 Office: Davis Wright Tremaine 1201 Third Ave Seattle WA 98101-3045

DAVIS, JOHN ROWLAND, academic administrator; b. Mpls., Dec. 19, 1927; s. Roland Owen and Dorothy (Norman) D.; m. Lois Marie Falk, Sept. 4, 1947; children— Joel C., Jacque L., Michele M., Robin E. BS, U. Minn., 1949, MS, 1951; postgrad., Purdue U., 1955-57; PhD, Mich. State U., 1959. Hydraulic engr. U.S. Geol. Survey, Lincoln, Nebr., 1950-51; instr. Mich. State U., 1951-55; asst. prof. Purdue U., 1955-57; lectr. U. Calif., Davis, 1957-62; hydraulic engr. Stanford Rsch. Inst., South Pasadena, Calif., 1962-64; prof. U. Nebr., Lincoln, 1964-65, dean coll. engrng. and architecture, 1965-71, faculty rep. intercollegiate athletics; prof., head dept. agrl. engrng. Oreg. State U., Corvallis, 1971-75, instl. athletic rep., 1972-87, dir. Agrl. Expt. Sta., assoc. dean Sch. Agr., 1975-85, dir. spl. programs Office of Academic Affairs, assoc. dir. athletics, 1987-89, prof. emeritus, assoc. dir. athletics, 1989—. Governing bd. Water Resources Research Inst., 1975-85; dir. Western Rural Devel. Center, 1975-85, Agrl. Research Found., Jackman Inst.; cons. Stanford Research Inst., Dept. Agr., Consortium for Internat. Devel.; dir. Engrs. Council Profl. Devel., 1966-72; pres. Pacific-10 Conf., 1978-79. Contbr. articles to profl. jours. Mem. budget commn. City of Corvallis, 2003—. With USNR, 1945-46. Fellow Am. Soc. Agrl. Engrs. (dir. 1971-73, Agrl. Engr. Yr. award Pacific N.W. region 1974), NCAA (v.p. 1979-83, sec.-treas. 1983-85, pres. 1985-87), Heartland Humane Soc. (pres. bd. dirs. 2002). Home: 2940 NW Aspen St Corvallis OR 97330-3307 Personal E-mail: davisjrd@aol.com.

DAVIS, JONATHAN, JR., broadcast executive; b. Aug. 7, 1971; Intern NBC, NYC; writers' asst. Politically Incorrect ABC; asst. DreamWorks TV; dir. alternative programming and latenight devel. Fox Broadcasting Co., Beverly Hills, Calif., 2002—05, dir. comedy devel., 2005—06, v.p. comedy devel., 2006—. Achievements include overseeing development of the TV series Til Death and Happy Hour. Office: Fox Broadcasting Co PO Box 900 Beverly Hills CA 90213

DAVIS, LANCE EDWIN, economics professor; b. Seattle, Nov. 3, 1928; s. Maurice L. and Marjorie Dee (Seibert) D.; m. Susan Elizabeth Gray, Dec. 2, 1977; 1 child, Maili. BA, U. Wash., Seattle, 1950; PhD (Ford Found. dissertation fellow summer 1956), Johns Hopkins U., 1956. Teaching asst. U. Wash., 1950-51, 52-53; teaching asst., then instr. Johns Hopkins U., 1953-55; from instr. to prof. econs. Purdue U., 1955-62; mem. faculty Calif. Inst. Tech., Pasadena, prof. econs., 1968—, Mary Stillman Harkness prof., 1980—; rsch. assoc. Nat. Bur. Econ. Rsch., 1979—. Author: The Growth of Industrial Enterprise, 1964; co-author: The Savings Bank of Baltimore, 1956, American Economic History: The Development of a National Economy, 2d rev. edit, 1968, Institutional Change and American Economic Growth, 1971, Mammon and the Pursuit of Empire: The Political Economy of British Imperialism, 1860-1912, 1987, Internat. Capital Markets and Economic Growth 1820-1914, 1994, In Pursuit of Leviathan: Technology, Institutions, Productivity and Profits in American Whaling, 1816-1906, 1997, Evolving Financial Markets and Foreign Capital Flows: Britain, the Americas, and Australia, 1870-1914, 1999; co-editor: American Economic Growth: An Economist's History of the United States, 1971; mem. bd. editors Jour. Econ. History, 1965-73, Explorations in Economic History, 1984-88, THESIS, Theory, and History of Econ. and Social Instns. and Structures, with Soviet and Western Scholars, 1991—. With USNR, 1945-48, 51-52. Recipient Arthur Cole prize Econ. History Assn., 1966, Alice Hanson Jones prize, 1998, Sanwa Monograph prize Ctr. for Japan-U.S. Bus. and Econ. Studies, 1995, Libr. Co. Phila. program in early Am. economy and society prize, 2000; Ford Found. Faculty fellow, 1959-60; Guggenheim fellow, 1964-65; fellow Ctr. for Advanced Study in Behavioral Scis., 1985-86. Fellow Am. Acad. Arts and Scis.; mem. Coun. 1 Rsch. Econ. History (chmn. 1973-74, 75-76), Econ. History Assn. (pres. 1978-79, trustee 1980-82, Alice Hanson Jones prize 1998), Anglo-Am. Hist. Assn. (gov. 1978-80), Econs. Inst. (policy and adv. bd. 1984-87), Cliometric Soc. (trustee 1993-97). Office: Calif Inst Tech Humanities And Social Scis Dv Pasadena CA 91125-0001 Home: 9717 Thistle Ct Fort Smith AR 72908-9242 Home Phone: 323-254-2046; Office Phone: 626-395-4092. Business E-Mail: led@hss.caltech.edu.

DAVIS, MARK E., chemical engineering educator; b. Ellwood City, Pa. m. Mary P. Davis; 3 children. BS, U. Ky., Lexington, 1977; MS, U. Ky., 1978, PhD in chem. engrng., 1981. Asst. prof., assoc. prof., to chaired prof. chem. engrng. Va. Poly. Inst. and State U., Blacksburg, 1981—91; prof. dept. chemistry Calif. Inst. Tech., Pasadena, prof. chem. engrng., 1991—93, Warren and Katharine Schlinger Prof. Chem. Engring., 1993—. Sci. adv. bd. Alnylam, NovoDynamics, Symyx; founder Insert Therapeutics, Pasadena, chief sci. adv., bd. dirs.; founding scientist Calando Pharms., Duarte, Calif.; mem. Exptl. Therapeutics Prog. City of Hope Comprehensive Cancer Ctr., Duarte; lectr. Co-editor Fundamentals Chem. Reaction Engring.; founding editor: CaTTech, assoc. editor: Chemistry of Materials, AIChE Jour.; contbr. articles sci. jours. Recipient Dow Outstanding Young Faculty award, Am. Soc. Engring. Edn., 1985, Presdl. Young Investigator award, 1985, Donald Breck award, Internat. Zeolite Assn., 1989, Alan T. Waterman award, NSF, 1990, Paul H. Emmett award, North Am. Catalysis Soc., 1995. Mem.: Materials Rsch. Soc., Am. Inst. Chem. Engrs. (Allan P. Colburn award 1989, Profl. Progress award 1999), Am. Chem. Soc. (Ipatieff prize 1992), NAS, NAE, Tau Beta Pi, Omega Chi Epsilon, Phi Eta Sigma. Achievements include pioneering work in the synthesis of new catalytic materials. Office: Calif Inst Tech Dept Chemistry 210-41 1200 E California Blvd Pasadena CA 91125-0001

DAVIS, MARK M., microbiologist, educator; b. Paris, Nov. 27, 1952; BA in Molecular Biology, Johns Hopkins U., 1974; PhD in Molecular Biology, Calif. Inst. Tech., 1981. Fellow lab. of immunology NIH, Bethesda, Md., 1980-82, staff fellow lab. of immunology, 1982-83; asst. prof. med. microbiology Stanford (Calif.) U. Sch. Medicine, 1983-86, assoc. prof. microbiology and immunology, 1986-91, prof. microbiology and immunology, 1991—, Burt & Marion Avery prof. immunology, dir. predoctoral program in immunology, 1994—, chair microbiology & immunology, 2002—04, dir. Stanford Inst. Immunity, Transplantation, & Infection, 2004—; assoc. investigator Howard Hughes Med. Inst., Stanford U., 1987-91, faculty coord., 1989—, investigator, 1991—. Instr. Cold Spring Harbor (N.Y.) Lab., 1983; mem. sci. adv. bd. Damon Runyon-Walter Cancer Found., 1985-88; co-organizer UCLA Symposium, 1987; mem. allergy and immunology study sect. divsn. rsch. grants NIH, 1988-92. Recipient Intra-Sci. Rsch. Found. award 1980, Youth Scientist award Passano Found., 1985, Eli Lilly award 1986, Kayden award N.Y. Acad. Scis., 1986, Howard Taylor Ricketts award U. Chgo., 1988, Gairdner Found. award, 1989, King Faisal Internat. prize 1995, Sloan prize Gen. Motors Rsch. Found., 1996; scholar PEW Found. 1985-89. Mem. Nat. Acad. Scis., Inst. Medicine (2004). Office: Howard Hughes Med Inst Beckman Ctr B221 279 Campus Dr Stanford CA 94305-5323

DAVIS, MARK R., state agency administrator; grad., JD, Stanford U. Divsn. dir. banking and securities Alaska Dept. Commerce, Cmty., and Econ. Devel., 2003—, dep. commr., 2005—. Office: Dept Commerce Cmty and Econ Devel Divsn Banking and Securities PO Box 110807 Juneau AK 99811-0807 Office Phone: 907-465-2521. Office Fax: 907-465-2549. E-mail: Mark_Davis@commerce.state.ak.us.

DAVIS, MEGAN J., consulting firm executive; b. 1967; Pres. The Davis Consulting Grp., Inc. Mem. Ariz. Humanities Coun., Women at the Top Bd.; adv. coun., Women's Studies U. Ariz. Chairwoman Jewish Fedn. Southern Ariz., Planned Parenthood Southern Ariz. Bd. Named one of 40 Under 40, Tucson Bus. Edge, 2006.

DAVIS, MIKE, state legislator; BA in Hist., U. NC, Charlotte; MPA, Calif. State U., Northridge; MA Behavioral Sci., Calif. State U., Dominguez Hills. California State Assemblyman, District 48, 2006-. Founder, The Images of Blacks in America Symposium at UCLA; sr. dep. dir. Supr. Yvonne Brathwaite Burke, LA; dist. dir. Assemblymember/US Rep. Maxine Waters. Chairman, Western Regional Social Action Committee, Kappa Alpha Psi Fraternity; past member, National Social Action Commission; past member, Black Advisory Committee, LA Police Department Commission. Democrat. Office: Administrative Offices West Dist 48 700 State Dr Los Angeles CA 90037-1210 Office Phone: 213-744-2111. Office Fax: 213-744-2122. Business E-Mail: Assemblymember.Davis@assembly.ca.gov.

DAVIS, NATHANIEL, humanities educator; b. Boston, Apr. 12, 1925; s. Harvey Nathaniel and Alice Marion (Rohde) Davis; m. Elizabeth Kirkbride Creese, Nov. 24, 1956; children: Margaret Morton Davis Mainardi, James Creese, Thomas Rohde, Helen Miller Davis Presley. Grad., Phillips Exeter Acad., 1942; AB, Brown U., 1944, LLD, 1970; MA, Fletcher Sch. Law and Diplomacy, 1947, PhD, 1960; postgrad., Columbia, Cornell U., Middlebury Coll., 1953—54, U. Central de Venezuela, 1961—62, Norwich U., 1989. Asst. history Tufts Coll., 1947; joined U.S. Fgn. Service, 1947; 3d sec. Prague, Czechoslovakia, 1947-49; vice consul Florence, Italy, 1949-52; 2d sec. Rome, 1952-53, Moscow, USSR, 1954-56; Soviet desk officer State Dept., 1956-60; 1st sec. Caracas, Venezuela, 1960-62; acting Peace Corps dir., Chile, 1962; spl. asst. to dir. Peace Corps, 1962-63, dept. assoc. dir., 1963-65; U.S. minister to Bulgaria, 1965-66; sr. staff Nat. Security Coun. (White House), 1966-68; U.S. amb. Guatemala, 1968-71, Chile, 1971-73; dir. gen. Fgn. Service, 1973-75, asst. sec. of state for African affairs, 1975; U.S. amb. Switzerland, 1975-77; State Dept advisor and Chester Nimitz prof. Naval War Coll., 1977-83; Alexander and Adelaide Hixon prof. humanities Harvey Mudd Coll., Claremont, Calif., 1983—2002, faculty exec. com., 1986-89, acting dean of faculty, 1990, emeritus prof., 2002—. Lectr. in field. Author: The Last Two Years of Salvador Allende, 1985, Equality and Equal Security in Soviet Foreign Policy, 1986, A Long Walk to Church: A Contemporary History of Russian Orthodoxy, 1995, 2d edit., 2003. Mem. ctrl. com. Calif. Dem. Party, 1987—90, 1991—, mem. exec. bd., 1993—, mem. bus. and profl. caucus, 1992—; mem. L.A. County Dem. Ctrl. Com., 1988—90, 1992—, regional vice chmn., 1994—96; del. Dem. Nat. Conv., 1988, 1992, 1996, 2000; del. So. Calif. conf. United Ch. of Christ, 1986—87. Lt. (j.g.) USNR, 1944—46. Recipient Cinco Aguilas Blancas Alpinism award, Venezuelan Andean Club, 1962, Disting. pub. Svc. award, USN, 1983, Elvira Roberti award for outstanding leadership, Los Angeles County Dem. Com., 1995, spl. merit award (as author), So. Calif. Motion Picture Coun., 1998, Prism award for nat., state, county and local svcs., Jerry Voorhis Claremont Dem. Club, 1999; Fulbright scholar, Moscow, 1996—97. Mem.: AAUP (pres. Claremont Coll. chpt. 1992—96, 1998), Am. Acad. Diplomacy, Coun. on Fgn. Rels., Am. Fgn. Svc. Assn. (bd. dirs., vice chmn. 1964), Cosmos Club, Phi Beta Kappa. Home: 1783 Longwood Ave Claremont CA 91711-3129 Office: Harvey Mudd Coll 301 E 12th St Claremont CA 91711-5901 Office Phone: 909-624-8022.

DAVIS, NICHOLAS HOMANS CLARK, finance company executive; b. NYC, Dec. 1, 1938; s. Feltz Cleveland and Loraine Vanderpool (Homans) D.; children from previous marriage: Loraine, Helen, Alexandra, Eleanor; m. Brenda Jean Molen, Dec. 18, 1982; children: Nicholas, Elizabeth. BA in Geology with honors, Princeton U., 1961; MBA in Fin., Stanford U., 1963. Chartered fin. analyst. Research analyst Fahnestock & Co., NYC, 1963-67; mgr. research Andresen & Co., NYC, 1967-71; dir. research Boettcher & Co., Denver, 1971-75; v.p. corp. fin. White Weld & Co., Denver, 1975-78; v.p. asset mgmt. Paine Webber Co., Denver, 1978-92; pres. Mont. Investment Advisors, Inc., Bozeman, 1991—. Trustee, investment officer Thenen Found., Montclair, N.J., 1966—. Bd. dirs. Eagle Mount Rehab. Ctr. Mem. Riverside Country Club, Rotary (pres. Bozeman Noon). Avocations: fly fishing, deepwater voyaging, writing, backpacking. Home: 85 Limestone Meadows Ln Bozeman MT 59715 Office: Mont Investment Advisors Inc 104 E Main St # 416 PO Box 7090 Bozeman MT 59771-7090

DAVIS, R. STEVEN, lawyer, telecommunications industry executive; m. Kim Davis; 2 children. BS, JD, U. Kans., Lawrence. Bar: Kans. 1978, Mo. 1981, Tex. 1986. Pvt. practice atty., Kans., 1978—81; v.p. law and state govt. affairs AT&T, Basking Ridge, NJ, 1981—2000; sr. v.p. policy and law, dep. gen. counsel Qwest Comm. Internat., Inc., Denver, 2000—. Office: Qwest Comm Internat Inc 1801 California St Denver CO 80202 Office Phone: 303-896-4200. Office Fax: 303-896-8515. E-mail: steve.davis@qwest.com.

DAVIS, RICHARD MALONE, economics professor; b. Hamilton, NY, June 2, 1918; s. Malone Crowell and Grace Edith (McQuade) Davis. AB, Colgate U., 1939; MA, Cornell U., 1941, PhD, 1949. From instr. to assoc. prof. econs. Lehigh U., Bethlehem, Pa., 1941-54; assoc. prof. econs. U. Oreg., Eugene, 1954-62, prof., 1962-83, prof. emeritus, 1983—. Contbr. articles to profl. jours. With US Army, 1942—45,

CBL Mem.: Phi Beta Kappa. Republican. Office: Univ Oreg Dept Econs Eugene OR 97403 Home: 786 Lake Shore Blvd Rochester NY 14617-1524 Office Phone: 541-345-1307.

DAVIS, ROGER LEWIS, lawyer; b. New Orleans, Jan. 27, 1946; s. Leon and Anada A. Davis; m. Annette Vucinich; 1 child, Alexandra. BA, Tulane U., 1967; MA, UCLA, 1969, PhD, 1971; JD, Harvard U., 1974. Bar: Calif. 1974. Assoc. Orrick, Herrington & Sutcliffe, L.L.P., San Francisco, 1974—79, ptnr., 1980—, chmn. pub. fin. dept., 1981—, mem. exec. com. Mem. mcpl. fiscal adv. com. Mayor of San Francisco; tech. adv. com. Calif. Debt & Investment Adv. Commn. Named a Dealmaker of the Yr., Am. Lawyer mag., 1999, 2006. Fellow: Am. Coll. Bond Counsel (bd. dirs.); mem.: Infrastructure Subcom of State, Calif. Pub. Securities Assn. (bd. dirs.), Nat. Assn. Bond Lawyers. Office: Orrick Herrington & Sutcliffe LLP The Orrick Building 405 Howard St San Francisco CA 94105 Business E-Mail: rogerdavis@orrick.com.

DAVIS, RONALD WAYNE, genetics researcher, biochemistry educator; b. Moroa, Ill., July 17, 1941; s. Lester and Gerzella Mary (Brown) D.; m. Janet L. Dafoe, May 2, 1949; children: Whitney Allen, Ashley Halcyon. BS, Ea. Ill. U., 1964; PhD, Calif. Inst. Tech., 1970. Postdoctoral fellow Harvard U., Cambridge, Mass., 1970-71; asst. prof. biochemistry Stanford (Calif.) U., 1972-77, assoc. prof., 1977-80, prof., 1980—. Mem. sci. adv. bd. Collaborative Rsch., Bedford, Mass., 1978—. Author: Manual for Genetic Engineering, 1980. Recipient Eli Lilly award in microbiology, 1976, U.S. Steel award in molecular biology, 1981, Louis S. Rosensthiel award Brandeis U., 1992. Mem. NAS. Avocation: backpacking. Office: Stanford U Dept Biochemistry 855 California Ave Stanford CA 94305

DAVIS, ROY KIM, otolaryngologist, retired health facility administrator; b. Logan, Utah, Jan. 20, 1947; m. JoNell Davis; children: Kimberly, Roy Neal, Tamralyn, Cynthia Joy, Mindy Anne, Ricks Eric. BS magna cum laude, Utah State U., 1972; MD, U. Utah, 1975. Diplomate Am. Bd. Otolaryngolgoy. Resident in prespeciality surgery Madigan Army Med. Ctr., 1975-76, resident in otolaryngology, 1976-79; fellow Boston U., Boston, 1979-80; instr. surgery Uniformed Svc. U. Health Sci., Bethesda, Md., 1980-81, asst. prof. surgery, 1981-83; asst. chief otolaryngology svc. Walter Reed Army Med. Ctr., 1980-83; from asst prof. to assoc. prof. U. Utah, Salt Lake City, 1983-85; chief otolaryngology head and neck surgery Salt Lake VA Med. Ctr., Salt Lake City, 1986-93, 99—; dir. John A. Dixon Laser Inst. U. UT, Utah, 1993-98. Adj. prof. comm. disorders U. Utah, 1993—, prof. surgery, 1993; course instr. Am. Acad. Otolaryngology; scientific dir. Rocky Mountain Cancer Data System, 1985-96; mem. head and neck com. SW Oncology Group, 1985—; vis. prof. Madigan Army Medical Ctr., 1980, Brooke Army Medical Ctr., 1981, Tripler Army Medical Ctr., 1982, U. N.C., 1986, U. Tex., 1988, Szent-Gyorgyi Albert Univ., Szeged, Hungary, 1989, First Pavlov Medical Inst., Leningrad, USSR, 1990, Univ. Keil, Germany, 1990, Georg-August U., Gottingen, Germany, 1990, 96, Wilhelm-Pieck Univ. Rostock, Germany, 1990, U. Indonesia, Jakarta, 1995, Bowman-Gray Med. Sch.-Wake Forest U., 1996; Univ. of Iowa, 1997, Cairo Un., 2001-2002; guest examiner Am. Bd. Otolaryngology, 1994-95, 99. Co-author numerous books and book chpts.; contbr. articles to profl. jours. Mem. Jon A. Huntsman Cancer Inst. Fellow Am. Acad. Otolaryngology, Am. Laryngological Assn., Am. Soc. Laser Medicine and Surgery, Am. Coll. Surgeons, Am. Soc. Head and Neck Surgery; Soc. Univ. Otolaryngolgoists, Utah Soc. Otolaryngology, Am. Laryngo., Rhinol. & Otol. Soc., Sec. of Am. Bronchoesophagol. Assoc., Soc. Univ. Otolaryngologists, Alpha Epsilon Delta, Am. Laryngo. Assn.

DAVIS, STEPHEN DARREL, biology professor, researcher; b. Santa Rosa, Calif., Sept. 15, 1944; s. Ivan Darrel and Maurine (Johnson) Davis; m. Janet Claire Moody, July 12, 1969; children: Jerel Clayton, Cindy Maurine. BS, Abilene Christian U., 1967, MS, 1968; PhD, Tex. A&M U., 1974. Asst. prof. biology Pepperdine U., Malibu, Calif., 1974-78, assoc. prof. biology, 1983-86, prof. biology, 1987—, disting. prof. biology, 1997—. Vis. scholar Stanford U., 1981—82, UCLA, 1989, U. Utah, 1996—97. Contbr. articles to profl. jours. With US Army, 1970—72. Recipient Profl. Devel. award, NSF, 1981, Robert Foster Cherry Award for Great Tchg., Baylor U., 2008; named Disting. Prof., 1997, 2002, 2007, Prof. of Yr., 2002; named to Golden Key Nat. Honor Soc.; Harriet and Charles Luckman Disting. Tchg. Fellow, 1990—95. Mem.: AAAS, Coun. on Undergraduate Rsch., Botanical Soc. Am., Ecological Soc. Am., Am. Inst. Biological Sci., Phi Sigma. Office: Pepperdine U Rockwell Academic Ctr 110 24255 Pacific Coast Hwy Malibu CA 90263 Office Phone: 310-456-4324. E-mail: stephen.davis@pepperdine.edu.

DAVIS, SUSAN A., United States Representative from California; b. Cambridge, Mass., Apr. 13, 1944; m. Steven Davis, 1970; 1 child, Jeffery; 1 child, Benjamin. BA in Sociology, U. Calif., Berkeley, 1965; MA in Social Work, U. NC, 1968. Devel. assoc. KPBS-FM, San Diego, 1977, KPBS-TV, San Diego, 1979—83; exec. dir. Aaron Price Fellowship Prog., San Diego, 1990—94; mem. Calif. State Assembly, 1994-2000, US Congress from 53rd Calif. dist., 2000—, mem. armed svcs. com., edn. & labor com., joint com. on printing. Mem., v.p., pres. San Diego Unified Sch. Dist. Bd. Edn., 1983—92; mem. Dem. Leadership Coun., San Diego Consortium & Pvt. Industry Coun., Nat. Conf. Christians & Jews; exec. bd. mem. New Dem. Coalition. Youth vol. United Way; vol. June Burnett Inst. Children & Families, San Diego. Mem.: San Diego League Women Voters (pres. 1977). Democrat. Jewish. Office: US Ho Reps 1224 Longworth House Office Bldb Washington DC 20515-0553

DAVIS, WAYNE ALTON, computer science educator; b. Ft. Macleod, Alta., Can., Nov. 16, 1931; s. Frederick and Anna Mary (Barr) D.; m. Audrey M. Zorolow, July 17, 1959 (div. 1989); children: Fredrick M., Peter W., Timothy M.; m. Patricia Ruth Syme, Mar. 24, 1990. BSE, George Washington U., 1960; MSc, U. Ottawa, 1963, PhD, 1967. Sci. officer Def. Resch. Bd., Ottawa, Ont., 1960-68; research scientist Dept. Comms., Ottawa, 1968-69; vis. scientist NRC, Ottawa, 1975-76; assoc. prof. U. Alta., Edmonton, 1969-77, prof. computing sci., 1977-91, prof. emeritus, 1991—, acting chmn. computing sci., 1982-83; acting dir. Alta. Centre for Machine Intelligence and Robotics, 1988-89. Lectr. U. Ottawa, 1965-69; sessional lectr. Carleton U., 1967; cons. Editor: The Barrs of Ardenville, 1978; editor Procs. Graphics Interface, 1994, 95, 96, 97, 98. Grantee NRC, 1970-78; rsch. grantee Natural Scis. and Engring. Rsch. Coun., 1978-92; strategic grantee Natural Scis. and Engring. Rsch. Coun., 1981-83; grantee Def. Rsch. Bd., 1974-76; hon. prof. Harbin Shipbldg. Engring. Inst., China, 1985. Mem. Can. Info. Processing Soc. (pres. 1978-79), Can. Human Computer Comms. Soc. (pres. 1981-96), Can. Soc. Computational Study of Intelligence (treas. 1976-86), Faculty Club. Anglican. Home: Box 817 605-21st St Fort Macleod AB Canada T0L 0Z0 Office: U Alta Dept Computing Sci Edmonton AB Canada T6G 2E8 Personal E-mail: waltondavis@mac.com.

DAVIS, WILLIAM ALBERT, parks director; b. New Haven, Sept. 10, 1946; s. Arthur Wilson Davis and Dorothy May (Hellyer) Jordan; m. Rebecca Marsden Haile, Apr. 8, 1965; children: William Albert Jr., Anna Catherine. BA in Profl. Arts, Brooks Inst. Photography, 1971; BSBA, San Diego State U., 1980. Photographer, owner Davis-Hixon Photography, Santa Ana, Calif., 1971-73; photographer Sea World, Inc., San Diego, 1973, sales rep., 1974-76, sales mgr., 1976-78, mktg. mgr. fast food subs., 1978-80, corp. planning assoc., 1980-81; dir. mktg. Sea World Ohio, Aurora, 1981-85, v.p. mktg., 1985-86, pres., 1986-88, Sea World Fla., Orlando, 1988-97; exec. v.p., gen. mgr. Sea World of Calif., 1997-2001; corp. v.p. guest svcs. Busch Entertainment Corp., St. Louis, 2001—03; mng. dir. Universal Mediterranea, Tarragona, Spain, 2003—04; v.p., gen. mgr. Six Flags Marine World, Vallejo, Calif., 2005—; pres., COO, Universal Orlando Resort, 2006—. Bd. dirs. Hubbs-Sea World Rsch. Inst., San Diego, Marine Rsch. Ctr., Sea World, Orlando, Calif. Travel and Tourism Commn. Bd. dirs., exec. com. Conv. and Visitors Bur. Orange County, Orlando, 1988-97, pres.-elect, 1990, pres., 1991, chmn., 1992-93; mem. bd. Efficient Transp. for Community Orlando, 1988-97; mem. adv. coun. Dick Pope Sr. Inst. Tourism Studies, Orlando, 1989-97; commr. Fla. Tourism Commn., 1991—; trustee United Arts of Ctrl. Fla., 1992—; mem. U. Ctrl. Fla. Found., 1994-97; mem. White House Com. on Tourism, 1995, mem. exec. com. San Diego Conv. and Visitors Bur., 1997—, Super Bowl XXXII Host com. Staff sgt. USAF, 1965-69, Vietnam. Fellow Am. Assn. Zool. Parks and Aquariums; mem. San Diego C. of C. Roundtable, Brooks Inst. Alumni Assn., Kiwanis (bd. dirs. Aurora club 1985-87, 1st v.p. 1987—) Avocations: golf, photography. Home: 210 Acadia Terr Celebration FL 34747-5004 Office: Six Flags Marine World 2001 Marine World Vallejo CA 94589 Office Phone: 407-224-6944. Business E-Mail: bill.davis@universalorlando.com.

DAVIS, WILLIAM F., state legislator; b. 1949; BS, U.S. Air Force Acad., 1970; MBA, U. N.Mex., JD, 1984. Bar: N.Mex. Practice of law; mem. N.Mex. State Senate, 1996—, mem. Indian and cultural affairs com., mem. judiciary com. Republican. Office: PO Box 6 Albuquerque NM 87103-0006 E-mail: wdavis@state.nm.us.

DAWKINS, BRIAN PATRICK, professional football player; b. Jacksonville, Fla., Oct. 13, 1973; m. Connie Dawkins; children: Brian Jr., Brionni, Chonni, Cionni. BEd, Clemson U., SC. Defensive back Phila. Eagles, 1996—2009, Denver Broncos, 2009—. Co-host The Brian Dawkins Show, 2007. Regional spokesman Juvenile Diabetes Rsch. Found. Recipient Fan's Choice award, NFL Players Assn.; named First Team All-Pro, AP, 2001, 2002, 2004, 2006, Man of Yr., Phila. Eagles, 2005, Father of Yr., Am. Diabetes Assn., 2007; named a Home Depot NFL Neighborhood MVP, 2007; named to Nat. Football Conf. Pro Bowl Team, NFL, 1999, 2001, 2002, 2004—06, 2008, Raines HS Hall of Fame, Jacksonville, 2004. Achievements include becoming the first player in NFL history to record a sack, an interception, a fumble recovery and a touchdown reception in a single game, 2002. Office: Denver Broncos 13655 Broncos Pky Englewood CO 80112*

DAWKINS, JOHNNY EARL, JR., men's college basketball coach; b. Washington, Sept. 28, 1963; m. Tracy Dawkins; children: Aubrey, Jillian, Blair, Sean. BA in polit. sci., Duke U., Durham, NC, 1986. Guard San Antonio Spurs, 1986—89, Phila. 76ers, 1989—94, Detroit Pistons, 1994—95; adminstrv. intern, dept. athletics Duke U. Blue Devils, 1996—97, asst. coach, assoc. head coach, 1999—2008; head coach Stanford U. Cardinals, 2008—. Radio color analyst Capitol Sports Network; player pers. dir. USA Basketball Sr. Nat. Team, 2006—08. Recipient Naismith Coll. Player of Yr. award, 1986; named to Duke Sports Hall of Fame, 1986, Legends of College Basketball, The Sporting News, 2002. Office: Stanford U Maples Pavillion 655 Campus Dr Stanford CA 94305

DAWSON, CHANDLER ROBERT, ophthalmologist, educator; b. Denver, Aug. 24, 1930; married; 3 children. AB, Princeton U., 1952; MD, Yale U., 1956. USPHS epidemiologist Communicable Disease Ctr., 1957-60; resident dept. ophthalmology Sch. Medicine U. Calif., San Francisco, 1960-63; asst. clin. prof. U. Calif., San Francisco, 1963-66, asst. prof. in residence, 1966-69, assoc. prof. opthalmology, 1969-75, prof. ophthalmology, 1975-97, prof. emeritus, assoc. dir. Francis I. Proctor Found., 1970-84, dir., 1984-95. Fellow Middlesex Hosp. Med. Sch., London, 1963-64; co-dir. WHO Collaborating Ctr. for Reference and Rsch. on Trachoma and other Chlamydial Infections, 1970-79, dir. Collaborating Ctr. for Prevention of Blindness and Trachoma, 1979—97. Recipient Knapp award AMA, 1967, 69, Medaille Trachome, 1978. Mem. Am. Soc. Microbiology, Am. Acad. Ophthalmology, Assn. Rsch. Vision & Ophthalmology. Achievements include rsch. in epidemiology of infectious eye diseases and cataracts; prevention of blindness; pathogenesis of virus diseases of the eyes; electron microscopy of eye diseases; clinical trials of treatment for trachoma and for herpes simplex eye infections. Office: U Calif San Francisco Francis I Proctor Found Rsch Ophthalmology San Francisco CA 94143-0412

DAWSON, JOHN JOSEPH, lawyer; b. Binghamton, NY, Mar. 9, 1947; s. Joseph John and Cecilia (O'Neill) D. BA, Siena Coll., 1968; JD, U. Notre Dame, 1971. Bar: Ariz. 1971, Nev. 1991, Calif. 1993, D.C. 1994, N.Y. 1996. Nat. practice group chair, bankruptcy and creditors rights practice group Quarles & Brady LLP, Phoenix. Reporter local rules ct. U.S. Bankruptcy Ct. for Dist. Ariz.; atty. rep. U.S. Ct. Appeals (9th cir.), 1992-95 Co-author: Advanced Chapter 11 Bankruptcy, 1991. Fellow Ariz. Bar Found.; mem. State Bar Ariz. (chmn. bankruptcy sect. 1976-77, 80-81), Am. Bankruptcy Inst. Republican. Roman Catholic. Avocations: sports, reading, movies, travel, writing. Office: Quarles & Brady LLP Renaissance One Two North Central Ave Phoenix AZ 85004-2391 Home Phone: 602-266-2769; Office Phone: 602-229-5414. Business E-Mail: jdawson@quarles.com.

DAWSON, PATRICIA LUCILLE, surgeon; b. Kingston, Jamaica, W.I., Sept. 30, 1949; arrived in U.S., 1950; d. Percival Gordon and Edna Claire (Overton) D.; children: Alexandria Zoe Hiserman, Wesley Gordon Hiserman BA in Sociology, Allegheny Coll., 1971; MD, N.J. Med. Sch., Newark, 1977; MA in Human and Orgn. Devel., The Fielding Inst., 1996, PhD in Human and Orgnl. Sys., 1998. Membership dir. N.J. ACLU, Newark, 1972; resident in surgery U. Medicine and Dentistry N.J. N.J. Med Sch., 1977-79; resident in surgery Virginia Mason Med. Ctr., Seattle, 1979-82; pvt. practice specializing in surgery Arlington, Wash., 1982-83; dir. med. staff diversity Group Health Coop., Seattle, 1993-98, staff surgeon, 1983-98; pvt. practice Seattle, 1998—2003; breast surgeon Swedish Cancer Inst., 2004—. Author: Forged by the Knife—The Experience of Surgical Residency from the Perspective of a Woman of Color, 1999 Fellow ACS, Seattle Surg. Soc.; mem. Physicians for Social Responsibility, Assn. Women Surgeons, Wash. Black Profls. in Health Care, NOW. Avocations: fiction, walking, cooking. Office: Cherry Hill Campus Comp Breast Ctr Jefferson Twr 1600 E Jefferson St Ste 300 Seattle WA 98122-5645 Home Phone: 206-725-1223; Office Phone: 206-320-4880.

DAWSON, PETER A., corporate financial executive; Exec. v.p. telecom. and indsl. bus. unit Bechtel Corp., sr. v.p., CFO, 2002—. Office: Bechtel Group 50 Beale St San Francisco CA 94105 also: PO Box 193965 San Francisco CA 94119 Office Phone: 415-768-1234. Office Fax: 415-768-9038.

DAY, GERALD W., wholesale grocery company executive; With Albertson's, Heber City, Utah, 1945-72; CEO Days Markets; chmn., bd. dirs. Associated Food Stores Inc. Office: Day's Market 890 S Main St Heber City UT 84032-2463

DAY, HOWARD WILMAN, geology educator; b. Burlington, Vt., Nov. 17, 1942; s. Wilman Forrest and Virginia Louise (Morton) D.; children: Kristina, Sarah, Susan; m. Judy Lynn Blevins. AB, Dartmouth Coll., 1964; MS, Brown U., 1968, PhD, 1971. Prof. geology U. Okla., Norman, 1970—76, U. Calif., Davis, 1976—, chmn. dept., 1990-96. Co-editor Jour. Metamorphic Geology, 1985-92; contbr. articles to profl. jours. Fulbright fellow, Norway, 1964, Alexander von Humboldt fellow, Fed. Republic Germany, 1977. Fellow Geol. Soc. Am., Mineral Soc. Am.; mem. Am. Geophys. Union. Office: U Calif Dept Geology Davis CA 95616 Business E-Mail: hwday@ucdavis.edu.

DAY, JAMES MCADAM, JR., lawyer; b. Detroit, Aug. 18, 1948; s. James McAdam and Mary Elizabeth (McGibbon); children: Cara McAdam, Brenna Marie, Michael James; m. Kathleen C. Henderson. AB, UCLA, 1970; JD magna cum laude, U. Pacific, Sacramento, 1973. Bar: Calif. 1973, US Dist. Ct. (no. dist.) Calif. 1973, US Ct. Appeals (9th cir.) 1975. Assoc. Downey, Brand, Seymour & Rohwer, Sacramento, 1973-78, ptnr., 1978—2006, chmn. natural resources dept., 1985—90; mng. ptnr. Downey, Brand, Seymour & Rohmer, Sacramento, 1990—94, chmn. nat. resources dept., 2002—03, mng. ptnr., 1997—2001; ptnr. Day Carter & Murphy LLP, Sacramento, 2006—. Contbr. articles to profl. jours. Pres., bd. dirs. Sacramento Soc. for Prevention of Cruelty to Animals, 1976-79, Children's Home Soc. of Calif., Sacramento, 1979-85; bd. dirs. Sta. KXPR/KXJZ, Inc. Pub. Radio, Sacramento, 1984-94, chmn., 1990-93; bd. dirs. Calif. State Libr. Found., 1995-2000, chmn., 1995-2000. Mem. ABA (natural resources sect. 1998), Calif. Bar Assn. (exec. com. 1985-89, chmn. real property law sect. 1988), Rocky Mountain Mineral Law Found., Sacramento Petroleum Assn., Calif. Mining Assn., U. Pacific McGeorge Law Sch. Alumni Assn. (bd. dirs. 1980-83). Avocations: yachting, fishing. Office: Day Carter & Murphy LLP 3620 Am River Dr Ste 205 Sacramento CA 95864 Home: 411 Burbank Way Sacramento CA 95864

DAY, LUCILLE LANG, museum administrator, educator, writer; b. Oakland, Calif., Dec. 5, 1947; d. Richard Allen and Evelyn Marietta (Hazard) Lang; m. Frank Lawrence Day, Nov. 6, 1965 (div. 1970); 1 child, Liana Sherrine; m. Theodore Herman Fleischman, June 23, 1974 (div. 1985); 1 child, Tamarind Channah Fleischman; m. Richard Michael Levine, Aug. 25, 2002. AB, U. Calif., Berkeley, 1971, MA, 1973, PhD, 1979; MA, San Francisco State U., 1999, MFA, 2004. Tchg. asst. U. Calif., Berkeley, 1971-72, 75-76, rsch. asst., 1975, 77-78; tchr. sci. Magic Mountain Sch., Berkeley, 1977; specialist math. and sci. Novato Unified Sch. Dist., Calif., 1979—81; sr. tech. writer, editor Schlage Electronics, Santa Clara, Calif., 1981—86; instr. sci. Project Bridge Laney Coll., Oakland, 1984-86; sci. writer and mgr. precoll. edn. programs Lawrence Berkeley Nat. Lab., 1986-90, life scis. staff coord., 1990-92, mgr. Hall of Health, Children's Hosp. & Rsch. Ctr. at Oakland, 1992—2004, dir. Hall of Health, 2004—. Lectr. St. Mary's Coll. Calif., Moraga, 1997—2000. Author: numerous poems, articles and book reviews; author: (with Joan Skolnick and Carol Langbort) How to Encourage Girls in Math and Science: Strategies for Parents and Educators, 1982; author: Self-Portrait with Hand Microscope, 1982, Fire in the Garden, 1997, Wild One, 2000, Lucille Lang Day, Greatest Hits, 1975-2000, 2001, Infinities, 2002, Chain Letter, 2005, The Book of Answers, 2006, God of the Jellyfish, 2007, The Curvature of Blue, 2009. Recipient Joseph Henry Jackson award in lit., San Francisco Found., 1982; Grad. fellow, NSF, 1972—75. Mem.: Women's Nat. Book Assn., Nat. Assn. Sci. Writers, No. Calif. Sci. Writers Assn., Phi Beta Kappa, Iota Sigma Pi. Home: 1057 Walker Ave Oakland CA 94610-1511 Office: Hall of Health 2230 Shattuck Ave Berkeley CA 94704-1416 Office Phone: 510-549-1564. Business E-Mail: lucyday@hallofhealth.org.

DAY, ROBERT WINSOR, preventive medicine physician, researcher; b. Framingham, Mass., Oct. 22, 1930; s. Raymond Albert and Mildred (Doty) Day; m. Jane Alice Boynton, Sept. 6, 1957 (div. Sept. 1977); m. Cynthia Taylor, Dec. 16, 1977; children: Christopher, Nathalia, Natalya, Julia. Student, Harvard U., 1949—51; MD, U. Chgo., 1956; MPH, U. Calif., Berkeley, 1958, PhD, 1962. With USPHS, 1956—57; resident U. Calif., Berkeley, 1958—60; research specialist Calif. Dept. Mental Hygiene, 1960—64; asst. prof. Sch. Pub. Health and Sch. Medicine UCLA, 1962—64; dep. dir. Calif. Dept. Pub. Health, Berkeley, 1965—67; prof., chmn. dept. health services Sch. Pub. Health and Community Medicine, U. Wash., Seattle, 1968—72, dean, 1972—82, prof., 1982—2005, emeritus prof. and dean, 2005—; pres., dir. Fred Hutchinson Cancer Rsch. Ctr., Seattle, 1981—97, pres., dir. emeritus, 1997—, mem. pub. health scis., 1997—. Mem. Nat. Cancer Adv. Bd., 1992—98, Nat. Cancer Policy Bd., 1996—2000; chief med. officer Epigenomics, Inc.; sci. dir. Internat. Consortium Rsch. Health Effects Radiation, 2001—04; founder, chmn. Targeted Growth, Inc., 1998—; chmn. Sci. and Mgmt. of Addictions, 2005—; mgr. Sci. Group, DLC, Investment Co.; cons. in field. Fellow: APHA, AAAS, Am. Coll. Preventive Medicine; mem.: AMA, Am. Soc. Addiction Medicine, King County Med. Soc., Wash. State Med. Assn., Am. Assn. Cancer Insts. (bd. dirs. 1983—87, v.p., pres., chmn. bd. dirs.), Assn. Schs. Pub. Health (pres. 1981—82), Am. Assn. Cancer Rsch., Am. Soc. Preventive Oncology, Am. Soc. Clin. Oncology. Office: 1872 E Hamlin St Seattle WA 98112 Office Phone: 206-954-9922. Personal E-mail: dlcllc@comcast.net.

DAY, VANCE D., former political organization administrator, lawyer; b. Willamette Valley, Ore. m. Mattie Day; children: Elizabeth, Daniel, Justin. Grad. magna cum laude, Warner Pacific Coll., 1984; attended, Inst. Holyland Studies, Jerusalem, Regent U.; JD, Willamette U., 1991. Bar: Ore. State Bar, admitted: US Dist. Ct. (Ore.), US Ct. Appeals (9th Cir.), US Supreme Ct. Tng. cons. Ritz Taipei Hotel, Overseas Radio and TV, Taiwan; news prodr., anchor nightly news hour Middle East TV; trial lawyer; vice chmn. Marion County Rep. Party, 1990—92, chmn., 1992—94; mem. exec. com. Oreg. Rep. Party, 1990—2002, state treas., 2003—05, chmn., 2005—09. Chmn. Oreg. Young Republicans, 1990—92; del. Rep. Nat. Conv., 1996; mem. Marion County Compensation Com., 1996—98; lectr. mil. history and leadership theory West Point, Oreg. State Police Acad., Lazard Lecture Series. Mem.: AAJ, Nat. Eagle Scout Assn., Ore. Trial Lawyers Assn. Republican.*

DAYTON, SKY, telecommunications company executive; b. NYC, Aug. 8, 1971; m. Arwen Elys; 3 children. Grad., Delphian Sch., 1988. Mgr. computer graphics dept. Mednick & Assocs., 1988-90; founder Cafe Mocha, LA, 1990-92; co-founder Dayton Walker Design, 1992-94; founder Earthlink Inc., Pasadena, Calif., 1994, CEO, 1994—96, chmn., 1994—2005; co-founder ECompanies, 1999—; founder, non-exec. chmn. Boingo Wireless, 2001—; CEO HELIO LLC (formerly SK-EarthLink), Westwood, Calif., 2005—08, chmn. bd. dirs., 2008—. Bd. dirs. Earthlink, Inc., 1994—2008, Business-.com, NeoPets; mem. adv. bd. Ctr. Pub. Leadership, John F. Kennedy Sch. Govt. Mem. Assn. Online Profls. (bd. dirs.), Internet Access Coalition. Avocations: surfing, snowboarding. Office: HELIO LLC 10960 Wilshire Blvd Ste 600 Los Angeles CA 90024

DCAMP, KATHRYN ACKER, human resources executive; b. Hartford, Conn., Jan. 12, 1956; d. Donald Jalmer and Virginia Ruth (Wainman) Acker; m. Glenn William DCamp, July 17, 1978; 1 child, Kristen Louise. AA, Ball State U., 1976, BS magna cum laude, 1978. Cert. compensation profl., sr. profl. in human resources. Actuarial/analyst pensions Aetna Life & Casualty, Hartford, Conn., 1980-81, compensation analyst, 1981-82, compensation cons., 1982-84, compensation adminstr., 1984-85, exec. compensation cons., 1985-86, sr. adminstr./exec. programs, 1986-88; compensation cons. The Assoc. Group, Indpls., 1988, compensation mgr., 1989-90, dir. exec. compensation benefits, 1990-93, dir. compensation, mgmt. edn. and exec. benefits, 1993-94; compensation leader GE Capital Corp., Stamford, Conn., 1994-2000; v.p., global compensation leader Cisco Sys., Inc., San Jose, Calif., 2000—01, sr. v.p. human resources, 2001—06, sr. exec. advisor, 2006—. Ind. cons., 1986-93, Motivation by Design, 1993-99; spkr. compensation topics; faculty advisor Univ. Evansville, Ind., 1990—; bd. dirs. Technology Solutions Co., 2007-; area rep. Ind. and Ky. World at Work, mem. nat. adv. bd. on exec. compensation, 1998-2000; columnist Talent Mgmt. Mag., 2006-. Co-author: Spot Gainsharing Personnel Journal, 1989. Mem.: Internat. Bar Assn., World at Work, Soc. Human Resources Mgmt. Lutheran. Office: Cisco Systems Inc 170 W Tasman Bldg 10 San Jose CA 95134-1619 Office Phone: 408-219-5391. E-mail: kdcamp@cisco.com.

DEA, PETER ALLEN, gas industry executive, geologist; b. Worchester, Mass., Aug. 28, 1953; s. Allen Pearson and Beverly Jane (Brown) Dea. BA in Geology, Western State Coll., Gunnison, Colo., 1976; MS in Geology, U. Mont., 1981. Geologist WGM, Inc., Anchorage, 1976—77, Novanda Exploration, Missoula, Mont., 1977, Converse Cons., Lakewood, Colo., 1980—81; prof. geology Western State Coll., Gunnison, 1980—82; sr. geologist Exxon Co., Corpus Christi, Tex.; positions through exec. v.p. exploration Barrett Resources Corp., vice chmn., CEO, 1994—2000, chmn., CEO, 2000—01; pres., CEO Western Gas Resources, Inc., 2001—. Bd. dirs. EchoStar Comm. Corp. Contbr. articles to profl. jours. Mem.: Corpus Christi Geol. Soc., Am. Assn. Petroleum Geologists. Avocations: skiing, sailing, mountain climbing, kayaking, writing.

DEADMARSH, ADAM, former professional hockey player; b. Trail, BC, Can., May 10, 1975; married; 2 children. Right wing Quebec Nordiques, 1994—95, Colo. Avalanche, Denver, 1995—2001, LA Kings, 2001—03. Mem. USA Olympic Hockey Team, Nagano, Japan, 1998, Salt Lake City, 2002. Achievements include being a member of Stanley Cup Champion Colorado Avalanche, 1996; being a member of silver medal winning USA Hockey Team, Salt Lake City Olympics, 2002.

DEAKTOR, DARRYL BARNETT, lawyer; b. Pitts., Feb. 2, 1942; s. Harry and Edith (Barnett) D.; children: Rachael Alexandra, Hallie Sarah. BA, Brandeis U., 1963; LLB, U. Pa., 1966; MBA, Columbia U., 1968. Bar: Pa. 1966, Fla. 1980, N.Y. 1980, Calif. 2003. Assoc. firm Goodis, Greenfield & Mann, Phila., 1968-70, ptnr., 1971; gen. counsel Life of Pa. Fin. Corp., Phila., 1972; asst. prof. U. Fla. Coll. Law, Gainesville, 1972-74, assoc. prof., 1974-80; with Mershon, Sawyer, Johnston, Dunwody & Cole, Miami, Fla., 1980-81, ptnr., 1981-84, Walker Ellis Gragg & Deaktor, Miami, 1984-86, White & Case LLP, Miami, 1987-95, Johannesburg, 1995-2000, Palo Alto, Calif., 2000—01, ret. ptnr., 2002—07, ptnr. of counsel Miami, 2007—. Mem. Dist. III (Fla.) Human Rights Advocacy Com. for Mentally Retarded Citizens, 1974-78, chmn., 1978-80; mem. adv. bd. Childbirth Edn. Assn. Alachua County, Fla., 1974-80; mem. resource devel. bd. Mailman Ctr. for Child Devel., 1981-88. Mem. Fla. Bar, NY Bar, Calif. Bar. Mailing: 1330 Mariposa Ave Boulder CO 80302-7842 Office Phone: 305-371-2700. E-mail: dbd@ionsky.com.

DE ALESSI, ROSS ALAN, lighting designer; b. San Francisco, Apr. 16, 1955; s. August Eugene De Alessi and Angela Maria (Caredio) Leonard; m. Susan Tracey Stearns, Aug. 11, 1990; 1 child, Chase Arthur. BFA, Stephens Coll., 1978. In-house lighting designer GUMP'S, San Francisco, 1981-84; prin. Ross De Alessi & Assoc., San Francisco, 1984-87, Luminae Lighting Design, San Francisco, 1987-93; prin., co-founder Ross De Alessi Lighting Design, Seattle, 1993—. Works include GUMP'S Christmas Windows, San Francisco (award of Distinction Gen. Electric, 1986, Spl. Citation 1989, Edwin F. Guth award Illuminating Engring. Soc. 1989, 90), TAB Products Showroom, L.A. (award of Distinction Gen. Electric 1987), St. Augustine's Ch., Pleasanton, Calif. (Sect. award Illuminating Engring. Soc. 1988), L.A. Quinta (Calif.) Resort Plz. Fountains (award of Excellence Gen. Electric 1988, Paul Waterbury award Illuminating Engring. Soc. 1989), McKesson Bldg. Lobby, San Francisco (award of excellence Gen. Electric 1988, Edwin F. Guth award Illuminating Engring. Soc. 1989), Brown & Bain, Phoenix (Merit award Gen. Electric 1989), Saxe Gallery, San Francisco (Edwin F. Guth award Illuminating Engring. Soc. 1989), Plz. Pk., San Jose, Calif. (Paul Waterbury Spl. Citation Illuminating Engring. Soc. 1990), The Palace Fine Arts, San Francisco (Edison Award Gen. Electric 1990, Paul Waterbury award Illuminating Engring. Soc. 1991, award of Excellence Internat. Assn. Lighting Designers 1991), Le Touessrok, Island of Mauritius (Merit award Gen. Electric 1993, Sect. Award Illuminating Engring. Soc. 1994, Paul Waterbury award 1994), St. Patrick's Sem., Menlo Park, Calif. (Edison award Gen. Electric 1993, Edwin F. Guth award Illuminating Engring. Soc. 1994, Citation Internat. Assn. Lighting Designers 1994), Palace of the Lost City, Republic of Boputhatswana (Award of Merit Gen. Electric 1992, Paul Waterbury award Internat. Assn. Lighting Designers 1993), Wells Fargo Bank-Flagship Bank, San Francisco (award of excellence Gen. Electric 1992, Merit award Illuminating Engring. Soc. 1993, citation Internat. Assn. Lighting Designers 1993), Santa Barbara County Courthouse, Santa Barbara (Paul Waterbury award Illuminating Engring. Soc. 1995, award of excellence Internat. Assn. Lighting Designers 1995), City of Bridges, Cleve. (Edison award 1995, Paul Waterbry award Illuminating Engring. Soc. 1997), MGM Grand Gateway of Entertainment, Las Vegas (award of excellence Gen. Elec. 1998, Edwin F. Guth award Illuminating Engring. Soc. 1999, Merit award Internat. Assn. Lighting Designers 1999), Helsinki Master Plan-Esplanade (Edison award 1999, Award of Distinction, Illuminating Engring. Soc. 2000, Merit award Internat. Assn. Lighting Designers), Space Needle (award of excellence Gen. Electric 2000, Illuminating Engring. Soc. 2001, Merit award Internat. Assn. Lighting Designers 2001), Forth Bridge (award of excellence Internat. Assn. Lighting Designers 2002), Montecasino (Merit award Gen. Electric 2001, Sect. award Internat. Assn. Design awards 2002). Mem. Internat. Assn. Lighting Designers (lighting cert.), Nat. Coun. on the Certification Lighting Profls., Illuminating Engring. Soc., Washington Athletic Club. Avocations: scuba diving, travel. Office: Ross De Alessi Lighting Design 2330 Magnolia Blvd W Seattle WA 98199-3813

DEAN, JAMES BENWELL, lawyer; b. Dodge City, Kans., May 23, 1941; s. James Harvey and Bess (Benwell) D.; m. Sharon Ann Carver, Sept. 1, 1962 (div. 1991); m. Patricia A. Bostick, Aug. 23, 1993 (div. 1999); children: Cynthia G. Dean Vosburgh, James M.; m. Gail M. Cohen, Sept. 21, 2002. Student, Southwestern Coll., 1959-60, U. Colo., 1961; BA, Kans. State U., 1962; JD, Harvard U., 1965. Bar: Colo. 1965, U.S. Dist. Ct. Colo. 1965, U.S. Tax Ct. 1966, Nebr. 1971, U.S. Ct. Appeals (10th cir.) 1971. From assoc. to ptnr. Tweedy & Mosley, Denver, 1965-71, Kutak Rock Cohen Campbell Garfinkle & Woodward, Omaha, 1971-73; ptnr. Mosley, Wells & Dean, Denver, 1973-77, Kutak Rock & Huie, Denver, 1977-81, James B. Dean, P.C., Denver, 1981-91, Dean, McClure, Eggleston & Husney, Denver, 1991-95, James B. Dean, PC, Denver, 1995-2000, Dean & Stern, LLC, Denver, 2001—05, Dean, Dunn & Phillips LLC, Denver, 2005—. Lectr. U. Ark. Law Sch., Fayetteville, 1982—86, C.C. Aurora, Colo., 1996—97; spl. asst. atty. gen. State of Colo., Denver, 1989—; assoc. reporter, drafting com. on uniform ltd. coop. assns. act Nat. Conf. Commrs. on Uniform State Laws, 2004—08. Co-editor Agricultural Law Jour., 1979-84; contbr. articles to profl. jours. Recipient Erwyn E. Witte Colo. Cooperator award, Colo. Coop. Coun., 1996. Mem.: ABA (advisor bd. forum com. on rural lawyers and agrl. bus. 1983—89), Am. Agrl. Law Assn. (bd. dirs. 1981—83, pres.-elect 1985—86, pres. 1986—87, strategic planning com. 2000—01, Disting. Svc. award 1989), Denver Bar Assn., Colo. Bar Assn. (bd. dirs. 1989—2001, sec. agrl. law sect. 1991—94, chair, Colo. coop. statute revision com. 1995—), Nebr. Bar Assn. Avocations: photography, woodworking, hiking, piano. Office: 650 S Cherry St Ste 620 Denver CO 80246 Home Phone: 303-756-8689; Office Phone: 303-756-6744. Business E-Mail: jim@lawatddp.com.

DEAN, JOHN WESLEY, III, investment banker, former federal official; b. Akron, OH, Oct. 14, 1938; m. Maureen (Mo) Dean, 1972; 1 child from previous marriage. Student, Colgate U.; BA, Coll. of Wooster, 1961; JD, Georgetown Univ., 1965. Law clk. Hollabaugh & Jacobs, 1964; jr. assoc. Welch & Morgan, Washington, 1965—66; chief minority counsel for Ho. Judiciary Com. US Congress, Washington, 1966—67; assoc. dep. atty. gen., Office Criminal Justice US Dept. Justice, Washington, 1969—70; counsel to Pres. The White House, Washington, 1970—73; private investment banker; writer; lectr.; columnist FindLaw. Assoc. dir. Nat. Commn. on Reform of Fed. Criminal Laws, Washington, 1967—68. Author: Blind Ambition, 1976, Lost Honor, 1982, The Rehnquist Choice: The Untold Story of the Nixon Appointment that Redefined the Supreme Court, 2001, Unmasking Deep Throat, 2002, Warren G. Harding (American Presidents Series), 2004; co-author (with Robertson Dean): Worse than Watergate: The Secret Presidency of George W. Bush, 2004; co-editor (with Barry M. Goldwater Jr.): Pure Goldwater, 2008. Key figure in Watergate scandal; pled guilty to obstruction of justice.

DEAN, LESLIE ALAN (CAP DEAN), international economic, social and political development consultant, interagency and defense analyst; b. Indpls., June 18, 1940; s. Henry Lloyd and Margaret Ann (Pfafman) Dean; m. Jeanne Louise Lambert, Apr. 14, 1962; children: David Richard, Laura Elizabeth. BA, U. Ill., 1963, MA, 1966; postgrad., U. Pitts., 1968-69. Internat. loan analyst Bank Calif., San Francisco, 1970; joined Fgn. Svc., 1970; devel. officer US AID, Washington, 1970, 77-79, Vientiane, Laos, 1971-75, Kathmandu, Nepal, 1975-77, Islamabad, Pakistan, 1979-83, Dar Es Salaam, Tanzania, 1983-85, asst. mission dir. Lusaka, Zambia, 1985-87, mission dir. sr. fgn. svc., 1988-90, office dir. Washington, 1990-92, mission dir. Pretoria, South Africa, 1992-96, dep. asst. adminstr. Africa Bur. Washington, 1996-98; dir. integrated devel. programs sub-Saharan Africa Internat. Found. Edn. and Self Help, Phoenix, 1999—2003, v.p. ops., 2003; regional coord. for Baghdad Coalition Provisional Authority, Baghdad, Iraq, 2004; interim mayor Baghdad, 2004; interim gov. Baghdad Province, 2004; internat. econ. and social devel. cons., 2004—05; sr. lead specialist, def. and interagency analyst Gen. Dynamics and US Joint Forces Command, 2005—06; dep. coord. econ. transition in Iraq, sr. advisor capacity devel. US Embassy, Baghdad, Iraq, 2007. Pres. Internat. Econ. and Social Devel. Cons., 2007—; elder Pinnacle Presbyn. Ch., 2002—, chair mission com., 2002—03, mem. mission com., 2004—; trustee Pinnacle Presbyn. Found., 2006—; bd. dirs. Operation Quality Time, 2008—. Capt. USAF, 1964—68. Recipient Disting. Spkrs. Program award, Trine U., 2008. Mem.: Phoenix Com. Fgn. Rels., Fgn. Policy Assn., Am. Fgn. Svc. Assn., Phi Eta Sigma. Avocations: swimming, reading, travel. Personal E-mail: cdean5000@aol.com.

DEAN, PAUL JOHN, magazine editor; b. Pitts., May 11, 1941; s. John Aloysius and Perle Elizabeth (Thompson) D.; m. Jo-ann Tillman, Aug. 19, 1972 (div. Mar. 1981); children: Jennifer Ann, Michael Paul. Student engring., Pa. State U., 1959-60. Gen. mgr. Civic Ctr. Honda Co., Pitts., 1965-68, Washington-Pitts. Cycle Co., Canonsburg, Pa., 1968-70; nat. svc. mgr. Yankee Motor Co., Schenectady, 1970-73. Competition congressman Am. Motorcyclist Assn., 1971, 72, trustee, sec. bd., 1988-91, chmn., 1991-97; bd. dirs. AMA ProRacing, 1997-2006; adv. bd., guest speaker L.A. Trade Tech. Coll., 1974-90; trustee Am. Motorcyclist Heritage Found., 1990-91. Engring. editor Cycle Guide mag., Compton, Calif., 1973-74, editor-in-chief, 1974-80, editorial dir., 1980-84; editor-in-chief Cycle World mag., Newport Beach, Calif., 1984-88, editorial dir. Cycle and Cycle World mags., 1988-92; v.p., editorial dir. Cycle World Mag. Group, 1992-2005, v.p., sr. editor, 2005—; author manuals. Served with AUS, 1964-65. Named to, Nat. Motorcycle Mus. and Hall of Fame, 2002. Home: 5915 Arabella St Lakewood CA 90713-1203 Office: Hachette Filipacchi Media US 1499 Monrovia Ave Newport Beach CA 92663-2752 Office Phone: 949-720-5386. E-mail: CW1Dean@aol.com.

DEAN, RICHARD ANTHONY, mechanical engineering executive; b. Bklyn., Dec. 22, 1935; s. Anthony David and Anne Mylod Dean; m. Sheila Elizabeth Grady, Oct. 5, 1957; children: Carolyn Anne, Julie Marie, Richard Drews. BSME, Ga. Inst. Tech., 1957; MSME, U. Pitts., 1963, PhDME, 1970. Registered profl. engr., Calif. From jr. engr. to mgr. thermal and hydraulic engring. Westinghouse Nuclear Energy Sys., 1959-70; v.p., tech. dir. water reactor fuels General Atomics, San Diego, 1970-74, v.p. uranium and light water reactor fuel, 1974-80, sr. v.p., 1980-92; pres. Leading Edge Engring., San Diego, 1993—; pres., CEO Cutting Edge Products, Inc., San Diego, 1997—. Cons. U.S. Congress Office Tech. Assessment. 1st lt. U.S. Army, 1957-59. Mem. AAAS, ASME (former chmn. nuclear fuels tech. com.), Am. Nuclear Soc. (gen. chmn. annual meeting 1993), Global Found. (bd. advisors), Internat. Thermonuclear Experimental Reactor (adv. bd.). Achievements include the develpoment of commercial nuclear power stations; advanced the understanding of boiling heat transfer phenomena; invention of advanced nuclear fuel assembly. Home: 6699 Via Estrada La Jolla CA 92037-6432 Office: Leading Edge Engineering 12555 High Bluff Dr Ste 100 San Diego CA 92130-3005 Office Phone: 858-513-1203. Business E-Mail: dean@leeinc.us.

DEAN, WILLIAM EVANS, aerospace engineer, engineering company executive, consultant; b. Greenville, Miss., July 6, 1930; s. George Thomas Dean and Martha Myrtle (Evans) Carlton; m. Dorothy Sue Hamilton, Oct. 14, 1953; children: Janet Lea, Jody Anne, Justin H. B in Aero. Engring., Ga. Inst. Tech., 1952; MBA, Pepperdine U., 1970; grad., USAF Air Command and Staff Coll., 1970. FAA cert. airplane and instrument flight instr. Commd. officer USAF, 1952, advanced through grades to maj., 1962; divsn. mgr., dir. Rockwell Internat. Corp., LA, 1962-67, v.p., divsn. gen. mgr., 1967-80; exec. v.p. Acurex Corp., Mountain View, Calif., 1981-82, pres., COO, 1982-83, pres., CEO, 1983-90, vice chmn., 1990-91; assoc. dir. Ames Rsch. Ctr. NASA, Moffett Field, Calif., 1991-93, dep. ctr. dir., 1994-97; v.p., dir. Univs. Space Rsch. Assn., Columbia, Md., 1997—2002; founder, mng. dir. The Dean Group, LLC, Santa Ana, Calif., 2002—. Lectr. Calif. State U., Chico, 1988, Santa Clara U., 1993-98, USAF Acad., 1961, 75. Contbr. articles on gen. mgmt. and aero. engring. to profl. jours. Bd. dirs. NCCJ, San Jose, Calif., 1984-97, co-chmn., 1988-91; bd. dirs. Santa Clara County Mfg. Group, San Jose, 1984-91, vice-chmn., 1988-91; bd. dirs. Saddleback Community Coll., Mission Viejo, Calif., 1976-77, United Fund, Orange County, Calif., 1971; United Way, Santa Clara County, San Jose, 1985-91; vice-chmn., bd. advisors Leavey Sch. Bus., Santa Clara U., 1987-97, vice chmn., 1989-91; tech. com. Orange County Bus. Coun., 1998-2000. Decorated Air Force Commendation medal with oak leaf cluster; recipient Spl. Svc. award United Way, 1986, NASA Astronaut Personal Achievement award, 1972, 84, Outstanding Contbn. to Manned Exploration of the Moon award, 1972, Medal for Outstanding Leadership, 1995, Group Achievement awards, 1995, Disting. Svc. medal, 1997; Silver Knight of Mgmt. award Nat. Mgmt. Assn., 1978, Commendation Cert. Calif. State Assembly, 1986, Pres. award Santa Clara U., 1993, Disting. Alumnus award Woodward Acad., 1999, Acad. Disting. Engring. Alumni award Ga. Inst. Tech., 1995; inducted to Engring. Hall of Fame, Ga. Inst. Tech., 1997. Fellow AIAA (bd. dirs. 1979-86, 91-95, fin. com. 1995—, Space Shuttle award 1984), Internat. Acad. Astronautics (Paris), Am. Astron. Soc., Nat. Space Soc.; mem. Am. Electronics Assn. (edn. found. 1982-88), Aircraft Owners and Pilots Assn. (command pilot), Air Force Assn. Republican. Baptist. Office: The Dean Group 13422 Laurinda Way North Tustin CA 92705-1926 Office Phone: 714-544-5020. Business E-Mail: wedean@thedeangroup.com.

DE ANTONI, EDWARD PAUL, retired lab administrator; b. San Francisco, Mar. 7, 1941; s. Attilio Mario and Zita Elizabeth (Lolich) DeA.; m. Karen Dolores Thode, Jan. 22, 1966; children: Marc Edward, Christopher Earl. AB, U. San Francisco, 1962; PhD, Cornell U., 1971. Vol. Peace Corps, Turkey, 1964-66; sr. analyst Planning Bur. State of S.D., Pierre, 1973-76; dir. health planning Dept. Health, 1976-81; asst. dir. Assoc. Sch. Bds. S.D., 1981-84; dir. cancer control program Colo. Dept. Health, 1986-90; rsch. dir. Cancer Ctr., Porter Meml. Hosp., Denver, 1991-92; chair genitourinary cancer control Southwest Oncology Group, 1991-97; rsch. dir. Prostate Cancer Edn. Coun., 1991-97; asst. prof. urology Health Sci. Ctr., U. Colo., Denver, 1992-99, sr. instr., 2000—06, sr. instr pathology/urology, 2001—06. Woodrow Wilson fellow, 1962-63; ESEA fellow, 1966-69 Personal E-mail: deantone7@msn.com.

DEAR, JOSEPH ALBERT, pension fund administrator; b. 1951; married; 2 children. BA in Polit. Economy, Evergreen State Coll., Olympia, Wash., 1976; grad. Program for Sr. Execs. in Govt., Harvard U., 1986. Founder, exec. dir. People for Fair Taxes, 1977—81; rsch. dir. Wash. State Labor Coun., 1981-85; dir. Wash. Dept. Labor and Industries, 1987—93; asst. sec. Occupl. Health & Safety Adminstrn. US Dept. Labor, 1993—97; chief of staff to Gov. State of Washington, Olympia, 1997—2001; govt. rels. officer Frank Russell Co., 2001—02; exec. dir. The Washington State Investment Bd. (WSIB), 2002—09; chief investment officer The Calif. Pub. Employees' Retirement Sys. (CalPERS), 2009—. Bd. trustees Washington State Investment Bd., 1987—92, chmn., 1989—91. Mem. Nat. Assn. Govtl. Labor Ofcls. (pres. 1990-91), Occupl. Safety and Health State Plan Assn. (bd. dirs. 1989-93). Office: Calif Pub Employees' Retirement Sys - CalPERS Lincoln Plz N 400 Q St Sacramento CA 95811*

DEASY, CORNELIUS MICHAEL, retired architect; b. Mineral Wells, Tex., July 19, 1918; s. Cornelius and Monetta (Palmo) D.; m. Lucille Laney, Sept. 14, 1941; children: Diana, Carol, Ann. BArch, U. So. Calif., 1941. Practice architecture, LA, 1946—76; ptnr. Robert D. Bolling, 1960—76, ret., 1976. Prin. works include prin. offices student union, Calif. State U., LA; author: Design for Human Affairs, 1974, Designing Places for People, 1985, Gifts From America, 2003. V.p. LA Beautiful; dir. Regional Plan Assn.; commr., LA Bd. Zoning Appeals, 1973-. Recipient numerous design awards, Nat. Endowment Arts award, 1983. Fellow AIA (past pres., dir. So. Calif. chpt., chmn. com. rsch.). Home and Office: Davenport Creek Farm 4979 Davenport Creek Rd San Luis Obispo CA 93401-8109 Personal E-mail: c_deasy@sbcglobal.net.

DEBERRY, DONNA, retail executive; b. 1955; Attended, Calif. State U. Worked with NFL, U.S. Olympic Com., The Oprah Winfrey Show; exec. v.p. global diversity and corp. affairs Wyndham Internat. Inc.; CEO, founder DRP Internat.; v.p. diversity Nike, Inc., 2006—. Bd. dirs. Nat. Hispanic Corp. Coun., U.S. Hispanic C. of C., Nat. Coalition of Black Meeting Planners, Nat. Assn. Black Hotel Owners, Operators and Developers; mem. adv. coun. eWomen Network Found.

DE BOER, JEFFREY B., auto dealership executive; Degree cum laude, Pomona Coll., 1988; MBA in Fin. and Investment Mgmt., London Bus. Sch., 1994. Internat. credit officer Fuki Bank Ltd., Tokyo, 1988-92; equity analyst, sector fund mgr. Fidelity Investments Japan, 1994-97; v.p. fin. and investor rels. Lithia Motors, Inc., Medford, Oreg., 1997-2000, sr. v.p., CFO, 2000—. Office: Lithia Motors Inc 360 E Jackson St Medford OR 97501

DE BOER, SIDNEY B., automotive executive; Attended, Stanford U., U. Oregon. Chmn., CEO Lithia Motors Inc., Medford, Oreg., 1968—. Mem. Presidents Club NADA; mem. DaimlerChrysler Nat. Dealer Council. Bd. mem. So. Oreg. Univ. Found., Oreg. Cmty. Found., Oreg. Shakespeare Festival. Recipient All-Star Dealer award, Sports Illustrated mag., 1990, Quality Dealer award, Time Mag., 1997. Office: Lithia Motors Inc 360 E Jackson St Medford OR 97501

DE BOOR, CARL-WILHELM R., mathematician; b. Stolp, Germany, Dec. 3, 1937; m. Matilda C. Friedrich, Feb. 6, 1960 (div. Sept. 12, 1984); children: C. Thomas, Elisabeth, Peter, Adam; m. Helen L. Bee, Jan. 2, 1991. Student, Universitaet Hamburg, 1956-59, Harvard U., 1959-60; PhD, U. Mich., 1966; doctorate in Sci. (hon.), Purdue U., 1993, Technion, 2002. Rsch. mathematician Gen. Motors Research Labs., 1960-64; asst. prof. math., computer sci. Purdue U., 1966-68, assoc. prof., 1968-72; prof. math., computer sci. U. Wis.-Madison, 1972—2003, prof. emeritus, 2003—. Vis. staff mem. Los Alamos Sci. Labs., 1970-95, affiliated prof. U. Wash., 2004-. Author: (with S. Conte) Elementary Numerical Analysis, 1972, 1980, A Practical Guide to Splines, 1978, 2001, (with J.B. Rosser) Pocket Calculator Supplement for Calculus, 1979, Spline Toolbox for Matlab, 1990, (with K. Höllig and S. Riemenschneider) Box Splines, 1993. Named John Von Neumann lectr. Soc. Indsl. and Applied Math., 1996, recipient Nat. medal of Sci., 2003, 05. Fellow Am. Acad. Arts and Scis.; mem. Nat. Acad. Engring., Nat. Acad. Sci., Soc. Indsl. and Applied Math., Polish Acad. Sci., Leopoldina, Phi Beta Kappa Office: PO Box 1076 Eastsound WA 98245

DE BRIER, DONALD PAUL, lawyer, oil industry executive; b. Atlantic City, Mar. 20, 1940; s. Daniel and Ethel de B.; m. Nancy Lee McElroy, Aug. 1, 1964; children: Lesley Anne, Rachel Wynne, Danielle Verne. BA in Hist., Princeton U., 1962; LLB with honors, U. Pa., 1967. Bar: NY 1967, Tex. 1977, Utah 1983, Ohio 1987. Assoc. firm Sullivan & Cromwell, NYC, 1967-70, Patterson, Belknap, Webb & Tyler, NYC, 1970-76; v.p., gen. counsel, dir. Gulf Resources & Chem. Corp., Houston, 1976-82; v.p. law Kennecott Corp. (former subs. BP America Inc.), Salt Lake City, 1983-89; assoc. gen. counsel BP America Inc., Cleve., 1987-89; gen. counsel BP Exploration Co. Ltd., London, 1989-93; exec. v.p., gen. counsel Occidental Petroleum Corp., LA, 1993—. Bd. dirs. LA Philharm., 1995—. Lt. USNR, 1962—64. Mem. Calif. Club, Riviera Tennis Club (chmn. adv. bd. govs. 2002-). Office: Occidental Petroleum Corp 10889 Wilshire Blvd Los Angeles CA 90024-4201

DEBRO, JULIUS, education educator, sociologist; b. Jackson, Miss., Sept. 25, 1931; s. Joseph and Seleana (Gaylor) Debro; m. Darlene Conley. BA in Polit. Sci., U. San Francisco, 1953; MA in Sociology, San Jose State U., 1967; PhD, U. Calif.-Berkeley, 1975. Research asst. U. Calif. Sch. Criminology, Berkeley, 1964-68; instr. dept. sociology Laney Coll., Alameda, Calif., 1968-69, Alameda Coll., Oakland, Calif., 1971, U. Md., College Park, 1971-72, asst. prof. Inst. for Criminal Justice and Criminology, 1972-79; mem. faculty Atlanta U., 1979-91, prof. criminal justice, 1979-91, chmn. dept. pub. adminstrn., 1979-80, chmn. dept. Criminal Justice Inst., 1979-89, chmn. dept. sociology, 1985-86; assoc. dean Grad. Sch., acting asst. provost U. Wash., Seattle, 1991—, prof. society and justice program, 1991—2000. Mem. adv. bd. dirs. Criminal Justice Rev., 1977—87; prin. investigator Joint Commn. on Criminology and Criminal Justice Edn. and Stds., 1978—79; v.p. Atlanta Met. Crime Commn., 1986, pres., 87; mem. investigative bd. Ga. Bar Assn., 1987. Assoc. editor Criminal Justice Quar., 1989—. Chmn. program evaluation com. Boys and Girls Home, Montgomery County, Md., 1979; bd. dirs. YMCA, Bethesda, Md., 1979, Totem Coun. Girl Scouts. Served to col. USAR, 1953—84. Recipient postdoctoral rsch. assoc., Narcotic and Drug Rsch. Inc., N.Y.C., 1989—90, Herbert Bloch award for Outstanding Svcs. to Criminal Justice Criminology, Am. Soc. Criminology; grantee, NIMH, 1974, Law Enforcement Assistance Adminstrn., 1979—81; fellow, NIMH, 1969—70, Ford, 1971, Inter-Univ. Seminar on Armed Forces and Soc., 1989, We. Soc. Criminology, 1989. Fellow: Narcotic Drug Rsch.; mem.: NAACP, Acad. Criminal Justice Sci., Am. Sociol. Assn., Nat. Assn. Black Sociologists, Nat. Assn. Blacks in Criminal Justice (editor quar. news mag. 1987—), Urban League, Rotary Club, Sigma Pi Phi (boule Alpha Omicron chpt.), Alpha Phi Alpha. Democrat. Office: U Wash 107 Gowen Box 353530 Seattle WA 98195-0001 E-mail: jdebro@u.washington.edu.

DE BRUYCKER, LLOYD HENRY, rancher, feedlot operator; b. Great Falls, Mont., Dec. 1, 1933; s. Achiel Henry and Rose Presperine (Emperor) De B.; m. Jane Crystal, July 2, 1954; 7 children. Grad. high sch., Dutton, Mont. Grain elevator laborer, 1954-59; rancher, 1959—. Home: Box 7700 Dutton MT 59433 Office: North Mt Feeders Inc PO Box 218 Choteau MT 59422-0218

DEBUCK, DONALD G., computer company executive; BA, U. Va.; MBA, George Washington U., 1984. From dir. to v.p., controller Computer Scis. Corp., El Segundo, Calif., 1979—2002, v.p., 2002—, controller, 2002—, interim CFO, 2008—. Office: Computer Sciences Corp 2200 E Grand Ave El Segundo CA 90245

DECARIA, KEN, state legislator; b. Ogden, Utah, Nov. 5, 1953; m. Peggy Decaria; 2 children. BS in Biology, U. Utah. Tchr.; mem. Wyo. House of Reps., 1997—98; mem. Dist. 15 Wyo. State Senate, 1999—, Minority Caucus Chmn., 2003—04, Minority Whip, 2005—06, Minority Fl. Leader, 2007—08. Democrat. Mailing: 202 Broken Circle Dr Evanston WY 82930 Office: 213 State Capitol Bldg Cheyenne WY 82002 Home Phone: 307-789-4616; Office Phone: 307-780-5499, 307-777-7881. Office Fax: 307-777-5466. Business E-Mail: kdecaria@wyoming.com.*

DECARLO, JOHN T., lawyer; b. Phila., Nov. 6, 1950; BS, Villanova U., 1972; JD, U. San Fernando Valley, 1975. Bar: Calif. 1976, US Dist. Ct., Cent. Dist. Calif. 1978, DC 1995, US Dist. Ct., DC 1996. Ptnr. DeCarlo & Connor, P.C., LA; gen. coun. United Brotherhood Carpenters & Joiners of Am. Mem.: ABA, LA County Bar Assn. Office: DeCarlo & Connor 9th Fl 533 S Fremont Ave Los Angeles CA 90071-1706

DE CASTRO, HUGO DANIEL, lawyer; b. Panama City, Sept. 12, 1935; arrived in U.S., 1947; s. Mauricio Fidanque and Armida Rebecca (Salas) de C.; m. Isabel Shapiro, July 25, 1958; children: Susan M., Teresa A., Andrea L., Michele L. BSBA in Econs. cum laude, UCLA, 1957, JD summa cum laude, 1960. CPA Calif.; bar: Calif. (ret.) 1961. Prin. de Castro, West, Chodorow, Glickfeld & Nass Inc., LA, 1961—2005. Lectr. UCLA, 1962-67, 68, counsel to dean Law Sch., 1963—; commr. tax adv. com. State Bar Calif. Editor UCLA Law Rev., 1959-60, Taxation for Lawyers, 1971-88; contbr. articles to profl. jours. Former trustee Stephen S. Wise Temple, Jewish Fedn. Cmty. Found.; trustee, bd. dir., chmn. fin. com. UCLA Found.; bd. dirs. Western LA Found., Hebrew Union Coll., Law Found.; bd. govs. Trustee Endowment Trusts. Mem. ABA chmn. taxation subcom.), ACLU, LA C. of C. (former chmn., dir.), LA World Affairs coun., Am. Jewish Com., Del Rey Yacht Club (Calif., former dir., officer), Founders of Music Ctr., Las Hadas Country Club (Mex.), Pi Lambda Phi. Office: 10877 Wilshire Blvd Ste 300C Los Angeles CA 90024 E-mail: hugo4ucla@gmail.com.

DECCIO, ALEXANDER A., state legislator; b. Walla Walla, Oct. 28, 1921; m. Lucille Deccio; 7 children. Mem. Wash. Senate, Dist. 14, Olympia, 1974—; Rep. whip Wash. Senate; mem. health and long-term care com. Wash. Legislature, Olympia, mem. legis. oversight com. on Seahawks Stadium, mem. Gov.'s Commn. on Early Childhood Edn. com. Bd. dirs. Providence Med. Ctr., Yakima Neighborhood Health Svcs., Yakima Vis. and Conv. Bur. Recipient 100 Percent Voting Record award Wash. State Farm Bur. Republican. Office: 407 Legislative Bldg Olympia WA 98504-0001

DECIL, STELLA WALTERS (DEL DECIL), artist; b. Indpls., Apr. 26, 1921; d. William Calvin and Hazel Jean (Konkle) Smith; m. John W. Walters, June 19, 1940 (div. Sept. 1945); m. Casimir R. Decil, Feb. 6, 1965. Grad., Indpls. Acad. Comml. Art, 1939, John Heron Art Inst., Indpls., 1941. Staff artist William H. Block Co., Indpls., 1945-50, art dir., 1952-62, Frank R. Jelleff Co., Washington, 1950-51, Diamonds Dept. Stores, Phoenix, 1962-67; freelance artist, 1967-70. Painting instr. various art groups in Ariz.-N.Mex, 1970—, Phoenix Art Mus., 1975—77; mem. visual arts bd. Prescott Fine Arts Assn., 1990—2000; original curator Mature Eye Bi-Ann. Prescott (Ariz.) Fine Arts Assn., 1996—2000; instr. Mountain Artists Guild, Prescott, 1995—97. One-woman shows include Cave Creek, Carefree, Scottsdale, Ariz., N.Mex., exhibited in group shows, Phoenix, Scottsdale, Las Cruces, N.Mex., Hoosier Salon, Folger Gallery, Indpls., Mammen II Gallery, Scottsdale, Thompson Gallery, Garelick Gallery, Hopkins Fine Art, Scottsdale, Ariz., Helen Vohl Gallery, Wickenburg, Ariz., Phippen Mus., Prescott, Ariz., Represented in permanent collections Continental Bank, Humana Hosp., Pueblo Grande Mus., VA Med. Ctr., Prescott, Mayo Ctr. Women's Health, Scottsdale, Proctor Bank Vt., Bank Rio Grande, Las Cruces, Detroit Inst. of Arts, Mich., Trevor Brown H.S., Phoenix, Ariz. State U., Tempe, Ind. State Archival Libr., pvt. collections in 20 states. Past pres. Scottsdale Art League, 1973. Recipient Maxine Cherrington Meml. award, Hoosier Salon, 1973; named Ad Woman of Yr., Indpls. Ad Club, 1958. Mem.: Ariz. Watercolor Assn. (Royal Scorpion Status, past pres.). Home: 9460 E Towago Dr Prescott Valley AZ 86314-7140 Office Phone: 928-775-5829.

DECIUTIIS, ALFRED CHARLES MARIA, oncologist, television producer; b. NYC, Oct. 16, 1945; s. Alfred Ralph and Theresa Elizabeth (Manko) deCiutiis; m. Catherine L. Gohn. BS summa cum laude, Fordham U., 1967; MD, Columbia U., 1971. Diplomate Am. Bd. Internal Medicine, Am. Bd. Med. Oncology. Intern N.Y. Hosp.-Cornell Med. Ctr., NYC, 1971-72, resident, 1972-74; fellow in clin. immunology Meml. Hosp.-Sloan Kettering Cancer Ctr., NYC, 1974-75, fellow in clin. oncology, 1975-76, spl. fellow in immunology, 1974-76; guest investigator, asst. physician exptl. hematology Rockefeller U., NYC, 1975-76; pvt. practice specializing in med. oncology LA, 1977—. Mem. adult bone marrow transplant team Memorial Sloan-Kettering Cancer Ctr., 1974—76; chief oncology svc. Misericordia Hosp. (now Mercy Hosp. Cornell Med. Ctr.), Bronx, NY, 1976; mem. med. adv. com. Olympics, 1984; co-founder Medtrina Med. Ctr., Torrance, Calif., physician asst. supr., 1984; mem. fgn. policy leadership project Ctr. Internat. Affairs, Harvard, Ill. Host cable TV shows, 1981—, med. editor Cable Health Network, 1983—, Lifetime Network, 1984—; syndicated columnist: Coast Media News, 1980; prodr.: numerous med. TV shows; interviewed: numerous stars; author: (Landmark sci. paper) Defects in the Alternate Pathway of Complement Activation post Splenectomy; contbr. articles to profl. jours. Mem. gov. bd. med. coun. Italian-Am. Found.; mem. Italian-Am. Civic Com., LA, 1983, Cath. League Civil and Rel. Liberty, World Affairs Coun., LA, Boston Mus. Fine Arts, Met. Mus.; founder Italian-Am. Med. Assn., 1982; co-founder Italian-Am. Legal Alliance, LA, 1982—; mem. UCLA Chancellor's Assocs. Served to capt. M.C. US Army, 1972—74. Leukemia Soc. Am. fellow, 1974—76. Fellow: ACP, Internat. Coll. Physicians and Surgeons; mem.: AAAS, AMA (Physician's Recognition award 1978—80, 1982—85, 1986—89, 1989—91, 1991—94, 1994—96, 1996—99, 1999—2002, 2002—04), Am. Soc. Hematology (emeritus), Internat. Platform Assn., Drug Info. Assn., Chinese Med. Assn., Am. Geriat. Soc., Am. Pub. Health Assn., N.Y. Acad. Sci. (life), Internat. Health Soc., Am. Union Physicians and Dentists, Los Angeles County Med. Assn., Calif. Med. Assn., Am. Soc. Clin. Oncology, Mensa, Smithsonian Instn., Nat. Geog. Soc. (life), Fondazione Giovanni Agnelli, Nature Conservancy, Nat. Wildlife Fedn., Sigma Xi, Alpha Omega Alpha, Phi Beta Kappa. Achievements include participated on some of the first bone marrow transplants in the USA; 1st comprehensive clinical description of chronic fatigue syndrome as a neuro-immunologic acquired disorder. Office: PO Box 384 Agoura Hills CA 91376-0384

DECKER, PETER RANDOLPH, rancher, retired state official; b. NYC, Oct. 1, 1934; s. Frank Randolph and Marjorie (Marony) D.; m. Dorothy Morss, Sept. 24, 1972; children: Karen, Christopher, Hilary. BA, Middlebury Coll., Vt., 1957; MA, Syracuse U., 1961; PhD, Columbia U., 1974. Tchr. Cate Sch., Carpinteria, Calif., 1961-63; sr. writer Congl. Quar., Washington, 1963-64; asst. to pres. Middlebury (Vt.) Coll., 1964-67; staff asst. Sen. Robert Kennedy, Washington, 1967-68; corr. AP, Laos, Vietnam, 1970; instr./lectr. Columbia U., NYC, 1972-74; asst. prof. Duke U., Durham, NC, 1974-80; owner, operator Double D Ranches, Ridgway, Colo., 1980—; commr. agr. State of Colo., Denver, 1987-89; pres. Decker & Assocs., Denver, 1989—. Dir. Nat. Western Stock Show, Denver, 1990—; bd. dirs. Fed. Res. Bd. Kansas City, Denver, 1992-98; bd. dirs. Western Colo. Bank, Montrose; pres. Telluride Bancorp, Inc., 1990-97; mem. adv. bd. Crow Canyon Archeol. Ctr., Fulcrum Press. Author: Fortunes and Failures, 1978, Old Fences, New Neighbors, 1998, The Utes Must Go, 2005; contbr. articles to profl. jours. and mags. Trustee Middlebury Coll., 1988-96, Fnt Lewis Coll., 2001-05, 2008-, Colo. Commn. on Higher Edn., 1985-93; chmn. Ouray County Planning Commn., 1981-85; chmn. Colo. Endowment Humanities, 1982-85; trustee Ft. Lewis Coll., 2002—. Lt. U.S. Army, 1957-60, capt. Res., 1960-67. English Speaking Union scholar, 1952-53; Nat. Endowment for Humanities fellow Yale U., 1977-78, Rockefeller Found. fellow, 1979-80. Mem. Colo. Livestock Assn., Denver Athletic Club, Mile High Club (Denver), Elks, Colo. Author's League, Angler's Club (Key Largo, Fla.), Columbia U. Club (N.Y.C), Commodore Ridgway (Co.) Yacht club. Democrat. Home: 395 Race St Denver CO 80206-4118

DECKER, RICHARD JEFFREY, lawyer; b. Manhasset, NY, Aug. 26, 1959; s. Alan B. and Shelley T. (Belkin) D.; m. Carrie Ann Gordon, Aug. 13, 1989. BA, Union Coll., Schenectady, NY, 1981; JD, Boston U., 1984. Bar: N.Y. 1985, Calif. 1985, Mass. 1985, U.S. Dist. Ct. (cen. dist.) Calif. 1985. Assoc. Turner, Gesterfeld, Wilk & Tigerman, Beverly Hills, Calif., 1985-86, Shapiro, Posell & Close, LA, 1986-90, Katten, Muchin, Zavis & Weitzman, LA, 1990-93; ptnr. Theodora Oringher Miller & Richman, LA, 1993—. Mem. Los Angeles County Bar Assn., Beverly Hills Bar Assn., Century City Bar Assn. Avocations: sports, guitar playing, travel, reading. Office: Theodora Oringher Miller & Richman 2029 Century Park E Ste 600 Los Angeles CA 90067-2907

DECKER, SUSAN LYNNE, former Internet company executive; b. Nov. 1962; married; 3 children. BS in Computer Sci. & Economics, Tufts U., 1984; MBA, Harvard U. Cert. Charterd Fin. Analyst. With Donaldson, Lufking & Jenrette (DLJ), 1986—2000, publ. and advtsg. rsch. anlayst, dir. global head rsch., 1998—2000; sr. v.p. fin. & adminstrn. Yahoo! Inc., Sunnyvale, Calif., 2000—02, CFO, 2000—07, exec. v.p. fin. & adminstrn., 2002—07, exec. v.p. head advt. & pub. group, 2007, pres., 2007—09. Mem. Fin. Acctg. Standards Adv. Coun., 2000—04; bd. dirs. Costco Wholesale Corp., 2004—, Pixar Animation Studios, 2004—06, Intel Corp., 2006—, Berkshire Hathaway, 2007—. Bd. dirs. Stanford Inst. Econ. & Policy Rsch., 2005—07. Named one of 50 Women to Watch, Wall St. Jour., 2006, 50 Who Matter Now, Business 2.0, 2007, 50 Most Powerful Women in Bus., Fortune mag., 2007, 2008, 100 Most Powerful Women, Forbes mag., 2008, Most Influential Women in Technology, Fast Company, 2009.*

DECKERT, RYAN, state legislator; b. Corpus Christi, Tex., Mar. 17, 1971; son of Ronald Irving Deckert & Linda DuBois D; single. Coordr, John Kitzhaber for Governor & Ron Wyden for United States Senate campaigns, formerly; Oregon State Representative, District 8, 1997-2001, vice chairman, Commerce Committee, 1997-2001, member, Agriculture & Forestry & General Govt Committees, 1997-2001, formerly, Oregon House Representative; Oregon State Senator, District 4, 2001-02; Oregon State Senator, District 14, 2003-, member Econ Develop Committee, currently, vice chairman, Education Committee, currently, chairman, Revenue Committee, currently, Oregon State Senator.Youth director, Living Enrichment Center, Wilsonville, formerly; job recruiter, Pvt Indust Coun, formerly. Democrat. Office: 900 Court St NE, S-219 Salem OR 97301 Office Phone: 503-986-1714. Fax: 503-643-6802. E-mail: sen.ryandeckert@state.or.us.

DEDERER, MICHAEL EUGENE, retired public relations executive; b. Seattle, Apr. 30, 1932; s. Michael and Clare (Collon) D.; separated; children— David M., Claira M. BA in Journalism, U. Wash., 1953. Account exec. Hugh A. Smith Mktg. & Pub. Relations Co., Seattle, 1956-59; account exec. Kraft, Smith & Ehrig, Inc., Seattle, 1959-63, Jay Rockey Pub. Relations and The Rockey Co., Inc., Seattle, 1963, v.p., 1970-78, exec. v.p., 1978-86, pres., 1986-94; vice chmn. The Rockey Co., Inc., Seattle, 1994-98, sr. cons., 1992—2002, ret., 2002. Served to 1st lt. U.S. Army, 1953-55. Mem. Pub. Rels. Soc. Am. (pres. Wash. chpt. 1970). Roman Catholic. Avocations: skiing, fly fishing. Office: Rockey Hill Knowlton 221 Yale Ave N Ste 530 Seattle WA 98109-5490

DEERING, THOMAS PHILLIPS, retired lawyer; b. Winfield, Kans., Feb. 15, 1929; s. Frederick Arthur and Lucile (Phillips) D.; m. Marilyn Marie Anderson, Sept. 6, 1952; children: Thomas P. Jr., Robert E., Paul A. BS, U. Colo., 1951, LLB, 1956. Bar: Oreg. 1956, Colo. 1956, U.S. Dist. Ct. Oreg. 1956. Assoc. Hart Spencer McCulloch Rockwood & Davies (now Stoel Rives), Portland, Oreg., 1956-62; ptnr. Stoel Rives LLP, Portland, 1962—99; ret., 1999. Mem. We. Pension and Benefits Conf., 1989-2002; mem. faculty Am. Law Inst.-ABA, 1985-96. Co-author: Tax Reform Act of 1986, 1987. Bd. dirs. Girl Scouts Columbia River Coun., Portland, 1961-70; trustee, moderator First Unitarian Ch., Portland, 1967-70; trustee, pres. Catlin Gabel Sch., Portland, 1970-76; bd. dirs., v.p. ACLU, Portland, 1966-71, 73-80; chmn. Multnomah County Task Force on Edgefield Manor, Portland, 1972-75; bd. dirs., treas. Portland Art Mus., Contemporary Arts Coun., 1986-88; mem. City County Task Fore on Svc. Evaluation, Portland, 1982-85, Citizen's Adv. Com. West Side Corridor Project, Portland, 1988-93; bd. govs. Pacific N.W. Coll. Art, 1991-2000, 2002-, chair, 1996-2000, chair presdl. search com. 2002-2003; mem. collections com. Portland Art Mus., 1992-96; trustee Oreg. Coll. Art and Craft Endowment, Portland, 1991-97. With U.S. Army, 1952-54. Recipient Disting. Mem. award We. Pension and Benefits Conf., 1999. Fellow Am. Coll. Benefits Counsel (emeritus); mem. ABA (tax sect., EB com. 1989-2000), City Club of Portland (bd. govs. 1968-70, 2000-03, rsch bd. 2003—). Democrat. Avocations: hiking, skiing, sailing, reading. Home: 5235 SW Burton Dr Portland OR 97221-2517 Office: Stoel Rives LLP 900 SW 5th Ave Ste 2600 Portland OR 97204-1268 Personal E-mail: tomdeering@comcast.net. Business E-Mail: tpdeering@stoel.com.

DEETS, DWAIN AARON, retired aerospace technology executive; b. Bell, Calif., Apr. 16, 1939; s. Kenneth Robert and Mildred Evelyn (Bergman) D.; m. Catherine Elizabeth Meister, June 18, 1961; children: Dennis Allen, Danelle Alaine. AB, Occidental Coll., 1961; MS in Physics, San Diego State U., 1964; ME, UCLA, 1978. Rsch. engr. Dryden Flight Rsch. Ctr. NASA, Edwards, Calif., 62-78, 79-85, hdqrs. liaison engr. Washington, 1978-79, mgr. Edwards, 1979-85; dir. rsch. engring. Dryden Flight Rsch. Ctr., Edwards, 1990-96, dir. aerospace projects, 1996-97, dir. flight rsch. R&T, 1997-99; hdqrs. mgr. flight rsch. NASA, Washington, 1988-89; ret., 1999. Chmn. Reusable Launch Vehicles Non-Advocate Rev., 1995-96. Editor-in-Chief: (mag.) Secular Nat., 2006-08, Atheist Alliance Internat., Architects and Engrs.; contbr. articles to profl. jours. Recipient Exceptional Svc. medal NASA, 1988, Pres. Rank award SES, 1998, Founders award

Atheists United, 2002. Fellow AIAA (assoc., Wright Bros. lectr. aeros. 1987); mem. Soc. Automotive Engrs. (chmn. aerospace control and guidance systems com. 1988-90), Occidental Coll. (bd. governors 2008-). Democrat. Home: 1770 Whitehall Rd Encinitas CA 92024-1036 Home Phone: 760-635-3719; Office Phone: 760-445-3242. E-mail: dadeets@cox.net.

DEFAZIO, LYNETTE STEVENS, dancer, choreographer, violinist, actress, educator; d. Honore and Mabel J. (Estavan) Stevens; children: J.H. Panganiban, Joanna Pang. Student, U. Calif., Berkeley, 1950—55, San Francisco State Coll., 1950—51; studied classical dance tchg. techniques and vocabulary with Gisella Caccialanza and Harold and Lew Christensen, San Francisco Ballet, 1952-56; D in Chiropractic, Life-West Chiropractic Coll., San Lorenzo, Calif., 1983; cert. techniques of tchg., U. Calif., 1985; BA in Humanities, New Coll. Calif., 1986, MFA, MA, New Coll. Calif., 2007. Lic. chiropracter, Mich.; diplomate Nat. Sci. Bd.; eminence in dance edn., Calif. C.C. dance specialist, std. svcs., childrens ctrs. credentials Calif. Dept. Edn., 1986. Contract child dancer Monogram Movie Studio, Hollywood, Calif., 1938-40; dance instr. San Francisco Ballet, 1953-65; performer San Francisco Opera Ring, 1960-67; performer, choreographer Oakland (Calif.) Civic Light Opera, 1963-70; dir. Ballet Arts Studio, Oakland, 1960; tchg. specialist Oakland Unified Sch. Dist., 1965-80; fgn. exch. dance dir. Academie de Danses-Salle Pleyel, Paris, 1966; instr. Peralta C.C. Dist., Oakland, 1971—, chmn. dance dept., 1985—. Cons., instr. ext. courses UCLA, Dirs. and Suprs. Assn., Pitts. Unified Sch. Dist., 1971-73, Tulare (Calif.) Sch. Dist., 1971-73; rschr. Ednl. Testing Svcs., HEW, Berkeley, 1974; resident choreographer San Francisco Childrens Opera, 1970—, Oakland Civic Theater; ballet mistress Dimensions Dance Theater, Oakland, 1977-80; cons. Gianchetta Sch. Dance, San Francisco, Robicheau Boston Ballet, TV series Patchwork Family, CBS, NYC; choreographer Ravel's Valses Nobles et Sentimentales, 1976. Author: Basic Music Outlines for Dance Classes, 1960, 1965, rev. edit., 1968, Teaching Techniques and Choreography for Advanced Dancers, 1965, Goals and Objectives in Improving Physical Capabilities, 1970, A Teacher's Guide for Ballet Techniques, 1970, Principle Procedures in Basic Curriculum, 1974, Objectives and Standards of Performance for Physical Development, 1975, Techniques of the Ballet School, 1970, rev. edit., 1974, The Opera Ballets: A Choreographic Manual Vols. I-V, 1986, 3rd Edit., 2008—09; assoc. music arranger: Le Ballet du Cirque, 1964, assoc. composer, lyricist: The Ballet of Mother Goose, 1968; choreographer Valses Nobles Et Sentimentales (Ravel), Transitions (Kashevaroff), 1991, The New Wizard of Oz, 1991, San Francisco Children's Opera (Gingold), Canon in D for Strings and Continuo (Pachelbel), 1979, Oakland Cmty. Orch. excerpts from Swan Lake, Faust, Sleeping Beauty, 1998, Rodeo, Alameda Coll. Cultural Affairs Program, 2000, The Gershwin Dances, 2004, The Christmas Party Ballet in 2 acts Based on Nutcracker, Laney Coll., 2007, solo dancer Three Stravinsky Etudes, Alameda Coll. Cultural Affairs Program, 1999, appeared in Flower Drum Song, 1993, Gigi, 1994, Fiddler on the Roof, 1996, The Music Man, 1996, Sayonara, 1997, Bye Bye Birdie, 2000, Barnum, the Circus Musical, 2001; musician (violinist): Oakland Cmty. Concert Orch., 1995—; condr.: Gil Gleason, coord.: Oakland Cmty. Orch., 2001—. Bd. dirs. Prodrs. Assocs., Inc., Oakland, 1999—; coord. Oakland (Calif.) Cmty. Orch., 2002—. Recipient Foremost Women of 20th Century, 1985, Merit award San Francisco Children's Opera, 1985, 90. Mem. Calif. State Tchrs. Assn., Bay Area Chiropractic Rsch. Soc., Profl. Dance Tchrs. Assn. Home and Office: 4923 Harbord Dr Oakland CA 94618-2506 Home Phone: 510-547-0477; Office Phone: 510-547-5477. Personal E-mail: LynetteDeFazio@comcast.net.

DEFAZIO, PETER ANTHONY, United States Representative from Oregon; b. Needham, Mass., May 27, 1947; m. Myrnie Daut. BA in Economics & Polit. Sci., Tufts U., Medford, Mass., 1969; postgraduate student, U. Oreg., Eugene, 1969-71, MS in Pub. Adminstrn. & Gerontology, 1977. Sr. issues specialist, caseworker dist. field office Staff of US Rep. Jim Weaver of Oreg., 1977-78, legis. asst. Washington office, 1978-80, dir. constituent svcs., 1980-82; mem. Lane County Commn., Oreg., 1982-86, chmn.; mem. US Congress from 4th Oreg. dist., 1987—, dean Oreg. del., mem. transp. and infrastructure com., mem. homeland security com., mem. natural resources com., chmn. subcommittee on hwys. and transit. Mem. Lane County Econ. Devel. com., Intergovtl. Relations com.; bd. dirs. Eugene-Springfield Met. Partnership; Lane County Dem. precinct person, 1982. Served in USAF, 1967—71. Recipient DC Disting. Alumnus award, U. Oreg. Alumni Assn., 1994, Congressional award, Mil. Prodn. Network, 1995, Human Lifetime Achievement award, Human Soc. US, 2002, Rail Leadership award, Am. Passenger Rail Coalition, 2006. Mem. Assn. Oreg. Counties (legis. com.), Nat. Assn. Counties (tax and fin. com.). Democrat. Roman Catholic. Office: US House Reps 2134 Rayburn House Office Bldg Washington DC 20515-0001 Office Phone: 202-225-6416.

DEFEBAUGH, JAMES E., IV, lawyer; b. 1954; BA, Mich. State U.; JD, Wayne State U., 1979. Bar: Mich. 1980. Atty. Kmart Holding Corp., Troy, Mich., 1983—92, div. counsel, comml. law, 1992—99, v.p., sec., 2000—02, sr. v.p., sec., chief compliance officer, 2002—04, sr. v.p., chief legal officer, 2004; v.p., gen. counsel, sec. Labor Ready, Inc., Tacoma, 2005—. Office: Labor Ready Inc 1015 A St Tacoma WA 98402 Office Phone: 253-680-8210. Business E-Mail: jdefebaugh@laborready.com.

DE FONVILLE, PAUL BLISS, monument and library administrator; b. Oakland, Calif., Mar. 3, 1923; s. Marion Yancey and Charlotte (Bliss) de F.; m. Virginia Harpell, June 17, 1967. Student, Calif. Poly. U., 1942-44, Michael Chekhov Group, 1947-52. Founder, pres. Cowboy Meml. and Libr., Caliente, Calif., 1969—; tchr. outdoor edn. Calif. State U., Bakersfield, 1980. Life mem. Presdl. Task Force, Washington, 1984—, Rep. Senatorial inner circle, Washington, 1989—, Nat. Rep. Congl. Com., Washington, 1990—, Rep. Nat. Com., 1987—, U.S. Senatorial Club, 1988—, Rep. Senatorial Commn., 1991, Presdl. Election Registry, 1992; del. Presdl. Trust, 1992; mem. Presdl. Commn. Am. Agenda; affiliate Lake Isabella Bd. Realtors, 1993; hon. marshall Lake Isabella, Kern County Christmas Parade, 1993. Recipient Slim Pickens award Calif. State Horsemen, 1980, Marshall-Working Western award Rose Parade, Pasadena, 1980, recognition Kern County, 1984, proclamations Mayor of Bakersfield, 1984, 85, Govt. of Calif., 1984, resolution Calif. Senate, 1988, Calif. Assembly, 1990, Presdl. Order of Merit, 1991, Congl. Cert. of Merit, 1992, Rep. Presdl. Legion of Merit award, 1992, Rep. Presdl. Legion of Merit award, 1992, document Gov. of Calif., 1993, Rep. Nat. Com. Cert. Recognition, 1992, Rep. Presdl. adv. Commn. Cert. award, 1993, Congl. Cert. Appreciation, 1993, Cert. Commendation Washington Legal Found., 1993, Rep. Presdl. award, 1994, Rep. Congl. Order of Liberty, 1993, Internat. Order of Merit medal, 1993, 20th Century award for achievement, 1993, Rep. Senatorial Medal of Freedom, 1994, Ronald Reagan Eternal Flame of Freedom medal and cert., 1995, Cmty. Svc. and Profl. Achievement medal, 1995, World Lifetime achievement award ABI-USA, 1996, Millennium medal of Freedom, 1999. Mem. SAG, NRA, Calif. State Horsemen (life), Equestrian Trails (life), Forty Niners (life), Calif. Rep. Assembly, Heritage Found., Cowboy Turtles Assn. (life), Rodeo Cowboys Assn. (life), Pro Rodeo Cowboys Assn. (life), Internat. Platform Assn., Lake Isabella C. of C., Kern County C. of C. Baptist. Avocations: anthropology, genealogy, history. Home: 40371 Cowboy Ln Caliente CA 93518-1405 Office Phone: 661-867-2410.

DE FRANCESCO, JOHN BLAZE, JR., public relations consultant, writer; b. Stamford, Conn., May 22, 1936; s. John Blaze and Mae (Matyscyk) DeF.; m. Louise C. Terlizzo, Nov. 1, 1958 (div. 1983); children: Daryl, Jay, Dana, Dorian; m. Diana Picchietti, Oct. 20, 1990. BS, U. Conn., 1958. Sr. v.p. Daniel J. Edelman, Inc., Chgo., 1967-77; exec. v.p. Ruder Finn & Rotman, Inc., Chgo., 1977-85; prin., CEO DeFrancesco/Goodfriend Pub. Relations, 1985-2001; exec. v.p. L.C. Williams & Assoc., Chgo., 2001—03; prin. DeFrancesco Artist and Writer, 2003—. Bd. dirs. Ill. Divsn. Vocat. Rehab., 1976-78; mem. pub. rels. adv. bd. Gov.'s State U., 1994-98. Comdr. USN, 1958-67; comdr. USNR; ret. 1979. Recipient 3 Silver Anvil awards Pub. Rels. Soc. Am., 6 Golden Trumpet awards Publicity Club, Chgo. Mem. Pub. Rels. Soc. Am., Navy League U.S., Mil. Officer Assn. Am. Roman Catholic. Home and Office: 18785 Saint Andrews Dr Monument CO 80132-8824

DE FRIES, JOHN CLARENCE, behavioral genetics educator, researcher; b. Delrey, Ill., Nov. 26, 1934; s. Walter C. and Irene Mary (Lyon) De F.; m. Marjorie Jacobs, Aug. 18, 1956; children: Craig Brian, Catherine Ann. BS, U. Ill., 1956, MS, 1958, PhD, 1961. Asst. prof. U. Ill., Urbana, 1961-66, assoc. prof., 1966-67; rsch. fellow U. Calif., Berkeley, 1963-64; assoc. prof. behavioral genetics and psychology U. Colo., Boulder, 1967-70, prof., 1970—, dir. Inst. for Behavioral Genetics, 1981-2001. Author: (with G.E. McClearn) Introduction to Behavioral Genetics, 1973, (with Plomin and McClearn) Behavioral Genetics: A Primer, 1980, 4th edit., 2001, (with R. Plomin) Origins of Individual Differences in Infancy, 1985; (with R. Plomin and D.W. Fulker) Nature and Nurture During Infancy and Early Childhood, 1988, Nature and Nurture During Middle Childhood, 1994, (with R. Plomin, I.W. Craig and P. McGuffin) Behavioral Genetics in the Postgenomic Era, 2003, (with S.A. Petrill, R. Plomin and J.K. Hewitt) Nature, Nurture and the Transition to Early Adolescence, 2003; co-founder Behavior Genetics jour., 1970, mem. editl. adv. bd. 1st lt. U.S. Army, 1957-65. Grantee in field. Fellow AAAS (sect. J), Internat. Acad. for Rsch. in Learning Disabilities; mem. Am. Psychol. Soc., Am. Soc. Human Genetics, Behavior Genetics Assn. (sec. 1974-77, pres. 1982-83, Th. Dobzhansky award for outstanding rsch. in field 1992), Internat. Dyslexia Assn., Rodin Remediation Acad. and Found. Office: U Colo Inst Behavioral Genetics 447 UCB Boulder CO 80309-0447

DEGENERES, ELLEN LEE, actress, comedienne, talk show host; b. Metairie, Jan. 26, 1958; d. Elliott and Betty DeGeneres; m. Portia de Rossi, Aug. 16, 2008. Began career as emcee local comedy club, New Orleans; performer various comedy clubs. Face of CoverGirl Cosmetics, 2008. Comedian (TV spls.) Young Comedians Reunion, HBO, Women of the Night, 1986, Command Performances: One Night Stand, 1989; author: My Point...And I Do Have One, 1995, The Funny Thing Is..., 2003; actor: (films) Coneheads, 1993, Mr. Wrong, 1996, Goodbye Lover, 1998, (voice) Dr. Doolittle, 1998, EDtv, 1999, The Love Letter, 1999, Reaching Normal, 1999, (voice of Dory) Finding Nemo, 2003 (Annie award for Outstanding Voice Acting in Animated Feature Prodn., 2004); writer, dir., actor (films) My Short Film, 2004; actor: (TV films) On the Edge, 2001; (TV series) Open House, 1989, Laurie Hill, 1992; actor, exec. prodr. (TV films) If These Walls Could Talk 2, 2000, (TV series) The Ellen Show, 2001—02, actor, prodr., writer Ellen (originally named These Friends of Mine from 1993-94), 1993—98 (Emmy award for Outstanding Writing for Comedy Series, 1997, Peabody award, 1997), host, exec. prodr. The Ellen DeGeneres Show, 2003— (Best Talk Show, Daytime Emmy award, Nat. Acad. TV Arts and Sciences, 2005, Best Talk Show Host, Daytime Emmy award, Nat. Acad. TV Arts and Sciences, 2005, People's Choice awards, favorite daytime talk show host, 2006, Outstanding Talk Show, Daytime Emmy award, Nat. Acad. TV Arts and Sciences, 2006, Outstanding Talk Show Host, Daytime Emmy awards, Nat. Acad. TV Arts and Sciences, 2006, 2007, Favorite Talk Show Host, People's Choice Awards, 2009), star, exec. prodr. (TV spls.) Ellen DeGeneres: The Beginning, 2000 (Am. Comedy award for Funniest Female Peformer in TV spl., 2001), Ellen DeGeneres: Here and Now, 2003, co-host 46th Annual Primetime Emmy Awards, 1994 (Am. Comedy award for Funniest Female Peformer in TV spl., 1995), host 53rd Annual Primetime Emmy Awards, 2001, 54th Annual Primetime Emmy Awards, 2002, 57th Annual Primetime Emmy Awards, 2005, 38th Annual Grammy Awards, 1996, 39th Annual Grammy Awards, 1997, VH1 Fashion Awards, 1998, VH1 Divas Las Vegas, 2002, 79th Annual Academy Awards, 2007, appeared as herself (documentaries) Wisecracks, 1991. Recipient Funniest Person Am. for videotaped club performances in New Orleans, Showtime, 1982, Am. Comedy award for Funniest Female Stand-Up Comic, 1991, Golden Apple award as Female Discovery Yr., Hollywood Women's Press Club, 1994, Lucy award, 2000, Enduring Spirit award, Amnesty Internat., 2000, Best Television Series or Specialty (Variety), The Producers Guild of Am., 2006; named Funny Female Star, People's Choice Awards, 2006, Favorite Talk Show Host & Funny Female Star, 2007, 2008; named one of 100 Most Influential People, Time Mag., 2006, The 100 Most Powerful Celebrities, Forbes.com, 2008. Office: c/o The Ellen DeGeneres Show PO Box 7788 Burbank CA 91523

DE GETTE, DIANA LOUISE, United States Representative from Colorado, lawyer; b. Tachikawa, Japan, July 29, 1957; arrived in US, 1957; d. Richard Louis and Patricia Anne (Rose) De Gette; m. Lino Sigismondo Lipinsky, Sept. 15, 1984; children: Raphaela Anne, Francesca Louise. BA in Polit. Sci., magna cum laude, Colo. Coll., 1979; JD, NYU Sch. Law, 1982. Bar: Colo. 1982, US Dist. Ct. Colo. 1982, US Ct. Appeals (10th cir.) 1984, US Supreme Ct. 1989. Dep. state pub. defender Colo. State Pub. Defender, Denver, 1982-84; assoc. Coghill & Goodspeed, P.C., Denver, 1984-86; sole practice Denver, 1986-93; of counsel McDermott & Hansen, Denver, 1993-96; mem. Colo. Ho. of Reps., 1992-96, asst. minority leader, 1995-96; mem. US Congress from 1st Colo. dist., 1996—, chief dep. whip, vice-chair energy & commerce com. Resolutions chair Denver Dem. Party, 1986; mem. Denver Women's Commn., Mayor's Mgmt. Review Commn. Social Svcs.; co-chair Congl. Bipartisan Pro-Choice Caucus, Congl. Diabetes Caucus; lead-whip State Children's Health Ins. Prog. Editor: Trial Talk mag., 1989—92. Bd. dirs. NYU Sch. Law Root-Tilden Prog., 1986—92, Planned Parenthood of Rocky Mountains. Recipient Vanderbilt medal, 1982; named a Root-Tilden scholar, NYU Sch. Law, 1979. Mem.: Denver Bar Assn., Colo. Women's Bar Assn., Colo. Trial Lawyers Assn. (bd. dirs., exec. com. 1986—92), Colo. Bar Assn. (bd. govs. 1989—91), Pi Gamma Mu, Phi Beta Kappa. Democrat. Avocations: reading, backpacking, gardening. Office: US Ho Reps 1527 Longworth Ho Office Bldg Washington DC 20515-0601

DE GEUS, AART J., computer software company executive; MSEE, Swiss Fedn. Polytech Inst.; PhD Electrical Engring., So. Meth. U. Chmn., CEO Synopsys, Mountain View, Calif., 1986—. Vice chmn., edn. supporter Silicon Valley Mfrs. Group; vice chmn. Electronic Design Automation Consortium. Fellow: IEEE (Indsl. Pioneer award, Robert N. Noyce medal 2007). Office: Synopsys 700 E Middlefield Rd Mountain View CA 94043-4033

DEGIORGIO, KENNETH D., lawyer, insurance company executive; BA with honors, Harvard U., Cambridge, Mass.; JD, MBA, UCLA. Atty. White & Case LLP, LA; regulatory and acquisition counsel First Am. Corp., Santa Ana, Calif., 1999—2001, v.p., assoc. gen. counsel, 2001—04, sr. v.p., gen. counsel, 2004—; exec. v.p. First Advantage Corp., 2003—. Bd. dirs. RP Data, 2006—. Office: First Am Corp 1 First American Way Santa Ana CA 92707 Office Phone: 714-250-3000.

DE GOFF, VICTORIA JOAN, lawyer; b. San Francisco, Mar. 2, 1945; d. Sidney Francis and Jean Frances (Alexander) De G.; m. Peter D. Coppelman, May 2, 1971 (div. Dec. 1978); m. Richard Sherman, June 16, 1980. BA in Math. with great distinction, U. Calif., Berkeley, 1967, JD, 1972. Bar: Calif. 1972, US Dist. Ct. (no. dist.) Calif. 1972, US Ct. Appeals 1972, US Supreme Ct. 1989; cert. appellate law specialist, 2006. Rsch. atty. Calif. Ct. Appeal, San Francisco, 1972-73; Reginald Heber Smith Found. fellow San Francisco Neighborhood Legal Assistance Found., 1973-74; assoc. Field, De Goff, Huppert & McGowan, San Francisco, 1974-77; pvt. practice Berkeley, Calif., 1977-80; ptnr. De Goff and Sherman, Berkeley, 1980—. Lectr. continuing edn. of bar, Calif., 1987, 90-92, U. Calif. Boalt Hall Sch. Law, Berkeley, 1981-85, dir. appellate advocacy, 1992; cons. Calif. Civil Practice Procedure, Bancroft Whitney, 1992; mem. Appellate Law Adv. Commn., 1995; apptd. applicant evaluation and nomination com. for State Bar Ct. by Calif. Supreme Ct., 1995, 2000; presented programs for Rutter Group Mastering Appellate Advocacy, 2004, Mastering the Stds. of Rev., 2005; apptd. by Chief Justice Calif. to Supreme Ct. Advisory Com. on publ. of ct. of appeals opinions, 2005-06; pvt. atty., clk. ct. com. Calif. Ct. Appeals, 1997-99; mem. com. on appellate practice ABA, 1997. Author: (with others) Matthew Bender's Treatise on California Torts, 1985. Apptd. to adv. com. Calif. Jud. Coun. on Implementing Proposition 32, 1984—85; mem. adv. bd. Hastings Coll. Trial and Appellate Adv., 1984—91; expert 20/20 vision project, commn. on future cts. Jud. Coun. Calif., 1993, apptd. to appellate standing adv. com., 1993—95; apptd. to Appellate Indigent Def. Oversight Adv. Com. State of Calif., 1995—2008; com. on appellate stds. of ABA Appellate Judges Conf., 1995—96; com. on appellate practice ABA, 1997; adv. bd. Witkin Legal Inst., Thompson Publishing Co., 1996—; adv. coun. Theltan E. Henderson Ctr. Social Justice, U. Calif., Berkeley Sch. Law, 2007—; appointee 9th Jud. Cir. Hist. Soc. Hon. Cecil Poole Biography Project, 1998; chair Roger Traynor State Moot Ct. Com., 1999—; bd. dirs. and officer Calif. Supreme Ct. Hist. Soc.; bd. dirs. State Bar Calif., 1996—2005; Appellate Law Cons. Group, 1994—95; bd. dirs. Ctr. for Youth Devel. Through Law, 2000—, officer, 2003—. Fellow Woodrow Wilson Found., 1967-68. Mem. Calif. Trial Lawyers Assn. (bd. govs. 1980-88, amicus-curiae com. 1981-87, editor-in-chief assn. mag. 1980-81, Presdl. award of merit 1980, 81), Calif. Acad. Appellate Lawyers (sec.-treas. 1989-90, 2d v.p. 1990-91, 1st v.p. 1991-92, pres. 1992-93), Am. Acad. Appellate Lawyers, Edward J. McFetridge Am. Inn of Cts. (counsellor 1990-91, edn. chmn. 1991-92, social chmn. 1992-93, v.p. 1993-94, pres. 1994-95), Boalt Hall Sch. Law U. Calif. Alumni Assn. (bd. dirs. 1989-91), Order of Coif. Jewish. Office: 1916 Los Angeles Ave Berkeley CA 94707-2419

DE GRASSI, LEONARD, art historian, educator; b. East Orange, NJ, Mar. 2, 1928; s. Romulus-William and Anna Sophia (Sannicolo) DeG.; m. Dolores Marie Welgoss, June 24, 1961; children: Maria Christina, Paul. BA, U. So. Calif., 1950, BFA, 1951, MA, 1956; postgrad., Harvard U., 1953, Istituto Centrale del Restauro di Roma, 1959-60, U. Rome, 1959-60, UCLA, 1970-73. Tchr. art Redlands Jr. HS, Calif., 1951—53, Toll Jr. HS, Glendale, Calif., 1953—61, Wilson Jr. HS, Glendale, 1961; mem. faculty Glendale Coll., 1962—, prof. art history, 1974-92, chmn. dept., 1972, 89, prof. emeritus, 1992—. Tchr. Cite U., Paris, 1992, Istituto /Schuola Leonardo da Vinci, Florence, Italy, 1992. Prin. works include: (paintings) high altar at Ch. St. Mary, Cook, Minn., altar screen at Ch. St. Andrew, El Segundo, Calif., 1965-71, 14 Stas. of the Cross Ch. St. Mary, Cook, Minn., altar screen at Ch. of the Descent of the Holy Spirit, Glendale, 14 Stas. of the Cross at Ch. of St. Benedict, Duluth, Minn., high altar at Holy Cross Ch., Orr, Minn.; research, artwork and dramatic work for Spaceship Earth exhbn. at Disney World, Orlando, Fla., 1980; refurnishing high altars, Holy Cross Ch. Orr, Minn. Decorated Knight Grand Cross Holy Sepluchre, knight St. John of Jerusalem, 1976, knight Order of Merit of Republic of Italy, Cross of Merit; recipient J. Walter Smith Svc. award, 2001; named First Disting. Faculty, 1987, Outstanding Educator of Am., 1971. Mem. Art Educators Assn., Am. Rsch. Ct. Egypt, Tau Kappa Alpha, Kappa Pi, Delta Sigma Rho. Office: 1500 N Verdugo Rd Glendale CA 91208-2809 Office Phone: 818-240-1000 ext. 5742. Business E-Mail: degrassi@glendale.edu.

DE HAAS, DAVID DANA, emergency physician; b. Hollywood, Calif., May 31, 1956; S. Martin and Norma (Deutsch) De H.; m. Mary Danuta Przybylowski, June 27, 1982; children: Lindsay Alexandra, Heather Brittany, Lance Austin. BS in Biochemistry, UCLA, Westwood, Calif., 1979; MD, Chgo. Med. Sch., 1983. Diplomate Am. Bd. Internal Medicine, Am. Bd. Emergency Medicine, Nat. Bd. Med. Examiners; cert. provider advanced trauma life support, ACLS, Pediatric Advanced Life Support, BCLS, Med. Disaster Response, instr. ACLS, Pediatric Advanced Life Support, Med. Disaster Response. Resident emergency medicine/internal medicine Kern Med. Ctr., Bakersfield, Calif., 1983-87; assoc. med. dir. Family Care Med. Assocs., Huntington Beach, Calif., 1987—; asst. clin. prof. medicine dept. internal medicine U. Calif.-Irvine Med. Ctr., Orange, 1989—; emergency physician St. Bernardine Med. Ctr., San Bernardino, Calif., 1991—; ptnr. Calif. Emergency Physicians Med. Group, San Bernardino, 1991—. Expert reviewer Med. Bd. Calif.; affiliate faculty ACLS, Pediatric Advanced Life Support, Am. Heart Assn.; vice chmn. dept. emergency medicine St. Bernardine Med. Ctr., ACLS dir., dir. quality assurance/continuous quality improvement dept. emergency medicine; mem. edn. com. Med. Disaster Response; ptnr.Calif. Emergency Physician Med. Group. Fellow ACP, Am. Coll. Emergency Physicians; mem. AMA, Calif. Med. Assn., Orange County Med. Soc., Soc. Orange County Emergency Physicians (bd. dirs.), Assn. Clin. Faculty U. Calif., Irvine Coll. Medicine. Avocations: gardening, pin collecting, reading. Home: 26882 Via La Mirada San Juan Capistrano CA 92675-4935 Office: St Bernardine Med Ctr 2101 N Waterman Ave San Bernardino CA 92404-4836

DEHAAS, JOHN NEFF, JR., retired architecture educator; b. Phila., July 4, 1926; s. John Neff and Sadie Lavinia (Hagel) DeH.; m. C. Bernice Wallace, Dec. 27, 1950; children: Kenneth Eric, Jocelyn Hilda. BArch, Tex. A&M U., 1948, MEd, 1950. Registered architect, Mont. Instr. Tex. A&M U., College Station, 1948-50, U. Tex., Austin, 1950-51; successively instr. to prof. Mont. State U., Bozeman, 1951-80. Supervisory architect Historic Am. Bldgs. Survey, summers San Francisco, 1962, Bozeman, 1963, 65, Milw., 1969; cons. Mont. Historic Preservation Office, Helena, 1977-78, mem. rev. bd., 1968-79. Author: Montana's Historic Structures, Vol. 1, 1864, Vol. 2, 1969, Historic Uptown Butte, 1977; editor quar. newsletter Mont. Ghost Town Preservation Soc., 1972— Bd. dirs. Mont. Assn. for Blind, Butte, 1984-95. Recipient Centennial Preservation award Mont. Historic Preservation Office, 1989, Dorothy Bridgman award for Outstanding Svc. to the Blind Montana Assn. for the Blind, 1990. Fellow AIA (com. on historic resources 1974—); mem. Mont. Hist. Soc. (trustee's award 1989). Republican. Methodist. Home: 2400 Durston Rd 50 Bozeman MT 59718

DE HERRERA, JUAN ABRAN (AGE), federal judicial security official; b. Costilla, N.Mex., Jan. 2, 1942; s. Gilbert and Maria (Arellano) De H.; m. Roberta Jo Vogel, June 22, 1959; 5 children. Grad., Nat. Crime Prevention Inst. Acad., 1975, Nat. FBI Acad., 1976; grad. in adminstrn. of jail facilities, U. Colo., 1977; BA in Edn., U. Wyo., 1993. Patrol officer Rawlins (Wyo.) Police Force, 1965-67, sgt. patrol divsn., 1968-71, lt. patrol divsn., 1972-76, chief of police, 1977-82, ret., 1986; U.S. marshal dist. of Wyo. apptd. by Pres. Clinton Dept. Justice, Cheyenne, 1996. Boxing coach Amateur Athletic Union, 1963-82. Mem. city counsel, 1987-92, Wyo. State Libr. Bd., 1988-91. Hearst Minority scholar U. Wyo., 1988, 89, 90, 91, Sundin scholar, 1988, 89, 90, 91, SEO scholar, 1990, Nat. Hispanic scholar, 1990, 91, 92; state and regional nat. Golden Gloves champion. Mem. Nat. FBI Acad. Assocs., Wyo. Peace Officers Assn., Rawlins Police Protective Assn., Pershing Elem. Sch. Parent Tchr. Assn. (life), K of C., Latin Am. Assn. Cheyenne. Roman Catholic. Avocations: family camping, cross country skiing, boating, hunting, walking. Home: 816 Skyline Dr Cheyenne WY 82009-3528 E-mail: juandeherrera@usdoj.gov.

DEHMELT, HANS GEORG, retired physicist; b. Görlitz, Germany, Sept. 9, 1922; arrived in U.S., 1952, naturalized, 1962; s. Georg Karl and Asta Ella (Klemmt) Dehmelt; m. Irmgard Lassow (dec.); 1 child, Gerd; m. Diana Elaine Dundore, Nov. 18, 1989. Grad., Graues Kloster, Berlin, Abitur, 1940; D Rerum Naturalium, U. Goettingen, 1950; D Rerum Naturalium (hon.), Ruprecht Karl-Universitat, Heidelberg, 1986; DSc (hon.), U. Chgo., 1987. Postdoctoral fellow U. Goettingen, Germany, 1950—52, Duke U., Durham, NC, 1952—55; vis. asst. prof. U. Wash., Seattle, 1955, asst. prof. physics, 1956, assoc. prof., 1957—61, prof., rsch. physicist, 1961—2002; ret. Cons. Varian Assocs., Palo Alto, Calif., 1956—76. Contbr. articles to profl. jours. Sr. pvt. German Army, 1940—45, (captured by US forces, POW to 1946). Recipient Humboldt prize, 1974, award in Basic Rsch., Internat. Soc. Magnetic Resonance, 1980, Rumford prize, Am. Acad. Arts and Scis., 1985, Nobel prize in Physics, 1989, Nat. medal of Sci., 1995; grantee NSF, 1958—. Fellow: Am. Phys. Soc. (Davisson-Germer prize 1970); mem.: NAS, Am. Optical Soc., Am. Acad. Arts and Scis., Sigma Xi.

DEIDE, DARREL A., state legislator; b. Sioux City, Iowa, Mar. 25, 1936; m. LaDonna Deide; children: Lori, Gina, David. BS in Biology, Albertson Coll. Idaho, 1960, MEd in Sch. Adminstrn. and Counseling, 1966. Sch. tchr., counselor, 1960-66; bldg. sch. adminstr., 1967-71; ctrl. office asst. supt., 1972-95; mem. Idaho Senate, Dist. 10, Boise, 1996—. Mem. agrl. affairs, commerce and human resources, edn., judiciary and rules, and transp. coms. Bd. dirs. Caldwell Edn. Found.; mem. Idaho Sch. Reform com.; mem. Caldwell Parks and Recreation Commn.; mem. Canyon County Rep. Ctrl. Com.; adv. bd. Salvation Army, mem. Caldwell Econ. Devel. Project; active Canyon Area United Way. With Idaho N.G., 1954-64. Recipient Disting. Citizen award, Idaho Statesman, Disting. Alumni award Caldwell H.S. Mem. Idaho Sch. Adminstrs. Assn., Idaho Profl. Stds. Assn., Caldwell (Idaho) Kiwanis (Kiwanian of Yr. 1986-87), Caldwell C. of C., Albertson Coll. Alumni Assn. Republican. Office: State Capitol PO Box 83720 Boise ID 83720-3720

DEITCHLE, GERALD WAYNE, restaurant company executive; b. Lockbourne AFB, Ohio, Sept. 19, 1951; BBA, Tex. A&M U., 1973; MBA, U. Tex., San Antonio, 1975. CPA, Tex. Div. controller Church's Fried Chicken Inc., San Antonio, 1978-80; asst. controller W. R. Grace and Co., San Antonio, 1980-84; v.p., controller Jerrico Inc., Lexington, Ky., 1984-87, sr. v.p. fin., 1987—; v.p. & CFO Cheesecake Factory Inc., Calabasas Hills, Calif. With USAF, 1974-78. Mem. AICPA, Tex. Soc. CPA's, Fin. Execs. Inst., Nat. Assn. Accts., Inst. Mgmt. Acctg., Nat. Assn. Securities Dealers Automated Quotations. Office: Cheesecake Factory Inc 26950 Agoura Rd Agoura Hills CA 91301 Address: Long John Silvers PO Box 11988 Lexington KY 40579-1988

DEKKER, GEORGE GILBERT, literature professor, writer, former academic administrator; b. Long Beach, Calif., Sept. 8, 1934; s. Gilbert J. and Laura (Barnes) D.; m. Linda Jo Bartholomew, Aug. 31, 1973; children by previous marriage: Anna Allegra, Clara Joy, Ruth Siobhan, Laura Daye. BA in English, U. Calif.-Santa Barbara, 1955; MA in English, 1958; M.Litt., Cambridge U., Eng., 1961; PhD in English, U. Essex, Eng., 1967. Lectr. U. Wales, Swansea, 1962-64; lectr. in lit. U. Essex, 1964-69, reader in lit., 1969-72, dean Sch. Comparative Studies, 1969-71; assoc. prof. English Stanford U., Calif., 1972-74, prof., 1974—2001, prof. emeritus, 2001—, chmn. dept., 1978-81, 84-85, Joseph S. Atha prof. humanities, 1988—, dir. program in Am. Studies, 1988-91, assoc. dean grad. policy, 1993—96, 2000—02. Author: Sailing After Knowledge, 1963, James Fenimore Cooper the Novelist, 1967, Coleridge and the Literature of Sensibility, 1978, The American Historical Romance, 1987, The Fictions of Romantic Tourism, 2005, Touching Fire: A Forestry Memoir, 2008; editor: Donald Davie: The Responsibilities of Literature, 1983 Nat. Endowment Humanities fellow, 1977; Inst. Advanced Studies in Humanities fellow U. Edinburgh (Scotland), 1982; hon. fellow, Clare Hall Cambridge, 1997, Stanford Humanities Ctr., 1997. Mem. Am. Lit. Assn. Democrat. Office: Stanford Univ Dept English Stanford CA 94305 Office Phone: 650-723-2635.

DEKMEJIAN, RICHARD HRAIR, political science professor; b. Aleppo, Syria, Aug. 3, 1933; came to U.S., 1950, naturalized, 1955; s. Hrant H. and Vahede V. (Matossian) D.; m. Anoush Hagopian, Sept. 19, 1954; children: Gregory, Armen, Haig. BA, U. Conn., 1959; MA, Boston U., 1960; Middle East Inst. cert., Columbia U., 1964, PhD, 1966. Mem. faculty SUNY, Binghamton, 1964-86; prof., chmn. dept. polit. sci. U. So. Calif., Los Angeles, 1986-90, prof. internat. bus. Marshall Sch. Bus.; also master Hinman Coll., 1971-72. Lectr. Fgn. Svc. Inst., Dept. Def., Dep. State, 1976-87; vis. prof. Columbia U., U. Pa., 1977-78; cons. Dept. State, AID, USIA, UN, Dept. Def. Author: Egypt Under Nasir, 1971, Patterns of Political Leadership, 1975, Islam in Revolution, 1985, 2nd edit., 1995, Ethnic Lobbies in U.S. Foreign Policy, 1997, Troubled Waters: The Geopolitics of the Caspian Region, 2001, The Just Prince: A Manual of Leadership, 2003, Spectrum of Terror, 2007; contbr. articles to profl. jours. Pres. So. Tier Civic Ballet Co., 1973-76. Served with AUS, 1955-57. Mem. Am. Polit. Sci. Assn., Middle East Inst., Middle East Studies Assn., Internat. Inst. Strategic Studies, Skull and Dagger, Pi Sigma Alpha, Phi Alpha Theta. Office: U So Calif Dept Polit Sci Los Angeles CA 90089-0044 Office Phone: 213-740-3619. Business E-Mail: dekmejia@usc.edu.

DELA CRUZ, ACELIA CASTRO, elementary school educator; m. Ray Dela Cruz; children: Austing, Celestial Jewel. Tchr. Tanapag Elem. Sch., Saipan, No. Marianas. Named No. Marianas Islands Tchr. of Yr., 2007. Office: Tanapag Elem Sch PO Box 501370 Saipan MP 96950 E-mail: aceliacdelacruz@yahoo.com.

DELA CRUZ, JOSE SANTOS, retired commonwealth supreme court justice; b. Saipan, Commonwealth No. Mariana Islands, July 18, 1948; s. Thomas Castro and Remedio Sablan (Santos) Dela C.; m. Rita Tenorio Sablan, Nov. 12, 1977; children: Roxanne, Renee, Rica Ann. BA, U. Guam, 1971; JD, U. Calif., Berkeley, 1974; cert., Nat. Jud. Coll., Reno, 1985. Bar: No. Mariana Islands, 1974, U.S. Dist. Ct. No. Mariana Islands 1978. Staff atty. Micro. Legal Svcs. Corp., Saipan, 1974-79; gen. counsel Marianas Pub. Land Corp., Saipan, 1979-81; liaison atty. CNMI Fed. Laws Commn., Saipan, 1981-83; ptnr. Borja & Dela Cruz, Saipan, 1983-85; assoc. judge Commonwealth Trial Ct., Saipan, 1985-89; commonwealth supreme ct. chief justice Supreme Ct. No. Mariana Islands, 1989—95; retired, 1995; gen. counsel No. Mariana Islands Port Authority, 1996—2003; sr. advisor Pacific Telecommunications, Inc., 2005—. Mem. Conf. of Chief Justices, 1989-95, Adv. Commn. on Judiciary, Saipan, 1980-82; chmn. Criminal Justice Planning Agy., Saipan, 1985-95. Mem. Coun. for Arts, Saipan, 1982-83; chmn. Bd. of Elections, Saipan, 1977-82; pres. Cath. Social Svcs., Saipan, 1982-85. Mem. No. Marianas Bar Assn. (pres. 1984-85). Roman Catholic. Avocations: golf, reading, walking. Personal E-mail: joedlc1@yahoo.com.

DE LA FUENTE, LAWRENCE EDWARD, artist; b. Chgo., Sept. 29, 1947; Student, Kansas City Art Inst., 1966-68. Exhbns. include San Francisco Art Commn., 1971, 72, Berkeley (Calif.) Art Ctr., 1973, San Jose (Calif.) State U., 1973, Gallery West, Mendocino, Calif., 1973, San Francisco Mus. Art, 1973, 74, 75, 76, 78, Mendocino Art Ctr., 1977, 80, 83, 93, Wilkinson-Cobb Gallery, Mendocino, 1977, Tucson (Ariz.) Mus. Art, 1977, Nat. Coll. Fine Art, Smithsonian, Washington, 1977, 80, mus. Mill Valley, Calif., 1978, Albuquerque Mus. Art, 1978, El Paso (Tex.) Mus. Art, 1978, Blaffer Gallery, U. Houston, 1978, Taylor Mus. Art, Colorado Springs, 1978, Everson Mus., Syracuse, N.Y., 1979, Witte Mus., San Antonio, 1979, Contemporary Arts Mus., Chgo., 1979, U. Ga., Athens, 1979, Tyler U., Phila., 1979, Palacio de Mineria, Mexico City, 1980, Internat. Sculpture Conf., Washington, 1980, Western States Fair, Pomona, Calif., 1980, Macintosh-Drysdale Gallery, Washington, 1981, Fondo del Sol Gallery, Wahsington, 1981, Alternative Mus., N.Y.C., 1982, P.S.1 Clocktower, N.Y.C., 1982, Ronald Feldman Gallery, N.Y.C., 1982, Knot Art Gallery, Mendocino, 1983, U. Houston, 1984, Cultural Arts Ctr. Santa Barbara, 1985, Pulsations, Phila., 1986, Retreti Art Ctr., Helsinki, 1987, Living Art Show, Mendocino, 1987, Philbrook Mus. Art, Tulsa, Okla., 1987, Chgo. Pub. Libr., 1988, Kohler Mus. Art, Sheboygan, Wis., 1989, Va. Mus. Fine Art, Richmond, 1989, Orlando (Fla.) Mus. Art, 1989, Tokyo Mus. Modern Art, 1990, Kyoto (Japan) Mus. Modern Art, 1990, Smithsonian Instn. Renwick Gallery, 1990, Calif. State U. Chico, 1993, Natural History Mus., L.A., 1994, Smithsonian Traveling Exhbn., 1994, others. NEA fellow 1980, 88, 95; recipient 1st prize Houston ArtCarr Parade, 2000. Home: PO Box 954 Mendocino CA 95460-0954 also: 41401 Comptche Ukiah Rd Mendocino CA 95460-9786

DELANEY, MARNIE PATRICIA, retail executive; b. Hartford, Conn., May 20, 1952; d. William Pride Delaney Jr. and Marian Patricia (Utley) Murphy. BA, Union Coll., Schenectady, NY, 1973. Adminstrv. asst. NY State Assembly, Albany, 1973-74; account exec. Foote, Cone & Belding, NYC, 1974-78; sr. account exec. Dailey & Assocs., LA, 1978-81; pub. rels. cons. NOW, Washington, 1981-83; account supr. BBDO/West, LA, 1983-85; v.p. Grey Advt., LA, 1985-87, San Francisco, 1987-89; sr. v.p. McCann-Erickson, San Francisco, 1989-95; sr. v.p., dir. advt./mktg. comms. Bank of Am., San Francisco, 1995-99; cons. Brand Strategy, 1999—2000; mng. dir. doodlebug LLC, San Anselmo, Calif., 2001—. Bd. trustees Marin Art and Garden Ctr. Del. Dem. Nat. Conv., San Francisco, 1984; bd. dirs. JED Found., Hartford, Conn., 1989—, Easter Seals Soc., Bay Area, 1995-97. Mem. NOW (v.p. L.A. chpt. 1980-83, pres. 1984, advisor 1985-87), Marin Assn. Female Execs., Contemporary Ceramics Studio Assn., Am. Spkty. Toy Retailers Assn., Craft and Hobby Assn., Toy Industry Assn., Marin Soc. Artists, Marin Needle Arts Guild, San Anselmo C. of C. (bd. dirs.).

DELANEY, WILLIAM FRANCIS, JR., reinsurance broker; s. William F. and Viola (Kelly) D.; m. Virginia Beers; children: Marcia, Gayle. Student, Ecole Albert de Mun, Nogent sur Marne, France, Douai Sch., Eng.; Oxford and Cambridge Sch. Cert.; AB, Princeton U.; LLB, Harvard U.; student, NYU, Practising Law Inst., Ins. Soc. N.Y.; Studied law, Paris. Bar: N.Y., U.S. Supreme Ct. Atty. Irving Trust Co., NYC; gen. counsel Am. Internat. Underwriters Group; N.Y. reins. mgr. Fairfield & Ellis; pres. Delaney Offices, Inc., NYC, 1954—. Founding mem., broker, N.Y. Ins. Exchange; reins. intermediary and cons. for U.S. and world wide; reins. lectr. Ins. Soc. N.Y. Author: Reinsurance Laws of South America and Mexico; contbr. articles to ins. publs. Mem. Ins. Soc. N.Y. Clubs: Princeton, Deal Golf. Roman Catholic.

DELAPP, TINA DAVIS, retired nursing educator; b. LA, Dec. 18, 1946; d. John George and Margaret Mary (Clark) Davis; m. John Robert DeLapp, May 31, 1969; children: Julia Ann, Sam, Scott Michael. Diploma, Good Samaritan Hosp., Phoenix, 1967; BSN, Ariz. State U., 1969; MS in Nursing, U. Colo., Denver, 1972; EdD in Post Secondary Edn., U. So. Calif., 1986. Health aide instr. Yukon-Kuskokwim Health Corp., Bethel, Alaska, 1970-71; asst. prof. nursing Bacone Coll., Muskogee, Okla., 1972-74; instr. nursing Alaska Meth. U., Anchorage, 1975-76; prof. nursing U. Alaska, Anchorage, 1976—84, assoc. dean nursing, 1984—96, dir. Sch. Nursing, 1996—2004, emeritus prof., 2004—. Mem. Alaska Bd. Nursing, 1989-92; cons. in field. Mem. editl. adv. bd. Jour. Nursing Edn., 2004—; contbr. articles to profl. jours. Treas. Alaska Nurses Found., 2004—. Recipient Chancellor's Tchg. award, 1994, emeritus award, Am. Assn. Coll. Nursing, 2005; named Legend of Nursing, Alaska March of Dimes, 2004. Fellow: We. Acad. Nursing; mem.: Alaska Nurses Found. (treas. 2004—), Am. Assn. Colls. Nursing (mem. nominating com. 2003, task force 2003—04, emeritus 2005), Nat. League for Nursing Accreditation Comn. (program evaluator 1986—, eval. review panel mem. 2000—05), We. Inst. Nursing (chair program com. 1994—95, sec.-treas. 1995—2005, gov.-at-large 2005—07, chair membership com 2006—, Jo Elinor Elliot Leadership award 2002, Anna Shannon Mentorship award 2006, Emeritus award 2007), Sigma Theta Tau (pres. chpt. 1986—88, v.p. 1988—93, counselor 1995—2000). Avocations: knitting, reading, politics. Personal E-mail: tdelapp@ak.net.

DE LA ROCHA, CASTULO, health services executive; b. Chihuahua, Mex., Dec. 1, 1948; s. Moises and Consuelo de la Roche; children: Marco Remi, Alexis, Milan. BA in Polit. Sci., U. Calif., Santa Barbara, 1972; JD, U. Calif., Berkeley, 1975. Cert. in Mgmt. Stanford U. Pres., CEO Alta Med. Health Svcs. Corp., LA, 1980—. Bd. dirs. Orthopaedic Hosp. of. So. Calif., Nat. Assn. Cmty. Health Ctrs.; mem. adv. bd. Edward R. Roybal Ctr. for Applied Gerontology, 1987, exec. com. mem. Latino Coalition for Healthy Calif. Bd. govs., treas. L.A. County Latino Coalition for Healthy Calif.; mem. bd. Latino Theater Co., The Theater Group. Recipient Nat. Project Health award US Commn. on Aging, 1986, Surgeon Gen.'s Gold medallion for pub. health, 1992, Chicano/Latino Med. Assn. award, 1991, Significant Achievement award Chicanos for Creative Medicine, 1995, Cmty. Svc. award Am. Diabetes Assn., 1995, Vantage award Vis. Nurses Found., 1996,; named Hispanic of Yr., Caminos, 1985, Program of Yr., United Way, 1982, #1 Nonprofit, Hispanic Bus. Mag.; named one of Top 10 Latinos in Healthcare LatinoLeaders mag., 2004 Office: Alta Med Health Svcs Corp 500 Citadel Dr Ste 490 Los Angeles CA 90040-1574

DELAVAR, MICHAEL, pilot; b. Winslow, Wash., Oct. 13, 1973; m. Katja Delavar, June 2000; 2 children. BFA summa cum laude, U. Colo., 1995. Lic. pilot US Air Force Acad. Aero Club. Pilot Capital City Air Carrier, 1998—2000; airline captain Horizon Airlines, 2000—. Republican. Office: Horizon Airlines 19300 International Blvd Seattle WA 98188

DELAWIE, HOMER TORRENCE, retired architect; b. Santa Barbara, Calif., Sept. 24, 1927; s. Fred Ely and Gertrude (Torrence) D.; m. Billie Carol Sparlin (div. 1969); m. Ethel Ann Mallinger, Sept. 3, 1973; children: Gregory, Claire, Shandell, Tracy, Stephanie, Scott. BS in Archtl. Engring., Calif. Poly. State U., San Luis Obispo, 1951. Registered architect, Calif. Pvt. practice architecture, San Diego, 1958-61; founder, CEO Delawie Wilkes Rodrigues Barker & Bretton Assocs., San Diego, 1961—98, ret., 1998, ptnr. emeritus, 1998—. Mem. Planning Commn., City of San Diego, 1969-82; adv. bd. KPBS Pub. TV. Recipient Award of Merit Calif. chpt. Am. Inst. Planners, Lay Citizens award Phi Delta Kappa, 1975, award Calif chpt. Am. Planning Assn., 1982; named Disting. Alumnus, Calif. Poly. State U., 1972. Fellow AIA (over 60 design awards 1973—, Architects Svc. award Calif. coun. 1973, spl. award San Diego chpt. 1978, Pub. Svc. award Calif. coun. 1981, Outstanding Firm award San Diego chpt. 1986, Calif. Coun. Lifetime Achievement award 1998). Democrat. Home: 2749 Azalea Dr San Diego CA 92106-1132 Office: Delawie Wilkes Rodrigues Barker & Bretton Assocs 2265 India St San Diego CA 92101-1725

DELBENE, KURT, computer software company executive; B in Indsl. Engring., U. Ariz.; MS, Stanford U.; MBA, U. Chgo. Software devel., systems engr. AT&T Bell Lab.; mgmt. cons. McKinsey & Co.; with Microsoft Corp., Redmond, Wash., 1992—, group mgr., systems divsn., group program mgr., Exchange client and schedule+, gen. mgr., Outlook, messaging and personal info. mgmt. application, v.p. authoring & collaboration svc. group, corp. v.p., Office Bus. Platform Group, 2006—08, sr. v.p., 2008—. Office: Microsoft Corp One Microsoft Way Redmond WA 98052-7329

DEL CALVO, JORGE A., lawyer; b. Havana, Cuba, Oct. 13, 1955; BA with distinction, Stanford Univ., 1977; MA Latin Am. history, UCLA, 1978; MA pub. policy, Harvard Univ., 1981, JD cum laude, 1981; ND, Univ. Philippines, 1982. Bar: Calif. 1982. Assoc. Pillsbury Winthrop Shaw Pittman, Palo Alto, Calif., 1982—90, ptnr., 1990—. Bd. dirs. Berkeley Process Control; mem. adv. bd. Linklore LLC. Editor (coord.): Venture Capital & Pub. Offering Negotiation. Mem.: ABA, HispanicNet, Asian Multicultural Assn., Indus Entrepreneurs, Phi Beta Kappa. Office: Pillsbury Winthrop Shaw Pittman 2475 Hanover St Palo Alto CA 94304-1114 Office Phone: 650-233-4537. Office Fax: 650-233-4545. Business E-Mail: jorge@pillsburylaw.com.

DE LEON, KEVIN, state legislator; b. Logan Heights, Calif. 1 child, Lluvia. Attended, U. Calif., Santa Barbara; B, Pitzer Coll. California State Assemblyman, District 45, 2006-, member, Arts, Entertainment, Sports, Tourism & Internet Media, Govt Organization, Health, Ins, Joint Committee on Legislature Budget Committees, 2007-.ESL & United States Citizenship teacher, formerly. California Teachers Association (formerly); Nat Education Association (senior associate, formerly). Democrat. Office: Dist 45 360 West Ave 26 Ste 121 Los Angeles CA 90031 Office Phone: 323-225-4545. Office Fax: 323-225-4500. Business E-Mail: Assemblymember.deLeon@assembly.ca.gov.

DELGADILLO, ROCKARD J. (ROCKY DELGADILLO), lawyer; b. LA, July 15, 1960; m. Michelle Delgadillo; children: Christian, Preston. BA with honors, Harvard U.; JD, Columbia U. Tchr., coach L.A. Unified Sch. Dist.; sr. atty. O'Melveny and Myers, LA; dir. bus. devel. Rebuild L.A.; dep. mayor econ. devel. City of L.A., city atty., 2001—, re-elected city atty., 2005. City Atty., LA, 2001—. Bd. dirs. Arnold's All-Stars, Para Los Niños, Cath. Big Bros., 1st AME Ch. Renaissance Program, Franklin HS Scholarship Found., Friends Jordan HS, Workforce L.A.; leader L.A. ann. salute to Latino Heritage Month, 1993—. Recipient medal of excellence, Columbia U., John F.

Kennedy Award, LA County Dem. Party, 2002; named Disting. Young Alumnus, Columbia U., 1998, Alumnus of the Yr., 2002; named an All-Am. Football Player. Office: 800 City Hall E 200 N Main St Los Angeles CA 90012-4131 Office Phone: 213-978-8100.

DE LINE, DONALD, former film company executive; b. LA; BA, UCLA. Casting and drama devel. exec. ABC Entertainment; dir. for prodn. filmed entertainment divsn. The Walt Disney Studios, 1985—86; v.p. prodn. The Disney Sunday Movie, 1986, pres. prodn., 1986, Snowback Prodns., 1987; v.p. prodn. Walt Disney Pictures, 1988; sr. v.p. Touchstone Pictures, 1990—91, exec. v.p., 1991—93, pres., 1993—98; with Paramount Pictures, Hollywood, Calif., 1998—2003, vice chmn. motion picture group, pres., 2004—05. Prodr.: (films) Domestic Disturbance, 2001, The Italian Job, 2003, The New Foon, 2004, Without a Paddle, 2004, The Stepford Wives (Remake), 2004.

DELISI, DONALD PAUL, geophysicist; b. Pitts., Nov. 15, 1944; s. Samuel P. and Jennie (Moffie) D.; m. Adele Pedicord Orr, Aug. 7, 1971; 1 child, Bergen Orr Delisi. BSE. magna cum laude, Princeton U., 1966; MS, U. Calif., Berkeley, 1967, PhD, 1972. Resident rsch. assoc. Geophys. Fluid Dynamics Lab./NOAA, Princeton, N.J., 1972-74; sr. rsch. scientist Flow Rsch., Inc., Kent, Wash., 1974-77; staff scientist Phys. Dynamics Inc., Bellevue, Wash., 1977-86; v.p., treas., sr. rsch. scientist N.W. Rsch. Assocs., Inc., Bellevue, 1986—. Contbr. articles to Jour. Geophys. Rsch., Jour. of the Atmospheric Scis., Pure and Applied Geophysics, AIAA Jour., Jour. of Aircraft. Mem. Am. Meteorol. Soc., Am. Geophys. Union, AIAA, Am. Inst. Physics. Achievements include research on stratified shear and vortex flows; on observational studies of atmospheric dynamics. Office: Northwest Research Associates Inc PO Box 3027 Bellevue WA 98009-3027

DE LISIO, STEPHEN SCOTT, lawyer, director, pastor; b. San Diego, Dec. 30, 1937; s. Anthony J. and Emma Irving (Cheney) DeL.; m. Margaret Irene Winter, June 26, 1964; children: Anthony W., Stephen Scott, Heather E. Student, Am. U., 1958-59; BA, Emory U., 1959; LLB, Albany Law Sch., 1962; LLM, Georgetown U., 1963. Bar: N.Y. 1963, D.C. 1963, Alaska 1964. Practice law, Fairbanks, Alaska, 1963-71, Anchorage, 1971—96; asst. dist. atty. Fairbanks, 1963-65; assoc. McNealy & Merdes, 1965-66; lectr. U. Alaska, 1965-67; ptnr. Staley, DeLisio & Cook, 1966-93, DeLisio, Moran, Geraghty & Zobel, Inc., 1994—2003; pastor Anchorage Bible Fellowship. Bd. dirs. Woodstock Property Co., Inc., Pasit Inc., Challenger Films Inc.; vice chmn. Crosstown CBMC, 1986—87, chmn., 1987—88, area coord., 1987—92; city atty., Fairbanks, 1967—70, Barrow, 1969—72, Ft. Yukon and North Pole, 1970—72; past sec. U. Alaska Heating Corp., Inc.; past sec.-treas. Trans-Alaska Electronics, Inc., Baker Aviation, Inc.; former arbitrator, mem. Alaska regional coun. Am. Arbitration Assn. Author: (with others) Law and Tactics in Federal Criminal Cases, 1964. Past pres. Tanana Valley State Fair Assn.; past v.p. Fairbanks Mental Health Assn., Fairbanks United Good Neighbors Fund; bd. dirs. Anchorage Cmty. Chorus, 1975—77, Common Sense for Alaska, 1987—94, Alaska chpt. Lupus Found., 1989—96; chmn. bd. Alaska Voluntary Health Assn., 1993—96; former bd. dirs. Greater Fairbanks Cmty. Hosp. Found.; met. dir. Christian Businessmen's Outreach, 1993—94, bd. dirs. Anchorage, 1985—92; met. dir. Alaska Christian Businessmen's Com. U.S.A., 1994—2000; rep. precinct committeeman, 1970—76; chmn. Alaska Rep. Rules Com. Anchorage Rep. Com, 1973; v.p. We the People, 1977—79; vice chmn. Alaska Libertarian Party, 1983—84; mem. nat. com. Libertarian Party, 1982—85; deacon Anchorage Bible Fellowship, 1986—90, elder, pastor, 1990—; Alaska coord. Crown Ministries, 1991—93; bd. dirs. Projects Fe, Inc., 2001—07. Recipient Jaycee Disting. Service award, 1968 Mem. Am. Trial Lawyers Assn., Am. Judicature Soc., Alaska Bar Assn., DC Bar Assn., Anchorage Bar Assn., Spenard Bar Assn. (pres. 1975-77), U.S. Jaycees (past dir.), Alaska Jaycees (past pres.), Fairbanks Jaycees (past pres.), Chi Phi, Pi Sigma Phi, Woodstock Golf Inc. Club (pres. 1984-2007). Home: 5102 Shorecrest Dr Anchorage AK 99502-1329 Office: Anchorage Bible Fellowship 7348 Elmore Rd Anchorage AK 99507 Home Phone: 907-243-5521. Personal E-mail: stevedabf@acsalasker.net.

DELL, CHERYL ELBRIGHT, publishing executive; b. Modesto, Calif., 1960; m. Brad Dell. Grad., Calif. State U., Sacramento. Advt. dir. Modesto Bee, Calif., 1997—99; v.p. sales and mktg. Fresno Bee, Calif., 1999—2000; pub. Tri-City Herald, Wash., 2000—04; pres., pub. News Tribune, Tacoma, 2004—08, Sacramento Bee, 2008—. Named one of 20 under 40 newspeople to watch, Presstime mag., 1999. Office: Sacramento Bee PO Box 15779 Sacramento CA 95826

DELL, ROBERT MICHAEL, lawyer; b. Chgo., Oct. 4, 1952; s. Michael A. and Bertha Dell; m. Ruth Celia Schiffman, May 29, 1976; children: David, Michael, Jessica. BGS, U. Mich., 1974; JD, U. Ill., 1977. Bar: US Dist. Ct. (no. dist.) Ill. 1977, US Ct. Appeals (7th cir.) 1977, US Dist. Ct. (no. dist.) Calif. 1990. Law clk. to justice US Ct. Appeals (7th cir.), Chgo., 1977—79; assoc. Latham & Watkins, Chgo., 1982—85, ptnr., 1985—, mng. ptnr. San Francisco office, 1990—94, firm chmn. and mng. ptnr., 1995—. Home: 19 Tamal Vista Ln Kentfield CA 94904-1005 Office: Latham & Watkins LLP 505 Montgomery St Ste 2000 San Francisco CA 94111-2552

DELLUMS, RONALD VERNIE, Mayor, Oakland, California, retired congressman; b. Oakland, Calif., Nov. 24, 1935; m. Cynthia Lewis; 4 children. AA, Oakland City Coll., 1958; BA, San Francisco State Coll., 1960; MSW., U. Calif., 1962. Psychiatric social worker Calif. Dept. Mental Hygiene, 1962-64; program dir. Bayview Community Ctr., San Francisco, 1964-65; from assoc. dir. to dir. Hunters Point Youth Opportunity Ctr., 1965-66; planning cons. Bay Area Social Planning Coun., 1966-67; dir. concentrated employment program San Francisco Econ. Opportunity Coun., 1967-68; sr. cons. Social Dynamics, Inc., 1968-70; mem. US Congresses from 9th Calif. Dist., 1971-98; former chmn. house com. on D.C.; former mem. permanent select com. on intelligence; chmn. house armed svcs. com., 1993; pres. Healthcare Internat. Mgmt., Washington, 1998—2001; founder, sr. ptnr. Dellums & Assocs., LLC, Washington, 2001—; mayor City of Oakland, Calif., 2007—. Lectr. San Francisco State Coll., U. Calif., Berkeley; mem. U.S. del. North Atlantic Assembly, ranking minority mem. Nat. Security Com.; former chmn. Congl. Black Caucus, Calif. Dem. Congl. Del. Author: Defense Sense: The Search For a Rational Military Policy, 1983; co-author (with H. Lee Halterman): Lying Down with the Lions: A Public Life from the Streets of Oakland to the Halls of Power, 2000. Mem. Berkeley City Coun., 1967-71; served in USMC, 1954-56. Democrat. Office: City Hall One Frank H Ogawa Plz Oakland CA 94612 Office Phone: 510-238-3141. Office Fax: 510-238-4731. E-mail: officeofthemayor@oaklandnet.com.*

DELMAN, MICHAEL, computer software company executive; BA, MBA, U. So. Calif. Mktg. exec. NW Ayer, First Interstate Bank; v.p. Ogilvy & Mather; dir. corp. comm. Microsoft Corp., Redmond, Wash., 1990, gen. mgr. MSN Internet access bus., corp. v.p. Global Mktg. Comm. Group, 2005—. Office: Microsoft Corp One Microsoft Way Redmond WA 98052-6399

DELNIK, ALEXANDER, engineering executive, consultant; b. Zhitomir, Ukraine, Nov. 10, 1961; arrived in US, 1991; s. Yefim and Bera (Nevelskaya) Delnik. MS, Civil Engring. Inst., Kiev, Ukraine, 1983, PhD, 1987; MBA, UCLA, 1997. Registered profl. engr., Calif. Engr. Civil Engring. Inst., Kiev, 1987-88, sr. rschr., lectr., 1988-91; engr., lab. supr. Soil Tech, Inc., Temecula, Calif., 1991-93; project mgr. Dames & Moore, Inc., LA, 1993-98; mgr. strategic planning and new bus. devel. Edison Internat., Rosemead, Calif., 1998—; pres. PTP Group Americas Inc., Studio City, Calif., 2003—. Editor: English-Russian-Ukrainian Geotechnical Dictionary, 1992; contbr. articles to profl. jours.; editl. bd. Ukrainian Jour. of Found. Engring., 1990-92. Recipient Diploma of Sr. Rschr., Coun. Ministers of USSR, 1990; Ministry of Higher Edn. Lenin's scholar, 1982-83, grantee, 1989-91. Achievements include research and development of numerical techniques to simulate soil-structure interaction; major design and construction projects worldwide; risk management, strategic planning and development of major business opportunities for a leading energy company; development of technology-based businesses. Home: 12745 Sarah St Studio City CA 91604 Personal E-mail: alex.delnik@usa.net.

DELORENZO, DAVID A., food products executive; b. 1947; BA, Colgate U.; MBA, U. Pa., 1970. With Dole Food Co., Inc., 1970—; pres. Dole Fresh Fruit Co., 1986—92, Dole Food Co., Inc., 1990—96, pres. internat. divsn., 1993—96, pres., COO, 1996—2001, vice chmn., 2001, cons., 2002—07, pres., CEO, 2007—. Bd. dirs. Dole Food Co., Inc. Office: Dole Food Co Inc 1 Dole Dr Westlake Village CA 91362-7300

DELORIA, PHILIP S. (SAM), lawyer; m. Vivian BA, JD, Yale Univ. Dir. Am. Indian Law Ctr., Albuquerque, 1972—. Lectr. Univ. N. Mex. Sch. Law; past sec. gen. World Council Indigenous Peoples. Co-founder Commn. State-Tribal Rels., N.Mex.; mem. Nat. Inst. Rev. Bd., Indian Health Svc. Mem.: Standing Rock Sioux. Office: American Indian Law Center PO Box 4456 Station A Albuquerque NM 87196 Office Phone: 505-277-5462. Business E-Mail: deloria@law.unm.edu.

DEL RIEGO, RUTILIO J., bishop; b. Valdesandinas, Spain, Sept. 21, 1940; arrived in US, 1964, naturalized, 1981; Grad., Sem. of Diocesan Labor Priests, Salamanca, Spain; ThL, Cath. U. of Am., M in Spanish. Ordained priest, 1965; Spanish language instr. St. Vincent Coll., Latrobe, Pa., 1966—69; dir. Spanish Cath. Apostolate Archdiocese of Washington, Washington, 1969—73; dir. Office of Vocations Archdiocese of San Antonio, Tex., 1975—78; dir. Office for Hispanics N.E. Pastoral Ctr., NY, 1978—92; pastor Santa Lucia Parish, El Paso, Tex., 1983—93, San Antonio Parish, El Paso, 1993—94; dir. Diocesan Laborer Priests House of Formation, Washington, 1994—99; vice rector Serra House Diocese of San Bernardino, Calif., 1999—2000; pastor Our Lady of Perpetual Help, Riverside, Calif., 2000—05; ordained bishop, 2005; aux. bishop Diocese of San Bernardino, 2005—. Roman Catholic. Office: Diocese of San Bernardino 1201 E Highland Ave San Bernardino CA 92404-4641 Office Phone: 909-475-5115. Office Fax: 909-475-5109. E-mail: rdelriego@sbdiocese.org.

DELSON, BRAD PHILLIP, musician; b. Calif., Dec. 1, 1977; m. Elisa Boren, Sept. 16, 2003; 1 child, Jonah Taylor. BA summa cum laude, UCLA, 1999. Founding mem., lead guitarist Linkin Park, 1996—; co-founder, A&R rep. Machine Shop Recordings, LA, 2002—. Musician: (albums) Hybrid Theory, 2000, Meteora, 2003, Live in Texas, 2003, Minutes to Midnight, 2007, Road to Revolution Live at Milton Keynes, 2008, (songs) Crawling, 2000 (Grammy award for Best Hard Rock Performance, 2002), In the End, 2000 (MTV Video Music award for Best Rock Video, 2002), Somewhere I Belong, 2003 (MTV Video Music award for Best Rock Video, 2003), Breaking the Habit, 2003 (MTV Video Music Viewer's Choice award, 2004), (with Jay-Z) Numb/Encore, 2004 (Grammy award for Best Rap/Sung Collaboration, 2006), What I've Done, 2007 (Top Modern Rock Track, Billboard Year-End Charts, 2007), Shadow of the Day, 2007 (MTV Video Music award for Best Rock Video, 2008). Recipient Best-Selling Rock Group award, World Music Awards, 2002, 2003, Favorite Alternative Artist award, Am. Music Awards, 2003, 2004, 2007, 2008; named Top Modern Rock Artist, Billboard Year-End Charts, 2001, 2004, 2007. Mem.: Phi Beta Kappa. Office: Linkin Park c/o Machine Shop Recordings PO Box 36915 Los Angeles CA 90036

DEL TORO, BENICIO, actor; b. Santurce, PR, Feb. 19, 1967; Actor: (films) Licence To Kill, 1989, China Moon, 1994, The Usual Suspects, 1995, The Funeral, 1996, The Fan, 1996, Joy Ride, 1996, Cannes Man, 1996, Basquiat, 1996, Excess Baggage, 1997, Fear and Loathing in Las Vegas, 1998, Snatch, 2000, The Way of the Gun, 2000, Traffic, 2000 (Acad. award best sup. actor, 2001, BAFTA award best sup. actor, 2001, Golden Globe award best sup. actor, 2001), The Pledge, 2001, The Hunted, 2003, 21 Grams, 2003 (Acad. Award nomination for best supporting actor, 2004, Screen Actors Guild Award nomination for best supporting actor, 2004), Sin City, 2005, Trailer for a Remake of Gore Vidal's Caligula, 2005, Things We Lost in the Fire, 2007, Che, 2008 (Best Actor, Festival de Cannes, 2008); prodr., writer: (films) Submission, 1995. TV appearances include Miami Vice, 1987, Private Eye, 1987, Tales from the Crypt, 1994, Fallen Angels, 1995, T4, 2004. Office: IFA Talent Agy 8730 W Sunset Blvd Ste 490 Los Angeles CA 90069-2248

DELUCE, RICHARD DAVID, lawyer; b. Nanaimo, BC, Can., Oct. 3, 1928; came to U.S., 1929; s. Robert and Myrtle (Hickey) DeL.; m. Joanne Strang, Sept. 10, 1955; children: David S., Amy Jane Eigner, Daniel R. AB, UCLA, 1950; JD, Stanford U., Palo Alto, Calif., 1955. Bar: Calif., 1955, U.S. Dist. Ct. (no. dist.) Calif. 1955, U.S. Ct. Appeals (9th cir.) 1955, U.S. Dist. Ct. (cen. dist.) Calif. 1956, U.S. Supreme Ct. 1963, U.S. Dist. Ct. (so. dist.) Calif. 1972. Rsch. atty. Calif. Supreme Ct., San Francisco, 1955-56; assoc. Lawler, Felix & Hall, LA, 1956-62, ptnr., 1962-90, Arter, Hadden, Lawler, Felix & Hall, LA, 1990—2000. Co-author: California Civil Writ Practice, 2d edit., 1987. Capt. U.S. Army, 1951-53, Korea. Fellow Am. Coll. Trial Lawyers, Am. Bar Found.; mem. Calif. Club. Home: 3617 Paseo Del Campo Palos Verdes Estates CA 90274-1161 Personal E-mail: richard.deluce@verizon.net.

DELUGACH, ALBERT LAWRENCE, journalist; b. Memphis, Oct. 27, 1925; s. Gilbert and Edna (Short) D.; m. Bernice Goldstein, June 11, 1950; children: Joy, David, Daniel, Sharon. B.J., U. Mo., 1951. Reporter Kansas City (Mo.) Star, 1951-60, St. Louis Globe Democrat, 1960-69, St. Louis Post Dispatch, 1969-70; investigative reporter Los Angeles Times, 1970-89. Served with USNR, 1943-46. Recipient Pulitzer prize for spl. local reporting, 1969, Gerald Loeb award for disting. bus. and fin. journalism, 1984 Home: 4313 Price St Los Angeles CA 90027-2815

DELUSTRO, FRANK ANTHONY, biomedical company executive, research immunologist; b. NYC, May 8, 1948; s. Frank and Yolanda (Lombardi) DeL.; m. Barbara Mary Cervini, May 4, 1974; 1 child, Laura Marie. BS, Fordham U., 1970; PhD, SUNY, Syracuse, 1976. Rsch. assoc. dept. immunology Med. U. S.C., Charleston, 1976-78, instr. dept. medicine, 1978-80, asst. prof. dept. medicine, 1980-83; mgr. immunology R & D Collagen Corp., Palo Alto, Calif., 1983-85, mgr. clin. sci., 1985-86, dir. med. affairs, 1986-88, program dir., 1988-90, v.p., 1990-91, sr. v.p., 1991-96; pres., CEO Cohesion Corp., Palo Alto, 1996-98; pres. Cohesion Technologies, Inc., Palo Alto, 1998—. Contbr. articles to profl. jours. Mem. Am. Assn. Immunology, Am. Urol. Assn., Soc. Biomaterials, Soc. Investigative Dermatology.

DE LUTIS, DONALD CONSE, investment advisor, consultant; b. Rome, NY, Apr. 25, 1934; s. Conse R. and Mary D.; m. Ruth L.; 1 child, Dante. BS in Econs., Niagara U., 1956; MBA, Boston Coll., 1962. V.p. John Nuveen & Co., Inc., San Francisco, 1968-74; acct. exec. Dean Witter & Co., London, 1975-77; sr. investment officer Buffalo Savs. Bank, NY, 1978-80; exec. v.p. Robert Brown & Co., Inc., San Francisco, 1980-89, Capitol Corp. Asset mgmt., 1989-91; exec. v.p., dir. Pacific Securities, Inc., San Francisco, 1980-91; mng. dir. Coast Ptnrs. Securities, Inc., 1998-99; chmn. Orrell Capital Mgmt., Inc., 1991-98, 2000—. Commr. San Francisco Bay Conservation and Devel. Commn., 1983-93, State of Calif. Commn. Housing and Community Devel., 1974-77. Served with USAF, 1957-58. Mem.: San Francisco Bond Club. Republican. Roman Catholic.

DEMAIO, CARL, councilman; Founder Performance Inst., 2000, Am. Strategic Mgmt. Inst. (ASMI), 2003; councilman, Dist. 5 San Diego City Coun., 2008—. Chmn. San Diego Citizens for Accountable Govt.; bd. dirs. SAFENOWProject. Office: 202 C St, MS #10A San Diego CA 92101 Office Phone: 619-236-6655. Office Fax: 619-238-0915. E-mail: carldemaio@sandiego.gov.*

DEMAREST, DAVID FRANKLIN, JR., banker, retired government official; b. Glen Ridge, NJ, Oct. 8, 1951; s. David Franklin Demarest and Alison (Clark) Fahrer; m. Leigh Ann Wisniewski, Feb. 5, 1977 (div. 1981); m. Sarah Tinsley, July 16, 1983; 2 children. BA, Upsala Coll., 1973. Dep. dir. local elections Republican Nat. Com., Washington, 1977-80; dir. pub. and intergovtl. affairs U.S. Trade Rep., Washington, 1981-84; asst. U.S. Trade Rep. Exec. Office of Pres., Washington, 1984; dep. undersec. U.S. Labor Dept., Washington, 1985-87, asst. sec. labor, 1987-88; dir. comm. George Bush for Pres. Com., 1988; dir. pub. affairs Presdl. Transition Office, 1988-89; asst. to pres. for comm. White House, Washington, 1989-92; sr. cons. Internat. Mgmt. and Devel. Group, Ltd., Alexandria, Va., 1993; dir. corp. comms., exec. v.p. Bank of Am., San Francisco, 1993-99; exec. v.p. global corp. rels. Visa Internat., San Francisco, 1999—. Presbyterian. Office: Visa Internat PO Box 8999 San Francisco CA 94128-8999

DEMARIA, ANTHONY NICHOLAS, cardiologist, educator; b. Elizabeth, NJ, Jan. 12, 1943; s. Anthony and Charlotte DeMaria; m. Delores Horn; children: Christine, Anthony, Jonathon. BA, Coll. Holy Cross, 1964; MD, N.J. Coll. Medicine, 1968; degree (hon.), Kagawa Med. U., Japan, U. Bordeaux, France. Diplomate Am. Bd. Internal Medicine, Am. Bd. Cardiovascular Disease, Am. Bd. Cardiovascular Medicine. Intern St. Vincent Hosp., Worcester, Mass., 1968-69; resident USPHS Hosp., Staten Island, NY, 1969-71; fellow cardiology U. Calif., Davis, 1969-73, asst. prof. medicine, 1972-77, assoc. prof. medicine, 1977-81, prof. medicine, 1977-81; prof. medicine, chief cardiology div. U. Ky., Lexington, 1981-92; dir. Ky. Heart Inst., Lexington, 1989—; prof. medicine, chief cardiology U. Calif. Sch. Medicine, San Diego, 1992—2004, vice chmn. internal medicine, 1998—2001, dir., Sulpizio Family Cardiovasc. Ctr., 2004—, Judith and Jack White chair cardiovasc. medicine. Mem. rev. bds. Vets. Adminstrn. Med. Research Merit in Cardiovascular Studies, Nat. Inst. Health, NSF, NIH, NHLBI, U. Calif., U.S. FDA; chmn. Diagnostic Radiology Study Sect. NIH; vice-chmn. dept. medicine U. Calif., San Diego, 1998-2001. Mem. editl. bd. Am. Heart Jour., Am. Jour. Cardiac Imaging, Circulation, Am. Jour. Cardiology, Jour. Am. Coll. Cardiology, Health News from New Eng. Jour. Medicine; assoc. editor, Jour. Am. Coll. Cardiology, editor-in-chief 2001—; editl. cons. Am. Jour. Physiology, Annals Internal Medicine, Archives Phys. Medicine and Rehab., Catheterization and Cardiovascular Diagnosis, Jour. Clin. Investigation, New Eng. Jour. Medicine; contbr. numerous articles to profl. jours.; host Cardiology Update, Lifetime Med. TV. Recipient Humanitarian award Theodore and Susan Cummings, 1978, Disting. Alumnus award Coll. Medicine and Dentistry of N.J., 1988, Echocardiography award Tufts U., 1988, award of excellence Am. Acad. Med. Adminstrs., 1994, William Harvey award Am. Med. Writers Assn., 1996; named one of Best Doctors in Am., Best Heart Doctors in Am., Good Housekeeping mag., 1996; Golden Empire Heart Assn. grantee, Am. Heart Assn. grantee, Ky. Heart Assn. grantee, Vet. Adminstrn. grantee, Nat. Heart, Lung and Blood Inst. grantee; teaching scholar Am. Heart Assn. Fellow ACP, Am. Coll. Cardiology (chmn. 27th ann. scientific session 1978, cardiovascular procedures com., govt. rels. com., v.p. elect 1986, pres. elect 1987-88, pres. 1988-89, active various coms., Young Investigator award 1976), Am. Coll. Chest Physicians; mem. Am. Heart Assn. (bd. dirs. work evaluation unit Yolo Sierra chpt., Ky. chapter, active various coms., Teaching scholar 1979-82), Am. Fedn. Clin. Rsch., Yolo County Med. Socs., Am. Inst. Ultrasound in Medicine (bd. dirs.), Am. Soc. Echocardiography (bd. dirs. 1975-87, v.p. 1983-85, pres. 1985-87, assoc. editor), N.Am. Soc. for Cardiac Radiology, Assn. U. Cardiologists. Roman Catholic. Office: U Calif San Diego Med Ctr Divsn Cardiology 200 W Arbor Dr #8411 San Diego CA 92103-8411 Office Phone: 619-543-6031, 619-543-6163. Business E-Mail: ademaria@ucsd.edu.

DE MASSA, JESSIE G., media specialist; b. Aliquippa, Pa. BJ, Temple U.; MLS, San Jose State U., 1967; postgrad., U. Okla., U. So. Calif. Tchr. Palo Alto Unified Sch. Dist., Calif., 1966; libr. Antelope Valley Joint Union HS Dist., Lancaster, Calif., 1966, ABC Unified Sch. Dist., Artesia, Calif., 1968—72; dist. libr. Tehachapi Unified Sch. Dist., Calif., 1972—81; media specialist, free lance writer, 1981—; assoc. Chris DeMassa & Assocs., 1988—. Author: (novel) The Haunting and Murder in Aruba, 2002; contbr. articles to profl. jours.

Active Statue of Liberty Ellis Island Found., Inc., Nat. Trust Hist. Preservation; founding mem. Nat. Campaign for Tolerance Wall of Tolerance, Montgomery, Ala., 2005; charter supporter US Holocaust Meml. Mus., Washington; supporting mem. US Holocaust Meml. Coun., Washington; founder Pacific Aviation Mus. Pearl Harbor at Ford Islands, Hawaii, 2006. Named Nat. Women's Hall Fame, 1995. Fellow Internat. Biog. Assn.; mem. Calif. Media Libr. Educators Assn., Calif. Assn. Sch. Librs. (exec. coun.), AAUW (bull. editor chpt., assoc. editor state bull., chmn. publicity, 1955-68), Nat. Mus. Women Arts (charter), Hon Fellows John F. Kennedy Libr. (founding mem.), Women's Roundtable Orange County, Nat. Writer's Assn. (so. Calif. chpt.), Calif. Retired Tchrs. Assn. (Harbor Beach divsn. 77), Heritage Found., Claremont Inst., Nat. Women's History Mus. (charter mem.), Libr. Congress (nat. charter mem.), Nat. World War II Meml. Nat. Mall (charter mem.), Nat. Trust Hist. Preservation. Home and Office: 9951 Garrett Cir Huntington Beach CA 92646-3604 Office Phone: 714-962-9810. Personal E-mail: jdwriter10@verizon.net.

DEMENT, WILLIAM CHARLES, medical researcher, educator; b. Wenatchee, Wash., July 29, 1928; s. Charles Frederick and Katheryn (Severyns) Dement; m. Eleanor Weber, Mar. 23, 1956; children: Catherine Lynn, Elizabeth Anne, John Nicholas. BS, U. Wash., 1951; MD, U. Chgo., 1955, PhD, 1957. Bd. cert. in clin. polysomography. Intern Mt. Sinai Hosp., NYC, 1957—58, rsch. fellow dept. psychiatry, 1958—63; assoc. prof. dept. psychiatry and behavioral scis. Stanford U., 1963—67, prof., 1967—; dir. Stanford Sleep Disorders Clinic and Lab., 1970—, Sleep Rsch. Lab., Stanford, Calif., 1963—. Chmn. U.S. Surgeon Gen.'s Joint Coord. Coun., Project Sleep, 1979—, Nat. Commn. on Sleep Disorders Rsch., 1990—92. Author: Some Must Watch While Some Must Sleep, 1972, The Sleep Watchers, 1992; editor-in-chief: Sleep, 1977—, mem. editl. bd.: Neurobiology of Aging, 1982—. Recipient medal, Intra-Sci. Rsch. Found., 1981, Disting. Svc. award, U. Chgo. Med. Alumni Assn., 1978. Mem.: Am. Phsyiol. Soc., Am. EEG Soc., Western EEG Soc., Soc. Neuroscience, Psychiat. Rsch. Found., Inst. Medicine of NAS, Assn. Sleep Disorders Ctrs. (pres. 1982, Nathaniel Kleitman prize), Sleep Rsch. Soc. (founder). Office: Stanford Sleep Disorders Ctr 701 Welch Rd Ste 2226 Palo Alto CA 94304-1711

DEMERS, PATRICIA A., English literature professor; BA, MA, McMaster Univ., Hamilton, Ont.; PhD, Univ. Ottawa. Assoc. dean, grad. studies Univ. Alberta, Edmonton, 1991—93, chmn. dept. English & film studies, 1995—98; v.p. Soc. Sci. and Humanities Rsch. Council of Canada, 1998—2002; prof. English Univ. Alberta, Edmonton. Author: Women as Interpreters of the Bible, Heaven Upon Earth: The Forms of Moral and Religious Children's Literature to 1850, P.L. Travers, Louis Hémon's Maria Chapdelaine, The World of Hannah Moore, Women's Writing in English: Early Modern England; editor: From Instruction to Delight: Children's Literature to 1850, A Garland from the Golden Age; contbr. articles to profl. jours. Mem.: Royal Soc. Canada (pres. 2005—07). Office: Univ Alberta English Dept 3-5 Humanities Ctr Edmonton AB T6G 2E5 Canada

DE MICHELE, O. MARK, real estate company executive; b. Syracuse, NY, Mar. 23, 1934; s. Aldo and Dora (Carno) De M.; m. Faye Ann Venturin, Nov. 8, 1957; children: Mark A., Christopher C., Michele M., Julianne; m. Barbara Joan Stanley, May 22, 1982; 1 child, Angela Marie. BS, Syracuse U., 1955; doctorate (hon.), No. Ariz. U., 1997. Mgr. Seal Right Co., Inc., Fulton, NY, 1955-58; v.p., gen. mgr. L.M. Harvey Co. Inc., Syracuse, 1958-62; v.p. Niagara Mohawk Power, Syracuse, 1962-78, Ariz. Pub. Svc., Phoenix, 1978-81, exec. v.p., 1981-82, pres., CEO, 1982-97, also bd. dirs.; pres., CEO Greater Phoenix Econ. Coun., 1997-98; chmn., CEO Urban Realty Ptnrs. LLC, 1998—. Bd. dirs. Ont. Power Generation. Pres. Jr. Achievement, Syracuse, 1974-75, Phoenix, 1982-83, United Way Ctrl. N.Y., Syracuse, 1978, Ariz. Opera Co., Phoenix, 1981-83, Phoenix Symphony, 1984-86, United Way Phoenix, 1985-86, Ariz. Mus. Sci. and Tech., 1988-90; pres. Children's Action Alliance, 1989-92; chmn. Valley Sun United Way, 1984-86, Phoenix Econ. Coun., 1991-94; chmn. Morrison Inst. Pub. Policy at Ariz. State U.; chmn. Ariz. Cities in Schs., 1994-97, Nat. Environ. Edn. Found., 1997—; pres. Episcopal Cmty. Svc. Found. Named Outstanding Young Man of Yr., Syracuse Jaycees, 1968, Phoenix Man of Yr., Phoenix Ad Club, 1992; recipient Humanitarian award Nat. Conf., 1995. Mem. Phoenix C. of C. (chmn. bd. 1986-87), Phoenix Country Club, Ariz. Club (Phoenix). Republican. Home: 1536 Glorietta Blvd Coronado CA 92118-2306 Office: Urban Realty Ptnrs LLC 2415 E Camelback Rd Ste 700 Phoenix AZ 85016-4245 E-mail: mdemichele@aol.com.

DEMIERI, JOSEPH L., retired bank executive; b. NYC, Aug. 31, 1940; s. Leo A. and Frances (Garone) DeM.; m. Anne Patricia McCue, May 15, 1965. BBA, Tex. A&M U., 1962. C.P.A., N.Y. With Peat, Marwick, Mitchell & Co., NYC, 1962-68; v.p., controller City Investing Co., NYC and Beverly Hills, Calif., 1968-82; exec. v.p. Motown Industries, Los Angeles, 1982-84; chmn., CEO Calif. Millworks Corp., Valencia, 1985-95; sr. v.p., CFO Western Security Bank, Burbank, Calif., 1995—2002. Home: 6259 Ebbtide Way Malibu CA 90265-3608

DEMING, JODY WHEELER, oceanography educator; b. Houston, July 2, 1952; d. Samuel Henry Wheeler and Laverne (Lewis) Kraft. BA in Biol. Scis., Smith Coll., 1974; PhD in Microbiology, U. Md., 1981. Rsch. asst. biology Sloan Found. Rsch. Smith Coll., Northampton, Mass., 1973; field biologist Water Quality Div. Md. State Dept. Natural Resources, Annapolis, 1974; rsch. technician Div. Infectious Diseases Tufts/New Eng. Med. Ctr. Hosp., Boston, 1974-75; rsch. assoc. Bioluminescence Lab. NASA/Goddard Space Flight Ctr., Greenbelt, Md., 1975-77; grad. teaching and rsch. asst. microbiology U. Md., College Park, 1977-81; NSF postdoctoral fellow Marine Biology Rsch. Div. Scripps Inst. Oceanography, La Jolla, Calif., 1981-82; NOAA postdoctoral fellow Office of Marine Pollution and Assessment, Rockville, Md., 1982-83; assoc. rsch. scientist Chesapeake Bay Inst. Johns Hopkins U., Shady Side, Md., 1981-86, rsch. scientist Chesapeake Bay Inst., 1986-88, asst. prof. biology, 1983-86; scientist Ctr. Marine Biotech., U. Md., Balt., 1986-88; dir., Marine Bioremediation Program U. Wash., Seattle, 1993—99; assoc. prof. U. Wash. Sch. Oceanography, Seattle, 1988—95, prof., 1995—, U. Wash. Astrobiology Program, 1998—. Mem. nat. com. ALVIN Rev. Com., 1984-87, internat. Arctic projects and steering coms., numerous proposal review panels for NOAA, NSF and others. Contbr. numerous chpts. to books and articles to profl. jours. Recipient award for Sci. Achievement in the Biol. Scis., Wash. Acad. Scis., 1987, Presdl. Young Investigator NSF award, 1989-94. Mem. AAAS, Am. Soc. for Microbiology, Am. Acad. of Microbiology, Am. Soc. of Limnology and Oceanography, Am. Geophys. Union, The Oceanography Soc., Sigma Xi. Achievements include patents for rapid quantitive determination of bacteria and their antibiotic susceptibilities in a variety of fluid samples. Office: U Wash Sch Oceanography Box 357940 Seattle WA 98195-0001 E-mail: jdeming@u.washington.edu.

DEMITRA, PAVOL, professional hockey player; b. Dubnica, Slovakia, Nov. 29, 1974; Right wing Ottawa Senators, 1993—96, St. Louis Blues, 1996—2005, LA Kings, 2005—06, Minn. Wild, 2006—08, Vancouver Canucks, 2008—. Mem. Slovakia Hockey Team, Olympic Games, Nagano, Japan, 1998. Recipient Lady Byng Meml. Trophy, 2000; named to NHL All-Star Game, 1999, 2000, 2002. Office: Vancouver Canucks GM Place 800 Griffiths Way Vancouver BC V6B 6G1 Canada

DEMME, JONATHAN, director, producer, writer; b. Baldwin, LI, NY, Feb. 22, 1944; m. Evelyn Purcell (div.); m. Joanne Howard; 3 children. Student, U. Fla.; degree (hon.), Wesleyan U., 1990. With Avco Embassy Films, 1966, Pathe Films, 1966-67; with publicity dept. United Artists, 1968-69; writer Film Daily, 1966-68. Actor: (films) The Incredible Melting Man, 1977, Into the Night, 1985; dir.: Crazy Mama, 1975, Handle with Care, 1977, Last Embrace, 1979, Melvin and Howard, 1980, Swing Shift, 1984, Swimming to Cambodia, 1987, Married to the Mob, 1988, Famous All Over Town, 1988, The Silence of the Lambs, 1991 (Acad. Award for best dir., 1992, Dir.'s Guild of Am. Award for Outstanding Directorial Achievement in Motion Pictures, 1992), Cousin Bobby, 1992, The Complex Sessions, 1994, Storefront Hitchcock, 1998, Rachel Getting Married, 2008; (TV films) Columbo: Murder Under Glass, 1978, Who Am I This Time?, 1982; (TV series) Alive From Off Center, 1984—87, Trying Times, 1987; exec. prodr.: (films) Amos & Andrew, 1993, Household Saints, 1993, Ray Cohn/Jack Smith, 1994, Devil in a Blue Dress, 1995, Shadrach, 1998, The Opportunists, 2000, Maangamizi: The Ancient One, 2001; prodr.: Miami Blues, 1990, One Foot On a Banana Peel, the Other Foot in the Grave: Secrets From the Dolly Madison Room, 1994, That Thing You Do! (also actor), 1996, Mandela, 1996, Into the Rope, 1996, Courage and Pain, 1996, The Uttmost, 1998, Adaptation, 2002, Beah: A Black Woman Speaks, 2003; (TV films) Women & Men 2: In Love There Are No Rules, 1991; writer (films) Black Mama, White Mama, 1972, Ladies and Gentlemen, the Fabulous Stains, 1981, cinematographer, dir., prodr. The Agronomist, 2003, dir., exec. prodr. (TV films) Subway Stories: Tales from the Underground, 1997, dir., prodr. (films) Something Wild, 1986, Philadelphia, 1993, Beloved, 1998, The Manchurian Candidate, 2004, Neil Young: Heart of Gold, 2006, dir., writer Caged Heat, 1974, Fighting Mad, 1976, Stop Making Sense, 1984, dir., prodr., writer The Truth About Charlie, 2002, Jimmy Carter Man from Plains, 2007, prodr., writer Angels Hard as They Come, 1971, The Hot Box, 1972; dir.: (Bruce Springsteen music video) Murder, Inc., 1995; co-dir.: Streets of Philadelphia. Recipient Billy Wilder Award for Excellence in Directing, Nat. Bd. Review, 2006. Mem.: Dirs. Guild Am.

DEMMEL, JAMES W., computer science educator; b. Pitts., Oct. 19, 1955; BS, Calif. Inst. Tech., 1975; PhD in Computer Sci., U. Calif., Berkeley, 1983. Prof. computer sci. NYU, 1983-90; prof. computer sci. divsn. U. Calif., Berkeley, 1990—. Recipient Presdl. Young Investigator award. Mem. NAE, IEEE, Am. Math. Soc., Math. Assn. Am., Soc. Indsl. and Applied Math. (J.H. Wilkinson prize). Office: U Calif Dept Math Berkeley CA 94710-1625

DEMOFF, MARVIN ALAN, lawyer; b. LA, Oct. 28, 1942; s. Max and Mildred (Tweer) D.; m. Patricia Caryn Abelov, June 16, 1968; children: Allison Leigh, Kevin Andrew. BA, UCLA, 1964; JD, Loyola U., LA, 1967. Bar: Calif. 1969. Asst. pub. defender Los Angeles County, 1968-72; ptnr. Steinberg & Demoff, LA, 1973-83, Craighill, Fentress & Demoff, L.A. and Washington, 1983-86; mng. dir. Neuberger Berman LLC, LA, 2002—08; of counsel Mitchell, Silberberg & Knupp, LA, 1987—2002, Morris Yorn Barnes Levine, LA, 2008—. Mem. citizens adv. bd. Olympic Organizing Com., L.A., 1982-84; bd. trustees Curtis Sch., L.A., 1985-94, chmn. bd. trustees, 1988-93; sports adv. bd. Constitution Rights Found., L.A., 1986—. Mem. ABA (mem. forum com. on entertainment and sports), Calif. Bar Assn., UCLA Alumni Assn., Phi Delta Phi. Avocations: sports, music, art. Office: 2000 Ave Stars 3rd fl N Tower Los Angeles CA 90067 Office Phone: 310-319-3980. Business E-Mail: mdemoff@bmkylaw.com, md@morrisyorn.com.

DEMPSEY, PATRICK, actor; b. Lewiston, Maine, Jan. 13, 1966; m. Rocky Parker, 1987 (div. 1994); m. Jillian Fink, July 31, 1999; children: Tallulah Fyfe, Darby Galen, Sullivan Patrick. Face of men's fragrance Avon, 2008. Actor: (films) Heaven Help Us, 1985, Meatballs III: Summer Job, 1986, Can't Buy Me Love, 1987, In the Mood, 1987, In a Shallow Grave, 1988, Some Girls, 1988, Loverboy, 1989, Happy Together, 1987, Coupe de Ville, 1990, Run, 1991, Mobsters, 1991, Face the Music, 1993, Bank Robber, 1993, Ava's Magical Adventure, 1994, With Honors, 1994, Bloodknot, 1995, Outbreak, 1995, Hugo Pool, 1997, Denial, 1998, The Treat, 1998, There's No Fish Food In Heaven, 1998, Me and Will, 1999, Scream 3, 2000, Rebellion, 2002, The Emperor's Club, 2002, Sweet Home Alabama, 2002, Shade, 2006, (voice) Brother Bear, 2006, Freedom Writers, 2007, Enchanted, 2007, Made of Honor, 2008; (TV films) A Fighting Choice, 1986, Merry Christmas Baby, 1991, For Better and for Worse, 1993, J.F.K.: Reckless Youth, 1993, The Right to Remain Silent, 1996, A Season in Purgatory, 1996, Odd Jobs, 1997, The Player, 1997, The Escape, 1997, 20,000 Leagues Under the Sea, 1997, Crime and Punishment, 1998, Jeremiah, 1998, Chestnut Hill, 2001, Blonde, 2001, Corsairs, 2002, About a Boy, 2003, Lucky 7, 2003, Iron Jawed Angels, 2004; (TV series) Fast Times, 1986, Grey's Anatomy, 2005— (Outstanding Performance by an Ensemble in a Drama Series, SAG, 2007), (guest appearances) Will & Grace, 2000, 2001, Once and Again, 2000, 2001, 2003, Karen Sisco, 2003, The Practice, 2004. Named Favorite Male TV Star, People's Choice Awards, 2007, 2008; named one of Barbara Walters-10 Most Fascinating People of 2006, The 100 Most Powerful Celebrities, Forbes.com, 2008. Office: c/o Grey's Anatomy Los Feliz Tower 4th Fl 4151 Prospect Ave Los Angeles CA 90027 also: c/o BWR Pub Rels Sixth Fl West Tower 9100 Wilshire Blvd Beverly Hills CA 90212

DEMPSEY, STANLEY (HOWARD STANLEY DEMPSEY), lawyer, mining and investment company executive; b. LaPorte, Ind., Aug. 12, 1939; s. Howard Taft and Katheryn Alice (Prichard) D.; m. Judith Rose Enyart, Aug. 20, 1960; children: Howard Stanley, Whitney Owen, Bradford Evan, Matthew Charles. Student, Colo. Sch. Mines, 1956-57; AB, U. Colo., 1960, JD, 1964; cert., Harvard Sch. Bus., 1969. Bar: Colo. 1964. Ind. mine operator, Colo. and Mont., 1957—60; from indsl. engr. to divsn. atty. western ops. Climax (Colo.) Molybdenum Co., 1960—70; gen. atty. law dept. western area, dir. environ. affairs AMAX Inc., Denver, 1970—81, v.p., 1977-83; ptnr. Arnold & Porter, Denver, 1983—86; pres. Denver Mining Fin. Co., 1987—; chmn., CEO Royal Gold, Inc., Denver, 1984—2008, also bd. dirs., chmn., 2007—; pres. Environ. Strategies, Inc., 1991—. Chmn. AMAX Australia Ltd., 1981-83; chmn., exec. com. AMAX Iron Ore, 1981-83; dep. chmn., exec. com. Australian Consol. Mines Ltd., 1981-83; bd. dirs. Mineral Info. Inst., World Gold Coun. Author: Mining the Summit, 1978; contbr. articles to profl. jours. Legal rsch. asst. Rocky Mountain Mineral Law Found., Boulder, Colo., 1962-64, trustee, pres., 1979-80; pres. Colo. Mining Assn., 1979-1980; bd. dirs. Colo. Hist. Found., 1997—, Gov. Nat. Mining Hall of Fame, 1997—Mem. Nat. Mining Assn. (chmn. public lands com. 1994-2000, 04, chmn. MINEPAC 2000-02), ABA (chmn. hard minerals com. 1975-77), Colo. Bar Assn. (coun. mem. mineral law sect. 1975-79), Colo. Natural Resources Law Ctr. (bd. dirs. 1998-2000), Continental Divide Bar Assn. (sec.-treas. 1967-68), Colo. Hist. Soc. (bd. dirs., chmn. 1991-94), Soc. Mining Law Antiquarians (co-founder), Mining and Metall. Soc. Am., Mining History Assn. (pres. 1992-94), Mountain States Employers Coun. (bd. dirs. 1990—), Rotary, Rollings Hills Country Club(Golden), Am. Alpine Club, Univ. Club, Harvard Club (NYC). Presbyterian. Office: Royal Gold Inc 1660 Wynkoop St Ste 1000 Denver CO 80202-1161 Office Phone: 303-573-1660.

DE MUNIZ, PAUL J., state supreme court chief justice; BS, Portland State U., 1972; JD, Willamette U., 1975. Bar: (Oreg. State Bar) 1975, (U.S. Dist. Ct.) 1977, (U.S. Ct. of Appeals, Ninth Circuit) 1980, (U.S. Supreme Ct.) 1981. Atty. Garret, Seideman, Hemann, Robertson & De Muniz, P.C., 1977—90; judge Oreg. Ct. Appeals, 1990—2001, presiding judge dept. one, 1997—2000; justice Oreg. Supreme Ct., 2001—, chief justice, 2006—. Mem. Jud. Fitness & Disability Commn., Supreme Ct. Access to Justice for All Com.; chair Com. to Implement Recommendations; mem. Oreg. Supreme Ct. Task Force on Racial/Ethnic Issues in Jud. System, Defense Advisory Com. on Women in Services, 1998—2001; former prof. Nat. Jud. Coll.; former mem., chair Oreg. Criminal Justice Council. Author (with others): Immigrants in Courts, 1999. Served in USAF, 1966—70. Mem.: Oreg. State Bar, ABA. Office: Supreme Ct 1163 State St Salem OR 97301

DEMURO, PAUL ROBERT, lawyer; b. Aberdeen, Md., Mar. 21, 1954; s. Paul Robert and Amelia C. DeMuro; m. Susan Taylor, May 26, 1990; children: Melissa Taylor, Natalie Lauren, Alanna Leigh. BA summa cum laude, U. Md., 1976; JD, Washington U., 1979; MBA, U. Calif., Berkeley, 1986. CPA Md.; bar: Md. 1979, US Dist. Ct. Md. 1979, DC 1980, US Dist. Ct. DC 1980, US Tax Ct. 1981, US Ct. Appeals (4th cir.) 1981, Calif. 1982, US Dist. Ct. (no. dist.) Calif. 1982, US Dist. Ct. (ea. dist.) Calif. 1986. Assoc. Ober, Grimes & Shriver, Balt., 1979-82; assoc. and ptnr. Carpenter et al, San Francisco, 1982-89; ptnr. McCutchen, Doyle, Brown & Enerson, San Francisco, 1989-93, Latham & Watkins, San Francisco, 1993—. Author: The Financial Managers Guide to Managed Care and Integrated Delivery Systems, 1995, The Fundamentals of Managed Care and Network Development, 1999; co-author: Health Care Mergers and Acquisitions: The Transactional Perspective, 1996, Health Care Executives' Guide to Fraud and Abuse, 1998; editor, contbg. author: Integrated Delivery Systems, 1994, article and rev. editor: Washington U. Law Quar., 1975—76. Mem. San Francisco Mus. Art, 1985—. Fellow: Am. Coll. Med. Practice Execs., Med. Group Mgmt. Assn. (cert. med. practice exec.), Healthcare Fin. Mgmt. Assn. (bd. dirs. No. Calif. chpt. 1990—93, nat. principles and practices bd. 1992—95, vice chair 1993—95, nat. bd. dirs. 1995—97, mem. exec. com. 1996—97, chair compliance officers forum adv. coun. 1998—2000, sec. 1999—2001, bd. dirs. No. Calif. chpt. 1999—2005, mem. nominating com. 2001—02, pres.-elect 2001—02, pres. 2002—03, mem. governance com. 2002—03); mem.: AICPA, ABA (chair transactional and bus. health care interest group 1998—2000, chair programs com. 2000—02, governing coun. 2000—08, chmn. mem. and mktg. com. 2002—04, vice chair coord. com. diversity 2002—, budget officer 2003—05, chair elect 2005—06, chair 2006—07, health law sect.), Md. Assn. CPAs, San Francisco Bar Assn., Health-care Compliance Assn. (cert. in health care compliance), Am. Coll. Healthcare Execs., Am. Health Lawyers Assn. (task force best practices in advising clients 1998—99, fraud and abuse and self-referral substantive law com. 1998—, task force on ENRON 2002), Calif. Bar Assn., LA County Bar Assn. (health law sect.). Republican. Office: Latham & Watkins LLP 505 Montgomery St Ste 2000 San Francisco CA 94111-2552 Office Phone: 415-395-8180. Business E-Mail: paul.demuro@lw.com.

DEMUTH, LAURENCE WHEELER, JR., lawyer, utilities executive; b. Boulder, Colo., Nov. 22; s. Laurence Wheeler and Eugenia Augusta (Roach) DeM.; m. Paula Phipps, Mar. 7, 1987; children: Debra Lynn, Laurence Wheeler III, Brant Hill. AB, U. Colo., 1951, LLB, 1953. Gen. atty. Mountain State Telephone and Telegraph Co., Denver, 1968, v.p., gen. counsel, 1968-84, sec., 1974-84; exec. v.p., gen. counsel, sec. U.S. West, Inc., Englewood, Colo., 1984-92, ret., 1992. Dist. capt. Rep. Precinct Com., 1957-70' trustee Lakewood (Colo.) Presbyn. Ch., 1965-68; bd. dirs. Colo. Epilepsy Assn., 1973-79; bd. litigation Mountain States Legal Found., 1980-89; Colo. Commr. on Uniform State of Laws, 1997—. Mem. ABA, Colo. Bar Assn. (chmn. ethics com. 1973-74, bd. govs., fellow found.), Denver Bar Assn., Am. Judicature Soc., Colo. Assn. Corp. Counsel (pres.), Order of Coif, Phi Beta Kappa, Pi Gamma Mu. Clubs: University, Metropolitan. Office: Att Broadband 183 Inverness Dr W Englewood CO 80112-5203

DENENBERG, ALAN F., lawyer; b. 1960; BA, McGill Univ., Montreal, 1982; LLB, Osgoode Hall Law Sch., Toronto, 1985; LLM, Columbia Law Sch., NYC, 1986. Bar: NY 1987, Calif. 1988. Ptnr. Shearman & Sterling, San Francisco, and mng. ptnr. Singapore; ptnr., global tech. group Davis Polk & Wardwell, Menlo Park, Calif., 2000—. Office: Davis Polk & Wardwell 1600 El Camino Real Menlo Park CA 94025 Office Phone: 650-752-2004. Office Fax: 650-752-3604. Business E-Mail: alan.denenberg@dpw.com.

DENEUVE, CATHERINE (CATHERINE DORLEAC), actress; b. Paris, Oct. 22, 1943; d. Maurice Dorleac and Renee Deneuve; m. David Bailey, 1965 (div. 1970); children: Christian Vadim, Chiara Mastroianni. Student, Lycée La Fontaine, Paris. Co-chair UNESCO campaign to protect World's Film Heritage, 1994—. Films include Les Petits Chats, 1956, Les Collegiennes, 1956, Les portes claquent, 1960, Les Parisiennes, 1961, Et Satan conduit le bal, 1962, Vacances portugaises, 1963, Le Vice et la Vertu, 1963, Les Parapluies de Cherbourg, 1964 (Golden Palm of Cannes Festival), La Chasse à l'homme, 1964, Les Plus belles escroqueries du monde, 1964, Un Monsieur de compagnie, 1964, Repulsion, 1965, Coeur à la gorge, 1965, Le Chant de Ronde, 1965, La Vie de Chateau, 1965, Les créatures, 1966, Les Demoiselles de Rochefort, 1966, Benjamin, 1967, Manon 70, 1967, Belle de Jour, 1967 (Golden Lion of Venice

Festival), Meyerling, 1967, La Chamade, 1968, The April Fools, 1968, La Sirène du Mississippi, 1968, Tristana, 1969, It Only Happens to Others, 1971, Dirty Money, Hustle, 1975, Lovers Like Us, 1975, Act of Aggression, 1976, March or Die, 1977, La Grande Bourgeoise, 1977, The Last Metro, 1980, A Second Chance, 1981, Reporters, 1982, The Hunger, 1983, Fort Saganne, Scene of the Crime, Agent Trouble, 1987, FM-Frequency Murder, 1988, Drole d'endroit Pour Une Rencontre, 1988, Helmut Newton: Frames from the Edge, 1989, Indochine, 1992 (César award Best Actress, Acad. award nominee for Best Actress), Ma Saison Preferee, 1993, La Partie d'Echecs, 1994, Les Cent et Une Nuits, 1995, Les Voleurs, 1996, Place Vendome, 1997, Gènèalogies d'un Crime, 1997, Pola X, 1998, Le Temps retrouvé, La Princesse de Clèves, 1999, The Last Napoleon, 1999, Est, ouest, 1999, Le Vent de la nuit, 1999, Belle Maman, 1999, Dancer in the Dark, 2000, Je rentre à la maison, 2001, Absolument fabuleux, 2001, The Musketeer, 2001, Le Petit poucet, 2001, 8 femmes, 2002 (Berlin Film Festival Silver Bear for Individual Artistic Contbn.), Au plus près du paradis, 2002, Um Filme Falado, 2003, Kings & Queen, 2004,Les Temps qui changent, 2004, Palais royal, 2005, Le Concile de pierre, 2006, Le Héros de la famille, 2006, Après lui, 2007, (voice) Persepolis, 2007, Un conte de Noël, 2008 (Spl. prize, Festival de Cannes, 2008), Je veux voir; TV movies include Les Liaisons dangereuses, 2003, Princesse Marie, 2004; prodr. A Strange Place to Meet, 1988. Recipient Berlin Film Festival Golden Bear for Lifetime Achievement, 1998, Venice Film Festival Silver Lion for Best Actress, 1998, Bangkok Internat. Film Festival Golden Kinnaree Career Achievement award, 2006. Office: 76 Rue Bonaparte 75006 Paris France

DENHAM, ROBERT EDWIN, lawyer; b. Dallas, Aug. 27, 1945; s. Wilburn H. and Anna Maria (Hughes) Denham; m. Carolyn Hunter, June 3, 1966; children: Jeffrey Hunter, Laura Maria. BA magna cum laude, U. Tex., 1966; MA, Harvard U., 1968, JD magna cum laude, 1971. Bar: Calif. 1972. Assoc. Munger Tolles & Olson LLP, LA, 1971—73, ptnr., 1973—85, 1992—93, 1998—, mng. ptnr., 1985—91; gen. counsel Salomon Inc, NYC, 1991—92, chmn., CEO, 1992—97. Bd. dirs. Chevron Corp., 2004—, Alcatel Lucent, 2006—, The NY Times Co., 2008—, Wesco Fin. Corp. Pres. Pasadena (Calif.) Ednl. Found., 1977—79; v.p. bd. trustees Poly. Sch. Pasadena, 1991—93; adv. bd. of the pres. Calif. State U., Sonoma, 1993—; trustee Poly. Sch. Pasadena, 1989—93, New Sch. U., 1995—, Natural Resources Def. Coun., 1992—2002, The Conf. Bd., 1994—2003, Russell Sage Found., 1997—; pub. mem. Ind. Stds. Bd., 1997—2000; former co-chmn. Subcoun. on Capital Allocation of the Competitiveness Policy Coun.; former mem. Bipartisan Commn. on Entitlement and Tax Reform; mem. bus. sector adv. group on corp. governance OECD; trustee Cathedral Corp. Diocese of L.A., 1986—92; bd. dirs. Pub. Counsel, L.A., 1981—84, United Way, NYC, 1994—97, U.S. Trust Co., AMKOR Tech., Inc., 1998—99, John D. & Catherine T.MacArthur Found. Mem.: ABA, L.A. County Bar (bus. and corps. exec. com. 1985—), State Bar Calif. Democrat. Episcopalian. Avocations: soccer, cooking, running. Office: Munger Tolles & Olson LLP 355 S Grand Ave # 3500 Los Angeles CA 90071-1560 E-mail: Robert.Denham@mto.com.

DENHARDT, ROBERT B., political science professor, director; PhD, U. Ky., 1968. Vice provost U. Mo.-Columbia; Charles P. Messick prof. pub. adminstrn. U. Del.; regents prof., Lincoln prof. of leadership and ethics., dir. Sch. Pub. Affairs Ariz. State U. Chair Mo. Gov.'s Adv. Coun. on Productivity. Author: The New Public Service Managing Human Behavior in Public and Nonprofit Organizations, The Pursuit of Significance, In the Shadow of Organization, Theories of Public Organization, Public Administration: An Action Orientation, Executive Leadership in the Public Service, The Revitalization of the Public Service, Pollution and Public Policy; contbr. articles to profl. jours. Fullbright Scholar, 1990. Mem.: Am. Soc. for Pub. Adminstrn. (past pres., Dwight Waldo Award 2004). Office: Ariz State U Sch Pub Affairs Tempe AZ 85289 Office Phone: 602-469-0450. E-mail: rbd@asu.edu.

DE NIRO, ROBERT, actor, film producer and director, restaurant owner; b. NYC, Aug. 17, 1943; s. Robert and Virginia De Niro; m. Diahnne Abbott, 1976 (div. 1988); 1 child, Raphael Eugene, 1 stepchild, Drina; m. Grace Hightower, June 17, 1997; 1 child, Elliot; 2 children, Aaron Kendric DeNiro, Julian Henry De Niro (with Toukie Smith). Studied acting with, Stella Adler, Lee Strasberg. Co-founder Tribeca Productions, 1988, Tribeca Film Festival, 2002; co-owner Tribeca Grill, 1990, Nobu, NYC, 1994, Rubicon, San Francisco, 1994; owner Ago, LA, 2008—. Actor: (films) The Wedding Party, 1969, Hi, Mom!, 1970, Bloody Mama, 1970, Jennifer On My Mind, 1971, Born to Win, 1971, The Gang That Couldn't Shoot Straight, 1971, Bang the Drum Slowly, 1973, Mean Streets, 1973, The Godfather, Part II, 1974 (Acad. award best supporting actor), The Last Tycoon, 1976, Nineteen Hundred, 1976, Taxi Driver, 1976, New York, New York, 1977, The Deer Hunter, 1978, Raging Bull, 1980 (Acad. award best actor), True Confessions, 1981, The King of Comedy, 1982, Once Upon a Time in America, 1984, Falling in Love, 1984, Brazil, 1984, The Mission, 1985, Angel Heart, 1987, The Untouchables, 1987, Midnight Run, 1988, Jacknife, 1989, Stanley & Iris, 1990, Goodfellas, 1990, Awakenings, 1991 (Acad. award nom.), Backdraft, 1991, Cape Fear, 1991, Guilty By Suspicion, 1991, Mistress, 1992, Night and the City, 1992, Mad Dog and Glory, 1993, This Boy's Life, 1993, Mary Shelley's Frankenstein, 1994, Casino, 1995, Heat, 1995, The Fan, 1996, Marvin's Room, 1996, Sleepers, 1996, Copland, 1997, Great Expectations, 1998, 15 Minutes, 1999, Analyze This, 1999, Flawless, 1999, The Score, 2001, Showtime, 2002, Analyze That, 2002, Godsend, 2004, (voice only) Shark Tale, 2004, Hide and Seek, 2005, (voice only) Arthur and the Invisibles, 2006, Stardust, 2007, Righteous Kill, 2008, What Just Happened?, 2008; actor, exec. prodr. (films) We're No Angels, 1989, Meet the Parents, 2000, actor, prodr. Wag the Dog, 1997, actor, dir. The Adventures of Rocky and Bullwinkle, 1999, Meet the Fockers, 2004, The Good Shepherd, 2006, A Bronx Tale, 1993, City by the Sea, 2002; actor: (plays) Strange Show, 1982; prodr.: (films) Entropy, 1999, About a Boy, 2002, Stage Beauty, 2004, Rent, 2005; co-prodr.: Thunderheart, 1992; exec. prodr.: (TV films) Tribeca, 1993, Holiday Heart, 2000; (films) Faithful, 1996, Navy Driver, 2000, Conjugating Niki, 2000; narrator (documentaries) Dear America: Letters Home From Vietnam, 1987, Lenny Bruce: Swear to Tell the Truth, 1998. Recipient Hasty Pudding award, Harvard U., 1979, D.W. Griffith award for best actor, 1990; named Greatest Living Movie Star, Empire Mag., 2004. Office: c/o Tribeca Productions 375 Greenwich St New York NY 10013

DENISH, DIANE D., Lieutenant Governor of New Mexico; d. Libby Donley and Jack Daniels; m. Herb Denish; 3 children. Assoc. pub., bus. devel. and advt. sales Starlight Pub. Ltd., Albuquerque Living and N.Mex Monthly, Albuquerque; state chmn. N.Mex Dem. Party, 1999—2001; former owner Target Group; lt. gov. State of N.Mex, Santa Fe, 2003—. Chair Children's Cabinet, Mortgage Fin. Authority, Mil. Base Planning Commn., Ind. Devel. Account Adv. Coun.; active Equal Pay Task Force, Spaceport Commn., Border Authority, Fin. Independence Task Force, Workforce Devel. Bd., Commn. on Volunteerism; trustee N.Mex. Mil. Inst. Found. Bd.; former chair N.Mex. First, N.Mex. Cmty. Found., N.Mex. Tech. Bd. Regents; former mem. N.Mex. Commn. on the Status of Women; former mem. nat. adv. bd. Small Bus. Adminstrn.; pres. N.Mex. State Senate; bd. mem. Daniels Fund. Named 2003 YWCA New Mexican of Vision; named one of Top 100 New Mexicans in honor of her cmty. leadership. Democrat. Office: Office Lt Governor State Capitol Ste 417 Santa Fe NM 87501

DENMAN, DAVID, actor; b. Calif., July 25, 1973; m. Nikki Boyer. BFA, Julliard Sch.; attended, Am. Conservatory Theatre, San Francisco. Actor: (films) The Replacements, 2000, Out Cold, 2001, The Singing Detective, 2003, Big Fish, 2003, When A Stranger Calls, 2006, The Nines, 2007, If I Had Known I Was a Genius, 2007, Cake, 2007, Take, 2007, Shutter, 2008, Smart People, 2008, Fanboys, 2008; (TV films) A Vow to Cherish, 1999, The '60s, 1999, The Perfect Husband: The Laci Peterson Story, 2004; (TV series) Angel, 2001—03, The Office, 2005— (SAG award outstanding performance by an ensemble in a comedy series, 2007), (appeared on) ER, 1997, Chicago Hope, 1997, The Pretender, 1998, The X Files, 1999, Arliss, 2000, CSI: Miami, 2002, Crossing Jordan, 2002, Without A Trace, 2004, Second Time Around, 2004, Night Stalker, 2005. Office: Hofflund Polone 9465 Wilshire Blvd Ste 420 Beverly Hills CA 90212-2603

DENMARK, BERNHARDT, manufacturing executive; b. Bklyn., June 6, 1917; s. William M. and Kate (Lazarus) D.; m. Muriel Schechter, Sept. 22, 1943; children: Richard J., Karen. AB, NYU, 1941; postgrad., Am. U., 1941-42, Nat. Inst. Pub. Affairs, 1941-42. Vice pres. sales Telecoin Corp., NYC, 1946-49; v.p. sales Internat. Latex Corp., NYC, 1949-55; mgr. mktg. Playtex Co., NYC, 1955-59, v.p., gen. mgr. family products div., 1959-63, v.p. mktg., 1963-65; pres. Playtex Co. Playtex div., 1965-67, Internat. Playtex Corp., NYC, 1968-69, chmn. bd., 1969; exec. v.p., dir., mem. exec. com. Glen Alden Corp., NYC, 1969-72; pres. Bevis Industries, Inc., White Plains, NY, 1972-76, Bus. Mktg. Corp. for N.Y.C., 1977-78; chmn. Denmark, Donovan & Oppel Inc., NYC, 1978-85; chmn. bd. dirs. Advanced Photonix, Inc., Camarillo, Calif., 1992—, Xsirius, Inc., Camarillo, 1992—. Bd. dirs. Stanley Warner Corp., Schenley Industries, BVD Corp., Kleinerts Inc., Advanced Photonics Inc. Served to capt. AUS, 1942-46. Mem.: Fairview Country (Greenwich, Conn.). Home: 870 United Nations Plz Apt 34B New York NY 10017-1820

DENNEHY, BRIAN, actor; b. Bridgeport, Conn., July 9, 1938; m. Judith Scheff, 1959 (div. 1974); 3 children; m. Jennifer Arnott, 1988; 1 adopted child. BFA, Columbia U.; postgrad., Yale U. Actor: (films) Semi-Tough, 1977, F.I.S.T., 1978, Foul Play, 1978, Butch and Sundance: The Early Days, 1979, 10, 1979, Little Miss Marker, 1980, Split Image, 1982, First Blood, 1982, Never Cry Wolf, 1983, Gorky Park, 1983, The River Rat, 1984, Silverado, 1985, Cocoon, 1985, Twice in a Lifetime, 1985, F/X, 1986, Legal Eagles, 1986, Best Seller, 1987, The Belly of an Architect, 1987, Return to Snowy River, 1988, Miles from Home, 1988, Cocoon: The Return, 1988, The Last of the Finest, Seven Minutes, Presumed Innocent, 1990, F/X 2, 1991, Gladiators, 1991, Midnight Movie, 1993, Gilligan's Island: The Movie, 1997, Tommy Boy, 1995, The Stars Fell on Henrietta, 1995, Romeo and Juliet, 1996, Dish Dogs, 1998, Out of the Cold, 1999, Deep River, Finders, Keepers, Looking for Mr. Goodbar, Summer Catch, 2001, Stolen Summer, 2002, She Hate Me, 2004, Assault on Precinct 13, 2005, 10th & Wolf, 2006, Welcome to Paradise, 2006, (voice) Everyone's Hero, 2006, (voice only) Ratatouille, 2007, War Eagle, 2007, Righteous Kill, 2008; theatre appearances include Streamers, off-Broadway, 1976, The Rat in the Skull, Death of a Salesman (Tony award 1999), Wisdom Bridge Theatre, Chgo., 1985, The Cherry Orchard, Bklyn. Acad. Music, 1988, The Iceman Cometh, Goodman Theatre, Chgo., 1990, Says I, Says He, Sea Plays, Bus Stop, Julius Caesar, Ivanov, The Front Page, Translations, Galileo, A Touch of the Poet, Goodman Theatre, Chgo., MacBeth, Romeo & Juliet, 1996, Long Days Journey into Night (Tony award winner for best actor), 2003, Death of a Salesman (Laurence Olivier award best actor, 2006), Inherit the Wind, 2007, Conversations in Tusculum, 2008, Desire Under the Elms, 2009, Goodman Theatre, Chgo.; TV series) Star of the Family, 1982-83, Birdland, 1993-94; (TV movies) Annie Oakley, Showtime Cable TV Tall Tales and Legends series, 1985, Acceptable Risk, 1986, The Lion of Africa, 1987, Perfect Witness, 1989 (Cable Ace nominee), The Last of the Finest, 1990, Shattered Vows, 1993, Murder in the Heartland, 1993 (Emmy nomination, Supporting Actor - Miniseries or Special, 1993), Prophet of Evil, 1993, Foreign Affair, 1993 (CableAce award, Best Actor in a movie or miniseries), Rising Son, Bloodfeud, Evergreen, Acceptable Risks, The Terrorist, A Rumor of War, In Broad Daylight, The Last Place on Earth, Teamster Boss: The Jackie Presser Story, Birdland, Leave of Absence, Jack Reed: An Honest Cop, Final Appeal, Pride and Extreme Prejudice, (miniseries) A Killing in a Small Town, 1990 (Emmy nominee for Outstanding Supporting Actor), To Catch a Killer, 1991 (Emmy nominee, Am TV awards nominee), The Burden of Proof, 1992 (Emmy nominee for Outstanding Supporting Actor), A Season in Purgatory, 1996, Nostromo, 1996, Dead Man's Walk, 1996, Day One, Undue Influence, 1996; dir., co-writer, actor, co-exec. prodr.: (TV movies) Jack Reed: Champion of the Cheap Homicide, Jack Reed: A Killer Amoungst Us, Jack Reed: One of Our Own, Shadow of A Doubt, Jack Reed: A Search for Justice, Jack Reed: Death and Vengeance, 1996, Netforce, 1999, Too Rich: The Secret Life of Doris Duke, Fail Safe, 2000, A Season on the Brink, 2002, Our Fathers, 2005; exec. prodr. (TV films) Three Blind Mice, 2001, Warden of Red Rock, 2001, Death of a Salesmean, 2000. With USMC, Vietnam. Mem.: Sigma Chi. Office: c/o Susan Smith Co 1344 N Wetherly Dr Los Angeles CA 90069

DENNEY, LAWERENCE E., state legislator; b. Councul, Idaho, Feb. 25, 1948; m. Donna Denney; 4 children. BS, U. Idaho, 1970. Farmer, 1972—; mem. Dist. 9 Idaho House of Reps., 1991—92, 1996—, spkr. of the house, 2006—, former majority leader, former asst. majority leader. With US Army, 1971—72. Republican. Office: State Capitol Bldg PO Box 83270 Boise ID 83720-0081 Office Phone: 208-332-1000. Office Fax: 208-334-5397. Business E-Mail: ldenney@house.idaho.gov.*

DENNING, PETER JAMES, computer scientist, engineer; b. NYC, Jan. 6, 1942; s. James Edwin and Catherine M. D.; m. Dorothy Elizabeth Robling, Jan. 24, 1974; children: Anne, Diana. BEE, Manhattan Coll., 1964, ScD (hon.), 1985; MS in Elec. Engring., MIT, 1965, PhD, 1968; LLD (hon.), Concordia U., 1984; PhD (hon.), Pace U., 2002. Asst. prof. elec. engring. Princeton U., 1968-72; assoc. prof. computer scis. Purdue U., 1972-75, prof., 1975-84, head dept., 1979-83; dir. Rsch. Inst. Advanced Computer Sci. NASA Ames Rsch. Ctr., Mountain View, Calif., 1983-90, rsch. fellow, 1990-91; assoc. dean, chair of computer sci. dept. George Mason U., 1991-97, dir. Ctr. for New Engr., 1993-98, vice provost for continuing profl. edn., 1997-98, univ. coord. for process reengring., 1998-2000, spl. asst. to v.p. for info. tech., 2000—02, chair of technology coun., 2001—02; prof., chmn. computer sci. dept. Naval Postgrad. Sch., 2002—, dir. Cebrowski Inst. Info. Superiority and Innovation, 2003—, disting. prof., 2006—. Co-founder CSNET, 1981; bd. dirs. Charles Babbage Inst., 2000-04, trustee, 1997—; bd. dirs. Ctr. for Nat. Software Studies, 1996—; mem. tech. adv. bd. Sequent Computer Corp., 1985-91, Hewlett-Packard Labs., 1989-93. Author: Professional Development Seminars, 1968—, also textbooks and numerous rsch. papers; columnist Am. Scientist mag., 1985-93, ACM Comm., 2001-. Bd. dirs. Philharmonic Baroque Orchestra, San Francisco, 1988—91. Recipient Outstanding Faculty award Princeton U. Engring. Assn., 1971, Best Paper award Am. Fedn. Info. Processing Socs., 1972, Disting. Svc. to Computing Rsch. award Computing Rsch. Assn., 1989, Centennial Engring. award Manhattan Coll., 1992, Commonwealth Va. Outstanding Educator award, 2003, Engring. Best Tchr. award George Mason U., 2002, Univ. Outstanding Faculty award 2002, Hall of Fame award Spl. Interest Group on Op. Sys., 2005; NSF fellow, 1964-67, NSF Disting. Edn. fellow, 2007. Fellow IEEE, AAAS, Assn. for Computing Machinery (pres. 1980-82, Karl Karlstrom Outstanding Educator award 1996, Outstanding Contbn. award 1998, Outstanding Computer Sci. Educator award 1999, Special award for Svc. 2007), Am. Soc. for Engring. Edn., Assn. for Computing Machinery (chmn. publs. bd. and leader digital libr. project 1992-98, chmn. edn. bd. 1998—2003, dir. info. tech. profession initiative 1999-2001, editor-in-chief Computing Surveys 1977-79, Comm. ACM 1983-92, Best Paper award 1968, Recognition of Svc. award 1974, Disting. Svc. award 1989), N.Y. Acad. Scis.; mem. Sigma Xi, Eta Kappa Nu, Tau Beta Pi. Achievements include development of a working set model for program behavior, an essential element of virtual memory, computer architecture and Internet caching; important extensions to operational analysis of network systems; discovery of eight foundational practices for innovation, formulation of great principles of computing. Office: Naval Postgrad Sch Code CS Monterey CA 93943 Home Phone: 831-455-0190; Office Phone: 831-656-3603. Business E-Mail: pjd@nps.edu.

DENNIS, DAVID L., management consultant; B Econs., San Diego State U.; MBA in Fin. and Corp. Strategy, UCLA. With def. attache office Am. Embassy, Lisbon, Portugal, 1973—76; with investment banking divsn. Merrill Lynch Capital Markets; mng. dir., co-head L.A. office Donaldson, Lufkin and Jenrette, 1989—2000; vice chmn., chief corp. officer, CFO Tenet Healthcare Corp., Santa Barbara, Calif., 2000—02; mng. ptnr. Pacific Venture Group, Encino, Calif., 2004—. Bd. dir. Westwood One, 1994—. With USAF, Vietnam. Office: Pacific Venture Group Ste 244 16830 Ventura Blvd Encino CA 91436

DENNIS, EDWARD ALAN, chemistry and biochemistry professor; b. Chgo., Ill., Aug. 10, 1941; s. Sol E. and Ruth (Marks) D.; m. Martha S. Greenberg; Mar. 30, 1969; children: Jennifer, Evan, Andrew. BA in Chemistry, Yale U., 1963; MA in Chemistry, Harvard U., 1965, PhD in Chemistry, 1968; postdoctoral in Biochemistry, Harvard Med. Sch., 1967—69. NIH predoctoral fellow, Dept. Chemistry Harvard U., 1963—67, tchg. fellow, Dept. Chemistry, 1966—67; NIH postdoctoral fellow, Dept. Biological Chemistry Harvard Med. Sch., Boston, 1967-69, vis. prof., 1983-84; asst. prof. chemistry U. Calif.-San Diego, La Jolla, 1970-75, assoc. prof., 1975-81, prof., Dept. Chemistry and Biochemistry, 1981—, vice chmn. Dept. Chemistry, 1984—87, vice chmn. dept. chemistry, 1992—99, chair dept. chemistry and biochemistry, 1999—2002, prof. dept. pharmacology, 1999—, prof. Dept Pharmacology, 2003—. Mem. NSF adv. panels, 1981-85; chmn. Faculty Acad. Senate U. Calif., 1987-88, mem. bd. overseers, 1988—; vis. scientist Brandeis U., 1984; cons. to pharm. industry; adj. prof., Dept. Immunology, Scripps Rsch. Inst., 1999-. Editor: Methods in Enzymology Cumulative Indexes, 1975-85, Phospholipases, 1991, Phospholipid Biosynthesis, 1992, Lipases, 1996, Handbook of Cell Signaling, 2003, Jour. Lipid Rsch., 2003; mem. editl. bd. Jour. Biol. Chemistry, 1988-93, Jour. Cellular Biochemistry, 1986—; contbr. over 250 articles to profl. jours.; patentee in field. Recipient Avanti award in lipid enzymology, 2000; Guggenheim fellow, 1983-84; grantee NSF, 1970—, NIH, 1970—. Fellow: AAAS; mem.: Internat. Assn. Colloid and Interface Scientists, Internat. Soc. on Toxinology, NY Acad. Sci., Am. Assn. Med. Grad. Depts. Biochemistry (bd. dir., pres.), Am. Soc. Biol. Chemists (membership com. 1979—81, program chair 1996), Am. Chem. Soc., Biophys. Soc. (chmn. biopolymers subgroup 1981—82), Alpha Chi Sigma Chemical, Protein Soc., Sigma Xi. Office: U Calif Dept Chemistry and Biochemistry 9500 Gilman Drive La Jolla CA 92093-0601 Office Phone: 858-534-3055. Office Fax: 858-534-7390. E-mail: edennis@ucsd.edu.

DENNIS, GIGI (GINETTE E. DENNIS), former state official; b. Kansas City, Mo., Nov. 28, 1961; m. Dean Dennis. Student, Adams State Coll., U. So. Colo., Harvard U. With Band of Monte Vista, 1982-87; customer svc. rep. Pub. Svc. Co. Colo., Alamosa, 1987-91, Pueblo, 1991-94; mem. Colo. State Senate from dist. 5, Denver, 1995—2001; dir. rural devel USDA, Denver, 2001—05; sec. state State of Colo., Denver, 2005—07. Bd. mem. El Pueblo Boys and Girls Ranch; active Sangre de Cristo Arts Ctr., Rosemount Mus.; sec., past sec. Rio Grande County Reps.; past chair Ho. Dist. 60; mem. Local, State and Nat. Campaign Com., 1984—. Mem. Pueblo Zool. Soc., Bel Nor Rep. Women, Monte Vista C. of C., Pueblo West Rotary, Colo. Cattle Assn. Republican. Roman Catholic.

DENNIS, KAREN MARIE, plastic surgeon; b. Cleve., Dec. 23, 1948; d. Chester and Adele (Wesley) D.; m. Miles Auslander, June 21, 1974; 1 child, Kristin. BS, Ohio State U., 1971, MD, 1974. Diplomate Am. Bd. Plastic Surgery, Am. Bd. Otolaryngology. Intern Kaiser Permanent, LA, 1974-75; resident in otolaryngology Roosevelt Hosp., NYC, 1976-79; resident in plastic surgery Ohio State Univ. Hosps., Columbus, 1979-81; pvt. practice Beverly Hills, Calif., 1981—. Mem. Am. Soc. Reconstructive and Plastic Surgeons, Calif. County Med. Assn., L.A. County med. Assn., L.A. Soc. Plastic Srugeons (sec. 1993-94), Phi Beta Kappa. Avocations: tennis, golf, travel, reading.

DENNISON, GEORGE MARSHEL, academic administrator; b. Buffalo, Ill., Aug. 11, 1935; s. Earl Fredrick and Irene Gladys (McWhorter) D.; m. Jane Irene Schroeder, Dec. 26, 1954; children: Robert Gene, Rick Steven. AA, Custer County (Mont.) Jr. Coll., 1960; BA, U. Mont., 1962, MA, 1963; PhD, U. Wash., 1967. Asst. prof. U.

Ark., Fayetteville, 1967-68; vis. asst. prof. U. Wash., Seattle, 1968-69; asst. prof. Colo. State U., Fort Collins, 1969-73, assoc. prof., 1973-77, assoc. dean Coll. Arts, Humanities and Social Sci., 1976-80, prof., 1977-87, acting acad. v.p., 1980-82, acting assoc. acad. v.p., 1982-86, assoc. acad. v.p., 1987; provost, v.p. acad. affairs Western Mich. U., Kalamazoo, 1987-90; pres. U. Mont., Missoula, 1990—. Cons. U.S. Dept. Justice, 1976-84; bd. dirs. Inst. Medicine and Humanities, Missoula, Internat. Heart Inst. Mont., Missoula. Author: The Dorr War, 1976; contbr. articles to jours. in field. Bd. dirs. Kalamazoo Ctr. for Med. Studies, 1989-90, Missoula Rocky Mountain Coll., Billings, Mont. Campus Compact, Internat; Maureen & Mike Mansfield Found.; bd. dirs., chair Student Exchange Program; chair Mont. Commn. Cmty. Svc.; presdl. appointee Nat. Security Edn. Bd. With USN, 1953-57. ABA grantee, 1969-70; Colo. State U. grantee, 1970-75, Nat. Trust for Hist. Preservation grantee, 1976-78; U.S. Agy. for Internat. Devel. grantee, 1979—; Colo. Commn. on Higher Edn. devel. grantee, 1985. Mem. Am. Hist. Assn., Orgn. Am. Historians, Am. Assn. Higher Edn., Am. Soc. for Legal History. Avocations: handball, cross country skiing. Office: U Montana Office of The Pres Univ UH 109 Missoula MT 59812-0001 Business E-Mail: dennisongm@mso.umt.edu.

DENNISON, RONALD WALTON, engineer; b. Oct. 23, 1944; s. S. Mason and Elizabeth Louise (Hatcher) D.; m. Deborah Ann Rutter, Aug. 10, 1991; children: Ronald, Frederick. BS in Physics and Math., San Jose State U., 1970, MS in Physics, 1972. Physicist Memorex, Santa Clara, 1970—71; sr. engr. AVCO, San Jose, Calif., 1972—73; advanced devel. engr. Perkin Elmer, Palo Alto, Calif., 1973—75; staff engr. Hewlett-Packard, Santa Rosa, Calif., 1975—79; program gen. mgr. Burroughs, Westlake Village, Calif., 1979—82; dir. engring., founder EIKON, Simi Valley, Calif., 1982—85; sr. staff technologist Maxtor Corp., San Jose, 1987—90; dir. engring. Toshiba Am. Info. Sys., 1990—93, cons. engr., 1994—. Author: tech. publs. Sgt. USAF, 1963—67. Mem.: IEEE, Internat. Comanche Soc., Aircraft Owners and Pilots Assn., Internat. Disk Drive Equipment and Materials Assn., Internat. Soc. Hybrid Microelectronics, Am. Vacuum Soc. Republican. Methodist. Home: 4050 Soelro Ct San Jose CA 95127-2711 Office Phone: 408-929-7023. E-mail: ron@rondennison.com.

DENNY, JAMES M., pharmaceutical and former retail executive; Former exec. v.p., chief fin. and planning officer G.D. Searle & Co.; former chmn. Pearle Heath Svcs. Inc., Dallas; former CFO & vice chmn. Sears, Roebuck & Co.; bd. dir. Gilead Sciences Inc., Foster City, Calif., 1996—, chmn., 2001—08, lead dir., 2008—. Former dir. Astra AB; sr. advisor William Blair Capital Partners, LLC, 1995—2000; bd. dirs. Allstate Corp., GATX Corp., ChoicePoint, Inc. Chnm. Northwestern Memorial Found. Office: Gilead Sciences Inc 333 Lakeside Dr Foster City CA 94404

DENSLEY, COLLEEN T., principal; b. Provo, Utah, Apr. 12, 1950; d. Floyd and Mary Lou (Dixon) Taylor; m. Steven T. Densley, July 23, 1968; children: Steven, Tiffany, Landon, Marianne, Wendy, Logan. BS in Elem. Edn., Brigham Young U., 1986, MEd in Tchg. and Learning, 1998. Cert. in elem. edn., K-12 adminstrn. Utah. Substitute tchr. Provo Sch. Dist., 1972-85, curriculum specialist, 1999-2001; tchr. 6th grade, mainstreaming program Canyon Crest Elem. Sch., Provo, 1985—94; instructional facilitator Campus Crest Elem., 1994—99; prin. Wasatch Elem. Sch., Provo, 2001—. Tchr. asst., math. tutor Brigham Young U., 1968—69; attendee World Gifted and Talented Conf., Salt Lake City, 1987, Tchr. Expectations and Student Achievement, 1988—89, Space Acad. for Educators, Huntsville, Ala., 1992; supr. coop. tchr. for practicum tchrs., 1987—90; co-chmn. accelerated learning and devel. com.; trainee working with handicapped students in mainstream classroom, 1989; mem. elem. sch. lang. arts curriculum devel. com., 90; mem. task force Thinking Strategies Curriculum, 1990—91; extensions specialist gifted and talented, 1990—91; math, 1991—; master tchr. Nat. Tchr. Tng. Inst., 1993. Co-author: (curricula) Provo Sch. Dist.'s Microorganism Sci. Kit, 1988, Arthropod Sci. Kit, 1988, Tchg. for Thinking, 1990—, PAWS Presents the Internet and the World Wide Web, 1997. Recipient Honor Young Mother of Yr. award, State of Utah, 1981, Mayor's award of Excellence, Provo, Utah, 2003; named Utah State Tchr. of the Yr., 1992. Mem.: NEA, Provo Edn. Assn. (Tchr. of the Yr. 1991—92), Internat. Space Edn. Initiative (adv. bd.), Utah Coun. Tchrs. Math., Utah Edn. Assn., Nat. Coun. Tchrs. Math. Republican. Mem. Lds Ch. Office: Wasatch Elem Sch 1080 N 900 E Provo UT 84604 Office Phone: 801-374-4910. Business E-Mail: colleend@provo.edu.

DENSON, CHARLES D., apparel executive; b. Corvallis, Oreg. BA in Bus., Utah State U., Logan, 1978. Asst. store mgr. The Athletic Dept., Portland, Oreg., 1979—80; East coast sports mktg. rep. coll. basketball, pro football and pro baseball Nike, Inc., Boston, 1980—81, Futures 1 customer svc. mgr. Western US Portland, 1981—82, sales rep. footwear & apparel LA, 1982—89, So. Calif. footwear sales mgr., 1989—90, strategic accounts apparel GMM Portland, 1990—91, Foot Locker Footwear GMM, 1991, head sales tng. & devel., 1992, dir. SAI (FootAction, TSA, JCP, TFL and TAF), 1993—94, dir. USA apparel sales, 1994, dir. US sales, 1994—97, v.p. European sales Hilversum, Netherlands, 1997—98, v.p., gen. mgr. NIKE Europe, 1998—2000, v.p., gen. mgr. NIKE USA, 2000—01, pres. NIKE Brand, 2001—. Named one of The Most Influential People in the World of Sports, Bus. Week, 2007. Office: Nike Inc One Bowerman Dr Beaverton OR 97005-6453 Office Phone: 503-671-6453.

DENSON, NIKKOLE E., beverage company executive, film producer; b. 1971; JD, U. San Francisco Law Sch. Prodn. asst. Paramount Studios, 1996—99; head movie divsn., fmr. LA Laker Earvin "Magic" Johnson, 1999—2004; dir. bus. devel. Starbucks Entertainment, 2004—. Prodr.: (films) Brown Sugar, 2002, Hair Show, 2004. Named a Maverick, Details mag., 2007. Office: Starbucks Corp Hdqs 2401 Utah Ave S Seattle WA 98134 Office Phone: 206-447-1575.

DENTON, CHARLES MANDAVILLE, corporate communications specialist, journalist; b. Glendale, Calif., June 22, 1924; s. Horace Bruce and Marguerite (Mandaville) D.; m. Jean Margaret Brady, Dec. 3, 1955; children— Charles Mandaville II, Margot Elizabeth. Student, U. Calif., 1942, Okla. A. and M. Coll., 1943; BA in Journalism, U. So. Calif., 1949. Reporter San Fernando Valley Times, N. Hollywood, Calif., 1949-50, U.P., Los Angeles, 1950-52; reporter, sportswriter, columnist I.N.S., Los Angeles, 1952-59; reporter, feature writer, TV editor-columnist Los Angeles Examiner, 1959-62; free-lance TV and mag. writer, 1962-63; reporter Los Angeles Times, 1963; columnist San Francisco Examiner, 1963-68; communications dir. Leslie Salt Co., San Francisco, 1968-73. Comm. dir. Crown Zellerbach Corp., San Francisco, 1973-83; v.p. Hilland Knowlton Inc., 1983-90. Author: (with Dr. W. Coda Martin) A Matter of Life, 1964. Pres. Greater Los Angeles Press Club Welfare Found., 1961. Served with USNR, 1943-46. Mem. Phi Beta Kappa, Phi Kappa Phi, Sigma Delta Chi, Blue Key. Clubs: Greater Los Angeles Press (pres. 1955-57), Tiburon Peninsula, Bohemian. Home and Office: 226 Monte Vista Ave Larkspur CA 94939-2026 Fax: (415) 435-0454. E-mail: chzdenton@aol.com.

DENTON, JAMES, actor; b. Nashville, Jan. 20, 1963; m. Jenna Lyn Ward (div. 2000); m. Erin O'Brien, 2002; children: Sheppard, Malin. Grad. with honors, U. Tenn., Knoxville. Actor: (films) Thieves Quartet, 1994, Hunter's Moon, 1995, That Old Feeling, 1997, Face/Off, 1997, Primary Colors, 1998, Jumbo Girl, 2004; (TV series, guest appearance) Moloney, 1996, Dark Skies, 1996, JAG, 1996, 2003, Two Guys, a Girl and a Pizza Place, 2000, Ally McBeal, 2000, The West Wing, 2000, The Pretender, 2000, Philly, 2001, The Drew Carey Show, 2002, Reba, 2005; (TV films) The Pretender 2001, 2001, The Pretender: Island of the Haunted, 2001; (TV series) Threat Matrix, 2003, Desperate Housewives, 2004— (Screen Actors Guild Award for outstanding performance by an ensemble in a comedy series, 2005, 2006, TV Choice Actor, Teen Choice Awards, 2006). Office: Desperate Housewives Touchstone Television 100 Universal City Plaza Bldg 2128 Ste G Universal City CA 91608

DENVER, THOMAS HR, lawyer; b. NYC, Oct. 29, 1944; s. Thomas H. Rorke and Eileen Ann Boland; m. Barbara Ann Denver, Dec. 19, 1987; children: Rorke, Nate. BS, Syracruse U., 1966; MS, U. Wash., 1967; JD, U. Calif., San Francisco, 1973. Bar: Calif. 1973, U.S. Dist. Ct. (no. dist.) Calif. 1973. From assoc. to mng. ptnr. Hoge, Fenton, Jones & Appel, Inc., San Jose, Calif., 1973—99. Judge pro tem Santa Clara County Superior Ct., San Jose, 1980—; instr. Stanford U. Law Sch. Advocacy Program; mem. faculty Hastings Coll. of Advocacy; mediator, arbitrator. Contbr. articles to profl. jours. Fellow Am. Coll. Trial Lawyers; mem. Am. Bd. Trial Advocates, Santa Clara County Civil Litigation Com., Santa Clara County Bar Assn Avocations: running, fishing, reading. Office: Mediation Masters 96 N Third St # 300 San Jose CA 95112 Office Phone: 408-535-3298. Business E-Mail: tdenver@mediationmasters.com.

DENZEL, NORA MANLEY, information technology executive; b. 1962; m. John M. Denzel. BS in Computer Sci., SUNY, Plattsburgh, 1984; MS in bus. admin., Santa Clara U., Calif. Various engring., mktg. and exec. roles to worldwide dir. storage software products IBM Corp., 1984—97; sr. v.p. product ops. Legato Systems, Inc., 1997—2000; gen. mgr., v.p. network storage solutions orgn. Hewlett Packard Co., 2000—02, sr. v.p., gen. mgr. software global bus. unit, 2002—06, sr. v.p. adaptive enterprises, 2004—05; ind. cons., 2006—08; sr. v.p. payroll svc. divsn. Intuit Inc., Mountain View, Calif., 2008—. Spkr. about computer technology and women's advancement in technology careers; mem. tech. adv. bd. of startup co.; bd. dirs. Overland Storage Inc., 2007—. Bd. trustees Anita Borg Inst. for Women & Tech., 2008—; mem. adv. bd. Santa Clara Univ. Bus. Sch., Women in Technology Internat., several private technology companies, Calif. C. of C.; mentors young executives in high tech careers WOMEN unlimited Program. Recipient Tribute to Women in Industry, YWCA, Santa Clara County; named Most Powerful People in Computer Networking, Networking World Mag.; named one of Top 20 Storage Movers and Shakers, Storage, Inc., Top 50 Tech. Women of the Next Millennium, Feminine Fortunes Mag., 50 Most Powerful People in Networking, Network World mag., 2003. Office: Intuit Inc 2632 Marine Way Mountain View CA 94043

DEOLALIKAR, ANIL B., economics professor, researcher; b. Baroda, India, Mar. 17, 1956; s. Bapu R. and Lata B. Deolalikar; m. Pama A. Khandekar; children: Nisha A., Sunil A. BA summa cum laude, Harvard Coll., Cambridge, Mass., 1977; PhD, Stanford U., Calif., 1981. Prof. economics U. Wash., Seattle, 1989—2002, U. Calif., Riverside, 2003—. Fellow: Am. Assn. Advancement Sci. Office: Univ California Dept Economics Sproul Hall 4120 900 Univ Ave Riverside CA 92521 Business E-Mail: anil.deolalikar@ucr.edu.

DE PALMA, BRIAN RUSSELL, film director; b. Newark, Sept. 11, 1940; s. Anthony Fredrick and Vivenne (Muti) DePalma; m. Nancy Allen, Jan. 12, 1979 (div. 1983); m. Gale Anne Hurd, July 20, 1991 (div.); 1 child, Lolita; m. Darnell Gregorio-De Palma, Oct. 11, 1995 (div. Apr. 18, 1997); 1 child, Piper. BA, Columbia Coll., 1962; MA, Sarah Lawrence Coll., 1964. Dir., prod., writer: (films) The Wedding Party, 1969, Home Movies, 1980, Body Double, 1984, Snake Eyes, 1998; dir., prod.: Carrie, 1976 (Avoriaz prize 1977), The Bonfire of the Vanities, 1990; dir., writer: Murder a la Mod, 1968, Greetings, 1968 (Silver Bear Berlin Film Festival award 1969), Hi Mom!, 1970, Sisters, 1973, Phantom of the Paradise, 1974 (Grand prize 1975), Obsession, 1976, Dressed to Kill, 1980, Blow Out, 1981, Raising Cain, 1992, Femme Fatale, 2002, Redacted, 2007; dir.: Get to Know Your Rabbit, 1972, The Fury, 1978, Blow Out, 1981, Scarface, 1983, Wise Guys, 1986, The Untouchables, 1987, Casualties of War, 1989, Carlito's Way, 1993, Mission Impossible, 1996, Mission to Mars, 2000, The Black Dahlia, 2006, Redacted, 2007; (short films) Icarus, 1960, 660124: The Story of an IBM Card, 1961, Woton's Wake, 1962 (Rosenthal Found. award 1963), Jennifer, 1964, Bridge That Gap, 1965, Show Me a Strong Town and I'll Show You a Strong Bank, 1966; (documentaries) The Responsive Eye, 1966, Dionysus in '69, 1970 Office: Creative Artists Agency 2000 Avenue Of The Stars Los Angeles CA 90067-4700

DE PASSE, SUZANNE, record company executive; b. NYC, 1947; m. Paul Le Mat. Student, Manhattan Cmty. Coll. Talent coord. Cheetah Disco, NYC; various positions including creative asst., prodr. Motown Prodns., LA, 1968-81, pres., 1981—89; CEO de Passe Entertainment (formerly Motown Prodns.), LA, 1989—. Acts signed and developed for Motown include The Commodores, The Jackson Five, Frankie Valli and the Four Seasons, Lionel Richie, Thelma Houston, Billy Preston, Teena Marie, Rick James, Stephanie Mills; co-author screenplay for film Lady Sings the Blues (Acad. award nomination); exec. producer: (TV miniseries) Lonesome Dove, (TV series) Motown on Showtime, Nightlife starring David Brenner, Motown Revue starring Smokey Robinson, Motown Returns to the Apollo (Emmy award, NAACP Image award), (TV spl.) Motown 25: Yesterday, Today, Forever (Emmy award, NAACP Image award); writer: (TV spls.) Happy Endings, Jackson 5 Goin' Back to Indiana, Diana; creative cons: Git on Broadway-Diana Ross & The Supremes & Temptations, TCB-Diana Ross & The Supremes & Temptations. Named to Black Filmmakers Hall of Fame, 1980, Power 150, Ebony mag., 2008. Mem.: Alpha Kappa Alpha Sorority, Inc. (hon.). Office: Releve Entertainment 6255 W Sunset Blvd Ste 923 Los Angeles CA 90028-7410

DEPATIE, DAVID HUDSON, motion picture company executive; b. LA, Dec. 24, 1930; s. Edmond LaVoie and Dorothy (Hudson) DeP.; m. Marcia Lee MacPherson, June 1972; children: David Hudson, Steven Linn, Michael Linn. Student, U. of South, 1947-48; AB, U. Calif.-Berkeley, 1951. With Warner Bros. Pictures, Inc., 1951-63, v.p., gen. mgr. comml. and cartoon films div., 1963; pres. DePatie-Freleng Enterprises, Inc., Van Nuys, Calif., 1963—; founder, proprietor The DePatie Vineyards, 1983-90. Producer: Pink Panther and Inspector theatrical cartoon series; TV series The New Mr. Magoo; TV live-action and animation spl. The Hoober Bloob Highway; TV spl. Clerow Wilson Great Escape; TV series The Houndcats and the Barkleys; Christmas TV spls. The Tiny Tree; ABC aftersch. spl. My Mom's Having a Baby (recipient Emmy award); Dr. Seuss spl. Halloween Is Grinch Night (recipient Emmy award), Fantastic Four, Spider-Woman, The Pink Panther Christmas Special, The Bugs Bunny Christmas Special, Spider-Man & his Amazing Friends, The Pink Panther in Pink at First Sight, Pink Panther & Sons, 1985; Dr. Seuss Spls. The Grinch Grinchesthe Cat-In-The-Hat (Emmy award 1982); others.; nominated for Emmy award 1974-75; exec. producer: The Incredible Hulk, Pandamonium, Meatballs and Spaghetti, Dungeons and Dragons. Recipient First award for the Lorax Zagreb Internat. Film Festival, 1972; recipient Emmy Award for Dr. Seus special The Grinch Grinches The Cat-in-the Hat, 1982; Calif. State Fair Double Gold award for Best Zinfandel Wine of 1983, 1985, Wine & Spirits Mag. Am. Champion Zinfandel wine of 1984, 1986. Mem. Acad. Motion Picture Arts and Scis. (Oscar award for Pink Panther 1964), Soc. Motion Picture Editors, Phi Gamma Delta. Republican. Episcopalian. Office: DePatie-Freleng Enterprises Inc 3425 Stiles Ave Camarillo CA 93010-3900

DEPINTO, DAVID J., public relations executive; BA in Polit. Sci., Brown U.; MBA, U. So. Calif. Dir. mktg., pub. rels., pub. affairs Coca-Cola Bottling Co., LA; exec. v.p. Pacific/West Comm. Group, LA; pres., CEO Stoorza Comm., Inc., San Diego. Mem. bd. dirs. L.A. Ednl. Partnership, Adopt-A-School-Coun. L.A. Unified Sch. Dist., Crescenta Youth Sports Assn.

DEPP, JOHNNY, actor; b. Owensboro, Ky., June 9, 1963; s. John and Betty Sue Depp; m. Lori Anne Allison Dec. 20, 1983 (div. 1985); children: Lily-Rose Melody, Jack. Guitarist; ex-member bands the Flame, the Kids, Rock City Angels, 1985; actor TV series 21 Jump Street, 1987-90; actor (films) A Nightmare on Elm Street, 1984, Private Resort, 1985, Platoon, 1986, Cry-Baby, 1990, Edward Scissorhands, 1990, Freddy's Dead: The Final Nightmare, 1991, American Dreamers, 1992, Benny & Joon, 1993, What's Eating Gilbert Grape, 1993, Ed Wood, 1994, Arizona Dreamer, Don Juan DeMarco, 1995, Dead Man, 1995, Nick of Time, 1996, Donnie Brasco, 1997, The Astronaut's Wife, 1998, L.A. Without a Map, 1998, Fear and Loathing in Las Vegas, 1998, The Source, 1999, The Ninth Gate, 1999, Just to Be Together, 1999, The Astronaut's Wife, 1999, Sleepy Hollow, 1999, The Source, 1999, The Man Who Cried, 2000, Chocolat, 2000, Blow, 2001, From Hell, 2001, Pirates of the Caribbean: The Curse of the Black Pearl, 2003 (Screen Actors Guild Award for best actor, 2004, Acad. Award nomination for best actor, 2004, Golden Globe nomination for best actor in a musical or comedy, 2004), Once Upon A Time in Mexico, 2003, Secret Window, 2004, Ils se marièrent et eurent beaucoup d'enfants, 2004, Finding Neverland, 2004, The Libertine, 2004, Charlie and the Chocolate Factory, 2005 (Choice Movie Actor: Comedy, Teen Choice awards, 2006), (voice) Corpse Bride, 2005, (narrator) Deep Sea 3D, 2006, Pirates of the Caribbean: Dead Man's Chest, 2006 (Choice Movie Actor: Drama/Action Adventure, Teen Choice awards, 2006, Best Performance, MTV Movie Awards, 2007), Pirates of the Caribbean: At World's End, 2007 (Choice Movie Actor: Action Adventure, Teen Choice Awards, 2007, Best Comedic Performance, MTV Movie Awards, 2008, Best Villain, 2008), Sweeney Todd: The Demon Barber of Fleet Street, 2007 (Best Performance by an Actor in a Motion Picture - Musical or Comedy, Golden Globe award, Hollywood Fgn. Press Assn., 2008, Choice Movie Villain, Teen Choice Awards, 2008); writer, dir., actor: The Brave, 1997; TV movies include Slow Burn, 1986; TV guest appearances include Lady Blue, 1985, Hotel, 1987, The Vicar of Dibley, 1999, (voice) King of the Hill, 2004; (video-voice) Kingdom Hearts II, 2005. Named Favorite Male Movie Star, People's Choice Awards, 2006, 2008, Favorite Male Star, Favorite Male Action Star & On-screen matchup (Keira Knightly), 2007, Favorite Movie Actor, Nickelodeon Kids Choice Awards, 2008; named one of Time Mag. 100 Most Influential People, 2005, 50 Most Powerful People in Hollywood, Premiere mag., 2004, 2005, 2006, The 100 Most Powerful Celebrities, Forbes.com, 2007, 2008, Top 25 Entertainers of Yr., Entertainment Weekly, 2007, 50 Smartest People in Hollywood, 2007. Office: 9100 Wilshire Blvd Ste 725E Beverly Hills CA 90212-3441

DEPRATU, ROBERT L., state legislator; b. Eureka, Mont., July 21, 1939; m. Beatrice DePratu. AA, Kinman Bus. Coll. Owner DePartu Ford, VW and Audi; mem. Mont. Senate, Dist. 40, Helena, 1996—; chair joint select com. on jobs and income; vice chair taxation com., mem. hwys. and transp. com.; mem. pub. health, welfare and safety com. Republican. Office: PO Box 1217 6331 Hwy 93 S Whitefish MT 59937-8236 E-mail: bobbe@digisys.net.

DEPUY, CHARLES HERBERT, chemist, educator; b. Detroit, Sept. 10, 1927; s. Carroll E. and Helen (Plehn) DeP.; m. Eleanor Burch, Dec. 21, 1949; children: David Gareth, Nancy Ellen, Stephen Baylie, Katherine Louise. BS, U. Calif., Berkeley, 1948; A.M., Columbia U., 1952; PhD, Yale U., 1953. Asst. prof. chemistry Iowa State U., 1953-59, asso. prof., 1959-62, prof., 1962-63; prof. chemistry U. Colo., Boulder, 1963-92, prof. emeritus, 1992—. Vis. prof. U. Ill., summer 1954, U. Calif., Berkeley, summer 1960; NIH sr. postdoctoral fellow U. Basel, Switzerland, 1969-70; cons. A.E. Staley Co., 1956-80, Marathon Oil Co., 1964-89. Author: (with Kenneth L. Rinehart) Introduction to Organic Chemistry, 1967, rev. edit., 1975, (with Orville L. Chapman) Molecular Reactions and Photochemistry, 1970, (with Robert H. Shapiro) Exercises in Organic Spectroscopy; contbr. articles profl. jours. Served wih AUS, 1946-47. John Simon Guggenheim fellow, 1977-78, 86-87; Alexander von Humboldt fellow, 1988-89, James Flack Norris Award, Am. Chem. Soc., 2001. Fellow AAAS; mem. Am. Chem. Soc. (exec. com. organic div., chmn. Colo. sect., mem. adv. bd. jour. 1987-92, gold medal), Sigma Xi, Nat. Acad of Sci., 1999, Am. Acad. of Arts and Sci., 2003. Home: 1509 Cascade Ave Boulder CO 80302-7631 Office: U Colo Boulder Dept Chemistry & Biochemistry PO Box 215 Boulder CO 80309-0215 Office Phone: 303-492-7652. Business E-Mail: charles.depuy@colorado.edu.

DER, DAVID F., family practice physician, retired general surgeon; married. MD, Howard Univ. Sr. ptnr., chief surgeon Bay Valley Med. Group, Hayward, Calif.; ret.; exec. dir. Chinese Am. Physicians' Soc.; currently family physician Alta Bates Summit Med. Ctr., Oakland, Calif. Asian Outreach Adv. Com. Alta Bates Summit Med. Ctr. Founder Asian Health Svcs., Oakland, 1974, Hong Fook Senior Health Care Ctr., Oakland, 1986. Recipient Benjamin Rush award for Citizenship and Comty. Svc., AMA, 2006. Mem.: Calif. Med. Assn. (bd. trustee 2006—08), Fedn. Chinese Am. and Chinese Canadian Med. Societies (sec.). Office: Prime Med Assocs Inc 817 Harrison St Oakland CA 94607 Office Phone: 510-451-8088. E-mail: daveder44@hotmail.com.

DERBES, DANIEL WILLIAM, manufacturing executive; b. Cin., Mar. 30, 1930; s. Earl Milton and Ruth Irene (Grauten) Derbes; m. Patricia Maloney, June 4, 1952; children: Donna Ann, Nancy Lynn(dec.), Stephen Paul. BS, U.S. Mil. Acad., 1952; MBA, Xavier U., Cin., 1963. Devel. engr. AiResearch Mfg. Co., Phoenix, 1956-58; with Garrett Corp., LA, 1958-80, v.p., gen. mgr., then exec. v.p., 1975-80, dir., 1976-87; pres. Signal Cos., Inc., La Jolla, Calif., 1980—82, Signal Advanced Tech Group, 1982—85, Allied-Signal Internat. Inc., 1985-88; exec. v.p. Allied-Signal, Inc., Morristown, NJ, 1985-88; pres. Signal Ventures, Solana Beach, Calif., 1990—2004. Chmn. bd. dirs. WD-40 Co.; bd. dirs. Sempra Energy, Oak Industries. Exec. bd. nat. coun. Boy Scouts Am., 1981—95; trustee U. San Diego, 1981—2005, vice-chmn., trustee, 1990—93, chmn., 1993—96, trustee emeritus, 2006. With US Army, 1952—56. Republican. Roman Catholic. Personal E-mail: dwderbes@aol.com.

DERBY, JILL TALBOT, anthropologist, educator, consultant; b. Lovelock, Nev., Apr. 19, 1940; d. Thomas R. and Helen Margaret (Moody) D.; m. Stephen C. Talbot, June 2, 1973; children: Ryan, Tobyn. BS, U. Calif., San Francisco, 1962; BA, U. Nev., Las Vegas, 1970; MA, U. Calif., Davis, 1974, PhD, 1988. Lic. dental hygienist, Calif., Nev. Dental hygienist, Berkeley, Oakland, Calif., 1962-65; lectr., clin. instr. U. Calif., San Francisco, 1965-66; health educator, tng. coord. Aramco, Dhahran, Saudi Arabia, 1966-69; dental hygienist Berkeley, Lake Tahoe, 1971-80; part-time instr. Western Nev. C.C., Carson City, 1974-76, Sierra Nev. Coll., Incline Village, 1977-79; dir. D & R Assocs., Genoa, Nev., 1982-90; regent Univ. and Cmty. Coll. System Nev., Reno, 1988—2006. Cons., lectr. Derby Enterprises, Gardnerville, Nev., 1980-94; conf. spkr., lectr. over 200 orgns., Nev., Calif., 1980-94. Contbr. articles to profl. jours. State chair Nev. Women's Polit. Caucus, 1979-81, mem. nat. steering com., Washington, 1979-82; appointee Judicial Selection Commn. State of Nev., Carson City, 1986, Supreme Ct. Gender Bias Task Force, Carson City, 1987; mem. leadership team Bi-State Coalition for Peace; chair Nev. State Dem. Party 2007-2008. Grad. scholar U. Calif., Nat. Episcopal Ch., 1972-77; recipient Woman Helping Women award Soroptimists Internat., 1988, Woman of Distinction award, 1990. Mem. Western Social Sci. Assn., Assn. Governing Bds., Assn. C.C. Trustees (state rep. 1991—), Assn. Jr. and C.C. Trustees, Rural Sociol. Soc., Phi Kappa Phi. Democrat. Episcopalian. Avocations: hiking, bicycling, cross country skiing. Home: 1298 Kingsbury Grade Gardnerville NV 89410-7714 Office: Univ & CC System Nev 2601 Enterprise Rd Reno NV 89512-1666

DERDENGER, PATRICK, lawyer; b. LA, June 29, 1946; s. Charles Patrick and Drucilla Marguerite (Lange) D.; m. Jo Lynn Dickins, Aug. 24, 1968; children: Kristin Lynn, Bryan Patrick, Timothy Patrick. BA, Loyola U., LA, 1968; MBA, U. So. Calif., 1971, JD, 1974; LLM in Taxation, George Washington U., 1977. Bar: Calif. 1974, US Ct. Claims 1975, Ariz. 1979, US Ct. Appeals (9th cir.) 1979, US Dist. Ct. Ariz. 1979, US Tax Ct. 1979, US Supreme Ct. 1979; cert. specialist in tax law. Trial atty. honors program US Dept. Justice, Washington, 1974—78; ptnr. Lewis and Roca, Phoenix, 1978—2000, Steptoe and Johnson, LLP, 2000—. Adj. prof. taxation Golden Gate U., Phoenix, 1983-87; mem. Ariz. State Tax Ct. Legis. Study Commn., Tax Law Specialist Commn., Ariz. Property Tax Oversight Commn.; appt. Ariz. Property Tax Oversight Commn., 1997—. Author: Arizona State and Local Taxation, Cases and Materials, 1983, Arizona Sales and Use Tax Guide, 1990, Advanced Arizona Sales and Use Tax, 1987-96, Arizona State and Local Taxation, 1989, 93, 96, Arizona Sales and Use Tax, 1988-96. Arizona Property Taxation, 1993-96, ABA Sales and Use Tax Deskbook, Property Tax Deskbook. Past pres., bd. dirs. North Scottsdale Little League; apptd. Ariz. Property Tax Oversight Commn. Served to capt. USAF, 1968-71. Recipient US Law Week award Bur. Nat. Affairs, 1974. Mem. ABA (taxation sect., various coms.), Ariz. Bar Assn. (taxation sect., former chair sect. taxation, former treas., chmn. state and local tax com., chmn. continuing legal edn. com., tax adv. com., others, mem. tax law specialist commn.), Maricopa County Bar Assn., Inst. Sales Taxation, Nat. Tax Assn., Inst. Property Taxation Met. C. of C., Ariz. C. of C. (chair tax com.), U. So. Calif. Alumni Club (past pres., bd. dirs.), Phi Delta Phi. Home: 10040 E Happy Valley Rd Scottsdale AZ 85255-2395 Office: Steptoe & Johnson LLP 201 E Washington St Fl 16 Phoenix AZ 85004-4453 Office Phone: 602-257-5209. Business E-Mail: pderdenger@steptoe.com.

DERENZO, STEPHEN E., electrical engineering and computer science educator, researcher; b. Chgo., Dec. 31, 1941; married, 1966; 2 children. BS in Physics, U. Chgo., 1963, MS in Physics, 1965, PhD in Physics, 1968. Rsch. asst. Enrico Fermi Inst. U. Chgo., 1964-68; physicist Lawrence Berkeley Lab. U. Calif., Berkeley, 1968-82, lectr. dept. physics, 1969-70, lectr. dept. elec. engring. and computer sci., 1979-87, sr. scientist Lawrence Berkeley Lab., 1982—, prof., 1988—. Grant application reviewer U.S. Dept. Energy, U.S. Nat. Insts. Health; co-chmn. Internat. Workshop on Bismuth Germanate, Princeton U., 1982; active numerous coms. Lawrence Berkeley Lab., U. Calif., mem. recreation adv. panel, 1984-87, mem. computer svc. adv. panel, 1985-88, quality assurance coord. bio-med divsn., 1986-88, asst. dir. rsch. medicine and radiation biophysics divsn., 1990-92, safety coord. rsch. medicine and radiation biophysics divsn., 1991-92, mem. mgmt. integration group, 1990—, authorized reviewer, quality assurance rep., environ. safety and health coord., and asst. dep. life scis. divsn., 1992—. Reviewer Jour. Cerebral Blood Flow and Metabolism, Physics in Medicine and Biology, Jour. Computer Assisted Tomography. Recipient Tech. Brief award NASA, 1973; grantee NIH, 1973—, IBM, 1986, U.S. Nat. Insts. Health, 1989—; Aargonne Nat. Lab. fellow Associated Midwest Univs., 1965-66, Shell Found. fellow, 1967-68; Ill. State scholar, 1959-62, U. Chgo. scholar, 1961-63. Mem. IEEE (sr., reviewer Transactions on Nuclear Sci., guest editor 1989, chair med. imaging conf. 1991, fellow award, radiation intrumentation achievement award, 01), Nuclear and Plasma Scis. Soc. of IEEE (mem. tech. com. on nuclear med. sci. 1983—, chair 1988-91, mem. adminstrv. com. 1988-91, Merit award 1992), Am. Phys. Soc., Materials Rsch. Soc. Avocations: long distance running, photography, astronomy. Office: U Calif Lawrence Berkeley Lab Berkeley CA 94720-0001

DERICCO, LAWRENCE ALBERT, retired college president; b. Stockton, Calif., Jan. 28, 1923; s. Giulio and Agnes (Giovacchini) DeR.; m. Alma Mezzetta, June 19, 1949; 1 child, Lawrence Paul. BA, U. Pacific, Stockton, Calif., 1949, MA, 1971, LLD (hon.), 1987. Bank clk. Bank of Am., Stockton, 1942-43; prin. Castle Sch. Dist., San Joaquin County, Calif., 1950-53; dist. supt., prin. Waverly Sch. Dist., Stockton, 1953-63; bus. mgr. San Joaquin Delta Jr. Coll. Dist., Stockton, 1963-65, asst. supt., bus. mgr., 1965-77, v.p. mgmt. services, 1977-81; pres., supt. San Joaquin Delta Coll., 1981-87, pres. emeritus, 1988—. Mem. Workforce Investment Bd. With AUS, 1943-46, PTO. Mem. NEA, Calif. Tchrs. Assn., Native Sons of Golden West (past pres.), Phi Delta Kappa Home: 6847 N Pershing Ave Stockton CA 95207-2524 Personal E-mail: ldericco@comcast.net.

DERISI, JOSEPH L., biochemist, educator; BA Biochemistry, U. Calif., Santa Cruz, 1992; PhD Biochemistry, Stanford U., 1999. Asst. prof. biochemistry, biophysics U. Calif., San Francisco, 2000—04, assoc. prof. biochemistry, biophysics, 2004—. Recipient JPMorgan Chase Health award; named a MacArthur Fellow, 2004. Fellow: The David & Lucille Packard Found., 2003. Achievements include invention of microarray known as the virus chip, a glass slide embedded with 12,096 snippets of viral DNA which has advanced the diagnosis and treatment of disease; along with colleagues, identified and characterized a novel coronavirus responsible for the outbreak of Severe Acute Respiratory Syndrome (SARS) in early 2003. Office: 513 Parnassus Ave Box 0448 San Francisco CA 94143 Business E-Mail: joe@desrilab.ucsf.edu.

DERKSEN, CHARLOTTE RUTH MEYNINK, librarian; b. Newberg, Oreg., Mar. 15, 1944; BS in Geology, Wheaton Coll., Ill., 1966; MA in Geology, U. Oreg., Eugene, 1968, MLS, 1973. Faculty and libr. Moeding Coll., Ootse, Botswana, 1968—71, head history dept., 1970-71; tchr. Jackson Pub. H.S., Minn., 1975-77; sci. libr. U. Wis., Oshkosh, 1977-80; libr. and bibliographer Stanford U., Calif., 1980—2004. Acting chief scis., 1985-86, head Sci. and Engring. Librs., 1992-97; cons. Am. Geol. Inst., 2004-.; sec. Pacific NW Mennohite Conf., 2008-. Contbg. author: Union List of Geologic Field Trip Guidebooks of North America; contbr. articles to profl. jours. Mem. ALA, Western Assn. Map Librs., Geosci. Info. Soc. (v.p. 1997-98, pres. 1998-99; first Mary B. Ansari Disting. Svc. award, 2005), Am. Geol. Inst. (mem. soc. coun. 2000-02), Geol. Soc. Am. (publ. com. 2002-05), Geoscience World (libr. adv. com., chair 2005-07). Republican. Mennonite. Office: Stanford U Branner Earth Scis Library Stanford CA 94305 Home: 12522C 26th Ave NE Seattle WA 98125-8803 Business E-Mail: cderksen@stanford.edu.

DERMANIS, PAUL RAYMOND, architect; b. Jelgava, Latvia, Aug. 2, 1932; came to U.S., 1949; s. Pauls and Milda (Argals) D. BArch, U. Wash., 1955; MArch, MIT, 1959. Registered arch., Wash. Arch. John Morse & Assocs., Seattle, 1961-62; assoc. Fred Bassetti & Co., Seattle, 1963-70; arch. Ibsen Nelsen & Assocs., Seattle, 1970-71; ptnr. Streeter/Dermanis & Assocs., Seattle, 1973-97; owner Paul Dermanis Archs., 1997—. Designs include Sunset house (citation 1984), treatment plant, 1992. Mem. Phinney Ridge Neighborhood Assn., Seattle, 1985—. With USN, 1955-57. Mem. AIA, Apt. Assn. Seattle and King County, U. Wash. Alumni Assn., MIT Club of Puget Sound, Phi Beta Kappa, Tau Sigma Delta. Democrat. Lutheran. Avocations: skiing, painting, photography. Home Phone: 206-783-3873; Office Phone: 206-783-0266. E-mail: pdermanis@comcast.net.

DE ROBERTIS, EDWARD M. F., research scientist, educator; MD, U. Uruguay; PhD in Chemistry, U. Buenos Aires. Postdoctoral tng. Med. Rsch. Coun. Lab. Molecular Biology, Cambridge, England; prof. U. Basel, Switzerland; investigator Howard Hughes Med. Inst., LA; Norman Sprague Prof. Biol. Chemistry UCLA Sch. Medicine. Fellow: Am. Acad. Arts and Scis.; mem.: Latin Am. Acad. Scis., Internat. Soc. Devel. Biology (ex-pres.), Iberoam. Molecular Biology Orgn., European Molecular Biology Orgn. Office: Howard Hughes Med Inst 5-748 MRL Bldg 675 Charles Dr Los Angeles CA 90095-1662

DERODES, ROBERT P., information technology executive; b. Wooster, Ohio; BSBA, St. Louis U., 1983; MBA, U. Tex., 1993. V.p. application systems, v.p. strategic planning Centerre Bancorporation, St. Louis, 1975—83; various positions including sr. v.p. bank ops. and tech. and v.p. fin. svcs. systems US Automobile Assn., 1983—93; pres. SABRE Devel. Svcs. SABRE Grp. (subsidiary of AMR Corp., the parent co. of Am. Airlines), 1993—95; sr. tech. officer card products grp. Citibank, 1995—99; chief info. officer Delta Air Lines, Inc., 1999—2002; pres., CEO Delta Tech., Inc., 1999—2002; exec. v.p., chief info. officer Home Depot, Inc., 2002—08; exec. v.p., CTO First Data Corp., Greenwood Village, 2008—. Named one of 25 Top Chief Tech. Officers, InfoWorld mag., 2006. Office: First Data Corp 6200 S Quebec St Greenwood Village CO 80111

DEROSA, DONALD V., academic administrator; b. New Rochelle, NY; m. Karen DeRosa; children: Michael, David;children from previous marriage: Carol, Joseph, Lauren. BA, Am. Internat. Coll., 1963; MA, Kent State U., PhD in Psychology, 1967. Prof. to dept. chair psychology Bowling Green State U., Ohio; dean Grad. Sch. U. NC, Greensboro, 1985—89, vice chancellor academic affairs, 1989—90, provost, 1990—95; pres. Univ. of the Pacific, Stockton, Calif., 1995—. Office: U of the Pacific Office of Pres 3601 Pacific Ave Stockton CA 95211

DEROUIN, JAMES GILBERT, lawyer; b. Eau Claire, Wis., July 11, 1944; BA cum laude, U. Wis., 1967, JD, 1968. Bar: Wis. 1968, Ariz. 1986. Ptnr. Steptoe & Johnson LLC, Phoenix, Ariz.; atty. Meyer, Hendricks, Victor, Osbonn & Maledon, Phoenix, Ariz.; ptnr. Dewitt, Ross & Stevens, Madison, Wis. Mem. bd. sci. counselors Agy. for Toxic Substances and Disease Registry, 2003—; mem. profl. task force Ariz. State Bar. Polychlorinatedbyphenol chair Wis. Dept. Natural Resources, 1976-78; mem. spl. com. on solid waste mgmt. Wis. Legis. Coun., 1976-79, ad hoc com. on hazardous waste mgmt., 1980-82, spl. com. on groundwater mgmt.; mem. Wis. Dept. Nat. Resources Metallic Mining Coun., 1978-85; chair Phoenix Environ. Quality Commn., 1986, Phoenix Environ. Quality Com., 1989-92; mem. Ariz. Govs. Regulatory Review Coun. 1986—; co-chair Ariz. Dept. Environ. Quality/Ariz. Dept. Water Resources Groundwater Task Force, 1996-97; mem. nat. adv. coun. superfun subcom. EPA. Chair. State Bar Ariz. (environ. and nat. resources law sect. 1989-90). Office: 201 E Washington St # 1600 Phoenix AZ 85004-2382

DERR, KENNETH TINDALL, retired oil industry executive; b. Wilkes-Barre, Pa., Aug. 4, 1936; m. Donna Mettler, Sept. 12, 1959; 3 children. BSME, Cornell U., 1959, MBA, 1960. Asst. to pres. Standard Oil Co. of Calif., San Francisco, 1969—72, v.p., 1972—79; pres. Chevron USA Inc., San Francisco, 1979—84; head merger program Chevron Corp. and Gulf Oil Corp., San Francisco, 1984—85; vice chmn. Chevron Corp., San Francisco, 1985—88, chmn., CEO, 1989—99; acting CEO Calpine Corp., San Jose, Calif., 2005, chmn., 2005—08. Bd. dirs. Chevron Corp. (formerly Standard Oil Co. of Calif.), 1981—99, Citigroup Inc., 1987—2009, AT&T Corp., 1995—2005, Calpine Corp., 2001—08, Halliburton Co., 2001—, Am. Productivity & Quality Ctr. Trustee emeritus Cornell U. Mem.: The Bus. Coun., Pacific Union Club, Orinda Country Club, San Francisco Golf Club.

DER TOROSSIAN, PAPKEN, engineering executive; B in Mech. Engring., MIT; M, Stanford U. Pres., CEO EVS Microsystems, Inc.; pres. Santa Cruz divsn., v.p. telephone products group Plantronics; pres. Silicon Valley Group, San Jose, Calif., 1984—, CEO, 1986—, chmn. bd. dirs., 1991—. Spkr. in field.

DE RUIZ, HECTOR J., information technology executive; b. Piedras Negras, Mex. BEE, MEE, U. Tex.; D in Electronics, Rice U., 1973. With Tex. Instruments, Dallas; pres. semicondr. products sector Motorola; pres. Advanced Micro Devices, Sunnyvale, Calif., 2002—06, chief operating officer, 2000—02, CEO, 2002—, chmn., 2004—. Mem. Gov.'s Task Force for Econ. Growth, Gov.'s Bus. Coun., Nat. Sec. Telecommunications Adv. Com.; bd. dirs. Eastman Kodak Co. Apptd. by Pres. George W. Bush Tex. Higher Edn. Coord. Bd., 1999; found. adv. coun. Coll. Engring., U. Tex.; bd. dirs. Soc. Hispanic Profl. Engrs.; mem. adv. bd. Tsinghua Sch. Econ. and Mgmt. Recipient inductee, Hispanic Nat. Achievement Awards Conf. Hall of Fame, 2000. Mem.: Semiconductor Industry Assn. (bd. dir.). Office: AMD 1 AMD Pl Sunnyvale CA 94088-3453

DERVAN, PETER BRENDAN, chemistry professor; b. Boston, July 28, 1945; s. Peter Brendan and Ellen (Comer) D.; m. Jackqueline K. Barton; children: Andrew, Elizabeth. BS in Chemistry, Boston Coll., 1967, DSc, 1997; PhD in Chemistry, Yale U., New Haven, Conn., 1972. NIH postdoctoral fellow Stanford U., 1973; asst. prof. chemistry Calif. Inst. Tech., Pasadena, 1973-79, assoc. prof. chemistry, 1979-82, prof. chemistry, 1982-88, Bren prof. chemistry, 1988—, chmn. div. chemistry & chem. engring., 1994—99. Adv. bd. ACS Monographs, Washington, 1979-81; vis. prof. for several internat. & domestic; mem. organizing com., nineteeth reaction mechanisms conf., 1982; co-organizer, workshop on reactive intermediates, NSF, 1984-85, mem. adv. panel for chemistry of life scis., 1985, mem. adv. com. for chemistry, 1986-88, chmn. adv. com. for chemistry, 1988-89; mem. bd. on chem. scis. and tech., NRC, 1988-90, chmn. bd. on chem. scis. and tech., 1991-94; mem. coun. Gordon Rsch. Conf., 1991-94; mem. adv. bd. Chem. & Engring. News, 1992-94. Mem. adv. bd. Jour. Organic Chemistry, Washington, 1981-85, Bioorganic Chemistry, 1983-, Chem. Rev. Jour., 1984-89, Nucleic Acids Res., 1986-88, Jour. Am. Chem. Soc., 1986-92, Accounts Chem. Res., 1987-89, Bioorganic Chem. Rev., 1988—, Catalysis Letters, 1988-89, Bioconjugate Chemistry, 1989—. Jour. Med. Chemistry, 1991-93, Tetrahedron, 1992-, Bioorganic and Medicinal Chemistry, 1993-, Chemical and Engineering News, 1992- Current Opinion in Drug Discovery and Develop., 1997-, Proceedings of NAS, 1999, Am. Chem. Soc. Chem. Biology, 2006-; contbr. articles to profl. jours. Alfred P. Sloan Rsch. fellow, 1977; Camille and Henry Dreyfus Tchr.-Scholar, 1978; John Simon Guggenheim Meml. Fellow, 1983; Arthur C. Cope Scholar award, 1986; recipient Maison de la Chimie Found. prize, 1996, Max Tishler prize, 1999; named 2006 Nat. Medal Sci. Laureate, NSF, 2007. Fellow Am. Acad. Scis.; mem. NAS(Class I membership com., 1994-96, 2005, nominating com., 1997), Am. Chem. Soc. (Nobel Laureate Signature award 1985, Harrison Howe award 1988, Arthur C. Cope award, 1993, Willard Gibbs medal, 1993, Rolf Sammet prize, 1993, William H. Nichols medal 1994, Kirkwood medal 1998, Alfred Bader award 1999, Achievement in Biomimetic Chemistry award, 2005, Ronald Breslow award, 2005), Inst. Medicine (Remsen award 1998, Linus Pauling medal 1999, Richard C. Tolman medal 1999), French Acad. Scis. (fgn., Tetrahedron prize 2000); mem. Am. Philos. Soc. (Harvey prize, Israel 2002), German Acad. Natural Scientists (Wilbur Cross medal 2005, Nat. Medal of Sci., 2006). Office: Calif Inst Tech Divsn Chemisty & Chem Engring 164-30 1201 E Calif Blvd Pasadena CA 91125-0001 Business E-Mail: dervan@caltech.edu.

DESAI, KAVIN HIRENDRA, pediatrician; b. Bombay, Oct. 8, 1963; MD, Wayne State U., 1988. Resident in pediatrics Stanford U., Palo Alto, Calif., 1989-91, fellow in pediatric cardiology, 1991—, staff pediat. cardiologist, 1994—. Recipient Clinician-Scientist award Am. Heart Assn., 1995-98. Office: Stanford U Pediat Cardio Divsn 750 Welch Rd Ste 305 Palo Alto CA 94304-1510

DESANTO, JOHN A., physicist, educator, mathematics professor; b. Wilkes-Barre, Pa., May 25, 1941; s. John and Esther DeSanto; m. Beverly DeSanto; children: John, Lauren, Andrea. BS in Physics, Villanova U., Pa., 1962, MA in Math., 1962; MS in Physics, U. Mich., Ann Arbor, 1963, PhD in Physics, 1967. Rsch. scientist Naval Rsch. Lab., Washington, 1967—81; sr. scientist Electromagnetic Applications Inc., Lakewood, Colo., 1981—82; prof. math. U. Denver, 1982—83, Colo. Sch. Mines, Golden, 1983—2006, prof. physics, 2006—, dir. Ctr. for Wave Phenomena, 1988—89. Mem. rev. panel Ocean Acoustic Tomography NSF, 1980; presenter in field. Author: Scalar Wave Theory, 1992; editor: Ocean Acoustics, 1979, Mathematical and Numerical Aspects of Wave Propagation, 1998; co-editor: Mathematical Methods and Applications of Scattering Theory, 1980; contbr. articles to profl. jours.; co-prodr.:. Fellow, NSF, 1962—67, Am. Physical Soc., Inst. Physics, Eng., Acoustical Soc. Am.; Woodrow Wilson fellow, 1962, Fulbright fellow, 1993, sr. postdoctoral fellow, NRC, 1994. Fellow: Am. Phys. Soc., Inst. Physics, Acoustical Soc. Am.; mem.: IEEE, Soc. for Indsl. and Applied Math. Home: 7692 S Saulsbury Ct Littleton CO 80128 Office: Colo Sch Mines Golden CO 80401 Business E-Mail: jdesanto@mines.edu.

DESAULNIER, MARK, state legislator; b. Lowell, Mass. 2 children. BA in History, Coll. Holy Cross. California State Assemblyman, District 11, 2006-08, member, Appropriations, Human Serv, Labor & Employment, Rules & Transportation Committees, 2007, chair, Select Committee on Growth Management, 2007-08; Mayor of Concord, formerly; Concord City Councilmember, 91-93. restaurant owner, currently; mem. Dist. 7, Calif. State Senate, 2009-. Contra Costa Co Bd of Supr (chairman, formerly, member, currently); Children & Families Committee of the Bd of Supr; Concord Planning Comn (formerly); Univ of California Toxic Substances Research & Teaching Prog Advisor Committee (formerly); AfterSchool4All; Future Fund; Association of Bay Area Govt (exec board, formerly); Bay Area Air Quality Management District (exec board, formerly); California Air Resources Bd; Metrop Transportation Comn (exec board, formerly); Regional Agency Coordinating Committee (chair, formerly). Democrat. Office: Dist 7 2801 Concord Blvd Concord CA 94519 Office Phone: 925-602-6593.

DESCHENE, CHRISTOPHER C., state legislator; b. Calif. married; 1 child. BS in Mech. Engring, US Naval Acad., Annapolis, 1993; MME, Ariz. State U., JD, 2005. Mil. rsch. engr. Lawrence Livermore Nat. Lab.; legal assoc. US Senate; co-founder & tribal atty. Schaff & Clark Deschene, LLC; mem. Dist. 2 Ariz. House of Reps., 2008—. Organizer Phoenix Urban Indian Summit Youth Conf., 2001—02; chmn. Apache County Dem. Party, Native Am. Dem. Caucus. From capt. to major USMC, 1995—2003. Mem.: Nat. Native Am. Law Student Assn. (former pres.). Democrat. Office: Capitol Complex 1700 W Washington Rm 325 Phoenix AZ 85007-2890 Office Phone: 602-926-5862. Office Fax: 602-417-3102. Business E-Mail: cdeschene@azleg.gov.*

DESHAZER, JAMES ARTHUR, biological engineer, educator, research administrator; b. Wash., July 18, 1938; s. Grant Arthur and Velma DeShazer; m. Alice Marie DeShazer, Apr. 5, 1969; children: Jean Marie, David James. BS in Agr., U. Md., Coll. Pk., 1960, BSME, 1961; MS, Rutgers U., New Brunswick, NJ, 1963; PhD, N.C. State U., Raleigh, 1967. Profl. engr., Idaho, Nebr. Assoc. prof. U. Nebr., Lincoln, 1967-75, prof., 1975-91, asst. dean, 1988-89; head agrl. engring. dept. U. Idaho, Moscow, 1991-95, head biol. and agrl. engring. dept., 1995—2001. Chair animal care and use com. U. Nebr., 1989—90; program coord. North Cen. Sustainable Agrl., Washington, 1988—89; nat. chair Modeling Responses of Swine CSRS, Washington, 1989-90, Sys. Approach to Poultry Prodn.-CSRS, Washington, 1990-91; dir. Idaho Rsch. Found., 1996—2001. Editor procs. Optics in Agr., 1990, Optics in Agr. & Forestry, 1992, Optics in Agr., Forestry & Biol. Processing, 1994, Optics in Agr., Forestry & Biol. Processing II, 1996, Precision Agriculture and Biological Quality, 1998, vol. II, 2000; contbr. chpt. in book. Trustee ASAE Found., 1996—2002; biol. and agr. engring. adv. bd. N.C. State U., 2002—04. Recipient Livestock Svc. award Walnut Grove, Iowa, 1988. Fellow: Am. Soc. Agrl. Engrs. (chair 1984—94, nat. medal 1979); mem.: NSPE (chpt. chair 1986—87, 1993—94, bd. dirs. 1994—2001, state pres. 1998—99, Young Engring. award 1974), Internat. Soc. Biometeorology, Am. Soc. Engring. Edn. (chair 1993—94), Lions (chpt. dir. 1995—97, 2002—04, club v.p. 2005—07, club pres. 2007—08, Lion of Yr. 2004—05), Alpha Gamma Rho (alumni bd. dirs. 1993—99, Alum of Yr. 2006). Home: 819 Nylarol St Moscow ID 83843-9313 Office: Biol & Agr Engring Dept Univ Idaho Moscow ID 83844-0904 Office Phone: 208-885-6182. Business E-Mail: Jades@uidaho.edu.

DESHPANDE, NILENDRA GANESH, physics professor; b. Karachi, Pakistan, Apr. 18, 1938; came to U.S., 1961; s. Ganesh V. and Myna G. (Junnarkar) D.; m. Kanchan S. Karnik, May 15, 1960; children: Pranay N., Rahul N. BS with honors, U. Madras, India, 1959, MA in Physics, 1960, MS in Physics, 1961; PhD, U. Pa., 1965. Asst. prof. physics Northwestern U., Evanston, Ill., 1967-73; assoc. prof U. Tex., Austin, 1973-75, U. Oreg., Eugene, 1975-83, prof., 1983—, head dept. physics, 1992-98, dir. Inst. Theoretical Sci., 1987-92, assoc. dean scis., 1998—2001. Contbr. articles to profl. jours. Named Outstanding Jr. Investigator, U.S. Dept. Energy, 1981-86; prin. investigator High Energy Physics Grant, U.S. Dept. Energy, 1981—. Fellow Am. Phys. Soc. (organizer annual meeting div. particles and fields 1985), Sigma Xi. Office: U Oreg Inst Theoretical Sci Eugene OR 97403 Home Phone: 541-344-9152; Office Phone: 541-346-5204. Business E-Mail: desh@uoregon.edu.

DESJARDIN, DENNIS E., plant pathologist, educator; b. Crescent City, Calif., May 18, 1950; 1 child, Spenser L. BS in Biology and Botany, San Francisco State U., 1983, MA in Ecology and Systematic Biology, 1985; PhD in Botany and Mycology, U. Tenn., 1989. Asst. prob. Oberlin (Ohio) Coll., 1989-90; asst. prof. San Francisco State U., 1990-93, assoc. prof., 1993-97, prof., 1997—, dir. H.D. Thiers Herbarium, 1991—. Bd. dirs. Sierra Nev. Field Campus; sci. adv. bd. Golden Gate Nat. Recreation Area; chief mycologist N.Am. Mycological Assn. Foray, 1998, Colo. Mycological Soc. Foray, 1998; cons. in field; presenter in field. Grantee NSF, 1986, 93, 96, 97, U. Tenn. Dept. Botany, 1991, San Fransisco State U., 1991, 94, U.S. Forest Svc., 1995, 97, others. Mem. Internat. Assn. for Plant Taxonomy, Mycological Soc. Am. (liaison with amateur socs. 1992-95, awards com. 1993-96, chair awards com. 1996, councilor for systematics and evolution nomenclature com. 1996-98, grad. fellow 1986, Alexopoulos prize 1998, William H. Weston award 1998), Am. Bryological and Lichenological Soc., Am. Inst. Biol. Scis., Biosystematists, Brit. Mycological Soc., Calif. Bot. Soc. (v.p. 1993-94), Mycological Soc. San Francisco (sci. advisor 1990—), Sigma Xi, Phi Kappa Phi. Office: San Francisco State U Dept Biology 1600 Holloway Ave San Francisco CA 94132 E-mail: ded@sfsu.edu.

DES JARDINS, TRACI, chef, restaurant owner; b. Calif. Student, U. Calif., Santa Cruz. Formerly mem. staff 7th St. Bistro, LA; former apprentice Michel and Pierre Troisgros, Lucas Carton, Alain Ducasse, Alain Passard, France; former mem. staff Montrachet, NYC; former chef de cuisine Patina, Calif.; former chef Aqua, San Francisco, Elka, San Francisco; exec. chef Rubicon, San Francisco, 1993—97; ptnr., chef Jardiniere, San Francisco, 1997—; exec. chef Mijita; consulting chef Acme Chophouse. Environ. activist. Named Rising Star Chef of Yr., James Beard Found., Best Chef: Pacific, 2007, Chef of Yr., San Francisco Mag.; named one of America's Best New Chefs, Food & Wine mag., 1995, Top 3 Chefs in Bay Area, San Francisco Chronicle. Office: Jardiniere 300 Grove St San Francisco CA 94102

DESMOND-HELLMANN, SUSAN, medical products manufacturing executive; b. 1958; BS in Pre-Medicine, U. Nev., MD; M in Epidemiology and Biostats., U. Calif. Sch. Pub. Health, Berkeley. Bd. cert. internal medicine and med. oncology. Trainee U. Calif., San Francisco; assoc. dir. clin. cancer rsch., project team leader Taxol Bristol-Myers Squibb Pharm. Rsch. Inst.; clin. scientist Genentech, Inc., South San Francisco, 1995-96, sr. dir. clin. sci., 1996, v.p. med. affairs, 1996, chief med. officer, 1996—97, v.p. devel., 1997, sr. v.p. devel., 1997, exec. v.p. devel. and product ops., 1999, pres., product devel., 2004—. Vis. faculty Uganda Cancer Inst.; asst. prof. hematology-oncology U. Calif. San Francisco, adj. assoc. prof. epidemiology and biostats; adv. com. regulatory reform, HHS, 2002; bd. dirs. Biotechnology Industry Orgn., 2001-, Am. Assn. Cancer Rsch., 2005-. Named Woman of Yr., Healthcare Businesswomen's Assn., 2006; named one of 50 Most Powerful Women in Bus., Fortune mag., 2001, 2003, 2004, 2006, 2007, 2008, 100 Most Powerful Women in World, Forbes Mag., 2005, Forbes mag., 2007, 2008, Top 50 Women to Watch, Wall St. Jour., 2004, 50 Women to Watch, 2005, 2006, Leading Women and Minority Scientists, NY Acad. Scis., 2005, 50 Who Matter Now, CNNMoney.com Bus. 2.0, 2006. Office: Genentech Inc One DNA Way South San Francisco CA 94080-4990 Office Fax: 650-225-6000.

DESOER, BARBARA JEAN, mortgage company executive; b. Nov. 4, 1952; m. Marc Desoer; 1 child. BA in Math., Mt. Holyoke Coll., South Hadley, Mass., 1974; MBA, U. Calif., Berkeley. Various positions to mng. strategy devel. and implementation, consumer banking unit Bank of America Corp., 1977—96, exec. v.p. Calif. retail banking grp., 1996—98, pres. No. Calif. banking, 1998, mktg. exec., 1999—2001, pres. consumer products, 2001—04, chief tech. and ops. officer, 2005—08, pres. consumer real estate ops. Countrywide Fin. Corp. Calabasas, Calif., 2008—. Chmn. internat. diversity adv. coun. Bank of America Corp.; mem. adv. coun. U. Calif. Haas Sch. Bus.; mem. bus. adv. coun. U. NC Belk Coll. Bus. Adminstrn., Charlotte. Bd. trustees Providence Day Sch., Charlotte, Mt. Holoyoke Coll.; bd. dirs. NC Dance Theatre, Presbyn. Hosp. Found., United Way Ctrl. Carolinas, Novant Healthcare. Named Bus. Leader of the Yr., U. Calif. Haas Sch. Bus., 2007; named one of 25 Most Powerful Women in Banking, US Banker, 2007, 50 Most Powerful Women in Bus., Fortune mag., 2008. Office: Bank of Am Corp 4500 Park Granada Calabasas CA 91302 Office Phone: 704-386-5681. Office Fax: 704-386-6699.

DESOER, CHARLES AUGUSTE, electrical engineer; b. Ixelles, Belgium, Jan. 11, 1926; came to U.S., 1949, naturalized, 1958; s. Jean Charles and Yvonne Louise (Peltzer) D.; m. Jacqueline K. Johnson, July 21, 1966; children: Marc J., Michele M., Craig M. Ingenieur Radio-Electricien, U. Liege, 1949, DSc (hon.), 1976; DSc in Elec. Engring, MIT, 1953. Rsch. asst. MIT, Cambridge, 1951—53; mem. tech. staff Bell Telephone Labs., Murray Hill, NJ, 1953—58; assoc. prof. elec. engring. and computer scis. U. Calif., Berkeley, 1958—62, prof., 1962—91, prof. emeritus, 1991—, Miller rsch. prof., 1970—71. Author: (with L. A. Zadeh) Linear System Theory, 1963, (with E. S. Kuh) Basic Circuit Theory, 1969, (with M. Vidyasagar) Feedback Systems: Input Output Properties, 1973, Notes for a Second Course on Linear Systems, 1970, (with F. M. Callier) Multivariable Feedback Systems, 1982, (with L.O. Chua and E.S. Kuh) Linear and Nonlinear Circuits, 1987, (with A.N. Gündes) Alegebraic Theory of Linear Feedback Systems with Full and Decentralized Compensation, 1990, (with F.M. Callier) Linear System Theory, 1991; contbr. numerous articles on systems and circuits to profl. jours. Served with Belgian Arty., 1944-45. Decorated Vol.'s medal; recipient Best Paper prize 2d Joint Automatic Control Conf., 1962, medal U. Liège, 1976, Disting. Tchg. award U. Calif., Berkeley, 1971, Prix Montefiore Inst. Montefiore, 1975; Field award in control sci. and engring., 1986, Am. Automatic Control Coun. Edn. award, 1983, Berkeley Citation, 1992; Guggenheim fellow, 1970-71. Fellow IEEE (Edn. medal 1975, Outstanding Paper award 1979), AAAS.; mem. IEEE Control Sys. Soc., IEEE Circuits and Systems Soc. (Mac Van Valkenburg award 1996), Nat. Acad. Engring., Am. Math. Soc. Office: Dept Elec Engring and Computer Sci Univ Calif Berkeley CA 94720-1770

DESOTO, LEWIS DAMIEN, artist, educator; b. San Bernardino, Calif., Jan. 3, 1954; s. Lewis Dan and Albertina (Quiroz) DeS. BA, U. Calif., Riverside, 1978; MFA, Claremont Grad. Sch., 1981. Tchr. Otis Parsons, LA, 1982-85; chmn. art dept. Cornish Coll. of Arts, Seattle, 1985-88; prof. art San Francisco State U., 1988—95; dir. grad. studies Calif. Coll. Arts and Crafts, Oakland, 1993-95; prof. art San Francisco State U., 1995—. Exhibitions include New Mus., N.Y.C., 1992, Centro Cultural De La Raza, San Diego, 1993, Moderna Museet, Stockholm, Sweden, 1993, Christopher Grimes Gallery, Santa Monica, Calif., 1994, Denver Art Mus., 1994, Columbus Mus. Art, 1994, Des Moines Art Ctr., 1995, Fundacao Serralves, Opporto, Portugal, 1995, Metronóm, Barcelona, Spain, 1997, Public Art Commn., San Francisco Courthouse, 1998, San Francisco Internat. Airport, 2000, San Jose Animal Care Ctr. Public Commn., Calif., 2004, U. Tex., San Antonio, 2003, Public Art Commn., List Visual Art Ctr., MIT, Cambridge, 1998, Bill Maynes Gallery, N.Y.C., 1999, 2000, Mus. of Contemporary Religious Art, St. Louis, 2000, Mus. Contemporary Art, San Diego, 2001, Worcester Art (Mass.) Mus., 2001, Bill Maynes Gallery, N.Y.C., 2002, Samek Art Ctr., Bucknell U., Lewisburg, Pa., 2002, N.C. Mus. Art, Raleigh, 2003, Newhouse Ctr. for Contemporary Art, S.I., 2003, Harn Mus. Art, Gainesville, Fla., 2003, Vanderbilt Art Gallery, Vanderbilt U., Nashville, 2003, San Diego Mus. Contemporary Aft, LaJolla, 2004, Columbus Mus. of Art, 2004, UCLA Fowler Art Mus., LA, 2006—, Aldrich Contemporary Art Mus., Ridgefield, Conn., 2006—, Oakland estuary channel project, Pub. Art Com., 2006—, one-man shows include Brian Gross Fine Art, San Francisco, 2006—. Mem. photo coun. Seattle Art Mus., 1987-88, Eureka Fellowship, vis. arts, 1999. Recipient New Genres award Calif. Arts Coun., 1992, NEA fellow, 1996, recipient Visual Arts award Flintridge Found., Pasadena, Calif., 2004. Mem. L.A. Ctr. for Photographic Studies (bd. dirs. 1983-85), CameraWork (exec. bd. dirs. 1991-93), Ctr. for Arts (adv. bd. 1993-95), Friends of Photography (peer award bd. 1991-96). Office: San Francisco State U Art Dept 1600 Holloway Ave San Francisco CA 94132-1722 Personal E-mail: Sotolux@sbcglobal.net.

DE SOTO, SIMON, mechanical engineer; b. NYC, Jan. 8, 1925; s. Albert and Esther (Eskenazi) de Soto; 1 child, Linda Jane. BME, CCNY, 1945; MME, Syracuse U., 1950; PhD, UCLA, 1965. Lic. profl. engr., Calif., N.Y. Engr. Johns-Manville Corp., NYC, 1946-48; instr. in engring. Syracuse U., 1948-50; research engr. Stratos-Fairchild Corp., Farmingdale, N.Y., 1950-54; research specialist Lockheed Missile Systems div. Lockheed Corp., Van Nuys, Calif., 1954-56; sr. tech. specialist Rocketdyne Rockwell Internat., Canoga Park, Calif., 1956-69; assoc. prof. mech. engring. Calif. State U., Long Beach, 1969-72, prof., 1972—. Lectr. UCLA, 1954—70; cons. engr.; dir., sec.-treas. Am. Engring. Devel. Co.; mem. tech. planning com. Pub. Policy Conf., 1973; founding mem. Calif. State U. and Colls.; cons. tech. assistance program Statewide Energy Consortium. Author: Thermostatics and Thermodynamics: An Instructor's Manual, 1963; contbr. articles to profl. jours. With U.S. Mcht. Marine, 1945—46. Mem.: SAG, AAAS, Am. Soc. Engring. Edn. (prof. recipients Outstanding Design award 1990), Pi Tau Sigma, Tau Beta Pi. Avocation: acting.

DESTEFANO, GARY M., apparel executive; b. Portsmouth, NH; married, 1978; 2 children. BS in Phys. Edn., U. NH, Durham, 1978; MBA, NH Coll., 1983. Customer svc. area mgr. Nike, Inc., 1982—84, asst. Ea. sales mgr. Footwear, 1984—88, nat. asst. Mid-West sales mgr. Apparel, 1988—89, dir. sports & fitness sales, 1989—92, divisional v.p. domestic sales, 1992—93, v.p. global sales, 1993—96, v.p. NIKE Asia Pacific, 1996—97, v.p., gen. mgr. Asia Pacific, 1997—2001, pres. USA ops., 2001—06, pres. global ops., 2006—. Avocations: running, golf, skiing, water-skiing, reading. Office: Nike Inc One Bowerman Dr Beaverton OR 97005-6453 Office Phone: 503-671-6453.

DETELS, ROGER, epidemiologist, retired dean; b. Bklyn., Oct. 14, 1936; s. Martin P. and Mary J. (Crooker) D.; m. Mary M. Doud, Sept. 14, 1963; children: Martin, Edward. BA, Harvard U., 1958; MD, NYU, 1962; MS in Preventive Medicine, U. Wash., 1966. Diplomate Am. Bd. Preventive Medicine. Intern U. Calif. Gen. Hosp., San Francisco, 1962—63; resident U. Wash., Seattle, 1963—66; med. officer, epidemiologist Nat. Inst. Neurol. Diseases, Bethesda, Md., 1969—71; assoc. prof. epidemiology Sch. Pub. Health UCLA, 1971—73, prof. Sch. Pub. Health, 1973—, dean, 1980—85, head divsn. epidemiology Sch. Pub. Health, 1972—80, chair, dept. epidemiology, 2001—05. Guest lectr. various univs., profl. confs. and med. orgns., 1969—; sci. adv. com. Am. Found AIDS Rsch.; dir. UCLA/Fogarty AIDS Internat. Tng. and Rsch. Program, 1988—, Tng. Program in Epidemiology of HIV/AIDS, 1995—; cons. Ministries of Health, Thailand, Myanmar, Philippines, 1989, Global Program on AIDS, 1995, Singapore, 1996, 2006, China, 2002-, WHO, 1999, U.S. AID, 1998, 99, 2000, 01, Cambodia, 1998, 99, 2000, 02, 03, 04, 05, 06, 07, UN Devel. Program, 2001, St. Thomas Med. Sch., London, 1993-94, Myanmar, 1997, UN Devel. Program, Myanmar, 2001, UNICEF, 2005; mem. Nat. Adv. Environ. Health Scis. Coun., 1990-94; com. to study transmission of HIV through blood products Inst. Medicine, 1994-95; external examiner Nat. U. Singapore, 1994, 2004. Editor: Oxford Textbook of Public Health, 1985, 2d edit. 1991, 3d edit., 1997, 4th edit., 2002; contbr. articles to profl. jours. Lt. comdr. M.C. USN, 1966-69. Grantee in field; recipient Sahametry award, Gov. Cambodia, 2007, Abraham Lilienfeld award, Am. Coll. Epidemiology, 2008. Fellow AAAS, Am. Coll. Preventive Medicine, Am. Coll. Epidemiology (coun. 1987-89), Faculty Pub. Health Medicine Royal Coll. Physicians of U.K. (hon.); mem. Am. Epidemiol. Soc., Soc. Epidemiologic Rsch. (pres. 1977-78), Assn. Tchrs. Preventive Medicine (chmn. essay com. 1969-75), APHA, Am. Assn. Cancer Edn. (membership com. 1978-85), Internat. Epidemiol. Assn. (exec. com. 1984-99, treas. 1984-90, pres. 1990-93), Assn. Schs. Pub. Health (sec.-treas. 1980-85), Sigma Xi, Delta Omega. Office: UCLA Dept Epidemiology Ctr for Health Scis Box 951772 Los Angeles CA 90095-1772 Office Fax: 310-206-6039. Business E-Mail: detels@ucla.edu.

DETERMAN, JOHN DAVID, lawyer; b. Mitchell, SD, Feb. 18, 1933; s. Alred John and Olive Gertrude (Lovinger) D.; m. Gloria Esther Rivas, Nov. 15, 1980; children by previous marriage: James Taylor, Mark Sterling. BEE cum laude, U. So. Calif., 1955; LLD magna cum laude, UCLA, 1961. Electronics engr. Hughes Aircraft Co., LA, 1955-60; sr. ptnr. Tuttle & Taylor, Inc., LA, 1961-86; gen. counsel Provena Foods Inc., Chino, Calif., 1986-92, CEO, 1992-98, chmn. bd., 1992—2004. Founder Carl D. Spaeth Scholarship Fund, Stanford U. Law Sch., 1972; mem. nat. panel arbitrators Am. Arbitration Assn., L.A., 1962—, mem. adv. coun., 1982—, mem. nat. panel of mediators, 1986—, mem. large complex case panel of arbitrators, 1993—. Mem. Am. Coll. Constrn. Arbitrators (charter 1982—), Order of Coif, Eta Kappa Nu, Tau Beta Pi. Home: 25 S El Molino St Alhambra CA 91801-4102

DETHERO, J. HAMBRIGHT, banker; b. Chattanooga, Jan. 2, 1932; s. Jacob Hambright and Rosalie Frances (Gasser) D.; m. Charlotte Nixon Lee, Sept. 19, 1959; children: Dinah Lee, Charles Drew. BS in Bus. Adminstrn., U. Fla., 1953; BFT, Am. Grad. Sch. Internat. Mgmt., Phoenix, 1958. With Citibank, NYC, P.R., Caracas, Venezuela, San Francisco, 1958-69; mgr. First Nat. City Bank (Internat.), San Francisco, until 1969; v.p. internat. div. Crocker Nat. Bank, San Francisco, 1969-75; sr. v.p. London, 1976-80, San Francisco, 1980-84, Bank America World Trade Corp., San Francisco, 1984-85; 1st v.p. Security Pacific Nat. Bank, Los Angeles, 1986-87; regional mgr. Calif. Export Fin. Office, Calif. State World Trade Commn., San Francisco, 1988-93; sr. v.p. Comml. Bank of San Francisco, 1994-98; sr. trade finance First Bank. Internat. bus. cons., instr., 1998-2007; adj. prof. Grad. Sch. Bus., St. Mary's Coll., Moraga, Calif., 1988-2000, John F. Kennedy U., Walnut Creek, Calif., 1997-2000. Author: Exporting Guide for California, 1993, 2d edit., 1999, 3rd edit., 2009. Bd. dirs. Calif. Coun. Internat. Trade, 1972-77, 82-98, pres., 1974-76; trustee World Affairs Coun. No. Calif., 1971-77, 88-93; chmn. dist. Export Coun. No. Calif., 1983-93; dir. Internat. Diplomacy Coun., San Francisco, 1995-2002, treas., 1997-2000, pres., 2000-01; mem. San Francisco Host Com., 2000-02, chair, past pres. Com., 2005-06. Lt. USN, 1953—57, with USNR. Recipient Export Citizen of the Year award No. Calif. Export Coun./San Francisco Bus. Times, 1996. Home and Office: 694 Old Jonas Hill Rd Lafayette CA 94549-5214 Personal E-mail: hamdethero@aol.com.

DETLEFSEN, WILLIAM DAVID, JR., chemicals executive; b. Scottsbluff, Nebr., Nov. 14, 1946; s. William David Sr. and Janette Fern (Tuttle) D.; m. Melba Kay Cunningham, Nov. 12, 1982; children: Michael David, Erika Lee, Whitney Anne. BS in Forestry, U. Idaho, 1970; PhD in Chemistry, U. Oreg., 1993. Chemist, applications technologist Borden, Adhesives and Resins, Springfield, Oreg., 1972-76, coord. tech. svc., 1976-78, supr. phenolic resins devel., 1983-87, mgr. R & D, 1987-94; dir. R & D, resins, adhesives specialties, 1994—; sr. devel. chemist Ga.-Pacific Resins, Crossett, Ark., 1978-83. Contbr. articles to profl. jours. 1st. lt. U.S. Army, 1970-72, Germany. Mem. AAAS, Am. Chem. Soc., Forest Products Rsch. Soc. Republican. Achievements include patents in field; co-discoverer first commercially feasible resins for gluing high moisture veneers into phenolic-bonded plywood. Office: Borden Chem Inc Adhesives & Resins Divsn 610 S 2nd St Springfield OR 97477-5398

DETTER, GERALD L., transportation executive; b. York, Pa. m. Iris Detter; 3 children. Student exec. mgmt. program, Columbia U. Dockman Consol. Freightways subs. CNF Transp. Svcs., York, 1964, line-haul dispatcher, various other positions, 1965, mgr. terminal Richfield, Ohio, 1971-76, divsn. mgr. Detroit, 1976-82, pres., CEO Con-Way Express, 1982, pres. CEO Con-Way Transp. Svcs., sr. v.p. Palo Alto, Calif. Active Mission of Hope Cancer Fund, Jackson, Mich., Boy Scouts of Am., Girl Scouts of Am., United Way. Office: Cnf Inc 2855 Campus Dr Ste 300 San Mateo CA 94403-2512

DETTERMAN, ROBERT LINWOOD, financial planner; b. Norfolk, Va., May 1, 1931; s. George William and Jeanneille (Watson) D.; m. Virginia Armstrong; children: Janine, Patricia, William Arthur. BS in Engring., Va. Poly. Inst., 1953; PhD in Nuclear Engring., Oak Ridge Sch. Reactor Tech., 1954, postgrad., 1954; cert. in fin. planning, Coll. Fin. Planning, Denver, 1986. Registered investment advisor, Calif. Engring. test dir. Foster Wheeler Co., NYC, 1954-59; sr. research engr. Atomics Internat. Co., Canoga Park, Calif., 1959-62; chief project engr. Rockwell Internat. Co., Canoga Park, Calif., 1962-68, dir. bus. devel., 1968-84, mgr. internat. program, 1984-87; pres. Bo-Gin Fin., Inc., Thousand Oaks, Calif., 1987—; owner Bo-Gin Arabians, Thousand Oaks, 1963—. Nuclear cons. Danish Govt., 1960, Lawrence Livermore Lab., Calif., 1959. Trustee, mem. exec. com. Morris Animal Found., Denver, 1984—, chmn., 1984-88, now trustee emeritus; mem. pres.' adv. com. Kellog Arabian Ranch, U. Calif. Poly., Pomona; treas., trustee Arabian Horse Trust, Denver, 1979-94, now trustee emeritus; chmn. Cal Bred Futurity. Named to Arabian Tent of Honor, Arabian Horse Trust, 1997. Mem. Nat. Assn. Personal Fin. Advisers, Fin. Planning Assn., Acad. Magical Arts, Am. Horse Shows Assn., Am. Horse Coun., Magic Castle Club, Internat. Arabian Horse Assn. Club, Tau Beta Phi, Eta Kappa Nu, Phi Kappa Phi. Republican. Avocations: stamp collecting/philately, gardening. Office: 3609 E Thousand Oaks Blvd Ste 220 Westlake Village CA 91362-6941 Home Phone: 805-495-1788; Office Phone: 805-494-1844. Business E-Mail: boginfin@aol.com.

DETTMAR, KEVIN JOHN HOFFMANN, literature and language professor, department chairman; b. Burbank, Calif., Dec. 24, 1958; s. Wilbur George and Joan Elizabeth (Fiddis) Dettmar; m. Robyn Hoffmann, Aug. 15, 1981; children: Emily Susan, Audrey Elizabeth, Esther Katherine, Colin Adam. BA in English and Psychology, U. Calif., Davis, 1981; postgrad. diploma, Trinity Coll., Dublin, Ireland, 1982; MA in English, UCLA, 1988, PhD in English, 1990. Teaching asst., assoc., fellow dept. English UCLA, 1984-90; vis. asst. prof. dept. English Loyola Marymount U., 1990-91; asst. prof. English Clemson U., SC, 1991-94, assoc. prof., asst. head dept. English SC, 1994—99, assoc. dean Coll. Architecture, Arts & Humanities SC; prod., chair Dept. English So. Ill. U., Carbondale, 1999—2008; W.M. Keck prof. English, chair Dept. English Pomona Coll., 2008—. Presenter in field. Author: The Illicit Joyce of Postmodernism: Reading Against the Grain, 1996, Is Rock Dead?, 2005; editor: Rereading the New: A Backward Glance at Modernism, 1992, Marketing Modernisms: Self-Promotion, Canonization, and Rereading, 1996, Reading Rock & Roll: Authenticity, Appropriation, Aesthetics, 1999, Blackwell Companion to British Literature and Culture, 2005; twentieth-century editor Oxford Encyclopedia of British Literature, 2005, mem. editl. team, gen. editor Longman Anthology of British Literature; contbr. articles to profl. jours. Fellow US Dept. Edn., 1986—87, Jacob K. Javits fellow, US Dept. Edn., 1987—88, 1988—89, 1989—90; NEH travel grantee, 1992—93, NEH summer stipend, 1994. Mem.: MLA, AAUP, Internat. Assn. for Study of Popular Music (bd. mem.), Modernist Studies Assn. (former pres.), Soc. Narrative Lit., Midwest MLA (pres. 2005—06, bd. mem.), James Joyce Found. Office: Pomona Coll Crookshank 103 333 N College Way Claremont CA 91711 Office Phone: 909-607-8032 78032.

DEUBLE, JOHN L., JR., environmental science and engineering services consultant; b. NYC, Oct. 2, 1932; s. John Lewis and Lucille (Klotzbach) D.; m. Thelma C. Honeychurch, Aug. 28, 1955; children: Deborah, Steven. AA, AS in Phys. Sci., Stockton Coll., 1957; BA, BS in Chemistry, U. Pacific, 1959. Cert. profl. chemist, profl. engr., environ. inspector; registered environ. profl., registered environ. assessor. Sr. chemist Aero-Gen Corp., Sacramento, Calif., 1959-67; asst. dir. rsch. Lockheed Propulsion Co., Redlands, Calif., 1968-73; asst. div. mgr. Systems, Sci. and Software, La Jolla, Calif., 1974-79; gen. mgr. Wright Energy Nev. Corp., Reno, Nev., 1980-81; v.p. Energy Resources Co., La Jolla, 1982-83; dir. hazardous waste Aerovironment Inc., Monrovia, Calif., 1984-85; sr. program mgr. Ogden Environ. and Energy Svcs., San Diego, 1989-96; environ. cons. Encinitas, Calif., 1986-88, 97—. Contbr. articles to profl. jours. With USAF, 1951-54. Recipient Tech. award Am. Ordnance Assn., 1969, Cert. of Achievement Am. Men and Women of Sci., 1986, Envrion. Registry, 1992. Fellow Am. Inst. Chemists; mem. ASTM, NSPE, Am. Chem. Soc., Am. Inst. Chem. Engrs., Am. Def. Inds. Assn., Air and Waste Mgmt. Assn., Calif. Inst. Chemists, N.Y. Acad. Scis., Environ. Assessors Assn. Republican. Lutheran. Achievements include development and pioneering use of chemical (non-radioactive) tracers--gaseous, aqueous, and particulate in environmental and energy applications. Home and Office: 7205 Savage Dr NE Albuquerque NM 87109 Office Phone: 505-823-6659.

DEUKMEJIAN, GEORGE, lawyer, Former Governor, California; b. Albany, NY, June 6, 1928; s. C. George and Alice (Gairdan) D.; m. Gloria M. Saatjian, 1957; children: Leslie Ann, George Krikor, Andrea Diane. BA, Siena Coll., 1949; JD, St. John's U., 1952. Bar: NY 1952, Calif. 1956, US Supreme Ct. 1970. Mem. Calif. Assembly, 1963-67, minority whip, 1965; mem. Calif. Senate, 1967-79, minority leader; atty. gen. State of Calif., 1979-82, gov., 1983-91, ret. gov.; former dep. county counsel Los Angeles County.; ptnr. Sidley & Austin, 1991-2000. Del. Rep. Nat. Conv., 1986, 80, 84, 88, 92, 96. Served with US Army, 1953—55. Republican. Episcopalian. Office: 5366 E Broadway Long Beach CA 90803-3549

DEUTSCH, BARRY JOSEPH, consulting and management development company executive; b. Gary, Ind., Aug. 10, 1941; s. Jack Elias and Helen Louise (La Rue) D. BS, U. So. Calif., 1969, MBA magna cum laude, 1970. Lectr. mgmt. U. So. Calif., LA, 1967-70; pres., founder The Deutsch Group, Inc., LA, 1970—; founder, CEO, chmn. bd., bd. dirs. Investment Planning Network, Inc., 1988—. Author: Leadership Techniques, 1969, Recruiting Techniques, 1970, The Art of Selling, 1973, Professional Real Estate Management, 1975, Strategic Planning, 1976, Employer/Employee: Making the Transition, 1979, Managing by Objectives, 1980, Conducting Effective Performance Appraisal, 1982, Advanced Supervisory Development, 1984, Managing a Successful Financial Planning Business, 1988, How to Franchise Your Business, 1991. Chmn. bd. govs. Am. Hist. Ctr., 1980—; mentor U. S.C. Career Advancement Program, 1999—. Mem. ASTD, Am. Mgmt. Assn., Am. Soc. Bus. and Mgmt. Cons., Internat. Mgmt. by Objectives Inst., Internat. Soc. for Performance Improvement, Organization Devel. Network, Planning Execs. Inst., Sponsors for Ednl. Advancement of Asians (bd. dirs.). Office: 1140 Highland Ave Ste 200 Manhattan Beach CA 90266-5335 Office Phone: 562-596-5544. E-mail: deutschbj@aol.com.

DEVAAN, JON S., computer software company executive; BS in Math. & Computer Sci., Oreg. State U., 1985. With Microsoft Corp., Redmond, Wash., 1985—, v.p., desktop applications, 1995—99, v.p., consumer and commerce, 1999, sr. v.p., consumer and commerce, 1999, sr. v.p. TV divsn., 1999—2002, sr. v.p. engring. excellence to sr. v.p. Windows Core Operating Sys. divsn., 2003—. Panelist UN World TV Forum, 2000; tech. advisor Oreg. Innovation Coun.; spkr. in field. Trustee Oreg. State Univ. Found.; amb. United Way of King County. Achievements include patents for simplifying user interface elements in PC applications. Office: One Microsoft Way Redmond WA 98052-6399

DEVENS, PAUL, retired lawyer; b. Gary, Ind., June 8, 1931; s. Zenove and Anna (Brilla) Dewenetz; m. Setsuko Sugihara, Aug. 14, 1955; children: Paula, Vladimir, Mignon. BA in Econs. cum laude, Ind. U., 1954; LLB, Columbia U., 1957. Bar: NY 1958, US Dist. Ct. Hawaii 1960, Hawaii 1961, US Ct. Appeals (9th cir.) 1962, US Ct. Internat. Trade 1963, US Supreme Ct. 1970. Pvt. practice law, NYC, 1958-60; ptnr. Lewis, Saunders & Key, Honolulu, 1960-69; corp. counsel City and County of Honolulu, 1969-72, mng. dir., 1973-75; ptnr. Devens, Nakano, Saito, Lee, Wong & Ching, Honolulu, 1975-94, of counsel, 1994—2006, ret., 2006. Judge Nuclear Claims Tribunal, Majuro, Republic of the Marshall Islands, 1988-90. Mem. Japan-Hawaii Econ. Coun., 1975-95, Honolulu Charter Reorgn. Com., 1979-80, Pacific and Asian Affairs Coun., 1983; trustee Japan-Am. Soc. Honolulu, 1981-2006, pres., 1987-89; chmn. bd. dirs. Nat. Assn. Japan-Am. Socs., 1989-91; mem. bd. govs. Japanese Cultural Ctr., Hawaii, 1989-94, mem. bd. dirs., v.p., 1994-96, chmn. bd. dirs., 1996-97. Decorated Imperial Order of the Sacred Treasure, Gold Rays with Neck ribbon Govt. of Japan, 1993. Mem.: Phi Beta Kappa. Democrat. Eastern Orthodox. Office: Devens Nakano Saito Lee Wong & Ching 220 S King St Ste 1600 Honolulu HI 96813-4597 Office Phone: 808-521-1456.

DEVENUTI, RICK (RICHARD R. DEVENUTI), former computer software company executive; b. 1958; BA in Acctg., U. Wash. With Microsoft Corp., Redmond, Wash., 1987—2007, gen. mgr. sales ops., dir. fin. analysis, U.S. contr., gen. mgr. N.Am. ops., v.p. worldwide ops., v.p., chief info. officer, 1999—2004, sr. v.p. worldwide svcs. & IT, 2004—07. Avocations: golf, skiing.

DEVI, AMRITANANDAMAYI (SRI MATA AMRITANANDAMAYI DEVI, AMMA), spiritual leader; b. Kerala, India, Sept. 27, 1953; d. Sugunanandan and Damayanti. Founder Amrita Inst. Med. Scis., Mata Amritanandamayi Mission Trust, Gujarat Earthquake Relief Effort; pres. Centenary Parliament of World Religions, Chgo.; spkr. UN. Subject of film, Darshan — The Embrace, Cannes Film Festival, 2005. Recipient Gandhi-King award for Non-Violence, 2002, James Parks Morton Interfaith award, Interfaith Ctr. NY, 2006. Office: Sri Mata Amma Amritapuri PO Kerala Kollum 690525 India also: MA Ctr PO Box 613 San Ramon CA 94583

DEVIN, IRENE K., state legislator, nurse; b. Sumter, SC, Jan. 24, 1943; m. Jerry Devin. BSN, U. Iowa, 1965. RN. Mem. Wyo. Ho. Rep., Cheyenne, 1992-96, Wyo. Senate, Dist. 10, Cheyenne, 1996—; mem. edn. com. Wyo. Senate, Cheyenne, mem. labor, health, and social svcs. com. Trustee Dist. Hosp., 1986-92, past pres.; mem. Laramie Econ. Devel. Corp., Friends of 4-H; pres. Ivinson Meml. Hosp. Found.; mem. state adv. bd. Medicaid, Rural Health TB Program; mem. adv. bd. Cmty. Pub. Health. Mem. Laramie C. of C., Soroptomists Internat. Republican. Home: 3601 Grays Gable Rd Laramie WY 82072-5032 Office: Wyo Senate State Capitol Cheyenne WY 82002-0001

DEVINE, BRIAN KIERNAN, pet food and supplies company executive; b. Wash., Mar. 1, 1942; s. William John and Rita Marie (Kiernan) D.; m. Silvija Viktorija Kutlets, June 13, 1964; children—Brian Jr., Brooke BA, Georgetown U., 1963; postgrad., Am. U., 1964-65, Yale U., 1965. Statis. adv. USPHS, Washington, 1963-70; with Toys "R" Us, 1970-88; gen. mgr. San Jose, Calif., 1970-75; regional gen. mgr. Chgo., 1975-77; v.p. Saddle Brook, N.J., 1977-82; sr. v.p. Rochelle Park, N.J., 1982-88; pres. of furniture mfr./retailer Krause's Sofa Factory, Fountain Valley, Calif., 1988-89; pres. Petco, San Diego, 1990—, CEO, 1990—2004, chmn., 1994—. Bd. dirs. Nat. Retail Fedn., Students in Free Enterprise, Wild Oats Markets, Inc.; mem. coll. bd. advisers, bd. regents Georgetown U. Contbr. articles to profl. publs. Mem. Internat. Mass Retail Assn. (bd. dirs.). Republican. Roman Catholic. Office: Petco 9125 Rehco Rd San Diego CA 92121-2270 Business E-Mail: briand@petco.com.

DEVINE, SHARON JEAN, lawyer; b. Milw., Feb. 27, 1948; d. George John Devine and Ethel May (Langworthy) Devine Chase; children: Devin Curtiss, Katharine Langworthy. BS in Linguistics magna cum laude, Georgetown U., 1970; JD, Boston U., 1975. Bar: Ohio, Colo. Staff atty. FTC, Cleve., 1975-79, asst. regional dir. Denver, 1982-84; atty. Mountain Bell, Denver, 1982-84, U.S. West Direct, 1984-85, assoc. gen. counsel, 1985-87, Landmark Pub. Co., Denver, 1987-88; antitrust counsel U.S. West, Denver, 1988-91, corp. counsel, 1991-99, assoc. gen. counsel, 1999-2000, 2 West Commns. Internat. Inc., 2000—. Dir. Denver Consortium, 1982-83, Ctr. for Applied Prevention, Boulder, Colo., 1982-90; dir. Legal Aid Found. of Colo., 1990-96, Suzuki Assn. of Colo., 1990-94. Active mem. Jr. League, Denver, 1980-87. Mem. Am. Corp. Counsel Assn. (dir. Colo. chpt. 1994-2000, pres. 1999-2000), Colo. Bar Assn., Denver Assn., Colo. Women's Bar Assn.- Office: 2West 1801 California St Ste 4900 Denver CO 80202-2610 Home: 979 Lipan St Denver CO 80204-3911 E-mail: sjdevine@qwest.com.

DEVLIN, GERRY, state legislator, farmer, rancher; b. Miles City, Mont., Sept. 11, 1932; m. Isabelle Devlin. Grad., Terry H.S. Farmer, rancher; mem. Mont. Ho. of Reps., 1981-88; chair taxation com., vice chair fish and game com.; mem. Mont. State Senate, 1988—, chair com. on taxes, chair taxation com., mem. agr., livestock and irrigation com. Served with U.S. Army, 1951-53. Republican. Home: 517 Mississippi Ave Miles City MT 59301-4137

DEVLIN, PATRICIA, lawyer; b. Vallejo, Calif., July 25, 1945; BA magna cum laude, U. Wash., 1968; JD, U. Calif., 1977. Bar: Calif. 1977, Hawaii 1978, U.S. Dist. Ct. Hawaii 1978. With Carlsmith Ball LLP, Honolulu. Mem. ABA, State Bar Calif., Hawaii Soc. Corp. Planners (pres. 1992-93), Phi Beta Kappa. Office: Carlsmith Ball LLP Pacific Tower # 2200 1001 Bishop St Honolulu HI 96813-3429 E-mail: pdevlin@carlsmith.com.

DEVLIN, RICHARD, state legislator; b. Eugene, Oreg., Sept. 9, 1952; m to Eliza; children: two. BS in Sci. in Admin. of Justice, Portland State U., 1976; MA in Mgmt., Pepperdine U., 1980. Mem., Tualatin Parks Advisor Com., 1982, Tualatin City Coun, 1984; chmn., Metro Area Comm. Com., 1987 & 1988; former mem. Dist. 24, Oreg. House of Reps., former vice chmn., House Rules & Redistricting & Public Affairs, former mem., Smart Growth & Commerce Committees; mem. Dist. 19, Oreg. State Senate, 2003-, Majority Leader. Legal investigator. Democrat. Roman Catholic. Mailing: 900 Court St NE, S-223 Salem OR 97301 Address: 10290 SW Anderson Ct Tualatin OR 97062 Office Phone: 503-691-2026, 503-986-1700. Fax: 503-986-1561. Business E-Mail: sen.richarddevlin@state.or.us.*

DEVRIES, KENNETH LAWRENCE, mechanical engineer, educator; b. Ogden, Utah, Oct. 27, 1933; s. Sam and Fern (Slater) DeVries; m. Kay M. McGee, Mar. 1, 1959; children: Kenneth, Susan. AS in Civil Engring., Weber State Coll., 1953; BSME, U. Utah, 1959, PhD in Physics, Mech. Engring., 1962. Registered profl. engr., Utah. Rsch. engr. hydraulic group Convair Aircraft Corp., Fort Worth, 1957-58; prof. dept. mech. engring. U. Utah, Salt Lake City, 1969-75, 1976-91, disting. prof., 1991—, chmn. dept., 1970-81, pres. acad. senate, 2004—05; sr. assoc. dean U. Utah Coll. Engring., Salt Lake City, 1983-97, acting dean, 1997-98. Program dir. div. materials rsch. NSF, Washington, 1975-76, pres. academic senate, 2004-05; materials cons. Browning, Morgan, Utah, 1972—; cons. 3M Co., Mpls., 1985—; tech. adv. bd. Emerson Electric, St. Louis, 1978-2002; mem. Utah Coun. Sci. and Tech., 1973-77; trustee Gordon Rsch. Conf., 1989-97, chair, 1992-93 Co-author: Analysis and Testing of Adhesive Bonds, 1978; contbr. chpts. to books, articles to profl. jours. Fellow ASME, Am. Phys. Soc.; mem. Am. Chem. Soc. (polymer div.), Am. Soc. for Engring. Edn. (nat. officer), Adhesion Soc. Mem. Lds Ch. Office: U Utah Coll Engring 50 S Central Campus Dr Salt Lake City UT 84112-9249 Office Phone: 801-581-7101. Business E-Mail: kldevries@mech.utah.edu, kldevries@eng.utah.edu.

DEW, BILL, construction executive; b. Utah; m. Jolene Dew. B in Fin., U. Utah, Salt Lake City, 1978. Bldg. contractor; founder, owner DewBury Homes. Humanitarian mission, Jordan. 1st lt. USAR, 1986. Republican. Office: DewBury Homes PO Box # 26491 Salt Lake City UT 84126 Office Phone: 801-201-3586. Office Fax: 801-968-8614.

DEW, WILLIAM WALDO, JR., bishop; b. Newport, Ky., Dec. 14, 1935; s. William Waldo and Thelma (Dittus) D.; m. Mae Marie Eggers, Jan. 5, 1958; children: Linda Dew-Hiersoux, William, Marilyn. BA, Union Coll., Barbourville, Ky., 1957; MDiv, Drew Theol. Sch., 1961; PhD (hon.), Rust Coll., 1991, Union Coll., 1992. Ordained to ministry United Meth. Ch. as deacon, 1958, as elder, 1963. Pastor Springville (Calif.) United Meth. Ch., 1961-64, Lindsay (Calif.) United Meth. Ch., 1964-67, Meml. United Meth. Ch., Clovis, Calif., 1967-72, Epworth United Meth. Ch., Berkeley, Calif., 1972-79; dist. supt. Cen. Dist. Calif.-Nev. Annual Conf., Modesto, Calif., 1979-84; pastor San Ramon Valley United Meth. Ch., Alamo, Calif., 1984-88; bishop United Meth. Ch., Portland, Oreg., 1988-96, United Meth. Ch. Desert S.W. Conf., Phoenix, 1996—. Lectr. Pacific Sch. Religion, Berkeley, 1976-79. Trustee Willamette U., Salem, Oreg., 1988-96, Alaska Pacific U., Anchorage, 1988-96, Claremont Sch. Theology, 1996—. Paul Harris fellow Rotary Internat., 1988. Democrat. Avocations: fishing, golf, reading, travel. Office: Claremont Sch of Theology 1325 North College Ave Claremont CA 91711

DEWEY, DONALD ODELL, dean, academic administrator; b. Portland, Oreg., July 9, 1930; s. Leslie Hamilton and Helen (Odell) D.; m. Charlotte Marion Neuber, Sept. 21, 1952; children: Leslie Helen, Catherine Dawn, Scott Hamilton. Student, Lewis and Clark Coll., Portland, Oreg., 1948—49; BA, U. Oreg., Eugene, 1952; MS, U. Utah, Salt Lake City, 1956; PhD, U. Chgo., 1960. Mng. editor Condon Globe-Times, Oreg., 1952-53; city editor Ashland Daily Tidings, Oreg., 1953-54; asst. editor, assoc. editor The Papers of James Madison, Chgo., 1957-62; instr. U. Chgo., 1960-62; from asst. prof. to prof. Calif. State U., LA, 1962-96, dean Sch. Letters and Sci., 1970-84, dean Sch. Natural and Social Sci., 1984-96, dean emeritus, prof. emeritus, 1996—; v.p. acad. affairs Trinity Coll. Grad. Studies, Anaheim, Calif., 2000—06. V.p. Calif. U. Emeritus and Retired Faculty Assn., 2005—06, pres., 2006—09. Author: The Continuing Dialogue, 2 vols., 1964, Union and Liberty: Documents in American Constitutionalism, 1969, Marshall versus Jefferson: The Political Background of Marbury v. Madison, 1970, Becoming Informed Citizens: Lessons on the Constitution for Junior High School Students, 1988, revised edit., 1995, Invitation to the Dance: An Introduction to Social Dance, 1991, Becoming Informed Citizens: The Bill of Rights and Limited Government, 1995, That's a Good One: Cal State L.A. at 50, 1997, The Federalist and Antifederalist Papers, 1998, Controversial Elections, 2001, James Madison: Defender of The Republic, 2009; contbr. chpts. to books. Recipient Outstanding Prof. award Calif. State U., 1976 Mem. Am. Hist. Assn. (exec. com. Pacific Coast br. 1971-74), Orgn. Am. Historians, Am. Soc. Legal History (adv. bd. Pacific Coast br. 1972-75), Gold Key, Calif. State U. Emeritus and Ret. Faculty Assn. (v.p. 2005-06, pres. 2006-), Phi Alpha Theta, Pi Sigma Alpha, Phi Kappa Phi, Sigma Delta Chi. Office: Calif State U Dept History 5151 State University Dr Los Angeles CA 90032-4226 Home Phone: 818-790-2673; Office Phone: 323-343-2022. Business E-Mail: ddewey@calstatela.edu.

DEWILDE, DAVID MICHAEL, management consultant, lawyer, finance company executive, retired recruiter; b. Bridgeton, NJ, Aug. 11, 1940; s. Louis and Dorothea (Donnelly) deW.; m. Katherine August, Dec. 30, 1984; children: Holland Stockdale, Christian DuCroix, Nicholas Alexander, Lucas Barrymore. AB, Dartmouth Coll., 1962; LLB, U. Va., 1967; MS in Mgmt., Stanford U., 1984. Bar: N.Y. 1968, D.C. 1972. Assoc. Curtis, Mallet-Prevost, Colt & Mosle, NYC, 1967-69; assoc. gen. counsel HUD, Washington, 1969-72; investment banker Lehman Bros., Washington, 1972-74; dep. commr. FHA, Washington, 1974-76; pres. Govt. Nat. Mortgage Assn., Washington, 1976-77; mng. dir. Lepercq DeNeuflize & Co., NYC, 1977-81; exec. v.p. policy and planning Fed. Nat. Mortgage Assn., Washington, 1981-82; pres. deWilde & Assocs., Washington, 1982-84; mng. dir., dir. fin. svcs. Boyden Internat., San Francisco, 1984-88; CEO Chartwell Ptnrs. Internat., San Francisco, 1989-97; mng. dir. LAI Worldwide, San Francisco, 1998-99; mng. ptnr. TMP Worldwide, San Francisco, 1999-2001; mgmt. cons., 2001—. Bd. dirs. Berkshire Realty Investment Trust, Fritzi of Calif., Silicon Valley Bankshares; bd. dirs. St. Luke's School, San Francisco, chair, 2001-03. Editor-in-chief Va. Jour. Internat. Law, 1966-67. Lt. USN, 1962-64. Mem. Pacific Union Club (San Francisco), Villa Taverna (San Francisco), Met. Club (Washington), Belvedere Tennis Club. Republican. Personal E-mail: ddewilde@pacbell.net.

DEWITT, BARBARA JANE, journalist; b. Glendale, Calif., Aug. 5, 1947; d. Clarence James and Irene Brezina; m. Don DeWitt, Apr. 21, 1974; children: Lisa, Scarlett. BA in Journalism, Calif. State U., Northridge, 1971. Features editor The Daily Ind. Newspaper, Ridgecrest, Calif., 1971-84; fashion editor The Daily Breeze, Torrance, Calif., 1984-89; freelance fashion reporter The Seattle Times,

1990; fashion editor, columnist The Los Angeles Daily News, LA, 1990—. Instr. fashion writing UCLA, 1988, Am. InterContinental U., L.A., 1996—. Dir. Miss Indian Wells Valley Scholarship Pageant, 1980-84. Recipient 1st Pl. Best Youth Page, Calif. Newspaper Pubs. Assn., 1980, 1st Pl. Best Fashion, Wash. Press Assn., 1989, The Internat. Aldo award for fashion journalism, 1995, 96. Republican. Lutheran. Avocations: antiques, reading, swimming. Office: The Daily News 21221 Oxnard St Woodland Hills CA 91367-5081 Home: PO Box 2518 Agoura Hills CA 91376-2518

DEWOLFE, CHRISTOPHER T., former Internet company executive; b. 1966; married. BA in Fin., U. Wash., 1988; MBA in Mktg., U. So. Calif., 1997. Mgr. merchant commerce divsn. First Bank Beverly Hills, v.p. mktg., 1997—99; pres. Euniverse, Inc., L.A.; v.p. mktg. Xdrive Technologies, Inc., Santa Monica, Calif., 1999—2001; CEO ResponseBase, LLC, Santa Monica, Calif., 2001—02, co-founder, pres., 2002—03; pres., CEO ResponseBase Mktg., LLC, 2002—03; co-founder MySpace.com, 2003, CEO, 2003—09. Bd. dirs. Fog Cutter Capital Grp., Inc., 2002—. Recipient Vanguard award, Prodrs. Guild America, 2009; co-recipient with Tom Anderson, Breakout of Yr., Webby award, Internat. Acad. Digital Arts and Scis., 2006; named one of The 100 Most Influential People in the World, TIME mag., 2006, with Tom Anderson, 25 Most Influential People in Web Music, Powergeek 25, 2007. Fellow: World Network Found. Achievements include MySpace.com being the most popular social networking website on the internet.*

DE YOUNG, DAVID SPENCER, astrophysicist, educator; b. Colorado Springs, Nov. 29, 1940; s. Henry C. and Zona L. (Church) DeY.; m. Mary Ellen Haney. BA, U. Colo., 1962; PhD, Cornell U., 1967. Rsch. physicist Los Alamos (N.Mex.) Nat. Labs., 1967-69; astronomer Nat. Radio Astronomy Obs., Charlottesville, Va., 1969-80, Kitt Peak Nat. Obs., Tucson, 1980—, assoc. dir., 1983-88, dir., 1988-94. Organizer numerous sci. confs.; mem. adv. bd. Aspen (Colo.) Ctr. Physics, 1977-, trustee, 1992—, pres., 2001-05; mem. exec. com. steering com. San Diego Supercomputer Ctr., 1985-98, chmn., 1989-91; mem. steering com. Nat. Virtual Obs., 2000—, project scientist, 2001-, exec. com., 2001—; mem. Nat. Optical Astronomy Obs., Tucson, 1982-, assoc. dir., 1988-94, 2007—; bd. dirs. WIYN Telescope Consortium, Tucson; mem. exec. com. Internat. Virtual Obs. Alliance, 2001—, vice chair, 2006—, chair, 2007-; mem. sci. adv. com. European Virtual Observatory, 2006—. Contbr. articles to profl. jours. NASA grantee. Fellow Am. Phys. Soc.; mem. Astron. Soc. Pacific, Am. Astron. Soc., Internat. Astron. Union, Internat. Union Radio Soc., Phi Beta Kappa. Office: Nat Optical Astronomy Observatory 950 N Cherry Ave Tucson AZ 85719-4933

DHIR, VIJAY K., engineering educator; b. Giddarbaha, Panjab, India, Apr. 14, 1943; arrived in US, 1969; s. Harnand Lal and Parsinni Devi (Sofat) D.; m. Komal Lata Khanna, Aug. 31, 1973; children: Vinita, Vashita. BScME, Punjab Engring. Coll., India, 1965; MTechME, Indian Inst. Tech., 1969; PhD in Mech. Engring., U. Ky., 1972. Asst. devel. engr. Jyoti Pumps, Ltd., Baroda, India, 1968-69; postgrad. engr. Engring. Rsch. Ctr. Tata Engring. & Locomotive Co., Poona, India, 1969; rsch. asst. U. Ky., Lexington, 1969-72, rsch. assoc., 1972-74; asst. prof. chem., nuclear & thermal engring. dept. UCLA, 1974-78, assoc. prof., 1978-82, prof. mech., aerospace & nuclear engring. dept., 1982—, vice chmn. mech., aerospace & nuclear engring. dept., 1988-91, chmn. dept., 1994-2000, assoc. dean Henry Samueli Sch. Engring. and Applied Sci., 2001—02, interim dean, 2002—03, dean, 2003—. Cons. Nuclear Regulatory Commn., Seabulk Corp., Ft. Lauderdale, Fla., Argonne (Ill.) Nat. Lab., Pickard, Lowe & Garrick, Inc., Irvine, Calif., Rockwell Internat., Canoga Park, Calif., GE Corp., San Jose, Calif., Battelle N.W. Lab., Richland, Wash., Phys. Rsch., Inc., Torrance, Calif., Nat. Bur. Stds., Gaithersburg, Md., Los Alamos (N.Mex.) Nat. Lab., Sci. Applications Inc., El Segundo, Calif., Brookhaven Nat. Lab., Upton, N.Y.; chmn. numerous conf. sessions. Contbr. over 150 articles to profl. jours., over 150 papers to procs./conf. & symposia records; assoc. editor Applied Mechs. Rev., 1985-88, Jour. Heat Transfer, Transactions ASME, 1993-96, editor, 2000—2005; assoc. editor ASME Symposium Vol., 1978; referee numerous jours. Recipient Max Jakob award, ASME/AIChE, 2004. Fellow: NAE (Thermal Hydraulic Divsn. Tech. Achievement award 2005), AIChE (Donald Q. Kern award 1999), ASME (sr. tech. editor Jour. Heat Transfer 2000—05, Heat Transfer Meml. Award Sci. Category 1992, Thurston Lecture award 2008), Am. Nuclear Soc. Office: Sch of Engring & Applied Sci Univ Calif 7400 Boelter Hall Los Angeles CA 90095 Business E-Mail: vdhir@seas.ucla.edu.

DIAB, MOHAMMAD, orthopedic surgeon; b. Cairo, May 6, 1964; B in Classics, Stanford U., Calif., B in Biology; MD, Stanford U. Sch. Medicine, Calif., 1990. Cert. in orthopaedic surgery 2000. Internship in orthopedics U. Wash. Sch. Medicine, Seattle, 1990—91, residency in orthopaedic surgery, 1993—97, asst. prof., dept. orthopedics, physician, 1998—2002; fellowship in pediatric orthopaedic surgery Harvard U., Boston, 1997—98; physician Children's Hosp. & Regional Med. Ctr., Seattle, 1998—2002, Overlake Hosp, Bellevue, Wash., 2000—02; assoc. prof. orthopaedic surgery and pediat. U. Calif., San Francisco, 2002—, paediatric orthopaedic surgeon, 2002—, chief, pediatric orthopedics. Mem.: AMA, Scoliosis Rsch. Soc., Pediatric Orthopedic Soc. North America, Am. Acad. Pediatrics, Am. Acad. Orthopedic Surgery. Office: Univ Calif San Francisco Dept Orthopaedic Surgery 500 Parnassus Ave San Francisco CA 94143 Office Phone: 415-476-1166.

DIAL, ELLEN CONEDERA, lawyer; b. Chgo., July 19, 1946; m. Joseph F. Dial. AB in English magna cum laude, Cornell U., 1968, JD magna cum laude, 1977. Bar: Washington 1979. Law clk. to Hon. Charles Horowitz Supreme Ct. Washington, 1977—79; ptnr. Perkins Coie LLP, Seattle. Pres. Wash. State Bar Assn., 2006—07, current immediate past pres., 2007—08. Bd. trustees YWCA Seattle, King County, Snohomish County; adv. bd. UW World Series Meany U. Wash. Recipient award merit, Wash. State Bar Assn., 2004; named one of Washington's Super Lawyers, Washington Law & Politics, 2003—07; named to Am. Leading Real Estate Lawyers, Chambers USA, 2003—07, Legal Women Leaders, Vault, 2006. Fellow: Am. Bar Found. Office: Perkins Coie LLP Ste 4800 1201 Third Ave Seattle WA 98101-3099 Office Phone: 206-359-8438. Office Fax: 206-359-9000.

DIAMA, BENJAMIN, retired secondary school educator, composer, writer; b. Hilo, Hawaii, Sept. 23, 1933; s. Agapito and Catalina (Buscas) D. BFA, Sch. Art Inst. Chgo., 1956. Cert. tchr., Hawaii. Tchr. art, basketball coach Waimea (Kauai, Hawaii) High Sch., 1963-67; tchr. music and art Campbell High Sch., Honolulu, 1967-68; tchr. math. and art Waipahu High Sch., Honolulu, 1968-69; tchr. art and music Palisades Elem. Sch., Honolulu, 1969-70; tchr. typing, history, art and music Honokaa (Hawaii) High Sch., 1970-73; tchr. music Kealakehe Sch., Kailua, 1973-74; ret., 1974. Spkr. Big Island Sci. Conf. State of Hawaii Govt., U. Hawaii, Hilo, 2003. Author, writer, composer: Hawaii, 1983; author: Poems of Faith, 1983-88, School One vs. School Two On The Same School Campus, 1983, The Calendar-Clock Theory of the Universe with Faith-Above and Beyond, 1984-90, Phonetic Sound-Musical Theory, 1990, The Calendar-Clock Theory of the Universe with Faith, Cambridge, 2008; contbg. author: Benjamin Diama-The Calendar Clock Theory of the Universe, 1991, 92, (poetry) Celebration of Poets, 1998, Poets Elite, Internat. Soc. of Poets, 2000, Labours of Love, Song of Honour, 2005; prodr., composer (Cassette) Hawaii I Love You, 1986; inventor universal clock, double floater boat, Gardener's Water Box, Full Court Half Court 6 vs. 6, 3 Offense-3 Defense Basketball Game. Recipient Achievement award Waimea Dept. Edn., 1964-67, Purchase award State Found. Arts on Culture and the Arts, 1984, State Found. Arts and Culture Acquisition Painting Art award State of Hawaii Govt. Art Collection, Lifetime Achievement award Internat. Biog. Ctr., 2005. Mem. NEA, Hawaii Tchrs. Assn., Hawaii Edn. Assn., AAAS, Nat. Geog. Soc., Smithsonian Assocs., ASCAP, N.Y. Acad. Scis., Nat. Libr. Poetry (assoc.), Internat. Soc. Poets, Am. Geophysical Union. Mem. Salvation Army. Achievements include design of slip on-pull a step lace walking aid foot or shoe slipper supporter. Avocations: singing, writing, basketball. Home: PO Box 2997 Kailua Kona HI 96745-2997 Home Phone: 808-329-9789.

DIAMOND, JARED MASON, biologist, writer; b. Boston, Sept. 10, 1937; m. Marie Cohen; children: Max, Joshua. BA in biochemical sciences, Harvard U., 1958; PhD in physiology, Cambridge U., Eng., 1961. Jr. fellow, Soc. Fellows Harvard U., 1962—65; assoc. in biophysics Harvard Med. Sch., 1965—66; assoc. prof. physiology UCLA Med. Sch., 1966—68, prof., 1968—; now prof. geography UCLA. Rsch. assoc. ornithology Am. Mus. Natural History, 1973—, LA County Mus. Natural History, 1985—; contbg. editor Discover mag., 1984—; bd. dirs. World Wildlife Fund, 1993—. Author: The Avifauna of the Eastern Highlands of New Guinea, 1972, The Third Chimpanzee: The Evolution and Future of the Human Animal, 1992 (Rhone-Poulenc Science Book Prize, 1992), Why is Sex Fun? The Evolution of Human Sexuality, 1997, Guns, Germs, and Steel: The Fates of Human Societies, 1997 (Phi Beta Kappa Sci. Book Prize, 1997, Pulitzer Prize, 1998, Cosmos Prize, Japan, 1998, Rhone-Poulenc Science Book Prize, 1998), Collapse: How Societies Choose to Fail or Succeed, 2004; co-author: Birds of New Guinea, 1986, The Birds of Northern Melanesia: Speciation, Ecology, and Biogeography, 2001; co-editor (with M.L. Cody): Ecology and Evolution of Communities, 1975; co-editor: (with T.J. Case) Community Ecology, 1986. Recipient Disting. Achievement Award, Am. Gastroent. Assn., 1975, Bowditch Prize, Am. Physiol. Soc., 1976, Burr Medal, Nat. Geog. Soc., 1979, Carr Medal, 1989, Coues Award, Am. Ornithologists' Union, 1998, Nat. Medal Science, 1999, Tyler Prize for Environ. Achievement, 2001; MacArthur Found. Fellowship, 1985. Fellow: Am. Acad. Arts and Scis.; mem.: NAS, Inst. Medicine, Am. Philos. Soc. Office: UCLA Med Ctr Dept of Physiology 10833 Le Conte Ave Los Angeles CA 90095-3075

DIAMOND, JASON BRETT, head, neck and facial plastic surgeon; b. NJ, Dec. 21, 1970; MD, U. Rochester Sch. Medicine, 1997. Diplomate Am. Bd. Facial Plastic and Reconstructive Surgery, Am. Bd. Otolaryngology. Fellow Am. Coll. Surgeon; pvt. practice Beverly Hills. Featured facelift, rhinoplasty and eyelid expert on Dr. 90210, 2005—, guest appearances Discovery Health Channel, Entertainment Tonight, NBC, and E! Channel, ABC, CBS, Access Hollywood, others, featured in Harpers Bazaar, Life & Style, People. Office: 9201 Sunset Blvd Los Angeles CA 90069 Office Fax: 310-859-9815. Business E-Mail: drdiamond@jasonbdiamond.com.

DIAMOND, LARRY, political scientist; BA, Stanford U., 1974, MA, 1978, PhD, 1980. Prof. Vanderbilt U., Nashville, 1980—85; sr. fellow Hoover Instn., Stanford, Calif., 1985—; prof. Stanford U., 1985—. Coord., Democracy Program Inst. Internat. Studies, Stanford U., Ctr. on Democracy, Devel. and the Rule of Law; co-dir. Forum Dem. Studies, Nat Endowment for Democracy; coord., Iran Democracy Project Hoover Instn.; Fulbright vis. lectr. Bayero U., Kano, Nigeria, 1982—83; vis. scholar Academia Sinica, Taiwan, 1997—98; cons. US Agency for Internat. Devel., 2001—02; sr. advisor Coalition Provisional Authority, Iraq, 2004. Co-editor: Journal of Democracy, 1990—; author: Developing Democracy: Toward Consolidation, 1999, Promoting Democracy in the 1990s: Actors and Instruments, Issues and Imperatives, 1999, Class, Ethnicity and Democracy in Nigeria: The Failure of the First Republic, 1988, Squandered Victory: The American Occupation and Bungled Effort to Bring Democracy to Iraq, 2005, The Spirit of Democracy: The Struggle to Build Free Societies Throughout the World, 2008; contbr. articles to profl jours. Recipient Dinkelspiel award, Stanford U., 2007; named Tchr. of Yr., Associated Students, Stanford U., 2007. Office: Hoover Instn Room 1202 Hoover Tower Stanford CA 94305-6010 Business E-Mail: diamond@hoover.stanford.edu.*

DIAMOND, MARIAN CLEEVES, neuroscientist, educator; b. Glendale, Calif., Nov. 11, 1926; d. Montague and Rosa Marian (Wamphler) Cleeves; m. Richard M. Diamond, Dec. 20, 1950 (div.); m. Arnold B. Scheibel, Sept. 14, 1982; children: Catherine, Richard, Jeffrey, Ann. AB, U. Calif., Berkeley, 1948, MA, 1949, PhD, 1953. With Harvard U., Cambridge, 1952-54, Cornell U., Ithaca, NY, 1954-58, U. Calif., San Francisco, 1959—62, prof. anatomy Berkeley, 1962—. Asst. dean U. Calif., Berkeley, 1967-70, assoc. dean, 1970-73, dir. The Lawrence Hall of Sci., 1990-95, dir. emeritus, 1995—; vis. scholar Australian Nat. U., 1978, Fudan U., Shanghai, China, 1985, U. Nairobi, Kenya, 1988. Author (with J. Hopson): Magic Trees of the Mind, 1998; author: Enriching Heredity, 1989; co-author: The Human Brain Coloring, 1985; editor: Contraceptive Hormones Estrogen and Human Welfare, 1978; contbr. over 155 articles to profl. jours. V.p. County Women Dems., Ithaca, 1957; bd. dirs. Unitarian Ch., Berkeley, 1969. Recipient Calif. Gifted award, 1989, C.A.S.E. Calif. Prof. of Yr. award, Nat. Gold medalist, 1990, Woman of Yr. award Zonta Internat., 1991, U. medal La. U. Del Zulia, Maricaibo, Venezuela, 1992, Alumna of the Yr. award U. Calif., Berkeley, 1995; Calif. Acad. Scis. fellow, 1991, Calif. Soc. Biomedical Rsch. Dist. Svc. award, 1998, Alumnae Resources-Women of Achievement Vision and Excellence award, 1999, Benjamin Ide Wheeler award 1999, Achievement award Calif. Child Devel. Adminstrs. Assn., 2001, LH Marshall Spl. Recognisation award, Soc. of Neuroscience, 2007; named Disting. Scholar America, Am. Assn. U. Women, 1997; named to Internat. Educators Hall of Fame, 1999, Fellow AAAS, AAUW (sr.; fellowship chair 1970-85); mem. Am. Assn. Anatomists, Soc. Neurosci., Philos. Soc. Washington, The Faculty Club (Berkeley, v.p. 1979-85, 90-95). Avocations: hiking, sports, painting. Home: 2583 Virginia St Berkeley CA 94709-1108 Office: U Calif Dept Integrative Biology 3060 Valley Life Sciences Bldg Berkeley CA 94720-3116 Office Phone: 510-642-4547. Business E-Mail: diamond@berkeley.edu.

DIAMOND, NEIL LESLIE, singer, composer; b. Bklyn., Jan. 24, 1941; m. Marcia Murphey, 1975; children: Jesse, Micah; children by previous marriage: Marjorie, Elyn. Student, NYU. Formerly with Bang Records, Uni, MCA Records, Los Angeles, now rec. artist, singer, composer, Columbia Records; songs include Solitary Man, Cherry, Cherry, Kentucky Woman, I'm a Believer, September Morn, Sweet Caroline, Holly Holy, A Little Bit Me, A Little Bit You, Longfellow Serenade, Song Sung Blue, America, I Am, I Said; albums include: The Feel of Neil Diamond, 1966, Just for You, 1967, Neil Diamond's Greatest Hits, 1968, Velvet Gloves and Spit, 1968, Touching You, Touching Me, 1969, Brother Love's Travelling Salvation Show, 1969, Gold, 1970, Tap Root Manuscript, 1970, Shilo, 1970, Stones, 1971, Do It!, 1971, Hot August Nights, 1972, Moods, 1972, Rainbow, 1973, Jonathan Livingston Seagull, 1973, Greatest Hits, 1974, Serenade, 1974, Gold 1, 1974, Gold 2, 1974, Diamonds, 1975, Focus On, 1975, Beautiful Noise, 1976, And the Singer Sings His Song, 1976, Live at the Greek, 1977, I'm Glad You're Here With Me Tonight, 1977, You Don't Bring Me Flowers, 1978, 20 Golden Greats, 1978, Neil Diamonds, 1979, September Morn, 1980, Jazz Singer, 1980, Best Of, 1981, Solitary, 1981, Love Songs, 1981, On the Way to the Sky, 1981, Live Diamond, 1982, Heart Light, 1982, Song Sung Blue, 1982, Primitive, 1984, Headed For the Future, 1986, Hot August Night II, 1987, The Best Years of Our Lives, 1989, Lovescape, 1991, Neil Diamond The Greatest Hits, 1966-92, 1992, The Christmas Album, 1992, Neil Diamond Glory Road 1968-72, 1992, Live in America, 1994, His 12 Greatest Hits, 1996, As Time Goes By-Movie Album, 1998, Best of Neil Diamond, 1999, Best of The Movie Album, 1999, Three Cord Opera, 2001, The Essential, 2001, Play Me, 2002, Gold, 2005, 12 Songs (prod. by Rick Rubin), 2005, Home Before Dark, 2008; (videos) Neil Diamond: Greatest Hits Live, 1988, Neil Diamond: Under a Tennessee Moon, 1996 (with others) Tennessee Moon, 1996; composer film scores Jonathan Livingston Seagull (Grammy award 1973), Every Which Way but Loose, 1978, The Jazz Singer (also actor), 1980; guest artist network TV shows; (TV specials) Neil Diamond's Christmas Special, HBO, 1992, ABC, 1993. Recipient 19 platinum albums, 28 gold albums.

DIAMOND, PHILIP ERNEST, lawyer; b. LA, Feb. 11, 1925; s. William and Elizabeth (Weizenhaus) D.; m. Dorae Seymour (dec.); children: William, Wendy, Nancy; m. 2d, Jenny White Carson. B.A., UCLA, 1949, M.A., 1950; J.D., U. Calif., Berkeley, 1953. Bar: Calif. 1953, U.S. Dist. Ct. (no., ea. and cen. dists.) Calif. 1953, U.S. Ct. Appeals (9th cir.) 1953. Law clk. to presiding justice Calif. Dist. Ct. Appeals, 1953-54; assoc. Landels & Weigel, San Francisco, 1954-60; ptnr. Landels Weigel & Ripley, San Francisco, 1960-62; sr. ptnr. Landels, Ripley & Diamond, San Francisco, 1962-93—; pres. Diamond Wine Mchts., San Francisco, 1976—; bd. dirs. Yasutomo & Co. Pres. Contra Costa Sch. Bd. Assn., 1966-68. With USN, 1943-46. Mem. ABA, Am. Arbitration Assn., Calif. State Bar Assn., San Francisco Bar Assn., Phi Beta Kappa. Democrat. Clubs: Commonwealth, Mchts. & Exch. Office: 350 The Embarcadero San Francisco CA 94105-1204

DIAMOND, STANLEY JAY, lawyer; b. LA, Nov. 27, 1927; s. Philip Alfred and Florence (Fadem) D.; m. Lois Jane Broida, June 22, 1969; children: Caryn Elaine, Diana Beth. BA, UCLA, 1949; JD, U. So. Calif., 1952. Bar: Calif. 1953. Practiced law, LA, 1953—; dep. Office of Calif. Atty. Gen., LA, 1953; ptnr. Diamond & Tilem, LA, 1957-60, Diamond, Tilem & Colden, LA, 1960-79, Diamond & Wilson, LA, 1979—. Lectr. music and entertainment law UCLA; mem. nat. panel arbitrators Am. Arbitration Assn. Bd. dirs. LA Suicide Prevention Ctr., 1971-76. Served with 349th Engr. Constrn. Bn. AUS, 1945-47. Mem. ABA, Calif. Bar Assn., Los Angeles County Bar Assn., Beverly Hills Bar Assn., Am. Judicature Soc., Calif. Copyright Conf., Nat. Acad. Rec. Arts and Scis., Zeta Beta Tau, Nu Beta Epsilon. Office: 12304 Santa Monica Blvd Fl 3D Los Angeles CA 90025-2551 Office Phone: 310-820-7808. E-mail: standimond@aol.com.

DIAZ, MARIA G., lawyer; BA, Stanford U., 1991, JD; MPP, Harvard U., 1994. Bar: Calif. Assoc., employment law practice Allred Maroko & Goldberg, LA. Recipient Wiley W. Manuel award, State Bar Calif., Outstanding Legal Services award, San Diego Volunteer Lawyer Program, Outstanding Service award, US Senator Barbara Boxer; named a Rising Star, So. Calif. Super Lawyers, 2005—06; Woodrow Wilson Nat. Fellow. Mem.: Calif. Employment Lawyers Assn., Mexican-Am. Bas Assn. LA, Latina Lawyers Bar Assn. LA, Nat. Employment Lawyers Assn., LA County Bar Assn. Office: Allred Maroko & Goldberg Ste 1500 6300 Wilshire Blvd Los Angeles CA 90048 Office Phone: 323-653-6530. Office Fax: 323-653-1660.

DIAZ, SHARON, education administrator; b. Bakersfield, Calif., July 29, 1946; d. Karl C. and Mildred (Lunn) Clark; m. Luis F. Diaz, Oct. 19, 1968; children: Daniel, David. BS, San Jose State U., 1969; MS, U. Calif., San Francisco, 1973; PhD (hon.), St. Mary's Coll. Calif., 1999. Nurse Kaiser Found. Hosp., Redwood City, Calif., 1969-73; lectr. San Jose (Calif.) State U., 1969-70; instr. St. Francis Meml. Hosp. Sch. Nursing, San Francisco, 1970—71; pub. health nurse San Mateo County, 1971—72; instr. Samuel Merritt Hosp. Sch. Nursing, Oakland, Calif., 1973—76, asst. dir., 1976—78, dir., 1978—84; founding pres. Samuel Merritt Coll., Oakland, 1984—; interim pres. Calif. Coll. Podiatric Medicine, 2001. V.p. East Bay Area Health Edn. Ctr., Oakland, 1980-87; mem. adv. com. Calif. Acad. Partnership Program, 1990-92; mem. nat. adv. com. Nursing Outcomes Project; bd. dirs. Calif. Workforce Initiative, U. Calif. San Francisco Ctr. for the Health Professions, 2000--. Bd. dirs. Head Royce Sch., 1990-98, vice-chair, 1993-95, chair, 1995-97; bd. dirs. Ladies Home Soc., 1992-2007, sec. 1994-95, treas., CFO 1995-97, 2d v.p. 1997-99, pres., 2006-07; bd. dirs. George Mark Children's House, 2001-07; adv. bd. Ethnic Health Inst., 1997—; com. minorities higher edn. Am. Coun. Edn., 1998—. Named Woman of Yr., Oakland YWCA, 1996. Mem. Am. Assn. Pres. Ind. Colls. and Univs., Sigma Theta Tau (bd. dirs. Nu Xi internat. chpt. at-large 2005-07, Leadership award Nu Xi chpt. 2001, Philanthropy award 2005). Office: Samuel Merritt Coll 450 30th St Oakland CA 94609-3302 E-mail: sdiaz@samuelmerritt.edu.

DICERCHIO, RICHARD D., wholesale distribution executive; b. 1945; V.p. ops. Costco Distbn. Corp., Issaquah, Wash., 1983—86, sr. v.p. merchandising, 1986—92, exec v.p., dir., 1992, exec. v.p., COO No. Divsn., 1992—94, now COO merchandising, distbn., constrn., also sr. exec., v.p., 1997—. Office: Costco Corp 999 Lake Dr Issaquah WA 98027*

DICICCIO, SAL, Councilman; b. Youngstown, Ohio, Jan. 26, 1958; s. Paul Oswald and Nicolina (Thomas) Florence; married; 2 children. BS in Bus., Ariz. State U., BSW. P. Carey Sch. Bus., 1981. Lic. real estate agent. Dist. coord. to US Congressman John McCain, Phoenix, 1981; dist. asst. to US Congressman John McCain, 1983—84; polit. dir. Ariz. Rep. Party, Phoenix, 1984—85; sheriff's adminstrv. aide Maricopa County Sheriff's Office, Phoenix, 1985—88; gen. mgr. ESI Corp., Phoenix, 1989; dir. sales Model Home Ctr., Phoenix, 1990—91; sales mgr. Am. Homebuyers, Phoenix, 1991; pres. Zenith Devel. Ariz. LLC; councilman, Dist. 6 Phoenix City Coun., 1994—2000, 2008—. Registration co-dir., Dist. 27 Rep. Party, 1980; former chmn. Internal Policy, Arts & Culture, Environ. & Natural Resources, Econ., Downtown & Sports Coms.; mem. Govs. Alt. Transp. Sys. Task Force; appointee Growing Smarter Working Adv. Com., 1998. Bd. dirs. Ariz. Ctr. for Blind, 1985—87; mem. Ariz. Mcpl. Tax Code Commn., State Land Conservation Task Force. Mem.: Rep. Caucus, Kiwanis Internat., Alpha Kappa Psi. Republican. Roman Catholic. Office: 200 W Washington St 11th Fl Phoenix AZ 85003-1611 Office Phone: 602-262-7491. Office Fax: 602-534-3574. Business E-Mail: council.district.6@phoenix.gov.*

DICK, BERTRAM GALE, JR., physics professor; b. Portland, Oreg., June 12, 1926; s. Bertram Gale and Helen (Meengs) D.; m. Ann Bradford Volkmann, June 23, 1956; children— Timothy Howe, Robin Berg, Stephen Gale. BA, Reed Coll., 1950, Wadham Coll., Oxford U., Eng., 1953, MA, 1958; PhD, Cornell U., 1958. Rsch. assoc. U. Ill., 1957-59; mem. faculty U. Utah, 1959-98, prof. physics, 1965-98, prof. emeritus, 1998—, Univ. prof., 1979-80, chmn. dept., 1964-67, dean grad. sch., 1987-93. Cons. Minn. Mining and Mfg. Co., 1960-67; vis. prof. Technische Hochschule, Munich, 1967-68; vis. scientist Max Planck Institut für Festkörperforschung, Stuttgart, Fed. Republic Germany, 1976-77; faculty Semester at Sea, fall 1983, 86. Mem. Alta Planning and Zoning Commn., 1972-76; pres. Chamber Music Salt Lake City, 1974-76; bd. trustees Citizen's Com. to Save Our Canyons, 1972—, Coalition for Utah's Future Project 2000, 1989-96. Served with USNR, 1944-46. Rhodes scholar, Oxford U., 1950—53. Fellow Am. Phys. Soc.; mem. Am. Alpine Club, Phi Beta Kappa, Sigma Xi. Achievements include research in solid state theory. Home: 1377 Butler Ave Salt Lake City UT 84102-1803 Home Phone: 801-359-5764. E-mail: gdick@xmission.com.

DICK, HENRY HENRY, minister; b. Russia, June 1, 1922; s. Henry Henry and Mary (Unger) D.; m. Erica Penner, May 25, 1946; children— Janet (Mrs. Arthur Enns), Judith (Mrs. Ron Brown), James, Henry. Th.B., Mennonite Brethren Bible Coll., 1950. Ordained to ministry Mennonite Brethren Ch., 1950; pastor in Orillia, Ont., Canada, 1950-54, Lodi, Calif., 1954-57, Shafter, Calif., 1958-69; faculty Tabor Coll., 1954-55; gen. sec. Mennonite Brethren Conf. of U.S.A., 1969-72; pres. Mennonite Brethren Bibl. Sem., Fresno, Calif., 1972-76; vice moderator Gen Conf. Mennonite Brethren Ch., 1975-78, moderator, 1979-84; pastor Reedley Mennonite Brethren Ch., 1976-88; ret., 1989; dir. ch. and constituency relations Mennonite Brethren Biblical Sem., 1987-89; dist. min. emeritus Mennonites, 2002—; min. pastoral care Mennonite Brethren, Dinuba, Calif., 2003—. Moderator Pacific Dist. Conf., 1959-60, 61-63, 75-77; mem. exec. com. Mennonite Central Com. Internat., 1967-75, mem. bd. reference and counsel, 1966-69, 72-75, mem. bd. missions and services, 1969-72; exec. sec. Bd. Edn. Mennonite Brethren, 1969-72; chmn. Bd. Missions and Services, 1985-91; pastor emeritus Reedley Mennonite Brethren Ch., 1987. Columnist bi-weekly publ. Christian Leader, 1969-75. Bd. dirs. Bob Wilson Meml. Hosp., Ulysses, Kans., 1969-72; dist. minister Pacific Dist. Conf. Mennonite Brethren, 1989—. Recipient Humanitarian award Shafter C. of C., 1969, Citation bd. dirs. Bibl. Sem. Mem.: Kiwanis, Reedley Rotary. Mem. Mennonite Brethren Ch. Home: 701 W Herbert # 36 Reedley CA 93654 Office: 1632 L St Reedley CA 93654-3340

DICKENSON, LARRY, aerospace transportation executive; b. 1943; BBA, Calif. State U.; attended, U. So. Calif. V.p. comml. sales Europe, Middle East and Africa McDonnell Douglas; v.p. aircraft programs Tex. Air Corp.; with Boeing Comml. Airplanes, 1983—, head Asia/Pacific sales, v.p. sales, 2006—. Bd. dirs. Fred Hutchinson Cancer Rsch. Ctr. Holiday Gala, Nat. Econ. Devel. Bd. Calif. State U. Fellow: Royal Aeronautical Soc. Office: Boeing Comml Airplanes PO Box 3707 Seattle WA 98124

DICKERSON, COLLEEN BERNICE PATTON, artist, educator; b. Cleburne, Tex., Sept. 17, 1922; d. Jennings Bryan and Alma Bernice (Clark) Patton; m. Arthur F. Dickerson; children: Sherry M., Chrystal Charmine. BA, Calif. State U., Northridge, 1980; studied with John Pike. Presenter, instr. in field. One-woman shows include Morro Bay Cmty. Bldg., Amandas Interiors, Arroyo Grande, Calif., 1996, Gt. Western Savs., San Luis Obispo, Calif.; exhibited in group shows including Aquarius Show Ctrl. Coast Watercolor Soc., Calif., 2003; represented in permanent collections, including Polk Ins. Co., San Luis Obispo, Med. Ctr. MDM Ins. Co., L.A. Mem. Ctrl. Coast Watercolor Soc. (pres. 1986-87, Svc. award 1998), Art Ctr., Oil Acrylic Pastel Group (chmn., co-chmn. 1989-98, prize Brush Strokes show 1999), Morro Bay Art Assn. (scholarship judge 1998), San Luis Obispo Art Ctr., Valley Watercolor Soc. (co-founder). Avocations: egyptology, chinese painting, art history, forensic anthropology. Home: 245 Hacienda Ave San Luis Obispo CA 93401-7967

DICKERSON, GARY E., former electronics executive; b. 1957; BS in Engring. Mgmt., U. Mo., Rolla; MBA, U. Mo., Kansas City. Head photo engring. sect. AT&T Techs.; various KLA-Tencor Corp., San Jose, Calif., 1986-99, COO, 1999—2004, pres., 2002—04.

DICKEY, GLENN ERNEST, JR., sportswriter; b. Virginia, Minn., Feb. 16, 1936; s. Glenn Ernest and Madlyn Marie (Emmert) D.; m. Nancy Jo McDaniel, Feb. 25, 1967; 1 son, Kevin Scott. BA, U. Calif., Berkeley, 1958. Sports editor Watsonville (Calif.) Register-Pajoronian, 1958-63; sports writer San Francisco Chronicle, 1963-71, sports columnist, 1971—. Author: The Jock Empire, 1974, The Great No-Hitters, 1976, Champs and Chumps, 1976, The History of National League Baseball, 1979, The History of American League Baseball, 1980, (with Dick Berg) Eavesdropping America, 1980, America Has a Better Team, 1982, The History of Professional Basketball, 1982, The History of the World Series, 1984, (with Jim Tunney) Impartial Judgment: The Dean of NFL Referees Calls Football As He Sees It, 1988, San Francisco Forty-Niners: The Super Year, 1989; (with Bill Walsh) Building a Champion, 1990; Just Win, Baby, Al Davis and His Raiders, 1991; Sports Hero Kevin Mitchell (juvenile), 1993, Sports Hero Jerry Rice (juvenile), 1993, San Francisco 49ers: 50 Years, 1995, San Francisco Giants: 40 Seasons, 1997, Glenn Dickey's 49ers, 2000, Champions: The History of the Oakland A's; contbr. stories to Best Sports Stories, 1962, 68, 71, 75, 76. Home: 120 Florence Ave Oakland CA 94618-2249 Office: Chronicle Pub Co 901 Mission St San Francisco CA 94103-2905

DICKEY, ROBERT MARVIN (RICK DICKEY), property manager; b. Charleston, SC, Dec. 3, 1950; s. John Lincoln II and Ruth (Marvin) D.; m. Teresa Ann Curry, Dec. 19, 1969 (div. 1979); 1 child, Gena Lynette; m. Martha Suzanne Coup, July 21, 1999; 1 child, Dylan Thomas. A of Computer Sci., USMC Degree Program, Washington, 1975. Cert. apt. property supr. Nat. Apt. Assn., Wash., occupancy specialist Nat. Ctr.for Housing Mgmt., Wash. Enlisted USMC, 1968, advanced through grades to staff sgt., 1968-78; shop mgr., bookkeeper Amalgamated Plant Co., Las Vegas, Nev., 1978-79; supr. constrn. Joseph Yousem Co., Las Vegas, 1979-80; apt. mgr. Robert A. McNeil Corp., Las Vegas, 1980, comml. bldg. mgr., leasing agt., 1980-82; asst. v.p., regional property mgr. Westminster Co., Las Vegas, 1982-87, Weyerhaeuser Mortgage Co., Las Vegas, 1988-89; pres., ptnr. Equinox Devel., Inc., Las Vegas, 1989-91; dir. residental properties R.W. Robideaux & Co., Spokane, Wash., 1992-97; mgr. residential divsn. Goodale & Barbieri Co. (formerly G&B Real Estate Svcs.), Spokane, 1997—. Contbr. articles to profl. jours. Mem. Nat. Assn. Realtors, Wash. Assn. Realtors, Spokane Assn. Realtors, Inst. Real Estate Mgmt. (accredited residential mgr., legis. chmn. 1987-88, Accredited Residential Mgr. award 1985, 86, 90), Nev. Apt. Assn. (v.p. 1985, pres. 1988—, bd. dirs.), So. Nev. Homebuilders Assn., Las Vegas Bd. Realtors (mgmt. legis. com. 1988). Personal E-mail: rdickey@g-b.com.

DICKEY, ROBERT PRESTON, writer, educator, poet; b. Flat River, Mo., Sept. 24, 1936; s. Delno Miren D. and Naomi Valentine (Jackson) D.; children: Georgia Rae, Shannon Ezra, Rain Dancer. BA, U. Mo., 1968, MA, 1969; PhD, Walden U., 1975. Instr. U. Mo., 1967-69; asst. prof. English and creative writing U. So. Colo., 1969-73; assoc. mem. faculty Pima Coll., Tucson, 1975-78. Author: (with Donald Justice, Thomas McAfee, Donald Drummond) poetry Four Poets, 1967, Running Lucky, 1969, Acting Immortal, 1970; Concise Dictionary of Lead River, Mo., 1972, The Basic Stuff of Poetry, 1972, Life Cycle of Seven Songs, 1972, McCabe Wants Chimes, 1973, Admitting Complicity, 1973; opera librettos Minnequa, 1976, The Witch of Tucson, 1976; Jimmie Cotton!, 1979, Way Out West, 1979, The Poetica Erotica of R.P. Dickey, 1989, The Little Book on Racism and Politics, 1990, The Way of Eternal Recurrence, 1994, Ode on Liberty, 1996, The Lee Poems, 1998, Self-Liberation, 1998, Exercise Anytime, 1998, Collected Poems, 1999, (with Lee Foster) Taos and Other Works of Art, 2002; contbr. poetry to popular mags., Poetry, Saturday Rev., Commonwealth, Prairie Schooner; founder, editor: The Poetry Bag quar., 1966-71; poetry editor: So. Colo. Std., 1973-74. With USAF, 1955-57. Recipient Mahan award for poetry U. Mo., 1965-66 Home: PO Box 87 Ranchos De Taos NM 87557-0087

DICKINSON, ELEANOR CREEKMORE, artist, educator; b. Knoxville, Tenn., Feb. 7, 1931; d. Robert Elmond and Evelyn Louise (Van Gilder) C.; m. Ben Wade Oakes Dickinson, June 12, 1952; children: Mark W., Katherine V.G., Peter S. BA, U. Tenn., 1952; postgrad., San Francisco Art Inst., 1961—63, Academié de la Grande Chaumière, Paris, 1971; MFA, Calif. Coll. Arts, Crafts, 1982, Golden Gate U., 1984. Cert. Recognition El Consejo Mundial de Artistas Plasticos, 1993. Escrow officer Security Nat. Bank, Santa Monica, Calif., 1953-54; mem. faculty Calif. Coll. of the Arts, Oakland, 1971—2001, assoc. prof. art, 1974—84, prof., 1984-2001, prof. emerita, 2001—, dir. galleries, 1975-85. Artist-in-residence U. Tenn., 1969, Ark. State U., 1993, Fine Arts Mus. of San Francisco, 2000, U. Alaska, 1991; faculty U. Calif. Ext., 1967-70; lectr. U. Calif., Berkeley, 1990—; interviewer Hatch, Billops, Collin, NY State Coun. for Arts, 2004; juror Interfaith Forum, Magnes Mus., 1986, Crocker Mus. Art, 1987, Sun Gallery, 1990, Caligraphy Rev., 1991, U. Alaska, 1991, San Francisco Women Arts, 1993, Pleasanton Art League, 1993, U. Tenn. Ann., 1997, Sierra Coll. Ann., 2000, Costal Art League, 2006, Commn. Status Women, 2006, Pacific Art League, 2006-07; lectr., juror in field. Author, illustrator: Elkmont: The Heart of the Great Smoky Mountains National Park, 2005; author (book) The History of the Women's Caucus for Art, BLAZE: Discourse on Art, Women, and Feminism, 2007; co-author, illustrator: Revival, 1974, That Old Time Religion, 1975; also mus. catalogs; illustrator: The Complete Fruit Cookbook, 1972, Human Sexuality: A Search for Understanding, 1984, Days Journey, 1985; commissions: U. San Francisco, 1990-2001; one-woman shows include San Francisco Mus. Modern Art, 1965, 68, Santa Barbara Mus., 1966, Corcoran Gallery Art, Washington, 1970, 74, Fine Arts Mus. San Francisco, 1969, 75, J.B. Speed Art Mus., 1972, Poindexter Gallery, NY, 1972, 74, U. Tenn. Ewing Gallery, 1976 Smithsonian Inst., 1975-81, U. Tenn. Downtown Gallery, 2005, Galeria de Arte y Libros, Monterrey, Mex., 1978, Oakland Mus., 1979, Interart Ctr., NY, 1980, Tenn. State Mus., 1981-82, Hatley Martin Gallery, San Francisco, 1986, 89, Michael Himovitz Gallery, Sacramento, Calif., 1988-89, 91, 93, 97-98, Gallery 10, Washington, 1989, Diverse Works, Houston, 1990, Ewing Gallery, U. Tenn., 1991, G.T.U. Gallery, U. Calif., Berkeley, 1991, Mus. Contemporary Religious Art, St. Louis, 1995, Coun. Creative Projects, NY, 1996, Thacher Gallery, U. San Francisco, 2000, Retrospective U. Tenn, 2005, Tenn. Regional Art Ctr., 2006, Retrospective Comma Gallery, Orlando, Fla, 2007, Retrospective Peninsula Mus. Art, Calif., 2007; represented in permanent collections Nat. Collection Fine Arts, Corcoran Gallery Art, Libr. of Congress, Smithsonian Instn., San Francisco Mus. Modern Art, Butler Inst. Am. Art, Oakland Mus., Santa Barbara Mus., Stanford Art Mus., The Oakland Mus., Tenn. State Mus., Mus. Contemporary Religious Art, St. Louis, Triton Mus., Santa Clara, Achenbach Found. Fine Arts Mus., San Francisco; prodr. (TV) The Art of the Matter-Professional Practices in Fine Arts, 1986—. Bd. dirs. Calif. Confedn. of the Arts, 1983-85; bd. dirs., v.p. Calif. Lawyers for the Arts, 1986—; mem. coun. bd. San Francisco Art Inst., 1966-91, trustee, 1964-67; sec., bd. dirs. YWCA, 1955-62; treas., bd. Westminster Ctr., 1955-59; bd. dirs. Children's Theater Assn., 1958-60, 93-94, Internat. Child Art Ctr., 1958-68. Recipient Disting. Alumni award San Francisco Art Inst., 1983, Master Drawing award Nat. Soc. Arts and Letters, 1983, Pres.'s award Nat. Women's Caucus for Art, 1995, Allgemeines Kunstlerfexidon, 2001, Lifetime Achivement award Nat. Women's Caucus for Art, 2003; grantee Zellerbach Family Fund, 1975, NEH, 1978, 80, 82-85, Thomas F. Stanley Found., 1985, Bay Area Video Coalition, 1988-92, PAS Graphics, 1988, San Francisco Cmty. TV Corp., 1990, Skaggs Found., 1991. Mem.: AAUW, NOW, Nat. Women's Caucus for Art (nat. Affirmative Action officer 1978—80, nat. bd. dirs. 2000—08, Pres.'s award 1995), Arts Advocates, Artists Equity Assn. (nat. v.p., dir. 1978—92), San Francisco Art Assn. (sec., dir. 1964—67), Calif. Lawyers for Arts (v.p. 1986—2004, bd. dirs. 1986—), Calif. Confederation of Arts (bd. dirs. 1983—89), Coll. Art Assn. (chair com. of Women in the Arts 2004—06), Coalition Women's Art Orgns. (dir. 1978—80, v.p. 2000—01), AAUP. Democrat. Episcopalian. Office: Calif Coll of the Arts 1111 8th St San Francisco CA 94107-2247 Office Phone: 415-260-6800. Personal E-mail: eleanordickinson@mac.com.

DICKINSON, JANET MAE WEBSTER, relocation consulting executive; b. Cleve., Oct. 2, 1929; d. Richard and Gizella (Keplinger) Fisher; m. Rodney Earl Dickinson, June 18, 1965 (div. 1976); 1 child, Kimberly Cae. Grad., Larson Coll. for Women, New Haven; student, Portland State Coll. Lic. broker, Oreg. Pub. rels./promotion dir. KPTV-Channel 27, Portland, Oreg., 1951-54; exec. dir. Exposition-Recreation Commn., Portland, 1954-58; v.p. Art Lutz & Co., Realtors, Portland, 1975-79, Lutz Relocation Mgmt., Portland, 1977-79; corp. relocation mgr. Ga. Pacific Corp., Portland, 1979-82; pres., broker Ga. Pacific Fin. Co., Portland, 1980-82; pres., chief exec. officer The Dickinson Cons. Group, Portland, 1982—; pres. Wheatherstone Press, Lake Oswego, Oreg., 1983—, The Relocation Ctr., Portland, 1984—. Cons. in field; lectr. in field; conductor workshops/seminars in field; advisory bd. Business Facilities Mag. Author: The Complete Guide to Family Relocation, The International Move, Building Your Dream House, Obtaining the Highest Price for Your Home, Have a Successful Garage Sale, Moving with Children, My Moving Coloring Book, The Group Move, Counseling the Transferee, Games to Play in the Car, Portland (Oreg.) Facts Book, Welcome to the United States, many others; contbr. articles to profl. jours. Mem. Pres.'s Com. to Employ Physically Handicapped, Oreg. Prison Assn.; established Women's Aux. for Waverly Baby Home; bd. dirs. Columbia River coun. Girl Scouts U.S.A., Salvation Army; active various polit. orgns.; chmn. ways and means com. Oreg. Symphony Soc., Portland Art Mus., Assistance League, Portland Jr. Symphony, March of Dimes, others. Mem.: Montgomery Adv. Bd. Internat. (prin. mentor), Directorship 100, Soc. Human Resource Mgr., Employee Relocation Coun., Internat. Platform Assn., Tualatin Valley Econ. Devel. Assn. (dir. 1988—), Forbes CEO Network, Multnomah Athletic Club, City Club. Republican. Episcopalian. Office: The Dickinson Cons Group Lincoln Ctr 10250 SW Greenburg Rd Ste 125 Portland OR 97223-5470 Office Phone: 503-244-8929. E-mail: jandickinson@comcast.net, relocntr@nwlink.com.

DICKINSON, MICHAEL HUGHES, physiologist, biotechnologist; ScB, Brown U., 1984; PhD, U. Wash., 1989. Postdoctoral trainee Roche Inst. Molecular Biology, 1990—91; mem. faculty dept. organismal biology and anatomy U. Chgo., 1991—96; prof. integrative biology U. Calif., Berkeley, 1996—2003, Williams prof. integrative biology; prof. bioengineering Calif. Inst. Tech., 2003—, Esther M. and Abe. M. Zarem prof. bioengineering. Vis. scholar Max Planck Inst. Biol. Cybernetics, 1991, 93. Recipient Larry Sandler award, Genetic Soc. Am., 1990, George Bartholomew award for physiology, Soc. Integrative and Comparative Biology, 1995; fellow, NSF, 1985, Packard Found., 1992; John D. and Catherine T. MacArthur fellow, 2001. Fellow: Am. Acad. Arts and Scis. Achievements include development of Flybot. Office: Calif Inst Tech M/C 138 78 1200 E California Blvd Pasadena CA 91125 Office Phone: 626-395-3906. Business E-Mail: flyman@caltech.edu.

DICKINSON, WADE, oil industry executive, educator; b. Sharon, Pa., Oct. 29, 1926; s. Ben Wade Orr and Gladys Grace (Oakes) D.; m. Eleanor Creekmore, June 12, 1952; children: Mark, Katherine, Peter. Student, Carnegie Inst. Tech., 1944-45; BS, U.S. Mil. Acad., 1949; postgrad., Oak Ridge Sch. Reactor Tech., 1950-51. Commd. 2d lt. USAF, 1949, advanced through grades to capt., 1954, resigned, 1954; cons. physicist RAND Corp., Santa Monica, Calif., 1952-54; engring. cons. Bechtel Group, Inc., San Francisco, 1954-87; tech. advisor U.S. Congress Joint Com. Atomic Energy, Washington, 1957-58; pres. Agrophysics, Inc., San Francisco, 1968—, Petrolphysics Inc., San Francisco, 1975—; ptnr. Radialphysics Ltd., San Francisco, 1980—, Robotphysics Ltd., San Francisco, 1983—. Lectr. engring. and bus. U. Calif., Berkeley, 1984—2004; cardiology cons. Mt. Zion Med. Ctr. U. Calif., San Francisco, 1970—99; chmn. bd. Calif. Med. Clin. Psychotherapy; mng. mem. Spark Group, 2000—08, Petro Jet, LLC, Solid Gas Techs., 2005—, Petrol Physics, Inc., Sequestration Co. LLC, 2007—, SEQ Energy LLC, 2004—. Contbr. articles to profl. jours; patentee in field. Trustee World Affair Coun., 1958-62; mem. San Francisco Com. Fgn. Rels., Young Republicans, Calif. Mem. Am. Phys. Soc., Am. Soc. Petroleum Engrs. Clubs: Bohemian (San Francisco), Chit Chat (San Francisco). Lodges: Masons, Guardsmen. Episcopalian. Home and Office: Petrolphysics Inc 2125 Broderick St San Francisco CA 94115-1627 Office: SEQ Energy LLC 1770 Post St Box 314 San Francisco CA 94115 Office Phone: 415-922-3733. Business E-Mail: wade@seqenergy.com.

DICKMAN, FRANCOIS MOUSSIEGT, former foreign service officer, educator; b. Iowa City, Dec. 23, 1924; s. Adolphe Jacques and Henriette Louise (Moussiegt) D.; m. Margaret Hoy, June 3, 1947; children: Christine, Paul. BA, U. Wyo., 1947; MA, Fletcher Sch. Law & Diplomacy, 1948; student, U.S. Army War Coll., Carlisle, Pa., 1968—69. Rsch. asst. Brookings Instn., Washington, 1950; with U.S. Fgn. Svc., 1951-84, consular/comml. officer Barranquilla, Colombia, 1952-54, Arabic lang. trainee Beirut, 1955-57, econ., comml., consular officer Khartoum, Sudan, 1957-60; Egyptian-Syrian affairs desk officer Dept. State, 1961-65, econ. officer Tunis, Tunisia, 1965-68; econ. counselor Jidda, Saudi Arabia, 1969-72; dir. Arabian Peninsula affairs Dept. State, 1972-76, amb. to United Arab Emirates, 1976-79, amb. to Kuwait, 1979-83; diplomat in residence Marquette U., 1984; adj. prof. polit. sci. U. Wyo., Laramie, 1985—2004. Lectr. in field. Served with AUS, 1943-46, 50-51. Recipient Dept. State Meritorious Honor award, 1965, Disting. Alumni award U. Wyo., 1980, Outstanding Achievement in Internat. Affairs, Citizens of Wyo., 2006; named Exemplary Alumnus U. Wyo., 1993. Mem. VFW, U.S. Army War Coll. Alumni Assn., U. Wyo. Alumni Assn., Phi Beta Kappa, Phi Kappa Phi. Office: U Wyo Polit Sci Dept Laramie WY 82071-3197 Personal E-mail: fmdmhd@aol.com.

DICKS, NORMAN DE VALOIS, United States Representative from Washington; b. Bremerton, Wash., Dec. 16, 1940; s. Horace D. and Eileen Cora Dicks; m. Suzanne Callison, Aug. 25, 1967; children: David, Ryan. BA, U. Wash., 1963; JD, U. Wash. Sch. Law, 1968; LLD (hon.), Gonzaga U., 1987. Bars: Wash. 1968, DC, 1978. Salesman Boise Cascade Corp., Seattle, 1963; labor negotiator Kaiser Gypsum Co., Seattle, 1964; legis. asst. Staff of US Senator Warren Magnuson of Wash., 1968-73, adminstrv. asst., 1973-76; mem. US Congress from 6th Wash. dist., 1977—, mem. homeland security com., mem.

appropriations com., ranking minority mem. interior and environment and related agencies subcommittee. Mem. U. Wash. Alumni Assn., Puget Sound Naval Bases Assn., Sigma Nu, Rotary (hon.), Kiwanis (hon.). Democrat. Lutheran. Office: US House Reps 2467 Rayburn House Office Bldg Washington DC 20515-0001 Office Phone: 202-225-5916.

DICKS, PATRICIA K., legislative staff member; b. Detroit, Nov. 22, 1951; BS, U. Colo., 1973. Sec. Colo. Senate, Denver, 1998—. Office: State Capitol 200 E Colfax Ave Ste 250 Denver CO 80203-1716

DIDION, JAMES J., real estate company executive; b. Sacramento; s. Frank R. D. and Eduene J. Didion. AB in Polit. Sci., U. Calif., Berkeley, 1962. With Coldwell Banker Co., 1962—, v.p., resident mgr. Sacramento, 1969-71, sr. v.p., regional mgr. Houston, from 1971; chmn., CEO, Coldwell Banker Comml. Group, LA; now chmn. Coldwell Banker, Carmel, Calif. Office: Coldwell Banker PO Box 1150 Carmel CA 93921-1150

DIEKMANN, GILMORE FREDERICK, JR., lawyer; b. Evansville, Ind., Jan. 14, 1946; s. Gilmore Frederick Sr. and Mabel Pauline (Daniel) K.; children: Anne Westlake, Andrew Gilmore, Matthew Frederick. BSBA, Northwestern U., 1968, JD, 1971. Bar: Calif. 1972, U.S. Dist. Ct. Calif. (no., ea., cen. and so. dists.) Calif. 1972, U.S. Ct. Appeals (9th cir.) 1972, U.S. Supreme Ct. 1978. Assoc. Bronson, Bronson & McKinnon, San Francisco, 1971-78, ptnr. labor and employment law, 1979-99, chmn., mng. ptnr., 1991-93, chmn. labor, employment dept., 1993-99; ptnr. Seyfarth Shaw, San Francisco, 1999—, chmn. no. Calif. labor dept., 1999—2005. Author and speaker in field. Mem. ABA, Def. Rsch. Inst., Am. Employment Law Coun., Order of Coif. Republican. Lutheran. Home: 901 Powell St # 6 San Francisco CA 94108 Office: Seyfarth Shaw 560 Mission St Fl 31 San Francisco CA 94105-2907 Office Phone: 415-544-1070. Business E-Mail: gdiekmann@seyfarth.com.

DIENES, LOUIS ROBERT, lawyer; b. New Brunswick, NJ, Apr. 17, 1966; s. Louis S. and Rosemary T. D. AB, U. Calif., Berkeley, 1990; JD, Stanford U., 1994. Bar: Calif. 1994. Ptnr. Alschuler Grossman Stein & Kahan, LLP, LA, 2005—06, Jeffer Mangels Butler & Marmaro LLP, 2006—09, TroyGould PC, 2009—. Mem. adv. bd. L.A. Bus. Tech. Ctr., LA, 2002—. Mem.: Century City Bar Assn. (pres. elect 2009), Pasadena Angels. Office: 1801 Century Pk E Ste 1600 Los Angeles CA 90067 Home Phone: 310-487-3503. Business E-Mail: lrd@troygould.com.

DIERCKMAN, THOMAS E., land use planner; Grad., U. Ill.; postgrad. U. Ca. Construction, facilities mgmt. U.S. Navy Civil Engr. Corps, 1971-82; The Newhall Land & Farming Co, Valencia, Ca., 1982, sr. v.p., Valencia Co., 1990—, pres., Valencia Co., 1994—. Bd dirs. L.A. Econ. Devel. Corp., Valencia Bank and Trust, Valencia Water Co., Boys and Girls Club Santa Clarita; chmn. Santa Clarita Valley United Way Campaign, 1997-98; mem. Urban Land Inst. Capt., Naval Reserve. Office: The Newhall Land & Farming Co 23823 Valencia Blvd Valencia CA 91355-2103

DIERKS, RICHARD ERNEST, veterinarian, academic administrator; b. Flandreau, SD, Mar. 11, 1934; s. Martin and Lillian Ester (Benedict) D.; m. Eveline Carol Amundson, July 20, 1956; children—Jeffrey Scott, Steven Eric, Joel Richard. Student, S.D. State U., 1952—55; BS, U. Minn., 1957, DVM, 1959, MPH, PhD, U. Minn., 1964; MBA, U. Ill., 1985. Diplomate Am. Coll. Vet. Microbiologists, Am. Coll. Vet. Preventive Medicine. Supervisory microbiologist Communicable Disease Ctr., Atlanta, 1964-68; prof. coll. veterinary medicine Iowa State U., Ames, 1968-74; head dept. veterinary sci. Mont. State U., Bozeman, 1974-76; dean Coll. Veterinary Medicine U. Ill., Urbana, 1976-89, prof., dean emeritus, 1989—; dean Coll. Veterinary Medicine U. Fla., Gainesville, 1989-97, prof., dean emeritus, 1997—. Mem. tng. grant rev. com. Nat. Inst. Allergy and Infectious Diseases, 1973-74 Contbr. articles on virology, immunology and epidemiology to profl. jours. Served with USPHS, 1964-67. Career Devel. awardee Nat. Inst. Allergy and Infectious Diseases, 1969-74, Nat. Acad. Practitioners, 1995. Mem. Am. Vet. Medicine Assn., Am. Soc. Virology, Am. Soc. Microbiologists, Am. Assn. Immunologists, Am. Assn. Vet. Lab. Diagnosis, Colo. Vet. Medicine Assn., Soc. Exptl. Biology and Medicine, Gamma Sigma Delta, Phi Kappa Phi, Phi Zeta. Clubs: Rotary. Republican. Lutheran. Office: 2409 Tyrrhenian Dr Longmont CO 80501 Home Phone: 303-774-1897; Office Phone: 303-774-1897. Personal E-mail: dierksrichardcar@msn.com, richcaro6@mesanetworks.net.

DIERS, JAMES ALAN, municipal official; b. Burnaby, BC, Can., Dec. 13, 1952; m. Sarah Driggs, 1975. BA in Third World Devel., Grinnell Coll., 1975, Doctorate (hon.), 2001. Organizer South End Seattle Comty. Orgn., 1976-82; asst. dir. for coop. affairs Group Health Coop. of Puget Sound, Wash., 1982-88; dir. Dept. of Neighborhoods, Seattle, 1988—. Founder Sr. Caucus and Nuclear Awareness Group, Ptnrs. for Health; dir. Seattle Little City Halls program, mgr. 57 cmty. gardens, and the Historic Preservation Program overseeing adminstrn. of 200 bldgs., seven hist. dists. Neighborhood Matching Fund under his adminstrn. named one of most innovative local govt. programs in nation, Ford Found. and Kennedy Sch. of Govt. Office: Dept Neighborhoods City of Seattle 700 3rd Ave Ste 400 Seattle WA 98104-1848

DIESEL, VIN (MARK VINCENT), actor; b. NYC, July 18, 1967; 1 child. Student, Hunter Coll. Actor, dir., prodr., writer: (films) Multi-facial, 1994; Strays, 1997; actor, exec. prodr. XXX, 2002; A Man Apart, 2003; actor, prodr. The Chronicles of Riddick, 2004; actor: Saving Private Ryan, 1998, (voice) The Iron Giant, 1999, Boiler Room, 2000, Pitch Black, 2000, The Fast and the Furious, 2001, Knockaround Guys, 2001, Be Cool, 2005, The Pacifier, 2005, Find Me Guilty, 2006, The Fast and the Furious: Tokyo Drift, 2006, Babylon A.D., 2008, Fast & Furious, 2009; exec. prodr.: Hitman, 2007; actor: (TV films) Into Pitch Black, 2000. Office: Endeavor Talent Agency 9601 Wilshire Blvd Ste 300 Beverly Hills CA 90210-5200

DIETERICH, JAMES H., geologist; b. Elgin, Ill., June 7, 1942; BS, U. Wash., 1964; MPh, Yale U., 1967, PhD in Geology and Geophysics, 1968. Dep. dir. US-USSR Coop. Exchange Agreement, 1982-94; with Nat. Earthquake Protection Coun., 1982-96, 96—; sr. scientist we. earthquake hazard team U.S. Geol. Survey, Menlo Park, Calif. Cons. Dept. State, U.S., Costa Rica, 1983, UN, Turkey, 1991; with Internat. Commn. Lithosphere, 1983-86; adv. coun. So. Calif. Earthquake Ctr., 1991— vis. prof., adj. prof. Tex. A&M Univ., 1987; with earthquake hazards reduction program. U.S. Geol. Survey, 1996—. Recipient Basic Rsch. award U.S. Nat. Com. Rock Med., 1985. Fellow Am. Geophys. Union (Walter H. Bucher medal 2000); mem. Internat. Assn. Seismology and Physics Earth's Interior (subcom. 1992—). Office: US Geol Survey 345 Middleford Rd MS 977 Menlo Park CA 94025-3591

DIETLER, CORTLANDT S., oil industry executive; b. Tulsa, Okla. Grad., U. Tulsa; degree (hon.), Hillsdale Coll. Founder, CEO Associated Natural Gas Corp.; chmn., CEO TransMontaigne Oil Co.; CEO TransMontaigne, Inc., Denver, 1995—99, chmn., 1995—2006. Dir. Hallador Petroleum Co., Cimarex Energy Co.; mem. Nat. Petroleum Council; dir. Am. Petroleum Inst.; former dir. Independent Petroleum Assn. of Am.; former pres. Rocky Mountain Oil & Gas Assn. Trustee Denver Art Museum, Denver Museum of Nature and Sci., Buffalo Bill Memorial Assn. Served in US Army.

DIETRICH, DEAN FORBES, academic administrator; b. Davenport, Iowa, Jan. 10, 1966; s. Dean Willis and Carolyn (Brandhorst) Dietrich. AB summa cum laude, Dartmouth Coll., 1988; MA, U. Va., 1990, PhD, 1997. Viewer info., ednl. svcs. asst. C-SPAN, Washington, 1988, 89; grad. instr. U. Va., Charlottesville, 1990-97, computer, video cons. Law Sch., 1995-97; vis. asst. prof. English Hanover (Ind.) Coll., 1998-99; sr. rschr. advancement SUNY, Stony Brook, 2000—03; prospect rsch. mgr. U. Nev., Reno, 2003—. Gov.'s fellow U. Va., 1990-91, 92-93. Mem. Assn. Profl. Rschrs. Advancement, Coun. Advancement and Support Edn., Greater N.Y. Assn. Profl. Rschrs. Advancement (sec. 2002-03), Phi Beta Kappa. Office: U Nev Devel & Alumni Rels Mail Stop 007 Reno NV 89557 Business E-Mail: ddietrich@unr.edu.

DIETRICH, WILLIAM ALAN, reporter, writer; b. Tacoma, Sept. 29, 1951; s. William Richard and Janice Lenore (Pooler) D.; m. Holly Susan Roberts, Dec. 19, 1970; children: Lisa, Heidi. BA, Western Wash. U., 1973. Reporter Bellingham (Wash.) Herald, 1973-76, Gannett News Svc., Washington, 1976-78, Vancouver (Wash.) Columbian, 1978-82, Seattle Times, 1982-97, 2002—; freelance writer, 1998—. Asst. prof. Western Wash. U., 2006—. Author: The Final Forest, 1992, Northwest Passage, 1995, Ice Reich, 1998, Getting Back, 2000, Dark Winter, 2001, Natural Grace, 2003, Hadrian's Wall, 2004, The Scourge of God, 2005, Napoleon's Pyramids, 2007. Recipient Paul Tobenkin award Columbia U., 1986, Pulitzer prize for nat. reporting, 1990; Nieman fellow Harvard U., 1987-88. Office Phone: 206-464-2373.

DIETZ, DIANE M., marketing executive; BA in Mktg. & Economics, No. Ill. U. Various brand mgmt. & mktg. positions The Procter & Gamble Co., Cin., 1989—2008; exec. v.p., chief mktg. officer Safeway Inc., Pleasanton, Calif., 2008—. Office: Safeway Inc Hdqs 5918 Stoneridge Mall Rd Pleasanton CA 94588 Office Phone: 925-467-3000. Office Fax: 925-467-3321.

DIFFIE, WHITFIELD (WHIT), computer and communications engineer; b. June 5, 1944; m. Mary L. Fischer. BS in Math., MIT, 1965; postgrad. in elec. engring., Stanford U., 1975-78; D in Tech. Scis. honoris causa, Swiss Fed. Inst. Tech., Zurich, 1992. Rsch. asst. The Mitre Corp., Bedford, Mass., 1965-69; rsch. programmer artificial intellingence lab. Stanford U., Palo Alto, Calif., 1969-73, rsch. asst., 1975-78, rsch. programmer, 1975; self-supported researcher in cryptography, 1973-74; mgr. secure syss. rsch. No. Telecom, Mountain View, Calif., 1978-91; disting. engr., adv. computer and comm. security Sun Microsystems, Palo Alto, Calif., 1991—, v.p., Sun fellow and chief security officer. Organizer conf. Crypto '81, '83; mem. program com. Crypto 89; mem. program com. Status and Prospects of Rsch. in Cryptography '93, First ACM Conf. on Comms. and Computer Security, 1993; mem. adv. bd. Electronic Privacy Info. Ctr.; presenter in field. Author (with Susan Landau) Privacy on the Line (Donald McGannon award for Social and Ethical Relevance in Comm. Policy Rsch. and the IEEE-USA award for Disting. Literary Contbn. Furthering Public Understanding of the Profession); Contbr. numerous articles to scientific jours.; featured in Sci.Am., Sci., Time, Omni, Newsweek, NY Times mag., others. G.C. Steward fellow Gonville and Caius Coll., 1996; recipient award for Disting. Contbn. to Consumer Protection Calif. State Psychol. Assn., 1978, Nat. Computer Sys. Security award Nat. Inst. Stds. and Tech. and Nat. Security Agy., 1996, Louis E. Levy medal Franklin Inst., 1997, First Paris Kanellakis award ACM, 1997, Fellow Marconi Found, 2000, Chairman's award for Innovation and Fellow Internat. Assn. for Cryptologic Rsch. 2004. Mem. IEEE (Info. Theory Soc. Paper award 1979, Donald G. Fink award 1981, conf. organizer 1983). Achievements include discovery of the concept of public key cryptography, 1975; devel. of Mathlab symbolic-manipulation sys., of Lisp 1.6 sys.; rsch. on interactive debugging and extensible compiling, proof of correctness of programs, proof checking and extensible compilers, on cryptography and its applications; patents (with Martin E. Hellman and Ralph Merkle) for cryptographic apparatus and method, 1980, (with Ashar Aziz) on security of mobile comm., 1993. Office: Sun Microsystems 4150 Network Cir Santa Clara CA 95054-1778

DIGORGIO, KENNETH, lawyer; MBA, JD, UCLA. Regulatory counsel First Am. Title Insurance Corp. (now The First Am. Corp.), Santa Ana, Calif., 1999—2003; exec. v.p., gen counsel First Advantage Corp. (subsidiary of First Am. Corp), 2003—04; gen. counsel The First Am. Corp., Santa Ana, Calif., 2004—. Office: First American Corp 1 First American Way Santa Ana CA 92707

DILFER, TRENT, professional football player; b. Santa Cruz, Ca, Mar. 13, 1972; m. Cassandra Dilfer; children: Madeleine, Victoria, Delaney, Trevin(dec.). Student, Fresno State U. Quarterback Tampa Bay Buccaneers, 1994—2000, Balt. Ravens, 2000, Seattle Seahawks, 2001—04, Cleve. Browns, 2005, San Francisco 49ers, 2006—08. Active Fellowship Christian Athletes, Athletes in Action, United Way, Big Bros./Big Sisters, Police Athletic League, Hardy's Huddle. Achievements include broke Doug Williams 1982 record by throwing 138 consecutive passes without interception.

DILL, GARY A., academic administrator; BA in Philos. and Religion, Houston Bapt. U.; PhD in Philosophy, U. Tex.; Doctorate in Ministry, Southern Theological Seminary; MDiv., Princeton Theol. Seminary. Pastor Price of Peace Ch. Brethren, South Bend, Ind., 1975—79; adj. staff Bethany Theological Seminary, 1978—82; pastor York Ctr. Ch. Brethren, Lombard, Ill., 1979—82; sr. v.p., prof. Schreiner Coll., Kerrville, Tex., 1991—96; pres. McPherson Coll., 1997—2002, Coll. S.W., N.Mex., 2002—. Former chmn. Tex. Arts and Crafts Ednl. Found.; mem. bd. dirs. Ptnrs. in Parenting Edn. Bd.; dir. cmty. svc. Noon Rotary Club, Kerrville. Office: Coll SW 6610 Lovington Hwy Hobbs NM 88240

DILL, LADDIE JOHN, artist; b. Long Beach, Calif., Sept. 14, 1943; s. James Melvin and Virginia (Crane) D.; children: Ariel, Jackson Caldwell. BFA, Chouinard Art Inst., 1968. Chmn. of visual arts The Studio Sch., Santa Monica, Calif. Lectr. painting and drawing UCLA, 1975-88. Exhibitions include San Francisco Mus. Modern Art, 1977—78, Albright Knox Mus., Buffalo, 1978—79, Charles Cowles Gallery, N.Y.C., 1983—85, Sonnabend Gallery, The First Show, L.A., Represented in permanent collections Mus. Modern Art, N.Y.C., Laguna Mus. Art, Los Angeles County Mus., Mus. Contemporary Art, L.A., Santa Barbara Mus., San Francisco Mus. Modern Art, Seattle Mus., Newport Harbor Art Mus., Oakland Mus., Smithsonian Instn., IBM, Nat. Mus., Seoul, Republic of Korea, San Diego Mus. Art, La. Mus., Denmark, Am. Embassy, Helsinki, Finland, Corcoran Gallery Art, Washington, Chgo. Art Inst., Greenville County (S.C.) Mus., Palm Springs Desert Mus., Phoenix Art Mus., William Rockhill Nelsen Mus., Kansas City, Phillips Collection. Nat. Endowment Arts grantee, 1975, 82; Guggenheim Found. fellow, 1979-80; Calif. Arts Council Commn. grantee, 1983-84

DILLARD, MICHAEL L., food products company executive; b. 1942; BS in Acctg., Miss. Coll., 1964. Various acctg. positions Chrysler Corp., Cape Canaveral, Fla., 1964-66; divsn. acct. Blue Goose Growers, Vero Beach, Fla., 1966-76; CFO Pure Gold, Redlands, Calif., 1976-85, Saticoy Lemon Assocs., Inc., Santa Paula, Calif., 1985—. Office: Saticoy Lemon Assoc Inc 103 N Pack Rd Santa Paula CA 93060

DILLENBERG, JACK, dean; b. NYC, Nov. 22, 1945; m. Marianna Dillenberg. BA in Psychology, Tulane U., 1967; DDS, NYU, 1971; MPH, Harvard Sch. Pub. Health, 1978. Dental officer USN, 1971—73; dentist Southbury (Conn.) Tng. Sch., 1973-75; mgr. dental clinic, Jamaica, 1975-77; vis. lectr. Cape Cod C.C., 1978-84; tutor dept. population scis. Harvard Sch. Pub. Health, 1978-81; cons. Mass. Dept. Mental Health, 1978-84; pvt. practice Beacon St. Dental Assocs., Brookline, Mass., 1980-84; instr. Harvard Sch. Dental Medicine, 1980-84; cons. Pan Am. Health Orgn., 1993-97; acting dir. Ariz. Dept. Health Services, 1993—94, dir., 1994—97; area health officer west area L.A. County Dept. Health Services, Santa Monica, Calif., 1997-99; assoc. dir. pub. health programs Calif. Dept. Health Services; dean Ariz. Sch. Dentistry and Oral Health A.T. Still U. of Health Sciences, 2001—; pres. Dillenberg & Friends Health Services Consulting. Cons. Dillenberg & Friends, Inc., 1979-84; pres. Dentanomics, Inc., 1984-86; pub. health cons. World Bank, 1978-99. Recipient Presdl. Citation ADA, 1992, Nat. Fluoridation award CDC, 1991, Alunmi award of Merit, Harvard Sch. Pub. Health, 1997; named Marketer of the Yr., Am. Mktg. Assn., 1997, CEO of Yr., Am. Pub. Adminstrn. Assn., 1997. Mem. ADA, Assn. State and Territorial Dental Dirs., Ariz. Pub. Health Assn. Office: AT Still U Health Scis Ariz Sch Dentistry & Oral Health 5850 East Still Cir Mesa AZ 85206 E-mail: jdillenberg@dhs.co.la.ca.us.

DILLEY, BARBARA JEAN, college administrator, choreographer, educator; b. Chgo., Mar. 13, 1938; d. Robert Vernon and Jean Phyllis (Fairweather) D.; m. Lewis Lloyd, May 1961 (div.); 1 child, Benjamin Lloyd; m. Brent Bondurant, Mar. 1977 (div.); 1 child, Owen Bondurant. BA, Mt. Holyoke Coll., 1960. Dancer Merce Cunningham Dance Co., NYC, 1963-68; ind. dancer, choreographer NYC and Boulder, Colo., 1966-82; dancer Yvonne Rainer Co., NYC, 1967-70; dancer, choreographer The Grand Union, NYC, 1970-76; mem. faculty dance program Naropa Inst., Boulder, 1974—, dir. dance program, 1974-84. Condr. pvt. workshops Toronto, Ont., Can., Montreal, Que., Can., Halifax, N.S., Can., The Netherlands, Eng., Switzerland, Germany, 1978—; vis. faculty European Dance Devel. Ctr., Arnheim, The Netherlands, 1993-94; artistic dir. Crystal Dance, Boulder, 1978-81; mem. vis. faculty NYU, Radcliffe Coll., Cornell U., U. Colo., George Washington U., others; dir. dance symposium, 1981; adjudicator S.W. divsn. Am. Coll. Dance Festival, Loretto Heights, Colo., 1986. Mem. grants selection panel Colo. Coun. of Arts and Humanities, 1981, mem. panel on policy devel. for individual grants, 1983. NEA Choreographic fellow, 1974, 76, 81; Boulder City Arts Coun. grantee, 1981. Democrat. Buddhist. Office: Naropa Inst 2130 Arapahoe Ave Boulder CO 80302-6697

DILLON, ADRIAN T., financial executive; BA summa cum laude, Amherst Coll. Sr. economist Eaton Corp., 1979-82, chief economist, 1982-86, mgr. corp. strategy, 1984-86, dir. fin. strategy, chief economist, 1986-88, asst. treas., 1988-91, v.p. planning, 1991-95, v.p., chief fin. and planning officer, 1995-97, exec. v.p., chief fin. and planning officer, 1997—2001; exec. v.p. fin. & adminstrn., CFO Agilent Technologies, Palo Alto, Calif., 2001—. Non-exec. chmn. Verigy Ltd.; bd. dir. Williams-Sonoma Inc. Chmn. Eaton's United Way Campaign, 1993, 94; exec. bd. mem. Boy Scouts Greater Cleve. Coun.; past chmn. bd. trustees Beech Brook; past vice-chmn. WVIZ & WCPN public radio, Cleve.; bd. mem. Castilleja Sch. Mem. Am. Econ. Assn., Conf. Bus. Economists, Coun. Fin. Execs. (mem. conf. bd.); past chmn. Conference Bd. Council of Fin. Executives. Office: Agilent Technologies Inc 5301 Stevens Creek Blvd Santa Clara CA 95051-7201

DILLON, CAROL K., lawyer; b. Honolulu; BA, Stanford U., 1975; JD, U. Calif. Berkeley, Boalt Hall, 1982. Bar: Calif. 1982. Ptnr. Bingham McCutchen LLP, Palo Alto, chairperson cmml. real estate practice group. Recipient Thelen Marrin Award Outstanding Legal Scholarship; named a No. Calif. Super Lawyer, Law & Politics & SF Magazine, 2004; named one of Silicon Valley Best Lawyers, San Jose Mag., 2002—04. Mem.: Nat. Assn. Coll. & U. Attys., State Bar Calif. Office: Bingham McCutchen LLP 1900 University Ave East Palo Alto CA 94303 Office Phone: 650-849-4812. Business E-Mail: carol.dillon@bingham.com.

DILLON, KEVIN, actor; b. Mamaroneck, NY, Aug. 19, 1965; s. Paul and Mary Ellen Dillon; m. Jane Stuart, Apr. 22, 2006; 1 child, Ava; 1 child, Amy. Actor: (TV films) No Big Deal, 1983, When He's Not a Stranger, 1989, Frankie's House, 1992, The Pathfinder, 1996, Gone in the Night, 1996, Medusa's Child, 1997; (films) Heaven Help Us, 1985, Platoon, 1986, Remote Control, 1988, The Rescue, 1988, The Blob, 1988, War Party, 1988, Immediate Family, 1989, The Doors, 1991, A Midnight Clear, 1992, No Escape, 1994, Criminal Hearts, 1995, True Crime, 1996, Stag, 1997, Hidden Agenda, 1998, Misbegotten, 1998, Interstate 84, 2000, Out for Blood, 2004, The Foursome, 2006, Poseidon, 2006, Hotel for Dogs, 2009; (TV series) St. Michael's Crossing, 1999, NYPD Blue, 1998—2000, 24, 2003, That's Life, 2000—05, Entourage, 2004—; voice (video game) Scarface: The World Is Yours, 2006. Office: c/o Evolution Entertainment Inc 901 N Highland Ave Los Angeles CA 90038

DILLON, MATTHEW, chef; b. San Bernardino, Calif., 1973; Grad., Seattle Ctrl. Cmty. Coll. Chef Salish Lodge, Snoqualmie, Wash., Supreme, The Herbfarm, Woodinville, Wash., Stumbling Goat Bistro, Seattle; owner, chef Sitka & Spruce, Seattle, 2006—. Named one of Best New Chefs, Food and Wine Mag., 2007. Avocation: foraging. Office: Sitka and Spruce 2238 Eastlake Ave E Seattle WA 98102 Office Phone: 206-324-0662.

DILLON, MICHAEL A. (MIKE), lawyer, information technology executive; BA in Comm. and Sociology, U. Calif., San Diego; JD, U. Santa Clara, Calif., 1984. Various positions Sun Microsystems, Inc., Santa Clara, Calif., 1993—99; v.p., gen. counsel ONI Systems Corp., San Jose, Calif., 1999—2002, sec., 2000—02; v.p. products law group Sun Microsystems, Inc., Santa Clara, Calif., 2002—04, sr. v.p., sec., 2004—06, gen. counsel, sec., 2004—, exec. v.p., 2006—. Office: Sun Microsystems Inc 4150 Network Cir Santa Clara CA 95054 Office Phone: 650-960-1300.

DILLON, MICHAEL EARL, mechanical engineering executive, educator; children: Bryan Douglas, Nicole Marie, Brendon McMichael. BA in Math., Calif. State U., Long Beach, 1978, postgrad. Registered profl. engr., Ala., Alaska, Ariz., Ark., Calif., Colo., Conn., Del., Fla., Ga., Hawaii, Idaho, Ill., Ind., Iowa, Kans., Ky., La., Md., Maine, Mass., Mich., Minn., Miss., Mo., Mont., Nebr., Nev., N.Mex., ND, NJ, NY, NC, Ohio, Okla., Oreg., Pa., SC, SD, Tenn., Tex., Utah, Va., Wash., W.Va., Wis., Wyo., chartered engr., U.K. Journeyman plumber Roy E. Dillon & Sons, Long Beach, 1967—69, ptnr., 1969—73; field supr. Dennis Mech., San Marino, 1973—74; chief mech. official City of Long Beach, 1974—79; mgr. engr. Southland Industries, Long Beach, 1979—83; v.p. Syska & Hennessy, LA and NY, 1983—87; prin. Robert M. Young & Assoc., Pasadena, Calif., 1987—89; pres. Dillon Cons. Engrs., Long Beach, 1989—. Mech. cons. in field; instr. in field; lectr. in field UCLA, U. Calif. San Diego, U. Calif., Irvine, U. So. Calif., U.S. Mil. Acad., West Point. Author: numerous poems; contbr. articles to profl. jours., chapters to books. Former chair Mechanical, Plumbing. Elec. and Energy CodeAdv. Commn. of Calif. Bldg. Stds. Commn.; former vice chmn. bd. examiners Appeals and Condemnations, Long Beach; mem. adv. bd. City of LA; mem. bus. adv. bd. City of Long Beach. Recipient Environ. Ozone Protection award, U.S. EPA, 1993, John Fies award, Internat. Conf. Bldg. Ofcls., 1995. Fellow Chartered Inst. Bldg. Svc. Engrs. Gt. Britain and Ireland, Inst. Refrigeration, Heating, Air Conditioning Engrs. of New Zealand, Inst. Advancement Engring.; mem. ASCE, ASME, IEEE, ISA, Internat. Soc. Fire Safety Sci., Nat. Inst. for Engring. Ethics, Nat. Fire Protection Assn., Internat. Assn. Bldg. Ofcls., Internat. Fire Code Inst., Internat. Code Coun., Soc. Fire Protection Engrs., Tau Beta Pi, Pi Tau Sigma, Chi Epsilon, others. Avocation: poetry. Office: Dillon Cons Engrs Inc 671 Quincy Ave Long Beach CA 90814-1818 Office Phone: 562-434-4640. Business E-Mail: medillon@dillon-consulting.com.

DILLOW, JOHN DAVID, lawyer; b. Bremerton, Wash., Aug. 17, 1946; s. Garold Maurice and Margaret (Roediger) D.; m. Alison Wenke, Sept. 19, 1977; children: Gwen, Jake, Claire BS magna cum laude, U. Wash., 1968; JD, Duke U., 1971. Bar: Calif. 1972, Wash. 1975, U.S. Dist. Ct. (Ctrl. Dist.) Wash. 1972, U.S. Dist. Ct. (We. Dist.) Calif. 1975, U.S. Ct. Appeals (9th Cir.) 1972, U.S. Supreme Ct. 1975, N.Y. 1981. Assoc. O'Melveny and Meyers, LA, 1971-75, Perkins Coie, LLP, Seattle, 1975-77, ptnr., Product Liability Area, 1977—. Editor Duke Law Jour. Bd. dirs. ARC King County, Seattle, 1987—; mem. coun. fund raising Duke U., Durham, N.C., 1975—. Mem. ABA (aviation & space law com.), Wash. State Bar Assn., King County Bar Assn., Barristers Club, Seattle Tennis Club, Order of Coif, Tau Beta Pi. Avocations: tennis, skiing. Office: Perkins Coie LLP 1201 3rd Ave Fl 40 Seattle WA 98101-3029 Office Phone: 206-359-8476. Office Fax: 206-359-9000. Business E-Mail: jdillow@perkinscoie.com.

DIMICK, NEIL FRANCIS, retired medical products wholesale executive; married; four children. BS in Acctg. summa cum laude, Brigham Young U. Corp. auditor Deloitte and Touche, 1973-77, mgr. tech. rsch. dept. NYC, 1977-80, ptnr., nat. dir. real estate industry divsn.; CFO Bergen Brunswig Corp., 1991—2001, exec. v.p., dir., CFO, 2001—02. Bd. dir. WebMD Corp., Thoratec Corp., Global Resources Professionals. Co-author: Real Estate Accounting and Reporting Manual. Bd. mem., past chair Orange County chpt. Nat. Multiple Sclerosis Soc.; adv. bd. mem. Am. Cancer Soc.; trustee Mardan Ctr. Ednl. Therapy, Irvine, Calif. Office: Thoratec Corp PO Box 9003 Pleasanton CA 94566-9003

DIMITRIADIS, ANDRE C., health care executive; b. Istanbul, Turkey, Sept. 29, 1940; s. Constantine N. and Terry D. BS, Robert Coll., Istanbul, 1964; MS, Princeton U., 1965; MBA, NYU, 1967, PhD, 1970. Analyst Mobil Oil Internat., NYC, 1965-67; mgr. TWA, NYC, 1967-73; dir. Pan Am. Airways, NYC, 1973-76, asst. treas., 1976-79; v.p., chief fin. officer Air Calif., Newport Beach, 1979-82; exec. v.p. fin. and adminstrn., chief fin. officer Western Airlines, Los Angeles, 1982-85, dir.; sr. v.p. (fin) Am. Med. Internat., from 1985, chief fin. officer, 1985-89, exec. v.p., 1988-89; dir., exec. v.p. fin., chief fin. officer Beverly Enterprises Inc., Ft. Smith, Ark., 1989-92; chmn., CEO LTC Properties, Inc., 1992—. Bd. dirs. Assisted Living Concepts, Inc. Democrat. Greek Orthodox. Home: 4470 Vista Del Preseas Malibu CA 90265-2540 Office: Ltc Properties Inc 31365 Oak Crest Dr Ste 200 Westlake Village CA 91361-5693

DIMITRIUS, JO-ELLAN, trial consultant; BS, Scripps Coll., Claremont, Calif., 1975; M, Claremont Grad. Sch., 1977, PhD in Criminology, 1984. With Litig. Scis. Inc., FTI, Vinson & Dimitrius, Dimitrius & Assocs., Pasadena, Calif. Co-author: Reading People, 1998, Put Your Best Foot Forward, 2000. Achievements include consulting on jury selection for the following high-profile trials: Night Stalker (Richard Ramirez), Rodney King, Reginald Denny, O.J. Simpson, Ken Lay, and Jeff Skilling. Office: Dimitrius & Assocs Ste 305 201 S Lake Ave Pasadena CA 91101 Office Phone: 626-431-2700. Office Fax: 626-431-2702. Business E-Mail: jed@dimita.com.

DIMMICK, CAROLYN REABER, federal judge; b. Seattle, Oct. 24, 1929; d. Maurice C. and Margaret T. (Taylor) Reaber; m. Cyrus Allen Dimmick, Sept. 10, 1955; children: Taylor, Dana. BA, U. Wash., 1951, JD, 1953; LLD, Gonzaga U., 1982, CUNY, 1987. Bar: Wash. 1953. Asst. atty. gen. State of Wash., Seattle, 1953-55; pros. atty. King County, Wash., 1955-59, 60-62; sole practice Seattle, 1959-60, 62-65; judge N.E. Dist. Ct. Wash., 1965-75, King County Superior Ct., 1976-80; justice Wash. Supreme Ct., 1981-85; judge U.S. Dist. Ct. (we. dist.) Wash., Seattle, 1985-94, chief judge, 1994-97, sr. judge, 1997—. Mem. Jud. Resources Com., 1987—94, chmn., 1991—94; mem. Jud. Conf. Com. to Rev. Cir. Coun. Conduct and Disability Orders, 2001—. Recipient Matrix Table award, 1981, World Plan Execs. Coun. award, 1981, Vanguard Honor award King County of Wash. Women Lawyers, 1996, Disting. Alumni award U. Wash. Law Sch., 1997, Outstanding Jurist award King County Bar Assn., 2003; named Wash. Women of Yr. Seattle U. Women's Law Caucus, 2004. Mem. ABA, Am. Judges Assn. (gov.), Nat. Assn. Women Judges, World Assn. Judges, Wash. Bar Assn., Am. Judicature Soc., Order of Coif (Wash. chpt.). Office: US Dist Ct 16134 US Courthouse 700 Stewart St Seattle WA 98101 Office Phone: 206-370-8850. E-mail: carolyn_dimmick@wawd.uscourts.gov.

DIMSDALE, JOEL EDWARD, psychiatry educator; b. Sioux City, Iowa, Apr. 16, 1947; s. Lewis J. and Phyllis (Green) D.; m. Nancy Kleinman, Sept. 17, 1978; 1 child, Jonathan Jared. BA in Biology, Carleton Coll., 1968; MA in Sociology, Stanford U., 1970, MD, 1973. Diplomate Am. Bd. Psychiatry. Resident in psychiatry Mass. Gen. Hosp., Boston, 1973-76; instr. psychiatry Harvard U. Sch. Medicine, Boston, 1976-80, asst. prof., 1980-84, assoc. prof., 1984-85; assoc. prof., disting. prof. psychiatry U. Calif., San Diego, 1985—, chair acad. senate, 2002—03. Cons. to Pres.'s Commn. on Mental Health, Washington, 1977-78, NIH, Washington, 1980—. Editor: Survivors, Victims and Perpetrators, 1980, Quality of Life in Behavior Medicine Rsch., 1995; editor-in-chief Psychosomatic Medicine, 1992-02; mem. editl. bd. Internat. Jour. Behavioral Medicine, 1993-2007, Applied Biobehavioral Rsch., 1994—, Am. Jour. Human Biology, 1994-2003, Psychosomatics, 1996—, taskforce on DSMV, Am. Psychiatry Assn., 2007-; contbr. articles to profl. jours. Fellow Am. Psychopathol. Assn., Acad. Behavioral Med. Rsch. (coun. 1988-91, 2004—, pres. 1991-92), Soc. of Behavioral Medicine (pres. 2000), Disting. fellow Am. Psychiat. Assn., Sleep Rsch. Soc. (chmn. rsch. com. 2005-08); mem. Am. Psychosomatic Soc. (coun. 1982-85, pres. 1999), Sigma Xi. Home: 4435 Ampudia St San Diego CA 92103 Office: Dept Psychiatry 0804 9500 Gilman Dr UCSD La Jolla CA 92093-0804 Office Phone: 619-543-5592. Business E-Mail: jdimsdale@ucsd.edu.

DINARELLO, CHARLES A., medical educator; b. Boston, 1943; MD, Boston U., 1969; Doctor Honoris Causa, U. Marseille, France, 1997. Clin. tng. Mass. Gen. Hosp.; clin. assoc. NIH, Bethesda, 1971—74, sr. investigator, 1975—77; prof. medicine and pediat. Tufts U. Sch. Medicine; staff physician New England Med. Ctr. Hosp., Boston; prof. medicine U. Colorado Sch. Medicine, Denver, 1996—. Sci. adv. bd. Senesco Technologies, Inc., 2002; mem. bd. scientific advisors Nat. Inst. Allergy and Infections Diseases; dir. Techne Corp. Mem. several editl. bds.; contbr. several articles to profl. jours. Recipient Ernst Jung prize in medicine, 1993, Ludwig Heilmeyer Gold medal, Soc. for Internal Medicine, 1996; co-recipient Crafoord prize in Polyarthritis, Royal Swedish Acad. Sciences, 2009. Mem.: NAS, Internat. Cytokine Soc. (pres. 1995—96), Am. Soc. Clin. Investigations (v.p. 1989—90), European Molecular Biology Organization (EMBO) (assoc.). Achievements include pioneering work with collegues to isolate interleukins, determine their properties and explore their role in the onset of inflammatory diseases. Office: Campus Box B168 U Colorado Sch Medicine 4200 E Ninth Ave Denver CO 80262 Office Phone: 303-724-4922.*

DINI, JOSEPH EDWARD, JR., state legislator; b. Yerington, Nev., Mar. 28, 1929; s. Giuseppe and Elvira (Castellani) D.; m. Mouryne Landing; children: Joseph, George, David, Michael. BSBA, U. Nev., Reno, 1951. Mem. Nev. State Assembly, Carson City, 1967—, majority leader, 1975, speaker, 1977, 87, 89, 91, 93, 97, 99, minority leader, 1985, interim fin. com. mem., 1985-01, speaker pro tem, 1973, co-spkr., 1995, chmn. water policy com. Western Legis. Conf., 1993-94, 96-00, speaker emeritus, 2001; pres. Dini's Lucky Club Casino, Yerington, Nev., 1972—. Mem. legis. com. Nev. State Assembly, 1971-77, 91, 93, 95, 97, vice chmn., 1981-82, 96-97, chmn., 1982-83, 93-94. Mem. Yerington Vol. Fire Dept.; mem. Lyon County Dem. Ctrl. Com., Nev. Am. Revolution Bicentennial Commn.; past dist. gov., active mem. 20-30 Club. Recipient Outstanding Citizen award Nev. Edn. Assn., 1973, Friend of Edn. award Nev. State Edn. Assn., 1986, Citizen of Yr. award Nev. Judges Assn., 1987, Dedicated and Valued Leadership award Nat. Conf. State Legislatures, 1989, Excellence in Pub. Svc. award Nev. Trial Lawyers Assn., 1990, Silver Plow award Nev. Farm Bur., 1991, Skill, Integrith, Responsibility award Assoc. Gen. Contractors, 1994, Guardian of Small Bus. award Nat. Fedn. Ind. Bus., 1996, Spl. Recognition award Nev. State Firefighters Assn., 1998, Appreciation award Nev. Emergency Preparedness Assn., 1998, Friendship Medal of Diplomacy, Taiwan, 2000; named Conservation Legislator of Yr. Nev. Wildlife Fedn., 1991, Alumni of Yr., U. Nev. Alumni Assn., 1997, Legislator of Yr., Nev. Rural Water Assn., 1999, Italian American of Yr. Augustus Soc. Las Vegas, 2001, Arts Advocate Nev. Arts Advocates, 2002. Mem. Mason Valley C. of C. (pres.), Rotary (pres. Yerington 1989), Lions (pres. Yerington chpt. 1975), Masons, Shriners, York Rite, Scottish Rite, Order Ea. Star, Gamma Sigma Delta, Phi Sigma Kappa (Disting. Alumna award 1993). Home: 104 N Mountain View St Yerington NV 89447-2239 Office: Dini's Lucky Club Inc 45 N Main St Yerington NV 89447-2230

DINKEL, JOHN GEORGE, automotive executive, consultant; b. Bklyn., Aug. 1, 1944; s. Charles Ernst and Loretta Gertrude D.; m. Leslie Hawkins, Oct. 25, 1969; children: Meredith Anne, Kevin Carter. BS in Mech. Engring, U. Mich., 1967, MS in Mech. Engring, 1969. Staff engr. Chrysler Corp., Highland Park, Mich., 1967-69; engring. editor Car Life Mag., Newport Beach, Calif., 1969-70, Road & Track Mag., Newport Beach, 1972-79, editor, 1979-88, editor in chief, 1988-91, editor at large, 1991-92; dir. product communications Hill-Holliday, 1991-92; pres. John Dinkel & Assocs., 1991—; editor-at-large Sports Car Internat., 1992—; v.p. editl. ops. Calcar, 1995-97; group mgr. member info. and comm. svcs. Automobile Club So. Calif., Costa Mesa, 1998-2000; pub. Westways, 1998-2000; v.p. pub. Driving Media, Inc./Driving.com, 2000—02; asst. pub. relations dir. Pirelli Tire and Saleen, Inc., 2002—05; exec. v.p. product planning, devel. and testing Visionary Vehicles, 2005—; L.A. bur. chief Auto Aficionado Mag., 2005—. Commencement spkr. U. Mich., Dearborn, 1987; hon. judge Meadow Brook Hall Concourse D'Elegance, 1985-86, Hillsborough Concourse D'Elegance, 1989, Palo Alto Concours D'Elegance, 1990; spkr. Direct Mktg. Club So. Calif., 1992; SCCA competition driving instr., 2000—. Author: Road & Track Auto Dictionary, 1977, Road & Track Illustrated Auto Dictionary, 2000; co-author: RX-7: Mazda's Legendary Sports Car, 1991, Mazda MX-5 Miata, 1998, The Mazda RX-8: World's First 4-Door, 4-Seat Sports Car, 2003; editor-at-large Westways, 2003—; contbg. editor No. New Eng. Journey, 2000—, European Car, 2003—; co-host daily radio show Auto Report, 1986-88; host weekly radio show Drive Time, 1996—; contbr. articles to profl. jours.; patentee method and sys. for adjusting settings of vehicle functions, 2000 Nat. chmn. U. Mich. Ann. Fund, 1988—; commr. Irvine (Calif.) Baseball Assn.; sec. Irvine Pony Baseball-Softball, 1995—; organizer clothing drive victims of Armenia earthquake, 1988; soccer coach AYSO, 1984-90, Irvine Soccer Club, 1991—; baseball coach Northwood Little League, 1994—; basketball coach Irvine Boys and Girls Club, 1993—; vol. mem. corp. alliance com. Orange County chpt. Nat. Multiple Sclerosis Soc., 2002. Honored by Colden Ctr. for the Performing Arts, Queens Coll., N.Y.C., 1990. Mem. SAE (panelist conf. on impacts of intelligent vehicle hwy. systems 1990, organizer, chmn. sessions on fuel economy and small cars 1978-79, chmn. pub. affairs Future Transp. Conf. 1997), Am. Racing Press Assn., Internat. Motor Press Assn., Sports Car Club Am., Internat. Motor Sports Assn., Motor Press Guild (pres. 1991), Road Racing Drivers Club (hon.)Pi Tau Sigma. Achievements include being the Four-time winner of SCCA Nelson Ledges 24-hour endurance auto race. E-mail: eleven-tenths@cox.net.

DINNERSTEIN, LEONARD, historian, educator; b. NYC, May 5, 1934; s. Abraham and Lillian (Kubrik) D.; m. Myra Anne Rosenberg, Aug. 20, 1961; children: Andrew, Julie. B of Social Scis., CCNY, 1955; MA, Columbia U., 1960, PhD, 1966. Instr. N.Y. Inst. Tech., NYC, 1960-65; asst. prof. Fairleigh Dickinson U., Teaneck, NJ, 1967-70; dir. Judaic studies U. Ariz., Tucson, 1993-2000, prof. Am. history, 1970—2004; ret. Adj. prof. Columbia U., summers 1969, 72, 74, 81, 87, 89, NYU, summers 1969-70, 82, 86. Author: The Leo Frank Case, 1968 (Anisfield-Wolf award 1969), 3rd edit., 2008, America and the Survivors of the Holocaust, 1982, Uneasy at Home, 1987; (with David M. Reimers) Ethnic Americans: A History of Immigration and Assimilation, 1997, 5th edit., 1999; (with R.L. Nichols, D.M. Reimers) Natives and Strangers, 1996, 4th edit., 2003, Antisemitism in America, 1994 (Nat. Jewish Book prize 1994); contbr. articles to profl. jours.; editor: (with Fred Jaher) The Aliens, 1970; (with Kenneth T. Jackson) American Vistas, 1971, 7th edit., 1995; (with Mary Dale Palsson) Jews in the South, 1973; (with Jean Christie) Decisions and Revisions: Interpretations of 20th Century American History, 1975, America Since World War II, 1976. Mem. Orgn. Am. Historians, Am. Hist. Assn., Am. Jewish Hist. Assn. Democrat. Jewish. Home: 1981 E Miraval Cuarto Tucson AZ 85718-3032 Home Phone: 520-615-8585. Business E-Mail: dinnerst@u.arizona.edu.

DION, PHILIP JOSEPH, consumer products and services executive, real estate and construction company executive; b. Chgo., Nov. 30, 1944; s. Philip J. and Loretta (Loftus) D.; m. Patricia Ann Reichert, June 24, 1967; children: Philip Joseph, David, Jaime. BA, St. Ambrose Coll., 1966; MBA, Loyola U., Chgo., 1968. Cons. Booz, Allen & Hamilton, Chgo., 1966-68; pres., gen. mgr. Cocrema Inc., Lorenzo DeMexico, Chgo., 1968-70; with Armour-Dial Inc., Phoenix, 1970-82, pres. subs., 1970-82; sr. v.p. fin. Del Webb Corp., Phoenix, 1982-83, exec.v.p., 1983-87, pres., 1987, chmn. bd., CEO, 1987-99, chmn., 1999—. Pres. coun. St. Ambrose U.; mem. Allendale Adv. Bd.; chmn. bd. dirs., dir. nat. bd. Boy's Hope; bd. dirs. United for Ariz., Scottsdale Meml. Found.; mem. Govs. Leadership Coun. Mem. Assn. Corp. Growth, Paradise Valley Country Club. Office: Del Webb Corp 15333 N Pima Rd Ste 300 Scottsdale AZ 85260-2782

DIRKS, LEE EDWARD, newspaper executive; b. Indpls., Aug. 4, 1935; s. Raymond Louis and Virginia Belle (Wagner) Dirks; m. Barbara Dee Nutt, June 16, 1956 (div. Jan. 1985); children: Stephen Merle, Deborah Virginia, David Louis; m. Judith Ann Putman, Dec. 28, 2001. BA, DePauw U., 1956; MA, Fletcher Sch. Law and Diplomacy, 1957. Reporter Boston Globe, 1957, Nat. Observer, Washington, 1962-65, news editor, 1966-68; securities analyst specializing in newspaper stocks Dirks Bros., Ltd., Washington, 1969-71, Delafield, Childs, Inc., Washington, 1971-75, C.S. McKee & Co., Washington, 1975-76; asst. to pres. Detroit Free Press, 1976-77, v.p., gen. mgr., 1977-80; chmn. Dirks, Van Essen & Murray, Santa Fe, N.Mex., 1980—. Author: Religion in Action, 1965; pub. Newspaper Newsletter, 1970-76. Bd. dirs. Nat. Ghost Ranch Found., Santa Fe, 1973-97, Santa Fe Opera, 1998-2004; pres. Georgia O'Keeffe Mus., Santa Fe, 2000-04. Named Religion Writer of Yr. Religious Newswriters Assn., 1964. Mem. Phi Beta Kappa, Lambda Chi Alpha, Nat. Press Club (Washington), Oakland Hills Country Club (Detroit), Las Campanas(Santa Fe). Presbyterian. Home: 11 E Arrowhead Cir Santa Fe NM 87506-8248 Office: 119 E Marcy St Ste 100 Santa Fe NM 87501-2046 Office Phone: 505-820-2700. E-mail: lee@dirksvanessen.com.

DIRZO, RODOLFO, biologist, educator, researcher; b. Cuernavaca, Mex., June 26, 1951; s. Felix and Antonia (Minjarez) D.; m. Bertha Guillermina Gomez, Dec. 18, 1986; 1 child, Arturo. BSc in Biology, U. Morelos, Cuernavaca, 1974; MSc in Ecology, U. Wales, Bangor, UK, 1977, PhD in Ecology, 1980. Rsch. asst. Nat. U. Mex., Mexico City, 1974-80, assoc. prof. ecology, 1980-83, prof. ecology, 1983-85; dir. Tropical Rsch. Sta., Veracruz, Mex., 1985-87; dep. chair Inst. Ecology, Nat. U. Mex., 1994-97, full prof. ecology, 1990—; Bing prof. environ. sci., dept. biol. scis. Stanford U., 2004. Prof., instr. Orgn. Tropical Studies, Costa Rica and U.S., 1982-; conservation & environment scholar Pew Charitable Trust, U.S., 1993; nat. rschr. Mex. Coun. Sci., Mexico City, 1990-; cons. Nat. Geographic Soc., Washington, 1995. Author, editor: Perspectives on Plant Population Ecology, 1984, Mexico Faces the Biodiversity Crisis, 1992, Tropical Forests: Biodiversity, 1996; mem. editl. bd. Trends in Ecology and Evolution, 1993—. Mem. Mex. Acad. Sci. (chair biology 1996-97), Ecol. Soc. Am. (mem. pub. affairs com. 1996-98, governing bd. 1999—), Internat. Geosphere-Biosphere Program (mem. scientific com. 1997—), Assn. Tropical Biology (pres. 1993-94), NAS (fgn. assoc.), Am. Acad. Arts & Sciences (hon. fgn.). Avocations: children's education, hiking, soccer, music, movies. Office: Stanford U Dept Biol Sciences Gilbert Hall Stanford CA 94305-5020 Business E-Mail: rdirzo@stanford.edu.

DISAIA, PHILIP JOHN, obstetrician, gynecologist, radiology educator; b. Providence, Aug. 14, 1937; s. George and Antoinette (Vastano) DiS.; children: John P., Steven D.; m. Patricia June; children: Dominic J., Vincent J. BS cum laude, Brown U., 1959; MD cum laude, Tufts U., 1963; MD (hon.), U. Genoa, Italy, 1999. Diplomate Am. Bd. Ob-Gyn. (examiner 1975—, bd. dirs. 1994, v.p. bd. dirs. 1997—), Am. Bd. Gynecologic Oncology (bd. dirs. 1987—). Intern Yale U. Sch. Medicine, New Haven Hosp., 1963-64, resident in ob-gyn., 1964-67, instr. ob-gyn., 1966-67; fellow in gynecologic oncology U. Tex. M.D. Anderson Hosp. and Tumor Inst., Houston, 1969-70, NIH sr. fellow, 1969-70, instr. ob-gyn., 1969-71; asst. prof. ob-gyn. and radiology U. So. Calif. Sch. Medicine, LA, 1971-74, assoc. prof., 1974-77; prof., chmn. dept. ob-gyn. U. Calif. Irvine Med. Ctr., Calif. Coll. Medicine, 1977-88, prof., 1977—, prof. radiology, radiation therapy div., 1978—, assoc. vice chancellor for health scis. Irvine Coll. Medicine, 1987-89, Dorothy Marsh chair of reproductive biology, 1989—; divsn. dir. cancer ctr. U. Calif. Irvine Med. Ctr.,

Calif. Coll. Medicine, 1989—; pres. med. staff U. Calif. Irvine Med. Ctr., Calif. Coll. Medicine, 1993-97; pres. UCI Clin. Practice Group, 1994—. Dir. div. gynecol. oncology Am. Bd. Obstetrics & Gynecology, 1995—, bd. dirs., 1994—, past chair, current pres.; bd. dirs. U. Calif. Irvine Med. Ctr., 1995, chair health sys. steering com., 1995, chair health sys. capital planning group, 1995, health sys. bd. dirs., 1995; clin. enterprise adv. coun. to pres. U. Calif., 1995; academic planning task force U. Calif. Irvine, 1994, continuing med. edn. com., 1991-94; cancer liaison commn. on cancer Am. Coll. Surgeons, 1981-94; bd. dirs., dir. at large Am. Cancer Soc., 1985—; clin. prof. dept. ob-gyn. U. Nev. Sch. Medicine, Reno, 1985—; chmn. site visit team for surgery br. Nat. Cancer Inst. NIH, 1983, subcom. surg. oncology rsch. devel., 1982-83, mem. sci. counselors div. cancer treatment, 1979-83; mem. gov.'s adv. coun. on cancer State of Calif., 1980-85; vis. prof., lectr., speaker various sci. meetings, confs., courses. Recipient Disting. Alumnus award M.D. Anderson Hosp. and Tumor Inst. U. Tex., 1980, Silver Apple award U. Calif. Med. Students, 1983, Lauds and Laurels Profl. Achievement award U. Calif. Alumni Assn., 1983, Hubert Haussel's award Long Beach Meml. Hosp., 1983, Dist. Faculty Lectureship award for Teaching, U. Calif. Irvine Acad. Senate, 1993-94, Robert Wood Johnson award, 2003, medal for excellence UIC, 2003, IGS award for excellence in gynecologic oncology Bristol Myers Squibb, 2004, Arise award UCI, 2005, award Women's Cancer Symposium, Amman, Jordan, 2005, Frederick Naptolin award SGI, 2007, also various rsch. awards. Fellow Am. Coll. Obstetricians and Gynecologists (com. on human rsch. for cancer 1979—, chmn. 1984—, chmn. subcom. on gynecologic oncology 1984-85, prolog editorial and adv. com. 1986—, v.p. 1997-99, various others), ACS (bd. govs. 1998—), Commn. on Cancer Liaison, Western Assn. Gynecologic Oncologists (founder 1971, pres. 1978-79), Am. Gynecol. and Obstet. Soc. (exec. coun. 1986—), Am. Gynecologic Soc., Pacific Coast Ob/Gyn Soc., South Atlantic Assn. Obstetricians and Gynecologists (hon.); mem. AMA, Am. Cancer Soc. (bd. dirs. L.A. County unit 1975-77, Orange County 1979, unit pres. 1993—; bd. dirs. Calif. div. 1985—, chmn. med. scientific com. 1993-94), Nat. Am. Cancer Soc. (dir.-at-large, bd. dirs. 1985—, chmn. program com. for nat. conf. 1986, vice-chmn. detection and treatment adv. group gynecol. cancer 1993-94, active in others), Am. Coll. Radiology (commn. on cancer 1984-85), Am. Soc. Clin. Oncologists, Soc. Gynecologic Oncologists (exec. coun. 1975-80, pres. 1982-83), Internat. Gynecologic Oncology Cancer Soc., Italian Soc. Ob-Gyn. (Camillo Golgi prof. U. Brescia 1991), Calif. Med. Assn., NCI, Ctrl. IRB, Academic Senate, (chair 2000-), Gynecologic Oncology Group, (chair 2002-), ABOG, (pres.2002-06, chmn. bd. 2006—), Alpha Omega Alpha. Office: U Calif Irvine Med Ctr 101 The City Dr S Bldg 56 Rm 265 Orange CA 92868-3201 Office Phone: 714-456-5220. E-mail: pjdisaia@uci.edu.

DISESSA, ANDREA A., education educator; b. June 3, 1947; m. Melinda M. diSessa; children: Kurt, Nicholas. AB in Physics, Princeton U., 1969; PhD in Physics, MIT, 1975. Mem. A.I. lab. logo group MIT, Cambridge, Mass., 1972—82, spl. lectr. edn., 1975—77, from asst. prof. to assoc. prof. edn., 1977—82, prin. scientist lab. for computer sci., 1982—84, sr. scientist lab. for computer sci., leader ednl. computing group, 1984—85; assoc. prof. edn. U. Calif., Berkeley, 1985—88, prof. edn., 1988—, chmn. SESAME grad. program, 1988—89, assoc. dean for acad. affairs Grad. Sch. Edn., 1989—91, chair cognition and devel. edn., 1998—2000. Vis. rschr. World Ctr. for Computers and Human Resources, Paris, 1982; spkr. divsn. edn. and math., sci. and tech. edn. U. Calif., Berkeley, 1992—93; vis. prof. media lab. MIT, Cambridge, 1993—94; convenor Ctr. for Study of Critical Transitions, 1997—2002; fellow Ctr. for Advanced Study in Behavioral Scis., 1997—98; cons. in field; founding mem. adv. bd. SIG in Edn. in Sci. and Tech., 1989—; mem. adv. bd. Handheld Assessment Project, 1999—. Contbg. editor: Jour. Math. Behavior, 1982—; editor: Instructional Science, 1984—89; mem. editl. bd.: Jour. Learning Scis., 1990—, Interactive Learning Environments, 1990, Jour. Sci. Edn. and Tech., 1993—. Recipient grants in field. Mem.: NAE, Math. Assn. Am., Jean Piaget Soc., Internat. Soc. of Learning Scis., Cognitive Sci. Soc., Am. Ednl. Rsch. Assn., Nat. Consortium on Uses of Computers in Math. Scis. Edn. (steering com. 1984—86), Phi Beta Kappa. Achievements include research in computers in education; learning genetic epistemology; instruction in physics and mathematics; programming languages for non-professionals. Office: 4533 Tolman Hall #1670 Grad Sch Edn U Calif Berkeley CA 94720-1670

DISHMAN, ROSE MARIE RICE, academic administrator, researcher; BS in Physics with honors, U. Mo., 1966; MS in Physics, U. Calif., Riverside, 1968, PhD, 1971; MBA, San Diego State U., 1979. Physics instr., elem. particle rsch. assoc. U. Tenn., Knoxville, Oak Ridge, 1968-71; computer programmer, analyst Signal Processing Divsn. Sys. Ctrl., Inc., Palo Alto, Calif., 1971-72; instr. physics San Diego State U., 1974-75; instr. algebra, calculus, physics San Diego C.C., Navy Tng. Ctr., Marine Corps Recruit Depot, 1975-78; instr. Grossmont Coll., San Diego, 1976-77; prof., dept. head Sch. Engring. and Applied Sci. U.S. Internat. U., San Diego, 1977-92, dean Sch. Engring. and Applied Sci., 1989-92, acting provost, v.p. acad. affairs, 1991-92; dean acad. affairs DeVry Inst. Tech., Pomona, Calif., 1992-94, pres. Pomona, Long Beach, Calif., 1994—. Supr. worldwide acad. progs. including campuses in Mex., Eng., Kenya, U.S. Internat. U., primary supr. deans Schs. of Edn., Bus., Visual and Performing Arts, Human Behavior, Hotel and Restaurant Mgmt., Libr., Learning Resource Ctr., developer civil engring., engring. mgmt., electronics tech., elec. engring. progs. resulting in Engring. Accreditation Commn. of the Accreditation Bd. for Engring. and Tech. accreditation for civil engring. prog. for San Diego, London campuses, mem. curriculum coun. for all univ. progs., advisor U.S. Internat. U. Engring. Club; elected mem. Calif. Engring. Liaison Com., pres. pvt. univ. segment. Named outstanting engring. educator Am. Soc. Engring. Edn., 1989; rsch. grantee Fulbright-Hayes, 1972-73, grantee Am. Soc. Engring. Edn., NASA, 1979, Am. Soc. Engring. Edn., Dept. Energy, 1981, 82, 1984-85, Fed. Emergency Mgmt. Agy., 1983, 86. Office: DeVry Inst Tech Univ Ctr 901 Corp Ctr Dr Pomona CA 91768-2642 Fax: 909-623-5666.

DISNEY, ROY EDWARD, broadcasting company executive; b. LA, Jan. 10, 1930; s. Roy Oliver and Edna (Francis) D.; m. Patricia Ann Dailey, Sept. 17, 1955; children: Roy Patrick, Susan Margaret, Abigail Edna, Timothy John. BA, Pomona Coll., 1951. Apprentice film editor Mark VII Prodns., Hollywood, 1942; guest relations exec. NBC, Hollywood, Calif., 1952; asst. film editor, cameraman prodn. asst., writer, producer Walt Disney Prodns., Burbank, Calif., 1954-77, dir., 1967—77; pres. Roy E. Disney Prodns. Inc., Burbank, 1978—; chmn. bd. dir. Shamrock Broadcasting Co., Hollywood, 1979—; chmn. bd. dir., founder Shamrock Holdings Inc., Burbank, 1980—; chmn. Walt Disney Animation, 1984—2003; vice chmn. Walt Disney Co., Burbank, 1984—2003, dir. emeritus, cons., 2005—. Trustee Calif. Inst. of the Arts, Valencia, 1967—. Author: novelized adaptation of Perri; producer (film) Pacific High, Mysteries of the Deep exec. producer Cheetah, 1989, The Little Mermaid, 1989, Beauty and the Beast, 1991, The Lion King, 1994, Pocahontas, 1995, Fantasia 2000;(TV show) Walt Disney's Wonderful World of Color, others; writer, dir., producer numerous TV prodns. Bd. dirs. Big Bros. of Greater Los Angeles, U.S. com. UNICEF, Ronald McDonald House charities, chmn. emeritus, Peregrine Fund; mem. adv. bd. dirs. St. Joseph Med. Ctr., Burbank; mem. U.S. Naval Acad. Sailing Squadron, Annapolis, Md.; fellow U. Ky. Recipient Acad. award nomination for Mysteries of the Deep, Mort Walker award for Outstanding Contbn. to the Cartoon Industry, Boca Raton Internat. Mus. of Cartoon Art, 1997, Internat. Creative Achievement award, Cinema Expo, 1997, Elizabeth Ann Seton award, Nat. Catholic Edn. Assn. 1999, Henry Bergh Humane award, ASPCA, 1999, Inaugural Environ. Leadership award, Audubon Soc. 2000, Lifetime Achievement in Animation, Santa Clarita Internat. Film Festival, 2002; named one of Forbes' Richest Americans, 2006. Mem. Dirs. Guild Am. West, Writers Guild Am. Clubs: 100, Confrerie des Chevaliers du Tastevin, St. Francis Yacht, Calif. Yacht, San Diego Yacht, Transpacific Yacht, Los Angeles Yacht. Republican.

DISTECHE, CHRISTINE M., geneticist; b. Liege, Belgium, July 22, 1949; PhD, U. Liege, Belgium, 1976. Genetics fellow Harvard U., Boston, 1977-80; now med. geneticist U. Wash. Hosp., Seattle. Prof. pathology U. Wash., Seattle. Office: U Wash Hosp Dept Pathology PO Box 357470 Seattle WA 98195-7470

DIVELY, DWIGHT DOUGLAS, finance director; b. Spokane, Wash., Sept. 24, 1958; s. Richard Lorraine and Marie Eleanor (Barnes) D.; m. Susan Lorraine Sederstrom, June 13, 1987; children: Nathan Douglas, Natalie Lorraine. BSChemE, Rose-Hulman Inst. Tech., 1980; MPA of Pub. Affairs, Princeton U., 1982; PhC in Civil Engring., U. Wash., 1986. Rsch. scientist Battelle, Seattle, 1982-84; policy analyst, staff dir. Wash. High Tech. Coord. Bd., Seattle, 1984-86; cons. Bellevue, Wash., 1986-87; legis. analyst Seattle City Coun., 1987-90, supervising analyst, 1990-92, staff dir., 1992-94; dir. Seattle Fin. Dept., 1994-96, Seattle Exec. Svcs. Dept., 1997—; CFO city of Seattle, 1999—. Cons. We. Interstate Commn. on Higher Edn., Boulder, Colo., 1986-91; affiliate prof. U. Wash., 1989—; instr. South Seattle C.C., 1992—; mem. faculty Cascade Ctr., Seattle, 1992—. Co-author: Benefit-Cost Analysis in Theory and Practice, 1994. Chmn. interview panel Truman Scholarship Found., Washington, 1989—. Recipient Elmer B. Staats award Truman Scholarship Found., 1994. Mem. Govt. Fin. Officers Assn. Lutheran. Avocations: cooking, gardening. Office: Exec Svcs Dept 600 4th Ave Ste 103 Seattle WA 98104-1874

DIVER, COLIN S., academic administrator, educator; b. 1943; BA, Amherst Coll., 1965; LLB, Harvard U., 1968; MA, U. Pa., 1989; LLD, Amherst Coll., 1990. Bar: Mass. 1968. Spl. counsel Office of the Mayor, Boston, 1968-71; asst. sec. consumer affairs Exec. Office Consumer Affairs, Boston, 1971-72; undersec. adminstrn. Exec. Office Adminstrn. and Fin., Boston, 1972-74; assoc. prof. Boston U., 1975-81, prof., 1981-89, from assoc. dean to dean, 1985-89; dean, Bernard G. Segal prof. U. Pa., Phila., 1989—99, Charles A. Heinbold, Jr., prof., 1999—2002; pres. Reed Coll., Portland, Oreg., 2002—. Cons. Adminstrv. Conf. of U.S., 1980-88. Chmn. Mass. State Ethics Com., 1983-89; mem. adv. com. on enforcement policy NRC, 1984-85. Office: Reed Coll 3203 SE Woodstock Blvd Portland OR 97202 Office Phone: 503-777-7500. Office Fax: 503-777-7701. E-mail: presidentsoffice@reed.edu.

DIXIT, VISHVA M., pathology educator; MD, U. Nairobi, Kenya, 1980; postgrad., Washington U., St. Louis, 1982-86. Intern dept. medicine Kenyatta Nat. Hosp., 1980-81; resident pathology and medicine Barnes Hosp., St. Louis, 1981-86; asst. prof. pathology Med. Sch. U. Mich., Ann Arbor, 1986-91, assoc. prof., 1991—, prof. pathology, 1995-97; dir. molecular oncology Genentech, San Francisco, 1997—. Contbr. articles to profl. jours. Recipient Best Pathology Student award Kenya Med. Assn., 1980, Best Overall Med. Student Kamala Meml. award, 1980, Warner-Lambert/Parke-Davis Exptl. Pathology award Am. Soc. Investigative Pathology, 1996; Josiah Macy Found. fellow, 1989. Office: Genentech 1 Dna Way South San Francisco CA 94080-4990

DIXON, GORDON HENRY, biochemist, educator; b. Durban, South Africa, Mar. 25, 1930; naturalized, Can., 1951; s. Walter James and Ruth (Nightingale) Dixon; m. Sylvia W. Gillen, Nov. 20, 1954; children: Frances Anne, Walter Timothy, Christopher James, Robin Jonathan. MA with honors, U. Cambridge, Eng., 1951; PhD, U. Toronto, 1956. Rsch. assoc. U. Wash., 1954-58, U. Oxford, England, 1958-59; asst. prof. biochemistry U. Toronto, 1959-61, assoc. prof., 1961-63; prof. U. B.C., 1963-72; prof., chmn. dept. biochemistry U. Sussex, England, 1972-74; prof. med. biochemistry U. Calgary, Alta., Canada, 1974-94; emeritus, 1994—; chmn. U. Calgary, Alta., Canada, 1983-88. Contbr. over 250 articles to prof. jours. Flying officer Royal Can. AFR 5001 Air Intelligence, 1952—54. Decorated officer Order of Can.; recipient Steacie prize, Steacie Found., 1966, Killam Meml. prize, Can. Coun., 1991, Queens Golden Jubilee medal, 2002. Fellow: Royal Soc. Can. (Flavelle medal 1980), Royal Soc. London; mem.: Internat. Union Biochemistry (mem. exec. coun. 1988—94), Pan-Am. Assn. Biochem. Socs. (v.p. 1984—87, pres. 1987—90), Can. Biochem. Soc. (pres. 1982—83, Ayerst award 1966). Avocations: hiking, gardening. Personal E-mail: gordon.dixon@shaw.ca.

DIXON, JACK EDWARD, biological chemistry professor, consultant; b. June 16, 1943; BA, UCLA, 1966; PhD, U. Calif., Santa Barbara, 1971. NSF Found. postdoctoral rsch. fellow U. Calif., San Diego, 1971—73; from asst. prof. to assoc. prof. biochemistry Purdue U., West Lafayette, Ind., 1973—82, prof. biochemistry, 1982—86, Harvey W. Wiley disting. prof. biochemistry, 1986—91; Minor J. Coon prof. biol. chemistry, chmn. dept. U. Mich., Ann Arbor, 1991—2003, co-dir. Life Scis. Inst., 2001—02, dir. Life Scis. Inst., 2002—03; prof. pharmacology, cellular medicine, chemistry and biochemistry U. Calif., San Diego, 2003—, dean sci. affairs Sch. Medicine, 2003—. Nathan O. Kaplan lectr. U. Calif., San Diego, 1991; Edmund Fischer lectr. U. Wash., Seattle, 1993; adj. prof. Salk Inst., 2003—; Baker lectr. U. Calif., Santa Barbara, 2003; Merck Award lectr. ASBMB, 2005; Dyer lectr. NIH, 2005. Recipient Merit award, NIH, 1987, 1996, 2004, William Rose award, ASBMB, 2003, Biochemistry and Molecular Biology award, Merck, 2003. Fellow: AAAS, Am. Acad. Arts and Sci., Mich. Soc. Fellows U. Mich. (sr.); mem.: Inst. Medicine, Nat. Acad. Sci., Am. Soc. Cell Biology, Am. Soc. Biochemistry and Molecular Biology (program chmn. 1994—, pres. 1996—97), Sigma Xi. Office: U Calif San Diego 9500 Gilman Dr 0602 La Jolla CA 92093-0602 Office Phone: 858-822-3529.

DIXON, PATRICK RICHARD, prosecutor; m. Diane Dixon; 1 child, Colleen. Grad., U. So. Calif., LA, 1971; law degree, U. San Diego. Bar: Calif. 1976. Dep. dist. atty., asst. head major crimes divsn. LA County Dist. Atty.'s Office, dep. dist. atty., head major crimes divsn. Spl. counsel to com. bar examiners State Bar Calif., 1986—89, 1999, mem. Commn. on Jud. Nominees Evaluation, 1990—92, mem. com. bar examiners, 1993—97, chair com. bar examiners, 1997, bd. govs. for LA County, Dist. 7, 2000—03. Named Prosecutor of Yr., Assn. Dep. Dist. Attys., 1994. Mem.: LA County Bar Assn. (vice chair jud. elections evaluation com. 1984—89, trustee 1993—95, chair criminal justice sect. 1994, mem. jud. appointments com. 1998—99, Prosecuting Atty. of Yr. (criminal justice sect.) 1998). Office: LA County Dist Attys Office 210 W Temple St Ste 18000 Los Angeles CA 90012 Office Phone: 213-974-3926.

DJERASSI, CARL, writer, retired chemistry professor; b. Vienna, Oct. 29, 1923; s. Samuel and Alice (Friedmann) Djerassi; m. Virginia Jeremiah (div. 1950); m. Norma Lundholm (div. 1976); children: Dale, Pamela(dec.); m. Diane W. Middlebrook, 1985 (dec. 2007). AB summa cum laude, Kenyon Coll., 1942, DSc (hon.), 1959; PhD, U. Wis., 1945, DSc (hon.), 1995, Nat. U. Mex., 1953, Fed. U., Rio de Janeiro, 1969, Worcester Poly. Inst., 1972, Wayne State U., 1974, Columbia U., 1975, Uppsala U., 1977, Coe Coll., 1978, U. Geneva, 1978, U. Ghent, 1985, U. Man., 1985, Adelphi U., 1993, U. S.C., 1995, Swiss Fed. Inst. Tech., 1995, U. Md.- Balt. County, 1997, Bulgarian Acad. Scis., 1998, U. Aberdeen, 2000, Polytechnic U., 2001, Cambridge U., 2005. Rsch. chemist Ciba Pharm. Products, Inc., Summit, NJ, 1942—43, 1945—49; assoc. dir. rsch. Syntex, Mexico City, 1949—52, rsch. v.p., 1957—60; v.p. Syntex Labs., Palo Alto, Calif., 1960—62, Syntex Rsch., 1962—68, pres., 1968—72, Zoecon Corp., 1968—83, chmn. bd. dirs., 1968—86; prof. chemistry Wayne State U., 1952—59, Stanford (Calif.) U., 1959—2002; ret., 2002. Founder Djerassi Resident Artists Program, Woodside, Calif. Author: The Futurist and Other Stories, 1988; author: (novels) Cantor's Dilemma, 1989, The Bourbaki Gambit, 1994, Marx Deceased, 1996, Menachem's Seed, 1997, NO, 1998; author: (poetry) The Clock Runs Backward, 1991; author: (plays) An Immaculate Misconception, 1998, BBC World Svc. Play of Week, 2000, ICSI--a pedagogic wordplay for 2 voices, 2002, Calculus, 2003, (musical version) Music Werner Schulze, 2005, Ego, 2003, Three on a Couch, 2004, Taboos, 2006, Phallacy, 2007, Four Jews on Parnassus, 2008; author: (with Roald Hoffmann) Oxygen, 2001, BBC World Svc.Play of Week, 2001; author: (with Pierre Laszlo) NO--a pedagogic wordplay for 3 voices, 2003; author: (autobiography) The Pill, Pygmy Chimps and Degas' Horse, 1992; author: (memoir) This Man's Pill, 2001; author: (with D. Pinner) Newton's Darkness: Two Dramatic Views, 2004; author: 9 other books; mem. editl. bd. Jour. Organic Chemistry, 1955—59, Tetrahedron, 1958—92, Steroids, 1963—2001, Procs. NAS, 1964—70, Jour. Am. Chem. Soc., 1966—75, Organic Mass Spectrometry, 1968—91, contbr. numerous articles to profl. jours., poems, memoirs and short stories to lit. publs. Decorated Austrian Cross of Honor 1st class, sci. & art, Great Cross of Merit Germany, Silver Cross of Honor Australia; recipient Intrasci. Rsch. Found. award, 1969, Freedman Patent award, Am. Inst. Chemists, 1970, Chem. Pioneer award, 1973, Nat. medal of Sci. for first synthesis of oral contraceptive, 1973, Wolf prize in chemistry, Israel, 1978, John and Samuel Bard award in Sci. and Medicine, 1983, Roussel prize, Paris, 1988, Discovers award, Pharm. Mfg. Assn., 1988, Nat. medal Tech. for new approaches to insect control, 1991, Nev. medal, 1992, Thomson medal, Internat. Soc. Mass Spectroscopy, 1994, Prince Mahidol award, Thailand, 1995, Sovereign Fund award, 1996, Othmer Gold medal, Chem. Heritage Found., 2000, Author's prize, German Chem. Soc., 2001, Erasmus medal, Acad. Europeae, 2003, Gold medal, Am. Inst. Chemists, 2004, Serono prize fiction, Rome, 2005, Lichtenberg medal, Göttingen Acad., 2005; named to Nat. Inventors Hall of Fame. Mem.: NAS (Indsl. Application of Sci. award 1990), Acad. Europeae, Bulgarian Acad. Scis. (fgn. mem.), Mex. Acad. Scis., Brazilian Acad. Scis., Royal Swedish Acad. Engring. (fgn. mem.), Royal Swedish Acad. Scis. (fgn. mem.), German Acad. Leopoldina, Am. Acad. Arts and Scis., Royal Soc. Chemistry (hon. fellow, Centenary lectr. 1964), Am. Chem. Soc. (award pure chemistry 1958, Baekeland medal 1959, Fritzsche award 1960, award for creative invention 1973, award in chemistry of contemporary tech. problems 1983, Esselen award 1989, Priestley medal 1992, Gibbs medal 1997), NAS Inst. Medicine, Am. Acad. Pharm. Scis. (hon.), Sigma Xi (Proctor prize for sci. achievement 1998), Phi Beta Kappa, Phi Lambda Upsilon (hon.). Office: Stanford U Dept Chemistry Stanford CA 94305-5080 Business E-Mail: djerassi@stanford.edu.

DJORDJEVICH, MIROSLAV-MICHAEL, bank executive; b. Belgrade, Yugoslavia, 1936; arrived in U.S., 1956; s. Dragoslav and Ruzica Georgevich; m. Marie Louise Hohman, 1963; children: Marie, Alexander, Michelle. BS, U. Calif., Berkeley, 1960; MBA, San Francisco State U., 1963; cert. advanced fin., U. Stanford. Fin. analyst Fireman's Fund Ins. Co., San Francisco, 1962-68, asst. v.p. investments, 1972-76, v.p. investments, 1976-78, v.p., treas., 1978-84; pres., CEO U.S. Fidelity and Guaranty Fin. Co., San Francisco, 1985-86; chmn., pres., CEO Capital Guaranty Ins. Co., San Francisco, 1986-94; pres., CEO Monad Fin., San Rafael, Calif., 1994-97, Bank S.E. Europe Internat., San Juan, 1997—2004; chmn. Devel. Bank of South-East Europe, Bosnia-Herzegovina, 2002—05; pres. Monad Fin. Co., San Rafael, Calif., 2005—, CEO, 2005—. Pres. Studenica Found., 1993—. Author: About Happy Living, 1985, Moral Society and Modern State, 2003, (poems) Pathways of a Yearning Sowl, 2007. State pres. Calif. Young Reps., 1965-66; commr. Statue of Liberty Ellis Island Centennial Commn., 1986; pres. Serbian Unity Congress, 1990-93, Coun. for Dem. Changes, 1998-01, Studenica Found., 1995-; dir. World Affairs Coun. of Am., 2002-04. With U.S. Army, 1961-63. Recipient Excellence award Am. Security Coun., 1967, Americanism medal Nat. Soc. DAR, 1969, medal of Yuboslav Flag II degree, 2003, medal of Nemanja, II degree, 2005. Mem.: First Serbian Benevolent Soc. (treas. 1978—82). Avocations: reading, tennis, politics. Office: Monad Fin 535 4th St Ste 203 San Rafael CA 94901-3314 Business E-Mail: info@monadfinancial.com.

DMYTRYSHYN, BASIL, historian, educator; b. Poland, Jan. 14, 1925; arrived in U.S., 1947, naturalized, 1951; s. Frank and Euphrosinia (Senchak) Dmytryshyn; m. Virginia Roehl, July 16, 1949; children: Sonia, Tania. BA, U. Ark., 1950; MA, U. Ark, 1951; PhD, U. Calif., Berkeley, 1955; diploma (hon.), U. Kiev-Mohyla Acad., 1993. Asst. prof. history Portland (Oreg.) State U., 1956-59, assoc. prof., 1959-64, prof., 1964-89, prof. emeritus, 1989—, assoc. dir. Internat. Trade and Commerce Inst., 1984-89. Vis. prof. U. Ill., 1964-65, Harvard U., 1971, U. Hawaii, 1976, Hokkaido U., Sapporo, Japan, 1978-79; adviser U. Kiev-Mohyla Acad., 1993. Author books including: Moscow and the Ukraine, 1918-1953, 1956, Medieval Russia, 900-1700, 4th edit., 2000, Imperial Russia, 1700-1917, 4th edit., 1999, Modernization of Russia Under Peter I and Catherine II, 1974,

Colonial Russian America 1817-1832, 1976, A History of Russia, 1977, U.S.S.R.: A Concise History, 4th edit., 1984, The End of Russian America, 1979, Civil and Savage Encounters, 1983, Russian Statecraft, 1985, Russian Conquest of Siberia 1558-1700, 1985, Russian Penetration of the North Pacific Archipelago, 1700-1799, 1987, The Soviet Union and the Middle East, 1917-1985, 1987, Russia's Colonies in North America, 1799-1867, 1988, The Soviet Union and the Arab World of the Fertile Crescent, 1918-1985, 1994, Imperial Russia, 1700-1917, 1999, Medieval Russia, 850-1700, 2000; contbr. articles to profl. jours. U.S., Can., Yugoslavia, Italy, South Korea, Fed. Republic Germany, France, Eng., Japan, Russia, Ukraine. State bd. dirs. PTA, Oreg., 1963-64; mem. World Affairs Coun., 1965-92. Named Hon. Rsch. Prof. Emeritus, Kyungnam U., 1989—; Fulbright-Hays fellow W. Germany, 1967-68; fellow Kennan Inst. Advanced Russian Studies, Washington, 1978; recipient John Mosser award Oreg. State Bd. Higher Edn., 1966, 67; Branford P. Millar award for faculty excellence Portland State U., 1985, Outstanding Retired Faculty award, 1994; Hillard scholar in the humanities U. Nev., Reno, 1992. Mem. Am. Assn. Advancement Slavic Studies (dir. 1972-75), Am. Hist. Assn., Western Slavic Assn. (pres. 1990-92), Can. Assn. Slavists, Oreg. Hist. Soc. (hon. mem. coun.), Nat. Geog. Soc., Conf. Slavic and East European History (nat. sec. 1972-75), Am. Assn. for Ukrainian Studies (pres. 1991-93), Ctr. Study of Russian Am. (hon.), Internat. Cultural Soc. Korea (hon.), Assn. Study Nationalities (bd. mem.-at-large USSR and Ea. Europe 1993—), Czechoslovak Soc. Arts and Scis., Soc. Jewish-Ukraine Contacts Assn., Salem City Club. Home: Apt 3011 5210 River Rd N Keizer OR 97303

DOAN, MARY FRANCES, advertising executive; b. Vallejo, Calif., Apr. 16, 1954; d. Larry E. and Dudley (Harbison) D.; m. Timothy Warren Hesselgren, Mar. 19, 1988; children: Edward Latimer, Clinton Robert. BA in Linguistics, U. Calif., Berkeley, 1976; M in Internat. Mgmt., Am. Grad. Sch. Internat. Mgmt., 1980. Trading asst. The Capital Group, LA, 1980-81; fin. analyst Litton Industries, Beverly Hills, 1981-82; account exec. Grey Advt., San Francisco, L.A., 1982-84, J. Walter Thompson, San Francisco, 1984-85, Lowe Marshalk, 1985-86; account supr. Young & Rubicam, 1986-89; acct. mgr. Saatchi & Saatchi, 1989—95, CEO, pres., 1995—96, worldwide dir. client svc. applications, 1997—98; cons., 1999; v.p. mktg. Roundl, San Francisco, 1999-2000; cons., 2001—02; v.p. mktg. and advt. Good Guys, 2002—04, cons., 2005—. Office Phone: 415-504-6977. Personal E-mail: mfdoan@hotmail.com.

DOAN, SHANE, professional hockey player; b. Halkirk, Alta., Can., Oct. 10, 1976; s. Bernie; m. Andrea Doan; children: Gracie, Joshua. Right wing Winnipeg Jets (now Phoenix Coyotes), 1995—96, Phoenix Coyotes, 1996—, capt., 2003—. Player Team Can., World Championships, 2003, Team Can., World Cup of Hockey, 2002. Charity work United Blood Svcs. Named to NHL All-Star Game, 2004, 2009. Achievements include winning gold medal with team Canada, World Championships, 2003; being a member of World Cup Champion Team Can., 2004. Avocations: golf, horseback riding. Office: Phoenix Coyotes Hockey Club 6751 N Sunset Blvd, #200 Glendale AZ 85305*

DOANE, W. ALLEN, water transportation executive; b. Jan. 17, 1948; BA, Brigham Young Univ., 1969; MBA, Harvard Univ., 1975. Mgmt. positions C. Brewer Co., 1975—85; group v.p. IU Internat. Corp., 1985—88; COO The Shidler Group, 1988—90; exec. v.p., COO A&B Hawaii Inc., Honolulu, 1991—95, pres., 1995—99, CEO, 1997—99; exec. v.p. Alexander & Baldwin Inc., Honolulu, 1998, pres., CEO, 1998—2006, chmn., pres., CEO, 2006—08, chmn., CEO, 2008—; chmn. Matson Navigation Co. Inc. Bd. dir. First Hawaiian Bank, BancWest Corp., Pacific Guardian Life Ins. Co. Officer USN. Office: Alexander & Baldwin Inc 822 Bishop St Honolulu HI 96813

DOBAY, SUSAN VILMA, artist; b. Budapest, Hungary, May 12, 1937; arrived in U.S., 1957; d. Otto and Lenke Stiasny Heltai; m. Endre Imre Dobay, Oct. 16, 1954; children: Vivian, Andrew. Diploma, Famous Artists Sch., Westport, Conn., 1963. One-woman shows include featured artist Vasarely Mus., Budapest, Hungary, 1993, Joslyn Arts Ctr., Torrance, Calif., 1994, Deri Mus., Hungary, 1999, BGH the Loft Gallery, Santa Monica, Calif., 2001, Lurdy House Gallery, Budapest, 2001, Hungarian Consulate, N.Y.C., 2001, one-woman shows include Mystic Sisters Gallery 2, Monrovia, Calif., 2002, 2003, Wall Art Gallery, Fernandina Beach, Fla., 2006, 2B Gallery, Budapest, 2006, Muzeul Judetean, Satu Mare, Transylvania, 2006, Mus. Szatmari, Mateszalka, Hungary, 2006, exhibited in group shows at Calif. Mus. Sci. and Industry, L.A., 1967, 1975, UN Woman Conf., Nairobi, Kenya, 1985, Jillian Coldirow Fine Art, South Pasadena, Calif., 1993—, Hungarian Consulate, N.Y.C., 1996—, Kortars Galleria, Budapest, 1996—, Mus. Downtown L.A., 1998—, Hungarian House, San Diego, 2003, exhibitions include 2B Gallery, Budapest, 2004, Lemplein Galleria, Hungary, 2004, Wall Art Gallery, 2006, Muzeul Jedetean Satu Mare, Sectia de Arta, Transylvania, 2006, Szatmari Mus., Mátészalka, Hungary, 2006, 2 B Gallery, Budapest, 2006, illustrator, Lloyd's Advt., L.A., 1963—64, fashion illustrator, Pasadena Star News, 1985, one-woman shows include Tibor Erno Galleria, Naqyucivad, Transylvania, 2007. Mem. World Fedn. Hungarian Artists, N.Y. Artists Equity, L.A. Artists Equity. Avocations: reading, travel, theater, movies, classical music. Home: 125 W Scenic Dr Monrovia CA 91016-1610 Personal E-mail: sedobay@altrionet.com.

DOBBS, DAN BYRON, lawyer, educator; b. Ft. Smith, Ark., Nov. 8, 1932; s. George Byron and Gladys Pauline (Stone) D.; m. Betty Jo Teeter, May 31, 1953 (div. 1978); children: Katherine, George, Rebecca, Jean. BA, LL.B., U. Ark., 1956; LL.M., U. Ill., 1961, J.S.D., 1966. Bar: Ark. 1956. Partner firm Dobbs, Pryor & Dobbs, Ft. Smith, 1956-60; asst. prof. law U. N.C., Chapel Hill, 1961-63, assoc. prof., 1963-66, prof., 1967, Aubrey L. Brooks prof. law, 1975-77; Rosenstiel prof. law U. Ariz., 1978—2008, Regents prof., 1992—2008, Regents and Rosential prof. emeritus, 2008—. Vis. asst. prof. U. Tex., summer 1961; vis. prof. U. Minn., 1966-67, Cornell Law Sch., 1968-69, U. Va. Law Sch., 1974, U. Ariz. Law Sch., 1977-78 Author: Handbook on the Law of Remedies, Damages, Equity, Restitution, 1973, Problems in Remedies, 1974, The Law of Remedies, 3 vols., 2d edit., 1993, The Law of Torts, 2000; co-author: Prosser and Keeton on Torts, 5th edit., 1984, Torts and Compensation, 1985, 6th edit., 2009, (with Paul Hayden & Ellen Bublick), 1997, (with Ellen Bublick) Economic and Dignitary Torts, 2006; contbr. articles to legal jours. Office: U Ariz Law Coll Tucson AZ 85721-0001 Office Phone: 520-621-7671. Business E-Mail: dobbs@law.arizona.edu.

DOBBS, GREGORY ALLAN, journalist; b. San Francisco, Oct. 9, 1946; s. Harold Stanley and Annette Rae (Lehrer) D.; m. Carol Lynn Walker, Nov. 25, 1973; children: Jason Walker, Alexander Adair. BA, U. Calif., Berkeley, 1968; MSJ, Northwestern U., 1969. Assignment editor, reporter Sta. KGO-TV, San Francisco, 1966-68; news dir. San Francisco Tourist Info. Program Service, 1968; editor ABC Radio, Chgo., 1969-71; prodr. ABC News, Chgo., 1971-73, corr., 1973-77, London, 1977-82, Paris, 1982-86, Denver, 1986-92; host The Greg Dobbs Show/Sta. KOA Radio, 1992—98; corr. Nat. Geographic TV, 2001—03; host The Greg Dobbs Morning Show KNRC Radio, Denver, 2002—04; host Colo. State of Mind Rocky Mt. PBS, 2003—09; sr. corr. HDNet TV, 2004—. Adj. prof. Northwestern U. Sch. Journalism, 1975, 76; prof. U. Colo. Sch. Journalism, 1996-2003; corr. Nat. Geog. TV. Columnist The Denver Post, 1996—2001, Rocky Mountain News, 2001—05, nationally syndicated columnist Scripps Howard, 2001—05, Sr. Correspondent HDNet " World Report", 2004—. Recipient Sigma Delta Chi Disting. Svc. award for TV reporting Soc. Profl. Journalists, 1980, Emmy award for the best news reporting on a network 1980, outstanding documentary, 1989, award of excellence Colo. Broadcasters Assn., 1993, 94, award for best talk show Colo. Soc. Profl. Journalists, 1994, Emmy Best Interview/Discussion program, 2003; Lippmann fellow Ford Found., 1975; named Best Talk Show Host in Denver, Westword Mag., 2002 Office: 1153 Bergen Pkwy Ste M150 Evergreen CO 80439-9501 Office Phone: 303-619-1977. E-mail: dobbs@newslike.com.

DOBEY, JAMES KENNETH, banker; b. Vallejo, Calif., June 20, 1919; s. Austin E. and Margaret (Hansen) D.; m. Jean Smith, Apr. 18, 1942 (dec. Feb. 2007); children: James A., Peter M. AB, U. Calif., Berkeley, 1940; postgrad., Rutgers U., 1956. With Shell Oil Co., Comml. Credit Corp., 1940-42, Wells Fargo and Co., San Francisco, 1946—72, exec. v.p., 1965—72, vice chmn. bd., 1973, chmn. bd., 1977—80, ret. Capt. airborne inf. AUS, 1942-46. Mem. Delta Chi. Mailing: Carmel Valley Manor 8545 Carmel Valley Rd Carmel CA 93923-9556

DOBLER, DONALD WILLIAM, retired procurement and materials executive, dean; b. Rocky Ford, Colo., Apr. 18, 1927; s. William L. and Anna (Nelson) Dobler; m. Elaine Carlson, Dec. 27, 1951; children: Kathleen, David, Daniel. BS in Engring., Colo State U., 1946-50; MBA, Stanford U., 1958, PhD, 1960. Application and sales engr. Westinghouse Elec. Corp., Pitts. and Phila., 1950-53; mgr. procurement and materials FMC Corp., Green River, Wyo., 1953-57; guest lectr. Stanford Sch. Bus., 1960; asst. prof. mgmt. State U. Utah, Logan, 1960-63, assoc. prof., 1964-66, head dept. bus. adminstrn., 1964-66; vis. prof. mgmt. Dartmouth Coll., 1963-64; dean Coll. Bus., Colo. State U., Ft. Collins, 1966-86; ind. mgmt. cons. Ft. Collins, 1986-91; corp. v.p. for cert. and program devel. Inst. Supply Mgmt., Tempe, Ariz., 1990-94; full time mgmt. cons. Ft. Collins, 1995—2000. Pres. Parklane Arms, Inc., 1967—77; part-time mgmt. cons., 1960—86; cons. European Logistics Mgmt. Program, 1970, 72, 77, European Fedn. Purchasing, 1970; faculty Mgmt. Ctr. Netherlands, 1972; mem. dean's adv. coun. logistics mgmt. program Ariz. State U., 1991—94; mem. adv. bd. Mgmt. Inst. U. Wis., 1992—97; past bd. dirs. U. Nat. Bank, Home Fed. Savs. Bank. Sr. author: Purchasing and Supply Management, 1965, 6th edit., 1996; co-author: The Purchasing Handbook, 1993; mem. editl. bd. European Jour. Purchasing and Supply Mgmt., 1993—; contbr. articles to profl. jours., chapters to books. Mem. Colo. Gov.'s Adv. Com., 1968—77, Ft. Collins Mayor's Budget Com., 1968—71; dist. chmn. Boy Scouts Am., 1974—77; mem. adv. coun. Colo. region SBA, 1973—79, mem. adv. coun. no. region Colo. divsn. employment, 1975—77; bd. dirs., divsn. chmn. Ft. Collins United Way, 1973—80, pres., 1977; bd. dirs. Ft. Collins Jr. Achievement, 1973—87, Colo. Assn. Commerce and Industry Ednl. Found., 1988—91. With USNR, 1945—46. Mem.: Am. Assn. Collegiate Schs. Bus. (nat. com. continuing accreditation 1972—78, nat. stds. commn. 1978—81, dir. 1980—83, chmn. fin. and audit com. 1983), Acad. Mgmt., Am. Prodn. and Inventory Control Soc., Denver Purchasing Mgmt. Assn. (dir. 1975—83, v.p. 1977, pres. 1979), Nat. Assn. Purchasing Mgmt. (assoc. editor Internat. Jour. Purchasing and Materials Mgmt. 1975—80, chmn. nat. acad. plan com. 1976—81, profl. cert. bd. 1981—86, chmn. 1985—86, editor 1980—97, Shipman medalist 1987), Green River Jr. C. of C. (pres. 1955), Rotary, Beta Gamma Sigma (nat. gov. 1975—78), Phi Kappa Phi (editl. cons. Nat. Forum 1988—94), Sigma Tau. Methodist.

DOBROTKA, DAVID ALLEN, protective services official; m.; 2 children. BS, MPA. With Minn. Police Dept., Mpls., 1976-94; chief Glendale (Ariz.) Police Dept., 1994—. Office: Glendale Police Dept 6835 N 57th Dr Glendale AZ 85301-3218

DOBROWOLSKI, JAMES PHILLIP, agriculturist, educator; b. LA, June 2, 1955; s. Joseph Adolph and Lois Ann (Hibbs) D.; m. Janet Ann Brown, Mar. 10, 1984; children: Jessica, Jonathan. BS, U. Calif., Davis, 1977; MS, Wash. State U., 1979; PhD, Tex. A&M U., 1985. Systems analyst The Norac Co., Inc., Azusa, Calif., 1980-81; W.G. Mills fellow in hydrology Tex. Water Resources Inst., College Station, 1981-83; Tom Slick fellow in Agr. Tex. A&M U., College Station, 1983-84; research asst. prof. Utah State U., Logan, 1984-85, asst. prof., 1985-91, assoc. prof., 1992—. Cons. Dern & Polk Cons., Belton, Tex., 1981; co-dir. Inst. Land Rehab., Logan, 1985—. Contbr. articles to profl. jours. Recipient Advisor of Yr. award Utah State U., 1989, Prof. of Yr. award, 1991. Mem. Soc. Range Mgmt., Am. Water Resources Assn., Am. Soc. Agrl. Engrs. (affiliate), Soc. Ecol. Restoration, Sigma Xi, Phi Kappa Phi. Avocations: cross country skiing, fishing, camping. Office: Utah State U Dept Range Sci Logan UT 84322-0001

DOBSON, DOROTHY LYNN WATTS, retired elementary school educator; b. Santa Monica, Calif., Nov. 29, 1954; d. Seymour Locke and Margaret (Cheeseman) Watts; m. J. Cody Dobson, June 5, 1982; children: Jeremiah, Hannah. BS, Utah State U., 1975; MEd, U. Utah, 1982. Cert. tchr. intellectually handicapped and behaviorally handicapped, elem., Utah. Tchr. San Juan Sch. Dist., Blanding, Utah, 1974-76; behavioral specialist Salt Lake Sch. Dist., Salt Lake City, 1976-77; tchr. Granite Sch. Dist., Salt Lake City, 1977-82; instr. Utah State U., Logan, 1987—2003; tchr. Edith Bowen Lab. Sch., Logan, 1982—2004. Team coord. First Amendment Schs., Bowen Lab. Sch., Logan, 2002—. Author: Utilizing Newspapers in Social Studies, Math. and Science and Language Arts, 1983; also articles. Mem. Nat. Coun. for Social Studies (bd. dirs. 1996-99, Nat. Elem. Tchr. of Yr. 1992, State Farm Good Neighbor award 1993), Utah Coun. for Social Studies (State Elem. Tchr. of Yr. 1991), Nat. Assn. Lab. Schs. Episcopalian. E-mail: dordob@direcway.com.

DOBSON, JAMES CLAYTON, evangelist, psychologist, author; b. Shreveport, La., Apr. 21, 1936; s. James Clayton Sr. and Myrtle Georgia (Dillingham) Dobson; m. Shirley Mae Deere, Aug. 27, 1960; children: Danae A., J. Ryan. BA in Psychology, Pasadena City Coll., Calif., 1958; MS, U. So. Calif., 1962, PhD in Child Devel., 1967; LLD, Pepperdine U., 1983; DHum (hon.), Franciscan U., 1988; DHL, Seattle Pacific U., 1988, Liberty U., 1993, Biola U., 1995; others. Psychometrist, tchr. Hudson Sch. Dist., Hacienda Heights, Calif., 1962-63; psychometrist, counselor Charter Oak HS, Covina, Calif., 1963-64; sch. psychologist, coord. pers. svcs. Charter Oak Unified Dist., Covina, 1964-66; asst. prof. pediatrics U. So. Calif. Sch. Medicine, LA, 1969-77, assoc. clin. prof., 1978-83; attending staff div. med. genetics Childrens Hosp. LA, 1969-83; pres., chmn Focus on the Family, Colorado Springs, Colo., 1977—2004, chmn., 2004—09. Bd. dirs. Focus on the Family, Vancouver, BC, Canada, 1982—2009, Family Rsch. Coun., 1992—. Author: Dare to Discipline, 1977, What Wives Wish Their Husbands Knew About Women, 1981, Preparing for Adolescence, 1980, Dr. Dobson Answers Your Questions About Raising Children, 1982, Emotions: Can You Trust Them?, 1984, Dr. Dobson Answers Your Questions about Feelings and Self-Esteem, 1986, Temper Your Child's Tantrums, 1986, Parenting Isn't for Cowards: Dealing Confidently With the Frustrations of Child-Rearing, 1987, The Strong-Willed Child, 1992, Straight Talk: What Men Should Know, What Women Need to Understand, 1995, The New Dare to Discipline, 1996, Solid Answers, 1997, Straight Talk to Men, 2000, Life on the Edge, 2000, The Complete Marriage and Family Home Reference Guide, 2000, When God Doesn't Make Sense, 2001, The New Hide or Seek: Building Confidence in Your Child, 2001, Parents' Answer Book, 2003, Bringing Up Boys: Practical Advice and Encouragement for Those Shaping the Next Generation of Men, 2003, Romantic Love: How to Be Head Over Heels and Still Land on Your Feet, 2004, Dr. James Dobson on Parenting, 2004, Love for a Lifetime: Building a Marriage That Will Go the Distance, 2004, Stories of Heart and Home, 2007, The New Strong-Willed Child, 2007, Love Must Be Tough: New Hope for Families in Crisis, 2007; co-author: The Focus on the Family Complete Book of Baby and Child Care, 1999, Judicial Tyranny: The New Kings of America?, 2004, Marriage Under Fire: Why We Must Win This Battle, 2007, Night Light: A Devotional for Couples, 2007, Night Light for Parents: A Devotional, 2007; contbr. articles to profl. jours., chapters to books. Del. White House Conf. on Families, 1980; mem. Nat. Adv. Commn. Juvenile Justice & Delinquency Prevention, 1982—84, US Army Task Force on Families, 1986—87, chmn., 1988; mem. Atty. Gen.'s Adv. Bd. Missing & Exploited Children, 1987—88, Dole Commn. Child & Family Welfare, 1994, Nat. Gambling Impact Study Commn., 1997. Served with US Army, 1958—59. Recipient Humanitarian award, Calif. State Psychol. Assn., 1988, Alumni Merit award, U. So. Calif., 1989; named one of 25 Most Influential Evangelicals in America, TIME mag., 2005, 25 Most Influential Republicans, Newsmax mag., 2008; grantee NIH, 1975—80, HHS. Office: Focus on the Family 8605 Explorer Dr Colorado Springs CO 80920-1051*

DOCTOR, KENNETH JAY, digital content consultant; b. LA, Jan. 5, 1950; s. Joseph and Ruth (Kazdoy) D.; m. Katherine Conant Francis, June 14, 1971; children: Jenika, Joseph, Katy. BA in Sociology, U. Calif., Santa Cruz, 1971; MS in Journalism, U. Oreg., 1979. Editor, pub. Willamette Valley Observer, Eugene, Oreg., 1975-82; mng. editor Oreg. Mag., Portland, 1982-84; mng. editor, features Boulder (Colo.) Daily Camera, 1984-86; assoc. editor, features St. Paul Pioneer Press, 1986-90, mng. editor, features, 1990-94, mng. editor, 1994-97; v.p. editl. Knight Ridder New Media, San Jose, Calif., 1997-99; v.p. strategy Knight-Ridder.com., 1999-2001; v.p. content svcs. Knight-Ridder Digital, 2001—05; pres. Content Bridges, LLC, 2005—; lead news industry analyst Outsell, Inc., 2006—. Chair Knight-Ridder Task Force on Family Readers, Miami, Fla., 1991, Knight-Ridder mgmt. devel. program, Harvard U., 1993. Pres. Alumni Assn. U. Calif., Santa Cruz. Recipient Achievement award Oreg. Civil Liberties Union, Eugene, 1982. Mem. Soc. Newspaper Design, Am. Soc. Newspaper Editors, U. Calif. Santa Cruz Alumni Assn. (pres. 2003-05), Santa Cruz Found. (trustee 2006-). Avocations: baseball, travel. Personal E-mail: kdoctor@gmail.com.

DODD, JAN EVE, lawyer; b. Kansas City, Mo., May 24, 1964; d. Raymond Thomas and Eva Faith (McCorkle) D. BA in Polit. Sci. & Journalism, U. Mo., Columbia, 1985; JD, U. Mo., Kansas City, 1988. Bar: Mo. 1988, Ill. 1989, U.S. Dist. Ct. (so. dist.) Ill. 1989, U.S. Dist. Ct. (ea. dist.) Mo. 1989, U.S. Ct. Appeals (7th cir.) 1991, U.S. Ct. Appeals (8th cir.) 1994. Rsch. asst. Prof. Jack M. Balkin, Kansas City, Mo., 1986-87; jud. law clk. Judge Edward D. Robertson Jr. Mo. Supreme Ct., Jefferson City, Mo., 1988-89; sr. assoc. def. litigation Sandberg, Phoenix & Von Gontard, St. Louis, 1989—; former special state atty gen. State of Mo.; now ptnr., litigation dept. Kaye Scholer, Los Angeles, Calif. Recipient diploma Nat. Inst. for Trial Adv., Mid-Am. Regional, 1994; named one of Litigation's Rising Stars, The Am. Lawyer, 2007. Mem. Def. Rsch. Inst., Bar Assn. Met. St. Louis, Tower Grove Neighborhood Assn. Office: Kaye Scholer 1999 Ave of Stars Ste 1700 Los Angeles CA 90067 Office Phone: 310-788-1000. Office Fax: 310-788-1200. Business E-Mail: jdodd@kayescholer.com.

DODDS, ROBERT JAMES, III, lawyer; b. San Antonio, Sept. 19, 1943; s. Robert James Jr. and Kathryn (Bechman) D.; m. Deborah N. Detchon, June 25, 1966 (div. Mar. 1989); children: Zachary Bechman, Seth Detchon; m. D.J. Knowles, Dec. 27, 1990. BA, Yale U., 1965; LLB, U. Pa., 1969. Assoc. Reed Smith Shaw & McClay, Pitts., 1969-77, ptnr., 1978-91, Davenport & Dodds, LLP, Santa Fe, 1992—. Bd. dirs. ATP Inc., Davison Sand & Gravel Co., Pitts.; pres. Homewood Cemetery, Pitts., 1980-91, bd. dirs. Trustee Mus. Art, Carnegie Inst, 1974-84, Westmoreland Mus. Art, Greensburg, Pa., YMCA of Pitts., Carnegie-Mellon U.; dir., pres. Pitts. Plan for Art, 1981-85; dir., chmn. West Pa. Hosp. Found., Carnegie Mellon Art Gallery; bd. dirs. Western Pa. Hosp., Western Pa. Healthcare Systems Inc., Pitts. Athletic Assn., Inst. Am. Indian Arts Found., Santa Fe; mus. panel Pa. Coun. on the Arts. Mem.: Yale Club (N.Y.C.), Duquesne Club (Pitts.). Democrat. Episcopalian. Home: 3101 Old Pecos Trl Unit 687 Santa Fe NM 87505-9547 Office: Davenport & Dodds LLP 721 Don Diego Ave Santa Fe NM 87505 Office Phone: 505-982-0080. E-mail: dod@newmexico.com.

DODGE, GEOFFREY A., information technology executive, former publishing executive; b. Newburyport, Mass., Aug. 14, 1960; s. Edward and Sandra (Whitley) Dodge. BA, Babson Coll., Wellesley, Mass., 1983. Ad sales rep. IDG, Boston, 1985-86; pub. Boston Computer News, 1986; sales rep. Fortune mag. Time Inc., NYC, 1987-89, Washington mgr., 1989-92, NY advt. dir., 1992-94, ea. advt. dir., 1994-95, pub. Money mag., 1995—2000; CEO Media Space Solutions, 2000—02; assoc. pub., v.p. US advt. BusinessWeek mag. McGraw-Hill Cos. Inc., NYC, 2002, pub. N. Am., v.p., 2004—07; sr. v.p. Salesforce.com, Inc., 2007—. Mem. exec. com. Jr. Achievement, NYC, 1988. Mem.: Rockefeller Ctr. Club, NY Athletic Club. Office: Salesforce Landmark @ One Market Ste 300 San Francisco CA 94105

DODGE, PETER HAMPTON, architect; b. Pasadena, Calif., July 1, 1929; s. Irving C. and Edna D. (Allison) D.; m. Janice Coor-Pender, Aug. 30, 1952; children: Susan Julia, Sarah Caroline. Student, Art Center Sch., Calif., 1947-49; AB with honors in Architecture, U. Calif., Berkeley, 1956. Cert. architect, Calif., Hawaii, Nev., Idaho, Colo., The Nat. Coun. of Archtl. Registration Bds., (NCARB). Apprentice Alvin Lustig (designer), Los Angeles, 1949-50; draftsman Joseph Esherick (AIA), 1956, architect, 1959-63; asso. architect Joseph Esherick and Assos. (architects), San Francisco, 1963-72; prin. Esherick, Homsey, Dodge and Davis (architects and planners, P.C.), San Francisco, 1972—, pres., 1979-85. Lectr. dept. architecture U. Calif., Berkeley, 1961-64, 71; vis. lectr. dept. design San Francisco Art Inst., 1965 Prin. archtl. works include grad. residence facility U. Calif.-Davis, 1970, Shortstop Inc. markets, office and warehouse, Benicia, Calif., 1976, Ekahi Village (297 condominium units) Wailea, Hawaii, 1976, TWA and Western Airlines at San Francisco Internat. Airport, 1977, Citizens Utility Ctr., Susanville, Calif., 1983, various projects Golden Gate U., San Francisco, 1984—, additions and renovation Forest Hill Mcpl. R.R. Sta., San Francisco, 1985, Life Sci. Bldg. Mills Coll., Oakland, Calif., 1986, showroom R.A.B. Motors Mercedes-Benz, San Rafael, Calif., 1986, U.S. Embassy, La Paz, Bolivia, 1979-87, boarding area "B" expansion San Francisco Internat. Airport, 1987, additions and renovations Mills. Coll. Art Ctr., Oakland, 1987, F.W. Olin Libr. Mills Coll., Oakland, 1989, Calif. State U. at Bakersfield Walter Stiern Libr., 1993, Mills Hall restoration, Olney Hall rehab. Mills Coll., 1994; mem. editorial bd. Architecture Calif. mag., 1984-88, chmn. bd., 1985-88, Landscape mag., 1986—. Mem. Rockridge Community Planning Council, Oakland, Calif., 1971. Served with C.E., U.S. Army, 1957-58. Firm recipient of highest nat. honor for archtl. firm. AIA, 1986. Fellow AIA (dir. Calif. council 1979-81, dir. San Francisco chpt. 1977-78, sec. 1979, v.p. 1980, pres. San Francisco chpt. 1981, Honor award 1970, Bartlett award 1970); mem. U. Calif. at Berkeley Coll. Environ. Design Alumni Assn. (mem. founding steering com., pres. 1990-91). Office: Esherick Homsey Dodge & Davis 500 Treat Ave Ste 201 San Francisco CA 94110-2014

DODS, WALTER ARTHUR, JR., bank executive; b. Honolulu, May 26, 1941; s. Walter Arthur Sr. and Mildred (Phillips) D.; m. Diane Lauren Nosse, Sept. 18, 1971; children: Walter A. III, Christopher L., Peter D., Lauren S. BBA, U. Hawaii, 1967. Mktg. officer 1st Hawaiian Bank, Honolulu, 1969, asst. v.p. mktg. div., 1969-71, v.p., chmn. mktg. and rsch. group, 1971-73, sr. v.p. mktg. and rsch. group, 1973-76, exec. v.p. retail banking group, 1976-78, exec. v.p. gen. banking group, 1978-84, pres., 1984-89, chmn., ceo, 1989—; chmn., pres., CEO First Hawaiian, Inc., 1989-90; chmn., CEO BancWest Corp, 1989—, First Hawaiian Creditcorp., 1989-92. Bd. dirs. First Hawaiian Inc., 1st Hawaiian Bank, First Hawaiian Creditcorp Inc., First Hawaiian Leading, Inc., Alexander & Baldwin Inc., A&B-Hawaii Inc., Duty Free Shoppers Adv. Bd., Matson Navigation Co. Inc., 1st Ins. Co. Hawaii Ltd., GTE Calif., GTE Hawaiian Telephone Co., GTE Northwest, Grace Pacific Corp., Oceanic Cablevision Inc., Pacific Guardian Life Ins. Co., Princeville Adv. Group, RHP, Inc., Restaurant Suntory USA, Inc., Suntory Resorts, Inc. Bd. dirs. Ahahui Koa Anuenue, East-West Ctr. Found.; past sec., treas. The Rehab. Hosp. of the Pacific; exec. bd. mem. Aloha Coun., Boy Scouts Am.; trustee, past chmn., trustee Blood Bank Hawaii; past chmn. bd. Aloha United Way; past chmn. Bd. Water Supply; bd. govs., v.p. fin. Ctr. for Internat. Comml. Dispute Resolution; bd. dirs., treas. Coalition for Drug-Free Hawaii; trustee Contemporary Mus. co-chmn. corp. campaign com.; mem. Duty Free Shoppers Adv. Bd.; past chmn. Gubernatorial Inauguration, 1974, 82; bd. govs. Hawaii Employers Coun.; trustee Hawaii Maritime Ctr; mem. Gov.'s Adv. Bd. Geothermal/Inter-Island Cable Project, Gov.'s Blue Ribbon Panel on the Future of Healthcare in Hawaii; dir., past chmn. Hawaii Visitors Bur.; exec. com. Hawaiian Open; past spl. dir. Homeless Kokua Week; bd. gov. Honolulu Country Club, Japanese Cultural Ctr. Hawaii, Pacific Peace Found.; trustee Japan-Am. Inst. Mgmt. Sci., The Nature Conservancy Hawaii, Punahou Sch.; Hawaii chmn. Japan-Hawaii Econ. Coun.; chmn., dir. Pacific Internat. Ctr. for High Tech. Rsch.; past co-chmn., chmn. bldg. fund St. Louis High Sch.; treas. The 200 Club; dir. World Cup Honolulu 1994. Named Outstanding Jaycee in Nation, 1963, Outstanding Young Man Am. from Hawaii, 1972, Marketer of Yr., Am. Mktg. Assn., 1987; recipient Riley Allen Individual Devel. award, 1964, Hawaii State Jaycees 3 Outstanding Young Men award, 1971, Am. Advt. Fedn. Silver medal, 1977, St. Louis High Sch.'s Outstanding Alumnus award, 1980. Mem. Am. Bankers Assn., Bank Mktg. Assn., Hawaii Bankers Assn., Hawaii Bus. Roundtable, C. of C. of Hawaii, Honolulu Press Club. Office: BancWest Corp PO Box 3200 Honolulu HI 96847-0001

DOEBLER, PAUL DICKERSON, publishing management executive; b. Milw., July 3, 1930; s. Paul Henry and Grace Elizabeth (Whittaker) D.; m. Aileen Mary Hunt, May 15, 1958 (dec. 1966); m. Terry Gerda Moss, Dec. 15, 1967 BS in Journalism, Northwestern U., 1953; BS in Printing Mgmt., Carnegie-Mellon U., 1956. Editor-in-chief Book Prodn. Industry mag. Penton Pub. Co., NYC, 1965-71; pub. mgmt. cons. NYC, 1972-80; mgr. bus. devel. R.R. Bowker subs. Xerox, NYC, 1980-82, editor-in-chief profl. books, 1983-84; pub. cons. Xerox Systems Group, El Segundo, Calif., 1984-85, mgr. documentation cons. services, 1985-86, mgr. documentation systems mktg., 1986-89; pres. Paul Doebler Enterprises, Camarillo, Calif., 1990—. Instr. Assn. Am. Pubs., 1985, CCNY, 1980-85; guest lectr. The Writing Program MIT, 1988-90; instr. learning Tree U., 1997—. Contbr. articles to mags. Mem. Carnegie Printers Alumni Assn. (pres. 1972) Home: 6343 Gitana Ave Camarillo CA 93012-8135

DOERR, JOHN (L. JOHN DOERR III), venture capitalist; b. St. Louis, June 29, 1951; m. Ann Doerr; 2 children. BS in Electrical Engring., Rice U., 1973, MSEE in Electrical Engring., 1974; MBA, Harvard U. Joined Intel Corp., 1974; ptnr. Kleiner Perkins Caulfield & Byers, Menlo Park, Calif., 1980—; founder, CEO Silicon Compilers, 1981—; adv. bd. mem. Generation Investment Mgmt., Inc., 2007—. Bd. dirs. Sun Microsystems Inc., 1982—2006, Intuit, 1990—, Netscape Communications Corp., 1994—, Amazon.com, 1996—, Drugstore.com, 1998—2004, Handspring Inc., 1998—2003, Homestore.com, 1998—, Google Inc., 1999—, Palm, Inc., 2003—, Zazzle.com, Inc., 2005—, Amyris Biotechnologies Inc, 2006—, iControl Networks Inc., 2008—; mem. President's Econ. Recovery Advisory Bd., 2009—. Named one of The 400 Richest Americans, Forbes mag., 2006, The 50 Most Important People on the Web, PC World, 2007. Office: Kleiner Perkins Caufield and Byers 2750 Sand Hill Rd Menlo Park CA 94025-7020 E-mail: johnd@kpcd.com.*

DOHERTY, SHANNEN, actress; b. Memphis, Apr. 12, 1971; d. Tom and Rosa D.; m. Ashley Hamilton, Sept. 24, 1993 (div. 1994); m. Rick Salomon, Jan. 25, 2003 (annulled 2003). Actor TV series Little House: A New Beginning, 1982-83, Our House, 1986-88, Beverly Hills, 90210, 1990-94, Charmed, 1998-2001, Scare Tactics, 2003, North Shore, 2004, Love, Inc., 2005, 90210, 2008-; TV movies The Other Lover, 1985, Robert Kennedy and His Times, 1985, Obsessed, 1992, Rebel Highway: Jailbreakers, Showtime, 1994, A Burning Passion: The Margaret Mitchell Story, 1994, Gone in the Night, 1996, Sleeping with the Devil, 1997, The Ticket, 1997, Satan's School for Girls, 2000, Another Day, 2001, Hell on Heels: The Battle of Mary Kay, 2002, Nightlight, 2003, Category 7: The End of the World, 2005, Christmas Caper, 2007, Kiss Me Deadly, 2008; host Breaking Up With Shannen Doherty, 2006; TV guest appearances include Father Murphy, 1981, Magnum, P.I., 1983, Airwolf, 1984, Highway to Heaven, 1985, 21 Jump Street, 1989, Life Goes On, 1989; films: Night Shift, 1982, (voice) The Secret of Nimh, 1982, Girls Just Want to Have Fun, 1985, Heathers, 1989, Blindfold: Acts of Obsession, 1993, Almost Dead, 1994, Mallrats, 1995, Nowhere, 1997, Striking Poses, 1999, The Rendering, 2002. Baptist. Office: Agency for the Performing Arts LA 405 S Beverly Dr Beverly Hills CA 90212-4425

DOHERTY, STEVE, lawyer, state legislator; b. Great Falls, Mont., May 5, 1952; s. Arthur Frederick and Myra M. Doherty. BA, U. Pa., 1975; JD, Lewis & Clark Law Sch., 1984. Assoc. Spears, Lubersky, Campbell, Bledsoe, Anderson & Young, Portland, 1984-86; from assoc. to ptnr. Graybill, Ostrem, Warner & Crotty, Great Falls, Mont., 1986-92; assoc. Smith & Guenther, Great Falls, Mont., 1992-97; mem. Mont. Senate, Dist. 24, Great Falls, 1991—2003; majority whip, chmn. jud. com. Mont. Senate, Great Falls, Mont., 1993-94, mem. taxation and nat. resources com., 1991-94, mem. environ. quality coun. com., 1991-94, mem. edn. com., 1995, mem. fish and game and ethics com., 1997, minority leader, 1999-2001, mem. rules com., 1999—2001; ptnr. Smith & Doherty, Great Falls, 1998—2002, Smith, Doherty & Belcourt, P.C., Great Falls, 2003—06, Smith & Doherty PC, Great Falls, 2006—. Chmn. Mont. Fish, Wildlife, and Parks Commn., 2005—. Mem. legis. del. to Taiwan, 2000, Mont. del. to Mnsfield Ctr. Conf. on Environment, Kumamoto, Japan, 2000; trainer Nat. Dem. Inst., Guiyang Province, China, 2004; bd. dirs. Rural Employment Opportunities, Helena, 1990—92. Recipient Conservation Eagle award, N.W. Energy Coalition, 1999, Pub. Svc. award, Mont. Trial Lawyers Assn., 2001; Flemming fellow, Ctr. for Policy Alts., 1998, Eleanor Roosevelt Global fellow, Chile, 2001. Mem. Great Falls Pub. Radio Assn. (bd. dirs. 1986-91). Democrat. Avocations: hunting, fishing, hiking, skiing, western history. Office: Smith Doherty PC 410 Central Ave Ste 608 Great Falls MT 59401-3128 Office Phone: 406-721-1070. Fax: 406-721-1799.

DOHRING, DOUG, marketing executive; m. Laurie Dohring; 5 children. Founder, chmn., CEO Dohring Co., Glendale, Calif., 1986—95, 1998—, NeoPets, Inc., Glendale, Calif., 2000—06. Office: Dohring Co PO Box 230 Glendale CA 91209

DOI, ROY HIROSHI, retired biochemist, educator; b. Sacramento, Mar. 26, 1933; s. Thomas Toshiteru and Ima (Sato) D.; m. Joyce Takahashi, Aug. 30, 1958 (div. 1992); children: Kathryn E., Douglas A.; m. Joan M. Saul, Feb. 14, 1992. BA in Physiology, U. Calif., Berkeley, 1953, BA in Bacteriology, 1957; MS in Bacteriology, U. Wis., Madison, 1958, PhD in Bacteriology, 1960. NIH postdoctoral fellow U. Ill., Urbana, 1960-63; asst. prof. Syracuse U., NY, 1963-65, U. Calif., Davis, 1965-66, assoc. prof., 1966-69, prof. biochemistry, 1969-92, chmn. dept. biochemistry and biophysics, 1974—77, dir. biotechnology prog., 1989-92, prof. molecular biology, 1992—2003, disting. prof. molecular biology, 2003—08. Cons. NIH, Bethesda, Md., 1975-79, 82-84, Syntro Corp., San Diego, 1983-88; treas. Internat. Spores Conf., Boston, 1980-89; mem. recombinant DNA adv. com. NIH, 1990-94; eminent scientist Riken Inst., Wako, Japan, 1998. Contbr. articles sci. jours.; editor: Microbiol. and Molecular Biology Revs., 1998—2006. With U.S. Army, 1953-55. Fellow NSF, 1971-72; recipient Sr. Scientist award, Alexander von Humboldt Found., Munich, 1978-79, vis. scholar award Naito Found, Tokyo. Fellow AAAS, Am. Acad. Microbiology; mem. NAS. Democrat. Avocations: photography, sports. Office Phone: 530-752-3191.

DOIG, IVAN, writer; b. White Sulphur Springs, Mont., June 27, 1939; s. Charles Campbell and Berneta (Ringer) D.; m. Carol Dean Muller, Apr. 17, 1965. BJ, Northwestern U., 1961, MS in Journalism, 1962; PhD in History, U. Wash., 1969; LittD (hon.), Montana State U., 1984, Lewis and Clark Coll., 1987. Editorial writer Lindsay-Schaub Newspapers, Decatur, Ill., 1963-64; asst. editor The Rotarian, Evanston, Ill., 1964-66. Author: (memoir) This House of Sky, 1978, Heart Earth, 1993, (non-fiction) Winter Brothers, 1980; (novels) The Sea Runners, 1982, English Creek, 1984, Dancing at the Rascal Fair, 1987, Ride With Me, Mariah Montana, 1990, Bucking the Sun, 1996, Mountain Time, 1999, The Whistling Season, 2006. Sgt. USAFR, 1962-69. Recipient Gov.'s Writers Day award, 1979, 81, 85, 88, award for lit. excellence Pacific N.W. Booksellers, 1979, 81, 83, 85, 88, 94, Disting. Achievement award Western Lit. Assn., 1989, Evans Biography award, 1992; fellow Nat. Endowment for Arts, 1985. Mem. Authors Guild, PEN Am. Ctr. Mailing: Author mail care Harcourt Pub Ste 1900 525 B St San Diego CA 92101

DOLAN, ANDREW KEVIN, retired lawyer; b. Chgo., Dec. 7, 1945; s. Andrew O. and Elsie Dolan; children: Andrew, Francesca, Melinda. BA, U. Ill., Chgo., 1967; JD, Columbia U., 1970, MPH, 1976, DPH, 1980. Bar: Wash. 1980. Asst. prof. law Rutgers-Camden Law Sch., N.J., 1970-72; assoc. prof. law U. So. Calif., LA, 1972-75; assoc. prof. pub. health U. Wash., Seattle, 1977-81; ptnr. Bogle & Gates, Seattle, 1988-93; pvt. practice law, 1993—2006. Commr. Civil Svc. Commn., Lake Forest Park, Wash., 1981; mcpl. judge City of Lake Forest Park, 1982-98. Russell Sage fellow, 1975. Mem. Order of Coif, Washington Athletic Club. Avocation: book collecting.

DOLAN, BRENDAN G., lawyer; b. Oct. 1959; m. Suzanne Dolan Dolan. BA, UC Berkeley, 1981; JD, U. San Francisco, 1986. Bar: Calif. 1986. Ptnr., asst. mng. labor & employment practice group Morgan, Lewis & Bockius LLP, San Francisco. Mem.: Bar Assn. San Francisco, McAuliffe Honor Soc. Office: Morgan Lewis & Bockius LLP Spear Street Tower One Market St San Francisco CA 94105 Office Phone: 415-442-1667. Office Fax: 415-415-1001. Business E-Mail: bdolan@morganlewis.com.

DOLAN, JAMES MICHAEL, JR., zoological park administrator; b. NYC, Feb. 27, 1937; s. James Michael and Emily Catherine (Wackerbauer) D. BS, Mt. St. Mary's Coll., Emmitsburg, Md., 1959; PhD, Inst. fur Haustierkunde, U. Kiel, Fed. Republic Germany, 1963. Asst. curator birds Zoological Soc. San Diego, The San Diego Zoo, 1963-64, assoc. curator birds, 1964-73, dir. animal sci., 1973-74; gen. curator Zoological Soc. San Diego, The San Diego Wild Animal Pk., 1974-81; gen. curator mammals Zoological Soc. San Diego, 1982-85, dir. collections, 1986—. Advisor Econ. Rsch. Assocs.; adj. prof. zoology San Diego State U.; tech. asst. UN in Malaysia, 1970, Indian Zool. Gardens, 1976, Kuwait Zool. Garden, 1978, Seoul (Korea) Zool. Garden; mem. Survival Svc. Commn., Faro, Portugal, 1978; zoo advisory for U.S. Fish & Wildlife Svc. to India, 1980; del. internat. confs. including Conv. on Internat. Trade in Endangered Species Wild Fauna and Flora, Buenos Aires, 1985, Internat. Conf. Rupricaprines, Japan, 1987. Collecting expdns. to Cen. Am. countries, 1965, Australia, 1966, Papua-New Guinea, 1966, Java and Borneo, 1969, Fiji, 1970, Costa Rica, 1976; participant giant eland capture expdn. Senegal and Mali, 1979; mem. adv. bd. Internat. Zoo Yearbook, London. Fellow Am. Assn. Zool. Pks. and Aquariums (coordinator Arabian oryx group species survival plan); mem. Internat. Union Dirs. Zool. Gardens, Internat. Union for Conservation of Nature & Natural Resources (active several species survival commn. specialist groups, del. meetings and confs. Eng., Australia, Czechoslovakia, Hong Kong 1980-84, Fed. Republic Germany, 1987, reintroduction program Przewalski's horse Republic of China and Tibet, 1987, conf. Arabian oryx Saudi Arabia, 1987, com. to review new Taipei Zoo 1987), Am. Pheasant and Waterfowl Assn., African Lovebird Soc., Avicultural Soc., Explorer's Club, Fauna Preservation Soc., Found. Protection and Preservation of Przewalski Horse, Internat. Crane Found., World Pheasant Assn., Zooculturists, German Soc. Mammalogists. Avocations: book collecting, aviculture. Home: 18836 Paradise Mountain Rd Valley Center CA 92082-7430 Office: San Diegi Zool Soc San Diego Zoo PO Box 120551 San Diego CA 92112-0551

DOLAN, MARY ANNE, journalist, columnist; b. Wash., May 1, 1947; d. William David and Christine (Shea) D. BA, Marymount Coll., Tarrytown, NY, 1968; HHD (hon.), Marymount Coll., %, 1984; student, Queen Mary, Royal Holloway colls., U. London, London Sch. Econs., Kings Coll., Cambridge U., 1966-68. Reporter, editor Washington Star, 1969-77; asst. mng. editor, 1976-77; mng. editor L.A. Herald Examiner, 1978-81, editor, 1981—, now commentator. Mem. Pulitzer Prize Journalism Jury, 1981—82; bd. selectors for Neiman Fellows Harvard U. Recipient Golden Flame award, Calif. Press Women, 1980, Woman Achiever award, Calif. Fed. Bus. and Profl. Women's Clubs, 1981. Mem.: Am. Soc. Newspaper Editors, NOW. Office: MAD Inc 1033 Gayley Ave Ste 205 Los Angeles CA 90024-3417

DOLAN, PETER BROWN, lawyer; b. Bklyn., Mar. 25, 1939; s. Daniel Arthur and Eileen Margaret (Brown) D.; m. Jacqueline Elizabeth Gruning, Sept. 9, 1961; children: Kerry Anne, Peter Brown Jr. BS, U.S. Naval Acad., 1960; JD, U. So. Calif., 1967. Bar: Calif. 1967, US Ct. Appeals (9th cir.) 1967, US Dist. Ct. (no. and ctrl. dists.) Calif. 1967, US Dist. Ct. (ea. dist.) Calif. 1972, US Dist. Ct. (so. dist.) Calif. 1973, US Claims Ct. 1982, US Supreme Ct. 1986. Dep. LA County counsel, 1967-69; assoc. Macdonald, Halsted & Laybourne, LA, 1969-71, ptnr., 1972-77, Overton, Lyman & Prince, LA, 1977-87, Morrison & Foerster, LA, 1987-93, Morgan, Lewis & Bockius LLP, LA, 1993-99; prin. The Dolan Law Firm, LA, 1999—. Active Pasadena (Calif.) Tournament Roses Assn., 1973-05; pres. West Pasadena Residents Assn., 1979-81. Served to lt. USN, 1960-64, comdr. USNR, 1964-86. Mem.: LA County Bar Assn., Assn. Bus. Trial Lawyers, State Bar Calif., Chancery (LA), Bel-Air Bay Club, Phi Delta Phi. Roman Catholic. Office Phone: 213-689-0333. Fax: 213-680-9889. Personal E-mail: peterbdolan@yahoo.com.

DOLBY, RAY MILTON, electrical engineer, company executive; b. Portland, Oreg., Jan. 18, 1933; s. Earl Milton and Esther Eufemia (Strand) Dolby; m. Dagmar Baumert, Aug. 19, 1966; 1 child, Thomas Eric; 1 child, David Earl. Student, San Jose State Coll., 1951-52, 55, Washington U., St. Louis, 1953—54; BSEE, Stanford U., 1957; PhD in Physics (Marshall scholar 1957-60, Draper's studentship 1959-61, NSF fellow 1960-61), Cambridge U., Eng., 1961, ScD (hon.), 1997; Doctor of the U. (hon.), U. York. Lic. Comml. pilot instrument rating FAA. Electronic technician/jr. engr. Ampex Corp., Redwood City, Calif., 1949—53, engr., 1955—57, sr. engr., 1957; PhD research student in physics Cavendish Lab., Cambridge U., 1957—61, research in long wavelength x-rays, 1957—63; fellow Pembroke Coll., 1961—63; cons. U.K. Atomic Energy Authority, 1962—63; UNESCO adviser Central Sci. Instruments Orgn., Chandigarh, Punjab, India, 1963—65; owner, chmn., CEO Dolby Labs., Inc., San Francisco and Wootton Bassett, U.K., 1965—. Mem. Marshall Scholarship selection com., 1979—85; Trustee Univ. High Sch., San Francisco, 1978—84; bd. dirs. San Francisco Opera; bd. govs. San Francisco Symphony. With US Army, 1953—54. Decorated officer Most Excellent Order of Brit. Empire; recipient Beech-Thompson award, Stanford U., 1956, Emmy award, 1957, 1989, Trendsetter award, Billboard, 1971, Emile Berliner Maker of the microphone award, Emile Berliner Assn., 1972, Lyre award, Inst. High Fidelity, 1972, Top 200 Execs. Bi-Centennial award, 1976, Sci. and Engring. award, Acad. Motion Picture Arts and Scis., 1979, Pioneer award, Internat. Teleprodn. Soc., 1988, Edward Rhein Ring award, Edward Rhein Found., 1988, Oscar award, 1989, Life Achievement award, Cinema Audio Soc., 1989, Grammy award, NARAS, 1995, Nat. medal Tech., U.S. Dept. Commerce, 1997, medal of Achievement, Am. Electronics Assn., 1997, Festival medal Cannes, Cannes Internat. Film Festival, 2004; named Man of Yr., Internat. Tape Assn., 1987, Nat. Inventors Hall of Fame, U.S. Patent and Trademark Office, 2004; named one of Forbes' Richest Americans, 2006; fellow Pembroke Coll., Cambridge U., 1983. Fellow: Inst. Broadcast Sound, Soc. Motion Picture and TV Engrs. (Samuel L. Warner award 1979, Alexander M. Poniatoff Gold medal 1982, Progress award 1983), Brit. Kinematograph, Sound and TV Soc. (Outstanding Tech. and Sci. award 1995), Audio Engring. Soc. (bd. govs. 1972-74 1979—84, Silver medal 1971, Gold medal 1992); mem.: NATAS (Charles F. Jenkins Lifetime award 2003), Consumer Electronics Assn. (Consumer Electronics Hall of Fame 2000), Internat. Broadcasting Conv. (John Tucker award 2000), IEEE (Ibuka award 1997), Pacific Union Club, St. Francis Yacht Club, Tau Beta Pi. Achievements include invention of Dolby Stereo, video tape recording, x-ray microanalysis, noise reduction and quality improvements in audio and video systems; more than 60 patents in the US Lab. Inc. Office: Dolby Labs 100 Potrero Ave San Francisco CA 94103-4886

DOLCOURT, JOHN (JACK) LAWRENCE, pediatrician; b. Denver, May 13, 1949; s. Benjamin and Nessie (Badion) D.; m. Joyce Linda Papper, Sept. 3, 1972; children: Bram, Cameron. BA, U. Colo., 1971, MD, 1975. Diplomate Am. Bd. Pediatrics, Am. Bd. Neonatal, Perinatal Medicine. Asst. prof. pediatrics U. Utah Sch. of Medicine, Salt Lake City, 1990-86, assoc. prof., 1986—. Med. dir. Ctr. for Pediatric Continuing Edn., Primary Childen's Med. Ctr., Salt Lake City, Utah, 1986—. Contbr. articles to profl. jours.; inventor percutaneously placed catheter. Bd. dirs. Jewish Reconstructionist Fedn.,

Phila., 1990-93, v.p., 1993—. Fellow Am. Acad. Pediatrics. Home: 509 Northmont Way Salt Lake City UT 84103-3324 Office: U Utah Sch Medicine Divsn Neonatology 50 N Medical Dr Ste 2a111 Salt Lake City UT 84132-0001

DOLENZ, MICKEY (GEORGE MICHAEL DOLENZ, MICKEY BRADDOCK), entertainer, actor, television producer; b. LA, Mar. 8, 1945; s. George and Janelle (Johnson) Dolenz; m. Samantha Just, 1967-1975 (div.) 1 daughter, m. Trina Dow, 1977-91 (div.) 3 daughters, m. Donna Quinter, 2002-. Student, Valley Coll., Los Angeles Tech. Inst. Ind. actor, musician, 1958-66; mem. The Monkees, 1966-70, 85—, star TV series, 1966-68; cartoon voice-over artist, actor, musician, 1970-77; TV dir., producer England, 1977-85; solo artist, 1990—92; actor theater productions; morning host CBS-FM 101.1, NYC, 2005. Rec. artist: (The Monkees: Dolenz, Mike Nesmith, Davey Jones, Peter Tork) The Monkees, 1966, More of the Monkees, 1967, Headquarters, Pisces, Aquarius, Capircorn & Jones Ltd., 1967, The Birds, the Bees & the Monkees, 1968, (film soundtrack) Head, 1968, Instant Replay, 1969, The Monkees Present, 1969, Changes, 1969, The Monkees Greatest Hits, 1969, The Monkees Golden Hits, (The Monkees: Dolenz, Jones, Tork) Then and Now, 1986, Missing Links, 1987, vol. 2, 1990, Listen To The Bard, 1991, JustUs, 1996; hit singles include Last Train to Clarksville, Daydream Believer, Valerie, Peter Percival and his Pet Pig Porky, I'm a Believer, Steppin' Stone, Pleasant Valley Sunday; other TV series appearances include My Three Sons, Adam 12, Pacific Blues, 1995; (cartoon series) Scooby Doo, Devlin, The Funky Phantom, 1971, The Tick, 1995; (TV movies) 33 1/3 Revolutions per Monkee, 1969, Hey, Hey, It's the Monkees, 1997, The Love Bug, 1997; (films) Head, 1968, Keep off my Grass!, 1971, Night of the Strangler, 1972, Keep Off! Keep Off!, 1975, Linda Lovelace for President, 1976, Deadfall, 1993, The Brady Bunch Movie, 1995, Mom, Can I keep Her?, 1998; stage appearances include Tom Sawyer, Sacramento, 1976, The Point by Harry Nilsson, London; author: I'm a Believer: My Life of Monkees, Music and Madness, 1993.

DOLGEN, JONATHAN L., former motion picture company executive, investor; b. NYC, Apr. 27, 1945; m. Susan Dolgen; children: Tamar, Lauren. Grad., Cornell U., 1966; JD, N.Y.U. Law Sch., 1969. Lawyer Fried, Frank, Harris, Shriver & Jacobson, NYC, 1969-76; asst. gen. counsel, deputy gen. counsel Columbia Pictures Industries, 1976-85, sr. v.p. Worldwide Bus. Affairs, 1979, exec. v.p., 1980, pres. Pay Cable & Home Entertainment Group, 1983—85; sr. exec. v.p. Fox Inc., 1985—88, pres. Beverly Hills, 1988—90, chmn. Twentieth Century TV, 1988—90; pres. Columbia Pictures, 1990-94; pres. motion picture group Sony Pictures Entertainment, 1991—94; chmn., CEO Viacom Entertainment Group, NYC, 1994—2004; prin. Wood River Ventures, LLC, 2004—; sr. adv. Viacom, Inc., 2004—; dir. Expedia, Inc., Bellevue, Wash., 2005; sr. cons. ArtistsDirect, Inc., 2006—. Bd. fellows Claremont U. Ctr. and Grad. Sch.; founder Friends of the Cornell U. Theater Arts Ctr.; mem. Alumni Coun. NYU Law Sch.; founding mem. Edn. First; adv. Calif. State Summer Sch. for the Arts.; bd. dirs. Sony Pictures, Charter Comm. Named Pioneer of Yr., Will Rogers Motion Picture Pioneers Found., 2002. Office: Expedia Inc 3150 139th Ave Bellevue WA 98005

DOLICH, ANDREW BRUCE, professional sports team executive; b. Bklyn., Feb. 18, 1947; s. Mac and Yetta (Weiselter) D.; m. Ellen Andrea Fass, June 11, 1972; children: Lindsey, Caryn, Cory. BA, Am. U., 1969; MEd, Ohio U., 1971. Adminstrv. asst. to gen. mgr. Phila. 76ers, 1971—74; v.p. Md. Arrows Lacrosse, Landover, 1974—76; mktg. dir. Washington Capitals, Landover, 1976—78; exec. v.p., gen. mgr. Washington Diplomats Soccer, 1978—80; v.p. bus. ops. Oakland Athletics, Calif., 1980—92, exec. v.p. bus. ops., 1993—95; pres., COO Golden State Warriors, Oakland, 1994—95; pres. Dolich & Assocs. Sports Mktg., Alameda, Calif., 1996—97; exec. v.p. sales and mktg. Tickets.com, 1998—2000; pres. bus. ops. Memphis Grizzlies, 2000—07; COO San Francisco 49ers, 2008—. Nat. fundraising chmn. sports adminstrs. prog. Ohio U., Athens, dir., 1978-82; lectr. sports mktg. U. Calif. Ext. Bd. dirs. Bay Area Sports Hall of Fame, 1982, Grizzlies Found, Sports Exec. Leadership Coun., 2000-04, San Francisco Conv. Visitors Bereau, Silicon Vally C. of C. Recipient Alumni of Yr. award Ohio U. Sports Adminstrs. Prog., Athens, 1982, Clio award Am. Advt. Fedn., 1982; Woodard fellow U. Oreg., 2006. Office: San Francisco 49ers 4949 Centennial Blvd Santa Clara CA 95054 Office Phone: 901-205-1234, 408-562-4949. Business E-Mail: andy.dolich@niners.nfl.net. E-mail: adolich@niners.nfl.net.

DOLINKO, ROBERT A., lawyer; b. NYC, Oct. 9, 1953; married; 2 children. BS in Indsl. & Labor Relations, Cornell U., 1974; JD, NYU, 1977. Bar: Calif. 1977. Assoc. Littler Mendelson, San Francisco, 1977—80; labor atty. Merck & Co. Inc., Whitehouse Station, NJ, 1980—82; assoc. Epstein, Becker & Green, San Francisco, 1982—86, ptnr., 1986—94; ptnr., labor & employment dept. Thelen Reid & Priest LLP, San Francisco. Lectr. Cornell U. Sch. Indsl. & Labor Relations, Ithaca, NY, 1980—82. Bd. trustees Seven Hills Sch., Walnut Creek, Calif., 1992—. Mem.: ABA (Labor Sect.), State Bar Calif. (Labor Sect.). Office: Thelen Reid & Priest LLP 101 Second St Ste 1800 San Francisco CA 94105-3606 Office Phone: 415-369-7180. Office Fax: 415-371-1211. Business E-Mail: radolinko@thelenreid.com.

DOLLARHIDE, MARY C., lawyer; b. Long Beach, Calif., Jan. 28, 1957; BA with distinction, Occidental Coll., 1979; OTH, Circle Sq. Theatre Sch., NYC, 1981; JD, U. So. Calif., 1988. Bar: Calif. 1988, D.C. 1991, Conn. 1996. Ptnr. Paul, Hastings, Janofsky & Walker LLP, San Diego. Master Wallace Inn of Ct., sec. Co-author: Reductions-in-Force Treatise; editor-in-chief: So. Calif. Law Rev. Named Top 26 women Attys., 2007; named a San Diego Super Lawyer, 2006; named one of Top Employment Lawyers in San Diego, 2005—06. Master: Wallace Inn Ct.; mem.: Assn. Bus. Trial Lawyers (bd. govs.), ABA. Avocations: baseball, sailing. Office: Paul Hastings Janofsky & Walker LLP 3579 Valley Center Dr San Diego CA 92130 Office Phone: 858-720-2660. Office Fax: 858-847-3660. Business E-Mail: marydollarhide@paulhastings.com.

DOLUCA, TUNC, electronics executive; b. 1957; Attended, Middle East Tech. U., Ankara; BSEE, Iowa State U.; MSEE, U. Calif., Santa Barbara. Mem., integrated cir. design devel. staff Maxim Integrated Products, Inc., Sunnyvale, Calif., 1984, v.p., rsch. and devel., 1994—2005, founder, vertical bus. unit, sr. v.p., group. pres., portable, computing, instrumentation electronics group., 2005—07, pres., CEO, 2007—. Bd. dirs. Maxim Integrated Products, Inc., 2007—. Achievements include patents in field of mixed signal design. Office: Maxim Integrated Products Inc 120 San Gabriel Dr Sunnyvale CA 94086 Office Phone: 408-737-7600. Office Fax: 408-737-7194.

DOMBEK, CURTIS MICHAEL, lawyer; b. St. Louis, July 3, 1958; AB in Stats. magna cum laude with highest honors, Harvard Coll., 1980; JD magna cum laude, Harvard U., 1983. Bar: Mo. 1983, Calif. 1984, D.C. 1995, U.S. Dist. Ct. (ea. dist.) Mo. 1983, U.S. Dist. Ct. (ctrl. dist.) Calif. 1984, U.S. Dist. Ct. D.C. 1996, U.S. Ct. Appeals (8th cir.)1983, U.S. Ct. Appeals (D.C. cir.) 1995, U.S. Supreme Ct. 1994. Assoc. Bryan, Cave, McPheeters & McRoberts, Mo., 1983-91; ptnr. Bryan Cave LLP, LA, 1992—, group leader Internat. Trade. Editor-in-chief Harvard Jour. Law and Pub. Policy, 1982-83; contbr. articles to profl. jours. Mem. ABA, Internat. Bar Assn., Internat. Inst. Space Law, London Comml. Bar Assn., L.A. County Bar Assn., Am. Arbitration Assn. (corp. counsel com.). Avocations: piano, languages. Office: Bryan Cave LLP 120 Broadway, Ste 300 Santa Monica CA 90401-2382 E-mail: cmdombek@bryancave.com.

DOMENICI, (PETE) VICHI, retired United States Senator from New Mexico; b. Albuquerque, May 7, 1932; s. Cherubino and Alda (Vichi) D.; m. Nancy Burk, Jan. 15, 1958; children: Lisa, Peter, Nella, Clare, David, Nanette, Helen, Paula. Student, U. Albuquerque, 1950-52; BS, U. N.Mex., 1954; LLB, Denver U., 1958; LLD (hon.), U. N.Mex., Georgetown U. Sch. Medicine; HHD (hon.), N.Mex. State U. Bar: N.Mex. 1958. Tchr. math. pub. schs., Albuquerque, 1954-55; ptnr. firm Domenici & Bonham, Albuquerque, 1958-72; chmn., ex-officio mayor Albuquerque, 1967; city commr., 1966-68; US Senator from N.Mex., 1973—2009. Mem. com. appropriations US Senate, com. budget, chmn. energy and natural resources, com. homeland security and governmental affairs, com. Indian affairs. Author: A Changing America: Conservatives View the '80's from teh US Senate, 1980; author: (with Sam Nunn) Ctr. Strategic and Internat. Studies, 1992. Mem. Gov.'s Policy Bd. for Law Enforcement, 1967-68; chmn. Model Cities Joint Adv. Com., 1967-68. Recipient Nat. League of Cities award Outstanding Performance in Congress; Disting. Svc. award Tax Found., 1986, Legislator of Yr. award Nat. Mental Health Assn., 1987, public sector leadership award, 1996, Award for Leadership in Reducing Threat of Nuclear Proliferation in former Soviet Union Ctr. Non-Proliferation Studies Monterey Inst. Internat. Studies, 1999, Champion Sci. and Engring. Rsch. award, Sci. Coalition, 1999, Erna and John Steinbruck award mental illness leadership N Street Village, 1999, Whitney Clinic award extraordinary public svc., 1999, Good Neighbor award US-Mexico C. of C., 2000, Henry DeWolfe Smyth Statesman award Am. Nuclear Soc. 2000, Public Svc. award, Am. Astronomical Soc., 2003, Pick and Gavel award Assn. Am. State Geologists, 2004, Public Svc. award Am. Chem. Soc., 2005. Mem. ABA, N.Mex. Bar Assn., Kiwanis, Nat. Sch. Bd. Assn., Nat. League Cities, Middle Rio Grande Council Govts. Republican. Roman Catholic. Office Phone: 202-224-6621, 505-346-6791. Office Fax: 202-228-3261, 505-346-6720. E-mail: senator_domenici@domenici.senate.gov.*

DOMEÑO, EUGENE TIMOTHY, elementary education educator, principal; b. LA, Oct. 22, 1938; s. Digno and Aurora Mary (Roldan) D. AA, Santa Monica City Coll., Calif., 1958; BA, Calif. State U., 1960, MA, 1966. Cert. elem. tchr., gen. sch svcs, special secondary tchr. Elem. tchr. L.A. Unified Sch. Dist., 1960-70; asst. prin. Pomona (Calif.) Unified Sch. Dist., 1970-71, prin., 1971—. Cons. testing and evaluation Pomona Unified Sch. Dist., 1990—. With USNR, 1958-65. Recipient PTA Hon. Svc. award Granada Elem. PTA, Granada Hills, Calif., 1960, Armstrong Sch. PTA, Diamond Bar, Calif., 1990, Calif. Disting. Sch. Calif. Dept. Edn., 1989, Nat. Blue Ribbon Sch. U.S. Dept. Edn., Washington, 1990, Prin. and Leadership award, 1990. Mem. ASCD, Nat. Assn, Elem. Sch. Prins. (Prin. of Leadership award with Nat. Safety Com., 1991), Nat. Assn. Year Round Sch., Assn. Calif. Sch. Administrs., Diamond Bar C. of C. (edn. com.). Avocations: golf, dance, church, flute. Office: Neil Armstrong Elem Sch 22750 Beaverhead Dr Diamond Bar CA 91765-1566 E-mail: auroratlc@aol.com.

DOMINGUEZ, EDDIE, artist; b. Tucumcari, N.Mex., Oct. 17, 1957; BFA, Cleve. Inst. Art, 1981; MFA, Alfred U., 1983. Grad. asst., ceramics and visual design courses Alfred (N.Y.) U., 1981-83; artist-in-residence, lectr. Ohio State U., Columbus, 1984; artist-in-edn. N.Mex. Arts Divsn., Santa Fe, 1985-86; artist-in-residence Cleve. Inst. Art, 1986; artist-in-residence, lectr. U. Mont., Missoula, 1988; asst. prof. art U. Nebr., Lincoln, 1998—. Lectr., presenter workshops, mem. panels Ill. Arts Coun., Chgo., 1994, NEA, Washington, 1994, Ariz. Commn. on the Arts, 1994, Concordia U., Montreal, Que., Can., 1994, Mass. Coll. Art, Boston, 1994, Bennington (Vt.) Coll., 1994, 95, 96, Peters Valley, Layton, N.J., 1994, Firehouse Art Ctr., Norman, Okla., 1994, Haystack Mountain Sch. Arts & Crafts, Deer Isle, Maine, 1994, Ghost Ranch, Abiquiu, N.Mex., 1995, We. States Arts Fedn., Santa Fe, 1995, Colo. Coun. on the Arts, Boulder, 1995, Durango (Colo.) Art Ctr., 1995, Tamarind Inst., Albuquerque, 1995, 96, Kansas City (Mo.) Ar Inst., 1995, Hallmark Cards, Kansas City, 1996, Wichita (Kans.) Ctr. Arts, 1996, La. State U., Baton Rouge, 1996, Idaho State Arts Coun. Grants, Boise, 1996, Mattie Rhodes Counseling and Art Ctr., Kansas City, 1996, Southwest Ctr. Crafts, San Antonio, 1997, Very Spl. Arts, Albuquerque, 197, Topeka (Kans.) and Shawnee County Pub. Libr., 1997, U. Alaska, Anchorage, 2000, Craft Guild of Tex., Dallas, RISD, 2001, S.W. Ctr. for Crafts, San Antonio, 2002, numerous others; mem. fellowship panelist Colo. Coun. on the Arts, Denver, Penland Sch. of Crafts, N.C., 2001. Solo exhbns. include Pro Art Gallery, St. Louis, 1990, Mobilia Gallery, Cambridge, Mass., 1990, Munson Gallery, Santa Fe, 1990, 92, 94, 95, 97, 99, 2001, Mariposa Gallery, Albuquerque, 1990, Joanne Rapp Gallery, Scottsdale, Ariz., 1991, 93, 95, Felicita Found., Escondido, Calif., 1991, Tucumcari (N.Mex.) Area Vocat. Sch., 1992, Manchester Art Ctr., Pitts., 1993, Wetsman Collection, Detroit, 1993, Clovis (N.Mex.) C.C., 1993, Firehouse Art Ctr., 1994, Kavesh Gallery, Sun Valley, Idaho, 1995, Jan Weiner Gallery, Kansas City, 1995, 96, 2000, Jan Weiner Gallery, 2000, Gallerymateria, Scotsdale, Ariz., 2001, Munson Gallery, Santa Fe, 2001, Univ. Tulsa, Okla., 2001, Roswell (N.Mex.) Mus. and Art Ctr., 2002, Mus. Nebr. Art, Kearny, 2005, Allene Lapides Gallery, Santa Fe, 2005numerous others; group exhbns. include Fred Jones Mus. Art, U. Okla., Norman, 1995, Roswell (N.Mex.) Mus. & Art Ctr., 1995, Nancy Margolis Gallery, N.Y.C., 1995, Sharadin Art Gallery, Kutztown (Pa.) U., 1995, Richard Kavesh Gallery, 1995, Jan Weiner Gallery, 1995, Ariz. State U. Art Mus., Tempe, 1995, Islip (N.Y.) Mus., 1995, Bruce Kapson Gallery, Santa Monica, Calif., 1996, Site Sante Fe Gallery, 1996, Johnston County C.C., Overland Parks, Kans., 1996, Jane Haslem Gallery, Washington, 1996, Karen Ruhlen Gallery, Santa Fe, 1996, Margo Jacobson Gallery, Portland, Oreg., 1996, Very Spl. Arts Gallery, Albuquerque, 1997, Joanne Rapp Gallery, 1997, Munson Gallery, 1999, numerous others; pub. art project include, among others, murals at Great Brook Valley Health Ctr., Worcester, Mass., 1994, Mass. Gen. Hosp., 1996, (mural) Island Nursing Home, Deer Isle, 2000, (mural) Big Red, Lincoln, Nebr., 2000, Washington Park, Albuquerque, 2002; represented in many permanent collections, including Sheldon Meml. Art Mus, Lincloln, Nebr., Mus. Nebr. Art, Kearney, Nebr., Cooper-Hewitt, N.Y.C., Mus. Fine Arts, Santa Fe, Cleve. Inst. Art, Fed. Reserve Bank, Dallas, Roswell Mus. and Art Ctr., Albuquerque Mus. Fine Arts, City of Tucson (Ariz.), Phoenix Airport, Renwick Gallery Nat. Mus. Am. Art Smithsonian Inst., Washington, Detroit Inst. Art, Hallmark Cards Corp., Kansas City, State Capitol Art Collection, Santa Fe, pvt. collections. Recipient numerous grants, including NEA fellowships, 1986, 88, Kohler Arts-in-Industry grant, Sheboygan, Wis., 1988, 2000, Percent for Art Project grant, Phoenix Arts Coun., 1990, 1992, artist-in-residence grantee Roswell (N.Mex.) Mus. and Art Found., 1986, 2001; recipient Govs. award for excellnece in the arts in sculpture State N.Mex., 2006. Office Phone: 402-472-5919. Business E-Mail: edominguez@unl.edu.

DOMINICK, PETER HOYT, JR., architect; b. NYC, June 9, 1941; s. Peter Hoyt and Nancy Parks D.; m. Philae M. Carver, Dec. 9, 1978; children: Philae M., James W. BA, Yale U., 1963; MArch, U. Pa., 1967. Registered architect, Colo. Project designer John R. Wild, Pty., Ltd., Papau, New Guinea, 1968-69, Spence Robinson, Hong Kong, 1969-71, W.C. Muchow & Ptnrs., Denver, 1971-74; pres. Wazee Design/Devel., Denver, 1973-75; prin. Dominick Architects, Denver, 1975-88; sr. prin. Urban Design Group, Inc. (now 4240 Arch., Inc.), Denver, 1988—. Pres., chmn. bd. Urban Design Group, Inc., 2001—. Trustee Downtown Denver, Inc., Civic Ventures, 1984-94, Met. Denver Arts Alliance, 1983-84; active Mayor's Commn. on the Arts, 1983; juror Gov.'s awards, Denver, 1982; nat. com., exec. com. Whitney Mus. Am. Art.; bd. trustees Denver Art Mus., 2002. Fellow AIA (nat. com. on design, bd. dirs.); mem. Colo. Soc. Architects, Yale Arch. Coun., Cactus Club, Arapahoe Tennis Club. Republican. Episcopalian. Office: 4240 Architecture Inc 3003 Larimer St Denver CO 80205-2310 Office Phone: 303-292-3388. E-mail: pdominick@4240arch.com.

DOMKE, DAVID S., communications educator; PhD in Mass Comm., U. Minn., 1996. With Orange County Register, Atlanta Jour.-Constn.; asst. prof. to assoc. prof. communication U. Wash., 1998—. Contbr. articles to profl. publs.; author: God Willing? Political Fundamentalism in the White House, the "War on Terror," and the Echoing Press, 2004. Recipient Catherine Covert award for Yr.'s Outstanding Article in Journalism and Mass Communication Hist., 1998, Hillier Krieghbaum Under-40 award for Outstanding Achievement in Rsch., Tchg. and Pub. Svc., Assn. Edn. in Journalism & Mass Communication, 2006, US Prof. of Yr. award, Carnegie Found. for Advancement of Tchg. and Coun. for Advancement and Support of Edn., 2006. Office: Dept Communication U Wash Box 353740 Seattle WA 98195-3740 Office Phone: 206-685-1739. Office Fax: 206-616-3762. E-mail: domke@u.washington.edu.

DONAHOE, JOHN JOSEPH, II, Internet company executive; b. 1960; m. Eileen Chamberlain; 4 children. AB in Econ. magna cum laude, Dartmouth Coll., 1982; MBA, Stanford U., 1986. With Salomon Brothers (now Citigroup Inc.), Rolm Corp.; mng. dir. Bain & Co., Inc., 2000—05; pres. eBay Marketplaces eBay, Inc., 2005—08, pres., CEO, 2008—. Bd. dirs. eBay, Inc., 2008—. Adv. bd. Stanford Grad. Sch. Bus., Backroads; trustee Sacred Heart HS, Atherton, Calif.; bd. trustees Dartmouth Coll., 2003—, vol. Mem.: Phi Beta Kappa. Office: eBay Inc 2145 Hamilton Ave San Jose CA 95125 Office Phone: 408-376-7400. Office Fax: 408-558-7401.*

DONALD, JACK C., gas industry executive; b. Edmonton, Alta., Can., Nov. 29, 1934; s. Archibald Scott and Margaret Catherine (Cameron) D.; m. Joan M. Schultz, Oct. 29, 1955. Student, Southern Alta. Inst. Tech., 1959. Owner, operator Parkdale Auto Svc., Edmonton, 1959—62; sales mgr. Sanford Oil Ltd., Edmonton, 1962—64, Pacific Petroleums, Edmonton, 1964—71; pres., gen. mgr. Parkland Oil Products, Red Deer, Alta., 1971—76; v.p. mktg. Turbo Resources, Calgary, Alta., 1977—2002; chmn. Parkland Industries Ltd., Red Deer, 1977—2004. Chmn., bd. dirs. Can. Western Bank, Edmonton, Can. Western Trust; v.p., bd. dirs. Deermart Equipment Sales Ltd., Red. Deer, Sifton Energy Inc., Calgary; bd. dirs. Ensign Energy Svcs., Inc., Can. Direct Ins.; past coun. Inst. Chartered Accts. Alta. Alderman City of Red Deer, 1971-77. Mem.: Rotary. Office: Parkland Properties Ltd Bridgeview Pl Ste 110 5102 58th St Red Deer AB Canada T4N 2L8 Business E-Mail: jackdonald@telus.net.

DONALD, JAMES LLOYD (JIM DONALD), former beverage service company executive; b. 1954; m. Laura L. Donald; 2 children. BBA, Century U. Trainee Publix Super Mkts., Inc., 1971-76; mgmt. exec. Fla., Ala. and Tex. divsns. Albertson's, 1976-91; with Wal-Mart Stores, Inc., 1991-94; sr. v.p., mgr. 130 store ea. divsns. Safeway, Inc., 1994-96; chmn., pres. CEO Pathmark Stores, Inc., Carteret, NJ, 1996—2002; pres, North Am. divsn. Starbucks Corp., Seattle, 2002—05, pres., CEO, 2005—08. Bd. dirs. Starbucks Corp., 2005-08, Rite Aid, 2008-. Bd. dirs. Rumson Country Sch.

DONALDSON, EDWARD MOSSOP, research scientist, marine biologist, consultant; b. Whitehaven, Cumbria, Eng., June 1939; arrived in Can., 1961; s. Edward D.; m. Judith Selwood, Aug. 8, 1964; 1 child, Heather. BSc with honors, Sheffield U., Eng., 1961, DSc, 1975; PhD, U. B.C., Vancouver, Can., 1964. Rsch. scientist Dept. Fisheries and Oceans, West Vancouver, B.C., 1965-97, sect. head fish culture rsch., 1981-89, sect. head biotech., genetics and nutrition, 1989-97, head Ctr. of Disciplinary Excellence for Biotech. and Genetics in Aquaculture, 1987-97, scientist emeritus, 1997—; cons. in aquaculture and the environment, 1997—; dir. Ed Donaldson & Assocs. Ltd. Aquaculture and Fisheries Cons., 2001—. Hon. rsch. assoc. U. B.C., 1979-88, adj. prof., 1988—; cons. finfish aquaculture FAO, UN Devel. Program, Can. Internat. Devel. Agy., Internat. Devel. Rsch. Ctrs., U.S. AID, Office of Tech. Assessment of the U.S. Congress, Can. Exec. Svc. Overseas, Sci. Com. on Problems of Environment, WHO, U.S. Seagrant, Portugese Ministry Sci. and Tech., 2002; mem. Nat. Scis. and Engring. Rsch. Coun. Can., mem. strategic grant selection com. for food agr. and aquaculture, 1988-93; mem., active in strategic planning for applied rsch. and knowledge com. biotech. B.C. Sci. Coun. Mem. editl. bd. Gen. and Comparative Endocrinology, 1971-78, Can. Jour. Fisheries and Aquatic Sci., 1985-88, Aquaculture, 1983—, physiology & endocrinology sect. editor, 1999—; mem. editl. bd. Can. Jour. Zoology, 1986-91, Revista Italiana de Acquacoltura, 1991-96; contbr. over 400 articles to sci. jours. and conf. procs.; contbr. to books on endocrinology, biotech. and aquaculture; patentee in field. Bd. dirs. Vancouver Aquarium Marine Sci. Ctr., 1992—. Recipient award for best publs. in Transactions of Am. Fisheries Soc., 1977, Ministerial Merit award Min. of Fisheries and Oceans, 1989, B.C. Sci. Coun. Gold medal, 1992, Commendation award Dep. Minister, 1997, Murray A. Newman award for Lifetime Achievement in Aquatic Rsch. and Conservation, Vancouver Aquarium Marine Sci. Ctr., 2006; B.C. Sugar Co. scholar,

1961; NIH fellow, 1964-65; recipient Thomas W. Eadie medal Royal Soc. Can., 1995. Fellow Acad. Sci. of Royal Soc. Can. (mem. Rowmanoswky medal com. 1994, Thomas W. Eadie medal com. 1995-96, life sci. fellowship selection com., 2001-04); mem. Can. Soc. Zoologists (councilor 1980-83), Aquaculture Assn. Can. (Rsch. Excellence award 2004, Lifetime Achievement award, 6th Internat. Symposium First Indo Crinology, 2008). Office: Dept Fisheries & Oceans 4160 Marine Dr Vancouver BC Canada V7V 1N6 Office Phone: 604-666-7928. Business E-Mail: ed.donaldson@dfo-mpo.gc.ca.

DONALDSON, ROGER, film director, film producer; b. Ballarat, Australia, Nov. 15, 1945; Co-founder New Zealand's Film Commn. Dir., prodr. (films): Sleeping Dogs, 1977, Smash Palace, 1981, Cadillac Man, 1990; dir. The Bounty, 1984, Marie, 1985, No Way Out, 1987, Cocktail, 1988, White Sands, 1992, The Getaway, 1994, Species, 1995, Dante's Peak, 1997, Thirteen Days, 2000, The Recruit, 2003, The Bank Job, 2008; dir., prodr., writer The World's Fastest Indian, 2005; (TV films) Fearless, 1999. Office: Creative Artists Agency 2000 Avenue Of The Stars Los Angeles CA 90067-4700

DONALDSON, SARAH SUSAN, radiologist; b. Portland, Oreg., Apr. 20, 1939; BS, RN, U. Oreg., 1961; MD, Harvard U., 1968. Intern U. Wash., 1968—69; resident in radiol. therapy Stanford Med. Ctr., Calif., 1969—72; fellow in pediatric oncology Inst. Gustave-Roussy, 1972—73; prof. radiol. oncology Stanford U. Sch. Medicine., 1973—, Catherine and Howard Avery prof., dept. radiation. Recipient Elizabeth Blackwell medal, Am. Med. Women's Assn., 2005. Mem.: NIH. Office: Stanford U Med Ctr Dept Radio/Oncology 875 Blake Wilbur Dr Stanford CA 94305-5847 Business E-Mail: sarah2@stanford.edu.*

DONDERO LOOP, MARILYN, state legislator; b. Las Vegas, Nev., 1951; married; children: Lindsey, Heather, Amy. BS in Elem. Edn., U. Nev., Las Vegas, MEd in Curriculum & Instrn. Library Media Specialist & Literacy Endorsement. Elem. sch. tchr. Harvey N. Dondero Elem., Laura Dearing Elem., Rose Warren Elem., R. Guild Gray Elem.; elem. sch. tchr. (ret. 2004) Elaine Wynn Elem.; mentor tchr. (new tchr. program); sales rep.; text book pub., 2004—; mem. Dist. 5 Nev. State Assembly, 2008—. Recipient Project Coordn. of the Year award; named a Southwest Region Distinguished Educator. Mem.: NEA. Democrat. Office: 401 South Carson St Room 4110 Carson City NV 89701 also: 3724 Emerald Bay Cir Las Vegas NV 89147 Office Phone: 775-684-8833. Fax: 702-240-7995. Business E-Mail: mdonderoloop@asm.state.nv.us.

DONE, ROBERT STACY, researcher, consultant; b. Tucson, Apr. 7, 1965; s. Richard Avon Done and Nancy Jane (Meeks) Burks; m. Michele Renae Barwick, May 17, 1987 (div. Mar. 1990); m. Elizabeth Evans Robinson, Feb. 20, 1993 (div. Jan. 2009); children: Rachel Evans, Ethan James. AS in Law Enforcement, Mo. So. State U., 1987, BS in Criminal Justice Adminstrn., 1987; MPA, U. Ariz., 1992, MS in Mgmt., 1998, PhD in Mgmt., 2000. Criminal investigator Pima County, Tucson, 1988-99; asst. rsch. prof. U. Ariz., 2000—02; evaluator The Partnership, 2003—06; sr. transp. planner Pima Assn. Govts., 2006—07, long range transp. planning team lead, 2007—08, resource mgmt. specialist, 2008—. Pres. Data Methods Corp., Tucson, 1984—. Contbr. articles to profl. jours. Mem. Inst. Transp. Engrs. Home: 808 N Camino Miramonte Tucson AZ 85716

DONEGAN, MARK, metal products executive; Pres., airfoil divsn. Precision Castparts Corp., pres., structural divsn., pres., Wyman-Gordon, 1999, pres., COO Portland, Oreg., 1999—2002, pres., CEO, dir., 2002—03, chmn., CEO, 2003—. Office: Precision Castparts Corp 4650 SW Macadam Ave Ste 440 Portland OR 97239-4262

DONG, NELSON G., lawyer; b. 1949; AB, Stanford U., 1971; JD, Yale U., 1974. Bar: Calif. 1974, Minn. 1992. Whitehouse fellow and spl. asst. to US atty. gen. Griffin B. Bell Dept Justice, Wasington, 1978—79, dpt. assoc. atty. gen., 1979—80; asst. US atty. Boston, 1980—82; ptnr., corp. dept. chair, Asian dept. Dorsey & Whitney LLP, Seattle. Legal counsel IEEE. Bd. trustees Stanford U., 1978—82; bd. dir. Com. 100, NYC, 1998—, gen. counsel, sec., 1999—2003; mem. pres.'s export coun. subcom. on export adminstrn. US Export Control Policy, 1999—2001; bd. dir. White House Fellows Assn., 2004—06. Grantee White House Fellow, 1978—79. Mem.: Yale Law Sch. Assn. (exec. com. 2006—), Asian Am. Bar Assn. (secy. 1984, bd. mem. 1985). Office: Dorsey & Whitney LLP Ste 3400 US Bank Ctr 1420 Fifth Ave Seattle WA 98101-4010 Office Phone: 206-903-8871. Office Fax: 206-903-8820. Business E-Mail: dong.nelson@dorsey.com.

DONLEY, DENNIS LEE, school librarian; b. Port Hueneme, Calif., July 19, 1950; s. Mickey Holt and Joan Elizabeth (Smith) D.; m. Ruth Ann Shank, June 10, 1972; children: Eric Holt, Evan Scott. AA, Ventura Coll., 1970; BA with honors, U. Calif., Santa Barbara, 1973; MLS, San Jose State U., 1976. Cert. secondary tchr. Calif. Tchr. libr. media San Diego Unified Sch. Dist., 1975—. Lectr. Calif. State U., L.A., 1987-89; libr. cons. San Diego C.C. Dist., 1990; chmn. sch. adv. com. Point Loma H.S., San Diego, 1986-87; coop. book rev. bd. San Diego County, 1984-86; creator adult sch. curriculum, 1984-86; contbr. Deadbase X, Deadbase 94, The Deadhead's Taping Compendium, Vols. 1-3, The Deadhead's Taping Addendum. Mem. ALA, Calif. Libr. Media Educators Assn. Avocations: reading, music, walking. Office: Hoover HS 4474 El Cajon Blvd San Diego CA 92115-4312 Office Phone: 619-283-6281 2179. Personal E-mail: dennisd@well.com. Business E-Mail: ddonley@sandi.net. E-mail: dennisdster@gmail.com.

DONLEY, RUSSELL LEE, III, small business owner, former state legislator; b. Salt Lake City, Feb. 3, 1939; s. R. Lee and Leona (Sherwood) Donley; m. Karen Kocherhans, June 4, 1960; children: Tammera Sue, Tonya Kay, Christina Lynn. BSCE with honors, U. Wyo., 1961; MS in Engring., U. Fla., 1962. From mem. to spkr. of house Wyo. Ho. of Reps., 1969-84; chmn. bd. Nat. Ctr. Constl. Studies, Wyo. region, 1983-87; CEO Constitution Schs. Inc., Casper, 1987—; owner Russell L. Donley & Assocs., 1988—2005. Chmn. appropriations com. Wyo. Ho. of Reps., 1975—78, chmn. legis. mgmt. coun., 1983—84. Pres. bd. dirs. YMCA, Casper, 1976—77; chmn. western region Coun. State Govts., 1982—83; Rep. candidate for Gov. Wyo., 1986; precinct committeeman Rep. Ctrl. Com., 1987—96, 2006—; chmn. Wyo. Young Reps., 1968; fin. chmn. Natrona County Rep. Ctrl. Com., 1970; state chmn. Initiative 3 dr. Invest in Wyo. not Wall St., 1994; missionary LDS Ch., 2005—06. Recipient award for engring. excellence, Am. Cons. Engrs. Coun., Legislator of the Yr. award, Nat. Rep. Legislators Assn., 1981; named Wyo. Outstanding Young Engr., Sigma Tau, 1974, Disting. Wyo. Engr., Tau Beta Pi, 1976. Republican. Mem. Lds Ch. Personal E-mail: russ-rlda@bresnan.net.

DONLON, TIMOTHY A., cytogeneticist; b. Pasadena, Calif., Apr. 16, 1952; PhD, U. Oreg., 1984. Med. genetics fellow Children's Hosp., Boston, 1984-86; chief molecular clin. cytogenetics Kapiolani Med. Ctr., Honolulu, 1992-98, dir., 1995; assoc. prof., rschr. Cancer Rsch. Ctr. of Hawaii, 1998—; dir., lab. molecular and cytogenetics Ohana Genetics, Honolulu, 1998-2000; dir. lab molecular genetics Queens Med. Ctr., Honolulu, 2000—. Assoc. prof. U. Hawaii Burns Sch. Medicine, Honolulu, 1992—. Office: Queens Med Ctr 1010 S King St Ste 201 Honolulu HI 96814-1701

DONNELLY, RUSSELL JAMES, physicist, educator; b. Hamilton, Ont., Can., Apr. 16, 1930; naturalized 2000; s. Clifford Ernest and Bessie (Harrison) D.; m. Marian Card, Jan. 21, 1956 (dec. 1999); 1 son, James. BSc, McMaster U., 1951, MSc, 1952, LLD, 1999; MS, Yale U., 1953, PhD, 1956. Faculty U. Chgo., 1956-66, prof. physics, 1965-66, U. Oreg., Eugene, 1966—, chmn. dept., 1966-72, 82-83; vis. prof. Niels Bohr Inst., Copenhagen, Denmark, 1972; co-founder Pine Mountain Obs., 1967. Cons. GM Co. Rsch. Labs., 1958—68, NSF, 1968—76, mem. adv. panel for physics, 1970—73, chmn., 1971—72, mem. adv. coms. on materials rsch., 1979—84; mem. task force on fundamental physics and chemistry in space, space sci. bd. NRC; cons. Jet Propulsion Lab., Calif. Inst. Tech., Pasadena, 1973—82; chmn. Sci. Adv. Com. Low Temp. Facilities in Space, 1990—91; mem. fluid dynamics discipline working group NASA, 1992—95; gen. chmn. 20th Internat. Conf. on Low Temp. Physics, 1993; Chia-Shun Yih lectr. U. Mich., 1995; Fritz London meml. lectr. Duke U., 1996; Howard Vollum award Reed Coll., 1997. Author: (with Parks, Glaberson) Experimental Superfluidity, 1967, (with Francis) Cryogenic Scienee and Technology: Contributions of Leo Dana, 1985, Quantized Vortices in Helium II, 1991; editor: (with Herman, Prigogine) Non-Equilibrium Thermodynamics Variational Techniques and Stability, 1966, High Reynolds Number Flows Using Liquid and Gaseous Helium, 1991, Procs. 20th Internat. Conf. Low Temperature Physics, Physica B, 1994, (prin. sci. cons. two-hour documentary) ABsolute Zero, 2008; editor: (with Sreenivasan) Flow at Ultra-High Reynolds and Rayleigh Numbers, (with Barenghi and Vinen) Quantized Vortex Dynamic and Superfluid Turbulence; mem. editl. bd. Physics of Fluids, 1966-68, Phys. Rev. E, 1978-84, assoc. editor, 1987-93; mem. editl. bd. Jour. Phys. and Chem. Ref. Data, 1989-92, Handbook of Chemistry and Physics, 1989-98, Royal Soc. London; contbr. articles to profl. jours. Bd. dirs. U. Oreg. Found., 1970-72, 88-91, investment com., 1990-91; bd. dirs. Oreg. Mus. Park Commn., 1975-87, chmn., 1975-82; bd. dirs. Oreg. Bach Festival, 1975-87, Oreg. Mozart Players, 1990-93. Recipient Disting. Alumnus award, McMaster U., 1992, Lars Onsager medal, Norwegian U. Sci. and Tech., 1996, Fritz London prize, Internat. Union Pure and Applied Physics, 2002; Alfred P. Sloan fellow, 1959—63, sr. vis. fellow, Sci. Rsch. Coun., Eng., 1978. Fellow: AAAS, Inst. of Physics (London), Am. Phys. Soc. (exec. com. divsn. fluid dynamics 1966—72, 1980—84, 1988—91, sec.-treas. 1967—70, 1988—91, chmn. 1971—72, 1983—83, Otto Laporte award 1974), Am. Acad. Arts and Scis.; mem.: Soc. Archtl. Historians, Nat. Trust for Scotland, Cosmos Club. Episcopalian. Achievements include research on physics of fluids, especially hydrodynamic stability, turbulence and superfluidity. Office: Univ Oreg Dept Physics Eugene OR 97403-1274 Home: 1975 Olive St #502/504 Eugene OR 97401 Office Phone: 541-346-4226. Business E-Mail: russ@vortex.uoregon.edu.

DONOGHUE, MILDRED RANSDORF, education educator; b. Cleve. d. James and Caroline (Sychra) Ransdorf; m. Charles K. Donoghue (dec.); children: Kathleen, James. EdD, UCLA, 1962; JD, Western State U., 1979. Asst. prof. edn. and reading Calif. State U., Fullerton, 1962-66, assoc. prof., 1966-71, prof., 1971—. Founder, dir. Donoghue Children's Lit. Ctr., Calif. State U., Fullerton, Calif., 2001—. Author: Foreign Languages and the Schools, 1967, Foreign Languages and the Elementary School Child, 1968, The Child and the English Language Arts, 1971, 75, 79, 85, 90, Using Literature Activities to Teach Content Areas to Emergent Readers, 2001, Language Arts: Integrating Skills for Classroom Teacing, 2009; co-author: Second Languages in Primary Education, 1979; contbr. articles to profl. jours. and Edni. Resources Info. Ctr. U.S. Dept. Edn. Mem. AAUP, AAUW, Nat. Network for Early Lang. Learning, Nat. Coun. Tchrs. English, Nat. Coun. Tchrs. Math., Nat. Coun. Social Studies, Nat. Sci. Tchrs. Assn., Am. Ednl. Rsch. Assn., Nat. Soc. for Study of Edn., Internat. Reading Assn., Nat. Assn. Edn. Young Children, Assn. for Childhood Edn. Internat., Phi Beta Kappa, Phi Kappa Phi, Pi Lambda Theta, Alpha Upsilon Alpha. Address: Calif State U 800 State Coll Blvd Fullerton CA 92834

DONOVAN, DENNIS MICHAEL, psychologist, researcher; b. Oregon City, June 7, 1948; s. Dennis Joseph Donovan and Josephine R. (Spees) Middleton; m. Anne Mary Waldock, Jan. 27, 1973; 1 child, Collin Thomas. BS, Seattle U., 1970; MA, Western Wash. U., 1972; PhD, U. Wash., 1980. Lic. psychologist, Wash. Asst. chief alcohol dependence treatment program VA Med. Ctr., Seattle, 1980-86, chief in-patient sect. addictions treatment ctr., 1986—, asst. chief addictions treatment ctr., 1987—. Assoc. prof. dept. psychiatry and behavioral scis. U. Wash. Sch. of Medicine, 1984—; cons., reviewer Nat. Inst. on Alcohol Abuse & Alcoholism, Rockville, Md., 1986—; assoc. editor Psychology of Addictive Behaviors, Chgo., 1990—. Editor: Assessment of Addictive Behaviors, 1988; field editor: Jour. of Studies on Alcohol, 1987—; contbr. numerous articles to profl. jours. Named one of Outstanding Young Man of Am., U.S. Jaycees, 1977. Mem. Am. Psychol. Assn., Assn. for the Advancement of Behavior Therapy, Rsch. Soc. on Alcoholism, Soc. Psychologists in Addictive Behavior (sec., treas. 1988—), Wash. State Psychol. Assn.

DONOVAN, JOHN ARTHUR, lawyer; b. NYC, Apr. 11, 1942; children: Lara, Alex. AB, Harvard U., 1965; JD, Fordham Law Sch., 1967. Bar: N.Y. 1967, U.S. Tax. Ct. 1968, U.S. Ct. Appeals (2nd cir) 1968, U.S. Dist. Ct. (so., no. dists.) N.Y. 1969, U.S. Supreme Ct. 1971, U.S. Ct. Appeals (10th cir.) 1972, U.S. Ct. Appeals (9th cir.) 1976, Calif. 1982, U.S. Dist. Ct. (so., no. dists.) Calif. 1982, U.S. Ct. Appeals (5th cir.) 1983, Alaska 1993. Assoc. Hughes, Hubbard & Reed, NYC, 1967-74, ptnr. NYC, L.A., 1974-85, Skadden, Arps, Slate, Meagher & Flom, LA, 1985—. Mem. adj. faculty law sch. U. So. Calif., L.A., 1986-87. Office: Skadden Arps Slate Meagher & Flom 300 S Grand Ave Ste 3400 Los Angeles CA 90071-3109

DONOVAN, TATE, actor; b. Tenefly, NJ, Sept. 25, 1963; m. Corinne Kingsbury, Nov. 26, 2005 (separated 2008). Actor: (films) No Small Affair, 1985, North Beach and Rawhide, 1985, Into thin Air, 1986, Spacecamp, 1986, Dangerous Curves, 1988, Clean and Sober, 1988, Dead-Bang, 1989, Memphis Belle, 1990, Little Noises, 1991, Inside Mickey Zetterland, 1992, Equinox, 1992, Love Potion #9, 1992, Ethan Fromme, 1993, Holy Matrimony, 1994, (voice only) Hercules, 1997, The Only Thrill, 1997, Murder at 1600, 1997, Waiting for Woody, 1998, The Thin Pink Line, 1998, October 22, 1998, 4 a.m. Open All Night, 1999, The Office Party, 2000, Jesus and Hutch, 2000, Drop Back Ten, 2000, Swordfish, 2001, Get Well Soon, 2001, West of Here, 2002, Exposed, 2003, The Pacifier, 2005, Good Night, and Good Luck, 2005, The Lather Effect, 2006, Shooter, 2007, Nancy Drew, 2007, Neal Cassady, 2007; (TV films) Not My Kid, 1985, Into Thin Air, 1985, A Case of Deadly Force, 1986, Rising Son, 1990, American Dream, 1996, Tempting Fate, 1998, Silver Bells, 2005, Painkiller Jane, 2005; (TV series) Philly Heat, 1994, Partners, 1995-96, (voice only) House of Mouse, 2001-02, Mister Sterling, 2003, The O.C., 2003-06, Damages, 2007-; (TV mini-series) Nutcracker: Money, Madness and Murder, 1987; (TV appearaces) Family Ties, 1984, Hill Street Blues, 1985, Magnum, P.I., 1986, Vietnam War Story II, 1988, Tales From the Crypt, 1994, America's Dream, 1996, Homicide: Life on the Street, 1997, Ally McBeal, 1997, Godzilla: The Series, 1998, Friends, 1998, Trinity, 1999, (voice only) Hercules, 1998, The Outer Limits, 2000, The Legend of Tarzan, 2001, The Guardian, 2002, Law & Order: Criminal Intent, 2007 Office: c/o United Talent Agy Inc 9560 Wilshire Blvd Ste 500 Beverly Hills CA 90212-2427

DONOVAN, TIMOTHY R., lawyer; b. 1955; BS, Ohio State U.; JD cum laude, Capital U., Columbus, OH, 1981. Bar: 1981. Assoc. Jenner & Block, ptnr., 1989—99, chmn. corp. securities group; sr. v.p. Tenneco Corp. (formerly Tenneco Automotive Inc.), Lake Forest, Ill., 1999—2001, gen. counsel, 1999—2007, exec. v.p., 2001—07, mng. dir. internat. group, 2001—07; exec. v.p., sec., gen. counsel Allied Waste Industries Inc., Phoenix, 2007—. Dir. John B. Sanfilippo Sons Inc. Mem.: Chgo. Bar Assn. (securities law com.), ABA. Office: Allied Waste Industries 18500 N Allied Way Phoenix AZ 85054

DONZE, JERRY LYNN, electrical engineer; b. Wauneta, Nebr., June 12, 1943; s. John Henry and Virgina May (Francis) D.; m. Marilyn Grace Bascue, Feb. 22, 1964 (div. May. 1980); children: Scott. L., Michele A.; m. Sandra Kay Morris, July 25, 1981. Cert. technician, Denver Inst. Tech., 1964; BSEE, U. Colo., 1972; postgrad., Advanced Metaphysics Inst. Religios Sci., 1986. Electronic technician A.B.M. Co., Lakewood, Colo., 1964-71; computer programmer Nat. Bur. Standards, Boulder, Colo., 1971-72; electronic engr. Autometrics Co., Boulder, Colo., 1972-76, Gates Research and Devel., Denver, 1976-77; devel. engr. Emerson Electric Co., Lakewood, 1977; engring. mgr. Storage Tech., Louisville, Colo., 1977—. Cons. Sun Co., Arvada, Colo., 1974-75. Patentee in field. Mem. IEEE Student Soc. (treas. 1971-72), Eta Kappa Nu. Republican. Religious Scientist. Avocation: giving workshops and presentations. Home: 7464 Isabell Cir Arvada CO 80007-7814 Office: Storagetek 500 Eldorado Blvd Broomfield CO 80021-3408

DOODY, GREGORY L., lawyer, former energy executive; b. 1964; BS in Mgmt., Tulane U., 1987; JD, Emory U., 1994. Staff acct. Price Waterhouse & Co., 1987—89; asst. mgr. Schlumberger Ltd., 1989—91; assoc. Walston Stabler Wells & Bains, Birmingham, Ala., 1994—96, Maynard Cooper & Gale, Birmingham, Ala., 1996—98; ptnr., CFO Hungry Man LLC, 1998—2000; ptnr. Balch & Bingham LLP, Birmingham, Ala., 2000—03; exec. v.p., gen. counsel, sec. HealthSouth Corp., 2003—06, Calpine Corp., San Francisco, 2006—08. Mem.: ABA, Birmingham Bar Assn., Ala. Bar Assn. Office Phone: 800-359-5115.

DOOGAN, MIKE, state legislator; b. Fairbanks, Alaska, June 7, 1948; m to Kathleen; children: Matthew & Amy. BA in English, U. San Francisco, 1970; MFA in Creative Writing/Literary Arts, U. Alaska, Anchorage, 1999. Alaska State Representative, District 25, 2007-; member, Budget and Audit, Transportation and Public Facil, Econ Develop, Trade and Tourism, Mil and Vet Affairs, Oil and Gas, Transportation Committees, 2007-, Alaska House Representative.editor, Anchorage Daily News, 85-90, columnist, 90-2004; self employed writer & novelist, 88-present; editor, Our Alaska; press secretary, House & Senate Democratic, Alaska Legislature, 2004-06. Author: How to Speak Alaskan, Fashion Means Your Fur Hat Is Dead, War Can Be Murder. Democrat. Address: 4800 Cambridge Way Anchorage AK 99503 Office: Dist 25 716 W 4th Ave Ste 320 Anchorage AK 99501-2133 also: State Capitol Rm 112 Juneau AK 99801-1182 Office Phone: 907-465-4998, 907-269-0216. Office Fax: 907-465-4419, 907-269-0218. Business E-Mail: Rep_Mike_Doogan@legis.state.ak.us.

DOOLEY, GEORGE JOSEPH, III, metallurgist; b. Greenwich, Conn., Aug. 8, 1941; s. George Joseph and Susan Marilyn (Robustelli) D.; children: Deborah Susan, Jennifer Ann, Daniel Paul; m. Marye Khrys Von Tellrop, Oct. 27, 1984; children: Samantha Joel, Charles Douglas, Anastacia Halley, James Huston, Cynthia Maureen, Sandra Robin, Karen Linn, Kimberly Marie. BS, U. Notre Dame, 1963; MS, Iowa State U., 1966; PhD, Oreg. State U., 1969. Research asst. Ames (Iowa) Lab. AEC, 1963-66; research metallurgist U.S. Bur. Mines, Albany, Oreg., 1966-68, dir. Albany Research Ctr., 1984—; research scientist Aerospace Research Labs. USAF, Wright Patterson AFB, Ohio, 1968-72; dir. research and devel. Oreg. Metall. Corp., Albany, 1974-83, dir. metall. and quality assurance, 1983-84. Mem. metallurgy adv. bd. Linn Benton Community Coll., Albany, 1976—. Contbr. articles to profl. jours. Served to capt. USAF, 1968-72. Democrat. Roman Catholic. Home: 8804 NW Arboretum Rd Corvallis OR 97330-9571 Office: US Dept Energy Albany Rsch Ctr 1450 Queen Ave SW Albany OR 97321-2152

DOOLEY, JAMES H., product company executive; BS in Agrl. Engring., Calif. Poly., San Luis Obispo, 1971; M in Engring., U. Calif., Davis, 1972; PhD in Forest Resources/Forest Engring., U. Wash., 2000. Registered profl. engr., Hawaii, Wash. Dir. control and devel. Puna Papaya Inc., Keaau, Hawaii, 1973-77; mgr. nursery, seed orchard and greenhouse sys. unit-silvicultural engring. dept. Weyerhaeuser Co., Tacoma, 1977-82, mgr., biomech. engring unit, diversified r & d, 1982-85, dir. rsch. and engring., nursery products div., 1986-89, product engring. mgr., sensor and simulation products div., 1989-90, program mgr., corp. r & d div., 1991-94, interim mgr. strategic biol. scis. program, 1994-95; pres., CEO Silverbrook Ltd., Federal Way, Wash., 1995—. Exptl. sta. com. on orgn. and policy Nat. Assn. State U. and Land Grant Colls., 1986, plant biol. engring., strategic planning com., 1989-94; task force on univ., industry and govt. coop. ASAE, 1989; emerging technologies devel. com. ASAE, 1994-95; emerging technologies adv. com. chair ASAE, 1995-96; adv. com. past chmn. biol. engring ASAE, 1992-93; engring and tech. accreditation com. ASAE, 1984—; comprehensive review team U.S. Dept. Agr., Coop. State Rsch. Svc., Auburn U., 1989, Pa. State U., 1991, U. Ga., 1993; adv. com. forest biology project Inst. Paper Sci. Tech., 1994; adv. group biol. engring. program indsl. adv. group Wash. State U., 1994—, agrl. engring. dept. Calif. Poly, 1992—; engring.

accreditation commn. ABET, 1990-95, sec., 2005-06; presenter in field Contbr. articles to profl. jours., local newspapers. Recipient Am. Soc. Agrl. Engrs. fellow award, 1996. Fellow Am. Soc. Agrl. Engrs. (Pres. Citation, 1994, Dirs. award, 1994, Dir. Citation, 1996, Fellow award 1996); mem. Inst. Biol. Engring. (pres. 2000), Licensing Execs. Soc. Achievements include patents for a Seed Planter a double-row vacuum precision sower for foresty and other densely planted seeds, Seed Supply Sytem for Multiple Row Sower a method of ensuring all rows of a sower run out of seed at the same time, engineered wood structure for watershed restoration, wood-strand erosion control material. Address: 1911 SW Campus Dr # 545 Federal Way WA 98023-6473 Office Phone: 253-838-7229. E-mail: jdooley@seanet.com.

DOOLITTLE, RUSSELL FRANCIS, biochemist, educator; b. New Haven, Jan. 10, 1931; s. Russell A. and Mary Catherine (Bohan) D.; m. Frances Ann Tynan, June 6, 1931; children: Lawrence Russell, William Edward. BA, Wesleyan U., 1952; MA, Trinity Coll., 1957; PhD, Harvard U., 1962. Instr. biochemistry Amherst (Mass.) Coll., 1961-62; asst. research biologist U. Calif.-San Diego, La Jolla, 1964-65, asst. prof. biochemistry, 1965-67, assoc. prof., 1967-72, prof., 1972—, chmn. dept. chemistry, 1981-84, rsch. prof. biology and chemistry, 1994—. Advisor Can. Inst. for Advanced Rsch. Author: of Urfs and Orfs, 1987; contbr. articles to profl. jours. Served as sgt. U.S. Army, 1952-54. Guggenheim fellow, 1984-85, Non-Resident fellow Salk Inst., 1990-98. Fellow AAAS; mem. NAS (John J. Carty award for the Advancement of Sci., 2006), Am. Soc. Biol. Chemistry, Am. Acad. Arts and Scis., Am. Philos. Soc. (Paul Ehrlich prize 1989, Stein and Moore award 1991). Office Phone: 858-534-4417. Business E-Mail: rdoolittle@ucsd.edu.

DOR, YORAM, accountant; b. Tel Aviv, Apr. 17, 1945; arrived in U.S., 1974; s. Simon and Shulamit (Remple) Dor; m. Ofra Lipshitz, Apr. 9, 1967; children: Gil, Ron. Diploma in Acctg., Hebrew U., Jerusalem, 1969; BA in Econs., Tel Aviv U., 1971; MBA, UCLA, 1977. CPA Calif. Sr. auditor Somekh Chaikin, CPA, Tel Aviv, 1969—72; CFO East African Hotels, Dar-es-Salaam, Tanzania, 1972—74; staff acct. Hyatt Med. Enterprises, Inc. (name now Nu Med., Inc.), Encino, Calif., 1974—75, asst. contr., 1975—77, corp. contr., 1977—79, v.p. fin., 1979—82, sr. v.p. fin., CFO, 1982—87, exec. v.p. fin., CFO, 1987—95; ptnr. Sloman and Dor, Encino, 1995—, also bd. dirs. Mem.: AICPA, Calif. Soc. CPA's. Office: Sloman & Dor 16633 Ventura Blvd Ste 913 Encino CA 91436-1849 Business E-Mail: yoramdor@slomananddor.com.

DORAN, TIMOTHY PATRICK, academic administrator; b. NYC, July 1, 1949; s. Joseph Anthony and Claire (Griffin) D.; m. Kathleen Matava, Aug. 1, 1981; children: Claire Marie, Bridget Anne. BA in Econs., Le Moyne Coll., 1971; MA in Tchg., U. Alaska, 1984, Edn. Specialist, 1990. Cert. type A secondary, econs., type B K-12 prin., supt. Svc. rep. Emigrant Savs. Bank, NYC, 1971-72; exec., dir. Project Equality Northwest, Seattle, 1972-73, Jesuit Vol. Corps., Portland, Oreg., 1973-75, adminstv. advisor Kaltag City (Alaska) coun., 1975-77; program developer Diocese Fairbanks, Alaska, 1978-81, adminstr., supt. St. Mary's Cath. H.S., 1981-83; prin. intern U. Alaska, Fairbanks, 1984, vis. instr., 1990-94; tchr. Anthony A. Andrews Sch., St. Michael, Alaska, 1984-86; prin., tchr. James C. Isabell Sch., Teller, Alaska, 1986-88; prin. Unalakleet (Alaska) Schs., 1988-90, Denali Elem. Sch., Fairbanks, 1992—. Acad. coord. U. Alaska, Fairbanks, summers, 1984—86; instr. Elderhostel, 1991—; docent U. Alaska Mus., 1991—; sch. edn. adv. bd. U. Alaska, 1998—, adj. instr., Anchorage, 2001—. Active nat. com. Campaign for Human Devel., 1980-83; mem. manpower planning coun. Tanana Chiefs Conf., 1976-77, parish coun. Sacred Heart Cathedral, 1979-81; Sunday Sch. tchr. St. Mark's Univ. Parish, 1990-97, adv. coun., 1998-2001; mem. com. chair Fairbanks Arts and Culture in Edn., 1995—; bd. dirs., v.p., pres. Literacy Coun. Alaska, 1997-2002. Recipient Merit awards Alaska Dept. Edn., 1986-90; named Alaska Disting. Prin., 1998, Fairbanks Elem. Prin. of Yr., 2003. Mem. ASCD, Nat. Assn. Elem. Sch. Prins., Alaska Assn. Elem. Sch. Prins. (v.p., pres.-elect, past pres. 2000-02, state rep. 2004-), Fairbanks Prins. Assn. (v.p. 1998-99, pres. 1999-00), Alaska Math. Consortium (bd. dirs. 1992-99), Alaska Coun. Sch. Adminstrs. (bd. dirs. 1998-2002, 04). Home: 512 Windsor Dr Fairbanks AK 99709-3439 Office: Denali Elem Sch 1042 Lathrop St Fairbanks AK 99701-4124 Office Phone: 907-452-2456. Business E-Mail: tdoran@northstar.k12.ak.us.

DORATO, PETER, electrical and computer engineering educator; b. NYC, Dec. 17, 1932; s. Fioretto and Rosina (Lachello) D.; m. Marie Madeleine Turlan, June 2, 1956; children: Christopher, Alexander, Sylvia, Veronica. BEE, CCNY, 1955; MSEE, Columbia U., 1956; DEE, Poly. Inst. N.Y., 1961. Registered profl. engr., Colo. Lectr. elec. engring. dept. CCNY, 1956-57; instr. elec. engring. Poly. Inst. N.Y., Bklyn., 1957-61, prof., 1961-72; prof. elec. engring., dir. Resource System Analysis U. Colo., Colorado Springs, 1972-76; Gardner-Zemke prof. elec. and computer engring. U. N.Mex., Albuquerque, 1984—2004, chmn. dept., 1976-84, prof. emeritus, 2005—. Hon. chaired prof. Nanjing Aero. Inst., 1989; vis. prof. Politecnico di Torino, Italy, 1991-921 dir. Ctr. for Intelligent Systems Engring. U. N.Mex., 2001. Author: Analytic Feedback Systems Design, 2000; co-author Linear Quadratic Control, 1995, Robust Control for Unstructured Perturbations, 1992, Robust Control-System Design, 1996, Italian Culture—A View from America, 2001; editor: Robust Control, Recent Results in Robust Control and Advances in Adaptive Control, reprint vols., 1987, 90, 91, IEEE Press Reprint Vol. Series, 1989-90; assoc. editor Automatica Jour., 1969-83, 89-92, editor rapid publs., 1994-98; assoc. editor IEEE Trans on Edn., 1989-91; contbr. articles on control systems theory to profl. jours. Recipient John R. Ragazzini edn. award Am. Automatic Control Coun., 1998 Fellow IEEE (3rd Millenium medal); mem. IEEE Control Systems Soc. (Disting. Mem. award)., World Automation Congress (Life Achievement award 2002). Democrat. Home: 1514 Roma Ave NE Albuquerque NM 87106-4513 Office: Dept Elec & Comp Engrs MSCOI 1100 1 Univ Mex Albuquerque NM 87131-0001 Business E-Mail: pdorato@ece.unm.edu.

DORCHAK, GLENDA MARY, computer software company executive; b. 1954; Various positions IBM Canada, 1974—92; dir. sales and svc. AMBRA, 1993; various exec. positions in sales, mktg. and planning IBM US, 1993; pres. Value Am., Inc., Charlottesville, Va., 1998—99; chmn., CEO Value America, Inc., 2000; v.p., COO Communications Group Intel Corp., v.p., Desktop Platforms Group, gen. mgr., Consumer Electronics Group; chmn., CEO Intrinsyc Software Internat., 2006—08; CEO VirtualLogix, Inc., Sunnyvale, Calif., 2009—. Bd. dirs. VirtualLogix, Inc., 2009—. Named one of The Top 25 Executives of the New Millennium, Computer Reseller News, 1999. Office: VirtualLogix Inc 292 Gibraltar Dr Bldg 104 Sunnyvale CA 94089*

DORER, FRED HAROLD, retired chemistry educator; b. Auburn, Calif., May 3, 1936; s. Fred H. and Mary E. (Fisher) D.; m. Marilyn Pearl Young, Sept. 6, 1958; children: Garrett Michael, Russell Kenneth. BS, Calif. State U.-Long Beach, 1961; PhD, U. Wash., 1965; postgrad., U. Freiburg, (Germany), 1965-66. Rsch. chemist Shell Devel. Co., Emeryville, Calif., 1966-67; prof. chemistry Calif. State U., Fullerton, 1967-75; assoc. program dir. chem. dynamics NSF, Washington, 1974-75; chmn., prof. chemistry San Francisco State U., 1975-81; dean natural sci. Sonoma State U., Rohnert Park, Calif., 1981-82, provost, v.p., 1982-84; acad. v.p. Calif. State U., Bakersfield, 1984-99, provost v.p., 1996-99, ret., 1999, emeritus provost, v.p. acad. affairs, 2000—. Contbr. articles to profl. jours. Served with USMC, 1954-57. Grantee Research Corp., 1968; grantee NSF, 1969-75, Petroleum Research Fund, 1978, 80; fellow NSF, 1965 Mem. AAAS, Am. Chem. Soc. Home: 5704 Muirfield Dr Bakersfield CA 93306-9518

DOREY, WILLIAM G., construction executive; BS in Constrn. Mgmt., Ariz. State U. Br. mgr. Granite Constrn., Inc., Santa Barbara, Calif., 1973-83, asst. divsn. mgr., br. divsn. mgr., sr. v.p., mgr. br. divsn., 1983—87; exec. v.p., COO Granite Constrn. Inc., 1998—2003, pres., COO, 2003—04, pres., CEO, 2004—. also: PO Box 50085 Watsonville CA 95077-5085 Office: Granite Constrn Inc PO Box 50085 Watsonville CA 95077-5085

DORF, RICHARD CARL, electrical engineering and management educator; b. NYC, Dec. 27, 1933; s. William Carl and Marion (Fraser) D.; m. Joy H. MacDonald, June 15, 1957; children: Christine, Renée. BS, Clarkson U., 1955; MS, U. Colo., 1957; PhD, U.S. Naval Postgrad. Sch., 1961. Registered profl. engr., Calif. Instr. Clarkson U., Potsdam, N.Y., 1956-58; instr., asst. prof. U.S. Naval Postgrad. Sch., Monterey, Calif., 1958-63; prof., chmn. U. Santa Clara, Calif., 1963-69; v.p. Ohio U., Athens, 1969-72; dean of extended learning U. Calif., Davis, 1972-81, prof. in mgmt. and elec. engring., 1972—. Lectr. U. Edinburgh, Scotland, 1961-62; cons. Lawrence Livermore (Calif.) Nat. Lab., 1981—; chmn. Sacramento Valley Venture Capital Forum, 1985-90. Author: The Mutual Fund Portfolio Planner, 1988, The New Mutual Fund Advisor, 1988, Electric Circuits, 5d edit., 2000, Modern Control Systems, 9th edit., 2000; editor: Ency. of Robotics, 1987, Circuits, Devices and Systems, 1991, Handbook of Electrical Engineering, 2d edit., 1997, Handbook of Manufacturing and Automation, 1994, Handbook of Technology Management, 1999, Technology, Humans and Society, 2001. Bd. dirs. Sta. KVIE, PBS, Sacramento, 1976-79; ruling elder Davis Cmty. Ch., 1973-76, 1999—; chmn. Sonoma Valley Econ. Devel. Assn., 1993-2000; mem. City Coun., City of Sonoma, 1994-98; vice mayor City of Sonoma, 1994, 98, mayor, 1996; chmn. Davis Open Space Commn., 2000—. With U.S. Army, 1956. Recipient Alumni award Clarkson U., 1979, Disting. Alumni award Colo. U., 1998. Fellow IEEE; mem. Am. Soc. Engring. Edn. (sr., chmn. div. 1980—), University Club (bd. dirs. 1988-91), Rotary (bd. dirs. 1978-80). Presbyterian. Office: U Calif Elec Engring Dept Davis CA 95616 E-mail: rcdorf@ucdavis.edu.

DORFAN, JONATHAN MANNIE, physicist, researcher; b. Cape Town, South Africa, Oct. 10, 1947; came to U.S., 1969; s. Charles Archie and Esther (Levine) D.; m. Renee Bing, Dec. 15, 1969; children: Nicole Michelle, Rachel Lauren. BS, U. Cape Town, 1969; PhD, U. Calif., Irvine, 1976. Rsch. assoc. Stanford Linear Accelerator Ctr., Calif., 1976-78, staff physicist Calif., 1978-83, assoc. prof. Calif., 1984-88, prof. physics Calif., 1989—, assoc. dir. Calif., 1994-99, dir. Calif., 1999—2007, dir. emeritus Calif., 2007—; asst. to pres. Stanford U., 2007—. Mem. high energy physics adv. panel U.S. Dept. Energy, 1991—94; mem. exec. bd. BaBar, 1994—99; mem. adv. coun. Princeton Plasma Physics Lab., 2000—; mem. sci. adv. bd. Max Planck Inst., 2000—; mem. Internat. Com. Future Accelerators, 2000—. Fellow: Am. Phys. Soc., Am. Acad. Arts & Scis. Office: Stanford Linear Accelerator Ctr Mail Stop 75 2575 Sand Hill Rd Menlo Park CA 94025 E-mail: jonathan.dorfan@slac.stanford.edu.

DORFMAN, WILLIAM M. (BILL DORFMAN), dentist; b. 1958; children: Anna, Charlotte, Georgia. Grad., UCLA, 1980; DDS, U. Pacific, San Francisco, 1983. Dental resident, Lausanne, Switzerland, 1983—85; pvt. practice aesthetic and gen. dentistry LA, 1985—; founder Discus Dental, Inc., LA, 1989—. Dental cons. ABC's Extreme Makeover, NBC's The Today Show, NBC's Entertainment Tonight, NBC's EXTRA, NBC's The Rosie O'Donnell Show, E! Entertainment TV; founder, program coord. P.A.C.-live, U. Pacific Dental Sch., San Francisco; lectr. in field. Author: The Smile Guide; past editor Jour. Am. Acad. Cosmetic Dentistry; contbr. articles to profl. jours.; guest appearances Channel 4 News, LA, Channel 7 News. Judge Miss S.C. beauty pageant; raised and donated with Crown Coun. of Dentists to St Jude's Children Rsch. Hosp., Children's Dental Ctr., & Garth Brooks' Teammates for Kids Found. Recipient Lifetime Achievement awards (2), Outstanding Sr. award, UCLA, 1980; named Best Aesthetic Dentist in L.A., L.A. Mag. Fellow: Am. Acad. Cosmetic Dentistry; mem.: ADA. Recognized as one of the country's leading dentists and is responsible for creating smiles for famous Hollywood stars; developed products such as: Nite White, Day White, Zoom!, Breath Rx. Office: Discus Dental Inc Century City Aesthetic Dentistry 2080 Century Park E Ste 1601 Los Angeles CA 90067 Office Phone: 310-277-5678. Office Fax: 310-277-3294. Business E-Mail: billd@discusdental.com.

DORIAN, BRETT J., federal judge; b. 1934; BA, San Francisco State U., 1959; JD, Boalt Hall, 1962. Apptd. bankruptcy judge ea. dist. U.S. Dist. Ct. Calif., 1988—. With U.S. Army, 1952-54. Office: 2656 US Courthouse 1130 O St Fresno CA 93721-2201 Fax: 209-498-7344.

DORLEAC, CATHERINE See DENEUVE, CATHERINE

DORMAN, ALBERT A., engineering executive, consultant, architect; b. Phila., Apr. 30, 1926; s. William and Edith (Kleiman) D.; m. Joan Bettie Heiten, July 29, 1950; children: Laura Jane, Kenneth Joseph, Richard Coleman. BS, Newark Coll. Engring., 1945; MS, U. So. Calif., 1962; ScD (hon.), N.J. Inst. Tech., 1999. Registered profl. engr., Calif., N.Y., Ill., Oreg., Ariz., Nev., registered architect, Calif., Oreg. Owner firm Albert A. Dorman, Hanford, Calif., 1954-66; v.p. Daniel, Mann, Johnson & Mendenhall, Los Angeles, 1967-73, pres., chief oper. officer, 1974-77, pres., chief exec. officer, 1977-84, chmn., chief exec. officer, 1984-91, chmn., 1991-99; chmn., chief exec. officer AECOM Tech. Corp., LA, 1984-91, chmn., 1991-92; founding chmn. AECOM Tech Corp., LA, 1992—; chmn. Holmes & Narver, Inc., Orange, Calif., 1991-97, Frederic R. Harris, Inc., NYC, 1988-91, Consoer, Townsend and Assocs., Inc., Chgo., 1988-91. Pres., chmn. bd. dirs. Hanford Savs. & Loan Assn., 1963-72; chair com. on bus strategies for pub. capital investment NRC, 2002-04; rsch. prof. U. So. Calif., Viterbi Sch. Engring., 2005—, distng. rsch. prof. NJIT, 2008-. Contbr. articles to profl. jours. Pres. Kings County Concerts Assn., 1962-64; past mem. bd. councilors Sch. Urban and Regional Planning, U. So. Calif., Viterbi Sch. Engring., U. So. Calif., 2004—; trustee Harvey Mudd Coll., 1988-2005, J. David Gladstone Found., 1988—, Nat. Found. Advancement in Arts, 1988-99; bd. overseers N.J. Inst. Tech., 1989—; vice chmn. Los Angeles County Earthquake Fact-Finding Commn., 1980. With U.S. Army, 1945-47. Recipient Civil Engring. Alumnus award U. So. Calif., 1976, Edward F. Weston medal N.J. Inst. Tech., 1986, Golden Beaver Engring. award, 1991, Eponym, Albert Dorman Honors Coll., N.J. Inst. Tech., 1993, Disting. Award of Merit, ACEC, 1996, Medal, U. Calif., San Francisco, 1996. Fellow AIA, ASCE (hon. mem., Harland Bartholomew award 1976, Opal Outstanding Lifetime Achievement award 2000, Parcel-Sverdrup Civil Engring. Mgmt. award 1987, pres. L.A. sect. 1984-85), Am. Cons. Engrs. Coun. (life); mem. NAE (elected mem.), Real Estate Constrn. Industries (Humanitarian award 1986), Am. Pub. Works Assn. (life), Cons. Engrs. Assn. Calif. (bd. dirs. 1982-88, pres. 1985-86), Am. Water Works Assn. (life), Water Pollution Control Fedn. (life), Calif. C. of C. (bd. dirs. 1986-94), L.A. Area C. of C. (bd. dirs. 1983-88, exec. com. 1985-87), Calif. Club, Met. Club, Kiwanis (pres. 1962), Tau Beta Pi, Chi Epsilon. Office: AECOM Tech Corp Ste 3700 555 S Flower St Los Angeles CA 90071-2300

DORMAN, CRAIG EMERY, oceanographer, academic administrator; b. Cambridge, Mass., Aug. 27, 1940; s. Carlton Earl and Sarah Elizabeth (Emery) D.; m. Cynthia Eileen Larson, Aug. 25, 1962; children: Clifford Ellery, Clark Evans, Curt Emerson. BA, Dartmouth Coll., 1962; MS, Navy Post Grad. Sch., 1969; PhD, MIT/WHOI Joint Prog. Oceanog., 1972. Commd. ensign USN, 1962, advanced through grades to rear adm., 1987, ret., 1989; CEO Woods Hole (Mass.) Oceanographic Instn., 1989-93; dep. dir. Def. Rsch. and Engring. for Lab. Mgmt., Washington, 1993-95; sr. scientist Applied Rsch. Lab. Pa. State U., 1995—2002; chief scientist, tech. dir. internat. field office Office Naval Rsch., 1995-98, ONROID, 1998-99; chief scientist ONR, 1999—2001; govt. coord., GSC chair Medea, 2000—02; chief scientist CH Internat. Assts., 2001—; v.p. rsch. and acad. affairs U. Alaska, Fairbanks, 2002—. Vis. prof. Imperial Coll., London, 1996-97. Decorated Legion of Merit (2). Mem. Russian Acad. Natural Sci. Office: University of Alaska Rsch & Acad Affairs Ste 202 Butrovich Fairbanks AK 99775-5320 Office Phone: 807-450-8018. E-mail: craig.dorman@alaska.edu.

DORMAN, DAVID W., management consultant, former telecommunications industry executive; b. Atlanta, Jan. 1954; m. Susan P. Dorman, 1971; 3 children. BS in Indsl. Mgmt., Ga. Inst. Tech., 1975. Pres. Sprint Bus. Services, 1990—94; chmn., pres., CEO Pacific Bell, 1994—97; exec. v.p. SBC Comm., 1997; chmn., pres., CEO PointCast Inc., 1997—98; CEO Concert Comm. Co., 1998—2000; pres. AT&T Corp., 2000—02, chmn., CEO, 2002—05; pres. AT&T Inc. (merger of SBC Comm. & AT&T Corp.), San Antonio, 2005—06; mng. dir., sr. adv. Warburg Pincus LLC, San Francisco, 2006—; non-exec. chmn. Motorola, Inc., Schaumburg, Ill., 2008—. Bd. dirs. AT&T Corp., 2002—05, AT&T Inc. (merger of SBC Comm. & AT&T Corp.), 2005—06, YUM! Brands, Inc., 2005—, CVS Corp., 2006—, Motorola Inc., 2006—. Bd. dirs. Episcopal H.S., Alexandria, Va.; Ga. Tech. Found. Office: Warburg Pincus LLC Ste 1250 1 Embarcadero Ctr San Francisco CA 94111

DORNAN, ROBERT KENNETH, former congressman; b. NYC, Apr. 3, 1933; s. Harry Joseph and Gertrude Consuelo (McFadden) D.; m. Sallie Hansen, Apr. 16, 1955; children: Robin Marie, Robert Kenneth II, Theresa Ann, Mark Douglas, Kathleen Regina. Student, Loyola U., Westchester, Calif., 1950-53. Nat. spokesman Citizens for Decency Through Law, 1973-76; mem. 95th-97th Congresses from 27th Calif. dist., 1977-83, 99th-103rd Congresses from 38th Calif. dist., 1985-93, 103rd Congress and 104th Congress from 46th Calif. dist., 1993—97. Chmn. Armed Svcs. Subcom. on Mil. Pers., chmn. Tech. and Tactical Intelligence Subcom., Permanent Select Intelligence Com., 1988-97. Host TV polit. talk shows in Los Angeles, 1965-73; host, prodr.: Robert K. Dornan Show, LA, 1970-73, (talk radio network) The Bob Dornan Show, 1999-05; combat photographer/broadcast journalist assigned 8 times to Laos-Cambodia-Vietnam, 1965-74; originator POW/MIA bracelet. Served to capt., fighter pilot USAF, 1953-58, fighter pilot, amphibian rescue pilot and intelligence officer USAFR, 1958-75. Mem. Am. Legion, Navy League, Air Force Assn., Res. Officers Assn., AMVET, Assn. Former Intelligence Officers, Am. Helicopter Soc. Special Forces Assn., AFTRA. Lodges: K.C. Republican. Roman Catholic.

DORNE, DAVID J., lawyer; b. Chgo., Dec. 9, 1946; BS magna cum laude, U. Ill., 1969; MSc, London Sch. Econs., 1970; JD cum laude, Boston U., 1973. Bar: N.Y. 1973, U.S. Ct. Appeals (2d cir.) 1973, U.S. Tax Ct. 1973, U.S. Dist. Ct. (so. dist.) N.Y. 1975, Calif. 1978. Mem. Seltzer Caplan McMahon Vitek P.C., San Diego. Mem. City of San Diego Charter Rev. Commn., 1989—. Mem. ABA (taxation sect., corp., banking and bus. law sect.), State Bar Calif. (taxation sect., real property law sect., chmn. personal income tax subcom. 1982-84), San Diego County Bar Assn., Assn. of Bar of City of N.Y. (taxation sect.), Beta Gamma Sigma. Office: Seltzer Caplan McMahon Vitek PC 2100 Symphony Tower 750 B St San Diego CA 92101-8114 Office Phone: 619-685-3003.

DORNFELD, DAVID ALAN, engineering educator; b. Horicon, Wis., Aug. 3, 1949; s. Harlan Edgar and Cleopatra D.; Barbara Ruth Dornfeld, Sept. 18, 1976. BS in Mech. Engring. with honors, U. Wis., 1972, MS in Mech. Engring., 1973, PhD in Mech. Engring., 1976. Asst. prof. dept. sys. design U. Wis., Milw., 1976-77; asst. prof. mfg. engring. U. Calif., Berkeley, 1977-83, assoc. prof. mfg. engring., 1983-89, vice-chmn. instrn. dept. mech. engring., 1987-88, dir. Engring. Sys. Rsch. Ctr., 1989-98, prof. mfg. engring., 1989—, Will C. Hall Family prof. engring., 1999—2008, assoc. dean interdisciplinary studies Coll. Engring., 2001—; assoc. dir. rsch. Ecole Nationale Superieure des Mines de Paris, Berkeley, 1983-84. Invited prof. Ecole Nationale Superieure D'Arts et Metiers, Paris, 1992-93; cons., expert witness for intellectual property issues, sensor systems, mfg. automation, sustainable mfg. Contbr. articles to profl. jours., chpts. in books; presenter numerous seminars, confs.; patentee in field. Recipient Dist. Svc. citation U. Wis. Coll. Engring. Madison, 2000. Fellow ASME (past editor, mem. editl. bd. Mfg. Rev. Jour., pres advisory com., Blackall Machine Tool and Gage Award 1990), Soc. Mfg. Engrs. (fellow editl. bd. Jour. Mfg. Systems, Outstanding Young Engr. award 1982, Frederick W. Taylor Rsch. medal 2004); mem. Am. Soc.

Precision Engring., Acoustic Emission Working Group, N.Am. Mfg. Rsch. Inst. (past pres., scientific com.), Japan Soc. Precision Engring. (Takagi award 2005), Coll. Internat. pour l'Etude Scientifique des Techniques de Production Mechanique (CIRP). Avocations: hiking, travel, reading. Office: U Calif Dept Mech Engring Berkeley CA 94720-1740 Home Phone: 510-524-8890; Office Phone: 510-642-0906. E-mail: dornfeld@berkeley.edu.

DORPAT, THEODORE LORENZ, psychoanalyst; b. Miles City, Mont., Mar. 25, 1925; s. Theodore Ertman and Eda (Christiansen) D.; married; 1 child, Joanne Katherine. BS, Whitworth Coll., 1948; MD, U. Wash., Seattle, 1952; grad., Seattle Psychoanalytic Inst., 1964. Resident in psychiatry Seattle VA Hosp., 1953-55, Cin. Gen. Hosp., 1955-56; instr. in psychiatry U. Wash., 1956-58, asst. prof. psychiatry, 1958-59, assoc. prof., 1969-75, prof., 1976—; practice medicine specializing in psychiatry Seattle, 1958-64; practice psychoanalysis, 1964; instr. Seattle Psychoanalytic Inst., 1966-71, tng. psychoanalyst, 1971—, dir., 1984. Chmn. Wash. Gov.'s Task Force for Commitment Law Reform; trustee Seattle Cmty. Psychiat. Clinic; pres., trustee Seattle Psychoanalytic Inst. Contbr. numerous articles, books, revs. to profl. jours. Served to ensign USNR, 1943-46. Fellow Am. Psychiat. Assn.; mem. Am. Psychoanalytic Assn., AMA, Seattle Psychoanalytic Soc. (sec.-treas. 1965-67, pres. 1972-73), AAAS, Alpha Omega Alpha, Sigma Xi. Home: 7700 E Green Lake Dr N Seattle WA 98103-4971 Office: Blakely Bldg 2271 NE 51st St Seattle WA 98105-5713 Home Phone: 206-526-8165; Office Phone: 206-522-8553.

DORR, AIMEE, dean, education educator; b. LA, Sept. 20, 1942; d. Thomas Osborn and Mary Alice (Perkey) D.; m. Larry John Leifer, Dec. 19, 1962 (div.); 1 child, Simeon Kel Leifer; m. Donald Warren Bremme, Aug. 6, 1977 (div.); 1 child, John Thomas Dorr-Bremme; m. Donald Ross Simpson, Feb. 19, 1989. BS, Stanford U., 1964, MA, 1966, PhD in Psychology, 1970. Acting asst. prof. communication Stanford U., 1967-70, research assoc. in psychiatry and communication, 1970-71, research assoc. in psychiatry, acting asst. prof. communication, childcare policy analyst in Pres.'s Office, 1971-72; asst. prof. edn. Harvard U., Cambridge, Mass., 1972-76, assoc. prof., 1976-78; assoc. prof. communications Annenberg Sch. Communication U. So. Calif., Los Angeles, 1978—81, prof., 1981; prof. edn. UCLA, 1981—, dean Sch. Edn. & Info. Systems, 2005—. Cons. Children's TV Workshop, NBC, KCET, Children's Advt. Rev. Unit, others. Author: Television and Children: A Special Medium for a Special Audience, 1986; editor: (with Edward L. Palmer) Children and the Faces of Television-Teaching, Violence, Selling, 1980, 2d edit., 1981; contbr. articles to profl. jours. Fellow Am. Psychol. Assn., Am. Ednl. Research Assn., Soc. Research in Child Devel., Internat. Communication Assn., Amnesty Internat., Friends Com. on Nat. Legis. Democrat.

DORR, LAWRENCE DOUGLAS, orthopedic surgeon; b. Storm Lake, Iowa, 1941; m. Marilyn Dorr. BA in English, Cornell Coll., 1963; MS, U. Iowa, 1965, MD, 1967. Cert. Orthopaedic Surgery, 1978. Intern, orthopedics LA County, U. So. Calif. Sch. Med., 1967—68, resident, joint replacement surgery, 1974—76; fellow Hosp. Spl. Surgery, NYC, 1976—77; founder (Calif. based inst.), med. dir. Dorr Inst., Centinela Hosp. Med. Ctr., Inglewood, Calif., 2001—; prof. U. So. Calif. Sch. Medicine, LA. Founder, med. staff mem. Operation Walk, 1994—; lectr. in field; researcher in field. Featured on Miracle Workers (ABC), 2006; contbr. articles to profl. jours. Bd. trustee Cornell Coll. Recipient Humanitarian Yr. award, Am. Acad. Orthopedic Surgeons for work with Operation Walk, 2005, Cornell Coll. Disting. Achievement award, 2003, Disting. Alumni award, U. Iowa, 2006. Mem.: Hip Soc. (pres. elect 2006). Office: Centinela Freeman Health Systems Arthritis Inst Centinela Campus 555 E Hardy St Inglewood CA 90301 Home Phone: 818-952-1281; Office Phone: 310-695-4800. E-mail: patriciajpaul@yahoo.com.

DORSEY, DOLORES FLORENCE, retired corporate treasurer, finance company executive; b. Buffalo, May 26, 1928; d. William G. and Florence R. D. BS, Coll. St. Elizabeth, 1950. With Aerojet-Gen. Corp., 1953—, asst. to treas. El Monte, Calif., 1972-74, asst. treas., 1974-79, treas., 1979—2001, ret., 2001. Mem. adv. bd. Scripps Ctr. for Integrative Medicine, 2001—. Mem. Cash Mgmt. Group San Diego (past pres.), Nat. Assn. Corp. Treas., Fin. Execs. Inst. (v.p.). Republican. Roman Catholic.

DORSEY, JACK, software architect; Attended, NYU. Worked with dispatch co., Manhattan, NY, 1999—2000; owner of co. to dispatch couriers, taxis and emergency services from the web Calif., 2000; co-founder Obvious Corp. (spun off Twitter, Inc.), 2006; creator Twitter.com, Calif., 2006; co-founder Twitter, Inc., Calif., 2007, CEO Calif., 2007—08, chmn. Calif., 2008—. Mem. adv. bd. Ustream.tv, 2009—. Named one of Technology's Best and Brightest Young Entrepreneurs, Bus. Week, The World's Most Influential People, TIME mag., 2009; named to TR35, an outstanding innovator under the age of 35, MIT Tech. Rev. Office: Twitter Inc 539 Bryant St Ste 402 San Francisco CA 94107*

DOSCHER, RICHARD JOHN, protective services official; b. Livermore, Calif., Aug. 31, 1952; s. Henry John and Violet Mary (Sutton) D.; m. Kathryn Laura Vierria, May 5, 1979; children: Cameron, Shannon. AS in Adminstrn. Justice with honors, Yuba C.C., Maryville, Calif., 1991; BPA with honors, U. San Francisco, 1991, MPA with honors, 1993. Chief of police Yuba City (Calif.) Police Dept., 1995—, peace officer, 1977—. Adj. prof. ethics and professionalism/history Yuba C.C., 1997--2003; adj. prof. law enforcement history Calif. State Jr. Coll., 1996-; pres. Calif. 911 adv. bd., 2005-; guest lectr. orgnl. behavior U. San Francisco, 1993-. Bd. dirs. Yuba/Sutter Easter Seal Soc., 1988-96; vol. Calif. Prune Festival, 1988—, Spl. Olympics, 1987—, Bok Kai Chinese Cultural Festival, 1993—, Yuba City Cmty. Theater, 1992—; adv. com. Adminstrn. of Justice Yuba Coll., 1993—; eucharistic min. St. Isidore's Cath. Ch., 1984—; hon. squadron comdr. security forces Beale AFB, 1998-, lt. col., With USAF, 1972-76. Decorated Air Force Commendation medal; recipient Helen Putnam award, League Calif. Cities Pub. Safety Com., 1995—, Diversity Recognition award, Sikh Cmty., 1996—, award, City Excellence Cmty. Svc. award, 2001, Dept. Life Saving medal, 2001, Dept. Meritorious Svc. medal, 2004, Police Unit Commendation, 2007; nominee Europe One of Twelve Outstanding Airman, USAF, 1974, Airman of Yr., 1974, Police Officer of Yr., RAF Lakenheath, 1974. Mem. Am. Soc. for Pub. Adminstrn., Calif. Assn. Police Tng. Officers, Calif. Police Chiefs Assn. (bd. dirs. 1998—, area rep. 1996-), Calif. Peace Officers Assn., Peace Officers' Rsch. Assn. Calif., Yuba City Police Officers Assn. (past officer 1978-80), League of Calif. Cities (pub. safety com. 1996--), Kiwanis Club (bd. dirs., 2d v.p. Yuba City), Yuba City Health and Racquet Club, Am. Quarter Horse Assn., Beale Mil. Liaison Com. Avocations: astronomy, horseback riding. Office: Yuba City Police Dept 1545 Poole Blvd Yuba City CA 95993-2615 Home Phone: 530-674-0166; Office Phone: 530-822-4664. Personal E-mail: rooscher@yubacity.net, richardd8@sbcglobal.net.

DOTI, JAMES L., academic administrator; Dean Chapman U., 1991—, pres., 1991—. Office: Chapman U Office of President 1 University Dr Orange CA 92866-1005

DOTOLO, VINNY, chef; b. Clearwater, Fla., 1979; Grad., Inst. Ft. Lauderdale. Chef The Strand restaurant, South Beach, Mark's, Café Maxx, The River House, Wildflower Restaurant, Vail, Chadwick Restaurant, LA; co-owner, exec. chef Animal Restaurant, LA, 2008—. Co-owner, chef catering bus. Chef (TV series) Two Dudes Catering, The Food Network; co-author: Two Dudes One Pan, 2008 (Top 10 Cookbooks of 2008, Nat. Pub. Radio). Named one of America's Best New Chefs, Food & Wine Mag., 2009. Office: Animal Restaurant 435 N Fairfax Ave Los Angeles CA 90036 Office Phone: 323-782-9225.*

DOTSON, NANCY JEAN DAVIS, secondary school educator; b. Houston, Feb. 5, 1941; d. Willie and Callie D. (Morris) Davis; m. Earl Leslie Dotson, Oct. 2, 1964; children: Lisa Chandra, Leslie Chan, Lamar Cedric. BS, So. Univ., Baton Rouge, 1962; MS, Pepperdine U., 1974; postgrad., U. So. Calif., U. Calif., LA. Cert. elem. tchr.; cert. secondary tchr.; cert. supervision K-12; cert. gen. adminstrn. Tchr. Houston Ind. Sch. Dist., 1962-64; math., sci. tchr. Gompers Jr. High Sch., LA, 1964-70, math. tchr., coord., 1970-72; math. area advisor Area C, Title I Office, L.A. USD, 1972-76; compensatory edn. coord. Drew Jr. High Sch L.A. USD, 1976-88, categorical programs advisor, coord., 1988—. Owner, dir., cons. Agape Resource Ctr., Carson, Calif., 1988—. Contbr. instructional bulls. and aids and other writings for profls. local schs. V.p. Wheatley West Alumni, Inc., Carson, 1982—; sec. Good Neighbors Fariman Dr. Block Club, Carson, 1984—; vol. Harbor Christian Ctr. Libr., Wilmington, Calif., 1979—. Recipient edn. grants Pepperdine U., 1973, 74; Recipient Thank you for Sharing and Caring plaque Calif. Congress of Parents and Tchrs., 1969. Mem. ASCD, Nat. Coun. Tchrs. Maths., Internat. Alliance for Invitational Edn., Nat. Staff Devel. Coun., Calif. Math. Coun. (southern section pres., speaker), L.A. City Tchrs. Maths. Assn. (pres., speaker), Calif. Staff Devel. Coun., Calif. Assn. Supervision and Curriculum, Basic Coun. Edn., Assn. Tchr. Educators (pres., speaker, Nat. Mid. Sch. Assn., Calif. League Mid. Schs., Computer Using Educators, Inc., State Calif. Assn. Tchr. Educators, Secondary Coords. Assn. (pres. 1981—, Outstanding Svc. plaque, 1981-83, engraved gavel, 1981-83). Avocations: collecting quotations, collecting butterflies, travel, reading.

DOTTEN, MICHAEL CHESTER, lawyer; b. Marathon, Ont., Can., Feb. 23, 1952; arrived in US, 1957, naturalized; s. William James and Ona Adelaide (Sheppard) D.; m. Kathleen Curtis, Aug. 17, 1974 (div. July 1991); children: Matthew Curtis, Tyler Ryan; m. Cheryl Calvin, Apr. 16, 1994. BS in Polit. Sci., U. Oreg., 1974, JD, 1977. Bar: Idaho 1977, Oreg. 1978, Washington. 2005, US Dist. Ct. Idaho 1977, US Dist. Ct. Oreg. 1978, US Ct. Appeals (9th cir.), US Ct. Appeals (DC cir.) 1987, US Ct. Claims 1986, US Supreme Ct. 1996. Staff asst. to Senator Bob Packwood, U.S. Senate, Washington, 1973-74; asst. atty. gen. State of Idaho, Boise, Idaho, 1977-78; chief rate counsel Bonneville Power Adminstrn., Portland, Oreg., 1978-83; spl. counsel Heller, Ehrman, White & McAuliffe, Portland, 1983-84, ptnr., 1985-98, 99—; gen. counsel PG&E Gas Transmission, N.W. Corp., Portland, 1998-99; co-chair Energy Nat. Practice Group, 2003—06. Utility com. mem. Ctr. for Pub. Resources, N.Y.C., 1992—; Nat. Panel Arbitrators, Am. Arbitration Assn., 2005-; Panel Arbitrators and Mediators, U.S. Arbitration and Mediation Oreg., 2005-. Coun. Emanual Hosp. Assocs., Portland, 1988-92; bd. dirs. William Temple House, 1995-99, chmn. devel. com., 1996-98, v.p., 1997-98, pres., 1998-99; active Portland Interneighborhood Trans. Rev. Commn., 1986-88; vestryman Christ Episcopal Ch., Lake Oswego, Oreg., 1999-03, sr. warden, 2001-03; bd. dirs. Health Bridges Internat., Inc., 2006-, treas., 2007—; pres. Arlington Club Toastmasters, 2006. Hunter Leadership scholar U. Oreg., 1973, Oreg. scholar, 1970. Mem. ABA (chmn. electric power com. sect. natural resources 1985-88, coun. liaison energy com. 1990-93, coordinating group on energy law 1992-96), Fed. Bar Assn. (pres. Oreg. chpt. 1989-90, Chpt. Activity award 1990, Pres. award 1988-89), Oreg. State Bar (chmn. dispute resolution com. 1986-87), U. Oreg. Law Sch. Alumni Assn. (pres. 1989-92), Am. Arbitration Assn., Arlington Club, Multnomah Athletic Club. Democrat. Episcopalian. Avocations: skiing, golf, hiking, travel, racquetball. Office: Heller Ehrman White & McAuliffe 701 Fifth Ave Seattle WA 98104 Office Phone: 206-389-6111, 503-795-7420. Business E-Mail: michael.dotten@hellerehrman.com.

DOUCET, DAVID, musician; Mem. band BeauSoleil, 1976—. Albums include The Spirit of Cajun Music, 1976, Parlez Nous au Boire, 1984, Louisiana Cajun Music, 1984, Zydeco Gris Gris, 1985, Allons a Laayette, 1986, Bayou Boogie, 1986, Bayou Cadillac, 1989, Live! From the Left Coast, 1989, Quand J'ai Parti, 1989, Deja Vu, 1990, Cajun Conja, 1991, La Danse de la Vie, 1993, L'Echo, 1994, L'Amour ou la Folie, 1995 (Grammy award for Best Traditional Folk Album, 1997), Arc de Triomphe Two-Step, Looking Back Tomorrow, 2001, Gitane Cajun, Live in Louisiana, 2006, Live At The 2008 New Orleans Jazz & Heritage Festival (Grammy award for Best Cajun Album, 2009), Alligator Purse, 2009. Recipient Big Easy Entertainment award for Best Cajun Band, 2005. Office: care Rosebud Agy PO Box 170429 San Francisco CA 94117-0429

DOUCET, MICHAEL, musician, songwriter; b. Scott, La., 1951; m. Sharon Arms; children: Melissa, Ezra, Matthew. BA in English, La. State U., 1973. With Coteau band, until 1977; Cajun fiddler, leader, solo artist BeauSoleil band, 1975—, extensive tours in Mid. East, Europe, N.Am., S.Am. Performer traditional, acoustic and rock bands, including Coteau, before 1977, Savoy-Doucet band. Albums (with BeauSoleil) include La Nuit, 1976, The Spirit of Cajun Music, 1977, Les Amis Cadjins, 1979 (reissued as Zydeco), Dit Beausoleil, 1981, Parlez-Nous au Boire, 1984, Louisiana Cajun Music, 1984, Allons a Lafayette, 1986, Belizaire the Cajun (original motion picture soundtrack, Grammy award nominee), 1986, Gris-Gris, 1986, Bayou Cadillac, 1988 (Grammy award nominee), Cajun Brew, 1988, Cajun Experience, 1988, Hot Chile Mama, 1988, Quand J'ai Parti, 1989, Cajun Jam Session, 1989, Two Step d'Amede, 1989, Live! From the Left Coast, 1989, Bayou Boogie, 1989, DeJa Vu, 1990, Beau Solo, 1990, J'ai Ete au Bal, 1990, Hoogie Boogie/French Music for Childen, 1991, Cajun Conja, 1991 (Grammy award nominee), Bayou Deluxe, 1993, Home Music with Spirits, 1993, La Danse de la Vie, 1993 (Grammy award nominee), L'Echo, 1994 (Grammy award nominee), L'Amour ou la Folie, 1995 (Grammy award for Best Traditional Folk Album, 1997), Arc de Triomphe Two-Step, 1997, Looking Back Tomorrow, 2001, Gitane Cajun, 2004, Live in Louisiana, 2006, Live at the 2008 New Orleans Jazz & Heritage Festival (Grammy award for Best Cajun Album, 2009), Alligator Purse, 2009, (with Savoy-Doucet) Les Harias Home Music, Two-step d'Amede, With Spirits, (with Danny Poullard) Cajun Jam Session, (solo albums) Cajun Jam Sessions, 1983, Dit Beausoleil, 1983, Christmas Bayou, 1986, Michael Doucet & Cajun Brew, 1988, Beau Solo, 1989, Le Hoogie Boogie: Louisiana French Music for Children, 1992, The Mad Reel, 1994, From Now On, 2008; numerous appearances on Prairie Home Companion radio show; performed at Pres. Carter's inaugural gala, 1977; composer, recorded music (with BeauSoleil) for films: Belizaire the Cajun, 1985, The Big Easy, 1987. Recipient 1st Clifton Chenier award, 1990, Big Easy award for Best Cajun Band, 2005; grantee Nat. Endowment for Arts, 1975, Nat. Heritage fellowship, Nat. Endowment for Arts, 2005. Office: care Rosebud Agy PO Box 170429 San Francisco CA 94117-0429

DOUD, JACQUELINE POWERS, academic administrator; V.p. acad. affairs Woodbury U., LA, until 1989, pres., 1989—. Office: Woodbury U 7500 N Glenoaks Blvd Burbank CA 91504-1099

DOUDNA, JENNIFER A., molecular biologist, educator; BA, Pomona Coll., 1985; PhD, Harvard U., 1989. Post-doctoral fellow Harvard Med. Sch., 1989-91, U. Colo., 1991-94; Henry Ford II prof. molecular biophysics and biochemistry Yale U., New Haven, 1994—2002, assoc. investigator Howard Hughes Med. Inst., 1997—; R. B. Woodward Visiting Prof. Harvard U., 2000—01; faculty scientist, physical biosciences div. Lawrence Berkeley Nat. Lab., 2003; faculty, biophysics grad. group U. of Calif., Berkeley, 2003—, prof. biochemistry and molecular biology, dept. chemistry, 2003—, prof. biochemistry and molecular biology, dept. molecular and cell biology, 2003—. Contbr. articles to profl. jours. Mem. bd. trustees Pomona Coll., 2001. Recipient award for initiatives in rsch., NAS, 1999, Alan T. Waterman award, NSF, 2000. Fellow: Am. Academy of Arts and Sciences; mem.: NAS. Achievements include structure and function of ribozymes and RNA-protein complexes. Office: UC Berkeley 305 Hildebrand Hall MS #3206 Berkeley CA 94720-3206

DOUGHERTY, BETSEY OLENICK, architect; b. Guanatamo Bay, Cuba, Oct. 25, 1950; (parents Am. citizens); d. Everett and Charlotte (Kristal) Olenick; m. Brian Paul Dougherty, Aug. 25, 1974; children: Gray Brenner, Megan Victoria. AB in Architecture, U. Calif., Berkeley, 1972, MArch, 1975. Registered architect, Calif.; cert. Nat. Coun. Archtl. Registration Bds. Designer, drafter Maxwell Starkman, LA, 1972-73, HO & K, San Francisco, 1975-76; job capt. Wm. Blurock & Ptnrs., Newport Beach, Calif., 1976-78; assoc. architect U. Calif., Irvine, 1978-79; arch. Dougherty & Dougherty Archs. LLP, Costa Mesa, 1979—. Author: Green Architecture, 1995; contbr. articles to profl. jours. Mem. Newport Beach Specific Area Plan Com., 1985, Career Edn. Adv. Com., Newport Beach, 1986; leader Orange County bd. Girl Scouts U.S.A., 1995-2001. Recipient Gold Nugget grand award Pacific Coast Builders Conf., 1998, Coalition for Adequate Sch. Housing award of excellence, 1992, 94, 96, Calif. Masonry award, 1992, So. Calif. Edison award of excellence, 1994, Disting. Svc. citation AIACC, 1994. Fellow AIA (pres. Orange County chpt. 1984, Calif. chpt. 1988, nat. bd. dirs. 1989-91, nat. sec. 1992-94, design awards Orange County chpt. 1981-86, 89-90, 98, Nathaniel Owings award Calif. Coun. 1997), Calif. Archtl. Found. (pres. 1995-97). Avocations: sailing, camping. Office: Dougherty & Dougherty Archs LLP 3194 Airport Loop Dr Ste D Costa Mesa CA 92626-3405

DOUGHERTY, DENNIS A., chemistry educator; b. Harrisburg, Pa., Dec. 4, 1952; s. John E. and Colleen (Canning) D.; m. Ellen M. Donnelly, June 3, 1973; children: Meghan, Kayla. BS, MS, Bucknell U., 1974; PhD, Princeton U., 1978. Postdoctoral fellow Yale U., New Haven, 1978-79; from asst. prof. to prof. Calif. Inst. Tech., Pasadena, 1979—2002, George Grant Hoag prof., 2002—. Contbr. articles to sci. jours. Recipient ICI Pharms. award for excellence in chemistry, 1991, Arthur C. Cope Scholar award, 1992; Alfred P. Sloan Found. fellow, 1983; Camille and Henry Dreyfus Tchr. scholar, 1984. Fellow AAAS, Am. Acad. Arts and Scis.; mem. Am. Chem. Soc., Biophys. Soc., Phi Beta Kappa. Home: 1817 Bushnell Ave South Pasadena CA 91030-4905 Office: Calif Inst Tech Div Chemistry & Chem Engring # 164-30 Pasadena CA 91125-0001

DOUGHERTY, ELMER LLOYD, JR., retired chemical engineering professor, consultant; b. Dorrance, Kans., Feb. 7, 1930; s. Elmer Lloyd and Nettie Linda (Anspaugh) Dougherty; m. Joan Victoria Benton, Nov. 25, 1952 (div. June 1963); children: Sharon, Victoria, Timothy, Michael(dec.); m. Ann Marie Da Silva (dec.). Student, Ft. Hays State Coll., 1946-48; BS in Chem. Engring., U. Kans., 1950; MS in Chem. Engring., U. Ill., 1952, PhD in Chem. Engring., 1955. Chem. engr. Esso Standard Oil Co., Baton Rouge, 1951-52; chem. engr. Dow Chem. Co., Freeport, Tex., 1955-58; research engr. Standard Oil of Calif., San Francisco, 1958-65; mgr. mgmt. sci. Union Carbide Corp., NYC, 1965-68; cons. chem. engring. Stamford, Conn. and Denver, 1968-71; founder and owner Maraco, Inc., Monarch Beach, Calif., 1980—; prof. chem. engring. U. So. Calif., LA, 1971-95, prof. emeritus, 1995—. Cons. OPEC, Vienna Austria, 1978-82, SANTOS, Ltd., Adelaide, Australia, 1980—, Kuwait Oil Co., 1995—, many others. Contbr. articles to profl. pubs. Named to, Kans. U. Hall of Fame, 2006. Mem. Soc. Petroleum Engrs. (Disting. mem., chmn. Los Angeles Basin sect. 1984-85, Ferguson medal 1964, J.J. Arps award 1989), Am. Inst. Chem. Engrs., Internat. Assn. Energy Economists, Inst. Mgmt. Sci., El Niguel Country (founder 1976, bd. dirs. 1976-78). Republican. Avocation: golf. Home and Office: Maraco Inc 33531 Marlinspike Dr Monarch Beach CA 92629-4426 Office Phone: 949-388-6193. Business E-Mail: eld@maraco.com.

DOUGHERTY, RALEIGH GORDON, manufacturer representative; b. Saginaw, Mich., Aug. 19, 1928; s. Raleigh Gordon and Helen Jean (McCrum) D.; 1 child, Karen Kealani. Salesman H.D. Hudson Mfg. Co., Chgo., 1946-48; field sales rep. Jensen Mfg. Co., Chgo., 1948-50; field sales mgr. Regency Idea, Indpls., 1950-54; mgr. Brenna & Browne, Honolulu, 1954-56; owner, pres. Dougherty Enterprises, Honolulu, 1956—. With U.S. Army, 1950-52. Mem. Hawaii Hotel Assn., Internat. Home Furnishings Reps. Assn., Air Force Assn., DAV (life), Navy League U.S., Am. Legion, Korean Vet., Elks (past trustee Hawaii). Republican. Methodist. Home: 115 Apolena Ave Newport Beach CA 92662-1213

DOUGLAS, BONNIE, state representative; b. Ill., Aug. 26, 1948; m. Ronald Douglas; 2 children. BA, U. Ill., 1970; student, U. Idaho. Lic. broker, ins. agt.; cons., bus. systems analyst various cos., 1970—82; office asst. Med. Office Ronald J. Douglas, 1982—; state rep. dist. 4A Idaho Ho. of Reps., Boise, 2002—. Leader La Leche League Internat., 1992—2002; treas. Kootenai County Dem. Ctrl. Com., 2000—02; bd.

dirs. ICARE, 2002. Mem.: Internat. Soc. Tech. in Edn., Fernan Elem. PTO (sec. 1995—96). Democrat. Roman Catholic. Office: State Capitol PO Box 83720 Boise ID 83720-0081

DOUGLAS, DIANE MIRIAM, museum director; b. Harrisburg, Pa., Mar. 25, 1957; d. David C. and Anna (Barron) D.; m. Steve I. Perlmutter, Jan. 23, 1983; 1 child, David Simon. BA, Brown U., 1979; MA, U. Del., 1982. Oral history editor Former Members of Congress, Washington, 1979-80; assoc. curator exhibitions John Michael Kohler Arts Ctr., Sheboygan, Wis., 1982-83; dir. arts ctr. Lill Street Gallery, Chgo., 1984-88; exec. dir. David Adler Cultural Ctr., Libertyville, Ill., 1988-91; dir. Bellevue (Wash.) Art Mus., 1992—. Program chair, exec. bd. nat. Coun. for Edn. in Ceramic Arts, Bandon, Oreg., 1990-93; nat. adv. bd. Friends of Fiber Art, 1992; artists adv. com. Pilchuck Glass Sch., 1993—; mem. bd. dirs. Archie Bray Found., Helena, Mont., 1995—.

DOUGLAS, JAMES, construction engineering educator; b. Uvalde, Tex., Oct. 1, 1914; s. Raymond C. and Mae (Savage) D.; m. Sarah Maria Bisset, July 22, 1941; children— Sarah A., Susan E., Bonnie B., James A. BS, US Naval Acad., 1938; BCE, Rensselaer Poly. Inst., 1942; MCE, 1943; PhD, Stanford U., Calif., 1963. Registered profl. engr., DC, Calif. Commd. ensign USN, 1938, advanced through grades to capt., 1956, in charge constrn. Cubi Point Naval Air Sta. Philippines, 1951-54, dir. Seabee div., 1954-58, in charge constrn. Antarctic bases Internat. Geophys. Yr., 1956-58; prof. constrn. engring. Stanford, 1963—. Cons. constrn. engring. Stanford Rsch. Inst., various corps., US and fgn. govts., 1963—; chmn. com. constrn. mgmt. Transp. Rsch. Bd., NRC, 1969-76 Author: Construction Equipment Policy, 1975, also numerous tech. articles. Active Boy Scouts Am., 1946—. Served with Armed Forces, World War II. Decorated Bronze Star; recipient Thomas Fitch Rowland prize ASCE, 1969, Constrn. Mgmt. award, 1975 Fellow ASCE (chmn. constrn. equipment com. 1960-65); mem. Tau Beta Pi, Sigma Xi, Chi Epsilon, Chi Phi. Republican. Episcopalian. Home and Office: 100 Thorndale Dr Apt 272 San Rafael CA 94903-4567 Office Phone: 415-492-2572. Personal E-mail: jdouglas38@juno.com.

DOUGLAS, JOEL BRUCE, lawyer; b. LA, Jan. 25, 1948; BA magna cum laude, Calif. State U., Northridge, 1970; postgrad., East L.A. Coll.; JD, Loyola U., LA, 1973. Bar: Calif. 1973, U.S. Dist. Ct. (ctrl. dist.) Calif. 1974, U.S. Ct. Appeals (9th cir.) 1978, U.S. Supreme Ct. 1979. Ptnr. Bonne, Bridges, Mueller, O'Keefe & Nichols P.C., LA. Adj. prof. sch. law Pepperdine U., Malibu, Calif., 1981-84; judge pro tempore L.A. Mcpl. Ct., 1980—, L.A. Superior Ct., 1988—. Assoc. editor Loyola U. L.A. Law Rev., 1972-73. Mem. ABA (litigation sect., tort and ins. practice sect.), State Bar Calif., L.A. County Bar Assn. (mem. legal-med. com. 1979-83, staff atty. med.-legal hot line 1979-82), Am. Bd. Trial Advocates, St. Thomas Moore Law Honor Soc., Phi Alpha Delta. Office: Bonne Bridges Mueller O'Keefe & Nichols PC 3699 Wilshire Blvd Fl 10 Los Angeles CA 90010-2719

DOUGLAS, KIMBERLY, university librarian; MA, Freie U., Germany, 1976; MS in Libr. Sci., Long Island U., Greenvale, NY, 1978. Position at Bigelow Lab. of Ocean Sci., Boothbay Harbor, Maine; dir. Hancock Libr. Biology & Oceanography U. So. Calif., LA, 1982—85, head Sci. & Engring. Libr., 1985—88; libr. staff Calif. Inst. Tech., Pasadena, 1988—, acting libr. dir., 2003—04, univ. libr., 2004—. Libr. adv. coun. IEEE; mem. vis. com. Goddard Space Flight Ctr. Libr. Mem.: Libr. Info. and Tech. Assn. Office: Building 1-43 Calif Inst Tech 1200 E California Blvd Pasadena CA 91125 Office Fax: 626-792-7540. E-mail: kdouglas@caltech.edu.

DOUGLAS, KIRK (ISSUR DANIELOVITCH), actor; b. Amsterdam, NY, Dec. 9, 1916; s. Harry and Bryna (Sanglel) Danielovitch; m. Diana Dill (div. Feb. 1950); children: Michael, Joel; m. Anne Buydens, May 29, 1954; children: Peter, Eric (dec. 2004) Anthony. AB, St. Lawrence U., 1938, DFA (hon.), 1958; student, Am. Acad. Dramatic Arts, 1939-41. Appeared on Broadway in Spring Again, Three Sisters, Kiss and Tell, Wind is Ninety, Alice in Arms, Man Bites Dog, One Flew Over the Cuckoo's Nest; actor: (films) The Strange Love of Martha Ivers, 1946, Morning Becomes Electra, 1947, I Walk Alone, 1947, Out of the Past, 1947, Walls of Jericho, 1948, My Dear Secretary, 1948, A Letter to Three Wives, 1948, Champion, 1949, Young Man with a Horn, 1950, The Glass Menagerie, Ace in the Hole, Along the Great Divide, Detective Story, 1951, The Big Sky, 1951, The Big Trees, The Bad and the Beautiful, 1952, Equilibrium, 1952, The Story of Three Loves, The Juggler, 1953, Act of Love, Ulysses, 20,000 Leagues Under the Sea, 1954, Man Without a Star, The Racers, 1954, Lust for Life, 1956, Top Secret Affair, Gunfight at O.K. Corral, Paths of Glory, 1957, Last Train for Gunhill, 1958, Strangers When We Meet, 1958, The Devil's Disciple, 1959, Town Without Pity, The Last Sunset, 1961, Two Weeks in Another Town, 1962, The List of Adrian Messenger, For Love or Money, The Hook, 1963, In Harm's Way, Heroes of Telemark, 1965, Cast a Giant Shadow, Is Paris Burning?, 1966, War Wagon, The Way West, 1967, A Lovely Way to Die, 1968, The Arrangement, 1969, There Was a Crooked Man, 1970, The Light at the Edge of the World, Catch Me A Spy, 1971, A Man To Respect, 1972, Master Touch, 1972, Jekyl & Hyde, 1973, Once is Not Enough, 1975, Holocaust 2000, 1977, The Fury, 1978, The Villain, 1979, Home Movies, 1979, Saturn 3, 1980, The Man from Snowy River, 1982, Eddie Macon's Run, 1983, Tough Guys, 1986, Oscar, 1991, Greedy, 1994, Welcome to Veraz, 1990, A Song for David, 1996; (TV mini-series) Queenie, 1987; (TV movies) Mousy, 1973, The Money Changers, Victory at Entebbe, 1976, Remembrance of Love, 1982, Draw!, 1984, Amos, 1985, Inherit the Wind, 1988, Touched by An Angel, 2000; actor, prodr.: (films) The Final Countdown, Indian Fighter, 1955, Vikings, 1964, Spartacus, 1960, The Last Sunset, 1961, Lonely are the Brave, 1962, Summertree, 1963, Seven Days in May, 1964, The Brotherhood, 1968, A Gunfight, 1971, Oscar, 1991, The Secret, 1991, Take Me Home Again, 1994, Diamonds, 1999, It Runs in the Family, 2003; dir. prodr.: (films) Scalawag, 1973, Posse, 1975; performer: (one man shows) Before I Forget, 2009; author: (autobiography) The Ragman's Son, 1988, Climbing the Mountain, 1997, My Stroke of Luck, 2002, Let's Face It, 2007; (novels) Dance with the Devil, 1990, The Gift, 1992, Last Tango in Brooklyn, 1994, The Broken Mirror, 1997, (juvenile) Young Heroes of the Bible, 1999. Nominated for Acad. Award, 1949, 52, 56; nominated for Emmy, 1985, 98, 2000; recipient N.Y. Film Critics award, 1956, Hollywood Fgn. Press award, 1956, Heart and Torch award Am. Heart Assn., 1956, Splendid Am. award of merit George Washington Carver Meml. Found., 1957, cited in Congl. Record for service as goodwill ambassador, 1964, Cecil B. DeMille award for contbns. in entertainment field, 1967, Presdl. Medal of Freedom, 1981, elected to Cowboy Hall of Fame, 1984, Lifetime Achievement award Am. Film Inst., 1991; decorated Legion of Honor (France), 1985, Chevalier de la Legion d'Honneur, 1985, Officer de la Legion d'Honneur, 1990; Kennedy Center Honor, 1994; Honorary Oscar, Lifetime Achievement, 1996, Meltzer award for breaking blacklist Writers Guild Am., 1999, Lifetime Achievement SAG, 1999, Golden Boot award, 1999, Spencer Tracy award Outstanding Achievement in Drama, 1999, Lifetime Achievement Jerusalem Film Festival, 2000, Golden Bear award Berlin Film Festival, 2001, Nat. medal of Arts, 2002, Excellence in Film award, Santa Barbara Internat. Film Festival, 2006. Mem. UN Assn. (dir. Los Angeles chpt.) Achievements include making State Dept.-USIA tours around world; Kirk Douglas High School named in his honor, 2000, Kirk Douglas Theatre named in his honor, 2004, Kirk Douglas Way named in his honor, 2004. E-mail: mnewberger@warrencowan.com.

DOUGLAS, MICHAEL LAWRENCE, state supreme court justice; b. LA, Mar. 13, 1948; s. Elmer Walter and Lottie Lee (Nelson) D.; m. Frankie Haws, 1968 (div. Dec. 1970); 1 child, Christine; m. A. Martha Douglas, Jan. 13, 1971. BA in Polit. Sci., Calif. State U., Long Beach, 1971; JD, U. Calif., San Francisco, 1974. Bar: Pa. 1981, US Dist. Ct. (ea. dist.) Pa. 1981, US Ct. Appeals (2d cir.) 1983, Nev. 1983, US Dist. Ct. Nev. 1983. Pvt. practice, Phila., 1981-82; directing atty. Nev. Legal Svcs., Las Vegas, 1982-84; dep. dist. atty. Clark County Dist. Atty., Las Vegas, 1984-96; dist. ct. judge State of Nev. 8th Dist. Ct., Las Vegas, 1996—2004, chief dist. ct. judge, 2003—04; justice Nev. Supreme Ct., 2004—. Instr. in law LA C.C. Dist., 1975-77; spkr. in field. Bd. dirs. Temporary Assistance for Domestic Crisis, 1983-85; mem. task force For Kids Sake/KLAS-TV, 1987-88; vol. Bridge Counseling, 1990-92; coach Ctrl. Valley Little League, 1991-95; bd. dirs. Nev. Law Found., 1991-93; mem. program com. H.P. Fitzgerald Sch., 1994-96. Recipient Svc. to Youth award YMCA LA, 1971, Proclamation for Svc. to Youth award City of LA, 1980, 81, Cmty. Svc. award Calif. State Assembly, 1981, Martin Luther King Com., LA, 1980, Proclamation for Cmty. Svc. award Clark County, 1989, Mark of Excellence award Nat. Fedn. Black Pub. Adminstrs., 1996. Mem. ABA, NAACP (fundraising com. 1990-96, freedom fund budget com. 1990-93), State Bar Nev.(atty. grievance rev. com. 1986-95, mem. disciplinary bd. 1988-95), Clark County Bar Assn., Nat. Bar Assn. (sec. Las Vegas chpt. 1985-87, pres. 1987-88, scholarship chmn. 1989-95, scholarship budget com. 1987-94, Las Vegas Svc. award 1987, 91, Pres. Appreciation award 1988, 89, 90), Pa. Bar Assn., Phila. Bar Assn., Nat. Dist. Atty.'s Assn., Nev. Gaming Attys., Hastings Coll. of Law Alumni Assn., Calif. State U.-Long Beach Alumni Assn., Sigma Pi Phi, Alpha Phi Alpha. Presbyterian. Avocations: outdoor sports, camping, coaching youth sports. Office: Nev Supreme Ct 200 Lewis Ave 17th Fl Las Vegas NV 89101 Home Phone: 702-521-4949; Office Phone: 702-486-3225, 775-684-1755. Office Fax: 702-486-3231. Business E-Mail: mdouglas@nvcourts.state.nv.us.

DOUGLASS, CRAIG BRUCE, computer technology executive; b. Santa Monica, Calif., July 3, 1956; s. W. Bruce and Frances A. (Ellingwood) D. AB, Dartmouth Coll., 1978; MBA, U. Chgo., 1980. Sr. bus. devel. analyst Bell & Howell Co., Chgo., 1980-82, product mgr., 1982-83, sr. product mgr., 1983, mgr. product and market devel., 1983-86, v.p. product and market devel. Torrance, Calif., 1986-89, Bell & Howell Quintar Co., 1989-94; v.p. mktg. & product devel. Quintar Co., Torrance, Calif., 1995-96, v.p. sales and bus. devel., 1996-98; mng. dir. Multifunction Peripherals Assn., 1998—; CEO Converging Systems, Inc., 1999—. Inventor digital film recording. Mem. Nat. Computer Graphics Assn. (pres. Ill. chpt. 1985-86, v.p. Los Angeles Orange County chpt. 1986—, nat. com. 1986—), Dartmouth Club of Chgo. (v.p. 1984-85), Dartmouth Club of L.A. (bd. dirs. 1986-2009, pres. 1993-2007). Avocations: yacht racing, skiing, scuba diving, wind surfing. Office: Converging Systems Inc 32420 Nautilus Dr Rancho Palos Verdes CA 90275-6002 Fax: 310-544-4787. Business E-Mail: cdouglass@convergingsystems.com.

DOUGLASS, DONALD ROBERT, banker; b. Evanston, Ill., Oct. 7, 1934; s. Robert William and Dorothy (Gibson) D.; m. Susan Douglass (dec.). BBA, U. N.Mex., 1959, MBA, 1966. With Security Pacific Nat. Bank, LA, 1961—, mgmt. trainee, 1962-63, asst. mgr. Vernon, Calif., 1963-64, Whittier, Calif., 1964, asst. v.p., 1965, asst. v.p., credit officer regional adminstrn. LA, 1966-69, v.p. San Francisco, 1969-74; mgr. corp. accts. credit adminstrn. No. Calif. Corp. Banking, 1974-77; group v.p. Annco Properties, Burlingame, Calif., 1977-79; v.p., sr. loan officer Borel Bank and Trust Co., San Mateo, Calif., 1979-83, sr. v.p., 1983-84, exec. v.p. mortgage banking divsn. comml. property sales Los Altos, Calif., 1984-87. Ptnr. Key Equities, Inc., San Mateo, Calif., 1987—; ptnr., broker Centre Fin. Group Inc., San Mateo, 1987—96, Centre Fin. Group South Inc., Menlo Park, Calif., 1987—96; pres., chmn., CEO ServiCtr. Mortgage, Inc., 1996—; pres. Sage Fin., Inc., 1999—2005; CFO La Fuenta Fin. Svcs., 2005—; instr. Am. Inst. Banking, 1963, Coll. San Mateo, 1982—; nat. adv. bd. Anderson Schs. Mgmt., U. N.Mex, Ellie Mae. With AUS, 1954-56. Mem. U. N.Mex. Alumni Assn., Sigma Alpha Epsilon, Delta Sigma Phi. Republican. Presbyterian. Home: 745 Celestial Ln San Mateo CA 94404-2771 Office Phone: 650-594-1117. Personal E-mail: ddougl2@aol.com.

DOUGLASS, EVA ROSE, retired accountant; b. Reynolds, Ind., Apr. 16, 1936; d. Kenneth and Marie (Burnett) Firth; AA, Bellevue (Wash.) C.C., 1973; m. Robert E. Douglass, July 8, 1955; children: Robert E., June E., Michele E. Acct., owner Douglass Bus. Svcs., Inc., Bellevue, 1974-92; acct. Tom Locks & Assocs., Mercer Island, Wash., 1974, Carmar Steel, Inc., Bellevue, 1973-74, ret. Mem. adv. bd., acctg. dept. Bellevue C.C. Mem. Wash. Assn. Accts. (Seattle chpt. sec.-treas. 1977-78, co-chmn. editl. and publs. com. 1979-80, chpt. v.p. 1981-82, pres.-elect 1982-83, pres. 1983-84, Wash. state treas. 1982-85), Am. Soc. Women Accts., Nat. Soc. Pub. Accts., Metro Women Bus. Enterprises. Home and Office: 18838 N Conquistador Dr Sun City West AZ 85375-4243

DOUMANI, LISSA, chef; m. Hiro Sone. Pastry apprentice Spago Hollywood, 1982, pastry chef, 1982; designer, pastry programs Sydney, Australia, 1983; pastry chef 385 North, LA; owner, pastry chef Terra, Napa Valley, 1988—, Ame, San Francisco, 2005—. Co-author: Cooking from the Heart of Napa Valley, 2000. Recipient Outstanding Svc. award (with Hiro Sone), James Beard Found., 2008. Office: Ame 689 Mission St San Francisco CA 94105

DOUPE, ALLISON JANE, psychaitry and physiology educator; b. May 13, 1954; MD, Harvard U., 1984. Cert. Psychiatry. Intern, psychiatry Mass. Gen. Hosp., Boston, 1984—85; fellow Calif. Inst. Tech., Pasadena, 1988—93; resident, neurological biology UCLA, 1985—88; asst. prof. to prof., psychiatry and physiology U. Calif., San Francisco, 1993—; faculty mem., computational neurosci. Marine Biol. Lab at Woods Hole, 1998—2000. Mem. editl. bd. Learning & Memory. Searle Scholar, 1993. Fellow: Am. Acad. Arts & Scis.; mem.: NAS. Office: Box 0444 513 Parnassus Ave HSE 818 University of California San Francisco San Francisco CA 94143-0444 Office Phone: 415-476-6446, 415-476-6415. Office Fax: 415-502-4848. Business E-Mail: ajd@phy.ucsf.edu, allison@phy.ucsf.edu.

DOVE, DONALD AUGUSTINE, city planner, educator; b. Waco, Tex., Aug. 7, 1930; s. Sebert Constantine and Amy Delmena (Stern) Dove; m. Cecelia Mae White, Feb. 9, 1957; children: Angela, Donald, Monica Gilstrap, Celine, Cathlyn, Dianna, Jennifer, Austin. BA, Calif. State U. L.A., 1951; MA in Pub. Adminstrn., U. So. Calif., 1966. Planning & devel. cons. D. Dove Assocs., LA, 1959—60; supr. demographic rsch. Calif. Dept. Pub. Works, LA, 1960—66; dir. transp. employment project State of Calif., LA, 1966—71, chief L.A. Region transp. study, 1975—84; chief environ. planning Calif. Dept. Transp., LA, 1972—75; dir. U. So. Calif., LA, 1984—87; panelist, advisor Pres. Conf. Aging, Washington, 1970—2000; environ. coord. Calif. Dept. Pub. Works, Sacramento, 1971—75; panelist, advisor Internat. Conf. Energy Use Mgmt., 1981; ret., 1993. Guest lectr. univs. We. U.S., 1969—. Author: Preserving Urban Environment, 1976, Small Area Population Forecasts, 1966. Chmn. Lynwood City Planning Commn., Calif., 1982—2004; pres. Area Pastoral Coun., LA, 1982—83; mem., del. Archdiocesan Pastoral Coun., LA, 1979—86, Compton Cmty. Devel. Bd., Calif., 1967—71; pres. Neighborhood Esteem/Enrichment Techniques Inst., 1992—93. With US Army, 1952—54. Mem.: LA County Dem. Ctrl. Com., Assn. Environ. Profls. (co-founder 1973), Am. Inst. Cert. Planners, Calif. Assn. Mgmt. (pres. 1987—88), Am. Inst. Planners (transp. chmn. 1972—73), Am. Planning Assn., Optimists Club (sec. 1978—79). Democrat. Roman Catholic. Home and Office: 11356 Ernestine Ave Lynwood CA 90262-3711 Home Phone: 310-603-9194. Business E-Mail: dondve@aol.com.

DOWDY, ROBERT ALAN, retired lawyer, director; b. June 12, 1941; s. Andrew Hunter and Helen Marie (Brandes) Dowdy; m. Lynne Bryant, June 18, 1966; children: Roger Alan, Douglas John. BA, U. Calif., Berkeley, JD, 1966. Bar: D.C. 1967, Calif. 1968, Wash. 1974. Atty. Am. Airlines, NYC, 1969—72, Weyerhaeuser Co., Tacoma, 1972—74, sr. legal counsel, 1974—86, asst. gen. counsel, 1986—91, dep. gen. counsel, 1991—97, v.p., gen. counsel, 1997—2004, sr. v.p., gen. counsel, 2004—06; ret., 2006. Dir. Green Arrow Motor Co., Tacoma; mem. Wash. Bd. Bar Examiners, 1982—; arbitrator King County Superior Ct., 1986—; vis. com. U. Wash. Sch. Law, Seattle, 1986—. Contbr. articles to profl. jours. Bd. dir. N.W. Chamber Orch., Seattle, 1975—76; trustee St. James Sch., Kent, Wash., 1982—84; elder St. Elizabeth Episcopal Ch., Burien, Wash., 1976—78. Capt. US Army, 1966—69. Decorated Army Commendation medal. Mem.: Am. Forest Products and Paper Assn. (gen. counsel com. 1997—), Assn. Gen. Counsel, Wash. Bar Assn. (exec. com. corp. sect. 1977—79, mem. legal edn. sect. 1982—84). Republican.

DOWELL, DAVID RAY, library administrator; b. Trenton, Mo., Nov. 14, 1942; s. Clarence Ray and Ruth Lucille (Adams) D.; m. Arlene Grace Taylor, May 9, 1964 (div. 1983); children: Deborah Ruth, Jonathan Ray; m. Denise Jaye Christie, Aug. 19, 1983; stepchildren: David Lee Smithey, Jason Alan Smithey. BA in History, Okla. Bapt. U., 1964; AM in History, U. Ill., 1966, MLS, 1972; PhD, U. NC, Chapel Hill, 1986. Tchr. Wilson Jr. High Sch., Tulsa, 1964-65; head library adminstrv. services Iowa State U., Ames, 1972-75; asst. univ. librarian Duke U., Durham, N.C., 1975-81; dir. libraries Ill. Inst. Tech., Chgo., 1981—90; libr. dir. & asst. dean Pasadena City Coll., Calif., 1991—95; dir. libr./learning resources Cuesta Coll., San Luis Obispo, Calif., 1995—. Cons. County Commr.'s Library Planning Com., Durham, 1976, Gov.'s Conf. on Libraries and Info. Services, Raleigh, NC, 1978, Biblioteca do Centro Batista, Goiania, Brazil, 1978. Contbr. articles to profl. jours. Trustee Glenwood-Lynwood Pub. Library Dist., Ill., 1985-87. Served to capt. USAF, 1967-71 Mem. ALA (chmn. profl. ethics com. 1977-78, chmn. election com. 1982-83, chmn. libr. personnel adv. com. 1979-80, career pathways task force, 2000-02, awards com. 2001-05, Libr. of Future award jury, 2002-03, chmn. 2003-04, edn. com., 2003-04, scholarship taskforce, 2004-05), Assn. Coll. and Research Libraries (nominat ing com. 1979-80, libr. tech. asst. training com., 1992-2005, chair 1993-95, academic status com., 1993-, instnl. priorities & faculty rewards task force, 1997, profl. devel. com, 1997-2001, Learning Resources Leadership award, 2007), Libr. Adminstrn. & Mgmt. Assn. (bd. dirs. 1981-83, membership com.& govtl. affairs task force, 1983-84, alternative finance task force, 1984-85, orientation com., 1985-87). Democrat. Baptist. Avocations: tennis, genealogy. Home: 2627 Laurel Ave Morro Bay CA 93442-1723 Office: Cuesta Coll PO Box 8106 San Luis Obispo CA 93403-8106 Office Phone: 805-546-3159. E-mail: ddowell@cuesta.edu.

DOWER, WILLIAM J., research company executive; Sr. dir. Affymax Rsch. Inst., Palo Alto, Calif. Recipient Newcomb-Cleve. prize, 1996-97. Office: Affymax Rsch Inst 4001 Miranda Ave Palo Alto CA 94304-1218

DOWIE, IAN JAMES, management consultant; b. London, Mar. 3, 1938; came to U.S., 1980; s. James George and Ethel (Walker) Dowie; m. Barbara Eva Page, Jan. 9, 1960 (div. 1991); children: Paul James, David Ian; m. Nancy M. Pollard, 1993 (div. 2004). BSEE, A.City & Guilds Inst., U. London, 1958. Registered profl. engr., Ont., Can. Seismic engr. Seismograph Svcs. Ltd., England, 1958-61; design engr. GE, Toronto, Ont., 1961-62; v.p., div. dir. IBM Can., Toronto, 1962-80; v.p. field ops. Exxon Office Systems, Stamford, Conn., 1980-82; pres. Aregon Internat. Inc., Stamford, 1983-84, Benchmark East, Westport, Conn., 1985-96, Park City, Utah, 1993-97, Benchmark Pub. Inc., Park City, Utah; developer Goshawk Ranch, Park City, Utah, 1997—2005, The Overlook, Park City, Utah, 2000—02, Turnberry Condos, Midway, Utah, 2003—. Pres. Benchmark-Goshawk, Inc., Park City, Utah; v.p. bus. develop. Interloci Inc., 2002—03. Pub. Once A Londoner, 1989, What's Love Got To Do With It?, 1993, From Womb to Tomb, 1994, Remuda Dust, 1994. Chmn. Credit Valley Assn. for Handicapped Children, Toronto, 1972-79. Mem. Shore and Country Club (Norwalk, Conn.), Jeremy Ranch Golf Club (Park City, Utah). Avocations: tennis, travel, skiing, golf. Office Phone: 435-640-0896. E-mail: ijd@benchmarkventures.com.

DOWLING, THOMAS ALLAN, retired mathematics professor; b. Little Rock, Feb. 19, 1941; s. Charles and Esther (Jensen) D.; m. Nancy Lenthe D.; children: Debra Lynn, David Thomas. BS, Creighton U., 1962; PhD, U. N.C., 1967. Research assoc. U. N.C.-Chapel Hill, 1967-69, asst. prof., 1969-72; assoc. prof. math. Ohio State U., Columbus, 1972-82, prof., 1982—. Ops. researcher U.S. Govt., Patrick AFB, Fla., 1963-64; conf. organizer U. N.C., 1967, 70, Ohio State U., 1978, 82, 88, 92, 94, 98, 00, 02, 03, 05. Editor: Combinatorial Mathematics and its Applications, 1967, 70; contbr. article to profl. jours.; discoverer Dowling lattices. NSF grantee, 1972-80; fellow NASA, 1968 Mem. AAUP, Am. Math. Soc., Math. Assn. Am., Inst. Combinatorics and Applications. Democrat. Home: 2423 High Lonesome Trl Lafayette CO 80026-9393 Personal E-mail: dowling.ta@gmail.com.

DOWNES, WILLIAM F., federal judge; b. 1946; BA, U. North Tex., 1968; JD, U. Houston, 1974. Ptnr. Clark and Downes, Green River, Wyo., 1976-78; mem. Brown & Drew, Casper, Wyo., 1978-94; dist. judge US Dist. Ct. Wyo., Casper, Wyo., 1994—, chief judge. Capt. USMC, 1968—71. Mem.: Natrona County Bar Assn., Wyo. State Bar. Office: US Dist Ct 111 S Wolcott St Rm 210 Casper WY 82601-2534

DOWNEY, ARTHUR HAROLD, JR., lawyer, mediator; b. NYC, Nov. 21, 1938; s. Arthur Harold Sr. and Charlotte (Bailey) D.; m. Gwen Vanden Berg, May 28, 1960; children: Anne Leigh, Neal Arthur, Drew Thomas. BA, Cen. Coll., Pella, Iowa, 1960; LLB, Cornell U., 1963. Bar: Colo. 1963, Wyo. 1991, U.S. Dist. Ct. Colo. 1963, U.S. Dist. Ct. Wyo. 1993, U.S. Ct. Appeals (10th cir.) 1963; diplomate Am. Bd. Forensic Examiners. From assoc. to ptnr. Weller, Friedrich, Ward & Andrew, Denver, 1963-82; ptnr., chief exec. officer Downey Law Firm P.C., Windsor, Colo., 1982—. Trustee panel Colo. Hosp. Assn., 1988-93; del. Nat. Congress Hosp. Trustees, Am. Hosp. Assn., 1988-93. Contbr. articles to profl. jours. Past pres. Columbine Village Homeowners Assn., Trails End Homeowners Assn., Upper Village Homeowners Assn., Powderhorn Condo. Homeowners Assn., Breckenridge, Colo.; chmn. Promontory Point Homeowners Com., 2004—; vice moderator Presbytery of Denver, 1972; chmn. bd. trustees Bethesda Psychealth Sys., Inc., 1990—93. Fellow Internat. Soc. Barristers (emeritus); mem. emeritus Colo. Bar Assn., Larimer County Bar Assn., Wyo. Bar Assn., Def. Rsch. Inst. (disting. svc. award), Nat. Inst. Trial Advocacy (teaching faculty, team leader 1973—), Colo. Def. Lawyers Assn. (pres. 1977-78), Am. Coll. Legal Medicine (assoc. in law), Nat. Bd. Trial Advocacy (cert. 1983-2008), Am. Arbitration Assn. Republican. Mem. Christian Reformed Ch. In Am. Avocations: photography, woodworking, reading. Office: Downey Law Firm PC 7688 Promontory Dr Windsor CO 80528-9305 Home Phone: 970-267-0921; Office Phone: 970-267-0925. E-mail: downeypc@comcast.net.

DOWNEY, SUSAN, film company executive; b. Nov. 6, 1973; m. Robert Downey, Jr., Aug. 27, 2005. Grad., U. So. Calif. Asst. to prodr. Threshold Entertainment; co-pres. Dark Castle Entertainment; v.p. prodn. to exec. v.p. prodn. Silver Pictures, 1999—. Co-prodr.: (films) Ghost Ship, 2002, Cradle 2 the Grave, 2003; prodr.: Gothika, 2003, House of Wax, 2005, The Reaping, 2007; exec. prodr.: Kiss Kiss Bang Bang, 2005. Office: Silver Pictures c/o Warner Bros Pictures 4000 Warner Blvd Bldg 90 Burbank CA 91522-0001

DOWNEY, TOM, museum director, former lawyer; m. Lori Fox; children: Cate, Ella, Meg. Grad., Coll. William and Mary; JD, Villanova Sch. Law. With various firms, Colo. and Md.; asst. atty. gen. Office Atty. Gen. Ken Salazar; exec. dir. Children's Mus. Denver, 2005—. Mem. editl. adv. bd.: Heritage 365 Mag. Mem. leadership bd. Mile High Montessori Cmty.; mem. citizens com. for bond expenditures Denver Pub. Schs., 2003, mem. capital needs com., 2006; bd. dirs. Denver Preschool Program, Mayor Hickenlooper's Leadership Team for Early Childhood Edn., LoDo Dist. Recipient Pro Bono Atty. award, Ballard Spahr, 2002, Anna Jo Haynes Care About Kids award, Mile High United Way, 2006; named a Livingston fellow, Bonfils Stanton Found., 2007; named one of Forty Under 40, Denver Bus. Jour., 2002. Mem.: Am. Assn. Mus. (co-chair Denver conf. host com. 2008), Colo. Nonprofit Assn. (bd. vice chair). Office: Children's Mus Denver 2121 Children's Mus Dr Denver CO 80211 Office Phone: 303-433-7444. Office Fax: 303-433-9520. Business E-Mail: tomd@cmdenver.org.

DOWNING, DAVID CHARLES, retired minister; b. South Gate, Calif., June 24, 1938; s. Kenneth Oliver and Edna Yesobel (Casaday) D.; m. Tommye Catherine Tew, July 11, 1959 (dec. Dec. 11, 1985), Eddie West, 2001; children: Sheri Lynn, Teresa Kay, Carla Jeane, Michael David. BA, N.W. Christian Coll., 1961; B in Divinity, Tex. Christian U., 1966, M in Theology, 1973; DMin, San Francisco Theol. Sem., 1987. Ordained to ministry Christian Ch., 1961. Min. Marcola (Oreg.) Ch. of Christ, 1958-59; assoc. min. First Christian Ch., Lebanon, Oreg., 1960-63, min. Ranger, Tex., 1963-65, Knox City, Tex., 1966-68, Fredonia, Kans., 1968-74, Ctrl. Christian Ch., Huntington, Ind., 1974-77; regional min., pres. Christian Ch. Greater Kansas City, Mo., 1978-94; sr. minister Univ. Christian Ch., Disciples of Christ, San Diego, 1994—2001; ret., 2001; moderator GLAD-PSWR, 2004—; mem. Nat. Disciples Peace Fellowship Exec. Com. Trustee Phillips Grad. Sem., Enid, Okla., 1988-94; bd. dirs. Ch. Fin. Coun., Indpls., Midwest Career Devel. Svc., Chgo.; v.p. bd. dirs. Midwest Christian Counseling Ctr., Kansas City. Author: A Contrast and Comparison of Pastoral Counseling in Rural and Urban Christian Churches, 1972, A Design for Enabling Urban Congregations to Cope with Their Fear of Displacement When Faced with Communities in Transition, 1987. Pres. Kansas City Interfaith Peace Alliance, 1980-82; interim regional min. Pacific S.W. Region Disciples Ch., 2002, vol. Mama's Kitchen and San Diego Natural History Mus. Democrat. Mem. Christian Ch. Avocations: swimming, camping, fishing, collecting chalices, music. Home: 4325 Caminito De La Escena San Diego CA 92108-4201 E-mail: davidd624@cox.net.

DOWS, DAVID ALAN, chemistry professor; b. San Francisco, July 25, 1928; s. Samuel Randall and Rita M. (Bowers) D.; m. Wena Hunt Waldner, July 29, 1950; children— Janet Louise, Carol Marie, Joyce Ellen. BS, U. Calif., Berkeley, 1952, PhD, 1954. Instr. chemistry Cornell U., 1954-56; instr. U. So. Calif., Los Angeles, 1956-57, asst. prof., 1957-59, assoc. prof., 1959-63, prof. chemistry, 1963—, chmn. dept., 1966-72; NATO prof., 1970. Contbr. articles profl. jours. NSF fellow, 1962-63 Mem. Am. Chem. Soc., Am. Phys. Soc., Phi Beta Kappa. Office: U So Calif Dept Chemistry University Park Los Angeles CA 90089-0482 Office Phone: 213-740-4121. Business E-Mail: dows@usc.edu.

DOYLE, DAN A., state representative; b. 1957; m. Victoria Doyle; children: Andrea, Martha, Kelly. BSBA, Ariz. State U.; JD, Willamette U. Coll. Law. State rep. Oreg. House Rep., Dist. 19, Salem, 2002—; pvt. practice Salem; ptnr. Connolly & Doyle, LLP, Salem. Vice chair sub-com. Ways and Means Pub. Safety; com. mem. Agr. and Forestry Rules, Redistricting and Pub. Affairs. Bd. mem. Providence Benedictine Nursing Ctr. Found.; chmn., bd. mem. Willamette Valley Hospice; chmn. parish coun. St. Vincent's Ch. Mem.: Aumsville C. of C., Stayton-Sublimity C. of C. Address: Capitol State House 900 Court St NE H-283 Salem OR 97301

DOYLE, DAVID C., lawyer; b. Nashville, Apr. 11, 1951; BA magna cum laude, U. Calif., San Diego, 1973; JD, UCLA, 1976. Bar: Calif. 1976. Law clk. to Hon. Gordon Thompson Jr. U.S. Dist. Ct. (so. dist.) Calif., 1976-78; asst. U.S. atty. So. Dist. of Calif., 1978-80; mem. Baker & McKenzie, San Diego; ptnr. Morrison & Foerster LLP, San Diego, co-leader patent practice group. Mem. editorial bd. UCLA Law Rev., 1974-76. Mem. State Bar Calif., San Diego County Bar Assn., Order of Coif.

DOYLE, FIONA MARY, dean, metallurgical engineer, educator; b. Newcastle upon Tyne, Eng., Sept. 27, 1956; came to the U.S., 1983; d. Vincent Thomas and Teresa Mary (Lockey) D.; m. Stephen Craig Blair, Aug. 5, 1990; children: Katherine Nicole Blair, Ian James Blair. BA in Metallurgy and Materials Sci., U. Cambridge, 1978, MA in Natural Sci., 1982; MSc in Extractive Metallurgy, Imperial Coll., 1979, PhD in Metallurgy, 1983. Chartered engr., Great Britain. Grad. trainee metals and minerals div. Davy McKee, Stockton-on-Tees, United Kingdom, 1983; asst. prof. materials sci. and mineral engring. U. Calif., Berkeley, 1983-88, assoc. prof., 1988-94, prof., 1994—, acting assoc. dean coll. engring., 1990, dir. Inst. Environmental Sci. and Engring., 2001—02, chair dept. materials sci. and engring., 2002—05, exec. assoc. dean Coll. Engring., 2005—. Cons. Placer Dome, U.S., San Francisco, 1989-90. Co-editor: Innovations in Materials Processing Using Aqueous Colloids and Surface Chemistry, 1989, Biotechnology in Minerals and Metal Processing, 1989, Mineral Processing and Extractive Metallury Rev., 1990—; editor: Mining and Mineral Processing Wastes, 1990; contbr. articles to profl. jours. Tech. cons. Sierra Club Legal Def. Fund, San Francisco, 1991. Grantee NSF, 1984, U.S. Dept. Interior, 1987, 91, U.S. Dept. Energy, 1990. Mem. Minerals, Metals and Materials Soc., Am. Inst. Mining, Metall. and Petroleum Engrs. (chair aqueous processing com. 1988-90), Instn. Mining and Metallurgy, Electrochem. Soc., Materials Rsch. Soc. Office: U Calif Berkeley Dept Materials Sci 325 Hearst Mining Bldg Berkeley CA 94720-1760 Home Phone: 510-451-0318; Office Phone: 510-642-7594.

DOYLE, MARY E., lawyer; B in Biology and Econs., U. Calif. Santa Cruz; JD, U. Calif. Berkeley, 1978. Litigator Manatt, Phelps & Phillips, LA, 1978—84; various positions including gen. counsel Teledyne Inc., 1984—96; gen. counsel Magic Inc., 1996—2003; sr. v.p., gen. counsel Palm Inc., Sunnyvale, Calif., 2003—. Office: Palm Inc 950 W Maude Ave Sunnyvale CA 94085

DOYLE, PATRICK JOHN, otolaryngologist, department chairman; b. Moose Jaw, Sask., Can., Nov. 17, 1926; s. William E. and Bertha L. (Fisher) D.; m. Irene Strilchuk, May 21, 1949; children: Sharon, Patrick, Robert, Barbara, Joseph, Kathleen. BSc, U. Alta., 1947, MD, 1949. Diplomate Am. Bd. Otolaryngology (bd. dirs., v.p. 1986-88, pres. 1988-90). Intern U. B.C. Hosp., 1949-50; resident in medicine and pediatrics, 1950-51; resident in otolaryngology U. Oreg. Hosp., 1958-61; asst. prof., then asso. prof. U. Oreg. Med. Sch., 1965-70; mem. faculty U. B.C. Med. Sch., 1963—, prof. otolaryngology, 1972-91, prof. otolaryngology emeritus, 1992—, head dept., 1972-91, program dir. residency tng. program, 1972-91. Head div. otolaryngology St. Paul's Hosp., mem. numerous nat. med. coms. Author numerous articles in field; mem. editorial bds. profl. jours. Fellow Royal Coll. Surgeons Can., Am. Laryngol., Rhinol. and Otol. Soc. (v.p. western sect. 1988, pres. 1994), Am. Laryngol. Soc., Am. Acad. Otolaryngology-Head and Neck Surgery (v.p. 1984, bd. dirs. 1985-87), Am. Otol. Soc.; mem. Can. Soc. Otolaryngology-Head and Neck Surgery (pres. 1987), Pacific Coast Oto-Ophthal. Soc. (pres. 1977), Soc. Univ. Otolaryngologists, U. Oreg. Otolaryngology Alumni Assn. (pres. 1968-70), Am. Otological Soc., Centurion Club, Tinnitus Rsch. Found. Roman Catholic. Office: # 301-5704 Balsam St Vancouver BC Canada V6M 4B9

DOYLE, PATRICK T., broadcast executive; Dir. taxes Hughes Electronics Corp., 1992; v.p. taxes DIRECTV Group, El Segundo, Calif., 1996—2000, v.p. corp. devel., 1997—2000, corp. v.p., 2000—01, contr., 2000—07, treas., 2001—07, sr. v.p., chief acctg. officer, 2001—07, sr. v.p., CFO, 2007—08, exec. v.p. fin., CFO, 2008—. Office: DIRECTV Group 2230 E Imperial Hwy El Segundo CA 90245 Office Phone: 310-964-5000.

DRACUP, KATHLEEN ANNE, dean, nursing educator; b. Santa Monica, Calif., Sept. 28, 1942; d. Paul Joseph and Lucy Elizabeth (Milligan) Molloy; children: Jeffrey, Jonathan, Joy, Jan, Brian. BS in Nursing, St. Xavier's Coll., Chgo., 1967; M of Nursing, U. Calif., LA, 1974; D of Nursing Sci., U. Calif., San Francisco, 1982. Clin. nurse Little Co. of Mary Hosp., Chgo., 1967-70, UCLA Med. Ctr., 1970-74; asst. clin. prof. U. Calif., 1974-78, rsch. fellow dept. medicine, 1979-81, asst. prof. to prof., 1982-99, dean Sch. Nursing San Francisco, 2000—; clin. nurse Sch. Nursing U. Calif. San Francisco Med. Ctr., 1979; pvt. practice psychotherapist, 1980—95. Editor Heart and Lung Jour., 1981-91, Am. Jour. Critical Care, 1991—; editor Critical Care Nursing Series; contbr. chpts. to books, articles to profl. jours. Recipient Eugene Brunwald Acad. Mentorship award Am. Heart Assn., 2003; Disting. Practitioner Nat. Acad., Washington, 1987; Fulbright Sr. scholar, 1995. Fellow Coun. Cardiovascular Nursing, Am. Heart Assn., Am. Assn. Cardiopulmonary Rehab.; mem. Inst. of Medicine, Am. Nurses' Assn., Am. Assn. Critical Care Nurses (life), Sigma Theta Tau. Office: U Calif San Francisco Sch Nursing 2 Koret Way Rm N319 San Francisco CA 94143-0604 Office Phone: 415-476-1805. Business E-Mail: kathydracup@nursing.ucsf.edu.

DRAIN, ALBERT STERLING, business management consultant; b. Decatur, Tex., July 5, 1925; s. Albert S. and Bessie (Burk) D.; m. Mauvaline Joyce Beam, Apr. 18, 1946; children: Ronald Dale, Deborah Kay Drain Crawford. Student, Bellville Jr. Coll., Ill., Tex. Christian U., Iowa U., Milsaps Coll., Pittsburg Coll., Kans. With Armour & Co., 1945-79, regional mgr. Pitts., 1966-67, mgr. pork div. Chgo., 1967-68, fresh meats div. mgr., 1968-69, corporate v.p., 1968-75, exec. v.p., 1971-73, group v.p. food marketing div., 1973-75; pres. Armour Foods, 1975-79; also dir.; exec. v.p. for Iowa Beef Processors Inc., Dakota City, Nebr., 1979-80; group v.p. Greyhound Corp., Phoenix, 1977—; pres. Sterling Mktg. Inc. (ind. bus. cons. to meat industry), Phoenix, 1980-91; pvt. practice mgmt. cons. meat packing Phoenix, 1991-94; pvt. practice Al Drain Mgmt. Cons., Phoenix, 1994—. Served with USNR, 1943-45. Mem. Am. Soc. Agrl. Cons., Masons, Shriners. Baptist. Home: 7550 N 16th St Apt 6128 Phoenix AZ 85020-7640 Fax: 602-266-4797.

DRAKE, CHARLES WHITNEY, physicist; b. South Portland, Maine, Mar. 8, 1926; s. Charles Whitney and Katharine Gabrielle (O'Neill) D.; m. Ellen Tan, June 15, 1952; children— Judith Ellen, Robert Charles, Linda Ann. BS, U. Maine, 1950; MA, Conn. Wesleyan U., 1952; PhD, Yale U., 1958. Scientist Westinghouse Atomic Power Div., 1952-53; instr. Yale U., New Haven, 1957-60, asst. prof., 1960-66, rsch. assoc., 1966-69; assoc. prof. Oreg. State U., 1966-74; prof., 1974-93; prof. emeritus, 1993—; chmn. dept. physics, 1976-84. Vis. prof. Oxford U. Clarendon Lab. and St. Peter's Coll., 1972-73, U. Tuebingen (W.Ger.), 1982. Contbr. articles to profl. jours. Served with USN, 1944-46. Recipient various fellowships and grants. Fellow Am. Phys. Soc.; mem. Am. Assn. Physics Tchrs., Sigma Xi, Tau Beta Pi, Sigma Pi Sigma. Office: Oreg State U Dept Physics Corvallis OR 97331 Personal E-mail: drakec@onid.orst.edu.

DRAKE, FRANK DONALD, radio astronomer, educator; b. Chgo., May 28, 1930; s. Richard Carvel and Winifred (Thompson) D.; m. Elizabeth Bell, Mar. 7, 1953 (div. 1977); children: Stephen, Richard, Paul; m. Amahl Zekin Shakhashiri, Mar. 4, 1978; children: Nadia, Leila. B in Engring. Physics, Cornell U., 1952; MA in Astronomy, Harvard U., 1956, PhD in Astronomy, 1958. Astronomer Nat. Radio Astron. Obs., Green Bank, W.Va., 1958-63; sect. chief Jet Propulsion Lab., Pasadena, Calif., 1963-64; prof. Cornell U., Ithaca, N.Y., 1964-84; dir. Nat. Astron. and Ionospace Ctr., Ithaca, 1971-81; dean natural sci. dept. U. Calif., Santa Cruz, 1984-88, prof. astronomy, 1984-95, prof. emeritus, 1995—; pres. SETI Inst., Mountain View, Calif., 1984-2000, chmn. bd. trustees, 2000—02; dir. Ctr. for Study of Life in the Universe, 2005—. Author: Intelligent Life in Space, 1962, Murmurs of Earth, 1978, Is Anyone Out There, The Scientific Search for Extraterrestrial Intelligence, 1992. Lt. USN, 1947-55. Fellow AAAS, Am. Acad. Arts and Scis.; mem. NAS, Internat. Astron. Union (chmn. U.S. nat. com.), Astron. Soc. Pacific (pres. 1988-90), Explorers Club. Avocation: jewelry making. Home: SETI Inst 515 N Whisman Rd Mountain View CA 94043 Office Phone: 650-960-4511. E-mail: drake@seti.org.

DRAKE, HUDSON BILLINGS, aerospace and electronics executive; b. LA, Mar. 3, 1935; s. Hudson C. and Blossom (Billings) Drake; m. Joan M. Johnson, Feb. 9, 1957 (dec. 1997); children: Howard Billings, Paul Marvin; m. Mary H. Vaugier, Nov. 1, 2000. BA in Econs., UCLA, 1957, grad. Exec. Program, 1991; MBA, Pepperdine U., Malibu, Calif., 1976. Mgr. autonetics divsn. N.Am. Aviation, Rockwell Inc., Anaheim, Calif., 1958-68; exec. dir. Pres.'s Commn. White House Fellows, Washington, 1969-70; dep. under sec. U.S. Dept. Commerce, Washington, 1970-72; v.p., gen. mgr. Teledyne Ryan Electronics, San Diego, 1972-80, pres., 1980-84; pres., group exec. Teledyne Ryan Aero., San Diego, 1984-88; pres. aerospace and electronics Teledyne Inc., LA, 1988—97; ltd. ptnr. Carlisle Enterprises, La Jolla, Calif., 1997—. Mem. Def. Procurement Adv. Com. Trade, Washington, 1988—93; cons. unmanned aerial systems Evergreen Internat. Aviation, 2004—; bd. dirs. Compass Aerospace Corp., Piper Aircraftt Co. Contbr. articles to profl. jours. Bd. dirs. Johnson Cancer Ctr. Found., UCLA, 1998—2005; vestry St. James by Sea, La Jolla, Calif., 1998—2002; trustee Children's Hosp., San Diego, 1981—86, chmn. rsch. corp., 1983—86; pres.'s coun. San Diego State U., 1984—90; bd. overseers U. Calif., San Diego, 1985—88. QMQ 2 Instructor USNR, 1953—61. Recipient Exec. of the Yr. award, Nat. Mgmt. Assn., 1995, San Diego Bd. Suprs. resolution, 1988; named Silver Knight of Mgmt., Nat. Mgmt. Assn., 1975, Gold Knight of Mgmt., 1986; White House fellow, 1968—69. Mem.: AIAA, IEEE, San Diego C. of C. (bd. dirs.), Inst. Navigation, Navy League (life), La Jolla Beach and Tennis Club, La Jolla Country Club. Republican. Episcopalian. Avocations: golf, fly fishing. Home: 1707 Soledad Ave La Jolla CA 92037 Personal E-mail: hdrake1@san.rr.com.

DRAKE, MICHAEL J., meteoriticist, planetary scientist, educator; b. Bristol, Eng., July 8, 1946; Am. citizen; married; 2 children. BSc, U. Manchester, 1967; PhD in Geology, U. Oreg., 1972. Rsch. assoc. lunar sci. Smithsonian Astrophys. Obs., 1972-73; from asst. prof. to assoc. prof. planetary sci. U. Ariz., Tucson, 1973-83, assoc. dir. Lunar and Planetary Lab., 1978-80, assoc. dean sci., 1986-87, prof. planetary sci., 1983—, prof. geosci., 1988—, head dept. planetary scis., dir. Lunar and Planetary Lab., 1994—. Mem. numerous coms. and working groups NASA. Assoc. editor Jour. Geophys. Rsch., 1982. Fellow Meteoritical Soc. (pres. 1999-2000), Am. Geophys. Union; mem. Am. Astron. Soc., Geochemical Soc. Office: Univ Ariz Lunar & Planetary Lab Tucson AZ 85721-0001

DRAKE, MICHAEL V., academic administrator, ophthalmologist, educator; b. NYC; AB, Stanford U.; BS, MD, U. Calif., San Francisco. Resident U. Calif., San Francisco, asst. prof. ophthalmology, 1979—87, chief eye clinic, 1979—91, assoc. prof., 1991—93, dir. vision care and clin. rsch. unit, asst. dean student affairs, 1991—93, prof., 1993—98, vice chmn. dept. ophthalmology, assoc. dean admissions and student programs, sr. assoc. dean admissions and extramural academic programs, 1998—2000, Stephen P. Shearing prof., 1998—2005, v.p. health affairs, 2000—05, chancellor, 2005—. Author: (with D.O. Harrington) The Visual Fields: Text and Atlas of Clinical Perimetry, 1990, (with R. Stamper and M. Lieberman) Becker-shaffer Diagnosis of glaucoma, 1999. Recipient Herbert W. Nickens award, Assn. Am. Med. Colls., 2004. Fellow: AAAS. Office: U Calif The Chancellor's Office Irvine CA 92697-1900 Office Phone: 949-824-5111. Office Fax: 949-824-2087.

DRAKE, ROGER ALLAN, psychology professor, neuroscience researcher; s. Theodore Francis and Quinica Venetta (Cram) D. Student, Calif. Inst. Tech.; BA, Western Washington U., 1966; MA, U. Iowa, 1969; PhD, U. Tenn., 1981. Prof. Western State Coll., Gunnison, Colo., 1969—. Fulbright lectr. Sheffield Polytech, Yorkshire, England, 1981-82; vis. prof. U. Colo., Boulder, 1984-85, sch. medicine Johns Hopkins U., Balt., 1988-89; vis. scholar Keck Sch. of Medicine, U. So. Calif., 2003-2004 Author: Cognitive Simplicity and Social Perceptual Errors, 1982; contbr. articles to profl. jours. Faculty senate We. State Coll., 1990-2006; bd. trustees University Press Colo., 1992—. Sabbatical Rsch. grantee Charles A. Dana Found., 1988-89, Internat. Rsch. grantee NATO, Berlin, 1987-91; recipient Rsch. Opportunity grantee NSF, 1984-85, NIH grantee, 2003-2005. Mem. Soc. Advancement Social Psychology (pres. 1989-94), Soc. Neurosci., Soc. for Personality and Social Psychology, Assn. Psycholol. Sci. Achievements include research on effects of selective lateral brain activation on optimism, aesthetic judgements, risk, mood, perceived control and causal attributions, understanding of persuasion and processing of arguments, including selective memory. Office: Western State Coll 217 Kelley Hall Gunnison CO 81231-0001 Business E-Mail: rdrake@western.edu.

DRAKE, SYLVIE (JURRAS), theater critic; b. Alexandria, Egypt, Dec. 18, 1930; arrived in U.S., 1949, naturalized, 1952; d. Robert and Simonette (Barda) Franco; m. Kenneth K. Drake, Apr. 29, 1952 (div. Dec. 1972); children: Jessica, Robert I.; m. Ty Jurras, June 16, 1973. M. Theater Arts, Pasadena Playhouse, 1969. Free-lance TV writer, 1962-68; theater critic Canyon Crier, LA, 1968-72; theater critic, columnist L.A. Times, 1971-91, chief theater critic, 1991-93, theatre critc emeritus, 1993—; lit. dir. Denver Ctr. Theatre Co., 1985; pres. L.A. Drama Critics Circle, 1979-81, free lance travel writer, translator, book reviewer. Mem. Pulitzer Prize Drama Jury, 1994; adv. bd. Nat. Arts Journalism Program, 1994-97. Dir. publs. Denver Ctr. for the Performing Arts, 1994—; artistic assoc. for spl. projects Denver Ctr. Theatre Co., 1994—. Mem.: Am. Theater Critics Assn. Office: Denver Ctr Performing Arts 1101 13th St Denver CO 80204-2100 Office Phone: 303-893-4000. Business E-Mail: sdrake@dcpa.org.

DRAPER, WILLIAM HENRY, III, venture capitalist; b. White Plains, NY, Jan. 1, 1928; s. William Henry and Katherine (Baum) Draper; m. Phyllis Culbertson, June 13, 1953; children: Rebecca, Polly, Timothy. BA, Yale U., 1950, MA (hon.), 1991; MBA, Harvard U., 1954; LLD (hon.), Southeastern U., 1985. With Inland Steel Co., Chgo., 1954-59, Draper, Gaither & Anderson, Palo Alto, Calif., 1959-62; pres. Draper & Johnson Investment Co., Palo Alto, 1962-65; founder, gen. ptnr. Sutter Hill Ventures, Palo Alto, 1965-81; pres., chmn. U.S. Export-Import Bank, Washington, 1981-86; adminstr., CEO, UN Devel. Programme, 1986-93; mng. dir. Draper Richards, San Francisco, 1994—, Draper Internat., San Francisco, 1994—. Bd. dirs. numerous cos. Nat. co-chmn. fin. com. George Bush for Pres., 1980; bd. dirs., former chmn. Rep. Alliance; chmn. bd. Am. Conservatory Theatre, 1980—81, bd. dirs., 1977—81; chmn. Internat. Inst. Edn. West, 1989—2000; vice chmn. Population Action Internat., 1993—; mem. adv. bd. Stanford Grad. Sch. Bus. Adminstrn., 1980—86; chmn. World Affairs Coun. No. Calif., 2000—02; trustee Yale U., 1991—98, George Bush Libr. Found., 1993—; bd. dirs. Population Crisis Com., 1976—81, Atlantic Coun., 1989—, World Rehab. Fund, 1988—92, Ctr. for Econ. Policy Rsch., Stanford U., 1988, Inst. Internat. Studies Stanford U. (FSI), 1997—, UN Assn.-USA, 2003—. With US Army, 1946—48, with US Army, 1951—52. Recipient Alumni Achievement award, Harvard Bus. Sch., 1982, medal of Honor, Ellis Island, 1992, Citizen Diplomacy award, Internat. Diplomacy Coun., 1996, Woodrow Wilson award for pub. svc., 2002, Vision award, SD Forum, 2005, Silicon Valley Fast 50 Lifetime Achievement award, 2006, Inst. Internat. Edn. Disting. Svc. award, 2006; named one of U.S.'s 50 New Corp. Elite, Bus. Week mag., 1985; named to, Dow Jones Venture Capital Hall of Fame, 2005. Mem.: Overseas Devel. Coun., Coun. Fgn. Rels., River Club, Chevy Chase Club, Met. Club, Bohemian Club, Pacific Union Club. Home: 91 Tallwood Ct Atherton CA 94027-6431 Office: Draper Richards 50 California St Ste 2925 San Francisco CA 94111-4726 Office Phone: 415-616-4050. E-mail: bill@draperrichards.com.

DRAYMAN, JOHN, Mayor, Glendale, California; MFA, New Theater Inc., NYC. Councilman City of Glendale, mayor, 2008—. Former chmn. Glendale Redevelopment Agy. Former v.p. Friends of Alex Theater; former treas. Glendale Regional Arts Coun.; pres. bd. dirs. Montrose Shopping Park Assn. Office: City Hall 613 E Broadway Glendale CA 91206 Office Phone: 818-548-4844. Office Fax: 818-547-6740. Business E-Mail: jdrayman@ci.glendale.ca.us.*

DR. DRE, (ANDRE RAMELLE YOUNG), rap musician, record producer; b. L.A., Feb. 18, 1965; s. Theodore and Verna Young; m. Nicole Threatt, 1996; children: Truth, Truly Co-founder Death Row Records, 1992—95; founder Aftermath Entertainment, 1996—. Singer: (albums with N.W.A.) Straight Outta Compton, 1989, 100 Miles and Runnin', 1990, Efil4zaggin, 1991, NWA Greatest Hits, 1996; (solo albums) The Chronic, 1993 (Grammy award Best Pop Solo for "Let Me Ride" 1994), Two Thousand and One, 1999, Detox, 2008; prodr.: (albums) Doggy Style, 1993, Murder Was the Case, 1994, U Can't Cee Me and California Love singles, 1996, Wild Wild West, 1999, The SLim SHady Lp, 1999, The Marshall Mathers LP, 2000, Death Row: Snoop Doggy Dogg at His Best, 2001, The Eminem Show, 2002; (soundtracks) Above the Rim, 1994; actor: (films) Who's The Man, 1993, Ride, 1998, Whiteboyz, 1999, The Wash, 2001, Training Day, 2001. Office: Aftermath Entertainment 10900 Wilshire Blvd Ste 1040 Los Angeles CA 90024-6501

DREHER, NICHOLAS C., lawyer; b. Michigan City, Ind., Nov. 15, 1948; AB magna cum laude, Harvard U., 1970; JD, Stanford U., 1973. Bar: Hawaii 1973. Ptnr. Cades Schutte Fleming & Wright, Honolulu, 1980—, chmn. of fin. and real estate dept., 1991—. Vice-chmn. local rules com. U.S. Bankruptcy Ct. Mem. ABA (mem. com. foreclosure and related remedies sect. real property, probate and trust law 1991—), Am. Bankruptcy Inst. (chmn. Hawaii membership com. 1989—, mem. adv. com. bankruptcy rules 1990—), Hawaii State Bar Assn. (v.p. bankruptcy law sect. 1990-91, pres. 1991—, bd. dirs. 1990—). Office: Cades Schutte Fleming & Wright PO Box 939 Honolulu HI 96808-0939 E-mail: ndreher@cades.com.

DREIER, DAVID TIMOTHY, United States Representative from California; b. Kansas City, Mo., July 5, 1952; s. H. Edward and Joyce (Yeomans) Dreier. BA in Polit. Sci., Claremont McKenna Coll., 1975; MA in Am. Govt., Claremont Grad. Sch., 1976. Dir. corp. rels. Claremont McKenna Coll., 1975-78; dir. mktg./govt. rels. Indsl. Hydrocorbons, San Dimas, Calif., 1979—80; mem. US Congress from 26th (formerly 33rd) Calif. dist., 1980—, mem. rules com., subcom. legis. & budget process; v.p. Dreier Devel. Co., Kansas City, Mo., 1985—. Co-chair Gov. Arnold Schwarzenegger's transition team, 2004, Zero Capital Gains Tax Caucus, US-Mex. Congl. Caucus; chair Calif. Congl. Rep. Del.; mem. Rep. Cyber-Security Team, Nat. Rep. Congl. Com., Rep. Policy Com., Rep. Steering Com. Recipient Golden Bulldog award, Watchdogs of Treasury, 1981—99, Clean Air Champion award, Sierra Club, 1988; named a Friend of Taxpayers, Nat. Union, 1981—99. Mem.: Coun. Fgn. Rels., Friar's Club, James Madison Soc. (bd. govs.). Republican. Office: US Ho Reps 233 Cannon Ho Office Bldg Washington DC 20515-0526

DREIER, R. CHAD (ROBERT CHAD DREIER), construction and mortgage company executive; b. 1947; BSBA, Loyola Marymount U., 1969. Exec. v.p. Golden West Holding Corp., LA, 1979-80; v.p., dir. devel. Daon Corp., 1980-85; exec. v.p., CFO Kaufman and Broad Home Corp., 1986; chmn. Kaufman & Broad Mortgage Corp.; pres., CEO The Ryland Group, Inc., Woodland Hills, Calif., 1993, chmn., pres., CEO, 1994—2008, chmn., CEO, 2008—. Bd. dirs. Occidental Petroleum Corp.; adv. bd. Joint Ctr. Housing Studies, Harvard U. Bd. trustees Loyola Marymount U., 1994—, chmn., 1998—. 1st lt. USAF, 1969—72. Recipient The Sedes Sapientiae Medallion, Loyola Marymount U., 2005. Avocation: sports. Office: Ryland Group Suite 400 24025 Park Sorrento Calabasas CA 91302*

DREILINGER, CHARLES LEWIS (CHIPS DREILINGER), dean; b. Bklyn., Feb. 19, 1945; s. Samuel Leonard and Harriet Karen (Kaplan) D.; m. Anna Douglas, Mar. 21, 1966; children: Sean Eric, Daniel Ethan, Seth Aaron. BA, Antioch Coll., 1967; MA, Claremont Grad. Sch., 1968. Assoc. for program devel. Union Experimenting Colls. and Univs., Yellow Springs, Ohio, 1968-70; asst. dean, assoc. dean Antioch Coll., Yellow Springs, 1970-73; assoc. dean, acting dean Hobart Coll., Geneva, N.Y., 1973-79; dean John Muir Coll. U. Calif.-San Diego, La Jolla, 1979—. Democrat. Avocation: horticulture.

DREISBACH, JOHN GUSTAVE, investment banker; b. Paterson, NJ, Apr. 24, 1939; s. Gustave John and Rose Catherine (Koehler) D.; m. Janice Lynn Petitjean; children: John Gustave Jr., Christopher Erik. BA, NYU, 1963. With Dreyfus & Co., 1959-62, Shields & Co., Inc., 1965-68, Model, Roland & Co., Inc., NYC, 1968-72, F. Eberstadt & Co., Inc., NYC, 1972-74; asst. v.p., trust officer Bessemer Trust Co., 1974—76; pres. Cmty. Housing Capital, Inc., 1978-80; chmn., pres. John G. Dreisbach, Inc., Santa Fe, 1980—, JDG Housing Corp., 1982—, JGD Mgmt. Corp., 1996—. Gen. ptnr. numerous real estate ltd. partnerships; bd. dirs., pres. The Santa Fe Investment Conf., 1986—; assoc. Sta. KNME-TV. Mem. Santa Fe Cmty. Devel. Commn. With USAR, with USAFR, 1964. Mem. Internat. Assn. for Fin. Planning, Nat. Assn. Securities Dealers, Inc., NYU Alumni Assn., N.Mex. First, Friends of Vieilles Maisons Francaises Inc., Mensa, Santa Fe C. of C., Augustan Soc., St. Bartholomew's Cmty. Club, Essex Club, Hartford Club, Amigos del Alcalde Club. Avocations: travel, marathoning, architecture, classical music, shotokan karate (1st dan). Office: 369 Montezuma Ave No 215 Santa Fe NM 87501-2626 Home: 72 Gras Lawn Barrack Rd Exeter Devon EX2 4SZ England Personal E-mail: john@dreisbach.freeserve.co.uk.

DRELL, PERSIS SYDNEY, physicist; b. Dec. 30, 1955; m. James Welch; 3 children. BA in Math. & Physics, Wellesley Coll., 1977; PhD in Atomic Physics, U. Calif., Berkeley, 1983. Postdoctoral rsch. assoc. in high-energy physics Lawrence Berkeley Nat. Lab., 1983—88; asst. prof. physics Cornell U., 1988—97, prof. physics, 1997—2002, head, high energy group, 2000—01, dep. dir., Lab. Nuclear Studies, 2001—02; mem. program adv. com. Stanford Linear Accelerator Ctr. (SLAC), Menlo Park, Calif., 1993—95, assoc. dir., rsch. divsn., 2002—07, prof. physics, 2002—, dep. project mgr., Gamma Ray Large Area Space Telescope, 2004, 2005, dep. dir., 2005—07, dir., particle and particle astrophysics, 2005, current chair, scientific policy com., acting dir., 2007, dir., 2007—. Leader of Cornell Group, Wilson Lab. CLEO (one of the world's most advanced particle detectors), 2000. Recipient Presdl. Young Investigator Award, NSF; named One of the 50 Most Important Women in Science, Discover Mag., 2002; grantee Guggenheim Fellowship. Fellow: Am. Physical Soc., Am. Acad. Arts & Scis. Office: Stanford Linear Accelerator Ctr 2575 Sand Hill Rd Menlo Park CA 94025 Address: Stanford Linear Accelerator Ctr PO Box 20450 Stanford CA 94309 Office Phone: 650-926-3300. E-mail: drell@slac.stanford.edu.

DRELL, SIDNEY DAVID, physicist, arms control and national security specialist; b. Atlantic City, Sept. 13, 1926; s. Tulla and Rose (White) D.; m. Harriet Stainback, Mar. 22, 1952; children: Daniel White, Persis Sydney, Joanna Harriet. AB, Princeton U., 1946; MA, U. Ill., 1947, PhD, 1949, DSc (hon.), 1981, Tel Aviv U., 2001, Weizman Inst. Sci., 2001. Rsch. assoc. U. Ill., 1949-50; instr. physics Stanford U., 1950-52, assoc. prof., 1956-60, prof., 1960-63, Lewis M. Terman prof. and fellow, 1979-84; co-dir. Stanford U. Ctr. for Internat. Security and Arms Control, 1983-89; prof. Stanford Linear Accelerator Ctr., 1963-98, dep. dir., 1969-98, exec. head theoretical physics, 1969-86, prof. emeritus, 1998—. Rsch. assoc. MIT, 1952-53, asst. prof., 1953-56, adv. bd. Lincoln Lab., 1985-90; vis. scientist Guggenheim fellow CERN Lab., Switzerland, 1961, U. Rome, 1972; vis. prof., Loeb lectr. Harvard U., 1962, 70; vis. Schrodinger prof. theoretical physics U. Vienna, 1975; vis. fellow All Souls Coll., Oxford, 1979; I.I. Rabi vis. prof. Columbia U., 1984; adj. prof. engring., pub. policy Carnegie Mellon U., 1989-96; cons. Office Sci. and Tech., 1960-73, Office Sci. and Tech. Policy, 1977-82, ACDA, 1969-81; adviser NSC, 1973-81, Office Tech. Assessment US Congress, 1975-90, House Armed Svcs. Com., 1990-93, Senate Select Com. on Intelligence, 1990-93; original mem. JASON, 1960—; mem. high energy physics adv. panel Dept. Energy, 1973-86, chmn., 1974-82, energy rsch. adv. bd., 1978-80; mem. Coun. on Foreign Rels. New York, 1980-2007; mem. Carnegie Commn. on Sci., Tech. and Govt., 1988-93, Pres.'s Fgn. Intelligence Adv. Bd., 1993-2001; Richtmyer lectr. Am. Assn. Physics Tchrs., San Francisco, 1978; Danz lectr. U. Wash., 1983; Hans Bethe lectr. Cornell U., 1988; chmn. U.C. pres. coun. on nat. labs., 1992-99; chmn. internat. adv. bd. Inst. Global Conflict and Cooperation, U. Calif., 1990-93; mem. bd. dirs. Internat. Sci. Found., 1993-96; Brickwedded lectr. John Hopkins U., 1997; chair sr. rev. bd. Intelligence Tech. Innovation Ctr., 2001-02; mem. adv. com. Nat. Nuc. Secuirty Adminstrn., 2001-03; mem. sr. adv. group LANL, 2003—; gov. Los Alamos Nat. Security, 2005-, Lawrence Livermore Nat. Lab., 2007-. Author: (books) Electromagnetic Structure of Nucleons, 1961, The Reagan Strategic Defense Initiative: a Technical, Political and Arms Control Assessment, 1985, In the Shadow of the bomb: Physics and Arms Control, 1993, The Gravest Danger: Nuclear Weapons, 2003; co-author (with J.D. Bjorken): Relitivistic Quantum Mechanics, 1964, Relitivistic Quantum Field, 1965, Facing the Threat of Nuclear Weapons, 1983, updated, 1989; co-author: (with Sergei P. Kapitza) Sakharov Remembered: A Tribute by Friends and Colleagues, 1991; co-author: others; editor: (books) The New Terror: Facing the Threat of Biological and Chemical Weapons, 1999; editor: (with James E. Goodby) The Gravest Danger, 2006; contbr. columns in newspapers. Trustee Inst. Advanced Study, Princeton, 1974-83; bd. govs. Weizmann Inst. Sci., Rehovoth, Israel, 1970—; bd. dirs. Ann. Revs., Inc., 1976-97; mem. Pres. Sci. Adv. Com., 1966-70. Recipient Ernest Orlando Lawrence Meml. award AEC, 1972, Alumni award U. Ill., 1973, Alumni Achievement award, 1988, Hilliard Roderick prize AAAS, 1993, Woodrow Wilson award Princeton U., 1994, Ettore Majorana-Erice Sci. for Peace prize, 1994, Gian Carlo Wick medal, 1996, Disting Assoc. award US Dept. Environ., 1997, I. Pomeranchuk prize, 1998, Linus Pauling medal Stanford U., 1999-2000, Enrico Fermi award, 2000, Presidential award, U. Calif., 2000, Heinz R. Pagels Human Rights of Scientists award, 2001, Nat. Intelligence Disting. Svc. medal, 2001, William O. Baker award Intelligence and Nat. Security Alliance, 2001, Heinz award, 2005, others; MacArthur fellow, 1984-89, Sr. fellow Hoover Instn., 1998—. Fellow Am. Phys. Soc. (pres. 1986, Leo Szilard award 1980); mem. AAAS, NAS, Am. Acad. Arts and Scis., Am. Philos. Soc., Arms Control Assn. (bd. dirs. 1978-93), Aspen Strategy Group (emeritus 1991), Academia Europaea. Office: Stanford Linear Accelerator Ctr 2575 Sand Hill Rd MS 80 Menlo Park CA 94025-7015 Office Phone: 650-926-2664. Business E-Mail: drell@slac.stanford.edu.

DRESHER, PAUL JOSEPH, composer, performer, educator; b. LA, Jan. 8, 1951; s. Melvin J. and Martha (Whitaker) D.; m. Robin Naomi Kirck, Mar. 8, 1986 (dec. 1999); 1 child, Cole Kirck Dresher; m. Philippa Kelly, Aug. 2, 2003. MusB, U. Calif., Berkeley, 1977; MA in Composition, U. Calif., La Jolla, 1979. Prof. music Cornish Inst. Arts, Seattle, 1980-83; artistic dir. Paul Dresher Ensemble, Berkeley, 1984—. Cons. Nat. Endowment for the Arts, Calif. Arts Coun., 1982-94, Meet the Composer, Rockefeller Found. Composer: (opera) Slow Fire, 1987, Power Failure, 1989, (music theater) Pioneer, 1989, (orchestral work) Reaction, 1984; (chamber orch.) Cornucopia, 1990; (dances) Shelf Life, 1987, Age of Unrest, 1991, The Gates, 1993, Outawak, 1997, Kalasam, 2000; (trio) Double Ikat, 1989; (chamber) Din of Iniquity, 1994; (solo piano) Blue Diamonds, 1995, Violin Concerto (chamber), 1996-97, Elapsed Time (for violin and piano), 1998, (music theater) Sound Stage, 2001, Snow in June, 2003, (chamber) Cello Concerto Unequal Distemperament, 2001, Chromatic Quadrachord, 2001, (dance) In the Name, 2001; works presented by numerous symphonic and other orchs. including N.Y. Philharm. Munich State Opera, London Internat. Festival of Theatre; recordings on New Albion, Lovely, Starkland and New World labels. Bd. dirs. New Langton Arts Orgn., San Francisco, 1984-2002, Am. Music Ctr., 1994-2000. Recipient numerous grants NEA, 1979-2003; Fulbright grantee, 1984; Goddard Lieberson fellow, 1982. Mem. Broadcast Music, Inc., Am. Music Ctr., Opera America, Chamber Music America. Home and Office: 51 Avenida Dr Berkeley CA 94708-2145 Home Phone: 510-644-9541; Office Phone: 510-834-4102. Business E-Mail: pauld@dresherensemble.org.

DRESSEL, MELANIE J., bank executive; m. Bob Dressel; children: Robb, Brent. BS in Polit. Sci., Univ. Wash. With Bank of Calif., 1974—78; dir. private banking Puget Sound Bank; sr. v.p., private banking Columbia Bank, Tacoma, 1993—97, exec. v.p. retail banking, 1997—2000, pres., 2000—; also CEO Columbia Banking System, Inc., Tacoma, 2003—. Chmn. Washington Bankers Assn. Bd. mem. Foss Waterway Devel.; chmn. Exec. Coun. Greater Tacoma; bd. mem. Washington Roundtable, Bellarmine Prep. Sch.; Mary Bridge Children's Found. Tacoma. Named one of 25 Most Powerful Women in Banking, US Banker, 2005, 2006. Office: Columbia Banking System Ste 800 1301 A St Tacoma WA 98402 Office Phone: 253-305-1900.

DRESSLER, ALAN MICHAEL, astronomer; b. Cin., Mar. 23, 1948; s. Charles and Gay (Stein) Dressler. BA in Physics, U. Calif., Berkeley, 1970; PhD in Astronomy, U. Calif., Santa Cruz, 1976. Carnegie Instn. of Washington fellow Hale Obs., Pasadena, Calif., 1976-78, Las Campanas fellow, 1978-81; sci. staff Carnegie Obs. (formerly Mt. Wilson and Las Campanas Obs., formerly Hale Obs.), Pasadena, 1981—, acting assoc. dir., 1988-89. Chair origins subcomS NASA, 2000—03. Contbr. to sci. jours. Recipient Pub. Svcs. medal NASA 1999. Fellow Am. Acad. Arts and Scis.; mem. NAS, Am. Astron. Soc. (councilor 1989-91, Pierce prize 1983), Internat. Astron. Union. Office: Carnegie Obs 813 Santa Barbara St Pasadena CA 91101-1232

DREW, CLIFFORD JAMES, dean, psychologist, educator; b. Eugene, Oregon, Mar. 9, 1943; s. Albert C. and Violet M. (Caskey) D. BS magna cum laude, Ea. Oreg. Coll., 1965; EdM, U.Ill., 1966; PhD (hon.), U. Oreg., 1968. Asst. prof. edn. Kent State U., Ohio, 1968-69; asst. prof. dir. rsch. and spl. edn. U. Tex., Austin, 1969-71; assoc. prof. spl. edn. U. Utah, Salt Lake City, 1971-76, prof., 1977—, asst. dean Grad. Sch. Edn., 1974-77, assoc. dean, 1977-79, 89-95, prof. spl. edn., ednl. psychology, 1979—, coord. instrnl. tech., acad. v.p. office, 1995-97, assoc. acad. v.p., 1997—2004, assoc. dean Coll. Edn., 2004—. Cons. HEW, 1969-80; Bd. dir. Far West Lab. Ednl. Rsch. and Devel., San Francisco, 1974-80; mem. exec. bd. Salt Lake County Assn. Retarded Children, 1971-72; mem. adv. com. Mental Retardation Counseling Svc., Tex. Dept. Mental Health Mental Retardation, 1969-70. Author: Intro. to Designing Rsch. and Evaluation, 2d edit., 1976, Designing and Conducting Behavioral Rsch., 1985; co-author (with B. Wampold): Theory and Application of Stats., 1990; co-author: (with M. Hardman and A. Hart) Designing and Conducting Rsch.: Inquiry in Edn. and Social Sci., 1996; co-author: (with M. Hardman) Mental Retardation: A Life Cycle Approach, 2000, 8th edit., 2004; co-author: (with D. Gelfand) Understanding Child Behavior Disorders, 2003; co-author: (with M. Hardman) Mental Retardation: A Life Cycle Approach to People with Intellectual Disabilities, 8th edit., 2004, Intellectual Disabilities Across the Lifespan, 2006, 9th edit., 2007; co-author: (with M. Hardman and W. Egan) Human Exceptionality: School, Community, and Family, 2006, 2008; co-author: (with M. Hardman and J. Hosp) Designing and Conducting Research in education, 2008; contbr. numerous articles to profl. jours. NDEA fellow, 1965-66; U.S. Office Edn. fellow, 1966-68. Fellow Am. Assn. on Intellectual and Devel. Disabilities; mem. Am. Psychol. Assn., Am. Ednl. Rsch. Assn. Office: U Utah Dean's Office 1705 Campus Center Dr Rm 225 Salt Lake City UT 84112-9007 Home Phone: 435-783-2743. Business E-Mail: cliff.drew@utah.edu.

DREW, PAUL S., entrepreneur; b. Detroit, Mar. 10, 1935; s. Harry and Elizabeth (Schneider) Schlachman; m. Dove Ann Austin, Sept. 9, 1961. BA, Wayne State U., Detroit, 1957. Disc jockey, Port Huron, Mich. and Atlanta, 1955-67; program dir. Sta. WQXI, Atlanta, 1966-67, Sta. CKLW, Detroit, 1967-68; program cons. Storer Broadcasting Co., Phila., 1968-69; program dir. RKO Radio stas. in, Detroit, San Francisco, Washington and L.A., 1970-73; v.p. programming RKO Radio stas., 1973-77; pres. Paul Drew Enterprises, LA, 1977—; dir. USIA-Radio Marti, 1984-85; pres. USA Japan Co., 1985—, The Mobotron Corp., Hollywood, Calif., 1988—, Fuzzmug Corp., 1991—, 2151 Corp., 1991—. Personal mgr. Pink Lady, outside Japan, 1978; ptnr. Teacup-Teaspoon Music Pub. Co., 1978; chmn. Billboard Internat. Programming Conf., 1976; commr. Calif. Motion Picture Coun., 1979-85. Del. Dem. Nat. Conv., 1976; mem. Dem. Nat. Com., Calif. Dem. Com., Dem. Nat. Fin. Council. Named DeeJay of Year Sixteen Mag., 1965; Program Dir. of Year Bill Gavin Report, 1967; recipient Superior Achievement award RKO Radio, 1973; also numerous gold records for contbs. toward million selling records. Mem. NARAS, Am. Advt. Fedn., Am. Film Inst., Hollywood Radio and TV Soc., L.A. World Affairs Coun., Town Hall Calif., Japan Am. Soc., Variety, Friars, Frat. of Friends, Music Ctr. Home and Office: 11663 Amestoy Ave Granada Hills CA 91344

DREXLER, JEROME, technology company executive; Chmn. bd., CEO Drexler Tech. Corp., Mountain View, Calif.

DREXLER, KENNETH, lawyer; b. Aug. 2, 1941; s. Fred and Martha Jane Drexler; m. Sarah Leach, Jan. 1, 1982; 1 child, Daniel Warren. BA, Stanford U., 1963; JD, UCLA, 1969. Bar: Calif. 1970. Assoc. David S. Smith, Beverly Hills, Calif., 1970, McCutchen, Doyle, Brown and Enersen, San Francisco, 1970-77, Chickering &

Gregory, San Francisco, 1977-80, ptnr., 1980-82, Drexler & Leach, San Rafael, Calif., 1982—2008; atty., 2009—. Served with AUS, 1964-66. Mem. Calif. State Bar (resolutions com. conf. of dels. 1979-83, chmn. 1982-83, adminstrn. justice com. 1983-89, chmn. 1987-88, adv. mem. 1990-2000), Marin County Bar Assn. (bd. dirs. 1985-87), Bar Assn. San Francisco (bd. dirs. 1980-81), San Francisco Barristers Club (pres. 1976, dir. 1975-76), Marin Conservation League (bd. dirs. 1985-97, 98—, treas. 2001—). Office: 1330 Lincoln Ave Ste 300 San Rafael CA 94901-2143 Office Phone: 415-485-1330. E-mail: kdrexler@svn.net.

DRIGGS, ADAM, state legislator; b. Ariz., Apr. 22, 1965; m. Leonore Mortensen, 1998; children: Emily, J.R., Charlie. BA in Portuguese, Brigham Young U., 1990; JD, Ariz. State U. Sch. Law, 1993. Prosecutor Maricopa County Atty.'s Office, Phoenix, 1995—97; pvt. practice atty., 1997—; mem. Dist. 11 Ariz. House of Reps., 2007—, chair judiciary com., mem. govt. com. Vol. Habitat for Humanity, Boy Scouts. Republican. Office: Ariz House Reps Capitol Complex 1700 W Washington Rm 222 Phoenix AZ 85007 Home Phone: 602-957-3761; Office Phone: 602-926-3016. Office Fax: 602-417-3007. Business E-Mail: adriggs@azleg.gov.*

DRINKWATER, PETER LOFTUS, airport executive; m. Joanne Loftus Drinkwater; children: Adam, Nathan. AA, U. N.H., 1975, BA, 1977; MPA, Golden Gate U., 1981. Enlisted USAF, 1971-75, advanced through grades to lt. col., 1977-98, ret., 1998; airport mgr. Ontario Internat. Airport, 1998—. Active Boy Scouts Am. With USAF. Mem. Exptl. Aircraft Assn. Avocation: licensed pilot. Office: Ontario Internat Airport Terminal Bldg Rm 200 Ontario CA 91761 E-mail: peterdrink@cs.com, peterdrink@la.org.

DRINNON, RICHARD, retired historian; b. Portland, Oreg., Jan. 4, 1925; s. John Henry and Emma (Tweed) D.; m. Anna Maria Faulise, Oct. 20, 1945; children: Donna Elizabeth, Jon Tweed. BA summa cum laude, Willamette U., 1950; MA, U. Minn., 1951, PhD, 1957. Instr. humanities U. Minn., 1952-53, social sci., 1955-57; instr. Am. history U. Calif., 1957-58, asst. prof., 1958-61; Bruern fellow in Am. studies U. Leeds, 1961-63; faculty research fellow Social Sci. Research Council, 1963-64; asso. prof. history Hobart and William Smith Colls., 1964-66; chmn. dept. history Bucknell U., 1966-74, prof. history, 1974-87, prof. emeritus, 1987—. Vis. prof. U. Paris, 1975 Author: Rebel in Paradise: a Biography of Emma Goldman, 1961, White Savage: The Case of John Dunn Hunter, 1972, Facing West: The Metaphysics of Indian-Hating and Empire-Building, 1980, 90, 97, Keeper of Concentration Camps: Dillon S. Myer and American Racism, 1987; co-editor: Nowhere at Home: Letters from Exile of Emma Goldman and Alexander Berkman, 1974; contbr. articles and revs. to profl. jours. and mags. Served with USNR, 1942-46. NEH sr. fellow, 1980-81 Office: PO Box 1001 Port Orford OR 97465-1001

DRISCOLL, CHARLES FREDERICK, physicist, educator; b. Tucson, Feb. 28, 1950; s. John Raymond Gozzi and Barbara Jean (Hamilton) Driscoll; m. Suzan C. Bain, Dec. 30, 1972; children: Thomas A., Robert A. BA in Physics summa cum laude, Cornell U., 1969; MS, U. Calif. San Diego, La Jolla, 1972, PhD, 1976. Staff scientist Gen. Atomics, San Diego, 1969; rsch. asst. U. Calif. San Diego, La Jolla, 1971-76, rsch. physicist, sr. lectr., 1976-96, prof. physics, 1996—, assoc. dir. Inst. for Pure and Applied Scis., 1998—. Cons. Sci. Applications, Inc., 1980-81; staff physicist, cons. Molecular Biosystems, Inc., 1981-82. Editor: Non-Neutral Plasma Physics, 1988; contbr. numerous articles to sci. jours. Fellow NSF, 1969-71. Fellow Am. Phys. Soc. (Excellence in Plasma Physics Rsch. award 1991, Disting. Lectr. divsn. plasma physics 1999-2000); mem. AAAS, Math. Assn. Am., Phi Beta Kappa. Achievements include development of quantitative analysis of magnetic targeting of microspheres in capillaries, experiments and theory on magnetized electron plasmas, new camera-diagnosed electron plasma apparatus, new laser-diagnosed ion plasma apparatus for in-situ transport measurements; establishment of magnetic containment characteristics of unneutralized plasmas; measurement of collisional transport of heat and particles to thermal equilibrium; observation of new 2D fluid instability and relaxation of 2D turbulence to vortex crystal states. Office: U Calif San Diego Dept Physics 0319 9500 Gilman Dr Dept 0319 La Jolla CA 92093-5004 E-mail: fdriscoll@ucsd.edu.

DRISCOLL, MICHAEL PATRICK, bishop; b. Long Beach, Calif., Aug. 8, 1939; Student, St. John's Sem., Camarillo, Calif.; STB, Cath. U. of Am., 1965; MSW, U. So. Calif., LA, 1975. Ordained priest Archdiocese of LA, Calif., 1965; aux. bishop Diocese of Orange, Calif., 1990-99; ordained bishop, 1990; bishop Diocese of Boise City, 1999—. Roman Catholic. Office: Boise Diocese 303 Federal Way Boise ID 83705-5925 Office Phone: 208-342-1311. Office Fax: 208-342-0224.

DRISKILL, JAMES LAWRENCE, minister; b. Rustburg, Va., Aug. 18, 1920; s. Elijah Hudnall and Annie Pharr (Carwile) D.; m. Ethel Lillian Cassel, May 28, 1949 (dec. Aug. 2004); children: Edward Lawrence, Mary Lillian; m. Edina de Rosa, Apr. 18, 2007. BA, Pa. State U., 1946; BD, San Francisco Theol. Sem., 1949; ThM, Princeton Sem., 1957; S.T.D., San Francisco Theol. Sem., 1969. Ordained minister in Presbyn. Ch. 1949. Missionary Presbyn. Ch. USA, Japan, 1949-72; stated supply pastor Madison Square Presbyn. Ch., San Antonio, 1973; minister Highland Presbyn. Ch., Maryville, Tenn., 1973-82; supply pastor of Japanese-Am. chs. Presbyn. Ch. USA, Long Beach, Calif., Hollywood, Calif., Altadena, Calif., 1984-99. Vis. prof. religion dept. Trinity U., 1972-73. Author: Adventures in Senior Living, 1997, Christmas Stories from Around the World, 1997, Worldwide Mission Stories for Young People, 1996, Cross-Cultural Marriages and the Church, 1995, Mission Stories from Around the World, 1994, Japan Diary, 1993, Mission Adventures in Many Lands, 1992; contbr. articles to profl. jours. Trustee Osaka (Japan) Girls Sch., 1952-65, Seikyo Gakuen Christian Sch., Japan, 1953-92. With USN, 1943-46. Mem. Am. Acad. Religion, Presbyn. Writers Guild, Sierra Club. Democrat. Presbyterian. Home and Office: 3716 Grace Ave Baldwin Park CA 91706

DRIVER, MICHAEL J., lawyer; b. Highland Park, Ill., Dec. 4, 1944; BA, Amherst Coll., 1967; JD, Univ. Denver, 1974. Bar: Colo. 1974. Ptnr., Public Policy, Legis. Affairs, Environ. Health & Safety practices, mem. exec. com. Patton Boggs LLP, Denver. Mem. Clinton for Pres. Nat. Exec. Com., Clinton Nat. Fin. Com., Pres. Inaugural Com., Clinton Transition Team Nat. Resources sect. Mem. Native Am. Rights Fund Nat. Sponsorship Com., John F. Kennedy Ctr for Performing Arts Adv. Com. on the Arts. Mem.: ABA, Colo. Bar Assn., Denver Bar Assn. Office: Patton Boggs LLP Suite 1900 1660 Lincoln St Denver CO 80264-1901 Office Phone: 303-830-1776. Office Fax: 303-894-9239. Business E-Mail: mdriver@pattonboggs.com.

DROOYAN, RICHARD E., lawyer; b. LA, 1950; BA summa cum laude, Claremont Men's Coll., 1972; JD cum laude, Harvard U., 1975. Bar: Calif. 1975. Assoc. Kadison, Pfaezler, Woodard, Quinn & Rossi, 1975; asst. atty. States Atty.'s Office, LA, 1978—84; cheif Criminal Complaints Unit, 1982, US State Office, 1982—84; chief asst. US Atty. Robert C. Bonner, 1984—88; mem. Skadden, Arps, Slate, Meagher & Flom, 1988—93; cheif, criminal divsn. US Atty.'s Office, LA, 1993—96; chief asst. US Atty. Nora Manella, 1997—99; ptnr. Munger, Tolles & Olson LLP, LA. Lectr. So. Calif. Law Ctr., Loyola Law Sch.; dep. gen. counsel Ind. Comm. LA Police Dept., 1991; gen. councel Rampart Ind. Rev. Panel., 2000. Mem. (bd. trustees) Camp Ronald McDonald Good Times; mem. Children's Law Ctr., LA. Mem. LA County Bar Assn.'s (bd. trustees) LACBA com., pres. LA Chpt. Fed. Bar Assn. Office: Munger Tolles & Olson LLP 355 S Grand Ave 35th Fl Los Angeles CA 90071-1560 Office Phone: 213-683-9136. Office Fax: 213-683-5136. Business E-Mail: richard.drooyan@mto.com.

DR. PHIL, (PHILLIP CALVIN MCGRAW), psychologist, television personality; b. Vinita, Okla., Sept. 1, 1950; s. Joseph and Jerri McGraw; m. Debbie Higgins, 1970 (div. 1973); m. Robin Jameson, 1976; children: Jay, Jordan. Student U. Tulsa; BA in Clin. Psychology, North Tex. State U., MA in Clin. Psychology, 1976, PhD in Clin. Psychology, 1979. Bd. cert. and licensed Clin. Psychologist 1978. Clin. psychologist, behavioral medicine practitioner; co-founder Courtroom Scis., Inc. (litigation consulting firm), Irving, Tex., 1989; regular commentator Oprah Winfrey Show, 1986—; host The Dr. Phil Show, 2001—, Dr. Phil's Prime Time Spl.-Escaping Addiction, 2006; monthly columnist O, the Oprah Magazine. Cons., MindFindBind with Dr. Phil match.com, 2006—; pub. spkr. in field. Author: Life Strategies: Doing What Works, Doing What Matters, 1999, Relationship Rescue: A Seven-Step Strategy for Reconnecting with Your Partner, 2000, Self Matters: Creating Your Life from the Inside Out, 2001, The Ultimate Weight Solution: The Seven Keys to Weight Loss Freedom, 2003, The Ultimate Weight Solution Food Guide, 2003, Family First: Your Step-by-Step Plan for Creating a Phenomenal Family, 2004 (Publishers Weekly Bestseller list, 2004), The Ultimate Weight Solution Cookbook: Recipes for Weight Loss Freedom, 2004, Real Life: Preparing for the 7 Most Challenging Days of Your Life, 2008; introduced themes to Dr. Phil Show such as: The Ultimate Weight Loss Challenge, Relationship Rescue Retreat Series, Brandon's Intervention; contbr. articles to profl. jours.; actor: (films) Scary Movie 4, 2006. Founder Dr. Phil Foundation, 2003—. Named one of Most Intriguing People of 2002, People mag., Ten Most Fascinating People, Barbara Walters TV special, 2002, The 100 Most Powerful Celebrities, Forbes.com, 2007, 2008. Avocations: golf, tennis, scuba diving, coaching Little League baseball. Office: The Dr Phil Show 5482 Wilshire Blvd 1902 Los Angeles CA 90036

DRUDGE, MATT (MATTHEW NATHAN DRUDGE), journalist, celebrity blogger; b. Oct. 27, 1967; s. Robert Drudge. Gift shop mgr. CBS-TV, LA; founder, editor The Drudge Report website, 1995—; host TV show Drudge, 1998—99; host radio show ABC Network, 1999—2000, Premiere Radio Networks, Inc., 2001—. Author: Drudge Manifesto, 2000. Named one of 100 Most Influential People, TIME mag., 2006, Top 25 Web Celebs, Forbes mag., 2006, 2007. Achievements include Drudge Report listing as #2 on the top 10 web moments that changed the world at the 1998 Webby awards for news break of the Monica Lewinsky scandel. Office: Premiere Radio Networks Inc 15260 Ventura Blvd 5th Fl Sherman Oaks CA 91403 Office Phone: 818-377-5300. Office Fax: 818-377-5333.*

DRUEHL, LOUIS DIX, biology professor; b. San Francisco, Oct. 9, 1936; naturalized Can. citizen, 1974; s. Louis Dix and Charlotte (Primrose) D.; m. Jo Ann Reeve, Aug. 17, 1967 (div. 1974); m. Rae Kristanne Randolph, Aug. 11, 1983. BSc, Wash. State U., 1958; MSc, U. Wash., 1962; PhD, U. B.C., Vancouver, B.C., 1966. Rsch. advisor Brazil Navy, Cabo Frio, 1975-77; cons. biomass program GE, Catalina, Calif., 1981-83; from asst. prof. to assoc. prof. Simon Fraser U., Burnaby, B.C., 1966-88, prof. biology, 1988—2002, prof. emeritus, 2002—, dir. Inst. Aquaculture Rsch., 1988-90; assoc. dir. Bamfield (B.C.) Marine Sta., 1992-96. Rsch. assoc. Inst. Algae Rsch. U. Hokkaido, 1972-73; pres. Can. Kelp Resources Ltd., Bamfield, 1982—. Mem. editorial bd. European Jour. Phycology, 1993-96; contbr. over 50 articles to profl. jours. Recipient Provasoli Best Paper award, Jour. Phycology, 1988. Mem. Western Soc. Naturalists (pres. 1988). Avocation: poetry. Home: 4 Port Desire Bamfield BC Canada V0R 1B0 Office: Bamfield Marine Sta Bamfield BC Canada V0R 1B0 Home Phone: 250-728-3297; Office Phone: 250-728-3301. E-mail: ldruehl@island.net.

DRUKER, BRIAN JAY, medical educator, researcher; b. St. Paul, Apr. 30, 1955; s. Jean S. Druker. MD, U. Calif.-San Diego, La Jolla, 1981. Internship and residency in internal medicine Barnes Hosp., Washington Sch. of Medicine, St. Louis; trained in oncology Harvard's Dana-Farber Cancer Inst.; prof. medicine Oreg. Health & Sci. U., Portland, 1993—2001, JELD-WEN chair, dir., leukemia ctr. Recipient medal of honor, Am. Cancer Soc., 2001, AACR-Richard and Hinda Rosenthal award, 2001, Dameshak prize, Am. Soc. Hematology, 2001, Warren Alpert Found. award, Harvard Med. Sch., 2001, John J. Kenney award, Leukemia and Lymphoma Soc., 2000, Brupbacher Found. Cancer Rsch. award, 2001, Emil J. Freireich award for clin. rsch., MD Anderson Cancer Ctr., 2001, Charles F. Kettering prize, GM Cancer Rsch. Found., 2002, Pioneer Survivorship award, Lance Armstrong Found., 2002. Mem.: NAS, Inst. Medicine, 2004. Avocations: running, bicycling. Office: Oreg Health and Sci U 3181 SW Sam Jackson Park Rd Portland OR 97201

DRUMMOND, DAVID C., information technology executive, lawyer; BA in History, Santa Clara U; JD, Stanford Law Sch., 1989. Former ptnr. corp. transactions group Wilson, Sonsini, Goodrich, & Rosati, 1998; exec. v.p. fin., CFO CBT Group PLC, 1999, SmartForce; v.p. corp. devel. Google Inc., Mountain View, Calif., 2002—, gen. counsel, 2002—06, sec., 2002—06, sr. v.p. corp. devel. Office: Google Inc 1600 Amphitheatre Pky Mountain View CA 94043 Office Phone: 650-623-4000. Office Fax: 650-618-1499.

DRUMMOND, MARSHALL EDWARD (MARK), academic administrator; b. Stanford, Calif., Sept. 14, 1941; s. Kirk Isaac and Fern Venice (McDeritt) D.; 2 children. BS, San Jose State U., 1964, MBA, 1969; EdD, U. San Francisco, 1979. Adj. prof. bus. and edn. U. San Francisco, 1975-81; adj. prof. bus. and info. systems San Francisco State U., 1981-82; prof. MIS, Ea. Wash. U., Cheney, 1985—98, exec. dir. info. resources, 1988, assoc. v.p. adminstrv. svcs., chief info. officer, 1988-89, v.p. adminstrv. svcs., 1989-90, exec. v.p., 1990, pres., 1990-98; chancellor L.A. C.C. Dist., 1999—2004, Calif. C.C. sys., 2004—. Cons. Sch. Bus., Harvard Coll., U. Ariz. Contbg. editor Diebold Series; contbr. articles to profl. jours. Democrat. Avocations: horse breeding and traing, equestrian sports. Office: Calif Cmty Colls Chancellor's Office 1102 Q St Sacramento CA 95814-6511 Home Phone: 916-444-7538; Office Phone: 916-322-4005. Business E-Mail: mdrummond@cccco.edu.

DRUMMY, KATHLEEN H., lawyer; BA, U. Calif., Berkeley, 1973; MA, UCLA, 1974, JD, 1977. Bar: Calif. 1977. Judicial internship Judge Harry Pregerson, US Dist Ct. ctrl dist. Calif., 1976; ptnr. Mucisk Peeler & Garrett LLP, McDermott Will & Emery, Memel Jacobs Pierno Gersh & Ellsworth; ptnr., health law practice Davis Wright Tremaine LLP, LA. Editor (exec.): UCLA Alaska Law Rev.; contbr. articles to profl. jours. Mem.: Am. Health Lawyers Assn., Calif. Bar Assn. Office: Davis Wright Tremaine LLP Ste 2400 865 S Figueroa St Los Angeles CA 90017-2566 Office Phone: 213-633-6800. Office Fax: 213-633-6899. Business E-Mail: kathydrummy@dwt.com.

DRYER, MURRAY, physicist, educator; b. Bridgeport, Conn., Nov. 4, 1925; s. Sol and Sarah (Shapiro) D.; m. Geraldine Gray Goodsell, May 12, 1955; children: Steven Michael, Lisa Dryer Travis. Student, U. Conn., 1943-44; BS, Stanford U., 1949, MS, 1950; PhD, Tel-Aviv U., 1971. Research asst. NACA-NASA Ames Research Ctr., Calif., 1949; aero. research scientist NACA-NASA Lewis Research Ctr., Cleve., 1950-59; assoc. research scientist Martin Marietta Corp., Denver, 1959-65; chief interplanetary physics Space Environ. Lab., NOAA Environ. Research Labs., Boulder, Colo., 1965-94, guest worker emeritus, 1994—; sr. scientist Coop. Inst. for Rsch. in Environ. Scis., U. Colo., Boulder, 1994-96; cons. Exploration Physics Internat., Inc., 1996—, Geophysical Inst. U., Fairbanks, Ala., 2001—. Lectr. dept. aerospace engrng. scis. U. Colo., 1963-76, dept. astrogeophysics, 1978; vis. assoc. prof. dept. mech. engring. Colo. State U., 1966-67; mem. com. solar terrestrial rsch. NAS, 1976-80, 84-91, com. geophys. data NAS, 1987-93. Author: (with others) Solar-Terrestrial Physics in the 1980's, 1981; editor: (with others) Solar Observations and Predictions of Solar Activity, 1972, Exploration of the Outer Solar System, 1976, Solar and Interplanetary Dynamics, 1980, Advances in Solar Connection wirh Interplanetary Phenomena, 1998; spl. issue editor Space Sci. Revs., 1976; contbr. articles to profl. jours. With U.S. Navy, 1944-46. Mem. Am. Phys. Soc., Am. Geophys. Union, AAAS, Sci. Com. Solar-Terrestrial Physics, Internat. Astron. Union, Com. Space Research, AIAA (Space Sci. award 1975), Sigma Xi Office: Space Environment Ctr NOAA NCEP NWS Mail Code R-E-SE Boulder CO 80305-3328 Home Phone: 303-798-1440; Office Phone: 303-497-3978. Personal E-mail: murraydryer@msn.com. Business E-Mail: murray.dryer@noaa.gov.

DUBÉ, SUSAN E., women's healthcare company executive; BA, Simmons Coll., 1969; MBA, Harvard U., 1981. V.p. ventures Brigham and Women's Hosp., Boston, 1985-91; exec. v.p., COO, v.p. bus. devel. Adeza Biomed., Inc., Sunnyvale, Calif., 1991-93; ind. cons. to numerous health cos., 1993-94; pres., CEO, BioIntervensions, Inc., Saratoga, Calif., 1994-95; cons. LifeSci. Econs., Inc., Menlo Park, Calif., 1995; v.p. mktg. and bus. devel., v.p. bus. devel. Imagyn Med., Inc., Laguna Niguel, Calif., 1996-97; sr. v.p. strategy and corp. devel. Imagyn Med. Techs., Inc., Newport Beach, Calif., 1997-98; jr. v.p., v.p. strategic planning and acquisitions Women First HealthCare, Inc., San Diego, 1998—. Fax: 619-509-1353.

DUBIN, MARK WILLIAM, neuroscientist, educator, academic administrator; b. NYC, Aug. 30, 1942; s. Sidney Stanley and Dorothy (Cirinsky) D.; m. Alma Hermine Heller, June 27, 1964; children: Lila Rachel, Miriam Rebecca AB in Biophysics, Amherst Coll., 1964; PhD in Biophysics, Johns Hopkins U., 1969. Research fellow Australian Nat. U., Canberra, 1969-71; asst. prof. dept. molecular, cellular and devel. biology U. Colo., Boulder, 1971-77, assoc. prof., 1977-82, prof., 1982—87, chmn. dept., 1983-87, assoc. chmn. dept., 2000—, assoc. vice chancellor for acad. affairs, 1988-97, chief info. officer, 1996-97, faculty fellow info. tech. svcs., 1997-98, dir. acad. devel. BP Ctr. for Visualization, 2003—05. Sci. cons. Wills Found., 1981-91; cons., mem. bd. sci. advisors Columbine Venture Fund, Denver, 1984-94, Photometrics, Tucson, 1987-89; founding ptnr. 3D Embodiment LLC; owner MWm Crafts, 1996—; co-founder 3D Embodiment, LLC, 2005—; mem. acad. adv. bd. higher edn. Apple Computing, 1997-98. Author: How the Brain Works; contbr. articles to profl. jours. Bd. dirs. Congregation Har Ha-Shem, Boulder, 1976-80, pres., 1978, 79, Cmty. Access TV of Boulder, 1996-97. Grantee NIH-Nat. Eye Inst., 1972-90, NSF, 1976-83, March of Dimes Found., 1982-83; Fight for Sight fellow Australian Nat. U., 1969-71 Mem. AAAS, AAUP, Soc. Neurosci., Sigma Xi. Democrat. Jewish. Avocation: woodworking. Home: 1010 Grape Ave Boulder CO 80304-2129 Office: Univ Colo Dept Molecular Cellular Biology PO Box 347 Boulder CO 80309-0347 Home Phone: 303-442-7818; Office Phone: 303-250-6668. Business E-Mail: dubin@colorado.edu.

DUBOFSKY, JEAN EBERHART, lawyer, retired state supreme court justice; b. 1942; m. Frank Dobofsky; children: Joshua, Matthew. BA, Stanford U., 1964; LLB, Harvard U., 1967. Admitted to Colo. bar, 1967. Legis. asst. to U.S. Senator Walter F. Mondale, 1967-69; atty. Colo. Rural Legal Services, Boulder, 1969-72, Legal Aid Soc. Met. Denver, 1972-73; ptnr. Kelley, Dubofsky, Haglund & Harnsey, Denver, 1973-75; dep. atty. gen. Colo., 1975-77; counsel Kelly, Haglund, Garnsey & Kahn, 1977-79, 88-90, Jean E. Dubofsky, P.C., Boulder, 1991—. Justice Colo. Supreme Ct., Denver, 1979-87; vis. prof. U. Colo. Law Sch., Boulder, 1987-88. Office: 1000 Rosehill Dr Boulder CO 80302-7148

DUBON, OSCAR D., JR., engineering educator; BS in Materials Engrng., UCLA, 1989; MS in Materials Sci. & Mineral Engrng., U. Calif., Berkeley, 1992, PhD in Materials Sci. & Mineral Engrng., 1996. Grad. student rsch. asst. U. Calif./Lawrence Berkeley Nat. Lab., 1989-96, vis. postdoctoral rsch. engr., 1996-97; postdoctoral fellow Harvard U., 1997-2000; asst. prof. dept. materials sci. and mineral engring. U. Calif., Berkeley, 2000—. Presenter in field. Contbr. articles to profl. jours. Recipient Robert Lansing Hardy gold medal Minerals, Metals and Materials Soc., 2000; ASM scholar, 1987; Nat. Phys. Sci. Consortium fellow, 1989-95, Japanese Soc. for the Promotion Sci. postdoctoral fellow, 1996. Mem. Am. Phys. Soc., Materials Rsch. Soc. Achievements include research on electronic materials processing, low-temperature molecular beam epitaxy, growth and properties of group IV alloys, synthesis of semiconductor nanostructures. Office: U Calif Berkeley Dept Materials Sci 587 Evans Hall #1760 Berkeley CA 94720-1760 E-mail: oddubon@socrates.berkeley.edn.

DUBOSE, GUY STEVEN, lawyer; b. Hollywood, Calif., June 12, 1954; s. Donald Thomas DuBose and Normalee Carol (Johnson) Farris. AB, U. So. Calif., 1976; JD, Whittier Coll., 1979; LLM, Cambridge U., Eng., 1981; cert., The Hague Acad. Internat. Law, The Netherlands, 1981. Bar: Calif. 1979, U.S. Dist. Ct. (cen. dist.) Calif. 1979. In house counsel Di-Line Corp., Orange, Calif., 1980-82; project contract adminstr. Rockwell Internat., Los Angeles, 1982-84; corp. counsel So. Calif. Savs., Beverly Hills, Calif., 1984-87; sr. v.p., gen. counsel Mercury Savs., Huntington Beach, Calif., 1987-91; COO, gen. counsel Guardian Fed., Huntington Beach, Calif., 1991-92; sr. v.p., gen. counsel Westcorp (Western Fin.), Irvine, Calif., 1992—. Mem. Orange County Bar Assn. Office: Westcorp 23 Pasteur Irvine CA 92618-3816 Office Phone: 949-727-1044.

DUBREUIL, FRANCIS W., lawyer; b. Westport, Mass., Sept. 15, 1948; m. Marcia Beall Dubreuil; children: Jessie Beall Dubreuil, Owen Beall Dubreuil, Ellen Beall Dubreuil. BA summa cum laude, Boston Coll., 1970; JD cum laude, Harvard U., 1974; MS, Stanford U., 1990. Bar: Mass. 1974, Calif. 1997, US Dist. Ct. Mass., US Dist. Ct. (no. dist.) Calif., US Ct. Appeals (1st cir.) 1974, US Ct. Appeals (9th cir.) 1997, US Tax Ct. 1997. Ptnr., chmn. estate planning dept., co-chmn. pvt. bus. grp., mem. exec. com. Goodwin Procter, LLP, Boston, 1974—96; ptnr., mem. estate planning and wealth mgmt. grp., chmn. tax svcs. grp. Wilson, Sonsini, Goodrich & Rosati, P.C., Palo Alto, Calif., 1996—2006; nat. mng. dir. Bernstein Global Wealth Mgmt., San Francisco, 2006—. Named one of Top 100 Attys., Worth mag., 2005—06. Fellow Am. Coll. Trust and Estate Counsel; mem. ABA (mem. corps., taxation, real property, probate, trust law sects.), Mass. Bar Assn., Boston Bar Assn., Calif. Bar Assn. Office: Bernstein Global Wealth Mgmt 555 California St Ste 4300 San Francisco CA 94104 Mailing: 2465 South Ct Palo Alto CA 94301-4239 Office Phone: 415-217-8072. Business E-Mail: francis.dubreuil@bernstein.com.

DUBROFF, HENRY ALLEN, editor, journalist, entrepreneur; b. Neptune, NJ, Nov. 28, 1950; s. Sol and Gilda (Burdman) D.; married, 1980 (div. 1986). AB in History and Lit., Lafayette Coll., 1972; MS in Journalism, Columbia U., 1982. Program analyst Dept. Health and Human Svcs., Washington, 1972-73; tchr. English Holyoke St. Sch., Mass., 1974-78; employment & tng. program mgr. Knoxville-Knox CY Community Action, Tenn., 1978-81; bus. writer, columnist Springfield Newspapers, Mass., 1982-85, The Denver Post, Colo., 1985-88, bus. editor, 1988-95; editor Denver Bus. Jour., Colo., 1995-99; founder, editor, chmn. Pacific Coast Bus. Times, 1999—. Contbg. writer CFO Mag., Boston, 1985-90; guest lectr. U. Wis., Madison, Calif. State U., Channel Islands, U. Colo., Denver, U. Calif., Santa Barbara. Contbr. articles to N.Y. Times, 1982-89. Vol. Russian Resettlement Program Jewish Family & Children's Svcs., Denver, 1989—90; mem. bd. United Way, 2005—; chmn. Santa Barbara County United Way Campaign, 2004—05; bd. dirs. Ventura County Econ. Devel. Assn., U. Calif. Santa Barbara Econ. Forecast Project, Ptnrs. in Edn., Santa Barbara, Jewish Fedn. Santa Barbara. Recipient NY Fin. Writers Assn. scholarship, 1982, Morton Margolin prize U. Denver, 1988, Bus. Story of Yr. award AP, 1989, Gen. Excellence award Am. City Bus. Jour., 1996, 1997, Human Svc. award Am. Jewish Com., 1999, Small Bus. of the Yr. Calif. Legis. 38th Dist., Blue Ribbon Shield Bus. award US C. of C. 2007, S. Coast Bus. Tech. award, 2006; finalist Gerald Loeb award, 1997; semi-finalist Ernest & Young Entrepreneur of Yr. award, LA, 2006; named Small Bus. Journalist of Yr., LA dist. US SBA, 2004. Mem. Soc. Am. Bus. Editors and Writers (past pres., bd. govs., Best in Bus. award 1995, 96, 98, 2000, 06). Avocations: writing, golf, restoring 1975 Porsche. Office: 14 E Carrillo St Ste A Santa Barbara CA 93101 Home (Summer): 1125 Vine St Denver CO 80206 Office Phone: 805-560-6950 ext. 222. Personal E-mail: hadubroff@aol.com.

DUCHENE, TODD MICHAEL, lawyer; b. Akron, Ohio, June 19, 1963; s. Glenn Robert DuChene and Judith Ann (Dipnall) Kehoe; m. Jennifer Lee Belt, May 25, 1990; children: Elizabeth, Margaret, Emily. BA in polit. sci. with honors, Coll. Wooster, 1985; JD, U. Mich., 1988. Bar: Ohio 1988. Assoc. Baker & Hostetler, Cleve., 1985-93; v.p., gen. counsel, asst. sec. Office Max, Inc., Shaker Heights, Ohio, 1994—95, sr. v.p., gen. counsel, sec., 1995—96; v.p., gen. counsel, sec. Fisher Sci. Internat. Inc., Hampton, NH, 1996—2005; exec. v.p., gen. counsel, sec. Solectron, 2005—. Mem.: New England Law Found., Ohio State Bar Assn. Office: Solectron Corp 847 Gibraltar Dr Milpitas CA 95035

DUCKER, BRUCE, writer, lawyer; b. NYC, Aug. 10, 1938; s. Allen and Lillian Ducker; m. Jaren Jones, Sept. 1, 1962; children: Foster, Penelope, John. AB, Dartmouth Coll., 1960; MA, Columbia U., 1963, LLB, 1964. Bar: Colo. 1964, U.S. Dist. Ct. Colo. 1964, U.S. Ct. Appeals (10th cir.) 1964. Gen. counsel Great Western United Corp., Denver, 1972-73; pres., chmn. bd. dirs. Great Western Cities Inc., Denver, 1974-75; pres. Ducker, Montgomery, Aronstein & Bess P.C., Denver, 1979—97, of counsel, 1998—. Author: (novels) Rule by Proxy, 1976, Failure at the Mission Trust, 1986, Bankroll, 1989, Marital Assets, 1993, Lead Us Not Into Penn Station, 1994, Bloodlines, 2000, Mooney in Flight, 2003; contbr. articles, poetry and short stories to lit. jours. Former trustee Legal Aid Found. of Colo., Denver Symphony Assn., Kent Denver Country Day Sch. Recipient Colo. Book award, Macallan Story Prize. Mem. ABA, PEN/America, Authors' Guild, Poetry Soc. Am., Denver Club, Cactus Club. Office: Ducker Montgomery et al 1560 Broadway Ste 1400 Denver CO 80202-5151 Office Phone: 303-861-2828. Business E-Mail: bducker@duckerlaw.com.

DUCKWORTH, SUSAN, state legislator; b. Oct. 18; m. Carl Duckworth. Attended, Salt Lake Cmty. Coll., U. Utah. Caregiver; mem. Magna C of C, Magna Cmty. Sheriff Coun., Citizen's Acad. Salt Lake Co.; assoc. mem. USWA; mem. Dist. 22 Utah House of Reps., 2009—. Democrat. Office: W030 State Capitol Complex Salt Lake City UT 84114 Mailing: 2901 Merton Way Magna UT 84044 Home Phone: 801-250-0728; Office Phone: 801-538-1029. Office Fax: 801-538-1908. Business E-Mail: sduckworth@utah.gov.

DUDZIAK, DONALD JOHN, nuclear engineer, educator; b. Alden, NY, Jan. 6, 1935; s. Joseph and Josephine Mary (Ratajczak) Dudziak; m. Judith Ann Staib, Aug. 22, 1959; children: Alan Joseph, Matthew John, Karin Marie. BS in Marine Engring., US Mcht. Marine Acad., 1956; MS in Radiation Biology/Radiol. Physics, U. Rochester, NY, 1957; PhD in Applied Math., U. Pitts., 1963. Registered profl. engr., Calif., USCG lic. engr. steam & diesel 1956-92. Commd. ensign USN, 1956, advanced through grades to capt.; sr. engr. Bettis Atomic Power Lab., Pitts., 1957-65; staff mem. U. Calif.-Los Alamos Nat. Lab., 1965-68, 69-74, assoc. and alt. group leader, 1974-78, group leader, 1978-82, theoretical divsn. tech. advisor, 1982, dep. group leader, sect. leader, 1983—88, lab. fellow, 1988—; ret. USN, 1995; prof., head dept. nuclear engring. NC State U., Raleigh, 1990—2001; pres. Pinorealosa Corp, 1989-90. Vis. prof. U. Va., Charlottesville, 1968-69; adj. prof. U. N.Mex., 1966, Kans. State U., 1989-90; guest scientist Swiss Fed. Inst. Reactor Rsch., Wuerenlingen, 1981-82; mem. lab. microfusion facility steering com. US Dept. Energy, 1986-90, inertial confinement fusion adv. com., 1992-96; vice-chair accelerator prodn. of tritium rev. panel Los Alamos Nat. Lab., 1995-98; chmn. fusion tech. working group Neutronics, Brookhaven, NY, 1975; mem. Nat. Nuc. Accrediting Bd., Nat. Acad. Nuc. Tng., 1998-2004; cons. nuc. power schs. USN, 1962-65; cons. Oak Ridge Nat. Lab., 1993-96, TSI Rsch. Co., 1992-, US Nuc. Regulatory Commn., 1997, Am. Coun. on Edn., 1995-, Duke U., 1997-98, Am.Electrical Power, 2004, TVA, 2008 Editor: Reactor Principles, 1964, Radiation Shielding, 1964, Progress in Nuclear Energy, 1992—; contbr. editor Fusion Tech., 1987-2001; contbr. articles to profl. jours. Vice-chmn. Los Alamos County Planning and Zoning Commn., 1969-74. Fellow Am. Nuc. Soc. (divsn. chair 1972-73, 77-78, 92-93, gen. chair fusion energy divsn. nat. meeting 1994); mem. Am. Soc. Engring. Edn., US Naval Inst., Los Alamos Sunrise Kiwanis (treas. 1987-89), Sigma Xi, Phi Kappa Phi. Libertarian. Avocations: hunting, hiking, skeet shooting, rifle shooting, pistol shooting. Office: Los Alamos Nat Lab Tech Assessment Group AET-2 MS E548 Los Alamos NM 87545 Business E-Mail: dudziak@lanl.gov.

DUDZIAK, MARY LOUISE, law educator; b. Oakland, Calif., June 15, 1956; d. Walter F. Dudziak and Barbara Ann Campbell; 1 child, Alicia. AB in Sociology with highest honors, U. Calif., Berkeley, 1978; JD, Yale Law Sch., 1984; MA, MPhil in Am. Studies, Yale U., 1986, PhD in Am. Studies, 1992. Adminstrv. asst. to dep. dir. Ctr. Ind. Living, Berkeley, 1978-80; law clk., nat. legal staff ACLU, NYC, 1983; law clk. Judge Sam J. Ervin, III Fourth Cir. Ct. Appeals, Morganton, N.C., 1984-85; assoc. prof. coll. law U. Iowa, Iowa City, 1986-90, prof. coll. law, 1990-98. Vis. prof. U. So. Calif., 1997-98, Harvard Law Sch., 2005-; prof. U. So. Calif., 1998-2002, Judge Edward J. and Ruey L. Guirado prof. law and history, 2002-; vis. scholar Kennedy Sch. Govt., Harvard U., 2006-; mem. faculty senate task force on faculty devel. U. Iowa, 1989-90, mem. faculty welfare com., 1990-92, mem. faculty senate task force on faculty spouses and ptnrs., 1991-92, mem. presdl. lecture com., 1992-95; v.p. rsch. adv. com. in social scis., 1992-94; fellow law and pub. affairs program Princeton U., 2002; presenter in field. Author: Cold War Civil Rights: Race and the Image of American Democracy, 2000; editor, co-author: September 11 in History: A Watershed Moment?, 2003; co-editor Legal Borderlands: Law and the Construction of American Borders, 2006, mem. bd. mng. editors Am. Quar., 2003—; contbr. articles to profl. jours. Bd. dirs. Iowa Civil Liberties Union, 1987-88; chairperson office svcs. for persons with disabilities program rev. com., U. Iowa, 1987-88, law sch. ombudsperson, 1991. Charlotte W. Newcombe Doctoral Dissertation fellow Woodrow Wilson Fellowship Found., 1985-86; Old Gold fellow U. Iowa, 1987, 88, 89, Moody Grant Lyndon Baines Johnson Fdn., 1998, Theodore C. Sorenson Fell., JFK Libr. Fdn., 1997, Orgn. Am. Historians-Japanese Assn. for Am. Studies fellow 2000; travel grantee Eisenhower World Affairs Inst., 1993; recipient Scholars Devel. award Harry S. Truman Libr. Inst., 1990. Fellow Am. Coun. on Learned Soc., 2006-, Mem. Am. Soc. Legal History (mem. com. on documentary preservation 1988-2000, mem. program com. for 1988 conf., mem. exec. com., bd. dirs. 1990-92, 95-97, chairperson program com. 1993, mem. nominating com. 1999-2001, chair nominating com. 2001), Am. Hist. Assn. (Littleton-Griswold rsch. grantee 1987), Am. Studies Assn. (mem. nominating com. 1999-2002, chair nominating com. 2002), Assn. Am. Law Schs. (sec.-treas. legal history sect. 1987, vice chair 1988, chair 1989), Law and Soc. Assn. (bd. trustees, 2005-, mem. com., 2004-06, mem. Hurst prize com. 1992), Orgn. Am. Historians, Soc. Am. Law Tchrs., Soc. for Historians Am. Fgn. Rels. Democrat. Office: U So Calif Law Sch Los Angeles CA 90089-0001

DUDZIAK, WALTER FRANCIS, physicist; b. Adams, Mass., Jan. 7, 1923; s. Michael Casimer and Mary (Piekielniak) D.; m. Barbara Ann Campbell, June 25, 1954; children: Diane, Mary, Daniel, Suzanne. BS, Rensselaer Poly. Inst., 1946, MS in Physics, 1947; PhD in Physics, U. Calif., Berkeley, 1954. Instr. physics Rensselaer Poly. Inst., Troy, 1946-48; aero scientist NASA, Cleve., 1948-49; rsch. assoc. U. Calif., Berkeley, 1949-54, lectr. physics Santa Barbara, 1954-60; mgr. computer sci. Gen. Electric Co., Santa Barbara, 1958-64; exec. v.p. Pan Fax Corp., Santa Barbara, 1964-68; pres. Info. Sci., Inc., Santa Barbara, 1968—. Rsch. analsyt Manhattan Dist. Project, Oak Ridge, Tenn., 1942-44, Carbon Carbide Corp., Oak Ridge, 1944-46. With U.S. Army, 1942-44. Recipient Livetime Achievement award Dept. of Def., 1998; dams scholar City of Adams. Mem. KC (grand knight 1974—), Elks. Roman Catholic. Office: 123 W Padre St Santa Barbara CA 93105-3960 Home: 29805 8th Pl S Federal Way WA 98003-3745

DUERDEN, JOHN H., apparel executive; b. 1941; With Xerox Corp., 1970-88; v.p. Reebok Internat. Ltd., 1989-90, pres., COO, 1990—95; pres., CEO Reebok Brands worldwide divsn., Stoughton, Mass., 1991-93, exec. v.p worldwide ops., 1993—95; chmn., CEO Dictaphone Corporation, 1995—2000; CEO Lernout & Hauspie, 2000—01; COO devel. divsn. Invensys plc, 2002—05; founder Chrysallis Group, 2006—09; pres., CEO Crocs Inc., 2009—. Bd. dirs. Sunglass Hunt Internat., 1992—2001, Telewest, 2004—06, Obago Medical Products Inc., 2007—, Crocs, Inc., 2009—. Office: Crocs Inc 6328 Monarch Pk Niwot CO 80503*

DUFF, WILLIAM LEROY, JR., retired dean, finance educator; b. Oakland, Calif., Sept. 14, 1938; s. William Leroy and Edna Francis (Gunderson) D.; m. Arline M. Wight, Sept. 1, 1962; children— Susan M., William Leroy III. BA, Calif. State U.-, San Francisco, 1963, postgrad., 1963-64; MSSc., Nat. Econs. Inst., U. Stockholm, 1965; PhD, UCLA, 1969. Rsch assoc. C.F. Kettering Found., 1967-69; asst. JOBS program Nat. Alliance Businessmen, 1969-70; prof. U. No. Colo., Greeley, 1970—, Bur Bus. and Pub. Research, 1972-75, dean Coll. Bus. Adminstrn., 1984—, interim v.p. acad. affairs, 1987, chmn. faculty senate, 1981-82. On leave as UN adviser to Govt. of Swaziland, 1975-77; cons. in field. Contbr. articles to profl. jours. Mem. Greeley Planning Commn., 1972-75, chmn., 1974-75; trustee U. No. Colo., 1983; mem. Greeley Water and Sewer Bd., 1994-98, Greeley City Coun., 2000; bd. dirs. Centennial Svcs., 2003, United Way of Weld County, 2003, exec. bd. and investment com., UNC Found., 2003, treas., mem. exec. com., investment com.; bd. dirs. Greeley Philharm., U. NC Found. With U.S. Army, 1958-60. Mem. Greeley Rotary Club (bd. dirs.), Greeley Area C. of C. (bd. dirs.). Home: 1614 Lakeside Dr Greeley CO 80631-5343 Office: U No Colo Coll Bus Adminstrn Kepner Greeley CO 80639-0001

DUFFIELD, DAVID A., application developer, former computer software company executive; b. Shaker Heights, OH, Sept. 21, 1940; m. Cheryl Duffield; 9 children. BS in Elec. Engring., Cornell U., 1962, MBA, 1964. Mktg. rep., sys. engr. IBM, 1964—69; co-founder Info. Assocs.; founder, chmn. Integral Systems Inc., Walnut Creek, Calif., 1972—87, PeopleSoft Inc., Pleasanton, Calif., 1987—2004, pres., 1987—99, CEO, 1987—99, 2004; co-founder Workday, Incline Village, Nev., 2005—. Co-founder Maddie's Fund, Alameda, Calif., 1999—. Named one of Forbes' Richest Americans, 2006.

DUFFIELD, THOMAS ANDREW, art director, production designer; b. Grosse Pointe, Mich., Sept. 8, 1951; s. Thomas A. Sr. and Grace A. (Schaefer) D. BArch, Calif. State Poly. U., San Luis Obispo, 1976. Set designer Universal Studios, LA, 1976-79; freelance designer LA, 1979-84, 87—; asst. art dir. Michael Landon Prodns., Culver City, Calif., 1984-86; art dir. Warner Bros., Burbank, Calif., 1986-87; prodn. designer Touchstone Pictures, LA, 1993—. Prodn. designer: (films) Ed Wood, 1994, The Ring, 2002, Welcome To The Jungle, 2003, Why Men Shouldn't Marry, 2003; art dir.: (films) The Lost Boys, 1987, The Accidental Tourist, 1988, Beetlejuice, 1988, Ghostbusters II, 1989, Joe Versus the Volcano, 1990, Edward Scissorhands, 1990, Batman Returns, 1992, Grand Canyon, 1991, Wolf, 1994, A Little Princess, 1995, The Bird Cage, 1996, Men In Black, 1996, Primary Colors, 1997, Wild, Wild West, 1998, What Planet are you From, 2000. Mem. SAG, Acad. Motion Picture Arts and Scis., Internat. Alliance Theatrical Stage Employees. Avocations: art, sports, photography, auto racing, investments. Home: 17031 Lisette St Granada Hills CA 91344-1435 Office: c/o Soc Motion Picture Art Dirs 11365 Ventura Blvd Studio City CA 91604-3148

DUFFY, JAMES EARL, JR., state supreme court justice; b. St. Paul, June 4, 1942; s. James Earl and Mary Elizabeth (Westbrook) Duffy; m. Jeanne Marie Ghiardi; children: Jennifer, Jessica. BA, Coll. St. Thomas, 1965; JD, Marquette U., 1968. Bar: Wis. 1968, Hawaii 1969. Assoc. Cobb & Gould, Honolulu, 1968—71, Chuck & Fujiyama, Honolulu, 1972—74; partner Fujiyama, Duffy & Fujiyama, Honolulu, 1975—2003; assoc. justice Hawaii Supreme Ct., 2003—. Mem. Am. Bd. Trial Advocates, med. ethical resources com. Kapiolani Children's Med. Ctr., 1984—. recipient Lifetime Achievement award, Consumer Lawyers of Hawaii, John S. Edmunds award for Civility & Vigorous Advocacy. mem. Hawaii Bar Found. (bd. dirs. 1984—), Hawaii Bar Assn. (pres. 1982, Lifetime Achievement award), Hawaii Trial Lawyers Assn. (pres. 1981), Hawaii Supreme Ct. Jud. Coun., Trial Lawyers Assn. Am. (bd. govs. 1982-85), Hawaii Acad. Plaintiff's Attys. (pres. 1986-93), Am. Inns of Court IV. Office: Ali'iolani Hale 417 S King St Honolulu HI 96813-2902

DUFTY, BEVAN, city supervisor; b. Feb. 1955; s. William Dufty and Maely Bartholomew. B in Polit. Sci. and Journalism, U. Calif., Berkeley. Sr. legis. asst. for edn. to Rep. Shirley Chisholm, NY; chief legis. asst. to Rep. Julian Dixon LA, 1979; chief of staff to supr. Susan Leal San Francisco, 1993; aide to mayor, coord. Office of Neighborhood Svcs. office Mayor Willie Brown, San Francisco; supr., Dist. 8 San Francisco Bd. Supervisors, 2003—, chair city ops. & neighborhood svcs. com., vice-chair city & sch. dist. com., mem. Transp. Authority. Mem. Golden Gate Bridge, Highway & Transp. Dist. Bd., Mental Health Bd. Active Friends of Noe Valley, Friends of Portola Park. Recipient Charles M. Holmes Individual Leadership award, Golden Gate Bus. Assn., 2004. Mem.: Upper Market & Castro Merchant Assn., Mt. Olympus Neighborhood Assn., Glen Park Assn., Eureka Valley Promotion Assn., Duboce Triangle Neighborhood Assn., Cole Valley Improvement Assn., Buena Vista Neighborhood Assn., San Francisco FrontRunners, Robert F Kennedy Dem. Club, Raoul Wallenberg Dem. Club, Alice B Toklas Dem. Club. Democrat. Office: 1 Dr Carlton B Goodlett Pl Rm 244 San Francisco CA 94102-4689 Office Phone: 415-554-6968. Fax: 415-554-6909. E-mail: Bevan.Dufty@sfgov.org.*

DUGAN, MICHAEL, communications executive; BSEE, Rochester Inst. Technology. Formerly with Xeros Corp.; former v.p. engring., dir. product mktg., engring. Tandon Corp.; former pres. Echostar Technologies; pres., chief opers. officer Echostar Comms., Littleton, Colo., chief tech. officer, 2005—06. Office: Echostar Comms 5701 S Santa Fe Littleton CO 80120

DUGAN, MICHAEL JOSEPH, former career officer, health agency executive; b. Albany, NY, Feb. 22, 1937; s. D. Joseph and Dorothy M. (Krebs) D.; m. Grace A. Robinson, Aug. 9, 1958; children: Colleen, Erin, Mike, Sean, Kathleen, Kevin. BS, U.S. Mil. Acad., 1958; MBA, U.Colo., 1972. Commd. officer USAF, 1958, advanced through grades to gen.; comdr.-in-chief U.S. Air Forces Europe, 1989—90; comdr. Allied Air Forces Cen. Europe, 1989—90; chief of staff USAF, 1990, ret., 1991; lectr. in strategic studies Johns Hopkins U., Washington, 1991—92; pres., CEO Nat. Multiple Sclerosis Soc., NYC, 1992—2005; ret., 2005. Decorated three D.S.M., Silver Star, two Legion of Merit, D.F.C., Purple Heart; Knight's Cross (Germany). Home: 36 James Ct Dillon CO 80435 E-mail: mike@mikedugan.net.

DUGAR, SUNDEEP, chemist; PhD, U. Calif., Davis, 1984. With Schering-Plough Rsch. Inst., Kenilworth, NJ, Bristol-Myers Squibb Pharmaceutical Rsch. Inst.; dir. chemistry Scios Inc., Fremont, Calif., 1999—2002, v.p. chemistry, 2002—. Recipient Thomas Alva Edison Patent award, R&D Council NJ, 2002; named a Hero of Chemistry, Am. Chem. Soc., 2004; named an Inventor of the Yr., Intellectual Property Owners Assn., 2005.

DUGONI, ARTHUR A., dean emeritus, orthodontics educator; b. San Francisco, June 29, 1925; s. Arthur B. and Lina Maria (Bianco) D.; m. Katherine Agnes Groo, Feb. 5, 1949; children: Steven, Michael, Russell, Mary, Diane, Arthur, James. DDS, Coll. Physicians and Surgeons, San Francisco, 1948; MSD, U. Wash., 1963; BS, Gonzaga U., 1986; DHL honoris causa, U. Detroit, 1997. Diplomate Am. Bd. Orthodontics (bd. dirs., pres. 1979-86). Clin. instr. operative dentistry Coll. Physicians and Surgeons, San Francisco, 1951-55, asst. clin. prof. operative dentistry, 1955-60, asst. clin. prof. orthodontics, 1963-64, chair dept. orthodontics, 1963-67; assoc. prof. orthodontics U. Pacific, San Francisco, 1966-77, prof., 1977—, dean Sch. Dentistry, 1978—2006, dean emeritus, 2006. Chair coun. deans Am. Assn. Dental Schs., 1985; active Pew Commn. for the Health Professions, 1993-96. Recipient Disting. Svc. award San Mateo County Dental Soc., 1971, 1990, Disting. Svc. award Pacific Coast Soc. Orthodontists, 1976, Merit award, 1976, 2001, Disting. Practitioner award Nat. Acads. Practice Press Club, 1987, Hinman medallion, 1989, medallion of distinction U. Pacific, 1989, Orthodontic Edn. and Rsch. Found. disting. merit award, 1993, Albert H. Ketcham award Am. Bd. Orthodontics, 1994, Chmn.'s award Am. Dental Trade Assn., 1994, Dr. Irving E. Gruber award, 1997, List of Honor of FDI World Dental

Fedn., 1998; named Person of Yr., South San Francisco, 1960, Alumnus of Yr., U. Pacific Sch. Dentistry, 1983, U. Wash., 1984, U. San Francisco, 1988, Gonzaga U., 1992, Gold medal Pierre Fauchard Acad., 1996, Callahan Internat. award Ohio Dental Assn., 1999, William J. Gies award Am. Coll. Dentists, 2001, Excellence in Dentistry award 13th Dist.'s Internat. Coll. Dentists, 2002, Willard C. Fleming Meritorious Svc. award No. Calif. sect. Am. Coll. Dentists, 2003, Arthur A. Dugoni Lifetime Achievement award Alumni Assn. U. Pacific, Arthur A. Dugoni Sch. Dentistry, 2006; named Arthur A. Dugoni Sch. Dentistry in his honor U. Pacific, 2004. Fellow Pierre Fauchard Acad., Acad. Dentistry Internat. (Internat. Dentist of Yr. 2005), Acad. Gen. Dentistry (hon.); mem. ADA (trustee 1984-87, treas. 1987-88, pres. 1988-89, Found. pres., Pres.'s citation 1994, 99, Disting. Svc. award 1995), Fedn. Dentaire Internat. (councilor 1989-98, treas. 1992-98, List of Honour 1999), Am. Assn. Dental Schs. (pres. 1995, Disting. Svc. award 2000), Calif. Dental Assn. (pres. 1982-83, Dist. Svc. award, 1978, Dale F. Redig Dist. Svc. award, 2003), Am. Dental Assn. (found. pres. 2003-), Peninsula Golf and Country Club, Phi Kappa Phi, Omicron Kappa Upsilon, Tau Kappa Omega, Xi Psi Phi. Republican. Roman Catholic. Avocation: golf. Office: U Pacific Arthur A Dugoni Sch Dentistry 2155 Webster St San Francisco CA 94115-2333 Business E-Mail: adugoni@pacific.edu.

DUHAMEL, JOSH (JOSHUA DAVID DUHAMEL), actor; b. Minot, ND, Nov. 14, 1972; s. Larry and Bonny Duhamel; m. Stacy Ferguson (Fergie), Jan. 10, 2009. BS, Minot State U. Co-owner 10 North Main restaurant, Minot, ND, 2005—. Actor: (TV series) All My Children, 1999—2002 (Emmy for Outstanding Supporting Actor in a Drama Series, 2002), Las Vegas, 2003—08, (guest appearance) Crossing Jordan, 2004, 2007,: (films) The Picture of Dorian Gray, 2004, Win a Date with Tad Hamilton!, 2004, Turistas, 2006, Transformers, 2007. Avocations: golf, skiing, football, basketball. Office: c/o Gersh Agency 232 N Canon Dr Beverly Hills CA 90210*

DUHL, LEONARD J., psychiatrist, educator; b. NYC, May 24, 1926; s. Louis and Rose (Josefsberg) D.; m. Lisa Shippee; children: Pamela, Nina, David, Susan, Aurora. BA, Columbia U., 1945; MD, Albany Med. Coll., 1948; postgrad., Menninger Sch. Psychiatry, 1949—54. Diplomate Am. Bd. Psychiatry and Neurology (examiner 1977, 85); cert. in psychoanalysis Wash. Psychoanalytic Inst., 1964. With USPHS, 1951-53, 54-72, med. dir., 1954-72; fellow Menninger Sch. Psychiatry Menninger Sch. Psychiatry, Winter VA Hosp., Topeka, 1949-51, resident psychiatry, 1953-54; asst. health officer Contra Costa County (Calif.) Health Dept., 1951-53; with USPHS, 1949-51, 53-54; psychiatrist profl. svcs. br., chief office planning NIMH, 1954-66; spl. asst. to sec. HUD, 1966-68; cons. Peace Corps, 1961-68; assoc. psychiatry George Washington Med. Sch., 1961-63, asst. clin. prof., 1963-68, assoc. prof., 1966-68; prof. public health Sch. Pub. Health U. Calif., Berkeley, 1968—93; prof. city planning Coll. Environ. Design U. Calif., Berkeley, 1968-92; dir. dual degree program in health and med. scis. U. Calif., Berkeley, 1971-77, clin. prof. psychiatry San Francisco, 1969—; pvt. practice psychiatry Berkeley. Sci. adv. coun. Calif. Legis., 1970-73, sr. cons. Assembly Office of Rsch., 1981-85; cons. Health Cities Program, Environ. Health, WHO, UNICEF, ICDC, Florence, Global Forum of Parliamentarians and Spiritual Leaders, 1989-98, Ctr. for Fgn. Journalists, 1987-90, Am. Hosp. Assn. Health Rsch. and Edn. Trust, 1995—. Author: Approaches to Research in Mental Retardation, 1959, The Urban Condition, 1963, (with R.L. Leopold) Mental Health and Urban Social Policy, 1969, Health Planning and Social Change, 1986, Social Entrepreneurship of Change, 1990, 1995, Health and the City, 1993; bd. editors Jour. Community Psychology, 1974, Jour. Cmty. Mental Health, 1974—, Jour. Mental Health Consultation and Edn., 1978—, Jour. Prevention, 1978—, Nat. Civic Rev., 1991—; contbr. articles to tech. lit. Trustee Robert F. Kennedy Found., 1971-83; bd. dirs. Citizens Policy Ctr., San Francisco, 1975-85, New World Alliance, 1980-84, Calif. Inst. for Integral Studies, 1991-95, Ptnrs. for Dem. Change, 1990-2002; chair First Internat. Healthy Cities Conf., San Francisco, 1993; exec. trustee Nat. Inst. for Citizen Participation and Negotiation, 1988-90; trustee Menninger Found., Topeka, Houston, 1994—, bd. dirs., 1995—; bd. dirs. Louis August Jonas Found. (Camp Rising Sun), 1990—, Ctr. for Transcultural Studies, 1996—; exec. dir. Internat. Healthy Cities Found., 1993—. Med. dir. USPHS, 1950—72. Recipient Albert Deutsh award, 1957, World Health Day award, WHO, 1996, Health Cities award for Coalition of Healthier Cities and Cmtys., 1999, A. Horwitz award Pan Am. Health Orgn., 2002. Fellow Am. Psychiat. Assn. (life), Am. Coll. Psychiatry (life), No. Calif. Psychiat. Soc. (disting. life), Group for Advancement in Psychiatry (chmn. com. preventive psychiatry 1962-66), APHA. Democrat. Jewish. Avocations: photography, woodcarving, snorkeling, painting, reading. Home: 1715 Elm Ave Richmond CA 94805-1615 Office Phone: 510-642-1715. Business E-Mail: lduhl@berkeley.edu.

DUKE, DONALD NORMAN, publishing executive; b. LA, Apr. 1, 1929; s. Roger V. and Mabel (Weineger) D. BA in Ednl. Psychology, Colo. Coll., 0951. Comml. photographer, Colorado Springs, Colo., 1951-53; pub. rels. Gen. Petroleum, LA, 1954-55; agt. Gen. S.S. Corp., Ltd., 1956-57; asst. mgr. retail advt., sales promotion Mobil Oil Co., 1958-63; pub. Golden West Books, Alhambra, Calif., 1964—. Dir. Pacific R.R. Publs., Inc., Athletic Press; pub. rels. cons. Santa Fe Rlwy., 1960-70. Author: The Pacific Electric: A History of Southern California Railroading, 1958, Southern Pacific Steam Locomotives, 1962, Santa Fe...Steel Rails to California, 1963, Night Train, 1961, American Narrow Gauge, 1978, RDC: the Budd Rail Diesel Car, 1989, The Brown Derby, 1990, Camp Cajon, 1991, Fred Harvey: Civilizer of the American West, 1994, editor: Water Trails West, 1977, Branding Iron, 1988-91, Santa Fe...The Railroad Gateway to the American West, Vol. 1, 1995, Vol. 2, 1997, Incline Railways of Los Angeles and Southern California, 1998, Electric Railroads of San Francisco Bay, Vols. 1 and 2, 1999, Pacific Electric Railway (The No. Divsn.), vol. 1, 2001, Pacific Electric Railway (The Ea. Divsn.), vol. 2, 2002, Pacific Electric Railway (The So. Divsn.), vol. 3, 2003, Pacific Electric Railway (The We. Divsn.), vol. 4, 2004, The Union Pacific in Southern California, 2005, Pacific Coast Interurbans, vol. 1, 2007, West Coast Interurbans, 2008. Recipient Spur award for Trails of the Iron Horse Western Writers Am., 1975. Mem. Rlwy. and Locomotive Hist. Soc. (dir. 1944-98), Western History Assn., Newcomen Soc., Lexington Group of Transp. History, Western Writers Am., PEN Internat. (v.p. 1975-77), Authors Guild Am., Book Pubs. Assn. So. Calif. (dir. 1968-77), Calif. Writers Guild (dir. 1976-77), Calif. Book Pubs. Assn. (dir. 1976-77), Westerners Internat. (hon., editor Branding Iron 1971-80, 88-91), Hist. Soc. So. Calif. (dir. 1972-75), Henry E./Arabella Huntington Soc., Kappa Sigma (lit. editor Caduceus 1968-80). Home: PO Box 80250 San Marino CA 91118-8250 Office: Golden West Books 525 N Electric Ave Alhambra CA 91801-2032 Office Phone: 626-458-8148. Personal E-mail: trainbook@earthlink.net.

DUKE, MICHAEL B., aerospace scientist; b. LA, Dec. 1, 1935; s. Leon and Eva (Siegel) D.; m. Julia Elizabeth Bartram, 1958 (div. 1966); children: Lisa, Stuart; m. Mary Carolyn Creamer, July 17, 1967; children: Kenneth, Donna. BS Geology, Calif. Inst. Tech., 1957, MS Geochemistry, 1961, PhD Geochemistry, 1963. Rsch. scientist U.S. Geol. Survey, Washington, 1963-70; lunar sample curator NASA, Houston, 1970-77, chief solar system exploration div., 1977-90, dep. for sci., moon/Mars exploration, 1990-95; sr. project coord. Lunar & Planetary Inst., Houston, 1995—2000; mem. rsch. faculty Colo. Sch. Mines, 1998—, dir. Ctr. for Comml. Applications of Combustion in Space, 2003—. Advisor manned space exploration.; founder Space Resources Roundtable, 1999. Organizer: Lunar Bases Symposia, 1984-88; contbr. articles to profl. jours. Adult leader Boy Scouts Am. Houston, 1980-90. Recipient Nininger Meteorite award, 1963, Presdl. Meritorious award, 1988. Fellow AIAA (Space Sci. award 1991), AAAS, Meteoritical Soc.; mem. Internat. Acad. Astronautics, Geol. Soc. Washington (D.C.). Office: Colo Sch Mines CCACS 1500 Illinois St Golden CO 80401 Office Phone: 303-384-2096. Business E-Mail: mduke@mines.edu.

DULBECCO, RENATO, biologist, educator; b. Catanzaro, Italy, Feb. 22, 1914; arrived in U.S., 1947, naturalized, 1953; s. Leonardo and Maria (Virdia) D.; m. Guiseppina Salvo, June 1, 1940 (div. 1963); children: Peter Leonard (dec.), Maria Vittoria; m. Maureen Rutherford Muir; 1 child, Fiona Linsey. MD, U. Torino, Italy, 1936; DSc (hon.), Yale U., 1968; LL.D., U. Glasgow, Scotland, 1970; DSc (hon.), Vrije Universiteit, Brussels, 1978, Ind. U., 1984, U. Bologna, 1988. Asst. U. Torino, 1940-47; research asso. Ind. U., 1947-49; sr. research fellow Calif. Inst. Tech., 1949-52, asso. prof., then prof. biology, 1952-63; sr. fellow Salk Inst. Biol. Studies, San Diego, 1963-71; asst. dir. research Imperial Cancer Research Fund, London, 1971-74, dep. dir. research, 1974-77; disting. research prof. Salk Inst., La Jolla, Calif., 1977—, pres., 1989-92, pres. emeritus, 1993—; prof. pathology and medicine U. Calif. at San Diego Med. Sch., La Jolla, 1977-81, mem. Cancer Ctr.; with Nat. Rsch. Coun., Milan, 1993—. Vis. prof. Royal Soc. G.B., 1963—64; Leeuwenhoek lectr., 1974; Clowes Meml. lectr., Atlantic City, 61; Harvey lectr. Harvey Soc., 1967; Dunham lectr. Harvard U., 1972; 11th Marjory Stephenson Meml. lectr., London, 73; Harden lectr., Wye, England, 73; Am. Soc. for Microbiology lectr., LA, 79; mem. Calif. Cancr Adv. Coun., 1963—67; mem. vis. com. Case Western Res. Sch. Medicine; adv. bd. Roche Inst., 1968—71, Inst. Immunology, Basel, Switzerland; esperto Italian Nat. Rsch. Coun.; trustee Am.-Italian Fedn. for Cancer Rsch.; bd. dirs. Scientific Counselors Dept. Etiology NCI; cons. Nat. Rsch. Coun. ESPERTO, 1994—. Trustee La Jolla Country Day Sch., Am.-Italian Fedn. for Cancer Rsch.; bd. mem. sci. counselors dept. etiology Nat. Cancer Inst.; mem. commissionary CCB Cariplo Found., Milan. Decorated grand ufficiale Italian Republic; recipient John Scott award City Phila., 1958, Kimball award Conf. Pub. Health Lab. Dirs., 1959, Albert and Mary Lasker Basic Med. Rsch. award, 1964, Howard Taylor Ricketts award, 1965, Paul Ehrlich-Ludwig Darmstaedter prize, 1967, Horwitz prize, Columbia U., 1973, Targa d'oro Villa San Giovanni, 1978, Mandel Gold medal, Czechoslovak Acad. Scis., 1982, Via de Condotti prize, 1990, Cavaliere di Gran Croce Italian Rep., 1991, Natale Di Roma prize, 1993, Columbus prize, 1993, S. Ambrogio medal, City of Milan, 1993, Spl. Oscar of Italian TV, 1999; co-recipient (with David Baltimore and Howard Martin Temin) Nobel prize in medicine, 1975; named Man of Yr., London, 1975, Italian Am. of Yr., San Diego County, 1978, hon. citizen, City of Imperia (Italy), 1983, City of Arezzo, City of Sommariva Perno, City of Catanzaro, City of Torino, hon. founder, Hebrew U., 1981; fellow Guggenheim and Fulbright fellow, 1957—58. Mem.: NAS, Am. Acad. Arts and Scis., Fedn. Am. Scientists, Royal Soc. (fgn.), Academia Nazionale del Lincei (fgn.), Am. Philos. Assn., Internat. Physicians for Prevention Nuclear War, Am. Assn. Cancer Rsch., Comitato di Collaborazione Culturale (hon.), Academia Ligure di Scienze e Lettre (hon.), Alpha Omega Alpha. Office: Salk Inst PO Box 85800 San Diego CA 92186-5800 also: National Research Council Piazzale Aldo Moro 7 00185 Rome Italy Office Phone: 858-453-4690.

DULL, DAVID A., lawyer; b. 1949; BA in Am. Studies with honors, Yale U., 1971, JD, 1982. Staff mem. UN Assn. U.S.A.; ptnr. Irell & Manella LLP, Century City, Silcon Valley, Calif., 1985—98; v.p. bus. affairs, gen. counsel Broadcom Corp., Irvine, Calif., 1998—. Bd. dirs. Magfusion. Office: Broadcom Corporation 5300 California Ave Irvine CA 92617-3038 Office Phone: 949-450-8700. Office Fax: 949-450-8710.

DULLEA, CHARLES W., university chancellor emeritus, priest; Joined S.J., ordained priest Roman Catholic Ch. Chancellor emeritus U. San Francisco. Office: U San Francisco Xavier Hall 650 Parker Ave San Francisco CA 94118-4267

DUMAINE, R. PIERRE, bishop emeritus; b. Aug. 2, 1931; Student, St. Joseph Coll., Mountain View, Calif., 1945-51, St. Patrick Sem., Menlo Park, Calif., 1951-57; PhD, Cath. U. Am., 1962. Ordained priest Archdiocese of San Francisco, 1957; asst. pastor Immaculate Heart Ch., Belmont, Calif., 1957-58; mem. faculty dept. edn. Cath. U. Am., Belmont, Calif., 1961-63; tchr. Serra High Sch., San Mateo, Calif., 1963-65; asst. supt. Cath. schs. Archdiocese of San Francisco, 1965-74, supt., 1974-78, aux. bishop, 1978—81; ordained bishop, 1978; bishop Diocese of San Jose, Calif., 1981—99, bishop emeritus Calif., 1999—. Dir. Archdiocesan Ednl. TV Ctr., Menlo Park, Calif., 1968-81. Mem. Pres.'s Nat. Adv. Council on Edn. of Disadvantaged Children, 1970-72. Bd. dirs. Cath. TV Network, 1968-81, pres. 1975-77; bd. dirs. Pub. Svc. Satellite Consortium, 1975-81. Mem. Nat. Cath. Edn. Assn., Assn. Cath. Broadcasters and Allied Communicators, Internat. Inst. Communications, Assn. Calif. Sch. Adminstrs. Roman Catholic. Office: 20 Willow Rd. Unit 43 Menlo Park CA 94025 E-mail: bishopdsj@aol.com.

DUMMETT, CLIFTON ORRIN, dentist, educator; b. Georgetown, British Guiana, May 20, 1919; s. Alexander Adolphus and Eglantine Annabella (Johnson) Dummett; m. Lois Maxine Doyle, Mar. 6, 1943; 1 child, Clifton Orrin Jr. BS in Psychology, Roosevelt U., Chgo., 1941; DDS, Northwestern U., 1941, MScD, 1942, DSc (hon.), 1976; MPH, U. Mich., 1947; ScD (hon.), U. Pa., 1978; DSc (hon.), Meharry Med. Coll., 2004. Diplomate Am. Bd. Periodontology, Am. Bd. Oral Medicine. Dean, prof. periodontology Meharry Med. Coll., Nashville, 1945-49; chief dental service VA Hosp., Tuskegee, Ala., 1949-65, assoc. chief staff for rsch. and edn., 1958-65, chief dental service Chgo., 1965-66; dental dir., dir. ctr. Watts Health Ctr., LA, 1966-69; assoc. dean, chmn. dept. cmty. dentistry U. So. Calif. Sch. Dentistry, LA, 1969-75, prof., 1969-89, prof. emeritus, 1989-96, disting. emeritus prof., 1997—. Adj. prof. Northwestern U. Dental Sch., 1989; vis. prof., cons. Sch. Vet. Medicine Tuskegee Inst., 1962—65; vis. prof. Meharry Med. Coll., 1989—; trustee Am. Fund Dental Health, Chgo., 1968—78; chem. devel. component rev. panel Calif. Regional Med. Programs, LA, 1975—77; mem. Pres.'s Com. Nat. Health Ins., 1977; sr. reviewer US Surgeon Gen. Report Oral Health, 2000. Author: Community Dentistry, 1974, Afro-Americans in Dentistry: Sequence and Consequence of Events, 1977, Charles Edwin Bentley, 1982, Dental Education at Meharry Medical College: Origin and Odyssey, 1992, Culture and Education in Dentistry at Northwestern University, 1993, NDA.II The Story of America's Second National Dental Association, 2000, (editl.) Nor Yet the Last, 1962 (W.J. Gies award, 1963), The Hillenbrand Era, 1986; editor: Nat. Dental Assn., 1953—75; contbr. chapters to books, more than 300 articles to profl. jours. Chmn. adv. bd. Econ. and Youth Opportunity Agy. Project Head Start, Tuskegee, Ala., 1964—65; mem. spl. health adv. com. Calif. Bd. Edn., LA, 1972—74; mem. L.A. regional hearing planning coun. Pres.'s Com. on Health Edn., LA, 1973—74. Lt. col. USAF, 1955—58. Recipient Alumni Merit award, Northwestern U., 1971, Fones Gold medal, Conn. Dental Assn., 1976, Pierre Fauchard Gold medal, Pierre Fauchard Acad., 1980, Lifetime Achievement award, U. Md., 2000, John R. Callahan award, Ohio Dental Assn., 2003; named to, U. So. Calif. Dental Hall of Fame, 1997. Fellow: AAAS (chmn. dental sect. 1975—76, 1987—88), APHA (v.p. for U.S. 1995—96, John W. Knutson Disting. Svc. award 1992), Am. Acad. History of Dentistry (pres. 1982—83, Hayden and Harris award 1987), Internat. Coll. Dentists; mem.: ADA (hon.), Am. Dental Edn. Assn. (Presdl. citation 2003), Inst. Medicine of NAS (sr. mem.), Nat. Acads. Practice (Disting. Practitioner 1987), Am. Assn. Dental Editors (editor 1963—72, pres. 1974—75, Disting. Svc. medal 1976), Assn. Mil. Surgeons (life), Internat. Assn. Dental Rsch. (pres. 1969—70), Am. Coll. Dentists (Wm. J. Gies award 1992, Salute of Coll. 1988), Sigma Xi, Omicron Kappa Upsilon (pres., founder Nashville chpt. 1947—49), Delta Omega, Alpha Phi Alpha, Sigma Pi Phi. Democrat. Episcopalian. Avocations: music, politics, track. Home: 5344 Highlight Pl Los Angeles CA 90016-5119 Office: U So Calif Sch Dentistry PO Box 77006 Los Angeles CA 90007-0006

DUMONT, JAMES KELTON, JR., actor, theater producer; b. Chgo., Aug. 12, 1965; s. James Kelton and Judith Katherine (Johnson) DuMont; m. Wendell Faith Hall, Dec. 14, 1968; children: Sinclair Marie, Kelton Hall. Student, Boston U., 1983-85. Field recruiter Nat. Rsch. Group, Hollywood, Calif., 1993-2000; pres., CEO DuMont Entertainment Group, Hollywood, 1994—; v.p. sales and mktg. PACE Am., Hollywood, 2000—04, website, 2005—. Mem. Ensemble Studio Theatre, NYC, 1989—, co-artistic dir. L.A. Project, 1996. Actor: (Broadway plays) Six Degrees of Separation, 1990—93, (off-Broadway play) Tony & Tina's Wedding, 1989—90; (films) Speed, 1993, Combination Platter, 1993, Bombshell, 1996, The Peacemaker, 1996, Primary Colors, 1996, Erasable You, 1997, In Quiet Night, 1997, Bellyfruit, 1998, Love & Basketball, 1999, Catch Me if You Can, 2002, S.W.A.T., 2003, Seabiscuit, 2003, Along Came Polly, 2003, Miss Congeniality 2, 2004, Dating Games People Play, 2004, War of the Worlds, 2005, The Sound, 2005, Statistics, 2006, Oceans 13, 2006; (TV series) NYPD Blue, 1995, Lois & Clark, 1996, Chgo. Sons, 1996, Tracy Takes on, 1995, Fallen Angels, 1995, The Client, 1995, Sweet Justice, 1995, Can't Hurry Love, 1995, Arliss, 1998, Then Came You, 1999, The West Wing, 2000, Becker, 2000, Titus, 2001, That's Life, 2001, That Was Then, 2002, Cold Case, 2003, C.S.I., 2003, ER, 2004, Joan of Arcadia, 2005, Close to Home, 2005, House, 2006; (TV films) Pentagon Wars, 1998, Winchell, 1999, Gotta Kick It Up, 2001, Pandemic (Part 1), 2006; prodr.: Satistics, 2006; prodr., actor: (films) The Confession, 1996; co-exec. prodr.: (TV films) The Sound, 2005. Democrat. Buddhist. Avocation: writing prose and short stories, plays and screenplays. Office: 5225 Wilshire Blvd # 410 Los Angeles CA 90036 E-mail: dumontentgrp@earthlink.net.

DUNAWAY, CAMMIE, marketing executive; b. 1962; m. Lendy Dunaway; 1 child, Davis. BS, U. Richmond, 1984; MBA, Harvard U., 1990. Mktg. analyst Martin Agency, Richmond, Va.; account exec. Howard Merrell and Ptnrs., NC; asst. brand mgr. Frito-Lay, Dallas, product mgr., v.p. sales for No. Calif., Wash., Ore., Alaska and Hawaii, head nat. sales force, v.p. for kids and teens mktg., 2001—03; chief mktg. officer, head customer experience divsn. Yahoo!, Inc., Sunnyvale, Calif., 2003—07; v.p. sales & mktg. Nintendo of Am. Inc., Redmond, Wash., 2007—. Co-founder TravelingChefs; bd. dirs. Brunswick Corp., 2006—. Vol. San Jose Tech Mus.; bd. mem. Jr. Achievement of Silicon Valley. Recipient Gold Reggie award, Promotional Mktg. Assn., 2006; named one of 100 Top Marketers, Advt. Age Mag. Mem.: Am. Mktg. Assn. Office: Nintendo of Am Inc 4820 150th Ave NE Redmond WA 98052

DUNCAN, DAVID EWING, editor, writer; b. 1958; Contbg. editor, writer Harper's, Atlantic Monthly, Smithsonian, Outside, NY Times, San Francisco Chronicle, Wired, Discover; chief corr. NPR Talk's Biotech Nation. Founder, editl. dir. BioAgenda; commentator Morning Edit. Nat. Pub. Radio; tchr. in field; visiting rschr. UC Berkeley Sch. of Journalism; blog writer MIT Tech. Review. Author: (book) Pedaling the Ends of the Earth, 1985, Calendar: Humanity's Epic Struggle to Determine a True and Accurate Year, 1998, Hernando de Soto: A Savage Quest in the Americas, 1996, Residents: The Perils and Promise of Educating Young Doctors, 1996, The Geneticist Who Played Hoops With My DNA, 2005, Masterminds: Genius, DNA and the Quest to Rewrite Life, 2005 (Best Book of Yr. selection, San Francisco Chronicle); dir.: Grotto Nights; spl. corr., prodr. (television) Nightline ABC, 20/20; prodr.: (television) Discovery TV; corr., writer (television) ScienceNow PBS Nova sci. mag. program. Recipient Mag. Story of Yr. award, Am. Assn. for Advancement Sci., 2003. Office Phone: 415-861-3795. E-mail: deduncan@literati.net.

DUNCAN, GREG JOHN, economics researcher; b. St. Paul, Sept. 17, 1948; s. Elwin Raymond and Selma Louisa (Elquist) Duncan; m. Dorothy Jo Telfer, June 24, 1983; children: Ellen Louisa, Mitchell Telfer. BA, Grinnell Coll., 1970; PhD in Econs., U. Mich., 1974; PhD (hon.), U. Essex, 1999. Asst. prof. Dept. Econs. U. Mich., Ann Arbor, 1977—80, adj. assoc. prof., 1983—87, prof., 1987—95; prof. Sch. Edn. and Social Policy Northwestern U., 1995—2002, faculty affiliate Inst. for Policy Rsch. (formerly Ctr. Urban Affairs and Policy Rsch.), 1995—2008, Edwina S. Tarry prof., 2002—08, adj. prof., 2008—; disting. prof. edn. U. Calif., Irvine, 2008—. Vis. scholar U. Bremen, 1993; vis. prof. Dept. Econs. U. Paris I (Sorbonne), 1996, 97, 98; dep. dir. Joint Ctr. Poverty Rsch. Northwestern U. / U. Chgo., 1997—2000, dir., 2000—03; vis. scholar Russell Sage Found., 2004—05; Roy Geary lectr. Econ. and Social Rsch. Inst., Dublin, 2005. Author: Year of Poverty, Years of Plenty, 1984; co-author (with Aletha Huston and Tom Weisner): Higher Ground: New Hope for the Working Poor and Their Children, 2007; co-editor (with Jeanne Brooks-Gunn): Consequences of Growing up Poor, 1997, Neighborhood Poverty, 1997; co-editor: (with Lindsay Chase Lansdale) For Better and For Worse:

Welfare Reform and the Well-Being of Children and Families, 2001; contbr. articles to profl. jours. Mem. MacArthur Network on Family and Economy, 1996—; mem. tech. adv. com. Head Start Impact Study, 2003—; nat. adv. bd. Nat. Poverty Ctr., 2003—; tech. working group Americorp Evaluation Study, 2006—; co-chair Nat. Forum on Early Childhood Program Evaluation, 2006—. Mem.: MacArthur Network on the Family and the Economy, Soc. for Rsch. on Child Devel., Midwest Econs. Assn. (pres. 2004—05), Inst. Scientific Info., Am. Acad. Arts & Scis., Population Assn. Am. (pres. 2007—08), Am. Econs. Assn. Office: U Calif Irvine 2062 Berkeley Place N Irvine CA 92697-5500 Office Phone: 949-824-7831. Office Fax: 949-824-2965. E-mail: gduncan@uci.edu.

DUNCAN, JAMES DANIEL, paper distribution company executive; b. LaSalle, Ill., June 12, 1941; s. Lawrence James and Margaret Mary (Brehm) D.; m. Sandra Ruth Crowe, Nov. 10, 1963; children: Lawrence, Brian, Stephen. BA in Journalism, U. Notre Dame, Ind., 1963; MBA in Mgmt., Xavier U., Cin., 1978. With sales dept. Campbell Soup Co., Chgo. and Mich., 1963-66; with sales and sales mgmt. depts. Weyerhaeuser Co., Chgo. and Houston, 1966-70; with sales mgmt. dept. Boise Cascade, Chgo. and Marion, Ind., 1970-71; with sales mgmt. and mgmt. depts. Internat. Paper Co., Pitts., NYC and Cin., 1971-82; exec. v.p., chief operating officer WWF Paper Corp., Phila., 1982-87, also bd. dirs.; pres. Grant Paper Co., Pennsauken, N.J., 1988-89; pres., chief exec. officer Sequoia Pacific Systems, Inc. (subs. Jefferson Smurfit Group), Exeter, Calif., 1989—. Mem. exec. com. Paper Distbn. Coun., N.Y., 1987—. Editor sales tng. manual, 1976. Mem. Nat. Paper Trade Assn. (printing paper com. 1986—). Republican. Roman Catholic. Avocations: golf, tennis, bridge.

DUNCAN, MICHAEL CLARKE, actor; b. Chgo., Dec. 10, 1957; s. Jean Duncan. Attended, Alcorn State U., Kankakee CC. Actor: (TV series) The Bold and the Beautiful, 1992—94, Skwids, 1996; (films) Friday, 1995, Back in Business, 1997, Caught Up, 1998, The Players Club, 1998, Bulworth, 1998, Armageddon, 1998, A Night at the Roxbury, 1998, Breakfast of Champions, 1999, The Green Mile, 1999, The Underground Comedy Movie, 1999, The Whole Nine Yards, 2000, Wrestlemania 2000, 2000, Soldier of Fortune, 2000, See Spot Run, 2001, The Immigrant Garden, 2001, Cats & Dogs, 2001, Planet of the Apes, 2001, They Call Me Sirr, 2001, Hollywood Digital Diaries, 2001, The Scorpion King, 2002, Daredevil, 2003, George and the Dragon, 2004, Pursued, 2004, (voice) Dinotopia: Curse of the Ruby Sunstone, 2004, Racing Stripes, 2005, American Crude, 2005, The Island, 2005, Sin City, 2005, Talladega Nights: The Ballad of Ricky Bobby, 2006, School for Scoundrels, 2006, The Last Mimzy, 2007, One Way, 2007, Slipstream, 2007, Welcome Home Roscoe Jenkins, 2008, (voice) Kung Fu Panda, 2008, Delgo, 2008, Street Fighter: The Legend of Chun-Li, 2009, numerous TV guest appearances. Office: Dolores Robinson Entertainment 3815 Hughes Ave # 3 Culver City CA 90232-2715

DUNCAN, RICHARD FREDRICK, JR., retired secondary school educator, consultant; b. Millry, Ala., July 12, 1947; s. Richard F. and Claire Louise (Wood) D.; m. Rebecca Susan Davis, July 14, 1973. AA, Okaloosa-Walton Jr. Coll., 1967; BS, Fla. State U., 1969, MS, 1971; postgrad., Ore. State U., 1981-82. Tchr. Gadsden County Sch. Bd., Quincy, Fla., 1970-71, Leon County Sch. Bd., Tallahassee, 1972-73, Beaverton (Oreg.) Sch. Dist. No. 48, 1973—2006, tchr. emeritus, 2006—. Microbiologist Washington County, Hillsboro, Ore., 1971-72; cons. on sci. edn. Northwest Regional Ednl. Lab., Portland, Ore., 1978-79; cons. on marine edn. Ore. Dept. Edn., Salem, 1980-81; adj. prof. Portland State U., 1981-2006. Recipient award for excellence in sci. teaching Ore. Mus. Sci. and Industry, Portland, 1984, Psdl. award, 1984. Mem. Assn. Presdl. Awardees in Sci. Teaching (nat. pres. 1987-88), Nat. Assn.Biology Tchrs. (Ore. Biology Tchr. of Year award 1981), Nat. Sci. Tchrs. Assn. (Presdl. award for excellence in sci. teaching, 1983, Sheldon award 1993, Nat. Disting. Svc. to Sci. award 2001), Oreg. Sci. Tchrs. Assn. (pres. 1980-81, Oreg. Jr. High Tchr. of Yr. award 1982), North Assn. Marine Educators (state dir. 1978-80), Masons, Shriners, Pi Lambda Theta. Democrat. Avocations: sports, photography, sailing, scuba diving, camping. Home: 1035 Northshore Pl Lake Oswego OR 97034-3722 Office: Beaverton School District 2180 SW 170th Ave Beaverton OR 97006-4348 Office Phone: 503-744-0794. Personal E-mail: r2duncan@comcast.net.

DUNCAN, RONALD A., telecommunications company executive; b. 1953; B in Econs., Johns Hopkins U.; MBA, Harvard U. Founder, pres. Alaskavision; ptnr. Lyall Assocs.; with Gen. Comm. Inc., Anchorage, exec. v.p., founder, pres., CEO, 1989—. Bd. dirs., past chmn. Anchorage Econ. Devel. Corp.; chmn. Alaska Sci. and Tech. Found.; asst. dir. Johns Hopkins U. Ctr. for Met. Planning andRsch.; spl. asst. to Congressman John Dow. Office: Gen Comm Inc 2550 Denali St Ste 1000 Anchorage AK 99503-2781

DUNDAS, DENNIS FRANKLIN, plastic surgeon; b. LA, Oct. 12, 1942; s. John Arthur and Wanda (Yoakum) D.; m. Zoe Lynn Anderson, Feb. 9, 1969; children: Gregory, Denise. BA, Johns Hopkins U., 1964; MD, U. So. Calif., 1968. Diplomate Am. Bd Plastic Surgery. Pvt. practice, Kirkland, Wash., 1978—. Lt. comdr. USN, 1978—. Fellow ACS; mem. Am. Soc. Plastic Surgeons. Office: 13114 120th Ave NE Kirkland WA 98034-3014

DUNFORD, DAVID JOSEPH, foreign service officer, ambassador; b. Glen Ridge, NJ, Feb. 24, 1943; s. Thomas Joseph and Katherine Celeste (Jahn) D.; m. Sandra Corbett Mitchell, Dec. 18, 1965; children: Gregory, Kristina. BS in Engring., MIT, 1964; MA in Polit. Sci., Stanford U., 1965, MA in Econs., 1976. Jr. officer Am. Embassy, Quito, Ecuador, 1967-68, econ.-commercial officer Helsinki, Finland, 1969-72; dir. planning and econ. analysis staff Dept. State, Washington, 1977-79, dir. Office of Devel. Fin., 1979-80; dep. asst. U.S. trade rep. Office of U.S. Trade Rep., Washington, 1980-81; minister-counselor for econ. affairs Am. Embassy, Cairo, 1981-84; dir. Egyptian affairs Dept. State, Washington, 1984-87; dep. chief of mission Am. Embassy, Riyadh, Saudi Arabia, 1988-92, amb. to Oman, Muscat, 1992-95; ret. from fgn. svc., 1995; adj. prof. dept. polit. sci. U. Ariz., 1995—; coord. transition team Menabank, Cairo, 1997-98; adj. prof. Am. Grad. Sch. Internat. Mgmt., 1998-00. Bd. mem. Assn. for Internat. Practical Tng. Recipient Presdl. Meritorious Svc. awards, 1991, 92, Disting. Citizen award U. Ariz. Alumni Assn., 1994. Mem. Am. Fgn. Svc. Assn. (Christian A. Herter award 1991). Avocations: skiing, bicycling, hiking, creative writing, photography.

DUNHAM, SCOTT H., lawyer; b. Seattle, May 7, 1950; BA with highest honors, Wash. State U., 1972; JD, U. Wash., 1975. Bar: Calif. 1975, U.S. Dist. Ct. (ctrl. dist.) Calif. 1976, U.S. Supreme Ct. 1977. Mem. O'Melveny & Myers, LLP, LA, chair labor and employment law group. Author: Avoiding and Defending Wrongful Discharge Claims, 1987, Designing an Effective Fair Hiring and Termination Compliance Program, 1992; contbr. chpts. to books; editor-in-chief Wash. Law Rev., 1974-75. Fellow Coll. Labor and Employment Lawyers; mem. ABA (mem. and co-chair com. occupational safety and health labor and employment law sect.), LA County Bar Assn. (tchr., lectr. Calif. Bus. Law Inst., ABA nat. Inst., Pers. and Indsl. Rels. Assn., Japan Bus. Assn., Inst. Applied Mgmt. and Law, Inc., Calif. Continuing Edn. Bar and various other employer assns.), Order of Coif, Phi Beta Kappa, Phi Kappa Phi, Omicron Delta Kappa, Phi Delta Phi (magister Ballinger inn chpt. 1974). Office: O'Melveny & Myers LLP 400 S Hope St Los Angeles CA 90071-2899

DUNIPACE, IAN DOUGLAS, lawyer; b. Tucson, Dec. 18, 1939; s. William Smith and Esther Morvyth (McGeorge) D.; m. Janet Mae Dailey, June 9, 1963; children: Kenneth Mark, Leslie Amanda. BA magna cum laude, U. Ariz., 1961, JD cum laude, 1966. Bar: Ariz. 1966, U.S. Supreme Ct. 1972, Nev. 1994, Colo. 1996. Reporter, critic Long Branch (N.J.) Daily Record, 1963; assoc. firm Jennings, Strouss, Salmon & Trask, Phoenix, 1966-69; assoc. Jennings, Strouss & Salmon, PLC, Phoenix, 1969-70, ptnr., 1971-93, mem., 1993—2003, chmn. comml. practice dept., 1998—2001; mem. I. Douglas Dunipace, PLC, Phoenix, 2004—. Comments editor Ariz. Law Rev., 1965-66. Reporter Phoenix Forward Edn. Com., 1969-70; mem. Phoenix Arts Commn., 1990-93, chmn., 1992-93; bd. mgmt. Downtown Phoenix YMCA, 1973-80, chmn. 1977-78; bd. dirs. Phoenix Met. YMCA, 1976-87, 1988-2005, chmn. 1984-85; bd. mgmt. Paradise Valley YMCA, 1979-82, chmn. 1980-81; bd. mgmt. Scottsdale/Paradise Valley YMCA, 1983, legal affairs com. Pacific Region YMCA, 1978-81; chmn. YMCA Ariz. State Youth and Govt. Com., 1989-95, cmty. resource bd., 2005—; bd. dirs. Schoolhouse Found. 1990-96, pres. 1990-94, Kids Voting, 1990-94, Beaver Valley Improvement Assn. 1977-79, Pi Kappa Alpha Holding Corp., 1968-72, Heard Mus. 1993-94, Ariz. Bar Found., 1996-2003, pres., 2001-02, Phoenix Kiwanis Charitable Found., 2001-06, pres., 2005-06, Phoenix Ctr. Cmty. Devel., 2002-04; trustee Paradise Valley Unified Dist. Employee Benefit Trust, 1980-93, chmn. 1987-93, Sch. Theology, Claremont, Calif. 1994-2006, chmn., 2004-06; bd. mgrs. Desert Schs. Fin. Svcs., 2003—; trustee First Meth. Found. Phoenix, 1984-93, 99—, pres., 2002-04; active Greater Paradise Valley Cmty. Coun., 1985-87; bd. dirs. Heard Mus. Coun., 1990-95, pres. 1993-94; mem. Ariz. Venture Capital Conf. Planning Com., 1994-2003, exec. com. 1997-2003, chmn., 2000; mem. Assn. for Corp. Growth, 1995-96, Ariz. Bus. Leadership Assn., 1996-2005, bd. dirs., 2001-04, sec.-treas., 2002-04, Ariz. Town Hall, 2003—; bd. vis. U. Ariz. Law Coll., 1996-2003; mem. met. Phoenix commn., Meth. Ch., 1968-71, lay leader, 1975-78, trustee, 1979-81, pres., 1981; mem. Pacific S.W. ann. Meth. Conf., 1969-79, lawyer commn., 1980-85, chancellor Desert S.W. ann. conf. 1985-2005. Capt. AUS, 1961-63. Mem. State Bar Ariz. (securities regulation sect. 1970-2004, chmn. 1991-92, mem. com. unauthorized practice of law 1972-84, chmn. 1975-83, mem. bus. law sect. 1981—, chmn. 1984-85), State Bar Nev., State Bar Colo., Am., Fed. (pres. Ariz. chpt. 1980-81), Maricopa County Bar Assns. (bd. dirs. Corp. Coun. divsn. 1996-99), U. Ariz. Law Coll. Assn. (bd. dirs. 1983-90, pres. 1985-86), U. Ariz. Alumni Assn. (bd. dirs. 1985-86), Masons, Kiwanis (pres. Phoenix 1984-85, disting. lt. gov. 1986-87, S.W. dist. cmty. svc. chmn. 1987-88, dist. activity com. coord. 1988-89, dist. laws and regulation chmn. 1989-90, 92-93, 95-96, 2002—, asst. to dist. gov. for club svcs. 1990-91, field dir. 1991-92, dist. conv. chmn. 1993-94, pub. rels. chmn. 1996-98, mem. internat. com. on Project 39, 1988-89, internat. com. On to Anaheim 1990-91, internat. com. on leadership tng. and devel. 1991-92, 93-94, trustee SW dist. found. 1987-92, 1st v.p. 1990-92), Orange Tree Club, Phi Beta Kappa, Phi Kappa Phi, Phi Delta Phi, Phi Alpha Theta, Sigma Delta Pi, Phi Eta Sigma, Pi Kappa Alpha (nat. counsel 1968-72). Democrat. Methodist. Home: 2527 E Vogel Ave Phoenix AZ 85028-4729 Office: I Douglas Dunipace PLC 3116 E Shea Blvd # 251 Phoenix AZ 85028 Office Phone: 602-370-6895. Personal E-mail: dunipaceplc@cox.net.

DUNKLIN, BETSY D., state legislator; b. Goshen, Va., Oct. 9, 1949; m. Charles F. Cole; 1 child, Kate. BA in English, Newberry Coll., 1971; postgrad., U. S.C., 1972-73; MSW, U. Md., Balt., 1981. Svcs. coord. Families Forward, Boise, 1986, dir., 1986-87, Women's and Children's Crisis Ctr., Boise, 1987-89; bd. pres. Idaho Women's Network, Inc., Boise, 1989-90, exec. dir., 1990-94; pub. affairs coord. Planned Parenthood of Idaho, Boise, 1995-96; mem. Idaho Senate, Dist. 19, Boise, 1996—. Mem. edn. and judiciary and rules com.; adj. faculty, Boise State U., 1988-89. Mem. Idaho Coun. Tech. and Learning, Hispanic Commn. Idaho, Baltimore City Tenants' Assn., United Farm Workers. Mem. Idaho Women's Network (founding mem.; Opal Brooten award), Idaho Rivers United, WCA of Boise (pres. we. states ctr.). Democrat. Unitarian-Universalist. Office: State Capitol PO Box 83720 Boise ID 83720-3720

DUNLAP, F. THOMAS, JR., lawyer, retired electronics executive; b. Pitts., Feb. 7, 1951; s. Francis Thomas and Margaret (Hubert) D.; m. Kathy Dunlap; children: Bridgette, Katie. BSE.E., U. Cin., 1974; JD, U. Santa Clara, Calif., 1979. Bar: Calif., 1979, U.S. Dist. Ct. (no. dist.) Calif. 1979. Mgr. engring. Intel Corp., Santa Clara, Calif., 1974-78, adminstr. tech. exchange, 1978-80, European counsel, 1980-81, sr. atty., 1981-83, gen. counsel, sec., 1983-87, v.p., gen. counsel, sec., 1987—2001, sr. v.p., gen. counsel, 2001—04. Drafter, lobbyist Semiconductor Chip Protection Act, 1984 Republican. Roman Catholic. Avocation: jogging.

DUNLEAVY, MIKE (MICHAEL JOSEPH DUNLEAVY JR.), professional basketball coach; b. Bklyn., Mar. 21, 1954; m. Emily Dunleavy; children: Michael, Jr., William Baker, James. Grad., U. SC, 1976. Player Phila. 76ers, 1976-77, Houston Rockets, 1977—82, San Antonio Spurs, 1982—83, Milw. Bucks, 1983—85, 1988—90, asst. coach, 1986—90, head coach, 1992—96, v.p. basketball ops., 1993-96, gen. mgr., 1993—97; player-coach All-Am. Basketball Alliance Carolina Lightning; head coach LA Lakers, 1990-92, Portland Trail Blazers, Oreg., 1997—2001, LA Clippers, 2003—, gen. mgr., 2008—. Named NBA Coach of Yr., 1989, 1999. Office: LA Clippers Staples Ctr 1111 S Figueroa St Ste 1100 Los Angeles CA 90015

DUNN, ARNOLD SAMUEL, biochemistry educator; b. Rochester, NY, Jan. 31, 1929; s. Alexander and Dora (Cohen) D.; m. Doris Ruth Frankel, Sept. 14, 1952; children: Jonathan Alexander, David Hillel. BS, George Washington U., 1950; PhD, U. Pa., 1955; LHD (hon.), Hebrew Union Coll., 1995. Research assoc. Michael Reese Hosp. Research Inst., Chgo., 1955-56; asst. prof. NYU Sch. Medicine, NYC, 1956-62; vis. prof. Weizmann Inst. Sci., Rehovot, Israel, 1972-73, 83-84, Hebrew U., Jerusalem, 1972-73; dir. molecular biology U. So. Calif., LA, 1982-90, assoc. dean, 1990-92; vis. fellow history sci. Princeton U., 1993; prof. molecular biology U. So. Calif., Los Angeles, 1962—2008, prof. emeritus, 2008. Contbr. articles to profl. jours.; mem. editorial bd.: Am. Jour. Physiology, 1979-, Analytical Biochemistry, 1980-. UPSHS fellow, 1972, 83; Meyerhoff fellow Weizmann Inst. Sci., 1983. MEm. Am. Physiol. Soc., Am. Soc. Biol. Chemists, Endocrine Soc., Phi Beta Kappa, Sigma Xi, Phi Kappa Phi, Golden Key. Home Phone: 310-454-9661. Business E-Mail: arnolddu@usc.edu.

DUNN, BOYD W., mayor, Chandler, Arizona, lawyer; m. Nancy Dunn; children: Andrew, Kevin. BA in Polit. Sci., Ariz. State U., JD. Bar: Ariz. 1979. Mem. Chandler City Coun., 1994—2002; pvt. practice; mayor City of Chandler, Ariz., 2002—. Mem. East Valley Behavioral Health Assn., Chandler Airport Commn.; mem., past chmn. Planning & Zoning Commn.; mem. transportation policy com. Maricopa Assn. Govts.; liaison City of Chandler's Fin., Pub. Safety & Cmty. Svcs. Coms. Treas., bd. dirs. Phoenix Coun. Navy League; charter mem. Downtown Chandler Cmty. Partnership; bd. dirs. Greater Phoenix Econ. Coun.; hon. adv. bd. dirs. United Food Bank. Mem.: Christian Legal Soc., Ariz. State U. Alumni Assn., Ariz. Parents Assn., US Naval Acad. Office: Office of Mayor and City Council Mail Stop 603 PO Box 4008 Chandler AZ 85244-4008 Office Phone: 480-782-2200. Office Fax: 480-782-2233. Business E-Mail: boyd.dunn@chandleraz.gov.*

DUNN, BRUCE SIDNEY, materials scientist, educator; m. Wendy Joan Rader, 1970; 1 child. BS in Ceramic Engring., Rutgers U., 1970; MS in Materials Sci., UCLA, 1972, PhD in Materials Sci., 1974. Staff scientist GE, Schenectady, NY, 1976-80; assoc. prof. materials sci. UCLA, 1981-85, prof., 1985—, Nippon Sheet Glass chair materials sci., 2003. Invited prof. U. Paris, 1986, 91-93, 98, U. Bordeaux, 2000; cons. in field Contbr. articles to profl. jours. Fulbright fellow, 1985-86. Fellow Am. Ceramic Soc.; mem. Electrochem. Soc., Materials Rsch. Soc. Achievements include patents in field.

DUNN, DAVID JOSEPH, investment company executive; b. Bklyn., July 30, 1930; s. David Joseph and Rose Marie (McLaughlon) Dunn; m. Marilyn Percaccia, June 1955 (div.); children: Susan, Steven, Linda; m. Marilyn Bell, Apr. 1994. BS, US Naval Acad., 1955; MBA, Harvard U., Cambridge, Mass., 1961. Investment banker G.H. Walker & Co., NYC, 1961-62; ptnr. J.H. Whitney & Co., NYC, 1962-70; mng. ptnr. Idanta Ptnrs., San Diego, 1971—. Chmn. bd. dirs. Munchkin, Inc.; bd. dirs. Engineous Software, NanoNexus. With USMC, 1950—51, with USMC, 1955—59. Mem.: Glenwild Country Club, Del Mar Country Club, Vintage Club, Univ. Club (NYC). Office: Idanta Ptnrs 12526 High Bluff Dr Ste 160 San Diego CA 92130

DUNN, FLOYD, biophysics and biomedical engineering professor; b. Kansas City, Mo., Apr. 14, 1924; s. Louis and Ida (Leibtag) Dunn; m. Elsa Tanya Levine, June 11, 1950; children: Andrea Susan, Louis Brook. Student, Kans. City Jr. Coll., 1941-42, Tex. A&M U., College Station, 1943; BS, U. Ill., Urbana, 1949, MS, 1951, PhD, 1956. Rsch. assoc. elec. engring. U. Ill., Urbana, 1954-57, rsch. asst. prof. elec. engring., 1957-61, assoc. prof. elec. engring. and biophysics, 1961-65, prof., 1965—95, prof. elec. engring., biophysics and bioengring., 1972-95, faculty mem. Beckman Inst. Advanced Sci. and Tech., prof. emeritus, 1995—, dir. bioacoustics rsch. lab., 1976-95, chmn. bioengring. faculty, 1978-82. Vis. prof. U. Coll., Cardiff, Wales, 1968—69, Inst. Chest Diseases and Cancer, Tohoku U., Sendai, Japan, 1989—90, U. Nanjing, China, 1983; mem. bioengring., radiation, diagnostic radiology and NIBIB study sects. NIH, 1970—81, 2008; steering com. workshop interaction ultrasound and biol. tissues NSF, 1971—72; vis. sr. scientist Inst. Cancer Rsch., Sutton, Surrey, England, 1975—76, Sutton, 1982—83, Sutton, 1990; chmn. working group health aspects exposure to ultrasound radiation WHO, London, 1976; mem. tech.-elec. products radiation stds. com. FDA, 1974—76; vis. prof. radiation oncology U. Ariz., Tucson, 1996—2008, vis. prof., radiology dept., 2008—; mem. Nat. Coun. Radiation Protection and Measurement, 1980—2003, fellow, 2003—; treas. Interscience Rsch. Inst., Champaign, Ill., 1957—58; mem. sci. adv. bd. Resonant Med. Inc., Montreal, 2005—. Mem. editl. bd. Jour. Acoustical Soc. Am., 1968—, Ultrasound Medicine and Biology, 1981—, Ultrasonics, 1981—2003, Encyclopedia of Acoustics, 1981—97, Encyclopedia of Applied Physics, 1981—, Am. Inst. Physics Series Modern Acoustics and Signal Processing, 1990—97; contbr. articles to profl. jours.; cons. Piezo Energy Technologies LLC, 2007—. Trustee Hensley Twp., Ill., 1980—81. With AUS, 1943—46. Recipient Spl. Merit medal, Acoustical Soc. Japan, 1988, History Med. Ultrasound Pioneer award, AIUM/WFUMB, 1988; Spl. Rsch. fellow, NIH, 1968—69, Eleanor Roosevelt-Internat. Cancer fellow, Am. Cancer Soc., 1975—76, 1982—83, Fulbright fellow, 1982—83, Japan Soc. Promotion Sci. fellow, 1982, 1996, Fogarty Internat. fellow, 1990. Fellow: AAAS, IEEE (life), Inst. Acoustics (U.K.), Am. Inst. Ultrasound in Medicine (William J. Fry meml. award 1984, Joseph H. Holmes Basic Sci. Pioneer award 1990), Acoustical Soc. Am. (assoc. editor Jour. 1968-, exec. coun. 1977-80, v.p. 1980-81, pres. 1985-86, chmn. pub. policy com. 1994-, Silver medal 1989, Gold medal 1998), Am. Inst. Med. Biol. Engring. (IEEE Engring. Medicine and Biology Soc. Career Achievement award 1995, Edison medal 1996, William J. & Francis J. Fry award 2008), Internat. Acad. Med. Biol. Engring.; mem.: NAE, NAS, Biophys. Soc., Rochester Soc. Biomed. Ultrasound (hon.), Japan Soc. Ultrasound in Medicine (hon.), Am. Inst. Physics (mem. editl. bd. series in modern acoustics and signal processing 1990—97, publs. policy com. 1992—2000), NCRP Alumni Assn., NIH Alumni Assn., Sigma Xi, Phi Sigma Phi, Phi Sigma, Pi Mu Epsilon, Tau Beta Pi, Eta Kappa Nu, Sigma Tau. Home: 13500 N Rancho Vistoso Blvd # 143 Tucson AZ 85755-5956 Personal E-mail: floyd@ece.arizona.edu.

DUNN, RANDALL LAWSON, judge; b. Gary, Ind., May 28, 1950; s. Jack Harold Wheeler and Doris Marjorie (Rose) D.; m. Laurie Marie Loomis, Sept. 17, 1954; children: Jonathan Loomis, Andrew Jack. BA with honors, Northwestern U., Evanston, Ill., 1972; JD, Stanford U., 1975. Bar: Oreg., Wash., U.S. Dist.Ct. Oreg., U.S. Dist. Ct. Utah, U.S. Ct. Appeals (9th and 10th cirs.), U.S. Dist. Ct. (ea. and we. dists.) Wash. Law clk. Hon. James J. Richards Chief Judge Superior Ct. Lake County, Hammond, Ind., 1973-74; assoc. Berman & Giauque, Salt Lake City, 1975-76; assoc., ptnr. to mng. ptnr. Copeland, Landye, Bennett & Wolf, Portland, Oreg., 1977—98; apptd. bankruptcy judge US Dist. Ct. Oreg., 1998—; apptd. bankruptcy appellate panel Ninth Cir., 2006—. Articles editor Stanford Law Rev., 1974-75; editor-in-chief Bankruptcy Briefs, 1991-95; cons. editor Fed. Bar News and Jour., 1994; editor-in-chief, author Oreg. Debtor Creditor Newsletter, 1988-95. Pres., treas., bd. dirs. Beaverton (Oreg.) Arts. Commn., 1986-92; pres., bd. dirs. Portland Festival Symphony, 1985—98; chmn. West Sylvan Mid. Sch. Funding Com.,

Portland, 1993. Mem. ABA (sects. on antitrust, corp. banking and bus. law), Oreg. State Bar Assn. (sects. on antitrust, debtor/creditor, treas. exec. com.), Fed. Bar Assn. (chmn. exec. com. bankruptcy sect. 1994-95), Wash. State Bar Assn. (sects. on creditor, debtor, corp., bus. and banking law), Am. Fedn. Musicians, Nat. Conf. Bankruptcy Judges(treas., sec., bd. govs.) Avocations: playing the clarinet, weight-lifting, reading, gardening. Office: 1001 SW 5th Ave Ste 700 Portland OR 97204-1141 Office Phone: 503-326-1538.

DUNN, RICHARD JOSEPH, retired investment advisor; b. Chgo., Apr. 5, 1924; s. Richard Joseph and Margaret Mary (Jennett) Dunn; m. Marygrace Calhoun, Oct. 13, 1951 (dec. May 2000); children: Richard, Robert(dec.), Marianne, Anthony, Gregory, Noelle. AB, Yale U., New Haven, Conn., 1948; JD, Harvard U., Cambridge, Mass., 1951; MBA, Stanford U., Calif., 1956. Bar: Tex. 1952. Mem. Carrington, Gowan, Johnson & Walker, Dallas, 1951-54; investment counselor Scudder, Stevens & Clark, San Francisco, 1956-84, gen. ptnr., 1974-84, ret., 1984. Mem. Sovereign Coun., Rome, 1999—2004. With AUS US Army, 1943—46. Decorated Combat Inf. badge, Purple Heart, Bronze Star, Bailiff Grand Cross of Honor and Devotion in Obedience of the Sovereign Mil. Hospitaller Order St. John of Jersusalem Rhodes and Malta, knight comdr. with star Papal Order St. Gregory; recipient Disting. Grad. award, Boston Latin Sch., 2008. Roman Catholic.

DUNNE, KEVIN JOSEPH, lawyer; b. Pitts., Sept. 22, 1941; s. Matthew S. and Marjorie (Whelan) D.; m. Heather Wright Dunne, Sept. 27, 1963; children: Erin, Kevin Jr., Patrick, Sean. BA, U. Conn., 1963; JD, Georgetown U., 1966. Bar: Calif. 1967, U.S. Dist. Ct. (no. dist.) Calif., 1967, U.S. Dist. Ct. (ea. dist.) Calif. 1969, U.S. Dist. Ct. (ctrl. dist.) Calif. 1971, U.S. Ct. Appeals (9th cir.) 1971. Assoc. Sedgwick, Detert, Moran & Arnold, San Francisco, 1968-75, ptnr., 1975—, chmn., 2001—. Adj. prof. U. San Francisco Sch. Law, 1980-86; bd. editorial advisors Bender's Drug Product Liability Reporter, 1988-92. Author: Dunne on Depositions, 1995; contbr. articles to profl. jours. Capt. U.S. Army, 1966-68, Vietnam. Recipient Bronze Star, Army Commendation medal; recipient Exceptional Performance award Def. Rsch. Inst., 1988. Fellow: Am. Coll. Trial Lawyers, Internat. Acad. Trial Lawyers; mem.: Lawyers for Civil Justice (pres. 1998—2000), Am. Bd. Trial Advocates, Internat. Assn. Def. Counsel (pres. 1994—95), No Calif. Assn. Def. Counsel (pres. 1987—88). Roman Catholic. Avocation: golf. Office: Sedgwick Detert Moran & Arnold Stewart Tower 8th Fl One Market Plz San Francisco CA 94105 Office Phone: 415-627-1475.

DUNNE, THOMAS, geology educator; b. Prestbury, U.K., Apr. 21, 1943; arrived in U.S., 1964; s. Thomas and Monica Mary (Whitter) D. BA with honors, Cambridge U., Eng., 1964; PhD, Johns Hopkins U., 1969. Rsch. assoc. USDA-Agrl. Rsch. Svc., Danville, Vt., 1966—68; rsch. hydrologist U.S. Geol. Survey, Washington, 1969; asst. prof. McGill U., Montreal, Que., Canada, 1969—73; from asst. prof. to prof. U. Wash., Seattle, 1973—95, chmn. dept., 1984—89; prof. Sch. Environ. Scis. & Mgmt. U. Calif., Santa Barbara, 1995—. Vis. prof. U. Nairobi, Kenya, 1969—71; cons. in field, 1970—. Author (with L.B. Leopold) Water in Environmental Planning; (with L.M. Reid) Rapid Evaluation of Sediment Budgets, 1996. Fulbright scholar 1984; grantee NSF, NASA, Rockefeller Found., 1969—; Guggenheim fellow, 1989-90. Fellow AAAS, Am. Acad. Arts and Scis., Am. Geophys. Union (Robert E. Horton award 1987, Langbein lectr. 2003), Calif. Acad. Scis.; mem. NAS (G.K. Warren prize in Fluviatile Geology 1998), Geol. Soc. Am. (Easterbrook Disting. Scientist award 2003), Sigma Xi. Office: U Calif Donald Bren Sch Environ Scis & Mgmt 3510 Bren Hall Santa Barbara CA 93106 Office Phone: 805-893-7557. Business E-Mail: tdunne@bren.ucsb.edu.

DUNNER, DAVID LOUIS, medical educator; b. Bklyn., May 27, 1940; s. Edward and Reichel (Connor) D.; m. Peggy Jane Zolbert, Dec. 27, 1964; children: Laura Louise, Jonathan Michael. AA, George Washington U., 1960; MD, Washington U., St. Louis, 1965. Diplomate Am. Bd. Psychiatry and Neurology. Intern Phila. Gen. Hosp., 1965-66; resident in psychiatry Barnes Renard Hosp. of Washington U., St. Louis, 1966-69; rsch. psychiatrist NY State Psychiat. Inst., NYC, 1971—79; from asst. prof. to assoc. prof. clin. psychiatry Columbia U., NYC, 1972-79; chief psychiatry Harborview Med. Ctr., Seattle, 1979-89, dir. outpatient psychiatry, 1989-97; prof. psychiatry and behavioral scis. U. Wash., Seattle, 1979—2006, prof. emeritus, 2006—, vice chmn. clin. svcs., 1989-97; dir. Ctr. for Anxiety & Depression, 1997—; pvt. practice psychiatry, 2006—. Cons. Found. for Depression and Manic Depression, NYC, 1974—. Editor-in-chief Comprehensive Psychiatry, 1997—; contbr. articles to profl. jours. Served to lt. comdr. USPHS, 1969-71. Fellow Am. Psychiat. Assn., Am. Psychopathol. Assn. (pres. 1986), Am. Coll. Neuropsychopharmacology, West Coast Coll. Biol. Psychiatry (charter, pres. 1987); mem. Psychiat. Research Soc. (pres. 1984). Office: Ctr for Anxiety & Depression 7525 SE 24th St Ste 400 Mercer Island WA 98040 Office Phone: 206-230-0330. Personal E-mail: dldunner@comcast.net.

DUNSTAN, LARRY KENNETH, endowment director; b. Payson, Utah, May 26, 1948; s. Kenneth Leroy Dunstan and Verna Matilda (Carter) Taylor; m. Betty K. Limb, Sept. 23, 1966 (div. June 1975); children: Tamara, Thane; m. Jacqueline Lee Darron, Oct. 7, 1975; children: Tessa, Matthew, Bennett, Spencer, Adam. CLU, CPCU, chartered fin. cons., registered health underwriter, life underwriter tng. council fellow. Mgr. Diamond Bar Inn Ranch, Jackson, Mont., 1972-73; agt. Prudential Ins. Co., Missoula, Mont., 1973-77, devel. mgr. Billings, Mont., 1977-78, div. mgr. Gt. Falls, Mont., 1978-83; pres. Multi-Tech Ins. Svcs., Inc., West Linn, Oreg., 1983—2005; agy. mgr. Beneficial Life Ins. Co., Portland, Oreg., 1983-88; dir. endowment Grand Teton Coun., 2006—. Mem. planning commn. City of West Linn, Oreg., 1985-87; mem. bishopric Ch. Jesus Christ of Latter Day Sts., West Linn, 1984-86, exec. sec. Lake Oswego Oreg. Stake, 1987-89; scouting coord. Boy Scouts Am., West Linn, 1984-86, scoutmaster various troops; pres. West Linn Youth Basketball Assn., 1991-97, West Linn/Wilsonville Youth Track Club, 1993-96. Fellow Life Underwriter Tng. Coun. (bd. dirs. local chpt. 1980-81); mem. Gen. Agts. and Mgrs. Assn. (bd. dirs. local chpt. 1981-82), Am. Soc. CLU (pres. local chpt. 1982-83). Republican. Avocations: sports, stamp collecting/philately, hunting, gardening, photography. Home: 3728 Deloy Dr 3 Idaho Falls ID 83401 Office: Boy Scouts Am Grand Teton Coun 574 4th St Idaho Falls ID 83401 Office Phone: 208-522-5155. Personal E-mail: lkdunstan@aol.com, ldunstan@grandtetoncouncil.org.

DUNYE, CHERYL, artist, filmmaker; b. Phila. BA, Temple U.; MFA, Rutgers U. Part-time instr. dept. media studies Pitzer Coll., Calif. Film maker (short film films) Greetings from Africa, 1994, (video films) The Potluck and the Passion, creator (films) The Watermelon Woman, contbr. articles to profl. jours. Recipient Major Artists award, MARMAF Pa., 1993; fellow, Rutgers U., 1990, 1991, Art Matters, Inc., 1992, grantee, Astrea Found., 1992, Frameline, 1992, NEA, 1995. Office: c/o Media Studies Pitzer Coll Scott Hall Basement 1050 N Mills Ave Claremont CA 91711-3908

DUQUE, HENRY MCARTHUR, utilities executive, consultant; b. LA, Nov. 23, 1931; s. Henry O'Melveny and Elizabeth (McArthur) D.; m. Judith Stadelman, Nov. 14, 1959; children: Adrienne, Carolyn, Susan, Henry Jr. AB, Stanford U., 1954; postgrad. in law, U. Calif., Berkeley, 1957-58. Asst. cashier Union Bank, LA, 1958-61; vice chmn. Western Fed. Savs., Marina Del Rey, Calif., 1961-83; sr. v.p. Calif. Fed. Bank, LA, 1983-90; v.p., sr. mktg. officer Trust Svcs. Am., LA, 1990—95; commr. Calif. Pub. Commn., 1995—2003; freelance utilities cons. Los Altos Hills, Calif., 2003—. Chmn. bd. dirs. Savs. Assns. Mktg. Co., Santa Clara, Calif. Chmn. Golden Gate chpg. ARC, San Francisco, 1990. 1st lt. USMC, 1954-57. Republican. Roman Catholic. Avocations: gardening, hunting, travel, sports. Office Phone: 650-948-5262.

DUQUETTE, DIANE RHEA, library director; b. Springfield, Mass., Dec. 15, 1951; d. Gerard Lawrence and Helen Yvette (St. Marie) Morneau; m. Thomas Frederick Duquette Jr., Mar. 17, 1973. BS in Sociology, Springfield Coll., 1975; MLS, Simmons Coll., 1978. Libr. asst. Springfield City Libr., 1975—78; reference libr. U. Mass., Amherst, 1978—81; head libr. Hopkins Acad., Hadley, Mass., 1980; instr. Colo. Mountain Coll., Steamboat Springs, 1981—83; dir. East Routt Libr. Dist., Steamboat Springs, 1981—84; agy. head Solono County Libr., Vallejo, Calif., 1984; dir. libr. svcs. Shasta County Libr., Redding, Calif., 1984—87; dir. librs. Kern County Libr., Bakersfield, Calif., 1987—. Chmn. San Joaquin Valley Libr. Sys., 1988. Contbr. articles to profl. jours. Active San Joaquin Valley Libr. Assn., Calif., 1987—. Recipient John Cotton Dana Spl. Pub. Rels. award, H.W. Wilson and ALA, 1989, 2nd ann. Pub. Libr. Mgmt. award of excellence, Urban Librs. Coun./Libr. Systems and Svcs., 2002. Mem. ALA, Calif. Libr. Assn. (mem. coun. 1987—), Calif. County Librs. Assn. (pres. 1990). Democrat. Roman Catholic. Achievements include serving as director of Kern County Library when it was awarded the John Cotton Dana award for Public Relations. Avocations: golf, skiing, bicycling, reading, gardening. Office: Kern County Libr 701 Truxtun Ave Bakersfield CA 93301-4800 Office Phone: 661-868-0789. Office Fax: 661-868-0799. Business E-Mail: duquette@kerncountylibrary.org.

DURAN, KARIN JEANINE, librarian; b. Burbank, Calif., Aug. 31, 1948; d. Jose Antonio and Sophia (Cortez) D.; m. Richard Mark Nupoll, Sept. 5, 1971. AA, L.A. Pierce Coll., Woodland Hills, Calif., 1968; BA, Calif. State U., 1970; MLS, U. So. Calif., 1972, PhD, 1986. Libr. Calif. State U., Northridge, 1972—. Lectr. Calif. State U., Northridge, 1977—. Mem. Comision Femenil San Fernando Valley, Calif., 1987-2009. Recipient Northridge Extraordinary Svc. Facility award, CSU, 2006, Svc. to Soc. Recognition, 2003; named Woman of Year Calif. Women Higher Edn., Northridge, 1989, Bicentennial Woman, L.A. Human Rels. Com., 1976. Mem. ALA, Nat. Assn. Chicano Studies, Calif. Acad. Rsch. Librs., REFORMA, Phi Kappa Phi. Avocations: travel, theater, reading. Office: Calif State U Northridge Libr 18111 Nordhoff St Northridge CA 91330-8327 Business E-Mail: karin.duran@csun.edu.

DURAN, MICHAEL CARL, bank executive; b. Colorado Springs, Aug. 27, 1953; s. Lawrence Herman and Jacqueline Carol (Ward) D. BS magna cum laude, Ariz. State U., 1980. With J.P. Morgan Chase Bank (formerly Bank One, Ariz., N.A.), Phoenix, 1976—2006; corp. credit trainee Bank One Ariz., Phoenix, 1984—85, comml. loan officer, 1985—86, br. mgr., asst. v.p., 1986—90, comml. banking officer, asst. v.p., 1990—93, credit mgr., v.p., 1993—99, relationship mgr., v.p., 1999—2004, v.p., credit rev. officer, 2004—. Cons. various schs. and orgns., 1986—; incorporator Avondale Neighborhood Housing Svcs., 1988. Mem. Cen. Bus. Dist. Revitalization Com., Avondale, Ariz., 1987-88, Ad-Hoc Econ. Devel. Com., 1988; coord. Avondale Litter Lifters, 1987-88; vol. United Way, Phoenix, 1984; bd. dirs. Jr. Achievement, Yuma, Ariz., 1989-91, vol., Phoenix, 1993—; yokefellow 1st So. Bapt. Ch. of Yuma, 1990-91; treas. Desert View Bapt. Ch., Gilbert, Ariz., 1998—. Recipient Outstanding Community Svc. award City of Avondale, 1988. Mem. Robert Morris Assocs., Ariz. State U. Alumni Assn. (life), Toastmasters, Kiwanis (local bd. dirs. 1986-88), Beta Gamma Sigma, Phi Kappa Phi, Phi Theta Kappa, Sigma Iota Epsilon. Democrat. Baptist. Avocations: art, photography, hiking, jogging. Home: 925 N Quartz St Gilbert AZ 85234-3661 Office: JP Morgan Chase 201 N Central Ave 7th Fl Phoenix AZ 85004 Office Phone: 602-221-1097. Personal E-mail: mcd7az@yahoo.com.

DURANTI, ALESSANDRO, anthropology professor; b. Rome, Sept. 17, 1950; Student, U. Rome; PhD in Linguistics, U. So. Calif., 1981. Post-doctoral fellow Australian Nat. U. Rsch. Sch. Pacific Studies, Canberra; asst. in lab. comparative human cognition U. Calif., San Diego; prof. Pitzer Coll., Claremont, Calif.; prof. comm. dept. U. Calif., San Diego; prof. anthropology UCLA, 1988—. Author: From Grammar to Politics: Linguistic Anthropology in a Western Samoan Village, 1994, Linguistic Anthropology, 1997, Linguistic Anthropology: A Reader, 2001, A Companion to Linguistic Anthropology, 2004, Etnopragmatica, 2007; contbr. articles to profl. jours. Recipient Distinguished Tchg. award, UCLA Alumni Assn., 1999; grantee Guggenheim Meml. Found. Fellowship, 1999—2001. Fellow: Am. Acad. Arts & Scis.; mem.: Am. Anthrop. Assn. (Mayfield Award for Excellence in undergrad. tchg. 2001). Office: UCLA Dept Anthropology 341 Haines Hall Box 951553 Los Angeles CA 90095 Office Phone: 310-825-5833. Office Fax: 310-206-7833. Business E-Mail: aduranti@anthro.ucla.edu.

DURCAN, MARK D., engineering executive; BS, Rice U., M in Chem. Engring. Diffusion engr. Micron Tech. Inc., 1984, various positions, process integration mgr., process R&D devel. mgr., v.p. process R&D, chief tech. officer Boise, 1996—. Office: Micron Tech Inc PO Box 6 8000 S Federal Way Boise ID 83707-0006

DURFY, SEAN, air transportation executive; b. Corner Brook, Nfld., Can. 2 children. B in Commerce, Dalhousie U. With GM Super Group, MacLaren Lintas, Honeywell Ltd., TransAlta Energy; pres., CEO ENMAX Energy Corp., bd. dirs., 1999—2004; exec. v.p. sales, mktg. and airports WestJet Airlines Ltd., Calgary, Alberta, Canada, 2004—06, pres., 2006—, CEO, 2007—. Named Marketer of Yr., 2004. Avocations: running, skiing. Office: WestJet Airlines Ltd 5055 11th St NE Calgary AB Canada T2E 8N4 Office Phone: 403-444-2600. Office Fax: 403-444-2301.

DURHAM, CHRISTINE MEADERS, state supreme court chief justice; b. LA, Aug. 3, 1945; d. William Anderson and Louise (Christensen) Meaders; m. George Homer Durham II, Dec. 29, 1966; children: Jennifer, Meghan, Troy, Melinda, Isaac. AB, Wellesley Coll., 1967; JD, Duke U., 1971. Bar: N.C. 1971, Utah 1974. Sole practice law, Durham, N.C., 1971-73; instr. legal medicine Duke U., Durham, 1971-73; adj. prof. law Brigham Young U., Provo, Utah, 1973-78; ptnr. Johnson, Durham & Moxley, Salt Lake City, 1974-78; judge Utah Dist. Ct., 1978-82; assoc. justice Utah Supreme Ct., 1982—2002, chief justice, 2002—. Pres. Women Judges Fund for Justice, 1987-88. Fellow Am. Bar Found.; mem. ABA (edn. com. appellate judges' conf.), Nat. Assn. Women Judges (pres. 1986-87), Utah Bar Assn., Am. Law Inst. (coun. mem.), Nat. Ctr. State Courts (bd. dirs.), Am. Inns of Ct. Found. (trustee). Office: Utah Supreme Ct PO Box 140210 Salt Lake City UT 84114-0210

DURHAM, HARRY BLAINE, III, lawyer; b. Denver, Sept. 16, 1946; s. Harry Blaine and Mary Frances (Oliver) Durham; m. Lynda L. Durham, Aug. 4, 1973; children: Christopher B., Laurel A. BA cum laude, Colo. Coll., 1969; JD, U. Colo., 1973. Bar: Wyo. 1973, U.S. Tax Ct. 1974, U.S. Ct. Appeals (10th cir.) 1976. Assoc. Brown, Drew, Apostolos, Massey & Sullivan, Casper, Wyo., 1973-77; ptnr. Brown & Drew, Casper, 1977-98, Brown, Drew & Massey, LLP, Casper, 1998—. Articles editor: U. Colo. Law Rev., 1972—73. Bd. dirs. Natrona County United Way, 1974—76, pres., 1975—76; mem. City of Casper Pks. and Recreation Commn., 1985—94, vice chmn., 1987—94; Rep. precinct committeeman, 1999—2002; bd. dirs. Casper Symphony Assn., 1974—88, vice chmn., 1979—82, pres., 1983—87. Recipient State Heroes award, Sporting Goods Mfg. Assn., 1997; named Permanent Class Pres., Class of 1969, Colo. Coll., Mem. Nat. Alumni Coun. Mem.: Nat. Assn. R.R. Trial Counsel, Natrona County Bar Assn., Wyo. Bar Assn. (Wyo. editor fifty state constrn. lien and bond law), Wyo. Amateur Hockey Assn. (bd. dirs., sec. 1974—85, pres. 1985—88), Casper Amateur Hockey Club (bd. dirs. 1970—77, sec. 1974—77), Phi Beta Kappa. Home: 3101 Hawthorne Ave Casper WY 82604-4975 Office: 159 N Wolcott St Ste 200 Casper WY 82601-7009 Office Phone: 307-234-1000.

DURHAM, ROBERT DONALD, JR., state supreme court justice; b. Lynwood, Calif., May 10, 1947; s. Robert Donald Durham and Rosemary Constance (Brennan) McKelvey; m. Linda Jo Rollins, Aug. 29, 1970; children: Melissa Brennan, Amy Elizabeth. BA, Whittier Coll., 1969; JD, U. Santa Clara, 1972; LLM in the Jud. Process, U. Va., 1998. Bar: Oreg. 1972, Calif. 1973, U.S. Dist. Ct. Oreg. 1974, U.S. Ct. Appeals (9th cir.) 1980, U.S. Supreme Ct. 1987. Law clk. Oreg. Supreme Ct., Salem, 1972-74; ptnr. Bennett & Durham, Portland, Oreg., 1974-91; assoc. judge Oreg. Ct. Appeals, Salem, 1991-94; assoc. justice Oreg. Supreme Ct., Salem, 1994—. Adv. com. Joint Interim Judiciary Com., 1984-86; chmn. Oreg. Commn. on Adminstrv. Hearings, 1988-89; faculty Nat. Jud. Coll., Reno, Nev., 1992; mem. Case Disposition Benchmarks Com., 1992-93, Coun. on Ct. Procedures, 1992-93, 95—; mem. Oreg. Rules of Appellate Procedure Com., 1998-2002; bd. dirs. Oreg. Law Inst.; chmn. commn. on jud. rule 4 Oreg. Supreme Ct., 1995-97, 2002-05. Mem. ACLU Lawyer's Com., Eugene and Portland, Oreg., 1978-91. Recipient award for civil rights litig. ACLU of Oreg., 1988, Ed Elliott Human Rights award Oreg. Edn. Assn., Portland, 1990. Mem. Am. Acad. Appellate Lawyers (ninth cir. screening com. 1991—, rules com. 1994, co-chair appellate cts. liaison com. 1994), Oreg. Appellate Judges Assn. (pres. 1996-97), Oreg. State Bar (chair labor law sect. 1983-84, adminstrv. law com. govt. law sect. 1986), Willamette Valley Inns of Ct. (master of bench, team leader 1994—). Office: Oreg Supreme Ct 1163 State St Salem OR 97301-2563 Home Phone: 503-274-2766; Office Phone: 503-986-5725. Business E-Mail: robert.d.durham@ojd.state.or.us.

DURIE, DARALYN J., lawyer; b. 1967; Degree, Stanford U., 1988; M, U. Calif. Berkeley, 1989; grad., Boalt Hall Sch. Law, U. Calif. Berkeley, 1992. Clerk US Ct. Appeals, DC Cir.; assoc. Keker & Van Nest, San Francisco, ptnr., 1999—. Co-chair Lawyer Representatives to Ninth Cir. Jud. Conf.; tchr. Nat. Inst. Trial Adv. Bd. dirs. Berkeley Montessori Sch. Named one of Best Intellectual Property Lawyers in Calif., Chambers & Partners, Top 75 Women Litigators in Calif., Daily Jour., Litigation's Rising Stars, The Am. Lawyer, 2007; named to Best Lawyers in Am. Mem.: Northern Calif. Assn. Bus. Trial Lawyers, Assn. Bus. Trial Lawyers, ABA. Office: Keker & Van Nest LLP 710 Sansome St San Francisco CA 94111 Office Phone: 415-391-5400. Office Fax: 415-397-7188.

DURITZ, ADAM, musician; b. Aug. 1, 1964; s. Gilbert and Linda Duritz. Student, U. Calif., Berkeley. Founder, lead singer Counting Crows, 1991—; founder E Pluribus Unum record label (bought by Geffen Records, 2000), 1997, Tyrannosaurus Records, 2007. Singer: (albums) August and Everything After, 1993, Recovering the Satellites, 1996, Across a Wire: Live in New York, 1998, This Desert Life, 1999, Hard Candy, 2002, Films About Ghosts: The Best Of, 2004, New Amsterdam: Live at Heineken Music Hall, 2006, Saturday Nights & Sunday Mornings, 2008, (songs) Accidentally in Love, 2004. Office: c/o DGC/Geffen Records 9130 W Sunset Blvd Los Angeles CA 90069-3110

DURNING, CHARLES, actor; b. Highland Falls, NY, Feb. 28, 1923; m. Carol Durning (div.); children: Michele, Douglas, Jeanine; m. Mary Ann Amelio, 1974. Former boxer, cab driver, waiter, iron-worker, constrn. worker, elevator operator. Profl. theatre debut with nat. co. of The Andersonville Trial, 1960; stage appearances include Measure for Measure, King John, Chronicles of Henry IV, N.Y. Shakespeare Festival That Championship Season (Drama Desk award 1972), Boom Boom Room, Child Buyer, Drat! The Cat!, Lemon Sky, Comedy of Errors, Au Pair Man, Knock Knock, Cat on a Hot Tin Roof, 1990, (Antoinette Perry award, 1990), Third, 2005 (Lucille Lortel award, outstanding featured actor, 2006); actor: (films) Harvey Middleman, Fireman, 1965, Stiletto, 1969, I Walk the Line, 1970, Hi, Mom!, 1970, Pursuit of Happiness, 1971, Dealing: Or the Berkeley-to-Boston Forty-Brick Lost-Bag Blues, 1972, Doomsday Voyage, 1972, Deadhead Miles, 1972, The Sting, 1973, Sisters, 1973, The Front Page, 1974, Hindenburg, 1975, Dog Day Afternoon, 1975, Harry & Walter Go to New York, 1976, Breakheart Pass, 1976, An Enemy of the People, 1977, Twilight's Last Gleaming, 1977, Choirboys, 1977, Tilt, 1978, The Greek Tycoon, 1978, The Fury, 1978, When A Stranger Calls, 1979, Starting Over, 1979, North Dallas Forty, 1979, The Muppet Movie, 1979, Die Laughing, 1980, The Final Countdown, 1980, True Confessions, 1981, Sharky's Machine, 1981, Tootsie, 1982, Best Little Whorehouse in Texas, 1982, To Be or Not To Be, 1983, Two of a Kind, 1983, Mass Appeal, 1984, Hadley's Rebellion, 1984, Stick, 1985, Stand Alone, 1985, The Man with One Red Shoe, 1985, Tough Guys, 1986, Big Trouble, 1986, Solar Babies,

1986, Where The River Runs Black, 1986, Meatballs III: Summer Job, 1986, Happy New Year, 1987, Rosary Murders, 1987, A Tiger's Tale, 1987, Etoile, 1988, Cop, 1988, Far North, 1988, Cat Chaser, 1989, Fatal Sky, 1990, Dick Tracy, 1990, V.I. Warshawski, 1991, Brenda Starr, 1992, The Music of Chance, 1993, The Hudsucker Proxy, 1994, I.Q., 1994, Home for the Holidays, 1995, The Last Supper, 1995, The Grass Harp, 1995, (voice only) The Land Before Time IV: Journey Through the Mists, 1996, Elmo Saves Christmas, 1996, Spy Hard, 1996, Recon, 1996, One Fine Day, 1996, Shelter, 1997, Secret Life of Algernon, 1997, Justice, 1998, Jerry & Tom, 1998, Hi-Life, 1998, State and Maine, 1999, Hunt for the Devil, 1999, Never Look Back, 2000, Lakeboat, 2000, O' Brother, Where Art Though?, 2000, Very Mean Men, 2000, The Last Producer, 2000, State and Main, 2000, Turn of Faith, 2001, L.A.P.D.: To Protect and to Serve, 2001, The Naked Run, 2002, The Last Man Club, 2002, Pride & Loyalty, 2002, Mother Ghost, 2002, One Last Ride, 2003, Dead Canaries, 2003, Death and Texas, 2004, River's End, 2005, Resurrection: The J.R. Richards Story, 2005, The L.A. Riot Spectacular, 2005, Dirty Deeds, 2005, Naked Run, 2006, Descansos, 2006, Miracle Dogs Too, 2006, Forget About It, 2006, Local Color, 2006, Jesus, Mary and Joey, 2006, Unbeatable Harold, 2006, The Waiter, 2007, Deal, 2007, Polycarp, 2007; (TV films) Look Homeward, Angel, 1972, The Connection, 1973, Rx for the Defense, 1973, The Trial of Chaplain Jensen, 1975, Queen of the Stardust Ballroom, 1975, The Rivalry, 1975, The Ashes of Mrs. Reasoner, 1976, Special Olympics, 1978, One of the Missing, 1979, Attica, 1979, A Perfect Match, 1980, Crisis at Central High, 1981, Casey Stengal, 1981, The Best Little Girl in the World, 1981, The Girls in Their Summer Dresses and Other Stories by Irwin Shaw, 1981, Dark Night of the Scarecrow, 1981, Working, 1982, Mister Roberts, 1984, Good Evening, He Lied, 1984, P.O.P., 1984, Death of a Salesman, 1985, Kenny Rogers as The Gambler, Part III: The Legend Continues, 1987, I Would Be Called John: Pope John XXIII, 1987, The Man Who Broke 1,000 Chains, 1987, Case Closed, 1988, Unholy Matrimony, 1988, It Nearly Wasn't Christmas, 1989, The Butter Battle Book, 1989, Prime Target, 1989, Dinner at Eight, 1989, The Return of Eliot Ness, 1991, The Story Lady, 1991, The Water Engine, 1991, Tales from Hollywood, 1992, When a Stranger Calls Back, 1993, Harlan & Merleen, 1993, Roomates, 1994, Texan, 1994, Leslie's Folly, 1994, Mrs. Santa Claus, 1996, A Chance of Snow, 1998, Hard Time, 1998, Hard Time: The Premonition, 1999, Justice, 1999, Hard Time: Hostage Hotel, 1999, Desperation, 1999, The Judge, 2001, Bleacher Burns, 2002, A Boyfriend for Christmas, 2004, A Very Married Christmas, 2004, Detective, 2005; (TV series) The Cop and the Kid, 1975, Evening Shade, 1990-94, Chicken Soup for the Soul, 1999, First Monday, 2002, Everybody Loves Raymond, 1998-2002, Rescue Me, 2004-; (TV appearances) East Side/West Side, 1963, The Nurses, 1965, N.Y.P.D., 1967, The High Chaparral, 1970, Madigan,1972, All in the Family, 1973, Switch, 1975, Cannon, 1975, Barnaby Jones, 1975, Baretta, 1975, Hawaii Five-0, 1975, Visions, 1977, Eye to Eye, 1985, Comedy Factory,1985, Amazing Stories, 1985, Tall Tales and Legends, 1987, Orleans, 1997, Homicide: Life on the Street, 1998, Cybill, 1998, The Hoop Life, 2000, The Practice, 1998, 2000, Early Edition, 1997, 2000, (voice only) Family Guy, 1999, 2001, 2005, Arli$$, 2001, Citizen Baines, 2001, Touched by an Angel, 2003, Navy NCIS: Naval Criminal Investigative Service, 2004, Everwood, 2006, Monk, 2007; (mini-series) Captains and the Kings, 1976, Studs Lonigan, 1979, The Kennedys of Massachusetts, 1990 (Golden Globe award for Best Actor in a Supporting Role, 1991), A Woman of Independent Means, 1995. With US Army. Decorated 3 Purple Hearts, Silver Star; recipient Lifetime Achievement award, SAG, 2008, Star on Hollywood Walk of Fame, 2008.

DURYEE, DAVID ANTHONY, management consultant; b. Tacoma, July 29, 1938; s. Schuyler L. and Edna R. (Muzzy) Duryee; m. Anne Getchell Peterson, Nov. 26, 1966; children: Tracy Anne, Tricia Marie. BA in Bus., U. Wash., 1961, MBA, 1969; diploma, Pacific Coast Banking Schs., Seattle, 1973. Lending officer Seattle 1st Nat. Bank, 1964-68, v.p., trust officer, 1970-80; cons., chmn. Mgmt. Adv. Svcs., Inc., Seattle, 1980-93; mng. prin. Moss Adams Adv. Svcs., Moss Adams LLP, 1994—2001; dir. Horizon Mgmt. Svcs. LLC, 2002—. Lectr. in field; expert witness, Wash., NY, Md., Calif., Mass., Ind., Fla.; bd. dirs. Lafromboise Newspapers, Inc. Author: The Business Owners Guide to Achieving Financial Success, 1994; contbr. articles to profl. jours. Capt. US Army, 1962—64. Mem.: Northwest Family Bus. Advisors, Estate Planning Coun. Seattle, Seattle Tennis Club. Avocations: tennis, golf. Home and Office: 3301 E John St Seattle WA 98112-4938 Home Phone: 206-329-6403; Office Phone: 206-329-4911. Personal E-mail: dduryee@comcast.net.

DUSCHA, JULIUS CARL, journalist; b. St. Paul, Nov. 4, 1924; s. Julius William and Anna (Perlowski) D.; m. Priscilla Ann McBride, Aug. 17, 1946 (dec. Sept. 1992); children: Fred C., Steve D., Suzanne, Sally Jean; m. Suzanne Van Den Heurk, June 21, 1997. Student, U. Minn., 1943—47; AB, Am. U., 1951; postgrad., Harvard Coll., 1955—56. Reporter St. Paul Pioneer Press, 1943-47, Congl. Quar., 1947—48; publicist Dem. Nat. Com., 1948, 52; writer Labor's League for Polit. Edn., AFL, 1949-52, Internat. Assn. Machinist, 1952-53; editl. writer Lindsay-Schaub Newspapers, Ill., 1954-58; nat. affairs reporter Washington Post, 1958-66; assoc. dir. profl. journalism fellowships program Stanford (Calif.) U., 1966-68; dir. Washington Journalism Ctr., 1968-90; columnist, freelance journalist, West Coast corr. Presstime mag., San Francisco, 1990-99; sr. corr. News Inc., San Francisco, 1998—. Mem. Commn. on Presdl. Press Confs., U. Va., 1981. Author: Taxpayer's Hayride: The Farm Problem from the New Deal to the Billie Sol Estes Case, 1964, Arms, Money and Politics, 1965, The Campus Press, 1973, From Pea Soup to Politics - A Memoir, 2005; editor: Defense Conversion Advisory; contbr. articles to mags., including Washingtonian, N.Y. Times Mag., Changing Times, Harper's, Reporter, Progressive, New Leader. Recipient award for Disting. Washington corr. Sigma Delta Chi, 1961 Mem.: Cosmos Club (Washington), Kappa Sigma. Home: 2200 Pacific Ave Apt 7D San Francisco CA 94115-1412 Personal E-mail: duschaduscha@sbcglobal.net.

DUSTER, TROY, sociology educator; b. Chgo., July 11, 1936; s. Benjamin Cecil and Alfred Margarita (Barnett) D.; m. Ellen Marie Johansson, May 16, 1964 (div. 1974) BS, Northwestern U., 1957, PhD, 1962; MA, UCLA, 1959; DSc (hon.), Northwestern U., 2005. Asst. prof. sociology U. Calif., Riverside, 1963-65, asst. research sociologist Berkeley, 1965-69, assoc. prof. sociology, 1970-78, prof. to Chancellor's prof., 1979—, chmn. dept., 1986—. Dir. Inst. for Study of Social Change, U. Calif., 1976—; Bernhard prof. anthropology and sociology Williams Coll., 1985; mem., chair adv. com. ethical, legal and social issues in human genome project NIH/DOE, 1996-98; dir. Am. Cultures Ctr. U. Calif., Berkeley, 2000-02; mem. adv. bd. Social Sci. Rsch. Coun., 2003-07; chmn. bd. dirs. Assn. Am. Colls. and Univs., 2003-04; Silver prof. sociology, dir. Inst. for the History of the Prodn. of Knowledge, NYU, 2005—. Author: Legislation of Morality, 1970, (monograph) Aims and Control of the Universities, 1972, Backdoor to Eugenics, 1990; co-editor: Cultural Perspectives on Biological Knowledge, 1984. Mem. assembly of behavioral and social scis. Nat. Acad. Scis., Washington, 1973-78; mem. research panel Pres.'s Commn. on Mental Health, Washington, 1977-78; cons., advisor Pres.'s Commn. for Study of Ethical Problems in Medicine, Washington, 1980; mem. bio-tech. adv. council State of Calif.; chmn. Ethical, Legal, and Social Issues Commn. Nat. Ctr. Human Genome Rsch., Washington, 1996—, Nat. Panel of the Am. Commitments Initiative Assn. Am. Colls. and Univs., Washington, 1993—, Com. Social and Ethical Impact of Advances in Biomedicine Inst. of Medicine, Nat. Acad. Scis., Washington, 1991-94, Spl. Commn. Meeting the Challenge of Diversity in an Acad. Democracy Assn. Am. Law Schs., Washington, 1991-95, Subcom. Protection of Human Subjects, Health and Environ. Rsch. Adv. Com. Dept. Energy, 1994; adv. bd. Ctr. for Study of Race, Crime, and Social Policy Swedish Govt. fellow Uppsala U., 1962-63; Guggenheim Found. fellow London Sch. Econs., 1971-72; Ford Found. fellow, 1978-79 Mem. Am. Sociol. Assn. (mem. exec. office of the budget coun. 1991-94, pres. 2004-05). Avocations: ceramics; photography; tennis; chess. Home: 3031 Benvenue Ave Berkeley CA 94705-2509 Office: U Calif-Berkeley Dept Sociology Berkeley CA 94720-0001 Business E-Mail: troy.duster@nyu.edu.

DUTILE, ROBERT ARTHUR, information technology manager; b. Stoneham, Mass., Dec. 26, 1959; s. Robert Arthur and Mary-Helene (Revane) D.; m. Ellen R. Ahearn, June 9, 1995. BS, Boston Coll., 1981. Cons. Monchik-Weber, Boston, 1981—83, Gately, Glew & Co., Wellesley, Mass., 1983—84; dir. MIS Reebok Internat., Ltd., Stoughton, Mass., 1984—91; sr. cons. Grant Thornton, LLP, Boston, 1992, mgr., 1992—95, sr. mgr., 1995—97, prin., 1997—99, Value Edge, Solon, Ohio, 2005—; exec. v.p. Key Corp., Cleve., 1999—2005; pres. Sharp End Enterprises LLC, 2005—; gen. mgr. UST Global, 2005—. Author: The Benchmarking Course, 1993. Mem. Am. Soc. Quality Control, Am. Mgmt. Assn., Am. Prodn. & Inventory Control Soc., Am. Mountain Guides Assn., Am. Alpine Club (life), Two/Ten Found. (life.). Avocations: writing, rock climbing, mountain climbing, golf. Home: 55 Brook Rd Amherst NH 03031 Office: UST Global 120 Vantis Aliso Viejo CA 92656 Home Phone: 603-673-6034; Office Phone: 216-410-0359. Business E-Mail: robert_dutile@valueedge.net, dutile@ameritech.net, robert_dutile@ust-global.com.

DUTSON, THAYNE R., dean; b. Idaho Falls, Oct. 3, 1942; s. Rollo and Thelma (Fugal) D.; m. Joyce Cook, Dec. 19, 1962 (div. 1980); 1 child, Bradley; m. Margaret McCallum, June 23, 1989; children: Taylor, Alexandra. BS, Utah State U., 1966; MS, Mich. State U., 1969, PhD, 1971. Postdoctoral fellow U. Nottingham, Sutton Bonnington, Eng., 1971-72; prof. Tex. A&M U., College Station, 1972-83; dept. head Mich. State U., East Lansing, Mich., 1983-87; dir. agrl. exptl. sta. Oreg. State U., Corvallis, 1987-93, dean, dir. Coll. Agrl. Sci., 1993—. Editor: Advances in Meat Research (11 vols.) 1985-97; contbr. articles to profl. jours. Scoutmaster Boy Scouts Am., Mich., 1966-71. Fellow Inst. Food Technologists; mem. Am. Meat Sci. Assn. (bd. dirs. 1979-81, Disting. Rsch. award 1985), Am. Soc. Animal Sci. (Meat Rsch. award 1981), Coun. for Agr. Sci. and Tech. (pres. 1988), Phi Kappa Phi, Sigma Xi. Avocations: skiing, running, exercise, golf.

DUUS, PETER, retired historian; b. Wilmington, Del., Dec. 27, 1933; s. Hans Christian and Mary Anita (Pennypacker) D.; m. Masayo Umezawa, Nov. 25, 1964; 1 child, Erik. AB magna cum laude, Harvard U., 1955, PhD, 1965; MA, U. Mich., 1959. Asst. prof. history Washington U., St. Louis, 1964-66, Harvard U., Cambridge, Mass., 1966-70; assoc. prof. history Claremont (Calif.) Grad. Sch., 1970-73, Stanford (Calif.) U., 1973-78, prof., 1978—2003, ret., 2003. Author: Party Rivalry and Political Change in Taishó Japan, 1968, Feudalism in Japan, 1969, The Rise of Modern Japan, 1976, The Cambridge History of Japan, Vol. 6: The Twentieth Century, 1989, The Japanese Informal Empire in China, 1989, The Abacus and the Sword: The Japanese Penetration of Korea, 1995, The Japanese Discovery of America, 1996, Modern Japan, 1997. Exec. sec. Inter-Univ. for Japanese Lang. Studies, Tokyo, 1974-90; bd. dirs. Com. for Internat. Exch. of Scholars, Washington, 1987-91. Served with U.S. Army, 1955-57. NEH sr. fellow, 1972-73, Japan Found. postdoctoral fellow, 1976-77, Fulbright rsch. fellow, 1981-82, 94-95, Japan Found. rsch. fellow, 1986-87. Fellow AAAS, mem. Assn. for Asian Studies (bd. dirs. 1972-75, nominating com. 1983, v.p. 1999-2000, pres. 2000-01), Am. Hist. Assn. (bd. editors 1984-87). Home: 818 Esplanada Way Palo Alto CA 94305-1015 Office: Stanford U History Dept Stanford CA 94305 Business E-Mail: pduus@stanford.edu.

DUVAL, JULIAN J., arboretum administrator; b. Oak Park, Ill., Feb. 15, 1947; s. Julian Adrian Duval and Isabel (Klawczyk) Luther; m. Becky Kotsarelis, Jan. 10, 1975 (div. Oct. 1980); m. Leslie Ann Berling, Feb. 5, 1990. AA, Coll. of Dupage, 1972; BS in Wildlife Mgmt., N.Mex. State U., 1974. Marine mammal trainer Brookfield Zoo, Chgo., 1965-71; curator, mammal and reptiles Parque Zool. Nat., Dominican Rep., 1975-78; adminstr. gen. Auto Safari Chapin, Guatemala, 1978-80; gen. curator Indpls. Zoo, 1980-87, v.p. zool. and botanical collections, 1987-94, v.p. scientific and program devel., 1994-95; exec. dir., CEO Quail Botanical Gardens, Encinitas, Calif., 1995—. Mem. IUCN Species Survival Commn., Conservation Breeding, Specialist Group. Co-host: (TV program) At the Zoo, WRTV/ABC Indpls. Channel 6, 1989-95. Dir. Encinitas C. of C. Mem. Encinitas Rotary. Avocations: horticulture, wildlife study, photography, herpetology. Office: Quail Botanical Gardens 230 Quail Gardens Dr PO Box 230005 Encinitas CA 92023-0005

DUVALL, MICHAEL D., state legislator; m. Susan Duvall; 2 children. California State Assemblyman, District 72, 2006-; member, Budget, Ins, Joint Legislature Budget Committees, 2007-, vice-chair, Transportation Committee, 2007-; City Councilman Yorba Linda, 2000-present, coun liaison to Chamber of Commerce, formerly. owner, local ins agency. Orange Co Transportation Authority; City Audit Committee; Yorba Linda Chamber of Commerce (president, formerly); Foothill/Eastern Corridor Joint Powers Authority; Orange Co Sanitation District; Ground Water Replenishment Syst (director); Santa Ana River Flood Protection Agency; Yorba Linda General Plan Steering Committee (chairman, formerly); Safe Streets Are for Everyone (co-chair, formerly). Republican. Office: Dist 72 210 W Birch St Ste 202 Brea CA 92821 Office Phone: 714-672-4784. Office Fax: 714-672-4737. Business E-Mail: Assemblymember.Duvall@assembly.ca.gov.

DUXBURY, THOMAS, planetary scientist; b. Fort Wayne, Ind. s. John and Justine D.; m. Natalia D.; children. BSEE, Purdue U., 1965, MSEE, 1966. Planetary scientist Jet Propulsion Lab., Pasadena, Calif., 1966—; mem. NASA Mariner mission sci. investigation of Mars, Venus and Mercury, 1969—74; mem. NASA Viking mission sci. team, Mars, Phobos and Deimos investigations, 1974—81; mem. NASA Voyage mission sci. teams, Jupiter and Saturn investigation, 1977—82; project sci. NASA Sci. Internet, 1984—86; mem. US-Russia Joint Working Group for Mars Exploration, 1987—97; mem. Soviet PHOBOS mission, interdisciplinary sci., 1988—89; mem. Clementine mission sci. team for lunar exploration, 1992—94; mem. Russian Mars 96 mission interdisciplinary sci., 1990—96; project mgr. NASA Stardust mission, 1999—2007; NASA Mars Global Surveyor mission sci. team, 1996—2007; mem. European Space Agy. Mars Express mission interdisciplinary sci., 1999—; sci. definition team dep. leader, Clementine II, 1997—98; cartography chair NASA Mars Program, 2002—; scientist Mars Odyssey THEMIS, 2006—; mem. sci. team Mars Reconnaissance Orbiter, 2007—; mem. sci. team Lunar Reconnaissance Orbiter, 2007—; project mgr. NASA NEXT, 2007—, NASA EPOXI, 2007—. Co-author: Television Investigations of Phobos, 1994. Recipient Sci. Achievement medal NASA, Washington, 1972, Burka award Inst. of Navigation, 1973, Achievement awards NASA, 1978-82, Soviet Space Mission Svc. medal, Lavochkin Assn., The Hague, Netherlands, 1991, Innovation award, Popular Mechanics 2006, Program Excellence award, Aviation Week, 2006, Nelson P. Jackson award, Nat. Space Club, 2007, Laureate award, Aviation award, 2007, Stellar award, Rotary Space Achievement, 2007, Nat. Air and Space Mus. Achievement trophy, 2008. Mem. Am. Geophysical Union, Am. Astronomical Soc., Russian Assn. for Space Sci. & Tech. Achievements include production of first map of another planet's moon; discovery of the Groove Network on Phobos (Mars moon); co-discovery of the Rings of Jupiter, co-discoverer of the Jupiter Lightning; produced the most precise cartographic maps of Mars landing sites for Viking, Pathfinder, Mars Polar Lander, Beagle 2 and MER Spirit and Opportunity; led the world's first planetary mission to return cometary samples to Earth. Office: Jet Propulsion Lab 4800 Oak Grove Dr 264-379 Pasadena CA 91109-8099 Office Phone: 818-354-4301. Business E-Mail: tduxbury@jpl.nasa.gov.

DWAN, DENNIS EDWIN, broadcast executive, photographer; b. St. Joseph, Mich., Oct. 6, 1958; s. Edwin O. and Elizabeth L. (Miller) D.; m. Tami L. Nixon, Oct. 13, 1984; children: Megan, Kaitlyn. BA, Mich. State U., 1981. Photographer Sta. WJIM-TV, Lansing, Mich., 1981-83, Sta. KAYU, Spokane, Wash., 1984-86, Sta. KREM-TV, Spokane, 1984-87; ops. mgr. Sta. KOMO-TV, Seattle, 1987—. Mem. Nat. Press Photographers Assn. E-mail: DennisD@Komotv.com.

DWORK, CYNTHIA, researcher; BSE with honors in Elec. Engring. and Computer Sci., Princeton U., 1979; MSc in Computer Sci., Cornell U., 1981, PhD in Computer Sci., 1983. Bantrell Postdoctoral Fellowship MIT Lab. for Computer Sci., 1983—85; rsch. staff mem. IBM Almanden Rsch. Ctr., 1985—2000; staff fellow Compaq Sys. Rsch. Ctr., 2000—01; prin. researcher Microsoft Rsch., Calif., 2001—. Vis. indsl. prof. Stanford U., 1988, consulting prof., 1997—2006; vis. scientist MIT Lab. for Computer Sci., 1989—90; chair steering com. Symposium on Principles of Distributed Computing, 1993—95; mem. external adv. bd. DIMACS (Ctr. for Discrete Math. and Theoretical Computer Sci.), 1996—2008; mem. sci. adv. bd. Bertinoro Internat. Ctr. for Informatics, 2004—; invited lectr. in field. Contbr. chapters to books, several articles to profl. jours. Recipient Charles Ira Young Tablet and Medal for Excellence in Independent Rsch., Dept. Elec. Engring. and Computer Sci., Princeton U., 1979, Edsger W. Dijkstra prize, 2007. Fellow: Am. Acad. Arts & Scis.; mem.: Internat. Assn. of Cryptologic Researchers (IACR) (mem. fellow com. 2004—), IEEE (program com. mem. Symposium on Founds. Computer Sci. 1988, 1992, 1995, 2001), Assn. Computer Machinery (program com. mem., Symposium on Principles of Distributed Computing 1985, 1986, 1988, 1989, 1990, 1993, 2003, program com. mem., 40th Ann. Symposium on Theory of Computing 2008), NAE. Achievements include patents in field. Office: Microsoft Research Silicon Valley Campus 1065 La Avenida Mountain View CA 94043 Office Phone: 650-693-3701. Business E-Mail: dwork@microsoft.com.

DWORKIN, SAMUEL FRANKLIN, dentist, educator, psychologist; b. Freedom, Ohio, Sept. 26, 1933; s. Louis and Minnie (Katz) D.; m. Mona Mae Moskowitz, Dec. 23, 1956; children: Adam, Ted. BS, CCNY, 1954; D.D.S., NYU, 1958, PhD, 1969. Practice dentistry, NYC, 1959—74; Nat. Inst. Dental Research spl. fellow, 1965-69; asst. prof. dept. preventive dentistry and community health NYU Coll. Dentistry, 1969-70; assoc. prof. div. preventive dentistry, dir. office of edn. and behavioral research Columbia U. Sch. Dental and Oral Surgery, 1970-74; prof. oral surgery, assoc. dean acad. affairs U. Wash. Sch. Dentistry, Seattle, 1974-77; prof. psychiatry and behavioral sci. U. Wash. Sch. Medicine, 1977—; prof. oral medicine, 1977—; dir. psychophysiologic liaison clinic dept. psychiatry and behavioral sci. U. Wash. Sch. Medicine, 1978-89, Washington dental svc. disting. prof. dentistry, 1999—. Clin. dir. Regional Clin. Dental Rsch. Ctr., U. Wash., 1992-99; cons. NIH, mem. behavioral medicine study sect., 1985-90, mem. rsch. adv. coun. 1999—; cons. ADA, Am. Dental Hygiene Assn. Cons. editor Jour. Dental Edn., 1976—, Jour. Dental Rsch., 1976—, Pain, 1984—, Clin. Jour. Pain, 1989—, Psychosomatic Medicine, 1989—; guest editor Jour. Preventive Dentistry, 1977, Jour. ADA, Pain; contbr. articles to profl. jours. Co-founder, pres. League of Parents of Hearing Impaired Infants, N.Y.C., 1966-70; v.p. N.Y. State Parents of Hearing Impaired Children, 1970-74; adv. coun. Lexington Sch. of Deaf, N.Y.C., 1970-74; bd. dirs. Seattle Pro-Musica, 1977, v.p., 1978-81, treas., 1991-98, pres. 1995-98, pres. emeritus, 1999. Grantee, NIH, 1979—. Fellow Internat. Assn. for Study of Pain, Am. Pain Soc.; mem. ADA (coun. dental health edn., coun. nat. bd. exams. 1974-79), AAAS, APA, Am. Assn. Dental Schs., Behavioral Scientists in Dental Rsch. (pres. 1975, 90), Internat. Assn. for Dental Rsch. (Disting. Scientist award behavior and health svcs. rsch., Dental Rsch. Giddon award), Internat. Soc. Clin. and Exptl. Hypnosis, Behavioral Scis. Group (Disting. Rschr. award), Behavioral and Health Svcs. Rsch. Group (pres. 1990-91). Office: U Wash Dept Psychiatry Seattle WA 98195-0001 E-mail: dworkin@u.washington.edu.

DWORSKY, DANIEL LEONARD, architect, educator; b. Mpls., Oct. 4, 1927; s. Lewis and Ida (Fineberg) D.; m. Sylvia Ann Taylor, Aug. 10, 1957; children: Douglas, Laurie, Nancy. BArch, U. Mich., 1950. Practice architecture as Dworsky Assocs., LA, 1953-2000, Cannon Dworsky, LA, 2000—03; design critic, lectr. architecture U. So. Calif., 1983—84, U. Mich., 1983—84, UCLA, 1983—84. Chmn. archtl. rev. panel Fed. Res. Bank. Recipient Design citation Progressive Arch. mag. 1967, Gov. Calif. award 1966, 3 LA Grand Prix awards So. Calif. AIA and City of LA 1967; prin. works include Angelus Plz. Elderly Housing, LA, 1981, Ontario (Calif.) City Hall, 1980, CBS Exec. Office Bldg., North Hollywood, Calif., 1970, UCLA

Stadium, 1969, Fed. Res. Bank Bldg., LA, 1987, U. Mich. Crisler Arena at Ann Arbor, 1966, Dominguez Hills State U. Theatre, 1977, Ventura County Govt. Ctr., 1979, Northrop Electronics Hdqrs., LA, 1983, Hewlett-Packard Region Office, North Hollywood, 1984, LA County Mcpl. Cts. Bldg., 1985, Tom Bradley Internat. Terminal LA Airport, 1984, City Tower, Orange, Calif., 1988, Fed. Office Bldg., Long Beach, Calif., 1992, Las Vegas Fed. Cts. Bldg., 2000. Disting. Alumnus award Coll. Architecture, U. Mich., 2005. Fellow AIA (more than 100 awards including 24 awards Calif. chpts., Nat. Honor award 1974, 68-69, Firm award Calif. chpt. 1985, L.A. Gold Medal award 1994, State of Calif. Lifetime Achievement award 2004). Home: 9225 Nightingale Dr Los Angeles CA 90069-1117 Home Phone: 310-271-2106; Office Phone: 310-271-2106. Business E-Mail: dandworsky@mac.com.

DWYER, CARRIE ELIZABETH, lawyer, investment company executive; b. San Mateo, Calif., Dec. 19, 1950; d. Robert Harold and Alice Marian (Daley) Dwyer; m. Richard M. Konecky, Feb. 12, 1977; children: Rachel Anne, Philip. BA in English, U. Santa Clara, 1973, JD, 1976. Bar: Calif., NY. Staff atty. Am. Stock Exchange, NYC, 1977-79, exec. asst. to exec. v.p. legal and regulatory affairs, 1979—81, asst. v.p., exec. asst. to pres., 1981—83, v.p., exec. asst. to pres., 1983—85, v.p., assoc. gen. counsel, 1985—87, sr. v.p., gen. counsel, 1987—89; contract lawyer Milbank, Tweed, Hadley & McCoy, NYC; sr. counsel to chmn. Arthur Levitt SEC, 1993—96; exec. v.p. corp. oversight The Charles Schwab Corp., San Francisco, 1996—, gen. counsel, 1998—. Named one of Bay Area's 100 Most Influential Women, San Francisco Bus. Women, 2007. Mem. ABA, The Assn. of Bar of City of NY, NY State Bar Assn., Investment Assn. Office: The Charles Schwab Corp 101 Montgomery St San Francisco CA 94104

DWYER, JOHN CHARLES, lawyer; b. San Francisco, Mar. 26, 1962; s. Richard Thomas and Dorothy (Blake) D. BS in Bus. Administrn. summa cum laude, U. Calif., Berkeley, 1984; JD magna cum laude, Harvard U., 1988. Bar: Calif. 1988, US Dist. Ct. (no. dist.) Calif. 1988, US Ct. of Appeals (9th cir.) 1988, US Supreme Ct. 1996, DC. Assoc. Jackson, Tufts, Cole & Black, San Francisco, 1989-93; dep. assoc. atty. gen. U.S. Dept. Justice, Washington, 1993-96. acting assoc. atty. gen., 1997; ptnr. Cooley Godward LLP, Palo Alto, Calif., 1998—. Auditor Arthur Andersen & Co. Recipient Calif. Lawyer of the Yr., Calif. Lawyer mag., 2005. Mem.: US Supreme Ct., ABA, Phi Beta Kappa. Democrat. Roman Catholic. Office: Cooley Godward LLP PA Square Bldg 5 Palo Alto Sq 3000 El Camino Real Palo Alto CA 94306-2155 Office Fax: 650-857-0663. Business E-Mail: dwyerjc@cooley.com.

DWYRE, WILLIAM PATRICK, journalist; b. Sheboygan, Wis., Apr. 7, 1944; s. George Leo and Mary Veronica (O'Brien) D.; m. Jill Ethlyn Jarvis, July 30, 1966; children— Amy, Patrick BA, U. Notre Dame, Ind. Sports copy editor Des Moines Register, 1966-68; sports writer, asst. sports editor, sports editor Milw. Jour., 1968-81: asst. sports editor, sports editor LA Times, 1981—2006, columnist sports, 2006—. Columnist Referee Mag., 1977-02; voting mem., bd. dir. Amateur Athletic Found. Nat. Sports Hall of Fame, 1981—. Bd. dir. Honda-Brockerick Cup Women's Collegiate Athlete of Yr.; bd. dir. Casa Colina Hosp. Rehab., Pomona. Named Sportswriter of Yr., Wis. Nat. Sportscasters and Sportswriters Assn., 1980; Nat. Editor of Yr., Nat. Press Found., 1985; recipient award Sustained Excellence by Individual, L.A. Times, 1985, Red Smith award AP sports Editors, 1996, Acad Literary award, 2004, Los Angeles Sports and Entertainment Commn. Ambassador award, 2005, Good Guy award, Calif. Golf Writers Assn., 2007. Mem. Nat. Sportscasters and Sportswriters Assn. (bd. dirs., Powerade Sport Story of Yr. award 1999), Assoc. Press Sports Editors (pres. 1989), LA Sports and Entertainment Commn. Amb. award, 2005, Subiaco (Ark.). Avocations: tennis, golf. Office: Los Angeles Times Times Mirror Sq Los Angeles CA 90012 E-mail: bill.dwyre@latimes.com.

DYCK, ANDREW ROY, philologist, educator; b. Chgo., May 24, 1947; s. Roy H. and Elizabeth (Beck) D.; m. Janis Mieko Fukuhara, Aug. 20, 1978. BA, U. Wisc., 1969; PhD, U. Chgo., 1975. Sessional lectr. U. Alta., Edmonton, Can., 1975-76; asst. prof. U. Minn., Mpls., 1977-78; vis. asst. prof. Classics UCLA, 1976-77, asst. prof., 1978-82, assoc. prof., 1982-87, prof., 1987—, chmn. dept. classics, 1988-91. Mem. Inst. for Advanced Study, Princeton, 1991-92; vis. fellow All Souls Coll., Oxford, 1998, Clare Hall, Cambridge, 1999. Author: A Commentary on Cicero, De Officiis, 1996; editor: Epimerismi Homerici, 2 vols., 1983, 95, Essays on Euripides and George of Pisidia and on Helidorus and Achilles Tatius (Michael Psellus), 1986, Cicero, De Natura Deorum I, 2003, LA Commentary on Cicero, De Legibus, 2004; co-editor: Studies in Classics: Outstanding Dissertations, 2002-. Alexander von Humboldt-Stiftung fellow, Bonn, Fed. Republic of Germany, 1980-89; NEH fellow, 1991-92. Mem. Am. Philol. Assn., Calif. Classical Assn., U.S. Nat. Com. on Byzantine Studies. Office: UCLA Classics Dept 405 Hilgard Ave Los Angeles CA 90095-9000 E-mail: dyck@humnet.ucla.edu.

DYEN, ISIDORE, linguistic scientist, educator; b. Phila., Aug. 16, 1913; s. Jacob and Dena (Bryzell) D.; m. Edith Brenner, June 11, 1939 (dec. 1976); children— Doris Jane, Mark Ross. BA, U. Pa., 1933, MA, 1934, PhD in Indo-European Linguistics, 1939; postgrad. Slavic, Columbia, 1938-39, Yale, 1939-40. Faculty Yale U., 1942-84, prof. Malayan langs., 1957-58, prof. Malayopolynesian and comparative linguistics, 1958-73, prof. comparative linguistics and Austronesian langs., 1973-84, prof. emeritus, 1984—, dir. grad. studies Indic and Far Eastern langs. and lit., 1960-62, Indic and Southeast Asia, 1960-66, dir. grad. studies linguistics, 1966-68; adj. prof. linguistics U. Hawaii, 1985-89; linguist Coordinated Investigation Micronesian Anthropology, Truk, 1947, Sci. Investigation Micronesia, Yap, 1949. Vis. prof. U. Padjadjaran, Bandung, 1960-61, U. Auckland, summer 1969, Australian Nat. U., fall 1971, U. Philippines, spring 1972, Inst. Study of Langs. and Cultures of Asia and Africa, Tokyo U. for Fgn. Langs., 1982-83; coordinator linguistics sect. 10th Pacific Sci. Congress, Honolulu, 1961; asso. prof. U. Chgo. and Linguistic Soc. Am. Summer Inst., 1955; prof. U. Mich. and Linguistic Soc. Am. Summer Inst., 1957; dir. SE Asia Linguistics Program, 28th Internat. Congress Orientalists, Canberra, 1971; organizing com. Conf. Genetic Lexicostatistics, New Haven, 1971; organizer 1st Eastern Conf. Austronesian Linguistics, New Haven, 1973; adv. com. 1st Internat. Conf. Comparative Austronesian Linguistics, Honolulu, 1974; mem. adv. bd. Oceanic Linguistics. Author: Spoken Malay, 2 vols., 1945, The Proto-Malayo-Polynesian Laryngeals, 1953, A Lexicostatistical Classification of the Austronesian Languages, 1965, A Sketch of Trukese Grammar, 1965, A Descriptive Indonesian Grammar, 1967, Beginning Indonesian, 4 vols., 1967, Lexicostatistics in Genetic Linguistics: Proc. of Yale Conf., 1973, (with David Aberle) Lexical Reconstruction: The Case of the Athapaskan Kinship System, 1974, Linguistic Subgrouping and Lexicostatistics, 1975, (with Guy Jucquois) Lexicostatistics in Genetic Linguistics II, 1976, (with Joseph B. Kruskal and Paul Black) An Indoeuropean Classification: A Lexicostatistical Experiment, 1992. Research fellow Slavic Am. Council Learned Socs., 1938-40; Guggenheim fellow, 1949, 64; Tri-Instl. Pacific Program grantee, 1956-57; NSF grantee, 1960-77 Mem. Linguistic Soc. Am., Am. Oriental Soc. (v.p. 1965-66), Am. Anthrop. Assn., Current Anthropology, Société de Linguistique de Paris, Koninklijk Instituut voor Taal-, Land-, en Volkenkunde, New Haven Oriental Club (pres. 1963-64, 74-76) Office: Univ Hawaii Manoa Dept Linguistics Honolulu HI 96822 also: Yale U Dept Linguistics Hall Grad Studies New Haven CT 06520

DYER, CHARLES RICHARD, law library director, educator; b. Richmond Heights, Mo., Aug. 20, 1947; s. Helmuth Kinner and Sue Anne (Stone) D.; m. Cecelia Ann Duncan, Dec. 20, 1969 (div. June 1982); m. Roberta Sharlyn Monroe, June 2, 1984; 1 child, Christina L. Floyd. BA, U. Tex., 1969, JD, 1974, MLS, 1975; MA, Northwestern U., 1971. Bar: Tex. 1974. Assoc. law libr., asst. prof. law St. Louis U., 1975-77; law libr., assoc. prof. U. Mo., Kansas City, 1977-87; dir. librs. San Diego County Pub. Law Libr., 1987—. Cons. in field. Editor Law Libr. Jour., 1972-74. Centre City adv. com. City of San Diego, 2000—02; chair relocation appeal bd. City of San Diego Redevel. Agy., 2001—05. Mem. Am. Assn. Law Librs., Mid-Am. Assn. Law Librs (sec.-treas. 1976-78), Southwestern Assn. Law Librs. (v.p. 1981-82, pres. 1982-83), So. Calif. Assn. Law Librs. (mem. exec. bd. 1991-93), Coun. Calif. County Law Librs. (pres. 1998-2000). Democrat. Unitarian Universalist. Office: San Diego County Pub Law Libr 1105 Front St San Diego CA 92101-3904 Home: 808 E Maple St Bellingham WA 98225-5225 Office Phone: 619-531-3904. Business E-Mail: cdyer@sdcpll.org.

DYER, PHILIP E., insurance company executive; b. Salem, Oreg., Feb. 10, 1953; s. William Connell Jr. and Clara Belle (Burnside) D.; m. Carolyn J. Pierce, Mar. 11, 1978; children: Pierce, Peyton. BS, Oreg. State U., 1976; grad., U.S. Army Command and Gen. Coll., Leavenworth, Kans., 1983. Cert. ins. counselor. Commd. 2d lt. U.S. Army Nat. Guard, 1971, advanced through grades to maj.; account exec. Marsh and McLennan, Inc., Seattle, 1977-80, 85-86; comml. mktg. rep. Indsl. Indemnity, Seattle, 1980-81; regional v.p. Ins. Corp. Am., Houston, 1981-85; pres. Doctor's Agy. Wash., Inc., Seattle, 1987-94; sr. v.p. Wash. Casualty Co., 1994-96; v.p. The Doctors' Co., Seattle, 1996—. Cons. Group Health Coop., Seattle, 1987. Pres. Eagle Ridge Homeowners Assn.; rep. 5th Legis. Dist. Wash. Ho. of Reps., Issaquah, chmn. health care com., 1994—; tech. advisor Wash. State Health Care Commn., Olympia, 1990-92; ranking minority mem. Ho. Reps. Health Care Com.; asst. ranking mem. Fin. Inst. Ins. Commn.; mem. legis. com. Liability Reform Coalition, Seattle, 1988—; precinct officer Rep. Com., Issaquah, 1991—; cons., mem. ins. com. Issaquah Sch. Dist., 1992; mem. youth div. staff Re-elect Pres. Ford Commn., Washington; staff researcher Oreg. Legislature; chmn. Health Care Com. Wash. Ho. of Reps.; mem. Wash. Health Policy Bd. Mem. Wash. Health Care Risk Mgmt. Soc. (com. chair 1989-90), Soc. Am. Mil. Engrs., Aircraft Owners and Pilot Assn., Profl. Liability Underwriting Soc. (bd. dirs. 1988-89), Issquah Valley Kiwanis. Republican. Episcopalian. Avocations: water-skiing, reading, flying, skiing. Office: Doctors Company 6100 219th St Sw Ste 580 Mountlake Terrace WA 98043

DYM, CLIVE LIONEL, engineering educator; b. Leeds, Eng., July 15, 1942; came to U.S., 1949, naturalized, 1954; s. Isaac and Anna (Hochmann) D.; children: Jordana, Miriam; m. Joan Dym, June 28, 1998. BCE, Cooper Union, 1962; MS, Poly. Inst. Bklyn., 1964; PhD, Stanford U., 1967. Asst. prof. SUNY, Buffalo, 1966-69; assoc. professorial lectr. George Washington U., Washington, 1969; research staff Inst. Def. Analyses, Arlington, Va., 1969-70; assoc. prof. Carnegie Mellon U., Pitts., 1970—74; vis. assoc. prof. TECHNION, Israel, 1971; sr. scientist Bolt Beranek and Newman, Inc., Cambridge, Mass., 1974-77; prof. U. Mass., Amherst, 1977-91, head dept. civil engring., 1977-85; Fletcher Jones prof. engring. design Harvey Mudd Coll., Claremont, Calif., 1991—, dir. Ctr. Design Edn., 1995—, chair dept. engring., 1999—2002. Vis. sr. rsch. fellow Inst. Sound and Vibration Rsch., U. Southampton, Eng., 1973; vis. scientist Xerox PARC, 1983-84; vis. prof. civil engring. Stanford U., 1983-84, Carnegie Mellon U., 1990; Eshbach vis. prof. Northwestern U., 1997-98, U. So. Calif., 2004; cons. Bell Aerospace Co., 1967-69, Dravo Corp., 1970-71, Salem Corp., 1972, Gen. Analytics Inc., 1972, ORI, Inc., 1979, BBN Inc., 1979, Avco, 1981-83, 85-86, TASC, 1985-86, D.H. Brown Assocs., 1991, Johnson Controls, 1996; vice chmn. adv. bd. Amerinex Artificial Intelligence, 1986-88. Author: (with I.H. Shames) Solid Mechanics: A Variational Approach, 1973, Introduction to the Theory of Shells, rev. edit. 1990, Stability Theory and Its Applications to Structural Mechanics, 1974, 2002, (with E.S. Ivey) Principles of Mathematical Modeling, 1980, (with I.H. Shames) Energy and Finite Element Methods in Structural Mechanics, 1985, (with R.E. Levitt) Knowledge-Based Systems in Engineering, 1990, Engineering Design: A Synthesis of Views, 1994, Structural Modeling and Analysis, 1997, (with P. Little, E.J. Orwin and R.E. Spjut) Engineering Design: A Project-Based Introduction, 1999, 2d edit., 2004, 3rd edit., 2008, (with P.D. Cha and J.J. Rosenberg), Fundamentals of Modeling and Analyzing Engineering Systems, 2000, Principles of Mathematical Modeling, 2nd edit., 2004, (with J.S. Rossmann), Introduction to Engineering Mechanics: A Continuum Approach, 2008; editor: (with A. Kalnins) Vibration: Beams, Plates, and Shells, 1977, Applications of Knowledge-Based Systems to Engineering Analysis and Design, 1985, Computing Futures in Engineering Design, 1997, Designing Design Education for the 21st Century, 1999, (with L. Winner) Social Dimensions of Engineering Design, 2001, Designing Engineering Education, 2003, Learning and Engring. Design, 2005, (with P.E. Ocepker) Design Engring. Edn. is a Flat, 2007, Artificial Intelligence for Engring. Design Analysis and Mfg., 1986-96; contbr. articles and tech. reports to profl. publs. NATO sr. fellow in sci., 1973; Boeing Outstanding Engring. Educator award (first-runnerup), 2001. Fellow Acoustical Soc. Am., ASME (Ruth and Joel Spira Outstanding Design Educator award 2004), ASCE (Walter L. Huber rsch. prize 1980), ASEE (Western Electric Fund award 1983, Fred Merryfield Design award 2002, Archie Higdon Disting. Educator award 2006). Jewish. Office: Harvey Mudd Coll Engring Dept 301 E 12th St Claremont CA 91711-5901 Office Phone: 909-621-8853.

DYMALLY, MERVYN MALCOLM, retired state legislator; b. Cedros, Trinidad, W.I., May 12, 1926; s. Hamid A. and Andreid S. (Richardson) D.; m. Alice M. Gueno; children: Mark, Lynn. BA in Edn., Calif. State U., 1954; MA in Govt., Calif. State U., Sacramento 1970; PhD in Human Behavior, U.S. Internat. U., 1978; LLD (hon.), U. W. L.A., 1970; JD (hon.), Lincoln U., Sacramento, 1975; LLD (hon.), Calif. Coll. Law, 1976; HLD (hon.), Shaw U., NC, 1981; PhD (hon.), Calif. Western. U., 1982; LLD (hon.), Lincoln U., San Francisco, 1984, Fla. Meml. Coll., 1987. Cert. elem., secondary and exceptional children tchr. Tchr. L.A. City Schs., 1955-61; coord. Calif. Disaster Office, 1961-62; mem. Calif. Assembly, 1962-66, 2002—08, Calif. Senate, 1967-74; lt. gov. Calif., 1975-79; mem. 97th-102nd Congresses from 31st Calif. dist., 1981-92; pres. Dymally Internat. Group Inc., Inglewood, Calif., 1992—; dir. Urban Health Inst.; prof. Coll. Medicine. Mem. Com. on Fgn. Affairs and its subcoms. on Internat. Ops., chmn. subcom. on Africa, 1989-92; mem. Com. on D.C. and chmn. subcom. on judiciary and edn., 1981-92; chmn. Congl. Task Force on Minority Set Asides, 1987-92; chmn. Senate Majority Caucus, Senate Select Com. on Children and Youth; chmn. Senate coms. on mil. and vets. affairs, social welfare, elections and reapportionment, subcom. on med. edn. and health needs; chmn. joint coms. on legal equality for women, on revision of election code; chmn. assembly com. on indsl. rels.; current mem. Congl. Hispanic Caucus, Congl. Caucus Women's Issues, Congl. Human Rights Caucus, Congl. Black Caucus and chmn. of its task force on Caribbean; chmn. Caribbean Action Lobby, Caribbean Am. Rsch. Inst.; founder Congl. Inst. for Space, Sci. and Tech., chmn. adv. bd.; past chmn. Calif. Commn. Econ. Devel., Commn. of Califs. (U.S., Baja Calif., Calif. Sur, Mex.); past vice chmn., Nat. Conf. Lt. Govs.; former Gov.'s designee U.S. Border States Commn.; past mem. State Lands Commn., others; lectr. Claremont (Calif.) Grad. Sch., Golden Gate U., Sacramento, Pepperdine U., L.A., Pomona (Calif.) Coll., U. Calif., Davis, Irvine, Whittier (Calif.) Coll., Shaw U., Raleigh, N.C.; Disting. prof. Ctrl. State U.; mem. faculty Drew U. Medicine and Sci.; adj. prof. Compton Coll.; cons. to chancellor L.A. C.C. Author: The Black Politician-His Struggle for Power, 1971; co-auhtor: (with Dr. Jeffrey Elliot) Fidel Castro: Nothing Can Stop the Course of History, 1986, also articles; former editor:The Black Politician (quar.) Mem. L.A. County Water Appeals Bd.; advisor to Calif. Assembly Spkr. for Cmty. Congress; chmn. Calif. Black Leadership Roundtable, Caribbean Am. Coalition; chair select com. cmty. colls. Prof. Charles Drew U. Medicine & Sci., 2009-; mem. Calif. Assembly, 2003-08. Recipient numerous awards including Chaconia Gold medal Govt. Trinidad and Tobago, Adam Clayton Powell award Congl. Black Caucus, Dr. Solomon P. Fuller award Black Psychiatrists of Am., others from Golden State Med. Assn., United Tchrs. L.A., Bd. Suprs. L.A., L.A. City Coun., various univs., colls., orgns. Mem. AAUP, NAACP, Am. Acad. Polit. Sci., Am. Polit. Sci. Assn., Am. Acad. Polit. and Social Sci., ACLU, Urban League, Phi Kappa Phi, Kappa Alpha Psi Democrat. Home Phone: 310-635-4641. Business E-Mail: mervyn.dymally@asm.ca.gov, mervyndymally@cdrewu.edu.

DYNES, ROBERT C., physics professor, former academic administrator; b. London, Ont., Can., Nov. 8, 1942; m. Ann P. Dynes. BS of Math. & Physics, U. Western Ont., 1964, LLD (hon.); MS of Physics, McMaster U., 1965, PhD of Phys., 1968, DSc (hon.); PhD (hon.), L'U. de Montréal. Postdoctoral fellow AT&T Bell Labs, Murray Hill, NJ, 1968—70, mem., technical staff, 1970—74, dept. head, semiconductor & chem. physics rsch., 1974—81, dept. head, solid state & physics of materials rsch., 1981—83, dir., chem. physics rsch., 1983—90; physics prof. U. Calif., San Diego, 1991—; chair, dept. physics U. Calif, San Diego, 1994—95; sr. vice chancellor, acad. affairs U. Calif., 1995—96, chancellor, 1996—2003; pres. U. Calif. Sys., Oakland, 2003—08; prof. physics U. Calif., Berkeley, 2008—. Founding mem. San Diego Sci. and Tech. Coun.; adv. bd. Tex. Ctr. Superconductivity U. Houston; spkr. in field. Contbr. articles to profl. jours. Dir. Calif. C. of C.; mem. Calif. Commn. Jobs and Econ. Growth. Recipient Fritz London award Low Temp. Physics, 1990. Fellow: Can. Inst. Advances Rsch., Am. Phys. Soc.; mem.: NAS, Am. Acad. Arts & Scis. Office: U Calif, Berkeley Dept Physics Berkeley CA 94720 E-mail: rdynes@berkeley.edu.

DYSON, ALLAN JUDGE, retired librarian; b. Lawrence, Mass., Mar. 28, 1942; s. Raymond Magan and Hilda D.; m. Susan Cooper, 1987; 1 child, Brenna Ruth. BA in Govt., Harvard U., 1964; MSLS, Simmons Coll., 1968. Asst. to dir. Columbia U. Librs., NYC, 1968-71; head Moffitt Undergrad. Libr. U. Calif., Berkeley, 1971-79, univ. libr. Santa Cruz, 1979—2003, ret., 2003. Editor Coll. and Rsch. Librs. News, 1973-74; chmn. editl. bd. Choice mag., 1978-80, Am. Librs., 1986-89. CFO Cabrillo (Calif.) Music Festival, 1985-86; chmn. No. Calif. Regional Libr. Bd., 1986-88, 94-98, U. Calif. Librs. Group, 1998-2001. Lt. U.S. Army, 1964-66. Decorated Army Commendation medal; Coun. on Libr. Resources fellow, 1973-74. Mem. ALA, ACLU, Librs. Assn. U. Calif. (pres. 1976), Sierra Club.

DYSON, FRED, state legislator; b. Vancouver, Can., Jan. 16, 1939; m. Jane Rae Dyson; children: Cindy, Wendy Shaw, Jana Oztergut. Studied, U. Wash. Supr. maintenance British Petroleum, 1972—84; coml. fisherman, 1976—99; owner, capt. Marine Charter Svc.; mem. Alaska House of Reps., 1996—2002, Alaska State Senate from Dist. I, 2002—. Columnist Anchorage Times, Anchorage Daily News; cons., tech. writer, 1985—; contbg. editor Alaska Boating Mag. Mem. Eagle River Cmty. Coun.; mem. area bd. Eagle River Ltd. Rd. Svc.; mem. Alaska State Human Rights Commn.; mem. citizens adv. bd. Chugach State Park; mem. Anchorage Libr. Commn., Anchorage Aquatic Resources Commn., Anchorage Mcpl. Assembly, 1985—91. Republican. Avocations: boating, reading, history, Outdoor Sports. Office: Dist I 10928 Eagle River Rd Ste 238 Eagle River AK 99577 also: State Capitol Rm 121 Juneau AK 99801 Office Phone: 907-694-1015, 907-465-2199. Office Fax: 907-694-6683, 907-465-4587. Business E-Mail: senator_fred_dyson@legis.state.ak.us.*

DZYALOSHINSKII, IGOR EKHIELIEVICH, physicist; b. Moscow, Feb. 1, 1931; s. Ekhiel Moiseevich and Maria Semionovna (Aseeva) D.; m. Elena Aronovna Lebedeva, Dec. 2, 1960; 1 child, Elena. MA in Physics, Moscow State U., 1953; PhD in Physics, Inst. for Phys. Problems, Moscow, 1957, DSc in Physics, 1962. Sr. rschr. Inst. for Phys. Problems, Moscow, 1957—65; head dept. magnetism Landau Inst. for Theoretical Physics, Moscow, 1965—91; prof. physics U. Calif., Irvine, 1992—2004, prof. emeritus, 2004—. Author: Methods of Quantum Field, Theory in Statistical Physics (in Russian, English, Japanese and Chinese), 1962, 3d edit., 1975, 2d Russian edit., 1998. Decorated Order of Red Banner of Labour, Order of Honor, Medal of Vet. of Labour, Govt. of Russia; recipient State prize Govt. USSR, 1984. Fellow AAAS, Am. Phys. Soc.; mem. Russian Acad. Scis. (Lomonosov prize 1962, Landau prize 1989), Am. Acad. Art and Scis. (hon. fgn. mem.). Achievements include research in theory of weak ferromagnetism; theory of van der Waals forces in condensed media; theory of one-dimensional metals. Office: Univ Calif Dept Physics Irvine CA 92697-0001

EARHART, DONALD MARION, management consultant, health care company executive; b. Hastings, Nebr., May 22, 1944; s. Donald Glen and Mary Elizabeth (Alber) E.; m. June 3, 1977 (dec. July 1988); children: Timothy, Daniel, Cynthia; m. Chelu Travieso, Nov. 22, 1988. BS Indsl. Engring., Ohio State U., 1967; MBA, Roosevelt U., 1979. Engr. Eastman Kodak Co., Rochester, N.Y., 1967-70; mgmt. cons. Peat, Marwick, Mitchell, Cleve., 1970-71; div. dir. Abbott Labs., North Chicago, I, 1971-78; corp. officer, v.p. Abbott Metals, Chgo., 1978-79; div. pres., corp. officer Bausch & Lomb, Rochester, 1979-86, Allergan Inc., Irvine, Calif., 1986-90; chmn., pres., CEO I-Flow Corp., Irvine, 1990—. Bd. dirs. AnPing, Ltd., Alamar Bioscis., Inc. Republican. Avocation: photography. Home and Office: 10 Delphinus Irvine CA 92612-5705 Office: I-Flow Corp 20202 Windrow Dr Lake Forest CA 92630

EARLE, SYLVIA ALICE, research biologist, oceanographer; b. Gibbstown, NJ, Aug. 30, 1935; d. Lewis Reade and Alice Freas (Richie) E. BS, Fla. State U., Tallahassee, 1955; MA, Duke U., Durham, NC, 1956, PhD, 1966, PhD (hon.), 1993, Monterey Inst. Internat. Studies, 1990, Ball State U., Muncie, Ind., 1991, George Wash. U., Washington, DC, 1992; grad., U. RI, Kingston, 1996, Plymouth State Coll., 1996; DSc (hon.), Ripon Coll., Wis., 1994, U. Conn., Storrs, 1994. Resident dir. Cape Haze Marine Lab., Sarasota, Fla., 1966-67; rsch. scholar Radcliffe Inst., 1967-69; rsch. fellow Farlow Herbarium, Harvard U., 1967-75, rschr., 1975—; rsch. assoc. in botany Natural History Mus. Los Angeles County, 1970-75; rsch. biologist, curator Calif. Acad. Scis., San Francisco, from 1976; rsch. assoc. U. Calif., Berkeley, 1969-75; fellow in botany Natural History Mus., 1989—; chief scientist U.S. NOAA, Washington, 1990-92, advisor to the adminstr., 1992-93; founder, pres., CEO, bd. dirs. Deep Ocean Engrs., Inc., Oakland, Calif., 1981-90; founder, chmn., CEO Deep Ocean Exploration and Rsch., Oakland, 1992—, bd. dirs., 1992—; advisor SeaWeb, 1996—2000. Bd. dirs. Dresser Industries, Oryx Energy, Inc.; explorer-in-residence Nat. Geog., 1998-; dir., Natl. Geographic Suatainable Seas Expedition, 1998—; chair, adv. coun. Harte Rsch. Inst., Tex. A&M U., Corpus Christi. Author: Exploring the Deep Frontier, 1980, Sea Change, 1995, Ocean: An Illustrated Atlas, 2008; editor: Scientific Results of the Tektite II Project, 1972-75; contbr. 150 articles to profl. jours. Trustee World Wildlife Fund US, 1976-82, mem. coun., 1984-90; trustee World Wildlife Fund Internat., 1979-81, mem. coun., 1981-95; trustee Charles A. Lindbergh Fund, pres., 1990-95; trustee Ctr. Marine Conservation, 1992-2000, Perry Found., chmn., 1993-95; mem. coun. Internat. Union for Conservation of Nature, 1979-81; corp. mem. Woods Hole Oceanographic Inst., trustee, 1996—; mem. Nat. Adv. Com. on Oceans and Atmosphere, 1980-94. Recipient Conservation Svc. award US Dept. Interior, 1970, Boston Sea Rovers award, 1972, 79, Nogi award Underwater Soc. Am., 1976, Conservation Svc. award Calif. Acad. Sci., 1979, Order of Golden Ark Prince Netherlands, 1980, David B. Stone medal New Eng. Aquarium, 1989, Gold medal Soc. Women Geographers, medal Radcliffe Coll., 1990, Pacon Internat. award, 1992, Dirs. award Natural Resources Coun. Am., 1992, Washburn award Boston Mus. Sci., 1995, Charles A. and Ann Morrow Lindbergh award, 1996, Julius Stratton Leadership award, 1997, Kilby award, 1997, Bal de la Mar Found. Sea Keeper award, 1997, Sea Space Environment award, 1997; Environmental Global 500 award, 1998; US Environmental award, 1998; named Woman of Yr. LA Times, 1970, Scientist of Yr., Calif. Mus. Sci. and Industry, 1981. National Women's Hall of Fame, 2000. Fellow AAAS, Marine Tech. Soc. (Compass award 1997), Calif. Acad. Scis., Calif. Acad. Sci., Explorers Club (hon., bd. dirs. 1989-, Lowell Thomas award 1980, Explorers medal 1996); mem. Internat. Phycological Soc. (sec. 1974-80), Phycological Soc. Am., Am. Soc. Ichthyologists and Herpetologists, Am. Inst. Biol. Scis., Brit. Phycological Soc., Ecol. Soc. Am., Internat. Soc. Plant Taxonomists. Planted a flag in the seafloor off Hawaii to mark the first solo dive to 1,250 feet without a support vessel, wearing hardened diving suit "JIM"; Set and still holds the depth record for women's solo dive:3,300 feet; lived for two weeks underwater with an all-female crew to test the effects of prolonged subsea habitation. Office: DOER 1827 Clement St Alameda CA 94501 Personal E-mail: saearle@aol.com.*

EARLING, DEBRA MAGPIE, writer, educator; Student, Spokane Falls Cmty. Coll., Univ. Calif., Berkeley; BA, Univ. Washington; MFA in Creative Writing, Cornell Univ., 1991. Assoc. prof., creative writing, Native Am. studies Univ. Mont., Missoula. Author: (novels) Perma Red, 2002 (Am. Book award, 2003, WILLA award, Spur award, Mountains and Plains Bestsellers Assn. award); contbr. chapters to books The Last Best Place: A Montana Anthology, Circle of Women: Anthology of Western Women Writers, Wild Women: Anthology of Women Writers, short stories to Talking Leaves: Contemporary Native American Short Stories. Mem. Confederated Salish and Kootenai Tribes of Mont. Address: Author Mail c/o Penguin USA Publicity 375 Hudson St New York NY 10014 Office Phone: 406-243-4963.

EARLY, ROBERT JOSEPH, magazine editor; b. Indpls., Sept. 22, 1936; s. Robert Paul and Helen Theresa (Schluttenhofer) E.; m. Gail Louise Horvath, Sept. 6, 1958; children: Mary Jane, Joseph Robert, Jill Ann. BA, U. Notre Dame, 1958. Reporter Indpls. Star, 1958-61, The Ariz. Republic, Phoenix, 1961-66, asst. city editor, 1966-69, city editor, 1969-77, asst. mng. editor, 1977-78, mng. editor, 1978-82; pres. Telesource Communication Svcs. Inc., Phoenix, 1982-90; editor Phoenix Mag., 1985-89, Ariz. Hwys., Phoenix, 1990—. Lectr. Ariz. State U., 1992, 94; editor in residence No. Ariz. U., 1992, 93, 94. Chmn. Victims Bill of Rights Task Force, Phoenix, 1989. Recipient Virg Hill Newsman of Yr. award Ariz. Press Club, 1976. Mem. Soc. Profl. Journalists. Republican. Roman Catholic. Office: Ariz Hwys 2039 W Lewis Ave Phoenix AZ 85009-2819

EARNHARDT, HAL J., III, automotive executive; b. Mar. 20, 1956; CEO, pres. Earnhardt's Motor Cos., Gilbert, Ariz., 1986. Office: Earnhardts Motor Cos 1301 N Arizona Ave Gilbert AZ 85233-1600

EAST, DANIEL K., small business owner; b. Las Cruces, N.Mex., Nov. 11, 1957; m. Nancy East; 7 children. BSc in Constrn. Mgmt., Colo. State U., 1988. V.p. RMCI, Inc., 1995—99; owner, operator Cone Constrn. Corp., Inc., Albuquerque, 1999—. Mem.: Nat. Utility Contractors Assn. (pres. 2003, sr. v.p. 2008). Republican. Office: Cone Constrn Corp Inc 515 Wheeler Ave SE Albuquerque NM 87102 Office Phone: 505-342-2898. Office Fax: 505-342-2205.

EASTAUGH, ROBERT L., state supreme court justice; b. Seattle, Nov. 12, 1943; BA in English Literature, Yale U., 1965; JD, U. Mich., 1968. Bar: Alaska 1968. Asst. atty. gen. State of Alaska, 1968—69, asst. dist. atty., 1969—72; lawyer Delaney, Wiles, Hayes, Reitman & Brubaker, Inc., 1972—94; assoc. justice Alaska Supreme Ct., 1994—. Charter mem. Advisory Com. on Rules of Practice & Internal Operating Procedures, Alaska Ninth Circuit Ct., 1983—92; mem. Alaska Supreme Ct. Appellate Rules Com., 1985—; co-chair Alaska Supreme Ct. Fairness & Access Implementation Com., 1998—. Mem.: Alaska Bar Assoc. (bar examiner). Office: Alaska Supreme Ct 303 K St Anchorage AK 99501-2048 Office Phone: 907-264-0624.

EASTHAM, JOHN D., marketing executive; Profl. Degree, Burnley Sch., Seattle, 1967. Mng. ptnr. EMB Ptnrs., Seattle, 1994—2002, Eastham Hinton & Simpson LLC, 2002—. Recipient Clio awards, 1986, Effie, Am. Mktg. Assn., 1991, Totem awards Pub. Rels. Soc. Am., 1982.

EASTHAM, THOMAS, retired foundation administrator; b. Attelboro, Mass., Aug. 21, 1923; s. John M. and Margaret (Marsden) Eastham; m. Berenice J. Hirsch, Oct. 12, 1946; children: Scott Thomas, Todd Robert. Student English, Northwestern U., 1946-52. With Chgo. American, 1945-56, asst. Sunday editor, 1953-54, feature writer, 1954-56; news editor San Francisco Call Bull., 1956-62, exec. editor, 1962-65; exec. editor, then D.C. bur. chief San Francisco Examiner, 1965-82; dir. pub. info, press sec. to mayor of San Francisco, 1982-88; v.p., western dir. William Randolph Hearst Founds., 1988—2005; ret., 2005. Active Nat. Trust Hist. Preservation; mem. Amnesty Internat.; mem. Pres.'s roundtable U. San Francisco. Recipient Disting. Achievement in Journalism award, Assn. Schs. Journalism and Mass Comm., 1994; finalist Pulitzer prize, 1955. Mem.: ACLU, San Francisco Planning and Urban Rsch. Assn., Coun. Founds., Ind. Sector, Nat. Press Club, White House Corrs. Assn., Am. Internat. Press Insts., Inter-Am. Press Assn., Am. Soc. Newspaper Editors, Peninsula Tennis Club, Commonwealth Club, Marine Meml. Club, Sigma Delta Chi. Office: Hearst Found 90 New Montgomery St Ste 1212 San Francisco CA 94105-4596 Home: 12127 Gatewater Dr Potomac MD 20854-2873 Personal E-mail: t.eastham@comcast.com. Business E-Mail: teastham@hearstfdn.com.

EASTIN, DELAINE ANDREE, education educator; b. San Diego, Aug. 20, 1947; d. Daniel Howard and Dorothy Barbara Eastin. BA in Polit. Sci., U. Calif., Davis, 1969; MA in Polit. Sci., U. Calif., Santa Barbara, 1971. Instr. Calif. Community Colls., various locations, 1971-79; acctg. mgr. Pacific Bell, San Francisco, 1979-84; corp. planner Pacific Telesis Group, San Francisco, 1984-86; assemblywoman Calif. State Legis., Sacramento, 1986-95; supt. of public instruction Calif. Edn. Dept., Sacramento, 1995—2003; exec. dir. Nat. Inst. Sch. Leadership, 2003—04; disting. prof. ednl. leadership Mills Coll., Oakland, Calif. Ex officio mem. bd. regents U. Calif., 1995—2003; ex officio mem. bd. trustees Calif. State U., 1995—2003. Bd. dirs. CEWAER, Sacramento, 1988-2003, Pence Gallery, 2003—, Internat. Assn. Fgn. Students Found., 2003—; commr. Commn. on Status of Women, Sacramento, 1990-2003; mem. coun. City of Union City, Calif., 1980-86; chair Alameda County Libr. Commn., Hayward, Calif., 1981-86; planning commr. City of Union City, 1976-80; mem., pres. Alameda County Solid Waste Mgmt. Authority, Oakland, Calif., 1980-86. Named Outstanding Pub. Ofcl. Calif. Tchrs. Assn., 1988, Cert. of Appreciation Calif. Assn. for Edn. of Young Children, 1988-92, Legislator of the Yr. Calif. Media Libr. Educators, 1991, Calif. Sch. Bd. Assn., 1991, 94, Ednl. Excellence award Calif. Assn. Counseling and Devel., 1992. Mem.: Am. Bus. Women's Assn. (Outstanding Bus. Woman 1988), The Internat. Alliance (21st Century award 1990), World Affairs Coun., Commonwealth Club. Democrat. Avocations: photography, hiking, reading, theater, travel. Home: 4228 Dogwood Pl Davis CA 95616-6066 Office Phone: 510-430-2365.

EASTWOOD, CLINT (CLINTON EASTWOOD JR.), actor, film director; b. San Francisco, May 31, 1930; s. Clinton and Margaret Ruth Eastwood; m. Maggie Johnson, Dec. 19, 1953 (div. May 14, 1984); children: Kyle, Alison; m. Dina Ruiz, March 31, 1996; children: Morgan; 1 child, (with Roxanne Tunis) Kimber; 1 child (with Frances Fisher) Fracesca Ruth Grad., Oakland Tech. High Sch., 1948; attended, LA City Coll.; DFA (hon.), Wesleyan U., 2000. Worked as lumberjack in Oreg. before being drafted into the Army. Owner Malpaso Records Co., Mission Ranch Resort, Carmel, Calif., Tehama Golf Club, Carmel, Calif; co-founder, ptnr. Tehama Inc.; co-owner Pebble Beach Co. Actor: (TV series) Rawhide, 1959-1966; (films) Revenge of the Creature, 1955, Francis in the Navy, 1955, Lady Godiva, 1955, Tarantula, 1955, Never Say Goodbye, 1956, The First Travelling Saleslady, 1956, Star in the Dust, 1956, Away All Boats, 1956, Escapade in Japan, 1957, Ambush at the Cimmaron Pass, 1958, Lafayette Escadrille, 1958, Ambush at Cimarron Pass, 1958, A Fistful of Dollars, 1964, For a Few Dollars More, 1965, The Good, the Bad and the Ugly, 1966, The Witches, 1967, Hang 'Em High, 1968, Coogan's Bluff, 1968, Where Eagles Dare, 1968, Paint Your Wagon, 1969, Two Mules for Sister Sara, 1970, Kelly's Heroes, 1970, The Beguiled, 1971, Dirty Harry, 1971, Joe Kidd, 1972, Magnum Force, 1973, Thunderbolt and Lightfoot, 1974, The Enforcer, 1976, Every Which Way But Loose, 1978, Escape from Alcatraz, 1979, Any Which Way You Can, 1980, City Heat, 1984, The Dead Pool, 1988, Pink Cadillac, 1989, In the Line of Fire, 1993; actor, dir.: (films) Play Misty For Me, 1971, High Plains Drifter, 1973, The Eiger Sanction, 1975, The Outlaw Josey Wales, 1976, The Gauntlet, 1977, Bronco Billy, 1980, The Rookie, 1990, Gran Torino, 2008 (Best Actor Nat. Bd. Review, 2008); actor, dir., prodr.: (films) Firefox, 1982, Honkeytonk Man, 1982, Sudden Impact, 1983, Pale Rider, 1985, Heartbreak Ridge, 1986, White Hunter Black Heart, 1990, Unforgiven, 1992 (Academy Award for Best Director & Best Picture, 1992, Golden Globe award for best director, 1993), A Perfect World, 1993, The Bridges of Madison County, 1995, Absolute Power, 1997, True Crime, 1999, Space Cowboys, 2000, Blood Work, 2002, Million Dollar Baby, 2004 (Golden Globe award for best director, 2005, Director's Guild award for best feature, 2005, Acad. award for Best Director & Best Picture, 2005); actor, prodr.: (films) Tightrope, 1984, The Exchange, 2008 (Spl. prize, Festival de Cannes, 2008); dir.: (films) Breezy, 1973; (TV episodes) Amazing Stories (Vanessa in the Garden episode), 1985; (TV miniseries) The Blues -(Piano Blues episode), 2003; dir., prodr.: (films) Bird, 1988, Midnight in the Garden of Good and Evil, 1997, Mystic River, 2003, Flags of Our Fathers, 2006 (Runner-up, Dir. of Yr., LA Film Critics Assn., 2006), Letter from Iwo Jima, 2006 (Best Picture of Yr., LA Film Critics Assn., 2006 & Runner-up, Dir. of Yr., 2006, Best Fgn. Film, Golden Globe award, Hollywood Fgn. Press Assn., 2007), Changeling, 2008; prodr.: (films) The Stars Fell on Henrietta, 1995; exec. prodr. (films) Thelonious Monk-Straight, No Chaser, 1989; singer: (singles) Unknown Girl, 1981, Rowdy, For You, For Me, For Evermore, Cowboy in a Three Piece Suit, 1981, (albums) Rawhide's Clint Eastwood Sings Cowboy Favorites, 1962, Mem. Nat. Coun. Arts, 1972-78; mem. bd. Monterey Jazz Festival; chmn. Monterey Peninsula Found.; hon. bd. governors Entertainment Industry Found.; mayor City of Carmel, Calif., 1986-88; Calif. State Parks commr. for Carmel, 2002-; vice-chair Calif. State Parks & Recreation Commn.; nat. spokesman Take Pride in Am., 2005-. Recipient Golden Globe award for world film favorite, Hollywood Fgn. Press. Assn., 1971, Cecil B. DeMille Award, 1988, Irving G. Thalberg Meml. award, Acad. Motion Picture Arts & Sciences, 1995, Life Achievement award, Film Soc. at Lincoln Ctr., 1996, Am. Film Inst., 1996, Kennedy Ctr. Honors, John F. Kennedy Ctr. Performing Arts, 2000, Lifetime Career Achievement award, NY Nat. Bd. Review, 2000, Hank award, Henry Mancini Inst., 2003, Lifetime Achievement Award, Screen Actors Guild, 2003, Milestone award, Producers Guild America, 2006, Lifetime Achievement Award, Directors Guild America, 2006, Stanley Kubrick Britannia award for Excellence in Film, British Acad. Film & Television Arts/LA, 2006, Golden Boot award, Motion Picture & Television Fund, 2006, Jack Valenti Humanitarian Award, Motion Picture Assn. Am., 2007, Legion d'Honneur order, Govt. of France, 2007, Career Achievement award, Palm Springs Internat. Film Soc., 2009, Modern Master award, Santa Barbara Film Festival, 2009, Golden Palm award, Cannes Film Festival, 2009; named Dir. of Yr., Hollywood Film Festival, 2008; named one of The 100 Most Influential People of 2005, TIME mag., 2005; named to The Calif. Hall of Fame, 2006. Office: c/o Leonard Hirshan 1680 Clearview Dr Beverly Hills CA 90210

EASTWOOD, KATHLEEN DEGIOIA, physics and astronomy professor; b. Palo Alto, Calif., July 22, 1954; d. Joseph Anthony DeGioia and Helen Nancy Runyan; m. John Douglas Eastwood; children: Erin Nancy, Megan Marie. AB in Physics, Dartmouth Coll., Hanover, NH, 1976; PhD in Physics, U. Wyo., Laramie, 1982. Asst. scientist U. Wis., Madison, 1983—87; asst. prof. physics and astronomy Northern Ariz. U., Flagstaff, 1988—94, assoc. prof., 1994—2001, prof., 2001—; program dir. NSF, Arlington, Va., 2001—03. Dir. Nat. Undergrad. Rsch. Obs., Flagstaff, 1989—; dir., young scholars in astronomy program Northern Ariz. U., 1989—90, dir., rsch. experiences undergrads. site, 1992—, site dir., tchr. resource agents program, 1994—96; vis. astronomer Lowell Obs., Flagstaff, 1995—96; vis. prof. U. de La Serena, Chile, 2006; vis. astronomer Cerro Tololo Interam. Obs., La Serena. Contbr. articles to profl. jours. Grantee, NASA/JPL, 1987, Rsch. Corp., 1988, NSF, 1988, 1991, 1995, 2000, 2005, NASA/Space Telescope Sci. Inst., 2003, 2005; Sr. Fellow, Dartmouth Coll., 1975-1976, Fulbright Scholar, U.S. Dept. State, 2006. Mem.: Astron. Soc. the Pacific, Internat. Astron. Union, Am. Astron. Soc. (editor, the com. on status women in astronomy newsletter 1988—93), Sigma Xi. Democrat. Congregationalist. Office: Northern Ariz Univ Dept Physics and Astronomy Flagstaff AZ 86011-6010 Office Fax: 928-523-1371. E-mail: kathy.eastwood@nau.edu.

EATMAN, LOUIS PERKINS, lawyer; b. Montgomery, Ala., Nov. 16, 1948; s. Jack Bernard and Margaret Worthington (Perkins) E. BS in Fgn. Svc., Georgetown U., 1970; MBA, JD, Stanford U., 1974. Bar: Calif. 1974. Ptnr. Loeb and Loeb, LA, 1974—94, Mayer, Brown, Rowe & Maw LLP, LA, 1994—, co-adminstr., nat. real estate practice group, 1994—96, ptnr.-in-charge, LA office, 1996—2007, co-leader global real estate practice group, 2002—04; pres. Constitutional Rights Found., 2004—06. Mem. Los Angeles County Bar Assn., Internat. Coun. Shopping Ctrs., Riviera Country Club, City Club on Bunker Hill. Phi Beta Kappa. Avocations: golf, fly fishing. Office: Mayer Brown Rowe & Maw LLP 25th Fl 350 S Grand Ave Los Angeles CA 90071-1503 Office Phone: 213-229-5144. Business E-Mail: leatman@mayerbrownrowe.com.

EATON, CURTIS HOWARTH, banker, lawyer; b. Twin Falls, Idaho, Sept. 3, 1945; s. Curtis Turner and Wilma (Howarth)E.; m. Mardo Ohisson, Aug. 2, 1969; 1 child, Dylan Alexander. BA, Stanford U., 1969; MPA, Johns Hopkins U., 1971; JD, U. Idaho, 1974. Bar: Idaho 1974. Atty. Idaho Atty. Gen.'s Office, Boise, 1974-76; ptnr. Stephan, Slavin, Eaton, Twin Falls, 1975-82; exec. v.p. Twin Falls Bank & Trust, 1982-84, area pres., from 1984, also bd. dirs., from 1984; former v.p., bd. dirs. 1st Security Bank at Idaho, Twin Falls, pres., 1992—; exec. dir. CSI Foundation (planning & devel.), Twin Falls, Idaho. Bd. dirs. San Francisco Fed. Res. Bank, Salt Lake City. Bd. dirs. United Way Magic Falley, 1978—, Sr. Citizens, 1978-82; mem. Idaho Bd. Edn., 1993—, now pres.; trustee YFCA, 1981—; pres. Coll. So. Idaho Found., 1986-88. Mem. ATLA, Idaho Bar Assn. Office: Coll So Idaho P O Box 1238 315 Falls Ave Twin Falls ID 83303-1238 Office Phone: 208-732-6242 6242. Business E-Mail: ceaton@csi.edu.

EATON, GARETH RICHARD, chemistry professor, dean; b. Lockport, NY, Nov. 3, 1940; s. Mark Dutcher and Ruth Emma (Ruston) E.; m. Sandra Shaw, Mar. 29, 1969. BA, Harvard U., 1962; PhD, MIT, 1972. Asst. prof. chemistry U. Denver, 1972-76, assoc. prof., 1976-80, prof., 1980-97, dean natural scis., 1984-88, vice provost for rsch., 1988-89, John Evans prof., 1997—. Organizer Internat. Electron-Paramagnetic Resonance Symposium. Author, editor: 7 books, mem. editl. bd.: 4 jours.; contbr. articles to profl. jours. Lt. USN, 1962-67. Mem. AAAS, Am. Chem. Soc., Royal Soc. Chemistry (London), Internat. Soc. Magnetic Resonance, Am. Phys. Soc., Internat. Electron Paramagnetic Resonance Soc. Office: U Denver Dept Chem/Biochem Denver CO 80208 Home Phone: 303-759-1932; Office Phone: 303-871-2980. Business E-Mail: geaton@du.edu.

EATON, GEORGE WESLEY, JR., petroleum engineer, oil company executive; b. Searcy, Ark., Aug. 3, 1924; s. George Wesley and Inez (Roberson) E.; m. Adriana Amin, Oct. 28, 1971; 1 child, Andrew. BS in Petroleum Engring., U. Okla., 1948. Registered profl. engr. Tex., N.Mex. Petroleum engr. Amoco, Longview, Ft. Worth, Tex., 1948-54, engring. supr. Roswell, N.Mex., 1954-59, dist. engr. Farmington, N.Mex., 1959-70; constrn. mgr. Amoco Egypt Oil Co., Cairo, 1970-81; ops. mgr. Amoco Norway Oil Co., Stavanger, 1981-84; petroleum cons. G.W. Eaton Cons., Albuquerque, 1984-94. Adj. prof. San Juan Coll., Farmington, 1968-70. Bd. dirs. Paradise Hills Civic Assn., Albuquerque, 1986-89; elder Rio Grande Presbyn. Ch., Albuquerque, 1987-90; mem. Rep. Nat. Com., Washington, 1986-92. Mem. N.Mex. Soc. Profl. Engrs. (bd. dirs. 1967-70), Soc. Petroleum Engrs. (Legion of Honor), Egyptian Soc. Petroleum Engrs. (chmn. 1980-81).

EATON, JERRY, television executive; b. LA, June 13, 1945; BS in Biology, Trinity Coll. V.p., gen. mgr. KYW, Phila., KPIX-TV, San Francisco, 1997—. Office: KPIX-TV 855 Battery St San Francisco CA 94111-1597

EATON, PAULINE, artist, educator; b. Neptune, NJ, Mar. 20, 1935; d. Paul A. and Florence Elizabeth (Rogers) Friedrich; m. Charles Adams Eaton, June 15, 1957; children: Gregory, Eric, Paul, Joy, Jane(dec.). BA, Dickinson Coll., Carlisle, Pa., 1957; MA, Northwestern U., Evanston, Ill., 1958. Lic. instr. Calif. Instr. Mira Costa Coll., Oceanside, Calif., 1980—82, Idyllwild Sch. Music and Arts, Calif., 1983—; instr. dept. continuing edn. U. N.Mex.; pres. Corrales Bosque Gallery, 2007—. Juror, demonstrator numerous art socs.; founder, dir. Corrales Art/Studio Tour, 1999—2006; dir. Art Expo, NYC, 2006. One-woman shows include Nat. Arts Club, NYC, 1977, Designs Recycled Gallery, Fullerton, Calif., 1978, 1980, 1984, San Diego Art Inst., 1980, Spectrum Gallery, San Diego, 1981, San Diego Jung Ctr., 1983, Marin Civic Ctr. Gallery, 1984, R. Mondayi Winery, 1987, exhibited in group shows at Am. Watercolor Soc., 1975, 1977, Butler Inst. Am. Art, Youngstown, Ohio, 1977—79, 1981, NAD, 1978, N.Mex Arts and Crafts Fair, 1994 (Best in Show award), Corrales Bosque Gallery, Art is OK Gallery, Albuquerque, N.Mex., 2004—08, Represented in permanent collections Butler Inst. Am. Art, St. Mary's Coll., Md., Mercy Hosp., San Diego, Sharp Hosp., Redlands Hosp., Riverside, N.Mex. Women in Arts, Albuquerque Mus.; work featured in: book Watercolor, The Creative Experience, 1978, Creative Seascape Painting, 1980, Painting the Spirit in Nature, 1984, Exploring Painting (Gerald Brommer); author: Crawling to the Light, An Artist in Transition, 1987; author: (with Mary Ann Beckwith) Best of Watercolor Texture, 1997; The Art of Layering: Making Connections, 2004; contbr. chapters to books. Trustee San Diego Art Inst., 1977—78, San Diego Mus. Art, 1982—83. Recipient award, Hollywood (Calif.) Form Arts, 1986, Grumbacker award, Conf. 96 Hill Country Art Ctr., 2d award, Tex. Friends and Neighbors, Irving, 2000, award of excellence, Ariz. Aqueous, 2002, Originals award, N.Mex. Women in Arts, Albuquerque Mus., 2003, Water US award, 2008. Mem.: Soc. Layerists Multi-Media (bd. dirs.), Eastbay Watercolor Soc. (v.p. 1988—90), West Coast Watercolor Soc. (exhbns. chmn. 1983—86, pres. 1989—92), We. Fedn. Watercolor Socs. (chmn. 1983, 3d prize 1982, Grumbacher Gold medal 1983), N.Mex Watercolor Soc. (Grumbacker award, Wingspread award 1999), San Diego Artists Guild (pres. 1982—83), Artists Equity (v.p. San Diego 1979—81), San Diego Watercolor Soc. (pres. 1976—77, workshop dir. 1977—80), Marin Arts Guild (instr. 1984—87), Internat. Soc. Exptl. Artists (Nautilus Merit award 1992, 1998), Watercolor West (Strathmore award 1979, Purchase award 1986), Rocky Mountain Watermedia Soc. (Golden award 1979, Mustard Seed award 1983), Nat. Watercolor Soc., Watercolor USA Soc. (hon. Veloy Vigil Meml. award 1986), Nat. Soc. Painters Acrylic and Casein (hon.). Democrat. Home: 68 Hop Tree Trl Corrales NM 87048-9613 Office Phone: 505-898-1573.

EATON, PHILIP W., academic administrator; m. sharon Eaton; children: Mark, Michael, Todd. BA, Whitworth Coll.; MA, PhD, Ariz. State Univ. Interim pres. Whitworth Coll., Spokane, Wash., 1992—93; v.p. acad. affairs Seattle Pacific Univ., Wash., 1993—95, provost Wash., 1995—96, pres. Wash., 1996—. Bd. dir. Independent Coll. Wash. Named one of 100 Most Influential People in Washington State, Washington CEO Mag., 2002, 50 US Coll. and U. Character-Bldg. Presidents, John Templeton Found., 2002. Avocations: golf, reading, sports. Office: Seattle Pacific Univ President's Office 3307 3d Ave W Seattle WA 98119-1997

EAVES, ALLEN CHARLES EDWARD, hematologist, health facility administrator; b. Ottawa, Ont., Can., Feb. 19, 1941; s. Charles and Margaret E.; m. Connie Jean Halperin, July 1, 1975; children: Neil, Rene, David, Sara. BSc, Acadia U., Wolfville, NS, Can., 1962; MSc, Dalhousie U., Halifax, NS, 1964, MD, 1969; PhD, U. Toronto, Ont., Can., 1974. Intern Dalhousie U., Halifax, N.S., Canada, 1968-69; resident in internal medicine Sunnybrook Hosp., Toronto, 1974-75, Vancouver Gen. Hosp., 1975-79; dir. Terry Fox Lab., Cancer Control Agy. B.C., Vancouver, Canada, 1980—; asst. prof. medicine U. B.C., 1979-83, assoc. prof., 1983-88, head div. hematology, 1985—2003, prof., 1988—; pres. StemCell Technologies Inc., Vancouver, 1993—, Malachite Mgmt. Inc., 1996—, StemSoft Software Inc., 2000—. Treas. Found. for Accreditation of Hematopoetic Cell Therapy, 1995-2002. Fellow Royal Coll. Physicians (Can.), ACP; mem. Internat. Soc. Hematotherapy and Graft Engrng. (pres. 1995-97), Am. Soc. Blood and Marrow Transplantation (pres. elect 1998-99, pres. 1999-2000). Office: The StemCell Group of Companies 570 W 7th Ave Ste 400 V5Z 1B3 Vancouver BC Canada Office Phone: 604-675-8125.

EBBELING, WILLIAM LEONARD, physician; b. Whitinsville, Mass., June 29, 1947; s. Titus Jr. and Agnes Ebbeling; m. Dianne Wilder, Apr. 10, 1976; children: Jennifer Lynn, Daniel Wilder. BS, Wheaton Coll., 1969; MD, Wake Forest U. Sch. Medicine, 1974. Commd. ensign USN, 1974, advanced through grades to capt., 1988; resident Naval Med. Ctr., Portsmouth, Va., 1974-77, pediatrician Naples, Italy, 1977-80; fellow in allergy Duke U. Med. Ctr., Durham, N.C., 1985-88; head ambulatory pediatrics, staff pediatrician Nat. Naval Med. Ctr., Bethesda, Md., 1981-85, head allery, immunology and clin. investigation dept., 1988-93; dep. chief med. corps for career planning Navy Bur. Medicine and Surgery, Washington, 1993-95; head direct med. care divsn. Naval Healthcare Support Office, San Diego, 1995-97; staff allergist Naval Tng. Ctr., Allergy Clinic, San Diego, 1997—. Fellow Am. Acad. Allergy, Asthma and Immunology, Am. Acad. Pediat.; mem. Am. Coll. Physician Execs., Assn. Mil. Allergists (chmn. 1996-97). Avocations: tennis, computers, fishing. Office: Naval Med Ctr Allergy Clinic at NTC 2650 Stockton Rd Bldg 624 San Diego CA 92106-6000 Home: 1495 E Carlyle Way Fresno CA 93720-3579

EBEL, DAVID M., federal judge; b. 1940; BA, Northwestern U., 1962; JD, U. Mich., 1965. Law clk. to Justice Byron White US Supreme Ct., Washington, 1965—66; pvt. practice Davis, Graham & Stubbs, Denver, 1966—88; judge US Ct. Appeals (10th cir.), Denver, 1988—2006, sr. judge, 2006—. Adj. prof. law U. Denver Law Sch., 1987—89; sr. lectr. fellow Duke U. Law Sch., 1992—94. Mem.: Jud. Conf. U.S. (com. on codes of conduct 1991—98, co-chair 10th cir. gender bias task force 1994—99), Colo. Bar Assn. (v.p. 1982), Am. Coll. Trial Lawyers. Office: US Ct Appeals 1823 Stout St Rm 109L Denver CO 80257-1823 E-mail: david_m_ebel@ca10.uscourts.gov

EBERHARDT, MARTY LAMPERT, botanical garden administrator; b. Albuquerque, Aug. 6, 1952; d. Charles Lampert and Mary Elizabeth (Marty) E.; m. Thomas George Schramski, Mar. 19, 1977 (div. May 1986); children: Paul, Sam; m. Philip Alan Hastings, Dec. 12, 1987. BA, Prescott Coll., 1974; MEd, U. Ariz., 1978. Program dir. Tumamoc Hill Environ. Edn. Ctr., Tucson, 1978-79; tchr. Cmty. Psychology and Edn. Svcs., Tucson, 1985-87; asst. dir./edn. coord. Tucson Bot. Gardens, 1986-88, exec. dir., 1988—. Reviewer grants Inst. Mus. and Libr. Svcs., Washington, 1994—; mem. adv. bd. Registree, 1993—. Mem. steering com. Nat. and Cultural Heritage Alliance of Pima County, 1996—; mem. exec. com. Intercultural Ctr. for Study of Deserts and Oceans, Puerto Peñasco, Mex., 1998—, Tucson Cmty. Found., 1997-99, Tucson Origins Project, 1999—. Recipient Women on the Move award YWCA, Tucson, 1993, various grants from corps. and founds., 1988—. Mem. Exec. Women's Coun., Strategic Leadership in Changing Environ., Am. Assn. Bot. Gardens and Arboreta (regional coord.), Am. Assn. Museums (reviewer grants 1994-98), Native Seeds/SEARCH. Avocations: hiking, backpacking, reading, gardening. Office: Tucson Bot Gardens 2150 N Alvernon Way Tucson AZ 85712-3153

EBERHART, RALPH E., retired military officer; BS in Polit. Sci., USAF Acad., 1968; grad., Squadron Officer Sch., 1973, Air Command and Staff Coll., 1974; MS in Polit. Sci., Troy State U., 1977; postgrad. studies, Nat. War Coll., Ft. Lesley J. McNair, Washington, 1987. Commd. 2d lt. USAF, 1968, advanced through grades to gen., 1997; forward air controller Tactical Air Support Squadron USAF, Plieka Air Base, S. Viet Nam, 1970; from instr. pilot to squadron hdqrs. comdr. 71st Flying Tng. Wing Air Tng. Command USAF, Vance AFB, Okla., 1970-74; flight commdr., instr. pilot 525th Tactical Fighter Squadron USAFs in Europe, Bitburg Air Base, Germany, 1975-77; instr. pilot. flight examiner, asst. chief evaluation 50th Tactical Fighter Wing, Hahn Air Base, Germany, 1977-78; action officer, chief exec. com. Air Force Budget team Hdqs. USAF, Washington, 1979-80; aide to comdr.-in-chief, comdr. Air Forces Ctrl. Europe USAF, Ramstein AFB, Germany, 1980-82; comdr. 10th tactical fighter squadron, asst. dep. comdr. ops. 50th tactical fighter wing USAF in Europe, Hahn Air Base, Germany, 1982—84; exec. officer to Air Force chief of staff Hdqs. USAF, Washington, 1984-86; vice comdr. to comdr. 363d tactical fighter wing Tactical Air Command USAF, Shaw AFB, S.C., 1987-90; dep. chief of staff, plans and ops. Hdqs. USAF, Washington, 1995-96; cmdr. U.S. Forces Japan, cmdr. 5th Air Force USAF, Yokota Air Base, Japan, 1996-97; vice chief of staff Hdqs. USAF, Washington, 1997—99; comdr. Air Combat Command, Langley AFB, Va., 1999—2000, Air Force Space Command, Peterson AFB, Colo., 2000—02; mgr. for manned space flight support ops. Dept. Def., Peterson AFB, Colo., 2000—02; comdr. in chief N.Am. Aerospace Def. Command and U.S. Space Command, Peterson AFB, Colo., 2000—04; comdr. U.S. Northern Command, Peterson AFB, Colo., 2002—04. Numerous decorations include: Legion of Merit with Oak Leaf cluster, Disting. Flying Cross, Air medal with 11 Oak Leaf clusters, Vietnam Svc. medal with 3 svc. stars, Humanitarian Svc. medal with svc. star, Republic of Vietnam Gallantry Cross with Palm, Republic of Vietnam Campaign medal, The Grand Cordon of the Order of the Sacred Treasure, Japan. and many others. Mem. Coun. of Fgn. Rels.

EBIE, WILLIAM D., retired museum director; s. William P. and Mary Louise (Karam) E.; m. Gwyn Anne Schumacher, Apr. 11, 1968 (div. Jan. 1988); children: Jason William, Alexandra Anne; m. Mary Teresa Hayes, June 10, 1989. BFA, Akron Art Inst., 1964; MFA, Calif. Coll. of Arts and Crafts, 1968. Graphic artist Alameda County Health Dept., Oakland, Calif., 1967-68; instr. painting Fla. A&M U., Tallahassee, 1968-69; instr. photography Lawrence (Kans.) Adult Edn. Program, 1969-70; asst. dir. Roswell (N.Mex.) Mus. & Art Ctr., 1971-87, dir., 1987-98, Millicent Rogers Mus., Taos, N.Mex., 1998—2002. Juror various art exhbns., 1971—; panelist N.Mex. Arts Divsn., Santa Fe, 1983-87; field reviewer Inst. for Mus. Svcs., 1988-90; mem. State Capitol Renovation Art Selection Com., Santa Fe, 1991-92; bd. dirs. Capitol Art Found., Santa Fe, 1992-2002, 2006-. Bd. dirs. Helene Wurlitzer Found., Taos, N.Mex., 1999—. Mem. Am. Assn. of Mus., Mountain Plains Mus. Assn., N.Mex. Assn. of Mus. Democrat. Avocations: photography, carpentry. Personal E-mail: billebie@earthlink.net, billebie@taosnet.com.

ECCLES, MATTHEW ALAN, landscape and golf course architect; b. Ft. Dodge, Iowa, Apr. 19, 1956; s. Guy Eldon Jr. and Mary Ellen (Baldwin) E.; m. Debra Kay Sorenson, Mar. 19, 1983; children: Stephanie Ann, Jason Alan. BS in Landscape Architecture, Iowa State U., 1978. Registered landscape architect, Kans., Minn. From project mgr. to dir. golf course design THK Assocs., Inc., Greenwood Village, Colo., 1980-94; pres. Eccles Design Inc., Englewood, Colo., 1994—. Mem. Am. Soc. Landscape Architects, U.S. Golf Assn., Golf Course Supts. Assn. Am., Nat. Golf Found., Nat. Ski Patrol, Tau Sigma Delta. Avocations: golf, skiing, fishing, photography. Office: Eccles Design Inc 8120 S Monaco Cir Englewood CO 80112-3022

ECCLES, SPENCER FOX, banker, director; b. Ogden, Utah, Aug. 24, 1934; s. Spencer Stoddard and Hope (Fox) E.; m. Cleone Emily Peterson, July 21, 1958; children: Clista Hope, Lisa Ellen, Katherine Ann, Spencer Peterson. BS, U. Utah, 1956; MA, Columbia U., 1959; degree in bus. (hon.), So. Utah State Coll., 1982; LLB (hon.), Westminster Coll., Salt Lake City, 1986. Trainee First Nat. City Bank, NYC, 1959-60; with First Security Bank of Utah, Salt Lake City, 1960-61, First Security Bank of Idaho, Boise, 1961-70; exec. v.p. First Security Corp., Salt Lake City, 1970-75, pres., 1975-86, COO, 1980-82, chmn. bd. dirs., CEO, 1982—. Dir. Union Pacific Corp., Anderson Lumber Co., Zions Corp., Merc. Instn.; mem. adv. council U. Utah Bus. Coll. 1st lt. U.S. Army. Recipient Pres.'s Circle award Presdl. Commn., 1984, Minuteman award Utah N.G., 1988; Named Disting. Alumni U. Utah, 1988. Mem. Am. Bankers Assn., Bankers Roundtable, Salt Lake Country Club, Alta Club. Office: Wells Fargo Bank NW 299 S Main St Salt Lake City UT 84111-2263

ECHAVESTE, MARIA, lobbyist, former federal official; b. Tex., 1954; m. Chris Edley. BA in Anthropology, Stanford U., 1976; JD, U. Calif., Berkeley, 1980. Assoc. Wyman Bautzer; spl. counsel Rosenman & Colin, 1989—93; dep. dir. pers. Pres. Bill Clinton's Transition Team, Washington, 1993; adminstr. wage & hour divsn. US Dept. Labor, Washington, 1993—97; asst. to Pres., dir. pub. liaison The White House, Washington, 1997-98, asst. to Pres., dep. chief staff, 1998—2001; sr. fellow Ctr. for Am. Progress; co-founder, ptnr. Nueva Vista Group LLC, 2000—. Lectr. in residence U. Calif. Berkeley Sch. Law; commentator To the Contrary; mem. exec. com. Dem. Nat. Com., 2001; sr. adv. Presdl. Campaign for Howard Dean, 2003. Bd. dirs. People for the Am. Way, Children's Law Ctr., CARE; mem. adv. bd. Woodrow Wilson Mexico Inst. Recipient Innovations in Govt. award, 1996, Dialogue on Diversity Leadership award, 2002, Nat. Hispana Leadership Inst. award, 2003; named an Outstanding Latina Leader in Govt., Latina mag., 1999. Jewish. Office: Nueva Vista Group LLC 1100 17th St NW Ste 902 Washington DC 20036 also: Center for American Progress 1333 H St NW 10th Fl Washington DC 20005 also: U Calif Berkeley 2440 Bancroft Way Office 303D Berkeley CA 94720 Office Phone: 510-643-9291. E-mail: mechaveste@law.berkeley.edu, mechaveste@americanprogress.org, mechaveste@nvgllc.com.

ECHEVESTE, JOHN ANTHONY, public relations consultant; b. Compton, Calif., Dec. 14, 1949; s. John Robert and Margaret (Suarez) E.; m. Patrician Ann Griffin, Sept. 28, 1985; childen: John Matthew, Michael Anthony. BA in Comm., Calif. State U., Fullerton, 1973. Reporter San Gabriel Valley Daily Tribune, West Covina, Calif., 1976; dir. comm. TELACU, LA, 1977-82, v.p. comm., 1985-88; adminstrv. asst. Rep. Matthew Martinez, Rosemead, Calif., 1982; mgr. pub. com. So. Calif. Assn. Govts., LA, 1982-85; ptnr. Valencia, Maldonado & Echeveste (now VPE Public Relations), Pasadena, Calif., 1988—. Chmn. East L.A. YMCA, 1993-94; mem. Calif. com. comms. Am. Cancer Soc., 1991; mem. cultural adv. bd. LA County Mus. Art, 1988; mem. L.A. Regional Family Planning Coun., 1990; chmn. comm. San Gabriel Valley chpt. United Way, 1991; bd. dirs. LA County Library Found., Bilingual Found. Arts. Mem. Hispanic Pub. Rels. Assn. (founder, pres., bd. dirs. 1982—). Democrat. Office: 1605 Hope St Ste 250 South Pasadena CA 91030-2671

ECHOHAWK, JOHN ERNEST, lawyer; b. Albuquerque, Aug. 11, 1945; s. Ernest V. and Emma Jane (Conrad) E.; m. Kathryn Suzanne Martin, Oct. 23, 1965; children: Christopher, Sarah. BA, U. N.Mex, 1967, JD, 1970. Bar: Colo. 1972, US Dist. Ct. Colo. 1972, US Appeals (8th Cir.) 1976, US Ct. Appeals (9th Cir.) 1980. Research assoc. Calif. Indian Legal Services, Escondido, 1970, Native Am. Rights Fund, Berkeley Calif. and Boulder, Colo., 1970-72, dep. dir. Boulder, 1972-73, 1975-77, exec. dir., 1973-75, 1977—. Mem. task force Am. Indian Policy Rev. Commn., US Senate, Washington, 1976-77; bd. dirs. Am. Indian Lawyer Tng. Program, Oakland, Calif., 1975—; bd. dirs. Assn. Am. Indian Affairs, 1980—, Nat. Com. Responsive Philanthropy, Washington, 1981-2000; mem. Clinton Adminstrn. Transition Team for Interior Dept., 1992-93, Pres.-elect Barack Obama's Transition Team, 2008. Presdl. appointee Western Water Policy Rev. Adv. Commn., 1995-97; Ind. Sector, Washington, 1986-92; mem. Natural Resources Def. Coun., NYC, 1988—; bd. dirs. Nat. Ctr. Enterprise Devel., 1988—, Keystone Ctr., 1993-99, Environ. and Energy Study Inst., 1994—. Recipient Disting. Svc. award Ams. for Indian Opportunity, 1982, Pres. Indian Svc. award Nat. Congress Am. Indians, 1984, Annual Indian Achievement award Indian Coun. Fire, 1987; named one of Most Influential Attys. Nat. Law Jour., 1988, 91, 94, 97, 2000. Mem. Native Am. Bar Assn., Colo. Indian Bar Assn. Democrat. Avocations: fishing, skiing. Office: Native Am Rights Fund 1506 Broadway St Boulder CO 80302-6217 Office Phone: 303-447-8760. Office Fax: 303-443-7776.

ECHOHAWK, LARRY, lawyer, former state attorney general; b. Cody, Wyo., Aug. 2, 1948; m. Terry Pries, 1968; children: Jennifer, Paul, Mark, Matthew, Emily, Michael. BS, Brigham Young U., 1970; JD, U. Utah, 1973; postgraduate, U. N.Mex., 1970, Stanford U., 1974—75, Catholic U., 1971. Bar: Utah 1973, Calif. 1974, Idaho 1979. With Calif. Indian Legal Svcs., Oakland; pvt. practice law Salt Lake City; chief gen. counsel Shoshone-Bannock Tribes, 1977-85; mem. Idaho House of Reps. from Dist. 33, 1983—84, Idaho House of Reps. from Dist. 27, 1985—86; prosecutor Bannock County, Idaho, 1986—91; atty. gen. State of Idaho, Boise, 1991—95; of counsel EchoHawk Law Offices PLLC, Pocatello, Idaho. Prof. law J. Reuben Clark Sch. Law, Brigham Young U., 1995—2001. Active Idaho Bd. Land Commissioners; mem. exec. com. Conf. Western Attys. Gen.; active Idaho Elder Care Coalition; mem. exec. bd. Ore-Ida Boy Scout Coun.; chmn. Idaho Job Tng. Coun., 1989-90; vice-chmn. Idaho Commn. for Children and Youth, 1989-90; speaker Dem. Nat. Conv., 1992; mem. steering com. Dem. Policy Commn., 1985-87; bd. visitors, J. Reuben Clark Law Sch. Served in USMC. Recipient Martin Luther King medal George Washington U., 1991, Disting. Alumni award U. Utah, 2003, NCAA Silver Anniversary award, Prof. of the Yr. award Brigham Young U. J. Reuben Clark Law Sch., Alumni Disting. Svc. award Brigham Young U., Am. Indian Disting. Achevement award; named one of 20 People to Watch Newsweek mag., 1991, The 20 Most Promising People in Politics USA Weekend Mem. ABA, Am. Indian Bar Assn., Calif. Bar Assn., Utah Bar Assn., Idaho Bar Assn. (Outstanding Svc. award 1986), Nat. Dist. Attorneys Assn., mem. Attys. Against Hunger Project, Nat. Assn. Attys. Gen. (mem. exec. com., v.p), Pawnee Tribe, Phi Delta Kappa (Friend of Edn. award 1985). Democrat. Lds. Achievements include the first Native American in US history to be elected attorney general of State of Idaho, 1991. Office: EchoHawk Law Offices PLLC 151 N 4th Ave Ste A PO Box 6119 Pocatello ID 83205 Office Phone: 208-478-1624. E-mail: echohawkl@echohawk.com.*

ECK, DOROTHY FRITZ, state legislator; b. Sequim, Wash., Jan. 23, 1924; d. Ira Edward and Ida (Hokanson) Fritz; m. Hugo Eck, Dec. 16, 1942 (dec. Feb. 1988); children: Laurence, Diana. BS in Secondary Edn., Mont. State U., 1961, MS in Applied Sci., 1966. Mgr. property mgmt. bus., 1955—; conf. coord. Am. Argl. Econs. Assn., 1967-68; state-local coord. Office of Gov. Mont., Helena, 1972-77; mem. Mont. State Senate, 1981—, Mont. Environ. Quality Coun., 1981-87. Bd. dirs. Meth. Youth Fellowship, 1960-64, Mont. Coun. for Effective Legislature, 1977-78, Rocky Mountain Environ. Coun., 1982—; del. Western v.p. Mont. Constl. Conv., 1971-72; chmn. Gov.'s Task Force on Citizen Participation, 1976-77; mem. adv. com. No. Rockies Resource and Tng. Ctr. (now No. Lights Inst.), 1979-81. Recipient Outstanding Alumna award Mont. State U., 1981, Centennial Faculty award, 1989. Mem. LWV (state pres. 1967-70), Common Cause, Nat. Women's Polit. Caucus. Democrat. Home: 10 W Garfield St Bozeman MT 59715-5602 Office: State Senate State Capitol Helena MT 59620

ECK, ROBERT EDWIN, retired physicist; b. Ames, Iowa, Nov. 28, 1938; s. John Clifford and Helen (Behrendt) E.; m. Carolyn Jennie Vodicka, May 11, 1974; children: David Michael, Elizabeth Claire. BA in Physics, Rutgers U., 1960; MS in Physics, U. Pa., 1962, PhD in Physics, 1966; MA in Econs., U. Calif., Santa Barbara, 1973. Sr. rsch. scientist Ford Motor Co., Newport Beach, Calif., 1966-69; project engr. Santa Barbara Rsch. Ctr., Goleta, Calif., 1969-73, asst. mgr. infrared components, 1974-81, mgr. major program, 1982-84, dir. tech., 1985-88, dir./mgr. engring., 1989-95; new bus. devel. mgr. R.G. Hansen & Assocs., Santa Barbara, Calif., 1995-96; program mgr. Optoelectronics-Textron, Petaluma, 1996-2000; adminstrv. dir. Enhancement Inst., Houston, 2002—03. Bd. dirs. Goleta Edn. Found. Mem. Goleta Noontime Rotary Club (pres. 1989-90). Achievements include patents on superconductors, infrared detector testing and magnetoresistor sensors.

ECKER, JOSEPH R., plant molecular and cellular biologist; BA in Biology and Chemistry, Coll. NJ, Ewing; PhD in Microbiol., Pa. State U. Coll. Medicine. Postdoctoral fellow Stanford U. Sch. Medicine, Calif.; faculty mem. U. Pa., 1987—2000; prof. plant biology lab. Salk Inst. Biol. Studies, La Jolla, 2000—, dir. genome analysis lab., 2000—. Contbr. articles to sci. jours.; editl. bd.: Pub. Libr. of Sci. Genetics. Recipient Kumho Sci. Internat. award in plant molecular biology and biotechnology, 2001, Disting. Rsch. award, Internat. Plant Growth Substances Assn., 2004, Martin Gibbs medal, Am. Soc. Plant

Biologists, 2005. Mem.: NAS (John J. Carty award for the Advancement of Sci. 2007), Internat. Soc. Plant Molecular Biology (pres.). Achievements include the sequencing of the common mustard seed Arabidopsis and the discovery of a method to identify its functional genes; being named a rsch. leader in agr. Sci. Am. 50, 2004. Office: Salk Inst for Biol Studies PO Box 85800 San Diego CA 92186-5800

ECKERT, RINDE, composer, librettist; m. Ellen McLaughlin. Librettist (musical theater prodns.) Slow Fire, 1986 (San Francisco Critics Cir. award, Best Solo Performance, 1988), Pioneer, 1990, Awed Behavior, 1993, author, composer Not For Real, 1987 (San Francisco Critics Cir. award, Best New Theater Performance, 1987), Romeo Sierra Tango, 1995, Power Failure, 1989, Ravenshead, 1998, author, composer, dir. Navigators, 1999, author, composer, performer And God Created Great Whales, 2000 (Obie award, 2000), An Idiot Divine, 2001, Highway Ulysses, 2003 (Eliot Norton award, 2003), Horizon, 2005 (Lucille Lontel award, 2008), Orpheus X, 2006 (Pulitzer Prize in Drama finalist, 2007); composer: (dance scores) Shelf Life, 1987 (Isadora Duncan award, 1988), Woman, Window, Square, 1990, The Gardening of Thomas D, 1992; musician: (albums) Finding My Way Home, 1992, Do the Day Over, 1995, Story In, Story Out, 1997, Sandhills Reunion, 2004. Recipient Marc Blitzstein award, AAAL, 2005, Aipert award, 2009; fellow Guggenheim Found., 2007. Office: c/o Susan Endrizzi Calif Artists Mgmt PO Box 2479 Mendocino CA 95460-2479 Office Phone: 707-937-4787. Business E-Mail: sue@calartists.com. E-mail: sue.endrizzi@gmail.com.

ECKERT, ROBERT A., consumer products company executive; m. Kathie Eckert; 4 children. BSBA, U. Ariz., 1976; MBA in Mktg. and Fin., Northwestern U., 1977. Various mktg. positions Kraft Foods, 1977-87, v.p. strategy and devel. grocery products divsn., 1987-89, v.p. mktg. refrigerated products, 1989-90, v.p., gen. mgr. cheese divsn., 1990-97, pres., CEO, 1997-2000; chmn. bd., CEO Mattel, Inc., 2000—. Bd. dirs. McDonalds Corp., 2003—; com. mem. Trilateral Commn. Active adv. bd. J.L. Kellogg Grad. Sch. Mgmt., Northwestern U.; bd. visitors, Anderson Sch., UCLA; bd. dirs., mem. exec. com. Met. Family Svcs.; trustee Ravinia Festival Assn., Art Inst. Chgo.; nat. trustee Lake Forest Coll. Bd. dirs., chmn. govt. affairs coun. Grocery Mfrs. Am.; bd. dirs. L.A. World Affairs Coun., Bus. Coun., Wash. D.C.; mem. Asia Society, Young Presidents' Org., L.A., Town Hall L.A. Office: Mattel Inc 333 Continental Blvd El Segundo CA 90245-5012 Fax: 310-252-2179.

ECKHART, AARON, actor; b. Cupertino, Calif., Mar. 12, 1968; BA, Brigham Young U., 1994. Actor: (films) Slaughter of the Innocents, 1994, In the Company of Men, 1997 (Ind. Spirit award for Best Debut Performance, 1998, Satellite Spl. Achievement award for Outstanding New Talent, 1998), Your Friends & Neighbors, 1998, Thursday, 1998, Molly, 1999, Any Given Sunday, 1999, Tumble, 2000, Erin Brockovich, 2000, Nurse Betty, 2000, The Pledge, 2001, Possession, 2002, The Core, 2003, The Missing, 2003, Paycheck, 2003, Suspect Zero, 2004, Conversations with Other Women, 2005, Thank You for Smoking, 2006, The Black Dahlia, 2006, The Wicker Man, 2006, No Reservations, 2007, The Dark Knight, 2008, Nothing Is Private, 2008, Towelhead, 2008; actor, co-prodr. (films) Neverwas, 2005; actor: (TV films) Double Jeopardy, 1992; (TV miniseries) Ancient Secrets of the Bible, Part II, 1993; (TV series) Aliens in the Family, 1996. Office: c/o Barry Hirsch and David Matlof 23rd Fl 10100 Santa Monica Blvd Los Angeles CA 90067

ECKHART, WALTER, molecular biologist, educator; b. Yonkers, NY, May 22, 1938; s. Walter and Jean E. BS, Yale U., 1960; postgrad., Cambridge U., Eng., 1960-61; PhD, U. Calif.-Berkeley, 1965. Postdoctoral fellow Salk Inst., San Diego, 1965-69, mem., 1970-73, assoc. prof. molecular biology, 1973-79, prof., 1979—, cancer ctr. dir., 1976—2007. Adj. prof. U. Calif.-San Diego, 1973-2003. Contbr. articles on molecular biology and virology to profl. jours. NIH research grantee, 1967-2008. Mem. AAAS, Am. Soc. Microbiology. Home: 951 Skylark Dr La Jolla CA 92037-7731 Office: Salk Inst PO Box 85800 San Diego CA 92186-5800 Home Phone: 858-454-6566; Office Phone: 858-453-4100 1386. Business E-Mail: eckhart@salk.edu.

ECKSTEIN, MIGUEL P., psychology professor; BS in Physic & Psychology, U. Calif., Berkeley, 1990; MA in Cognitive Psychology, U. Calif., LA, 1991, PhD in Vision, 1994. Rsch. assoc. scientist Cedars-Sinai Med. Ctr., Dept. Med. Physics; prof., psychology U. Calif., Santa-Barbara. Contbr. several articles to profl. publications. Co-recipient Troland Rsch. award, NAS, 2008. Office: Dept Psychology U California Santa Barbara Psychology East Building 251 Room 3806 Santa Barbara CA 93106-9660 Office Phone: 805-893-2255. Office Fax: 805-893-4303. Business E-Mail: eckstein@psych.ucsb.edu.

ECKSTROM, JOHN, health facility administrator; b. San Francisco; Diploma in Psychology, San Francisco State U. Various exec. positions TRW, Bank of Am., Charles Schwab; CEO Haight Ashbury Free Clinics, Inc., San Francisco, 2006—. Vol. drug treatment program counselor, East Contra Costa County, Calif.; crisis counselor Ctrl. Emergency Hosp., San Francisco. Office: Haight Ashbury Free Clinics Inc PO Box 29917 San Francisco CA 94129 Office Phone: 415-552-2114. Office Fax: 415-552-2243.

ECKSTUT, MICHAEL KAUDER, management consultant; b. Prague, Czechoslovakia, Mar. 13, 1952; came to U.S., 1960; s. Robert and Erika Kauder (Neumann) E.; m. Mary Jane Haymond, May 21, 1978; children: Martina, Robert. BS in Chem. Engring., Rensselaer Poly., 1973, MS in Chem. Engring., 1974; MBA, Harvard U., 1978. Chem. engr. E.I. DuPont de Nemours, Wilmington, Del., 1974-76; assoc. Idanta Ptnrs., La Jolla, Calif., 1978-79; v.p. Booz, Allen & Hamilton, Inc., NYC, 1979-93, A.T. Kearney Inc., NYC, 1993-99; sr. v.p. bus. devel. Chemconnect, San Francisco, 1999—. Home: 110 Las Lomas Ln Belvedere Tiburon CA 94920-1960

ECTON, DONNA R., business executive; b. Kansas City, Mo., May 10, 1947; d. Allen Howard and Marguerite E.; m. Victor H. Maragni, June 16, 1986; children: Mark, Gregory. BA (Durant Scholar), Wellesley Coll., 1969; MBA, Harvard U., 1971. V.p. Chem. Bank, NYC, 1972-79, Citibank, N.A., NYC, 1979-81; pres. MBA Resources, Inc., NYC, 1981-83; v.p. adminstrn., officer Campbell Soup Co., Camden, NJ, 1983-89; chmn. Triangle Mfg. Corp. subs. Campbell Soup Co., Raleigh, NC, 1984-87; sr. v.p., officer Nutri/System, Inc., Willow Grove, Pa., 1989-91; pres., CEO Van Houten N.Am., Delavan, Wis., 1991-94, Andes Candies Inc., Delavan, 1991-94; chmn., pres., CEO Bus. Mail Express, Inc., Malvern, Pa., 1995-96; bd. dirs. PETsMART, Inc., Phoenix, 1994—98, COO, 1996-98; chmn., pres., CEO EEI Inc., Paradise Valley, 1998—. Commencement spkr. Pa. State U., 1987; bd. dirs. Johns Hopkins' JHPIEGO, Balt., 2004—07, CVR GP LLC, Houston, 2008—. Bd. overseers Harvard U., 1984-90; mem. Coun. Fgn. Rels., NYC, 1987—; trustee Inst. for Advancement of Health, 1988-92. Named one of 80 Women to Watch in the 80's, Ms. mag., 1980, one of All Time Top 10 of Last Decade, Glamour mag., 1984, one of 50 Women to Watch, Bus. Week mag., 1987, one of 100 Women to Watch, Bus. Month mag., 1989; recipient Wellesley Alumnae Achievement award, 1987; Fred Sheldon Fund fellow Harvard U., 1971-72; Margaret Rudkin scholar Harvard U., 1969-71. Mem. Harvard Bus. Sch. Assn. (pres. exec. council 1983-84), Harvard Bus. Sch. Club Greater N.Y. (pres. 1979-80), Wellesley Coll. Nat. Alumnae Assn. (bd. dirs., 1st v.p. 1977-80). Avocations: public speaking, art, gardening, reading, bicycling.

EDDY, ALLISON, nephrologist, educator; b. Can. arrived in US, 1997, naturalized, 2008; MD, McMaster U., Hamilton, Ontario, 1975. Diplomate Am. Bd. Pediat., 1981, in pediatric nephrology Am. Bd. Pediat., 1985. Instr. U. Minn., Mpls., 1984—85; asst. prof. U. Toronto, Ont., Canada, 1985—92, assoc. prof., 1992—97, with Inst. Med. Sci., 1993—97; dir. postgraduate edn. in pediatric nephrology Hosp. Sick Children, Toronto, 1991—97; scientist Rsch. Inst., 1996—97; vis. assoc. prof. McMaster U., Hamilton, 1995—96; head divsn. pediatric nephrology Children's Hosp. and Regional Med. Ctr., Seattle, 1997—; prof. U. Wash., Seattle, 1997—, program dir., pediat. nephrology fellowship, 2001—08, Dr. Robert O. Hickman endowed chair in pediatric nephrology, 2007—; dir., Ctr. Tissue and Cell Biology Seattle Children's Hosp. Rsch. Inst., 2007—. Grantee Rsch. grant, NIH/NIDDK, 1999—, NIH/NICHD, 2003—, Children's Hosp. and Regional Med. Ctr., 2006—08, Basic Rsch. Steering Com. award, NIH/NIDDK, 2002—, Rsch. grant, Puget Sound Partners for Global Health, 2007—09; grant, Cystinosis Rsch. Found., 2008—. Mem.: Internat. Pediatric Nephrology Assn., Can. Assn. Pediatric Nephrologists, Women in Nephrology, NW Renal Soc., King County Med. Soc., Am. Pediatric Soc., Royal Coll. Physicians and Surgeons Can., Internat. Soc. Nephrology, Am. Soc. Nephrology, Am. Soc. Pediatric Nephrology, Am. Assn. Pathologists, Nat. Kidney Found., Am. Assn. Immunologists, Am. Physiol. Soc., Australian and New Zealand Soc. Nephrology (hon.). Avocations: skiing, hiking, squash. Office: Children's Hosp 4800 Sand Point Way NE A-7931 Seattle WA 98105 Office Phone: 206-987-2524. Office Fax: 206-987-2636. Business E-Mail: allison.eddy@seattlechildrens.org.

EDDY, DAVID MAXON, health policy and management advisor; BA, Stanford U., Calif., 1964, PhD with great distinction, 1978; MD, U. Va., 1968. Gen. surg. intern Stanford U. Med. Ctr., 1968-69, resident, postdoct. fellow cardiovascular surgery, 1969-71, acting asst. prof., 1976-78; asst. prof. dept. engring.-econ. sys. Stanford U., 1978-80, prof., 1980-81; J. Alexander McMahon prof. health policy and mgmt. Duke U., 1986-90, prof. health policy and mgmt., 1980—95; dir. WHO Collaborating Ctr. for Rsch. in Cancer Policy, 1984-95. Sr. advisor health policy, mgmt. Kaiser Permanente So. Calif. Region, 1991—; columnist Jour. of the AMA, 1990—; spl. govt. employee Hillary Rodham Clinton's Health Care Task Force, 1993; expert adv. panel on cancer WHO, 1981-96; founder, dir. Archimedes, Inc., San Francisco, Calif.; cons. numerous cos., orgns. and assns. Author: A Manual for Assessing Health Practices and Designing Practice Policies, 1992, FAST*PRO: Software for Meta-Analysis by the Confidence Profile Method, 1992, The Synthesis of Statistical Evidence: meta-Analysis by the Confidence Profile Method, 1992, Common Screening Tests, 1991, Screening for Cancer: Theory, Analysis and Design, 1980, (Lanchester Prize, 1981), Clinical Decision Making: From Theory to Practice, 1996; contbr. articles to profl. jours. Recipient Sci. and Technol. Achievement award EPA, 1993, FHP Prize Internat. Soc. of Tech. Assessment in Health Care, 1991, USQA Quality Algorithm award, 1995, Novartis Outcomes Leadership award, 1997, Founders award Am. Coll. Med. Quality, 1998, Disting. Achievement award, CDC, 2005. Mem. Inst. of Medicine, Nat. Acad. Scis.

EDDY, DEBORAH H., state legislator; m. Jon Eddy; 3 children. BS, W.Va. U., 1976; JD, U. NC, 1979. City coun. mem. City of Kirkland, 1994—2000, mayor; exec. dir. Suburban Cities Assn.; mem. Dist. 48 Wash. House of Reps., 2006—, majority caucus vice chair, 2009—. Founding bd. mem. Eastside Domestic Violence Program. Fellow: Cascadia Ctr. for Regional Transp. Democrat. Office: 132D Legislative Bldg PO Box 40600 Olympia WA 98504 Office Phone: 360-786-7848. E-mail: eddy.deb@leg.wa.gov.

EDELBROCK, O. VICTOR, automotive part manfacturing executive; m. Nancy E.; 1 child, Cathleen. Chmn., CEO Edelbrock Corp., Torrance, Calif., 1962—. Office: Edelbrock Corp 2700 California St Torrance CA 90503

EDELMAN, GERALD MAURICE, biochemist, neuroscientist, educator; b. NYC, July 1, 1929; s. Edward and Anna (Freedman) Edelman; m. Maxine Morrison, June 11, 1950; children: Eric, David, Judith. BS, Ursinus Coll., 1950, ScD, 1974; MD, U. Pa., 1954, DSc, 1973; MD (hon.), U. Siena, Italy, 1974; DSc (hon.), Gustavus Adolphus Coll., 1975, Williams Coll., 1976, U. Paris, 1989; LSc (hon.), U. Cagliari, 1989; DSc (hon.), Georgetown U., 1989, U. degli Studi di Napoli, 1990, Tulane U., 1991, U. Miami, 1995, Adelphi U., 1995, U. Bologna, 1998, U. Minn., 2000, Academiae Moscovlensis, Moscow State U., 2008, Rockefeller U., 2008, PhD, 1960; MD (hon.), U de A Coruña, Spain, 2000. Med. house officer Mass. Gen. Hosp., 1954—55; asst. physician hosp. of Rockefeller U., 1957—60, mem. faculty, 1960—92, assoc. dean grad. studies, 1963—66, prof., 1966—74, Vincent Astor disting. prof., 1974—92; mem. faculty and chmn. dept. neurobiology Scripps Rsch. Inst., La Jolla, Calif., 1992—. Mem. biophysics and biophys. chemistry study sect. NIH, 1964—67; mem. Sci. Council Ctr. for Theoretical Studies, 1970—72, assoc., sci. chmn. Neurosciences Research Program, 1980—, dir. Neuroscis. Inst., 1981—; mem. adv. bd. Basel Inst. Immunology, 1970—77, chmn., 1975—77; non-resident fellow, trustee Salk Inst., 1973—85; bd. overseers Faculty Arts and Scis. U. Pa., 1976—83; trustee, mem. adv. com. Carnegie Inst., Washington, 1980—87; bd. govs. Weizman Inst. Sci., 1971—87, mem. emeritus; researcher structure of antibodies, molecular and devel. biology. Author: The Mindful Brain, 1978, Neural Darwinism, 1987, Topobiology, 1988, The Remembered Present, 1989, Bright Air, Brilliant Fire, 1992, A Universe of Consciousness: How Matter Becomes Imagination, 2000, Wider than the Sky: The Phenomenal Gift of Consciousness, 2004, Second Nature: Brain Science and Human Knowledge, 2006. Trustee Rockefeller Bros. Found., 1972—82. Capt. M.C. US Army, 1955—57. Recipient Spencer Morris award U. Pa., U. Pa., 1954, Ann. Alumni award, Ursinus Coll., 1969, Nobel prize for physiology or medicine, 1972, Albert Einstein Commemorative award, Yeshiva U., 1974, Buchman Meml. award, Calif. Inst. Tech., 1975, Rabbi Shai Shacknai meml. prize, Hebrew U.-Hadassah Med. Sch., Jerusalem, 1977, Regents medal Excellence, N.Y. State, 1984, Hans Neurath prize, U. Wash., 1986, Sesquicentennial Commemorative award, Nat. Libr. Medicine, 1986, Cécile and Oskar Vogt award, U. Dusseldorf, 1988, Disting. Grad. award, U. Pa., 1990, Personnalité de l'année, Paris, 1990, Warren Triennial Prize award, Mass. Gen. Hosp., 1992, C.V. Ariens-Kappers medal, 1999, medal of the Presidency of the Italian Republic, 1999, medaille de la Ville de Paris, 2002, Cátedra Santiago Grisolia prize, Spain, 2003, Caianiello Internat. award, INNS, 2003, Calabria award, Italy, 2003. Fellow: AAAS, N.Y. Acad. Medicine, N.Y. Acad. Scis.; mem.: NAS, Am. Chem. Soc. (Eli Lilly award biol. chemistry 1965), Century Assn., Coun. Fgn. Rels., Soc. Developmental Biology, Acad. Scis. of Inst. France (fgn.), Am. Soc. Cell Biology, Japanese Biochem. Soc. (hon.), Pharm. Soc. Japan (hon.), Am. Acad. Arts and Scis., Harvey Soc. (pres. 1976—77), Genetics Soc. Am., Am. Assn. Immunologists, Am. Soc. Biol. Chemists, Am. Philos. Soc., Cosmos Club, Alpha Omega Alpha, Sigma Xi, Phi Beta Kappa. Office: Scripps Rsch Inst Dept Neurobiol SBR-14 10550 N Torrey Pines Rd La Jolla CA 92037-1000

EDELMAN, LAUREN B., sociologist, law educator; d. Murray J. and Bacia Edelman. JD, Boalt Hall, 1986; PhD, Stanford U., 1986. Asst. to assoc. prof. U. Wis., Madison, 1986—96; Agnes Roddy Robb prof. law and prof. sociology U. Calif., Berkeley, 1996—. Fellow, Guggenheim Found., 2000, Ctr. for Advanced Study in the Behavioral Scis., 2003—04, 2005—06. Mem.: Am. Sociol. Assn. (chair, sociology of law sect. 1993—94, Dist. Scholarship award 1995), Law and Soc. Assn. (pres. 2002—03). Achievements include research in analyses of relationship between employment law and organizational governance. Office: JSP Program/ UC Berkeley 2240 Piedmont Ave Berkeley CA 94720-2150 Office Fax: 510-642-2951. Business E-Mail: ledelman@law.berkeley.edu.

EDELMAN, SCOTT ALAN, lawyer; b. Mar. 25, 1959; BA with distinction, Stanford U., 1981; JD, U. Calif., 1984. Bar: Calif. 1984. Law clk. to Hon. Jesse W. Curtis US Dist. Ct. (ctrl. dist.) Calif., 1984—85; co-chair Media and Entertainment Practice Group Gibson, Dunn & Crutcher LLP, LA, ptnr. Litigation Dept. and Intellectual Property Group, Nat. Pro Bono coord. Contbr. chapters to books. Chmn. bd. dir. KCET Pub. TV, exec. com.; bd. dir. Bet Tzedek Legal Svcs., past pres. Named one of Best Lawyers in Am., Am. Lawyer Media, Am. Leading Lawyers for Bus., Chambers USA, 2006, Hollywood's Top Litigators, Daily Variety, 2007, 100 Power Lawyers, Hollywood Reporter, 2007; named to LA Super Lawyers, LA Mag. Office: Gibson Dunn & Crutcher LLP 1043 Roscomare Rd Los Angeles CA 90077-2227 Office Phone: 310-557-8061. Office Fax: 310-552-7041. Business E-Mail: sedelman@gibsondunn.com.

EDELSTEIN, CHARLES BRUCE, investment banker, education company executive; b. Chgo., Dec. 30, 1959; s. Paul Harold and Lois Jean (Resnick) E. BS in Acctg., U. Ill., 1982; MBA, Harvard U., 1987. CPA, Ill. Cons. Price Waterhouse, Chgo., 1982-84, sr. cons., 1984-85; assoc. in investment banking Credit Suisse (The First Boston Corp.), Chgo., 1987-91; v.p. Credit Suisse, 1991—98, mng. dir., head global services group, investment banking div., 1998—2008; CEO Apollo Group, Inc., Phoenix, 2008—09, joint CEO, 2009—. Baker Scholar. Avocations: piano, tennis. Office: Apollo Group 4025 S Riverpoint Pkwy Phoenix AZ 85040*

EDELSTEIN, MARK GERSON, college president; BA in English, Colby Coll., 1968; MA in English, U. N.H., 1971; PhD in English, SUNY, Stony Brook, 1982. English faculty Palomar C.C., 1976-85; exec. dir. intersegmental coordinating coun. Coll. of Redwoods, 1987-91, v.p. acad. affairs, 1991-96; pres. Diablo Valley Coll., 1996—. Pres. acad. senate Calif. C.C.; spkr. in field. Co-author: Inside Writing. Office: Diablo Valley Coll 321 Golf Club Rd Pleasant Hill CA 94523-1529

EDENS, GARY DENTON, broadcast executive; b. Asheville, NC, Jan. 6, 1942; s. James Edwin and Pauline Amanda (New) E.; m. Hannah Suellen Walter, Aug. 21, 1965; children: Ashley Elizabeth, Emily Blair. BS, U. N.C., 1964. Account exec. PAMS Prodns., Dallas, 1965-67, Sta. WKIX, Raleigh, NC, 1967-69; gen. mgr. Sta. KOY, Phoenix, 1970-81; sr. v.p. Harte-Hanks Raido, Inc., Phoenix, 1978-81, pres., CEO, 1981-84; chmn., CEO Edens Broadcasting, Inc., 1984-95. Dir. Citibank Ariz., 1986—, Inter-Tel, Inc., 1994-2007; chmn. The Hanover Cos., Inc., 1995—; chair fin. seminar Chief Execs. Orgn./World Pres. Orgn., N.Y.C., 1998. Bd. dirs. Valley Big Bros., 1972-80, Ariz. State U. Found., 1979—, COMPAS, 1979—, Men's Arts Coun., 1975-78. Named one of Three Outstanding Young Men, Phoenix Jaycees, 1973; entrepreneurial fellow U. Ariz., 1989; inducted into Ariz. Broadcasters Assn. Hall of Fame, 2000. Mem. Phoenix Execs. Club (pres. 1976), Nat. Radio Broadcasters Assn. (dir. 1981-86), Radio Advt. Bur. (dir. 1981—), Young Pres. Orgn. (chmn. Ariz. chpt. 1989-90), Chief Execs. Orgn., Ariz. Pres. Orgn. Republican. Methodist. Office: 5112 N 40th St Ste 102 Phoenix AZ 85018-2142 E-mail: ge@garyedens.com.

EDGAR, JAMES MACMILLAN, JR., management consultant; b. NYC, Nov. 7, 1936; s. James Macmillan Edgar and Lilyan (McCann) E.; m. Judith Frances Storey, June 28, 1958; children: Suzanne Lynn Randolph, James Macmillan III, Gordon Stuart. B in Chem. Engring., Cornell U., 1959, MBA with distinction, 1960. CPA; cert. mgmt. cons. New product rep. E.I. duPont Nemours, Wilmington, Del., 1960-63, mktg. svcs. rep., 1963-64; with Touche Ross & Co., 1964-78, mgr. Detroit, 1966-68, ptnr. in charge, mgt. svcs. ops. for No. Calif. and Hawaii San Francisco, 1971-78, ptnr. Western regional mgmt. svcs., 1978; sr. ptnr. Edgar, Dunn & Co., San Francisco, 1978-2000; ind. mgmt. cons., 2000—. Bd. dirs. Assoc. Oreg. Industries Svcs. Corp.; ptnr. Global Brand Positioning LLC, 2001—; owner Western Sport Shop, San Rafael, Calif., Santa Rosa, Calif. Patentee nonwoven fabrice. Active San Francisco Mayor's Fin. Adv. Com., 1976-2001, exec. com., 1978-2001, Blue Ribbon com. for Bus., 1987-88, Alumnae Resources adv. bd., 1986-94, San Francisco Planning and Urban Rsch. Bd., 1986-89, adv. bd., 1989-93; alumni exec. coun. Johnson Grad. Sch. Mgmt. Cornell U., Cornell Coun., 1970-73; steering com. Bay Area Coun., 1989-95, program adv. com., 1996-2001, bd. dirs., 1999-2001; chmn. San Francisco Libr. Found., 1989-96; bd. dirs. Rosenberg Found., 1996-2004, chmn. bd. dirs., 2001-02; bd. dirs. Harding Lawson Assoc. Group, 1996-2000, Golden Gate U., 1997-99; mem. San Francisco Com. on Jobs, 1994-2000; trustee The Buck Inst. Age Rsch., 2007—. Recipient Merit award for outstanding pub. svc. City and County of San Francisco, 1978, Honor award for outstanding contbns. to profl. mgmt. Johnson Grad. Sch. Mgmt., Cornell U., 1978. Mem. AICPA, Assn. Corp. Growth (v.p. membership San Francisco chpt. 1979-81, v.p. programs 1981-82, pres. 1982-83, nat. bd. dirs. 1983-86), Calif. Soc. CPAs, Inst. Mgmt. Cons. (regional v.p. 1973-80, bd. dirs. 1975-77, v.p. 1977-80), San Francisco C. of C. (bd. dirs. 1987-89, 1991-2003, mem. exec. com. 1988-89, 91-95, chmn. mktg. San Francisco program 1991-92, membership devel. 1993, chmn. bd. dirs. 1994, dir. emeritus 1995-2003), Pacific Union Club, Marin Rod and Gun Club, Tau Beta Pi. Home: 10 Buckeye Way San Rafael CA 94904-2602 Office: James Edgar Mgmt Cons 10 Buckeye Way Kentfield CA 94904-2602 Office Phone: 415-279-4107. Personal E-mail: jedgarconsulting@aol.com, jedgar7777@aol.com.

EDGERTON, BRADFORD WHEATLY, plastic surgeon; b. Phila., May 8, 1947; s. Milton Thomas and Patricia Jane (Jones) E.; children: Bradford Wheatly Jr., Lauren Harrington; m. Louise Dungan Edgerton; stepchildren: Catherine Kelleher, Robert Kelleher. BA in Chemistry, Vanderbilt U., 1969, MD, 1973. Diplomate Am. Bd. Plastic Surgery, Am. Bd. Hand Surgery. Intern U. Calif., San Francisco, 1973-74; resident U. Va., Charlottesville, 1974-78; resident in plastic surgery Columbia-Presbyn., NY, 1979-81; fellow in hand surgery NYU, 1981-82, clin. instr. plastic surgery, 1981-89; ptnr. So. Calif. Permanente Med. Group, LA, 1989—; assoc. prof. clin. plastic surgery U. So. Calif., LA, 1989—. Mem. Pacific Coun. Internat. Policy. Trustee Harvard-Westlake Sch., L.A., 2001—; pres. Edgerton Found., Beverly Hills, Calif, 2001-. Mem. Am. Assn. Hand Surgery, Am. Soc. Plastic and Reconstructive Surgery, Am. Soc. Surgery of Hand, L.A. (Calif.) Tennis Club, L.A. (Calif.) Country Club Episcopal. Home: 494 S Spalding Dr Beverly Hills CA 90212-4104 Office: 6041 Cadillac Ave Los Angeles CA 90034-1702

EDGINGTON, THOMAS S., pathologist, molecular and vascular biologist, educator; b. LA, Feb. 10, 1932; BA in Biol. Scis., Stanford U., 1953, MD, 1957. Diplomate Am. Bd. Pathology, spl. cert. immunopathology. Intern Hosp. Univ. Pa., Phila., 1957—58; resident Ctr. Health Scis. UCLA, 1958—60; sr. postdoctoral fellow immunology Scripps Clinic & Rsch. Found., La Jolla, Calif., 1965—68, assoc. mem. dept. exptl. pathology, 1968—71; founder, head dept. anatomic pathology and lab. medicine Scripps Clinic and Rsch. Found., La Jolla, 1968—74, prof. depts. immunology and vascular biology, 1971—; asst. prof., surg. pathologist dept. pathology UCLA Sch. Medicine, 1962—65; assoc. adj. prof. pathology U. Calif., San Diego, La Jolla, 1968—75, adj. prof., 1975—. Cons. Centocor, 1993—95, Eli Lilly, 1982—85, Becton-Dickinson, 1977—80; founder, bd. dirs. Corvas Internat., NuVas. Contbr. numerous articles to profl. jours. Recipient Coll. de France medal, 1981, John A. Lynch Molecular Biology award, U. Notre Dame, 1992, Rous-Whipple prize, Am. Soc. Investigative Pathology, 1995, Disting. Career award, Internat. Soc. Thrombosis and Hemostatis, 1995. Fellow: AAAS; mem.: Inst. of Medicine of NAS, Thrombosis Inst. (bd. sci. govs. 1995—), Internat. Soc. Thrombosis and Hemostatis, Fedn. Am. Socs. Exptl. Biology (pres. 1990—91, chmn. bd. 1990—91). Office: The Scripps Rsch Inst C-204 10550 N Torrey Pines Rd # C204 La Jolla CA 92037-1000 E-mail: tsedgington@hotmail.com.

EDGINTON, JOHN ARTHUR, lawyer; b. Kingsburg, Calif., July 23, 1935; s. Arthur George and Pochantas Clementina (Ball) E.; m. Jane Ann Simmons, June 25, 1960. AA, U. Calif., Berkeley, 1955, AB in Econs., 1957, JD, 1963. Bar: Calif. 1964, No. Marianas 1969, US Ct. Claims 1969, US Ct. Appeals (9th cir.) 1969, US Supreme Ct. 1969. Assoc. Graham & James, San Francisco, 1964-71, ptnr., 1971-94, Dezurick Edginton & Harrington LLP, Emeryville, Calif., 1994-98, Booth Banning LLP, San Francisco, 1999-2000; pvt. practice Point Richmond, Calif., 2000—. Author: Maritime Bankruptcy, 1989, Benedict on Admiralty, vol. 3B and 3C; editor-in-chief Maritime Practice and Procedure, vol. 29 Moore's Federal Practice, 1997, Benedict's Maritime Bull., 2003; editor Maritime Desk Reference, Benedict on Admiralty, vol. 8, 2001; contbr. articles to profl. jours. Bd. dirs. Richmond Conv. and Visitors Bur., 2004—, pres., 2005—06. With USN, 1957—60. Mem.: U. Calif., Bentley Band Alumni Assn. (Coun. 1958—2007), Bowles Hall Alumni Assn., U. Calif. (bd. dir. & group. sec. 2005—), East Bay Model Engrs. Soc. (bd. dirs. 1996—2002, pres. 2000—02), Swedish-Am. C. of C. (bd. dirs. 1971—, pres. Western Nat. 1988—90, nat. vice chmn. 1988—90, pres. Western Nat. 1998—2000, bd. dirs. 1998—2003, CFO 1999—2000, corp. sec. 2000—03), Maritime Law Assn. (chmn. practice and procedure com. 1991—95, bd. dirs. 1993—96), Golden State Model R.R. Mus. (corp. sec., bd. dirs. 1995—), Sierra Club (nat. outing com. 1964—, chmn. ins. com. 1991—, internat. trips 1992—95, outing governance com. 1992—2006), U. Calif. Alumni Order Golden Bear. (permanent class pres. 1957—). Democrat. Methodist. Avocations: mountain climbing, hiking, photography, model railroads. Office: Law Office of John A Edginton 124 Washington Ave Ste A-1 Point Richmond CA 94801-3979 Home Phone: 510-843-6966; Office Phone: 510-232-7180. Office Fax: 510-232-7181. Business E-Mail: jedginton@edg-law.com.

EDGMON, BRYCE, state legislator; Alaska State Representative, District 37, 2007-; member, Fish and Game, Education and Early Develop, Fisheries, Resources Committees, 2007-, Alaska House Representative. Democrat. Address: PO Box 84 Dillingham AK 99576 Office: Dist 37 716 W 4th Ave Ste 380 Anchorage AK 99501 also: State Capitol Rm 424 Juneau AK 99801 Home Phone: 907-842-1729; Office Phone: 907-465-4451, 907-269-0275. Office Fax: 907-465-3445, 907-269-0274. Business E-Mail: Rep_Bryce_Edgmon@legis.state.ak.us.

EDIGER, ROBERT IKE, botanist, educator; b. Hutchinson, Kans., Apr. 2, 1937; s. Peter F. and Martha (Friesen) E.; m. Patricia L. Dickerson, Feb. 7, 1981; children: Madeline, Maureen, Alan, Shelly. BA, Bethel Coll., 1959; MS, Emporia State U., 1964; PhD, Kans. State U., 1967. Tchr. public schs., Ford, Kans., 1959-62, Hays, Kans., 1962-63; teaching and research asst. Kans. State U., 1964-67; asst. prof. dept. biol. scis. Calif. State U., Chico, 1967-71, asso. prof., 1971-74, prof., 1975-99, chmn. dept. biol. scis., 1974-77, dir.Eagle Lake field sta., 1967-73; ret., 1999. Mem. Am. Soc. Plant Taxonomists, Orgn. Biol. Field Stas. (pres. 1975), Calif. Bot. Soc., Calif. Native Plant Soc. Methodist. Home: 5359 Royal Oaks Dr Oroville CA 95966-3837 Office: Calif State U Dept Biol Scis Chico CA 95929-0001 E-mail: bpediger@aol.com.

EDLEY, CHRISTOPHER FAIRCHILD, JR., dean, law educator; b. Boston, Jan. 13, 1953; s. Christopher Fairchild and Zaida (Coles) Edley; m. Tana Pesso, Sept. 23, 1983 (div.); 1 child, Christopher Fairchild III; m. Maria Echaveste; children: Zara, Elias. BA, Swarthmore Coll., 1973; JD, MPP, Harvard U., 1978. Bar: DC 1980. Asst. dir. Domestic Policy Staff The White House, Washington, 1978-79; spl. asst. to sec. US Dept. Health Edn. & Welfare, Washington, 1979-80; assoc. asst. to the Pres., Office Chief of Staff The White House, Washington, 1980; asst. prof. Harvard Law Sch., Cambridge, Mass., 1981-87, prof., 1987—2004; assoc. dir. Office Mgmt. & Budget, Exec. Office of the Pres., Washington, 1993—95; spl. counsel to Pres. The White House, Washington, 1995; dean, prof. law U. Calif., Boalt Hall Law Sch., Berkeley, 2004—. Mem. U.S. Civil Rights Commn., 1999—2005, Nat. Commn. on Fed. Election Reform. Editor and officer Harvard Law Review; author: Administrative Law: Rethinking Judicial Control of Bureaucracy, 1990, Not All Black and White: Affirmative Action, Race and American Values, 1996. Nat. Issues Dir. Dukakis for Pres. Campaign, Boston, 1987-88; co-founder, Civil Rights Project, 1996-; spl. con. to Pres. Clinton on Race Initiative, 1997-99. Named one of 100 Most Influential Lawyers, Nat. Law Jour., 2006. Fellow: Am. Acad. Arts & Scis.; mem.: Divsn. on Behavioral and Social Scis. and Edn. Nat. Academies Scis. (adv. bd. exec. com.), Coun. on Fgn. Relations, Nat. Acad. of Pub. Adminstrn. Office: The Civil Rights Project 125 Mt Auburn St 3rd Fl Cambridge MA 02138 also: U Calif 215 Boalt Hall Berkeley CA 94720-7200 Office Phone: 510-642-6483. E-mail: edley@law.berkeley.edu.

EDLICH, RICHARD FRENCH, biomedical engineer, educator; b. NYC, Jan. 19, 1939; MD, NYU, 1962; PhD, U. Minn., 1973. From instr. to assoc. prof. U. Va. Sch. Medicine, Charlottesville, 1971-76, prof. plastic surgery and biomed. engring., dist. prof. emergency medicine, 1976-82, disting. prof. plastic and maxillofacial surgery and biomed. engring., 1983-96, Raymoon F. Morgan prof. plastic surgery and disting. prof. biomed. engring., 1996—2001; dir. Trauma Prevention, Rsch. and Edn. Trauma Specialist LLP of Legacy Emanuel Hosp., Portland, 2004—. Founder dept. emergency medicine U. Va., 1973, DeCamp Burn and wound Healing Ctr., 1974—85, Pegasus Air Med. Transp. Sys., 1984; physician tech. adviser Bur. Emergency Svc., HEW, 1974—79; cons. Divsn. Health Manpower and Nat. Ctr. Health Svc. Rsch., 1977—79; founder North Fork Rsch. Pk., Charlottesville, Va., 1991. Editor-in-chief: Jour. Long-Term Effects Med. Implants, 2000—06. Recipient Disting. Pub. Svc. award for Contbns. to Emergency Medicine, USPHS, 1979, Outstanding Tchg. award, U. Va., 1989, Thomas Jefferson award, 1991, Outstanding Faculty award, Commonwealth of Va. Coun. Higher Edn., 1989, Disting. Alumni award, U. Minn. Med. Alumni Assn., 2005, The Lawn Soc., U. Va., 2006; named 5th Ann. David Boyd Lectr. in Emergency Medicine, U. Va., 2001, Richard Edlich rsch. prof. plastic surgery, U. Va. Health Sys., 1984, Endowed Edlich Henderson Inventor of Yr., U. Va. Patent Found., 2002—. Mem.: ACS, Am. Surg. Assn., Am. Coll. Emergency Physicians (James D. Mills Outstanding Contbn. Emergency Medicine award, 2008), Soc. Acad. Emergency Medicine, Am. Soc. Plastic and Reconstructive Surgeons, Univ. Assn. Emergency Medicine, Am. Burn Assn. (Harvey Stuart Allen award 2000), Am. Assn. Surg. Trauma, Soc. Univ. Surgeons, U. Va. Lawn Soc., Alpha Omega Alpha. Achievements include research in biology of wound repair and infection, systems approach to emergency medical and trauma care; development of Edlich gastric lavage; reinforced steri-strip; CSM gram stain procedure; Shur-Clens; stabilized topical pharmaceutical preperations. Home and Office: 22500 NE 128th Cir Brush Prairie WA 98606 Office Phone: 360-944-7641. Office Fax: 360-944-7612. Personal E-mail: richardedlichmd@gmail.com.

EDMONDS, CHARLES HENRY, retired publisher; b. Lakewood, Ohio, Sept. 4, 1919; m. Ruth Audrey Windfelder, Nov. 4, 1938; children: Joan Dickey, Charles Henry, Carolyn Anne, Dianne Marie. Attended, Woodbury Bus. Coll., 1939—40. Owner Shoreline Transp. Co., LA, 1946—58; mgr. transp. Purity Food Stores, Burlingame, Calif., 1958—61; supr. Calif. Motor Express, San Jose, 1961—64; account exec. Don Wright Assocs., Oakland, Calif., 1964—65; sales mgr. Western U.S. Shippers Guide Co., Chgo., 1965—70; pub. No. Calif. Retailer, San Jose, 1970—83, Retail Observer, 1990—2007; v.p. Kasmar Publs., 1983—88; ret., 2008. Contbr. articles to profl. jours. Recipient journalism awards, various orgns. Republican. Roman Catholic. Home: 1442 Sierra Creek Way San Jose CA 95132-3618 Personal E-mail: retailobs@aol.com.

EDMONDS, JIM (JAMES PATRICK EDMONDS), professional baseball player; b. Fullerton, Calif., June 27, 1970; children: Haylee, Lauren. Outfielder Calif. Angels (now Anaheim Angels), 1993—99, St. Louis Cardinals, 2000—07, San Diego Padres, 2008—. Recipient Gold Glove Award, 1997—98, 2000—05, Silver Slugger award, 2004; named to Am. League All-Star Team, 1995, Nat. League All-Star Team, 2000, 2003, 2005. Achievements include setting the National League record for strikeouts by a lefty in a season with 167 in 2000; being a member of the World Series Champion St. Louis Cardinals, 2006. Avocations: water sports, ice skating. Mailing: c/o San Diego Padres PETCO Pk 100 Park Blvd San Diego CA 92101

EDMONSON, TRACY K., lawyer; BA, Rice U., 1985; JD, U. Calif., Berkeley, 1988. Bar: Calif. 1988. Ptnr., corp. fin. Latham & Watkins LLP, San Francisco, chair, San Francisco corp. dept., 2002—, and head, Bay Area Corp. Fin. practice group, 1998—. Frequent public speaker. Named one of Top 20 Under 40, Daily Jour., 2003, No. Calif. Superlawyers, San Francisco Mag., 2004. Office: Latham & Watkins LLP Ste 2000 505 Montgomery St San Francisco CA 94111-2562 Office Phone: 415-391-0600. Office Fax: 415-395-8095. Business E-Mail: tracy.edmonson@lw.com.

EDMUNSON, JAMES L., political organization administrator; b. Eugene, Oreg., 1951; m. Ellen Edmunson; 2 children. BS, Oreg. State U.; JD, U. Oreg., 1983. Chmn. Oreg. Dem. Party, Portland, 2001—; rep. 39th dist. State of Oreg., 1987—95; lawyer, appellate counsel Malagon, Moore & Johnson; pvt. practice Eugene, Oreg. Office: Democratic Party Oregon 232 NE 9th Ave Portland OR 97232-2915 Fax: 503-224-5335.

EDSELL, PATRICK L., computer company executive; Pres. Spectra-Physics, Mountain View, Calif. Office: Spectra-Physics PO Box 7013 1335 Terra Bella Ave Mountain View CA 94039-7013

EDSON, WILLIAM ALDEN, retired electrical engineer, researcher; b. Burchard, Nebr., Oct. 30, 1912; s. William Henry and Pearl (Montgomery) E.; m. Saralou Peterson, Aug. 23, 1942; children: Judith Lynne, Margaret Jane, Carolyn Louise. BS (Summerfield scholar), U. Kans., 1934, MS, 1935; D.Sc. (Gordon McKay scholar), Harvard U., 1937. Mem. tech. staff Bell Telephone Labs., Inc., NYC, 1937-41, supr., 1943-45; asst. prof. elec. engring. Ill. Inst. Tech., Chgo., 1941-43; prof. physics Ga. Inst. Tech., Atlanta, 1945-46, prof. elec. engring., 1946-51, dir. sch. elec. engring., 1951-52; vis. prof., research asso. Stanford U., 1952-56, cons. prof., 1956; mgr. Klystron sub-sect. Gen. Electric Microwave Lab., Palo Alto, Calif., 1955-61; v.p., dir. research Electromagnetic Tech. Corp., Palo Alto, 1961-62, pres., 1962-70; sr. scientist Vidar Corp., Mountain View, Calif., 1970— 71; from staff mem. to sr. staff scientist, assoc. dir. Radio Physics Lab of SRI Internat., Menlo Park, Calif., 1971—2004. Cons. high frequency sect. Nat. Bur. Standards, 1951-64; dir. Western Electronic Show and Conv., 1975-79 Author: (with Robert I. Sarbacher) Hyper and Ultra-High Frequency Engineering, 1943, Vacuum-Tube Oscillators, 1953. Life fellow IEEE (chmn. San Francisco sect. 1963-64, com. standards piezoelectricity 1950-67); mem. Am. Phys. Soc., Sigma Xi, Tau Beta Pi, Sigma Tau, Phi Kappa Phi, Eta Kappa Nu, Pi Mu Epsilon. Home: 2350 E Estates Dr #106 Fairfield CA 94533 Home Phone: 707-422-1420.

EDWARDS, BRUCE GEORGE, retired ophthalmologist, military officer; b. Idaho Springs, Colo., Apr. 6, 1942; s. Bruce Norwood and Evelyn Alice (Kohut) Edwards. BA, U. Colo., 1964; MD, U. Colo., Denver, 1968. Diplomate Am. Acad. Ophthalmology. Commd. ensign USN, 1964; advanced through grades to capt. US Naval Hosp., 1980, intern San Diego, 1968-69; USN med. officer USS Long Beach (CGN-9), 1969-70; gen. med. officer US Naval Hosp., Taipei, Taiwan, 1970-72, US Naval Dispensary Treasure Island, San Francisco, 1972-73; resident in ophthalmology US Naval Hosp., Oakland, Calif., 1973-76, mem. ophthalmology staff Camp Pendleton, Calif., 1976—83, ophthalmologist, chief of med. staff Naples, Italy, 1983—85; resident in ophthalmology U. Calif., San Francisco, 1973-76; ophthalmology head Camp Pendleton Naval Hosp., 1985-97, dir. surg. svcs., 1990-92, physician advisor quality assurance, 1985-86, ret., 1997. Vol. Internat. Eye Found., Harar, Ethiopia, 1975. Fellow Am. Acad. Ophthalmology (diplomate); mem. AMA, Calif. Med. Assn., Calif. Assn. Ophthalmologists, Am. Soc. Contemporary Ophthalmologists, Assn. U.S. Mil. Surgeons, Pan Am. Assn. Ophthalmology, Order of DeMolay (Colo. DeMolay of Yr. 1961, Idaho Springs Chevalier, Colo. State sec. 1961-62). Republican. Methodist. Avocations: piano, camping, hiking, bicycling, travel.

EDWARDS, GEORGE KENT, lawyer; b. Ogden, Utah, Oct. 3, 1939; s. George and S. Ruth Edwards; m. Linda E. Brown; children: Scott M., Stacey R., Mark D. BA, Occidental Coll., 1961; JD, U. Calif.-Berkeley, 1964. Bar: Calif. 1965, Alaska 1966. Legislative counsel Alaska Legislature, 1964-66; ptnr. law firm Stevens, Savage, Holland, Erwin & Edwards, Anchorage, 1966-67; dep. atty. gen. Alaska, 1967-68; atty. gen., 1968-70; U.S. atty. Dist. Alaska, 1971-77; pvt. practice, 1977-81; shareholder Hartig Rhodes Norman Mahoney & Edwards, Anchorage, 1981—. Mem. Nat. Conf. Commrs. Uniform State Laws, 1968-70; chmn. Gov. Alaska Planning Coun. Adminstrn. Criminal Justice, 1968-70; guest lectr. bus. law U. Alaska, 1981-82; guest editorial columnist Anchorage Times, 1982-88. Co-author: Considerations in Buying or Selling a Business in Alaska, 1992. Pres. Greater Anchorage Area Young Reps., 1967; chmn. Carrs Great Alaska Shootout, 1995; pres. bd. dirs. Miss Alask Scholarship Pageant, 1980-84; bd. dirs. Anchorage Crime Stoppers, 1981-85; pres. Common Sense Alaska, 1982-85, 91—; bd. dirs., 1986—. Mem. ABA, Calif. Bar Assn., Alaska Bar Assn., Nat. Assn. Attys. Gen., Nat. Assn. Former U.S. Attys. (bd. dirs., pres.), Anchorage C. of C. (bd. dirs. 1989-96), Rotary (scholarship chair 1993, 95-98), Phi Delta Phi, Sigma Alpha Epsilon (Outstanding Sr. award Calif. Epsilon chpt. 1961). Office: 717 K St Anchorage AK 99501-3330

EDWARDS, GLEN R., metallurgist; b. Monte Vista, Colo., July 21, 1939; married, 1959; 2 children. BS, Colo. Sch. Mines, 1961; MS, U. N.Mex., 1967; PhD in Math. Sci., Stanford U., 1971. Staff plutonium metall. Los Alamos (N.Mex.) Sci. Lab., 1963-67; asst. instr. math./sci. Stanford (Calif.) U., 1967-71; from asst. to assoc. prof. Naval Postgrad. Sch., 1971-76; assoc. prof. metall. engring. Colo. Sch. Mines, Golden, 1976-79, prof. metall. engring., 1979—, dir. ctr. welding and joining rsch., 1987—. Fellow Am. Soc. Metals Internat.; mem. Am. Inst. Mining & Metall. Engrs., Am. Welding Soc., Internat. Inst. Welding, Sigma Xi. Office: Colo Sch Mines Ctr Welding Joining Rs Golden CO 80401

EDWARDS, GLENN THOMAS, history educator; b. Portland, Oreg., June 14, 1931; s. Glenn Thomas E. and Marie Ann (Cheska) McMullen; m. Nannette Wilhelmina McAndie, June 15, 1957; children: Randall Thomas, Stephanie Lynn. BA, Willamette U., 1953; MA, U. Oreg., 1960, PhD, 1963. Asst. prof. San Jose State U., 1962-64, Whitman Coll., Walla Walla, Wash., 1964-68, assoc. prof., 1968-75, prof., 1976-98, ret., 1998. Cons. TV documentary Yakima Valley Mus. on William O. Douglas, Yakima, Wash., 1981-82; trustee Wash. Commn. of Humanities, Olympia, 1980-86. Author: Sowing Good Seeds: The Northwest Suffrage Campaigns of Susan B. Anthony, 1990, The Triumph of Tradition: The Emergence of Whitman College, 1859-1924, 1992; co-editor: Experiences in a Promised Land: Essays on Pacific Northwest History, 1986; contbr. articles to profl. jours. Mem. pub. edn. adv. com. State Supt. of Pub. Instrn., Olympia, 1975-78; mem. bd. trustees Wash. State Hist. Soc., 1983-92, Wash. Commn. for Humanities. Served with U.S. Army, 1954-56. Grantee Am Philos. Soc., 1971 Mem. Orgn. Am. Historians, Western History Assn., Oreg. Hist. Soc., Washington Hist. Soc. (photography cons. 1980). Congregationalist. Office: Whitman Coll Dept History Walla Walla WA 99362 E-mail: tomed@spiretech.edu.

EDWARDS, JAMES ROBERT, minister, educator; b. Colorado Springs, Oct. 28, 1945; s. Robert Emery and Mary Eleanor (Callison) E.; m. Mary Jane Pryor, June 22, 1968; children: Corrie, Mark. BA in History, cum laude, Whitworth U., Spokane, Wash., 1963; MDiv, Princeton Sem., 1970; PhD, Fuller Sem., Pasadena, Calif., 1978. Youth min. First Presbyn. Ch., Colorado Springs, 1971-78; prof. religion Jamestown (N.D.) Coll., 1978—97, Whitworth U., 1997—. Mem. spkrs. bur. N.D. Humanities Coun., 1983-84; rsch. scholar U. Tuebingen, Germany, 1988, Tyndale House, Cambridge, England, 2000; mem. Ctr. for Theol. Inquiry, Princeton, NJ, 2007; spkr. in field. Author: (with others) The Layman's Overview of the Bible, 1987, Commentary on Romans, 1992, The Divine Intruder, 2000, Commentary on Gospel of Mark, 2002, Is Jesus the Only Savior?, 2005 (named Book of Yr., Christianity Today 2006); contbg. editor Christianity Today, 1993—, Scottish Jour. Theology, 2006—; contbr. articles to profl. jours. Recipient several tchg. awards; Templeton grantee in sci. and religion, 1996; scholar German Acad. Exch., 1993 Mem. Soc. Bibl. Lit. Office: Whitworth Univ Dept Theology Spokane WA 99251 Business E-Mail: jedwards@whitworth.edu.

EDWARDS, KENNETH NEIL, chemical engineering executive; b. Hollywood, Calif., June 8, 1932; s. Arthur Carl and Ann Vera (Gomez) E.; children: Neil James, Peter Graham, John Evan. BA in Chemistry, Occidental Coll., 1954; MS in Chem. and Metall. Engring., U. Mich., 1955. Prin. chemist Battelle Meml. Inst., Columbus, Ohio, 1955-58; dir. new products rsch. and devel. Dunn-Edwards Corp., LA, 1958-72; sr. lectr. organic coatings and pigments dept. chem. engring. U. So. Calif., LA, 1976-80; CEO Dunn-Edwards Corp., 2001—. Bd. dirs. Dunn-Edwards Corp., LA; co-chair indsl. adv. coun., mem. pres.'s cir. Calif. Poly. U., San Luis Obispo. Contbr. articles to sci. jours. Recipient Judo Masters belt (6th dan), Korean Judo Assn., 2000, 38th

Western Regional Indsl. Innovations award, 2003. Mem. Am. Chem. Soc. (chmn. divisional activities 1988-89, exec. com. divsn. polymeric materials sci. and engring. 1963—, chair divsn. 1970, mem. devel. adv. com. 1996-99, Disting. Svc. award 1996, chair Disting. Svc. award selection 1997—, chair So. Calif. local sect. 1999), Alpha Chi Sigma (chmn. L.A. profl. chpt. 1962, counselor Pacific dist. 1967-70, grand profl. alchemist nat. v.p. 1970-76, grand master alchemist nat. pres. 1976-78, nat. adv. com. 1978—). Achievements include patents for air-dried polyester coatings and application, for process and apparatus for dispensing liquid colorants into a paint can, fluidic fillers, and for mechanical mixers. Home: Bottle Bay Rd Sagle ID 83860 also: 2926 Graceland Way Glendale CA 91206-1331 Office: Dunn Edwards Corp 136 W Walnut Ave Monrovia CA 91016-3444 Personal E-mail: kneatde@aol.com.

EDWARDS, KIRK LEWIS, medical services company executive; b. Berkeley, Calif., July 30, 1950; s. Austin Lewis and Betty (Drury) E.; m. Randi Edwards, Feb. 14, 1998; children: Elliott Tyler, Jonathan Bentley. BA in Rhetoric and Pub. Address, U. Wash., Seattle, 1972; postgrad., Shoreline Coll., 1976. Cert. bus. broker. From salesperson to mgr. Rede Realty, Lynnwood, Wash., 1973-77; br. mgr. Century 21/North Homes Realty, Lynnwood, Wash., 1977-79, Snohomish, Wash., 1979-81; pres., owner Century 21/Champion Realty, Everett, Wash., 1981-82, Champion Computers, Walker/Edwards Investments, Everett, 1981-82; br. mgr. Advance Properties, Everett, 1982-87; exec. v.p. Bruch & Vedrich Better Homes & Garden, Everett, 1987-88, dir. career devel., 1988-90; pres., CEO Century 21/Champion Realty, Everett, 1991-95, KR Bus. Brokers, Kirkland, Wash., 1995—; pres. Exec. Med. Svcs., Bellevue, Wash., 2001—. V.p. Edwards Med. Svcs., Inc., 2003—05; ptnr. Hayes Auto Rebuild, 2003—, KR Bus. Brokers, Bellevue, Wash., 1995—, Exec. Med. Svcs., 2001—03. Named Top Business Broker In Washington Investment Brokers Assn., 1994-96. Mem. Snohomish County Camano Bd. Realtors (chmn. 1987-88), Snohomish County C. of C., Hidden Harbor Yacht Club, Mill Creek Country Club. Republican. Avocations: travel, water-skiing, scuba diving. Office: KR Business Brokers 2285 116th Ave NE # 100 Bellevue WA 98004 E-mail: mrbzns@hotmail.com.

EDWARDS, LINDA L., former elementary education educator; Tchr. Highland Park Elem. Sch., Lewistown, Mont.; ret., 1999. Named Mont. State Elem. Tchr. of Yr., 1993. Office: Highland Park Elem Sch 1312 7th Ave N Lewistown MT 59457-2112

EDWARDS, NOKIE, musician; b. Lahoma, Okla., May 9, 1935; m. Judy Edwards; children: Tina, Kim(dec.), Patrick, Seth. Lead guitarist The Ventures, 1960—69, 1972—85; founder HitchHiker Guitars, 2002. Musician: (albums) (with The Ventures) Bobby Vee Meets the Ventures, 1962, Let's Go!, 1963, The Ventures Play the Country Classics, 1963, Runnin' Strong, 1966, Christmas Joy, 2002, (solo albums) Nokie, 1971, Again, 1972, King of Guitars, 1973, A Surf 'n' Swing Fren 'n' String, 2001, Hitchhiker Heals Hearts, 2005, Adventure in Country Swing, 2005, Guitar Band Classics, 2005, Guitars Over, 2005, Hitchhiker Heals Hearts, vol. 2, 2006. Served in USAR, 1956—60. Recipient Key to the City of Mesquite, Tex., 2003, cert. of appreciation, Fgn. Minister of Japan, 2004; named to Rock & Roll Hall of Fame, 2008. Office: Taylor Wilson & Assocs Inc PO Box 372021 Reseda CA 91337-2021 also: Nokie Edwards Fan Club 13280 S Orlando Rd Yuma AZ 85365-4838

EDWARDS, RALPH M., librarian; b. Shelley, Idaho, Apr. 17, 1933; s. Edward William and Maude Estella (Munsee) E.; m. Winifred Wylie, Dec. 25, 1969; children: Dylan, Nathan, Stephen. BA, U. Wash., 1957, MLS, 1960; DLS, U. Calif.-Berkeley, 1971. Libr. NY Pub. Libr., NYC, 1960-61; catalog libr. U. Ill. Libr., Urbana, 1961-62; br. libr. Multnomah County Libr., Portland, Oreg., 1964-67; asst. prof. Western Mich. U., Kalamazoo, 1970-74; chief Ctl. Libr. Dallas Pub. Libr., 1975-81; city libr. Phoenix Pub. Libr., 1981-95, ret., 1996—. Author: Role of the Beginning Librarian in University Libraries, 1975. U. Calif. doctoral fellow, 1967-70; library mgmt. internship Council on Library Resources, 1974-75 Mem. ALA, Pub. Library Assn. Democrat. Home: 2884 Spring Blvd Eugene OR 97403-1662 E-mail: rme33@comcast.net.

EDWARDS, RANDALL, former state treasurer; b. Eugene, Oreg., Aug. 13, 1961; m. Jill Brim-Edwards; 3 children. BA in Econs., Colo. Coll., 1983; MBA, George Washington Univ., 1990. Legis. aide US Senate, 1983—87; internat. trade analyst US Dept. Commerce, 1987—91; sr. adv. Oreg. State Treasury, 1992—96; mng. ptnr. EDJE Cons., 1996—2000; state treas. State of Oreg., 2000—09. Rep. Oreg. Ho. Reps., 1996—2000. Mem.: Nat. Assn. State Treas. (pres. 2006). Democrat. Office Phone: 503-378-4329. Office Fax: 503-378-2870. Business E-Mail: oregon.treasurer@state.or.us.

EDWARDS, RICHARD ALAN, retired lawyer; b. Portland, Oreg., June 28, 1938; s. Howard A. and Kay E. (Sheldon) E.; m. Renee Rosier, June 18, 1960; children: Teri Edwards Obye, Lisa Edwards Smith, Steve. BS, Oreg. State U., 1960; JD summa cum laude, Willamette U., 1968. Bar: Oreg. 1968, U.S. Dist. Ct. Oreg. 1968, U.S. Ct. Appeals (9th cir.) 1969. Various positions 1st Interstate Bank of Oreg., Portland, 1960-65; assoc. Miller, Nash, Wiener, Hager & Carlsen, Portland, 1968-74, ptnr., 1974—99, mng. ptnr., 1991-96. Editor Willamette Law Jour., 1967-68. Mem. ABA (litig. sect. 1972), Oreg. State Bar (chairperson debtor-creditor sect. 1981-82, mem. various coms.). Republican. Presbyterian. Personal E-mail: richardaedwards@verizon.net.

EDWARDS, ROBERT L., corporate financial executive; BA, MBA, Brigham Young U. Various exec. positions Santa Fe Pacific Corp.; sr. v.p., CFO, chief adminstrv. officer Imation Corp., 1998—2003; exec. v.p., CFO Maxtor, Milipitas, Calif., 2003—04, Safeway Inc., 2004—. Office: Safeway Inc 5918 Stoneridge Mall Rd Pleasanton CA 94588

EDWARDS, ROBIN MORSE, lawyer; b. Glens Falls, NY, Dec. 9, 1947; d. Daniel and Harriet Morse; m. Richard Charles Edwards, Aug. 30, 1970; children: Michael Alan, Jonathan Philip. BA, Mt. Holyoke Coll., 1969; JD, U. Calif., Berkeley, 1972. Bar: Calif. 1972. Assoc. Donahue, Gallagher, Thomas & Woods, Oakland, Calif., 1972—77, ptnr., 1977—89, Sonnenschein, Nath & Rosenthal, San Francisco, 1989—, mgmt. com., 1998—2008. Bd. dirs. Temple Sinai, 1997-2002. Mem. ABA, Calif. Bar Assn., Alameda County Bar Assn. (bd. dirs. 1978-84, v.p. 1982, pres. 1983), Alameda County Bar Found. (bd. dirs. 1998-2000), K.E.E.N.S.F. (bd. dirs. 2007-), Forum Women Entrepreneurs & Execs. Jewish. Avocations: skiing, cooking, travel. Office: Sonnenschein Nath Rosenthal 525 Market St 26th Fl San Francisco CA 94105-2708 Office Phone: 415-882-5019. Business E-Mail: redwards@sonnenschein.com.

EDWARDS, SUSAN M., hotel executive; b. Bristol, Eng., Jan. 2, 1953; Student in English lit., 1970. Office mgr. Godfrey Davis Internat., San Francisco, 1970's; dir. sales Karageorgis Cruises, San Francisco, 1980's; regional sales dir., then nat. sales dir. Aston Hotels and Resorts, Hawaii, 1981-91, assoc. v.p. Hawaii, 1981-91; pres. Delfin Hotels & Resorts, Santa Cruz, Calif., 1991—. Avocation: dogs.

EDWARDS, TREVOR, apparel executive; b. London; With Colgate-Palmolive; joined Nike, Inc., Beaverton, Oreg., 1992, v.p. brand mgmt. Europe, Middle East and Africa, dir. mktg. Ams., v.p, US brand mgmt., corp. v.p. global brand and category mgmt., chief mktg. officer, 2002—. Office: Nike One Bowerman Dr Beaverton OR 97005-6453

EFFEL, LAURA, lawyer; b. Dallas, May 9, 1945; d. Louis E. and Fay (Lee) Ray; m. Marc J. Patterson, Sept. 19, 1992 (dec. July 30, 2002); 1 child, Stephen Patterson; m. Robert A. Miltner, Aug. 26, 2006; BA, U. Calif., Berkeley, 1971; JD, U. Md., 1975. Bar: NY 1976, US Dist. Ct. (so. and ea. dists.) NY 1976, US Ct. Appeals (2d cir.) 1980, US Supreme Ct. 1980, DC 1993, NC 1998, Va. 2001; cert. mediator Judicial Coun. Va., 2004. Assoc. Burns Jackson Miller Summit & Jacoby, NYC, 1975-78, Pincus Munzer Bizar & D'Alessandro, NYC, 1978-80; v.p., sr. assoc. counsel Chase Manhattan Bank, N.A., NYC, 1980-96; counsel Baker & McKenzie, NYC, 1996-99; gen. counsel Garban Cos., 1999-2000; counsel LeClair Ryan Flippin Densmore, Roanoke, Va., 2000—02, ptnr., 2002—06, ind. neutral, 2006—07; of counsel Jackson Lewis, LLP, Richmond, Va., 2007—. Mem. nat. roster of neutrals Am. Arbitration Assn. Meml. editl. bd.: Alternatives to the High Cost of Litigation. Mem. Workforce Devel. Com., New Century Tech. Coun., 2001-06; bd. dirs. Bklyn. Legal Svcs. Corp. A, 1992-2000, Blue Ridge Pub. TV, 2001-06. Named one of Best Lawyers in Am., 2005—07, Va. Legal Elite, 2006—08; named to Va. Super Lawyers, 2006—08. Mem.: ABA, DC Bar Assn., NC Bar Assn. Office: Jackson Lewis LLP 321 W Franklin St Richmond VA 23220 Home Phone: 415-924-7229; Office Phone: 804-517-8756. Personal E-mail: laura.effel@gmail.com.

EFFREN, GARY ROSS, financial executive; b. Jersey City, Feb. 27, 1956; s. Ronald Lewis and Ethel Frances (Ross) E.; m. Francine Oberfest, May 24, 1980; children: Jessica Leigh, Jenna Ashlee. BS summa cum laude, Rider Coll., 1978; postgrad., U. Miami, Coral Gables, Fla., 1984-89. CPA, Fla. Sr. auditor Peat, Marwick, Mitchell & Co., Miami, 1978—80; sr. fin. acct. Knight-Ridder, Inc., Miami, Fla., 1980—82, mgr. fin. reporting, 1982—84, dir. corp. acctg., 1986—88, asst. to v.p./finance, 1988—95; bus. mgr. Viewdata Corp. Am., Miami Beach, Fla., 1984—86; v.p., contr. Knight Ridder, Inc., San Jose, Calif., 1995—2001, sr. v.p. fin., CFO, 2001—04, v.p. fin., 2004—. Mem. Am. Inst. CPA's, Fla. Inst. CPA's. Jewish. Avocations: guitar playing, racquetball. Office: Knight-Ridder Inc 50 W San Fernando St San Jose CA 95113-2413 E-mail: geffren@knightridder.com.

EFFROS, MICHELLE, electrical engineer, educator; b. NYC, Sept. 7, 1967; d. Richard Matthew and Gail (Hochman) E. BSEE, Stanford U., 1989, MSEE, 1990, PhD, 1994. Elec. engr. Info. Systems Lab., Stanford (Calif.) U.; asst. prof. elec. engring. Calif. Inst. Tech., Pasadena, Calif., 1994—2000, assoc. prof. elec. engring., 2000—05, prof. elec. engring., 2005—, dir. data compression lab. Editor: (newsletter) IEEE Info. Theory Soc., 1995—98. Masters fellow Hughes Aircraft Co., L.A., 1989-90; NSF grad. fellow, Washington, 1990-93; named AT&T Bell Labs. PhD scholar, NJ, 1993, Frederick Emmons Terman Engring. Scholastic award, Stanford u., 1989, NSF Career award, 1995, Charles Lee Powell Found. award, 1997, Richard Feynman-Hughes Fellowship, 1997, named among the World's Top 100 Young Innovators in Tech. and bus. Tech. Review mag, 2002. Mem. Sigma Xi, Phi Beta Kappa, Tau Beta Pi (chpt. pres. 1988-89). Office: M/C 136-93 162A Moore Calif Inst Tech 1200 E California Blvd Pasadena CA 91125

EFRON, BRADLEY, statistician, educator; b. St. Paul, May 24, 1938; s. Miles Jack and Esther (Kaufman) Efron; m. Gael Guerin, July 1969 (div.); 1 child, Miles James; m. Nancy Troup, June 1986 (div.). BS in Math., Calif. Inst. Tech., 1960; PhD, Stanford U., 1964; DSc (hon.), U. Chgo., 1995; D (hon.), U. Carlos III de Madrid, 1998; DSc (hon.), U. Oslo, 2002. Asst. and assoc. prof. stats. Stanford U., Calif., 1965-72, chmn. dept. stats. Calif., 1976-79, 1991-1994, chmn. math. scis. Calif., 1981—, prof. stats. and of health rsch. and policy Calif., 1974—, assoc. dean humanities and scis. Calif., 1987-90, endowed chair Max H. Stein prof. humanities and scis. Calif., 1991-94. Statis. cons. Alza Corp., 1971—, Rand Corp., 1962—. Author: Bootstrap Methods, 1979, Biostatistics Casebook, 1980. MacArthur Found. fellow, 1983; named Outstanding Statistician of Yr. Chgo. Statis. Assn., 1981; Wald and Rietz Lectr. Inst. Math. Stats., 1977, 81; recipient Fisher award, Chgo., 1996, Parzen prize for statis. innovation, 1998, Rao prize, 2003, Noether prize, 2006, 2005 Nat. Medal Sci., NSF, 2005. Fellow Inst. Math. Stats. (pres. 1987), Am. Statis. Assn. (pres. 2004, Wilks medal 1990, Noether prize); mem. NAS, Am. Acad. Arts and Scis., Internat. Statis. Assn. Achievements include invention of the bootstrap method. Office: Stanford U Dept Stats Sequoia Hall 390 Serra Mall Stanford CA 94305-4065

EFRON, ZAC, actor, singer; b. San Luis Obispo, Calif., Oct. 18, 1987; s. David and Starla Efron. Actor: (TV films) The Big Wide World of Carl Laemke, 2003, Triple Play, 2004, Miracle Run, 2004, If You Lived Here, You'd Be Home Now, 2006, High School Musical (Choice Breakout Star award & Choice Chemistry award, Teen Choice Awards, 2006), High School Musical 2, 2007; (TV series) Summerland, 2004—05; (films) The Derby Stallion, 2005, Hairspray, 2007 (Young Hollywood "One to Watch" award, 2007, Ensemble of Yr. award, Hollywood Film Festival, 2007, Breakthrough Performance, MTV Movie Awards, 2008), High School Musical 3: Senior Year, 2008, 17 Again, 2009; singer: (albums) High School Musical, 2006, Hairspray, 2007, High School Musical 2, 2007 (Favorite Soundtrack Album, Am. Music Awards, 2007), High School Musical 3: Senior Year, 2008. Named one of Top 25 Entertainers of Yr., Entertainment Weekly, 2007, The 100 Most Powerful Celebrities, Forbes.com, 2008, The World's Most Influential People, TIME mag., 2009. Office: c/o Jason Barett Alchemy Entertainment 9229 Sunset Blvd Ste 720 Los Angeles CA 90069 also: Creative Artists Agency 2000 Ave of the Stars Los Angeles CA 90067 Office Phone: 424-288-2000, 310-278-8889.*

EGAN, TIMOTHY K., writer, journalist; b. Seattle; m. Joni Balter; 2 children. BA in Journalism, U. Washington; LHD (hon.), Whitman Coll., 2000. Reporter Seattle Post-Intelligencer; pacific northwest corr. NY Times, nat. enterprise reporter. Commentator Letters from America series BBC. Author: (novels) The Good Rain: Across Time and Terrain in the Pacific Northwest, 1991 (Pacific Northwest Booksellers award, Washington State Book award, 1991), Lasso The Wind: Away to the New West, 1998 (Mountains and Plains Booksellers award, Gov. Writing award, 1999, Notable Book of Yr. NY Times Sunday Book Rev., 1999, Washington State Book award, 1999), The Winemaker's Daughter, The Worst Hard Time: The Untold Story of Those Who Survived the Great American Dust Bowl, 2006 (Nat. Book award nonfiction, 2006, Washington State Book award, 2006); co-author: How Race is Lived in America, 2001 (Pulitzer prize, 2001).

EGBERT, PETER ROY, ophthalmologist, educator; b. Indpls., Dec. 6, 1941; BA magna cum laude, DePauw U., Greencastle, Ind., 1963; MD, Yale U., 1967. Diplomate Nat. Bd. Med. Examiners, Am. Bd. Ophthalmology. Intern Cleve. Met. Gen. Hosp., 1967—68; resident in ophthalmology Yale U., New Haven, 1968—69; acting asst. prof. surgery (ophthalmology Stanford (Calif.) U., 1973—74, dir. Ophthalmic Pathology Lab., 1973—, asst. prof. surgery, 1974—81; acting head divsn. ophthalmology Stanford U. Med. Ctr., 1980—82, assoc. prof. surgery, 1981—88, prof. ophthalmology, 1988—, chmn. dept. ophthalmology, 1992—97; resident in ophthalmology Yale U., New Haven, 1971—73. Recipient Bordon prize, DePauw U., 1960. Mem.: Verhoeff Ophthalmic Pathology Soc., Peninsula Eye Soc., Michael Hogan Eye Pathology Soc., Am. Intra-Ocular Implant Soc., Am. Assn. Ophthalmic Pathologists, Am. Acad. Ophthalmology (Outstanding Humanitarian Svc. award 2004), Phi Beta Kappa, Alpha Omega Alpha. Office: Stanford U Sch Medicine 300 Pasteur Dr Stanford CA 94305-5308

EGLEE, CHARLES HAMILTON, scriptwriter, film and television producer; b. Boston, Nov. 27, 1951; s. Donald Read and Nancy (Hamilton) E.; m. Madeline Dalton, Feb. 29, 1984; children: Blythe Dalton, Eli Hamilton. BA in English, Yale U., 1974. Teaching asst. Yale U., New Haven, 1976; producer, writer for film Deadly Eyes Warner Bros., LA, 1982; story editor for TV series St. Elsewhere MTM Prodns., Studio City, Calif., 1984-86; exec. story cons. for TV series Moonlighting ABC Circle Films, LA, 1986-87, prodr. for TV series Moonlighting, 1987-89; prodr. 20th Century Fox TV, 1989-91; writer, co-exec. producer "Civil Wars" Steven Bochco Prodns., 1991-93; writer L.A. Law, 1992; co-creator, exec. producer The Byrds of Paradise (Steven Bochco Prodns.), 1993-94; co-exec. producer N.Y.P.D. Blue (Steven Bochco Prodns.), 1994-95; co-creator, exec. prodr. Murder One (Steven Bochco Prodns.), 1995-97, Total Security (Steven Bochco Prodns.), 1997-98; co-creator, exec. prodr. TV series Dark Angel Cameron-Eglee Prodns., 1999—2002; writer, exec. prodr. The Shield, FX, 2003—07, Dexter Showtime, 2008—. Story editor (St. Elsewhere episode) Bye George, 1985 (Humanitas prize); co-writer (St. Elsewhere episode) Haunted, 1986 (Emmy nomination, Salute to Excellence Award nominee NAACP 1986), (Moonlighting episode) I Am Curious, Maddie, 1987 (Emmy nomination), N.Y.P.D. Blue, 1994 (Emmy award for best drama), Murder One, 1996 (People's Choice award for best new drama, Emmy nomination, best writing in one hour drama, pilot episode 1996, Golden Globe nomination 1996, best fgn. drama Brit. Acad. Film and TV, 1996, nominee Best Drama award Writers Guild Am., 1996), Dark Angel, 2001 (People's Choice award for best new drama 2001), The Shield (Peabody award 2005). Mem. Acad. TV Arts and Scis., Writers Guild Am., Yale U. Alumni Fund, Mory's Assn. (New Haven). Democrat. Avocations: sailing, skiing, pottery, gardening, hip hop.

EGOLF, BRIAN F., state legislator; m. Kelly Egolf. B in Diplomacy and Public Service, Georgetown U.; JD, U. N.Mex. Atty.; mem. Dist. 47 N. Mex. House of Reps., 2009—. Democrat. Home: 128 Grant Ave 301 Santa Fe NM 87501 Office: House of Representatives The State Capitol North Rm 203FCN Santa Fe NM 87503 Home Phone: 505-986-1782; Office Phone: 505-986-9641. E-mail: brian@brianegolf.com.

EGUCHI, YASU, artist; b. Japan, Nov. 30, 1938; came to U.S., 1967; s. Chihaku and Kiku (Koga) E.; m. Anita Phillips, Feb. 24, 1968. Student, Horie Art Acad., Japan, 1958-65. Exhibited exhbns., Tokyo Mus. Art, 1963, 66, Santa Barbara Mus. Art, Calif., 1972-74, 85, Everson Mus. Art, Syracuse, N.Y., 1980, Nat. Acad. Art, N.Y.C., 1980—; one-man shows include Austin Gallery, Scottsdale, Ariz., 1968-87, Joy Tash Gallery, Scottsdale, 1989-99, Greystone Galleries, Cambria, Calif., 1969, 70, 72, Copenhagen Galleries, Calif., 1970-78, Charles and Emma Frye Art Mus., Seattle, 1974, 84, 98, Hammer Galleries, N.Y.C., 1977, 79, 81, 93, 2001, 2002, City of Heidenheim, Germany, 1980, Artique Ltd., Anchorage, 1981—, Heidenheim Mus. Art, 2000; pub. and pvt. collections, Voith Gmbh, Germany, City of Giengen and City of Heidenheim, Germany, represented, Deer Valley, Utah, Hunter Resources, Santa Barbara, Am. Embassy, Paris, Charles and Emma Frye Art Mus., Seattle, Nat. Acad. Art; author: Der Brenz Entlang, 1980; author: Yasu Eguchi, Kunstmuseum Heidenheim, 2000; contbr. to jours in field. Active Guide Dogs for the Blind, San Raphael, Calif., 1976, City of Santa Barbara Arts Coun., 1979, The Eye Bank for Sight Restoration, NY, 1981, Anchorage Arts Coun., 1981, Santa Barbara Mus. Natural History, 1989, Kinder & Kunst Artist Projecti, Heidenheim, Forest Lawn Mus., 2006. Recipient Selective Artist award Yokohama Citizen Gallery, 1965; recipient Artist of Yr. award Santa Barbara Arts Council, 1979, Hon. Citizen award City of Heidenheim, 1980, The Adolph and Clara Obrig prize NAD, 1983, Cert. of Merit NAD, 1985, 87. Home: PO Box 30206 Santa Barbara CA 93130-0206

EHMANN, ANTHONY VALENTINE, lawyer; b. Chgo., Sept. 5, 1935; s. Anthony E. and Frances (Verweil) E.; m. Alice A. Avina, Nov. 27, 1959; children: Ann, Thomas, Jerome, Gregory, Rose, Robert. BS, Ariz. State U., 1957; JD, U. Ariz., 1960. Bar: Ariz. 1960, U.S. Tax Ct. 1960, U.S. Supreme Ct. 1968; CPA, Ariz.; cert. tax specialist, trusts and estates specialist. Spl. asst. atty. gen., 1961-68; mem. Ehmann and Hiller, Phoenix, 1969—2004, Fennemore Craig, Phoenix, 2004—. Rep. dist. chmn. Ariz., 1964; pres. Grand Canyon coun. Boy Scouts Am., 1987-89, mem. exec. com., 1981—, v.p. western region, 1991-99; bd. dirs. Nat. Cath. Com. on Scouting, 1995—. Recipient Silver Beaver award Boy Scouts Am., 1982, Bronze Pelican award Cath. Com. on Scouting, 1981, Silver Antelope award Boy Scouts Am., 1994. Fellow Am. Coll. Trusts and Estate Counsel; mem. State Bar Ariz. (chmn. tax sect. 1968, 69), Ctrl. Ariz. Estate Planning Coun. (pres. 1968, 69), Rotary Club, KC (grand knight Glendale, Ariz. 1964, 65), Serra Internat. (pres. Phoenix 1992-93, dist. gov. ariz. 1993-95), Knight of Holy Sepulchre, Knight of Malta, Legatus. Republican. Roman Catholic. Office: Fennemore Craig 3003 N Central Ste 2600 Phoenix AZ 85012 Office Phone: 602-916-5416. Business E-Mail: ehmann@fclaw.com.

EHRHORN, RICHARD WILLIAM, electronics executive; b. Marshalltown, Iowa, Jan. 21, 1934; s. Theodore Raymond and Zelda Elizabeth (Axtell) E.; m. Marilyn Patrick, Aug. 1, 1959; children: Scott Patrick, Kimberlee Dawn. BSEE, U. Minn., 1955; MSEE, Calif. Inst. Tech., 1958. Sr. engr. Gen. Dynamics Corp., Pomona, Calif., 1956-60; sr. rsch. engr. Calif. Inst. Tech. Jet Propulsion Lab., Pasedena, 1960-63; mgr. advanced devel. lab. Electronic Communications Inc., St. Petersburg, Fla., 1963-68; gen. mgr. Signal/One div., 1968-70; chmn., CEO Ehrhorn Tech. Ops., Inc., Colorado Springs, Colo., 1970-95; vice chmn. ASTeX/ETO, Inc., Colorado Springs, 1996-99; regent Liberty U., 1995—; chmn., CEO Alpha/Power, Inc., Longmont, Colo., 1996-2000; ptnr. Alpha Radio Products, LLC, Boulder, Colo., 2005—. Author: (with others) Principles of Electronic Warfare, 1959; patentee in field. Mem.: IEEE (sr. life), Am. Radio Relay League (life).

EHRLICH, ANNE HOWLAND, research biologist; b. Des Moines, Nov. 17, 1933; d. Winston Densmore and Virginia Lippincott (Fitzhugh) Howland; m. Paul Ralph Ehrlich, Dec. 18, 1954; 1 child: Lisa Marie Daniel. Student, U. Kans., 1952-55; LLD (hon.), Bethany Coll., 1990; doctorate (hon.), Oreg. State U., 1999. Technician dept. entomology U. Kans., Lawrence, 1955; rsch. asst. dept. biol. scis. Stanford (Calif.) U., 1959-72, rsch. assoc., 1972-75, sr. rsch. assoc., 1975—, assoc. dir. Ctr. for Conservation Biology, 1987—. Bd. dirs. Pacific Inst., Ploughshares Fund. Author: (with others) Ecoscience: Population, Resources, Environment, 1977, The Golden Door, 1979, Extinction, 1981, Earth, 1987, The Population Explosion, 1990, Healing the Planet, 1991, The Stork and the Plow, 1995, Betrayal of Science and Reason, 1996, One With Ninevah, 2004; contbr. articles to profl. jours. Named to Global 500 Roll of Honour for Environ. Achievement, UN, 1989, UNEP-Sasekawa prize, 1994, Heinz award, 1995, Tyler prize, 1998. Fellow Am. Acad. Arts & Scis., Calif. Acad. Scis. (hon.); mem. Am. Humanists Assn. (hon. life, Disting. Svc. 1985, Raymond B. Bragg award 1985). Avocations: fly fishing, hiking, reading. Home: Pine Hill Stanford CA 94305 Office: Stanford U Dept Biol Scis Stanford CA 94305

EHRLICH, ANNETTE, psychologist, educator; b. NYC, Mar. 23, 1931; d. Alexander and Henrietta (Frant) Goldhirsch; m. Daniel Ehrlich, June 1956 (div. 1963). BA, Bklyn. Coll., 1954; MA, CUNY, 1956; PhD, McGill U., Montreal, 1960. Rsch. assoc. Med. Sch., Northwestern U., Chgo., 1960-64; asst. prof. Bowling Green (Ohio) State U., 1966-69; from asst. prof. to assoc. prof. Calif. State U., LA, 1969-75, prof., 1975—94; emeritus prof., 1994—. Cons. in rsch. design, L.A., 1982—. Contbr. articles to profl. jours. Columbia U. fellow, 1975-76; Rsch. grantee NIMH, 1969-73, The Grant Found. N.Y., 1973. Mem. Am. Soc. Primatologists, Internat. Primatological Soc. Avocations: photography, folk dance.

EHRLICH, KENNETH JAMES, television producer; b. Cleve., May 11; s. Arthur A. and Lucile Ehrlich; m. Harriet Stromberg, Feb. 19, 1967; children: Mathew, Dori. BS in Journalism, Ohio U., 1964. Pres. Comminique, Chgo., 1970-72; dir. devel. Sta. WTTW-TV, Chgo., 1972-76; pres. Ken Ehrlich Prodns., Los Angeles, 1976—. Exec. producer (series) Showtime Coast to Coast, numerous spls. with Paul Simon, Stevie Wonder, Phil Collins, Elton John, Eric Clapton, Shania Twain, Faith HIll, Celine Dion, Christina Aguilera, Ricky Martin, Ray Charles, Patti LaBelle others, intimate portrait (9 episodes), 1997-2001; exec. prodr. or producer Grammy Awards Show, 1980—, Blockbuster Awards, 1995-2001, Latin Grammys, Alma Awards, 2002, Primetime Emmy awards, 2005-; producer Soundstage (creator), writer, dir. 1974-83, Fame, 1983-85; producer Soundstage (creator), Nelson Mandela Freedom Fest, 1988. Recipient Golden Rose of Montreax (Switzerland) Montreax Film Fest, 1975, Golden Globe award Hollywood Fgn. Press Assn., Los Angeles, 1983, Emmy award Acad. of TV Arts and Scis., Los Angeles, 1984, Emmy award nominations, 1986, 88, Visionary award, Producers Guild of Am., 2007. Mem. Nat. Assn. Cable TV (bd. dirs.). Avocations: golf, music, writing. Office: Ken Ehrlich Prodns 17200 Oak View Dr Encino CA 91316-4014

EHRLICH, PAUL RALPH, biology professor; b. Phila., May 29, 1932; s. William and Ruth (Rosenberg) E.; m. Anne Fitzhugh Howland, Dec. 18, 1954; 1 child, Lisa Marie. AB, U. Pa., 1953; AM, U. Kans., 1955, PhD, 1957. Rsch assoc. U. Kans., Lawrence, 1958—59; asst. prof. biol. scis. Stanford U., 1959—62, assoc. prof., 1962—66, prof., 1966—, Bing prof. population studies, 1976—, dir. grad. study dept. biol. scis., 1966—69, pres. Ctr. for Conservation Biology, 1988—, dir. grad. study dept. biol. scis., 1974—76. Cons. Behavioral Rsch. Labs., 1963—67; corr. NBC News, 1989—92. Author: How to Know the Butterflies, 1961, Process of Evolution, 1963, Principles of Modern Biology, 1968, Population Bomb, 1968, Population Bomb, 2d edit., 1971, Population, Resources, Environment: Issues in Human Ecology, 1970, Population, Resources, Environment: Issues in Human Ecology, 2d edit. 1972, How to Be a Survivor, 1971, Global Ecology: Readings Toward a Rational Strategy for Man, 1971, Man and the Ecosphere, 1971, Introductory Biology, 1973, Human Ecology: Problems and Solutions, 1973, Ark II: Social Response to Environmental Imperatives, 1974, The End of Affluence: A Blueprint for the Future, 1974, Biology and Society, 1976, Race Bomb, 1977, Ecoscience: Population, Resources, Environment, 1977, Insect Biology, 1978, The Golden Door: International Migration, Mexico, and the U.S., 1979, Extinction: The Causes and Consequences of the Disappearance of Species, 1981, The Machinery of Nature, 1986, Earth, 1987, The Science of Ecology, 1987, The Birder's Handbook, 1988, New World/New Mind, 1989, The Population Explosion, 1990, Healing the Planet, 1991, Birds in Jeopardy, 1992, The Birdwatchers Handbook, 1994, The Stork & the Plow, 1995, Betrayal of Science and Reason, 1996, World of Wounds, 1997, Human Natures, 2000, Wild Solutions, 2001, Butterflies: Ecology and Evolution Taking Flight, 2003, On the Wings of Checkerspots, 2004, One with Nineveh, 2004, The Dominant Animal: Human Evolution on the Environment, 2008; contbr. articles to profl. jours. Recipient World Wildlife Fedn. medal, 1987, Volvo Environ. prize, 1993, World Ecology medal, Internat. Ctr. Tropical Ecology, 1993, UN Sasakawa Environ. prize, 1994, Heinz prize for the environment, 1995, Tyler Environ. prize, 1998, Heineken prize for environ. sci., 1998, Blue Plant prize, 1999, Disting. Achievement award, Kansas U. Alumni, 2003; co-recipient Crafoord prize in population biology and conservation biol. diversity, 1990; fellow MacArthur Prize fellow, 1990—95. Fellow: AAAS, Entomology Soc. Am., Am. Philos. Soc., Am. Acad. Arts and Scis., Calif. Acad. Scis. (Fellows medal 2003); mem.: NAS, Lepidopterists Soc., Am. Mus. Natural History (hon.), Am. Mus. Natural History (life), Brit. Ecol. Soc. (hon.), Am. Soc. Naturalists, Soc. Systematic Biology, Soc. for Study of Evolution, Ecol. Soc. Am. (Eminent Ecologist award 2001). Office: Stanford U Dept Biol Scis Stanford CA 94305

EHRLICH, THOMAS, law educator; b. Cambridge, Mass., Mar. 4, 1934; s. William and Evelyn (Seltzer) E.; m. Ellen (Rome), June 18, 1957; children: David, Elizabeth, Paul. AB, Harvard U., Cambridge, Mass., 1956, LLB, 1959; LLD (hon.), Villanova U., 1979, Notre Dame U., 1980, Pa. State U., 1987. Bar: Wis., 1959. Law clk. Judge Learned Hand U.S. Ct. Appeals 2d. Cir., 1959-60; spl. asst. to legal adviser U.S. State Dept., 1962-64, spl. asst. to under-sec., 1964-65; assoc. prof. law Stanford U., Stanford, Calif., 1965-68; prof. Stanford U., Stanford, Calif., 1968-75; dean Stanford U., Stanford, Calif., 1971-75, Richard E. Lang dean and prof., 1973-75; pres. Legal Services Corp., Washington, 1976-79; dir. Internat. Devel. Coop. Agy., Washington, 1979-81; provost, prof. law U. Penn., Phila., 1981-87; pres., prof. law Ind. U., Bloomington and Indpls., Ind., 1987-94; vis. prof. Duke U., Durham, NC, 1994; disting. Univ. scholar U. Calif., San Francisco, 1995-2000. Vis. prof. Stanford Law Sch., 1994-99; sr. scholar, Carnegie Found. for Advancement of Tchg., 1997—. Author: (with Abram Chayes and Andreas F. Lowenfeld) The Internat. Legal Process, 3 vols., 1968; (with Herbert L. Packer) New Directions in Legal Edn., 1972, Internat. Crises and the Role of Law, Cyprus, 1958-67, 1974; editor: (with Geoffrey C. Hazard Jr.) Going to Law School?, 1975; (with Mary Ellen O'Connell) Internat. Law and the Use of Force, 1993, The Courage to Inquire, 1995, Philanthropy and the Nonprofit Sector in a Changing Am., 1998, Civic Responsibility and Higher Edn., 2000; (with Jane V. Wellman) How the Student Hour Shapes Higher Education: The Tie that Binds, 2003; (with others) Educating Citizens: Preparing America's Undergraduates for Lives of Moral and Civic Responsibility, 2003, (with Ray Bacchetti) Reconnecting Education & Foundations: Turning Good Intentions Into Educational Capital, 2006, (with others) Educating for Democracy: Preparing Undergraduates for Responsible Political Engagement, 2007. Office: Carnegie Found Advancement Tchg 51 Vista Ln Stanford CA 94305-8703 Home Phone: 650-853-8608; Office Phone: 650-566-5137. E-mail: ehrlich@carnegiefoundation.org.

EIBERGER, CARL FREDERICK, lawyer; b. Denver, Jan. 17, 1931; s. Carl Frederick and Madeleine Anastasia (Ries) E.; children: Eileen, Carl III, Mary, James. BS in Chemistry magna cum laude, U. Notre Dame, 1952, JD magna cum laude, 1954; MBA, Denver U., 1959. Sole practice, 1954-55; ptnr. Rovira, DeMuth & Eiberger, Denver, 1957—79, Eiberger, Stacy, Smith & Martin, Denver, 1979-96; prin. Carl F. Eiberger & Assocs., Denver, 1996—. Chmn. CBA/DBA/Econs. of Law Practice Coms.; co-founder CBA/Steering Com. Labor Law Com., Denver; arbitrator Am. Arbitration Assn.; asst. bar examiner, 1963-68; lectr. on continuing legal edn. Contbr. articles to legal jours. Bd. dirs. Colo. Assn. Commerce and Industry; pres. Prospect Recreation and Park Dist.; founder Applewood Athletic Club, Jefferson County; gen. counsel Denver Symphony Orch. Recipient merit award Jefferson County Commrs., merit cert. Jefferson County Homeowners, McCafferty Disting Svc. award U. Notre Dame Law Sch.; named Man of the Yr. Notre Dame Club of Denver, Vol. of Yr. Channel 9TV, Denver., Citizen of Yr., Lions Club Internat., Citizen Amb. of US, Silent Hero of Notre Dame, 2006; Prospect Dist. Pk. named in his honor. Mem. ABA, Colo. Bar Assn. (bd. govs.), Denver Bar Assn. (nominated pres.), Notre Dame Law Assn. (bd. dirs. 1965—, exec. com. 1998—), Gov. Adv. Coun. to Colo dept. of labor, Notre Dame Club (pres., bd. dirs.), Athletic Club (Denver). Roman Catholic. Home and Office: 14330 Fairview Ln Golden CO 80401-2050 Office Phone: 303-278-0707. Fax: 303-278-0113.

EICHELBERGER, JOHN CHARLES, volcanologist, educator; b. Syracuse, NY, Oct. 3, 1948; s. William Custer and Esther (Dorr) E.; m. Alice Palen, Dec. 27, 1969 (div. 1993); children: Laura Palen, Nathan William; m. Gail Davidson, Sept. 3, 1994; stepchildren: Jennifer Ruth March, Jody Elizabeth March. BS, MS in Geology, MIT, 1971; PhD in Geology, Stanford U., 1974. Staff mem. Los Alamos (N.Mex.) Nat. Lab., 1974-79; mem. tech. staff Sandia Nat. Labs., Albuquerque, 1979-89, disting. mem. tech. staff, 1989-90, supr. geochem. divsn., 1990-91; prof. volcanology U. Alaska, Fairbanks, 1991—. Group leader volcanology Geophys. Inst., 1991—; coord. scientist Alaska Volcano Obs., 1991—; chief scientist Katmai (Alaska) Sci. Drilling Project, 1988-94, Inyo Sci. Drilling Project, Mammoth Lake, Calif., 1983-88; adj. prof. geochemistry N.Mex. Inst. Mines and Tech., Socorro, 1989-91. Editor Volcanology of Eos, Transactions of the Am. Geophys. Union, 1985-88; assoc. editor Jour. Geophys. Rsch., 1998—; contbr. more than 60 articles to profl. jours. Fellow Geol. Soc. Am.; mem. Am. Geophys. Union (life). Office: U Alaska Alaska Volcano Observatory Geophysical Inst Fairbanks AK 99775 E-mail: eich@gi.alaska.edu.

EICHINGER, MARILYNNE KATZEN, museum administrator; children: Ryan, Kara, Julia, Jessica, Talik. BA in Anthropology and Sociology magna cum laude, Boston U., 1965; MA, Mich. State U., 1971. With emergency and outpatient staff Ingham County Mental Health Ctr., 1972; founder, pres., exec. dir. Impression 5 Sci. and Art Mus., Lansing, Mich., 1973-85; pres. Oreg. Mus. Sci. and Industry, Portland, 1985-95; bd. dirs. Portland Visitors Assn., 1985-95; pres. Informal Edn. Products Ltd., 1995—, Portland, 1995—. Bd. dirs. N.W. Regional Edn. Labs., 1991-97; instr. Lansing (Mich.) C.C., 1978; ptnr. Eyrie Studio, 1982-85; condr. numerous workshops in interactive exhibit design, adminstrn. and fund devel. for schs., orgns., profl. socs. Author: (with Jane Mack) Lexington Montessori School Survey, 1969, Manual on the Five Senses, 1974; pub. Mich. edit. Boing mag. Founder Cambridge Montessori Sch., 1964; bd. dirs. Lexington Montessori Sch., 1969, Mid-Mich. South Health Sys. Agy., 1978-81, Cmty. Referral Ctr., 1981-85, Sta. WKAR, 1981-85; active Lansing "Riverfest" Lighted Boat Parade, 1980; mem. state Health Coordinating Coun., 1980-82; mem. pres.'s adv. coun. Portland State U., 1986—90, mem. pres.' adv. bd., 1987-91; bd. dirs. Portland Visitors Assn., 1994-97, Friends of Tryon Creek State Pk., 2001-06. Recipient Diana Cert. Leadership, YWCA, 1976-77, Woman of Achievement award, 1991, Cmty. Svc. award Portland State U., 1992, Cataloguer of Yr. award Catalog Success, 2005. Mem. Am. Assn. Mus., Oreg. Mus. Assn., Assn. Sci. and Tech. Ctrs. (bd. dirs. 1980-84, 88-93), Mus. Store Assn., Direct Mktg. Assn., Zonta Lodge (founder, bd. dirs. East Lansing club 1978), Internat. Women's Forum, Woman Pres. Orgn., Portland C. of C. Office: Informal Edn Products Ltd 2517 SE Mailwell Dr Milwaukie OR 97222 Home Phone: 503-224-6374. Business E-Mail: sales@museumtour.com.

EICKHOFF, THEODORE CARL, infectious disease physician, epidemiologist; b. Cleve., Sept. 13, 1931; s. Theodore Henry and Clara (Strasen) E.; m. Margaret Heinecke, Aug. 24, 1952; children: Stephen, Mark, Philip. BA, Valparaiso U., 1953; MD, Case Western Res. U., 1957. Diplomate Am. Bd. Internal Medicine. Intern, then resident Harvard Med. Svcs., Boston City Hosp., 1957-59; fellow in medicine Harvard Med. Sch.-Boston City Hosp., 1961-64; epidemiologist Ctr. for Disease Control, 1964-67; prof. medicine U. Colo. Med. Ctr., 1975—2003, prof. emeritus, 2003—, head divsn. infectious disease, 1967-80, vice chmn. dept. medicine, 1976-81; dir. medicine Denver Gen. Hosp., 1978-81; dir. internal medicine Presbyn./St. Luke's Med. Ctr., 1981-92. Cons. FDA, CDC, Am. Hosp. Assn.; mem. nat. commn. orphan diseases HHS, 1986-90, mem. vaccines adv. com., 1995-99. Contbr. over 150 articles to med. jours. Served with USPHS, 1959-67. Recipient Commr.'s Spl. Citation, FDA, 1990, Trustee's award Am. Hosp. Assn., 1993. Master ACP (Disting. Internist award Colo. chpt. 1995); mem. Am. Fedn. Clin. Rsch., Am. Soc. Clin. Investigation, Assn. Am. Physicians, Infectious Diseases Soc. Am. (sec. 1978-82, pres. 1983-84, Finland Lectureship award 1995), Am. Epidemiol. Soc. (pres. 1985-86). Home: 5114 Long Meadow Cir Greenwood Village CO 80111-3436 Office: Univ Colo Health Sci Ctr 12700 E 19th Ave Arvada CO 80004 Home Phone: 303-789-0194; Office Phone: 303-724-4928. Business E-Mail: theodore.eickhoff@ucdenver.edu.

EID, ALLISON HARTWELL, state supreme court justice; b. Spokane, Wash. m. Troy Eid; 2 children. BA in Am. Studies with honors, Stanford U., 1987; JD, U. Chgo., 1991; Temple Bar scholar, London. Bar: 1991. Former special asst. and speechwriter US Dept. Edn.; clk. to Judge Jerry E. Smith US Ct. of Appeals for Fifth Circuit, Houston, 1991; clk. to Justice Clarence Thomas US Supreme Ct., 1993; former atty. Arnold & Porter, Denver; assoc. prof. law U. Colo., 1998—2005; former chief legal officer Colo. Atty. Gen.; solicitor gen. State of Colo., 2005—06; justice Colo. Supreme Ct., 2006—. Mem. Permanent Com. for Oliver Wendell Holmes Devise, 2002—. Mem.: Am. Law Inst., Order of the Coif, Phi Beta Kappa. Office: Colo Supreme Ct 2 E 14th Ave Fourth Fl Denver CO 80203 Office Phone: 303-837-3790.

EID, TROY A., lawyer, former prosecutor; b. Chgo., Nov. 2, 1963; m. Allison Eid; 2 children. BA, Stanford U., 1986; JD, U. Chgo., 1991. Bar: Colo. 1991, US Ct. Appeals (5th Cir.), US Dist. Ct. Colo. Law clk. to Hon. Edith H. Jones US Ct. Appeals (5th cir.), 1991—92; assoc. Holme Roberts & Owen, LLP, Denver, 1992—94; COO, gen. counsel InfoTEST Internat., 1994—98; chief legal counsel to Gov. State of Colo., Denver, 1999—2001, sec. pers. & adminstrn., 2001—03; ptnr. Greenberg Traurig LLP, Denver, 2003—06, 2009—; US atty. Dist. Colo. US Dept. Justice, Denver, 2006—09. Adj. prof. Am. Indian law U. Colo. Recipient Coloradan of the Yr. award, Colo. Jaycees, Outstanding Govt. Advocate of the Yr. award, US Hispanic C of C; grantee Am. Marshall Meml. Fellowship, German Marshall Fund US. Mem.: Navajo Nation Bar Assn., Am. Law Inst., Colo. Bar Found., Colo. Bar Assn. Office: Greenberg Traurig LLP 1200 17th St Ste 2400 Denver CO 80202 Office Phone: 303-572-6500. Office Fax: 303-572-6540. E-mail: eidt@gtlaw.com.*

EIDE, TRACEY J., state legislator; m. Mark Eide; children: Joanna, Matthew. Grad. sr. execs. in state and local govt. program, Harvard U. JFK Sch. Govt., Mass. Small bus. owner; mem. Wash. House of Reps., Olympia, 1993—94; mem. Dist. 30 Wash. State Senate, Olympia, 1998—, majority fl. leader, 2005—. Mem.: Federal Way Lions Club. Democrat. Office: 305 Legislative Bldg PO Box 40430 Olympia WA 98504-0430 Office Phone: 360-786-7658. Office Fax: 360-786-1999. Business E-Mail: eide.tracey@leg.wa.gov.*

EIFLER, KAREN ELIZABETH, language educator; b. Des Moines, Oct. 17, 1960; d. Clyde Andrew and Marilyn Elizabeth (Quinn) Perlenfein; m. Mark Eifler. BA magna cum laude in Study of Religion, UCLA, 1982; PhD in Adminstrn., Curriculum and Instrn., U. Nebr., Lincoln, 1997. Clear multiple subject tchg. credential Holy Names Coll., Calif., 1986. Tchr. Our Lady of Peace Sch., Sepulveda, Calif., 1983—86, St. Mary's Jr. HS, Walnut Creek, Calif., 1986—90, Sch. of the Madeleine Jr. HS, Berkeley, Calif., 1990—92; grad. lectr. U. Nebr., Kearney, 1993—98; asst. prof. edn. U. Portland, Oreg., 1998—2004, assoc. prof., 2004—. Writing cons. U. Calif., Berkeley, Diocese of Oakland, Calif., 1989-90; lectr. St. Mary's Coll., Moraga, Calif., 1990. Contbr. articles to profl. jours.; prodr. video presentation Magnificat Anima, 1990. Bd. dirs. Garaventa Ctr. Cath. Intellectual Life and Am. Culture, 2005—. Recipient Assn. Liberal Arts Colls. for Tchr. Edn. Scholar award, US Prof. of Yr. award, Carnegie Found. for Advancement of Tchg. and Coun. for Advancement and Support of Edn., 2006. Mem.: Assn. Liberal Arts Colls. for Tchr. Edn., Am. Assn. Colls. of Tchr. Edn., Assn. Supervision and Curriculum Devel., Am. Ednl. Rsch. Assn., Nat. Assn. Multicultural Edn., Kappa Delta Pi, Phi Beta Kappa. Roman Catholic. Avocations: reading, sewing, crafts, hiking. Office: Sch Edn U Portland 5000 N Willamette Blvd Portland OR 97203-5798 Office Phone: 503-943-8014. E-mail: eifler@up.edu.

EIGNER, WILLIAM WHITLING, lawyer; b. Dover, Ohio, Feb. 4, 1959; s. Stanley Spencer and Jeraldine (Lippy) E. BA, Stanford U., 1981; JD, U. Va., 1986. Bar: Calif. 1986, U.S. Dist. Ct. (so. dist.) Calif. 1986. Jud. intern U.S. Supreme Ct., Washington, 1981; assoc. Higgs, Fletcher & Mack, San Diego, 1986-89, Procopio, Cory, Hargreaves & Savitch LLP, San Diego, 1989-95, ptnr., 1995—. Bd. dirs. Mundoval Fund, CommNexus San Diego; bd. advisors QuantumThink Group, Inc., Bioelectric Med. Solutions, Inc., Am. Eco-Energy, Bluedominoes Inc., Iselfstore mem. San Diego Venture Group. Contbr. articles to profl. jours. Trustee, La Jolla (Calif.) Town Coun., 1988-92, chmn. land use com., 1988-90; trustee La Jolla Country Day Sch., 2004-08 Recipient spl. commendation San Diego City Coun., Vol. Advocate of Yr., San Diego Regional C. of C., 2004, named Top Atty. San Diego Com., 2008. Mem. ABA, State Bar Calif., San Diego County Bar Assn. (bus. sect.), San Diego Regional C. of C. (bd. dirs. 1998-2001, 03-06, 08-, chmn. bus. recognition and awards com. 1989-98, chmn. emerging bus. com. 1998-00, pub. policy com.). Republican. Jewish. Avocations: tennis, Civil War history. Office: Procopio Cory Hargreaves & Savitch LLP 530 B St Ste 2100 San Diego CA 92101-4496 Office Phone: 619-515-3210. Business E-Mail: wwe@procopio.com.

EIGSTI, ROGER HARRY, retired insurance company executive; b. Vancouver, Wash., Apr. 17, 1942; s. Harry A. and Alice E. (Huber) E.; m. Mary Lou Nelson, June 8, 1963; children: Gregory, Ann. BS, Linfield Coll., 1964. CPA, Oreg., Wash. Staff CPA Touche Ross and Co., Portland, Oreg., 1964-72; asst. to controller Safeco Corp., Seattle, 1972-78, controller, 1980, Safeco Life Ins. Co., Seattle, 1978-80; pres. Safeco Credit Co., Seattle, 1980-81, Safeco Life Ins. Co., Seattle, 1981-85; exec. v.p., CFO Safeco Corp., Seattle, 1985, CEO, chmn., 1985-2001. Bd. dirs. Ind. Colls. of Wash., Seattle, 1981-87, bus. dir. Seattle Repertory Theatre, 1981—, bd. dirs. 1981—. Mem. Am. Inst. CPA's, Life Office Mgmt. Assn. (bd. dirs. 1983—), Seattle C. of C. (chmn. metro budget rev. com. 1984—). Clubs: Mercer Island (Wash.) Country (treas., bd. dirs. 1981-84); Central Park Tennis. Republican. Home: 1503 Parkside Dr E Seattle WA 98112-3719

EILENBERG, LAWRENCE IRA, theater educator, artistic director; b. Bklyn., May 26, 1947; s. Jerome and Dorothy Vera (Natleson) E.; m. Diane Marie Eliasof, Nov. 25, 1973 (dec. Dec. 1984); children: David Joseph, Benjamin Alan; m. Judith Heiner, Nov. 10, 1990 (dec. Nov. 1994), Kathleen O'ttara, Jan. 06, 2008. BA, Cornell U., 1968; MPhil, Yale U., 1971, PhD, 1975. Jr. fellow Davenport Coll., Yale U., New Haven, 1971-72; asst. prof. theatre dept. Cornell U., Ithaca, N.Y., 1972-75; vis. asst. prof. in theatre U. Mich., Ann Arbor, 1975-77; asst. prof., then assoc. prof. U. Denver, 1977-82, 83; prof. San Francisco State U., 1983—, chmn. theatre arts dept., 1984-92; artistic dir. Magic Theatre, San Francisco, 1992-93, 1998—2003, dramaturg, 1997—98. Theatre corr. Sta. KCFR (NPR), Denver, 1979-82; literary mgr. Denver Ctr. Theatre Co., 1981-83; artistic dir. San Francisco New Vaudeville Festival, 1985-89; dramaturg One Act Theatre Co., San Francisco, 1986-88; bd. dirs. Theatre Bay Area, San Francisco, 1985-90, pres., 1987-89; co-dir. Congress of Clowns, 1994; speaker, lectr. in field. Editor Stage/Space mag., 1981-83; contbr. articles, book and theater revs. to profl. publs. U.S. del. Podium Festival of USSR, Moscow, 1989. Grantee Lilly Found., 1981, Idaho Humanities Assn., 1983, 84, 85, NEA, 1986, 92, Calif. Arts Coun., 1987, 88, 92; recipient Best Broadcast award Colo. Broadcasters Assn., 1982. Mem. Literary Mgrs. and Dramaturgs Am. (v.p. 1989-90), Nat. Assn. Schs. of Theatre (bd. accreditation, 1990-91, evaluator 1986—). Office: San Francisco State U Theatre Arts Dept 1600 Holloway Ave San Francisco CA 94132-1722 Home: 642 Amaranth Blvd Mill Valley CA 94941-2605 Office Phone: 415-338-1341. Business E-Mail: leilenbe@sfsu.edu.

EINSTEIN, ALBERT See BROOKS, ALBERT

EINSTEIN, CLIFFORD JAY, advertising executive; b. LA, May 4, 1939; s. Harry and Thelma (Bernstein) E.; m. Madeline Mandel, Jan. 28, 1962; children: Harold Jay, Karen Holly. BA in English, UCLA, 1961; PhD, DFA, Otis Coll. Art and Design, 2002. Writer Norman, Craig and Kummel, NYC, 1961-62, Foote, Cone and Belding, LA, 1962-64; ptnr. Silverman and Einstein, LA, 1965-67; pres., creative dir. Dailey and Assos., LA, 1968-93, chmn., 1994—, also bd dirs. Dir. Campaign '80, advt. agy. Reagan for Pres., 1980; lectr. various colls.; founder First Coastal Bank; bd. dirs. Cost Plus World Market, Mapleton Comm., Mcht. House Internat. Contbr. articles to Advertising Age; prodr.: (play) Whatever Happened to Georgie Tapps, L.A. and San Francisco, 1980; film appearances include Real Life, Modern Romance, Defending Your Life, Face/Off, 1997; T.V. appearance in Bizarre, Super Dave Show. Bd. dirs. Discovery Fund for Eye Rsch.; chmn. Emeritus Mus. Contemporary Art, L.A.; with U.S. Army, 1957. Recipient Am. Advt. award, 1968, 73, 79, Clio award, 1973, Internat. Broadcast Pub. Svc. award, 1970, 85, Nat. Addy award, 1979, Gov.'s award, 1987; named Creative Dir. of the West, Adweek Poll, 1982, Exec. of West, 1986, Western States Assn. Advt. Agys. Leader of Yr., 1992, Leader of the West, Am. Advt. Fedn., 2002. Mem. AFTRA, ASCAP, SAG, Dirs. Guild Am., Hillcrest Country Club, Calif. Club.

EINSTEIN, STEPHEN JAN, rabbi; b. LA, Nov. 15, 1945; s. Syd C. and Selma (Rothenberg) E.; m. Robin Susan Kessler, Sept. 9, 1967; children: Rebecca Yael, Jennifer Melissa, Heath Isaac, Zachary Shane. AB, UCLA, 1967; BHL, Hebrew Union Coll., LA, 1968, DHL, 1995, DD (hon.), 1996; MAHL, Hebrew Union Coll., Cin., 1971. Ordained rabbi. Rabbi Temple Beth Am, Parsippany, NJ, 1971-74, Temple Beth David, Westminster, Calif., 1974-76, Congregation B'nai Tzedek, Fountain Valley, Calif., 1976—. Lectr. Calif. State U., Fullerton. Co-author: Every Person's Guide to Judaism, 1989; co-editor: Introduction to Judaism, 1983. Pres., trustee Fountain Valley (Calif.) Sch. Bd., 1984—90; chmn. pers. commn. Fountain Valley Sch. Dist., 1991—; pres. Retinoblatoma Internat., 2000—01; chaplain Fountain Valley Police Dept.; pres. Greater Huntington Beach Inter-Faith Coun., 2001—02; active Anti Defamation League, Am. Jewish Com.; co-chmn. Commn. on Outreach and Synagogue Cmty., 1999—; regional bd. dirs. Nat. Conf. Cmty. and Justice, 2001—06; co-chair, cmty. adv. bd. KOCE-TV. Recipient Micah Award for Interfaith Activities, Am. Jewish Com., 1988. Mem.: Inst. for Character Edn. (exec. adv. bd.), Clergy for Choice, Orange County Bur. Jewish Edn. (v.p. 1982—84, 1992—94, pres. 1994—97, honored for Maj. Contbns. to Jewish Learning 1986), Jewish Educators Assn. Orange County (pres. 1979—81), Orange County Bd. Rabbis (pres. 1976—79, 1997—98), Pacific Assn. Reform Rabbis (exec. bd. 1987—91, 1998—2002, pres. 2002—03), Ctrl. Conf. Am. Rabbis (exec. bd. 1989—91, ethics com. 1993—98, 2006, chair 2007—), Alzheimers Assn. (religious adv. com.), Am. Cancer Soc. (v.p. West Orange County dist. 1994—98), Phi Beta Kappa. Democrat. Office: Congregation Bnai Tzedek 9669 Talbert Ave Fountain Valley CA 92708 Home Phone: 714-963-0285; Office Phone: 714-963-4611. Personal E-mail: rebgiraffe@aol.com.

EISEN, MICHAEL B., research scientist, educator; Degree in Math., Harvard U., 1989, PhD in Biophysics, 1996. Post-doctoral fellow Stanford U.; scientist, life sciences divsn. Ernest Orlando Lawrence Berkeley Nat. Lab, 2000—; adj. asst. prof., dept. molecular and cellular biology U. Calif., Berkeley, 2000—. Co-founder, bd. dir. Pub. Libr. Sci. (PLoS), 2003—. Recipient Benjamin Franklin award in Bioinformatics, 2002. Fellow: World Tech. Network (World Tech. Network award (Media and Journalism) 2005). Office: Lawrence Berkeley Nat Lab Mailstop 84-171 One Cyclotron Rd Berkeley CA 94720 Address: Pub Libr Sci (PLoS) 185 Berry St Ste San Francisco CA 94107 Office Phone: 510-486-5214. Office Fax: 786-549-0137. Business E-Mail: mbeisen@lbl.gov.

EISENBERG, DAVID SAMUEL, molecular biologist, educator; b. Chgo., Mar. 15, 1939; s. George and Ruth E.; m. Lucy Tuchman, Aug. 25, 1963; children: Jenny, Nell. AB, Harvard U., 1961; Phil.D., Oxford U., Eng., 1964. NSF postdoctoral fellow Princeton U., 1964-66; research fellow chemistry Calif. Inst. Tech., Pasadena, 1966-69; asst. prof. UCLA, 1968-71, assoc. prof., 1971-76, prof. chemistry, biochemistry, 1976—, assoc. dir. Molecular Biology Inst., 1981-85; dir. UCLA-DOE Ctr. for Genomics and Proteomics, 1993—; investigator Howard Hughes Med. Inst., 2001—. Author: (with W. Kauzmann) Structure and Properties of Water, 1969, (with D.M. Crothers) Physical Chemistry with Applications in the Life Sciences, 1979. Chmn. Citizens for the West L.A. Veloway, 1977—2001; bd. dirs. Westlake Sch., 1983—89, Harvard-Westlake Sch., 1990—91. Recipient USPHS Career Devel. awardee, 1972-77; Rhodes scholar, 1961-64; Guggenheim fellow, 1985, Stein & Moore award, 1996, Repligen award, 1998. Fellow Biophys. Soc.; mem. NAS, Am. Acad. Arts and Scis., Am. Soc. Biol. Chemists, Am. Crystallographic Assn., Biophys. Soc. (councillor 1977-80), The Protein Soc. (pres. 1987-89, councillor 1989-94). Office: UCLA-DOE Ctr for Genomics and Proteomics PO Box 951570 Los Angeles CA 90095-1570

EISENBERG, MELVIN A., law educator; b. NY, Dec. 3, 1934; s. Max and Laura (Wallance) E.; m. Helen Garlitz, Feb. 5, 1956; children: Bronwyn, David Abram (dec. 1997). AB, SCL, Columbia U., 1956; LLB, SCL, Harvard U., 1959, Faye Diploma in Law, 1959; LLD (hon.), U. Milan, 1998; LLD (hon.), U. Cologne, 2004. Bar: N.Y. 1960. Assoc. Kaye Scholer Fierman Hays & Handler, 1959-63, 64-66; corp. counsel City of N.Y., 1966; acting prof. U. Calif.-Berkeley, 1966-69, prof. law, 1969-83, Koret prof. law, 1983—. Vis. prof. Harvard U., 1969-70; vis. prof. law Columbia U., 1998—, Stephen and Barbara Friedman vis. prof. law, 2005—; asst. counsel Pres. Commn. on Assassination Pres. Kennedy, Warren Commn., 1964; counsel mayor's task force on reorgn N.Y.C. govt., 1966; mem. mayor's task force on N.Y.C. transp. reorgn., 1966; mem. mayors' task force on mcpl. collective bargaining, 1966; reporter Am. Law Inst., principles of corporate governance: analysis and recommendations, 1980-84, chief reporter, 1984-94, Ammi Cutter chair, 1991-93; adviser, restatement 3d of agy. 1996-2005; adviser, restatement 3d of restitution, 1998—; prof.-in-residence, Cologne U., 1984, U. Milan, 1992; mem. and cons. ABA com. on corp. laws, 1992—; U. Iowa Inaugural lectr., 1987, Roy R. Ray lectr. So. Meth. U., 1993, Robert L. Levine Distg. lectr., Fordham U., 1993; Pillegi lectr. Weidener U., 2004; chmn. AALS contracts sect., 1989, AALS contracts workshop, 1986; chmn. AALS bus. assns. sect., 1998; visitor-in-residence U. Murdoch, U. Western Australia, 1992, McGill U., 1981; Sobeloff lectr. U. Md., 1994; Freehill, Hollingsdale and Page vis. fellow U. New South Wales, Australia, 1994. Author: The Structure of the Corporation, 1977 (Coif Triennial Book award honorable mention 1980), The Nature of the Common Law, 1988, Cases and Materials on Corporations and Other Business Organization, 2005, (with L. Fuller) Basic Contract Law, 2006; also numerous articles. Pres. Queen's Child Guidance Ctr., 1963-66. Guggenheim fellow, 1971-72, Canterbury vis. fellow U. Canterbury, New Zealand, 1988, Kimber fellow York U., Toronto, 1989, Rabin fellow Yale Sch. Law, vis. fellow Doshisha U., Kyoto, Japan, 2003—; Fulbright Sr. scholar, Australia, 1987, Disting. Mellon scholar U. Pitts., 1989, Manuel F. Cohen vis. scholar George Washington U. Sch. Law; Cooley lectr. U. Mich., 1985; Baron de Hirsch Meyer lectr. U. Miami Sch. Law, 1983, Wythe lectr. William and Mary Law Sch., 1999, TePoel lectr. Creighton U. Sch. Law, 1982; recipient Faye Diploma Harvard U. Law Sch., Rutter Outstanding Tchg. award Boalt Hall Law Sch., 2002, Disting. Tchg. award U. Calif., Berkeley, 1990. Fellow AAAS; mem. Am. Law Inst., Am. Assn. Law Schs. (chair contracts sect. 1989, chair bus. assns. sect. 1999), Phi Beta Kappa. Office: U Calif Sch Law 331 Boalt Hl Berkeley CA 94720-0001 also: Columbia U Law Sch 435 W 116th St New York NY 10027-7201 Home: 1197 Keeler Ave Berkeley CA 94708-1753 Office Phone: 510-642-1799. Business E-Mail: eisenberg@law.berkeley.edu.

EISENBERG, PAUL RICHARD, cardiologist, consultant, educator; b. Rome, Mar. 9, 1955; came to US, 1956; s. David Marvin and Sonia Maria (Benedetti) Eisenberg; m. Patricia Lynn Goodman, Apr. 25, 1982; 1 child, Jamie. BS, Tulane U., New Orleans, 1975, MPH, 1980; MD, NY Med. Coll., Valhalla, 1980. Diplomate Am. Bd. Internal Medicine, Am. Bd. Cardiology. Intern in internal medicine Barnes Hosp., St. Louis, 1980-83, fellow in cardiology, pulmonary medicine, 1983-85, asst. dir. CCU, 1986-91, dir. CCU, 1991-98; asst. prof. Washington U., St. Louis, 1985-91, assoc. prof., 1991-97, prof., 1997-98; med. dir. cardiovasc. therapeutics Eli Lilly & Co., Indpls., 1998-2000, exec. dir. cardiovasc. discovery, 2000—01, v.p. med., 2001—02, v.p. global drug safety, 2003—05; v.p. Amgen Global Safety, Thousand Oaks, Calif., 2005—06, v.p. Global Regulatory Affairs Safety, 2007—, sr. v.p. Global Regulatory Affairs Safety, 2008. Asst. editor: Medical Management of Heart Disease; contbr. over 100 articles to profl. jours. Fellow Am. Heart Assn. (clin. cardiology), Am. Coll. Chest Physicians, Am. Coll. Cardiology; mem. Am. Fedn. Clin. Rsch., Internat. Soc. Thrombosis and Haemostasis. Office: Amgen 1 Amgen Ctr Dr Thousand Oaks CA 91320 Home Phone: 805-670-1944; Office Phone: 805-447-6453. Personal E-mail: piesenberg@attglobal.net.

EISENBUD, DAVID, mathematics professor; b. NYC, Apr. 8, 1947; s. Leonard and Ruth-Jean (Rubinstein) E.; m. Monika Margarete Schwabe, June 3, 1970; children: Daniel, Alina. BS, U. Chgo., 1966, MS, 1967, PhD, 1970. Lectr. Brandeis U., Waltham, Mass., 1970-72, asst. prof., 1972—73, assoc. prof., 1976-80, prof., 1980—97, chmn. dept. of math., 1982-84, 1992—94; prof. math. U. Calif., Berkeley, 1997—. Vis. scholar, Harvard U., 1973-74; vis. prof. U. Bonn, Fed. Republic of Germany, 1979-80, Math. Sciences Rsch. Inst. (MSRI), Berkeley, 1986-87, Harvard U., 1987-88, 1994; Chercheur Associ'e a l'Institut Henri Poincar'e, Centre Nat. de la Recherche Scientifique, Paris, 1995; mem. adv. panel in maths. NSF, 1978-81; dir. Math. Sciences Rsch. Inst.(MSRI), Berkeley, 1997-2007; mem. bd. math. sci. and applications NRC, 2001-03. Editor: Procs. of Am. Math. Soc., 1978-82, Asterisque, 1983-88, (book series) Wadsworth Advanced, 1985-92, Jour. Algebraic Geometry, 1990—, Annals of Math, 2001-2004, Springer Algorithms and Computation in Math.; serves on several editl. boards; contbr. numerous books and articles to profl. jours. Alfred P. Sloan Found. fellow, 1973-75, Institut des Hautes Etudes Scientifiques (IHES-Bures-Sur-Yvette), 1974-75; NSF grantee, 1970—. Mem. Am. Math. Soc. (coun., pres. 2003-05, editor Bull. 1996-98, Bull. Sci. Math. 2000—), Soc. Indsl. and Applied Math., Assn. for Women in Math., Math. Assn. Am.; fellow Am. Acad. Arts & Sciences Avocations: flute, vocalist, juggling, hiking, music. Office: MSRI 17 Gauss Way Berkeley CA 94720 Business E-Mail: de@msri.org.

EISENSTADT, PAULINE DOREEN BAUMAN, state legislator; b. NYC, Dec. 31, 1938; d. Morris and Anne (Lautenberg) Bauman; m. Melvin M. Eisenstadt, Nov. 20, 1960; children: Todd Alan, Keith Mark. BA, U. Fla., 1960; MS, U. Ariz., 1965; postgrad., U. N.Mex. Tchr., Ariz., 1961—65, PR, 1972—73; adminstrv. asst. Inst. Social Rsch. U. N.Mex., 1973—74; founder, 1st exec. dir. Energy Consumers N.Mex., 1977—81; chmn. consumer affairs adv. com. Dept. Energy, 1979—80; v.p. tech. bd. Nat. Ctr. Appropriate Tech., 1980—; pres. Eisenstadt Enterprises, investments, 1983—; mem. N.Mex. House of Reps., 1985—92, chairwoman majority caucus, chair rules com., 1987—, chair sub. com. on children and youth, 1987; mem. N.Mex. State Senate, 1996—2000, mem. senate fin. com., com. higher edn., com. econ. devel., sci. & tech., water & natural resources, electric deregulation com., chair conservation co, mem. senate fin. com., com. higher edn., com. econ. devel., sci. & tech., water & natural resources, electric deregulation com., chair conservation com. Mem. exec. com., vice chair pvt. coun. Nat. Conf. State Legislators, 1987; vice chmn. Sandoval County (N.Mex.) Dem. Party, 1981—; mem. N.Mex. Dem. State Ctrl. Com., 1981—; N.Mex. del. Dem. Nat. Platform Com., 1984, Dem. Nat. Conv., 1984; mem. cmty. adv. bd. Intel Corp., 2004. Dir., host (TV program) Consumer Viewpoint, 1980—82, host N.Mex. Today and Tomorrow, 1992—, exec. prodr., host Tech Talks, 2001—; author: Corrales, Portrait of a Changing Village, 1980; painter (gallery and art show), 2005. Pres. Anti Defamation League, N.Mex., 1994—95; mem. N.Mex. First; pres. Sandoval County Dem. Women's Assn., 1979—81; vice chmn. N.Mex. Dem. Platform Com., 1984—; mem. Sandoval County Redistricting Task Force, 1983—84, Rio Rancho Ednl. Study Com., 1984—. Recipient Gov.'s award Outstanding N. Mex. Women, Commn. on the Status of Women and Gov. Bruce King, 1992; named Outstanding Senator, N.Mex. Tech. Showcase, 2000; named to Miami Beach Sr. HS Hall of Fame, 2000; grantee, NSF, 1965. Mem.: Rio Rancho Rotary Club (pres. 1995—, Rotarian of Yr. 1995), Kiwanis (1st woman mem. local club). Home: PO Box 658 Corrales NM 87048-0658 E-mail: peisenstadt@aol.com.

EISERMAN, RICK, marketing executive; b. 1973; BS in Advt., Art Inst. So. Calif. Account mgmt. Young & Rubicam Brands, NY; founding mem., CEO BrandBuzz, NYC, 2000—06; North Am. mng. ptnr., global client ptnr. lead Young & Rubicam Brands, So. Calif., 2006—08; CEO Trailer Park, Berns Comm. Grp., Hollywood, Calif., 2008—. Launch splty. unit within WPP BIG Cons., Bounce Entertainment & Events. Office: 6922 Hollywood Blvd Los Angeles CA 90028 also: 1741 Ivar Ave Los Angeles CA 90028

EISMANN, DANIEL T., state supreme court chief justice; b. Eugene, Oreg. m. Sheila Wood, 1982; 1 child, Matthew stepchildren: Catherine Richardson, Christine Putz. Grad. cum laude, U. Idaho, 1976. Former law clerk to justice Donaldson Idaho State Supreme Ct., Boise; magistrate judge Owyhee County, 1986—95; dist. judge Fourth Jud. Dist., 1995—98, adminstrv. dist. judge, 1998—2000; justice Idaho Supreme Ct., Boise, 2001—, chief justice, 2007—. Chair Idaho State Supreme Ct. Civil Rules Com., Idaho State Supreme Ct. Criminal Jury Instructions Com., Idaho State Supreme Ct. Drug Court Coordinating Com. Mem. Ada County Domestic Violence Task Force, Region III Coun. for Children and Youth; judge Ada County Drug Ct. With USAR. Decorated 2 Purple Hearts. Mem.: Inns of Ct. (Boise Chpt.), Idaho Bar Assn. (mem. Bar Exam Preparation Com.). Office: Idaho Supreme Ct PO Box 83720 Boise ID 83720

EISNER, ELLIOT W., education educator; MA in Art and Edn., Roosevelt U., 1954; MS in Art Edn., Ill. Inst. Tech., 1955; MA in Edn., U. Chgo., 1958, PhD in Edn., 1962. HS art tchr., Chgo., 1956—58; art tchr. U. Chgo., 1958—60, instr. edn., 1961—62, asst. prof. edn., 1962—65; instr., art edn. Ohio State U., 1960—61; assoc. prof. edn. & art Stanford U., 1965—70, edn. & art prof., 1970—. Consulting editor Curriculum Perspectives, 1981—; mem. editl. bd. Kappan, 1995—2000; mem. editl. advisory bd. Just & Caring Edn., 1995—2000; mem. editl. bd. Critical Inquiry into Curriculum & Instruction, 1998—. Contbr. articles various profl. jours.; co-author (with David W. Ecker): Readings in Art Education, 1966; co-author: (with Alan Peshkin) Qualitative Inquiry in Education: The Continuing Debate, 1990; co-author: (with Elizabeth Vallance) Conflicting Conceptions of Curriculum series on Contemporary Educational Issues, 1974; author: Confronting Curriculum Reform, 1971, Educating Artistic Vision, 1972, The Arts, Human Development, and Education, 1976, The Education Imagination: On the Design and Evaluation of School Programs, 1979, The Art of Educational Evaluation: A Personal View, 1985, The Role of Discipline-Based Art Education in America's Schools, 1988, The Enlightened Eye: Qualitative Inquiry and the Enhancement of Educational Practice, 1991, Cognition and Curriculum Reconsidered, 1994, Evaluating and Assessing the Visual Arts in Education: International Perspectives, 1996, The Kind of Schools We Need: Personal Essays, 1998, The Arts and the Creation of the Mind, 2002 (The Grawemeyer award for Edn., U. Louisville, 2005). Recipient Harold McGraw Jr. prize in Edn., Nat. Art Edn. Assn., 1998. Mem.: Nat. Acad. of Edn., John Dewey Soc. (pres. 1998—2000), J. Paul Getty Ctr. for Edn. in the Arts. Achievements include research in the rold of artistic thinking in the conduct of social sci. rsch., programs to further arts edn. in Am. schs., the role of artistry in ednl. theory and practice. Office: Stanford U Sch of Edn 485 Lasuen Mall Stanford CA 94305-3096 E-mail: eisner@stanford.edu.

EISNER, MICHAEL DAMMANN, investment and former entertainment company executive; b. Mt. Kisco, NY, Mar. 7, 1942; s. Lester and Margaret (Dammann) E.; m. Jane Breckenridge, 1967; children: Breck, Eric, Anders. BA, Denison U., 1964. Began career in programming dept. CBS; asst. to nat. programming dir. ABC, 1966-68, mgr. spls. and talent, dir. program devel.-East Coast, 1968-71, dir. program devel. East Coast, 1968-71, dir. feature films and program devel., 1969, v.p. daytime programming, 1971-75, v.p. program planning and devel., 1975-76, sr. v.p. prime time prodn. and devel., 1976; pres., COO Paramount Pictures Corp., 1976-84; chmn. Walt Disney Co., Burbank, Calif., 1984—2004, CEO, 1984—2005; founder The Tornante Co., LLC, Beverly Hills, Calif., 2005—; host, Conversations with Michael Eisner CNBC, 2006—. Bd. dirs. The Walt Disney Co., 1984-2005, Veoh Networks, Inc., 2006-; gov. Mighty Ducks of Anaheim, 1993; mem. bus. steering com. Global Business Dialogue on Electronic Commerce; founder, The Eisner Found., 1996-; lectr. in field Author (with Tony Schwartz): Work in Progress: Risking Failure, Surviving Success, 1998; author: Camp, 2005. Trustee Denison U., Calif. Inst. Arts; bd. dirs. Am. Hosp. of Paris Found., UCLA Exec. Bd. for Med. Sci. Office: The Tornante Co LLC 233 Beverly Dr S Beverly Hills CA 90212 also: The Eisner Found 9401 Wilshire Found Ste 760 Beverly Hills CA 90212

EKANGER, LAURIE, retired state official, consultant; b. Salt Lake City, Mar. 4, 1949; d. Bernard and Mary (Dearth) E.; m. William J. Shupe, Nov. 6, 1973; children: Ben, Robert. BA in English, U. Oreg., 1973. Various pos. Mont. State Employment & Tng. Divsn., Helena, 1975-80, dep. adminstr., 1980-82; adminstr. Mont. State Purchasing Divsn., Helena, 1982-85, Mont. State Personnel Divsn., Helena, 1985-93; labor commr. Mont. Dept. Labor and Ind., Helena, 1993-97; dir. Mont. Dept. Pub. Health and Human Svcs., 1997-2000; rsch., analysis and pers. mgmt. projects, 2000—. Council chair State Employee Group Benefits Coun., 1985-93; bd. dirs. Pub. Employee Retirement Bd., 1988; mem. various state adv. couns. health and human svcs. Home: 80 Pinecrest Rd Clancy MT 59634-9505

EKEGREN, E. PETER (PETE EKEGREN), state legislator; Farm implement dealer; mem. Mont. Senate, Dist. 44, Helena, 1998—; mem. bills and jour. com., taxation com., fish and game com. Mont. State Senate, mem. agr., livestock and irrigation com. Republican. Office: PO Box 862 Choteau MT 59422-0862

EKLUND, CARL ANDREW, lawyer; b. Aug. 12, 1943; s. John M. and Zara (Zerbst) E.; m. Nancy Jane Griggs, Sept. 7, 1968; children: Kristin, Jessica, Peter. BA, U. Colo., 1967, JD, 1971. Colo. 1971, D.C. 2001. Dep. dist. atty. Denver Dist. Attys. Office, 1971-73; ptnr.

DiManna, Eklund, Ciancio & Jackson, Denver, 1975-81, Smart, DeFurio, Brooks & Eklund, Denver, 1982-84, Roath & Brega, P.C., Denver, 1984-88, Faegre & Benson, Denver, 1988-94, LeBoeuf, Lamb, Greene & MacRae LLP, Denver, 1994—2003, Ballard Spahr Andrews & Ingersoll, LLP, Denver, 2003—. Mem. local rules com. Bankruptcy Ct. D.C., 1979-80; reporter Nat. Bankruptcy Conf., 1981-82; lectr. ann. spring meeting Am. Bankruptcy Inst., Rocky Mountain Bankruptcy Conf., Continuing Legal Edn. Colo., Inc., Colo. Practice Inst., Colo. Bar Assn., Nat. Ctr. Continuing Legal Edn., Inc., Profl. Edn. Sys., Inc., Comml. Law Inst. Am., Law Edn. Inst., Inc., Bur. Nat. Affairs, Inc., Practising Law Inst., So. Meth. U. Sch. Law, Continuing Edn. Svcs., Law Seminars Internat., Lorman Bus. Ctr., Inc, adv. bd. Am. Bankruptcy Inst. Law Review 1993-1999. Author: The Problem with Creditors' Committees in Chapter 11: How to Manage the Inherent Conflicts without Loss of Function; contbg. author: Collier's Bankruptcy Practice Guide, Representing Debtors in Bankruptcy, Letters Formbook and Legal Opinion, Advanced Chapter 11 Bankruptcy Practice, mem. adv. bd. ABI Law Rev., 1993-2000; contbr. to law jours. Best Lawyers in Am., Who's Who in Am., Who's Who Legal, Law & politics Colorado Super Lawyer 2006. Fellow Am. Coll. Bankruptcy; mem. ABA (bus. law and corp. banking sect. 1977—, bus. bankruptcy com. 1982—, subcom. on rules 1981—), Colo. Bar Assn. (bd. govs. 1980-82, corp. banking and bus. law sect. 1977—, ethics com. 1981-82, subcom. bankruptcy cts.), Am. Bankruptcy Inst. (dir. Rocky Mountain Bankruptcy Conf.), Denver Bar Assn. (trustee 1983-86), mem. Faculty Fed. Advocates & trustee 1999-2001. Office: Leboeuf Lamb Greene Macrae Llp 50 N Laura St Ste 2800 Jacksonville FL 32202-3656 also: Ballard Spahr Andrews & Ingersoll, LLP Ste 2300 1225 17th St Denver CO 80202-5596 Office Phone: 303-299-7330. Office Fax: 303-382-4630. Business E-Mail: eklundc@ballardspahr.com.

ELACHI, CHARLES, aerospace engineer; b. Beirut, Apr. 18, 1947; m. Valerie Gifford; 2 children. BS, U. Grenoble, France, 1968; MS, Calif. Inst. Tech., 1969, PhD in Elec. Sci., 1971; MBA, U. So. Calif., 1978; MS, UCLA, 1983. Rsch. fellow Calif. Inst. Tech., Pasadena, 1971-74, leader Radar Remote Sensing Team, 1974-80, asst. lab. dir. space and sci. instruments, 1987-95, prof. elec. engring., 1982—2000, dir. & v.p., 2001—; sr. rsch. scientist CIT Jet Propulsion Lab., Pasadena, 1981—87, dir. space and earth sci. programs, 1995—2000, dir., 2000—. Prin. investigator NASA, 1973-87, mem. Solar Sys. Exploration Com. Coun., 1988—, Astrophysics Coun., 1988—; mem. Electromagnetic Acad., 1990-95; participant in archeological expeditions; spkr. in field. Contbr. over 200 articles to profl. jours.; mem. editl. adv. bd. Scientific American Chmn. JPL United Way Campaign. Recipient Prof. R.W.P. King award for outstanding contbrn. in field of electromagnetics, 1973, Nev. Medal Outstanding Achievement in Sci. and Engring., Desert Rsch. Inst., 1995, Wernher Von Braun award, 2000, Takeda award, 2002, Mem. AIAA (Dryden Lecturship in Rsch., 2000), NAE(councillor 2007-), IEEE (Geosensing and Remote Sensing Disting. Achievement award 1987, Engring. Excellence medal 1992), Am. Astronautical Soc., Electromagnetic Soc., Am. Geophys. Union, Planetary Soc., Internat. Acad. Astronautics, Sigma Xi. Achievements include development of a series of imaging radar systems for the Space Shuttle that allowed scientists to study the earth and other planets of the solar system; patents in field. Avocations: skiing, woodworking, travel, history. Office: Jet Propulsion Lab MS 180-704 4800 Oak Grove Dr Pasadena CA 91109-8001 also: M/C JPL 180-904 Pasadena CA 91109 E-mail: charles.elachi@jpl.nasa.gov.

EL-BIALY, TAREK H., orthodontist, biomedical engineer; b. Al-Mahallah Al Kubra, Gharbia, Egypt, Apr. 28, 1965; s. Hessin A. El-Bialy; m. Tayhreed G. Hodaya; children: Rowan T., Ahmed T., Moh'd T., Omar T. B in Dental Sci., Tanta U., Egypt, 1987, MS in Orthodontics, 1993; MS in Oral Scis., U. Ill., Chgo., 2000, PhD in Bioengineering, 2001. Law lic. cert. in gen. law: Tanta U. 1994; cert. Orthodontics U. Ill. Chgo., 2001. Undergraduate lab. instr., dept. orthodontics, faculty dentistry Tanta U., 1989—93, asst. lectr., dept. orthodontics, faculty dentistry, 1993—97, lectr. orthodontics, 2001—; rsch. asst. prof. dept bioengring. U. Ill., Chgo., 2001—02; asst. prof. orthodontics and bioengring., dentistry, preventative dental services, clinic dir., orthodontics King Abdul Aziz U., Jeddah, Saudi Arabia, 2002—05; assoc. prof. orthodontics U. Alberta, 2005—. Orthodontic clinic dir. faculty dentistry King Abdul Aziz U., Jeddah, 2002—. Reviewer Am. Jour. Orthodontics and Dentofacial Orthopedics, Am. Assn. Orthodontists, Rsch., 1999—2004; contbr. articles to profl. jours. Recipient Rsch. award, Chgo. Odontographic Soc., 1999—2000; Biomedical Rsch. grant, Am. Assn. Orthodontists Found., 1999—2001, Campus Rsch. Bd. grant, U. Ill., Chgo., 2001—03. Mem.: World Fedn. Orthodontists, Internat. Assn. for Dental Rsch., Egyptian Orthodontic Soc., Canadian Assn. Orthodontists, Arab Orthodontic Soc., Am. Bd. Orthodontics, Am. Assn. Orthodontics, Am. Assn. for Dental Rsch., Alberta Soc. Orthodontists, Saudi Orthodontic Club (assoc.). Achievements include first to treat human tooth root resorption after orthodontic treatment non-invasively; discovery of enhancing lower jaw (mandibular) growth without surgery, or orthopedic appliances with ultrasound only; patents for New Technique to monitor bone healing and bone health; patents pending for Ultrasound Stimulation Devices. Office: Univ Alberta Grad Orthodontic Program Faculty Medicine and Dentistry 4051 Dent/Pharm Bldg Edmonton AB T6G 2N8 Canada Office Fax: +966-2640-3316, 780-492-1624. Business E-Mail: telbialy@ualberta.ca. E-mail: telbialy@hotmail.com.

ELDER, REX ALFRED, civil engineer; b. Pa., Oct. 4, 1917; s. George Alfred and Harriet Jane (White) E.; m. Janet Stevens Alger, Aug. 10, 1940; children: John A., Carol S., Susan A., William P. BSCE, Carnegie Inst. Tech., 1940; MS, Oreg. State Coll., 1942. Hydraulic engr. TVA, Norris, Tenn., 1942-48, dir. hydraulic lab., 1948-61, dir. engring. lab., 1961-73; engring. mgr. Bechtel Civil & Minerals Inc., San Francisco, 1973-85; cons. hydraulic engr., 1986—. Contbr. numerous articles on hydraulic structures, hydraulic model studies, reservoir stratification and water quality, hydraulic research and hydraulic machinery to profl. jours. Served with USN, 1945-46. Fellow ASCE (hon. 1993, James Laurie prize 1949, Hunter Rouse lectr. 1984, Hydraulic Structures medal 1991), NAE, Internat. Assn. Hydraulic Rsch. (hon.). Home and Office: 501 Via Casitas Apt 424 Greenbrae CA 94904-1947

ELDER, ROBERT LAURIE, newspaper editor; b. Nashville, June 23, 1938; s. Charles Jerome and Dorothea Eloise (Calhoun) E.; m. Betty Ann Doak, Sept. 1, 1958 (div. May 1969); children— Mark Christopher, Jeffrey Cathcart. BA, Washington and Lee U., 1960; MA, Vanderbilt U., 1966; postgrad., Stanford U., 1976-77. Reporter Nashville Tennessean, 1964-68; asst. dir. So. Newspaper Pubs. Assn. Found., Atlanta, 1969; reporter The Miami Herald, Fla., 1970-76; editor San Jose (Calif.) Mercury News, 1978—, v.p. editor, 1987—. Bd. dirs. RLM Ptnrs. Author: Crash, 1977. Bd. dirs. Santa Clara U. Ctr. for Applied Ethics, 1987—, Alliance for Cmty. Care, 1997, Nonprofit Devel. Ctr., 1997—. 1st lt. U.S. Army, 1960-62. Recipient Disting. Achievement award Fla. Soc. Newspaper Editors, 1973, White House Conf. on Librs. Pub. award, 1994, Pres. award Calif. Libr. Assn., 1995. Episcopalian. Office: San Jose Mercury News 750 Ridder Park Dr San Jose CA 95190-0001

ELDREDGE, BRUCE BEARD, museum director; b. Van Wert, Ohio, July 1, 1952; s. Thomas Harte and Barbara Louise (Beard) E.; m. Janet Duncan Roth, May 17, 1975; children: Lindsay Katherine, Barbara Roth. BA, Ohio Wesleyan U., 1974; MA, Tex. Tech U., 1976; postgrad., SUNY, 1980-81. Dir. Geneva (N.Y.) Hist. Soc. and Mus., 1976-78, Schenectady (N.Y.) Mus., 1978-80; coord. art and humanities Capital Dist. Humanities Program, SUNY, Albany, 1980-81; dir. Frederic Remington Art Mus., Ogdensburg, N.Y., 1981-84, Muskegon (Mich.) Mus. Art, 1984-87, Tucson Mus. Art, 1987-89, Portsmouth (Va.) Mus's., 1991-93, Stark Mus. Art, Orange, Tex., 1993-96, Hubbard Mus. Am. West (formerly Mus. of the Horse), Ruidoso Downs, N.Mex., 1996—. Presenter Gov.'s Conf. on Tourism, Phoenix, 1989; mem. coun. Midwest Mus. Assn., 1986-87, chmn. program ann. meeting, Grand Rapids, Mich., 1987; chmn. Ruidoso Arts Commn., 1996—, Village Visioning Process, 1997—. Vice pres. Schenectady County coun. Boy Scouts Am., 1979-81, Seaway Valley coun., Canton, N.Y., 1982-84, West Mich. Shores coun., Grand Rapids, 1985-87, dist. com. Three Rivers coun., 1992-96, v.p. Three Rivers coun., 1995-96; bd. dirs. Orange Cmty. Concert Assn., 1995-96. Mem. Am. Assn. Mus., Tex. Assn. Mus. (sourcebook editor 1993-96), N.Mex. Mus. Assn. (membership chair), Kokopelli Club, Cree Meadows C.C., Rotary. Republican. Presbyterian. Office: The Hubbard Mus PO Box 40 Ruidoso Downs NM 88346-0040 Home: 920 Meadow Lane Ave Cody WY 82414-4518 E-mail: bruce@ruidoso.k12.nm.us, eldredge@zianet.com.

EL-ERIAN, MOHAMED A., investment company executive; b. NYC, Aug. 19, 1958; BA in Economics, Cambridge U., 1980; MA, Oxford U., PhD in Economics, 1983. Dep. dir. IMF, 1983—97, mem. Capital Markets Consultative Group; mng. dir. econ. rsch. Salomon Smith Barney, London, 1997—99; mng. dir., sr. mem. portfolio mgmt. and investment strategy group Pacific Investment Mgmt. Co. LLC (PIMCO), 1999—2005, co-CEO, chief investment officer, 2008, CEO, 2008—, Harvard Mgmt. Co., Boston, 2005—07. Author: When Markets Collide: Investment Strategies for the Age of Global Economic Change, 2008 (Fin. Times Goldman Sachs Bus. Book of Yr., 2008). Mem.: Emerging Markets Creditors Assn., Emerging Market Traders Assn. Office: Pacific Investment Mgmt Co LLC (PIMCO) 84 Newport Ctr Dr Ste 100 Newport Beach CA 92660 also: 1345 Ave of the Americas New York NY 10105-4800 E-mail: el-erian@pimco.com.*

ELEY, HUNTER R., lawyer; b. Williamsburg, Va. BA, Univ. Va., 1995; JD, Coll. William & Mary, 2000. Bar: Va. 2000, Calif. 2003. Judicial extern Justice Lawrence L. Koontz, Va. Supreme Ct.; law clk. Judge James C. Turk, US Dist. Ct. We. Va.; atty. Gibson Dunn & Crutcher LLP, LA, Browne Woods & George LLP, Beverly Hills, Calif.; ptnr., bus. & entertainment litigation Doll Amir & Eley LLP, LA. Named a Rising Star, So. Calif. Super Lawyers, 2006. Office: Doll Amir & Eley LLP Ste 1106 1888 Century Park E Los Angeles CA 90067 Office Phone: 310-557-9100. Office Fax: 310-557-9101. Business E-Mail: heley@dollamir.com.

EL FATTAH, YOUSRI M., computer scientist; arrived in U.S., 1984; BSc in Aero. Engring., Cairo U., Egypt, 1967, PhD, 1972, U. Calif., Irvine, 1993. Bd. cert. control sys. engr., Calif. Owner Artificial Intelligence Tng., Tustin, Calif., 1986—91; lectr. Nat. U., Irvine, Calif., 1986—92, U. Calif. Irvine U. Ext., 1988—93, Calif. State U., Long Beach, 1988—93; vis. rschr. U. Vienna, 1994—95; rsch. scientist U. Calif., Irvine, 1995—96, Rockwell Sci., Thousand Oaks, Calif., 1996—99, sr. scientist, 1999—2009; owner Causal Computing, Santa Monica, Calif., 2009—. Cons. UN McDonnel Douglas. Mem.: Am. Assn. Artificial Intelligence. Avocations: painting, writing, hiking, martial arts, travel. Home: 824 4th St 102 Santa Monica CA 90403 Office: Teledyne Sci 1049 Camino dos Rios Thousand Oaks CA 91360 Personal E-mail: yousri_el_fattah@hotmail.com. Business E-Mail: yousri@causalcomputing.com.

ELFMAN, DANNY, composer; b. Amarillo, Tex., May 29, 1953; m. Bridget Fonda, Nov. 29, 2003; 3 children. Lead singer, songwriter (band) Oingo Boingo, 1979—. Albums (with Oingo Boingo): Oingo Boingo, 1980, Only a Lad, 1981, Nothing to Fear, 1982, Good for Your Soul, 1984, Dead Man's Party, 1986, Boi-ngo, 1987, Boingo Alive, 1988, Skeletons in the Closet, 1988, Dark at the End of the Tunnel, 1990, Best O' Boingo, 1991, Boingo, 1994; composer: (film scores) Forbidden Zone, 1980, Back to School, 1985, Pee-wee's Big Adventure, 1985, Wisdom, 1987, Summer School, 1987, Beetlejuice, 1988, Hot to Trot, 1988, Midnight Run, 1988, Scrooged, 1988, Batman 1989 (Grammy award), Dick Tracy, 1990, Darkman, 1990, Edward Scissorhands, 1990, Nightbreed, 1990, Pure Luck, 1991, Article 99, 1992, Batman Returns, 1992, Somersby, 1993, March of the Dead Theme (Army of Darkness), 1993, The Nightmare Before Christmas, 1993, Black Beauty, 1994, Dolores Claiborne, 1995, Mission Impossible, 1996, The Frighteners, 1996, Bordello of Blood, 1996, Extreme Measures, 1996, Mars Attacks!, 1996, Men in Black, 1997 (Oscar nomination), Flubber, 1997, Good Will Hunting, 1997 (Oscar nomination), A Civil Action, 1998, Instinct, 1999, Sleepy Hollow, 1999, Proof of Life, 2000, The Family Man, 2000, Spy Kids, 2001, Planet of the Apes, 2001, Novocaine, 2001, Spiderman, 2002, Men in Black II, 2002, Red Dragon, 2002, Chicago, 2002, Hulk, 2003, Big Fish, 2003, Spider-Man 2, 2004, Charlie and the Chocolate Factory, 2005, Corpse Bride, 2005, Nacho Libre, 2006, Charlotte's Web, 2006, Meet the Ronsinsons, 2007, The Kingdom, 2007, Standard Operating Procedure, 2008, Wanted, 2008, Hellboy II: The Golden Army, 2008, Milk, 2008; (TV series score, Grammy nomination) The Simpsons (Emmy nomination), (TV) Tales of the Crypt, Pee-wee's Playhouse, 1986, Amazing Stories (2), Alfred Hitchcock Presents (1), Fast Times, 1986, Sledgehammer, 1986, Beetlejuice (animated), 1989, The Flash, 1990, Family Dog, 1992, Batman, 1992, Weird Science, 1994, Perversions of Science, 1997, Dilbert, 1999, Desperate Housewives, 2004; (albums) So-lo, 1984, Music for a Darkened Theatre, 1990. Office: The Kraft-Engel Management 15233 Ventura Blvd Ste 200 Sherman Oaks CA 91403

ELFRINK, WIM, computer company executive; V.p. customer advocacy Cisco Systems, Inc., San Jose, Calif., 1997—2000, sr. v.p. customer advocacy, 2000—06, chief globalization officer, 2006—, exec. v.p. Cisco Svcs., 2007—. Office: Cisco Systems Inc 170 W Tasman Dr Bldg 10 San Jose CA 95134-1706

ELFVING, DON C., horticulturist, educator; b. Albany, Calif., June 20, 1941; BS in Botany, U. Calif., Davis, 1964, MS in Horticulture, 1966; PhD in Plant Physiology, U. Calif., Riverside, 1971. From asst. prof. to assoc. prof. pomology Cornell U., Ithaca, NY, 1972-79; rsch. scientist Hort. Rsch. Inst. Ontario, Simcoe, Canada, 1979-91, mgr. rsch. programs Vineland, Canada, 1991-93; supt. tree fruit rsch. and extension ctr. Wash. State U., Wenatchee, 1993-97, horticulturist, prof., 1997—. Cons. U.S. AID, 1977; cons. Internat. Agrl. Devel. Svc., Ark., 1981-82. Author: Training and Pruning of Apple and Pear Trees, 1992. Recipient U.P. Hedrick 1st Pl. award Am. Pomological Soc., 1992. Fellow Am. Soc. Hort. Sci.; mem. Am. Soc. for Hort. Sci. (bd. dirs. 1993-95, chair publs. com. 1993-95), Internat. Fruit Tree Assn. (R.F. Carlson Disting. lectr. 1993). Office: Tree Fruit Rsch & Ext Ctr 1100 N Western Ave Wenatchee WA 98801-1230 Business E-Mail: delfving@wsu.edu.

ELGER, WILLIAM ROBERT, JR., accountant; b. Chgo., Mar. 20, 1950; s. William Robert and Grace G. (LaVaque) E.; m. Kathryn Michele Johnson, July 10, 1971; children: Kimberly, William, Kristin, Joseph. AS in Applied Sci., Coll. of DuPage, Glen Ellyn, Ill., 1970; BS magna cum laude, U. Ill.-Chgo., 1972. CPA, Ill. Staff acct. Ernst & Whinney, Chgo., 1973, in-charge acct., 1973-74, sr. acct., 1974-78, mgr., 1978-82, sr. mgr., 1982-88; chief fin. officer U. Ill. Eye and Ear Infirmary, 1988-89; CFO U. Mich. Med. Sch., Ann Arbor, 1989—99, exec. dir. adminstrn., CFO, 2000—08. Chair fin. controls frame work task force U. Mich., 1999—2004, chmn. internal controls adv. group, 2005—; presenter various confs. in field.; sr. assoc. dean for Adminstr. and Finance U. Ariz. Coll. Medicine, 2008—09; exec. v.p. and cheif bus. and fin. officer U. Tex. Med. Br., 2009—. Author, developer: (tng. course) Auditing Third Party Reimbursement, 1986, 87; Author: Managing Resources in a Better Way: A New Financial Management Approach for the University of MIchigan Medical School, 2006. Active Union League Civic and Arts Found., Chgo., 1982-89, Union League Found. for Boys and Girls Clubs, Chgo., 1982-89; treas. Newport Assn., Carol Stream, Ill., 1982-83; coach Tri-City Soccer Assn., St. Charles, Ill., 1984, 87, Saline Soccer Assn., 1990, 91, 93, 94, 95, Saline H.S. Soccer Club, 1996, 97. Mem. AICPA, Healthcare Fin. Mgmt. Assn. (advanced mem., acctg. and reimbursement com. 1982-87, chpt. task force com. 1986, 87, auditing com. 1986, 87, Spl. Recognition award 1986, Follmer Bronze Merit award 1999), Ill. Soc. CPAs (mem. long term healthcare com. 1983, hosps. com. 1988-89), Nat. Coun. Univ. Rsch. Adminstrs., Med. Group Mgmt. Assn., Assn. Am. Med. Colls. (group on bus. affairs steering com. 2004, chair Midwest region 2004, profl. devel. com. 2004-, group on bus. affairs nat. chair 2006-2007). Methodist. Avocation: golf. Office: 1501 N Campbell Ave PO Box 245017 Tucson AZ 85724 Home Phone: 734-846-6799, 520-395-1346; Office Phone: 406-266-2007, 520-626-5394. Business E-Mail: welger@utmb.edu, welger@email.arizona.edu.

ELGIN, RON ALAN, advertising executive; b. Milw., Sept. 15, 1941; s. Carl John and Vivian Elaine (Phillips) E.; m. Bonnie Kay Visintainer, Dec. 3, 1968; 1 child, Alison. BA in Advt., U. Wash., 1965. With Cole & Weber, Seattle, 1965-81; pres. Elgin Syferd, Seattle, 1981-89; chmn. Elgin Syferd/Drake, Boise, Idaho, 1987—2007; pres. DDB Needham Retail, Seattle, 2000—. Chmn. Hornall Anderson Design Works, Seattle, 1982-91; ptnr. Christiansen & Fritsch Direct, Seattle, 1988-96; bd. dirs. Hart Crowser; bd. dirs. Knowledge Anywhere, Impart Media, 2006—, Just Cause, Inc., 2006—, Haas Found., 2007—. Bd. dirs. Ronald McDonald House, Seattle, 1984—, Big Bros., Seattle, 1986—, Spl. Olympics, Seattle, 1987-90, Pacific N.W. Ballet, Seattle, 1988-98, Poncho, Seattle, 1991—, Odyssey, 1993-99, Swedish Hosp., 1995-2000; mem. adv. bd. U. Wash., Wash. State U. Lt. U.S. Army, 1965-69. Mem. Am. Assn. Advt. Agencies, Am. Mktg. Assn., Mktg. Comm. Execs. Internat. Office: DDB Seattle 1000 2nd Ave Seattle WA 98104-1004 Office Phone: 206-442-9900. Business E-Mail: ron.elgin@sea.ddb.com.

ELIASSEN, JON ERIC, retired corporate financial and utilities executive; b. Omak, Wash., Mar. 10, 1947; s. Marvin G. and Helen G. (Meyer) E.; m. Valerie A. Foyle, Aug. 14, 1971; 1 child, Michael T. BA in Bus., Wash. State U., 1970. Staff acct. Wash. Water Power Co., Spokane, 1970-73, tax acct., 1973-76, fin. analyst, 1976-80, treas., 1980-86, v.p. fin., CFO, 1986-96; sr. v.p., CFO Avista Corp., Spokane, 1996—2003; ret., 2003. Bd. dirs. Itron Corp., Red Lion Hotels, Inc., IT Lifeline, Inc., 2003—07; pres., CEO Spokane Area Econ. Devel. Coun. Trustee Wash. State U. Found., Pullman, 1987-99, N.W. Mus. Art and Culture, 1998-2003; treas. Wash. State U. Found., 1995-97; trustee Spokane Symphony, 1989-95, treas., 1990-95, mem. symphony endowment bd., pres. 2002-04; pres., trustee Spokane Intercollegiate Rsch. and Tech. Inst. Found., 1996-2000; bd. dirs. Western Energy Inst., chair, 2001-02; bd. dirs. Wash. Tech. Ctr., 2002—, Wash. State U. Rsch. Found., 2002—. Mem. Fin. Exec. Inst. (Seattle chpt. 1983—). Episcopalian. Avocations: skiing, travel, bicycling, photography. Office: Terrapin Capital Group LLC 827 W 1st St Ste 317 Spokane WA 99201

ELINSON, HENRY DAVID, artist, language educator; b. Leningrad, USSR, Dec. 14, 1935; arrived in U.S., 1973; s. David Moses and Fraida Zelma (Ufa) Elinson; m. Ludmila Nicholas Tepina, Oct. 7, 1955; 1 child, Maria Henry. Attended, Herzen State Pedagogical U., Leningrad, 1954—57; BA, Pedagogical Inst., Novgorod, USSR, 1958; MA, Pedagogical Inst., Moscow, 1963. Cert. educator. Spl. edn. tchr. Leningrad Sch. Spl. Edn., 1961-64; supr. dept. speech therapy Psychoneurological Dispensary, Leningrad, 1964-73; instr. Russian lang. Yale U., New Haven, 1975-76, Def. Lang. Inst., Presidio of Monterey, Calif., 1976-94. One-man shows include Light and Motion Transmutation Galleries, N.Y.C., 1974, Thor Gallery, Louisville, 1974, Monterey Peninsula Art Mus., 1977, U. Calif. Nelson Gallery, Davis, 1978, Nahamkin Gallery, N.Y.C., 1978, Nahamkin Fine Arts, 1980, Gallery Paule Anglim, San Francisco, 1981, 1985, 1987, Gallery Puale Anglim, 1991, 1993, 1996, 1999, 2000, Dostoevsky's Mus., St. Petersburg, Russia, 1992, Mus. Art Santa Cruz, Calif., 1994, Duke U. Mus. Art, 1996, Mead Art Mus., 1998, Mus. Non Conformist Art, St. Petersburg, 2000, Russian Mus., 2002, exhibited in group shows at Ctrl. Exhbn. Hall St. Petersburg, 2004, Bklyn. Coll. Art Ctr., 1974, CUNY, 1974, Galleria II Punto, Genoa, Italy, 1975, New Art From Soviet Union, Washington, 1977, Gallery Hardy, Paris, 1978, Mus. Fine Art, San Francisco, 1979, Santa Cruz Mus. Fine Arts, 1994, V. Morlan Gallery Transylvania U., Lexington, Ky., 1995, Art Gallery, Adriondack CC, Queensbury, N.Y., 2002, A.P.E. Gallery, Northampton, Mass., 2003, others, Represented in permanent collections Mus. Fine Arts, San Francisco, Yale U. Art Gallery, Monterey Mus. Art, U. Calif. Art Mus., Berkeley, Bochum Mus., Germany, Check Point Charlie Mus., Berlin, State Russian Mus., Leningrad, Zimmerly Art Mus., Rutgers U., N.J., Duke U. Mus. Art, Mead Art Mus., Mus. St. Petersburg History, Mus. Non Conformist Art, State Hermitage, St.

Petersburg, Visual Arts Gallery Adirondack CC, N.Y., A.P.E. Gallery, Northampton. Mem. Underground Anti-Soviet Govt. Students' Orgn., 1957. Recipient Gold medal Art Achievement, City of Milan, 1975. Avocations: travel, writing. Home: 997 Benito Ct Pacific Grove CA 93950-5333 Personal E-mail: lelinson1973@cs.com.

ELIOT, THEODORE LYMAN, JR., former ambassador, consultant; m. Patricia P. Peters. BA, Harvard U., 1948, M.P.A., 1956; LL.D., U. Nebr., Omaha, 1975. With U.S. Fgn. Svc., 1949-78; spl. asst. to under sec. of state; to sec. treasury; country dir. for Iran Dept. State; exec. sec. State Dept.; also spl. asst. to sec. of state Dept. State; ambassador to Afghanistan; insp. gen. Dept. State., Washington; dean Fletcher Sch. Law and Diplomacy, Tufts U., 1979-85; exec. dir. Ctr. for Asian Pacific Affairs Asia Found., San Francisco, 1985-87. Bd. dirs. Neurobiol. Tech. Trustee Asia Found., Bd. Cmty. Found., Sonoma County. Mem. Am. Acad. Diplomacy.

ELKINS, GLEN RAY, retired diversified management services company executive; b. Winnsboro, La., May 23, 1933; s. Ceicel Herbert and Edna Mae (Lewallen) E.; m. Irene Kay Hildebrand, Aug. 25, 1951 (div. 1990); children: Steven Breen, Douglas Charles, Karen Anne, Michael Glen; m. Diane Hodgson, Mar. 2, 1992. AA in Indsl. Mgmt., Coll. San Mateo, 1958. Successively mgr. prodn. control, mgr. logistics, plant mgr., asst. v.p. ops. Aircraft Engring. and Maintenance Co., 1957-64; from mgr. field ops. to pres. Internat. Atlas Svc. Co., Princeton, NJ, 1964-85; sr. v.p. Atlas Corp., Princeton, NJ; chmn., CEO, dir. Global Assoc., 1973-85; pres. Global Assoc. Internat. Ltd., 1975-84; pres., CEO Triad Am. Svc. Corp., 1985-2000; pres. Pacific Mgmt. Svc. Corp., TASC Enterprises Inc., dba, Gottschall Engraving Co., 1993-2000; ret., 2000. Area chmn. Easter Seals drive, 1974; bd. dirs. Utah Children's Mus. With USN, 1950—54. Mem. Nat. Mgmt. Assn., Electronic Industries Assn., Lakeview Club, Willow Creek Country Club (past pres.). Home: 1445 Harvard Ave Salt Lake City UT 84105-1917 Personal E-mail: grelkinsut@msn.com.

ELLEGOOD, DONALD RUSSELL, publishing executive; b. Lawton, Okla., June 21, 1924; s. Claude Jennings and Iva Claire (Richards) E.; m. Bettie Jane Dixon, Dec. 11, 1947; children—Elizabeth Nemi, Francis Hunter, Kyle Richards, Sarah Helen. BA, U. Okla., 1948, MA, 1950. Asst. editor U. Okla. Press, 1950-51; editor Johns Hopkins Press, 1951-54; dir. La. State U. Press, 1954-63, U. Wash. Press, Seattle, 1963—96. Contbr. articles to profl. jours. Served to 1st lt. USAAF, 1943-46. Decorated Air medal, D.F.C. Mem. Am. Univ. Pubs. Group London (dir.), Am. Assn. Univ. Presses (pres.), Phi Beta Kappa. Office: U Wash Press PO Box 50096 Seattle WA 98145-5096 E-mail: DREedit@aol.com.

ELLER, MARLIN, security firm executive; BA in Math. and Physics magna cum laude, U. Wash., 1979. Mgr. software devel. Microsoft Corp., 1982—95; founder, CEO, pres. Sunhawk.com, Seattle, 1995—. Vis. instr. in computer sci. Williams Coll., 1980—82; bd. dir. Fire Donations, Gig Harbor, Wash. Co-author: Barbarians Led by Bill Gates, 1998. Office: Sunhawk.com Corp 1463 E Republican St Seattle WA 98112-4517

ELLICKSON, BRYAN CARL, economics professor; b. Bklyn., Feb. 12, 1941; s. Raymond Thorwald and Loene (Gibson) E.; m. Phyllis Lynn Rutter, June 19, 1965; 1 child, Paul Bryan. BA, U. Oreg., 1963; PhD, MIT, 1970. From asst. prof. to assoc. prof. UCLA, 1968-83, prof., 1983—, chair econs. dept., 1996-99. Cons. Rand, Santa Monica, Calif., 1970—. Author: Competitive Equilibrium, 1993; contbr. articles to profl. jours. Rsch. grantee HUD, 1979-81, NSF, 1982-87. Mem. Am. Econ. Assn., Econometric Soc. Avocation: scuba diving. Home: 18409 Wakecrest Dr Malibu CA 90265-5620 Office: UCLA Dept Econs 405 Hilgard Ave Los Angeles CA 90095-1477 Home Phone: 310-459-6798; Office Phone: 310-825-4556. Business E-Mail: ellickson@econ.ucla.edu.

ELLIFF, J(OHN) ERIC, lawyer; b. Sterling, Colo., Dec. 28, 1961; s. John Edgar and Gladys Vera (Cline) E. BS, Washington U., 1984; JD, U. Colo., 1987. Bar: Colo. 1987, U.S. Dist. Ct. Colo. 1987, U.S. Ct. Appeals (10th cir.), 1987, N.Y. 2004. Assoc. Morrison & Foerster LLP, Denver, 1987, ptnr. Instr. legal writing U. Colo., Boulder, 1986. Bd. dirs. Scenic Am. Recipient Am. Jurisprudence award, 1987. Mem. ABA, ASCE, Colo. Bar Assn., Denver Bar Assn., N.Y. State Bar Assn., Order of Coif. Democrat. Avocations: skiing, antique automobiles. Office: Morrison & Foerster LLP 5200 Republic Plz 370 Seventeenth St Denver CO 80202-5638 Office Phone: 303-592-2240. Office Fax: 303-592-1510. Business E-Mail: jelliff@mofo.com.

ELLINGSEN, RICHARD D., lawyer; BA magna cum laude, U. Wash., 1976; JD with distinction, Duke U., Durham, NC, 1979. Bar: Calif. 1979. Ptnr. Ellingsen, Christensen & Steinberg, 1985—90, Davis Wright Tremaine L.L.P., LA, 1990—, mng. ptnr., 2002—. Mem.: Calif. State Bar Assn., Phi Beta Kappa. Office: Davis Wright Tremaine LLP 865 S Figueroa St Ste 2400 Los Angeles CA 90017-2566 Office Phone: 213-633-6800. Office Fax: 213-633-6899. E-mail: rickellingsen@dwt.com.

ELLINGSON, JON ERIC, state legislator; b. Rochester, NY, Aug. 21, 1948; m. Kathy Ellingson; 3 children. BA, Harvard U., 1970; MA, U. Mont., 1972; JD, U. Calif., 1974. Vol. Vista, 1970; atty., pvt. practice of law, 1975—; mem. Mont. Ho. of Reps., 1995-98, Mont. Senate, Dist. 33, Helena, 1998—; mem. taxation com., mem. edn. and cultural resources com. Mont. State Senate; mem. fish and game com. Mont. State Sanate. Formerly bd. dirs. Missioula Specialized Transp. Sys., Regional Chem. Dependency Program; formerly bd. dirs. Missoula Mus. Arts; mem. adv. coun. Mont. Dept. Family Svcs. Democrat. Home: 430 Ryman St Missoula MT 59802-4249 E-mail: jee@mssl.uswest.net.

ELLINGTON, JAMES WILLARD, retired mechanical engineer; b. Richmond, Ind., May 26, 1927; s. Oscar Willard and Leola Lenora (Sanderson) E.; m. Sondra Elaine Darnell, Dec. 6, 1952 (dec. Jan. 1997); children: Ronald, Roxanna; m. Vada M. Jellsey, Oct. 10, 1998. BSME summa cum laude, West Coast U., LA, 1978. Designer NATCO, Richmond, 1954—67; design engr. Burgmaster, Gardena, Calif., 1967—69; sr. mfg. engr. Xerox Co., El Segundo, Calif., 1969—84, cons. mem. engring. staff Monrovia, 1984—87; staff engr. Photonic Automation, Santa Ana, Calif., 1987—88; sr. mech. engr. Optical Radiation Co., Azusa, Calif., 1988; sr. staff engr. Omnichrome, Chino, Calif., 1988—96, ret., 1996. With USN, 1945-52. Mem. Soc. Mfg. Engrs. (sec. 1984). Republican. Baptist. Avocation: gardening.

ELLIOTT, CHARLES HAROLD, clinical psychologist; b. Kansas City, Mo., Dec. 30, 1948; s. Joseph Bond and Suzanne (Wider) E.; 1 child, Brian Douglas. BA, U. Kans., 1971, MA, 1974, PhD, 1976. Cert. clin. psychologist, N. Mex. Asst. prof. East Ctrl. U., Ada, Okla., 1976-79, U. Okla. Health Scis., 1979-85; assoc. prof. dept. psychiatry U. Okla., 1983-85, U. N. Mex. Sch. Medicine, Albuquerque, 1985-87; adj. assoc. prof. dept. psychology U. N.Mex., Albuquerque, 1986—; faculty full appointment Fielding Inst., Santa Barbara, Calif., 1987—. Consulting editor Jour. Clin. Child Psychology, 1987-89; ad hoc reviewer to profl. jours., 1983—; cognitive therapist NIMH Collaborative Study of Depression, Okla. City, 1980-85. Co-author: (with Maureen K. Lassen) Why Can't I Get What I Want, 1998, (with Laura L. Smith) Why Can't I Be the Parent I Want to Be?, 1999, (with Laura L. Smith) Hollow Kids: Recapturing the Soul of a Generation Lost to the Self-Esteem Movement, 2001; guest editor Psychiatric Annals, 1992; contbr. numerous articles to profl. jours. Fellow Acad. Cognitive Therapy (founding); mem. APA, Biofeedback and Behavioral Medicine Soc. N.Mex. (pres. 1988), Assn. for Advancement of Behavior Therapy, Assn. for Advancement Psychology, Soc. Behavioral Medicine, Soc. Pediat. Psychology, N.Mex. Psychol. Assn. (bd. dirs. 1992-96). Home: 156 Tierra Encantada Corrales NM 87048-6806

ELLIOTT, DAVID DUNCAN, III, science company executive; b. LA, Aug. 4, 1930; s. David Duncan Elliott II and Mildred B. (Young) Mack; m. Arline L. Leckrone, Aug. 18, 1962; 1 child, Lauren Elliott Croft. BS, Stanford U., Calif., 1951; MS, Calif. Inst. Tech., Pasadena, 1953, PhD, 1959. Mem. tech. staff Lockheed Rsch. Lab., Palo Alto, Calif., 1959-61; postdoctoral fellow U. Paris., 1962; dept. head Aerospace Corp., El Segundo, Calif., 1962—70; sci. advisor Nat. Aeronautics and Space Coun., Washington, 1970-72; sr. staff mem. exec. office of pres. NSC, Washington, 1972-77; v.p. SRI Internat., Menlo Park, Calif., 1977-86; sr. v.p. Sci. Applications Internat. Corp., San Diego, 1986-91, Syst Control Tech., Palo Alto, Calif., 1991-94; corp. v.p. Sci. Applications Internat. Corp., Palo Alto, Calif., 1994-95; cons., 1995-99; cons. prof. Ctr. Internat. Security & Coop., Stanford U., Calif., 1999—. Mem. Army Sci. Bd., The Pentagon, Washington, 1982-89; cons. NRC, NAS, 1988—; mem. bd. visitors U. Calif., Davis, 1997-2003. Mem. editl. bd. Jour. Def. Rsch., 1988—. Recipient Outstanding Civilian Svc. award US Army, 1989. Mem. AIAA, AAAS, Am. Phys. Soc., Am. Geophys. Union. Home: 2434 Sharon Oaks Dr Menlo Park CA 94025-6829 Office: CISAC Encina Hall Stanford CA 94305-6165 Personal E-mail: ddelliott3@aol.com.

ELLIOTT, GERRI, computer software company executive; V.p. distbn. sector for North and South Am. IBM, v.p. sales and mktg. solutions for Asian Pacific Region Toyko; joined Microsoft Corp., 2001, corp. v.p. Enterprise Group, corp. v.p. Worldwide Public Sector, 2004—. Mem. Sec. of Edn.'s Commn. on Future of Edn., 2005, Women's Sr. Leadership Program, Kellogg Sch. Mgmt., Catalyst Western Region Adv. Bd., World Economic Forum's Global Edn. Initiative. Bd. mem. Operation Hope Inc. Office: Microsoft Corp One Microsoft Way Redmond WA 98052-6399

ELLIOTT, JIM, state legislator; b. Montgomery County, Pa., Dec. 26, 1942; m to Leslie; children: two. Montana State Representative, District 51, 1989-94, District 72, 1995-97; Montana State Senator, District 36, 2001-2005, District 7, 2005-, Montana State Senate.Supvr, Green Mountain Conserv District, formerly; rancher, currently. Democrat. Mailing: 100 Trout Creek Rd Trout Creek MT 59874-9609

ELLIOTT, LEE ANN, company executive, former government official; b. June 26, 1927; BA, U. Ill. V.p. Bishop, Bryant amd Assocs., Inc., 1979-81; mem. Fed. Election Commn., Washington, 1981-2000, chmn., 1884, 90, 96; pres. Form Meets Function Enterprises, Inc., Chandler, Ariz., 2000—. Lectr., author and inventor in field. Bd. dirs., pres. Chgo. Area Pub. Affairs Group; bd. dirs. Kids Voting, USA. Mem. Am. Med. Polit. Action Com. (asst. dir. 1961-70, assoc. exec. dir. 1970-79), Am. Assn. Polit. Cons. (bd. dirs.), Nat. Assn. Mfrs. (award of excellence), U.S. C. of C. (pub. affairs com.). Office: Form Meets Function Enterprises Inc 820 W Warner Rd Ste 123 Chandler AZ 85225-2940

ELLIOTT, SCOTT D., lawyer; BA in Econs., U. Calif. Berkeley, 1988; JD, Hastings Coll. Law, 1992. Bar: Calif. 1992. Ptnr. Orrick, Herrington & Sutcliffe, Menlo Park, Calif., Ropes & Gray LLP, San Francisco, 2006—. Mem.: Calif. Bar Assn. Office: Ropes & Gray LLP One Embarcadero Ctr Ste 2200 San Francisco CA 94111-3627 Office Phone: 415-315-6379. Office Fax: 415-315-4834.

ELLIOTT, WARREN G., lawyer; b. Pueblo, Colo., Jan. 3, 1927; s. Wallace Ford and Hazel (Ellsworth) E.; m. Martha McCabe, June 20, 1953 (div. Sept. 1980); children: Mark, Winthrop, Carolyn, Byron. Student, U. Nebr., 1944-45, U. Colo., 1947-49, AB, 1973; JD, U. Mich., 1952. Bar: Colo. 1952, Conn. 1976, D.C. bar 1978. Asst. city mgr., city atty., Pueblo, 1952-55; adminstrv. asst., legislative counsel U.S. Senator Gordon Allott, 1956-61; asst. gen. counsel Life Ins. Assn. Am., Washington, 1961-68; gen. counsel Aetna Life & Casualty Co., Hartford, Conn., 1968-78; mem. firm Hedrick & Lane, Washington, 1978-79; ptnr. Nossaman, Guthner, Knox & Elliott, Washington, 1979-85, of counsel, 1986—, Epstein, Becker & Green, P.C., Washington, 1986—. Bd. dirs. Friends of the Hopkins Ctr., VISTAS; trustee Opera North. Served with USAAC, 1944-46. Mem. ABA, Fed. Bar Assn., Phi Gamma Delta, Phi Alpha Delta. Office: 3703 Dixon St Santa Barbara CA 93105-2462 Home Phone: 805-687-8302; Office Phone: 805-687-8302. E-mail: warrengelliott@hotmail.com.

ELLIS, ALVIN, state legislator, farmer, rancher; b. Red Lodge, Mont., July 11, 1936; m. Maureen Ellis. BS in Animal Scis. Farmer, rancher; mem. Mont. State Ho. of Reps., 1991-98, Mont. Senate, Dist. 12, Helena, 1998—; mem. labor and employment rels. com., mem. taxation com. Mont. Senate; mem. edn. and cultural resources com. Mont. State Senate. Served to 2d lt. U.S. Army, also Res. Trustee Sch. Bd. Republican. Home: HC 50 Box 4840 Red Lodge MT 59068-9724

ELLIS, ELDON EUGENE, retired surgeon; b. Washington, Ind., July 2, 1922; s. Osman Polson and Ina Lucretia (Cochran) E.; m. Irene Eaves Clay, June 26, 1948 (dec. 1968); m. Priscilla Dean Strong, Sept. 20, 1969 (dec. Feb. 1990); children: Paul Addison, Kathe Lynn, Jonathan Clay, Sharon Anne, Eldon Eugene, Rebecca Deborah; m. Virginia Michael Ellis, Aug. 22, 1992. BA, U. Rochester, NY, 1946, MD, 1949. Intern surgery Stanford U. Hosp., San Francisco, 1949—50, resident and fellow surgery, 1950—52, 1955; Schilling fellow pathology San Francisco Gen. Hosp., 1955; ptnr. Redwood Med. Clinic, Redwood City, Calif., 1955—87, med. dir., 1984—87, Peninsula Occupl. Health Assocs., San Carlos, Calif., 1991—94, physician, 1995—99, Sequoia Med. Clinic, Redwood City, 1999—2006; ret., 2006. Asst. clin. prof. surgery Stanford U., 1970-80; dir. Sequoia Hosp., Redwood City, 1974-82. Pres. Sequoia Hosp. Found., 1983-92, bd. dirs.; pres., chmn. bd. dirs. Bay Chamber Symphony Orch., San Mateo, Calif., 1988-91; mem. Nat. Bd. Benevolence Evang. Covenant Ch., Chgo., 1988-93; mem. mgmt. com. The Samarkand Retirement Cmty., Santa Barbara, Calif., 1991-2000; past pres. Project Hope Nat. Alumni Assn., 1992-94, bd. dirs., 1994—; med. advisor Project Hope, Russia Commonwealth Ind. States, 1992. With USNR, 1942-46, 50-52. Recipient Disting. Svc. award, San Mateo County Med. Assn., 2005; named Outstanding Citizen of Yr., Redwood City, 1987. Mem.: AMA, Calif. Thoracic Soc., Cardiovasc. Coun., San Mateo Individual Practice Assn. (treas. 1984—97), Stanford Surg. Soc., San Mateo Surg. Soc., San Mateo County Comprehensive Health Planning Coun. (v.p. 1969—70), San Mateo Med. Soc. (pres. 1969—70, Disting. Svc. award 2005), San Mateo County Heart Assn. (pres. 1961—63), Calif. Heart Assn. (pres. 1965—66), Am. Heart Assn. (v.p. 1974—75), Am. Coll. Chest Physicians, Calif. Med. Assn. Republican. Mem. Peninsula Convenant Ch. Home: 2305 Wooster Ave Belmont CA 94002-1549 Personal E-mail: eldonellis@hotmail.com.

ELLIS, GEORGE RICHARD, museum administrator; b. Birmingham, Ala., Dec. 9, 1937; s. Richard Paul and Dorsie (Gibbs) E.; m. Sherroll Edwards, June 20, 1961 (dec. 1973); m. Nancy Enderson, Aug. 27, 1975; 1 son, Joshua. BA, U. Chgo., 1959, MFA, 1961; postgrad., UCLA, 1971. Art supr. Jefferson County Schs., Birmingham, 1962-64; asst. dir. Birmingham Mus. Art, 1964-66, UCLA Mus. Cultural History, 1971-81, assoc. dir., 1981-82; dir. Honolulu Acad. Arts, 1981—. Author various works on non-western art, 1971—. Bd. dirs. Children's Lit. Hawaii, Japan Am. Soc.; humanities adv. com. mem. Hawaii Pacific U., 1995—; cmty. adv. bd. Japanese Cultural Ctr., 1997—; sec.-treas. Social Sci. Club, 1985—. Recipient Ralph Altman award UCLA, 1968; recipient Outstanding Achievement award UCLA, 1980; fellow Kress Found., 1971 Mem. Pacific Arts Assn. (v.p. 1985-89, exec. bd. 1989—), Hawaii Mus. Assn. (v.p. 1986-87, pres. 1987-88, pres. 1996-97, 97-98), Assn. Art Mus. Dirs., Am. Assn. Mus., L.A. Ethnic Arts Coun. (hon.), Friends of Iolani Palace (bd. dirs.), Pacific Club. Office: Honolulu Academy Arts 900 S Beretania St Honolulu HI 96814-1495 Home: 1320 Pleasant Way S Saint Petersburg FL 33705-6131

ELLIS, JAMES REED, retired lawyer; b. Oakland, Calif., Aug. 5, 1921; s. Floyd E. and Hazel (Reed) E.; m. Mary Lou Earling, Nov. 18, 1944 (dec.); children: Robert Lee, Judith Ann (dec.), Lynn Earling, Steven Reed. BS, Yale, 1942; JD, U. Wash., 1948; LLD (hon.), Lewis and Clark U., 1968, Seattle U., 1981; PSD (hon.), Whitman Coll., 1992. Bar: Wash. 1949, D.C. 1971. Ptnr. Preston, Thorgrimson, Horowitz, Starin & Ellis, Seattle, 1952-69, Preston, Thorgrimson, Starin, Ellis & Holman, Seattle, 1969-72, Preston, Thorgrimson, Ellis, Holman & Fletcher, Seattle, 1972-79; sr. ptnr. Preston, Thorgrimson, Ellis & Holman, Seattle, 1979-90, Preston, Thorgrimson, Shidler, Gates & Ellis, Seattle, 1990-92; of counsel Preston, Gates & Ellis, Seattle, 1992—2002; chmn., CEO Wash. State Convention and Trade Ctr., Seattle, 1986—2002. Dep. pros. atty. King County, 1952; gen. counsel Municipality of Met. Seattle, 1958-79; dir., mem. exec. com. Key Bank of Wash., 1969-94, KIRO, Inc., 1965-95; dir. Blue Cross of Wash. and Alaska, 1989-98. Mem. Nat. Water Commn., 1970-73; mem. urban transp. adv. council U.S. Dept. Transp., 1970-71; mem. Wash. Planning Adv. Council, 1965-72; mem. Washington State Growth Strategies Commn., 1989-90; pres. Forward Thrust Inc., 1966-73; chmn. Mayors Com. on Rapid Transit, 1964-65; trustee Ford Found., 1970-82, mem. exec. com., 1978-82; bd. regents U. Wash., 1965-77, pres., 1972-73; trustee Resources for the Future, 1983-92; mem. council Nat. Mcpl. League, 1968-76, v.p., 1972-76; chmn. Save our Local Farmlands Com., 1978-79, King County Farmlands Adv. Commn., 1980-82; pres. Friends of Freeway Park, 1976-99; bd. dirs. Nat. Park and Recreation Assn., 1979-82; trustee Lewis and Clark U., 1988-94; pres. Mountains to Sound Greenway Trust, Inc., 1991-2001; trustee Henry M. Jackson Found., 1992—. 1st lt. USAAF, 1943-46. Recipient Bellevue First Citizen award, 1968, Seattle First Citizen award, 1968, Nat. Conservation award Am. Motors, 1968, Distinguished Service award Wash. State Dept. Parks and Recreation, 1968, Distinguished Citizen award Nat. Municipal League, 1969, King County Distinguished Citizen award, 1970, La Guardia award Center N.Y.C. Affairs, 1975, Environ. Quality award EPA, 1977, Am. Inst. for Public Service Nat. Jefferson award, 1974, State Merit medal State of Wash., 1990, Nat. Founders award Local Initiatives Support Corp., 1992, Henry M. Jackson Disting. Pub. Svc. medal, 1998, U. Wash. Alumnus Summa Laude Dignatus award, 1999, Lifetime Achievement award, The Am. Lawyer mag., 2005. Fellow: Am. Bar Found.; mem.: ABA (ho. dels. 1978—82, past chmn. urban, state and local govt. law sect.), AIA (hon.), Acad. Pub. Adminstrn., Am. Judicature Soc., D.C. Bar Assn., Seattle Bar Assn. (Pres.'s award 1993), Wash. Bar Assn., Nat. Assn. Bond Lawyers (com. stds. of practice), Mcpl. League Seattle and King County (past pres.), Coun. Fgn. Rels., Rainier Club (Seattle), Order of Coif (hon.), Phi Gamma Delta, Phi Delta Phi. Home: 903 Shoreland Dr SE Bellevue WA 98004-6738 Office: 925 4th Ave Seattle WA 98104-1158 Office Fax: 206-623-7022.

ELLIS, JOHN MARTIN, German literature educator; b. London, May 31, 1936; came to U.S., 1966, naturalized, 1972; s. John Albert and Emily (Silvey) E.; m. Barbara Stephanie Rhoades, June 28, 1978; children: J. Richard, Andrew W., Katherine M., Jill E. BA with 1st class honours, U. London, 1959, PhD, 1965. Tutorial asst. German Univ. Coll., Wales, Aberystwyth, 1959-60; asst. lectr. U. Leicester, Eng., 1960-63; asst. prof. U. Alta., Edmonton, Can., 1963-66; mem. faculty U. Calif., Santa Cruz, 1966—, prof. German, 1970-94, prof. emeritus, 1994, dean grad. div., 1977-86. Vis. prof. U. Kent, Canterbury, Eng., 1970-71 Author: Schiller's Kalliasbriefe and the Study of His Aesthetic Theory, 1969, Kleist's Prinz Friedrich von Homburg: A Critical Study, 1970, Narration in the German Novelle, 1974, The Theory of Literary Criticism: A Logical Analysis, 1974, Heinrich von Kleist: Studies in the Character and Meaning of His Writings, 1979, One Fairy Story Too Many: The Brothers Grimm and Their Tales, 1983, Against Deconstruction, 1989, Language, Thought and Logic, 1993, Literature Lost: Social Agendas and the Corruption of the Humanities, 1997 (Peter Shaw Meml. award). Served with Brit. Army, 1954-56. Fellow Guggenheim Found., 1970-71; Fellow NEH, 1975-76, 92. Mem. NAS, Am. Assn. Tchrs. German, Assn. Lit. Scholars and Critics (sec.-treas. 1994-2002). E-mail: john.ellis@earthlink.net.

ELLIS, JOHN W., professional baseball team and utilities executive; b. Seattle, Sept. 14, 1928; s. Floyd E. and Hazel (Reed) R.; m. Doris Stearns, Sept. 1, 1953; children: Thomas R., John, Barbara, Jim. BS, U. Wash., 1952, JD, 1953. Bar: Wash. State bar 1953. Ptnr. Perkins, Coie, Stone, Olsen & Williams, Seattle, 1953-70; with Puget Sound

Power & Light Co., Bellevue, Wash., 1970—, exec. v.p., 1973-76, pres., CEO, 1976-87, also dir., chmn., CEO, 1987-92, chmn. bd., 1992—, bd. dirs., 1993—; dir., chmn. Seattle br. Fed. Res. Bank of San Francisco, 1982-88; CEO, Seattle Mariners, 1992-99, chmn. emeritus, 1999—. Mem. Wash. Gov.'s Spl. Com. Energy Curtailment, 1973-74; mem. Wash. Gov.'s Coun. on Edn., 1991—; chmn. Pacific N.W. Utilities Coordinating Com., 1976-82; bd. dirs. Wash. Mut. Savs. Bank, Seattle, SAFECO Corp., Nat. Energy Found., 1985-87, FlowMole Corp., Assoc. Electric & Gas Ins. Svcs. Ltd.; chmn. Electric Power Rsch. Inst., 1984—; chmn., CEO, The Baseball Club of Seattle, L.P.; regent Wash. State U., 1992—. Pres. Bellevue Boys and Girls Club, 1969-71, Seattle/King County Econ. Devel. Council, 1984—; mem. exec. dirs. Seattle/King County Boys and Girls Club, 1972-75; bd. dirs. Overlake Hosp., Bellevue, 1974—, United Way King County, 1977—, Seattle Sci. Found., 1977—, Seattle Sailing Found., Evergreen Safety Council, 1981, Assn. Wash. Bus., 1980-81, Govs. Adv. Council on Econ. Devel., 1984—; chmn. bd. Wash. State Bus. Round Table, 1983; pres. United for Washington; adv. bd. Grad. Sch. Bus. Adminstrn. U. Wash., 1982—, Wash. State Econ. Ptnrship., 1984—; chmn. Seattle Regional Panel White Ho. Fellows, 1985—; trustee Seattle U., 1986—. Mem. ABA, Wash. Bar Assn., King County Bar Assn., Nat. Assn. Elec. Cos. (dir. 1977-79), Edison Electric Inst. (dir. 1978-80, exec. com. 1982, 2d vice chmn. 1987, 1st vice chmn. 1988, now chmn.), Assn. Edison Illuminating Cos. (exec. com. 1979-81), Seattle C. of C. (dir. 1980—, 1st vice chmn. 1987-88, chmn. 1988—), Phi Gamma Delta, Phi Delta Phi. Clubs: Rainier (Seattle) (sec. 1972, v.p. 1984, pres. 1985), Seattle Yacht (Seattle), Corinthian Yacht (Seattle); Meydenbauer Bay Yacht (Bellevue), Bellevue Athletic. Lodges: Rotary (Seattle). Home: 901 Shoreland Dr SE Bellevue WA 98004-6738 also: Puget Sound Power & Light Co PO Box 97034 Bldg Bellevue WA 98009-9734

ELLIS, JOHNNY, state legislator; b. Springfield, Mo., Mar. 13, 1960; Attended, U. Alaska, Anchorage, 1978—79; BA, Claremont McKenna Coll., 1979—82. Alaska State Representative, District 12-B, 86-92, chairman, Health, Education & Social Serv, 88-99, member, Judiciary Committee, formerly, Alaska House Representative; Alaska State Senator, District H, 1992-2002, member, Committee on Committees, Judiciary & Rules Committees, currently, Alaska State Senate; member, Mental Health Parity Task Force, 98, Anchorage Waterways Coun, Fairview Community Coun, Anchorage Econ Develop Corp & Mt View Community Center Fundraising Drive, currently; Alaska State Senator, District L, 2003-, minority leader, formerly, majority leader, currently, Alaska State Senate. Mkt research, Suddock & Suddock Assocs, 83-85; co-owner, Macuir Co, 89-; owner, Alaska Natural, currently. Outstanding Representative, STAR, 88; Friend of ARCA, 90; Golden Key Award, ARCA, 90; Advisor Alaska's Children Award, 98. America Mkg Association; Friends of the Musk Ox. Democrat. Avocations: travel, reading, history, politics. Office: Dist L 716 W Fourth Ave Ste 440 Anchorage AK 99501 also: State Capitol Rm 9 Juneau AK 99801 Office Phone: 907-269-0169, 907-465-3704. Office Fax: 907-269-0172, 907-465-2529. Business E-Mail: Senator_Johnny_Ellis@legis.state.ak.us.*

ELLIS, MONTA, professional basketball player; b. Oct. 26, 1985; s. Rosa Ellis. Diploma, Lanier HS, Jackson, Miss., 2005. Player Golden State Warriors, Calif., 2005—. Named EA Sports Player of Yr., 2005, Mr. Basketball, Miss., 2005, Nat. Co-Player of Yr., Parade Mag., 2005, Most Improved Player, NBA, 2007. Mailing: Golden State Warriors 1011 Broadway Oakland CA 94607

ELLIS, ROBERT HARRY, retired broadcast executive, academic administrator; b. Cleve., Mar. 2, 1928; s. John George Ellis and Grace Bernice (Lewis) Ellis Kline; m. Frankie Jo Lanter, Aug. 7, 1954; children: Robert Harry Jr., Kimberley Kay Ellis Murphy, Shana Ellis Antonio. BA, Ariz. State U., 1953; MA, Case Western Res. U., 1962. Newswriter, announcer Sta. KOY, Phoenix, 1953-55, continuity dir., 1955-61; dir., radio ops. Ariz. State U., Tempe, 1959-61; gen. mgr. Sta. KAET-TV, Tempe, 1961-87; assoc. v.p. Ariz. State U., Tempe, 1986-90. Exec. com. bd. dirs. Pub. Broadcasting Svc., Washington, 1972-77, 80-86; founder Pacific Mountain Network, Denver, 1972, pres., 1973-75; mem. ednl. telecomm. com. Nat. Assn. Ednl. Broadcasters, Washington, 1973-77, 80-86. Mem. Sister City, Tempe, Tempe Ctr. For the Handicapped, East Valley Mental Health Alliance, Mesa, Ariz., Ariz. Acad., State Ariz. Behavior Health Bd. of Examiners, 1991-92. Recipient Bd. Govs. award Pacific Mountain Network, 1987, achievement award Ariz. State U., 1997; named to Ariz. Broadcasters Hall of Fame, 1999. Mem. Nat. Assn. TV Arts and Scis. (life, v.p., bd. trustees 1969-70, bd. dirs. Phoenix chpt. 1986, silver circle award 1992), Nat. Assn. Pub. TV Stas. (bd. dirs. 1988-94), Tempe C. of C. (diplomate, bd. dirs. 1987-90), Sundome Performing Arts Assn. (bd. dirs. 1986-90), Ariz. Zool. Soc. (bd. dirs., sec. 1984-90), Ariz. State U. Alumni Assn. (life), Ariz. State U. Retirees Assn. (founder, pres. 1991-92), Tempe Conv. and Visitors Bur. (founder, sec./treas. 1988-93), Tempe Sports Authority (founder 1989-95), ASU Faculty Emeritus Orgn. (pres. 1992-93). Methodist. Avocations: tennis, bridge. Personal E-mail: bobhellis@cox.net.

ELLIS, STEPHEN CHARLES, lawyer; b. Portland, Oreg., Apr. 17, 1945; s. Donald E. Ellis and Francis E. (Shainholts) Cordiner; m. Helen Stevens, Jan. 1, 1981; children: Donald, Peter. BA cum laude, U. Wash., 1967; JD cum laude, U. Mich., 1970. Bar: Wash., 1970, U.S. Dist. Ct. (We. dist. Wash.). Assoc. Reed McClure Moceri & Thonn, Seattle, 1970—73, ptnr., 1973—86; mng. ptnr., pres. Weiss Jensen Ellis & Botteri (later Weiss Jensen Ellis & Howard, combined with offices Holland & Knight LLP), Seattle, 1986—2001; ptnr. Holland & Knight LLP, Seattle, profl. devel. and recruiting. Chmn. Com. of Law Examiners, Seattle, 1983-86; mem. WSBA Character and Fitness Com., Seattle, 1985-91. Contbr. articles to profl. jours. Bd. trustee Seattle Children's Home, 1987-91, King County Bar Found., 2004—; bd. trustee, sec. N.W. Theol. Union, Seattle, 1986-1994; bd. dir., pres. Village Theatre Issaquah, Wash., 1994-2002 Mem. ABA (mem., sect. on corp., banking and bus. law), Wash. State Bar Assn. (bar examiners com. mem. 1975-86, chmn., com. law examiners, 1983-86, law clerk com. 1983-97, corp., banking law and internat. law, sect. mem., character and fitness com. 1986-91), Seattle-King County Bar Assn., King County Bar Found. (trustee 2004—), Athletic Club, Harbor Club. Avocations: racquetball, book collecting, writing. Home: 12225 188th St SE Snohomish WA 98296-8153 Office Phone: 206-340-9573. Business E-Mail: stephen.ellis@hklaw.com.

ELLISON, CYRIL LEE, literary agent, retired publishing executive; b. NYC, Dec. 11, 1916; m. Anne N. Nottonson, June 4, 1942 (dec. June 2000). Assoc. pub., v.p. Watson-Guptill Publs., 1939-69, v.p., advt. dir., 1939-69, assoc. pub. Am. Artist mag.; exec. v.p. Communication Channels, Inc., NYC, 1969-88; pub. emeritus Fence Industry, Access Control, Pension World, Trusts & Estates, Nat. Real Estate Investor, Shopping Center World; pres. Lee Comms., 1980—; assoc. Kids Countrywide, Inc., 1987-94; literary agent, 1994—. Pub. cons., book rep., advt. and mktg. cons., 1987-94; assoc. Mark Clements Rsch. N.Y., Inc., 1994—; pub. cons. Mag. Rsch. Co., 1994—; assoc. publisher Plants, Sites & Parks. Served with USAAF, 1942-46, PTO. Named Gray-Russo Advt. Man of Year Ad Men's Post Am. Legion, 1954; recipient Hall of Fame award Internat. Fence Industry Assn., 1985. Mem. Nat. Art Material Trade Assn. (v.p., cons.), Amateur Artists Assn. Am., Am. Legion (life, comdr. advt. men's post 1954, 64). Home: 6839 N 29th Ave Phoenix AZ 85017-1213 Office: Lee Communications 5060 N 19th Ave Phoenix AZ 85015-3210 Home Phone: 602-249-6008. Business E-Mail: intern@azpra.org.

ELLISON, DAVID R., career officer; BS, U.S. Naval Acad., 1970; MS, George Washington U., 1975; PhD in Bus. Adminstrn., Pa. State U., 1984; postgrad., Harvard U., 1989. asst. prof. U.S. Naval Acad., 1973-76. Ensign USN, 1970, advanced through ranks to rear adm.; various assignments to superintendent Naval Postgrad. Sch., 2000—. Decorated Def. Superior Svc. medal, Legion of Merit (3 awards), Bronze Star (with Combat V), Meritorious Svc. medal (3 awards), Navy Commendation medal, Navy Achievement medal, Coast Guard Achievement medal, others; fellow CNO Strategic Studies Group, Naval War Coll.

ELLISON, HERBERT JAY, retired historian, educator; b. Portland, Oreg., Oct. 3, 1929; s. Benjamin F. and Esther (Anderson) Ellison; m. Alberta M. Moore, June 13, 1952; children: Valery, Pamela. BA, U. Wash., 1951, MA, 1952; PhD (Fulbright fellow), U. London, 1955. Instr. history U. Wash., 1955—56, prof. Russian and Ea. European studies, 1968—2008, dir. divsn. internat. programs, 1968—72, vice provost for ednl. devel., 1969—72, dir. Inst. Comparative and Fgn. Area Studies, 1973—78, chmn. Russian and East European studies, 1979—83; asst. prof. U. Okla., 1956—62; assoc. prof. history, chmn. Slavic studies program U. Kans., 1962—67, prof., 1965—68, dir. NDEA Lang. and Area Ctr. Slavic Studies, 1965—67, assoc. dean faculties internat. programs, 1967—68; sec. Kennan Inst. Advanced Russian Studies, Washington, 1983—85. Trustee Nat. Coun. Russian and E. European Rsch., 1983—87; dir. Russian rsch. Nat. Bur. Asian Rsch., 1990—2008, bd. dirs., 1993—2008; chmn. bd. dirs. Internat. Rsch. and Exchs. Bd., 1992—98; dir. new Russia in Asia rsch. and conf. project, 1993—96; chmn. acad. coun. Kennan Inst. Advanced Russian Studies, 1997—2001; bd. govs. Blakemore Found., 1998—2008. Author: History of Russia, 1964, Sino-Soviet Conflict, 1982, Soviet Policy Toward Western Europe, 1983, Japan and the Pacific Quadrille, 1987, Boris Yelstin and Russian Democratization, 2006; co-author: Twentieth Century Russia, 1999; contbr. articles to profl. jours.; chief cons., exec. dir. (TV series) Messengers from Moscow, 1995, Yeltsin, 2000. Named Ellison Ctr. Russian, East European and Ctrl. Asian Studies Ctr. and Ellison Disting. Professorship Russian History, U. Wash., 2005. Mem.: AAUP, Am. Assn. Advancement Slavic Studies, Am. Hist. Assn., Univ. Club. Home: 12127 SE 15th St Bellevue WA 98005-3821 Home Phone: 425-644-9416. Business E-Mail: hellison@u.washington.edu.

ELLISON, LARRY (LAWRENCE JOSEPH ELLISON), computer software company executive; b. Chgo., Aug. 17, 1944; m. Ada Quinn, 1967 (div. 1974); m. Nancy Wheeler, 1976 (div. 1977); m. Barbara Boothe, 1983 (div. 1986); m. Melanie Craft, Dec. 18, 2003; 2 children. Student, U. Ill., U. Chgo. With Amdahl, Inc., Santa Clara, Calif., 1967—71, systems arch.; pres. systems divsn. Omex Corp., 1972—77; co-founder (with Bob Miner & Ed Oates) Oracle Corp. (formerly Software Devel. Labs.), Redwood, Calif., 1977; CEO Oracle Corp., Redwood, Calif., 1977—, pres., 1978—96, chmn., 1990—92, 1995—2004. Bd. dirs. Oracle Corp., 1977—, Apple Computer, Inc., 1997—2002; trustee US Coun. Internat. Bus. Recipient Leadership award for Global Integration, 1994, Disting. Info. Scis. award, Assn. Info. Tech. Profls., 1996, Industry Achievement award, 1997; named Entrepreneur of Yr., Harvard Sch. Bus., 1990, Bio-IT Champion, Bio-ITWorld, 2002; named one of World's Richest People, Forbes Mag., 1999—, Forbes Richest Americans, 2006, 50 Who Matter Now, CNNMoney.com Bus. 2.0, 2006. Avocation: yachting. Office: Oracle Corp 500 Oracle Pky Redwood Shores CA 94065-1675*

ELLISON, LUTHER FREDERICK, oil industry executive; b. Monroe, La., Jan. 2, 1925; s. Luther and Gertrude (Hudson) E.; m. Frances Williams, July 18, 1948 (dec.); children: Constance Elizabeth, Carolyn Williams; m. Patsy Hunter, Nov. 23, 1996. Student, Emory U., 1943-44; BS in Petroleum Engring., Tex. A&M U., 1949, BS in Geol. Engring., 1950. Registered profl. engr., Tex., La. Jr. petroleum engr. Sun Prodn. Co., Kilgore and McAllen, Tex., 1950-52, area petroleum engr. Garcia Field, Tex., 1952-54, Delhi (La.) unit engr., 1954-60, asst. region supt. Dallas, 1960-62, dist. drilling engr. Corpus Christi, 1962-63, dist. engr. McAllen, 1963-65, supr. engring. Dallas, 1965-66, div. chief petroleum engr., 1966-70, regional mgr. engring., 1970-75, region mgr., 1975-78, dir. devel., 1978-80, v.p. devel., 1980-84; div. v.p., dir. Sun Exploration and Prodn. Co., 1984-86, pres., bd. dirs., 1986—, Dallas C. of C., 1975—88; pres., chief exec. officer Oil & Gas Experts, Inc., Dallas, 1986—, Am. Energy Enterprises Inc., Dallas, 1988—. Pres., dir., mem. exec. com. Nabors-Sun Drilling Co.; dir., mem. exec. com. East Tex. Salt & Water Disposal Co.; CEO, pres. Oil & Gas Experts Inc., 1986; spkr. and writer in field. V.p. Northwood Jr. H.S. PTA, Dallas, 1967—68, pres., 1968—69; elder, trustee Preston Hollow Presbyn. Ch. Found.; sr. trustee, 2005—; bd. dirs. Glen Lakes Assn. With USN, 1943—46. Mem. Tex.-Mid-Continent Oil and Gas Assn. (Outstanding Achievement award 1964, chmn. area 1964-65, mgr. north region, operating com., Outstanding Performance award 1985—), Am. Petroleum Inst., Soc. Petroleum Engrs., Dallas Engrs. Club, Petroleum Engrs. Club, Dallas Petroleum Club, Park City Club, Northwood Club (Dallas), Lions Club, Premier Club (Dallas), Parents League, Sigma Alpha Epsilon (pres. 1944-45). Home: 526 Preston Trail Loop Kerrville TX 78028-6406 Office: PO Box 219 High Rolls Mountain Park NM 88325 Office Phone: 210-218-4150.

ELLMAN, JONATHON ANTHONY, chemist; BS in Chemistry, MIT, 1984; PhD in Organic Chemistry, Harvard U., 1989. NSF postdoctoral fellow U. Calif., Berkeley, 1989-92, asst. prof., 1992-97, assoc. prof., 1997-98, prof., 1999—. Co-organizer NAS Symposium on Combinatorial Chemistry, 1997; sci. co-founder Sunesis Pharms., 1998; bd. dirs. Lake Tahoe Symposia. Assoc. editor Jour. Combinatorial Chemistry, 1998; guest editor spl. issue Combinatorial Chemistry, Accounts Chem. Rsch., 1996, Current Opinion in Chem. Biology, 1998; mem. editl. bd. Molecular Diversity, 1996-98. Recipient Burroughs Wellcome 1993 Hitchings award for drug design and discovery, 1993-97, Young Investigator award Arnold and Mabel Beckman Found., 1993-95, Young Investigator award NSF, 1993-98, Young Investigator award Office Naval Rsch., 1994-97, Cyanamid Faculty award, 1994, Burroughs Wellcome Fund New Initiatives in Malaria Rsch. award, 1997; named Procter and Gamble Young Investigator, 1994-96; grantee Eli Lilly, 1994-96; Predoctoral fellow NSF, 1984-87, postdoctoral fellow NSF, 1989-91, Alfred P. Sloan fellow, 1994-96; James Bryant Conant scholar, 1984, Texaco Philanthropist scholar, 1984. Mem. Am. Chem. Soc. (mem. long range planning com. medicinal chemistry divsn. 1996-98, Arthur C. Cope Scholar award 2000). Office: Dept Chemistry Univ Calif Berkeley CA 94704

ELLMAN, MARK, chef, restaurant owner; b. LA, Aug. 26, 1955; married; three children. Cook Texas Tommy's Hamburger Stand, San Fernando Valley, 1969; owner Can't Rock and Roll But Sure Can Cook, LA, 1975, Avalon Restaurant, Maui, 1989, Maui Tacos, 1995—. Avocations: sailing, movies. Office: Ste 102 834 Front St Lahaina HI 96761-2501

ELLNER, CAROLYN LIPTON, non-profit organization executive, dean, consultant; b. Jan. 17, 1932; d. Robert Mitchell and Rose (Pearlman) Lipton; m. Richard Ellner, June 21, 1953; children: D. Lipton, Alison Lipton. AB cum laude, Mt. Holyoke Coll., 1953; AM, Columbia Tchrs. Coll., 1957; PhD with distinction, UCLA, 1968. Tchr., prof., administr. N.Y. and Md., 1957-62; prof. dir. tchr. edn., assoc. dean Claremont Grad. Sch., Calif., 1967-82; prof., dean sch. edn. Calif. State U., Northridge, 1982-98, dean emerita, 1998—. Ret., CEO On-the-Job Parenting. Co-author: Schoolmaking, 1977, Studies of College Teaching, 1983 (Orange County Authors award 1984). Trustee Ctr. for Early Edn., L.A., 1968-71, Oakwood Sch., L.A., 1972-78, Mt. Holyoke Coll., South Hadley, Mass., 1979-84, Pacific Oaks Coll. and Children's Sch., 2004-09; commr. Economy and Efficiency com., L.A., 1974-82, Calif. Commn. Tchr. Credentialing, 1987-90, 93—, vice chair, 1995-96, chair, 1996-98; bd. dirs. Found. for Effective Govt., L.A., 1982, Calif. Coalition for Pub. Edn., 1985-88, Valley Hosp. Found., 1992-94, Mt. Holyoke Alumnae Assn. Bd., 1993-96; founding dir. Decade of Edn., 1990; assoc. dir. New Devel. in Sci. Project NSF, 1985-94; bd. dirs., chair edn. com. Valley Industry and Commerce Assn., 1990-93, v.p. 1993-94; co-prin. dir. Mid South Calif. Arts Project, 1991-98; mem. coun., trustees L.A. Alliance for Restructing Now (LEARN), 1992-2000; bd. dirs. Inner City Arts Found., 1993-96; involved with L.A. Annenberg Met. Project (LAAMP); exec. bd. DELTA, 1995—, Calif. Subject Matter Projects, 1998—. Ford Found. fellow 1964-67, fellow Ednl. Policy Fellowship Program, 1989-90; recipient Office of Edn. award U.S. Office of Edn., 1969-72, Alumnae medal of honor Mt. Holyoke Coll., 1998; W.M. Keck Found. grantee, 1983, 94. Mem. ASCD, Am. Edn. Rsch. Assn., Am. Assn. Colls. for Tchr. Edn., Nat. Soc. for Study of Edn. Home: 1205 S Oak Knoll Ave Pasadena CA 91106-4442

ELLSTRAND, NORMAN CARL, plant genetics, conservation and evolution educator; b. Elmhurst, Ill., Jan. 1, 1952; s. Edwin August and Beverly (Singer) Ellstrand; m. Tracy Lynn Kahn, July 2, 1983; 1 child, Nathan. BS, U. Ill., 1974; PhD, U. Tex., 1978. Assoc. Duke U., 1978—79; asst. prof. genetics U. Calif., Riverside, 1979—86, assoc. prof., 1986—91, prof., 1991—, vice chmn. dept. botany and plant scis., 1994—96, chmn. conservation biology program, 1995—97. Founder, dir. Ctr. Conservation Biology, 1997—98, Biotechnology Impacts Center, 2003—08; adj. prof. Keck Grad. Inst., 2006—. Contbr. articles to profl. jours.; author: (book) Dangerous Liasons? When Cultivated Plants Mate With Their Wild Relatives, 2003. Recipient Honor award, Calif. Cherimoya Assn., 1992, Highly Cited, Inst. Sci. Info., 2006—; named Mid-Career Fellow, NSF, 1992, Rschr. of Yr., Calif. Rare Fruit Growers Assn., 1984, Eminent Ecologist, W.K. Kellogg Biol. Sta., 1988, Dissortation Mentor of Yr., U. Calif., 2004; grantee, NSF, Dept. Agr., Environ. Protection Agy.; Fulbright grantee, 1993, fellow, Am. Assn. Advancement Sci., 2000—. Mem.: Soc. Conservation Biology, Am. Soc. Naturalists, Soc. Study Evolution, Phi Kappa Phi, Phi Beta Kappa. Office: U Calif Dept Botany And Scis Riverside CA 92521-0124

ELLSWORTH, FRANK L., not-for-profit executive; b. Wooster, Ohio, May 20, 1943; s. Clayton Sumner and Frances (Fuller) E.; 1 child, Kirstin Lynne. BA, Western Res. Coll., 1965; MEd, Pa. State U., 1967; MA, Columbia U., 1969; PhD, U. Chgo., 1976; LLD, Pepperdine U., 1997, Southwestern U., 2004. Asst. dir. devel. Columbia Law Sch., 1968-70; dir. spl. projects, prof. lit. Sarah Lawrence Coll., NY, 1971; asst. dean Law Sch., U. Chgo., 1971-79, instr. social sci. collegiate div., 1975-79; pres., prof. polit. sci. Pitzer Coll., Claremont, Calif., 1979-91; pres. Ind. Colls. So. Calif., LA, 1991-97; v.p. Capital Rsch. & Mgmt. Co., 1997—2003; pres. Japan Soc., 2003—06, Ellsworth Collection, 2006—. Author: The Foundation of the 21st Century, 2002, Law on the Midway, 1977, Student Activism in American Higher Education; contbr. articles to profl. jours. Trustee Japanese Am. Nat. Mus., Give2Asia, Southwestern U.; chmn. Global Ptnrs. Inst., Can., Give2Asia Coll.; trustee Am. Friends Nat., Portrait Gallery, London. Recipient Disting. Young Alumnus award Case Western Res. U., 1981, Tree of Life award United Jewish Fund, 1991. Mem. Grolier Soc., Young Pres.'s Orgn., Asia Soc., Japanese Art Soc. Home: 2935 Sequoia Dr S Palm Springs CA 92262

ELLWOOD, PAUL MURDOCK, JR., health policy analyst, consultant; b. San Francisco, July 16, 1926; s. Paul and Rebecca May (Logan) Ellwood; m. Barbara Ellwood; children: David, Cynthia, Deborah. BA, Stanford U., 1949, MD, 1953. Dir. Kenny Rehab. Inst., Mpls., 1962—63; exec. dir. Am. Rehab. Found., Mpls., 1963—73; dir. Inst. Interdisciplinary Studies, Mpls., 1970—73; pres. InterStudy, health policy analysis Excelsior, Minn., 1973—85; pres. Paul Ellwood & Assocs., Excelsior, 1985—87; chmn. bd., pres. InterStudy, 1987—92; pres. Jackson Hole Group, Teton Village, Wyo., 1992—; founding dir. Found. for Accountability/Quality Measure for Healthcare, Portland, Oreg., 1997—. Dir., mem. exec. com. Jackson Hole Ski Corp., Wyo., 1972—87; clin. prof. phys. medicine and rehab., neurology and pediat. U. Minn. Med. Sch.; cons. in health and delivery systems. Co-author: Assuring the Quality of Health Care, 1973; co-editor: Handbook of Physical Medicine and Rehabilitation, 1971. With USNR, 1944—46. Recipient award, Ministry Pub. Health, Republic Argentina, 1957, 1st award sci. exhibit, Am. Acad. Neurology, 1958, citation, Pres.'s Com. Employment Handicapped, 1962, Gold Key award, Am. Congress Rehab., 1971; named Disting. fellow, Am. Rehab. Found., 1973. Mem.: Group Health Assn. Am. (dir. 1975—76), Assn. Rehab. Ctrs. (pres. 1960—61, U.S. Healthcare Quality award 1991), Nat. Health Coun. (dir. 1971—76), Inst. Medicine NAS. Home: PO Box 15 Bondurant WY 82922-0015

EL MALLAKH, DOROTHEA HENDRY, editor, publishing executive; b. Emmett, Idaho, July 16, 1938; d. David Lovell Parker and Lygia Teressa (Dalton) Hendry; m. Ragaei William El Mallakh, Aug.

26, 1962 (dec. Mar. 19, 1987); children: Helen Alise, Nadia Irene. BA in Modern Langs., Lewis and Clark Coll., 1960; MA in History, U. Colo., 1962, PhD in History, 1972; postgrad., Georgetown U., 1962-63. Exec. adminstr., treas. Internat. Rsch. Ctr. Energy & Econ. Devel., Boulder, Colo., 1973-87, exec. dir., 1987—. Assoc. editor Jour. Energy & Devel., Boulder, 1975-87, mng. editor, 1987—; bd. dirs. Rocky Mountain Eye Found., Boulder. Author: The Slovak Autonomy Movement, 1979; author (with others): The Genius of Arab Civilization, 1983, Gulf Oil in the Aftermath of the Iraq War: Strategies and Policies, 2005; editor: The Energy Watchers I-IX, 1990-98; author and editor: Saudi Arabia, 1982. Perrine Meml. fellow, U. Colo., 1960-61, Rare Lang. fellow, U.S. Govt., U. Colo., 1961-62, Rotary Internat. fellow, Boise, Idaho, 1962. Mem. Internat. Assn. Energy Econs. (v.p. internat. affairs 1989-91, sec. 1988-89). Office: ICEED 850 Willowbrook Rd Boulder CO 80302-7439 Office Phone: 303-442-4014. Business E-Mail: iceed@colorado.edu.

EL-MOSLIMANY, ANN PAXTON, paleoecologist, educator, writer; b. Fullerton, Calif., Aug. 2, 1937; d. Donald Dorn and Sarah Frances (Turman) Paxton; m. Mohammed Ahmad El-Moslimany, May 31, 1962 (dec.); children: Samia, Ramsey, Rasheed. BS, N.Mex. State U., 1959; MS, Am. U., Beirut, 1961; PhD, U. Wash., 1983. Tchr. various schs., 1959-83, Kuwait U., 1984—86, Seattle Ctrl. C.C., 1986-90; prin., tchr. Islamic Sch. Seattle, 1989-99, curriculum coord., 1999—. Paleoecological rschr. Palynological Consultants, 1987—; founding dir. Islamic Sch. of Seattle; adv. bd. Islamic Sch. League Am. Author: Zaki's Ramadan Fast, 1994; contbr. articles to sci. jours.; mem. adv. bd. Aziah mag. Speaker Children of Abraham Organization. Mem. Amnesty Internat., Am. Quaternary Assn., Islamic Sch. League. Muslim. Avocations: travel, literature, history. Office: Islamic Sch Seattle 720 25th Ave Seattle WA 98122-4902 Mailing: PO Box 367 Seahurst WA 98062 Personal E-mail: annelmoslimany@yahoo.com.

ELOP, STEPHEN A., computer software company executive; b. Canada, 1963; m. Nancy M. Elop; 5 children. B in computer engring. & mgmt., McMaster U., Hamilton, Ont., 1986. Mgmt. positions Soma Inc., Canada; dir. cons. services group Lotus Development Corp., 1992—94; sr. v.p. systems, CIO Boston Chicken Inc., 1994—98; CIO Macromedia Inc., 1998—99, gen. mgr. ebusiness div., 1999—2001, exec. v.p. worldwide field ops., 2001—04, COO, 2004—05, pres., CEO, 2005; pres. worldwide field ops. Adobe Systems Inc., 2005—06; COO Juniper Networks, Inc., Sunnyvale, Calif., 2007—08; pres. bus. divsn. Microsoft Corp., Redmond, Wash., 2008—. Office: Microsoft Corp 1 Microsoft Way Redmond WA 98052-6399

ELROD, LU, music professor emerita, actress; b. Chattanooga, Apr. 23, 1935; d. John C. Elrod and Helen Pauline (Kohn). MusB, Ga. State U., 1960; M in Music Edn., U. Ga., 1970, EdD, 1971; PhD, U. London, 1975. Prof. music, music coach U. Md., Balt., 1972-78, Calif. State U., LA, 1978—2004, prof. emerita, 2003. Singer with Dallas Opera, 1957. Appeared in movies Charly, 1969, Brewster's Millions, 1986, Major Pettigrew and Me, 1976, Seduction of Joe Tynan, 1977, Atlanta Child Murders, 1985, Children Don't Tell, 1986, For Love or Money, 1986, High School High, 1996, Wag the Dog, 1997, The Big Lebowski, 1998, Primary Colors, 1998, Lloyd the Ugly Kid, 1999, Beautiful, 1999, Glory Days, 2001, Freaky Friday, 2004, Kicking and Screaming, 2005, A River Reborn, 2006, The Achievers, 2008; appeared on TV in Lazarus Syndrome, 1980, Hill Street Blues (Emmy award), 1988, Superior Court, 1988, TV Bloopers, 1989, Beakman's World (Emmy award), Dream On, 1993, Misery Loves Company, 1995, Caroline in the City, 1995, Louie, 1996, George and Alana, 1996, Maggie, 1998, Two Guys and a Girl, 2000, Glory Days, 2001, I Love the 90's, 2004; appeared in TV commls Recipient Gold medal, Silver medal swimming Am. Atheletic Union, 1955, Leadership Devel. award Ford Found., 1967, Leadership Fellows award Ford Found., 1968, Nat. Philanthropy award, 2006; Tift Coll. voice scholar, 1953, Baylor U. voice scholar, 1956; Lu Elrod scholarship named at Calif. State U., LA, 1989; named to Calif. State U., L.A. Wall of Fame, 1993; named Disting. Prof. Arts and Letters, 1993. Mem. AAUP, AFTRA, SAG, Am. Guild Variety Artists, Calif. Faculty Assn., Coll. Music Soc. Achievements include established 32 music, theatre, communication studies scholarships through fundraising activities, collective bargaining, social work, and athletics 1978-2006. Office: Calif State Univ 5151 State University Dr Los Angeles CA 90032-4226 Business E-Mail: lelrod@calstatela.edu.

ELSBERND, SEAN R., city supervisor; b. San Francisco, Feb. 7, 1976; m. Jennifer Johnston. BA, Claremont McKenna Coll., Calif., 1997; JD, U. Calif. Hastings Coll. Law, 2000. Bar: Calif. 2000. Law clk. San Francisco Dist Atty.'s Office, 1998—99, Nielsen, Merksamer, Parinello, Mueller & Naylor LLP, 1999—2000; chief legis. aide to supr. Tony Hall, 2000—03; supr., Dist. 7 San Francisco Bd. Supervisors, 2004—, chair city & sch. dist. com., vice-chair rules com., mem. budget & fin. com. Mem. Health Svc. Sys. Bd., Retirement Bd.; co-dir. Congl. Human Rights Caucus. Vol. St. Thomas More Parish. Mem.: U. Calif. Hastings Coll. Law Alumni Assn., St. Ignatius Alumni Assn. Democrat. Roman Catholic. Office: City Hall 1 Dr Carlton B Goodlet Pl Rm 244 San Francisco CA 94102-4689 Office Phone: 415-554-6516. Fax: 415-554-6546. E-mail: Sean.Elsbernd@sfgov.org.*

ELSBREE, LANGDON, English language educator; b. Trenton, NJ, June 23, 1929; s. Wayland Hoyt and Miriam (Jenkins) E.; m. Aimee Desiree Wildman, June 9, 1952; 1 child, Anita. BA, Earlham Coll., 1952; MA, Cornell U., 1954; PhD, Claremont Grad. Sch., 1963. Instr. in English Miami U., Oxford, Ohio, 1954-57, Harvey Mudd Coll., Claremont, Calif., 1958-59; instr. humanities Scripps Coll., Claremont, Calif., 1959-60; instr., prof. Claremont McKenna Coll., 1960-94, prof. emeritus, 1994; mem. grad. faculty Claremont Grad. Sch., 1965—. Lectr. Calif. State U., L.A., 1968-70; vis. prof. Carleton Coll., 1987, Claremont McKenna Coll., 1995-2000. Author: The Rituals of Life, 1982, Ritual Passages and Narrative Structures, 1991; co-author: Heath College Handbook, 6th-12th edits., 1967-90; guest editor D.H. Lawrence Rev., 1975, 87. Bd. dirs. Claremont Civic Assn., 1964-66; mem. founding com. Quaker Studies in Human Betterment, Greensboro, N.C., 1987. Fulbright Commn. lectr., 1966-67; grantee NEH, 1975, Claremont McKenna Coll., 1980, 82, 87. Mem.: MLA, Sci. Fiction Rsch. Assn., Virginia Woolf Soc., Friends Assn. Higher Edn., D.H. Lawrence Soc. (exec. bd. 1990), Phi Beta Kappa. Democrat. Soc. Of Friends. Avocations: travel, reading, swimming, films, photography. Personal E-mail: le.ade@verozen.net.

ELTON, KIM, state legislator; b. Havre, Mont., Apr. 9, 1948; m to Marylou. Attended, St. Olaf Coll., 1966—68, U. Alaska, Fairbanks, 1972—76. Member, Juneau Borough Assembly, 90-94; asst state ombudsman, formerly; director policy, Off of Lieutenant Governor Terry Miller, fomerly; member, Alaska State Salary Comn; Alaska State Representative, District 3, formerly; Alaska State Senator, District B, 99-, member, Resources, Community and Reg Affaris & Legislature Ethics Committees, currently, Alaska State Senate. Ed, Juneau Empire, 76-78; exec director, Alaska Seafood Mkt Inst, formerly; Commercial fisherman, formerly; newspaper reporter/ed, Anchorage Times & Fairbanks Daily News-Miner, formerly; contractor & writer, currently. Served in US Army, 1969—71, Vietnam. Democrat. Office: State Capitol Rm 506 Juneau AK 99801-1182 Office Phone: 907-465-4947. Office Fax: 907-465-2108. Business E-Mail: Senator_Kim_Elton@legis.state.ak.us.*

ELWAY, JOHN ALBERT, professional sports team executive, retired professional football player; b. Port Angeles, Wash., June 28, 1960; s. John Albert and Janet (Jordan) Elway; m. Janet Elway, Mar. 3, 1984 (div. Dec. 29, 2003); children: Jessica Gwen, Jordan Marie, Juliana, Jack. BA in Econs., Stanford U., 1983. Quarterback Denver Broncos, 1983—98; ret., 1998; owner, CEO Colo. Crush, Arena Football League, 2002—; owner John Elway AutoNation, Elway's, Denver, 2004—, Crown Toyota, Ontario, Calif., 2004—; quarterbacks coach Cherry Creek HS, Greenwood Village, Colo., 2007—. Mem. exec. com. Arena Football League, competition com. (TV appearances) Home Improvement, 1994, Las Vegas, 2004, (film appearances) Resurrecting the Champ, 2007. Founder The Elway Found.; mem. Mayor's Coun. on Phys. Fitness City of Denver; chmn. Rocky Mountain Regional Nat. Kidney Found. Recipient Founders award, Arena Football League; named NFL All-Pro, 1986, 1987, 1993, 1996, 1997, NFL MVP/Player of Yr., AP, 1987, Am. Football Conf. Offensive MVP/Player of Yr., 1987, 1993, Edge NFL Man of Yr., 1992, Super Bowl XXXIII MVP, 1998, Exec. of Yr., Arena Football League, 2007; named to Sporting News Coll. All-Am. Team, 1980, 1982, Sporting News NFL All-Pro Team, 1987, Am. Football Conf. Pro Bowl Team, 1986, 1987, 1989, 1991, 1993, 1994, 1996, 1997, 1998, 1990's All-Decade Team, Colo. Sports Hall of Fame, 1999, NFL Hall of Fame, 2004. Achievements include being the the first overall selection in the 1983 NFL Draft; being a member of Super Bowl Championship winning Denver Broncos, 1998, 1999. Avocations: hunting, fishing, golf. Office: Cherry Creek HS Football Program 9300 E Union Ave Greenwood Village CO 80111 also: Colo Crush Pepsi Ctr 901 Auraria Pky Denver CO 80202 Office Phone: 720-554-2285.

ELY, GARY G., utilities company executive; Grad., Brigham Young U.; postgrad., U. Idaho, Stanford U., Edison Elec. Inst. Leadership. With Avista Corp., Spokane, Wash., 1967—, v.p. mktg., 1986-91, v.p. natural gas, 1991-95, sr. v.p., 1996-97, chmn., CEO, 1997—. Mem. State Bldg. Code Coun. Mem. Pacific Coast Gas Assn. (chmn. gas mgmt. exec. com., chmn. mktg. exec. com., bd. dirs.), N.W. Electric Light and Power Assn. (bd. dirs.), Spokane Valley C. of C. (exec. bd.), N.W. Gas Assn. (bd. dirs.). Office: Avista Corp 1411 E Mission Ave Spokane WA 99220-3727

ELY, PARRY HAINES, dermatologist, educator; b. Washington, Sept. 19, 1945; s. Northcutt and Marica (McCann) E.; m. Elizabeth Magee, June 24, 1969 (div. June 1998); children: Sims, Rebecca, Meredith, Tess; m. Kathleen O'Brien, May 3, 2000 AB, Stanford U., 1967; MD, U. So. Calif., 1971. Diplomate Am. Bd. Dermatology, Am. Bd. Pathology; lic. dermatologist, Calif. Intern medicine U. So. Calif.-L.A. County Med. Ctr., 1971—72, resident dermatology, 1972—75; clin. prof. dermatology U. Calif., Davis, 1975—. Bd. dirs. Nevada City Wineries Mem. editl. bd. Calif. Physician, 1994—; manuscript reviewer Archives Internal Medicine, 1988—, Annals Internal Medicine, 1980—, Archives Dermatology, 1977—; contbr. articles to med. jours Fellow Am. Acad. Dermatology (asst. editor jour. 1988-94, manuscript reviewer 1994—), Am. Soc. Dermatopathology; mem. AMA, Internat. Soc. Tropical Dermatology, Am. Fedn. Clin. Rsch., Am. Soc. Dermatologic Surgery, N.Am. Clin. Dermatologic Soc., Calif. Med. Assn. (alt. del. 1995—, rep. to Calif. Telehealth/Telemedicine coord. project planning com. 1996—), Pacific Dermatologic Soc. (Nelson Paul Anderson Meml. Essay 1st pl. award 1979, Mini Presentation of Yr. award 1984), Noah Worcester Dermatol. Soc., Cutaneous Therapy Soc., Soc. Investigative Dermatology, Sacramento Valley Dermatol. Soc. (pres. 1990-91), Placer Nev. Med. Soc. (bd. dirs. 1978-79, 91-93, v.p. 1994, pres. 1995), Skin Cancer Found. (med. coun. 1987—), Tri-County Am. Cancer Soc. (bd. dirs. 1978-79, 91-92), Royal Soc. Medicine (London), Dermatology Found., Space Dermatology Found. (founding), Shivas Irons Soc. (founding) Office: 565 Brunswick Rd Ste 7 Grass Valley CA 95945-9053 E-mail: haines@netshel.net.

EMANUEL, ARI (ARIEL Z. EMANUEL), talent agent; b. Chgo., 1961; s. Benjamin and Marsha Emanuel; m. Sarah Emanuel; 3 children. Grad., Macalester Coll. Agent trainee Creative Artists Agency; sr. agent Internat. Creative Mgmt.; ptnr. InterTalent; co-founder, ptnr. Endeavor Agy., Beverly Hills, Calif., 1995—. Blog contbr. The Huffington Post. Named one of The 50 Smartest People in Hollywood, Entertainment Weekly, 2007. Democrat. Office: Endeavor Agency 9601 Wilshire Blvd Beverly Hills CA 90210 Office Phone: 310-248-2000. Office Fax: 310-248-2020.

EMENHISER, JEDON ALLEN, retired political science professor, dean; b. Clovis, N.Mex., May 19, 1933; s. Glen Allen and Mary Opal (Sasser); m. Patricia Ellen Burke, Jan. 27, 1954; 1 child, Melissa Mary Emenhiser Westerfield. Student, Am. U., Washington, DC, 1954; BA, U. Redlands, Calif., 1955; PhD, U. Minn., 1962. Cert. community coll. adminstr. Calif. Instr. to prof. polit. sci. Utah State U., Logan, 1960-77, acting dean, 1973-74; prof. Humboldt State U., Arcata, Calif., 1977—2009, dean, 1977-86, acting v.p., 1984; chair Social Sci. Rsch. and Instrnl. Coun. Calif. State U., 1994-95; prof. Jr. Statesmen Summer Sch., Stanford U., 1989—2002, 2005. Vis. instr. U. Redlands, Calif., 1959—60; vis. prof. U. Saigon, Vietnam, 1964—65, U. Mons-Hainaut, Belgium, 2003; dir. Bur. Govt. and Opinion Rsch., Logan, 1965—70; staff dir. Utah Legislature, Salt Lake City, 1967, cons., 1968—77, USCG, McKinleyville, Calif., 1982; v.p. Exch. Bank, New Franklin, Mo., 1970—76; asst. dean Colgate U., Hamilton, NY, 1972—73; reader advanced placement exam. US Govt. Coll. Bd., 1990—98; vis. fellow govt. divsn. Congl. Rsch. Svc., Libr. of Congress, 1996; vis. fellow Nat. U. Ireland, Galway, 2002; vis. prof. Am. studies Royal Libr., Belgium, 2003. Author: Utah's Governments, 1964, Freedom and Power in California, 1987; editor, contbr. Dragon on the Hill, 1970, Rocky Mountain Urban Politics, 1971; producer, dir. TV broadcasts The Hawks and the Doves, 1965-66; contbr. articles to profl. jours. Sec. Cache County Dem. Party, Logan, 1962-63; chmn. Mayor's Commn. on Govt. Orgn., Logan, 1973-74; campaign mgr. various candidates and issues, Logan, 1965-75; bd. dirs. Humboldt Connections, Eureka, Calif., 1986-96, pres., 1989-92; elder Presbyn. ch. Sr. Fulbright-Hays lectr. Com. Internat. Exch. of Persons, Vietnam, 1964-65; Adminstrv. fellow Am. Coun. Edn., Colgate U., 1972-73; Paul Harris fellow Rotary Internat.; Fulbright prof., Belgium, 2003. Mem.: Phi Beta Kappa, Omicron Delta Kappa. Presbyterian. Avocations: gardening, photography, travel. Home: 2898 Sand Pointe Dr Mckinleyville CA 95519 Office Phone: 707-826-4117. Business E-Mail: jae1@humboldt.edu.

EMERALD, MARTI, councilwomen, reporter; married; 1 child. BS magna cum laude, Nat. U. Freelancer reporter AP Radio Network, Washington, 1978; reporter, anchor KSDO, San Diego; troubleshooter, investigative reporter 10News, 1985—; councilwomen, Dist. 7 San Diego City Coun., 2008—. Office: 202 C St, MS #10A San Diego CA 92101 Office Phone: 619-236-6677. Office Fax: 619-238-1360. E-mail: martiemerald@sandiego.gov.*

EMERSON, ALTON CALVIN, retired physical therapist; b. Webster, NY, Sept. 29, 1934; s. Homer Douglas and Pluma (Babcock) E.; m. Nancy Ann Poarch, Dec. 20, 1955 (div. 1972); children: Marcia Ann, Mark Alton; m. Barbara Irene Stewart, Oct. 6, 1972. BS in Vertibrate Zoology, U. Utah, 1957; cert. phys. therapy, U. So. Calif., 1959. Staff phys. therapist Los Angeles County Crippled Children's Services, 1958-65; pvt. practice phys. therapy Los Angeles, 1966-98; ret., 1998. Cons. City of Hope, Duarte, Calif., 1962-72; trustee Wolcott Found. Inc., St. Louis, 1972-86, chmn. bd. trustees, 1980-85. Recipient Cert. of Achievement, George Washington U., Washington, 1986. Mem. Masons (pres. Temple City High Twelve Club 1971, master Camellia 1973 (Hiram award Conejo Valley Lodge 2001), pres. Calif. Assn. High Twelve Clubs 1986, internat. pres. High Twelve 1990-91, mem. High Twelve Internat., Pasadena Scottish Rite Bodies, Venerable Master, Lodge of Perfection 1998, KCCH, Legion Merit, coroneted 33, 2001), Royal Order Scotland, Al Malaikah Tmeple, Ancient Arabic order Nobles Mystic Shrine, DeMolay Legion of Honor, Order of DeMolay (hon. internat. supreme coun.), Conejo-Westlake Shrine Club (pres. 1996, 2002), Conejo Valley High Twelve Club 2000 (pres.), Divan 2000, Sigma Phi Epsilon. Home and Office: 287 W Avenida De Las Flores Thousand Oaks CA 91360-1808

EMERSON, BARRY D., computer company executive; b. 1958; BS in Acctg. (hons.), Calif. State U. Long Beach; MBA, UCLA Sch. Mgmt. CPA Arthur Anderson & Co.; mgr. corp. acctg. Wyle, 1984-86, corp. dir. fin. reporting, 1986-90, asst. corp. controller, 1990-92, controller, 1992-95, v.p., 1995—. Office: Elite Information Group Inc 5100 W Goldleaf Cir Ste 50 Los Angeles CA 90056

EMERSON, R. CLARK, priest; b. LA, Mar. 9, 1945; s. George Heins and Irma Furney (Sorter) E.; m. Katharine Ann Lawrence, June 27, 1980; children: Cynthia, Holly, Angela, William, Richard. BA, San Jose State U., 1966; MDiv, Ch. Div. Sch. of Pacific, 1972. Ordained deacon Episcopal Ch., 1972, ordained priest, 1973; cert. secondary tchr., Calif. Comml. tchr. Middletown (Calif.) High Sch., 1967-69; asst. to rector St. Francis Ch., Palos Verdes, Calif., 1972-76; adminstr. Power Transistor Co., Torrance, Calif., 1977-85; priest assoc. St. John's Ch., LA, 1976-85; adminstr. Richard B. Belli Accountancy, San Jose, Calif., 1988-96; priest assoc. St. Luke's Ch., Los Gatos, Calif., 1985—. Contr. St. John's Well Child Ctr., L.A., 1985. Republican. Episcopalian. Avocations: steam railroading, antique automobiles.

EMERSON, SHIRLEY, retired professor counseling; b. Houston, Dec. 29, 1930; d. Riley C. and Neola (Pinckney) Armstrong; m. David W. Emerson, Sept. 4, 1954; children: Richard, Eric, Ellen. BA, Rice U., 1953; MA, U. Mich., 1966, PhD, 1977. Lic. marriage and family therapist, Nev. Emeritus prof. counseling U. Nev., Las Vegas, 1984—2008. Contbr. articles to profl. jours. Pres. Nev. State Bd. Marriage and Family Therapist Examiners, 1989—. Mem. Am. Assn. Marriage and Family Therapists (clin. mem., approved supr.). Home: 4240 Woodcrest Rd Las Vegas NV 89121-4942 Business E-Mail: semer@unlv.nevada.edu.

EMERT, GEORGE HENRY, former academic administrator, biochemist; b. Tenn., Dec. 15, 1938; s. Victor K. Emert and Hazel G. (Shultz) Ridley; m. Billie M. Bush, June 10, 1967; children: Debra Lea Lipp, Ann Lanie Taylor, Laurie Elizabeth, Jamie Marie. BA, U. Colo., 1962; MA, Colo. State U., 1970; PhD, Va. Tech. U., 1973. Registered profl. chem. engr. Microbiologist Colo. Dept. Pub. Health, Denver, 1967-70; post doctoral fellow U. Colo., Boulder, 1973-74; dir. biochem. tech. Gulf Oil Corp., Merriam, Kans., 1974-79; prof. biochemistry, dir. biomass rsch. ctr. U. Ark., Fayetteville, 1979-84; exec. v.p. Auburn (Ala.) U., 1984-92; pres. Utah State U., Logan, 1992—2000, pres. emeritus, porf. biochemistry, 2001—. Adj. prof. microbiology U. Kans., Lawrence, 1975-79. Editor, author: Fuels from Biomass and Wastes, 1981; author book chpt.; contbr. articles to profl. jours.; poet. Mem. So. Tech. Coun., Raleigh, N.C., 1985-92; dir. Ala. Supercomputer Authority, Montgomery, 1987-92, Blue Cross Blue Shield Utah, 1996—, Utah Partnership Econ. Devel.; trustee, adv. bd. First Security Bank. Capt. U.S. Army, 1963-66, Vietnam. Named to Educators Hall of Fame, Lincoln Meml. U., 1988. Fellow Am. Inst. Chemists; mem. Rotary (Paul Harris fellow, pres., v.p. 1989-90), Phi Kappa Phi, Sigma Xi. Republican. Achievements include patent for method for enzyme reutilization.

EMIN, DAVID, physicist; b. NYC, Oct. 2, 1941; s. Irving and Sonia Emin; m. Shirley Lynne Hirshey, Aug. 15, 1963. Student, U. Chgo., 1958—60; AB in Physics, Fla. State U., 1961—62; PhD, U. Pitts., 1968. Asst. rsch. physicist UCLA, 1968—69; mem. tech. staff Sandia Nat. Labs., Albuquerque, 1969—83, disting. mem. tech. staff, 1983—97; rsch. prof. U. N.Mex, Albuquerque, 1997—. Author: 212 refereed jour. articles and book chpts. Recipient Significant Implications for Dept. of Energy Related Technologies, U.S. Dept. Energy, 1988. Fellow: Am. Phys. Soc. (life Outstanding Referee award). Achievements include research in theory of polaron formation and motion; electronic and thermal transport in boron-rich solids; polaron transport in magnetic semiconductors; theory of Hall Effect for hopping conduction; theory of light interstitial diffusion in metals; theory of the Seebeck Effect in hopping conduction; theory of superconductivity of large bipolarons; small-polarons in noncrystalline semiconductors; patents for fast opening switch; radiation tolerant icosahedral boride beta-voltaic cell. Office: Univ New Mexico Dept Physics and Astronomy MSC07 4220, 1 Univ of New Mexico Albuquerque NM 87131 Office Fax: 505-277-1520. Business E-Mail: emin@unm.edu.

EMINEM, (MARSHALL MATHERS III), rap artist; b. St. Joseph, Mo., Oct. 17, 1973; m. Kimberly Ann Scott, June 14, 1999 (div. Oct. 11, 2001), remarried Jan. 14, 2006 (div. Dec. 19, 2006); 1 child Hailie Jade. Founder Shady Records, NYC, 1999—; performer D12. Performer: (albums) Infinite, 1997, The Slim Shady LP, 1999, The Marshall Mathers LP, 2000, The Eminem Show, 2002 (Best Selling Album in U.S., 2002), Encore, 2004, Curtain Call, 2005, The Re-Up, 2006, with D12: (albums) Devil's Night, 2001, D12 World, 2004; prodr.: albums My Band (D12), 2004; actor: (films) 8 Mile, 2002; author: (autobiography) Way I Am, 2008. Recipient 2 Grammy awards, 1999, 3 Grammy awards, 2000, 2 Grammy awards, 2002, Favorite Male Rap Artist, Am. Music Awards, 2005, 2006, Best-Selling Pop/Rock Artist, World Music Awards, 2005, Best-Selling Rap/Hip-Hop Artist, Favorite Hip-Hop Song-Shake That, People's Choice Awards, 2007; nominee 5 Grammy awards, 2003. Office: Interscope Records 2220 Colorado Ave Santa Monica CA 90404

EMMANOUILIDES, GEORGE CHRISTOS, physician, educator; b. Drama, Greece, Dec. 17, 1926; came to U.S., 1955; s. Christos Nicholas and Vassiliki (Jordanopoulos) E.; married; children: Nicholas, Elizabeth, Christopher, Martha, Sophia MD, Aristotelion U., 1951; MS in Physiology, UCLA, 1963. Diplomate in pediatric cardiology and neonatal-perinatal medicine Am. Bd. Pediat. Asst. prof. UCLA, 1963-69, assoc. prof., 1969-73, prof., 1973-95, prof. emeritus, 1995—. Chief divsn. pediat. cardiology Harbor UCLA Med. Ctr., Torrance, Calif., 1963-95 Co-author: Practical Pediatric Electrocardiography, 1973; co-editor: Heart Disease in Infants, Children and Adolescents, 2d edit., 1977, Moss' Heart Disease in Infants, Children and Adolescents, 5th edit., 1995, Neonatal Cardiopulmonary Distress, 1988; contbr. more than 70 articles to profl. jours. and 25 chpts. to books Served as 2d lt. M.C., Greek Army, 1953-55 Recipient Sherman Mellincoff award UCLA Sch. Medicine, 1982, Rsch. award Am. Heart Assn., 1965-83. Fellow Am. Acad. Pediat. (cardiology sect., chmn. 1978-80, Founders award 1996), Am. Coll. Cardiology; mem. Am. Pediatric Soc., Soc. for Pediatric Rsch., Hellenic-Am. Med. Soc. (pres.), Acad. of Athens (corr.), Hellenic Univ. Club (LA, bd. dirs.) Democrat. Greek Orthodox. Avocation: gardening. Home: 4619 Browndeer Ln Rolling Hills Estates CA 90275-3911 Office: Harbor-UCLA Med Ctr 1000 W Carson St Torrance CA 90502-2004 Home Phone: 310-377-6643; Office Phone: 310-222-4000. Business E-Mail: akrevoe@live.com.

EMMANUEL, JORGE AGUSTIN, chemical engineer, environmental consultant; b. Manila, Philippines, Aug. 28, 1954; came to U.S., 1970; s. Benjamin Elmido and Lourdes (Orozco) E.; 1 child, Andres Layanglawin. BS in Chemistry, N.C. State U., 1976, MSChemE, 1978; PhD in Chem. Engring., U. Mich., 1988. Registered profl. engr., Calif., environ. profl.; cert. hazardous materials mgmt. U. Calif., Berkeley, 1993; cert. pub. health U. Iowa, 2006. Process engr. Perry Electronics, Raleigh, N.C., 1973-74; rsch. asst. N.C. State U., Raleigh, 1977-78; rsch. chem. engr. GE Corp. R & D Ctr., Schenectady, N.Y., 1978-81; Amoco rsch. fellow U. Mich., Ann Arbor, 1981-84; sr. environ. analyst TEM Assocs., Inc., Emeryville, Calif., 1988-91; pres. Environ. & Engring. Rsch. Group, Pinole, Calif., 1991—. Environ. cons. to the Philippines, UN Devel. Program, 1992, 94; rsch. assoc. U. Calif., Berkeley, 1988-90; adj. prof. chem. engring. U. Philippines-Diliman. Contbr. articles to profl. jours. Mem. Assn. for Asian Studies, Ann Arbor, 1982-88; sec. Alliance for Philippine Concerns, L.A., 1983-91; assoc. Philippine Resource Ctr., Berkeley, 1988-92; bd. dirs. ARC-Ecology, San Francisco, 1990-2005, Asia Pacific Ctr., Washington, 1995-2000; bd. advisors Urban Habitat, 1995-2002; chmn. bd. Filipino-Am. Coalition for Environ. Solutions, 2001-03; internat. cons. WHO, UN Devel. Program, Healthcare Without Harm, 2005—. Grantee, NC State U., 1976; Phoenix grant, U. Mich., 1982. Mem. NSPE, AAAS, APHA, Air and Waste Mgmt. Assn., Assn. Profl. in Infection Control and Epidemiology, Calif., Scis., N.Y. Acad. Sci., Filipino-Am. Soc. Architects and Engrs. (exec. sec. 1989-90, Svc. award 1990). Avocations: classical guitar, ethnomusicology, asian studies. Office: Environ & Engring Rsch Group 2550 Appian Way Ste 202 Pinole CA 94564 Office Phone: 510-758-2525.

EMMELUTH, BRUCE PALMER, investment company executive, venture capitalist; b. LA, Nov. 30, 1940; s. William J. and Elizabeth L. (Palmer) E.; children: William J. II (dec.), Bruce Palmer Jr., Carrie Elaine; m. Canda S. Samuels, Mar. 29, 1987. Sr. investment analyst corp. fin. dept. Prudential Ins. Co. Am., LA, 1965—70; with Seidler Amdec Securities, Inc., 1970—90, sr. v.p., mgr. corp. fin. dept., 1974—90; gen. ptnr. VK Ventures, VK Capital, 1990—99; exec. v.p., sr. mng. dir. investment banking Van Kasper & Co., LA, 1990—99, First Security Van Kasper, 1999—2000; exec. v.p., sr. mng. dir. Wells Fargo Van Kasper, LA, 2000—01; exec. v.p., sr. mng. dir. investment banking Wells Fargo Securities, 2001—03; pvt. investor, 2004—. Pres., bd. dirs. SAS Capital Corp., venture capital subs. Seidler Amdec Securities, 1974-90; bd. advisors Entreprenurial Studies program Anderson Grad. Sch. Mgmt. UCLA, 1985-2006. With U.S. Army N.G., 1965-71. Presbyterian. Home: 16 Augusta Ln Santa Barbara CA 93108

EMMER, MAURICE STANLEY, lawyer; b. Oklahoma City, June 26, 1947; s. Milton and Miriam (Rubin) E.; m. Jamie Lappin, Dec. 18, 1971; children: Jackson Allan, Monte Edward. BS, U. Pa., 1969; JD, U. Chgo., 1978. Bar: Calif., Ill.; CPA, Okla., Ill. Acct. Arthur Young & Co., Oklahoma City, 1970-72; ptnr. Baker & McKenzie, Chgo., L.A., Palo Alto, 1978—2001; prin. Deloitte & Touche, San Jose, Calif., 2001—. Mem. ABA (tax sect.), AICPAs, Internat. Fiscal Assn. Office: Deloitte & Touche 225 W Santa Clara St San Jose CA 95113 Office Phone: 408-704-4418. Office Fax: 408-704-8417. E-mail: memmer@deloitte.com.

EMMERSON, ARCHIE ALDIS (RED EMMERSON, A.A. EMMERSON), sawmill owner; b. 1929; Mgr. R.H. Emmerson & Son, 1949—52, 1954—69; pres. Sierra Pacific Industries, Redding, Calif. Recipient Harry A. Merlo award, 2002; named one of Forbes' Richest Americans, 2006. Office: Sierra Pacific Industries 19794 Riverside Ave Redding CA 96007 also: PO Box 496028 Redding CA 96049-6028

EMMERSON, BILL, state legislator; b. Oakland, Calif. m Nan; children: Kate, Caroline. BA in History/Polit. Sci., La Sierra U., Riverside, Calif., 1969; MS, DDS, Loma Linda U. California State Assemblyman, District 63, 2005-; vice chairman, Local Govn; member, Approp, Waters, Parks & Wildlife, Ways & Means comts, currently.Orthodontist, Educator. Republican. Office: Dist 63 10681 Foothill Blvd Ste 325 Rancho Cucamonga CA 91730 Office Phone: 909-466-9096. Office Fax: 909-466-9892. Business E-Mail: assemblymember.emmerson@assembly.ca.gov.

EMMERT, MARK ALLEN, academic administrator, educator; b. Tacoma, Dec. 16, 1952; s. Chester Eugene and Naomi Abigale E.; m. DeLaine Sharon Smith, June 24, 1977; children: Stephen Kenneth, Jennifer Ashley. BA in Polit. Sci., U. Wash., 1975; MPA, Syracuse U., 1976, PhD in Pub. Adminstrn., 1983. Fellow, rsch. asst. Syracuse U., 1980—83; asst. prof. dept. polit. studies Northern Ill. U., DeKalb, 1983-85; assoc. dean grad. sch. pub. affairs U. Colo., Denver, assoc., asst. prof., grad. sch. pub. affairs, assoc. vice chancellor academic affairs, 1985—92; provost, v.p. academic affairs Mont. State U., Bozeman, 1992—95; chancellor, prof. U. Conn., Storrs, 1994-99, La. State U., Baton Rouge, 1999—2004; pres. U. Wash., Seattle, 2004—, prof. Evans Sch. Pub. Affairs, 2004—. Bd. dirs. Weyerhaeuser Co., 2008—. Contbr. articles to profl. jours. Bd. dirs. Boy Scouts Am., Baton Rouge, 1999, La. Rsch. Park, 1999, LUMCON, 1999—; coun. chmn. Nat. Assn. State Univ. and Land Grant Coll., 1998-99; mem. Seattle Cmty. Devel. Roundtable, 2005-, Governor's Global Competitiveness Coun., 2005-; co-chair Prosperity Partnership, 2005-; bd. trustees Greater Seattle Chamber of Commerce, 2006- Am. Coun. on Edn. fellow U. Colo., 1988, Fulbright fellow, Germany, 1990-91; recipient Good Growth award, Baton Rouge Bus. Report & Growth Coun., 2003; named Marketer of Yr., Sales and Mktg. Executives Assn., 2003 Mem. Rotary, Phi Kappa Phi, Golden Key Honor Soc., Alpha Lambda Delta, Assn. Am. Universities, Coun. Presidents, Am. Coun. on Edn., Coun. Fellows, Assn. Governing Boards of Universities and Colleges Avocations: reading, golf, scuba diving, fly fishing. Office: Office of the Pres Box 351230 301 Gerberding Hall Seattle WA 98195-1230 E-mail: pres@u.washington.edu.

EMMETT, BRIAN, software developer; b. Herndon, Va. B in Computer Sci., Va. Polytechnic Inst. and State Univ. (Va. Tech.), 1998. Intern Boeing; sr. software developer, endoscopy divsn. Stryker Corp., San Jose, Calif. Won the 2005 Oracle Space Sweepstakes (N.Am.) once-in-a-lifetime trip 62 miles above the surface of the Earth, but decided to forfeit the Grand Prize because of the cost of taxes on the contest prize. Second chance to receive such an opportunity by serving as a test passenger (free ride) for a space flight in 2008 through the company Benson Space Company. Office: Stryker Endoscopy 5900 Optical Ct San Jose CA 95138 Office Phone: 408-754-2000.

EMMONS, ROBERT JOHN, corporate executive, poet; b. Trenton, NJ, Sept. 18, 1934; s. Charles Glunk and Ruth Marie (Heilhecker) E.; m. Christine Young Bebb, July 13, 1980; children: Bradley Thomas, Cathy Lynne, Christopher Robert, Ryan Hunter. AB in Econs, U. Mich., 1956, MBA, 1960, JD, 1964. V.p. Baskin-Robbins Co., Burbank, Calif., 1964-68; pres. United Rent-All, Los Angeles, 1968-69, Master Host Internat., Los Angeles, 1969-71; prof. Grad. Sch. Bus., U. So. Calif., 1971-82; pres. LTI Corp., Monterey, Calif., 1982-84; chmn., CEO, dir. Casino USA/SFI Corp., Santa Barbara, Calif., 1984-98; mng. ptnr. Emmons Capital Investments, Santa Barbara, Calif., 1999—. Author: The American Franchise Revolution, 1970, The American Marketing Revolution, 1980; poetry Other Places, Other Times, 1974, Love and Other Minor Tragedies, 1980, The Road to Paradise, 2003, The Wanderer, A Poet's Journey, 2005, Seafarer, Poems of the Sea, 2007. Mem. AAUP, Am. Mktg. Assn., European Mktg. Assn., Am. Econ. Assn., Calif. Yacht Club (L.A.), Hawaii Yacht Club (Honolulu), The Valley Club of Montecito (Calif.), Useppa Island Club (Fla.), St. Petersburg Yacht Club (Fla.), The Calif. Club (LA), Ocean Reef Club (Fla.), Beta Gamma Sigma, Pi Kappa Alpha. Office: Emmons Capital Investments PO Box 50243 Santa Barbara CA 93150-0243

EMORY, MEADE, lawyer; b. Seattle, Feb. 26, 1931; s. DeWolfe and Marion (Burton) E.; m. Deborah Carley, Apr. 30, 1959; children: Ann, Campbell, Elizabeth. AB, George Washington U., 1954, LL.B., 1957; LL.M. in Taxation, Boston U., 1963. Bar: D.C. 1958, Wash. 1958, Iowa 1966. Trial atty. IRS, Boston, 1961-64; teaching fellow N.Y.U. Sch. Law, 1964-65; mem. faculty U. Iowa Sch. Law, 1965-70; legislation atty. Joint Com. on Taxation, U.S. Congress, 1970-72; mem. faculty U. Calif. Sch. Law, Davis, 1972-75; asst. to commr. IRS, 1975-77; ptnr. firm LeSourd & Patten, Seattle, 1978-90; of counsel Lane Powell Spears Lubersky, Seattle, 1991—; prof. law and dir. grad. program in taxation U. Wash. Sch. Law, Seattle, 1995—2005, prof. emeritus law, 2005—. Vis. prof. law UCLA, 1987, Tulane U. Law Sch., 1990, Duke U., 1991, 92, Northwestern U. Sch. of Law, 1993, Georgetown U. Law, 1993, U. Pa. 1995; Mason Ladd dist. vis. prof. U. Iowa Law, 1994; Earl Dunlap dist. vis. prof. U. Nebr. Law, 1994; Charles S. Lyon vis. prof. taxation from practice NYU, 1989. Co-author: Federal Income Taxation of Corporations and Shareholders-Forms, 1981, rev. edit., 1989; mem. bd. editors Jour. Taxation. Trustee Seattle Symphony Orch., 1978-89; bd. dirs. Cornish Inst. Art, Seattle, 1979—. Recipient Commr.'s award IRS 1976. Mem. Am. Bar Assn., Am. Law Inst. Clubs: Rainier (Seattle), Seattle Tennis (Seattle), Univ. (Seattle); Cosmos (Washington). Office: U Wash William Gates Hall Box 353020 Seattle WA 98195-3020 Business E-Mail: memory@u.washington.edu.

EMUNAH, RENEE, drama therapist, professor; d. Mandel Fisch and Helene Aylon; children: Melea Rose, Gavi Lev. BA in Drama Therapy, Antioch U. West, San Francisco, 1976; MA in Theatre and Psychology, San Francisco State U., 1979; PhD in Clin. Psychology, Union Inst., Cin., 1996. Registered drama therapist Nat. Assn. Drama Therapy, 1982, cert. drama therapists trainer Nat. Assn. Drama Therapy, 1995. Drama therapist Pacific Med. Ctr., San Francisco, 1976—85, Gladman Meml. Hosp. Day Treatment and Youth Ctrs., Oakland, Calif., 1976—90; founder, dir. drama therapy program Antioch U., San Francisco, 1983—89; founder, dir., prof. drama therapy Calif. Inst. Integral Studies, San Francisco, 1989—. Founder, dir. Beyond Analysis Theater Co., San Francisco, 1979—85. Author: (book in English, Japanese and Chinese) Acting for Real, 1994 (translated in 2007); editl. bd. mem. Internat. Jour. Arts in Psychotherapy, Pergamon Press, 1985—2002. Recipient Commendation award, San Francisco Bd. Suprs., 1981. Mem.: Nat. Assn. Drama Therapy (life; pres. 1985—87, bd. dirs. 1983—91, Gertrud Schattner Disting. Svc. award for outstanding contbn. to drama therapy 1996). Democrat. Jewish. Achievements include being among the first four drama therapists to be officially registered in the US. Avocations: photography, creative writing. Office: Calif Inst Integral Studies 1453 Mission St San Francisco CA 94103 Business E-Mail: remunah@ciis.edu.

ENDERS, ALLEN COFFIN, anatomy educator; b. Wooster, Ohio, Aug. 5, 1928; s. Robert Kendal and Abbie Gertrude (Crandell) E.; m. Alice Hay, June 15, 1950 (div. Dec. 1975); children: Robert H., George C., Richard S., Gregory H.; m. Sandra Jean Schlafke, Aug. 5, 1976. AB, Swarthmore Coll., 1950; AM, Harvard U., 1952, PhD, 1955. From asst. prof. to assoc. prof Rice Inst., Houston, 1954-63; from assoc. prof. to prof. Washington U., St. Louis, 1963-75; prof., chmn. dept. human anatomy U. Calif., Davis, 1976-86, prof. cell biology and human anatomy, 1986—. Cons. NIH, Bethesda, Md., 1964-68, 70-73, 76-80, 83-93. Author: (with others) Bailey's Microscopic Anatomy, 1984; editor: Delayed Implantation, 1964; contbr. numerous articles on anatomy and reproduction to profl. jours. Nat. pres. Perinatal Rsch. Soc., 1981. Grantee NIH, 1959-99. Fellow AAAS; mem. Am. Assn. Anatomists (v.p. 1980-82, pres. 1983-84), Pioneer Reprodn. Res. Home: 39707 Barry Rd Davis CA 95616-9415 Office: U Calif Sch Medicine Cell Biology & Anatomy Davis CA 95616

ENDICOTT, WILLIAM F., journalist; b. Harrodsburg, Ky., Aug. 26, 1935; s. William O. and Evelyn E.; m. Mary Frances Thomas, Dec. 27, 1956; children: Gene, Fran, Greg. Student, Am. U., 1955; BA in Polit. Sci., Transylvania U., 1957. With Lexington (Ky.) Leader, 1957; sports writer Louisville Courier-Jour., 1958-62; reporter Tulare (Calif.) Advance-Register, 1963; reporter, city editor Modesto (Calif.) Bee, 1963-66; city editor Sacramento Union, 1966-67; with Los Angeles Times, 1968-85; Capitol bur. chief Sacramento Bee, 1985-95, asst. mng. editor, 1995-98, dep. mng. editor, 1998-2000, ret. Hearst vis. profl. U. Tex., 1993. Served with USMCR, 1957-58. Recipient various journalism awards Disting. Alumnus award Transylvania U., 1980 Episcopalian.

ENG, LAWRENCE FOOK, biochemistry educator, neurochemist; b. Spokane, Wash., Feb. 19, 1931; s. On Kee and Shee (Hue) E.; m. Jeanne Leong, Aug. 30, 1957; children: Douglas, Alice, Steven, Shirley. BS in Chemistry, Wash. State U., 1952; MS in Chemistry, Stanford U., 1954, PhD in Chemistry, 1962. Chief chemistry sect. path. and lab. med. svc. PAVA Health Care Sys., Palo Alto, Calif., 1961—; rsch. assoc. dept. pathology Sch. Medicine Stanford (Calif.) U., 1966-70, sr. scientist dept. pathology Sch. of Medicine, 1970-75, adj. prof., 1975-82, prof. dept. pathology Sch. of Medicine, 1982—. Mem. ad hoc neurol. sci. study sect. and neurology B study sect. NIH, 1976-79, mem. neurol. sci. study sect., 1978-83; mem. adv. bd. VA Office of Regeneration Rsch. Program, 1985-89; mem. VA Merit Rev. Bd. for Neurobiology, 1987-90; mem. Nat. Adv. Neurol. Disorders and Stroke Coun., 1991-94. Mem. editorial bd. Neurobiology, 1970-75, Jour. of Neurochemistry, 1978-85, Jour. of Neuroimmunology, 1980-83, Molecular and Chem. Neuropathology, 1982-98, Glia, 1987-2001, Jour. for Neurosci. Rsch., 1991—, Neurochemical Rsch., 1993-2000. Capt. USAF, 1952—57. Mem. Am. Soc. for Neurochemistry (coun. 1979-83, 85-87, 93—, sec. 1987-93), Am. Soc. Biochemistry and Molecular Biology, Internat. Soc. for Neurochemistry, Soc. for Neurosci. Office: VAPA Health Care System Path & Lab Med Svc 3801 Miranda Ave Palo Alto CA 94304-1207 E-mail: lfeng@stanford.edu.

ENGDAHL, TODD PHILIP, editor; b. Jamestown, NY, Feb. 8, 1950; s. George Philip and Janice Marie (Wallin) E.; m. Caroline C.N. Schomp, Dec. 29, 1973; children: Anders Justus Schomp, Mats Philip Schomp. BA, Pomona Coll., 1971; MS, Northwestern U., 1972. Reporter Oregonian, Portland, 1972—75, Denver Post, 1975—80, asst. city editor, 1980—83, night city editor, 1983—85, Sunday editor, 1985—86, city editor, 1986—90, exec. city editor, 1990—95, website editor, 1995—2003, perspective editor, 2003—07; editor Edu. News, Colo., 2008—. Lectr. journalism Portland State U., 1974. Democrat. Lutheran. Avocations: reading, gardening, woodworking. Personal E-mail: tengdahl@comcast.net.

ENGEL, BARBARA ALPERN, history professor; BA in Russian Studies, CCNY, 1965; MA in Russian Studies, Harvard U., 1967; PhD in Rusian History, Columbia U., 1974. Part-time instr. Drew U., Madison, NJ, 1972—73; instr. Columbia U., NYC, 1974; asst. prof. Sarah Lawrence Coll., 1974—76, U. Colo., Boulder, 1976—82, assoc. prof., 1982—92, prof., 1992—, disting. prof., dir. Ctrl. and Ea. European studies, 1993—95, chair dept. history, 1995—98. Author, co-editor: Five Sisters: Women Against the Tsar, 1975; author: Spanish transl., 1980, new edit., 1992, Mothers and Daughters: Women of the Intelligentsia in Nineteenth Century Russia, 1983; author, co-editor: Russia's Women: Accomodation, Resistance, Transformation, 1991; author: Between the Fields and the City: Women, Work and Family in Russia, 1861-1914, 1994, paperback edit., 1996; co-editor: A Revolution of their Own. Voices of Women in Soviet History, 1998; cons. editor Feminist Studies, 1979—98, mem. editl. bd. Frontiers, 1980—86, Slavic Rev., 1996—2001; contbr. articles. Recipient Heldt Article award, 1991, cert. tchg. excellence, Mortar Bd. Sr. Honor Soc., 1994, Heldt prize for Outstanding Achievement in Slavic Studies, AWSS, 1996, numerous other awards, grants; Wallenberg fellow, Rutgers Ctr. Hist. Analysis, 1995, fellow, John Simon Guggenheim Meml. Found., 2003, Sr. Exch. grant with the Soviet Union, IREX, 1985, 1987, 1991, Fulbright-Hays tng. grant, Faculty Rsch. Abroad program, 1987, Woodrow Wilson fellow, 1991, John D. and Catherine T. MacArthur Found. grantee, 1993—95, NEH fellow, 2003—. Mem.: Am. Assn. for Advancement of Slavic Studies, We. Assn. Women Historians (book prize com. 1990), Internat. Fedn. Socs. Rsch. Women's History (mem. U.S. com. 1988—91), Am. Hist. Assn. (com. on women historians 1987—89, mem. profl. divsn. 1990—92, mem. program com. 1994—95), Phi Beta Kappa. Office: Univ Colo Dept History 234 UCB Boulder CO 80309-0234 Office Phone: 303-492-6831. E-mail: barbara.engel@colorado.edu.

ENGEL, THOMAS WALTER, chemistry professor; b. Yokohama, Japan, Apr. 2, 1942; came to U.S., 1947; s. George Walter and Juliane (Urban) E.; m. Esther Neeser, Aug. 23, 1979; 1 child, Alex. BS, Johns Hopkins U., 1963, MS, 1964; PhD, U. Chgo., 1969; Dr. rer. nat. habil., U. Munich, Fed. Republic Germany, 1979. Instr. Tech. U. Clausthal, Clausthal-Zellerfeld, Fed. Republic Germany, 1969-75, U. Munich, 1975-78; staff mem. IBM Rsch. Lab., Zurich, Switzerland, 1978-80; assoc. prof. chemistry U. Wash., Seattle, 1979-84, prof., 1984—, chmn. dept. chemistry, 1987-90. Contbr. papers and book chpts. to profl. publs. Recipient numerous grants NSF, Air Force Office Sci. Rsch., Office Naval Rsch, Am. Chem Soc. award in Colloid or Surface Chemistry, 1995; sr. rsch. award, Alexander von Humboldt Found. Mem. Am. Chem. Soc. (Surface Chemistry award 1995), Am. Vacuum Soc. Office: U Wash Dept Chemistry Box 1700 Seattle WA 98195 Business E-Mail: engel@chem.washington.edu.

ENGELBART, DOUGLAS C., engineering executive; b. Portland, Oreg., Jan. 30, 1925; BSEE, Oreg. State U., 1948, PhD (hon.), 1994; B in Engring., U. Calif., Berkeley, 1952; PhD in Elec. Engring. and Computer Sci., U. Calif., 1955; PhD (hon.), Santa Clara U., 2001. Electronic/radar tech. USN, 1944-46; elec. engr. NACA Ames Lab. (now NASA), Mountain View, Calif., 1948-51; asst. prof. elec. engring. U. Calif., Berkeley, 1955-56; rschr. Stanford Rsch. Inst. (now SRI Internat.), Calif., 1957-59, dir. augmentation rsch. ctr. Calif., 1959-77; sr. scientist Tymshare, Inc., Cupertino, Calif., 1977-84, McDonnell Douglas ISG, San Jose, Calif., 1984-89; dir. Bootstrap Project Stanford U., 1989-90; dir. Bootstrap Project, Palo Alto, Calif., 1989—90, Bootstrap Inst., Fremont, Calif., 1990—. Vis. scholar

Stanford U.; spkr. in field. Contbr. numerous articles to profl. jours. Recipient E.B. Lemon Disting. Alumni award, 1987, Lifetime Achievement award for Tech. Excellence, PC Mag., 1987, Disting. Alumni of Yr. award Oreg. State U., 1987, Disting. Svc. and Outstanding Contbns. in Field citation Sigma Phi Epsilon, St. Louis, 1989, Lifetime Achievement award for Vision, Inspiration and Contbn., Electronic Networking Assn., San Francisco, 1990, Software Sys. award Assn. Computing Machinery, 1990, Am. Ingenuity award Nat. Assn. Mfrs.' Congress of Am. Industry, Washington, 1991, Disting. Alumnus award U. Calif., Berkeley, 1991, Lifetime Achievement award Dominican Coll. of San Rafael, Calif., 1991, Lifetime Achievement award Price Waterhouse, Washington, 1994, cert. of appreciation Smart Valley, Inc., 1994, Editors' Choice award MacUser Awards Ceremony, 1995, SoftQuad Web award World Wide Web Conf., Boston, 1995, cert. of merit The Franklin Inst. Com. on Sci. and the Arts, 1996, Disting. Engring. Alumnus, 1996, Spl. award, Am. Soc. for Info. Sci., 1996, Jerome H. Lemelson-MIT prize for excellence in invention and innovation, 1997, A.M. Turing award, Assn. Computing Machinery, 1997, George R. Stibitz Computer Pioneer award, Am. Computer Mus. with Computer Sci. Dept. Montana State U., 1998, Ronald H. Brown Am. Innovators award, US Dept. Commerce & the Patent and Trademark Office, 1998, Weldon B. "Hoot" Gibson Achievement award, 1999, Benjamin Frankin medal in Computer and Cognitive Sci., 1999, Software Visionary award, 1999, Webby Lifetime Achievement award, 2001, Lovelace medal, British Computer Soc., 2001, Fellow award, Computer History Mus., 2005, Cert. of Spl. Congl. Recognition, 2005; named Pioneer of the Electronic Frontier, Electronic Frontier Found., Washington, 1992; named to Discovery Online Hackers Hall of Fame, 1997, Nat. Inventors Hall of Fame, 1998, Oregon State U. Engring. Hall of Fame, 1998, Computer Hall of Fame, 2000, Industry Hall of Fame, 2001, Computer Human Interaction, Assn. Computing Machinery, 2002, Silicon Valley Engring. Coun. Hall of Fame, 2005; Engelbart award established in his honor Internat. Conf. on Hypertext and Hypermedia, 1994; named in honor of Douglas C. Engelbart Room, Cyberia Corp. Services Tng. Room, 2001, Douglas C. Engelbart Day, Oregon State, Jan. 24, 2002. Fellow Nat. Acad. Arts and Scis.; mem. IEEE (treas., vice chmn., chmn. San Francisco chpt. profl. group on electronic computers 1957-59, Computer Pioneer award 1993, John Von Neumann medal award, 1999), NAS (panel on future role of computers in rsch. librs. 1968-70, com. on augmentation of human intellect 1989), NAE, Computer Profls. for Social Responsibility (adv. bd.), The Tech. Ctr. of Silicon Valley (adv. coun.), Phi Kappa Phi, Tau Beta Pi, Sigma Tau, Eta Kappa Nu, Blue Key, Sigma Xi. Achievements include visionary and pioneering work in organizational augmentation, including strategies for continuous improvement, human-tool coevolution and interactive collaborative hypermedia computing to support the knowledge-intensive work of groups and individuals; 7 patents relating to bi-stable gaseous plasma digital devices, 12 patents relating to all-magnetic digital devices, 1 patent for invention of the Mouse. Home: 89 Catalpa Dr Atherton CA 94027-2167 Office: Bootstrap Inst 6505 Kaiser Dr Fremont CA 94555-3614

ENGELBRECHT, RUDOLF, electrical engineering educator; b. Atlanta, Apr. 18, 1928; s. Walter and Dorothea Engelbrecht; m. Christel M. Kluth, Sept. 10, 1050; children: Richard, Rolf, Erika. BS, Ga. Inst. Tech., 1951, MSEE, 1953; PhD in Elec. Engring., Oreg. State U., 1979. Mem. tech. staff Bell Labs., Whippany, N.J., 1953—60, supr. Murray Hill, N.J., 1961—63, dept. head, 1964—69; dir. RCA Tech. Ctr., Somerville, N.J., 1970—72; group leader RCA Labs., Zurich, Switzerland, 1972—77; assoc. prof. Oreg. State U., Corvallis, 1977—93. Co-author: Microwave Devices, 1969; contbr. articles to profl. jours. Named to Oreg. State U. Engring. Hall of Fame, 1998. Fellow: IEEE (life Centennial award 1984, Third Millennium medal 2000); mem.: Sigma Xi. Achievements include patents in field. Office: Oreg State U Dept Elec Computer Eng Corvallis OR 97331

ENGELHARDT, ALBERT GEORGE, physicist; b. Toronto, Ont., Can., Mar. 17, 1935; came to U.S., 1957, naturalized, 1965; s. Samuel and Rose (Menkes) E.; m. Elzbieta Szajkowska, June 14, 1960; children— Frederick, Leonard, Michael. BASc., U. Toronto, 1958; MS, U. Ill., 1959, PhD (grad. fellow), 1961. Rsch. asst. elec. engring. U. Ill., Urbana, 1958-61; staff rsch. and devel. ctr. engr. Westinghouse Electric Co., Pitts., 1961-70, mgr., 1966-69, fellow scientist, 1969-70; sr. rsch. scientist, group leader Hydro-Que. Rsch. Inst., Varennes, Canada, 1970-74; mem. staff Los Alamos Sci. Lab., 1974-86; adj. prof. elec. engring. Tex. Tech. U., Lubbock, 1976—; pres., chief exec. officer, founder Enfitek, Inc., Los Alamos, N.Mex., 1982—. Vis. prof. U. Que., 1970-77 Contbr. articles to profl. jours. Group leader Boy Scouts Can., 1972-74. Mem. IEEE Nuclear and Plasma Scis. Soc., Am. Phys. Soc. Home and Office: 549 Bryce Ave Los Alamos NM 87544-3607

ENGESTRÖM, JYRI, Internet company executive; b. Helsinki, Finland, Oct. 19, 1977; Attended, U. Montreal, Lancaster U.; M in Social Sci., U. Helsinki. New media designer To the Point, 1994—98; concept designer Satama Interactive, 1998—2000; cons. Tera Group, 2000—01; co-founder ShiftControl Finland, 2001—02; founder, vice chmn. Aula Network, 2000; founder, CEO Aula Design Oy, 2005; co-founder, chmn. Jaiku; product mgr. Goggle, 2007—. Office: Google Inc 1600 Amphitheatre Parkway Mountain View CA 94043

ENGFER, SUSAN MARVEL, zoological park executive; b. Mpls., Dec. 6, 1943; d. Frederick Paul and Dorothy M. Engfer. BS, Albion Coll., 1965; MS, U. Wyo., 1968; postgrad., U. Calif., Santa Barbara, 1975-76; dipl., Sch. Profl. Mgmt. Devel. for Zoo and Aquarium Pers., 1981. Ranger, naturalist Grand Teton Nat. Park, Moose, Wyo., 1967; cancer rsch. technician U. Calif., Santa Barbara, 1967-68; zoo keeper Santa Barbara Zool. Gardens, 1968-70, edn. curator, 1970-72, asst. dir., 1972-88; pres., CEO Cheyenne Mountain Zool. Park, Colorado Springs, Colo., 1988—. Cons. oiled bird rehab. Union Oil and Standard Oil Co., 1968-70; master plan cons. Moorpark (Calif.) Coll., 1986-88; instr., bd. regents Sch. Profl. Mgmt. Devel. Zoo and Aquarium Pers., Wheeling, W.V., 1984-87. Author: North American Regional Studbook, Asian Small-Clawed Otter (Aonyx cinerea), 1987—. Fellow Am. Assn. Zool. Pks. and Aquariums (profl., bd. dirs. 1987-90, mem. accreditation commn. 1990—, chmn. accreditation commn. 1994-95); mem. Internat. Union Dirs. Zool. Gardens, Internat. Union Conservation of Nature and Natural Resources (mem. otter specialist group), Soc. Conservation Biology, Colo. Women's Forum, Rotary. Office: Cheyenne Mountain Zool Pk 4250 Cheyenne Mountain Zoo Rd Colorado Springs CO 80906-5755

ENGLE, KATHLEEN FAYE, elementary education educator; b. Rapid City, SD, July 8, 1958; d. Frank Denton and Marie Lucille (Coffield) Packard; m. Steven S. Engle, June 1, 1984; children: Kirstin Marie, Kalin Kathleen. BS in Edn., Black Hill State Coll., 1980. Tchr. physical edn. Campbell County Sch. Dist., Gillette, Wyo., 1980-84, Weston County Sch. Dist., Newcastle, Wyo., 1985—. Mem. evaluatin team Conestiga Rep., Gillette, 1982-83; mem. adv. team Newcastle Mid. Sch., 1981—, evaluation team, 1992—. Middle Sch. Physical Edn. Teacher or the Year, Nat. Assn. for Sport & Phys. Edn., 1995. Mem. Wyo. Edn. Assn., Wyo. Alliance Physical Edn. Health Recreation and Dance, Wyo. Coaching Assn., Newcastle Edn. Assn., Delta Kappa Gamma. Avocations: aerobics, weightlifting. Office: Newcastle Mid Sch 116 Casper Ave Newcastle WY 82701-2705

ENGLE, STEVEN B., biotechnology company executive; BSEE, MSEE, U. Tex. Mgmt. cons. Strategic Decisions Group, 1979—84, SRI Internat., 1979—84; v.p. mktg. and divsnl. gen. mgr. Micro Power Systems, 1984—87; CEO Quantum Mgmt. Co., 1987—91; v.p. mktg. Cygnus Inc., 1991—93; exec. v.p., COO La Jolla Pharm. Co., San Diego, 1993—94, pres., dir., sec., 1994—95, CEO, 1995—2006, chmn. bd., 1997—2006. Chmn. BIOCOM; dir. CareLinc Corp.

ENGLEMAN, EPHRAIM PHILIP, rheumatologist; b. San Jose, Calif., Mar. 24, 1911; s. Maurice and Tillie (Rosenberg) E.; m. Jean Sinton, Mar. 2, 1941; children: Ephraim Philip, Edgar George, Jill. BA, Stanford U., 1933; MD, Columbia U., 1937. Intern Mt. Zion Hosp., San Francisco; resident U. Calif., San Francisco, Jos. Pratt Diagnostic Hosp., Boston; rsch. fellow Mass. Gen. Hosp., Boston, 1937-42; practice medicine specializing in rheumatology San Francisco, 1948—; mem. faculty U. Calif. Med. Ctr., San Francisco, 1949—, clin. prof. medicine, 1965—; dir. Rosalind Russell Arthritis Ctr., 1979—. Staff U. Calif. Hosp.; chmn. Nat. Commn. Arthritis and Related Diseases, 1975-76. Author: The Book on Arthritis: A Guide for Patients and Their Families, 1979; also articles, chpts. in books. Served to maj. M.C. USMCR, 1942—47. Recipient medal of Honor, U. Calif., San Francisco, 1999, citation Arthritis Found., 1973, Gold medal for excellence in clin. medicine Columbia U. P&S Alumni, 2007; Ephraim P. Engleman Disting. Professorship in Rheumatology named in his honor U. Calif., San Francisco, 1991; Nat. Inst. Arthritis grantee. Fellow ACP; mem. Internat. League Against Rheumatism (pres. 1981-85), Am. Coll. Rheumatology (founding fellow, master, pres. 1962-63, Presdl. Gold medal 2002), Nat. Soc. Clin. Rheumatologists, AMA, Am. Fedn. Clin. Rsch.; mem. Japanese Rheumatism Soc. (hon.), Spanish Rheumatism Soc., Uruguay Rheumatism Soc., Australian Rheumatism Assn., Chinese Med. Assn., French Soc. Rheumatology, Internat. League against Rheumatism, Gold-Headed Cane Soc. (U. Calif. San Francisco), Family Club (San Francisco). Republican. Jewish. Office: U Calif Rosalind Russell Med Rsch Ctr Arthritis 350 Parnassus Ave Ste 600 San Francisco CA 94117-3608 Business E-Mail: ephraim.engleman@ucsf.edu.

ENGLERT, PETER, academic administrator, director; Grad., U. Cologne, Germany. Faculty mem., adminstr. San Jose State U., Calif.; pro vice chancellor, dean sci., architecture and design Victoria U., Wellington, New Zealand, 1995—2002; CEO, chancellor U. Hawaii, Manoa, 2002—05, faculty mem., geophysics and planetology, 2005—. Founder support group Maori and Pacific nation students U. Victoria; adminstrv. bd. Internat. Assn. Univs. (IAU), 2004—08. Office: U Hawaii Hawai Inst Geophysics and Plan 1680 E-W Rd, Post 602 Honolulu HI 96822 Home Phone: 808-595-0119; Office Phone: 808-956-5033. Office Fax: 808-965-6322. Business E-Mail: penglert@hawaii.edu.

ENGLERT, WALTER GEORGE, classics and humanities educator; b. Oakland, Calif., June 30, 1952; s. Walter George and Isobel Ann (O'Hearne) E.; m. Mary Ellen Mecchi; children: Francesca, Molly. BA summa cum laude, St. Mary's Coll. Calif., 1974; MA, U. Calif. Santa Barbara, 1976; postgrad., Am. Sch. Classical Studies, Athens, 1979; PhD, Stanford U., 1981. Teaching asst. U. Calif., Santa Barbara, 1974-76, Stanford U., 1977-78; vis. lectr. U. Mich., Ann Arbor, 1980-81; vis. assoc. prof. U. Calif., Berkeley, 1986, Intercollegiate Ctr. Classical Studies, Rome, 1992-93, 2007—; Omar and Althea Hoskins prof. Reed Coll., Portland, Oreg., 1981—. Organizer and lectr. Reed Latin Symposium for H.S. Students, 1988-2006; participant TAG Spring Interdisciplinary confs., 1988; tchr. Paideia Class, 1989, 91, 96, 97, Reed MALS Seminar, 1988, 93, 97, 2001, 05, Reed Elderhostel Program, 1989; mem. faculty Reed Alumni Coll., 1989, 95; lectr. Seattle Reed Alumni Group, 1991; guest Town Hall TV show, 1991. Contbr. articles to profl. jours. Grantee NEH, 1983, 95, Mellon Faculty Seminar, 1986-87, Sloan Found., 1987-88. Office: Reed Coll 3203 SE Woodstock Blvd Portland OR 97202-8138 Home Phone: 503-775-8470; Office Phone: 503-517-7310. Business E-Mail: walter.englert@reed.edu.

ENGLISH, DIANE, television producer, writer, communications executive; b. Buffalo, 1948; d. Richard and Anne English; m. Joel Shukovsky. Grad., Buffalo State Coll., 1970. Tchr. high sch. English, Buffalo, 1970-71; with Theatre In Am. series Sta. WNET-TV, NYC, assoc. dir. TV lab.; TV columnist Vogue Mag., NYC, 1977-80; exec. prodr., ptnr. Shukovsky English Entertainment, 1981. Writer (TV films) The Lathe of Heaven, 1980, Her Life as a Man, 1984, Classified Love, 1986; prodr.: (TV series) Foley Square, 1985; prodr., writer (TV series) My Sister Sam, 1986, Double Rush, 1995, exec. prodr., writer Murphy Brown, 1988—98, Ink, 1996, writer Love & War, 1992; exec. prodr.: (TV series) The Louie Show, 1996, Living in Captivity, 1998; writer, prodr. (films) Women, 2008. Recipient 3 Emmy awards, Golden Globe award, 1989, Outstanding Writing in a Comedy Series award Writers Guild, 1990, 92, Genie award Am. Women in Radio and TV, 1990, Commrs.' award Nat. Commn. on Working Women, Peabody award, 1991. Office: c/o Shukovsky-English Entertainment 4605 Lankershim Blvd Ste 510 North Hollywood CA 91602

ENGLISH, STEPHEN FRANCIS, lawyer; b. Portland, Oreg., Jan. 17, 1948; BA, Hons. Coll., U. Oreg., 1970; JD, U. Calif., San Francisco, 1973. Bar: Oreg. 1973; U.S. Dist. Ct. Oreg. 1973; U.S. Ct. Appeals (9th cir.) Oreg. 1980; U.S. Supreme Ct. 1982. Ptnr. Bullivant Houser Bailey, Portland, Oreg., 1983—. Mem. faculty Hastings Coll. Trial Advocacy, 1998—; mem. Bus. Litigation Inst., 2000; bd. dirs. Dr. Martens AirWair USA, 2002—, Fellow Am. Coll. Trial Lawyers; Mem. ABA (vice-chair products liability com., 1996—, chair self insurers and risk mgrs. com. 1994-95, editor Self Insurers Newsletter 1987-89, chair non-profit, charitable and religious orgns. com. 1990-92, mem. Tort and Insurance Practice Sect.), Multnomah County Bar Assn., Oreg. State Bar Assn. (chair litigation sect. 1990-91, exec. com. 1987-91), Am. Bd. Trial Adv. (treas. Oreg. chpt. 1996-98, bd. dirs. 1997—, sec. 1998—, pres. 2002-, pres. Oreg. chpt., 2003-04), Oreg. Assn. Def. Counsel (chair products liability practice group 1997-98), Def. Rsch. Inst., Oreg. State Bar Masters of Trial Advocacy. Office: Bullivant Houser Bailey 300 Pioneer Tower 888 SW 5th Ave Portland OR 97204-2089 E-mail: steve.english@bullivant.com.

ENGLISH, STEPHEN RAYMOND, lawyer; b. Key West, Fla., Nov. 25, 1946; s. Jack Raymond and Jean Clyde (Peightal) E.; m. Molly Munger, Oct. 7, 1978; children: Nicholas, Alfred. BA, UCLA, 1975; JD, Harvard U., 1975. Bar: Calif. 1975, U.S. Dist. Ct. (ctrl. dist.) Calif. 1976, U.S. Dist. Ct. (so. dist.) Calif. 1978, U.S. Dist. Ct. (ea. dist.) Calif. 1988, U.S. Ct. Appeals (9th cir.) 1992. Assoc. Agnew, Miller & Carlson, LA, 1975-78, Morgan, Lewis & Bockius, LA, 1978-85, ptnr., 1985-98, English, Munger & Rice, LA, 1998—, co-dir. Advancement Project, 2000—. Lawyer rep. Ninth Cir. Jud. Conf., 1996-97. Pres. bd. dirs. Pub. Counsel, L.A., 1988-89, Inner City Law Ctr., L.A., 1992-93; mem. L.A. Legal Aid Found., pres., 2006-07. Mem. L.A. County Bar Assn. (mem. barristers exec. com. 1980-82, trustee 1990-92, chair pro bono coun. 1990-92, chair legal svcs. for poor 1993-95, mem. exec. com. litig. sect. 1994-2005, chair litig. sect. 2003-04), L.A. County Bar Found. (pres. 1998-99).

ENGLUND, ROBERT, actor, director, producer; b. Glendale, Calif., June 6, 1949; s. C. Kent and Janice (McDonald) E.; m. Nancy Ellen Booth, Oct. 1, 1988. Student, Oakland U., U. Calif., Northridge, UCLA, Royal Acad. Dramatic Arts, Rochester, Mich. Actor, dir., producer; resident artist Meadow Brook Theatre, Rochester, 1969-72, guest artist, 1973; resident actor Gt. Lakes Shakespeare Festival, Cleve., 1970—71; resident actor Judas in Godspell, Cleve., 1971. Appeared as Freddy Krueger in A Nightmare on Elm Street, 1984, A Nightmare on Elm Street, Part 2: Freddy's Revenge, 1985, A Nightmare on Elm Street 3: Dream Warriors, 1987, A Nightmare on Elm Street 4: The Dream Master 1988, A Nightmare on Elm Street 5: The Dream Child, 1989, Freddy's Dead: The Final Nightmare, 1991, Wes Craven's New Nightmare, 1994, Freddy vs Jason, 2003; also appeared in films Buster and Billie, 1973, Hustle, 1974, Last of the Cowboys, 1976, Stay Hungry, 1975, A Star Is Born, 1976, Bloodbrothers, 1977, Big Wednesday, 1978, Galaxy of Terror, 1980, Dead and Buried, 1981, Don't Cry, It's Only Thunder, 1982, Never Too Young to Die, 1986, Phantom of the Opera, 1989, Dance Macabre, 1992, Steven King's The Mangler, 1995, Tobe Hoopers Night Dreams, 1992, Ford Fairlane, 1990, Killer Tongue, 1996, Wishmaster, 1997, Disney's Meet the Deedles, 1997, Dee Snyder's Strangeland, 1997, Urban Legend, 1998, Nobody Knows Anything, 1999, The Prince and the Surfer, 1999, Wish You Were Dead, 2000, The Return of Caligostro, 2000, Python, 2000, Cold Sweat, 2000, Windfall, 2001, Like A Bad Dream, 2002, 2001 Maniacs, 2002, Behind The Mask, 2004, Hatchet, 2005, Heart STopper, 2005, Jack Brooks: Monster Slayer, 2006, Red, 2006, others; dir. 976-EVIL, 1988; appeared on TV in series Downtown, 1986-87, Freddy's Nighymares, 1987-89, Nightmare Cafe, 1992-93, Young Joe, the Forgotten Kennedy, 1977, The Ordeal of Patty Hearst, 1979, V, 1983, Hobson's Choice, 1983, I Want to Live, 1983, Hunter, 1985, Knight Rider, 1986, MacGyver, 1986, also on Police Woman, Soap, Charlie's Angels, Police Story, Married With Children, also others; TV films Mortal Fear, 1995, Unspoken Truth, 1996; dir. (films) Killer Pad, 2006; master of horror Showtime, 2005; also stage actor and producer. Mem. SAG, AFTRA, Actors Equity Assn., Dirs. Guild Am.

ENNIS, WILLIAM LEE, physics educator; b. Houston, Aug. 10, 1949; s. Arthur Lee and Helen Ennis; m. Constance Elizabeth Livsey, July 20, 1991. BS, Auburn U., Ala., 1974, BA, 1978. Rsch. tech. Nat. Tillage Lab., Auburn, Ala., 1974-76; tchr. Stanford Jr. H.S., Hillsborough, N.C., 1979-81; physics tchr., chmn. sci. dept. East H.S., Anchorage, 1981—. Chmn. Anchorage Sch. Dist. Physics Tchrs.; curriculum devel. sci. cons. Copper River Schs., Anchorage, 1991. Recipient Nat. Tchr. award Milken Family Found., 1999; named Tandy Tech. Outstanding Tchr., 1989-90, Tchr. of Excellence Brit. Petroleum, 1996, Brit. Petroleum Tchr. of Yr., 1996, Disting. Tchr., White House Commn. on Presdl. Scholars; Fermi Lab. scholar U.S. Dept. Energy, 1991; grantee MIT/Lemelson Found. Inventeam, 2003-. Mem. AAAS, Am. Assn. Physics Tchrs., Am. Phys. Soc., Nat. Sci. Tchrs. Assn., Alaska Sci. Tchrs. (life), Am. Mountain Guides Assn., Am. Alpine Club. Avocations: mountain climbing, outdoor activities, sailing, computers. Office: East HS 4025 E Northern Lights Blvd Anchorage AK 99508-3588 Office Phone: 907-742-2100. E-mail: ennis_williams@asdk12.org.

ENOCH, JAY MARTIN, optometrist, research scientist, educator; b. NYC, Apr. 20, 1929; s. Jerome Dee and Stella Sarah (Nathan) E.; m. Rebekah Ann Feiss, June 24, 1951; children: Harold Owen, Barbara Diane, Ann Allison. BS in Optics and Optometry, Columbia U., 1950; post grad., Inst. Optics U. Rochester, 1953; PhD in Physiol. Optics, Ohio State U., 1956; DSc (hon.), SUNY, 1993, U. Politecnica Catalunya, Barcelona, Spain, 2002. Asst. prof. physiol. optics Ohio State U., Columbus, 1956-58; assoc. supr. Ohio State U. (Mapping and Charting Rsch. Lab.), 1957-58; fellow Nat. Phys. Lab., Teddington, England, 1959-60; rsch. instr. dept. ophthalmology Washington U. Sch. Medicine, St. Louis, 1958-59, rsch. asst. prof., 1959-64, rsch. assoc. prof., 1965-70, rsch. prof., 1970-74; fellow Barnes Hosp., St. Louis, 1960-64, cons. ophthalmology, 1964-74; rsch. prof. dept. psychology Washington U., St. Louis, 1970-74; grad. rsch. prof. ophthalmology and psychology Coll. Medicine U. Fla., Gainesville, 1974-80, grad. rsch. prof. physics, 1979-80; dir. Ctr. for Sensory Studies, 1976-80; dean Sch. Optometry, chmn. Grad. Group in Vision Sci. U. Calif., Berkeley, Calif., 1980-92, prof. optometry and vision sci., 1980-94, prof. of Grad. Sch., 1994—; prof. physiol. optics in ophthalmology U. Calif., San Francisco, 1980—. Exec. sec. subcom. on vision and its disorders of nat. adv. Neurol. Diseases and Blindness Coun., NIH, 1963-66; chmn. subcom. contact lens stds. Am. Nat. Std. Inst., 1970-77; nat. adv. eye coun. Nat. Eye Inst., NIH, 1975-77, 80-84; exec. com., com. on vision NAS-NRC, 1973-76; mem. US Nat. Com. Internat. Commn. Optics, 1976-79, health sci. com. Systemwide Adminstrn. U. Calif., 1989-93, co-chmn. subcom. on immigrant health in Calif., 1993-94, sci. adv. bd. Fight-for-Sight, 1988-92, Allergan Corp., 1991-95, mem. Lighthouse Internat., NY, 1991-95, 2001-05, chair, 1995, Pisart award com., bd. dir. 2001-06, com. on Refractive Errors WHO, 2002-; founder Elite Sch. Optometry, Chennai, Tamil Nadu, India, dedication lectr., 1985, plenary spkr. 20th Ann., 2005, Pahlkivala Foundation Oration, Chennai, Tamil Nadu, 2008; Enoch Lecture on Vision Sci., Washington U. Med. Sch., St. Louis, 2007-. Mem. editl. bd.: Investigative Ophthalmology and Vision Sci., 1965—75, 1983—88, Vision Rsch., 1974—80, Sight-Saving Rev., 1974—84, Sensory Processes, 1974—80, Internat. Ophthalmology, 1977—93, mem. editl. bd. optical scis.: Springer-Verlag, 1978—87, mem. editl. bd.: Binocular Vision, 1984—2004, Clin. Vision Sci., 1986—93, Biomed. Optics, 1988—90, mem. editl. bd. biomed. scis.: Springer-Verlag, 1988—95, mem. editl. bd.: Annals of Ophthalmology, 1997—2006, assoc. editor for vision: Handbook of Optics, Optical Soc. Am., 1997—, mem. internat. editl. bd.: Ophthalmic and Physiol. Optics, 2002—; contbr. articles to profl. jours., chapters to books. Nat. sci. adv. bd. Retinitis Pigmentosa Found., 1977-95; US rep. Internat. Perimetric Soc., 1974-90, also exec. com., chmn. Rsch. Group Standards; bd. dirs. Friends of Eye Rsch.,

1977-88, Lighting Rsch. Bd., 1988-95; trustee Illuminating Engring. Rsch. Inst., 1977-81; mem. bd. counselors U. Calif. San Francisco Sch. Dentistry, 1995-2003. 2d lt. US Army, 1951-52. Recipient Career Devel. award, NIH, 1963—73, Everett Kinsey award, Contact Lens Soc. Ophthalmologists, 1991, Berkeley citation, Festschrift U. Calif. Berkeley, 1996, Pisart award, Lighthouse Internat., 2001, Gaspar de Portola award, U. Calif. and Govt. of Catalunya, 2001, 2004, US Congl. Recognition award, 2005, Spl. Recognition award, Friends Indo-Am. Cmty., 2005, Glenn A. Fry medal, Ohio State U., 2007; named one of 250 Alumni Ahead of Their Time, Columbia Univ., 2004. Fellow AAAS, Am. Acad. Optometry (co-founder eye disease sect., Glenn A. Fry award 1972, Charles F. Prentice medal award 1974, 50 Yr. award 2004), Optical Soc. Am. (chmn. vision tech. sect. 1974-76, mem. book pub. com. 1996-2000), Am. Acad. Ophthalmology (low-vision com., honor award 1985); mem. Assn. for Rsch. in Vision and Ophthalmology (trustee 1967-73, pres. 1972-73, Francis I. Proctor medal 1977, elected fellow 2009), Concilium Ophthalmologicum Universale (chmn. visual functions com. 1982-86), Am. Optometric Assn. (low vision sect., Vision Care award 1987), Internat. Perimetric Soc. (hon. mem., chair com. stds.), Ocular Heritage Soc. (medal 1997), Cogan Ophthalmic History Soc., Optometric Hist. Soc. (trustee 2000-02, 2006—, v.p. 2002-04, pres. 2005), Cosmos Club (Washington), Sigma Xi. Achievements include research in visual sci., photoreceptor optics, perimetry, contact lenses, infant and aged vision, myopia, history of earliest lenses and mirrors. Office: U Calif Sch Optometry Berkeley CA 94720-2020 Home Phone: 925-631-0198; Office Phone: 510-642-9694. Business E-Mail: jmenoch@berkeley.edu.

ENOS, KELLY D., telecommunications company financial executive; V.p. Sutro & Co., 1991-94, Oppenheimer & Co., Inc., 1994-95, Fortune Fin., 1995-96; ind. cons. mcht. banking field, 1996; CFO, Telecom., Inc., Santa Barbara, Calif., 1996—, treas., 1997—. Office: Star Telecommunications 2544 Joshua Ct Oxnard CA 93036-6204 Fax: 805-899-2972.

ENQUIST, BRIAN JOSEPH, ecologist, educator; b. Mar. 4, 1969; BA in Biology with distinction, Colo. Coll., Colo. Springs, 1991; MS in Biology, U. N.Mex., Albuquerque, 1994, PhD in Biology, 1998. Rsch. asst. prof. dept. biology U. N.Mex., 1998—2001; NSF postdoctoral fellow Santa Fe Inst., 1998—99; NSF postdoctoral fellow Nat. Ctr. Ecol. Analysis and Synthesis U. Calif., Santa Barbara, 1999—2000; asst. prof. dept. ecology and evolutionary biology U. Ariz., Tucson, 2001—05, assoc. prof., 2005—. Contbr. articles to sci. jours. Recipient CAREER award, NSF, 2002—; named an Brilliant 10, Popular Sci. mag., 2004. Mem.: Bot. Soc. Am. (mem. ecol. and tropical biology sects.), Ecol. Soc. Am. (mem. theoretical sect., George C. Mercer award 2001), Am. Soc. Naturalists, AAAS. Office: Dept Ecology and Evolutionary Biology U Ariz BioSciences West Tucson AZ 85721 Office Phone: 520-626-3329. Office Fax: 520-621-9190. E-mail: benquist@u.arizona.edu.

ENRICO, ROGER A., film company executive, retired food and beverage company executive; b. Chisholm, Minn., Nov. 11, 1944; m. Rosemary Margo, 1969; 1 child. BA, Babson Coll., 1965. Former v.p. sales and mktg. Pepsi-Cola Metropol Bottling Co. Inc., Purchase, NY; chmn., CEO PepsiCo Worldwide Beverages, Purchase, 1987, PepsiCo, Inc., 1996—2001, vice-chmn, 2001—02; chmn. DreamWorks Animation SKG Inc., 2004—. Bd. dirs. Belo Corp., 1995—, Electronic Data Systems Corp., 2000—. Office: Dream Works Animation SKG Inc 1000 Flower St Glendale CA 91201

ENRIGHT, CYNTHIA LEE, illustrator; b. Denver, July 6, 1950; d. Darrel Lee and Iris Arlene (Flodquist) E. BA in Elem. Edn., U. No. Colo., Greeley, 1972; student, Minn. Sch. Art and Design, Mpls., 1975-76. Tchr. 3d grade Littleton Sch. Dist., Colo., 1972-75; graphics artist Sta. KCNC TV, Denver, 1978-79; illustrator No Coast Graphics, Denver, 1979-87; editorial artist The Denver Post, 1987—. Illustrator, editor "Tiny Tales" The Denver Post, 1991-94. Recipient Print mag. Regional Design Ann. awards, 1984, 85, 87, Phoenix Art Mus. Biannual award, 1979, third pl. Best of the West award for illustration, 2004. Democrat. Home: 1210 Ivanhoe St Denver CO 80220-2640 Office: The Denver Post 101 W Colfax Ave Denver CO 80202-5177

ENRIGHT, WILLIAM BENNER, judge; b. NYC, July 12, 1925; s. Arthur Joseph and Anna Beatrice (Plante) E.; m. Bette Lou Card, Apr. 13, 1951; children— Kevin A., Kimberly A., Kerry K. BA, Dartmouth, 1947; LLB, Loyola U. at L.A., 1950. Bar: Calif. 1951; diplomate: Am. Bd. Trial Advs. Dep. dist. atty., San Diego County, 1951-54; ptnr. Enright, Levitt, Knutson & Tobin, San Diego, 1954-72; judge U.S. Dist. Ct. (so. dist.) Calif., San Diego, 1972-90, sr. judge, 1990—. Mem. adv. bd. Joint Legis. Com. for Revision Penal Code, 1970-72, Calif. Bd. Legal Specialization, 1970-72; mem. Jud. Council, 1972; Bd. dirs. Defenders, 1965-72, pres., 1972 Served as ensign USNR, 1943-46. Recipient Honor award San Diego County Bar, 1970; Extraordinary Service to Legal Professions award Mcpl. Ct. San Diego Jud. Dist., 1971 Fellow Am. Coll. Trial Lawyers, Am. Bar Found.; mem. ABA, San Diego County Bar Assn. (dir. 1963-65, pres. 1965), State Bar Calif. (gov. 1967-70, v.p. 1970, exec. com. law in a free soc. 1970—), Dartmouth Club San Diego, Am. Judicature Soc., Alpha Sigma Nu, Phi Delta Phi. Clubs: Rotarian. Office: US Dist Ct 4145 US Courthouse 940 Front St San Diego CA 92101-8994

ENRIQUEZ, CAROLA RUPERT, museum director; b. Washington, Jan. 2, 1954; d. Jack Burns and Shirley Ann (Orcutt) Rupert; m. John Enriquez, Jr., Dec. 30, 1989. BA in History cum laude, Bryn Mawr Coll., 1976; MA, U. Del., 1978, cert. in mus. studies, 1978. Pers. mgmt. trainee Naval Material Command, Arlington, Va., 1972-76; tchg. asst. dept. history U. Del., Newark, 1976-77; asst. curator/exhibit specialist Hist. Soc. Del., Wilmington, 1977-78; dir. Macon County Mus. Complex, Decatur, Ill., 1978-81, Kern County Mus., Bakersfield, Calif., 1981—. Pres. Kern County Mus Found., 1991-02; advisor Kern County Heritage Commn., 1981-88; chmn. Hist. Records Commn., 1981-88; sec.-treas. Arts Coun. of Kern, 1984-86, pres., 1986-88; county co-chmn. United Way, 1981, 82; chmn. steering com. Calif. State Bakersfield Co-op Program, 1982-83; mem. cmty. adv. bd. Calif. State U.-Bakersfield Anthrop. Soc., 1986-88; bd. dirs. Mgmt. Coun., 1983-86, v.p., 1987, pres., 1988; bd. dirs. Calif. Coun. for Promotion of History, 1984-86, v.p., 1987-88, pres., 1988-90; mem. cmty. adv. bd. Calif. State U.-Bakersifled Sociology Dept., 1986-88; mem. women's adv. com. Girls Scouts U.S., 1989-91; bd. dirs. Greater Bakersfield Conv. and Visitors Bur., 1993-95; co-chair 34th St. Neighborhood Partnership, 1994-01. Hagley fellow Eleutherian Mills-Hagley found., 1977-78; Bryn Mawr alumnae reg. scholar, 1972-76. Mem. Calif. Assn. Mus. (regional rep. 1991—2002, v.p. legis. affairs 1992—2002), Am. Assn. State and Local History (chair awards com. Calif. chpt. 1990, regional vice chair 1999—2002). Presbyterian. Office: Kern County Museum 3801 Chester Ave Bakersfield CA 93301-1345

ENSIGN, DONALD H., landscape architect; b. Salt Lake City, Sept. 5, 1936; s. C. Wesley and Mildred (Harker) E.; m. Kay Bateman, Sept. 9, 1959 (div. 1970); m. Nancy Ensign; children: Philip Wesley, Craig Allen, Michael Donald. B in Landscape Architecture, Utah State U., 1963; M in Landscape Architecture, U. Mich., 1968. Registered landscape architect, Mich., N.C. Landscape architect Frehner and Assocs., Salt Lake City, 1961-62; planner Roswell/Ensign and Assocs., Salt Lake City, 1962-66; instr. dept. landscape architecture and environ. planning Utah State U., Logan, 1963-66; planner Richard B. Wilkinson and Assocs., Ann Arbor, Mich., 1966-68; prin. Design Workshop, Inc., Aspen, Colo., 1970—; assoc. prof. sch. design N.C. State U., 1968-74, dir. basic design program, 1971-73. Prin. works include Aspen Inst., Grand Valley High Sch., Marolt Ranch, U. Mich., Utah State U., Estrella Lake Parks, Goodyear, Ariz., Fox River, Geneva, Ill., Lauder Residence, Aspen, Resort at Squaw Creek, Squaw Valley, Calif., 700 East Main, Aspen, Snowmass (Colo.) Club, Blackcomb Resort, Whistler, British Columbia, Early Winters Resort, Mazama, Wash., Grand Champions Resort, Aspen, many others. Avocations: hunting, cross country skiing, painting, golf, hiking. Office: Design Workshop 120 E Main St Aspen CO 81611-1714

ENSIGN, JOHN ERIC, United States Senator from Nevada, former United States Representative from Nevada; b. Roseville, Calif., Mar. 25, 1958; s. Mike and Sharon Ensign; m. Darlene Sciarretta; 3 children. Student, U. Nev., Las Vegas, 1979; BS in Gen. Sci., Oreg. State U., 1981; D of Veterinary Medicine, Colo. State U., 1985. Intern West LA Vet. Med. Group; owner West Flamingo Animal Hosp., Las Vegas, 1987—94, South Shores Animal Hosp., Las Vegas, 1994—; gen. mgr. Gold Strike Hotel & Casino, 1991, Nev. Landing Hotel & Casino, 1992; mem. US Congress from 1st Nev. Dist., Washington, 1995—99; US Senator from Nev., 2001—. Mem. US Senate Health, Edn., Labor & Pensions Com., US Senate Commerce, Sci., Transp. Com., US Senate Budget Com., US Senate Fin. Com.; chmn. Nat. Republican Senatorial Com. (NRSC), 2007—09, US Senate Republican Policy Com., 2009—. Recipient Taxpayers' Friend award, Nat. Taxpayers Union, 2003, Thomas Jefferson award, Food Marketing Inst. and Internat. Foodservice Distributors Assn., 2004, Legis. of Yr., Info. Tech. Industry Coun., 2004, Cyber Champion award, Bus. Software Alliance, 2005. Republican. Christian. Office: US Senate 356 Russell Senate Office Building Washington DC 20510 also: Lloyd George Federal Bldg Ste 8203 333 Las Vegas Bvld South Las Vegas NV 89101 Office Phone: 202-224-6244, 702-388-6605. Office Fax: 202-224-2193, 702-338-6501.*

ENSIGN, MICHAEL S., resort company executive; Gen. mgr. Circus Circus-Las Vegas; COO, exec. v.p. Circus-Circus Enterprises; also bd. dirs.; rejoined as COO, vice-chmn., 1995-98; CEO, chmn., 1998; CEO, COO, chmn. Mandalay Resort Group, Las Vegas, 1998—. Office: Mandalay Resort Group 3950 Las Vegas Blvd S Las Vegas NV 89119

ENSTROM, JAMES EUGENE, epidemiologist; b. Alhambra, Calif., June 20, 1943; s. Elmer Melvin, Jr. and Klea Elizabeth (Bissell) E.; m. Marta Eugenia Villanea, Sept. 3, 1978. BS, Harvey Mudd Coll., Claremont, Calif., 1965; MS, Stanford U., 1967; PhD in Physics, 1970; M.P.H., UCLA, 1976. Research assoc. Stanford Linear Accelerator Center, 1970-71; research physicist, cons. Lawrence Berkeley Lab. U. Calif., 1971-75; Celeste Durand Rogers cancer research fellow Sch. Pub. Health, UCLA, 1973-75; Nat. Cancer Inst. postdoctoral trainee, 1975-76; cancer epidemiology researcher, 1976-81; assoc. research prof., 1981—. Program dir. for cancer control epidemiology Jonsson Comprehensive Cancer Center, 1978-88, research epidemiologist, 1988—, sci. dir. tumor registry, 1984-87, mem. dean's council, 1976—; cons. epidemiologist Linus Pauling Inst. Sci. and Medicine, 1976-94; cons. physicist Rand Corp., 1969-73, R&D Assos., 1971-75; mem. sci. bd. Am. Council on Sci. and Health, 1984—. Author papers in field. NSF predoctoral trainee, 1965-66; grantee Am. Cancer Soc., 1973—, Nat. Cancer Inst., 1979—; Preventive Oncology Acad. award, 1981-87. Fellow Am. Coll. Epidemiology; mem. Soc. Epidemiologic Research, Am. Heart Assn., Am. Pub. Health Assn., Am. Phys. Soc., AAAS, N.Y. Acad. Scis., Galileo Soc. Office: U Calif Sch Pub Health Los Angeles CA 90024

ENTHOVEN, ALAIN CHARLES, economist, educator; b. Seattlle, Sept. 10, 1930; s. Richard Frederick and Jacqueline E.; m. Rosemary Fenech, July 28, 1956; children: Eleanor, Richard, Andrew, Martha, Nicholas, Daniel. BA in Econs., Stanford U., 1952; M.Phil. (Rhodes scholar), Oxford U., Eng., 1954; PhD in Econs, MIT, 1956; PhD in Public Pol. (hon.), RAND Graduate Sch., 2008. Instr. econs. MIT, Cambridge, 1955-56; economist The RAND Corp., Santa Monica, Calif., 1956-60; ops. research analyst Office of Dir. Def. Research and Engring., Dept. Def., Washington, 1960; dep. comptroller, dep. asst. sec. U.S. Dept. Def., Washington, 1961-65, asst. sec. for systems analysis, 1965-69; v.p. for econ. planning Litton Industries, Beverly Hills, Calif., 1969-71; pres. Litton Med. Products, Beverly Hills, 1971-73; Marriner S. Eccles prof. pub. and pvt. mgmt. Grad. Sch. Bus. Stanford (Calif.) U., 1973-2000, prof. health care econs. Sch. Medicine, 1973-2000; sr. fellow Ctr. for Health Policy, Stanford U., 2000—. Cons. The Brookings Instn., 1956-60; vis. assoc. prof. econs. U. Wash., 1958; mem. Stanford Computer Sci. Adv. Com., 1968-73; cons. The RAND Corp., 1969—; mem. vis. com. in econs. MIT, 1971-78; mem. vis. com. on environ. quality lab. Calif. Inst. Tech., 1972-77; mem. Inst. Medicine, Nat. Acad. Scis., 1972—; mem. vis. com. Harvard U. Sch. Pub. Health, 1974-80; cons. Kaiser Found. Health Plan, Inc., 1973—; vis. prof. U. Paris, 1985, London Sch. Hygiene and Tropical Medicine, 1998-99; vis. fellow St. Catherine's Coll., Oxford U., Eng., 1985, New Coll., 1998-99; dir. Hotel Investors Trust, 1986-87, PCS Inc., 1987-90, Caresoft, 1996-2002, Rx Intelligence, 2000-03, eBenX Inc, 2001-03. Author: (with K. Wayne Smith) How Much is Enough? Shaping the Defense Program 1961-69, 71, 2d edit., 2005, Health Plan: The Only Practical Solution to the Soaring Cost of Medical Care, 1980; editor: (with A. Myrick Freeman III) Pollution, Resources and the Environment, 1973, Theory and Practice of Managed Competition in Health Care Finance, 1988, In Pursuit of an Improving National Health Service, 1999, (with Laura A. Tollen) Toward a 21st Century Health System: The Contributions and Promise of Prepaid Group Practice, 2004; contbr. articles to profl. jours. Bd. dirs. Georgetown U., Washington, 1968-73, Jackson Hole Group, 1993-96; bd. regents St. John's Hosp., Santa Monica, 1971-73; chmn. Gov's Taskforce Managed Health Care Improvement, 1997-98, vis. com. Harvard U. Kennedy Sch. Govt., 1998-2003. Recipient President's award for disting. fed. civilian svc., 1963, Disting. Pub. Svc. medal Dept. Def., 1968, Baxter prize for health svcs. rsch., 1994, Bd. Dirs.' award Healthcare Fin. Mgmt. Assn., 1995, Ellwood award Found. for Accountability, 1998, Rock Carling fellow, Nuffield Trust, 1999. Mem. Am. Assn. Rhodes Scholars, Am. Acad. Arts and Scis., Integrated Healthcare Assn. (bd. dirs. 1999—), Phi Beta Kappa. Home: 1 McCormick Ln Atherton CA 94027-3033 Office: Stanford Univ Grad Sch Business 518 Memorial Way Stanford CA 94305-5015 Office Phone: 650-723-0641. Business E-Mail: enthoven@stanford.edu.

ENZI, MICHAEL BRADLEY, United States Senator from Wyoming, accountant; b. Bremerton, Wash., Feb. 1, 1944; s. Elmer Jacob and Dorothy (Bradley) E.; m. Diana Buckley, June 7, 1969; children: Amy, Bradley, Emily. BBA, George Wash. U., 1966; MBA, Denver U., 1968. Cert. profl. human resources, 1994. Mayor City of Gillette, Wyo., 1975—82; pres. NZ Shoes, Inc., Gillette, Wyo., 1969-95, NZ Shoes of Sheridan, Inc., Wyo., 1983-96; acctg. mgr. Dunbar Well Svc., Inc., Gillette, 1985-97; mem. Wyo. Ho. of Reps., Cheyne, 1986—91, Wyo. State Senate, Cheyenne, 1991-96; commr. Western Interstate Commn. for Higher Edn., 1995—96; US Senator from Wyo., 1997—; chmn. US Senate Health Edn. Labor & Pensions Com., 2005—07; mem. US Senate Fin. Com., 2009—. Mem. Edn. Commn. of States, 1989—93, Western Interstate Commn. Higher Edn., 1995—96. Pres. Wyo. Assn. Mcpls., Cheyenne, 1980-82; chmn. bd. dirs. 1st Wyo. Bank, Gillette, 1978-88, bd. dirs. Black Hills Corp., 1992-96. Served as Sgt. Wyo. Air NG, 1967—73. Recipient W. Stuart Symington award, Air Force Assn., 2001, Small Investor Empowerment award, Nat. Assn. Real Estate Investment Trusts, 2002, Legis. of Yr., Am. Soc. Consultant Pharmacists, 2004, Biotechnology Industry Orgn., 2005, Congressional Leadership award, Food Industry Assn., 2005, Leadership award, Nat. Orgn. Fetal Alcohol Syndrome, 2005, Policy Maker of Yr., Assn. Career and Technical Edn., 2005, TechNet Founders Cir. award, 2005. Mem. Wyo. Order of DeMolay (state master councilor 1963-64), Wyo. Jaycees (state pres. 1973-74), Masons (Sheridan and Gillette lodges), Scottish Rite, Shriners, Lions, Sigma Chi. Republican. Presbyn. Avocations: fishing, bicycling, soccer, hunting. Office: US Senate 379A Senate Russell Bldg Washington DC 20510-0001 also: District Office Ste 303 400 South Kendrick Ave Gillette WY 82716-3803 Office Phone: 202-224-3424, 307-682-6268. Office Fax: 202-228-0359, 307-682-6501. Business E-Mail: senator@enzi.senate.gov.*

EPEL, DAVID, biologist, educator; b. Detroit, Mar. 26, 1937; s. Jacob A. and Anna K. E.; m. Lois S. Ambush, Dec. 18, 1960; children: Andrea, Sharon, Elissa. AB, Wayne State U., 1958; PhD, U. Calif.-Berkeley, 1963. Postdoctoral fellow Johnson Research Found., U. Pa., 1963-65; asst. prof. Hopkins Marine Sta., 1965-70; assoc. prof., then prof. Scripps Instn. Oceanography, 1970-77; Jane and Marshall Steel Jr. prof. marine scis. Hopkins Marine Sta., Stanford U., Pacific Grove, Calif., 1977—; acting dir. Hopkins Marine Sta., Pacific Grove, 1984—88. Co-dir. embryology course Marine Biol. Lab, Woods Hole, 1974—77. Mem. editl. bd. Zygote. Bd. dirs. Monterey Bay Aquarium Rsch. Inst., 1987-89, trustee, 1985-88. Guggenheim fellow, 1976-77, Overseas fellow Churchill Coll., Cambridge, Eng., 1976-77, Dist. Fellow Calif. State U., 2004; recipient Allen Cox medal for fostering excellence in undergrad. rsch. Stanford U., 1995, Ed Ricketts award for lifetime contbn. to marine sci., 2006. Fellow AAAS (mem.-at-large, sect. G 1979-84, chmn. sect. on biol. scis. 1998—), Calif. Acad. Scis.; mem. Am. Soc. Cell Biology (mem. council 1978-80), Soc. Devel. Biology, Internat. Soc. Devel. Biology, Soc. Integrative and Comparative Biology (chairperson devel. and cell biology sect. 1990-92).

EPP, TIMOTHY LEE, lawyer; BS, Iowa State U., 1981; MBA, San Diego State U., 1989; JD, UCLA, 1992. Bar: Calif. 1993, US Ct. Appeals (9th cir.), US Dist. Ct. (ctrl. dist.) Calif., US Patent and Trademark Office. Legal extern to Hon. David R. Thompson US Ct. Appeals (9th cir.), 1992; v.p., gen counsel, sec. Taylor Made-adidas Golf Co.; ptnr. Intellectual Property Practice Group Sheppard, Mullin, Richter & Hampton, LLP, Costa Mesa, Calif. Mem.: ABA, Am. Corp. Counsel Assn., Orange County Patent Law Assn., Am. Intellectual Property Law Assn., Orange County Bar Assn. Office: Sheppard Mullin Richter & Hampton, LLP 4th Fl 650 Town Center Dr Costa Mesa CA 92626 Office Phone: 714-424-2892. Office Fax: 714-513-5130. E-mail: tepp@sheppardmullin.com.

EPPERSON, ERIC ROBERT, finance executive, film producer; b. Oregon City, Oreg., Dec. 10, 1949; s. Robert Max and Margaret Joan (Crawford) E.; m. Lyla Gene Harris, Aug. 21, 1969; 1 child, Marcie. BS, Brigham Young U., 1973, M of Acctg., 1974; MBA, Golden Gate U., 1977, JD, 1981. Instr. acctg. Brigham Young U., Provo, Utah, 1973-74; supr. domestic taxation Bechtel Corp., San Francisco, 1974-78; supr. internat. taxation Bechtel Power Corp., San Francisco, 1978-80; mgr. internat. tax planning Del Monte Corp., San Francisco, 1980-82, mgr. internat. taxes, 1982-85; internat. tax specialist Touche Ross & Co., San Francisco, 1985-87; dir. internat. tax Coopers & Lybrand, Portland, Oreg., 1987-89; exec. v.p., CFO Epperson Dayton Sorenson Prodns., Inc., Salt Lake City, 1989-90, Epperson Prodns., 1990-92; exec. dir. The Oreg. Trail Found., Inc., Oregon City, 1992-93; pres., chmn. bd. MFD Ltd., Portland, 1993—; pres. Oreg. Trail Films, Ltd., 1998—, Morgan's Ferry Prodns., LLC, 1988—2007, Lakeboat Prodns., LLC, 1999—2007, Oregon Trail TV, Ltd., 1999—2006, Oregon Trail Promotions, Ltd., 1999—2006; COO, CFO Whitlock Training Group Corp., 2006—. Estate executor in field, 2005—; CFO/COO Crimeline and Whitlock Training Group Corp., 2006. Author: (with T. Gilbert) Interfacing of the Securities and Exchange Commission with the Accounting Profession: 1968 to 1973, 1974; prodr. (film) Without Evidence, 1995, Morgan's Ferry, 1999, Lakeboat, 2000; exec. prodr. (film) Dream Machine, 1989, Live & Learn, 2001, (TV series) Live & Learn, 2000, Dixie Chick Fly Tour, 2000. Scoutmaster Boy Scouts Am., Provo, 1971-73, troop committeeman, 1973-74, 83—, vice-chmn. ranch devel. com., Butte Creek; mem. IRS Vol. Income Tax Assistance Program, 1972-75; pres. Youth First Found. Inc., 2000-, Mut. Improvement Assn., Ch. Jesus Christ of Latter-day Saints, 1972-74, pres. Sunday sch., 1977-79, tchr., 1974-80, ward clk., 1980-83, bishopric, 1983-87; bd. dirs. Oreg. Art Inst. Film Ctr., Oreg. Trail Coordinating Coun., Hist. Preservation League of Oreg. Mem. World Affairs Coun., Japan/Am. Soc., Internat. Tax Planning Assn., Internat. Fiscal Assn., Oreg. Trail Coordinating Coun. (exec. bd.), Oreg. Hist. Soc., U.S. Rowing Assn., Oreg. Calif. Trail Assn., Royal Photog. Soc., Commonwealth Club, Multnomah Athletic Club, Exec. Officers Club. Republican. Office: PMB 180 25 NW 23d Pl Ste 6 Portland OR 97210-5599

EPPERSON, STUART W., religious raido broadcaster; b. 1935; m. Atsinger Nancy Epperson; 4 children. BA in Radio/TV Broadcasting, Bob Jones U., Greenville, SC, MA in Comm. Co-founder, chmn. Salem Comm., 1986—. Mem. bd. of dir. Nat. Religious Broadcasters

Assoc. Mem. Coun. Nat. Policy, 1996—. Named one of 25 Most Influential Evangelicals in America, Time Mag. Baptist. Achievements include being the leading U.S. radio broadcaster focused on religious and family themed programming with 92 radio stations in 36 radio markets. Office: Salem Comm Corp 4880 Santa Rosa Rd Camarillo CA 93012 Office Phone: 805-987-0400. Office Fax: 805-384-4520.

EPPLER, JEROME CANNON, investment advisor; b. Englewood, NJ, Mar. 16, 1924; s. William E. and Aileen (Vaughan) E.; m. Debora Nye Eppler; children: Stephen Vaughan, William Durand, Margaret Nye, Elizabeth Scott, Edward Curtis. BSME, Tex. A&M U., 1946; MBA, U. Pa., 1949. Mem. N.Y. Stock Exch. With Gen. Electric Supply Corp., Newark, 1949-50; investment banker Equitable Securities Corp., Nashville, mgr. Houston, 1950—53; gen. ptnr. Cyrus J. Lawrence & Sons, NYC, 1953—61; owner Eppler & Co., Denver, 1961; chmn. bd. United Screen Arts, Inc., LA, 1966—73; chmn. bd. dir. Life Ins. Co. Calif., 1967—77, I.S.I. Corp., 1967—77, Tessco Techs. Inc., Hunt Valley, Md., 1982—2007, World Wide Life Assurance Co., London, 1972—77; ltd. ptnr. Alex Brown & Sons, Balt., 1982—84; prin. Olympic Capital Ptnrs., Seattle, 1995—2000. Mem. indsl. adv. com. U. Calif., San Diego, 1978—93; mem. N.Y. Stock Exch.; chmn. Global Leadership Coun. Coll. Bus. Colo. State U., Ft. Collins, Colo.; dir. emeritus Tessco Techs. Inc., Hunt Valley. Trustee emeritus Scripps Clinic and Research Found., La Jolla; former trustee Drew U. (N.J.), 1966-67, Morris Mus. Arts & Scis. (N.J.), 1954-76, Met. Opera Assn., 1980-82, Wharton Grad. Sch. Bus. N.Y., 1972-86. Lt. (j.g.) USNR, 1942-46. Mem. Wharton Grad. Bus. Sch. Club, Castle Pines Golf Club, River Bend Country Club (Tequesta, Fla.). Presbyterian. Home: 2800 S University Blvd #22 Denver CO 80210

EPPS, MARY ELLEN, state legislator; b. Copperhill, Tenn., Dec. 25, 1934; Student, Regis Coll.; BS, Colo. Christian U. Former bus. owner; nurse/physician asst.; owner, founder Future Visions Video Prodn. Co.; mem. Colo. Ho. of Reps., Dist. 19, 1986-98, Colo. Senate, Dist. 11, Denver, 1998—; chair health, environment, welfare and instns. com.; mem. judiciary com., mem. transp. com. Edn. com. chair Am. Legis. Exch. Coun., Criminal Justice Task Force; leader Girl Scouts; active El Paso County Planning Commn.; vice-chair Social Svcs. Consumer Rev. Bd. Mem. AARP, VFW, Nat. Conf. State Legislatures (arts and tourism com.), Security Lioness Club, Optimists Club, Fountain Valley Lions Club, Am. Legion Aux., ENT Aero Club, Fountain Valley Teen Club. Republican.

EPPS, OMAR, actor; b. Bklyn., July 23, 1973; m. Keisha Spivey; 1 child, K'mari Mae. Actor: (films) Juice, 1992, The Program, 1993, Major League II, 1994, Higher Learning, 1995, Don't Be a Menace to South Central While Drinking Your Juice in the Hood, 1996, Blossoms and Veils, 1997, Scream 2, 1997, Breakfast of Champions, 1999, The Mod Squad, 1999, The Wood, 1999, In Too Deep, 1999, Love & Basketball, 2000, Brother, 2000, Dracula 2000, 2000, Perfume, 2001, Big Trouble, 2002, Against the Ropes, 2004, Alfie, 2004, (TV films) Daybreak, 1993, Deadly Voyage, 1996, First Time Felon, 1997, Conviction, 2004 (TV series) House M.D., 2004-(Outstanding Supporting Actor in a Drama Series, NAACP Image award, 2007, 2008); TV appearances include Here and Now, 1992, Street Justice, 1993, ER, 1996, 97. Office: The Gersh Agy 232 N Canon Dr Beverly Hills CA 90210-5302

EPSEN, ROBERT A., lawyer; b. Omaha, May 25, 1939; AB, Princeton U., 1961; JD, Stanford U., 1971. Bar: Calif. 1971. Atty. Heller, Ehrman, White & McAuliffe, San Francisco, 1971—, gen. coun. Mem. ABA. Office: Heller Ehrman White & McAuliffe 333 Bush St San Francisco CA 94104-2806 Office Phone: 415-772-6042. Office Fax: 415-772-6268. E-mail: repsen@hewm.com.

EPSTEIN, CHARLES JOSEPH, pediatrician, geneticist, biochemist, educator; b. Phila., Sept. 3, 1933; s. Jacob C. and Frieda (Savransky) E.; m. Lois Barth, June 10, 1956; children: David Alexander, Jonathan Akiba, Paul Michael, Joanna Marguerite. AB, Harvard U., 1955, MD, 1959; DS, Northeastern Ohio U., 1997. Diplomate Am. Bd. Med. Genetics. Intern in medicine Peter Bent Brigham Hosp., Boston, 1959-60, asst. resident in medicine, 1960-61; research assoc., med. officer and sect. chief Nat. Heart Inst. and Nat. Inst. Arthritis and Metabolic Diseases, NIH, Bethesda, Md., 1961-67; rsch. fellow in med. genetics U. Wash., 1963-64; assoc. prof. pediat. and biochemistry U. Calif., San Francisco, 1967-72, prof., 1972—2005, prof. emeritus, 2005—, chief divsn. med. genetics. dept. pediat. San Francisco, 1967—2007, co-dir. program in human genetics, 1997—2004. Investigator Howard Hughes Med. Inst., 1976-81; mem. human embryology and devel. study sect. NIH, 1971-75; mem. mental retardation rsch. com. Nat. Inst. Child Health and Devel., 1979-83, chmn., 1981-83; mem. com. for study inborn errors of metabolism NRC, 1972-75; mem. sci. adv. bd. Nat. Down Syndrome Soc., 1981-99, chmn., 1984-99, mem. nat. adv. bd., 1999-2006, hon. bd. govs., 2007—, also bd. dirs.; mem. recombinant DNA adv. com. NIH, 1985-90, mem. human gene therapy subcom., 1987-91, chmn. residency rev. com. med. genetics, 1993-99; mem. sci. adv. bd. Buck Inst., 2002-, chmn., 2004-, trustee, 2004-; mem. sci. steering com., Pediatric Biobank, 2006-07; Stanley Wright Meml. lectr. Western Soc. Pediatric Rsch., 1986; William Potter lectr. Thomas Jefferson U., 1987; George H. Fetterman lectr. U. Pitts., 1989; faculty rsch. lectr. U. Calif., San Francisco, 1994; Mary Hulings Edens lectr. U. Tex. Med. Br., Galveston, 1996; Ida Cordelia Beam lectr. U. Iowa, 1998; Donald L. Thurston meml. lectr. Washington U., St. Louis, 1999, others. Author: The Consequences of Chromosome Imbalance: Principles, Mechanisms and Models, 1986; editor: Human Genetics, 1984-95, The Neurobiology of Down Syndrome, 1986, Oncology and Immunology of Down Syndrome, 1987, Am. Jour. Human Genetics, 1987-93, Molecular and Cytogenetic Studies of Non-disjunction, 1989, Molecular Genetics of Chromosome 21 and Down Syndrome, 1990, Morphogenesis of Down Syndrome, 1991, Down Syndrome and Alzheimer Disease, 1992, Phenotypic Mapping of Down Syndrome and other Aneuploid Conditions, 1993, Etiology and Pathogenesis of Down Syndrome, 1995, Inborn Errors of Development. The Molecular Basis of Clinical Disorders of Morphogenesis, 2004, 2nd edit., 2008; assoc. editor Rudolph's Textbook of Pediatrics, 18th edit., 1986, 20th edit., 1996; mem. editl. bd. Biology Reproduction, 1974-78, Cytogenetics and Cell Genetics, 1975-80; mem. editl. bd. Am. Jour. Med. Genetics, 1977-95, sr. editor, 1995-99, adv. editor, 2000—; mem. editl. bd. Devel. Genetics, 1983-85, Jour. Embryology and Exptl. Morphology, 1983-85, Human Gene Therapy, 1990-98, Human Mutation, 1992-99, Human Genetics, 1995-99, Down Syndrome Quar., 1996—2004, Trends in Genetics, 1997—, Cmty. Genetics, 1998-2007, Ann. Rev. of Human Genetics and Genomics, 1999-2004, Mechanisms of Aging and Devel., 2000—, Pub. health genetics, 2008-; contbr. numerous rsch. articles on human and med. genetics, devel. genetics and biochemistry to profl. publs. Served with USPHS, 1961-63. Recipient Henry A. Christian award, Harvard Med. Sch., 1959, Rsch. Career Devel. award, NIH, 1967—72, Nancy and Daniel Weisman Charitable Found. award, 1990, Lifetime Achievement award in genetic scis., March of Dimes Birth Defects Found., Col. Harland Sanders, 1995, 6th World Congress on Down Syndrome award, 1997, Disting. Rsch. award, The Arc of the U.S., 1998, Premio Internat. Phoenix-Anni Verdi Perle Rsch. Geneticha, Italian Soc. Human Genetics, 1999, Allan award, Am. Soc. Human Genetics, 2001; named to Hall of Fame, Central High Sch. of Phila., 2001. Fellow AAAS, Am. Acad. Arts and Scis.; mem. AMA, Am. Bd. Med. Genetics (bd. dir. 1988-93, v.p. 1989, pres. 1990-91), Genetics Soc. Am., Am. Fedn. Clin. Rsch., Am. Soc. Human Genetics (bd. dir. 1972-75, 87-93, 97-98, pres.-elect 1995, pres. 1996), Am. Soc. Biochemistry and Molecular Biology, Soc. Pediatric Rsch. (coun. 1972-75), Am. Coll. Med. Genetics (pres.-elect 2001-02, pres. 2003-05, past pres., 2005-07), Western Soc. Clin. Investigation, Western Soc. Pediatric Rsch., Am. Soc. Clin. Investigation, Am. Soc. Cell Biology, Soc. Devel. Biology, Am. Pediatric Soc., Western Assn. Physicians (coun. 1993-95), Assn. Am. Physicians, Soc. Inherited Metabolic Disorders, Inst. Medicine of NAS, Calif. Acad. Medicine (exec. com. 2002-, v.p. 2004-05, pres. 2006-07), Phi Beta Kappa, Alpha Omega Alpha. Jewish. Office: U Calif Dept Pediat Rock Hall RH584B 1550 4th St San Francisco CA 94143-2911 Home Phone: 415-435-1919; Office Phone: 415-476-2981.

EPSTEIN, DANIEL J., management consultant; Chmn., CEO Con Am Mgmt. Corp., San Diego, 1995—. Office: Con Am Mgmt Corp 3990 Ruffin Rd #100 San Diego CA 92123-1826

EPSTEIN, EDWARD LOUIS, lawyer; b. Walla Walla, Wash., Jan. 10, 1936; s. Louis and Marie (Barger) E.; m. Marilyn K. Young, Dec. 29, 1962; children: Lisa Marie, Rachel Ann. BA with great distinction, Stanford U., 1958; LLB magna cum laude, Harvard U., 1961. Bar: Oreg. 1962, U.S. Dist. Ct. Oreg. 1962, U.S. Ct. Appeals (9th cir.) 1963. Assoc. Stoel Rives LLP, Portland, Oreg., 1962-67, ptnr., 1967—2008. Past sec., bd. dirs. Portland Hosp. Facilities Authority; trustee Good Samaritan Hosp. and Med. Ctr., Portland, 1972-78, pres., 1978; past trustee Morrison Ctr. for Youth and Family Svcs., Oreg. Assn. Hosps. Found.; bd. dirs. Banner Corp., Banner Bank, Neurocom Internat. Inc, Lib. Found. Mem. ABA, Am. Bar Found., Am. Health Lawyers Assn., Oreg. Bar Assn., Multnomah County Bar Assn., Multnomah Athletic Club, Univ. Club, Harvard Law Rev., Phi Beta Kappa. Office: Stoel Rives LLP 900 SW 5th Ave Ste 2600 Portland OR 97204-1268 Home Phone: 503-223-1790; Office Phone: 503-294-9245. Business E-Mail: elepstein@stoel.com.

EPSTEIN, EMANUEL, plant physiologist; b. Duisburg, Germany, Nov. 5, 1916; came to U.S., 1938, naturalized, 1946; s. Harry and Bertha (Lowe) E.; m. Hazel L. Leask, Nov. 26, 1943; children: Jared H. (dec.), Jonathan H. BS, U. Calif., Davis, 1940, MS, 1941; PhD, U. Calif., Berkeley, 1950. Plant physiologist Dept. Agr., Beltsville, Md., 1950-58; lectr., assoc. plant physiologist U. Calif.-Davis, 1958-65, prof. plant nutrition, plant physiologist, 1965-87, faculty rsch. lectr., 1980, prof. botany, 1974-87, prof. and plant physiologist emeritus (active), 1987—. Cons. in field. Author: Mineral Nutrition of Plants: Principles and Perspectives, 1972, 2d edit. (with A.J. Bloom), 2005; mem. editl. bd. Plant Physiology, 1962-71, 76-92, CRC Handbook Series in Nutrition and Food, 1975-84, The Biosaline Concept: An Approach to the Utilization of Underexploited Resources, 1978, Saline Agriculture: Salt-Tolerant Plants for Developing Countries, 1990, Plant Sci., 1981-89, Advances in Plant Nutrition, 1981-88; contbr. articles to profl. jours. With US Army, 1943—46. Recipient Gold medal Pisa (Italy) U., 1962; Guggenheim fellow, 1958; Fulbright sr. research scholar, 1965-66, 74-75, award of honor, Am. Soc. Agronomy Calif. Chapter, 2002. Fellow AAAS (pres. Pacific divsn. 1990, Fifty-Yr. Life mem. award 1999); mem. Nat. Acad. Scis., Am. Soc. Plant Biologists (Charles Reid Barnes Hon. Life Membership award 1986), Am. Soc. Agronomy Calif. (award of honor, 2002), Common Cause, Save-the-Redwoods League, U. Calif. Davis Club, Calif. Aggie Alumni Assn. (Alumni citation for Excellence, 1999), Nature Conservancy, Sigma Xi. Achievements include rsch. in ion transport in plants, mineral nutrition and salt rels. of plants, salt tolerant crops, and silicon in plant biology. Office: UC Soils & Biogeochemistry-Land Air & Water Resources One Shields Ave Davis CA 95616-8627 Home Phone: 530-753-2620; Office Phone: 530-752-0197. Business E-Mail: eqepstein@ucdavis.edu.

EPSTEIN, JEFFREY EMANUEL, computer software company executive; b. Mineola, NY, Aug. 17, 1956; s. Morris and Joan Ruth (Scherl) E.; m. Sue Ellen Hoover, May 9, 1982; children: Sam, Eric, Alison. BA summa cum laude, Yale Coll., 1977; MBA, Stanford U., 1979. Cons. Boston Consulting Group, Menlo Park, Calif., 1979-82; dir. bus. devel. Washington Post Co., Washington, 1982-84; v.p. First Boston Corp., NYC, 1984-88; CFO King World Prodns., Inc., NYC, 1988—94; exec. v.p. CUC, 1995—96; CFO DoubleClick, 1998—2001, The Nielsen Co. US Inc., 2002—04; pres., CEO Revonet, Inc., 2004—05; CFO Valassis Direct Mail, Inc., 2005—07; exec. v.p., CFO Oberon Media, 2007—08, Oracle Corp., Redwood Shores, Calif., 2008—. Arjay Miller scholar, Stanford U., 1979. Mem. Phi Beta Kappa. Office: Oracle Corp 500 Oracle Pkwy Redwood Shores CA 94065

EPSTEIN, JOHN HOWARD, dermatologist; b. San Francisco, Dec. 29, 1926; s. Norman Neman and Gertrude (Hirsch) E.; m. Alice Thompson, Nov. 1953; children: Norman H., Janice A., Beverly A. BA, U. Calif., Berkeley, 1949, MD, 1952; MS, U. Minn., 1956. Diplomate Am. Bd. Dermatology (dir. 1974-84, pres. 1981-82). Intern Stanford U. Med. Ctr., 1952-53; resident in dermatology Mayo Clinic, Rochester, Minn., 1953-56; practice medicine specializing in dermatology San Francisco, 1956—; chief dermatology Mt. Zion Hosp., 1970-80. Clin. prof. U. Calif. Med. Sch., San Francisco, 1972—; cons. Letterman Army Med. Center, U.S. Naval Hosp., San Diego. Chief editor Archives of Dermatology, 1973-78; asst. editor Jour. Am. Acad. Dermatology, 1978-88; contbr. over 275 articles to profl. jours. With USNR, 1944-46. Recipient Finsen medal, Internat. Soc. Photobiology, 2004. Fellow ACP; mem. Am. Acad. Dermatology (pres. 1981-82, Silver award for exhibit 1962, Gold award 1969), Soc. Investigative Dermatology (v.p. 1979-80), Am. Dermatol. Assn. (bd. dirs. 1983-88, pres. 1990-91), N.Am. Dermatology Soc., Pacific Dermatol. Assn. (pres. 1985-86), Brit. Dermatol. Soc., Danish Dermatol. Soc., Polish Dermatol. Soc., San Francisco Dermatol. Soc. (pres. 1963-64), Am. Soc. Photobiology (councilor 1983-86), Academia Mexicana and Dermatologia (hon.), European Acad. Dermatology and Venerology (hon.), La Societe Francaise de Dermatologie & de Syphiligraphie, Spanish Dermatol. Soc. Office: 450 Sutter St Rm 1306 San Francisco CA 94108-4002 Office Phone: 415-781-4083.

EPSTEIN, MARSHA ANN, public health service officer, physician; b. Chgo., Feb. 4, 1945; 1 child, Lee Rashad Mahmood. BA, Reed Coll., 1965; MD, U. Calif., San Francisco, 1969; MPH, U. Calif., Berkeley, 1971. Diplomate Am. Bd. Preventive Medicine. Intern French Hosp., San Francisco, 1969-70; resident in preventive medicine Sch. Pub. Health, U. Calif., Berkeley, 1971-73; fellow in family planning dept. ob-gyn. UCLA, 1973-74; med. dir. Herself Health Clinic, 1974-79; pvt. adult gen. practitioner, 1978-82; dist. health officer LA County Pub. Health, 1982—2001, area med. dir., 2001—07, chief special projects, chronic disease and injury prevention, 2007—. Part-time physician U. Calif. Student Health, Berkeley, 1970—73; co-med. dir. Monsenior Oscar Romero Free Clinic, LA, 1992—93. Mem.: APHA, Calif. Acad. Preventive Medicine, So. Calif. Pub. Health Assn., LA-Am. Med. Women's Assn., Am. Med. Women's Assn., Am. Coll. Physician Execs. Democrat. Jewish. Avocations: dance, native plants, meditation. Office: South Tower 14 Fl 695 S Vermont Ave Los Angeles CA 90005 Home Phone: 310-390-6430. Business E-Mail: mepstein@ph.lacounty.gov.

ERASMUS, CHARLES JOHN, anthropologist, educator; b. Pitts., Sept. 23, 1921; s. Percy Thomas and Alice E.; m. Helen Marjorie O'Brien, Feb. 18, 1943; children: Thomas Glen, Gwendolyn. BA, UCLA, 1942; MA, U. Calif., Berkeley, 1950, PhD, 1955. Field ethnologist Smithsonian Instn., Colombia, 1950-52; applied anthropologist AID, Western S.Am., 1952-54; research assoc. culture exchange project U. Ill., Champaign-Urbana, 1955-59; vis. prof. anthropology Yale U., New Haven, 1959-60; assoc. prof. U. N.C., Chapel Hill, 1960-62, U. Calif., Santa Barbara, 1962-64, prof., 1964-87, prof. emeritus, 1987—, chmn. dept. anthropology, 1964-68. Author: Man Takes Control: Cultural Development and American Aid, 1961, In Search of the Common Good: Utopian Experiments Past and Future, 1977, Contemporary Change in Traditional Communities of Mexico and Peru, 1978. Served with USN, 1942-45. Home: 6190 Barrington Dr Santa Barbara CA 93117-1758 Office: U Calif Dept Anthropology Santa Barbara CA 93106

ERB, RICHARD A., state legislator, real estate company executive; b. Chariton, Iowa, Dec. 26, 1928; married. BA in Bus. Mgmt., Eckerd Coll. Mem. Wyo. Ho. Reps., Cheyenne, 1992-96, Wyo. Senate, Dist. 24, Cheyenne, 1996—; mem. minerals, bus. and econ. devel. com. Wyo. Senate, Cheyenne, mem. corps., elections and polit. subdivisions com. Mem. Campbell County Airport Bd. Mem. Am. Legion, Rotary. Republican. Home: 1100 Warren Ave Gillette WY 82716-4804 Office: Wyo Senate State Capitol Cheyenne WY 82002-0001

ERGEN, CHARLES W. (CHARLIE ERGEN), communications executive; b. Oak Ridge, Tenn., Mar. 1, 1953; m. Cantey Ergen; 5 children. BS in Bus. and Acctg., U. Tenn., Knoxville; MBA, Wake Forest U. Fin. analyst Frito-Lay; profl. blackjack player Las Vegas, Nev.; founder, chmn., CEO Echostar Communications Corp. (DISH Network), Littleton, Colo., 1980—. Co-founder Satellite Broadcasting Comm. Assoc. Recipient Star award, Home Satellite TV Assn., 1988; named Rocky Mountain region Master Entrepreneur of Yr., INC. Mag., 1991, Bus. Person of Yr., Rocky Mountain News, 1996, 2001, Space Industry Bus. Man of Yr., Aviation Week Mag., 2000, CEO of Yr., Frost & Sullivan, 2001; named one of Forbes Richest Americans, 1999—, World's Richest People, Forbes Mag., 2000—. Achievements include spearheading the movement for the Satellite Home Viewer Improvement Act in 1999 which gave American consumers the right to watch local TV channels via satellite; testifying before Congress regarding other video competition issues on several occasions. Avocations: mountain climbing, poker, basketball. Office: Echostar Comms 5701 S Santa Fe Littleton CO 80120

ERICHSEN, PETER CHRISTIAN, b. Kentfield, Calif., Aug. 4, 1956; s. Hans Skabo and Ruth Elsie (Henderson) E. AB magna cum laude, Harvard U., 1978, JD cum laude, 1981. Bar: Mass. 1981, Pa. 2000. Assoc. Ropes & Gray, Boston, 1981-90, ptnr., 1990-93, 2007—; dep. asst. atty. gen. U.S. Dept. Justice, Washington, 1993-96; assoc. counsel to Pres. The White House, 1996-97; v.p., gen. counsel U. Pa., U. Pa. Health Sys., 1997—2001; v.p., gen. counsel, sec. J. Paul Getty Trust, 2001—07. Bd. govs. Phila. Stock Exch., 1999—; bd. dirs. Music Ctr. Performing Arts Ctr., LA, 2004-07; mem. exec. com. LA Appleseed, Appleseed Found., Washington, DC, 2003-06, Recording for Blind and Dyslexic, Inc., NJ, 2005-; trustee Samuel Courtauld Trust, London, 2003-07; dir. Claymore Western Asset Treas. Inflation Protected Securities Funds, 2004-07. Vestryman Trinity Ch., Boston, 1987-91, 92-93; founding dir. Trinity Hospice, Boston, 1988-93. Office Phone: 617-951-7098. E-mail: peter.erichsen@ropesgray.com.

ERICKSEN, JERALD LAVERNE, retired science engineering educator; b. Portland, Oreg., Dec. 20, 1924; s. Adolph and Ethel Rebecca (Correy) E.; m. Marion Ella Pook, Feb. 24, 1946; children: Lynn Christine, Randolph Peder. BS, U. Wash., 1947; MA, Oreg. State Coll., 1949; PhD, Ind. U., 1951; DSc (hon.), Nat. U. Ireland, 1984, Heriot-Watt U., 1988. Mathematician, solid state physicist U.S. Naval Rsch. Lab., 1951-57; faculty Johns Hopkins U., 1957-83, prof. theoretical mechanics, 1960-83; prof. mechanics and math. U. Minn., Mpls., 1983-90; cons. Florence, Oreg., 1990—. Served with USNR, 1943-46. Recipient Bingham medal, 1968, Timoshenko medal, 1979, Engring. Sci. medal, 1987. Mem. Internat. Liquid Crystal Soc. (hon.), NAE, Soc. Rheology (Panetti-Ferrari prize and Gold medal 2003), Soc. Natural Philosophy, Soc. Interaction Mechanics and Math., Soc. Engring. Sci., Royal Irish Acad. (hon.). Home: 5378 Buckskin Bob Dr Florence OR 97439-8320

ERICKSON, ARTHUR CHARLES, architect; b. Vancouver, BC, Can., June 14, 1924; s. Oscar and Myrtle (Chatterson) Erickson. Student, U. BC, Vancouver, 1942-44, LittD (hon.), 1985; BArch, McGill U., Montreal, Que., Can., 1950, DEng (hon.), 1971; LLD (hon.), Simon Fraser U., Vancouver, 1973, U. Man., Winnipeg, Can., 1978, Lethbridge U., 1981; LittD (hon.), Frank Lloyd Wright Sch. Arch., 2001, MArch (hon.), 2001. Asst. prof. U. Oreg., Eugene, 1955-56; assoc. prof. U. B.C., 1956-63; ptnr. Erickson-Massey Architects, Vancouver, 1963-72; prin. Arthur Erickson Architects, Vancouver, 1972-91, Toronto, Ont., Can., 1981-91, Los Angeles, 1981-91, Arthur Erickson Archtl. Corp., Vancouver, 1991—. Prin. works include, Simon Fraser U., Lethbridge U. Alta., Bloedel Bldg., Can. Pavilion Expo '70, Osaka (1st prize nat. competition, Archtl. Inst. Japan award for best pavillion), Robson Sq./Law Cts. (honor award), Mus. Anthropology (honor award), Eppich Residence (honor award), Habitat Pavillion (honor award), Sikh Temple (award of merit), Champlain Heights Cmty. Sch. (award of merit), San Diego Conv. Ctr., Calif. Plz., LA, Fresno City Hall, Can. Embassy, Washington, Roy Thompson Hall, Toronto, Bank of Can., Ottawa, Koerner Libr., Liu Internat. Conf. Ctr., U. BC, Scotibank Dance Ctr., Internat. Glass Mus., Tacoma, 2003. Mem. com. urban devel. Coun. of Can.,

1971; bd. dirs. Can. Conf. Arts, 1972; mem. design adv. coun. Portland Devel. Commn., Can. Coun. Urban Rsch.; trustee Inst. Rsch. Pub. Policy; mem. internat. coun. Mus. Modern Art, NYC, 1982—86. Capt. Can. Intelligence Corps., 1945—46. Decorated officer Order of Can., companion; recipient Molson prize, Can. Coun. Arts, 1967, Triangle award, Nat. Soc. Interior Design, Royal Bank Can. award, 1971, Gold medal, Tau Sigma Delta, 1973, Residential Design award, Can. Housing Coun., 1975, August Perret award, Internat. Union Archs. Congress, 1975, Pres. award Excellence, Am. Soc. Landscape Archs., 1979, Chgo. Architecture award, 1984, Gold medal, French Acad. Architecture, 1984. Fellow: AIA (Pan Pacific citation Hawaiian chpt. 1963, Gold medal 1986), Royal Archtl. Inst. Can. (award 1980, Gold medal 1984), Royal Inst. Scottish Archs. (hon.), Royal Inst. Brit. Archs. (hon.), Frank Lloyd Wright Found. (hon.); mem.: Royal Can. Acad. Arts (academician), ARCAB Wash. State Archtl. Assn., Coll. d'arquitectos de España (hon.), Coll. d'architectos de Mex. (hon.), Archtl. Inst. BC, S.F.U. Faculty Club. Office: Arthur Erickson Archtl Corp 303-375 W 5th Ave Vancouver BC Canada V5Y 1J6 Office Phone: 604-737-6091. E-mail: arthurerickson@lynx.bc.ca, arthurerickson@telut.net.

ERICKSON, DENNIS, college football coach, former professional football coach; b. Everett, Wash., Mar. 24, 1947; m. Marilyn Erickson; children: Bryce, Ryan. BS Phys. Educ., Montana State U. Grad. asst. coach Montana State U. Bobcats, 1969, backfield coach, 1971-73; grad. asst. coach Washington State U. Cougars, 1970; head football coach Billings Central H.S., Billings, Mont., 1970; offensive coord., head football coach U. Idaho Vandals, 1974-75, 1982-85; offensive coord. Fresno State U. Bulldogs, 1976-78, San Jose State U. Spartans, 1979-81; head football coach U. Wyoming Cowboys, 1986, Washington State U. Cougars, 1987-88, U. Miami Hurricanes, 1989-95, Seattle Seahawks, 1995-98, Oreg. State U. Beavers, 1999—2003, S.F. 49ers, 2003—04, U. Idaho Vandals, 2006, Ariz State U. Sun Devils, Tempe, 2007—. won Nat. Championship, 1989, 1991. Office: Ariz State U 1200 S Forest Ave Tempe AZ 85281

ERICKSON, LEIF B., federal judge; b. 1942; Law clk. Mont. Supreme Ct., 1967-68, pub. defender, 1969-70, dep. county atty., 1970-75, deputy city atty., 1979-85, judge 11th jud. dist., 1985-91; apptd. magistrate judge U.S. Dist. Ct. Mont., 1992. Office: Russell Smith Federal Bldg 201 E Broadway St Missoula MT 59802-4506 Fax: 406-542-7292. E-mail: leiferickson@9dc.mt.missoula.

ERICKSON, WILLIAM HURT, retired state supreme court justice; b. Denver, May 11, 1924; s. Arthur Xavier and Virginia (Hurt) E.; m. Doris Rogers, Dec. 24, 1953; children: Barbara Ann, Virginia Lee, Stephen Arthur, William Taylor. Degree in petroleum engring., Colo. Sch. Mines, 1947; student, U. Mich., 1949; LLB, U. Va., 1950; PhD in Engring. (hon.), Colo. Sch. of Mines, 2002. Bar: Colo. 1951. Pvt. practice, Denver; state supreme ct. justice Colo. Supreme Ct., 1971-96, state supreme ct. chief justice, 1983-86; faculty NYU Appellate Judges Sch., 1972-85. Mem. exec. Commn. on Accreditation of Law Enforcement Agys., 1980-83; chmn. Pres.'s Nat. Commn. for Rev. of Fed. and State Laws Relating to Wiretapping and Electronic Surveillance, 1976. Chmn. Erickson Commn., 1997, Limitations on use Deadly Force by Police; chmn. gov.'s Columbine Rev. Commn., 1999-2001. With USAAF, 1943. Recipient Disting. Achievement medal Colo. Sch. Mines, 1990. Fellow Internat. Acad. Trial Lawyers (former sec.), Am. Coll. Trial Lawyers (state chmn. 1970), Am. Bar Found. (chmn. 1985), Internat. Soc. Barristers (pres. 1971); mem. ABA, (bd. govs. 1975-79, former chmn. com. on standards criminal justice, former chmn. coun. criminal law sect., former chmn. com. to implement standards criminal justice, mem. long-range planning com., action com. to reduce ct. cost and delay), Colo. Bar Assn. (award of merit 1989), Denver Bar Assn. (past pres., trustee), Am. Law Inst. (coun. 1973—), Practising Law Inst. (nat. adv. coun., bd. govs. Colo.), Freedoms Found. at Valley Forge (nat. coun. trustees, 1986—), Order of Coif, Scribes (pres. 1978). Home: 6391 S Zenobia Ct Littleton CO 80123-6740 Personal E-mail: bnderickson@yahoo.com.

ERICSON, BRUCE ALAN, lawyer; b. Buffalo, Feb. 28, 1952; s. Carl H. and Jean (Herman) E.; m. Elizabeth Whitney Burton, Feb. 6, 1988; children: John Cotton, Whitney Burton. AB, U. Pa., 1974; JD, Harvard U., 1977. Bar: Calif. 1977, U.S. Dist. Ct. (no. dist.) Calif, 1977, U.S. Dist. Ct. (ea. dist. and so. dist.) Calif. 1988, U.S. Dist. Ct. Ariz. 1992, U.S. Ct. Appeals (9th cir.) 1981, U.S. Ct. Appeals (11th cir.), 1991, U.S. Ct. Appeals (D.C. cir.) 1994, U.S. Supreme Ct. 1982. Assoc. Pillsbury, Madison & Sutro, San Francisco, 1977-84, ptnr., 1985—2001, Pillsbury Winthrop LLP, San Francisco, 2001—05; ptnr., chmn. Securities Litigation practice, head litig. sect. Pillsbury Winthrop Shaw Pittman, San Francisco, 2005—. Judge pro tem. San Francisco Mcpl. Ct., 1984—. Contbr. articles to profl. jours. Named No. Calif. Super Lawyer, San Francisco mag., 2004, 2006. Mem. ABA, San Francisco Bar Assn., Phi Beta Kappa. Clubs: Olympic (San Francisco). Republican. Avocation: skiing. Office: Pillsbury Winthrop Shaw Pittman 50 Fremont St San Francisco CA 94105 Office Phone: 415-983-1560. Office Fax: 415-983-1200. Business E-Mail: bruce.ericson@pillsburylaw.com.

ERISMAN, FRANK, lawyer; b. Lackawanna, NY, Mar. 6, 1943; s. Henry S. and Mary Lorraine (Conlin) E.; m. Judith A. Milano, Feb. 18, 1984; children: Porter, Melanie, Lindsay, Jacob. Degree in metall. engring., Colo. Sch. Mines, 1965; JD, U. Denver, 1968. Bar: Colo., 1968. Law clk. U.S. Ct. Appeals (5th cir.), Jacksonville, Fla., 1968-69; ptnr. Holme Roberts & Owen, L.L.P., Denver, 1969—. Mem. editorial bd. American Law of Mining, 2d edit., 1984; chmn. editorial bd. (periodical) The Public Land Resources Law Digest, 1985-88. Pres. bd. trustees Colo. Sch. Mines, Golden, 1996—; chmn. Colo. Sch. Mines Ann. Fund, 1990-91, Colo. Sch. Mines Pres.'s Coun., 1991-93; trustee Western Mus. of Mining & Industry, Colorado Springs, 1991-93. Recipient Disting. Achievement medal Colo. Sch. Mines, 1993. Mem. ABA (chmn. sect. of natural resources, energy and environ. law 1993-94), Colo. Bar Assn. (chmn. mineral law sect. 1991-92), Colo. Mining Assn. (bd. dirs. 1990-92), Rocky Mountain Mineral Law Found. (trustee, exec. bd. dirs. 1986-93, pres. 1997-98), Mining and Metallurgical Soc. Am. Avocations: gardening, hiking, fishing. Office: Holme Roberts & Owen LLP 1700 Lincoln St Ste 4100 Denver CO 80203-4541

ERNST, DAVID A., lawyer; b. Portland, Oreg., Oct. 2, 1960; BS, Oreg. State U., 1982; JD, Lewis & Clark Coll., 1985. Bar: Oreg. 1985, U.S. Dist. Ct. Oreg. 1985, Wash. 1990, U.S. Dist. Ct. Wash. (we. dist.). Shareholder, bd.dirs. Bullivant Houser Bailey PC, Portland, Oreg., 1997—2002, 2006—, shareholder in charge, 2002—05, pres., 2006—, chmn. food & beverage industry group. Pres. Fed. Bar Assn. (Oreg. Chpt.), 1996—97; chmn. 9th Cir. Lawyer Representatives, 2001; pres. alumni bd. Lewis and Clark Law Sch., 2001—02; program chmn. First Ann. DRI Conf. on Food Liability, St. Louis, 2005; bd. dirs. Multnomah Bar Found., Northwest Bus. Culture and Arts; bd. visitors Lewis and Clark Law Sch.; spkr. in field. Office: Bullivant Houser Bailey PC 300 Pioneer Tower 888 SW Fifth Ave Portland OR 97204-2089 Office Phone: 503-499-4634. Office Fax: 503-295-0915. E-mail: dave.ernst@bullivant.com.

ERNST, DONALD WILLIAM, producer; b. LA, Jan. 25, 1934; s. William McKinley and Dorothy Elizabeth (Hast) E.; m. Janice Elaine Barber, Apr. 16, 1966; children: Stacey Dawn, Darci Lynn. BS in Civil Engring., UCLA, 1956. Apprentice editor Telemat, LA, 1956-61; asst. editor Columbia Pictures, LA, 1961-62, Metro-Goldwyn-Mayer, Culver City, Calif., 1962-64; film editor CBS, Studio City, Calif., 1964-72, Bakshi Prodns., LA, 1972-79; sound editor Echo Films, LA, 1979-82, Horta Editorial, Burbank, Calif., 1982-88; film editor Walt Disney Pictures, Glendale, Calif., 1988-89, prodn. exec., 1989—. Prodr.: (animated film) Roller Coaster Rabbit, 1990, Spirited Away, 2002; co-prodr.: (animated film) Aladdin, 1992; exec. prodr.: (live action film) Homeward Bound: The Incredible Journey, 1993; producer Fantasia, 2000. Recipient Emmy awards TV Acad. Arts and Scis., 1977, 82. Mem. Am. Cinema Editors, Acad. Motion Picture Arts and Scis. Home: 25686 Moore Ln Stevenson Ranch CA 91381-1404

ERNST, WALLACE GARY, geology educator, dean; b. St. Louis, Dec. 14, 1931; BA, Carleton Coll., 1953; MS, U. Minn., 1955; PhD, Johns Hopkins U., 1959. Geologist U.S. Geol. Survey, Washington, 1955-56; fellow (Geophys. Lab.), Washington, 1956-59; mem. faculty UCLA, 1960-89, prof. geology and geophysics, 1968-89, chmn. geology dept. (now earth and space scis. dept.), 1970-74, 78-82, dir. Inst. Geophysics and Planetary Physics, 1987-89; dean Stanford Sch. of Earth Scis., 1989-94; prof. geol. and environ. scis. Stanford (Calif.) U., 1989—, Benjamin M. Page prof., 1999—, dean Sch. of Earth Scis., 1989-94. Author: Amphiboles, 1968, Earth Materials, 1969, Metamorphism and Plate Tectonic Regimes, 1975, Subduction Zone Metamorphism, 1975, Petrologic Phase Equilibria, 1976, The Geotectonic Development of California, 1981, The Environment of the Deep Sea, 1982, Energy for Ourselves and Our Posterity, 1985, Cenozoic Basin Development of Coastal California, 1987, Metamorphic and Crustal Evolution of the Western Cordillera, 1988, The Dynamic Planet, 1990, Integrated Earth and Environmental Evolution of the Southwestern United States, 1998, Planetary Petrology and Geochemistry, 1999; editor: Earth Systems: Processes and Issues, 2000, (with R.G. Coleman) Tectonic Studies of Asia and the Pacific Rim--A Tribute to Benjamin M. Page, 2000, (with J.G. Liou) Ultrahigh-Pressure Metamorphism and Geodynamics in Collision-Type Orogenic Belts, 2000, Frontiers in Geochemistry, 2002, (with S.L. Klemperer) The Lithosphere of Western North America, 2004, Serpentite and Serpentinites, 2004. Trustee Carnegie Instn. of Washington, 1990—. Recipient Miyashiro medal Geol. Soc. Japan, 1998, Penrose medal, Geol. Soc. Am., 2004, Roebling medal, Mineralogical Soc. Am., 2006. Mem. NAS (chmn. geology sect. 1979-82, chair class I 2000—), AAAS, Am. Philos. Soc., Am. Geophys. Union, Am. Geol. Inst., Geol. Soc. Am. (pres. 1985-86), Am. Acad. Arts and Sci., Geochem. Soc., Mineral Soc. Am. (recipient award 1969, pres. 1979-80). Office: Stanford U Dept Earth & Environ Scis Green Earth Sci #209 Palo Alto CA 94303-1823

ERSKINE, JOHN MORSE, surgeon; b. San Francisco, Sept. 10, 1920; s. Morse and Dorothy (Ward) E. BS, Harvard U., 1942, MD, 1945. Diplomate Am. Bd. Surgery. Surg. intern U. Calif. Hosp., San Francisco, 1945-46; surg. researcher Mass. Gen. Hosp., Boston, 1948; resident in surgery Peter Bent Brigham Hosp., Boston, 1948-53; George Gorham Peters fellow St. Mary's Hosp., London, 1952; pvt. practice in medicine specializing in surgery San Francisco, 1954-98; asst. clin. prof. Stanford Med. Sch., San Francisco, 1956-59; asst., assoc. clin. prof. U. Calif. Med. Sch., San Francisco, 1959—. Surg. cons. San Francisco Vets. Hosp., 1959-73. Contbr. articles to profl. jours., chpts. to books. Founder No. Calif. Artery Bank, 1954-58, Irwin Meml. Blood Bank, San Francisco, commr., pres., 1969-74; bd. dirs. People for Open Space-Greenbelt Alliance, 1984-98, adv. coun., 1998—; chmn. adv. coun. Dorothy Erskine Open Space Fund. Capt. with U.S. Army, 1946-48. Fellow ACS; mem. San Francisco Med. Soc. (bd. dirs. 1968-72), San Francisco Surg. Soc. (v.p. 1984), Pacific Coast Surg. Assn., Am. Cancer Soc. (bd. dirs. San Francisco br. 1965-75), Calif. Med. Assn., Olympic Club, Sierra Club. Democrat. Unitarian Universalist. Avocations: mountains, tree farming, gardening, walking, reading, music. Office: 233 Chestnut St San Francisco CA 94133-2452 Office Phone: 415-781-4847. Personal E-mail: john.m.erskine@gmail.com.

ERWIN, DONALD CARROLL, plant pathology educator; b. Concord, Nebr., Nov. 24, 1920; s. Robert James and Carol Erwin; m. Veora Marie Endres, Aug. 15, 1948; children: Daniel Erwin, Myriam Erwin Casey. Student, Wayne State Coll., Nebr., 1938-39; BSc, U. Nebr., 1949, MA, 1950; PhD, U. Calif.-Davis, 1953. Jr. plant pathologist U. Calif., Riverside, 1953-54, asst. plant pathologist, 1954-60, assoc. plant pathologist, 1960-66, prof. plant pathology, 1966—, emeritus prof., 1991. Sr. author: Phytophthora Diseases Worldwide, 1996; editor: Phytophthora: Its Biology, Taxonomy, Ecology and Pathology, 1983; contbr. articles to profl. jours. With U.S. Army, 1942-46; ETO. Nathan Gold fellow, 1949, Guggenheim fellow, 1959 Mem.: Am. Phytopathol. Soc. (fellow), Sigma Xi.

ERWIN, JOAN LENORE, artist, educator; b. Berkeley, Calif., Feb. 12, 1932; d. Ralph Albert and Dorothy Christine (Wuhrman) Potter; m. Byron W. Crider, Jan. 28, 1956 (div. May 1975); children: Susan Lynne Crider Adams, Gayle Leann Crider; m. Joseph G. Erwin Jr., May 28, 1976; children: Terry, Ray, Steve, Tim. BS, U. So. Calif., 1954; MS in Sch. Adminstrn., Pepperdine U., 1975. Cert. tchr., Calif.; registered occupational therapist, Calif. Occupational therapist Calif. State Hosp., Camarillo, 1955-56, Harlan Shoemaker Sch., San Pedro, Calif., 1956-57; tchr. Norwalk (Calif.) Sch. Dist., 1957-59, Tustin (Calif.) Sch. Dist., 1966-68, Garden Grove (Calif.) Sch. Dist., 1968-92; freelance artist Phelan, Calif., 1976—; comml. artist Morningstar Creations, Fullerton, Calif., 1982-92; substitute tchr. Snowline Sch. Dist., Phelan, Calif., 1994—2007; owner, artist Plumfrog Creations, Phelan, 2000—03. Artist Y.U.G.O., Los Alamitos, 1977-87; organizer 34th Annual Open Internat. Exbhn. Art, San Bernardino County Mus., 1999; resident artist High Desert Ctr. for the Arts, Victorville, 2000-2004; pvt. tchr. art, tutor, 1994—. One-woman shows include Victorville C. of C., 2004, Redlands Art Gallery, 2005, exhibited in group shows at San Bernardino County Mus., Redlands, Calif., Riverside Art Mus., Wildlife Artist Assn., American West Art Show, Norco, Calif., 2004—06 (premiere artist, 2004, 2005, 1st Pl. Profl. Divsn. Watercolor, 2007); pet portrait artist, U.S. and Eng., 1978—85, author, artist Biblical coloring books, 1985—90. Bd. dirs. San Bernardino County Mus., Fine Arts Inst.; juror county fair San Bernardino, Calif., 2003-07. Named Premier Artist, City of Norco Annual Show, 2005; grantee, Ford Found., 1957—58, Mentor Tchr. Program, 1986; Calif. Elks scholar, 1952—53. Republican. Baptist. Avocations: gardening, travel. Home: 10080 Monte Vista Rd Phelan CA 92371-8371 Office Phone: 760-868-5523. Personal E-mail: jaybird92371@yahoo.com.

ERWIN, ROBERT LESTER, biotechnology company executive; b. Tallahassee, Sept. 30, 1953; s. Walter Lambuth and Flora (Bailey) E.; m. Marti Nelson, Oct. 30, 1986. BS, La. State U., 1976, MS, 1979. Rsch. assoc. U. Ala., Birmingham, 1978-79; staff scientist Abbott Labs., North Chicago, Ill., 1979-80, Internat. Plant Rsch. Inst., San Carlos, Calif., 1980-81; v.p. rsch. and devel. Sungene Technologies, Inc., Palo Alto, Calif., 1981-87; pres., chief exec. officer Biosource Genetics Corp., Vacaville, Calif., 1987-91, chmn., chief exec. officer, 1991—. Advisor indsl. biotech. adv. com. Iowa State U., Ames, 1985-89. Mem. Am. Chem. Soc., N.Y. Acad. Scis., Calif. Tissue Culture Assn. (exec. com. 1987-90), Ind. Inst. (bd. dirs. 1992—). Achievements include patents for Glucan/Collagen Therapeutic Eye Shields; Melanin Biosynthesis; Neurotherapeutics. Office: Biosource Genetics 3333 Vaca Valley Pkwy Ste 1000 Vacaville CA 95688-9420

ESBER, EDWARD MICHAEL, JR., software company executive; b. Cleve., June 22, 1952; s. Edward Michael and Joanne Helen (Saah) E.; m. Margaret Renfrow, July 19, 1980; children: Dianne Michelle, Paul Andrew, Alexander Joseph. BS in Computer Engring., Case Western Res. U., Cleve., 1974; MSEE, Syracuse U., NYC, 1976; MBA, Harvard U., Cambridge, 1978. Assoc. engr. IBM, Poughkeepsie, N.Y., 1974-76; mktg. mgr. Tex. Instruments, Lubbock, Tex., 1978-79; v.p. mktg. Visi Corp., San Jose, Calif., 1979-83; exec. v.p. mktg. and sales Ashton-Tate, Torrance, Calif., 1984, pres., COO, 1984—, pres., chief exec. officer, 1984—, chmn., chief exec. officer, 1986-90; pres., COO Creative Labs, Milpitas, Calif., 1993-94; chmn., CEO Creative Insights, Sunnyvale, Calif., 1994-95; CEO, pres. Solo Point, Los Gatos, Calif., 1995—98, chmn., 1995—98; CEO The Esber Group, Los Gatos, 1990; chmn. Esber Group, Los Altos Hills, Calif., 1990—. Bd. dirs. Quantum Inc. Republican. Office: The Esber Group 13430 Country Way Los Altos CA 94022-2434

ESHLEMAN, VON RUSSEL, electrical engineering educator, aerospace scientist; b. Darke County, Ohio, Sept. 17, 1924; married; 4 children. BEE, George Washington U., 1949; MS, Stanford U., 1950, PhD in Elec. Engring., 1952. Rsch. assoc. Radio Propagation Lab. Stanford (Calif.) U., 1952-56, from instr. to prof. elec. engring., 1956-61, prof. elec. engring., co-dir. Ctr. Radar Astronomy, 1961-82, dir. Radioscience Lab., 1974-83. Cons. NAS, Nat. Bur. Stds., SRI Internat., Jet Propulsion Lab.; mem. Internat. Astronaut Congress, Internat. Astron. Union, Internat. Sci. Radio Union; dir. emeritus Watkins-Johnson Co.; mem. radio sci. teams for Viking, Pioneer, Mariner, Voyager, Galileo spacecraft studies of the planets. Fellow AAAS, IEEE, Am. Geophys. Union, Royal Astronomy Soc.; mem. NAE. Achievements include rsch. in radar astronomy, planetary exploration, ionospheric and plasma physics, radio wave propagation, astronautics. Office: Stanford U Radar Astronomy Ctr Packard EE Bldg 309 Stanford CA 94305-9515 E-mail: eshleman@stanford.edu.

ESHOO, ANNA GEORGES, United States Representative from California; b. New Britain, Conn., Dec. 13, 1942; d. Fred and Alice Alexandre Georges; children: Karen Elizabeth, Paul Frederick. AA in English, with honors, Canada Coll., 1975. With Alcoa, Inc., 1963—66, Arcata Nat. Corp., 1966—70; chair San Mateo Dem. Party, 1978—82; mem. San Mateo County Bd. Suprs., 1982—92, pres., 1986; mem. US Congress from 14th Calif. dist., 1992—, Dem. whip, 2003—; mem. energy and commerce com., intelligence com. Chief-of-staff Calif. assembly spkr. Leo McCarthy, 1981; mem. Nat. Com. Presdl. Nominations, 1981, Dem. Nat. Com., 1981—92; former mem. Bay Conservation & Devel. Commn.; co-chair Congl. E-911 Caucus, Dem. Task Force Health Care, Info. Tech. Round Table, Med. Tech. Caucus; vice chair Dem. Budget Grp.; mem. New Dem. Coalition, Nat. Women's Polit. Caucus, Dem. Congl. Campaign Com.; co-founder Internet Caucus. Co-founder San Mateo Women's Hall of Fame; chair bd. dirs. San Mateo County Gen. Hosp., 1984—92. Mem.: League Women Voters, League Conservation Voters, Dem. Activists for Women Now, Jr. League Palo Alto. Democrat. Roman Catholic. Office: US House Reps 205 Cannon House Office Bldg Washington DC 20515-0514

ESKRIDGE, GEORGE E., state legislator; m. Jenise Eskridge. Ret. exec. Bonneville Power; real estate agent; mem. Dist. 1 Idaho House of Reps., Boise, 2000—. Republican. Office: Dist Office PO Box 112 Dover ID 83825 also: Legis Services Office PO Box 83720 Boise ID 83720 Office Phone: 208-265-0123.*

ESLAMBOLCHI, HOSSEIN, communications executive; BSEE with highest honors, U. Calif., San Diego, MSEE, PhD in Elec. Engring. Joined AT&T Bell Labs., 1986—; v.p. network ops. and chief compliance officer AT&T Corp., v.p., AT&T Data and Network Svcs., 2000, sr. v.p., Packet and Optical Network Svcs., 2000—01, interim pres. Excite@Home Broadband Networks, 2001, pres., AT&T labs, 2001—, pres., AT&T Global Networking Tech. Svcs., chief tech. officer, 2001—, chief information officer, chief tech. officer, 2001—05; chmn., CEO Divvio Inc., Menlo Park, Calif., 2006—; chmn. 2020 Venture Partners, Menlo Park, Calif. Bd. dirs. Mindspeed Techs., Inc., 2003—, Nat. Action Coun. for Minorities in Engring., Wytec; mem. adv. bd., bd. dir. Nat. Alliance Bus.; serves as AT&T's Accessibility Champion President's Com. on Employment of People with Disabilities; bd. advisor The Catalyst Group, Inc., Pacific Broadband Comm., Conexant; bd. tech. advisors Compaq Computer Corp.; spkr. in field. Mem. editl. bd.: IEEE Jour. Network and Sys. Mgmt.; contbr. articles to profl. jours.; author: 2020 Vision: Business Transformation Through Technology. Mem. adv. coun. John Hopkins U. Whiting Sch. Engring. Recipient Thomas Alva Edison award, NJ R&D Coun., 1997; named Inventor of Yr., NJ Inventors Hall of Fame, 2001, Alumnus of Yr., U. Calif. San Diego, 2002; named one of Top Ten Innovators "Ten award", Exec. Coun. NY, 2003, 10 Internet Bus. Leaders, Cisco IQ Mag., 2003, Premiere 100 IT Leaders, Computerworld, 2004, Top 25 Most Influential CTOs of 2005, InfoWorld; AT&T Fellow, 1999. Achievements include patents in field; invention of FASTAR (Fast Automated Restoration System), which instantly reroutes service on AT&T's SONET rings, eliminating or minimizing service outages for customers. Office: Divvio Inc Ste 116 3705 Haven Ave Menlo Park CA 94025

ESPARZA, RICHARD R., museum director; b. Washington; m. Lauraine Brekke, Oct. 24, 1992; 4 children. BA in Philosophy, Calif. State U., Hayward, 1969; student, Met. State Coll., 1972-73. Asst.

curator Colo. State Mus. Colo. State Hist. Soc., Denver, 1972-73; exec. dir. South Park City Mus., Fairplay, Colo., 1973-74, Ventura (Calif.) County Mus. History and Art, 1974-80, San Diego Hist. Soc., 1980-87, Santa Barbara (Calif.) Hist. Museums, 1987-89, Nev. Mus. Art, Reno, 1991-95; dir. Riverside (Calif.) Mcpl. Mus., 1995—. Faculty U. Calif. Santa Barbara Inst. Local History, 1981, Small Mus. Adminstrn. UCLA ext., 1981, Williamsburg Seminar for Historic Adminstrn., 1984. Mem. Riverside Downtown Assn. (bd. dirs.), Mission Inn Found. (bd. dirs.), Calif. Assn. Museums (bd. dirs.). Office: Riverside Mcpl Mus 3580 Mission Inn Ave Riverside CA 92501-3307

ESPINOZA, EDGARD O'NIEL, forensic chemist; b. Concepcion, Chile, Dec. 24, 1953; came to U.S., 1975; s. Alberto and Rhoda (Cameron) E. BS in Med. Tech., Loma Linda U., Calif., 1978; M in Forensic Sci., U. Calif., Berkeley, 1984, D in Forensic Sci., 1988. Sr. forensic specialist Nat. Fish & Wildlife Forensic lab., Ashland, Oreg., 1988-90, chief criminalistics sect., 1990-95, lab. dep. dir. and forensic science branch chief. Presenter in field. Contbr. articles to Jour. for Sci., The Microscope, Assn. Firearms and Toolmark Examienrs Jour., Current Rsch. in the Pleistocene, Hepatology, Jour. Am. Inst. for Conservation, Jour. Lipid Rsch., Analytica Chemica Acta, Archeozoology. Recipient Best Conf. Paper, Forensic Sci. Soc., Australia, 1990. Achievements include research in the bear bile trade, trade items of zoological origen, computer program to estimate time of death of deer. Home: PO Box 3107 Ashland OR 97520-0304 Office: Nat Fish & Wildlife Svc Nat Forensic Lab 1490 E Main St Ashland OR 97520-1310 Office Phone: 541-482-4191. Office Fax: 541-482-4989. Business E-Mail: ed_espinoza@fws.gov.

ESPLIN, J. KIMO, chemicals executive; BS in Acctg., Brigham Young U., Provo, Utah; MBA, Northwestern U. V.p. Investment Banking Divsn. Bankers Trust Co.; v.p., treas. Huntsman Corp., Salt Lake City, 1994—96, sr. v.p. to exec. v.p., CFO, 1997—. Dir. Nutraceutical Internat. Corp., 2004—. Office: Huntsman Corp 500 Huntsman Way Salt Lake City UT 84108 Office Phone: 801-584-5700.

ESPOSITO, JOSEPH JOHN, publishing company executive; b. Englewood, NJ, June 19, 1951; s. Ross and Ann (Tamborinno) E.; m. Kim Ann Loretucci. AB, Rutgers U., 1973, MA, 1977, M in Philosophy, 1978. Editor Rutgers U. Press, New Brunswick, N.J., 1978-81, Dover Publs., NYC, 1981-82; v.p. spl. projects New Am. Libr., NYC, 1982-85; pres. reference div. Simon & Schuster, NYC, 1985-88; v.p. reference, pres. Fodor's Travel Publs. Random House Pub. Co., NYC, 1988-90; with Ency. Britannica, 1990-96; pres. Merriam-Webster sub., 1990; CEO Ency. Britannica, 1995-96; pres., CEO Tribal Voice, Scotts Valley, Calif., 1997—. Mem. mgmt. bd. MIT Press. Mem. ACLU, Dictionary Soc. N.Am.

ESQUIBEL, FLOYD AMARANTE, state legislator; b. Mora, NM, Aug. 27, 1938; son of Martin Edwardo Esquibel & Gertrude Garcia E; married 1964 to Jacqueline Vigil; children: Stephanie Terese, Daniel Martin & Jacqueline Noelle. Social work supr. State Wyo. Dept. Social Svc., 1975—83, hearing officer, 1983—86; compliance officer, supr., State of Wyo. Dept. Labor, 1989—95; Wyo. State Rep. District 44, 1997—2008; mem. Dist. 08 Wyo. State Senate, 2009—; atty. Social Worker of Year, State of Wyo. Dept. Social Svcs., 1977. Kiwanis; Nat Fedn; Latin Am. Assn. (pres., 1995-97). Democrat. Catholic. Mailing: 1222 W 31st St Cheyenne WY 82001 Office: 213 State Capitol Bldg Cheyenne WY 82002 Home Phone: 307-638-6529; Office Phone: 307-777-7881. Fax: 307-632-6518; Office Fax: 307-777-5466. Business E-Mail: fesquibel@wyoming.com.

ESQUIVEL, JOE G., food products executive; b. 1938; With Hanson Farms, Salinas, Calif., 1967-83; pres. Adobe Packing Co., Salinas, Calif., 1983—. Office: Adobe Packing Co PO Box 4940 Salinas CA 93912-4940

ESSER, LUKE, political organization administrator; b. Seattle, 1961; BS in Acctg., U. Wash., 1985, BS in Editl. Jour., 1985, JD, 1989. Sports writer, mem. Pro Football Writers Am.; law clk., bailiff King County Superior Ct.; spl. dep. prosecutor King County Juvenile Ct.; policy dir. King County Councilmember Rob McKenna; outreach dir. State Atty Gen.'s Office; rep. Wash. House Representatives, 1999—2002; senator Wash. State Senate, 2003—06, majority fl. leader, 2003—04, Rep. fl. leader, 2003—06; chmn. Wash. Rep. Party, 2007—. Co-vice chair capital budget com. Wash. House Representatives, 1999—2001; chmn. tech. and comm. com. Wash. State Senate, 2003; mem. Boeing 7E7 Five Corners Alliance, 2003, Regional Transp. Leadership Group, 2005. Recipient Guardian Small Bus. award, Nat. Fedn. Ind. Bus., 2000, 2004, Star award, Bellevue Cmty. Coll. Trustees, 2001, Housing Supporter award, Low-Income Housing Congress, 2001, Cert. Appreciation, Wash. Parks & Recreation Assn., 2004, Cert. Recognition, Soc. Profl. Engring. Employees in Aerospace, 2004, Cert. Thanks, Wash. State Coalition Against Domestic Violence, 2004, Gold medal award, Ind. Bus. Assn., 2004, Cornerstone award, Assn. Wash. Bus., 2005, Citation of Merit, Wash. Wildlife & Recreation Coalition, 2005; named Legislator of Yr., Wash. Tow Truck Assn., 2003, State Official of Yr., Nat. Assn. Home Builders, 2004, Legislator of Yr., Wash. Coun. Police & Sheriffs, 2006. Republican. Roman Catholic. Office: Wash Rep Party 16400 Southcenter Pkw Ste 200 Seattle WA 98188 Office Phone: 206-575-2900. Business E-Mail: luke@wsrp.org.

ESSEX, LAUREN S., women's health care company executive; BA in Psychology and Bus., U. Rochester; MS in Mgmt., Northwestern U. Various brand mgmt. positions Helene Curtis, 1984-94, br. mgr., 1991-94; v.p. personal care products, sales and customer svc. La Costa Products Internat., 1994-96; v.p. mktg. Cosmederm Tech.s, Inc., 1996-98; v.p. mktg. self-care products Women First HealthCare, Inc., San Diego, 1998—.

ESTABROOK, REED, artist, educator; b. Boston, May 31, 1944; s. F. Reed and Nancy (Vogel) E.; 1 son, August. BFA, R.I. Sch. Design, Providence, 1969; MFA, Art Inst. Chgo., 1971. Instr. U. Ill., 1971-74; asst. prof. U. No. Iowa, Cedar Falls, 1974-78, assoc. prof., 1978-83, head dept. photog. program, 1974-83; advisor visual arts Iowa Arts Coun., Des Moines, 1977-78, mem. art purchase com., 1977-78; chmn. photog. dept. Kansas City (Mo.) Art Inst., 1983—84, prof., coord. photography, 1984—92, 2005—; prof., coord. photo dept. San Jose (Calif.) State U., 1984—89. Bd. dirs. San Francisco Camera Work, 1987-90; Fulbright exch. tchr. Sheffield Poly., Eng., 1990-91. One-man shows include Sioux City Art Ctr., Iowa, 1981, Klein Gallery, Chgo., 1982, James Madison U., Harrisonburg, Va., 1983, Orange Coast Coll., Costa Mesa, Calif., 1983, Portland State U., Oreg., 1983, others, group shows, Isetan Mus. of Art, Tokyo, 1993, U. Colo., Boulder, 1977, 82, Mus. Modern Art, NYC, 1978, 82, 84, Santa Barbara Mus. Art, Calif., 1979, San Francisco Mus. Modern Art, 1982, 90, Hokkaido Obihito Mus. Art, Tokyo, 1993, Royal Coll. Art, London, 1994, Mus. Fine Art, Santa Fe, N.Mex., 1994, 96, San Jose Inst. Contemporary Art, 1996, San Francisco Mus. Modern Art, 1996, Sheppard Gallery U. Nev., Reno, others; represented permanent collections, Mus. Modern Art, NYC, Mpls. Inst. Arts, Hallmark Collection, Kansas City, Mo., Boise Gallery Art, Idaho, Walker Art Ctr., Mpls., RI Sch. Design, U. Colo., Fogg Mus. Art, Harvard U., Spencer Mus. Art, U. Kans., Lawrence, Internat. Mus. Photography, Rochester, NY, Art Inst. Chgo., Humbolt State U., Arcata, Calif., Smithsonian Instn., Washington, San Francisco Mus. Modern Art, J. Paul Getty Mus., Santa Monica, Calif., Honolulu Acad. Arts. W.R. French fellow Art Inst. Chgo., 1971; Nat. Endowment for Arts fellow, 1976. Fellow Soc. Contemporary Photo; mem. Soc. for Photog. Edn. Home: 482 Chetwood St Oakland CA 94610-2649 Office: San Jose State U Sch Art & Design San Jose CA 95192-0089 Home Phone: 510-763-0450. Personal E-mail: reed@reedestabrook.net.

ESTEP, JOHN HAYES, religious organization administrator, clergyman; b. Bellwood, Pa., June 30, 1930; s. Kenneth and Anna Emily Estep; m. Dorothy L. Nash, Aug. 21, 1951; children: Heidi Ann, John H. Jr. BA, Wheaton Coll., Ill., 1953; MDiv, Denver Sem., 1956, DD (hon.), 1980. Ordained to ministry Bapt. Ch., 1956. Asst. pastor Forest City Bapt. Ch., Rockford, Ill., 1956-62; pastor, sr. min. Calvary Bapt. Ch., Longmont, Colo., 1962-69; dir. ch. rels. Mission to the Americas, Wheaton, 1969-80, CEO, 1980-95; exec. adminstr. CB Am., 1996—2004; exec. pastor Castle Pines Cmty. Ch., 2004—. Bd. dirs. Colo. Christian U., Denver, 1964-71, Denver Sem., 1968-70. Mem. Nat. Assn. Evangelicals (officer 1988-96), Nat. Black Evang. Assn. (bd. dirs. 1992—). Baptist. Avocations: golf, travel, reading, music. Home Phone: 303-346-5303.

ESTES, CARROLL LYNN, sociologist, educator; b. Ft. Worth, May 30, 1938; d. Joe Ewing and Carroll (Cox) E.; 1 child, Duskie Lynn Gelfand Estes. AB, STanford U., 1959; MA, So. Meth. U., 1961; PhD, U. Calif., San Diego, 1972; DHL (hon.), Russell Sage Coll., 1986. Rsch. asst., asst. study dir. Brandeis U. Social Welfare Rsch. Ctr., 1962-63, rsch. assoc., 1964-65, project dir., 1965-67; vis. lectr. Florence Heller Grad. Sch., 1964-65; rsch. dir. Simmons Coll., 1963-64; asst. prof. social work San Diego State Coll., 1967-72; asst. prof. in residence dept. psychiatry U. Calif., San Francisco, 1972-75, assoc. prof. dept. social and behavioral scis., 1975-79, prof., 1979-92, chair dept. social and behavioral scis., 1981-93, coord. human devel. tng. program, 1974-75; dir. Aging Health Policy Rsch. Ctr., 1979-85, Inst. for Health and Aging, 1985-99. Faculty rsch. lectr. U. Calif., 1993; LaSor lectr. Oreg. Health Scis. U, 2005; co-founder Concerned Scientists in Aging, 2005, founder Estes scholars program, Inst. Health Aging, U. Calif., San Fransisco, 2008. Author: The Decision-Makers: The Power Structure of Dallas, 1963; co-author: Protective Services for Older People, 1972, U.S. Senate Special Committee on Aging Report, Paperwork and the Older Americans Act, 1978, The Aging Enterprise, 1979 Fiscal Austerity and Aging, 1983, Long Term Care of the Elderly, 1985, Political Economy, Health and Aging, 1984, The Long Term Care Crisis, 1993, The Nation's Health, 2001, 7th edit., 2003, Critical Gerontology, 1999, Social Policy and Aging, 2001, Social Theory, Social Policy and Aging, 2003, Health Policy, 5th edit., 2008, Social Justice of Social Insurance, 2009; contbr. articles to profl. jours. Mem. Calif. Commn. on Aging, 1974-77; cons. U.S. Senate Spl. Com. on Aging from 1976, Notch Commn. U.S. Commn. Social Security, 1993-94; bd. dir. Nat. Com. to Preserve Social Security and Medicare, 2002—, vice chair, 2006-08, chair 2009-, NC Found., 2009. Recipient Matrix award Theta Sigma Phi, 1964, award for contbns. to lives of older Californians, Calif. Commn. on Aging, 1977, Helen Nahm Rsch. award U. Calif., San Francisco, 1986, Woman Who Would Be Pres. League of Women Voters, 1998, Lifetime Achievement award Nat. Com. to Preserve Social Security and Medicare, 2006, Improvement of Status of Women award, U. Calif. San Francisco, 2007. Fellow Am. Acad. Nursing (hon.); Mem. Inst. Medicine of NAS, ACLU, Am. Pub. Health Assn.(Weiler award 2008), Am. Sociol. Assn. (Disting. Scholar award Aging and Life Course 2000), Assn. Gerontology in Higher Edn. (pres. 1980-81, recipient Beverly award 1993, Tibbitts award 2000), Am. Soc. on Aging (pres. 1982-84, Leadership award 1986, Hall of Fame award, 2007), Geronotol. Soc. Am. (Kent award 1992, pres. 1995-96), Older Women's League (v.p. 1994-97), Sociologists Women Soc. (Feminist Activist award 2008), Soc. Study Social Problems, Alpha Kappa Delta, Pi Beta Phi. Office: U Calif San Francisco Inst Health & Aging 3333 California St Ste 340 San Francisco CA 94118-1944 Office Phone: 415-476-3236. Business E-Mail: carroll.estes@ucsf.edu.

ESTEVEZ, RAMON See **SHEEN, MARTIN**

ESTRIN, GERALD, computer scientist, engineering educator, academic administrator; b. NYC, Sept. 9, 1921; married; 3 children BS, U. Wis., 1948, MS, 1949, PhD in Elec. Engring., 1951. Rsch. engr. electronic computer project Inst. Advanced Study, Princeton, 1950-53, 55-56; dir. electronic computing project Weizmann Inst. Sci., Israel, 1953-55; assoc. prof. engring. UCLA, 1956-58, prof., 1958-91, prof. emeritus, 1991—, chmn. dept. computer sci., 1979-82, 85-88. Mem. adv. bd. applied math. div. Argonne Nat. Lab., 1966-68, mem. assoc. univs. rev. com. for chmn., 1976-77, mem. adv. bd. applied math. div., 1974-80, adv. com. NASA Space Applications, 1983-86; dir. Computer Communications, Inc., 1966-67, Systems Engring. Labs., 1977-80; mem. internat. program com. Internat. Fedn. Info. Processing Congress, 1968; internat. program chmn. Jerusalem Conf. Info. Tech., 1971; mem. math. and computer sci. research adv. com. AEC; mem. sci. com., operating bd. Gould, Inc., Rolling Meadows, Ill., 1981-86; bd. govs. Weizmann Inst. Sci., 1971-96, gov. emeritus, 1996—. Lipsky fellow, 1954, Guggenheim fellow, 1963, 67; recipient Disting. Svc. award U. Wis., 1975, Jerusalem Conf. on Info. Tech. Spl. Recognition award, 1978, NASA Commendation, 1986, Computer Pioneer award IEEE Computer Soc., 1995, Israeli Software Ind. Pioneer award, 2005 Fellow AAAS, IEEE (disting. spkr. 1980), Assn. Computing Machinery (nat. lectr. 1966-67). Office: UCLA BH3726 Dept Computer Sci Los Angeles CA 90095-0001 E-mail: estrin@cs.ucla.edu.

ESTRIN, JUDITH, computer company executive; m. Bill Carrico. BS in Maths. and Computer Sci., UCLA; MSEE, Stanford U. Co-founder Bridge Comms.; pres., CEO Network Computing Devices; chief tech. officer, sr. v.p. Cisco Sys., Inc., San Jose; chmn. Packet Design, Palo Alto, 2002—. Bd. dirs. Fed. Express, Sun Microsystems, Walt Disney Co. Named to, Women in Tech. Internat. Hall Fame. Office: Packet Design Inc 2455 Augustine Dr Ste 200 Santa Clara CA 95054-3052 Fax: 408-526-4100.

ETCHEMENDY, JOHN, academic administrator, educator; b. Reno; m. Nancy Etchemendy; 1 child, Max. Bachelors Degree, Masters Degree, U. Nev.; PhD, Stanford U., 1982. Lectr. Princeton U., 1981—82, asst. prof., 1982—83; faculty philosophy dept. Stanford U., 1983—, sr. assoc. dean Sch. Humanities and Scis., 1993—97, provost, 2000—, mem. Symbolic Systems Program, sr. rschr. Ctr. for Study of Language and Info. Faculty mem. Symbolic Sys. Program Stanford U., sr. rschr. Ctr. for the Study of Lang. and Info. Author: Hyperproof, 1994, Language, Proof and Logic, 1999; editor: Jour. Symbolic Logic; mem. editl. bd. Synthese, Philosophia Mathematica. Mem.: Assn. for Symbolic Logic (mem. governing coun.), Am. Philos. Assn. Office: Office of the Provost Bldg 10 Stanford Univ Stanford CA 94305-2061 Office Phone: 650-724-4074. Office Fax: 650-725-1347. E-mail: etch@csli.stanford.edu.

ETCHESON, WARREN WADE, business administration educator; b. Bainbridge, Ind., May 15, 1920; s. Raymond W. and Rosetta (Evans) E.; m. Marianne Newgent, May 30, 1947; children: Denise Elene, Crayton Wade. BS, Ind. U., 1943; MA, U. Iowa, 1951, PhD, 1956. Adminstrv. sec., exec. sec., nat. sec. Delta Chi Nat. Fraternity, 1946-56; lectr. Santo Tomas U., Manila, 1946, U. Iowa, 1951-54; asst. prof. U. Wash., 1954-56, assoc. prof., 1956-60, prof. Sch. Bus. Adminstrn., 1960-90, assoc. dean Bus. Adminstrn., 1974-87, prof. emeritus, 1990—. Fulbright prof. Istanbul, Turkey, 1963-64. Author: Pazarlama, 1964, Consumerism, 1972. Served to lt. U.S. Army, 1942-46. Mem. Alpha Kappa Psi, Phi Eta Sigma, Beta Gamma Sigma, Delta Chi. Home: 6625 NE 132nd St Kirkland WA 98034-1614

ETH, JORDAN DAVID, lawyer; BA, Swarthmore Coll., 1980; JD, Stanford U., 1985. Bar: Calif. 1985. Law clerk to Chief Judge Robert F. Peckham U.S. Dist. Ct. Calif. (No. dist.), 1985—86; economist U.S. Dept. Energy, U.S. Ho. of Reps., 1980—82; assoc. Morrison & Foerster LLP, San Francisco, 1986—92, ptnr., 1992—. Spkr. in field. Contbr. articles to profl. jours. Office: Morrison & Foerster LLP 425 Market St San Francisco CA 94105-2482 Office Phone: 415-268-7126. Office Fax: 415-268-7522. E-mail: jeth@mofo.com.

ETRA, DONALD, lawyer; b. NYC, July 23, 1947; s. Harry and Blanche (Goldman) E.; m. Paula Renee Wiener, Dec. 28, 1985; children: Harry, Dorothy, Anna, Jonathan. BA, Yale U., 1968; MBA, JD, Columbia U., 1971. Atty. to Ralph Nader, Washington, 1971-73; trial atty. U.S. Dept. Justice, Washington, 1973-77, asst. U.S. atty. LA, 1978-81; ptnr. Sidley & Austin, LA, 1983-95, Law Offices of Donald Etra, LA, 1995—. Co-author: Citibank, 1973. E-mail: etralaw@aol.com.

ETTENGER, ROBERT BRUCE, physician, pediatric nephrologist; b. Phila., Sept. 17, 1942; s. Ervin Earl and Sylvia (Goodstein) W.; m. Angela Joan Castellano; children: Allison, Jessica. BA, U. Pa., 1964; MD, 1968. Asst. prof. pediat. Children's Hosp. LA, 1976-80, Sch. Medicine UCLA, 1980-84, asst. prof., 1984-89, prof., 1989—, Casey Lee Ball Disting. prof. pediat., 2005—, head divsn. pediat. nephrology dept. pediat., 1990—2004, vice chmn. clin. affairs, 1990—2004; med. dir. pediat. renal transplant program UCLA Med. Ctr., 1983—, dir. historcompatibility lab., 1987—2001, vice chief med. staff, 2002—04, chief med. staff, 2004—06. Mem., chair sub-bd. nephrology Am. Bd. Pediat., Chapel Hill, N.C., 1986-91; cons. Immunosuppressive Adv. Com. Food and Drug Adminstrn., Bethesda, Md., 1994—, Biologics and Immune Response Modifiers, Food and Drug Adminstrn., Bethesda, 1994—; mem. biol. sci. adv. com. U.S. Renal Data Sys., Ann Arbor, Mich., 1993-2000, Data Safety Monitoring Bd., Dept. Transplantation, Nat. Inst. Immunology Transplant Adv. Group, U.S. Sec. Health and Human Svcs., Am. Soc. Nephrology; mem. Adv. Com. Transplantation. Assoc. editor Am. Jour. Transplantation; mem. editl. bd. Transplantation, Pediat. Nephrology, Pediat. Transplantation; contbr. articles to profl. jours. Coach, mem. exec. bd. AYSO Soccer, Santa Monica, Calif., 1994-2001, Bobby Sox Softball, 1995-97, YWCA Basketball, 1995-2000; mem. med. adv. bd. Nat. Kidney Found., LA, 1993—. Maj. US Army, 1971—73. Recipient Ortho Biotech Lectureship Urologic Soc. for Transplantation, 1990, Continuing Svc. award Nat. Kidney Found., L.A., 1991, 92, 94. Fellow Internat. Soc. Nephrology, Internat. Pediat. Nephrology Assn., Am. Acad. Pediat., Am. Soc. Transplant Physicians (pres. 1984-85), Am. Pediat. Soc., Am. Soc. of Nephrology, Am. Soc. Pediat. Nephrology, Soc. Pediat. Rsch., Transplantation Soc. (Best Drs. in Am. 1992-06, Am.'s Top Drs. 1998-06), United Network Organ Sharing (regional councillor at region 5, bd. dirs. 2000-02). Jewish. Avocations: distance running, youth sports. Office: UCLA Med Ctr A2-383 Dept Pediatrics 10833 Le Conte Ave Los Angeles CA 90095-3075

ETTINGER, HARRY JOSEPH, retired industrial hygiene engineer, consultant; b. NYC, July 20, 1934; s. Morris and Pauline (Waxman) E.; m. June Kopf, June 14, 1958; children: Linda E., Steven E., Robert A. BCE, CCNY, 1956; MCE, NYU, 1958. Registered profl. engr., N.Mex.; cert. indsl. hygienist. San. engr. USPHS, Bethesda, Md., 1958-61; staff mem. Los Alamos (N.Mex.) Nat. Lab., 1961-71, alt. group leader, 1971-74, group leader, 1974-80, program mgr., 1981-87, tech. rsch. coord., 1989-91, program mgr., 1991-93, chief scientist environ., safety and health divsn., 1993-97, acting dep. divsn. dir., 1995-96, lab. assoc., 1997-99, cons., 1999—2004; project dir. Occupl. Safety and Health Adminstrn., Washington, 1987-89. Cons. divsn. reactor licensing USAEC, 1970-71, cons. EPA, 1972-74, various industries, 1970—; cons. to adv. com. on nuc. facility safety DOE, 1990-91; mem. adj. faculty U. Ark., Little Rock, 1969-90, San Diego State U., 1981-86; vis. faculty Tex. A&M U., College Station, 1981-99; faculty affiliate Colo. State U., Ft. Collins, 1983-2004; mem. exec. com. toxic substances rsch. and tchg. program U. Calif., 1984-90; mem. stds. steering group DOE Lab. Dirs. Environ. and Occupl. Health, 1990-96; mem. liaison com. NIOSH Nat. Occupl. Rsch. Agenda, 2000-03; reviewer Inst. Medicine, 2006. Mem. editl. bd. Jour. Occupl. and Environ. Hygiene, 2004-; contbr. jour. articles and tech. reports on indsl. hygiene, aerosol physics, respiratory protection. Active Los Alamos County Utility Bd., 1968-70, 78-82, chmn., 1970; vice chmn. Los Alamos County Planning and Zoning Commn., 1974-76, mem., 1972-76, 97-2001, 2004-2006. Fellow: Am. Indsl. Hygiene Assn. (chmn. aerosol tech. com. 1968—70, mem. aerosol tech. com. 1968—78, editl. rev. bd. 1979—87, aerosol tech. com. 1980—84, bd. dirs. 1987—90, editl. rev. bd. 1990—91, v.p. 1991—92, pres.-elect 1992—93, pres. 1993—94, editl. rev. bd. 1995—2003, respirator com. 1995—, Edward Baier award 1990, Donald Cummings Lectr. and award 2003, Henry Smyth Lectr. and award 2004); mem.: Internat. Occupl. Hygiene Assn. (bd. dirs. 1994—97), Internat. Soc. Respiratory Protection (bd. dirs. 1985—88, 1995—97, mem. editl. bd. NSC Jour. safety rsch. 2001—07), Am. Conf. Govtl. Indsl. Hygiene (Meritorious Achievement award 1985),

Am. Bd. Indsl. Hygiene (bd. dirs. 1979—85, chmn. 1983—85), Am. Acad. Indsl. Hygiene (editor newsletter 1997—2001). Democrat. Jewish. Office Phone: 505-662-7132. Personal E-mail: junee@rt66.com.

ETTLICH, WILLIAM F., electrical engineer; b. Spokane, Wash., Jan. 7, 1936; s. Fred Ernest Ettlich and Dorothy Sue (Olney) Nicholls; m. Alice Dianne Lawton, Aug. 24, 1958; children: Pamela, Daniel. BS, Oreg. State U.; PMD-25, Harvard U. Registered profl. engr., Oreg., Calif., Nev., Colo., Ohio. Project engr. CH2M-Hill Corp., Corvallis, Oreg., 1959-65; pres. Neptune Microfloc, Corvallis, 1965-74; v.p. Culp Wesner Culp, Cameron Park, Calif., 1974-86; exec. v.p. HDR Engring., Inc., Folsom, 1986—. Pres. Cameron Estates CSD, Cameron Park, 1977-80. Contbr. tech. articles to jours.; patentee in field. Bd. dirs. Marshall Hosp.; trustee emeritus Marshall Hosp. Found. and Hosp. Bd. Mem. IEEE (sr.), Instrument Soc. Am., Rotary (pres. Cameron Park club 1987-88). Republican. Presbyterian. Avocations: skiing, woodworking. Home: 101 Flindell Way Folsom CA 95630 Office: HDR Engring 2365 Iron Point Rd Folsom CA 95630 Business E-Mail: bill.ettlich@hdrinc.com.

EUSTACE, ALAN, information technology executive; BS, MS, U. Ctrl. Fla., PhD in Computer Sci. With Western Rsch. Lab., Hewlett Packard, 1987—2002, dir., 1999—2002; v.p. engring. Google Inc., Mountain View, Calif., 2002—06, sr. v.p. engring & rsch., 2006—. Vol. Harvest Food Bank, Anita Borg Scholarship Fund. Mem.: Internet Soc. Avocations: flying, bicycling. Office: Google Inc 1600 Amphitheatre Pkwy Mountain View CA 94043 Office Phone: 650-253-0000. Office Fax: 650-253-0001.

EUSTIS, ROBERT HENRY, design company executive, mechanical engineer; b. Mpls., Apr. 18, 1920; s. Ralph Warren and Florence Louise E.; m. Katherine Vik Johnson, Mar. 20, 1943; children: Jeffrey Nelson, Karen V. B in Mech. Engring., U. Minn., 1942, MS, 1944; ScD, MIT, 1953. Instr. U. Minn., 1942-44; rsch. scientist NASA, 1944-47; asst. prof. MIT, 1947-51; chief engr. Thermal Rsch. and Engring. Corp., 1951-53; mgr. heat and mech. sect. S.R.I. Internat., 1953-55; mem. faculty dept. mech. engring. Stanford (Calif.) U., 1955-90, prof., 1962, dir. high temperature gasdynamics lab., 1961-80, assoc. dean engring., 1984-88; pres. Menlo Furniture Designs, 2004—. Chmn. tech. adv. coun. Emerson Electric Corp.; prin. Eustis Designs, 1990-00. Contbr. articles to profl. jours. Recipient medal Soviet Sci. Acad., 1973. Fellow: AAAS, ASME, AIAA. Home: 862 Lathrop Dr Palo Alto CA 94305-1053 Office: Stanford Univ Dept Mech Engring Stanford CA 94305 Home Phone: 650-857-0623. Business E-Mail: rheustis@stanford.edu.

EVANS, ANTHONY HOWARD, retired university president; b. Clay County, Ark., Sept. 24, 1936; s. William Raymond and Thelma Fay (Crews) E.; m. Lois Fay Kirkham, Aug. 29, 1959. BA, East Tex. Bapt. Coll., Marshall, 1959; MA, U. Hawaii, 1961; PhD, U. Calif.-Berkeley, 1966. Program officer Peace Corps, Seoul, Korea, 1970-72, chief program planning Washington, 1972-73, dir. planning office, 1973-75; asst. to pres. Eastern Mich. U., Ypsilanti, 1975-76, exec. v.p., 1976-79, acting pres., 1978-79, provost, v.p. acad. affairs, 1979-82; pres. Calif. State U., San Bernardino, 1982-97. Mem. Orgn. Am. Historians, Phi Kappa Phi Home: 79 Wild Turkey Trl Hendersonville NC 28792-8030

EVANS, BARTON, JR., retired analytical instrument company executive; b. Washington, Dec. 11, 1947; s. Barton and Viola (Gompf) E.; m. Harriet Andrea Neves, Nov. 20, 1983. BA in Econs., Claremont McKenna Coll., Calif., 1970; BS in Engring., MS in Engring., Stanford U., Calif., 1972. Sr. instr. Ctrl. Tex. Coll., 1974—75; sr. engr. Lockheed Missiles and Space Co., Sunnyvale, Calif., 1976-77, Dionex Corp., Sunnyvale, 1977-79, engring. mgr., 1979-81, dir. engring., 1981-83, v.p. engring., 1983-84, v.p. ops., 1984-93, sr. v.p. ops., 1993-2001, exec. v.p. and COO, 2001—05; pvt. practice, 2005—. Trustee Claremont McKenna Coll., 2005—, chair Info. Tech. adv. bd., 2005—; treas. San Francisco Lyric Opera, Calif., 2008—. 1st lt. US Army, 1972—75, col. USAR, 1976—2002, ret. Mem.: ASME, Res. Officers Assn., Assn. U.S. Army, Psychol. Ops. Assn., Civil Affairs Assn. (dir.). Progressive. Achievements include co-inventor conductivity detector. Home Phone: 650-357-6971. Personal E-mail: barton.evans@comcast.net.

EVANS, BERNARD WILLIAM, geologist, educator; b. London, July 16, 1934; came to U.S., 1961, naturalized, 1977; s. Albert Edward and Marjorie (Jordan) E.; m. Sheila Campbell Nolan, Nov. 19, 1962. BSc, U. London, 1955; DPhil, Oxford U., Eng., 1959. Asst. U. Glasgow, Scotland, 1958-59; departmental demonstrator U. Oxford, 1959-61; asst. research prof. U. Calif., Berkeley, 1961-65, asst. prof., 1965-66, assoc. prof., 1966-69; prof. geology U. Wash., Seattle, 1969—2001, chmn. dept. geol. scis., 1974-79; emeritus prof. U. Washington, 2001—. Contbr. articles to profl. jours. Recipient U.S. Sr. Scientist award Humboldt Found., Fed. Republic Germany, 1988-89; Fulbright travel award, France, 1995-96. Fellow Geol. Soc. Am., Mineral Soc. Am. (pres. 1993-94, award 1970, Roebling medal, 2008), Geochem. Soc., Geol. Soc. London, Mineral. Soc. Gt. Britain. Home: 8001 Sand Point Way NE Apt C55 Seattle WA 98115-6399 Office: U Wash Dept Earth and Space Scis PO Box 351310 Seattle WA 98195-1310 Office Phone: 206-543-1163. Business E-Mail: bwevans@u.washington.edu.

EVANS, BEVERLY ANN, state legislator, school system administrator; b. Tod Park, Utah, Jan. 26, 1944; d. Elias Wilbur and Geraldine Vilate (Rigby) Cook; m. Stephen R. Evans, July 31, 1965; children: Lorie Ann, James. BS, Utah State U., 1965, MS, 1974. Tchr. Duchesne (Utah) Sch. Dist., 1965-70; instr. Utah Basin Applied Tech. Ctr., Roosevelt, Utah, 1970-73, adminstr., 1973—; instr. Utah State U., Logan, 1968—; mem. Utah Ho. of Reps., Salt Lake City, 1986-98, Nat. Nuclear Waste Task Force, 1987-88, Utah Senate, Dist. 26, Salt Lake City, 1998—. Cons. Utah State U., 1980—. Recipient Award of Merit, Nat. Safety Coun., Chgo., 1985-87, Alumni award Nat. 4-H, 1989, Bus. Woman of Yr award Utah BPW, 1990, Pub. Servant award Duchesne County C. of C., 1993. Mem., Amer. Vocational Assoc., Uintah Basin Education Ctr., Chamber of Commerce,Wasatch & Duchesne Counties. Republican. Mem. Lds Ch. Avocations: computers, outdoor activities, writing. Office: State Capitol Salt Lake City UT 84111 Home: 10073 Homecoming Ave South Jordan UT 84095-4542

EVANS, BILL (JAMES WILLIAM EVANS), dance professor, academic administrator, choreographer; b. Lehi, Utah, Apr. 11, 1940; s. William Ferdinand and Lila (Snape) E.; married, Aug. 27, 1962 (div. 1965); 1 child, Thaïs. BA in English, U. Utah, 1963, MFA in Modern Dance, 1970; dance student various pvt. dance schs. and studios; cert. in laban and bartenieff, U. Utah, 1997. Apprentice Harkness Ballet Co., NYC, 1966; mem. Chgo. Ballet and Lyric Opera Ballet, 1966-67; teaching asst. dept. ballet and modern dance U. Utah, 1967-68, faculty Virginia Tanner Creative Dance Program, 1968-73, asst. prof. modern dance, 1974-76, dancer, tchr., choreographer, artistic coordinator, mem. Repertory Dance Theatre, 1967-74; artistic dir. Dance Theatre Seattle, 1976-83; artistic dir., resident tchr., choreographer Winnipeg's Contemporary Dancers, Man., Can., 1983-84; assoc. prof., coord. dance program dept. kinesiology Ind. U., Bloomington, 1986-87, 87-88, artistic dir. Ind. Dance Theatre, 1986-88; head dance program dept. theatre and dance U. N.Mex., Albuquerque, 1988-93; prof. dance, 1993—; artistic dir. univ. Contemporary Dance Ensemble U. N.Mex., Albuquerque, 1989-93, dir., founder Univ. Youth Dance Camp, 1990, dir., founder Magnificio Youth Dance Groups, 1991-96. Artistic dir. Bill Evans Dance Co., toured U.S., Europe, Mex. 1975-99; Bill Evans Summer Insts. of Dance and Summer Festivals of Dance, Bill Evans Solo Dance Repertory, 1976—, Bill Evans Dance Co. Sch., Seattle; vis. prof. dance div. U. Wash., 1976-81; artistic advisor Fairmount Dance Theatre, Cleve., 1974-75; guest artist in residence Dance Dept., U. Utah; artist in resident Ill. U., Harvard U. Summer Sch., choreographer in residence Repertory Dance Theater; dir., choreographer N.Mex. Repertory Theatre, Santa Fe and Albuquerque; mem. Artists in Edn. Bank, Utah arts council; dance/movement specialist Artist-in-Schs. program Nat. Endowment for Arts; founder, dir. Celebrate Youth Summer Dance Inst., 1993-98; artistic coord. SW Am. Coll. Dance Festival, 1994; guest artist Kala Chhaya Cultural Ctr., India, 1993—; toured Karnataka, Maharastra, India. Free-lance dancer, 1969—, including Berlin Ballet, 1969, Jacob's Pillow Dance Festival, Lee, Mass., 1973, Harvard U., 1973, 74, 90; choreographer over 170 works for various ballet and modern dance cos., 1967—; mem. editl. bd. Dance Connections, 1997. Am. Arts Alliance rep. before House and Senate appropriations coms., 1979. Served as officer U.S. Army, 1963-65. Recipient various choreographic awards, grants and fellowships from Nat. Endowment for Arts, 1972-75, 77-83, Utah Bicentennial Com., 1976, Art Found., Western States Arts Fedn., Wash. Arts Commn., King County Arts Commn., Seattle Arts Commn., Man. Arts Council, Ind. Arts Commn., N.Mex. Arts Div., U. N.Mex. Found., U. N.Mex. Coll. Fine Arts, Ind. U., Multidisciplinary Ventures Fund, U. N.Mex. Rsch. Allocations Com., City of Albuquerque, BRAVO award Albuquerque Arts Alliance, 1997, 2003, N.Mex. Gov.'s award for excellence and achievement in the arts, 2001; Guggenheim fellow, 1976-77, Am. Coll. Dance Fest., regional awards, 1986,87, 89-90, nat., 1986, 90; recipient Teaching Plaudit award nat. Dance Assn., 1981, scholar artist, 1997; named adjudicator and guest artist 1st Nat. Ballet Festival Regional Dance Am., 1997-99. Mem. Dancers, Inc. (adv. bd.), Nat. Dance Assn. (chair performance divsn. 1993—), Am. Coll. Dance Festival Assn. (bd. dirs. 1992—, U.S. rep. 1st internat. coll. dance festival Japan 1993). Office: U NM Fine Arts Dept 1 Univ NM MSC 04 2570 Albuquerque NM 87131-0001 E-mail: beran@unm.edu.

EVANS, CHARLES ALBERT, microbiology educator; b. Mpls., Feb. 18, 1912; s. Albert Grant and Susan Briery (Thompson) E.; m. Allie Ann Christman, Dec. 22, 1939; children: Nicholas J. (dec.), Susan Ethel, Thomas Charles, Carol Ann. BS, U. Minn., 1935, MD, 1937, PhD, 1943. Diplomate Am. Bd. Med. Microbiology. NRC fellow U. Rochester, 1941-42; rsch. supr. Minn. State Dept. Conservation, Mpls., 1942-43; asst. prof. dept. bacteriology U. Minn., Mpls., 1942-44, assoc. prof. dept. bacteriology, 1944-46; assoc. dir. Fred Hutchinson Cancer Rsch. Ctr., Seattle, 1971-75; prof. dept. microbiology U. Wash., Seattle, 1946-82, chmn., 1946-70, prof. emeritus, 1982—. Mem. nat. cancer coun. USPHS, Bethesda, Md., 1958-59,64-67; chmn. rsch. adv. coun. Am. Cancer Soc., 1967-70. Contbr. over 100 articles to profl. jours. Recipient numerous rsch. grants from NIH and Am. Cancer Soc. Mem. Am. Soc. for Microbiology (hon., pres. 1959-60), Soc. for Infectious Diseases (emeritus), Am. Assn. for Cancer Rsch. (emeritus), Am. Acad. Microbiology (mem. bd. govs. 1959-65, chmn. 1960-61). Avocations: birdwatching, photography. Home: 7739 29th Ave NE Seattle WA 98115-4616 Office: U Wash Sch Medicine Dept Microbiology Seattle WA 98195-0001 E-mail: evansmic@u.washington.edu.

EVANS, DANIEL JACKSON, former senator, management consultant; b. Seattle, Oct. 16, 1925; s. Daniel Lester and Irma (Ide) E.; m. Nancy Ann Bell, June 6, 1959; children: Daniel Jackson, Mark L., Bruce M. BS in Civil Engring, U. Wash., 1948, MS, 1949. Registered profl. engr., Wash. With Assoc. Gen. Contractors, Seattle, 1953-59; cons. civil engr. Seattle, 1949-51; ptnr. Gray & Evans, structural and civil engrs., Seattle, 1961-65; mem. Wash. Ho. of Reps. from, King County, 1956-65; Republican floor leader Wash. Ho. of Reps., 1961-65; gov. State of Wash., 1965-77; pres. Evergreen State Coll., Olympia, 1977-83; mem. US Senator from Wash., 1983-89; now involved in environ. work, pub. appearances; chmn. Daniel J. Evans & Assocs., Seattle, 1989—; dir. Costco Wholesale Corp., Issaquah, Wash., 2003—; co-founder Seattle Initiative for Global Devel. Chmn. Pacific N.W. Electric Power and Conservation Planning Coun., 1981-83; bd. dirs. Puget Sound Energy, Tera Computer Co., Santa Fe, Inc., Flow Internat., Attachmate, Western Wireless Corp., NIC Inc. Keynote speaker Rep. Nat. Conv., 1968; chmn. Nat. Gov.'s Conf., 1973-74; chmn. Com. on Policy Options for Global Warming, NAS, 1989-90; regent U. Wash., 1993—. Lt. USNR, 1943-46, 51-53. Recipient Disting. Eagle Scout award, Silver Beaver award, Silver Antelope award Boy Scouts Am., Disting. Citizen award Nat. Mcpl. League, 1977, First Citizen award, Seattle-King County Assn. Realtors, 2003, Legacy award, Rainier Inst., 2004. Congregationalist. Office: 111 3d Ave Ste 3400 Seattle WA 98104

EVANS, DON A., healthcare company executive; b. Jerome, Ariz., June 22, 1948; s. Rulon Cooper and Berniece (Ensign) E.; m. Susan Dahl, June 3, 1972; children: Emily, Austin, Adrienne, Alan. BS, Ariz. State U., Tempe, 1972; MS, U. Colo., 1974. Asst. adminstr. Nat. Jewish Hosp., Denver, 1974-80, LDS Hosp., Salt Lake City, 1980-84, COO, 1984-88; CEO Luth. Healthcare Network, Mesa, Ariz., 1988—; sr. group v.p. Banner Health Ariz., Mesa, 1999-2000, COO Phoenix, 2000—; CEO Banner Baywood Med. Ctr., 2001—. Adj. prof. U. Minn., 1985-86. Fellow Am. Coll. Healthcare Execs. (regent for Ariz.); mem. Ariz. Hosp. Assn. (bd. dirs., chmn. bd. 1998-99). Republican. Office: 6644 E Baywood Ave Mesa AZ 85205 Home Phone: 480-924-3575; Office Phone: 480-981-4100. Business E-Mail: don.evans@bannerhealth.com.

EVANS, ERSEL ARTHUR, engineering executive, consultant; b. Trenton, Nebr., July 17, 1922; s. Arthur E. and Mattie Agnes (Perkins) E.; m. Patricia A. Powers, Oct. 11, 1945 (div.); children: Debra Lynn (dec.), Paul Arthur. BA, Reed Coll., Portland, Oreg., 1947; PhD, Oreg. State U., 1950. Registered profl. engr., Calif. With Gen. Electric Co., 1951-67, supr. ceramics research and devel. Hanford, Wash., 1961-64; mgr. plutonium devel. Vallecitos Lab., Pleasanton, Calif., 1964-67; mgr. fuels and materials dept. Battelle Meml. Inst., Richland, Wash., 1967-70; with Westinghouse Electric Corp., 1970-87; v.p. Westinghouse Hanford Co., Richland, 1972-87, v.p., lab. tech. dir., 1985-87, ret., 1987, cons., 1987—. Mem. Tech. Assistance Adv. Group for Three Mile Island Recovery, 1981-86; mem. rev. Com. EBR-II, U. Chgo., 1989-91, 94—; mem. Japan Tech. Panel for Nuclear Power, NSF, 1989-90; mem. alt. applications of laser isotope separations tech. com. NRC, 1991-92, separations and tech. study, 1991-95, 96; del. Atlantic Coun. U.S.-Japan Conf. on Global Energy Issues, Maui, 1994, 96. Chmn. vis. com. U. Wash. With USNR, 1943—45. Recipient Westinghouse Order of Merit; DuPont fellow, 1950-51; recipient Mishima award Am. Nuclear Soc., 1995, Inaugural Class award Wash. State Acad. Scis., 2008 Fellow Am. Nuclear Soc. (Spl. Merit award 1964, Spl. Performance award 1980 Presidential Design Achievement award 1991, Walker Cisler medal 2001), Am. Inst. Chemists, Am. Soc. Metals, Am. Ceramic Soc.; mem. NAE, Phi Kappa Phi, Sigma Xi. Achievements include patents in field. Home and Office: 4152 Providence Point Dr SE 106 Issaquah WA 98029 Office Phone: 425-369-2320. Personal E-mail: ersel3@gmail.com.

EVANS, GERALDINE ANN, former academic administrator; b. Zumbrota, Minn., Feb. 24, 1939; d. Wallace William and Elda Ida (Tiedemann) Whipple; m. John Lyle Evans, June 21, 1963; children: John David, Paul William. AA, Rochester Community Coll., 1958; BS, U. Minn., 1960, MA, 1963, PhD, 1968. Cert. tchr., counselor, prin. and supt., Minn. Tchr. Hopkins (Minn.) Pub. Schs., 1960-63; counselor Anoka (Minn.) Pub. Schs., 1963-66; cons. in edn. Mpls., 1966-78; policy analyst Minn. Dept. Edn., St. Paul, 1978-79; dir. pers. Minn. CC Sys., St. Paul, 1979-82, chancellor, 1992-94; pres. Rochester (Minn.) CC, 1982-92; exec. dir. Ill. CC Bd., Springfield, 1994-96; chancellor San Jose (Calif.) Evergreen CC Dist., 1996—2004; ret., 2004. Mem. San Jose Workforce Investment Bd., 2000—; mem. legis. and adv. com. Calif. C.C. League, 1998-2002. Mem. Gov.'s Job Tng. Coun., St. Paul, 1983—94, chair, 1992—94; mem. Silicon Valley Pvt. Industry Coun., 1997—2000, Workforce Silicon Valley, 1998—2002; trustee Golden Gate U., 1997—; chair Rochester (Minn.) United Way, 1985—86; mem. campaign cabinet United Way of Silicon Valley, 2003—04; moderator Mizpah United Ch. Christ, Hopkins, 1982; mem. complete count com. U.S. Census, Santa Clara County, 2000; vice chair, bd. dirs. Wayzata (Minn.) Sch. Bd., 1980—83; bd. dirs. Minn. Tech. Ctr., Rochester, 1991—92; bd. mem. Boy Scouts San Clara Coun., 2004; sec.-treas. Coun. North Ctrl. Cmty. and Jr. Colls., 1990—92; mem. ACE Commn. on Edn. Credit and Credentials, 1992—96. Winner Rochester C. of C. Athena award, 1990, San Jose YWCA Exec. award, 1998; Inst. Ednl. Leadership fellow, Washington, 1978-79. Mem. Nat. League Nursing (bd. assoc. degree accreditation rev. 1990-93, exec. com. 1993-96), Am. Assn. Cmty. Colls. (workforce commn. 2000-03), Am. Assn. Cmty. Jr. Colls. (bd. dirs. 1984-87), North Ctrl. Assn. Cmty. and Jr. Colls. (evaluator 1985-96), Silicon Valley C. of C. (bd. dirs. 2001-04). Congregationalist. Avocations: travel, gardening. Personal E-mail: gevans@mm.com.

EVANS, GREGORY HINOJOSA, lawyer; BS in Pub. Affairs, U. So. Calif., 1984; MSW, U. Calif., Berkeley, 1986; JD, U. Notre Dame, 1989. Bar: Calif. 1990, US Dist. Ct. (all dists. Calif.), US Ct. Appeals (7th and 9th cirs.), Calif. Supreme Ct., Wash. Supreme Ct. Dep. counsel Nat. Coalition Homeless, Washington; ptnr. Orrick, Herrington & Sutcliffe, LLP, LA, Milbank, Tweed, Hadley & McCloy, LLP, LA, 2006—. Fellowship US Dept. Justice, 1987; mem. Nat. Assn. Elected and Appointed Officials Ednl. Fund; bd. dirs. Leadership for Environment and Devel., USA. Contbr. articles to law jours. Bd. trustees Cath. Charities LA; bd. dirs. YMCA, San Francisco, NAACP Legal Def. and Ednl. Fund, Inc., LA County Bar Found. Named one of Am. Top 45 Young Lawyers, The Am. Lawyer mag., 2003. Mem.: Nat. Assn. Latino Elected and Apptd. Ofcls., State Bar Calif. (Wiley W. Manuel award 1993). Office: Milbank Tweed Hadley & McCloy LLP 601 S Figueroa St 30th Fl Los Angeles CA 90017 Office Phone: 213-892-4488. E-mail: gevans@milbank.com.

EVANS, JAMES HANDEL, academic administrator, architect; b. Bolton, Eng., June 14, 1938; came to U.S., 1965. s. Arthur Handel and Ellen Bowen (Ramsden) E.; m. Carol L. Mulligan, Sept. 10, 1966; children: Jonathan, Sarah. Diploma of Architecture, U. Manchester, Eng., 1965; MArch., U. Oreg., 1967; postgrad., Cambridge U., Eng., 1969-70. Registered architect, Calif., U.K.; cert. NCARB. Assoc. dean. prof. architecture Calif. Poly. State U., San Luis Obispo, 1967-78; prof. art and design San Jose (Calif.) State U., 1979—, assoc. exec. v.p., 1978-81, interim exec. v.p., 1981-82, exec. v.p., 1982-91, interim pres., 1991-92, pres., 1992-95; sr. adminstr. Calif. State U., Monterey Bay, 1991—94; vice chancellor Calif. State U System, Long Beach, Calif., 1995-96; planning pres. Calif. State U. Channel Islands, Ventura, 1996-2001; pres. HE Cons. Inc., 2001—. Cons. Ibiza Nueva, Ibiza, Spain, 1977-80; vis. prof. Ciudad Universitaria, Madrid, 1977; vis. lectr. Herriott Watt U., Edinburgh, 1970; mem. adv. com. Army Command Staff Coll., Ft. Leavenworth, Kans., 1988. Trustee Good Samaritan Hosp., San Jose, 1987-90; bd. dirs. San Jose Shelter, 1988-90; dir. San Jose C. of C., 1991-94, Ventura County Mus. History and Art. Sci. Rsch. Coun. fellow Cambridge U., 1969-70. Fellow AIA; mem. Royal Inst. Brit. Architects, Assn. Univ. Architects. Avocation: golf. Home Phone: 805-384-8151. Personal E-mail: jhevans@adelphia.net. Business E-Mail: hevans@vcccd.edu.

EVANS, JOHN, state legislator, lawyer, educator; m. Mary Ann; children, Evan, John-Paul. BA, U. Denver; MEd, PhD, Ga. State U.; JD, Valparaiso U. Bar: Colo., Ill, Ind., U.S. Supreme Ct. Mem. Colo. Senate, Dist. 30, Denver, 1998—2006; asst. majority leader edn., vice chair fin. com., chair legal svcs. com.; vice-chair health, environ., welfare and instns. com.; mem. judiciary com., mem. transp. com. Active Colo. State Bd. Edn.; chair, pres. Western Inst. for Agrl. Land Use; adv. bd. Gov.'s Manpower Devel. Commn.; organizer Rep. Leaders Initiative Forum; founder First Friday Breakfast Club, Rep. Forum Douglas County. Recipient Commendation medal Mil. Police Corps. Army, Cmty. Svc. award Optimist. Fellow Nat. Endowment for the Humanities; mem. Colo. Bar Assn. (bd. govs.), Nat. Orgn. on Legal Problems in Edn., Rotary Club. Republican. Avocations: skiing, fly fishing, hiking, carpentry. E-mail: evansjo@sni.net.

EVANS, JOHN DECOURCEY, real estate company officer; B in Commerce, U. BC. Sr. v.p., dir. Intrawest Properties Ltd.; pres., dir. Strand Properties Corp.; pres., founding ptnr. Trilogy Properties Corp., Vancouver, BC. Pres. Urban Devel. Inst. Can., 1984—85, pres. Pacific Region, 1984—85; trustee Urban Devel. Inst. Pacific Region Edn. Trust Fund, 1993—; trustee, chmn. investment com. Can. Hotel Income Properties Real Estate Investment Trust, Toronto Stock Exchange, 1997—2007; chmn. U. Victoria Properties Investments Inc., 2005—; mem. bd. govs. U. Victoria, 2005—. Chmn. Can. Craft

Mus., 1990—94; trustee Vancouver Art Gallery, 1996—2001; co-chmn. Capital Fundraising Campaign Dr. Peter HIV/AIDS Found., 2000—01, chmn., 2007—. Mem.: Can. Cancer Soc. (dir. BC and Yukon Divsn. 1989—92). Office: Trilogy Properties Corp Ste 1268 Bentall 5 550 Burrard St Vancouver BC Canada V6C 2B5

EVANS, KEITH EDWARD, government official, researcher; b. Pueblo, Colo., Apr. 26, 1940; s. C. Leslie and Clarabelle (Hammond) E.; m. Betty J. Watson, Aug. 21, 1960; children: Susan E., Steven C. BS in Wildlife Sci., Colo. State U., 1962, MS in Wildlife Sci., 1964; PhD in Wildlife Sci., Cornell U., 1971; postgrad., Fed. Exec. Inst., Charlottesville, Va., 1991. Range conservationist USDA Forest Svc., Rapid City, S.D., 1964-65, wildlife rsch. biologist, 1965-72, wildlife rsch. biologist, project leader Columbia, Mo., 1972-81, Am. Polit. Sci. Congl. fellow Washington, 1985-86, legis. asst., 1986-87, nat. range, wildlife and fish leader, 1987-89, asst. dir. Ogden, Utah, 1981-85, 89—. Contbr. over 50 articles to sci. jours. Recipient pub. svc. award North Utah Pub. Svc. Orgns., 1994. Mem. Nat. Audubon Soc. (past chpt. pres. and bd. dirs.). Avocations: birdwatching, photography. Office: US Forest Svc Intermountain Rsch Sta 324 25th St Ste 4013 Ogden UT 84401-2394

EVANS, LOUISE, investor, retired psychologist; b. San Antonio; d. Henry Daniel and Adela (Pariser) E.; m. Thomas Ross Gambrell, Feb. 23, 1960. BS, Northwestern U., 1949; MS in Clin. Psychology, Purdue U., 1952, PhD in Clin. Psychology, 1955. Lic. marriage, family and child counselor Calif.; Nat. Register of Health Svc. Providers in Psychology; lic. psychologist, Calif., N.Y. (inactive); diplomate Clin. Psychology, Am. Bd. Profl. Psychology. Intern clin. psychology Menninger Found. Topeka (Kans.) State Hosp., 1952-53; postdoctoral fellow clin. child psychology Menninger Clinic, Topeka, 1955-56; staff psychologist Kankakee (Ill.) State Hosp., 1954-55; head staff psychologist child guidance clinic Kings County Hosp., Bklyn., 1957-58; dir. psychology clinic Barnes-Renard Hosp.; instr. med. psychology Sch. Medicine Washington U., 1959-60; clin. rsch. cons. Episc. City Diocese, St. Louis, 1959-60; pvt. practice Fullerton, Calif., 1960—93; fellow Internat. Coun. Sex Edn. and Parenthood, 1984, Am. U., Washington. Psychol. cons. Fullerton Cmty. Hosp., 1961-81; staff cons. clin. psychology Martin Luther Hosp., Anaheim, Calif., 1963-70; chair, participant psychol. symposiums, 1956—; spkr., lectr. in field. Contbr. articles on clin. psychology to profl. publs. Elected to Hall of Fame Ctrl. H.S., Evansville, Ind., 1966; recipient Svc. award Yuma County (Ariz.) Head Start Program, 1972, Statue of Victory Personality of Yr. award Centro Studi E. Ricerche Delle Nazioni, Italy, 1985, Alumni Merit award Northwestern U. Coll. Arts and Scis., 1997; named Miss Heritage, Heritage Publs., 1965. Fellow AAAS (emeritus), APA (Soc. for the Psychology of Women, Psychotherapy Internat. Psychology Recognition award for lifelong contbns. to advancement of psychology internationally 2002), Soc. Clin. Psychology, Soc. Cons. Psychology (dir. exec. bd. 1976-79), Acad. Clin. Psychology, Am. Assn. Applied and Preventive Psychology (charter), Royal Soc. Pub. Health Eng. (emeritus), Internat. Coun. Psychologists (dir. 1977-79, sec. 1962-64, 73-76, 2 awards 2003, recognition for pioneering leadership in internat. psychology, named amb. for life award 2003), Am. Orthopsychiat. Assn. (life), World Wide Acad. Scholars of N.Z. (life), Assn. Psychol. Sci. (charter), L.A. Soc. Clin. Psychologists (exec. bd. 1966-67), Internat. Coun. Psychologists; mem. AAUP (emeritus), Calif. Psychol. Assn. (life, ins. com. 1961-65), LA County Psychol. Assn. (emeritus), Orange County Psychol. Assn. (charter founder, exec. bd. 1961-62), Am. Pub. Health Assn. (emeritus), Internat. Platform Assn., NY Acad. Scis. (emeritus), Purdue U. Alumni Assn. (life, past pres. coun., mem. dean's club, Citizenship award 1975, Disting. Alumni award 1993, Old Master 1993), Northwestern U. Past 1851 Soc. (Coll. Arts and Scis. Merit award 1997), Ctr. Study Presidency, Soc. Jewelry Historians USA (charter), Alumni Assn. Menninger Sch. Psychiatry, Sigma Xi (emeritus). Achievements include development of innovative theories and techniques of clinical practice; acknowledged pioneer in development of psychology as science and profession both nationally and internationally, and in marital and family therapy, and in consulting to hospitals and clinics. Office: PO Box 6067 Beverly Hills CA 90212-1067 Office Phone: 310-474-1361. Office Fax: 310-474-1361.

EVANS, MAX JAY, historical society administrator; b. Lehi, Utah, May 11, 1943; s. Karl Robinson and Lucile (Johnson) E.; m. Mary Wheatley, June 16, 1967; children: David Max, Joseph Michael, Katherine Anne, Laura, Emily. BS, U. Utah, 1968; MS, Utah State U., 1971. Archivist LDS Ch. Hist. Dept., Salt Lake City, 1971-75; asst. ch. librarian, archivist Mormon Ch. Hist. Dept., Salt Lake City, 1975-77; dep. state archivist State Hist. Soc. Wis., Madison, 1977-86, library dir., 1986; dir. Utah State Hist. Soc., Salt Lake City, 1986—; acting dir. Utah State Archives, Salt Lake City, 1986-88. Archival cons. N.Y. State Archives, Albany, 1981, Wyo Dept. Archives and Hist., Cheyenne, 1982. Co-author: MARC for Archives and Manuscripts: A Compendium of Practice, 1985 (SAA Coker award 1986); articles in field. Trustee Middleton (Wis.) Pub. Libr., 1974-86, Am. West Heritage Found., 1995—; exec. sec. Utah Statehood Centennial Commn., 1988-93, Utah Pioneer Sesquicentennial Celebration Coord. Coun., 1994-98; chair Utah State Rcds. com., 1992—; bd. dirs. Rsch. Librs. Group, 1991-92; coun. mem. Am. Assn. for State and Local History, 1997—. Fellow Soc. Am. Archivists; mem. Utah State Hist. Soc. Mem. Lds Ch. Avocations: skiing, bicycling, hiking, reading, movies. Office: Utah State Hist Soc 300 Rio Grande St Salt Lake City UT 84101-1106

EVANS, R. MONT, state legislator; b. Montpelier, Idaho, Jan. 9, 1947; m. Cheryl Evans; 4 children. BA in Polit. Sci. and History, Brigham Young U.; MSW, U. Utah. Social worker, adminstr. Utah Dept. Corrections; mem. Utah Ho. of Reps., 1986-96, Utah State Senate, 1996—, mem. transp. and pub. safety com., mem. transp. and environ. quality appropriations com., chair state and local affairs com. Mem. Riverton (Utah) City Coun., 1983-86; trustee, chmn. Riverton Arts Coun., 1983-87; trustee Riverton Hist. Soc.; mem., chmn. Riverton City Planing and Zoning Commn., 1982-84. Recipient Total Citizen award Utah C. of C., 1992. Republican. Mem. Lds Ch. Home: 1599 Big Var Way Riverton UT 84065-4003

EVANS, ROBERT VINCENT, sales and marketing executive; b. Mobile, Ala., Sept. 21, 1958; s. William Alexander Evans and Katherine Barbara (Doerr) Davidson; children: James Vernon, Chelsea Marie; m. Elise Ann Brackmann; children: Layla Annelise, Alexander Robert. BS in Computer Info. Systems, Regis U., Denver, 1987, BS in Tech. Mgmt., 1987; postgrad. in Mgmt., U. Wash., 1995. Electrician Climax Molybdenum Co., Colo., 1978—82; applications engr. Honeywell, Inc., Englewood, Colo., 1982—83, sales engr., 1983—87; sys. engr. Apple Computer, Inc., Seattle, 1987—88, mgr. regional sys. engring. Portland, Oreg., 1988—96, dist. sales mgr. Seattle, 1997—2002; v.p. Bulldog Beach Interactive, Seattle, 2002—04; sales enablement mgr. BEA Sys., Inc., Kirkland, Wash., 2004—. Author: Anthology of American Poets, 1981. Dir. Operation Lookout, Seattle, 1989; mem. Rep. Nat. Com.; commr. dist. chmn. Boy Scouts Am. Recipient USMC Blues award, Marine Corps Assn. Leatherneck award, 1977, Denver Post Outstanding Svc. award, 1983, N.Y. Zool. Soc. Hon. medal, James West fellowship award, Paul Harris fellowship award, Silver Beaver award Boy Scouts Am., 1998. Mem. Am. Mgmt. Assn., Am. Platform Assn., Mensa, Rotary, Kiwanis. Republican. Avocations: reading, church ministry. Office: BEA Systems Inc 10230 NE Points Dr Kirkland WA 98033 E-mail: rvevans@gmail.com.

EVANS, RONALD ALLEN, lodging chain executive; b. Louisville, Apr. 5, 1940; s. William Francis and Helen Maxine (Hart) E.; m. Lynne Anne Ingraham, Aug. 25, 1979; children: Nicole Louise, Michele Lynne, Christopher Hart BS in Mgmt., Ariz. State U., 1963. Vice pres. Electronic Data Systems, Dallas, 1969-73; vice pres. First Fed. Savs., Phoenix, 1973-77, Community Fin. Corp., Scottsdale, Ariz., 1977-78; pres. Evans Mgmt. Services, Inc., Phoenix, 1978-84; pres., CEO Best Western Internat., Inc., Phoenix, 1979-98; dean Sch. Hotel and Restaurant Mgmt. No. Ariz. U., Flagstaff, 1998—. Served to lt. USNR, 1963-66 Decorated Bronze Star Mem.: Masons (32 deg.), KT, Shriner. Republican. Episcopalian. Office: No Ariz U Sch Hotel & Restaurant Mgmt PO Box 5638 Flagstaff AZ 86011-0001

EVANS, RONALD M., microbiologist, educator; BA in Bacteriology, UCLA, 1970, PhD in Microbiology and Immunology, 1974. Asst. rsch. prof. dept. molecular cell biology Rockefeller U., NYC, 1975—78; from asst. to assoc. prof. tumor virology lab. Salk Inst. Biol. Studies Howard Hughes Med. Inst., La Jolla, Calif., 1978—84, sr. mem. molecular biology and virology lab. Salk Inst. Biol. Studies, 1984—86, prof. gene expression lab Salk Inst. Biol. Studies, 1986—, investigator, 1985—; prof. Salk Institute for Biol. Studies, San Diego. Adj. prof. dept. biology U. Calif., San Francisco, 1985—, adj. prof. dept. biomedical scis. Sch. Medicine, San Diego, 1989—, adj. prof. dept. neurosciences, 1995—; chmn. faculty Salk Inst. Biol. Studies Howard Hughes Med. Inst., La Jolla, 1993—94, La Jolla, 1997—98; mem. sci. adv. bd. SIBIA, 1983—; mem. external sci. adv. com. City of Hope, 1987; mem. molecular biology study sect. NIH, 1983—86, mem. molecular neurobiology study sect., 1984—85; mem. nat. adv. com. Pew Scholars Program in Biomedical Scis., 1987—2000; founder and chair sci. adv. bd. Ligand Pharm., 1988—; mem. program com. Searle Scholars, 1989—91; mem. Alfred P. Sloan Jr. selection com. GM Cancer Rsch. Found., 1991; organizer numerous confs. in field; mem. external sci. adv. bd. Mass. Gen. Hosp., 1996—; mem. sci. adv. bd. Dana Farber Cancer Inst., 1996—, Osaka Bioscience Inst., 1999—; S. Richard Hill, Jr. vis. prof. U. Ala., 1995; Woodward vis. prof. Meml. Sloan-Kettering, 1996; Burroughs Wellcome vis. prof. U. Mass., 1998; spkr. in field, lectr.; March of Dimes chair in Molecular and Developmental Neurobiology Salk Inst., La Jolla, Calif. Editor: Molecular Endocrinology, 1993—97; editor: (assoc. editor) Molecular Brain Rsch., 1985—93, Jour. Neuroscience, 1985—90, Neuron, 1987—93; mem. editl. bd. Receptors and Channels, 1992—93, Genes and Development, 1992—, Hormones and Signalling, 1996—; co-editor: Current Opinion in Cell Biology, 1993. Mem. fellowship screening com. Am. Cancer Soc., 1987—90. Recipient Gregory Pincus medal, Laurentian Soc., 1988, Louis S. Goodman and Alfred Gilman award, Am. Soc. Pharmacology and Exptl. Therapeutics, 1988, Van Meter/Rorer Pharm. prize, Am. Thyroid Assn., 1989, Gregory Pincus Meml. award, Worcester Found. Exptl. Biology, 1991, Rita Levi Montalcini award, Fidia Rsch. Found. Neuroscience, 1991, Osborne and Mendel award, Am. Inst. Nutrition, 1992, award for cancer rsch., Robert J. and Claire Pasarow Found., 1993, Transatlantic medal, Soc. Endocrinology, 1994, Dickson prize in medicine, U. Pitts., 1994—95, Morton award, U. Liverpool, Biochemical Soc., 1996, Gerald Aurbach Meml. award, Assn. Bone and Mineral Rsch., 1997, Fred Conrad Koch award, Endocrine Soc., 1999, award for disting. achievement in metabolic rsch., Bristol-Myers Squibb, 2000, Alfred P. Sloan Jr. prize, GM Cancer Rsch. Found., 2003, Albert Lasker award for Basic Medical Rsch., 2004, Gairdner Found. Internat. award, 2006, Grande Médaille d'Or, France, 2005, Glenn T. Seaborg medal, 2005, Harvey prize, 2006, Albany Med. Ctr. prize in Medicine and Biomedical Rsch., 2007; named Calif. Scientist of Yr., Calif. Mus. Sci., 1994, most cited researcher, Inst. Scientific Info., 1997; fellow, NIH, 1975—78; Rsch. Assoc. fellow, Cancer Rsch. Com. Calif., 1975. Mem.: NAS, Inst. Medicine, 2004, Am. Assn. Cancer Rsch. (chair cancer rsch. com. 2001, Pezcoller Internat. award 2001, Eleventh C.P. Rhoads Meml. award 1990), Am. Acad. Arts and Scis. (fellow), Harvey Soc., Am. Acad. Microbiology, Am. Soc. Microbiology (fellow), Soc. Neuroscience, Soc. Devel. Biology, Endocrine Soc. (Edwin B. Astwood Lectureship award 1993). Office: Salk Inst Biol Studies Howard Hughes Med Inst 10010 N Torrey Pines Rd La Jolla CA 92037 Office Phone: 858-453-4100 ext. 1302. Office Fax: 858-455-1349. Business E-Mail: evans@salk.edu.*

EVANS, THOMAS EDGAR, JR., title insurance agency executive; b. Toronto, Ohio, Apr. 17, 1940; s. Thomas Edgar and Sarah Ellen (Bauer) E.; m. Cynthia Lee Johnson, Feb. 23; children: Thomas Edgar, Douglas, Melinda, Jennifer. BA, Mt. Union Coll., 1963. Tchr., Lodi, Ohio, 1963-64; salesman Simpson-Evans Realty, Steubenville, Ohio, 1964-65, Shadron Realty, Tucson, 1965-67; real estate broker, co-owner Double E Realty, Tucson, 1967-69; escrow officer, br. mgr., asst. county mgr., v.p. Ariz. Title Ins., Tucson, 1969-80; pres. Commonwealth Land Title Agy., Tucson, 1980-82, dir.; pres. Fidelity Nat. Title Agy., 1982—90; bd. govs. Calif. Land Title Assn., 1990—; exec. v.p. Fidelity Nat. Title Ins. Co., 1990-92; v.p. Inland Empire Divsn. Fidelity Nat. Title, 1991-93, pres. Orange County divsn., 1993-2000, exec. v.p., regional mgr., 2000—08; exec. v.p. Fidelity Nat. Title Group, 2008—. Bd. dirs. Western Fin. Trust Co., Fidelity Nat. Fin. Inc., Fidelity Nat. Title Ins. Co., The Griffin Co., Computer Market Place, Inc., e Market Place, Chgo. Title Ins. Co.; bd. dirs., chmn. bd. Cochise Title Agy., TIPCO; v.p., dir. A.P.C. Corp. Named Boss Yr., El Chaparral chpt. Am. Bus. Women's Assn., 1977. Mem. Calif. Land Title Assn. (pres. 1995-96), So. Ariz. Escrow Assn., So. Ariz. Mortgage Bankers Assn. (bd. dirs. 1982-85), Ariz. Mktg. Bankers Assn., Old Pueblo Businessmen's Assn. Tucson, Tucson Bd. Realtors, Ariz. Assn. Real Estate Exchangors (bd. dirs. 1968-69), Land Title Assn. Ariz. (pres. 1984), So. Ariz. Homebuilders Assn., Tucson Real Estate Exchangors (pres. 1968), Pacific Club, Ctr. Club, Old Pueblo Courthouse Club, La Paloma Club, Ventana Country Club, Centre Ct. Club, Coto de Casa Country Club, Montecito Country Club, Elks Club, Pima Jaycees (dir. 1966), Sertoma (charter pres., chmn. bd. Midtown sect. 1968-70), Sunrise Rotary, Old Pueblo Club, South Coast Repertory (trustee 1996-2000), Blue Key, Sigma Nu. Home: 3260 Braemar Dr Santa Barbara CA 93109 Office: 4050 Calle Real Ste 210 Santa Barbara CA 93110-3413

EVEN, RANDOLPH M., lawyer; b. 1943; BS, U. Calif.; JD, Calif. Western Sch. Law. Bar: Calif. 1969. Atty. Even, Crandall, Wade, & Lowe and predecessor firm Genson, Even, Crandall & Wade, P.C., Woodland Hills, Calif., Randolph M. Even & Assocs., PLC, 2002—. Mem. legal com. Calif.; lectr. in field. With Calif. Med. Legal Com., 2005—. Mem. Am. Bd. Trial Advocates (diplomate), Assn. So. Calif. Def. Counsel (bd. dirs. 1978-80, 93-98). Office: 5550 Topanga Canyon Blvd STE 280 Woodland Hills CA 91367-7471 Office Phone: 818-226-5444.

EVENHUIS, HENK J., research company executive; b. Ontario, Calif., Apr. 10, 1943; s. Kornelus and Harmina (Vermeer) E.; m. Cynthia Wheelus, Jan. 31, 1964; children: John, Karen. BS in Acctg., Calif. State Poly. U., Pomona, 1967; MBA in Fin., U. Santa Clara, 1976. V.p., CFO, Ferix Corp., Fremont, Calif., 1983-85, Trimedia Corp., Fremont, 1985-86, Corvus Systems Corp., San Jose, Calif., 1986-87; sr. v.p., CFO, Lam Rsch. Corp., Fremont, 1987—. Bd. dirs. Credence Corp., Fremont. Mem. Fin. Execs. Inst. (bd. dirs. Santa Clara, Calif. 1988-90). Avocations: skiing, golf. Office: Fair Isaac & Co Inc 120 N Redwood Dr San Rafael CA 94903

EVERETT, JUDITH, merchandising educator; d. Culbertson; m. Christopher Everett. BS, Kent State U., Ohio, 1972; MA, Kent State U., Kent, Ohio, 1974; MBA, Ariz. State U., Tempe, 1987. Asst. prof. Western Mich. U., 1977—79; prof. No. Ariz. U., Flagstaff, Ariz., 1979—. Author: Guide to Producing a Fashion Show, 2004, Promotion in the Merchandising Environment, 2007, Writing for the Fashion Business, 2008—; dir.: (fashion shows) Student productions, 2000—06 (NAU's Svc. Learning awards, 2000, 2006). Charter bd. mem. Fashion Group Internat., Phoenix/Scottsdale, Ariz., 1995—2004. Recipient Lifetime Achievement award, Sch. of Comm., 2003. Mem.: Am. Collegiate Retailing Assn., Fashion Group Internat. Office: No Arizona Univ Box 5619 Flagstaff AZ 86011

EVERETTE, BRUCE L., retail executive; Joined Richmond Divsn. Safeway, Inc., 1968, dist. mgr. Okla. and Va., retail ops. mgr. Phoenix, 1991, divsn. mgr., 1995—98, Calif., 1998—2001, exec. v.p. retail ops. Pleasanton, Calif., 2001—. Office: Safeway Inc 5918 Stoneridge Mall Rd Pleasanton CA 94588

EVERHART, THOMAS EUGENE, retired academic administrator, engineering educator; b. Kansas City, Mo., Feb. 15, 1932; s. William Elliott and Elizabeth Ann (West) E.; m. Doris Arleen Wentz, June 21, 1953; children: Janet Sue, Nancy Jean, David William, John Thomas. AB in Physics magna cum laude, Harvard, 1953; MSc, UCLA, 1955; PhD in Engring., Cambridge U., Eng., 1958. Mem. tech. staff Hughes Research Labs., Culver City, Calif., 1953—55; mem. faculty U. Calif., Berkeley, 1958—78, prof. elec. engring. and computer scis., 1967—78, Miller research prof., 1969—70, chmn. dept., 1972—77; prof. elec. engring., Joseph Silbert dean engring. Cornell U., Ithaca, 1979—84; prof. elec. and computer engring., chancellor U. Ill., Urbana-Champaign, 1984—87; prof. elec. engring. and applied physics, pres. Calif. Inst. Tech., Pasadena, 1987—97, pres. emeritus, 1997—. Fellow scientist Westinghouse Rsch. Labs., Pitts., 1962-63; guest prof. Inst. Applied Physics, U. Tuebingen, Germany, 1966-67, Waseda U., Tokyo, Osaka U., 1974; vis. fellow Clare Hall, Cambridge, U., 1975; chmn. Electron, Ion and Photon Beam Symposium, 1977; cons. in field; sci. and edn. adv. com. Lawrence Berkeley Lab., 1978-85, chmn., 1980-85; mem. sci. adv. com. GM, 1980-89, chmn., 1984-89; bd. dirs. Saint-Gobain Corp., Acorn Techs., Novelx, Inc.; tech. adv. com. R.R. Donnelly & Sons, 1981-89; sr. sci. advisor W.M. Keck Found., 1997—, dir., 2006-; pro-vice chancellor Cambridge U., 1998; dir. Kavli Found., 2002-. Chmn. Sec. of Energy Adv. Bd., 1990-93; bd. dirs. KCET, 1989-97, Corp. for Nat. Rsch. Initiatives; trustee Calif. Inst. Tech., 1998—; mem. bd. overseers Harvard U., 1999-2005, pres., 2004-05. Marshall scholar Cambridge U., 1955-58, NSF sr. fellow, 1966-67, Guggenheim fellow, 1974-75. Fellow IEEE (Founder's Award medal 2002), AAAS, ASEE, Royal Acad. Engring.; mem. Okawa Found. (Okawa award 2002), NAE (ednl. adv. bd. 1984-88, mem. com. 1984-89, chmn. 1988, coun. 1988-94, 96-2002), Microbeam Analysis Soc. Am., Electron Microscopy Soc. Am. (coun. 1970-72, pres. 1977), Coun. on Competitiveness (vice-chmn. 1990-96), Assn. Marshall Scholars and Alumni (pres. 1965-68), Athenaeum Club, California Club, Sigma Xi, Eta Kappa Nu. Home: PO Box 1639 Goleta CA 93116 Business E-Mail: everhart@caltech.edu.

EVERROAD, JOHN DAVID, lawyer; b. Columbus, Ind., Jan. 6, 1940; s. Henry and Margaret L. (Eckleman) E.; m. Patricia Diane Hayworth, June 10, 1967; children: Andrew Quinn, Matthew Oldham. BA, Vanderbilt U., 1962, JD, 1969. Bar: Ariz. 1970, Calif. 1997. Atty. Fennemore Craig PC, Phoenix, 1969—. Mem. panels Nat. Inst. Trial Advocacy programs; lawyer Com. Uniform Jury Standards State of Ariz.; mem. faculty Continuing Edn. Legal Programs. Pres. Parochial Sch. Bd., Phoenix, 1972-78; mem. Christ Luth. Ch., Phoenix, 1969—, sec., 1986, 88-89, pres., 1979-80; bd. dirs. Combined Metro. Phoenix Arts and Scis., 1996-98. With USMC, 1962-66. Fellow ABA, Ariz. Bar Found. (founder), Maricopa County Bar Found. (founder), Am. Coll. Trial Lawyers; mem. Am. Bd. Trial Advocates, Maricopa County Bar Assn. (pres. 1992-93), Ariz. State Bar Assn. (chmn. edit. bd. Jour., com. revisions uniform jury instructions 1984-89, Disciplinary com. 1984-90), Phi Delta Phi. Republican. Lutheran. Avocations: scuba diving, fishing, bow hunting. Office: Fennemore Craig PC 3003 N Central Ste 2600 Phoenix AZ 85012-2913 Home: 33 E Coulter Ave Phoenix AZ 85012 Home Phone: 602-274-3139; Office Phone: 602-916-5302. Business E-Mail: jeverroa@fclaw.com.

EVERS, WILLIAMSON MOORE (BILL EVERS), education policy analyst, former federal agency administrator; b. San Francisco, Oct. 18, 1948; s. Henry Kaspar and Emily Stout Evers; m. Leslie Carver Johnson (div.); m. Mary Therese Gingell (div.); m. M. Anna Bryson; children: Daniel Kenneth, Pamela Ruth. BA in Polit. Sci., Stanford U., 1972, MA in Polit. Sci., 1978, PhD in Polit. Sci., 1987. Editor-in-chief Inquiry Mag., San Francisco, 1976—80; vis. asst. prof. Emory U., Atlanta, 1987—88; nat. and vis. fellow The Hoover Instn., Stanford U., 1988—94, rsch. fellow, 1995—; sr. edn. adv. to Amb. Paul Bremer Coalition Provisional Authority, Baghdad, Iraq, 2003; sr. adv. to Sec. Margaret Spellings US Dept. Edn., Washington, 2007, asst. sec. for planning, evaluation & policy devel., 2007—09. Adj. assoc. prof. Santa Clara (Calif.) U., 1995—98; commr. State Calif. Commn. for the Establishment Academic Content and Performance Stds., Sacramento, 1996—98; mem. math. content rev. panel State Calif. Standardized Testing and Reporting Program, Sacramento, 1998—2007, mem. history-social sci. content rev. panel, 1999—2007; mem. adv. bd. Calif. History-Social Sci. Project, Davis, 1999—2007; mem. Koret Task Force on K-12 Edn., Hoover Instn., Stanford, 1999—, Nat. Ednl. Rsch. Policy and Priorities Bd., Washington, 2001—02; commr. White House Commn. on Presdl. Scholars, Washington, 2001—07; mem. content rev. panel, history textbook adoption State of Calif., 2005; mem. Math. Sci. Review Panel, Inst. Edn. Sci., US Dept. Edn., Washington, 2005—06; mem. editl. bd. Edn. Next Mag., Stanford, Calif., 2000—07. Author: (public policy research) Victims' Rights, 1996; editor, contbr.: public policy research National Service: Pro & Con, 1990, What's Gone Wrong in America's Classrooms, 1998; co-editor: School Reform: The Critical Issues, 2001, School Accountability, 2002, Teacher Quality, 2002, Testing Student Learning, Evaluating Teaching Effectiveness, 2004. Mem. edn. adv. com. Bush-Cheney Transition, 2000—01; edn. policy advisor Richard Riordan Gubernatorial Campaign, 2001—02, William Simon Gubernatorial Campaign, 2002, George W. Bush Presidential Campaign, 2000, co-chmn. Calif. Edn. Coalition, 2000, co-vice-chmn. Calif. Edn. Coalition, 2004, mem. Nat. Steering Com., Nat. Edn. Coalition, 2004; co-chmn. Gov. Schwarzenegger's Coalition for Edn. Reform, 2005; co-chmn edn. coalition Arnold Schwarzenegger Gubernatorial Campaign, 2006; mem. bd. dirs. East Palo Alto Charter Sch., Calif., 1997—2004, pres., 2003—04; trustee Santa Clara County Bd. Edn., 2004—07. Co-recipient Koret Prize, 2002. Episcopalian. Office: The Hoover Institution Stanford U 434 Galvez Mall Stanford CA 94305-6010*

EWALD, ROBERT HANSEN (BO EWALD), computer software company executive; b. 1947; BS, U. Nev., 1969; MS, U. Colo., 1970. With U. Colo., 1970—76, Sperry Univac, 1976—77; at Los Alamos Nat. Lab., 1977-84; with Cray Rsch. Inc., Eagan, Minn., 1984—, v.p. Mendota Heights, Minn., 1985-89, exec. v.p. Chippewa Falls, Wis., 1989—, chief tech. officer, 1992-93, pres., COO, 1994—97, 1994—; exec. v.p., computer systems Silicon Graphics, Inc, 1997, exec. v.p., COO, 1997—98; pres., CEO E-Stamp Corp., 1999—2001; exec. chmn. Learn2 Corp., 2001—02; chmn., CEO Scale Eight, Inc., 2002—03; exec. v.p., pres. Ceridian Human Resources Ceridian Corp., 2003—05; chmn., CEO Linux Network, Inc., 2005—07; CEO Silicon Graphics, Inc. (SGI), Sunnyvale, Calif., 2007—. Mem. Pres. Info. Tech. Adv. Com., 1997—2001; bd. dirs. Ceridian Corp., 1997—2005, Silicon Graphics, Inc. (SGI), 2007—. Office: Silicon Graphics Inc 1140 E Arques Ave Sunnyvale CA 94085

EWELL, CHARLES MUSE, health care industry executive, consultant, publisher, educator; b. Richmond, Va., Jan. 12, 1937; s. Charles Muse Sr. and Virginia (Causey) E.; m. Loretta Ann Morris, Feb. 1960 (div. 1967); children— Charles Daniel, Elizabeth Morris; m. Valerie Ann White, Aug. 29, 1984 BS, MHA, Va. Commonwealth U.; PhD, U. Wis. Adminstr. for various hosps. in Midwest and East Coast, 1964-74; ptnr. Arthur Young & Co., Los Angeles, 1974-84; pres., chief exec. officer Am. Health Care Systems, San Diego, 1984-86; chmn. The Governance Inst., 1986—. Contbr. articles to profl. jours.; mem. editorial bd. various profl. jours. Chmn. men's bd. L.A. Philharm., 1982-83; bd. dirs. San Diego Symphony, 1986-90, Sharp Meml. Hosp., 1988-99. Mem. Valley Club (Sun Valley, Idaho), La Jolla Beach Club, La Jolla Country Club. Republican.

EWELL, MIRANDA JUAN, journalist; b. Beijing, Apr. 25, 1948; d. Vei-Chow and Hsien-fang Yolanda (Sun) J.; m. John Woodruff Ewell Jr., Feb. 20, 1971; children: Emily, David, Jonah. BA summa cum laude, Smith Coll., 1969; postgrad., Princeton U., 1971, U. Calif., Berkeley, 1981-82. Staff writer The Montclarion, Oakland, Calif., 1982-83; with San Jose (Calif.) Mercury News, 1984-99, staff writer; now correspondent San Jose (Calif.) Mercury News, San Francisco Bureau, 1990-95; correspondent in bus. San Jose Mercury News, 1997-99. Recipient Elsa Knight Thompson award Media Alliance, San Francisco, 1984, George Polk award L.I. U., N.Y., 1989, Heywood Broun award Newspaper Guild, Washington, 1989; Knight fellow Stanford U., 1995. Mem. Asian-Am. Journalists Assn.

EWY, GORDON ALLEN, cardiologist, researcher, educator; b. Brenham, Kans., Aug. 5, 1933; s. Marvin John and Hazel Miller (Allen) E.; m. Priscilla Ruth Weldon; children: Kim Elizabeth (dec.), Gordon Stuart, Mark Allen. BA, U. Kans., 1955, MD, 1961. Resident, house officer Georgetown U. Hosp., Washington, 1961-64, cardiology fellow, 1964-65; instr. medicine Georgetown U., Washington, 1965-68, asst. prof., 1968-69, U. Ariz., Tucson, 1969-70, assoc. prof., 1970-75, prof. medicine, 1975—, chief cardiology, dir. cardiology fellowship program, 1982—, assoc. head dept. medicine, 1986-94, dir. Sarver Heart Ctr., 1991—, The Gordon A. Ewy MD Disting. Endowed Chair Cardiovasc. Medicine, 2002—. Editor: Cardiovascular Drugs and Management of Heart Disease, 1982, 93, Current Cardiovascular Drug Therapy, 1984, Manual of Cardiovascular Diagnosis and Therapy, 5th edit., 2002; author numerous sci. publs.; contbr. numerous revs. to profl. jours., chpts. to books. Lt. (j.g.) USNR, 1955-57. Fellow ACP, Am. Heart Assn. (mem. clin. coun., nat. faculty advanced cardiac life support 1982-84, chmn. nat. programs subcom. 1982, bd. dirs. Ariz. chpt. 1975-82, 84-89, tchg. fellow 1970-75), Am. Coll. Cardiology (chmn. learning ctr. com. 1988-91, trustee 1992-97). Republican. Developed continuous chest compression CPR and Cardiocerebral Resuscitation. Office: Ariz Health Scis Ctr 1501 N Campbell Ave Tucson AZ 85724-0001 Office Phone: 520-626-2000. Personal E-mail: gaewy@aol.com.

EYMANN, RICHARD CHARLES, lawyer; b. Hanover, NH, June 6, 1945; BS, U. Oreg., 1968; JD, Gonzaga U., 1976. Bar: Wash. 1976, U.S. Dist. Ct. (ea. dist.) Wash. 1978, U.S. Ct. Appeals (9th cir.) 1987, U.S. Dist. Ct. (we. dist.) Wash. 1989, U.S. Supreme Ct. 1995. Ptnr. Eymann, Allison, Hunter Jones, P.S., Spokane, Wash. Mem. ABA, Am. Assoc. Justice, Wash. State Bar Assn. (bd. govs. 1997-98, pres. elect 1998-99, pres. 1999-2000), Wash. State Trial Lawyers Assn. (bd. govs. 1984-86, 88-95, v.p. East 1991-92, Trial Lawyer of Yr. 1995, pres. 1996-97), Wash. Trial Lawyers for Pub. Justice (bd. dirs. 1994-98), Am. Bd. Trial Advocates, Spokane County Bar Assn., Am. Inns of Ct.1991-93, Damage Attys. Round Table (2001-). Office: Eymann Allison Et Al 2208 W 2nd Ave Spokane WA 99201-5417 E-mail: eymann@eahjlaw.com.

EYRE, DAVID R., orthopedics educator; BS in Biochemistry, U. Leeds, Eng., 1966; PhD, U. Leeds, 1969. Prof., dir. rsch. U. Wash. Med. Ctr., Seattle. Mem. AAAS, Internat. Soc. Matrix Biology (founder), Am. Acad. Orthopaedic Surgeons (assoc.), Orthopaedic Rsch. Soc., Biochem. Soc., Conn. Tissue Soc., Protein Soc., East Coast Connective Tissue Club. Achievements include research on connective tissue biochemistry, collagen chemistry, inborn skeletal diseaease, cartilage pathology, biochemistry of intervertebral disc, bone resorption and osteoporosis. Office: U Wash Med Ctr Dept Orthopaedics Box 356500 1959 NE Pacific St Seattle WA 98195-0001

EYRING, HENRY BENNION, head of religious order; b. Princeton, NJ, May 31, 1933; s. Henry and Mildred (Bennion) E.; m. Kathleen Johnson, July 27, 1962; children: Henry J., Stuart J., Matthew J., John B., Elizabeth, Mary Kathleen. BS, U. Utah, 1955; MBA, Harvard U., 1959, DBA, 1963; DHum (hon.), Brigham Young U., 1985. Asst., then assoc. prof. Stanford U., Palo Alto, Calif., 1962—71; pres. Ricks Coll., Rexburg, Idaho, 1972—77; dep. commr. edn., then commr. LDS Ch., Salt Lake City, 1977—85, presiding bishopric, 1985—92, mem. 1st Quorum of the Seventy, 1992—95, mem. Quorum of the Twelve, 1995—2007, Second Counselor in First Presidency, 2007—08, First Counselor in First Presidency, 2008—. Author: To Draw Closer to God, 1997, Because He First Loved Us, 2002; co-author: The Organizational World, 1973. With USAF, 1955—57. Recipient Sloan faculty fellowship, MIT, 1963—64. Avocations: painting, woodcarving. Office: LDS Ch First Presidency 47 E South Temple Salt Lake City UT 84150-9701

EZRA, DAVID ALAN, federal judge; b. 1947; BBA magna cum laude, St. Mary's U., 1969, JD, 1972. Law clk. Office of Corp. Counsel City and County Honolulu, 1972; mem. firm Greenstein, Cowen & Frey, 1972-73, Anthony, Hoddick, Reinwald & O'Connor, 1973-80, Ezra, O'Connor, Moon & Tam, 1980-88; judge US Dist. Ct. (Hawaii dist.), 1988—, chief judge, 1998—. Adj. prof. law Wm. S. Richardson Sch. Law, 1978—; exec. com. 9th cir. Jud. Conf. Co-editor, author: Hwaii Construction Law - What to Do and When, 1987; editor: Hawaii Collection Practices Manual. 1st lt. USAR 1971-77. Daugherty Fund scholar, 1971, San Antonio Bar Assn. Aux. scholar, 1972. Mem. ABA, U.S. Fed. Judges Assn. (bd. dirs., exec. com.), Dist. Judges Assn. (v.p. 9th cir.), Hawaii State Bar, Am. Arbitration Assn., Delta Epsilon Sigma, Phi Delta Phi. Office: US Dist Ct 300 Alamoana Blvd C-400 Honolulu HI 96850

FAAL, EDI M. O., lawyer; b. Gambia, Africa, 1954; came to U.S., 1974; BS, Fla. Internat. U.; Barrister at Law, Mid. Temple Inns Ct., London; JD, Western State U., Fullerton, Calif., 1982. Bar: U.K., Wales, Calif., Ind., U.S. Supreme Ct. Adj. prof. U. So. Calif. Law Ctr., LA. Named Lawyer of Yr., Langston Bar Assn. L.A., 1994; recipient Pres.'s award L.A. Criminal Cts. Bar Assn., Legal Champion award Ohio Criminal Def. Bar Assn.

FAATZ, JEANNE RYAN, councilwoman; b. Cumberland, Md., July 30, 1941; d Charles Keith Ryan & Elizabeth McIntyre R; divorced; children: Kristin & Susan. BS, U. Ill., 1962; MA, U. Colo., Denver, 1985. Colorado State Representative, District 1, formerly, Assistant Majority Leader, formerly, member, Transportation & Energy Committee, formerly, Colorado House Representative; director, Sch-to-Career, Gov's Office, Colorado, currently; city councilwoman, Denver, currently.Teacher Eng & speech, Urbana Public Sch, 1963-66, Cherry Creek Sch, Englewood Colorado, 1966-67; secretary to Senate Majority Leader, 1976-78; col speech instructor, Metrop State Col, 1985-98. Former ho. asst. majority leader. Past pres. S.W. Denver YWCA Adult Edn. Club; former mem. bd. mgrs. S.W. Denver YMCA; past pres. Harvey Park (Colo.) Homeowners Assn. Denver Post Gallery of Fame, 1976; Gates Fellow to Harvard/JFK Sch Govt, Sr Exec Prog for State & Local Off, 1984; Woman of Year in Transportation, 1986; Health Sci Center Alumni Legislature Recognition Award, Colorado Univ, 1991; Guardian of Small Bus, Colorado, 1992; Taxpayer Champion, Colorado Union Taxpayers, 1998. Harvey Park Improvement Association (president, formerly). Republican. Home: 2903 S Quitman St Denver CO 80236-2208 Home Phone: 303-935-6915; Office Phone: 303-763-8562.

FABE, DANA ANDERSON, state supreme court chief justice; b. Cin., Mar. 29, 1951; d. George and Mary Lawrence (Van Antwerp) F.; m. Randall Gene Simpson, Jan. 1, 1983; 1 child, Amelia Fabe Simpson. BA, Cornell U., 1973; JD, Northeastern U., 1976. Bar: Alaska 1977, U.S. Supreme Ct. 1981. Law clk. to justice Alaska Supreme Ct., 1976-77; staff atty. pub. defenders State of Alaska, 1977-81; dir. Alaska Pub. Defender Agy., Anchorage, 1981—88; judge Superior Ct., Anchorage, 1988—92; deputy presiding judge Third Judicial Dist., 1992—95; justice Alaska Supreme Ct., Anchorage, 1996—, chief justice, 2000—03, 2006—. Chair Alaska Supreme Ct. Civil Rules Com., Alaska Supreme Ct. Judicial Outreach Commn., Alaska Ct. System Law Day Steering Comm., Alaska Teaching Justice Network. Named alumna of yr. Northeastern Sch. Law, 1983; recipient Northeastern Sch. Law Alumni Pub. Svc. award, 1991. Mem.: Am. Judicature Soc. (bd. dirs.), Alaska Bar Assoc. (bd. govs. 1987—88, co-chair Gender Equality Sect.). Office: Alaska Supreme Ct 303 K St Fl 5 Anchorage AK 99501-2013 Office Phone: 907-264-0622.

FABER, GEORGE DONALD, retired communications executive; b. Mpls., June 17, 1921; s. Morris William and Lowella (Whitman) F.; m. Marjorie Alice Knodel; children: Kathie Diane Goodman, Michael William, Patricia Netzley. Student, Wis. Coll. Music, 1940; BA, Northwestern U., 1941; PhD, Colo. State U., 1969. Writer, announcer, actor Sta. WHBL, Sheboygan, Wis., 1937-39; prodn. mgr. Sta. WMFD, Wilmington, NC, 1939-41; columnist and author Behind the Mike series, Cape Fear Pub. Co., Wilmington, NC, 1940-41; news editor NBC, Chgo., 1943-46; news dir., writer CBS, 1946-56; internat. mgr. CBS films, LA, 1956-71; internat. dir. client rels. Viacom Prodsn. divsn. Paramount TV, 1971—2000. Dir. comm., bd. dir. Callahan and Assocs. LA Vol. fundraising Childrens Hosp. Recipient 2 Emmys. Mem. Internat. Photo Journalists (hon. life), TV Programs Execs. Com. (publicity), Sigma Delta Chi. Avocations: photography, fundraising for charities. Home: 10760 Cushdon Ave Los Angeles CA 90064-3219 Personal E-mail: georgedfaber@aol.com.

FABER, MICHAEL WARREN, lawyer; b. NYC, June 7, 1943; s. Carl Faber and Harriet Ruth Cohen; m. Adele Zolot, Apr. 16, 1975; children: Evan, Jenna. AB, Hunter Coll., 1964; JD, Fordham U., 1967. Bar: N.Y. 1967, D.C. 1972, U.S. Ct. Claims, 1972, U.S. Supreme Ct. 1972, Colo. 1993. Gen. atty. FCC, Washington, 1967-69, trial atty., 1969-71, atty. advisor to Commr. T.J. Houser, 1971; assoc. Peabody, Rivlin, Lambert & Meyers, Washington, 1971-73; ptnr. Peabody, Lambert & Meyers, Washington, 1973-84, Reid and Priest, Washington, 1984-93, mem. exec. com., 1986-92; prin. The Faber Group, Cascade, Colo., 1993-94; pres. USA Volleyball Ctrs. LLC, Colorado Springs, Colo., 1995-96; owner The Pantry Restaurant, Green Mountain Falls, Colo., 1996—2001; prin. Crossroads Cons., LLC, Cascade, 2001—. Dir. Workforce Partnership study Pikes Peak Workforce Investment Bd., Colorado Springs, 2003; cons. White House Office Telecom. Policy, 1971; chmn. organizing com. Nat. Volleyball League. Bd. dirs. Washington Very Spl. Arts, 1986-93; chair Telecom. Policy Adv. Com., Colo. Springs, 2002—, SAFE Com., Colo. Springs, 2002—; v.p. devel. Pikes Peak United Way, 2003-04, dirs. campaign, 2003. Mem. NY Bar Assn., DC Bar Assn., Fed. Comm. Bar Assn., Colo. Bar Assn., Manitou Springs Edn. Assn. (pres. 2002-04), Ct. Care Pikes Peak Region (bd. dirs. 2006-).

FABER, SANDRA MOORE, astronomer, educator; b. Boston, Dec. 28, 1944; d. Donald Edwin and Elizabeth Mackenzie (Borwick) Moore; m. Andrew L. Faber, June 9, 1967; children: Robin, Holly. BA, Swarthmore Coll., 1966, DSc (hon.), 1986; PhD, Harvard U., 1972; DSc with honors, Williams Coll., 1996, Chgo. U., 2006. Asst. prof., astronomer Lick Obs., U. Calif., Santa Cruz, 1972-77, assoc. prof., astronomer, 1977-79, prof., astronomer, 1979—; Univ. Prof. U. Calif., Santa Cruz, 1996—. Mem. astronomy adv. panel NSF, 1975-77; vis. prof. Princeton U., 1978, U. Hawaii, 1983, Ariz. State U., 1985; Phillips visitor Haverford Coll., 1982; Feshbach lectr. MIT, Cambridge, Mass., 1990; Darwin lectr. Royal Astron. Soc., 1991; Marker lectr. Pa. State U., 1992; Bunyan lectr. Stanford U., 1992; Tomkins lectr. U. Calif., San Francisco, 1992; Mohler lectr. U. Mich., 1994; mem. Nat. Acad. Astronomy Survey Panel, 1979-81Nfat. Acad. Com. on Astronomy and Astrophysics 1993-1995; chmn. vis. com. Space Telescope Sci. Inst., 1983-84, co-chmn. TAC rev. commn., 2002, mem. treas. program adv. commn., 2002-; co-chmn. sci. steering com. Keck Obs., 1987-92, leader DEIMOS spectrograph team, 1993—; mem. Wide Field Camera team Hubble Space Telescope, 1985-97, user's com., 1990-92, mem. advanced radial camera selection team, 1995,co-chmn. TAC review comm., 2002; mem. treas. pgm. advis. comm. 2002-; mem. Calif. Coun. on Sci. and Tech., 1989-94,; Com. on Future Smithsonian Instn., 1994-95; mem. White House Space Sci. Workshop, 1996, Waterman Awards Com., NSF, 1997-99, Nat. Medal of Sci. selection com., 1999-2001; mem. Plumian Prof. selection com. Cambridge U., 1998—, Ceclia Payne Gaposchkin lectr. Howard Coll. Obs., 2004, Halley lectr. astronomy dept., Oxford U., 2004, Miller visiting prof., U. Calif., 2005, Sackler lectr. physics dept., Princeton U., 2005, Einstein lectr. Hebrew U., Jerusalem, 2006, bd. overseas Howard U., 2006-. Assoc. editor: Astrophys. Jour. Letters, 1982-87; editorial bd.: Ann. Revs. Astronomy and Astrophysics, 1982-87; contbr. articles to profl. jours. Trustee Carnegie Instn., Washington, 1985—; bd. dirs. Ann. Revs., 1989—, SETI Inst., 1997-2006; editl. affairs com. Ann. Revs., 1996—; exec. com. Ann. Revs., 1998—; Scripps Instn. Oceanography Coun., 2000-08; bd. overseers Fermilab, 2002-06. Recipient Bart J. Bok prize Harvard U., 1978, Director's Distinguished Lectr. award Livermore Nat. Lab., 1986; NASA Group Achievement award, 1993, DeVaucouleurs medal U. Tex., 1997, Medaille de l'Institute d' Astophysique de Paris, 2006, Centennial medal Howard Grad. Sch. Arts Scis., 2006; Carnegie Lectr. Carnegie Inst. Washington, 1988, 99; NSF fellow, 1966-71; Woodrow Wilson fellow, 1966-71; Alfred P. Sloan fellow, 1977-81; listed among 100 best Am. scientists under 40, Sci. Digest, 1984, listed among 50 best Am. Women scientists, Discover Mag., 2002; Tetelman fellow, Yale U., 1987. Fellow Calif. Coun. on Sci. and Tech., Am. Assn. Advancement Sci.; mem. NAS (vice chair adv. panel on cosmology 1993, rsch. in astronomy commn. on orgn. and mgmt. astrophysics 2001, chair Spitzer Space Telescope Time Assignment Comm. 2008, chair astronomy sect.), Am. Philos. Soc. Am. Acad. Arts and Scis., Calif. Acad. Scis., 1998—, Am. Astron. Soc. (councilor 1982-84, Dannie Heineman prize 1986), Internat. Astron. Union, Am. Philos. Soc., Phi Beta Kappa, Sigma Xi. Office: U Calif Lick Obs Santa Cruz CA 95064 E-mail: faber@ucolick.org.

FABREGAS, J. ROBERT, retail appearel executive; M in Bus. Adminstrn., Rutgers U. Exec. v.p. Credit Suisse, Los Angeles; exec. v.p., head corp. fin. Am. Savings Bank; pres., founder Stonepine Holdings, Ltd.; CFO, exec. v.p. Easyriders, Inc., 1999—. Office: Easyriders Inc 28210 Dorothy Dr Agoura Hills CA 91301

FACTOR, MAX, III, mediator, arbitrator; b. LA, Sept. 25, 1945; s. Sidney B. and Dorothy F.; BA in Econs. magna cum laude, Harvard U., 1966; JD, Yale U., 1969. Bar: Calif. 1970, US Ct. Appeals (6th cir.) 1971, US Dist. Ct. (ctrl. dist.) Calif. 1971. Law clk. US Ct. Appeals (6th cir.), 1969-71; exec. dir. Calif. Law Ctr., LA, 1973-74; dir. Consumer Protection Sect., Los Angeles City Atty., 1974-77; pvt. practice Factor & Agay, Beverly Hills, Calif, 1978-94; full-time neutral Factor Mediation and Arbitration Svcs., 2000-. Expert witness numerous state and fed. bds., 1974-78; guest lectr. UCLA, U. So. Calif., LA County Bar Assn., Calif. Dept. Consumer Affairs, 1974-76; hearing examiner City of LA, 1975. Contbr. articles to profl. jours. Bd. dirs. Western Law Ctr. for Handicapped, LA, 1977-79, Beverly Hills Unified Sch. Dist., 1979-83; pres. Beverly Hills Bd. Edn., 1983; bd. councilors U. Southern Calif. Law Ctr., LA, 1983—; chmn. Beverly Hills Visitors Bur., 1989-90. Recipient scholarship award Harvard Coll., 1965; Max Factor III Day proclaimed in his honor Beverly Hills City Council, 1979; recipient Disting. Service to Pub. Edn. award Beverly Hills Bd. Edn., 1979; named one of Southern Calif. Top Neutrals, Best Lawyers Am. and Super Lawyers, 2005, 06, 07. Fellow Internat. Acad. Mediators; mem. State Bar Calif. (chair com. on adminstrn. of justice 2006-07), LA County Bar Assn. (chmn. various coms. 1976-78), Southern Calif. Mediation Assn. (pres. 2005-06), Beverly Hills C. of C. (pres. 1987-88), Beverly Hills Edn. Found. (pres. 1977-79). Office: Factor Mediation and Arbitration Svcs 21355 Pacific Coast Hwy Ste 200 Malibu CA 90265 Office Phone: 310-456-3500. Business E-Mail: max@factormediation.com.

FADELL, TONY (ANTHONY M. FADELL), computer company executive; b. 1969; m. Danielle Lambert. BS in Computer Engring., U. Mich., 1991. Software engr., salesman, tech. support engr. Quality Computers, Inc., Grosse Point, Calif., 1986—89; design engr. Ronan, Inc., Woodland Hills, Calif., 1989; founder, sys. dir., rschr. U. Mich., Ann Arbor, Mich., 1988—91; founder, pres., ASIC HW engr. ASIC Enterprises, Inc., Westlake Village, Calif., 1989—92; founder, pres. Constructive Instruments, Inc., Ann Arbor, Mich., 1991—92; diagnostics engr. General Magic, Inc., Sunnyvale, Calif., 1992, hardware & software engr., 1992—94, system architect, 1994—95; contractor, sr. SW engr. Rocket Science, Inc., 1994—95; founder, CTO, dir. engring., dir. bus. develop. Phillips Consumer Electronics, Mobile Computing Group, 1995—98; v.p. bus. develop. Phillips Consumer Electronics, Strategy & Ventures U.S.A., 1998—99; independent mgmt. cons. Beatnik, Inc., 1999; founder, CEO Fuse Systems, Inc., 1999—2000; contractor Apple Inc. (formerly Apple Computer, Inc.), Cupertino, Calif., 2001, sr. dir., iPod & other spl. projects, 2001—04, v.p., iPod engring., 2004—06, sr. v.p., iPod divsn., 2006—08, adv. to CEO, 2008—. Named one of 50 Who Matter Now, Business 2.0, 2007. Achievements include patents in field. Office: Apple Inc 1 Infinite Loop Cupertino CA 95014 Fax: 650-233-8247. E-mail: tony@fadell.ca.

FAERBER, CHARLES N., editor; b. Wakefield, RI, July 11, 1944; BA, Dartmouth Coll., 1966; MS, San Diego State U., 1977. Newspaper reporter/editor, 1972-78; v.p. legis. affairs Nat. Notary Assn. Editor Nat. Notary mag., Notary Bull. Served with USN, 1967-72. Office: Nat Notary Assn Box 2402 9350 DeSoto Ave Chatsworth CA 91313-2402

FAGAN, TUCKER, legislative staff member, former state agency administrator; Commd. USAF, advanced through grades to vice comdr. 20th Air Force, rep. to Sec. of Def., chief Air Force Manpower and Orgn. divsn., head Joint Chiefs of Staff Office, Nuc. War Plan, wing comdr. 90th wing Cheyenne, Wyo.; ret., 1998; dir. Wyo. Dept. Commerce, 1998—2000; CEO Wyo. Bus. Coun., Cheyenne, 2000; campaign mgr. Cynthia Lummis's Congl. Campaign, 2008; chief of staff to Rep. Cynthia Lummis US House of Reps., Washington, 2009—. Bd. dirs. Meals on Wheels, United Med. Ctr. Found., Cheyenne Frontier Days. Republican. Office: Office of Congresswomen Cynthia Lummis 100 E B St, Ste 4003 Casper WY 82602 also: 1004 Longworth House Office Bldg Washington DC 20515 Office Phone: 307-772-2595. E-mail: tucker.fagan@mail.house.gov.*

FAGEL, BRUCE G., lawyer, former emergency physician; b. Chgo., Oct. 11, 1946; BA with high honors, U. Ill., 1968; MD, U. Ill. Coll. Medicine, 1972; JD with high honors, Whittier Coll. Sch. Law, LA, 1982. Bar: Calif. 1982; lic. to practice medicine Ill., 1973, Calif., 1975. Practiced emergency medicine, 1972—82; atty. Bruce G. Fagel & Associates., Beverly Hills, Calif., 1982—. Seminar spkr. Consumer Attys. Calif., Consumer Attys. Assocs. LA. Author: Liberty on Hold, Families of Victims Need Help Not Lawsuits; guest appearances on CBS, NBC & ABC, featured in LA Times, Sacramento Bee, Oakland Tribune. Mem. Birth Trauma Litigation Group, Inner Circle of Advocates. Capt., medical corps. USAF, 1974—76. Named one of Top 10 Litigators, Nat. Law Jour., 2003; nominee Trial Lawyer of Yr. (6 Times). Fellow: Am. Coll. of Law and Medicine; mem.: LA County Med. Assn., Calif. Med. Assn., Assn. of Trial Lawyers Am., ABA, President's Club of Consumer Attorneys Assn. of LA, Calif., Phi Beta Kappa. Office: Bruce G Fagel Assocs 100 N Cresent Dr Ste 360 Beverly Hills CA 90210 Office Phone: 310-281-8700. Business E-Mail: bgfagel@aol.com.

FAGG, RUSSELL, judge, lawyer; b. Billings, Mont., June 26, 1960; s. Harrison Grover and Darlene (Bohling) F.; m. Karen Barclay, Feb. 15, 1992. BA, Whitman Coll., 1983; JD, U. Mont., 1986; MJS, U. Nev., 1999. Law clk. Mont. Supreme Ct., Helena, 1986-87; atty. Sandall Law Firm, Billings, 1987-89; city prosecutor City of Billings, 1989-91; dep. atty. Yellowstone County, Billings, 1991-94; mem. Mont. State Legislature, Helena, 1991-94; judge State Dist. Ct. (13th dist.) Mont., Billings, 1995—. Dir. Midland Empire Pachyderm Club, 1988-94, pres. 1990-91; chmn. judiciary com. House of Reps., 1993-94. Named Outstanding Young Montanan, Mont. Jaycees, 1994; recipient Young Life Spirit award Billings Young Life, 2002. Avocations: hiking, skiing, reading, tennis. Office: PO Box 35027 Billings MT 59107-5027 Home: 3053 Thousand Oaks St Billings MT 59102 Office Phone: 406-256-2906.

FAGGIN, FEDERICO, electronics executive; b. Vicenza, Italy, Dec. 1, 1941; arrived in U.S., 1968, naturalized, 1978; s. Giuseppe and Emma (Munari) Faggin; m. Elvia Sardei, Sept. 2, 1967; children: Marzia, Marc, Eric. Grad., Perito Industriale Instituto A. Rossi, Vicenza, 1960; D.Physics, U. Padua, Italy, 1965. Sect. head Fairchild Camera & Instrument Co., Palo Alto, Calif., 1968-70; dept. mgr. Intel Corp., Santa Clara, Calif., 1970-74; founder, pres. Zilog Inc., Cupertino, Calif., 1974-80; v.p. computer systems group Exxon Enterprises, NYC, 1981; co-founder, pres. Cygnet Techs., Inc., Sunnyvale, Calif., 1982-86; co-founder, CEO Synaptics, Inc., San Jose, Calif., 1986-99, chmn., 1999—; pres., CEO Foveon, Inc., 2003—. Recipient W. Wallace McDowell award, IEEE Computer Soc., 1994, Kyoto prize, 1997, Lifetime Achievement award, European Patent Office, 2006; named to Nat. Inventor's Hall of Fame, 1996; Marconi Fellowship award, 1988. Achievements include development of silicon gate technology for MOS fabrication, first microprocessor, Intel 4004, Intel8080, Intel4040, Intel8008, Intel 2102A, Zilog Z80 and Z8 microprocessors. Office: 2880 Junction Ave San Jose CA 95134 Business E-Mail: federico.faggin@foveon.com.

FAGIN, DAVID KYLE, mining executive; s. Kyle Marshall and Frances Margaret (Gaston) F.; m. Margaret Anne Hazlett, Jan. 24, 1959 (dec. July 1999); children: David Kyle, Scott Edward; m. Terry Lee Craig, Dec. 6, 2002. BS in Petroleum Engring., U. Okla., 1960; postgrad., Am. Inst. Banking, So. Meth. U. Grad. Sch. Bus. Adminstrn. Registered profl. engr., La., Okla., Tex. Trainee Exxon-Mobil (formerly Magnolia Petroleum Co.), 1955—56; jr. engr., engr., then ptnr. W.C. Bednar Petroleum Cons., Dallas, 1958—65; petroleum engr. Bank of Am. N.A. (formerly First Nat. Bank Dallas), Dallas, 1965—68; v.p. Rosario Resources Corp. (merged 1980 with AMAX Inc.), NYC, 1968—75; pres. Alamo Petroleum Corp., 1968—82; exec. v.p. Rosario Resources Corp. (now Freeport McMoran Gold), NYC, 1975—77, dir., 1975—80, pres., COO, 1977—82; chmn., dir., pres., CEO Fagin Exploration Co., Denver, 1982—86; pres., COO, bd. dirs. Homestake Mining Co. (now Barrick Gold), Toronto, Ont., Canada, 1986—91; CEO & chmn. Golden Star Resources Ltd., Denver, 1992—96, dir., 1992—; chmn., CEO Western Exploration and Devel. Ltd., Denver, 1997—2000, dir., 1997—2001. Bd. dirs. T. Rowe Price Pub. Mut. Funds, Balt., Golden Star Resources Corp., Denver, Canyon Resources Corp., Denver, chmn. bd., 2007—. Bd. dirs. Denver Area coun. Boy Scouts Am., 1993—, Mineral Info. Inst.; bd. visitors U. Okla. Sch. Engring., 1995-98, 99—, chmn., 2002—04; Nat. Mining Hall of Fame and Mus., 1997—. Mem. AIME (chmn. Dallas sect. of Soc. Petroleum Engrs. 1975, chmn. investment fund 1979-82), Soc. Mining, Metallurgy and Exploration (dir. 1996-97), Soc. Petroleum Engrs., Mining and Metall. Soc. Am., Internat. Mining Profls. Soc. (dir., exec. com., v.p. 1999, pres. 2001-2002). Business E-Mail: dkfagin@aol.com.

FAGUNDO, ANA MARIA, language educator; b. Santa Cruz de Tenerife, Spain, Mar. 13, 1938; came to U.S., 1958; d. Ramón Fagundo and Candelaria Guerra de Fagundo. BA in English and Spanish, U. Redlands, 1962; MA in Spanish, U. Wash., 1964, PhD in Comparative Lit., 1967. Prof. contemporary lit. of Spain and creative writing U. Calif., Riverside, 1967—. Vis. lectr. Occidental Coll., Calif., 1967; vis. prof. Stanford U., 1984. Author 11 books of poetry including Invention de la Luz, 1977 (Carbala de Oro Poetry prize Barcelona 1977), Obra Poetica: 1965-90, 1990, Isla En Si., 1992, Antologia, 1994, El Sol, La Sombra En El Instante, 1994, La Miriada de Los Sonambulos, 1994, Trasterrado Marzo, 1999, Pacabras Sobre Las Dias, 2004, The Poetry of Ana Maria Fagundo: A Bilingual Anthology, 2005; founder, editor Alaluz, 1969—. Grantee Creative Arts Inst., 1970-71, Humanities Inst., 1973-74; Summer faculty fellow U. Calif., 1968, 77; Humanities fellow, 1969. Mem. Am. Assn. Tchrs. Spanish and Portuguese, Sociedad Gen. de Autores de Espana. Roman Catholic. Avocations: tennis, jogging, walking. Office: U Calif Spanish Dept Riverside CA 92521-0001 Home: Valdevarnes 13 5o D 28039 Madrid Spain

FAHEY, JOHN LESLIE, immunologist; b. Cleve., Sept. 8, 1924; MS, Wayne State U., 1949; MD, Harvard U., 1951. Intern medicine Columbia-Presbyn. Hosp., NYC, 1951-52, asst. resident, 1952-53; clin. assoc. Nat. Cancer Inst., NIH, 1953-54, sr. investigator metabolism, 1954-63, chief immunology br., 1964-71; prof. medicine, microbiology and immunology, chmn. dept. Sch. Medicine UCLA, 1971-81; dir. Ctr. Interdisciplinary Rsch. Immunological Diseases UCLA, 1978—. Recipient Abbott Laboratories award Am. Society for Microbiology, 1995 Mem. Assn. Immunologists, Assn. Am. Physicians, Am. Soc. Microbiology, Clin. Immunology Soc. (founding pres.), Clin. Immunology Com. (pres.), Internat. Union Immunological Socs., Am. Assn. Cancer Rsch. Achievements include rsch. in immunology, AIDS, oncology. Office: UCLA Sch Medicine Dept Microbiology & Immunology Factor Bldg 12-262 Los Angeles CA 90095-0001

FAIRBANK, ROBERT HAROLD, lawyer; b. Northampton, Mass., Mar. 4, 1948; s. William Martin and Jane (Davenport) F.; m. Valerie Baker; children: Sarah Julia, David Kivy. AB in Polit. Sci., Stanford U., 1972; MLS, U. Calif.-Berkeley, 1973; JD, NYU, 1977. Bar: Calif. 1977, US Dist. Ct. (cen. and no. dists.) Calif. 1978, US Dist. Ct. (so. dist.) Calif. 1993. Assoc. Gibson, Dunn & Crutcher, LA, 1977-84, ptnr., 1985-96; co-founding ptnr. Fairbank & Vincent, 1996—. Lawyer rep., co-chair 9th cir. Jud. Conf. Ctrl. Dist., 2000—02; bd. dirs. 9th Jud. Cir. Hist. Soc.; lectr. law U. So. Calif. Law Sch., 2004—, Stanford U. Sch. Law, 2007. Author: Effective Pretrial and Trial Motions, 1983, California Practice Guide: Civil Trials and Evidence (The Rutter Group 1993, with yearly updates); mem. editl. bd. NYU Law Rev., 1975-76. Named One of Top 100 Bus. Lawyers in LA, LA Bus. Jour., 1995. Mem. Assn. Bus. Trial Lawyers (co-founder San Francisco and Orange County chpts., bd. govs. 1984-85, treas. 1986-87, sec. 1987-88, v.p. 1988-89, pres. 1989-90), LA County Bar Assn. (fed. cts. com. 1983-85), Jud. Coun. Calif. Adv. Com. on Local Rules (subcom. chair on civil trial rules). Office: 444 S Flower St Ste 3860 Los Angeles CA 90071-2938 Office Phone: 310-996-5520. E-mail: rfairbank@fairbankvincent.com.

FAIREY, SHEPARD, printmaker; b. Charleston, SC, Feb. 15, 1970; BA in illustration, RI Sch. Design, 1992. Founder Obey Giant campaign, LA, 1990—. Prin. works include iconic posters of Andre the Giant and Barack Obama, one-man shows include Tin Man Alley Gallery, New Hope, Pa., 2001, 1300 Gallery, Cleve., Milk, San Francisco, 2003, Merry Karnowsky Gallery, LA, 2004, 2005, 2007, Toy Room Gallery, Sacramento, 2004, 2005, 2007, Back Room Gallery, Phila., 2005, White Walls Gallery, San Francisco, 2006, 2008, Jonathan LeVine Gallery, Bklyn., 2007, Stolen Space Gallery, London, 2007, Inst. Contemporary Art, Boston, 2009. Named one of Men of the Yr., GQ Mag., 2008. Office: Obey Giant Art PO Box 741299 Los Angeles CA 90004 also: Merry Karnowsky Gallery 1st Fl 170 S La Brea Ave Los Angeles CA 90036 also: Jonathan LeVine Gallery 529 W 20th St 9E New York NY 10011

FAIRFULL, THOMAS MCDONALD, museum director; b. Greensburg, Pa., Nov. 28, 1942; s. Tom and Margaret Jane (Heasley) F. BA, U. Pitts., 1964; MA, Duke U., 1972. Dir. 82d Airborne Divsn. Mus., Fort Bragg, N.C., 1975-78; instr. Campbell U., Buies Creek, N.C., 1976-78; dir. U.S. Army Mus. Hawaii, Honolulu, 1978—. Co-author: (with William R. Porter) History of the 3d Brigade 82d Airborne Divsn. 1969. Served to capt. U.S. Army, 1965-74, Vietnam. Recipient Bronze Star with oak leaf cluster, USA. Mem. Am. Mil. Inst., Hawaii Mus. Assn., Coun. Am.'s Mil. Past. Home: 1950 A 9th Ave Honolulu HI 96816-2906 Office: US Army Museum of Hawaii Stop 319 APVG-GAR-LM CRD DCA USAG Fort Shafter HI 96858

FAIRHURST, MARY E., state supreme court justice; b. 1957; BA in Polit. Sci. cum laude, Gonzaga U., 1979, JD magna cum laude, 1984. Bar: Wash. 1984. Jud. clk. to Hon. William H. Williams Wash. Supreme Ct., 1984, jud. clk. to Hon. William C. Goodloe, 1986; chief revenue, bankruptcy and collections divsn. Wash. Atty. Gen.'s Office, 1986—2002; judge Wash. Supreme Ct., Olympia, 2003—. Mem. Wash. Supreme Ct. Gender and Justice Commn., Access to Justice Bd. Com. Established Lawyers and Students Engaged in Resolution Program; mem. Girl Scouts Bd. of Pacific Peak Council; mem. bd. advisors Gonzaga Law Sch. Recipient Steward of Justice award, 1998, Allies for Justice award, LEGALS, P.S., 1999. Mem.: Wash. Women Lawyers (past pres., Passing the Torch award 1999), Wash. State Bar Assn. (past. pres., mem. bd. govs.). Office: Wash Supreme Ct PO Box 40929 415 12th Ave SW Olympia WA 98504-0929 Business E-Mail: J_M_Fairhurst@courts.wa.gov.

FAIRLEY, DARLENE, state legislator; b. Seattle; m to Michael; children: Andrew. City councilwoman, Lake Forest Park, formerly; volunteer victim advisor, Seattle Police Department, formerly; Washington State Senator, District 32, 94-, chairwoman, Labor & Workforce Develop Committee, currently, member, Energy, Technology & Telecommunications & Ways & Means Committees, currently, Washington State Senate.Owner, Fairlook Antiques, currently. Democrat. Mailing: State Senate 425 John A Cherberg Bldg, PO Box 40432 Olympia WA 98504-0482 Fax: 360-786-1999. E-mail: fairley_da@leg.wa.gov.

FAISS, ROBERT DEAN, lawyer; b. Centralia, Ill., Sept. 19, 1934; s. Wilbur and Theresa Ella (Watts) F.; m. Linda Louise Chambers, Mar. 30, 1991; children: Michael Dean Faiss, Marcy Faiss Ayres, Robert Mitchell Faiss, Philip Grant Faiss, Justin Cooper. BA in Journalism, Am. U., 1969, JD, 1972. Bar: Nev. 1972, D.C. 1972, U.S. Dist. Ct. Nev. 1973, U.S. Supreme Ct. 1977, U.S. Ct. Appeals (9th cir.) 1978. City editor Las Vegas (Nev.) Sun, 1957-59; pub. info. officer Nev. Dept. Employment Security, 1959-61; asst. exec. sec. Nev. Gaming Commn., Carson City, 1961-63; exec. asst. to gov. State of Nev., Carson City, 1963-67; staff asst. U.S. Pres. Lyndon B. Johnson, White House, Washington, 1968-69; asst. to exec. dir. U.S. Travel Adminstrn., Washington, 1969-72; ptnr., chmn. adminstrv. law dept. Lionel, Sawyer & Collins, Las Vegas, 1973—. Mem. bank secrecy Act Adv. Group U.S. Treasury. Co-author: Legalized Gaming in Nevada, 1961, Nevada Gaming License Guide, 1988, Nevada Gaming Law, 1991, 95, 98. Recipient Bronze medal Dept. Commerce, 1972, Chris Schaller award We Can, Las Vegas, 1995, Lifetime Achievement award Nev. Gaming Attys. Assn., 1997; named One of 100 Most Influential Lawyers in Am. and premier U.S. gaming atty., Nat. Law Jour., 1997. Mem. ABA (chmn. gaming law com. 1985-86), Internat. Assn. Gaming Attys. (founding, pres. 1980), Nev. Gaming Attys. Office: Lionel Sawyer & Collins 300 S 4th St Ste 1700 Las Vegas NV 89101-6053

FAIT, GLENN A., lawyer, educator; BA, Calif. State Univ., Sacramento; JD, Univ. Pacific. Assoc. dean McGeorge Sch. Law, Univ. Pacific, spl. counsel; dir. Inst. for Adminstrv. Justice, Univ. Pacific. Former mayor City of Folsom, Calif. Office: University of the Pacific McGeorge School of Law 3200 Fifth Ave Sacramento CA 95817 Office Phone: 916-739-7049.

FAKE, CATERINA, Internet company executive; b. Pitts. m. Stewart Butterfield; 1 child, Sonnet Beatrice. BA with honors, Vassar Coll. Lead designer Organic Online; art dir. Salon.com; mem. rsch. staff Interval Rsch.; creative dir. Yellowball; co-founder, v.p. mktg. and cmty. Ludicorp, Vancouver, 2002—05; co-founder Flickr, 2004; with Yahoo!, San Francisco. Co-recipient with Stewart Butterfield, Webby Breakout of Yr. award, 2005; named one of 100 Most Influential People, Time mag., 2006, 50 Who Matter Now, CNNMoney.com Bus. 2.0, 2006, Most Influential Women in Technology, Fast Company, 2009. Office: Yahoo Inc 701 1st Ave Sunnyvale CA 94089 E-mail: caterina@ludicorp.com.*

FALCO, CHARLES MAURICE, physicist, researcher; b. Ft. Dodge, Iowa, Aug. 17, 1948; s. Joe and Mavis Margaret (Mickelson) F.; m. Dale Wendy Miller, May 5, 1973; children: Lia Denise, Amelia Claire. BA, U. Calif., Irvine, 1970, MA, 1971, PhD, 1974. Trainee NSF, 1970-74; asst. physicist Argonne (Ill.) Nat. Lab., 1974-77, physicist, 1977-82, group leader superconductivity and novel materials, 1978-82; prof. physics and optical scis., research prof. U. Ariz., Tucson, 1982-97, prof. optical scis., chair condensed matter physics, 1998—, dir. lab. x-ray optics, 1986—. Vis. prof. U. Paris Sud, 1979, 86, U. Aachen, 1989; lectr., 1974—; mem. panel on artificially structured materials NRC, 1984-85; co-organizer numerous internat. confs. in field, 1978—; mem. spl. rev. panel on high temperature superconductivity Applied Physics Letters, 1987—; mem. panel on superconductivity Inst. Def. Analysis, 1988—; researcher on artificial metallic superlattices, X-ray optics, auperconductivity, condensed matter physics, electronic materials; curatorial advisor Solomon R. Guggenheim Mus., 1997—, co-curator The Art of the Motorcycle exhbn. Editor: Future Trends in Superconductive Electronics, 1978, Materials for Magneto-Optic Data Storage, 1989; contbr. articles to profl. jours.; patentee in field. Mem. divsn. condensed matter physics Exec. Com. Arts, 1992-94. Alexander von Humboldt Found. sr. disting. grantee, 1989; recipient Art Motorcycle Exbhn. award Internat. Assn. Art Critics, 1999. Fellow IEEE, SPIE, Optical Soc. Am., Am. Phys. Soc. (counselor 1992-94, exec. com. div. condensed matter physics 1992-94, exec. com. div. internat. physics 1994-98); mem. Materials Rsch. Soc., Coll. Optical Scis., Sigma Xi. Achievements include rsch. on artificial metallic superlattices, X-ray optics, superconductivity, condensed matter physics, electronic materials. Home: 13005 E Cape Horn Dr Tucson AZ 85749-9734 Office: U Ariz Optical Scis Ctr Box 210077 Tucson AZ 85721-0077 Office Phone: 520-621-6771.

FALCO, EDIE, actress; b. Northport, NY, July 5, 1963; d. Frank Falco and Judith M. Anderson; adopted children: Anderson, Macy. BFA, SUNY, Purchase, NY, 1986. Actress: (films) Sweet Lorraine, 1987, The Unbelievable Truth, 1990, Trust, 1990, Time Expired, 1992, Laws of Gravity, 1992, I Was on Mars, 1992, Bullets Over Broadway, 1994, Backfire!, 1995, The Addiction, 1995, Layin' Low, 1996, The Funeral, 1996, Breathing Room, 1996, Firehouse, 1997, Cost of Living, 1997, Cop Land, 1997, Trouble on the Corner, 1997, A Price Above Rubies, 1998, Hurrican Streets, 1998, Judy Berlin, 1999, Random Hearts, 1999, Overnight Sensation, 2000, Death of a Dog, 2000, Sunshine State, 2002 (Best Supporting Acress award LA Film Critics Assn. 2002, Golden Satellite award best supporting actress 2003), Family of the Year, 2004, The Girl from Monday, 2005, The Great New Wonderful, 2005, The Quiet, 2005, Freedomland, 2006; (TV movies) The Sunshine Boys, 1995, Jenifer, 2001, Fargo, 2003; (TV series) Oz, 1997-99, The Sopranos, 1999-2007 (Golden Globe award best actress in a drama 2000, 2003, Emmy for best actress 1999, 2001, 2003, Actor of Yr., Am. Film Inst. 2001, Golden Satellite award 2002, Outstanding Performance by a Female Actor in a Drama Series, SAG, 2003, 2008, Outstanding Performance by an Ensemble in a Drama Series, SAG, 2008); TV guest appearances include Homicide: Life on the Street, 1993-94, 97, Law & Order, 1993-94, 97, New York Undercover, 1995; film dir. Rift, 1993; TV prodr. Stringer, 1999; theater appearances include Side Man, 2000, The Vagina Monologues, 2001, Frankie and Johnny in the Clair de Lune, 2002.

FALCONE, PATRICIA JEANNE LALIM, investor, foundation administrator; b. Montevideo, Minn., Oct. 12; d. Clarence I. and Eva (Corneliusen) Lalim; m. Alfonso Benjamin Falcone, Oct. 22; children: Christopher Lalim Falcone, Steven Lalim Falcone. BS, U. Minn.; MS, PhD, U. Wis. Former libr. asst. U. Minn., St. Paul; former singer/performer Mpls.; former asst. prog. dir. U. Wis. Meml. Union, Madison; former instr. U. Wis., Madison; med. exec. A.B. Falcone, M.D., Ph.D., Fresno, Calif.; pres. Dr. A.B. Falcone Meml. Found. U. Calif. Berkeley. Pvt. investor lectr. in field Patricia Lalim Falcone; spkr., presenter in field. Contbr. articles to profl. jours.;, author various ednl. and profl. pamphlets; former artist/craftsman (textile designs) U. Wis. Traveling exhibit. Bd. dirs. Fresno/Madera Med. Polit. Action Com., Med. Soc., 1985-89, 1990, treas. 1997-2001; bd. dirs. Philip Lorenz Meml. Keyboard Concert, Profl. Exch. Svc. Corp., 2006—; mem. Supts. Roundtable, Fresno Unified Sch. Dist., 1989; chmn. U. Calif., Fresno com. to bring UC campus to Fresno area, 1987—; chmn. Parent Adv. Com. for Gifted and Talented, Fresno Unified Sch. Dist., 1985; citizens adv. coun. U. Calif., San Joaquin, 1991—. Fellow U. Wis.; scholar. Mem.: AAUW, VesterHeim Mus. Decorah, De Young Mus., San Francisco (legion of honor), Pacific Legal Found., Edison Computech Assn., Assn. Acad. Excellence (chmn. 1988—91), Med. Alliance of Fresno/Madera County Med. Soc. (exec. bd. 1989—), Danish Am. Ctr. at Danebo Mpls., U.S. English, Am. Scandinavian Found., Sharada Sangeet Sadan, Med. Ministries Internat., Fresno/Verona, Italy Sister City (com. 2001—), St. George Greek Orthodox Ch. Cmty. Luth. Brotherhood, Phi Delta Gamma, Pi Lambda Theta, Kappa Omicron Nu. Avocations: genealogy, swimming, travel, cross country skiing. Office: PO Box 14030 Pinedale CA 93650-4030 also: Riverview Tower # 1707 1920 First St South Minneapolis MN 55454-1055

FALK, JEROME B., JR., lawyer; b. May 25, 1940; AB with honors, Univ. Calif., Berkeley, 1962, JD, 1965. Bar: Calif. 1966, US Supreme Ct. Law clk. Justice William O. Douglas, U.S. Supreme Ct.; sr. dir., civil & appellate litigation Howard Rice Nemerovski Canady Falk & Rabkin, San Francisco. Adj. prof. Univ. Calif. Berkeley, 1968—78; mem. Ninth Cir. Com. Judicial Evaluation, 1980; lawyer rep. Ninth Cir. Judicial Conf., 1983—85; lectr. CLE programs. Bd. chmn. KQED Inc., 1999—2001. Named Order of Coif, U. Calif., Berkeley. Mem.:

Calif. Acad. Appellate Lawyers (pres. 1994—95), Assn. Bus. Trial Lawyers No. Calif. (pres. 1993—94), Bar Assn. San Francisco (pres. 1985). Office: Howard Rice Nemerovski Canady Falk & Rabkin 7th Fl 3 Embarcadero Ctr San Francisco CA 94111-4024 Office Phone: 415-434-1600. Office Fax: 415-217-5910. Business E-Mail: jfalk@howardrice.com.

FALK, JULIA S., linguist, educator, dean; b. Englewood, NJ, Sept. 21, 1941; d. Charles Joseph and Stella Sableski; m. Thomas Heinrich, Jan. 20, 1967; 1 child, Tatiana Prentice. BS, Georgetown U., 1963; MA, U. Wash., 1964, PhD, 1968. Instr. linguistics Mich. State U., East Lansing, 1966-68, asst. prof., 1968-71, assoc. prof., 1971-78, prof., 1978-2001, asst. dean Coll. of Arts and Letters, 1979-81, assoc. dean Coll. Arts and Letters, 1981-86, prof. emerita, 2001—. Vis. scholar U. Calif., San Diego, 2000—; cons. on lang. and law, lang. and gender, bias-free communication. Author: Linguistics and Language, 1973, 2d revised edit., 1978, Women, Language and Linguistics, 1999; contbr. articles on history of linguistics to profl. jours. Fellow Woodrow Wilson Found., 1963, NDEA Title IV, 1963-66, NSF, 1965; recipient Paul Varg Alumni award for Tchg., 1993, Faculty Profl. Women's Assn. Outstanding U. Woman Faculty award, 1999. Mem.: N.Am. Assn. History of Lang. Scis. (pres. 2000), Linguistic Soc. Am. Home: 8939 Caminito Verano La Jolla CA 92037-1606

FALK, STEVEN B., newspaper publishing executive; Various positions Gannett Newspapers, 1983—87; various positions, including circ. dir. San Francisco (Calif.) Newspaper Agy., 1987—98, pres., CEO, 1998—2000; pres., assoc. pub. & COO San Francisco (Calif.) Chronicle, 2000—03, pres. & pub., 2003—. Office: San Francisco Chronicle 901 Mission St San Francisco CA 94103-2905

FALKNER, JAMES GEORGE, SR., foundation executive; b. Spokane, Wash., Dec. 24, 1952; s. Albert Andrew and Amanda Rosalia (Reisinger) F.; m. Joleen Rae Ann Brown, June 22, 1974; children: James Jr., Jayson, Jerin, Jarret. BS in Acctg., U. Wash., 1975. CPA, Wash. CPA LeMaster & Daniels, Spokane, 1975-80; treas. Dominican Sisters Spokane, 1980-95; pres. Dominican Outreach Found., Spokane, 1995—. Bd. dirs. Providence Health Care, chmn. fin. com., exec. com., 2002—; mem. bishop's fin. coun. Diocese of Spokane, 1990-96; mem. investment adv. com. Gonzaga Prep. H.S., 1995-99, Sinsinawa Dominican Sisters, 1995—; mem. investment adv. com. Spokane Cath. Investment Trust, 1997—, chmn. investment com.; bd. dirs. Transitions, treas. exec. com., 2003-05 Bd. dirs. sch. bd. St. Mary's Ch., Veradale, Wash., 1986-89, 90, sch. found., 1987-2000; mem. acctg. dept. adv. com. Spokane Falls C.C., 1989-2004. Mem.: Wash. Soc. CPAs (state bd. dirs. 2005—), Nat. Notary Assn., Wash. State Soc. CPAs (Spokane bd. dirs., pres. 1998—2002, strategic planning com. 2001—03), AICPA, Healthcare Fin. Mgmt. Assn. (bd. dirs. 1982—85). Avocations: coaching baseball, golf, soccer, carpentry. Office: Dominican Outreach Found 3102 W Fort George Wright Dr Spokane WA 99224-5203

FALKOW, STANLEY, microbiologist, educator; b. Albany, NY, Jan. 24, 1934; s. Jacob and Mollie (Gingold) F.; children from previous marriage: Lynn Beth, Jill Stuart; m. Lucy Stuart Tompkins, Dec. 3, 1983. BS in Bacteriology cum laude, U. Maine, 1955, DSc (hon.), 1979; MS in Biology, Brown U., 1960, PhD, 1961; MD (hon.), U. Umea, Sweden, 1989. Asst. chief dept. bacterial immunity Walter Reed Army Inst. Rsch., Washington, 1963-66; prof. microbiology Med. Sch. Georgetown U., 1966-72; prof. microbiology and medicine U. Wash., Seattle, 1972-81; prof., chmn. dept. med. microbiology Stanford U., Calif., 1981-85, prof. microbiology, immunology & medicine Calif., 1981—, Robert W. and Vivian K. Cahill prof. in cancer rsch. Calif. Karl H. Beyer vis. prof. U. Wis., 1978-79; Sommer lectr. U. Oreg. Sch. Medicine, 1979, Kinyoun lectr. NIH, 1980; Rubbro orator Australian Soc. Microbiology, 1981; Stanhope Bayne-Jones lectr. Johns Hopkins U., 1982; mem. Recombinant DNA Molecule Com, task force on antibiotics in animal feeds FDA, microbiology test com. Nat. Bd. Med. Examiners. Author: Infectious Multiple Drug Resistance, 1975; editor: Jour. Infection and Immunity, Jour. Infectious Agents and Diseases. Recipient Ehrlich prize, 1981, Altemeier medal Surg. Infectious Diseases Soc., 1990, Disting. Achievement in Infectious Disease Rsch. award Bristol-Myers Squibb, 1997, Lasker Koshland Spl. Achievement award in Med. Sci., Albert and Mary Lasker Found., 2008; Bristol-Myers Squibb unrestricted infectious disease grantee. Fellow Am. Acad. Microbiology; mem. Inst. Medicine, AAAS, Infectious Disease Soc. Am. (Squibb award 1979), Am. Soc. Microbiology (Becton-Dickinson award in Clin. Microbiology, 1986, Abbott-ASM Lifetime Achievement award, 2003), Genetics Soc. Am., NAS, Royal Soc. UK (fgn.), Sigma Xi. Office: Stanford U Dept Microbiology and Immunology 299 Campus Dr Stanford CA 94305-5402 Office Phone: 650-723-9187, 650-723-2671. Office Fax: 650-725-7282. E-mail: falkow@stanford.edu.

FALLER, JAMES ELLIOT, physicist, researcher; b. Mishawaka, Ind., Jan. 17, 1934; s. Elmer Edward and Leona Maxine (Forstbauer) F.; m. Jocelyne T. Bellenger, March 7, 1996; children: William Edward, Peter James. AB summa cum laude, Ind. U., 1955; MA, Princeton U., 1957, PhD, 1963; MA (hon.), Wesleyan U., Middletown, Conn., 1972. Instr. Princeton U., 1959-62; mem. Joint Inst. Lab. Astrophysics, Boulder, Colo., 1963-66, fellow, 1972—; asst. prof. physics Wesleyan U., 1966-68, assoc. prof. physics, 1968-71, prof., 1971-72. Nat. Acad. Sci./NRC postdoctoral fellow, 1963-64; Sloan fellow, 1972-73; recipient Precision Measurement award Nat. Bur. Standards, 1970, Arnold O. Beckman award Instrument Soc. Am., 1970, Exceptional Sci. Achievement medal NASA, 1973, Gold medal Dept. Commerce, 1990, Fed. Lab. Consortium Tech. Transfer award, 1992, Joseph F. Keithley award, 2001, Presdl. Rank award, 2006. Fellow: Am. Phys. Soc.; mem.: AAAS, Internat. Astron. Union, Optical Soc. Am., Am. Geophysical Union, Sigma Xi, Phi Beta Kappa. Home: 303 Hollyberry Ln Boulder CO 80305-5230 Office: JILA Univ Colorado Boulder CO 80309-0001 Office Phone: 303-492-8509. Business E-Mail: fallerj@jila.colorado.edu.

FALLER, THOMPSON MASON, philosophy educator; b. Louisville, Apr. 26, 1938; s. Louis Joseph and Katherine Thompson Faller; m. Madeleine O'Brien, Aug. 22, 1969; 1 child, Thompson Mason II. BA, St. Mary's Coll., 1962; MA, Xavier U., 1964; PhD, U. Salzburg, Austria, 1969. From instr. to prof. U. Portland, Oreg., 1964—. Instnl. rev. bd. mem. Providence Health Sys., Portland, Oreg., 1990—, chair, privacy bd., 2003—; vis. prof./animal rsch. rev. com. mem. Oreg. Health Scis. U., Portland, 1991—. Authro: Axiology: F. Brentano, 1983; contbr. chpts. to books. Chair com. for scholars Reagan/Bush Election Com., Washington, 1984, 88; pres. Portland-Sapporo Sister City Assn., 1997-99, bd. dir. 1987—; com. mem. Portland Sister City Coun., 1998-2005; v.p. Cascade Coun. Boy Scouts, Portland, 2000—; bd. dir. Nat. Cath. Ednl. Assn., 1994-. Recipient Pilgrim shell, Patriach of Jerusalem, Jerusalem, 1996, named Danforth Assoc., Danforth Found., St. Louis, 1976, J.F. Kennedy Man of Yr., KC, Portland, 1993, Fulbright fellow, Washington, 1968—69, Silver Beaver, Boy Scouts Am., 2003, Alumnus of the Yr., St. Xavier Prep. HS, 2003. Mem. AAUP, Nat. Assn. Bds. Cath. Edn. (chair exec. com. 1991-2001, 2006—, exec. com. 1991—), Nat. Assn. Fgn. Student Affairs, Blue Key Internat. Hon. Soc. (pres., chair bd. 2003—), Internat. Ho. of Japan, Knights of Malta (knight), Knights of the Holy Sepulchre (knight), Delta Epsilon Sigma. Roman Catholic. Avocations: raquetball, classical music, football, travel. Home: 4684 NW Brassie Pl Portland OR 97229-0901 Office: Univ Portland 5000 N Willamette Blvd Portland OR 97203-5798 Office Phone: 503-943-7144. Personal E-mail: faller@up.edu.

FALLON, JIMMY THOMAS, actor, talk show host; b. Bklyn., Sept. 19, 1974; s. Jim and Gloria Fallon; m. Nancy Juvonen, Dec. 22, 2007. BA in Comm., Coll. St. Rose, 2009. Actor: (TV series) Saturday Night Live, 1998—2006; (TV films) Sex and the Matrix, 2000; (TV miniseries) Band of Brothers, 2001, (guest appearance): (TV series) Spin City, 1998,; (films) Almost Famous, 2000, Anything Else, 2003, The Entrepreneurs, 2003, Taxi, 2004, Fever Pitch, 2005, (voice) Doogal, 2006, Arthur and the Invisibles, 2006, Factory Girl, 2006, The Year of Getting to Know Us, 2008; co-author (with Gloria Fallon): (book) I Hate This Place: The Pessimist's Guide to Life, 1999; performer: (comedy album) The Bathroom Wall, 2003; host (TV series) Late Night with Jimmy Fallon, 2009—. Named one of The 50 Most Beautiful People in the World, People mag., 2002. Office: c/o Creative Artist Agy 9830 Wilshire Blvd Beverly Hills CA 90212

FALSTRUP, ASGER, electronics executive; V.p. No. European region Ingram Micro, 1996-2000; sr. v.p. Ingram Micro, Inc., 2000—; pres. Ingram Micro Can., 2000—. Office: Ingram Micro Inc 1600 E St Andrew Pl Santa Ana CA 92705

FALUDI, SUSAN C., journalist, scholarly writer; Formerly with West Mag., San Jose, Calif., Mercury News; with San Francisco Bur., Wall St. Jour. Spkr. in field. Author: Backlash: The Undeclared War Against American Women, 1991 (National Book Critics Circle award for general non-fiction 1992); contbr. articles to mags. Recipient Pulitzer Prize for explanatory journalism, 1991. Office: care Sandra Dijkstra Literary Agy 1155 Camino Del Mar PMB 515 Del Mar CA 92014-2605

FAN, SHANHUI, engineering educator; b. 1972; Student, U. Sci. and Tech. China, 1988—92; PhD in Physics, MIT, 1997. Tchg. asst. MIT, 1992—94, rsch. asst., 1994—97, postdoctoral rsch. assoc., physics, 1997—99, rsch. scientist, Rsch. Lab. Electronics, 1999—2001; asst. prof., dept. elec. engring. Stanford U., Calif., 2001—. Cons. Claredon Photonics, 1999—2001, mem. tech. adv. bd., 2001—; invited spkr. in field. Contbr. articles to profl. jours., chapters to books; reviewer for leading scientific jours. in the optics field. Recipient NAS award for Initiatives in Rsch., 2007; David and Lucile Packard Fellowship in Sci. and Engring., 2003. Mem.: NSF (mem. review panels 2001—03), Optical Soc. Am., Am. Phys. Soc. Achievements include patents in field. Office: AP 273 Ginzton Laboratory Stanford CA 94305 Office Phone: 650-724-4759. Office Fax: 650-725-2533. Business E-Mail: shanhui@stanford.edu.

FAN, XIAOHUI, astrophysicist, educator; b. Beijing; m. Jinyoung Serena Kim, 1995; 1 child. BS, Nanjing U., China, 1992; MS, Chinese Acad. Scis. Beijing Astron. Obs., 1995; PhD, Princeton U., 2000. Mem. Inst. Advanced Study, Princeton, NJ, 2000—02; astronomer Steward Obs. U. Ariz., Tucson, 2002—, asst. prof. dept. astronomy, 2002—05, assoc. prof., 2005—. Contbr. articles to sci. jours. Recipient Newton Lacy Pierce prize, Am. Astron. Soc., 2003; named one of Brilliant 10, Popular Sci. mag., 2003; Alfred P. Sloan Rsch. fellow, 2003, David and Lucile Packard Fellow in Sci. and Engring., 2004. Office: Steward Obs Rm 310 U Ariz 933 N Cherry Ave Tucson AZ 85721-0065 Office Phone: 520-626-7558. E-mail: fan@as.arizona.edu.

FANCHER, MICHAEL REILLY, editor, publishing executive; b. Long Beach, Calif., July 13, 1946; s. Eugene Arthur and Ruth Leone (Dickson) F.; m. Nancy Helen Edens, Nov. 3, 1967 (div. 1982); children: Jason Michael, Patrick Reilly; m. 2d Carolyn Elaine Bowers, Mar. 25, 1983; Katherine Claire, Elizabeth Lynn. BA, U. Oreg., 1968; MS, Kans. State U., 1971; MBA, U. Wash., 1986. Reporter, asst. city editor Kansas City Star, Mo., 1970-76, city editor Mo., 1976-78; reporter Seattle Times, 1978-79, night city editor, 1979-80, asst. mng. editor, 1980-81, mng. editor, 1981-86, exec. editor, 1987—2006, v.p., 1989—95, sr. v.p., 1995—, editor at large, 2006—. Bd. dirs. Blethen Maine Newspapers, Walla Walla Union-Bulletin, Yakima Herald Rep. Ruhl fellow Hall of Achievement, U. Oreg., 1983 Mem. Am. Soc. Newspaper Editors, Soc. Profl. Journalists, Nat. Press Photographers Assn. (Editor of Yr. 1986); v.p., Washington Coalition open Govt. Office: Seattle Times PO Box 70 1120 John St Seattle WA 98111-0070 Business E-Mail: mfancher@seattletimes.com.

FANG, GUOWEI, science educator; BS in Biochemistry, Nanjing U., 1987; PhD in Biochemistry, U. Colo., 1993. Asst. prof. biol. scis. Stanford U., Calif. Office: Gilbert Hall Stanford U Stanford CA 94305

FANSELOW, MICHAEL SCOTT, psychology professor; b. Bklyn, May 2, 1954; BS magna cum laude with honors, CUNY, Bklyn., 1976; PhD in Behavioral Psychology, U. Wash., 1980. Asst. prof. Rensselaer Poly. Inst., Troy, N.Y., 1980-81, Dartmouth Coll., Hanover, N.H., 1981-86, assoc. prof., 1986-88, UCLA, 1988-89, prof., 1989—. Recipient Troland Rsch. award NAS, 1995. Fellow AAAS, APA (Edwin B. Newman award 1979, D.O. Heb Young Scientist award 1983, Disting. Sci. award 1985). Office: UCLA Dept Psychology PO Box 951563 Los Angeles CA 90095-1563

FANTINO, EDMUND, psychology professor; b. NYC, June 30, 1939; s. Claudio Fantino and Mary Lentini; m. Stephanie Stolarz, Sept. 22, 1977; children: Ramona Emily, Marin Antonia. BA, Cornell U., 1961; PhD, Harvard U., 1964. Asst. prof. psychology Yale U., New Haven, 1964—67; disting. prof. psychology and neuroscis. group U. Calif., San Diego, 1967—. Pres. Soc. for Exptl. Analysis of Behavior, 1985—87. Author: Introduction to Contemporary Psychology, 1975, The Experimental Analysis of Behavior: A Biological Perspective, 1979, Behaving Well: Strategies for Celebrating Life In The Face of Illness, 2007; contbr. over 100 articles to profl. jours.; editor: Jour. Exptl. Analysis of Behavior, 1987—91. Grantee, NIMH, NSF, 1965—. Office: U Calif San Diego Dept Psychology La Jolla CA 92093-0109 Business E-Mail: efantino@ucsd.edu.

FARBER, STEVEN W., lawyer; BA, U. Colo., 1965, JD, 1968. Bar: Colo. Founding ptnr. Brownstein Hyatt Farber Schreck, Denver. Commr. Colo. Commn. on Higher Edn., 1992—96; chmn. Colo. Gov. Roy Romer gubernatorial campaigns; mem. site advisory com. Dem. Nat. Conv., 2000, co-chair, mem. exec. com., Host Com., 08; commr. Colo. U. Blue Ribbon Commn. on Diversity; mem. Citywide Banks; fellow Coll. Law Practice Mgmt., Am. Bar Found., Colo. Bar Found. Mem. Comm. Civil Svc. Reform; mem. bd. dirs. Denver Metro C. of C., Colo. Black C. of C.; mem. bd. trustees Anti-Defamation League, Race to Erase M.S. Found., Children's Hosp. Found.; mem. bd. dirs. Allied Jewish Fedn., campaign chmn., 1984, 1985, pres., 1986; founder Am. Transplant Found.; chmn. exec. com. Colo. Concern; chmn. bd. trustees Rose Cmty. Found.; mem. bd. trustees Children's Diabetes Found., U. Denver; mem. bd. dirs. U. Colo. Hosp. Found., Fresh Start; mem. bd. trustees Denver Metro Chamber Found., mem. bd. dirs., 1997—2003; co-chmn. Colo. Coll.; chmn. bd. trustees Rose Health Care Systems; chmn. Rose Med. Ctr.; mem. bd. dirs. Denver Health Bd. Recipient Del Hock Lifetime Achievement award, Metro Denver C. of C., 2004, Disting. Alumni award for Pvt. Practice, U. Colo. Law Sch., 2007, Barbara Davis High Hopes award, 2007; named Businessperson of Yr., Rocky Mountain Times, 2008. Mem.: Colo. Bar Assn., Denver Bar Assn., ABA. Democrat. Office: Brownstein Hyatt Farber Schreck 410 Seventeenth St Ste 2200 Denver CO 80202-4432 Office Phone: 303-223-1109. Office Fax: 303-223-0909. Business E-Mail: sfarber@bhfs.com.*

FARGO, THOMAS BOULTON, retired career military officer; b. San Diego, 1948; Grad., U.S. Naval Acad., 1970. Commd. ensign USN, 1970, advanced through ranks to adm.; various assignments to comd. U.S. Naval Forces, Cen. Command/Comdr., U.S. Fifth Fleet; dep. chief of naval opers., comdr. U.S. Pacific Fleet; comdr. U.S. Pacific Command, Honolulu, 2002—05. Decorated Disting. Svc. medal (4 times), Def. Superior Svc. medal, Legion of Merit (3 times), others; recipient James Bond Stockdale award for Inspirational Leadership, 1989.

FARHANG, ALI J., lawyer; b. 1971; BA, U. Ariz., 1993; JD, U. Denver, 1997. Tucson atty. rep. US Dist. Ct.; atty. Fennemore Craig Law Firm. Mem., Fed. Bar Tech. Com. Dist. Ariz.; chmn., Fall Employment Seminar Ariz. State Bar, 2005—06. Student mentor U. Ariz. Law Coll.; bd. mem. Metro. YMCA; mem. Fiesta Bowl Com. Named one of 40 Under 40, Tucson Bus. Edge, 2006. Mem.: Iranian Assn. of Tucson (bd. mem.), State Bar of Ariz. (Exec. Coun., Labor and Employment Sect., chair, Employment and Labor Law Continuing Legal Edn. Sect.), Pima County Bar Assn., State Bar of Colo., Young Lawyers Divsn., Ariz. Def. Lawyers Assn., Ariz. Minority Bar Assn., Morris K. Udall Inn of Ct. Office: Fennemore Craig One S Church Ave Ste 1000 Tucson AZ 85707 Office Phone: 520-879-6402. Office Fax: 520-879-6884.

FARIDI, ABBAS M., physics professor; b. Teheran, Iran, Mar. 8, 1940; m. Lillian F. Koskinen, Dec. 23, 1966; children: Andrea M. Majd-Farid, Sara L. Majd-Farid, David A. Majd-Farid, Leila Marie F. Majd-Farid. BS in Physics, Fairleigh Dickenson U., Teaneck, NJ, 1968; PhD, NY U., NYC, 1976. Prof., physics Shiraz U., Iran, 1976—82, Calif. State U., Dominguez Hills, 1987—89, Orange Coast Coll., Costa Mesa, Calif., 1989—; asst. prof., physics U. Calif., Santa Barbara, Calif., 1983—87. Advisor Persian Club, Costa Mesa, 1994—; mentor Physics Club, Costa Mesa, 1995—. Contbr. articles to profl. jours. Mem. Amer Fedn. Tchrs., Costa Mesa, 1989—. Finalist Best Tchr. of Yr., Orange Coast Coll., 2007. Mem.: Vis. Scholars, Calif. Tchrs. Assn., Am. Assn. Physics Tchrs., Am. Phys. Soc. Avocations: cooking, gardening. Office: Orange Coast Coll 2701 Fairview Rd PO Box 5005 Costa Mesa CA 92628-5005 Office Phone: 714-432-5888. Business E-Mail: afaridi@occ.cccd.edu.

FARIS, ANNA MAY, actress; b. Baltimore, Nov. 29, 1976; d. Jack and Karen Faris; m. Ben Indra, June 3, 2004 (div. Feb. 19, 2008). Degree in English Lit., U. Wash. Actress (TV films) Deception: A Mother's Secret, 1991, Blue Skies, 2005, (films) Eden, 1996, Lovers Lane, 1999, Skanks, 1999, Scary Movie, 2000, May, 2000, The Hot Chick, 2002, Winter Break, 2003, Lost in Translation, 2003, Scary Movie 3, 2003, Spelling Bee, 2004, Southern Belles, 2005, Waiting, 2005, Brokeback Mountain, 2005, 3 & 3, 2005, Just Friends, 2005, Scary Movie 4, 2006, My Super Ex-Girlfriend, 2006, Smiley Face, 2007, Mama's Boy, 2007, Observe and Report, 2009, actress, exec. prodr. The House Bunny, 2008, actress (TV appearances) Friends, 2004, Entourage, 2007. Office: c/o Raw Talent 9615 Brighton Way Beverly Hills CA 90210

FARKAS, DANIEL FREDERICK, food science and technology educator; b. Boston, June 20, 1933; m. Alice Bridgetta Brady, Jan. 25, 1959; children: Brian Emerson, Douglas Frederick. BS, MIT, 1954, MS, 1955, PhD, 1960. Lic. chem. engr., Calif. Commd. U.S. Army, 1954, advanced through grades to major, 1968, ret., 1974; staff scientist Arthur D. Little, Cambridge, Mass., 1960-62; asst. prof. Cornell U. Agrl Expt. Sta., Geneva, NY, 1962-66; rsch. leader We. regional rsch. ctr. USDA, Albany, Calif., 1967-80; prin. Daniel F. Farkas Assocs., 1976—; prof., chair dept. food sci. U. Del., Newark, 1980-87; v.p. process R & D Campbell Soup Co., Camden, NJ, 1987-90; Jacobs-Root prof., head dept. food sci. and tech. Oreg. State U., Corvalis, 1990-2000, prof. emeritus, 2000—. Contbr. more than 50 articles to peer-reviewed sci. and tech. jours. Fellow Inst. Food Technologists (Nicholas Appert medal 2002); mem. AIChE, Am. Chem. Soc. (profl.), Sigma Xi. Achievements include 5 U.S. patents for centrifugal fluidized bed food drying system, application of ultra-high hydrostatic pressure to food preservation.

FARLEY, JAMES NEWTON, retired manufacturing executive, electrical engineer; b. Hutchinson, Kans., Nov. 8, 1928; s. James N. Farley and Elizabeth (Martin) Sanders; m. Nancy J. Hollabaugh, Apr. 30, 1956; children: Sarah Huskey, Timothy, Barbara Carré, James, Stuart. BSEE, Northwestern U., 1950. Registered profl. engr., Ill. Test engr. GE, Schenectady, NY, 1950-51; sales engr. Allen Bradley Co., Milw., 1953-54, Chgo., 1954-60; sales mgr. SpeedFam Corp., Skokie, Ill., 1960-64, pres. Des Plaines, Ill., 1964-87, chmn. bd. dirs., 1987-97; pres., CEO SpeedFam-IPEC, Inc., Chandler, Ariz., 1987-92, CEO, chmn. bd. dirs., 1992-97, chmn. bd. dirs., 1997-2001, chmn. emeritus, 2001—02, ret., 2002—. Bd. dirs. Lovejoy, Inc., Downers Grove, Ill., imortgage.com, Scottsdale, Ariz. Trustee Scottsdale Healthcare Found.; mem. McCormick adv. com. Northwestern U.; mem. adv. bd. Am. Precision Mus., Windsor, Vt. With U.S. Army, 1951-53. Recipient Alumni Merit award Northwestern U., 1996. Mem. Assn. for Mfg. Tech., Oriental Order of Groundhogs, Kappa Sigma. Democrat. Episcopalian. Office: JNF Group 7702 E Doubletree Ranch Rd Ste 300 Scottsdale AZ 85258 Home: 6404 N 52d Pl Paradise Valley AZ 85253

FARLEY, KENNETH A., geochemist, educator; m. Kristen Farley; children: Scott, Ryan. BS, Yale U.; PhD, U. Calif., San Diego, 1991. Prof. geochemistry Calif. Inst. Tech. Divsn. Geol. and Planetary Scis., Pasadena, W.M. Keck Found. prof. geochemistry, divsn. chair. Recipient James B. Macelwane medal, 1999, award for initiatives in sci. NAS, 2000. Avocation: long distance running. Office: Calif Inst Tech Divsn Geol & Planetary Scis MS 170-25 Pasadena CA 91125 Office Fax: 626-568-0935. Business E-Mail: farley@gps.caltech.edu.

FARLEY, STEVE, state legislator; b. Upland, Calif., Dec. 24, 1962; m. Regina Kelly Farley; children: Amelia, Genevieve. BA in Polit. Sci., Williams Coll., Mass., 1985. Owner Steve Farley Design, 1991—; mem. Dist. 28 Ariz. House of Reps., 2007—, mem. transp. & infrastructure com., ways & means com. Graphics tchr. multimedia prog. Tucson-Pima Arts Coun., 1997—99; resident artist Ariz. Dept. Juvenile Corrections, 2001; roster artist Ariz. Commn. Arts, 2002—; vice-chair regional transp. plan task force Pima Assn. Govt.'s, 2003—05. Founder Tucsonans for Sensible Transp., 2001; mem. social activism com. Grace St. Paul's Episcopal Ch., 2005—; bd. dirs. Tucson Downtown Alliance, 1999—. Named a Legis. Champion, Ariz. League Cities & Towns; named an Arts Hero, Ariz. Citizen Action for Arts. Mem.: Graphic Artists Guild, Blenman-Elm Neighborhood Assn., Stonewall Dems., Dem. Nucleus Club. Democrat. Episcopalian. Office: Ariz House Reps Capitol Complex 1700 W Washington Rm 119 Phoenix AZ 85007 Office Phone: 602-926-3022. Office Fax: 602-417-3128. Business E-Mail: sfarley@azleg.gov.*

FARMER, DIANA LEE, pediatric surgeon; b. Chgo., Nov. 28, 1955; married. BA in Biology, Wellesley Coll., Mass., 1977; premed., Harvard Coll., Coll. Idaho; MD, U. Wash. Sch. Medicine, Seattle, 1983. Cert. Am. Bd. Surgery, 2004, in pediatric surgery Am. Bd. Surgery, 2005. Internship in surgery U. Wash. Sch. Medicine, 1986—87; fellowship in surg. oncology U. Calif. Sch. Medicine, San Francisco, 1987—89, residency in gen. surgery, 1990—91, sr. resident, gen. surgery, 1991—92, chief resident, gen. surgery, 1992—93, assoc. prof. surgery to prof. clin. surgery, pediat., ob-gyn and reproductive sciences; fellowship Children's Hosp., Detroit, 1993—95, pediatric surgeon, 1995—98, Henry Ford Hosp., Detroit, 1995—98, St. John's Hosp., Detroit, 1995—98; asst. prof. surgery Wayne State U. Sch. Medicine, Detroit, 1995—98; hosp. appointment in pediatric surgery U. Calif. Med. Ctr., 1998, Calif. Pacific Med. Ctr., 1998—, Kaiser Permanente Med. Ctr., 1998; chief pediatric surgery U. Calif. Children's Hosp., San Francisco, vice-chair dept. surgery, divsn. chief pediatric surgery, co-dir. fetal treatment ctr. Rschr. Woods Hole Oceanographic Inst., Stanford, Calif., Bermuda; asst. med. dir. cancer immunology DuPont Pharm., Wilmington, Del. Contbr. articles to profl. jours. Rhodes Scholar finalist, Luce Scholar, Nat. U., Singapore. Office: Univ Calif San Francisco Sch Medicine Campus Box 0570 513 Parnassus Ave San Francisco CA 94143-0570 Office Phone: 415-476-2538. Office Fax: 415-476-2929. Business E-Mail: pedsurg@surgery.ucsf.edu.

FARMER, KENNETH LLOYD, JR., health system administrator, retired military officer; b. Leeds, Ala., Apr. 13, 1950; married; 4 children. BS, Auburn U.; MD, U. Ala., 1975; grad., Army Command Gen. Staff Coll., Army War Coll. Diplomate Am. Bd. Family Practice. Commd. 2d lt. U.S. Army, advanced through grades to maj. gen., 2002, ret., 2006; early assignments include Madigan Army Med. Ctr., Ft. Lewis, Wash., 9th Med. Detachment and Health Clinic, Heilbronn, Germany, 1976-79; chief of family practice dept. Keller Army Hosp., West Pt., NY; divsn. surgeon 101st Airborne divsn., Ft. Campbell, Ky.; dep. comdr. clin. svcs. Ft. Campbell Hosp.; comdr. 85th Evacuation Hosp., Dhahran, Saudi Arabia, 1990-91, 22nd Support Group (provisional), 1990—91; dept. chief of family practice residency program Eisenhower Army Med. Ctr., Ft. Gordon, Ga.; comdr. Bayne-Jones Army Cmty. Hosp., Ft. Polk, Darnall Army Cmty. Hosp. and U.S. Army Med. Dept. Activity, Ft. Hood, Tex.; command surgeon U.S. European Command, Stuttgart, Germany, 1994-97; dir. Healthcare Svcs. and surgeon 18th Airborne Corps. Ft. Bragg, NC; comdg. gen. 44th Med. Brigade, Ft. Bragg, NC, 1999-2000, Western Regional Med. Command, Tacoma, 2000—02, TRICARE NW Region, Ft. Lewis, 2000—02; dep. surg. gen., chief of staff US Army Med. Commd., 2002—04; commdg. gen. N. Atlantic Regional Med. Command & Walter Reed Army Med. Ctr., Washington, 2004—06; exec. v.p., COO TriWest Healthcare Alliance, Phoenix, 2006—. Decorated Disting. Svc. medal with oak leaf cluster, Def. Superior Svc. medal, Legion of Merit with 3 oak leaf clusters, Bronze Star, Meritorious Svc. medal with 4 oak leaf clusters, Order of Mil. Med. Merit. Fellow Am. Acad. Family Physicians (Robert Graham Physician Exec. award 2001). Office: TriWest Healthcare Alliance 16010 N 28th Ave Phoenix AZ 85053

FARMER, ROBERT LINDSAY, lawyer; b. Portland, Oreg., Sept. 29, 1922; s. Paul C. and Irma (Lindsay) F.; m. Carmen E. Engebretson, Sept. 8, 1943; children: Cort W., Scott L., Eric C. BS, UCLA, 1946; LLB, U. So. Calif., 1949. Bar: Calif. 1949. Since practiced in, LA; mem. Farmer & Ridley, LA, 1949—. Trustee Edward James Found., West Dean Estate, Chichester, Eng. Served with AUS, 1943-46. Mem. ABA, Los Angeles County Bar Assn., Order of Coif, Beta Gamma Sigma, Kappa Sigma, Phi Delta Phi, Annandale Golf Club (Pasadena, Calif.). Home: 251 S Orange Grove Blvd Apt 1 Pasadena CA 91105-1766 Office: 333 S Hope St Los Angeles CA 90071

FARNSWORTH, ELIZABETH, broadcast journalist; b. Mpls., Dec. 23, 1943; d. H. Bernerd and Jane (Mills) Fink; m. Charles E. Farnsworth, June 20, 1966; children: Jennifer Farnsworth Fellows, Samuel. BA, Middlebury Coll., 1965; MA in History, Stanford U., 1966; LLD (hon.), Colby Coll., 2002. Reporter, panelist PBS World Press, KQED, San Francisco, 1975-77; reporter InterNews, Berkeley, Calif., 1977-80; freelance TV and print reporter, San Francisco, 1980-91; fgn. corr. MacNeil/Lehrer News Hour, San Francisco, 1991-95; chief corr., prin. substitute anchor News Hour with Jim Lehrer, Arlington, Va., 1995-97, San Francisco, 1997-99, sr. corr., 1999—2004, spl. corr., 2005—. Co-author: El Bloqueo Invisible, 1974; prodr., dir. documentary Thanh's War, 1991 (Cine Golden Eagle award); contbr. articles to various publs. Mem. adv. bd. Berkeley Edn. Found., 1990-95, U. Calif. Sch. Journalism, Berkeley; mem. nat. adv. bd. Ctr. Investigative Reporting, 2001-; bd. dirs. Data Ctr., Oakland, Calif., 1993-95. Recipient Golden Gate award San Francisco Film Festival, 1984, Best Investigative Reporting award No. Calif. Radio, TV News Dirs.' Assn., 1986, Blue Ribbon, Am. Film and Video Festival, 1991, Silver World medal N.Y. Film Festivals, 2001; nominee Emmy award, 2002. Mem. AFTRA, NATAS, World Affairs Coun. No. Calif. (bd. dirs. 1998-2004), Nat. Adv. Writers Corps, Phi Beta Kappa. Presbyterian. Avocations: gardening, hiking, poetry.

FARQUHAR, JOHN WILLIAM, physician, educator; b. Winnipeg, Man., Can., June 13, 1927; arrived in U.S., 1934; s. John Giles and Marjorie Victoria (Roberts) Farquhar; m. Christine Louise Johnson, July 14, 1968; children: Margaret F., John C.M.;children from previous marriage: Bruce E., Douglas G. AB, U. Calif., Berkeley, 1949; MD, U. Calif., San Francisco, 1952. Intern U. Calif. Hosp., San Francisco, 1952—53, resident, 1953—54, 1957—58, postdoctoral fellow, 1955—57; resident U. Minn., Mpls., 1954—55; rsch. assoc. Rockefeller U., NYC, 1958—62; asst. prof. medicine Stanford (Calif.) U., 1962—66, assoc. prof., 1966—73, prof., 1978—, C.F. Rehnborg prof. in disease prevention, 1989—2000; dir. Stanford Ctr. Rsch. in Disease Prevention, 1973—98; dir. collaborating ctr. for chronic disease prevention WHO, 1985—99; prof. health rsch. and policy, 1988—. Mem. staff Stanford U. Hosp.; chair Victoria Declaration Implementation com. Author: The American Way of Life Need Not Be Hazardous to Your Health, 1978, 1987; author: (with Gene Spiller) The Last Puff, 1990; author: The Victoria Declaration for Heart Health, 1992, How to Reduce Your Risk of Heart Disease, 1994, The Catalonia Declaration: Investing in Heart Health, 1996, Worldwide Efforts to Improve Heart Disease, 1997; author: (with Spiller) Diagnosis Heart Disease: Answers to Your Questions about Recovery and Lasting Health, 2001; contbr. articles to profl. jours. With US Army, 1944—46. Recipient James D. Bruce award, ACP, 1983, Myrdal prize, 1986, Dana award for Pioneering Achievement in Health, Dana Found., 1990, Nat. Cholesterol award for Pub. Edn., Nat. Cholesterol Edn. Program of NIH, 1991, Rsch. Achievement award, Am. Heart Assn., 1992, Order of St. George for Svc. to Autonomous Govt. of Catalonia, 1996, Joseph Stokes Preventive Cardiology award, Am. Soc. Preventive Cardiology, 1999, Ancel Keys Meml. lectureship, Am. Heart Assn., 2000, Fries prize Improving Health, 2005. Mem.: Internat. Heart Health Soc., Soc. Behavioral Medicine (pres. 1991—92), Am. Heart Assn. (coun. epidemiology and prevention), Am. Soc. Clin. Investigation, Inst. Medicine NAS, Gold Headed Cane Soc., Alpha Omega Alpha, Sigma Xi. Episcopalian. Office: Stanford U Sch of Medicine Stanford Prevention Rsch Ctr 211 Quarry Rd Stanford CA 94305-5705 Business E-Mail: John.Farquhar@stanford.edu.

FARQUHAR, MARILYN GIST, cell biologist, pathologist, educator; b. Tulare, Calif., July 11, 1928; d. Brooks DeWitt and Alta (Green) Gist; m. John W. Farquhar, June 4, 1952; children: Bruce, Douglas (div. 1968); m. George Palade, June 7, 1970. AB, U. Calif., Berkeley, 1949, MA, 1952, PhD, 1955. Asst. rsch. pathologist Sch. Medicine U. Calif., San Francisco, 1956—58, assoc. rsch. pathologist, 1962—64, assoc. prof., 1964—68, prof. pathology, 1968—70; rsch. assoc. Rockefeller U., NYC, 1958—62, prof. cell biology, 1970—73, Sch. Medicine Yale U., New Haven, 1973—87, Sterling prof. cell biology and pathology, 1987—90; prof. pathology cell molecular medicine U. Calif., San Diego, 1990—, chair divsn. cellular and molecular medicine, 1991—99, prof. cellular & molecular medicine, chair dept. cellular & molecular medicine, 1999—. Mem. editorial bd. numerous sci. jours.; contbr. articles to profl. jours. Recipient Career Devel. award NIH, 1968-73, Disting. Sci. medal Electron Microscope Soc., 1987, Gomori medal Histochem. Soc., 1999, A.N. Richards award Internat. Soc. Nephrology, 2003, FASAB Excellence Sci. award, 2006. Mem.: NAS, Internat. Soc. Nephrology (A.N. Richards award 2003), Am. Soc. Nephrology (Homer Smith award 1988, Gottschalk award 2002), Am. Assn. Investigative Pathology (Rous Whipple award 2001), Am. Soc. Cell Biology (pres. 1981—82, E.B. Wilson medal 1987), Am. Acad. Arts and Scis. Home and Office: U Calif San Diego Sch Med 12894 Via Latina Del Mar CA 92014-3730

FARR, KEVIN M., consumer products executive; BS in Acctg., Mich. State U.; MBA in Fin. and Mktg., Northwestern U. CPA. With PricewaterhouseCoopers; sr. v.p., corp. contr. Mattell, Inc., El Segundo, Calif., 1991-2000, CFO, 2000—. Bd. dirs., treas. Children Affected by AIDS Found. Mem. AICPA, Calif. Soc. of CPAs. Office: Mattel Inc 333 Continental Blvd El Segundo CA 90245-5012

FARR, ROSS, lawyer; b. Eugene, Ore., Feb. 8, 1970; BA, Evergreen State Coll., 1992; JD magna cum laude, Seattle Univ., 2001. Bar: Wash. 2001. Former judicial clerk Wash. State Ct. Appeals; assoc. atty., gen. litig. Ogden Murphy Wallace, P.L.L.C., Seattle. Contbr. articles to numerous profl. jours.; content editor: Wash. Lawyers Practice Manual. Named Wash. Rising Star, SuperLawyer Mag., 2006. Mem.: King Co. Bar Assn. (legal clinician), Wash. State Bar Assn. Office: Ogden Murphy Wallace Ste 2100 1601 Fifth Ave Seattle WA 98101-1686

FARR, SAM, United States Representative from California; b. San Francisco, July 4, 1941; m. Shary Baldwin; 1 child, Jessica. BS in Biology, Willamette U., Salem, Oreg., 1963; student, Monterey Inst. Internat. Studies, U. Santa Clara Law Sch. Vol. US Peace Corps, Colombia, 1963-65; budget analyst, com. cons. Calif. State Legislature, 1969—75; mem. Monterey County Bd. Suprs., Calif., 1975—80; rep. Calif. State Assembly, 1980-93; mem. US Congress from 17th Calif. dist., 1993—, mem. appropriations com., drug adminstrn. and related agencies com., agr. and military constrn. subcoms. Vice chair Environ. Caucus; mem. Ho. Appropriations Com., 1999—; co-chair Unexploded Ordnance Caucus, House/Senate Internat. Edn. Study Grp., Travel & Tourism Caucus, 1997—, Ocean Caucus, 1997—, Organics Caucus, 2003—. Active NAACP, Ctr. for Non-Proliferation, Natividad Hosp. Found. Named Calif. Legislator of Yr. Mem.: Returned Peace Corps Volunteers Assn. Democrat. Episcopalian. Avocations: photography, skiing, fly fishing, spanish. Office: US House of Reps 1126 Longworth House Office Bldg Washington DC 20515-0517

FARRAR, JOHN EDSON, II, finance company executive, consultant, investment advisor; b. Williamsport, Pa., Oct. 9, 1938; s. John Edson and Ruth (Price) F.; children: John Edson III, Jamie, Ryan. BA in Psychology, Pasadena Coll., 1963; postgrad., Claremont Grad. Sch., 1963-64, U. Calgary, Canada, 1967; MA in Early Childhood Edn., U. Calgary; postgrad., U. Calif., Riverside, 1968-71. Cert. in pub. rels. U. Calif., 1972, in mktg. practice U. Calif., 1972, profl. accreditation in pub. rels. practice Pub. Rels. Soc. Am., 1975, registered investment advisor Calif., 1993. Evaluating social svcs. dir. Head Start Dental Rsch. Project Loma Linda Sch. Dentistry, Calif., 1966-67; coord. Head Start Riverside County Econ. Opportunity Bd., Riverside, Calif., 1967; dir. cmty. rels. San Bernardino County Welfare and Probation Depts., Calif., 1968-73; publicity and promotions coord. in charge tourism and indsl. devel. San Bernardino County Econ. Devel. Dept., 1973; dir. pub. rels. Mid. East Boeing Comml. Airplane Co., Seattle, 1973-76, Northwest Hosp., Seattle, 1976-77; owner Craig & Farrar Pub. Rels. and Advt., 1977-80, Aamco Transmissions Ctr. Bremerton, Wash., 1982-86; exec. v.p. Environ. Rsch. and Devel. Corp., Seattle, 1980-82; stockbroker Prudential-Bache Securities, Seattle, 1984-86; ind. fin. and bus. cons. and broker Kent, Wash., 1987-93; pres. Professionally Managed Portfolios, Acton, Calif., 1993—. Lectr. mktg. pub. rels., investment techniques and options strategies Coll. of Canyons, Valencia, Calif.; former chmn. dept. pub. rels. and advt. U. Wash., Sch. Comm., Seattle; instr. pub. rels. City Coll., Seattle; cons. in field. Pres. bd. dirs. Frazee Cmty. Ctr., 1970-71; bd. dirs., pub. relations chmn. Chief Seattle council Boy Scouts Am., promotions chmn. for camping in Southwestern US; exec. bd. Seattle-King County Visitors and Conv. Bur.; mem. Rep. Presdl. Task Force, 1982-84; chmn. March of Dimes WalkAmerica, 1995-96. Recipient Distinction award, San Bernardino County Bd. Suprs., 1973, Outstanding Achievement award, Boeing Co., 1974. Mem. Pub. Rels. Soc. Am. (chpt. pres. 1971, 72, dist. chmn. govt. sect., Recognition of Distinction for Pub. Rels. Excellence 1974), Calif. Social Workers Orgn. (v.p. 1970-71), Soc. for Internat. Devel., Nat. Pub. Rels. Coun. Health and Welfare Svcs., Internat. Pub. Rels. Assn., US-Arab C. of C., Rotary. Lutheran. Avocations: photography, coin collecting/numismatics. Business E-Mail: john@pmpmanagement.com.

FARRELL, DAVID MICHAEL, musician; b. Plymouth, Mass., Feb. 8, 1977; Attended, UCLA. Bassist Linkin Park. Musician: (albums) Meteora, 2003, Minutes to Midnight, 2007, Road to Revolution Live at Milton Keynes, 2008, (songs) Somewhere I Belong, 2003 (MTV Video Music award for Best Rock Video, 2003), Breaking the Habit, 2003 (MTV Video Music award for Viewers' Choice, 2004), (with Jay-Z) Numb/Encore, 2004 (Grammy award for Best Rap/Sung Collaboration, 2006), What I've Done, 2007 (Top Modern Rock Track, Billboard Year-End Charts, 2007), Shadow of the Day, 2007 (MTV Video Music award for Best Rock Video, 2008). Recipient Best-Selling Rock Group award, World Music Awards, 2003, Favorite Alternative Artist award, Am. Music Awards, 2003, 2004, 2007, 2008; named Top Modern Rock Artist, Billboard Year-End Charts, 2004, 2007. Office: Linkin Park c/o Machine Shop Recordings PO Box 36915 Los Angeles CA 90036

FARRELL, JOSEPH, film producer and company executive, financial analyst; b. NYC, Sept. 11, 1935; s. John Joseph and Mildred Veronica (Dwyer) F. AB summa cum laude, St. John's Coll., 1958; A.M., U. Notre Dame, 1959; JD, Harvard U., 1965. Bar: N.Y. 1965. With firm Milbank, Tweed, Hadley & McCloy, NYC, 1964-65; exec. assoc. Carnegie Corp. N.Y., 1965-66; exec. v.p., chief oper. officer Am. Council of Arts, 1966-71; cons. Rockefeller Bros. Fund, Spl. Projects, 1966-74, exec. v.p., 1974-77; vice chmn. Louis Harris & Assocs. (Harris Poll), NYC, 1978; chmn., CEO, Nat. Rsch. Group, Inc., subs. VNU, L.A., London and Tokyo, 1978—. Movie market analyst and cons., 1978—; movie exec. producer, 1986—; sculptor, 1958—; designer Farbino Furniture, 1982—. Author, editor: Americans and the Arts, 1973, 75, Museums: USA, 1973, The Cultural Consumer, 1973, The U.S. Arts and Cultural Trend Data System, 1977; author: (novel) Birds of Prey, 1998; screenwriter The Foundation, Second Son, 1990—. Mem. Gov. N.Y. Task Force on Arts, 1975; founder, bd. dirs. Vol. Lawyers for Arts, 1968-76; bd. dirs. Arts and Bus. Coun. N.Y., 1973-76; bd. advisors Actors Studio, 1983-90. Woodrow Wilson fellow, 1958; named among Top 100 Influential People in Hollywood, Premiere mag., 1998, 99. Office: 6255 W Sunset Blvd #19TH-FLR Los Angeles CA 90028-7403

FARRELL, THOMAS JOSEPH, insurance company executive, consultant; b. Butte, Mont., June 10, 1926; s. Bartholomew J. and Lavinia H. (Collins) F.; m. Evelyn Irene Southam, July 29, 1951; children: Brien J., Susan M., Leslie A., Jerome T. Student, U. San Francisco, 1949. CLU. Ptnr. Affiliated-Gen. Ins. Adjusters, Santa Rosa, Calif., 1949-54; agt. Lincoln Nat. Life Ins. Co., Santa Rosa, 1954-57, supr., 1957-59, gen. agt., 1959-74; pres. Thomas J. Farrell & Assocs., 1974-76, 7 Flags Ins. Mktg. Corp., 1976-81, Farrell-Dranginis & Assocs., 1981-88, 88-90, cons., 1990. Specialist Dept. of Devel. Svcs., Calif.; pres., bd. dirs. Lincoln Nat. Bank, Santa Rosa, San Rafael. Pres. Redwood Empire Estate Planning Coun., 1981-82, Sonoma County Coun. for Retarded Children, 1956-59, Sonoma County Assn. for Retarded Citizens, City Santa Rosa Traffic and Parking Commn., 1963; specialist State of Calif. Dept. Devel. Svcs., 1990—; del. Calif. State Conf. Sml. Bus., 1980; mem. Santa Rosa City Schs. Compensatory Edn. Adv. Bd.; bd. dirs. Santa Rosa City Schs. Consumer Edn. Adv. Bd.; pres., nat. dir. United Cerebral Palsy Assn., 1954-55; nat. coord. C. of C. - Rotary Symposia on Employment of People with Disabilities, 1985-87; v.p. Vigil Light, Inc; chmn. bd. dirs. Nat. Barrier Awareness for People with Disabilities Found., Inc.; pres. Commn. on Employment of People with Disabilities, 1986-92; mem. Pres.'s Com. on Mental Retardation, 1982-86; chmn. Santa Rosa Cmty. Rels. Com., 1973-76; pres. Sonoma County Young Reps., 1953; past bd. dirs. Sonoma County Fair and Expn., Inc.; bd. dirs. Sonoma County Family Svc. Agy., Eldridge Found., North Bay Regional Ctr. for Developmentally Disabled; trustee Sonoma State Hosp. for Mentally Retarded. Recipient cert. Nat. Assn. Retarded Children, 1962, Region 9 U.S. HHS Cmty. Svc. award, 1985, Sonoma County Vendor's Human Svc. award 1986, Individual Achievement award Cmty. Affirmative Action Forum of Sonoma County, 1986. Mem. Nat. Assn. Life Underwriters, Redwood Empire Assn. CLU's (pres. 1974-75), Japanese-Am. Citizens League, Jaycees (Outstanding Young Man of Yr. 1961, v.p. 1955), Santa Rosa C. of C. (bd. dirs. 1974-75), Calif. PTA (hon. life), Rotary (Svc. Above Self award 1996). Home: 963 Wyoming Dr Santa Rosa CA 95405-7342

FARRELLY, BOBBY (ROBERT LEO RARRELLY JR.), scriptwriter, film director and producer; b. Cumberland, RI, 1958; m. Nancy Farrelly; 2 children. Student, Rensselaer Poly. Inst. Writer, prodr. Outside Providence, 1999; writer, co-prodr., dir. Dumb and Dumber, 1994; exec. prodr., writer, dir. There's Something About Mary, 1998; writer, prodr., dir. Me, Myself and Irene, 2000, Shallow Hall, 2001. Stuck on You, 2003; writer Bushwacked, 1995; dir. Kingpin, 1996; dir., prodr. Osmosis Jones, 2001; prodr. Say It Isn't So, 2001; exec. prodr. The Ringer, 2005, (TV series) Ozzy & Drix, 2002; dir. Fever Pitch, 2005; dir., writer, The Heartbreak Kid, 2007. Recipient Screenwriter of Yr. ShoWest Conv., 1999.

FARRELLY, PETER JOHN, screenwriter; b. Phoenixville, Pa., Dec. 17, 1956; s. Robert Leo and Mariann (Neary) F. BA, Providence Coll., 1979; MFA, Columbia U., 1987. Salesman U.S. Lines, Inc., Boston, 1979-81; bartender various libationary locales, Boston, 1981-85; screenwriter Paramount Columbia and Disney Studios, Los Angeles, 1985—. Author Outside Providence, 1988; co-writer (TV spls.) Our Planet Tonight, 1987, Paul Reiser: Out on a Whim, 1987; writer (film) Dumb & Dumber, 1994, Bushwhacked, 1995, There's Something About Mary, 1998; dir. (film) Dumb & Dumber, 1994, Kingpin, 1996, There's Something About Mary, 1998, Fever Pitch, 2005; prodr. There's Something About Mary, 1998, Outside Providence, 1999; writer, co-dir, prodr.: Me, Myself & Irene, 2000, Shallow Hal, 2002; dir., writer The Heartbreak Kid, 2007; exec. prodr. (TV series) Oxxy & Drix, 2002; writer, dir., prodr. Stuck on You, 2003. Mem. Writers Guild Am. West. Roman Catholic.

FARRER, CLAIRE ANNE RAFFERTY, anthropologist, educator; b. NYC, Dec. 26, 1936; d. Francis Michael and Clara Anna (Guerra) Rafferty; 1 child, Suzanne Claire. BA in Anthropology, U. Calif., Berkeley, 1970; MA in Anthropology and Folklore, U. Tex., 1974, PhD in Anthropology and Folklore, 1977. Various positions, 1953-73; fellow Whitney M. Young Jr. Meml. Found., NYC, 1974-75; arts specialist, grant adminstr. Nat. Endowment for Arts, Washington, 1976-77; Weatherhead resident fellow Sch. Am. Rsch., Santa Fe, 1977-78; asst. prof. anthropology U. Ill., Urbana, 1978-85; assoc. prof., coord. applied anthropology Calif. State U., Chico, 1985-89, prof., 1989—2001, prof. emerita, 2002—, dir. Multicultural and Gender Studies, 1994. Cons. in field, 1974—; mem. film and video adv. panel Ill. Arts Coun., 1980-82; mem. Ill. Humanities Coun., 1980-82; vis. prof. U. Ghent, Belgium, 1990; vis. prof. Southwestern studies Colo. Coll., Colorado Springs, 2002-06, Hulbert chair in Southwestern studies, 1997; bus. mgr. Calif. Folklore Soc., 1994-99; NEH and Harry J. Gray disting. vis. prof. in humanities U. Hartford, Conn., 2002-03. Author: Play and Inter-Ethnic Communication, 1990, Living Life's Circle: Mescalero Apache Cosmovision, 1991, Thunder Rides a Black Horse: Mescalero Apaches and the Mythic Present, 1994, 96, others; co-founder, co-editor Folklore Women's Commn., 1972; editor spl. issue Jour. Am. Folklore, 1975, 1st rev. edit., 1986; co-editor: Forms of Play of Native North Americans, 1979, Earth and Sky: Visions of the Cosmos in Native North American Folklore, 1992; contbr. numerous articles to profl. jours., mags. and newspapers, chpts. to books. Recipient J. Gordon prize in S.W. Studies, Colo.Coll.; numerous fellowships and grants. Fellow Am. Anthrop. Assn.; mem. Authors Guild, Am. Ethnol. Soc., Am. Folklore Soc., Am. Soc. Ethnohistory, Astronomy in Culture. Home: PO Box 50293 Colorado Springs CO 80949-0293 Personal E-mail: crfarrer@earthlink.net. Business E-Mail: crfarrer@coloradocollege.edu.

FARRINGTON, GREGORY C., museum director, former academic administrator; b. Bronxville, NY, Aug. 4, 1946; m. Jean Farrington. B in Chemistry, Clarkson U., 1968; AM in Chemistry, Harvard U., 1970, PhD in Chemistry, 1972; degree (hon.), U. Uppsala, Sweden, 1984. Staff sci. GE, Schenectady, NY, 1972-79; assoc. prof. materials sci. and engring. U. Pa., 1979-84, prof., 1984, chair dept. materials sci. and engring., 1984-87, dir. Lab. for Rsch. on Structure of Matter, 1987-90, dean Sch. Engring. and Applied Sci., 1990-98; pres. Lehigh U., Bethlehem, 1998—2006, pres. emeritus, prof., 2006—07; exec. dir. Calif. Acad. Sciences, San Francisco, 2007—. Bd. trustees St. Luke Hosp. & Health Network, Nat. Mus. of Indsl. History, Lehigh Valley Partnership, Lehigh Valley Econ. Devel. Corp. Contbr. chapters to books, articles 100 articles to tech. jours. Achievements include holding or sharing more than two dozen patents. Office: California Academy Of Sciences 55 Music Concourse Dr San Francisco CA 94118-4503 Office Phone: 415-321-8000. E-mail: info@calacademy.org.

FARRIS, JEROME, federal judge; b. Birmingham, Ala., Mar. 4, 1930; s. William J. and Elizabeth Farris; 2 children. BS, Morehouse Coll., 1951, LLD, 1978; MSW, Atlanta U., 1955; JD, U. Wash., 1958. Bar: Wash. 1958. Mem. Weyer, Roderick, Schroeter and Sterne, Seattle, 1958—59; ptnr. Weyer, Schroeter, Sterne & Farris and successor firms, Seattle, 1959—61, Schroeter & Farris, Seattle, 1961—63, Schroeter, Farris, Bangs & Horowitz, Seattle, 1963—65, Farris, Bangs & Horowitz, Seattle, 1965—69; judge Wash. State Ct. of Appeals, Seattle, 1969—79, US Ct. Appeals (9th cir.), Seattle, 1979—95, sr. judge, 1995—. Lectr. U. Wash. Law Sch. and Sch. Social Work, 1976—; mem. faculty Nat. Coll. State Judiciary, U. Nev., 1973; adv. bd. Nat. Ctr. for State Cts. Appellate Justice Project, 1978—81; founder First Union Nat. Bank, Seattle, 1965, dir., 1965—69; mem. Jud. Wellness III Com., 2005—, US Supreme Ct. Jud. Fellows Commn., 1996—2002, Jud. Conf. Com. on Internat. Jud. Rels., 1997—2000; chmn. Ninth Circuit Judicial Conf. Com., Ninth Circuit Standing Com. on Fed. Pub. Defenders. Del. The White House Conf. on Children and Youth, 1970; mem. King County (Wash.) Youth Commn., 1969—70; vis. com. U. Wash. Sch. Social Work, 1977—90; mem. King County Mental Health-Mental Retardation Bd., 1967—69; past bd. dirs. Seattle United Way; mem. Tyee Bd. Advisers, U. Wash., 1984—88, bd. regents, 1985—97, pres., 1990—91; trustee U. Law Sch. Found., 1978—84, Morehouse Coll., 1999—; mem. vis. com. Harvard Law Sch., 1996—2005. With Signal Corps US Army, 1952—53. Recipient Disting. Svc. award, Seattle Jaycees, 1965, Clayton Frost award, 1966. Fellow: Am. Bar Found. (chair of fellows 2000, bd. dirs. 1987, exec. com. 1989—97); mem.: ABA (exec. com. appellate judges conf. 1978—84, chmn. conf. 1982—83, exec. com. appellate judges conf. 1987—88, del. jud. adminstrn. coun. 1987—88, sr. lawyers divsn. coun. 1998—), State-Fed. Jud. Coun. State Wash. (vice-chmn. 1977—78, chmn. 1983—87), Wash. Coun. on Crime and Delinquency (chmn. 1970—72), U. Wash. Law Sch., Order of Coif (mem. law rev.).

FARROW, MIA, actress; b. L.A., Feb. 9, 1945; d. John Villiers and Maureen Paula (O'Sullivan) Farrow; m. Frank Sinatra, July 19, 1966 (div. Aug. 16, 1968); m. Andre Previn, Sept. 10, 1970 (div. Feb. 1979); children: Sascha Villiers, Matthew Phineas, Fletcher; adopted children: Lark(dec.), Daisy, Soon-Yi, Moses Amadeus, Dylan O'Sullivan, Satchel O'Sullivan, Tam(dec.), Isaiah, Gabriel Wilk. Actress: (TV series) Peyton Place, 1964-65; (films) John Paul Jones, 1959, Guns at Batasi, 1964, A Dandy in Aspic, 1968, Rosemary's Baby, 1968, Secret Ceremony, 1968, John and Mary, 1969, See No Evil, 1971, The Public Eye, 1972, High Heels, 1972, The Great Gatsby, 1974, Full Circle, 1977, A Wedding, 1978, Avalanche, 1978, Death on the Nile, 1978, Hurricane, 1979, A Midsummer Night's Sex Comedy, 1982, Zelig, 1983, The Purple Rose of Cairo, 1985, Broadway Danny Rose, 1984, Supergirl, 1984, Hannah and Her Sisters, 1986, September, 1987, Radio Days, 1987, Another Woman, 1988, New York Stories (Oedipus Wrecks segment), 1989, Crimes and Misdemeanors, 1989, Alice, 1990, Shadows and Fog, 1992, Husbands and Wives, 1992, Widows' Peak, 1994, Miami Rhapsody, 1995, Reckless, 1995, Angela Mooney, 1996, Private Parts, 1997, Coming Soon, 1999, Purpose, 2002, The Omen, 2006, Be Kind Rewind, 2008; (TV films) Johnny Belinda, 1967, Goodbye, Raggedy Ann, 1971, Peter Pan, 1976, Sarah, 1982, Miracle at Midnight, 1998, Forget Me Never, 1999, A Girl Thing, 2001, Julie Lydecker, 2002, The Secret Life of Zoey, 2002, Samantha: An American Girl Holiday, 2004; appeared in stage plays The Importance of Being Earnest, NYC, 1964, Romantic Comedy, Mary Rose, The Three Sisters, The House of Bernarda Alba, Ivanov, Fran's Bed, 2005; joined Royal Shakespeare Co., London, 1974. Recipient Golden Globe award, 1967, Best Actress award, French Acad., 1969, Rio de Janeiro Film Festival award, 1969, Italian Academy award, 1970, D. W. Griffith award for best actress, 1990; named one of The 100 Most Influential People in the World, TIME mag., 2008. Office: Hofflund Polone 9465 Wilshire Blvd Ste 420 Beverly Hills CA 90212-2603

FARSHIDI, ARDESHIR B., cardiologist, educator; b. Kerman, Iran, June 13, 1945; arrived in U.S., 1972, naturalized, 1977; s. Jamshid and Farangis Farshidi; m. Katayoon Kavoussi, Jan. 2, 1982. MD, Tehran U., 1969. Diplomate Am. Bd. Internal Medicine, Am. Bd. Cardiovasc. Disease, Am. Bd. Cardiac Electrophysiology. Intern, Washington, 1972—73; resident U. Pa., Phila., 1973—75, resident in cardiology, 1975—77, electrophysiologist, 1977—78; asst. prof., assoc. prof. medicine U. Conn., Farmington, 1978—84; dir. electrophysiology LA Heart Inst., 1984—90; dir. arrhythmia ctr. Los Robles Regional Med. Ctr., 1990—. Dir. electrophysiologist U. Conn., Farmington, 1982—84, attending cardiologist, 1982—84; co-dir. electrophysiology, asst. prof. medicine Yale U., 1979—82; attending cardiologist Yale U. Hosp., 1979—82; chief cardiology sect. VA Hosp., Newington, Conn., 1982—84. Rschr. Am. Heart Assn., 1981. Lt. Iranian Army, 1969—72. Fellow: ACP, Am. Heart Assn., Am. Coll. Cardiology; mem.: Am. Electrophysiologic Soc., Am. Fedn. Clin. Rsch. Achievements include research in clin. cardiac electrophysiology and arrhythmia. Home: 3011 Grandoaks Dr Westlake Village CA 91361-5563 Office: 2100 Lynn Rd Ste 220 Thousand Oaks CA 91360-8036 Home Phone: 818-865-1286; Office Phone: 805-449-9990.

FARSON, RICHARD EVANS, psychologist; b. Chgo., Nov. 16, 1926; s. Duke Mendenhall and Mary Gladys (Clark) F.; m. Elizabeth Lee Grimes, May 21, 1954 (div. 1962); children: Lisa Page, Clark Douglas; m. 2d Dawn Jackson Cooper, Jan. 4, 1964 (div. 1990); children: Joel Andrew, Ashley Dawn, Jeremy Richard. BA, Occidental Coll., LA, 1947, MA, 1951; postgrad., UCLA, 1948-50; PhD, U. Chgo., 1955. Faculty human rels. Haward Bus. Sch., 1953—54; dean Sch. Design Calif. Inst. Arts, Valencia, 1969-73; pres. Esalen Inst., Big Sur and San Francisco, 1973-75; faculty Saybrook Inst., San Francisco, 1975-79; pres. Western Behavioral Scis. Inst., La Jolla, Calif., 1958-68; chmn. bd. Western Behavior Scis. Inst., La Jolla, Calif., 1968-79, pres., 1979—. Dir. Internat. Design Conf. in Aspen, Colo., 1971-2001, pres. 1976-80, 94-97; pub. dir. AIA, 1999-2001. Editor: Science and Human Affairs, 1967; author: Birthrights: A Bill of Rights for Children, 1974, Management of the Absurd: Paradoxes in Leadership, 1996; (with others) The Future of the Family, 1969; (with Ralph Keyes) Whoever Makes the Most Mistakes Wins: The Paradox of Innovation, 2002, The Power of Design: A Force for Transforming Everything, 2008. Served to lt. j.g. USNR, 1955-57. Fellow, Ford Found., 1953—54, World Acad. Art and Sci., Design Futures Coun. Mem.: APA. Home: 7520 Mar Ave La Jolla CA 92037 Office Phone: 858-454-2048. Personal E-mail: rfarson@wbsi.org.

FARWELL, HERMON WALDO, JR., parliamentarian and speech educator; b. Englewood, NJ, Oct. 24, 1918; s. Hermon Waldo and Elizabeth (Whitcomb) Farwell; m. Martha Carey Matthews, Jan. 3, 1942. AB, Columbia U., 1940; MA, Pa. State U., 1964. Commd. USAF, 1940, advanced through grades to maj., various positions, 1940—66, ret., 1966; instr. aerial photography Escola Tecnica de Aviaçao, Brazil, 1946—48; mem. faculty Colo. State U., Pueblo, 1966—84, prof. emeritus speech comm., 1984—; cons., tchr. parliamentary procedure. Author: Point of Opinion: The Majority Rules - A Manual of Procedure for Most Groups: Parliamentary Motions: Majority Motions; editor: The Parliamentary Jour., 1981—87, 1991—93; contbr. articles to profl. jours. Mem.: VFW, Nat. Assn. Parliamentarians, Ret. Officers Assn., Commn. on Am. Parliamentary Practice (chmn. 1976), Am. Inst. Parliamentarians (nat. dir. 1977—87), Air Force Assn., Am. Legion. Home and Office: 65 MacAlester Rd Pueblo CO 81001-2052 Home Phone: 719-542-7028. Personal E-mail: hymartco@earthlink.net.

FASI, FRANK FRANCIS, state legislator; b. East Hartford, Conn., Aug. 27, 1920; BS, Trinity Coll., Hartford, 1942. Mem. Hawaii Senate, 1959—; Dem. mayor City and County of Honolulu, 1969-81, Rep. mayor, 1985-94; resigned, 1994; owner Property & Bus., Honolulu, 1995. Mem. Dem. Nat. Com. for Hawaii, 1952-56; del. 2d Constl. Conv., 1968; mem.-at-large Honolulu City Coun., 1965-69; non-partisan candidate for Mayor of Honolulu, 2000. Served to capt. USMCR. Mem. Pacific-Asian Congress Municipalities (founder, past pres., exec. dir.), VFW (former comdr. Hawaii dept.), AFTRA (past v.p.). Home: 2054 Makiki St Honolulu HI 96822-2038

FATE, HUGH, state representative; b. Mountain View, Calif., Dec. 4, 1929; m. Mary Jane Fate; children: Janine, Jennifer, Julie, Al H. Woods. Student, U. Wash., 1948—49, U. Alaska, 1954—57; D in Pub. Svc. (hon.); BS, U. Oreg., 1959; DMD, 1962. Diplomate Internat. Coll. Dentists. Gold miner; coml. fisherman; heavy equipment oper., oil driller; real estate developer; dentist; mem. Alaska Ho. of Reps., 2000—. Past pres. Alaska State Bd. Dental Examiners. Chair Energy Coun., Gov. Task Force Rural Hire; chair adv. com. Alaska Land Use Coun.; past pres. Alaska Local Boundary Commn.; trustee U. Alaska Found.; past pres. Bd. Regents U. Alaska; vice-chair Alaska Rep. Party; chair Rep. Dist. 33. With US Army. Mem.: North Pole C. of C., Fairbanks C. of C. (past chair), Alaska C. of C. (bd. dirs., past exec. com.), Alaska Dental Soc. (past pres.), Rotary. Republican. Avocation: flying. Address: 100 N Cushman Ste 501 Fairbanks AK 99707

FATEMI, KHUSROW, academic administrator, economics educator; BA, Abadan Inst. Tech., Iran; MBA, Univ. So. Calif., PhD in internat. rels. Sr. economist Nat. Iranian Oil Co., 1972—79; asst. prof. Middle Tenn. State Univ., 1979—82; prof. internat. bus. Tex. A&M Univ., 1982—90, dean coll. bus., grad. sch. internat. trade & bus. adminstrn., 1990—98; dean, prof. internat. bus. San Diego State Univ., Imperial Valley, 1998—2004; pres. Ea. Oreg. Univ., La Grande, 2004—. Editor (founding): Global Economy Quarterly, The Internat. Trade Jour.; contbr. articles to profl. jours. Bd. dir. U.S.-Mex. C. of C. Mem.: Internat. Mgmt. Develop. Assn. (past pres., Internat. Dean of the Year 1999). Office: Eastern Oregon Univ Office of the President 1 University Blvd La Grande OR 97850-2899

FATHAUER, THEODORE FREDERICK, meteorologist; b. Oak Park, Ill., June 5, 1946; s. Arthur Theodore and Helen Ann (Mashek) Fathauer; m. Mary Ann Neesan, Aug. 8, 1981. BA, U. Chgo., 1968. Cert. cons. meteorologist. Rsch. aide USDA No. Devel. Labs., Peoria, Ill., 1966, Cloud Physics Lab., Chgo., 1967; meteorologist Sta. WLW Radio/TV, Cin., 1967-68, Nat. Meteorol. Ctr., Washington, 1968-70, Nat. Weather Svc., Anchorage, 1970-80, meteorologist-in-charge Fairbanks, Alaska, 1980-98, lead forecaster, 1998—. Instr. USCG Aux., Fairbanks, Anchorage, 1974—97, U. Alaska, Fairbanks, 1975—76, Osher Lifelong Learning Inst., Fairbanks, 2008; specialist in Alaska meteorology. Co-author: Denali's West Buttress, 1997, Living with the Coast of Alaska, 1997, (column) Weatherwatch, Weatherwise Mag., 2003—; contbr. articles to mags. and jours. Bd. dirs. Fairbanks Concert Assn., 1988—, Friends U. Alaska Mus., 1993—, pres., 1993—95, sec., 1997—98; bd. dirs. Fairbanks Symphony Assn., 1994—, sec., 1994—2001, treas., 2001—; trustee U. Alaska Found., 1997—, mem. coll. fellows, 1993—, mem. exec. com., 1997—, vice chair, 1998—99, chair, 2000—01; mem. adv. bd. Salvation Army, Fairbanks, 1997—; bd. dirs. No. Alaska Combined Fed. Campaign, 1996—2008, campaign chmn., 1996—97; bd. dirs. Alaska Statewide Combined Fed. Campaign, 2008—; bd. visitors U. Alaska, Fairbanks, 1995—; mem. KUAC Pub. Radio Leadership Coun., 2006—. Recipient Fed. Employee of the Yr. award, Fed. Exec. Assn., Anchorage, 1978. Fellow: Royal Meteorol. Soc., Am. Meteorol. Soc. (mem. sci. and tech. adv. com. coastal environments 1998—2004, co-chmn. Conf. Coastal Environment 2003, TV and radio seals approval); mem.: AAAS, Oceanography Soc. (charter mem.), Nat. Weather Assn. (charter mem.), Am. Sailing Assn., Can. Meteorol. and Oceanog. Soc., Arctic Inst. N.Am. (exec. sec. U.S. Corp. 1998—2003, bd. govs. U.S. Corp. 2003—), Western Snow Conf., Am. Geophys. Union, Am. Polar Soc., Greater Fairbanks C. of C. Catholic. Achievements include being a member of the science team on the voyage of the CCGS "Sir Wilfrid Laurier" from Victoria, BC to Barrow, Alaska, July 2006. Avocations: reading, music, skiing, canoeing. Home: 1738 Chena Ridge Rd PO Box 80210 Fairbanks AK 99708-0210 Office: Nat Weather Svc Forecast Office Internat Arctic Rsch Ctr U Alaska PO Box 757345 Fairbanks AK 99775-7345 Office Phone: 907-474-5606. Business E-Mail: ted.fathauer@gi.alaska.edu.

FATHI, BEN, computer software company executive; married; 1 child. Bachelor's Degree in Computer Sci. and Psychology, U. Mass., Master's Degree in Computer Sci. Dir., Operating Systems Silicon Graphics, Inc.; with Microsoft Corp., Redmond, Wash., 1998—, gen. mgr., storage and high availability, Windows divsn., gen. mgr., security tech. unit, 2006—07, corp v.p. develop., Windows Core Op. Sys, div., 2007—. Avocation: photography. Office: Microsoft Corp One Microsoft Way Redmond WA 98052-6399

FAULCONER, KEVIN, councilman; m. Katherine Faulconer; children: Jack, Lauren. Grad., San Diego State U. Councilman, Dist. 2 San Diego City Coun., 2006—, chair Audit Com., vice chair Com. on Budget & Fin., mem. Pub. Safety & Neighborhood Services Com., pres. pro tem. Former mem. City of San Diego Park & Recreation Bd. Office: 202 C St MS #10A San Diego CA 92101 Office Phone: 619-236-6622. Fax: 619-236-6996. E-mail: kevinfaulconer@sandiego.gov.*

FAULSTICH, JAMES R., retired bank executive; b. St. Louis, Dec. 19, 1933; s. Robert C. and Eva D. (Mueller) F.; m. Gretchen Felthouse, July 28, 1956; children: Robert, Julie, Clairann. BS, Ind. U., 1958; JD, U. Chgo., 1961. Dep. legis. counsel State Oreg., Salem, 1961-67, ins. commr., 1967-69, asst. to gov., 1969-71; v.p. industry rels. Nat. Assn. Ind. Insurers, Des Plaines, Ill., 1971-77, dir. rsch., sr. v.p. industry rels., 1977-79; pres., CEO Fed. Home Loan Bank Seattle, 1979-99. Bd. dirs. Pentegra. Treas. Bd. of Social Compact, Washington; bd. dirs. Housing Partnership, Seattle, Seattle Ctr. Found.; mem. Higher Edn. Coordinating Bd.; trustee Seattle Opera. Mem. ABA, Am. Judicature Soc., Oreg. Bar Assn., Wash. Athletic Club, Rainier Club, Downtown Seattle Assn., Columbia Tower Club, Rotary. Home: 8101 SE 48th St Mercer Island WA 98040-4301 Office: Fed Home Loan Bank 1501 4th Ave Ste 1900 Seattle WA 98101-1693

FAUSCH, KURT DANIEL, fisheries ecologist, educator; b. Crookston, Minn., Jan. 17, 1955; s. Homer David and Guinevere Jean (Smythe) F.; m. Deborah Anne Eisenhauer, Dec. 20, 1975; children: Emily Rebecca, Benjamin Thomas. BS in Zoology, U. Minn., Duluth, 1976; MS in Fisheries and Wildlife, Mich. State U., 1978, PhD in Fisheries and Wildlife, 1981. Postdoctoral fellow U. Ill., Champaign, 1981-82; asst. prof. fishery biology Colo. State U., Ft. Collins, 1982-87, assoc. prof., 1987-92, prof., 1992—, chmn. fishery biology major, 1991-93, 95-97, 1998-2000, advising faculty grad. degree program in ecology, 1995—. Vis. assoc. prof. U. B.C., 1990; invited rsch. fellow Japanese Soc. for Promotion of Sci., 1994, 2001; vis. sr. scientist, US Forest Svc., Boise, Idaho, 2004; vis. prof. U. Otago, New Zealand, 1997, Monash U. and Griffith U., Australia, 2005; mem organizing com. Internat. Meeting Atlantic Salmon, Scotland, 1997; invited external PhD examiner U. Lyon, France, 1994, U. B.C., 1996, 98, 2007, U. Wyo., 2002, Swiss Fed. Tech. U., 2005, U. Canberra, Australia, 2006; invited keynote talks: Spanish Limnological Soc., Barcelona, 2006, Fisheries Soc. British Isles, Exeter, UK, 2007, Freshwater Biol. Assn. British Isles, Windemere, UK, 2008, World Fisheries Congress, Yokohama, Japan, 2008. Co-editor: Fish Biology in Japan, 1998; expert panel reviewer for Instream Flow Needs, Electric Power Rsch. Inst., 1986, NRC report on endangered fishes in the Klamath River Basin, 2003, internat. expert panel to review multidisciplinary rsch. on causes of fish declines in Switzerland. Swiss Fed. Inst. Environ. Rsch.(EAWAG), 2003, rehabilitation of rare native brook trout populations in Lake Superior, US Fish and Wildlife Service, 2003, NSF (US and Japan) 11th US-Japan Conf. on Global Change, 2005, Fisheries Conservation Found. (Am. Fisheries Soc.) sci. team mem. 2005-, Colo. River Cutthroat Trout Status Endangered Species Act Review, US Fish and Wildlife Service, 2006, Cascade-Siskyou Nat. Monument Livestock Impacts publications, Ecological Soc. America, 2007, Cache la Poudre River flow regulation, City of Fort Collins, The Nature Conservancy, US Corps of Engineers, 2007-2009; contbr. 6 chpts. to books, 80 articles to profl. jours.; exec. prodr. (documentary film) RiverWebs, PBS (shown at 6 film festivals) & over 20 universities and profl. mtgs. (won two awards) & broadcast to over 50 million homes on PBS. Recipient US Forest Svc. Nat. Rise-to-the-Future Rsch. Achievement award, 2008, 1st Internat. Sci. prize, World Coun. Fisheries Socs., 2008; named Outstanding Sr. in Biology, U. Minn.-Duluth, 1976. Mem. Am. Fisheries Soc. (assoc. editor 1988-90, Albert S. Hazzard award 1982, best paper awards at profl. mtgs. 1989, 1992), Ecol. Soc. Am. (bd. editors Ecol. Applications 2000-03), Am. Inst. Biol. Scis., Fisheries Soc. British Isles, Japanese Soc. Ichthyology (editl. adv. bd. 1996-), N.Am. Benthol. Soc., Nature Conservancy Colo. (sci. adv. bd. 1995-2001). Office: Colo State U Dept Fish, Wildlife & Conservation Biol Fort Collins CO 80523-1474 E-mail: kurtf@cnr.colostate.edu.

FAVREAU, JON, actor, film director, film producer; b. Queens, NY, Oct. 19, 1966; m. Joya Tillem, Nov. 24, 2000; children: Max, Madelaine, Brighton Rose. Actor: (films) Folks!, 1992, Hoffa, 1992, Rudy, 1993, PCU, 1994, Mrs. Parker and the Vicious Circle, 1994, Batman Forever, 1995, Notes From Underground, 1995, Just Your Luck, 1996, Persons Unknown, 1996, Dogtown, 1996, Deep Impact, 1998, Very Bad Things, 1998, Love & Sex, 2000, The Replacements,

2000, Daredevil, 2003, Something's Gotta Give, 2003, Wimbledon, 2004, The Break-Up, 2006, (voice) Open Season, 2006, Iron Man, 2008, Four Christmases, 2008, I Love You, Man, 2009; (TV films) Grandpa's Funeral, 1994, Rocky Marciano, 1999; (TV series) Ain't It Cool News, 2001, (TV appearances) Seinfeld, 1994, Chicago Hope, 1994, The Larry Sanders Show, 1995, Tracey Takes On..., 1996, Friends, 1997, Hercules, 1999, Dilbert, 2000, The Sopranos, 2000, (voice only) Buzz Lightyear of Star Command, 2000, The King of Queens, 2004, My Names Is Earl, 2006; actor, prodr., writer: (films) Swingers, 1996; actor, prodr., writer, dir. Made, 2001; actor, prodr. The Big Empty, 2003; actor, dir. Elf, 2003; dir.: Zathura, 2005; writer, dir., prodr.: (TV films) Smog, 1999; dir.: Life on Parole, 2003; prodr.: (TV series) Undeclared, 2001; exec. prodr., host (TV series) Dinner for Five, 2001—; exec. prodr.: (TV films) Hooligans, 2005; writer: (films) The First $20 Million Is Always the Hardest, 2002. Office: c/o Creative Artists Agy Inc 9830 Wilshire Blvd Beverly Hills CA 90212

FAWCETT, MATTHEW KNOWLTON, lawyer; b. NYC; m. Christine Anderson; children: Paxton, Ainsley. B in rhetoric, U. Calif. Berkeley, 1989; LLD, UCLA, 1992. With Proskauer Rose, San Francisco, 1992—94, Morrison & Foerster, 1994—97, Fujitsu Am. Inc., 1997—99, E-Tech Dynamics, 1999—2000, JDS Uniphase Corp., San Francisco, 2000—, v.p., gen. counsel. Office: JDS Uniphase 430 N Mccarthy BLVD Ste 100 Milpitas CA 95035-5112

FAY, ABBOTT EASTMAN, history professor; b. Scottsbluff, Nebr., July 19, 1926; s. Abbott Eastman and Ethel (Lambert) F.; m. Joan D. Richardson, Nov. 26, 1953; children: Rand, Diana, Collin. Grad., Scottsbluff Jr. Coll., Nebr.; BA, Colo. State Coll. Edn., 1949, MA, 1953; postgrad., U. Denver, 1961-63; cert. advanced study, Western State U., 1963. Tchr. Leadville (Colo.) Pub. Schs., 1950-52, elem. prin., 1952-54; prin. Leadville Jr. H.S., 1954-55; pub. info. dir., instr. history Mesa Coll., Grand Junction, Colo., 1955-64; asst. prof. history Western State Coll., Gunnison, Colo., 1964-76, assoc. prof. history, 1976-82, assoc. prof. emeritus, 1982—. Adj. faculty Adams State Coll., Alamosa, Colo., Mesa State Coll., Grand Junction, Colo., 1989—; propr. Mountaintop Books, Paonia, Colo.; bd. dirs. Colo. Assoc. Univ. Press; dir. hist. tours; columnist Valley Chronicle, Paonia, Beacon, Grand Junction, Free Press, Grand Junction, The Historian, Fruita, Colo., Grand Mesa Byway News, Delta, Colo.; profl. speaker in field; cons. Colo. Welcome Ctr., 1997—. Author: Mountain Academia, 1968, Writing Good History Research Papers, 1980, Ski Tracks in the Rockies, 1984, Famous Coloradans, 1990, I Never Knew That About Colorado, 1993, Beyond The Great Divide, 1999, To Think That This Happened in Grand County!, 1999, A History of Skiing in Colorado, 2000, More That I Never Knew About Colorado, 2000, The Story of Colorado Wines, 2002, Grand Mesa Country, 2005; playwright: Thunder Mountain Lives Tonight!; contbr. articles to profl. jours.; freelance writer popular mags. Founder, coord. Nat. Energy Conservation Challenge; travel cons. Colo. State Welcome Ctr., 1997-99; project reviewer NEH, Colo. Hist. Soc.; steering com. West Elk Scenic & Historic Byway, Colo., 1994—; founder Leadville (Colo.) Assembly, pres., 1953-54; mem. Advs. of Lifelong Learning, 1994—. Named Top Prof. Western State Coll., 1969, 70, 71; fellow Hamline U. Inst. Asian Studies, 1975, 79; recipient Colo. Ind. Pubs. award, 1998. Mem. Western Writers Am., Rocky Mountain Social Sci. Assn. (sec. 1961-63), Am. Hist. Assn., Assn. Asian Studies, Western History Assn., Western State Coll. Alumni Assn. (pres. 1971-73), Internat. Platform Assn. Profl. Guides Assn. Am. (cert.), Rocky Mountain Guides Assn., Colo. Antiquarian Booksellers Assn., Am. Legion (Outstanding Historian award 1981), Phi Alpha Theta, Phi Kappa Delta, Delta Kappa Pi. Home: 2709 F1/2 Rd #402 Grand Junction CO 81506

FAY, THOMAS F., library director; BA in Fine Arts, U. Nev., Las Vegas. Page Overton Libr., 1983; various positions including computer technician, network specialist and network mgr. Las Vegas-Clark County Libr. Dist.; computer network specialist Cooperative Librs. Automated Network; info. tech. mgr. Henderson Dist. Pub. Librs., Nev., dir. Nev., 2004—. Mem.: Nev. Libr. Assn. (Scholarship 2000). Office: Henderson Dist Pub Librs Adminstrn 280 S Green Valley Pky Henderson NV 89012 Office Phone: 702-492-6595. Office Fax: 702-492-1711. E-mail: tffay@hdpl.org.

FAYER, MICHAEL DAVID, chemist, educator; b. LA, Sept. 12, 1947; s. William and Frieda Fayer; m. Terry Wolfe, Dec. 21, 1968; children: Victoria, William. BS, U. Calif., Berkeley, 1969, PhD, 1974. Asst. prof. chemistry Stanford U., 1974—80, assoc. prof. chemistry, 1980—84, prof. chemistry, 1984—2000, David Mulvane Ehrsam and Edward Curtis Franklin prof. of chemistry, 2000—. Prof. physics U. Grenoble, France, 1982; invited lectr. in field. Author: (book) Elements of Quantum Mechanics, 2001; contbr. articles to sci. jours.; mem. editl. bd. Jour. Chem. Physics, 1987—90, mem. adv. bd. Jour. Phys. Chemistry, 1986—89, adv. editor Chem. Physics Letters, 1984—, Chem. Physics, 1985—, assoc. editor Jour. Luminescence, 1988—. Recipient E. Bright Wilson award in Spectroscopy, Am. Chem. Soc., 2007; fellow Alfred P. Sloan fellow, Sloan Found., 1977, Camille & Henry Dreyfus Found. fellow, Dreyfus Found., 1977, Guggenheim Found. Fellow, 1983—84. Fellow: Am. Acad. Arts and Sciences, Am. Phys. Soc. (Earl K. Pyler prize for molecular spectroscopy 2000); mem.: NAS, Phi Beta Kappa, Sigma Xi. Office: Dept Chemistry KECK 113 Stanford University Stanford CA 94305-5080 Office Fax: 650-723-4817. E-mail: fayer@stanford.edu.

FAY-SCHMIDT, PATRICIA ANN, paralegal; b. Waukegan, Ill., Dec. 25, 1941; d. John William and Agnes Alice (Semerad) Fay; m. Dennis A. Schmidt, Nov. 3, 1962 (div. Dec. 1987); children: Kristin Fay Schmidt, John Andrew Schmidt. Student, L.A. Pierce Coll., 1959-60; BA in Theater Arts, U. San Jose, 1962; postgrad., Western State U. of Law, Fullerton, Calif., 1991-92. Cert. legal asst., Calif. Paralegal Rasner & Rasner, Costa Mesa, Calif., 1979-82; paralegal, adminstr. Law Offices of Manuel Ortega, Santa Ana, Calif., 1982-92; sabbatical, 1992-94. Mem. editorial adv. bd. James Pub. Co., Costa Mesa, 1984-88. Contbg. author: Journal of the Citizen Ambassador Paralegal Delegation to the Soviet Union, 1990. Treas., Republican Women, Tustin, Calif., 1990-91; past regent, 1st vice regent, 2d vice regent NSDAR, Tustin, 1967—; docent Richard M. Nixon Libr. and Birthplace, 1993—, bd. dirs. Docent Guild, 1994-99; docent Orange County Courthouse Mus., 1992-94; chmn. Am. History Essay, 1999—. Mem. Orange County Paralegal Assn. (hospitality chair 1985-87). Roman Catholic. Avocations: theater, dance. Home: 13571 Hewes Ave Santa Ana CA 92705-2215 Business E-Mail: gabriellx@pacbell.net.

FEARING, GEORGE B., lawyer; b. Hinsdale, Ill., Oct. 24, 1957; 1 child, George. BBA magna cum laude, Walla Walla Coll., College Place, Wash., 1979; JD, U. Wash. Sch. Law, Seattle, 1982. Bar: US Dist. Ct. (ea. dist. Wash.), Ct. of Appeals (9th cir.) 1998, Ct. of Fed. Claims 2000. Ptnr. Leavy, Schultz, Davis & Fearing PS, 1982—. Lectr. Wash. State U. Author: My Year with Bush, 2002, Water Gate, 2004, Why I Hate 911, 2005. Mem. Franklin County Democratic Ctrl. Com., 1998—2006; candidate, dist. 16 Wash. State House of Representatives, 2006. Mem.: NRA, ACLU, NAACP, Wash. State Bar Assn. (disciplinary bd. 2000—03), Benton Franklin County Bar Assn., Wash. State Trial Lawyers Assn. Democrat. Office: Leavy Schultz Davis & Fearing PS 2415 West Falls Ave Kennewick WA 99336 Office Phone: 509-736-1330. Office Fax: 509-736-1580. Business E-Mail: gfearing@tricitylaw.com.

FEARON, LEE CHARLES, chemist; b. Tulsa, Nov. 22, 1938; s. Robert Earl and Ruth Belle (Strothers) F.; m. Wanda Sue Williams, Nov. 30, 1971 (div. June 1998); m. Shirlene Olsen, Dec. 9, 2000. Student, Rensselaer Polytech. Inst., 1957-59; BS in Physics, Okla. State U., Stillwater, 1961, BA in Chemistry, 1962, MS in Analytical Chemistry, 1969. Rsch. chemist Houston process lab. Shell Oil Co., Deer Park, Tex., 1968-70; chief chemist Pollution Engring. Internat., Inc., Houston, 1970-76; rsch. chemist M-I Drilling Fluids Co., Houston, 1976-83; cons. chemist Profl. Engr. Assocs., Inc., Tulsa, 1983-84; chemist Anacon, Inc., Houston, 1984-85; scientist III Bionetics Corp., Rockville, Md., 1985-86; sr. chemist L.A. County Sanitation Dist., Whittier, Calif., 1986; chemist Test Am., West Sacramento, Calif., 1986-87; cons. chemist Branham Industries, Inc., Conroe, Tex., 1987-89; chemist 4, Lab Accreditation unit EAP, Wash. State Dept. Ecology, Manchester, 1989—. Cons. chemist Terra-Kleen, Okmulgee, Okla., 1988—94, Excel Pacific, Inc. & Precision Works, Inc., Camarillo, Calif., 1993—96, 2002—, Precision Works, Inc., 2002—. With US Army, 1962—65. Fellow: Am. Inst. Chemists; mem.: AAAS, Am. Chem. Soc. Achievements include patents for environ. soil remediation tech. Avocations: photography, travel. Home: PO Box 514 Manchester WA 98353-0514 Office: PO Box 488 Manchester WA 98353-0488 Personal E-mail: limafox@wavecable.com. Business E-Mail: lfea461@ecy.wa.gov.

FEATHERSTONE, BRUCE ALAN, lawyer; b. Detroit, Mar. 2, 1953; s. Ronald A. and Lois R. (Bosshart) F.; children: Leigh Allison, Edward Alan, Rex Saunders. BA cum laude with distinction in Econs., Yale U., 1974; JD magna cum laude, U. Mich., 1977. Bar: Ill. 1977, Colo. 1983, U.S. Dist. Ct. (no. dist.) Ill. 1977, U.S. Dist. Ct. Colo. 1983, U.S. Ct. Appeals (5th cir.) 1980, U.S. Ct. Appeals (7th cir.) 1981, U.S. Ct. Appeals (10th cir.) 1983, U.S. Ct. Appeals (9th cir.) 1990, U.S. Ct. Appeals (fed. cir.), U.S. Supreme Ct. 1984, others. Assoc. Kirkland & Ellis, Denver, 1977-83, ptnr., 1983-96, Featherstone & Shea, LLP, Denver, 1996-99, Featherstone DeSisto LLP, Denver, 1999—. Articles editor U. Mich. Law Rev., 1976-77. Mem. ABA (litigation sect., tort and ins. practice sect., prof. liability sect., antitrust sect.), ATLA, Colo. Bar Assn., Colo. Trial Lawyers Assn., Denver Bar Assn., Order of Coif. Home: 725 Saint Paul St Denver CO 80206-3912 also: PO Box 1467 Denver CO 80201-1467 Office: Featherstone DeSisto LLP 600-17th St Ste 2400 Denver CO 80202-5402 Office Phone: 303-626-7125. E-mail: bfeatherstone@featherstonelaw.com.

FEATHERSTONE, DIANE L., utilities executive; B in Econs. and History, Towson U., Md.; M in Econs., U. Va., Charlottesville. CPA; cert. fraud examiner. Various positions in human resources, fin. and acctg. Balt. Gas and Electric Co.; with Constellation, 1976; mng. dir. strategic planning Constellation Power Source; pres., CEO Constellation Energy Source; v.p. mgmt. consulting and auditing Constellation Energy Group, Balt.; v.p., gen. auditor Edison Internat., Rosemead, Calif., 2002, v.p., gen. auditor So. Calif. Edison subs., 2002, sr. v.p. human resources, sr. v.p. human resources So. Calif. Edison subs. Office: Edison Internat 2244 Walnut Grove Ave Rosemead CA 91770-3714 Office Phone: 626-302-1212.

FEE, WILLARD EDWARD, JR., otolaryngologist; b. Portchester, June 10, 1943; s. Willard E. and Jane Frances (Cromwell) F.; m. Caroline Fee, June 13, 1965; children: Heather, Adam. BS cum laude, U. San Francisco, 1965; MD magna cum laude, U. Colo., 1969. Cert. Am. Bd. Otolaryngology, 1974. Intern Harbor Gen. Hosp., Torrance, Calif., 1969-70; resident in gen. surgery Wadsworth VA Hosp., LA, 1970-71; resident in head and neck surgery UCLA Sch. Medicine, 1971-74; asst. prof. Stanford (Calif.) U. Med. Ctr., 1974-80, assoc. prof. otolaryngology, 1980-86, prof., 1986—, Edward C. & Amy H. Sewall prof., 1995—, chmn. dept., 1980-00. Dir. Am. Bd. of Otolaryngology, Houston, 1985-2003; chmn. med. sch. faculty senate Stanford U., 1992-94. Editl. bd. Archives in Otolaryngology, Chgo., 1984-95; contbr. numerous articles to profl. jours. Mem. Collegium ORLAS-US (chmn. 1995-2001), Paul H. Ward Soc., Inc. (pres. 1988-89), Am. Soc. Head and Neck Surgery (pres. 1989-90), Am. Acad. Otolaryngology and Head and Neck Surgery, Calif. Soc. Otolaryngology (pres. 1995-99), Alpha Omega Alpha. Home: 907 Clark Way Palo Alto CA 94304 Office: 875 Blake Wilbur Dr Cancer Ctr Rm 2227 Stanford CA 94305-5826 Office Phone: 650-725-6500.

FEEHAN, CHRISTINE, writer; b. Calif. m. Richard Feehan; 11 children. Author (Dark series): Dark Prince, 1999 (three Pearl Paranormal awards for for Romantic Lit., 1999), Dark Desire, 1999, Dark Gold, 2000, Dark Magic, 2000, Dark Challenge, 2000, Dark Fire, 2001 (two Pearl Paranormal Excellence awards, 2001, Reviewer's Choice award for best vampire, Romantic Times, 2001), Dark Dream, 2001, Dark Legend, 2002, Dark Guardian, 2002 (Pearl Paranormal Excellence award, 2002, two Golden Rose Readers Choice awards, 2002), Dark Symphony, 2003, Dark Descent, 2003, Dark Melody, 2003, Dark Destiny, 2004, Dark Hunger, 2004, Dark Secret, 2005, Dark Demon, 2006, Dark Celebration, 2006, Dark Possession, 2007, Dark Curse, 2008 (No. 1 Publishers Weekly bestseller); author: (Drake Sisters series) The Twilight Before Christmas, 2003, Magic in the Wind, 2005, Oceans of Fire, 2005, Dangerous Tides, 2006, Safe Harbor, 2007, Turbulent Sea, 2008 (Publishers Weekly bestseller); author: (Ghostwalkers series) Shadow Game, 2003, Mind Game, 2004 (Rio award of Excellence for sci-fi romance, 2004, Pearl award for best fantasy, 2004, Hughey award for best paranormal romance, 2004), Night Game, 2005, Conspiracy Game, 2006, Deadly Game, 2007, Predatory Game, 2008, Murder Game, 2008 (Publishers Weekly bestseller); author: (Leopard series) The Awakening in Fantasy, 2003, Wild Rain, 2004 (No. 1 Waldenbooks bestseller); author: (other works) The Scarletti Curse, 2001, Lair of the Lion, 2002 (Reviewer Choice award for best historical paranormal, Romantic Times); contbr. numerous stories to anthologies. Recipient Career Achievement award, Romantic Times, 2003. Mailing: Christine Feehan Prodns PO Box 181 Mendocino CA 95460 Business E-Mail: christine@christinefeehan.com.

FEELEY, MICHAEL F., state legislator; b. Hackensack, NJ, 1953; m. Lesley A. Dahlkemper. B in Econs. magna cum laude, U. Colo., 1977; JD, U. Denver, 1982. Ptnr. Overton & Feeley; mem. Colo. State Senate, 1992, minority leader, mem. svcs. com., mem. legis. coun. Mem. gender and justice com. Colo. Supreme Ct. Active Gov.'s Colo. Edn. Goals Panel; ad hoc mem. Children's Campaign Legis. Com.; bd. mem. Colo. Guaranteed Student Loan Program, West Metro Fire Protection Dist. Sgt. USMC, 1971-74. Named Outstanding Legislator, Colo. Bankers Assn., Domestic Violence Coun., Bldg. and Constrn. Trades Coun. Roman Catholic. Avocations: tennis, reading, cu football. Address: 13486 W Center Dr Lakewood CO 80228-2452 Office: State Capitol 200 E Colfax Ave Ste 274 Denver CO 80203-1716 also: 1120 Lincoln St Denver CO 80203-2139 Fax: 303-866-4543. E-mail: mike.freeley@state.co.us.

FEENEY, FLOYD FULTON, law educator; b. Franklin, Ind., Sept. 26, 1933; s. Burla L. and Ona Marie (McMillin) F.; m. Peggy Ann Ballard, June 15, 1956; children: Elizabeth, Linda. BS in History with honors, Davidson Coll., 1955; LLB, NYU, 1960. Bar: N.C. 1960, D.C. 1961. Law clk. U.S. Supreme Ct., 1961-62; spl. asst. to solicitor Dept. Labor, 1962-63; dep. spl. counsel Pres.'s Com. on Equal Employment Opportunity, 1963; asst. dir. Pres.'s Crime Commn., 1966-67; spl. asst. to adminstr. AID, 1963-68; prof. law U. Calif.-Davis, 1968—; mem. Calif. Atty. Gen.'s Research Adv. Council, 1985-90. Cons. Nat. Ctr. for State Cts., Nat. Inst. Justice, Brit. Home Office. Author: The Police and Pretrial Release, 1982, (with Roger Baron) Juvenile Diversion Through Family Counseling, 1976, (with Dill and Weir) Arrests Without Conviction, 1983, (with Philip Dubois) Lawmaking by Initiative, 1998. Served to 1st lt. U.S. Army, 1956-58. Fulbright scholar, 1995-96; recipient Pepperdine award, 1978 Mem. ABA, Am. Assn. Law Schs., Am. Law Inst., D.C. Bar Assn., N.C. Bar Assn., Assn. for Criminal Justice Research Calif. Home: 1228 Colby Dr Davis CA 95616-1719 Office Phone: 530-752-2893. Business E-Mail: fffeeney@ucdavis.edu.

FEHER, GEORGE, biophysicist, educator; b. Czechoslovakia, May 29, 1924; s. Ferdinand and Sylvia (Schwartz) Feher; m. Elsa Rosenvasser, June 18, 1961; children: Laurie, Shoshanah, Paoli. BS in Engring. Physics, U. Calif., Berkeley, 1950, MSEE, 1951, PhD in Physics, 1954; PhD (hon.), Hebrew U. Jerusalem, 1994. Rsch. physicist Bell Tel. Labs., Murray Hill, NJ, 1954-60; vis. assoc. prof. Columbia U., NYC, 1959-60; prof. physics U. Calif., San Diego, 1960—92, rsch. prof. physics, 1993—. Vis. prof. biology MIT, Cambridge, 1967-68; William Draper Hawkins lectr. U Chgo., May 1986; Raymond and Beverly Sackler disting. lectr. U. Tel-Aviv, June 1986; vis. prof. Hebrew U. Jerusalem, Israel, spring 1989, 93; bd. govs. Weizmann Inst. Sci., Rehovot, Israel, 1988-, Technion-Israel Inst. Tech., Haifa, 1968-. Author: Electron Paramagnetic Resonance with Applications to Selected Problems in Biology, 1970; contbr. articles to profl. jous., chpts. to books. Recipient Oliver E. Buckley Solid State Physics prize, 1976, Inaugural Ann. award Internat. Electron Spin Resonance Soc., 1991; co-recipient 2006/2007 Wolf Found. Prize in Chemistry, Israel; NSF fellow, 1967-68. Fellow AAAS, Internat. EPR/ESR Soc. (Zavoisky award 1996), Biophysical Soc.; mem. Am. Phys. Soc. (prize 1960, biophysics prize, 1982), Biophys. Soc. (nat. lectr. 1983), NAS, Am. Acad. Arts & Scis. (Rumford medal 1992), Sigma Xi. Office: Dept Physics U Calif 9500 Gilman Dr Dept 319 La Jolla CA 92093-0319 E-mail: gfeher@physics.ucsd.edu.

FEHIR, KIM MICHELE, oncologist, hematologist; b. Chgo., Aug. 31, 1947; d. William Frank and Beatric Mae (Mc Glaughlin) Debelak; m. John Stephen Fehir, Dec. 24, 1974. BS, Mich. State U., 1969; MS, U. Ill., Chgo., 1973, PhD, 1975; MD, Rush Med. Sch., Chgo., 1978. Diplomate Am. Bd. Internal Medicine. Intern, resident John Hopkins Hosp., Balt., 1978-81; fellow in oncology Meml. Sloan Kettering Cancer Ctr., NYC, 1981-83; dir. med. oncology Stehlin Oncology Clin., Houston, 1983—. Asst. prof. medicine Bayler Coll., Houston, 1983-98. Contbr. to profl. jours. Mem. AMA, Am. Med. Soc. Hematologist, Am. Med. Soc. Clin. Oncology. Republican. Avocations: running, climbing, skiing. Office: Med Assocs of Johnson County 497 W Lott St Buffalo WY 82834-1609 E-mail: kfehir@wyoming.com.

FEHR, JOHN WILLIAM, newspaper editor; b. Long Beach, Calif., Mar. 8, 1926; s. John and Evelyn (James) F.; m. Cynthia Moore, Sept. 4, 1951; children— Michael John, Martha Ann BA in English, U. Utah, 1951. City editor Salt Lake City Tribune, 1964-80, mng. editor, 1980-81, editor, 1981-91. Served to 1st lt. USAF, 1951-53 Mem. Am. Soc. Newpaper Editors, Sigma Chi Home: 468 13th Ave Salt Lake City UT 84103-3229

FEHR, LOLA MAE, health facility administrator; b. Hastings, Nebr., Sept. 29, 1936; d. Leland R. and Edith (Wunderlich) Gaymon; m. Harry E. Fehr, Aug. 15, 1972; children: Dawn, Cheryl, Michael. RN, St. Luke's Hosp., Denver, 1958; BSN magna cum laude, U. Denver, 1959; MS, U. Colo., Boulder, 1975. Dir. staff devel. Weld County Gen. Hosp., Greeley, Colo., 1972-76, dir. nursing, 1976-80; exec. dir. Colo. Nurses Assn., Denver, 1980-89; dir. membership Assn. Oper. Rm. Nurses, Inc., Denver, 1989-90, exec. dir., 1990-99; pres. Fehr Cons. Resources, 1999—; exec. dir. Am. Soc. Bariatric Physicians, 2000—01; program dir. Colo. Ctr. for Nursing Excellence, 2003; exec. dir. N.Y. State Nurses Assn., 2003—. Editor: Colo. Nurse, 1980—89. Recipient U. Colo. Alumni award, Colo. Nurses Assn. Profl. Nurse of Yr. award. Mem. Am. Acad. Nursing, Nat. Assn. Parliamentarians, Am. Soc. Assn. Execs., N.Y. State Nurses Assn., Sigma Theta Tau. Office Phone: 518-782-9400 ext. 201. Business E-Mail: lolafehr@gmail.com.

FEICHTINGER, MARK R., career officer; b. Eugene, Oreg., May 31, 1948; m. Nancy G. Feichtinger. Grad. with distinction, Northwestern U., Evanston, Ill., 1970; JD, U. Mich., 1978. Commd. ensign USN, 1970; advanced through ranks to rear adm. USNR; various assignments to sr. inspector, asst./mission effect.; dep. comdr. submarine force U.S. Pacific Fleet; ptnr. Stoel Rives LLP. Chair Clark County United Way Campaign, 1991-92; active 4-county United Way Bd.; chmn. bd. Clark County's Econ. Devel. Coun.; pres. Cmty. Found. for Southwest Washington. Decorated Navy Meritorious Svc. medal (4 times), Navy Commendation medal (2 times), Navy Achievement medal. Mem. Phi Beta Kappa. Avocations: bicycling, reading, railroading, attending auto races. Home: 7680 SW Northshire St Portland OR 97225-2764

FEIG, STEPHEN ARTHUR, pediatrician, hematologist, oncologist, educator; b. NYC, Dec. 24, 1937; s. Irving L. and Janet (Oppenheimer) F.; m. Judith Bergman, Aug. 28, 1960; children: Laura, Daniel, Andrew. AB in Biology, Princeton U., NJ, 1959; MD, Columbia U.,

NYC, 1963. Diplomate Am. Bd. Pediat., Am. Bd. Hematology-Oncology. Intern Mt. Sinai Hosp., NYC, 1963-64, resident in pediat., 1964-66; hematology fellow Children's Hosp. Med. Ctr., Boston, 1968-71, assoc. in medicine, 1971-72; asst. prof. pediat. UCLA, 1972-77, chief divsn. hematology and oncology Sch. Medicine, 1977—2005, assoc. prof., 1977-82, prof., 1982—2005, exec. vice chmn. dept. pediat. Sch. Medicine, 1994—2004, prof. emeritus, 2005—. Trustee LA chpt. Leukemia Soc. Am., 1978—2004, trustee, 1984—2004; chair exec. com. subsect. hemotology/oncology Am. Acad. Pediat., 2005-09; mem. Coun. Pediat. Subspltys., 2006—; bd. dirs. Camp Ronald McDonald for Good Times; active numerous other pediatric hosp. and med. sch. coms Reviewer Am. Jour. Pediatric Hematology/Oncology, Blood, Pediat., Pediatric Rsch., Jour. Pediat.; contbr. articles to profl. jours.; editl. bd. Jour. Pediat. Hematology & Oncology. Served with USNR, 1966-68. Mem. Am. Soc. Hematology, Soc. Pediatric Rsch., Am. Pediatric Soc., Internat. Soc. Exptl. Hematology, Am. Assn. Cancer Rsch. Jewish. Avocation: native arts. Office: UCLA Sch Medicine Dept Pediatrics 10833 Le Conte Ave Los Angeles CA 90095-3075

FEIGENBAUM, EDWARD ALBERT, retired computer science educator; b. Weehawken, NJ, Jan. 20, 1936; s. Fred J. and Sara Rachman; m. H. Penny Nii, 1975. BEE, Carnegie Inst. Tech., 1956, PhD in Indsl. Adminstrn., 1960; DSc (hon.), Aston U., UK, 1989. From asst. prof. to assoc. prof. bus. adminstrn. U. Calif., Berkeley, 1960—65; from assoc. prof. computer sci. to prof. Stanford U., 1965—95, prin. investigator heuristic programming project and knowledge sys. lab., 1965—2001, chmn. dept. computer sci., 1976-81, dir. Computation Ctr., 1965-68, Kumagai prof. computer sci., 1995—2001, emeritus, 2001—; pres. Intelli Genetics Inc., 1980—82, mem. tech. adv. bd., 1983-86; chmn., dir. Teknowledge, Inc., 1981-82; dir. IntelliCorp, 1984-90; chief scientist USAF, 1994-97. Mem. computer and biomath. scis. study sect. NIH, 1968-72, adv. com. on artificial intelligence in medicine, 1974-92; mem. Math. Social Sci. Bd., 1975-78, Internat. Joint Coun. on Artificial Intellignece, 1973-83; computer sci. adv. com. NSF, 1977-80; chief scientist, USAF, 1994-97; sci. adv. bd. USAF, 1997-2000; sci. advisor Air Force Office Sci. Rsch., 2000-07; trustee Computer History Mus., 2005-; cons. in field. Author: (with others) Information Processing Language V Manual, 1961, (with P. McCorduck) The Fifth Generation, 1983; author: (with R. Lindsay, B. Buchanan, J. Lederberg) Applications of Artificial Intelligence to Organic Chemistry: the Dendral Project, 1980; Editor: (with J. Feldman) Computers and Thought, 1963, (with A. Barr and P. Cohen) Handbook of Artificial Intelligence, 1981, 82, 89, (with Pamela McCorduck and H. Penny Nii) The Rise of the Expert Company: How Visionary Companies are using Artificial Intelligence to Achieve Higher Productivity and Profits, 1988, The Japanese Entrepreneur: Making the Desert Bloom, 2002; mem. editorial bd.: Jour. Artificial Intelligence, 1970-88. Trustee Charles Babbage Found. History of Info. Processing, U. Minn., 2000-03, 2004-; mem. Feigenbaum-Nii Found., 2000—. Feigenbaum medal named in his honor World Congress on Expert Systems, 1991. Fellow AAAI, AAAS, Am. Coll. Med. Informatics, Am. Inst. Med. and Biol. Engring.; mem. NAE, Assn. Computing Machinery (nat. coun. 1966-68, chmn. spl. interest group on biol. applications 1973-76, A.M. Turing award 1994), Am. Assn. Artificial Intelligence (pres. 1980-81, Robert S. Engelmore Meml. award 2004), Am. Acad. Arts and Scis., Cognitive Sci. Soc. (coun. 1979-82), Sigma Xi, Tau Beta Pi, Eta Kappa Nu, Pi Delta Epsilon. Home: 1017 Cathcart Way Palo Alto CA 94305-1048 Office: Stanford U Knowledge Systems Lab Gates Computer Sci Rm 220 Stanford CA 94305-9020 Business E-Mail: feigenbaum@cs.stanford.edu.

FEIGIN, JOEL, composer, educator; b. NYC, May 23, 1951; s. Irwin and Mollie Kanowitz Feigin; m. Severine Neff, 1986. BA, Columbia U., 1968—72; MA, Juilliard Sch., 1977; DMA, 1982. Mellon post doctoral fellowship Cornell U., 1983—85; asst. prof. U. Ut., 1985—87; faculty Manhattan Sch., 1988—92; asst. prof. U. Calif., 1992—97, assoc. prof., 1997—2002, prof., 2002—. Composer: (Operas) Mysteries of Eleusis, 1986, The Ferryman, 1997, Twelfth Night, 2004, (chamber music) variations of violin, piano and string quartet (speculum musicae and auros group for new music composition competitions, 1998), Veränderungen, 1995, Transcience, 1996 (third place internat. chamber music competition, 1997), vocal and choral music, (video soundtrack) Music for Mountains and Rivers, 1996. Andrew D. Mellon post-doctoral fellow, Cornell U., 1983—85, Guggenheim fellow, 1985—86, Sr. Fulbright fellow, Moscow State Conservatory, 1998—99, winner, NYCO Vox Competition, 2004, Opera Am. Showcase, 2006. Avocations: reading, sitting zaren. Office: U Calif Music Dept Rm 1121 Santa Barbara CA 93105

FEIMAN, THOMAS E., investment company executive; b. Canton, Ohio, Dec. 21, 1940; s. Daniel Thaviu and Adrienne (Silver) F.; m. Marilyn Judith Miller, June 26, 1966; children: Sheri, Michael. BS in Econs., U. Pa., 1962; MBA, Northwestern U., 1963. CPA, Calif. Staff acct. Arthur Young & Co., LA, 1963-66; field auditor IRS, LA, 1966-68; pvt. practice acctg. Thomas Feiman, C.P.A., LA, 1968-69; ptnr. Wideman & Feiman, C.P.A.s, LA, 1969-74; pres. Wideman, Feiman, Levy, Sapin & Ko, LA, 1974-93; investment mgr., v.p. Schroder Wertheim & Co., Inc., 1993-96; CFO Spinal Home Health Systems, Inc., LA, 1983-85; fin. cons., v.p. Merrill Lynch, 1996—2004, UBS, 2004—; pres., dir. Urol. Scis. Rsch. Found., 1993—. Sr. instr. UCLA Extension, 1967-84. Trustee Temple Israel of Hollywood, Calif., 1981-83, treas., 1983-84. Recipient cert. of award IRS, 1967. Mem. AICPA, Calif. Soc. CPAs, Northwestern Bus. So. Calif. Club (pres. 1977-80), Northwestern Alumni of So. Calif. Club (trustee 1977-92, treas. 1977-90 L.A.). Republican. Jewish. Office: UBS Financial Svcs 21650 Oxnard St Woodland Hills CA 91367-4907 Personal E-mail: thomasfeiman@yahoo.com. Business E-Mail: thomasfeiman@ubs.com.

FEIN, RONALD LAWRENCE, lawyer; b. Detroit, Aug. 26, 1943; s. Lee Allen and Billie Doreen (Thomas) F.; m. Sandra Siegel, March 21, 2006; children: Samantha, Mark. AB with honors, UCLA, 1966; JD with honors, U. San Diego, 1969. Bar: Calif. 1970, U.S. Dist. Ct. (cen. dist.) Calif. 1970. Assoc. Gibson, Dunn & Crutcher, Los Angeles, 1969-75; chief dep. commr. of corps. State of Calif., Los Angeles, 1975-78; ptnr., mem. firmwide adv. com., chmn. corp. fin./mergers and acquisitions sect., chmn. corp. dept. Jones, Day, Reavis & Pogue, Los Angeles, 1978-87; ptnr., mem. exec. com., chmn. gen. bus. dept. Wyman, Bautzer, Kuchel & Silbert, LA, 1987-91; sr. ptnr. Stutman, Treister & Glatt, 1991—2007; pres. & CEO R. L. Fein, Inc., 2007—. Bd. dirs. Executours, Inc., Los Angeles, Lottery Info., North Hollywood, Calif., Malibu Grand Prix, Woodland Hills, Calif.; adj. prof. law Loyola U., Los Angeles, 1976; mem. Commr.'s Circle Adv. Com. to the Calif. Commr. of Corps., Fin. Lawyers Conf.; mem. adv. bd. Inst. Corp. Counsel U. S.C Articles editor San Diego Law Rev., 1969; contbr. articles to profl. jours. Co-dir. protocol for boxing Los Angeles Olympic Organizing Com., 1984. Lt. USAF, to 1966-69. Mem. ABA (corp., banking and bus. law sect., mem. ad hoc com. on merit regulation, mem. fed. regulation of securities com., mem. ad hoc com. on the Uniform Limited Offering Exemption, com. on Counsel Responsibility, mem. ad hoc com. on Regulation D, mem. subcom. on Registration Statements—1933 Act, vice chmn. state regulation securities com., chmn. pvt. offering exemption and simplification of capital formation subcom., chmn. NASAA Omnibus guideline subcom.), Calif. Bar Assn. (bus. law sect.), Los Angeles County Bar Assn. (mem. exec. com. bus. and corps. law sect.), Nat. Assn. Securities Dealers, Inc. (mem. subcom. on indemnification, mem. arbitration panel, mem. adv. bd. Prentice-Hall West coast mergers and acquisitions panels), Mountaingate Country Club. Avocations: sports, reading, theater. Home: 455 N Oakhurst Dr Beverly Hills CA 90210-3911 Office: FL 12 1901 Avenue of the Stars Los Angeles CA 90067-6013 Home Phone: 310-274-5206; Office Phone: 310-228-5780. Business E-Mail: ron@rlfein.com. E-mail: ron@rlfein.coin.

FEINBERG, LARRY J., museum director, curator; m. Starr Siegele. BA with distinction, Northwestern U., MBA; MA, PhD, Harvard U.; MBA, Northwestern U. Curator Allen Art Mus., Oberlin Coll., Ohio, Frick Collection, NYC, Nat. Gallery Art, Washington; with Art Inst. Chgo., 1991—2007, Patrick G. and Shirley W. Ryan curator, 1997—2007; exec. dir. Santa Barbara Mus. Art, 2008—. Bd. dirs. Art Resources in Teaching, Chgo., 1998—2000, chmn., 2000—06; asst. to under-secretary-general Olara Otunnu UN, 2004, 05. Exhibitions include Girodet: Romantic Rebel, The Medici Michelangelo and the Art of Late Renaissance Florence, Gustave Moreau: Between Epic and Dream (named one of Mus. Exhbns. of Yr., Art News). Mem.: Old Masters Soc. (dir. 1993, 2005, 2006—07), Phi Beta Kappa. Office: Santa Barbara Mus Art 1130 State St Santa Barbara CA 93101

FEINBERG, LAWRENCE BERNARD, dean, psychologist; b. Bklyn., June 2, 1940; s. Robert Erwin and Geraldine F.; m. Lynn J. Feinberg; children: Ronald, Nancy, Jillian. BA, U. Buffalo, 1961; MS, SUNY, Buffalo, 1963, PhD, 1966. Lic. psychologist, Calif. cert. rehab. counselor. Lectr. dept. counselor edn. SUNY, Buffalo, 1965-66; prof. spl. edn. and rehab. Syracuse U., 1966-77, dir. rehab. edn., 1967-77; prof. counselor edn. San Diego State U., 1977—2002, adj. prof. public health, 1981-96, assoc. dean grad. div. and research, 1977-98, acting dean Coll. Edn., 1984-85, acting dean grad. div. and research, 1986-87, exec. dir internat. programs, 1988-98, assoc. v.p. for rsch. and tech., 1998—2002, prof. emeritus, 2002—. Cons. psychologist VA Hosp., Syracuse, 1970-77; cons. Rehab. Services Adminstrn., HEW, Washington, 1976-77, Nat. Inst. Handicapped Research, U.S. Dept. Edn., 1982; chmn. Nat. Commn. Accreditation of Rehab. Edn., 1974-76; bd. dirs. Nat. Commn. Rehab. Counselor Cert., 1973-77 Author: (with others) Rehabilitation and Poverty: Bridging the Gap, 1969, Rehabilitation in the Inner City, 1970, Education for the Rehabilitation Services, 1974; cons. editor 6 profl. jours.; contbr. articles to profl. jours. Recipient 20 fed. grants, 4 nat. profl. service awards Fellow Am. Psychol. Assn. (treas. div. rehab. psychology 1980-83, pres. div. rehab. psychology 1984-85), Am. Psychol. Soc.; mem. Am. Rehab. Counseling Assn. (pres. 1973, dir. 1980-83), Am. Personnel and Guidance Assn. (dir. 1974), N.Y. State Rehab. Counseling Assn. (pres. 1970), Council Rehab. Counselor Educators (regional dir. 1969-71), Phi Beta Delta (pres. Delta chpt. 1987-89). Home: 5021 Bluff Pl El Cajon CA 92020-8212 Office: San Diego State U ARPE San Diego CA 92182

FEINER, EDWARD A., architect; BArch, Cooper Union, NYC, 1969; MArch, Cath. U. Am., Washington, DC, 1971. Project coord. Gruen Assocs. Inc.; dir. master planning program USN; dep. dir. design and constrn. GSA, DC, chief arch., 1996—2005; dir. Skidmore, Owings and Merill, DC, 2005—08; sr. v.p., chief arch. Las Vegas Sands Corp., Nev., 2008—. Lectr. Harvard Grad. Sch. Design. Recipient Cooper Union Presdl. award, 1997, Nat. Design award, Cooper-Hewitt Design Mus., 2003, Client of Yr. award, Soc. Mktg. Profl. Svcs., 2004. Fellow: AIA (Thomas Jefferson award Pub. Architecture 1996); mem.: Nat. Inst. Bldg. Svcs. Office: Las Vegas Sands Corp 3355 Las Vegas Blvd S 1A Las Vegas NV 89109

FEINGOLD, BENJAMIN S., broadcast executive; BA, Brandeis U.; MA, London Sch. Econs.; JD, U. Calif., San Francisco. With Kaye, Scholer, Fierman, Hays & Handler, NYC; corp. counsel, securities lawyer Sony Pictures Entertainment, 1988, v.p. entertainment transactions, 1989, sr. v.p. corp. devel.; pres. Sony Pictures Entertainment Columbia TriStar Home Video, Culver City, Calif., 1994—. Office: Sony Pictures Entertainment Columbia Tristar Home Video 10202 Washington Blvd Culver City CA 90232-3119

FEINSTEIN, DIANNE, United States Senator from California; b. San Francisco, June 22, 1933; d. Leon and Betty (Rosenburg) Goldman; m. Bertram Feinstein, Nov. 11, 1962 (dec. 1978); 1 child, Katherine Anne; m. Richard C. Blum, Jan. 20, 1980. BA History, Stanford U., 1955; LLB (hon.), Golden Gate U., 1977; D Pub. Adminstrn. (hon.), U. Manila, 1981; D Pub. Service (hon.), U. Santa Clara, 1981; JD (hon.), Antioch U., 1983, Mills Coll., 1985; LHD (hon.), U. San Francisco, 1988. Fellow Coro Found., San Francisco, 1955-56; with Calif. Women's Bd. Terms & Parole, 1960-66; mem. Mayor's com. on crime, chmn. adv. com. Adult Detention, 1967-69; mem. San Francisco Bd. Supervisors, San Francisco, 1970-78, pres., 1970-71, 74-75, 78; mayor City of San Francisco, 1978-88; US Senator from Calif., 1992—; mem. US Senate Rules & Adminstrn. Com., US Senate Judiciary Com., US Senate Appropriations Com.; chair US Senate Rules & Adminstrn. Com., 2007—09, US Senate Select Com. on Intelligence, 2009—, Joint Com. on the Library, 2007, Joint Com. on Printing, 2009—, Joint Com. on Inaugural Ceremonies, 2009—. Mem. exec. com. US Conf. of Mayors, 1983-88; Dem. nominee for Gov. of Calif., 1990; mem. Nat. Com. on U.S.-China Rels. Mem. Bay Area Conservation & Devel. Commn., 1973-78. Recipient Woman of Achievement award Bus. and Profl. Women's Clubs San Francisco, 1970, Disting. Woman award San Francisco Examiner, 1970, Coro Found. award, 1979, Scopus award Am. Friends Hebrew U., 1981, French Legion of Honor, 1984, Brotherhood/Sisterhood award NCCJ, 1986, Comdr.'s award U.S. Army, 1986, Disting. Civilian award USN, 1987, Coro Leadership award, 1988, Pres. medal U. Calif., San Francisco, 1988, Lifetime Achievement award, Nat. AIDS Found., 1993, Awareness Achievement award, Bd. of Sponsors Breast Cancer Awareness, 1995, Donald Santarelli award, Nat. Orgn. for Victims Assistance, 1996, Congl. Excellence award, MADD, 1997, Paul E. Tsongas award, Lymphoma Rsch. Assn. of Am., 1997, Abraham Lincoln award, Ill. Coun. Against Handgun Violence, 1998, Congl. award, Nat. Assn. Police Orgn., 1999, Celebration of Courage award, Handgun Control, Inc., 1999, Congl. Champion award, Coalition Cancer Rsch., 1999, Winning Spirit award, Women's Info. Network Against Breast Cancer, 2000, Recognition award, Susan G. Komen Breast Cancer Found., 2000, Woodrow Wilson award, Woodrow Wilson Internat. Ctr. Scholars, 2001, Torch of Liberty award, Anti-Defamation League, 2002, Dr. Nathan Davis award, AMA, 2002, Pub. Svc. award, Am. Soc. Hematology, 2003, Leadership award, Alta Med Health Svcs. Corp., 2004, Pat Brown Legacy award, 2004, Lifetime of Idealism award, City Yr., 2004, Legislator of Yr. award, Calif. Sch. Resource Officer's Assn., 2004, Nat. Disting. Advocacy award, Am. Cancer Soc., 2004, Women of Achievement award, Century City Chamber of Commerce, 2004, Friend of Watershed award, Ventura County Assn. of Water Agencies, 2004, Outstanding Mem. US Senate award, Nat. Narcotic Officers Assn. Coalition, 2005; named Number One Mayor All-Pro City Mgmt. Team City and State Mag., 1987, Person of Yr., Nat. Guard Assn. Calif., 1995, Funding Hero, Breast Cancer Rsch. Found., 2004; named one of Congl. Quarterly's Top 50 Mem. of Congress, 2000, Most Powerful Women, Forbes mag., 2005. Mem. Trilateral Commn., Japan Soc. of No. Calif. (pres. 1988-89), Inter-Am. Dialogue, Nat. Com. on U.S.-China Rels. Democrat. Jewish. Office: US Senate 331 Hart Senate Office Bldg Washington DC 20510-0001 also: District Office Ste 2450 One Post Street San Francisco CA 94104 Office Phone: 202-224-3841, 415-393-0707. Office Fax: 202-228-3954, 415-393-0710. E-mail: senator@feinstein.senate.gov.*

FEINSTEIN, MICHAEL JAY, singer, pianist, musicologist, actor; b. Columbus, Ohio, Sept. 7, 1956; s. Edward and Florence Mazie (Cohen) F. Grad. high sch., Columbus, 1974. Personal archivist Ira Gershwin, LA, 1977-83; asst. Harry Warren, LA, 1979-81; recorded with Elektra, Angel. Accompanist Liza Minnelli, Rosemary Clooney, John Bubbles, Rose Marie, Jessie Matthews, Estelle Reiner, Leona Mitchell, 1980-84; singer, pianist Le Mondrian Hotel, West Hollywood, 1984-85, 87, York Hotel, San Francisco, 1985-87, Algonquin Hotel, N.Y.C., 1986, 87, The White House, Washington, 1986, 88, 89, Ritz Hotel, 1986, Mondavi Festival, 1986, Singers Salute to the Songwriter, L.A., 1986, 87, 88, 50th Anniversary George Gershwin Celebration, Hollywood Bowl, L.A., 1987, 100th Birthday Celebration for Irving Berlin, Hollywood Bowl, L.A., 1988 and Carnegie Hall, N.Y., 1988, Royal Command Performance, Palace Theatre, London, 1988, Dominion Theatre, London, 1989; Libr. of Congress Gerswhin Concert, 1989; performed with Houston Pops Orch., 1987, San Francisco Symphony & Pops Orch., 1987, 88, Liza Minnelli in European tour, 1987, Atlanta Symphony, 1988, Aspen Music Festival, Colo., 1988; appeared on Broadway and across country in show Michael Feinstein in Concert: Isn't it Romantic, 1988-89, Piano and Voice, 1990, Cole Porter 100th Birthday Concert Carnegie Hall, 1991; toured with Rosemary Clooney, 1991—; TV appearances include A Musical Toast: The Stars Shine for Pub. TV, 1986, Broadway Sings: The Music of Jule Styne, 1987, George Gershwin Remembered, 1987, Celebrating Gershwin: 'SWonderful, 1987, thirtysomething, 1987, The Two Mrs. Grenvilles, 1987, Nightline, 1988, A Grand Night: The Performing Arts Salute Pub. TV, 1988, Omnibus, 1989, An All-Star Salute to the Pres., 1989, Pat Sajak Show, 1989, Nightwatch, 1989, Royal Command Performance, BBS-TV, 1988, London TV Michael Feinstein in Concert BBC-TV, 1989, PBS-TV, Michael Feinstein in Concert, 1991, Wolf Trap 20th Anniversary Concert, 1991, PBS, Am. Masters-Cole Porter, 1990, others; film, Scenes from the Class Struggle in Beverly Hills; albums include Pure Gershwin, 1985, Live at the Algonquin, 1986, Remember: Michael Feinstein Sings Irving Berlin, 1987, Isn't it Romantic, 1987, Over There: Songs of War and Peace c. 1900-1920, 1989, The M-G-M Album, 1989, Michael Feinstein Sings the Burton Lane Songbook Vol. One, 1990, Michael Feinstein Sings the Jule Styne Songbook, 1991, Pure Imagination, 1991, Michael & George, 1998, Big City Rhythms, 1999, Hopeless Romantics, 2005; editor: Ira Gershwin Songbook; contbr. articles to Washington Post, N.Y. Times. Recipient Golden Laurel award San Francisco Coun. on Entertainment, 1985, 87, 88, N.Y.C. Seal of Recognition, 1987, Drama Desk award, 1988, Outer Critics Circle award, 1988; scholarships in his honor were established at Calif. State, Los Angeles and Queens Coll., N.Y.C. Mem. ASCAP, AFTRA, SAG, Am. Fedn. Musicians, Actor's Equity, Players Club. Office: c/o Buddy Morra Morra Brezner & Steinberg Los Angeles CA 90028

FEISS, GEORGE JAMES, III, financial services company executive; b. Cleve., June 24, 1950; s. George James Jr. and Bettie (Kalish) F.; m. Susan Margaret Cassel, May 30, 1981; children: Kalish Ilana Cassel-Feiss, Nika Catherine Cassel-Feiss. BA in Social Studies, Antioch Coll., 1973; MBA in Internat. Fin., Am. Grad. Sch. Internat. Mgmt., Phoenix, 1975; MPA in Economics, Harvard U., 2007. Registered investment advisor, Wash.; CFP Coll. Fin. Planning, Denver. Ptnr. Healthcare Cons., Seattle, 1976-80; pres. M2 Inc., Seattle, 1980—. Pres., CEO, Vivid Image Co., San Diego, 1994—; cons. Sta. KRAB, Seattle, 1988-89, Zion Christian Acad., Seattle, 1990—; sr. fellow Harvard U. Kennedy Sch. Govt., 2007-. Author: Mind Therapies/Body Therapies, 1979, Hope & Death in Exile - The Economics and Politics of Cancer in the United States, 1981. Bd. dirs. B'nai Brith, Seattle, 1988-91; mem. fin. com. Univ. Child Devel. Sch., Seattle, 1989—; mem. social action com. Am. Jewish Com., Seattle, 1992. Fellowship, Ctr. Bus. Govs., Harvard U., 2007—. Mem. Eastside Estate Planning Coun., Inst. CFPs, Social Investment Forum, Social Venture Network. Avocations: sailing, skiing, travel, writing, sculpture. Office: M2 Inc 1122 E Pike St Seattle WA 98122-3916 Personal E-mail: gfeiss@hotmail.com.

FEJER, MARTIN M., physics professor; BA in Physics, Cornell U., 1977; PhD in Applied Physics, Stanford U., 1986. Acting asst. prof. applied physics Stanford (Calif.) U., 1986-89, asst. prof. applied physics, 1989-93, rsch. assoc. phys. sci., 1993-94, assoc. prof., 1994-2000, prof., 2000—, chair applied physics, 2002—, co-dir. Stanford Photonics Rsch. Ctr. Fellow Optical Soc. Am. (W.R. Wood prize 1998); mem. IEEE, Am. Phys. Soc. Achievements include research on nonlinear optical materials and devices, guided waveoptics, microstructured ferroelectrics and semiconductors, photorefractive phenomena, optical characterization of materials and material synthesis processes. Office: Stanford U EL Ginzton Lab 316 Via Pueblo Mall Stanford CA 94305-4085 E-mail: fejer@stanford.edu.

FELD, DONALD H., network consultant; b. Marshalltown, Iowa, Mar. 12, 1945; s. Donald C. and Wanda L. (Morgan) F.; m. Ruth L. Hensley, Aug. 29, 1965; children: Donald O., Derrick H. BSEE, Iowa State U., 1968; ME in Indsl. Engring./Ops. Rsch., U. Fla., 1975. Commd. 2d lt. USAF, 1968-94, advanced through grades to col., 1989, comdr. 95th Reconnaissance Squadron RAF Alconbury, U.K., 1985-87; chief tactical sys. divsn. USAF Ctr. for Studies and Analysis, Pentagon, Washington, 1987-90, dir. resources directorate, 1990-91; chief flying tng. divsn. Air Edn. and Tng. Command, Randolph AFB, Tex., 1991-94; ret., 1994; v.p. Commonwealth Cons. Corp., Arlington, Va., 1994-96; network cons. Make Systems, Inc., Mountain View,

Calif., 1996-99; dir. Nat. Lab., Enterprise Networking Sys., Inc., Redwood City, Calif., 1999—. Decorated DFC with 1 oak leaf cluster, Air Medal with 10 oak leaf clusters, Legion of Merit. Mem. IEEE, Air Force Assn. Avocations: water and snow skiing, computers, camping, golf, antique restoration. Office: Enterprise Networking Sys Inc 100 Headquarters Dr San Jose CA 95134-1370 also: Make Systems 12121 Wilshire Blvd Ste 600 Los Angeles CA 90025-1188

FELDBERG, HARLEY, marketing professional; B in history and polit. sci., U. Md. Sales mgr. Time Electronics, Balt., 1982, v.p. sales and mktg.; served as pres. of the interconnect, passive, and electro-mechanical product bus. group Avnet, Inc., 1996—99, named pres. and dir. Avnet Electronics mktg. Americas' product bus. groups, 1999—2002, corp. v.p., 1999—2004, pres. Avnet Electronics mktg. Asia, 2000—02, pres. Avnet Electronics Mktg. Am. Phoenix, 2002—04, pres. Avnet Electronics Mktg., 2004—. Office: Avnet Inc 2211 S 47th St Phoenix AZ 85034

FELDHAMER, THELMA LEAH, retired architect; b. Bklyn., May 10, 1925; d. Frank and Anna Pearl (Shapiro) Sitzer; m. Carl Feldhamer, Aug. 27, 1950 (dec. Apr. 1990); children: Raquel Alexander, Mark David. BArch, Cooper Union for Advancement, Sci. and Arts, 1978. Registered architect Colo. Prin. Thelma Feldhamer, P.C. Aia Architect, Denver, 1980—2007; ret., 2007. Active Pres. Council of Denver; pres.-elect to Colo. State Drafting Tech. Com. State Bd. Community Colls. and Occupational Edn., City and County of Denver Dept. Pub. Works Affirmative Action Office and Goals com. Pres. nat. women's com. Brandeis U., 1998—2003; vol. Denver Dumb Friend League, 1994—; treas. Denver chpt. Haddassah, 1998—2006, bd. mem., 2008—; mem. adv. bd. Emily Griffith Opportunity Sch. Lt. col., pers. officer Colo. Wing CAP, Lowry AFB, 1979—2002, ret., 2002. Mem. AIA, Women in Architecture (Denver chpt.), Bus. and Profl. Women's Club, Denver, Inc. (pres. 1974-76, 89-90, treas. 1987-89, 91-2003), Denver C. of C., Altrusa Club (wd v.p., bd. dirs. Denver 1984), El Mejdel Temple, Daus. of Nile. Democrat. Jewish.

FELDMAN, BORIS, lawyer; b. South Bend, Ind., 1955; BA in history summa cum laude, Yale U., 1977; JD, Yale Law Sch., 1980. Law clk. to Judge Abraham D. Sofaer, US Dist. Ct. for So. Dist. NY, 1980—81; assoc. Arnold & Porter, Washington, 1981—85; spl. asst. to legal adviser US Dept. State, 1985—86; atty. Wilson Sonsini Goodrich & Rosati, Palo Alto, Calif., 1986—, mem. exec. mgmt. com., chair policy com. Note & topics editor Yale Law Jour., Vol. 89; mem. Ninth Circuit Lawyer Rep. Coordinating Com.; co-chair lawyer rep. to No. Dist. Calif.; bd. dirs. Silicon Valley Campaign for Legal Svcs.; mem. Santa Clara County Superior Ct. Task Force on Complex Lit.; mem. adv. bd. Securities Regulation Inst. Author: 20 articles on various disclosure topics. Named one of Top 45 Lawyers in Country Under Age of 45, Am. Lawyer, 1995, 100 Most Influential Lawyers in Calif., LA Daily Jour., 2002, Top Ten Lawyers in Bay Area, San Francisco Chronicle. Mem.: Phi Beta Kappa. Office: 650 Page Mill Rd Palo Alto CA 94304 Office Fax: 650-493-6811.

FELDMAN, JOEL SHALOM, mathematician; b. Ottawa, Ont., Can., June 14, 1949; s. Keiva and Anna (Ain) F. BS, U. Toronto, Ont., 1970; AM, Harvard U., 1971, PhD, 1974. Rsch. fellow Harvard U., Cambridge, Mass., 1974-75; Moore instr. MIT, Cambridge, 1975-77; prof. U. B.C., Vancouver, Can., 1977—; Aisenstadt chair lectr., Ctr. Rsch. Math. U. Montréal, 1999—2000. Assoc. editor Revs. Math. Physics, 1988—, Can. Jour. Math., 1994-98, Can. Math. Bull., 1994-98, Math Phys. EJ, 1995—, Ann. Henri Poincaré, 2000—, Jour. Math. Physics, 2005—; contbr. articles to profl. jours. Recipient Killam Rsch. prize U. B.C., 1988, Jeffery-Williams prize CMS, 2004, Faculty of Sci. Achievement award for Tchg., U. B.C., 2004, Killan Tchg. prize Faculty of Sci., 2006-07, prize in theoretical and math. physics Can. Assn. Physicists-Ctr. Rsch. Math., 2007, Ctr. Rsch. Math.-Fields-Pacific Inst. for Math. Scis. prize, 2007; Woodrow Wilson fellow, 1970. Fellow: Royal Soc. Can. (John L. Synge award). Office: U BC Dept Math Vancouver BC Canada V6T 1Z2

FELDMAN, LARRY ROBERT, lawyer; BS, San Fernando Valley State Coll., 1966; JD, Loyola U., 1969. Ptnr. Kaye Scholler LLP. Named an 100 Power Lawyers, Hollywood Reporter, 2007. Fellow: Am. Coll. of Trial Lawyers; mem.: Assn. of Bus. Trial Lawyers (bd. of govs.), Am. Bd. of Trial Advocates (v.p.), Internat. Acad. of Trial Lawyers, Calif. Trial Lawyers Assn. (bd. of govs. 1981), LA County Bar Assn. (pres. 1987—88), LA Trial Lawyers Assn. (pres. 1984). Office: Kaye Scholler LLP 1999 Ave of the Stars Ste 1700 Los Angeles CA 90067 Office Phone: 310-788-1090. Office Fax: 310-788-1200. E-mail: larryfeldman@kayescholer.com.

FELDMAN, LEWIS G., lawyer; b. NYC, Feb. 13, 1956; BA with highest honors, U. Calif., Santa Cruz, 1978; JD, U. Calif., Davis, 1982. Bar: Calif. 1982. Ptnr. Goodwin Procter LLP, LA. Chair Goodwin Proctor LLP, chair pub.pvt. devel. practice; bd. mem. City of Hope Real Estate Industry Council, Univ. So. Calif. Lusk Ctr. for Real Estate Devel. Editor (exec.): UC Davis Law Rev.; contbr. articles to newspapers & profl. jours.; mem. editl. adv. bd. Real Estate So. Calif. Bd. mem. United Way of Greater LA. Mem.: ABA, Nat. Assn. Bond Lawyers, Nat. Assn. Real Estate Investment Trusts, Urban Land Inst., LA Bar Assn., Beverly Hills Bar Assn. Office: Goodwin Procter LLP 21st Fl MGM Tower 10250 Constellation Blvd Los Angeles CA 90067-6221 Office Phone: 310-788-5188. Business E-Mail: lfeldman@goodwinprocter.com.

FELDMAN, ROBERT C. (BOB), public relations executive; b. NYC, Oct. 22, 1956; BA, Syracuse U., 1978. Gen. mgr. Sta. WPNR-FM Utica Coll. Syracuse U., 1976-78; from asst. acct. exec. to sr. v.p., group mgr. Burson-Marsteller, 1978-88; sr. v.p. Ketchum Pub. Rels., NYC, 1988-97; pres., CEO GCI Group, Inc., 1997—2005; head corp. comms. DreamWorks Animation SKG, Glendale, Calif., 2005—07; founder, mng. ptnr., CEO Feldman & Ptnrs., LA, 2007—. Adj. prof. corp. reputation U. So. Calif.; lectr. in field. Contbr. articles to profl. jours. Bd. dirs. Thurgood Marshall Scholarship Fund; bd. trustees Pub. Rels. Inst. Mem.: Arthur Page Soc., Coun. Pub. Rels. Firms (bd. dirs.), Pub. Rels. Seminar, Pub. Rels. Soc. Am. Office: Feldman & Ptnrs Ste 2000 8491 Sunset Blvd Los Angeles CA 90069 Office Phone: 310-360-0211. Office Fax: 310-360-0250. E-mail: bob@feldmanandpartners.com.

FELDMAN, ROBERT PAUL, lawyer; b. Flushing, NY, Mar. 28, 1951; BA, SUNY Buffalo, 1972; JD, Columbia U., 1975. Bar: Calif. 1976. Mng. editor Columbia Law Review, 1974—75; law clk. to Hon. Samuel P. King US Dist. Ct. Dist. Hawaii, 1976; asst. US atty. (no. dist.) Calif., mem. spl. prosecutions unit US Dept. Justice, San Francisco, 1979—84; ptnr. Wilson Sonsini Goodrich & Rosati, Palo Alto, Calif., 1985—2007, chmn. litig. dept., 2000—04, co-chmn. compensation com., 2004—07; ptnr. Quinn Emanuel Urquhart Oliver & Hedges, LLP, San Francisco, 2007—. Lawyer-delegate 9th Cir. Judicial Conf., 1985—88. Trustee Portola Valley Sch. Dist., 1996—2000. Mem.: ABA, State Bar Calif., Am. Coll. Trial Lawyers. Office: Quinn Emanuel Urquhart Oliver & Hedges LLP 50 California St 22nd Fl San Francisco CA 94111

FELDMAN, ROGER LAWRENCE, artist, educator; b. Spokane, Wash., Nov. 19, 1949; s. Marvin Lawrence and Mary Elizabeth (Shafer) Feldman; m. Astrid Lunde, Dec. 16, 1972; children: Kirsten B., Kyle Lawrence. BA in Art Edn., U. Wash., 1972; postgrad., Fuller Theol. Sem., Pasadena, Calif., 1972—73, Regent Coll., Vancouver, B.C., 1974; MFA in Sculpture, Claremont Grad. U., Calif., 1977. Tchg. asst. Claremont Grad. U.; prof. art Biola U., La Mirada, Calif., 1989-2000, Seattle Pacific U., 2000—. Adj. instr. Seattle Pacific U., 1979-80, 82-83, Linfield Coll., 1978, Edmonds C.C., 1978-80, Shoreline C.C., 1978; guest artist and lectr. One-man shows include Art Ctr. Gallery, Seattle Pacific U., 1977, 83, 84, Linfield Coll., McMinnville, Oreg., 1979, Blackfish Gallery, Portland, 1982, Lynn McAllister Gallery, Seattle, 1986, Biola U., 1989, 93, Coll. Gallery, La. Coll., Pineville, 1990, Gallery W, Sacramento, 1991, 96, Aughinbaugh Gallery, Grantham, Pa., 1992, Riverside Art Mus., 1994, Azusa Pacific U., 1995, Cornerstone '96, Bushnell, Ill., 1996, Barnsdall Art Park, LA, 1996, Davison Gallery Roberts Wesleyan Coll., Rochester, NY, 1997, Concordia U., Irvine, Calif., 1999, Northwestern Coll., St. Paul, 2000, Union U., Jackson, Tenn., 2001, F. Schaeffer Inst., St. Louis, 2001, G. Fox U., Newberg, Oreg., 2001, Seattle Pacific U., 2002, Suyama Space, Seattle, 2005, Schloss Mittersill, Austria, 2005, Beyond Malibu, Princess Louisa Inlet, BC, Can., 2007, Friesen Gallery, NNU, Nampa, Idaho, 2008; numerous group shows including most recently Weaver Art Gallery, Bethel Coll., Mishawaka, Ind., 1998-, Concordia U. Art Gallery, Mequon, Wis., 1999, Palos Verdes Art Ctr., Calif., 1999, Grand Canyon U., Phoenix, 2000, Tryon Ctr. Visual Arts, Charlotte, NC, 2001, U. Dallas, 2001, Weaver Gallery, 2001, John Brown U., Siloam Springs, Ark., 2001, Sweetwater Ctr. for the Arts, Sewickley, Pa., 2002, Ind. Wesleyan U., Marion, 2002, Tacoma Art Mus., 2004, Mus. Bibl. Art, NYC, 2005, Gordon Coll., Wenham, Mass., 2006, Schloss Mittersill, Austria, 2007; comms. Wheaton, Pasadena, Calif., 1999, Renton Vocat. Tech Inst., 1987-89. Recipient King County Arts Commn. Individual Artist Project award, Seattle, 1988, Natl. Endowment for the Arts Individual Artist fellowship in Sculpture, 1986, David Gaiser award for sculpture Cheney Cowles Mus., 1980, Disting. award for Harborview Med. Ctr. "Viewpoint", Soc. for Tech. Comm., 1987, Design award for "Seafirst News", Internat. Assn. Bus. Comm., 1987, Pace Setter award, 1987, Prescott Sculpture award Christians in the Visual Arts, 2005, others; Connemara Sculpture grant, 1990, Biola U., 1991; Faculty Rsch. grantee Seattle Pacific U., 2001-02, Sr. Faculty Rsch. grantee, 2005-06, Faculty Rsch. grantee, 2007-08. Office: Seattle Pacific U 3307 Third Ave West Seattle WA 98119 Office Phone: 206-281-3442. Business E-Mail: rfeldman@spu.edu. E-mail: rakfeldman2@comcast.net.

FELDMAN, STANLEY GEORGE, lawyer; b. NYC, Mar. 9, 1933; s. Meyer and Esther Betty (Golden) F.; m. Norma Arambula; 1 dau., Elizabeth L. Student, UCLA, 1950—51; LLB, U. Ariz., 1956. Bar: Ariz. 1956. Practiced in, Tucson, 1956-81; ptnr. Miller, Pitt & Feldman, 1968-81; justice Ariz. Supreme Ct., Phoenix, 1982—2002, chief justice, 1992-97; of counsel Haralson, Miller, Pitt Feldman & McAnally. Lectr. Coll. Law, U. Ariz., 1965-76, adj. prof., 1976-81, 2000, 03, 05, 06. Bd. dirs. Tucson Jewish Community Council, U. Ariz. Found., 1999-2005. Mem. ABA, Am. Bd. Trial Advocates (past pres. So. Ariz. chpt.), Ariz. Bar Assn. (pres. 1974-75, bd. govs. 1967-76), Pima County Bar Assn. (past pres.), Am. Trial Lawyers Assn. (dir. chpt. 1967-76), U. Ariz. Law Coll. Assn., Ariz. Trial Lawyers Assn. (bd. dirs. 2006-), United Policy Holders (bd. dirs. 2007-), Ariz. Ctr. for Law in pub. interest (bd. dirs. 2008-). Democrat. Jewish. Office: 1 S Church Ave Ste 900 Tucson AZ 85701-1620 Office Phone: 520-792-3836. E-mail: sfeldman@hmpmlaw.com.

FELDMAN NEBENZAHL, BERNARDO, composer, educator; b. Mexico City, Sept. 28, 1955; s. Jaime Feldman Shtiglick and Felicie Nebenzahl de Feldman; children: Kendahl May Goldwater-Feldman, Gisèle Aliyah Goldwater-Feldman. Advanced Musical Studies, Nat. Conservatory of Music, Mexico City, 1969—78; BA, BS Sci. and Humanities, Mex. Nat. U., Mexico City, 1979; BFA, Calif. Inst. of the Arts, Valencia, 1983; MFA, Calif. Inst. Arts, Valencia, 1985; PhD, UCLA, 1992—2000. Pres. Soc. for Electro-Acoustic Music in the U.S., Los Angeles Chapter, Calif., 1987—90; music faculty Calif. Inst. of the Arts, Valencia, Calif., 1988—99; chmn., dept. of music Coll. of the Canyons, Santa Clarita, Calif., 1989—. Faculty mem. Calif. Inst. of the Arts, Valencia, Calif., 1988—99. Composer (libretist): (electro-rock opera) Fractured Stories (Am. Soc. for Composers, Authors, and Publishers, 2005); composer: (sound designer) (film) Paris is a Woman (Best Short Film at the NY Internat. Ind. Film Festival, 2003); composer: (music producer) (multi-media) Creatures of Habit (Pew Charitable Trust & Lila Wallace-Reader's Digest Award, 1994); composer: (symphonic score) In Red and Black (Am. Soc. for Composers, Authors and Publishers, 1986). Panelist Cultural Affairs Dept., LA, Calif., 2002—03. Recipient Meet the Composer, Meet the Composer, Inc., 1986, 1988, 1992, 1996. Achievements include Innovative performances involving live musicians interacting with electronics. Avocations: outdoors activities, films, soccer. Home: 121 Strand St Ste #9 Santa Monica CA 90405 Office: Santa Clarita Cmty Coll Dist 26455 Rockwell Canyon Rd Santa Clarita CA 91355 Office Fax: 661-259-8302; Home Fax: 661-259-8302. Personal E-mail: feldman_b@canyons.edu.

FELDSTEIN, PAUL JOSEPH, management educator; b. NYC, Oct. 4, 1933; s. Nathan and Sarah Feldstein; m. Anna Martha Lee, Dec. 24, 1968; children: Julie, Jennifer. BA in Econs., CCNY, 1955; MBA in Fin., U. Chgo., 1957, PhD in Econs., 1961. Dir. divsn. rsch. Am. Hosp. Assn., Chgo., 1961-64; prof. Sch. Pub. Health U. Mich., Ann Arbor, 1964-87; prof. Paul Merage Sch. Bus. U. Calif., Irvine, 1987—. Author: Health Policy Issues: An Economic Perspective on Health Reform, 4th edit., 2007, Health Care Economics, 6th edit., 2005, The Politics of Health Legislation, 3d edit., 2006; contbr. articles to profl. jours. 1st lt. inf. US Army. Mem. Am. Econs. Assn. Office: Univ Calif Paul Merage Sch Business Irvine CA 92697-0001 Office Phone: 949-824-8157. Business E-Mail: pfeldste@uci.edu.

FELIX, RICHARD E., academic administrator; Pres. Azusa (Calif.) Pacific U., 1985—2000, pres. emeritus, 2000—. Office: Azusa Pacific U Office of President 901 E Alosta Ave Azusa CA 91702-2769

FELLER, LLOYD HARRIS, lawyer; b. New Brunswick, NJ, Aug. 27, 1942; s. Alexander and Freda (Kaminsky) F.; m. Susan Sydney Weinberg, Aug. 6, 1967; children: Jennifer, Andrew. BS in Econs., U. Pa., 1964; LLB, NYU, 1967. Bar: N.Y. 1967, D.C. 1980. Assoc. Rubin, Wachtel, Baum & Levin, 1967—70; trial atty. organized crime sect., divsn. enforcement SEC, Washington, 1970—72, legal asst. Commr. A. Sydney Herlong, Jr., 1972—73, legal asst. Commr. A.A. Sommer, Jr., 1973—76; chief counsel Office of the Chief Acct., 1976—77; assoc. dif. divsn. market regulation Office of Market Structure and Trading Practices, 1977—79, of counsel, 1979—81; ptnr. Morgan, Lewis & Bockius LLP, Washington, 1981—99, mem. governing bd., 1996—99, mem. exec. com., 1989—99, mem. allocations com., 1999—; sr. v.p., sec., gen. counsel SoundView Tech. Group, Inc., San Francisco, 1999—.

FELLER, RALPH PAUL, dentist, educator; b. Quincy, Mass., Aug. 31, 1934; s. Paul Frederich and Frances Elizabeth (Hubert) F.; children: Lynne Anne Feller Grenier, Paul Herbert, Wendy Elizabeth. BS, Tufts U., 1956, DMD, 1964; MS, U. Tex., Houston, 1975; MPH, Loma Linda U., 1981. Asst. prof. Harvard U., Boston, 1965-71; assoc. prof. U. Tex. Med. Br., Houston, 1971-75; clin. investigator VA Med. Ctr., Houston, 1971-75, chief dental svc. Lyons, N.J., 1975-77, Loma Linda, Calif., 1977-95; assoc. prof. Fairleigh Dickinson U., Hackensack, N.J., 1975-77; prof., dir. clin. rsch. ctr. Loma Linda U. Sch. Dentistry, 1995—. Cons. Johnson & Johnson, East Windsor, N.J., 1980-85, Oral-B Labs., Inc., Redwood City, Calif., 1986-92, Richardson-Vicks, Shelton, Conn., 1988-92, Colgate-Polmolive Co., Piscataway, N.J., 1988—. Contbr. articles to profl. jours. Col. USAR, 1960-95, ret. Mem. ADA (Achievement award 1995), Internat. Assn. Dental Rsch. (numerous offices 1964—), am. Coll. Prosthodontists, Am. Assn. Dental Schs., Calif. Dental Assn., Assn. Mil. Surgeons U.S., Rotary. Avocations: boating, golf. Home: 30832 Alta Mira Dr Redlands CA 92373-7402 Office: Loma Linda U Sch Dentistry Loma Linda CA 92350-0001 Fax: (909) 558-0328. E-mail: rpfeller@aol.com.

FELLOWS, GERALD LEE, lawyer; b. Joliet, Ill., Mar. 21, 1962; s. Barbara Ann Gast; children: Christopher Lee, Anna Elisabeth. BS, U. Ill., 1984; MS, Pa. State U., 1989; JD, Marquette U., 1992. Bar: U.S. Patent & Trademark Office 1992. Engr., foundry supr. GM, Saginaw, Mich., 1985—87; assoc. Reinhart Boerner Van Deuren, Milw., 1991—98; ptnr. Michael Best & Friedrich LLP, 1998—, Milw. office mng. ptnr., 2005—07; ptnr. Greenberg Traurig LLP, Phoenix, 2007—. Adj. asst. prof. Marquette U. Law Sch., Milw., 1993—98. Chair Flood Remediation Task Force, Elm Grove, Wis., 2000—01; commr. Police and Fire Commn., Elm Grove, 2003—06. Recipient AV rating, Martindale-Hubbel, 2002—; named one of Best Lawyers in Am., 2005—. Mem.: State Bar Wis. (chair intellectual property sect.), Soc. Automotive Engrs. (chair Milw. chpt. 1999—2000). Office: Greenberg Traurig LLP 2375 E Camelback Rd Ste 700 Phoenix AZ 85016 Office Fax: 602-445-8100. Business E-Mail: fellowsj@gtlaw.com.

FELSENSTEIN, JOSEPH, science educator; b. Phila., Pa., May 9, 1942; BS (honors) in Zoology, U. Wis., Madison, 1964; PhD in Zoology, U. Chgo., 1968; DSc (hon.), U. Edinburgh, 2005. NIH trainee (genetics tchg. grant) U. Chgo., 1964—67; NIH Postdoctoral Rsch. Fellow Inst. Animal Genetics, U. Edinburgh, Scotland, 1967—68; asst. prof., dept. genetics U. Wash., Seattle, 1967—73, assoc. prof., dept. genetics, 1973—78, prof., dept. genetics, 1978—2001, prof., dept. genome sciences, 2001—, prof., dept. zoology (on joint basis with genome sciences), 2002—03, prof., dept. biology (on joint basis with genome sciences), 2003—. Adj. prof., statistics U. Wash., Seattle, 1981—, adj. prof., dept. zoology, 1990—2002, adj. prof., dept. computer sci. and engring., 2003—, coord., program in computational molecular biology, 2001—06; sabbatical leave, dept. genetics U. Edinburgh, Scotland, 1982—83. Contbr. several articles to profl. jours.; assoc. editor Genetics, 1974, Theoretical Population Biology, 1975—86, 1995—98, 2003—, Evolution, 1978—79, 1981—83, Journal of Classification, 1984—, mem. editl. com. Annual Review of Ecology and Systematics, 1982—86, mem. editl. bd. Molecular Phylogenetics and Evolution, 1992—, Journal of Molecular Evolution, 1993—, Journal of Computational Biology, 1994—, Evolutionary Bioinformatics, 2005—; co-editor: A Bibliography Theoretical Population Genetics, 1973; author: Inferring Phylogenies, 2004, Theoretical Evolutionary Genetics, 2005. Recipient Sewall Wright award, Am. Soc. Naturalists, 1993, Weldon Meml. prize, U. Oxford, 2000, Darwin-Wallace medal, Linnean Soc. London, 2008. Mem.: Soc. Molecular Biology and Evolution, Soc. Systematic Biology (President's award for Excellence in Systematics 2002), Am. Acad. Arts & Sciences, Wash. State Acad. Sciences, Soc. for the Study of Evolution (v.p. II 1986, pres. 2003, pres.-elect 1992, retiring pres. 1994), NAS (John. J. Carty award for the Advancement of Sci. 2009). Office: U Washington Foege S420B Box 355065 Seattle WA 98195-5065 Office Phone: 206-543-0150. Office Fax: 206-543-0754. Business E-Mail: joe@gs.washington.edu.*

FELSINGER, DONALD E., utilities corporation executive; BSME, U. Ariz. Exec. v.p. SDG&E (subs. Enova Corp.), 1993-96, pres., CEO, 1996-98, Enova Corp., 1998; group pres., unregulated affils. Sempra Energy (merger of Pacific Enterprises/Enova Corp.), San Diego, 1998—2004; pres., COO Sempra Energy, 2004—06, chmn., CEO, 2006—. Bd. dirs. Edison Electric Inst. Bd. dirs. U.S.-Mexico C. of C., Greater San Diego C. of C., Inst. of the Americas, San Diego Holiday Bowl. Office: Sempra Energy 101 Ash St San Diego CA 92101-3017

FELSTINER, JOHN, literature educator, translator; b. Mt. Vernon, NY, July 5, 1936; s. Louis John Felstiner and Gertrude Robison Shiman; m. Mary Lowenthal, Feb. 19, 1966; children: Sarah Alexandra, Aleksandr Lowenthal. BA, Harvard Coll., 1958; PhD, Harvard U., 1965. Vis. prof. of English The Hebrew U., Jerusalem, 1974—75; vis. prof. of comparative lit. Yale U., New Haven, 1990—90; vis. faculty Ny State Summer Writers Inst., Saratoga Springs, NY, 1997—99; vis. prof. of English Yale U., New Haven, 2002—02; fulbright-Hays prof. in Am. lit. U. Chile, Santiago, Chile, 1967—68; prof. of English Stanford U., Stanford, Calif., 1965—. Cons./evaluator publs., jours., univ. depts., founds., 1965—; judge Am. PEN, MLA, Helen and Kurt Wolff Lit. Prize, 1980—2003; v.p. Ctr. Art Transl., San Francisco, 2000—. Author: (book) The Lies of Art: Max Beerbohm's Parody and Caricature, Paul Celan: Poet, Survivor, Jew (Truman Capote award for lit. criticism, 1997), (poetry) Twenty Questions I Wish I'd Asked My Father (Mass. rev.), The Runners in the Luxembourg Gardens (Paris rev.), (scholarly study) Translating Neruda: The Way to Macchu Picchu (Calif. commonwealth club gold medal, 1981); translator: (literary translation) The Dark Room and Other Poems by Enrique Lihn, (anthology) Selected Poems and Prose of Paul Celan, 2001, (bibliophile edition) Heights of Macchu Picchu/Alturas De Macchu Picchu, Deathfugue/Todesfuge; co-editor:

(book) Jewish American Literature: A Norton Anthology, 2000; contbr. articles to profl. jours.; author: (book) Can Poetry Save the Earth, A Field Guide to Nature Poems, 2009. Bd. dirs. Holocaust Ctr. No. Calif., San Francisco, 1979—2003. Lt. USN, 1958—61. Recipient Kenyon Rev. prize for Lit. Criticism, 1967, publ., Brit. Comparative Lit. Assn., Gold medal, Coun. Advancement and Support Edn., 1991, Translation prize, Brit. Comparative Lit. Assn., Lois Roth prize, MLA, 2001, transl. prize, 2001, ATA, 2001, Pen West Transl., 2001, citation, Nat. Book Critics Cir., 1995; named resident in Yaddo, Macdowell, Djerassi, Rockefeller, Bellagio, Millay, Mesa Refuge and Jentel Artist colonies, 1993—2002; finalist James Russell Lowell prize, MLA, 1997, Nat. Book Critics Cir., 1996; Guggenheim fellow, Rockefeller fellow, NEH fellow, NEA fellow, Stanford Humanities Ctr. fellow, 1983—2005. Mem.: Am. Acad. Arts and Scis., Paul Celan Soc. Democrat. Jewish. Avocations: book and map collecting, acappella singing, hiking, running. Office: English Dept Stanford U Building 460 Stanford CA 94305-2087 Business E-Mail: felstiner@stanford.edu.

FELSTINER, MARY LOWENTHAL, retired history professor; b. Pitts., Feb. 19, 1941; d. Alexander and Anne Lowenthal; m. John Felstiner, Feb. 19, 1966; children: Sarah Alexandra, Aleksandr. BA, Harvard U., 1963; MA, Columbia U., 1966; PhD, Stanford U., 1971. Prof. history San Francisco State U., 1972—2006, prof. emeritus, 2006—; vis prof. history Stanford U., 2007—. Author: To Paint Her Life, 1994, Out of Joint, 2005. Recipient prize in women's history, Am. Hist. Assn., 1995. Mem.: Phi Beta Kappa.

FELTER, EDWIN LESTER, JR., judge; b. Washington, Aug. 11, 1941; s. Edwin L. Felter and Bertha (Peters) Brekke; m. Yoko Yamauchi-Koito, Dec. 26, 1969. BA, U. Tex., 1964; JD, Cath. U. of Am., 1967. Bar: Colo. 1970, U.S. Dist. Ct. Colo. 1970, U.S. Ct. Appeals (10th cir.) 1971, U.S. Supreme Ct. 1973, U.S. Tax Ct. 1979, U.S. Ct. Claims 1979, U.S. Ct. Internat. Trade 1979. Dep. pub. defender State of Colo., Ft. Collins, 1971-75; asst. atty. gen. Office of the Atty. Gen., Denver, 1975-80; state adminstrv. law judge Colo. Office Adminstrv. Cts., Denver, 1980-83, chief adminstrv. law judge, 1983-98, sr. adminstr., law judge, 1998—. Disciplinary prosecutor Supreme Ct. Grievance Com., 1975-78; mem. faculty Nat. Jud. Coll., 1999—; cons. Star Viet Nam, Hanoi, 2003, 2006-; adj. prof. law U. Denver Coll. Law., 2006-. Contbg. editor Internat. Franchising, 1970. Mem. Colo. State Mgmt. Cert. Steering Com., 1983-86; No. Colo. Criminal Justice Planning Coun., Ft. Collins, 1973-75; bd. dirs., vice chmn. The Point Cmty. Crisis Ctr., Ft. Collins, 1971-73; mem. Denver County Dem. Party Steering Com., 1978-79, chmn. 12th legis. dist., 1978-79; bd. dirs., pres. Denver Internat. Program, 1989-90. Fellow: ABA (advisor to nat. com. on state laws 2004—, mem. standing com. ethics and profl. responsibility 2006—), Am. Inns Ct.; mem.: Rhone Brackett Inn (pres. 2008—), Canadian Coun. and Adminstrn. Tribunals, Internat. Bar Assn., Colo. Bar Assn. (chmn. grievance policy com. 1991—94, interprofl. com. 1995—), Nat. Assn. Adminstrv. Law Judges (pres. Colo. chpt. 1982—84, chair fellowship com. 1996—2006, Fellowship winner 1994), Denver Bar Assn., Arapahoe County Bar Assn., Nat. Conf. Adminstrv. Law Judiciary (chair 2000—01). Office: Colo Office Adminstrv Cts Ste 1300 633 17th St Denver CO 80202 Office Phone: 303-866-5676. Business E-Mail: ed.felter@state.co.us.

FELTHEIMER, JON, entertainment company executive; B in Economics, Washington Un. Pres., CEO New World Entertainment, 1989—97; exec. v.p. Sony Pictures Entertainment Inc., 1997—99; pres. Columbia Tristar TV; CEO Lions Gate Entertainment, 2000—, co-chmn. bd. dirs. Named one of 50 Most Powerful People in Hollywood, Premiere mag., 2006. Office: Lions Gate Entertainment Inc 2700 Colorado Blvd Santa Monica CA 90404

FENIGER, SUSAN, chef, television personality, writer; Former mem. staff Le Perroquet, Chgo., Ma Maison, LA, L'Oasis, France; formerly chef, co-owner City Cafe, LA; chef, co-owner CITY, LA, 1985—94, Border Grill, LA, 1985—91, Santa Monica, 1990—, Las Vegas, 1998—, Ciudad, LA, 1998—. Co-host (TV series) Too Hot Tamales, 1995—, Tamales' World Tour, (radio show) Good Food; co-author: City Cuisine, 1989, Mesa Mexicana, 1994, Cantina, 1996, Cooking with Too Hot Tamales, 1997, Mexican Cooking for Dummies; guest appearances (TV series) Oprah Winfrey Show, Maury Povich, Today Show, Sabrina the Teenage Witch, featured in USA Today, People Mag., Entertainment Weekly. Active Scleroderma Rsch. Found. Named Chef of Yr., Calif. Restaurant Writers, 1993. Mem.: Chef's Collaborative 2000, Women Chefs and Restaurateurs. Office: Border Grill Santa Monica 445 S Figueroa St Ste 2950 Los Angeles CA 90071-1634

FENIMORE, GEORGE WILEY, management consultant; b. Bertrand, Mo., 1921; BBA in Fin., Northwestern U., 1941; JD, Harvard U., 1947; postgrad., UCLA, 1955; LLD (hon.), Southwestern U., 1992. Bar: Mich. 1948. Asst. to dir. planning Ford Motor Co., Dearborn, Mich., 1947-48; exec. to v.p. and gen. mgr. Hughes Aircraft Co., Culver City, Calif., 1948-53; adminstrv. mgr. tech. products Packard Bell Electronics Co., 1954-55; with TRW, Inc., LA, 1955-64; v.p., gen. mgr. TRW Internat., LA, 1959-64; v.p. internat. ops. Bunker Ramo Corp., LA, 1964-65; dir. pub. rels., then corp. sec. Litton Industries, Inc., Beverly Hills, Calif., 1965-73, v.p., corp. sec., 1973-81, sr. v.p., corp. sec., 1981-86, mgmt. cons., 1986—. Past chmn. bd. Southwestern U. Sch. Law; mem. Calif. Tchrs. Retirement Bd.; cons. JCM Group. Bd. dirs. Children's Bur. L.A., Child Shelter Homes a Rescue Effort; sec. French Found. for Alzheimer's Rsch.; past mem. Calif. Fair Polit. Practices Commn., 1986-91; mem. United Way Emergency Food Sys. Study Task Force; elder, chmn. fin. com. Westwood Presbyn. Ch.; past trustee Sheldon Jackson Coll., Sitka, Alaska; mem. Beverly Hills Mayor's Econ. Adv. Com. and MOVE com., Calif. Fraud Assessment Commn. Maj. USAAF, WW II. Recipient Citizen of Yr. award, Beverly Hills Lions Club, 1976, Spirit Honoree, Beverly Hills Edn. Found., 1986, Beverly Hills YMCA, 1988, Brentwood/San Vicente C. of C., 1987, Hon. Citizen award, Beverly Hills City Coun., 1986, Guardian Angel award, Child S.H.A.R.E., 1989, Lifetime Achievement award, 2001, Highest award for Lifetime Svc. to Cmty., Key to City of Beverly Hills, 1990, State Gold award, Calif. Tchrs. Assn., 1993. Mem. Am. Soc. Corp. Secs. (dir., past nat. dir., past pres. L.A. Group), Beverly Hills C. of C. (past pres., Citizen of Yr. award 1979, chmn. edn. com., bd. dirs., David Orgell Meml. award 1990), Mandeville Canyon Assn. (past pres.), Bar Assn. Mich., L.A. Country Club, Rotary (past pres. Beverly Hills, Paul Harris fellow, William C. Ackerman trophy 1986), Shriners. Presbyterian. Office Phone: 310-472-9264. Personal E-mail: fenimore98@aol.com.

FENNELL, LAURA A., lawyer; BA, Calif. State U.; JD, Santa Clara U. Assoc. Wilson Sonsini, Goodrich and Rosati; v.p. corp. legal recourses, acting gen. counsel Sun Microsystems; v.p., gen. counsel, sec. Intuit Inc., Mountain View, Calif., 2004—. Office: Intuit 2700 Coast Ave Mountain View CA 94043

FENNELLY, JANE COREY, lawyer; b. NYC, Dec. 12, 1942; d. Joseph and Josephine (Corey) F. BA, Cornell U., 1964; MLS, UCLA, 1968; JD, Loyola U., LA, 1974. Bar: Calif. 1974, U.S. Dist. Ct. (ctrl. and so. dists.) Calif. 1974, U.S. Dist. Ct. (ea. dist.) Calif. 1977, U.S. Dist. Ct. (no. dist.) Calif. 1980, N.Y. 1982, Colo. 1993, Ariz. 1995. Ptnr. Graham & James, 1976-83; with legal dept. Bank of Am., LA, 1973-76, Wyman, Bautzer, Kuchel & Silbert, LA, 1983-87, Dennis, Shafer, Fennelly & Creim (merged with Bronson & McKinnon), LA, 1987-96; with Squire, Sanders & Dempsey, Phoenix, 1996—98; prin. Jane C. Fennelly, P.C., Phoenix, 1998—; of counsel Creim, Macias & Koenig LLP, LA, 1999—. Mem. L.A. County Bar Assn. (bd. dirs., mem. exec. com. comml. law and bankruptcy sect. 1989-92). Home: 15356 W Pasadena Dr Surprise AZ 85374 Office: #610 Ste 101 15508 W Bell Rd Surprise AZ 85374 Office Phone: 602-909-1855. Personal E-mail: jane.fennelly@azbar.org.

FENNER, PETER DAVID, communications executive; b. Newark, Apr. 18, 1936; s. John David and Janice (Gleason) F.; m. Nancy Carrell Royce, Aug. 1958; children: Guy David, Karl Gleason, James Andrew. BS in Indsl. Engring., Lehigh U., 1958; MSBA, MIT, 1975. Field engr. Factory Mut.Engring., Montclair, N.J., 1958-61; assignments in engring., d.p., and software devel. Western Electric Co., Inc., N.J., N.Y., Mo., Colo., Calif., Mass., 1961-82; regional v.p. AT&T Network Systems (now Lucent Techs.), Balt. and Bethesda, Md., 1982-85; v.p. product planning, Morristown AT&T Network Systems, Balt. and Bethesda, Md., 1986-88, pres. Transmission Systems, 1989-92; mgmt. cons., 1993-95; CEO, COM 21, Milpitas, Calif., 1996-2001. Bd. dirs. SBS Techs., Albuquerque, BitMicro, Fremont, Calif., Active Strategies, Pa. Sloan fellow MIT, Cambridge, 1974-75. Mem. Westhampton Yacht Squadron, Westhampton Country Club. Avocations: sailing, tennis. Home: 3570 SW River Pkwy Unit 2401 Portland OR 97239-4548

FENNESSEY, PAUL VINCENT, pediatrics and pharmacology educator, researcher; b. Oct. 3, 1942; m. Susan Blackwell; children: Shirley, Karl, Shaun. BS in Chemistry, U. Okla., 1964; PhD of Organic Analytical Chemistry, MIT, 1968. Rsch. asst. U. Okla., Norman, 1963-64; predoctoral fellow MIT, Cambridge, 1964-69; asst. prof. pediat. and pharmacology U. Colo. Health Sci. Ctr., Denver, 1975-81, co-dir. mass spectral ctr., 1980, assoc. prof. pediat. and pharmacology, 1981-90, prof. pediat. and pharmacology, 1990—, vice chair pediat., 1991—. Contbr. articles to profl. jours. Asst. program scientist Viking Project, Martin Marietta Corp., Denver, 1969-72, program scientist, 1972-74. Recipient NSF Undergrad. Rsch. award, 1963-64, Merck award in Organic Chemistry, 1963; fellow Woodrow Wilson, 1964-65, NIH, 1964-68. Mem. Am. Chem. Soc., Am. Soc. Mass Spectrometry, Nat. Acad. Clin. Biochemists, Soc. Inherited Metabolic Diseases, Am. Soc. Pharmacology and Exptl. Therapeutics, Internat. Soc. Study Xenobiotics, Sigma Xi. Home: 13009 S Parker Ave Pine CO 80470-9617 Office: Children's Hosp 13123 East 16th Ave B-065 Aurora CO 80045 Home Phone: 303-838-4359; Office Phone: 303-315-7286, 720-777-7286. Business E-Mail: paul.fennessey@uchsc.edu.

FENNESSY, RICHARD A., information technology executive; BS, Mich. State Univ. Mgmt. positions IBM, 1987—2004, gen. mgr. worldwide PC direct, v.p. worldwide mktg. PC div., gen. mgr. worldwide ibm.com; pres., CEO Insight Enterprises, Inc., Tempe, Ariz., 2004—, bd. dir., 2005—. Office: Insight Enterprises Inc 1305 W Auto Dr Tempe AZ 85284 Office Phone: 480-902-1001. Office Fax: 480-902-1157.

FENNING, LISA HILL, lawyer, mediator, retired judge; b. Chgo., Feb. 22, 1952; d. Ivan Byron and Joan Hill; m. Alan Mark Fenning, Apr. 3, 1977; 4 children. BA with honors, Wellesley Coll., 1971; JD, Yale U., 1974. Bar: Ill. 1975, Calif. 1979, U.S. Dist. Ct. (no. dist.) Ill., U.S. Dist. Ct. (no., ea., so. & cen. dists.) Calif., U.S. Ct. Appeals (6th, 7th & 9th cirs.), U.S. Supreme Ct. 1989. Law clk. U.S. Ct. Appeals 7th cir., Chgo., 1974-75; assoc. Jenner and Block, Chgo., 1975-77, O'Melveny and Myers, LA, 1977-85; judge U.S. Bankruptcy Ct. Cen. Dist. Calif., LA, 1985-2000; mediator JAMS, Orange, Calif., 2000-01; ptnr. Dewey Ballantine LLP, LA, 2001—07, Dewey and LeBoeuf, 2007—. Bd. govs. Nat. Conf. Bankruptcy Judges, 1989-92; pres. Nat. Conf. of Women's Bar Assns., N.C., 1987-88, pres.-elect, 1986-87, v.p., 1985-86, bd. dirs.; lectr., program coord. in field; bd. govs. Nat. Conf. Bankruptcy Judges Endowment for Edn., 1992-97, Am. Bankruptcy Inst., 1994-2000; mem., bd. advisors Nat. Jud. Edn. Program to Promote Equality for Women and Men in the Cts., 1994-99. Mem., bd. advisors: Lawyer Hiring & Training Report, 1985-87; contbr. articles to profl. jours. Durant scholar Wellesley Coll., 1971; named one of Am's. 100 Most Important Women Ladies Home Jour., 1988, LA's 50 Most Powerful Women Lawyers LA Bus. Jour., 1998, So. Calif. Superlawyers LA Mag., 2005, 06. Fellow Am. Bar Found., Am. Coll. Bankruptcy (bd. regents 1995-98); mem. ABA (standing com. on fed. jud. improvements 1995-98, mem. commn. on women in the profession 1987-91), Individual Rights and Responsibilities sect. 1984—, bus. law sect. 1986—, bus. bankruptcy com.), Nat. Assn. Women Judges (nat. task force gender bias in the cts. 1986-87, 93-94), Nat. Conf. Bankruptcy Judges (chair endowment edn. bd. 1994-95), Am. Bankruptcy Inst. (nominating com. 1994-95, bd. steering com. stats. project 1994-96), Calif. State Bar Assn. (chair com. on women in law 1986-87), Women Lawyers' Assn. L.A. (ex officio mem., bd. dirs., chmn., founder com. on status of women lawyers 1984-85, officer nominating com. 1986, founder, mem. Do-It-Yourself Mentor Network 1986-96), Phi Beta Kappa. Democrat. Office: Dewey & LeBoeuf LLP 333 S Grand Ave 26th Fl Los Angeles CA 90071 Office Phone: 213-621-6000. Business E-Mail: lfenning@deweyleboeuf.com, lfenning@dl.com.

FENSTERSHEIB, MARTIN, city health department administrator; b. Pitts., 1949; MD, U. Autonoma de Guadalajara, 1975. Internist MC Pa. Hosp., Phila., 1975—77; resident, pediat. Milw. Children's Hosp., 1977—79; fellow, preventive medicine U. Calif., Berkeley, 1981—82; clin. practice Ira Greene Positive PACE Clinic; health officer, pub. health med. dir. Santa Clara Co. Pub. Health Dept., San Jose, Calif., 1994—. Chair, dept. cmty. health and preventive medicine Valley Med. Ctr. Mem.: Santa Clara Co. Med. Assn. (v.p., cmty. health), Calif. Conf. of Local Health Officers (past pres.).

FENTON, DENNIS MICHAEL, retired medical products executive; b. Roslyn, NY, Nov. 2, 1951; s. Robert Edward and Catherine (O'Dwyer) F.; m. Linda Marie Owens, June 30, 1974. BS in Biology, Manhattan Coll., 1973; PhD in Microbiology, Rutgers U., NJ, 1977. Rsch. scientist Pfizer Co., Groton, Conn., 1977-81, AmGen, Inc., Thousand Oaks, Calif., 1982-84, head lab., 1984—85, dir. pilot plant ops., 1985—88, v.p. pilot plant ops. and clin. mfg., 1988—91, v.p. process devel., facilities and mfg. svcs., 1991—92, sr. v.p. sales and mktg., 1992—95, sr. v.p. ops., 1995—2000, exec. v.p. ops., 2000—07. Bd. dirs. Biotechnology Industry Orgn. Contbr. articles to profl. jours.; patentee in field. Bd. trustees Keck Grad. Inst., Rutgers U.; bd. regents Calif. Luth. U. Mem. Am. Chem. Soc., Soc. Indsl. Microbiology, Am. Soc. Microbiology, Parenteral Drug Assn. Avocations: sports, music, hiking, camping.

FENTON, NOEL JOHN, venture capitalist; b. New Haven, May 24, 1938; s. Arnold Alexander and Carla (Mathiasen) F.; m. Sarah Jane Hamilton, Aug. 14, 1965; children: Wendy, Devon, Peter, Lance. BS, Cornell U., 1959; MBA, Stanford U., 1963. Research asst. Stanford (Calif.) U., 1963-64; v.p. Mail Systems Corp., Redwood City, Calif., 1964-66; v.p., gen. mgr. products div. Acurex Corp., Mountain View, Calif., 1966-72, pres., chief exec. officer, dir., 1972-83, Covalent Systems Corp., Sunnyvale, Calif., 1983-86; mng. gen. ptnr. Trinity Ventures Ltd., 1986—. Bd. dirs. Multifamily Tech. Solutions, Inc., LoopNet, Inc., SciQuest, Inc., ID Analytics, Inc., Blue Tarp Fin., Blue Stripe Software, Inc. Mem. adv. coun. resource Ctr. for Women, chmn. bd. dirs. 1987-88; mem. San Jose Econ. Devel. Task Force, 1983, Young Pres.'s Orgn., 1976-88, Pres. Reagan's Bus. Adv. Panel; mem. World Pres.'s Orgn., 1988—, dir., 1994-2000; mem. athletic bd. Stanford U., 2003—. Lt. (j.g.) USN, 1959-61. Mem. Am. Electronics Assn. (chmn. 1978-79, dir. 1976-80), Santa Clara County Mfrs. Group (dir. 1980-83), Chief Execs. Orgn., Stanford Bus. Sch. Alumni Assn. (pres. 1976-77, dir. 1971-76), Stanford Alumni Assn. (exec. bd. 1985-89). Republican. Episcopalian. Home: 247 Mapache Dr Portola Valley CA 94028-7354 Office: Trinity Ventures Bldg 4 3000 Sand Hill Rd Ste 160 Menlo Park CA 94025-7113 Business E-Mail: noel@trinityventures.com.

FENVES, GREGORY L., engineering educator; PhD, U. Calif. Berkeley. Prof. civil engring. U. Calif. Berkeley, T.Y. and Margaret Lin Prof. Engring., chair, dept. civil and environmental engring. Asst. dir. industry programs Pacific Earthquake Engring. Rsch. Ctr. U. of Calif. Berkeley; mem. Ctr. for Information Technol. Rsch. in the Interest of Society. Recipient Walter L. Huber Civil Engring. Rsch. prize ASCE, 1995. Office: U Calif Berkeley Dept Civil Engring MC 1710 Berkeley CA 94720-1710

FENWICK, JAMES HENRY, editor, writer, columnist; b. South Shields, Eng., Mar. 17, 1937; came to U.S., 1965; s. James Henry and Ellen (Tinmouth) F.; m. Suzanne Helene Hatch, Jan. 27, 1968. BA, Oxford U., Eng., 1960. Freelance lectr., writer, 1960-65; assoc. editor Playboy mag., Chgo., 1965-71; planning and features editor Radio Times, BBC, London, 1971-77, U.S. rep. NYC, 1978-87; sr. editor Modern Maturity mag., Lakewood, Calif., 1987-90, exec. editor, 1990-91, editor, 1991-98; contbg. editor Get Up and Go!, Age Wave Comm., Lakewood, Calif., 1998-99; editor Next Mag., Palm Springs, Calif., 2000—01, Desert Mag., Palm Springs, 2002—04, food columnist, 2004—, The Desert Sun, Calif., 2004—. Author (with Eric Wadlund): Palm Springs Flavors, 2007. Business E-Mail: fenwickfood@aol.com.

FENZL, TERRY EARLE, lawyer; b. Milw., Mar. 19, 1945; s. Earle A. and Elaine A. (Chandler) F.; m. Barbara Louise Pool, June 24, 1967; children: Allison, Andrew, Ashley. BBA, U. Wis., 1966; JD, U. Mich., 1969. Bar: Ariz. 1970, U.S. Dist. Ct. Ariz. 1970, U.S. Ct. Claims 1970, U.S. Ct. Appeals (9th cir.) 1973, U.S. Supreme Ct. 1973, U.S. Dist. Ct. (no. dist.) Calif. 1983. Assoc. Brown & Bain, P.A. and predecessor firms, Phoenix, 1969-74; ptnr. Perkins Coie Brown & Bain, P.A. and predecessor firms, Phoenix, 1975—2007. Mem. Ariz. State Bar Assn., Ariz. Town Hall. Democrat. Mem. United Ch. of Christ. Home: 6610 N Central Ave Phoenix AZ 85012-1014 Office: Ariz Atty Gen Office Chief of Staff 1275 W Washington Phoenix AZ 85007 Office Phone: 602-542-7711. Business E-Mail: terry.fenzl@azag.gov.

FEO, EDWIN F., lawyer; b. LA, 1952; BA, UCLA, 1974, JD, 1977. Bar: Calif. 1977. Ptnr., co-chmn. utility & energy practice & mem. global exec. com. Milbank Tweed Hadley & McCloy, LA. Trustee Calif. Sci. Ctr. Found.; bd. gov. Aquarium of the Pacific. Mem.: Am. Wind Energy Assn., Western Energy Inst., Independent Energy Producers Assn., Am. Council on Renewable Energy, Order of the Coif, Phi Beta Kappa. Office: Milbank Tweed Hadley & McCloy 30th Fl 601 S Figueroa St Los Angeles CA 90017-5735 Office Phone: 213-892-4417. Office Fax: 213-629-5063. Business E-Mail: efeo@milbank.com.

FEOLA, LOUIS, broadcast executive; Pres. MCA/Universal Home Video, Inc., North Hollywood, Calif., 1983-98, Universal Family & Home Entertainment Prodn., North Hollywood, 1998—.

FERBER, NORMAN ALAN, retail executive; b. NYC, Aug. 25, 1948; m. Rosine Abergel; children: Robert, Lauren, Richard. Student, Bklyn. Coll., 1965-68, L.I.U., 1968-70. Buyer, mdse. mgr. Atherton Industries, NYC, 1976-79; v.p., mdse. mgr. Raxton Corp., NYC, 1979-82; v.p. Fashion World, NYC, 1982; v.p merchandising, mktg. and distbn. Ross Stores Inc., Newark, Calif., 1984-87, pres., COO, 1987-88, pres., CEO, 1988-93, chmn., CEO, 1993-96, chmn., 1996—. Office: Ross Stores Inc 4440 Rosewood Dr Pleasanton CA 94588

FERGIE, (STACY ANN FERGUSON), singer; b. Whittier, Calif., Mar. 27, 1975; d. Terri and Pat Ferguson; m. Josh Duhamel, Jan. 10, 2009. Band mem. Wild Orchid, 1996—2002, Black Eyed Peas, 2003—. Singer: (albums with Wild Orchid) Wild Orchid, 1997, Oxygen, 1998, Fire, 2001, (albums with Black Eyed Peas) Elephunk, 2003, Monkey Business, 2005 (Favorite Rap/Hip-Hop Album, Am. Music Awards, 2006), (solo albums) The Dutchess, 2006, (songs) (with Wild Orchid) At Night I Pray, 1996, Talk to Me, 1997, Supernatural, 1997, Be Mine, 1998, Stuttering (Don't Say), 2001, (with Black Eyed Peas) Where is the Love?, 2003, Shut Up, 2003, Let's Get It Started, 2004 (Grammy, Best Rap Performance, 2005), Hey Mama, 2004 (MTV Music Video Award), Don't Phunk with My Heart, 2005 (Grammy award, Best Rap Group Performance, 2006), Don't Lie, 2005 (Grammy award for Best Group Pop Vocal Performance, 2007), My Humps, 2005 (MTV Video Music award for Best Hip-Hop Video, 2006), (as solo artist) London Bridge, 2006; actor: (films) Be Cool, 2005, Poseidon, 2006, Grindhouse (Planet Terror segment), 2007; (TV series) Kids Incorporated, 1984—89, The

Charlie Brown & Snoopy Show, 1984—85, Great Pretenders, 1999. Recipient MTV Europe award for Best Pop Act (with Black Eyed Peas), 2004, 2005, Favorite Pop Group & Rap Group, Am. Music Awards, 2005, Favorite Soul/Rhythm & Blues Group, 2006, Favorite Rap/Hip-Hop Group, 2006, Favorite Female Pop Artist, 2007, Female Artist of Yr., MTV Video Music Awards, 2007; named one of 50 Most Beautiful People in the World, People mag., 2004. Office: c/o Sara Ramaker Paradigm LA 360 N Crescent Dr N Bldg Beverly Hills CA 90210*

FERGUSON, CRAIG, actor, television personality; b. Glasgow, Scotland, May 17, 1962; m. Sascha Ferguson, July 18, 1998 (div. 2004); 1 child, Milo; m. Megan Wallace-Cunningham. Actor (tv series) The Ferguson Theory, 1994, Freakazoid!, 1995, Maybe This Time, 1995, The Drew Carey Show, 1996—2003, (film) Modern Vampyres, 1999, The Big Tease, 1999, Born Romantic, 2000, Saving Grace, 2000, Chain of Fools, 2000; writer (film): The Tease, 1999; tv guest appearances include: Red Dwarf, 1988, Chelmsford 123, 1988, Have I Got News for You, 1991, The Brain Drain, 1993, Almost Perfect, 1995; co-writer, co-prodr., actor: Je M'Appelle Crawford; comedian, comic actor in one-man shows, U.K.; writer (screenplay): All American Man, (with others) Saving Grace, The Ferguson Theory; host: The Late Late Show with Craig Ferguson, 2005-; author: (novels) Between the Bridge and the River, 2006. Office: c/o William Morris Agy 151 S El Camino Dr Beverly Hills CA 90212-2775

FERGUSON, ELDON EARL, retired physicist; b. Rawlins, Wyo., Apr. 23, 1926; s. George Earl and Bess (Pierce) F. BS, Okla. U., 1949, MS, 1950, PhD, 1953. Physicist U.S. Naval Research Lab., Washington, 1954-57; prof. physics U. Tex., Austin, 1957-62; dir. aeronomy lab. NOAA, Dept. Commerce, Boulder, Colo., 1962-95, ret., 1995. Served with U.S. Army, 1944-45. Guggenheim Found. fellow, 1960; Humboldt fellow, 1979-80; recipient Will Allis prize Am. Physical Society, 1994 Mem. Am. Phys. Soc., Am. Geophys. Union. Office: 325 Broadway St Boulder CO 80305-3337

FERGUSON, JOHN, JR., professional sports team executive; b. Montreal, July 7, 1969; m. Stephanie Ferguson; children: Emily, John, Grace. BA magna cum laude, Providence Coll.; JD, Suffolk U. Bar: Mass. 1989. Player agent NHL, with hockey ops. and legal depts., 1994, 1995; mem. scouting staff Ottawa Senators, 1993—96; asst. gen. mgr. St. Louis Blues, 1997—2001, v.p. hockey ops., 2001—03; pres., gen. mgr. Worcester IceCats; v.p., gen. mgr. Toronto Maple Leafs, 2003—08; scout Hockey Can., 2008; dir. pro scouting San Jose Sharks, 2008—. Former chmn. Am. Hockey League's Competition Com. Office: San Jose Sharks 525 W Santa Clara St San Jose CA 95113

FERGUSON, MARGARET ANN, tax specialist, consultant; b. Steuben County, Ind., Mar. 24, 1933; d. Leo C. and Ruth Virginia (Engle) Wolf; m. Billy Hugh Ferguson, Feb. 15, 1955 (dec. Oct. 1971); children: Theresa Ruth, Scott Earl, Wade Leo, Luke, Angela, Cynthia, Brenda. AA in Psychology/Social Svs., Palomar Coll., San Marcos, Calif., 1977; BA in Behavioral Sci., Nat. U., Vista, Calif., 1980. Enrolled agt. Office mgr., adminstr. asst. Better Bus. Bur., San Diego, 1979-82; tax technician IRS, Oceanside, Calif., 1982-84, problem resolution tax specialist, 1985-87, revenue agt., 1987-90; pvt. cons. Vista, Calif., 1991—2008. Instr. adult edn. Vista Unified Sch. Dist., 1990-99; mem. adv. com. of nat. cemetery sys. Dept. Vet. Affairs, 1991-98; adv. coun. IRS, 1999-2001, mem. taxpayer advocate panel, 2005-08. Mem. AAUW (treas.), Calif. Assn. Ind. Accts., Calif. Soc. Enrolled Agts. (dir. Palomar chpt. 1993-95, 2000-01, 1st v.p. 1998-2000), Inland Soc. Tax Cons., Assn. Homebased Bus., Gold Star Wives Am., Inc. (regional pres. 1989-90, chpt. pres. 1992-93, 96-97, nat. pres. 1993-95, chmn. nat. bd. dirs. 2004-06). Avocations: lace making, needle work, gardening, writing. Home and Office: 1161 Tower Dr Vista CA 92083-7144 Personal E-mail: gswtax@sbcglobal.net.

FERINI, ROBERT PAT, agricultural products company executive; b. 1963; With Betteravia Farms, Santa Maria, Calif.; now ptnr. Office: Betteravia Farms PO Box 5845 Santa Maria CA 93456-5845

FERNANDEZ, FERDINAND FRANCIS, federal judge; b. 1937; BS, U. So. Calif., 1958, JD, 1963; LLM, Harvard U., 1963. Bar: Calif. 1963, US Dist. Ct. (cen. dist.) Calif. 1963, US Ct. Appeals (9th cir.) 1963, US Supreme Ct. 1967. Elec. engr. Hughes Aircraft Co., Culver City, Calif., 1958-62; law clk. to dist. judge US Dist. Ct. (ctrl. dist.) Calif., 1963-64; pvt. practice law Allard, Shelton & O'Connor, Pomona, Calif., 1964-80; judge Calif. Superior Ct. San Bernardino County, Calif., 1980-85, US Dist. Ct. (ctrl. dist.) Calif., LA, 1985-89, US Ct. Appeals (9th cir.), LA, 1989—2002, sr. judge, 2002—. Lester Roth lectr. U. So. Calif. Law Sch., 1992. Contbr. articles to profl. jours. Vice chmn. City of La Verne Commn. on Environ. Quality, 1971-73; chmn. City of Claremont Environ. Quality Bd., 1972-73; bd. trustees Pomona Coll., 1990-05. Fellow Am. Coll. Trust and Estate Counsel; mem. ABA, State Bar of Calif. (fed. cts. com. 1966-69, ad hoc com. on attachments 1971-85, chmn. com. on adminstrn. of justice 1976-77, exec. com. taxation sect. 1977-80, spl. com. on mandatory fee arbitration 1978-79), Calif. Judges Assn. (chmn. juvenile cts. com. 1983-84, faculty mem. Calif. Jud. Coll. 1982-83, faculty mem. jurisprudence and humanities course 1983-85), L.A. County Bar Assn. (bull. com. 1974-75), San Bernardino County Bar Assn., Pomona Valley Bar Assn. (co-editor Newsletter 1970-72, trustee 1971-78, sec.-treas. 1973-74, 2d v.p. 1974-75, 1st v.p. 1975-76, pres. 1976-77), Estate Planning Coun. Pomona Valley (sec. 1966-76), Order of Coif, Phi Kappa Phi, Tau Beta Pi, Eta Kappa Nu. Office: US Ct Appeals 9th Cir 125 S Grand Ave Ste 602 Pasadena CA 91105-1621

FERRANDINO, MARK, state legislator; b. Nyack, NY; life ptnr. Greg Wertsch. BA in Polit. Sci., U. Rochester, 1999, MA in Pub. Policy Analysis, 2000. Sr. budget analyst Colo. Dept. Health Care Policy & Financing; program analyst US Dept. Justice Office of Inspector Gen.; policy analyst White House Office Mgmt. & Budget; mem. Dist. 2 Colo. House of Reps., Denver, 2007—. Treas. Colo. Dem. Party, 2005—07; co-capt. House Dist. 2A; co-chmn. Colo. Stonewall Dems. CFO Clandestine Chef Experience. Named Colo. Young Dem. of Yr., Colo. Dem. Party. Mem.: Baker Hist. Neighborhood Assn. Democrat. Office: State House 200 E Colfax Denver CO 80203 Office Phone: 303-866-2911. Business E-Mail: mferrandino@yahoo.com.*

FERREIRA, ARMANDO THOMAS, sculptor, educator; b. Charleston, W.Va., Jan. 8, 1932; s. Maximiliano and Placeres (Sanchez) F.; children: Lisa, Teresa. Student, Chouinard Art Inst., 1949—50, Long Beach City Coll., 1950—53; BA, UCLA, 1954, MA, 1956. Asst. prof. art Mt. St. Mary's Coll., 1956-57; mem. faculty dept. art Calif. State U., Long Beach, 1957—, prof., 1967—, chmn. dept. art, 1971-77, assoc. dean Sch. Fine Arts, acting dean Coll. Arts. Lectr., cons. on art adminstrn. to art schs. and univs., Brazilian Ministry Edn. One-man shows include, Pasadena Mus., 1959, Long Beach Mus., 1959, 69, Eccles Mus., 1967, Clay and Fiber Gallery, Taos, 1972; exhibited in group shows at L.A. County Art Mus., 1958, 66, Wichita Art Mus., 1959, Everson Mus., 1960, 66, San Diego Mus. Fine Arts, 1969, 73, Fairtree Gallery, N.Y.C., 1971, 74, L.A. Inst. Contemporary Art, 1977, Utah Art Mus., 1978, Bowers Mus., Santa Ana, Calif., 1980, No. Ill. U., 1986, Beckstrand Gallery, Palos Verdes (Calif.) Art Ctr., 1987, U. Madrid, 1993; permanent collections include Utah Mus. Art, Wichita Art Mus., Long Beach (Calif.) Mus. Art, State of Calif. Collection, Fred Jones Jr. Mus. Art U. Okla., U. Okla. Art Mus.; vis. artist, U. N.D., 1974. Fulbright lectr. Brazil, 1981. Fellow: Nat. Assn. Schs. Art and Design (bd. dirs.). Personal E-mail: atferreira@msn.com.

FERRELL, CONCHATA GALEN, actress, performing arts educator; b. Charleston, W.Va., Mar. 28, 1943; d. Luther Martin and Mescal Loraine (George) F.; m. Arnold A. Anderson; 1 dau., Samantha. Student, W.Va. U., 1961-64, Marshall U., 1967-68. Actor: (NY theater appearances) The Hot L Baltimore, 1973, The Sea Horse, 1973—74 (OBIE award and Drama Desk award, 1974), Battle of Angels, 1975; (plays) Getting Out, 1978, Here Wait, 1980, Picnic, 1986; (TV series) The Hot L Baltimore, 1975, B.J. and the Bear, 1979, McClain's Law, 1981, E.R., 1984, A Peaceable Kingdom, 1989, L.A. Law, 1991, Hearts Afire, 1993—94, Townies, 1996, Teen Angel, 1997, Push, Nevada, 2002, Two & 1/2 Men, 2003—, (movies) Network, 1975, Dangerous Hero, 1975, Heartland, 1981, Where the River Runs Black, 1986, For Keeps, 1987, Mystic Pizza, 1987, Witches of Eastwick, 1987, Chains of Gold, 1990, Edward Scissorhands, 1990, Family Prayers, 1993, True Romance, 1993, Samurai Cowboy, 1993, Heaven and Earth, 1993, Freeway, 1995, Touch, 1996, My Fellow Americans, 1996, Erin Brokovich, 2000, Crime and Punishment-High School, 2000, Stranger Inside, 2001, K-Pax, 2001, Mr. Deeds, 2002, Kabluey, 2007—08, (TV movies) A Girl Called Hatter Fox, 1977, A Death in Canaan, 1977, The Orchard Children, 1978, Before and After, 1979, Bliss, 1979, Reunion, 1980, The Rideout Case, 1980, The Great Gilley Hopkins, 1981, Life of the Party, 1982, Emergency Room, 1983, Nadia, 1984, Miss Lonely Hearts, 1985, Samaritan, 1986, Northbeach and Rawhide, 1986, Picnic, 1986, Eye on the Sparrow, 1987, Runaway Ralph, 1987, Goodbye Miss Liberty (Disney Channel), 1988, Running Mates, 1990, Deadly Intentions, Again, 1990, Back Field in Motion, 1991, 120 Volt Miracle, 1992, Forget Me Not, 1996, Sweetdreams, 1996, Amy and Isabelle, 2001. Recipient Wrangler award Nat. Cowboy Hall of Fame, 1981, Most Promising Newcomer award Theatre World, 1974, Emmy award nomination, 1991-92, 2004-2005, 2006-07. Mem. AFTRA, ACLU, NOW, SAG, Actors Equity Assn., Women in Films, Circle West. Democrat. Office: PO Box 7010 Santa Monica CA 90406 Personal E-mail: chattagail@hotmail.com.

FERRERA, AMERICA GEORGINE, actress; b. LA, Apr. 18, 1984; Student in Internat. Rels. and Theater, U. So. Calif. Actor: (films) Real Women Have Curves, 2002 (Best Actress, Sundance Jury award), The Sisterhood of the Traveling Pants, 2005, Lords of Dogtown, 2005, How the Garcia Girls Spent Their Summer, 2005, 3:52, 2005, Steel City, 2006, Muertas, 2007, Towards Darkness, 2007, La misma luna, 2007, The Sisterhood of the Traveling Pants 2, 2008; (TV films) Gotta Kick It Up!, 2002, $5.15/Hr., 2004, Plainsong, 2004; (TV series, 1 episode) Touched by an Angel, 2002, CSI: Crime Scene Investigation, 2004; (TV series) Ugly Betty, 2006— (Best Performance by an Actress in a TV Series, Comedy, Golden Globe award, Hollywood Fgn. Press Assn., 2007, Outstanding Performance by a Female Actor in a Comedy Series, SAG, 2007, Choice TV: Breakout, Teen Choice Awards, 2007, Primetime Emmy for Outstanding Lead Actress in a Comedy Series, Acad. TV Arts and Scis., 2007, Outstanding Actress in a Comedy Series, NAACP Image award, 2008); (plays, off-Broadway) Dog Sees God: Confessions of a Teenage Blockhead, 2005. Recipient Movieline Breakthrough award, 2005; named Hispanic Woman of Yr., Hollywood Reporter and Billboard, 2007, Entertainer of yr., ALMA Awards, 2008; named one of The World's Most Influential People, TIME mag., 2007. Mailing: Ugly Betty Raleigh Studios 5300 Melrose Ave Los Angeles CA 90038

FERRETTI, DANTE, display designer; b. Macerata, Italy, Feb. 26, 1943; m. Francesca LoSchiavo; 1 child, Edoardo. Prodn. designer: (films) The Working Class Goes to Heaven, 1971, (with Nicola Tamburro) Medea, 1971, The Decameron, 1971, Sbatti il Mostro in Prima Pagina, 1972, The Canterbury Tales, 1972, Storie Scellerate, 1973, Il Fiore della Mille e una Notte, 1974, Crime of Love, 1974, The Night Porter, 1974, Salo: One Hundred Days of Sodom, 1975, Todo Modo, 1976, Bye Bye Monkey, 1978, Il Gatto, 1978, Eutanasia di un amore, 1978, Orchestral Rehearsal, 1979, Till Marriage Do Us Part, 1979, Arabian Nights, 1980, Il Minestrone, 1980, City of Women, 1980, La Pelle, 1981, Oltra la Porta, 1982, Desire, 1983, La Nuit de Varennes, 1983, Tales of Ordinary Madness, 1983, And the Ship Sails On, 1983, Pianoforte, 1984, Il Futuro e Donna, 1984, Le Bon Roi Dagobert, 1984, The Name of the Rose, 1986, Ginger and Fred, 1986, Il Secreto del Sahara, 1987, The Adventures of Baron Munchausen, 1989 (Academy award nomination best art direction 1989), The Voice of the Moon, 1990, Hamlet, 1990 (Academy award nomination best art direction 1990), (with Francesca Lo Schiavo) The Sleazy Uncle, 1991, (with Wolfgang Hundhammer) Club Extinction, 1991, The Age of Innocence, 1993 (Academy award nomination best art direction 1993), Interview with the Vampire, 1994 (Academy award nomination best art direction 1994), Casino, 1995, Kundun, 1997, Meet Joe Black, 1998, Bringing Out the Dead, 1999, Titus, 1999, Gangs of New York, 2002, Cold Mountain, 2003, The Aviator, 2004 (Acad. award for Best Art Direction, 2005), (with Francesca Lo Schiavo) Sweeney Todd: The Demon Barber of Fleet Street, 2007 (Acad. award for Best Art Direction, 2008; set designer: (operas) The Fly, 2008. Office: Sandra Marsh Mgt 9150 Wilshire Blvd Ste 220 Beverly Hills CA 90212-3429

FERRILLO, PATRICK J., JR., dean, endodontist; b. St. Louis, Mar. 4, 1941; s. Patrick J. Ferrillo Sr. BS in biology, Georgetown U., 1973; DDS, Baylor U., 1976, cert., 1978. Instr. Baylor Coll. of Dentistry, Dallas, 1976-78; clin. asst. prof. So. Ill. U. Sch. Dental Medicine, Alton, 1978-79, asst. prof., 1979-84, sect. head, 1979-87, dir. current affairs, 1982-87, acting chmn., 1984-85, chairperson, 1985-87, acting dean, 1986-87, dean, assoc. prof., 1987—2002; dean Sch. Dental Medicine Univ. of Nevada, Las Vegas, 2002—, vice provost divsn. health sciences, 2002—. Pres. Am. Assn. Dental Schs., Washington, DC, 1999—2000. Fellow Am. Coll. Dentists, Internat. Coll. Dentists; mem. Omicron Kappa Upsilon (v.p. 1988-89, pres. 1989-91), Phi Kappa Phi. Office: Univ Nevada Sch Dentistry 4505 Maryland Pkwy Box 453055 Las Vegas NV 89154 Office Phone: 702-895-2952. Business E-Mail: pat.ferrillo@ccmail.nevada.edu.

FERRIOLI, TED, state legislator; b. Spokane, Wash., Feb. 15, 1951; m to Mary; children: John & Talia. Member, Creswell City Coun, formerly; Oregon State Senator, District 28, formerly, Assistant Majority Leader, formerly, chairman, Ways & Means Subcomt, formerly, co-chmn, Joint Stream Restoration & Species Recovery Committee, formerly, member, Agriculture & Natural Resources, Transportation & Ways & Means Committees, formerly, Oregon State Senate; Oregon State Senator, District 30, 2003-, Republican Leader, currently, member, Legislature Counsel Committee, currently, vice chairman, Rules Committee, currently, Oregon State Senate.Exec director, Malheur Timber Operators, Inc, currently. Republican. Office: 900 Court St NE, S-323 Salem OR 97301 Office Phone: 503-986-1950. E-mail: sen.tedferrioli@state.or.us.

FERRY, DAVID KEANE, electrical engineering educator; b. San Antonio, Oct. 25, 1940; s. Joseph Jules and Elizabeth (Keane) F. m. Darleen Heitkamp; Aug. 25, 1962; children: Lara Annette, Linda Renee. BSEE, Tex. Tech U., 1962, MSEE, 1963; PhD, U. Tex., 1966. Lectr. U. Tex., Austin, 1966; postdoctoral fellow U. Vienna, 1966-67; asst. prof., then assoc. prof. Tex. Tech. U., Lubbock, 1967-73; sci. officer Office Naval Rsch., Arlington, Va., 1973-77; prof., head elec. engring. Colo. State U., Ft. Collins, 1977-83; Regent's prof., dir. Ctr. for Solid State Electronics Rsch. Ariz. State U., Tempe, 1983-89, Regent's prof., chair elec. computing engring., 1989-92, Regent's prof., 1992—. Mem. microelectronics panel NRC, Washington, 1977-79; mem. materials rsch. coun. Def. Advanced Rsch. Projects Agy., Arlington, 1982-98; mem. supercomputer adv. group NSF, Washington, 1984-87. Author (with D.R. Fannin): Physical Electronics, 1971; author: (with L.A. Akers and E.W. Greeneich) Ultra Large Scale Integrated Microelectronics, 1988, Semiconductors, 1991; author: (with R.O. Grondin) Physics of Submicron Devices, 1991, Quantum Mechanics, 1995, 2d edit., 2000; author: (with S.M. Goodnick) Transport in Nanostructures, 1997; author: (with J.P. Bird) Electronic Materials and Devices, 2001, Semiconductor Transport, 2001; numerous pub. sci. articles; editor: GaAs Technology, 1985, GaAs Technology II, 1989; editor: (with J.R. Barker and C. Jacoboni) Physics of Nonlinear Transport in Semiconductors, 1979, Granular Nonelectronics, 1991; editor: (with C. Jacoboni) Quantum Transport in Semiconductors, 1992; editor: (with C. Jacoboni, A.P. Jauho, H.L. Grubin) Quantum Transport in Ultrasmall Devices, 1995; editor: (with S. Ota) Silicon Nanoelectronics, 2005; patentee in field. Fellow IEEE (Cledo Brunetti prize for advancements in nanoelectronics 1999), Am. Phys. Soc., Inst. Physics (Eng.); mem. Sigma Xi. Avocations: photography, skiing. Office: Ariz State U Elec Dept Tempe AZ 85287

FERRY, FRANK, mayor, Santa Clarita, California, principal; children: Nick, Jake. BA in govtl. comm., Calif. State U.; BA in law, JD. Cert. Calif. Teacher Alemany High Sch., Santa Clarita, Calif., principal; mayor City of Santa Clarita City Council, Calif., 1998—. Co-founder City's Visions in Progress Youth Adv. Com., Blue Ribbon Task Force for Youth; mem. 2000 Census Com., Calif. Contract Cities Com.; Regional Planning Com.; William S. Hart Ed. Com. Achievements include the building of the Youth Grove in Ctrl. Pk. Office: City of Clarita Mayor's Office 23920 Valencia Blvd Valencia CA 91355 Office Phone: 661-255-4309. Office Fax: 661-259-8125. Business E-Mail: fferry@santa-clarita.com, mayordude@santa-clarita.com.*

FERRY, MILES YEOMAN, state legislator; b. Brigham City, Utah, Sept. 22, 1932; s. John Yeoman and Alda (Cheney) F.; m. Suzanne Call, May 19, 1952; children: John, Jane Ferry Stewart, Ben, Sue Ferry Thorpe; foster children: Helen and Nora Buck. BS, Utah State U., 1954. Rancher, Corinne, Utah, 1952; pres. J.Y. Ferry & Son, Inc.; mem. Utah Ho. of Reps., 1965-66, Utah Senate, 1967-84, minority whip, 1975-76, minority leader, 1977-78, pres. senate, 1979-84; mem. presdl. advisor commn. on intergovtl. affairs, 1984; mem. governing bd. Council State Govts., 1983-84. V.p. Legis./Exec. Consulting Firm, 1994—; chmn. Corinne Cemetery Dist., 1989—. Pres. Brigham Jr. C. of C., 1956-61, Nat. Conf. of State Legislators, 1984, v.p., 1982, pres.-elect, 1983, pres., 1984; v.p. Utah Jr. C. of C., 1960-61; nat. dir. Utah Jaycees, 1961-62; pres. Farm Bur. Box Elder County, 1958-59; food and agr. commr. USDA, commr. agr. State of Utah, 1985-93. Recipient award of merit Boy Scouts Am., 1976, Alumnusi of Yr. award Utah State U., 1981, award of merit Utah Vocat. Assn., 1981, Friend of Agr. award Utah Farm Bur., 1988, Cert. Appreciation USDA, 1988, Contbn. to Agr. award Utah-Idaho Farmers Union, 1989, Disting. Svc. award Utah State U., 1993, 94; named Outstanding Young Man of Yr., Brigham City Jr. C. of C., 1957, Outstanding Nat. Dir. U.S. Jaycees, 1963, Outstanding Young Man in Utah, Utah Jr. C. of C., 1961, Outstanding Young Farmer, 1958, One of 3 Outstanding Young Men of Utah, 1962, Rep. Legislator of Yr., 1984, One of 10 Outstanding Legislators of Yr., 1984. Mem. SAR, Sons Utah Pioneers, Gov.'s Cabinet, Utah Commn. Agr., Fed. Rsch. Com., Nat. Assn. State Depts. Agr. (bd. dirs. 1989), Western Assn. of State Depts. of Agr. (v.p. 1990-91, pres. 1991-92), Western U.S. Agr. Trade Assn. (sec. treas- elect 1987-88, pres. 1989-90), Utah Cattlemen's Assn., Nat. Golden Spike Assn. (dir. 1958—), Phi Kappa Phi, Pi Kappa Alpha. Republican. Address: 815 N 6800 W Corinne UT 84307-9737 Office Phone: 435-744-2258. Personal E-mail: lec23@comcast.net.

FETTER, ALEXANDER LEES, theoretical physicist, educator; b. Phila., May 16, 1937; s. Ferdinand and Elizabeth Lean Fields (Head) F.; m. Jean Holmes, Aug. 4, 1962 (div. Dec. 1994); children: Anne Lindsay, Andrew James; m. Lynn Bunim, Sept. 10, 2004. AB, Williams Coll., 1958; BA, Balliol Coll., Oxford U., 1960; PhD, Harvard U., 1963. Miller rsch. fellow U. Calif., Berkeley, 1963-65; mem. faculty dept. physics Stanford U., 1965—, prof., 1974—, chmn. dept. physics, 1985-90, assoc. chmn. dept. physics, 1998-99, asso. dean undergrad. studies, 1976-79, assoc. dean humanities and sci., 1990-93, dir. Hansen Exptl. Physics Lab., 1996-97, dir. lab. for adv. materials, 1999—2002; vis. prof. Cambridge U., 1970-71; Nordita vis. prof. Tech. U., Helsinki, Finland, 1976. Author: (with J.D. Walecka) Quantum Theory of Many Particle Systems, 1971, Theoretical Mechanics of Particles and Continua, 1980, Nonlinear Mechanics, 2006. Alumni trustee Williams Coll., 1974-79. Rhodes scholar, 1958-60; NSF fellow, 1960-63; Sloan Found. fellow, 1968-72; Recipient W.J. Gores award for excellence in teaching Stanford U., 1974 Fellow Am. Physics Soc. (chmn. div. condensed matter physics 1991), AAAS; mem. Sigma Xi. Home: 904 Mears Ct Palo Alto CA 94305-1029 Office: Stanford U Physics Dept Stanford CA 94305-4045 E-mail: fetter@stanford.edu.

FETTERLY, LYNN LAWRENCE, real estate broker and manager; b. Ogdensburg, NY, Oct. 21, 1947; s. Keith C. and Florence E. Fetterly; m. Melody Bulriss, July 23, 1971; children: Kim Marie, Adam Lynn. AAS, Canton Coll., NY, 1967; BS, SUNY, Albany, 1969; MA, U. Detroit, 1972; cert. in mgmt., U. So. Calif., LA, 1984. Auditor Arthur Andersen & Co., Rochester, N.Y., 1969-70; asst. v.p. Security Pacific Nat. Bank, LA, 1972-75, Security Pacific Corp., LA, 1976-77, Citibank, N.A., Rochester, 1977-81; v.p. regional mgr. Security Pacific Nat. Bank, NYC, 1981-84; pres., CEO Security Pacific EuroFinance, Inc., London, 1984-88; vice chmn. Security Pacific Fin. Svcs. Sys., Inc., San Diego, 1988-90; pres., COO Security Pacific Fin. Svcs. System, Inc., San Diego, 1991-92; ind. real estate broker/developer, gen. contractor, 1993—. With USAR, 1969-75. Republican. Presbyterian. Avocations: golf, tennis.

FETTERMAN, DAVID MARK, anthropologist, educator, evaluator; b. Danielson, Conn., Jan. 24, 1954; s. Irving and Elsie (Blumenthal) F.; m. Summer Fetterman; 2 child, Sarah Rachel, David Fetterman II. BA, BS, U. Conn., 1976; MA in Anthropology, Stanford U., 1977, MA in Edn., 1979, PhD in Anthropology, 1981. Cert. tchr. Calif., Conn. Tchr. Richard C. Lee High Sch., New Haven, 1975-76; dir. Office of Econ. Opportunity Anti-Poverty, Danielson, 1976; tchr. Beth Am and Beth David, Cupertino and Palo Alto, Calif., 1976-78; sr. assoc., project dir. RMC Rsch. Corp., Mountain View, Calif., 1978-82; prin. rsch. scientist Am. Insts. Rsch., Stanford, Calif., 1982-91; dir. MA policy analysis and evaluation Stanford U., 1993—2003, dir. evaluation tng. program, 1993—, dir. evaluation, career devel. and alumni rels., 2003—04, dir. evaluation Sch. Medicine Calif., 2005—; dir. rsch. and evaluation Calif. Inst. Integral Studies, San Francisco, 1993—97; collaborating prof. Colegio de Postgrad., Mexico, 2007—; prof. edn. U. Ark., Pine Bluff, 2007—; disting. vis. prof. San Jose State U., 2006—. Mem. adv. bd. Ednl. Leadership, U.S. Dept. Edn., Washington, 1987—89, mem. adv. bd. Nat. Rsch. Ctr. Gifted and Talented; trustee Nueva Learning Ctr., Hillsborough, Calif., 1990—2001; accreditation team Calif. Inst. Integral Studies, San Francisco, 1994—. Author: Empowerment Evaluation Principles in Practice, 2005, Excellence and Equality, 1988 (Mensa award 1990), Ethnography: Step by Step, 1989, (G. & L. Spindler award Am. Anthropol. Assn., 1990), 2d edit., 1998, Foundations of Empowerment Evaluation, 2002 (Paul Lazarsfield award for contbns. to evaluation theory, Am. Evaluation Assn. 2002); editor: Speaking the Language of Power, 1993, Empowerment Evaluation, 1995. Pres. Mini-Infant Day Care Ctr., Palo Alto, 1992-93. Recipient Outstanding Higher Edn. Profl., 2008. Fellow Am. Anthrop. Assn. (bd. dirs. 1993), Soc. Applied Anthropology (liaison 1989); mem. Am. Evaluation Assn. (pres. 1992-94, Myrdal award 1999), Coun. Anthropology and Edn. (life, pres. 1988-92, Ethnographic Evaluation award 1988), Collaborative, Participatory, and Empowerment Group (chair 1995—, Pres.'s prize 1984). Avocations: computers, internet, digital video production. Office: Stanford U Sch Medicine Stanford CA 94305 Home: 566 Hopkins St Menlo Park CA 94025-3593 Office Phone: 650-269-5689. Personal E-mail: fettermanassociates@gmail.com.

FETTERS, NORMAN CRAIG, II, retired banker; b. Pitts., Aug. 27, 1942; s. Karl Leroy and Hazel (Lower) F.; m. Linda Wood, Aug. 14, 1965; children— Eric Craig, Kevin Edward, Brian Allan AB, Westminster Coll., 1964; MBA, U. Pitts., 1965. Various positions to v.p. Security Pacific Nat. Bank, Los Angeles, 1965-66, 69-74, v.p., 1974-82; sr. v.p. Rainier Bank, Security Pacific Bank Washington, Seattle, 1982-92, SeaFirst Bank, Seattle, 1992-93; sr. v.p., dir. Security Pacific Savs. Bank, Seattle, 1993-94; v.p. Key Bank of Wash., Seattle, 1994-96, sr. v.p., 1996-99; v.p., credit officer Fed. Home Loan Bank Seattle, 1999—2003, v.p., credit analysis mgr., 2003—05, ret., 2005. Served to lt. US Army, 1966—69. Decorated Commendation medal US Army. Mem. Risk Mgmt. Assocs., Lions Club (pres. 1988-89, 05-06, Melvin Jones fellow). Presbyterian (elder). Avocations: cross country skiing, travel, hiking, photography. Home Phone: 206-236-1634. Personal E-mail: ncfetters@aol.com.

FEUER, MICHAEL, state legislator; b. San Bernadino, Calif. m to Gail Ruderman; children: Aaron & Danielle. BA, JD, Harvard U. City councilman, District 5, Los Angeles, California, 1995-2002, member, Ad Hoc Committee Gangs & Juv Justice, Ad Hoc Committee Substandard Housing, Ad Hoc Committee Welfare Reform & Task Force on Info Access, Budget & Finance Committee, formerly, vice chairman, Public Safety Committee, formerly, chairman, Arts, Health & Humanities Committee, Los Angeles City Coun; California State Assemblyman, District 42, 2006-, California State Assembly.Atty, Hofstedler, Miller, Carlson & Beardsley, Los Angeles, formerly; exec director, Bet Tzedek Legal Serv, formerly; practiced law; teacher, UCLA Sch Public Affairs & UCLA Law Sch, formerly. Courageous Leadership Award, Women Against Gun Violence; Education Advocacy Award, America Civil Liberties Union; FAMMY Award, Jewish Family Services Los Angeles; John Harvard Public Svc Award, Harvard Club of Southern California; Justice Award, Los Angeles Center for Law & Justice; Community Leadership Award; Named California 100 Most Influential Attorneys, Los Angeles Daily Journal; Outstanding Leadership award, Legal Community Against Violence; Angel of Peace award, Violence Prevention Coalition of Greater Los Angeles; Man of the Year, Rotary Club of Century City; Leaf Award, Children's Nature Inst; Sheldon W. Anderson award, Alternative Living for the Aging; Award for Public Svc, Valley Non-Profit Alliance; Award for Commitment to Children and Families of Los Angeles, The H.E.L.P. Group. Democrat. Address: 9544 Cresta Dr Los Angeles CA 90035 Office: Dist 42 9200 Sunset Blvd PH 15 Los Angeles CA 90069 also: State Capitol PO Box 942849 Sacramento CA 94249-0042 Office Phone: 916-319-2042, 310-285-5490. Office Fax: 916-319-2142, 310-285-5499. Business E-Mail: Assemblymember.Feuer@assembly.ca.gov.

FEUERSTEIN, HOWARD M., lawyer; b. Memphis, Sept. 16, 1939; s. Leon and Lillian (Kapell) F.; m. Tamra Lynn Saperstein, May 19, 1968; children: Laurie, Leon. BA, Vanderbilt U., 1961, JD, 1963. Bar: Tenn. 1963, Oreg. 1965. Law clk. to justice US Ct. Appeals (5th cir.), Montgomery, Ala., 1963-64; teaching fellow Stanford U., 1964-65; assoc. Davies, Biggs et al (now Stoel Rives LLP), Portland, Oreg., 1965-71; ptnr. Stoel Rives LLP, Portland, 1971—. Mem. Oreg. Gov.'s Task Force on Land Devel. Law, 1974; bd. realtors Condominium Study Com., Oreg., 1975-76. Editor-in-chief Vanderbilt Law Rev., 1962-63. Trustee Congregation Beth Israel, Portland, 1977-83; bd. dirs. Jewish Family & Child Service, Portland, 1975-81, Young Musicians and Artists Inc., 1991-96. Recipient Founder's medal Vanderbilt Law Sch., 1963. Mem. ABA, Oreg. State Bar, Community Assn. Inst. (bd. dirs. Oreg. chpt. 1980-86), Am. Coll. Real Estate Lawyers. Office: Stoel Rives LLP 900 SW 5th Ave Ste 2600 Portland OR 97204-1268 Office Phone: 503-294-9215. Business E-Mail: hmfeuerstein@stoel.com.

FIBIGER, JOHN ANDREW, life insurance company executive; b. Copenhagen, Apr. 27, 1932; came to U.S., 1934, naturalized, 1953; s. Borge Rottboll and Ruth Elizabeth (Wadmond) F.; m. Barbara Mae Stuart, June 22, 1956; children: Karen Ruth McCarthy, Katherine Louise. BA, U. Minn., 1953, MA, 1954; postgrad., U. Wis. With Lincoln Nat. Life Ins. Co., Ft. Wayne, Ind., 1956-57; with Bankers Life Ins. Co. Nebr., Lincoln, 1959-73, sr. v.p. group, 1972-73; with New Eng. Mut. Life Ins. Co., Boston, 1973-89, vice chmn., pres., chief operating officer, 1981-89; with Transam Life Cos., 1991-94; exec. v.p., CFO, then pres. Transamerica Occidental Life Ins. Co., LA, 1994-95, chmn., 1995-97. Past vice chmn. Actuarial Bd. for Counseling and Discipline; bd. dirs. Fidelity Life Assn., Genworth Pvt. Asset Mgmt., Contra Fund. Life trustee, past chmn. Mus. Sci., Boston, 1989-91; past overseer New Eng. Med. Ctr., Boston Symphony Orch.; bd. dirs. Menninger Found., past v.p.; mem. fin. com., strategic planning com. L.A. Chamber Orch.; past chmn. Menninger Fund; past bd. dirs. U. So. Calif. Sch. Gerontology; bd. dirs. Austin Symphony Orch.; past trustee Calif. Mus. Sci. and Industry; bd. visitors, chmn. Menninger Baylor Meth. Found.; past chmn. Assn. Calif Life Insurance Co.; past founding dir. Boston Classical Orch., mem. fin. acctg. standards bd. adv. comm., 1984-88. With chem. corps US Army, 1957—59. Fellow Soc. Actuaries (past bd. dirs.); mem. Nat. Acad. Social Ins. (founding mem.), Am. Acad. Actuaries (past pres.). Personal E-mail: fibij@aol.com.

FIDEL, JOSEPH A., state legislator; b. Bibo, N.Mex., Oct. 14, 1923; married. Grad., St. Michael's H.S. Real estate broker; bank dir., ins. agt.; mem. N.Mex. Senate, Dist. 30, Sante Fe, 1972—. Vice chair fin. com. N.Mex. Senate, chmn. fin. com., 2005—. County assessor, 1950-54, 62-66; mem. City Coun., 1953-60; mem. Sch. Bd., 1959-71. Mem. Elks (life), K.C. (charter mem.). Democrat. Office: PO Box 968 Grants NM 87020-0968 Office Phone: 505-287-4432. Business E-Mail: dagvilar@1cities.net.

FIDEL, RAYA, information science educator; b. Tel Aviv, Jan. 18, 1945; came to U.S., 1977; BSc, Tel Aviv U., 1970; MLS, Hebrew U., Jerusalem, 1976; PhD, U. Md., 1982. Tchr. Adult Edn. Ctr., Jerusalem, 1971-72; br. libr. Hebrew U., Jerusalem, 1972-77; asst. prof. libr. sci. U. Wash., Seattle, 1982-87, assoc. prof. libr. sci., 1987-2000, prof. Info. Sch., 2000—, head Ctr. Human-Info. Interaction The Info. Sch., 2003—. Vis. libr. Duke U. Libr., Durham, N.C., 1992-93. Author: Database Design, 1987; editor Advances in Classification, 1991-94 (award 1992-94); contbr. articles to profl. publs. Recipient Research award Am. Society for Information Science, 1994 Mem. AAUP (chair U. Wash. chpt. 1990-92, pres. state conf. 1992-97), Assn. Computing Machinery, Am. Soc. Info. Sci. (dir.-at-large 2000-02). Home: 5801 Phinney Ave N Seattle WA 98103-5862

FIEDLER, FRED EDWARD, retired organizational psychology educator, consultant; b. Vienna, July 13, 1922; arrived in US, 1938; s. Victor and Hilda (Schallinger) F.; m. Judith Joseph, Apr. 14, 1946; children: Decky, Ellen Victoria, Carol Ann. AM, U. Chgo., 1947, PhD, 1949. Clin. psychol. trainee US VA, Chgo., 1947-50; rsch. assoc., instr. U. Chgo., 1949-51; asst. prof. psychology to prof. U. Ill., Urbana, 1951-69; prof. U. Wash., 1969-93, prof. emeritus psychology, 1993—. Vis. prof. U. Amsterdam, 1958-59; guest prof. U. Louvain, Belgium, 1963-64; vis. rsch. fellow Templeton Coll., Oxford, 1986; cons. State of Wash., 1981-84, King County, Wash., 1970-80; cons. various govt., mil., pvt. orgns., U.S., Europe, 1953—; apptd. to SLA Marshall chair U.S. Army Rsch. Inst., 1988-89. Author: Boards, Management and Company Success, 1959; A Theory of Leadership Effectiveness, 1967; Improving Leadership Effectiveness, 1976; Leadership and Effective Management, 1974; New Approaches to Effective Leadership—Cognitive Resources and Organizational Performance, 1987; contbr. numerous articles to profl. jours. Mem. Wash. Gov.'s Transition Team, 1980, Task Force on Pers. Selection of Apptd. Ofcls; co-chmn. Tech. Transfer, State of Wash., 1980-81; pub. mem. State Med. Disciplinary Bd., 1981-85. With Med. Dept. and Mil. Govt. br. U.S. Army, 1942-45. Recipient Outstanding Rsch. award Am. Pers. and Guidance Assn., 1953, Stogdill award for disting. contbns. to leadership, 1978, award Outstanding Sci. Contbns. to Mil. Psychology, 1979, Walter F. Ulmer Jr. Applied Rsch. award Ctr. Creative Leadership, 2005; named Disting. Bicentennial lectr. U. Ga., 1985; Claremont Grad. Sch. and Claremont-McKenna Coll. 1991 Leadership Conf. dedicated to him. Fellow APA (Rsch. award in cons. psychology 1971), Soc. for Indsl./Orgnl. Psychology (Disting. Sci. Contbns. award 1996), Am. Psychol. Soc. (James McKeen Caltell award 1999), Am. Acad. Mgmt. (Disting. Educator award), Internat. Assn. Applied Psychology (Disting. Contrbns. award 2002), Internat. Assn. Applied Psychology (past pres. orgnl. psychology divsn.), Soc. Orgnl. Behavior. Office: U Wash Dept Psychology 351525 Seattle WA 98195-0001 Office Phone: 206-232-8360.

FIELD, JOHN LOUIS, architect; b. Mpls., Jan. 18, 1930; s. Harold David and Gladys Ruth (Jacobs) F.; m. Carol Helen Hart, July 23, 1961; children: Matthew Hart, Alison Ellen. BA, Yale U., 1952, MArch, 1955. Individual practice architecture, San Francisco, 1959-68; v.p. firm Bull, Field, Volkmann, Stockwell, Architects, San Francisco, 1968-83; ptnr. Field/Gruzen, Architects, San Francisco, 1983-86, Field Paoli Architects, San Francisco, 1986—. Guest lectr. Stanford, 1970; chmn. archtl. council San Francisco Mus. Art, 1969-71; mem. San Francisco Bay Conservation and Devel. Commn., Design Rev. Bd., 1980-84; founding chmn. San Francisco Bay Architects Review, 1977-80 Co-author, producer, dir.: film Cities for People (Broadcast Media award 1975, Golden Gate award San Francisco Internat. Film Festival 1975, Ohio State award 1976); film The Urban Preserve (Calif. Council AIA Commendation of excellence 1982); co-design architect design for New Alaska Capital City (winner design competition). Bd. dir. Berkley Repertory Theatre; bd. mem. Ctr. for Urban Edn. About Sustainable Agriculture. Recipient Archtl. Record award, 1961, 1972; AIA, Sunset mag. awards, 1962, 64, 69; No. Calif. AIA awards, 1967, 82; Calif. Council AIA award, 1982; certificate excellence Calif. Gov.'s Design awards, 1966; Homes for Better Living awards, 1962, 66, 69, 71, 77; Albert J. Evers award, 1974, Best Bldg. award Napa (Calif.) C. of C., 1987, Design award Internat. Council Shopping Ctrs., 1988, Stores of Excellence award Nat. Mall Monitor, 1989, 92, 93, Pacific Coast Builders Gold Nugget award, 1989, 91, Urban Design award Calif. Coun. AIA, 1991, 93; Density Myth Competition winner Boston Soc. Architects, 2003. Fellow AIA (com. on design, mem. coun. Calif. arch., Lifetime Achievement award, 2005); mem. Nat. Coun. Archtl. Registration Bds., Urban Land Inst. (Design award 1995), Yale Club, Lambda Alpha. Office: Field Paoli Architects 150 California St 7th Fl San Francisco CA 94111-1315 Home Phone: 415-922-0373; Office Phone: 415-788-6606. Business E-Mail: jlf@fieldpaoli.com.

FIELD, TED (FREDERICK), film company and recording industry executive; b. Chgo. s. Marshall Field IV and Katherine W. Fanning; 8 children. Student, U. Chgo., Pomona Coll. Former race car driver; chmn., CEO Radar Pictures, 2002—; chmn. Artistdirect, Inc.; chmn., CEO Artistdirect Recs.; founder Interscope Communications; co-founder Interscope Records; former co-owner Field Enterprises, Chgo.; owner Panavision, 1985-87. Co-prodr.: (films) Critical Condition, 1987, Outrageous Fortune, 1987, Three Men and a Baby, 1987, Revenge of the Nerds II, 1987, Cocktail, 1988, The Seventh Sign, 1988, An Innocent Man, 1989; co-exec. prodr. (films) Bill and Ted's Excellent Adventure, 1989, Renegades, 1989; prodr. Revenge of the Nerds, 1984, Turk 182, 1985, Three Men and a Little Lady, Class Action, Jumanji, 1995, Mr. Holland's Opus, 1996, Runaway Bride, 1999; exec. prodr. The First Power, 1990, Bird on a Wire, 1990, The Hand That Rocks the Cradle, 1992, What Dreams May Come, 1998, Very Bad Things, 1998, Pitch Black, 2000, Texas Chainsaw Massacre, 2003, The Last Samurai, 2003, Le Divorce, 2003, The Amityville Horror, 2005, Zathura, 2005, The Heartbreak Kid, 2007; co-exec. prodr.: (TV films) The Father Clements Story, Everybody's Baby: The Rescue of Jessica McClure, A Mother's Courage; exec. prodr.: (feature film) Waist Deep, 2006. Avocations: chess, martial arts. Office: Radar Pictures 10900 Wilshire Blvd Ste 1400 Los Angeles CA 90024-6532

FIELDER, DAVID R., medical research administrator; V.p. rsch. Calif. Pacific Med. Ctr. Research Inst., San Francisco, Calif. Office: Calif Pacific Med Ctr Rsch Inst 2340 Clay St San Francisco CA 94115-1932

FIELDING, ELIZABETH BROWN, education educator; b. Ligonier, Ind., Feb. 17, 1918; d. Herbert Benjamin and Roberta (Franklin) B.; m. Frederick Allan Fielding, May 23, 1942 (wid. July 1962); children: Elizabeth Enndriss Fielding, Frederick Allan Fielding, Jr. BA, Smith Coll., 1939; MA, U. San Francisco, 1975. Cert. tchr. com. colls., Calif. Field staff mem. San Francisco Bay Girl Scout Assn. Coun., 1963-69; exec. dir. Tri-City Project on Aging, Rodeo, Calif., 1970-73; tchr., cons. various univs., 1974—. Mem. curriculum com. U. Calif., Berkeley, 1979-80; chair edn. programs Diablo Valley Found. on Aging, Walnut Creek, Calif., 1980s. Author: The Memory Manual: 10 Simple Things You Can Do to Improve Your Memory After 50, 1999, Teacher's Guide to The Memory Manual, 2000; contbr. articles to profl. jours. Chair Mental Health Task Force, County Coun. for Aging, Contra Costa County, 1974-76; mem. Sr. Svcs. Commn., City of Lafayette, Calif., 1981-2003; pres. bd. dirs. Calif. Specialists on Aging, Calif., 1976-79. Mem. Western Gerontol. Assn. (now Am. Soc. on Aging), Authors Guild, Calif. Writers Club. Avocations: writing, genealogy, art, birdwatching. Home: 1824 Stanley Dollar Dr 4A Walnut Creek CA 94595

FIELDING, JONATHAN EVAN, county health department administrator, pediatrician; b. Oct. 4, 1942; BA, Williams Coll., 1964; MA, MD, Harvard Coll., 1969, MPH, 1971; MBA, U. Pa., 1977. Diplomate Am. Bd. Pediats., Am. Bd. Preventive Medicine. Josiah Macy fellow Harvard U., Cambridge, Mass., 1969; intern, resident Boston Children's Hosp., 1969-71; fellow Harvard U., Boston, 1971; resident in pediats. Georgetown U. Med. Ctr., Washington, 1971-72, prin. med. svcs. nat. officer Job Corps, 1971-73; commr. pub. health Commonwealth of Mass., 1975-79; prof. health svcs. & pediats. UCLA, 1979—; dir. pub. health L.A. County, 1997—. Spl. asst. to dir. Bur. Cmty. Health Svcs. Health Svcs. & Mental Health Adminstrn. HEW, 1971-73; co-dir. Ctr. Health Enhancement Edn. & Rsch., 1979-84; co-dir. Ctr. for Healthier Children, Families & Cmtys., 1995-2004; lectr. Harvard U., Boston, 1973-75, Boston U., 1975-79, Brandeis U., 1975-79, Northwestern U., 1975-79; vis. lectr. UCLA, 1977; rsch. assoc. Urban Rsch. Ctr. Hunter Coll. CUNY, 1978; vis. prof. Nordic Sch. Pub. Health, Sweden, 1980, 83, 93. Editor: Ann. Revs. Pub. Health, 1995—; asst. editor Mercy-Rosenau Pub. Health and Preventive Medicine 1992-98, 14th edit. Vice-chair Partnership for Prevention, 1997—2002, chmn., 2002—, U.S. Cmty. Preventive Svcs. Task Force, 1996—, chair, 2001—. Mem. Am. Legacy Found. (bd. dir. 2005-), Sec.'s adv. com. health objectives nation (chair 2008), Pub. Health Adv. Com., Calif.; Fellow Assn. Health Svcs.; mem. NAS Inst. Medicine, Am. Acad. Pediats., Am. Assn. Pub. Health Physicians, Am. Med. Peer Rev. Assn., Am. Pub. Health Assn., Assn. Health Svcs. Medicine, Am. Heart Assn., Am. Coll. Preventive Medicine (pres. 1997-99). Office: UCLA Sch Pub Health Ctr Health Sci 61 253A Los Angeles CA 90095-0001

FIELDS, ANTHONY LINDSAY AUSTIN, health facility administrator, oncologist, educator; b. St. Michael, Barbados, Oct. 21, 1943; arrived in Can., 1968; s. Vernon Bruce and Marjorie F.; m. Patricia Jane Stewart, Aug. 5, 1967. MA, U. Cambridge, 1969; MD, U. Alta., 1974. Diplomate Am. Bd. Internal Medicine. Sr. specialist Cross Cancer Inst., Edmonton, Alta., Canada, 1980-85, dir. dept. medicine, 1985-88, dir., 1988-2000; v.p. med. affairs and cmty. oncology Alta. Cancer Bd., 2000—. Asst. prof. medicine U. Alta., Edmonton, 1980-84, assoc. prof., 1984-98, prof., 1998—, dir. divsn. med. oncology, 1985-89, dir. divsn. oncology, 1988-93; v.p. Nat. Cancer Inst. Can., 2000-02. pres., 2002-04. Fellow ACP, Royal Coll. Physicians and Surgeons Can. (specialist cert. med. oncology, internal medicine); mem. Can. Assn. Med. Oncologists (pres. 1994-96), Am. Soc. Clin. Oncology, Can. Soc. for Clin. Investigation, Can. Med. Assn. Avocation: photography. Office: # 1220 10405 Jasper Ave Edmonton AB Canada T5J 3N4

FIELDS, BERTRAM HARRIS, lawyer; b. LA, Mar. 31, 1929; s. H. Maxwell Fields and Mildred Arlyn (Ruben); m. Lydia Ellen Minevitch, Oct. 22, 1960 (dec. Sept. 1986); 1 child, James Eldar; m. Barbara Guggenheim, Feb. 21, 1991. BA, UCLA, 1949; JD magna cum laude, Harvard U., 1952. Bar: Calif. 1953. Assoc. firm Shearer, Fields, Rohner & Shearer, and predecessor firms, 1955—57, mem. firm, 1957—82; ptnr. Greenberg, Glusker, Fields, Claman & Machtinger, LA, 1982—. Mem. editl. bd.: Harvard Law Rev., 1953—55; author (as D. Kincaid): The Sunset Bomber, 1986; author: The Lawyer's Tale, 1992; author: (as B. Fields) Royal Blood Richard III and the Mystery of the Princes, 1998, Players-The Shakespeare Mystery, 2005. 1st lt. USAF, 1953—55, Korea. Recipient Legal Aid Soc. Access to Justice award. Mem.: ABA, Coun. Fgn. Rels., LA County Bar Assn. Achievements include being the subject of profiles Calif. Mag., Nov. 1987; Avenue Mag., Mar. 1989; Am. Film Mag., Dec. 1989; Vanity Fair Mag., Dec. 1993; Harvard Law Sch. Bull., spring 1998; London Sunday Telegraph, June 1999; Sunday New York Post, July 1999; W Mag., Apr. 2002; L.A. Times, Apr. 2003; London Sunday Times, Apr. 2003; NY Times, May 2005; New Yorker Mag., July 2006. Office: Greenberg Glusker Fields Claman & Machtinger Ste 2000 1900 Avenue Of The Stars Los Angeles CA 90067-4590 Business E-Mail: bfields@ggfirm.com.

FIELDS, DEBBI (DEBRA FIELDS ROSE), cookie franchise executive; b. Oakland, Calif. m. Randy Fields (div.); children: Jessica, Jenessa, Jennifer, Ashley, McKenzie; m. Michael Rose, Nov. 29, 1997. Profl. water-skier Marine World; founder Mrs. Fields Chocolate Chippery (now Mrs. Fields Inc.), Palo Alto, 1977, Mrs. Fields Inc., Park City, Utah, 1978—, pres., CEO, 1977—93. Bd. dirs. Outback Steakhouse, 1996—, WKNO, The Orpheum Theater. Author: (cookbook) 100 Recipes from the Kitchen of Debbi Fields, I Love Chocolate, 1994, Debbi Fields Great American Desserts, (autobiography) One Smart Cookie. Mem.: Soc. Entrepreneurs. Office: Mrs Fields Original Cookies 2855 Cottonwood Pkwy Ste 400 Salt Lake City UT 84121-7050

FIELDS, HENRY MICHAEL, lawyer; b. NYC, Feb. 11, 1946; s. Jack and Sylvia (Eggert) F.; m. Barbara Ann Schinman, June 20, 1971; children: Alexandra Wynne, Matthew Wyatt. BA magna cum laude, Harvard U., 1968; JD, Yale U., 1972. Bar: N.Y. 1973, N.J. 1974, Calif. 1981. Law clk. to presiding judge U.S. Dist. Ct. N.J. and U.S. Ct. Appeals (3d cir.), Newark, 1972-73; assoc. Cleary, Gottlieb, Steen & Hamilton, NYC and Paris, 1973-80, Morrison & Foerster, LA, 1980—81, ptnr., 1981—, mem. exec. com. Lectr. banking law various orgns., chair, Inst. for Corp. Counsel, 2000-01. Mng. editor Yale U. Law Rev., 1971-72; contbr. articles to profl. jours. Tower fellow Harvard U., 1968. Phi Beta Kappa. Clubs: Harvard-Radcliffe So. Calif. University (Los Angeles). Avocations: tennis, photography. Office: Morrison & Foerster LLP 555 W 5th St Ste 3500 Los Angeles CA 90013-1024 Office Phone: 213-892-5275. Office Fax: 213-892-5454. Business E-Mail: hfields@mofo.com.

FIELDS, HOWARD LINCOLN, neurologist, physiologist, educator; b. Chgo., Dec. 12, 1939; s. Charles and Mae (Pinkert) Fields; m. Carol Margaret Felts, Dec. 31, 1966; children: Rima Margaret Johnson, Gabriel Charles. BS, U. Chgo., 1960; MD, Stanford U., 1965, PhD in Neuroscience, 1966. Research neurologist Walter Reed Research Inst., Washington, 1967-70; clin. fellow Harvard Med. Sch., Boston, 1970-72; asst. prof. U. Calif., San Francisco, 1973-78, assoc. prof., 1978-82, prof., 1982—; vice chmn. neurology, 1993—; dir. Wheeler Ctr. for Neurobiology of Addiction. Cons. NIH, Bethesda, 1979—84; vis. fellow Clare Hall Coll. Cambridge U., England, 1979; vis. prof. Royal Soc. Medicine, 1988. Editor: Recent Advances in Pain Research and Therapy, 1985, Core Curriculum for Professional Education in Pain, 1991, 2d edit., 1995; author: Pain, 1987, Pain Syndromes in Neurology, 1990, Pharmacotherapy of Pain, 1994; contbr. articles to profl. jours. Recipient Rsch. Career Devel. award, NIH, Merit award, Nat. Inst. Drug Abuse, Kerr award, Am. Pain Soc., 1997. Mem.: Inst. Medicine of NAS, Soc. Neuroscience, Am. Neurol. Assn. (councillor 1991, mem. program com. 1991, R.D. Adams award 2006), Am. Acad. Neurology (Cotzias lectr. award 2000), Am. Soc. Clin. Investigation, Internat. Assn. Study Pain (program chmn. 1981—84, sec. 1990—93, editor-in-chief IASP Press 1993—2003). Office: U Calif Dept Neurology 5858 Horton St Ste 200 Emeryville CA 94608 Business E-Mail: hlf@phy.ucsf.edu.

FIELDS, ROBIN, reporter; Investigative writer LA Times. Co-recipient Ursula & Gilbert Farfel prize for investigative reporting, Scripps Howard Found., 2006, Local Watchdog Reporting award, Am. Soc. Newspaper Editors, 2006. Office: LA Times 202 W 1st St Los Angeles CA 90012 Office Phone: 213-237-7847. Office Fax: 213-237-4712. E-mail: robin.fields@latimes.com.

FIFER, SALLY JO, broadcast executive, editor; b. Albuquerque, May 22, 1958; d. Reginald Dekoven and Shirley Rae (Canaday) F. BA in Art History, U. Calif., 1981. Dir. mktg., sales Serious Bus. Co., Oakland, Calif., 1981-84; program devel. dir., editor video news San Francisco, 1984—92; exec. dir. Bay Area Video Coalition, San Francisco, 1992—2001; pres. & CEO Ind. TV Svc. (ITVS), San Francisco, 2001—. Bd. dirs. Video Refuses, San Francisco, Marin County Regional Occupational Program. Editor: Art Video, Video Networks, Videomaker; exec. prodr.: (documentaries) The Education of Shelby Knox, 2005, A Lion in the House, 2006, The World According to Sesame Street, 2006; (TV series) Independent Lens, 2002—. Recipient Best Documentary award for Independent Lens: Be Good, Smile Pretty, News & Documentary Emmy Awards, 2004, Alfred I. duPont-Columbia award for Independent Lens: Seoul Train, 2007. Office: ITVS Ste 410 651 Brannan St San Francisco CA 94107 Office Phone: 415-356-8383 ext. 233. Office Fax: 415-356-8391. E-mail: sally_fifer@itvs.org.

FIFIELD, MARVIN G., psychologist, educator; BA in Music, Idaho State U., 1956, MEd in Ednl. Adminstrn., 1958; EdD in Counseling, Wash. State U., 1963. Lic. psychologist, Idaho; cert. sch. psychologist, Utah, Idaho; cert. sch. counselor, Utah, Idaho. Dir. rsch. and spl. svcs. Pocatello (Idaho) Sch. Dist., 1964-66; dir. Ctr. for MR Study Idaho State U., Pocatello, 1967-69; postdoctoral fellow Columbia Tchr. Coll., NYC, summer 1970; chmn. dept. spl. edn. Utah State U., Logan, 1969-72, dir. Affiliated Devel. Ctr. for Handicapped Persons, 1972-86; profl. staff mem. Com. on Labor and Human Resources U.S. Senate, Washington, 1986-87; dir. Ctr. for Persons with Disabilities Utah State U., Logan, 1987—2000, dir. Utah Assistive Tech. Program, 1989—, prof., then prof. emeritus dept. spl. edn. and psychology, 1989—. Vocat. expert HEW/Social Security Adminstrn., Washington, 1968—; UAF liaison cons. HEW/OHDS Divsn. Devel. Disabilities, Washington, 1975-78; expert cons., tchr. trainer WHO Pan Am. Sanitary Bur., Santiago, Chile, 1979; cons. in evaluation tng. and psychol. svcs. Diné Ctr. for Human Devel., Navajo C.C., Ariz., 1980-86; curriculum and psychol. cons. Assn. Venezolena de Padres y Amigos de Ninos Excepcionales, Caracas, 1981-86. Contbr. articles to profl. jours.; author 18 books, chpts. in books, monographs. Vice chmn. Idaho Mental Retardation and Mental Health Planning Coun., 1963-65; adv. bd. Intermountain Regional Med. Program, 1972-76; mem. Utah Gov.'s Coun. for Persons with Disabilities, 1978—; chmn. Senator Hatch's Adv. Com. on Disability Issues, 1981—; chmn. bd. dirs. OPTIONS for Independence, No. Utah, 1987-91; exec. com. Utah Legis. Task Force on Svcs. for Persons with Handicaps, 1990-91; bd. dirs. Utah Legal Ctr. for Persons with Disabilities, 1991—; active ARC. Mem. APA (mem. divsn. counseling psychology, ednl. psychology and sch. psychology), Am. Assn. Univ. Affiliated Proglrams (pres. 1984-85, bd. dirs. 1995—), Rehab. Engring. Soc. N.Am. (co-chair ann. conv. 1996), Am. Assn. on Mental Retardation, Nat. Assn. Retarded Citizens, Utah Cerebral Palsy Assn., Phi Delta Kappa. Office: Utah State U Ctr Persons with Disabilities UMC 680C Logan UT 84322-0001 E-mail: marv@cpo2.usu.edu.

FIFKOVA, EVA, behavioral neuroscience educator; b. Prague, Czechoslovakia, May 21, 1932; came to U.S., 1968; d. Ivan and Maria Fifka. MD, Charles U., Prague, 1957; PhD, Inst. Physiology Czechoslovakia Acad. Scis., Prague, 1963. Lectr. Charles U., 1954-60; mem. staff Czechosolvakia Acad. Scis., 1960-68; research assoc. Calif. Inst. Tech., Pasadena, 1968-74; asst. prof. behavioral neuroscis. U. Colo., Boulder, 1974-75, assoc. prof., 1975-78, prof., 1978—. Mem. neurobiology adv. panel NSF, Washington, 1982-85; alcohol biomed. rsch. rev. com. Nat. Inst. Alcohol Abuse and Alcoholism, 1988-89; mem. neurology study sect. NIH, 1990-94; mem. rev. bd. Bionat. Sci. Found., 1992—. Contbr. numerous articles to profl. jours. U. Colo. Faculty fellow, Boulder, 1979, 84; research grantee Nat. Inst. Aging, Bethesda, Md., 1984—, Nat. Inst. Alcohol, 1983—, Nat. Inst. Mental Health, 1988—. Mem. AAAS, Am. Physiol. Soc., Soc. Neurosci., Am. Assn. Anatomists, Electron Microscopy Soc. Am., Inst. Brain Rsch. Orgn. Clubs: Cajal (Denver). Office: U Colo Dept Psychology PO Box 345 Boulder CO 80309-0345 Office Phone: 303-492-8729.

FIFLIS, TED JAMES, lawyer, educator; b. Chgo., Feb. 20, 1933; s. James P. and Christine (Karakitsos) F.; m. Vasilike Pantelakos, July 3, 1955 (dec.); children: Christina Eason, Antonia Fowler, Andreanna Lawson. BS, Northwestern U., 1954; LLB, Harvard U., 1957. Bar: Ill. 1957, Colo. 1975, U.S. Supreme Ct. 1984. Pvt. practice law, Chgo., 1957-65; emeritus prof. U. Colo. Law Sch., Boulder, 1965—, prof., 1968—. Vis. prof. NYU, 1968, U. Calif., Davis, 1973, U. Chgo., 1976, U. Va., 1979, Duke U., 1980, Georgetown U., 1982, U. Pa., 1983, Am. U., 1983, Harvard U., 1988; Lehmann disting. vis. prof. Washington U., St. Louis, 1991; cons. Rice U.; arbitrator AT&T divesture disputes, 1984-87. Author: (with Homer Kripke, Paul Foster) Accounting for Business Lawyers, 1970, 3rd edit., 1984, Accounting Issues for Lawyers, 1991; editor-in-chief Corp. Law Rev., 1977-88; contbr. articles to profl. jours. Mem. ABA, Am. Assn. Law Schs. (past chmn. bus. law sect.), Colo. Bar Assn. (mem. coun. sect. of corp., banking and bus. law 1974-75), Am. Law Inst. (life, chmn. com. on rsch. proposed fed. securities code), Colo. Assn. Corp. Counsel (pres. 1998-99). Greek Orthodox. Home: 1602 Columbine Ave Boulder CO 80302-7832 Office: Univ Of Colo Law Sch Boulder CO 80309-0401 Office Phone: 303-443-4753. E-mail: ted.fiflis@colorado.edu, vasited@aol.com.

FIFTY CENT, (CURTIS JAMES JACKSON), rap artist; b. Queens, NY, July 6, 1976; Performer: (songs) How to Rob, 1999, Wanksta, 2002, In Da Club, 2003 (Top R&B/Hip-Hop Song, ASCAP, 2004, Top Rap Song, ASCAP, 2004, Pop Songwriter of Yr., ASCAP, 2004), (albums) Power of the Dollar, 2000, Guess Who's Back, 2001, 50 Cent is the Future, 2001, Get Rich or Die Tryin', 2003, Massacre, 2005 (Am. Music Awards Favorite Rap Album, 2005, Billboard Album of Yr., 2005, Billboard 200 Album of Yr., 2005), God's Plan, 2006, No Mercy No Fear, 2006, Before I Self Destruct, 2007, Curtis, 2007; performer: (with G-Unit) Beg for Mercy, 2003; author (with Kris Ex): (autobiography) From Pieces to Weight, 2005; actor: (films) Get Rich or Die Tryin', 2005, Righteous Kill, 2008. Recipient Artist of Yr., Hip-Hop Artist of Yr., Rap Artist of Yr., Hot 100 Artist of Yr., Billboard Music Awards, 2005, Best Male Pop Artist, World Music Awards, 2005, Best Rap/Hip-Hop Artist, 2007; named one of The 100 Most Powerful Celebrities, Forbes.com, 2008. Office: c/o Cara Lewis William Morris Agy 1325 Ave of the Americas New York NY 10019 also: c/o Jim Wiatt William Morris Agy 1 William Morris Pl Beverly Hills CA 90212

FIGGINS, CHONE (DESMOND DECHONE FIGGINS), professional baseball player; b. Leary, Ga., Jan. 22, 1978; Infielder, outfielder Anaheim Angels, 2002—04, LA Angels of Anaheim, 2005—. Recipient Cool Papa Bell award, Negro Leagues Baseball Mus., 2005. Achievements include member of the World Series Championship winning Anaheim Angels, 2002; leading the American League in: stolen bases (62), 2005. Office: LA Angels of Anaheim Angels Stadium 2000 Gene Autry Way Anaheim CA 92806*

FIGLIN, ROBERT ALAN, hematologist, oncologist; b. Phila., June 22, 1949; s. Jack and Helen Figlin; 1 child, Jonathan B. BA in Chemistry, Temple U., Phila., 1970; postgrad. in inorganic chemistry, Temple U., 1972; MD, Med. Coll. Pa., 1976. Diplomate Am. Bd. Internal Medicine, Am. Bd. Med. Oncology, Nat. Bd. Med. Examiners; lic. physician, Calif. Med. intern, resident in medicine Cedars-Sinai Med. Ctr., LA, 1976-79, chief resident in medicine, 1979-80; fellow in hematology-oncology UCLA, 1980-82, dir., hematology-oncology fellowship program, divsn. hematology-oncology, dept. medicine, 1992—2003, co-dir., oncology program area divsn. hematology-oncology, dept. medicine, 1993—95; asst. prof. medicine, divsn. hematology-oncology, dept. medicine UCLA Sch. Medicine, 1982-88, assoc. prof., divsn. hematology-oncology, dept. medicine, 1988-94, med. dir., thoracic oncology program, dept. medicine and surgery, divsns. hematology-oncology and thoracic surgery, 1994—2006, med. dir., genitourinary oncology, dept. medicine and surgery, divsns. hematology-oncology and urology, 1995—2006, Henry Alvin and Carrie L. Meinhardt chair in urol. oncology, 2000—06; prof. medicine, divsn. hematology-oncology, dept. medicine UCLA David Geffen Sch. Medicine, 1994—2006, prof. clin. urology, divsn. urologic oncology, dept. urology, 2000—06; asst. dir., Bowyer Multidisciplinary Oncology Clinic Jonsson Comprehensive Cancer Ctr., UCLA, 1985—90, dir. Bowyer Oncology Ctr., dir. outpatient clin. rsch. unit, 1990-92, dir. clin. rsch. unit, 1993-98, dir. hematology/oncology fellowship program, 1995—2003, assoc. program dir., solid tumor oncology, 1996—97, program dir., solid tumor oncology, 1997—98, program dir., solid tumor develop. therapeutics, 1998—2001, co-dir., genitourinary oncology, 2004—06, co-dir., lung cancer rsch. program, 2005; assoc. dir. clin. rsch., Comprehensive Cancer Ctr. City of Hope, Duarte, Calif., 2006—, chair, divsn. med. oncology & exptl. therapeutics rsch., 2006—, Arthur and Rosalie Kaplan prof. med. oncology, 2006—, acting dir., Comprehensive Cancer Ctr., 2008—. Co-principal investigator, mem. exec. bd. Lung Cancer Study Group, UCLA, 1982—89; co-principal investigator, mem. genitourinary com., mem. kidney cancer subcommittee Eastern Cooperative Oncology Group, 1988—93; mem. exec. bd. UCLA Med./Surgical Oncology Ctr., 1989—95; FDA cons., 1990—92; prin. investigator UCLA S.W. Oncology Group, 1990—2000, mem. lung com., 1990—2003, bd. gov., 1990—2000, mem. genito-urinary com., 1990—2003; mem. med. adv. bd. Nat. Kidney Cancer Assn., 1993—; med. dir. U. Calif. Preferred Oncology Networks of Calif., 1994—95; sci. founder Agensys, 1996—; chmn. instl. rev. bd., mem. human rsch. policy bd. UCLA, 1998—; co-prin. investigator, clin. dir. NCI Specialized Program of Rsch. Excellence, Lung Cancer, 2000—, NCI Bladder Cancer Prevention, 2003—06; co-dir. Lung Cancer Rsch. Program, 2003—; chmn. scientific adv. bd. Phase One Found., 2005—. Editor: Interferons in cytokines, 1988—90, Kidney Cancer Jour., 1993—94, Current Clin. Trials, 1992—96; UCLA Cancer Trials Newsletter, 1990—96, Seminars on Oncology-Kidney Cancer, 1995, Cancer Therapeutics, 1997, Cancer Biotherapy and Radio Pharms., 1997; contbr. articles and revs.; editor: Renal & Adrenal Tumors, 2002, Kidney Cancer Jour., 2003—. Named one of Best Doctors in Am., 1994-, America's Top Doctors for Cancer 2006. Fellow ACP, Internat. Soc. for Biologic Therapy; mem. Am. Soc. Clin. Oncology, Am. Fedn. Clin. Rsch., Am. Assn. for Cancer Rsch., Soc. for Biologic Therapy (chmn. ann. scientific meeting 1997, pres. cancer panel 1997, S.W. Oncology Group, Assn. Subspecialty Profs., Am. Urological Assn., Internat. Assn. for Study of Lung Cancer. Office: City of Hope 1500 E Duarte Rd Duarte CA 91010 Office Phone: 626-471-9290. Business E-Mail: rfiglin@coh.org.

FIGUEROA, FRANCISCO ARMANDO, aerospace defence executive, chief financial officer; b. Del Rio, Tex., Feb. 4, 1945; s. Armando Garz and Flavia (Aldrete) F.; m. Sharon Marie Sanislo, Dec. 14, 1968; children: Derek Armando, Adam Joseph. BSEE, Tex. Tech. U., 1967; MS in Astronautics, Air Force Inst. Tech., 1969; MS in Systems Mgmt., USC, 1973; postgrad., Indsl. Coll. Armed Forces, Fort McNair, DC, 1983-84. PMP;CPA;CFP. USAF Officer, 1967-1987, commissioned 2nd Lt in Lubbock, Texas. Commd. officer USAF, 1967, advanced to lt. col., various positions, 1969-79; staff officer Pentagon, Arlington, Va., 1979-83; mgmt. dir. HQ SD, Denver, 1984-86, ops. dir., 1986-87; ret. USAF, 1987; former bus. mgr. Martin Marietta, Denver, 1987; owner F.A. Figueroa, CPA, Aurora, Colo., 1984—; now v.p., bus. mgmt. & facilities svc, CFO Sandia Nat. Labs., Albuquerque. Test Engr. and Launch Contr., Vandenberg AFB, Calif. 1969-1974, Chief Launch Integrations and Chief Fin. Mgmt AFS, Calif., 1974-1979, Pentagon Staff Officer and Chief Mgmt. Support Office, Washington, DC, 1979-1983, Dir.Mgmt. and Dir. Operations, Buckley AFB, Colo., 1984-1987, V.P. Infrastructure Svc. and Bus. Mgmt. chief Fin. Officer, Sandia Nat. Lab. Albuquerque, New Mexico, 1997-2007, Pres.and Gen. Mgr., Mission Support Alliance, Richland, Washington, 2007-. V.p. Lompoc (Calif.) Chpt. Jaycees, 1970-72; mem. Community Svcs. Commn., Denver, 1992—. Recipient Hispanic Engring. Nat.Achievement award for Mgmt. excellence, 2002; named Disting. Engr., Tex. Tech U., 2006; named one of 50 Most Important Hispanics in Govt., Edn., Hispanic Engineer and Info. Tech. mag., 2005. Mem. PMI, AICPA, AIAA, Colo. Soc. CPAs, Air Force Assn., Tau Beta Pi, Eta Kappa Nu. Avocations: reading, writing, poetry, mountain climbing, running. Home: PO Box 11337 Albuquerque NM 87192-0337 Office: Sandia Nat Labs PO Box 5800 Albuquerque NM 87185 also: 1981 Synder St Richland WA 99354 Office Phone: 209-376-1310.

FIGUEROA, GUILLERMO, conductor; Studied under Pablo Casals; studied under Oscar Shumsky, Felix Galimir, Juilliard Sch; tng., Conservatory of Music, PR. Music dir. New Mex. Symphony, 2001—, PR Symphony Orch., 2001—07, prin. guest conductor, 2007—. Guest conductor Iceland Symphony, NJ Symphony, N.Mex. Symphony, Orquestra Sinfonica do Teatro Municipal, Ballet Memphis, Cayuga Chmaber Orch., N.Y.C. Ballet, El Salvador Symphony, Rio de Janeiro. Conductor Colo. Symphony, Kansas City Symphony, Iceland Symphony, Four Seasons, (collaborated) with Janos Starker, Vladimir Feltsman, Glenn Dicterow, Horacio Guttierrez, Paul Neubauer, concertmaster N.Y.C. Ballet Orch., 1992, soloist (violin concerts) Brahms, Berg, Glass, Barber, Mikhail Baryshnikov, Deutsche Grammophon, Reverie, Bourgeois Getilhomme, Violin Concerto, Duo Fantasy, Synchronisms No.9; musician: Scherzo-Tarantelle, Liebesleid, Concertino for violin and chamber orch., premiere of John Adams' violin concert, premiere of two sonatas for violin and piano written by German Caceres, perfomed with Houston de Camera Latin Am. Festival, Music in the Vineyard Chamber music festival, Pro Arts Chamber Music Soc. Recipient Victor Herbert prize, Julliard Sch., 1st prize, Washington Internat. Competition, 1979. Mem.: Orpheus Chamber Orch. (concertmaster, soloist U.S., Europe, Asia). Office: N Mex Symphony Orch 4407 Menaul Blvd NE Albuquerque NM 87110

FIGUEROA, LIZ, former state senator; b. San Francisco; children: AnaLisa, Aaron. Student, Coll. San Mateo. Owner, oeprator Figueroa Employment Cons., 1981-98; mem. Union Sanitary Dist., pres., 1985; mem. Calif. State Senate, 1998—2007, mem. bus. and professions com.; mem. Calif. Unemployment Ins. Appeals Bd., 2007—. Mem. Hispanic Cmty. Affairs Coun.; mem. Fermont Adult Sch. Adv. Bd.; bd. dirs. Legal Assistance for Srs.; local bd. dirs. Selective Svc. Sys.; mem. adv. bd. Peninsula Coll. Law. Named Outstanding Legislator by several orgns. Mem. Calif. Elected Women's Assn. for Edn. and Rsch. (bd. dirs.). Democrat. Office: Calif State Senate State Capitol Rm 2057 Sacramento CA 95814 also: Liz Figueroa Senator 43801 Mission Blvd Ste 103 Fremont CA 94539-6217

FILIPPENKO, ALEXEI VLADIMIR, astrophysicist, educator; b. Oakland, Calif., July 25, 1958; s. Vladimir Ivan and Alexandra (Karmansky) F.; m. Diana Louise Lee, Aug. 5, 1989; children: Zoe, Simon. BA in Physics, U. Calif., Santa Barbara, 1979; PhD in Astronomy, Calif. Inst. Tech., 1984. Asst. prof. astronomy U. Calif., Berkeley, 1986-88, assoc. prof. astronomy, 1988-92, prof. astronomy, 1992—. Lectr. in field. Co-author (with Jay M. Pasachoff): The Cosmos: Astronomy in the New Millennium, 2001; contbr. articles to profl. jours. Recipient Robert M. Petrie prize, Can. Astron. Soc., 1997, Guggenheim fellow, 2001, US Professors of Yr. Award for Outstanding Doctoral and Rsch. Universities Prof., Carnegie Found. for Advancement of Tchg. and Coun. for Advancement and Support of Edn., 2006, Richtmyer Meml. Award, Am. Assn. Physics Tchrs., 2007; named Presdl. Young Investigator, NSF, 1989—94; Miller fellow, U. Calif., Berkeley, 1984—86, rsch. fellow astronomy, Calif. Tech. Inst., 1984. Mem. Am. Astron. Soc. (Newton Lacy Pierce prize 1992), Astron. Soc. Pacific, Internat. Astron. Union. Achievements include discovery of new type of exploding str; found that many nearby galaxies show low-level nonstellar activity similar to that of quasars; discovery of several probable black holes in the milky way galaxy; contributed to the discovery that the expansion of the universe appears to be accelerating; development of a robotic telescope. Office: U Calif Dept Astronomy 439 Campbell Hall Berkeley CA 94720-3411 Office Phone: 510-642-1813. Fax: 510-642-3411. E-mail: alex@astro.berkeley.edu.

FILIPPOU, FILIP C., engineering educator; b. Thessaloniki, Greece, July 14, 1955; m. Lucia L. Longhi, 1984; children: Pauline, Romina. Diploma, Tech. U., Munich, Germany, 1978; PhD in Civil Engring., U. Calif., Berkeley, 1983. Asst. prof. U. Calif., Berkeley, 1983-89, assoc. prof. structural engring., 1989-98, prof. structural engring., 1998—, dept. vice chair for rsch. and tech. support, 1999—2003, Roy W. Carlson Disting. Prof. of civil engring., 2004—. Engr. Tylin Int, 1983-84; NSF presdl. young investigator, 1987; vis. prof. U. Rome, Italy, 1988, Ecole Normale Superieure, Cachan, France, 1999, 2000. Fellow Am. Concrete Inst.; mem. ASCE (Alfred Noble prize 1988, Walter L. Huber Civil Engring. rsch. prize 1994), Prestressed Concrete Inst., Earthquake Engring. Rsch. Inst. Achievements include research in analysis and behavior of reinforced and prestressed concrete structures under normal and extreme loadings;

development of models and effective simulation strategies; design guidelines for structures, particularly, under earthquake loads. Office: U Calif Dept Civil Engring 731 Davis Hall Berkeley CA 94720-1711 E-mail: filippou@ce.berkeley.edu.

FILNER, BOB (ROBERT FILNER), United States Representative from California; b. Pitts., Sept. 4, 1942; m. Jane Merrill; children: Erin, Adam. BA in Chemistry, Cornell U., 1963; MA in Hist., U. Del., 1969; PhD in Hist., Cornell U., 1973. Prof. hist. San Diego State U., 1970-92; legis. asst. to Senator Hubert Humphrey US Senate, 1974; legis. asst. to Rep.Don Fraser US Congress, 1975, spl. asst. to Rep. Jim Bates, 1984; city councilman 8th dist. City of San Diego, 1987-92, dep. mayor, 1992; mem. US Congress from 50st Calif. dist., 1993—2003, US Congress from 51st Calif. dist., 2003—; chmn. US House Veterans Affairs Com., 2007—; mem. US House Transp. & Infrastructure. Mem. San Diego Bd. Edn., 1979—83, pres., 1982; chmn. San Diego Schs. of Future Commn., 1986—87; mem. Econ. Conversion Coun., Nat. Writing Project, Common Cause; exec. com. Dem. Study Grp.; co-chair US-Philippines Caucus. Mem.: NAACP, Navy League, Mex. Am. Polit. Assn., Am. Civil Liberties Union, Anti-Defamation League, Freedom Riders, Gray Panthers, Sierra Club. Democrat. Jewish. Office: US Congress 2428 Rayburn House Office Bldg Washington DC 20515-0551 also: Ste A 333 F St Chula Vista CA 91910 also: Ste D 1101 Airport Rd Imperial CA 92251 Office Phone: 619-422-5963, 760-355-8800. Office Fax: 619-422-7290, 760-355-8802.*

FILO, DAVID, Internet company executive; b. Moss Bluff, La. BS in Computer Engring., Tulane U.; MSEE, Stanford U., 1990, PhD studies in Elec. Engring. Co-creator online navigational guide Yahoo!, Calif., 1994—; co-founder, chief Yahoo! Inc., Calif., 1995—, dir., 1995—96. Co-author (with Jerry Yang, Karen Heyman): (books) Yahoo! Unplugged: Your Discovery Guide to the Webb, 1995; co-author: (with Richard Raucci, Elizabeth Crane, Jerry Yang) Yahoo-ligans!: Way Cool Web Sites, 1996. Named one of 400 Richest Americans, Forbes mag., 2004, 2005, 2006; named one of 50 Most Important People on the Web, PC World, 2007. Named company YAHOO! (acronym for Yet Another Hierarchical Officious Oracle). Office: Yahoo! Inc 701 First Ave Sunnyvale CA 94089

FILOSA, GARY FAIRMONT RANDOLPH, II, film and television producer; b. Wilder, Vt., Feb. 22, 1931; s. Gary F.R. de Marco de Varra and Rosaline M. (Falzaran) F.; m. Catherine Moray Stewart (dec.); children: Marc Christian Bazire de Villadon III, Gary Fairmont Randolph de Varra III. Grad., Mt. Hermon Sch., 1950; PhB, U. Chgo., 1954; BA, U. Americas, Mex., 1967; MA, Calif. Western U., 1968; PhD, U.S. Internat. U., 1970. Sports reporter Claremont Daily Eagle, Rutland Herald, Vt. Informer, 1947-52; pub. The Chicagoan, 1950—54; account exec., editor house publs. Robertson, Buckley & Gotsch, Inc., Chgo., 1953-54; account exec. Fuller, Smith & Ross, Inc., NYC, 1955; prodr./host Weekend KCET Channel 13, NYC, 1956—67; editor Apparel Arts mag. (now Gentlemen's Quar.), Esquire, Inc., NYC, 1955-56; chmn. bd., CEO, pres. Filosa Publs. Internat., NYC, 1957—65; pub. Teenage, Rustic Rhythm, Teen Life, Mystery Digest, Top Talent, Rock & Roll Roundup, Celebrities, Stardust, Personalities, Campus monthly mags.; pres., chmn. bd. Teenarama Records, Inc., NYC, 1956-62; chmn. bd., pres. Producciones Mexicanes Internationales (S.A.), Mexico City, 1958—70; assoc. pub. Laundromatic Age, NYC, 1958-59; ptnr. with Warner LeRoy purchase of Broadway plays for Hollywood films, NYC, 1958—64; pres. Montclair Sch., 1958-60, Pacific Registry, Inc., LA, 1959-61; exec. prodr. Desilu Studios, Inc., Hollywood, Calif., 1958—62; exec. asst. to Benjamin A. Javits, 1963—64; propr. Gino's of Hollywood, 1961-70; dean adminstrn. Postgrad. Ctr. for Mental Health, NYC, 1962-64; chmn. bd., CEO Filosa Films Internat., Glendale, Calif., 1962—; pres. Amateur Athletes Internat., Iowa City, 1996-2000; chmn. bd., pres. Cinematografica Americana Internationale (S.A.), Mexico City, 1964-84; pres. Casa Filosa Corp., Palm Beach, Fla., 1982-87; dir. Cmty. Savs., North Palm Beach, Fla., 1982-87. V.p. acad. affairs World Acad., San Francisco, 1967-68; asst. to provost Calif. Western U., San Diego, 1968-69; assoc. prof. philosophy Art Coll., San Francisco, 1969-70; v.p. acad. affairs, dean of faculty Internat. Inst., Phoenix, 1968-73; chmn. bd. dirs., pres. Universite Universelle, 1970-73, 2000-03; bd. dirs., v.p. acad. affairs, dean Summer Sch., Internat. C.C., L.A., 1970-72; chmn. bd., pres. Social Directory Calif., 1967-75, Am. Assn. Social Registries, L.A., 1970-76; pres. Social Directory U.S., N.Y.C., 1974-76; pres. Herbert Hoover Forum, Iowa City, 1996-2000; chmn. bd. dirs. Internat. Soc. Social Registers, Paris, 1974-2007; surfing coach U. Calif. at Irvine, 1975-77; v.p. Xerox-Systemic, 1979-80; CEO Internat. Surfing League, Palm Beach, 1987-95, Santa Barbara, Calif., 1996—; pres. Amateur Athletes Internat., Iowa City; internat. syndicated columnist Conservations with Am., 1997-. Editor: Sci. Digest, 1961-62; composer: (lyrics) The Night Discovers Love, 1952, That Certain Something, 1953, Bolero of Love, 1956; author: (stage play) Let Me Call Ethel, 1955, The Bisexual, 1961, Technology Enters 21st Century, 1966, (mus.) Feather Light, 1966, No Public Funds for Nonpublic Schools, 1968, Creative Function of the College President, 1969, The Surfers Almanac, 1977, The Filosa Newsletter, 1986-92, The Sexual Continuum, 1990, Traveltalk, 1991, God's Own Prince, 1995, Holy Hawai'i, 1996, (biography) A Plague on Paradise, 1994, (TV series) Danny Thomas Show, 1963, Surfing USA, 1977, Payne of Florida, 1985, rev. new series, 2007, Honolulu, 1991, The Gym, 1992, Sales Pitch, 1992, 810 Ocean Avenue, 1992, One Feather, 1992, Conversations with America, 1989, All American Beach Party, 1989, Riding High, 2000, Dreamsport, 2000, Icons, 2000; contbr. numerous articles, editorials, to profl. jours., newspapers, and encys., including Life, Look, Sci. Digest, Ency. of Sports, World Book Ency., New York Times, Cedar Rapids Gazete, L.A. Times, others. Trustee Univ. of the Ams., Pueblo, Mex., 1986-2000; candidate for L.A. City Coun., 1959; chmn. Educators for Re-election of Ivy Baker Pirest, 1970; mem. So. Calif. Com. for Olympic Games, 1977-84. With AUS, 1954-55. Recipient DAR Citizenship award, 1959, Silver Conquistador award Am. Assn. Social Registers, 1970, Ambassador's Cup U. Ams., 1967, resolution Calif. State Legis., 1977, Duke Kahanamoku Classic surfing trophy, 1977, gold pendant Japan Surfing Assn., 1978, Father of Olympic Surfing award Internat. Athletic Union, 1995, Father of Surfing trophy Amateur Athletes Internat., 1997, Father of Surfing trophy Internat. Surfing Fedn., 2000; inducted into Rock & Roll Mus. & Hall of Fame, Cleve., 1995. Mem. NAACP, NCAA (bd. dels. 1977-82), AAU (gov. 1978-82), Am. Acad. Motion Picture Arts and Scis., Internat. Surfing Com., U.S. Surfing Com. (founder 1960—), Internat. Surfing League (founder, chmn., CEO 1988—), Internat. Surfing Fedn. (pres. 1960—), Am. Assn. UN, Authors League, Authors Guild, Alumni Assn. U. Ams. (pres. 1967-70), Surf Club of the Palm Beaches (pres. 1983-94), Sierra Club, Surfing Hui of Hawaii, Internat. Soc. Bibliotherapists (Paris, pres. 1997-2007), Lords Corybantes (Berlin) (life pres. 1966—), Commonwealth Club (San Francisco), Town Hall (L.A.), Calif. Club (L.A.), Palm Beach Surf Club, Sigma Omicron Lambda (founder, pres. 1965-92). Episcopalian. Office: PO Box 251324 Glendale CA 91225-1324 Business E-Mail: ffilm@att.net.

FILS-AIME, REGGIE, electronics executive; b. Brentwood, NY, Mar. 25, 1961; divorced; 3 children. BS in Applied Economics, Cornell U., Ithaca, NY, 1983. With Proctor and Gamble, 1983—91; sr. dir. Panda Mgmt. Co.; sr. dir. nat. mktg. Pizza Hut; US mktg. chief Guiness Import Co.; chief mktg. officer, acting mng. dir. UK ops. Derby Cycle Corp.; sr. v.p. mktg. VH1 MTV Networks, 2001—03; exec. v.p. sales, mktg. Nintendo of Am., Inc., Redmond, Wash., 2003—06, pres., COO, 2006—. Recipient Clio, 2 Gold EFFFIES, NY Am. Mktg. Assn., award for Advertising Excellence, AICP, Silver Edison, Am. Mktg. Inst.; named Grand Marketer of Yr., BrandWeek, 2007; named to Mktg. 100, Advertising Age, 1998. Achievements include first American to hold the position of President, COO at Nintendo of America. Home: Nintendo of Am Inc 4820 150th Ave NE Redmond WA 98052

FINBERG, JAMES MICHAEL, lawyer; b. Balt., Sept. 6, 1958; s. Laurence and Harriet (Levinson) Finberg; m. Melanie Piech; children: Joseph, John. BA, Brown U., 1980; JD, U. Chgo., 1983. Bar: Calif. 1984, U.S. Dist. Ct. (no. dist.) Calif. 1984, U.S. Dist. Ct. (ea. dist.) Calif. 1987, U.S. Ct. Appeals (9th and fed. cirs.) 1987, U.S. Dist. Ct. Hawaii, 1988, U.S. Supreme Ct. 1994. Law clk. to assoc. justice Mich. Supreme Ct., 1983-84; assoc. Feldman, Waldman and Kline, San Francisco, 1984-87, Morrison and Foerster, 1987-90; ptnr. Lieff, Cabraser, Heimann & Bernstein, L.L.P., San Francisco, 1991—2006, Altshuler Berzon, San Francisco, 2007—. Mem. adv. com. local rules for securities cases US Dist. Ct., Calif., 1996; lawyer rep. to 9th Jud. Conf., 1999-2001; chair No. Calif. del. 2000-01; adj. law prof. Hastings College of Law. Exec. editor U. Chgo. Law Rev., 1982-83. Bd. mem. Legal Aid Soc. / Employment Law Ctr. San Francisco, 2006—. Named Lawyer of Yr., Calif., 2009; named one of Best Lawyers in Am., 2005—08, Top 100 Superlawyers in San Francisco Bay Area, 2005—09, Top 100 Lawyers in Calif., 2006. Fellow: Am. Coll. Labor and Employment Lawyers; mem.: ACLU (bd. dirs. No. Calif. chpt. 1995), ABA (chmn. securities subcom. class and derivative action com. 1998—2006, plaintiff's program chair equal employment opportunity com. 1999—2001), U. Chgo. Law Sch. (bd. dirs. 2008—), Lawyers Com. for Civil Rights of San Francisco Bay Area (fin. chmn. 1992—95, bd. dirs. 1992—98, sec. 1996, co-chmn. 1997—98, bd. 2008—), Calif. Bar Assn. (mem. standing com. on legal svcs. to poor 1990—94, vice-chmn. 1993—94), Bar Assn. San Francisco (jud. evaluation com. 1994, bd. dirs. 1999—2000, sec. 2002, treas. 2003, pres.-elect. 2004, pres. 2005). Office: Altshuler Berzon 177 Post St Ste 300 San Francisco CA 94108 Office Phone: 415-421-7151. Business E-Mail: jfinberg@altshulerberzon.com.

FINCH, CALEB ELLICOTT, neurobiologist, educator; b. London, July 4, 1939; came to U.S., 1939; s. Benjamin F. and Faith (Stratton) Campbell; m. Doris Nossamen, Oct. 11, 1975; stepsons: Michael, Alec Tsongas. BS, Yale U., 1961; PhD, Rockefeller U., 1969. Guest investigator Rockefeller U., NYC, 1969-70; asst. prof. Cornell U. Med. Coll., NYC, 1970-72; asst. prof. biology, gerontology U. So. Calif., LA, 1972-75, assoc. prof., 1975-78, prof., 1978—, ARCO and William Kieschnick prof. neurobiology of aging, 1985—, Univ. prof., 1989—. Mem. edit. bd. Jour. Gerontology, 1979-86, Neurobiology of Aging, 1982—, Synapse, 1992—, Exp. Gerontol., 1997—; contbr. more than 350 articles to profl. jours.; author: Longevity, Senescence and the Genome, 1990, (with R. Ricklefs) Aging: A Natural History, 1995, (with T. Kirkwood) Chance, Development and Aging, 2000. Recipient Allied Signal Inc. award Achievement in Biomed. Aging, 1988, Rsch. award Alzheimer's Assn. L.A., 1989, Am. Aging Assn., 1994, Cherkin award UCLA, 1991, Sandoz Premier prize IAG, 1996, prize for longevity rsch. IPSEN Found., 1996, award for leadership in comms. IASIA, 1996, Irving Wright award AFAR, 1999; NIH rsch. grantee, 1972—. Fellow AAAS, Gerontol. Soc. Am. (chmn. biology sect. 1992-93, Robert W. Kleemeier award 1984); mem. Neurosci. Soc., Endocrine Soc., Neuroendocrine Soc., Psychoneuroendocrine Soc., Iron Mountain String Band (fiddler 1963—). Home: 2144 Crescent Dr Altadena CA 91001-2112 Office: U So Calif Gerontology Ctr University Park Los Angeles CA 90007

FINCHER, DAVID, film director and producer; b. Denver, Aug. 28, 1962; m. Donya Fiorentino (div.); 1 child. With Industrial Light & Magic, 1981—83; co-founder Propaganda Films, 1987. Dir.: (films) Alien 3, 1992, Seven, 1995, The Game, 1997, The Fight Club, 1999, Panic Room, 2002, Zodiac, 2007, The Curious Case of Benjamin Button, 2008 (Best Dir. Nat. Bd. Review, 2008, Dir. of Yr., London Film Critics' Cir. Awards, 2009); (music videos) Don Henley, Sting, The Wallflowers, Paula Abdul, Aerosmith, Madonna, Michael Jackson, George Michael, Rolling Stones (Grammy award for best music video "Love is Strong", 1995), Steve Winwood, The Motels, Iggy Pop, Billy Idol, A Perfect Circle; exec. prodr. (films) Ambush, 2001, Chosen, 2001, The Follow, 2001, Star, 2001, Powder Keg, 2001, The Ticker, 2002, Lords of Dogtown, 2005, Love and Other Disasters, 2006; dir. (TV commericals) for Nike, Coca-Cola, Budweiser, Heinekin, Pepsi, Levi's, Converse, AT & T, and Chanel. Office: c/o Anonymous Content 3532 Hayden Ave Culver City CA 90232

FINDLEY, JOHN ALLEN, JR., publishing executive; b. Fulton, Mo., Feb. 25, 1951; s. John Allen and Naomi Joan (Reker) F.; m. Oneida Lynn Blackwell, Dec. 4, 1993; children: John III, Hugh. AB, Westminster Coll., 1973. Sales rep. Kingdom Daily News, Fulton, 1973-74; advt. dir. Colo. Daily, Boulder, 1973-74; advt. sales rep. Dallas Times Herald, 1976-77, advt. sales mgr., 1977-80, dir. consumer mktg., 1981-83, dir. circulation, 1983, dir. retail advt., 1983-84; regional sales mgr. Times Mirror Nat. Mktg., 1984-86; v.p. mktg. So. Conn. Newspapers, Stamford, 1986-88, sr. v.p. mktg. and prodn., 1989-93; pres. Charleston (W.Va.) Newspapers, 1993-97; pub., CEO Long Beach (Calif.) Press-Telegram, 1998—2001; v.p. newspaper rels. Parade Mag., LA, 2002—03, sr. v.p., 2003—. Bd. govs. Calif. State U., Long Beach; bd. dirs. Long Beach Found., Long Beach Venture Forum, Nat. Conf. Cmty. and Justice. Mem. Newspaper Assn. Am., Internat. Newspaper Promotion Assn., Sigma Chi. Office: 6300 Wilshire Blvd Los Angeles CA 90048

FINE, ARTHUR I., philosopher, educator; b. Lowell, Mass., Nov. 11, 1937; s. David Fine and Rae (Silverberg) Mintz; m. Helen S. Feldberg, June 16, 1957 (div. May 1980); children: Dana S. Mintz, Sharon D. Mintz; m. Micky Forbes, July 11, 1980. Student, Harvard U., 1955-56; BS, U. Chgo., 1958; MS, Ill. Inst. Tech., 1960; PhD, U. Chgo., 1963. Asst. prof. math and philosophy Ill. Inst. Tech., Chgo., 1961—63; asst. prof. philosophy U. Ill., Urbana, 1963—65; assoc. prof. philosophy Cornell U., Ithaca, NY, 1967—71, prof. philosophy, 1971—72, U. Ill., Chgo., 1972—82, Northwestern U., Evanston, Ill., 1982—85, John Evans prof. philosophy, 1985—2001; prof. philosophy U. Wash., Seattle, 2001—, adj. prof. physics, 2003—, adj. prof. history, 2003—. Mem. nat. com. Internat. Union History and Philosophy Sci. NAS, 1973—77; mem. adv. panel History and Philosophy Sci. NSF, 1975—77, 1987—88, 1992—93. Author: The Shaky Game, 1986, 2d edit., 1996; co-editor: Philosophical Rev., 1969—71; editor (with others): PSA, 1986, PSA, vols. I and II, 1990; subject editor: Philosophy fo Science Routledge Encyclopedia of Philosophy, 1993—98; contbr. articles to profl. jours. Fellow, Ctr. Advanced Study Behavioral Scis. Stanford, 1985—86; NSF fellow, 1966—67, NSF grantee, 1968, 1973, 1978, 1980, 1989, sr. fellow, NEH, 1974—75, Gugenheim fellow, 1982—83, vis. fellow, Dibner Inst., MIT, 1996. Mem.: Am. Philos. Assn. (ctrl. divsn. pres. 1997—98), Philosophy Sci. Assn. (pres. 1986—88). Office: U Wash Philosophy Dept Box 353350 Seattle WA 98195-3350 Business E-Mail: afine@u.washington.edu.

FINE, CHARLES LEON, lawyer; b. Waukegan, Ill., Jan. 30, 1932; s. David M. and Henrietta (Goodman) F.; m. Penny J. Haines, Aug. 30, 1958; children: Karen L., Andrew H. BS, U. Wis., 1955; LLB, JD, Am. U., 1961. Bar: Mich. 1962, Ariz. 1981, U.S. Supreme Ct. 1971. Newscaster, news editor WKOW Radio and TV, Madison, Wis., 1953-58; editor, writer U.S. Bur. Pub. Roads, Washington, 1958-61; trial, staff atty. U.S. NLRB, Washington, Detroit, 1961-63; atty, assoc. Griffith & Griffith law firm, Detroit, 1963-69; atty., ptnr. Clark, Hardy, Lewis & Fine, Detroit, Birmingham, 1969-81; assoc. prof. law U. Detroit Sch. Law, 1976-80; ptnr. O'Connor, Cavanagh, et al, Phoenix, 1981-96, Streich Lang, 1996-2000, Littler Mendelson, 2000—. Cons. Met. Detoit Bur. Sch. Studies, 1970-80, Employer's Assn. Detroit, 1970-80. Assoc. editor Washington Coll. Law Rev., 1960; co-editor, author: Ariz. Employment Law Handbook, 1994-; contbr. articles to legal jours. and chpts. to books. Mem. Ariz. Supreme Ct. Commn. on Minorities, 1996-2000; pres. Meadowlake Homeowners Assn., Birmingham, Mich., 1972-73; bd. dirs. Sch. Law Inst., Detroit, 1976-77; atty., advisor Gov.'s Office, Mich., 1979-80; cons. Cmty. Legal Svcs., Phoenix, 1986—. 1st lt. U.S. Army, 1955-57. Recipient Best Advocate award Nat. Moot Ct. Competition, Washington, 1960, Order of Barristers award Nat. Honor Soc., 1978; scholarship fund in his name U. Detroit Sch. of Law, 1979. Fellow Coll. Labor and Employment Lawyers; mem. Am. Employment Law Coun., Ariz. Bar Assn., Mich. Bar Assn., Am. Arbitration Assn. (arbitrator, employment arbitration panelist 1995—), Ariz. Insl. Rels. Assn. Avocations: badminton, hiking, swimming, reading. Home: 9041 N 33rd Way Phoenix AZ 85028-4968 Office: Littler Mendelson 2425 E Camelback Rd Ste 900 Phoenix AZ 85016 Office Phone: 602-996-6697. E-mail: CFINE@Littler.com.

FINE, JAMES STEPHEN, physician; b. St. Paul, June 14, 1946; s. Ralph Irving and Beverlee Lois (Rockler) F.; m. Meredith Ann Blehert, June 20, 1970; children: Zachary, Esther, Gabriel. BA in Math., U. Minn., 1968, MD, 1972, MS in Biometry, Health Info. Systems, 1977. Intern in medicine St. Paul-Ramsey Hosp., 1972-73; residency U. Minn., Mpls., 1973-77; assoc. prof., dir. info. and specimen processing div. U. Wash. Hosp., Seattle, 1977-94, chmn. lab. medicine, 1994—. CIO U. Wash. Medicine, Seattle, 2005—. Mem. Am. Assn. Clin. Chemistry, Acad. Clin. Lab. Physicians and Scientists (Gerald T. Evans award 2001), Computer Soc. IEEE, Assn. Pathology (chmn.), Am. Med. Informatics Assn., Wash. State Med. Assn., King County Med. Soc. Office: U Wash Med Ctr Box 357110 1959 NE Pacific Ave NW 120 Seattle WA 98195-7110 Home Phone: 206-323-8417; Office Phone: 206-598-6137. Business E-Mail: jsfine@u.washington.edu.

FINE, MARJORIE LYNN, lawyer; b. Bklyn., Aug. 14, 1950; m. John Kent Markley, May 6, 1979; children: Jessica Paige Markley, Laura Anne Markley. BA, Smith Coll., 1972; JD, U. Calif., 1977. Bar: Calif. 1977. Assoc. to ptnr. Donahue Gallagher Woods, Oakland, Calif., 1977-87; sr. counsel Bank of Am., San Francisco, 1987-89; assoc., gen. counsel Shaklee Corp., San Francisco, 1989-90; gen. counsel, v.p. Shaklee U.S., Inc., San Francisco, 1990-94, Shaklee U.S., Shaklee Technica, 1995-99, Yamanouchi Pharma Techs., Inc., 1999-2001; gen. counsel, sr. v.p. Shaklee Corp., 2001—05, gen. counsel, exec. v.p., sec., 2005—. Judge pro tem Oakland Piedmont Emeryville Mcpl. Ct., 1982-89; fee arbitrator Alameda Co. Bar Assn., 1980-87. Mem. ABA, Calif. Bar Assn., Calif. Employment Law Coun. (bd. dirs. 1993-03, 05—). Jewish. Office: Shaklee Corp 4747 Willow Rd Pleasanton CA 94588-2740

FINE, RICHARD ISAAC, lawyer; b. Milw., Jan. 22, 1940; s. Jack and Frieda F.; m. Maryellen Olman, Nov. 25, 1982; 1 child, Victoria Elizabeth. BS, U. Wis., Madison, 1961; JD, U. Chgo., 1964; PhD in Internat. Law, U. London, 1967; diplôme supérieur in Comparative Law, Faculté Internat. pour l'Enseignment du Droit Comparé, Strasbourg, France, 1967. Bar: Ill. 1964, DC 1972, Calif. 1973, cert.: Internat. U. Comparative Sci. (comparative law) 1965, Hague Acad. Internat. Law, The Netherlands (pvt. internat. law) 1965, Hague Acad. Internat. Law, The Netherlands 1966. Trial atty. fgn. commerce sect. antitrust divsn. US Dept. Justice, 1968-72; chief antitrust divsn. LA City Atty.'s Office, also spl. counsel gov. efficiency com., 1973-74; prof. internat., comparative and EEC antitrust law U. Syracuse Law Sch. (overseas program), NY, 1970-72; individual practice Richard I. Fine and Assocs., LA, 1974—. Mem. antitrust adv. bd. Bur. Nat. Affairs, 1981—; bd. dirs. Am. Friends London Sch. Econ. and Polit. Sci., 1984—, chmn. So. Calif. chpt., 1984—2005, chmn. LA adv. com.; mem. internat. cir. LA World Affairs Coun., 1990—, founder internat. cir.; vis. com. U. Chgo. Law Sch., 1992—95. Contbr. articles to legal publs. Bd. dirs. Retinitis Pigmentosa Internat., 1985-90, Citizens Island Bridge Co., Ltd., 1992-; founder LA Music Ctr. Named Atty. of the Decades, Calif. Black Rep. Women's Coun. and Judea-Christian Alliance, 2006. Mem. ABA (chmn. subcom. internat. antitrust and trade regulation, internat. law sect. 1972-77, co-chmn. com. internat. econ. orgn. 1977-79), ATLA, Am. Soc. Internat. Law (co-chmn. com. corp. membership 1978-83, exec. coun. 1984-87, budget com. 1992-97, regional coord. for L.A. 1994—, 1995 ann. program com. 1994-95, corr. editor Internat. Legal Materials 1983—), Am. Fgn. Law Assn., Internat. Law Assn., Brit. Inst. Internat. and Comparative Law, State Bar Calif. (chmn. antitrust and trade regulation law sect. 1981-84, exec. com. 1981-87), L.A. County Bar Assn. (chmn. antitrust sect. 1977-78, exec. com. sect. internat. law 1993—, treas. 1997, chmn. 2003-04), Ill. Bar Assn., Phi Delta Phi. Office: Ste 200 468 N Camden Dr Beverly Hills CA 90210 Home Phone: 818-996-8512; Office Phone: 310-277-5833. Business E-Mail: rifinelaw@earthlink.net.

FINEGAN, COLE, lawyer; b. Tulsa, Oct. 1, 1956; s. Philip Cole and Margaret (Hudson) F.; m. Robin Fudge, Dec. 29, 1984; children: Jordan Nicole, Ryan Andrew. BA in English, U. Notre Dame, Ind., 1978; JD, Georgetown U., 1987. Legis. asst., adminstrv. asst. Ctrl. Dist.-1st Dist. Okla., Tulsa and Washington, 1978-87; assoc. Brownstein Hyatt Farber & Strickland, Denver, 1987-91, shareholder, 1993—2003; dir. Office Policy and Initiatives Gov. State of Colo., Denver, 1991-93; city atty. City and County, Denver, 2003—06; atty. Hogan & Hartson LLP, Denver, 2007—. Chief of staff to Mayor John W. Hichinloafer, 2005—. Staff mem. The Tax Lawyer, 1984-86. Bd. mem. Greater Denver Corp., 1993-96, State Bd. of Agr., 1997-98, I Have A Dream Found.; bd. trustees State Colls. Colo., 1993-97; bd. mem. Auvaria Higher Edn. Commn., 1993-95; co-chair Downtown Denver Area Plan. Mem.: Urban Land Inst. Democrat. Roman Catholic. Home: 1934 Forest Pkwy Denver CO 80220-1337 Office: Hogan & Hartson LLP One Tabor Ctr Ste 1500 1200 Seventeenth St Denver CO 80202 Office Phone: 720-865-8600. Fax: 303-899-7333; Office Fax: 720-865-8796. E-mail: city.attorney@ci.denver.co.us.

FINEGOLD, SYDNEY MARTIN, microbiology educator; b. NYC, Aug. 12, 1921; s. Samuel Joseph and Jennie (Stein) F.; m. Mary Louise Saunders, Feb. 8, 1947 (dec. June 1994); children: Joseph, Patricia, Michael; m. Gloria Weiss, Feb. 18, 1996. AB, UCLA, 1943; MD, U. Tex., 1949. Diplomate: Am. Bd. Med. Microbiology (mem. bd. 1979-85), Am. Bd. Internal Medicine. Intern USPHS, Galveston, Tex., 1949-50; fellow in medicine U. Minn. Med. Sch., 1950-52, research fellow, 1951-52; resident medicine Wadsworth Hosp., VA Ctr., Los Angeles, 1953-54; instr. medicine U. Calif. Med. Ctr., Los Angeles, 1955-57, asst. clin. prof., 1957-59, asst. prof., 1959-62, assoc. prof., 1962-68, prof., 1968—2000, emeritus, 2000—, prof. microbiology and immunology, 1983—2000, emeritus, 2000—; chief chest and infectious disease sect. Wadsworth Hosp., 1957-61, chief infectious disease sect., 1961-86, assoc. chief staff for research and devel., 1986-92; staff physician infectious disease sect. VA Med. Ctr., LA, 1992—. Mem. pulmonary disease rsch. program com. VA, 1961-62, infectious disease rsch. program com., 1961-65, merit rev. bd. (infectious diseases), 1972-74, med. rsch. program specialist, 1974-76, adv. com. on infectious disease, 1974-87; mem. NRC-Nat. Acad. Sci. Drug Efficacy Study Group, 1966-69; mem. subcom. on gram-negative anaerobic bacilli Internat. Com. on Nomenclature Bacteria, 1966—, chmn., 1972-78; mem. adv. panel U.S. Pharmacopoeia, 1970-75; chmn. working group on anaerobic susceptibility test methods Nat. Com. Clin. Lab. Standards, 1987-97, advisor, 1998-2002. Mem. editl. bd. Calif. Medicine, 1966-73, Applied Microbiology, 1973-74, Western Jour. Medicine, 1974-77, Am. Rev. Respiratory Disease, 1974-76, Jour. Clin. Microbiology, 1975-85, Infection, 1976—, Jour. Infectious Disease, 1979-82, 84-85, Antimicrobial Agts. Chemotherapy, 1980-89, Diagnostic Microbiology and Infectious Diseases, 1982-90; editor Revs. of Infectious Diseases, 1990-91, Clin. Infectious Diseases, 1992-2000; sect. editor: infectious diseases vols. Clin. Medicine, 1978-82, Microbiol. Ecology in Health and Disease, 1987-90; assoc. editor, consulting editor Anaerobe, 1994—. editor-in-chief, 1998—. Vice chmn. UCLA Acad. Senate, 1986-87, chair, 1987-88. Served with USMCR, with USNR, 1943-46, to 1st. lt. AUS, 1952-53. Co-recipient V.A. William S. Middleton award for biomed. rsch., 1984; recipient Profl. Achievement award UCLA, 1987, Mayo Soley award Western Soc. Clin. Investigation, 1988, Disting. Alumnus award U. Tex. Med. Br., 1988, UCLA Med. Alumni Assn. Med. Scis. award, 1990, Hoechst Roussel award Am. Soc. Microbiology, 1992, medal Helsinki U., Finland, 1996, Lifetime Achievement award Infectious Disease Assn. Calif., 1995, Wm. H. Oldendorf Lifetime Achievement awrd VA Med. Ctr., 1996, Lifetime Achievement award Internat. Soc. Anaerobic Bacteriology, 1998, Lifetime Achievement award, Anaerobic Soc. America, 2006, Becton Dickinson award in Clin. Microbiology, 1999; organism named Finegoldia magna, 1999; new species named Alistipes finegoldii, 2003; new species named Bacteriology Finegoldii, 2006; Dickinson Emeritus proffessorship award, UCLA, 2007. Master ACP; fellow APHA, AAAS, Am. Acad. Microbiology, Infectious Diseases Soc. Am. (councilor 1976-79, pres.-elect 1980-81, pres. 1981-82, exec. com. 1980-83, Bristol award 1987, Soc. citation 1999); mem. Assn. Am. Physicians, Am. Soc. Microbiology (chmn. subcom. on taxonomy of Bacteroidaceae 1971-74, 1st annual Alex Sonnenwirth award 1986), Am. Thoracic Soc., Western Soc. Clin. Rsch., Western Assn. Physicians, Wadsworth Med. Alumni Assn. (past pres.), Anaerobe Soc. of the Ams. (interim pres. 1992-94, pres. 1994-96), Soc. Intestinal Microbiology Ecology and Disease (interim pres. 1982-83, pres. 1983-87), Va. Soc. Physician in Infectious Diseases (pres. 1986-88), Am. Fedn. Clin. Rsch., Sigma Xi, Alpha Omega Alpha. Democrat. Jewish. Office: Infectious Disease Sect VA Med Ctr Wilshire & Sawtelle Blvds Los Angeles CA 90073 Home: 13082 Mindanao Way #17 Marina Del Rey CA 90292 Office Phone: 310-268-3678. Personal E-mail: sidfinegol@aol.com.

FINGARETTE, HERBERT, philosopher, educator; b. Bklyn., Jan. 20, 1921; m. Leslie J. Swabacker, Jan. 23, 1945; 1 dau., Ann Hasse. BA, UCLA, 1947, PhD, 1949; LHD, St. Bonaventure U., 1993. Mem. faculty U. Calif.-Santa Barbara, 1948—, Phi Beta Kappa Romanell prof. philosophy, 1983—; William James lectr. religion Harvard U., 1971; W.T. Jones lectr. philosophy Pomona Coll., 1974; Evans-Wentz lectr. Oriental religions Stanford U., 1977; Gramlich lectr. human nature Dartmouth Coll., 1978; cons. NEH; Raphael Demos lectr. Vanderbilt U., 1985. Disting. tchr. U. Calif.-Santa Barbara, 1985, faculty rsch. lectr., 1977. Author: The Self in Transformation, 1963, On Responsibility, 1967, Self Deception, 1969, Confucius: The Secular as Sacred, 1972, The Meaning of Criminal Insanity, 1972, Mental Disabilities and Criminals Responsibility, 1979, Heavy Drinking: The Myth of Alcoholism as a Disease, 1988, Rules, Rituals, and Responsibility: Essays Dedicated to Herbert Fingarette, 1991, Death: Philosophical Soundings, 1996, Mapping Responsibility, 2004; free choice, current psychology, volume 27, 2008. Washington and Lee U. Lewis law scholar, 1980; fellow NEH, NIMH, Walter Meyer Law Rsch. Inst., Battelle Rsch. Ctr., Addiction Rsch. Ctr., Inst. Psychiatry, London; fellow Ctr. for Advanced Studies in Behavioral Sci., Stanford, 1985-86. Mem. Am. Philos. Assn. (pres. Pacific divsn. 1977-78). Office: U Calif Dept Philosophy Santa Barbara CA 93106 Home: 1611 Rose St Berkeley CA 94703-1010

FINK, JOSEPH RICHARD, academic administrator; b. Newark, Mar. 20, 1943; s. Joseph Richard and Jean (Chorazy) F.; m. Donna Gibson, 1965 (div. 1986); children: Michael, Taryn; m. Christine Gaudenzi, Oct. 4, 1992 (div. 2003); children: Madison, Joseph; m. Denise Riley, Nov. 17, 2006. AB, Rider U., 1963; PhD in Am. History, Rutgers U., 1971; DLitt (hon.), Rider U., 1982, Coll. of Misericordia, 1992, Golden Gate U., 1994. Asst. then assoc. prof history Immaculata (Pa.) Coll., 1964-72, adminstrv. asst. to pres., 1969-72; dean of Arts & Scis. City Colls. Chgo., 1972-74; pres. Raritan Valley Coll., Somerville, NJ, 1974-79, Coll. Misericordia, Dallas, 1979-88, Dominican U of Calif, San Rafael, 1988—. Pres. Regional Planning Coun. Higher Edn., Region 3/Northeastern Pa., 1986-88. Mem. exec. com. Philharm. Soc. Northeastern Pa., 1986-89; bd. dirs. Marin Symphony, 1989-2004, San Francisco Ballet, 1994-97, Ind. Coll. No. Calif., 1992—1999, Marin Forum, 1991—, Guide Dogs for the Blind, 1994-97, Alonzo Kings Lines Ballet, 2006—; bd. dirs. Am. Land Conservancy, 1995—2007, exec. com.; mem. campaign cabinet United Way San Francisco, 1990; bd. dirs. North Bay Coun., 1993—, chmn., 1996, exec. com. Mem. Nat. Assn. Ind. Colls. and Univs. (secretariat 1986), Nat. Assn. Intercollegiate Athletics (pres.'s adv. coun. 1986), Am. Coun. on Higher Edn. (commn. leadership devel. higher edn. 1978-82, commn. on internat. edn. 1993-96, acad. adminstrn. fellow 1974-75), Assn. Mercy Colls. (pres. 1985-87, exec. com. 1981-87), Coun. for Ind. Colls. (bd. dirs. 1989-92), Am. Hist. Assn., World Affairs Coun. No. Calif. (bd. dirs. 1990-96), Commonwealth Club Calif. (quar. chmn. 1989, chmn. Marin County chpt. 1989—2001, bd. dirs. 1992—, exec. com. 1997—, pres., 2003). Office: Dominican U Calif 50 Acacia Ave San Rafael CA 94901-2230 Business E-Mail: jrf@dominican.edu.

FINK, RICHARD A., lawyer; b. 1940; BA, MBA, Stanford U. Sr. exec. v.p., dir. corp. devel. Glendale (Calif.) Fed. Bank; dir. corp. devel. Glendale Fed. Bank, Glendale. Office: Glendale Fed Bank 414 N Central Ave Glendale CA 91203-2002

FINK, ROBERT RUSSELL, music educator and theorist, retired dean; b. Belding, Mich., Jan. 31, 1933; s. Russell Foster and Frances (Thornton) F.; m. Ruth Joan Bauerle, June 19, 1955; children: Denise Lyn, Daniel Robert. B.Mus., Mich. State U., 1955, M.Mus., 1956, PhD, 1965. Instr. music SUNY, Fredonia, 1956-57; instr. Western Mich. U., Kalamazoo, 1957-62, asst. prof., 1962-66, assoc. prof., 1966-71, prof., 1971-78, chmn. dept. music, 1972-78; dean Coll. Music U. Colo., Boulder, 1978-93; retired, 1994. Prin. horn Kalamazoo Symphony Orch., 1957-67; accreditation examiner Nat. Assn. Schs. Music, Reston, Va., 1973-92, grad. commr., 1981-89, chmn. grad. commn., 1987-89, assoc. chmn. accreditation commn., 1990-91, chmn., 1992. Author: Directory of Michigan Composers, 1972, The Language of 20th Century Music, 1975; composer: Modal Suite, 1959, Four Modes for Winds, 1967, Songs for High School Chorus, 1967; contbr. articles to profl. jours. Bd. dirs. Kalamazoo Symphony Orch., 1974-78, Boulder Bach Festival, 1983-90. Mem. Coll. Music Soc., Soc. Music Theory, Mich. Orch. Assn. (pres.), Phi Mu Alpha Sinfonia (province gov.), Pi Kappa Lambda. Home: 643 Furman Way Boulder CO 80305-5614 Business E-Mail: robert.fink@colorado.edu.

FINK, SCOTT ALAN, lawyer; b. Aurora, Ill., Sept. 18, 1953; s. Harold Lawrence and Lois (Franch) F.; m. Kathy Ellen Klein, May 14, 1978; children: Lindsay Klein, Anna Klein. AB, Stanford U., 1974; JD, U. Mich., 1978. Bar: Calif. 1978, U.S. Dist. Ct. (no. dist.) Calif. 1978, U.S. Ct. Appeals 9th cir.) 1981, U.S. Supreme Ct. 1985. Assoc. Heller, Ehrman, White & McAuliffe, San Francisco, 1978-84, ptnr., 1985-87, Gibson, Dunn & Crutcher, San Francisco, 1987—. Office: Gibson Dunn Crutcher 1 Montgomery St Fl 31 San Francisco CA 94104-4505 Office Phone: 415-393-8200. Business E-Mail: sfink@gibsondunn.com.

FINKEL, EVAN, lawyer; b. Bklyn., Oct. 7, 1956; BS, Harpur Coll., SUNY, Binghampton, 1978; JD, Univ. Calif., Hastings, 1981. Bar: Calif. 1981, U.S. Patent & Trademark Office, U.S. Dist. Ct., (Calif. & Mich.), U.S. Ct. Appeals (9th, Fed. cir.), U.S. Supreme Ct. 1988, U.S. Dist. Ct. (Eastern Dist. Mich.). Ptnr., chmn. LA Intellectual Property group Pillsbury Winthrop Shaw Pittman, LA. Named a So. Calif. Super Lawyer, LA Mag., 2004. Mem.: USPTO, Intellectual Property Assn., Phi Beta Kappa, Order of the Coif, Thurston Soc. Office: Pillsbury Winthrop Shaw Pittman Suite 2800 725 S Figueroa St Los Angeles CA 90017 Office Phone: 213-488-7307. Office Fax: 213-629-1033. Business E-Mail: evan.finkel@pillsburylaw.com.

FINKELSTEIN, JAMES ARTHUR, management consultant; b. NYC, Dec. 6, 1952; s. Harold Nathan and Lilyan (Crystal) F.; m. Lynn Marie Gould, Mar. 24, 1984; children: Matthew, Brett. BA, Trinity Coll., Hartford, Conn., 1974; MBA, U. Pa., 1976. Cons. Towers, Perrin, Forster & Crosby, Boston, 1976-78; mgr. compensation Pepsi-Cola Co., Purchase, NY, 1978-80; mgr. employee info. systems Am. Can. Co., Greenwich, Conn., 1980; mgr. bus. analysis Emery Airfreight, Wilton, Conn., 1980-81; v.p. Meidinger, Inc., Balt., 1981-83; prin. The Wyatt Co., San Diego, 1983-88; pres., chief exec. officer W. F. Corroon, San Francisco, 1988-95; founder, CEO FutureSense, Inc., 1995—97, chmn., CEO, 2001—; founder TallyUp Software, 1996—98; dir. En Wisen, Inc., 1996-98; ptnr. Andersen LLP, San Francisco, 1997-2001. Mem. regional adv. bd. Mchts. and Mfrs. Assn., San Diego, 1986-88; instr. U. Calif., San Diego, 1984-88. Mem. camp com. State YMCA of Mass. and R.I., Framingham, 1982-86; pres. Torrey Pines Child Care Consortium, La Jolla, Calif., 1987-88; founder, pres., CEO, Marin Football Club, Inc., 2003—; vice chmn. La Jolla YMCA, 1986-88; chmn. fin. com. YMCA, San Francisco, 1992-95, vice chmn., 1993-95, chmn., 1995-97, bd. dirs., 1988-2004; bd. dirs. San Domenico Sch., 1994-2000; trustee World Affairs Coun., 1998-2004; bd. dirs. Becket Chimney Corners YMCA, 1999—2003, 2008-; treas. Ctrl. Marin Competitive Soccer Club, 2000-05. Avocations: soccer coaching and refereeing, music, theater, sports, camping. Home: 17 Bracken Ct San Rafael CA 94901-1587 Office: FutureSense Inc 369 B 3d St # 181 San Rafael CA 94901-3581 Personal E-mail: futuresense@yahoo.com.

FINLAY, JAMES CAMPBELL, retired museum director; b. Russell, Man., Can., June 12, 1931; s. William Hugh and Grace Muriel F.; m. Audrey Joy Barton, June 18, 1955; children: Barton Brett, Warren Hugh, Rhonda Marie. BSc, Brandon U., 1952; MSc in Zoology, U. Alta., Can., 1968. Geophysicist Frontier Geophys. Ltd., Alta., 1952-53; geologist, then dist. geologist Shell Can., Ltd., 1954-64; chief park naturalist and biologist Elk Island (Can.) Nat. Pk., 1965-67; dir. hist. devel. and archives, dir. hist. and sci. svc., dir. Nature Ctr., dir. interpretation and recreation City of Edmonton, Alta., 1967-92; ret., 1992; founder Fedn. Alta. Naturalists, 1969. Author: A Nature Guide to Alberta, Bird Finding Guide to Canada; (with Joy Finlay) Ocean to Alpine-A British Columbia Nature Guide, A Guide to Alberta Parks. Recipient Order of the Bighorn, Govt. of Atla., 1987, Heritage award Environment Can., 1990, Loran Goulden award Fedn. Alta. Naturalists, 1991, Can. 125th Anniversary award, 1993, Greenways Achievement award, BC Province Capital Commn., 2001, Douglas Pimlott award Nature Can., 1991; named to Edmonton Hist. Hall of Fame, 1976. Mem. Can. Mus. Assn. (pres. 1976-78), Alta. Mus. Assn. (founding mem., past pres.), Am. Mus. Assn. (past coun.), Am. Ornithol. Union. Home: 270 Trevlac Pl RR 3 Victoria BC Canada V9E 2C4 Personal E-mail: joyandcamfinlay@shaw.ca.

FINLAYSON, BRUCE ALAN, retired chemical engineering professor; b. Waterloo, Iowa, July 18, 1939; s. Rodney Alan and Donna Elizabeth (Gilbert) F.; m. Patricia Lynn Hills, June 9, 1961; children: Mark, Catherine, Christine. BA, Rice U., 1961, MS, 1963; PhD, U. Minn., 1965. Asst. prof. to prof. U. Wash., Seattle, 1967—2005, prof. dept. chem. engring. and applied math., 1977-82, Rehnberg prof., 1989—2005, chmn. dept. chem. engring., 1989-98; prof. emeritus, 2005—. Vis. prof. Univ. Coll., Swansea, Wales, 1975—76, Denmark Tekniske Hojskole, Lyngby, 1976, Universidad Nacional del Sur, Bahia, Argentina, 1980, Carnegie Mellon U., 1986; mem. editl. bd. Internat. Jour. Numerical Methods in Fluids, Swansea, Wales, 1980—, Numerical Heat Transfer, 1981—2002, Numerical Methods for Partial Differential Equations, 1984—2007, Chem. Engring. Edn., 1991—2007; trustee Computer Aids to Chem. Engring. Edn., Austin, Tex., 1980—92; mem. bd. on chem. sci. and tech. NRC, 1990—92; fellow Am. Inst. Chem. Engineers, 1993—, vice pres., 1999, pres., 2000. Author: (books) The Method of Weighted Residuals and Variational Principles, 1972, Nonlinear Analysis in Chemical Engineering, 1980, Numerical Methods for Problems with Moving Fronts, 1992, Introduction to Chemical Engineering Computing, 2006. Lt. USNR, 1965—67. Fellow AIChE (CAST divsn. programming 1981-85, William H. Walker award 1983, bd. dirs. CAST divsn. 1984-86, vice chmn. 1987-88, chmn. 1989, bd. dirs. 1992-94, editorial bd. 1985-91, v.p. 1999, pres. 2000, past pres. 2001); mem. Am. Chem. Soc. (bd. dirs. Petroleum Rsch. Fund 1998-2004), Am. Soc. Engring. Edn. (dir. Summer Sch. for Chem. Engring. Faculty 1997, Martin award Ch.E. divsn. 1994, Dow Lectureship award, 2005), CACHE Award for Excellence in Computing in Chem. Engring. Edn., Chem. Engring. Divsn., ASEE, June, 2008), Soc. Indsl. and Applied Math., Soc. Rheology, Nat. Acad. Engring., N.Am. Alliance of Chem. Engrs. (pres. 2001). Avocations: cello, running. Home: 6315 22nd Ave NE Seattle WA 98115-6919 Office: U Wash Dept Chem Engring PO Box 351750 Seattle WA 98195-1750 Office Phone: 206-685-1634. Personal E-mail: bafinlayson@mindspring.com. Business E-Mail: finlayso@u.washington.edu.

FINLEY, DOROTHY HUNT, beverage distribution company executive; b. Douglas, Ariz. d. John P. and Salley E. (Stewart) Hunt; m. Harold Walter Finley, June 29, 1946 (dec. 1983); 1 child, John H. BA, MEd, U. Ariz. Cert. tchr., sch. adminstr., Ariz. Tchr. Tucson Unified Sch. Dist., 1943-46, 55-58, supervising tchr., 1958-60, sch. prin., 1960-80; pres., dir. Finley Distbg. Co., Inc., Tucson, 1983—. Bd. dirs. Tucson YWCA, 1984, Tucson area Girl Souts U.S., 1985, Tucson chpt. Planned Parenthood, 1987; founder, pres. Women's Studies Orgn. U. Ariz., Tucson, 1986; chair Met. Tucson Conv. and Visitors Bur. Mem. Ariz. Whgolesale Beer and Liquor Assn., Pima County Wholesale Beer and Liquor Assn., Tucson Key Club, U. Ariz. Alumni Club, Pi Lambda Theta, Delta Kappa Gamma. Republican. Episcopalian. Avocations: golf, cards, needlepoint, travel. Office: Finley Distbg Co Inc 2104 S Euclid Ave Tucson AZ 85713-3653

FINLEY, MORDECAI, rabbi; m. Meirav Finley; children: Lev, Kayitz, Shulamitz, Avigayil. PhD in Religion and Social Ethics, U. So. Calif. Cert. Rabbinic Ordination Hebrew Union Coll.-Jewish Inst. of Religion. Co-founder, co-CEO, Rabbi Ohr HaTorah Temple, LA, 1994—. Provost, prof. Liturgy and Jewish Ethics Acad. Jewish Religion, Calif., former pres.; faculty mem. Wexner Heritage Found.; mem. dept. Continuing Edn. U. Judaism; also taught Hebrew Union Coll.-Jewish Inst. Religion, Loyola Law Sch., Shalom Hartman Inst., Jerusalem. Actor: Fathers and Sons, 2005. Named one of The Top 50 Rabbis in America, Newsweek Mag., 2007. Office: Ohr Hatorah 11827 Venice Blvd Los Angeles CA 90066-3903 Office Phone: 818-769-8223, 310-278-9049. Fax: 818-278-9049. Business E-Mail: rabbifinley@ohrhatorah.org.

FINN, FRED, state legislator; b. NYC, Aug. 24, 1945; m. Bonnie Finn; 3 children. BA, Johns Hopkins U.; JD, Fordham U. Sch. Law. Bar: Washington State. Atty. KXXO radio station, 1998; owner Lynch Paint Co., 1990—2004; mgr. AMS Real Estate, 1998—2008; mem. Dist. 35 Wash. House of Reps., 2008—, asst. majority whip. Mem. Washington Conservation Voters, South Puget Sound Rotary Club; bd. dirs. Mason General Hosp. Found., Griffin Sch. Found. Served US Army, 1968—71. Democrat. Office: 430 John L O'Brien Bldg PO Box 40600 Olympia WA 98504 Office Phone: 360-786-7902. E-mail: finn.fred@leg.wa.gov.

FINNEGAN, CYRIL VINCENT, retired dean, zoology educator; b. Dover, NH, July 17, 1922; emigrated to Can., 1958; s. Cyril Vincent and Hilda A. (McClintock) F.; children: Maureen A., Patrick S., Cathaleen C., Kevin S., Eileen D., Gormlaith R., Michaeleen S., Mairead B., Conal E. BS, Bates Coll., Lewiston, Maine, 1946; MS, U. Notre Dame, 1948, PhD, 1951. From instr. to asst. prof. St. Louis U., 1952-56; asst. prof. U. Notre Dame, South Bend, Ind., 1956-58; from asst. prof. to prof. zoology U. B.C., Vancouver, 1958-88, emeritus, 1988—, assoc. dean sci., 1972-79, dean sci., 1979-85, dean emeritus, 1988—, assoc. acad. v.p., 1986-88. Contbr. articles to profl. jours. Served to sgt F.A. and C.E. AUS, 1942-45, NATOUSA, CBI. Postdoctoral research fellow NIH, 1952-53; Killum sr. fellow, 1968-69. Mem. Soc. Devel. Biology, Can. Soc. Cell Biology, Tissue Culture Assn., Internat. Soc. Develop. Biology, Sigma Xi Roman Catholic. Office: U BC Dept Zoology Faculty of Science Vancouver BC Canada V6T 1Z4

FINNEGAN, MICHAEL J., lawyer; b. LA, Dec. 14, 1962; BA cum laude, Loyola Marymount Univ., 1985; JD with honors, Loyola Law Sch., 1988. Bar: Calif. 1988. Ptnr., Litigation practice, mem. mng. bd. Pillsbury Winthrop Shaw Pittman, LA. Bd. dir. Public Counsel. Mem.: ABA, Am. Arbitration Assn., LA Bus. Trial Lawyers Assn., LA County Bar Assn. Office: Pillsbury Winthrop Shaw Pittman Suite 2800 725 S Figueroa St Los Angeles CA 90017 Office Phone: 213-488-7272. Office Fax: 213-629-1033. Business E-Mail: michael.finnegan@pillsburylaw.com.

FINNELL, MICHAEL HARTMAN, mining executive; b. LA, Jan. 27, 1927; s. Jules Bertram and Maribel Hartman (Schumacher) F.; m. Grace Vogel, Sept. 11, 1954 (div. June 1964); children: Lesley Finnell Blanchard, Carter Hartman, Hunter Vogel. BA, U. Toronto, 1950; MBA, Harvard U., Cambridge, Mass., 1952; HHD (hon.), Capital U., Columbus, Ohio, 1980. Sec.-treas. Triad Oil Co. Ltd., 1952-62, v.p., dir., 1962-65; pres. Devon-Palmer Oils Ltd., 1966—70; v.p., dir. Can. Hydrocarbons, Ltd., 1970, pres., 1970—, Montreal River Internat. Silver Mines Ltd., 1972—. Trustee Capital U., Columbus, 1982—94; life trustee Columbus Mus. of Art. Mem. Calif. Club, Annandale Golf Club, Ranchmen's Club, Calgary Petroleum Club, Calgary Golf and

Country Club, Nantucket Yacht Club, Calif. Club LA. Home: 724 Holladay Rd Pasadena CA 91106-4115 Office: 625 Fair Oaks Ave Ste 288 South Pasadena CA 91030 Office Phone: 626-403-9588. Personal E-mail: finnellmh@yahoo.com.

FINNIE, IAIN, mechanical engineer, educator; b. Hong Kong, July 18, 1928; s. John and Jessie Ferguson (Mackenzie) F.; m. Joan Elizabeth Roth, July 28, 1969; 1 dau., Shauna. BS with honors, U. Glasgow, 1949; MS, MIT, 1951, M.E., 1952, Sc.D., 1954; D.Sc. (hon.), U. Glasgow, 1974. With Shell Devel. Co., 1954-61, engr., to 1961; mem. faculty dept. mech. engring. U. Calif., Berkeley, 1961—, prof., 1963—92. Vis. prof. Cath. U. Chile, 1965, Ecole Polytechnique, Lausanne, Switzerland, 1976, 87. Author: Creep of Engineering Materials, 1959; contbr. articles to profl. jours. Guggenheim Found. fellow, 1967-68 Mem. Nat. Acad. Engring., ASME (hon., Nadai award 1982). Home: 2901 Avalon Ave Berkeley CA 94705-1401 Office: U Calif 6179 Etcheverry Berkeley CA 94720-0001 Office Phone: 510-642-1496. Business E-Mail: finnie@me.berkeley.edu.

FINNIGAN, ROBERT EMMET, retired small business owner; b. Buffalo, May 27, 1927; s. Charles M. and Marie F. (Jacobs) F.; m. Bette E. van Horn, Apr. 1, 1950; children: Michael, Patrick, Robert E. Jr., Joan, Shawn, Thomas, Matthew. BS, U.S. Naval Acad., 1949; MS, U. Ill., 1954, PhD, 1957. Commd. lt. USAF, 1949, advanced through grades to capt., 1954; sr. scientist Livermore Lab., U. Calif., 1959, U. Calif. Lawrence Livermore Lab., 1957-62; sr. rsch. scientist Stanford Rsch. Inst., Menlo Park, Calif., 1962-63; dir. Electronic Assocs. Inc., Palo Alto, Calif., 1963-67; founder, vice chmn., sr. v.p., chief strategic officer Finnigan Corp., San Jose, Calif., 1967-92, vice chmn. emeritus, cons., 1992—. Mem. panel NAS, Washington, 1986—89; bd. dirs. Pacific Nanotechnology, Inc., Santa Clara, Calif. Author: Identification and Analysis of Organic Pollutants in Water, 1976, Advances in Identification and Analysis of Organic Pollutants in Water, 1981. Chmn., co-founder U.S. Nat. Working Group on Pollution, Internat. Orgn. for Legal Metrology, Washington, 1982-87; mem. pres.'s coun., U. Ill., Urbana, 2002—; mem. bd. overseers Chem. Heritage Found., Phila., 2005—. Recipient Alumni Honor award, Coll. of Engring., U. Ill., 1980, Disting. Alumnus award, U. Ill. Dept. Elec. Engring., 1975, Robert Finnigan professorship established, Keck Grad. Inst. Applied Life. Sci., Claremont, Calif., 2002; named Pioneer in Analytical Instrumentation-Mass Spectrometry, Soc. Analytical Chemists of Pitts. and Pitts. Conf. on Analytical Chemistry, 1994; named to Instrumentation Hall of Fame, Pitts. Conf. on Analytical Chemistry and Analytical Chem. Soc., 1999, Legend, Am. Chem. Soc., 2008. Mem. IEEE (sr.), Am. Soc. Mass Spectrometry (bd. dirs.), Am. Electronic Assn. (bd. dirs. 1982-84, 87, chmn., co-founder environ. and occupational health com.), U.S. Naval Acad. Alumni Assn. (pres.'s cir. 1996—), Sigma Xi. Avocations: wine, hiking, snowshoeing.

FIORE, NICHOLAS FRANCIS, metal products executive; b. Pitts., Sept. 24, 1939; s. William H. and Margaret (Scinto) F.; m. Sylvia M. Chinque, Aug. 13, 1960; children: Maria L., Nicholas F., Kristin M., Anthony T. BS, Carnegie-Mellon U., 1960, MS, 1963, PhD, 1964. Asst. prof. metall. engring. and materials sci. U. Notre Dame, Ind., 1966-69, prof. Ind., 1969-81, chmn. dept. Ind., 1969-72, 80-81; v.p. Cabot Corp., Boston, 1982-89; mng. dir. materials and applied physics Arthur D. Little, Inc., Cambridge, Mass., 1989-90; v.p. Carpenter Tech. Corp., Reading, Pa., 1990-93, sr. v.p., 1993-2000; CEO Walsin USA, Henderson, Nev., 2000—. Vis. scientist Argonne (Ill.) Nat. Labs., 1974-75. Co-author: Binding of Solute to Dislocations, 1967, Hydrogen Related Embrittlement of High Temperature Materials, 1975; editor: (with B.J. Berkowitz) Advanced Techniques for Characterizing Hydrogen in Metals, 1982; contbr. articles to profl. jours. Trustee Albright Coll.; sci. and tech. edn. com. New Eng. Coun. Capt. U.S. Army, 1964-66. Fellow Am. Soc. Metals (trustee); mem. AIME, Alpha Sigma Mu. Home: 2294 Feathertree Ave Henderson NV 89052 Office: Walsin USA 701 N Green Valley Ste 200 Henderson NV 89074 Office Phone: 702-379-8654. Personal E-mail: nffsr@aol.com. Business E-Mail: fiore@walsinusa.com.

FIRE, ANDREW Z., pathologist, geneticist, educator; b. Santa Clara, Calif., 1959; BA in Math., U. Calif., Berkeley, 1978; PhD in Biology, MIT, 1983; postdoctoral studies, Med. Rsch. Coun. Lab., Cambridge, UK, 1983—86. Microbiologist, dept. embryology Carnegie Instn., Washington, 1986—2003; adj. prof., biology Johns Hopkins U., Balt., 2000—; prof., depts. pathology and genetics Stanford U. Sch. Medicine, Calif., 2003—. Adj. prof. biology Johns Hopkins U., 1986—2003. Contbr. articles in profl. jours. Recipient Maryland Disting. Young Scientist award, 1997, medal, Genetics Soc. Am., 2002, Wiley Prize, Rockefeller U., 2003, Dr. H.P. Heineken prize in biochemistry and biophysics, Netherlands Acad. Arts and Sci., 2004, Gairdner Found. Internat. award, 2005; co-recipient Nobel Prize in Physiology or Medicine, Nobel Found., 2006. Fellow: Am. Acad. Arts and Scis.; mem.: Inst. Medicine, NAS (award in Molecular Biology 2003). Achievements include discovery of process now known as RNAi (with Craig C. Mello), that double-stranded RNA can quash the activity of specific genes. Office: Dept Pathology and Genetics Stanford Univ Sch Medicine 300 Pasteur Dr L235 Stanford CA 94305-5324 Office Phone: 650-723-2885. Office Fax: 650-725-6902, 650-724-9070. Business E-Mail: afire@stanford.edu.*

FIRESTONE, MORTON H., finance company executive; b. Chgo., Feb. 4, 1935; s. William and Lillian (Kliot) F.; m. Roberta (Bobbie) Schwartz, Feb. 3, 1957; children: Jeffrey, Scott, Dan. BS, U. Calif., Davis, 1957; MBA, U. So. Calif., 1971. V.p. Security Pacific Nat. Bank, Los Angeles, 1957-77; chmn. bd., chief fin. officer, corp. sec. Elixir Industries, 1977-87, also dir.; pres. Garden Ins., 1978-87, Club Wholesale Concepts, Inc., 1986-87; chmn. bd., chief exec. officer Rondure Industries, 1987-90; pres. Lin Mor Corp., Woodland Hills, Calif., 1990—. Bd. dirs. Robert Burns & Sons, Inc. Past chmn. Los Angeles-Eilat Sister City Com. Mem. Fin. Execs. Inst., Beta Gamma Sigma. Lodges: Optimist (past pres. Hollywood), Kiwanis (past pres. West Hollywood). Office: Lin Mor Corp PO Box 571025 Tarzana CA 91357-1025 E-mail: mort@linmorcorp.com.

FIRMAGE, EDWIN BROWN, lawyer, educator; b. Utah, Oct. 01; s. Edwin Raddon and Mary Myrtice (Brown) F.; children: Edwin James, Miriam, Sarah, Zina, Joseph, Jonathan, David. BS, Brigham Young U., 1960, MS, 1962; JD, U. Chgo., 1963, LLM, SJD, 1964. Bar: Utah, US Supreme Ct. Staff v.p. Hubert Humphrey White House, Washington, 1965-66; assoc, asst. prof. U. Utah Law Sch., Salt Lake City, 1966-70, prof. of law, 1970—. Vis. scholar UN, NYC, 1970-71; internat. affairs fellow Coun. Fgn. Rels., Geneva, Switzerland, 1970-71; fellow in law and humanities Harvard Law Sch., Cambridge, 1974-75; sr. fellow Keynes Coll. U. Kent, Canterbury, Eng., 1987; vis. prof. U. Tex. Sch. of Law, Austin, summer 1979, Clark Law Sch., Brigham Young U., Provo, summer 1983, 86, U. London, 1992; Reynold's lectr. U. Utah, 1987; Lane lectr. Creighton U. Law Sch., 1992; Kellogg lectr. Episcopal Div. Sch., Cambridge, Mass., 1993. Author: Zion in the Courts: A Legal History of the Church of Jesus Christ of Latter-Day Saints, 1988 (Alpha Sigma Nu book award 1989), To Chain the Dog of War: The War Power of Congress in History of Law, 1989, Religion and the Law: Biblical, Jewish & Islamic Perspectives, 1990; editor: The International Legal System: Cases and Materials, 1995. Found. pres. Utah Opera Co., 1976-80, Utahn's United Against Nuclear Arms Race, 1981-84. Recipient Gov.'s award in the Humanities, 1989, Rosenblatt prize U. Utah, 1991; named Samuel D. Thurman prof. of Law Utah Law Sch., 1990. Mem. ABA, Am. Soc. Internat. Law, Utah Bar Assn., Phi Alpha Delta, Phi Kappa Phi, Pi Sigma Alpha. Achievements include working actively with refugees and others in exile in Vietnam, Thailand, Hong Kong, India, China, Russia and Tibet; working with parliament and cabinet of His Holiness since early 1980's; working with His Holiness the Dalai Lama since late 1990's. Office: U Utah Coll Law Bldg Salt Lake City UT 84112 Home Phone: 801-364-2023; Office Phone: 801-581-7819. Personal E-mail: ed.firmage@comcast.net.

FIRSTENBERG, JEAN PICKER, retired film institute executive; b. NYC, Mar. 13, 1936; d. Eugene and Sylvia (Moses) Picker; m. Paul Firstenberg, Aug. 9, 1956 (div. July 1980); children: Debra, Douglas BS summa cum laude, Boston U., 1958. Asst. producer Altman Prodns., Washington, 1965-66; media advisor J. Walter Thompson, NYC, 1969-72; asst. for spl. projects Princeton U., NJ, 1972-74, dir. publs. NJ, 1974-76; program officer John & Mary R. Markle Found., NYC, 1976—80; pres., CEO Am. Film Inst., L.A., Washington, 1980—2007, pres. emeritus, 2007—. Mem. Citizens' Stamp Advisory Com., US Postal Svc., 2002-; bd. dirs. Trans-Lux Corp.; former chmn. nat. adv. bd. Peabody Broadcasting Awards; bd. dirs. Trans-Lux Corp. Former trustee Boston U.; mem. adv. bd. Will Rogers Inst., N.Y.C.; chmn., bd. advisors Film Dept. N.C. Sch. of Arts; lifetime trustee, Am. Film Inst., 2007- Recipient Alumni award for disting. service to profession Boston U., 1982, Lifetime Achievement award Am. Film Inst., 2007; seminar and prodn. chairs at directing workshop for women named in her honor Am. Film Inst., 1986 Mem. Women in Film (Crystal award 1990), Trusteeship for Betterment of Women, Acad. Motion Picture Arts and Scis. Office: Am Film Inst 2021 N Western Ave Los Angeles CA 90027-1657 Office Phone: 323-856-7677.

FIRTH, COLIN ANDREW, actor; b. Grayshott, Eng., Sept. 10, 1960; m. Livia Giuggioli, June 21, 1997; children: Luca, Mateo; 1 child, Will. Attended, Barton Peveri Coll. Actor: (films) Another Country, 1981, Dutch Girls, 1985, 1919, 1985, A Month in the Country, 1987, Apartment Zero, 1988, Valmont, 1989, Wings of Fame, 1990, Femme Fatale, 1991, The Hour of the Pig, 1993, The Deep Blue Sea, 1994, Playmaker, 1994, Circle of Friends, 1995, The English Patient, 1996, Fever Pitch, 1997, A Thousand Acres, 1997, Shakespeare in Love, 1998, My Life So Far, 1999, The Secret Laughter of Women, 1999, Blackadder Back & Forth, 1999, Relative Values, 2000, Bridget Jones's Diary, 2001, The Importance of Being Earnest, 2002, Hope Springs, 2003, What a Girls Wants, 2003, Girl with the Pearl Earings, 2003, Love Actually, 2003, Bridget Jones: The Edge of Reason, 2004, Where the Truth Lies, 2005, Nanny McPhee, 2005, The Last Legion, 2007, And When Did You Last See Your Father?, 2007, Then She Found Me, 2007, Mamma Mia!, 2008; (TV films) Camille, 1984, Tales from the Hollywood Hills: Pat Hobby Teamed with Genius, 1987, The Secret Garden, 1987, Tumbledown, 1989 (Royal Television Soc. Best Actor award), Out of the Blue, 1991, Hostages, 1993, The Deep Blue Sea, 1994, Master of the Moor, 1994, The Widowing of Mrs. Holroyd, 1995, Conspiracy, 2001; (TV miniseries) Lost Empires, 1986, Pride and Prejudice, 1995, Nostromo, 1997; (plays) Another Country, 1983, The Lonely Road, 1985, Desire Under the Elms, 1987, The Caretaker, 1991, Chatsky, 1993, Three Days of Rain, 1999—2000; guest host Saturday Night Live, 2004. Mem.: Royal Shakespeare Co. Office: c/o Chris Andrews Creative Artists Agy LLC 2000 Ave of the Stars Los Angeles CA 90067 Office Phone: 212-556-5600.

FISCH, MICHAEL J., publisher; b. Fairmont, Minn., 1952; Pres., CEO THe Bakersfield Californian, 1992; pres., publisher Honolulu Advt. Inc., 1998—. Office: PO Box 3110 Honolulu HI 96802-3110

FISCHER, ALFRED GEORGE, geology educator; b. Rothenburg, Germany, Dec. 10, 1920; arrived in US, 1935; s. George Erwin and Thea (Freise) F.; m. Winnifred Varney, Aug. 26, 1939; children: Joseph Fred, George William, Lenore Ruth. Student, Northwestern Coll., Watertown, Wis., 1935-37; BA, U. Wis., 1939, MA, 1941; PhD, Columbia U., 1950. Instr. Va. Poly. Inst. and State U., Blacksburg, 1941-43; geologist Stanolind Oil & Gas Co., Kans. and Fla., 1943-46; instr. U. Rochester, NY, 1947-48; from instr. to asst. prof. U. Kans., Lawrence, 1948-51; sr. geologist Internat. Petroleum, Peru, 1951-56; prof. geology Princeton (N.J.) U., 1956-84, U. So. Calif., LA, 1984, now prof. emeritus. Co-Author: Invertebrate Fossils, 1952, The Permian Reef Complex, 1953, Electron Micrographs of Limestone, 1967; editor: Petroleum and Global Tectonics, 1975. Recipient Verrill medal Yale U. Fellow Geol. Soc. Am. (Penrose medal 1993), Geol. Soc. London (hon., Lyell medal 1992), Soc. Econ. Paleontologists (hon., Twenhofel medal); mem. AAAS, NAS(Mary Clark Thompson medal, 2009), U.S. Nat. Acad. Sci., Am. Assn. Petroleum Geologists, Paleontol. Soc. (medal 1995), German Geol. Soc. (Leopold von Buch medal), Geol. Union (Gustav Steinmann medal 1992), Mainz Acad. Sci. Lit. (corr.), Lincei Acad. Rome (fgn.), U.S. Nat. Acad. Sci.(Thompson medal 2009), Sigma Xi. Home: 1736 Perch St San Pedro CA 90732-4218 Office: U So Calif Dept Earth Scis Zumberge Hall of Sci 117 Univ Park Los Angeles CA 90089-0001

FISCHER, BRADLEY J., film company executive; b. Sept. 8, 1976; Grad. in Film Studies and Psych., Columbia U., NYC, 1998. Intern Brillstein-Grey, NYC; exec. asst. to Mike Medavoy Phoenix Pictures, 1998—99, dir. devel., 1999—2002, v.p. prodn., 2002—04, sr. v.p. prodn., 2004—. Co-exec. prodr.: (films) Basic, 2003; exec. prodr.: Pathfinder, 2007; prodr.: Resurrecting the Champ, 2007, Zodiac, 2007. Office: Phoenix Pictures Inc Frankovitch Bldg 10202 W Washington Blvd Culver City CA 90232 Office Phone: 310-244-6540. E-mail: bfischer@phoenixpictures.com.

FISCHER, EDMOND HENRI, biochemistry educator; b. Shanghai, Apr. 6, 1920; arrived in U.S., 1953, naturalized; s. Oscar and Renée (Tapernoux) Fischer. Lic. es Sciences Chimiques et Biologiques, U. Geneva, 1943, Diplome d'Ingenieur Chimiste, 1944, PhD, 1947; D (hon.), U. Montpellier, France, 1985, U. Basel, Switzerland, 1988, Med. Coll. of Ohio, 1993, Ind. U., 1993, U. Bochum, Germany, 1994. Pvt. docent biochemistry U. Geneva, 1950—53; research assoc. biology Calif. Inst. Tech., Pasadena, 1953; asst. prof. biochemistry U. Wash., Seattle, 1953—56, assoc. prof., 1956—61, prof., 1961—90, prof. emeritus, 1990—. Mem. exec. com. Pacific Slope Biochem. Conf., 1958—59, pres., 1975; mem. biochemistry study sect. NIH, 1959—64; symposium co-chmn. Battelle Seattle Rsch. Ctr., 1970, 73, 78; mem. sci. adv. bd. Biozentrum, U. Basel, Switzerland, 1982—86, Weizmann Inst. Sci., Rehovot, Israel, 1998—, bd. govs., 1997—; mem. sci. adv. bd. Principe Felipe Sci. Mus., Valencia, Spain, 1998—, Friedrich Miescher Inst., Ciba-Geigy, Basel, 1976—84, chmn., 1981—84; mem. bd. sci. govs. Scripps Rsch. Inst., La Jolla, Calif., 1987—; mem. scientific adv. bd. Basel Inst. for Immunology, 1996—2001; bd. sci. govs. Scripps Rsch. Inst., La Jolla, Calif. Contbr. numerous articles to sci. jours. Mem. sci. council on basic sci. Am. Heart Assn., 1977—80; sci. adv. com. Muscular Dystrophy Assn., 1980—88. Recipient Lederle Med. Faculty award, 1956—59, Guggenheim Found. award, 1963—64, Disting. Lectr. award, U. Wash., 1983, Laureate Passano Found. award, 1988, Steven C. Beering award, 1991, Nobel prize in physiology or medicine, 1992. Fellow: Am. Acad. Arts and Scis.; mem.: AAUP, NAS, AAS, Am. Chem. Soc. (editl. adv. bd. Biochemistry 1961—66, adv. bd. biochemistry divsn. 1962, assoc. editor 1966—91, exec. com. divsn. biology 1969—72, monograph adv. bd. 1971—73), fgn. acads. (hon.), Korean Acad. Sci. and Tech. (hon.), Japanese Biochem. Soc. (hon.), Spanish Royal Acad. Scis. (assoc.; fgn.), Venice Inst. Sci., Arts and Letters (assoc.; fgn.), Royal Acad. Medicine and Surgery (hon.; Cadiz, Spain), European Acad. Scis. (hon.), Am. Soc. Biol. Chemists (coun. 1989—93). Achievements include cellular regulation by phosphorylation/dephosphorylation cycle. Office: U Washington Med Sch PO Box 357350 Seattle WA 98195-7350 E-mail: efischer@u.washington.edu.

FISCHER, JOEL, social work educator; b. Chgo., Apr. 22, 1939; s. Sam and Ruth (Feiges) F.; m. Renee H. Furuyama; children: Lisa, Nicole. BS, U. Ill., 1961, MSW, 1964; D in Social Welfare, U. Calif., Berkeley, 1970. Prof. sch. social work U. Hawaii, Honolulu, 1970—. Vis. prof. George Warren Brown Sch. Social Work, Washington U., St. Louis, 1977, U. Wis. Sch. Social Welfare, Milw., 1978-79, U. Natal, South Africa, 1982, U. Hong Kong, 1986; cons. various orgns. and univs. Author: (with Harvey L. Gochros) Planned Behavior Change: Behavior Modification in Social Work, 1973, Handbook of Behavior Therapy with Sexual Problems, vol. I, 1977, vol. II, 1977, Analyzing Research, 1975, Interpersonal Helping: Emerging Approaches for Social Work Practice, 1973, The Effectiveness of Social Casework, 1976; (with D. Sanders and O. Kurren) Fundamentals of Social Work Practice, 1982, Effective Casework Practice: An Eclectic Approach, 1978, (with H. Gochros) Treat Yourself to a Better Sex Life, 1980; (with H. Gochros and J. Gochros) Helping the Sexually Oppressed, 1985; (with Martin Bloom) Evaluating Practice: Guidelines for the Helping Professional, 1982; (with Kevin Corcoran) Measures for Clinical Practice and Research, 1987, 3d edit, vol. 2, 2006, Couples, Children and Families, Adults, vol. 2, 2000, East-West Connections: Social Work Practice Traditions and Change, 1992, Measures for Clinical Practice and Research, vol. 1, 2006, Couples, Children and Families, vol. 2, 2006; (with Daniel Sanders) Visions for the Future: Social Work and Pacific-Asian Perspectives, 1988; (with Martin Bloom and John Orme) Evaluating Practice, 2d edit., 1995, 5th edit., 2006, Instructor's Manual for Evaluating Practice, 1999, 3rd edit., 2006; mem. editl. bd. 12 profl. jours.; contbr. over 150 articles to profl. jours. Bd. dirs. U. Hawaii Profl. Assembly, Hawaii Peoples' Fund, Greenpeace; precinct pres. Dem. Party. With U.S. Army, 1958-61. Mem. NASW (Social Worker of Year for Social Justice 2005), ACLU, Hawaii Com. for Africa, Coun. Social Work Edn., Acad. Cert. Social Workers, Nat. Conf. Social Welfare, AAUP, Unity Organizing Com., Hawaii People's Legis. Coalition, People for the Ethical Treatment of Animals (bd. dirs.), Stop/The U. Utah Animal Rights Coalition, Bertha Reynold Soc., Amnesty Internat., Sierra Club. Democrat. Office: U Hawaii Sch Social Work Henke Hall Honolulu HI 96822-2217 Home Phone: 808-735-7582. Business E-Mail: jfischer@hawaii.edu.

FISCHER, MICHAEL LUDWIG, environmental executive; b. Dubuque, Iowa, May 29, 1940; s. Carl Michael and Therese Marie (Stadler) F.; m. Jane Pughe Rogers; children: Christina Marie, Steven Michael. BA in Polit. Sci., Santa Clara U., 1964; M in City and Regional Planning, U. Calif., Berkeley, 1967; grad. exec. program in environ. mgmt., Harvard U., 1980. Planner City of Mountain View, Calif., 1960-65; planner assoc. Bay Area Govts., 1966-67; planner County of San Mateo, Calif., 1967-69; assoc. dir. San Francisco Planning and Urban Rsch. Assn., nonprofit civc orgn., 1969-73; exec. dir. North Cen. region Calif. Coastal Zone Conservation Commn., San Rafael, 1973-76; chief dep. dir. Gov.'s Office Planning and Rsch., Sacramento, 1976-78; exec. dir. Calif. Coastal Commn., San Francisco, 1978-85; sr. assoc. Sedway Cooke Assocs., environ. cons., San Francisco, 1985-87; exec. dir. Sierra Club, San Francisco, 1987-93; resident fellow John F. Kennedy Sch. Govt., Inst. Politics, Harvard U., Cambridge, Mass., 1993; sr. cons. Natural Resources Def. Coun., San Francisco, 1993-95; exec. officer Calif. Coastal Conservancy, Oakland, 1994-97; program dir. environ. William & Flora Hewlett Found., Menlo Park, Calif., 1997—2002, sr. fellow, 2002—03; environ. and mgmt. cons., 2003—07; sr. advisor Green Burial Coun., 2003—07; exec. dir. Consultative Group on Biol. Diversity, 2008—. Lectr. dept. city and regional planning U. Calif., Berkeley, 1984; mem., co-chair environ. com. adv. coun. Calvert Social Investment Fund, 1989—2005; mem. Harvard Commn. Global Change Info. Policy, 1993—95; mem. com. on impact of maritime facility devel. NAS/NRC, 1975—78; mem. nat. sea grant rev. panel NOAA, 1998—2001; mem. adv. bd. Sustainable Conservation, 2003—, Coastal States Stewardship Found., 2005—07; mem. steering com. Travel Just, 2003—07. Co-author Calif. state plan, An Urban Strategy for Calif., 1978, Building a New Municipal Railway, 1973, Oral History, Coastal Commn. Yrs., 1973-85, Oral History, Sierra Club Yrs., 1987-93; author intro. Ansel Adams: Yosemite, 1995; contbr. papers to profl. publs. Bd. dirs. High Country News Found., 2000—05, Resources for Cmty. Collaboration, 1999—2006, Am. Youth Hostels, Inc., 1985—87, Yosemite Restoration Trust, 1990—97, pres., 1995—97. Recipient Life Achievement award, Assn. Environ. Profls., 1986, Disting. Leadership award, Am. Soc. Pub. Adminstrn., 1987, Outstanding Nat. Leadership award, Coastal States Orgn., 1990, David Brower award for environ. leadership, Conservation Laborers Against Wrong, 1993, Exemplary Pub. Svc. award, San Francisco Bay Conservation and Devel. Commn., 1997, Spl. Recognition award, Calif. State Legis., 1998, Coastal Champion award, Nat. Resources Def. Coun. and Sierra Club, Calif., 2003, Coastal Hero award, Calif. Coastal Commn., 2005, Disting. Alumnus medal, U. Calif., Berkeley, Coll. Environ. Design, 2007. Fellow: Inst. Journalism and Nat. Resources (disting.); mem.: Calif. Planning and Conservation League (bd. dirs. 1970—76), Friends of the Earth (bd. dirs. 1988—94), The Oceanic Soc. (bd. dirs. 1983—88), Alliance Ethnic and Environ. Orgn. (founding bd. dirs. 1991—93), Sierra Club, Lambda Alpha Phi Theta Kappa. Achievements include making Renaissance keyboard instruments. E-mail: fischer@igc.org.

FISCHER, RANDY, state legislator; m. Kathy Fischer. BS, Colo. State U., Ft. Collins. Owner engring. cons. bus.; mem. Dist. 53 Colo. House of Reps., Denver, 2007—, dep. majority whip. Mem. Larimer County Rural Land Use Adv. Bd., Colo. State U. Coll. Natural Resources Alumni Bd., Ft. Collins Water Bd., Storm Drainage Bd., Natural Resources Adv. Bd., Legacy Land Trust Bd., Ft. Collins City Plan Update Com., Poudre Sch. Dist. Outdoor Edn. Program. Democrat. Office: Colo State Capitol 200 E Colfax Denver CO 80203 Office Phone: 303-866-2917. Business E-Mail: randy.fischer.house@state.co.us.*

FISCHER, THOMAS COVELL, law educator, consultant, writer; b. May 2, 1938; s. Vilas Uber and Elizabeth Mary (Holland) Fischer; m. Katherine Brenda Andrew, Sept. 29, 1972. AB, U. Cin., 1960; postgrad., U. Wash., 1960-62, Loyola U., Chgo., 1964-66; JD, Georgetown U., 1966. Asst. dir. U. Ill., Chgo., 1964-66; asst. dean Georgetown U. Law Ctr., 1966-72; cons. Antioch Sch. Law, 1972-73; asst. exec. dir. Am. Bar Found., Chgo., 1974-76; assoc. dean, prof. law U. Dayton, 1976-78; dean, prof. law New Eng. Sch. Law, Boston, 1978—81, prof., 1981—2003, prof. emeritus, 2003—; disting. acad. in residence Seattle U. Law Sch., 2003—. Vis. scholar, Cambridge, 1991, Exeter, 91, Edinburgh, 91, Konstanz U., 1993, Muenster U., 1993, U. Auckland, 1996; fellow Inst. Advanced Legal Studies, U. London, English Inns of Court, 1997; vis. fellow Wolfson Coll., Cambridge, England, 1997; sr. vis. fellow, LLM program U. Southampton Law Faculty, 2001, sr. vis. tutor, 02; cons. in field. Author: Due Process in the Student/Institutional Relationship, 1970; author: (with Duscha) The Campus Press: Freedom and Responsibility, 1973; author: (with Zenhle) Introduction to Law and Legal Reasoning, 1977, Legal Education, Law Practice and the Economy: A New England Study, 1990, The Europeanization of America: What Americans Need to Know About the European Union, 1996, The United States, the European Union, and the Globilization of World Trade: Allies or Adversaries?, 2000; author: (with Cox) Quick Review of Conflict of Laws, 3rd edit., 2001; author: Sum & Substance of Conflict of Laws, 4th edit., 2007, What's Wrong With Globalization!?, 2009, Quick Riview of Conflict of Laws, 2009. Project dir. Commn. Legal Edn. and Practice and Econ. New Eng. Recipient Elaine R. Maham award, U. Cin., 1960, Pub. Svc. award, Access to Justice Inst., 2006; Pi Kappa Alpha Meml. scholar, 1960—62. Fellow: Inns of Ct.; mem.: Phi Alpha Theta, Pi Delta Epsilon, Delta Theta Phi. Roman Catholic. Office: Seattle U Sch Law 901 12th Ave PO Box 222000 Seattle WA 98122 Office Phone: 206-398-4034. Business E-Mail: fischert@seattleu.edu.

FISCHL, ERIC, artist; b. NYC, 1948; BFA, Calif. Inst. Arts, 1972. Lectr, painting Nova Scotia Coll. Art & Design, 1974—78. Exhibitions include Dalhousie Art Gallery, Halifax, Canada, 1975, Studio, 1976, Galerie B., Montreal, Canada, 1976, 1978, Edward Thorp Gallery, New York, 1980, 1981—82, Emily Davis Art Gallery, Akron, OH, 1980, Sable-Castelli Gallery, Toronto, Canada, 1981—82, 1985, 1987, Sir George Williams Gallery, Montreal, Canada, 1983, Saidye Bronfman Centre, 1983, Larry Gagosian Gallery, Los Angeles, 1983, 1986, Mario Diacono Gallery, Rome, 1983, Boston, 1985, 1999, Multiples/Marian Goodman Inc., New York, 1983, Nigel Greenwood Gallery, London, 1983, Mendel Art Gallery, Saskatoon, Cananda, 1985, Stedelijk Van Abbe Museum, The Netherlands, 1985, Kunsthalle Basel, Basel, Switzerland, 1985, Institute of Contemporary Art, London, 1985, Art Gallery of Ontario, Toronto, Canada, 1985, Whitney Museum of Am. Art, New York, 1986, Mary Boone Gallery, 1984, 1986—88, 1990, 1992, 1994, 1996, 1999—2000, Daniel Weinberg Gallery, Los Angeles, 1986, Galerie Michael Werner, Koln, West Germany, 1988, Waddington Galleries, London, 1989, Akademie der Bildenden Kunste, Vienna, Austria, 1990, Musee Cantonal des Beaux-Arts de Lausanne, Lausanne, Switzerland, 1990, Aarhus Kunstmuseum, Aarhus, Denmark, 1991, Louisiana Museum of Modern Art, Humlebaek, Denmark, 1991, Michael Kohn Gallery, Santa Monica, CA, 1992, Center for the Fine Arts, Miami, FL, 1992, Galeria Soledad Lorenzo, Madrid, Spain, 1993, Galerie Daniel Templon, Paris, France, 1994, 1999, Daniel Weinberg Gallery, San Francisco, CA, 1994, Michael Nagy Fine Art, Potts Point, Australia, 1995, Baldwin Gallery, Aspen, CO, 1997, Gagosian Gallery, New York, 1998, London, 2000, Galleria Lawrence Rubin, Milan, Italy, 1998. Named National Academician, Nat. Acad. of Design, 1994. Mem.: Am. Acad. Arts and Letters. Office: c/o Baldwin Gallery 209 S Galena St Aspen CO 81611 also: c/o Mary Boone Gallery 745 Fifth Ave New York NY 10151 Office Phone: 970-920-9797, 212-752-2929. Office Fax: 970-920-1821, 212-752-3939.

FISETTE, SCOTT MICHAEL, landscape and golf course architect; b. Orange, Tex., May 17, 1963; s. Roderick John and Addie Faye (Byrnes) F.; m. Keali'i Kane; children: Shane Roderick, Hayley Kaimalie. BS in Landscape Architecture, Tex. A&M U., 1985. Registered landscape architect, Tex., Hawaii, Commonwealth of No. Mariana Islands. Project architect Dick Nugent Assocs., Long Grove, Ill., 1985-90; prin., pres. Fisette Golf Designs, Kaneohe, Hawaii, 1991—. Mem. Golf Course Supts. Assn. Am., Am. Soc. Landscape Architects, Nat. Golf Found., Hawaii Turf Grass Assn. (bd. dirs. 1991-96), Donald Ross Soc. Avocations: golf, fishing, water-skiing, softball. Office: Fisette Golf Designs PO Box 1433 Kaneohe HI 96744-1433

FISHBACK, DENNIS, information technology executive; Mgmt. Va. Power; with Calif. Ind. Sys. Operator; sr. v.p. & chief info. officer Calpine Corp., San Jose, Calif., 2001—. Named one of the Premier 100 IT Leaders, Computerworld mag., 2004. Office: SVP & CIO Calpine Corp 50 W San Fernando St San Jose CA 95113

FISHBURNE, LAURENCE, actor; b. Augusta, Ga., July 30, 1961; s. Laurence John Jr. and Hattie Bell Crawford F.; m. Hajna O. Moss, July 1, 1985 (div.); children: Langston Issa, Montana Isis; m. Gina Torres Sept. 20, 2002; 1 child, Delilah Stage appearances include Section D, 1975, Eden, 1976, Short Eyes, 1984, Loose Ends, 1988, Urban Blight, 1988, Two Trains Running, 1992 (Best Featured Actor Tony award 1992), Fences, 2006, Thurgood, 2008 (Drama Desk award for Outstanding Solo Performance, 2008); actor: (films) Cornbread, Earl and Me, 1975, Apocalypse Now, 1979, Fast Break, 1979, Willie and Phil, 1980, Death Wish II, 1982, Rumble Fish, 1983, The Cotton Club, 1984, The Color Purple, 1985, Band of the Hand, 1986, Quicksilver, 1986, Gardens of Stone, 1987, Cherry 2000, 1987, A Nightmare on Elm Street 3: Dream Warriors, 1987, School Daze, 1988, Red Heat, 1988, King of New York, 1990, Cadence, 1991, Class Action, 1991, Boyz N the Hood, 1991, Deep Cover, 1992, What's Love Got To Do With It, 1993, Searching For Bobby Fischer, 1993, Higher Learning, 1995, Bad Company, 1995, Just Cause, 1995, Othello, 1995, Fled, 1996, Event Horizon, 1997, The Matrix, 1999, (voice only) Osmosis Jones, 2001, Biker Boyz, 2003, The Matrix Reloaded, 2003, Mystic River, 2003, The Matrix Revolutions, 2003, Assault on Precinct 13, 2005, Mission Impossible III, 2006, Bobby, 2006, (voice only) TMNT, 2007, (voice only) 4: Rise of the Silver Surfer, 2007, The Death and Life of Bobby Z, 2007, Twenty-One, 2008; (TV films) If You Give a Dance, You Gotta Pay the Band, 1972, A Rumor of War, 1980, I Take These Men, 1983, For Us the Living: The Medgar Evers Story, 1983, The Father Clements Story, 1987, Decoration Day, 1990, Before Your Eyes, 1996; (TV series) The Six O'Clock Follies, 1980, CSI: Crime Scene Investigation, 2008-; (TV appearances) Trapper John, M.D., 1981, Strike Force, 1982, M*A*S*H, 1982, Hill Street Blues, 1981, Miami Vice, 1986, Pee-wee's Playhouse, 1986, 1987, Spenser: For Hire, 1987, The Equalizer, 1989, Tribeca, 1993; actor, dir., prodr., writer (films) Once in the Life, 2000; actor, exec. prod. Hoodlum, 1997, Akeelah and the Bee, 2006, Akeelah and the Bee, 2006; (TV films) Miss Ever's Boys, 1997, Always Outnumbered, 1998 Recipient Emmy award, 1993, 97, Image award, 1996, 98. Mailing: Landmark Artist & Mgmt 4116 W Magnolia Blvd, Ste 101 Burbank CA 91505

FISHER, DELBERT ARTHUR, pediatric endocrinologist, educator, retired health facility administrator; b. Placerville, Calif., Aug. 12, 1928; s. Arthur Lloyd and Thelma (Johnson) Fisher; m. Beverly Carne Fisher, Jan. 28, 1951; children: David Arthur(dec.), Thomas Martin, Mary Kathryn. BA, U. Calif., Berkeley, 1950; MD, U. Calif., San Francisco, 1953. Diplomate Am. Bd. Pediat., Sub Bd. Pediatric Endocrinology. Intern, resident in pediat. U. Calif. Med. Ctr., San Francisco, 1953—55; resident in pediat. U. Oreg. Hosp., Portland, 1957—58; Irwin Meml. fellow in pediatric endocrinology, 1958—60; from asst. prof. to prof. pediat. Med. Sch. U. Ark., Little Rock, 1960—68; prof. pediat. UCLA Med. Sch., LA, 1968—73, prof. pediat. and internal medicine, 1973—91, prof. pediat. and internal medicine emeritus, 1991—; chief, pediat. endocrinology Harbor-UCLA Med. Ctr., 1968—75, rsch. prof. devel. and perinatal biology, 1975—85, chmn. pediat., 1985—89, sr. scientist Rsch. and Edn. Inst., 1991—, chmn. bd. Rsch. and Edn. Inst., 2001—02; dir. Walter Martin Rsch. Ctr., 1986—91; pres. Nichols Inst. Reference Labs, San Juan Capistrano, Calif., 1991—93; pres. acad. assocs., chief sci. officer Nichols Inst., San Juan Capistrano, Calif., 1993—94, Quest Diagnostics-Nichols Inst., San Juan Capistrano, Calif., 1994—97, sr. sci. officer, 1997—98, chief sci. officer, 1998—99; v.p. sci. and innovation Quest Diagnostics Inc., 1999—2005, sr. sci. officer, 2005—07, acad. assoc., 2007—. Cons. genetic disease sect. Calif. Dept. Health Svcs., 1978—98; mem. organizing com. Internat. Conf. Newborn Thyroid Screening, 1977—88; examiner Am. Bd. Pediat., 1971—80, mem. subcom. on pediat. endocrinology, 1976—79. Co-editor: Pediatric Thyroidology, 1985, 10 other books; editor-in-chief: Jour. Clin. Endocrinology and Metabolism, 1978—83, Pediat. Rsch., 1984—89; contbr. over 450 articles to profl. jours., over 100 chpts. to books. Capt. M.C. USAF, 1955—57. Recipient Career Devel. award, NIH, 1964—68; named to Hall of Honor, NICHHD, NIH, 2003. Master: Am. Coll. Endocrinology; mem.: Am. Assn. Clin. Chemistry (So. Calif. sect., Albert L. Nichols award 2004), Clin. Ligand Assay Soc. (Disting. Scientist award 2001), Western Soc. Pediat. Rsch. (pres. 1982—83), Lawson Wilkins Pediatric Endocrine Soc. (pres. 1982—83, Van Wyk award 2008), Assn. Am. Physicians, Am. Soc. Clin. Investigation, Am. Thyroid Assn. (pres. 1988—89, Disting. Lectr. 1982), Endocrine Soc. (pres. 1983—84, Leadership award 1998), Am. Pediat. Soc. (pres. 1992—93, John Howland medal 2001), Soc. Pediat. Rsch. (v.p. 1973—74), Am. Acad. Pediat. (Borden award 1981), Nat. Acad. Clin. Biochemistry, Inst. Medicine of NAS, Alpha Omega Alpha, Phi Beta Kappa. Home: 24582 Santa Clara Ave Dana Point CA 92629-3031 Personal E-mail: fisherd1@cox.net.

FISHER, DONALD G., retail executive; b. 1928; m. Doris Fisher. BS, U. Calif., 1950. With M. Fisher & Son, 1950-57; former ptnr. Fisher Property Investment Co.; co-founder Gap Stores, San Bruno, Calif., 1969; chmn. Gap Inc., San Bruno, Calif., 1969—2004, pres., 1969—83. Mem. adv. coun. Office of US Trade Rep., 1987—98. Dir Schwab Charles Corp.; trustee Presidio Trust, 1997—; bd. mem. Calif. State Bd. Ed. Named one of Top 200 Collectors, ARTnews Mag., 2004—08, Forbes Richest Americans, 2006. Avocation: art collector. Office: Gap Inc 2 Folsom St San Francisco CA 94105 Address: 3456 Washington St San Francisco CA 94118

FISHER, DORIS, retail executive; m. Donald G. Fisher; 1 child, Robert J. Co-founder Gap, Inc., 1969, merchandiser, 1969—2003, bd. dir., 1969—. Trustee Stanford U. Named one of top 200 collectors, ARTnews, 2004—08, most powerful women, Forbes mag., 2005. Office: Gap Inc Two Folsom St San Francisco CA 94105 Office Phone: 650-952-4400.

FISHER, ERIC O'NEILL, economist; b. NYC, Feb. 9, 1954; s. Leonard and Lora (Segall) Porter; m. Kathryn G. Marshall, June 15, 1991; children: Jane Marshall, Marshall Havard. AB in Philosophy, Princeton U., NJ, 1974; MA in Internat. Rels., Johns Hopkins U., Washington, 1979; PhD, U. Calif., Berkeley, 1985. Economist bd. govs. FRS, Washington, 1984—87; asst. prof. Cornell U., Ithaca, NY, 1987—93; asst. then assoc. prof. Ohio State U., Columbus, 1993—2006; prof., dir. econs. lab. Calif. Poly. State U., San Luis Obispo, 2006—. Vis. fellow Inst. Internat. Econ. Studies, Stockholm, 1987, Australian Nat. U., Canberra, 1994, Tinbergen Inst., Rotterdam, 1993; vis. prof. U. Sao Paulo, 1990, Va. Polytech. Inst., 2004, U. Calif., Santa Barbara, 2005-08, Chulalongkorn U., 2007-08; vis. asst. prof. U. Chgo., 1990-91; vis. fgn. scholar Inst. Social and Econ. Rsch., U. Osaka, Japan, 1998; Associazione Generale Italiana di Petrol prof. Johns Hopkins U., 2002-03; Jean Monnet fellow European U. Inst, 2002-03; rsch. assoc. Fed. Res. Bank, Cleve., 2003-2006, vis. scholar, Fed. Res. Bank, San Francisco, 2007-; mem. editl. coun. Rev. Internat. Econs., 1994—; mem. editl. bd. Jour. Econ. Integration, 1994-2000; mem. COTA Legacy Coun., 2000-04; assoc. editor Jour. Internat. Econs., 2004—, Jour. Money, Credit and Banking, 2005—. Contbr. articles to profl. jours. Vol. Peace Corps, Morocco, 1975-77; mem. City of Ithaca Rep. Com., 1991-93; village coun. Riverlea, Ohio, 2000-02; mem. staff Amnesty Internat., USA, 1978; mem. vestry, St. Stephen's Ch. Recipient Outstanding Tchr. award, Sigma Chi Fraternity, Ohio State U. chpt., 1993—94, Srs. Recognition Outstanding Faculty, Ohio State U., 1995; fellow, Found. Def. Democracies, 2003; scholar, Fed. Res. Bank, San Francisco, 2007. Mem. Econometric Soc., Am. Econ. Assn., Internat. Econs. and Fin. Soc. (sec. 1998-2000). Republican. Episcopalian. Avocation: fly fishing. Office: Calif Poly State Univ Orfalea Coll Bus 1 Grand Ave San Luis Obispo CA 93407 Home: 522 Stoneridge Dr San Luis Obispo CA 93401-5669 Office Phone: 805-756-2764. Office Fax: 805-756-1473. Personal E-mail: eric.on.fisher@gmail.com.

FISHER, (DONALD) GARTH, plastic surgeon; b. Sacto, MS, May 24, 1958; s. Donald Fisher; m. Brooke Burke, 2001 (div. 2005); children Neriah, Sierra Sky; m. Jessica Canseco, 2007. BA in Biology, U. Miss., Oxford, 1980; MD, U. Miss., Jackson, 1984. Diplomate Am. Bd. Plastic Surgery, Am. Bd. Surgery. Intern in gen. surgery U. Calif., Irvine, 1984-85, resident in gen. surgery, 1985-89, resident in plastic surgery, 1989-91; fellow in aesthetic plastic surgery Santa Ana, Calif., 1991; pvt. practice Beverly Hills, Calif., 1991—. Instr. dept. surgery U. Miss. Sch. Medicine, 1980, dept. anatomy, 1980; lectr. in field; consulted extensively for many TV, news and magazine interviews. Author: (5 part ednl. video series) The Naked Truth About Plastic Surgery, The Informed Patient; contbr. articles to sci. and profl. jours.; appeared in: (TV series) Extreme Makeover; guest appearances Good Morning America, Oprah, Today Show, CBS Evening News, NBC Evening News, CNN, Entertainment Tonight, Access Hollywood, EXTRA, E!, and the Discovery Channel, featured in Elle, Allure, GQ, People, Details, In Touch, LA Mag., Town & Country, TV Guide, Wall Street Journal, US Weekly, Parade, LA Times, and USA Today. Fellow ACS; mem. AMA, Calif. Med. Assn., Los Angeles County Med. Assn., L.A. Soc. Plastic Surgeons. Achievements include first plastic surgeon selected to appear on ABC's hit show "Extreme Makeover". Office: 120 S Spalding Dr Ste 222 Beverly Hills CA 90212-1840 Office Phone: 310-273-5995. Office Fax: 310-273-9079. Personal E-mail: garthmd@earthlink.net.

FISHER, GEORGE ALBERT, JR., internist, oncologist; b. Worcester, Mass., Mar. 9, 1954; PhD, Stanford U. Sch. Medicine, MD, 1987. Cert. Med. Oncology. Intern, internal medicine Stanford U. Sch. Med., Calif., 1988, resident, med. oncology Calif., 1989, fellow Calif., 1993, assoc. prof. medicine Calif. Dir. Cancer Clin. Trial Office, Standford; program leader GI Oncology, Standford. Contbr. several articles to profl. jours. Mem.: Am. Cancer Soc. (pres. Calif. divsn. 2009). Office: Stanford Comprehensive Cancer Ctr MC 5826 875 Blake Wilbur Dr Stanford CA 94305 Office Phone: 650-725-9057. Business E-Mail: georgeaf@stanford.edu.

FISHER, JEFFREY L., lawyer; b. 1970; BA in English, Duke U., 1992; JD, U. Mich. Law Sch., 1997. Bar: Wash. 2000. Law clk. to Justice John Paul Stevens U.S. Supreme Ct., Washington; law clk. to Hon. Stephen Reinhardt US Ct. Appeals (9th cir.); assoc. Davis Wright Tremaine LLP, Seattle, 1999—2004, ptnr., 2005—; assoc. prof. Stanford Law Sch., Palo Alto, Calif., 2006—, co-dir. Supreme Ct. Litig. Clinic Palo Alto., Calif., 2006. Vis. lectr. U. Wash. Law Sch.; vice chair, amicus com., co-chair supreme ct. oral argument com. Nat. Assn. Criminal Def. Lawyers; spkr. in field. Contbr. articles to profl. jours. Recipient Professionalism award, Wash. Young Lawyers Divsn., Wash. State Bar, 2004, William O. Douglas Award, Wash. Assn. of Criminal Defense Lawyers; named one of Top 40 Lawyers Under 40, Nat. Law Jour., 2005, Top 100 Influential Lawyers, 2006, Litigation's Rising Stars, The Am. Lawyer, 2007. Mem.: Wash. State Bar Assn., ACLU of Washington (mem. legal com.). Office: Davis Wright Tremaine LLP 2600 Century Sq 1501 Fourth Ave Seattle WA 98101-1688 Office Phone: 206-622-3150. Business E-Mail: jefffisher@dwt.com.

FISHER, JOEL MARSHALL, political scientist, educator, wine consultant; b. Chgo., June 24, 1935; s. Dan and Nell (Kolvin) F.; children: Sara Melinda, Matthew Nicholas. AB, U. So. Calif., 1955; LLB, MA, U. Calif.-Berkeley; PhD in Govt., Claremont Grad. U., 1968. Orgn. dir. Republican Citizens Com. of U.S., Washington, 1964-65; dir. arts and scis. state legis. divs. Rep. Nat. Com., Washington, 1968-69; asst. dep. counsel to pres. U.S. White House, 1969-70; dep. asst. sec. econ. and social affairs U.S. Dept. State, Washington, 1969-71; vis. prof. comparative and internat. law Loyola U. Sch. Law, LA, 1972-73; dir. World Bus. Inst., LA, 1974-75; prof. constl. law Southwestern U. Sch. Law, LA, 1974-76; dir. World Trade Inst. So. Calif., 1976-84; prof. internat. law, asst. dean Whitter Coll. Sch. Law, LA, 1977-80; prin. Ziskind, Greene and Assocs., 1980-83; v.p. Wells Internat., 1983-84; pres. LawSearch Inc., 1984-91; v.p. Clarke Cos., 1991-93; pres. Fisher Group, 1993—; adj. prof. Calif. Internat. U., LA, 1993-99. Spl. projects Hollywood Palace, 1998—2002, pub. affairs, 2002—; ofcl. visitor The European Cmtys., 1974, 76; wine instr. AILA/culinary arts, 1999—2006, Cordon Bleu Program CSCA, 2007—; mem. US dels. UN confs., 1969—71; chmn. Strategy for Peace Conf. Panel on US and UN, 1972—; coord. Series on the Contemporary Am. Presidency, 1972—73; cons. Robert Taft Inst., 1977—82, World Trade Inst., NY, 1977—80; chair Bid Renewal Steering Com., Hollywood Entertainment Dist.; pres. Hollywood United Neighborhood Coun., 2000—06; chair Bid Security Com., 2001—03, 2003—06; bd. dirs., treas. Hollywood Bus. Improvement Dist., 2001—08, v.p., 2003—05, 2006; organizer, pres. Lawine Fest, Inc., 2005—. Co-author three books; contbr. articles to profl. jours. Steering com. Calif. Com. Reelection of Pres., 1972; nat chmn. Cmty. Leaders Ford, 1976; trustee Rep. Assocs., 1978—, exec. com., 1986—; mem. vestry, sr. warden St. Michael and All Angeles Ch., Studio City, Calif., 1983-86, 89-93, mem. diocesan coun. L.A., 1986-88, chmn. budget com. 1987; bd. dirs. Corp. of the Cathedral, 1988-91, com. on constn. and canons, 1993—; mem. bd. dirs. Hollywood-Wilshire YMCA, 2005-. Fellow Nobel Found., 1958; Falk fellow, 1961-62 Mem. Am. Polit. Sci. Assn. (state legis. fellow 1970-73). Home: 4358 Mammoth Ave Unit 26 Sherman Oaks CA 91423-3692 Office: 1735 Vine St Hollywood CA 90028-5248 Office Phone: 818-429-6770. Personal E-mail: jmfisher@aol.com.

FISHER, LAWRENCE N., lawyer, engineering and construction management company executive; BA, U. So. Calif., LA, 1965, JD, 1968. Bar: Calif. 1969. Assoc. ptnr. Hahn & Hahn, Pasadena, Calif., 1969-74; tax atty. Fluor Corp., 1974-76; sr. tax counsel Flour Corp., 1976-78; v.p. adminstrn. Fluor Arabia Ltd., 1978-79; v.p. corp. law, asst. sec. Fluor Corp., 1984—96, sr. v.p. law, corp. sec., chief legal officer, 1996—2007. Pres. Nat. Constructor's Assn. Tax Com., 1983—84. Fluor's bd. rep. Orange County Performing Arts Ctr.

FISHER, LOUIS MCLANE, JR., management consultant; b. Balt., July 25, 1938; s. Louis McLane and Betty Taylor (Griswold) F.; m. Sue Jane Roderick, Jan. 2, 1977; children: Kathy, Mark, Matthew, Andy; stepchildren: Rolf (dec.), Sonja, Kirsten. BA magna cum laude, Hampden-Sydney Coll., 1961; postgrad., U. Va., 1961-62; MBA, U. Oreg., 1963. Exec. trainee First Nat. Bank Oreg., Portland, 1963, investment analyst, 1964; owner. Bus. Consulting Svcs., Corvallis, Oreg., 1964-65; administrv. mgr. CH2M HILL, Denver, 1965-70, treas., 1970-75, exec. v.p., 1975-94; pres. Quaere, Littleton, Colo.,

1995—. Guest lectr. Oreg. State U.; bd. dirs. Open Door Inc., Iotech Inc., OMI Inc., Indsl. Design Corp., Power Interests Holding Corp., Coleman Sperryn-Jones, Mariott Resort, Bahamas, GCSI Tissuscan Tech., Grand Masters of Lacrosse, PSMA, Merrick Engring., Woodard & Curran Inc., Psomas Assocs. Contbr. articles to profl. jours. Bd. dirs. Corvallis Arts Ctr. Fellow Profl. Svcs. Mgmt. Assn. (cert. profl. svcs. mgr.; bd. dirs. 1975-78, pres. 1976-77, chmn. coll. fellows 1980—); mem. Am. Mgmt. Assn., Am. Cons. Engrs. Coun., Alliance Profl. Consultants, Nat. Assn. Corp. Dirs., Fin. Execs. Inst., Western Regional Coun. (treas. 1987-88), Denver C. of C., Corvallis Area C. of C. (bd. dirs., v.p. 1971), Met. Club, Chaîne de Rôtisseurs. Republican. Episcopalian.

FISHER, LUCY, film producer; b. NYC, Oct. 2, 1949; d. Arthur Bertram and Naomi (Kislak) F.; m. Douglas Z. Wick, Feb. 16, 1986; children: Sarah, Julia, Tessa. BA in English, cum laude, Harvard U., 1971. Reader United Artists; v.p. prodn. 20th Century Fox, LA, 1979-80; v.p. worldwide prodns. Zoetrope Studios, Burbank, Calif., 1980-81; v.p., sr. prodn. exec. Warner Bros. Pictures, Burbank, 1981-87, sr. v.p., 1987-89, exec. v.p. prodn., 1989-96; vice chmn. Columbia Tristar Motion Picture Co., Culver City, Calif., 1996-2000; prodr. Red Wagon Productions, Culver City, Calif., 2000—, pres. Prodr.: (films) Stuart Little 2, 2002, Peter Pan, 2003, Win a Date with Tad Hamilton!, 2004, Bewitched, 2005, Jarhead, 2005, Memoirs of a Geisha, 2005, Stuart Little 3: Call of the Wild, 2005; exec. prodr.: (TV series) Stuart Little, 2003. Recipient Crystal award, 1998, David O. Selznick Achievement award in Theatrical Motion Pictures, Producers Guild Am., 2007. Office: Red Wagon Entertainment Hepburn West 10202 Washington Blvd Culver City CA 90232-3119

FISHER, MARK JAY, neurologist, neuroscientist, educator; b. Bklyn., Aug. 23, 1949; s. Ralph Aaron and Dorothy Ann (Weissman) F.; m. Janeth Godeau, Aug. 5, 1994. BA in Polit. Sci., UCLA, 1970; MA in Polit. Sci., U. S.D., 1972; MD, U. Cin., 1975; JD, Loyola U., 1997. Diplomate Am. Bd. Psychiatry and Neurology. Intern UCLA Sepulveda VA Hosp., 1975-76; resident UCLA Wadsworth VA Med. Ctr., 1976-79, chief resident, 1979-80; faculty mem., dir. stroke rsch. program U. So. Calif. Sch. of Medicine, LA, 1980-98, prof. neurology, 1995-98; dir. residency tng. program U. So. Calif. Sch. Medicine, LA, 1992-96; chmn. dept. neurology U. Calif. at Irvine, Orange, 1998—2006, prof. neurology and anatomy and neurobiology, 1998—, prof. polit. sci., 2003—. Editor: Medical Therapy of Acute Stroke, 1989. Recipient Tchr. Investigator award NIH, Bethesda, Md., 1984-89, Program Project grantee, 1994-99. Mem.: Internat. Soc. Polit. Psychology, Am. Polit. Sci. Assn., State Bar Calif., Internat. Soc. for Thrombosis and Haemostasis, Am. Polit. Sci. Assn., Am. Heart Assn. (stroke coun.), Am. Neurol. Assn., Am. Acad. Neurology. Office: U Calif Irvine Dept Neurology 101 The City Dr S Orange CA 92868-3201

FISHER, MATTHEW P. A., physicist; Rsch. physicist Inst. Theoretical Physics, Santa Barbar, Calif. Recipient Initiatives in Rsch. award NAS, 1997. Office: U California Inst Theoretical Physics 522 University Rd Santa Barbara CA 93106-0002

FISHER, NANCY LOUISE, pediatrician, geneticist, retired nurse; b. Cleve., July 4, 1944; d. Nelson Leopold and Catherine (Harris) F.; m. Larry William Larson, May 30, 1976 (div. Oct. 2000); 1 child, Jonathan Raymond. Student, Notre Dame Coll., Cleve., 1962-64; BSN, Wayne State U., 1967; postgrad., Calif. State U., Hayward, 1971-72; MD, Baylor Coll. of Medicine, 1976; M in Pub. Health, U. Wash., 1982, certificate in ethics, 1993. Diplomate Am. Bd. Pediatrics, Am. Bd. Med. Genetics. RN coronary care unit and med. intensive care unit Highland Gen. Hosp., Oakland, Calif., 1970-72; RN coronary care unit Alameda (Calif.) Hosp., 1972-73; intern in pediatrics Baylor Coll. of Medicine, Houston, 1976-77, resident in pediatrics, 1977-78; attending physician, pediatric clinic Harborview Med. Ctr., Seattle, 1980-81; staff physician children and adolescent health care clinic Columbia Health Ctr., Seattle, 1981-87, founder, dir. of med. genetics clinic, 1984-89; maternal child health policy cons. King County div. Seattle King County Dept Pub. Health, 1983-85; dir. genetic svcs. Va. Mason Clinic, 1986-89; dir. med. genetic svcs. Swedish Hosp., 1989-94; pvt. practice Seattle, 1994-97; med. cons. supr. office of managed care Wash. State Dept. Social and Health Svcs., Olympia, 1996-97; med. dir. Medicaid Dept. of Social and Health Svcs., Wash., 1997-99; assoc. med. dir. Govt. Programs Regence Blue Shield, 1999; med. dir. Regence Blue Shield, 2000—02; chief med. officer Wash. State Health Care Authority, 2003—. Nurses aide psychiatry Sinai Hosp., Detroit, 1966—67; charge nurse Women's Hosp., Cleve., 1967; rsch. asst. to Dr. Shelly Liss, 76; with Baylor Housestaff Assn., Baylor Coll. Medicine, 1980—81; clin. asst. prof. grad. sch. nursing U. Wash., Seattle, 1981—85, clin. asst. prof. dept. pediat., 1982—92, clin. assoc. prof. dept. pediat., 1992—; com. appointments include Seattle CCS Cleft Palate Panel, 1984—97; bd. dirs., first v.p. King County Assn. Sickle Cell Disease, 1985—86, acting pres., 1986, pres., 1986—87; hosp. affiliation include Childrens Orthopedic Hosp. and Med. Ctr., Seattle, 1981—, Virginia Mason Hosp., Seattle, 1985—89, Harborview Hosp., Seattle, 1986—89; mem. Wash. State Steering Coun. Stroke and Heart Disease, 2006—, Wash. State Vaccine Adv. Com., 2006—. Contbr. articles to profl. jours. Active Seattle Urban League, 1982-96, 101 Black Women, 1986-94; bd. dirs. Seattle Sickle Cell Affected Family Assn., 1984-85, Am. Heart Assn., 2001—, March of Dimes 2002—; mem. People to People Citizen Ambassador Group; sec. Health and Human Svcs. Com. on Infant Mortality, 1993—2003; mem. Twins Com. Inst. of Medicine, 1995-2000; Evaluation, Rsch. and Planning Group Ethical Legal and Social Implications Nat. Human Gerome Rsch. Inst., 1997-2000. Served to lt. USN Nurse Corps, 1966-70; active State Steering Com. on Heart Disease and Stroke, 2005—, Washington State Govs. Coun. on Disparities, 2006—. Fellow Am. Coll. Medicine Genetics (founder); mem. AMA, APHA, Am. Heart Assn. (bd. dirs. King County 2001—, Pacific NW affiliate bd. 2006—, Physician of Yr.), Am. Acad. Physician Execs., Student Governing Body and Graduating Policy Com. Baylor Coll. Medicine (founding mem. 1973-76), Loans and Scholarship Com. Baylor Coll. Medicine (voting mem. 1973-76), Am. Med. Student Assn., Student Nat. Med. Assn., Admission Com. Baylor Coll. Medicine (voting mem. 1974-76), Am. Med. Women's Assn., Am. Acad. Pediatrics, Am. Soc. Human Genetics, Nat. Spkrs. Assn., Nat. Quality Found. (steering com.), Wash. State Assn. Black Providers of Health Care, Soc. Health and Human Values, Wash. State Soc. Pediatrics, Wash. State Med. Assn. (women in medicine com., intersplty. coun., fin. com.), Seattle C. of C. (mem. Leadership Tomorrow 1988—), Sigma Gamma Rho, Phi Delta Epsilon. Office: Wash State HCA 676 Woodland Sq Loop SE MS-42701 Olympia WA 98504-2701 Office Phone: 360-923-2709. Business E-Mail: nancy.fisher@hca.wa.gov.

FISHER, ORA T., lawyer; BS in Econ., Univ. Pa., 1984; JD cum laude, Univ. Mich., 1991. Bar: Calif. 1991. Internal cons. and public fin. banking officer JPMorgan, NYC; atty. Latham & Watkins LLP, San Francisco, 1991—97, atty., Silicon Valley office Menlo Park, 1997—2004, mng. ptnr. Silicon Valley office, 2004—, and co-chair, venture & tech. practice group. Mem.: ABA, San Francisco Bar Assn., State Bar of Calif. Office: Latham & Watkins LLP 140 Scott Dr Menlo Park CA 94025-1008

FISHER, RAYMOND CORLEY, federal judge; b. Oakland, Calif., July 12, 1939; s. Raymond Henry and Mary Elizabeth (Corley) Fisher; m. Nancy Leigh Fairchilds, Jan. 22, 1961; children: Jeffrey, Amy. BA, U. Calif., Santa Barbara, 1961; LLB, Stanford U., 1966. Bar: Calif. 1967, U.S. Supreme Ct. 1967. Law clk. to Hon. J. Skelly Wright US Ct. Appeals (DC cir.), Washington, 1966—67; law clk. to Hon. William J. Brennan US Supreme Ct., Washington, 1967—68; ptnr. Tuttle & Taylor, L.A., LA, 1968—88, Heller, Ehrman, White & McAuliffe, LA, 1988—97; assoc. atty. gen. US Dept. of Justice, Washington, 1997—99; judge US Ct. Appeals (9th cir.), 1999—. Pres.: Stanford Law Rev., 1965—66. Dir. Constl. Rights Found., LA, 1978—, pres., 1983—87, LA City Bd. Civil Svc. Commn., 1987—88; dep. gen. counsel Christopher Commn., LA, 1991—92; pres. LA City Bd. Police Commrs., 1996—97; dir. Western Justice Ctr. Found., 2000—; spl. asst. to Gov. of Calif., 1975. With USAR, 1957—64. Fellow: Am. Bar Found., Am. Coll. Trial Lawyers; mem.: Am. Law Inst., Calif. State Bar, Fed. Bar Assn. (exec. com. 1990—96), Chancery Club, Order of Coif. Office: US Ct Appeals 125 S Grand Ave Rm 400 Pasadena CA 91105

FISHER, ROBERT ALAN, laser physicist; b. Berkeley, Calif., Apr. 19, 1943; s. Leon Harold and Phyllis (Kahn) F.; children: Andrew Leon, Derek Martin. AB, U. Calif., Berkeley, 1965, MA, 1967, PhD, 1971. Programmer Stanford (Calif.) linear accelerator Stanford U., 1965; staff mem. Granger Assocs., Palo Alto, Calif., 1966; lectr. U. Calif., Davis, 1972-74; physicist Lawrence Livermore Lab., Calif., 1971-74; laser physicist Los Alamos (N.Mex.) Nat. Lab., 1974-86. Cons. R.A. Fisher Assocs., Santa Fe, 1986—; instr. Engring. Tech., Inc., 1982—; mem. Air Force ABCD Panel, 1982; program com. mem. Internat. Quantum Electronics Conf., 1982, 86; program com. CLEO Conf., 2002—05, chair subcom. nonlinear optics, 2006—07; vice chmn. Gordon Conf. on Lasers and Non-linear Optics, 1981; chmn. Soc. Photo-Optical Instrumentation Engrs. Conf. on Optical Phase Conjugation/Beam Combining/Diagnostics, 1987—; mem. Air Force Red Team for Space-Based Laser, 1983—86, HEDS II SDI Red Team, 1986, U.S. Ballistic Missile Office Options Team, 1986; mem. secretariat SDI Red/Blue Sensor Teams, 1986, SDI GBL Red/Blue Team Interaction, 1987—88; mem. architecture panel SDI SDS Phase I, 1990, Air Force Laser 21 Working Group, 1990. Assoc. editor Optics Letters, 1984-86, Applied Optics, 1984-91, Topical Edit. Optics Letters, 2002-04; editor: Optical Phase Conjugation, 1973; contbr. articles to profl. jours. Vol. coach elem. sch. chess team Pojoaque Elem. Sch. (winner nat. elem. championship 1984), Santa Fe, 1984. Fellow Optical Soc. Am. (guest editor jour. spl. issue on optical phase conjugation, mem. Engring. Excellence award com. 2003, chmn. 2004), SPIE (bd. dirs. 2002-04, scholarship com. 2001-04, edn. com. 2004-); mem. IEEE (sr.), Optical Soc. Am. Found. Avocation: performing and teaching bluegrass and fiddle tune music. Home and Office: 2996 Plaza Blanca Santa Fe NM 87507-5340 Office Phone: 505-992-3930.

FISHER, ROBERT J., retail executive; b. 1954; s. Donald G. and Doris (Feigenbaum) Fisher; married; 3 children. BA, BS, Princeton U., NJ, 1976; MBA, Stanford U., Calif., 1980. Store mgr. Gap, Inc., 1980-85, exec. v.p. mdse. Banana Republic, 1985-89, pres. Banana Republic, 1989-90, exec. v.p., 1992—99, COO, 1992—93, 1995—97, CFO, 1993-95, pres. Gap Brand, 1997—2004, non-exec. chmn., 2004—07, interim CEO, 2007—. Bd. dirs. The Gap, Inc., 1990—, Sun Microsystems, Inc., 1995—2006. Chair exec. com. Conservation Internat.; vice chair bd. Natural Resources Def. Coun.; bd. mem. San Francisco Mus. Modern Art. Named one of Forbes' Richest Ams., 2006. Office: Gap Inc 2 Folsom St San Francisco CA 94105 Office Phone: 650-952-4400.

FISHER, ROBERT MORTON, foundation and academic administrator; b. St. Paul, Oct. 15, 1938; s. S.S. and Jean Fisher; m. Elinor C. Schectman, June 19, 1960; children: Laurie, Jonathan. AB magna cum laude, Harvard Coll., 1960; JD, Harvard U., 1963; PhD, London Sch. Econs, Polit. Sci., 1967; LLD, West Coast U., LA, 1981; DHL, Profl. Sch. Psychology, San Francisco, 1986; DPS, John F. Kennedy U., Orinda, Calif., 1988. Rsch. assoc. Mass. Mental Health Ctr., Cambridge, 1957-62; rsch. asst. Ctr. Study Juvenile Delinquency, Cambridge, 1961-63; spl. asst. to chief psychologist British Prison Dept. Home Office, London, 1963-67; prof. Sch. Criminology U. Calif., Berkeley, 1965-71; profl. race car driver, 1972-77; pres. John F. Kennedy U., Orinda, Calif., 1974-85; exec. dir. 92d St. YMHA, NYC, 1984-85; dir., CEO The San Francisco Found., 1987-97; pres. nonprofit edn. and founds. Rushal, Loscavio & LoPresto Exec. Search, San Francisco, 2005—. Mayor, councilman Lafayette, Calif., 1968-76; mem. Minn. and Calif. Bar Specialty: charitable gift planning; CEO Fisher Cos., 1997—; exec. dir. Alonzo King's Line Ballet, 2003-04; prin. cons. Robert Fisher Assocs. Non-Profit Cons., 2003—. Scholar-in-residence Rockefeller Found., Bellagio, 1994; Polit. Sci. vis. fellow London Sch. Econs. and Polit. Sci., 1994; named Outstanding Fundraising Exec. Nat. Soc. Fund Raising Execs. Home: 85 Southwood Dr Orinda CA 94563-3026 Office: Rusher Loscavio Exec Search 100 Spear St # 935 San Francisco CA 94105 Home Phone: 925-254-1566; Office Phone: 415-765-6584. E-mail: rmfisher@earthlink.net.

FISHER, STEVEN KAY, neurobiology educator; b. Rochester, Ind., July 18, 1942; s. Stewart King and Hazel Madeline (Howell) F.; m. Dinah Dawn Marschall, May 2, 1971; children: Jenni Dawn, Brian Andrew, Steven William. BS, Purdue U., 1964, MS, 1966; postgrad., Johns Hopkins U., 1967—69; PhD, Purdue U., 1969. Postdoctoral fellow Johns Hopkins U., Balt., 1969-71; prof. U. Calif., Santa Barbara, 1971—, dir. Inst. Environ. Stress, 1985-88, dir. Neurosci. Rsch. Inst., 1989-2001. Cons. Ultrastructure Tech., Goleta, Calif., 1984—, Regeneron Pharms., Inc., 1993, 94, Amgen, Inc., 1994, 95; mem. NIH Visual Scis. A2 Study Sect. Contbr. numerous articles to profl. jours. Recipient Devel. award, NIH, 1980—84, M.E.R.I.T. award, 1989—99, Ludwig von Sallmann prize for vision rsch., 2002, Faculty Research Lecture award, U. Calif., Santa Barbara, 2007; grantee, NIH, 1971—, NSF, 2003. Mem. Assn. Rsch. in Vision and Ophthalmology (mem. program com. 1979-80, K-12 edn. com. 1997-2001), Internat. Soc. for Eye Rsch., Soc. Neurosci. Avocations: music, gardening, guitar, literature, weightlifting. Home: 6890 Sabado Tarde Rd Goleta CA 93117-4305 Office: U Calif Neurosci Rsch Inst Santa Barbara CA 93106-5060 E-mail: fisher@lifesci.ucsb.edu.

FISHER, THOMAS E., energy company executive; BSME, Tex. A&M U., 1966. Various engring. and mgmt. positions Unocal Corp., El Segundo, Calif., 1966-87, divsn. v.p., 1987-94, sr. v.p. corp. new ventures, comml. affairs, 1994—.

FISHMAN, ROBERT ALLEN, retired neurologist, educator, department chair; b. NYC, May 30, 1924; s. Samuel Benjamin and Miriam (Brinkin) F.; m. Margery Ann Satz, Jan. 29, 1956 (dec. May 29, 1980); children: Mary Beth, Alice Ellen, Elizabeth Ann.; m. Mary Craig Wilson, Jan. 7, 1983. AB, Columbia U., 1944; MD, U. Pa., 1947. Mem. faculty Columbia Coll. Physicians and Surgeons, 1954-66, asso. prof. neurology, 1962-66; asst. attending neurologist N.Y. State Psychiat. Inst., 1955-66, Neurol. Inst. Presbyn. Hosp., NYC, 1955-61, asso., 1961-66; co-dir. Neurol. Clin. Research Center, Neurol. Inst., Columbia-Presbyn. Med. Ctr., 1961-66; prof. neurology U. Calif. Med. Ctr., San Francisco, 1966-94, chmn. dept. neurology, 1966-92, prof. emeritus, 1994—; ret., 2005. Cons. neurologist San Francisco Gen. Hosp., San Francisco VA Hosp., Letterman Gen. Hosp.; dir. Am. Bd. Psychiatry and Neurology, 1981-88, v.p., 1986, pres., 1987 Author: Cerebrospinal Fluid in Diseases of the Nervous System, 1992; chief editor Annals of Neurology, 1993-97; contbr. articles to profl. jours. Nat. Multiple Sclerosis Soc. fellow, 1956-57; John and Mary R. Markle scholar in med. sci., 1960-65; recipient Disting. Alumnus award U. Pa. 1996. Mem. Am. Neurol. Assn. (pres. 1983-84), Am. Fedn. for Clin. Research, Assn. for Research in Nervous and Mental Diseases, Am. Acad. Neurology (v.p. 1971-73, pres. 1975-77), Am. Assn. Physicians, Am. Soc. for Neurochemistry, Soc. for Neurosci., N.Y. Neurol. Soc., Am. Assn. Univ. Profs. Neurology (pres. 1972-73), AAAS, Am. Epilepsy Soc., N.Y. Acad. Scis., AMA (sec. sect. on nervous and mental diseases 1964-67, v.p. 1967-68, pres. 1968-69), Alpha Omega Alpha (hon. faculty mem.), NAS Insts. Medicine. Home: 205 Paradise Dr Belvedere Tiburon CA 94920-2534 Personal E-mail: raf530@comcast.net.

FISKE, NEIL S., retail executive; b. Colo. Degree in Polit. Economy, Williams Coll.; MBA, Harvard U. Polit. speechwriter; bus. cons. Boston Consulting Group, 1989—99, mng. ptnr., 2000—02; CEO Bath & Body Works, Inc., Reynoldsburg, Ohio, 2003—07; pres., CEO Eddie Bauer Holdings, Inc., Redmond, Wash., 2007—. Bd. dirs. Eddie Bauer Holdings, Inc., 2007—. Co-author (with Michael Silverstein): Trading Up: The New American Luxury, 2003. Past legis. adv. Congressman and Senator Timothy E. Wirth. Office: Eddie Bauer 10401 NE 8th St # 500 Bellevue WA 98004-4346

FISKER, HENRIK, automobile designer and company executive; b. Denmark, Aug. 10, 1963; Grad., Art Ctr. Coll. Design, Calif., 1989. Designer BMW Technik GmbH, Munich, 1989—97; pres., CEO DesignworksUSA (subs. BMW Grp.), Munich, 2000; design dir. Aston Martin; creative dir. Ingeni Ford Motor Co., London, 2001—03, dir. Global Advanced Design Studio (CAPC) Irvine, Calif., 2003—04; co-founder, CEO Fisker Coachbuild, LLC, 2004—. Named a Maverick, Details mag., 2008. Achievements include design of BMW Z8, Aston Martin DB9, Aston Martin V8 Vantage; Z07 concept car showcased at the Tokyo Motor Show. Office: Fisker Coachbuild LLC 2811 McGaw Ave Ste B Irvine CA 92614 Office Phone: 949-274-8588.

FITIAL, BENÍGNO REPEKI, Governor of Northern Mariana Islands; b. No. Mariana Islands, Nov. 27, 1945; m. Josie P. Fitial; 6 children. BA, U. Guam, 1976. Budget officer Commonwealth No. Mariana Islands Legislature, 1978—80, rep. Dist. 3, 1980—2006, spkr., 1982—84, 2000—02, 2004—06, minority leader, 1980—82, 1984—86, chmn. Commn. on Fed. Laws, 1985—88, vice spkr., 1986—88; gov. Commonwealth No. Mariana Islands, 2006—. News dir. KJQR Radio Station; chmn. Bank of Saipan, 1990—94; cons. Tan Holdings Corp.; pres. Century Ins. Co., 1988—96, Century Travel Corp., Consolidated Transp. Svcs. Inc., Pacific Oriental Inc., Home Improvement. Chmn. Trusteeship Termination Task Force, Civil Svc. Commn., Saipan Mcpl. Scholarship Bd.; founder Covenant Party; delegatge 1st No. Marianas Constl. Convention, chmn. Tax, Pub. Dept, Edn. and Local Govt. Com.; mem. Tax Task Force, Rep. Presdl. Task Force; chmn. No. Marianas Rep. Party, Zoning Bd., Bush for Pres. Com. for Commonwealth No. Mariana Islands. Recipient Disting. Alumni Award, U. Guam, 1982. Mem.: Oxford Club. Catholic. Office: Office of Gov Caller Box 10007 Saipan MP 96950 Office Fax: 670-233-5112. E-mail: fitial@vzpacifica.net.

FITZGERALD, JAMES MICHAEL, federal judge; b. Portland, Oreg., Oct. 7, 1920; s. Thomas and Florence (Linderman) F.; m. Karin Rose Benton, Jan. 19, 1950; children: Dennis James, Denise Lyn, Debra Jo, Kevin Thomas. BA, Willamette U., 1950, LLB, 1951; postgrad., U. Wash., 1952. Bar: Alaska 1953. Asst. U.S. atty., Ketchikan and Anchorage, Alaska, 1952-56; city atty. City of Anchorage, 1956-59; legal counsel to Gov. Alaska, Anchorage, 1959; commr. pub. safety State of Alaska, 1959; judge Alaska Superior Ct., 3d Jud. Dist., 1959-69, presiding judge, 1969-72; assoc. justice Alaska Supreme Ct., Anchorage, 1972-75; judge U.S. Dist. Ct. for Alaska, Anchorage, from 1975, formerly chief judge, now sr. judge. Mem. advisory bd. Salvation Army, Anchorage, 1962—, chmn., 1965-66; mem. Anchorage Parks and Recreation Bd., 1965-77, chmn., 1966. Served with AUS, 1940-41; Served with USMCR, 1942-46. Office: US Dist Ct 222 W 7th Ave Box 50 Anchorage AK 99513-7564

FITZ-GERALD, JOAN, state legislator; b. NYC, June 2, 1948; m 72 to John Fitz-Gerald; children: Matthew & Patrick. Clerk, recorder, Jefferson Co, Colorado, 91-99; member, Motor Vehicle Licensing Bd, formerly; vice president, Motor Vehicle Dealer Bd, formerly; Colorado State Senator, District 13, 2001-02; Colorado State Senator, District 16, 2003-, chairwoman, Exec Committee Legislature Coun, Legislature Coun, Senate Serv, currently, member, State, Veterans & Military Affairs Committee, currently, Colorado State Senate; president, Colorado State Senate, currently. Named Bus Woman of the Yr, Golden Bus and Prof Women Association, 95. Democrat. Home: 942 Sleepy Hollow Golden CO 80401 Mailing: 200 E Colfax Rm 330 Denver CO 80203 Office Phone: 303-866-2318. Fax: 303-866-4543. E-mail: joan.fitzgerald.senate@state.co.us.

FITZGERALD, JOHN CHARLES, JR., investment banker; b. Sacramento, May 23, 1941; s. John Charles and Geraldine Edith (McNabb) F.; m. Mildred Ann Kilpatrick, June 26, 1965; children: Geraldine Kathrine, Erec John. BS, Calif. State U., Sacramento, 1964; MBA, Cornell U., 1965. Dir. corp. planning Bekins Co., LA, 1966-73; mgr. corp. planning Ridder Publs., Inc., LA, 1973-75; CFO City of

Inglewood, Calif., 1975-77; treas./contr. Inglewood Redevel. Agy., 1975-77; v.p. mcpl. fin. White, Weld & Co., Inc., LA, 1977-78; v.p. pub. fin. Paine Webber Jackson & Curtis, LA, 1978-79; v.p. and mgr. for Western region, mcpl. fin. dept. Merrill Lynch Capital Markets, LA, 1979-82, mng. dir. Western region, mcpl. fin. dept., 1982-86; mng. dir. Seidler-Fitzgerald Pub. Fin., LA, 1986—2002; sr. v.p. The Seidler Cos., Inc., LA, 1986—2002; mng. dir. John C. Fitzgerald & Assocs., a divsn. of Wulff, Hansen & Co., 2002—. Instr. fin./adminstrn. El Camino Coll., Torrance, Calif., 1977-80. Chmn. bd. dirs., exec. com., treas., chmn. fundraising com. L.a. chpt. Am. Heart Assn., 1977—; bd. dirs. Daniel Freeman Hosps. Inc., Corondelet Health Care corp.; trustee Mt. St. Mary's Coll., L.A., 1992-2001, regent, 2004—; bd. dirs. Tau Kappa Epsilon Ednl. Found., Indpls., 1995-2003; bd. dirs. Calif. Soc. for Biomed. Rsch., 1998; alumni coun. mem. Johnson Grad. Sch. Mgmt. Cornell U., real estate coun. Mem. Fin. Execs. Inst., Mcpl. fin. Officers, League Calif. Cities, So. Calif. Corp. Planners Assn. (past pres.), L.A. Bond, Lido Isle Yacht Club, Jonathan Club, The Calif. Club, Lake Arrowhead Country Club, Rotary, Navy League, Beta Gamma Sigma. Address: PO Box 765 27447 Bayshore Dr Lake Arrowhead CA 92352 Office Phone: 213-955-5977.

FITZGERALD, LARRY DARNELL, JR., professional football player; b. Mpls., Aug. 31, 1983; s. Larry Darnell and Carol Fitzgerald. Attended, Univ. Pitts., 2002—04. Wide receiver Ariz. Cardinals, 2004—. Participant NFL-USO Tour, Persian Gulf, 2009. Recipient Walter Camp Player of Yr. award, 2003, Fred Biletnikoff award, 2003; named 1st Team All-Pro, AP, 2008, NFL Pro Bowl MVP, 2009; named to All-Am. Team, NCAA, 2003, Nat. Football Conf. Pro Bowl Team, NFL, 2005, 2007, 2008. Achievements include leading the NFL in: receptions, 2005; receiving touchdowns (12), 2008. Office: Ariz Cardinals PO Box 888 Phoenix AZ 85001-0888*

FITZGERALD, TIKHON (LEE R. H. FITZGERALD), bishop; b. Detroit, Nov. 14, 1932; s. LeRoy and Dorothy Kaeding (Higgins) F. AB, Wayne State U., 1958. Ordained deacon, 1971, priest, 1978, bishop Eastern Orthodox, 1987. Enlisted U.S. Army, 1954-57; commd. 2 lt. USAF, 1960, advanced through grades to capt., 1971; air staff, 1966-71; released, 1971; protodeacon Holy Virgin Mary Russian Orthodox Cathedral, LA, 1972-78, rector, archpriest, 1979-87; bishop of San Francisco and the West Orthodox Ch. in Am., LA, 1987—. Recipient Order of St. Vladimir II Class, Patriarch Aleksy of Moscow, 1993. Democrat. Russian Orthodox. Home: 649 Robinson St Los Angeles CA 90026-3612 Office: Orthodox Ch Am Diocese of the West 650 Micheltorena St Los Angeles CA 90026-3623

FITZ-PATRICK, DAVID, endocrinologist, educator; b. Burnley, Lancashire, England, Sept. 1, 1951; came to U.S., 1975; s. Malcolm Milligan and Ada (Maguire) F.; m. Elizabeth Joaquin, Dec. 30, 1972; children: Ian Rodney, Claire Larissa. MB, BS, U. Newcastle-Upon-Tyne, England, 1974. House officer Newcastle (England) Gen. Hosp., 1974-75; resident in internal medicine U. Md. Hosp., Balt., 1975-77; fellow in endocrinology McGill U., Montreal, Que., Can., 1977-81; cons. physician Straub Clinic and Hosp, Honolulu, 1981-91, chief of endocrinology, 1986-91; asst. clin. prof. medicine John Burns Sch. Medicine, Honolulu, 1982-95, assoc. clin. prof., 1995—; med. dir. Diabetes and Hormone Ctr. of Pacific, Honolulu, 1990—, East-West Med. Rsch. Inst., 1999—. Mem. house of dels. Hawaii Med. Assn., 1987-90; med. adv. com. Bd. Med. Examiners, Hawaii, 1989—; founding mem., bd. dirs. Juvenile Diabetes Found., Honolulu, 1989-92 (Geraldine Fleming Meml. fellowship 1980-81); dir. East-West Med. Rsch. Inst., 1999—. Mem. editl. bd. Endocrine Practice, 2000-08; contbr. articles to profl. jours.; founder, editor Diabetes & Endocrinology Home Page on Internet. Dir. The Straub Found., Honolulu, 1984-90. Rsch. scholar McGill U., 1979-80. Fellow Am. Coll. Physicians (mem. coun. 1990-93, Gov's. prize 1986), Am. Coll. Endocrinology; mem. Am. Diabetes Assn. (pres. 1984-86, 93-94), The Endocrine Soc., Am. Soc. Internal Medicine, Am. Assn. Clin. Endocrinologists (state chair 1992-96, 98—). Avocations: reading, piano, golf. Office: 1585 Kapiolani Blvd Ste 1500 Honolulu HI 96814-Office Phone: 808-531-6886.

FITZPATRICK, LOIS ANN, library administrator; b. Yonkers, NY, Mar. 27, 1952; d. Thomas Joseph and Dorothy Ann (Nealy) Sullivan; m. William George Fitzpatrick, Jr., Dec. 1, 1973; children: Jennifer Ann, Amy Ann. BS in Sociology, Mercy Coll., 1974; MLS, Pratt Inst., 1975. Clk. Yonkers Pub. Libr., 1970-73, libr. trainee, 1973-75, libr. I, 1975-76; reference libr. Carroll Coll. Libr., Helena, Mont., 1976-79, acting dir., 1979, dir., 1980—; asst. prof. Carroll Coll., Helena, 1979-89, assoc. prof., 1989-99, prof., 2000—. Bd. dirs. Mont. Shares 2000-; chmn. arrangements Mont. Gov.'s Pre White House Conf. on Libraries, Helena, 1977-78; mem. steering com. Reference Point coop. program for librs., 1991; mem. adv. com. Helena Coll. of Tech. Libr., 1994—; adv. coun. Mont. Libr. Svcs., 1996-2000; mem. Networking Task Force, 1998-2003, Laws Revision Task Force, 1998-2001, Not Ready for Prime Time Freedom Fighters, 2004-; pres. elect Helena Area Health Sci. Libraries Cons., 1979-84, pres., 1984-88; bd. dirs. Mont. FAXNET; chair govt. affairs Mont. Libr. Assn., 1997-2005, 2006-. Co-chmn. interst group OCLC; chmn. local arrangements Mont. Gov.'s Pre White House Conf.; mem. Soroptimist Internat. of Helena, 1977-, Mont. Race for the Cure, 1998-2004; bd. dirs. ACLU-MT, 1998—2007, pres., 2005-2007; mem. adv. com. Am. Cancer Soc. Lewis and Clark County; bd. dir. Montana Shares, 2004-07, legis. ambassador Am. Cancer Soc., 2003-, legis. contact, Mont. Am. Libr. Assn. Recipient Women Helping Women award, Soroptimist Internat. Helena, 1986, Spl. Recognition award, Mont. Libr. Assn., 1999. Mem. Mont. Libr. Assn. (task force for White House conf. 1991, chair govt. affairs com. 1997-2003, 2005-, EdLINK-MT 1997-99, 2000-01, spl. recognition award 1999), Soroptimist Internat. of Helena (2d v.p. 1984-85, pres. 1986-87, Women Helping Women award 1988), Am. Cancer Soc. (mem. lapel program, 2005—, mem. Cancer Advocacy Network program, 2005—, legislative ambassador, 2007-); Mont. Cancer Control Coalition (mem. adv. bd. 2005-, steering com., 2006-, chair legislative work group, 2006-). Home: 1308 Shirley Rd Helena MT 59602-6635 Office: Carroll Coll Jack & Sallie Corette Libr 1601 N Benton Ave Helena MT 59625-0001 Home Phone: 406-431-6122; Office Phone: 406-447-4341. Business E-Mail: lfitzpat@carroll.edu.

FITZPATRICK, THOMAS MARK, lawyer; b. Anaconda, Mont., June 12, 1951; s. Marcus Leo and Natalie Stephanie (Trbovich) F. BA, U. Mont., 1973; JD, U. Chgo., 1976. Bar: Ill. 1976, Wash. 1978. Asst. to pres.-elect ABA, Chgo., 1976-77, asst. to pres., 1977-78; assoc. Karr, Tuttle, Campbell, Seattle, 1978-85, ptnr., 1985-89, Stafford, Frey, Cooper, Seattle, 1989-99; asst. chief civil divsn. Snohomish County Prosecuting Atty.'s Office, Everett, Wash., 1999—2005; exec. dir. Snohomish County County Exec. Office, Everett, 2005—06; ptnr. Talmadge Law Group PLLC, Tukwila, Wash., 2006—. Editor: ABA: A Century of Service, 1979. Fellow Am. Bar Found.; mem. ABA (chmn. lawyer and media conf. 1985-88, profl. discipline com. 1988-94, LRIS com. 1994-97, ethics com. 2001-04, chmn. nat. conf. groups 1982-85, ho. of dels. 1990—, state del. 1993-98, bd. govs. 1998-2001), Wash. Bar Assn. (pres. young lawyer divsn. 1986-87), Snohomish County Bar Assn., Seattle-King County Bar Assn., U. Chgo. Law Sch. Alumni Assn. (bd. dirs., Seattle regional pres. 1980-86). Roman Catholic. Home: 7345 13th Ave NW Seattle WA 98117-5306 Office: Talmadge Law Group PLLC 18010 Souteastern Pkwy Tukwila WA 98188 Office Phone: 206-574-6661. Business E-Mail: tom@talmadgelg.com.

FIX, WILBUR JAMES, department store executive; b. Velva, ND, Aug. 14, 1927; s. Jack J. and Beatrice D. (Wasson) F.; m. Beverly A. Corcoran, Sept. 20, 1953; children: Kathleen M., Michael B., Jenifer L. BA, U. Wash., 1950. Credit mgr. Bon Marche, Yakima, Wash., 1951-54, controller, ops. mgr. Boise, Idaho, 1954-58, sr. v.p. Seattle, 1970-76, exec. v.p., 1976-77, pres., chief exec. officer, 1978-87; chmn., chief exec. officer, sr. v.p. Allied Stores Corp., 1987-93; chmn. Fix Mgmt. Group, 1993—; ret., 2004. Chmn. Wash. Retail Coun., 1983-84; mem. adv. coun. Inst. for Retail Studies, Col. of the Desert, Palm Desert, Calif., Corp. Coun. of the Arts, Seattle. Mem. pres.'s adv. com. Allied Stores Corp., N.Y., 1968-72; mem. citizens adv. com. Seattle Pub. Schs., 1970-71; v.p. Citizens Council Against Crime; chmn. Seattle King County Conv. & Visitors Bur., 1990. With AUS, 1946-47. Mem.: Mission Hills Country Club (Rancho Mirage, Calif.), Wash. Athletic Club, Wash. Round Table, Downtown Seattle Devel. Assn., Assn. Wash. Bus., Seattle C. of C., Western States Regional Controllers Congress, Fin. Execs. Inst., Seattle Retail Controllers Group, Controllers Congress, Nat. Retail Mcts. Assn., Phi Theta Kappa, Pi Kappa Alpha. Episcopalian. Office: The Bon Marché 3rd And Pine St Seattle WA 98181-0001 Home: 1500 4th Ave # 3 Seattle WA 98101-1666 E-mail: b2fix@aol.com.

FIXMAN, MARSHALL, chemist, educator; b. St. Louis, Sept. 21, 1930; s. Benjamin and Dorothy (Finkel) F.; m. Marian Ruth Beatman, July 5, 1959 (dec. Sept. 1969); children: Laura Beth, Susan Ilene, Andrew Richard; m. Branka Ladanyi, Dec. 7, 1974. AB, Washington U., 1950; PhD, MIT, 1954. Jewett postdoctoral fellow chemistry Yale U., 1953-54; instr. chemistry Harvard U., 1956-59; sr. fellow Mellon Inst., Pitts., 1959-61; prof. chemistry, dir. Inst. Theoretical Sci., U. Oreg., 1961-64, prof. chemistry, research asso. inst., 1964-65; prof. chemistry Yale U., New Haven, 1965-79; prof. chemistry and physics Colo. State U., Ft. Collins, 1979-2000, prof. emeritus, 2000—. Mem. editorial bd. Jour. Chem. Physics, 1962-64, Jour. Phys. Chemistry, 1970-74, Macromolecules, 1970-74, Accounts Chem. Rsch. 1982-85, Jour. Polymer Sci. B, 1991-93; assoc. editor Jour. Chem. Physics, 1994—2006. Wwith U.S. Army, 1954-56. Fellow Alfred P. Sloan Found., 1961-63; recipient Governor's award Oreg. Mus. Sci. and Industry, 1964 Mem. NAS, Am. Acad. Arts and Scis., Am. Chem. Soc. (award pure chemistry 1964, award polymer chemistry 1991), Am. Phys. Soc. (high polymer physics award 1980), Fedn. Am. Scientists. Office: Colo State U Dept Chemistry Fort Collins CO 80523-0001 Business E-Mail: mf@fibm.mfbl.colostate.edu.

FLACHMANN, MICHAEL CHARLES, English language educator; b. St. Louis, Nov. 3, 1942; s. Charles Randall and Charlotte W. (Widen) F.; m. Josephine Kumbera Marschel, June 30, 1969; children: Christopher Michael, Laura Marschel. BA, U. of the South, 1964; MA, U. Va., 1965; PhD, U. Chgo., 1972. Asst. prof. English So. Ill. U., Edwardsville, 1965-68; from asst. prof. to prof. English Calif. State U., Bakersfield, 1972—, chair honors consortium, 1995—. Dir. univ. honors programs Calif. State U., 1985—; dir. Camp Shakespeare Utah Shakespearean Festival, 1986—, company-dramaturg, 1985—; vis. prof. Calif. Inst. Arts, Valencia, 1988; mem. Western Region Adv. Coun. Shakespeare Globe Ctr., 1983—; mem. Internat. Com. for the Bibliography of Shakespeare Quarterly, 1985—. Author: Shakespeare's Lovers, 1983, Shakespeare's Women, 1986, The Prose Reader, 1986, Teaching Excellence, 1998, Beware the Cat, 1988, Shakespeare: From Page to Stage, 2005, eight edit., 2007; editor: Image of Idleness, 1990; contbr. articles to profl. jours. Named CSU System-Wide Outstanding Prof., 1993, Carnegie Found. U.S. Prof. of Yr., 1995; recipient Wang Tchg. Excellence award Calif. State U., 2001. Mem. MLA, Shakespeare Assn. Am., Early English Text Soc., Renaissance Soc. Am., Assn. for Theatre in Higher Edn., Shakespeare Theatre Assn. Am. Avocations: Judo (Fifth Degree Black Belt), tennis. Home: 1236 Fairway Dr Bakersfield CA 93309-2422 Office: Calif State Univ Dept English 9001 Stockdale Hwy Bakersfield CA 93311-1022 Office Phone: 661-654-2121. Business E-Mail: mflachmann@csub.edu.

FLAGAN, RICHARD CHARLES, chemical engineering educator; b. Spokane, Wash., June 12, 1947; s. Robert and Frances F.; m. Aulikki Pekkala, Aug. 4, 1979; children: Mikko, Suvi, Taru. BSE in Mech. Engring., U. Mich., 1969; MS, MIT, 1971, PhD, 1973; TechD (hon.), Lund Tech U., Sweden, 2004. Research assoc. MIT, Cambridge, 1973-75; asst. prof. environ. engring. sci. Calif. Inst. Tech., Pasadena, 1975—81, assoc. prof., 1981—84, assoc. prof., environ. engring. and mech. engring., 1984—85, prof., 1986—90, prof. chem. engring., 1990—2000, Irma and Ross McCollum prof. chem. engring., 2000—, prof. environ. sci. and engring., 2003—04, William H. Corcoran prof. chem. engring., 2004—, acting exec. officer, chem. engring., 1996, exec. officer, chem. engring., 1997, 2004—. Vis. prof. Helsinki U. Tech., 1987. Assoc. editor Aerosol Sci. and Tech.; editor-in-chief Aerosol Sci. and Tech., 2003—. Recipient NASA Cert. of Recognition for Creative Develop., 1984, 1989; Japan Soc. for the Promotion of Sci. Fellow, 1992. Mem. AIChE (Thomas Baron award in fluid particle sys. 1997), Am. Assn. Aerosol Rsch. (pres. 1996-97, David Sinclair award 1993, Nicholas Fuchs award 2006), Am. Chem. Soc. (Divsn. Environ. Chemistry Outstanding Paper award 1987, ACS award for creative advances in environ. chemistry 2007), Gesellschaft fur Aerosolforschung (Marion Smoluchowski award for Aerosol Rsch., 1990). Office: Calif Inst of Tech Dept Chem Engring 213 Spalding Mail Code 210-41 Pasadena CA 91125 Business E-Mail: flagan@cheme.caltech.edu, flagan@caltech.edu.

FLAGEL, MARK ALAN, lawyer; b. LA, Sept. 18, 1958; s. Bertram Flagel and Wendy Moloshco; m. Sandra Elizabeth Williams, Apr. 20, 1991; children: Christina, Matthew William, Cameron David. BA magna cum laude, U. Calif., LA, 1980; JD, U. Calif., Berkeley, Calif., 1983. Bar: Calif. 1983, U.S. Dist. Ct. (ctrl. dist.) Calif. 1984, U.S. Ct. Appeals (fed. cir.) 1991, U.S. Ct. Appeals (9th cir.) 1986, U.S. Supreme Ct. 1995. Litig. assoc. Munger, Tolles & Olson, LA, 1983—84, Reboul, MacMurray, Hewitt, Maynard & Kristol, LA, 1984—87, Irell & Manella, LA, 1987—90, litig. ptnr., 1991—96, Latham & Watkins LLP, LA, 1996—. Adj. prof. Loyola Law Sch., LA, 2003—05; spkr. in field. Vol. lawyer Kayne-ERAS Ctr., Culver City, Calif., 1994—. Mem.: ABA, Order of Coif. Home: 450 South Camden Drive Beverly Hills CA 90212 Office: Latham Watkins 355 S Grand Ave Los Angeles CA 90071-1560 Office Fax: 213-891-8763. Business E-Mail: mark.flagel@lw.com.

FLAGG, NORMAN LEE, retired advertising executive; b. Detroit, Jan. 21, 1932; s. Frank and Harriet (Brown) F.; m. Carolanne Flagg; children: James, Suzanne. BFA, U. Miami, Miami, Fla., 1958. Advt. supr. Smithkline Beckman, Phila., 1970-75, creative dir., 1975-80; owner Illusions Restaurants, Bryn Mawr, Pa., 1979—87, Illusions Restaurant, Tucson, 1984-88. Author: Shooting Blanks, 1994. With USMC, 1954-56. Recipient Diana awards Whlse Druggest Assn. 1977, Aesculapius award Modern Medicine 1978. Mem. Acad. Magical Arts.

FLAHERTY, LAUREN PATRICIA, marketing executive; BA, Syracuse U. V.p. worldwide mktg., small bus. IBM Corp., dir. advt., brand imaging, 1993—97, v.p worldwide mktg., global bus.; chief mktg. officer Nortel Networks Corp., 2006—08; exec. v.p., chief mktg. officer Juniper Networks, Inc., Sunnyvale, Calif., 2009—. Spkr. at events sponsored by Am. Mktg. Assoc., CMO Coun., Columbia U. MBA prog. Named one of Best Marketers, BtoB Mag., 2006, 2008; named to The Top 100, Women's Exec. Network, 2007, 2008. Office: Juniper Networks Inc 1194 N Mathilda Ave Sunnyvale CA 94086*

FLAKE, JEFF, United States Representative from Arizona; b. Snowflake, Ariz., Dec. 31, 1962; m. Cheryl, 15 yrs.; 5 children. BA in Internat. Rels., Brigham Young U., 1986, MA in Polit. Sci., 1987. Worked in pub. rels., Wash., DC, 1987; exec. dir. Found. Democracy, Nambia, Goldwater Instit., Ariz., 1992; mem. U.S. Congress from 1st Ariz. dist., 2001—. Mem. House Judiciary com.; serving on House Internat. Rels. com. Republican. Mem. Lds Ch. Office: US House Reps 240 Cannon House Office Bldg Washington DC 20515-0306 Office Phone: 202-225-2635. Office Fax: 202-226-4386. E-mail: jeff.flake@mail.house.gov.

FLANAGAN, FIONNULA MANON, actress, writer, theater director; b. Dublin; came to U.S., 1968; d. Terence Niall and Rosanna (McGuirk) F.; m. Garrett O'Connor, Nov. 26, 1972; 2 stepchildren. C.I.H.E., U. Fribourg, Switzerland, 1962; student, Abbey Theatre Sch., Dublin, 1964-66. Pres. The Rejoycing Co., 1978—. Stage appearances include: Ulysses in Nighttown, N.Y.C., 1974, Lovers, 1968, Ghosts, 1989, Happy Days, 1991, Unfinished Stories, 1992, Countess Cathleen, 1992, Summerhouse, 1994; author, actress one-woman shows: James Joyce's Women, 1977 (L.A. Drama Critics award, San Francisco Theatre Critics award, Drama-Logue award); films include: Ulysses, 1967, In the Region of Ice, 1980, Mr. Patman, 1980, James Joyce's Women, 1984, Reflections, 1984, Chain Reaction, 1985, Death Dreams, 1992, Mad at the Moon, 1992, Money for Nothing, 1993, Some Mother's Son, 1996, Waking Ned Devine, 1998, With or Without You, 1999, The Others, 2000, Divine Secrets of the Ya-Ya Sisterhood, 2002, Tears of the Sun, 2003, One of the Oldest Con Games, 2004, Blessed, 2004, Man About Dog, 2004, Transamerica, 2005, Four Brothers, 2005; TV appearances include: The Picture of Dorian Gray, 1973, The Legend of Lizzie Borden, 1975, Rich Man Poor Man, 1976 (Emmy award for most outstanding support role 1976), How the West Was Won, 1977-79 (Emmy nominee 1978), A Winner Never Quits, 1986, White Mile, 1994, Kings in Grass Castles, 1998, To Have and To Hold, 1998, For Love or Country: The Arturo Sandoval Story, 2000, Murder She Wrote: The Celtic Riddle, 2003, Revelations, 2005; dir. Freedom of the City, Theatre West L.A., 1988 (Dramalogue award), Faith Healer, 1989, Away Alone, Court Theatre, L.A., 1991, Abbey Theatre, Dublin, 1992, A Secret Affair, 1999, Havana Nocturne, 2000; TV guest appearances include: Chicago Hope, 1999, Enterprise, 2002, Law & Order: Special Victims Unit, 2003, Nip/Tuck, 2004. Mem. AFTRA, SAG, Actors' Equity, Irish Actors Equity. Office: Don Buchwald & Assocs 6500 Wilshire Blvd Ste 2200 Los Angeles CA 90048-4942

FLANAGAN, JOHN MICHAEL, editor, publisher; b. Bangor, Maine, Mar. 8, 1946; s. Joseph F. and Dorothy Elizabeth (Albert) F.; m. Mary Katherine Fastenau, June 22, 1990. Student, U. Notre Dame, 1963-65; BJ, U. Mo., 1971. With The News-Jour. papers, Wilmington, Del., 1971-84, mng. editor, 1982-84; editor Marin Ind. Jour., San Rafael, Calif., 1984-87; exec. editor Honolulu Star-Bulletin, 1987-93; editor, pub. Honolulu Star-Bull., 1993—. With U.S. Army, 1965-68. Office: Honolulu Star Bull Unit 210 500 Ala Moana Blvd Honolulu HI 96813-4914

FLANAGAN, NORMAN PATRICK, lawyer; b. Pitts., Feb. 3, 1953; s. Norman Patrick and Janice (Smith) F.; m. Caroline E.E. Reverdin, Aug. 2, 1975; children: Erin Elizabeth, Sean Patrick. BS in Edn., Duquesne U., 1975; JD, Calif. Western U., 1978. Bar: Pa., Nev., U.S. Dist. Ct. Nev., U.S. Ct. Appeals (9th cir.), U.S. Supreme Ct. Dep. pub. defender Washoe County Pub. Defender's Office, Reno, 1979-81; asst. pub. defender Pub. Defender's Office, Reno, 1982—90; atty. Hale, Lane, Peek, Dennison & Howord, 1990—. Mem. Nev. State Bar Assn. (continuing legal edn. sect., pres-elect, 2002-03), Legal Def. Fund (capital litigation sect.). Republican. Roman Catholic. Avocations: tennis, cross country skiing. E-mail: pflanagan@halelane.com.

FLANAGAN, ROBERT JOSEPH, economics professor; b. New Haven, Dec. 16, 1941; s. Russell Joseph and Anne (Macauley) F.; m. Susan Rae Mendelsohn, Aug. 23, 1986. BA, Yale U., 1963; MA, U. Calif., 1966, PhD, 1970. Economist U.S. Dept. Labor, Washington, 1963-64; asst. prof. labor econs. Grad. Sch. Bus. U. Chgo., 1969-75; assoc. prof. labor econs. Grad. Sch. Bus. Stanford (Calif.) U., 1975-86; sr. staff economist Coun. of Econ. Advisors, Washington, 1978-79; sr. fellow The Brookings Instn., Washington, 1983-84; prof. labor econs. Grad. Sch. Bus., Stanford (Calif.) U., 1987-92, Matsushita prof. internat. labor econs. and econ. policy, 1993—, assoc. dean, 1996-99. Cons. OECD, Paris, 1988, U.S. Civil Rights Commn., Washington, 1982-83, NOAA, Washington, 1981; vis. scholar IMF, 1994, Australian Nat. U., 1990, 2000. Author: Labor Relations and Litigation Explosion, 1987, Globalization and Labor Conditions, 2006; (with others) Unionism, Economic Stabilization and Income Policy, 1982, Economics of the Employment Relationship, 1989, numerous others; contbr. articles to profl. jours. Mem. Am. Econs. Assn., Indls. Rels. Rsch. Assn., Soc. Labor Economists. Office: Stanford U Grad Sch Bus Palo Alto CA 94305

FLANAGAN, THOMAS JAMES, medical products executive; Grad., US Naval Acad., Annapolis, Md., MIT, Cambridge, US Naval War Coll., Newport, RI, Harvard U. John F. Kennedy Sch. Govt., Cambridge. Officer USN; various exec. positions including chief info. officer and sr. v.p. global svc. delivery MCI, 1995—2004; v.p. info. systems Amgen, Inc., Thousand Oaks, Calif., 2004—05, head global enterprise resource planning program, 2005—06, sr. v.p., chief info. officer. Office: Amgen Inc One Amgen Center dr Thousand Oaks CA 91320-1799 Office Phone: 805-447-1000. Office Fax: 805-447-1010.

FLANIGAN, JAMES J(OSEPH), journalist; b. NYC, June 6, 1936; s. James and Jane (Whyte) F.; m. Patricia Quatrine, Nov. 28, 1997; children: Michael, Siobhan Jane. BA, Manhattan Coll., 1961. Fin. writer N.Y. Herald Tribune, 1957-66; bur. chief, asst. mng. editor Forbes Mag., 1966-86; bus. columnist, sr. econs. editor L.A. Times, 1986—. Office: LA Times 202 W 1st St Los Angeles CA 90012 Office Phone: 213-237-7167. E-mail: jim.flanigan@latimes.com.

FLATTERY, THOMAS LONG, lawyer, administrator; b. Detroit, Nov. 14, 1922; s. Thomas J. and Rosemary (Long) F.; m. Gloria M. Hughes, June 10, 1947 (dec.); children: Constance Marie, Carol Dianne Lee, Michael Patrick, Thomas Hughes, Dennis Jerome, Betsy Ann Sprecher m. Barbara J. Balfour, Oct. 4, 1986; children: Laura B. Lundquist, Linda B. Flint, William D. Balfour III. BS, U.S. Mil. Acad., 1947; JD, UCLA, 1955; LLM, U. So. Calif., 1965. Bar: Calif. 1955, U.S. Patent and Trademark Office 1957, U.S. Customs Ct. 1968, U.S. Supreme Ct. 1974, Conn. 1983, N.Y. 1984. With Motor Products Corp., Detroit, 1950, Equitable Life Assurance Soc., Detroit, 1951, Bohn Aluminum & Brass Co., Hamtramck, Mich., 1952; mem. legal staff, asst. contract adminstr. Radioplane Co. (divsn. Northrop Corp.), Van Nuys, Calif., 1955—57; gen. counsel, asst. sec. McCulloch Corp., LA, 1957—64; sec., corp. counsel Technicolor, Inc., Hollywood, Calif., 1964—70; v.p., sec. and gen. counsel Amcord, Inc., Newport Beach, Calif., 1970—72; v.p., sec., gen. counsel Schick Inc., LA, 1972—75; counsel, asst. sec. C.F. Braun & Co., Alhambra, Calif., 1975—76; sr. v.p., sec., gen. counsel Automation Industries, Inc. (now PCC Tech. Industries Inc. a unit of Penn Ctrl. Corp.), Greenwich, Conn., 1976—86; v.p., gen. counsel G&H Tech., Inc. (a unit of Penn Ctrl. Corp.), Santa Monica, Calif., 1986—93; temp. judge Superior Ct. Calif. L.A. Jud. Dist. and Santa Monica Unified Cts., 1987—; settlement officer L.A. Superior Ct., 1991—; pvt. practice Palisades, Calif., 1993—. Panelist Am. Arbitration Assn., 1991—; jud. arbitrator and mediator Alternative Dispute Resolution Programs LA Superior Ct., 1993—, Calif. Ct. Appeals 2d Appellate Dist., 1999—; alternative dispute resolution com. LA Superior Ct., 2001-07. Contbr. articles to profl. jours. Served to 1st lt. AUS, 1942-50. Master L.A. West Am. Inns Court, mem. ABA, Nat. Assn. Securities Dealers (bd. arbitrators 1996, bd. mediators 1997), State Bar Calif. (co-chmn. corp. law dept. com. 1978-79, lectr. continuing legal edn. program, mandatory fee arbitrator 2001—), L.A. County Bar Assn. (chmn. corp. law dept. com. 1966-67, dispute resolution svcs. atty.-client fee dispute arbitrator and mediator 1993—), Century City Bar Assn. (chmn. corp. law dept. com. 1979-80), Conn. Bar Assn., Santa Monica Bar Assn. (trustee 1999-2003, chmn. alt. dispute resolution sect. 2000-2007, atty.-client fee dispute arbitrator and mediator), N.Y. State Bar Assn., Am. Soc. Corp. Secs. (L.A. regional group pres. 1973-74), L.A. Intellectual Property Law Assn., Irish-Am. Bar Assn. Calif., Am. Ednl. League (trustee 1988—, sec. 1998-2007), Am. Legion (life), West Point Alumni Assn., Army Athletic Assn., Friendly Sons St. Patrick, Jonathan Club (dir. 1996-99, 2d v.p. 1997-98, Trumbull award 2005), Phi Alpha Delta Law Fraternity. Roman Catholic. Home and Office: 439 Via De La Paz Pacific Palisades CA 90272-4633 Office Phone: 310-454-3768. Personal E-mail: flatterytl@verizon.net.

FLAUM, KEITH AVERY, lawyer; b. Bklyn., Aug. 14, 1963; married. BA, UCLA, 1986; JD, U. Calif., Davis, 1989. Bar: Calif. 1989, Colo. 1993. Assoc. Cooley Godward LLP, Palo Alto, Calif., 1995—97, ptnr. Bus. Dept., 1997—. Author: Antitrust Provisions: A Dealmaker's Guide; contbr. articles to law jours.; spkr. in field. Named Top 20 Calif. Lawyers Under the Age of 40, Calif. Law Bus., 1999; named a Dealmaker of the Yr., Am. Lawyer Mag., 2006; named one of Calif. Lawyer/Attys. of Yr. (CLAY), Calif. Lawyer mag., 2005. Mem.: ABA (Com. on Negotiated Acquisitions), Colo. Bar Assn., State Bar Calif. Office: Cooley Godward LLP Five Palo Alto Sq 3000 El Camino Real Palo Alto CA 94306-2155 Office Phone: 650-843-5141. Office Fax: 650-849-7400. E-mail: flaumka@cooley.com.

FLAXMAN, JON E., computer company executive; B in Fin., U. Ill. Urbana-Champaign; MBA, Washington U., St. Louis. Cost acct. Hewlett-Packard Co., Palo Alto, Calif., 1981, v.p., CFO Bus. Customer Orgn., 1999—2001, v.p., contr., 2001—02, sr. v.p., contr., 2002—07, exec. v.p., chief adminstrv. officer, 2007—08, mem. exec. council leadership team, 2007—. Office: Hewlett Packard Co 3000 Hanover St Palo Alto CA 94304-1185

FLEISCHAKER, GORDON HENRY, JR., pediatrician; b. Louisville, July 1, 1928; s. Gordon H. and Agnes Rose (Shatzen) F.; m. Barbara Lorraine Draeger, Aug. 15, 1954 (dec. 1998); children: Rachel, Judith, James. BA in Zoology, U. Louisville, 1949, MD, 1953. Diplomate Am. Bd. Pediatrics, 1960. Intern Univ. Hosp., Madison, Wis., 1953-54; resident in pediat. The Children's Hosps., Denver, 1956-58; fellow in pediatric rheumatology State U. Iowa, Iowa City, 1958-60; practice medicine specializing in pediat. Denver, 1960—. Assoc. clin. prof. pediat. U. Colo. Sch. Medicine, Denver, 1960—; mem. active med. staff The Children's Hosp., Denver. Served to capt. MC, USAF, 1953-56. Fellow Am. Acad. Pediat.; mem. AMA, AAAS, Colo. Med. Soc., Clear Creek Valley Med. Soc. (pres. 2002-03). Office: G H Fleischaker MD 4485 Wadsworth Blvd Wheat Ridge CO 80033-3318 Office Phone: 303-421-0194. Personal E-mail: PeeDaTrx@aol.com.

FLEISCHER, EVERLY BORAH, academic administrator, department chairman; b. Salt Lake City, June 5, 1936; s. Arthur and Clare (Katzenstein) F.; m. Harriet Eve Perlysky, June 14, 1959; children: Deborah, Adam Joseph. BS, Yale U., 1958, MS, 1959, PhD, 1961. Asst. prof., then assoc. prof. chemistry U. Chgo., 1961-69; prof. U. Calif., Irvine, 1970-80, dean phys. sci., 1975-80, exec. vice chancellor, prof. chemistry Riverside, 1988-94; prof. chemistry, dean Coll. Arts and Scis. U. Colo., Boulder, 1980-88; program exec. Am. Acad. Arts and Scis., Western Ctr., 1996; project dir. NSF Math. Sci. Partnership Focus! grant, 2003—05; interim chair Dept. Environ., Health, Sci. and Policy, 2006—. Author articles on metalloporphyrins, bioinorganic chemistry. NSF fellow, 1959-61; Alfred P. Sloan fellow, 1962-66; recipient Univ. Svc. award U. Calif., Irvine, 1980. Fellow AAAS; mem. Am. Chem. Soc., Sigma Xi, Alpha Chi Sigma. Office: Univ California Dept Chemistry Irvine CA 92697-0001 Home: 62 Shade Tree Ln Irvine CA 92603 Business E-Mail: ebfleisc@chem.ps.uci.edu.

FLEISCHER, GERALD ALBERT, industrial engineer, educator; b. St. Louis, Jan. 7, 1933; s. Louis Saul and Rita Bashkow F.; m. Ann Ivancic, Dec. 17, 1960 (div. 1992); children: Laural Andrea, Adam Steven; m. Carolyn M. Boyum, Apr. 13, 1993. BS, St. Louis U., 1954; MS, U. Calif., Berkeley, 1959; PhD, Stanford U., Calif., 1962. Ops. analyst Consolidated Freightways, Menlo Park, Calif., 1959-60; instr. Stanford U., Calif., 1961-63; asst. prof. U. Mich., Ann Arbor, 1963-64; assoc. prof. engring. U. So. Calif., Los Angeles, 1964-71, prof. engring., 1971-97, univ. marshal, 1981-87, pres. faculty senate, 1986-87, prof. emeritus, 1998—. Author: Capital Allocation Theory, 1969, Risk and Uncertainty, 1975, Contingency Table Analysis, 1981, Engineering Economy, 1984, Introduction to Engineering Economy, 1994; contbr. to Handbook of Industrial Engineering, 2001, Industrial Engineering Handbook, 2001, Manufacturing Engineering Handbook, 2004. Served to lt. (j.g.) USN, 1954-57 Ford Found. fellow, 1960-62, Fulbright sr. lectr. Ecuador, 1974; fellow Inst. Advancement of Engring., 1976 Fellow Inst. Indsl. Engrs. (region v.p. 1984-86); mem. Am. Soc. Engring. Edn., Inst. Mgmt. Scis. Home: 4449 Chateau Dr Loveland CO 80538-1591 Business E-Mail: fleische@usc.edu.

FLEISCHMAN, PAUL, children's author; BA, Univ. of N.Mex., 1977. Author: The Birthday Tree, 1979, The Half-a-Moon Inn, 1980 (Silver medal Commonwealth of Calif. 1980, Golden Kite honor book Soc. Children's Book Writers 1980), Graven Images: Three Stories, 1982 (Newbery honor book 1983), The Animal Hedge, 1983, Finzel the Farsighted, 1983, Path of the Pale Horse, 1983 (Golden Kite honor book Soc. Children's Book Writers 1983, Parents' Choice award Parents' Choice Found. 1983), Phoebe Danger, Detective, in the Case of the Two-Minute Cough, 1983, Coming-and-Going Men: Four Tales, 1985, I Am Phoenix: Poems for Two Voices, 1985, Rear-View Mirrors, 1986, Rondo in C, 1988, Joyful Noise: Poems for Two Voices, 1988 (John Newbery medal 1989), Saturnalia, 1990, Shadow Play, 1990, Time Train, 1991, The Borning Room, 1991, Townsend's Warbler, 1992, Copier Creations, 1993, Bull Run, 1993 (Scott O'Dell award), Dateline: Troy, 1996, A Fate Totally Worse than Death, 1997, Seedfolks, 1997, Whirligig, 1998, Weslandia, 1999 (Pen West Lit. award, Calif. Young Readers medal), Mind's Eye, 1999, Cannibal in the Mirror, 2000, Big Talk: Poems for Four Voices, 2000, Lost!: A Story in String, 2000, Seek, 2001, Sidewalk Circus, 2003, 04, Animal Hedge, 2003, Breakout, 2003 (Nat. Book award finalist), Zap, 2005. Office: PO Box 646 Aromas CA 95004

FLEISCHMANN, ERNEST MARTIN, performing arts executive, consultant; b. Frankfurt, Germany, Dec. 7, 1924; came to U.S., 1969; s. Gustav and Antonia (Koch) F.; children: Stephanie, Martin, Jessica. B of Commerce, U. Cape Town, South Africa, 1950, MusB, 1954; postgrad., South African Coll. Music, 1954-56; MusD (hon.), Cleve. Inst. Music, 1987. Gen mgr. London Symphony Orch., 1959-67; dir. Europe CBS Masterworks, 1967-69; exec. v.p., mng. dir. LA Philharm. Assn. and Hollywood Bowl, 1969-98; artistic cons. LA Philharm. Assn., 1998—; pres. Fleischmann Arts, Internat. Arts Mgmt. Cons. Svc., 1998—. Mem. French Govt. Commn. Reform of Paris Opera, 1967-68; steering com. U.S. nat. commn. UNESCO Conf. Future of Arts, 1975; artistic dir. Ojai Festival, 1998-03; bd. counselors U. So. Calif. Thornton Sch. Music; bd. dirs. Monday Evening Concerts.; hon. lifetime dir. LA Philharm. bd. of visitors Columbia Sch. for Performing Arts; bd dirs. Masika Angelica. Debut as condr. Johannesburg (Republic of South Africa) Symphony Orch., 1942; asst. condr. South African Nat. Opera, 1948-51, Cape Town U. Opera, 1950-54; condr. South African Coll. Music Choir, 1950-52, Labia Grand Opera Co., Cape Town, 1953-55; music organizer Van Riebeeck Festival Cape Town, 1952; dir. music and drama Johannesburg Festival, 1956; contbr. to music publs. Decorated officier Ordre des Arts et Lettres (France), comdrs. cross Order of Merit (Germany), knight 1st class Order of the White Rose (Finland); recipient award of Merit, L.A. Jr. C. of C., John Steinway award, Friends of Music award, Disting. Arts Leadership award U. So. Calif., 1989, L.A. Honors award, L.A. Arts Coun., 1989, Live Music award Am. Fedn. Musicians Local 47, 1991, Disting. Authors/Artists award U. Judaism, 1994, Treasures of L.A. award, Ctrl. City Assn. L.A., 1996, Los Amigos de Los Angeles award, L.A. Conv. and Vis. Bur., 1996; honored Mayor and City Coun. as First Living Cultural Treasure of L.A., 1998, Gold Baton award Am. Symphony Orch. League, 1999. Mem. Assn. Calif. Symphony Orchs., L.A. Philharm. Assn. (bd. dirs. 1984—), Salzburg Seminar/Alberto Vilar Conf. on Orch. Mgmt. (co-chmn. 2002). Office: Fleischmann Arts 2225 Maravilla Dr Los Angeles CA 90068 Office Phone: 323-851-5822. Business E-Mail: efleischmann@laphil.org.

FLEISHER, ARTHUR A., II, physician; b. Phila., Sept. 7, 1932; s. Oscar Teller and Beatrice Naomi (Rosenzweig) F.; m. Francine Queenth, June 26, 1955; children: Rebecca, Martin Q., Arthur III, Carolyn B. BS, U. Miami, Fla., 1954; MD, U. Miami, 1958. Diplomate Am. Bd. Obstetrics and Gynecology. Resident in obstetrics and gynecology Jackson Meml. Hosp., Miami, Fla., 1959-62; obstetrician/gynecologist So. Calif. Permanente Med. Group, Panorama City, Calif., 1962—, chief dept. ob-gyn, 1975-81; assoc. clin. prof. ob-gyn L.A. County/U. So. Calif. Med. Ctr., Los Angeles, 1972—; clin. prof.; assoc. clin. prof. ob-gyn UCLA, 1964-83. Fellow Am. Coll. Ob-Gyn, ACS, Los Angeles Ob-Gyn Soc. (pres. 1997-98). Office: So Calif Permanente Med Group 13652 Cantara St Panorama City CA 91402-5423

FLEISHMAN, SUSAN NAHLEY, entertainment company executive; b. Charlottesville, Va., Sept. 26, 1960; d. Richard and Mary Daniels Nahley; m. Eric Philip Fleishman, Dec. 28, 1995; 1 child, Henry Richard. BA in Am. Lit., Middlebury Coll., 1982. Copywriter Macy's, NYC, 1984—86; dir. Interbrand, NYC, 1986—87; asst. v.p. Continental Ins., NYC, 1987—93; dir., pub. affairs Sony Corp. Am., NYC, 1993—95; v.p. corp. comm. and pub. affairs Universal Studios, LA, 1995—2000, sr. v.p. corp. comm. & pub. affairs Los Angeles, Calif., 2000—05; exec. v.p. corp. comm. Warner Bros. Entertainment Inc., Burbank, Calif., 2005—. Bd. dirs. Workplace, Hollywood, LA, 2001—, St. Joseph's Hosp., Burbank, Calif., 2002—; trustee The Cantry Sch., Valley Village, Calif. Office: Warner Bros Entertainment Inc 4000 Warner Blvd Burbank CA 91522

FLEMING, ARTHUR WALLACE, physician, surgeon; b. Johnson City, Tenn., Oct. 1, 1935; s. Smith Goerge and Vivian (Richardson) F.; m. Dolores E. Caffey, Apr. 8, 1978; children: Arthur Jr., Robyn, Jon, Mark, Bernadette, Robert, Erik. Student, Ill. State U., 1953-54; BA, Wayne State U., 1958-61; MD cum laude, U. Mich., 1961-65. Diplomate Am. Bd. Surgery, Am. Bd. Thoracic Surgery. Intern Walter Reed Gen. Hosp., Washington, 1965-66, resident in gen. surgery, 1966-70, resident in thoracic and cardiovascular surgery, 1970-72; research tng. fellowship Walter Reed Army Inst. of Research, Walter Reed Army Med. Ctr., Washington, 1973-74, mem. staff dept. surgery, 1974-76, chief div. exptl. surgery, 1976-77, dir. dept. surgery, 1977-83; assoc. prof. surgery Uniformed Service U. of Health Scis., Bethesda, Md., 1978-83, clin. assoc. prof. surgery, 1983—; program dir. gen. surgery residency tng. program Martin L. King, Jr./Drew Med. Ctr., Los Angeles, 1983—, dir. trauma ctr., 1983-99, chief surgery, 1983—; clin. prof. surgery UCLA, 1983—; chmn. dept. surgery, prof. surgery Charles R. Drew U. Medicine & Sci., Los Angeles, 1983—. Contbr. numerous articles to profl. jours. Served with USN, 1954-62. Recipient Hoff Medal, 1974, Gold Medal for paper Southeastern Surg. Congress, 1977, Letter of Commendation Commanding Gen. U.S. Army Med. Research and Devel. Command, 1981, Surgeon Gen's. "A" prefix, 1981, Commendation Compton City Council, 1985, Recognition award King-Drew Hosp. Social Service, 1985. Mem. ACS., Nat. Assn. Minority Med. Educators (western region), Golden State Med. Soc., Nat. Med. Assn., Charles R. Drew Med. Soc., Am. Heart Assn., Soc. Surg. Chmn., Assn. Program Dirs. in Surgery, Soc. Thoracic Surgeons, Assn. Acad. Surgery, Am. Assn. Blood Banks, Southeastern Surg. Congress, Am. Fedn. Clin. Research, Assn. Mil. Surgeons. Democrat. Roman Catholic. Avocations: golf, classical music, carpentry. Office: Charles R Drew U Medicine & Sci 12021 Wilmington Ave Los Angeles CA 90059-3019

FLEMING, BRICE NOEL, retired philosophy educator; b. Hutchinson, Kans., July 29, 1928; s. Augustus Brice and Anna (Noel) F.; m. Barbara Warr, Dec. 20, 1965. BA, Harvard U., 1950; D.Phil., Oxford U., Eng., 1961. Asst. lectr. Manchester (Eng.) U., 1956-57; instr. Yale U., 1957-59, 1960-62; asst. prof. U. Calif. at Santa Barbara, 1962-65, assoc. prof., 1965-69, prof., 1969-91, prof. emeritus, 1991—. Served with AUS, 1951-53. Office: U Calif Dept Philosophy Santa Barbara CA 93106

FLEMING, CAROLYN ELIZABETH, religious organization administrator, interior designer; b. Sept. 24, 1946; d. Jerry J. and Mary Josephine (Korten) Maly; m. Roger Earl Fleming, May 26, 1974; children: Karl Joseph, Briana Danika. Student, Texarkana Jr. Coll., 1963-65, Okla. State U., 1965-66; BS in Interior Design, U. Tex., 1970. Asst. to designer Planning/Design Cons., Inc., Tulsa, 1970-72; pvt. cons. Texarkana, Tex., 1972-73; with Anchorage Neuro-Spinal Clinic, 1987-90, 91-96; sec. Nat. Tchg. Com. Bahais of Alaska, Anchorage, 1976—84, mem., 1989-92, Baha'i materials promotion com., Anchorage, 1987-89, Nat. Spirituality Assembly, Bahais of Alaska, 1992-97, sec. gen., CEO, 1994-96; chmn. Anchorage Bahais Local Spiritual Assembly, 1990-92; mem. Texarkana Bahai Local Spirituality Assembly, 1985, Oceanview (Alaska) Bahai Local Spiritual Assembly, 1986-87; rec. sec. Chena Valley (Alaska) Local Spiritual Assembly Bahais, 1997; mem. internat. goals com. Nat. Spiritual Assembly Bahais of Alaska, Inc., 1997-2000; adminstrv. asst. to treas. in corp. offices Alaska Comm. Sys. Group, Inc., 2000—, adminstrv. asst. to treas. and v.p., 2000, adminstrv. asst. to v.p. investor rels., 2000-2001, adminstrv. asst. to CFO and treas., 2001—, v.p. investor rels., 2001—, v.p. sales and mktg.-Corp. office, 2001—. Coord. Interdenominational Cultural Unity Conf. for Anchorage Area, 1986. Vol. Rural Comty. Action Program, 1986-87, Alaska Coun. on Prevention Alcohol and Drug Abuse, 1987, Spirit Days, 1987-88; trainee Parent and Youth Mediation Program, 1990; mem. Anchorage Local Spiritual Assembly, 1998; asst. aux. bd. for Bahai Oceanview Comty., 1989-92; mem. Arts Coun., Valdez, Alaska, 1974-76, Beyond Beijing Coalition, Anchorage, 1995-96. Mem. ACS (contbns. and donations com. 2000-2001), Assn. Interior Designers, Alaska Women's Network (chmn. 2001-02, vice-chmn. 2000-01, v.p. 2000—), Internat. Assn. of Adminstrv. Profls., Bus. and Profl. Women's Orgn., Beta Sigma Phi. Mem. Baha'I Faith.

FLEMING, GRAHAM RICHARD, chemistry educator; b. Barrow-in-Furness, Lancashire, Eng., Dec. 3, 1949; came to U.S., 1979; s. Maurice Norman and Ena (Winter) F.; m. Jean McKenzie, Sept. 16, 1977; 1 child, Matthew. BS with honors, U. Bristol, Eng., 1971; PhD in Phys. Chemistry, U. London, 1974. Rsch. fellow Calif. Inst. Tech., Pasadena, 1974-75; univ. rsch. fellow U. Melbourne, Australia, 1975, Australian Rsch. Grants Commn. rsch. asst., 1976; Leverhulme fellow Royal Instn., London, 1977-79; asst. prof. U. Chgo., 1979-83, assoc. prof., 1983-85, prof., 1985-87, A.H. Compton Disting. Svc. prof., 1987-97, chmn. dept. chemistry, 1988-90; prof. U. Calif., Berkeley, 1997—, Melvin Calvin disting. prof., 2002—; dir. phys. bioscis. divsn. Lawrence Berkeley Nat. Lab., 1997—, assoc. lab. dir. for phys. sci., 2002—. Co-chmn. Ultrafast Phenomena V Meeting, Snowmass, Colo., 1986; co-dir. Inst. Bioengring., Biotech., Quantitative Biomedicine, U. Calif., Berkeley, San Francisco, Santa Cruz. Author: Chemical Applications of Ultrafast Spectroscopy, 1986; mem. editl. bd. Chem. Physics Letters, Jour. of Phys. Chemistry, Chem. Physics; contbr. 235 rsch. articles to profl. publs. Recipient Coblentz award, Coblentz Soc., 1985, Earle K. Plyler award, Am. Phys. Soc., 2002; fellow Alfred P. Sloan Found. fellow, 1981, J.S. Guggenheim fellow, 1987; scholar Dreyfus tchr.-scholar, 1982. Fellow Am. Acad. Arts and Scis., Royal Soc. London; mem. Optical Soc. Am., Inter-Am. Photochem. Soc. (award 1996), Royal Soc. Chemistry (Marlow medal 1981, Tilden medal 1991, Centenary medal 1996), Am. Chem. Soc. (Nobel Laureate Signature award for grad. edn. in chemistry 1995, Peter Debye award in phys. chemistry 1998, Harrison Howe award 1999, Ahmed Zewail award, 2008), NAS. Avocation: mountain climbing. Office: Univ of Calif-Berkeley Dept Chemistry B77 Hildebrand Hall Berkeley CA 94720-0001 Office Phone: 510-643-7609. Office Fax: 510-643-7012.

FLEMING, JAYNE ELIZABETH, lawyer; children: Anthony, Isabel. BA in Polit. Sci., U. Calif., Berkeley, 1994; JD, U. Calif. Boalt Hall Sch. Law. Bar: Calif. 2000. Assoc. Crosby Heafey Roach & May LLP (merged with Reed Smith LLP), 2000—03, Reed Smith LLP, Oakland, Calif., 2003—, pro bono counsel. Pro bono counsel, leader human rights team Reed Smith LLP. Recipient Sean Halpin award, Reed Smith LLP, 2005, Father Moriarity award, Lawyers Com. for Civil Rights, 2005; named Calif. Lawyer Atty. of Yr., Calif. Lawyer mag., 2005; named one of The 50 Most Influential Women Lawyers in Am., Nat. Law Jour., 2007. Mem.: ABA, Lawyers' Com. Civil Rights San Francisco Bay Area, First Dist. Appellate Project, Ctr. Gender & Refugee Studies, San Francisco Bar Assn.: Internat. Human Rights Section. Office: Reed Smith LLP 1999 Harrison St Ste 2400 Oakland CA 94612 Office Phone: 510-466-6847. Home Fax: 510-273-8832. E-mail: jfleming@reedsmith.com.

FLEMING, PATRICIA V., state legislator; b. Mexico, Mont., Mar. 10, 1949; m. Robert L. Fleming; children: Kevin, Kyle. BA in Bus Mgmt., U. Phoenix, 1984. Budget analyst US Army, 1983—94, 1997—2000, manpower mgmt. analyst, 1994—97, 2000—05; mem. Dist. 25 Ariz. House of Reps., 2008—, mem. mil. affairs & pub. safety com., natural resources & rural affairs com. Chair Cochise County Dem. Party, 2007. Treas., trustee Sierra Vista Cmty. United Ch. Christ Coun., 2005—06. Mem.: Am. Assn. Mil. Comptrollers, Am. Fedn. Govt. Employees, Nat. Assn. Retired Fed. Employees, Cochise County League Women Voters, Southwest Assn. Buffalo Soldiers.

Democrat. Office: Ariz House Reps Capitol Complex 1700 W Washington Rm 125 Phoenix AZ 85007 Office Phone: 602-926-5836. Office Fax: 602-417-3125. Business E-Mail: pfleming@azleg.gov.*

FLEMING, REX JAMES, meteorologist; b. Omaha, Apr. 25, 1940; s. Robert Leonard and Doris Mae (Burrows) F.; m. Kathleen Joyce Ferry, Sept. 3, 1969; children: Thane, Manon, Mark, Noel. BS, Creighton U., 1963; MS, U. Mich., 1968, PhD, 1970. Commd. lt. U.S. Air Force, 1963, advanced through grades to capt., 1972; research scientist Offutt AFB, Nebr., 1963-67; sci. liaison to Nat. Weather Service for Air Weather Service, Suitland, Md., 1970-72; resigned, 1972; mgr. applications mktg. advanced sci. computer Tex. Instruments, Inc., Austin, 1972-75; dir. U.S. Project Office for Global Weather Expt., NOAA, Rockville, Md., 1975-80, Spl. Research Projects Office, 1980-82, Office of Climate and Atmospheric Research, 1983-84, Internat. Tropical Ocean and Global Atmosphere Project Office and Nat. Storm Program Office, 1984-86; pres. Tycho Tech. Inc., Boulder, Colo., 1986-87, Creative Concepts, Boulder, Colo., 1987-91; sr. mgr., coord. FAA rsch. Nat. Ctr. for Atmospheric Rsch., 1991-92, vis. scientist, 1987-88; NOAA, Boulder, 1993-2001; program mgr. U. Corp. for Atmospheric Rsch., 2001—04; pres. Global Aerospace, LLC, Boulder, Colo., 2005—. Contbr. articles to profl. jours. Recipient Gold Medal award Dept. Commerce, 1980 Fellow AAAS; mem. Am. Meteorol. Soc. (chmn. probability and statistics com. 1976-77), The Planetary Soc., Am. Geophys. Union (sec. atmospheric scis. sect. 1984-86). Republican. Patents for aerial sampler system, temperature sensor system for mobile patrforms; atmospheric turbulence analysis system and method, airplane system for an atmospheric trubulence analysis system. Home: 7225 Spring Dr Boulder CO 80303-5115 Office: NCAR PO Box 3000 Boulder CO 80307-3000

FLEMMING, STANLEY LALIT KUMAR, physician, mayor, state legislator; b. Rosebud, SD, Mar. 30, 1953; s. Homer W. and Evelyn C. (Misra) F.; m. Martha Susan Light, July 2, 1977; children: Emily Drisana, Drew Anil, Claire Elizabeth Misra. AAS, Pierce Coll., 1973; BS in Zoology, U. Wash., 1976; MA in Social Psychology, Pacific Luth. U., 1979; DO, Western U., 1985; degree in Def. Strategy, Army War Coll., 1998; MA in Strategic Planning, Nat. Def., Naval War Coll., 2007. Diplomate Am. Coll. Family Practice; cert. ATLS. Intern Pacific Hosp. Long Beach (Calif.), 1985-86; resident in family practice Pacific Hosp. Long Beach, 1986-88; fellow in adolescent medicine Children's Hosp. L.A., 1988-90; clin. preceptor Family Practice Residency Program Calif. Med. Ctr., U. So. Calif., LA, 1989—; clin. instr. Sch. Medicine U. So. Calif., LA, 1989-90; clin. instr. Western U. Health Sci., Pomona, Calif., 1989-90, clin. asst. prof. Family Medicine, 1987—; exam. commr., expert examiner Calif. Osteo. Med. Bd., 1987-89; med. dir. Cmty. Health Care Delivery Sys. Pierce County, Tacoma, 1990—99, Cmty. Clinics Pierce County, 1999—2001; chief med. officer NW Phys. Network, 2004—; pres. Pacific NW U. Health Sci., 2007—. Clin. instr. U. Wash. Sch. Medicine, 1990—; bd. dirs. Calif. State Bd. Osteo. Physicians Examiners, 1989—, cons., 1989; chmn. Evergreen State Coll., 1997-2007. Mayor, City of University Place, Wash. Brig. gen., US Army, 1976—, Named one of Outstanding Young Men of Am., U.S. Jaycees, 1983, 85, Intern of Yr. Western U. Health Sci. Coll., 1986, Resident of Yr., Greater Long Beach Assn., 1988, Alumnus of Yr., Pierce Coll., 1993, 97; recipient Pumerantz-Weiss award, 1985. Mem. Fedn. State Bds. Licensing, Am. Osteopathic Assn., Am. Acad. Family Practice, Soc. Adolescent Medicine, Assn. Military Surgeons U.S., Assn. U.S. Army (chpt. pres.), Soc. Am. Military Engrs. (chpt. v.p.), Calif. Med. Assn., Wash. Osteopathic Med. Assn. (Physician of Yr. 1993), Calif. Family Practice Soc., Long Beach Med. Assn. (com. mem.), N.Y. Acad. Sci., Calif. Med. Review Inc., Sigma Sigma Phi, Am. Legion. Episcopalian. Home: 7619 Chambers Creek Rd W University Place WA 98467-2015 Office: Northwest Physicians Network Tacoma WA 98402 E-mail: stanflemming@hotmail.com.

FLESSNER, PAUL, computer software company executive; b. Roberts, IL, Jan. 1959; m. Sue Flessner; children: Andy, Jonathan. BS in Computer Sci. & Bus. Adminstrn., Ill. State U., 1981. With Microsoft Corp., Redmond, Wash., 1994—, prog. mgr., gen. mgr. SQL Server, v.p. SQL Server, sr. v.p., enterprise servers divsn., sr. v.p., server applications. Mem. bus. leadership team Microsoft, leader devel. & coord. combined enterprise bus. strategy plan. Bd. mem. Cystic Fibrosis Found. Office: One Microsoft Way Redmond WA 98052-6399

FLETCHER, BETTY BINNS, federal judge; b. Tacoma, Mar. 29, 1923; BA, Stanford U., 1943; LLB, U. Wash., 1956. Bar: Wash. 1956. Mem. firm Preston, Thorgrimson, Ellis, Holman & Fletcher, Seattle, 1956—79; judge US Ct. Appeals (9th cir.), Seattle, 1979—98, sr. judge, 1998—. Mem.: ABA (Margaret Brent award 1992), Fed. Judges Assn. (past pres.), Am. Law Inst., Wash. State Bar Assn., Phi Beta Kappa, Order of Coif. Office: US Ct Appeals 9th Cir 1200 6th Ave 21st Fl Seattle WA 98101

FLETCHER, NATHAN, state legislator; m. Mindy Fletcher; 1 child, Zach. Grad., Calif. Bapt. U. Counter intelligence/human intelligence specialist US Marine Corps Reserves; apptd. to San Diego County Veterans Adv. Coun.; mem. Dist. 75 Calif. State Assembly, Calif., 2008—. Republican. Bapt. Office: State Capital Room 2111 PO Box 942849 Sacramento CA 95814 also: 9909 Mira Mesa Blvd Ste 130 San Diego CA 92131 Office Phone: 858-689-6290, 916-319-2075. Office Fax: 858-689-6296, 916-319-2175.*

FLETCHER, WILLIAM A., federal judge, educator; b. June 6, 1945; BA, Harvard U., 1968, Oxford U., 1970; JD, Yale U., 1975. Law clk. to presiding justice US Dist. Ct. Calif., San Francisco, 1975—76; law clk. to Justice William J. Brennan US Supreme Ct., Washington, 1976—77; acting prof. law U. Calif., Berkeley, 1977—84, prof. law, 1984—98; judge US Ct. Appeals (9th cir.), San Francisco, 1998—. With Office of Emergency Preparedness, Exec. Office of the Pres., 1970—72; prof. Salzburg Seminar on Am. Legal Institutions; mem. Am. Law Inst. Lieutenant USN, 1970—72. Mem.: Calif. Bar Assn. Office: 95 7th St San Francisco CA 94103

FLETTNER, MARIANNE, opera administrator; b. Frankfurt, Germany, Aug. 9, 1933; d. Bernhard J. and Kaethe E. (Halbritter) F. Bus. diploma, Hessel Bus. Coll., 1953. Sec. various cos., 1953-61, Pontiac Motor Div., Burlingame, Calif., 1961-63, Met. Opera, NY, 1963-74, asst. co. mgr. NY, 1974-79; artistic adminstr. San Diego Opera, 1979—. Avocations: travel, hiking, swimming, cooking. Home: 4015 Crown Point Dr San Diego CA 92109-6270 Office: San Diego Opera 1200 Third Ave 18th Fl San Diego CA 92101-4112 Office Phone: 619-232-7636, 619-533-7004. Business E-Mail: mflettner@sdopera.com.

FLINN, PAUL ANTHONY, materials scientist; b. NYC, Mar. 25, 1926; s. Richard A. and Anna M. (Weber) F.; m. Mary Ellen Hoffman, Aug. 20, 1949; children: Juliana, Margaret, Donald, Anthony, Patrick. AB, Columbia Coll., 1948, MA, 1949; ScD, MIT, 1952. Asst. prof. Wayne U., Detroit, 1953-54; research staff Westinghouse Research Lab., Pitts., 1954-63; prof. Carnegie-Mellon U., Pitts., 1964-78; sr. staff scientist Intel Corp., Santa Clara, Calif., 1978-95; cons. prof. dept. material sci. and engring. Stanford (Calif.) U., 1985—. Vis. prof. U. Nancy, France, 1967-68, U. Fed. do Rio Grand du Sol, Porto Allegro, Brazil, 1975, Argonne (Ill.) Nat. Lab., 1977-78, Stanford (Calif.) U., 1984-85. Contbr. sci. articles to profl. jours. Served with USN, 1944-46, PTO. Fellow Am. Phys. Soc.; mem. Metall. Soc., Materials Rsch. Soc., Phi Beta Kappa, Tau Beta Pi.

FLORES, CANDACE, special events director; b. 1974; Owner The Stillwell House; special events dir. El Charro Cafe. Mem. Big Brothers/ Big Sisters, Humane Soc. Southern Ariz., Angel Charities, Jr. League, Tu Nidito. Named one of 40 Under 40, Tucson Bus. Edge, 2006.

FLORES, LINDA, state legislator; Oregon State Representative, District 51, 2003-.partner, GreenPro Yard Serv; legal asst, Robert M Mercer, attorney; exec asst, GeoTrust, Inc. Republican. Office: 900 Court St NE H-287 Salem OR 97301 Office Phone: 503-986-1451. E-mail: rep.lindaflores@state.or.us.

FLORY, CURT ALAN, research physicist; b. 1953; BS in Physics with distinction, Stanford U., 1975; MS in Physics, U. Wash., 1977; PhD in Physics, U. Calif., Berkeley, 1981. R&D fellow, rsch. physicist Agilent Technologies, Palo Alto, Calif., 1984—; postdoc. SLAC, 1981-84. Recipient Indsl. Physics prize Am. Inst. Physics, 1993-94. Fellow Am. Phys. Soc.

FLOSS, HEINZ G., chemistry professor, researcher; b. Berlin, Aug. 28, 1934; s. Friedrich and Annemarie F.; m. Inge Sauberlich, July 17, 1956; children: Christine, Peter, Helmut, Hanna. BS in Chemistry, Technische Universitat, Berlin, 1956, MS in Organic Chemistry, 1959; PhD in Organic Chemistry, Technische Universitat, Munich, W. Ger., 1961, Habilitation in Biochemistry, 1966; DSc (hon.), Purdue U., 1986; Dr. (h.c.), U. Bonn, 2001. Hilfsassistent Technische Universitat, Berlin, 1958-59; hilfsassistent Technische Hochschule, Munich, 1959-61, wissenschaftlicher asst. and dozent, 1961-66; on leave of absence at dept. biochemistry and biophysics U. Calif.-Davis, 1964-65; assoc. prof. Purdue U., 1966-69, prof., 1969-77, Lilly Disting. prof., 1977-82, head dept. medicinal chemistry, 1968-69, 74-79; prof. chemistry Ohio State U., Columbus, 1982-87, chmn. dept. chemistry, 1982-86; prof. chemistry U. Wash., Seattle, 1987—, adj. prof. medicinal chemistry and microbiology, 1988—, adj. prof. biochemistry, 1988-99, prof. emeritus, 2001—. Vis. scientist ETH Zurich, 1970; vis. prof. Tech. U. Munich, 1980, 86, 95; mem. bio-organic and natural products study sect. NIH, 1989-93; mem. internat. adv. Natural Product Reports, 1997—. Mem. editorial bd. Lloydia-Jour. Natural Products, 1971—2002, BBP-Biochemie und Physiologie der Pflanzen, 1971-84, Applied and Environ. Microbiology, 1974-84, Planta Medica, 1978-83, Jour. Medicinal Chemistry, 1979-83, Applied Microbiology and Biotech., 1984-88, Jour. Basic Microbiology, 1989-95. Recipient Lederle faculty award, 1967, Mead Johnson Undergrad. Rsch. award, 1968, rsch. career and devel. award USPHS, 1969-74, Volwiler award, 1979, Humboldt sr. scientist, 1980, Newby-McCoy award 1981, award in microbial chemistry Kitasato Inst. and Kitasato U., 1988, White Magnolia Commemoration award and medal, Shanghai, 1995, honorable mention Kitasato Inst. Fellow Acad. Pharm. Scis. (Research Achievement award in natural products 1976), AAAS; mem. Am. Chem. Soc., Am. Soc. Biol. Chemistry and Molecular Biology, Am. Soc. Microbiology, Am. Soc. Pharmacognosy (Rsch. award 1988), Phytochem. Soc. N.Am., Sigma Xi (Faculty Research award 1976) Office: Univ Wash Dept Chemistry Box 351700 Seattle WA 98195-1700 Office Phone: 206-543-0310. Office Fax: 206-543-8665. E-mail: floss@chem.washington.edu.

FLOURNOY, JOHN CHARLES, SR., retired civilian military employee, officer; b. Florala, Ala., Nov. 30, 1936; s. Q. P. and Alice Ruby (Cope) Flournoy; m. Charlene Reneé Lett, June 7, 1957; children: Jamie Lynn, John Charles Jr., Jeffrey Allan. BS, Auburn U., 1959. Commd. 2d lt. USAF, 1959, advanced through grades to col., dep. chief of staff for ops. 23rd Air Force Hurlburt Field, Fla., 1983—88; site mgr., tng. mgr. Raytheon Sys., Kirkland AFB, N.Mex., 1988-98, tng. analyst, Air Force Rsch. Lab. Albuquerque, 1998—99; tng. cons. Air Force Rsch Lab, Mesa, 2000—06. Decorated Legion Merit; recipient German Gratitude medal, Fed. Republic of Germany, 1962. Mem.: Vietnam Helicopter Pilots Assn., Pedro Rescue Helicopter Assn. (member at large), Air Rescue Assn. (mem. at large), Air Commando Assn., USAF Helicopter Pilot Assn., Tanker/Airlift Assn., Jolly Green Assn. (1st v.p. 1983—84, pres. 1985—86), Order of Daedalians (former vice flight capt.). Republican. Avocations: fishing, walking, coin collecting/numismatics, NASCAR, ballooning. Home: 6817 Medinah Ln NE Albuquerque NM 87111-6419 Personal E-mail: jflournoy2@comcast.net.

FLOWERS, DAVID J., corporate financial executive; Grad., Carleton Coll. V.p. Liberty Media Corp., Englewood, Colo., 1995—97, v.p., treas., 1997—2000, sr. v.p., treas., 2000—06, sr. v.p., treas., CFO, 2006—. Office: Liberty Media 9197 S Peoria St Englewood CO 80112

FLOWERS, ROBERT SWAIM, medical educator, surgeon; b. Greenville, Ala., Sept. 13, 1934; m. Susan Flowers; children: Swain, Rob, Christian, Jonathan. BS in Chemistry and Biology, U. Ala., 1955, MD, 1960. Diplomate Am. Bd. Plastic Surgery. Intern U.S. Army Tripler Med. Ctr., 1960-61; battle group surgeon U.S. Army, 1961-63; resident gen. surgery Cleve. Clinic, Ohio, 1963-66, resident plastic surgery Ohio, 1966-68; chmn. plastic surgery sect. Straub Clinic, Honolulu, 1968-72; chmn. dept. plastic surgery Queen's Med. Ctr., Honolulu, 1972-74; asst. clinical prof. plastic surgery U. Hawaii, 1971—; dir., prin. surgeon Plastic Surgery Ctr. of the Pacific Inc., Honolulu, 1975-93; surgeon, dir. Flowers Clinic, Honolulu, 1993—. Chief, dir. Hawaii Fellowship Prog. Aesthetic Surgery; co-founder Gender Identity Clinic, Hawaii U.; vis. prof., lectr. Stanford U., U. Miami, 1975, U. Calif., 1976, Emory U., 1976, U. Zagreb, Yugoslavia, 1977, U. Munich, Germany, 1979, Columbia Presbyn. U., 1983, Duke U., 1985—86, Cleve. Clinic, 1985, UCLA, 1987, U. Louisville, 1988—90, U. Ala., 1990, Saarland U., Germany, 1993, U. Colo., 1994, U. Toronto, 1995. Contbr. articles to profl. jours., chapters to books. Pres. congregation, ch. coun., choir dir. Calvary By The Sea Luth. Ch., Honolulu, liturgist, lay minister, 1969—; bd. dirs. Honolulu Symphony, 1986—88. Fellow: Am. Coll. Surgeons; mem.: AMA, Pan-Pacific Surgical Assn., Internat. Soc. Clinical Plastic Surgeons, Internat. Soc. Aesthetic Plastic Surgeons, Honolulu County Med. Soc. (bd. govs. 1990—94), Hawaii Plastic Surgical Socs., Hawaii Med. Assn., Southeastern Soc. Plastic Surgeons (hon.), Australasian Soc. Aesthetics Plastic Surgery (hon.), Northwest Soc. Plastic Surgeons (hon.), Can. Soc. Aesthetic Plastic Surgeons, Calif. Soc. Plastic Surgeons, Asian Soc. of Aesthetics, Am. Soc. Plastic Surgeons, Am. Assn. Plastic Surgeons, Ala. Med. Soc., Honolulu Club, Waikiki Yacht Club, Outrigger Canoe Club. Avocations: drawing, painting, writing, sailing, singing. Office: Flowers Clinic 677 Ala Moana Blvd Ste 1011 Honolulu HI 96813-5415 Home: 726 Kahiau Loop Honolulu HI 96821-2542 Office Phone: 808-521-1999. Office Fax: 808-599-2972. Business E-Mail: info@flowersclinic.com.

FLOWERS, WILLIAM HAROLD, JR., lawyer; b. Chgo., Mar. 22, 1946; s. William Harold Sr. and Ruth Lolita (Cave) Flowers; m. Pamela Ann Mays, Sept. 13, 1980. BA, U. Colo., 1967, JD, 1971. Bar: Colo. 1973, U.S. Ct. Appeals (10th cir.) 1973, U.S. Dist. Ct. Colo. 1973, U.S. Supreme Ct. 1985, U.S. Ct. Appeals (4th cir.) 1994. Atty. Pikes Peak Legal Svcs., Colorado Springs, Colo., 1973; ptnr. Tate, Tate & Flowers, Denver, 1973-76; dep. dist. atty. Office Adams County Dist. Atty., Brighton, Colo., 1977-78; ptnr. Taussig & Flowers, Boulder, 1978-81; pvt. practice Boulder, 1981-89; ptnr. Holland & Hart, LLP, Denver, 1989-97, Hurth Yeager, Sisk & Blakemore LLP, Boulder, 1997—. Mem. Boulder County Cmty. Corrections Bd., 1985—90. Mem. Boulder Bd. Zoning Adjustment, 1973-78, chmn., 1977-78; mem. Boulder Growth Task Force, 1980-82; mem. exec. bd. Longs Peak coun. Boy Scouts Am., 1983-98; bd. dirs. Sta. KGNU, Boulder County Broadcasting, 1981-84, Coloradans Against the Death Penalty, 2001-04; trustee Nat. Coll. Advocacy, 2002-06. Mem.: AAJ (chair Coun. of Pres. 2001—02, exec. com. 2001—03, chair state dels. 2002—03, bd. govs. 2002—04), Am. Bd. Trial Advs. ABOTA, Colo. Bar Assn. (bd. govs. 2000, v.p. 2002—03), U. Colo. Found. (bd. dirs. 1995—2002), U. Colo. Boulder Alumni Assn. (bd. dirs. 1987—96, pres. 1994—95), Sam Cary Bar Assn. (pres. 1987), Boulder County Bar Assn. (civil litig. com. 1978—, criminal law com. 1979—, bd. dirs. 2003—, pres. 2007—08), Colo. Trial Lawyers Assn. (bd. dirs. 1989—, exec. com. 1996—, pres. 1999—2000), Colo. Criminal Def. Bar (bd. dirs. 1982—83), Nat. Bar Assn. (regional dir. 1983—86, bd. govs. 1983—96, v.p. 1990—91). Democrat. Methodist. Office: Hurth Yeager Sisk & Blakemore LLP PO Box 17850 4860 Riverbend Rd Boulder CO 80308 Office Phone: 303-443-7900.

FLOYD, TIM, men's college basketball coach, former professional basketball coach; b. Hattiesburg, Miss. s. Lee Floyd; m. Beverly Floyd; 1 child, Shannon. BS in Health & Phys. Edn., La. Tech. U., 1977. Student asst. La. Tech. U. Bulldogs, 1977; asst. coach U. Tex. El Paso Miners, 1978—86; head basketball coach U. Idaho Vandals, 1986-88, U. New Orleans Privateers, 1989—94, Iowa State U. Cyclones, 1994-98; dir. ops Chgo. Bulls, 1998, head basketball coach, 1999—2001, New Orleans Hornets, 2003—04, U. So. Calif. Trojans, 2005—. Basketball advisor: Glory Road, 2006. Named Coach of Yr., Am. South Conf., 1989, Sun Belt Conf., 1993, Big Eight Conf., 1996. Office: c/o USC Athletic Dept 3501 Watt Way HER 203 A Los Angeles CA 90089*

FLYNN, JOAN MAYHEW, librarian; b. Mpls., Sept. 13, 1927; d. Oscar Koehler and Mabel Victoria (Stein) Mayhew; m. Elliot Colter Dick, Jr., Aug. 19, 1950 (div. May 1966); children: Emily Diane Dick Tuttle, Elliot Mayhew Dick; m. Paul James Flynn, Nov. 4, 1967. BMus, U. Minn., 1950; MLS, U. Hawaii, 1972, cert. in advanced libr. and info. studies, 1986. Circulation clk., 1972-75; reference libr., 1975-85; dir. acad. support svcs., head Sullivan Libr. Chaminade U. of Honolulu, 1986—. Mem. Interlibr. Cooperation Coun., 1990, 91; supr. vocal music Forest Lake (Minn.) Pub. Schs. Asst. dir. races Norman Tamanaha Meml., 1982, dir. 1983; bd. dirs. Hawaii Kai Fun Runners. Mem. ALA, Hawaii Libr. Assn., MidPac Road Runners Assn. (bd. dirs.), Hawaii Masters Track Club, Beta Phi Mu, Pi Lambda Theta, Sigma Alpha Iota. Avocations: running, bicycling, swimming, weightlifting, reading. Office: Chaminade U 3140 Waialae Ave Honolulu HI 96816-1578 Home: 8927 N Fitzgerald Ln Tucson AZ 85742-4451

FLYNT, LARRY CLAXTON, JR., publisher; b. Magoffin County, Ky., Nov. 1, 1942; s. Larry Claxton and Edith (Arnett) F.; m. Kathy Barr, Dec. 1968 (div. 1969); m. Althea Leasure, Aug. 21, 1976 (dec. June 27, 1987); m. Elizabeth Berrios, June 20, 1998; children: Tonya, Lisa, Teresa, Larry Claxton, III. Student public schs., Saylersville, Ky. Factory worker Gen. Motors Co., Dayton, Ohio, 1958, 64-65; owner, operator Hustler Club, Dayton, Columbus, Toledo, Akron and Cleve., 1970-74; owner, pub. Hustler and Chic magazines, L.A., 1974—; owner, operator Larry Flynt Publications, L.A., 1976—. Actor: (films) The People vs. Larry Flynt, 1996; appeared in (documentaries) Larry Flynt: The Right to Be Left Alone, 2008; author: An Unseemly Man: My Life as a Pornographer, Pundit, and Social Outcast, 1996, Sex, Lies and Politics: The Naked Truth, 2004. Served with U.S. Army, 1958-59; Served with USN, 1960-64. Democrat.

FOCHT, MICHAEL HARRISON, health care industry executive; b. Reading, Pa., Sept. 16, 1942; s. Benjamin Harrison and Mary (Hannahoe) F.; m. Sandra Lee Scholwin, May 14, 1964; 1 child, Michael Harrison Archtl. estimator Caloric Corp., Topton, Pa., 1964-65, cost acct., 1965-66, indsl. engr., 1966-68, mgr. wage rates and standards, 1968-70; indsl. engr. Am. Medicorp. Inc., Fort Lauderdale, Fla., 1970-71, exec. dir. midwest region Chgo., 1977-78; asst. adminstr. Cypress Community Hosp., Pompano Beach, Fla., 1971-73, adminstr., 1975-77, Doctor's Hosp. Hollywood, Fla., 1973-75; v.p. Medfield Corp., St. Petersburg, Fla., 1978-79; v.p. ops. hosp. group Nat. Med. Enterprises, Inc., Los Angeles, 1979-81, regional sr. v.p. hosp. group Tampa, Fla., 1981-83, pres., chief exec. officer internat. group Los Angeles, 1983-86, pres. chief exec. officer hosp. group, 1986-91, sr. exec. v.p., dir. ops., 1991-93, pres., 1993-95; pres., COO Tenet Healthcare Corp., Santa Barbara, 1995—. Mem. Fedn. Am. Hosps. (bd. govs. 1983—), Fla. League Hosps. (bd. dirs. 1982-83) Republican. Roman Catholic. Home: PO Box 703 Santa Ynez CA 93460-0703 Office: Tenet Healthcare 13737 Noel Rd Ste 100 Dallas TX 75240-2017

FODOR, PETER BELA, plastic surgeon, educator; b. Cluj, Romania, May 14, 1942; MD, U. Wis. Med. Sch., 1966. Cert. Am. Bd. Surgery, Am. Bd. Plastic Surgery, lic. Colo., Conn., Mich., NY, Calif., Wis. Intern, gen. surgery Parkland Meml. Hosp., Dallas, 1966—67; resident, plastic surgery Columbia-Presbyn. Med. Ctr., 1967—68; resident St. Luke's Hosp., NYC, 1974—76; faculty, plastic surgery St. Luke's-Roosevelt Hosp.; faculty, reconstructive plastic surgery and gen. surgery Columbia U. Coll. Physicians and Surgeons; assoc. clin. prof. plastic surgery UCLA Med. Ctr., LA; practicing plastic surgeon, dir. Century Aesthetics, LA. Hosp. appointment Santa Monica/UCLA Med. Ctr.; staff mem., plastic surgery Century City Doctors Hosp., LA, Olympia Hosp., LA, St. John's Hosp., Santa Monica, Calif.;

mem. adv. bd., exec. editl. cons., round table moderator Consumer Guide to Plastic Surgery. Contbr. scientific papers to peer-reviewed jours., chapters to books; medical editor Be Your Best: A Comprehensive Guide to Aesthetic Plastic Surgery, 2006. Bd. mem., patron Coun. of Children's Burn Found., Helen Keller Manhattan League for the Blind, Music Ctr. LA, Sonance-House Ear Inst., LA Wild Beat Soc., Music Ctr.-Fraternity of Friends, Peterson Auto Mus. Checker 200, Thalians-President's Club, Bel Air Navy League, Calif. Hwy. Patrol Found. Capt. USAF. Recipient Ellis Island Medal of Honor. Fellow: Internat. Coll. Surgeons Plastic Surgery, ACS; mem.: Semmelweiss Scientific Soc. (past pres.), Royal Soc. Medicine, Northeastern Soc. Plastic Surgeons (founding mem.), NY Acad. Medicine, NY County Med. Soc., NY Regional Soc. Plastic and Reconstructive Surgeons, LA Soc. Plastic Surgeons, Lipoplasty Soc. N.Am. (immediate past pres., past treas.), Internat. Soc. Aesthetic Plastic Surgery, Conn. Soc. Plastic and Reconstructive Surgeons (founding mem.), Conn. State Med. Soc., Calif. Soc. Plastic Surgeons (past sec.), Bay Surgical Soc., Am. Soc. Plastic Surgeons, Am. Soc. for Aesthetic Plastic Surgery (past pres., past v.p., past treas., past clin. investigator), Am. Assn. Plastic Surgeons. Office: Century Aesthetics 2080 Century Park E Ste 710 Los Angeles CA 90067 Office Phone: 866-370-9042. Office Fax: 310-203-9798. Business E-Mail: pbfodor@centurysurgery.com.

FODOR, STEPHEN P. A., chemical company executive; BS in Biology, Wash. State U., 1978, MS in Biochemistry, 1981; MA in Chemistry, Princeton U., 1983, PhD in Chemistry, 1985. NIH postdoctoral fellow dept. chemistry U. Calif., Berkeley, 1986-89; sr. scientist optical techs. Affymax Rsch. Inst., Palo Alto, Calif., 1989-92, dir. phys. scis., 1992-93; chmn., CEO Affymetrix, Inc., Santa Clara, Calif., 1993—. Contbr. over 40 articles to profl. jours. Recipient Chemistry Tchg. award Princeton U., 1982, Assn. Princeton Grad. Alumni Tchg. honor, 1983, Postdoctoral fellow NIH, 1986-89, Alumni Achievement award Wash. State U., 1992, Intellectual Property Owner's Disting. Inventor of Yr. award, 1993, Chiron Corp. Biotechnology Rsch. award Am. Acad. Microbiology, 1997, Gabbay award in Biotech. in Medicine, 1998, Achievement award Assn. for Lab. Automation, 1998. Mem. AAAS (Newcomb-Cleveland award 1992), Am. Chem. Soc., Biophysical Soc. Office: Affymetrix Inc 3380 Central Expy Santa Clara CA 95051-0704

FOGARTY, THOMAS JAMES, surgery educator; b. Cin., Feb. 25, 1934; s. William Henry and Anna Isabella (Ruthemeyer) F.; m. Rosalee Mae Brennan, Aug. 28, 1965; children: Thomas James Jr., Heather Brennan, Patrick Erin, Jonathan David. BS in Biology, Xavier U., 1956; MD, U. Cin., 1960; D (hon.), Xavier U., 1987. Intern U. Oreg. Med. Sch., Portland, 1960-61, resident, 1962-65, instr. surgery, 1967-68; chief resident, instr. surgery divsn. cardiovascular surgery Stanford (Calif.) U. Med. Ctr., 1969-70, asst. prof. surgery, 1970-71, asst. clin. prof. surgery, 1971-73; cardiovascular surgeon pvt. practice, Stanford, 1973-78; pres. med. staff Stanford U. Med. Ctr., 1977-79; cardiovascular surgeon pvt. practice, Redwood City, Calif., 1978-93; dir. cardiovascular surgery Sequoia Hosp., Redwood City, Calif., 1980-93; clin. prof. surgery Stanford U. Med. Ctr., 1993—. Bd. dirs. Acorn Cardiovascular Inc., Satellite Dialysis Ctrs., Inc.; co-founder, bd. dirs. AneuRx, Inc., Biopsys Med., Inc., Cardiac Pathways, Inc., Emergency Med. Sys., Windy Hill Tech., Inc., Gen. Surg. Innovations, Inc., LocalMed, Inc., Vital Insite, Inc., Raytel Med. Corp., Cardiovascular Imaging Sys., Inc., Devices for Vascular Intervention, Inc., Hancock Labs., Imagyn Med., Inc., Physiometrix, Inc., Ventritex, Inc., Xenotech; mem. scientific adv. bd. Autogenics, BioLink Corp., Cardio Thoracic Sys., Inc., bd. dirs.; pres., founder Fogarty Engring., Inc.; co-founder, sr. ptnr. Three Arch Ptnrs., Baccitus Vascular, Novare Surg., Vascular Archs. Safety; founder, proprietor Thomas Fogarty Winery, 1981-. Portrait included in Bay Area Hon. Mus., 1998; contbr. articles to profl. jours.; patentee in field. Fellow U. Cin. Coll. Medicine, Good Samaritan Hosp., 1961-62, Nat. Heart Inst. Surgery br., Bethesda, Md., 1965-67, rsch. fellow divsn. cardiovascular surgery Stanford Med. Ctr., 1968-69; recipient AstroLobe award Roger Bacon High Sch., 1974, Disting. Alumnus award U. Cin. Med. Sch., 1989, Lifetime Achievement award Phoenix Hall of Fame, 1997, No. Calif. 1998 Entrepreneur of Yr. award Ernst & Young, 1998, Lemelson-MIT $500, 000 Prize invention and innovation, 2000, Assn. Advancement Med. Instrumentation's Found.'s Ann. Laufman-Greatbatch prize, 2000, Sci. Leadership award Nat. Breast Cancer Coalition, 2000, Internat. Soc. award Excellence in Endovascular Innovation Internat. Soc. Endovascular Specialists, 2001, Jacobson Innovation award Am. coll. Surgeons, 2001; named Inventor of Yr., San Francisco Patent and Trademark Assn., 1980; inducted into the Nat. Inventors Hall of Fame, 2001. Mem. AMA, ACS, Am. Assn. Thoracic Surgery, Am. Bd. Thoracic Surgery, Am. Coll. Physican Inventors, Am. Heart Assn. (grantee), Am. Inst. Med. and Biol. Engring., Assn. for Advancement Med. Instrumentation, Med. Device Mfrs. Assn., Am. Med. Polit. Action Com., Am. Surg. Assn., Internat. Soc. Specialists Surgery, Western Thoracic Surg. Soc., Calif. Med. Soc., Pacific Coast Surg. Assn., San Francisco Surg. Soc., San Mateo County Med. Assn., Santa Clara County Med. Assn. (Achievement award in medicine), Internat. Soc. Cardiovascular Surg. (N.Am. chpt.), Soc. Clin. Vascular Surgery, Soc. Vascular Tech., Soc. Thoracic Surgeons, Soc. Vascular Surgery (past pres. 1995), Copco Lake Sportsmen Assn., Santa Cruz Mountain Winegrowers Assn., South Skyline Assn., Sports Car Club Am., Rapley Trail Improvement Assn., Soc. Med. Friends of Wine. Republican. Achievements include invention of balloon embolectomy catheter. Avocations: hunting, fishing, pond gardening, woodworking, genealogy. Office: 3274 Alpine Rd Portola Valley CA 94028 also: Thomas Fogarty Winery 3270 Alpine Rd Portola Valley CA 94028

FOGEL, JEREMY DON, judge; b. San Francisco, Sept. 17, 1949; s. Daniel and Gladys (Caplan) F.; m. Kathleen Ann Wilcox, Aug. 20, 1977; children: Megan, Nathaniel. AB, Stanford U., Palo Alto, Calif., 1971; JD, Harvard U., 1974. Bar: Calif. 1974, U.S. Dist. Ct. (no. dist.) Calif. 1974. Atty. Smith, Johnson, Fogel and Ramo, San Jose, 1974-78; dir. atty. Mental Health Advocacy Project, San Jose, 1978-81; exec. dir. Santa Clara County Bar Assn. Law Found., San Jose, 1980-81; judge Santa Clara County Mcpl. Ct., San Jose, 1981-86, Santa Clara County Superior Ct., San Jose, 1986-98, U.S. Dist. Ct. (no. dist.) Calif., 1998—. Lectr., Stanford Law Sch., 2003—; faculty Calif. Continuing Jud. Studies Prog., Berkeley, 1987—; trainer of judges and lawyers in case mgmt. and mediation, Jordan, Bangladesh, Hong Kong, Israel, 1989-2001. Contbr. articles to profl. jours. Recipient Service award, Mental Health Assn., Santa Clara County, 1980, Honors award Legal Advocates Children and Youth, 1997, Spl. award for exemplary leadership and professionalism Santa Clara County Bar Assn., 2002; named Judge of Yr., Consumer Attys. Calif., 1997. Mem. Calif. Judges Assn. (v.p. 1990-91, exec. bd. 1988-91, chair jud. ethics com. 1987-88, discipline and disability com. 1991-93, jud. discipline adv. panel 1992-98, Pres.'s award 1997). Office: US Dist Ct 280 S 1st St Rm 4050 San Jose CA 95113-3095 Business E-Mail: jeremy_fogel@cand.uscourts.gov.

FOGEL, PAUL DAVID, lawyer; b. Santa Monica, Calif., Sept. 19, 1949; s. Phillip and Betty (Distler) Fogel; m. Yvette Chalom, Feb. 11, 1981; 1 child, Daniele. AB, U. Calif.-Berkeley, 1971; postgrad., U. Paris II, 1972-73; JD, UCLA, 1976. Bar: Calif. 1976, US Dist. Ct. (ctrl. dist.) Calif. 1977, US Dist. Ct. (no. dist.) Calif. 1987, US Supreme Ct. 1990, US Ct. Appeals (9th cir.) 1981, US Ct. Appeals (DC cir.) 2004, US Ct. Appeals (7th cir.) 2006. Grad. fellow Ctr. for Law in Pub. Interest, LA, 1976-77; dep. state pub. def. State Pub. Defender, LA, 1977-79; Fulbright fellow U. Paris II Law Sch., 1979-80; dep. state pub. def. State Pub. Def., San Francisco, 1980-82; sr. supervising atty. Calif. Supreme Ct., San Francisco, 1982-87; assoc. Hinton & Alfert, Walnut Creek, Calif., 1987-88, Crosby, Heafey, Roach & May, San Francisco, 1988-89, ptnr., 1990—2002, Reed Smith LLP, San Francisco, 2003—. Lectr. Am. law U.S. State Dept., Washington, 1980, 87, 99, 2006; lectr. U. Calif. Berkeley Boalt Hall Sch. Law, 1995, practitioner-advisor, 1991-94, 96—. Fellow Am. Acad. Appellate Lawyers, Calif. Acad. Appellate Lawyers (sec., treas. 2003-04, 2d v.p. 2004-05, 1st v.p. 2005-06, pres. 2006-07); mem. Calif. State Bar Assn. (chmn. appellate cts. com. 1990-91), Bar Assn. San Francisco (chair appellate practice sect. 1999-2000), 9th cir. rules com. 1999-2005, appellate rules task force 1998-2004, Calif. jud. coun., appellate adv. com. 2004-, Amnesty Internat. Office: Reed Smith LLP 2 Embarcadero Ctr Ste 2000 San Francisco CA 94111-4191 Home Phone: 510-540-8402; Office Phone: 415-543-8700, 415-659-5929. Business E-Mail: pfogel@reedsmith.com.

FOGELMAN, ALAN MARCUS, internist; b. Bklyn., 1940; BA in Zoology, UCLA, 1962, MD, 1966. Diplomate Am. Bd. Internal Medicine. Intern UCLA Hosp., 1966-67, resident, 1967-68, 70-71, fellow cardiology, 1971-73, prof. medicine, exec. chair dept. medicine. With USN, 1968-70. Mem. ACP, Am. Coll. Cardiology. Office: UCLA Sch Medicine 10833 Le Conte Ave Los Angeles CA 90095-3075

FOGERTY, JOHN CAMERON, musician, composer; b. Berkeley, Calif., May 28, 1945; s. Lucile and Galen Robert Fogerty; m. Martha Paiz, Sept. 4, 1965 (div.); 3 children; m. Julie Lebiedzinski, Apr. 20, 1991; 4 children. Singer, guitarist Creedence Clearwater Revival, 1968—72; solo performer, 1973—. Albums include (with Creedence Clearwater Revival) Creedence Clearwater Revival, 1968, Bayou Country, 1969, Willy & the Poor Boys, 1969, Green River, 1969, Cosmo's Factory, 1970, Pendulum, 1970, Creedence Gold, 1972, Mardi Gras, 1972, More Creedence Gold, 1973, Live in Europe, 1973, Chronicle, Vol. 1, 1976, Vol. 2, 1986, Down on the Corner, 1976, Hot Stuff, 1977, Greatest Hits, 1979, Concert, 1980, Creedence Country, 1981, Rollin' on the River, 1988, Travelin' Band, 1990, At the Movies, 1999, Chronicles, 1999, Keep on Chooglin', 1999, Best of Creedence Clearwater Revival, 2003, Platinum, 2004, Greatest Hits, 2005, Absolute Originals, 2006; (solo albums) Blue Ridge Rangers, 1973, John Fogerty, 1975, Hoodoo, 1976, Centerfield, 1985, Knockin' on Your Door, 1986, Eye of the Zombie, 1986, Blue Moon Swamp, 1997 (Grammy award for Best Rock Album, 1998), Deja Vu All Over Again, 2004, Revival, 2007; prodr. (soundtracks) Big Chill, 1984, American Flyers, 1985, My Girl, 1991, Blue Chips, 1994, My Fellow Americans, 1996, Prefontaine, 1997, Remember the Titans, 2000, Songs & Artists that Inspired Fahrenheit 9/11, 2004, We Are Marshall, 2007. Inducted to Rock and Roll Hall of Fame, 1993, Songwriters Hall of Fame, 2005; recipient: Golden Plate award, Acad. Achievement, 2005. Office: John Fogerty Ste 3517 4570 Van Nuys Blvd Sherman Oaks CA 91403 also: c/o Rob Light Creative Artists Agy 2000 Ave of the Stars Los Angeles CA 90067

FOGG, RICHARD LLOYD, food products executive; b. Boston, Jan. 22, 1937; s. Lloyd Clark and Mildred Ann (Cass) F.; m. Carolyn Ann Kane, Feb. 12, 1966; children— Amanda C., Jennifer S., Timothy L. AB, Bowdoin Coll., Brunswick, Maine, 1959; MBA, Cornell U., 1961. With brand mgmt. dept. Procter & Gamble Co., Cin., 1961-66; dir. mktg. mgmt. Hunt-Wesson Foods, Fullerton, Calif., 1967-76; sr. v.p. Amfac Food Group, Portland, Oreg., 1977; pres. subs. Fisher Cheese Co., Wapakoneta, Ohio, 1978-83; group v.p., COO Land O'Lakes Dairy Foods, Mpls., 1983-93; pres., CEO Orval Kent Food Co., Wheeling, Ill., 1994-96; pvt. investor, 1997—. Office Phone: 707-996-1991. Office Fax: 707-939-7859. Personal E-mail: sonomafogg@aol.com.

FOHRER, ALAN J., utilities company executive; BS, MS, U. So. Calif.; MBA, Calif. State U., Los Angeles. V.p., treas., CFO Southern Calif. Edison (SCE), 1991—93; sr. v.p., treas., CFO Edison Internat., SCE, Rosemead, Calif., 1993; chmn., pres., CEO Edison Mission Energy, Irvine, Calif., 2000—02; CEO Southern Calif. Edison (SCE), 2002—. Office: So Calif Edison 2244 Walnut Grove Ave Rosemead CA 91770

FOHRMAN, BURTON H., lawyer; b. Chgo., July 9, 1939; s. Max and Helen (Naparty) F.; m. Raleigh S. Newman, Dec. 12, 1975. AB cum laude, U. So. Calif., Los Angeles, 1960; JD, UCLA, 1963. Bar: Calif. 1964. Pvt. practice, Riverside, Calif., 1964-66; mng. ptnr. Redwine and Sherrill, Riverside, 1966-83; ptnr. Jones, Day, Reavis and Pogue, LA, 1983-92, former chmn. gen. real estate sect.; ptnr. White & Case, 1992—. Editor Calif. Real Property Jour., 1978-83. Mem. State Bar Calif. (chmn. real property sect. 1983), Los Angeles County Bar Assn. (chmn. real property fin. com. 1979-80, exec. com. real property sect. 1980-83), Daini Bar Assn. Office: Three Embarcadero Ctr Ste 2210 San Francisco CA 94111-3162 E-mail: bfohrman@whitecase.com.

FOK, AGNES KWAN, retired cell biologist, educator; b. Hong Kong, China, Dec. 11, 1940; came to US, 1962; d. Sun and Yau (Ng) Kwan; m. Fok, June 8, 1965; children: Licie Chiu-Jane, Edna Chiu-Joan. BA in Chemistry, U. Great Falls, 1965; MS in Plant Nutrition and Biochemistry, Utah State U., 1966; PhD in Biochemistry, U. Tex., 1971. Asst. rsch. prof. pathology U. Hawaii, Honolulu, 1973-74, Ford Found. postdoctoral fellow, anatomy dept., 1975, asst. rsch. prof., 1975-82, assoc. rsch. prof., 1982—88, rsch. prof. Pacific Biomed. Rsch. Ctr., 1988-96, grad. faculty, dept. microbiology, 1977—2003, dir., 1994-96, dir., prof. biology program, 1996—2003, prof. emeritus, 2003—. Contbr. articles to profl. jours. Mem. Soc. for Protozoologists, Sigma Xi (treas. Hawaii chpt. 1979-2002). Avocations: reading, gardening, hiking, sewing. Office: U Hawaii Biology Program Honolulu HI 96822 Business E-Mail: fok@hawaii.edu.

FOLBERG, HAROLD JAY, lawyer, educator, dean, mediator; b. East St. Louis, Ill., July 7, 1941; s. Louis and Matilda (Ross) F.; m. Diana L. Taylor, May 1, 1983; children: Lisa, Rachel, Ross. BA, San Francisco State U., 1963; JD, U. Calif., Berkeley, 1968. Bar: Oreg. 1968. Assoc. Rives & Schwab, Portland, Oreg., 1968-69; dir. Legal Aid Service, Portland, 1970-72; exec. dir. Assn. Family and Conciliation Cts., Portland, 1974-80; prof. law Lewis and Clark Law Sch., Portland, 1972-89; clin. asst. prof. child psychiatry U. Oreg. Med. Sch., 1976-89; judge pro-tem Oreg. Trial Cts., 1974-89; dean, prof. U. San Francisco Sch. Law, 1989-99, prof. law, 1999—. Chair jud. coun. Calif. Task Force on Alternative Dispute Resolution and the Jud. Sys., 1998-99, Calif. Blue Ribbon Panel Experts on Arbitration Ethics, 2001-2002, chair jud. coun.; Rockefeller Found. scholar in residence Bellagio, Italy, 1996; vis. prof. U. Wash. Sch. Law, 1985-86; mem. vis. faculty Nat. Jud. Coll., 1975-88; mem. Nat. Commn. on Accreditation for Marriage and Family Therapists, 1984-90; cons. Calif. Jud. Coun., U.S. Dist. Ct. (no. dist.) Calif., JAMS. Author: Joint Custody and Shared Parenting, 1984, 2d edit., 1991; (with Taylor) Mediation-A Comprehensive Guide to Resolving Conflicts without Litigation, 1984; (with Milne) Divorce Mediation, 1988; (with others) Divorce and Family Mediation: Models, Techniques and Applications, 2004, Resolving Disputes: Theory, Practice and Law, 2005, (with Golann) Lawyer Negotiation, 2006; mem. editl. bd. Family Counts Rev., Jour. of Divorce, Conflict Resolution Quar.; contbr. articles to profl. jours. Bd. dirs. Internat. Bioethics Inst., 1989-95, Oreg. Dispute Resolution Adv. Coun., 1988-89. Recipient Bernard E. Witkin award, Jud. Coun. Calif., 2002. Mem. ABA (chmn. mediation and arbitration com. family law sect. 1980-82, chmn. ethics com. dispute resolution sect. 2002-04), Oreg. State Bar Assn. (chmn. family and juvenile law sect. 1979-80), Am. Bd. Trial Advs., Multnomah Bar Assn. (chmn. bd. dirs. legal aid svc. 1973-76), Assn. Family and Conciliation Cts. (pres. 1983-84), Assn. Marriage and Family Therapists (disting. mem.), Am. Assn. Law Schs. (chmn. alternative dispute resolution sect. 1988), Acad. Family Mediators (bd. dirs., pres. 1988), CPR Inst. (panel disting. mediators), World Assn. Law Profs. (sec.-gen. 1995-2000). Office: Jams Two Embarcadero Ste 1500 San Francisco CA 94111 Office Phone: 415-774-2699, 415-834-1363. Business E-Mail: jfolberg@jamsadr.com.

FOLDVARY, FRED EMANUEL, economist, educator; b. Haifa, Israel, May 11, 1946; came to U.S., 1952; s. Otto and Tina (Klein) F.; m. Janet Waara. BA in Econs./Computer Sci., U. Calif., Berkeley, 1970; MA in Econs., George Mason U., 1990, PhD in Econs., 1992. Editor Topical Time mag., 1981-87; prof. U. Latvia, Riga, 1993, Latvian U. Agr., Jelgava, 1992-93; prof. econs. Mary Washington Coll., Fredericksburg, Va., 1994, Va. Poly. Inst. and State U., Blacksburg, 1994-95, Calif. State U., Hayward, 1995—98; lectr. econ. Santa Clara U., 1998—. Dir. Embarcadero Fed. Credit Union, San Francisco, 1979-81. Author: Soul of Liberty, 1980, Public Goods and Private Communities, 1994, Dictionary of Free MarketEconomics, 1998. Chmn. Libertarian party, Alameda County, Calif., 1981-82. Bradley fellow Ctr. for Study of Pub. Choice, George Mason U., 1989-91. Mem. Am. Econ. Assn., Congress Polit. Economists, Common Ground Va. Office: Dept Economics Santa Clara Univ 500 El Camino Real Santa Clara CA 95053 Office Phone: 408-554-6968. Office Fax: 408-554-2331. Business E-Mail: ffoldvary@scu.edu.

FOLEY, JACK (JOHN WAYNE HAROLD FOLEY), poet, writer, editor-in-chief; b. Neptune, NJ, Aug. 9, 1940; s. John Harold and Juana (Terio) F.; m. Adelle Joan Abramowitz, Dec. 21, 1961; 1 child, Sean Ezra. BA, Cornell U., 1963; MA, U. Calif., Berkeley, 1965. Exec. prodr.-in-charge poetry program Sta. KPFA-FM, Berkeley, 1988—; editor-in-chief Poetry USA, Oakland, Calif., 1990-95. Resident artist The Djerassi Program, 1994. Author: (poetry and prose) Letters/Lights-Words for Adelle, 1987, (poetry) Gershwin, 1991, Exiles, 1996, (prose) O Her Blackness Sparkles! The Life and Times of the Batman Art Gallery, San Francisco, 1960-1965, 1995, O Powerful Western Star, 2000, Foley's Books: California Rebels, Beats and Radicals, 2000, (prose and poetry) The Dancer & the Dance: A Book of Distinctions, 2008—, (poetry) Greatest Hits 1974-2003, 2004; editor, contbr. The Fallen Western Star Wars, 2001, editor ALL: A James Broughton Reader, 2006, (with Ivan Arquelles) (poetry) New Poetry From California: Dead, Requiem, 1998, editor Advice to the Lovelorn, 1998, (translations from the French) Some Songs by Georges Brassens, 2001; contbr. (film jour.) Bright Lights; contbg. editor Poetry Flash, 1992—, performances of poetry with wife Adelle, 1985—, columnist Foley's books, The Alsop Rev., 1998—; co-author (with Adelle Foley): (poetry) Fennel in The Rain, 2007. Woodrow Wilson fellow U. Calif., 1963-65; Poetry grant Oakland Arts Coun., 1992-95. Mem. MLA, Poets and Writers, Nat. Poetry Assn. (sec. San Francisco 1989-95), PEN Oakland (program dir. 1990-97). Avocations: playing guitar, tap dancing, writing songs. Home and Office: 2569 Maxwell Ave Oakland CA 94601-5521 E-mail: jandafoley@sbcglobal.net.

FOLEY, JAMES, film director; b. NYC, Dec. 28, 1953; Attended, U. So. Calif. Film Sch. Dir. (films) Reckless, 1984, At Close Range, 1986, Who's That Girl, 1987, Glengarry Glen Ross, 1992, Two Bits, 1995, No Fear, 1996, The Chamber, 1996, The Corruptor, 1999, Confidence, 2003, Perfect Stranger, 2007; screenwriter, dir.: (films) After Dark, My Sweet, 1990. Office: Creative Artists Agency 2000 Avenue Of The Stars Los Angeles CA 90067-4700

FOLEY, JOHN V., water company executive; Chmn. Met. Water Dist. of So. Calif., LA, bd. dirs. Office: Office of the Bd of Dirs PO 54153 Los Angeles CA 90054-0153

FOLEY, L(EWIS) MICHAEL, real estate company officer; s. Raymond B. and Mabel F.; m. Pamela Wagner, June 16, 1962; children: Michael D., Kimberly B., Robin E. BS in Sci. Engring., U. Mich., 1960; MBA in Fin. and Mktg., Harvard U., 1964. Pres. Econ. Devel. Corp., Detroit, 1969-71; v.p. Chrysler Realty Corp., Troy, Mich., 1972-77; exec. v.p. Bell and Howell Video Group, Chgo., 1977-79; v.p. fin., chief fin. officer Bell and Howell Corp., Chgo., 1979-80; sr. v.p. Homart Devel. Co., Chgo., 1981-84, exec. v.p., 1984-93; sr. exec. v.p. Coldwell Banker Real Estate Group Inc., Chgo., 1986-93; chmn., CEO Sears Savs. Bank, Chgo., 1989-93; sr. v.p., CFO Coldwell Banker Corp., 1995-96. Chmn. Borrowers Choice Corp., 1992-93; ret. non exec. chmn. bd. BRE Properties, Inc.; Chmn., Internat. Coun. Shopping Ctr. Found. Author: Management of Racial Integration in Business, 1965. Former vestry, jr. warden St. James by the Sea Episcopal Ch. Mem. Internat. Coun. Shopping Ctrs. (former v.p., trustee), Sigma Alpha Epsilon. Episcopalian. Office: 5824 Camino de la Costa La Jolla CA 92037-6551 Home Phone: 858-459-7095.

FOLEY, RIDGWAY KNIGHT, JR., lawyer, writer; b. Portland, Oreg., Oct. 7, 1937; s. Ridgway Knight and Eunice Alberta (Ammer) F. BS magna cum laude, with honors, Lewis & Clark Coll., 1959; JD, U. Oreg., 1963. Bar: Oreg. 1963. Assoc. Mautz, Souther, Spaulding,

Kinsey & Williamson, Portland, 1964-71; gen. ptnr. Schwabe, Williamson & Wyatt (and predecessor firms), Portland, 1972-84, sr. ptnr., 1985-92; ptnr., shareholder Foley & Duncan, P.C., Portland, 1993-96; of counsel Greene & Markley PC, Portland, 1997—, med. office mgr., 1999—2004. Com. mem. Multnomah Lawyer Com., 1964-68, 90-93, chair, 1992-93. Contbr. more than 100 articles, essays to profl. jours. Trustee Found. Econ. Edn., Inc., Irvington-on-Hudson, N.Y., 1974-91, 93-96; founding dir. Paulist Fathers Cath. Ctr., Portland, 1978-85. Mem. ABA, Oreg. State Bar, Multnomah County Bar (dir. 1993-97), Univ. Club (Portland), Mt. Hood Philos. Soc. (founding trustee, officer 1972-85), Lang Syne Soc., Order of Coif. Episcopalian. Avocations: writing, lecturing, genealogy, publishing, golden retrievers. Office: Greene & Markley PC 1515 SW 5th Ave Ste 600 Portland OR 97201-5449 Office Phone: 503-295-2668. Business E-Mail: ridgway.foley@greenemarkley.com.

FOLEY, SYLVESTER ROBERT, JR., science administrator, retired military officer; b. Manchester, NH, Sept. 19, 1928; s. Sylvester Robert and Gladys Nancy (Cameron) F.; m. Kathleen MacDonald, June 23, 1951; children— Robert, Maureen, Brenda, Christopher BS, U.S. Naval Acad., 1950; postgrad., Naval War Coll., 1961; MS in Internat. Affairs, George Washington U., 1968. Commd. ensign USN, 1950, advanced through grades to adm., 1982; instr. U.S. Naval Acad., 1956-59; mem. staff Comdr. in Chief U.S. Naval Forces, Europe, 1962-65; exec. officer Attack Squadron 106, 1965-66, comdr., 1966-67; comdr. Carrier Air Wing Eleven USS Kitty Hawk, 1968-69; mem. air weapons systems analysis staff, tactical aircraft plans officer Office Naval Ops., Dept. Navy, Washington, 1969-71; comdr. USS Coronado, 1971-72, USS Midway, 1972-73; chief of staff to comdr. 7th Fleet, 1973-74; dep. dir. Strategic Plans, Policy, Nuclear Systems and NSC Affairs Div. OPNAV, 1974-76; comdr. Carrier Group 7 Flagship Enterprise, 1976-78; comdr. 7th Fleet, 1978-80; dep. chief naval ops., plans and policy Dept Navy, Washington, 1980-82; comdr. in chief US Pacific Fleet, 1982-85; asst. sec. energy US Dept. Energy, Washington, 1985-87; v.p. Am. Capital & Rsch., 1987-88; pres. Advanced Tech. Group ICF Kaiser Engrs., Fairfax, Va., 1988—91; v.p. comml. mktg., pres. Raytheon Japan, v.p. Asian ops. Raytheon Internat., Inc. Raytheon Co., 1991; v.p. lab. mgmt. U. Calif., Oakland, 2003—. Bd. dirs. Intel Fat Gen. Corp.; trustee Navy War Coll. Found. Decorated Disting. Service medal (3), Legion of Merit, D.F.C., Bronze Star, Air medal, Navy Commendation medal with gold star, others; French Legion of Honor, others from Japan, Korea and Brazil Mem. U.S. Naval Inst., Council of Fgn. Relations Clubs: Bohemian (San Francisco), Army-Navy (Washington). Roman Catholic. Office: U Calif Lab Mgmt 1111 Franklin, #5301 Oakland CA 94607 E-mail: Bob.Foley@ucop.edu.

FOLEY, WILLIAM PATRICK, II, insurance company executive; b. Austin, Tex., Dec. 29, 1944; s. Robert P. Foley; m. Carol J. Johnson, Nov. 15 1969; children: Lindsay, Robert P. II, Courtney Diane, William P. III. BS, U.S. Mil. Acad., 1967; MBA, Seattle U., 1970; JD, U. Wash., 1974. Assoc. Streich, Lang, Weeks, Cardon & French P.A., Phoenix, 1974-76; ptnr., pres., dir. Foley, Clark & Nye P.A., Phoenix, 1976-84; pres., CEO Land Resources Corp., Scottsdale, Ariz., 1983-84; chmn., pres., CEO Fidelity Nat. Fin. Inc., Jacksonville, Fla., 1981—2007, chmn., 2007—, Checkers Drive-In Restaurants, Inc., Clearwater, Fla. Chmn. bd., dir., pres., chief exec. officer Fidelity Nat. Fin., Inc., Fidelity Nat. Title Ins. Co. of Calif., Fidelity Nat. Title Ins. Co. of Tenn., Fidelity Nat. Title Ins. Co. of Tex., So. Title Holding Co., Pacific Western Aviation, Inc., Western Am. Exch. Corp., Western Pacific Property & Casualty Agy., Inc., Fidelity Appraisal Group, Inc., Folco Devel. Corp., Western Pacific Acquisitions, Inc., Bristol Investment Corp.; chmn. bd., dir. Western Fin. Trust Co., Rocky Mountain Aviation, Inc.; chmn. bd. dir., chief exec. officer Fidelity Nat. Title Agy., Inc. Fidelity Nat. Title Agy. of Maricopa County, Inc., Fidelity Nat. Title Agy. of Pinal County, Inc., Fidelity Nat. Title Co. of El Paso, Fidelity Nat. Title Co. of Oreg., Ramada Inn Old Town Mgmt., Inc.; numerous other chairmanships and directorships in fin. industry; founder & mng. ptnr. Foley Estates Vineyard & Winery of Calif.; founder & mng. ptnr. LinCourt Vineyards of Calif.; chmn. bd. CKE Restaurants Inc. Mem. Jacksonville C. of C., Fla.; del. Rep. Nat. Conv., 1996; adv. bd. mem. U. Wash. Sch. Law; trustee Found. Bd. U. Calif. Santa Barbara. Capt. USAF. Recipient Semper Fidelis award, Marine Corps Scholarship Found., 1997. Avocations: golf, chess, winemaking. Office: Fidelity Nat Fin Inc 601 Riverside Ave Jacksonville FL 32204-2950

FOLICK, JEFFREY M., healthcare systems company executive; married; three children. BS in Bus., Calif. State U., LA. Chief fin. officer Vly. Presbyn. Hosp.; pres. Peak Health Plan, Calif.; v.p. Secure Horizons PacifiCare Health Sys., 1989-94, exec. v.p., chief fin. officer, 1994-98, pres., COO Santa Ana, Calif., 1998—. Chmn. allocation com., bd. dirs. PacifiCare Found.; bd. dirs. Long Term Health Group. Office: PacifiCare Health Sys 3120 W Lake Center Dr Santa Ana CA 92704-6917

FOLKMAN, DAVID H., retail, wholesale and consumer products consultant; b. Jackson, Mich., Nov. 6, 1934; s. Jerome D. and Bessie (Schomer) F.; m. Susan Kleppner, June 22, 1958; children: Louis, Sarah, Karen, Jeffrey. AB, Harvard U., 1957, MBA, 1960. Mdse. mgr. Foley's, Houston, 1957-69; v.p. dir. stores Famous-Barr, St. Louis, 1969-74; sr. v.p., gen. mdse. mgr. Macy's Calif., San Francisco, 1974-82; pres., chief exec. officer Emporium Capwell, San Francisco, 1982-87; gen. ptnr. U.S. Venture Ptnrs., Menlo Park, Calif., 1987-90; venture ptnr., 1991-93; pres., chief exec. officer Laurel Burch, Inc., San Francisco, 1990-91; retail investor, cons., 1991-93; CEO Esprit de Corp, San Francisco, 1993-95; mng. dir. Regent Pacific Mgmt. Corp., San Francisco, 1995—. Instr. U. Houston, 1968—69, Washington U., St. Louis, 1970—73; bd. dirs. Regent Pacific Mgmt. Corp.; MBA students mentor Ctr. Entrepreneurial Studies, Stanford Grad. Sch. Bus., 2005—; cons. Harvard Bus. Sch., Cmty. Ptnrs. Projects, 2006—. Mem. Harvard Club (N.Y.C.). Office: Regent Pacific Mgmt Corp 433 California St Ste 210 San Francisco CA 94104 Office Phone: 415-391-8500. Business E-Mail: dfolkman@regent-pacific.com.

FOLLETT, ROBERT JOHN RICHARD, publisher; b. Oak Park, Ill., July 4, 1928; s. Dwight W. and Mildred (Johnson) F.; m. Nancy L. Crouthamel, Dec. 30, 1950; children: Brian L., Kathryn R., Jean A., Lisa W. AB, Brown U., 1950; postgrad., Columbia U., 1950-51. Editor Follett Pub. Co., Chgo., 1951-55, sales mgr., 1955-58, gen. mgr. edn1. divsn., developer first multi-racial textbook program, first textbooks for disadvantaged, first beginning-to-read books, 1958-68, pres., 1968-78; chmn., dir. Follett Corp., 1979-94. Pres. Alpine Guild, Inc., 1977—; dir. Assn. Am. Pubs., 1972—79; chmn. Sch. Pubs., 1971—73; dir. Edn1. Sys. Corp.; mem. Ill. Gov.'s Commn. on Schs, 1972; pres. Alpine Rsch. Inst., Adv. Coun. on Edn. Stats., 1975—77; chmn. Book Distbn. Task Force of Book Industry, 1978—81; adv. coun. Krannert Sch. of Mgmt., 1988—93; pres. Soda Creek Open Space Assn. Inc., 1994—; dir. Continental Divide Land Trust, 1996—2002; chmn. Rocky Mountain Resource Ctr., Inc., 1997—2002; lectr. Denver U. Pub. Inst., 1997—; mem. adv. bd. Ctr. for Living Democracy, 1997—2000; mem. Consortium on Renewing Edn., 1997—2000; chmn. Open Space for Summit, 1999; pres. Snake River Cmty. Assoc., 2001—, Continental Divide Land Trust, 2001—03; dir. Keystone Ctr., 2006—09. Author: Your Wonderful Body, 1961, What to Take Backpacking and Why, 1977, How to Keep Score in Business, 1978, The Financial Side of Book Publishing, 1982, rev. edit., 1988, Financial Feasibility in Book Publishing, 1988, rev. edit., 1996, Wolf Trapped: The Death of a Young Artist in Hitler's Europe, 2006. Bd. dirs. Village Mgr. Assn., 1964-84, Cmty. Found. Oak Park and River Forest, 1959-86, Fund for Justice, 1974-77, For Character, 1983-93, Ctr. Book Rsch., 1985-88; trustee Inst. Ednl. Data Sys., 1965-; trustee, pres. Rotary Found., 2000-06; elected mem. Rep. State Com. from 7th dist. Ill., 1982-90, vice chmn., 1986-90; chmn. Ill. Reps. Strategic Planning Com., 1986-87; Presdl. Elector, 1988; pres. Keystone Citizens League, 1997-2004; mem. Keystone Mountain Responsibility Team, 1998-2000; mem. adv. coun. Colo. Mountain Coll., 2003-; hon. co-chair Colo. Mountain Coll. Campaign, 1998-99; mem. Wildlife/Wetlands Citizens Adv. Group, 2001-02; mem. adv. com. Keystone Sci. Sch., 2003—; sustaining bd. Nat. Repertory Orch. Endowment, 2006-; trustee NRO; adj. prof. U. Denver, 2002-. Served in AUS, 1951-53. sgt. Psychol. Warfare Sch. Recipient Citizen of Yr. award, Summit County, 1999, Philanthropist of Yr. award, 2003; named one of Torchbearers, Olympics, 2004. Mem.: Soc. Midland Authors, Ill. C. of C. (chmn. edn. com. 1977—79), Am. Book Coun. (v.p. 1987—88), Rocky Mountain Book Pubs. Assn., Mid.-Am. Pubs. Assn. (mng. dir. 1987—88, dir. 1988—93), Chgo. Pubs. Assn (pres. 1976—94), Rotary Club Summit County, River Forest Tennis Club, Sierra Club. Office: Alpine Guild Inc PO Box 4848 Dillon CO 80435-4848 Home: 0160 Kinnikinnik Rd Keystone CO Home Phone: 970-262-1038. Business E-Mail: bob@alpineguild.com.

FOLLETT, RONALD FRANCIS, soil scientist; b. Laramie, Wyo., June 26, 1939; s. Roy Lawrence and Frances (Hunter) F.; m. Dorothy Mae Spangle, Jan. 1, 1967; children: William, Jennifer, Michael. BS, Colo. State U., 1961, MS, 1963; PhD, Purdue U., 1966. Rsch. soil scientist Agrl. Rsch. Svc., USDA, Mandan, ND, 1968-75, nat. rsch. program leader Beltsville (Md.) and Ft. Collins (Colo.), 1976-86, rsch. leader soil-plant-nutrient rsch. unit Ft. Collins, 1986—; postdoctoral rsch. U.S. Plant-Soil-Nutrition Lab., Ithaca, NY, 1975-76. Co-author: The Potential of U.S. Cropland to Sequester Carbon and Mitigate the Greenhouse Effect, 1998; editor: Soil Erosion & Crop Productivity, 1985, Soil Fertility and Organic Matter as Critical Components of Production Systems, 1987, Nitrogen Management and Ground Water Protection, 1989, Managing Nitrogen for Ground Water Quality and Farm Profitability, 1991, Soil Processes & The Carbon Cycle, 1997, Soil Properties & Their Management for Carbon Sequestration, 1997, The Potential of U.S. Grazing Lands to Sequester Carbon and Mitigate the Greenhouse Effect, 2000, Nitrogen in the Environment, Sources, Problems and Management, 2001, 2008, Agricultural Practices and Policies for Carbon Sequestration in Soil, 2002, Soil Carbon Management-Economic, Environmental and Societal Benefits, 2007; guest editor spl. issue Jour. Containment Hydrol., 1995, Soil & Tillage Rsch., 2005; contbr. over 150 articles to profl. jours. Officer 1st Presbyn. Ch., Mandan, then Ft. Collins; adult leader local Boy Scouts Am., Beltsville, then Ft. Collins. Capt. arty., U.S. Army, 1966-68; maj. Res. Recipient Disting. Svc. award, USDA, 1984, 1992, Superior Svc. award, 2000, Appreciation cert., Soil Conservation Svc./USDA, 1992, Merit cert., Agr. Rsch. Svc./USDA, 1990, 1996, 1999—2003, 2005—09, U.S. Presdl. Rank Meritorious Svc. award, 2004, Innovator award, No-Till Farmer Magazine, 2007; named Scientist of Yr., Agr. Rsch. Svc./USDA, 2005. Fellow Soil Sci. Soc. Am. (divsn. chmn. bd. dirs. 1985-88), Am. Soc. Agronomy, Soil and Water Conservation Soc. Am. (pres. Colo. chpt. 1993, 2006, bd. dir. 2006, 07, Colo. chpt. Presdl. citation 2002, Nat. citation 2007). Avocations: working with youth, skiing, fishing, gardening, woodworking. Office: USDA Agrl Rsch Svc Soil-Plant-Nutrient Rsch Unit 2150 Centre Ave Bldg D Ste 100 Fort Collins CO 80526-8119 Office Phone: 970-492-7220. Business E-Mail: ronald.follett@ars.usda.gov.

FOLLETTE, WILLIAM ALBERT, electronics company executive; b. Tampa, Fla., Dec. 29, 1946; s. Harold Albert and Louise Olga (Mehm) F.; m. Barbara Ann Cunneen, June 8, 1968; children: Kelly, James, William T. BBA, U. Notre Dame, 1968; MBA, Ariz. State U., 1978. Prodn. control analyst Motorola, Mesa, Ariz., 1974-77; successively bus. planner, bus. planning mgr., dir. strategic planning Sperry Corp., Phoenix, 1977-87; dir. bus. and strategic planning, group dir. quality Honeywell Inc., Phoenix, 1987—. Pres. Phoenix chpt. Planning Forum. Maj. USAFR, 1968-90. Republican. Roman Catholic. Avocations: skiing, golf, flying. Home: 5041 E Cortez Dr Scottsdale AZ 85254-4634 Office: Honeywell Inc Comml Flight Sys Group 21111 N 19th Ave Phoenix AZ 85027-2700

FOLLICK, EDWIN DUANE, law educator, dean, chiropractor; b. Glendale, Calif., Feb. 4, 1935; s. Edwin Fulfford and Esther Agnes (Catherwood) Follick; m. Marilyn K. Sherk, Mar. 24, 1986. BA in Social Sci., Calif. State U., LA, 1956, MA in Edn., 1961; MA in Social Sci., Pepperdine U., 1957, MPA, 1977; PhD in Social Sci., Sem. Free Prot. Episc. Ch., London, 1958, DTh, 1958; MS in LS, U. So. Calif., 1963, MEd in Instrnl. Materials, 1964, AdvMEd in Edn. Adminstrn., 1969; postgrad., Calif. Coll. Law, 1965; LLB, Blackstone Law Sch., 1966, JD, 1967; DC, Cleve. Chiropractic Coll., LA, 1972; PhD in Eccles. Law, Academia Theatina, Pescara, 1978; MA in Orgnl. Mgmt., Antioch U., LA, 1990. Tchr., libr. adminstr. L.A. City Schs., 1957-68; law libr. Glendale U. Coll. Law, 1968-69; coll. libr. Cleve. Chiropractic Coll., LA, 1969-74, dir. edn. and admissions, 1974-84, prof. jurisprudence, 1975—2003, dean student affairs, 1976-92, coll. chaplain, 1985—2003, dean of edn., 1989—2003, rector, 2003—04, rector emeritus, 2004—; assoc. prof. Newport U., 1982; extern prof. St. Andrews Theol. Coll., London, 1961; dir. West Valley Chiropractic Health Ctr., 1972-2000, West Valley Chiropractic Consulting, 2001—04; cons. instnl. chaplain, 2004—; libr. dir. South Baylo U., 2004—, u. chaplain, 2004—; libr. dir. Calif. U. Mgmt. and Sci., 2004—. Adj. prof. law Calif. U. Mgmt. and Sci., 2004—, univ. chaplain, 2004—. Contbr. articles to profl. jours. Chaplain's asst. US Army, 1958—60. Decorated cavaliere Internat. Order Legion of Honor of Immaculata (Italy); Knight of Malta, Sovereign Order of St. John of Jerusalem; Knight Grand Prelate, comdr. with star, Order of Signum Fidei; comdr. chevalier Byzantine Imperial Order of Constantine the Gt.; comdr. ritter Order St. Gereon; chevalier Mil. and Hospitaller Order of St. Lazarus of Jerusalem (Malta), Chaplain to the Order of St. Stanislas; numerous others. Mem. ALA, NEA, Am. Assn. Sch. Librarians, LA Sch. Libr. Assn., Calif. Sch. Libr. Assn., Assn. Coll. and Rsch. Librarians, Am. Assn. Law Librarians, Am. Chiropractic Assn., Internat. Chiropractors Assn., Nat. Geog. Soc., Internat. Platform Assn., Phi Delta Kappa, Sigma Chi Psi, Delta Tau Alpha. Democrat. Episcopalian. Home: 6435 Jumilla Ave Woodland Hills CA 91367-2833 Office: 590 N Vermont Ave Los Angeles CA 90004-2115 also: 7022 Owensmouth Ave Canoga Park CA 91303-2005 Address: 1126 N Brookhurst St Anaheim CA 92801 Office Phone: 323-906-2114, 714-533-6077. Business E-Mail: edwin.follick@cleveland.edu, edfollick@southbaylo.edu.

FOLTZ, CRAIG B., astronomer, educator; b. Shamokin, Pa., June 28, 1952; m. Sharon Burrier, Aug. 30, 1980; children: Rachel Elizabeth, Robin Amelia. BA in Physics summa cum laude, Dartmouth Coll., 1974; PhD in Astronomy, Ohio State U., 1979. Postdoctoral fellow dept. astronomy Ohio State U., 1979-80, instr. dept. physics, 1980, instr. dept. astronomy, 1980, rsch. assoc. dept. astronomy, 1981; rsch. assoc. Steward Obs., U. Ariz., 1983, astronomer, 1990—; asst. prof. dept. astronomy U. Ill., 1983-84; staff astronomer Multiple Mirror Telescope Obs., U. Ariz., Tucson, 1984-90, acting dir., 1990-91, 96-97, dep. dir., 1990-96, dir., 1997—. Project scientist 6.5m Telescope Project, 1989-94, dir., 1996—; vis. scholar Inst. Astronomy, Cambridge U., 1995; astroner Smithsonian Astrophys. Obs., 1990—; lectr. in field. Contbr. articles to profl. jours. Grantee NSF, 1987-90, 90-94, 92-95, 94-98, 94-98, 1998-2001, NASA, 1991-92, STScI, 1993-96, 94-96, 94-96, 96-97, 1999-2000, Smithsonian, 1994-99; Alfred P. Sloan scholar Dartmouth Coll., 1970-74; univ. fellow Ohio State U., 1974-78. Mem. Internat. Astron. Union, Am. Astron. Soc., Astron. Soc. of the Pacific, Phi Beta Kappa, Phi Kappa Phi. Achievements include research of QSO absorption lines and the intergalactic medium, distribution of Quasi-Stellar objects, gravitational lenses, emission lines in QSOs and active galactic nuclei, astronomical instrumentation. E-mai. Office: Multiple Mirror Telescope Obs Rm 460a Steward Obs Bldg Univ Ariz Tucson AZ 85721-0465 Fax: 520-670-5740. E-mail: cfoltz@as.arizona.edu, cfoltz@cfa.harvard.edu.

FONG, KEVIN MURRAY, lawyer; AB magna cum laude, Harvard U., 1976, JD cum laude, 1979. Bar: Calif. 1979. Law clk. Judge Constance Baker Motley, U.S. Dist. Ct. (so. dist.) N.Y., NYC, 1979-80; ptnr. Pillsbury, Madison & Sutro LLP, San Francisco, 1980—2001, Pillsbury Winthrop LLP, 2001—05; ptnr. litigation practice, co-leader appellate practice, chmn. diversity com. Pillsbury Winthrop Shaw Pittman LLP, 2005—. Editor-in-chief Law Rev. Harvard civil rights-civil liberties, 1979. Mem. ABA (mem. com. racial and ethnic diversity 2004-07), Calif. Acad. Appellate Lawyers (v.p.), Asian Am. Bar Assn. (pres. 1989), Asian Pacific Bar Calif. (pres. 1990), Bar Assn. San Francisco (bd. dirs. 1991-92), Legal Aid Soc. San Francisco (treas. 1995-97, mem. exec. com.). Democrat. Office: Pillsbury Winthrop Shaw Pittman LLP 50 Fremont St San Francisco CA 94105 Office Phone: 415-983-1270. Office Fax: 415-983-1200. Business E-Mail: kevin.fong@pillsburylaw.com.

FONG, MATTHEW KIPLING, state official; b. Oakland, Calif., Nov. 20, 1953; s. Chester and March Fong; m. Paula Fong, May 28, 1978; children: Matthew II, Jade. Grad., U.S. Air Force Acad., 1975; MBA, Pepperdine U., 1982; JD, Southwestern Law. Sch., 1985. Former vice chmn. State Bd. Equalization; treas. State Calif., LA, 1999; atty. LA, 1999—. Regent Pepperdine U., Children's Hosp. L.A.; Rep. nominee State Controller, 1990. Lt. col. Air Force Res. Office: Sheppard Mullin Richter & Hampton 333 S Hope St Fl 48 Los Angeles CA 90071-1406

FONG, PAUL, state legislator; m. Grace Fong; children: Sydney, Nicole, Sean. BA in Sociology, San Jose State U., MPA; MAEd, U. San Francisco. Owner with wife Flowers Cottage, Sunnyvale; mem. Dist. 22 Calif. State Assembly, 2008—. Democrat. Office: 274 Castro St Ste 202 Mountain View CA 94041 also: PO Box 942849 Rm 5135 Sacramento CA 94249-0022 Office Phone: 650-210-2000, 916-319-2022, 408-277-2003. Office Fax: 650-210-2005, 916-319-2122, 408-277-2084. Business E-Mail: Assemblymember.Fong@assembly.ca.gov.*

FOOSE, CHIP, automotive designer, television personality; b. Santa Barbara, Calif., Oct. 6, 1963; s. Sam Foose; m. Lynne Foose; children: Brock, Katie. Grad., Art Ctr. Coll. Design, 1990. Staff designer, fabricator Asha Corp., 1986—89, dir., 1989; automotive designer Stehrenberger Design; chief designer, fabricator Baker Sportronics; automotive designer Project Design; with Hot Rods by Boyd, 1990—98, mng. dir., pres.; founder Foose Design, Huntington Beach, Calif., 1998—. Host (TV series) Overhaulin, 2004—. Vice chmn. Progeria Rsch. Found. Calif. Chpt. Recipient Good Guys Trendsetter award, 1998, America's Most Beautiful Roadster award, 1995, 1996, 1999, 2000, 2001, 2003, 2006, Detroit Autorama Ridler award, 2002, 2003, 2005, 7 Good Guy Streetcar of Yr. awards; inductee, Hot Rod Hall of Fame, 1997, Darryl Starbird Rod &Custom Car Mus. Hall of Fame, 2002, Grand Nat. Roadster Show Hall of Fame, 2003, San Francisco Rod and Custom Motorcycle Hall of Fame, 2004. Office: Foose Design Inc 17811 Sampson Ln Huntington Beach CA 92647

FOOTE, ADAM, professional hockey player; b. Whitby, Ont., Can., July 10, 1971; m. Jennifer Foote; children: Callan, Nolan. Defenseman Que. Nordiques, Canada, 1991—95, Colo. Avalanche, 1995—2005, 2008—, Columbus Blue Jackets, 2005—08, capt., 2005—08. Mem. Can. World Cup Team, 1996, 2004, Can. Olympic Team, Nagano, 1998, Salt Lake City, 2002. Achievements include being a member of Stanley Cup Champion Colorado Avalanche, 1996, 2001; being a member of gold medal Canadian Hockey team, Salt Lake City Olympic Games, 2002; being a member of World Cup Champion Team Canada, 2004. Office: Colo Avalanche Hockey Club Pepsi Ctr 1000 Chopper Circle Denver CO 80204

FORBES, BRIAN L., lawyer; BA, Univ. Calif., Berkeley, 1970; JD, Univ. Calif., Hastings, 1974. Bar: Calif. 1974, Tex., US Dist. Ct. (so. dist. Calif.) 1974, US Dist. Ct. (no. dist. Calif.) 1989, US Ct. Appeals (9th cir.) 1990, US Tax Ct. 1989, US Supreme Ct. 1980. Gen. counsel Gray Cary & Freidenrich, 1999—2004; profl. responsibility ptnr. DLA Piper Rudnick Gray Cary, San Diego, 2005—. Mem.: Thurston Soc., Order of the Coif. Office: DLA Piper Rudnick Gray Cary Suite 1100 4365 Executive Dr San Diego CA 92121 Office Phone: 858-638-6842. Office Fax: 858-677-1401. Business E-Mail: brian.forbes@dlapiper.com.

FORBES, DAVID CRAIG, musician; b. Seattle, Feb. 12, 1938; s. Douglas James and Ruby A. (Niles) F.; m. Sylvia Sterling, Aug. 29, 1965 (div. Apr. 1973); 1 child, Angela Rose. Grad., USN Sch. Music, 1957; student, Western Wash. U., 1960-64. Prin. horn La Jolla (Calif.) Civic Orch., 1958-60, Seattle Worlds Fair Band, 1962, Seattle Opera Co., 1964—, Pacific Northwest Ballet, Seattle, 1964—; asst. prin.

horn Seattle Symphony Orch., 1964—2003, ret., 2003; prin. horn Pacific Northwest Wagner Fest., Seattle, 1975—. Instr. horn Western Wash. State U., 1969-81, Cornish Inst., Seattle, 1964-78. Served with USN, 1956-60. Mem. NARAS, Internat. Horn Soc. Avocations: piano, golf, fishing. Home: 19630 Ashcrest Loop NE Apt 23 Poulsbo WA 98370-7556 E-mail: DavidForbes@webtv.net.

FORCE, RONALD WAYNE, retired librarian; b. Sioux City, Iowa, Sept. 7, 1941; s. Robert N. and Madeline (Heine) F.; m. Jo Ellen Hitch, May 31, 1964; children: Emily, Alicia. BS, Iowa State U., 1963; MA, U. Minn., 1968; MS, Ohio State U., 1975. Asst. to head dept. librs. Ohio State U., Columbus, 1968-70, head engring. librs., 1970-72, head edn./psychology libr., 1972-79; asst. dir. pub. svcs. Wash. State U. Librs., Pullman, 1979-82; asst. sci. libr. U. Idaho Libr., Moscow, 1982-84, pub. svcs. libr., 1984-85, humanities libr., 1985-88, assoc. dean libr. svcs., 1988-91, dean libr. svcs., 1991—2006; ret., 2006. Mem. adv. coun. Libr. Svcs. and Constrn. Act. Author: Guide to Literature on Biomedical Engineering, 1972; contbr. articles to profl. jours. Mem. Sacajawea Coun. Campfire Bd., 1980-85, mem. Pullman Dist. Campfire Com., fin. com., 1980-82, chair, 1983-84, treas., 1985, Sacajawea County Self-Study Com., 1986; mem. adv. bd. N.W. Net Info. Resources, 1994-95, 2000—; mem. Idaho Network Adv. Com., 1993-95; mem. LSCA Adv. Coun., 1989-95; mem. Libraries Linking Idaho Bd., 2000—. Mem. ALA, Idaho Libr. Assn. (2d v.p. 1997-98, 1st v.p. 1998-99, pres. 1999-2000). Home: 545 N Blaine St Moscow ID 83843-3626

FORD, BETTY ANN (ELIZABETH ANN FORD), former First Lady of the United States, health facility executive; b. Chgo., Apr. 8, 1918; d. William Stephenson and Hortence (Neahr) Bloomer; m. William G. Warren, 1942 (div. 1947); m. Gerald R. Ford (38th Pres. US), Oct. 15, 1948; children: Michael Gerald, John Gardner, Steven Meigs, Susan Elizabeth. Studied, Bennington Sch. of Dance, 1936-37; studied with Martha Graham, Graham Sch. of Dance, NYC, 1937; LL.D. (hon.), U. Mich., 1976. Dancer Martha Graham Concert Group, NYC, 1939-41; fashion dir. Herpolscheimer's Dept. Store, Grand Rapids, Mich., 1943-48; dance instr. Grand Rapids, 1932-48; First Lady of the United States, 1974—77. Co-founder Susan G. Komen Found., 1982; co-founder (with Leonard Firestone), chmn. The Betty Ford Ctr., Rancho Mirage, Calif., 1982—. Author: (autobiography) The Times of My Life, 1978, Betty: A Glad Awakening, 1987. Bd. dirs. Nat. Arthritis Found. (hon.); trustee Martha Graham Dance Ctr., Eisenhower Med. Ctr., Rancho Mirage; hon. chmn. Palm Springs Desert Mus.; nat. trustee Nat. Symphony Orch.; bd. dirs. The Lambs, Libertyville, Ill. Recipient Presdl. Medal of Freedom, 1991, Living Legacy award, Women's Internat. Ctr., 1998, Congl. Gold Medal, 1999, C. Everett Koop Health award, Am. Hosp. Assn., 1999, Woodrow Wilson Pub. Svc. award, 2003; named to Mich. Women's Hall of Fame, 1987. Republican. Episcopalian. Office: Gerald R Ford Library 1000 Beal Ave Ann Arbor MI 48109

FORD, CELESTE VOLZ, aerospace engineer; b. Washington, May 24, 1956; d. Frederick and Jeannine Bradley Volz; m. Kevin Edward Ford, June 17, 1978; children: Miranda, Nathan, Hillary. BS in Aerospace Engring., U. Notre Dame, 1978; MS in Aerospace Engring., Stanford U., 1980. Project mgr. Aerospace Corp., Sunnyvale, Calif., 1980-84; v.p. Scitor Corp., Sunnyvale, 1984-95; CEO Stellar Solutions, Inc., Palo Alto, Calif., 1995—. Mem. Coun. on Civil and Comml. Space, Sunnyvale, 1996; bd. dirs. Calif. Space Authority. Bd. dirs. Portola Valley (Calif.) Sch. Found., 1995. Recipeint Coll. Engring. Hoor award U. Notre Dame, South Bend, Ind., 1993, Woman's award achievement U. Notre Dame, South Bend, 1997, Working Woman Entrepreneurial award, 2000, Women of Distinction Bus. Services Award Silicon Valley Business Jour. & NAWBO; named Bay Area Dynamic Woman, 2000. Mem. AIAA, Nat. Assn. Woman Bus. Owners, Internat. Coun. on Sys. Engring., U. Notre Dame Engring. Adv. Coun. Roman Catholic. Avocation: bike riding. Office: Stellar Solutions Inc 250 Cambridge Ave Ste 204 Palo Alto CA 94306-1555 Fax: 650-473-9867. E-mail: cford@stelalrsolutions.com.*

FORD, NEVILLE F., clinical pharmacologist; b. Greenock, Scotland, Nov. 30, 1934; m. Branka P. Ford, May 19, 1978. BSc, U. Bristol, England, 1955, PhD, 1958, DSc, 1975; MD, Washington U., St. Louis, 1985. Sr. chemist Ciba Pharm., Summit, NJ, 1960—68, dir. chem. rsch., 1969—71; exec. dir. pharm. divsn. Ciba-Geigy, Summit, 1971—81; assoc. dir. clin. pharm. Bristol-Myers Squibb, Princeton, NJ, 1988—90, dir. clin. pharmacology, 1991—97, exec. dir. clin. pharmacology, 1998—2000; pres. Woodfield Clin. Cons., Lawrenceville, NJ, 2000—05, Green Valley, Ariz., 2005—. Cln. assoc. prof. medicine U. Medicine and Dentistry NJ, New Brunswick, 2000—. Recipient Vol. Faculty Tchg. award, U. Medicine and Dentistry NJ, 2005. Fellow: ACP, Am. Coll. Clin. Pharmacology. Presbyterian. Office: Woodfield Clin Cons LLC 5481 S Acacia Creek Dr Green Valley AZ 85622 Office Phone: 520-648-2713. Business E-Mail: neville@woodfieldclinical.com.

FORD, PETER C., chemistry professor; b. Salinas, Calif., July 10, 1941; s. Clifford and Thelma (Martin) F.; children: Vincent, Jonathan; m. Mary E. Howe-Grant. BS with honors, Calif. Inst. Tech., 1962; MS, Yale U., 1963, PhD, 1966. Postdoctoral fellow Stanford U., 1966-67; asst. prof. chemistry U. Calif., Santa Barbara, 1967-72, assoc. prof. chemistry, 1972-77, prof. chemistry, 1977—. Grad. advisor dept. chemistry U. Calif., 1980-81, co-grad. advisor, 1985-92, 99—, chmn., 1994-96; vis. fellow Australian Nat. U., 1974; guest prof. H.C. Oersted Inst., Denmark, 1981; lectr. U. Berne, Switzerland, 1989, MITI-ASTI, Japan, 1990; guest investigator radiation biology br. Nat. Cancer Inst., 1994. Contbr. to profl. jours. Fellow NIH, 1963-66, NSF, 1966-67, Sterling fellow Yale U., 1963, sr. fellow Fulbright Found., 1974; Dreyfus Found. Tchr. scholar, 1971-76; recipient Alexander von Humboldt-Stiftung U.S. Sr. Scientist Rsch. award, 1992, Richard C. Tolman medal Am. Chem. Soc., 1993. Fellow: AAAS; mem.: Inter-Am. Photochem. Soc. (v.p. 2002—04, pres. 2004—). Achievements include research in the photochemical, photocatalytic and photophysical mechanisms of transition metal complexes and with homogeneous catalysis mechanisms as probed by modern kinetics techniques; the bioinorganic chemistry of metal nitrosyl complexes. Office: Univ of California Dept of Chemistry 552 University Rd Santa Barbara CA 93106-0001

FORD, RICHARD THOMPSON, law educator; b. 1966; AB in Polit. Sci., Stanford U., 1988; JD cum laude, Harvard U., 1991. Housing policy cons. City of Cambridge, Mass., 1990—91; litig. assoc. Morrison & Foerster, San Francisco, 1991—93; Reginald Lewis Fellow Harvard Law Sch., Cambridge, Mass., 1993—94; assoc. prof. law Stanford Law Sch., 1994—99, prof., 1999—, Justin M. Roach, Jr. faculty scholar, 2003—04, George E. Osborne prof. law, 2004—. Vis. prof. law Columbia Law Sch., NYC, 2000; commr. Housing Authority of the City and County of San Francisco, 1997—98. Author: (book) The Race Card, 2008. Office: Stanford Law Sch Crown Quadrangle 559 Nathan Abbott Way Stanford CA 94305-8610 Office Phone: 650-723-2796. Business E-Mail: rford@stanford.edu.

FORD, TOM, apparel designer and executive; b. Austin, Tex., Aug. 27, 1962; Student, NYU, Parsons Sch. Design, NY, Paris. Sr. designer Cathy Hardwick, 1986—88; design dir. Perry Ellis Women's Am. Divsn., 1988—90; chief women's ready-to-wear designer Gucci, 1990—92, design dir., 1992—94, creative dir., 1994—2004, creative dir. Yves Saint Laurent Rive Gauche, YSL Beauté line, 2000—04; CEO, pres. Tom Ford Co., 2005—. Collaborator fragrance and beauty products line Tom Ford for Estee Lauder, 2005—. Recipient Style Icon award, Elle Style Awards, 1999, Commitment to Life award, AIDS Project, LA, 1999, Superstar award, Fashion Group Internat. Night Stars, 2000; named Future's Best New Designer, VH1/Vogue Fashion Awards, 1995, Menswear Designer of Yr., 1996, Womenswear Designer of Yr., 1996, 1999, Designer of Yr. for Yves Saint Laurent Rive Gauche, 2002, Internat. Designer of Yr., Fashion Editor's Club Japan, 1996, Best Designer of Yr., 2001, Internat. Man of Yr., British GQ, 2000, Best Fashion Designer, Time Mag., 2001, Designer of Yr., GQ Am., 2001, Internat. Designer of Yr., Coun. Fashion Designers America, 1996, Womenswear Designer of Yr., 2001, Accessory Designer of Yr., 2002, Menswear Designer of Yr., 2008; named a Maverick, Details mag., 2007.

FORDIS, JEAN BURKE, lawyer; b. Ashiya AFB, Japan, Feb. 25, 1956; BA in Biology with distinction, Calif. State U., 1978; JD cum laude, Am. U., 1985. Bar: Md. 1985, US Ct. Appeals (Fed. Cir.) 1986, DC 1988, US Supreme Ct. 1993, Calif. 2005, registered: US Patent & Trademark Office. Law clk. to Hon. Philip Nichols Jr., Sr. Cir. Judge US Ct. Appeals (Fed. Cir.), 1985—86; biologist Nat. Inst. Health, Uniformed Services U. for Health Sci.; ptnr. Finnegan, Henderson, Farabow, Garret & Dunner LLP, Palo Alto, Calif., mng. ptnr. Pa. office. Mem. Am. U. Law Rev., 1983—85. Mem.: Md. Patent Law Assn. (sec. 1990—92, v.p. 1993—94, pres. 1995—97), Licensing Exec. Soc., Am. Intellectual Property Law Assn. (chmn. awards com. 1988—90), Phi Kappa Phi. Office: Finnegan Henderson Farabow Garrett & Dunner LLP 3300 Hillview Ave Palo Alto CA 94304-1203 Office Phone: 650-849-6600. Office Fax: 650-849-6666. Business E-Mail: jean.fordis@finnegan.com.

FORE, JOHN A., lawyer; b. NYC, Oct. 3, 1956; BA cum laude, Yale U., 1979; JD, NYU, 1983. Bar: NY, Calif. Ptnr. Wilson Sonsini Goldrich & Rosati, Palo Alto, Calif., 1991—, chmn. fin. dept. Mem.: NY State Bar, State Bar Calif., Bus. Law Sect. (corporations com.). Office: Wilson Sonsini Godrich & Rosati 650 Page Mill Rd Palo Alto CA 94304-1050 Office Phone: 650-493-9300. Office Fax: 650-493-6811. Business E-Mail: jfore@wsgr.com.

FOREMAN, DALE MELVIN, lawyer, state official; b. LA, May 1, 1948; s. C. Melvin and Sylvia (Ahnlund) F.; m. Gail Burgener, June 24, 1972; children: Mari Elizabeth, Ann Marie, James Sterling. AB cum laude, Harvard U., 1970, JD, 1975. Bar: Wash. 1976, U.S. Dist. Ct. (we. dist.) Wash. 1977, U.S. Ct. Claims 1977, U.S. Dist. Ct. (ea. dist.) Wash. 1981, U.S. Ct. Appeals (9th cir.) 1981, Calif. 1986, U.S. Ct. Appeals (3rd cir.) 1987. Ptnr. Jeffers, Danielson & Foreman, Wenatchee, Wash., 1975-81, Jardine, Foreman & Arch, Wenatchee, 1981-88; sr. ptnr. Foreman, Arch, Dodge, Volyn & Zimmerman, Wenatchee, 1988—; mem. 12th legis. dist. Wash. Ho. of Reps., 1993-96, majority leader, 1995-97; owner Law Offices of Dale M. Foreman, Wenatchee, Wash. Mem. Spl. Adv. Commn. on Pub. Opinion, U.S. Dept. of State, 1970-72, elected chmn. Wash. State Rep. Party, elected Rep. Nat. Com. Author: Whiplash and the Jaw Joint: TMJ Injury - 1st (1985) 2nd (1991) edits., Washington Trial Handbook, 1988, Dental Law, 1989, How to Become an Expert Witness, 1989, Crucify Him! A Lawyer Looks at the Trial of Jesus, 1989, contbd artical to profl. jour. Chmn. Chelan County Rep. Cen. Com., Wenatchee, 1977-79, 82-84; bd. dirs. Am. and Fgn. Christian Union, N.Y.C., 1985—, Greater Wenatchee Community Found., 1987-, chmn. Wash. Apple Commn., bd. mem. US Apple Assn. Mem. ABA, Assn. Trial Lawyers Am., Wash. State Bar Assn., State Bar Calif., bd. govs. Wash. State Trial Lawyers Assn. 1990-, Harvard Club, Rotary. Republican. Presbyterian. Avocation: horticulture. Home: 323 Chatham Hill Rd Wenatchee WA 98801-5931 Office: Law Offices Dale M Foreman Ste A 124 N Wenatchee Ave Wenatchee WA 98801 Office Phone: 509-662-9602. Office Fax: 509-662-9606. Business E-Mail: dale@daleforeman.com.

FORET, MICKEY PHILLIP, retired air transportation executive; b. McComb, Miss., Oct. 23, 1945; s. Fadias Phillip and Christine (Brown) F.; m. Mary Ann Tramonte, Aug. 12, 1966; 1 child, Keri. BS in Fin., MBA in Fin., La. State U., 1971. Dir. credit/interim dir. internal audit Tex. (Houston) Internat. Airlines, 1975-77, dir. cash mgmt., 1977-78, asst. treas., 1978-81, v.p. fin. svcs., 1981-82; v.p., treas. Continental Airlines, LA, 1982-84, v.p., chief fin. officer, 1984-86, also bd. dirs.; sr. v.p. fin. and internat. Eastern Airlines, Miami, Fla., 1987-88, v.p., chief fin. officer, 1986—, also bd. dirs.; sr. v.p. Tex. (Houston) Air Corp., 1988—; exec. v.p. fin. and planning Continental Airlines, Houston, 1988-89, pres., 1989-90; exec. v.p., CFO Northwest Airlines, 1992-96; pres. Atlas Air, Inc., 1996-1997; spec. projects offcr. Northwest Airlines, 1998, CFO, exec. v.p., 1998—2002. Chmn. bd. dirs., chief exec. officer Chelsea Catering Co., Houston; bd. dir. URS Corp. 2003- Pres. Clear Wood Improvement Assn., Houston, 1975-78; coach Friendswood (Tex.) Girls Softball Team, 1981. Served with USAF, 1966-69, Vietnam. Mem. Phi Kappa Phi, Beta Gamma Sigma. Republican. Baptist. Avocations: boating, water-skiing, bicycling. Mailing: URS Corp Bd Directors 600 Montgomery St San Francisco CA 94111-2728

FORGAN, DAVID WALLER, retired career officer; b. Chgo., Sept. 28, 1933; s. Harold Nye and Ruth Ada (Waller) F.; m. Shirley Dobbins, Oct. 18, 1958; children— Bruce Dobbins, Todd Macmillan. BS in Mktg., U. Colo., 1955; MS in Mgmt., George Washington U., 1966. Commd. 2d lt. U.S. Air Force, 1956, advanced through grades to maj. gen., 1985, various positions worldwide, 1956-77, dir. programs hdqrs. tactical air command Langley AFB, Va., 1977-79, dir. force devel. Washington, 1979-80, dep. comdr. spl. ops. command Fort Bragg, N.C., 1980-82; asst. chief staff ops. Allied Forces Central Europe, Brunssum, The Netherlands, 1982-85; dep. chief staff ops. U.S. Air Force Europe, Ramstein Air Base, Fed. Republic Germany, 1985-87; comdr. Sheppard Tech. Tng. Ctr. Sheppard AFB, Tex., 1987-89; ret., 1989. Decorated Silver Star, D.F.C. (3), Legion of Merit, Air medal, Def. Disting. Svc. medal, Def. Superior Svc. medal; Aero Cross of Merit (Spain). Mem. Delta Tau Delta Republican. Avocations: military history, skiing, golf. Personal E-mail: dforgan@aol.com.

FORGANG, DAVID M., curator; b. NYC, Mar. 26, 1947; s. Joseph Hyman and Clarice (Ishbia) F.; m. Joyce Enid Blumenthal, June 15, 1968 (div. May 1979); children: Adam, Bradley. B in Anthropology, U. Ariz., 1968, M in Anthropology, 1971. Mus. curator So. Ariz. Group Nat. Pk. Svc., Phoenix, 1971-77, regional curator we. region San Francisco, 1977-82, curator Yosemite (Calif.) Mus., 1982—. Pres. Yosemite Renaissance Art Competition, 1983-94; dir. Yosemite Artist in Residence Program, 1985—. Mariposa County advisor El Portal (Calif.) Town Planning Adv. Bd., 1984-94. Recipient Unit Award citation US Dept. Interior, 1974. Democrat. Jewish. Avocations: fishing, canoeing, hunting, gardening. Office: Nat Pk Svc PO Box 577 Yosemite National Park CA 95389-0577

FORMBY, BENT CLARK, immunologist; b. Copenhagen, Apr. 3, 1940; naturalized, 1991; s. John K. and Gudrun A. (Dinesen) F.; m. Irene Menck-Thygesen, June 28, 1963 (div. May 1980); children: Rasmus, Mikkel; m. Florence G. Schmid, June 28, 1980. BA in Philosophy summa cum laude, U. Copenhagen, 1959, PhD in Biochemistry, 1968, DSc, 1976. Asst. prof. U. Copenhagen, 1969-73, assoc. prof., 1973-79, prof., 1979-83; vis. prof. U. Calif., San Francisco, 1979-84; sr. scientist, dir. lab. of immunology Sansum Med. Rsch. Found., Santa Barbara, Calif., 1984-99; dir. rsch. The Rasmus Inst. Med. Rsch., Santa Barbara, Calif., 2000—; chmn., CEO Rasmus Pharms. Inc., 2002—. Cons. Cell Tech., Inc., Boulder, Colo., 1989—, Immunex Corp., Seattle, 1989—; med. adv. bd. Biocellular Rsch. Orgn., Ltd., London, Childrens Hosp. of Orange County, Lautenburg Ctr. for Gen. and Tumor Immunology, Hebrew U., Hadassah Med. Sch., Jerusalem, 1993—. Co-author: Lightsout, 2000, Sex, Lies and Menopause: The Choking Truth About HRT, 2003; editor: Fetal Islet Transplantation, 1988, 2d edit. 1995; contbr. articles to profl. jours.; patentee on non-invasive glucose measurement; BH55 Hyaluronidase. Grantee, Juvenile Diabetes Found., 1987, 1988, E.L. Wiegand Found., 1993, Santa Barbara Cottage Hosp. Rsch. Found., 1993—94, 2001—02, U. Calif. Breast Cancer Rsch. Found., 1995—98. Mem.: N.Y. Acad. Scis., Am. Diabetes Assn. (pres. Santa Barbara chpt. 1995, grantee 1985, 1986, 1989), Am. Fedn. Clin. Rsch., European Assn. for the Study of Diabetes, European Menopause and Andropause Soc., N.Am. Menopause Soc. (mem. rsch. com. 2007—). Avocations: painting, swimming. Office: Rasmus Pharmaceuticals Inc 1625 Overlook Ln Santa Barbara CA 93103-2812 Office Phone: 805-895-3055. Personal E-mail: bcformby@aol.com.

FORSBERG, PETER, professional hockey player; b. Ornskoldsvik, Sweden, July 20, 1973; Center MoDo, Swedish Elite League, Sweden, 1990-94, 2004—05, Quebec Nordiques, Colo. Avalanche, 1994—2005, 2008, Phila. Flyers, 2005—07, Nashville Predators, 2007. Mem. Swedish Olympic Hockey Team, Lillehammer, Norway, 1994, Nagano, Japan, 98, Torino, Italy, 2006, Team Sweden, World Cup of Hockey, 1996, 2004. Recipient Calder Trophy, 1995, Art Ross Trophy, 2003, Hart Memorial Trophy, 2003; named NHL First Team All-Star, 1998, 1999, 2003; named to NHL All-Rookie Team, 1995, NHL All-Star game, 1996, 1998, 1999, 2001, 2003. Achievements include being a member of gold medal Swedish Hockey Team, Lillehammer Olympics, Norway, 1994, Torino Olympics, Italy, 2006; being a member of Stanley Cup Champion Colorado Avalanche, 1996, 2001.

FORST, DAVID L., lawyer; b. LA, Dec. 26, 1967; AB cum laude, Princeton Univ., 1989; JD with distinction, Stanford Univ., 1992. Bar: Calif. 1993. Ptnr., tax group Fenwick & West LLP, Mountain View, Calif. Taught law sch. courses. Contbr. articles to profl. jours.; editor: Journal of Taxation. Top tax advisors in the Western U.S. by Internat. Tax Rev. Mem.: Phi Beta Kappa. Editor: Jour. of Taxation. Office: Fenwick & West LLP Silicon Valley Ctr 801 Calif St Mountain View CA 94041 Office Phone: 650-335-7254, 650-988-8500. Office Fax: 650-938-5200. Business E-Mail: dforst@fenwick.com.

FORSTER, MERLIN HENRY, foreign languages educator, writer, researcher; b. Delta, Utah, Feb. 24, 1928; s. Henry and Ila Almeda (Rawlinson) F.; m. Vilda Mae Naegle, Apr. 25, 1952; children: Celia Marlene, David Merlin, Angela, Daniel Conrad, Elena Marie. BA, Brigham Young U., 1956; MA, U. Ill., 1957, PhD, 1960. Instr. in Spanish U. Tex., Austin, 1960-61, asst. prof., 1961-62; asst. prof. Spanish and Portuguese U. Ill., Urbana, 1962-65, assoc. prof., 1965-69, prof., 1969-78, dir. Latin Am. studies, 1972-78; prof., chmn. dept. Spanish and Portuguese, U. Tex., Austin, 1978-87; disting. prof. Latin Am. lit. Brigham Young U., Provo, Utah, 1987-98, chmn. dept. Spanish and Portuguese, 1989-93, prof. emeritus, 1998—. Dir. summer seminars NEH, 1978, 89, 90, 93, 96, 98. Author: Los Contemporáneos, 1964, Fire and Ice, 1976, Historia de la poesía hispanoamericana, 1981, The Committed Word: Studies in Spanish American Poetry, 2002, Many Stages: Studies in Latin American Drama, 2004, Arbol de imágenes: Nueva historia de la poesía hispanoamericana, 2007; editor: Index to Mexican Journals, 1966, Tradition and Renewal, 1975, De la Crónica a la Nueva Narrativa, 1986, Vanguardism in Latin American Literature: An Annotated Bibliographical Guide, 1990, La vanguardia literaria en México y la América Central, 2001. Rsch. grantee Social Sci. Rsch. Coun., Mexico City, 1965, Fulbright-Hays, Buenos Aires, 1971, NEH, Austin, 1986-87, Am. Coun. Learned Socs. and German Acad. Exch. Svc., 1993-94; fellow Ctr. for Advanced Study, Urbana, 1976-77. Mem. MLA, Latin Am. Studies Assn., Am. Assn. Tchrs. Spanish and Portuguese, Internat. Inst. Iberoam. Lit. (pres. 1981-83, 94-96). Mem. Lds Ch. Avocations: classical music, quartet singing, gardening, woodworking. Personal E-mail: merlinforster@yahoo.com.

FORSYTH, BEN RALPH, retired academic administrator, medical educator; b. NYC, Mar. 8, 1934; s. Martin and Eva Forsyth; m. Elizabeth Held, Aug. 19, 1962; children: Jennifer, Beverly, Jonathan. Attended, Cornell U., 1950-53; MD, NYU, 1957. Diplomate Am. Bd. Internal Medicine. Intern, then resident Yale Hosp., New Haven, 1957-60; postdoctoral fellow Harvard U. Med. Sch., Boston, 1960-61; rsch. assoc. NIH, Bethesda, Md., 1963-66; assoc. prof. med. microbiology and prof. medicine U. Vt., Burlington, 1966—90, prof. emeritus medicine, 1990; sr. exec. asst. to pres. Ariz. State U., Tempe, 1990—2002, pres., 2002—, prof. health adminstrn. and policy, 1992—2002, prof. emeritus health adminstrn. and policy, 2002—. Sr. cons. Univ. Health Ctr., Burlington, 1986-90; sr. adv. Ctr. Future Ariz., Phoenix, Ariz., 2003—. Contbr. articles to profl. jours. V.p., chmn. United Way Planning Com., Burlington, 1974—75, mem. ops. com., 1975—76, bd. dirs., officer, 1977—89; mem. New Eng. Bd. Higher

Edn. Com., Burlington, 1985—89; chmn. U. Vt. China Project Adv. Bd., Burlington, 1989—90; trustee U. Vt., Burlington, 1996—2002. Lt. comdr. USN, 1962—63. Sinsheimer Found. faculty fellow, 1966-71. Fellow ACP, Infectious Diseases Soc. Am.; mem. Phi Beta Kappa, Alpha Omega Alpha. Avocations: hiking, gardening, travel. E-mail: forsyth@asu.edu.

FORSYTH, G. FRED, electronics executive; BS magna cum laude, U. N.H.; MBA, Babson Coll. Former corp. sr. v.p., pres. Profl. Products Divsn. Iomega Corp.; former sr. exec. Apple Computers, Digital Equipment Corp., GE; corp. v.p., pres. Solectron Ams. Solectron Corp., Milpitas, Calif., 1999—. Office: Solectron Corp 847 Gibraltar Dr Milpitas CA 95035

FORTE, WILL (ORVILLE WILLIS FORTE IV), actor, scriptwriter; b. Calif., June 17, 1970; Mem. Groundlings comedy troupe, LA. Writer (TV Specials) MTV Movie Awards, 1997—2003, 2005, 2007, MTV Video Music Awards, 2004—05, (TV films) Castaway Dick, 2001, Panic Room with Will Ferrell, 2002, (TV series) The Jenny McCarthy Show, 1997, Late Show with David Letterman, 1997—98, 3rd Rock from the Sun, 2000—01, (films) Extreme Movie, 2008, writer, prodr. (TV series) That 70's Show, 2001—02, actor, writer Clone High, 2002—03, (films) The Brothers Solomon, 2007; actor: (TV series) Saturday Night Live, 2002—; (films) Around the World in 80 Days, 2004, Beerfest, 2006, Baby Mama, 2008; appearances on (TV series) Campus Ladies, 2006, Drawn Together, 2006, Aqua Teen Hunger Force, 2006, 30 Rock, 2007, The Flight of the Conchords, 2007, Tim and Eric Nite Live, 2007, Tim and Eric Awesome Show, Great Job!, 2007—08. Office: c/o Mosaic Media Group 9200 W Sunset Blvd 10th Fl Los Angeles CA 90069

FORTMANN, STEPHEN PAUL, medical educator, researcher, epidemiologist; b. Burbank, Calif., Oct. 13, 1948; s. Daniel John and Mary (Van Halteren) F.; married; children: Nicolas, Michele. AB, Stanford U., 1970; MD, U. Calif., San Francisco, 1974. Diplomate Am. Bd. Internal Medicine, Am. Coll. Epidemiology. Clin. instr. Stanford (Calif.) U. Sch. Medicine, 1979-83, asst. prof., 1983-90, assoc. prof., 1990-99, prof., 1999—. Advisor World Health Orgn., Geneva, 1980-86. Contbr. articles to profl. jours; co-author: The Blood Pressure Book, 2001. Fellow ACP, Am. Heart Assn. (coun. on epidemiology and prevention), Am. Coll.Epidemiology, Soc. Behavioral Medicine; mem. Inst. Medicine. Avocations: photography, running.

FORTSON, EDWARD NORVAL, physics educator; b. Atlanta, June 16, 1936; s. Charles Wellborn and Virginia (Norval) F.; m. Alix Madge Hawkins, Apr. 3, 1960; children— Edward Norval, Lucy Frear, Amy Lewis BS, Duke U., 1957; PhD, Harvard U., 1963. Research fellow U. Bonn., Federal Rep. Germany, 1965-66; research asst. prof. physics U. Wash., Seattle, 1963-65, asst. prof., 1966-69, assoc. prof., 1969-74, prof., 1974—. Fulbright travel grantee, 1965-66; Nat. Research Council fellow Oxford, Eng., 1977; Guggenheim fellow, 1980-81 Fellow AAAS, Am. Phys. Soc.; mem. NAS. Office: U Wash Dept Physics PO Box 351560 Seattle WA 98195-1560

FOSSLAND, JOEANN JONES, real estate company executive; b. Balt., Mar. 21, 1948; d. Milton Francis and Clementine (Bowen) Jones; m. Richard E. Yellott III, 1966 (div. 1970); children: Richard E. IV, Dawn Joeann; m. Robert Gerard Fossland Jr., Nov. 25, 1982. Student, Johns Hopkins U., 1966—67; cert., Hogan's Sch. Real Estate, 1982. Cert. values coach, behaviors coach, 1998, GRI; master cert. coach. Owner Kobble Shop, Indiatlantic, Fla., 1968-70, Downstairs, Atlanta, 1971; seamstress Aspen (Colo.) Leather, 1972-75; owner Backporch Feather & Leather, Aspen and Tucson, 1975-81; area mgr. Welcome Wagon, Tucson, 1982; realtor assoc. Tucson Realty & Trust, 1983-85; mgr. Home Illustrated mag., Tucson, 1985-87; asst. pub., gen. mgr. Phoenix, Scottsdale, Albuquerque, Tricities Tucson Homes Illustrated, 1990-93; pres. Advantage Solutions Group, Cortaro, Ariz., 1993—. Power leader Darryl Davis Seminars Power Program, 1995—; personal and profl. coach.; instr. Women's Coun. Realtors, 1999—. Designer leather goods (Tucson Mus. Art award 1978, Crested Butte Art Fair Best of Show award 1980); author: Personal and Professional Coaching: Coach University, Certified Training Program, 1996. Voter registrar Recorder's Office City of Tucson, 1985-91; bd. dirs. Hearth Found., Tucson, 1987-96, pres., 1994; bd. dirs. Ariz. Integrated Residential & Ednl. Svcs., Inc., 1989-95, pres. 1994-95. Mem. NAFE, Internat. Fedn. Coaches (master cert. coach), Women's Coun. Realtors (leadership tng. grad. designation, pres. Tucson chpt. 1995, Ariz. state gov. 1997-98, v.p. Region IV, 2000, Tucson Affiliate of Yr. award 1991, Ariz. State Mem. of Yr. 1999), Tucson Assn. Realtors (Affiliate of Yr. award 1988). Democrat. Presbyterian. Avocations: tennis, gardening, reading, travel, public speaking. Office: Advantage Solutions Group PO Box 133 Cortaro AZ 85652-0133 Office Phone: 520-744-8731. E-mail: joeann@joeann.com.

FOSTER, BOB **See FOSTER, ROBERT**

FOSTER, CAROL MARVEL, pediatric endocrinologist; b. Detroit, Sept. 12, 1952; d. Howard and Margaret (Paulson) Marvel; m. Norman L. Foster, Nov. 19, 1977; children: Daniel, Sarah. BS, Purdue U., 1974; MD, Washington U., St. Louis, 1978. Lic. physician Md., Mich., cert. Am. Bd. Pediat., 1983, in pediatric endocrinology 1983. Pediat. intern U. Utah, Salt Lake City, 1978—79, pediatric endocrinology resident, 1979—81; NIH fellow U. Mich., Ann Arbor, 1981—84, asst. prof. pediatric endocrinology, 1985—93, assoc. prof. pediatric endocrinology, 1993—99, prof. pediatric endocrinology, 1999, dir., divsn. endocrinology, assoc. dir. pediat. programs, Cin. Rsch. Ctr.; prof. pediat., divsn. pediat. endocrinology Utah Diabetes Ctr. Prof. U. Utah Health Scis. Ctr. and Primary Children's Med. Ctr. Contbr. articles to profl. jours. Recipient Am. Diabetes Assn. rsch. award, 1987; NIH grantee, 1991. Mem. Endocrine Soc., Soc. Pediatric Rsch., Am. Fedn. for Clin. Rsch., Lawson Wilkins Pediatric Endocrine Soc., Phi Beta Kappa, Phi Kappa Phi. Achievements include research on mechanisms involved in initiation of puberty, mechansims of action of growth hormone, nature of steroid hormone receptors in transformed cells. Office: Utah Diabetes Ctr 615 Arapeen Dr Ste 100 Salt Lake City UT 84108 Office Phone: 801-581-7761. Office Fax: 801-587-3920. Business E-Mail: carol.foster@hsc.utah.edu.

FOSTER, DAVID SCOTT, lawyer; b. White Plains, NY, July 13, 1938; s. William James and Ruth Elizabeth (Seltzer) F.; m. Eleanore Stalker, Dec. 21, 1959; children: David Scott, Robert McEachron. BA in Physics, Amherst Coll., 1960; LLB, Harvard U., 1963. Bar: NY 1963, DC 1977, Calif. 1978. Jud. law clk. US Dist. Ct. (so. dist.) N.Y., 1963-64; assoc. Debevoise & Plimpton, NYC, 1964-72; from atty.-advisor to internat. tax counsel US Treasury Dept., Washington, 1972-77; ptnr. Brobeck, Phleger & Harrison, San Francisco, 1978-90, Coudert Bros., San Francisco, 1990-91, Thelen LLP, San Francisco, 1991—2008, Nixon Peabody LLP, 2008—. Mem. ABA, San Francisco Bar Assn., Western Pension and Benefits Conf., St. Francis Yacht Club (San Francisco), Phi Beta Kappa, Sigma Xi. Presbyterian. Office: Nixon Peabody LLP Ste 1800 One Embarcadero Ctr San Francisco CA 94111-3600 Office Phone: 415-984-8331. Business E-Mail: dfoster@nixonpeabody.com.

FOSTER, ELYSE, cardiologist, educator; b. Bklyn., Mar. 4, 1952; MD, Tufts U. Sch. Medicine, 1977. Cert. Internal Medicine, Cardiovascular Disease. Intern, internal medicine Boston U. Hosp., Mass., 1977—78, resident, internal medicine Mass., 1978—79; resident, cardiology Boston Med. Ctr., Mass., 1979—80, fellow, cardiovascular disease Mass., 1983, hosp. appointment Mass.; asst. prof. Boston U. Sch. Medicine, Mass.; prof., medicine, divsn. cardiology U. Calif., San Francisco, dir., adult echocardiography lab., dir., adult congenital heart disease svc. Mem.: Am. Coll. Cardiology (mem., women in cardiology com.), Internat. Soc. Adult Congenital Heart Diseases (mem. exec. com.). Office: U Calif San Francisco Divsn Cardiology 505 Parnassus Ave San Francisco CA 94143-0214 Office Phone: 415-353-9156. Office Fax: 415-353-8687.

FOSTER, JAMES HENRY, advertising and public relations executive; b. Kansas City, Mo., May 14, 1933; s. Wendell F. and Lillian M. (East) F. BA, Drake U., 1955, postgrad., 1957. Reporter, editor Des Moines Register, 1951-61; pub. rels. and advt. exec. J. Walter Thompson Co., NYC, 1961-73, 79-99, v.p., 1970-73; sr. v.p., gen. mgr. Brouillard Comm. divsn., NYC, 1979-81, exec. v.p., gen. mgr., 1981-84, pres., CEO, 1984-94; chmn., CEO Brouillard Comm., 1994-97, chmn., 1997-99, chmn. emeritus, 1999—2003; v.p. pub. affairs Western Union Corp., Upper Saddle River, 1973-79; pres. Reputation Mgmt. Strategies, Durango, Colo., 1999—; bd. dirs. Music in the Mountains, Inc., Durango, 1999—, pres., 2000—03. Bd. dirs. Fort Lewis Coll. Found., 2004-, sec., 2005-06, v.p., 2006-07, pres., 2008-. Mem. Union League Club (N.Y.C.), Petroleum Club, Rocky Mountain PBS (bd. dirs., 2008-), Glacier Club. Presbyterian. Office: Reputation Mgmt Strategies 1472 E Third Ave Durango CO 81301-5244

FOSTER, JODIE (ALICIA CHRISTIAN FOSTER), actress, film director, producer; b. LA, Nov. 19, 1962; d. Lucius and Evelyn (Almond) F.; children: Charles, Kit BA in Lit. cum laude, Yale U., 1985, DFA (hon.), 1997; DArts (hon.), U. Penn., 2006; Degree (hon.), Smith Coll., 2000. Owner, chair Egg Pictures Prodn. Co., LA, 1990—2001. Actress: (films) Napoleon and Samantha, 1972, Kansas City Bomber, 1972, One Little Indian, 1973, Tom Sawyer, 1973, Alice Doesn't Live Here Anymore, 1974, Taxi Driver, 1976 (Acad. award nominee for Best Supporting Actress), Echoes of a Summer, 1976, Bugsy Malone, 1976, Freaky Friday, 1976, Moi, Fleur Bleue, 1977, Casotto, 1977, The Little Girl Who Lives Down the Lane, 1977, Candleshoe, 1977, Foxes, 1980, Carny, 1980, O'Hara's Wife, 1982, The Hotel New Hampshire, 1984, The Blood of Others, 1984, Five Corners, 1987, Siesta, 1987, Stealing Home, 1988, The Accused, 1988 (Acad. award for Best Actress, 1989, Golden Globe award for Best Performance by an Actress, 1989), Backtrack, 1989, The Silence of the Lambs, 1991 (Golden Globe award for Best Actress in Drama, 1992, Acad. award for Best Actress, 1992, BAFTA award for Best Actress, 1992), Shadows and Fog, 1992, Sommersby, 1993, Maverick, 1994, Contact, 1997, Anna and The King, 1999, Panic Room, 2002, A Very Long Engagement, 2004, Flightplan, 2005, Inside Man, 2006, The Brave One, 2007, Nim's Island, 2008; (TV movies) Menace on the Mountain, 1970, My Sister Hank, 1972, Alexander, 1973, Rookie of the Year, 1973, Smile, Jenny, You're Dead, 1974, The Secret Life of T.K. Dearing, 1975, Svengali, 1983; (TV appearances) The Doris Day show, 1969, Julia, 1969, Mayberry, R.F.D, 1969, Gunsmoke, 1969, '71, '72, The Courtship of Eddie's Father, 1969, '70, '71, Disneyland, 1970, Nanny and the Professor, 1970, Daniel Boone, 1970, Adam-12, 1970, My Three Sons, 1971 The Paul Lunde Show, 1972, Ghost Story, 1972, Ironside, 1972, Bonanza, 1972, The Amazing Chan and the Chan Clan, 1972, The Partridge Family, 1973, Kung Fu, 1973, The Addams Family, 1973, Bob & Carol & Ted & Alice, 1973, The New Perry Mason, 1973, Love Story, 1973, Paper Moon, 1974, Medical Center, 1975, Frasier, 1996, The X-Files, 1997; actress, dir. (films) Little Man Tate, 1991; actress, prodr. (films) Mesmerized, 1986, Nell, 1994 (Acad. award nominee for Best Actress 1995), The Dangerous Lives of Altar Boys, 2002, The Brave One, 2007; dir., prodr. (films) Home For the Holidays, 1995; dir. (TV episode) Tales from the Darkside, 1988; exec. prodr. (TV movies) The Baby Dance, 1998; (films) Waking the Dead, 2000. Recipient Sherry Lansing Leadership award, Hollywood Reporter, 2007; named one of 50 Smartest People in Hollywood, Entertainment Weekly, 2007. Office: c/o Pat Kingsley PMK/HBH Public Rels 700 San Vicente Ave #G-910 West Hollywood CA 90069

FOSTER, JOHN STUART, JR., physicist, former defense industry executive; b. New Haven, Sept. 18, 1922; s. John Stuart and Flora (Curtis) F.; m. Frances Schnell, Dec. 28, 1978; children: Susan, Bruce, Scott, John. BS, McGill U., 1948; PhD in Physics, U. Calif., Berkeley, 1952; DSc (hon.), U. Mon., 1979. Dir. Lawrence Livermore (Calif.) Lab., 1952-65; dir. def. rsch. and engring. Dept. Def., Washington, 1965-73; v.p. TRW Energy Systems Group, Redondo Beach, Calif., 1973-79; v.p. sci. and tech. TRW Inc., Cleve., 1979-88, also bd. dirs. Chmn. Def. Sci. Bd., 1989-93; chmn. GKN Aerospace Transparency Sys.; ptnr. Tech. Strategies & Alliances. Decorated knight comdr.'s cross, badge and star Order of Merit (Germany); comdr. Legion of Honor (France); recipient Ernst Orlando Lawrence Meml. award AEC, 1960, Disting. Pub. Svc. medal Dept. Def., 1969, 73, 93, Crowell medal, 1972, Enrico Fermi Award, U.S. Dept. of Energy, 1992, Eugene Fubini award, U.S. Dept. Def., 1998. Mem. NAE (Founders award 1989), AIAA, Am. Def. Preparedness Assn., Nat. Security Indsl. Assn. Office: Northrop Grumman 1 Space Park Bldg E1-5010 Redondo Beach CA 90278-1071

FOSTER, JOYCE, state legislator; b. Benton Harbor, Mich. m. Steven Foster; 3 children. Mem. Denver City Coun., 1993—2003; mem. Dist. 35 Colo. State Senate, 2008—. Former bd. mem. Denver Regional Coun. Govts. Mem.: Denver Kids (mentor). Democrat. Office: State House 200 E Colfax Denver CO 80203 Office Phone: 303-866-4875. Business E-Mail: joyce.foster.senate@state.co.us.*

FOSTER, KENNITH EARL, life sciences educator; b. Lamesa, Tex., Jan. 20, 1945; s. John Hugh and Mamie (Hyatt) F.; children: Sherry, Kristi. BS, Tex. Tech. U., 1967; MS, U. Ariz., 1969, PhD, 1972. Prof. and dir. Office of Arid Lands Studies, U. Ariz., Tucson, 1983—. Contbr. articles to profl. jours. Grantee NASA, NSF, USDA, U.S. AID, industry, 1983—. Home: 651 S Avenida Princesa Tucson AZ 85748-6858 Office: Univ of Ariz Office of Arid Lands Studies 1955 E 6th St Tucson AZ 85719-5224

FOSTER, KENT B., retired information technology executive; b. 1944; BS in Elec. Engring., NC State U.; MS in Mgmt., U. SC. Bd. dirs. GTE Corp., Irving, Calif., 1992—99, vice chmn. bd., 1993—99, pres., 1995—99; chmn., pres., CEO Ingram Micro Inc., Santa Ana, Calif., 2000—05, non-exec. chmn., 2005—07. Bd. dir. Campbell Soup Co., J.C. Penney Co., NY Life Ins. Co. Bd. mem. Dallas Opera, Dallas Symphony. Capt. USAF, 1966—70. Named Forbes' America's Most Powerful People.

FOSTER, LAWRENCE, concert and opera conductor; b. LA, 1941; Student, Bayreuth Festival Masterclasses; studied with, Fritz Zweig. Debut as condr., Young Musicians' Found., Debut Orch., 1960; condr., mus. dir., 1960-64, condr., San Francisco Ballet, 1961-65, asst. condr., Los Angeles Philharmonic Orch., 1965-68, chief guest condr., Royal Philharmonic Orch., Eng., 1969-75, guest condr., Houston Symphony, 1970-71, condr. in chief, 1971-72, music dir., 1972-78, Orch. Philharmonique of Monte Carlo, 1979, gen. music dir., Duisburg & Dusseldorf Opera (Ger.), 1982-86, former music dir. Lausanne Chamber Orch., 1991-96, Aspen (Colo.) Music Festival and Sch.; prin. guest condr. Orquestra Ciutat de Barcelona; music dir. Gulbenkian Orch., Lisbon; music adviser Jerusalem Symphony-Orch.; artistic dir. Bucharest Festival and Competition; guest condr. orchs. in, U.S., Europe, Australia and Japan; recorded, condr. world premiere Paul McCartney's Standing Stone, 1997; (Recipient Koussevitsky Meml. Conducting prize 1966, Eleanor R. Crane Meml. prize Berkshire Festival, Tanglewood, Mass. 1966); regular guest condr. Deutsche Opera, Berlin, L.A. Opera.

FOSTER, MARY CHRISTINE, film producer, writer; b. LA, Mar. 19, 1943; d. Ernest Albert and Mary Ada (Quilici) Foster; m. Paul Hunter, July 24, 1982. BA, Immaculate Heart Coll., LA, 1967; M in TV News Documentary, UCLA, 1968. Dir. R & D Metromedia Producers Corp., LA, 1968-71; dir. devel. and prodn. svcs. Wolper Prodns., LA, 1971-76; mgr. film programs NBC-TV, Burbank, Calif., 1976-77; v.p. movies and mini series Columbia Pictures TV, Burbank, 1977-81, v.p. series programs, 1981; v.p. program devel. Group W. Prodns., LA, 1981-87; agt. The Agency, LA, 1988-90, Shapiro-Lichtman Agy., LA, 1990-99; ind. prodr., 1999—. Lectr. in field. Creator (TV series) Sullivan, 1985, Auntie Mom, 1986; author: Immaculate Heart High School: Memories of 100 Years 1906-2006, 2005. Trustee Immaculate Heart H.S., LA, 1980—; exec. com. Humanitas awards Human Family Inst., 1985—; cmty. devel. com. Immaculate Heart Cmty., 2001—; exec. com. LA Roman Cath. Archdiocesan Comm. Commn., 1986—90; bd. dirs., treas. Catholics in Media, 1992—2004; vol. com., writer tour script, vis. book, newsletter and website Cathedral of Our Lady of Angels, 2002—; chmn. pastorial coun. St. Francis of Assisi, 2003—05, chmn. stewardship com. and renovation com. Democrat. Personal E-mail: fosterc@aol.com.

FOSTER, NORMAN HOLLAND, geologist; b. Iowa City, Oct. 2, 1934; s. Holland and Dora Lucinda (Ransom) F.; m. Janet Lee Grecian, Mar. 25, 1956; children: Kimberly Ann, Stephen Norman. BA, U. Iowa, 1957, MS, 1960; PhD, U. Kans., 1963. Instr. geology U. Iowa, 1958-60; sr. geologist, geol. specialist, exploration team supr. Sinclair Oil Corp. and Atlantic Richfield Co., Casper, Wyo., also Denver, 1962-69; dist. geologist Trend Exploration Ltd., 1969-72, v.p., 1972-79; ind. geologist Denver, 1979—; instr. geology U. Kans., 1960-62. Chmn., pres., CEO Voyager Exploration, Inc., Denver, 1995—; guest lectr. geology Colo. Sch. Mines, 1972—, U. Colo., 1972—, U. Iowa, 1975—, U. Kans., 1975—; adv. bd. U. Kans., 1982—, U. Iowa, 1988—, U. Colo., 1990—; chmn. fin. com. 28th Internat. Geol. Congress, 1987-89, ofcl. U.S. rep., Washington, 1989; dir. MarkWest Hydrocarbon, Inc., Denver, 1996—. Assoc. editor Guidebook to Geology and Energy Resources of Piceance Basin, Colorado, 1974, Mountain Geologist, 1967-68, 71-85, editor, 1968-70; co-editor, compiler Treatise of Petroleum Geology, 1984—; contbr. papers on geology to profl. publs. Served to capt. inf. AUS, 1957. Recipient Haworth Disting. Alumni award dept. geology U. Kans., 1977, Disting. Alumni award dept. geology U. Iowa, 1992. Fellow Geol. Soc. Am.; mem. Am. Assn. Petroleum Geologists (del. 1972-75, 79-82, disting. lectr. 1976-77, pres. Rocky Mountain sect. 1979-80, treas. 1982-84, adv. coun. 1985-88, chmn. astrogeology com. 1984-88, nat. pres. 1988-89, found. trustee 1979—, hon. mem. 1993—, Levorsen award 1980, Disting. Svc. award 1985, founder astrogeology com. 1984, mem. 1984—, mem. resource evaluation com. 1992—), Rocky Mountain Assn. Geologists (sec. 1970, 1st v.p. 1974, pres. 1977, best paper award 1975, Explorer of Yr. award 1980, Disting. Svc. award 1981, hon. mem. 1983—), Soc. Econ. Paleontologists and Mineralogists, Am. Inst. Profl. Geologists, Soc. Ind. Profl. Earth Scientists, Soc. Exploration Geophysicists, Soc. Petroleum Engrs., Nat. Acad. Scis. (bd. earth scis. and resources, U.S. nat. com. geology, com. earth resources, com. adv. to U.S. Geol. Survey 1989-92), Colo. Sci. Soc., Sigma Xi, Sigma Gamma Epsilon. Republican. Mem. Christian Ch. Office: 1625 Broadway Ste 370 Denver CO 80202-4746

FOSTER, RICHARD, state legislator; b. Nome, Alaska, Aug. 9, 1946; m to Cathy; children: Neal, Jimmy, Myria, Justin, Tiffany, Richard, Nathan, Ramsey & Chandler. BBA, U. Alaska, Fairbanks, 1964—68. Alaska State Representative, District 23, 88-92, District 38, 1992-2002, vice chairman, Community & Regional Affairs Committee, formerly, chairman, Transportation Committee, currently, member, Resources Committee & Special Committee Mil & Vet Affairs, formerly, co-chmn, Finance Committee, Majority Whip, 1991-, Alaska House Representative; member, Federal Selective Serv Bd, Nome Planning & Zoning Comn, Nome Sch Bd & Nome City Coun, currently; member, Bush Caucus, formerly; Alaska State Representative, District 39, 2003-. Air taxi, ret; board member, Nome Community Center, Norton Sound Health Corp & NW Community Col, formerly; board member, Sitnasuak Native Corp, Bering Straits Native Corp & Nome Eskimo Community (IRA coun), currently. Capt. US Army. Decorated Vietnam Svc. medal, Bronze Star medal, Commendation medals. Rotary; Lions; Pioneer Igloo No 1. Democrat. Office: Dist 39 103 E Front St Nome AK 99762 also: State Capitol Rm 410 Juneau AK 99801 Office Phone: 907-443-5036, 907-465-3789. Office Fax: 907-443-2162, 907-465-3242. Business E-Mail: Rep_Richard_Foster@legis.state.ak.us.*

FOSTER, ROBERT G. (BOB FOSTER), Mayor, Long Beach, California; b. Brooklyn, Jan. 1, 1947; BS in Pub. adminstrn., San Jose State University. Formerly with Calif. State Senate, Calif. Energy Commn.; with So. Calif. Edison, 1984—2006, v.p. pub. affairs,

1993—96, sr. v.p. pub. affairs, 1996—2001, sr. v.p. external affairs, 2001—02, Edison Internat., 2001—02; pres. So. Calif. Edison, 2002—06; mayor City of Long Beach, Calif., 2006—. Dep. dir. Calif. State Energy Resources Conservation Commn.; bd. dirs. Calif. Inst., Calif. Found. on the Environment and Economy, Long Beach Aquarium of the Pacific; trustee Calif. State Univ. Sys.; bd. dirs. Pub. Corp. for the Arts' CEO Leadership Bd.; mem. spkrs. com. on initiative reform Govs. Work Force Investment Bd.; mem. L.A. World Airports Bus. Coun. Trustee Calif. State U.; mem. Long Beach Public Library Found.; bd. mem. Long Beach Aquarium; adv. bd. mem. Long Beach Memorial Miller Children's Hosp. Office: 333 W Ocean Blvd 14th Fl Long Beach CA 90802 Office Phone: 562-570-6801. Office Fax: 562-570-6538.*

FOSTER, RONALD C., electronics executive; BA in Econs., Whitman Coll.; MBA, U. Chgo. With Hewlett-Packard, Applied Materials, Novell, JDS Uniphase; CFO FormFactor, Inc.; bd. dirs. Micron Tech. Inc., Boise, Idaho, 2004—05, v.p. fin., CFO, 2008—. Office: Micron Tech, Inc 8000 S Federal Way PO Box 6 Boise ID 83707-0006 Office Phone: 208-368-4000. Office Fax: 208-368-4435.

FOSTER, SUSAN EILEEN, lawyer; b. Olympia, Wash., Apr. 16, 1961; m. Maurice Joseph Pirio; children: Alex Pirio, Haley Pirio. BA, Pacific Luth. U., Tacoma, 1984; JD, U. Puget Sound, Tacoma, 1988. Bar: Wash. 1988, US Dist. Ct. (western dist.) Wash. 1988, US Dist. Ct. (eastern dist.) Wash. 1989, US Ct. Appeals (10th cir.) 1993, US Dist. Ct. (eastern dist.) Mich. Assoc. Perkins Coie, Seattle, 1988—94, ptnr., 1994—. Spkr. in field. Contbr. articles to profl. jours. Gen. counsel bd. dirs. Pacific NW Ballet, Seattle, 1993—2002, trustee, 1997—2002; mem. adv. bd. Hate Free Zone, 2002—03; mem. assocs. program Corp. Coun. Arts, 1993—96. Named King County Vol. of Month, King County Bar Assn., 2002. Mem.: ABA (co-chmn. Pacific NW divsn.), Wash. State Bar Assn. (mem. exec. com. consumer protection, antitrust and unfair bus. practic 1994—2003, chmn. 2000—01). Office: Perkins Coie LLP 1201 3d Ave Ste 4800 Seattle WA 98101-3099

FOSTER-BARBER, AUDREY ELIZABETH, neurologist, educator; BS in Biology with high honors, Harvard College; MD in Biochemistry, U. Calif. Sch. Medicine, San Francisco, 1999. Cert. in neurology, in child neurology 2006. Pediat. resident U. Calif., San Francisco, 2002, child neurology resident, 2005, from clin. instr. neurology to asst. prof.; chief neurology resident U. Calif. Med. Ctr., San Francisco. Recipient Exceptional Physician award, U. Calif. San Fransisco Med. Ctr., 2005, Pediat. Dept. Fellow Tchg. award; grantee, Acad. Med. Educators, 2006—; A. P. Giannini Med. Rsch. fellowship, Bank of America. Mem.: Am. Acad. Pediat., Child Neurology Soc., Am. Acad. Neurology. Office: U Calif Box 0137 350 Parnassus Ave #609 609 San Francisco CA 94143 Office Phone: 415-353-4149. Office Fax: 415-353-2400. Business E-Mail: fostera@neuropeds.ucsf.edu.

FOTSCH, DAN ROBERT, retired elementary school educator; b. St. Louis, May 17, 1947; s. Robert Jarrel and Margaret Louise (Zimmermann) F.; m. Jacquelyn Sue Rotter, June 12, 1971; children: Kyla Michelle, Jeffrey Scott, Michael David. BS in Edn. cum laude, U. Mo., 1970; MS in Edn., Colo. State U., 1973. Cert. K-12 phys. edn. and health tchr. Mo., Colo. Tchr. phys. edn., coach North Callaway Schs., Auxvasse, Mo., 1970-71; grad. teaching asst., asst. track coach Colo. State U., Ft. Collins, 1971-73; tchr. elem. phys. edn., coach Poudre R-1 Sch. Dist., Ft. Collins, 1973—; tchr. on spl. assignment Elem. Phys. Edn. Resource, 1990; adminstrv. asst. Moore Sch., Ft. Collins, 1990—, acting prin., 1997, tchr. on spl. assignment dist. phys. edn. coord., 1998, k-12 coord. dist. phys. edn., 1998—; whole child facilitator K-6 art K-12 phys. edn., 2007—. Co-dir. Colo. State U. Handicapped Clinic, Ft. Collins, 1973-93; dir. Moore Elem. Lab. Sch., Ft. Collins, 1979—; dir. Colo. State U. Super Day Camp, 1979—; affiliate faculty mem. Colo. State U. Dept. Health and Exercise Sci., 1980-00, Dept. Edn., 2000-02; presenter for conf. in field; prin. Summer Sch., 2003-04, 05-06; univ. supr. student tchrs. Colo. state U. Coll., 2006—. Contbr. articles to profl. jours. State dir. Jump Rope for Heart Project, Denver, 1981. Recipient Scott Key Acad. award, Sigma Phi Epsilon, 1969, Honor Alumni award, Coll. of Profl. Studies of Colo. State U., 1983; grantee Colo. Heart Assn., 1985; recipient Coaching Excellence award Ft. Collins Soccer Club, 1991-92. Mem. NEA, AAHPERD (exec. bd. mem. coun. on phys. edn. for children 1983-86, reviewer Jour. Phys. Edn., Recreation and Dance 1984—, fitness chairperson, conv. planner 1986), ASCD, Poudre Edn. Assn., Colo. Edn. Assn., Colo. Assn. Health, Phys. Edn., Recreation and Dance (pres. 1979-82, Tchr. award 1977, Honor award 1985), Internat. Platform Assn., Ctrl. Dist. Alliance for Health, Phys. Edn., Recreation and Dance (elem. divsn. chairperson for phys. edn. 1989—), Phi Delta Kappa (found. rep. 1985), Phi Epsilon Kappa (v.p. 1969, pres. 1970). Republican. Avocations: marathons, triathlons, racquetball, volleyball, swimming. Home: 2807 Blackstone Dr Fort Collins CO 80525-6190 Personal E-mail: jackiefotsch@msn.com.

FOURATT, GREGORY J., prosecutor; Grad., N.Mex. State U.; JD, Tex. Tech Sch. Law. Clk. to Judge William D. Browning US Dist. Ct., Tucson; atty. JAG; US atty. Dist. N.Mex. US Dept. Justice, 2008—. Maj. USAFR. Office: US Attys Office PO Box 607 Albuquerque NM 87103 also: 201 3rd St NW Albuquerque NM 87102 Office Phone: 505-346-7274. Office Fax: 505-346-7296. E-mail: greg.fouratt@usdoj.gov.

FOWLER, JAMES H., political science professor; BA cum laude, Harvard U., Cambridge, Mass., 1992, MA in Govt., 2001, PhD in Govt., 2003; MA in Internat. Rels., Yale U., New Haven, 1997. ESL, health promotion tchr. US Peace Corps, Ecuador, 1992—94; lectr. Yale U., New Haven, 1996—97, Harvard U., Cambridge, Mass., 1999—2003; asst. prof. polit. sci. U. Calif. San Diego, La Jolla, 2003—06, assoc. prof. polit. sci., 2006—; lectr. U. Calif., Calif., 2004—06, UCLA, 2007, Duke U., Durham, NC, 2008. Faculty Empirical Implications Theoretical Models Summer Inst., 2006—08; mem. adv. bd., Political Behavior: Cognition, Psychology, & Behavior Social Sci. Rsch. Network, 2007—; mem. editl. bd. Polit. Analysis, 2007—, Jour. Politics, 2009—; co-founder Polit. Networks, 2008—; rep. Am. Acad. Arts & Sciences, 2008—, Am. Polit. Sci. Assn., 2008—. Contbr. articles to profl. jours., chapters to books. Named Most Original Thinker, The McLaughlin Group, 2008; named to Seminole HS Hall of Fame, 2008, Nifty Fifty, most inspiring scientists, San Diego Sci. Festival, 2009; Harvard scholar, 1988—90, 1991—92, John Harvard scholar, 1990—91, Yale U. fellow, 1995—97, Buttenweiser fellow, Harvard U., 1998—99, Nebel fellow, 1999—2000. Office: Univ Calif San Diego Dept Polit Sci 0521 Social Sci Bldg 383 9500 Gilman Dr La Jolla CA 92093-0521 Office Phone: 858-534-6807. Office Fax: 858-534-7130. Business E-Mail: jhfowler@ucsd.edu.*

FOWLER, JOHN, information technology executive; Various engrng. mgmt. positions Java Software, Solaris, Unix Desktop and Graphics Sun Microsystems, Inc., dir. engrng. Software Devel. Tools, chief tech. officer Software, exec. v.p. x64 Systems Group, exec. v.p. systems. Office: Sun Microsystems Inc 4150 Network Cir Santa Clara CA 95054 Office Phone: 650-960-1300.

FOWLER, RAYMOND DALTON, psychologist, educator; b. Jasper, Ala., Dec. 22, 1930; s. Raymond Dalton and Willie (Sanders) F.; m. Nancy Allebach, Aug. 13, 1955 (dec.); children: Karen Sydney, Derek Tyson, Michael Allan; m. Sandra Mumford, May 5, 1984. Student, Vanderbilt U., 1948-50; BA, U. Ala., 1952, MA, 1953; PhD, Pa. State U., 1957. Diplomate in clin. psychology Am. Bd. Profl. Psychology; lic. psychologist, Ala. Rsch. asst. Psychoacoustics Lab., Pa. State U., University Park, 1953-54; fellow USPHS, 1954-56; asst. prof. psychology, asst. dir. Psychol. Clinic, U. Ala., Tuscaloosa, 1956-59, assoc. prof., dir. Psychol. Clinic Birmingham, 1959-65, prof., chmn. dept., 1965-83, prof. (on leave), 1983-86, prof. emeritus, 1986—; sr. cons. Psych. Sys. and Nat. Computer Sys., Balt. and Washington, 1983-86; prof. psychology, head dept. U. Tenn., Knoxville, 1986-89; exec. v.p., CEO APA, Washington, 1989—2002. Participant White House Conf. on Health, 1965, Nat. Conf. on Criminal Justice Stds. and Goals, 1973; mem. nat. adv. com. on alcoholism HEW, 1970-72, chmn. com. on rsch., 1970; mem. task panel on manpower and pers. President's Commn. on Mental Health, 1977-78; mem. Ala. Gov.'s Adv. Com. on Alcoholism and Drug Abuse, 1973-82; vice chmn. program com. N.Am. Congress on Alcohol and Drug Addiction, 1974; mem. sci. adv. com. Nat. Coun. on Alcoholism, 1974-78; mem. rsch. tng. rev. com. Nat. Inst. Alcohol Abuse and Alcoholism, 1975-78; dir. Ala. Prison Classification Project, 1976-77; chmn. So. Sch. Alcohol Studies, 1960-62; cons. Ala. Commn. on Alcoholism, 1958-70, VA, 1959-65, Estate of Howard R. Hughes, 1976-84; prin. cons. Roche Psychiat. Svc. Inst., Nutley, N.J., 1966-77, Med. Computer Svc., Basel, Switzerland, 1968-76, Med. Computer Svc., Hans Huber Verlag, Berne, Switzerland, 1976-89; cons. to adminstr. Law Enforcement Assistance Adminstrn., U.S. Dept. Justice, Washington, 1971-73; program cons. div. alcoholism Ala. Dept. Mental Health, 1973-75; sr. cons. Nat. Computer Sys., Mpls., 1983-89 Contbg. author: Assessment for Decision, 1987, Handbook of Psychological Assessment, 1990; editor Am. Psychologist, 1989-2002; contbr. articles and revs. to profl. jours. Vice pres. Ala. Coun. on Human Rels., 1965-68, Rehab. Rsch. Found., 1965-80; alumni fellow Pa. State U., 1988—; bd. dirs. Rosalynn Carter Inst. for Human Devel., 1988-98. Named Disting. Practitioner, Nat. Acad. Practice, 1986; recipient significant Minn. Multiphasic Personality Inventory contbn. award U. Minn., 1988; grantee Ala. Commn. on Alcoholism, 1962-63, 64-68, NIMH, 1963-64, Roche Psychiat. Svc. Inst., 1967-76, Ala. Dept. Mental Health, 1969-70, U.S. Dept. Justice, 1971-82, Ala. Bd. Corrections, 1972-73, Ala. Law Enforcement Planning Agy., 1972-74, Nat. Inst. Alcohol Abuse and Alcoholism, 1973-83. Fellow APA (pres. div. 13, 1978-79, coun. reps. 1965-68, 70-73, 75-78, bd. dirs. 1979—, treas. 1983-87, pres.-elect 1987-88, pres. 1988-89, presdl. citation 1990), Soc. for Personality Assessment; mem. AAUP (pres. U. Ala. chpt. 1969-70), Southeastern Psychol. Assn. (pres. 1971-72, dir. continuing edn. 1973-89, dist. speaker 1982, 87), Ala. Psychol. Assn. (pres. 1962, award for outstanding contbns. 1979), Alcohol and Drug Problems Assn. N.Am. (program chmn. 1974-76, bd. dirs. 1975-77), Internat. Assn. Applied Psychology (pres.-elect 2006—), Sigma Xi (life), Psi Chi (nat. v.p. 1980-84, disting. speaker 1977, 88), Omicron Delta Kappa, Phi Kappa Phi. Democrat. Avocations: running, gardening, cooking. Home: 8276 Caminito Maritimo La Jolla CA 92037

FOWLER, THOMAS KENNETH, physicist; b. Thomaston, Ga., Mar. 27, 1931; s. Albert Grady and Susie (Glynn) F.; m. Carol Ellen Winter, Aug. 18, 1956; children: Kenneth, John, Ellen. BS in Engring, Vanderbilt U., 1953, MS in Physics, 1955; PhD in Physics, U. Wis., 1957. Staff physicist Oak Ridge Nat. Lab., 1957-65, group leader plasma theory, 1961-65; staff physicist Gen. Atomic Co., San Diego, 1965-67, head plasma physics divsn., 1967; group leader plasma theory Lawrence Livermore Lab., Livermore, Calif., 1967-69, div. leader, 1969-70, assoc. dir. magnetic fusion, 1970-87; prof., chmn. dept. nuclear engrng. U. Calif., Berkeley, 1988-94, prof. emeritus, 1995—. Calif. Coun. Sci. Tech. fellow, 1997—. Fellow Am. Phys. Soc. (chmn. plasma physics div. 1970); mem. Nat. Acad. Scis., Sigma Xi, Sigma Nu. Home: 221 Grover Ln Walnut Creek CA 94596-6310 Office: U Calif Dept Nuclear Engring Berkeley CA 94720-1730 Business E-Mail: fowler@nuc.berkeley.edu.

FOWLER, VINCENT R., dermatologist; b. South Bend, Ind., Dec. 15, 1944; s. Vincent R. and Miriam Frances (Alward) F.; m. Madeline M. Morales, Apr. 26, 1975; children: Debra, Michael, Peter. BA in Pscyhology, Calif. State U., LA, 1969; MD, U. Autonoma Guadalajara, Mex., 1973. Diplomate Am. Bd. Dermatology; lic. Calif. Intern Long Beach (Calif.) Med. Ctr., 1974-75; resident in internal medicine SUNY Med. Ctr., Stonybrook, N.Y., 1975-78; resident in dermatology Letterman Army Med. Ctr., Presido San Francisco, Calif., 1978-80; chief medicine/dermatology Reynolds Army Hosp., Fort Sill, Okla., 1980-82; chief dermatology W. L.A. Kaiser Med. Ctr., 1982—. Asst. clin. prof. UCLA Sch. Medicine, 1984—. Major Army Med. Corps., 1978-82. Fellow Am. Acad. Dermatology; mem. L.A. Met. Dermatol. Soc. Avocations: surfing, skiing, tennis. Office: Kaiser W LA Med Ctr 5971 Venice Blvd Los Angeles CA 90034-1713 Home: 7225 Crescent Park W Apt 408 Playa Vista CA 90094-2721

FOWLER, WILLIAM MAYO, JR., rehabilitation medicine physician; b. Bklyn., June 16, 1926; BS, Springfield Coll., 1948, MEd, 1949; MD, U. So. Calif., LA, 1957. Diplomate Am. Bd. Phys. Medicine and Rehab. Intern UCLA, 1958, resident in pediatrics, 1959, resident in phys. medicine, rehab., 1963; chmn. dept. phys. medicine, rehab. U. Calif., Davis, 1968-82, mem. faculty dept. phys. medicine, rehab., 1972-91, prof. emeritus, 1991—. Fellow Am. Acad. Phys. Medicine and Rehab. (pres. 1981, Krusen award 1994), Am. Coll. Sports Medicine; mem. Assn. Acad. Physiatrists. Office: U Calif Davis Dept Phys Med Rehab One Shields Ave Davis CA 95616

FOX, GALEN W., state representative; b. Hilo, Feb. 24, 1943; children: Derek, MeiMei. BA, U. Redlands, 1965; MPA, Princeton U., 1967, PhD, 1978. Fgn. svc. officer U.S. Dept. of State, 1966—82; rsch. fellow East-West Ctr., Honolulu, 1982—84; exec. asst. Mayor of Honolulu, 1985—91; chief bus. devel. and mkrg. divsn. Hawaii Dept. of Econ. Devel., 1991—96; mem. Hawaii State Ho. of Reps., 1996—, Rep. whip, 1998—2000, Rep. leader, 2000—05. Chair Sec. of State's Open Forum, 1978—79; sec. Am. Fgn. Svc. Assn., 1979—81; chair, vice chair Neighborhood Bd. #3, 1989—96. Mem., treas. Oahu Pvt. Industry Coun., 1985—91; pres. Hawaii Cmty. Svcs. Coun., 1995—96; sec., treas. exec. com. East-West Ctr. Internat. Alumni, 1995—2000; mem. allocations com. Aloha United Way, 1996—; exec. bd. Ch. of the Crossroads, 2001—04. Mem.: Waikiki Residents Assn., Waikiki Improvement Assn. Republican. United Ch. Of Christ. Home Phone: 808-946-5223; Office Phone: 808-586-8520. E-mail: repfox@capitol.hawaii.gov.

FOX, JAMES MICHAEL, orthopedic surgeon; b. Milw., July 20, 1942; m. Ellen Fox. BS, U. Wis., 1964, MD, 1968. Diplomate Nat. Bd. Med. Examiners, Am. Bd. Orthop. Surgery. Intern Bronx (N.Y.) Mcpl. Hosp./Albert Einstein Coll. Medicine, 1968-69, surg. resident, 1969-70, orthop. surgery resident, 1970-72, chief resident orthop. surgery, 1972-73; asst. instr. orthop. surgery Albert Einstein Coll. Medicine, 1972-73; sports medicine fellow Nat. Athletic Health Inst., Inglewood, Calif., 1973-74, mem. med. adv. bd., 1974—; pvt. practice Sherman Oaks, Calif., 1976-81, So. Calif. Orthop. Inst., Van Nuys, Calif., 1981—. Mem. staff Centinela Valley Cmty. Hosp., Inglewood, 1973-74, Daniel Freeman Hosp., Inglewood, 1973-74, View Park Hosp., L.A., 1973-74, Keesler Med. Ctr., Keesler AFB, Miss., 1974-76, Encino (Calif.) Hosp., 1976-81, Sherman Oaks Cmty. Hosp., 1976-83, Valley Presbyn. Hosp., 1981—; med. cons. sports medicine video cassettes VCI-Nat. Athletic Health Inst., 1974-76; cons. cmty. outreach program on emergency treatment of athletic injuries Sherman Oaks Cmty. Hosp., 1978-80; cons., presenter in field; cons. Youth Soccer Mag.; med. dir. Ctr. for Disorders of Knee, Van Nuys; mem. Ctr. for Sports Medicine, Calif. State U., Northridge, 1990; med. examiner State of Calif. Dept. Indsl. Rels., 1993-95. Author: Save Your Knees; co-editor: Patello-Ferral Joint; mem. editl. bd. Jour. of Arthroscopy, 1989-93, video supplement, 1989, The Knee, 1994. Mem. Summer Olympics, 1984. Maj. Med. Corps USAF, 1974-76. Fellow ACS; mem. Am. Athletic Trainers Adv. Assn. and Cert. Bd. Inc. (mem. com.), Arthroscopy Assn. N.Am. (mem. rsch. com. 1986-89, bd. dirs. 1989-91, chmn. pub. rels. com. 1989, program chmn. 1993, sec. 1994-97), Calif. Med. Assn. Office: 7230 Medical Center Dr Ste 503 West Hills CA 91307-4030 Home Phone: 310-428-3172; Office Phone: 818-444-5100. Business E-Mail: dfox@scoi.com, jfox@synergyperformancehealth.com.

FOX, JEREMY, chef; m. Deanie Hickox Fox, 2006. Studied, Johnson & Wales U. Cook Anson, Charleston, SC; chef de cuisine Mumbo Jumbo, Atlanta; stage De Snippe, Belgium; cook Rubicon, San Francisco, 2001, Charles Nob Hill, San Francisco, Manresa, Los Gatos, Calif., 2003—04, chef de cuisine; stage Gordon Ramsay, London, 2004, St. John, London; exec. chef Ubuntu, Napa, Calif., 2007—. Named one of America's Best New Chefs, Food & Wine Mag., 2008. Avocations: music, baseball, reading. Office: Ubuntu 1140 Main St Napa CA 94559

FOX, JOHN, film company executive; b. May 13, 1974; B in English, UCLA. Intern Baumgarten/Prophet Entertainment; prodn. asst. Timecop ABC; asst. to prodn. head Casey La Scala Gaylord Films; dir. devel. DreamWorks, 2002—04, v.p. devel., 2004—. Achievements include overseeing development and production for Anchorman: The Legend of Ron Burgundy, 2004, and the upcoming releases Norbit and Transformers.

FOX, MEGAN DENISE, actress; b. Rockwood, Tenn., May 16, 1986; Actress (films) Holiday in the Sun, 2001, Confessions of a Teenage Drama Queen, 2004, Transformers, 2007, How to Lose Friends and Alienate People, 2008, (TV series) Ocean Ave, 2002—, The Help, 2004, Hope & Faith, 2004—06, (TV films) Crimes of Fashion, 2004, appearances on (TV series) What I Like About You, 2003, Two and a Half Men, 2004, Jimmy Kimmel Live!, 2007, Entertainment Tonight, 2007, voice (video game) Transformers: The Game, 2007. Recipient modeling awards, American Modeling and Talent Conv., 1999. Office: c/o Teitelbaum Artists Group 8840 Wilshire Blvd Beverly Hills CA 90211

FOX, MICHAEL J., museum director; Pres., CEO Mus. of No. Ariz., Flagstaff. Office: Mus of No Ariz 3101 N Fort Valley Rd Flagstaff AZ 86001-8348

FOX, MITCHELL B., publishing executive; b. Mar. 24, 1955; s. Myron C. and Millicent Fox; m. Katherine Angela Maurer, June 21, 1981; 3 children. BS in Polit. Sci., SUNY, Stonybrook. Grp. mgr. retail advt. NY Times; sr. v.p. sales and promotion Bergdorf Goodman; pub. Details mag. Condé Nast Publs., 1989—94, pub. Vanity Fair mag. NYC, 1994—97, v.p., 1997—99, sr. v.p., corp. sales, 1999—2000, exec. v.p. sales and mktg., 2000—01, pres. Golf Digest Cos., 2001—05, CEO, 2001—05, pres. Golf Digest mag., 2005—08, pres. Fairchild Fashion Grp., 2006—08, pres. Bridal Grp., pres. W mag., 2006—08; pres. 8020 Pub., San Francisco, 2008—. Adv. coun. Telluride Film Festival; nat. trustee The First Tee. Mem.: Mag. Pubs. America (bd. dirs., exec. com.). Office: 8020 Pub 199 Fremont St San Francisco CA 94105

FOX, NED, professional sports team owner; BS in Acctg., U. So. Calif., 1969, MBA, 1971. With real estate Arthur Andersen & Co., 1971-78; sr. ptnr. Maguire Thomas Ptnrs., 1978-93. Founder, co-mng. dir. CommonWealth Ptnrs., L.A., 1993—; adv. com. U. So. Calif. Grad. Sch. Bus.; adv. coun. U. So. Calif. Sch. Arts & Architecture. Exec. com., bd. dirs. L.A. Convention & Vis. Bur., 1993—; chmn. real estate/constrn. com. L.A. County Music Ctr Unified Fund Campaign, 1992-93; urban devel./mixed-use coun. Urban Land Inst.; vol. Boy Scouts Am. Mem. Am. Inst. Cert. CPAs. Office: Sacramento Kings One Sports Pkwy Sacramento CA 95834 also: Commonwealth Ptnrs 633 W 5th St Ste 5610 Los Angeles CA 90071-3502

FOX, STEVE, editor-in-chief; B in English, Yale U. Mng. editor Omni mag.; with Popular Mechanics, IEEE; editor-in-chief The Web Mag., 1996—98; various editl. positions PC World mag., 1991—96, editor, 1998—99; editor in chief pcworld.com, 1999; editl. dir. CNET, 1999—2003; editor-in-chief InfoWorld Media Group, 2003—. Spkr. in field. Office: Inforworld Media Group 501 Second St San Francisco CA 94107 Office Fax: 415-978-3120. Business E-Mail: stevefox@inforworld.com.

FOX, STUART IRA, physiologist; b. Bklyn., June 21, 1945; s. Sam and Bess Fox; m. Ellen Diane Berley; 1 child, Laura Elizabeth. BA, UCLA, 1967; MA, Calif. State U., LA, 1967; postgrad., U. Calif., Santa Barbara, 1969; PhD, U. So. Calif., 1978. Rsch. assoc. Children's Hosp., LA, 1972; prof. physiology LA City Coll., 1972-85, Calif. State U., Northridge, 1979-84, Pierce Coll., 1986—. Cons.

McGraw-Hill, 1976—. Author: Computer-Assisted Instruction in Human Physiology, 1979, Laboratory Guide to Human Physiology, 10th edit., 2003, 13th edit., 2009, Textbook of Human Physiology, 1986, 11th edit., 2009, Human Anatomy and Physiology, 1986, Perspectives on Human Biology, 1991, Laboratory Manual for Anatomy and Physiology, 1986;: 5th edit., 1999, Fundamentals of Human Physiology, 2008; co-author: Biology, 5th edit., 1999, Synopsis of Anatomy and Physiology, 1997. Mem.: AAAS, Am. Anatomy and Physiology Soc., Am. Physiol. Soc., Sigma Xi. Home: 5556 Forest Cove Ln Agoura Hills CA 91301-4047 Office Phone: 818-710-2832. Business E-Mail: Foxsi@piercecollege.edu.

FOXE, MARYE ANNE, academic administrator; b. Canton, Ohio, Dec. 9, 1947; m. James K. Whitesell, 1990; stepchildren: Christopher Whitesell, Robert Whitesell; children: Robert Fox, Michael Fox, Matthew Fox. BS, Notre Dame Coll. of Ohio, 1969; MS, Cleve. State U., 1970; PhD, Dartmouth Coll., 1974; postgrad., U. Md., 1974-76; DSc (hon.), Notre Dame Coll., 1994, Cleve. State U., 1998; JD (hon.), Sandhills Cmty. Coll., 2000; degree (hon.), Universite Pierre et Marie Curie, 2001; LHD (hon.), Texas A&M, 2002; degree (hon.), Universidad Nacional de Educacion a Distancia, Madrid, 2003. Prof. chemistry U. Tex., Austin, 1976-91, Rowland Pettit Centennial prof., 1986-92, M. June and J. Virgil Waggoner regents chair chemistry, 1992-98, v.p. rsch., 1994-98; chancellor N.C. State U., Raleigh, 1998—2004, U. Calif. San Diego, 2004—. Mem. Nat. Sci. Bd., 1991-96, vice-chair, 1994-96; bd. dirs. Kenan Inst. Engring., Tech., and Sci., 1998—, Microelectric Ctr., NC, 1998—, mem. sci. adv. bd. Robert A. Welch Found., 1998—, David and Lucile Packard Found., 1998—; mem. Coun. on Competitiveness, 1999—; bd. trustees Nat. Inst. Statistical Sciences, 2000—; bd. dirs. Nat. Inst. Environment, 2001—, Boston Sci. Inc., 2001—, mem. President's Adv. Coun. of Advisors on Sci. and Tech., 2001—; bd. dirs. NC Bd. Sci. and Tech., 2002—, PPD Inc., 2002—, Red Hat Inc., 2002, Nat. Assn. State Universities and Land Grant Coll., 2003— Assoc. editor Jour. Am. Chem. Soc., 1986-94; mem. adv. bd. Jour. Organic Chemistry, Chem. Engring. News, Chem. Rev. Bd. trustees U. Notre Dame, 2002—; bd. dirs. N.C. Citizens for Bus. and Industry, 2003—. Recipient Agnes Faye Morgan Rsch. award Iota Sigma Pi, 1984, Arthur C. Cope scholar award Am. Chem. Soc., 1988; Garvan medal Am. Chem. Soc., 1988, Havinga medal Leiden U., 1991, Monie A. Ferst award, 1996; named to Hall of Excellence, Ohio Found. Ind. Colls., 1987, The Best of the New Generation, Esquire Mag., 1984; Alfred P. Sloan Rsch. fellow, 1980-82, Camille and Henry Dreyfus tchr. scholar, 1981-85. Fellow AAAS, Assn. Women in Sci.; mem. NAS (co-chair, Govt.-Univ.-Industry Rsch. Roundtable, 1999-), Am. Acad. Arts and Sci., Am. Philos. Soc., Sigma Xi (pres. 2001-02). Office: U Calif San Diego Chancellors Office 9500 Gilman Sr La Jolla CA 92093-0005

FOXLEY, CECELIA HARRISON, commissioner; BA in English, Utah State U., 1964; MA in English, U. Utah, 1965, PhD in Ednl. Psychology, 1968. English tchr. Olympus H.S., Salt Lake City, 1965-66; asst. prof. edn., assoc. dir. student activities U. Minn., Mpls., 1968-71; from asst. prof. to assoc. prof., asst. dean Coll. Edn. U. Iowa, Iowa City, 1971-81; prof. psychology Utah State U., Logan, 1981-85, from asst. v.p. student svcs. to assoc. v.p. for student svcs. and acad. affairs, 1981-85; assoc. commr. for acad. affairs Utah State Bd. Regents, Salt Lake City, 1985-93, commr., 1993—. Utah rep. Am. Coun. on Edn. Office Women in Higher Edn., 1982-92; mem. nat. adv. coun. on nurse tng. U.S. Dept. Health and Human Svcs., 1987-91; mem. nat. adv. bd. S.W. Regional Ctr. for Drug Free Schs., 1988-93; mem. edn. bd. Utah Alliance for Edn. and Humanities, 1989-93; mem. prevention subcom. Utah Substance Abuse Coordinating Coun., 1991-93; mem. exec. bd. U.S. West Comm., 1995—; mem. adv. bd. Salt Lake Buzz, 1995—; active Consortium for Women in Higher Edn. Bd., 1981-85, Utah State Libr. Bd., 1990-93, Compact for Faculty Diversity, 1994—; presenter in field; cons. in field. Author: Recruiting Women and Minority Faculty, 1972, Locating, Recruiting, and Employing Women, 1976, Non-Sexist Counseling: Helping Women and Men Redefine Their Roles, 1979; co-author: The Human Relations Experience, 1982; editor: Applying Management Techniques, 1980; co-editor: Multicultural Nonsexist Education, 1979; author chpts. to books; contbr. articles to profl. jours. Grantee Utah State Dept. Social Svcs., 1984-85, 85-86; recipient Pres. Leadership award Assn. Utah Women Edn. Adminstrs., 1990, Disting. Alumni award Utah State U., 1991. Mem. APA, Am. Assn. Counseling and Devel., Am. Coll. Pers. Assn., Nat. Forum Sys. Chief Acad. Officers, State Higher Edn. Exec. Officers (mem. exec. com. 1994—), Western Interstate Cooperative Higher Edn. (mem. exec. com. 1994—).

FOXLEY, WILLIAM COLEMAN, cattleman; b. St. Paul, Jan. 7, 1935; s. William Joseph and Eileen (Conroy) F. BA, U. Notre Dame, 1957. Pres., chmn. bd. Foxley Cattle Co., Omaha, 1960—. Chmn. bd. Mus. Western Art, Denver. Served with USMCR, 1957-60. Republican. Roman Catholic. Office: 6106 Camino De La Costa La Jolla CA 92037-6520

FOXX, JAMIE (ERIC BISHOP), actor, comedian; b. Terrell, Tex., Dec. 13, 1967; s. Shaheed Abdulah and Louise Annette D.(div.); raised by great grandparents Mark and Ester Talley. Student, U.S. Internat. U., San Diego, 1986—88; studied classical piano, Juliard Sch. Fine Arts. Host, The Foxxhole Sirius Radio. Actor: (TV series) In Living Color, 1991—94; actor, dir., prodr., writer (TV series) The Jamie Foxx Show, 1996 (NAACP Image award for Outstanding Lead Actor in a Comedy Series, 1997), comedian, exec. prodr., writer (TV Spl.) Jamie Foxx: I Might Need Security, 2002; actor: (films) Toys, 1992, The Truth About Cats and Dogs, 1996, The Great White Hype, 1996, Booty Call, 1997, The Players Club, 1998, Held Up, 1999, Any Given Sunday, 1999, Bait, 2000, Date from Hell, 2001, Ali, 2001 (NAACP Image award for Outstanding Supporting Actor in a Motion Picture, 2002), Shade, 2003, Breakin' All the Rules, 2004, Collateral, 2004, Ray, 2004 (Named Best Actor Nat. Bd. Rev. Motion Pictures, 2004, Best Actor, Washington, DC Film Critics award, 2004, Best Actor, Boston Film Critics award, 2004, Golden Globe award for best actor musical or comedy, 2005, Screen Actors Guild Award, outstanding performance by male actor in leading role, 2005, Academy award for best actor in a leading role, 2005), Stealth, 2005, Jarhead, 2005, Miami Vice, 2006, Dreamgirls, 2006, The Kingdom, 2007, The Soloist, 2009; (TV films) Redemption: The Stan Tookie Williams Story, 2004, (voice only): (TV series) C-Bear and Jamal, 1996; host MTV Video Music Awards, 2001, ESPY Awards, 2003; singer: (albums) Peep This, 1994, Unpredictable, 2005 (Best Album, Soul Train awards, 2007), Intuition, 2008, (songs) (with Kanye West) Gold Digger, 2005 (Best Duet & Video of Yr., BET awards, 2006). Recipient Outstanding Male Artist, NAACP Image awards, 2006, 2009, Favorite Male Artist, Soul/Rhythm & Blues, Am. Music awards, 2006; named one of The 100 Most Influential People in the World, TIME mag., 2005, The 10 Most Fascinating People of 2005, Barbara Walters Special. Office: c/o The Gersh Agy 232 N Canon Dr Beverly Hills CA 90210*

FOY, THOMAS PAUL, lawyer, retired state legislator, bank executive; b. Silver City, N.Mex., Oct. 19, 1914; s. Thomas J. and Mary V. Foy; m. Joan Carney, Nov. 17, 1948 (dec. June 1994); children: Celia, Thomas Paul Jr. (dec.), Muffet (Mary Ann), J. Carney, James B. BS in Commerce, Notre Dame U., 1938, JD, 1939; DHL (hon.), Western N.Mex U., 2004. Bar: N.Mex. 1946. Dist. atty. N.Mex. 6th Jud. Dist., Silver City, 1949-57; atty. Village of Bayard, N.Mex., 1954-68, Village of Ctrl., N.Mex., 1960-70; v.p., counsel, bd. dirs. Sunwest Bank, Silver City, 1946-84, chmn. bd. dirs., 1969-84, chmn. emeritus, 1971—98; state rep. Dist. 39 State of N.Mex., Grant-Hidalgo, 1984—97; chmn. jud. com. N.Mex. State Legis., Santa Fe, 1984-98; pres. Foy & Vesely and Foy, Foy & Castillo, Silver City, 1946-99, Foy Law Firm PC, 1999—. 1st lt. U.S. Army, 1941-46; prisoner of war, PTO, 1942-45. Decorated Bronze Star, Purple Heart, Asiatic-Pacific Ribbon with 3 oak leaf clusters; recipient Citizen of Yr. award Silver City-Grant County C. of C., 1965, Dedication to Advancement award Trial Lawyers Assn., 1993, N.Mex. Disting. Svc. medal, 1994. Mem. ABA, N.Mex. Bar Assn. (bar commr. 1967-85, v.p. N.Mex. bar commn. 1978-79, Disting. Svc. of Laws award 1987), Am. Judicature Soc., Bataan Vets. Orgn. (state comdr. 1965-66, 98-99, 2004—), KC (Grand Knight 1936-37), VFW (state comdr. 1959-60), Lions (dist. gov. 1956-57), Elks. Democrat. Roman Catholic. Avocations: football, baseball, travel, conventions. Office: Box 266 Bayard NM 88023-2660 Home: PO Box 266 Bayard NM 88023-0266 Office Phone: 505-537-3355.

FRACKMAN, RUSSELL JAY, lawyer; b. NYC, July 3, 1946; s. Sam and Doris (Wasserberg) F.; m. Myrna D. Morganstern, Aug. 3, 1980; children: Steven Howard, Abigail Zoe. BA in History, Northwestern U., 1967; JD cum laude, Columbia U., 1970. Bar: Calif. 1971, U.S. Dist. Ct. (ctrl., ea. and no. dists.) Calif., U.S. Ct. Appeals (2d and 9th cirs.), U.S. Supreme Ct. Assoc. Mitchell, Silberberg & Knupp LLP, LA, 1970-76, ptnr., 1976—, chmn. litigation dept., 1994-96. Lectr. on intellectual property and entertainment law various instns. including Practising Law Inst., L.A. Copyright Soc., Beverly Hills Bar Assn., U. So. Calif. Sch. Law, Am. Film Mktg. Assn., Calif. Copyright Conf. Bd. editors Columbia Law Rev., 1969-70; contbr. articles and revs. to legal jours. Co-chmn. internat. leadership devel. forum CARE, 1990; bd. trustees CARE Found., 1991—, Twitty, Milsap, Sterban Found., 1988-92. Named Entertainment Lawyer of the Year, Beverly Hills Bar Assn.; named one of Top 100 Most Influential Lawyers in Calif., Calif. Law Bus., Los Angeles' Top 50 Litigators, Los Angeles Bus. Jour., Best Lawyers in Am., Entertainment Law, The Best Lawyers in Am., Los Angeles Mag., 2005, 2006, 100 Most Influential Lawyers, Nat. Law Jour., 2006. Mem. ABA (chmn. copyright subcom. litigation sect. 1990-93, lectr. various confs.), Am. Film Mktg. Assn. (mem. arbitration tribunal). Democrat. Jewish. Office: Mitchell Silberberg & Knupp LLP 11377 W Olympic Blvd Los Angeles CA 90064-1625 Home Phone: 310-471-2787; Office Phone: 310-312-3119.

FRADELLA, HENRY F., law educator; b. NYC, Feb. 11, 1969; s. Diana Dressel and Anthony Peter. BA, Clark U., 1990; M Forensic Sci., The George Washington U., 1993, JD, 1993; PhD, Ariz. State U., 1997. Bar: Ariz. 1995; US Dist. Ct. Ariz., 1995. Jud. law clk. US Dist. Ct., Phoenix, 1993-94; assoc. Kaye, Scholar, Fierman, Hays & Handler, 1990; law clk., summer assoc. Squire, Sanders & Dempsey, Washington, 1991; instr. Ariz. State U., Tempe, 1994—97; prof. law and justice The Coll. of NJ, Ewing, 1997—2007; prof., chair dept. criminal justice Calif. State U., Long Beach, 2007—. Dir. Fradella Forensic Cons., 1997—. Author: (books) Key Cases, Comments, and Questions on Substantive Criminal Law, 2000, Forensic Psychology, 2008, Defenses of Excuse in Contemporary American Law, 2007, From Insanity to Diminished Capacity, 2007, Criminal Procedure for the Criminal Justice Professional, 2008; legal lit. editor Criminal Law Bulletin, 2005—; contbr. articles to profl. jours. Mem. Am. Soc. Criminology, Acad. Criminal Justice Scis., ABA, Am. Judicature Soc., Lambda Legal Def. and Edn. Fund/US, Human Rights Campaign, Phi Beta Kappa. Avocations: movies, music, singing, travel, cooking. Office: Calif State Univ Long Beach Dept Criminal Justice 1250 Bell Flower Blvd Long Beach CA 90840 Office Phone: 562-985-2669.

FRAGNER, MATTHEW CHARLES, lawyer; b. NYC, Jan. 12, 1954; s. Berwyn N. and Marcia R. (Salkind) F.; m. Mariann Donahue, June 19, 1983; children: Rachel Jade, Jaron Roark, Bailyn Natalie, Talia Colby. BA, Yale U., 1975; JD, U. Calif., Berkeley, 1978. Bar: Calif. 1978, U.S. Tax Ct. 1979, U.S. Ct. Appeals (9th crct.) 1979. Atty. Thomas Shafran & Wasser, LA, 1978-83; ptnr. Shafran & Fragner, LA, 1984-87, Lane & Edson, LA, 1987-88, Mayer Brown & Platt, LA, 1989-92, Sonnenschein Nath & Rosenthal, LA, 1992-2000; pres. Somnolence, Inc., LA, 1989—96; gen. cousel, dir. investments Citadel Capital Mgmt. Corp., 2000—02; founder, chmn. Tools to Talent Non Profit Corp., 2001—; ptnr. Liner Yankelevitz Sunshine & Regenstreif, Santa Monica, Calif., 2002—03; prin. Fragner & Pace Law Corp., Los Angeles, 2003—05; ptnr. Fragner Seifert Pace & Winograd, LLP, LA, 2005—; gen. counsel CIM Group, LA, 2006—. Lectr. U. So. Calif., 1994—99. Active Berkeley (Calif.) Law Found., 1978-83. Mem. Los Angeles County Bar Assn. (chair comml. devel. and leasing subsect.). Office: Fragner Seifert Pace & Winograd LLP 300 S Grand Ave 14th Fl Los Angeles CA 90071 Office Phone: 213-687-2320. Business E-Mail: mfragner@fspwlaw.com.

FRAKES, RODNEY VANCE, plant geneticist, educator; b. Ontario, Oreg., July 20, 1930; s. Wylie and Pearl (Richardson) F.; m. Ruby L. Morey, Nov. 27, 1952; children: Laura Ann, Cody Joe. BS, Oreg. State U., 1956, MS, 1957; PhD, Purdue U., 1960. Instr. dept. agronomy Purdue U., West Lafayette, Ind., 1959-60; asst. prof. dept. crop sci. Oreg. State U., Corvallis, 1960-64, assoc. prof., 1964-69, prof., 1969—, assoc. dean research, 1981-88, emeritus dean of rsch., prof. emeritus crop sci., 1989—. Author numerous papers and abstracts; contbr. to books in field Served with USCG, 1950-53 Named Man of Yr., Pacific Seedsmen's Assn., 1972; recipient Elizabeth P. Ritchie Disting. Prof. award Oreg. State U., 1980. Fellow Am. Soc. Agronomy, Crop Sci. Soc. Am.; mem. AAAS, Soc. Research Adminstrs., Nat. Council Univ. Research Adminstrs., Western Soc. Crop Sci. (pres. 1978), Model A Ford Club of Am., Model T Ford Club of Am., Rotary. Avocations: antiques, history, amateur radio. Home: 2615 NW Linnan Cir Corvallis OR 97330-1221 Office: Oreg State U Rsch Office Corvallis OR 97331

FRAKNOI, ANDREW, astronomer, educator; b. Budapest, Hungary, Aug. 24, 1948; came to US, 1959; naturalized; s. Emery I. and Katherine H. (Schmidt) F.; m. Lola Goldstein, Aug. 16, 1992; 1 child, Alexander. BA in Astronomy, Harvard U., 1970; MA in Astrophysics, U. Calif., Berkeley, 1972. Instr. astronomy and physics Cañada Coll., Redwood City, Calif., 1972-78; exec. dir. Astron. Soc. Pacific, San Francisco, 1978-92; chmn. dept. astronomy Foothill Coll., Los Altos, Calif., 1992—. Prof. San Francisco State U., 1980-92; fellow Com. for Sci. Investigation of Claims of Paranormal, 1984—; bd. dirs. Search for Extra Terrestrial Intelligence Inst., Mountain View, Calif.; host radio prog. Exploring the Universe Sta. KGO-FM, San Francisco, 1983-84. Author: Resource Book for the Teaching of Astronomy, 1978; (with others) Effective Astronomy Teaching and Student Reasoning Ability, 1978, Universe in the Classroom, 1985; (with T. Robertson) Instructor's Guide to the Universe, 1991, (with others) Exploration of the Universe, 1995; (with others) Voyages Through the Universe, 1997, Voyages to the Planets, 2000, Voyages to the Stars and Galaxies, 2004, Disney's Wonderful World of Space, 2007; editor: The Planets, 1985, Interdisciplinary Approaches to Astronomy, 1985, The Universe, 1987, The Universe at Your Fingertips Resource Notebook, 1995, Cosmos in the Classroom, 2000; editor Mercury Mag., 1978-92, The Universe in the Classroom Newsletter, 1985-92, Astronomy Education Review, 2002—; assoc. editor: The Planetarian, 1986-88. Bd. dirs. Bay Area Skeptics, San Francisco, 1982-91. Recipient award of merit Astron. Assn. No. Calif., 1980, award Astron. League, 1993, Klumpke-Roberts award, 1994, Annenberg Found. prize in astronomy edn., 1994, Carl Sagan prize for sci. popularization, 2002; Asteroid 4859 named Asteroid Fraknoi, 1992. Fellow Calif. Acad. Scis.; mem. AAAS (astronomy sect. com. 1988-92), Am. Astron. Soc. (astronomy edn. adv. bd. 1988-2004), Astron. Soc. Pacific (Richard H. Emmons award for Excellence in Coll. Astronomy Tchg. 2007), Am. Assn. Physics Tchrs., Nat. Assn. Sci. Writers. Avocations: music, astronomy, science, literature. Office: Foothill Coll Dept Astronomy 12345 El Monte Rd Los Altos CA 94022-4504 Office Phone: 650-949-7288. E-mail: fraknoiandrew@fhda.edu.

FRAME, LARRY A., electronics executive; BSEE, U. Wyo.; MBA, Santa Clara U. Mgr. test equipment design Lockheed Missiles and Space Co.; with Litton Industries, Inc., Woodland Hills, Calif., 1964-67, v.p. Salt Lake City, 1967-87, v.p. program mgmt. Woodland Hills, Calif., 1987-90, corp. v.p., 1990-94, sr. v.p., group exec. navigation, guidance & control sys., 1994—. Office: Litton Industries Inc 21240 Burbank Blvd Woodland Hills CA 91367-6675

FRANCESCONI, LOUISE L., defense equipment manufacturing company executive; b. Calif., Mar. 1953; BA, Scripps Coll., 1975; MBA, UCLA, 1978. With Hughes Missile Systems Co., 1976—98, CFO, 1993, pres., 1996—98; sr. v.p. Raytheon Systems Co., 1998—99; v.p. Raytheon Co., 1999—; dep. gen. mgr. Raytheon Missile Systems, Tucson, 1998—99, gen. mgr., 1999—2002, pres., 2002—. Bd. dirs. Stryker Corp., 2006—; bd. trustees Tucson Med. Ctr. Healthcare, Tucson Airport Authority. Mem. Ariz. Gov.'s Coun. on Innovation and Tech., 2003—; nat. bd. advisors Eller Coll. Bus. and Pub. Adminstn., U. Ariz.; bd. trustees Tucson Med. Ctr. Healthcare, Tucson Airport Authority. Recipient Lifetime Achievement award, Women in Aerospace, 2005; named Tech. Exec. of the Yr., Eller Coll. & U. Ariz. Coll. Engring. & MInes, 2002. Office: Raytheon Missile Systems 1151 E Hermans Rd Tucson AZ 85706

FRANCHINI, GENE EDWARD, state supreme court justice; b. Albuquerque, May 19, 1935; s. Mario and Lena (Vaio) F.; m. Glynn Hatchell, Mar. 22, 1969; children: Pamela, Lori (dec.), Gina, Joseph James, Nancy. BBA, Loyola U., 1955; degree in adminstrn., U. N.Mex., 1957; JD, Georgetown U., 1960; LLM, U. Va., 1995. Bar: N.Mex. 1960, U.S. Dist. Ct. N.Mex. 1961, U.S. Ct. Appeals (10th cir.) 1970, U.S. Supreme Ct. 1973. Ptnr. Matteucci, Gutierrez & Franchini, Albuquerque, 1960-70, Matteucci, Franchini & Calkins, Albuquerque, 1970-75; judge State of N.Mex. 2d Jud. Dist., Albuquerque, 1975-81; atty.-at-large Franchini, Wagner, Oliver, Franchini & Curtis, Albuquerque, 1982-90; chief justice N.Mex. Supreme Ct., Santa Fe, 1990-99, justice, 1999—2003. V.p. bd. dirs. Conf. Chief Justices, 1997-98. Chmn. Albuquerque Pers. Bd., 1972, Albuquerque Labor Rels. Bd., 1972, Albuquerque Interim Bd. Ethics, 1972. Capt. USAF, 1960-66. Recipient Highest award Albuquerque Human Rights Bd., 1999. Mem. Am. Bd. Trial Advocates, N.Mex. Trial Lawyers (pres. 1967-68), N.Mex. Bar Assn. (bd. dirs. 1976-78), Albuquerque Bar Assn. (bd. dirs. 1976-78, Outstanding Judge award 1997). Democrat. Roman Catholic. Avocations: fishing, hunting, golf, mushroom hunting. Home: 4901 Laurene Ct NW Albuquerque NM 87120-1026

FRANCIS, CHARLES K., medical educator; b. Newark, May 24, 1939; BA, Dartmouth Coll., 1961; MD, Jefferson Med. Coll., 1965. Med. intern Phila. Gen. Hosp., 1965—66; med. resident Boston City Hosp., Tufts U., 1969—70; clin. fellow cardiology Tufts Circulation Lab., 1970—71; clin. and rsch. fellow cardiology Mass. Gen. Hosp., 1971—72, sr. med. resident, 1972-73; chief cardiac catheterization lab. divsn. cardiology Martin Luther King Jr. Gen. Hosp., LA, 1973—74, chief cardiology divsn., 1974—77; dir. cardiology divsn. Mt. Sinai Hosp., Hartford, Conn., 1977—80; assoc. dir. hypertension svc., assoc. prof. medicine, dir. cardiac catheterization lab. Yale Med. Sch., Hartford, Conn., 1980-87; dir. dept. medicine Harlem Hosp. Ctr., NYC, 1987—98; prof. clin. medicine Columbia U. Coll. Physicians and Surgeons, 1987—98; pres. Charles R. Drew U. Med. and Sci., 1998—. Clin. instr. medicine Sch. Medicine Tufts U., 1970—71; tchg. fellow Harvard Med. Sch., 1971—72, clin. fellow, 1972—73; asst. prof. medicine Charles R. Drew Postgrad. Med. Sch. & Sch. Medicine U. Calif., 1973—75; asst. prof. medicine, dir. Burgdorf Hypertension Clin., Med. Sch. U. Conn., 1977—80; mem. cardiac adv. com. Nat. Heart, Lung & Blood Inst., NIH, 1977—79; asst. prof. medicine Sch. Medicine Yale U., 1980—81, assoc. prof., 1981—87; pres. Am. Coll. of Physicians, 2004—05. Fellow: ACP, Am. Coll. Cardiology; mem.: Assn. Black Cardiologists (chmn. bd. 1994—), Am. Heart Assn., Am. Fedn. Clin. Rsch., Inst. Medicine-NAS. Address: Charles Drew U Med & Sci 1621 E 120th St Los Angeles CA 90059-3025

FRANCIS, MERRILL RICHARD, lawyer; b. Iowa City; children: Kerry L., David M., Robin A. BA magna cum laude, Pomona Coll., 1954; JD, Stanford U., 1959. Bar: Calif. 1960, Supreme Ct. 1970. Ptnr. Sheppard, Mullin, Richter & Hampton, LA, 1959-00, of counsel, 2001—. Mem. Fellows of Contemporary Art, 1980—. Served to lt. (j.g.) U.S. Navy, 1954-56. Fellow Am. Bar Found., Am. Coll. Bankruptcy (chmn. 9th cir. admissions coun. 1992-95, bd. dirs. 1995—, chair bd. regents 1995-01); mem. ABA (bus. law sect., chmn. secured creditors com. 1981-85, chmn. bus. bankruptcy com. 1986-89, chmn. Task Force on Fed. Ct. Structure 1990-93, mem. Coun. Bus. Law sect. 1991-95, chmn. ad hoc com. on brown bag programs

1994-97, chmn. ad hoc com. bankruptcy ct. structure and insolvency process com. 2001-, sr. lawyers divsn., chmn. sr. housing and real estate practice com. 2001—), State Bar of Calif. (mem. debtor/creditor and bankruptcy com. of bus. law sect. 1978-79), L.A. County Bar Assn. (mem. real property sect., exec. com. 1970-80, mem. comml. law and bankruptcy sect., sect. chmn. 1976-77), Fin. Lawyers Conf. (bd. govs. 1970—, pres. 1972-73), La Canada-Flintridge C. of C. and Cmty. Assn. (pres. 1971-72), Order of the Coif, Jonathan Club, Phi Beta Kappa. Office: Sheppard Mullin Richter & Hampton 333 S Hope St Fl 48 Los Angeles CA 90071-1406 Business E-Mail: mfrancis@sheppardmullin.com.

FRANCIS, PHILIP L., retail executive; BS, U. Ill.; MBA, Ind. U. Sr. leadership positions Cardinal Health, Jewel Cos.; corp. v.p. wholesale Roundy's, Pewaukee, Wis., 1988—91; pres., COO Shaw's Supermkts., E. Bridgewater, Mass., 1991-98; dir. PetSmart Inc., Phoenix, 1989—, chmn., pres., CEO, 1999—2001, chmn., CEO, 1999—. Mem. Greater Phoenix Leadership. Office: PetsMart 19601 N 27th Ave Phoenix AZ 85027

FRANCIS, TIMOTHY DUANE, chiropractor; b. Chgo., Mar. 1, 1956; s. Joseph Duane and Barbara Jane (Sigwalt) F. Student, U. Nev., 1974—80, We. Nev. C.C., 1978; BS, L.A. Coll. Chiropractic, 1982, DC magna cum laude, 1984; postgrad., Clark County C.C., 1986—; MS in Bio/Nutrition, U. Bridgeport, 1990. Diplomate Internat. Coll. Applied Kinesiology, Am. Acad. Pain Mgmt., Am. Naturopathic Med. Bd.; cert. kinesiologist, applied kinesiology tchr.; lic. chiropractor, Calif., Nev. Instr. dept. recreation and phys. edn. U. Nev., Reno, 1976-80; from tchng. asst. to lead instr. dept. principles & practice L.A. Coll. Chiropractic, 1983-85; pvt. practice Las Vegas, 1985—. Asst. instr. Internat. Coll. Applied Kinesiology, 1990, chmn. exam review com., 1993, chmn. syllabus review com., 1994; adj. faculty The Union Inst. Coll. of Undergrad. Studies, 1993; joint study participant Nat. Olympic Tng. Ctr., Beijing, China, 1990. Mem. edtl. rev. bd. Alternative Medicine Rev., 1996; contbr. articles to profl. jours. including Internat. Coll. Applied Kinesiology. Charles F. Cutts scholar, 1980. Fellow Internat. Acad. Clin. Acupuncture, British Inst. Homeopathy (homeopathy diploma 1993); mem. Am. Chiropractic Assn. (couns. on sports injuries, nutrition, roentgenology, technic, and mental health), Nev. State Chiropractic Assn., Nat. Strength and Conditioning Assn., Gonsted Clin. Studies Soc., Found. for Chiropractic Edn. and Rsch., Internat. Chiropractors Assn., Internat. Coll. Applied Kinesiology, Internat. Fedn. Practitioners Natural Therapeutics, Nat. Inst. Chiropractic Rsch., Nat. Strength and Conditioning Assn., Am. Naturopathic Med. Assn., Nat. Acad. Rsch. Biochemists, Phi Beta Kappa, Phi Kappa Phi (v.p. 1979-80, Scholar of the Yr. award, 1980), Delta Signa. Republican. Roman Catholic. Avocations: Karate, weightlifting. Home: 7473 Lake Mead Blvd Las Vegas NV 89128 Office Phone: 702-221-8870.

FRANCKE, UTA, geneticist, educator; b. Wiesbaden, Germany, Sept. 9, 1942; arrived in U.S., 1969; d. Kurt and Gertrud Muller; m. Bertold Richard Francke, May 27, 1967 (div. 1982); m. Heinz Furthmayr, July 27, 1986. MD, U. Munich, Fed. Republic Germany, 1967; MS, Yale U., 1985. Diplomate Am. Bd. Pediatrics, Am. Bd. Med. Genetics (bd. dirs. 1981-84). Asst. prof. U. Calif., San Diego, 1973—78; assoc. prof. Yale U., New Haven, 1978—85, prof., 1985—88; prof. genetics Stanford (Calif.) U., 1989—. Investigator Howard Hughes Med. Inst., Stanford, 1989—2000, mem. sci. rev. bd., Bethesda, Md., 1986—88; mem. mammalian genetics study sect. NIH, Bethesda, 1990—94. Profl. advisor March of Dimes Birth Defects Found., White Plains, NY, 1990, Marfan Assn., Port Washington, NY, 1991. Mem.: Am. Soc. Human Genetics (pres. 1999, bd. dirs. Rockville, Md. chpt. 1981—84), Soc. for Inherited Metabolic Disorders, Soc. for Pediatric Rsch., Human Genome Orgn., Inst. Medicine of NAS (assoc.). Avocation: piloting. Office: Stanford U Med Sch Beckman Ctr Stanford CA 94305-5323 Office Phone: 650-725-8089. Business E-Mail: ufrancke@stanford.edu.

FRANGAS, K. JERRY, state legislator; b. Denver, Oct. 24, 1966; m. Gregoria Frangas; 3 children. BSW, Metro State U.; MSW, U. Denver; MPA, Cleve. State U. Counselor Denver Dept. Human Services; mem. Dist. 4 Colo. House of Reps., Denver, 2002—. Pres. North Denver Neighbors Alliance, West Highlands Neighborhood Assn. Democrat. Office: Colo State Capitol 200 E Colfax Rm 271 Denver CO 80203 Office Phone: 303-866-2954. Business E-Mail: kjerry.frangas.house@state.co.us.*

FRANK, ANTHONY MELCHIOR, federal official, former financial executive; b. Berlin, May 21, 1931; came to U.S., 1937, naturalized, 1943; s. Lothar and Elisabeth (Roth) F.; m. Gay Palmer, Oct. 16, 1954; children: Tracy, Randall BA, Dartmouth Coll., 1953, MBA, 1954; postgrad. in fin., U. Vienna, 1956. Asst. to pres., bond portfolio mgr. Glendale Fed. Savs. Assn., Calif., 1958-61; v.p., treas. Far West Fin. Corp., Los Angeles, 1962; adminstrv. v.p., v.p. savs. First Charter Fin. Corp., Beverly Hills, Calif., 1962-66; pres. State Mut. Savs. and Loan Assn., Los Angeles, 1966-68, Titan Group, Inc., NYC and Los Angeles, 1968-70, INA Properties, Inc., 1970-71, Citizens Savs. & Loan, San Francisco, 1971-73, vice chmn., chief exec. officer, 1973-74; chmn. bd., pres., chief exec. officer FN Fin. Corp., 1974-88; postmaster gen. U.S. Postal Svc., 1988-92; founding chmn. Belvedere Capital Ptnrs., San Francisco. Also pres., vice chmn., industry dir. Fed. Home Loan Bank San Francisco, 1972-77; trustee, treas. Blue Shield of Calif., from 1976-88; bd. dirs. Temple Inland, Schwab, Bedford Property Investors Inc., Crescent Real Estate Equities. Chmn., bd. dirs. Calif. Housing Fin. Agy., Sacramento, 1978-86; trustee Am. Conservatory Theater; chmn. bd. visitors Sch. Architecture and Planning UCLA, 1971-86; bd. overseers Tuck Sch.; del. Calif. Dem. Conv., 1968. Served with AUS, 1954-56 Mem. SAG, Chief Execs. Orgn., World Bus. Forum, Dartmouth Club No. Calif., Bohemian Club. Democrat. Office: Belvedere Capital Ptnrs One Maritime Plz Ste 825 San Francisco CA 94111-6114 Home Phone: 415-435-2709; Office Phone: 415-434-1236.

FRANK, PETER SOLOMON, art historian, curator, critic; b. NYC, July 3, 1950; s. Reuven and Bernice (Kaplow) F. BA in Art History, Columbia U., 1972, MA in Art History, 1974. Art critic SoHo Weekly News, NYC, 1973-76; chief art critic Village Voice, NYC, 1977-79; art critic, columnist L.A. Weekly, 1988—; critic Long Beach Press-Telegram, 1993-96; L.A. corr. Contemporanea, 1989-91; curatorial assoc. Ind. Curators Inc., NYC and Washington, 1974—; co-curator Documenta VI, Kassel, W. Ger., 1976-77; assoc. editor Nat. Arts Guide, Chgo., 1979-81, Art Express, NYC, 1980-81; curator Exxon Nat. Exhbn. of Am. Artists, Guggenheim Mus., NYC, 1980-81, Dokumenta, Kassel, Germany, 1981; art critic Diversion mag., 1983-90; former editor Visions Art Quarterly; columnist Angeleno mag. Mem. faculty New Sch. for Social Rsch., 1974, Pratt Inst., 1975-76, Columbia U. Sch. Arts, 1978, Claremont Grad. Sch., 1989, 92-94, 95-97, U. Calif., Irvine, 1988-90, Calif. State U., Fullerton, 1990-91, U. Calif., Santa Barbara, 1994, Tyler Sch. Art; Am. curatorial advisor Documenta 8, 1986-87; organizer numerous theme and survey shows; co-curator "On Ramps: Moments of Transition in California Art", Pasadena Mus., California Art and "Fluxus Film and Video", Museo Reina Sofia, Madrid. Author: The Travelogues, 1982, Something Else Press: An Annotated Bibliography, 1983; co-author: New, Used and Improved: Art in the '80s, 1987; assoc. editor Tracks mag., 1974-76; editor Re Dact, 1983-85, contbg. editor Art Economist, 1981-84; contbr. articles to art periodicals including ARTnews and Art on Paper; writer on intermedia and Fluxus artists, many catalogues to one person and group exhbns.; edited Ken Friedman:Events for Jaap Rietmann, Inc. Nat. Endowment for Arts art critics travel fellow, 1978; critics project fellow, 1981; Royal Norwegian Ministry of Fgn. Affairs Fluxus rsch. fellow, 1987. Mem. Internat. Assn. Art Critics (v.p.), Coll. Art Assn., Internationale Künstlers Gremium Home: PO Box 24a36 Los Angeles CA 90024-1036

FRANKLE, DIANE HOLT, lawyer; BA, Coll. of Wooster, 1975; JD magna cum laude, Georgetown Univ., 1979. Bar: DC 1979, Md. 1980, Calif. 1985. Law clk. Judge R. Dorsey Watkins, US Dist Ct. (Md. Dist.), 1979—81; assoc. Ginsburg, Feldman & Bress, Washington, 1981—84; ptnr., co-chmn., mergers and acquisitions practice group DLA Piper Rudnick Gray Cary, East Palo Alto, Calif. Faculty mem. ABA Nat. Inst., 1997—, Practising Law Inst., 1995—. Editor (in chief): Guide to Calif. Securities Law Practice, 2004; contbr. articles to profl. jours. Mem. adv. bd. Corp. Counsel Inst., Georgetown Univ., 2003—04; mem. Cmty. Working group, Opportunity Ctr., Palo Alto, Calif. Named a No. Calif. Super Lawyer, San Francisco mag. Mem.: ABA (co-chmn. task force on pub. co. acquisitions 1995—, com. corp. laws, com. negotiated acquisitions), State Bar Calif., Phi Beta Kappa. Office: DLA Piper Rudnick Gray Cary 2000 University Ave East Palo Alto CA 94303 Office Phone: 650-833-2026. Office Fax: 650-833-2001. Business E-Mail: diane.frankle@dlapiper.com.

FRANKLIN, EVE, state legislator; b. NY, Aug. 14, 1954; m to Les Nilson. Montana State Senator, District 17, 1991-94, District 21, 1995-2002, Minority Whip, 1997-2002, Montana State Senate; Montana State Representative, District 42, 2003-05, District 24, 2005-, Montana House Representative.Nurse & educator, currently. Democrat. Address: PO Box 6057 Great Falls MT 59406-6507 Mailing: State Capitol PO Box 201706 Helena MT 59620-1702 Office Phone: 406-761-6815.

FRANKLIN, GENE FARTHING, engineering educator, consultant; b. Banner Elk, NC, July 25, 1927; s. Burnie D. and Delia (Farthing) F.; m. Gertrude Stritch, Jan. 1952; children: David M., Carole Lea. BSEE, Ga. Inst. Tech., 1950; MSEE, MIT, 1952; DEngSc, Columbia U., 1955. Asst. prof. Columbia U., NYC, 1955-57; prof. elec. engrng. Stanford (Calif.) U., 1957-95, prof. emeritus, 1995—. Cons. IBM, Rochester, Minn., 1982-94. Author: Sampled-Data Control, 1958, Digital Control, 1980, 3d edit., 1997, Feedback Control, 1986, 5th edit., 2006. With USN, 1945—47. Recipient Edn. award Am. Automatic Control Coun., 1985, Bellman Award, 2005. Fellow IEEE (life), Control Soc. of IEEE (Bode lectr. 1994). Democrat. Avocations: travel, writing. Office: Stanford U Dept Elec Engring 252 Packard Bldg Stanford CA 94305 Business E-Mail: franklin@ee.stanford.edu.

FRANKLIN, JOEL NICHOLAS, mathematician, educator; b. Chgo., Apr. 4, 1930; m. Patricia Anne; 1 dau., Sarah Jane. BS, Stanford, 1950, PhD, 1953. Research asso. N.Y. U., 1953-55; asst. prof. math. U. Wash, 1955; mem. faculty Calif. Inst. Tech., 1957—, prof. applied sci., 1966-69, prof. applied math., 1969—. Author: Matrix Theory, 1968, Methods of Mathematical Economics, 1980, also articles. Mem. Am. Math. Soc., Soc. Indsl. and Applied Math., Phi Beta Kappa. Home: 1763 Alta Crest Dr Altadena CA 91001-2130 Office: Calif Inst Tech 217 50 Pasadena CA 91125-0001

FRANKLIN, MARC ADAM, law educator; b. Bklyn., Mar. 9, 1932; s. Louis A. and Rose (Rosenthal) Franklin; m. Ruth E. Korzenik, June 29, 1958 (dec. Dec. 2000); children: Jonathan, Alison. AB, Cornell U., 1953, LLB, 1956. Bar: N.Y. 1956. Assoc. Proskauer Rose Goetz & Mendelsohn, NYC, 1956-57; law clk to Hon. Carroll C. Hincks, New Haven, 1957-58; prof. law Stanford U., Calif., 1962-76, Frederick I. Richman prof. law, 1976—2001, emeritus, 2001—; prof. law Columbia U., 1959-62; law clk to to Earl Warren, U.S. Supreme Ct., Washington, 1958-59. Author: Biography of a Legal Dispute, 1968, Dynamics of American Law, 1968, Cases and Materials on Tort Law and Alternatives, 1971; co-author (with R.L. Rabin and M.D. Green): 8th edit., 2006; author: Mass Media Law, 1977; co-author (with D.A. Anderson and L.C.B. Lidsky): 7th edit., 2005; author: The First Amendment and the Fourth Estate, 1977; co-author (with T.B. Carter and J.B. Wright): The First Amendment and the Fourth Estate, 9th edit., 2005; author: The First Amendment and the Fifth Estate, 1986; co-author (with T.B. Carter and J.B. Wright): The First Amendment and the Fifth Estate, 7th edit., 2008. Fellow Ctr. for Advanced Study in Behavioral Scis., 1968—69; scholar Fulbright, Victoria U., 1973. Office: Stanford U Law Sch Nathan Abbott Way Stanford CA 94305 Home: 1001 NW Lovejoy St Unit 1001 Portland OR 97209 Business E-Mail: marcf@stanford.edu.

FRANKLIN, MICHAEL HAROLD, arbitrator, lawyer, consultant; b. LA, Dec. 25, 1923; m. Betty Chernow, 1989; children from previous marriage: Barbara, John, James, Robert. AB, UCLA, 1948; LL.B., U. So. Calif., 1951. Bar: Calif. 1951. Practiced in, Los Angeles, 1951-52; pvt. practice, 1951-52; atty. CBS, 1952-54, Paramount Pictures Corp., 1954-58; exec. dir. Writers Guild Am. West, Inc., 1958-78; nat. exec. dir. Dirs. Guild Am., Inc., 1978-88. Mem. Fed. Cable Adv. Commn. Served with C.E. AUS, 1942-46. Mem. Order of Coif.

FRANKLIN, ROSA, state legislator; m. to James; children: three, three grandchildren. Washington State Representative, District 29, 91-92; Washington State Senator, District 29, 93-, President Pro Tempore, currently, vchairwoman, Labor & Workforce Develop Committee, currently, member, Health & Long Terme Care, Human Serv & Corrections & Rules Committees, currently, vpresPro Tempore, formerly, Democratic Whip, 97, Minority Whip, 98, Washington State Senate.Registered nurse, 42 years. Thurgood Marshall Award; Outstanding Non Vet, 95; Ever Active Tribute to Excellence Award, 95. Pierce Co Nurses Association; League Women Voters; Urban League; Women in Govt; NAACP; Safe Streets; S End Neighborhood for Family Safety; AHEC. Democrat. Baptist. Address: Tacoma WA Mailing: State Senate 312 Legislative Bldg PO Box 40429 Olympia WA 98504-0482 Office Phone: 360-786-7656. Fax: 360-786-7524. E-mail: franklin_ro@leg.wa.gov.

FRANKLIN, WILLIAM EMERY, international business educator; b. Sedalia, Mo., Apr. 6, 1933; s. Russell George and Edith Mae (Van Dyke) Franklin; m. Beverly Jean Feig, Mar. 25, 1933 (div. 1963); children: Stephen, Julia, Angela. BS in Bus., U. Mo., 1954; postgrad., Harvard U., 1982. With forestry ops. Weyerhaeuser Co., Longview, Wash., 1954; pres. Weyerhaeuser Far East Ltd., Hong Kong, 1980-96, Franklin Internat., Ltd., Seattle, 1996—. Chmn. Weyerhaeuser China Ltd.; pres. Weyerhaeuser Korea; mem. U.S.-Japan Bus. Coun., Pacific Basin Econ. Coun.; bd. dirs. NCR Japan Ltd.; mem. Eisenhower Fellowship Com., adv. com. on investment and devel. U.S. Dept. State; past chmn. forestry working group industry coop. program of UN-FAO, com. on internat. trade U.S. Dept. Commerce; adj. prof. U. Puget Sound, Am. Grad. Sch. Internat. Mgmt.; guest lectr. U. Internat. Bus. Econs., Beijing, Columbia U., Internat. U. of Japan, Seattle U. Trustee Pacific N.W. Ballet; chmn. Far East Coun. Friends of Scouting. Mem. Am. C. of C. in Japan (pres.), Yomiuri Internat. Econ. Soc. (bd. dirs.), Coun. Fgn. Rels., World Affairs Coun., U.S.-Asian Bus. Coun., Fgn. Corrs. Club, Tokyo Lawn Tennis Club, Tokyo Club. Avocations: tennis, music, sailing. E-mail: franklininternational@msn.com.

FRANKS, TRENT, United States Representative from Arizona; b. Uravan, Colo., June 19, 1957; m. Josephine Franks, 1980. Student, Ottawa U. Mem. Ariz. Ho. Reps., 1985—87, vice-chmn. commerce com., chmn. sub-com. on child protection and family preservation, mem. human resources com., mem. agr. com., mem. judiciary com.; head Ariz. Govs. Office for Children, 1987; exec. dir. Ariz. Family Rsch. Inst.; pres. Strategic Consulting and Liberty Petroleum Corp.; mem. U.S. Congress from 2nd Ariz. dist., 2003—. Pres. Children's Hope Scholarship Assn.; active North Phoenix Bapt. Ch. Republican. Office: US Ho Reps 1237 Longworth House Office Bldg Washington DC 20515-0302 also: Ste 200 7121 W Bell Rd Glendale AZ 85308

FRANSE, R. NELSON, lawyer; b. Clovis, N.Mex, Feb. 5, 1961; s. Roy and Jerrie Lou Franse; m. M. Marie McCulloch; 1 child, Colson Brack. BS in U. Studies, U. N. Mex., 1984, JD, 1987. Bar: N. Mex. 1987, U.S. Dist. Ct., Dist. N. Mex. 1987, U.S. Ct. Appeals, tenth cir. 1987. Ptnr. Rodey, Dickason, Sloan, Akin & Robb PA, Albuquerque, leader profl. liability sect. Rep. to ABA, Law Student Div. U. N. Mex., 1985—87. Named one of best lawyers in Am., 2003—04. Mem.: Am. Bd. Liability Atty. (diplomat with spl. competence in area of legal profl. liability), Profl. Liability Underwriting Soc., State Bar N.Mex., ABA, Albuquerque Bar Assn. Baptist. Avocations: monday morning quarterbacking, Monday morning quarterbacking. Office: Rodey Dickason Sloan Akin & Robb PA 201 Third St NW Ste 2200 PO Box 1888 Albuquerque NM 87103 Office Phone: 505-765-5900. Business E-Mail: nfranse@rodey.com.

FRANZ, THOMAS R., computer company executive; b. Pa. B in Elec. Engring., Cornell U., 1980. Various positions and several divsns. Intel Corp., Folsom, Calif., 1980, Santa Clara, v.p., 1987—99, v.p., gen. mgr. applied computing products divsn., 1999, v.p., gen. mgr. comm. infrastructure group, 1999—. Office: Intel Corp 2200 Mission Coll Blvd Santa Clara CA 95052

FRANZKE, RICHARD ALBERT, lawyer; b. Lewistown, Mont., Mar. 7, 1935; s. Arthur A. and Senta (Clark) F.; divorced; children: Mark, Jean, Robert. BA in Polit. Sci., Willamette U., 1958, JD with honors, 1960. Bar: Oreg. 1960, U.S. Dist. Ct. Oreg., 1960, U.S. Supreme Ct., 1961. Ptnr. Stoel, Rives, Portland, 1960—. Bd. dirs., chmn. various coms. Assn. Gen. Contractors Am., Portland, 1972-79; mem. com. on legis. affairs Assn. Builders & Contractors, Portland, 1983—. Author: A Study of the Construct by Contract Issue, 1979. Mem. Gov.'s Task Force on Reform of Worker's Compensation, Salem, Oreg., 1980-81; atty. gen.'s com. on Pub. Contracting. Recipient SIR award Assn. Gen. Contractors, 1979, Nat. Winner Outstanding Oral Argument award U.S. Moot Ct., 1959. Mem. ABA (sect. pub. contract law), Oreg. Bar (law sch. liaison, com. on practice and procedure specialization), Multnomah County Bar Assn. Republican. Avocations: antique autos, antique furniture, boating. Home: 14980 SW 133rd Ave Tigard OR 97224-1646 Office: Stoel Rives 900 SW 5th Ave Ste 2300 Portland OR 97204-1229 E-mail: franzkehill@comcast.com.

FRASCA, ROBERT JOHN, architect; b. Niagara Falls, NY, May 10, 1933; s. John and Jean Marie (Delgross) F.; m. Marilyn Margaret Buys, Sept. 23, 1937; children: Jason Robert, Andrea Melina. BArch, U. Mich., 1957; M in City Planning, MIT, 1959. Registered architect, Oreg., Wash., Calif., N.Y., Ariz., Utah. Ptnr. in charge of design Zimmer Gunsul Frasca Partnership, Portland, Oreg., 1966—, chief exec. officer, 1979—. Design commn. U. Wash.; vis. prof. architecture U. Mich., U. Calif., Berkeley; design juror numerous nat., state and chpt. AIA awards programs. Prin. works include Justice Ctr., 1983, KOIN Ctr., 1985, Vollum Inst. for Advanced Biomed. Rsch., 1986, Oreg. Conv. Ctr., 1990, Oreg. Mus. of Sci. and Industry, 1992, Fred Hutchinson Cancer Rsch. Ctr., 1993; contbr. articles to profl. jours. and mags. Charter adv. bd. mem. Portland State U., 1987—; trustee Nat. Bldg. Mus., Washington; bd. dirs. Assn. for Portland Progress. Fellow AIA; mem. Arlington Club (Portland), Multnomah Athletic Club, Century Club (N.Y.). Clubs: Arlington (Portland), Multnomah Athletic. Office: Zimmer Gunsul Frasca 320 SW Oak St Ste 500 Portland OR 97204-2737

FRASER, BRENDAN, actor; b. Indpls., Dec. 3, 1968; s. Peter and Carol Fraser; m. Afton Smith, Sept. 27, 1998 (separated Dec. 2007); children: Griffin Arthur, Holden Fletcher, Leland Francis. BFA, Cornish Coll. Arts, Seattle. Actor: (films) Dogfight, 1991, Encino Man, 1992, School Ties, 1992, Twenty Bucks, 1993, Son in Law, 1993, Younger and Younger, 1993, With Honors, 1994, In the Army Now, 1994, Airheads, 1994, The Scout, 1994, The Passion of Darkly Noon, 1995, (voice only) Balto, 1995, Now and Then, 1995, Kids in the Hall: Brain Candy, 1996, Mrs. Winterbourne, 1996, Glory Daze, 1996, George of the Jungle, 1997, Still Breathing, 1998, Gods and Monsters, 1998, (voice only) Sinbad: Beyond the Veil of Mists, 1999, Ringside, 1999, Monkey Bone, 1999, Blast from the Past, 1999, The Mummy, 1999, Dudley Do-Right, 1999, Bedazzled, 2000, The Mummy Returns, 2001, The Quiet American, 2002, Looney Tunes: Back in Action, 2003, Revenge of the Mummy: The Ride, 2004, Crash, 2004 (recipient, Outstanding Performance by a Cast in a Motion Picture, 2006), (voice only) Beach Bunny, 2005, The Last Time, 2006, The Air I Breathe, 2007, Journey to the Center of the Earth, 2008, The Mummy: Tomb of the Dragon Emperor, 2008, Inkheart, 2008; actor, exec. prodr. (films) Journey 3-D, 2008; actor: (TV films) My Old School, 1991, Child of Darkness, Child of Light, 1991, Guilty Until Proven Innocent, 1991, Journey to the End of the

Night, 2006, (TV appearances) Fallen Angels, 1995, Scrubs, 2002, 2004, (voice only) The Simpsons, 1998, King of the Hill, 2000, 2005. Office: William Morris Agy 151 El Camino Dr Beverly Hills CA 90212

FRASER, BRUCE DOUGLAS, JR., architect, artist; b. Corvallis, Oreg., Dec. 1, 1948; s. Bruce Douglas and Betty Adele (Lively) F.; m. Laura Jane Wells, June 18, 1972. BArch, Calif. Poly. State U., 1972. Registered architect, Calif. Artist, illustrator Hopkins Assocs., San Luis Obispo, Calif., 1972-73; planner U.S. Peace Corps, Mashhad, Iran, 1973-75; mem. archtl. staff Meyer-Merriam Assocs., San Luis Obispo, 1975-77; prin. MDW Assocs., San Luis Obispo, 1977-85, Merriam-Fraser Architecture and Planning, San Luis Obispo, 1985-87, Archtl. Office Bruce Fraser, San Luis Obispo, 1987—. Chair Bldg. Appeals Bd., Pismo Beach, Calif., 1990, Planning Commn., Pismo Beach, 1991-92, vice chair, 1990. Recipient various design awards Obispo Beautiful Assn., 1977—, Downtown Assn., 1990—. Mem. AIA (v.p. Calif. Ctrl. Coast chpt. 1985, pres. 1986). Office: Archtl Office of Bruce Fraser AIA 971 Osos St San Luis Obispo CA 93401-3212

FRASER, KAREN, state legislator; b. Seattle, Sept. 12, 1944; m to Tim Malone; children: Hiromi. City councilwoman, Lacey, 73-80; mayor, Lacey, Washington, 76-80; commissioner, Thurston County, Washington, 81-88; president, Washington State Association of Counties, formerly; legislation liaison for three state agencies, formerly; Washington State Representative, District 22, formerly; Washington State Senator, District 22, 93-, co-chairwoman, Legislature Int Caucus, currently, chairwoman, Environ Qual & Water Resources Committee, currently, member, Technology & Telecommunications & Ways & Means Committees, currently, Washington State Senate; member, Coun State Govt & Coun River Governance, 98-; board member, Washington Wildlife & Recreation Coalition, 98- & Olympic Trials Legacy Committee, 98-. Legislator of Year, Washington Fedn State Employees, 93; Silver Beaver Award, Boy Scouts; Outstanding Leadership Award, Washington State Boating Safety Officers Association, 93; Toll Fellow, Coun State Govt, 93; Woman of Distinction, Girl Scouts, 95; Legislator of Year, People for Puget Sound, 95; Legislator of Year, Washington Health Care Association, 96; Cert Appreciation, Washington Fedn State Employees, 98; Distinguished Leadership Recognition, Association Washington Housing Authorities, 98; Prog Leadership Award, Nisqually River Management Prog, 98; Legislature Citation Merit, Washington Recreation & Parks Association, 98. Democrat. Office: State Senate 404 Legislative Bldg PO Box 40422 Olympia WA 98504 Fax: 360-786-7450. E-mail: fraser_ka@leg.wa.gov.

FRASER, KATHLEEN JOY, poet, creative writing professor; b. Tulsa, Mar. 22, 1935; d. James Ian and Marjorie Joy (Axtell) F.; m. Jack Marshall, July 10, 1960 (div. 1970); 1 child, David Ian; m. Arthur Kalmer Bierman, June 30, 1984 BA in English Lit., Occidental Coll., 1958; doctoral equivalency, San Francisco State U., 1976. Vis. prof. writing, lectr. in poetry The Writer's Workshop, U. Iowa, Iowa City, 1969-71; writer in residence Reed Coll., Portland, Oreg., 1971-72; dir. Poetry Center San Francisco State U., 1972-75, prof. creative writing, 1972-92. Founder-dir. Am. Poetry Archives, San Francisco, 1973-75; founder-editor How(ever), Jour. for poets/scholars interested in modernism and women's innovative writing, 1983-91. Author: (children's book) Stilts, Somersaults and Headstands, 1967; (poetry) What I Want (New and Selected Poems), 1974, New Shoes, 1978, Something (even human voices in the foreground) A Lake, 1984, Notes Preceding Trust, 1988, When New Time Folds Up, 1993, Il Cuore: The Heart, Selected Poems 1970-95, 1997, Discrete Categories Forced Into Coupling, 2004, (essays) Translating the Unspeakable: Poetry and the Innovative Necessity, 2000. Recipient Frank O'Hara Poetry prize, 1964; Nat. Endowment for Arts fellow, 1978, Guggenheim fellow, 1981.

FRASIER, S. DOUGLAS, medical educator; b. LA, Nov. 29, 1932; m. Robin D'Arvin; children: Karen Lynn, Eric Marc, Sara Leslie. BA, U. Calif., LA, 1953; MD with highest honors, U. Calif., 1958. Diplomate Am. Bd. Pediatrics (chair sub-bd. endocrinology, 1997-98). Intern in pediat. Strong Meml. Rochester (N.Y.) Mcpl. Hosps., 1958-59; asst. resident pediat. U. Calif. Hosps., LA, 1959-61; postdoc. trainee U. Calif., LA, 1963-65; from asst. prof. to prof. pediat. U. So. Calif. Sch. Medicine, LA, 1965-86; prof. pediat. UCLA Sch. Medicine, LA, 1986—. Attending physician Children's Mercy Hosp., Kansas City, Mo., 1962-63, L.A. county-Harbor Gen. Hosp., Torrance, Calif., 1965-67; endocrine cons. Pacific State Hosp., Pomona, Calif., 1965-69, tng. cons., 1965-70; med. adv. Human Growth Found. L.A. Chpt., 1967-74, chmn. adv. com., 1967-72, co-chmn. rsch. com., 1972-75; med. adv. bd. Nat. Pituitary Agy., 1971-74; chief divsn. pediat. endocrinology, L.A. County-U. So. Calif. Med. Ctr., 1967-86, physician, 1967-86, dir. pediat. endocrine and diabetic clinics., 1967-72; exec. asst. Calif. Student Health Project, L.A., 1967-68, faculty dir., 1968-69; coord. curriculum U. So. Calif. Sch. Medicine, L.A., 1969-76, assoc. dean student affairs, 1970-76, vice-chair dept. pediat., 1986—; assoc. attending physician divsn. endocrinology/metabolism children's Hosp. L.A., 1976-79, cons., 1979-82; cons. Calbiochem Corp., 1969-78, Hoechst-Roussel Pharmaceutical Corp., 1978-79, maternal and child health br. genetics disease sect. Calif. Dept. Health Scis., 1978—, Soreno Labs., Inc., 1979-94, growth hormone program Can. Med. Rsch. Coun., 1981, program on drugs AMA, 1985; endocrine cons. Lanterman State Hosp., Pomona, 1980-82; chief pediat. Olive View-UCLA Med. Ctr., Sylmar, Calif., 1986—; mem. med. staff UCLA Med. Ctr., L.A., 1986—; vis. lectr. Milwaukee Children's Hosp., 1977; vis. prof. U. Ariz. Sch. Medicine, 1978, Kapiolani/Children's Med. Ctr., Honolulu, 1983, U. Montreal/Hosp. Sainte-Justine, 1988, Australasian Pediat. Endocrine Group, 1990, Tripler Army Hosp., Honolulu, 1993; mem., chmn. various other hosp. coms. Mem. editl. bd. Jour. Pediat. Endocrinology; rev. Pediats., Jour. Pediats., Jour. Clin. Endocrinology and Metabolism, Am. Jour. Diseases Children, Pediat. Rsch., Med. Letter, Metabolism, Endocrine Revs. Capt. U.S. Army Med. Corps, 1961-63. Fellow U. Calif. Sch. Medicine, L.A., 1955-56, Cecil E. Vesy scholar, 1956-58; recipient Sheard-Sanford prize Am. Soc. Clin. Pathologists, 1958. Mem. L.A. Pediat. Soc., Am. Acad. Pediat., Western Soc. Pediat. Rsch. (chmn. nominating com. 1975-76), Endocrine Soc., Lawson Wilkins Pediat. Endocrine Soc. (membership com. 1971-74, chmn. membership com. 1973-74, dir. 1978-82, ad hoc com. uses human growth hormone 1981-87, 88-90, pres.-elect 1988-89, chmn. awards com. 1988—, pres. 1989-90, past pres. 1990-91, chmn. drug and therapeutic com., 1990-94), Soc. Pediat. Rsch., Am. Pediat. Soc. Home: 10428 Lorenzo Pl Los Angeles CA 90064-4449 Office: UCLA-Ssch of Med Dept Pediatrics/Endocrin 10833 Le Conte Ave Los Angeles CA 90095-3075

FRASURE, EVAN S., state legislator; b. Pocatello, Idaho, Mar. 20, 1951; m. Analyn Frasure; children: Kent, Evan, Lena, Jessica. BA in Edn., Idaho State U. Grocery store owner, 1981-83; real estate broker, mgr. Coldwell Banker, 1983-87; exec. dir. Melaleuca, Inc., 1987—; elected rep. Idaho Ho. of Reps., Boise, 1990-92; mem. Idaho Senate, Dist. 34, Boise, 1992—. Chair transp. com., mem. local govt. and tax., fin., and resources and environment coms.; vice chair, energy and transp. com., Nat. Conf. State Legislators. Mem. Am. Legis. Exch. Coun. Republican. Mem. Lds Ch. Office: State Capitol PO Box 83720 Boise ID 83720-3720

FRAUENFELDER, MARK, editor-in-chief, blogger, illustrator; m. Carla Sinclair; 2 children. Editor-in-chief Make Mag.; co-founder boING boING Mag. Creator, blogger Boing Boing; editor: Wired, 1993—98; columnist Wired, Playboy mag., NY Times Mag.; co-editor: The Happy Mutant Handbook, 1995; author: The Mad Professor, 2002, Rule The Web: How To Do Anything And Everything on the Internet-Better, Faster, Easier, 2007; design columnist Mobile PC; contbg. editor: TheFeature. Named one of Top 25 Web Celebs, Forbes mag., 2007. Business E-Mail: mark@boingboing.net, markf@oreilly.com.

FRAUNFELDER, FREDERICK THEODORE, ophthalmologist, educator; b. Pasadena, Calif., Aug. 16, 1934; s. Reinhart and Freida Fraunfelder; m. Yvonne Marie Halliday, June 21, 1959; children—Yvette Marie, Helene, Nina, Frederick, Nicholas. BS, U. Oreg., 1956, MD, 1960, postgrad. (NIH postdoctoral fellow), 1962. Diplomate Am. Bd. Ophthalmology (bd. dirs. 1982-90). Intern U. Chgo., 1961; resident U. Oreg. Med. Sch., 1964-66; NIH postdoctoral fellow Wilmer Eye Inst., Johns Hopkins U., 1967; chmn. dept. ophthalmology U. Ark. Health Scis. Ctr., 78-98, prof., 1978—; prof., chmn. dept. ophthalmology Oreg. Health Scis. U. Dir. Casey Eye Inst., 1992-98, Nat. Registry Drug-Induced Ocular Side Effects, 1976—; vis. prof. ophthalmology Moorfields Eye Hosp., London, 1974. Author: Drug-Induced Ocular Side Effects and Drug Interactions, 1976, 6th edit., 2008, Current Ocular Therapy, 1985, 6th edit., 2008, Recent Advances in Ophthalmology, 8th edit., 1985; assoc. editor: Retirement Rx, 2008, Clin. Ocular Toxicology, 2008, Retire Right, 2009, Jour. Toxicology: Cutaneous and Ocular, 1984-2002; mem. editl. bd. Am. Jour. Ophthalmology, 1982-92, Ophthalmic Forum, 1983-90, Ophthalmology, 1984-89; contbr. over 200 articles on ocular toxicology or ocular cancer to med. jours. Served with U.S. Army, 1962-64. FDA grantee, 1976-86; Nat. Eye Inst. grantee, 1970-87; named Best Doc. in Am., 2005 Mem. AMA, ACS, Am. Acad. Ophthaolmology, Assn. Univ. Profs. in Ophthalmology (pres. 1976), Am. Ophthalmol. Soc., Am. Coll. Cryosurgery (pres. 1977), Assn. Research in Ophthalmology. Clubs: Lions, Elks. Home: 13 Cellini Ct Lake Oswego OR 97035-1307 Office: Casey Eye Inst 3375 SW Terwilliger Blvd Portland OR 97239-4197 Home Phone: 503-636-7229; Office Phone: 503-494-5686. Business E-Mail: fraunfel@ohsu.edu.

FRAUTSCHI, STEVEN CLARK, physicist, researcher; b. Madison, Wis., Dec. 6, 1933; s. Lowell Emil and Grace (Clark) F.; m. Mie Okamura, Feb. 16, 1967; children: Laura, Jennifer. BA, Harvard U., 1954; PhD, Stanford U., 1958. Rsch. fellow Kyoto (Japan) U., 1958-59, U. Calif.-Berkeley, 1959-61; mem. faculty Cornell U., 1961-62, Calif. Inst. Tech., Pasadena, 1962—, prof. theoretical physics, 1966—2006, exec. officer physics, 1988-97, master student houses, 1997—2002, prof. emeritus, 2006—. Vis. prof. U. Paris, Orsay, 1977-78, Pohang U. Sci. and Tech., Republic of Korea, 2007. Author: Regge Poles and S-Matrix Theory, 1963, The Mechanical Universe, 1986. Guggenheim fellow, 1971-72. Mem. Am. Phys. Soc. Achievements include research and publications on Regge poles, bootstrap theory, cosmology. Home: 1561 Crest Dr Altadena CA 91001-1838 Office: 1201 E California Blvd Pasadena CA 91125-0001

FRAZIER, G. REX, real estate executive; Grad., U. Utah. CPA, Utah. Audit supr. Touche Ross & Co.; dir. fin. Fairfax, v.p. fin., exec. v.p., pres., COO, 1986—; pres., COO, JP Realty Inc., Salt Lake City, 1993—, also bd. dirs. Office: Jp Realty 230 E South Temple Salt Lake City UT 84111-1205

FRÉCHET, JEAN, chemistry professor; came to U.S., 1967; 2 children. MSc, SUNY, Syracuse, 1969, PhD, 1971, Syracuse U., 1971; Doctorate (hon.), U. Lyon, 2002, U. Ottawa, 2004. Asst. prof. chemistry U. Ottawa, Canada, 1973-78, assoc. prof. chemistry, 1978-82, prof. chemistry, 1982-87; IBM prof. chemistry Cornell U., Ithaca, NY, 1987-95, P.J. Debye chair chemistry, 1996—98; prof. chemistry U. Calif., Berkeley, 1996—, H. Rapoport chair organic chemistry, 2003—; head materials synthesis Lawrence Berkeley Nat. Lab., 1999—. Vis. scientist IBM Rsch. Lab., San Jose, Calif., 1979, 83; vice dean grad. studies and rsch. U. Ottawa, 1983-87; cons. Kodak, 1997-05, Xenoport, 2000—, Intermolecular, 2005-, Nanomix, 2006-, ICI, 2004-; bd. dirs. Ont. Ctr. for Materials Rsch., Toronto, Dendritic Nanotechnologies, Inc, NOVOMER, NTERYX. Contbr. numerous articles to profl. jours.; patentee in field. Recipient Internat. Union Pure and Applied Chemistry award, 1983, Polymer Soc. Japan, 1986, A.K. Doolittle award, 1986, Coop. Rsch. award Am. Chem. Soc., 1994, Applied Polymer Chem. award Am. Chem. Soc., 1996, 00, Kosar Meml. award Soc. Imaging Sci. Tech., 1999, Salute to Excellence award Am. Chem. Soc., 2001, Esselen award chemistry pub. svc., 2005, medal Macro Group UK, 2006, Arthur C. Cope award, Am. Chem. Soc., 2007; A.C. Cope scholar Am. Chem. Soc., 2001; numerous rsch. grants. Fellow AAAS; mem. NAS, NAE, Am. Acad. Arts and Scis. Avocation: oenophile. Office: U Calif Coll Chemistry 718 Latimer Berkeley CA 94720-1460 Home Phone: 510-594-1573; Office Phone: 510-643-3077.

FREDERICK, DOLLIVER H., investment banker; b. Edmonton, Alta, Can., Apr. 2, 1944; m. Joan B. Dickau. Student, Alta Coll., U. Alta; No. Alta Inst. Tech., 1965. With Imperial Oil Ltd., Edmonton, 1965-72; sr. analyst mktg. Toronto, Canada, 1972—73; corp. devel. mgr. Hees Internat. (formerly Bovis Corp. Ltd.), 1973-75, copr. v.p., 1975-79; pres., chief operating officer Gen. Supply Co. Ltd., Canada, 1975—79, Equipment Fed. Que. Ltd., 1975-79; pres. CEO, dir. CanWest Investment Corp., Toronto, Ont., 1979-81; chmn. exec. com., dir. Na-Churs Plant Food Co., Marion, Ohio, 1979-81, Macleod-Stedman, Inc., Winnipeg and Toronto, 1980-81; chmn., pres. CEO, dir. Cochran-Dunlop Lt., 1982-87, Frederick Capital Corp. Inc., Canada, 1981—; pres., CEO, dir. Comterm Inc., 1989-90, Electrohome Ltd., 1985-87. Mem. Can. Coun. Christians and Jews, dir. the Nat. Conf., 1997—. Mem. Engineers Club of Toronto, Assn. Corp. Growth, World Pres.'s Orgn., CChief Executive Org., Nat., Can. Club N.Y., Pacific Club. Republican. Office: Frederick Capital Corp 5000 Birch St Ste 3000 Newport Beach CA 92660-2140 Office Phone: 949-476-3720. Office Fax: 949-476-3683. Business E-Mail: dhfrederick@frederickcapital.com.

FREDERICK, TILLIAN, casting director; b. 1975; d. Jude and Charles Jameson; m. Albert Frederick. BA in Drama, U. Ariz., 1997, MA in Drama Edn., 1999. Asst. dir. U. Ariz. Drama Student Theater, 1995—97; adj. prof. U. Ariz. Drama Dept., 1998—2004; jr. dir. Meriks Drama Ctr, 1999—2003, dir., 2004—06, sr. casting dir., 2007—. Actress Sunlight Theater, 2000—. Author: Drama Free Theater, 2000; dir.: (plays) The Life & Times of Melinda, 2004, The Night at the Diner, 2006. Mem. Raise Your Voice, 2004—. Office: Meriks Drama Ctr 2509 N Campbell St #311 Tucson AZ 85719

FREDERICKS, DALE EDWARD, communications company executive; b. Springfield, Ill., Mar. 12, 1943; m. Jean Schmidt, June 8, 1968; children: Michael J., Amy C. BS with honors, Bradley U., 1965; JD, U. Ill., 1968. Bar: D.C. 1969, Calif. 1971, U.S. Supreme Ct. 1978. Gen. counsel Summit Fidelity and Surety Co., Minneapolis, 1988-93, Hampton Ct. Holdings, Inc., San Francisco, 1989-93; ptnr. Sheppard, Mullin, Richter & Hampton, 1991-96, mng. ptnr. San Francisco office, 1993-95; CEO C5 Comm. LLC, Incline Village, Nev., 1999—. Pres. Sangamon Properties Co., Incline Village, Nev., Sangamon Devel. Co., Sangamon Energy Co., Lafayette, Calif. Capt. USMCR, 1968-72. Mem. ABA (antitrust law and litigation sects.), Calif. Bar Assn., San Francisco Bar Assn., Internat. Bar Assn., World Trace Club. Republican. Avocations: golf, real estate.

FREDERICKS, PATRICIA ANN, real estate executive; b. Durand, Mich., June 5, 1941; d. Willis Edward and Dorothy (Plowman) Sexton; m. Ward Arthur Fredericks, June 12, 1960; children: Corrine Ellen, Lorraine Lee, Ward Arthur II. BA, Mich. State U., 1962; cert. mediator, U. Calif., 1999. Cert. Grad. Real Estate Inst., residential broker, residential salesperson; cert. real estate broker. Assoc. Stand Brough, Des Moines, 1976-80; broker Denton, Tucson, 1980-83; broker-trainer Coldwell Banker, Westlake Village, Calif., 1984-90; broker, br. mgr. Brown, Newbury Park, Calif., 1990-94; dir. tng. Brown Real Estate, Westlake Village, Calif., 1994-95; gen. mgr., dir. mktg. Coldwell Banker Town & Country Real Estate, Newbury Park, Calif., 1994—; dir. mktg. Coldwell Banker Town and Country, 1995—2004; broker mgr. First Team Becker & Becker, 2004—06; gen. mgr. First Team Real Estate, LaQuinta, Calif., 2004—06; dir., exec. devel. Realty Exec. Descent Cities, 2008. Bd. sec. Mixtec Corp., Thousand Oaks, Calif., 1984—; pres. Mixtec Real Estate Tng. Contbr. articles to profl. jours. Pres. Inner Wheel, Thousand Oaks, 1991, 96-97; bd. dir. Community Leaders Club, Thousand Oaks, 1991, Conejo Future Found., Thousand Oaks, 1989-92, Wellness Community Ventura Valley, 1994—. Mem. ABA, Calif. Assn. Realtors (dir. 1988-95 regional chair 1995, vice-chair expn. 1997, chair Calif. Expo 1998, presdl. liason officer 2004), Calif. Assn. Edn. (com. chair 2003), Conejo Valley Assn. Realtors (sec., v.p., pres.-elect 1989-92, pres. 1993, Realtor of Yr. 1991), Calif. Desert Assn. Realtors (bd. dir. 2003-, pres. 2005), Pres.'s Club Mich. State U., Com. 100, Cmty. Concerts Assn., Alliance for the Arts, Conejo Valley Symphony Guild, Wellness Cmty., Indian Wells Country Club, North Ranch Country Club, Sherwood Country Club, Aviation Country Club Calif., Jaquar Club N.Am. Personal E-mail: classybker@aol.com. Business E-Mail: patfredricks@yahoo.com.

FREDERICKS, WARD ARTHUR, venture capitalist; b. Tarrytown, NY, Dec. 24, 1939; s. Arthur George and Evelyn (Smith) F.; m. Patricia A. Sexton, June 12, 1960; children: Corrine E., Lorrine L., Ward A. BS cum laude, Mich. State U., 1962, MBA, 1963, PhD. Assoc. dir. Technics Group, Grand Rapids, Mich., 1964-68; gen. mgr. logistics systems Massey-Ferguson, Inc., Toronto, Ont., Canada, 1968-69, v.p. mgmt. svcs., comptr., 1969-73, sr. v.p. fin., dir. fin. Americas, 1975—; comptr. Massey-Ferguson Ltd., Toronto, Ont., Canada, 1973-75; prin. W.B. Saunders & Co., Washington, 1962—64; sr. v.p. mktg. Massey.Ferguson, Inc., 1975-78, also pres., gen. mgr. tractor divsn., 1978-80; gen. mgr. Rockwell Graphic Sys., 1980-82; pres. Goss Co., Chgo.; v.p. ops. Rockwell Internat., Pitts., 1980-84; v.p. Fed. MOG, 1983-84; chmn. MIXTEC Group LLC, 1998—2002; also dir., chmn.; prin. Venture Assocs., 1993—. Dir. Polyfet RF, Inc., Venture Assocs., Badger Horthland, Inc., MST, Inc., Calif., Tech-Mark Group, Inc., Spectra Tech., Inc., Mixtec Group-Venture Capital, Inc., Unicorn Corp., Mixtec Food Group Calif., Mixtec Signal Tech., Harry Ferguson, Inc., M.F. Credit Corp., M.F. Credit Co. Can Ltd.; chmn. ProduceCareers.com., 2000-02. Author: (with Edward Smykay) Physical Distribution Management, 1974; author: Management Vision, 1988, Competitive Advantage in Technology Organizations, 1986, Competitive Advantage in Technology Firms, 1996; contbr. articles to profl. jours. Bd. dirs., mem. exec. com. Des Moines Symphony, 1975-79; pres. Conejo Symphony, 1988-90, Westlake Village Cultural Found., 1991, Conejo Valley Indsl. Assn., 1990, 93, Aviation CC Calif., 2001, Indian Wells Desert Symphony, 2002, bd. dirs., 2001-02; mem. exec. com. Alliance for Arts, vice chair; mem. Constn. Bicentennial Com., 1987-88, Ventura County Airport Commn., 1995-99, La Quinta Arts Found.; mem. World Affairs Coun. of Desert, pres., 2001-06, chmn. 2006—; bd. dirs. Ventura County Bus. Incubator, 1996-99, Cochella Valley Cmty. Concerts Assn., 1992-95, Coll. The Desert Found., 2002—, chmn. investment com., 2004, v.p., 2006, pres., 2007-; v.p. Com. Leaders Club, 1988, pres., 1989-90; bd. regents Calif. Luth. U., 1990-99, chmn. acad. affairs, 1992-99, exec. com., 1992-99, vice chmn., 1997-98; pres. coun. McCallun Theater, Palm Desert; mem. Pres.'s circle Coll. of Desert, Palm Desert; mem. rep. ctrl. com. State Calif., 1993-98; pres. World Affairs Coun. of Desert, 2001-06, chmn., 2006; bd. dirs. Boys and Girls Club Coachella Valley, 2003-; pres. Fredericks Found., 2002—; chmn. Westlake Village C. of C., 1990; nat. councillor World Affairs Coun., Washington, 2004—, dir., 2006—; chair investment com. COD Found., 2002—, exec. com., 2005-, v.p., 2006, pres. 2007-. Fellow Am. Transp. Assn.; mem. AAAS, IEEE, SAR, Am. Mktg. Assn., Nat. Coun. Phys. Distbn. Mgmt. (exec. com. 1974), Produce Mktg. Assn., United Fresh Fruit and Vegetable Assn., Internat. Fresh-Cut Produce Assn., Soc. Automotive Engrs., US Strategic Inst., Tech. Execs. Forum (Tech. Corridor 100 award 1989), Internat. Food Mfg. Assn., Produce Mktg. Assn., Toronto Bd. Trade, English-Speaking Union (bd. dirs. 2004-06), Westlake Village C. of C. (chmn. 1990), Old Crows, Assn. Advanced Tech. Edn., Air Force Assn., Aerospace Soc., Exptl. Aircraft Assn., Mil. Order World Wars, Conf. Air Force (Col.), Westlake Village C. of C. (chmn. bd. 1990-91), Cmty. Leaders Club, Pres.'s Club Mich. State U., Pres.'s Circle/Coll. of the Desert, English-Spkg. Union, Friends of Parliament, Old Bold Pilots Club, Indian Wells Country Club, Sherwood Country Club, St. Georges Club (UK), Aviation Country Club of Calif. (v.p. 1999, pres. 2000), Sandstone Club (Vail, Colo.), Rotary (dir. 2003—), Flying Rotarians, World Affairs Coun. (nat. bd. dir. 2007-), Beta Gamma Sigma. Lutheran. Home: 75375 Painted Desert Dr Indian Wells CA 92210 Office: 709 E Colorado Blvd Pasadena CA 91101

FREDMANN, MARTIN, ballet company artistic director, educator, choreographer; b. Balt., Feb. 3, 1943; s. Martin Joseph and Hilda Adele (Miller) Fredmann; m. Kaleriya Fedicheva Fredmann (div. Jan. 2, 1978); m. Patricia Renzetti, June 12, 1980. Student, Nat. Ballet Sch., Washington DC, 1962-64, Vaganova Sch., Leningrad, 1972. Prin. dancer The Md. Ballet, Balt., 1961-64; dancer The Pa. Ballet, Phila., 1964-65, Ballet of the Met. Opera Co., NYC, 1965-66; prin. dancer Dortmund (Fed. Republic Germany) Ballet, 1973-75, Scapino Ballet, Amsterdam, Holland, 1975-76; tchr. German Opera Ballet, West Berlin, Germany, 1979—82, Netherlands Dance Theater, 1979, Royal Swedish Ballet, 1980, San Francisco Ballet, 1981; tchr., coach Australian Ballet, 1982; tchr. Tokyo City Ballet, Hong Kong Ballet, 1985, 86, 87, London Festival Ballet, 1981-83; dir. ballet Teatro Comunale, Florence, Italy, 1984-85; artistic dir. Tampa Ballet, Fla., 1984—90, Colo. Ballet, Denver, 1987—2005; assoc. prof. Taipei Nat. U. of Arts, 2007—. Tchr. German Opera Ballet, 1982, Ballet Rambert, London, 1983, Bat Dor summer course, Israel, 1983, Cullberg Ballet, Sweden, 1983, Hong Kong Acad. For Performing Arts, 1985—89, 1991, Tokyo City Ballet, 1985—90, Ballet West, 1990, Nat. Ballet Korea, 1991, Dance Divsn. Tsoying High Sch., Kaohsiung, Taiwan, 1992; guest lectr., tchr. Cen. Ballet China, Beijing Dancing Acad., P.L.A. Arts Coll., Beijing, 1990; tchr. Legat Sch., 1978, examiner, 80; tchr. Eglevsky Sch., NYC, 1980; asst. dir. ballet master Niavaron Cultural ctr., Tehran, Iran, 1978; tchr. Ballet Arts Sch. Carnegie Hall, NYC, 1979—81; choreographer Estonia Nat. Theatre, Russia, 1991; dir. Marin Ballet., Calif., 1981, Japan Grand Prix, 2003—. Choreographer Romeo and Juliet, 1983, Sachertorte, 1984, A Little Love, 1984, Ricordanza, 1986, Cinderella, 1986, Coppelia, 1987, The Nutcracker, 1987, Beauty and the Beast, 1988, Masquerade Suite, 1989, Silent Woods, 1989, The Last Songs, 1991, Centenial Suite, 1994. Recipient Recipient Mayor's award, Denver, 1996, Dance Mag. award, 1999, Bonfils-Stanton Found. award, 2000, Order of the Rising Sun, Gold Rays with Rosette, Govt of Japan, 2005. Mem.: Nat. Assn. Regional Ballet., Fla. State Dance Assn, Am. Guild Mus. Artists. Avocations: cooking, cook book collecting, travel, opera. Office: 836 E 17th Ave Apt 3A Denver CO 80218-1449 Home Phone: 303-837-9433; Office Phone: 303-837-9433.

FREDRICKSON, GLENN HAROLD, chemical engineering and materials educator; b. Washington, May 8, 1959; BS with honors in Chem. Engring., U. Fla., 1980; MS in Chem. Engring., Stanford U., Calif., 1981, PhD in Chem. Engring., 1984. Mem. tech. staff AT&T Bell Labs., Murray Hill, NJ, 1984-89, disting. mem. tech. staff, 1989-90; assoc. prof. dept. chem. engring. and engring. materials dept. U. Calif., Santa Barbara, 1990-91, dir. Macromolecular Sci. and Engring. Ctr., prof. dept. chem. engring. and engring. materials dept., 1991—, vice-chair chem. engring., 1996-98, chair chem. engring., 1998—2001, founding dir. Mitsubishi Chem. Ctr. Advanced Materials, 2001—, dir. Complex Fluids Design Consortium, 2002—, assoc. dir. Materials Rsch. Lab., 2004—, Mitsubishi chem. chair functional materials, 2004—. Allan P. Colburn lectr. U. Del., 1991; George T. Piercy disting prof. chem. engring. and materials sci. U. Minn., Mpls., 1992; vis. rsch. prof. Miller Inst. U. Calif., Berkeley, 1993; lectr. in field. Contbr. articles to sci. jours.; mem. editl. bd. Jour. Polymer Sci. physics edit., 1992—, Macromolecules, 1994-96; mem. internat. editl. adv. bd. Acta Polymerica, 1992—. Exxon Tchg. fellow Stanford U., 1982-84, Alfred P. Sloan Rsch. fellow, 1992; recipient Presdl. Young Investigator award NSF, 1990, Camille and Henry Dreyfus Tchr.-Scholar award, 1991. Fellow Am. Phys. Soc. (publs. com. 1992-94, John H. Dillon medal Divsn. High Polymer Physics 1992, Polymer Physics prize 2007), AIChE, 1999 (Alpha Chi Sigma award); mem. Phi Kappa Phi, NAE. Office: Mitsubishi Chem Ctr Advanced Materials U Calif 3105 MRL Bldg Santa Barbara CA 93106-5080 Office Phone: 805-893-8308. Office Fax: 805-893-8797. E-mail: ghf@mrl.ucsb.edu.

FREED, PETER QUENTIN, amusement park executive; b. Salt Lake City, Jan. 8, 1921; s. Lester David and Jasmine (Young) F.; children: David Wicker, Michael Stahle, Howard Eldred, Anne, Kristen, Jennifer. BA with hons., U. Utah, 1947. Pres. Freed Co., 1952-74; exec. v.p. Amusement Svc., Salt Lake City, 1947—. V.p. Terrace Co., Salt Lake City, from 1952; exec. v.p. Patio Gardens, Farmington, Utah, from 1956; v.p. Westworld Corp., Salt Lake City, from 1974, Pioneer Village Campground, Farmington, from 1975; dir. Pioneer Village, Farmington; pres. Lagoon Corp., Salt Lake City, 1974—. Mem. Union Sta. Theatre Bd. With USNR, 1942-45. Mem. Nat. Assn. Amusement Parks, Utah Mus. Assn., Salt Lake Tennis Club, New Yorker Club. Republican. Christian Scientist. Home: 642 Aloha Rd Salt Lake City UT 84103-3329 Office: Lagoon Theme Park 375 N Lagoon Dr Farmington UT 84025-2554

FREEDMAN, JONATHAN BORWICK, journalist, writer, educator; b. Rochester, NY, Apr. 11, 1950; s. Marshall Arthur and Betty (Borwick) F.; children: Madigan, Nicholas; m. Isabelle Rooney, 1999; children: Genevieve, Lincoln. AB in Lit. cum laude, Columbia Coll., NYC, 1972. Reporter AP of Brazil, Sao Paulo and Rio de Janeiro, 1974-75; editorial writer The Tribune, San Diego, 1981-90; syndicated columnist Copley News Service, San Diego, 1987-89; free-lance opinion writer L.A. Times, 1990—; free-lance editorial writer N.Y. Times, 1990-91; dir. Hope Lit. Project, 1998—. Dist. vis. lectr. and adj. faculty San Diego State U., 1990—; mem. U.S.-Japan Journalists Exch. Program, Internat. Press Inst., 1985. Author, illustrator: The Man Who'd Bounce the World, 1979; author: The Editorials and Essays of Jonathan Freedman, 1988, Wall of Fame, 2000; contbg. author: Best Newspaper Writing, From Contemporary Culture, 1991, (nonfiction) From Cradle to Grave: The Human Face of Poverty in America, 1993; freelance columnist, 1979-81; dir. (TV documentary) Pedaling Hope, 1998; contbr. articles to N.Y. Times, Chgo. Tribune, San Francisco Examiner, Oakland Tribune, others. Moderator PBS, San Diego, 1988; bd. dirs. Schs. of the Future Commn., San Diego, 1987. Recipient Copley Ring of Truth award, 1983, Sigma Delta Chi award, 1983, San Diego Press Club award, 1984, Spl. citation Columbia Grad. Sch. Journalism, 1985, Disting. Writing award Am. Soc. Newspaper Editors, 1986, Pulitzer prize in Disting. Editorial Writing, 1987; Cornell Woolrich Writing fellow Columbia U., 1972, Eugene C. Pullian Editorial Writing fellow Sigma Delta Chi Found., 1986, Media fellow Hoover Instn., Stanford, Calif., 1991, Kaiser Media fellow, 1995, Peacemaker award San Diego Mediation Ctr., 1999, one of 45 Am. Heroes, Esquire mag., 1998. Mem. Soc. Profl. Journalists (Disting. Svc. award 1985, Casey medal for meritorious journalism 1994), Nat. Conf. Editl. Writers, Authors Guild, Phi Beta Kappa. Jewish. Avocations: skiing, tai chi. Office: 755 Genter St La Jolla CA 92037-5459 Office Phone: 619-236-0991. Personal E-mail: jonathan_freedman@earthlink.net.

FREEDMAN, MARC, think-tank executive; b. 1958; married. Grad., Swarthmore Coll., Pa., 1980; MBA, Yale U., New Haven. V.p. Pub./Pvt. Ventures; co-founder Experience Corps; founder, CEO Civic Ventures, 1998—. Vis. fellow Kings Coll., U. London. Author: The Kindness of Strangers: Adult Mentors, Urban Youth, and the New Volunteerism, 1993, Prime Time: How Baby Boomers Will Revolutionize Retirement and Transform America, 1999, Encore: Finding Work That Matters in the Second Half of Life, 2007. Recipient Prime Mover award, Hunt Alternatives Fund, Maxwell A. Pollack award, Gerontol. Soc. Am., Jack Ossofsky award, Nat. Coun. Aging; named one of Nation's Leading Social Entrepreneurs, Fast Co. Mag.; Atlantic Fellowship in Pub. Policy, Ashoka Sr. Fellowship. Office: Civic Ventures 114 Sansome St Ste 850 San Francisco CA 94104 Office Phone: 415-222-7480. Business E-Mail: mfreedman@civicventures.org.

FREEDMAN, MICHAEL HARTLEY, mathematician, educator, researcher; b. LA, Apr. 21, 1951; s. Benedict and Nancy (Mars) Freedman; m. Leslie Blair Howland, Sept. 18, 1983; children: Hartley, Whitney, Jake. PhD, Princeton U., 1973. Lectr. U. Calif., Berkeley, 1973—75; faculty mem. Inst. Advanced Study, Princeton, NJ, 1980—81, mem., 1975—76; asst. prof. U. Calif., San Diego, 1976—79, assoc. prof., 1979—80, prof., 1982—85, Charles Lee Powell chair math., 1985—; sr. rsch. scientist Theory Group Microsoft Rsch., Microsoft Station Q, U. Calif., Santa Barbara, 1997—. Author: Classification of Four Dimensional Spaces, 1982; author: (assoc. editor) Jour. Differntial Geometry, Math. Rsch. Letters and Topology, 1982—, Annals of Math., 1984—91, Jour. Am. Math. Soc., 1987—. Recipient Veblen prize, Am. Math. Soc., 1986, Fields medal, Internat. Congress of Mathematicians, 1986, Nat. medal of Sci., 1987, Humboldt Award, 1994; named Calif. Scientist of Yr., Calif. Mus. Assn., 1984; fellow MacArthur Found., 1984—89, Guggenheim, 1989, 1994. Mem.: NAS, N.Y. Acad. Scis., Am. Assn. Arts and Scis. Avocation: rock climbing. Office: Univ Calif San Diego Dept Math 0112 9500 Gilman Dr La Jolla CA 92093-0112 also: Microsoft Station Q Elings Hall, Office 2243 U Calif Santa Barbara CA 93106 E-mail: mfreedman@ucsd.edu.

FREEDMAN, SARAH WARSHAUER, education educator; b. Wilmington, NC, Feb. 23, 1946; d. Samuel Edward and Miriam Warshauer; m. S. Robert Freedman, Aug. 20, 1967; 1 child, Rachel Karen. BA in English, U. Pa., 1967; MA in English, U. Chgo., 1970; MA in Linguistics, Stanford U., 1976, PhD in Edn., 1977. Tchr. English Phila. Sch. Dist., 1967-68, Lower Merion H.S., 1968-69; instr. English U. N.C., Wilmington, 1970-71; instr. English and linguistics Stanford U., 1972-76; asst. and assoc. prof. English San Francisco State U., 1977-81; asst. prof. edn. U. Calif., Berkeley, 1981-83, assoc. prof. edn., 1983-89, dir. Nat. Ctr for Study of Writing and Literacy, 1985-96, prof. edn., 1989—, sr. rschr. Human Rights Ctr., 2001—06. Resident Bellagio Conf. and Study Ctr., Rockefeller Found., 1997; mem. nat. task force Nat. Writing Project, 1998—. Author: Response to Student Writing, 1987, Exchanging Writing, Exchanging Cultures, Lessons in School Reform from the United States and Great Britain, 1994, (with E.R. Simons, J.S. Kalnin, A. Casareno and M-Class teams) Inside City Schools, Investigating Literacy in Multi-cultural Classrooms, 1999; editor: The Acquisition of Written Language: Response and Revision, 1985, (with A. Ball) Bakhtinian Perspectives on Language, Literacy, and Learning, 2004; contbr. chpts. to books and articles to profl. jours. Recipient Multicultural Book award Nat. Assn. Multicultural Edn., 2000, Alan Purves award, 2006; fellow Nat. Conf. Rsch. in English, 1986-, Ctr. Advanced Studies in Behavioral Scis., 1999-2000, 06-07; grantee Spencer Found. 1996-2003, Nat. Ctr. Study of Writing and Literacy, Office Edni. Rsch. and Improvement, 1985-95, Minority Undergrad. Rsch. Program U. Calif., 1988, 89, 92, 93, US Inst. Peace, 2003-06, numerous other grants. Mem. Nat. Coun. Tchrs. English (standing com. on rsch. 1981-87, ex-officio 1987-96, Richard Meade award for Pub. Rsch. in Tchr. Edn. 1989, 94, chair bd. trustees rsch. found. 1990-93, Ed Fry book award, 1996, 2000, co-chair rsch. assembly 1999-2001, chmn. 2003-06), Am. Ednl. Rsch. Assn. (chair spl. interest group on rsch. in writing 1983-85, numerous other coms.) Office: U Calif Dept Edn Berkeley CA 94720-0001

FREEDMAN, STANLEY MARVIN, manufacturing executive; b. Frederick, Md., Aug. 26, 1923; s. Jacob Menaham and Ethel (Freiman) F.; m. Lynn Maureen Katchen, Apr. 24, 1957 (dec.); children: Rita, Lynn, Michael, Richard, Jon, Jack; m. Lottie Carnell, Dec. 31, 1994 (div.); m. Barbara Lucking Aug. 27, 2007. Student, Georgetown U., 1944; AB in English, High Point Coll., 1946. Owner, operator retail bus., Bound Brook, N.J., 1949-63; dir. mktg. Franklin State Bank, Somerset, N.J., 1963-65; program dir. mktg. div. Am. Mgmt. Assn. N.Y.C., 1965-67; exec. dir. Internat. Bus. Forms Industries, Washington, 1967-69; dir. communications, dir. office machines group Bus. Equipment Mfrs. Assn., Washington, 1969-72; div. pres. Litton Industries, Hampton, Va., 1972-74, group v.p., paper, printing and forms group Virginia Beach, Va., 1974-86. Cons. bus. planning and devel; univ. lectr., 1986-91; dir. Somerset County Savs. & Loan; exec. in residence U. Wis. Grad. Sch. Bus., 1973; entrepreneur in residence U. of the Pacific, Stockton, Calif., 1996. Mem. Bound Brook Bd. Edn., 1955-63; trustee Raritan Valley Hosp., Somerset, N.J., 1960-62; chmn. Urban Devel., Bound Brook, N.J., 1963; mem. def. conversion team AID, Warsaw, Poland, 1995-96. Served with U.S. Army, 1943-46, PTO. Mem. Am. Mgmt. Assn. Home and Office: 7501 E Thompson Peak Pkwy Scottsdale AZ 85255 Personal E-mail: stanrlmrjj@msn.com, sfreedman2@cox.net.

FREEDMAN, STUART JAY, nuclear science educator; BS, U. Calif., Berkeley, 1965, MS, 1967, PhD, 1972. Rsch. asst. U. Calif., Berkeley, 1970-72, mem. faculty to Luis W. Alvarez Meml. Chair exptl. physics, 1991—; instr. Princeton U., NJ, 1972-75, lectr., 1975-76; asst. prof. Stanford U., Calif., 1976-82; staff physicist Argonne Nat. Lab., Ill., 1982-87, sr. physicist, 1987-91, sr. scientist, 1991—; prof. U. Chgo. Enrico Fermi Inst., 1987-91; sr. scientist U. Calif. Berkeley/Lawrence Berkeley Nat. Lab., Calif., 1991—. Contbr. articles to profl. jours. Recipient Kraft award, 1962, T.W. Bonner prize in nuc. physics, 2007; NDEA fellow, 1965—69, Sloan Found. fellow, 1978—82. Fellow: AAAS, Am. Acad. Arts and Scis., Am. Phys. Soc. (Tom W. Bonner prize in Nuc. Physics 2007); mem.: Nat. Acad. Sci., Tau Beta Pi, Phi Beta Kappa. Office: Dept Physics U Calif Berkeley 366 LeConte Hall Berkeley CA 94720-7300 Office Phone: 510-486-7850. E-mail: sjfreedman@lbl.gov.

FREEDMAN, WENDY LAUREL, astronomer, educator, director; b. Toronto, Ont., Can., July 17, 1957; arrived in US, 1984, naturalized, 1998; d. Harvey Bernard and Sonya Lynn Freedman; m. Barry F. Madore, June 23, 1985; children: Rachael, Daniel. BSc, U. Toronto, 1979, MSc, 1980, PhD in Astronomy and Astrophysics, 1984. Fellow Observatories of Carnegie Instn., Pasadena, Calif., 1984-87, staff mem., 1987—, Crawford H. Greenewalt chair dir., 2003—. Mem. Astronomy and Astrophysics adv. com., 2005—. Contbr. articles to sci. jours. Recipient Marc Aaronson Lectureship and prize, 1994, John P. McGovern award, 2000, Helen Sawyer Hogg award, 2000. Fellow Am. Acad. Arts & Scis.; mem. Am Philos. Soc. (Megellanic Premium award 2002), Am. Astron. Soc., Am. Phys. Soc., Can. Astron. Soc., Astron. Soc. of the Pacific, NAS. Office: Observatories of Carnegie Inst 813 Santa Barbara St Pasadena CA 91101 Office Phone: 626-577-1122, 626-304-0204. Business E-Mail: wendy@ociw.edu.

FREEHLING, ALLEN ISAAC, rabbi; b. Chgo., Jan. 8, 1932; s. Jerome Edward and Marion Ruth (Wilson) F.; m. Lori Golden; children: Shira Freehling Cramer, David Matthew, Jonathan Andrew. Student, U. Ala., 1949-51; AB, U. Miami, Fla., 1953; B of Hebrew Letters, Hebrew Union Coll., 1965, MA, 1967, DD (hon.), 1992. Ordained rabbi, 1967. Asst. to pres. Stylaneze, Inc., 1953-54, Univ. Miami, 1954-56; exec. dir. Temple Israel, Miami, 1956-57; asst. to pres. Stevens Markets, Inc., 1957-59; acct. exec. Hank Meyer Assocs., 1959-60; exec. dir. Temple Emanu-El, Miami Beach, Fla., 1960-62; assoc. rabbi The Temple, Toledo, 1967-72; sr. rabbi Univ. Synagogue, LA, 1972—2002, rabbi emeritus, 2002—; exec. dir. City L.A. Human Rels. Commn., 2002—. Adj. prof. Loyola-Marymount U., St. Mary's Coll.; v.p. Westside Ecumenical Coun., 1979-81; v.p. Bd. Rabbis of So. Calif., 1981-85, pres., 1985-87; mem. com. on rabbinic growth Cen. Conf. Am. Rabbis; chair Regional Synagogue Coun., 1984-86; bd. dirs., mem. several coms. and commns. Jewish Fedn. Coun.; cons. social actions Union of Am. Hebrew Congregations, mem. nat. and Pacific-S.W. region coms. on AIDS; mem. Rabbinic Cabinet, United Jewish Appeal; bd. dirs. Israel Bonds Orgn., Nat. Jewish Fund; bd. govs. Synagogue Coun. Am.; bd. dirs., newsletter editor Am. Jewish Com. Guest columnist L.A. Herald Examiner (Silver Angel award Religion in Media, 1987, 88); guest religion progs. Sta. KCBS, KABC; radio/TV host Nat. Conf. Christians and Jews. Chaplain L.A. Police Dept., 1974-86; bd. dirs., mem. exec. com., chair com. on pub. policy, chair govt. affairs com. AIDS Project L.A.; founding chair, exec. com. chmn. AIDS Interfaith Coun. So. Calif.; adv. bd. L.A. AIDS Hospice Com., Westside Children's Mus., Interreligious Info. Ctr.; apptd. mem., founding chair L.A. County Commn. on AIDS, 1987-89, chair svcs. com., 1989-91, L.A. County Commn. on Mental Health, 1992-95; AIDS-related grants proposal rev. com. Robert Wood Johnson Found., AIDS Task Force of United Way; com. on ethics, medicine and humanity Santa Monica Hosp., L.A. County Commn. on Pub. Social Svcs., 1984-86, Gateways Hosp. bd dirs., 1992-95, Jewish Big Bros., 1994—; City of L.A. Task Force on Diversity of Families, Commn. to Draft Ethics Code for L.A. City Govt.; mem. L.A. County Commn. on Juvenile Delinquency and Adult Crime, 1991—; bd. dirs. Jewish Homes for Aging of Greater L.A., NCCJ, 1989, exec. com., 2000—; chmn. com. on fed. legislation commn. on law and legislation L.A. Jewish Cmty. Rels. Com., trustee; chair Ctrl. Conf. Am. Rabbi's/Union Am. Hebrew Congregations com. on HIV AIDS, Progressive Religious Alliance, City of L.A. 1998; Vol. Restival adv. com. Internat. Conf. on Allocation of Health Resources, Washington, 1997, Vienna, 1999, Cairo, 2000; mem. exec. com., treas. sec., chair nominating com., bd. dirs. Heal the Bay; adv. com. Disability Rights Advocates; founding mem. Calif. Commn. Fair Adminstrn. Justice; hon. bd. dirs. Jewish Fedn. Western Region. Recipient Bishop Daniel Corrigan commendation Episcopal Diocese, 1987, Humanitarian award NCCJ, 1988, Social Responsibility award L.A. Urban League, 1988, Nat. Friendship award Parents and Friends of Lesbians and Gays, 1989, AIDS Hospice Found. Gene La Pietra Leadership award, 1989, Cath. Archdiocese's Serra Tribute award, 1989, Univ. Synagogue's Avodah award for Cmty. Svc., 1990, Am. Jewish Congress Tzedek award for Cmty. Leadership and Svc., 1990, Crystal Achievement award AIDS Project L.A., 1996, Planned Parenthood Disting. Svc. award, 1996, Cmty. Leadership award Beth Chayim Chadashim Congregation. Mem. Am. Jewish Congress (pres. 1977-80, 82-84), Ams. for Dem. Action, Internat. Assn. Physicians in AIDS Care (chmn. bd. dirs.), AIDS Nat. Interfaith Network (bd. dirs.), Ctr. Govtl. Studies (vice chair), Jr. C. of C. (chair internat. rels. com.), Sigma Alpha Mu, Omnicron Delta Kappa, Phi Mu Alpha. Jewish. Office: Human Rels Commn City of LA 200 N Spring St #1625 Los Angeles CA 90012 Office Phone: 213-978-1660. Business E-Mail: rabbi.allen.freehling@lacity.org.

FREEMAN, DOUGLAS K., lawyer; AB with distinction, Stanford U., Calif., 1967; JD, UCLA, 1970; LLM in Taxation, U. San Diego, 1984. Bar: Calif. 1971, US Supreme Ct., US Tax Ct., US Dist. Ct. (9th cir.), US Ct. Mil. Appeals, cert.: State Bar Calif. (specialist in taxation). Chmn., nat. mng. ptnr. IFF Advs., LLC, Irvine, Calif.; founding ptnr. estate and charitable planning practice dept. Freeman, Freeman & Smiley, Irvine, Calif. Co-author: A Founder's Guide to Family Foundation; contbr. articles to profl. publs. Chmn. bd. trustees U. Calif. Irvine Found. Named one of Top 100 Attys., Worth, 2005—06. Mem.: Coun. Founds., Nat. Com. Planned Giving, ABA. Office: Iff Advisors Llc 18101 Von Karman Ave Ste 700 Irvine CA 92612-0145 Office Phone: 494-833-1112. E-mail: doug@iffadvisors.com.

FREEMAN, JANE A., publishing executive; b. 1953; BA in Math. & Chemistry, Cornell U., MBA with distinction, 1978. Cert. in Applied Economics U. Louvain, Belgium. Investments, portfolio mgr. Scudder, Stevens and Clark, 1978—88; global asset allocation, mgmt. bd. Rockefeller & Co., 1988—98; v.p., fin., treas. Scientific Learning Corp., 1999, v.p. bus. devel., 1999—2000, CFO, 2000—, sr. v.p., 2004—07, exec. v.p., CFO, 2007—. Dir. mutual funds Harding Loevner, LLP, chair, audit cmty. Office: Scientific Learning Corp 300 Frank H Ogawa Plaza Ste 600 Oakland CA 94612

FREEMAN, LINTON CLARKE, sociologist, educator; b. Chgo., July 4, 1927; s. Willis and Kathryn Clarke (Kieffer) Freeman; m. Sue Carole Feinberg, Aug. 2, 1958; children: Stacey Elizabeth Vanhanswyk, Michael Andrew. BA, Roosevelt U., Chgo., 1952; MA, U. Hawaii, 1953; PhD, Northwestern U., 1956. From asst. prof. to assoc. prof. sociology Syracuse (N.Y.) U., 1956-67; prof. sociology and computer sci. U. Pitts., 1967-69; prof. sociology and info. sci. U. Hawaii, 1969-72; Lucy G. Moses distinguished prof. sociology Lehigh U., Bethlehem, Pa., 1973-79; prof. Sch. Social Scis., U. Calif., Irvine, 1979—, dean, 1979-82; Killam sr. lectr. sociology and anthropology Dalhousie U., Halifax, N.S., Canada, 1972; directeur d'Etudes Associé Maison des Sciences de l'Homme, Paris, 1991. Ward supr. Onodaga County Bd. Suprs., NY, 1966—68. Author: Elementary Applied Statistics, 1965, Patterns of Local Community Leadership, 1968; co-author: Residential Segregation Patterns, 1970, The Development of Social Network Analysis, 2004; editor: Social Networks; contbr. articles to profl. jours. With USNR, 1944—46. Office: U Calif Sch Social Scis Irvine CA 92697-1500 Home Phone: 949-494-6139; Office Phone: 949-824-6698. Business E-Mail: lin@aris.ss.uci.edu.

FREEMAN, MATT, advertising executive; m. Robin Freeman; children: Sawyer, Colby. BA in English, Art Hist., Dartmouth Coll., Hanover, NH; grad., NY Sch. Visual Arts. Writer MTV Networks; ptnr., exec. creative dir. Poppe Tyson, 1995—97; exec. creative dir. Modem Media / Poppe Tyson (merged when acquired by Digitas, Inc.), 1997—98; founder, CEO Tribal DDB Worldwide, 1998—2008; CEO GoFish Corp., 2008—. Founder, chmn. agy. bd. Interactive Advt. Bureau; served as judge Cannes Internat. Advt. Festival; served as chmn. Clio awards, Internat. ANDY awards, The One Show; bd. dirs. GoFish Corp., 2008—. Mktg. adv. bd. mem. Modern Mus. Art, NYC. Named to Hall of Achievement, Am. Advt. Fedn. Mem.: Am. Assn. Advt. Agencies (bd. mem.), Advt. Club (bd. mem.). Office: GoFish Corp Hdqs 706 Mission St 10th Fl San Francisco CA 94103 Office Phone: 415-738-8706.

FREEMAN, MILTON MALCOLM ROLAND, anthropology educator; b. London, Apr. 23, 1934; arrived in Can., 1958; s. Louis and Fay (Bomberg) F.; m. Mini Christina Aodla; children: Graham, Elaine, Malcolm. BS, Reading U., Eng., 1958; postgrad., U. Coll., London, 1962-64; PhD, McGill U., 1965. Research scientist No. Affairs Dept., Ottawa, Ont., Canada, 1965-67; asst. prof. Meml. U., St. John's, Nfld., Canada, 1967-71, assoc. prof., 1971-72; dir. Inuit Land Use Study, Hamilton, Ont., Canada, 1973-75; prof. anthropology McMaster U., Hamilton, 1976-81; Henry Marshall Tory prof. U. Alta., Edmonton, Canada, 1982-99, prof. emeritus, 1999—, adj. prof. East Asian studies, 1993—99. Adj. prof. environ. studies U. Waterloo, Ont., 1977-81; sr. sci. advisor Indian and No. Affairs, Ottawa, 1979-81; sr. rsch. scholar Can. Circumpolar Inst., U. Alta., 1990—; McLean prof. Trent U., Peterborough, Can., 1995; chmn. UNESCO-MAB No. Sci. Network, 1983-88. Author: People Pollution, 1974, Cultural Anthropology of Whaling, 1989, Recovering Rights, 1992, Inuit, Whaling, and Sustainability, 1998; editor: Inuit Land Use and Occupancy Report, 1976, Procs. Internat. Symposium on Renewable Resources and the Economy of the North, 1981, Japanese Small-type Coastal Whaling, 1988, Endangered Peoples of the Arctic, 2000; co-editor: Adaptive Management of Marine Resources in the Pacific, 1991, Elephants and Whales: Resources for Whom?, 1994, Conservation Hunting: People and Wildlife in Canada's North, 2005 Bd. dirs. Sci. Inst. N.W.T., 1985-87; chmn. adv. bd. Can. Circumpolar Inst., 1990-2001; chmn. Man-Environ. Commn., Internat. Union Anthrop. and Ethnol. Scis., 1977-82. Fellow: Soc. Applied Anthropology, Arctic Inst. N.Am., Am. Anthropol. Assn.; mem.: Soc. Applied Anthropology Can. (pres. 1984—85). Office: U Alta Can Circumpolar Inst Edmonton AB Canada T6G 2E1 Home Phone: 780-439-8248; Office Phone: 780-492-4682. E-mail: milton.freeman@ualberta.ca.

FREEMAN, PATRICIA ELIZABETH, multi-media specialist, educational consultant; b. El Dorado, Ark., Nov. 30, 1924; d. Herbert A. and M. Elizabeth (Pryor) Harper; m. Jack Freeman, June 15, 1949; 3 children. BA, Centenary Coll., 1943; postgrad., Fine Arts Ctr., 1942—46, Art Students League, 1944—45; BSLS, La. State U., 1946; postgrad., Calif. State U., 1959—61, U. N.Mex., 1964—74; EdS, Vanderbilt U., 1975. Libr. U. Calif., Berkeley, 1946-47; libr. Albuquerque Pub. Schs., 1964-67, ind. sch. libr. media ctr. cons., 1967—. One-woman shows include La. State Exhibit Bldg., 1948; author: Pathfinder: An Operational Guide for the School Librarian, 1975, Southeast Heights Neighborhoods of Albuquerque, 1993; compiler, editor: Elizabeth Pryor Harper's Twenty-One Southern Families, 1985; editor: SEHNA Gazette, 1988—93. Mem. task force Goals for Dallas-Environ., 1977—82; pres. Friends Sch. Librs., Dallas, 1979—83; v.p., editor S.E. Heights Neighborhood Assn., 1988—93. With USAF, 1948—49. Recipient Vol. award for Outstanding Svc., Dallas Ind. Sch. Dist., 1978; named honoree, AAUW Ednl. Found., 1979, 1996; AAUW Pub. Svc. grantee, 1980. Mem.: LWV (sec. Dallas 1982—83, editor Albuquerque 1984—86, editor Albuquerque/Bernalillo County Voters' Guide 1986, 1988, editor N.Mex. 2004—07, editor, Albuquerque 2005—08), AAUW (bd. dirs. Dallas 1976—82, bd. dirs. Albuquerque 1983—85, dir. N.Mex. editor 1999—2005, bd. dirs. Albuquerque 2003—06, editor), ALA, N.Mex Symphony Guild, Nat. Trust Historic Preservation, Friends Pub. Libr., Colorado Springs Fine Arts Ctr., Alpha Xi Delta. Home: 612 Ridgecrest Dr SE Albuquerque NM 87108-3365

FREEMAN, PETER A., dean; PhD in Computer Sci., Carnegie-Mellon U., 1970. Asst. prof. to prof. info. and computer sci. U. Calif., Irvine, 1971-90; divsn. dir. Computer and Computation Rsch. NSF, 1987-89; vis. disting. prof. info. tech. George Mason U., Fairfax, Va., 1989-90; dean, Coll. Computing Ga. Inst. Tech., Atlanta, 1990—2002, John P. Imlay, Jr. Dean of Computing; asst. dir. NSF, Arlington, Va., 2002—07; dir. Washington Adv. Group, 2007—. Former Chief Info. Officer, Ga. Inst. Tech.; bd. dirs. Computing Rsch. Assn., 1988-2002; rev. com. IRS and FAA; chair vis. com. Schlumberger Austin Rsch.; cons. in field. Author: Software Perspectives: The System is the Message, 1987, Software System Principles, 1975; editor, co-editor: Software Design Techniques, Software Reusability; founding editor McGraw-Hill Series in Software Engineering and Technology; contbr. articles to profl. jours. Fellow IEEE (past chairi IEEE/CS Tech. Com. on Software Engring.), AAAS, Assn. Computing Machinery. Office: Washington Adv Group 1725 Eye St NW Ste 800 Washington DC 20006 Office Phone: 202-682-0164. Business E-Mail: pfreeman@theadvisorygroup.com.

FREEMAN, RALPH CARTER, investment banker, management consultant; b. La Grange, Ga. s. Ralph Carter and Alice (Cordell) F.; m. Carole Stephens, July 31, 1957 (div. 1977); children: Carter III, Allyson (dec.), Stephens, LeAnna; m. Nancy Lynn Brown, Apr. 8, 1977. BBA, Emory U., 1959. CPA, Mont.; cert. mgmt. cons.; real estate broker, Calif. Acct., cons. Pannell Kerr Forster, Atlanta, Honolulu, 1959—72, ptnr., 1967—72; co-founder Freeman & Noll Accts. and Auditors, 1962—66; mgmt. cons. Touche Ross & Co., Honolulu, Am. Samoa, Asia, South Pacific, 1972-75; pres. FP Industries, Inc., Hawaii, Mont., Ga., Ala., 1975-85, Janas Consulting, Inc., Huntsville, Ala. and San Francisco, Calif., 1986—95, chmn., Janas Assoc., Investment Bankers and Cons., Pasadena, Calif., 1995—, Janas Assoc., Investment Bankers and Cons., US, China, S.E. Asia, Honolulu, Corp. Janas Assoc., Janas Assn. Ltd., Hong Kong, China; ceo Janas Capital Corp., Las Vegas, 1990—. Founder Peoples Bank, LaGrange, Ga., 1966; founding investor Bank of Honolulu, 1973, Bank of Newnan, Ga., 1988, Profl. Bus. Bank, Pasadena, Calif., 2001; mem. Emory U., Atlanta. Contbr. articles to profl. jours. and nat. trade mags. Presbyn. San Marino Cmty. Ch.; dir. Found. San Marino Cmty. Ch., treas. Mem. Inst. Mgmt. Cons. (cert., bd. dirs., treas. 1999-00), Hong Kong Assn., Calif. Capital Market Pl., Sigma Alpha Epsilon Frat., Chapman Woods Assn. (dir., treas)., University Club (chmn. alternatives com., mem. long range planning) Avocations: fishing, tennis, camping. Office: 225 S Lake Ave Ste 610 Pasadena CA 91101-3027 Office Phone: 626-432-7000. Business E-Mail: rcf@janascorp.com.

FREEMAN, TIM J., state legislator; b. Oakland, Oreg. m. Angelia Freeman, 1984; 2 children. Field mechanic Don Whitaker Logging; owner Freeman's Garden Valley Shell, 1991—; mem. Roseburg City Budget Com., 2001—08, Roseburg City Coun., 2003—08, pres; mem. Dist. 2 Oreg. House of Reps., 2008—. Republican. Office: 900 Court St NE H-371 Salem OR 97301 Office Phone: 503-986-1402. Business E-Mail: rep.timfreeman@state.or.us.

FREEMAN, TOM M., lawyer; b. Wauwatosa, Wis., Oct. 5, 1952; s. Max and Betty J. (Zimmerman) F.; m. Judith Casper, June 23, 1974; children: Sarah Carolyn, Benjamin Robert. BA with honors, U. Wis., 1974; JD cum laude, Harvard U., 1977. Bar: Wis. 1977, Ill. 1978, Calif. 1980, US Dist. Ct. (we. dist.) Wis. 1977, US Ct. Appeals (7th cir.) 1978, US Dist. Ct. (no. dist.) Calif. 1980, US Ct. Appeals (9th cir.) 1982. Law clk. Wis. Supreme Ct., Madison, 1977-78; staff atty. US Ct. Appeals (7th cir.), Chgo., 1978-80; assoc. Brobeck, Phleger, Harrison, LLP, San Francisco, 1980-85, ptnr., 1985—2003, Morgan, Lewis & Bockius LLP, 2003—05; cons. pvt. practice, 2005—. Mem.: Phi Kappa Phi, Phi Beta Kappa. Republican. Jewish. Office: PO Box 63 Lafayette CA 94549 Home Phone: 925-284-1634; Office Phone: 925-283-4877. Business E-Mail: tfreeman@freemanlegal.net.

FREER, RANDY, broadcast executive; Grad. in bus. and history, St. Joseph's Coll., North Windham, Maine. Sr. v.p. entertainment sales Turner Broadcasting, NYC, 1985—92, exec. v.p. entertainment sales, 1992—94; sr. vice pres. bus. affairs Active Entertainment, 1994—97; various bus. positions Fox Sports Network, LA, 1997—2001, COO bus. devel., ops., 2001—07, pres. regional cable sports networks, 2007—. Bd. dirs. Big Ten Network. Named one of Most Influential People in Sports, Sports Bus. Jour., Most Influential People in the World of Sports, Bus. Week, 2007, 2008. Office: Fox Sports Fox Sports TV Group FNC/Bldg 101/5th Fl 10201 W Pico Blvd Los Angeles CA 90035 Office Phone: 310-369-6000. Business E-Mail: rfreer@foxsports.net.

FREESTONE, THOMAS LAWRENCE, state legislator; b. Mesa, Ariz., July 15, 1938; s. Herbert L. and Margaret (Heywood) F.; m. Phyllis Rogers, Jan. 14, 1961; children: Jeanne Freestone Palmer, Crystal Freestone Davis, Michael, Phillip. Student, Brigham Young U., 1956-57, Ariz. State U., 1957-58, Mesa C.C., 1964. Constable East Mesa Justice precinct Maricopa County, 1968-72, chief dep. recorder, 1972-74; mgr. Maricopa County Auto Lic. Bur., Mesa, 1972-74; recorder Maricopa County, 1974-78, memb. bd. suprs., 1978—; pres. Freestone Travels, Inc., Mesa, 1979-83. Mem. Ariz. Jail Assn., Ariz. Jail Standards Adv. Com., various Ariz. Joint Legis. Coms.; past chmn. Rep. State Election Bd.; past precinct committeeman Dist. 29, 21.; del. Conf. on Security and Cooperation in Europe. Mem. Ariz. State Legis. Jt. Study Com. on County Issues, Corp. Commn. Citizens Com.; active Mesa United Way; bd. dirs. Mesa Hist. and Archaeol. Soc., Morrison Found., Mesa, PreHab Found., Mesa, Luth. Healthcare Network, Mesa, Mesa Community Coll. Ho-Chief Found., Cystic Fibrosis Found., March of Dimes, Mesa YMCA; scoutmaster, explorer post advisor Boy Scouts Am. Recipient Outstanding Citizen award Valley Radio, United Way award, 1981, MARC Ctr. award for Outstanding Svc., 1981, Key to City of Mesa, 1992; named Outstanding Citizen of Yr., 1990. Mem. Nat. Assn. Counties (criminal justice and pub. safety steering com. 1884—), Ariz. Assn. Counties, Maricopa Assn. Govts., Nat. Recorders and Clerks Assn., Ariz. Assn. County Recorders (legis. steering com.), Nat. Assn. Election County Officials, Trunk 'N Tusk Club, Mesa C. of C., Chandler C. of C. Republican. Mem. Ch. of Jesus Christ of Latter-Day Saints. Avocations: racquetball, football, bodybuilding. Office: Ariz Senate 1700 W Washington St Phoenix AZ 85007-2812

FREI, BRENT R., computer software executive; BS in Engring., Dartmouth Coll., NH, 1989, MS. Mech. engr. Motorola Corp., 1989-90; progammer analyst Microsoft Info. Tech. Group, 1991-94; dir. ONYX, 1994—, pres., sec., treas., 1995-98, pres., CEO, Chmn., 1998—.

FREIER, ELLIOT G., lawyer; b. Huntington, NY, Apr. 2, 1961; s. Walter and Sondra J. Freier; children: Matthew V., Aaron M. BA in Econs., U. Va., 1983; JD, Yale U., 1986. Bar: Calif. 1986. Assoc. Irell & Manella LLP, LA, 1986—92, ptnr., 1993—2006, counsel, 2007—; prin. The Roy Funds, LLC, 2005—. Adv. bd. The M&A Tax Report, 1992—96. Mem. editl. adv. bd.: Mergers and Acquisitions: The Monthly Tax Jour., 2000—03. Named to Am.'s Leading Lawyers, Chambers USA, Who's Who Legal, Best Lawyers in Am. Mem.: ABA (chmn. affiliated and related corps. com. 1996—97, tax sect.), Phi Beta Kappa. Avocations: tennis, skiing. Office: Irell & Manella LLP Ste 900 1800 Avenue of The Stars Los Angeles CA 90067 E-mail: efreier@irell.com.

FREIMAN, PAUL E., pharmaceutical company executive; b. 1932; BS, Fordham U., 1955. Formely exec. v.p. pharm. and agribusiness Syntex USA Inc., pres., co-chief exec. officer, now pres., chief exec. officer, bd. dirs.; also pres. Syntex Corp., Palo Alto, Calif.; pres. and CEO Neurobiological Technologies Inc., Richmond, CA, 1997—. Office: Neurobiological Technologies Inc Ste 500 3260 Blume Dr Richmond CA 94806-5715

FREIMARK, ROBERT (BOB FREIMARK), artist; b. Doster, Mich., Jan. 27, 1922; s. Alvin O. and Nora (Shinaver) F.; m. Mary Carvin (dec.); 1 child, Matisse Jon; m. Lillian Tihlarik (dec. 2005); 1 child, Christine Gay. B.E., U. Toledo, 1950; M.F.A., Cranbrook Acad. Art, 1951. Prof. art emeritus San Jose State U., 1964-86; W.I.C.H.E. prof. Soledad State Prison, 1967. Established artist in residence program Yosemite Nat. Park,1984-85, Fire Clay and Tile, Aromas, Calif., 1998; artist in residence Museo Regla, Cuba, 2000, Ferencsik Janos Zeneskola, L. Balaton, Hungary, 2002; panelist SECOLAS S.E. conf. Latin Am. Studies, Vera Cruz, Mex., NC U., Santa Domingo. Guest artist Harvard U., 1972-73; first Am. to make tapestries in Art Protis technique at Atelier Vlnena, Brno, Czechoslovakia.; contbr. to profl. publs.; One-man shows include Northamerican Cultural Inst., Mexico City, 1963, Minn. Inst. Arts, Toledo Mus. Art, Salpeter Gallery, Morris Gallery, NYC, Des Moines Art Ctr., Santa Barbara Mus., Moravska Mus., Czechoslovakia, Brunel U., London, Amerika Haus, Munich, Stuttgart, Regensburg, Joslyn Ctr. for Arts, Torrance, Calif, Stanford U., San Jose (Calif.) Mus. Art, Triton Mus., Santa Clara, Calif., Guatemalteco, Guatemala City, Dum Umeni Brno, CSFR, Strahov Closter, Prague, 1990, Walter Bischoff Gallery, Stuttgart, 1990, Kunstler aus den USA, Kunsthaus Ostbayern and Amerika Haus, Stuttgart, 1991, Max Planck Inst., Munich, The Gag Theatre, Prague, 1992, Haus Wiegand, Munich, 1993, San Jose State U., 1964, 1967-68, 1981, 1994, Viva!, Tokyo, 1994, Gallery Q, Sacramento, 1997, Parish Gallery, DC, 1997, 02, Barton Gallery, Sacramento, 1997, 2002-03, 05; Galeria Galiano Havana, 1998, Galerie Weber, Viechtach, Germany, 1998, Point Gall., Brno, Czech Rep., 1998, Galerie Divadlo, Uherske Hradiste, C.R., 1998, Marco Polo Galleries, Carmel, Calif., 2001, Colton Hall Mus., Monterey, Calif., 2002, Hart Galleries, Palm Desert, Calif., 2003, Morgan Hill Cmty. Cultural Ctr., 2004, Mexican Heritage Plz., San Jose, 2007, Quilts & Textiles, 2007; exhibited in group shows at Art Inst. Chgo., 1952, Pa. Acad. Fine Arts, 1953 (Lambert Fund prize), Detroit Inst. Arts, 1950, 56, Mich. State U., 1956 (Purchase award), N.A.D., 1956, Boston Print Symposium, 1997, Portland Art Mus., Oreg., 1997 (Purchase award), Honolulu Acad. Art, 1998, Internat. Graphic Triennial, Krakow, Poland, 1998, Internat. Small Engraving Salon, Florean Mus., Romania, Art Expo, NYC, 2000, Internat. Woodprint Assn., Kyoto, Japan, 1999, Bklyn. Mus. (Purchase award), Mus. Modern Art, Michael Stone Collection, DC, Contempo Collection, Tokyo, Havana Bienale, 2000, others; exhbn. 50 States toured, European Mus., 1970-71; represented in collections including Pa. Acad. Fine Art, Boston Mus. Fine Arts, Fogg Mus., Butler Inst. Am. Art, Ford Motor Co., South Bend Art Assn., Joslyn Art Mus., Seattle Art Mus., Ga. Mus., Huntington Gallery, Des Moines Art Center, Smithsonian Instn., Libr. Congress, LA County Art Inst., Brit. Mus., Nat. Gallery, Prague, Birmingham (Eng.) Mus., Moravske Mus., Brno, Czechoslovakia, Bibliotheque Nationale, Paris, Harn Mus., Gainsville, Fla., Portland Mus. Art (over 500 prints), Nat. Mus., Washington, Natl. Mus. Cuba, La Habana, Nat. Mus. Costa Rica, San Jose, Nat. Mus. Egypt, Cairo, Mus. Arte Contemporaneo, Bahia Blanca, Mus. Genaro Perez, Cordoba, Mus. de Bellas Artes, Cordoba, Argentina, Mus. Guayasamin, Quito, Ecuador, Mus. Nat., Panama City, Panama, others; tapestries in pub. and pvt. collections including Mus. of Quilts and Textiles, San Jose, Calif.,History San Jose, created tapestry representing U.S. for Olympic Games, Moscow, 1980, Parish Gallery, Washington, Triad Gallery, Seal Rock, Oreg., Haus Wiegand, Munich, Art Foundry Gallery, Sacramento, Greg Barlon Gallery, Sacramento, Hart Gallery, Palm Desert and Carmel, Calif.; prodr. video documentary: Arte Cubano (Contemporary Art and Culture in Cuba, 1999, 2000, 1st award, San Francisco Throwback Film Festival, Los Desaparecidos--The Disappeared Ones, 2003 (Freedom award Dahlonega Film Festival, also Best Documentary Short and Best of Show, Accolade Competition, Best Documentary Spl. Gold statuette, World Fest, Houston, Dirs. Citation award Black Maria Film Festival 2006, 20 Internat. Festivals); guest artist Joslyn Meml. Mus., 1961, instr. painting and drawing, Ohio U., 1955-59, artist in residence, Des Moines Art Center, 1959-63, dir., Crystal Lake Art Ctr., Frankfort, Mich., (1955-57), guest lectr.,one man show, Columbia U., 1963; guest artist Riverside Art Ctr., 1964, Agora Vienna, Austria, 1994, MuseoGuayasamin, Quito, Ecuador, 2002; curated exhibit Stuttgart, 1993; founder Bob & Lil Freimark Collection Portland Art Mus.; artist in residence MuseoRegla, Cuba, 2002, Lake Balaton, Hungary, 2002; Am. corollary to Dakar Bienale, 5 works, Senegal, 2002, Art Workshop, Dakar, others; contbr. to craft and fibre publs. With Western Interstate Commn. Higher Edn., Soledad State Prison, 1967. Coxwain USN, 1939—46, Pacific. Recipient 2d award for oil Northwest Territorial exhibit, 1954, Roulet medal Toledo Mus. Art, 1957, 1st award Print Exhbn., 1958, purchase award Midwest Biennial and Northwest Printmakers, Jurors award Berkeley Art Ctr, 1996; Calif. State Coll. Sys. spl. creative leave edit. serigraphs; elected to New Talent in U.S.A., 1957; Ohio U. rsch. grantee, 1958-59, Ford Found. grantee, 1965; Western Interstate Commn. for Higher Edn. grantee, 1967, San Jose State Coll. Found. grantee, 1966, 67, 68, 69, 70, 71, 85; designated ofcl. U.S. Bicentennial Exhbn. Amerika Hausen, Fed. Republic Germany, 1976. Independent. Avocations: hunting, fishing, reading, films, cooking. Home: 539A Dougherty Ave Morgan Hill CA 95037-9241 Office: Grass Valley Studios Morgan Hill CA 95037 Personal E-mail: Bob_Freimark@hughes.net.

FRENCH, HOLLIS, state legislator; b. Newton, Mass., Oct. 11, 1958; m to Peggy Pepper French; children: Christopher. Attended, U. Colo., 1976—77; BA in English, U. Alaska, 1986—90; JD, Cornell U., Ithaca, NY, 1992—95. Alaska State Senator, District M, 2003-; Assistant District Atty, 1996-2002; Law clerk to superior court judge, 1995-96.Co-owner, French Apts, 1989-; Lead operator, ARCO, 1991-92, production operator, 1984-90; production operator, Shell Oil Co, 1980-84. Pvt. USMC, 1977—78. Victims for Justice, High 5 award, 2002; MADD Vol award, 1999; climbed to the summit of Mt McKinley twice. Alaska Bar Association; Big Bros/Big Sisters; Challenge Alaska; Access Alaska; MADD; Underage Drinking Task Force. Democrat. Office: State Capitol Rm 417 Juneau AK 99801-1182 also: Dist M 716 W 4th Ave Ste 420 Anchorage AK 99501 Office Phone: 907-465-3892, 907-269-0234. Office Fax: 907-465-6595, 907-269-0238. Business E-Mail: senator_hollis_french@legis.state.ak.us.*

FREUDENBERGER, KENT W., freight company executive; Exec. v.p. mktg. Airborne Freight Corp., Seattle, 1989—. Office: Airborne Freight Corp PO Box 662 3101 Western Ave Seattle WA 98111-0662

FREUDENTHAL, DAVE (DAVID D. FREUDENTHAL), Governor of Wyoming; b. Thermopolis, Wyo., Oct. 12, 1950; m. Nancy Freudenthal; children: Don, Hillary, Bret, Katrina. BA, Amherst Coll., 1973; JD, U. Wyo. Coll. Law, 1980. Economist Wyo. Dept. Econ. Planning & Devel., 1973—75; state planning coord. State of Wyo., 1975—77; pvt. law practice, 1980—93; U.S. atty. for Wyo. U.S. Dept. Justice, Cheyenne, 1994—2001; gov. State of Wyo., Cheyenne, 2003—. Chmn. Wyo. State Demo. Ctrl. Com., 1981—85; mem. Wyo. Futures Project, 1984—87, Econ. Devel. & Stabilization Bd., 1985—89, Edn. Policy Implementation Coun., 1989—90, Gov. Substance Abuse and Violent crime Adv. Bd., 1994—2001. Democrat. Office: Office of Governor State Capitol 200 West 24th St Cheyenne WY 82002-0010 Office Phone: 307-777-7434. Office Fax: 307-632-3909. Business E-Mail: governor@state.wy.us.

FREUDENTHAL, STEVEN FRANKLIN, lawyer, political organization worker; b. Thermopolis, Wyo., June 8, 1949; s. Lewis Franklin and Lucille Iola (Love) F.; m. Janet Mae Mansfield, Aug. 30, 1969 (div. Sept. 1996); children: Lynn Marie, Kristen Lee; m. Barbara A. Crofts, Jan. 1, 1998; stepchildren: Shane C., Jeanne N. BA, Trinity Coll., Hartford, Conn., 1971; JD, Vanderbilt U., 1975. Bar: Wyo. 1975, U.S. Supreme Ct. 1981. Tax acct. Conn. Gen. Life Ins. Co., Hartford, Conn., 1971-72; asst. atty. gen. Wyo. Cheyenne, 1975-77; atty. gen. Wyo., 1981-82; state planning coordinator Office Gov. Wyo., Cheyenne, 1977-78; dep. under sec. Dept. Interior, Washington, 1978-79, exec. asst. to sec., 1979-80; ptnr Sherman & Howard, Cheyenne, Wyo., 1980-81; ptnr. Freudenthal & Bonds, Cheyenne,

1983—; mem. Wyo. Ho. Reps., 1987-91. Trustee United Med. Ctr., 1990-97, pres., 1993-96; bd. dirs. Cheyenne LEADS, 1990-93; chmn. Wyo. Dem. Party, 1999-2001. Office: 123 E 17th St Cheyenne WY 82003-0387 Office Phone: 307-634-2240. Business E-Mail: steve@wyolaw.com.

FREUND, FREDRIC S., real estate broker and manager; b. Denver, Sept. 23, 1930; AB, Brown U., 1952. Sr. v.p. Hanford, Freund & Co., San Francisco, 1956—. Past adv. dir. Western Investment Real Estate Trust; bd. dirs. Berkeley Antibody Co.; instr. real estate mgmt. U. Calif. Ext.; guest lectr. Stanford U. Sch. Bus. Adminstrn. Commr. Calif. Senate Adv. Commn. on Cost Control in State Govt.; chair code adv. com. Bldg. Inspection Dept., San Francisco. Mem. Am. Soc. Real Estate Counselors (CRE, pres. no. Calif. 1987-88), San Francisco Assn. Realtors (pres. 1974-75, Realtor of Yr. 1975), Bldg. Owners & Mgrs. Assn. San Francisco, Realtors Nat. Mktg. Inst. (CCIM), Inst. Real Estate Mgmt. (CPM). Office: Hanford Freund & Co 47 Kearny St Ste 300 San Francisco CA 94108-5582 Home: 112 Alta St San Francisco CA 94133 Home Phone: 415-291-9309; Office Phone: 415-981-5780. Fax: 415-296-0725. E-mail: ffreund@hanfordfreund.com.

FREYD, JENNIFER JOY, psychology professor; b. Providence, Oct. 16, 1957; d. Peter John and Pamela (Parker) F.; m. John Q. Johnson, June 9, 1984; children: Theodore, Philip, Alexandra. BA in Anthropology magna cum laude, U. Pa., Phila., 1979; PhD in Psychology, Stanford U., Calif., 1983. Asst. prof. psychology Cornell U., 1983-87, mem. faculty coun. reps., 1986-87; assoc. prof. psychology U. Oreg., Eugene, 1987-92, mem. exec. com. Inst. Cognitive and Decision Scis., 1991—94, prof., 1992—, mem. dean's adv. com., 1990-91, 92-93, mem. exec. com. Ctr. for the Study of Women in Soc., 1991-93, mem. child care com., 1987-89, 90-91, mem. instnl. rev. bd., 2002—05, dir. undergrad. studies dept. psychology, 2004—08, mem. exec. com. dept. psychology, 2006—08. Author: Betrayal Trauma: The Logic of Forgetting Childhood Abuse, 1996 (Disting. Publ. award Assn. of Women in Psychology 1997, Pierre Janet award Internat. Soc. for Study Dissociation 1997), Spanish edit., 2003; co-editor: (with A.P. De Prince) Trauma and Cognitive Science: A Meeting of Minds, Science, and Human Experience, 2001; mem. editl. bd. Jour. Exptl. Psychology: Learning, Memory, and Cognition, 1989-91, Gestalt Theory, 1985—, Jour. of Aggression, Maltreatment, and Trauma, 1997—, Jour. of Psychopathology and Behavioral Assessment, 2001-03, Jour. Psychological Trauma, 2003—, Jour. of Trauma and Dissociation, 1999-2005, assoc. editor, 2004, editor, 2005—; guest reviewer Am. Jour. Psychology, Am. Psychologist, others; contbr. over 100 articles to profl. jours. including Sci. Mag. Grad. fellowship NSF, 1979-82, Univ. fellowship Stanford U., 1982-83, Erskine fellowship, U. Canterbury, 2009, Presdl. Young Investigator award NSF, 1985-90, IBM Faculty Devel. award, 1985-87, fellowship Ctr. for Advanced Study in the Behavioral Scis., 1989-90, John Simon Meml. fellowship Guggenheim Found., 1989-90, Rsch. Scientist Devel. award NIMH, 1989-94, Pierre Janet award Internat. Soc. Study of Dissociation, 1997, 05, Psychologist-Scientist of Yr. award Lane County Psychologists Assn., 2006, Rsch. Innovation award, U. Oreg. 2009 Fellow AAAS, APA (liaison divsn. 35 to sci. directorate 1998-2000, liaison divsn. 56 to sci. dir. 2006-, chair sci. com. trauma psychology divsn. 2006—), Am. Psychol. Soc., Psychonomic Soc.; mem. Internat. Soc. Study of Traumatic Stress, Cannon Inst. (rsch. com. mem.), Brisbane, Sigma Xi. Office: Dept Psychology 1227 U Oreg Eugene OR 97403-1227 Office Phone: 541-346-4950. Business E-Mail: jjf@dynamic.uoregon.edu.

FREYD, WILLIAM PATTINSON, not-for-profit fundraiser, director; b. Chgo., Apr. 1, 1933; s. Paul Robert Freyd and Pauline Margaret (Pattinson) Gardiner; m. Diane Marie Carlson, May 19, 1984. BS in Fgn. Svc., Georgetown U., 1960. Field rep. Georgetown U., Washington, 1965-67; campaign dir. Tamblyn and Brown, NYC, 1967-70; dir. devel. St. George's Ch., NYC, 1971; assoc. Browning Assocs., Newark, 1972-73; regional v.p. C.W. Shaver Co., NYC, 1973-74; founder IDC, Henderson, Nev., 1974—. Founder, treas., prodr. SFS Entertainment, 2005. Prodr.: A Chorus Line, 2005; prodr.: Cabaret, 2006; prodr.: Best Little Whorehouse in Texas, 2006. Bd. dirs. Nev. Symphony Orch., 1994-99, NJ Symphony Orch., 1991-94, Las Vegas Philharm., 2004, exec. com., 2005, pres., 2006; bd. dirs. Nev. Opera Theater, 2004; apptd. Nev. Charitable Solicitation Task Force, 1994, pres.'s circle adv. coun. U.S. Naval Acad., 2003. Mem. SAG, Assn. Fundraising Profls. (nat. treas. 1980-81, pres. NY chpt. 1974-76, cert. 1982), Am. Assn. Fund Raising Counsel (sec. 1984-86, designated Sage 2000), World Fund Raising Coun. (bd. dirs. 1995-99, treas. 1998-99), Georgetown U. (regional club coun.), NY Yacht Club, Union League Club NY, Masons, Nassau Club, Circumnavigators Club. Achievements include invention of Phone Mail program. Office: IDC IDC Ctr 2500 Paseo Verde Pky Henderson NV 89074 Personal E-mail: wfreyd@aol.com. E-mail: wfreyd@goidc.com.

FREYERMUTH, CLIFFORD L., structural engineering consultant; BS in Civil Engring., State U. Iowa, 1956, MS in Structural Engring., 1958. Registered structural engr., Ariz. Consulting engr. structural design Ned L. Ashton, 1955-57; grad. teaching asst. structural mechanics State U. Iowa, 1957-58; with bridge divsn. Ariz. State Hwy. Dept., 1958-64; with Portland Cement Assn., Chgo., Skokie, Ill., 1964-71; dir. post-tensioning divsn. Prestessed Concrete Inst., 1971-76; mgr. Post-Tensioning Inst., 1976-88, Am. Segmental Bridge Inst., 1989—2008; pres. Clifford L. Freyermuth, Inc., 1988—. Mem. cable-stayed bridges com. Post-Tensioning Inst, editor various publs.; prin. investigator Nat. Coop. Hwy Rsch. Project, Washington, 1988. Contbr. articles to profl. jours. Recipient Martin P. Korn award Prestressed Concrete Inst., 1969, George C. Zollman award Precast/Prestressed Concrete Inst., 1999. Fellow Am. Concrete Inst. (prestressed concrete com., standard bldg. code com., bd. dirs. 1991—, Henry C. Turner medal 1992, Arthur R. Anderson award 2004, ASBI Leadership award, 2008); mem. ASCE (prestressed concrete com.), Structural Engrs. Assn. Ariz., Chi Epsilon. Office: Clifford L Freyermuth Inc 2375 E Camelbook Ste 500 Phoenix AZ 85016 Office Phone: 602-263-4770. Personal E-mail: asbi@earthlink.net. Business E-Mail: clifffreyermuth@olfinc.net.

FRIBERG, GEORGE JOSEPH, electronics company executive, entrepreneur; m. Mary Seymour; children: Fane George, Felicia Lynn Friberg Clark. BSME, U. N.Mex., 1962, MBA, 1982, postgrad. Sales engr. Honeywell, LA, 1962-64; liaison engr. ACF Industries, Albuquerque, 1964-66; quality assurance mgr. data sys. divsn. Gulton Industries Inc., Albuquerque, 1966-72, mgr. mfg. Femco divsn. Irwin (Pa.), High Point (N.C.), 1972-77, v.p. mfg. data sys. divsn. Albuquerque, 1977-86; pres., CEO Tetra Corp., Albuquerque, 1986-92, also bd. dirs.; pres., CEO Laguna Industries Inc., Albuquerque, 1992-96; sr. dir. Tech. Ventures Corp., Albuquerque, 1996—. Adj. prof. U. N.Mex. Mgmt. Tech., 1998—2005, 2008-; bd. dir. Noonday, Inc. Mem. editl. bd. N.Mex. Bus. Jour., 1989-91 Mem. N.Mex. R&D Gross Receipts Task Force, 1988-89; mem. Econ. Forum of Albuquerque; bd. dir. Technet, 1983-97, pres., 1983-84, 88-89; bd. dir. Lovelace Insts., 1988-99, U. N.Mex. R.O. Anderson Bus. Sch. Found., 1988-92, N.Mex. Bus. Innovation Ctr., 1986-92, U. N.Mex. Found., 1999—, N.Mex. Golden Apple Found., 1998-2007, pres., 2003—04; mem. coun. trustees Lovelace Respiratory Rsch. Insts., 1999-2006, chmn, 2004-; bd. dir. N.Mex. Natural History Mus. Found., 1999-2005, sec. 2002-05; bd. dir. N.Mex. First, 2001—05, United Way, N.Mex., 2001-02, Samaritan Counseling Found., 2007-; pres. Licensing Exec. Soc. New Mex. Chpt., 2008-; chmn. Law Enforcement Tech. Commercial Coun., 1999-2008; grad. Leadership N.Mex., 1998; mem. mech. engring. adv. coun. U. N.Mex., 1999— Inducted Anderson Sch. of Bus. Hall of Fame, 1996, U. N.Mex. Athletic Hall of Honor, 2003; recipient Zia award U. N.Mex., 1998, Erna Ferguson Alumni award UNM, 2009, Regents medal U. N.Mex., 1998, Lockheed Martin Nova award, 1998, Albuquerque High Harrington award, 2000; named to All-Time Football Team Albuquerque HS, 2001, Albuquerque HS Hall of Fame, 2004. Mem. Albuquerque C. of C. (bd. dirs. 1985-92, polit. action com. 1983-84, chair Buy N.Mex. chpt. 1986-87, vice chmn. econ. affairs planning coun. 1987—, chmn. bd. 1990-91), N.Mex. Alumni Lettermen's Club, U. N.Mex. Alumni Assn. (bd. dirs. 1995-2001, pres.-elect 1997, pres. 1997-98, chair legis. com. 2000-2007) Home: 13234 Sunset Canyon Dr NE Albuquerque NM 87111-4220 Business E-Mail: george.j.friberg@lmco.com.

FRICK, OSCAR LIONEL, pediatrician, educator; b. NYC, Mar. 12, 1923; s. Oscar and Elizabeth (Ringger) F.; m. Mary Hubbard, Sept. 2, 1954. AB, Cornell U., 1944, MD, 1946; M.Med. Sci., U. Pa., 1960; PhD, Stanford U., 1964. Diplomate: Am. Bd. Allergy and Immunology (chmn. 1967-72). Intern Babies Hosp., Columbia Coll. Physicians and Surgeons, NYC, 1946-47; resident Children's Hosp., Buffalo, 1950-51; pvt. practice medicine specializing in pediatrics Huntington, NY, 1951-58; fellow in allergy and immunology Royal Victoria Hosp., Montreal, Que., Canada, 1958-59; fellow in allergy U. Calif.-San Francisco, 1959-60, asst. prof. pediatrics, 1964-67, assoc. prof., 1967-72, prof., 1972—, dir. allergy tng. program, 1964—; fellow immunology Inst. d'Immunobiologie, Hosp. Broussais, Paris, 1960-62. Contbr. articles papers to profl. publs. Served with M.C., USNR, 1947-49. Mem. Am. Assn. Immunologists, Am. Acad. Pediatrics (chmn. allergy sect. 1971-72, Bret Ratner award 1982), Am. Acad. Allergy (exec. com. 1972—, pres. 1977-78), Internat. Assn. Allergology and Clin. Immunology (exec. com. 1970-73, sec. gen. 1985—), Am. Pediatric Soc. Clubs: Masons. Home: 370 Parnassus Ave San Francisco CA 94117-3609

FRIED, JOHN H., chemist; b. Leipzig, Germany, Oct. 7, 1929; s. Abraham and Frieda F.; m. Heléne Gellen, June 26, 1955; children: David, Linda, Deborah. AB, Cornell U., 1951, PhD, 1955. Steroid chemist, research assoc. Merck and Co., Rahway, NJ, 1956-64; with Syntex Research, Palo Alto, Calif., 1964-92, dir. inst. organic chemistry, 1967-74, exec. v.p., 1974-76, pres., 1976-92; sr. v.p. Syntex Corp., 1981-86, vice chmn., 1986-92; dir. Corvas Internat., Inc., 1992-99, chmn., 1997-99. Chmn. Alexion Pharms., Inc., 1992-2002; pres. Fried & Co., 1992—. Mem. Am. Chem. Soc. Office: 20 Faxon Forest Atherton CA 94027-4067

FRIEDEN, CLIFFORD E., lawyer; b. LA, Mar. 8, 1949; s. Sidney S. and Norma (Stern) Frieden; m. Dinah S. Baumring, June 20, 1971; children: Jamie, Kari, Curtis. BA, UCLA, 1971; JD, U. Calif., Berkeley, 1974. Bar: Calif. 1974, US Dist. Ct. (so. dist.) Calif. 1974, US Dist. Ct. (ctrl. dist.) Calif. 1977. Ptnr. Rutan & Tucker, Costa Mesa, Calif., 1974—. Dir. Nat. Football Found. and Coll. Hall of Fame, Orange County, Calif., 2005—; mem. Orange County chpt. ARC, 1995—2001. Mem.: Orange County Bar Assn. (del. state conv. 1983—95, chair judiciary com. 1987—88, bd. dirs. 1989—91), Phi Beta Kappa, Order of Coif. Avocation: sports. Office: Rutan and Tucker PO Box 1950 611 Anton Blvd Ste 1400 Costa Mesa CA 92626-1931 Office Phone: 714-641-5100. Business E-Mail: cfrieden@rutan.com.

FRIEDEN, ILONA JOSEPHINE, pediatric dermatologist; b. Oakland, Calif., Oct. 12, 1949; d. Michael and Evelyn Judith (Fargo) F.; m. Mark Andrew Jacobson, Apr. 17, 1987; children: Michael, Sarai. AB, Boston U., 1973; MD, U. Calif., San Francisco, 1977. Diplomate Am. Bd. Pediats., Am. Bd. Dermatology. Residency in pediat. U. Calif., San Francisco, residency in dermatology, asst. prof., 1990-93, assoc. prof., 1993-97, prof. clin. dermatology, dept. dermatology and pediat., 1997—; staff dermatologist Kaiser Permanent, Oakland, Calif., 1983-89. Founder, dir. U. Calif. Vascular Anomalies Clinic, San Francisco, 1991—; founder Hemangioma Investigator Group; bd. dirs. Am. Bd. Dermatology, past pres. Author: (with others) Pediatric Dermatology, 1995, Rudolph's Textbook of Pediatrics, 1995, Textbook of Dermatology, 1996; mem. editl. bd. Current Problems in Dermatology, 1994—, Pediat. Dermatology, 1998—; editor-in-chief, co-editor Neonatal Dermatology; contbr. over 75 articles to profl. jours. Recipient Chancellor's award, Women of Distinction, U. Calif. San Francisco, Mentor of Yr. award, Women's Dermatologic Soc.; named Nancy B. Esterly Lectr., Wis. Dermatology Soc., Williams Moores Lectr., Ind. Dermatology Soc., Cawley Lectr., U. Va., Harold Perry Lectr., Mayo Clinic, Tchr. of Yr., U. Calif. San Francisco; named to Best Doctors, Bay Area, Best Doctors, USA. Mem. Am. Acad. Dermatology (mem. editl. bd. 1998—), Soc. Pediat. Dermatology (Founders Lectr., bd. dirs. 1990-93, past pres.). Office: Univ Calif PO Box 316 San Francisco CA 94143-0001 Office Phone: 415-353-7883. Business E-Mail: friedeni@derm.ucsf.edu.

FRIEDENBERG, RICHARD MYRON, radiologist, physician, educator; b. NYC, May 6, 1926; s. Charles and Dorothy (Steg) F.; m. Gloria Geshwind, Jan. 22, 1950; children: Lisa, Peter, Amy. AB, Columbia, 1946; MD, L.I. Coll. Medicine, 1949. Diplomate: Am. Bd. Radiology. Intern in medicine Maimonides Hosp., Bklyn., 1949-50; resident in radiology Bellevue Hosp., NYC, 1950-51, Nat. Cancer fellow, 1951-52; fellow radiology Columbia-Presbyn. Hosp., 1952-53; cons. radiologist 3d Air Force, London, Eng., 1953-55; asst. prof. radiology Albert Einstein Coll. Medicine, 1955-66, assoc. clin. prof. radiology, 1966-68; dir., chmn. dept. radiology Bronx Lebanon Hosp. Center, 1957-68; prof., chmn. dept. radiology N.Y. Med. Coll., 1968-80; prof., chmn. dept. radiol. scis. U. Calif., Irvine, 1980—92, emeritus prof. radiol. scis., 1992—. Dir. radiology Flower Fifth Ave. Hosp., Met. Hosp. Ctr., Bird S. Coler Hosp., NYC, Westchester County Med. Ctr., 1968—80. Author: (with Charles Ney) Radiographic Atlas of the Genitourinary System, 1966, 2d edit., 1981; Contbr. (with Charles Ney) articles to profl. jours. Fellow Am. Coll. Radiology, N.Y. Acad. Medicine; mem. Assn. Univ. Radiologists, Radiol. Soc. N.Am., Am. Roentgen Ray Soc., N.Y. Acad. Scis., Assn. Am. Med. Colls., AMA, Soc. Chairmen Acad. Radiology Depts. (past pres.), N.Y. Roentgen Soc. (past pres.), Orange CTY Radiology Soc. (past pres.). Home: 18961 Castlegate Ln Santa Ana CA 92705-2801 Office: U Calif Dept Radiology Irvine CA 92697-0001 Office Phone: 714-456-5303. Business E-Mail: rmfriede@uci.edu.

FRIEDLANDER, SAUL, historian, educator; b. Prague, Czechoslovakia, Oct. 11, 1932; Degree, Inst. d'Etudes Politiques, Paris, 1955; PhD, Grad. Inst. Internat. Studies, Geneva, 1963. Asst. to Vice Min. Def., 1959-61; tchr. Hebrew U., Jerusalem, Grad. Inst. Internat. Studies, Geneva, U. Calif., LA, Tel Aviv U. Author: Pius XII and the Third Reich, 1965, Kurt Gerstein, 1970, History and Psychoanalysis, 1979, When Memory Comes, 1979, Reflections of Nazism, 1984, History, Memory, and the Extermination of the Jews, 1993, Nazi Germany and the Jews, Volume One: The Years of Persecution, 1933-1939, 1999, The Years of Extermination, 1939-1945, 2007 (Pulitzer prize for general nonfiction 2008); sr. editor History and Memory. Mem. Israel Def. Forces, 1951-53. Recipient Israel prize for history, 1983. Office: UCLA Dept History 6265 Bunche Hall PO Box 951473 Los Angeles CA 90095-1473

FRIEDMAN, ALAN E., lawyer; b. NYC, May 5, 1946; BA, Amherst Coll., 1967; JD, Stanford U., 1970. Bar: Calif. 1971. Ptnr. Tuttle & Taylor, LA, 1970—. Note editor: Stanford Law Rev., 1969-70 Office: Ste 4600 555 W 5th St Los Angeles CA 90013-3002

FRIEDMAN, ALEXANDER STEPHEN, foundation administrator, investment banker; BA in Politics, Princeton U., NJ; MBA, Columbia U., NYC, JD, 1997. Small-claims ct. and family mediator, NYC; White House fellow US Dept. Def., 1998—99, asst. to sec. for spl. projects; head corp. devel. Medarex; mergers and acquisitions specialist, co-head fin. sponsor group Lazard Freres & Co.; CFO Bill & Melinda Gates Found., Seattle, 2007—. Co-founder Adventa.com; founder, pres. Accelerated Clin.; founder 21st Century Roundtable; cons. Harvard Ctr. Internat. Devel. Founder Climb for the Cure, 1993; bd. mem. Lower Manhattan Cultural Coun., NetAid. Mem.: Coun. Fgn. Rels. Office: Bill & Melinda Gates Found PO Box 23350 Seattle WA 98102 Office Phone: 206-709-3100.

FRIEDMAN, ARTHUR DANIEL, electrical engineer, computer scientist, investment company executive, educator; b. Bronx, NY, Apr. 24, 1940; s. Henry and Yetta Friedman; m. Barbara Bernstein, Mar. 31, 1968; children: Michael Kenneth, Steven David. BA, Columbia U., 1961, BS, 1962, MEE, 1963, PhD, 1965. Tech. staff Bell Labs., Murray Hill, NJ, 1965-72; assoc. prof. elec. engring. and computer sci. U. So. Calif., LA, 1972-77; prof. George Washington U., Washington, 1977-97, dept. chmn., 1980-84, prof. emeritus, 1997—. Vis. prof. U. Calif., San Diego, 1999, 2002-04, mem. Chancellor's Assocs., 1999-2005; chmn. bd., co-founder Computer Sci. Press (acquired by WH Freeman Co.), Rockville, Md., 1974-88, co-editor-in-chief, 1988-89; co-founder, pres. investment mgmt. co. ABF Enterprises, 1988—, Friedman Family Found. Inc., ABF Capital Mgmt.; founder, pres. Market Mavens, 1998-2001; gen. ptnr. Potomac Ptnrs. LP, 1991; mem. Aztec Venture Networks, 2000-01, Tech Coast Angels, 1999-2001; mem. TIE 2002-03; mem. adv. com. on elec. engring. San Diego State U., 2003—, mem. adv. com. dept. elec. engring., mem. adv. bd. Entrepreneurial Soc. Author: (with Premanchandra Menon) Fault Detection in Digital Circuits, 1971, Theory and Design of Switching Circuits, 1975, Russian trans., Logical Design of Digital Systems, 1975 (translated into Russian, 1978), Fundamentals of Logic Design and Switching Theory, 1986; (with Melvin Breuer) Diagnosis of Digital Systems, 1976; (with Miron Abramovici and Melvin Breuer) Digital System Testing and Testable Design, 1990, 2d edit., 1995, Chinese trans., 2006. Judge San Diego (Calif.) Sci. and Engring. Fair San Diego State U., 2003—, judge venture challenge competition, 2002—06; pres. Friedman Family Found. Fellow IEEE. Avocations: reading, swimming, travel, writing, cooking. Home: 4969 Beauchamp Court San Diego CA 92130-2742

FRIEDMAN, GARY, plastic surgeon; BS, MD, Ohio State U. Diplomate Am. Bd. Plastic Surgery, cert. Advanced Edn. Cosmetic Surgery Am. Soc. Aesthetic Plastic Surgery. Intern Mt. Zion Hosp., San Francisco; gen. surgery resident Marquette U., Milw.; plastic surgery resident St. Francis Hosp., San Francisco; pvt. practice San Francisco, 1973—. Chief plastic surgery Calif. Pacific Med. Ctr.; clinical instr. St. Francis Hosp., 1973—98. Contbr. articles to profl. jours., chapters to books. Recipient Physician Recognition award, Continuing Medical Edn., Am. Med Assn. Mem.: AMA (Physician Recognition award in Continuing Med. Edn.), San Francisco Med. Soc., Calif. Soc. Plastic Surgeons, Calif. Med. Assn., Am. Soc. Aesthetic Plastic Surgery, Am. Soc. Plastic & Reconstructive Surgeons. Office: 525 Spruce St San Francisco CA 94118 Office Phone: 866-677-8587. E-mail: gdf@sf-plasticsurgeon.com.

FRIEDMAN, GARY DAVID, epidemiologist; b. Cleve., Mar. 8, 1934; s. Howard N. and Cema C. F.; m. Ruth Helen Schleien, June 22, 1958; children: Emily, Justin, Richard. Student, Antioch Coll., 1951-53; BS in Biol. Sci., U. Chgo., 1956, MD with honors, 1959; MS in Biostats., Harvard Sch. Pub. Health, 1965. Diplomate Am. Bd. Internal Medicine. Intern, resident Harvard Med. Svcs., Boston City Hosp., 1959-61; 2d yr. resident Univ. Hosps. Cleve., 1961-62; med. officer heart disease epidemiology study Nat. Heart Inst., Framingham, Mass., 1962-66; chief epidemiology unit, field and tng. sta., heart disease ctrl. program USPHS, San Francisco, 1966-68; sr. epidemiologist divsn. rsch. Kaiser Permanente Med. Care Program, Oakland, Calif., 1968-76, asst. dir. epidemiology and biostats., 1976-91, dir., 1991-98, sr. investigator, 1998-99, adj. investigator, 1999—; cons. prof. Dept. Health Rsch. and Policy Stanford U. Sch. Medicine, 1998—. Rsch. fellow, then rsch. assoc. preventive medicine Harvard Med. Sch., 1962-66; lectr. dept. biomed. and environ. health scis., sch. pub. health U. Calif. Berkeley, 1968-95; lectr. epidemiology and biostats. U. Calif. Sch. Medicine, San Francisco, 1980-2000, asst. clin. prof. 1967-75, assoc. clin. prof., 1975-92 depts. medicine and family and cmty. medicine; US-USSR working group sudden cardiac death NHLBI, 1975-82, com. on epidemiology and veterans follow-up studies Nat. Rsch. Coun., 1980-85, subcom. on twins, 1980-94, epidemiology and disease ctrl. study sect. NIH, 1982-86, US Preventive Svcs. Task Force, 1984-88, scientific rev. panel on toxic air contaminants State of Calif., 1988—, adv. com. Merck Found./Soc. Epidemiol. Rsch., Clin. Epidemiology Fellowships, 1990-94; sr. advisor expert panel on preventive svcs. USPHS, 1991-96; mem. instl. rev. bd. Kaiser Permanente, 1997—. Author: Primer of Epidemiology, 1974, 5th edit. 2004; assoc. editor, then editor Am. Jour. Epidemiology, 1988-96, 99—; mem. editl. bd. HMO Practice, 1991-98, Jour. Med. Screening, 1997—; contbr. over 300 articles to profl. jours., chpts. to books; composer: Autumn for oboe and piano (First prize Composers Today Competition Music Tchrs. Assn. Calif. 1999),

Fugue for Four Winds (Second prize Music Tchrs. Assn. Calif. 2000). Oboist San Francisco Civic Symphony, 1990—, Symphony Parnassus, 1994-2004, Bohemian Club Band, 1994—, Coll. Marin Orch., 2004—; bd. dirs. Chamber Musicians No. Calif., Oakland, 1991-98. Sr. surgeon USPHS, 1962-68. Recipient Roche award for Outstanding Performance as Med. Student; Merit grantee Nat. Cancer Inst., 1987, Outstanding Investigator grantee, 1989, 94; named to Disting. Alumni Hall of Fame Cleve. Heights High Sch., 1991. Fellow Am. Heart Assn. (chmn. com. on criteria and methods 1969-71, chmn. program com. 1973-76, coun. epidemiol.), Am. Coll. Physicians; mem. APHA, Am. Epidemiol. Soc. (mem. com. 1982-86, pres. 1999-2000), Am. Soc. Preventive Oncology, Internat. Epidemiol. Assn., Soc. Epidemiologic Rsch. (exec. com. 1998-2001), Med. Biol. Alumni Assn. U. Chgo. (Disting. Svc. award 2000), Phi Beta Kappa, Alpha Omega Alpha, Delta Omega. Achievements include research on cancer, cardiovascular disease, gallbladder disease, effects of smoking, alcohol and medicinal drugs, evaluation of health screening tests. Office: Stanford U Sch Medicine Dept Health Rsch and Policy Redwood Bldg Rm T210 Stanford CA 94305-5405 E-mail: gdf@stanford.edu.

FRIEDMAN, GEORGE JERRY, aerospace engineering executive; b. NYC, Mar. 22, 1928; s. Sander and Ruth (Oberlander) F.; m. Ruthanne Goldstein, Sept. 7, 1953; children— Sanford, Gary, David BS, U. Calif.-Berkeley, 1949; MS, UCLA, 1956, PhD, 1967. Registered profl. mech. engr., controls engr., Calif. Mech. engring. assoc. Dept. Water and Power, Los Angeles, 1949-56; devel. engr. Servo Mechanisms, Hawthorne, Calif., 1956-60; v.p. Northrop Corp., Los Angeles, 1960-94; exec. v.p., rsch. dir. Space Studies Inst., Princeton, NJ, 1994—. Mem. indsl. adv. group NATO, Brussels, 1977-78; guest lectr. UCLA, 1983—, Calif. State U., Northridge, 1983—, dir. trust fund, 1984-89; cons. to sci. adv. bd. USAF, Washington, 1985—, bd. govs. Aerospace and Elec. Sys. Soc., L.A., 1985—, v.p. publs., 1995-; adj. prof. U. So. Calif., L.A., 1994—; pres. Internat. Coun. on Sys. Engring., 1994, fellow 1998. Contbr. articles to profl. jours. Served as pfc. U.S. Army, 1950-52 Recipient Engring. Excellence award San Fernando Valley Engring. Council, 1983 Fellow IEEE (Baker award 1970), AIAA (assoc.; chmn. planetary def. subcom. 1995-97); mem. Am. Def. Preparedness Assn. (exec. com., preparedness award 1985). Democrat. Jewish. Home and Office: 5084 Gloria Ave Encino CA 91436-1529 E-mail: gfriedma@usc.edu.

FRIEDMAN, K. BRUCE, lawyer; b. Buffalo, Jan. 1, 1929; s. Bennett and Florence Ruth (Israel) Friedman; m. Lois G. Rosoff, June 15, 1986. AB, Harvard U., Cambridge, Mass., 1950; LLB, Yale U., New Haven, Conn., 1953. Bar: NY 1955, DC 1956, Calif. 1958. Atty. CAB, Washington, 1955—57; pvt. practice San Francisco, 1958—; mem. Zang, Friedman & Damir, 1969—78, Cotton, Seligman & Ray, 1978—79, Friedman, McCubbin, Spalding, Bilter, Roosevelt, & Montgomery, San Francisco, 1980—. Pres. Econ. Roundtable San Francisco, 1964; lectr. law U. Calif., Berkley, 1966—76. Trustee World Affairs Coun. No. Calif., San Francisco, 1970—76; pres. San Francisco Estate Planning Coun., 1973—74; bd. dirs. Am. Coll. Trust and Estate Counsel Found., 2000—06; bd. dirs. San Francisco chpt. Am. Jewish Com., 1960—76; regional dir. No. Calif. Harvard Alumni Assn., 1981—84. With US Army, 1953—55. Fellow: Am. Bar Found., Am. Coll. Trust and Estate Counsel; mem.: ABA, U. Calif. San Francisco Found., San Francisco Com. Fgn. Rels., Am. Law Inst., Internat. Acad. Estate and Trust Law (treas. 1996—2006), San Francisco Bar Assn., State Bar Calif., Harvard Club San Francisco (pres. 1976—78), Commonwealth Club Calif., Calif. Tennis Club, Univ. Club. Jewish. Office: Friedman McCubbin Spalding Bilter Roosevelt & Montgomery 425 California St Ste 2500 San Francisco CA 94104-2207 Business E-Mail: kbrucefriedman@fomlaw.com.

FRIEDMAN, LAWRENCE M., law educator; b. Chgo., Apr. 2, 1930; s. I. M. and Ethel (Shapiro) F.; m. Leah Feigenbaum, Mar. 27, 1955; children: Jane, Amy. AB, U. Chgo., 1948, JD, 1951, LLM, 1953; LLD (hon.), U. Puget Sound, 1977, CUNY, 1989, U. Lund, Sweden, 1993, John Marshall Law Sch., 1995, U. Macerata, Italy, 1998, U. Milan, 2006. Mem. faculty St. Louis U., 1957-61, U. Wis., 1961-68; prof. law Stanford U., 1968—, Marion Rice Kirkwood prof., 1976—; David Stouffer Meml. lectr. Rutgers U. Law Sch., 1969; Sibley lectr. U. Ga. Law Sch., 1976; Wayne Morse lectr. U. Oreg., 1985; Childress meml. lectr. St. Louis U., 1987. Jefferson Meml. lectr. U. Calif., 1994; Higgins vis. prof. Lewis and Clark U., 1998; Tucker lectr. Washington and Lee U., 2000, Charter lectr. U. Ga, 2004; Johnson lectr. Vanderbilt U., 2005. Author: Contract Law in America, 1965, Government and Slum Housing, 1968, A History of American Law, 1973, 3d edit., 2005, The Legal System: A Social Science Perspective, 1975, Law and Society: An Introduction, 1977, American Law, 1984, Total Justice, 1985, Your Time Will Come, 1985, The Republic of Choice, 1990, Crime and Punishment in American History, 1993, The Horizontal Society, 1999, Law in America: A Short History, 2002, American Law in The 20th Century, 2002, Private Lives: Families, Individuals, and The Law, 2004, Guarding Life's Dark Secrets, 2007; author: (with Robert V. Percival) The Roots of Justice, 1981; author: (with Stewart Macaulay and Elizabeth Mertz) Law in Action, 2007; co-editor (with Stewart Macaulay): Law and the Behavioral Sciences, 1969, 2d edit., 1977; co-editor: (with Stewart Macaulay and John Stookey) Law and Society: Readings on the Social Study of Law, 1995; co-editor: (with Harry N. Scheiber) American Law and the Constitutional Order, 1978; co-editor: Legal Culture and the Legal Profession, 1996; co-editor: (with George Fisher) The Crime Conundrum, 1997; co-editor: (with Rogelio Prerz-Perdomo) Legal Culture in the Age of Globalization: Latin America and Mediterranean Europe, 2003; contbr. articles to profl. jours. Served with U.S. Army, 1953-54. Recipient Triennial award Order of Coif, 1976, Willard Hurst prize, 1982, Harry Kalven prize, 1992, Silver Gavel award ABA, 1994, Rsch. award Am. Bar. Found., 2000-01; Ctr. for Advanced Study in Behavioral Sci. fellow, 1974-75, Inst. Advanced Study fellow, Berlin, 1985. Mem. Law and Soc. Assn. (pres. 1979-81), Am. Acad. Arts and Scis., Am. Soc. for Legal History (v.p. 1987-89, pres. 1990-91), Soc. Am. Historians, Rsch. Com. Sociology of Law (hon. life, pres. 2003-06). Home: 724 Frenchmans Rd Palo Alto CA 94305-1005 Office: Stanford U Law Sch Nathan Abbott Way Stanford CA 94305-9991 Business E-Mail: lmf@stanford.edu.

FRIEDMAN, MORTON LEE, retired lawyer; b. Aberdeen, SD, Aug. 4, 1932; s. Philip and Rebecca (Feinstein) F.; m. Marcine Lichter, Dec. 20, 1955; children— Mark, Philip, Jeffrey. Student, U. Mich., 1950-53; AB, Stanford U., 1954, LL.B., 1956. Bar: Calif. bar 1956. Mem. firm Kimble, Thomas, Snell, Jamison & Russell, Fresno, 1957, Busick & Busick, Sacramento, 1957-59; sr. ptnr. firm Friedman, Collard & Panneton, Sacramento, 1959—2006, ret., 2006. Lectr. various law schs. and seminars; mem. Calif. Bd. Continuing Edn. Pres. Mosaic Law Congregation, 1977-80, 97-99; v.p. Sacramento Jewish Fedn., 1980-82; chmn. Sacramento campaign United Jewish Appeal, 1981; bd. dirs., former nat. v.p. Am. Israel Pub. Affairs Com.; mem. bd. Calif. State U. Inst., 1995-99; bd. dirs. Nat. Bd. AntiDefamation League. 1st lt. USAF, 1956. Recipient Sacramento Businessman of Yr. award Sacramento Met. C. of C., 1991, Best Lawyers in Am. award, Outstanding Philanthropists award Nat. Soc. Fund Raising Execs., 1999, Sacramentan of Yr., 2006, Sacramento C. of C.; Fulbright candidate Stanford Law Sch., 1956. Fellow Am. Coll. Trial Lawyers; mem. ABA, ATLA, Calif. Bar Assn., Sacramento County Bar Assn. (pres. 1976, Lawyer of Yr. 1999), Calif. Trial Lawyers Assn. (v.p. 1973-75), Capitol City Lawyers Club (past pres.), Am. Bd. Trial Advocates (adv., pres. 1977, Calif. Trial Lawyer of Yr. 1988, SCALE award 2002), West Sacramento C. of C. (dir.), Order of Coif. Democrat. Home: 1620 McClaren Dr Carmichael CA 95608-5936 Office: 3610 American River Dr Ste 100 Sacramento CA 95864 Office Phone: 916-979-9199. Business E-Mail: mort@fulcrumproperty.com.

FRIEDMAN, PAUL JAY, retired radiologist; b. NYC, Jan. 20, 1937; s. Louis Alexander and Rose (Solomon) Friedman; m. Elisabeth Clare Richardson, June 18, 1960; children: Elizabeth Ruth Coley, Deborah Anne Yeager, Matthew Alexander Xu-Friedman, Rachel Clare Lentz. BS, U. Wis., 1955; postgrad., Oxford U., Eng., 1957—58; MD, Yale U., 1960. Diplomate Am. Bd Radiology. Intern Einstein Med. Sch., NYC, 1960-61; resident in radiology Columbia-Presbyn. Hosp., NYC, 1961-64; from asst. prof. to assoc. prof. U. Calif. San Diego Med. Sch., 1968-75, prof. radiology, 1975-2001, prof. emeritus, 2001—, from assoc. dean to dean acad. affairs, 1982-95; Hans Kende lectr. Mich. State U., 2008; cons. Nat. U. Singapore, 2007; sec. EMERITI Assn., UCSD, 2007—09. Cons. VA Hosp., 1971—2001; vis. scholar Inst. Med./NAS, AAMC, 1988—89; mem. adv. com. rsch. integrity HHS, 1991—93; cons. 26th, 27th, and 28th edit. Stedman's Med. Dictionary; specialist in chest radiology, rsch. ethics, acad. pers. issues; bd. dirs. Am. Coun. Edn., 1996—97. Mem. editl. bd. Investigative Radiology, 1976—87, Am. Jour. Roentgenology, 1986—88; contbr. articles to profl. jours. Bd. dirs. La Jolla Symphony Assn., 1987—92. Lt. cmdr. MC USNR, 1964—66. Markle scholar acad. medicine, 1969—74, Picker Found. Advanced Acad. fellow and scholar, 1966—69. Fellow: Am. Coll. Radiology, Am. Coll. Chest Physicians; mem.: Roentgen Ray Soc. (emeritus), Radiol. Soc. N.Am. (emeritus), Assn. Univ. Radiologists (emeritus), Internat. Soc. Magnetic Resonance Medicine (emeritus), Assn. Am. Med. Colls. (disting. svc. mem.), Fleischner Soc. (pres. 1994—95), Phi Beta Kappa, Alpha Omega Alpha. Avocations: singing, computers, gardening. Home: 5644 Soledad Rd La Jolla CA 92037-7048 Office: U Calif Sch Medicine Dept Radiology 200 W Arbor Dr San Diego CA 92103-8756 Office Phone: 619-543-5206. Business E-Mail: pfriedman@ucsd.edu.

FRIEDMAN, ROBERT GLENN, film company executive; b. 1950; s. Stuart S. and Sonia K. Friedman; m. Shari Ann Bernstein, July 17, 2004. With Warner Brothers, 1970—89, pres. worldwide advt. and publicity, 1989—96; vice chmn. Paramount Motion Picture Group, LA, 1997—2005; COO Paramount Pictures, LA, 2002—05; CEO Summit Entertainment L.L.C., 2007—. Office: Summit Entertainment LLC 1630 Stewart St Santa Monica CA 90404

FRIEDMAN, ROBERT LEE, film company executive; s. Edward A. and Claire (Seidenberg) F.; m. Marlene Saltz; children: Marc, Lisa. Sales Universal Pictures, NYC, 1948-52, 54-59; exec. v.p., distbn. & mktg. United Artists Corp., NYC, 1959-79; pres., distbn. Columbia Pictures, Burbank, Calif., 1979-82; pres. AMC Entertainment Internat., LA, 1984-92, pres. motion picture group, 1992-99; pres. RLF Entertainment, Beverly Hills, Calif., 1999—; CEO, pres. Stereo Vision Entertainment, Beverly Hills, 2000—. Radio announcer The Bob Friedman Hour, 1952-54; cons. RLF Prodns., Beverly Hills, Calif., 1982-84; sr. entertainment advisor, cons. Chanin Capital Ptnrs.; mem. bd. advisors Smart Video Tech.; ptnr. Media Entertainment Group LLC; bd. adv. MCorp and Roar Entertainment. Exec. prodr., appeared in film 9 Deaths of the Ninja, 1984; appeared in film Stardust Memories, 1980; prodr. film Girls Gone Wild. Bd. dirs., chmn. Entertainment Industry com. Century City C. of C., LA, 1988—; chmn. Will Rogers Hosp., 1980-81, also bd. dirs.; bd. dirs. Dare Am.; mem. vision fund The Lighthouse for the Blind. With US Army, 1952—54. Named Man of Yr. NY State Nat. Assn. Theatre Owners, 1981, Va., Md., Washington DC Assn. Theatre Owners, 1980. Mem. Acad. Motion Picture Arts & Scis. (bd. dirs. endowment fund, 1979—), Variety Club Am. (LA), Motion Picture Pioneers Am., Motion Picture Assocs. Found. (pres. 1970-73), LA-Century City C. of C. (Citizen of Yr., 1994) Avocations: photography, movies, tennis, exercise. Office: RLF Entertainment 2216 Summitridge Dr Beverly Hills CA 90210-1526 Personal E-mail: rlfblz@aol.com.

FRIEDMAN, SYDNEY M., anatomist, educator, medical researcher; b. Montreal, Que., Can., Feb. 17, 1916; s. Jacob and Minnie (Signer) F.; m. Constance Livingstone, Sept. 23, 1940. B.Sc., McGill U., Montreal, Can., 1938, MD, C.M., 1940, M.Sc., 1941, PhD, 1946. Med. licentiate, Que. Teaching fellow anatomy McGill U., Montreal, Que., Can., 1940-42, asst. prof. anatomy, 1944-48, assoc. prof. anatomy, 1948-50; prof., head dept. anatomy U. B.C., Vancouver, Can., 1950-81, prof. anatomy, 1981-85, prof. emeritus, 1985—. Mem. panel on shock Def. Research Bd., Ottawa, Can., 1955-57; sci. subcom. Can. Heart Found., 1962-66, Am. Heart Assn., 1966-68, B.C. Heart Found., Vancouver, founding mem. Author: Visual Anatomy, 1950, 2d edit., 1970; contbr. more than 200 articles to profl. publs. Served as flight lt. RCAF, 1943-44. Recipient Premier award for rsch. in aging CIBA Found., 1955, Outstanding Svc. award Heart Found. Can., 1981, Disting. Achievement award Can. Hypertension Soc., 1987; Commemorative medal 125th Anniversary Can. Confedn.; Pfizer travel fellow Clin. Rsch. Inst., Montreal, 1971. Fellow AAAS, Royal Soc. Can., Coun. High Blood Pressure Rsch.; mem. Am. Anatomical Assn. (exec. com. 1970-74), Can. Assn. Anatomists (pres. 1965-66, J.C.B. Grant award 1982), Internat. Soc. Hypertension, Am. Physiol. Soc., Royal Vancouver Yacht Club, Vancouver Club, Alpha Omega Alpha. Avocation: painting. Home: 4916 Chancellor Blvd Vancouver BC Canada V6T 1E1

FRIEDMAN, TULLY MICHAEL, finance company executive; b. Chgo., Jan. 9, 1942; s. Louis P. and Dorothy G. Friedman; m. Elise Woolsey Dorsey; children: Albert Evans Walker (dec.), Abigail Fay, Alexander Louis, Allegra Woolsey. AB, Stanford U., Calif., 1962; JD, Harvard U., Cambridge, Mass., 1965. Bar: Calif. 1965, Ill. 1967. With Charles Percy for Senator Com., Chgo., 1966; assoc. Sidley & Austin, Chgo., 1967-70; corp. fin. assoc. Salomon Bros., NYC, 1970-71, v.p., dir. West Coast corp. fin. San Francisco, 1972-79, gen. ptnr., 1979-81, mng. dir., 1981-84; founding ptnr. Hellman & Friedman, San Francisco, 1984-97; chmn., CEO Friedman, Fleischer & Lowe, LLC, San Francisco, 1997—. Bd. dirs. Clorox Co., Mattel, Inc., Kool Smiles Holding Co. Trustee, treas. Am. Enterprise Inst., 1988—; dir. Telluride Cmty. Found., 2001-. Home Phone: 415-441-1071; Office Phone: 415-402-2101.

FRIEDMANN, THEODORE, physician; b. Vienna, June 16, 1935; s. Eric and Rochelle (Behar) Friedmann; m. Ingrid Anna Stromberg, Jan. 3, 1965; children: Eric, Carl. BA, U. Pa., 1956, MD, 1960, MA, 1994. Diplomate Nat. Bd. Med. Examiners. Staff scientist NIH, Bethesda, Md., 1965-68; from asst. to full prof. pediatrics U. Calif. San Diego, La Jolla, 1970—, prof. pediatrics, dir. gene therapy, bd. dirs. Newton Abraham vis. prof., fellow Lincoln Coll., U. Oxford, England, 1994; mem. Congrl. Biomed. Ethics Adv. Com., U.S. Congress, Washington, 1988—92, Exptl. Virology Study Sect./NIH, 1986—90; Muriel Jeannette Whitehill chair biomed. ethics U. Calif., San Diego, 1989—; mem. com. on human cloning State of Calif., 2000—; mem. com. on medicine, health & rsch. IOC, World Anti Doping Agy., 2000—; mem. Recombinant DNA Adv. Bd./NIH, 1998—, chmn., 2002—. Author: (monograph) Gene Therapy: Fact and Fiction, 1993; editor: (book series) Molecular Genetic Medicine, 1989—; patentee in gene therapy. Recipient H.C. Jacobeaus prize, Nordic Rsch. Com., Sweden, 1995, Cross of Honor for Sci. and the Arts, Austria, 1996. Mem.: AAAS (chmn. adv. com. germ line gene therapy 1995—), NIH (chmn. DNA adv. com. 2001—). Avocation: music. E-mail: tfriedmann@ucsd.edu.

FRIEMAN, EDWARD ALLAN, academic administrator, educator; b. NYC, Jan. 19, 1926; s. Joseph and Belle (Davidson) F.; m. Ruth Paula Rodman, June 19, 1949 (dec. May 1966); children: Jonathan, Michael, Joshua; m. Joy Fields, Sept. 17, 1967; children: Linda Gatchell, Wendy. BS, Columbia U., 1946, MS in Physics, 1948; PhD in Physics, Poly. Inst. Bklyn., 1952. Prof. astrophys. scis., dep. dir. Plasma Physics Lab. Princeton U., N.J., 1953-79; dir. energy rsch. Dept. Energy, Washington, 1979-81; exec. v.p. Sci. Applications Internat. Corp., La Jolla, Calif., 1981—99; dir. Scripps Instn. Oceanography, La Jolla, 1986-96, rsch. prof., dir. emeritus San Diego, 1996—; vice-chancellor marine scis. U. Calif., San Diego, 1986-96. Vice-chmn. White House Sci. Coun., 1981-89, Def. Sci. Bd., Washington, 1984-90; mem. Joint Oceanog. Insts., Inc., 1986—, chmn., 1991—; chmn. supercollider site evaluation com. NRC, 1987-89; sci. adv. com. GM, 1987-93, corp. Charles Stark Draper Lab., Inc., 1989—, Sec. Energy Adv. Bd., 1990—, v.p. Space Policy adv. bd., 1992—; bd. dirs. Sci. Applications Internat. Corp.; chmn. NASA Earth Observing Sys. Engring. Rev., 1991-92, v.p.'s space policy adv. bd., 1992—; chmn. Pres.'s Com. on Nat. Medal Sci., 1992-93; chmn. bd. global change NAS/NRC, 1993-94, chmn. bd. on sustainable devel., 1995—; active Joint Oceanog. Insts., Inc., 1986—, chmn., 1991-94; spl. study group NRAC, 1995—; mem. law and policy adv. bd. Ctr. for Oceans, 1994—; mem. Def. Sci. Bd. Task Force on Future Submarines, 1997—. Contbr. articles to profl. jours. With USN, 1943-46, PTO. Recipient Disting. Service medal Dept. Energy, Compass Disting. Achievement Award, Marine Technology Soc., 1995; Disting. Alumni award Poly. Inst. Bklyn.; NSF sr. postdoctoral fellow; Guggenheim fellow Fellow Am. Phys. Soc. (Richtmyer award); mem. AAAS, NAS, Am. Philos. Soc., Cosmos Club (Washington). Avocations: piano, tennis, literature. Home: 1001 Genter St Ph 6 La Jolla CA 92037-5539 Office: Univ Calif San Diego Inst Geophys & Plan Physics 1241 Cave St La Jolla CA 92037-3602

FRIEND, STEPHEN H., biotechnology company executive; BA in Philosophy, Ind. U., MD, PhD in Biochemistry. Faculty Mass. Gen. Hosp., Boston, 1990—95, Harvard Med. Sch., Cambridge, Mass., 1987—95; co-founder, co-dir. Seattle Project Fred Hutchinson Cancer Rsch. Ctr., 1995—2000, vis. scientist, then head dept. molecular pharmacology, 1994—2000; pres. Inpharmatics, Kirkland, Wash., 1996—. Office: 401 Terry Ave N Seattle WA 98109-5234

FRIENDLY, DAVID T., film executive, producer; b. NYC, May 1, 1956; s. Fred W. and Dorothy Friendly; m. Priscilla Nedd-Friendly; 1 child. BA in Journalism, Northwestern U., 1978. Reporter, corr. Newsweek mag., NYC, LA, 1978-86; sr. v.p. motion pictures Imagine Films Entertainment, LA, 1987—91, pres. prodn., 1991; pres. Davis Entertainment, 1994; co-founder Deep River Prodns., 2000—. Columnist: First Look, LA Times, 1985—87; developer, supr.: (films) The Burbs, 1988; The Dream Team, 1988; Opportunity Knocks, 1989; Kindergarten Cop, 1990; exec. prodr.: My Girl, 1991, For Love or Money, 1993, My Girl 2, 1994, Greedy, 1994, The Chamber, 1996, Digging to China, 1998; prodr.: Courage Under Fire, 1996, Daylight, 1996, Out to Sea, 1997, Dr. Doolittle, 1998, Here on Earth, 2000, Big Momma's House, 2000, Laws of Attraction, 2004, The Honeymooners, 2005, Big Momma's House 2, 2006, Little Miss Sunshine, 2006 (Darryl F. Zanuck Prodr. of Yr. award in Theatrical Motion Pictures, Prodrs. Guild of Am., 2007). Bd. dirs. US-Ireland Alliance. Avocations: golf, tennis, music. Office: Deep River Productions 8733 W Sunset Blvd Ste 205 West Hollywood CA 90069-2244

FRIERY, THOMAS P., city treasurer; m. Linda Friery; three children. BS in Acctg., Dyke Coll., 1965; Corp. Cash Mgmt. Cert., Wharton Sch.'s Entrepreneurial, Ctr. Cert. Calif. Mcpl. Treas. Fin. and investment specialist State Auditor Gen., Calif., 1974-76; treasury divsn. mgr. Washington Pub. Power Supply System, Richland, 1976-78; city treas. City of Sacramento, 1978—. Mem. Calif. Mcpl. Treas. Assn. (past prest., chair legis. com.). Avocations: golf, fishing. Home: 915 I St Sacramento CA 95814-2604

FRIES, JAMES A., academic administrator; BS in Chem. Edn., U. SD, 1965; MS in Phys. Chem., U. Iowa, 1968, PhD in Phys. Chem., 1969. Tchg. and rsch. asst. U. Iowa; prof. chemistry Northern State Coll., 1969—78, sr. devel. officer, asst. to pres./dir. devel., 1978—85; acting pres. and v.p. adminstrn. SD State U., 1985—86; pres., CEO Coll. Santa Fe, 1986—2000, pres. emeritus; interim pres. N.Mex. Highlands U., Las Vegas, N.Mex., 2001—02, pres., 2007—; exec. dir. GROW Santa Fe Cmty. Coll. V.p. Santa Fe Econ. Devel., Santa Fe Chamber of Commerce; co-chair Higher Edn. Transition Team, 2002. Mem. bd. dirs. Golden Apple Found.; mem. Coun. Ind. Colleges and Universities on N.Mex.; involved with Santa Fe Symphony. Office: New Mexico Highlands University Office of President Box 9000 Las Vegas NM 87701 Office Phone: 505-454-3269. Office Fax: 505-454-3069.

FRIES, JAMES FRANKLIN, internal medicine educator; b. Normal, Ill., Aug. 25, 1938; s. Albert Charles and Orpha (Hair) F.; m. Sarah Elizabeth Tilton, Aug. 27, 1960; children: Elizabeth Ann, Gregory James. AB, Stanford U., 1960; MD, Johns Hopkins U., 1964. Diplomate Am. Bd. Internal Medicine. Intern Johns Hopkins Hosp., Balt., 1964-65, resident in medicine, 1965-66, fellow connective tissue disease divsn., 1966-68; resident in medicine Stanford (Calif.)

U. Sch. Medicine, 1968-69, instr. in medicine, 1969-71, asst. prof. medicine, 1971-77, assoc. prof. medicine, 1978-93, prof. medicine, 1993—. Dir. Arthritis, Rheumatism, Aging Med. Info. Sys., Stanford, 1975—; chmn. bd. dirs. Fries Found., Menlo Park, Calif.; chmn. Healthtrac, Inc., 1984-2001; exec. com. The Health Project, 1992—. Author: Take Care of Yourself, 1975, 2004, Prognosis, 1981, Living Well, 1997, 1999, 2004, Taking Care of Your Child, 2005, The Arthritis Helpbook, 2005, Arthritis, 2005; mem. editl. bd. Jour. Rheumatology, Jour. Clin. Rheumatology. Recipient C. Everett Koop Nat. Health award, 1994; named Best Med. Specialist in U.S., Town and Country mag., 1984, Best Dr. in U.S., Good Housekeeping mag., 1991, Rsch. Hero, Arthritis Found., 2001, Highly Cited Rschr., ISI, 2008; named one of Best Drs. in Am., Woodward-White, 1995. Master Am. Coll. Rheumatology (Clin. Rsch. award 2005); fellow ACP, Am. Coll. Med. Info. Avocations: skiing, running, expedition mountain climbing. Home: 135 Farm Rd Woodside CA 94062-1210 Office: Stanford U Sch Medicine 1000 Welch Rd Ste 203 Palo Alto CA 94304-1808 Office Phone: 650-723-6003. Business E-Mail: jff@stanford.edu.

FRIES, MICHAEL T., communications executive; BA, Wesleyan Univ.; MBA, Columbia Univ. Mgmt. positions with UnitedGlobal-Com, 1990—95, head Asia Pacific ops., 1995—98, pres., COO, 1998—2004, pres., CEO, 2004—05, Liberty Global Inc., Englewood, Colo., 2005—. Mem. Colo. Gov. Commn. on Sci. & Tech. Mem.: Young Presidents' Org. Office: Liberty Global Inc 12300 Liberty Blvd Englewood CO 80112

FRIESE, ROBERT CHARLES, lawyer; b. Chgo., Apr. 29, 1943; s. Earl Matthew and Laura Barbara (Mayer) F.; m. Chandra Ullom; children: Matthew Robert, Mark Earl, Laura Moore. AB in Internat. Rels., Stanford U., 1964; JD, Northwestern U., 1970. Bar: Calif. 1972. Dir. Tutor Applied Linguistics Ctr., Geneva, 1964-66; atty. Bronson, Bronson & McKinnon, San Francisco, 1970-71, SEC, San Francisco, 1971-75; ptnr. Shartsis, Friese & Ginsburg, San Francisco, 1975—. Pres., bd. dirs. Custom Diversification Fund Mgmt., Inc., 1993—; dir.-co-founder Internat. Plant Rsch. Inst., Inc., San Carlos, Calif., 1978-86 Chmn. bd. suprs. Task Force on Noise Control, 1972-78; chmn. San Franciscans for Cleaner City, 1977; exec. dir. Nob Hill Neighbors, 1972-81; bd. dirs. Nob Hill Assn., 1976-78, Palace Fine Arts, 1992-94, San Francisco Beautiful, 1986—, pres., 1988-2000, chmn. 2008-; chmn. Citizens Adv. Com. for Embarcadero Project, 1991-98; mem. major gifts com. Stanford U.; bd. dirs. Presidio Heights Neighborhood Assn., 1993—, pres., 1996-98; bd. dirs. Inst. of Range and the American Mustang, 1990—, Worldwatch Inst., 2005, chmn. nominating com., 2006, vice-chmn. 2008-, bd. dir., 2008-. Mem. ABA (co-chmn., sec. enforcement subcom., litigation sect., 2005-), Assn. Bus. Trial Lawyers (bd. dirs.), Calif. Bar Assn., Bar Assn. San Francisco (bd. dirs. 1982-85, chmn. bus. litigation com. 1978-79, chmn. state ct. civil litigation com. 1983-90, new courthouse com. 1993-95), Assn. SEC Alumni (bd. dirs. 1995—, pres. 2005-07), Lawyers Club of San Francisco, Mensa, Calif. Hist. Soc., Commonwealth Club, Swiss-Am. Friendship League (chmn. 1971-79). Office: Shartsis Friese LLP 1 Maritime Plz Fl 18 San Francisco CA 94111-3404 Home Phone: 415-773-7244. Business E-Mail: rfriese@sflaw.com.

FRIESECKE, RAYMOND FRANCIS, health company executive, president; b. Mar. 12, 1937; s. Bernhard P. K. and Josephine (De Tomi) F. BS in Chemistry, Boston Coll., 1959; MSCE, MIT, 1961. Product specialist Dewey & Almy Chem. divsn. W. R. Grace & Co., Inc., Cambridge, Mass., 1963-66; market planning specialist USM Corp., Boston, 1966-71; mgmt. cons. Boston, 1971-74; dir. planning and devel. Schweitzer divsn. Kimberly-Clark Corp., Lee, Mass., 1974-78; v.p. corp. planning Butler Automatic, Inc., Canton, Mass., 1978-80; pres. Butler-Europe Inc., Greenwich and Munich, Conn., Germany, 1980; v.p. mktg. and planning Butler Greenwich Inc., 1980-81; pres. Strategic Mgmt. Assocs., San Rafael, Calif., 1981-96; chmn. Beyond Health Corp., 1994—, Health-E-America Found., 2000—; pres. TPED Found., 2008. Bd. dirs. Better Physiology, Ltd., 2000-05; corp. clk., v.p. Bldg. R&D, Inc., Cambridge, 1966-68. Host, prodr. Beyond Health Show, Sta. KEST, San Francisco, 1994—98, WWNN, 1995—, Sta. KBZS, 1998—2001, Stas. WRPT and WSRO, 1999—2001; host, prodr. KYCY, 2001—05; host, prodr. KRLA, KSBN, KFNX, 2003—05, KNTS, 2005—, KKNT, 2006—; pub.: Beyond Health News, 1995—; author: Management by Relative Product Quality, 1982, The New Way to Manage, 1983, Never Be Sick Again, 2002, Never Be Fat Again, 2007; contbr. articles to profl. jours. State chmn. Citizens for Fair Taxation, 1972-73; state co-chmn. Mass. Young Reps., 1967-69; chmn. Ward 7 Rep. Com., Cambridge, 1968-70; vice-chmn. Cambridge Rep. City Com., 1966-68; bd. dirs. Kentfield Rehab. Hosp. Found., 1986-88, chmn., 1988-91; Rep. candidate Mass. Ho. of Reps., 1964, 66; pres. Marin Rep. Coun., 1986-91; chmn. Calif. Acad., 1986-88; sec. Navy League Marin Coun., 1984-91, v.p., 1994-2000; bd. dirs. The Marin Ballet, 1996-98; bd. dirs. Insts. for Behavioral Physiology, Seattle, 1999-2000; nat. chmn. Project to End Disease, 2005—. 1st lt. U.S. Army, 1961-63. Named Businessman of Yr., Bus. Adv. Coun., 2006. Mem. NRA, Nat. Health Fedn., Am. Chem. Soc., Physicians Com. for Responsible Medicine, Marin Philos. Soc. (v.p. 1991-92), Ctr. for Sci. in Pub. Interest, Health Medicine Forum, Assn. of Am. Physicians and Surgeons, Orthomolecular Health Medicine Soc., The World Affairs Coun., Am. Holistic Health Assn., Naval Inst., Milt. Officers Assn. Am., Am. Legion. Office: 777 Grand Ave Ste 205 San Rafael CA 94901-3509

FRIMMER, PAUL NORMAN, lawyer; b. NYC, June 8, 1945; s. William and Irene (Alper) F.; m. Carol S. Zucker, June 9, 1968; children: Tracey, Scott. BS, Queens Coll., NYC, 1966; JD cum laude, Fordham U., 1969. Bar: N.Y. 1969, Calif. 1971. Assoc. Stroock and Stroock, and Lavan, NYC, 1969-71; ptnr. Irell and Manella, LA, 1971—. Panelist Calif. Continuing Edn. of Bar, 1972, co-chmn. various sects. 73, 75, 76, 80, 86; instr. advanced profl. program U. So. Calif., 1977-80; lectr. 6th and 14th Insts. Estate Planning U. Miami Law Ctr., 1972, 80, Practicing Law Inst.-ABA programs, 1973-91, 31st Inst. Fed. Taxation U. So. Calif., 1979, other bar assn. groups on estate planning, probate, taxation, charitable giving and community property. Contbr. numerous articles to profl. jours. Nat. trustee, asst. sec. Leukemia Soc. Am., Inc., 1976-86, 91—, trustee, chmn. planned giving com. L.A. chpt., chpt. pres., 1973-86; trustee L.A. Children's Mus., 1982-86. Fellow Am. Coll. Trust and Estate Counsel, Internat. Acad. Probate and Trust Law; mem. ABA (real property, probate and trust law sect. com. charitable giving, trusts and founds., chmn. disclaimer task force), Calif. Bar Assn. Avocations: tennis, skiing. Office: Irell & Manella 1800 Avenue Of The Stars Los Angeles CA 90067-4276

FRISBEE, DON CALVIN, retired utilities executive; b. San Francisco, Dec. 13, 1923; s. Ira Nobles and Helen (Sheets) F.; m. Emilie Ford, Feb. 5, 1947; children: Ann, Robert, Peter, Dean. BA, Pomona Coll., 1947; MBA, Harvard U., 1949. Sr. investment analyst, asst. cashier investment analysis dept. 1st Interstate Bank Oreg., N.A., Portland, 1949-52; treas. PacifiCorp, Portland, 1958-60, then v.p., exec. v.p., pres., 1966-73, chief exec. officer, 1973-89, chmn., 1973-94; chmn. emeritus PacifiCorp., Portland, 1994-97. Bd. dirs. Wells Fargo Bank. Trustee Reed Coll.; former trustee Safari Game Search Found., High Desert Mus.; mem. cabinet Columbia Pacific coun. Boy Scouts Am.; founder Oreg. chpt. Am. Leadership Forum. 1st lt. AUS, 1943-46. Mem. Arlington Club, Univ. Club Multnomah Athletic Club, City Club. Home Fax: 503-224-1199.

FRISON, GEORGE CARR, education educator; BA, U. Wyo., 1963; MA, U. Mich., 1965, PhD, 1967. Prof. of anthropology U. Wyo., 1967-95, prof. emeritus, 1995—; dir. archeol. excavations State of Wyo. Mem. NAS, Soc. for Am. Archaeology (pres. 1983-85).

FRITZ, ETHEL MAE HENDRICKSON, writer; b. Gibbon, Nebr., Feb. 4, 1925; d. Walter Earl and Alice Hazel (Mickish) Hendrickson; m. C. Wayne Fritz, Feb. 25, 1950; children: Linda Sue, Krista Jane. BS, Iowa State U., Ames, 1949. Accredited master flower show judge. Dist. home economist Internat. Harvester Co., Des Moines, 1949-50; writer Wallace's Farmer mag., Des Moines, 1960-64; freelance writer, 1960—. Author: The Story of an Amana Winemaker, 1984, Prairie Kitchen Sampler, 1988, The Family of Hy-Vee, 1989. Chmn. Ariz. Coun. Flower Show Judges, 1983-85; medial rels. Presdl. Inaugural Com., 1988; mem. PEO. Mem. AAUW, Assn. for Women in Comm. (pres. Phoenix profl. chpt., nat. task force com. 1980-82), PEO, Am. Soc. Profl. and Exec. Women, Am. Assn. Family and Consumer Sci., Consumer Sci. Bus. Profls., S.W. Writer's Conf., Ariz. Authors Assn., Phi Upsilon Omicron, Kappa Delta. Republican. Methodist. Office Phone: 602-906-1953, 906-602-1953.

FRITZ, RENE EUGENE, manufacturing executive; b. Prineville, Oreg., Feb. 24, 1943; s. Rene and Ruth Pauline (Munson) Fritz; m. Sharyn Ann Fife, June 27, 1964; children: Rene Scott, Lanz Eugene, Shay Steven, Case McGarrett. BSBA, Oreg. State U., 1965. Sales mgr. Renal Corp., Albany, Oreg., 1965-66, Albany Machine and Supply, 1965-66; pres. Albany Internat. Industries Inc., 1966-85, Wood Yield Tech. Corp., 1972-85, Albany Internat. DISC, 1972-85, Automation Controls Internat. Inc., 1975-85; co-founder, chmn. Albany Titanium Inc., 1981-89; prin. Torwest Capital, 1989; founder, pres. WY Tech. Corp., 1984-89, R. Fritz & Assocs., 1987-89; prin., owner Engaging Media, Inc., 2006—. Pres. Chief Execs. Forum, 1989—, Fritz Grup, Inc., 1989—; fin. planner, investment banker M&A, Vancouver, Wash., 1991—; chmn. Stormwater Treatment LLC, CSF Treatment Sys., NTP, Wilsonville, Oreg., 1999—, Dentamax, Inc., Vancouver, 1999—, Human Capital Oreg./Wash., Vancouver, 1999—, MindNautilus, Inc., Portland, 2000—, Engaging Media, Inc., Rustic Canyon Entertainment, Inc. Patentee computer controlled machinery. Pres. Oreg. World Trade Coun., 1982—; trustee US Naval Acad. Found., Annapolis, Md., 1988—2004. Mem.: Forest Products Rsch. Soc., Young Pres. Orgn., Oreg. State Alumni, Elks, Rotary. Presbyterian.

FROEBE, GERALD ALLEN, lawyer; b. The Dalles, Oreg., Feb. 16, 1935; s. Earl Wayne and Ethelene Alvina (Ogle) F.; m. Olivia Ann Tharaldson, Aug. 31, 1958; children: Dana Lynn, Heidi Ann. BBA, U. Oreg., 1956, LLB, 1961; LLM, NYU, 1962. Bar: N.Y. 1962, Oreg. 1962, U.S. Dist. Ct. Oreg. 1962. Auditor Arthur Andersen & Co., Seattle, 1956-58; lawyer, ptnr. Miller, Nash, Wiener, Hager & Carlsen, Portland, Oreg., 1962—99. Editor-in-chief Oreg. Law Rev., Eugene, 1960-61. Republican. Christian. Avocations: hiking, travel. Office: 1109 SW Ardmore Ave Portland OR 97205

FROHNMAYER, DAVID BRADEN, academic administrator; b. Medford, Oreg., July 9, 1940; s. Otto J. and MarAbel (Braden) F.; m. Lynn Diane Johnson, Dec. 30, 1970; children: Kirsten (dec.), Mark, Kathryn (dec.), Jonathan, Amy. AB magna cum laude, Harvard U., 1962; BA, Oxford U., Eng., 1964, MA (Rhodes scholar), 1971; JD, U. Calif., Berkeley, 1967; LLD (hon.), Willamette U., 1988; D Pub. Svc. (hon.), U. Portland, 1989. Bar: Calif. 1967, US Dist. Ct. (no. dist.) Calif. 1967, Oreg. 1971, US Dist. Ct. Oreg. 1971, US Supreme Ct. 1981. Assoc. Pillsbury, Madison & Sutro, San Francisco, 1967-69; asst. to sec. Dept. HEW, 1969-70; prof. law U. Oreg., 1971-81, spl. asst. to univ. pres., 1971-79; atty. gen. State of Oreg., 1981-91; dean Sch. Law U. Oreg., 1992-94, pres., 1994—. Chmn. Conf. Western Attys. Gen., 1985-86; chmn. Am. Coun. Edn. Govtl. Rels. commn, 1996-98; bd. dirs. Umpqua Holding Co. Mem. Oreg. Ho. of Reps, 1975-81; mem. coun. pub. reps. NIH, 1999-00; bd. dirs. Fred Hutchinson Cancer Rsch. Ctr., 1994-00, Nat. Marrow Donor Program, 1987-99, Fanconi Anemia Rsch. Fund, Inc., Ford Family Found., 2004-, Assn. Am. U., 2004-; active Oreg. Progress Bd., 1991-04. Fellow Am. Acad. Arts and Scis.; mem. ABA (Ross essay winner 1980), Oreg. Bar Assn., Calif. Bar Assn., Nat. Assn. Attys. Gen. (pres. 1987, Wyman award 1987), Round Table Eugene, Order of Coif, Phi Beta Kappa, Rotary. Republican. Presbyterian. Home: 2315 McMorran St Eugene OR 97403-1750 Office: Office of Pres 110 Johnson Hall 1226 University of Oregon Eugene OR 97403-1226 Office Phone: 541-346-3036. Office Fax: 541-346-3017. Business E-Mail: pres@uoregon.edu.

FROHNMAYER, JOHN EDWARD, lawyer, writer; b. Medford, Oreg., June 1, 1942; s. Otto J. and MarAbel (Braden) F.; m. Leah Thorpe, June 10, 1967; children: Jason Otto, Jonathan Aaron. BA in Am. History, Stanford U., 1964; MA in Christian Ethics, U. Chgo., 1969; JD, U. Oreg., 1972. Bar: Oreg. 1972, Mont. 1995. Assoc. Johnson, Harrang & Mercer, Eugene, Oreg., 1972-75; ptnr. Tonkon, Torp, Galen, Marmaduke & Booth, Portland, Oreg., 1975-89; 5th chmn. Nat. Endowment for the Arts, Washington, 1989-92; writer, lectr. on art, ethics and politics, 1992—; pvt. practice Oreg., 1972-89, Bozeman, Mont., 1995—2005. Mem. Oreg. Arts Commn., 1978-85, chmn., 1980-84; bd. dirs. Internat. Sculpture Symposium, eugene, 1974; chmn. screening com. Oreg. State Capitol Bldg., 1977; affiliate prof. liberal arts Oreg. STate U., 2004—. Author: Leaving Town Alive, 1993, Out of Tune: Listening to The First Amendment, 1994; editor-in-chief Oreg. Law Rev., 1971-72; singer; appeared in recital, oratorio, mus. comedy and various other mus. prodns. Trustee Holladay Park Pla.; founding mem. chamber choir Novum Cantorum; bd. dirs. Chamber Music Northwest, Western States Arts Found.; mem. Nat. Endowment for the Arts Opera-Mus. Theater, 1982, 83. With USN, 1966-69. Active USNR, 1966—69, Vietnam. Sr. fellow Freedom Forum, 1993; recipient People for the Am. Way Ann. 1st Amendment award, 1992, Oreg. Gov. Arts award, 1993, Intellectual Freedom award Mont. Libr. Assn., 1997, Citation of Merit Mu Phi Epsilon, 1998, Lifetime Achievement award World Arts Fedn., 2006, Oreg. Lit. Arts award, 2007. Fellow Am. Leadership Forum; mem. ABA (com. comml. trans. litig.), Oreg. State Bar Assn. (chmn. bar com. domestic law 1975-76, procedure and practice com. 1984-85), Multnomah County Bar Assn., City Club Portland (program com.), Sta. L. Rowing Club (sec.), Corvallis Rowing Club, Order of the Coif (legal hon. 1972). Avocations: rowing, singing. Home and Office: 1335 SW Timian St Corvallis OR 97333 Business E-Mail: john.frohnmayer@oregonstate.edu.

FROMAN, SANDRA SUE, lawyer; b. San Francisco, June 15, 1949; d. Jay and Beatrice Froman. AB with honors, Stanford U., 1971; JD, Harvard U., 1974. Bar: Calif. 1974, U.S. Dist. Ct. (cen. dist.) Calif. 1974, U.S. Dist. Ct. (so. dist.) Calif. 1976, U.S. Dist. Ct. (no. dist.) Calif., U.S. Ct. Claims 1979, U.S. Tax Ct. 1984, Ariz. 1985, U.S. Dist. Ct. Ariz. 1985, U.S. Ct. Appeals (9th cir.) 1986, U.S. Supreme Ct. 1986. Assoc. Loeb & Loeb, LA, 1974-80, ptnr., 1981-84; assoc. Bilby & Schoenhair, P.C., Tucson, 1985, shareholder, 1986-89; ptnr. Snell & Wilmer, Tucson, 1989-99. Vis. asst. prof. law U. Santa Clara, Calif., 1983-85; mem. Pima County Commn. on Trial Ct. Appointments, 1996-98. Trustee NRA Civil Rights Def. Fund, 1992-98, NRA Found., pres. 1997-2000; bd. dirs. NRA, 1992-, pres. 2005-07, exec. coun. Mem. Ariz. Bar Found. (pres. 1996), Nat. 4-H Shooting Sports Found. (pres. 2002-04), Wildlife for Tomorrow Found. (pres. 1999-02). Office: Ste 140 200 W Magee Rd Tucson AZ 85704-6492 Address: NRA 11250 Waples Mill Rd Fairfax VA 22030

FRONTERA, MICHAEL P., municipal official; b. Newburgh, NY, May 22, 1969; BA, SUNY, Binghamton, 1991; JD, U. Ariz., 1994. Election specialist City Clk.'s Office City of Tucson (Ariz.), 1993-95; info. dir. Denver Election Commn. City of Denver, 1996-97, exec. dir. Denver Election Commn., 1997-99; client support mgr. Sequoia Pacific, Denver, 1999—, installation mgr. Mem. Election Ctr. 96. Recipient Am. Jurisprudence award in Constl. Law Lawyers Coop. Publishing, 1991. Mem. ABA, Colo. Bar Assn., Denver Bar Assn., Internat. Assn. Clks., Recorders, Election Officials & Treasurers, Colo. State Assn. County Clks. & Recorders. Office: Sequoia Pacific 410 17th St Ste 1950 Denver CO 80202-4432

FROST, EVERETT LLOYD, academic administrator, anthropologist; b. Salt Lake City, Oct. 17, 1942; s. Henry Hoag Jr. and Ruth Salome (Smith) F.; m. Janet Owens, Mar. 26, 1967; children: Noreen Karyn, Joyce Lida. BA in Anthropology, U. Utah, 1965; PhD in Anthropology, U. Oreg., 1970. Field rschr. in cultural anthropology, Taveuni, Fiji, 1968-69; asst. prof. in anthropology Ea. N.Mex. U., Portales, 1970-74, assoc. prof., 1974-76, asst. dean Coll. Liberal Arts and Scis., 1976-78, dean acad. affairs and grad. studies, 1978-80, v.p. for planning and analysis, dean rsch., 1980-91, dean grad. studies, 1983-88, pres., 1991-2001, pres. emeritus, prof. anthropology emeritus, 2001—. Cons., evaluator N. Ctrl. Assn. Accreditation Agy. for Higher Edn., 1989-93—, mem. rev. bd., 1993-95—; commr., past chair Western Interstate Commn. for Higher Edn., 1993-; pres. Lone Star Athletic Conf. Pres.'s Commn., 1992-93. Chmn. N.Mex. Humanities Coun., 1980-88; mem. N.Mex. Gov.'s Commn. on Higher Edn., 1983-86; mem. exec. bd. N.Mex. First, 1987-92, chmn. rsch. com., 1989-91, exec. bd. emeritus, 1992-; bd. dirs. Roosevelt Gen. Hosp., Portales, 1989-92; pres. bd. dirs. San Juan County Mus. Assn., Farmington, 1979-82; vice chair Portales Pub. Schs. Facilities Com., 1990-91, Eastern N.Mex Local Growth Mgmt. Orgn., 2007. NDEA fellow, 1969-70; grantee NEW, 1979-80, NSF, 1968-69, Fiji Forbes, Ltd., 1975-76, others. Fellow Am. Anthropol. Assn., Am. Assn. Higher Edn., Soc. Coll. and Univ. Planning, Assn. Social Anthropologists Oceania, Anthrop. Soc. Wash., Sch. Am. Rsch., Western Assn. Grad. Deans, Current Anthropology (assoc.) Polynesian Soc., Phi Kappa Phi. Office: Ea NMex Univ Dept Anthropolog Sta 3 Portales NM 88130 Home Phone: 575-356-3609; Office Phone: 575-562-2883. Business E-Mail: everett.frost@enmu.edu.

FROST, STERLING NEWELL, arbitrator, mediator, management consultant; b. Oklahoma City, Dec. 21, 1935; s. Sterling Johnson and Eula Dove (Whitford) F.; m. Patricia Joyce Rose, Aug. 18, 1957; children: Patricia Diane Wiscarson, Richard Sterling, Lindy Layne Harrington. BS Indsl. Engring., U. Okla., Norman, 1957; MS Indsl. Engring., Okla. State U., 1966. Registered profl. engr., Okla., Calif. Asst. mgr. acctg. Western Electric, Balt., 1972-73; mgr. indsl. engring. Chgo., 1973-75; mgr. devel. engring., 1975-76; mgr. acct. mgmt. San Francisco, 1976-78; dir. staff Morristown, N.J., 1978-79; gen. mgr. distbn. & repair AT&T Techs., Sunnyvale, Calif., 1979-85; area v.p. material mgmt. svcs. AT&T Info. Systems, Oakland, Calif., 1985-87; ops. v.p. material mgmt. svcs. San Francisco, 1988-89; dir. configuration ops. Businessland, Inc., San Jose, Calif., 1989-90; dir. svcs. support, 1990-91; exec. v.p. Isotek, Tiburon, Calif., 1991; v.p., gen. mgr. Tree Fresh, San Francisco, 1991-92; CFO Prima Pacific, Iinc., Tiburon, 1992-93; mgmt. cons., arbitrator/mediator Sterling Solutions, Santa Cruz, 1992—. Bd. dirs. Contract Office Group, San Jose, 1983-2001, chmn., 1984-2001; arbitrator FINRA (formerly NASD and NY Stock Exch.) 1992-; contbr. Calif. State Mediation and Conciliation Svcs., 1992-2007; mediator US Postal Svc., 1998—. Bd. dirs. Santa Clara County YMCA, San Jose, Calif., 1981-84, No. Calif. Mediation Assn., 1995-99. Recipient Man of Day citation Sta. WAIT Radio, Chgo. Mem. NSPE (chmn. edn. com. 1969-70), Am. Inst. Indsl. Engrs. (pres. bd. dirs. 1966-68), Okla. Soc. Profl. Engrs. (v.p. 1968-69), No. Calif. Mediation Assn. (bd. dirs. 1996-98), Am. Arbitration Assn. Republican. Office Phone: 831-458-9213. Personal E-mail: snfrost@sbcglobal.net.

FROT-COUTAZ, CECILE, television producer; b. Chambery, France, Apr. 18, 1966; m. M. Eliot Charles, Dec. 29, 2001; 1 child, Amelie. BA in Bus., ESSEC, 1988; MBA, INSEAD, 1994. Assoc. Mercer Mgmt. Consulting, London, 1988—93; exec. corp. strategy Pearson TV, London, 1994—98, dep. chief exec. officer So. Europe, mng. dir. France Paris, 1998—2000, head digital media, 2000—01; exec. v.p. comml. and ops. FremantleMedia North America, LA, 2001—02, COO Santa Monica, Calif., 2002—05, CEO prodn., 2005—, exec. prodr. Am. Idol, 2002—05, mem. operating bd. Named one of The 100 Most Powerful Women in Entertainment, Hollywood Reporter, 2007.

FRUCHTER, JONATHAN SEWELL, research scientist, geochemist; b. San Antonio, June 5, 1945; s. Benjamin and Dorothy Ann (Sewell) F.; m. Cecelia Ann Smith, Mar. 31, 1973; children: Diane, Daniel. BS in Chemistry, U. Tex., 1966; PhD in Geochemistry, U. Calif., San Diego, 1971. Research assoc. U. Oreg., Eugene, 1971-74; research scientist Battelle Pacific Northwest Nat. Lab., Richland, Wash., 1974—79, mgr. research and devel., 1979—87, staff scientist, 1987—91, 1994—, tech. group leader, 1991—94. Contbr. numerous articles to profl. jours. Recipient R&D 100 Awd., 1998. Mem. AAAS,

Am. Chem. Soc., Phi Beta Kappa, Phi Kappa Phi. Avocations: fishing, skiing, boating. Office: Pacific Northwest Nat Lab PO Box 999 Richland WA 99352-0999 Office Phone: 509-371-7075.

FRUCHTERMAN, JAMES ROBERT, JR., computer company and not-for-profit executive; b. Washington, May 1, 1959; s. James R. Sr. and Ellen Patricia (Fallon) F.; m. Virginia Belwood, Aug. 11, 1984; children: James David, Richard Andrew, Katherine Elizabeth. BS in Engring., Calif. Inst. Tech., Pasadena, 1980, MS in Applied Physics, 1980; doctoral studies, Stanford U., Calif., 1980—81. Co-founder, v.p. Calera Recognition Systems, Inc. (formerly Palantir Corp.), Santa Clara, Calif., 1982—89; v.p. mktg. The Palantir Corp., Santa Clara, Calif., 1987-89; co-founder, CFO RAF Tech., Inc., Redmond, Wash., 1989—2004; chmn. Arkenstone, Inc., Moffett Field, Calif., 1989-2000; chmn., CEO, pres. Benetech Initiative, Palo Alto, Calif., 2000—. Dir. Zero Divide Foundation, 2007-; chief elec. engr. 1st pvt. US launch vehicle venture. Mem. fed. adv. com. on telecomm. access, 1996-97; mem. Electronic and Info. Tech. Access Fed. Adv. Comm., 1998-99; social dir. Enterprise Alliance, 2000—; mem. adv. com. Rehab. Engring. Rsch. Ctr. on Telecom. Access, U. Wis./Gallaudet U., 2001. Recipient Access award, Am. Found. Blind, Robert S. Bray award, Am. Coun. Blind; fellow, MacArthur Found., 2006. Mem.: AIAA, AAAS, IEEE, Assn. Computing Machinery. Achievements include development of the most accurate optical character recognition technology in the world, and of leading reading machine for the blind and people with reading disabilities. Office: Benetech Initiative 480 California Ave Ste 201 Palo Alto CA 94306-1609

FRUMKIN, SIMON, political organization worker, writer; b. Kaunas, Lithuania, Nov. 5, 1930; came to U.S., 1949; s. Nicholas and Zila (Oster) F.; m. Rhoda Hirsch, June 1953 (div. 1978); children: Michael Alan, Larry Martin; m. Kathy Elizabeth Hoopes, June 22, 1981 (dec. 1994); m. Ella Zousman, Dec. 11, 1995. BA, NYU, 1953; MA in History, Calif. State U., Northridge, 1964. Pres., chief exec. officer Universal Drapery Fabrics, Inc., Los Angeles, 1953-87; chmn. Southern Calif. Council for Soviet Jews, Studio City, 1969—. Lectr. Simon Wiesenthal Ctr. for Holocaust Studies, Los Angeles, 1980—; chmn. Union of Councils for Soviet Jews, 1972-73. Columnist Heritage, numerous other So. Calif. newspapers, 1980—; corr. to columnist Panorama, U.S.A. Russian Lang., 1985—; contbr. articles to newspapers. Pres. Media Analysis Found., Los Angeles, 1988; chmn. Ams. for Peace and Justice, 1972-74; mem. Pres.' Senatorial Inner Circle, U.S. Senatorial Club. Honored by Calif. Govt., Los Angeles City Council, Los Angeles Office of City Atty., numerous Jewish orgns. Mem. Assn. Soviet Jewish Emigre's (pres. 1987—), Zionist Orgn. Am., Am. Israel Polit. Action Com., Russian Republican Club, Mensa. Avocations: writing, photography, skiing, exercise. Home and Office: 3755 Goodland Ave Studio City CA 91604-2313 Office Phone: 818-769-8862. E-mail: esfrumkin@roadrunner.com.

FRY, DAVID, electronics executive; CFO, CIO Fry's Electronics, Inc., San Jose, Calif. Mng. gen. ptnr. San Jose SaberCats. Office: Fry's Electronics Inc 600 E Brokaw Rd San Jose CA 95112

FRY, EARL HOWARD, political scientist, educator; b. Oakland, Calif., May 19, 1947; s. Harvey Wallace and Alice (Horlacher) F.; m. Elaine Fisher, May 29, 1971; children: Christopher, Lisa, Leanna, Kimberly, Steven, Kristen. BA, BA, Brigham Young U., 1971, MA, 1972; PhD, UCLA, 1976. Fulbright prof. U. Sorbonne, Paris, 1974-75; asst. prof. Boise State U., Idaho, 1976-79; assoc. prof. SUNY, Plattsburgh, 1979-80, Brigham Young U., Provo, Utah, 1980-83, prof. dept. Polit. Sci., Endowed prof. Canadian studies, 1989—, dir. the Washington Seminar, 1999-2000; spl. asst. Office U.S. Trade Rep., Washington, 1983-84. Asst. dir. Brigham Young U.-U Grenoble Semester Abroad Program, 1972; vis. rschr. UN, Geneva, 1974; asst. prof. Boise State U., 1976-79; chmn. BSU Faculty Rsch. com., 1977-78; vis. prof. U. B.C., 1977; prin. investigator Idaho Internat. Trade directory Pacific N.W. Regional Commn., 1979; assoc. prof. SUNY Plattsburgh, 1979-80, dir. Internat. Edn., Canadian Studies, 1979-80; vis. prof. U. Montreal, 1989, Ecole des Hautes Etudes en Scis. Sociales, Paris, 1990; rev. com. Internat. Proposals U.S. Dept. Edn., 1985-88; Utah State Tax Commn. Task Force on Unitary Taxation, 1985; chmn. Can. studies, Brigham Young U., 1980—; Univ. rep. Atlantic Coun. U.S., 1987—; fellowship com. Coun. Fgn. Rels., 1989-93, fellow 1983-84; dir. Grad. Studies, Rsch., Publs., David M. Kennedy Ctr. Internat. Studies, 1987-90; Fulbright Commn. rev. com., 1991; vis. fellow Ams. Soc., N.Y.C., 1991-93; acad. assoc. Atlantic Coun., Washington, 1987—; dir. The Washington Seminar, 1999-2000; scholar-in-residence in urban studies U. Calif., San Diego, 2003; lectr., cons. and spkr. in field. Author: Financial Invasion of the U.S.A., 1980, Canadian Government and Politics in Comparative Perspective, 1983, The Canadian Political System, 1991, Canada's Unity Crisis: Implications for U.S.-Canadian Economic Relations, 1992; co-author Idaho's Foreign Relations: The Transgovernmental Linkages of an American State, 1978, The Other Western Europe: A Comparative Analysis of the Smaller Democracies, 1980, The Other Western Europe, 1983, America the Vincible: U.S. Foreign Policy for the Twenty-First Century, 1994, The Expanding Role of State and Local Governments in U.S. Foreign Affairs, 1998; co-editor The Canada/U.S. Free Trade Agreement: The Impact on Service Industries, 1988, Investment in the North American Free Trade Area: Opportunities and Challenges, 1992; gen. editor Canadian Studies Curriculum Guide, 1980; contbr. numerous articles to profl. jours. Bd. dirs. Fulbright Assn., 1995-98. Recipient Can. Studies Sr. Fellowship award, 1983, Karl G. Maeser Rsch. and Creative Arts award, 1989; rsch. grantee Coll. Family, Home and Social Scis., 1986, 88, 89, 92; rsch. and conf. grantee Can. govt., 1985-92; Fulbright lectr. U. Paris (La Sorbonne), 1974-75; Bissell-Hyde-Fulbright chair U. Toronto, 1995-96; Elliot/Winant Lecture fellow UK, 1993, Coun. Fgn. Rels. Internat. Affairs fellow, 1983, David M. Kennedy Rsch. fellow Brigham Young U., 1985-86, Rsch. grantee, 1987-89; Atlantic Coun. Travel grantee, 1988; Presdl. fellow Am. Grad. Sch. Internat. Mgmt., 1993; Thomas O. Enders fellow McGill U., 2002. Mem. Internat. Polit. Sci. Assn., Assn. Can. Studies in U.S. (Washington v.p. 1989-91, pres. 1991-93, exec. coun. 1985—, Bissell-Hyde Fulbright chair U. Toronto 1995-96), Fulbright Assn. (bd. dirs. 1995-97), Coun. Fgn. Rels. Mem. Lds Ch. Office: Brigham Young U Dept Pol Scis Provo UT 84602 E-mail: earl_fry@byu.edu.

FRY, JOHN C., electronics executive; s. Charles; m. Ramune Ambrozaitis. BS in Math, Santa Clara Univ. Founder, CEO Fry's Electronics Inc., San Jose, Calif., 1985—; gen. ptnr. San Jose SaberCats, 1994—. Office: Frys Electronics Inc 600 E Brokaw Rd San Jose CA 95112-1006

FRY, MICHAEL GRAHAM, historian, educator; b. Brierley, Eng., Nov. 5, 1934; s. Cyril Victor and Margaret Mary (Copley) F.; m. Anna Maria Fulgoni; children: Michael Gareth, Gabrielle, Margaret Louise. B.Sc. in Econs. with honors, U. London, 1956, PhD, 1963. Dir. Norman Paterson Sch. Internat. Affairs, Carleton U., Ottawa, Ont., 1973-77; dean, prof. internat. relations Grad. Sch. Internat. Studies, U. Denver, 1978-81; dir., prof. Sch. Internat. Relations, U. So. Calif., Los Angeles, 1981—. Vis. prof. Middle East Center, U. Utah, 1979, U. Leningrad, 1976 Author: Illusions of Security: North Atlantic Diplomacy, 1918-1922, 1972, Freedom and Change, 1975, Lloyd George and Foreign Policy, Vol. I, The Education of a Statesman, 1890-1916, 1977, Despatches from Damascus, 1933-39, 1986, History and International Studies, 1987, History, The White House and the Kremlin: Statesmen as Historians, 1991, Power, Personalities and Policies, 1992, The North Pacific Triangle: Canada Japan and the U.S. at Century's End, 1998, Guide to International Relations and Diplomacy, 2002. NATO rsch. fellow, 1970-71, rsch. fellow Annenberg Program, Washington, 1986-87; grantee Can. Coun. Fellow: Royal Hist. Soc. Roman Catholic. Home: 7555 Eads Ave Unit 18 La Jolla CA 92037-4856

FRYE, DONNA, councilwoman; b. Jan. 20, 1952; m. Skip Frye. Grad., Nat. U. Councilwoman, Dist. 6 San Diego City Coun., 2001—. Co-founder S.T.O.P. - Surfers Tired of Pollution. Recipient San Diego Environ. Champion Award, San Diego League of Conservation Voters, 2005. Office: 202 C St MS 10A San Diego CA 92101 Office Phone: 619-236-6616. Fax: 619-236-7329. E-mail: donnafrye@sandiego.gov.*

FRYE, HELEN JACKSON, federal judge; b. Klamath Falls, Oreg., Dec. 10, 1930; d. Earl and Elizabeth (Kirkpatrick) Jackson; m. William Frye, Sept. 7, 1952; children: Eric, Karen, Heidi; 1 adopted child, Hedy; m. Perry Holloman, July 10, 1980 (dec. Sept. 1991). BA in English with honors, U. Oreg., 1953, MA, 1960, JD, 1966. Bar: Oreg. 1966. Public sch. tchr., Oreg., 1956-63; with Riddlesberger, Pederson, Brownhill & Young, 1966-67, Husband & Johnson, Eugene, 1968-71; trial judge State of Oreg., 1971-80; U.S. dist judge Dist. Oreg. Portland, 1980-95; sr. judge U.S. Dist. Ct., Portland, 1995—. Coll. Arts and Sci. Alumni Fellow, Univ. Oreg., 1997—98. Mem. Phi Beta Kappa.

FRYXELL, DAVID ALLEN, publishing executive; b. Sioux Falls, SD, Mar. 8, 1956; s. Donald Raymond and Lucy (Dickinson) F.; m. Lisa Duaine Forman, June 16, 1978; 1 child, Courtney Elizabeth. BA, Augustana Coll., 1978. Assoc.-sr. editor TWA Ambassador, St. Paul, 1978-80, mng. editor, 1980-81; sr. editor Horizon, Tuscaloosa, Ala., 1981-82; circuit writer Telegraph Herald, Dubuque, Iowa, 1982-85; contbg. editor Horizon mag., 1982-85; dir. publs., exec. editor Pitt mag. U. Pitts., 1985-90; editl. dir. Quad/Creative Group Milwaukee Mag., 1991-92; exec. features editor, dir. new ventures St. Paul Pioneer Press, 1992-95, sr. editor technology and new ventures, 1995-96; sr. editor bus. and tech., 1996; exec. producer Twin Cities Sidewalk Microsoft Corp., 1996-98; mag. editl. dir. F & W Publs., Cin., 1998—2001, editor-in-chief, 2001—03; editor, pub. Desert Exposure, 2003—; pub. Gila Books, 2005—; pres. Continental Divide Pub. LLC, 2005—. Chief judge mags. Golden Quill awards, Pitts., 1980; nonfiction columnist Writer's Digest, 1994—2006; faculty Maui Writers Conf., 2000—, dir., 2006—. Author: Double-Parked on Main Street, 1988, How to Write Fast While Writing Well, 1992, Elements of Article Writing: Structure and Flow, 1996, Write Faster, Write Better, 2004, The Best in Health & Nutrition, 2007; editor: Family Tree Mag., 2000-03, Comair Navigator Mag., 2001-02, Tufts University Guide to Healthy Living, 2004-05; mng. editor Tufts Health and Nutrition Letter, 2004—; contbr. articles to mags. including Travel & Leisure, Playboy, Passages, AAA World, Savvy, Online Access, Diversion, Easy Living, Readers Digest, Link Up, others. Chief writer Anderson for Pres. Com., Minn., 1978. Recipient Merit award for editing, Chgo. Art Dir. Club, 1981, 2d award master columnist, Iowa Newspaper Assn., 1983, 2d award best feature writing, 1983, 2d award best series, 1983, Periodicals Improvement award, Coun. for Advancement and Support of Edn., 1987, 1990, 1991, Top Ten Mag. award, 1990, 1991, Articles of Yr. award, 1990, Institutional Relations Publications award, 1991, Periodical Special Issues award, 1991, Periodical Resource Mgmt. award, 1990, 1991, Golden Triangle award, Internat. Assn. Bus. Communicators, 1997, 1989, Best Special Pub. award, 1988, Matrix award, Women in Comm., 1990, Hon. Mention, 1990, 1991, Gen. Excellence award, City and Regional Mgr. Assn., 1992, Special Sect. award, 1992, Commentary award, 1992, Investigative Writing award, 1992, 2d Gen. Excellence award, Mo. Lifestyle awards, 1994, 1995, Notable Essays of Yr., Best Am. Essays, 2004, 2005. Mem.: Augustana Alumni Assn. (Decades of Leadership award 1978), Augustana Coll. Fellows, Blue Key. Democrat. Unitarian Universalist. Office: PO Box 191 Silver City NM 88062 Office Phone: 575-538-4374. Business E-Mail: editor@desertexposure.com.

FU, LEE-LUENG, oceanographer; b. Taipei, Republic of China, Oct. 10, 1950; s. Yi-Chin and Er-Lan (Chen) F.; m. Cecilia C. Liu, Mar. 26, 1977; 1 child, Christine. BS, Nat. Taiwan U., Taipei, 1972; PhD, MIT, 1980. Postdoctoral assoc. MIT, Cambridge, Mass., 1980; mem. tech. staff Jet Propulsion Lab., Pasadena, Calif., 1981-85, tech. group supr., Topex/Poseidon, 1986-93, project scientist, 1988—, lead scientist/ocean scis., 1994, sr. rsch. scientist, 1994. Chmn. Jason sci. working team NASA, Washington, 1988—; vis. prof. Ocean U. Qingdao, China, 2002. Editor: Satellite Altimetry and Earth Sciences, 2001; contbr. articles to profl. publs. Recipient Laurels award Aviation Week and Space Tech., 1993, CNES medal French Space Agy., 1994, Exceptional Scientific Achievement medal NASA, 1996, Outstanding Leadership Medal, 2004, Space Sys. Team award, Am. Inst. Aeronautics and Astronautics, 2006. Fellow: Am. Meteorol. Soc. (Editor's award 2005, Verner E. Suomi award 2002), Am. Geophys. Union; mem.: Oceanography Soc. Office: Jet Propulsion Lab MS 300-323 4800 Oak Grove Dr Pasadena CA 91109-8001 Business E-Mail: llf@pacific.jpl.nasa.gov.

FUCALORO, ANTHONY FRANK, dean; b. Bklyn., Apr. 17, 1943; s. Gaetano Atillio and Josepina (Noto) F.; m. Liliane Marie-Louise Rigas, June 25, 1967; children: Nicole Antionette, Cristina Veronique. BS, Poly. Inst., Bklyn., 1964; PhD, U. Ariz., 1969. Assoc. N.Mex. State U., Las Cruces, 1969-71; vis. asst. prof. U. New Orleans, 1971-74; prof. chemistry Claremont (Calif.) McKenna Coll., 1974-93, v.p., pres., dean faculty, 1991—. Cons. Occidental Petroleum, Irvine, Calif., Ill. Tool Works, Chgo., Jet Propulsion Lab., Pasadena, Calif. Contbr. articles to profl. jours. Mem. Am. Chem. Soc. (soc. advisor to Congressman David Dreier). Office: Claremont McKenna Coll Bauer Ctr 500 E 9th St Claremont CA 91711-5903

FUCHS, VICTOR ROBERT, economist, educator; b. NYC, Jan. 31, 1924; s. Alfred and Frances Sarah (Scheiber) Fuchs; m. Beverly (Beck), Aug. 29, 1948; children: Nancy, Frederic, Paula, Kenneth. BS, N.Y. Univ., 1947; MA, Columbia Univ., 1951, PhD, 1955. Internat. fur broker, 1946—50; lectr. Columbia Univ., NYC, 1953—54, instr., 1954—55, asst. prof. econ., 1955—59; assoc. prof. econ. N.Y. Univ., NYC, 1959—60; program assoc. Ford Found. Program in econ., devel., and adminstrn., 1960—62; mem. sr. rsch staff Nat. Bur. Econ. Rsch., 1962—; prof. econ. Grad. Ctr. City Univ. of N.Y., NYC, 1968—74; prof. cmty. medicine Mt. Sinai Sch. Medicine, 1968-74; v.p. rsch. Nat. Bur. Econ. Rsch., 1968—78; prof. econ. Stanford U., Stanford Med. Sch., 1974—95; Henry J. Kaiser Jr. prof. Stanford U., Stanford Med. Sch., 1988—95, prof. emeritus, 1995—. Author: The Economics of the Fur Industry, 1957; co-author (with Aaron Warner): Concepts and Cases in Econ. Analysis, 1958; author: Changes in the Location of Mfg. in the U.S. Since 1929, 1962, The Svc. Economy, 1968, Prodn. and Productivity in the Svc. Industries, 1969, Policy Issues and Rsch. Opportunities in Indsl. Orgn., 1972, Essays on the Economics of Health and Med. Care, 1972, Who Shall Live? Health, Economics, and Social Choice, 1975; co-author (with Joseph Newhouse): The Economics of Physician and Patient Behavior, 1978; author: Economic Aspects of Health, 1982, How We Live, 1983, The Health Economy, 1986, Women's Quest for Econ. Equality, 1988, The Future of Health Policy, 1993, Individual and Social Responsibility: Child Care Edn., Med. Care, and Long-term Care in Am., 1996, Who Shall Live? Health, Economics and Social Choice, expanded edit., 1998; contbr. articles to profl. jour. Served in USAF, 1943—46. Fellow: Am. Econ. Assn. (disting., pres. 1995), Am. Acad. Arts and Sci.; mem.: Am. Philos. Soc. (John R. Commons award), Am. Inst. Medicine of NAS, Beta Gamma Sigma, Sigma Xi. Home: 796 Cedro Way Stanford CA 94305-1032 Office: NBER 30 Alta Rd Stanford CA 94305-8006 Office Phone: 650-326-7639.

FUENTES, BRIAN CHRISTOPHER, professional baseball player; b. Merced, Calif., Aug. 9, 1975; m. Barbara Fuentes; 1 child, Giovanni Paolo. Grad., Merced Jr. Coll., 1996. Draft pick Seattle Mariners, 1995, pitcher, 2001, Colo. Rockies, 2001—08; relief pitcher LA Angles of Anaheim, 2008—. Mem. US nat. team World Baseball Classic, 2009. Named to Nat. League All-Star Team, Maj. League Baseball, 2005—07. Office: LA Angels of Anaheim Angel Stadium 2000 Gene Autry Way Anaheim CA 92806*

FUENTES, FELIPE, state legislator; m. Lena Wu; 1 child, Iliana Flor. Grad., UCLA, Pepperdine U., Graziadio Sch. Bus. Deputy mayor City of San Fernando Valley, Calif.; chief of staff for President Alex Padilla LA City Coun., Calif.; mem. Dist. 39 Calif. State Assembly, San Fernando Valley, Calif., 2007—. Democrat. Office: PO Box 942849 Rm 5136 Sacramento CA 94249-0039 Address: 9300 Laurel Canyon Blvd Pacoima CA 91331-4314 Office Phone: 916-319-2039, 818-504-3911. Business E-Mail: Assemblymember.fuentes@assembly.ca.gov.*

FUERSTENAU, DOUGLAS WINSTON, mineral engineering educator; b. Hazel, SD, Dec. 6, 1928; s. Erwin Arnold and Hazel Fuerstenau; m. Margaret Ann Pellett, Aug. 29, 1953; children: Linda(dec.), Lucy, Sarah, Stephen. BS, S.D. Sch. Mines and Tech., 1949; MS, Mont. Sch. Mines, 1950; ScD, MIT, 1953; Mineral Engr., Mont. Coll. Mineral Sci. and Tech., 1968; doctorate (hon.), U. Liege, Belgium, 1989; DTech (hon.), Lulea U. Tech., Sweden, 2001. Asst. prof. mineral engring. MIT, 1953-56; sect. leader, metals research lab. Union Carbide Metals Co., Niagara Falls, NY, 1956-58; mgr. mineral engring. lab Kaiser Aluminum & Chem. Corp., Permanente, Calif., 1958-59; assoc. prof. metallurgy U. Calif., Berkeley, 1959-62, prof. metallurgy, 1962-86, P. Malozemoff prof. of mineral engring., 1987-93, prof. grad. sch., 1994—, Miller rsch. prof., 1969-70, chmn. dept. materials sci. and mineral engring., 1970-78; hon. prof. Huainan Inst. Tech., 2000—, Ctrl. South U., Changsha, China, 2008—. Guest prof. Imperial Coll. London, 1966, U. Karlsruhe, Germany, 1973, Tech. U. Clausthal, Germany, 1984; mem. Nat. Mineral Bd., 1975—78; Am. rep. Internat. Mineral Processing Congress Com., 1978—97; mem. adv. bd. Korea Inst. for Interfacial Sci. and Engring., 1992—97. Editor: Froth Flotation-50th Anniversary Vol., 1962; co-editor-in-chief: Internat. Jour. Mineral Processing, 1974—98, hon. editor-in-chief:, 1998—, adv. editor: Elsevier Monograph Series on Advances in Mineral Processing, 1975—99, chmn. editl. bd. for the Ams.: KONA-Particle Tech., 1997—; contbr. articles to profl. jours. Trustee SD Sch. Mines Found., 1997—. Recipient Guy E. March Silver medal, SD Sch. Mines, 1979, Disting. Alumnus award, 2002, Alexander von Humboldt Sr. Am. Scientist award, Germany, 1984, Frank F. Aplan award, Engring. Found., 1990, Lifetime Achievement award, Internat. Mineral Processing Congress, 1995, Council award, 2008; named Douglas W. Fuerstenau professorship at S.D. Sch. of Mines and Tech., 1998; named to S.D. Hall of Fame, 2005; Rsch. fellow, Japan Soc. Promotion Sci., 1993, Consiglio Nationalle delle Ricerche, Italy, 1995. Fellow: Indian Nat. Acad. Engring. (fgn.), Australian Acad. Tech. Scis. and Engring. (fgn.); mem.: AIChE (Particle Tech. Forum Lifetime Achievement award 2006), NAE, Russian Fedn. Acad. Natural Scis. (fgn. mem.), Am. Chem. Soc., Soc. Mining Engrs. (bd. dirs. 1968—71, Disting. mem.), Am. Inst. Mining and Metall. Engrs. (chmn. mineral processing divsn. 1967, Robert Lansing Hardy gold medal 1957, Rossiter W. Raymond award 1961, Robert H. Richards award 1975, Antoine M. Gaudin award 1978, Mineral Industry Edn. award 1983, Henry Krumb disting. lectr. 1989, hon. 1989), The Berkeley Fellows, Sigma Xi, Theta Tau. Congregationalist. Home: 1440 Le Roy Ave Berkeley CA 94708-1912 Office Phone: 510-642-3826. Business E-Mail: dwfuerst@berkeley.edu.

FUERSTENAU, M(AURICE) C(LARK), metallurgical engineer; b. Watertown, SD, June 6, 1933; m. 1953; 4 children. BS, S.D. Sch. Mines & Tech., 1955; MS, MIT, 1957, ScD in Metallurgy, 1961. Rsch. engr. N. Mex. Bur Mines, Socorro, 1961—63; from asst. prof. to assoc. prof. Colo. Sch. Mines, 1963-68; from assoc. prof. to prof. U. Utah, 1968-70; prof., dept. head S.D. Sch. Mines & Tech., 1970-87, interim v.p., 1987-88, acting head mech. engring., 1994-96; prof. U. Nev., Reno, 1988—2005, prof. emeritus, 2005—. Contbr. articles to profl. jours. Recipient Frank F. Aplan award, United Engring. Found., 2000; named to SD Hall of Fame, 2006. Mem. Nat. Acad Engrs., Am. Inst. Mining (v.p. 1983, Robert H. Richards award 1982, Mineral Industry Edn. award 1989), Soc. Mining Engrs. (pres. 1982, Arthur F. Taggart award 1978, Antoine M. Gaudin award 1979). Office: Univ Nevada Dept Chem & Metall Engring Reno NV 89557-0001 Home Phone: 775-333-9134; Office Phone: 775-784-4310. Business E-Mail: mcf@unr.edu.

FUGATE, IVAN DEE, banker; b. Blackwell, Okla., Dec. 9, 1928; s. Hugh D. and Iva (Holmes) F.; m. Lois Unita Rossow, June 3, 1966; children: Vickie Michelle, Roberta Jeanne, Douglas B., Thomas P.

AB, Pittsburg State U., Kans., 1949; LLB, U. Denver, 1952, JD, 1970. Bar: Colo. 1952. Exec. sec., mgr. Jr. C. of C. of Denver, 1950-52; also sec. Colo. Jr. C. of C.; individual practice law Denver, 1954—; chmn. bd., pres. Green Mountain Bank, Lakewood, Colo., 1975-82; chmn., pres. Western Nat. Bank Denver (now Vectra Bank of Colorado); chmn. exec. com. North Valley Bank, Thornton, Colo., 1962—, chmn., pres., 1981-2000, chmn., 2000—; founder, chmn. emeritus Ind. State Bank of Colo. (now Bankers Bank of West), 1978—, Ind. Bankers of Colo., 1973—. Former bd. dirs. Kit Carson State Bank, Colo.; sec. First Nat. Bank, Burlington, Colo.; owner, farms, ranches, Kans., Colo.; instr. U. Denver Coll. Law, 1955-60; mem. Colo. Treas's. Com. Investment State Funds, 1975—. Treas. to Rep. Assos., Colo., 1959-61, trustee, 1959-64. Maj. USAR, 1952-54. Mem. ABA, Colo. Bar Assn., Denver Bar Assn. (trustee 1962-65), Colo. Bankers Assn. (bd. dirs.), Colo. Cattlemen's Assn., Ind. Bankers Assn. Am. (pres. 1978, adminstrv. com., exec. coun. 1976—, bd. dirs. fed. legis. com., chmn. spl. tax com., instr. One Bank Holding Co. seminars 1976—), Lakewood Country Club, Phi Alpha Delta. Methodist. Home: 12015 W 26th Ave Lakewood CO 80215-1110

FUJII, SHARON M., federal agency administrator; BA, U. Washington, 1966, M in Social Work, 1969; PhD, Brandeis U., 1975. Sr. v.p. Gerontological Planning Assn., 1975-77; prin. investigator Pacific-Asian Elderly Rsch. Project, 1977-79; program analyst Office of Refugee Resettlement, 1978-79, regional dir., 1979-80; regional dir., adminstrn. for children and families Dept. Health and Human Svcs., 1980-86; regional adminstr., adminstrn. for children and families, 1986—. Mem. Pres. Fed. Coun. on Aging, 1975-78. Health, Edn. and Welfare fellow, 1978-79. Office: Dept Health & Human Svcs 50 United Nations Plz Rm 450 San Francisco CA 94102-4912

FUJINAMI, ROBERT SHIN, pathologist, researcher; b. Salt Lake City, Dec. 8, 1949; BA, U. Utah, 1972; PhD, Northwestern U., Chgo., 1977. Instr. microbiology and immunology Northwestern U., Chgo., 1973-76; rsch. fellow immunopathology Scripps Clinic and Rsch. Found., La Jolla, Calif., 1977-80, rsch. assoc. immunopathology, 1980-81, asst. mem., asst. prof. dept. immunology, 1981-85, vis. investigator dept. immunology, 1985-89; vis. investigator dept. neuropharmacology divsn. virology Scripps Rsch. Inst. (formerly Scripps Clinic and Rsch. Found.), La Jolla, 1989-90; rsch. immunopathologist dept. pathology U. Calif., San Diego, 1980-82, assoc. prof. pathology, 1985-90; prof. neurology U. Utah, Salt Lake City, 1990—2007, adj. prof. dept. pathology divsn. cell biology and immunology, 1991—2007, prof. pathology, adj. prof. neurology. Mem. Weber immunology adv. com., dept. pathology U. Utah, Salt Lake City, 1991—, mem. neurosci. steering com., 1992-96, mem. biosafety com., 1992-96, chmn., 1994-96, chmn. safety com., dept. neurology, 19932007, chmn. promotion, retention and tenure com., 1993-96, mem. univ. promotions and tenure adv. com., 1995-98, chair oversight com. Fluorescence Activated Cell Sorter (FACS) Sch. Medicine, 1996-99, mem. univ. rsch. com., 1999—2004, disting. rsch. award subcom., 1999—2001, senate task force on RPT procedures, 1999—2000, adv. com. core facilities Huntsman Cancer Inst., 1999—2000, dir. grad. studies pathology PhD program, 1999—2002, chmn. tenured faculty rev. com., dept. neurology, 1999—2000. Contbr. chpts. to books, 165 articles to profl. jours. Recipient New Investigator award NIH, 1981-83; NIH scholar, 1989-96. Fellow AAAS; mem. Nat. Multiple Sclerosis Soc. (bd. dirs. Utah chpt. 1992-99—, Hary M. Weaver Neurosci. award 1982-86).NIH CNBT Study Sec. Office: U Utah Dept Pathology 30 N 1900 E 3R330 SOM Salt Lake City UT 84132-0001 Home Phone: 801-582-8002; Office Phone: 801-585-3305. Business E-Mail: Robert.Fujimami@hsc.utah.edu.

FUJIOKA, ROGER SADAO, microbiologist, researcher; b. Pearl City, Hawaii, May 11, 1938; s. Nobuichi and Hisayo (Iboshi) F.; m. Ruby Nanaye Yamashita, July 2, 1966; 1 child, Ryan Makoto. BS in Med. Tech., U. Hawaii, 1960, MS in Microbiology, 1966; PhD in Virology, U. Mich., 1970. Assoc. research U. Hawaii, Honolulu, 1963-66, rsch. microbiologist, 1972—; predoctoral fellow U. Mich., Ann Arbor, 1966-70; postdoctoral fellow Baylor Coll. Medicine, Houston, 1970-71. Sec.-treas. Hawaii Water Pollution Control, Honolulu, 1986—; mem. com. Standard Methods, Washington, 1986—. Contbr. articles to profl. jours. Served to capt. USAR, 1960-66. Grantee Sea Grant Coll. Program, 1976-84, Office Water United States Geol. Survey, 1978—, Office Naval Research, 1985—, Dept. Health, 1986—, all in Honolulu. Mem. AAAS, Am. Soc. Microbiology, Water Environment Fedn., Am. Water Works Assn., Soc. for Applied Bacteriology, Internat. Assn. on Water Quality. Avocation: tennis. Office: U Hawaii Water Resources Research Ctr Holmes Hall 283 2540 Dole St Honolulu HI 96822-2303

FUKUDA, NOBUO, chef; b. Tokyo, 1959; With Yamakasa, Phoenix; sushi chef Hapa, Scottsdale, Ariz.; co-owner, chef Sea Saw, Scottsdale, Ariz.; owner Shell Shock bar. Named Best Chef: Southwest, James Beard Found., 2007; named one of America's Best New Chefs, Food & Wine mag., 2003. Office: Sea Saw 7133 E Stetson Dr Scottsdale AZ 85251 Office Phone: 480-481-9463. Office Fax: 480-946-3055.

FULGINITI, VINCENT, dean; b. Phila., 1931; AB in Psychology, Temple U., 1953, MD, 1957, MS in pediatrics, 1961. Intern Phila. Gen. Hosp., 1957-58; resident in pediatrics Christophers Hosp. for Children, 1958-61, chief resident, 1960-61; NIH fellow pediatric infectious diseases U. Colo. Sch. Medicine, Denver, 1961-62, from asst. prof. to assoc. prof. pediatrics, 1962-69; prof., chmn. dept. pediatrics U. Ariz. Coll. Med., Tucson, 1969-85, vice dean for acad. affairs, 1985-89, acting dean, 1988-89; dean Tulane U. Sch. Medicine, New Orleans, 1989-93; chancellor U. Colo. Health Sci. Ctr., Denver, 1993-98, prof. pediats., 1998—. Editor Am. Jour. Diseases of Children, 1983-93. Chmn. Nat. Vaccine Adv. Com., 1990-94. Mem. AAAS, AMA, Am. Pediatric Soc. (pres. 1990), Am. Assn. Physician., Am. Pub. Health Assn., Soc. Pediatric Rsch.

FULKERSON, RICHARD J., state agency administrator; BA in Bus. Adminstrn., Chadron State Coll., 1974; postgraduate student, U. Nebr., Omaha, 1981—83, cert. in Bus. Computing, 1986. Nat. accreditation fed. thrift regulator. Mgr. Chgo. Lumber Co., Omaha, 1977—82; v.p., contr. Midwest Fed. Savs. and Loan Assn., Nebraska City, Nebr., 1983—86; asst. dir. Fed. Home Loan Bank Topeka, 1986—89, Office Thrift Supervision, Overland Park, Kans., 1989—95; dir. exams. Colo. Divsn. Banking, Denver, 1995—96; Colo. State Bank commr. Dept. Regulatory Agys., Denver, 1996—. Office: Divsn Banking Colo Dept Regulatory Agys 1560 Broadway Ste 975 Denver CO 80202 Office Phone: 303-894-7575. Office Fax: 303-894-7570. E-mail: banking@dora.state.co.us.

FULKERSON, WILLIAM MEASEY, JR., college president; b. Moberly, Mo., Oct. 18, 1940; s. William Measey and Edna Frances (Pendleton) F.; m. Grace Carolyn Wisdom, May 26, 1962; children: Carl Franklin, Carolyn Sue. BA, William Jewell Coll., 1962; MA, Temple U., 1964; PhD, Mich. State U., 1969. Asst. to assoc. prof. Calif. State U., Fresno, 1981—; asst. to pres. Calif. State U.-Fresno, 1971-73; assoc. exec. dir. Am. Assn. State Colls., Washington, 1973-77; acad. v.p. Phillips U., Enid, Okla., 1977-81; pres. Adams State Coll., Alamosa, Colo., 1981-94, State Colls. in Colo., 1994—. Interim pres. Met. State Coll., Denver, 1987-88, Western State Coll., 1996. Author: Planning for Financial Exigency, 1973; contbr. articles to profl. jours. Commr. North Ctrl. Assn., Chgo., 1980—; bd. dirs. Acad. Collective Bargaining Info. Svc., Washington, 1976, Office for Advancement Pub. Negro Colls., Atlanta, 1973-77, Colo. Endowment for Humanities, 1988-2000, pres., 1998-99. Named Disting. Alumni William Jewell Coll., 1982, Outstanding Alumnus Mich. State U. Coll. Comm., Arts & Scis., 1987. Mem. Am. Assn. State Colls. and Univs. (parliamentarian, bd. dirs. 1992-94), Am. Coun. on Edn. (bd. dirs.), Assn. Pub. Coll.s and Univs. Pres.s (pres. 1994-95), Nat. Assn. Sys. Heads, Alamosa C. of C. (dir., pres. 1984 Citizen Yr. award), Rotary.

FULLENWIDER, NANCY VRANA, composer, dancer, musician, educator; b. Sheridan, Wyo., May 9, 1940; d. Jacob Allen and Edith Martha (Tripp) Fullenwider; m. Linsfred Leroy Vrana, Apr. 26, 1980. BA summa cum laude, U. Denver, 1962, MA, 1971, postgrad., 1974. Prin. dancer, instr. Colo. Ballet and Colo. Ballet Ctr., Denver, 1958-80; owner, instr. Idaho Springs (Colo.) Sch. Ballet, 1962-67, Sch. Ballet, Parker, Colo., 1974-79. Curriculum developer Career Edn. Ctr., Denver Pub. Schs., 1973; grad. asst. U. Denver, 1974; guest artist, choreographer, composer Young Audiences, Denver, 1975-80; instr. ballet Ballet Arts Ctr., Denver, 1992-98, Colo. Dance Ctr., Littleton, 1992—; music dir., accompanist for Western Chamber Ballet, Denver, 1994-98, Colo. Ballet, 1999, Arvada Ctr., 1998, Ballet Arts, 1998, Internat. Sch. Ballet, 2000. Composer (CD's) To the Pointe, 1997, Brava!, 1999, Curtain Call, 2000, Inner Dance, 2002, Prepare!, 2005; commissioned ballet works performed at Auditorium Theatre, Denver, 2000, Arvada Ctr. for Performing Arts, Colo., 1991, Aurora (Colo.) Fox Arts Ctr., 1989-92, Buell Theatre, Colo., 1993, Cleo Parker Robinson Dance Theatre, Colo., 1992, 2003, 04, Colo. Springs Fine Arts Ctr., 1991, Houston Fine Arts Ctr., Colo., 1971, San Luis Arts Festival, Colo., 1990, Bonfils Theatre, Colo., 1971, Denver Civic Theatre, 2000, Auditorium Theatre, Denver, 2000, 01, (TV series) Providence, 2000; pianist theatre restaurant Denver Ctr. Performing Arts, Denver, Colo., 2003-04. Grantee Douglas County Schs., Colo., 1998. Mem. ASCAP, Phi Beta Kappa, Alpha Lambda Delta. Avocations: hiking, fly fishing, theater, concerts.

FULLER, DALE L., software security company executive; V.p., gen. mgr. portable computer divsn. NEC Technologies, Inc.; gen. mgr., v.p. powerbook divsn. Apple Computer, Inc.; pres., CEO WhoWhere? Inc.; dir. Software and Info. Industry Assn.; interim pres., CEO Borland Software Corp., 1999—2000, pres., CEO, 2000—05; interim CEO, pres. McAfee, Inc., 2005—.

FULLER, KATHY J., special education educator, consultant, researcher; b. Lamar, Colo., Oct. 24, 1957; d. Alfred L. and Leona M. Fuller; 1 child, Samantha Devon Blake. MA in Elem. Edn., Emphasis Early Childhood, Calif. State U. Northridge, 1993; PhD in Psychol. Studies Edn., UCLA, 2004; BAE in Elem. Edn. and Special Edn. Music Minor, U. North Colo. Tchg. cert. edn. specialist mild to moderate disabilities. Lectr. UCLA ext., 2002—, prof., 1999—, Pacific Oaks Coll., Pasadena, Calif., 2002—, core faculty, 2002—; cons. L.A. County of Edn., 2002—; coord. Intern Program PO, 2001—. Tchr. Pasadena Unified Sch. Dist., Calif., 1992—94; tchr., full inclusion specialist LA Unified Sch. Dist., 1994—2000; adj. prof. Calif. State U., LA, 1997—, field supr. for student tchr., 1998—, prof., 1999—2002, lectr., 2002—, supr., ext., 2002—; owner Teacher Talk, 2003—; reviewer Nat. Assn. Alternative Cert. Online Jour., 2005—. Musician: (singer) New Life - Kora Music for the 21st Century (Prince Diabate CD); poet Helpless Hoping (Editor's Choice award); contbg. author: Rescued Tails, 2005; contbr. articles to profl. jours.; presenter (numerous conf. presentations). Pet therapist Love on 4 Paws, LA, 2002; edn. dir. Beagles and Buddies, Orange County Cavy Haven; vol. pet therapist Vitas Hospice, 2006—, Ronald McDonald Houses; vol. Calif. State Performance Personal Devel. Com., 2006—08, State Leadership Com., 2006—08; rschr. Tng. Shelter Dogs. Recipient 1st place Edn. award, 2001, 2d place Behavioral/Social Scis. award, 2002; Nat. Rsch. grantee, Nat. Assn. Alternative Cert., 1999—. Mem.: Calif. Assn. Special Edn. Prof. (state membership coord.), Calif. State Leadership Com., Callif. State Performance and Pers. Devel. Plan, Spl. Edn. Rsch., Nat. Assn. Alternative Edn., Am. Ednl. Rsch. Assn., Coun. Exceptional Children, Phi Lambda Theta. Achievements include design of Fuller-Blake Academic Inventory. Avocations: swimming, sailing, surfing, scuba diving, painting. Home: 790 Monterey Rd South Pasadena CA 91030 Personal E-mail: kfullerbla@aol.com.

FULLER, ROBERT KENNETH, architect, urban designer; b. Denver, Oct. 6, 1942; s. Kenneth Roller and Gertrude Ailene (Heid) F.; m. Virginia Louise Elkin, Aug. 23, 1969; children: Kimberly Kirsten, Kelsey Christa. BArch, U. Colo., 1967; MArch and Urban Design, Washington U., St. Louis, 1974. Registered profl. arch., Colo. Archtl. designer Fuller & Fuller, Denver, Marvin Hatami Assocs., 1968-69; architect, planner Urban Research and Design Ctr., St. Louis, 1970-72; urban designer Victor Gruen & Assocs., 1973-75; prin. Fuller & Fuller Assocs., Denver, 1975—. Past pres. Denver East Ctrl. Civic Assn., Country Club Hist. Dist.; bd. dirs. Cherry Creek Steering Com.; treas. Cherry Creek Found.; pres. Horizon Adventures, Inc.; permanent sec.-treas. Archtl. Edn. Found., AIA Colo. Sgt. USMCR, 1964-70. Mem.: AIA (past pres. Denver chpt.), Rocky Mountain Vintage Racing Assn., Colo. Arlberg Club (past pres.), Delta Phi Delta, Phi Gamma Delta. Home: 2244 E 4th Ave Denver CO 80206-4107 Office: 3320 E 2nd Ave Denver CO 80206-5302 Office Phone: 303-333-3320.

FULLER, WILLIAM P., foundation administrator; b. Calif. BA, Stanford U., 1960, MA in Polit. Sci., 1964, PhD in Devel. Econs. and Edn., 1970; MBA, Harvard U., 1962. Program officer UNICEF, Cairo, Egypt, 1962-64, planning officer and asst. to dep. dir. NYC, 1964-66, regional planning officer Beirut, Lebanon, 1966-67; cons. economist for Nigeria, Ghana, Morocco World Bank/UNESCO Program, Paris, 1970-71; planning and rsch. advisor funded by Ford Found. Nat. Edn. Commn., Bangkok, Thailand, 1971-76; vis. lectr. U. Chgo., 1976; rep. Ford Found., Dhaka, Bangladesh, 1977-81; mission dir. Sr. Fgn. Svc. USAID, Indonesia, 1981-87, dep. asst. adminstr. bur. for Asia and Near East Washington, 1987-89; pres. The Asia Found., San Francisco, 1989—. Bd. dirs. Overseas Devel. Coun., Washington, Inst. for the Future, Stanford, Calif.; vice chmn. World Affairs Coun. No. Calif., San Francisco. Recipient Pres.'s Meritorious Svc. award, 1985, '87. Fellow Asia Pacific Ctr., Stanford U.; mem. Nat. Com. U.S.-China Rels. Office: The Asia Found 465 California St Fl 14 San Francisco CA 94104-1804

FULLMER, DANIEL WARREN, former psychologist, educator; b. Spoon River, Ill., Dec. 12, 1922; s. Daniel Floyd and Sarah Louisa (Essex) F.; m. Janet Satomi Saito, June 1980; children: Daniel William, Mark Warren. BS, Western Ill. U., 1947, MS, 1952; PhD, U. Denver, 1955. Post-doctoral intern psychiat. div. U. Oreg. Med. Sch., 1958-61; mem. faculty U. Oreg., 1955-66; prof. psychology Oreg. System of Higher Edn., 1958-66; faculty Coll. Edn. U. Hawaii, Honolulu, 1966-95, retired, 1995, prof. emeritus, 1974—; pvt. practice psychol. counseling. Cons. psychologist Grambling State U., 1960-81; founder Free-Family Counseling Ctrs., Portland, Oreg., 1959-66, Honolulu, 1966-74; co-founder Child and Family Counseling Ctr., Waianae, Oahu, Hawaii, Kilohana United Meth. Ch., Oahu, 1992, v.p., sec., 1992; pres. Human Resources Devel. Ctr., Inc., 1974—; chmn. Hawaii State Bd. to License Psychologists, 1973-78. Author: Counseling: Group Theory & System, 2d. edit., 1978, The Family Therapy Dictionary Text, 1991, MANABU, Diagnosis and Treatment of a Japanese Boy with a Visual Anomaly, 1991; co-author: Principles of Guidance, 2d. edit., 1977; author (counselor/cons. training manuals) Counseling: Content and Process, 1964, Family Consultation Therapy, 1968, The School Counselor-Consultant, 1972, Family Therapy as the Rites of Passage, 1998; editor: Bulletin, Oreg. Coop Testing Service, 1955-57, Hawaii P&G Jour., 1970-76; assoc. editor: Educational Perspectives, U. Hawaii Coll. Edn. Served with USNR, 1944-46. Recipient Francis E. Clark award Hawaii Pers. Guidance Assn., 1972, Thomas Jefferson award for Outstanding Pub. Svc., 1993; named Hall of Fame Grambling State U., 1987. Mem. Am. Psychol. Assn., Am. Counseling Assn. (Nancy C. Wimmer award 1963), Masons. Methodist. Office: 1750 Kalakaua Ave Apt 809 Honolulu HI 96826-3725 Office Phone: 808-942-2072.

FULTON, DANIEL S., paper company executive; b. 1948; BA in Econs., Miami U., Ohio, 1970; MBA, U. Wash., 1976; grad. exec. program, Stanford U., 2001. Former officer USN Supply Corps; mem. investment evaluation dept. Weyerhaeuser Co., 1976—78; planning mgr. Weyerhaeuser Real Estate Co., 1978—79; investment mgr. Weyerhaeuser Venture Co., 1978—87; CEO Cornerstone Columbia Devel. Co., 1987—88; chief investment officer Weyerhaeuser Realty Investors, Inc., 1994—95, COO, 1996—97, pres., CEO, 1998—2000, Weyerhaeuser Real Estate Co., 2001—07; pres. Weyerhaeuser Co., 2008, pres., CEO, 2008—. Bd. dirs. Weyerhaeuser Co., 2008—. Bd. dirs. United Way of King County; mem. adv. bd. U. Wash. Bus. Sch.; bd. govs. Lambda Alpha Internat. Land Econs. Soc., High Prodn. Homebuilder Coun. of Nat. Assn. Homebuilders. Office: Weyerhaeuser Co 33663 Weyerhaeuser Way S Federal Way WA 98063-9777

FULTON, KENNETH RAY, professional association administrator; b. Cleve., Dec. 22, 1948; BS in Social Scis., U. Md., 1973; MPA in Mgmt., Am. U., 1977. Mem. staff Nat. Acad. Scis., Washington, 1971-80, dir. membership, 1980-84, spl. asst. to pres., 1984-93, exec. dir., 1993—; exec. dir. Nat. Academies Corp., 2007—. Mgr. membership and program activities Nat. Acad. Scis.; organizer numerous sci. confs. and symposia, art exhibitions and cultural programs; mem. U.S. delegation to Codex Alimentarius Commn. UN, 1977-80, com. on dissemination of sci. info. Internat. Coun. for Sci., 1998-2004. Publisher Proceedings of the Nat. Acad. Scis., 1995-. With U.S. Navy. Fellow AAAS, Am. Soc. Assn. Execs., NY Acad. Sci., Cosmos Club. Office: National Academy of Sciences The Beckman Ctr 100 Academy Irvine CA 92617 Office Phone: 949-721-2257. Business E-Mail: kfulton@nas.edu.

FUNG, INEZ Y., science educator; SB in Applied Math., MIT, 1971, ScD in Meteorology, 1977. Richard and Rhonda Goldman Disting. Prof. Phys. Scis. U. Calif., Berkeley, 1997—2002; prof. atmospheric sci., dept. earth & planetary sci., dept. environ. sci., policy and mgmt. U. Calif., Berkeley Inst. Environ., co-dir. Contbr. to the 2007 Nobel Peace Prize awarded to the UN Environ. Programme Intergovernmental Panel for Climate Change; spkr. in field. Featured in Women's Adventures in Sci.; contbr. several articles to profl. jours. Recipient NASA Goddard Inst. for Space Studies Peer award, 1987, 1993, NASA Exceptional Scientific Achievement medal, 1989, NASA Goddard Inst. for Space Studies Most Valuable Paper award, 1990, 1996, NOAA Disting. Authorship award, 1991, Nat. Ctr. for Atmospheric Rsch. Cmty. Climate Sys. Model Disting. Achievement award, 2007; named Scientist of the Month, Ms. Maggie Owens, 2nd grade class, Marin Elem. Sch., Albany, Calif., 2006; named one of Scientific American 50, 2005; NASA Goddard Sr. Fellow, 1992—97. Fellow: World Tech. Network (World Tech. award-Environment 2006), Am. Meterological Soc., Am. Geophysical Union (Roger Revelle medal 2004); mem.: NAS. Office: 307 McCone Mail Code 4767 University of California Berkeley Berkeley CA 94708-4767 also: Office 399 McCone 355 Hilgard University of California Berkeley Berkeley CA 94708-4767 Office Phone: 510-643-9367. Office Fax: 510-643-9980. Business E-Mail: ifung@berkeley.edu. E-mail: inez@atmos.berkeley.edu.

FUNG, YUAN-CHENG BERTRAM, bioengineering educator, writer; b. Yuhong, Changchow, Kiangsu, China, Sept. 15, 1919; arrived in U.S., 1945, naturalized, 1957; s. Chung-Kwang and Lien (Hu) F.; m. Luna Hsien-Shih Yu, Dec. 22, 1949; children: Conrad Antung, Brenda Pingsi. BS, Nat. Ctrl. U., Chungking, China, 1941, MS, 1943, DSc (hon.), 2002; PhD, Calif. Inst. Tech., 1948; DSc (hon.), Hong Kong U. Sci. and Tech., 1992, Drexel U., 2001, Sichuan U., 2002, Nat. Cheng Kung U., 2003, Northwestern U., 2004. Rsch. fellow Bur. Aero. Rsch. China, 1943-45; rsch. asst., then rsch. fellow Calif. Inst. Tech., 1946-51, mem. faculty, 1951-66, prof. aerospace, 1959-66; prof. bioengring. and applied mechanics U. Calif., San Diego, 1966—2000, prof. emeritus bioengineering, 2000—. Cons. aerospace indsl. firms, 1949—; hon. prof. 15 univs., China; hon. chair World Coun. Biomechanics, 1998. Author: The Theory of Aeroelasticity, 1955, 69, 93, Foundations of Solid Mechanics, 1965, A First Course in Continuum Mechanics, 1969, 77, 93, Biomechanics, 1972, Biomechanics: Mechanical Properties of Living Tissues, 1980, 1993, Biodynamics: Circulation, 1984, Biomechanics: Circulation, 1996, Biomechanics: Motion, Flow, Stress and Growth, 1990, Selected Works on Biomechanics and Aeroelasticity by Y.C. Fung, 1997, Classical and Computational Solid Mechanics, 2001, Introduction to Bioengineering, 2001; also papers; editor Jour. Biorheology, Jour. Biomech. Engring. Hon. bd. trustees Chongqing U.; hon. chair, bd. trustees Nanjing U., China. Recipient Achievement award Chinese Inst. Engrs., 1965, 68, 93, Lifetime Achievement award of Asian Ams.

in Engring., 2004, Landis award Microcirculatory Soc., 1975, Poiseuille medal Internat. Soc. Biorheology, 1986, Engr. of Yr. award San Diego Engring. Soc., 1986, von Karman medal ASCE, 1976, ALZA award Biomed. Engring. Soc., 1989, Borelli award Am. Soc. Biomechanics, 1992, US Nat. Medal of Sci., 2000.; Guggenheim fellow, 1958-59. Fellow AIAA, ASME (hon., Lissner award 1978, Centennial medal 1978, Worcester Reed Warner medal 1984, Timoshenko medal 1991, Melville medal 1994); mem. Japan Soc. Mech. Engrs. (Bioengring. award 1995), NAS, NAE(Founders award, 1998, Fritz J. and Dolores H. Russ prize, 2007), Inst. Medicine, Soc. Engring. Sci., Microcirculatory Soc., Am. Physiol. Soc., Nat. Heart Assn., Acad. Sinica, Chinese Acad. Scis. (fgn. mem.), Basic Sci. Coun., Sigma Xi. Achievements include contributing to tissue engineering for the treatment of burns and other severe tissue injuries and the development of engineered blood vessels. Office: U Calif Dept Bioengring 9500 Gilman Dr La Jolla CA 92093-0412

FUNK, WILLIAM HENRY, retired environmental engineering educator; b. Ephraim, Utah, June 10, 1933; s. William George and Henrietta (Hackwell) F.; m. Ruth Sherry Mellor, Sept. 19, 1964 (dec.); 1 dau., Cynthia Lynn; m. Lynn Bridget Robson, Mar. 30, 1996. BS in Biol. Sci, U. Utah, 1955, MS in Zoology, 1963, PhD in Limnology, 1966. Tchr. sci., math. Salt Lake City Schs., 1957-60; research asst. U. Utah, Salt Lake City, 1961-63; head sci. dept. N.W. Jr. High Sch., Salt Lake City, 1961-63; mem. faculty Wash. State U., Pullman, 1966-99, assoc. prof. environ. engring., 1971-75, prof., 1975-99, chmn. environ. sci./regional planning program, 1979-81; dir. Environ. Research Center, 1980-83, State of Wash. Water Research Ctr., 1981-99; ret., 1999. Cons. U.S. Army C.E., Walla Walla, Wash., 1970—74, Harstad Engrs., Seattle, 1971—72, Boise Cascade Corp., Seattle, 1971—72, Wash. Dept. Ecology, Olympia, 1971—72, ORB Corp., Renton, Wash., 1972—73, U.S. Civil Svc., Seattle, Chgo., 1972—74; mem. High Level Nuclear Waste Bd., Wash., 1986—89, Wash. 2010 Com., 1989, Pure Water 2000 Steering Com., 1990; co-dir. Inst. Resource Mgmt.; co-founder Terrene Inst., Washington, 1991, pres., 1993—2002. Contbr. articles to profl. jours. Bd. mem. Manti-Ephraim Airport, 2006—. Capt. USNR, 1955—76. Grantee NSF Summer Inst., 1961, U.S. Army C.E., 1970-74, 94-96, 97-98, Office Water Resources Rsch., 1971-72, 73-76, EPA, 1980-83, 93-94, 95-96, U.S. Geol. Survey, 1983-94, 95-96, 97-98, 99-00, Nat. Parks Svc., 1985-87, Colville Confederated Tribes, 1990-92, Nez Pierce Tribe, 1992-95, Wash. Conservation Commn., 1992-95, Clearwater Co., 1992-93, Idaho Dept. Environ. Quality, 1995-96, U.S. Bur. Reclamation, 1995-98; USPHS fellow, 1963; recipient Pres.'s Disting. Faculty award Wash. State U., 1984. Mem. Naval Res. Officers Assn. (chpt. pres. 1969), N.Am. Lake Mgmt. Soc. (pres. 1984-85, Secchi Disk award 1988), Pacific N.W. Pollution Control Assn. (editor 1969-77, pres.-elect 1982-83, pres. 1983-84), Water Pollution Control Fedn. (Arthur S. Bedell award Pacific N.W. assn. 1976, nat. bd. dirs. 1978-81, bd. dirs. Rsch. Found. 1990-92), Nat. Assn. Water Inst. Dirs. (chair 1985-87, bd. dirs. univ. council on water resources 1986-89), Wash. Lakes Protection Assn. (co-founder 1986, Friend of Lakes award 1999), Am. Water Resources Assn. (v.p. Wash. sect. 1988), Am. Soc. Limnology and Oceanography, Am. Micros. Soc., N.W. Sci. Assn., North Am. Lake Mgmt. Soc. (co-founder 1972), Sigma Xi, Phi Sigma. Achievements include research in water pollution control and lake restoration. Avocations: flying, photography, boating, waterskiing, gardening. Home: 202 W 200 South Manti UT 84642-1309 Personal E-mail: wfwhf@mail.manti.com.

FURBUSH, DAVID MALCOLM, lawyer; b. Palo Alto, Calif., Mar. 25, 1954; s. Malcolm Harvey and Margaret (McKittrick) F. BA, Harvard U., 1975, JD, 1978. Bar: Calif. 1978, U.S. Dist. Ct. (no. dist.) Calif. 1978, U.S. Ct. Appeals (9th cir.) 1987, U.S. Supreme Ct. 1990. Assoc. Chickering & Gregory, San Francisco, 1978-81, Brobeck, Phleger & Harrison, San Francisco, 1981-85, ptnr. Palo Alto, Calif., 1985—2003, O'Melveny & Myers, LLP, Menlo Park, Calif., 2003—07; ptnr., co-leader securities litig. team Pillsbury Winthrop Shaw Pittman LLP, Palo Alto, Calif., 2007—. Mem.: ABA, San Francisco Bar Assn., Calif. Bar Assn. Office: Pillsbury Winthrop Shaw Pittman LLP 2475 Hanover St Palo Alto CA 94304 Office Phone: 650-233-4623. Office Fax: 650-233-4545. Business E-Mail: david.furbush@pillsburylaw.com.

FURCAL, RAFAEL, professional baseball player; b. Loma de Cabrera, Dominican Republic, Aug. 24, 1978; Short stop Atlanta Braves, 2000—05, LA Dodgers, 2005—. Recipient NL Rookie Yr. award, MLB, 2000; named to Nat. League All-Star Team, 2003. Achievements include leading the National League in: triples (10), 2003. Office: Los Angeles Dodgers 1000 Elysian Park Ave Los Angeles CA 90012*

FURLOTTI, ALEXANDER AMATO, real estate and investment company executive; b. Milan, Apr. 21, 1948; came to U.S., 1957; s. Amato and Polonia Concepcion (Lopez) F.; m. Nancy Elizabeth Swift, June 27, 1976; children: Michael Alexander, Patrick Swift, Allison Nicole. BA in Econs., U. Calif. Berkeley, Berkeley, 1970; JD, UCLA, 1973. Bar: Calif. 1973, U.S. Dist. Ct. (9th cir.) 1973. Assoc. Alexander, Inman, Kravetz & Tanzer, Beverly Hills, Calif., 1973-77, ptnr., 1978-80, Kravetz & Furlotti, Century City, Calif., 1981-83; pres. Quorum Properties, LA, 1984—, Quorum Funds, LA, 2000—. Trustee Harvard-Westlake Sch., L.A., 1989-97, Yosemite Nat. Inst., San Francisco, 1990-92. Recipient Grand award Pacific Coast Bldrs. Conf., 1993, 98, Golden Nugget award, 1993, 98, Grand award Nat. Assn. Home Builders, 1993, Platinum award, 1997, Best Attached Housing award, 1998, Residential Project of Yr., 1998; finalist Pillars of Industry award Nat. Assn. Homebuilders, 2004 Mem. Am. Bar Assn., Urban Land Inst., The Beach Club, Calif. Club, Bohemian Club. Republican. Episcopalian. Personal E-mail: af@qfuds.net.

FURTH, FREDERICK PAUL, lawyer; b. West Harvey, Ill., Apr. 12, 1934; s. Fred P. and Mamie (Stelmach) F.; children: Darby, Ben Anthony, Megan Louise; m. Peggy Wollerman, July 19, 1986. Student, Drake U., 1952-53; BA, U. Mich., 1956, JD, 1959; postgrad., U. Berlin, 1959, U. Munich, Fed. Republic Germany, 1960. Bar: Mich. 1959, N.Y. 1961, D.C. 1965, U.S. Supreme Ct. 1965, Calif. 1966. Assoc. Cahill, Gordon, Reindel & Ohl, NYC, 1960-64; with Kellogg Co., Battle Creek, Mich., 1964-65; assoc. Joseph L. Alioto, San Francisco, 1965-66; sr. ptnr. The Furth Firm LLP, San Francisco, 1966—. Bd. dirs. Robert Half Internat.; chmn., propr. Chalk Hill Winery. Trustee, chmn. bd. Furth Family Found., San Francisco; bd. dirs. Franklin and Eleanor Roosevelt Inst., 1996—, The Ctr. for Democracy, Washington; chmn. Internat. Jud. Conf., Strasbourg, France, 1992-. Mem. ABA, Internat. Bar Assn., N.Y. Bar Assn., San Francisco Bar Assn., State Bar Calif., Assn. of Bar of City of N.Y., St. Francis Yacht Club, Olympic Club. Office: The Furth Firm Llp 10300 Chalk Hill Rd Healdsburg CA 95448-9558 E-mail: fpfurth@aol.com.

FURUTANI, WARREN T., state legislator; BA, Antioch U. Bd. mem. LA Unified Sch. & CC Dist.; pres., chief exec. Asian Pacific Policy & Planning Coun.; mem. Bd. Trustees LA CC; mem. Dist. 55 Calif. State Assembly, 2008—. Democrat. Mailing: PO Box 942849 Room 3126 Sacramento CA 94249-0055 Address: 4201 Long Beach Blvd Ste 327 Long Beach CA 90807 Office Phone: 919-319-2055, 562-989-2919. Office Fax: 562-989-5494. Business E-Mail: Assemblymember.Furutani@assembly.ca.gov.*

FUSCO, JACK A., energy executive; BSME, Calif. State Univ., Sacramento. Exec. dir. internat. develop. & ops. PG&E; v.p., power Goldman Sachs; pres., CEO, dir. Orion Power Holdings, 1998—2002; energy investment adv. Texas Pacific Group, 2002—04; chmn., CEO Texas Genco LLC, 2004—06; pres., CEO Calpine Corp., San Jose, Calif., 2008—. Bd. dir. Foster Wheeler Ltd., Graphic Packaging Holding Co., Calpine Corp. Office: Calpine Corp 50 W San Fernando St San Jose CA 95113 Office Phone: 408-995-5115. Office Fax: 408-995-0505.

FUTAMI, NORMAN, lawyer; b. Hermosa Beach, Calif., Jan. 5, 1960; arrived in Japan, 1993; s. Akimasa and Reiko (Nobe) F.; m. Jean Kiyoko Kashiwabara, July 11, 1987; 1 child, Gregory Minoru. BA, Yale U., New Haven, Conn., 1981; JD, Harvard U., Cambridge, Mass., 1984. Bar: Calif. 1984, Japan 1993. Assoc. Paul, Hastings, Janofsky & Walker LLP, LA, 1984-92, ptnr. Tokyo, 1988—90, 1993—95, LA, 1990—93, 1995—, vice chmn. mgmt.-L.A. Office. Office: Paul Hastings Janofsky & Walker LLP 515 S Flower St Los Angeles CA 90071-2228 Office Phone: 213-683-6321. Office Fax: 213-627-0705. Business E-Mail: normanfutami@paulhastings.com.

FUTCH, MICHAEL, lawyer, construction executive; b. Monroe, La., Sept. 7, 1947; BSCE, So. U., 1970; MSCE, U. Calif., Berkeley, 1975; JD, Cornell U., 1981. Cert. engr., Calif., 1975. Structural engr. Western Div. Naval Facilities Engring. Command, San Bruno, Calif., 1972—76; sr. structural engr. Parsons Brinckerhoff, San Francisco, 1976—78; assoc. Cox, Castle & Nicholson, Los Angeles; gen. counsel, sec. Kasler Corp., San Bernadino, 1983—86; v.p., gen counsel Penhall Internat., 1986—88; of counsel Robinson & Pearman, 1988—96; v.p., gen. counsel Granite Construction Inc., 1996—. Sgt. US Army, 1970—72. Mem.: ABA, Am. Soc. Corp. Secs., Am. Corp. Counsel Assn., Nat. Bar Assn. Office: Granite Construction Inc 585 W Beach St PO Box 50085 Watsonville CA 95077-5805 Office Phone: 831-761-4708.

GABAY, JANIS T., literature and language educator; b. Honolulu, 1953; BA, San Diego State Univ., 1972, MA, 1978. Tchr. English lang. Junipero Serra High Sch., San Diego, 1980—; advanced placement English tchr., staff developer Preuss Sch., Univ. Calif. San Diego. Reg. dir. Calif. Lit. Project. Recipient Nat. Tchr. of Yr. award, 1990. Office: The Preuss Sch UCSD 9500 Gilman Dr La Jolla CA 92093-0536 Business E-Mail: jgabay@ucsd.edu.

GABBARD, MIKE (GERALD MIKE GABBARD), state legislator; b. Fagatogo, American Samoa, Jan. 15, 1948; m. Carol Gabbard; children: Bhakti, Jai, Ryan, Tulsi, Vrindavan. BA in English, Calif. State U., Sanoma, 1971; MEd in Adult Edn., Oreg. State U., Corvallis, 1980. Profl. tennis player; tchr. Faga'Itua High Sch., 1971—72; program dir., instr. Samoana High Sch., 1972—73; tchr. America Samoa Cmty. Coll., 1973—74, guidance counselor, 1974—76, asst. dean of instruction, 1976—77, dean of adult and continuing edn., 1980—83; owner, operator Mike's Sport Shop, 1974—78; headmaster, tchr. Ponomauloa Sch., 1983—87; owner, operator The Natural Deli, 1988—92, MC Svcs., 1994—, Hawaiian Toffee Treasures, 1998—; owner Infotech Comm., 2002—04; councilman Dist. 1 Honolulu City Coun., 2003—05; substitute tchr. West Oahu, 2005—; mem. Dist. 19 Hawaii State Senate, 2007—. Co-founder Stand Up For America, Healthy Hawaii Coalition; chair Ewa Transp. Coalition, 2003—05; founder Alliance for Traditional Marriage & Values. Singer (musician): Stand As One (E Kupono me ke Aloha). Mem.: Small Bus. Hawaii, Navy League of US, KC, Filipino C. of C., Kapolei City Lions Club. Democrat. Catholic. Avocations: golf, tennis. Office: Hawaii State Capitol 415 South Beretania St Rm 201 Honolulu HI 96813 Office Phone: 808-586-6830. Office Fax: 808-586-6679. Business E-Mail: sengabbard@Capitol.hawaii.gov.

GABEL, KATHERINE, retired academic administrator; b. Rochester, NY, Apr. 9, 1938; d. M. Wren and Esther (Conger) G.; m. Seth Devore Strickland, June 24, 1961 (div. 1965). AB, Smith Coll., Northampton, Mass., 1959; MSW, Simmons Coll., 1961; PhD, Syracuse U., 1967; JD, Union U., 1970; bus. program, Stanford U., 1984. Psychol. social worker Cen. Island Mental Health Ctr., Uniondale, NY, 1961-62; psychol. social worker, supt. Ga. State Tng. Sch. for Girls, Atlanta, 1962-64; cons. N.Y. State Crime Control Coun., Albany, 1968-70; faculty Ariz. State U., Tempe, 1972-76; supt. Ariz. Dept. of Corrections, Phoenix, 1970-76; dean, prof. Smith Coll., 1976-85; pres. Pacific Oaks Coll. and Children's Sch., Pasadena, Calif., 1985-98; western region v.p. Casey Family Program, Pasadena, 1998—2001; pvt. practice, 2001—. Advisor, del. UN, Geneva, 1977; mem. So. Calif. Youth Authority, 1986-91; west region dir. Lambda LegalDef. Fund, LA, 2003— Editor: Master Teacher and Supervisor in Clinical Social Work, 1982; author report Legal Issues of Female Inmates, 1981, model for rsch. Diversion program Female Inmates, 1984, Children of Incarcerated Parents, 1995. Vice chair United Way, Northampton, 1982-83; chair Mayor's Task Force, Northampton, 1981. Mem. Nat. Assn. Social Work, Acad. Cert. Social Workers, Nat. Assn. Edn. Young Children, Western Assn. Schs. and Colls., Pasadena C. of C., Athenaeum, Pasadena Rotary Club. Democrat. Presbyterian. Avocation: collecting south west Indian art, aviary. Personal E-mail: gabelk@prodigy.net.

GABLER, ELIZABETH BRAND, film company executive; m. Lee Gabler. Agent motion picture literary dept. ICM; creative exec. Columbia Pictures; v.p. prodn. United Artists; with 20th Century Fox, Beverly Hills, Calif., 1988—, exec. v.p. prodn.; pres. Fox 2000 Pictures, 1999—. Mem. adv. bd. Ctr. Film, TV and New Media U. Calif., Santa Barbara. Named one of The 100 Most Powerful Women in Entertainment, Hollywood Reporter, 2004, 2005, 2006, 2007. Office: 20th Century Fox PO Box 900 Beverly Hills CA 90213-0900

GABLER, LEE, talent agency executive; m. Elizabeth Gabler. Agent Ashley Steiner Famous Artists (now Internat. Creative Mgmt.), NYC, 1964—68, v.p., 1968—70; exec. v.p., head of worldwide TV Internat. Creative Mgmt., Calif., 1970—83; ptnr., co-chmn. Creative Artists Agy., LA, 1983—2007; with Worldwide Pants Inc., 2007—. Bd. dirs. Mus. TV & Radio; bd. councilors U. So. Calif. Sch. Cinema; v.p. Hollywood Radio & TV Soc., 1994—97.

GABOW, PATRICIA ANNE, internist, health facility executive; b. Starke, Fla., Jan. 8, 1944; m. Harold N. Gabow, June 21, 1971; children: Tenaya Louise, Aaron Patrick. BA in Biology, Seton Hill Coll., 1965; MD, U. Pa. Sch. Medicine, 1969. Diplomate Am. Bd. Internal Medicine, Am. Bd. Nephrology, Nat. Bd. Med. Examiners; lic. Colo. Internship in medicine Hosp. of U. of Pa., 1969-70; residency in internal medicine Harbor Gen. Hosp., 1970-71; renal fellowship San Francisco Gen. Hosp. and Hosp. of U. Pa., 1971-72, 72-73; instr. medicine divsn. renal diseases, asst. prof. U. Colo. Health Scis. Ctr., 1973-74, 74-79, assoc. prof. medicine divsn. renal diseases, prof., 1979-87; chief renal disease, clin. dir. dept. medicine Denver Gen. Hosp., 1973-81, 76-81, dir. med. svcs., 1981-91; CEO, med. dir. Denver Health and Hosps., 1992—2008; CEO Denver Health, 2008—. Intensive care com. Denver Gen. Hosp., 1976-81, med. records com., 1979-80, ind. rev. com., 1978-81, continuing med. edn. com., 1981-83, animal care com., 1979-83; student adv. com. U. Colo. Health Scis. Ctr., 1982-87, faculty senate, 1985, 86, internship adv. com., 1977-92; exec. com. Denver Gen. Hosp., 1981—, chmn. health resources com., 1988-90, chmn. pathology search com., 1989, chmn. faculty practice plan steering com., 1990-92. Mem. editorial bd. EMERGINDEX, 1983-93, Am. Jour. of Kidney Disease, 1984-96, Western Jour. of Medicine, 1987-98, Annals of Internal Medicine, 1988-91, Jour. of the Am. Soc. of Nephrology, 1990-97; contbr. numerous articles, revs. and editorials to profl. publs., chpts. to books. Mem. Mayor's Safe City Task Force, 1993; mem. sci. adv. bd. Polycystic Kidney Rsch. Found., 1984-96, chmn., 1991; mem. sci. adv. bd. Nat. Kidney Found., 1991-94; mem. Nat. Pub. Health and Hosps. Inst. Bd., 1993-2001, 03—. Recipient Sullivan award for Highest Acad. Average in Graduating Class, Seton Hill Coll., 1965, Pa. State Senatorial scholarship, 1961-65, Kaiser Permanente award for Excellence in Tchg., 1976, Ann. award to Outstanding Woman Physician, 1982, Kaiser Permanente Nominee for Excellence in Tchg. award, 1983, Seton Hill Coll. Disting. Alumna Leadership award, 1990, Florence Rena Sabin award U. Colo., 2000, Nathan Davis award AMA, 2000, Good Housekeeping Women in Govt. award, 2002; named one of The Best Doctors in Am., 1994-95, 2002; grantee Bonfils Found., 1985-86, NIH, 1985-90, 91-96, 96-00, W.K. Kellogg Found., 1997—, AHRQ, 2000-03; named to Colo. Women's Hall of Fame, 2004, One of the Top 25 Women in Healthcare, 2005, 100 Most Influential People in Healthcare in Modern Healthcare, Women Who Make a Difference International Women's Forum, 2005, Unique Woman Colo., 2007. Mem. Denver Med. Soc., Colo. Med. Soc., Polycystic Kidney Disease Rsch. Found. (sci. advisor 1984-96), Nat. Kidney Found. (sci. adv. bd. 1987-91), Women's Forum of Colo., Inc., Assn. Am. Physicians. Roman Catholic. Office: Denver Health 660 Bannock St Denver CO 80204-4506 Address: Denver Health 777 Bannock St Denver CO 80204

GABRIEL, DONALD EUGENE, science educator; b. Brush, Colo., May 24, 1944; s. Max and Vera Ellen (Coleman) G.; m. Evonne Kay Asheim, Sept. 27, 1964; children: Shawn Lee, Dawn Kay. AA, Northeastern Jr. Coll., Sterling, Colo., 1964; BA, Colo. State Coll., 1967; MA, U. No. Colo., 1972. Cert. secondary chemistry tchr. Tchr. sci. and math. Brush (Colo.) H.S., 1967—. Adv. bd. mem. Colo. Sci. and Engring. Fair, Fort Collins, 1980—; ea. zone chairperson Colo.-Wyo. Jr. Acad. Sci., Fort Morgan, Colo., 1980—; co-dir. Morgan-Washington BiCounty Sci. Fair, Fort Morgan, 1975—. Contbr. articles to profl. jours. Pres. South Platte Valley BOCES, Fort Morgan, 1993-99, v.p., 1991-93; Eagle Scout reviewer Boy Scouts Am., Fort Morgan, 1990—; sec., treas. Brush Pub. Schs., 1995-99. Grantee Tandy Corp., 1989, Joslin Needhams Found., 1990; recipient Presdl. award NSF, 1994; named Milken Nat. Educator, Milken Found., 1991, Tandy Tech. Scholars Outstanding Tchr., 1994-95, Pub. Svc. Co. of Colo. Classroom Connection awards, 1993-99, S. Platte Valley Bd. of Coop. Ednl. Svcs. grants, 1995-98. Mem. Nat. Sci. Tchrs. Assn. (Presdl. award 1994), Colo. Assn. Sci. Tchrs. (regional dir. 1993-96, Outstanding Tchr. 1990). Republican. Lutheran. Avocations: arrowhead hunting, rock hounding. Home: 26137 MCR S 2 Brush CO 80723 Office: Brush HS PO Box 585 Brush CO 80723-0585

GADDES, RICHARD, former opera company director; b. Wallsend, Northumberland, Eng., May 23, 1942; s. Thomas and Emilie Jane (Rickard) G. L.T.C.L. in piano, L.T.C.L. for sch. music; G.T.C.L., Trinity Coll. Music, London, 1964; D. Mus. Arts (hon.), St. Louis Conservatory, 1983; D.F.A. (hon.), U. Mo.-St. Louis, 1984; D.Arts (hon.), Webster U., 1986. Founder, mgr. Wigmore Hall Lunchtime Concerts, 1965; dir. Christopher Hunt and Richard Gaddes Artists Mgmt., London, 1965-66; bookings mgr. Artists Internat. Mgmt., London, 1967-69; artistic adminstr. Santa Fe Opera, 1969—75, assoc. gen. dir., 1995—2000, gen. dir., 2000—08, Opera Theatre of St. Louis, 1975-85, life bd. dirs., 1985—. Bd. dirs., emeritus mem. Grand Ctr., Inc., 1988—, pres., 1988-95; emeritus bd. dirs. William Matheus Sullivan Found.; chmn. bd. Oprah America, 2004-08. Mem. bd. advs. Royal Oak Found.; bd. dirs. Pulitzer Found. for the Arts. Recipient Lamplighter award, 1982, Mo. Arts award, 1983, St. Louis award, 1983, Human Relations award Jewish-Am. Com., St. Louis, 1985, Nat. Inst. for Music Theatre award, 1986, Cultural Achievement award Young Audiences, 1987, Arts Mgmt. Career Svc. Award., 1997. Office: Santa Fe Opera PO Box 2408 Santa Fe NM 87504-2408 E-mail: director@santafeopera.org.

GADRE, ANIL, information technology executive; BSEE, Stanford U., Calif.; M of Mgmt., Northwestern U. With Hewlett-Packard, Apollo Computer; v.p. software mktg. Sun Microsystems, Inc., gen. mgr. Solaris group, v.p. North Am. field mktg., v.p. product mktg., exec. v.p., chief mktg. officer. Office: Sun Microsystems Inc 4150 Network Cir Santa Clara CA 95054 Office Phone: 650-960-1300.

GAEDE, JAMES ERNEST, physician, educator; b. Calgary, Alta., Can., July 2, 1953; s. John Ernest and Florence Eleanor (Hilmer) G.; married, Dec. 23, 1994; children: Graham, Jason, Nikki, Mary Frances, Sydney, Camille. BA, Augustana Coll., 1975, MA, 1976; MD, U. S.D., 1980. Diplomate Am. Bd. Family Practice. Staff physician Queen of Peace, Mitchell, SD, 1983—2001, chief of staff, 1988, med. dir., 1988-89, St. Joe's Med. Assn., Howard, SD, 1988—2000, Women's Health Clinic, Mitchell, SD, 1983—2000; assoc. prof. U. S.D. Sch. Medicine; 2005med. dir. Desert Regional Med. Ctr., Palm Springs, Calif., 2001—05; med. dir. Tenet Home Health, 2005; CEO Physiogard LLC, 2005—. Presenter U.S. Senate, Washington, 1991; med. dir. Cave South Home Health, 2005, Sleep Disorders of Palm Springs, 2005 Contbr. articles to profl. jours. Bd. dirs. Dakota Weslayan U., Mitchell, 1986-89, Dakota Mental Health, Mitchell, 1988-90; mem. Commn. 2000 S.D., Sioux Falls, 1988-00; pub. health officer City of Mitchell, 1983-01. Named one of Top 100 Family Physicians in U.S., Consumer Rsch. Coun., Washington, Top 70 Drs. in 35 Specialties, Caste Connolly Med. Ltd. Fellow Am. Acad. Family Practice (Active Tchrs. award 1984—); mem. AMA, Calif.

Acad. Family Practice, S.D. Assn. Family Practice, S.D. State Med. Assn. (del. 1983-2000, sec. 1998-99, v.p. 1999, pres. 2000), Calif. State Med. Assn., Mitchell C. of C., Mayo Alumni Assn., Doctors Mayo Soc. Avocations: sailing, music, auto restoration. Home: 31240 Calle Cayuga Cathedral City CA 92234-0100 Office Phone: 760-218-7662.

GAFFNEY, DONALD LEE, lawyer; b. Dallas, July 7, 1952; s. Leroy H. and Myriam (Brazeal) G.; m. Debby Dunn, May 31, 1974; children: Brian, Colin, Caitlin. BA, Austin Coll., 1974; JD, U. Tex., 1977. Bar: Ariz. 1979, U.S. Ct. Appeals (9th cir.) 1979, U.S. Ct. Appeals (10th cir.) 1984, U.S. Supreme Ct. 1984. Ptnr. Streich & Lang, Phoenix, 1977-89, Snell & Wilmer L.L.P., Phoenix, 1988—; consumer privacy ombudsman US Bankruptcy Ct. Ariz., 2006—. Adj. prof. Ariz. State U. Law Sch., Tempe, 1983-84; dean's council U. Tex. Law Sch., 2005—; atty. rep. 9th Cir. Ct. Appeals Judicial Conf. Co-author: Bankruptcy, 1987; note comment and book review editor: Tex. Law Review 1976-77; contbr. to profl. jours. Mem. Gov.'s Task Force Ctrl. Ariz. Project, 1993. Austin scholar. Mem. ABA, Am. Arbitration Assn. (com. panel), Comml. Law League of Am. (bankruptcy com. 1980-84), State Bar Ariz. (chmn. bankruptcy sect., 1982-84, com. on bankruptcy rules 1979-81, uniform comml. code com. 1980—), Phi Delta Phi. Democrat. Presbyterian. Office: Snell & Wilmer LLP 1 Arizona Ctr Phoenix AZ 85004-0001

GAFFNEY, JOHN T., lawyer; b. Poughkeepsie, NY, May 10, 1960; BA, George Washington Univ., 1982; MBA, JD, NYU, 1986. Bar: NY 1987. Assoc. Cravath Swaine & Moore LLP, NYC, 1986—93, ptnr., corp., 1993—2008; exec. v.p., gen. counsel First Solar, Inc., Phoenix, 2008—. Mem.: NY State Bar Assn., Assn. of Bar of City of NY. Office: First Solar Inc 4050 E Cotton Center Blvd #6-68 Phoenix AZ 85040 Business E-Mail: jgaffney@firstsolar.com.

GAFFNEY, JOSEPH M., lawyer; b. 1944; BCS in Acctg., Seattle U., 1967; JD, U. Calif., 1972; LLM in Tax., NYU, 1975. Bar: Wash. 1972. Atty., tax, bus., estate planning Dorsey & Whitney LLP, 2000—03, ptnr.-in-charge, Seattle, tax, estate planning group Seattle, 2003—, mem., mgmt. com.; and officer & dir. Dorsey & Whitney Trust Co. Bd. trustees Seattle Univ., Wash. Edn. Found., Wash. Assn. Ind. Coll. & Univ., Nesholm Family Found., 1989—. Bd. trustees Arts Fund, Seattle; adv. bd. ElderHealth Northwest. Recipient Disting. Alumni award, Seattle Univ., 1991; named a Super Lawyer, Wash. Law & Politics. Fellow: Am. Coll. Trust & Estate Counsel; mem.: King Co. Bar Assn., Wash. State Bar Assn., Seattle Estate Planning Coun., Order of Coif. Office: Dorsey & Whitney LLP Ste 3400 US Bank Ctr 1420 Fifth Ave Seattle WA 98101-4010 Office Phone: 206-903-5448. Office Fax: 206-903-8820. Business E-Mail: gaffney.joe@dorsey.com.

GAGE, FRED H., neuroscientist, educator; BS, U. Fla.; PhD, Johns Hopkins U., Balt. Assoc. prof. dept. histology U. Lund, Sweden; prof. dept. neuroscience U. Calif., San Diego; prof. Lab. Genetics Salk Inst. Biol. Studies, San Diego, 1995—. Contbr. articles to profl. jours. Recipient MERIT award, NIH, Decade of the Brain medal, Neurosciences award, Pew Found., Neuroscience Rsch. award, Bristol-Myers Squibb, 1987, IPSEN prize, Neuronal Plasticity, 1990, Charles A. Dana award, Pioneering Achievements in Health and Edn., 1993, Christopher Reeve Rsch. medal, 1997, Max Planck Rsch. prize, 1999, Robert J. and Claire Pasarow Found. award, 1999, Award, Med. Rsch., MetLife, 2002, Klaus Joachim Zulch prize, Max Planck Soc., 2003; grantee Predoctoral fellowship, NIMH. Fellow: NAS Inst. Medicine, Am. Acad. Arts & Sci., NAS; mem.: Soc. Neuroscience (pres. 2001). Achievements include first successful strategies to stimulate recovery of function following brain and spinal cord injuries. Office: Salk Inst Biol Studies PO Box 85800 San Diego CA 92186-5800 E-mail: gage@salk.edu.

GAGLIARDI, SARA, state legislator; m. Jack Gagliardi; children: Gordon, Chris, Anthony. LPN, Iowa Lakes CC, Estherville, 1977. Med. surg. nurse Emmetsburg Cmty. Hosp., Iowa; lic. practical nurse at various hospitals and clinics in obstetrics, pediat., surgery, orthopedics trauma and dermatology Colo.; mem. Dist. 27 Colo. House of Reps., Denver, 2007—. Active Jefferson County Democrats; mem. accountability com. Vanderhoof Elem. Sch., Drake Mid. Sch.; treas. Arvada Northwest Bus. & Profl Women's Group; union steward Svc. Employees Internat. Union Local 105; tchr., LBC classes Spirit of Christ Cmty. Ch. Mem.: League of Women Voter's. Democrat. Office: Colo State Capitol 200 E Colfax Denver CO 80203 Office Phone: 303-866-2962. Business E-Mail: sara.gagliardi.house@state.co.us.*

GAILLARD, MARY KATHARINE, physicist, educator; b. New Brunswick, NJ, Apr. 1, 1939; d. Philip Lee and Marion Catharine (Wiedemayer) Ralph; children: Alain, Dominique, Bruno. BA, Hollins Coll., Va., 1960; MA, Columbia U., 1961; Dr du Troiseme Cycle, U. Paris, Orsay, France, 1964, Dr-es-Sciences d'Etat, 1968. With Ctr. Nat. Rsch. Sci., Orsay and Annecy-le-Vieux, France, 1964-84, head rsch. Orsay, 1973-80, Annecy-le-Vieux, 1979-80, dir. rsch., 1980-84; prof. physics, sr. faculty staff Lawrence Berkeley lab. U. Calif., Berkeley, 1981—. Morris Loeb lectr. Harvard U., Cambridge, Mass., 1980; Chancellor's Disting. lectr., U. Calif., Berkeley, 1981; Warner-Lambert lectr. U. Mich., Ann Arbor, 1984; vis. scientist Fermi Nat. Accelerator Lab., Batavia, Ill., 1973-74, Inst. for Advanced Studies, Santa Barbara, Calif., 1984, U. Calif., Santa Barbara, 1985; group leader L.A.P.P., Theory Group, France, 1979-81, Theory Physics div. LBL, Berkeley, 1985-87; sci. dir. Les Houches (France) Summer Sch., 1981; cons., mem. adv. panels U.S. Dept. Energy, Washington; cons. Nat. Sci. Bd., 1996-97, 2002, bd. dirs., 1997-2002. Co-editor: Weak Interactions, 1977, Gauge Theories in High Energy Physics, 1983; contr. articles to profl. jours. Recipient Thibaux prize U. Lyons (France) Acad. Art and Sci., 1977, E.O. Lawrence award, 1988, J.J. Sakurai prize for theoretical particle physics, APS, 1993; Guggenheim fellow, 1989-90. Fellow Am. Acad. Arts and Scis., Am. Phys. Soc. (mem. various coms., chair com. on women, J.J. Saburai prize 1993); mem. AAAS, NAS, Am. Philos. Soc. Office: U Calif Dept Physics Berkeley CA 94720-7300

GAINES, FRANCIS PENDLETON, III, judge; b. Lexington, Va., Sept. 24, 1944; s. Francis Pendleton Jr. and Dorothy Ruth (Bloomhardt) G.; m. Mary Chilton, Dec. 19, 1967 (div. Aug. 1992); children: Elizabeth Chilton, Edmund Pendleton, Andrew Cavett. Grad., Woodberry Forest Sch., Va., 1962; BA in Hist., U. Ariz., 1967; LLB, U. Va., 1969. Bar: U.S. Dist. Ct. (Ariz.) 1969, Ariz. 1969, U.S. Ct. Appeals (9th cir.) 1972, U.S. Supreme Ct. 1975. Assoc. Evans, Kitchel & Jenckes, Phoenix, 1969-75, ptnr., 1975-89, Fennemore Craig, Phoenix, 1989-99; judge Superior Ct. of Ariz., Phoenix, 1999—; assoc. presiding civil judge Maricopa County Superior Ct., 2001—05, Maricopa County Complex Civil Litigation Ct., 2003—08. Panel arbitrators N.Y. Stock Exch., 1984-99, NASD, 1984-99; judge pro tem Ariz. Ct. Appeals, 1994-95, 2006-07, Maricopa County (Ariz.) Superior Ct., 1994-99; mem. State Bar Disciplinary Hearing Com., 1991-94, chair, 1995-97; mem. nat. litig. panel U. Va. Sch. Law; mem. Ariz. Commn. on Judicial Performance Review, 2001-08; lectr. and panelist CLE programs. Author: Punitive Damages-A Railroad Trial Lawyers Guide, 1985. Chmn. bd. govs. All Saints' Episcopal Day Sch., Phoenix, 1990—91; sr. warden All Saints' Episcopal Ch., 1994—97, parish chancellor, 1997—99, diversity preceptor, 1999—2003; standing com. Episcopal Diocese of Ariz., 1997—2001. Recipient Outstanding Alumnus award, U. Az., 2002; named one of 500 Leading Judges in Am., Lawdragon mag., 2006. Fellow: Ariz. Bar Found., Am. Bar Found.; mem.: ABA, Am. Coll. Bus. and Comml. Ct. Judges, Nat. Conf. State Trial Judges (coms. on jury mgmt. and bus. and comml. cts.), Securities Industry Assn., Nat. Assn. R.R. Trial Counsel (exec. com. Pacific Region, v.p. 1997—98), Maricopa County Bar Assn., State Bar Ariz. (civil practice and procedure com. 2000—, professionalism course oversight com. 2001—), U. Ariz. Pres.'s Club, Univ. Club. Republican. Episcopalian. Office: Superior Ct Ariz 201 W Jefferson St Phoenix AZ 85003-2205 Home Phone: 602-943-6219; Office Phone: 602-506-3940. Business E-Mail: pgaines@superiorcourt.maricopa.gov.

GAINES, LA DONNA ADRIAN See SUMMER, DONNA

GAINES, TED, state legislator; b. Roseville, Calif. m. Beth Gaines, 1985; 6 children. BA in Bus. Adminstrn., Lewis & Clark Coll., Portland, Oreg. California State Assemblyman, District 4, 2006-, member, Health, Labor & Employment Committees, currently, vice chair, Banking & Finance Committee, currently; City of Roseville's Planning Comn, 97-99; Placer Co Bd of Supr, 2000 & 2004. owner, Point West Ins. Auburn Dam Coalition (formerly); Golden Sierra Job Training Partnership (formerly); Placer Co Transportation Agency (formerly); Sacramento Area Coun of Govts (formerly); Sacramento Area Commerce & Trade Organization (formerly); Roseville Rotary Club (honorary member); Roseville Chamber Leadership Prog (grad); Bayside Covenant Church; South Placer Nat Day of Prayer Breakfast (chair, 2004); Peace for Families Capitol Campaign (honorary comt); Independent Ins Agents & Brokers of Sacramento (president, formerly). Republican. Office: Dist 4 1700 Eureka Rd Ste 160 Roseville CA 95661 Office Phone: 916-774-4430. Office Fax: 916-774-4433. Business E-Mail: Assemblymember.Gaines@assembly.ca.gov.

GAITHER, JAMES C., lawyer; b. Oakland, Calif., Sept. 3, 1937; s. Horace Rowan Jr. and Charlotte Cameron (Castle) G.; m. Susan Good, Apr. 30, 1960; children: James Jr., Whitaker, Reed, Kendra. BA in Econs., Princeton U., 1959; JD, Stanford U., 1964. Bar: Calif. 1964, U.S. Dist. Ct. D.C. 1965, U.S. Dist. Ct. (no. dist.) Calif. 1965, U.S. Ct. Appeals (D.C. cir., 7th cir., 9th cir.), 1965, U.S. Supreme Ct. Law clk. to chief justice Earl Warren, Washington, 1964-65; spl. asst. to asst. atty. gen. John W. Douglas, Washington, 1965-66; staff asst. Pres. Lyndon B. Johnson, Washington, 1966-69; atty. Cooley Godward Kronish LLP, San Francisco, 1969-71, ptnr., 1971—2000, mng. ptnr., 1984-90, sr. counsel, 2000—; mng. dir. Sutter Hill Ventures, 2000—. Cons. to sec. HEW, 1977, chmn. ethics adv. bd., 1977—80; bd. dirs. Kineto, Milpitas, Calif., nVidia Corp., Santa Clara, Satmetrix, Foster City, Calif., Hewlett Found., SeeSaw Networks, San Francisco; chair Carnegie Endowment for Internat. Peace; former trustee The RAND Corp. Editor: Stanford Law Rev., 1963—64. Former pres. bd. trustees, Stanford (Calif.) U.; mem. exec. com. bd. vis. Sch. Law Stanford U.; former chmn. bd. trustees Branson Sch., Ross, Calif., Ctr. for Biotech. Rsch. San Francisco; past trustee Family Svc. Agy. San Francisco, St. Stephens Parish Day Sch., Belvedere, Calif., The Scripps Rsch. Inst.; past trustee, chmn. protem Marin Cmty. Found, Marin County, Calif.; past pres. bd. trustees Marin County Day Sch., Corte Madera; past pres. bd. trustees Marin Ednl. Found., San Rafael; past treas., trustee Rosenberg Found.; past v.p., trustee, vice chmn. San Francisco Devel. Fund; past chmn. Dean's Adv. Coun. Stanford Law Sch., chmn. capital campaign; Inst. Capt. USMC, 1959-61. Recipient Disting. Pub. Svc. award HEW, 1977, Stanford Assocs. award Stanford U., 1989, 97, Uncommon Man award, Stanford U., 2006; named Entrepreneur of Yr. Harvard Bus. Sch., 1979. Fellow Am. Acad. Arts and Scis.; mem. ABA, Calif. Bar Assn., San Francisco Bar Assn., Order of Coif, Phi Delta Phi (province 12). Democrat. Presbyn. Avocations: tennis, hiking, camping, fishing, photography. Home and Office: Sutter Hill Ventures 755 Page Mill Rd # A-200 Palo Alto CA 94304

GALANTI, RICHARD A., wholesale business executive; BS, U. Pa. Wharton Sch.; MBA, Stanford U. Grad. Sch. Bus., Calif., 1982. Assoc. Donaldson Lufkin & Jenrette Securities Corp., 1978—84; v.p. fin. Costco Wholesale, Corp., Issaquah, Wash., 1984—85, sr. v.p., treas., CFO, 1985—93, exec. v.p., CFO, 1993—, dir., 1995—. Office: Costco Wholesale 999 Lake Dr Ste 200 Issaquah WA 98027-5367*

GALBRAITH, JAMES MARSHALL, lawyer, corporate executive; b. Iowa City, Oct. 4, 1942; s. John Semple and Laura (Huddleston) G.; m. Margaret Rodi, Aug. 19, 1966; children: Margaret Laura, Katherine Lou, Robert James. BA, Pomona Coll., 1964; JD, Stanford U., 1967. Bar: Calif. 1968. Assoc. Gibson, Dunn & Crutcher, Los Angeles, 1967-68; ptnr. Rodi, Pollock, Pettker, Galbraith & Cahill, Los Angeles, 1968-84, of counsel, 1984—2003; pres. Bell Helmets Internat., Inc., 1980-84; ptnr. Palm Properties Co., 1979—2001. Pres., dir. Van de Kamp's Bakers, Inc., 1984—87; ptnr. Huntington Hotel Assocs., San Marino, 1986—95; pres. Crestmont Investments, LLC, 1991—. Author: In the Name of the People, 1977, The Money Tree, 1982, Fear of Failure, 1993, Patient Power, 1995; mem. bd. editors Stanford Law Rev., 1965-67. Trustee Pomona Coll., 1987-89, trustee emeritus, 1989—; trustee, mem. exec. com. Childrens Hosp. L.A., 1986-91, hon. trustee, 1991—; mem. Soc. of Fellows, Huntington Libr. Art Gallery and Bot. Gardens, 1982—; mem. Young Pres. Orgn., 1979-93. Mem. State Bar Calif., Phi Beta Kappa. Clubs: California (L.A.), Valley Hunt (Pasadena). Episcopalian. Home: 1640 Oak Grove Ave San Marino CA 91108-1109 Office: 2600 Mission St San Marino CA 91108-1676

GALBRAITH, JOHN ROBERT, insurance company executive; b. Portland, Oreg., Oct. 18, 1938; s. Maurice Kerr and Margaret Ione (Veach) G.; m. Maureen McKovich, Oct. 2, 1971 (div. Mar. 1978); children: Margaret Maureen, Marc Ryan; m. Betty Jean Irelan, Dec. 11, 1987. BA, Willamette U., 1960; MBA, U. Washington, 1962. CPA, Oreg. Staff acct. Ernst & Young, Portland, 1962-65; treas. First Pacific Corp., Portland, 1965-71; v.p., treas. Geo McKovich Cos., Palm Beach, Fla. and L.A., 1971-80; v.p., chief fin. officer SAIF Corp., Salem, Oreg., 1980-82; exec. v.p., CFO Liberty N.W. Ins. Corp., Portland, 1983—, bd. dir. Bd. dir. Helmsman Mgmt. Svcs. N.W., Inc., Portland, 1987—. Bd. dirs. Liberty Health Plan, Inc., Portland, 1992—. With Army N.G., 1957-66. Mem. AICPAs, Fin. Exec. Inst., Fla. Ins. CPAs, Calif. Soc. CPAs, Oreg. Soc. CPAs, Multnomah Athletic Club. Republican. Home: 8004 Castlehill Rd Birmingham AL 35242-7226

GALE, ARNOLD DAVID, pediatric neurologist, consultant; b. Chgo., Nov. 2, 1949; s. Benjamin and Revelle Frances (Steinman) G.; m. Sharon Ann Stone, 1997. AB summa cum laude, Stanford U., 1971; MD, Johns Hopkins U., 1976. Diplomate Am. Bd. Pediat., Nat. Bd. Med. Examiners; med. lic., Calif. Resident in pediat. Mass. Gen. Hosp., Boston, 1976-78; postdoctoral fellow Johns Hopkins Hosp., Balt., 1978-79, resident in neurology, 1979-82; asst. prof. pediat. and neurology George Washington U. Sch. Medicine, Washington, 1982-89; dir. neurology tng. program Children's Hosp. Nat. Med. Ctr., Washington, 1982-89; clin. assoc. prof. neurology, neurological scis. and pediat. Sch. of Med. Stanford U., Stanford, Calif., 1989—; med. info. officer Muscular Dystrophy Assn., Tucson, 1992—. Cons. neurologist Vaccine Injury Program U.S. Dept. HHS, Rockville, Md., 1989—, Inst. Vaccine Saftey, Bloomberg Sch. Pub. Health Johns Hopkins U., Balt., 1998—, Anthrax Vaccine Expert Com., 1999—; mem. adv. panel FDA, Rockville, 1983—89; vis. lectr. U. Pitts. Sch. Medicine, 1981—89; cons. Office Human Rsch. Protection U.S. Dept. Health and Human Svcs., 2003—; cons. Brighton Collaboration, Ctrs. for Disease Control, Atlanta, 2003—; mem. Clin. Expert Immunization Com. US Dept. Health and Human Svcs., Rockville, Md., 2003—; cons. Federal Trade commn., Washington, 2008—. Author: Pediatric Emergency Medicine, 1989; contbr. articles to profl. jours. Support group coord. Muscular Dystrophy Assn., San Jose, Calif., 1989—; mem. Pres.'s Com. Employment of People Disabilities, Washington, 1992—; med. adv. bd. Multiple Sclerosis Soc., Santa Clara, Calif., 1990—; v.p. Muscular Dystrophy Assn., Tucson, 1992-94, bd. dirs., 1993-96; med. vol. disaster preparedness, Dept Pub. health, Santa Clara County, Calif., 2005-. Recipient Nat. Rehab. award, Allied Svcs., Scranton, Pa., 1994, Exceptional Civilian Svc. award, US Dept. Defense, 2004, Adminstrs. citation, Health Resources and Svcs. Adminstrn., 2004, Heritage award, Johns Hopkins U., 2005. Fellow Am. Acad. Pediat.; mem. Am. Acad. Neurology, Am. Soc. Neurol. Investigation (founding mem.), Am. Acad. Immunotherapy, Child Neurology Soc., Calif. Children's Lobby, Nat. Alumni Coun. (Johns Hopkins U.), Phi Beta Kappa, Alpha Omega Alpha. Jewish. Avocations: writing, travel. Office Phone: 408-261-8765. E-mail: adgale@jhu.edu.

GALE, ROBERT PETER, physician, scientist, researcher; b. NYC, Oct. 11, 1945; s. Harvey Thomas and Evelyn (Klein) G.; m. Tamar Tishler, June 2, 1976; children: Tal, Shir, Elan. BA, Hobart Coll., 1966; MD, SUNY, Buffalo, 1970; PhD, UCLA, 1976; DSc (hon.), Albany Med. Coll., 1987; LHD (hon.), Hobart Coll., 1987; D of Pub. Svc. (hon.), MacMurray Coll., 1988. Diplomate Am. Bd. Internal Medicine, Am. Bd. Med. Oncology, Am. Bd. Hematology. Resident in hematology and oncology UCLA, 1972-74, prof. medicine, 1974—; dir. bone marrow and stem cell transplantation Salick Health Care, Inc., 1993—. Chmn. Internat. Bone Marrow Transplant Registry, Milw., 1982—; pres. Armand Hammer Ctr. for Advanced Studies in Nuc. Energy and Health; sci. dir. Ctr. for Advanced Studies in Leukemia, L.A.; mem. Am. Com. on U.S.-Soviet Rels. Author 20 books, 700 articles on hematology, oncology, immunology and transplantation. Recipient Presdl. award N.Y. Acad. Scis., 1986, Olender Peace prize, 1986, Emmy award NATAS, Scientist of Distinction award Weizmann Inst. Sci., 1988; Bogart fellow and scholar Leukemia Soc. Am., 1976-81. Fellow ACP; mem. Transplantation Soc., Am. Soc. Hematology, Am. Assn. Immunology, Internat. Soc. Hematology, Soc. Exptl. Hematology, Am. Soc. Clin. Oncology, Am. Assn. Cancer Rsch., Russian Acad. Med. Sci. (hon.). Office: 11693 San Vicente Blvd # 335 Los Angeles CA 90049-5105 Home: 980 Bluegrass Ln Los Angeles CA 90049-1433

GALEL, SUSAN ALPERT, transfusion medicine physician; MD, Harvard U., 1979. Diplomate Am. Bd. Pediat., Am. Bd. Pediatric Hematology/Oncology. Dir. clin. ops. Stanford Med. Sch. Blood Ctr., Palo Alto, Calif., 1987—. Office: Stanford Med Sch Blood Ctr 3373 Hillview Ave Palo Alto CA 94304

GALL, DONALD ALAN, data processing executive; s. Clarence Oliver and Evelyn Louise Gall; m. Elizabeth Olmstead, June 25, 1960 (div. 1972); children: Christopher, Keith, Elizabeth; m. Kathleen Marie Insogna, Oct. 13, 1973 (div. 2004); 1 child, Kelly Marie; m. Margaret Andersen, May 24, 2007. BSME, U. Ill., 1956; SM, MIT, 1958, ME, 1960, ScD, 1964. Rsch. engr. GM, Detroit, 1956—57; staff engr. Dynatech Corp., Cambridge, Mass., 1959—60, mgr. ctr. sys., 1962—63; asst., assoc. prof. Carnegie-Mellon U., Pitts., 1964—69; rsch. assoc. prof. surgery and anesthesiology U. Pitts. Sch. Medicine, 1969—73; vis. fellow IBM Rsch. Lab., Rueschlikon, Switzerland, 1970—71; pres. Omega Computer Sys., Inc., Phoenix, 1973—; CEO Omega Legal Sys., Inc., Phoenix, 1995—; bd. dirs. TTI Technologies, Inc., Omaha. Contbr. articles to profl. jours.; inventor fuel injection system. Bd. dirs. Scottsdale Boys and Girls Club, 1978—87; mem. Verde Vaqueros, 1987—; mem. alumni adv. bd. dept. mech. and indsl. engring. U. Ill., 2001—, bd. visitors Coll. Engring., 2009—. Recipient Taylor medal, Internat. Conf. Prodn. Rsch., 1970, Disting. Alumnus award dept. mech. and indsl. engring., U. Ill., 1997, Alumni Honor award, Coll. Engring., U. Ill., 2009. Mem.: ASME (life), M Tech. Assn. (exec. dir., bd. dirs. 1996—98, chmn. bd. dirs. 1998—2001), Sigma Xi, Phi Kappa Phi, Tau Beta Pi, Pi Tau Sigma. Avocations: horseback riding, skiing, golf. Home: 8675 E Via de McCormick Scottsdale AZ 85258 Office: Omega Computer Sys Inc 3875 N 44th St Ste 200 Phoenix AZ 85018-5486 Office Phone: 602-952-5240. Business E-Mail: dgall@omegalegal.com.

GALL, MEREDITH (MARK) DAMIEN, education professor emeritus, writer; b. New Britain, Conn., Feb. 18, 1942; s. Theodore A. and Ray G.; m. Joyce Pershing, June 12, 1968; 1 child, Jonathan. AB, EdM, Harvard U., 1963; PhD, U. Calif., Berkeley, 1968. Sr. research assoc. Far West Lab. for Ednl. Research and Devel., San Francisco, 1968-75; assoc. prof. edn. U. Oreg., Eugene, 1975-79, prof., 1980—2005, dept. head for tchr. edn., 2002—05; ret., 2005. Author: Handbook for Evaluating and Selecting Curriculum Materials, 1981; author: (with J.P. Gall) Making the Grade, 1993; author: (with W.R. Borg and J.P. Gall) Educational Research: An Introduction, 8th edit., 2007; author: (with J.P. Gall, D.R. Jacobsen, and T.L. Bullock) Tools for Learning: A Guide to Teaching Study Skills, 1990; author: (with W.R. Borg and J.P. Gall) Applying Educational Research, 5th edit., 2005; co-author: Clinical Supervision and Teacher Development, 5th edit., 2003; editor (with B.A. Ward): Critical Issues in Educational Psychology, 1974; cons. editor: Jour. Rsch. in Rural Edn., Forum for Reading, Elem. Sch. Jour. Grantee, USPH, 1963—64. Fellow Am.

Psychol. Assn.; mem. ASCD, Am. Ednl. Research Assn., Phi Delta Kappa (Dist. I Meritorious award 1978). Home: 4810 Mahalo Dr Eugene OR 97405-4609 Business E-Mail: mgall@uoregon.edu.

GALLAGHER, DENNIS JOSEPH, municipal official, state senator, educator; b. July 1, 1939; s. William Joseph and Ellen Philomena (Flaherty) G.; children: Meaghan Kathleen, Daniel Patrick. BA, Regis Coll., 1961; MA, Cath. U. Am., 1968; postgrad. (Eagleton fellow), Rutgers U., 1972-86. With locals of Internat. Assn. Theatrical and Stage Employees, Denver and Washington, 1956-63; tchr. St. John's Coll. H.S., Washington, 1964-66, Heights Study Ctr., Washington, 1965-67, Regis U., Denver, 1967—2003; mem. Colo. Ho. of Reps. from 4th Dist., 1970-74, Colo. Senate, 1974-95; councilman dist. 1, Denver, 1995—2003. Chmn. Dem. Caucus, 1982-84, Dem. Whip, 1985-87. Mem. Platte Area Reclamation Com., 1973-75; mem. Denver Anti-Crime Coun., 1976-77; trustee Denver Art Mus.; bd. dirs. Cath. Cmty. Svcs.; past mem. Colo. Commn. on Aging; past mem. Colo. State Adv. Coun. on Career Edn.; mem. Victim Assistance Law Enforcement Bd., Denver, 1984-88; bd. dirs. Denver Am. Ireland Fund. Named Gates Found. fellow Harvard U.; recipient Jacques Ellul award Media Ecology Assn., 2001. Mem.: Nat. Comm. Assn., Gerard Manley Hopkins S.J. Soc. Regis (conf. co-dir.), Western States Comm. Assn., Rocky Mountain Comm. Assn., James Joyce Reading Soc., Colo. History Group, Colo. Calligrapher's Guild, Colo. Fedn. Tchrs. (pres. local 1333 1972—74). Democrat. Catholic. Home: 5097 Meade St Denver CO 80221-1033 Office: Denver Auditor's Office 201 W Colfax Ave Sept 705 Denver CO 80202 E-mail: dennis.gallagher@ci.denver.co.us.

GALLAGHER, JOSEPH FRANCIS, marketing executive; b. NYC, May 15, 1926; s. Joseph O'Neil and Nora (Shea) G.; m. Anne Decker, June 17, 1950; children: June, Virginia, Aline. Student, U. Va., 1947-50. Advanced to pres., dir. Erwin Wasey, Inc., Los Angeles, 1968-80; pres. JFG, Inc., Oildale, Calif., 1981—. Served with USNR, 1944-46. Mem. Phi Gamma Delta, Delta Sigma Rho. Office: JFG Inc Bakersfield CA 93388

GALLAGHER, M. CATHERINE, English literature educator; b. Denver, Feb. 16, 1945; d. John Martin and Mary Catherine Sullivan; m. Martin Evan Jay, July 6, 1974; children: Margaret Shana, Rebecca Erin. BA, U. Calif., Berkeley, 1972, MA, 1974, PhD, 1979. Asst. prof. U. Denver, 1979-80, U. Calif., Berkeley, 1980-84, assoc. prof., 1984-90, prof., 1990—. Author: The Industrial Reformation of English Fiction, 1985, Nobody's Story, 1994, The Body Economic, 2005; co-author: The Making of the Modern Body, 1987, Practicing New Historicism, 2000; editor Representation, 1983—. Guggenheim fellow Guggenheim Found., 1989; fellow NEH, 1990, ACLS, 1990, Mem. MLA (del. assembly mem. 1985-86, exec. com. lit. criticism divsn. 1991-94), Am. Acad. Arts and Scis., Acad. Lit. Studies, Brit. Studies Assn., The Dickens Soc. Office: U Calif Dept English Berkeley CA 94720-0001 Business E-Mail: cgall@berkeley.edu.

GALLAGHER, MICHAEL L., lawyer; b. LeMars, Iowa, Apr. 14, 1944; BA, Ariz. State U., 1966, JD, 1970. Bar: Ariz. 1970. Maj. league scout N.Y. Mets, 1967—70; atty. Snell & Wilmer, Phoenix, 1970—78, Gallagher & Kennedy, Phoenix, 1978—. Judge pro tem Maricopa County Superior Ct., 1979, Ariz. Ct. Appeals, 1985; Amerco, U-Haul; bd. dirs. Ariz. Pub. Svc. Co., Omaha World-Herald Co., Pinnacle West Capital Corp. Chmn. gov.'s adv. com. profl. football, 1981-87, mayor's adv. com. profl. sports, 1984-91; bd. dirs. Maricopa County Sports Authority, 1989; bd. visitors law sch. Ariz. State U., 1979; dir. Valley of the Sun YMCA, chmn., 1995; trustee Peter Kiewit Found. Fellow Internat. Acad. Trial Lawyers. Office: Gallagher & Kennedy PA 2575 E Camelback Rd Phoenix AZ 85016-9225 Home Phone: 602-277-9462; Office Phone: 602-530-8000. Business E-Mail: mlg@gknet.com.

GALLAGHER, THOMAS EDMUND, hotel executive, lawyer; b. Detroit, Dec. 10, 1944; s. Edmund James and Monica F. Gallagher; m. Mary Kay Stoegbauer; children: Meighan, Kevin, Erin, Ryan. AB magna cum laude, Holy Cross Coll., 1966; JD cum laude, Harvard Univ., 1969. Bar: Calif. 1970. Assoc. Gibson, Dunn and Crutcher, 1969—70, 1973—77, ptnr., 1977—92, with LA, 1977—79, London, 1979—83, Riyadh, 1983—87, NYC, 1988—92; legis. asst. US Senate, 1970—72; pres., CEO The Griffin Group, Inc., 1992—97; pres., CEO Resorts Internat./Griffin Gaming and Entertainment, Atlantic City, 1995—96; exec. v.p., chief adminstrv. officer, gen. counsel Hilton Hotels Corp., Beverly Hills, Calif., 1997-2000; pres. & CEO Park Place Entertainment Corp. (NYSE-PPE), Las Vegas, 2000—. Dir., chmn. exec. com. Resorts Internat., Atlantic City, 1993-95; dir., chmn. comp. com. Players Internat. Inc., Las Vegas, Nev., and Atlantic City, 1992-97. Trustee Greylock Found., N.Y.C., 1992—. Mem. Urban Land Inst. Office: Park Place Entertainment 2100 Caesars Palace Dr Las Vegas NV 89109-8969

GALLEGLY, ELTON WILLIAM, United States Representative from California; b. Huntington Park, Calif., Mar. 7, 1944; m. Janice Shrader; 4 children. Student, Calif. State U., LA. Mem. Simi Valley City Coun., 1979; mayor City of Simi Valley, 1980-86; mem. US Congress from 21st (now 24th) Calif. dist., 1986—, mem. fgn. affairs com., internat. rels. com., judiciary com., natural resources com., select com. intelligence. Chair Task Force Urban Search/Rescue; mem. Ho. Rep. Rsch. Com. Bd. dirs. Moorpark Coll. Found. Mem.: Ventura County Assn. Govts. Republican. Office: US House Reps 2309 Rayburn House Office Bldg Washington DC 20515-0524

GALLINGER, LORRAINE D., prosecutor; b. Sept. 2, 1948; BS, U. Wyo., 1970; JD, Cath. U. Am., 1975. Bar: D.C., Mont. 1st asst. U.S. atty. Dept. Justice, Billings, Mont., 1976-85, 91, sr. litigation counsel, chief civil divsn., 1985-91, acting U.S. atty., 1991-93; first asst. U.S. Attys. Office, Billings, Mont., 1993—. Instr. Atty. Gen. Advocacy Inst. Recipient Dir.'s Superior Performance award AUSA, 1988. Office: US Attys Office PO Box 1478 Billings MT 59103-1478

GALLIVAN, JOHN WILLIAM, retired publishing executive; b. Salt Lake City, June 28, 1915; s. Daniel and Frances (Wilson) G.; m. Grace Mary Ivers, June 30, 1938 (dec.); children: Gay, John W. Jr., Michael D., Timothy. BA, U. Notre Dame, 1937. With Salt Lake Tribune, 1937—, promotion mgr., 1942-48, asst. pub., 1948-60, pub., 1960-84; pres. Kearns-Tribune Corp., 1960-86, chmn. bd., 1984-99; dir., exec. com. Tele-Communications, Inc., 1989-2000, ret., 2000—. Pres. Silver King Mining Co., 1960-97. Pres. Utah Symphony, 1964-65. Mem. Sigma Delta Chi, Bohemian Club (San Francisco). Clubs: Nat. Press (Washington); Alta (Salt Lake City), Salt Lake Country (Salt Lake City), Rotary (Salt Lake City). Home and Office: 1665 White Pine Canyon Rd Park City UT 84060 Personal E-mail: jwgallivan@comcast.net.

GALLO, JOAN ROSENBERG, lawyer; b. Newark, Apr. 28, 1940; BA in Psychology, Boston U., Mass., 1965; postgrad., We. Md. Coll., Westminster, 1966—67; postgrad, We. Grad. Sch. Psychology, 1966—67; JD magna cum laude, U. Santa Clara, 1975. Bar: Calif. 1975. Assoc. with Cynthia Mertens U, Santa Clara, Calif., 1975-76; sr. law clk. US Dist. Ct., Calif., 1976-78; assoc. Decker and Collins, San Jose, Calif., 1978-79; from dep. city atty. to city atty. City of San Jose, 1979-2000; ptnr. Terra Law LLP, San Jose, 2000—02, Realty Law, LLP, San Jose, 2002—03; of counsel Hopkins & Carley, 2004—. Mem.: Psi Chi. Office: Hopkins & Carley 70 S First St San Jose CA 95113 Office Phone: 408-286-9800. Business E-Mail: jgallo@hopkinscarley.com.

GALLO, JON JOSEPH, lawyer; b. Santa Monica, Calif., Apr. 19, 1942; s. Philip S. and Josephine (Sarazan) G.; m. Jo Ann Broome, June 13, 1964 (div. 1984); children: Valerie Ann, Donald Philip; m. Eileen Florence, July 4, 1985; 1 child, Kevin Jon. BA, Occidental Coll., 1964; JD, UCLA, 1967. Bar: Calif. 1968, U.S. Ct. Appeals (9th cir.) 1968, U.S. Tax Ct. 1969. Assoc. Greenberg, Glusker, Fields, Claman & Machtinger, LA, 1967-75, ptnr., 1975—. Bd. dirs. USC Probate and Trust Conf., L.A., 1980—; bd. dirs. UCLA Estate Planning Inst., chmn. 1992—99. Contbr. articles to profl. jours. Fellow Am. Coll. Trust and Estate Counsel; mem. ABA (chair generation skipping taxation com. 1992-95, co-chair life ins. com. 1995-2000, chair psychol. and emotional issues of estate planning 2001—), Internat. Acad. Estate and Trust Law, Assn. for Advanced Life Underwriting (assoc.). Avocation: photography. Office: Greenberg Glusker Fields Claman & Machtinger LLP Ste 2100 1900 Avenue Of The Stars Los Angeles CA 90067-4502

GALLO, JOSEPH E., vintner; b. 1941; Various positions E&J Gallo Winery, South San Francisco, 1962—, now co-pres. & CEO. Office: E & J Gallo Winery 600 Yosemite Blvd Modesto CA 95354

GALLO, MARTA IRENE, retired literature and language educator; b. Córdoba, Argentina, Oct. 20, 1926; d. Gregorio and María Luisa (Teodoro) Gallo. Grad., U. Buenos Aires, 1951. Rschr. Inst. de Filologia, U. Buenos Aires, 1960—66, asst. prof. lit. theory, 1964—66; vis. prof. U. P.R., 1967-68; prof. Spanish U. Calif., Santa Barbara, 1968-91, prof. emeritus, 1991—. Author: Novela Hispoamericana del siglo XIX, Reflexiones sobre espejos; contbr. articles to profl. jours. Mem.: MLA, Linguistic Soc. Am., Internat. Assn. Semiotic Studies, Asociación Internat. de Hispanistas, Inst. Internat. de Literatura Iberoamericana, Asociación Española de Semiótica. Home: 2948 Kenmore Pl Santa Barbara CA 93105-2224 Personal E-mail: martagallo@earthlink.net.

GALLOWAY, PATRICIA DENESE, civil engineer; b. Lexington, Ky., June 14, 1957; d. Howard John and Maudine Lou (Jones) Frisby; m. Kris Richard Nielsen, Mar. 16, 1987. BS in Civil Engring., Purdue U., 1978; MBA, NY Inst. Tech., 1984; PhD in Civil Engring., Kochi U. Tech., Japan, 2005. Registered profl. engr. Ky., NY, NJ, Ariz., Wis., Wyo., Fla., Wash., Colo., Pa., Man., Can., Australia. Project engr., insp. CH2M Hill, Milw., 1978-79, master program scheduler, 1979-81; sr. cons. Nielsen-Wurster Group, NYC, 1981-83, sr. engr., 1983-84, v.p., 1984-85, prin., exec. v.p., 1985-99, pres., 1999-2000, CEO, pres., 2001—04, CEO, 2004—. Lectr. Columbia U., U. Wis.-Madison; vis. prof. Kochi U. Tech.; presenter to numerous orgns; ptnr. Unionville Vineyards, Ringoes, NJ; pres. Unionville Ranch, L.L.C., Wash.; chief exec. Nielsen-Wurster Asia Pacific, Melbourne, Australia, 2001—, bd. dirs., mem. adv. bd. Contbr. articles to profl. jours. Named one of Top 10 Women in Constrn., Engring. New Record, 1986, one of Top 10 Women, Glamour Mag., 1987, 88, White House fellow regional finalist, 1990, Ky. Col., Gov. Patten, Sts. of Ky., 2002; named to Lafayette H.S. Hall of Fame, 2001; recipient Nat. Leadership Coun. Capital award, 1990, Engr. of Yr. award Mercer County Profl. Engrs., 1990, Nat. Leadership award Profl. Women in Constrn., 1995, Fed. Infrature Design award Whitehouse Commn., 1999, Upward Mobility award Soc. Women Engrs., 2003, Tribute to Women in Industry award, YWCA, 2004; named Disting. Engring. Alumnus, Purdue U., 1992, Celebration of Women, NAE, 2000. Fellow ASCE (instr. constrn. claims course, bd. chair task com. on women in civil engring. 1998—2000, internat. dir., bd. dirs. 1992-95, chmn. membership com. 2001—, pres.-elect 2003—, pres., bd. dirs. 2004 (1st woman); mem. NSF (dir. engring. 2004-), Nat. Sci. Bd., 2006—, YWCA (Tribute to Women award), Am. Assn. Engring Socs., Nat. Soc. Professional Engrs., Am. Arbitration Assn., Professional Women in Construction, The Acad. Experts, UK, The Inst. Engrs., Australian Fellow, Soc. Women Engrs. (pres. Wis. chpt. 1980, pres. NY chpt. 1982, Disting. New Engr. 1980, Mobility award 2003-), Project Mgmt. Inst. (dir. pub. bd.), Am. Assn. Cost Engrs., Am. Nuclear Soc., Garden State Wine Growers Assn. (pres. 1990-92), Somerset County C. of C. (most outstanding woman in bus. and industry 1987), Purdue Engring. Alumni Assn. (bd. dirs., 1975-2001), Toastmasters, Sigma Kappa (fin. com. 1993-97), Tau Beta Pi. Republican. Methodist. Avocations: scuba diving, cross country skiing, hiking, horseback riding, wine making. Office: The Nielsen Wurster Group 1301 5th Ave Ste 1900 Seattle WA 98101-2682 Office Phone: 509-857-2235. Office Fax: 609-497-3412. Personal E-mail: patnwg@aol.com.

GALSTER, RICHARD W., engineering geologist; b. Seattle, May 13, 1930; BS in Geology, U. Wash., 1951, MS, 1956. Geologist Grant County (Wash.) Pub. Utilities Dist., 1954-55; geologist Seattle dist. U.S. Army Corps. Engrs., 1955-85; dist. geologist, 1973-85; cons. engring. geologist, 1985—. Recipient Dept. of Army Decoration for Meritorious Civilian Svc., 1985. Fellow Geol. Soc. Am. (chmn. engring. geology divsn. 1978-79, E.B. Burwell award 1993, Disting. Practice award 1995), Assn. Engring. Geologists (hon., pres. 1982-83, Claire P. Holdredge award 1991). Home: 546 Alder St Apt 206 Edmonds WA 98020-3441 E-mail: georichgal@connectexpress.com.

GALUTERIA, BRICKWOOD, state legislator; b. Kaka'ako, Hawaii; m. Abigail Galuteria; 5 children. Acct. exec. & tour dir. Hawaii Airlines; founder No'eau Consulting LLC; mem. Dist. 12 Hawaii State Senate, 2008—. Broadcaster KCCN 1420AM, Hawaiian 105 KINE, KCCN-FM 100; host AM940 KKNE Morning Show, Hawaii's Kitchen, Treasures; spokesperson Bank of Hawaii, Mike McKenna's Windward Ford, Hawaii Visitors & Convention Bur., Hawaii Dept. Agr.; performer Royal Hawaiian Hotel. Pres. & bd. mem. Hawaii Acad. Recording Arts; bd. mem. Hawaii Assn. Retarded Citizens & Life Found., Hawaii Book & Music Festival, Hawaiian Music Hall of Fame, Hawaii Spl. Olympics, Native Hawaiian Culture & Arts Program. Mem.: Dem. Nat. Com., Polynesian Voyaging Soc. (bd. mem.). Democrat. Office: State Capitol 415 S Beretania St Rm 208 Honolulu HI 96813 Office Phone: 808-586-6740. Office Fax: 808-586-6829. Business E-Mail: sengaluteria@capitol.hawaii.gov.

GALVAN, JOE H., federal judge; Bar: N.Mex. Magistrate judge for N.Mex., U.S. Magistrate Ct., Las Cruces, 1991—. Office: US Magistrate Ct B-201C US Courthouse 200 E Griggs Ave Las Cruces NM 88001-3523

GALVIN, PATRICK, Commissioner Department Revenue, Alaska; m. Alyse Galvin; 4 children. B in Visual Arts and Quantitative Econ., U. Calif. San Diego; JD, U. San Diego; MBA, San Diego State U. Atty. pvt. practice; dir. Divsn. Governmental Coord., Ala.; petroleum land mgr. Alaska Dept. Nat. Resources Divsn. Oil and Gas; commr. Alaska Dept. Revenue, 2006—. Office: Alaska Dept Revenue PO Box 110400 333 W Willoughby 11th Fl SOB Juneau AK 99811-0400

GAMBLE, GEOFFREY, academic administrator; Degree in English, Fresno State Coll., 1965, M Linguistics, 1971; PhD Linguistics, U. Calif., Berkeley, 1975. Cert. specialist in Native Am. linguistics. Chair, anthropology chair Washington State U., dir. mus. anthropology, dir. summer session, interim vice provost, vice provost; provost, sr. v.p. U. Vt.; pres. Mont. State U.-Bozeman, 2000—. Grantee Nat. Endowment of Arts, Nat. Endowment for Humanities. Office: Mont State U-Bozeman 211 Montana Hall Bozeman MT 59717-2420

GAMBLE, PATRICK K., retired military officer, rail transportation executive; BA in Math., Tex. A&M U., 1967; MBA, Auburn U., 1978; Grad., Air Command and Staff Coll., Maxwell AFB, 1978; Disting. Grad., Air War Coll., Maxwell AFB, 1984. Commd. 2d lt. USAF, 1967, advanced through ranks to gen., 1998; various assignments to dep. chief of staff air/space opers. Hdqtrs. USAF/The Pentagon, Washington, 1997-98; comdr. Pacific Air Forces, Hickam AFB, 1998—2001; pres., CEO Alaska R.R. Corp., Anchorage, 2001—. Contbr. articles to profl. jours. Decorated Def. Disting. Svc. medal with one oak leaf cluster, Disting. Svc. medal with one oak leak cluster, Legion of Merit, Disting. Flying Cross, Meritorious Svc. medal with two oak leaf clusters, Air medal with 13 oak leaf clusters, Air Force Commendation medal, Presdl. Unit citation with oak leaf cluster, Vietnam Svc. medal with three svc. stars, Republic of Vietnam Gallantry Cross with svc. star, Republic of Vietnam Gallantry Cross with Palm, NATO medal, others. Office: PO Box 107500 Anchorage AK 99510

GAMBLE, SHAWNA, marriage and family therapist, psychologist; b. Dec. 24, 1966; d. Melinda and Moses Fass; m. Sean Gamble; children: Sean Jr., Gwen, Dana. BA in Psychology, U. Utah, 1988, MA in Marriage Counseling, 1990, PhD in Clinical Psychology, 1993. Cert. in Marriage Therapy Utah, 1992. Asst. sex counselor Summit Medical Group, 1994—96, marriage therapist, 1996—2001; group therapist Meriks Matchmakers, Salt Lake City, 2002—, applicant screener, 2004—, couples sex therapist, 2006—. Psychology dept. intern Annex Rush Hospital, 1987—89. Author: Sex, Your Marriage and Cheating, 1999, Finding Love Through the Broken Glass, 2003, An Brokenhearted Girls' Guide to Finding "The One", 2006 (Cosmopolitan's Best Advice Book, 2006). Democrat. Roman Catholic. Office: Meriks Matchmakers 3353 S Main St #288 Salt Lake City UT 84115

GAMBLE, STEVEN G., academic administrator; BA in Am. History, Tex. Tech. U., 1967, MA in Am. History, 1968, PhD in Am. History, 1976. Part-time instr. Tex. Tech U., 1973—76, admission officer, 1976—79; dean admissions, prof. history Angelo St. U., 1979—86; dean enrollment mgmt., prof. history W. Tex. A&M U., 1986—87, v.p. acad. affairs, 1987—92; pres. Southern Ark. U., Magnolia, 1992—2001, Ea. N.Mex. U., Portales, 2001—. With USAF, 1968—72, with USAFR, 1972—95. Office: Eastern New Mexico State U 1200 W University Portales NM 88130

GAMBRELL, THOMAS ROSS, investor, retired physician, surgeon; b. Lockhart, Tex., Mar. 17, 1934; s. Sidney Spivey and Nora Katherine (Rheinlander) G.; m. Louise Evans, Feb. 23, 1960. Student summa cum laude, U. Tex., 1953, MD, 1957. Intern Kings County Hosp., Bklyn., 1957-58; company physician Hughes Aircraft, Fullerton, Calif., 1958-65, Chrysler Corp., Anaheim, Calif., 1962-65, L.A. Angels Baseball Team, Fullerton, 1962-64; pvt. practice medicine Fullerton, 1958-91. Attending staff, St. Jude Hosp., Anaheim Meml. Hosp., Fullerton Cmty. Hosp., Martin Luther Hosp.; mem. utilization rev. com. physician St. Mary's Convalescent Hosp., North Orange County, 1960-1990, Fullerton Convalescent Hosp., Sunhaven and Fairway Convalescent Hosp.; developer, Ranching (Citrus) & Comml. Devel., Ariz., Tex., N.Y., 1962-94. Author: An Ancestral History, 8 B.C. to 1986, 2001, History, rev. and expanded edit., 2004; contbr. articles to profl. jours. Organizer of care for needy elderly, North Orange County, 1962-65; sponsor numerous charity events. Fellow Am. Acad. Family Physicians; mem. AMA, Am. Geriats. Soc., Calif. Med. Assn., Tex. Med. Assn., Tex. U. Alumni Assn., Orange County Med. Assn., Mayflower Soc., Plantagenet Soc., Sons of Confederacy, SAR, Order Royal Descendants Living in Am. (col., listed in Living Descendants of Blood Royal), Order Crown (col.), Baronial Order Magna Carta, Order of Aesculaepius, Phi Eta Sigma, Delta Kappa Epsilon, Phi Chi. Avocations: collecting, travel, history. Office: PO Box 6067 Beverly Hills CA 90212-1067 Personal E-mail: thomasgambrell@msn.com.

GAMSON, JOSHUA PAUL, sociology educator, writer; b. Ann Arbor, Mich., Nov. 16, 1962; s. William Anthony and Zelda (Finkelstein) G. BA, Swarthmore Coll., 1985; MA, U. Calif., Berkeley, 1988, PhD, 1992. Asst. editor Moment Mag., Boston, 1985-86; tchr. h.s. The Cambridge Sch., Weston, Mass., 1986-87; instr. U. Calif., Berkeley, 1992, lectr., 1993; asst. prof. Yale U., New Haven, 1993—98, assoc. prof., 1998—2002, U. San Francisco, 2002—. Author: Claims to Fame: Celebrity in Contemporary America, 1994, Freaks Talk Back: Tabloid Talk Shows and Sexual Nonconformity, 1998, Fabulous Sylvester, 2005; contbr. articles to profl. jours. Activist, media coord. Act Up/San Francisco, 1988-90. Spencer fellow Woodrow Wilson Nat. Fellowship Found., 1991-92, Regents-Intern fellow U. Calif., 1987-92, program on non-profit orgns. fellow Yale U., 1994. Mem. Am. Sociol. Assn. (coun. mem. coun. on stats. of lesbians, gays and bisexuals in sociology 1995—, Fund for the Advancement of the Discipline award 1995), Ea. Sociol. Assn. Office: Univ San Francisco 2130 Fulton Street San Francisco CA 94117

GANAS, PERRY SPIROS, physicist; b. Brisbane, Australia, June 20, 1937; came to U.S., 1968, naturalized, 1975; s. Arthur and Lula (Grivas) G. BS, U. Queensland, Australia, 1961; PhD, U. Sydney, 1968. Tchg. fellow U. Sydney, 1967; postdoctoral rsch. assoc., instr. U. Fla., 1968-70, vis. asst. rsch. prof., 1972, vis. assoc. rsch. prof., 1978, vis. assoc. prof. physics, 1979—80, 1981; prof. physics Calif. State U., LA, 1970—2001, emeritus prof., 2001—. Adj. faculty U. So. Calif., 1985-86, East L.A. Coll., 1988-2004; vis. prof. physics UCLA, summer 1987, 91, 92; referee Astrophys. Jour., Astron. and Astrophysics. Contbr. articles to profl. jours. Mem. AAUP, Congress of Faculty Assns., Am. Phys. Soc., Sigma Xi. Home: 11790 Radio Dr Los Angeles CA 90064-3615 Office: Calif State U Physics Dept Los Angeles CA 90032 Office Phone: 323-343-2121. Business E-Mail: pganas@calstatela.edu.

GANDARA, DANIEL, lawyer; b. LA, July 7, 1948; s. Henry and Cecilia (Contreras) G.; m. Juleann Cottini, Aug. 26, 1972; children: Mario, Enrico. BA, UCLA, 1970; JD, Harvard U., 1974. Bar: Calif. 1974, Wash. 1978. Asst. city atty. City of L.A., 1974-77; staff atty. FTC, Seattle, 1977-79; ptnr. Lane, Powell, Moss & Miller, Seattle, 1979-87, Graham & Dunn, Seattle, 1987-93, Vandeberg, Johnson & Gandara, Seattle, 1993—. Mem. bd. Visitors Seattle U. Sch. Law & U. Wash. Law Sch., King County Healthy Families Task Force, mem. King County Pers. bd., past pres. CHHIP. Recipient Outstanding Lawyer Award, King County Bar Assn., 2006, Affirmative Action Award, wash. state bar assn. bd. gov., 1995, Lawyer of the Year, Wash. State Hispanic Bar Assn., 1997. Mem. ABA, Wash. State Bar Assn., King County Bar Assn. (v.p., former Trustee), past pres. King County Bar Found., Hispanic Nat. Bar Assn., Wash. State Hispanic C. of C., Seattle Athletic Club, mem. Bar Secs. Intellectual (Property, Internat. Law, & Litig.). Democrat. Roman Catholic. Home: 2010 E Lynn St Seattle WA 98112-2620 Office: Vandeberg Johnson & Gandara Ste 2424 600 University St 1 Union Sq Seattle WA 98101-1192 Office Fax: 206-464-0484.

GANDHI, OM PARKASH, electrical engineer; b. Multan, Pakistan, Sept. 23, 1934; came to U.S., 1967, naturalized, 1975; s. Gopal Das and Devi Bai (Patney) G.; m. Santosh Nayar, Oct. 28, 1963; children: Rajesh Timmy, Monica, Lena. BS with honors, Delhi U., India, 1952; MSE, U. Mich., 1957, Sc.D., 1961. Rsch. specialist Philco Corp., Blue Bell, Pa., 1960-62; asst. dir. Cen. Electronics Engring. Rsch. Inst., Pilani, Rajasthan, India, 1962-65, dep. dir., 1965-67; prof. elec. engring., rsch. prof. bioengring. U. Utah, Salt Lake City, 1967—, chmn. elec. engring., 1992-2000. Cons. U.S. Army Med. R&D Command, Washington, 1973-77; cons. to microwave and telecom. industry and govtl. health and safety orgns.; mem. Commns. B and K, Internation Union Radio Sci.; mem. study sect. on diagnostic radiology NIH, 1978-81; mem. rsch. team identifying adverse effects of wireless comm. devices Nat. Acads. Ctr., 2007 Author: Microwave Engineering and Applications, 1981; editor: Engineering in Medicine and Biology mag., 1987, Electromagnetic Biointeraction, 1989, Biological Effects and Medical Applications of Electromagnetic Energy, 1990; contbr. over 200 articles to profl. jours. Recipient Disting. Rsch. award U. Utah, 1979-80. Microwave Pioneer award IEEE-MTT Soc., 2001, Gov.'s medal for sci. and tech. State of Utah, 2002; grantee NSF, NIH, EPA, USAF, U.S. Army, USN, N.Y. State Dept. Health, others. Fellow IEEE (editor spl. issue Procs. IEEE 1980, co-chmn. com. on RF safety stds. 1988-97, Tech. Achievement award Utah sect. 1975, Utah Engr. of Yr. 1995), Am. Inst. for Med. and Biol. Engring.; mem. Electromagnetics Acad., Bioelectromagnetics Soc. (bd. dirs. 1979-82, 87-90, v.p., pres. 1991-94, d'Arsonval award 1995). Office: Univ Utah Dept Elec Engring 3280 Merrill Engring Salt Lake City UT 84112 Office Phone: 801-581-7743. Business E-Mail: gandhi@ece.utah.edu.

GANDOLFINI, JAMES, actor; b. Westwood, NJ, Sept. 18, 1961; m. Marcy Wudarski, 1999 (div. 2002); 1 child; m. Deborah Lin, Aug. 30, 2008. BA in Comm., Rutgers U., 1983. Actor: (films) A Stranger Among Us, 1992, Mr. Wonderful, 1993, Italian Movie, 1993, True Romance, 1993, Money for Nothing, 1993, Angie, 1994, Terminal Velocity, 1994, Le Nouveau Monde, 1995, Crimson Tide, 1995, Get Shorty, 1995, The Juror, 1995, Night Falls on Manhattan, 1997, She's So Lovely, 1997, Perdita Durango, 1997, Fallen, 1998, The Mighty, 1998, A Civil Action, 1998, Wild Flowers, 1999, 8MM, 1999, A Whole New Day, 1999, The Mexican, 2001, The Man Who Wasn't There, 2001, The Last Castle, 2001, Surviving Christmas, 2004, Stories of Lost Souls, 2005, Romance & Cigarettes, 2005, Lonely Hearts, 2006, All the King's Men, 2006, Club Soda, 2006; (TV films) 12 Angry Men, 1997; (TV series) Gun, 1997, The Sopranos, 1999—2007 (Emmy award best actor drama, 2000, 2001, 2003, Golden Globe best actor drama, 2000, Outstanding Performance by a Male Actor in a Drama Series, SAG, 2000, 2003, 2008, TV Critics Assoc. award, 1999, 2000, 2001, Outstanding Performance by an Ensemble in a Drama Series, SAG, 2008); (plays) A Streetcar Named Desire, 1992, On the Waterfront, 1995; (Broadway plays) God of Carnage, 2009; exec. prodr.: (documentaries) Alive Day Memories: Home From Iraq, 2007; led Mardi Gras parade, New Orleans, 2007. Recipient Joe DiMaggio award, Xaverian HS, 2005; named one of Top 20 Entertainers of 2001, E!.

GANEM, DONALD E., immunologist; AB, MA, Harvard U., 1972, MD, 1977. Asst. prof. microbiology, immunology and medicine U. Calif., San Francisco, 1982—88, assoc. prof. microbiology and medicine, 1988—90, prof. microbiology and medicine, 1990—, vice-chair, Dept. Microbiology & Immunology, 1995—; assoc. investigator Howard Hughes Med. Inst., San Francisco, 1991—94, investigator, 1995—. Recipient Soma Weiss award for med. student rsch., Harvard Med. Sch., 1975, Leon Resnick prize for rsch., 1977, Kaiser award for excellence in basic sci. tchr., 1986, Acad. Senate Tchg. award, U. Calif., 1986, 2d Yr. Students' Tchg. award for small group tchg., 1986, 2d Yr. Students' Tchg. award for excellence in lecturing, 1987, 1989, 1991; scholar Harkness scholar, Harvard Med. Sch., 1972. Fellow: Am. Acad. Arts and Scis.; mem.: Am. Soc. Clin. Investigation (v.p. 1997), Assn. Am. Physicians, Inst. of Medicine (life), Am. Acad. Microbiology, Alpha Omega Alpha. Office: UCSF Box 0552 San Francisco CA 94143-0552 Office Phone: 415-476-2826. Office Fax: 415-476-0939. E-mail: ganem@cgl.ucsf.edu.

GANGL, KENNETH R., automotive executive; Grad., U. Ill., Urbana-Champaign, 1967. Pres. CNH Capital Am. LLC; pres., CEO Case Credit Corp.; v.p. fin. svcs. PACCAR, Bellevue, Wash., 1999—2005, sr. v.p., 2005—08, v.p., treas., 2008—. Mem. bus. adv. coun. U. Ill. Urbana-Champaign. Office: PACCAR PO Box 1518 Bellevue WA 98009

GANIS, SIDNEY, motion picture association executive, film company executive; b. Bklyn., Jan. 8, 1940; m. Nancy Ganis; children: Chloe, Kristina. Student, Bklyn. Coll. Staff writer, newspaper & wire svc. contact 20th Century Fox, 1961—62; publicity mgr. Seven Arts Productions, 1965—69; prodn. publicity mgr. Warners Seven Arts, 1969—70; studio publicity dir. Cinema Center Films, 1970—74; dir. advt. Warner Bros., 1974—77, v.p. worldwide advt. & publicity, 1977—79; sr. v.p. Lucasfilm Ltd., 1979—86; exec. v.p., pres. worldwide mktg. Paramount Pictures, 1986—88, pres. motion picture group, 1988—91; exec. v.p. Columbia/TriStar Motion Pictures, 1991—96, pres. worldwide mktg., 1992—96; founder Out of the Blue Entertainment, 1996—. Bd. dirs. Marvel Entertainment, Inc., 1999—. Actor: (films) All the President's Men, 1976, Little Nicky, 2000, Anger Management, 2003, Montgomery West and the Wings of Death, 2003, Click, 2006; actor, prodr.: Mr. Deeds, 2002; Akeelah and the Bee, 2006; exec. prodr.: (TV films) Great Movie Stunts: Raiders of the Lost Ark, 1981, The Making of Raiders of the Lost Ark, 1981 (Emmy award for Outstanding Informational Spl., 1982), The Making of Indiana Jones and the Temple of Doom, 1984; prodr.: (films) Deuce Bigalow: Male Gigolo, 1999, Big Daddy, 1999, The Master of Disguise, 2002. Recipient NATO Chmn.'s Mktg. award, 1983. Mem.: Acad. Motion Picture Arts and Scis. (bd. govs. 1973—77, 1979—81, 1992—2001, 2002—, pres. 2005—). Office: Acad Motion Picture Arts and Scis 8949 Wilshire Blvd Beverly Hills CA 90211-1972*

GANN, PAMELA BROOKS, academic administrator; b. 1948; BA, U. NC, 1970; JD, Duke U., 1973. Bar: Ga. 1973, NC 1974. Assoc. King & Spalding, Atlanta, 1973; 1975assoc. Robinson, Bradshaw & Hinson, P.A., Charlotte, 1974; asst. prof. Duke U. Sch. Law, Durham, 1975—78, assoc. prof., 1978—80, prof., 1980—99, dean, 1988—99; pres. Claremont McKenna Coll., Claremont, Calif., 1999—. Vis. asst. prof. U. Mich. Law Sch., 1977; vis. assoc. prof. U. Va., 1980 Author: (with D. Kahn) Corporate Taxation and Taxation of Partnerships and Partners, 1979, 83, 89; article editor Duke Law Jour. Mem. Am. Law Inst., Coun. Fgn. Rels., Order of Coif, Phi Beta Kappa Office: Claremont McKenna Coll Office Pres 500 E 9th St Claremont CA 91711-5903 Office Phone: 909-621-8111. Business E-Mail: pamela.gann@cmc.edu.

GANTZ, DAVID ALFRED, law educator, academic administrator; b. Columbus, Ohio, July 30, 1942; s. Harry Samuel and Edwina G.; m. Susan Beare, Aug. 26, 1967 (div. Feb. 1989); children: Stephen David, Julie Lorraine; m. Catherine Fagan, Mar. 28, 1992. AB, Harvard U., 1964; JD, Stanford U., 1967, M in Jud. Sci., 1970. Bar: Ohio 1967, D.C. 1971, U.S. Ct. Internat. Trade 1983, U.S. Ct. Appeals (9th cir.) 1972, U.S. Supreme Ct. 1972. Asst. prof. law U. Costa Rica, San Jose, 1967-69; law clk. U.S. Ct. Appeals, San Francisco, 1969-70; asst. legal advisor U.S. Dept. State, Washington, 1970-77; ptnr. Cole & Corrette, Washington, 1977-83, Oppenheimer Wolff & Donnelly, Washington, 1983-90, Reid & Priest, Washington, 1990-93, of counsel, 1993-97, Dorsey & Whitney, 1997-99; Samuel M. Fegtly prof. law, dir. inter trade law program U. Ariz. Coll. Law, Tucson, 1993—; assoc. dir. Nat. Law Ctr. for Inter-Am. Free Trade, 1993—. Panelist US-Can. Free Trade Agreement, 1989-92, NAFTA, 1994-2007; judge OAS Adminstrv. Tribunal, 1987-95; adj. prof. Georgetown U. Law Ctr., 1982-93; vis. prof. law George Washington U., 2003-04. Contbr. articles to profl. jours. Pres. Potomac River Sports Found., 1992-94. Mem. Am. Soc. Internat. Law, Potomac Boat Club (Washington, bd. dirs. 1986-93). Office: Ariz James E Rogers Coll Law 1201 E Speedway Blvd Tucson AZ 85721 Home Phone: 520-319-1859; Office Phone: 520-621-1801. Business E-Mail: gantz@law.arizona.edu.

GANULIN, JUDY, public relations professional; b. Chgo., May 2, 1937; d. Alvin and Sadie (Reingold) Landis; m. James Ganulin, June 23, 1957; children: Stacy Ganulin Clark, Amy Ganulin Lowenstein. BA in Journalism, U. Calif., Berkeley, 1958. Copywriter-sec. Joe Connor Advt., Berkeley, 1958; exec. sec. Prescolite Mfg. Co., Berkeley, 1958-59; info. officer Office of Consumer Counsel, Sacramento, 1959-61; pub. rels. positions various polit. campaigns, Fresno, Calif., 1966; adminstrv. asst., editor, mktg. Valley Pubs., Fresno, 1971-80; staff asst. to county supr. Bd. Suprs., Fresno, 1980-82; field rep. Assemblyman Bruce Bronzan, Fresno, 1982-84; prin. Judy Ganulin Pub. Rels., Fresno, 1984—. Speaker new bus. workshop SBA/Svc. Corps Ret. Execs., Fresno, 1990—. Active Hadassah, Fresno, 1975—; pres. Temple Beth Israel Sisterhood, Fresno, 1976; panelist campaign workshop Nat. Women's Polit. Caucus, Fresno, 1994, 2001, publicity chmn. ctrl. Calif. chpt., 1999—2000; mem. C. of C. Art and Wine Festival Com., 1999—2000, Juvenile Justice Ctr. Task Force, 2001, Valley Women's Polit. Fund; bd. dirs. Temple Beth Israel, Fresno, 1972—75, Planned Parenthood Ctrl. Calif., Fresno, 1986—91, Empty Bowls, Sr. Companion Program. Mem. Pub. Rels. Soc. Am. (accredited pub. rels. practitioner, pres. Fresno/Ctrl. Valley chpt. 1994), Am. Mktg. Assn. (pres. ctrl. Calif. chpt. 1987-88), Calif. Press Women, Fresno Advt. Fedn., Fresno Comm. Network (v.p., pres. 1991-93), Fresno C. of C. (mem. mktg. com. 1988-), Fresno Comm. Network (formerly Pub. Rels. Roundtable). Democrat. Avocations: travel, reading, cooking. Office: Judy Ganulin Pub Rels 1117 W San Jose Ave Fresno CA 93711-3112 Home Phone: 559-227-5122; Office Phone: 559-222-7411. Personal E-mail: jganulin@comcast.net.

GANZ, LOWELL, scriptwriter, television producer; b. NYC, Aug. 31, 1948; s. Irving and Jean (Farber) G.; m. Jeanne Russo, Dec. 26, 1976; 3 children. Student, Queens Coll., NYC. Adj. prof.grad. film screenwriting USC. TV work includes: story editor The Odd Couple, ABC, 1972-74, producer Happy Days, ABC, 1975, 79-81, Laverne & Shirley, ABC, 1976-78, exec. producer Busting Loose, 1978-79, Joanie Loves Chachi (also dir.), 1982, all Paramount TV, (with Babaloo Mandel) Makin' It, ABC, 1979, Gung Ho, ABC, 1986, Knight and Daye, NBC, 1986, A League of Their Own, CBS, 1993, (pilots) Herndon, NBC, 1983, Take Five, CBS, 1987, Channel 99, CBS, 1987, Hiller and Diller, 1997; dir. TV series The Bad News Bears, 1979; screenwriter: (with Babaloo Mandel) Night Shift, 1982, Splash (Nat. Film Critics Screenplay of Yr. award), 1984, Spies Like Us, 1985, Gung Ho, 1986, Vibes, 1988, Parenthood, 1989, City Slickers, 1991, A League of Their Own, 1992, Mr. Saturday Night, 1992, Greedy, 1994, (with Dan Aykroyd and Babaloo Mandel), City Slickers II: The Legend of Curly's Gold, 1994, Forget Paris, 1995, Multiplicity, 1996, Father's Day, 1997, Edtv, 1999, Where the Heart Is, 2000, Robots, 2005, Fever Pitch, 2005.

GARABEDIAN, CHARLES, artist; b. Detroit, 1923; MFA, UCLA, 1961. Solo shows include LaJolla (Calif.) Mus. Art, 1966, CeJee Gallery, N.Y., 1966, 67, Eugenia Butler Gallery, L.A., 1970, Newspace Gallery, L.A., 1974, Whitney Mus. Am. Art, N.Y.C., 1976, Broxton Gallery, L.A., 1976, L.A. Louver Gallery, Venice, Calif., 1979, 83, 86, 89, 90, 92, 94, 96, 2004, LaJolla Mus. Contemporary Art, 1981, Ruth S. Schaffner Gallery, Santa Barbara, Calif., 1982, Rose Art Mus., Waltham, Mass., 1983, Hirschl & Adler Modern Mus., N.Y.C., 1984, Gallery Paule Anglim, San Francisco, 1985, 93, 98, numerous others; exhibited in group shows at numerous mus. including Rose Art Mus., The High Mus., Atlanta, 1980, Emanuel Walter Gallery, San Francisco, 1981, LaJolla Mus. Contemporary Art, 1981, Mizumo Gallery, L.A., 1981, Mandeville Art Gallery, San Diego, Oakland Mus. Art, 1981, Brooke Alexander Gallery, N.Y., 1982, Kunst Mus., Luzern, 1983, Fresno Art Ctr., 1983, Tibor de Nagy Gallery, N.Y.C., 1983, Hirshhorn Mus. and Sculpture Garden, Smithsonian Instn., Washington, 1984, Newport Harbor Art Mus., Calif., 1984, El Museo Rufino Tamayo, Mexico City, 1984, L.A. Mcpl. Art Gallery, 1984, L.A. Louver, Venice, 1985, Whitney Mus. Art, 1986, DiLaurenti Gallery, N.Y., 1986, R.C. Erpf Gallery, N.Y., 1987, N.Y. State Mus., Albany, 1987, Richard Green Gallery, 1988, Bklyn. Mus. Art, 1989, James Corcoran Gallery, 1991, Riva Yares Gallery, Scottsdale, Ariz., 1994, Hirschl & Adler Mus., 1996, Mcpl. Art Gallery L.A., 1997; pub. collections include Met. Mus. Art, N.Y.C., Whitney Mus. Am. Art, Mus. Contemporary Art, L.A., Rose Art Mus., San Diego Mus. Contemporary Art, L.A. County Mus. Art Staff sgt. USAF, 1942-45. John Simon Guggenheim Meml. Found. fellow, 1979, Nat. Endowment for the Arts fellow, 1977. Dealer: L A Louver 45 Venice Blvd Venice CA 90291 Office Phone: 310-822-4955.

GARAMENDI, JOHN R., Lieutenant Governor of California, former state legislator; b. Mokelumne Hill, Calif., 1945; m. Patricia Wilkinson; 6 children. BA in Bus., U. Calif.-Berkeley; MBA, Harvard Bus. Sch. Rancher nr. Sacramento County; former mem. Calif. Assembly, 1974—76; senator Calif. State Senate, 1976—91; chmn. revenue and taxation Joint Com. on Sci. and Tech.; insurance commr. State of Calif., 1991—94, 2002—06; dep. sec. Dept. Interior, 1995—98; ptnr. Yucaipa Companies, 1998; lt. gov. State of Calif., 2007—. Chair Joint Com. on Sci. and Tech., Senate Health and Welfare Com., Senate Revenue and Taxation Com. Vol. US Peace Corps, Ethiopia, 1966—68. Democrat. Office: Lieutenant Governor State Capitol Rm 1114 Sacramento CA 95814 Office Phone: 916-445-8994.

GARBACZ, GREGORY A., lawyer; b. Columbus, Ind., May 21, 1967; s. Gerald G. and Jane Elizabeth (Snyder) Garbacz; m. Lauren Krause, Sept. 17, 1995; children: Luke, Matthew, Juliet Grace. BA in Govt. and Law, Lafayette Coll., Easton, Pa., 1989; JD, Wash. and Lee U., Lexington, Va., 1993. Shareholder, COO Klinedinst PC, San Diego, 1993—2002, mng. shareholder LA, 2002—05, COO, 2006—. Contbr. articles to profl. jours. Office: Klinedinst PC 777 S Figueroa Ste 4700 Los Angeles CA 90017-3584 also: Klinedinst PC 501 W Broadway San Diego CA 92101 Business E-Mail: ggarbacz@klinedinstlaw.com.

GARBARINO, JOSEPH WILLIAM, labor arbitrator, economics and business educator; b. Medina, NY, Dec. 7, 1919; s. Joseph Francis and Savina M. (Volpone) G.; m. Mary Jane Godward, Sept. 18, 1948; children: Ann, Joan, Susan, Ellen. BA, Duquesne U., 1942; MA, Harvard U., 1947, PhD, 1949. Faculty U. Calif., Berkeley, 1949—, prof., 1960-88, dir. Inst. Bus. and Econ. Research, 1962-88, prof. emeritus, 1988—. Vis. lectr. Cornell U., 1959-60, UCLA, 1949, SUNY, Buffalo, 1972; Fulbright lectr. U. Glasgow, Scotland, 1969; vis. scholar U. Warwick; mem. staff Brookings Instn., 1959-60; vis. lectr. U. Minn., 1978; labor arbitrator. Author: Health Plans and Collective Bargaining, 1960, Wage Policy and Long Term Contracts, 1962, Faculty Bargaining: Change and Conflict, 1975, Faculty Bargaining in Unions in Transition. Served with U.S. Army, 1942-45, 51-53. Decorated Bronze Star. Democrat. Roman Catholic. Home: 7708 Ricardo Ct El Cerrito CA 94530-3344

GARBER, ALAN MICHAEL, internist, educator, economist; s. Harry Garber; m. Anne Yahanda, Oct. 9, 1988. AB in Econs. summa cum laude, Harvard Coll., 1976, AM in Econs., 1977, PhD in Econs., 1982; MD, Stanford U., 1983. Diplomate Am. Bd. Internal Medicine. Cons. Inst. Medicine, Washington, 1979-80; clin. fellow Med. Sch. Harvard U., Boston, 1983-86, rsch. fellow John F. Kennedy Sch. Govt. Cambridge, Mass., 1986; staff physician VA Palo Alto Health Care System, Calif., 1986—; rsch. assoc. Nat. Bur. Econ. Rsch., Palo Alto, Calif., 1986—, dir. health care program Cambridge, 1990—; asst. prof. Stanford U., Calif., 1986-93, assoc. prof., 1993-98, dir. Ctr. Health Policy/Ctr. Primary Care and Outcomes Rsch., 1997—, prof. medicine, 1998—, Henry J. Kaiser jr. prof., endowed chair; contractor Office Tech. Assessment, Washington, 1987-88, 89-92. Chair Medicare Coverage Adv. Com., 2005—07; mem. Nat. Adv. Coun. Aging, 2004—07. Grad. fellow NSF, 1976, Henry J. Kaiser faculty fellow Kaiser Found., 1989-92. Fellow ACP, Acad. Health; mem. Inst. Medicine of NAS, Soc. Med. Decision Making (trustee 1989-91), Am. Econ. Assn., Am. Fedn. Clin. Rsch. (nat. councillor 1991-96), Soc. Gen. Internal Medicine, Am. Soc. for Clin. Investigation, Assn. Am. Physicians, Internat. Health Econs. Assn. Office: Primary Care Outcomes Rsch Ctr Health Policy 117 Encina Commons Stanford CA 94305-6019 Business E-Mail: garber@stanford.edu.*

GARCHIK, LEAH LIEBERMAN, journalist; b. Bklyn., May 2, 1945; d. Arthur Louis and Mildred (Steinberg) Lieberman; m. Jerome Marcus Garchik, Aug. 11, 1968; children— Samuel, Jacob BA, Bklyn. Coll., 1966. Editorial asst. San Francisco Chronicle, 1972-79, writer, editor, 1979-83, editor This World, 1983-84, columnist, 1984—; also author numerous book and movie reviews, features and profiles. Author: San Francisco: The City's Sights and Secrets, 1995, Real Life Romance, 2008; panelist (radio quiz show) Minds Over Matter; contbr. articles to mags. Vice pres. Golden Gate Kindergarten Assn., San Francisco, 1978; pres. Performing Arts Workshop, San Francisco, 1977-79; bd. dirs. Home Away From Homelessness, 1994-99. Recipient 1st prize Nat. Soc. Newspaper Columnists, 1992. Mem. Newspaper Guild. Democrat. Jewish. Home: 156 Baker St San Francisco CA 94117-2111 Office: San Francisco Chronicle 901 Mission St San Francisco CA 94103-2905 Home Phone: 415-626-0993. Business E-Mail: lgarchik@sfchronicle.com.

GARCIA, CARLOS M., financial services company executive; BS summa cum laude, Calif. State Univ., Long Beach. CPA. V.p. fin., chief acctg. officer Countrwide Credit Ind., Inc., Calabasas, Calif., 1984-86, sr. v.p., 1986-90, mng. dir., chief acctg. officer, 1990-95, mng. dir. fin., CFO, CAO, 1995-99, COO, mng. dir. fin., 1999-00; chmn. Countrywide Bank N.A.; exec. mng. dir. Countrywide Fin. Group, 2001—. Office: Countrywide Fin Group 4500 Park Granada Calabasas CA 91302-1613

GARCIA, CHRISTINE, academic administrator, educator, researcher; B in Govt., U.Nex., 1961, M in Polit. Sci. and Edn., 1964; PhD in Polit. Sci., U. Calif., Davis, 1972. Prof. polit. sci. U. N.Mex., 1970—, asst. dir. divsn. govt. rsch., 1970—72, asst., assoc. dean Coll. Arts and Scis., 1975—80, dean coll. Arts and Scis., 1980—86, v.p. acad. affairs, 1987—90, interim provost, v.p. acad. affairs, 1993, 1998—2000, pres., 2002—. Tchr. various us.; rschr. in field. Author (editor): 10 books, 50 monographs; contbr. articles, chapters to books. Office: U NMex 115 Civic Plz Dr Taos NM 87571

GARCIA, DAVID, agricultural products executive; b. 1953; Grad., U. Wyo., 1975. With We. Nuclear Mining, Lander, Wyo., 1976-78, Diamond Fruit Growers, Inc., Hood River, Oreg., 1978—; now contr. Office: Diamond Fruit Growers Inc PO Box 185 Odell OR 97044-0185

GARCIA, EDWARD J., federal judge; b. 1928; AA, Sacramento City Coll., 1951; LLB, U. Pacific, 1958. Dep. dist. atty. Sacramento County, 1959-64, supervising dep. dist. atty., 1964-69, chief dep. dist. atty., 1969-72; judge Sacramento Mcpl. Ct., 1972-84, U.S. Dist. Ct. (ea. dist.) Calif., Sacramento, 1984-96, sr. judge, 1996—. Served with U.S. Army Air Corps, 1946-49. Office: US Dist Ct US Courthouse Clk Office 501 I St Rm 4-200 Sacramento CA 95814-7300

GARCIA, F. CHRIS, academic administrator, political scientist, educator; b. Albuquerque, Apr. 15, 1940; s. Flaviano P. and Crucita A. Garcia; m. Sandra D. Garcia; children: Elaine L., Tanya C. BA, U. N.Mex., 1961, MA in Govt., 1964; PhD in Polit. Sci., U. Calif., Davis, 1972. Prof. U. N.Mex., Albuquerque, 1970—, dean arts coll., 1980—87, acad. v.p., 1987—90, provost, 1993, 1998—2000, pres., 2002—03, disting. prof., 2005—; founder Zia Rsch. Assocs., Inc., Albuquerque, 1973-94, also chmn. bd. dirs. Cons.-evaluator North Ctrl. Assn. Higher Learning Commn., 1994-06; bd. dirs. Think N.Mex., 2005—. Author: Political Socialization of Chicano Children, 1973, La Causa Politica, 1974, The Chicano Political Experience, 1977, State and Local Government in New Mexico, 1979, New Mexico Government, 1976, 81, 94, Latinos and the Political System, 1988, Latino Voices, 1992, Pursuing Power, 1997, Governing New Mexico, 2006, Hispanics And The US Political System, 2008 Charter rev. com. City of Albuquerque, 1999, Albuquerque goals commn., 1985—87; bd. dirs. Nat. Hispanic Cultural Ctr., 2002—04. With N.Mex. Air N.G., 1957—63, hon. comdr., 2005—. Recipient Disting. Svc. award, Am. Polit. Sci. Assn., 2001. Mem. Western Polit. Sci. Assn. (pres. 1977-78), Am. Polit. Sci. Assn. (v.p. 1994-95, exec. coun. 1984-86, sec. 1992-93, Disting. Svc. award 2001), Am. Assn. Pub. Opinion Rsch., Coun. Colls. of Arts and Sci. (bd. dirs. 1982-85), Nat. Assn. State Univs. and Land Grant Colls. (coun. acad. affairs 1987-90, exec. com. 1989), Western Social Sci. Assn. (exec. coun. 1973-76), Phi Beta Kappa, Phi Kappa Phi, Gold Key. Home: 1409 Snowdrop Pl NE Albuquerque NM 87112-6331 Office: U N Mex Polt Sci Dept 1 Univ NM MSC 05 3070 Albuquerque NM 87131-0001 Office Phone: 505-277-5217. Business E-Mail: cgarcia@unm.edu.

GARCIA, JEFF (JEFFREY JASON GARCIA), professional football player; b. Gilroy, Calif., Feb. 24, 1970; s. Bob and Linda Garcia; m. Carmela DeCesare, Apr. 21, 2007. Postgrad in bus. & mktg., San Jose State U. Quarterback Calgary Stampede CFL, 1994—99, San Francisco 49ers, 1999—2003, Cleve. Browns, 2004, Detroit Lions, 2005—06, Phila. Eagles, 2006—07, Tampa Bay Buccaneers, 2007—09, Oakland Raiders, 2009—. Recipient Jeff Nicklin Meml. Trophy, Can. Football League, 1997; named to Nat. Football Conf. Pro-Bowl Team, NFL, 2000—02, 2007. Achievements include becoming one of seven NFL QBs to throw 30-plus TDs in consecutive years. Office: Oakland Raiders 1220 Harbor Bay Pky Alameda CA 94502*

GARCIA, JORGE LUIS, state legislator; b. Nogales, Sonora, Mex., Sept. 10, 1953; m. Maria Garcia; children: Yvette, Dominique, Rolando. BA in Sociology, U. Ariz., 1975; MSW, Ariz. State U., 1981. Dep. dir. El Rio Health Ctr., Tucson, 1980—84; clin. mgr. Maricopa Med. Ctr., Phoenix, 1984—87, emergency rm. social worker, 1998—2000; social worker Univ. Med. Ctr., 1991—93, Univ. Physicians, Inc., 2005—; mem. Dist. 11 Ariz. House of Reps., 1993—97; mem. Dist. 27 Ariz. State Senate, 2003—, minority leader, 2007—. Bd. dirs. Pima Prevention Partnership, 1994—, El Rio Health Ctr., 1998—. Mem.: Nat. Assn. Social Workers. Democrat. Roman Catholic. Office: Ariz State Senate Capitol Complex 1700 W Washington Rm 213 Phoenix AZ 85007 Office Phone: 602-926-4171. Office Fax: 602-417-3262. Business E-Mail: jgarcia@azleg.gov.*

GARCIA, JUNE MARIE, librarian; b. Bryn Mawr, Pa., Sept. 12, 1947; d. Roland Ernest and Marion Brill (Hummel) Traynor; m. Teodosio Garcia, July 17, 1928; children: Gretchen, Adrian. BA, Douglass Coll., 1969; MLS, Rutgers U., 1970. Reference libr. New Brunswick (N.J.) Pub. Libr., 1970-72, Plainfield (N.J.) Pub. Libr., 1972-75; br. mgr. Phoenix Pub. Libr., 1975-80, extension svcs. adminstr., 1980-93; dir. San Antonio Pub. Libr., 1993-99; CEO, CARL Corp., Denver, 1999-2001; v.p., chief amb. TLC/CARL, Denver, 2001—02; mng. ptnr. Dubberly Garcia Assocs., 2002—08, E-Learn Librs., Inc., Nashville and Denver, 2004—, June Garcia Consultation Inc., 2008—. Recipient Productivity Innovator award, City of Phoenix, 1981. Mem. ALA (life, coun. 1986-90, 93-2001, pres. Pub. Libr. Assn. 1991-92, new stds. task force 1983-87, goals, guidelines and stds. com. 1986-90, chairperson 1987-90, resource allocation com. 1998-99), Freedom to Read Found. (bd. dirs.), Ariz. State Libr. Assn. (pres. 1984-85, Libr. of Yr. award 1986, Pres.'s award 1990), Pub. Libr. Internat. Network (exec. dir.), Beta Phi Mu. Office: 1195 S Harrison St Denver CO 80210 Home Phone: 303-757-7420; Office Phone: 303-757-7420. Business E-Mail: june@junegarcia.com.

GARCIA, LORENZO F., federal judge; b. 1947; BA with honors, Coll. of Santa Fe, 1969; JD, U. N.Mex., 1973. Bar: N.Mex. Judge N.Mex. Dist. Ct., Santa Fe, N.Mex. Ct. Appeals, Santa Fe; designated justice N.Mex. Supreme Ct.; magistrate judge for N.Mex., U.S. Dist. Ct., Albuquerque, 1992—. Mem. editl. bd. N.Mex. Law Rev. With U.S. Army. Office: US Dist Ct US Courthouse 333 Lomas Blvd NW Albuquerque NM 87102-2272

GARCIA, MARTHA, state legislator; b. Tempe, Ariz., July 13, 1945; 3 children. Student, Estrella Mountain Cmty. Coll., Avondale, Ariz. Cmty. mobilization mgr. Maricopa County Dept. Health, Phoenix, 2004; mem. Dist. 13 Ariz. House of Reps., 2004—, mem. rules com., environ. com. Exec. dir. Valley-Cmty. Revitalization Project, 1998—2006; pres. Cartwright Elem. Sch. Bd., 1998—. Pres. Cartwright Edn. Found., Maryvale Village Block Watch Alliance, Phoenix; bd. trustees Maryvale Hosp. Recipient Award of Distinction, League Ariz. Cities & Towns, 2005, Qwest Alliance award, 2005; named Maryvale Woman of Yr., 2003. Mem.: Nat. Sch. Bd.'s Assn. Democrat. Office: Ariz House Reps Capitol Complex 1700 W Washington Rm 335 Phoenix AZ 85007 Office Phone: 602-926-5830. Office Fax: 602-417-3113. Business E-Mail: mgarcia@azleg.gov.*

GARCIA, MARY HELEN, state legislator; b. Las Cruces, N.Mex., July 14, 1937; m. George Garcia (dec. Jan. 18, 2009); 2 children. BS, N.Mex. State U., 1960, M, 1976. Tchr. Gadsden (N.Mex.) Pub. Schs., 1960—61, Las Cruces Pub. Schs., 1967—92, dir. instr., 1993—99, elem. sch. prin., 1984—93, 1999—; vice chair, voters and elections com., mem. appropriations and fin. com. N.Mex. House of Reps., Santa Fe, state rep. dist. 34, 2002—. Co-chair United Fund Campaign, 1971; chair Methens March of Dimes., N.Mex. and Dist. Dem. Party, 1997—. Mem.: NEA, Internat. Assn. Reading, Dona Ana Arts Coun., Assn. Curriculum and Design, Pan Am. Round Table, La Casa Shelter for Domestic Violence, Las Cruces Jr. Women's Club, Phi Delta Kappa. Democrat. Roman Catholic. Office: State Capitol Room 413D Santa Fe NM 87503 Office Phone: 505-986-4435. E-mail: maryhelen.garcia@nmlegis.gov, maryhelen.garcia@nmlegis.gov.*

GARCIA, MARY JANE MADRID, state legislator; b. Dona Ana, N. Mex., Dec. 24, 1936; d. Isaac C. and Victoria M. Garcia. AA, San Francisco City Coll., 1956; BS, N.Mex. State U., 1982, BA in Anthropology, 1983, MA in Anthropology, 1985. Interpretor, translator to USAF Capt., Hotel Balboa, Madrid, 1962-63; exec. sec. to city mgr. City of Las Cruces, N.Mex., 1964-65; adminstrv. asst. RMK-BRJ, Saigon, Socialist Rep. Vietnam, 1966-72; owner Billy the Kid Gift Shop, Mesilla, N.Mex., 1972-81; pres., owner Victoria's Night Club, Las Cruces, 1981—; candidate US House of Reps., 1998; mem. Dist. 36 N.Mex. State Senate, 1988—. With archaeol. excavations N.Mex. State U. Anthropology Dept., summer 1982, spring 1983; bd. dirs., sec-treas. Dona Anna Mutual Domestic Water Assn.; mem. Subarea Council Health Systems Agy., 1979; bd. dirs. Sun Country Savings Bank, Las Cruses, 1985; treas. Toney Anaya for U.S. Senate, 1978; active Toney Anaya for N.Mex. Gov., 1979-82. Mem. N.Mex. Retail Liquor Assn. Democrat. Roman Catholic. Address: Majority Whip 226 Issac Garcia Rd PO Box 22 Dona Ana NM 88032-0022 Office Phone: 505-986-4726. E-mail: maryjane.garcia@nmlegis.gov.*

GARCIA, MICHAEL, state legislator; b. Fort Bragg, NC, Jan. 1974; son of Juan & Elizabeth Garcia; Legislature asst, Representative Solomon Ortiz, 98-99; Colorado State Representative, District 42, 2000-, asst majority leader, currently, member, Appropriations, Finance & Legislature Coun Committees, currently, Colorado House Representative.Coordr, Youth Coun for Public Policy, currently. Bus Legislator of Year Award, CACI, 95. Democrat. Roman Catholic. Mailing: 200 E Colfax Room 271 Denver CO 80203 Office Phone: 303-866-3911.

GARCIA, MIGUEL P., state legislator; b. NM, Jan. 19, 1951; divorced; children: Four. New Mexico State Representative, 1996-, District 14, 2003-.Director, Casa Armijo Community Center, 1979-85; real estate broker, Anasazi Realty, 1985-92; teacher, Albuquerque Public Sch, 1989-. Democrat. Roman Catholic. Address: 1118 La Font Rd SW Albuquerque NM 87105 Mailing: State Capitol, Room #203AN Santa Fe NM 87503 E-mail: miguel.garcia@nmlegis.gov.

GARCIA, RICHARD JOHN, bishop; b. Jan. 24, 1947; M.Div., St. Patrick's, 1973; STL, Pontifical U. of St. Thomas, 1982. Ordained priest Archdiocese of San Francisco, 1973; aux. bishop Diocese of Sacramento, 1997—2006; ordained bishop, 1997; bishop Diocese of Monterey, Calif., 2007—. Roman Catholic. Office: Diocese Of Monterey 425 Church St Monterey CA 93940-3207 Office Phone: 831-373-4345. Office Fax: 831-373-1175.

GARCIA, VERONICA, school system administrator; BA, MA, U. N.Mex, EdD in Edn. Leadership. Exec. dir. N.Mex Coalition of Sch. Adminstrs.; supt. Santa Fe Pub. Schs.; regional supt. Albuquerque Pub. Schs.; sec. edn. N.Mex Pub. Edn. Dept., 2003—. Recipient Educator of Yr., N.Mex Rsch. and Study Coun., 2003, Lifetime Achievement award, Hispanic Mag., 2004; named one of Top Ten Hispanic Woman in N.Mex, N.Mex Legis., 2000. Office: NMex Pub Edn Dept 300 Don Gaspar Ave Santa Fe NM 87501-2786 Office Fax: 505-827-6696. E-mail: veronica.garcia@state.nm.us.

GARCIAPARRA, NOMAR (ANTHONY NOMAR GARCIAPARRA), professional baseball player; b. Whittier, Calif., July 23, 1973; m. Mia Hamm, Nov. 22, 2003; 2 children. Student, Ga. Tech. Shortstop Fla. St. League, Sarasota, Fla., 1994, Ea. League, Trenton, NJ, 1995, Internat. League, Pawtucket, 1996, Boston Red Sox, 1996—2004, Chicago Cubs, 2004—05; infielder LA Dodgers, 2005—. Named Am. League Rookie Player of the Yr., The Sporting News, 1997, Baseball Writers' Assn. Am., 1997, Player's Choice Am. League Outstanding Rookie, AL Batting Champion, 1999, 2000, NL Comeback Player Yr, Players Choice Awards, 2006; named to Am. League All-Star Team, 1997, 1999, 2000, 2002, 2003, Nat. League All-Star Team, 2006, Cape Cod League Hall of Fame, 2002. Achievements include being a mem. of U.S. Olympic Baseball Team, 1992; led Am. League in Batting Avg., 1999 (.357), 2000 (.372); led Am. League in Hits (209), 1997. Office: LA Dodgers 1000 Elysian Park Ave Los Angeles CA 90012

GARD, GARY LEE, chemistry professor, researcher; b. Goodland, Kans., Nov. 17, 1937; s. Edward and Grace O. (Campbell) G.; m. Elizabeth Ann Kester; children: Timothy Lee, Dolores Ann, Julie Ann; m. Christina Huprich, Mar. 18, 1972; 1 child, Jason Lee. AA, Clark Coll., 1957; BA in Edn., U. Wash., 1959, BS in Chemistry, 1960, PhD in Chemistry, 1964. Sr. rsch. chemist Allied Chem. Co., Morristown, N.J., 1964-66; asst. prof. Portland State U., 1966-70, assoc. prof., 1970-75, prof., 1975—99, head dept. chemistry, 1971—77, 1992—94, acting dean Coll. Sci., 1979—81, emeritus prof., 1999—. Cons. C3S, 1983—96. Contbr. more than 220 articles to profl. jours. Recipient Fulbright Sr. Prof. award, 1989-90, Branford Price Millar award, Portland State U., 1990-91; Camille and Henry Dreyfus Sr. Scientist Mentor, 2003—. Mem. Am. Men. and Women of Sci., Sigma Xi., Phi Delta Kappa, Phi Theta Kappa, Phi Kappa Phi. Avocations: fishing, reading, sports exercise. Office: Portland State U Dept Chemistry PO Box 751 Portland OR 97207-0751 Office Phone: 503-725-4274. Personal E-mail: gard37@comcast.net. Business E-Mail: gardg@pdx.edu.

GARDINER, DAVID M., biologist, educator; AB with honors, Occidental Coll., LA, 1971; PhD, Scripps Institution of Oceanography, U. Calif. San Diego, 1976. Rsch. assoc., lectr., Marine Biology, Dept. Biology Occidental Coll., LA, 1976—78, vis. asst. prof., biology, 1976—80, assoc. dir. marine sciences, 1978—80; postdoctoral tng. U. Calif. Davis, 1980—82, vis. asst. prof. zoology and develop. biology, 1980—82; asst. rsch. biologist, Develop. Biology Ctr. U. Calif. Irvine, 1982—84, course coord., develop. and cell biology, 1995—96, assoc. rsch. biologist, Develop. Biology Ctr., 1994—2000, asst. dean for corp. rels, sch. biol. sciences, 1999—2000, rsch. biologist, dept. develop. and cell biology, Develop. Biology Ctr., 2000—. Faculty adv. bd. U. Calif. Irvine-Santa Ana Teachers Inst., 2000—; bd. dir. Orange County Sci. and Engring. Fair, 2000—. Contbr. articles to profl. jours. Mem.: AAAS, Am. Soc. for Cell Biology, Soc. for Develop. Biology. Office: Dept Develop and Cell Biology Develop Biology Ctr Univ Calif Irvine 4111 Natural Sciences II Mail Code 2305 Irvine CA 92697-2275 Office Phone: 949-824-2792. Business E-Mail: dmgardin@uci.edu.

GARDINER, JOHN JACOB, writer, educator, philosopher; b. Tel Aviv, Feb. 6, 1946; arrived in U.S., 1952; s. Leon and Zipora Zucker; m. Joanna Meredith Winslow, 1967 (div. 1998); children: James, Katharine. BA, U. Fla., 1967, PhD, 1973; postgrad., U. Oreg., 1978, Stanford U., 1983. Tchr., dept. chair Keystone Heights (Fla.) Sch., 1968-72; instr., asst. to v.p. acad. affairs U. Fla., Gainesville, 1973-75; asst. prof. edn. The Citadel, Charleston, SC, 1975-77; prof., dept. chair Okla. State U., Stillwater, 1979-91, Seattle U., 1991—. Assoc. in edn. Harvard U., 1985; vis. asst. prof. Fla. State U., Tallahassee, 1977-78, U. Oreg., Eugene, 1978-79; chair bd. Pacific N.W. Postdoctoral Inst., Seattle, 1995-99; bd. dir. Internat. Leadership Assn., Conflict Resolution Inst., Human Connection Inst., Ctr. for Advanced Study of Leadership, U. Md., College Park; co-founder All Russia Leadership Devel. Ctr., Novosibirsk, 1999-2000; mem. exec. com. Internat. Leadership Assn., 2001-03. Co-author: UNESCO Guide, 1991, Insights on Leadership, 1998, Building Leadership Bridges, 2003. Recipient Svc. to State award Gov. and Ho. of Reps., 1991; fellow W. K. Kellogg Found., 1972-73; grantee James McGregor Burns Leadership Acad. Ctr. for Advanced Study of Leadership, 1998. Mem. Am. Coun. Edn. (bd. dirs. Nat. Leadership Group 1985-96), Assn. Study of Higher Edn. (bd. dirs. 1983-85), Am. Ednl. Rsch. Assn. (bd. dirs. divsn. J 1983-85), Vashon Island Rotary Club (pres. 2000-01, dist. 5030 gov. 2003-04, permanent fund chair dist. 5030, 1996-2002, strategic advisor ann. program fund Zone 33, 2005-2008). Avocations: walking, reading, gardening, public speaking. Office: Seattle U 413 Loyola Hall Broadway and Madison Seattle WA 98122 Office Phone: 206-296-6171. Business E-Mail: gardiner@seattleu.edu.

GARDINER, LESTER RAYMOND, JR., retired lawyer; b. Salt Lake City, Aug. 20, 1931; s. Lester Raymond and Sarah Lucille (Kener) G.; m. Janet Ruth Thatcher, Apr. 11, 1955; children: Allison Gardiner Bigelow, John Alfred, Annette Gardiner Weed, Leslie Gardiner Crandall, Robert Thatcher, Lisa Gardiner West, James Raymond, Elizabeth Gardiner Smith, David William, Sarah Janet Gardiner Boyden. BS with honors, U. Utah, Salt Lake City, 1954; JD, U. Mich., Ann Arbor, 1959. Bar: Utah 1959, U.S. Dist. Ct. Utah 1959, U.S. Ct. Appeals (10th cir.) 1960. Law clk. U.S. Dist. Ct., 1959; assoc. then ptnr. Van Cott, Bagley, Cornwall & McCarthy, Salt Lake City, 1960—67; ptnr. Gardiner & Johnson, Salt Lake City, 1967—72, Christensen, Gardiner, Jensen & Evans, 1972—78, Fox, Edwards, Gardiner & Brown, Salt Lake City, 1978—87, Chapman & Cutler, 1987—89, Gardiner & Hintze, 1990—92; CEO and pres. Snowbird Ski and Summer Resort, Snowbird Corp., 1993—97; prin., mgmt. cons. Ray Gardiner Assocs., 1998—2003; ret. Reporter, mem. Utah Sup. Ct. Com. on Adoption of Uniform Rules of Evidence, 1970-73, mem. com. on revision of criminal code, 1975-78; master of the bench Am. Inn of Ct. I, 1980-90; mem. com. bar examiners Utah State Bar, 1973; instr. bus. law U. Utah, 1965-66; adj. prof. law Brigham Young U., 1984-85. Mem. Republican State Central Com. Utah, 1967-72, mem. exec. com. Utah Rep. Party, 1975-78, chmn. state convs., 1976, 77; mem. Salt Lake City Bd. Edn., 1971-72; bd. dirs. Salt Lake City Pub. Library, 1974-75; trustee Utah Sports Found., 1987-91; bd. dirs. and exec. com. Salt Lake City Visitors and Conv. Bur., 1988-91, 93-98; mem., chmn. bd. dirs. Inst. Outdoor Recreation and Tourism Utah State U., 1997-03. Served to 1st lt. USAF, 1954—56. Mem.: Utah State Bar Assn. Mem. Lds Ch. Avocations: art, golf, gardening.

GARDINER, T(HOMAS) MICHAEL, artist; b. Seattle, Feb. 5, 1946; s. Thomas Scott Gardiner and Carolyn Virginia (Harmer) Bolin; m. Kelly Michelle Floyd, Mar. 7, 1981 (div. Dec. 1983); m. Diana Phyllis Shurtlieff Rainwater, Sept. 26, 1986; children: Rita Em, Nigel Gus. BA in Philosophy, Sulpician Sem. N.W., Kenmore, Wash., 1969; student, Cornish Inst. Arts, 1971—73. Seaman Tidewater Barge, Camas, Wash., 1969; pari-mutuel clk. Longacres Racetrack, Renton, Wash., 1969-92; dock worker Sealand, Inc., Seattle, 1970. Tchr. Coyote Jr. H.S., Seattle, 1989-95, Sch. Visual Concepts, Seattle, 1990-95; tchr., vis. artist Ctrl. Wash. U., Ellensburg, 1991; installer fine art Artech, Seattle, 1999—. Represented in permanent collections Tacoma Art Mus., Ballard HS, Seattle, Microsoft Corp., Stoel Rives LLP, Stokes Lawrence PS, Seattle Water Dept., Nordstrom, Seattle City Light, Mus. of N.W. Art, LaConner, Wash., Sultan (Wash.) Sch. Dist., King County Portable Works Collection, SAFECO Ins. Co., Seattle, City of Portland Collection, 1988, Highline Sch. Dist., Seattle, U. Wash. Med. Ctr.; commns. include ARTp Metro Art Project, Seattle, interior painting Villa del Lupo restaurant, Vancouver, B.C., Can.; illustrations included in New Yorker Mag., Am. Illustration 13, Seattle Times. Recipient Best Design award Print Mag., 1985; Nat. Endowment for Arts fellow, 1989; grantee Gottlieb Found., 2007. Democrat. Roman Catholic. Home and Office: 3023 NW 63rd St Seattle WA 98107-2566 E-mail: gardiner@speakeasy.net.

GARDNER, BOB B., state legislator; m. LeAnn Gardner. Atty.; mem. Dist. 21 Colo. House of Reps., Denver, 2007—. Republican. Office: Colo State Capitol 200 E Colfax Denver CO 80203 Office Phone: 303-866-2191. Business E-Mail: bob.gardner.house@state.co.us.*

GARDNER, BOOTH, former governor; b. Tacoma, Aug. 21, 1936; m. Jean Gardner; children: Doug, Gail BA in Bus., U. Wash., 1958; MBA, Harvard U., 1963. Asst. to dean Sch. Bus. Adminstrn., Harvard U., Cambridge, Mass., 1966—67; dir. Sch. Bus. and Econs., U. Puget Sound, Tacoma, 1967-72; pres. Laird Norton County, 1972-80; mem. Wash. Senate from 26th Dist., 1970-73; county exec. Pierce County, Tacoma, 1981-84; gov. State of Wash., 1985—93; amb. WTO, 1994—98; chmn. emeritus bd. dirs. & advisors Total Living Choices, Seattle. Co-founder Central Area Youth Assn. Seattle; chmn. emeritus Northwest Parkinson's Found., Mcpl. Golf Club Seattle; mem. adv. coun. Casey Found.; trustee U. Puget Sound. Recipient Harold W. McGraw, Jr. prize in edn., McGraw-Hill, 1993. Mem.: Nat. Governors Assn. (former chmn.), Western Governors Assn. (chmn. 1987—88). Democrat. Office: Total Living Choices 1633 Westlake Ave N Ste 170 Seattle WA 98109-6227

GARDNER, CORY, state legislator; Mem. Dist. 63 Colo. House of Reps., Denver, 2007—; minority whip. Republican. Office: Colo State Capitol 200 E Colfax Denver CO 80203 Office Phone: 303-866-2906. Business E-Mail: cory.gardner.house@state.co.us.*

GARDNER, EMERSON N., JR., military officer; b. Chestertown, Md., Oct. 16, 1951; Grad. cum laude, Duke U., 1973; grad., Basic Sch., Def. Lang. Inst., Command and Staff Coll., Armed Forces Staff Coll., Norwegian Def. Coll. Commd. 2d lt. USMC, 1972, advanced through grades to lt. gen., 2005, helicopter pilot; White Ho. liaison officer, presdl. helicopter commd. pilot, 1980-85; commdg. officer 26th MEU, 1996-98; staff officer 9th Marine Amphibious Brigade, Okinawa, Japan, 1986-87; asst. chief of staff for ops. and logistics Allied Forces No. Europe, Kolsas, Norway and High Wycombe, England, 1993-95, High Wycombe, Eng., 1994-95; asst. dep. chief of staff aviation USMC, 1998-2000, dep. comdr. Marine Forces Atlantic, 2000—02, dir. ops. U.S. Pacific Command, 2002—04, dep. commandant for programs and resources, 2005—. Decorated Def. Superior Svc. medal., Legion of Merit with Gold star, Def. Meritorious Svc. medal, Air medal; Olmsted scholar, 1978, Germany.

GARDNER, JAMES HARKINS, venture capitalist; b. Evanston, Ill., July 15, 1943; s. James Floyd and Charlotte (Hoban) Gardner; m. Shirley Jane Bisset, June 22, 1968 (div. 1980); 1 child, Warren Lee; m. Shannon Lee Greer, Nov. 19, 1982; 1 child, Charlotte Greer. BS, Purdue U., 1965; MBA, Harvard U., 1968. V.p. Geomet, Inc., Rockville, Md., 1970—78; pres. Risk Mgmt. Resources, Inc., San Francisco, Calif., 1979—91; COO KinderCare Learning Centers, Inc., Montgomery, Ala., 1991—93; pres., COO, dir. Discovery Zone, Inc., 1994—95; mng. gen. ptnr. Media Venture Ptnrs., 1995—; CEO HBS Funding, Inc. dba Great City Traders, 1998—. Treas. No. Calif. With USPHS, 1968—70; del. White House Conf. on Small Bus., 1986. Mem.: Ind. Adminstrs. Assn. (bd. dirs. 1989—91, v.p. 1991), Nat. Fedn. Ind. Bus. (fed. liasion 1988—91, Calif. guardian coun., dir. Calif. polit. action com.), Commonwealth Club Calif. (San Francisco), Masons, Sigma Nu. Home: 21704 Broadway Sonoma CA 95476-8219

GARDNER, MURRAY BRIGGS, pathologist, educator; b. Lafayette, Ind., Oct. 5, 1929; s. Max William and Margaret (Briggs) G.; m. Alice E. Danielson, June 20, 1961; children: Suzanna, Martin, Danielson, Andrew. BA, U. Calif., Berkeley, 1951; MD, U. Calif., San Francisco, 1954. Intern Moffitt Hosp., San Francisco, 1954-55; resident in gen. practice Sonoma County Hosp., Santa Rosa, Calif., 1957-59; resident in pathology U. Calif. hosps., San Francisco, 1959-63; faculty U. So. Calif. Sch. Medicine, Los Angeles, 1963-81, prof. pathology, 1973-81, U. Calif., Davis Sch. Medicine, 1981—, chmn. dept. pathology, 1982-90. Contbr. chpts. to books, numerous articles in field to profl. jours. Served to lt. M.C. USNR, 1957-59. Grantee NIH, 1968— Fellow AAAS; mem. Coll. Am. Pathologists, Internat. Acad. Pathology, Am. Coll. Vet. Pathologists (hon.). Home: 8313 Maxwell Ln Dixon CA 95620-9662 Office: Ctr of Comparative Medicine U Calif Davis Davis CA 95616 Office Phone: 530-752-1245. Business E-Mail: mbgardner@ucdavis.edu.

GARDNER, SHERYL PAIGE, gynecologist; b. Bremerton, Wash., Jan. 24, 1945; d. Edwin Gerald and Dorothy Elizabeth (Herman) G.; m. James Alva Beat, June 20, 1986. BA in Biology, U. Oreg., 1967, MD cum laude, 1971. Diplomate Am. Bd. Ob-Gyn. Intern L.A. County Harbor Gen. Hosp., Torrance, Calif., 1971-72, resident in ob-gyn., 1972-75; physician Group Health Assn., Washington, 1975-87; pvt. practice Mililani, Hawaii, 1987—; chmn. dept. ob-gyn. Wahiawa Gen. Hosp., 1996—2007. Med. staff sec. Wahiawa (Hawaii) Gen. Hosp., 1994-95. Mem. Am. Coll. Ob-Gyn., Am. Soc. Colposcopy and Cervical Pathology, N.Am. Menopause Soc., Sigma Kappa, Alpha Omega Alpha, Hawaii Med. Assn. Democrat. Office: 95-1249 Meheula Pkwy Ste 127 Mililani HI 96789-1763 Office Phone: 808-625-5277. Business E-Mail: sgardner@my.team.praxis.com.

GARDNER, WILFORD ROBERT, physicist, researcher; b. Logan, Utah, Oct. 19, 1925; s. Robert and Nellie (Barker) G.; m. Marjorie Louise Cole, June 9, 1949; children: Patricia, Robert, Caroline. BS, Utah State U., 1949; MS, Iowa State U., 1951, PhD, 1953; DSc honoris causa (hon.), Ohio State U., 2002. Physicist U.S. Salinity Lab., Riverside, Calif., 1953-66; prof. U. Wis., Madison, 1966-80; physicist, prof., head dept. soil and water sci. U. Ariz., Tucson, 1980-87; dean coll. natural resources U. Calif., Berkeley, 1987-94, dean emeritus, 1994—; adj. prof. Utah State U., 1995—. Hon. prof. Nanjing U., China, 1984. Author: Soil Physics, 1972. Served with U.S. Army, 1943-46. Recipient Hon. Faculty award, U. Ghent, Belgium, 1972, Centennial Alumnus award, Utah State U., 1986; NSF Sr. fellow, 1959, Fulbright fellow, 1971—72, Haight travel fellow, U. East Asia, 1978, Macalaster fellow, Australia. Fellow: AAAS, Am. Soc. Agronomy; mem.: NAS, Soil Sci. Soc. Am. (pres. 1990, Rsch. award 1962), Internat. Union Soil Sci. (hon.), Internat. Soil Sci. Soc. (pres. physics commn. 1968—74). Office Phone: 801-981-9568. Personal E-mail: colegardner@comcast.net.

GARDOM, GARDE BASIL, former lieutenant governor of British Columbia; b. Banff, Alta., Can., July 17, 1924; s. Basil and Gabrielle Gwladys (Bell) G.; m. Theresa Helen Eileen Mackenzie, Feb. 11, 1956; children: Kim Gardom Allen, Karen Gardom MacDonald, Edward, Brione Gardom, Brita Gardom McLaughlin. BA, LLB, U. BC, Vancouver, Can., 1949; LLD (hon.), U. B.C., 2003, U. Victoria, 2004. Called to bar 1949. With Campbell, Brazier & Co., 1949; sr. ptnr. Gardom & Co., Vancouver, 1960-75; apptd. Queen's Counsel, 1975; mem. BC Legis. Assembly for Vancouver-Point Grey, 1966-87; atty. gen. BC, 1975-79; min. intergovtl. rels., 1979-86; policy cons. Office of Premier, 1986-87; agt. gen. BC, 1987-92, Europe; mem. Premier's Econ. Adv. Coun., 1988-91; lt.-gov. BC, 1995—2001; dir. Brouwer Claims Can., 2002—. Dir. Justitute Inst. BC. Hon. dir. Boys and Girls Club Vancouver; hon. chmn. Bibl. Mus. Can.; hon. patron Pacific Alzheimer Rsch. Found.; former mem. adv. coun. BC Cmty. Achievement awards. Decorated Order of BC; named to BC Sports Hall of Fame, 1995; named Freeman of City of London, 1992; hon. col. BC Regiment. Mem. Can. Bar Assn., BC Law Soc., Heraldry Soc. Can., Royal United Svcs. Inst. Vancouver, Govt. House Garden Soc., Brock House Soc., Royal Commonwealth Soc., Vancouver Lawn Tennis and Badminton Club (hon. life), Union Club BC, Knight of Justice, Order St. John, Royal Overseas Club, Can. Club Vancouver (life), Vancouver Club, Phi Delta Theta. Anglican. Home Phone: 604-263-7450; Office Phone: 604-267-9507. Home Fax: 604-267-9525. Personal E-mail: heggbg@shaw.ca.

GARFIELD, ERNEST, bank executive, consultant; b. Colorado River, Ariz., July 14, 1932; s. Emil and Carmen (Ybarra) G.; m. Betty Ann Redden, Apr. 18, 1953; children: Laural, Jeffery Alan. BS, U. Ariz., 1975; B of Internat. Mgmt., Am. Grad. Sch., Phoenix, 1975, M of Internat. Mgmt., 1976. Owner Garfield Ins. Agy., Tucson, 1962-70; senator State of Ariz., Phoenix, 1967-68, dep. treas., 1970-71, treas., 1971-74; commr. Ariz. Corp. Commn., Phoenix, 1974-79; chmn. United Bancorp Systems, Inc., Phoenix, 1979—, Interstate Bank Developers, Inc., Scottsdale, 1994—. Chmn. The White House Conf. on Energy, Com. on Energy Policy of Nat. Assn. Regulatory Utility Commn.; pres. Western Conf. Pub. Svc. Commns.; mem. Ad Hoc Com. on Regulatory Reform, Electric and Nuclear Energy Com., bd. dirs. East Valley Inst. Tech. Edn. Found., 2004—; chmn. Ariz. Fin. Insts. Task Force; apptd. mem. Ariz. Skill Stds. Commn., 2007. Mem. Ariz. Kidney Found., Multiple Sclerosis Soc., Rep. Senatorial Inner Circle, 1989; mem. Pres. Bush Task Force, 1989; mem. adv. bd. St. Joseph's Hosp., Phoenix; mem. establishment com. Pima County Jr. Coll., Tucson; mem. orgn. com. Pima County Halfway House, Tucson; chmn. Ariz. Gov. Commn. on Rape Prevention, 1988, Nat. Commn. on Rape Prevention, 1990—; commr. Ariz. Gov. Commn. on Violence Against Women, 1993-03; active Ariz. Gov.'s Sexual Assault Task Force; dir. Ariz. Sexual Assault Network; bd. dirs. Ariz. Cactus-Pine coun. Girl Scouts U.S.; mem. Men Against Violence Network; chmn. Ariz. Fin. Instns. Task Force, 2007—. With U.S. Army, 1952-55. Recipient Outstanding Young Men Ariz. award, Press Club award; named to U.S. Arty. Hall of Fame, 1999. Mem.: Thunderbird Internat. Banking Inst. (mem. adv. coun. 1990—), Ariz-Mex. C. of C. Republican. Roman Catholic. Avocation: graphology. Home and Office: 8442 N 72nd Pl Scottsdale AZ 85258-2762 Home Phone: 480-348-0505; Office Phone: 480-348-0404. E-mail: egarfield@qwest.net.

GARFIELD, LEONARD, museum director; Archtl. hist. Wash. State Office Archaeology and Hist. Preservation, preservation programs coord.; mgr. King County Office Cultural Resources; exec. dir. Mus. History and Industry, Seattle, 1998—. Instr. Am. archtl. history U. Mich.; instr. hist. preservation planning U. Wash. Co-author: Built in Washington, 1990; contbr. articles to profl. jours. Mem.: Wash. Trust for Hist. Preservation (pres.). Office: Mus of History & Industry 2700 24th Ave E Seattle WA 98112-2031 Office Phone: 206-324-1126 ext. 32. Business E-Mail: leonard.garfield@seattlehistory.org.

GARG, AKASH, Internet company executive; BS, Stanford U., MS in Computer Sci. Software engr. Reactivity; co-founder, chief tech. officer hi5 Networks, Inc., 2003—. Spkr. in field. Office: hi5 Networks, Inc 55 Second St, Ste 300 San Francisco CA 94105 Office Phone: 415-404-6094. Office Fax: 415-704-3482.

GARLAND, CEDRIC FRANK, epidemiologist, educator; b. La Jolla, Calif., Nov. 10, 1946; s. Cedric and Eva (Caldwell) Garagliano. BA, U. So. Calif., 1967; MPH, UCLA, 1970, DrPH, 1974. Asst. prof. Johns Hopkins U., Balt., 1974-81; prof. Sch. Medicine U. Calif., La Jolla, 1981—. Contbr. chpts. to books, articles to profl. jours. Recipient Aristotle award for acad. excellence UCLA, 1974, Golden Apple award for Tchg. Excellence Johns Hopkins U., 1980, Environ. Health Coalition Disting. Svc. award, 1984, NIH Rsch. Career award, 1982. Fellow Am. Coll. Epidemiology; mem. Physicians for Social Responsibility (chmn. info. resources 1982—), Soc. Epidemiol. Rsch., Sierra Club (chmn. Save Our Shore 1982—, Disting. Achievement award 1984). Roman Catholic. Achievements include work with Dr. Frank Garland and Dr. Edward Gorham who together played a role in establishing the association between deficiency of vitamin D and calcium, and risk of intestinal, breast and ovarian cancer and melanoma; this group also played the central role in establishing that ultraviolet A is a cause of human melanoma. Office: U Calif Dept 0631C Dept Family & Preventive Medicine 9500 Gilman Dr La Jolla CA 92093-0631 Business E-Mail: cgarland@ucsd.edu.

GARMANY, CATHARINE DOREMUS, astronomer; b. NYC, Mar. 6, 1946; d. Edwin and Janet (MacMaster) Doremus; children: Richard, Jeffrey. BS, Ind. U., 1966; MS, U. Va., 1968, PhD, 1971. Rsch. assoc. U. Va., Charlottesville, 1971-73; rsch. assoc. Joint Inst. for Lab Astrophys. U. Colo., Boulder, 1977-84, sr. rsch. assoc. Joint Inst. for Lab Astrophys., 1984-2000; dir. Fiske Planetarium, 1991-2000; dir. astronomy Astronomy, Oracle, Ariz., 2000—03, Nat. Optical Astronomy Observatory, 2004—. Contbr. articles to profl. jours. Recipient Annie J. Cannon award AAUW, AAS, 1976; grantee NASA, NSF. E-mail: garmany@noao.edu.

GARN, EDWIN JACOB (JAKE GARN), former senator; b. Richfield, Utah, Oct. 12, 1932; s. Jacob Edwin and Fern (Christensen) G.; m. Hazel Rhae Thompson, Feb. 2, 1957 (dec. 1976); children: Jacob Wayne, Susan Rhae, Ellen Marie, Jeffrey Paul; m. Kathleen Brewerton, Apr. 8, 1977; children: Matthew Spencer, Christopher Brook, Jennifer Kathleen. BS, U. Utah, 1955. City commr., Salt Lake City, 1968-72; mayor, 1972-74; U.S. Senator from Utah, 1974-93; vice chmn. Huntsman Corp., Salt Lake City, 1993-99; mng. dir. Summit Ventures LLC, Salt Lake City, 1999—. Bd. dirs. Dean Witter InterCapital, N.Y.C., Franklin Covey, Salt Lake City. Served to lt. USNR, 1956-60; brig. gen. Utah Air N.G., 1963-79; payload specialist, space shuttle mission 51D, 1985. Recipient Tom McCoy award Utah League Cities and Towns, 1972, Wright Bros. Meml. trophy, 1992. Mem. Utah League Cities and Towns (pres. 1971-72, dir. 1968—), Nat. League Cities (1st v.p. 1973-74, hon. pres. 1975), Sigma Chi. Mem. Lds Ch. Office: Summit Ventures LLC 1 Utah Ctr #600 201 S Main St Salt Lake City UT 84111-2215

GARN, STANLEY MARION, physical anthropologist, educator; b. 1922; AB, Harvard U., 1942, AM, 1947, PhD, 1948. Rsch. assoc. chem. engring. Chem. Warfare Svc. Devel. Lab. MIT, 1942-44; tech. editor Polaroid Co., 1944-46; cons. applied anthropology, 1946-47; rsch. fellow cardiology Mass. Gen. Hosp., Boston, 1946-52; instr. anthropology Harvard U., 1948-52; anthropologist Forsyth Dental Infirmary, Boston, 1947-52; dir. Forsyth face size project Army Chem. Corps, 1950-52; chmn. dept. growth and genetics Fels Rsch. Inst., Yellow Springs, Ohio, 1952-68; fellow Ctr. Human Growth and Devel. U. Mich., Ann Arbor, also prof. nutrition and anthropology, 1968-92, prof. emeritus, 1993—. Raymond Pearl lectr. Human Biol. Coun., 1992—; E.B.D. Neuhauser lectr. Soc. Pediatric Radiology, 1981. Author: Human Races, 1970, Gain and Loss of Cortical Bone, 1970; also contbr. over 1000 articles to profl. jours.; editorial bds. numerous jours. Recipient Disting. Svc. award, U. Mich., Charles Darwin Lifetime Achievement award, Am. Assn. Phys. Anthropologists, 1994, Franz Boas award, Human Biol. Coun., 2002. Fellow AAAS, Am. Acad. Pediatrics (hon. assoc.), Am. Anthropol. Assn., Am. Acad. Arts and Scis., Human Biology Coun., Am. Soc. Clin. Nutrition, Am. Soc. Nutrition Scis.; mem. NAS, Am. Assn. Phys. Anthropologists, Internat. Assn. Dental Rsch., Internat. Orgn. Study Human Devel., Am. Soc. Naturalists, Internat. Assn. Human Biologists (coun.).

GARNER, CARLENE ANN, not-for-profit fundraiser, consultant; b. Dec. 17, 1945; d. Carl A. and Ruth E. (Mathison) Timblin; m. Adelbert L. Garner, Feb. 17, 1964; children: Bruce A., Brent A. BA, U. Puget Sound, 1983. Adminstrv. dir. Balletacoma, 1984-87; exec. dir. Tacoma Symphony, 1987-95; prin. New Horizon Cons., Tacoma, 1995-98; co-owner Stewardship Devel., 1998—. Cons. Wash. PAVE, Tacoma, 1983-84. Treas. Coalition for the Devel. of the Arts, 1992-94; pres. Wilson High Sch. PTA, Tacoma, 1983-85; chmn. Tacoma Sch. Vol. Adv. Bd., 1985-87; pres. Emmanuel Luth. Ch., Tacoma, 1984-86, chmn. future steering com., 1987-93; sec.-treas. Tacoma-Narrows Conf., 1987-98; vice chmn. Tacoma Luth. Home, 1996-98; pub. mem. Wash. State Bd. Pharmacy, 1993-98. Mem. N.W. Devel. Officers Assn. (chair Tacoma/Pierce County com. 1994-96), Jr. Women's Club Tacoma (pres. 1975-76, pres. Peninsula dist. 1984-86), Gen. Fedn. Women's Club-Wash. State (treas. 1988-90, 3d v.p. 1990-92, 2d v.p. 1992-94, 1st v.p. 1994-96, pres. 1996-98, Clubwoman of Yr. 1977, Outstanding FREE chmn. Gen. Fedn. 1982), Commencement Bay Woman's Club (pres. 1990-92), Gen. Fedn. of Women's Club (bd. dirs., chair nat. conv. 1995, state pres. 1996-98, chair cmty. improvement program 1998-2000, treas. 2000—02, rec. sec. 2002-04, 2d v.p. 2004-06, 1st v.p. 2006-08, pres. elect 2008-). Lutheran.

GARNER, DONALD K., lawyer; b. 1944; BS, MBA, U. So. Calif. Bar: Calif. 1971. Ptnr. Bryan Cave LLP, Santa Monica, Calif. Office: Bryan Cave LLP 120 Broadway Ste 500 Santa Monica CA 90401-2386

GARNER, JENNIFER ANNE, actress; b. Houston, Apr. 17, 1972; d. Bill and Pat Garner; m. Scott Foley, Oct. 19, 2000 (div. Mar. 30, 2003); m. Ben Affleck, June 29, 2005; children: Violet Anne, Seraphina Rose Elizabeth. BFA, Dennison U., 1994. Actor: (TV miniseries) Danielle Steele's Zoya, 1995, Dead Man's Walk, 1996; (TV films) Harvest of Fire, 1996, The Player, 1997, Rose Hill, 1997, Aftershock: Earthquake in New York, 1999; (TV series) Swift Justice, 1996, Law & Order, 1996, Spin City, 1996, Fantasy Island, 1998, The Pretender, 1999, Significant Others, 1998, The Time of Your Life, 1999—2000, Alias, 2001—06 (Emmy nominee for outstanding lead actress in a drama, 2002, 2003, 2004, 2005, Golden Globe award for best actress in a television series, 2001, Saturn award for best actress in a television series, 2003, SAG award for outstanding performance in a drama series, 2005); (films) Deconstructing Harry, 1997, Washington Square, 1997, Mr. Magoo, 1997, In Harm's Way, 1997, Nineteen Ninety-Nine, 1998, Dude, Where's My Car, 2000, Pearl Harbor, 2001, Rennie's Landing, 2001, Catch Me if You Can, 2002, Daredevil, 2003, 13 Going On 30, 2004, Elektra, 2005, Catch and Release, 2006, (voice) Charlotte's Web, 2006, The Kingdom, 2007, Juno, 2007, Ghosts of Girlfriends Past, 2009; (Broadway plays) Cyrano de Bergerac, 2007. Recipient People's Choice award, favorite female TV star, 2006, People's Choice award, favorite female action star, 2006; named West Virginian of Yr., Sunday Gazette-Mail, 2007.

GARNER, SCOTT, communications executive; b. 1970; Positions with Nickelodeon, Children's TV Workshop; dir. rsch. Cartoon Network; exec. dir., Planning and Scheduling Disney Channel, dir. rsch., sr. v.p., Programming. Named one of 40 Executives Under 40, Multichannel News, 2006. Office: Disney Channel Worldwide 500 S Buena Vista St Burbank CA 91521-6078 Office Phone: 818-560-1000. Office Fax: 818-560-1930.

GAROFALO, DAVID P., publishing executive, former mayor; s. Phyllis Garofalo; 1 child, Kevin James. BA, Ariz. State U., 1967; MA, U. Calif., Long Beach, 1982. Owner, CEO Garofalo & Associates, Inc., 1984—2007; owner The Local News, 1991—2007; mem. city coun. City of Huntington Beach, Calif., 1994, mayor, 1999—2000. Chmn. Numerous Non-Profits, 1970—2007; bd. dirs. Pacific Liberty Bank, 1997—2000; founding pres. Orange County Cancer Found., Fountain Valley, Calif., 1997—2000. Founding pres. Orange County Cancer Found., 1997—2000. Sergeant USMC, 1967—69. Roman Catholic. Avocations: politics, cooking. Office: The Local News 5901 Warner Ave Ste 429 Huntington Beach CA 92649 E-mail: hbnews1@aol.com.

GAROFALO, JANEANE, actress, comedienne; b. Newton, NJ, Sept. 28, 1964; d. Carmine Garofalo; m. Robert Cohen, Aug. 16, 1991 (separated). BA in Hist. and Am. Studies, Providence Coll. Co-anchor Majority Report Air America Radio, 2004—06. Actress (films) Late for Dinner, 1991, That's What Women Want, 1992, Armistead Maupin's Tales of the City, 1993, Suspicious, 1994, Reality Bites, 1994, Bye Bye Love, 1995, I Shot a Man in Vegas, 1995, Cold-blooded, 1995, Now and Then, 1995, Sweethearts, 1996, The Truth About Cats & Dogs, 1996, The Cable Guy, 1996, Larger Than Life, 1996, HBO 1 Hour Special, 1997, Touch, 1997, Romy and Michele's High School Reunion, 1997, Cop Land, 1997, The MatchMaker, 1997, The Thin Pink Line, 1998, Half Baked, 1998, Thick as Thieves, 1998, Permanent Midnight, 1998, Dog Park, 1998, Clay Pigeons, 1998, Can't Stop Dancing, 1999, The Minus Man, 1999, 200 Cigarettes, 1999, Dogma, 1999, Mystery Men, 1999, The Bumblebee Flies Anyway, 1999, The Cherry Picker, 2000, Steal This Movie, 2000, The Independent, 2000, The Adventures of Rocky & Bullwinkle, 2000, Titan A.E., 2000, Wet Hot American Summer, 2001, The Search for John Gissing, 2001, The Laramie Project, 2002, Martin & Orloff, 2002, Big Trouble, 2002, Manhood, 2003, Ash Tuesday, 2003, Wonderland, 2003, Nobody Knows Anything!, 2003, Junebug and Hurricane, 2004, Jiminy Glick in Lalawood, 2004, Duane Hopwood, 2005, Stay, 2005, Southland Tales, 2005, The Wild (voice), 2006, Ratatouille (voice), 2007, The Ten, 2007, Girl's Best Friend, 2008, (TV films) Slice o' Life, 2003, Nadine in Date Land, 2005, (TV appearances) The Ben Stiller Show, 1992—93, The Larry Sanders Show, 1992—97, Saturday Night Live, 1994—95, Comedy Product, 1995, Mr. Show with Bob and David: Fantastic Newness, 1996, Ellen, 1996, Seinfeld, 1996, Home Improvement, 1997, Law & Order, 1997, The Simpsons, 1998, Felicity, 1999, Mad About You, 1999, Jimmy Kimmel Live, 2003, The King of Queens, 2004, The West Wing, 2006, King of the Hill, 2003; co-author (with Ben Stiller): Feel This Book: An Essential Guide to Self-Empowerment, Spiritual Supremacy, and Sexual Satisfaction, 2000. Named one of Comedy Ctrl.'s 100 Greatest Standups of All Time, 2004.*

GARON, CLAUDE FRANCIS, laboratory administrator, researcher; b. Baton Rouge, Nov. 5, 1942; s. Ivy Joseph and Janith (Latil) G.; m. Sally Sheffield; children: Michele, Anne, Julie. BS, La. State U., 1964, MS, 1966; PhD, Georgetown U., 1970. Predoctoral fellowship La. State U., Baton Rouge, 1964-66; predoctoral traineeship Georgetown U., Washington, 1966-69; postdoctoral fellowship Nat. Inst. Allergy and Inf. Diseases, Bethesda, Md., 1971-73, staff fellowship, 1971-73, sr. staff fellowship, 1973-74, rsch. microbiologist, 1974-81; head electron microscopy Rocky Mountain Labs., Hamilton, Mont., 1981-85, chief pathobiology, 1985-89, chief lab. vectors and pathogens, 1989-94, chief microscopy br., 1994—. Bd. govs. Ctr. Excellence in Biotech., Missoula, Mont., 1988—; faculty affiliate U. Mont., 1989—. Mem. editorial bd. Jour. Clin. Microbiology, 1993; assoc. editor Jour. Spirochetal and Tick-borne Diseases, 1993. Bd. dirs. Internat. Heart Inst. of Mont. Found., 1995. Recipient award of merit NIH, 1979, Dirs. award, 1988, Lyme Disease Found prize, 1996. Mem. Am. Soc. for Microbiology, Am. Soc. Biochemistry and Molecular Biology, Microscopy Soc. Am., Am. Soc. Rickettsiology, Pacific N.W. Electron Microscopy Soc., Lions (pres. Hamilton 1989-90). E-mail: claude_garon@nih.gov.

GARRARD, WILLIAM ROBERT, radio station owner; b. Rochester, NY, May 10, 1940; s. Burdette Koplin and Helen Elizabeth (Van Sickle) G.; m. Sharon Lee Kincaid, Dec. 17, 1987; children: Kimerly, Katherine, Candace, Michael. Grad. high sch., Rochester. Announcer KAGO Radio, Klamath Falls, Oreg., 1962-81, owner, mgr., 1987—; sta. mgr. KFAX Radio, San Francisco, 1981-84; owner, mgr. KUKI/KIAH Radio, Ukiah, Calif., 1984-87. Small marker radio cons. stereo broadcasting, Fresno, Calif., 1984—; pres. Key Broadcasting; v.p. KUKI/KIAH Inc., 1983-89; gen. mgr., v.p. Turnaround Radio Sta., 1986. Mem. adv. bd. Small Bus. Devel. Assn., Klamath Falls, 1987—. With USAF, 1958-62, Japan. Named Top Sportscaster Oreg. Assn. of Broadcasters, 1971-75. Mem. Rotary (bd. dirs. Ukiah chpt. 1985-86). Republican. Presbyterian. Avocations: flying aircraft, fishing.

GARRETT, BRAD, actor, comedian; b. Woodland Hills, Calif., Apr. 14, 1960; s. Al and Barbara Gerstenfeld; m. Jill Diven, May 18, 1999 (separated); children: Maxwell Brady, Hope. Actor in films including: Jetsons: The Movie (voice), 1990, Casper (voice), 1995, Suicide Kings, 1997, George B., 1997, Postal Worker, 1998, Postal Worker, 1998, A Bug's Life (voice), 1999, Sweet and Lowdown, 1999, An Extremely Goofy Movie (voice), 2000, Facade, 2000, Stuart Little 2, 2002, The Country Bears (voice), 2002, Finding Nemo (voice), 2003, The Trailer, Garfield (voice), 2004, The Moguls, 2005, The Pacifier, 2005, Asterix and the Vikings (voice), 2006, Night at the Museum (voice), 2006, Music and Lyrics, 2007, Ratatouille (voice), 2007; TV films include: The Bears Who Saved Christmas, 1994, Don King: Only in America, 1997, Hooves of Fire (voice), 1999, Club Land, 2001, Bleacher Bums, 2002, Gleason, 2002, Legend of the Lost Tribe, 2002; TV series include: The Transformers (voice), 1984, Rock 'n' Wrestling (voice), 1985, First Impressions, 1988, Where's Waldo (voice), 1991, Eek! the Cat (voice), 1992, Biker Mice From Mars (voice), 1993, Bonkers (voice), 1993, 2 Stupid Dogs (voice), 1993, Pursuit of Happiness, 1995, Project G.e.e.K.e.R. (voice), 1996, Mighty Ducks (voice), 1996, Everybody Loves Raymond, 1996-2005 (Emmy award outstanding supporting actor comedy series, 2002, 2003, 2005), Nightmare Ned, 1997, Toonsylvania (voice), 1998, 'Til Death (also prodr.), 2006-; TV guest appearances include: Roseanne, 1991, The Fresh Prince of Bel-Air, 1994, Lois & Clark: The New Adventures of Superman, 1996, Mad About You, 1996, Seinfeld, 1996, Superman (voice), 1996, 97, Murphy Brown, 1998, The King of Queens, 1998, Batman: The Animated Series, 1992; appeared on Broadway in Chicago, 2002, The Odd Couple, 2005 & 2006.

GARRETT, ELIZABETH, law educator, academic administrator; b. Oklahoma City, June 30, 1963; d. Robert D. and Jane (Thompson) Garrett. BA in History with spl. distinction, U. Okla., Norman, 1985; JD, U. Va., Charlottesville, 1988. Bar: Tex. 1988, DC 1989. Law clk. to Hon. Stephen Williams US Ct. Appeals (D.C. cir.), Washington, 1988—89; law clk. to Hon. Thurgood Marshall US Supreme Ct., Washington, 1989—90; legal adviser to Hon. Howard M. Holtzman Iran-U.S. Claims Tribunal, The Hague, Netherlands, 1990—91; legal counsel, tax counsel Senator David L. Boren, Washington, 1991—93, legis. dir., tax counsel, 1993—94; vis. assoc. prof. U. Va., Charlottesville, 1994—95; asst. prof. U. Chgo. Law Sch., 1995—99, prof., 1999—2003, dep. dean, 1999—2001; vis. asst. prof. Harvard U., 1998; vis. prof. Ctrl. European U., Budapest, Hungary, 1999—2003, Interdisciplinary Ctr. Law Sch., Tel Aviv, 2001, Calif. Inst. Tech., Pasadena, 2004, U. Va., 2001, U. So. Calif. Law Sch., LA, 2002; dir. Caltech Ctr. Study Law & Politics U. So. Calif., LA, 2003—, vice provost acad. affairs, 2005—06, v.p. academic planning and budget, 2005—, Sydney M. Irma prof. pub. interest law, legal ethics and polit. Sci. Pasadena, 2005—. Bd. dir. Initiative & Referendum Inst.; articles editor U. Va. Law Rev.; mem. editl. bd. Election Law Jour. Contbr. articles to profl. jours. Vice chair nat. governing bd. Common Cause, 2006—. Fellow: Am. Bar Found.; mem.: ABA, DC Bar Assn., Tex. Bar Assn., Am. Law, Econ. Assn., Phi Beta Kappa, Mortar Bd., Order of Coif, Chi Omega. Office: Univ So Calif Rm 103 Bovard Adminstrn Bldg Los Angeles CA 90089-4019 Office Phone: 213-740-0064. Business E-Mail: vpapb@usc.edu.

GARRETT, JAMES JOSEPH, lawyer; b. LA, Dec. 17, 1939; s. Joseph Robert and Catherine Agnes (Cavanaugh) G.; m. Mary Isabel McNeil, June 22, 1963 (div.); children: Sean, Drew, Craig; m. Maria Pamela Rivera, July 26, 1980; children: Joshua, Matthew. AB, Stanford U., 1961; JD, Harvard U., 1964. Bar: Calif. 1965. Ptnr. Morrison & Foerster, San Francisco, 1966—. Author: Antitrust Compliance, 1978; gen. editor and contbg. author: World Antitrust Law and Practice, 1995; author chpt.: A Guide to Foreign Investment in the United States, 1992. Capt. U.S. Army, 1964-66. Mem. ABA, Calif. Bar Assn. Roman Catholic. Avocations: collecting newspapers, running, fly fishing, backpacking. Office: Morrison & Foerster Ste 450 101 Ygnacio Valley Rd Walnut Creek CA 94596-4094

GARRETT, SCOTT T., medical products executive; BS in Mech. Engring., Valparaiso U.; MBA, Lake Forest Grad. Sch. Mgmt. Various positions Baxter Internat., Am. Hosp. Supply Corp.; chmn. Dade Behring, 1994—97; interim CEO Kendro Lab. Products, L.P., 2000; CEO Garrett Capital Advisors; pres., clin. diagnostic divsn. Beckman Coulter, Inc., Fullerton, Calif., 2002—03, pres., COO, 2003—05, pres., CEO, 2005—09, chmn., pres., CEO, 2009—. Chmn. LifeStream Internat.; vice chmn. Kendro Lab. Products; dir. Inovision Holdings, Sunol Molecular Corp., Biotrin Holdings plc, Ability One Corp., Lake Forest Hosp. Found.; mem., adv. bd. Radius Ventures. Office: Beckman Coulter 4300 N Harbor Blvd PO Box 3100 Fullerton CA 92834-3100*

GARRISON, P. GREGORY, diversified financial services company executive; BSBA, Univ. Mo.; MBA, Harvard Univ. Joined Price Waterhouse L.L.P.-U.S., St. Louis, 1976, chmn. entertainment, media and comm., also mng. ptnr. LA, leader, Assurance Svcs. Practice. Adv. bd. Univ. Mo. Sch. Acctg. Mem.: AICPA, Calif. Soc. CPA, Mo. Soc. CPA. Office: Price Waterhouse Cooper 350 S Grand Ave Los Angeles CA 90071-3406

GARRISON, WILLIAM LOUIS, civil engineering educator; b. Nashville, Apr. 20, 1924; s. Sidney Clarence and Sara (Elisabeth) McMurry; s. Marcia Fordyce Stanley, Aug. 31, 1938; children: Sara, Ann, Helen, Deborah, James, Jane, John. BS, Peabody Coll., 1946, MS, 1947; PhD, Northwestern U., 1950. From asst. prof. to prof. dept. geography U. Wash., Seattle, 1950-60; prof. dept. geography, civil engring. Northwestern U., Evanston, Ill., 1960-67, dir. transp. ctr., 1965-67; dir. ctr. for urban studies U. Ill., Chgo., 1967-69; Weidlein Prof. Environ. Engring. U. Pitts., 1969-73; dir. Inst. for Transp. Studies U. Calif., Berkeley, 1973-81, prof. civil engring., 1981—. Cons. U.S. Bur. Pub. Rds., Washington, 1960-68; bd. govs. Regional Sci. Rsch. Inst., Phila., 1964—; adv. com. on econs. NSF, Washington, 1958-63; panel on values of social sci. rsch. Nat. Sci. Bd., Washington, 1963-64. Author: Geographical Impact of Highway Improvements, 1960, Tomorrow's Transportation, 2000; author, editor Jour. Transp. Tech., 1985, The Transportation Experience, 2005; editor: Quantitative Geography, 1969; articles in field. Served to capt. USAF, 1943-46. Recipient Disting. award U. Coun. of Transp. Rsch. Ctrs., 1999. Mem. AAAS, ASCE, Transp. Rsch. Bd. (chmn. 1972-73, Roy C. Crum award 1973), Regional Sci. Assn. (pres. 1960), Assn. Am. Geographers (Outstanding Rsch. award 1958). Home: 10 Rancho Diablo Dr Lafayette CA 94549-2722 Office: U Calif Dept Civil Engring Berkeley CA 94720 Business E-Mail: garrison@newton.berkeley.edu.

GARRUTO, JOHN ANTHONY, cosmetics executive; b. Johnson City, NY, June 18, 1952; children: James, Christopher, Catherine, Gabrielle, Sofia. BS in Chemistry, SUNY, Binghamton, 1974; AAS in Bus. Adminstrn., Broome Coll., 1976. Rsch. chemist Lander Co. Inc., Binghamton, 1974-77, rsch. dir. St. Louis, 1977-79, Olde Worlde Products, High Point, N.C., 1979-81; v.p. rsch. and devel. LaCosta Products Internat., Carlsbad, Calif., 1981-89; chief ops. officer Randall Products Internat., Carlsbad, 1989-91; pres. Dermasearch Internat., 1991-92; chief tech. officer Innovative Bioscis. Corp., Oceanside, Calif., 1992-95; v.p. rsch. Garden Botanika, Oceanside, Calif., 1995-99; pres., founder Free Radical Tech., 1999—. Cons. Trans-Atlantic Mktg., Binghamton, 1975-78; instr. cosmetic sci UCLA, 1991—, UCLA Ext.; lectr. to cosmetic industry. Patentee in field. Mem. AAAS, Soc. Cosmetic Chemists (newsletter editor 1980-81, feature editor, 2004—, publicity chmn. 1984—, edn. chmn. 1987, employment chmn. 1994—, chmn. elect 1999-2000, chmn. 2000, nat. elections com. 2001—, nominations com., 2006—, lab lorn editor, 2004—), Am. Chem. Soc., Inst. for Food Technologists (sec. beauty industry west), Pacific Tech. Exch., Fedn. Am. Scientists, N.Y. Acad. Scis., Cosmetic, Toiletry and Fragrance Assn. (sci. adv. com.).

GARRY, JAMES B., historian, naturalist, storyteller, writer; b. Taylor, Tex., Apr. 28, 1947; s. Mahon Barker and Grace (Dellinger) G. BS, U. Mich., 1970, MS, 1975. Part-time wilderness guide, naturalist Triangle X Ranch, Moose, Wyo., 1969-75; community organizer, media cons., tchr. Hobart St. Project, Detroit, 1974-75; media specialist, lobbyist Powder River Basin Resource Coun., Sheridan, Wyo., 1975-76; pvt. practice media and polit. cons. Big Horn, Wyo., 1976-78; video and film artist-in-residence Wyo. Coun. on the Arts/Sheridan Coll., Sheridan, 1978-80; mem. staff Great Plains Lore and Natural History, Big Horn, 1980—. Storyteller Buffalo Bill Hist. Ctr., Cody, Wyo., 1980—; tchr. Yellowstone (Wyo.) Inst., 1986—; tour study leader, rsch. collaborator Smithsonian Instn., Washington, 1984—. Co-author: Writing About Wildlife, 1974; author, editor: Buck: Stories by Lloyd Buck Bader, 1984, This Ol' Drought Ain't Broke Us Yet But We're All Bent Pretty Bad, 1992, The First Liar Never Has a Chance: Curly, Jack and Bill (and Other Characters of the Hills, Brush and Plains), 1994; storyteller in field. 2d lt. U.S. Army, 1970. Recipient Spl. Heritage award Old West Trail Found., 1983; named one of Individual Humanist of Yr., Wyo. Coun. for Humanities, 1986. Democrat. Roman Catholic. Avocation: nature. Office: PO Box 2165 Cody WY 82414-2165

GARSH, THOMAS BURTON, publisher; b. New Rochelle, NY, Dec. 12, 1931; s. Harry and Matilda (Smith) G.; m. Beatrice J. Schmidt; children: Carol Jean, Thomas Burton, Janice Lynn. BS, U. Md., 1955. Edn. rep. McGraw Hill Book Co., NYC, 1959-68; mktg. mgr. D.C. Heath & Co., Boston, 1969-71; dir. mktg. Economy Co., Oklahoma City, 1971-72; sr. v.p. Macmillan Pub. Co., NYC, 1972-78; pres. Am. Book Co., NYC, 1978-81; founder, pres., dir. Am. Ednl. Computer, Inc., Palo Alto, Calif., 1981-86. Founder, chmn., chief exec. officer OmnyEd Corp., Palo Alto, 1987-91; pres. Silver Burdett & Ginn divsn. of Simon and Schuster, 1991-92; dir. Fifty Plus Fitness Assn., Palo Alto, Calif. Publ. Homes and Land of Santa Clara, 1998—. Mem. county council Boy Scouts Am., 1963-65; mem. ch. council on Interracial Affairs, 1966-68, pres., 1967; vice-chmn. Madison County Democratic Party, 1967. Mem. Assn. Am. Pubs., Profl. Bookman's Assn., Omicron Delta Kappa, Sigma Alpha Epsilon. Clubs: Cazenovia Country (founder). Home: 401 Old Spanish Trl Portola Valley CA 94028 E-mail: tnb401@aol.com.

GARSTANG, ROY HENRY, astrophysicist, educator; b. Southport, Eng., Sept. 18, 1925; came to U.S., 1964; s. Percy Brocklehurst and Eunice (Gledhill) G.; m. Ann Clemence Hawk, Aug. 11, 1959; children: Jennifer Katherine, Susan Veronica. BA, U. Cambridge, 1946, MA, 1950, PhD, 1954, Sc.D., 1983. Research assoc. U. Chgo., 1951-52; lectr. astronomy U. Coll., London, 1952-60; reader astronomy U. London, 1960-64, asst. dir. Obs., 1959-64; prof. astrophysics U. Colo., Boulder, 1964-94, chair faculty assembly, 1988-89, prof. emeritus, 1994—; chmn. Joint Inst. for Lab. Astrophysics, 1966-67. Cons. Nat. Bur. Standards, 1964—73, Internat. Commn. Illumination, 1990—; v.p. commn. 14 Internat. Astron. Union, 1970—73, pres., 1973—76; Erskine vis. fellow U. Canterbury, New Zealand, 1971; vis. prof. U. Calif., Santa Cruz, 1971. Editor: Observatory, 1953-60; Contbr. numerous articles to tech. jours. Recipient Excellence in Svc. award, U. Colo., 1990. Fellow Am. Phys. Soc., AAAS, Optical Soc. Am., Brit. Inst. Physics, Royal Astron. Soc.; mem. Am. Astron. Soc., Royal Soc. Scis. Liege (Belgium). Achievements include rsch. on atomic physics and astrophys. applications; calculation of atomic transition probabilities, atomic spectra in very high magnetic fields and magnetic white dwarf stars; modelling of light pollution. Home: 830 8th St Boulder CO 80302-7409 Office: U Colo Boulder CO 80309-0440 Home Phone: 303-444-3606; Office Phone: 303-492-7795. Personal E-mail: garstang@earthlink.net.

GARTEN, DAVID BURTON, lawyer; BA in Econs., summa cum laude, Yale U., 1974, JD, 1977. Bar: Ill. 1979. Law clk. to Hon. Anthony M. Kennedy U.S. Ct. Appeals (9th cir.), Sacramento, 1977-78; assoc. Kirkland & Ellis, Chgo., 1979-84, ptnr., 1984-90; v.p., gen. counsel NL Industries Inc., Houston, 1990—2004, Chevron Corp., San Ramon, Calif., 2004—. Mem. Phi Beta Kappa. Office: Chevron Corp 6001 Bollinger Canyon Rd T3046 A7 San Ramon CA 94583 Office Phone: 925-842-3232. Office Fax: 925-842-2022.

GARTMAN, JOHN E., lawyer; BS in Elec. Engring. with highest honors, U. Tex., 1983, JD with honors, 1986. Bar: Calif., Va., DC. Judicial clk. to Honorable Giles S. Rich, US Ct. Appeals Fed. Circuit, 1988—90; ptnr. Brown & Bain, P.A., Fish & Richardson, 1993—98, mng. prin. San Diego, 1998—. Adj. prof. law Santa Clara U. Sch. Law, 1995—96. Contb. patents editor Fed. Circuit Bar Jour., 1990—98; contbr. articles to jour. Named one of Nation's Magnificent 7, IP's Best Young Trial Lawyers, IP Worldwide, 2002, Calif. Top 25 IP Lawyers, Daily Jour., Top 25 Intellectual Property Atty. Calif., 2003, 2004. Office: 12390 El Camino Real San Diego CA 92130 Home Phone: 858-793-1750; Office Phone: 858-678-4313. Business E-Mail: gartman@fr.com.

GARVENS, ELLEN JO, artist, educator; b. Omro, Wis., Aug. 15, 1955; d. Leonard Kenneth and Eugenia Mary (Wetter) G.; m. James Patrick Phalen, Oct. 18, 1988; children: Cole Garvens Phalen, Mason Garvens Phalen. BS in Art, U. Wis., 1979; MA, U. N. Mex., 1982, MFA, 1987. Asst. prof. of art Oberlin (Ohio) Coll., 1990-94; assoc. prof. art U. Wash., Seattle, 1994—. Artist: one person shows include: Humboldt State, 2000, Jayne H. Baum Gallery, N.Y.C., 1986, 89, 93, Wooster (Ohio) Mus. of Art, U. R.I., Kingston. Recipient Wis. Women in Arts award Madison, 1978, Fullbright Hays scholarship Internat. Comm. Agy., Washington, 1979-80; grantee, NEA, Washington, 1986, HC Powers grant, Oberlin Coll., 1991, Royalty Rsch. Fund grant, U. Wash., 1996, Artist Trust Washington State fellowship, 2000—. Home: 19518 67th Ave NE Kenmore WA 98028-3447 Office: U Wash Sch of Art PO Box 353440 Seattle WA 98195-3440 E-mail: elgarv@u.washington.edu.

GARVEY, DANIEL CYRIL, mechanical engineer; b. Chgo., Nov. 25, 1940; s. Cyril and Genei Marie (McCarthy) G; children: Michael Daniel, Erin T. BSME, Marquette U., Milw., 1963; MSME, IIT, Chgo., 1965. With Kearney & Trecker Corp., Milw., 1960-63, A C Electronics div. Gen. Mtrs. Corp., Milw., 1965-68; vibration and control sys. engr. Woodward Governor Co., Ft. Collins, Colo., 1970-99; cons. engr. DCG Power Systems, 1999—. Reviewer tech. papers IEEE, 1980—; contbr. articles to profl. jours.; patentee in field. Recipient Arch T. Colwell Merit award, SAE, 1984, Internal Combustion Engine award ASME, 1990. Mem. IEEE (sr.), Soc. Automotive Engrs., Instrument Soc. Am. Home: 5205 Mail Creek Ln Fort Collins CO 80525-3812

GARVEY, DANIEL EDWARD, foundation administrator, educator; b. Westfield, Mass., Apr. 25, 1950; s. John Henry and Ruth Marie (Long) G.; m. Barbara Nelson, Apr. 28, 1973; children: Kathryn, Connor. BA in Sociology, Worcester State Coll., 1973; MA in Social Change, Cambridge Goddard Coll., 1974; PhD in Edn., U. Colo., 1990. Dir. Upward Bound U. NH, Durham, 1974-79, assoc. dean students, 1979-88, adj. assoc. prof., 1988; exec. dir. Assn. for Exptl. Edn., Boulder, Colo., 1988-91; v.p. Am. Youth Found., Ossipee, NH, 1991; pres. Prescott Coll., 2001—. Adj. assoc. prof. Moscow State U.; dean, semeseter at sea prog., U. Pitts., mem., exec. com. AmeriCorps, trustee, Nat. Outdoor Leadership Sch., mem., bd. dirs., Project Am., Ariz. State Commn. Svc. and Volunteerism Guest editor Multi-Cultural Issues in Edn., 1992; author Management Development Directory, 1989; contbr. articles to profl. jours. Coach Youth Soccer, South Berwick, Maine; vol. Volunteers in Svc. to Am. Recipient Kurt Hahn award, 1997, Outstanding Teaching award, UNH Sch. Health Studies, 1998, Julian Smith award, 2002. Mem.: Assn. Experiential Edn. (pres., exec. dir.). Avocations: music, woodworking. Office: Prescott Coll Office of Pres 220 Grove Ave Prescott AZ 86301

GARVEY, JOANNE MARIE, lawyer; b. Oakland, Calif., Apr. 23, 1935; d. James M. and Marian A. (Dean) Garvey. AB with honors, U. Calif., Berkeley, 1956, MA, 1957, JD, 1961. Bar: Calif. 1962. Assoc. Cavaletto, Webster, Mullen & McCaughey, Santa Barbara, Calif., 1961-63, Jordan, Keeler & Seligman, San Francisco, 1963-67, ptnr., 1968-88, Heller, Ehrman, White & McAuliffe, San Francisco, 1988—. Bd. dirs. Mex.-Am. Legal Def. and Ednl. Fund; chmn. Law in Free Soc., Continuing Edn. Bar; mem. bd. councillors U. So. Calif. Law Ctr. Recipient Paul Veazy award, YMCA, 1973, Internat. Women's Yr. award, Queen's Bench, 1975, honors, Advs. Women, 1978, CRLA award, Boalt Hall Citation award, 1998, Judge Lowell Jensen Cmty. Svc. award, 2001, Margaret Brent award, 2003, Latcham State and Local Disting. Svc. award, 2003, Lifetime Achievement award, The Am. Lawyer mag., 2006, Jim Pfeiffer award, CDCBA, 2008. Fellow: Am. Bar Found.; mem.: ABA (gov., state del., chmn. SCLAID, chmn.delivery legal svcs., chmn. 10LTA), Calif. Women Lawyers (founder), Am. Law Inst., San Francisco Bar Assn. (pres., pres. Barristers), Calif. State Bar (v.p., gov., tax sect., del., Jud Klein award, Joanne Garvey award), Phi Beta Kappa, Order of Coif. Democrat. Roman Catholic. Home: 16 Kensington Ct Kensington CA 94707-1010 Office: 333 Bush St San Francisco CA 94104-2806 Office Phone: 415-772-6729. Business E-Mail: joanne.garvey@hellerehrman.com.

GARVEY, TONI, library director; m. Kevin Garvey; children: Brendan, Tess. BA, Western Mich. U., 1975, MLS, 1977. Children's libr. Tucson-Pima Pub. Libr., Ariz., 1979; dep. dir. Loudoun County Pub. Libr., Leesburg, Va., 1987, dir. libr. svcs.; city libr. Phoenix Pub. Libr., 1996—; dir. Phoenix Libr. Dept., 2002—. Pres. Pub. Libr. Assn., 2002; bd. mem. Librs. for the Future. Named Libr. of Yr., Libr. Jour., 2004. Mem.: ALA. Office: Phoenix Pub Libr 1221 N Central Ave Phoenix AZ 85004 E-mail: toni.garvey@phoenix.gov.

GARVIN, SAM SCOTT, marketing executive; b. Pitts., Aug. 16, 1964; s. Sam Landis and Mary Ann Garvin; m. Rita Garvin; 3 children. BA, U. Pitts., 1983; M of Internat. Mgmt., Am. Graduate Sch., 1988. Sales rep. Heinz U.S.A., Pitts., 1983-85; dir. bus. devel. ACS Mktg., Portland, Oreg., 1988; founder Continental Promotion Group Inc., Scottsdale, Ariz., 1989—, chmn., CEO, 1989—2005. Bd. dirs. Printseeker.com, ReligiousWarehouse.com, AliLaur LLC; bd. dirs., investor Phoenix Suns. Mem. Rep. Nat. Com., 1988; bd. dirs. Phoenix Country Day Sch. Recipient Cert. of Commendation U.S.-Western German Govts., 1983. Mem. Am. Mktg. Assn., Promo Mktg. Assn. Am. Clubs: ASGIM German (Phoenix) (pres. 1987-88); German (Pitts.) (pres. 1982-84). Avocations: travel, entrepreneural ventures. Office: Cpg 1120 W Warner Rd Tempe AZ 85284-2816

GARZA, ELIZEO, director solid waste management, Tucson; b. Chgo., July 21, 1951; BA, U. Tex., 1972; MEd, Antioch U., 1976. Asst. dir. neighborhood ctr. City of Tucson, 1974-79, planner, dep. asst. dir., 1979-93, dir. solid waste mgmt., 1993—. Mem. Solid Waste Assn. N. Am. Office: City Tucson Office Solid Waste Mgmt PO Box 27210 Tucson AZ 85726-7210

GASICH, WELKO ELTON, retired aerospace defense executive, management consultant; b. Cupertino, Calif., Mar. 28, 1922; s. Elija J. and Catherine (Paviso) Gasich; m. Patricia Ann Gudgel, Dec. 28, 1973; 1 child, Mark David. AB cum laude in Mech. Engring. (Bacon scholar), Stanford U., 1943, MS in Mech. Engring., 1947, cert. in fin. and econs. (Sloan exec. fellow), 1967; Aero. Engr., Calif. Inst. Tech., 1948. Aerodynamicist Douglas Aircraft Co., 1943-44, supr. aeroelastics, 1947-51; chief aero design Rand Corp., 1951-53; chief preliminary design aircraft divsn. Northrop Corp., LA, 1953-56, dir. advanced systems, 1956-61, v.p., asst. gen. mgr. tech., 1961-66, corp. v.p., gen. mgr. Northrop Ventura divsn., 1967-71, corp. v.p., gen. mgr. aircraft divsn., 1971-76, corp. v.p., group exec. aircraft group, 1976-79, sr. v.p. advanced projects, 1979-85, exec. v.p. programs, 1985-88, ret., 1988; aerospace cons. Encino, Calif., 1988—. Author: (book) 40 Years of Ferrari V-12 Engines, 1990. Chmn. adv. coun. Stanford Sch. Engring., 1981—83; past. mem. adv. coun. Stanford Grad. Sch. Bus.; chmn. United Way, 1964; chmn. Scout-O-Rama, L.A. coun. Boy Scouts Am., 1964, chmn. explorer scout exec. com., 1963—64. Served to lt. USN, 1944—46. Fellow: AIAA, Soc. Automotive Engrs.; mem.: NAE, Navy League, Stanford Grad. Sch. Bus. Alumni Assn. (pres. 1971), Bel Air Country Club, Conquistadores del Cielo Club. Republican. Achievements include patents in field.

GASOL, PAU, professional basketball player; b. Barcelona, July 6, 1980; s. Agusti and Marisa Gasol. Student in medicine, U. Barcelona. Forward, ctr. F.C. Barcelona, 1999—2001, Memphis Grizzlies, 2001—08, LA Lakers, 2008—. Mem. Spanish nat. team Summer Olympic Games, Athens, Greece, 2004, Beijing, 08, Internat. Basketball Fedn. World Championships, 2006. Amb., Spanish com. UNICEF, 2003. Recipient Good Sportsman award, Found. for Help Against Drug Addiction, 2002—03, Gold medal, Internat. Basketball Fedn. World Championships, 2006, Silver medal, men's basketball, Beijing Olympic Games, 2008; named Finals MVP, Spanish League, 2001, MVP, Spanish King's Cup, 2001, Internat. Basketball Fedn. World Championships, 2006, Rookie of Yr., NBA, 2002; named to All-Rookie First Team, 2002, Western Conf. All-Star Team, 2006, 2009. Office: LA Lakers 555 N Nash St El Segundo CA 90245*

GASPIN, JEFFREY M., broadcast executive; b. Bayside, NY, Dec. 29, 1960; m. Karen Gaspin; children: Max, Ben, Samantha. BS in Orgnl. Psych., SUNY, Binghamton, 1982; MBA, NYU. Fin. planner NBC News, acting CFO, 1988—89, v.p. prime time programming & devel., 1989—94; sr. v.p. programming QVC, 1994—96; sr. v.p. programming & prodn. VH1, 1996—98, exec. v.p. programming & prodn., 1998—2001; exec. v.p. alternative series, longform, specials & program strategy NBC, 2001—02; pres. Bravo, 2002—04; pres. cable entertainment & cross-network strategy NBC Universal, 2004—07, pres. cable & digital content, 2007, pres. COO Universal Television Group, 2007—. Bd. dirs. Nat. Cable & Telecommunication Assn. Creator (TV series) Behind the Music, Pop-Up Video, Rock & Roll Jeopardy, Storytellers, Before They Were Rock Stars, Divas Live. Recipient GE Leadership award, 2003; named a Rising Exec., Entertainment Weekly, 2003. Office: NBC Universal Television Group 30 Rockefeller Plz New York NY 10112 also: 100 Universal City Plz Universal City CA 91608

GASS, JOHN D., oil industry executive; b. Key Biscayne, Fla., Apr. 1952; BCE, Vanderbilt U., Nashville, 1974; MCE, Tulane U., New Orleans, 1980. Design engr. to positions of increasing responsibility in engring., ops. and mgmt. Chevron Corp., La., Calif., 1974—88; ops. mgr. Amoseas Indonesia Inc., Jakarta, Indonesia, 1988—91; project mgr. Alba Field devel., North Sea, UK Chevron Corp., 1991—94; profit ctr. mgr. Chevron USA Prodn. Co., Bay Marchand, La., 1994—96; mng. dir. Chevron Australia Pty. Ltd., Perth, 1996—2001; mng. dir., Southern Africa strategic bus. unit Chevron Corp., Luanda, Angola, 2001—03, corp. v.p., pres., Chevron Global Gas, 2003—. Bd. dirs. Sasol Chevron. Bd. dirs. Nat. Bur. Asian Rsch. Mem.: ASCE, Soc. Petroleum Engrs. Office: Chevron Corp Hdqs 6001 Bollinger Canyon Rd San Ramon CA 94583

GASS, MICHELLE PETKERS, beverage service company executive, marketing executive; b. Maine, 1968; BS in Chem. Engring., Worcester Poly. Inst., Mass., 1990; MBA, U. Washington, 1999. Mem. healthcare products group The Procter & Gamble Co., 1990—96; category mgr. blended beverages Starbucks Corp., Seattle, 1996—2001, v.p. beverage category, 2001—03, v.p. category mgmt., 2003—04, sr. v.p. category mgmt., 2004—08, sr. v.p. global strategy, 2008—. Bd. dirs. Ann Taylor Stores Corp., 2008—. Recipient Ichabod Washburn Young Alumni for Prof. Achievement, Worcester Poly. Inst., 2005; named a Woman to Watch, Advt. Age, 2007. Office: Starbucks Corp 2401 Utah Ave S Seattle WA 98134 Office Phone: 206-447-1575. Office Fax: 206-682-7570.

GASSNER, HOLGER GUENTHER, surgeon, consultant; b. Erlangen, Germany, Feb. 6, 1972; s. Dieter Siegmund and Anneliese Gassner; m. Jordana Rae Knecht, Sept. 17, 2005; children: Jonathan Patric Knecht, Daniel Johann. MD, U. Erlangen, 1998. Diplomate Am. Bd. Otorhinolaryngology, 2007, German Acad. Otorhinolaryngology. Rsch. fellow Mayo Clinic, Rochester, Minn., 1998—99, resident physician, 2001—06, U. Erlangen, 2000—01; fellow Am. Acad. Facial Plastic Surgery, Seattle, 2006—07; staff cons. U. Regensburg, Germany, 2007—, head divsn. facial plastic surgery, 2007—. Contbr. scientific papers to profl. pubs. Fellow: Am. Acad. Facial Plastic Surgery (Ben Schuster award 2000, Sir Howard Delf Gillies award 2007, Ben Schuster award 2006); mem.: European Acad. Facial Plastic Surgery (internet com. mem. 2008—), Am. Acad. Otorhinolaryngology, Head and Neck Surgery. Achievements include patents for new method to improve the appearance of cutaneous scars; use of Botulinum toxin to immobilize skin wounds in order to improve scarring and description of simultaneous use of Botulinum toxin with local anaesthetic agent in order to improve predictability of Botulinum toxin injections; first to desribe previously unknown anatomic structures in the face, including sublevator space and sublevator extension of buccal fat pad. Office: Univ Washington Dept Otorhinolaryngology Seattle WA 98195-6515 Office Fax: 206-386-3553; Home Fax: +49-941-6083437. Business E-Mail: info@drgassner.eu.

GASSON, JUDITH C., research scientist; m. David Kronemyer; children: Andrew, Lauren. BS in microbiology, Colo. State Coll., 1973; PhD in physiology, U. Colo., 1979; postdoctoral, Salk Inst., 1979—82. With UCLA Jonsson Comprehensive Cancer Ctr., 1983—, dir., 1995—; prof. medicine and biol. chemistry UCLA Sch. Medicine; and co-dir. UCLA Inst. Stem Cell Biology and Medicine, 2005—. Pres. Jonsson Cancer Ctr. Found., 1995—. Recipient Scholar award, Leukemia Soc. Am., 1988, Stohlman Scholar award, 1991, Women of Sci. award, UCLA, 1991, Am. Soc. Clin. Investigation award, 1994. Office: UCLA Jonsson Comprehensive Cancer Ctr 8-684 Factor Bldg 10833 Le Conte Ave Box 951781 Los Angeles CA 90095-1781

GASTIL, RUSSELL GORDON, geologist, educator; b. San Diego, June 25, 1928; s. Russell Chester and Frances (Duncan) G.; m. Emily Janet Manly, Sept. 13, 1958; children— Garth Manly, Mary Margaret, George Christopher, John Webster. A.B, U. Calif., Berkeley, 1950, PhD, 1954. With Shell Oil Co., 1954, Canadian Javelin Co., 1956-58; lectr. U. Calif. at Los Angeles, 1958-59; faculty San Diego State U., 1959—, prof. geology, 1965—, chmn. dept., 1969-72. AuthorL Follow the Sun, 2006; pub.: We Can Save San Diego, 1975; contbr. papers to profl. lit. Democratic candidate U.S. Ho. of Reps., 1976; mem. Calif. Dem. Central Com., 1977-78; coordinator 41st Congl. dist. Common Cause, 1977; pres. Grossmont-Mt. Helix Improvement Assn., 1978-80; mem. San Diego County Air Pollution Hearing Bd., 1977-80; trustee Friends com. on legislation edn. com., 1994-01. Recipient 2002 Dibblee medalist for outstanding geologic field mapping. Fellow Geol. Soc. Am. (vice chmn. Cordilleran sect. 1967, gen. chmn. ann. meeting San Diego 1991); mem. Soc. Econ. Mineralogists and Paleontologists, Am. Geophys. Union. Home: 9435 Alto Dr La Mesa CA 91941-4226 Office: San Diego State U Dept Geol Scis San Diego CA 92182 Personal E-mail: jgastil@sbcglobal.net.

GATES, ANTONIO, professional football player; b. Detroit, June 18, 1980; Grad., Kent State U. Tight end San Diego Chargers, 2003—. Named First Team All-Pro, AP, 2004—06; named to Am. Football Conf. Pro Bowl Team, NFL, 2004—08. Office: c/o San Diego Chargers 4020 Murphy Canyon Rd San Diego CA 92123

GATES, BILL (WILLIAM HENRY GATES III), computer software company executive; b. Seattle, Oct. 28, 1955; s. William H. and Mary M. (Maxwell) Gates; m. Melinda French, Jan. 1, 1994; children: Jennifer Katherine, Rory John, Phoebe Adele. Student, Harvard U., LLD (hon.), 2007. Co-founder Traf-O-Data Co., Seattle, 1972—73, Microsoft Corp. (formerly Micro Soft), Albuquerque, 1975, gen. ptnr. Redmond, Wash., 1975—77, pres., 1977—82, chmn. bd., 1981—, exec. v.p. development activities, 1982—83, CEO, 1981—2000, chief software architect, 2000—06. Founder Corbis, 1989; bd. dirs. ICOS Corp., 1990—, Berkshire Hathaway Inc., 2004—; spkr. Consumer Electronics Show, 2006, 08; spkr. in field. Author: The Future, 1994, The Road Ahead, 1995 (No. 1 NY Times bestseller), Business at the Speed of Thought, 1999 (NY Times, USA Today, Wall St. Jour., Amazon.com bestsellers). Founder William H. Gates Found., 1994—2000; co-founder Gates Learning Found. (formerly Gates Library Found.), 1997—2000, Bill and Melinda Gates Found., 2000—; pledged $900 million to fight tuberculosis, 2006; sponsor Code4Bill, a contest to identify software students in India, offering as top prize an internship with the Microsoft tech. team for a year., 2005; Bill and Melinda Gates Found. will give a $9.7 million grant to the Elizabeth Glaser Pediatric AIDS Found. to study ways to prevent HIV/AIDS transmission via breast milk, 2007. Recipient Howard Vollum award, Reed Coll., Portland, Oreg., 1984, Nat. Tech. Medal, US Dept. Commerce, 1992; named CEO of Yr., Chief Exec. mag., 1994; named a Knight Comdr. of the British Empire (KBE), Her Majesty Queen Elizabeth II, 2005; named one of Top 200 Collectors, ARTnews mag., 2004, The Three Persons of Yr., TIME mag., 2005, The 100 Most Influential People in the World, 2005, 2006, The World's Richest People, Forbes Mag., 1996—, The Richest Americans, Forbes mag., 2006, 50 Who Matter Now, CNNMoney.com Bus. 2.0, 2006, The 25 Most Powerful People in Bus., Fortune Mag., 2007, The Global Elite, Newsweek mag., 2008. Avocations: Collector 19th Century Am. Art, reading, golf, bridge, tennis. Office: Microsoft Corp 1 Microsoft Way Redmond WA 98052-8300*

GATES, BRUCE CLARK, chemical engineer, educator; b. Richmond, Calif., July 5, 1940; s. George Laurence and Frances Genevieve (Wilson) G.; m. Jutta M. Reichert, July 17, 1967; children: Robert Clark, Andrea Margarete. BS, U. Calif., Berkeley, 1961; PhD in Chem. Engring., U. Wash., Seattle, 1966. Rsch. engr. Chevron Rsch. Co., Richmond, Calif., 1967-69; asst. prof. to assoc. prof. U. Del., Newark, Del., 1969-77, prof. chem. engring., 1977-85, assoc. dir. Ctr. Catalytic Sci. & Tech., 1977-81, dir. Catalytic Ctr. Sci. & Tech., 1981-88, H. Rodney Sharp prof., 1985-92; prof. chem. engring. U. Calif., Davis, 1992—2003, disting. prof., chmn. engring., 2003—. Basic energy sci. adv. com. Dept. Energy, 2004—. Author: Catalytic Chemistry, 1992; co-author: Chemistry of Catalytic Processes, 1979; co-editor: Metal Clusters in Catalysis, 1986, Surface Organometallic Chemistry, 1988, Advances in Catalysis, 1996—. Recipient Sr. Rsch. award Humboldt Found., U. Munich, 1998-99, 2002; R.W. Moutlon medal, Disting. Alumnus award, Dept. Chem. Engring., U. Wash., 2005; Pruitt award Coun. Chem. Rsch., 2006; Fulbright Rsch. grantee Inst. Phys. Chemistry U. Munich, 1966-67, 75-76, 83-84, 90-91. Mem.: NAE, AIChE (Alpha Chi Sigma award 1989, William H. Walker award 1995, R.H. Wilhelm award 2002), Catalysis Soc. N.Am. (bd. dirs. 1997—), Am. Chem. Soc. (Del. sect. award 1985, Petroleum Chemistry award 1993, G.A. Somorjai award for creative rsch. in catalysis 2004). Achievements include research in catalysis, surface chemistry and reaction kinetics, chemical reaction engineering, petroleum and petrochemical processes, catalysis by solid acids, zeolites, soluble and supported transition-metal complexes and clusters, catalytic hydroprocessing. Office: Dept Chem Engring & Materials Sci U Calif 3102 Bainer Hall Davis CA 95616 Office Phone: 530-752-3953. E-mail: bcgates@ucdavis.edu.

GATES, MELINDA FRENCH, foundation administrator; b. Dallas, Aug. 15, 1964; d. Raymond French; m. Bill Gates, Jan. 1, 1994; 3 children. BS in Computer Sci. & Economics, Duke U., 1986, MBA, 1987. Gen. mgr. info. products Microsoft Corp., Redmond, Wash., 1987—96; co-founder Bill & Melinda Gates Found., Seattle, 2000—. Bd. dir. drugstore.com, The Wash. Post Co., 2004—. Bd. trustee Duke U., 1996—2003; former co-chair Wash. State Gov. Commn. on Early Learning. Named one of The 100 Most Powerful Women, Forbes mag., 2005—08, The Three Persons of Yr., TIME mag., 2005, The World's 100 Most Influential People, 2006, 50 Women to Watch, The Wall St. Jour., 2006, The Global Elite, Newsweek mag., 2008. Mem.: Bilderberg Group. Roman Catholic. Avocation: running. Office: Bill & Melinda Gates Found PO Box 23350 Seattle WA 98102*

GATES, MILO SEDGWICK, retired construction company executive; b. Omaha, Apr. 25, 1923; s. Milo Talmage and Virginia (Offutt) G.; m. Anne Phleger, Oct. 14, 1950 (dec. Apr. 1987); children: Elena Motlow, Susan Gates Suman, Virginia Lewis, Anne Symington, Milo T.; m. Robin Templeton Quist, June 18, 1988; stepchildren: Robert L. Quist, Catherine Brisbin, Sarah Mazzocco. Student, Calif. Inst. Tech., 1943-44; BS, Stanford U., 1944, MBA, 1948. With Swinerton & Walberg Co., San Francisco, 1955—, pres., 1976—, chmn., 1988-96, ret. Bd. dirs., trustee Children's Hosp. San Francisco; trustee Grace Cathedral, San Francisco; bd. dirs. Calif. Acad. Scis. Lt. (j.g.), USNR, 1944-46. Mem. Pacific-Union Club, Bohemian Club. Republican. Home: 7 Vineyard Hill Rd Woodside CA 94062-2531

GATES, MIMI GARDNER, museum director; b. Dayton, Ohio, July 30, 1942; BA in Asian History, Stanford U.; diploma in Chinese Langs. and Culture, Ecole Nationale des Langues Orientales Vivantes, Paris; MA in Oriental and Chinese studies, U. Iowa; PhD in Art History, Yale U. Curator Asian art Yale U. Art Gallery, New Haven, 1975—87, dir., 1987—94; Illsley Ball Nordstrom dir. Seattle Art Mus., Wash., 1994—. Mem. governing bd. Yale U. Art Gallery; instr. Chinese art history and mus. studies Yale U.; faculty mem. U. Wash.; chair Fed. Indemnity panel The Nat. Endowment, 1999—2002; bd. mem. Northwest African Am. Mus. Contbr. Bones of Jade, Soul of Ice: The Flowering Plum in Chinese Art, 1985, co-curator Stories of Porcelain, From China to Europe, 2000, Ancient Sichuan: Treasures from a Lost Civilization, 2001. Bd. mem. Downtown Seattle Assn., Greater Seattle YWCA, Copper Canyon Press; mem. adv. bd. Getty Leadership Inst. Mem.: Assn. Art Mus. Dirs. (past pres., trustee). Office: Seattle Art Mus 1300 First Ave Seattle WA 98101 Office Phone: 206-625-8900. Office Fax: 206-654-3135.

GATES, R. JORDAN, delivery service executive; From Europe controller to exec. v.p., CFO, treas. Expeditors Internat. of Washington, Seattle, 1991—2000, exec. v.p., 2000—07, CFO, 2000—07, treas., 2000—07, pres., COO, 2008—. Office: Expeditors International of Washington 1015 3rd Ave 12th Fl Seattle WA 98104

GATES, SUSAN INEZ, magazine publisher; b. San Francisco, Jan. 14, 1956; d. Milo Sedgewick and Anne (Phelger) Gates. BA in English, French magna cum laude (hon.), U. Colo., 1978; MS in Journalism, Columbia U., 1983. With GEO Mag., NYC, 1978—79, New York Mag., NYC, 1981—82, Ladd Assoc., NYC, 1983—85, Mc Namee Cons., NYC, 1986—88; founding pub. BUZZ Mag., LA, 1989—97; co-founder, prin. Mind Over Media, LLC, LA, 1997—. Mem.: Phi Beta Kappa. Business E-Mail: susan@mindovermedia.net.

GATTI, JIM, editor; b. Detroit, July 4, 1943; m. Carol A. Gatti; children: Theresa, Julie, Thomas, John. BA in English, Wayne State U., 1966. News editor Detroit News, city editor, asst. mng. editor, dep. mng. editor; editor Honolulu Advertiser, 1995—. With U.S. Army, 1966-68. Recipient Silver Gavel, ABA, Robert F. Kennedy Pub. Svc. award. Office: Honolulu Advertiser 605 Kapiolani Blvd Honolulu HI 96813-5129

GATTO, CARL, state legislator; b. NYC, Dec. 29, 1937; m to Cathy Gatto; children: Kip, Antonia, Samantha & Gabe. BA in Mech. Engring., Bklyn. Polytech, 1960; BA in Physical Sci., U. Calif., San Jose, 1968, BA in Biology, 1968; MS in Biology, Northern Ariz. U., Flagstaff, 1973; AA in Paramedicine, U. Alaska, Anchorage, 1975. Cert. Tchg. High Sch. and Spl. Edn.; Fire Instr. I, II, III. Alaska State Representative, District 13, 2003-. Farm irrigation engr; Mil jet engr; civilian liaison officer; tchr, high sch sci, formerly; Paramedic, firefighter, formerly. Mem. Alaska Commn. on Post Secondary Edn., NCSL Com. on Agr. and Rural Devel., NCSL Com. on Edn. Mem. Palmer C. of C.; ch. outreach counselor Yukon River Trips, Internat. Trips for Teens; mem. bd. trustees Valley Hosp.; bd. mem. Matanuska-Susitna Parks & Recreation; mem. Wasilla C. of C.; basketball coach; soccer coach; cross country team photographer. NRA; Nat Right to Life; Alaska Right to Life; Local sch board (vice-pres). Republican. Avocations: hunting, fishing, flying. Office: State Capitol Rm 108 Juneau AK 99801-1182 Office Phone: 907-465-3743. Office Fax: 907-465-2381. Business E-Mail: representative_carl_gatto@legis.state.ak.us.*

GAULT, POLLY L., utilities executive; Grad. magna cum laude, Mt. Holyoke Coll., South Hadley, Mass., 1975. Legis. asst. US Senator Richard S. Schweiker of Pa., 1977—80; staff dir. US Senate Edn., Arts and Humanities Subcommittee, 1981—87; mem. Presdl. Commn. on HIV Epidemic, 1987—88; exec. dir. Presdl. Commn. Exec., Legis. and Jud. Salaries; chief of staff Dept. Energy, 1989—93; prin. dir., exec. v.p. Wexler Group; with So. Calif. Edison subs. Edison Internat., 1997—, exec. v.p. pub. affairs, 2006—, exec. v.p. pub. affairs So. Calif. Edison subs., 2006—. Mem.: Phi Beta Kappa. Office: Edison Internat 2244 Walnut Grove Ave Rosemead CA 91770-3714

GAVALAS, GEORGE R., chemical engineering educator; b. Athens, Greece, Oct. 7, 1936; s. Lazaros R. and Belouso A. (Matha) G. BS, Nat. Tech. U., 1958; MS, U. Minn., 1962, PhD, 1964. Asst. prof. chem. engring. Calif. Inst. Tech., 1964-67, asso. prof., 1967-75, prof., 1975, prof. emeritus, 2005. Cons. in field. Author: Nonlinear Differential Equations of Chemically Reacting Systems, 1968, Coal Pyrolysis, 1983; contbr. articles to profl. jours. Mem. AIChE (Tech. award 1968, Wilhelm award 1983), Am. Chem. Soc., N.Am. Membrane Soc. Home: 707 S Orange Blvd # F Pasadena CA 91105-1779 Office: Caltech 210-41 Pasadena CA 91125-0001 E-mail: garalas@cheme.caltech.edu.

GAVIOLA, KAREN Z., television director; Dir.: (TV series, episodes) NYPD Blue (3 episodes), 1999—2001, Providence (1 episode), 2002, Strong Medicine (1 episode), 2002, CSI: Miami (12 episodes), 2003—, Cold Case (2 episodes), 2004, The Inside (1 episode), 2005, CSI: NY (1 episode), 2005, Medical Investigation (1 episode), 2005, Close to Home (1 episode), 2005, Crossing Jordan (1 episode), 2006, Lost: The Whole Truth, 2006 (NAACP Image award, Dir. of a drama series, 2007), Alias (1 episode), 2006, Justice (1 episode), 2006, Bones (1 episode), 2006, Prison Break (1 episode), 2006, Lincoln Heights (1 episode), 2007; (TV series) The Unit (1 episode), 2007. Mem.: Dirs. Guild Am. Office: Metropolitan Talent Agency 4500 Wilshire Blvd Fl 3 Los Angeles CA 90010-3861 E-mail: gavvy2000@yahoo.com.

GAY, E(MIL) LAURENCE, lawyer; b. Bridgeport, Conn., Aug. 10, 1923; s. Emil Daniel and Helen Lillian (Mihalich) Gulyassy; m. Harriet A. Ripley, Aug. 2, 1952; children: Noel L., Peter C., Marguerite S., Georgette A. BS, Yale U., 1946; JD magna cum laude, Harvard U., 1949. Bar: Hawaii 1988. Mem. bar NY, Conn. & Calif.; assoc. Root, Ballantine, Harlan, Bushby & Palmer, NYC, 1949—52; mem. legal staff U.S. High Commr. Germany, 1952—53; law sec. fo David W. Peck, presiding justice appellate divsn. 1st dept. N.Y. Supreme Ct., NYC, 1953—54; assoc. Debevoise, Plimpton & McLean, NYC, 1954—58; v.p., sec.-treas., gen. counsel Hewitt-Robins, Inc., Stamford, Conn., 1958—65; pres. Litton Gt. Lakes Corp., NYC, 1965—67; sr. v.p. fin. AMFAC, Inc., Honolulu, 1967—73, vice chmn., 1974—78; fin. cons. Burlingame, Calif., 1979-82; of counsel Pettit & Martin, San Francisco, 1982—88, Goodsill, Anderson, Quinn & Stifel, Honolulu, 1988—. Editor: Harvard Law Rev., 1948—49. Pres. Honolulu Symphony Soc., 1974—78; officer, dir. numerous arts and ednl. orgns.; bd. dirs. Loyola Marymount U., 1977—80, San Francisco Chamber Soloists, 1981—86, Honolulu Chamber Music Series, 1988—. 1st lt. US Army,

1943—46. Mem.: ABA, Hawaii State Bar Assn., Phi Beta Kappa. Republican. Roman Catholic. Avocations: music, literature. Home: 1159 Maunawili Rd Kailua HI 96734-4641 Office: Goodsill Anderson Quinn & Stifel 1099 Alakea St #1800 Honolulu HI 96814 Office Phone: 808-547-5641. Business E-Mail: egay@goodsill.com.

GAYNOR, C.W., paper company executive; BS, Iowa State U.; MBA, Ariz. State U., 1974. Fin. mgr. Weyerhaeuser Co., Tacoma, Wash., 1974, v.p. gen. mgr. Saskatchewan disvn., sr. v.p. Canada, 1998—. Dir. exec. com. Coun. Forest Industries. Served in U.S. Navy. Mem. Can. Pulp & Paper Assn. (bd. dirs.).

GAYNOR, JOSEPH, chemical engineer, management consultant; b. NYC, Nov. 15, 1925; s. Morris and Rebecca (Schnapper) G.; m. Elaine Bauer, Aug. 19, 1951; children: Barbara Lynne, Martin Scott, Paul David, Andrew Douglas. B in Chem. Engring., Poly. Inst., 1950; MS, Case Western Res. U., 1952, PhD, 1955. Rsch. asst. Case Inst., Cleve., 1952-55; with Gen. Engring. Labs. GE, Schenectady, NY, 1955-66, mgr. R & D sect., 1962-66; group v.p. rsch. Bell & Howell Co., 1966-72; mgr. comml. devel. group, mem. pres.' office Horizons Rsch., Inc., Cleve., 1972-73; pres. Innovative Tech. Assocs., Ventura, Calif., 1973—; mem. nat. materials adv. bd. com. NAS; chmn. conf. com. 2d internat. conf. on bus. graphics, 1979; program chmn. 1st internat. congress on advances in non-impact printing techs., 1981; mem. adv. com. 2d internat. congress on advances in non-impact printing techs., 1984; chmn. publs. com. 3rd internat. congress on advances in non-impact printing techs., 1986; chmn. internat. conf. on hard copy media, materials and processes, 1990. Editor: Electronic Imaging, 1991, Procs. Advances in Non-Impact Printing Technologies, Vol. I, 1983, Vol. II, 1988, 3 spl. issues Jour. Imaging Tech., Proc. Hard Copy Materials Media and Processes Internat. Conf., 1990; delivered invited keynote address NIP-17 Digital Printing Techs. Internat. Conf., 2001; patentee in field. Served with U.S. Army, 1944-46. Fellow AAAS, AIChE, Imaging Sci. and Tech. Soc. (sr., gen. chmn. 2nd internat. conf. on electrophotography 1973, chmn. bus. graphics tech. sect. 1976—, chmn. edn. com. L.A. chpt. 1978—), Am. Soc. Photobiology, Sigma Xi, Tau Beta Pi, Phi Lambda Upsilon, Alpha Chi Sigma. Home: 108 La Brea St Oxnard CA 93035-3928 Office: Innovative Tech Assocs 3639 Harbor Blvd Ste 203E Ventura CA 93001-4255 Office Phone: 805-650-9353. Personal E-mail: joseph.gaynor@roadrunner.com.

GAZELL, JAMES ALBERT, public administration educator; b. Chgo., Mar. 17, 1942; s. Albert James and Ann Marion (Bloch) G. BA in Polit. Sci. with honors, Roosevelt U., 1963, MA in Polit. Sci., 1966; PhD in Govt., So. Ill. U., 1968. Instr. Roosevelt U., Chgo., 1965, 67, So. Ill. U., Carbondale, 1966-68; asst. prof. San Diego State U., 1968-72, assoc. prof., 1972-75, prof., 1975—2008, prof. emeritus, 2008—. Cons. County San Diego, 1973, Ernst and Ernst, Detroit, 1973, Wadsworth Pub. Co., 1995, McGraw-Hill Pub. Co., 1997. Author books; contbr. articles to profl. jours.; assoc. editor Encyclopedia of Public Administration and Public Policy, 1999; mem. editl. bd. Internat. Jour. Pub. Adminstrn., Internat. Jour. Orgnl. Theory and Behavior. Mem. ACLU, Am. Soc. Pub. Adminstrn., Nat. Ctr. for State Cts., Nat. Assn. Ct. Mgmt., Nat. Assn. for Ct. Mgmt. Home: 4319 Hilldale Rd San Diego CA 92116-2135 Office: San Diego State U 5500 Campanile Dr San Diego CA 92182-4505 Home Phone: 619-283-3317; Office Phone: 619-594-4604. Business E-Mail: jgazell@mail.sdsu.edu.

GAZZALE, BOB, film institute executive; b. 1965; m. Mimi Gazzale; children: Nicholas, Ella. BA, U. Va., 1987. Founder Va. Festival of Am. Film; joined Am. Film Inst. (AFI), LA, 1992, head nat. programs NYC, dir. productions LA, pres., CEO, 2007—. Prodr.: AFI's 100 Years, 100 Laughs: America's Funniest Movies, 2000; prodr., writer AFI Life Achievement Award: A Tribute to Barbra Streisand, 2001, AFI's 100 Years, 100 Thrills: America's Most Heart-Pounding Movies, 2001, AFI's 100 Years...100 Passions, 2002, AFI Life Achievement Award: A Tribute to Tom Hanks, 2002, AFI's 100 Years...100 Heroes & Villains, 2003, AFI's 100 Years, 100 'Movie Quotes': The Greatest Lines from American Film, 2005, AFI's 100 Years...100 Cheers: America's Most Inspiring Movies, 2006, exec. prodr., writer AFI Life Achievement Award: A Tribute to Robert De Niro, 2003, AFI Tribute to Meryl Streep, 2003, AFI Tribute to George Lucas, 2005, AFI Life Achievement Award: A Tribute to Sean Connery, 2006. Nominee Emmy Award, 2002, 2003, 2004, 2007. Office: Am Film Inst 2021 N Western Ave Los Angeles CA 90027-1657 Office Phone: 232-856-7600. Office Fax: 323-467-4578.

GEBB, SHELDON ALEXANDER, lawyer; b. Long Beach, Calif., Jan. 12, 1935; AB, U. Calif., Berkeley, 1957; LLB, U. Calif., 1963. Bar: Calif. 1964. Mng. ptnr. Baker & Hostetler, L.A., Long Beach and Beverly Hills, Silicon Valley, Calif. Chmn. bd. trustees Southwestern U. Sch. Law, 1985-91 Mem. ABA, State Bar Calif., Maritime Law Assn. U.S. Office: Baker & Hostetler 600 Wilshire Blvd Los Angeles CA 90017-3212

GEBLER, DAVID B., finance company executive; b. Binghamton, NY, Oct. 6, 1949; s. Norman Frederick and Dorothy (Dedrick) G.; m. Catherine Hopkins, Oct. 7, 1978; children: Anna, Kathleen. BS, Clarkson U., 1971; postgrad., U. N.C., 1971-72; Dde, U. Mich., 1977, MS, 1979. Various positions Ford Motor Co./Ford Motor Credit Co., Dearborn, Mich., 1972-81; mgr. Ford Motor Credit Co., Dearborn, 1981-89; pres. U.S. Airlease Inc./U.S. Leasing Internat., San Francisco, 1989-90; exec. v.p. Transp. Financing/U.S. Leasing Internat., San Francisco, 1990—; pres. Airlease Ltd., San Francisco, 1989—. Capt. U.S. Army, 1971-81. Mem. Nat. Assn. Security Dealers (registered rep.). Office: Airlease Ltd 555 California St San Francisco CA 94104

GECKLE, TIMOTHY J., lawyer; b. 1952; m. Bernadette Geckle; children: Caroline, Noelle. BA in religion, Catholic U. Am., 1974, MA in religion, 1979; JD, U. San Francisco, 1984. Bar: 1985. Lawyer Piper & Marbury, 1985—91; corp. counsel The Ryland Group, Calabasas, Calif., 1991-95, v.p., dep. gen. counsel, 1995-97, v.p., corp. counsel, sec., 1997, sr. v.p., gen. counsel, sec., 1997—. Office: The Ryland Group Inc 24025 Pk Sorrento Ste 400 Calabasas CA 91302 Office Phone: 410-715-7000.

GEDDES, GARY LEE, wildlife park director; b. Peoria, Ill., Aug. 23, 1950; s. Robert and Mary O. (McCartney) G.; m. Debbie L. Lush, Sept. 7, 1974; children: Jake Austin, Cody Robert, Katelyn Jane. AS, Ill. Cen. Jr. Coll., 1970; BA in Zoology, So. Ill. U., 1972. Dir. Wildlife Prairie Park, Hanna City, Ill., 1973-81, N.W. Trek Wildlife Park, Eatonville, Wash., 1981—, Point Defiance Zoo & Aquarium, Tacoma, Wash. Co-chmn. bd. dirs. Region 6 Tourism Coun., Olympia, Wash., 1984-86; vice chmn. Bates Vocat. Sch. Tourism Adv. Bd.; exec. bd. mem. Regional Tourism Coun., Olympia, Wash., 1983-88. Leader Boy Scouts Am.; bd. dirs. Ctr. for Wildlife Conservation. Fellow Am. Assn. Zool. Parks and Aquariums, Audobon Soc. (bd. dirs. Tahoma chpt.). Avocations: mountain climbing, camping, cross country skiing, gardening. Office: Northwest Trek Wildlife Pk 11610 Trek Dr E Eatonville WA 98328-9502 Address: Point Defiance Zoo & Aquarium 5400 N Pearl St Tacoma WA 98407

GEDDES, ROBERT L., state legislator; b. Preston, Idaho, Nov. 14, 1955; m. Tammy Geddes; 5 children. Attended, Ricks Coll.; BS in Geology, Utah State U., 1981. Farmer, 1981—; geologist Conda Partnership, 1981—85; environ. engr. Monsanto, 1985—; mem. Dist. 31 Idaho State Senate, 1996—, pres. pro tem., 2000—. Nat Acad. Republican. Mem. Lds Ch. Office: State Capitol Bldg PO Box 83720 Boise ID 83720-0081 Office Phone: 208-334-2475. Office Fax: 208-334-2125.*

GEE, CHUCK YIM, dean; b. San Francisco, Aug. 28, 1933; s. Don Yow Elsie (Lee) G. AA, City Coll. of San Francisco, 1953; BSBA, U. Denver, 1957; MA, Mich. State U., 1958; PhD (hon.), China Acad. Chinese Cultural U., 1972; D of Pub. Svc. (hon.), U. Denver, 1991. Assoc. dir. Sch. of Hotel and Restaurant Adminstrn. U. Denver, 1958-68; cons. East West Ctr., Honolulu, 1968-74; assoc. dean and prof. Sch. of Travel Industry Mgmt. U. Hawaii, 1968-75, dean and prof. Sch. Travel Industry Mgmt., 1976-99, interim dean Coll. Bus. Adminstrn., 1998-99, dean emeritus, 2000—; regent, bd. regents U. Hawaii Sys., 2009—. Vis. prof. Sch Bus. and Commerce, Oreg. State U., 1975; hon. prof. Nankai U., Tianjin, China, 1987—, Beijing U. Internat. Studies, 1985-, Shanghai Inst. Tourism, 1994-03, Dept. Tourism Huaqiao U., Xiamen, China, 1995—, Shanghai Normal U., 2004—, Shunde Poly. U., Guangdong, China, 2005—, Hubei Coll., 2006—; cons. Internat. Sci. and Tech. Inst., Washington, 1986-90, cons. on tourism devel., Jiaojuo, Henan Province, Xiamen City, Fujian Province, China, 2004—, Xiaogen City, Hubei Province, 2006—; trustee Pacific Asia Travel Assn. Found., San Francisco; chmn. Govs. Tourism Tng. Coun., Honolulu, 1989-92, chmn., 1992-96, chmn. industry coun. PATA, 1994-96, PATA Human Resource Devel. Coun., 1996-99, chmn. PATA Coun. on Ednl. Devel. and Certification, 2000-02; mem. State Workforce Devel. Coun., 1997-98, Pacific Asia Travel Assn. Human Resource Devel. Coun, 1996-98; acad. Inst. Cert. Travel Agts., Wellesley, Mass., 1989—; mem. Coun. on Hotel, Restaurant Edn., 1967-00, Honolulu Commn. on Fgn. Rels., 1979-98; mem. Pacific Asian Affairs Coun.; sr. acad. adv. China Tourism Assn. Cons., Inc., 1993-2000; adv. World Tourism Orgn. Internat. Tourism Edn. and Tng. Ctr., 1991-2000; external examiner sch. accountancy and bus. Nanyang Tech. U., Singapore, 1996-98; bd. dirs. Projecton-Net.com; bus. advisor Che Che NY, 2004—, Grand Cafe, Honolulu, 2004-07. Author: Resort Devel. and Mgmt., 1988, 2d edit., The Story of PATA, 2d edit., co-editor, 2001; co-author: The Travel Industry, 1988, 3d edit., 1997, Profl. Travel Agency Mgmt., 1990, Internat. Hotels: Devel. and Mgmt., 1994; editor: Internat. Tourism: A Global Perspective, 1997; founding dir., Hong Kong, China, Hawaii Chamber of Commerce, 1998-; mem. adv. bd. Asian Hotelier mag., 1997-99, Get2Hawaii.com, 2001-04. Bd. dirs. Hawaii Visitors Bur., 1993-95, Kaukini Med. Ctr., Honolulu, 1986-95, 96-2005; mem. Travel and Tourism Adv. Bd., U.S. Dept. Commerce, Washington, 1982-90, Pacific Rim Found., Honolulu, 1987-93, vice-chmn. Tourism Policy Adv. Coun., Dept. Bus. and Econ. Devel., Honolulu, 1978-92; chmn. Kuakini Geriat. Care, Inc., bd. dirs., 1992-95; trustee Pata Found., 1984-95, Kuakini Health System, 1988-2003, 05—, fin. com., 2007-; mem. exec. com. Kuakini Med. Ctr., 2006-, fin. com.; consulting com. Beijing Inst. Tourism, 1992—; v.p. Hawaii Vision 2020, 1992-93; mem. Mayor's Task Force on Waikiki Master Plan, 1992-93; devel. bd. Miss Hawaii Scholarship Pageant, 1993-2009; workforce devel. coun. Hawaii Dept. of Labor and Indsl. Rels., 1996-98; bd. dirs., Cmty. Enterprises, Hawaii Dept. Edn., 1997—, Hong Kong Hawaii C. of C., 1999—; mem. Mayor's Adv. Com. on Oahu Strategic Tourism Plan, 2005-07. Served with U.S. Army, 1953-55. Recipient NOAH award, Acad. Tourism Orgns., 1987, Gov.'s Proclamation honors, Office of Gov., State of Hawaii, 1998, 1999, 2003, Dean Chuck Yim Gee Excellence in Creative Film Achievements award, China-Hawaii C. of C., 2004; named State Mgr. of Yr., Office of Gov., State of Hawaii, 1995; named one of 100 Who Made a Difference in Hawaii during 20th Century, Star Bull., 1999; grantee Chuck Yim Gee-Hawaii Scholarship Endowment established in his honor, Nat. Tourism Found., 2001; Chuck Yim Gee Tech. Learning Ctr. at U. Hawaii named in his honor, Travel Industry Mgmt. Internat., Inc. U. Hawaii Found., 2003. Mem. Acad. for Study of Tourism (emeritus), Pacific Asia Travel Assn. (hon. life Hawaii chpt., bd. dirs. 1993-96, chmn. industry coun. 1994-96, 50th Anniversary Hall of Honors, 2001, Grand award 1991, Life award 1990, Presdl. award 1986), Travel Industry Am. (Travel Industry Hall of Leaders award 1988), China Tourism Assn. (award of excellence 1992), China-Hawaii C. of C. (founding dir. 1998), Hong Kong-China-Hawaii C. of C. (bd. dirs. 1999—), Golden Key. Office: U Hawaii Sch Travel Industry Mgmt 2560 Campus Rd Honolulu HI 96822-2217 Home Phone: 808-524-5510. Business E-Mail: cgee@hawaii.edu.

GEE, GAVIN M., state agency administrator; b. Idaho; m. Libby Gee; 4 children. BA in Polit. Sci., Brigham Young U.; JD, U. Idaho Coll. Law. Securities examiner Idaho Dept. Fin., Boise, 1977—78, dep. atty. gen., 1978—81, securities bur. chief, 1981—86, fin. instns. bur. chief, 1986—95, acting dir., 1995—96, dir., 1996—. Vice chmn. Idaho Endowment Fund Investment Bd. Youth sports coach; numerous leadership positions Boy Scouts of Am., Ch. Mem.: Nat. Assn. State Credit Union Suprs. (bd. dirs. 1991—95, chmn. 1993—94, Pierre Jay award 2000), Conf. State Bank Suprs. (bd. dirs., chmn. 2002—03), Idaho State Bar Assn. (mem. corp. and securities law sect.), Fed. Fin. Instns. Exam. Coun. (chmn., mem. state liaison com. 1994—99). Avocations: mountain biking, white-water rafting, snow and water skiing, hiking, tennis. Office: Idaho Dept Fin PO Box 83720 Boise ID 83720-0031 Office Phone: 208-332-8010. E-mail: ggee@finance.idaho.gov.

GEFFEN, DAVID LAWRENCE, film company executive; b. Bklyn., Feb. 21, 1943; s. Abraham and Batya (Volovskaya) Geffen. Student, U. Tex., 1961—63, Bklyn. Coll. With William Morris Agy., NYC, 1964—68, Ashley Famous Agy., 1968; exec. v.p., agt. Creative Mgmt. Assocs., 1969; founder (with Laura Nyro) and pres. Tuna Fish Pub. Co.; pres. Geffen-Roberts, Inc., 1970—71, Asylum Records, 1970—73, Elektra-Asylum Records, 1973—76; vice-chmn. & chief asst. to chmn. Warner Bros. Pictures, 1974—75; founder, pres., chmn. Geffen Records & Geffen Film Co., LA, 1980—89; founder, pres. David Geffen Co., 1990—95; co-founder (with Jeffrey Katzenberg & Steven Spielberg) DreamWorks SKG, Universal City, Calif., 1994—2008, chmn., 1994—2006, co-chmn. Glendale, Calif., 2006—08. Mem. faculty Yale U., 1978; apptd. Regent U. Calif., Govt. Calif., 1980—87; bd. councilors USC Sch. Cinema-TV. Prodr.: (films) Personal Best, 1982, Risky Business, 1983, After Hours, 1985, Lost in America, 1985, Little Shop of Horrors, 1986, Beetlejuice, 1988, Men Don't Leave, 1990, Interview with the Vampire, 1994; co-prodr.: Dreamgirls, 2006; (plays) Master Harold...and the Boys, 1982, Cats, 1982, Good, 1982, Dreamgirls, 1983, Social Security, 1986, Madam Butterfly, 1988 (9 Tony awards including best play), Jack: A Night on the Town with John Barrymore, 1996, Hedda Gabler, 2001, By Jeeves, 2001, Little Shop of Horrors (revival), 2003. Bds. dirs. Los Angeles County Art Mus. Named one of Forbes' Richest Americans, 1999—, World's Richest People, Forbes mag., 2001—, Top 200 Collectors, ARTnews Mag., 2004—08, 50 Most Powerful People in Hollywood, Premiere mag., 2005—06. Democrat. Avocation: Collector of Modern and Contemporary Art, especially Abstract Expressionism.

GEHRY, FRANK OWEN, architect; b. Toronto, Ont., Can., Feb. 28, 1929; arrived in U.S., 1947; s. Irving and Thelma (Caplan) Gehry; m. Berta Aguilera, Sept. 11, 1975; children: Alejandro, Samuel; children: Leslie, Brina. BArch, U. So. Calif., 1954; postgrad., Harvard U., 1956—57; DFA (hon.), RI Sch. Design, 1987, Otis Art Inst. at Parsons Sch. Design, 1989; Doctorate of Visual Arts (hon.), Calif. Inst. Arts, 1987; DEng (hon.), Tech. U. Nova Scotia, 1989; HHD (hon.), Occidental Coll., 1993; doctorate (hon.), Whittier Coll., 1995, Calif. Coll. Arts and Crafts, Southern Calif. Inst. Architecture, 1997; LLD (hon.), U. Toronto, 1998; doctorate (hon.), U. Southern Calif., 2000, Yale U., 2000, Harvard U., 2000, U. Edinburgh, 2000. Registered profl. architect, Calif. Designer Victor Gruen Assocs., LA, 1953—54, planning, design and project dir., 1958—61; project designer, planner Pereira & Luckman, LA, 1957—58; prin. Frank O. Gehry & Assocs. (succeeded by Gehry & Krueger, Inc., now Gehry Partners, LLP), Santa Monica, Calif., 1962—. William Bishop chair Yale U, 1979, Charlotte Davenport Professorship in Architecture, 82, 85, 1987—89, 1999; Eliot Noyes chair Harvard U., 1984; vis. scholar Fed. Inst. Tech., Zürich, Switzerland, 1996—97; vis. prof. UCLA, 1998. Prin. works include Loyola Law Sch., LA, 1978—92, Temporary Contemporary Mus., 1983, Calif. Aerospace Mus., 1984, Frances Goldwyn Regional Br. Libr., Hollywood, Calif., 1986, U.C.I. Info. and Computer Sci./Engring. Rsch. Lab. and Engring Ctr., Irvine, Calif., 1986—88, Vitra Internat. Mfg. Facility and Design Mus., Weil am Rhein, Germany, 1989, Chiat/Day Hdqs., Venice, Calif., 1991, Advanced Tech. Labs. Bldg., U. Iowa, Iowa City, 1992, U. Toledo Ctr. for Visual Arts, Toledo, Ohio, 1992, Walt Disney Concert Hall, LA, 1993, Frederick R. Weisman Art Mus., Mpls., 1993, Vitra Internat. Hdqs., Basel, Switzerland, 1994, Am. Ctr., Paris, 1994, Team Disneyland Adminstrn. Bldg., Anaheim, Calif., 1995, EMR Communication and Tech. Ctr., Bad Oeynhausen, Germany, 1995, Nationale-Nederlanden Bldg., Prague, Czech Republic, 1996, Guggenheim Mus., Bilbao, Spain, 1997, Vontz Ctr. for Molecular Studies, U. Cin., Ohio, 1999, Der Neue Zolihof, Dusseldorf, Germany, 1999, DG Bank Hdqrs., Berlin, Germany, 2000, Experience Music Project, Seattle, 2000, Bard Coll. Ctr. for the Performing Arts, Annandale-on-Hudson, NY, 2001, The Walt Disney Concert Hall, LA, 2002, Peter B. Lewis Weatherhead Sch. Mgmt. Case Western Reserve U., Cleve., 2003, Ray and Maria Stata Ctr., MIT, Cambridge, Mass., 2003, Pritzker Pavilion, Millennium Pk., Chgo., Ill., 2004, MARTa, Headford, Germany, 2005, IAC/Interactive Corp. West Coast Hdqs., L.A., Calif., 2005, Marqués de Riscal Winery, Elciego, Spain, 2006, IAC/Interactive Corp. East Coast Hdqs., NYC, 2007, and several others, selected exhbn. designs, Art Treasures of Japan, LA County Mus. Art, 1965, Assyrian Reliefs, 1966, Billy Al Bengston Retrospective, 1968, Treasures of Tutankhamen, 1978, Avant-Garde of Russia 1910-1930, 1980, Seventeen Artists in the Sixties, 1981, German Expressionist Sculpture, 1983, Degenerate Art, 1994, Exiles & Emigrés, 1997, The Art of the Motorcycle, Solomon R. Guggenheim Mus., NY, 1998, Guggenheim Mus., Bilbao, Spain, 1999; work featured in major architectural publs. including Newsweek, Time, Forbes, Economist, Vanity Fair, Art in America, Wall Street Jour., NY Times, LA Times, Washington Post, Le Monde, L'Express, El Correo and Frankfurter Allgemeine. Trustee Hereditary Disease Found., Santa Monica, Calif., 1970—. Recipient Pritzker Architecture prize, The Hyatt Found., 1989, Wolf prize in art, Wolf Found., 1992, Praemium Imperiale award, Japan Art Assn., 1992, Dorothy and Lilian Gish award, 1994, Nat. Medal of Arts, Nat. Endowment of the Arts, 1998, Friedrich Kiesler prize, Friedrich Kiesler Found., 1998, Gold medal, Royal Architectural Inst. Canada, 1998, Lotus medal of Merit, Lotos Club, 1999, Lifetime Achievement award, Am. for the Arts, 2000, Golden Lion for Lifetime Achievement, Found. La Biennale di Venezia, 2008; named Hon. Consul, City of Bilbao, Spain, 1997, Chancellor, 1998. Fellow: Am. Inst. Architects (Gold medal 1999), AAAS, AAAL (Arnold W. Brunner Meml. prize in architecture 1983); mem.: Royal Acad. Arts (hon. academician 1998), Nat. Acad. Design (academician 1994), Am. Acad. Rome (trustee 1989). Office: Gehry Partners LLP 12541 Beatrice St Los Angeles CA 90066*

GEIGER, BETH C., freelance/self-employed journalist; Contbr. articles on Washington's geologic attractions to AAA Journey, Sunset mag., Current Sci. mag., others. Recipient AAAS Sci. Journalism award for children's sci. news, 2006. Mem.: NW Sci. Writers Assn.

GEISEN, MICHAEL, science educator; b. Seattle, Apr. 27, 1973; m. Jennifer Geisen; 2 children. BS magna cum laude, U. Wash., 1996; MA in Tchg., So. Oreg. U., 2001. Forester, Wash.; tchg. asst. experimental forest U. Wash., 1996—97; student tchr. North Middle Sch., 2001, Grants Pass HS, 2000—01; sci. tchr. Crook County Middle Sch., Prineville, Oreg., 2001—, sci. dept. chair, goal team leader, 2004—, dist. leadership team, tech. implementation team, 2007—. Named Oregon Tchr. of Yr., Coun. Chief State Sch. Officers, 2007—08, Nat. Tchr. of Yr., 2008. Mem.: NAE, Crook County Edn. Assn. (bldg. rep.), Oreg. Edn. Assn., Nat. Sci. Tchrs. Assn. Office: Crook County Middle Sch 100 NE Knowledge St Prineville OR 97754 Office Phone: 541-447-6283. E-mail: ntoy2008@ccsso.org.

GEISER, THOMAS CHRISTOPHER, lawyer, insurance company executive; b. Bern, Switzerland, Aug. 13, 1950; came to U.S., 1952; s. Henry Abraham and Pia Margaret (Tschudin) G.; m. Catherine Barlow Yeakle, Oct. 20, 1973 (div. Mar. 1983); m. Donna Lea Schweers, Jan. 3, 1987; 1 child, Kelsey Schweers. BA, U. Redlands, 1972; JD, U. Calif., San Francisco, 1977. Bar: Calif. 1978. Atty. Internat. Bur. Fiscal Documentation, Amsterdam, Netherlands, 1977—78; assoc., ptnr. Hanson, Bridgett, Marcus, Vlahos & Stromberg, San Francisco, 1979—85; ptnr. Epstein, Becker, Stromberg & Green, San Francisco, 1985—90, Brobeck, Phleger & Harrison, San Francisco, 1990—93; sr. v.p., gen. counsel, sec. WellPoint Health Networks Inc., Woodland Hills, Calif., 1993—96, exec. v.p., gen. counsel, sec., 1996—2005; sr. advisor Tex. Pacific Group, Santa Monica, Calif., 2006—. Mem. Am. Health Lawyers Assn., Calif. Soc.

Health Care Attys., Order of Coif. Office: TPG 1733 Ocean Ave Ste 325 Santa Monica CA 90401 Office Phone: 310-656-9580. Personal E-mail: thomasgeiser@aol.com. Business E-Mail: tgeiser@northbp.com.

GEISTFELD, RONALD ELWOOD, retired dental educator; b. St. James, Minn., Nov. 9, 1933; s. Victor E. and Viola (Becker) G.; m. Lois N. Tolzman Wilkens, June 15, 1955 (div. June 1974); m. Annette L. Swenson, Jan. 14, 1977; children: Shari, Mark, Steven, Ann, Leah, Erik. AA, Bethany Jr. Coll., 1952; BS, U. Minn., 1954, DDS, 1957. Pvt. practice dentistry, Northfield, Minn., 1959-72; clin. asst. prof. dentistry U. Minn. Sch. Dentistry, Mpls., 1969-72, assoc. prof., 1972-82, chmn. dept. operative dentistry, 1978-87, prof., 1982-97, prof. emeritus, 1997; dir. quality programs Pentegra Dental Group, Inc., 1998-2000. Dental cons. Hennepin County Med. Ctr., Mpls., 1975-96, VA Hosp., Mpls., 1977-96, VA Hosp., St. Cloud, Minn., 1978-96, Human Performance and Informatics Inst., Atama, Japan, 1990-95, K-9 Dental Sys. Quidnunc Australia Pty. Ltd., 1994-95, Metro Dental Group, Mpls., 1995-2000, The Dentists Ins. Co., 1995-99, VGM Expert Systems, 1996-98, Met. Life Ins. Co., 1996—, Pentegra Ltd., 1997-2000; mem. resource faculty for Bush faculty devel. program on excellence and diversity in teaching U. Minn., 1993-94; founder Global Network for Systematic Healthcare, 2003. Pres. PTA, Northfield, 1965, Arts Guild, Northfield, 1968; bd. dirs., chairperson Rice County Health and Sanitation Bd., Faribault, Minn., 1966-74; bd. dirs. Northfield Bd. Edn., 1969-74; pres. Roseville Luth. Ch., 1987-88. Capt. U.S. Army, 1957-59. Am. Coll. Dentists fellow, 1972; recipient Prof. of Yr. award Century Club, 1996-97. Mem. Am. Dental Assn. (chairperson operative dentistry sect. 1979-80, curriculum cons. 1981-88, grants and spl. projects request evaluator 1988-92, Am. fund for Dental Health, edit. review bd. JADA 1992-96), Minn. Dental Assn. (ethics com. 1969-76, chairperson sci. and ann. sessions com. 1984-86, spkr. house del. 1992-96, del. to ADA 1992-96, bd. dirs. 1992-96), Mpls. Dist. Dental Soc. (program chairperson 1978-79, peer rev. com. 1988-92, bd. dirs. 1979-80, 87-89, MDA del. 1989-92), Minn. Acad. Restorative Dentistry (pres. 1979-80), Minn. Acad. Gnathological Rsch. (pres. 1986-87), Am. Assn. Dental Schs. (chairperson operative dentistry sect. 1984-85, edit. rev. bd. 1984-88), Acad. Operative Dentistry (exec. council 1978-81, rsch. com. 1987-89), Am. Acad. Gold Foil Operators, Northfield C. of C. (treas. and chairperson 1968-70), Delta Sigma Delta, Omicron Kappa Upsilon (Theta chpt.). Lodges: Rotary (pres. Northfield 1972-73). Personal E-mail: RAGeist@comcast.net.

GELBER, DON JEFFREY, lawyer; b. LA, Mar. 10, 1940; s. Oscar and Betty Sheila (Chernitsky) G.; m. Jessica Jeasun Song, May 15, 1967; children: Victoria, Jonathan, Rebecca, Robert. Student UCLA, 1957-58, Reed Coll., 1958-59; AB, Stanford U., 1961, JD, 1963. Bar: Calif. 1964, Hawaii 1964, US Dist. Ct. (cen. and no. dists. Calif.) 1964, US Dist. Ct. Hawaii 1964, US Ct. Appeals (9th cir.) 1964, US Supreme Ct. 1991. Assoc. Greenstein, Yamane & Cowan, Honolulu, 1964-67; reporter Penal Law Revision Project, Hawaii Jud. Council, Honolulu, 1967-69; assoc. H. William Burgess, Honolulu, 1969-72; ptnr. Burgess & Gelber, Honolulu, 1972-73; prin. Law Offices of Don Jeffrey Gelber, Honolulu, 1974-77; pres. Gelber, Gelber & Ingersoll, 1978-; legal counsel Hawaii State Senate Judiciary Com., 1965; adminstrv. asst. to majority floor leader Hawaii State Senate, 1966, legal counsel Edn. Com., 1967, 68; majority counsel Hawaii Ho. of Reps., 1974; spl. counsel Hawaii State Senate, 1983. Contbr. articles to legal publs. Mem. State Bar Calif., ABA (sect. bus. law), Fed. Bar Assn., Am. Bankruptcy Inst., Hawaii State Bar Assn. (sect. bankruptcy law, bd. dirs. 1991-93, pres. 1993). Clubs: Pacific, Plaza (Honolulu). Office: Gelber Gelber and Ingersoll 745 Fort Street Mall Ste 1400 Honolulu HI 96813-3877 Office Phone: 808-524-0155.

GELFAND, HOWARD MICHAEL, history professor; b. New Brunswick, NJ, Dec. 20, 1967; s. Elayne Phyllis and Gerald Gelfand. AB, U. Ga., Athens, 1989, MA, 1994, U. Ky., Lexington, 1991; PhD, U. Ariz., Tucson, 2002. Prof. U. Ariz. Hist. Dept., Tucson, 2001—05, Ariz. State U. Hist. Dept., Tempe, Ariz., 2003; prof. hist. and interdisciplinary liberal studies James Madison U. Hist. Dept., Harrisonburg, Va., 2005—. Analyst U. S. Air Force Air Combat Command, Hampton, Va., 1995—2000; advisor U. of Ariz. Delta Tau Delta Frat., Tucson, 1994—2006, James Madison U. Frat., Sorority Life Adv. Com., Harrisonburg, Va., 2005—06, James Madison U. Sigma Chi Frat., 2006—. Author: (book) Seachange At Annapolis: The United States Naval Academy, 1949-2000. Recipient Faculty Excellence in Tchg. award, U. Ariz., 2004, Outstanding Tchg. award, U. Ariz. Found., 2002. Mem.: Pi Kappa Phi (advisor 2008—), Sigma Chi (advisor 2006—07). Jewish. Avocations: surfing, swimming, skateboarding, weightlifting. Office: James Madison U Dept Hist 210 Jackson Hall Harrisonburg VA 22807 Personal E-mail: hgelfand@hotmail.com. Business E-Mail: gelfanhm@jmu.edu.

GELLER, GLENN, broadcast executive; b. Jan. 24, 1972; MA, Northwestern U. Exec. drama dept. 20th Century Fox TV, 1999; with CBS Paramount Network TV, LA, 2001—, v.p. current programming, 2004—06, sr. v.p. current programming, 2006—. Achievements include working on such shows as Judging Amy, Joan of Arcadia and CSI:Crime Scene Investigation.

GELLER, KENNETH ALLEN, otolaryngologist; b. Bklyn., Feb. 5, 1948; MD, U. So. Calif., 1972. Cert. in otolaryngology. Intern L.A. County-U. So. Calif. Med. Ctr., LA, 1972-73; resident in gen. surgery Wadsworth VA Hosp., LA, 1973-75; resident in otolaryngology UCLA Health Scis. Ctr., LA, 1975-78; active Childrens Hosp., LA, 1978—; courtesy Huntington Meml. Hosp., 1993—. Assoc. clin. prof. U. So. Calif. Mem. ACS, Am. Acad. Otolaryngology-Head and Neck Surgery, Am. Acad. Pediatrics, Am. Bronco-Esophagological Assn., Am. Soc. Pediat. Otolaryngology. Office: Childrens Hosp Divsn Otolaryngology # 58 4650 Sunset Blvd Los Angeles CA 90027-6062 Office Phone: 323-361-2145. E-mail: kgeller@chla.usc.edu.

GELLER, STEPHEN ARTHUR, pathologist, educator; b. Bklyn., Apr. 26, 1939; s. Sam John and Alice (Podber) G.; m. Kate Eleanor DeJong, June 24, 1962; children: David Phillip, Jennifer Lee. BA, Bklyn. Coll., 1959; MD, Howard U., 1964. Diplomate Am. Bd. Pathology, Nat. Bd. Med. Examiners. Intern Lenox Hill Hosp., NYC, 1964-65; resident in pathology Mt. Sinai Hosp., NYC, 1965-69; chief lab. Naval Hosp., Beaufort, SC, 1969-71; asst. prof. pathology Mt. Sinai Med. Ctr., NYC, 1971-75, assoc. prof., 1975-78, prof., 1978-84; chmn. dept. pathology Cedars-Sinai Med. Ctr., LA, 1984—2006, chmn. emeritus Dept. Pathology, 2006—; prof. pathology UCLA, 1984—. Co-author: Histopathology, 1989, Biopsy Interpretation of the Liver, 2004; contbr. articles to profl. jours. Recipient Excellence in Teaching award CUNY, 1974, Golden Apple tchg. award Cedars-Sinai Med. Ctr., 1986, 2000, 02, 04, 05. Fellow Coll. Am. Pathologists, Am. Soc. Clin. Pathologists; mem. Am. Assn. Study of Liver Diseases, Hans Popper Hepatopathology Soc., Calif. Soc. Pathologists (sec. 1989-91, v.p. 1991-93, pres. 1994-96), L.A. Soc. Pathologists (v.p. 1989-91, pres. 1992), N.Y. Pathol. Soc., Alpha Omega Alpha. Democrat. Jewish. Avocations: music, photography, writing fiction. Office: Cedars Sinai Med Ctr 8700 Beverly Blvd Los Angeles CA 90048-1865 Office Phone: 310-423-6632. Business E-Mail: geller@cshs.org.

GELLERT, JAY M., health and medical products executive; b. Mar. 13, 1954; BA, Stanford U., 1975. Dir. health services, County of San Mateo Calif. Dept. of Health Services; sr. v.p., COO Calif. Healthcare System, 1985-88; pres., CEO Bay Pacific Health Corp., 1988-91; dir. strategic advisory engagements Shattuck Hammond Ptnrs. Inc.; pres., COO Health Systems Internat. Inc. (merged with Found. Health. Corp. in 1996), 1996—97, Health Net, Inc. (formerly Found. Health Systems), 1997—98; pres., CEO Health Net, Inc., 1998—, bd. dirs., 1999—. Chmn., admin. simplification com. Coun. Affordable Quality Healthcare; bd. dirs. Am. Assoc. Health Plans, MedUnite, Inc., Miavita, Inc. Office: Health Net Life Insurance Co 21281 Burbank Blvd Woodland Hills CA 91367-6607

GELLIN, GERALD ALAN, dermatologist; b. Bklyn., May 24, 1934; m. Lucille E. Gellin. AB, U. Pa., 1954; MD, NYU, 1958. Diplomate Am. Bd. Dermatology. Chief sect. dermatology VA Hosp., Bklyn., 1964-67; clin. prof. U. Calif. Med. Ctr., San Francisco, 1969—. Chief dermatology divsn. VA Hosp., Bklyn., 1963-67, San Francisco Gen. Hosp., 1969-73, Calif. Pacific Med. Ctr., 1986—2003. Contbr. articles to profl. jours. With USPHS, 1967-69. Fellow ACP. Office: 3838 California St San Francisco CA 94118-1522 Office Phone: 415-668-2400.

GELL-MANN, MURRAY, theoretical physicist, educator; b. NYC, Sept. 15, 1929; s. Arthur and Pauline (Reichstein) Gell-Mann; m. J. Margaret Dow, Apr. 19, 1955 (dec. 1981); children: Elizabeth Sarah, Nicholas Webster. BS in Physics, Yale U., 1948; PhD in Physics, MIT, 1951; ScD (hon.), Yale U., 1959, U. Chgo., 1967, U. Ill., 1968, Wesleyan U., 1968, U. Turin, Italy, 1969, U. Utah, 1970, Columbia U., 1977, Cambridge U., 1980, Oxford U., Eng., 1992, So. Ill. U., 1993; ScD in Natural Resources (hon.), U. Fla., 1994; ScD (hon.), So. Meth. U., 1999. Mem. Inst. for Advanced Study, Princeton, NJ, 1951, 1955, 1967—68; instr. U. Chgo., 1952—53, asst. prof., 1953—54, assoc. prof., 1954, prof., 1956; assoc. prof. Calif. Inst. Tech., Pasadena, 1955—56, prof., 1956—67, Robert Andrews Millikan prof. physics, 1967—93, Robert Andrews Millikan prof. emeritus, 1993—; co-chmn. sci. bd. Santa Fe Inst., 1985-2000, visitor, 1992—93, disting. fellow, 1993—. Vis. prof. MIT, 1963, CERN, Geneva, 1971—72, Geneva, 1979—80, U. N.Mex., 1995—; vis. assoc. prof. Columbia U., 1954; overseas fellow Churchill Coll., 1966; mem. Pres.'s Sci. Adv. Com., 1969—72, Pres.'s Coun. of Advisors on Sci. and Tech., 1994—2001; mem. sci. and grants com. Leakey Found., 1976—88, mem. sci. adv. com., 1988—; chmn. bd. trustees Aspen Ctr. for Physics, 1973—79; founding mem. Santa Fe Inst., 1982, bd. trustee, 1984—, chmn. bd. dir., 1984—85, co-chmn. sci. bd., 1985—2000, prof. and disting. fellow, 1993—, prof., disting. fellow, 1993—; cons. Inst. Def. Analysis, Arlington, Va., 1961—70, Rand Corp., Santa Monica, Calif., 1956; mem. physics panel NASA, 1964, Coun. Fgn. Rels., 1975—, Los Alamos Sci. Lab., N.Mex., 1956—, visitor, N.Mex., 1975, 1992—93, Lab. fellow, N.Mex., 1982—; mem. adv. bd. Network Physics, 1999—; fel. Com. for the Scientific Investigation of Claims of the Paranormal, 1985—. Author (with Y. Ne'eman): Eightfold Way, 1964; author: The Quark and the Jaguar: Adventures in the Simple and the Complex, 1994; author: (with S. Lloyd) Entropy: Interdisciplinary Applications, 2004. Citizen regent Smithsonian Instn., 1974—88; trustee Wildlife Conservation Soc., 1994—; dir. J.D. and C.T. MacArthur Found., 1979—2002, chmn., World Environ. & Resources Com., 1982—97; bd. dirs. Calif. Nature Conservancy, 1984—93, Aero Vironment, Inc., 1971—, So. Calif. Skeptics, 1985—91, Lovelace Insts., 1993—95; mem. sci. adv. com. Conservation Internat., 1993—. Recipient E. O. Lawrence Meml. award, AEC, 1966, Franklin medal, Franklin Inst. Phila., 1967, Rsch. Corp. award, 1969, Nobel prize in Physics, 1969, Ellis Island Family Heritage award in Sci., Statue of Liberty-Ellis Island Found., Inc., 2005, Albert Einstein medal, Albert Einstein Soc., 2005; co-recipient Erice "Science For Peace" prize, 1989; named to UN Environ. Program Roll of Honor for Environ. Achievement, 1988; fellow NSF postdoctoral, vis. prof., Coll. de France and U. Paris, 1959—60. Fellow: Am. Acad. Arts and Scis. (v.p. 1970—76, chmn. We. ctr. 1970—76), Am. Phys. Soc. (Dannie Heineman prize 1959); mem.: AAAS, NAS (John J. Carty medal 1968), Irish Acad. Scis., Russian Acad. Scis. (fgn. 1993—), Indian Acad. Scis. (fgn. 1985—), Pakistan Acad. Scis. (fgn. 1985—), French Phys. Soc. (hon.), Royal Soc. London (fgn. 1975—), Conservation Internat. (sci. adv. com. 1993), Am. Philos. Soc., Coun. on Fgn. Rels., Athenaeum, Century Assn., Cosmos Club, NY Explorers Club, Phi Beta Kappa, Sigma Xi (Procter Sci. Achievement prize 2004). Achievements include contributions and discoveries concerning the classification of elementary particles and their interactions. Address: Santa Fe Institute 1399 Hyde Park Rd Santa Fe NM 87501 Office Phone: 505-984-8800. Office Fax: 505-982-0565. E-mail: mgm@santafe.edu.

GELPI, ALBERT JOSEPH, language educator, department chairman, critic; b. New Orleans, July 19, 1931; s. Albert Joseph and Alice Marie (Delaup) G.; m. Barbara Charlesworth, June 14, 1965; children: Christopher Francis Cecil, Adrienne Catherine Ardelle. AB, Loyola U., New Orleans, 1951; MA, Tulane U., 1956; PhD, Harvard U., 1962. Asst. prof. Harvard U., 1962-68; assoc. prof. Stanford U., 1968-74, prof. Am. lit., 1974-99, Wm. Robertson Coe prof. Am. lit., 1978-99, Coe prof. emeritus, 1999—, chmn. Am. studies program, 1980-83, 94-97, asso. dean grad. study and research, 1980-85, chmn. English dept., 1985-88. Author: Emily Dickinson: The Mind of the Poet, 1965, The Tenth Muse: The Psyche of the American Poet, 1975, A Coherent Splendor: The American Poetic Renaissance 1910-1950, 1987; editor: The Poet in America: 1650 to the Present, 1974, (with Barbara Charlesworth Gelpi) Adrienne Rich's Poetry, 1975, Wallace Stevens: The Poetics of Modernism, 1985, (with Barbara Charlesworth Gelpi) Adrienne Rich's Poetry and Prose, 1993, Denise Levertov: Selected Criticism, 1993, The Blood of the Poet: Selected Poems of William Everson, 1994; editor Cambridge Studies in American Literature and Culture, 1981-91, Living in Time: The Poetry of C. Day Lewis, 1998, The Wild God of the World: An Anthology of Robinson Jeffers, 2003, Wild God of Eros: A William Everson Reader, 2003, (with Robert J. Bertholf) The Letters of Robert Duncan and Denise Levertov, 2004, Robert Duncan and Denise Levertov: The Poetry of Politics, The Politics of Poetry, 2006. Served with U.S. Army, 1951-53. Guggenheim fellow, 1977-78 Mem. MLA, Am. Lit. Assn. Democrat. Roman Catholic. Home: 870 Tolman Dr Palo Alto CA 94305-1026 Office: Stanford U Dept English Stanford CA 94305

GELWIX, MAX D., chemical company executive; BS, Colo. State U. Exec. v.p. Arthur J. Gallagher & Co., 1979-96; pres. Maxell Enterprises, 1996-97; v.p. Eco Soil Sys., Inc., San Diego, 1998-00, pres., COO, 2000—. Office: Eco Soil Sys Inc PO Box 7740 Burbank CA 91510-7740

GEMELLO, JOHN MICHAEL, economics professor, consultant, academic administrator; b. Palo Alto, Calif., Feb. 3, 1946; s. Mario John and Kathryn Marie (Volarvich) G.; m. Linda Marino, Sept. 17, 1966; children: Matthew, Gina. BA, U. Santa Clara, 1967; PhD, Stanford U., 1975. Asst. prof. econs. U. Toronto, Ont., Canada, 1972—75, San Francisco State U., 1976—82, assoc. prof., 1982—86, prof., 1986—90, chmn. dept. econs., 1986—90, assoc. v.p. for acad. resources, 1990—2002, interim v.p., acad. affairs, 2002—03, provost, v.p. academic affairs, 2003—. Cons. Calif. State Teaching Commn. on Teaching Profession, 1985, Inst. Rsch. on Ednl. Fin. and Governance, Stanford U., 1981-82. Mem. planning commn. City of Millbrae, Calif., 1979-83. Capt. USAR, 1973-75. Mem. Am. Econ. Assn., Western Econ. Assn., Western Regional Sci. Assn. Democrat. Roman Catholic. Office: San Francisco State U 1600 Holloway Ave San Francisco CA 94132-1722 Home Phone: 650-342-4170; Office Phone: 415-338-1141. E-mail: jgemello@sfsu.edu.

GENGA, JOHN MICHAEL, lawyer; b. Detroit, Apr. 28, 1962; BA, Stanford U., 1983; JD, U. Mich., 1986. Bar: Calif. 1986, U.S. Dist. Ct. (ctrl. and ea. dists.) Calif. 1987, U.S. Dist. Ct. (no. and so. dists.) Calif. 1988, U.S. Ct. Appeals (9th cir.) 1988, U.S. Supreme Ct. 1993, U.S. Ct. Appeals (10th cir.) 1997. Assoc. Jones, Day, Reavis & Pogue, LA, 1986-88, Hill Wynne Troop & Meisinger, LA, 1988-93; ptnr. Troop Steuber Pasich Reddick & Tobey, LLP, LA, 1994—2000, Paul, Hastings, Janofsky & Walker LLP, San Francisco, chmn. entertainment practice group; founder, owner Genga & Assocs., Encino, 2004—. Mem. ABA, State Bar Calif., L.A. County Bar Assn. Office: Genga Associates Pc 15260 Ventura Blvd Ste 200 Sherman Oaks CA 91403-5325 Office Phone: 818-444-4580. Business E-Mail: jgenga@gengalaw.com.

GENGLER, SUE WONG, health educator, consultant, speaker, trainer; b. Hong Kong, Apr. 6, 1959; came to U.S., 1966; d. Tin Ho and Yuet Kum (Chan) Wong; m. Clayton J. Gengler, 1995. BS, UCLA, 1981; MPH, Loma Linda U., Calif., 1990; DrPH, Loma Linda U., 1995. Cert. health edn. specialist. Asst. to the dir. Project Asia Campus Crusade for Christ, San Bernardino, Calif., 1982-83, Campus Crusade for Christ-Internat. Pers., San Bernardino, 1983-90; health educator San Bernardino County Pub. Health, 1990-92; community lab. instr., rsch. asst. dept. health promotion and edn. Loma Linda (Calif.) U. Sch. Pub. Health, 1992-95; behaviorist/educator Anaheim Hills Med. Group/St. Jude Heritage Med. Group, Anaheim, Calif., 1995-96; direct svcs. dir. Alternatives to Domestic Violence, Riverside, Calif., 1997—2001; evaluation cons., domestic violence sect. Maternal and Child Health br. Calif. Dept. Health Svcs., 1999—2001; health edn. mgr. Inland Empire Health Plan, San Bernardino, Calif., 2001—. Mem. Minority Health Coalition, San Bernardino, 1990-92, Com. for the Culturally Diverse, San Bernardino, 1990-92; vol. Am. Cancer Soc.; chair Gt. Am. Smokeout, Inland Empire, 1991; bd. dirs. Family Svcs. Agy., San Bernardino, 1994-96. Selma Andrews scholar Loma Linda U., 1994; named Outstanding Young Woman of Yr., 1983, Hulda Crooke Scholar, Loma Linda U., 1989; recipient Am. Cancer Soc. Rose award, 1991 (Calif.), Gaspar award, 1991 (nat.), Chief's award of Excellence Corona Police Dept. Mem. APHA, Nat. Coun. for Internat. Health, Soc. Pub. Health Edn. Avocations: travel, reading, volleyball, calligraphy, music. Office Phone: 909-890-2039. Business E-Mail: gengler-s@iehp.org.

GENINI, RONALD WALTER, retired history educator; b. Oakland, Calif., Dec. 5, 1946; s. William Angelo and Irma Lea (Gays) G.; m. Roberta Mae Tucker, Dec. 20, 1969; children: Thomas, Justin, Nicholas. BA, U. San Francisco, 1968, MA, 1969. Cert. secondary edn. tchr., Calif.; adminstrv. svcs. credential. Tchr. Ctrl. Unified Sch. Dist., Fresno, Calif., 1970—2004, ret., 2004—. Judge State History Day, Sacramento, 1986-94; mem. U.S. history exam. devel. team Golden State, San Diego, 1989-93; securer placement of state-registered landmarks; guest appearance History Channel program "UFO Hotspots,", Jan. 2003; guest contbr. Time Line Films, 2006. Author: Romualdo Pacheco, 1985, Darn Right It's Butch, 1994, Theda Bara, 1996; editl. asst. The Invincible Quest, 2007; contbr. articles to profl. jours.; cited as authority on Theda Bara by Ency. Brit. Online Am. Women in History, 1999, also on Romualdo Pacheco by Biog. Directory of Am. Congress. Bd. dirs. Fresno Area 6 Neighborhood Coun., 1973-74, Fresno City and County Hist. Soc., 1975-78, St. Anthony's sch. bd., Fresno, 1980-84; active Good Company Players, Fresno, 2000-01. Named one of Outstanding Young Educators Am., Fresno Jaycees, 1978; recipient recognition for Tchr. Cares award Calif. State Assembly and Fresno City Coun., 1996. Mem.: Mt. Vernon Ladies Assn., Calif. Ret. Tchrs. Assn., Smithsonian Inst., Carmel Bach Festival, Utah Shakespeare Festival, San Joaquin Pkwy. and Conservation Trust, Arte de Americas. Independent. Roman Catholic. Avocations: writing history, motion picture scriptwriting, commercial acting. Home: 1486 W Menlo Ave Fresno CA 93711-1305 E-mail: r_genini@yahoo.com.

GENN, NANCY, artist; b. San Francisco; d. Morley P. and Ruth W. Thompson; m. Vernon Chathburton Genn; children: Cynthia, Sarah, Peter. Student, San Francisco Art Inst., U. Calif., Berkeley. Lectr. on art and papermaking Am. Ctrs. in Osaka, Japan, Nagoya, Japan, Kyoto, Japan, 1979-80; guest lectr. various univs. and art mus. in U.S., 1975—; vis. artist Am. Acad. in Rome, 1989, 94, 2001. One-woman shows include, De Young Mus., San Francisco, 1955, 63, Gumps Gallery, San Francisco, 1955, 57, 59, San Francisco Mus. Art, 1961, U. Calif., Santa Cruz, 1966-68, Richmond Art Center, 1970, Calif., Oakland Mus., 1971, Linda/Farris Gallery, Seattle, 1974, 76, 78, 81, LA Inst. Contemporary Art, 1976, Susan Caldwell Gallery, NYC, 1976-77, 79, 81, Nina Freudenheim Gallery, Buffalo, 1977, 81, Annely Juda Fine Art, London, 1978, Inoue Gallery, Tokyo, 1980, Toni Birckhead Gallery, Cin., 1982, Kala Inst. Gallery, Berkeley, Calif., 1983, Ivory/Kimpton Gallery, San Francisco, 1984, 86, Eve Mannes Gallery, Atlanta, 1985, Richard Iri Gallery, LA, 1990, Harcourts Modern and Contemporary Art, San Francisco, 1991, 93, 96, Am. Assn. Advancement of Sci., Washington, 1994, Anne Reed Gallery, Ketchum, Id., 1995, Michael Petronko Gallery, NY, 1997, Mills Coll. Art Mus., Oakland, Calif., 1999, Takada Gallery, San Francisco, 1999-00, 03, Ulivi Gallery, Prato, Italy, 2002, Fresno Art

Mus., Calif., 2003, Bolinas Mus., Calif., 2003, Inst. Italiano di Cultura, Chgo., LA, 2004, Inst. Italiano Di Cultura/Chgo. Art Inst., Flatfile Galleries, Chgo., 2005, Burtan Marinkouich Fine Art, Washington, DC, 2008; group exhbns. include San Francisco Mus. Art, 1971, Aldrich Mus., Ridgefield, Conn., 1972-73, Santa Barbara Mus., Calif., 1974-75, Oakland Mus. Art, 1975, Susan Caldwell, Inc., NYC, 1974-75, Mus. Modern Art, NYC, 1976, traveling exhbn. Arts Coun. Gt. Britain, 1983-84, Inst. Contemporary Arts, Boston, 1977, J.J.Brookings Gallery, San Francisco, 1997, Portland Art Mus., Oreg., 1997—, Takada Gallery, San Francisco, 1999-00, Leighton Glalery, Blue Hill, Maine, 2005; represented in permanent collections Frederick Weisman Art Mus., U. Minn., Mpls., NYC Pub. Lib., Mus. Modern Art, NYC, NY Pub. Libr., Achenback Found., Palace of the Legion of Honour, San Francisco, Albright-Knox Art Gallery, Buffalo, Libr. of Congress, Washington, Nat. Mus. for Am. Art, Washington, LA County Mus. Art, Art Mus. U. Calif., Berkeley, McCrory Corp., NYC, Mus. Art, Auckland, NZ, Aldrich Mus., Ridgefield, Conn., (collection) Bklyn. Mus., (collection) U. Tex., El Paso, Internat. Ctr. Aesthetic Rsch., Torino, Italy, Cin. Art Mus., San Francisco Mus. Modern Art, Oakland Art Mus., LA County Mus., City of San Francisco Hall of Justice, Harris Bank, Chgo., Chase Manhattan Bank, NYC, Modern Art Gallery of Ascoli Piceno, Italy, Mills Coll. Art Mus., Oakland, Calif., Mills Coll. Art, Oakland, Calif., various mfg. cos., also numerous pvt. collections; commd. works include, Bronze lectern and 5 bronze sculptures for chancel table, 1st Unitarian Ch., Berkeley, Calif., 1961, 64, bronze fountain, Cowell Coll., U. Calif., Santa Cruz, bronze menorah, Temple Beth Am, Los Altos Hills, Calif., 17, murals and 2 bronze fountain sculptures, Sterling Vineyards, Calistoga, Calif., fountain sculpture, Expo 1974, Spokane, Wash; vis. artist Am. Acad., Rome, 1989. U.S./Japan Creative Arts fellow, 1978-79; recipient Ellen Branston award, 1952; Phelan award De Young Mus., 1963; honor award HUD, 1968 Home: 1515 La Loma Ave Berkeley CA 94708-2033 Home Phone: 510-848-2891; Office Phone: 510-849-4366.

GENNARO, ANTONIO L., biology professor; b. Raton, N.Mex., Mar. 18, 1934; s. Paul and Mary Lou (Gasperetti) G.; m. Virginia Marie Sullivan, May 15, 1955 (div. 1979); children: Theresa Ann, Carrie Marie, Janelle Elizabeth; m. Marjorie Lou Cox, Sept. 27, 1980. BS, N.Mex. State U., 1957, MS, 1961, PhD, 1965. Tchr. biology Las Cruces (N.Mex.) H.S., 1957-58; asst. prof. biology St. John's U., Collegeville, Minn., 1964-65; prof. biology Eastern N.Mex. U., Portales, 1965—. Bd. trustees N.Mex. Mus. Natural History, 1996—. Served to capt. U.S. Army, 1958-59; USAR, 1959-66. Recipient presdl. faculty award Eastern N.Mex. U., 1970, pres.'s faculty award for excellence in rsch., 1988, spirit of east award, 1995, outstanding sci. award N.Mex. Acad. Sci., 1975, disting. faculty emeritus, 1998. Mem. Southwestern Naturalists (treas. 1974-78), Am. Soc. Mammalogists, Herpetologists League, Sigma Xi, Phi Kappa Phi (pres. 1970-74).

GENRICH, MARK L., corporate communications director; b. Buffalo, Aug. 28, 1943; m. Allison Forbes, 1967; children: Audrey, Liza, Colby. BA, Bucknell U., 1966. Editl. writer Palladium-Item, Richmond, Ind., 1970; writing exec. Bruce Eberle & Assocs., Inc., Vienna, Va., 1975-77; dep. editor editl. pgs. Phoenix Gazette, 1977-96; editl. writer, columnist The Ariz. Republic, Phoenix, 1996-98; dir. Warne Ctr. Goldwater Inst., Phoenix, 1998-2000; pub. rels. dir. Qwest Comm. Internat., Inc., 2000—02; dir. Ariz. Affairs, 2002—, U. Club. Ariz. Voice Crime Victims, 2006—. Participant U.S. Army War Coll., Carlisle, Pa., U.S. Naval War Coll., Newport, R.I.; participant arms control, disarmament programs including Space & Arms talks, Geneva; chmn. New Tech. Com., Journalism in Edn. Com.; mem. various coms. Creator, host cable TV program focus on polit. figures; regional editor The Masthead. Grantee European Cmty. Visitor Programme, 1993; recipient highest honors editl. writing, newspaper design Ariz., Western Region; highest honor Maricopa County Bar Assn.; Hoover Inst. media fellow, 1985. Mem. Nat. Conf. Editl. Writers (bd. dirs., included vol. Editl. Excellence), First Amendment Cong. (bd. dirs.), Soc. Profl. Journalists/Sigma Delta Chi, ABA (com. prisons, sentencing). Home: 130 W Pine Valley Dr Phoenix AZ 85023-5283 Office: Qwest Comm Internat Inc 4041 N Central Ave 11th Fl Phoenix AZ 85012

GENSLER, M. ARTHUR, JR., architect; b. NYC, July 12, 1935; s. M. Arthur and Gertrude (Wilson) G.; m. Drucilla Cortell, Sept. 7, 1957; children— David, Robert, Kenneth, Douglas BA in Architecture, Cornell U., 1957. Lic. architect, 38 states. Jr. designer Shreve, Lamb & Harmon, NYC, 1958-59; project mgr. Norman & Dawbarn, Kingston, Jamaica, 1959-60, Albert Sigal & Assocs., NYC and San Francisco, 1961-63, Wurster, Bernardi & Emmons, San Francisco, 1963-65; pres., founder Gensler & Assocs., Architects, San Francisco, 1966—, now chmn. Mem. adv. council, mem. bldgs. and properties com. Coll. Architecture, Cornell U., Ithaca, N.Y., 1981-83. Co-author: A Rational Approach to Office Planning. Bd. dirs. World Coll. West, Petaluma, Calif., 1984-87; bd. overseers U. Calif., San Francisco; trustee World Affairs Coun., 1990—. Wity C.E., U.S. Army, 1958. Recipient Charles Goodwin Sands award Cornell U. Coll. Architecture, 1958; named charter mem. Interior Design mag. Hall of Fame, Cornell Enterpeneurs of Yr., 1995. Fellow AIA, Internat. Interior Design Assn.; mem. Inst. Bus. Designers (Star award 1992), San Francisco Planning and Urban Rsch. Assn., Bldg. Mgrs. and Owners Assn., Bay Area Coun., Urban Land Inst., San Francisco C. of C. (bd. dirs. 1984-86, 94—), Bohemian Club, Univ. Club, Bankers Club, Presidio Club. Republican. Congregationalist. Office: 2 Harrison St Ste 400 San Francisco CA 94105

GENTILE, DOMINIC P., lawyer; b. Chgo., Mar. 25, 1946; BS, DePaul U., 1968, JD, 1972. Bar: Ill. 1972, U.S. Supreme Ct. 1975, Nev. 1979. Pvt. practice Dominic P. Gentile, Ltd., Las Vegas. Adj. prof. law U. Nev., Las Vegas, mem. law sch. adv. com.; assoc. dean. nat. coll. criminal def. U. Houston, 1977—78; with faculty Yeshiva U.; guest faculty Harvard Law Sch., Cambridge, Mass.; spkr. in field. Author: various publications. Mem.: First Amendment Lawyers Assn., Libel Def. Resource Ctr., Nat. Assn. Criminal Def. Lawyers, Ill. State Bar Assn., State Bar Nev. (mem. bd. govs. 1991—96). Office: Dominic P Gentile Ltd 3960 Howard Hughes Pky Las Vegas NV 89109 Office Phone: 702-386-0066. Office Fax: 702-382-9309.

GENTILE, JOSEPH F., lawyer, educator; b. San Pedro, Calif., Jan. 15, 1934; s. Ernest B. and Icy Otie (Martin) Gentile; children: Kim Yvonne, Kevin James, Kelly Michele, Kristien Elyse, Kerri Nicole. BA cum laude, San Jose State U., 1955; JD, San Fernando Valley U., 1966; cert. in indsl. rels., UCLA, 1959; teaching credential, Calif. C.C., 1972; M.Pub. Adminstrn., U. So. Calif., 1976. Bar: Calif. 1967, U.S. Supreme Ct. 1972. Mem. indsl. relations staff Kaiser Steel Corp., Fontana Works, 1957-62; labor relations counsel Calif. Trucking Assn., Burlingame, Calif., 1964-68; acting dir. indsl. relations, labor relations counsel McDonnell Douglas Corp., Santa Monica, Calif., 1968-70; sr. partner Nelson, Kirshman, Goldstein, Gentile & Rexon, Los Angeles, 1970-76; individual practice, 1976—. Arbitration panel Fed. Mediation and Conciliation Svc., Calif. Counciliation Service; instr. bus. econs., indsl. rels. U. Calif. Ext., 1969-94, personnel and indsl. rels. San Bernardino Valley Coll., 1960-62, transp. Mt. San Antonio Coll., 1972-74; lectr. Loyola U., 1973-74, U. So. Calif., 1976-80; adj. prof. law Pepperdine U., 1981-2001; chmn. employee rels. commn. LA (Calif.) County, 1979—; employee rels. bd. City of LA, 2001—. Contbr. articles to profl. jours. Served with AUS, 1955-57. Mem. ABA, Calif. Bar Assn., Los Angeles County Bar Assn. (past chmn. exec. com. labor law sect.), Am. Arbitration Assn. (chmn. regional adv. coun., arbitration panel, nat. bd. dirs. 1985-91), Phi Sigma Alpha, Phi Alpha Delta. Office: PO Box 7418 Thousand Oaks CA 91359-7418 Office Phone: 805-499-4282.

GENTILE, LIZ, state legislator; b. Detroit, Jan. 2, 1958; m to Zachary Gentile; children: Christie & Patrick. Candidate for State Representative, District 36, 2000; Wyoming State Representative, District 36, 2002-04, 2007-, member, education, management audit comts.Acct manager, KGWC-TV, Casper, Wyoming, 1999-2000, KTWO-TV, Casper, 2000-. Democrat. Office Phone: 307-473-9062. E-mail: wotbca@vcn.com.

GENTRY, ALVIN, professional basketball coach; b. Nov. 5, 1954; m. Suzanne Gentry; children: Ryan Marcus, Matthew Jackson, Alexis. BA in Mgmt., Appalachian State U., Boone, NC, 1977. Asst. coach U. Colo. Buffaloes, 1977—78, 1981—85, Baylor U. Bears, 1980—81, U. Kans. Jayhawks, 1985—88, San Antonio Spurs, 1988—90, LA Clippers, 1990—91, head coach, 2000—03; asst. coach Miami Heat, 1991—95, interim head coach, 1995; asst. coach Detroit Pistons, 1995—97, interim head coach, 1997—98, head coach, 1998—99; asst. coach New Orleans Hornets, 2003—04, Phoenix Suns, 2004—09, interim head coach, 2009—. Asst. coach USA Basketball Men's Sr. Nat. Team, 2006. Office: Phoenix Suns 201 E Jefferson St Phoenix AZ 85004*

GENTRY, DONALD WILLIAM, engineering executive, mining engineer; b. St. Louis, Jan. 18, 1943; s. William Henry and Roberta Elizabeth (Bardelmeier) G.; m. Sheila Carol Schuepbach, Aug. 21, 1965; children: Tara Cassandre, Chad Ryan. BSE., U. Ill., 1965; MS, U. Nev., 1967; PhD, U. Ariz., 1972, DEng (hon.), 2002. From asst. prof. mining engrng. to prof. Colo. Sch. Mines, Golden, 1972—78, prof. mining engrng., 1978—2003, dean undergrad. studies, 1983—90, dean engrng. and undergrad. studies, 2001, head dept. mining engrng., 1995-98; pres., CEO Terra Nova Resources, Golden, 1990—2004; pres., CEO, bd. dirs. PolyMet Mining Corp., Golden, 1998—2003. Bd. dirs. Gryphon Gold Corp., 2005—, Constellation Copper Corp., 2006—. Contbr. articles to profl. jours. Mem. Soc. Mining Engrs. of AIME (pres. 1993), AIME (dir. Colo. sect. 1982-83, Krumb lectr. 1987, pres. 1996, Mineral Industry Edn. award 1991, Daniel C. Jackling award 1998), Nat. Acad. Engrng. (elected 1996). Republican. Lutheran. Personal E-mail: dwgentry@cox.net.

GENTRY, JAMES ROBERT, education educator; b. Evanston, Ill., Nov. 15, 1945; s. Lonnie W Gentry and Goldie Lee Brumback-Gentry; m. Barbara June Wolfer, Nov. 29, 1968; children: Robin June Angemi, Dale James. AA in social sci., Citrus Coll., 1964; BS in social sci., Calif. State Poly. U., 1966; MA in hist., Calif. State U. at LA, 1968; PhD in hist., U. of Utah, 1985. Instr. of history Cascade Coll., Portland, Oreg., 1968—69; prof. of history Coll. of So. Idaho, 1969—, chmn. social sci. dept., 1997—. Contbr. articles to jours. Mem. Twin Falls County Hist. Preservation Commn., Idaho, 1987—2007. Mem.: Am. Hist. Assn. (corr.), Phi Alpha Theta (corr.). Am. Bapt. Achievements include assisting in development and implementation of a J.A. & Kathryn Albertson grant under the Recreating Idaho colleges and schools of education initiative. Avocations: walking, movies, reading, canoeing. Home: 675 Alturas Dr N Twin Falls ID 83301-4334 Office: College Of Southern Idaho 315 Falls Ave Twin Falls ID 83301 Business E-Mail: jgentry@csi.edu.

GEOFFRION, ARTHUR MINOT, management scientist; b. NYC, Sept. 19, 1937; s. Arthur Joseph and Dorothy Arline (Senter) Geoffrion; m. Helen Mathilda Hamer, Dec. 22, 1962; children: Susan, Deborah. BME, Cornell U., 1960, M in Indsl. Engring., 1961; PhD, Stanford U., 1965; Dr.rer.pol. in Econ. and Social Scis. honoris causa, RWTH Aachen U., 2005. Asst. prof. in ops.rsch. UCLA, 1965-67, assoc. prof., 1968-70, prof. Grad. Sch. Mgmt., 1971-97; chair in mgmt. James A. Collins, 1998—. Bd. dirs. Insight, Inc. Author: Perspectives on Optimization, 1972; contbr. chapters to books, articles to profl. jours. Recipient Sys. Sci. prize, NATO, 1976, Harold Larnder Meml. prize, Can. Operational Rsch. Soc., 2002; fellow, Internat. Acad. Mgmt., 1996; Faculty Rsch. fellow, Ford Found., 1967—68, Rsch. grantee, 1969—72, NSF, 1968—91, Office Naval Rsch., 1972—90. Mem.: NAE, Inst. Ops. Rsch. and Mgmt. Scis. (pres. 1997, George E. Kimball medal 2000, fellow 2002), Ops. Rsch. Soc. Am., Inst. Mgmt. Scis. (pres. 1981—82, Disting. Svc. medal 1992), Omega Rho (hon.). Achievements include research in optimization theory (parametric concave programming, integer programming, multicriterion optimation, large-scale, decompostion, duality theory); optimization applications to logistics, production, finance; aggregation; foundations of modeling; analytical methods for e-business. Home: 322 24th St Santa Monica CA 90402-2518 Office: The UCLA Anderson Sch Mgmt Box 951481 Los Angeles CA 90095-1481

GEORGE, AUBREY WESTMORELAND, library director; b. Marshall, Tex., May 20, 1950; BA, Stephen F. Austin U., 1972, MA in Polit. Sci., 1974; MLS, N. Tex. State U., 1975. Asst. dir. Corpus Christi (Tex.) Pub. Libr., 1975-91; mgr. pub. svc. Spokane (Wash.) Pub. Libr., 1991-96, dep. dir., 1996, dir., 1996—. Mem. Am. Libr. Assn., Wash. Libr. Assn. Office: Spokane Pub Libr 906 W Main Ave Spokane WA 99201-0976

GEORGE, DILEEP, electrical engineer; BEE, Indian Inst. Tech., Bombay; MEE, Stanford U., PhD in Elec. Engring. Prin. engr. in several communications related start-up companies; grad. rsch. fellow Redwood Neuroscience Inst., 2003; co-founder, prin. architect Numenta, Inc., Menlo Park, Calif., 2005—. Achievements include patents pending in field; Numenta Inc. is creating a new pattern recognition software called Hierarchical Temporal Memory modeled on the human brain's neocortex. Office: Numenta Inc 1010 El Camino Real Ste 380 Menlo Park CA 94025 Office Phone: 650-321-8282. Office Fax: 650-321-8585.

GEORGE, DONALD WARNER, online columnist and editor, freelance writer; b. Middlebury, Conn., June 24, 1953; s. Lloyd Foster and Vivian (Minor) G.; m. Kuniko Ninomiya, Apr. 24, 1982; children: Jennifer Ayako, Jeremy Naoki. BA, Princeton U., 1975; MA, Hollins Coll., Va., 1977. Tchg. fellow Athens (Greece) Coll., 1975-76, Internat. Christian U., Tokyo, 1977-79; TV talk show host Japan Broadcasting Corp., Tokyo, 1977-79; freelance writer, 1980-81; travel writer San Francisco Examiner, 1981-82, sr. editor Calif. Living mag., 1982-85, sr. editor Image mag., 1985-87, travel editor, 1987-95; cyber columnist, Global Network Navigator American Online, Berkeley, Calif., 1995-96; editor Salon Wanderlust Online Travel Mag., 1997-2000; global travel editor Lonely Planet Publs., 2001—. Editor: Wanderlust: Real-Life Tales of Adventure and Romance, 2000, A House Somewhere: Tales of Life Abroad, 2002, The Kindness of Strangers, 2003 (Best Travel Book of 2003, Ind. Publishers Assn., Bronze Medal in best travel book competition, Soc. Am.Travel Writers, 2003), By the Seat of My Pants: Humorous Tales of Travel & Misadventure, 2005; co-author (with Amy Greimann Carlson): Travelers' Tales: Japan, 2005. Recipient gold award Pacific Asia Travel Assn., 1987-94, 2001. Mem. Soc. Am. Travel Writers (Lowell Thomas award 1987-94, 2002). Office: Lonely Planet 150 Linden St Oakland CA 94607 E-mail: dgeorge@lonelyplanet.com.

GEORGE, GARY, state legislator; b. Dos Palos, Calif., Nov. 17, 1943; m to Kathy; children: five. Oregon State Senator, District 2, 1997-2002, chairman, Agriculture & Natural Resources Committee, formerly, member, Education, Transportation, Water & Land Use & Ways & Means Subcomt on Agriculture & Natural Resources, currently, Oregon State Senate; Oregon State Senator, District 12, 2003-.Farmer, currently. Republican. Office: 900 Court St NE, S-214 Salem OR 97301 E-mail: sen.garygeorge@state.or.us.

GEORGE, GRANT, computer software company executive; BA in German & bus. adminstrn., Calif. State U., Fullerton. Test engr., test mgr. Tandem Computers; prin., owner Coop. Solutions Inc.; test engr. Taligent; with Microsoft Corp., Redmond, Wash., 1994—, test mgr. office product unit, corp. v.p. testing & ops., Windows Experience group, 2006—. Office: One Microsoft Way Redmond WA 98052-6399

GEORGE, KATTUNILATHU OOMMEN, physician, educator; Diploma in Medicine and Surgery, C.H. Med. Coll. and Hosp., 1965; Bachelor of Medicine and Surgery, Coun. Homoeopathic Medicine West Bengal, India, 1975; MSW, Am. Christian Theol. Sem., 1980; M in Marriage, Family and Child Counseling, Calif. Christian Inst., 1982; grad., Acupuncture Acad. Oriental Medicine, Fla., 1983; Diploma in Acupuncture, Acupuncture Rsch. Inst., LA, 1986. Resident Hahnemann Mission Hosp., Quilon, Kerala, India, 1965-67, med. officer, 1965-67; chief med. examiner pharmacology, clin. medicine and pharmacy Travancore-Cochin Med. Coun. Homoeopathic Medicine, Kerala, 1967-76; chief med. officer Fellowship Hosp., India; chief med. officer, dir. Fellowship Clinic and Pharm., India; resident Pub. Health Ctr., LA, 1978-80, Family Svcs. Am., Tustin, Calif., 1979-80; practicing homoeopathic physician; founding pres., dean, dir., prof. homoeopathic medicine with health scis. Samuel Hahnemann Sch. Homoeopathic Medicine, L.A. Internat. U., 1983—; pres. Hahnemannian Rsch. Ctr., Inc., Irvine, Calif., 1985—. Nutrition cons. Biochemical Analysis Clinic, 1978-80, Shaw Health Ctr., 1982—; instr. homoeopathic medicine Calif. Acupuncture Coll., Westwood, 1979-80; counselor, cons. New Hope Counseling Ctr., Garden Grove, Calif., 1980-81; mem. faculty coll. acupuncture L.A. U., 1980-81, Western U., Phoenix, 1982, grad. sch. Calif. Christian Inst., 1982-87; cons. Indsl. Med. Clinic and Potner's Med. Group, L.A., 1981-88; instr., bd. dirs. Acupuncture Rsch. Inst., 1982—; conductor seminars, trainer in field. Author: Twelve Energy Supplements for Health and Nutrition, 1979, A Comprehensive Therapeutics in Homoeopathy for Physicians, 1984, Twelve Energy Medicine, 1980, How to Balance your Body Dynamically, Ways to Change the Health Care Crisis in America, 1985; contbr. articles to profl. jours. Mem. Homoeopathic Med. Assn. Am. (founding pres., bd. dirs. 1988—), Nat. Ctr. Homoeopathy (bd. dirs. 1988), Homoeopathic Med. Assn. India, All-India Homoeopathic Med. Assn., All-India Homoeopathic Pharm. Assn. (exec. adv. mem.), Hahnemann Med. Soc. Am., Fla. State Soc. Homoeopathic Physicians, Internat. Homoeopathic Med. Orgn., Med. Acupuncture Rsch. Inst. (bd. dirs. 1977—), Internat. Homoeopathic Med. League, Soc. Ultramolecular Medicine. Office: Hahnemannian Research 18818 Teller Ave Ste 170 Irvine CA 92612-8884

GEORGE, ROBERT D., technology corporation executive; b. 1956; BA in Econs., Drew U.; MBA, Duke U. Various fin. and opers. positions Zurn Industries, Elgin Electronics, and Xerox Corp.; treas., controller Esterline Technologies Corp., Bellevue, Wash., 1997-99, chief fin. officer, v.p., 1999—.

GEORGE, RONALD M., state supreme court chief justice; b. LA, Mar. 11, 1940; AB, Princeton U., 1961; JD, Stanford U., 1964. Bar: Calif. 1965. Dep. atty. gen. Calif. Dept. Justice, 1965-72; judge L.A. Mcpl. Ct., L.A. County, 1972-77, Superior Ct. Calif., L.A. County, 1977-87, supervising judge criminal divsn., 1983-84; assoc. justice 2d dist., divsn. 4 Calif. Ct. Appeal, LA, 1987-91; assoc. justice Calif. Supreme Ct., San Francisco, 1991-96, chief justice, 1996—. Recipient St. Thomas More Medallion award, St. Thomas More Law Honor Soc., 1997, Judge Learned Hand award, 2000, Found. of the State Bar's Justice award, 2000, William H. Rehnquist award for Judicial Excellence, 2002, James Madison Freedom of Information award, Soc. of Professional Journalists, 2003, George Moscone award for Outstanding Public Service, Consumer Attorneys of L.A., 2003, William O. Douglas award, 2004; named Trial Judge of the Yr., L.A. Metropolitan News, 1983, Appellate Justice of the Yr., L.A. Trial Lawyers Assn., 1991, Person of the Yr., L.A. Metropolitan News, 1996. Mem. Calif. Judges Assn. (pres. 1982-83), Conf. Chief Justices (pres. 2003-04). Avocations: hiking, skiing, running. Office: Calif Supreme Court 350 McAllister St Fl 5 San Francisco CA 94102-4797 Office Phone: 415-865-7060.

GEORGE, RUSSELL LLOYD, lawyer, former state legislator; b. Rifle, Colo., May 28, 1946; s. Walter Mallory and Eleanora (Michel) G.; m. Neal Ellen Moore, Nov. 24, 1972; children: Russell, Charles, Thomas, Andrew. BS in Econs., Colo. State U., 1968; JD, Harvard Law Sch., 1971. Bar: Colo 1972, Mont. 1975. Shareholder Stuver & George, P.C., Rifle, 1976—; dir. Co. Div. Wildlife, Denver, 2000—04; exec. dir. Colo. Dept. of Natural Resources, Denver, 2004—. State rep. dist. 57 Colo. Gen. Assembly, 1993—., speaker of the House, Colo Gen.Assembly. Recipient Boettcher Scholar, 1968; named Legislator of Yr., by Associated Press capitol reporter, 1994, 1996. Fellow Colo. Bar Found.; mem. Colo. Bar Assn., Rotary Internat., Masonic

Lodge. Republican. Methodist. Office: Colo Dept of Natural Resources 1313 Sherman St Rm 718 Denver CO 80203 Office Phone: 303-866-3311. Office Fax: 303-866-2115.

GEORGE, SARAH B., museum director; Dir. Utah Mus. of Natural History, Salt Lake City. Office: Utah Mus Natural History U Utah 1390 E Pres Cir Salt Lake City UT 84112 E-mail: sgeorge@umnh.utah.edu.

GEORGE, THOM RITTER, conductor, composer; b. Detroit, June 23, 1942; s. Robert Murray and Virginia Flowers (Ritter) G.; m. Patricia Imogene Dengler, Aug. 14, 1965; children: Samantha, Clara, Alexander. MusB, Eastman Sch. Music, 1964, MusM, 1968; D in Mus. Arts, The Cath. U. Am., 1970. Lectr. music The Cath. U. Am., Washington, 1966-70; music dir., condr. Quincy (Ill.) Symphony Orch., 1970-83; lectr. music John Wood Community Coll., Quincy, 1980-83; music dir., condr. Idaho State Civic Symphony, Pocatello, 1983—; assoc. prof. Idaho State U., Pocatello, 1983-88, prof., 1988—. Composer: Concerto for Bass Trombone, 1964, Proclamations, 1965, Sextet, 1981, Five Brass Quintets, Sonatas for all orchestral instruments, numerous others. Bd. dirs. Civic Music Assn., Quincy, 1970-74; bd. sec. Vol. Action Ctr., Quincy, 1976-78. Served with USN, 1966-70. Recipient citation Quincy Coll., 1973, Sigvald Thompson award Fargo (N.D.) Moorhead Symphony, 1975, Composer-in-Residence Elkhorn Music Festival, Sun. Gov.'s award for excellence in the arts, State of Idaho, 1998. Mem. ASCAP, Am. String Tchrs. Assn., Nat. Band Assn. Lodges: Rotary (Quincy membership chmn. 1975-83, mem. Pocatello fine arts com. 1985—). Avocations: reading, travel, photography. Office: Idaho State U Dept Music PO Box 8099 Pocatello ID 83209-8099

GEORGE, TIMOTHY G., metallurgist; BS in Metallurgy, U. Pitts., 1980; postgrad., U. N.Mex.; M in Mgmt./Human Rels./Orgnl. Behavior, U. Phoenix, 1990. With Kennametal Inc. Latrobe Rsch. Lab.; joined Dept. Energy Los Alamos (N.Mex.) Nat. Lab., 1983, head Actinide Ceramics Group, 1993, head Radioisotope Heat Source Program, 1993, head Cassini Heat Source Prodn. Project, 1993, project leader Nuc. Fuels Demonstration, 1997, acting dep. dir. Nuc. Materials Tech. Divsn., dir. Nuc. Materials Tech. Divsn., 1999—. Contbr. articles to profl. jours. Recipient James F. Lincoln Arc Welding Found. award, 1995; co-recipient Schreiber-Spence Space Achievement award Inst. for Space and Nuc. Power Studies, 1998. Office: Los Alamos Nat Lab Nuc Materials Divsn PO Box 1663 MSE500 NMT-DO Los Alamos NM 87545 E-mail: tgeorge@lanl.gov.

GEORGES, ROBERT AUGUSTUS, retired folklore and mythology educator, researcher, writer; b. Sewickley, Pa., May 1, 1933; s. John Thomas and Pauline Pantzis G.; m. Mary Virginia Ruth, Aug. 11, 1956; 1 child, Jonathan Gregory. BS, Ind. U. of Pa., 1954; MA, U. Pa., 1961; PhD, Indiana U., 1964. Tchr. Bound Brook HS, NJ, 1954-56, Southern Regional HS, Manahawkin, NJ, 1958-60; asst. prof. U. Kans., Lawrence, 1963-66, UCLA, 1966-70, assoc. prof., 1970-76, prof., 1976-94; prof. emeritus, 1994—. Vice chmn. Folklore and Mythology Program UCLA, 1966-82, chmn. 1983-86. Author: Greek-American Folk Beliefs and Narratives, 1980; co-author: People Studying People: The Human Element in Fieldwork, 1980, American and Canadian Immigrant and Ethnic Folkore: An Annotated Bibliography; co-author: Folkloristics: An Introduction, 1996; editor: Studies on Mythology, 1968; translator: Two Studies on Modern Greek, Folklore by Stilpon P. Kyriakides, 1968; contbr. numerous articles to folklore periodicals. With U.S. Army, 1956-58. NDEA fellow, 1962-63, Guggenheim fellow, 1969-70. Fellow Am. Folklore Soc.; mem. Calif. Folklore Soc. Home: 906 Fiske St Pacific Palisades CA 90272-3841 E-mail: rgeorges@ucla.edu.

GERACI, RICHARD V., military officer, government agency administrator; BS in Mgmt., Park Coll.; M.Mgmt., Webster U.; MS in Systems Mgmt., Fla. Inst. Tech.; MA in Nat. Security Affairs and Strategic Studies, U.S. Naval War Coll. Commd. 2d lt. U.S. Army, 1975—, advanced through grades to brig. gen.; platoon leader, battery exec. officer, asst. ops. officer 3d Battalion 32nd Army Air Def. Command, Germany; Patriot plans and future war plans officer, G3 32d AADCOM; battalion ops. officer 1st Bn. 7th ADA (PATRIOT; brigade ops. officer and dep. brigade comdr. 94th ADA Brigade; battalion ops. officer 3d Battalion 1st ADA, Tng. Brigade, Ft. Bliss, Tex.; garrison ops., plans, tng., mobilization officer Installation Support Activity, U.S. Army, Aberdeen Proving Grounds, Md.; dep. commdg. gen. Army Space Command and Ops., U.S. Army Space and Missile Def. Command, Colorado Springs, Colo. Decorated Legion of Merit, Meritorious Svc. medal, silver and 2 bronze oak leaf clusters, Army Commendation medal with 2 oak leaf clusters, Army Achievement medal with 1 oak leaf cluster, S.W. Asia Svc. medal, Saudi-Kuwaiti Liberation medal, Kuwaiti Liberation medal.

GERAGHTY, JOHN VINCENT, public relations consultant; b. Seattle, Feb. 23, 1934; s. John V. and Gladys I (Johnson) G.; children: Marcella Maile, Sheila Leek, Brigid Krause, Nora Lipton. BA in Comm., U. Wash., 1956; MPA (hon.), Ea. Washington U., 1994. Reporter Spokane (Wash.) Daily Chronicle, 1959-62; sec. to mayor/coun. City of Spokane, 1962-64; county commr. Spokane (Wash.) County, 1964-71; vp. guest rels. EXPO '74 Corp., Spokane, 1971-74; publisher, owner The Falls Newspaper, Spokane, 1974-76; v.p. Haworth & Anderson, Inc., Spokane, 1976-83; owner, pres. Jack Geraghty & Assocs., Spokane, 1983—; prin. Alliance Pacific, Inc., Spokane, 1985—; mayor City of Spokane, 1994-98. Bd. dirs., past pres. Future Spokane, 1983-89; cons. Citizens League of Greater Spokane. Bd. dirs. and past pres., Spokane Comty. Mental Health Ctr., 1980-95; mem. and past chmn. bd. trustees Ea. Wash. U., Cheney, Wash., 1985-97; mem. and vice chair Spokane Centennial Projects Com., 1988. Mem. Pub. Rels Soc. Am. (pres. Spokane chpt. 1983), Spokane Pub. Rels. Coun. (past pres.), Spokane Club, Beta Theta Pi. Democrat. Roman Catholic. Avocations: golf, sailing, cooking. Office: PO Box 251 Spokane WA 99210-0251

GERAGOS, MARK JOHN, lawyer; b. LA, Oct. 5, 1957; BA, Haverford Coll., 1979; JD, Loyola Marymount U., 1982. Pvt. practice, LA; with Calif. Legis. Assembly Resolution, 2003; mng. ptnr. Geragos & Geragos, P.C., LA. Legal cons. CNBC, MSNBC, Fox News Svc., CNN; spkr. in field. Guest, legal commentator Today Show, Good Morning America, Dateline NBC, Larry King Live, Greta Van Susteren's On the Record, 60 Minutes, 48 Hours. Recipient Jerry Giesler Meml. award, Criminal Cts. Bar Assn., 1999, Humanitarian of Yr. award, Mexican Am. Grocers Assn., 2001, Resolution award for pioneering work in internet TV, Calif. Legis. Assembly, 2003, Profl. of Yr. award, Am. Profl. Soc., 2004, Calif. Lawyer of Yr. award, Civil Litig., 2006; named Trial Lawyer of Yr., LA Criminal Cts. Bar Assn., 2006; named one of 100 Most Influential Attys. in Calif., Calif. Bus. Law mag., LA's Superlawyers. Mem.: LA County Bar Assn. (mem. jud. appointments com., mem. outstanding trial jurist award com. 1992—93, jud. com. 1994—), State Bar Calif. Office: Geragos & Geragos PC 644 S Figueroa St Los Angeles CA 90017 Office Phone: 213-625-3900. Office Fax: 213-625-1600. E-mail: geragos@geragos.com.

GERARD, JAMES WILSON, publishing consultant; b. Chgo., May 16, 1935; s. Ralph Waldo and Margaret (Wilson) G. Student, U. Vt., 1955, Roosevelt U., 1955-59. Ptnr. UNIPUB, NYC, 1962-77; pres. Brookfield (Vt.) Pub. Co., 1977—. Bd. dirs. Renouf Pub. Co., Ltd. Mem. Am. Assn. Scholarly Pub., Les Ambassadeurs Club. Democrat. Home: 1347 Primavera Dr W Palm Springs CA 92264-8447 Office Phone: 760-320-8663. Personal E-mail: jgerard@dc.rr.com.

GERARD, SUSAN E., state agency administrator, former state senator; b. Englewood, NJ, June 13, 1950; d. Frederick McAdam Muir and Margaret Morley Green; m. Philip Charles Gerard, Nov. 25, 1972; children: Randall McAdam, Megan Elizabeth. BA, Drake U., Des Moines, 1972; MBA, Ariz. State U., 1977. State rep. Ariz. Ho. of Reps., Phoenix, 1989—2000; senator State of Ariz., Phoenix, 2000—02; health care policy advisor to Ariz. Gov. Napolitano, 2002—05; state health dir. Ariz. Dept. Health Svcs., Phoenix, 2005—. Mem. Nat. Campaign to Prevent Teen Pregnancy, Nat. Forum for State Health Policy Leadership; chmn. City of Phoenix AIDS Task Force; mem. Inst. for Mental Health Rsch., Ariz. Supreme Court Juvenile Justice Com.; Madison Edn. Found.; mem. Long Term Care Task Force. Named Legislator of the Yr., Am. Hosp. Assn., Coalition for Tobacco Free Ariz., Ariz. Psychol. Assn., Women in Mcpl. Govt. Republican. Methodist. Avocations: gardening, decorative painting. Office: Dept Health Svcs 150 N 18th Ave Phoenix AZ 85007

GERATY, LAWRENCE THOMAS, academic administrator, archaeologist, educator; b. St. Helena, Calif., Apr. 21, 1940; s. Thomas Sinclair and Hazel Mae (McVicker) G.; m. Gillian Anne Keough, Aug. 5, 1962; children: Brent, Julie. BA, Pacific Union Coll., 1962; MA, Andrews U., 1963, BD, 1965; PhD, Harvard U., 1972. Pastor 7th Day Adventist Ch., Calif., 1962-66; instr. old testament Andrews U., Berrien Springs, Mich., 1966-72, asst. prof. archaeology and history, 1972-76, assoc. prof. archaeology and history, 1976-80, prof., 1980-85; curator S.H. Horn Archaeol. Mus., Berrien Springs, Mich., 1976-85; dir. Inst. Archaeology Andrews U., Berrien Springs, 1981-85; pres. Atlantic Union Coll., Lancaster, Mass., 1985-93, La Sierra U., Riverside, Calif., 1993—. Project dir. Excavation of Tell Hesban, Jordan, 1973-76, Madaba Plains Project, Jordan, 1984—; v.p. Am. Ctr. of Oriental Rsch., Amman, 1985-03; pres. Am. Schs. Oriental Rsch., Boston, 2003-07. Editor, contbr. articles to profl. jours. Bd. dirs. Thayer Symphony Orch., Lancaster, Mass., 1985-93; mem. Edn. Forum of Clinton, Mass., 1990-93. Fulbright fellow, 1970-71, Robert H. Pfeiffer fellow, 1970-71; grantee Ford Found., 1969-70, Ctr. Field Rsch., 1976, NEH, 1979. Mem. Soc. Bibl. Literature (pres. 1988-90), Archeol. Inst. Am., Am. Schs. Oriental Rsch., Clinton C. of C. (bd. dirs. 1985-92), Riverside C. of C. (bd. dirs. 1996—), Raincross Club, Employers Group (bd. dirs. 1996-, chair 2006-07), United Way (chair 2003-04), Monday Morning Group. Seventh-Day Adventist. Office: La Sierra U Office of Pres 4500 Riverwalk Pkwy Riverside CA 92515 Home Phone: 951-689-7562; Office Phone: 951-785-2020. Business E-Mail: lgeraty@lasierra.edu.

GERBA, CHARLES PETER, microbiologist, educator; b. Blue Island, Ill., Sept. 10, 1945; s. Peter and Virginia (Roulo) G.; m. Peggy Louise Scheitlin, June 6, 1970; children: Peter, Phillip. BS in Microbiology, Ariz. State U., 1969; PhD in Microbiology, U. Miami, 1973. Postdoctoral fellow Baylor Coll. Medicine, Houston, 1973-74, asst. prof. microbiology, 1974-81; assoc. prof. U. Ariz., Tucson, 1981-85, prof., 1985—. Cons. EPA, Tucson, 1980—, World Health Orgn., Pan Am. Health Orgn., 1989—; advisor CRC Press, Boca Raton, Fla., 1981—. Editor: Methods in Environmental Virology, 1982, Groundwater Pollution Microbiology, 1984, Phage Ecology, 1987, Pollution Sci., 1996; contbr. numerous articles to profl. and sci. jours. Mem. Pima County Bd. Health, 1986-92; mem. sci. adv. bd. EPA, 1987-95. Recipient McKee medal Water Environ. Fedn., 1996; named Outstanding Research Scientist U. Ariz., 1984, 92, Outstanding Rsch. Team, 1994. Fellow AAAS (environ. sci. and engring.), Am. Acad. Microbiology, Am. Soc. Microbiology (divsn. chmn. 1982-83, 87-88, pres. Ariz. chpt. 1984-85, councilor 1985-88); mem. Internat. Assn. Water Pollution Rsch. (sr. del. 1985-91), Am. Water Works Assn. (A.P. Black award 1997), Water Quality Assn. (Hon. Mem. award 1998). Achievements include research in environmental microbiology, colloid transport in ground water, wastewater reuse and risk assessment. Home: 1980 W Paseo Monserrat Tucson AZ 85704-1329 Office: U Ariz Dept Microbiol & Immunol Wat Tucson AZ 85721-0001 Office Phone: 520-621-6906. Business E-Mail: gerba@ag.arizona.edu.

GERBER, ROBERT SCOTT, lawyer; b. Lansing, Mich. s. Arnold William and Carol L. Gerber. BA with high honors, U. Mich., 1984, M of Pub. Policy, 1985; JD cum laude, Harvard U., 1988. Bar: Calif. 1988, US Dist. Ct. (so. dist.) Calif. 1989, US Dist. Ct. (ctrl. dist.) Calif. 1991, US Ct. Appeals (9th cir.) 1992, US Dist. Ct. Ariz. 1994, US Supreme Ct. 2000, US Dist. Ct. (no. dist., Calif.), 2001. Econ. devel. analyst Mich. Dept. Commerce, 1984-85, City of San Diego, 1985; summer assoc. Riker, Danzig, Scherer, Hyland & Perretti, Morristown, NJ, 1986, Lillick, McHose & Charles, San Diego, 1987, Debevoise & Plimpton, NYC, 1987; law clk. Hon. Rudi M. Brewster U.S. Dist. Ct. (so. dist.) Calif., San Diego, 1988-89; assoc. Sheppard, Mullin, Richter & Hampton LLP, San Diego, 1989-97, ptnr., 1997—. Contbr. articles to profl. jours. Active San Diego Vol. Lawyer Program, 1989—; judge pro tempore Small Claims Ct., Mspl. Ct. Calif., San Diego Jud. Dist., 1994—2001; mem. Calif. Jud. Nominees Evaluation Commn., 2004—06; bd. dirs. ch. coun. Christ Evang. Luth. Ch., Pacific Beach, Calif., 1991—94, 1995—96, long range planning com., 1994—95. Master: Am. Inns of Ct. (bd. trustees 2005—); mem.: ABA (asst. editor-in-chief profl. liability com. newsletter 1994—), San Diego Def. Lawyers, Assn. Bus. Trial Lawyers, State Bar Calif. (fed. rules subcom. 1991—92, ct. rules com. 1992—, exec. com. litig. sect. 1995—, treas. 1996—97, sec. 1997—, vice chair 1998—99, chair 1999—2000). Avocations: fine wines, collecting movies, golf. Office: Sheppard, Mullin, Richter & Hampton LLP Ste 200 12275 El Camino Real San Diego CA 92130 Office Phone: 858-720-8907. Office Fax: 858-509-3691. Business E-Mail: rgerber@sheppardmullin.com, rgerber@smrh.com.

GERBER, ROBIN, history and social sciences educator; b. Miles City, Mont. AA, Miles CC; BA in Anthropology and Hist., U. Mont., Missoula, MA in Hist. Mem. faculty to instr. hist. and social scis. Miles CC, Miles City, Mont., 1998—. Author: A Long Way From Anywhere - A History of Miles City, MT - For Kids, 2006. Recipient US Prof. of Yr. award, Carnegie Found. for Advancement of Tchg. and Coun. for Advancement and Support of Edn., 2006. Office: Hist and Social Scis Miles CC 2715 Dickinson Miles City MT 59301-4774 Office Phone: 406-874-6193. E-mail: gerberr@milescc.edu.

GERBER, WILLIAM NORMAN, motion picture executive; b. Las Vegas, Apr. 30, 1957; s. Roy Herbert and Constance Doris Gerber. West coast dir. Nemporer Records, LA, 1978—79; exec. v.p. Lookout Mgmt., LA, 1979—84; prin. owner Gerber/Rodkin Co., LA, 1985—86; v.p. theatrical prodn. divsn. Warner Bros., Inc., Burbank, Calif., 1986—98, co-pres. worldwide theatrical prodn., 1998; prodr. Gerber Pictures, 1998—. Office: Gerber Pictures 9465 Wilshire Blvd Beverly Hills CA 90212-2612

GERBERDING, WILLIAM PASSAVANT, retired university president; b. Fargo, ND, Sept. 9, 1929; s. William Passavant and Esther Elizabeth Ann (Habighorst) G.; m. Ruth Alice Albrecht, Mar. 25, 1952; children: David Michael, Steven Henry, Elizabeth Ann, John Martin. BA, Macalester Coll., 1951; MA, U. Chgo., 1956, PhD, 1959. Congl. fellow Am. Polit. Sci. Assn., Washington, 1958-59; instr. Colgate U., Hamilton, N.Y., 1959-60; research asst. Senator E.J. McCarthy, Washington, 1960-61; staff Rep. Frank Thompson, Jr., Washington, 1961; faculty UCLA, 1961-72, prof., chmn. dept. polit. sci., 1970-72; dean faculty, v.p. for acad. affairs Occidental Coll., Los Angeles, 1972-75; exec. vice chancellor UCLA, 1975-77; chancellor U. Ill., Urbana-Champaign, 1978-79; pres. U. Wash., Seattle, 1979-95. Cons. Dept. Def., 1962, Calif. Assembly, 1965. Author: United States Foreign Policy: Perspectives and Analysis, 1966; co-editor, contbg. author: The Radical Left: The Abuse of Discontent, 1970. Trustee Macalester Coll., 1980—83, 1996—2001, Gates Cambridge Trust, U. Cambridge, England, 2000—. With USN, 1951—55. Recipient Distinguished Teaching award U. Calif., Los Angeles, 1966; Ford Found. grantee, 1967-68 Office: Univ Wash PO Box 352800 Seattle WA 98195-2800

GERE, RICHARD, actor; b. Phila., Aug. 31, 1949; s. Homer and Doris Gere; m. Cindy Crawford, Dec. 12, 1991 (div. 1995); m. Carey Lowell, Nov. 9, 2002; 1 child, Homer James Jigme. Attended, U. Mass. Played trumpet, piano, guitar and bass and composed music with various musical groups. acting appearances with Provincetown Playhouse in Great God Brown, Camino Real, Rosencrantz and Guildenstern are Dead; off-Broadway prodn. Killer's Head, Richard Farina: Long Time Coming and Long Time Gone, Back Bog Beast Bait; in Broadway prodn. Taming of the Shrew, Midsummer Night's Dream, Habeas Corpus, Bent, Grease; appeared in and composed music for Volpone at Seattle Repertory Theatre; actor: (films) Report to the Commissioner, 1975, Baby Blue Marine, 1976, Looking for Mr. Goodbar, 1977, Days of Heaven, 1978, Blood Brothers, 1978, Yanks, 1979, American Gigolo, 1980, An Officer and a Gentleman, 1982, Breathless, 1983, Beyond the Limit, 1983, The Cotton Club, 1984, King David, 1985, Power, 1986, No Mercy, 1986, Miles from Home, 1988, Internal Affairs, 1990, Pretty Woman, 1990, Rhapsody in August, 1991, Sommersby, 1993, Mr. Jones, 1993, Intersection, 1994, First Knight, 1995, Primal Fear, 1996, Red Corner, 1997, The Jackal, 1997, An Alan Smithee Film: Burn Hollywood Burn, 1998, Runaway Bride, 1999, Autumn in New York, 2000, Dr. T and the Women, 2000, The Mothman Prophecies, 2002, Unfaithful, 2002, Chicago, 2002, Shall We Dance?, 2004, Bee Season, 2005, The Hoax, 2007, The Hunting Party, 2007, I'm Not There, 2007, Nights in Rodanthe, 2008; (TV movies) Strike Force, 1975, And the Band Played On, 1993; (TV appearances) Kojak, 1973; actor, exec. prodr. (films) Final Analysis, 1992, Mr. Jones, 1993, Sommersby, 1993; author: Pilgrim Photo Collection, 1998 Recipient Marian Anderson award, City of Phila., 2007, Joel Siegel Humanitarian award, Critics Choice Awards, 2009. Office: Gere Found Hirsch Wallerstein Hayum Matlof LLP 10100 Santa Monica Blvd Ste 1700 Los Angeles CA 90067

GEREN, BOB (ROBERT PETER GEREN), professional baseball manager; b. San Diego, Calif., Sept. 22, 1961; Catcher NY Yankees, 1988—91, San Diego Padres, 1993; mgr. Sacramento River Cats, 2000—02; bench coach Oakland Athletics, 2003—06, mgr., 2006—. Achievements include being bench coach Am. League All-Star Team, 2005. Office: Oakland Athletics 7000 Colliseum Way Oakland CA 94621

GERHARDT, HEINZ ADOLF AUGUST, retired aircraft design engineer; b. Biedenkopf, Hessen, Germany, Jan. 31, 1934; came to U.S., 1962; s. Heinrich Ludwig and Emilie Henriette (Schuechler) G.; m. Heide Hanne Waltraud von Ryschkowsky, Sept. 3, 1962; children: Heinrich, Friederike, Helmar. MS in Mech. Engring., Tech. U. Darmstadt, Germany, 1961. Engr. Heinkel AG, Munich, 1962; from engr. to mgr. advanced aerodesign Northrop Corp., Hawthorne, Calif., 1962-91, prin. engr., 1991-99; ret., 1999. Patentee in field. Recipient Otto Lilienthal prize Wissenschaftliche Gesellschaft fuer Luftfahrt, 1954, Aerodynamic award Am. Inst. of Aeronautics and Astronautics, 1994 Mem. AIAA (assoc. fellow, Aerodynamics award 1994), Soc. Automotive Engrs., Deutsche Gesellschaft fuer Luft und Raumfahrt. Avocations: flying, sailplanes, swimming, hiking.

GERINGER, JAMES E., former governor; b. Wheatland, Wyo., Apr. 24, 1944; m. Sherri Geringer; children: Jen, Val, Rob, Meri, Beckie. BS in Mechanical Engring., Kans. State U., 1967. Commd. officer USAF; with contract administration Mo. Basin Power Project's Laramie River Sta., 1977-79; elected mem. Wyo. Legislature, 1982; farm owner, 1977—; gov. State of Wyo., 1994—2002. Participant in various space devel. programs, Calif., devel. variety Air Force and NASA space boosters including launches of reconnaissance satellites, the NASA Viking Mars lander, an upper stage booster for the space shuttle and the Global Positioning Satellite System; chief of computer programming at a ground receiving station for early warning satellites. Mem. Nat. Fedn. Ind. Bus., Am. Legion, Farm Bur., Farmer's Union, Rotary, Lions, Ducks Unlimited, Pheasants Forever, C. of C. Republican. Lutheran. Home: 1507 Road 215 Cheyenne WY 82009-9755

GERKEN, WALTER BLAND, insurance company executive; b. NYC, Aug. 14, 1922; s. Walter Adam and Virginia (Bland) G.; m. Darlene Stolt, Sept. 6, 1952; children: Walter C., Ellen M., Beth L., Daniel J., Andrew P., David A. BA, Wesleyan U., 1948; MPA, Maxwell Sch. Citizenship and Pub. Affairs, Syracuse, 1958. Supr. budget and adminstrv. analysis, Wis., Madison, 1950-54; mgr. investments Northwestern Mut. Life Ins. Co., Milw., 1954-67; v.p. finance Pacific Mut. Life Ins. Co., LA, 1967-69, exec. v.p., 1969-72, pres., 1972-75, chmn. bd., 1975-87, chmn. exec. com. Los Angeles, 1987-95, also dir.; ret. sr. advisor Boston Consulting Group. Bd. dirs. Mullin Cons., Inc.; vice-chmn. Global Fin. Group, 2000—. Bd. dirs. Keck Found.; trustee emeritus Occidental Coll. L.A., Wesleyan U., Middletown, Conn.; bd. dirs. Nature Conservancy Calif.; mem. Calif. Citizens Budget Com., Calif. Commn. Campaign Fin. Reform, Calif. Commn. on Higher Edn.; bd. dirs., former chair Exec. Svc. Corps. So. Calif.; v.p. Orange County Cmty. Found.; mem. adv. bd. The Maxwell Sch. Citizenship and Pub. Affairs, Syracuse U. Decorated D.F.C., Air medal. Mem. Calif. Club, Dairymen's Country Club (Boulder Junction, Wis.), Automobile Club So. Calif. (bd. dirs.), Pauma Valley Country Club, Edison Internat., Times Mirror Co. Office: Pimco Advisors LP 800 Newport Center Dr Newport Beach CA 92660-6309 E-mail: wgerken@pimcoadvisors.com.

GERMAN, DONALD FREDERICK, physician; b. San Francisco, Oct. 2, 1935; m. Marilyn Sue King; children: Susan, Charles, Donald. BS, U. San Francisco, 1956; MD, U. Calif., San Francisco, 1960. Diplomate Am. Bd. Pediats., Am. Bd. Allergy and Immunology. Intern Kaiser Found. Hosp., San Francisco, 1960-61, resident in pediats., 1963-65, fellow in allergy, 1966-68; staff pediatrician Kaiser Med. Ctr., Santa Clara, Calif., 1965-66, staff allergist, 1968-69; chief dept. allergy Kaiser Permanente Med. Ctr., San Francisco, 1969-99, allergy staff physician, 1999—. Clin. prof. pediatrics U. Calif. Med. Sch., San Francisco, 1991—; bd. dirs. Asthma, Allergy and Immunology Found. No. Calif. Capt. USAF, 1961-63. Fellow Am. Acad. Pediats., Am. Coll. Allergy and Immunology, Am. Acad. Allergy and Immunology; mem. Calif. Soc. Allergy and Immunology (past pres.). Avocations: running, hiking, fly fishing, travel. Address: 1030 Sir Francis Drake Blvd Ste 110 Kentfield CA 94904 Office Phone: 415-460-6686. Personal E-mail: dfgerman2@yahoo.com.

GERMAN, WILLIAM, newspaper editor; b. NYC, Jan. 4, 1919; s. Sam and Celia (Norack) G.; m. Gertrude Pasenkoff, Oct. 12, 1940 (dec. 1998); children: David, Ellen, Stephen. BA, Bklyn. Coll., 1939; MS, Columbia U., 1940; Nieman fellow, Harvard U., 1950. Mng. editor KQED, Newspaper of the Air, 1968; editor Chronicle Fgn. Service, 1960-77; reporter, asst. fgn., news, mng., exec. editor, editor San Francisco Chronicle, 1940-2000, editor emeritus, 2000—. Lectr. U. Calif., Berkeley, 1946-47, 68-70 Editor: San Francisco Chronicle Reader, 1962. Bd. trustees World Affairs Coun. Served with AUS, 1943-45. Mem. AP Mng. Editors Assn., Am. Soc. Newspaper Editors, Commonwealth Club of Calif. (pres. 1995). Office: San Francisco Chronicle 901 Mission St San Francisco CA 94103-2905 Home: 300 Deer Valley Rd #1B San Rafael CA 94903 Business E-Mail: wgerman@sfchronicle.com.

GEROU, CHERI, state legislator; b. Wyo. m. Phil Gerou; children: Greg, Sara. BA in Fine Arts, U. Colo. Mem. Dist. 25 Colo. House of Reps., 2008—. Bd. sec. State Licensing Bd. Architects, Profl. Engrs. & Profl. Land Surveyors, vice chmn. Survey Quorum Profl. Land Surveyors. Mem. Nat. Coun. Architectural Registration Bds.; former mem. Profl. Devel. Com. Mem.: Constructors & Designers Alliance (chmn.), AIA Denver Chpt. (former pres.), AIA Colo. Chpt. (former pres.). Republican. Office: State House 200 E Colfax Denver CO 80203 Office Phone: 303-866-2582. Business E-Mail: cheri.gerou@gmail.com.*

GEROU, PHILLIP HOWARD, architect; b. Natick, Mass., July 20, 1951; s. James Francis and Enid (Meymaris) G.; m. Cheri Rodgers, Nov. 24, 1979; children: Gregory Bedford, Sara Christine. BArch, U. Nebr., 1974, MArch, 1975. Designer, owner Gerou & Assocs. Ltd., Evergreen, Colo., 1986—. Design cons. Kilimanjaro Children's Hosp., Tanzania, 1988-91, World Alpine Ski Championships, Vail, Colo., 1988. Pres. Colo. Soc. of Architects Ednl. Fund., Denver, 1986; del. State Rep. Assembly, Denver, 1986; trustee Rockland Community Ch., Denver, 1986-89. Recipient Citation award Nat. Assn. of Remodeling Industry, 1991, 96, Design Excellence Wood, Inc., 1990, Citation award, 1990. Fellow AIA (pres. Colo. chpt. 1986, bd. dirs. 1981-87, nat. dir. 1991-94, nat. v.p. 1995, dir. Nat. Ethics Coun. 1997—2002, chmn., 2001—02, conf. chair Western Mountain region design conf. 1990, Spl. Recognition award 1990), Nat. Coun. Archtl. Adminstrn. Bds. (examiner 1985). Republican. Mem. United Ch. of Christ. Avocations: skiing, travel, architectural design. Home Phone: 303-670-4587; Office Phone: 303-674-4177. E-mail: phil@gerou.net.

GERRARD, KEITH, lawyer; b. Malden, Mass., Feb. 8, 1935; s. William Francis and Mary Ethel (Compton) Gerrard; children: Jessica, Beth stepchildren: Elizabeth Perera, Jonathan Perera. AB, Harvard U., 1956; LLB, Harvard U. Law Sch., 1963. Bar: Wash. 1963. Assoc. Perkins Coie, Seattle, 1963—70, ptnr., 1970—. Trustee Mus. Flight, 1998—2008. Served to lt. USAF, 1956—59. Fellow: Am. Coll. Trial Lawyers; mem.: ABA, Seattle-King County Bar Assn., Wash. State Bar Assn. Office: Perkins Coie 1201 3rd Ave Fl 40 Seattle WA 98101-3029 Office Phone: 206-359-8462. Business E-Mail: kgerrard@perkinscoie.com.

GERRITSEN, MARY ELLEN, vascular and cell biologist; b. Calgary, Alta., Can., Sept. 20, 1953; arrived in US, 1978; d. Thomas Clayton and Alice Irene (Minton) Cooper; m. Paul William Gerritsen, May 24, 1975 (div. 1977); m. Thomas Patrick Parks, Oct. 11, 1980; children: Kristen, Madelene. BSc summa cum laude, U. Calgary, 1975, PhD, 1978. Postdoctoral fellow U. Calif., San Diego, 1978-80; asst. prof. N.Y. Med. Coll., Valhalla, 1981-86, assoc. prof., 1986-90; sr. staff scientist Pharm. divsn. Bayer Corp., West Haven, Conn., 1990-93, head inflammation exploratory rsch., 1990-96, prin. staff scientist, 1993-97; vis. scientist Harvard U., 1996; assoc. dir. cardiovasc. rsch. Genentech, South San Francisco, 1997—2001; sr. dir. Millennium Pharms., South San Francisco, 2003—04; exec. dir. Molecular and Cellular Pharm., Exelixis Inc., South San Francisco, 2004—. Cons. Insite Vision, Alameda, Calif., 1987-89, Boehringer Ingelheim Pharms., Ridgefield, Conn., 1985-88, Xoma, Berkeley, Calif, 2003-04, Frazier Health Care Ventures, Palo Alto, Calif, 2003—, Macusight, Union City, Calif., 2004—; adj. assoc. prof. N.Y. Med. Coll., 1990-99. Co-author: Masdevallias: Gems of the Orchid World, 2005, Calochortus, Mariposa Lilies and Their Relatives, 2007; editor: N.Am. Vascular Biology Orgn. Newsletter, —; mem. editl. bd. Microvascular Rsch., 1988—96, Am. Jour. Physiology, 1983—90, Am. Jour. Cardiovasc. Pathology, 1996—98, Circulation Rsch., 1997—99, Endothelium, 1999—, editor-in-chief Microcirculation, 1993—98, cons. editor, 1998—; contbr. articles to profl. jours. Fellow I. W. Killam Found. 1976, Med. Rsch. Coun. Can. 1978-80; scholar Province Alb., Sinsheimer Scholar; recipient Kurt Weiderman award, Rsch. Career Devel. award NIH. Mem. Am. Soc. for Pharmacology and Exptl. Therapeutics, Am. Physiol. Soc., Am. Soc. Investigational Pathology, Microcirculatory Soc. (mem. coun. 1989-92, chairperson publs. com. 1991-93, Mary Weideman award 1985, Young Investigator award 1984), N.Am. Vascular Biology Orgn. (mem. steering com. 1993, mem. coun. 1994-97, editor-in-chief newsletter 1994-97, sec.-treas. 1997-99, pres. 1999, chair devel. com., 2004-05), Peninsula Orchid Soc. (bd. dirs. 2001, v.p. 2005-07, pres. 2008), Am. Orchid Soc., San Francisco Orchid Soc., Pleurothallid Alliance, Orchid Digest. Avocations: orchids, horticulture, photography. Personal E-mail: meg570@comcast.net.

GERSHON, GINA, actress; b. LA, Calif., June 10, 1962; Actress: (films) Pretty in Pink, 1986, 3:15, the Moment of Truth, 1986, Cocktail, 1988, Red Heat, 1988, Voodoo Dawn, 1991, City of Hope, 1991, The Player, 1992, Joey Breaker, 1993, Flinch, 1994, Showgirls, 1995, Bound, 1996, Touch, 1997, Face/Off, 1997, This World, Then the Fireworks, 1997, Palmetto, 1998, Lulu on the Bridge, 1998, I'm Losing You, 1998, One Tough Cop, 1998, Prague Duet, 1998, Guinevere, 1999, The Insider, 1999, Black and White, 1999, Driven, 2001, Picture Claire, 2001, Slackers, 2002, Demonlover, 2002, Borderline, 2002, Prey for Rock & Roll, 2003, Out of Season, 2004, Three Way, 2004, One Last Thing, 2005, Dreamland, 2006, Man About Town, 2006, Kettle of Fish, 2006, Delirious, 2006, What Love Is, 2007, P.S. I Love You, 2007, Beer for my Horses, 2008; (TV miniseries) Sinatra, 1992; (TV series) The Days and Nights of Molly Dodd, 1989, Melrose Place, 1993, Snoops, 1999-2000, Tripping the Rift, 2004, Ugly Betty, 2006-07, Rescue Me, 2007, Curb Your Enthusiasm, 2004, 2007; (voice) Batman, 2004-07; (Broadway plays) Cabaret, 2001, Boeing-Boeing, 2008 (Drama Desk award for Oustanding Revival of a Play, 2008); appeared in plays at Long Wharf Theatre, New Haven, 1986, 90. Office: United Talent Agy 9560 Wilshire Blvd Ste 500 Beverly Hills CA 90212-2427

GERSTELL, A. FREDERICK, manufacturing executive; b. 1938; AB, Princeton U., 1960. Vice pres. mktg., dir. Alpha Portland Cement Co., 1960-75; v.p. Calif. Portland Cement Co., LA, 1975-81, pres., chief operating officer, 1981-84, CalMat Co., LA, 1984-88, pres., chief exec. officer, chief operating officer, 1988-90, chmn.bd., pres., chief exec. officer/chief operating officer, 1990-96, chmn. bd., CEO, 1996-98, vice chmn., dir., 1998—. Trustee emeritus The Lawrenceville (N.J.) Sch. With USAR 1960-66. Mem. Merchants and Mfrs. Assn. (dir.), Nat. Stone Assn. (bd. dirs., vice chmn., exec. com.), Calif. C. of C. (bd. dirs.), Ameron, Inc. (dir.). Office: CalMat Co 3200 N San Fernando Rd Los Angeles CA 90065-1415

GERSTENBERGER, DONNA LORINE, humanities educator; b. Wichita Falls, Tex., Dec. 26, 1929; d. Donald Fayette and Mabel G. AB, Whitman Coll., 1951; MA, U. Okla., 1952, PhD, 1958. Asst. prof. English U. Colo., Boulder, 1958-60; prof. U. Wash., 1960-96, prof. emeritus, 1996—, chmn. undergrad. studies, 1971-74, assoc. dean Coll. Arts and Scis., dir. Coll. Honors and Office Undergrad. Studies, 1974-76, chmn. dept. English, 1976-83, vice chmn. faculty senate, 1984-85, chmn. faculty senate, 1985-86. Cons. in field; bd. dirs. Am. Lit. Classics; mem. grants-in-aid com. Am. Coun. Learned Socs.; chmn. region VII, Mellon Fellowships in Humanities, 1982-92; mem. adv. com. Grad. Record Exams, 1990-93, Coun. Internat. Exch. of Scholars, 1992-95. Author: J.M. Synge, 1964, 2d edition, 1988, The American Novel: A Checklist of Twentieth Century Criticism, vols. I and II, 1970, Directory of Periodicals, 1974, The Complex Configuration: Modern Verse Drama, 1973, Iris Murdoch, 1974, Richard Hugo, 1983; editor: Microcosm, 1969, Swallow Series in Bibliography, 1974—; assoc. editor: Abstracts of English Studies, 1958-68; founder, editor jour. Seattle Rev., 1983-96. Bd. dirs. N.W. Chamber Orch., Seattle, 1975-78, Wash. Friends Humanities, 1991—; trustee Wash. Commn. Humanities, 1985-91, pres., 1988-90; mem. vis. com. Lehigh U., 1987-92; pres. Am. Commn. for Irish Studies/West, 1989-91. Grantee Am. Council Learned Socs., 1962, 88, Am. Philos. Soc., 1963 Mem. MLA, Am. Com. Irish Studies. Office: U Wash Box 354330 Dept English Seattle WA 98195-4330

GERSTING, JUDITH LEE, computer scientist, educator, researcher; b. Springfield, Vt., Aug. 20, 1940; d. Harold H. and Dorothy V. (Kinney) MacKenzie; m. John M. Gersting, Jr., Aug. 17, 1962; children: Adam, Jason. BS, Stetson U., 1962; MA, Ariz. State U., 1964, PhD, 1969. Assoc. prof. computer sci. U. Ctrl. Fla., Orlando, 1980—81; asst. prof. Ind. U./Purdue U., Indpls., 1970—73, assoc. prof., 1974—79, prof., 1981—93, U. Hawaii, Hilo, 1994—. Staff scientist Indpls. Ctr. Advanced Rsch., 1982—84. Author: Mathematical Structures for Computer Science, 2006; contbr. articles to sci. jours. Mem.: Assn. Computing Machinery. Avocations: youth soccer, reading. Office: U Hawaii 200 W Kawili St Hilo HI 96720-4075 Business E-Mail: gersting@hawaii.edu.

GERTH, DONALD ROGERS, retired university president, educator; b. Chgo., Dec. 4, 1928; s. George C. and Madeleine (Canavan) G.; m. Beverly J. Hollman, Oct. 15, 1955; children: Annette, Deborah. BA, U. Chgo., 1947, AM, 1951, PhD, 1963. Field rep. S.E. Asia World Univ. Svc., 1950; asst. to pres. Shimer Coll., 1951; Admissions counselor U. Chgo., 1956-58; assoc. dean students, admissions and records, mem. dept. polit. sci. San Francisco St. U., San Francisco, 1958-63; assoc. dean instnl. relations and student affairs Calif. State U., 1963-64, chmn. commn. on extended edn., 1977-82, dean of students Chico, 1964-68, prof. polit. sci., 1964-76, assoc. v.p. acad. affairs, dir. internat. programs, 1969-70, v.p. acad. affairs, 1970-76, pres., prof. polit. sci. Dominguez Hills, 1976-84, pres., prof. pub. policy and adminstrn. Sacramento, 1984—2003, pres., prof. emeritus, 2003—; co-dir. Danforth Found. Research Project, 1968-69; coordinator Inst. Local Govt. and Public Service, 1968-70. Past chair Accrediting Commn. for Sr. Colls. and Univs. of Western Coll. Assn.; chmn. admissions coun. Calif. State U., 1974-03; bd. dirs. Ombudsman Found., L.A., 1968-71; lectr. U. Philippines, 1953-54, Claremont Grad. Sch. and Univ. Ctr., 1965-69; mem. World Trade Ctr. No. Calif., 1996, chair, 1996-03; chmn. Calif. State U. Inst., 1997-98; pres. Internat. Assn. Univ. Pres. 1996-99; mem. governing bd. UN Univ. Coun., 1998-2004, vice chair, 2002-04; mem. Am. Coun. for the UN Univ., 1998—, chair, 2004—. Co-author: The Learning Society, 1969; author, editor: An Invisible Giant, 1971; contbg. editor Education for the Public Service, 1970, Papers on the Ombudsman in Higher Education, 1979. Mem. pers. commn. Chico Unified Sch. Dist., 1969-76, chmn., 1971-74; adv. com. justice pgorams Butte Coll., 1970-76; mem. Varsity Scouting Coun., 1980-84; chmn. United Way campaign Calif. State Univs., LA County, 1981-82; bd. dirs. Sacramento Area United Way, campaign chmn., 1991-92, exec. com., 1991-96, vice chmn., 1992-94, chmn.-elect, 1994-95, chmn., 1995-96; bd. dirs. South Bay Hosp. Found., 1979-82; mem. Cultural Commn., LA, 1981-84; mem. com. govtl. rels. Am. Coun. Edn. Active USAF, 1952—56, released as capt. USAF, 1956. Mem. Internat. Assn. Univ. Pres. (pres. 1996-99), Am. Polit. Sci. Assn., Am. Soc. Pub. Adminstrn., Soc. Coll. and Univ. Planning, Western Govtl. Rsch. Assn., World Affairs Coun. No. Calif., Assn. Pub. Adminstrn. Edn. (chmn. 1973-74), Western Polit. Sci. Assn., Am. Assn. State Colls. and Univs. (bd. dirs.), Calif. State C. of C. (edn. com.), Calif. State U. Inst. (chmn. bd. dirs.), UN Ednl., Sci. and Cultural Orgn. (mem. adv. com.), UN U. Coun. (governing bd. 1998-04, vice chair 2001-04), Am. Coun. UN U. (chair 2004-). Democrat. Episcopalian. Avocations: tennis, skiing, reading. Mailing: 7132 Secret Garden Loop Roseville CA 95747-8041 Office: Calif State U Rm 3022 Libr 2000 State University Dr East Sacramento CA 95819-6039 Office Phone: 916-278-7400. Business E-Mail: dongerth@csus.edu.

GESCHKE, CHARLES M., computer company executive; b. Cleve., Sept. 11, 1939; married, 1964; 3 children. AB in Classics, Xavier U., 1962, MS in Math., 1963; PhD in Computer Sci., Carnegie-Mellon U., 1972. Instr. math. John Carroll U., 1963—68; rsch. scientist computer sci. LAB. Palo Alto Rsch. Ctr., Xerox Corp., 1972—80, mgr. Imaging Sci. Lab., 1980—87; co-founder Adobe Sys. Inc., Mountain View, Calif., 1982, pres., chmn. bd., 1987—2000, co-chmn. bd., 2000—. Bd. dirs. Rambus, Inc.; computer sci. adv. bd. Carnegie-Mellon U., Princeton U.; mem. Govt.-Univ. Industry Rsch. Roundtable NAS. Bd. govs. San Francisco Symphony; bd. trustees U. San Francisco. Recipient award, Assn. Computing Machinery, Nat. Computer Graphics Assn., Rochester Inst. Tech., Fellow award, Computer History Mus., 2002; named 7th most influential graphics person of last millennium, Graphic Exch. Mag., 2000. Fellow: Am. Acad. Arts & Scis.; mem.: NAE, IEEE (hon.), Math. Assn. Am., Assn. Computer Math. Achievements include research in programming languages; machine design for efficient emulation of higher level languages; computer imaging and graphics.

GESHELL, RICHARD STEVEN, lawyer; b. Colorado Springs, Colo., Aug. 6, 1943; s. Peter Steven and Ann Elizabeth (Irwin) G.; m. Carol Ann Reed, Sept. 6, 1965; 1 child, Carmen Marie. BA in Chemistry, Ariz. State U., 1965; JD, U. Nebr., 1968. Bar: Nebr. 1968, U.S. Dist. Ct. Nebr. 1968, Hawaii 1983, U.S. Dist. Ct. Hawaii 1983, U.S. Ct. Appeals (9th cir.) 1984, U.S. Supreme Ct. 1986. With Robak and Geshell, Columbus, Nebr., 1968-83; ptnr. R. Steven Geshell, Honolulu, 1983—. Lawyer; b. Colorado Springs, Colo., Aug. 6, 1943; s. Peter Steven and Ann Elizabeth (Irwin) G.; m. Carol Ann Reed, Sept. 6, 1965; 1 child, Carmen Marie. BA in Chemistry, Ariz. State U., 1965; JD, U. Nebr., 1968. Bar: Nebr. 1968, U.S. Dist. Ct. Nebr. 1968, Hawaii 1983, U.S. Dist. Ct. Hawaii 1983, U.S. Ct. Appeals (9th cir.) 1984, U.S. Supreme Ct. 1986. Mem. Robak and Geshell, Columbus, Nebr., 1968-83; ptnr. R. Steven Geshell, Honolulu, 1983—. Served to capt. USAR, 1974-83. Mem. Hawaii Bar Assn., Blue Key (pres. 1964-65), Elks (chief forum 1984, trustee), Phi Sigma Kappa. Republican. Capt. USAR, 1974-83. Mem. Hawaii Bar Assn., Blue Key (pres. 1964-65), Elks (chief forum 1984, trustee), Phi Sigma Kappa. Republican. Home: 1155 Kaluanui Rd Honolulu HI 96825-1357 Office: Ste #116 6600 Kalanianaole Hwy Honolulu HI 96825 Home Phone: 808-396-8261; Office Phone: 808-396-7701. Personal E-mail: geshell@lava.net.

GEST, HOWARD DAVID, lawyer; b. Bergenfield, NJ, Jan. 24, 1952; m. Lucy Acevedo; 1 child, Aaron. AB in Econs., U. Calif., Berkeley, 1974; JD, Hastings Coll., 1977. Bar: Calif. 1977. Staff atty. US Ct. Appeals (9th cir.), San Francisco, 1977-78; asst. U.S. atty. Cen. Dist. Calif., LA, 1978-83; assoc. Sidley & Austin, LA, 1983—86, ptnr., 1986—99, Burhenn & Gest, LA, 2000—. Office: Burhenn & Gest LLP Ste 2200 624 S Grand Ave Los Angeles CA 90017 Home Phone: 310-458-6258; Office Phone: 213-688-7715. Business E-Mail: hgest@burhenngest.com.

GESTON, MARK SYMINGTON, lawyer; b. Atlantic City, June 20, 1946; s. John Charles and Mary Tobiatha (Simmington) G.; m. Gayle Francis Howard, June 12, 1971 (div. Aug. 1972); m. Marijke Havinga, Aug. 14, 1976; children: Camille LaCroix, Robert L. LaCroix, Emily S. Geston. AB in History (with honors), Kenyon Coll., 1968; JD, NYU, 1971. Bar: Idaho, U.S. Ct. Appeals (9th cir.). With Eberle and Berlin, 1971—2003; atty. Stoel Rives LLP, Boise, Idaho, 2003—. Author: Lords of the Starship, 1967, Out of the Mouth of the Dragon, 1969, The Day Star, 1972, The Seige of Wonder, 1975, Mirror to the Sky, 1992, The Stronghold If, 1973; contbr. stories to Amazing Stories, Fantasy and Sci. Fiction. Recipient Kenyon Rev. prize for achievement in lit., Kenyon Coll., 1968; named Root-Tilden fellow NYU, 1968-71. Mem. Idaho State Bar Assn., Phi Beta Kappa. Avocation: writing. Office: Stoel Rives LLP 101 S Capitol Blvd Boise ID 83702 Home Phone: 208-343-0559; Office Phone: 208-387-4291. Business E-Mail: msgeston@stoel.com.

GETCHES, DAVID HARDING, lawyer, educator, dean; b. Abington, Pa., Aug. 17, 1942; s. George Winslow Getches and Ruth Erskine (Harding) Fossette; m. Ann Marks, June 26, 1964; children: Matthew, Catherine, Elizabeth. AB, Occidental Coll., 1964; JD, U. So. Calif., 1967. Bar: Calif. 1968, U.S. Supreme Ct. 1971, D.C. 1972, Colo. 1973. Assoc. Luce, Forward, Hamilton & Scripps, San Diego, 1967-69; directing atty. Calif. Indian Legal Services, Escondido, 1969-70; founding dir. Native Am. Rights Fund, Boulder, Colo., 1970-76; ptnr. Getches & Greene, Boulder, Colo., 1976-78; assoc. prof. U. Colo. Law Sch., Boulder, Colo., 1979—87, prof., 1987—94, Raphael J. Moses Prof. of Natural Resources Law, 1994—, interim dir. Natural Resources Law Ctr., 1995, dean, 2003—; exec. dir. Colo. Dept. Natural Resources, Denver, 1983-87; spl. consultant to sec. U.S. Dept. Interior, Washington, 1996. Ptnr. MB Land Co., Centro Bldg. Devel. Co. Author: Water Law in a Nutshell, 1997; co-author: Cases and Materials on Federal Indian Law, 2005, Water Resources Management, 5th edit., 2002; contbr. articles to profl. jours. Bd. trustees Rocky Mountain Mineral Law Fedn. Mem. Wilderness Soc. (governing coun.), Defenders of Wildlife (bd. dirs.). Democrat. Office: University Colorado School of Law Fleming Law Building 401 UCB Boulder CO 80309-0401 Home Phone: 303-449-4869; Office Phone: 303-492-3084. Business E-Mail: lawdean@colorado.edu.

GETIS, ARTHUR, geography educator; b. Phila., July 6, 1934; s. Samuel J. and Sophie Getis; m. Judith M. Marckwardt, July 23, 1961; children: Hilary Hope Tarazi, Victoria Lynn, Anne Patterson Tibbetts. BS, Pa. State U., University Park, 1956, MS, 1958; PhD, U. Wash., Seattle, 1961. Asst. instr. geography U. Wash., 1960-61; asst. prof. Mich. State U., 1961-63; faculty Rutgers U., New Brunswick, NJ, 1963-77, prof. geography, 1969-77, dir. grad. programs in geography, 1970-73, chmn. New Brunswick geography dept., 1971-73; prof. geography U. Ill., Urbana-Champaign, 1977-90, San Diego State U., 1990—, doctoral program coord., 1990-92, Stephen/Mary Birch Found. endowed chair geog. studies, 1992—2004, disting. prof. geography, 2004—, Albert W. Johnson univ. rsch. lectr., 1995; head dept. U. Ill., 1977-83, dir. Sch. Social Scis., 1983-84; centennial fellow Pa. State U., 1996, E. Willard Miller Lectr., 2007; A. Robinson lectr. Ohio State U., 1999. Vis. lectr. Bristol U., Eng., 1966-67, UCLA, summers 1968, 74, U. BC, 1969; vis. prof. Princeton U., 1971-74; vis. disting. prof. San Diego State U., 1989; mem. Regional Sci. Rsch. Group, Harvard U., 1970; panelist NSF, 1981-83 Author (with B.

Boot): Models of Spatial Processes, 1978, Point Pattern Analysis, 1988; author: (with J. Getis and J.D. Fellmann) Geography, 1981; author: (with J. Getis and J.D. Fellman) Human Geography, 10th edit., 2008, Introduction to Geography, 12th edit., 2008; author: (edited with J. Getis and J.D. Fellmann) The United States and Canada, 1995, 2d edit., 2001, The Tyranny of Data, 1996; author: (edited with M.M. Fischer) Recent Developments in Spatial Analysis, 1997; author: (with J. Mur and H. Zoller) Spatial Econometrics and Spatial Statistics, 2004; editor-in-chief: Jour. Geog. Sys., 1992—2008, hon. editor:, 2008, contbg. editor, assoc. editor: Jour. Geography, 1972—74, mem. editl. bd.: Nat. Geog. Rsch., 1984—90, Rsch. and Exploration, 1991—95, Geog. Analysis, 1991—, Papers in Regional Sci., 1999—2002, Annals of Regional Sci., 1999—, Regional Rsch. Inst., 2003—; contbr. articles to profl. jours. Mem. Urbana Zoning Bd. Appeals, 1980-84; co-pres. Univ. High Sch. Parent-Faculty Orgn., 1982-83; bd. dirs. Univ. Consortium for Geog. Info. Scis., 1997-2004, pres.-elect, 2000-02, pres. 2002-03. Rutgers U. faculty fellow, 1970; East-West Center sr. fellow, 1974; NSF grantee, 1983-85, 1992-94, 99-2007, NIH grantee, 1999—; recipient Walter Isard award N.Am. Regional Sci. Coun., 1997. Fellow Western Regional Sci. Assn. (bd. dirs. 1992-97, pres. 1998-99), Regional Sci. Assn. Internat. (pres. N.E. sect. 1973-74, bd. dirs. 1998-2007); mem. Assn. Am. Geographers (grantee 1964-65, vis. scientist 1970-72, chair math. models and quantitative methods splty. group 1991-92, honors for disting. scholarship 2002, Robert T. Aangeenbrug Disting. Career award), Internat. Inst. Brit. Geographers, Internat. Geog. Union (sec. commn. math. models 1988-96), Sigma Xi. Home: 5135 Jumilla St San Diego CA 92124-1503 Office: San Diego State U Dept Geography San Diego CA 92182 Business E-Mail: arthur.getis@sdsu.edu.

GETREU, SANFORD, retired city planner; b. Mar. 9, 1930; s. Isadore and Tillie (Kuchinsky) G.; m. Gara Eileen Smith, Dec. 8, 1952 (div. Feb. 1983); children: David Bruce, Gary Benjamin, Allen Dana; m. Kelly Heim, Aug. 8, 1988. BA in Arch., Ohio State U., 1953; MA in Regional Planning, Cornell U., 1955. Resident planner Mackesey & Reps., consultants, Rome, N.Y., 1955-56; planning dir. Rome, 1956-57; dir. gen. planning Syracuse, NY, 1957-59; dep. commr. planning, 1959-62; commr. planning Syracuse, 1962—65; planning dir. San Jose, Calif., 1965-74; urban planning cons., 1974—2008. Pres. Sanford Getreu, AICP, Inc., vis. lectr., critic Cornell U., 1960-65, Syracuse U., 1962-65, Stanford, 1965, San Jose State Coll., 1965, Santa Clara U., Calif. State Poly. Coll., DeAnza Coll., San Jose City Coll., U. Calif. at Berkeley; pres. planning dept. League of Calif. Cities, 1973-74; advisor State of Calif. Office of Planning and Research. Past bd. dirs. Theater Guild, San Jose, Triton Mus., San Jose. Mem. Am. Soc. Cons. Planners, Am. Planning Assn., Am. Inst. Cert. Planners, Bay Area Planning Dirs. Assn. (v.p. 1965-74, mem. exec. com. 1973-74), Assn. Bay Area Govts. (regional planning com. 1967-74), Rotary. Home and Office: PO Box 685 Pebble Beach CA 93953-0685

GETTO, ERNEST JOHN, lawyer; b. DuBois, Pa., May 24, 1944; s. Ernest F. and Olga (Gagliardi) G.; m. Judith Payne, Aug. 19, 1967; children: Matthew Payne, Christopher Ernest, Sarah Elizabeth. BA, Cornell U., 1966; JD, Vanderbilt U., 1969. Bar: NY 1970, Calif. 1973. Assoc. Simpson Thacher & Bartlett, NYC, 1969-73; from assoc. to ptnr. Kadison, Pfaelzer, Woodard, Quinn & Rossi, LA, 1973-80; ptnr. Latham & Watkins LLP, San Francisco & LA, 1980—, chair litig. dept., 1991—95. Past bd. dirs. Calif. Pediatric and Family Med. Ctr., LA, Children's Hosp. of LA Rsch. Inst. Named one of 100 Power Lawyers, Hollywood Reporter, 2007. Fellow Am. Coll. Trial Lawyers; mem. ABA, Calif. Bar Assn., LA Bar Assn., NY State Bar Assn., Assn. Bus. Trial Lawyers, Calif. Club, Valley Club Montecito, Lake Merced Golf Club. Republican. Roman Catholic. Office: Latham & Watkins Ste 2000 505 Montgomery St San Francisco CA 94111-2562 Office Phone: 415-395-8189. Office Fax: 415-395-8095. E-mail: ernie.getto@lw.com.

GETTY, BALTHAZAR, actor; b. LA, Jan. 22, 1975; s. Paul and Gisela Getty; m. Rosetta Millington, May 3, 2000 (separated); 4 children. Former fashion model Calvin Klien, Tommy Hilfiger, Versace. Actor: (films) Lord of the Flies, 1990, Young Guns II, 1990, My Heroes Have Always Been Cowboys, 1991, The Pope Must Diet, 1991, Where the Day Takes You, 1992, Natural Born Killers, 1994, Judge Dredd, 1995, White Squall, 1996, Lost Highway, 1997, Habitat, 1997, Fait Accompli, 1998, Out in Fifty, 1999, Big City Blues, 1999, Shadow Hours, 2000, Four Dogs Playing Poker, 2000, Sol Goode, 2001, MacArthur Park, 2001, The Center of the World, 2001, Run for the Money, 2002, Deuces Wild, 2002, Ladder 49, 2004, Slingshot, 2005, Feast, 2005, (TV films) The Turn of the Screw, 1990, Corsairs, 2002, Dirtbags, 2006, (TV miniseries) Traffic, 2004, Into the West, 2005, (TV series) Charmed, 2003-04, Alias, 2005-06, Brothers & Sisters, 2006-.

GETTY, GORDON PETER, composer, philanthropist; b. LA, Dec. 20, 1933; s. J. Paul and Ann Rork (Light) G.; m. Ann Getty; 4 children. Studied with Easton Kent, studied with Robert Vetlesen, studied with Sol Joseph, 1961-62; BS, San Francisco Conservatory Music, degree (hon.) in music, 1981, Pepperdine U., 1985; doctorate (hon.), Mannes Coll. Music, NYC, 1986. Former cons. Getty Oil Co., dir.; former chmn. LSB Leakey Found., Pasadena, Calif., now trustee. Works include opera in two acts Plump Jack, commnd. by Globe Shakespeare Ctr., London, performed by San Francisco Symphony, 1985, also Scene One broadcast live from Davies Symphony Hall, San Francisco, Mar. 1985; Emily Dickinson Song Cycle The White Election, 30 performances U.S. and abroad, 1981-85, also broadcast live from Nat. Gallery Art, Washington, 1985; Victorian Scenes, performed San Francisco Girls Chorus U. Calif., Berkeley, WInifred Baker Choral, 1985; Nine Piano Pieces performed by Stewart Gordon, 1985; A Cappella Choruses and Piano Works broadcast live Georgetown U., Washington, Apr., 1985; author monograph on White Election, poems My Uncle's House, 1984, other poetry. Adv. dir. Met. Opera, 1977—; trustee Mannes Coll. Music, 1982—; dir. San Francisco Symphony, 1979—. Recipient Golden Plate award Am. Acad. Achievement, 1985, Achievement Arts award Northwood Inst., 1985; named on of Forbes' Richest Americans, 2006. Office: Rork Music Publ 1 Embarcadero Ctr Ste 1050 San Francisco CA 94111-3698

GETZ, BERT ATWATER, investment company executive; b. Chgo., May 7, 1937; s. George Fulmer Jr. and Olive Cox (Atwater) G.; m. Sandra Maclean, July 17, 1958; children: Lynn Getz, George F., Bert A. Jr. BSBA, U. Mich., 1959. V.p. Globe Corp., Scottsdale, Ariz., 1960-74, pres., bd. dirs., 1974—, CEO, 1992—. Bd. dirs. Bank of Am., Ill., Dean Foods Co., Franklin Park, Ill., Ameritas Life Ins. Corp., Lincoln, bd. trustees, Mayo Found., Rochester (chmn. 2002—), dir. and pres. Globe Found., Arthur R. Merch Found. Bd. dirs. Western Golf Assn., Golf, Ill., Ind. U. Found., Bloomington, Nat. Hist. Fire Found.; chmn. bd. govs. Merit Club, Libertyville, Ill.; trustee Lawrenceville (N.J.) Sch., 1972—, pres. bd. dirs. 1984-90, trustee emeritus, 1990; trustee Ariz. Cmty. Found., Phoenix, 1978—, chmn. bd. dirs., 1981-89, chmn. emeritus, 1989. Mem. Phoenix Thunderbirds, Paradise Valley Country Club, John Gardiners Tennis Ranch, Merit Club, Sigma Chi, Theta Theta. Republican. Episcopalian. Avocations: tennis, golf. Home: 6335 W Highway 120 Libertyville IL 60048-9788 Office: Globe Corp 6730 N Scottsdale Rd Ste 250 Scottsdale AZ 85253-4416

GETZLAF, RYAN, professional hockey player; b. Regina, Sask., Can., May 10, 1985; Center Anaheim Ducks (formerly Mighty Ducks of Anaheim), 2005—. Mem. Team Canada, World Junior Championships, Grand Forks, ND, 2005. Named to NHL YoungStars Game, 2007, NHL All-Star Game, 2008, 2009. Achievements include being a member of Gold Medal Team Canada, World Junior Championships, 2005; being a member of Stanley Cup Champion Anaheim Ducks, 2007. Office: Anaheim Ducks 2695 E Katella Ave Anaheim CA 92806*

GEWERTZ, BRUCE LABE, surgeon, educator; b. Phila., Aug. 27, 1949; s. Milton and Shirley (Charen) G.; children: Samantha, Barton, Alexis; m. Diane Weiss, Aug. 31, 1997. BS, Pa. State U., State Coll., 1968; MD, Jefferson Med. Coll., Phila., 1972. Diplomate Am. Bd. Surgery. Surg. resident U. Mich., Ann Arbor, 1972-77; asst. prof. U. Tex., Dallas, 1977-81; assoc. prof. U. Chgo., 1981-87, prof. surgery, 1988—, faculty dean med. edn., 1989-92, Dallas Phemister prof., chmn. dept. surgery, 1992—2006; chmn. dept. surgery, surgeon-in-chief, v.p. Cedars-Sinai Med. Ctr., LA, 2006—. Tchg. scholar Am. Heart Assn., Dallas, 1980-83; pres. Assn. Surg. Edn., 1983-84; dir. vascular surgery bd. Am. Bd. Surgery, 2001—. Author: Atlas of Vascular Surgery, 1989, 2005, Surgery of the Aorta and its Branches, 2000; editor Jour. Surg. Rsch., 1987-2002; patentee removable vascular filter. Recipient Jobst award Coller Surg. Soc., 1975, Coller award Mich. chpt. Am. Coll. Surgeons, 1975, Outstanding Sci. Alumnus award Pa. State U., 2003. Mem. Soc. Vascular Surgery, Midwestern Vascular Soc. (pres. 1994-95), Soc. Clin. Surgery, Soc. Univ. Surgeons, Chgo. Surg. Soc. (pres. 2005), Western Surg. Assn. (pres. 2007-08), Am. Surg. Assn. Office: Cedars-Sinai Med Ctr 8700 Beverly Blvd Los Angeles CA 90048 Office Phone: 310-423-5884. Business E-Mail: bruce.gewertz@cshs.org.

GEYMAN, JOHN PAYNE, physician, educator; b. Santa Barbara, Calif., Feb. 9, 1931; s. Milton John and Betsy (Payne) Geyman; m. Eugenia Clark Deichler, June 9, 1956; children: John Matthew, James Caleb, William Sabin. AB in Geology, Princeton U., 1952; MD, U. Calif., San Francisco, 1960. Diplomate Am. Bd. Family Practice. Intern L.A. County Gen. Hosp., 1960—61; resident in gen. practice Sonoma County Hosp., Santa Rosa, Calif., 1961—63; pvt. practice specializing in family practice Mt. Shasta, Calif., 1963—69; dir. family practice residency program Cmty. Hosp. Sonoma County, Santa Rosa, 1969—71; assoc. prof. family practice, chmn. divsn. family practice U. Utah, 1971—72; prof., vice chmn. dept. family practice U. Calif., Davis, 1972—77; prof., chmn. dept. family medicine U. Wash., 1977—90, prof. family medicine, 1990—93, prof. family medicine emeritus, 1993—. Author: The Modern Family Doctor and Changing Medical Practice, 1971, Family Practice: Foundation of Changing Health Care, 1980, 2d edit., 1985, Flight as a Lifetime Passion: Adventures, Misadventures and Lessons, 2000, Falling Through the Safety Net: Americans Without Health Insurance, 2005; editor: Content of Family Practice, 1976, Family Practice in the Medical School, 1977, Research in Family Practice, 1978, Preventive Medicine in Family Practice, 1979, Profile of the Residency Trained Family Physician in the U.S, 1970—79, Funding of Patient Care, Education and Research in Family Practice, 1981, The Content of Family Practice: Current Status and Future Trends, 1982, Archives of Family Practice, 1980—82, Family Practice: An International Perspective in Developed Countries, 1983, Jour. Am. Bd. Family Practice, 1990—2003; founding editor Jour. Family Practice, 1973—90; co-editor: Behavioral Science in Family Practice, 1980, Evidence-Based Clinical Practice: Concepts and Approaches, 2000, Textbook of Rural Medicine, 2000, Health Care in America: Can Our Ailing System Be Healed?, 2002, The Corporate Transformation of Health Care: Can the Public Interest Still be Served?, 2004, Shredding of the Social Contract: The Privatization of Medicare, 2006, An Open Cockpit Biplane Dream: Honey Bee III, 2005, The Corrosion of Medicine: Can the Profession Reclaim Its moral Legacy, 2008, Do Not Resuscitate Why the Health Insurance Industry is Dying and How We Must Replace It, 2008. Pres. Physicians for Nat. Health Program, 2005—07. Served to lt. (j.g.) USN, 1952—55, PTO. Recipient Gold-Headed Cane award, U. Calif. Sch. Medicine, 1960, Alumnus of Yr. award, 1998. Mem.: Inst. Medicine NAS, Soc. Tchrs. Family Medicine, Am. Acad. Family Physicians. Unitarian Universalist. Home: 53 Avian Ridge Ln Friday Harbor WA 98250-8895 Business E-Mail: jgeyman@u.washington.edu.

GHAUSI, MOHAMMED SHUAIB, retired dean, electrical engineer, educator; b. Kabul, Afghanistan, Feb. 16, 1930; came to U.S., 1951, naturalized, 1963; s. Mohammed Omar; m. Marilyn Buchwold, June 12, 1961; children: Nadjya, Simine. BS summa cum laude, U. Calif., Berkeley, 1956, MS, 1957, PhD, 1960. Prof. elec. engring. NYU, 1960-72; head elec. scis. sect. NSF, Washington, 1972-74; prof., chmn. elec. engring. dept. Wayne State U., Detroit, 1974-77; John F. Dodge prof. Oakland U., Rochester, Mich., 1978-83, dean Sch. Engring. and Computer Sci., 1978-83; dean Coll. Engring., U. Calif., Davis, 1983-96, interim vice chancellor rsch., vice provost, dean grad., 1996-97; ret., 1997. Mem. adv. panel NSF, 1989. Author, co-author: Principles and Design of Linear Active Circuits, 1965, Introduction to Distributed-Parameter Networks, 1968, Electronic Circuits, 1971, Modern Filter Design: Active RC and Switched Capacitor, 1981, Electronic Devices and Circuits: Discrete and Integrated, 1985, Design of Analog Filters, 1990, Introduction to Electronic Circuit Design, 2003, also numerous articles.; cons. editor Van Nostrand Rinehold Pub. Co., 1968-71. Mem. disting. alumni rev. panel Elec. Engring. and Computer Sci. programs U. Calif., Berkeley, 1973; mem. external bd. visitors U. Pa., 1974. Recipient Outstanding Alumnus award in Elec. Engring. and Computer Sci., U. Calif., 1998. Fellow IEEE (chmn. edn. medal com. 1990-92, Centennial medal, Alexander von Humboldt prize 1983, circuits and systems soc. edn. award); mem. Circuits and System Soc. (v.p. 1970-72, pres. 1976), N.Y. Acad. Scis., Engring. Soc. Detroit, Sigma Xi, Phi Beta Kappa, Tau Beta Pi, Eta Kappa Nu. Business E-Mail: msghausi@comcast.net.

GHEZ, ANDREA MIA, astronomy and physics educator; b. NYC, June 16, 1965; d. Gilbert and Susanne Ghez; m. Tom LaTourette, May 1, 1993; 1 child, Evan LaTourette-Ghez. BS, MIT, 1987; MS, Calif. Inst. Tech., 1989, PhD in Physics, 1992. Hubble postdoctoral fellow U. Ariz., Tucson, 1992-93; vis. rsch. scholar Inst. Astronomy, Cambridge, England, 1994; asst. prof. physics and astronomy UCLA, 1994-97, assoc. prof., 1997—2000, prof., 2000—. Contbr. articles to profl. jours. Recipient Amelia Earhart award, 1987, Young Investigator award, NSF, 1994, Fullam/Dudley award, 1995, Maria Goeppert-Mayer award, Am. Phys. Soc., 1999, Sackler prize, U. Tel Aviv, 2004; named a MacArthur Fellow, The John D. and Catherine T. MacArthur Found., 2008; grantee Pacific Telesis fellowship, 1991, Alfred P. Sloan Rsch. fellowship, 1996, David and Lucile Packard fellowship, 1996. Fellow: Am. Acad. Arts & Scis.; mem.: AAUW, Am. Astron. Soc. (Annie Jump Cannon award 1994, Newton Lacy Pierce prize 1998), NAS, Phi Beta Kappa. Achievements include discovery of formation of young low mass stars in multiple star systems; production of the first diffraction-limited image with the keck 10-m telescope (the largest telescope in the world); measurement of stellar motions which indicate the presence of a supermassive black hole at the center of our own galaxy. Office: UCLA Divsn Astronomy and Astrophysics Physics and Astronomy Bldg 430 Portola Plz Box 951547 Los Angeles CA 90095-1547 Office Phone: 310-206-0420. E-mail: ghez@astro.ucla.edu.

GHOSH, SAMBHUNATH (SAM), environmental engineer, educator; BS, U. Calcutta, 1956; MS, U. Ill., 1963; PhD, Ga. Inst. Tech., Atlanta, 1970. Engr. Wiedeman & Singleton, Atlanta, 1963—65; mgr. bioengring. rsch. Gas Tech. Inst., Chgo., 1971—85; prof. civil engring. U. Utah, Salt Lake City, 1985—2000; prof. civil, agrl. and geol. engring. N.Mex State U., Las Cruces, 2000—01; pres. EnviroEnergetics, Salt Lake City, 1988—, EnviroEnergetics of Wis., Inc., 2005—. Recipient Ill. Energy award, 1985, Utah Gov.'s award for energy innovation, 1986, John Ericsson award and Gold medal in Renewable Energy, U.S. Dept. Energy, 1994, George Bradley Gascoigne medal, Water Environment Fedn., 1996, Thomas R. Camp medal, Water Environment Fedn., Alexandria, Va., 2001. Home: 1281 E Federal Heights Dr Salt Lake City UT 84103-4325 Office Phone: 801-355-1429. Personal E-mail: sambhughosh@aol.com.

GIAMBI, JASON GILBERT, professional baseball player; b. West Covina, Calif., Jan. 8, 1971; s. John and Jeanne Giambi; m. Dana Mandela, Nov. 9, 1996 (div.); m. Kristian Rice, Feb. 2002. Grad., Long Beach State U. 1st baseman Oakland Athletics, Calif., 1995—2001, 1st baseman, designated hitter, 2009—, NY Yankees, 2002—08. Spokesman CAP Cure; contbr. The Zone, Mount Sinai Hosp., NYC. Named Am. League MVP, 2000, Am. League Comeback Player of Yr., 2005; named to US Olympic Baseball team, Barcelona, 1992, Am. League All-star team, 2000, 2001, 2002, 2003, 2004. Avocations: off-roading, WWF. Office: c/o Oakland A's 7677 Oakport St Ste 200 Oakland CA 94621-1933*

GIANCARLO, CHARLES H., investment company executive, former computer systems network executive; b. 1957; m. Dianne Giancarlo. BSEE, Brown U., 1978; MSEE, U. Calif., Berkeley; MBA, Harvard U. Co-founder, former v.p. mktg. Adaptive Corp.; v.p. mktg. and corp. devel. Kalpana, Inc. (acquired by Cisco Systems, Inc.), 1993—94; dir. bus. devel. to v.p. Cisco Systems, Inc., San Jose, Calif., 1994—98, v.p. global alliances, 1997—99, sr. v.p. global alliances, 1998—99, sr. v.p., commercial line of bus., 1999—2001, sr. v.p., gen. mgr., access, aggregation, ethernet switching and wireless groups, 2001—02, sr. v.p. switching, voice and storage groups, 2002—03, chief tech. officer, 2004—05, sr. v.p., 2005—07, chief develop. officer, 2005—07, exec. v.p., 2007; pres. Cisco Systems-Linksys, LLC, 2003—07; chair Cisco Enterprise Bus. Coun.; mng. ptnr. Silver Lake, Menlo Park, Calif., 2008—. Founder ATM Forum; leader, Voice Technology and Global Gov. Solutions Cisco Systems, Inc.; former head Cisco Service Provider Bus. Coun.; co-chair Cisco Enterprise Bus. Coun.; bd. dirs. Netflix, Inc., 2007—. Patentee in field. Named one of The Top 50 Most Powerful People in Networking, Network World, 2003—07. Achievements include holding multiple patents in the areas of ATM and voice technologies. Office: Silver Lake 2775 Sand Hill Rd Ste 100 Menlo Park CA 94025

GIANNINI, VALERIO LOUIS, investment banker; b. NYC, Feb. 7, 1938; s. Gabriel M. and Luisa M. (Casazza) G.; m. Linda Martin, Oct. 6, 1979; children: Martin Louis, Alexander Elliot, Charles Gabriel. BSE, Princeton U., 1959. With Kidder Peabody & Co., NYC, 1961-64; sr. cons. IIT Rsch. Inst., Chgo., 1964-66; sec. Giannini-Voltex, LA, 1966-68; pres. V.L. Giannini & Co., LA, 1968-76; CEO Namco Chems., Inc., 1975; dir. White House ops., Washington, 1977-78; dep. spl. asst. to Pres. for adminstrn. White House, 1979-80; dep. asst. sec. Dept. Commerce, Washington, 1980-81; prin. Cumberland Investment Group, NYC, 1981-87; pres. Numex Corp., 1986-87; CEO, Geneva Bus. Network, Inc., Irvine, Calif., 1987-90. Adj. prof. Argyros Sch. Bus., Chapman U., 2001; founder Eurosearch Ptnr., Newport Beach, Calif., 1990; prin. Newcap Ptnr., 1995; bd. dir. Dudek & Assoc., Pro-Dex, Inc., 2002—09. Pres. Lido Jr. Sailing Found., 2000-03. Lt. USNR, 1959-61 Mem. N.Y. Yacht Club, Newport Harbor Yacht Club. Office: 1122 Bristol St Costa Mesa CA 92626 Office Phone: 714-241-8686. Business E-Mail: vgiannini@att.net.

GIANNOTTA, STEVEN LOUIS, neurosurgery educator; b. Detroit, Apr. 4, 1947; s. Louis D. and Betty Jane (Root) G.; m. Sharon Danielak, June 13, 1970; children: Brent, Nicole, Robyn. Student, U. Detroit, 1965-68; MD, U. Mich., 1972. Diplomate Am. Bd. Neurol. Surgeons. Surg. intern U. Mich., Ann Arbor, 1972-73, neurosurg. resident, 1973-78; asst. prof. neurosurgery UCLA, 1978-80; asst. prof. neurosurgery Sch. Medicine U. So. Calif., LA, 1980-83, assoc. prof. neurosurgery Sch. Medicine, 1983-89, prof. neurosurgery Sch. Medicine, 1989—, chmn. dept. neurosurgery, 2004—. Bd. dirs. Am. Bd. Neurol. Surgery, 1995—2001, sec., 1999—2000, chmn., 2000—01. Fellow ACS, Am. Heart Assn. (stroke coun., rsch. grantee 1980, 84), So. Calif. Neurol. Soc. (pres. 1993-94), Congress Neurol. Surgeons (sec. 1986-89, v.p. 1993) Soc. Clin. Neuroscis. (L.A. pres. 1992-93), Am. Assn. Neurol. Surgeons (bd. dirs. 2001-). Democrat. Roman Catholic. Avocations: golf, skiing, sports cars. Office: Neurosurgery Ste 5046 1200 N State St Los Angeles CA 90033-1029 Office Phone: 323-442-5720.

GIANNULLI, MOSSIMO, designer, apparel business executive; b. June 4, 1963; s. Gene and Nancy; m. Chris Clausen, 1988 (div. 1995); 1 child, Gianni; m. Lori Loughlin, 1997; children: Isabella Rose, Olivia Jade. Student, Orange Coast Cmty. Coll., U. So. Calif. Founder Mossimo Inc., Irvine, Calif., 1987, chmn. bd., 1988—, pres., 1988—98, 2000—02, CEO, 1995—96, 2000—; designer, exclusive clothing line Target, 2000—. Appeared in (music video) Janet Jackson's "You Want This?", 1994. Recipient Orange County Entrepreneur of Yr. award, 1992, Fashion Performance award, 1996. Office: Mossimo Inc 2016 Broadway Blvd Santa Monica CA 90404

GIANOPULOS, JIM, film company executive; b. Bklyn., 1952; m. Anne Gianopulos. JD, Fordham U., 1976. Bus. affairs RCA/Columbia Pictures Internat. Video, RCA Selectavision; sr. v.p. bus. affairs and internat. video divsn. Paramount Pictures, 1988—91; exec. v.p. internat. Carolco Pictures, 1991—92; pres. Twentieth Internat. TV, 1992—94, Twentieth Century Fox Internat. and Pay TV, 1994—2000; co-chmn., CEO Fox Filmed Entertainment, Inc., L.A., 2000—. Named one of The 50 Most Powerful People in Hollywood, Premiere mag., 2004—06. Office: Fox Filmed Entertainment Inc 10201 W Pico Blvd Los Angeles CA 90035 Office Phone: 310-277-2211. Office Fax: 310-203-1558.*

GIBBARD, BEN, singer, musician; b. Bremerton, Wash., Aug. 11, 1976; Attended, Western Wash. U. Founding mem., lead singer Death Cab for Cutie, 1997—, The Postal Service, 2001—; founder solo project All-Time Quarterback, 1999—. Singer: (albums) (with Death Cab for Cutie) Something About Airplanes, 1999, We Have the Facts and We're Voting Yes, 2000, The Photo Album, 2001, Transatlanticism, 2003, Plans, 2005, Narrow Stairs, 2008, (with All-Time Quarterback) All-Time Quarterback, 1999, (with The Postal Service) Give Up, 2003, (songs) (with Death Cab for Cutie) I Will Possess Your Heart, 2008 (MTV Video Music award for Best Editing, 2008). Office: c/o Zeitgeist Artist Mgmt Ste 216 660 W York St San Francisco CA 94110 also: c/o Zeitgeist Artist Mgmt Ste 408 39 W 14th St New York NY 10011 E-mail: info@deathcabforcutie.com.

GIBBONS, BILLY F., musician; b. Houston, Dec. 16, 1949; Mem. band, musician The Saints, The Coachmen, Billy G. and the Ten Blue Flames, The Moving Sidewalks, 1967-70, ZZ Top, 1969—. Albums include First Album, 1970, Rio Grande Mud, 1972, Tres Hombres, 1973, Fandango, 1975, Tejas, 1976, The Best of ZZ Top, 1977, Deguello, 1979, El Loco, 1981, Eliminator, 1983, Afterburner, 1985, The ZZ Top Sixpack, 1988, Greatest Hits, 1992, One Foot in the Blues, 1994, Antenna, 1994, Rythmeen, 1996, XXX, 1999, Mescalero, 2003, Live from Texas, 2008; author: (books) Rock + Roll Gearhead, 2005. Co-recipient MTV Video Music award, Best Group Video for Legs, 1984. inducted Rock and Roll Hall of Fame, 2004. Office: care Warner Bros Records 3300 Warner Blvd Burbank CA 91505-4632

GIBBONS, JAMES FRANKLIN, electrical engineering educator; b. Leavenworth, Kans., Sept. 19, 1931; s. Clifford Hugh and Mary Jewel (Petty) G.; m. Mary Lynn Krywick; children: Robert, Sally, Laura BS, Northwestern U., 1953; PhD, Stanford U., 1956. Prof. elec. engring. Stanford U., Calif., 1956—84, Calif., 1996—2002, Reid Weaver Dennis prof. elec. engring. Calif., 1983-84, 96—, dean Sch. Engring. Calif., 1984-96, Frederick Emmons Terman prof. engring., 1984-96. Bd. dirs. Centigram, Cisco Systems, El Paso (Tex.) Energy; founder, chmn. Sera Learning Techs.; cons. Shockley Transistor Corp., 1957-63, Fairchild Semiconductor, 1964-71, Avantek, Inc., 1964-91; chmn. grad. fellowship panel NSF, 1967-70; mem. Newman com. HEW Task Force on Higher Edn., 1969-74; mem. ednl. tech. panel Pres. Sci. Adv. Com., 1971-73; Fulbright guest lectr. European univs.; vis. prof. nuclear physics dept. Oxford U., 1970-71; vis. prof. U. Tokyo, 1971; cons. electronics br. Atomic Energy Research Establishment, 1971; mem. sci. team for exchanges on ion implanation and beam processing U.S. Nat. Acad. Scis., 1971, 76, 77, 79, 81. Author: (with J. G. Linvill) Transistors and Active Circuits, 1961, (with P. E. Gray, D. DeWitt and A. R. Boothroyd) SEEC Vol. 2: Physical Electronics and Models of Transistors, 1964, Semiconductor Electronics, 1966; editor: Fundamentals of Electronic Science, 1970-78; contbr. articles to profl. jours.; inventor tutored video instruction technique Recipient Western Electric Fund award Am. Soc. Engring. Edn., 1971, award for Outstanding Achievement, No. Calif. Solar Energy Assn., 1975, Founder's prize Tex. Instruments, 1983, Outstanding Alumni award Northwestern U., 1985, Rappaport award IEEE Electron Devices Soc., 1990, Univ. Rsch. award Semicondr. Industry Assn., 1996, Medal of Achievement award Am. Electronics Assn., 1966; NSF and NAS fellow, 1953-56; Fulbright fellow Cambridge (Eng.) U., 1956-57; NSF postdoctoral fellow, 1963-64; inducted Santa Clara County Bus. Hall of Fame, 1997, Silicon Valley Engring. Hall of Fame, 1997; Prof. James Gibbons award established by Internat. Conf. on Advanced Thermal Processing of Semicondrs., 1999. Fellow IEEE (Jack A. Morton award 1980, Edn. medal 1985, Solid State Sci. and Tech. award Electrochem. Soc. 1989, 3d Millenium medal 2001); mem. Nat. Acad. Engring., Nat. Acad. Sci., Swedish Acad. Engring. Scis., Norwegian Acad. Tech. Scis., Am. Acad. Arts and Scis., Sigma Xi, Tau Beta Pi (award for outstanding undergrad. engring. teaching 1976), Eta Kappa Nu. Office: Elec Engring Dept CISX-201X Paul G Allen Bldg Stanford CA 94305-4075 Home: 15 Red Berry Rdg Portola Valley CA 94028-8077

GIBBONS, JIM (JAMES ARTHUR GIBBONS), Governor of Nevada, former United States Representative from Nevada; b. Sparks, Nev., Dec. 16, 1944; s. Leonard A. and Matilda (Hancock) Gibbons; m. T. Dawn Sanders-Snelling, June 21, 1986 (separated 2008); children: Christopher, Jennifer, James A. Jr. BS in Geology, U. Nev., Reno, 1967, MS in Mining and Geology, 1973; JD, Southwestern U. Sch. Law, LA, 1979; postgrad., U. So. Calif. Bar: Nev. 1982, admitted to practice: US Dist. Ct. Nev. 1982. Hydrologist Office of Fed. Watermaster, Reno, 1963-67; mining geologist Union Carbide Co., Reno, 1971—73; comml. pilot Western Airlines, LA, 1979—87; sr. land mgr., atty. Homestake Mining Co., Reno, 1980-82; lawyer Haase, Harris & Morrison, Reno, 1982—84; atty. pvt. practice, 1984—86; pilot Delta Airlines, Salt Lake City, 1987—97; mem. Nev. State Assembly, 1989—93, US Congress from 2nd Nev. Dist., 1997—2006; gov. State of Nev., Carson City, 2007—. Mem. armed svcs. com. US Congress, mem. homeland security com., mem. resources com., chmn. subcomittee energy and mineral resources. Contbr. articles to profl. pubs.; co-author (with Dawn): Gibbon Tax Restraint Initiative. Bd. dirs. Nev. Coun. Econ. Edn., 1984-1987, co-chmn., The Congressional Mining Caucus, The House Gaming Caucas. Col. USAF, 1967—71, col. Nev. Air Nat. Guard, 1975—96, vice comdr. Nev. Air Nat. Guard, 1990—96, col. USAF Res., 1996—98. Decorated Legion of Merit, DFC, Air Medal with Two Oak Leaf Clusters, Aerial Achievement medal, Air Force Commendation Medal with One Oak Leaf Cluster; recipient Outstanding Freshman Legislator, 1988; named Mackay Sch. Mines Alumnus of Yr, 1999. Mem. Assn. Trial Lawyers of Am., Nev. Trial Lawyers Assn., Rocky Mt. Mineral Law Found., Comml. Law League Am., Am. Inst. Mining Engrs., Nev. Landman's Assn. (chmn. 1981-82, consulting atty. 1982-83), Congressional Sportsmen's Caucus, The Western Caucus, Rural Caucus, Air Force Caucus, Nat. Guard and Reserve Components Caucus, Travel and Tourism Caucus, Caucus on Cmty. Health Ctr. Republican. Achievements include first to elected to represent Nevada's 2nd District in the House of Representatives in 1996 and re-elected to a fifth term in 2004. Avocation: flying. Office: Office of Gov Capitol Bldg 101 N Carson St Carson City NV 89701

GIBBONS, MARK, state supreme court justice; BA, U. Calif., Irvine, 1972; JD, Loyola U., LA, 1975. Assoc. atty. Woofter & Bilbray, 1975—86; partner Bilbray & Gibbons, 1976—85, Gibbons & Berman, 1985—90, Oshins & Gibbons, 1990—95; of counsel Streich Lang, 1995—96; judge Clark County Dist. Ct., Nev., 1996—98, presiding judge civil divsn. Nev., 1998—2001; chief judge 8th Jud. Dist. Ct., Nev., 2001—02; assoc. justice Nev. Supreme Ct., Carson City, 2003—. Advisory mem. Senior Citizens Law Project Las Vegas City Council, 1995, chair of advisory mem. Senior Citizens Law Project, 1998—2001. Mem.: Nev. Bar Assn., Clark County Bar Assn. Office: Nev Supreme Ct 201 Carson St Carson City NV 89701-4702 Office Phone: 775-684-1500.

GIBBONS, TOM, computer software company executive; married; 2 children. BA, Bowdoin Coll. Tchr. of English, Osaka, Japan; with Microsoft Corp., Redmond, Wash., 1996—, gen. mgr. hardware bus., corp. v.p. specialized devices & applications group, mem. entertainment & devices div. exec. team. Office: Microsoft Corp 1 Microsoft Way Redmond WA 98052-6399

GIBBS, DAN, state legislator; B, Western Slope Coll. Office dir., Rep. Mark Udall US House of Reps., Western Slope, Colo.; mem. Dist. 56 Colo. House of Reps., Denver, 2007; mem. Dist. 16 Colo. State Senate, Denver, 2007—. Bd. mem. Club 20, High Country Conservation Ctr.; diplomat Summit C. of C.; mem. Rocky Mountain Elk Found., Trout Unlimited, Ducks Unlimited, Habitat for Humanity, Eagle River Clean Up, I-70 Clean Up Team; coach Battle Mountain HS Cross-Country Ski Team. Mem.: Vail-Eagle Valley Rotary Club. Democrat. Office: Colo State Capitol 200 E Colfax Denver CO 80203 Office Phone: 303-866-4873. Business E-Mail: dan.gibbs.senate@state.co.us.*

GIBBS, MARC, state legislator; m. Bonne Gibbs; 2 children. BA in Fin. Mgmt., Utah State U. Owner Gibbs Farms LLC; mem. Dist. 31 Idaho House of Reps., 2008—. Mem. Bear River Commn., Idaho Fish & Game Commn.; bd. dirs. Last Chance Canal Co. Mem.: NRA, Idaho Crop Improvement Assn. (bd. dirs.), Bear River Water Users Assn. (former pres.). Republican. Office: Capitol Annex PO Box 83720 Boise ID 83720-0054 also: 632 Hwy 34 Grace ID 83241 Office Phone: 208-334-2475, 208-425-3385. Office Fax: 208-334-2125, 208-425-3329. Business E-Mail: mgibbs@house.idaho.gov.*

GIBBS, RONALD STEVEN, obstetrician, gynecologist, educator; b. Phila., Mar. 31, 1943; MD, U. Pa., 1969. Intern Hartford (Conn.) Hosp., 1969-70; resident ob.-gyn. U. Pa. Hosp., Phila., 1970-74; fellow maternal-fetal medicine U. Tex. Health Ctr., San Antonio, 1976-78; obstetrician-gynecologist Univ. Hosp. U. Colo., Denver, 1989—; prof., chmn. dept. ob.-gyn. U. Colo., Denver, 1989—, E. Stewart Taylor chair ob-gyn. Dir., treas, Am. Bd. of Obstetric and Gyn., 1999-2004, Residency Review Com., 1997-2003. Mem. ACOG, AMA, Am. Gynecologic and Obstetric Soc. (pres. 2004-05), Infectious Disease Soc. Am., Infectious Disease Soc. Ob.-gyn. (pres. 1992-94), Soc. Gynecologic Investigation, Soc. Perinatal Obstet. (bd. dirs.).

GIBLETT, ELOISE ROSALIE, retired hematologist; b. Tacoma, Jan. 17, 1921; d. William Richard and Rose (Godfrey) Giblett. BS, U. Wash., 1942, MS, 1947, MD with honors, 1951. Mem. faculty U. Wash. Sch. Medicine, 1957—, research prof., 1967—87, emeritus research prof., 1987—. Assoc. dir., head immunogenetics Puget Sound Blood Ctr., 1957—79, exec. dir., 1979—87, emeritus exec. dir., 1987—; former mem. several rsch. coms. NIH. Author: Genetic Markers in Human Blood, 1969; mem. editl. bd. numerous jours. including: Blood, Am. Jour. Human Genetics, Transfusion, Vox Sanguinis; contbr. over 200 articles to profl. jours. Recipient fellowships, grants Emily Cooley, Karl Landsteiner, Philip Levine and Alexander Wiener immunohematology awards, disting. alumna award, U. Wash. Sch. Medicine, 1987. Fellow: AAAS; mem.: NAS, Assn. Am. Physicians, Western Assn. Physicians, Am. Fedn. Clin. Rsch., Internat. Soc. Hematologists, Brit. Soc. Immunology, Am. Assn. Immunologists, Am. Soc. Hematology, Am. Soc. Human Genetics (pres. 1973), Alpha Omega Alpha, Sigma Xi. Home: 6533 53rd Ave NE Seattle WA 98115-7748 Office: Puget Sound Blood Ctr 921 Terry Ave Seattle WA 98104-1256

GIBSON, ARTHUR CHARLES, biologist, educator; b. Bronx, NY, Oct. 16, 1947; s. Richard Goodwin and Rosalie (Reinhardt) G.; m. Linda Lee Corey, Aug. 15, 1970; children: Heather Elizabeth, Erin Kathryn. BA in Botany, Miami U., Ohio, 1969; PhD in Botany, Claremont U., Calif., 1973. Asst. prof. U. Ariz., Tucson, 1973-79, assoc. prof., 1979-80, UCLA, 1980-82, prof., 1982—. Dir. Mildred E. Mathias Bot. Garden. Author: (with J.H. Brown) Biogeography, 1983, (with P.S. Nobel) The Cactus Primer, 1986, (with P.W. Rundel) Ecological Communities and Processes in a Mojave Desert Ecosystem, 1996, Structure-Function Relations of Warm Desert Plants, 1996; editor: Neotropical Biodiversity and Conservation, 1996; contbr. articles to profl. jours. Fellow Cactus and Succulent Soc. Am. Office: UCLA Mildred E Mathias Bot Garden Botany Bldg Gdn Rm 124 Los Angeles CA 90095-0001

GIBSON, BENJAMIN FRANKLIN, physicist; b. Madisonville, Tex., Sept. 3, 1938; s. Mitchell Osler and Christine (Bennett) G.; m. Margaret Alice Ferguson, July 20, 1968; children: James M., Michael W., Stuart W. BA, Rice U., Houston, 1961; PhD, Stanford U., Calif., 1966. Postdoctoral fellow Lawrence Livermore Nat. Lab., Calif., 1966-68; rsch. assoc. NAS, Nat. Bur. Stds., Gaithersburg, Md., 1968-70, CUNY, Bklyn., 1970-72; group leader, T-5 Los Alamos Nat. Lab., N.Mex., 1982-86, staff mem. N.Mex., 1972—; detailee Dept. of Energy Divsn. Nuclear Physics, 1980-81. Program adv. com. MIT Bates Electron Accelerator, Boston, 1985-89, 98-2003; mem. subatomic physics grant selection com. Can. Natural Scis. and Engring. Rsch. Coun., 1994-96, theory rev. panel NSF, 1997, 98, 2006. Co-editor: Three-body Force in the Three-Nucleon System, 1986, Procs. of LAMPF Workshop on pi K Physics, 1991, New Vistas in Physics with High-Energy Pion Beams, 1993, Properties and Interactions of Hyperons, 1994, Baryons '95, 1996, 20 Years of Meson Factory Physics: Accomplishments and Prospects, 1997, Internat. Symposium on New Facet of Three Nucleon Force, 50 Yrs. Fujita Miyazawa Three Nucleon Force, 2008; assoc. editor Phys. Review C, 1988-02, editor, 2002—, mem. editl. bd., 1978-79, 87-88; mem. editl. bd. FEW Body Sys., 1986—; contbr. articles to profl. jours. Recipient Sr. Scientist Rsch. award Alexander von Humboldt Found., 1992; Japan Soc. Promotion of Sci. rsch. fellow Tohoku U., 1984; vis. fellow U. Melbourne, Australia, 1986, Flinders U., Adelaide, Australia, 1987, Murdoch fellow Inst. for Nuclear Theory, U. Wash., Seattle, 1992. Fellow Am. Phys. Soc., Few-Body Sys. Topical Group (vice chmn. 1990-92, chmn. 1992-93, exec. com. 2004-06), Divsn. Nuc. Physics (sec.-treas. 1995—). Achievements include patents in field of epithermal-neutron well logging. Office: T-2 MS-B283 Los Alamos NM 87545-0001 Home Phone: 505-672-3609; Office Phone: 505-667-5059. Business E-Mail: bfgibson@lanl.gov.

GIBSON, JAMES B., mayor, Henderson, Nevada; b. Las Vegas, 1948; BA, Brigham Young U., 1972; JD, Calif. Western, 1975. Gen. counsel Am. Pacific Corp.; ptnr. Rooker and Gibson Law Firm; mayor City of Henderson, Nev., 1997—. Bd. dirs. Las Vegas (Nev.) Monorail; bd. dir. Las Vegas (Nev.) Convention and Visitors Authority; mem. City of Henderson (Nev.) Redevelopment Agy.; alternate So. Nev. Water Authority; mem. regional trans. com. City of Henderson. Recipient Good Scout award, Boulder Dam Area Coun., 2002, Silver Beaver award, 2004, Humanitarian award, Nat. Jewish Med. and Rsch. Ctr., 2002, Pres. medal, Nev. State Coll., 2007, Vision award, Comml. Mgr. Group, 2009; named Outstanding Citizen, Henderson Cmty. Found., 2005, Person of Yr., City of Henderson, 2008. Mem.: Hendersn C. of C. (named Outstanding Mem. 1994). Office: City Hall 240 S Water St Rm 203 Henderson NV 89015-7296 Office Phone: 702-267-2085. Office Fax: 702-267-2081. Business E-Mail: Jim.Gibson@cityofhenderson.com.*

GIBSON, KIRK HAROLD, professional baseball coach, retired professional baseball player; b. Pontiac, Mich., May 28, 1957; s. Robert and Barbara Gibson; m. Joanne Sklarski, Dec. 21, 1985; children: Kirk Robert, Kevin Louis, Colleen, Cameron. Student, Mich. State U., 1975-78. Outfielder Lakeland Tigers, Fla., 1978, Evansville Triplets, Ind., 1979, Detroit Tigers, 1979-88, 1993—95, broadcast analyst, 1998—2002, bench coach, 2003—05; outfielder LA Dodgers, 1988-90, Kansas City Royals, 1990—92, Pitts. Pirates, 1992; bench coach Ariz. Diamondbacks, 2007—. Recipient Silver Slugger award, 1988; named Am. League Championship Series MVP, Maj. League Baseball, 1984, Nat. League MVP, 1988. Achievements include member of Major League Baseball World Series Championship winning Detroit Tigers, 1984, LA Dodgers, 1988. Office: Ariz Diamondbacks Chase Field 401 E Jefferson St Phoenix AZ 85001*

GIBSON, MEL, actor, film director and producer; b. Peekskill, NY, Jan. 3, 1956; emigrated to Australia, 1968; s. Hutton and Anne Gibson; m. Robyn Moore June 7, 1980 (separated 2009); children: Hannah, Edward, Christian, Willie, Louis, Milo, Tommy. Grad., Nat. Inst. Dramatic Art, Sydney, Australia, 1977; LHD (hon.), Loyola Marymount U., 2003. Founder Icon Prodns. Actor: (films) Summer City, 1977, Mad Max, 1979, Tim, 1979, Attack Force Z, Gallipoli, 1981, Mad Max II: The Road Warrior, 1982, The Year of Living Dangerously, 1983, The Bounty, 1984, The River, 1984, Mrs. Soffel, 1984, Mad Max Beyond Thunderdome, 1985, Lethal Weapon, 1987, Tequila Sunrise, 1988, Lethal Weapon II, 1988, Bird on a Wire, 1989, Hamlet, 1990, Air America, 1990, Lethal Weapon III, 1992, Forever Young, 1992, Maverick, 1994, Pocahontas, 1995 (voice only), Ransom, 1996, Father's Day, 1997, Conspiracy Theory, 1997, Lethal Weapon 4, 1998, The Million Dollar Hotel, 1999, Payback, 1999, Chicken Run, 2000 (voice only), The Patriot, 2000, What Women Want, 2000, Signs, 2002, We Were Soldiers, 2003, The Singing Detective, 2003; actor, dir.: The Man Without a Face, 1993; actor, dir., prodr.: Braveheart, 1995 (Golden Globe award for best dir. of film 1996, Acad. award for best dir. 1996, Acad. award for best picture of yr. 1996, Outstanding Directorial Achievement in Motion Picture award nominee Dir. Guild Am. 1996, Oscar award for Best Dir.); dir., screenwriter, prodr.: The Passion of the Christ, 2004, Apocalypto, 2006; performed with Nimrod Theatre Co. in plays including Death of a Salesman, Romeo and Juliet, with South Australian Theatre Co., from 1978, appeared in plays including Oedipus, Henry IV, Cedoona; work in TV series includes The Sullivans, The Oracle (Australia); exec. prodr. (TV) The Three Stooges, 2000, Complete Savages, 2004-05, Clubhouse, 2004-05. Favorite Movie Actor, People's Choice award, 1997, Outstanding Contribution to World Cinema award, Irish Film and TV awards, 2008; named one of 50 Most Power People in Hollywood Premiere mag. 2003-06. Roman Catholic.

GIBSON, VIRGINIA LEE, lawyer; b. Independence, Mo., Mar. 5, 1946; BA, U. Calif., Berkeley, 1972; JD, U. Calif., San Francisco, 1977. Bar: Calif. 1981. Assoc. Pillsbury, Madison & Sutro, San Francisco, 1980-83; ptnr. Chickering & Gregory, San Francisco, 1983-85, Baker & McKenzie, San Francisco, 1985—2001, White & Case, LLP, Palo Alto and San Francisco, 2001—. Mem. ABA (internat. law and practice sect., labor and employment law sect.), Nat. Assn. Stock Plan Profls., Nat. Ctr. for Employee Ownership, Calif. Bar Assn. (exec. com. tax sect. 1985-88), San Francisco Bar Assn. (internat. taxation sect.), Western Pension and Benefits Conf. (pres. San Francisco chpt. 1989-91, program com. 1984-88). Office: White & Case LLP 5 Palo Alto Sq 3000 El Camino Real Palo Alto CA 94306 also: 1155 Avenue Of The Americas Fl 9 New York NY 10036-2711

GIEDT, BRUCE ALAN, paper company executive; b. Fargo, ND, May 7, 1937; s. Alexander and Alice Mildred (Rognaldson) G.; m. Suzanna Tae Abbott, Apr. 30, 1963; children: Alex, Jeffrey, Marybeth; m. 2d, Gail Ann Platt. BA, U. Wash., 1959; MBA, Harvard U., 1965. From regional sales mgr. to v.p. service products bus. units Crown Zellerbach Corp., San Francisco, 1965—; pres. Champion Paper Distbrs., Inc., Riverside, Calif., 1981-87, Pioneer Packaging, Phoenix, 1987—. Author: The Future of Commercial Arbitration, 1965. V.p. exec. com. Keep Riverside AHead, econ. devel. com., bd. dirs.; exec. com. mem. Riverside C. of C., devel. com. Served to Capt. USAF, 1959-63. Evans scholar Western Golf Assn., 1967. Mem. Am. Paper Inst. (past com. chmn.), Elks. Republican. Lutheran. Home: 704 Foothills East cir Payson AZ 85541 Office: 730 E University Dr Phoenix AZ 85034-6509 Personal E-mail: bgiedt@q.com. Business E-Mail: bruceg@pioneerpackaging.com.

GIESELMAN, JON, advertising executive; married; 3 children. BA, Boston Coll.; MBA, St. John Fisher Coll., Rochester, NY. Staff, asst. senator Daniel Patrick Moynihan, NY; N.Am. brand mgr. Ray-Ban Sunglasses; v.p. advt., pub. rels. and brand devel. Home Shopping Network; v.p. advt./publicity Kmart Corp.; sr. v.p. advt./pub. rels. DIRECTV Inc., 2005—. Named to Advt. Hall of Achievement, Am. Advt. Fedn., 2008. Office: DIRECTV Grp Hdqs 2230 E Imperial Hwy El Segundo CA 90245

GIFFIN, GLENN ORLANDO, II, music critic, writer, newspaper editor; b. Denver, Feb. 27, 1943; s. Glenn Orlando and E. Louise (Mosler) G. B.Mus., U. Colo., 1965; MA in Librarianship, U. Denver, 1967. Scriptwriter, broadcaster radio Sta. KRNW-FM, Boulder, 1965-

67; asst. music critic San Francisco Chronicle, 1968; asst. music librarian Norlin libraries U. Colo., 1968-70; music critic, staff writer Denver Post, 1970-73, music editor, 1973-88, book page editor, music critic, 1988-98, editor Colo. Living, Writing/Entertainment, 1998—, entertainment columnist. Host Soundings, Sta. KOA Radio 1985-86; curator Carson-Brierly Dance Library U. Denver, 1986—. Rockefeller Found. fellow, 1966-68; Corbett Found. fellow, 1969; Nat. Endowment for Arts grantee Dance Criticism Inst., Conn. Coll., summer 1971; named Outstanding Alumnus U. Colo., 1985. Mem. Music Library Assn., Am. Musicol. Soc., Dance Critics Assn., Music Critics Assn., Sigma Delta Chi. Office: Denver Post PO Box 1709 1560 Broadway Denver CO 80202

GIFFIN, SANDRA LEE, nursing administrator; b. Tacoma, July 16, 1957; d. Clayton Eugene and Carol Lee (Fisher) Peterson; m. Herbert Kent Giffin, May 6, 1989. Diploma, Tacoma Gen. Hosp. Sch. Nursing, 1978; BSN magna cum laude, Pacific Luth. U., 1980; MS, Oreg. Health Scis. U., 1994. Cert. in nursing adminstrn. Staff nurse Mary Bridge Children's Hosp., 1978-81, evening nurse supr., infection control nurse, 1981-83, asst. med./surg. nurse mgr., 1983-84, med./surg. nurse mgr. Tacoma, 1984-89; dept. dir. Oreg. Poison Ctr. Oreg. Health Scis. U., Portland, 1989—, instr., Sch. Nursing, 1994—, dept. dir. nurse cons. program, 1995-2000, interim dir. physician cons. program, 2000. Presenter in field. Author/presenter abstracts in field. Sec. Rocky Butte Neighborhood Assn., 1996; sec. bd. dirs. Make A Wish Found. Oreg., 1989-96; mem. adv. bd. Oreg. Safe Kids Coalition; active Oreg. Interagy. Hazardous Comm. Coun., Oreg. Sch. Health Edn. Coalition. Grantee Agy. for Toxic Substances and Disease Registry/Am. Assn. Poison Control Ctrs., 1992, Oreg. State Health Divsn., 1993-94. Mem. Am. Acad. Ambulatory Care Nursing, Am. Assn. Poison Control Ctrs., N.W. Orgn. Nursing Execs. (apptd. mem. commn. on health care policy 2000). Avocations: skiing, reading, bicycling, travel, cooking. Office: Oreg Poison Ctr 3181 SW Sam Jackson Park Rd Portland OR 97201-3011

GIFFORD, GERALD FREDERIC, retired science educator; b. Chanute, Kans., Oct. 24, 1939; s. Gerald Leo and Marion Lou (Browne) Gifford; m. Cinda Jean Lowman, June 26, 1982. Student, Kans. U., 1957-60; BS in Range Mgmt., Utah State U., 1962, MS in Watershed Mgmt., 1964, PhD in Watershed Sci., 1968. Asst. prof. watershed sci. Utah State U., Logan, 1967-72, assoc. prof., 1972-80, prof., 1980-84, chmn. watershed sci. unit, 1967-84, dir. Inst. Land Reclamation, 1982-84; head range, wildlife and forestry U. Nev., Reno, 1984-92, chmn. environ. and resource sci. dept., 1992—94, prof. hydrology and natural resource mgmt., 1994—2000, ret., 2000. Exch. scientist NSF, Canberra, Australia, 1974; cons. in field. Author: (book) Rangeland Hydrology, 1981; assoc. editor: Jour. Range Mgmt., 1982—87, 1991—95, Arid Soil Rsch. and Rehab., 1985—90; contbr. scientific papers to profl. pubs. Mem.: Soil and Water Conservation Soc., Am. Water Resources Assn. Avocations: racquetball, antiques, garage sales. Home: 3880 Squaw Valley Cir Reno NV 89509-5663 Office Phone: 775-826-7932. Personal E-mail: fredandcinda@sbcglobal.net.

GIFFORD, MARILYN JOYCE, emergency physician, consultant; b. Denver, Aug. 3, 1943; m. Leslie Arthur and Dorothy Marianne (Stevens) G.; m. Robert Bruce Caplan (div.); children: Eric Louis Caplan, Brian Matthew Caplan; m. Daniel Patrick McKenna, July 17, 1992. AA, Stephens Coll., Columbia, Mo., 1963; BS, Mich. State U., 1965; MD, Mt. Sinai Sch. Medicine, NYC, 1971. Diplomate Am. Bd. Emergency Medicine. Emergency physician Longmont (Colo.) United Hosp., 1974-80, Boulder (Colo.) Cmty. Hosp., 1976-78; dir. emergency svcs. Meml. Hosp., Colorado Springs, Colo., 1980—. Physician advisor Colorado Springs Fire Dept., 1980—; bd. dirs. Nat. Registry Emergency Med. Technicians, Columbus, Ohio, 1983—. Co-author: Protocols for Prehospital Emergency Medical Care, 1984, Prehospital Emergency Care, 1996. Advisor E-911 Authority Bd., Colorado Springs, 1996—. Lt. USNR, 1971-72. Recipient Kim Langstaff Meml. award for excellence Region IV EMs Coun., 1986, Val. Wolhauer award for physician excellence Emergency Med. Technician Assn. Colo., 1982, Pres.'s Leadership award Nat. Assn. Emergency Med. Technicians, 1983, ACEP contbn. in EMS, 2001. Fellow Am. Coll. Emergency Physicians (chair EMS com. 1979-81, Colo. coun. 1978-85); mem. El Paso County Med. Soc. (pres. 1993-94). Avocation: skiing. Office: Meml Hosp 1400 E Boulder St Colorado Springs CO 80909-5599 Home Phone: 719-576-8608; Office Phone: 719-365-2000. Personal E-mail: marilyngifford@hotmail.com.

GIFFORD, RAYMOND L., state agency administrator; married; 2 children. BA, St. John's Coll.; JD, U. Chgo., 1992. Law clk. U.S. Dist. Ct., Colo.; mem. staff Kirkland & Ellis; atty. gen. Colo.; mem. staff Baker & Hostetler; chmn. Colo. Dept. Regulatory Agy., Denver, 1999—. Lectr. U. Colo. Mem.: Federalist Soc. (law practice group), Nat. Assn. Regulatory Utility Commr. (telecomm. com.).

GIFFORDS, GABRIELLE, United States Representative from Arizona, former state senator; b. Tucson, June 8, 1970; m. Mark E. Kelly. BA in Sociology and Latin Am. History, Scripps Coll., 1993; M in Regional Planning, Cornell U., 1997. Rschr. Am. Friends Svc. Com., San Diego, 1995; planner bi-national bus. develop. San Diego Dialogue U. San Diego, 1995; assoc. regional econ. develop. Price Waterhouse LLP, NYC, 1996; pres. El Campo Tires Warehouses, Inc., Tucson, 1996—2000; mng. ptnr. Giffords Capital Mgmt. LLC, Tucson, 2000—07; mem. Ariz. Ho. of Reps from Dist. 13, 2001—03, Ariz. State Senate from Dist. 28, 2003—05, US Congress from 8th Ariz. dist., 2007—, mem. armed services com., fgn. affairs com., sci. & tech. com. Bd. adv. U. Ariz. Coll. Bus. and Pub. Adminstrn.; bd. dirs. Met. YMCA, Tucson, Ariz. Friends of Small Bus., 162nd Air Nat. Guard Minuteman Com., Ariz. Prevention Resource Ctr. Adv. Coun., Tohono Chul Pk., Anti-Defamation League, Ariz. Cultural Develop., Women's Campaign Sch. Yale, Tucson Regional Water Coun., Pres. Coun. Cornell Women, Breast Cancer Boot Camp, Friends Saguaro Nat. Pk., Arts Reach Inc. Recipient Top 10 Tech award, Arizona Tech. Coun., 2003, 2004, Award of Distinction, League Ariz. Cities and Towns, 2005, 100% Rating, League Conservation Voters, 2005, Golden Eagle award, Independent Ins. Agents and Brokers Ariz., 2005, Eagle Enterprise award, Ariz. Small Bus. Assn., 2005, Women on the Move, YWCA Tucson, 2005; named Legis. of Yr., Ariz. Planning Assn., 2003, Ariz. Coalition to Prevent Homelessness, 2003, Mental Health Assn. Ariz., 2004, Most Valuable Player at Ariz. Legis., Sierra Club, 2005, Woman of Yr., Tucson Bus. Edge, 2005; named a Young Leader Worth Watching, Gannett News Svc., 2004; named an Outstanding Legis., Ariz. Family Literacy, 2003, Outstanding Alumna, Scripps Coll., 2004; William J. Fulbright scholar, Chihualhua, Mexico, 1993—94, Fannie Mae fellow, Harvard U. Kennedy Sch. Exec. Mgmt., 2003, Eagleton Inst. Rutgers U. fellow, 2003. Mem.: Hadassah (life). Democrat. Jewish. Achievements include becoming youngest woman elected to Arizona State Senate. Avocation: reading. Office: 502 Cannon House Office Bldg Washington DC 20515 also: 1661 N Swam Ste 112 Tucson AZ 85712

GIGUERE, JEAN-SEBASTIEN, professional hockey player; b. Montreal, Que., Can., May 16, 1977; m. Kristen Giguere; 1 child, Maxime Olivier. Goaltender Hartford Whalers, 1996—97, Calgary Flames, 1998—2000, Anaheim Ducks (formerly Mighty Ducks of Anaheim), 2000—. Recipient Harry Holmes Meml. Trophy, Am. Hockey League, 1998, Conn Smythe Trophy, 2003; named to NHL All-Star Game, 2009. Achievements include being a member of Stanley Cup Champion Anaheim Ducks, 2007. Office: Anaheim Ducks 2695 E Katella Ave Anaheim CA 92806*

GILBERT, DONALD ROY, lawyer; b. Phila., June 6, 1946; BA, Stanford U., 1968; JD, U. Calif., 1971. Bar: Calif. 1972, Ariz. 1972. Ptnr., dir. Fennemore Craig, Phoenix, 1972—. Mem. ABA, State Bar Ariz., State Bar Calif., Maricopa County Bar Assn. Office: Fennemore Craig 3003 N Central Ste 2600 Phoenix AZ 85012-2913

GILBERT, JAMES FREEMAN, geophysics educator; b. Vincennes, Ind., Aug. 9, 1931; s. James Freeman and Gladys (Paugh) G.; m. Sally Bonney, June 19, 1959; children: Cynthia, Sarah, James. BS, MIT, 1953, PhD, 1956; D honoris causa, Utrecht U., 1994; D in Engring. (hon.), Colo. Sch. Mines, 2004. Research assoc. MIT, Cambridge, 1956-57; asst. research geophysicist Inst. Geophysics and Planetary Physics at UCLA, 1957, asst. prof. geophysics, 1958-59; sr. research geophysicist Tex. Instruments, Dallas, 1960-61; prof. Inst. Geophysics and Planetary Physics, U. Calif. San Diego, La Jolla, 1961—2001, assoc. dir., 1976-88, prof. emeritus, 2001—; chmn. grad. dept. Scripps Inst. Oceanography, La Jolla, 1988-91. Chmn. steering com. San Diego Supercomputer, 1984-86. Contbr. numerous articles to profl. jours. Recipient Arthur L. Day medal Geol. Soc. Am., 1985, Internat. Balzan prize, 1990; Fairchild scholar Calif. Inst. Tech., Pasadena, 1987; fellow NSF, 1956, Guggenheim, 1964-65, 72-73, Overseas fellow Churchill Coll. U. Cambridge, Eng., 1972-73. Fellow AAAS, Am. Geophys. Union (William Bowie med. 1999); Nat. Acad. Scis., European Union Geoscis. (hon.); mem. Seismology Soc. Am. (medal 2004), Am. Math. Soc., Royal Astron. Soc. (recipient Gold medal 1981), Acad. Nat. dei Lincei (fgn.), Sigma Xi. Home: 780 Kalamath Dr Del Mar CA 92014-2630 Office: U Calif Inst Geophysics Planetary Physics 0225 La Jolla CA 92093-0225 Home Phone: 858-755-9287; Office Phone: 858-534-2470. Business E-Mail: fgilbert@ucsd.edu.

GILBERT, JEROME B., consulting environmental engineer; Pvt. practice, Orinda, Calif., 1991—. Gordon Fair award Am. Acad. Environ. Engring., 1993. Mem. Nat. Acad. Engring. Office: 324 Tappan Ter Orinda CA 94563-1343

GILBERT, LUCIA ALBINO, psychology professor; d. William V. and Carmelina (Cutro) Albino; m. John Carl Gilbert, Dec. 18, 1965; 1 child, Melissa Carlotta. BA, Wells Coll., 1963; MS, Yale U., 1964; PhD, U. Tex., 1974. Lic. psychologist, Tex. Supr. research info. G.S. Gilmore Research Lab., New Haven, 1964-67; tchr. St. Stephen Sch., Austin, Tex., 1967-69; asst. prof. Iowa State U., Ames, 1974-76, U. Tex., Austin, 1976-81, assoc. prof., 1981-86, prof., 1986—2006, dir. women's studies, 1994—99, vice provost undergrad. studies, 1999—2006; provost, acad. v.p., prof. psychology Santa Clara U., 2006—. Author: Men in Dual Career Families, 1985, Sharing It All: The Rewards and Struggles of Two-Career Families, 1988, Two Careers/One Family: The Promise of Gender Equality, 1993, Gender and Sex in Counseling and Psychotherapy, 1999; editor spl. issue Parenting, Dual Career Families; assoc. editor Psychology of Women Quarterly, 1987—. Recipient Excellence in Teaching award U. Tex., 1981-86, Holland award, 1989, Carolyn Sherif award, 1998. Fellow AAUW, Am. Psychol. Soc., Am. Psychol. Assn. (rep. council 1980-83, 86-89, 93—96); mem. Assn. Women in Psychology. Avocations: swimming, progressive country music, ecology, theater. Office: Santa Clara U 204 Walsh Hall 500 El Camino Real Santa Clara CA 95053 Office Phone: 408-554-4533. Office Fax: 408-551-6075. E-mail: lgilbert@scu.edu.

GILBERT, MELISSA, former actors guild executive, actress; b. LA, May 8, 1964; d. Paul and Barbara (Crane) G.; m. Bo Brinkman, 1988 (div. 1994); 1 son, Dakota; m. Bruce Boxleitner, Jan. 1, 1995; 1 son, Michael; stepchildren: Lee, Sam. Student, U. So. Calif. Actress: (TV movies) Little House on the Prairie, 1974, Christmas Miracle in Caulfield, U.S.A., 1977, The Miracle Worker, 1979, The Diary of Anne Frank, 1980, Splendor in the Grass, 1981, Little House: Look Back to Yesterday, 1983, Choices of the Heart, 1983, Little House: Bless All the Dear Children, 1984, Family Secrets, 1984, Little House: The Last Farewell, 1984, Choices, 1986, Penalty Phase, 1986, Family Secrets, Killer Instincts, Without Her Consent, Forbidden Nights, 1990, Blood Vows: The Story of a Mafia Wife, Joshua's Heart, 1990, Donor, The Lookalike, 1990, Conspiracy of Silence: The Shari Karney Story, 1992, With Hostile Intent, 1993, Shattered Trust, 1993, House of Secrets, 1993, Dying to Remember, 1993, Cries From the Heart, 1994, Against Her Will: The Carrie Buck Story, 1994, The Babymaker: The Dr. Cecil Jacobson Story, 1994, Danielle Steel's 'Zoya', 1995, Christmas in My Hometown, 1996, Seduction in a Small Town, 1996, Childhood Sweetheart, 1997, Her Own Rules, 1998, Murder at 75 Birch, 1999, Switched at Birth, 1999, A Vision of Murder: The Story of Donielle, 2000, Sanctuary, 2001, Then Came Jones, 2003; (TV series) Little House on the Prairie, 1974-82, Little House: A New Beginning, 1983, Stand By Your Man, 1992, Sweet Justice, 1994-95 (TV spls.) Battle of the Network Stars, 1978, 79, 81, 82, Celebrity Challenge of the Sexes, 1980, Circus Lions, Tigers and Melissa, Too, 1977, Dean Martin Celebrity Roast, 1984, (stage prodns.) Night of 100 Stars, 1982, The Glass Menagerie, 1985, A Shayna Maidel, 1987 (Outer Critics Circle Award), (feature films) Nutcracker Fantasy, 1979, Sylvester, 1985, Ice House, 1989. Mem.: SAG (pres. 2001—05).

GILBERT, NEIL ROBIN, social work educator, writer, consultant; b. NYC, Sept. 18, 1940; s. Alan and Ida (Bedzin) G.; children: Evan Mallory, Jesse Arthur; m. Rebecca A. Van Voorhis, 2002; children: George Nathaniel, Nicole. BA, Bklyn. Coll., 1963; MSW, U. Pitts., 1965, PhD, 1968. Caseworker Interdepartmental Service Ctr., NYC, 1963; dir. research Mayor's Com. on Human Resources, Pitts., 1967-69; prof. sch. social welfare U. Calif., Berkeley, 1969—, chmn. doctoral program, 1983—, acting dean sch. social welfare, 1986, 95-97, Milton and Gertrude Chernin prof. social welfare and social svcs., 1989—. Advisor Jour. Social Policy, 1982—. Author: Clients or Constituents, 1970, Capitalism and the Welfare State, 1983, (with others) Dimensions of Social Welfare Policy, 1974, 2d rev. edit., 1986, Dynamics of Community Planning, 1978, (with Barbara Gilbert) The Enabling State, 1989, Protecting Young Children from Sexual Abuse, 1989, Practical Program Evaluation, 1990, (with Jill Berrick) With the Best of Intentions, 1992, Welfare Justice, 1995, Transformation of the Welfare State, 2002, A Mother's Work, 2008; editor: (with Rebecca Van Voorhis) Activating the Unemployed; editor Social Welfare Series, 1977-83, Social Worker and Social Welfare Series, 1977—. Trustee Head Royce Sch., 1990-96; chair bd. dirs. Seneca Ctr. Fellow NIMH, 1966, U.N. Research Inst. for Social Devel., 1975; Fulbright scholar, U.S. Info. Agy, 1981; Fulbright Research fellow, London, 1981, Fulbright Western European scholar, 1987; recipient Medallion of Distinction U. Pitts., 1987. Mem. Nat. Assn. Social Workers, Assn. Pub. Policy Analysis and Mgmt. Avocations: skiing, mountain climbing. Office: U Calif Sch Social Welfare Haviland Hl Berkeley CA 94720-0001

GILBERT, PAUL H., engineering executive, consultant; b. Healdsburg, Calif., Apr. 23, 1936; s. Lindley D. and Beatrice Gilbert; m. Elizabeth A. Gilbert, July 13, 1963; children: Christopher, Gregory, Kevin. BSCE, U. Calif., Berkeley, 1959, MSCE, 1960. Registered profl. engr., in 17 states. Project mgr. Calif. State Water Project, Sacramento, 1959-68; officer U.S. Army Corp Engrs., Heidleberg, Germany, 1960-61, capt., 1961-68; project mgr. Parsons Brinckerhoff, NYC, 1969-73, regional mgr./ptnr. San Francisco, 1973-85, dir. NYC, 1973-98, sr. v.p., 1973—; vice chmn. Parsons Brinckerhoff Internat. Inc., 1973—99; chmn. bd. Parsons Brinckerhoff, Quade & Douglas, Inc., NYC, 1990-98; project dir. supercollider design and constrn. Parsons Brinckerhoff, Dallas, 1990-95. Prin.-in-charge award winning projects Glenwood Canyon I-70 tunnels, San Francisco Ocean Outfall, Seattle Bus. Tunnel, Hood Canal Floating Bridge and West Seattle High Level and Low Level Swing Bridges, others; reviewer Laser Interferometer Gravitational-Wave Obs. NSF, Washington, 1992—99; mem. faculties sub-com. for advising orgn. and mgmt. of major rsch. equipment & facilities contracting for NSF; program mgmt. advisor Railtrack West Coast Modernization Project, London, GM Design Ctr. Modernization, Warren, Mich.; mem. U. Calif. Pres.'s Coun.; chmn. project mgmt. panel U. Calif. Nat. Labs., 2000—07; chmn., AUI oversight com. for nat. radio astronomy obs. Atacama Large Millimeter Array Radio Astronomy Obs., 2000—; mem. com. sci. tech. countering terrorism NRC, 2001—05, spl. com. rev. oversight project mgmt. program, 1999—2002, chair bd., infrastructure constructed environ., 2002—05, mem., NAE Grainger Challenge Com., 2004—07, mem. organizing com. post-Katrina workshop, 2005; mem. Thirty Meter Optical Telescope External Adv. Panel, 2004—. Trustee Assoc. Univs., Inc., 1998—. Recipient Lincoln Art Welding award, 1966; named Disting. Engring. Alumnus, U. Calif., Berkeley, 1998. Fellow: ASCE (Rickey medal 1969, Constrn. Mgmt. award 1994); mem.: Washington State Acad. Sci, Nat. Acad. Engring., Moles, Project Mgmt. Inst. Republican. Roman Catholic. Office: Parsons Brinckerhoff 999 3rd Ave Ste 2200 Seattle WA 98104-4020 Office Phone: 206-382-6357. Business E-Mail: gilbert@pbworld.com.

GILBERT, RICHARD, broadcast executive; BS in Math., U. Calif.; MS in Computer Sci., Stanford U. Sr. mgr. IBM Corp., Vitalink Comm. Corp., Make Sys.; pres. ADC Kentrox, Portland, Oreg.; pres., CEO Copper Mountain Networks, Inc., Palo Alto, Calif., 1998—.

GILBERT, RICHARD JOSEPH, economics professor; b. NYC, Jan. 14, 1945; s. Michael N. and Esther (Dillon) G.; m. Sandra S. Waknitz, Sept. 7, 1974; children: Alison, David. BEE with honors, Cornell U., 1966, MEE, 1967; MA in Econs., Stanford U., 1976, PhD, 1976. Rsch. assoc. Stanford U., Calif., 1975-76, assoc. prof engring-econ. systems, 1982-83; from assist. prof. to assoc. prof. econs. U. Calif., Berkeley, 1976-83, prof. econs., 1983—, dir. energy rsch. inst., 1983-93, prof. bus. adminstrn., 1990—, chmn. dept. econ., 2002—; dep. asst. atty. gen. antitrust divsn. U.S. Dept. Justice, 1993-95. Prin. Law & Econ. Cons. Group, Berkeley, 1989—, dir. Univ. Calif. Energy Inst., 1984-2003. Contbr. numerous articles to profl. jours.; editor scholarly jours. Adv. U.S. Dept. Energy, Washington, 1983—, World Bank, Washington, 1980—, NSF, Washington, 1985—, Calif. Inst. Energy Efficiency, Berkeley, 1990—. Fulbright scholar Washington, 1989; vis. scholar Cambridge U., 1979, Oxford U., 1979. Mem. Tau Beta Pi, Eta Kappa Nu, Sigma Xi. Office: U Calif Dept Economics Berkeley CA 94720-0001

GILBERTSON, OSWALD IRVING, marketing executive; b. Bklyn., Mar. 23, 1927; s. Olaf and Ingeborg Gabrielsen (Aase) Gilbertson; m. Magnhild Hompland, Sept. 11, 1954; children: Erik Olaf, Jan Ivar. Cert. electrotechnician, Sorlandets Tekniske Skole, Norway, 1947; BSEE, Stockholms Tekniska Inst., 1956. Registered profl. engr., Vt. Planning engr. test equipment design and devel. Western Electric Co., Inc., Kearny, N.J., 1957-61, planning engr. new prodn., 1963-67, engring. supr. test equipment, 63-67, engring. supr. submarine repeaters and equalizers, 1967-69; engring. mgr. comm. cables ITT Corp., Oslo, Norway, 1969-71; mktg. mgr. for ITT's Norwegian co. Std. Telefon og Kabelfabrik A/S (STK), 1971-87, STK factory rep., 1987-89, Alcatel Kabel Norge AS Factory rep., 1989-92, Alcatel Can. Wire Inc. Factory rep., 1992-95; divsn. mgr. Eswa Heating Sys., Inc., 1980-87, pres., 1987-89. Author: Electrical Cables for Power and Signal Transmission, 2000, Sånn va dae då i Kvinesdal, 1999, Visions, 2006, Visjoner, 2006. With AUS, 1948-52. Named Hon. Norwegian Consul, 1981-2004; apptd. Knight 1st Class Norwegian Order Merit, 1989. Mem. IEEE, Norwegian Soc. Profl. Engrs., Soc. Norwegian Am. Engrs., Sons of Norway. Achievements include patents in field. Home and Office: 6240 Brynwood Ct San Diego CA 92120-3805 Personal E-mail: osgil@cox.net.

GILBERTSON, ROBERT G., computer company executive; b. Madison, Wis., May 18, 1941; s. Palmer B. and Agnes E. (Ericson) G.; m. Ellen L. Podell; children: David Scott, Jeffrey Allan. Student, MIT, 1959-62; MBA, U. Chgo., 1970; PhD, Stanford U., 1973. Arch. designer various firms, 1963-66; mktg. exec. IBM, Chgo., White Plains, N.Y., 1966-71; asst. prof. Harvard Grad. Sch. Bus., Cambridge, Mass., 1973-78; sr. v.p. Data Archs. Inc., Waltham, Mass., 1978-83; pres., CEO, Channel Net Corp., Southport, Conn., 1983-85, Data Switch Corp., Shelton, Conn., 1985-92, CMX Sys. Inc., Wallingford, Conn., 1993-96, also bd. dirs.; pres., CEO Network Computing Devices, Inc., Mountain View, Calif., 1996—. Bd. dirs. Network Computing Devices, DSL.Net; adj. prof. Brandeis U., Walthama, 1976-80. Contbr. articles to profl. jours. Bd. dirs. Griffin Hosp., Seymour, Conn., 1987-92, Conn. Bus. Industry Assn., 1995-96; bd. dirs., vice chmn. Mfr. Assn. Conn., 1992-96. Named Turnaround Mgr. of Yr., 1988. Mem. IEEE, Am. Electronics Assn. (treas., sec., chmn. 1991-92), Assn. for Computing Machinery, Soc. Info. Mgmt., Inst. Mgmt. Scis., Conn. Com. Bus. Opportunity, Def. Diversified and Indsl. Policy, S.W. Area Commerce and Industry Assn. (bd. dirs. 1988-93 (chmn. regional transp. coun. 1990-93). Lutheran. Avocations: tennis, racquetball, skiing, golf, bridge.

GILBERTSON, ROBERT LEONARD, plant pathology educator; BS, U. Mass., 1978, MS, 1981; PhD, Colo. State U., 1985. Contbr. numerous articles to profl. jours. Recipient Novartis award Am. Phytopathol. Soc., 1998. Achievements include research in the molecular characterization, detection, and genetics of plant viruses, particularly geminiviruses. Office: U Calif 4208 Storer Hall 1 Shields Ave Davis CA 95616-5200 E-mail: rlgilbertson@ucdavis.edu.

GILBERTZ, LARRY E., former state legislator, entrepreneur; b. Gillette, Wyo., Feb. 3, 1929; s. Jacob A. and Lena E. (Schlautmann) G.; m. Verna Ann Howell, June 18, 1955; children: Katerine, L.D., Susan, Jay. Mgr. Gilbertz Ranch, Gillette, 1953-62, owner, 1963—; sr. ptnr. Gilbertz Co., Gillette, 1971—; pres. Gilbertz Enterprises, Gillette, 1988—; mem. Wyo. Senate, Cheyenne, 1993—98. Chmn. U. Wyo. Exptl. Farm, Campbell County, 1970-74. Treas. Sch. Bd. Dist. # 9, Campbell County, 1969-71; active Sch. Dist. Reorgn., Campbell County, 1970, Wyo. Ct. Reform, 1971. With U.S. Army, 1951-53, PTO. Recipient Performance Testing award U. Wyo., 1969-74, Chem. Weed Control award, 1969-74. Mem. Am. Farm Bur., Am. Legis. Exch. Coun., Am. Legion. Republican. Roman Catholic. Avocation: travel. Home: 3934 Highway 50 Gillette WY 82718-9201

GILCHRIST, DEBRA L., college librarian; BS, Calif. State U., Northridge, 1977; MLS, U. Denver, 1983; MS, SD State U., 1987; PhD, Oreg. State U., 2007. Asst. reference libr. & asst. prof. SD State U., 1984—87; asst. prof. & instr. libr. Pacific Lutheran U., Tacoma, 1987—91; dean libr. & media svcs. Pierce Coll. Dist., Lakewood & Puyallup, Wash., 1991—. Mem.: ALA (councilor-at-large 1995—2001), Assn. Coll. & Rsch. Librs. (faculty mem. Inst. Info. Literacy Immersion 1998—, chair Appts. com. 2001—02, ACRL Task Force on the Future 2001—02, dean faculty Inst. Info. Literacy Immersion 2001—, co-chair Virtual Conf. com. 2005—, Miriam Dudley Instruction Libr. award 2007). Office: Pierce Coll Libr Fort Steilacoom Cascade 400F 9401 Farwest Dr SW Lakewood WA 98498 also: Pierce Coll Libr Puyallup 1601 39th Ave SE Puyallup WA 98374 Office Phone: 253-964-6553. E-mail: dgilchrist@pierce.ctc.edu.

GILCHRIST, JAMES BEARDSLEE, banker; b. Cleve., Apr. 1, 1939; s. Hart D. and Alice (Beardslee) G.; m. Lewayne Dorman, Sept. 14, 1963; children: Hart D., Matthew J. AB, Dartmouth Coll., 1961; LLB, Stanford U., 1964; grad. with honors, Pacific Coast Banking Sch., U. Wash., 1970. Bar: Wash. 1964, Colo. 1964. Dep. pros. atty., King County, Wash., 1964-65; with Seattle First Nat. Bank, 1965-93, v.p., 1973-93, trust officer, 1970-77, corp. sec., 1977-82; sec. Seafirst Corp., 1977-82, mgr. instl. trust dept., 1982-85, mgr. personal trust dept., 1985-93; ptnr. Trust Concepts, 1993—. Instr. Am. Inst. Banking, Seattle Community Coll., 1976-78 Mem. candidate evaluation team Seattle Mcpl. League, 1976-79, chmn., 1979; mem. adv. com. Mercer Island Sch. Bd., 1979-81; bd. dirs. Mercer Island Schs. Found., 1981-85; mem. Dartmouth Coll. Alumni Coun., 1987-90. Mem. Wash. Bar Assn., Am. Soc. Corp. Secs. (chpt. pres. 1980-81, corp. practices com. 1981-83, dir. 1982-84), Corp. Trustees Assn. of Wash. (chmn. 1988-91), Seattle Estate Planning Coun. (mem. exec. com. 1987-89, chmn. seminar 1975).

GILCHRIST, RICHARD IRWIN, real estate developer; b. LA, Mar. 6, 1946; s. Dennis Samuel and Norma Elizabeth (Irwin) G.; m. Nina Newsom, June 21, 1969; children: Katherine Claire, Kimberly Ann, Brian Roy, Bradley Richard. Student, U. Copenhagen, Denmark, 1967; BA, Whittier Coll., Calif., 1968; JD, UCLA, 1971. Bar: Calif. 1972, U.S. Supreme Ct. 1972. Assoc. Flint & MacKay, LA, 1972-74, ptnr., 1974-81, Thomas, Shafran, Wasser & Childs, LA, 1981-83; founding ptnr. Gilchrist & Rutter, Santa Monica, Calif., 1983, of counsel, 1984—; gen. counsel Maguire Thomas Ptnrs., Santa Monica, Calif., 1983-85, ptnr., 1985-88, sr. ptnr., 1988-95; co-owner Sacramento Kings NBA Team, 1992—; prin. founding ptnr. Common Wealth Ptnrs., LA, 1995-99, Alexandria, Va., 1999—; pres., CEO Commonwealth Atlantic Properties, Washington, 1997—; pres., co-chief exec. Maguire Properties Inc.; pres. Irvine Co. Office, Newport Beach, Calif., 2006. Instr. bus. law Calif. State U., L.A., 1973-74, chief exec. & founder of pub. & pvt. real estate co. U.S. Bd. dirs. Weingardt Ctr., 1993—, L.A. Met. YMCAs, 1993—; trustee Whittier Coll., 1996—. Mem. ABA, Calif. Bar Assn., Whittier Coll. Alumni Assn., UCLA Alumni Assn., Arltington (Va.) County C. of C. (bd. dirs. 1998—). Avocations: running, sports, travel. Office: Irvine Co 550 Newport Ctr Dr Newport Beach CA 92660 Office Phone: 949-720-2000.

GILDRED, THEODORE E., former diplomat, real estate developer; b. Mexico City, 1935; m. Heidi Copin. Grad., Stanford U., 1959; postgrad., Sorbonne, U. Heidelberg; grad. Sch. Internat. Rels. and Pacific Area Studies, U. Calif. Pres. Gildred Found., 1967; founder Torrey Pines Bank (now Wells Fargo Bank), San Diego, 1979; U.S. amb. to Argentina, 1986-89; founder, chmn. bd. The Lomas Santa Fe Group, San Diego, 1989—. Bd. dirs. N.Am. Airlines, Grad. Sch. Internat. Rels. and Pacific Area Studies, U. Calif., San Diego, Security Pacific Nat. Bank; spkr. in field. Recipient hon. command pilot wings Ecuadorian Air Force, Orden de Mayo al Mèrito, en Grado de Gran Cruz, Pres. Carlos Menem, Argentina, 1992. Office: 265 Santa Helena Ste 200 Solana Beach CA 92075-1547 Fax: 858-755-6821. E-mail: Tegildred@lsfg.com.

GILES, ROBERT EDWARD, JR., lawyer; b. Bremerton, Wash., Dec. 17, 1949; s. Robert Edward Sr. and Alice Louise (Morton) G.; m. Barbara Susan Miller, Aug. 21, 1971; children: Steven, William, Thomas, James. BA in Fin., summa cum laude, U. Washington, 1971, JD, 1974. Bar: Wash. 1974, US Tax Ct. 1974. From assoc. to fin. ptnr. Perkins Coie, Seattle, 1974-86, mng. ptnr., 1986—, chmn. mgmt. com. Bd. dirs. Jr. Achievement, Seattle, 1984—; bd. dirs., sec. Wash. Coun. Econ. Edn., 1981—91; v.p., chief Seattle coun. Boy Scouts Am., 1996—2002; pres. Seattle Sports Commn., 2005—06. Capt. US Army, 1974. Mem.: ABA, Seattle C. of C. (trustee 1994—97, 2000—02), Wash. State Bar Assn. Avocations: hiking, climbing. Office: Perkins Coie 1201 3rd Ave 48th Fl Seattle WA 98101-3029 Office Phone: 206-359-8536. Office Fax: 206-359-9536. Business E-Mail: rgiles@perkinscoie.com.

GILHOOLY, DAVID JAMES, III, artist; b. Auburn, Calif., Apr. 15, 1943; s. David James and Gladys Catherine (Schulte) G.; m. Camille Margot Chang, Aug. 23, 1983; children: David James, Andrea Elizabeth, Abigail Margaret, Peter Rodney, Hakan Yuatutsu, Kiril Shintora, Sorqan Subetei. BA, U. Calif., Davis, 1965, MA, 1967. Tchr. San Jose (Calif.) State Coll., 1967-69, U. Sask. (Can.), Regina, 1969-71, York U., Toronto, Ont., Can., 1971-75, 76-77, U. Calif.-Davis, summer 1971, 75-76, Calif. State U.-Sacramento, summers 1978-79; lectr. in field. One-man shows include San Francisco Museum Art, 1967, M. H. deYoung Meml. Mus., San Francisco, 1968, Matrix Gallery, Wadsworth Athenuem, Hartford, Conn., 1976, Mus. Contemporary Art, Chgo., 1976, Vancouver (B.C., Can.), Art Gallery, 1976, ARCO Ctr. for Visual Arts, L.A., 1977, Mus. Contemporary Craft, N.Y.C., 1977, E.B. Crocker Art Mus., Sacramento, 1980, St. Louis Mus. Art, 1981, Smith-Anderson Gallery, Palo Alto, 1985, San Jose Mus. Art, 1992, De Saisset Mus., Santa Clara U., 1999, Hallie Ford Mus. Art, Salem, Oreg., 2000, Micaela Art Gallery, San Francisco, 2006; group shows include U. Calif.-Berkeley Art Mus., 1967, Inst. Contemporary Art, Boston, 1967, Whitney Mus. Am. Art, N.Y.C., 1970, 74, 81, Musee d'art de la Ville Paris, 1973, Chgo. Art Inst., 1975, San Francisco Mus. Art and Nat. Collection Fine Art, Washington, 1976-77, Stedelijk Mus., Amsterdam, Netherlands, 1979, Everson Mus. Art, Syracuse, N.Y., 1979, Whitney Mus. Am. Art, N.Y.C., 1981, Palm Springs Desert Art Mus., 1984, Oakland Mus., 1985, Stanford Mus. Art, 1987, Inst. Contemporary Art, Boston, 1994, Mus. Glass, Tacoma, 2005, Pence Art Mus., Davis, Calif., 2005; represented in permanent collections S. Bronfman Collection Can. Art, Montreal, Que., San Francisco Mus. Art, Phila. Mus. Art, Vancouver Art Gallery, Art Gallery Greater Victoria (B.C.), Albright-Knox Art Gallery, Buffalo, San Antonio Mus. Art, Oakland (Calif.) Mus. Art, Stedelijk Mus., Stanford U., Palo Alto, Calif., Australian Nat. Gallery, Canberra, Govt. Can., Calgary, Alta., Whitney Mus. Am. Art, Eugene (Oreg.) Ctr. Performing Arts. Can. Coun. grantee, 1975, 78. Mem. Royal Can. Acad. Republican. Mem. Ch. of Scientology. Office: 4385 Yaquina Bay Rd Newport OR 97365-9618 Personal E-mail: dgilhooly@earthlink.net.

GILL, GEORGE WILHELM, retired anthropologist; b. Sterling, Kans., June 28, 1941; s. George Laurance and Florence Louise (Jones) Gill; m. Carol Anne Livesay, Aug. 11, 1962 (div. 1974); children: George Scott, John Ashton; m. Pamela Jo Mills, July 26, 1975 (div. 1988); children: Bryce Thomas, Jennifer Florence; m. Denise Ann Royer, Oct. 30, 2001. BA in Zoology with honors (NSF grantee), U. Kans., 1963, MPhil Anthropology (NDEA fellow, NSF grantee), 1970, PhD in Anthropology, 1971. Diplomate Am. Bd. Forensic Anthropology, 1978. Mem. faculty U. Wyo., Laramie, 1971—, dir. Anthropology Mus., 1979—87, prof. anthropology, 1985—2006, chmn. dept. anthropology, 1993—96, prof. emeritus anthropology, 2006—. Forensic anthropologist law enforcement agys., 1972—; sci. leader Easter Island Anthrop. Expdn., 1981; chmn. Rapa Nui Rendezvous: Internat. Conf. Easter Island Rsch., U. Wyo., 1993. Author: articles, monographs; editor: (with S. Rhine) Skeletal Attribution of Race, 1990. Capt. US Army, 1963—67. Recipient J.P. Ellbogen meritorious classroom tchg. award, 1983; rsch. grantee U. Wyo., 1972, 78, 82, Nat. Geog. Soc., 1980, Ctr. for Field Rsch. 1980, Kon-Tiki Mus., Oslo, 1987, 89, 94, 96, World Monuments Fund, 1989, Mus. Inventory and Curation co-grantee BLM, Bur. Reclamation, Wyo. DOT, Fish and Wildlife Svc., 1994-99, Disting. Emeritus Prof., Coll. Arts & Sci., 2007. Fellow: Am. Acad. Forensic Scis. (sec. phys. anthropology sect. 1985—87, chmn. 1987—88); mem.: Wyo. Archaeol. Soc., Plains Anthrop. Soc., Am. Assn. Phys. Anthropologists. Republican. Unitarian. Office: U Wyo Dept Anthropology Laramie WY 82071 Office Phone: 307-766-5136. Business E-Mail: ggill@uwyo.edu.

GILL, GORDON N., medical educator; b. Dec. 19, 1937; BA in Chemistry and Lit., Vanderbilt U., 1960, MD, 1963. Diplomate Am. Bd. Internal Medicine with subspecialty in endocrinology and metabolism. Internal medicine intern Vanderbilt U. Hosp., Nashville, 1963-64; resident Yale-New Haven Hosp., 1964-66; fellow postdoctoral fellow metabolism/endocrinology NIH/Yale U., 1966-68; spl. postdoctoral rsch. fellow NIH/U. Calif., San Diego, 1968-69; asst. prof. medicine U. Calif., San Diego, 1969-73, assoc. prof., 1973-78, prof. medicine, 1978—, prof. cellular and molecular medicine, 2000—, chief divsn. endocrinology dept. medicine, 1971-83, chief divsn. endocrinology/metabolism, 1983-95, assoc. chair sci. affairs, 1992-95, chmn. faculty basic biomed. scis., 1995—2002, dean sci. affairs, 2001—03, interim dir. Moores/UCSD Cancer Ctr., 2003, dean translational medicine, dir. Coll. Integrated Life Scis., 2006—. Chmn. endocrinology study sect. NIH, 1979-80, chmn. task force on endocrinology, 1978, dir. tng. grant on exptl. endocrinology and metabolism, 1978-; prin. investigator interdisciplinary program to study macromolecules regulating growth and oncogenesis U. Calif., San Diego, 1988-95; chmn. Gordon Conf. on Hormone Action, 1979, Gordon Conf. on Peptide Growth Factors, 1990; mem. sci. adv. bd. BioCryst, 1990-; sci. and med. adv. bd. chair Whittier Inst., 1991-95; sci. adv. bd. Liver Ctr., U. Calif., San Francisco, 1991-95, Charles E. Culpepper Found., 1992—2001, Coun. for Tobacco Rsch. USA, 1991-97, ICN Pharms., 1992-; internat. adv. bd. dept. molecular and structural biology U. Grenoble, France, 1993-98; S. Richardson Hill vis. prof. U. Ala., Birmingham, 1991; Berlin lectr. Northwestern U. Sch. Medicine, 1994, sci. adv. bd. Chau, Kirsch Found., 2001-04. Mem. editl. bd. Jour. Cyclic Nucleotide and Protein Phosphorylation Rsch., 1974-84, Endocrinology, 1978-82, Am. Jour. Physiology, Cell Physiology, 1981-87, Jour. Biol. Chemistry, 1983-88, Jour. Cellular Biochemistry, 1984-89, Ann. Rev. Medicine, 1986-91, Analytical Biochemistry, 1980-92; editor Molecular and Cellular Endocrinology, 1974-92; cons. editor Jour. Clin. Investigation, 1992-97; sect. editor: Endocrinology, Best and Taylor Physiological Basis of Medical Practice, 11th-12th edits., Endocrinology and Metabolism, Cecil's Textbook of Medicine, 20th-22nd edit. Bd. dirs. Med. Rsch. and Edn. Found., The Agouron Inst., 1985—; mem. biochemistry and endocrinology sci. adv. com. Am. Cancer Soc., 1989-91; adv. com. Markey Charitable Trust, 1990-97; peer rev. com. Am. Heart Assn., 1991-96. Helen Hay Whitney Found. fellow, 1969-73; NIH Rsch. Career Devel. awardee, 1969-73, Merit award. Fellow ACP, Am. Acad. Arts and Scis.; mem. AAAS, Assn. Am. Physicians, Am. Fedn. Clin. Rsch., Am. Soc. Clin. Investigation, Am. Soc. Biol. Chemistry and Molecular Biology, Endocrine Soc., Western Assn. Physicians, Western Soc. for Clin. Investigation, Am. Soc. for Cell Biology, Phi Beta Kappa, Alpha Omega Alpha. Office: Univ Calif 9500 Gilman Dr La Jolla CA 92093-0650 Office Phone: 858-534-4310.

GILL, LIBBY, television executive; BA in Theater magna cum laude, Calif. State U., Long Beach. Mgr., publicist Embassy Comm. and Columbia Pictures TV, Calif., 1986-89; dir. primetime publicity Columbia Pictures TV/TriStar TV, Calif., 1989-92; v.p. publicity and promotion Sony Pictures Entertainment TV Group, Calif., 1992-94; v.p. pub. rels. west coast Turner Entertainment Group, Calif., 1994-96; sr. v.p. media rels. Universal TV Group, Universal City, Calif., 1996—. Pub. rels. cons. for non-profit orgns., including Deaf Arts Coun. Mem. TV Publicity Execs. Com. (former chmn.).

GILL, MARGARET GASKINS, lawyer; b. St. Louis, Mar. 2, 1940; d. Richard Williams and Margaret (Cambage) Gaskins; m. Stephen Paschall Gill, Dec. 21, 1961; children: Elizabeth, Richard. BA, Wellesley Coll., 1962; JD, U. Calif., Berkeley, 1965. Bar: Calif. 1966. Assoc. Pillsbury, Madison & Sutro, San Francisco, 1966-72, ptnr., 1973-94, mem. mgmt. com., 1973-94, head corp. securities group, mem. assoc., rev. com., 1981-91, chair assoc., rev. com., 1988-91; sr. v.p. legal, external affairs & sec. AirTouch Communications, San Francisco, 1994—. Referee Calif. State Bar Ct., 1979-82; bd. dirs. Consolidated Freightways. Mem. steering com. Trinity Episcopal Ch., Menlo Park, Calif., 1980-82, com. to revise constitution, Diocese Calif., 1981-82; trustee St. Luke's Hosp. Found., San Francisco, 1983-93; mem. adv. coun. Ch. div. Sch. of the Pacific, 1986; bd. dirs. Episcopal Diocese Calif., 1989—; trustee San Francisco Ballet, 1991—; bd. dirs., gen. counsel United Way Bay Area, San Francisco, 1993-94. Fellow Am. Bar Found.; mem. ABA (spl. com. on internat. practice 1979-82, spl. com. negotiated acquisition 1988-90), Calif. Bar Assn. (corp. com. 1982-85, chairperson 1985, exec. com. 1985-88, vice chairperson 1987-88, chair nominating com. bus. law sect. 1988), San Francisco Bar Assn. Republican. Episcopalian.

GILL, STEPHEN PASCHALL, retired physicist, mathematician; b. Balt., Nov. 13, 1938; s. Robert Lee and Charlotte (Olmsted) G.; m. Margaret Ann Gaskins, Dec. 21, 1961; children: Elizabeth Olmsted, Richard Paschall. BS, MIT, 1960; MA, Harvard U., 1961, PhD, 1964. Cons. hypersonic aerodynamics Raytheon Corp., Bedford, Mass., 1963-64; research physicist Stanford Research Inst., Menlo Park, Calif., 1964-65, head high energy gasdynamics, 1965-68, Physics Internat. Co., San Leandro, Calif., 1968-70, mgr. shock dynamics dept., 1970-72; founder, pres. Artec Assocs., Inc., Hayward, Calif., 1972-77, chief scientist, 1977-91; founder, pres. Votan Corp., Hayward, Calif., 1979-91, chief scientist, 1981—99, chmn. bd., 1981—85; ret., 1999. Founder, chief scientist Magnetic Pulse Inc., 1985-99; founder, dir., CFO Stephen & Margaret Gill Family Found., 1999-. Mem. San Francisco Symphony Assn.; mem. San Francisco Mus. Art. Mem. IEEE, Am. Phys. Soc., Am. Math. Soc., MIT Alumni Assn., Sigma Xi, Delta Kappa Epsilon. Clubs: MIT. Republican. Episcopalian. Home: 32 Flood Cir Atherton CA 94027-2151 Personal E-mail: stephen@gillfamily.name.

GILLESPIE, GERALD ERNEST PAUL, comparative literature educator, writer; b. Cleve., July 12, 1933; s. Francis and Nora Veronica (Quinn) G.; m. Adrienne Amalia Galante, Sept. 5, 1959. AB, Harvard U., 1956; postgrad., U. Tübingen, Germany, 1956—57; MA, Ohio State U., 1958, PhD, 1961; postgrad., U. Munich, 1960—61. Asst. prof. U. So. Calif., LA, 1961-65; from assoc. prof. to prof. SUNY, Binghamton, 1965-74; prof. Stanford (Calif.) U., 1974—. Vis. prof. U. Pa., Phila, 1969, NYU, 1970, U. Minn., Mpls., 1978, Peking U., Beijing, 1985, U. East Anglia, Norwich, Eng., 1988, U. Munich, 1993, U. Hagen, Germany, 2002; hon. prof., Liaoning U., China. Author: Lohenstein's Historical Tragedies, 1965, German Baroque Poetry, 1972, Evolution of the European Novel, 1987, Garden and Labyrinth of Time, 1988, Proust, Mann, Joyce in the Modernist Context, 2003, By Way of Comparison, 2004, Echoland: Readings from Humanism to Postmodernism, 2006; author, editor: Herkommen und Erneuerung, 1976, Studien zum Werk D.C. von Lohenstein, 1983, German Theater Before 1750, 1992, Romantic Drama, 1994, Narrative Ironies, 1997, Mallarmé in the Twentieth Century, 1998, Romantic Nonfictional Prose, 2004, Romantic Prose Fiction, 2008; translator, editor: Night Watches, 1972, Puss-in-Boots, 1974, Bohemian Lights, 1976; editor: Littérature Comparée, Littérature Mondiale, 1991, Visions in History, 1995, Powers of Narration, 1995; mem. editl. bd.: Comparative Lit., 1977—, Internationales Archiv, 1975—, Utrecht Studies in Comparative Lit., 1987-2004, Recherche Littéraire, 1991—, Literary Imagination, 1998-2004; co-editor: German Life and Letters, 1987-2004, advisor, 2005—. Andrew Mellon Found. fellow, 1966—67, John S. Guggenheim Found. fellow, 1967—68, NEH sr. fellow, 1973—74, vis. fellow Clare Hall, Cambridge U., Eng., 1979. Mem.: MLA (exec. com. comparative studies in romanticism and the 19th century 1982—87, mem. nat. program com. 1985—88, mem. exec. com. classical studies and modern lit. 1986—91), Calif. Assn. Scholars (bd. dirs. 1992—), Assn. Lit. Scholars and Critics (coun. 1998—2001), Renaissance Soc. Am., Brit. Comparative Lit. Assn., Am. Comparative Lit. Assn., Internat. Comparative Lit. Assn. (sec. 1979—85, mem. editl. bd. bull. 1979—85, v.p. 1985—88, pres. 1994—97), Berliner Wissenschaftliche Gesellschaft (corr.). Office Phone: 650-723-3266.

GILLETTE, FRANKIE JACOBS, retired savings and loan association executive, federal agency administrator, social worker; b. Norfolk, Va., Apr. 1, 1925; d. Frank Walter and Natalie (Taylor) Jacobs; m. Maxwell Claude Gillette, June 19, 1976. BS, Hampton U., 1946; MSW, Howard U., 1948. Lic. clin. social worker; cert. jr. coll. tchr., life. Youth dir. YWCA, Passaic, N.J., 1948-50; dir. program Ada S. McKinley Community Ctr., Chgo., 1950-53; program dir. Sophie Wright Settlement, Detroit, 1953-64; dir. Concerted Services Project, Pittsburg, Calif., 1964-66, Job Corps Staff Devel., U. Calif., Berkeley, 1966-69; spl. program coordinator U.S. Community Services Adminstrn., San Francisco, 1969-83; pres. G & G Enterprises, San Francisco, 1985—. Chmn. bd. dirs. Time Savs. and Loan Assn., San Francisco, 1986-87. Commr. San Francisco Human Rights Commn., 1988-93; bd. dirs. Urban Econ. Devel. Corp., 1980-93, San Francisco Conv. and Visitors Bur.; trustee Fine Arts Mus. of San Francisco, 1993—; chmn. San Francisco-Abidjan Sister City Com., 1990—; founding bd. dirs. Mus. African Diaspora, 2002—. Mem. Nat. Assn. Negro Bus. and Profl. Women's Clubs (pres. 1983-87), The Links, Inc., Delta Sigma Theta, Inc. Office: G & G Enterprises 85 Cleary Ct Apt 4 San Francisco CA 94109-6518

GILLETTE, NANCY E., entomologist, researcher; b. Calif. BA in Fine Arts, U. Calif., Berkeley, 1969, PhD in Forest Entomology, 1987. Post-doctoral fellow Inst. Nat. de la Recherche Agronomique, Orleans, France, 1989; rsch. entomologist USDA Forest Svc. Rsch., Berkeley, Calif., 1991—. Interagency liaison (biopesticides) USDA Forest Svc.-EPA, 1996; arthropod taxa expert Northeast Forest Plan, 1997—. Contbr. articles to profl. jours. including Canadian Jour. Forest Rsch., Jour. Chem. Ecology, Environ. Entomology, Jour. Econ. Entomology. Office Fax: 510-559-6499. E-mail: ngillette@fs.fed.us.*

GILLETTE, PATRICIA K., lawyer; b. LA, Aug. 7, 1951; AB, Occidental Coll., 1973; JD cum laude, U. San Francisco, 1976. Bar: Calif., Am. Bar Assoc. In-house counsel Bank of Am.; atty. private practice; ptnr. Heller Ehrman LLP, San Francisco, 1990—. Co-chmn. labor and employment practice group Heller Ehrman LLP, co-chmn. gender diversity com., 2006—. Office: Heller Ehrman LLP 333 Bush St San Francisco CA 94104-2806 Office Phone: 415-772-6456. Business E-Mail: pgillette@hewm.com.

GILLETTE, ROBERT J., aerospace transportation executive; BS in Fin., Ind. U. With GE Plastics; v.p., gen. mgr. AlliedSignal Engring. Plastics; v.p. strategic growth, v.p., gen. mgr. Asia Worldwide aftermarket Garrett Engine Boosting Sys., pres., 2000—01; pres., CEO Honeywell Transp. Systems Honeywell Internat. Inc., Torrance, Calif., 2001—04, pres., CEO, Honeywell Aerospace Phoenix, 2005—. Office: Honeywell Aerospace 1944 E Sky Harbor Cir N Phoenix AZ 85034

GILLETTE, W. MICHAEL, state supreme court justice; b. Seattle, Dec. 29, 1941; s. Elton George and Hazel Irene (Hand) G.; children: Kevin, Saima. AB cum laude in German, Polit. Sci., Whitman Coll., 1963; LLB, Harvard U., 1966. Bar: Oreg. 1966, U.S. Dist. Ct. Oreg. 1966, U.S. Ct. Appeals (9th cir.) 1966, Samoa 1969, U.S. Supreme Ct. 1970, U.S. Dist. Ct. Vt. 1973. Assoc. Rives & Rogers, Portland, Oreg., 1966-67; dep. dist. atty. Multnomah County, Portland, 1967-69; asst. atty. gen. Govt. of Am. Samoa, 1969-71, State of Oreg., Salem, 1971-77; judge Oreg. Ct. Appeals, Salem, 1977-86; justice Oreg. Supreme Ct., Salem, 1986—. Instructor constitutional and criminal law Portland State U., 1971—74; mem. bd. Oreg. Law-Related Education Project, 1980—88; mem. advisory com. Scholars for Constitution Project, 1984; prof. administrative, constitutional, and consumer law Nat. Jud. Coll. Bd. trustees Oreg. Museum of Science and Industry, 1977—80. Avocation: basketball. Office: Oreg Supreme Ct Supreme Ct Bldg 1163 State St Salem OR 97310-1331 Office Phone: 503-986-5705.

GILLIAM, FRANKLIN D., JR., dean, political science professor; BA, Drake U., 1977; MA, U. Iowa, 1978, PhD, 1983. Asst. prof. Dept. Polit. Sci. U. Wis., Parkside, 1982—83, asst. prof. Dept. Polit. Sci., Dept. Afro-Am. Studies Robert M. LaFollette Inst. Pub. Affairs Madison, 1983—86; asst. prof. Dept. Polit. Sci. UCLA, 1986—91, chair BA and MA programs Ctr. for African-Am. Studies, 1992, assoc. prof., 1991—95, assoc. dir. Ctr. for Study of Am. Politics and Pub. Policy, 1993—98, founding dir. Ctr. for Comm. and Cmty., 1999—, prof., 1996—, assoc. vice chancellor cmty. partnerships, founding dir. Ctr. for Cmty. Partnerships, 2002—08, dean Sch. Pub. Affairs, 2008—. Vis. lectr. Grinnell Coll., 1982; rsch. dir. Commn. on Status of African-Am. Males, State of Calif., 1993—96; vis. prof. Dept. Polit. Sci. U. Dar Es-Salaam, Tanzania, 1997; vis. scholar Heller Sch., Brandeis U., 2001—04; lectr. in field. Contbr. articles to profl. jours. Recipient Mark O. Hatfield Nat. Scholar Award, Portland State U., 2004, Double D Award, Drake U., 2006. Mem.: Western Polit. Sci. Assn., Nat. Conf. of Black Polit. Scientists, Midwest Polit. Sci. Assn., Am. Polit. Sci. Assn. Office: UCLA Sch Pub Affairs 3284 Sch Pub Affairs Bldg 337 Charles Young Dr E Los Angeles CA 90095-1656 Office Phone: 310-206-3487. Office Fax: 310-206-5773. E-mail: fgilliam@spa.ucla.edu.*

GILLIS, CHRISTINE DIEST-LORGION, retired certified financial planner, stockbroker; b. San Francisco, Apr. 26, 1923; d. Evert Jan and Christine Helen (Radcliffe) Diest-Lorgion; children: Barbara Gillis Pieper and Suzanne Gillis Seymour (twins). BS in Bus. Adminstrn., U. Calif., Berkeley, 1944; MS in Edn., U. So. Calif., 1968. Cert. fin. planner, 1978. Account exec. Winslow, Cohu & Stetson, NYC, 1962-63, Paine Webber, NYC, 1964-65; sr. investment exec. Shearson Hammill, Beverly Hills, Calif., 1966-72; fin. planner, asst. v.p. E.F. Hutton, LA, 1972-87; 2d v.p. Shearson Lehman Hutton, Glendale, Calif., 1988; v.p. investments Dean Witter Reynolds, Glendale, Calif., 1988-90. Mem. AAUW (life; trustee ednl. found.), Town Hall. of Calif. (life; corp. sec. 1974-75, dir., gov. 1976-80), Women Stockbrokers Assn. (founding pres. N.Y.C. 1963), Women of Wall Street West (founder, pres. 1979-84), Navy League (life), U. Calif. Berkeley Alumni Assn. (life), U. So. Calif. Alumni Assn. (life), Town and Gown (life). Episcopalian. Home: 7820 Suncup Way Unit 209 Carlsbad CA 92009-6878

GILLIS, EDWIN, information technology executive; BA in Govt., Clark U.; MA in Internat. Rels., U. So. Calif.; MBA, Harvard Bus. Sch. CPA, gen. practice ptnr. Coopers & Lybrand, 1976—91; CFO Lotus Devel. Corp., 1991—95; exec. v.p., CFO Parametric Tech. Corp., 1995—2002, VERITAS Software Corp., Mountain View, Calif., 2002—. Office: VERITAS Software Corp 350 Ellis St Mountain View CA 94043

GILLIS, JOHN SIMON, retired psychologist, educator; b. Washington, Mar. 21, 1937; s. Simon John and Rita Veronica (Moran) G.; m. Mary Ann Wesolowski, Aug. 29, 1959; children: Holly Ann, Mark, Scott. BA, Stanford U., 1959; MS (fellow), Cornell U., 1961; PhD (NIMH fellow), U. Colo., 1965. Lectr. dept. psychology Australian Nat. U., Canberra, 1968-70; sr. psychologist Mendocino (Calif.) State Hosp., 1971-72; asso. prof. dept. psychology Tex. Tech U., Lubbock, 1972-76; prof. psychology Oreg. State U., Corvallis, 1976—2004, chmn. dept. psychology, 1976—84, 1997—2004; ret., 2004. Cons. VA, Ciba-Geigy Pharms., USIA, UN High Commn. for Refugees; commentator Oreg. Ednl. and Pub. Broadcasting System, 1978-79; Fulbright lectr., India, 1982-83, Greece, 1992, Kyrgyzstan, 2001; vis. prof. U. Karachi, 1984, 86, U. Punjab, Pakistan, 1985, Am. U., Cairo, 1984-86. Contbr. articles to profl. jours. Served with USAF, 1968-72. Ciba-Geigy Pharms. grantee, 1971-82 Roman Catholic. Home: 7520 NW Mountain View Dr Corvallis OR 97330-9106 Office: Oreg State U Dept Psychology Corvallis OR 97331 Business E-Mail: jgillis@orst.edu.

GILLIS, MIKE (MICHAEL DAVID GILLIS), professional sports team executive, retired professional hockey player; b. Sudbury, Ont., Can., Dec. 1, 1958; m. Diane Gillis; 3 children. Attended, Northeastern U., Boston Coll.; LLB, Queen's U., 1990. Left wing Colorado Rockies, 1978—81, Boston Bruins, 1981—84; founder, player agent M.D. Gillis and Assocs. Ltd., Kingston, Ont., Canada, 1994—2008; player agent Assante Sports Mgmt. Group, 2000, head hockey practice, 2001; gen. mgr. Vancouver Canucks, 2008—. Mem.: Sports Lawyers Assn. Office: Vancouver Canucks 800 Griffiths Way Vancouver BC V6B 6G1 Canada

GILLIS, STEVEN, biotechnology company executive; b. Phila., Apr. 25, 1953; s. Herbert and Rosalie Henrietta (Segal) G.; m. Anne Cynthia Edgar, June 26, 1976; children: Sarah Milne, Bradley Stirling. BA cum laude, Williams Coll., 1975; PhD, Dartmouth Coll., 1978. Lectr. in biology Dartmouth Coll., Hanover, N.H., 1977-78; research assoc. Dartmouth Med. Sch., Hanover, 1978-79; assoc. researcher Meml. Sloan-Kettering, NYC, 1979-80; asst. prof. U. Wash., Seattle, 1980-83; exec. v.p., dir. R & D Immunex Corp., Seattle, 1982—, pres., chief oper. officer, 1988—, chief exec. officer, 1990-94, also bd. dirs.; adj. prof. U. WA, Seattle, 1990-97; pres and CEO Corixa Corp., Seattle, 19946, 1994—. Adj. assoc. prof. U. Wsah., 1982-90, adj. prof., 1990—. Editor: Lymphokines, 1985, Recombinant Lymphokines and Their Receptors, 1987; contbr. articles to profl. jours. Asst. mem. Fred Hutchinson Cancer Ctr., Seattle, 1980-82, affiliate investigator, 1982—. Recipient Internat. Immunopharmacology award, 1983. Mem. Am. Assn. Immunologists, N.Y. Acad. Scis., Am. Assn. Arts and Scis., Columbia Tower Club (Seattle). Avocations: golf, swimming. Office: Corixa Corporation 1900 9th Ave Ste 1100 Seattle WA 98101-1325

GILLMOR, HELEN, federal judge; BA, Queen's Coll. of CUNY, 1965; LLB magna cum laude, Boston U., 1968. With Ropes & Gray, Boston, 1968-69, Law Offices of Alexander R. Gillmor, Camden, Maine, 1970, Torkildson, Katz, Jossem, Fonseca, Jaffe, Moore & Hetherington, Honolulu, 1971-72; law clk. to Chief Justice William S. Richardson Hawaii State Supreme Ct., 1972; dep. pub. defender Office of Pub. Defender, Honolulu, 1972-74; dist. ct. judge per diem Family Ct. (1st cir.) Hawaii, 1977-83; per diem judge Dist. Ct., 1st circuit, 1983-85; pvt. practice Honolulu, 1985-94; district judge U.S. Dist. Ct. Hawaii, 9th circuit, 1994—2005, chief dist. judge, 2005—. Counsel El Paso Real Estate Investment Trust, 1969; lectr. U.S. Agy. Internat. Devel., Seoul, South Korea, 1969-70, Univ. Hawaii, 1975. Office: Prince J K Kuhio Fed Bldg 300 Ala Moana Blvd Rm C-400 Honolulu HI 96850-0400

GILLUM, GARY PAUL, retired librarian; b. Indpls., June 12, 1944; s. Paul Brane and Ruth Janeve (Hansing) G.; m. Lynn Ann Ruhland, July 12, 1969 (dec. July 1977); children: Grant, Adina; m. Elizabeth Bayliss, Oct. 11, 1977 (dec. Apr. 1986); children: Bonnie, David, Annalyn, Timothy; m. Signe Marie Slangerup, Dec. 19, 1987; children: Mary Jane, Amy, Emily, Kathryn, Lucy, Karl, Judith, Jed, Elizabeth, Jacob, Joseph. AA, St. John's Coll., Winfield, Kans., 1966; BA, Concordia Sr. Coll., Ft. Wayne, Ind., 1968; MLS, Brigham Young U., 1971. Music libr. Indpls.-Marion County Libr., 1968-69; gen. reference libr. Brigham Young U., Provo, 1971-75, humanities libr., 1975-80, ancient studies bibliographer, 1980-85, religion libr., 1985—, chmn. history-religion reference dept. Harold B. Lee Libr., 1990—; ret., 2008. Editor: Of All Things! A Nibley Quote Book, 1981. Bd. dirs., treas. Utah Valley Symphony Orch., Provo, 1994—. Mem. Mormon History Assn., Phi Kappa Phi. Republican. Mem. Los Ch. Avocations: singing, playing piano, aviation, Native American culture, camping. Home: 165 N 1300 E Springville UT 84663-1745 Personal E-mail: gsgillum@comcast.com.

GILMAN, GEORGE L., state legislator; b. Portland, Oreg. Oregon State Representative, District 50, formerly; Oregon State Representative, District 55, 2003-. Republican. Mailing: 452 Beall Ln Central Point OR 97502 also: 900 Court St NE H-493 Salem OR 97301 Office Phone: 503-986-1455. E-mail: rep.georgegilman@state.or.us.

GILMAN, JOHN JOSEPH, research scientist; b. St. Paul, Dec. 22, 1925; s. Alexander Falk and Florence Grace (Colby) G.; m. Pauline Marie Harms, June 17, 1950 (div. Dec. 1968); children: Pamela Ann, Gregory George, Cheryl Elizabeth; m. Gretchen Marie Sutter, June 12, 1976; 1 son, Brian Alexander. BS, Ill. Inst. Tech., 1946, MS, 1948; PhD, Columbia, 1952. Research metallurgist Gen. Electric Co., Schenectady, 1952-60; prof. engring. Brown U., Providence, 1960-63; prof. physics and metallurgy U. Ill., Urbana, 1963-68; dir. Materials Research Center Allied Chem. Corp., Morristown, N.J., 1968-78; dir. Corp. Devel. Center, 1978-80; mgr. corp. research Amoco Co. (Ind.), Naperville, Ill., 1980-85; assoc. dir. Lawrence Berkeley Lab./U. Calif., Calif., 1985-87; sr. scientist Lawrence Berkeley Lab., Calif., 1987-93; adj. prof. UCLA, 1993—. Author: Micromechanics of Flow in Solids, 1969, Inventivity-The Art and Science of Research Management, 1992, Electronic Basis of the Strength of Materials, 2003; editor: The Art and Science of Growing Crystals, 1963, Fracture of Solids (with D.C. Drucker), 1963, Atomic and Electronic Structures of Metals, 1967, Metallic Glasses, 1973, Energetic Materials, 1993; editl. bd. Jour. Applied Physics, 1969-72; contbg. editor Materials Tech., 1994-99; contbr. over 325 papers, articles to tech. jours. Served as Ensign USNR, 1943-46. Recipient Mathewson gold medal Am. Inst. Metal Engrs., 1959, Disting. Service award Alumni Assn. Ill. Inst. Tech., 1962, Application to Practice award, 1985. Fellow AAAS, Am. Phys. Soc., The Materials Soc., Am. Soc. for Metals (Campbell lectr. 1966); mem. Nat. Acad. Engring., Phi Kappa Phi, Tau Beta Pi. Home: 2852 Forrester Dr Los Angeles CA 90064-4662 Office: UCLA 6532 Boelter Hl Los Angeles CA 90095-0001

GILMAN, NELSON JAY, library director; b. LA, Mar. 30, 1938; s. Louis L. and Alice (Cohen) G.; children: Justine C., Seth F.; m. Lixia Zhao. BS, U. So. Calif., 1959, MS, 1960; MLS, U. Calif., Berkeley, 1964. Tchr. math. dept. Pasadena (Calif.) H.S., 1960-61, Tamalpais H.S., Mill Valley, Calif., 1962-63; intern library adminstrn. UCLA, 1964-65, asst. to librarian, 1965-66, asst. to biomedical librarian, 1966-67, asst. biomedical librarian, 1967-69; assoc. dir. Pacific Southwest Regional Med. Library Svc., UCLA, 1969-71; dir. L.A. County/U. So. Calif. Med. Ctr. Libraries, 1974-79; asst. prof. dept. med. edn. U. So. Calif. Sch. Medicine, LA, 1971—, dir. Norris Med. Library, 1971—, dir. Health Scis. Librs., 1984—, assoc. dir. devel. and demonstration ctr., 1981—; assoc. dean librs., dir. planning for teaching libr. U. So. Calif., 1989-90; interim dir. Ctrl. Libr. System, 1990-91. Cons. HEW, San Francisco, 1973-76, NIH, Washington, 1970-71. Assoc. editor U. So. Calif. Sch. Medicine Info. Systems Research Program, 1984-87; contbr. articles to profl. jours. With USAR, 1961-67. Mem. Am. Library Assn., Am. Soc. Info. Sci., Assn. Acad. Health Scis. Library Dirs. (bd. dirs. 1980-83), Med. Library Assn. (bd. dirs. 1977-79). Democrat. Jewish. Avocation: gardening. Home: 615 22nd St Santa Monica CA 90402-3121 Office: U So Calif Norris Med Library 2003 Zonal Ave Los Angeles CA 90089-0001

GILMORE, DANNY D., state legislator; m. Cindi Gilmore; children: Damon, Deanna. Grad., Palomar CC, Calif. Hwy. Patrol Acad., 1972, Police Officers Std. Training program. With Calif. Highway Patrol, 1972—2003; mem. Dist. 30 Calif. State Assembly, 2008—. Republican. Office: 1489 W Lacey Blvd Ste 103 Hanford CA 93230 also: PO Box 942849 Rm 5126 Sacramento CA 94249-0030 Office Phone: 559-585-7170, 916-319-2030. Office Fax: 559-585-7175.*

GILMORE, DENNIS J., insurance company executive; BBA, San Diego State U.; MBA, Loyola Marymount U. With TRTS Data Svcs. (acquired by First Am. Corp. in 1991), 1988—91; v.p., area mgr. First Am. Corp., 1991—93, regional v.p., 1993—96, regional v.p., nat. dir., 1996—98, pres. First Am. Real Estate Solutions LLC, 1998, COO. Office: First Am Corp 1 First American Way Santa Ana CA 92707 Office Phone: 714-250-3000.

GILMORE, MIKE, state legislator; b. Oakland, Calif., July 9, 1945; m. Mary Gilmore; 2 children. Mem. Dist. 59 Wyo. House of Reps., 2009—. Democrat. Office: 213 State Capitol Bldg Cheyenne WY 82002 also: 1992 Chamberlin Rd Casper WY 82604 Office Phone: 307-777-7881, 307-266-0023. Office Fax: 307-777-5466. Business E-Mail: michaelgilmore@wyoming.com.

GILMORE, TIMOTHY JONATHAN, paralegal, consultant; b. Orange, Calif., June 24, 1949; s. James and Margaret (Swanson) G.; m. Blanche Jean Panter, Sept. 3, 1984; children: Erin, Sean and Brian (twins). BA, St. Mary's Coll., Moraga, Calif., 1971; grad., Denver Paralegal Inst., 1996. Adminstrv. asst. Gov. Ronald Reagan, Sacramento, 1971-73; salesman Penn Mutual, Anaheim, Calif., 1973-76; asst. devel. dir. St. Mary's Coll., Moraga, 1976-81; devel. dir. St. Alphonsus Hosp., Boise, Idaho, 1981-83; adminstr. Blaine County Hosp., Hailey, Idaho, 1983-86; exec. dir. Poudre Hosp. Found., Ft. Collins, Colo., 1986-87; nat. recruiting dir. Power Securities Corp., Denver, 1987-89; cons. Horn, Fagan & Lund Exec. Search Cons., Ft. Collins, 1989; v.p. Jackson & Coker Locum Tenens, Inc., Denver, 1990-93; pres. Gilmore and Assocs., Ft. Collins, Colo., 1993-98; paralegal, legis. specialist Brownstein, Hyatt & Farber Schreck LLP, Denver, 1998—. Republican. Mem. Lds Ch. Avocation: fishing. Home and Office: 2460 West 107th Dr Westminster CO 80234 Home Phone: 303-469-3073; Office Phone: 303-223-1346. Business E-Mail: tgilmore@bhfs.com.

GILMORE, W. FRANKLIN (FRANK), academic administrator; BS, Va. Mil. Inst.; PhD in Organic Chemistry, MIT; postdoctoral study, Inst. Molecular Biophysics, Fla. State U. Prof., dept. chmn., rsch. prof. med. chemistry dept. U. Miss.; exec. v.p. W.Va. U. Inst. Tech.; chancellor Mont. Tech, U. Mont., Butte. Mem. Goldwater Scholarship Selection Com.; mem. NAPLEX steering com. Nat. Assn. Boards of Pharmacy. With USMCR, 1952—55, capt. USAR, 1957—65. Mem.: Sigma Xi (past pres.). Office: Montana Tech Office of the Chancellor 1300 W Park St Butte MT 59701-8997 Office Phone: 406-496-4129. Business E-Mail: fgilmore@mtech.edu.

GILROY, TONY, scriptwriter, film director; b. NYC, Sept. 11, 1956; s. Frank D. Gilroy; children: Sam, John, Tony. Screenwriter (films) The Cutting Edge, 1992, Dolores Claiborne, 1995, Extreme Measures, 1996, The Devil's Advocate, 1997, Armageddon, 1998, The Bourne Identity, 2002, The Bourne Supremacy, 2004, The Bourne Ultimatum, 2007, screenwriter, exec. prodr. Bait, 2000, Proof of Life, 2000, dir., screenwriter Michael Clayton, 2007 (Edgar award for best motion picture screenplay, 2008), Duplicity, 2009. Office: ICM Los Angeles 10250 Constellation Blvd Los Angeles CA 90067

GILTNER, PHIL (F. PHILLIPS GILTNER III), food distributing executive; BSBA, U. Nebr.; MS in Acctg., U. Pa., Phila. CPA Ariz. Various auditing positions Deloitte, Price Waterhouse; v.p., CFO Wells Fargo Credit Corp.; v.p., asst. to chmn. Inertia Dynamics Corp.; CFO, sr. v.p. Shamrock Foods, Phoenix. Bd. dirs., mem. audit com. Poore Bros., Inc., 2003—. Mem. Ariz. Bus. Leadership Assn. (founding pres., spkr.). Office: Shamrock Foods 2540 N 29th Ave Phoenix AZ 85009 Office Phone: 602-233-6400.

GIMON, JULIETTE, foundation administrator, volunteer; d. Eleanor Hewlett Gimon. BA in Anthropology, Columbia U. Mem. family council Flora Family Found.; fellow, trustee William and Flora Hewlett Found., 2000—; former instructor WorldTeach, Quito, Ecuador; former recycling prog. designer Fundación Natura; co-founder, outreach and develop. coordinator Global Philanthropy Forum (now project of World Affairs Council of No. Calif.). Bd. dirs. Synergos Inst., Global Fund for Children; adv. com. mem. Youth Philanthropy Worldwide, Global Philanthropy Forum. Office: Global Philanthropy Forum World Affairs Ctr 312 Sutter St Ste 200 San Francisco CA 94108

GINGER, ANN FAGAN, lawyer; b. Nov. 25, 1925; Exec. dir. Meiklejohn Civil Liberties Inst., Berkeley. Vis. prof. law Univ. Calif. Hastings Coll., Univ. San Francisco, Univ. Santa Clara, New Coll. Calif., Univ. Puget Sound. Author: Calif. Criminal Law Practice (vol. I & II), Jury Selection in Civil & Criminal Trials, & other books and articles on civil liberties law. Office: Meiklejohn Civil Liberties Institute PO Box 673 Berkeley CA 94701-0673

GINN, SAM L., telephone company executive; b. Saint Clair, Ala., Apr. 3, 1937; s. James Harold and Myra Ruby (Smith) G.; m. Meriann Lanford Vance, Feb. 2, 1963; children: Matthew, Michael, Samantha. BS, Auburn U., 1959; postgrad., Stanford U. Grad. Sch. Bus., 1968. Various positions AT&T, 1960-78; with Pacific Tel. & Tel. Co., 1978—, exec. v.p. network San Francisco, 1979-81, exec. v.p. services, 1981-82, exec. v.p. network services, 1982, exec. v.p., strategic planning and adminstrn., 1983, vice chmn. bd., strategic planning and adminstrn., 1983-84; vice chmn. bd., group v.p. PacTel Cos. Pacific Telesis Group, San Francisco, 1984-86; pres. Air Touch Commn., San Francisco, 1984-87; vice chmn. bd., pres., chief exec. officer PacTel Corp. Pacific Telesis Group, San Francisco, 1986; pres., chief operating officer Pacific Telesis Group, San Francisco, 1987-88, former chmn., pres., chief exec. officer; chmn. Air Touch Commn., San Francisco, 1993—, now chmn. bd., CEO. Mem. adv. bd. Sloan program Stanford U. Grad. Sch. Bus., 1978-85, mem. internat. adv. council Inst. Internat. Studies; bd. dir. 1st Interstate Bank, Chevron Corp., Safeway, Inc. Trustee Mills Coll., 1982—. Served to capt. U.S. Army, 1959-60. Sloan fellow, 1968 Mem.: Blackhawk Country (Danville, Calif.); World Trade, Pacific-Union; Rams Hill Country (Borrego Springs, Calif.), Bankers. Republican. Office: Ste 1400 400 S El Camino Real San Mateo CA 94402-1740

GINORIO, ANGELA BEATRIZ, university research administrator, educator; b. Hato Rey, PR, Jan. 30, 1947; d. Melquiades Alejandro and Juana del Carmen (Morales) G.; m. Charles H. Muller; 1 child, Emilia Beatriz Muller-Ginorio. BA, U. P.R., 1968, MA, 1971; PhD, Fordham U., 1979. Instr. U. P.R., Rio Piedras, 1970-71; asst. prof. Bowling Green (Ohio) State U., 1978-80; counselor Office of Minority Affairs, Seattle, 1981-82; dir. Women's Info. Ctr., Seattle, 1983-87; dir. N.W. Ctr. for Rsch. on Women and Women's Info. Ctr. U. Wash., Seattle, 1987-92, affiliate asst. prof. psychology, 1986-93, dir. N.W. Ctr. Rsch. on Women, 1993—99, asst. prof. women studies, adj. asst. prof. psychology, 1993—99, assoc. prof., adj. prof., 1999—. Cons. U. Hawaii, Honolulu, 1989, AAUW Rsch. Found., 1994—. Mem. editl. bd. Internat. Jour. of Intercultural Rels., Sex Roles, Signs; co-editor: (spl. issue) Women's Studies Quar., 1990; author: (monograph) Warming the Climate for Woman in Academic Science, Si, se puede! Yes We Can! Bd. dirs. Mexican Am. Women Nat. Assn.-N.W., Seattle, 1988-89, Planned Parenthood, King County, Wash., 1991-93; mem. Wash. state com. Nat. Mus. Women in the Arts, 1989-92. Recipient Travel awards NIMH, 1979, APA/NSF, 1981; named Woman of Yr., Bus. and Profl. Women Campus chpt., 1986; grantee for evaluation Ford Found., 1989-91, grantee for summer sci. camp Discuren Found., 1992-93, NSF grantee, 1994-97. Fellow APA (bd. ethnic and minority affairs 1987-90); mem. Sociologists for Women in Soc. Office: Univ Wash Padel Ford Hall 35-4345 Seattle WA 98195-4345

GINSBURG, GERALD J., lawyer, management consultant; b. Poughkeepsie, NY, Aug. 29, 1930; s. Abraham and Anna (Murkoff) G.; children: Jason Andrew, Stephanie Carla. BS, Syracuse U., 1952; JD, Bklyn. Law Sch., 1958. Bar: N.Y. 1959. Pub. acct., 1954-59; v.p. fin. and ops., dir. Sheffield Watch Corp., NYC, 1959-70, dir., 1967-70; exec. v.p., dir. Kurt Orban Co., Wayne, NJ, 1971-83; pres., dir. Pacific Marine Holdings Corp., 1983-87; pres. J&S Cons., Walnut Creek, Calif. Dir. Ramapo Fin. Corp., Pilgrim State Bank Served with USNR, 1952-53. Mem. ABA, N.Y. Bar Assn. Office: PO Box 5314 Walnut Creek CA 94596-1314

GIOTTONINI, JAMES B., city official; b. Stockton, Calif., 1945; BS, Calif. State U., San Jose, 1968; MBA, Calif. State U., Sacramento, 1977. Dir. pub. works Town of Morgan Hill, Calif., 1978-82; city engr. City of Stockton, Calif., 1982-89, acting dir. pub. works, 1989, dir. pub. works, 1989—. Mem. ASCE. Office: City Stockton Dept Pub Works Rm 317 425 N El Dorado St Stockton CA 95202-1997

GIOVANIELLI, DAMON VINCENT, physicist, consultant; b. Teaneck, NJ, May 8, 1943; s. Dominick John and Marie Concetta (Conti) G.; m. Eleanor Ruth Rand, Aug. 18, 1968; children: Kira, Tina. AB, Princeton U., 1965; PhD in Physics, Dartmouth Coll., 1970. Instr. dept. engring. and applied sci. Yale U., New Haven, 1970-72; with Los Alamos (N.Mex.) Nat. Lab., 1972-93, leader physics divsn., 1987—93; ret., 1993; pres. Sumner Assocs., Sante Fe, 1993—; chmn. bd. dirs. La Mancha Co., 1997—. With J. Robert Oppenheimer Meml. Com. Contbr. articles to profl. jours. Mem. alumni schs. com. Princeton U.; trustee Coll. Santa Fe. Fellow AAAS; mem. Am. Phys. Soc., Fusion Power Assocs., Sigma Xi. Episcopalian. Home: 12 Loma Del Escolar Los Alamos NM 87544-2524 Office: Sumner Assocs 100 Cienega St Ste D Santa Fe NM 87501-2003

GIOVINCO, JOSEPH, non profit agency administrator, writer; b. San Francisco, Oct. 12, 1942; s. Joseph Bivona and Jean Andrews Giovinco; m. Sally Garey, Aug. 31, 1970 (div. Mar. 1982); 1 child, Gina Lorraine. BA, U. Oreg., 1964; MA in History, San Francisco State U., 1968; PhD in History, U. Calif., Berkeley, 1973. Asst. prof. history SUNY, Albany, 1974-76; instr. multicultural studies Sonoma State U., Cotati, Calif., 1976-79; exec. dir. Hist. Mus. Found., Sonoma County, Santa Rosa, Calif., 1977-80; exec. dir. no. Calif. affiliate Am. Diabetes Assn., San Francisco, 1980-81; exec. dir. San Francisco Sch. Vols., 1981-85, Calif. Hist. Soc., San Francisco, 1985-87; dir. Ctr. Advancement & Renewal of Educators, San Francisco, 1988—. Contbr. articles to profl. publs. Recipient Covello prize, Italian Am. Hist. Assn., 1976; named Alumnus of the Yr., San Francisco State U., 1987; fellow, NEH, Harvard U., 1973; scholar, U. Minn. Ctr. Immigration History, 1975; Rockefeller Found. grantee, 1977. Roman Catholic. Avocations: rose gardening, classical music. Home and Office: PO Box 395 Ross CA 94957

GIRARD, NETTABELL, lawyer; b. Pocatello, Idaho, Feb. 24, 1938; d. George and Arranetta (Bell) Girard. Student, Idaho State U., 1957—58; BS, U. Wyo., 1959, JD, 1961. Bar: Wyo. 1961, D.C. 1969, U.S. Supreme Ct. 1969. Practiced in, Riverton, Wyo., 1963-69; atty.-adviser on gen. counsel's staff HUD; assigned Office Interstate Land Sales Registration, Washington, 1969-70; sect. chief interstate land sales Office Gen. Counsel, 1970-73; ptnr. Larson & Larson, Riverton, 1973-85; pvt. practice Riverton, 1985—. Condr. course on women and law; lectr. in field. Editor Wyoming Clubwoman, 1966-68; bd. editors Wyo. Law Jour., 1959-61; writer Obiter Dictum column Women Lawyers Jour., Dear Legal Advisor column Solutions for Seniors, 1988-94; featured in Riverton Ranger, 1994; also articles in legal jours. Chmn. fund dr. Wind River chpt., ARC, 1965; chmn. Citizens Com. for Better Hosp. Improvement, 1965; chmn. subcom. on polit. legal rights and responsibilities Gov.'s Commn. on Status Women, 1965—69, mem. adv. com., 1973—93; local chmn. Law Day, 1966, 1967, county chmn., 1994—97; mem. state bd. Wyo Girl Scouts USA, sec., 1974—89, bd. dirs., 2001—04; state vol. adv. Nat. Found. March of Dimes, 1967—69; legal counsel Wyo. Women's Conf., 1977; gov. apptd. State Wyo. Indsl. Siting Coun., 1995—2001; rep. Nat. Conf. Govs. Commn., Washington, 1966. Recipient Spl. Achievement award HUD, 1972, Disting. Leadership award Girl Scouts USA, 1973, Franklin D. Roosevelt award Wyo. chpt. March of Dimes, 1985, Thanks Badge award Girl Scout Coun., 1987, Women Helping Women award Riverton Club Soroptimist Internat., 1990, Spl. award 27 yrs. svc. Wyo. Commn. for Women, 1964-92, Appreciation award Wyo. Sr. Citizens and Solutions for Srs., 1994, Arts in Action Pierrot award for outstanding musician, 1998, Disting. Svc. award Wyo. Music Edn. Assn., 2003, Leadership award 9th Jud. Dist., Wyo. Bar Assn., 2005. Mem. AAUW (br. pres., condr. seminar on law for layman Riverton br. 1965), Wyo. Bar Assn., Fremont County Bar Assn. (Spl. Recognition cert. 1997), DC Bar Assn., Women's Bar Assn. DC, Wyo. Trial Lawyers Assn., Nat. Assn. Women Lawyers (del. Wyo., nat. sec. 1969-70, v.p. 1970-71, pres. 1972-73), Wyo. Fedn. Women's Clubs (state editor, pres.-elect 1968-69, treas. 1974-76), Prog. Women's Club (pres.-elect. 1994-95), Riverton Chautauqua Club (pres. 1965-67, 2000-01), Riverton Civic League (pres. 1987-89), Kappa Delta, Delta Kappa Gamma (state chpt. hon.). Home: PO Box 687 Riverton WY 82501-0687 Office: 513 E Main St Riverton WY 82501-4440 Home Phone: 307-856-5048; Office Phone: 307-856-9339. Business E-Mail: ngirard@tcinc.net.

GIRARD, ROBERT DAVID, lawyer; b. Pitts., Aug. 2, 1946; s. Oscar L. and Ruth (Alpern) G. AB, UCLA, 1967; LLB, Yale U., 1970. Bar: Calif. 1971, U.S. Dist. Ct. (ctrl. dist.) Calif. 1971. Ptnr. Musick, Peeler & Garrett, LA, 1970-85, Girard, Ellingsen, Christensen & West, LA, 1985-88, Jones, Day, Reavis & Pogue, LA, 1988-92, Musick Peeler & Garrett, LA, 1992—97; with Sonnenschein Nath & Rosenthal LLP, LA, 1997—. Bd. dirs. Eisner Pediatric and Family Med. Ctr., L.A., 1980—, chmn., 1998-2002. Mem. ABA, L.A. County Bar Assn., Am. Health Lawyers Assn., Calif. Health Care Lawyers Assn. (bd. dirs. 1982-85), Phi Beta Kappa. Office: Sonnenschein Nath & Rosenthal LLP 601 S Figueroa St Ste 2500 Los Angeles CA 90017-5720 Office Phone: 213-892-5074. Business E-Mail: rgirard@sonnenschein.com.

GIRARDEAU, MARVIN DENHAM, physics professor; b. Lakewood, Ohio, Oct. 3, 1930; s. Marvin Denham and Maude Irene (Miller) G.; m. Susan Jessica Brown, June 30, 1956; children: Ellen, Catherine, Laura. BS, Case Inst. Tech., 1952; MS, U. Ill., 1954; PhD, Syracuse U., 1958. NSF postdoctoral fellow Inst. Advanced Study, Princeton, NJ, 1958—59; rsch. assoc. Brandeis U., 1959—60; staff mem. Boeing Sci. Rsch. Labs., 1960—61; rsch. assoc. Enrico Fermi Inst. Nuc. Studies, U. Chgo., 1961—63; assoc. prof. physics, rsch. assoc. Inst. Theoretical Sci., U. Oreg., Eugene, 1963—67, prof. physics, rsch. assoc., 1967—95, dir., 1967—69, chmn. dept. physics, 1974—76, prof. emeritus, 1995—; rsch. prof. optical scis. U. Ariz., 2000—. Contbr. articles to profl. jours. Recipient Humboldt Sr. U.S. Scientist award, 1984-85. NSF rsch. grantee, 1965-79; ONR rsch. grantee, 1981-87, 99—2007, ARO Rsch. grant, 2009-. Fellow Am. Phys. Soc.; mem. AAUP. Achievements include research on quantum-mech. many-body problems, statis. mechanics, atomic, molecular and chem. physics; Bose-Einstein condensation of atomic vapors, coherent control of quantum systems. Home: 288 N Bent Ridge Dr Green Valley AZ 85614-5949 Office: Optical Scis Ctr Univ Arizona Tucson AZ 85721-0001 Business E-Mail: girardeau@optics.arizona.edu.

GIRARDELLI, RONALD K., food products executive; b. 1949; BA, Oreg. State U., 1971. With Blue Cross, Portland, Oreg., 1971-73; pres. Diamond Fruit Growers, Inc., 1973—. Office: Diamond Fruit Growers Inc PO Box 185 Odell OR 97044-0185

GIRVIGIAN, RAYMOND, architect; b. Detroit, Nov. 27, 1926; s. Manoug and Margaret G.; m. Beverly Rae Bennett, Sept. 23, 1967; 1 son, Michael Raymond. AA, UCLA, 1947; BA with honors, U. Calif., Berkeley, 1950; MA in Architecture, U. Calif.-Berkeley, 1951. With Hutchason Architects, LA, 1952-57; owner, prin. Raymond Girvigian, LA, 1957-68, South Pasadena, Calif., 1968—. Co-founder, advisor LA Cultural Heritage Bd., 1961—; vice chmn. Hist. Am. Bldgs. Survey, Nat. Park Svc., Washington, 1967-71; co-founder Calif. Hist. Resources Commn., 1970-78; co-founder, chmn. governing bd. Calif. Hist. Bldgs. Code, 1976-91, chmn. adminstrv. law, 1992—, chmn. emeritus, 1993—; co-founder, chmn. Calif. State Capitol Commn., 1985-98, chmn. emeritus, 1998—. Co-editor, producer: film Architecture of Southern California for Los Angeles City Sch., 1965; hist. monographs of HABS Landmarks, Los Angeles, 1958-80; historical monographs of Calif. State Capitol, 1974, Pan Pacific Auditorium, 1980, LA Meml. Coliseum, 1984, Powell Meml. Libr., UCLA, 1989; designed: city halls for Pico Rivera, 1963, LaPuente, 1966, Rosemead, 1968, Lawndale, 1970 (all Calif.); hist. architect for restoration of Calif. State Capitol, 1975-82, Workman/Temple Hist. Complex, City of Industry, Calif., 1974-81, Robinson Gardens Landmarks, Beverly Hills, Calif., 1983-92, Pasadena (Calif.) Ctrl. Libr., 1982-92, 95—, Mt. Pleasant House Mus., Heritage Sq., LA, 1972-95. Mem. St. James' Episcopal Ch., S. Pasadena, Calif. With US Army, 1944—46. Recipient Outstanding Achievement in Architecture award City of Pico Rivera, Calif., 1968, Preservationist of Yr. award Calif. Preservation Found., 1987, LA Mayor's award for archtl. preservation, 1987, Gold Crown award Pasadena Arts Coun., 1990, Golden Palm award Hollywood Heritage, 1990, Design award for Oaklawn Bridge Rehab., Merit award Heritage Coalition of So. Calif., 2003, Cert. Spl. Congl. Recognition award, Cert. Spl. Recognition award Calif. State Assembly, 2006, Proclamation Commendation award City of South Pasadena, Calif., 2006; named Hist. Architect Emeritus Calif. State Capitol, Calif. Legislature, 1998, Commendation award Calif. Legislature, 1998; co-recipient honor award rehab. Los Altos Apts., Calif. Preservation Found., 1999, Lifetime Achievement award Calif. Preservation Found., 2007. Mem. AIA (mem. Coll. Fellows 1972, Calif. state preservation chmn. 1970-75, state preservation coord. 1970-89, co-recipient Nat. Honor award for Restoration Calif. State Capitol 1983, co-recipient Honor award for Restoration Pasadena Cen. Libr., Pasadena chpt. 1988, Regional and Urban Design award Pasadena and Foothill chpts., 2005); mem. Soc. Archtl. Historians, Nat. Trust for Historic Preservation, Calif. Preservation Found., Calif. Hist. Soc. (Neasham award 1982), Xi Alpha Kappa. Office: PO Box 220 South Pasadena CA 91031-0220

GIST, RICHARD D., federal judge; b. 1940; BS, U. Wyo., 1963, JD, 1965. Pvt. practice, Casper, Wyo., Lander, Wyo., 1970; U.S. magistrate judge, 1971—; alt. judge Lander Mcpl. Ct., 1974-79; commr. Wyo. Dist. Ct. 9th Jud. Dist., Fremont County, 1982-92. With U.S. Army, 1966-70. Home: 277 Lincoln St Lander WY 82520-2847 Fax: 307-332-2759.

GITTINGER, D. WAYNE, lawyer; b. Kellogg, Idaho, Jan. 22, 1933; s. Daniel Reese and Evelyn Caroline (Knudson) G.; 1 child, Marni; m. Anne Elizabeth Nordstrom, Dec. 17, 1984; stepchildren: John Hopen, Susan Dunn. BA, U. Wash., 1955, JD, 1957. Bar: Wash. 1957, U.S. Ct. Appeals (9th cir.) 1957, Tax Ct. of U.S., U.S. Supreme Ct. Teaching assoc. Northwestern U. Law Sch., Chgo., 1957-58; ptnr. Lane Powell PC, Seattle, 1959—. Active U. Wash. Alumni Assn., 1965—; bd. dirs. Seattle Sports Commn., First Tee Greater Seattle. Lt. USCGR, 1958-67. Mem. Vintage Club, Seattle Golf Club, Seattle Yacht Club, 101 Club, Overlake Golf and Country Club (past pres. 1978-79). Republican. Avocations: golf, yachting. Office: Lane Powell PC 1420 5th Ave Ste 4100 Seattle WA 98101-2338 Office Phone: 206-223-7053. E-mail: gittingerw@lanepowell.com.

GIULIANI, DAVID, personal care products company executive; BEE summa cum laude, U. Calif., Berkeley; grad. in Electrical Engring. and Bus., Stanford U. Co-founder Internat. Biomedics; co-founder, CEO Optiva Corp. (now Philips Oral Healthcare, Inc.), Bellevue, Wash., 1988—2000; co-founder (withDavid Engel and Roy Martin) GEMTech, 1987; co-founder, chmn. Pacific Bioscience. Featured spkr. White House Conf. on Corp. Responsibility, 1997. Chmn. Wash. Tech. Ctr. Recipient Small Bus. Person of Yr. award, US Bus. Adminstrn., 1997; named Entrepreneur of Yr. for US, 1997. Achievements include over 12 patents in field; development of Sonicare toothbrush in 1992. Office: Pacific Bioscience Laboratories 13222 SE 30th St #A1 Bellevue WA 98005

GIULIANO, NEIL GERARD, civil rights organization executive, former mayor; b. Bloomfield, NJ, Oct. 26, 1956; s. Jacqueline Ann (Enright) G. BA, Ariz. State U., 1979, MEd, 1983. Pres. Circle K. Internat., Chgo., 1977-78, conv. cons., 1983-91; counselor disabled students Ariz. State U., Tempe, 1980-81, pres. associated students, 1982-83, coord. leadership devel., 1983-87, constituent dir., 1988-91, dir. fed. and community rels., 1991; pres. Valley Achievement, Tempe, 1987—; mem. Tempe City Coun., 1990—94; vice mayor City of Tempe, 1992—94, mayor, 1994—2004; pres. Gay & Lesbian Alliance Against Defamation, 2005—. Speaker, trainer in field. Bd. dirs. Tempe Community Coun., 1990—2003, Valley Big Bros.-Big Sisters, Tempe, 1987—; pres. Tempe Leadership, Inc., 1990-91; mem. gov.'s task force on drug abuse, 1990—. Recipient Selected Participant award Ctr. for the Study of the Presidency Symposium, Washington, 1983. Mem. Tempe C. of C., Kiwanis (pres. 1986-87), Sigma Nu (conv. cons. 1988), Key Club Internat. (conv. cons. 1983-87). Republican. Roman Catholic. Avocations: reading, rock climbing, tennis. Office: GLAAD 5455 Wilshire Blvd Ste 1500 Los Angeles CA 90036 E-mail: Giuliano@glaad.org.*

GIVEN, DOUGLASS BRUCE, physician; b. Mpls., Feb. 29, 1952; s. Everet Herdman Jr. and E. June (Daggett) G.; m. Kim Susan Delamater, Nov. 24, 1984; children: Katherine, Anne. PhD, U. Chgo., 1979, MD, 1980. Diplomate Am. Bd. Internal Medicine. Fellow Harvard Med. Sch., Boston, 1980-84; med. cons. Lilly, Indpls., 1983-84, clin. scientist, 1984-85, med. advisor, 1985-86; v.p. Searle, Chgo., 1986-89, Schering-Plough Corp., Kenilworth, N.J., 1989—. Asst. prof. medicine Ind. U. Sch. Medicine, Indpls., 1985-87. Author: (book) Vancomycin, 1986; contbr. articles to Jour. Virology, 1976-80. Office: Neorx Acquisition 300 Elliott Ave W Ste 500 Seattle WA 98119-4114

GLAD, SUZANNE LOCKLEY, retired museum director; b. Rochester, NY, Oct. 2, 1929; d. Alfred Allen and Lucille A. (Watson) Lockley; m. Edward Newman Glad, Nov. 7, 1953; children: Amy, Lisanne Glad Lantz, William E. BA, Sweet Briar Coll., 1951; MA, Columbia U., 1952. Exec. dir. New York State Young Reps., NYC, 1951-57; mem. pub. rels. staff Dolphin Group, LA, 1974-83; scheduling sec. Gov.'s Office, Sacramento, 1983-87; dep. dir. Calif. Mus. Sci. and Industry, LA, 1987-94; ret. Mem. Calif. Rep. League, Pasadena, 1969—; mem. Assistance League of Flintridge, 1970—, Flintridge Guild Children's Hosp., 1969-89. Mem. Sweet Briar Alumnae of So. Calif. (pres. 1972), Phi Beta Kappa, Tau Phi. Episcopalian. Avocations: reading, gardening.

GLADWELL, DAVID L., state legislator; b. Ogden, Utah, Apr. 19, 1947; m. Ruth Ann. BA in English, U. Utah, 1971, JD, 1974. Atty., 1974—; mem. Utah State Senate, Sale Lake City, 2001—. Mem. Utah State Bar Assn. Office: 3159 N 1075 E Ogden UT 84414-1779 Fax: 801-626-2423. E-mail: dgladwel@le.sate.ut.us.

GLANCY, DOROTHY JEAN, lawyer, educator; b. Glendale, Calif., Sept. 24, 1944; d. Walter Perry and Elva T. (Douglas) G.; m. Jon Tobias Anderson, June 8, 1979. BA, Wellesley Coll., 1967; JD, Harvard Law Sch., 1970. Bar: D.C. 1971, Calif. 1976, U.S. Dist. Ct. D.C. 1971, U.S. Ct. Appeals (D.C. cir.) 1972. Assoc. Hogan & Hartson, Wash., 1971-73; counsel U.S. Senate Judiciary Subcomm. on Constitutional Rights, Wash., 1973-74; fellow in Law & Humanities Harvard U., Cambridge, Mass., 1974-75; asst. to assoc. prof. law Santa Clara U., Calif., 1975-82, prof. law Calif., 1984—; vis. prof. law U. Arizona, Tucson, 1979; asst. gen. counsel U.S. Dept. of Agr., 1982-83; cons. US DOT Vehicle Infrastructure Integration, 2006. Cons. Commn. Fed. Paperwork, Wash., 1976; dir. summer Law Study Program in Hong Kong, 1985-90; advisor Restatement, Third Property: Servitudes, 1986-97; mem. ct. tech. adv. com. Calif. Jud. Coun. Dir. legal rsch. project regarding privacy and intelligent trnsp. systems Fed. Hwy. Adminstrn., 1993-95; bd. dirs. Presidio Hts. Assn. Neighbors, 1990—. Stevens fellow Wellesley Coll., fellow law and humanities Harvard U. Mem. ABA (chair ethics com. of sect. on natural resources, energy and environ. law, 1993-95, coun. mem. 1995-98), State Bar Calif. (mem. environ. law sect., adv. exec. com. 1993-96, advisor 1996—), Am. Assn. Law Schs. (chair environ. law sect. 1992-93, chair property sect. 1996-97, chair defamation and privacy sec., 1997-98), Am. Law Inst., Calif. Women Lawers, Soc. Am. Law Tchrs., Phi Beta Kappa. Democrat. Avocations: gardening, travel. Office: Santa Clara U Sch Law Santa Clara CA 95053-0001 Home Phone: 415-922-4495. Business E-Mail: dglancy@scu.edu.

GLANVILLE, JERRY, college football coach, former professional football coach; b. Detroit, Oct. 14, 1941; m. Brenda Glanville; 1 child, Justin. Student, Mont. State U.; BS, No. Mich. U., 1964; MS, Western Ky. U. Defensive coord. We. Ky. U. Hilltoppers, 1967; defensive ends & outside linebackers coach Ga. Tech. U. Yellow Jackets, Atlanta, 1968-74; spl. teams coach, defensive asst. Detroit Lions, 1974-77; defensive backs coach Atlanta Falcons, 1977—78, defensive coord., 1979—82; defensive backfield coach Buffalo Bills, 1983; defensive coord. Houston Oilers, 1984-85, head coach, 1986-90, Atlanta Falcons, 1990-94; defensive coord. U. Hawaii Warriors, Honolulu, 2005—07; head coach Portland State U. Vikings, Oreg., 2007—; sports analyst NFL Today, CBS, Inside the NFL, Home Box Office, 1994—2005. Co-author (with J. David Miler): Elvis Don't like Football: The Life and Times of the NFL's Most Outspoken Coach, 1990. Recipient Disting. Alumnus award, No. Mich. U.; named to The No. Mich. U. Hall of Fame, 1992. Office: Portland State U PO Box 751 Portland OR 97207

GLASER, DONALD ARTHUR, physicist; b. Cleve., Sept. 21, 1926; s. William Joseph Glaser; m. Lynn Bercouitz, 1975. BS, Case Inst. Tech., 1946, ScD (hon.), 1959; PhD, Calif. Inst. Tech., 1949; ScD (hon.), U. Mich., 2002. Prof. physics U. Mich., 1949—59; prof. physics U. Calif., Berkeley, 1959—, prof. grad. sch., divsn. neurobiology, 1964—. Recipient Henry Russel award, U. Mich., 1955, Charles V. Boys prize, Phys. Soc., London, 1958, Nobel prize in Physics, 1960, Gold medal, Case Inst. Tech., 1967, Golden Plate award, Am. Acad. of Achievement, 1989; fellow NSF, 1961, Guggenheim, 1961—62, Smith-Kettlewell Inst. for Vision Rsch., 1983—84. Fellow: AAAS, Am. Physics Soc. (prize 1959), Neuroscis. Inst., Royal Swedish Acad. Sci., Royal Soc. Sci., Assn. Rsch. Vision and Ophthalmology, The Exploratorium (bd. dirs.), Fedn. Am. Scientists; mem.: NAS, Am. Philos. Soc., Internat. Acad. Sci., N.Y. Acad. Scis., Am. Assn. Artificial Intelligence, Sigma Xi, Theta Tau, Tau Kappa Alpha. Achievements include invention of the Bubble Chamber. Office: U Calif 221 Donner Lab Dept Physics and Neurobio 237 Hildebrand Hall #3206 Berkeley CA 94720-3206 Business E-Mail: glaser@berkeley.edu.

GLASER, PATRICIA L., lawyer; b. Charleston, W.Va., Sept. 15, 1947; d. Richard Stanley and Tilda Jane (Rosen) G.; m. Samuel Hunter Mudie, May 19, 1978; stepchildren: Heather and Jason Mudie. BA, Am. U., 1969; JD, Rutgers U., 1973. Bar: Calif. 1973, U.S. Dist. Ct. (no. and cen. dists.) Calif. 1973, U.S. Dist. Ct. (so. dist.) 1976, U.S. Ct. Appeals (9th cir.), U.S. Supreme Ct. Law clk. to presiding justice US Dist. Ct.; from assoc. to ptnr. Wyman, Bautzer, Rothman, Kuchel & Silbert, LA, 1973—88; ptnr. Christensen, Glaser, Fink, Jacobs, Weil & Shapiro, LLP, LA, 1988—. Judge pro tem West br. LA Mcpl. Ct., panelist legal continuing edn. programs. Mem. fund-raising com. Deukmejian for Gov. of Calif.; participant Parole-Aide program. Named one of 100 Power Lawyers, Hollywood Reporter, 2007. Mem. LA County Bar Assn. (fed. cts. and practices com.). Avocations: travel, skiing, tennis, reading. Office: Christensen Glaser Fink Jacobs Weil & Shapiro LLP 10250 Constellation Blvd 19th Fl Los Angeles CA 90067

GLASER, ROBERT, communications executive; BA in Econ., MA in Econ., Yale U., BS in Computer Sci. CEO and chmn. Progressive Networks, Seattle; various pos. Microsoft Corp., 1983—93; founder, CEO, chmn. RealNetworks, Seattle, 1995—. Adv. com. on pub. interest Pres. Clinton; spkr. in field. Editor: Yale Daily News. Office: Real Networks 2601 Elliott Ave Ste 1000 Seattle WA 98121

GLASER, WILLIAM, state legislator; b. Long Beach, Calif., Jan. 4, 1940; m to Patsy; children: six. Montana State Representative, District 98, 1985-90, District 44, 2005-, Montana House Representative; Montana State Senator, District 8, 1997-2004, vice chairman, Education & Cult Resources Committee, formerly, member, Local Govt & Taxation Committees & Select Committee on Implementation, formerly, Montana State Senate.Contractor, currently. Republican. Home: 1402 Indian Creek Frontage Rd Huntley MT 59037-9338 Mailing: State Capitol Helena MT 59620

GLASGOW, WILLIAM JACOB, lawyer, venture capitalist, business executive; b. Portland, Oreg., Sept. 29, 1946; s. Joseph Glasgow and Lena (Friedman) Schiff; m. Renée Vonfeld, Aug. 30, 1969; children: Joshua, Andrew. BS in econ. magna cum laude, U. Pa., 1968; JD magna cum laude, Harvard U., 1972. Bar: Oreg. 1972, U.S. Dist. Ct. Oreg. 1972, U.S. Ct. Appeals (9th cir.) 1978. Assoc. Rives, Bonyhadi & Drummond, Portland, 1972-76, ptnr., 1976-79; mng. ptnr. Perkins Coie, Portland, 1983-88; sr. v.p., gen. counsel PacifiCorp Fin. Svcs. Inc., Portland, 1988-89, chmn., CEO, 1989-95; sr. v.p. PacifiCorp, Portland, 1992-93, sr. v.p., CFO, 1993-95; pres. PacifiCorp Holdings Inc., Portland, 1992-95; pres., dir. NERCO, Inc., Portland, 1992-93; dir. Pacific-Telecom, Inc., 1992-93; ret. PacifiCorp, Portland, 1996; co-chmn. Shaw, Glasgow & Co. LLC, 1995-96; pres., CEO BCN Data Sys. (a Bechtel/CellNet Data Sys. joint venture), Portland, 1996-2000, Madrona Venture Group LLP, Portland, 2000—03; coo Fish & Neave LLP/Ropes & Gray LLP, NYC, 2003—05; ptnr. Perkins Coie LLP, Portland, Oreg., 2005—. Pres. bd. trustees Oreg. Mus. Sci. and Industry, Portland, 1976-82; mem. exec. com. bd. Portland C. of C. 1982-1983; pres. N.W. Fin. Symposium, Portland, 1985; trustee Oreg. Art Inst., 1990-92, 94-, Oreg. Grad. Inst. Sci. and Tech., 1991-97, Discovery Inst., 1992-; pres. Portland Met. Sports Authority, 1992-; trustee Portland Art Mus. 1992-1997; v.p. NIKE World Masters Games, 1994-; bd. dirs. Internat. World Masters Games, 1994-, pres., bd. trustees, chmn. emeritus Oreg. Sports Authority 1992-1998. Mem. Oreg. Bar Assn., Portland C. of C. (bd. dirs. 1983), Harvard Law Sch. Alumni Assn. (pres. Oreg. chpt. 1981). Democrat. Office: Perkins Coie LLP 1120 NW Couch St 10th Fl Portland OR 97209-4128 Office Phone: 503-727-2118. Office Fax: 503-346-2118. Business E-Mail: wglasgow@perkinscoie.com.

GLASKY, ALVIN JERALD, retired medical research scientist; b. Chgo., June 16, 1933; s. Oscar and Bessie (Akwa) G.; m. Rosalie Anne Hanfling, Aug. 25, 1957; children: Michelle S., Karen R., Mark J., Ira D. BS in Pharmacy, U. Ill., Chgo., 1954, PhD in Biochemistry, 1958. Dir. biochem. research Michael Reese Hosp., Chgo., 1959-61; research pharmacologist Abbott Labs., North Chicago, Ill., 1961-66; v.p. research ICN, Burbank, Calif., 1966-68; pres., CEO Newport Pharms., Inc., Newport Beach, Calif., 1968—86, Neo Therapeutics, Inc., Irvine, Calif., 1987—2002; regents prof. U. Calif., Irvine, 1998—2000. Contbr. articles to profl. jours. Mem. AAAS, Am. Pharm. Assn., Calif. Pharm. Assn., Am. Soc. Microbiology, Am. Chem. Soc., Rho Chi. Jewish. Avocations: tennis, swimming, theater, wine. Home: 28872 Alanya Mission Viejo CA 92692-4965

GLASS, DAVID J., lawyer; b. Union, NJ; BA, U. Pa., 1990; JD, Villanova U., 1996; PhD in Clin. Psychology, Drexel U., 1997. Bar: Pa. 1996, NJ 1996, Calif. 2003. Internship in clinical psychology Albert Einstein Coll. Medicine, Bronx, NY; atty. Schnader Harrison Segal & Lewis, Pa., Kolodny & Anteau, Beverly Hills, Calif., Law Offices of Alexandra Leichter, Beverly Hills, Calif.; prin., family law practice Glass Family Law, Beverly Hills, Calif. Co-editor: Ziskin's Coping with Psychiatric and Psychological Testimony, 2000 Supplement; co-author: Family Law chapter in Practicing Therapeutic Jurisprudence: The Law as a Helping Profession; editor (mng.): Villanova Law Rev. Named a Rising Star, So. Calif. Super Lawyers, 2005—06. Mem.: Am. Psychological Assn., LA Psychological Assn., Beverly Hills Bar Assn., LA County Bar Assn. Office: Glass Family Law 3d Fl 499 N Canon Dr Beverly Hills CA 90210 Office Phone: 310-777-5206. Office Fax: 310-777-5266. Business E-Mail: info@glassfamilylaw.com.

GLASSHEIM, JEFFREY WAYNE, allergist, immunologist, pediatrician; b. Far Rockaway, NY, Sept. 16, 1958; s. Ronald Alan and Glenda (Deitch) G.; m. Paulette Renèe, Apr. 16, 1989; children: Elyssa Gwen, Brenna Chase. BA cum laude, Temple U., 1980; DO in Osteo. Medicine (hon.), U. New. Eng., 1984. Diplomate Am. Bd. Pediatrics, 1989, Am. Bd. Allergy and Clin. Immunology, 1995. Commd. 2d lt. U.S. Army, 1980, advanced through grades to maj., 1989; intern pediat. Winthrop-Univ. Hosp., Mineola, NY, 1984-85; resident pediat. Madigan Army Med. Ctr., Tacoma, 1985-87; fellow allergy/immunology Fitzsimons Army Med. Ctr. and Nat. Jewish Med. Ctr., Denver, 1990—92, chief fellow allergy-clin. immunology, 1990—92; chief allergy-clin. immunology and immunizations svcs. Silas B. Hays Army Community Hosp., Fort Ord, Calif., 1992—93; resigned commn. USAR, 1993; dir. allergy-immunology Pediatric Med. Group of Fresno, Calif., 1994-95, Northwest Med. Group, Fresno, 1995-97; pvt. practice allergy and immunology Fresno, Calif., 1997—2005, Oshkosh, Wis., 2005—06; dir. allergy, asthma and immunology Theda Care Physicians, Inc., Oshkosh, 2006—08; dir. allergy, asthama and clin. immunology Childrens Hosp., Wis., 2008—; asst. prof. dept. pediat. Med. Coll. Wis., 2008—. Cons. numerous pharm. companies. Contbr. articles to profl. jours.; mem. editl. adv. bd. Unique Opportunites, 1998—, contbg. editor, 2004—. Bd. dirs. Am. Lung Assn. Ctrl. Calif., 1999—2002. Fellow Am. Acad. Allergy Asthma and Immunology, Am. Coll. Allergy, Asthma and Immunology; mem. AMA, Am. Osteo. Assn., Am. Physicians Fellowship for Medicine in Israel, Wis. Med. Soc., Winnebago County Med. Soc., Wis. Asthma Coalition, Wis. Assn. for Osteopathic Physicians and Surgeons. Republican. Jewish. Avocations: meteorology, sports, reading, gardening, walking. Home Phone: 920-385-0028; Office Phone: 920-738-6444, 920-969-7970. Personal E-mail: glasjw@juno.com.

GLAUTHIER, T. J., management consultant; b. Durham, NC, Jan. 3, 1944; s. Theodore and Martha May (Myers) G.; m. Carrie L. Bostrom, June 11, 1966 (div. 1973); children: Jeff, Paul, Tad; m. M. Brigid O'Farrell, July 9, 1977; 1 child, Patrick O. AB, Claremont McKenna Coll., Calif., 1965; MBA, Harvard Bus. Sch., 1967. Cons. Peat, Marwick, Livingston, LA, 1967-68; with Applied Computer Tech., LA, 1968-70; cons. Applied Decision Systems, Cambridge, Mass., 1970-74; v.p. Temple, Barker & Sloane, Inc., Lexington, Mass., 1974-90; head Pub. Policy Practice, 1980-90; head Washington office, 1986-90; dir. energy and climate change World Wildlife Fund, Washington, 1990-93; assoc. dir. nat. resources, energy and sci. U.S. Office Mgmt. and Budget, Exec. Office of Pres., Washington, 1993-98; dep. sec., COO U.S. Dept. Energy, 1999-2001; pres., CEO Electricity Innovation Inst., Palo Alto, Calif., 2001—04; pres. TJG Energy Assocs., LLC, Moss Beach, 2005—. Bd. dirs. Union Drilling, Inc., 2006—, San Mateo County Resource Conservation Dist., 2006—. Pres. Lake Barcroft Assn., 1989—94; assoc. Lake Barcroft Watershed Improvement Dist., 1989—2001; del. Va. State Dem. Conv., 1993, 1997. Democrat. Unitarian. Home: 1001 Ocean Blvd Moss Beach CA 94038 Office Phone: 650-353-6061. Personal E-mail: tjglauthier@aol.com.

GLAVIN, EDWARD P., television producer; b. Phila., Sept. 8, 1963; s. Maurice Denis and Maureen Elizabeth Glavin; m. Deborah Harwick, Aug. 22, 1992; childrens, Emily, Maureen, Sean. Degree, Glassboro Coll., NJ, 1985. Mem. staff KYW-TV, 1985-88, CNBC, Ft. Lee, NJ, 1988-92, Donahue Shoe, NYC, 1990-92; exec. prodr. Jenny Jones Show, Warner Bros., LA, 1992, Caroline Rhea Show, 2002, Change of Heart, 2003, The Ellen Degeneres Show, 2004—. Recipient Best Television Series or Special (Variety), The Producers Guild Am., 2006, 6 Emmy awards. Mem. NATAS. Office: The Ellen Degeneres Show 3000 Alameda Ave Burbank CA 91523

GLAZER, GARY MARK, radiology educator; b. Feb. 13, 1950; m. Diane Glazer; children: Daniel I., David A. AB, U. Mich., 1972; MD, Case Western Res. U., 1976. Intern in internal medicine U. Calif., San Francisco, 1976-77, resident in diagnostic radiology, 1977-80, clin. instr., fellow in diagnostic radiology, 1980-81; asst. prof. radiology, dir. div. body computed tomography U. Mich., Ann Arbor, 1981-84, assoc. prof. radiology, 1984-87, dir. divs. magnet resonance imaging and body computed tomography, 1984-89, assoc. prof. cancer ctr., 1986-87, prof. radiology, prof. cancer ctr., 1987-89; prof., chmn. dept. radiology Stanford (Calif.) Sch. Medicine, 1989—. Cons., assoc. editor, reviewer Radiology; cons., reviewer Jour. Computer Assisted Tomogrphy; cons., chmn., reviewer, mem. editorial bd. Radiographics; contbr. articles to profl. publs. Fellow Am. Cancer Soc., 1980-82, Clarence Heller Found., 1980-81. Mem. Am. Roentgen Ray Soc., Radiology Soc. N.Am., Soc. Magnetic Resonance in Medicine, Fred Jenner Hodges Soc., Soc. Magnetic Resonance Imaging, Internat. Soc. for Strategic Studies in Radiology (pres. 2003-05), Alpha Omega Alpha. Office: Stanford Sch Med Dept Radiology Stanford CA 94305 Office Phone: 650-723-7863. E-mail: glazer@stanford.edu.

GLAZER, MICHAEL, lawyer; b. LA, Oct. 10, 1940; BS, Stanford U., 1962; MBA, Harvard U., 1964; JD, U. Calif., LA, 1967. Bar: Calif. 1967. Law clk. to Hon. Roger J. Traynor Calif. Supreme Ct., 1967-68; commr. L.A. Dept. of Water & Power, 1973-76; chmn. Calif. Water Commn., 1976-78; asst. adminstr. nat. oceanic and atmospheric adminstrn. U.S. Dept. of Commerce, 1978-80; dir. Met. Water Dist. of So. Calif., 1984-91; ptnr. Paul, Hastings, Janofsky & Walker LLP, LA. Articles editor U. Calif. at L.A. Law Rev., 1966-67. Mem. State Bar Calif. (com. on corps. 1986-87), L.A. County Bar Assn. (chair fed. securities regulation com. 1988-90, chair exec. com. bus. and corp. law sect. 1995-96), Order of the Coif, Phi Beta Kappa. Office: Paul Hastings Janofsky & Walker LLP 515 S Flower St Los Angeles CA 90071-2300

GLEASON, JOANNA, actress; b. Toronto, Ont., Can., June 2, 1950; d. Monty and Marilyn (Plotell) Hall. Grad., UCLA. Broadway debut I Love My Wife, Ethel Barrymore Theatre, 1977; Broadway appearances include Hey! Look Me Over, 1981, The Real Thing, 1984, A Hell of a Town, 1984, A Day in the Death of Joe Egg, 1985, It's Only a Play, 1985, Social Security, 1986, Into the Woods, Old Globe Theatre, San Diego and Martin Beck Theatre, NYC, 1987 (Antoinette Perry award for leading actress in a mus., NY Outer Critics Circle award, Drama Desk award), Nick and Nora, 1991, Dirty Rotten Scoundrels, 2005-06; other stage appearances include Eleemosynary, 1989, The Normal Heart, 2004, The Cartells, 2006, Something You Did, 2008; appeared in films Heartburn, 1986, Hannah and Her Sisters, 1986, Crimes and Misdemeanors, 1989, FX2: The Deadly Art of Illusion, 1991, Mr. Holland's Opus, 1995, Boogie Nights, 1997, American Perfekt, 1997, Road Ends, 1997, Let the Devil Wear Black, The Wedding Planner, 2001, Fathers & Sons, 2005, The Pleasure of Your Company, 2006, The Girl in the Park, 2007; TV appearances include Why Us?, 1981, Great Day, 1983, Still the Beaver, 1983, Life Under Water, 1989, The Boys, 1991, For Richer, For Poorer, 1992, Born Too Soon, 1993, For The Love of Aaron, 1994, series Hello, Larry, 1979-80, Chain Reaction, 1980, Love and War, 1992, Temporarily Yours, 1997, Bette, 2000-01 The West Wing, 2001-02; dir. (plays) Call Waiting, 2001, A Letter from Ethel Kennedy, 2002. Mem. Actors' Equity Assn. Office: care Connie Tavel 9171 Wilshire Blvd Ste 406 Beverly Hills CA 90210

GLEASON, JOHN H., real estate development company executive; BS in Mktg., U. So. Calif. Gen. contractor, Ariz., Calif., Nev., Tex., Southeast states, 29 years; pres. The Foothills Del Webb Corp., Phoenix, 1988-90, sr. v.p. project planning & devel. Office: Del Webb Corp 15333 N Pima Rd Ste 300 Scottsdale AZ 85260-2782

GLEESON, JOSEPH, science educator; BA in Chem. and Econs., U. Calif., San Diego, 1986; MD, U. Chgo., 1991. Resident in pediats. Children's Hosp., Boston, 1991—93, resident in child neurology, 1993—95; postdoctoral fellow Harvard Med. Sch., 1995—99; instr., child neurologist Children's Hosp., Boston, 1996—99; asst. prof. dept. neurosci. U. Calif., La Jolla. Office: UCSD Sch Medicine MTF 312 9500 Gilman Dr La Jolla CA 92093

GLEICH, GERALD JOSEPH, immunologist, researcher, educator; b. Escanaba, Mich., May 14, 1931; s. Gordon Joseph and Agnes (Ederer) G.; m. Elizabeth Louise Hearn, Aug. 16, 1955 (div. 1976); children: Elizabeth Genevieve, Martin Christopher (dec.), Julia Katherine; m. Kristin Marie Leiferman, Sept. 25, 1976; children: Stephen Joseph, David Francis, Caroline Louise, William Gerald. BA, U. Mich., 1953, MD, 1956. Diplomate Am. Bd. Internal Medicine, Am. Bd. Allergy and Immunology. Intern Phila. Gen. Hosp., 1956-57; resident Jackson Meml. Hosp., Miami, Fla., 1959-61; instr. in medicine and microbiology U. Rochester, NY, 1961—65; cons. in medicine, prof. immunology and medicine Mayo Clinic-Med. Sch., Rochester, Minn., 1965—2001; chmn. dept. immunology Mayo Clinic, Rochester, Minn., 1982-90, George M. Eisenberg prof., 1995—2001; disting. investigator Mayo Found., Rochester, 1988—2001; prof. medicine & dermatology U. Utah, Salt Lake City, 2001—. Mem. bd. sci. counselors Nat. Inst. Allergy and Infectious Disease, 1981-83; chmn. subcom. on standardization allergens WHO, Geneva, 1974-75; lectr. Am. Acad. Allergy, 1976, 82; mem., chmn. immunological scis. study sect. NIH, 1984-87; John M. Sheldon Meml. lectr., 1976, 82, 88; Steve Lang Meml. Lectureship, 1980, Stoll-Stunkard lectr. Am. Soc. Parasitologists, 1986, David Talmage Meml. lectureship, 1987, Disting. lectr. Med. Scis. Mayo Clinic, 1988; original mem. Highly Cited Rschrs. Database, 2002. Contbr. articles on eosinophilic leukocyte to profl. jours. Served to capt. USAF, 1957-59. Recipient Landmark in Allergy award, 1990; grantee Nat. Inst. Allergy and Infectious Disease, 1970—; AAAS fellow for studies of structure, biol. properties and role in pathogenesis of disease of basic proteins present in cytoplasmic granules of eosinophilic leukocytes, 1993. Fellow ACP, Am. Acad. Allergy and Immunology (hon. fellow award 1992), AAAS; mem. Am. Soc. Clin. Investigation, Am. Assn. Immunologists, Assn. Am. Physicians, Phi Beta Kappa, Phi Kappa Phi, Alpha Omega Alpha. Roman Catholic. Office: Univ Utah 4B454 Sch Medicine 30 North 1900 East Salt Lake City UT 84132-2409 Office Phone: 801-581-6465. Business E-Mail: gerald.gleich@hsc.utah.edu.

GLENN, CONSTANCE WHITE, art museum director, educator, consultant; b. Topeka, Oct. 4, 1933; d. Henry A. and Madeline (Stewart) White; m. Jack W. Glenn, June 19, 1955; children: Laurie Glenn Buckle, Caroline Glenn Galey, John Christopher. BFA, U. Kans., 1955; grad., U. Mo., 1969; MA, Calif. State U., 1974. Dir. U. Art Mus. & Mus. Studies program, from lectr. to prof. Calif. State U., Long Beach, 1973—2004, prof. and dir. emeritus, U. Art Mus. and Mus. Studies program, 2004—. Art cons. Archtl. Digest, L.A., 1980-89. Author: Jim Dine Drawings, 1984, Roy Lichtenstein: Landscape Sketches, 1986, Wayne Thiebaud: Private Drawings, 1988, Robert Motherwell: The Dedalus Sketches, 1988, James Rosenquist: Time Dust: The Complete Graphics 1962-92, 1993, The Great American Pop Art Store: Multiples of the Sixties, 1997, The Artist Observed: Photographs by Sidney B. Felsen, 2003, Candida Höfer: Architecture of Absence, 2004, Tom Wesselmann; contbg. author: Encyclopedia Americana, 1995-, The Grove Dictionary of Art, 1989-, Carrie Mae Weems: The Hampton Project, 2000, Double Vision: Photographs from the Strauss Collection, 2001, Tom Wesselmann, 2005. Vice-chair Adv. Com. for Pub. Art, Long Beach, 1990-95; chair So. Calif. adv. bd. Archives Am. Art, LA, 1980-90; mem. adv. bd. ART/LA, 1986-94, chair, 1992. Recipient Outstanding Contbn. to Profession award Calif. Mus. Photography, 1986, Women of Distinction award Soroptimist Internat., 1999. Mem. Am. Assn. Mus., Assn. Art Mus. Dirs. (trustee 2000-02, emeritus 2004—), Coll. Art Assn., Art Table, Long Beach Pub. Corp. for the Arts (Arts Adminstr. of Yr. 1989), Kappa Alpha Theta. Office Phone: 949-715-0933. Personal E-mail: connieglenn@hotmail.com. Business E-Mail: cglenn@csulb.edu.

GLENN, EVELYN NAKANO, social sciences educator; b. Sacramento, Aug. 20, 1940; d. Makoto and Haru (Ito) Nakano; m. Gary Anthony Glenn, Nov. 20, 1962; children: Sara Haruye, Antonia Grace, Patrick Alexander. BA, U. Calif., Berkeley, 1962; PhD, Harvard Coll., 1971. Asst. prof. sociology Boston U., 1972-84; assoc. prof. sociology Fla. State U., Tallahassee, 1984-86; prof. sociology SUNY, Binghamton, 1986-90; prof. sociology women's and ethnic studies U. Calif., Berkeley, 1990—. Mem. bd. scholars Am. Nat. Mus., L.A., 1989—; vis. rsch. scholar Murray Rsch. Ctr., Radcliffe Coll., 1989-90. Author: Issei, Nisei, Warbride, 1986, Unequal Freedom: How Race and Gender Shaped American Citizenship and Labor, 2002; editor: Mothering: Ideology, Experience and Agency, 1994; adv. editor Gender and Soc., 1986-90, Frontiers, 1991-93, Editl. Collective Feminist Studies, 1999-; dep. editor Am. Sociol. Rev., 1999-2003; contbr. articles to profl. publs. Named Japanese Am. of Biennum, Japanese Am. Citizens League, 1994; recipient Article prize Assn. Black Women Historians, 1993. Mem. Am. Sociol. Assn. (mem. coun. 1990-94), Soc. for Study of Social Problems (pres. 1998-99, v.p. 1988-90, bd. dirs. 1984-87). Office: Univ Calif Dept Women's Studies 3408 Dwinelle Hall, #1070 Berkeley CA 94720-1070 Office Phone: 510-643-2444. E-mail: englenn@berkeley.edu.

GLENNEN, ROBERT EUGENE, JR., retired academic administrator; b. Omaha, Mar. 31, 1933; s. Robert E. and La Verda (Elledge) G.; m. Mary C. O'Brien, Apr. 17, 1958; children: Maureen, Bobby, Colleen, Billy, Barry, Katie, Molly, Kerry AB, U. Portland, 1955, M.Ed., 1957; PhD, U. Notre Dame, 1962. Asst. prof. U. Portland, 1956-60; asst. prof., assoc. prof. Eastern Mont. Coll., Billings, 1962-65; assoc. dean U. Notre Dame, South Bend, Ind., 1965-72; dean, v.p. U. Nev.-Las Vegas, 1972-80; pres. Western N.Mex. U., Silver City, 1980-84, Emporia (Kans.) State U., 1984-97; acting vice-chancellor U. Ark., Montecello, 1999; interim provost U. So. Colo., 1999-2000, interim pres., 2001—02. Bd. dirs. Emporia Enterprises; cons. HEW, Washington, 1964-84 Author: Guidance: An Orientation, 1966. Contbr. articles to profl. jours. Pres. PTA, South Bend, Ind., 1970-71; bd. trustees Am. Coll. Testing Corp., Iowa City, 1977-80; chmn. Kans. Regents Coun. of Pres., 1986-87, 92-93, 95-96. Recipient award of excellence Nat. Acad. Advising Assn., Disting. Alumnus award U. Portland, 1993, Kans. Master Tchr. award, 1994; named Coach of Yr., Coach and Athletic mag., 1958, Pub. Adminstr. of Yr., 1994, Athletic Hall of Fame, Portland, 1995; Rotary Paul Harris fellow, 1995, Ford Found. fellow, 1961-62. Mem. Kans. C. of C. (bd. dirs.), Emporia C. of C. Regional Devel. Assn. (bd. dirs., Bank IV), Am. Personnel and Guidance Assn., Am. Assn. State Colls. and Univs. (chair pres's. commn. on tchr. edn.), Am. Assn. Higher Edn., Nev. Personnel and Guidance Assn., Assn. Counselor Educators and Suprs., Am. Assn. Counseling and Devel., Nat. Assn. Student Personnel Adminstrs. Republican. Roman Catholic. Avocations: walking, reading. Home: 1591 Meadow Hills Dr Richland WA 99352

GLICK, MILTON DON, academic administrator, chemist; b. Memphis, July 30, 1937; s. Lewis S. and Sylvia (Kleinman) G.; m. Peggy M., June 22, 1965; children: David, Sander. AB cum laude, Augustana Coll., 1959; PhD, U. Wis., 1965. Asst. prof. chemistry Wayne State U., Detroit, 1966-70, assoc. prof., 1970-74, prof., 1974-83, chmn. dept., 1978-83; dean arts & scis. U. Mo., Columbia, 1983-88; provost Iowa State U., Ames, 1988-91, interim pres., 1990-91; sr. v.p., provost Ariz. State U., Tempe, 1991—2002, exec. v.p., provost, 2002—06; pres. U. Nev., Reno, 2006—. Contbr. articles to profl. jours. Fellow dept. chemistry Cornell U., Ithaca, N.Y., 1964-66. Office: Office of President Univ Nev Reno/001 Reno NV 89557-0154 Office Phone: 775-784-4805. Office Fax: 775-784-6429. Business E-Mail: glick@unr.edu.

GLICKMAN, DANIEL ROBERT, motion picture association executive, former United States Secretary of Agriculture; b. Wichita, Kans., Nov. 24, 1944; s. Milton and Gladys Anne (Kopelman) G.; m. Rhoda Joyce Yura, Aug. 21, 1966; children: Jonathan, Amy. BA, U. Mich., Ann Arbor, 1966; JD, George Washington U., Washington, 1969. Bar: Kans. 1969, Mich. 1970. Trial atty. SEC, 1969-70; assoc. Sargent, Klenda & Glickman, Wichita, 1971—73, ptnr., 1973—76; mem. US Congress from 4th Kans. Dist., 1977-95, mem. agrl. com., mem. judiciary, sci., space and tech. coms., chmn. permanent select com. on intelligence; sec. USDA, Washington, 1995-2001; sr. adv. pub. law & policy group Akin Gump Strauss Hauer & Feld LLP, Washington, 2001—04; dir. Inst. Politics, John F. Kennedy Sch. Govt.

Harvard U., 2002—04; pres. Motion Picture Assoc. America, Encino, Calif., 2004—. Mem. Wichita Bd. Edn., 1973-76, pres., 1975-76. Mem. Order of Coif, Phi Delta Phi, Sigma Alpha Mu. Democrat. Jewish.

GLOCK, CHARLES YOUNG, retired sociologist, writer; b. NYC, Oct. 17, 1919; s. Charles and Philippine (Young) G.; m. Margaret Schleef, Sept. 12, 1950; children: Susan Young, James William. BS, N.Y. U., 1940; MBA, Boston U., 1941; PhD, Columbia U., 1952. Research asst. Bur. Applied Social Research, Columbia U., 1946-51, dir., 1951-58, lectr., then prof. sociology, 1956-58; prof. sociology U. Calif. at Berkeley, 1958-79, prof. emeritus, 1979—2008, chmn., 1967-68, 69-71; dir. Survey Research Center, 1958-67; adj. prof. Grad. Theol. Union, 1971-79; Luther Weigle vis. lectr. Yale U., 1968. Co-author: American Piety, 1968, Wayward Shepherds, 1971, Anti-Semitism in America, 1979, The Anatomy of Racial Attitudes, 1983; author (sr.): Religion and Society in Tension, 1965, Christian Beliefs and Anti-Semitism, 1966, To Comfort and To Challenge, 1967, Adolescent Prejudice, 1968, The Apathetic Majority, 1975; contbg. editor: Rev. Religious Rsch. Sociol. Analysis; editor: Survey Research in the Social Sciences, 1967, Prejudice U.S.A., 1969, Beyond the Classics, 1973, Religion in Sociological Perspective, 1973, The New Religious Consciousness, 1975, Unison-Newsletter of One Voice, 1990—96; contbr. numerous articles on social scis. Active parish edn. Luth. Ch. Am., 1970-72; mem. mgmt. com. Office Rsch. and Planning, 1973-80; bd. dirs. Pacific Luth. Theol. Sem., 1962-74, 80-86, Inst. Rsch. in Social Behavior, 1962-90, Interplayers, 1990-92, Sandpoint Christian Connection, 1995-97; pres. Cornerhouse Fund, 1982-92, One Voice, 1994-95, bd. dirs., 1995-97; mem. adv. com. Office Rsch. and Evaluation Evang. Luth. Ch. Am., 1988-94; mem. history com. Soc. Study of Religion, 1993-94; v.p. Sandpoint chpt. Idaho Writers' League, 2003—. Capt. USAAF, 1942-46. Decorated Bronze Star, Legion of Merit; recipient Roots of Freedom award Pacific bd. Anti-Defamation League, 1977, Garman-Hidy award for Disting. Contbn. to Life of Luth. Ch. in the West, 1999; Berkeley citation U. Calif., Berkeley, 1979; Rockefeller fellow, 1941-42; fellow Center Advanced Study Behavioral Scis., 1957-58; fellow Soc. for Religion in Higher Edn., 1968-69 Fellow Soc. Sci. Study Religion (Western rep., pres. 1968-69); mem. Am. Assn. Pub. Opinion Research (v.p., pres. 1962-64, pres. Pacific chpt. 1959-60), Am. Sociol. Assn. (v.p. 1978-79), Religious Research Assn., Sociol. Research Assn. Home: 319 S 4th Ave Sandpoint ID 83864-1219 Personal E-mail: chyogl@yahoo.com.

GLORIA, TODD, councilman; Grad. summa cum laude, U. San Diego. With County of San Diego's Health and Human Svcs. Agency; dist. dir., housing advisor to US Congresswoman Susan A. Davis, 2000—08; commr. San Diego Housing Commn., 2005—08; councilman, Dist. 3 San Diego City Coun., 2008—. Named Harry S. Truman Scholar, 1999; named one of Top 40 Under Forty, San Diego Met. Mag., 2005, 50 People to Watch, San Diego Mag., 2008. Democrat. Office: 202 C St, MS #10A San Diego CA 92101 Office Phone: 619-236-6633. Office Fax: 619-595-1481. E-mail: toddgloria@sandiego.gov.*

GLOTFELTY, CHERYLL, literature and language professor; m. Steve Glotfelty; 1 child, Rosa Ramona. BA, U. Calif., Davis; MA, PhD, Cornell U., Ithaca, NY. Assoc. prof. lit. and the environment U. Nev., Reno, Sanford Disting. prof. humanities, 2000—02. Contbr. articles to profl. jours., chapters to books; co-editor: The Ecocriticism Reader: Landmarks in Literary Ecology, 1996. Recipient US Prof. of Yr. award, Carnegie Found. for Advancement of Tchg. and Coun. for Advancement and Support of Edn., 2006. Mem.: Assn. for Study of Lit. and Environment (founder). Avocations: reading, rock climbing, hiking, basket weaving. Office: English Dept 098 U Nev Reno Reno NV 89557 Office Phone: 775-682-6395. Office Fax: 775-784-6266. E-mail: glotfelt@unr.edu.

GLOVER, FRED WILLIAM, information scientist, director, educator; b. Kansas City, Mo., Mar. 8, 1937; s. William Cain and Mary Ruth (Baxter) G.; m. Diane Tatham, June 4, 1988; 1 child, Lauren Glover; children from previous marriage: Dana Reynolds, Paul Glover. BBA, U. Mo., 1960; PhD, Carnegie-Mellon U., 1965; DSc (hon.), Nat. Acad. Sci., Ukraine, 2006. Asst. prof. U. Calif., Berkeley, 1965-66; assoc. prof. U. Tex., Austin, 1966-69; prof. U. Minn., Mpls., 1969-70, U. Colo., Boulder, 1970—, Media One chair in sys. sci., 1998—; rsch. dir. Artificial Intelligence Ctr., Boulder, 1984-90; disting. prof. U. Colo. Sys., 2006—. Bd. dirs. Heuristec, Boulder, OptTek, Boulder, Decision Analysis, Rsch. & Computation, Austin. Author: Netform Decision Models, 1983 (DIS award 1984), Tabu Search I, 1989, Tabu Search II, 1990, Tabu Search (book and special vols.) 1993, 97, 98, 2003, Ghost Image Processes for Neural Networks, 1993, Linkages with Artificial Intelligence, 1990, Network Models in Optimization and Their Application in Practice, 1992, Handbook of Metaheuristics, 2003, others; contbr. over 350 articles on math. optimization and artificial intelligence to profl. jours. Recipient Internat. Achievement award Inst. Mgmt. Scis., 1982, Energy Rsch. award Energy Rsch. Inst., 1983, Univ. Disting. Rsch. Lectr. award U. Colo., 1988, Rsch. Excellence prize Ops. Rsch. Soc., 1989, Nat. Best Theoretical/Empirical Rsch. Paper award Decision Scis. Inst., 1993, Computer Sci. Rsch. Excellence award Ops. Rsch. Soc. Am., 1994, Nat. Rsch. Excellence award Comp. Sci. Ops. Rsch. Soc., 1994, John Von Neumann Theory award Inst. Ops. Rsch. Mgmt. Sci., 1998, Spl. Recognition award Inst. Ops. Rsch. and Mgmt. Scis., 2004; named first U.S. West Disting. fellow, 1987. Fellow: AAAS, ICC Inst., Am. Assn. Collegiate Schs. Bus., Am. Inst. Decision Scis. (lectr. 1984, Outstanding Achievement award 1984); mem.: NAE, Alpha Iota Delta. Achievements include invention of tabu search methodology for optimization, design of software systems used throughout the U.S. and abroad. Office: U Colo Coll Bus Box 419 Boulder CO 80309-0419 Home Phone: 303-442-3559; Office Phone: 303-492-8589. Business E-Mail: fred.glover@colorado.edu.

GLOVER, JAMES TODD, manufacturing executive; b. Aberdeen, SD, Apr. 30, 1939; s. Fay and Vi (Bruns) G.; m. Joann Elizabeth House; children: Jason, Jeffrey, Jamie. Student, S.D. State U.; BS in Math., No. State Coll., Aberdeen, 1961. Inside sales engr. Aberdeen Ops. Safeguard, 1961-64, asst. sales engr., 1965-67, mktg. mgr., 1968-72, gen. mgr., 1973-77; v.p. ops. Safeguard PowerTech Systems, Aberdeen, 1978-83, exec. v.p., 1984-85, pres., 1986-89; pres., chief exec. officer, chief ops. officer, dir. Hub City, Inc., Aberdeen, 1989—. Officer Safeguard Sci. Co., Inc.; v.p. corp. devel. Regal-Beloit (Wis.) Corp., 1990-93; v.p. HQ Cos., Mpls., 1993-98, gen. mgr. Pixall Ltd. Partnership, Clear Lake, Wis., 1993-98; pres. JTG Solutions, Inc., Peoria, Ariz., 1998--. Bd. mem. S.D. Swimming Assn.; S.D. Dist. Export Council. Export Devel. Authority; bd. dirs. No. State Found., James River Water Devel.; bd. mem., chmn. James River Water Devel. Dist. Recipient Ernie Gunderson award S.D. Swimming Assn. Mem. Power Transmission Distbrs. Assn. (past bd. dirs., past chmn. allied adv. bd.), Power Transmission Rep. Assn. (past bd. dirs., past chmn. allied adv. bd.), Aberdeen C. of C., S.D. Mfrs. Assn. (past dir.). Republican. Roman Catholic. Avocations: hunting, fishing, music.

GLOVER, KAREN ELAINE, lawyer; b. Nampa, Idaho, Apr. 14, 1950; d. Gordon Ellsworth and Cora (Frazier) G.; m. Thaddas L. Alston, Aug. 17, 1979; children: Samantha Glover Alston, Evan Glover Alston. AB magna cum laude, Whitman Coll., 1972; JD cum laude, Harvard U., 1975. Bar: Wash. 1975, U.S. Dist. Ct. (we. dist.) Wash. 1975. Assoc. Preston, Thorgrimson Ellis & Holman, Seattle, 1975-80; ptnr. Preston Gates & Ellis LLP, Seattle, 1981—2006, mng. ptnr., 2005—06; global integration ptnr. K&L Gates, Seattle, 2007—. Bd. dirs. Adaptis, Inc. Chmn. bd. dirs. United Way King County, Seattle, 1993-94; chmn. trustees Whitman Coll., Walla Walla, Wash., 2004-06; bd. trustees King County Libr. Sys., Seattle, 1992-01. Mem. Wash. State Bar Assn. (corp. and health sects.), Columbia Tower Club, Rainier Club. Episcopalian. Office: K&L Gates 925 4th Ave Ste 2900 Seattle WA 98104-1158 Office Phone: 206-370-7624. Business E-Mail: kari.glover@klgates.com.

GLOVER, THOMAS T., federal judge; Apptd. chief bankruptcy judge we. dist. U.S. Dist. Ct. Wash., 1985. Office: 315 Park Place Bldg 1200 6th Ave Seattle WA 98101-3123 Fax: 206-553-0187.

GLOVSKY, MYRON MICHAEL, medical educator; b. Boston, Aug. 15, 1936; divorced; five children. BS magna cum laude, Tufts U., 1957, MD, 1962. Bd. cert. Nat. Bd. Med. Examiners, Am. Bd. Allergy & Immunology, Am. Bd. Diagnostic Lab. Immunology. Intern Balt. (Md.) City Hosp., 1962-63; resident New Eng. Med. Ctr., Boston, 1965-66; spl. NIH fellow allergy and immunology Walter Reed Army Inst. Rsch., Washington, 1966-68; fellow hematology and immunology U. Calif., San Francisco, 1968-69; staff physician dept. internal medicine So. Calif. Permanente Med. Group, LA, 1969-72, dir. allergy & immunology lab., 1970-84, chief dept. allergy and clin. immunology, co-dir. residency program in allergy & clin. immunology, 1974-84, dir. pheresis unit, 1978-80; dir. L.A. County Gen. Hosp./U. So. Calif. Asthma Clinic; prof. medicine, head allergy and immunology labs. pulmonary divsn., head allergy and clin. immunology divsn. pulmonary medicine. U. So. Calif., Sch. Medicine, 1984-89, prof. pathology, 1986-89; clin. prof. medicine, clin. prof. pathology U. So. Calif., 1989—2003; dir. asthma and allergy referral ctr. Huntington Meml. Hosp., Pasadena, 1989—2003. Head fellowship and career devel. program Nat. Heart Inst., NIH, Bethesda, Md., 1963-65, fellowship bd. mem., 1964-65; vis. assoc. in chemistry Calif. Inst. Tech., Pasadena, 1977—; acad. assoc. complement and allergy Nichols Inst., San Juan Capistrano, Calif., 1980-2003, med. dir. immunology, 1980-89, 2003-06; clin. prof. medicine UCLA, 1983-84; vis. prof. clin. scholars program Eli Lilly & Co., Indpls., 1988; mem. steering com. Aspen Allergy Conf., 1988—. With USPHS, 1963-65. Fellow Am. Acad. Allergy; mem. AAAS, Am. Assn. Immunologists, Am. Thoracic Soc., Am. Fedn. for Clin. Rsch., Am. Coll. Allergy, L.A. Soc. Allergy and Clin. Immunology (pres. 1979-80), Collegium Internat. Allergolicum. Home: 287 Grace Dr South Pasadena CA 91030 Office: Huntington Asthma & Allergy Ctr 960 E Green St Pasadena CA 91106 Home Phone: 626-755-7783; Office Phone: 626-793-6680. Business E-Mail: yksvolg@caltech.edu.

GLUECKMAN, ALAN JAY, Internet company executive; BA in Econs., U. Mich., 1966; MBA in Mktg., Columbia U., 1968. Product mgr. Gen. Foods, 1969; copywriter BBDO, 1970—71; copywriter, prodr. McCaffrey and McCall, 1971—73; creative dir. Ted Bates Hellas, Athens, Greece, 1974—76, Ted Bates, NYC, 1977; writer, dir. Am.-Internat. Pictures, 1979; screenwriter Universal Pictures, Universal City, Calif., 1980, Melvin Simon Prodns., 1980, 1982, Walt Disney Prodns., LA, 1981, Ray Stark Prodns., LA, 1983—84, Paramount Pictures, LA, 1984, 86, Columbia Pictures, LA, 1985; pres. Glueckman Entertainment, LA, 1984—92, Glueckman Intertainment, LA, 1992—2002; chmn., pres. eJamming Inc., 2002—. Bd. dirs. (alt.) Writers Guild America, 1988—89; co-regional rep. Am. Coaster Enthusiasts, 2002—07. Writer, dir. (film) Pickup starring Glenn Close, 1977; screenwriter: Night Warning, 1982 (Best Horror Film award 1982), Russkies, 1987, Gross Anatomy, 1989, Crash Course (NBC), 1988, The Face of Fear (CBS), 1990; screenwriter, producer: It Almost Wasn't Christmas (LBS), 1989; screenwriter, exec. producer The Fear Inside, 1991; prodr. Ravager, 1997; creator, exec. prodr. (TV series) Scoring, 2002; co-creator, writer and site arch.: Mission Impossible: The Web Adventure, 1997; developer: You're Gotta Believe Me (MSN), Disco-Rama (EntertainNet); book-writer & lyricist (stage musicals) Starr Struck: A Musical Investigation, 1999, Stalag 17: The Musical, 2001, Friday Saturday Sunday, 2004. Mem. Writers Guild Am. West. Business E-Mail: info@ejamming.com, aglueckman@ejamming.com.

GLYNN, ROBERT D., JR., former electric power and gas industry executive; b. Orange, NJ, 1942; BSME, Manhattan Coll.; MS in Nuclear Engring., L.I. U.; postgrad., U. Mich., Harvard U. With L.I. Lighting Co., 1964-72; exec. v.p., prin., dir. Woodward Clyde Cons., 1972-84; with PG&E Corp., San Francisco, 1984—, pres., COO, 1997, CEO, 1997—, chmn. bd., 1998—2006, Pacific Gas and Electric Co. (subsidiary of PG&E Corp.), 2005—06. Mem. Bus. Council, Calif. Commn. for Jobs and Economic Growth. Bd. govs. San Francisco Symphony.

GOBAR, ALFRED JULIAN, retired economic consultant, investor, educator; b. Lucerne Valley, Calif., July 12, 1932; s. Julian Smith and Hilda (Millbank) G.; m. Sally Ann Randall, June 17, 1957, (dec. 2005); children: Wendy Lee, Curtis Julian, Joseph Julian; m. Cathleen Jane Anderson, Feb. 26, 2006, (div. 2009). BA in Econs., Whittier Coll., 1953, MA in History, 1955; postgrad., Claremont Grad. Sch., 1953-54; PhD in Econs., U. So. Calif., 1963; LHD (hon.), Whitter Coll., 2005. Asst. pres. Microdot Inc., Pasadena, Calif., 1953—57; regional sales mgr. Sutorbilt Corp., LA, 1957—59; mktg. rsch. assoc. Beckman Instrument Inc., Fullerton, Calif., 1959—64; sr. mktg. cons. We. Mgmt. Consultants Inc., San Diego, 1964—66; ptnr., prin., chmn. bd. Darley/Gobar Assocs., Inc., San Diego, 1966—73; pres., chmn. bd. Alfred Gobar Assocs., Inc., Anaheim, 1973—. Asst. prof. finance U. So. Calif., LA, 1963-64; assoc. prof. bus. Calif. State U., LA, 1963-68, 70-79, assoc. prof. Calif. State U.-Fullerton, 1968-69; mktg., fin. adviser 1957—; pub. spkr. seminars and convs. Contbr. articles to profl. publs. Trustee Whittier Coll., 1992—. Office: 300 S Harbor Blvd Anaheim CA 92805-3721 Office Phone: 714-772-8900 ext. 309. Business E-Mail: al@gobar.com.

GOCKLEY, DAVID (RICHARD DAVID GOCKLEY), opera company director; b. Phila., July 13, 1943; s. Warren and Elizabeth S. Gockley; children: Meredith, Lauren, Adam. BA, Brown U., 1965, DFA (hon.), 1993; MBA, Columbia U., 1970; DHL (hon.), U. Houston, 1992. Dir. music Newark Acad., 1965-67; dir. drama Buckley Sch., NYC, 1967-69; mgr. box office Santa Fe Opera, 1969-70; bus. mgr. Houston Grand Opera, 1970-71, assoc. dir., 1971-72, gen. dir., 1972—2005, San Francisco Opera, 2006—. Co-founder Houston Opera Studio, 1977. Prodr. (operas): Nixon in China (Emmy award 1988), Harvey Milk, Florencia en el Amazonas, Porgy and Bess (Tony award, Grammy award 1977), Treemonisha, A Quiet Place, Willie Stark, Resurrection, Carmen. Bd. dirs. Tex. Inst. Arts in Edn.; past pres. OPERA Am.; past chmn. Houston Theater Dist. Recipient Tony award League of N.Y Theaters and Producers, 1977, Dean's award Columbia Bus. Sch., 1982, Music Theater award Nat. Inst. Music Theater, 1985, William Rogers award, Brown U., 1995; named one of Outstanding Men Am., Nat. Jr. C. of C., 1976. Mem. OPERA Am. Avocation: tennis. Office: San Francisco Opera 301 Van Ness Ave San Francisco CA 94102 Office Phone: 713-546-0200, 415-551-6271. Business E-Mail: dgockley@sfopera.com.

GODAGER, JANE ANN, retired social worker; b. Blue River, Wis., Nov. 29, 1943; d. Roy and Elmyra Marie G. BA, U. Wis., 1965; MSW, Fla. State U., 1969. LCSW, diplomate Acad. Cert. Social Workers. Social worker III State of Wis. Dept Corrections, Wales, 1965—71; supervising psychiat. social worker I State of Calif., San Bernardino, 1972—75, La Mesa, 1975—77, psychiat. social worker San Bernardino, 1978—85; supr. mental health svcs. Riverside County Dept. Mental Health, Calif., 1985—86; mental health counselor Superior Ct. San Bernardino County, 1986—2001; staff asst. to dist. dir. Calif. State Assembly, 2002, ret., 2002. Former mem. adv. bd. Grad. Sch. Social Work Calif. State U., San Bernardino, Mental Health Assn.; mem. County Hosp. Re-Use Com. Mem. commn. sr. affairs City of San Bernardino, Calif.; mem. County Mental Health Commn.; sr. assemblyperson Calif. Sr. Legislature; legis. com. Mayor's Blue Ribbon Com.; bd. dirs. Sr. & Disabled Fund. Mem.: NASW, Acad. Cert. Social Workers, Kappa Kappa Gamma Alumnae Assn. Avocations: travel, reading, music.

GODBEY, ROBERT CARSON, lawyer; b. Houston, June 7, 1953; s. Charles Perry and Bobbye Lee Godbey; m. Ellen Carson, June 2, 1979. BS, BSEE magna cum laude, So. Meth. U., 1975; JD cum laude, Harvard U., 1980. Bar: U.S. Patent Office, 1981, Hawaii 1988. Telecom. engr. Southwestern Bell, Dallas, 1975—76, Tex. Instruments, Dallas, 1976—77; assoc. Peabody, Lambert & Meyers, Washington, 1980—84; asst. U.S. atty. U.S. Dept. Justice, Washington, 1984—87, Honolulu, 1987—91; ptnr. Godbey Griffiths LLLP, 1991—. Mem. ABA, IEEE, Hawaii State Bar Assn. (past chmn. intellectual property sect. 1994-96, past chmn. tech. com., 1995-97), Phi Beta Kappa, Tau Beta Pi. Office: 2300 Pauahi Tower 1003 Bishop St Honolulu HI 96813-3429 Office Phone: 808-523-8894.

GODDARD, JOE DEAN, chemical engineering educator, researcher; b. Buncombe, Ill., July 13, 1936; s. Bon Andrew and Helen May (Hudgens) G.; m. Shirley May Keltner, Sept. 1, 1957; children: Paul, Suzanne, Anna P., Andrew, Jessica. BS in Chem. Engring., U. Ill., 1957; PhD in Chemistry, U. Calif.-Berkeley, 1962. NATO postdoctoral fellow, Paris, 1961-63; asst. prof. to prof. chem. engring. U. Mich., Ann Arbor, Mich., 1963-76; R.J. Fluor prof., chmn. dept. chem. engring. U. So. Calif., Los Angeles, Calif., 1976-91; prof. dept. mech. and aerospace engring. sci. U. Calif., San Diego, 1991—. Cons. Dow Chem. Co., Midland, Mich., 1964, Hercules, Inc., Parlin, NJ, 1964-66, Jet Propulsion Lab., Pasadena, Calif., 1979; D.L. Katz lectr. U. Mich., Ann Arbor, 1983 Former mem. editl. bd. Ann. Rev. Fluid Mechanics, Continuum Mechanics and Thermodynamics; mem. editl. bd. Jour. Non-Newtonian Fluid Mechanics, Internat. Jour. Engring. Sci.; contbr. articles to profl. jour. NSF postdoctoral fellow Cambridge, Eng., 1971; Fulbright fellow, Belgium, 1984 Mem. AIChE (past mem. editl. bd. AIChe Jour.), Am. Soc. Rheology (v.p. 1990-91, pres. 1992-93, past pres. 1994-95), Brit. Soc. Rheology, Am. Math. Soc. Am. Phys. Soc. Office: Univ Calif San Diego Dept Mech & Aero Engring La Jolla CA 92093-0411 Home Phone: 858-551-9887; Office Phone: 858-534-4508. Business E-Mail: jgoddard@ucsd.edu.

GODDARD, JOHN WESLEY, cable television company executive; b. Aberdeen, Wash., May 4, 1941; s. Fred G. and Winifred (Vaughan) G.; m. Susan Ehrhart, Dec. 29, 1962 (div. Oct. 1978); 1 child, John Wesley Jr.; m. Joan Marie McGiff, Sept. 13, 1980. Grad., Stanford U.; MBA in Fin., U. Calif., Berkeley. Asst. mgr. Tele-Vue Systems Inc., Dublin, Calif., 1966, mgr., 1967-69, contr., 1969-74, pres., 1974-78; exec. v.p. Viacom Cable, Pleasanton, Calif., 1978-80, pres., 1980—. Dir. Viacom Internat. Inc., N.Y.C., 1983-87; treas. Nat. Cable TV Assn., Washington, 1984, sec., 1985-86, vice chmn., 1987, chmn., 1988, bd. dirs., 1981—. Republican. Episcopalian. Office: Viacom Cable 2166 Rheem Dr Pleasanton CA 94588-2613

GODDARD, KENNETH WILLIAM, forensic scientist, writer; b. San Diego, July 6, 1946; s. Joseph William and Bernice Elizabeth (Cahoon) G.; m. Georgene Shitara, June 22, 1968; 1 child, Michelle Suni. BS in Biochemistry, U. Calif., Riverside, 1968; MS in Criminalistics, Calif. State U., LA, 1971. Criminalist Riverside County Sheriff's Office, 1968-69; criminalist, dep. sheriff San Bernadino County (Calif.) Sheriff's Dept., 1969-72; chief criminalist Huntington Beach (Calif.) Police Dept., 1972-79; chief forensics br. U.S. Fish and Wildlife Svc., Washington, 1979-87; lab. dir. Nat. Fish and Wildlife Forensics Lab., Ashland, Oreg., 1987—. Adj. prof. So. Oreg. State Coll., Ashland, 1991—, mem. sci. adv. bd., 1990—. Author: Crime Scene Investigation, 1972, Balefire, 1983, The Alchemist, 1985, Digger, 1990, Prey, 1992, Wildfire, 1994, Cheater, 1997, Double Blind, 1997, First Evidence, 1999, Outer Perimeter, 2001. Fellow Am. Acad. Forensic Scis.; mem. Am. Assn. Crime Lab Dirs. (charter) Authors Guild, Mystery Writers Am. Achievements include development of first national and international wildlife crime laboratory in the world. Office: US Fish & Wildlife Svc Nat Forensics Lab 1490 E Main St Ashland OR 97520-1310 Office Phone: 503-482-4191. Office Fax: 541-482-4989. Business E-Mail: ken_goddard@fws.gov. E-mail: KenGoddard@aol.com.

GODDARD, TERRY, state attorney general; BA, Harvard U., 1969; JD, Ariz. State U., 1976. Bar: Ariz. 1976, U.S. Ct. Appeals (9th cir.) 1980, U.S. Supreme Ct. 2003. Mayor City of Phoenix, 1983-90; of counsel Bryan Cave, Phoenix, 1990-94; atty. gen. State of Ariz., 2003—. Bd. dirs. Ariz Theatre Co.; former pres. Nat. League of Cities, 1989; former chmn. Ariz Mcpl. Water Users Assn., Maricopa Assn. Govts., Regional Pub. Transp. Authority, Rebuild Am. Coalition; adv. bd. State and Local Legal Ctr. With USNR, 1970—98. Mem.: ABA,

Maricopa County Bar Assn., Ariz. State Bar Assn. Democrat. Office: Office of Atty General 1275 W Washington St Phoenix AZ 85007 Office Phone: 602-542-4266. E-mail: ag.inquiries@azag.gov.*

GODDEN, JEAN W., columnist; b. Stamford, Conn., Oct. 1, 1933; d. Maurice Albert and Bernice Elizabeth (Warvel) Hecht; m. Robert W. Godden, Nov. 7, 1952 (dec. Dec. 1985); children: Glenn Scott, Jeffrey Wayne. BA, U. Wash., 1974. News editor Univ. Dist. Herald, Seattle, 1951-53; bookkeeper Omniarts Inc., Seattle, 1963-71; writer editorial page Seattle Post-Intelligencer, Seattle, 1974-80, editorial page editor, 1980-81, bus. editor, 1981-83, city columnist, 1983-91, Seattle Times, 1991—. Author: The Will to Win, 1980, Hasty Put Ins, 1981. Communicator of the Yr. U. Wash. Sch. of Comm., 1995. Mem. LWV (dir. 1969-71), Wash. Press Assn. (Superior Performance award 1979), Soc. Profl. Journalists, Mortarboard, City Club, Phi Beta Kappa. Office: The Seattle Times PO Box 70 Seattle WA 98111-0070

GOE, DOUGLAS E., lawyer; b. Loma Linda, Calif., Apr. 28, 1955; BS, Lewis & Clark Coll., 1977; JD cum laude, Willamette U., 1981. Bar: Oreg. 1981, Wash. 1988. Law clk. to Hon. George A. Van Hoomissen Oreg. Ct. Appeals, 1981—82; assoc. Ragen, Roberts, Tremaine, Kriegar, Schmeer, O'Scannlain & Neill; mem. exec. com. Ater Wynne LLP, chmn. pub. fin. group; ptnr. Orrick, Herrington & Sutcliffe LLP, Portland, Oreg., vice chmn. pub. fin. group, office leader-Pacific Northwest/Portland/Seattle. Author: Low Cost Industrial Revenue Bonds Still Available to Bus., 1990, Great Western & Legis. Aftermath: Unconstl. Usurpation of Ct.'s Power?, 1980; co-author: Oreg. Sch. Bond Manual (revised). Mem.: Nat. Assn. Bond Lawyers, Oregon State Bar (treas. Indian law sect., professsionalism com.), ABA, Wash. State Bar Assn. (Indian law sect.), Multnomah County Bar Assn. (professionalism com.), Met. Youth Symphony (pres. devel. bd. 1994—96). Office: Orrick Herrington Sutcliffe 1120 NW Couch St Ste 200 Portland OR 97209-4163 Office Phone: 503-943-4810. Office Fax: 503-943-4801. Business E-Mail: dgoe@orrick.com.

GOEDDE, JOHN W., state legislator; married; children: Brian, Melissa(dec.). BA, Wash. State U., 1972. Mgr. Hayden Lake Country Club, 1973-79; agent, Panhandle Ins. and Realty, 1979-1983; pres. Panhandle Ins. Agy. Inc., 1983-; Trustee, Sch District 271, 1997-2000; Idaho State Senator, District 3, formerly; Idaho State Senator, District 4, 2000-. Ed Abbott Award. Coeur d'Alene Chamber of Commerce (commodores, legislation & transportation & local government comts, currently, president, chairman, formerly); Rotary; Coeur d'Alene Ins Agents Association (president, chairman, formerly); Idaho State Jaycee (treasurer, formerly). Republican. Office: State Capitol Bldg PO Box 83720 Boise ID 83720-0081 Mailing: 1010 E Mullan Unit 203 Coeur D' Alene ID 83814 Home Phone: 208-664-9223; Office Phone: 208-664-9223. Fax: 208-664-9336.

GOELTZ, THOMAS A., lawyer; BA in Econs. summa cum laude, DePauw U., 1969; JD magna cum laude, Mich. U., 1973. Assoc. Riddell, Williams, Ivie, Bullitt & Walkinshaw, Seattle, 1973-75; dep. prosecuting atty. civil divsn. King County Prosecuting Atty.'s Office, Seattle, 1976-79; prin. Cohen, Keegan & Goeltz, Seattle, 1979-86; ptnr. Davis Wright Tremaine, Seattle, 1986—. Cons. state and local govt. agencies on environ. land use issues; adv. shoreline mgmt. City of Seattle; part-time lectr. Law Sch. U. Wash., Seattle, 1976-79. Editor Mich. Law Rev. Active Gov. Task Force on Regulatory Reform, 1993-95. Mem. ABA (urban, state & local govt. law sect.), Wash. State Bar Assn. (real property sect., past chair land use and environ. law sect.), Seattle-King County Bar Assn., Am. Coll. Real Estate Lawyers, Nat. Assn. Indsl. and Office Park, ICSC, Order of Coif. Office: Davis Wright Tremaine 2600 Century Sq 1501 4th Ave Seattle WA 98101-1688

GOEN, BOB, television show host; b. Long Beach, Calif., Dec. 1, 1954; Grad., San Diego State U., 1976. DJ Stint Sta. KPRO-FM, Riverside, Calif., 1977-81; anchor, reporter, prodr., writer, editor Sta. KESQ-TV, Palm Springs, Calif., 1981—86; game show host Perfect Match, 1986, The Home Shopping Game, Blackout; daytime host Wheel of Fortune, 1989-92; game show host The Hollywood Game, 1992; corr., weekend anchor Entertainment Tonight, 1993—96, co-host, 1996—2004. Host Miss Universe, Miss USA, Miss Teen USA, 1993-96. Named to, Long Beach City Coll. Hall of Fame.

GOFORTH, NATHAN DAN, retired protective services official; b. Phoenix, Sept. 12, 1951; s. Nathan and Mabel Lettie (Deal) G.; m. Lori Ann Petersen (div. 1984). AA in Bus. Adminstrn., Glendale Community Coll., Ariz., 1974, AA in Adminstrn. Justice, 1976; BS in Pub. Programs, Ariz. State U., 1985. Second asst. mgr. Smittys Big Town, Phoenix, 1967-73, sales rep., 1975-76; sr. inventory auditor Motorola Semiconductor, Phoenix, 1973-74; police officer City Glendale, Ariz., 1976—2008. Interpreter for deaf Glendale Police Dept., 1976—, peer counselor, 1989—, field tng. officer, 1980—; vol. tchr. Glendale Community Coll. Police Res. Acad., 1989-94; pub. safety vol. program, coord. Glendale Police Dept., 2001-. Res. hwy. patrolman Ariz. Dept. Pub. Safety, Phoenix, 1975-76; advisor Glendale Explorer Post 469, 1978—, instl. head, 1992; bd. dirs. Theater Works, 1994-97, v.p., 1995-97; hon. mem. Ariz. Rangers, 2005—. Recipient Dedication to DAV award, 1990-91, Cert. of Appreciation award Independence High Sch., 1990, Outstanding Vol. Svc. award MADD, 1991, Spl. Recognition Hon. Mention award for Work Done with D.U.I Task Force, 2005. Mem. Ariz. State U. Alumni Assn., Internat. Police Assn., Frat. order of Police (treas. 1990-94, v.p. 1994-95, 96-00, trustee 1995—), Critical Incident Stress Debriefing (S.W. region), Sons of Am. Legion. Avocations: volleyball, racquetball, camping, travel. Office: Glendale Police Dept 6835 N 57th Dr Glendale AZ 85301-3218

GOIN, PETER JACKSON, art educator; b. Madison, Wis., Nov. 26, 1951; children: Kari, Dana. BA, Hamline U., 1973; MA, U. Iowa, 1975, MFA, 1976. Found. prof. art U. Nev., Reno, 1984—. Author: Tracing the Line: A Photographic Survey of the Mexican-American Border, 1987, Nuclear Landscapes, 1991, Arid Waters: Photographs from the Water in the West Project, 1992, Stopping Time: A Rephotographic Survey of Lake Tahoe, 1992, Humanature, 1996, Atlas of the New West, 1997, A Doubtful River, 2000, Changing Mines in America, 2004, Lake Tahoe, 2005, Black Rock, 2005, Lake Tahoe, 2006; one-man shows include Duke U. Mus. Art, Durham, N.C., 1992, Phoenix Mus. Art, 1992, Indpls. Mus. Art, 1992, Savannah (Ga.) Coll. Art and Design, 1992, Nev. Humanities Com. Traveling Exhibit, 1992, NICA, Las Vegas, Nev., 1997, Mus. for Photographie, Braunschweig, Germany, 1997, U. Oreg. Mus. of Art, Eugene, 1997, Nev. Mus. Art, Reno, 1996, 99, 2005-06, Princeton (N.J.) U. Art Mus., 1996, Whitney Mus. Am. Art, N.Y.C., 1996, Museet for Fotographie, Denmark, 1999. Recipient Millennium award for Excellence in Arts, Nev., 1999; named Outstanding Rschr. of Yr., U. Nev., Reno, 2007; grantee NEA, 1982, 90. Office: Univ Nev Dept Art Reno NV 89557-0007 Office Phone: 775-784-4994. Business E-Mail: pgoin@unr.edu.

GOIN, SUZANNE, chef; b. LA, Sept. 25, 1966; m. David Lentz. BA in History, Brown U.; apprenticeship, Ma Maison, LA. Line cook Chez Panisse, Berkeley, Calif., 1990-92, Arpege Brigade, Paris, 1993; sous chef Olives, Boston, 1993; exec. chef Alloro, Boston, 1994-96, Campanile, LA, 1997-98; co-owner, exec. chef Lucques, West Hollywood, 1998—, A.O.C., 2002—, The Hungry Cat, 2005—. Author (with Teri Gelber): (cookbooks) Sunday Suppers at Lucques, 2005 (James Beard award, 2006). Named Best Creative Chef Boston mag., 1994, One of America's Best New Chefs, Food & Wine mag., 1999, Best Chef award nominee, 2003, 2004, 2005, Best Chef: Calif. award of Excellence, James Beard Found., 2006. Office: Lucques 8474 Melrose Ave West Hollywood CA 90069-5313

GOLAY, FRANK H., JR., lawyer; b. Chgo., 1948; BA, Cornell U., 1970, MAT, 1972, JD, 1977. Bar: N.Y. 1978. Ptnr. Sullivan & Cromwell, LA. Office: Sullivan & Cromwell 1888 Century Park E Los Angeles CA 90067-1702

GOLD, ANNE MARIE, library director; b. NYC, Feb. 24, 1949; d. James Raymond and Marion Rita (Magner) Scully; m. Steven Louis Gold, Aug. 9, 1974; 1 child, Lauren Z. BA in English, St. Lawrence U., Canton, NY, 1971; MS in Libr. Svc., Columbia U., NYC, 1972. Libr. NY Pub. Libr., NYC, 1972—74, Oakland Pub. Libr., Calif., 1975—80; dir. libr. svcs. Solano County Libr., Fairfield, Calif., 1980—90; county libr. Contra Costa County Libr., Pleasant Hill, Calif., 1990—98; interim mgr. Libr. Calif., Calif. State Libr., Sacramento, 1999; exec. dir. Stanford-Calif. State Libr. Inst. 21st Century Librarianship, Calif., 1999—2001; dir. Sacramento Pub. Libr. Authority, 2002—. Guest lectr. U. Calif., Berkeley Grad. Sch. Libr. Sci., 1975—85, San Jose State U. Sch. Libr. and Info. Sci., 1994—; bd. dirs. Califa, 2004—08; mem. coun. Online Computer Libr. Ctr., 2006—. Contbr. articles to profl. jours. Bd. trustees Lafayette Sch., 1993-97; mem. adv. com. San Jose State U. Sch. Libr. and Info. Sci., 2002-07. Recipient Award for Excellence, Contra Costa County Bd. Suprs., 1997. Mem. ALA, Pub. Libr. Assn. (bd. dirs. 1992-93, 2004-07, met. librs. sect., pres. 1992-93), Libr. Adminstrn. and Mgmt. Assn. (various coms.), Calif. Libr. Assn. (coun. mem. 1985-87, 90-92, exec. bd. 1991-92, co-chair legis. com. 1992-94, pres. 1998, Mem. of Yr. award, 1994), Calif. Inst. Librs. (v.p. 1990-91), Restructuring Calif. Pub. Librs. Task Force (1994-95), Calif. County Librs. Assn. (pres. 1996), Urban Librs. Coun. Office: Sacramento Pub Libr 828 I St Sacramento CA 95814 Office Phone: 916-264-2830. Office Fax: 916-264-2755. E-mail: amgold@saclibrary.org.

GOLD, ARNOLD HENRY, judge; b. Santa Monica, Calif., Apr. 12, 1932; s. Louis and Rose (Shalat) G.; m. Gloria Victor; children: Jeffrey Alan, Kenneth Clarke, Susan Elizabeth. AB with distinction, Stanford U., 1953, JD, 1955. Bar: Calif. 1955, U.S. Dist. Ct. (so., ctrl. and no. dists.) Calif. 1955, U.S. Ct. Appeals (9th cir.) 1955, U.S. Supreme Ct. 1955. Law clk. to Hon. John W. Shenk Supreme Ct. of Calif., San Francisco, 1955-56; assoc. atty. Loeb & Loeb, LA, 1956-61; pvt. practice Beverly Hills, Calif., 1961-70; ptnr. Pachter, Gold & Schaffer, and predecessors, LA, 1970-88; judge Calif. Superior Ct. for County of L.A., 1988-2001, supervising judge probate dept., 1993-94. Mem. Calif. Atty. Gen.'s Com. on Charitable Reporting Stds., 1970—71; mem. exec. com. Stanford Law Soc. So. Calif., 1973—77; mem. Calif. Atty. Gen.'s Task Force on Charitable Solicitation Legis., 1975—78; chmn. probate and mental health com. Calif. Judges Assn., 1995—96; pres. bd. trustees Los Angeles County Law Libr., 1998—2000; Calif. rep. Nat. Coll. Probate Judges, 2003—; bd. dirs. Dispute Resolution Svcs., 2003—04; mem. adv. com. Calif. Jud. Coun. Probate and Mental Health, 1997—2004, advisor, adv. com., 2005—; lectr. in field. Co-author: Probate Module, California Civil Practice, 1993-; contbg. author: California Family Law Handbook, California Nonprofit Corporations Handbooks; mng. editor, bd. editors Stanford Law Rev., 1954-55. Mem. ABA, State Bar Calif. (vice chmn. conf. dels. 1986-87), L.A. County Bar Assn. (trustee 1981-83), Los Angeles County Bar Found. (bd. dirs. 1985-91), Mulholland Tennis Club, Phi Beta Kappa, Alpha Epsilon Pi, Phi Alpha Delta, Delta Sigma Rho. Office: 10842 Alta View Dr Studio City CA 91604-3901 Home Phone: 323-654-4307; Office Phone: 213-891-1501, 310-284-8224. Personal E-mail: judgeagold@aol.com.

GOLD, BETTY VIRGINIA, artist; b. Austin, Tex., Feb. 15, 1935; d. Julius Ulisses and Jeffie Mae (Meek) Lee; 1 child, Laura Lee Gold Bousquet. Student (hon.), U. Tex. Lectr. Gazi U., Ankara, Turkey, 1988, Nishida Gallery, Nara, Japan, 1989, Met. State Coll. Denver, 1992, Downey Mus., Calif., 1993, Foothills Art Ctr., Golden, Colo., 1994, Triskel Art Ctr., Cork, Ireland, 1994, ARmand Hammer Mus., LA, 1994, Austin Art Mus., 1996. One-woman shows include Sol Del Rio Gallery, San Antonio, 1971, Parkcrest Gallery, Austin, 1972, Rubicon Gallery, LA, 1973, Downtown Gallery, Honolulu, 1974, Esther Robles Gallery, LA, 1975, Laguna Gloria Art Mus., Austin, 1976, Charles W. Bowers Meml. Mus., Santa Ana, Calif., 1977, Phoenix Art Mus., 1979, Baum-Silverman Gallery, LA, 1988, Del. Art Mus., Wilmington, 1981, Univ. Art Mus., Austin, 1981, Decias Art, LaJolla, Calif., 1982, Patrick Gallery, Austin, 1983, Jan Baum Gallery, LA, 1984, Boise State U., 1985, Purdue U., West Lafayette, Ind., 1986, Walker Hill Art Ctr., Seoul, Korea, 1987, Nishida Gallery, 1989, Armeson Fine Arts, Ltd., Vail, Colo., 1991, Downey Mus., Calif., 1993, Art Mus. South Tex., Corpus Christi, 1995, Austin Art Mus., Austin, 1996, Czech Mus. Fine Arts, Prague, 1998, Elite Gallery, Venice, 1998, Gebert Gallery Venice, Calif., 2009; retrospectives include Palma-Mallorca, Spain, 2005, Buschlen Mowatt Gallery, Palm Desert, Calif., 2006, others; group shows include Enhol Gallery, Dallas, 1971, Bestart Fallery, Houston, 1972, Gargoyle, Inc., Aspen, Colo., 1975, Aronson Gallery, Atlanta, 1976, Shidoni Gallery, Sante Fe, N.Mex., 1977, Elaine Horwich Gallery, Scottsdale, Ariz., 1981, Fordham U., Bronx, 1983, Nat. Mus. Contemporary Art, Seoul, 1987, John Thomas Gallery, Santa Monica, Calif., 1989, La Quinta Sculpture Park, Calif., 1994, Bova Gallery, LA, 1995, Museo Nacional Centro de Arte Reina Sofia, Madrid, Spain, 1997, Threshold Gallery, Santa Monica, 1998, others; represented in permanent installations at RCA Bldg., Chgo., Cedars Sinai Hosp., LA, Sinai Temple, LA, Hawaii State Fond. Arts, Apollo Plastic Corp., Chgo., Houston First Savs., Pepperdine U., Malibu, Calif., Northern Ill. U., Dekalb, Mus. Nacional-Centro de Arte Reina Sofia, Madrid, Texas U., Austin, City of Palma de Mallorca, 1999, Spain, Duke U. Med. Ctr., 1999, Mary Baldwin Coll., Staunton, Va., 2001, Baylor U., Waco, Tex., 2002, Pres. Garden, Slovakia Republic (gift from US Embassy), Pepperdine U., Malibu, Calif, 2003, Esbaulard Mus., Palma de Mallorca, Spain, 2004, Palm Springs Desert Mus., Beinnale, Vancouver, 2006-07, Madi Mus. Geometric Art, Dallas, Va. Commonwealth U., Richmond, others. Fax: 310-399-3745. E-mail: bgold1324@earthlink.com.

GOLD, CAROL SAPIN, international management consultant, speaker, writer; b. NYC; d. Cerf Saul and Muriel Louise (Fudin) Rosenberg; children: Kevin Bart Sapin, Craig Paul Sapin, Courtney Byrens Sapin. BA, U. Calif., Berkeley, 1955. Asst. credit mgr. Union Oil Co., 1956; with U.S. Dept. State, 1964—66; mem. dept. pub. rels. Braun & Co., LA, 1964—66; corp. dir. pers. tng. Gt. We. Fin. Corp., LA, 1967—71; pres. Carol Sapin Gold & Assocs., LA, 1971—. Bd. dirs. Marathon Nat. Bank, L.A.; host radio program The Competitive Edge; mem. expdn. to Syria and Jordan, 1994, to Morocco, 1995; mem. WORID Bus. Acad.; instr. Learning Annex; instr. Asian program U. So. Calif., 1998; presenter, cons., spkr. in field. Author: Solid Gold Customer Relations and Success Secrets, Travel for Scholars, Paris, 1999; featured in tng. films Power of Words; author: Cassette Libraries, How to Present Seminars, Sound Selling. Bd. dirs. Ctr. Theatre Group, Town Hall, Music Ctr., Odyssey Theater; asst. dir. Burnhill Prodns., 1992—, asst. dir. Cabaret, Palisades Theatre; dir. Improv Corp.; vol. Exec. Svc. Corp., 1996—, CEO Leadership Forum, Lacma Coun. Mem. ASTD, Am. Film Inst. Assn., Sales and Mktg. Execs., Nat. Spkrs. Assn., Nat. Platform Assn., Women in Bus., KCET Women's Coun., Exec. Svc. Corps, World Affairs Coun., Blue Ribbon, Women in Arts, Women in Film, Manuscript Soc. Forum Scotland, Plato Soc., Brandeis U. Women, Sierra Club (Toure de Mt. Blanc), Supreme Ct. Hist. Soc., Dispute Resolution Svcs., Faces of History, Women of LA, Marina Del Rey C. of C., Internat. CEO Exec. Forum, Manuscript Soc., Brandeis Film Group, LACMA (vol. svcs.), OSHA, UCLA, Beach Film Buffs Westside Dem. Club. Avocations: collecting famous manuscripts, music, theater, writing. Office: PO Box 11447 Marina Del Rey CA 90295 Office Phone: 310-823-0202. Personal E-mail: cconsult@aol.com.

GOLD, CHRISTINA A., data processing company executive; b. Can., 1947; d. Peter. BA, Carleton U., Ottawa, 1969; degree (hon.), U. Montreal, 1991. With human resources, sales, mktg., fin. and mgmt. depts. Avon Can., 1970-89, pres., CEO, 1989-93, head oper. bus. unit, 1993; sr. v.p., pres. Avon North Am., NYC, 1993-98; exec. v.p. Global Direct Selling Devel., NYC, 1997-98; co-CEO Teleglobe, Inc.; CEO Beaconsfield Group, 1998—99; chmn., pres., CEO Excel Comm., Inc., Dallas, 1999—2002; sr. exec. v.p. First Data Corp., 2002—06; pres. The Western Union Co. (divsn. First Data Corp.), Greenwood Village, Colo., 2002—06; pres., CEO The Western Union Co., Greenwood Village, Colo., 2006—. Bd. dirs. Meredith Corp., 1999—2001, The Torstar Corp., The Conf. Bd., ITT Industries, NY Life Investment Mgmt. LLC, Western Union Co., 2006—. Named one of 50 Most Powerful Women in Bus., Fortune mag., 2006, 2008, 50 Women to Watch, Wall St. Jour., 2006, 100 Most Powerful Women, Forbes mag., 2007, 2008. Mem.: Direct Selling Assn. (bd. dirs.), Conf. Bd. NY and Can. (bd. dirs). Office: Western Union Co PO Box 6992 Greenwood Village CO 80155

GOLD, RICK L., water resources consultant; b. Rexburg, Idaho, June 25, 1946; s. Raymond Russell and Thelma (Lee) G.; m. Anamarie Sanone, May 14, 1988; children: Nanette Phillips, Russell. BSCE, Utah State U., 1968, MSCE, 1970. Registered profl. engr., Colo., Mont., Utah. Hydraulic engr. U.S. Bur. Reclamation, Provo, Utah, 1969-73, project hydrologist Durango, Colo., 1973-75, regional hydrologist Billings, Mont., 1975-81, spl. asst. to regional dir. Washington, 1981-82, asst. planning officer Billings, 1982-83, projects mgr. Durango, Colo., 1983-88, regional planning officer Salt Lake City, 1988-90, asst. regional dir., 1990-94, dep. regional dir., 1994—2000, regional dir., 2001—07, ret. fed. svc., 2007; mgr. Gold H2O Pro., L.C., 2007—. Mem. water quality com. Internat. Joint Commn. Study on Garrison Divsn. Unit, Billings, 1975-77; fed. negotiator Cost Sharing and Indian Water Rights Settlement, Durango, 1986-88; chmn. Cooperating Agy. on Glen Canyon Dam EIS, Salt Lake City, 1990-94. Contbr. articles to profl. jours.; author papers. Mem. Rotary Internat., Durango, 1985-87; bd. dirs. United Way of La Plata County, Durango, 1983-88; chmn. Combined Fed. Campaign, La Plata County, 1985; bd. dirs. U.S. Com. on Irrigation and Drainage, 1994-2000. Mem. ASCE. Office Phone: 801-931-7103. Business E-Mail: goldh2opro@comcast.net.

GOLDBERG, CATHERINE T., lawyer; b. Devils Lake, ND, June 28, 1950; AB summa cum laude, U. ND, 1971; JD magna cum laude, U. N. Mex., 1975. Bar: N. Mex. 1975. Law clk. to Hon. Howard C. Bratton U.S. Dist. Ct., Dist. N. Mex., 1975—76; dir. Rodey, Dickason, Sloan, Akin & Robb PA, Albuquerque. Named to Best Lawyers in Am. in real estate and banking, 1995—, Chamber's America's Leading Lawyers for Bus., 2004, 2005. Mem.: Albuquerque Mus. Art, History & Sci. (found. bd. 1987—93, 1994—2000, art adv. com. 1996—, bd. trustees 2000—), Albuquerque Econ. Devel. Forum, Albuquerque Bar Assn. (former pres.), ABA (real property probate & trust law sect., bus. law sect.), Am. Coll. Mortgage Attys. (trustee, opinions com.), Am. Coll. Real Estate Lawyers (new mem.'s com.), Phi Beta Kappa, Order of Coif. Office: Rodey Dickason Sloan Akin & Robb PA 201 Third St NW Ste 2200 PO Box 1888 Albuquerque NM 87103 Office Phone: 505-768-7318. Business E-Mail: ctgoldberg@rodey.com.

GOLDBERG, DAVID THEO, law educator, writer; b. Pretoria, South Africa, Jan. 8, 1952; came to U.S., 1978; s. Isidore and Florence (Lief) G.; m. Alena Luter, June 25, 1984; 1 child, Gabriel Dylan. BA in Econs. and Philosophy, U. Cape Town, South Africa, 1973, BA in Philosophy with honors, 1975, MA in Philosophy, 1978; PhD in Philosophy, CUNY, 1985. Adj. asst. prof. NYU, NYC, 1984-87, Hunter Coll., CUNY, 1984-87; co-pres. Metafilms, NYC, 1982-88; asst. prof. Drexel U., Phila., 1987-90; asst. prof. justice studies Ariz. State U., Tempe, 1990-92, assoc. prof., 1992-94, prof., dir., chair Sch. Justice Studies, 1995-2000; dir. Humanities Rsch. Inst. U. Calif., 2000—, prof. African Am. studies and criminology, law and soc. Irvine, 2000—. Author: Ethical Theory and Social Issues, 1989, Racist Culture: Philosophy and the Politics of Meaning, 1993, Racial Subjects: Writing on Race in America, 1997, The Racial State, 2001; editor: Anatomy of Racism, 1990, Multiculturalism: A Critical Reader, 1994; co-editor: Social Identities: A Journal of Race, Nation and Culture, Jewish Identity, 1993, Race Critical Themes, 2001, Blackwell Companion to Racial and Ethnic Studies, 2001, Between Law and Culture, 2001; co-dir. film The Island, 1982. Grantee N.Y. State Coun. on Arts, 1981, NSF, 1991, ACLS, 1988. Mem. Am. Philos. Assn. (mem. com. on Blacks 1992—), Law and Soc. Assn., Greater Phila. Philosophy Consortium (colloquia com. 1989-90), Soc. for Philosophy and Pub. Affairs (exec. com. 1987-88). Avocations: reading, swimming, surfing.

GOLDBERG, JACKIE, councilwoman; b. LA; 1 child, Brian. Tchr. Compton and L.A. Unified Sch. Dists.; instr. Calif. State U.; city councilwoman City of L.A., 1993—2000; mem. Calif. Ho. of Reps., 2000—. Chairwoman Personnel Com.; vice chairwoman Intergovt. Rels. Office: PO Box 942849 Sacramento CA 94249

GOLDBERG, MARK ARTHUR, neurologist; b. NYC, Sept. 4, 1934; s. Jacob and Bertha (Grushlawska) G.; 1 child, Jonathan. BS, Columbia U., 1955; PhD, U. Chgo., 1959, MD, 1962. Resident neurology NY Neurol. Inst., NYC, 1963-66; asst. prof. neurology Columbia U. Coll. Phys. and Surgs., NYC, 1968-71; assoc. prof. neurology and pharmacology UCLA, 1971-77, emeritus prof. neurology and pharmacology, 1977—; chair dept. neurology Harbor UCLA Med. Ctr., Torrance, 1977—2005. Contbr. articles to profl. jours., chpts. to books. Capt. US Army, 1966-68. Fellow Am. Neurol. Assn., Am. Acad. Neurology; mem. L.A. Neurol. Soc., Palos Verdes Land Conservancy. Avocation: oriental cusine. E-mail: mrkgldbrg@yahoo.com.

GOLDBERG, MITCHEL R., federal judge; b. 1943; BA, U. Colo., 1965, JD, 1968. With Rosen & Goldberg, Santa Ana, Calif., 1971-80; pvt. practice, 1981-88; apptd. bankruptcy judge cen. dist. U.S. Dist. Ct. Calif., 1988. With U.S. Army, 1969-70. Office: 3420 12th St Riverside CA 92501-3801

GOLDBERG, MORRIS, internist; b. Jan. 23, 1928; s. Saul and Lena (Schanberg) G.; m. Elaine Shaw, June 24, 1956; children: Alan Neil, Seth David, Nancy Beth. BS in Chemistry cum laude, Poly. Inst. Bklyn., 1951; MD, SUNY, Bklyn., 1956. Diplomate Am. Bd. Internal Medicine. Intern Jewish Hosp., Bklyn., 1956-57, resident, 1957-58, 61-62, renal fellow, 1958-59; practice medicine specializing in internal medicine NYC, 1962-71, Phoenix, 1971—. Instr. to asst. clin. prof. internal medicine State U. N.Y. Coll. Medicine, Bklyn., 1962-71; clin. investigator, metabolic research unit Jewish Hosp. Bklyn., 1962-71; cons. in field; mem. staff Phoenix Bapt., St. Joseph's Hosp., Vets. Affairs Med. Ctr., Phoenix. Contbr. articles to med. jours. Capt. M.C., U.S. Army, 1959-61. Fellow ACP; mem. AMA, Am. Soc. Internal Medicine, Am. Coll. Nuclear Physicians (charter mem.), Am. Soc. Nephrology, Am. Soc. Hypertension (charter mem.), Ariz. Med. Assn., 38th Parallel Med. Soc., S. Korea, Ariz., Maricopa County Med. Assn., Sigma Xi, Phi Lambda Upsilon, Alpha Omega Alpha. Office: Vets Affairs Med Ctr 650 E Indian School Rd Phoenix AZ 85012-1839 Office Phone: 602-277-5551. Personal E-mail: mgmd28@cox.net.

GOLDBERG, ROBERT B., molecular biologist, educator; b. Cleve., May 28, 1944; BS in botany, Ohio Univ., Athens, OH, 1966; MS in genetics, Univ. Ariz., Tucson, 1969, PhD in genetics, 1971. Asst. prof. Wayne State U., Detroit, 1973—76, UCLA, 1976—78, assoc. prof., 1978—83, prof., 1983—96, Disting. Prof. Molecular, Cell, and Devel. Biology, 1996—. Program dir. Genetic Mechanisms for Crop Improvement USDA, 1983, program dir. Plant Genetics and Molecular Biology, 84; chmn. Divsn. Cell, Molecular and Plant Biology UCLA, 1983, dir. Plant Molecular Biology Program, 1991—96, dir. Multicampus Seed Inst., 1986—; chair Edn. Found. Am. Soc. Plant Biologists, 1998—2002; co-founder and dir. Ceres Inc., Malibu, Calif., 1996—. Edtl. bd. (jour.) Developmental Genetics, 1981—84, Plant Molecular Biology, 1982—87, Molecular and General Genetics, 1982—87, Science, 1986—89, Sexual Plant Reproduction, 1998—, founding editor and editor-in-chief The Plant Cell, 1988—93. Recipient Recognition Disting. Tchg. and Rsch., Ohio House Rep., 1991, Disting. Svc. Award, Am. Soc. Plant Physiologists, 1993, Nat. Order Sci. Merit, Pres. of Brazil, 1998, Gold Shield Award, UCLA, 1998; named to NAS, 2001; grantee Professorship, Howard Hughes Med. Inst., 2002—. Office: UCLA Life Sciences Building 2835 Los Angeles CA 90095 Office Phone: 310-825-9093, 310-825-3270. E-mail: bobg@ucla.edu.

GOLDBERG, STEVEN MURRAY, lawyer; b. San Francisco, Feb. 25, 1957; s. Daniel T. and Tanette Goldberg; m. Renée Miguel, Aug. 25, 1984; children: Rachel, Sarah. BA in Journalism, San Jose State U., 1979; JD, U. Calif., Berkeley, 1984. Bar: Calif. 1984, US Dist. Ct. (no. dist. Calif.) 1984. Assoc. Schwab & Hibser, San Francisco, 1985-89, Goldberg & Brauer, San Francisco, 1989-92, Ropers, Majeski, Kohn & Bentley, Santa Rosa, Calif., 1992-96, Lanahan & Reilly, Santa Rosa, Calif., 1997; ptnr. Friedemann Goldberg, Santa Rosa, Calif. Mem. Redwood Empire estate planning coun., Santa Rosa, 1993—. Contbr. articles to profl. publs. Pres. bd. dirs. Village in the Park Homeowners Assn., Daly City, Calif., 1991-92; mem. estate planning subcommittee Marin and Sonoma Jewish Cmty. Fedn., San Rafael, Calif., 1992—. Named a Super Lawyer, No. Calif. Super Lawyers, 2006; named one of Top 100 Attys., Worth mag., 2005, 2006. Mem. State Bar of Calif. (estate planning and taxation sects. 1989—), Sonoma Bar Assn. Avocations: fiction writing, science, astronomy, sports. Office: Friedemann Goldberg LLP Ste 201 420 Aviation Blvd Santa Rosa CA 95403 Office Phone: 707-543-4900. Office Fax: 707-543-4910. E-mail: sgoldberg@frigolaw.com.

GOLDEN, T. MICHAEL, state supreme court justice; b. 1942; BA in History, U. Wyo., 1964, JD, 1967; LLM, U. Va., 1992. Bar: Wyo. 1967, U.S. Dist. Ct. 1967, U.S. Ct. Appeals (10th cir.) 1967, U.S. Supreme Ct. 1970. Mem. firm Brimmer, MacPherson & Golden, Rawlins, Wyo., 1971-83, Williams, Porter, Day & Neville, Casper, Wyo., 1983-88; chief justice Wyo. Supreme Ct., Cheyenne, 1994—96, justice, 1988—. Mem. Wyo. State Bd. Law Examiners, 1977-82, 86-88. Capt. US Army, 1967—71. Mem.: Wyo. State Bar Assn. Office: Wyo Supreme Ct Bldg 2301 Capitol Ave Cheyenne WY 82001

GOLDFARB, ROBERT PAUL, neurological surgeon; b. St. Paul, July 17, 1936; s. Jack and Frances S. (Singer) G.; m. Lesley G. Zatz, Aug. 11, 1963; children: Jill, Pam. BA with distinction, U. Ariz., 1958; MD, Tulane U., 1962. Diplomate Am. Bd. Neurol. Surgery. Intern Michael Reese Hosp., Chgo., 1962-63; resident gen. surgery Presbyn. St. Luke's Hosp., Chgo., 1963-64; resident neurol. surgery U. Ill. Rsch. Hosp., Chgo., 1963-67; pres. med. staff Crippled Children's Svc. So. Ariz., Tucson, 1973-75; chief staff Tucson Med. Ctr., 1978-80; neurol. surgeon Western Neurosurgery, Ltd., Tucson, 1980—. Bd. disr. S.W. Physician Network; neurosurg. cons. U. Ariz. athletic teams, Tucson, 1980—; trustee El Dorado Hosp., 1999—2005; mem. Ariz. Bd. Med. Examiners, 2002—, bd. sec., 2003-04, chmn. bd., 2006. Maj. USAFR, 1962-70. Baird scholar U. Ariz., 1958. Fellow ACS; mem. Am. Assn. Neurol. Surgeons, Congress Neurol. Surgeons, Am. Coll. Physician Exec., Rocky Mountain Neurosurg. Soc. (v.p. 1979). Office: Western Neurosurgery Ltd 6567 E Carondelet Dr Ste 305 Tucson AZ 85710

GOLDFARB, TIMOTHY MOORE, hospital administrator; b. Jerome, Ariz., Dec. 15, 1949; married. B, Ariz. State U., 1975, MHA, 1978. Adminstrv. resident Univ. Med. Ctr., Tucson, 1977-78, mgr. patient accts., 1978-79; asst. adminstr. Tucson Gen. Hosp., 1979, Univ. Med. Ctr., Tucson, 1979-83, assoc. adminstr., 1983-84; assoc. hosp. dir. Oreg. Health Scis. Univ. Hosp., Portland, 1984-89, health care sys. dir., 1989—. Office: Oreg Health Scis Univ Hosp 3181 SW Sam Jackson Park Rd Portland OR 97201-3011

GOLDFIELD, EMILY DAWSON, finance company executive, artist; b. Bklyn., May 31, 1947; d. Martin and Renee (Solow) Dawson; m. Stephen Gary Goldfield, June 17, 1973; children: Stacy Rose, Daniel James. BS, U. Mich., 1969; MEd, Pa. State U., 1971; PhD, U. So. Calif., 1977. Chmn. bd. Union Home Loan, Inc. Author: The Value of Creative Dance, 1971; Development of Creative Dance, 1977. U. Mich. scholar, 1969; Pa. State U. fellow, 1970, U. So. Calif. fellow, 1972. Mem.: Nat. Notary Assn., Pastel Soc. Gold Coast, Allied Artists of the Santa Monica Mountains, Pastel Soc. of the West Coast, Calif. Art Club, Calif. Mortgage Assn. Office: 23586 Calabasas Rd Ste 201 Calabasas CA 91302-1322

GOLDHABER, GERSON, astrophysicist, researcher; b. Chemnitz, Germany, Feb. 20, 1924; came to US, 1948, naturalized, 1953; s. Charles and Ethel (Frisch) G.; m. Judith Margoshes, May 30, 1969; children: Amos Nathaniel, Michaela Shally, Shaya Alexandra M.Sc., Hebrew U., Jerusalem, 1947; PhD, U. Wis., 1950; PhD honoris causus, U. Stockholm, 1986. Instr. Columbia U., NYC, 1950-53; acting asst. prof. physics U. Calif., Berkeley, 1953-54, asst. prof., 1954-58, assoc. prof., 1958-63, prof. physics, 1963-92, prof. physics emeritus, 1992—; Miller research prof. Miller Inst. Basic Sci. U. Calif.-Berkeley, 1958-59, 75-76, 84-85, prof. Grad. Sch., 1994—; Morris Loeb lectr. in physics Harvard U., 1976-77. Co-author (with R.N. Cahn): (textbook) The Experimental Foundations of Particle Physics, 2008. Named Calif. Scientist of Yr., 1977, Sci. Assoc., CERN, 1986. Gruber prize in Cosmology, 2007; Ford Found. fellow CERN, 1960-61; Guggenheim fellow CERN, 1972-73. Fellow Am. Phys. Soc. (Panofsky prize 1991, co-recipient Gruber prize 2007), Sigma Xi; mem. Am. Astron. Soc., Royal Swedish Acad. Sci. (fgn.), Nat. Acad. Sci. Achievements include discovery of the antiproton annihilation process; Bose-Einstein nature of Pions; J/Psi and Psion spectroscopy; charmed Mesons; dark energy. Avocations: drawing, painting. Office: Lawrence Berkeley Nat Lab Physics Ms 50 R5008 Berkeley CA 94720-0001 Office Phone: 510-486-6210. Business E-Mail: gerson@lbl.gov.

GOLDING, SUSAN G., former mayor; b. Muskogee, Okla., Aug. 18, 1945; d. Brage and Hinda Fay (Wolf) G.; children: Samuel, Vanessa. Cert. Pratique de Langue Francaise, U. Paris, 1965; BA in Govt. and Internat. Rels., Carleton Coll., 1966; MA in Romance Philology, Columbia U., 1974. Assoc. editor Columbia U. Jour. of Internat. Affairs, NYC, 1968-69; teaching fellow Emory U., Atlanta, 1973-74; instr. San Diego Community Coll. Dist., 1978; assoc. pub., gen. mgr. The News Press Group, San Diego, 1978-80; city council mem. City of San Diego, 1981-83; dep. sec. bus., transp., housing State of Calif., Sacramento, 1983-84; county supr. dist. 3 County of San Diego, 1984-92; mayor City of San Diego, 1992—2000; pres. & CEO The Golding Group, Inc., San Diego, 2000—; head Homeland Security Office, Titan Corp., San Diego, 2000—. Chmn. San Diego Drug Strike Force, 1987-88, Calif. Housing Fin. Agy., Calif. Coastal Commn.; bd. dirs. San Diego County Water Authority; trustee So. Calif. Water Com., Inc.; founder Mid City Comml. Revitalization Task Force, Strategic Trade Alliance, 1993, Calif. Big 10 City Mayors, 1993; mem. Gov. Calif. Mil. Base Reuse Task Force, 1994; established San Diego World Trade Ctr., 1993, San Diego City/State/County Regional Permit Assistance Ctr., 1994; mem. adv. bd. U.S. Conf. of Mayors, 1994; chair Gov. Wilson's Commn. on Local Governance for 21st Century. Bd. dirs. Child Abuse Prevention Found., San Diego Conv. and Vis. Bur., Crime Victims Fund, United Cerebral Palsy, San Diego Air Quality Bd., San Diego March of Dimes, Rep. Assocs.; adv. bd. Girl Scouts U.S.; trustee So. Calif. Water Comm.; mem. Rep. State Cen. Com.; co-chair com. Presidency George Bush Media Fund, Calif.; chair San Diego County Regional Criminal Justice Coun., race rels. com. Citizens Adv. Com. on Racial Intergration, San Diego Unified Sch. Dist.; hon. chair Am. Cancer Soc's. Residential Crusade, 1988. Recipient Alice Paul award Nat. Women's Polit. Caucus, 1987, Calif. Women in Govt. Achievement award, 1988, Willie Velasquez Polit. award Mex. Am. Bus. and Profl. Assn., 1988, Catalyst of Chance award Greater San Diego C. of C., 1994, Woman Who Means Bus. award San Diego Bus. Jour., 1994, Internat. Citizen award World Affairs Coun., 1994; named One of San Diego's Ten Outstanding Young Citizens, 1981, One of Ten Outstanding Rep. County Ofcls. in U.S.A., Rep. Nat. Com., 1987, San Diego Woman of Achievement Soroptimists Internat., 1988. Mem. Nat. Assn. of Counties (chair Op. Fair Share, mem. taxation and fin. com.), Nat. Women's Forum. Republican. Jewish. Office: The Golding Group Inc 7770 Regents Rd Ste 113 San Diego CA 92122 E-mail: commerce@golding.org.

GOLDMAN, ALLAN BAILEY, lawyer; b. Auburn, NY, Jan. 1, 1937; s. Charles and Rose Hortense (Abrahams) G.; m. Eleanor Ruth Levy, May 26, 1963; children: Jennifer Brooke Horwitz, Andrea Allison Gellert. AB magna cum laude, Harvard U., 1958, JD, 1963; LHD (hon.), Hebrew Union Coll.-Jewish Inst. Religion, 1992. Bar: Calif. 1964, D.C. 1977, U.S. Supreme Ct. 1977. Assoc. Wyman, Bautzer, Kuchel & Silbert, Beverly Hills, Calif., 1963-67, ptnr. LA, 1967-91, Katten Muchin Rosenman, LLP, LA, 1991—. Judge pro-tem Calif. Mcpl. and Small Claims Cts.; arbitrator Calif. Superior Ct. Contbr. articles to profl. jours. Chmn. Attys. for Brown for Gov., officer Brown for Pres., 1976; founder LA Com. for Civil Rights Under Law, Mus. Contemporary Art., LA, Fraternity of Friends of LA Music Ctr.; trustee Calif. Mus. Sci. and Industry, 1981-89, St. John's Hosp. and Health Ctr. Found., 1978—, exec. com., 1979-89, 2006-, chmn., 2008-, bd. dirs., 1989-95, 2006—, treas., 1990-94, chmn., 1994-95; chmn. nat. bd. trustees Union of Am. Hebrew Congregations, 1987-91, trustee, 1977-, officer, 1985-; bd. govs. Hebrew Union Coll.-Jewish Inst. Religion, 1988-, bd. overseers LA campus, 1981-85, 1988-2007, vice chair, 1997-2007; trustee HUC Skirball Cultural Ctr., 1997—; pres. Leo Baeck Temple, LA, 1975-77; mem. Conf. Pres.'s Major Jewish Orgns., 1987-91; mem. synagogue funding com. Jewish Fedn. Coun. of Greater LA, 1979, chmn., 1985-88; Calif. Commn. Jud. Nominees Evaluation, 1999-2002. Lt. USN, 1958—60. Named Humanitarian of Yr., NCCJ, 1995. Mem. Calif. Bar Assn., D.C. Bar Assn. Democrat. Jewish. Avocations: trekking, tennis. Home: 347 Conway Ave Los Angeles CA 90024-2603 Office: Katten Muchin Rosenman LLP 2029 Century Park E Ste 2600 Los Angeles CA 90067 Home Phone: 310-475-5621; Office Phone: 310-788-4520. Business E-Mail: allan.goldman@kattenlaw.com.

GOLDMAN, BENJAMIN EDWARD, lawyer; b. NYC, Feb. 25, 1940; s. William Wolfe and Blanche (Kallenburg) G.; m. Lynda Ann Schwartz, July 27, 1950; children: Brian Edward, Victoria Beth, Adam Edward BS, NYU, 1965; JD, Fordham U., 1968; LLM, Georgetown U., 1970. Bar: N.Y. 1968, D.C. 1972, U.S. Dist. D.C., U.S. Ct. Appeals (D.C., 4th, 5th and 9th cirs.), Calif. 1986, U.S. Dist. Ct. (cen. dist.) Calif. 1986. Atty., advisor to chmn. NLRB, Washington, 1968-72; assoc. Arent, Fox, Kitner, Plotkin, Kahn, Washington, 1972-75; ptnr. Feldman, Krieger, Goldman, Tisch, Washington, 1976-83, Memel, Jacobs, Pierno, Gersh & Ellsworth, LA, 1984-87, Graham and James, LA, 1987-2001, Squire, Sanders & Dempsey LLP, LA, 2001—07, Squire Sanders, LA, 2007—. Mem. com. on devel. law under NLRB Act, 1968—; speaker Healthcare Fin. Mgmt. Assn., Calif., 1987, Nat. Health Edn. Conf. on AIDS, 1987, Inst. Corp. Counsel, 1986, Hosp. Coun. N. Calif., 1985, others. Contbr. articles to profl. jours. Mem. ABA (forum com. on health law 1983, mem. labor and employment law sect. 1968—), Nat. Health Lawyers Assn. (speaker ann. healthlaw update 1985), Calif. Bar Assn., N.Y. Bar Assn., D.C. Bar Assn., Am. Acad. Hosp. Attys. Office: Squire Sanders Ste 3100 555 S Flower St Los Angeles CA 90071-2300 Home Phone: 310-375-4521; Office Phone: 213-624-2500. Office Fax: 213-623-4581. E-mail: bgoldman@ssd.com.

GOLDMAN, DONALD AARON, lawyer; b. NYC, Sept. 11, 1947; BA, UCLA, 1969, JD, 1972. Bar: Calif. 1972. Dep. atty. gen. Calif. Dept. Justice, LA, 1972-79; ptnr. Memel, Jacobs & Ellsworth, LA, 1979-87; ptnr., mem. firm exec. mgmt. com., chmn. firm compensation com. McDermott, Will & Emery LLP, LA, 1987—. Mem. Nat. Health Lawyers. Avocations: golf, music. Office: McDermott Will & Emery LLP 2049 Century Park E Los Angeles CA 90067-3101 Office Phone: 310-551-9319. Office Fax: 310-277-4730. Business E-Mail: dogoldman@mwe.com.

GOLDMAN, GERALD HILLIS, beverage distribution company executive; b. Omaha, July 26, 1947; s. Lester Jack and Lilyan Haykin (Weiskopf) G.; m. Cathy Evelyn Brightman, Dec. 15, 1973; children: Lori, Jeffrey. BSBA, U. Nebr., 1969; MBA, U. So. Calif., 1975. C.P.A., Calif., Nebr. Sr. acct. Arthur Andersen & Co., Los Angeles, 1969-72; exec. v.p., CFO CORE-MARK Internat., Inc., Richmond, B.C., Can., 1972-86, exec. v.p., 1986-87; pres. Gen. Acceptance Corp., Los Angeles, 1986-87; CFO, sr. v.p. fin. and ops. Alaska Distbrs., Inc., Seattle, 1987—. Mem. AICPA, Calif. Soc. CPAs, Fin. Execs. Inst.

GOLDMAN, JOEL A., lawyer; b. NYC, May 27, 1942; s. Solomon and Lee Goldman; m. Shirley Ann Curnow, Jan. 15, 1967; children: David Abraham, Nanette Francis, Jonathan Michael. BA, Grinnell Coll., Iowa, 1964; JD, U. So. Calif., LA, 1967. Bar: Calif. Assoc. Getz, Akins & Manning, LA, 1967—71; ptnr. Buchalter, Nemer, Fields, LA, 1971—94, Heenan Blaikie, Beverly Hills, Calif., 1994—95, Stephens Berg & Lasater McKenna & Cuneo, LA, 1995—2002, Russ, August & Kabat, LA, 2002—03, Lewis Brisbois Bisgaard & Smith LLP, LA, 2004—. Mem. grants com. Robert Russell Found., Miami, Fla., 1984—; v.p. Bell Canyon Assn., 1999—2002; bd. dirs. Encino Property Owners' Assn., Calif., 1978—94, Bell Canyon Assn., Calif., 1999—2002. Younker Acad. scholar, Grinnell Coll., 1960—64. Mem.: Comm. Law League Am., Assn. Bus. Trial Lawyers, LA Complex Litigation Inn of Ct., LA County Bar Assn. (comm. law and bankruptcy sect.), Calif. Bar Assn. (com. adminstrn. justice, litigation sect.). Jewish. Avocations: fishing, sports. Office: Lewis Brisbois Bisgaard & Smith LLP 221 N Figueroa St Ste 1200 Los Angeles CA 90012

GOLDMAN, RICHARD N., foundation administrator; b. San Francisco, Apr. 16, 1920; s. Richard and Alice Goldman; m. Rhoda Haas (dec.); children: Richard (dec.), John, Douglas, Susan. BA, U. Calif., Berkeley, 1941, postgrad. Chmn. Goldman Ins. Svcs.; pres. Richard and Rhoda Goldman Fund. Former mem. port commn., pub. utilities commn., chief of protocol City and County of San Francisco. Trustee World Fine Arts Mus. San Francisco, Nat. Symphony, U. Calif.-Berkeley Berkeley Found., Washington Inst. for Near East Policy, World Affairs Coun. No. Calif.; bd. dirs. Am. Jewish History Soc., Internat. House, Berkeley, Jerusalem Found., League to Save Lake Tahoe, San Francisco Ballet; mem. coun. Yosemite Fund; mem. exec. com. Bay Area Internat. Forum; mem. dv. com. Bus. Execs. for Nat. Security; bd. visitors Inst. for Internat. Studies, Stanford U.; bd. dirs., former pres. Jewish Cmty. Fedn., San Francisco; mem. adv. coun. Pacific Grad. Sch. Psychology; mem. governing coun. Save-the-Redwoods League; mem. pres.' adv. coun. San Francisco State U. With U.S. Army, 1942-46. Recipient The Chairman's Medal, Heinz Awards, 2005. Mem. San Francisco Planning and Urban Renewal Assn. (mem. adv. coun.), Concordia-Argonaut Club, The Family, Villa Taverna, Calif. Tennis Club. Office: Richard Rhoda Goldman Fund PO Box 29924 San Francisco CA 94129-0924

GOLDMAN, RONALD L.M., lawyer; b. NY, Nov. 21, 1937; s. George and Susan Goldman; m. Elizabeth H. Shenk, 1958 (div. 1972); children: Randall, Cheryl; m. Mary D. Petrinovich, 1985 (div. 1986); m. Judith Marlane, Sept. 7, 1990. BSL, U. Southern Calif., LA, 1960, JD, 1962. Cert.: Nat. Bd. Trial Advocacy (civil trial adv.), registered:, bar: Ctrl. Dist. Calif. (US Dist. Ct.) 1963, cert.: Northern Dist. Ill. 2006, Eastern Dist. Calif. 2006, Ctrl. Dist. Ill. 2008, Tenth Cir. (US Ct Appeals) 1970, (US Supreme Ct.) 1971, US Ct. Fed. Claims 1974, bar: US Ct. Appeals (9th cir.) 1973, US Ct. Appeals (2nd cir.) 1977, US Ct. Appeals (6th cir.) 1982, US Ct. Appeals (3rd cir.) 2008, Dist. Ct. Columbia 1979, Calif. (US Dist. Ct. (no. dist.)) 1983, NY (US Dist. Cts. (we. and ea. dists.)) 2009. Spl. guest lectr. NY Law Conf., Manila Law Conf., Madrid Law Conf., Christchurch Poly. Sch. Broadcasting, New Zealand, Shanghai Sch. Social Scis.; lectr. Belli Seminars, Town Hall; owner Ronald L. Goldman Assoc., LA, 1963, 1968—72; ptnr. Fields Goldman Gessler, LA, 1963—68, Goldman, Gangloff Boehme, LA, 1972—76; pres. RLMG, ALC, LA, 1976—; adj. prof., law Pepperdine U. Sch. Law, 1968—89; shareholder Baum Hedlund Aristei Goldman, LA, 2003—. Mediator LA Superior Ct., arbitrator, Am. Arbitration Assn., 1994. Contbr. articles to profl. jours. Gen. coun. Family Assistance Program Hollywood; gen. coun. and founder Women Clinic, LA. Named one of Bar Register of Preeminent Lawyers; named to Super Lawyer, Southern Calif., 2005—09. Mem.: ABA, Pub. Justice, Plaintiffs Steering Com., Tort Litig., Internat. Bar Assn., Aviation Law Com., LA County Bar Assn., Consumer Attys. Assn. LA, Consumer Attys. Calif., World Assn. Law Professors, World Peace Through Law Ctr. (founding mem.), World Jurist Assn., Lawyer-Pilots Bar Assn., Am. Assn. Justice, Ostriches Anonymous Assn. (life). Office: Baum Hedlund Aristei Goldman 12100 Wilshire Blvd Ste 950 Los Angeles CA 90025-7107

GOLDMAN, TYLER, Internet company executive, lawyer; BA, Dartmouth Coll.; JD, Northwestern U., MBA with honors. Atty. Wilson, Sonsini, Goodrich & Rosati, Steinberg & Moorad; founder, CEO, pres. Broadband Sports, Inc. (BSS), 1998; sr. v.p. bus. and corp. devel. Movielink, 2002—05; bd. mem., acting pres. Feedster; CEO Buzznet, 2007—. Office: Buzznet 6464 Sunset Blvd 6th Fl Hollywood CA 90028 also: 555 Fifth Ave 14th Fl New York NY 10017 Office Phone: 213-252-8999, 212-918-0690. Office Fax: 323-466-0150.

GOLDMAN, WILLIAM, writer, scriptwriter; b. Chgo., Aug. 12, 1931; s. M. Clarence and Marion (Well) Goldman; m. Ilene Jones, Apr. 15, 1961; children: Jenny, Susanna. BA, Oberlin Coll., 1952; MA, Columbia U., 1956. Author: (novels) The Temple of Gold, 1957, Your Turn to Curtsy, My Turn to Bow, 1958, Soldier in the Rain, 1960, Boys and Girls Together, 1964, No Way to Treat a Lady, 1964, The Thing of It Is, 1967, Father's Day, 1971, The Princess Bride, 1973, Marathon Man, 1974, Wigger, 1974, Magic, 1976, Tinsel, 1979, Control, 1982, The Silent Gondoliers, 1983, The Color of Light, 1984, Heat, 1985, Brothers, 1987, (non-fiction) The Season: A Candid Look at Broadway, 1969, Adventures in the Screen Trade, 1983; author: (with Mike Lupica) Wait Until Next year, 1988, Hype and Glory, 1990, Four Screenplays, 1995, Five Screenplays, 1997, Which Lie Did I Tell, 2000; author: (essays) The Big Picture, 1999; author: (with James Goldman) (plays) Blood Sweat and Stanley Poole, 1961; author: (with James Goldman and John Kander) (musical) A Family Affair, 1962; author: (films) Masquerade, 1965, Harper, 1966, Butch Cassidy and the Sundance Kid, 1969 (Acad. award Best Original Screenplay, 1970), The Hot Rock, 1972, The Stepford Wives, 1974, The Great Waldo Pepper, 1975, Marathon Man, 1976, All the President's Men, 1976 (Acad. award Best Screenplay Adaptation, 1977), A Bridge Too Far, 1977, Magic, 1978, The Princess Bride, 1987, Heat, 1987, Misery, 1990, The Year of the Comet, 1992, Memoirs of an Invisible Man, 1992, Chaplin, 1992, Maverick, 1994, Ghost and the Darkness, 1996, Absolute Power, 1997, Hearts in Atlantis, 2001, Dreamcatcher, 2003. Recipient Laurel award for Lifetime Achievement in Screenwriting, 1983. Personal E-mail: longbaugh@aol.com.

GOLDREICH, PETER MARTIN, astrophysics and planetary physics educator; b. NYC, July 14, 1939; s. Paul and Edith (Rosenfield) Goldreich; m. Susan Kroll, June 14, 1960; children: Eric, Daniel. BS in Engring. Physics, Cornell U., Ithaca, NY, 1960, PhD in Physics, 1963. Part-time instr. Cornell U., 1961—63; postdoctoral fellow Cambridge U., 1963—64; asst. prof. astronomy and geophysics UCLA, 1964—66; assoc. prof. planetary sci. and astronomy Calif. Inst. Tech., Pasadena, 1966—69, prof., 1969—81, Lee A. DuBridge prof. astrophysics and planetary physics, 1981—, emeritus prof., 2003—; prof. sch. natural scis. Inst. Advanced Study, Princeton, NJ, 2003—. Recipient Chapman medal, Royal Astron. Soc., 1985, Gold medal, 1990, Nat. Medal of Sci., 1995, Antoinette de Vaucouleurs medal, U. Tex., 1999, Grande médaille, French Acad. Scis., 2006, Shaw prize, Astronomy, Shaw Prize Found., Hong Kong, 2007; named Calif. Scientist of Yr., 1981; grantee Woodrow Wilson Hon. fellowship, 1960—61; fellow NSF, 1961—63, Sloan Found., 1968—70. Fellow: NAS, Am. Acad. Arts and Scis.; mem.: Royal Soc. (foreign mem. 2003—), Am. Astron. Soc. (Henry Norris Russell lectr., Dick Brouwer award 1986, George P. Kuiper prize divsn. planetary sci. 1992). Office: Calif Inst Tech Msc 150-21 1200 E California Blvd Pasadena CA 91125-0001 also: Sch Natural Scis Inst Advanced Study Einstein Dr Princeton NJ 08540 Office Phone: 626-395-6193, 609-734-8016. Office Fax: 609-951-4402. E-mail: pmg@ias.edu.

GOLDSCHLAGER, NORA FOX, internist, cardiologist, educator; b. NYC, 1939; MD, NYU, 1965. Diplomate Am. Bd. Internal Medicine, Am. Bd. Cardiovasc. Medicine. Intern Montefiore Hosp., NYC, 1965-66, resident, 1966-67, Henry Ford Hosp., Detroit, 1967-68; fellow in cardiology Wayne State U., Detroit, 1968-69, Pacific Med. Ctr., Calif., 1969-70; prof. clin. medicine U. Calif., San Francisco, 1983—. Mem. staff San Francisco Gen. Hosp., 1978—. Master ACP; Fellow Am. Coll. Cardiology, Heart Rhythm Soc., Am. Heart Assn. Office: San Francisco Gen Hosp Dept Cardiology San Francisco CA 94110-2897

GOLDSMITH, BRAM, banker; b. Chgo., Feb. 22, 1923; s. Max L. and Bertha (Gittelsohn) G.; m. Elaine Maltz; children: Bruce, Russell. Student, Herzl Jr. Coll., 1940, U. Ill., 1941—42. Asst. v.p. Pioneer-Atlas Liquor Co., Chgo., 1945-47; pres. Winston Lumber and Supply Co., East Chicago, Ind., 1947-50; v.p. Medal Distilled Products, Inc., Beverly Hills, Calif., 1950-75; pres. Buckeye Realty and Mgmt. Corp., Beverly Hills, 1952-75; exec. v.p. Buckeye Constrn. Co., Inc., Beverly Hills, 1952-75; chmn. bd., CEO City Nat. Corp., Beverly Hills, 1975-95; CEO City Nat. Bank, 1975-96, chmn., 1975-95, City Nat. Corp., 1995—. Mem., bd. dirs. L.A. Philharm. Assn.; bd. dirs. Cedars/Sinai Med. Ctr.; pres. Jewish Fedn. Coun. Greater L.A., 1969-70; nat. chmn. United Jewish Appeal, 1970-74; regional chmn. United Crusade, 1976; co-chmn. bd. dirs. NCCJ; chmn. Am. com. Weizman Inst. Sci. With signal corps U.S. Army, 1942-45. Mem. Masons, Hillcrest Country Club, Balboa Bay Club. Office: City Nat Corp 400 N Roxbury Dr Beverly Hills CA 90210 Business E-Mail: bram.goldmith@cnb.com.

GOLDSMITH, DONALD WILLIAM, lawyer, astronomer, writer; b. Washington, Feb. 24, 1943; s. Raymond William and Selma Evelyn (Fine) G.; m. Rose Marien, Apr. 10, 1975 (div. 1978); 1 child, Rachel Evelyn. BA, Harvard U., 1963; PhD, U. Calif., Berkeley, 1969, JD, 1983. Asst. prof. earth and space sci. SUNY, Stony Brook, 1972-74; vis. prof. Niels Bohr Inst., Copenhagen, 1977; vis. instr. physics Stanford (Calif.) U., 1983; vis. lectr. astronomy U. Calif., Berkeley, 1980-88, vis. assoc. prof., 1990-93; assoc. Pillsbury, Madison and Sutro, San Francisco, 1985-87. Cons. Cosmos TV program, Los Angeles, 1978-80; pres. Interstellar Media Publs., Berkeley, 1978—. Author: Nemesis, 1985, The Evolving Universe, 1985, Supernova!, 1989, Space Telescope, 1989, The Astronomers, 1991, The Hunt for Life on Mars, 1997, Worlds Unnumbered, 1997, The Ultimate Einstein, 1997, The Ultimate Planets, 1998, Voyage to the Milky Way, 1999, The Runaway Universe, 2000; (with others) The Search for Life in the Universe, 1980, 2d edit. 1992, Cosmic Horizons, 1982, Mysteries of the Milky Way, 1991; co-writer (TV programs) Is Anybody Out there, 1986, The Astronomers, 1991. Recipient 1st prize popular essays in astronomy Griffith Obs./Hughes Aircraft Corp., L.A., 1983, Best Popular Writing by a Scientist award Am. Inst. Physics, 1986, Klumpke-Roberts award for lifetime achievement Astronomy Soc. Pacific, 1990, Annenberg Found. award for edn. Am. Astron. Soc., 1995. Home: 2153 Russell St Berkeley CA 94705-1006

GOLDSMITH, STEPHEN ERNEST, lawyer; b. NYC, Dec. 25, 1944; s. Ernest and Charlotte Caroline Marie (Krohn) Goldsmith. BA, Marietta Coll., 1968; JD, Okla. City U., 1976. Bar: Hawaii 1977, US Dist. Ct. Hawaii 1977, US Ct. Appeals (9th cir.) 1977. Assoc. atty. James Krueger Atty. Law, Wailuku, Hawaii, 1977—81; pvt. practice Wailuku, 1981—, Maui, 1981—. Bd. dirs. Maui Philharmonic Soc., 1984—85. Mem.: Western Trial Lawyers (past pres. 1994—95, bd. mem. 1996—), Consumer Lawyers Hawaii (bd. dirs. 1995—), Maui County Bar Assn. (bd. dirs. 1984, adminstrv. v.p., pres. 1986—87), Hawaii Bar Assn., Assn. Plaintiff Lawyers Hawaii (bd. dirs. 1988—89), Assn. Trial Lawyers America (state del. 1984—93), Phi Delta Phi. Office: 24 N Church St PO Box 687 Wailuku HI 96793 Office Phone: 808-244-0080.

GOLDSTEIN, AVRAM, pharmacology educator; b. NYC, July 3, 1919; s. Israel and Bertha (Markowitz) Goldstein; m. Dora Benedict, Aug. 29, 1947; children: Margaret, Daniel, Joshua, Michael. AB, Harvard, 1940, MD, 1943. Intern Mt. Sinai Hosp., NYC, 1944; successively instr., assoc., asst. prof. pharmacology Harvard U., 1947—55; prof. dept. pharmacology Stanford U., Palo Alto, Calif., 1955—89, exec. head dept., 1955—70, prof. emeritus, 1989—. Dir. Addiction Rsch. Found., Palo Alto, Calif., 1973—87. Author: Biostatistics, Principles of Drug Action, 1965, ADDICTION: From Biology to Drug Policy, 2001. Served from 1st lt. to capt., Med. Corps US Army, 1944—46. Mem.: AAAS, Am. Soc. Biol. Chemists, Am. Soc. Pharmacology and Exptl. Therapeutics, Am. Acad. Arts and Scis., Inst. Medicine NAS.

GOLDSTEIN, DAVID BAIRD, energy executive, physicist; b. Cleve., June 29, 1951; s. Laurence and Gloria Reta (Baumgarten) G.; m. Julia Beth Vetromile, May 17, 1980; children: Elianna Louise, Abraham Micah. AB in Physics, U. Calif., Berkeley, 1973; PhD in Physics, U. Calif., 1978. Rsch. asst. Lawrence Berkeley (Calif.) Lab., 1975-78, staff scientist, 1978-80; sr. scientist, dir. energy program Natural Resources Def. Coun., San Francisco, 1980—. Sub-com. chair standing standards project com. 90.1 ASHRAE, Atlanta, 1983-96; vice-chmn. bd. Consortium for Energy Efficiency, Inc., Sacramento. 1991-93, 99-02, 06-, bd. dirs., 2002—, advisor, 1993-96; initiator and advisor Super Efficient Refrigerator Program, Inc., 1991-96. Author: Saving Energy, Growing Jobs, 2007; contbr. articles to profl. jours. Recipient Champion of Energy Efficiency award Am. Coun. for an Energy Efficient Economy, 1988, 94, Excellence in Achievement award Calif. Alumni Assn., 2003; MacArthur Found. fellow, 2002. Fellow: Am. Phys. Soc. (Leo Szilard award 1998); mem.: Sigma Xi, Phi Beta Kappa. Jewish. Avocations: travel, hiking, music, photography. Home: 1240 Washington St San Francisco CA 94108-1041 Office: Natural Resources Def Coun 111 Sutter 20th Fl San Francisco CA 94104 Home Phone: 415-771-7959; Office Phone: 415-875-6100. Business E-Mail: dgoldstein@nrdc.org.

GOLDSTEIN, EDWARD DAVID, lawyer, former glass company executive; b. NYC, July 12, 1927; s. Michael and Leah (Kirsh) G.; m. Rhoda Gordon, Apr. 18, 1950; children: Linda, Ellen, Ruth, Michael. BA, U. Mich., 1950, JD with distinction, 1952. Bar: Calif. 1952. Assoc. Orrick, Dahlquist, Herrington & Sutcliffe, San Francisco, 1952-54, Johnston & Johnston, San Francisco, 1954-56; with legal dept. Ohio Match Co., Hunt Foods & Industries, 1956-58; asst. gen. mgr., sales mgr. Glass Containers Corp., Fullerton, Calif., 1958-62, v.p., gen. mgr., 1962-68, pres., CEO, 1968-83. Chmn. bd. Knox Glass Co., Fairmount Glass Cos., 1967-68; gen. counsel FHP, Internat., FHP, Inc., 1985-87. Chmn. bd. trustees St. Jude Hosp., Fullerton, 1984-88. Served with USNR, 1945-46. Mem. ABA, State Bar Calif., Orange County Bar Assn., Nat. Health Lawyers Assn., Am. Arbitration Assn., Calif. Soc. Healthcare Attys. Home: 2230 Yucca Ave Fullerton CA 92835-3320 Office: 110 E Wilshire Ave STe 305 Fullerton CA 92832-1900 Office Phone: 714-525-5055. Personal E-mail: edgatty@aol.com.

GOLDSTEIN, JACK, biopharmaceutical executive, microbiologist; b. NYC, June 7, 1947; s. Arnold L. and Rachel (Vogel) G.; m. Laurie Ann Sacks, Aug. 28, 1969; 1 child, Justin T. BA, Rider U., Trenton, NJ, 1969; MS, St. John's U., Jamaica, NY, 1974, PhD, 1976. Diplomate Am. Bd. Med. Microbiology. Asst. dir. microbiology Queens Hosp. Ctr., Jamaica, 1976-81; dir. diagnostic labs. API div. Sherwood Med. Co., Plainview, NY, 1981-83; v.p. research and devel. MicroScan div. Baxter, Sacramento, 1983-86; group v.p. Ortho Diagnostic Systems Inc. div. Johnson & Johnson Co., Raritan, NJ, 1986-88; group v.p., gen. mgr. infectious disease bus. Ortho Diagnostic Systems, Inc. div. Johnson & Johnson Co., Raritan, NJ, 1988-92; exec. v.p. worldwide Ortho Diagnostic Sys. Inc. divsn. Johnson & Johnson Co., Raritan, NJ, 1992-93, pres. Ortho Diagnostic Sys. Inc. divsn., 1993-97; pres., CEO Applied Imaging Corp., Santa Clara, Calif., 1997-2001, chmn. bd., 2001—02; gen. ptnr. Windamere Venture Ptnrs., San Diego, 2001—02; pres. blood testing divsn. Chiron Corp., Emeryville, Calif., 2002—04, interim COO, 2004—05, pres., COO, 2005—. Mem. exam. com. Am. Bd. Med. Microbiology, Washington, 1984-91. Mem. editl. bd. Jour. Clin. Microbiology, Wasington, 1983-91; contbr. articles to profl. jours. Mem. Am. Soc. Microbiology, Am. Soc. Clin. Chemistry, Beta Beta Beta. Avocations: reading, skiing. Office: Chiron Corp 4560 Horton St Emeryville CA 94608-2916 Office Phone: 510-923-3850. E-mail: jack_goldstein@chiron.com.

GOLDSTEIN, KENNETH F., entertainment and publishing company executive; b. Detroit, Mar. 10, 1962; s. Earl Goldstein and Sarita (Bow) Snow; m. Shelley Wood, 2007. BA in Philosophy and Theater, Yale U., 1984. Freelance writer, TV and film producer, LA, 1984-89; writer, producer Cinemaware Corp., Westlake Village, Calif., 1989-91; designer, producer Philips Interactive Media, LA, 1991-92; exec. publisher Carmen Sandiego series Brøderbund Software, Inc., Novato, Calif., 1992-96, v.p. entertainment, gen. mgr. divsn. Red Orb Entertainment Myst, Riven Series, 1996-98, Journeyman Project series, Warlords series, 1996-98; sr. v.p., gen. mgr. Disney Online, 1998-2000; exec. v.p., mng. dir. Walt Disney Internet Group, 2000—06; chmn., CEO shop.com, 2006—. Author: (screenplays) 8; designer (software programs) Carmen Sandiego: Jr. Detective Edition, 1994 (Software Publs. Assn. award 1995), Reading Galaxy, 1994 (Family PC, Mac World awards 1996), In the 1st Degree, 1995 (Software Publs. Assn. award 1996); pub. Blast, 1998-06, FamilyFun Online, 1999-06, Disney's Toontown Online, 2002-06, Playhouse Disney Preschool Time Online, 2005-06, Movies.com website, 2002-06, Pirates of the Caribbean Online, 2006. Vol. Olive Crest Treatment Ctr., 1986, Free Arts Abused Children, 1988; sec. bd. trustees Full Circle Programs, Marin County, Calif., 1992-98; vice chmn. bd. trustees Hathaway Children and Family Svcs, 2002-05; bd. trustees Hathaway-Sycamores Child and Family Svcs., 2005—; bd. advs. Mediascope, 2002-04; bd. dirs. LA Make-A-Wish Found., 2005—; chair exec. com. Berit Mexia Peace Inst., 2006-; bd. advisors, Mustard Seed Youth Svsc. 2007-; adv. bd. Champlain Coll. Comm. and Creative Media Divsn., 2008-, Editl. bd., ACM Computers, 2005-. Recipient Pub. Svc. awards, Olive Crest Treatment Ctrs., 1986, Free Arts for Abused Children, 1988; named one of Top 100 Multimedia Producers, Multimedia Producer Mag., 1995, Best of What's New in Computers, Electronics, Popular Sci. Mag., 1995, Upside Mag. Elite 100, Digital Entertainment, 1998, Best of Festival award Internat. Web Awards, 2000, Web Mktg. Assn. Web Awards Best Game, Family, Movie, Entertainment Sites award 2001, Modalis Rsch. Excellence award, 2001, Outstanding Achievement award Web Mktg. Assn., 2002, 03, Web Internet Visionary award, Best of the Web, 2001, All Star Software award Software Rev., 2003, People's Voice award kids' category Webby Awards, 2003, Internet Safety award WiredKids website, 2005. Mem. Writers Guild of Am. West, Acad. Interactive Arts and Scis (founding mem., bd. govs. L.A.), Yale Univ. Alumni (schs. com. 1988—), Internat. Game Developers Assn. Office: shop-.com Bldg 1 Ste 210 1 Lower Ragsdale Dr Monterey CA 93940

GOLDSTEIN, MARY KANE, physician; b. NYC, Oct. 24, 1950; d. Edwin Patrick and Mary Kane; m. Yonkel Noah Goldstein, June 24, 1979; children: Keira, Gavi. Degree in Philosophy, Barnard Coll., 1973; MD, Columbia U., 1977; MS in Health Svcs. Rsch., Stanford U., Calif., 1994. Resident Duke U. Med. Ctr., Durham, NC, 1977-80; asst. prof. medicine U. Calif., San Francisco, 1980-84; clin. instr. dept. family and cmty. preventive medicine Stanford U., 1984-85, dir. grad. med. edn. divsn. gerontology, 1986-93, Agy. for Health Care Policy Rsch. fellow Sch. Medicine, 1991-94, asst. prof. medicine Med. Ctr. Line, 1996—99, with Ctr. Primary Care and Outcomes Rsch., 1998—, assoc. prof. medicine Med. Ctr. Line, 1999—2005, faculty fellow Inst. for Rsch. on Women and Gender, 2000—01, prof. medicine Med. Ctr. Line, 2005—; staff physician Mid-Peninsula Health Svc., Palo Alto, Calif., 1986-88; sect. chief for gen. internal medicine Palo Alto VA Med. Ctr., 1994-96, rsch. assoc. health svcs. R & D, 1996—2002; assoc. dir. clin. svcs. VA Geriatric Rsch. Edn. and Clinical Ctr., Palo Alto, 1999—. Editor Computer Ctr. Pubs., N.Y.C., 1971-72; computer programmer Columbia U., N.Y.C., 1972-73; governing coun. evidence-based practice ctr. U. Calif., Stanford, 1998—; automated decision support VA Health Svc. Rsch. & Devel., 2004, VISN collaborative for hypertension, 2005. Author chpt. to book; contbr. articles to profl. jours. Recipient Clin. Practice Guildelines for Hypertension award, VA Health Svc. R & D, 1997, Automated Decision Support Hypertension award, 2004, Practice Guidelines Multisite Study award, 2000, Dissemination Supplement to Drug Therapy Hypertension Multisite Study award, 2004, VA Intelligent Critiquing of Med. Records award, NIH/NLM, 2001, Disutility of Functional Limitations award NIH/NIA, 2001, VA Hosp., VISN Collaborative Improving Hypertension Mgmt. with ATHENA-HTN award, 2006-. Fellow: Am. Geriat. Soc. (bd. dirs. 1997—2002); mem.: Coll. Physicians and Surgeons. Office: VA Palo Alto Health Care Sys GRECC 182B 3801 Miranda Ave Palo Alto CA 94304-1290 Business E-Mail: goldstein@stanford.edu.

GOLDSTEIN, MICHAEL GERALD, lawyer, director; b. St. Louis, Sept. 21, 1946; s. Joseph and Sara G. (Finkelstein) G.; m. Ilene Marcia Ballin, July 19, 1970; children: Stephen Eric, Rebecca Leigh. BA, Tulane U., 1968; JD, U. Mo., 1971; LLM in Taxation, Washington U., 1972. Bar: Mo. 1971, U.S. Dist. Ct. (ea. dist.) Mo. 1972, U.S. Tax Ct. 1972, U.S. Ct. Appeals (8th cir.) 1974, U.S. Supreme Ct. 1976. Atty. Morris A. Shenker, St. Louis, 1972—78; ptnr. Lashly, Caruthers, Baer & Hamel and predecessor, St. Louis, 1978—84, Suelthaus & Kaplan, P.C. and predecessors, St. Louis, 1984—91; ptnr., chmn. dept. tax & estate planning Husch & Eppenberger, 1991—99; pres., CEO 1st Fin. Resources, 1999—2001; sr. v.p. EPS Fin. Solutions Corp., 1999—2000; sr. v.p., gen. counsel The Benefits Group, Inc., 2001—03; pres., COO Benefits Group Worldwide, 2003—05; sr. v.p. and counsel The Newport Group, 2005—. Adj. prof. tax law Washington U. Sch. Law, 1986-97; planning com. Mid-Am. Tax Confs., chmn. ALI/ABA Tax Seminar; lectr. in field. Author: BNA Tax Mgmt. Portfolios, ABA The Insurance Counselor Books; contbr. articles to profl. jours. Bd. dirs. Jewish Family and Children's Svc. St. Louis, 1980—, Maccabi USA/Sports for Israel, 2008-, pres., 1986-88; bd. dirs. Jewish Fedn. of St. Louis; trustee United Hebrew Temple, 1986-88; grad. Jewish Fedn. St. Louis Leadership Devel. Coun.; co-chmn. lawyers divsn. Jewish Fedn. St. Louis Campaign, 1981-82, Leadership St. Louis, 1988-89. Capt. USAR, 1970—78. Recipient Kenneth Black Jr. Jour. Author award, Jour. Fin. Svc. Profl., 2001. Fellow Am. Bar Found., Am. Coll. Tax Counsel, Am. Coll. Trust and Estate Counsel; mem. ABA (chmn. tax seminar, group editor newsletter taxation sect. 1989-97, books editor real property, probate and trust sects. 1998—), Am. Law Inst., Mo. Bar Assn., Bar Assn. Met. St. Louis, St. Louis County Bar Assn. Office: 2011 Yacht Mischief Newport Beach CA 92660-6713 Office Phone: 949-760-9098. Business E-Mail: mgoldstein@newportgroup.com.

GOLDSTEIN, MICHAEL L., neurologist; b. Chgo., June 14, 1945; s. Charles and Dorothy (Mack) G.; m. Barbara Joan Kaplan, June 18, 1967; children: Rachel, Elizabeth, Adam. AB, Princeton, 1966; MD, U. Chgo., 1970. Cert. Am. Bd. Neurology and Psychiatry with spl. comptence in child neurology. Intern Stanford U., 1970-71; resident in neurology Beth Israel Hosp., Boston, 1971-74; fellow in neurology Harvard U. Med. Sch., 1971-74; chief resident in neurology Children's Hosp., Boston, 1973-74; with Western Neurol. Assoc., Salt Lake City. Cons. Soc. Sec., Balt., 1990-91; bd. dirs., edn. comm. chmn. Rowland Hall, St. Marks Sch., Salt Lake City, 1986-92; examiner Am. Bd. Psychiatry and Neurology, 1987—; clin. assoc. prof. U. Utah Med. Sch., Salt Lake City, 1977—. Co-author: Managing Attention Disorders, 1990, Parent's Guide to ADD, 1993; co-producer: Educating Inattentive Children, 1992, It's Just Attention Disorder, 1993; acad. officer, Neurology. Pres. synagogue, Salt Lake City, 1985-86. Fellow Am. Acad. Pediat., Am. Acad. Neurology (chair practice com., 1995-2000, treas. 2001, v.p. 2007-). Office: Western Neurol Associates PC 1151 E 3900 S Ste B150 Salt Lake City UT 84124 Office Phone: 801-262-3441. Office Fax: 801-269-9005.

GOLDSTEIN, MORRIS, retired consumer products company executive; b. Pitts., Feb. 2, 1945; s. Irving and Clara (Caplan) G.; m. Diane Donna Davis, Aug. 21, 1966 (div. Nov. 1985); children: Jonathan, Julie; m. Kathy Evelyn Niemeier, July 7, 1990. BS, Carnegie Inst. Tech., 1967; MBA, U. Pa., 1979. Sales rep. computer divsn. RCA, Cherry Hill, NJ, 1968-70; sales mgr. Sedgwick Printout Sys., Princeton, NJ, 1970-76, pres., 1976-80; v.p. Courier-Jour. Louisville Times, 1980-81; mgr. bus. devel. Ziff-Davis Pub., NYC, 1982-2000; pres. Information Access Corp. divsn., Foster City, Calif., 1982-2000; pres., COO Imagination Network Inc., Oakhurst, Calif., 1994; sr. v.p. Ziff-Davis Pub., Foster City, Calif., 1994; CEO Info. Access Co., A Thomson Corp. Co., Foster City, Calif., 1995-96,

Thomson Tech. Ventures, San Mateo, Calif., 1997; pres., CEO Alliance Gaming Inc, Las Vegas, Nev., 1997-99; pres. entertainment bus. divsn. InnoVentry LLC, Las Vegas, 1999-2000; ret., 2000; exec. v.p. Global Cash Access, Las Vegas, 2001—03; prin., owner Nev. Slots and Supplies. Founder Nev. Slots and Supplies, Las Vegas, 2002. Dep mayor Mt. Laurel Twp., N.J., 1974-78. Home: 3581 E Maule Ave Las Vegas NV 89120-2918 Office: Nevada Slots and Supplies 2245 N Green Valley Pkwy Ste 283 Henderson NV 89120 Office Phone: 702-596-8609.

GOLDSTEIN, SIR NORMAN, dermatologist; b. Bklyn., July 14, 1934; s. Joseph H. and Bertha (Docteroff) Goldstein; m. Ramsay Goldstein, Feb. 14, 1980; children: Richard, Heidi. BA, Columbia Coll., 1955; MD, SUNY, 1959. Intern Maimonides Hosp., NYC, 1959—60; resident Skin and Cancer Hosp., 1960—61, Bellevue Hosp., 1961—62, N.Y.U. Postgrad. Ctr., 1962—63; ptnr. Honolulu Med. Group, 1967—72; pvt. practice dermatology Honolulu, 1972—; clin. prof. dermatology U. Hawaii Sch. Medicine, 1973—. Bd. dir. Pacific Laser, Skin Cancer Found.; trustee Dermatol. Found., 1979—82; pres. Hawaii Med. Libr., 1987. Editor (emeritus): Hawaii Med. Jour.; contbr. articles to profl. jours. Pres. Hawaii Theater Ctr., 1985—89; mem. Oahu Heritage Council, 1986—94, Hawaii Govs. Blue Ribbon Panel on Living and Dying with Dignity. With US Army, 1960—67. Recipient Henry Silver award, Dermatol. Soc. Greater N.Y., 1963, Husik award, NYU, 1963, Spl. award, Acad. Dermatologia Hawaiiana, 1971, Outstanding Scientific Exhibit award, Calif. Med. Assn., 1979, Spl. Exhibit award, Am. Urologic Assn., 1980, Svc. to Hawaii's Youth award, Adult Friends for Youth, 1991, Nat. Cosmetic Tattoo Assn. award, 1993, Cmty. Svc. award, Am. Acad. Dermatology, 1993, Nat. Leadership award and hon., Physians Adv. Bd., Washington, 2003; named Physician of Yr., Hawaii Med. Assn., 1993, 2003, Physcians Adv. Coun., 2003, Businessman of Yr., Bus. Adv. Coun., 2003. Fellow: ACP (Laureate award 2005, Laureate award 2005), Royal Soc. Medicine, Am. Soc. Lasers Medicine & Surgery, Am. Acad. Dermatology (Silver award 1972); mem.: AAAS, Internat. Soc. Dermatology (bd. dirs.), Hawaii Public Health Assn., Hawaii Dermatol. Soc. (sec.-pres.), Am. Coll. Sports Medicine, Honolulu County Med. Soc. (gov.), Pacific Health Research Inst., Pacific Dermatol. Assn., Hawaii State Med. Assn. (mem. public affairs com.), Am. Soc. Preventive Oncology, Internat. Soc. Dermatol. Surgery, Am. Coll. Cryosurgery, Physicians Exchange of Hawaii (bd. dir.), Am. Med. Writers Assn., Am. Soc. Micropigmentation Surgery, Internat. Soc. Cryosurgery, Am. Soc. Photobiology, Soc. Investigative Dermatologists, Internat. Soc. Tropical Dermatologists (Hist. and Culture award), C. of C., Pacific Telecom Council, Soc. for Computer Medicine, Pacific and Asian Affairs Council, Health Sci. Communication Assn., Am. Assn. for Med. Systems and Info., Biol. Photog. Assn., Assn. Hawaii Artists, Chancellor's Club, Plaza Club, Outrigger Canoe Club (pres. bd. dir. 1990—92), Ancient Gaelic Nobility Soc. (named Knight of the Niadh Nask 1995), Hemlock Soc. USA (mem. bd.), Rotary, Preservation Action, Nat. Wildlife Fedn., Japan Am. Soc. Hawaii (bd. dir.), Navy League. Office: Suite 400 550 S Beretania St Honolulu HI 96813 Office Phone: 808-544-2530. Personal E-mail: skinyouluv@aol.com.

GOLDSTEIN, PAUL, lawyer, educator; b. Mount Vernon, NY, Jan. 14, 1943; s. Martin and Nan Goldstein; m. Jan Thompson, Aug. 28, 1977. BA, Brandeis U., 1964; LLB Columbia U., 1967. Bar: NY 1968, Calif. 1978. Asst. prof. law SUNY-Buffalo, 1967-69, assoc. prof., 1969-71, prof., 1972-75; vis. assoc. prof. Stanford U., Calif., 1972-73, prof. law Calif., 1975—, Stella W. and Ira S. Lillick prof. law Calif., 1985—; of counsel Morrison and Foerster, San Francisco, 1988—. Author: Changing the American Schoolbook--Law, Politics and Technology, 1978, Real Estate Transactions--Cases and Materials on Land Transfer, Development and Finance, 1980, 3d edit. (with G. Korngold), 1993, Real Property, 1984, Copyright, 4 vols., 3d edit., 2005, Copyright, Patent, Trademark and Related State Doctrines--Cases and Materials on the Law of Intellectual Property, revised 5th edit., 2002, Copyright's Highway: From Gutenberg to the Celestial Jukebox, 1995, revised edit., 2003, International Copyright Law, 2001, International Intellectual Property Law, 2001, Errors and Omissions, 2006. Mem. Assn. Litteraire et Artistique Internationale, Copyright Soc. U.S.A. Office: Stanford U Law Sch Nathan Abbott Way Stanford CA 94305 Office Phone: 650-723-0313. E-mail: paulgold@stanford.edu.

GOLDSTEIN, REY, accountant; b. 1959; s. Shelia and Marc Goldstein; m. Maggie Goldstein (div. 1979); 6 children; life ptnr. Shmuel LaTova. BA in Accounting, U. Calif., 1981, MA in Accounting, 1983. CPA Calif., 1983. Acctg. dept. intern Mack & Ro Inc., 1981—82, jr. acct., 1984—87, sr. acct., 1988—2000; head acct. Meriks Phone Co., San Diego, 2001—06, v.p. acctg. dept., 2006—. Acctg. tutor U. Calif. Learning Ctr., 1979—81. Liberal. Jewish. Office: Meriks Phone Co 1380 Garnet Ave Ste E-278 San Diego CA 92109

GOLDSTEIN, STUART WOLF, lawyer; b. Buffalo, Sept. 9, 1931; s. Joseph and Esther (Wolf) G.; m. Myra Saft Stuart, June 1960 (dec. Aug. 1981); children: Jeffrey, Jonathan, Meryl; m. Nancy Baynes Lux, 1993. Student, U. Buffalo, 1949-52, JD, 1955; postgrad., U. Va., 1956. Bar: NY 1956, Fla. 1974, Ariz. 1977, US Supreme Ct. 1960, US Dist. Ct. (we. dist.) NY 1956, US Ct. Mil. Appeals 1957, US Ct. Appeals (2d cir.) NY, 1978, US Dist. Ct. Ariz. 1981. Sole practice, Buffalo, 1960-79, 82-85, Phoenix, 1980-82, 85—. Pres., founder Cystic Fibrosis Found., Buffalo, 1960; fund-raiser United Fund, United Jewish Appeal; pres. Boys League; active Erie County Spl. Task Force on Energy, Buffalo, 1978. 1st lt. JAG, US Army, 1956-60. Fellow Ariz. Bar Found.; mem. Am. Assn. Justice, Ariz. State Bar Assn., NY Trial Lawyers Assn., NY State Bar Assn., Fla. Bar Assn., Maricopa County Bar Assn. Avocations: astronomy, breeding boston terriers. Office: 2700 N 3rd St Ste 2010 Phoenix AZ 85004-4602 Office Phone: 602-279-1666. Personal E-mail: stugoldstn@aol.com. Business E-Mail: stuart@stuartgoldsteinlaw.com.

GOLDSTEIN, WALTER ELLIOTT, biotechnology executive; m. Paula G. Copen. BS in Chem. Engring., Ill. Inst. Tech., 1961; MBA, Mich. State U., 1968; MSChemE, U. Notre Dame, 1971, PhDChemE, 1973. Registered profl. engr., Ind. Process devel. engr. Linde div. Union Carbide, Tonawanda, NY, 1961-64; assoc. project engr. Miles Labs., Elkhart, Ind., 1964-67, assoc. rsch. scientist, 1967-72, rsch. scientist, 1972-73, rsch. supr., 1973-76; mgr. chem. engring. rsch. & pilot svcs. Chem. Engring. Rsch. & Pilot Svcs., Elkhart, Ind., 1976-78, dir., 1978-82; chem. engring. rsch. v.p. Biotech. Group, Elkhart, 1982-87; v.p. R&D ESCAgenetics Corp., San Carlos, Calif., 1987-94; pres. Goldstein Cons. Co., Foster City, Calif., 1994—; co-founder Transcyte Corp., Inc., 1996—, Phytonic Corp., 2001—; coord. Biotech. Ctr., Shadowlane Campus, U. Nev., Las Vegas, 2003—. Adj. prof. chem. engring. U. Notre Dame, 1974-75, San Jose State U., 1995—; cons. Bernard Wolnak, Chgo., 1987 Contbr. chpts. to books; inventions and publs. in chem. engring., pharm., food, diagnostics and biotech. field. Vice-pres. B'nai B'rith, South Bend., Ind., 1978-89. Mem. AAAS, Am. Chem. Soc., Am. Soc. Pharmacognosy, Soc. for Competitive Intelligence Profls., Am. Inst. Chem. Engrs., N.Y. Acad. Scis., Inst. Food Technologists, Sigma Xi. Avocations: reading, computers, sports, charitable causes. Office Phone: 702-774-2325, 702-804-5952. E-mail: goldconsul@aol.com, walter.goldstein@ccmail.nevada.edu.

GOLDSTINE, STEPHEN JOSEPH, art educator; b. San Francisco, Nov. 16, 1937; s. Edgar Nathan and Regina Thelma (Benno) G.; m. Emily Raechel Miller Keeler, Apr. 12, 1981; children: Rachel, Bettina, Simone Massimiliana Student, Calif. Sch. Fine Arts, 1951-58; BA, U. Calif., Berkeley, 1961, postgrad. in philosophy, 1962-67. Teaching asst. rhetoric dept. U. Calif., Berkeley, 1963-66; asst. prof. St. Mary's Coll., Moraga, Calif., 1964-70, chmn. art dept., 1969-70; cons. Freeman & Gossage, San Francisco, 1967-69; dir. neighborhood arts program Art Commn. City and County San Francisco, 1970-77; exec. sec. Mayor's Interagency Com. for Arts, San Francisco, 1971-75; founding dir. Performing Arts for the Third Age, San Francisco, 1973; co-dir. Rockefeller Tng. Fellowships in Mus. Edn., San Francisco, 1975; pres. San Francisco Art Inst., 1977-86; dir. grad. programs Calif. Coll. Arts and Crafts, 1983—2003, Dennis Leon prof. grad. studies, 2002—; vis. faculty San Francisco State U. Sr. cons. Daniel Solomon Architects and Planners, 1988; mem. chancellor's adv. bd. Univ. Art Mus., U. Calif., Berkeley, 1979—; exec. com., trustee San Francisco Arts Edn. Found., 1985—; mem. Oakland Cultural Affairs Commn., 2002—; mem. prominent orgns. panel Calif. Arts Coun., 1981, vice chmn., 1983, chmn., 1985-87; chmn. invited session Am. Philos. Assn. (Pacific divsn.), 1986, lectr. UCLA, 1976, Stanford U., 1966, Harvard U., 1976, 71; docent Lycee Internat. Franco-Am., 1993—. Editor: Western Round Table on Modern Art, 1993; co-prodr., co-dir. (film) Walz um die Wände hoch zu gehen, 1999. Condr. The Art Orch., Calif. Palace of the Legion of Honor, 1997. Democrat. Jewish. Home: 1331 Green St San Francisco CA 94109-1926 Office: Calif Coll Arts Crafts 1111 Eighth St San Francisco CA 94107-2206 Home Phone: 415-474-0838; Office Phone: 415-264-0439. E-mail: mrgoldstine@earthlink.net.

GOLDSTON, MARK R., Internet company executive; BSBA in Mktg. and Fin., Ohio State U.; MBA, Northwest U. V.p. mktg. worldwide Revlon, Inc.; chief mktg. officer Reebok; pres. Faberge USA, Inc.; prin. Odyssey Partners, L.P.; pres., COO LA Gear; pres., CEO Einstein/Noah Bagel Corp.; chmn., CEO Goldston Group, NetZero, Inc., United Online, Inc., 2001—, pres., 2006, 2007—; chmn., pres., CEO Classmates Media Corp. Mem. dean's adv. bd. J.L. Kellogg Sch., Northwestern U., Ohio State U. Fisher Sch. Bus. Author: The Turnaround Prescription, 1992. Achievements include patents for inflatable pump athletic shoes, lighted footwear, and Internet electronic delivery method. Office: Classmates Media Corp 21301 Burbank Blvd Woodland Hills CA 91367-6677

GOLDWATER, BERT M., federal judge; Apptd. bankruptcy judge U.S. Dist. Ct. Nev., 1995. Office: Fed Bldg US Courthouse 300 Booth St Rm 1109 Reno NV 85909

GOLDWYN, JOHN, film company executive; b. LA, Aug. 10, 1958; s. Samuel Goldwyn Jr. and Peggy Elliot Goldwyn; m. Colleen Camp. Exec. v.p. prodn. Paramount Pictures, LA, 1990, pres. motion pictures group/prodn., 1991—97, pres. motion picture group, 1997—2002, vice-chmn. motion picture group, 2002—, pres., 2002—. Exec. prodr.: (films) Police Academy 2: Their First Assignment, 1985. Office: Paramount Pictures 5555 Melrose Ave Los Angeles CA 90038

GOLIAN-LUI, LINDA MARIE, librarian; b. Woodbridge, NJ, Mar. 27, 1962; d. Joseph John Golian and Mary Grace (Juba) Rodriguez; m. Gary S. Lui, Oct. 6, 1988; 1 child, Katherine Jana Lui-Golian. BA, U. Miami, 1986; MLIS, Fla. State, 1988; EdS, Fla. Atlantic U., 1995, EdD, 1998; postgrad., Fla. Gulf Coast U., 1999—2002. Libr. tech. asst. U. Miami, 1981-86; serials control libr. U. Miami Law Sch., 1986-89; serials dept. head Fla. Atlantic U., Boca Raton, 1990-97; univ. libr. Fla. Gulf Coast U., Ft. Myers, 1997—2002, adj. instr. Coll. Arts and Scis., 1999—2002; libr. dir. U. Hawaii, Hilo, 2002—. Adj. instr. Fla. Atlantic U. Coll. Continuing & Distance Edn., 1993-97, U. So. Fla. Coll. Libr. Sci., 1995-2002; program specialist Marriott Statford Ctr. Sr. Living Cmty., Boca Raton, 1994-96. Vol. storyteller Aid to Victims of Domestic Assault, Delray Beach, Fla., 1994—96. Recipient Mover and Shaker award, Libr. Jour.; named Hawaii County Woman of Yr., 2005. Mem. NOW, AAUW (by laws chair Hawaii and Pacific chpt. 2005—), NAFE, ALA, Hawaii Libr. Assn. (state chpt. councilor 2003-), Spl. Libr. Assn., N.Am. Serials Interest Group (co-chair mentoring com. 1996-97), ASCD, Southeastern Libr. Assn., Assn. Libr. and Info. Sci. Educators, Am. Libr. Assn., Am. Assn. Higher Edn., Assn. Libr. Collection & Tech. Svcs., Libr., Adminstrn. & Mgmt. Assn., Reference & User Svcs. Assn. (continuing libr. edn. network & exch. round table, intellectual freedom round table, libr. instruction round table, new members round table, staff orgn. round table, women's studies sect. comm. com. 1994—, serials nomination com. 1993, Miami local arrangements com. 1994, chair libr. sch. outreach 1994—, pres. 1998-99, 3M profl. devel. grantee 1995), Assn. Coll. Rsch. Libr. (Lazerow rsch. fellow 1997), Laubach Literary Vols. of Am., Am. Assn. Adult and Continuing Edn., Fla. Libr. Assn. (serials libr. or yr. 1994, grantee 1987, Libr. Jour. Mover and Shaker 2005), Am. Coun. Edn. Hilo Chpt. Women in Edn., Zonta (fellowship com. 2002—). Roman Catholic. Avocations: reading, fishing, ceramics, tennis. Office: U HI Hilo Edwin H Mookini Lib & Graphic Ser 200 W Kawili St Hilo HI 96720-4091 Office Phone: 808-933-3132. Business E-Mail: golianlu@hawaii.edu.

GOLITZ, LOREN EUGENE, dermatologist, pathologist, medical association administrator; b. Apr. 7, 1941; s. Ross Winston and Helen Francis (Schupp) G.; m. Deborah Burd Frazier, June 18, 1966; children: Carrie Campbell, Matthew Ross. MD, U. Mo., 1966. Diplomate Am. Bd. Dermatology, Nat. Bd. Med. Examiners. Intern USPHS Hosp., San Francisco, 1966—67, med. resident, 1967—69, resident in dermatology SI, 1969—71, dep. chief dermatology, 1972—73; vis. fellow dermatology Columbia-Presbyn. Med. Ctr., NYC, 1971—72; asst. in dermatology Coll. Physicians Surgeons, Columbia, 1972—73; vice-chmn. Residency Rev. Com. for Dermatology, 1983—85; assoc. prof. dermatology, pathology Med. Sch. U. Colo., Denver, 1974—88, prof., 1988—97, clin. prof. pathology, dermatology, 1997—. Chief dermatology Denver Gen. Hosp., 1974-97; med. dir. Ambulatory Care Ctr., Denver Gen. Hosp., 1991-97. Mem. editl. bd. Jour. Cutaneous Pathology, Jour. Am. Acad. Dermatology, Advances in Dermatology (editl. bd. Current Opinion in Dermatology); contbr. articles to med. jours. Fellow Royal Soc. Medicine; mem. AMA (residency rev. com. for dermatology 1982-89, dermatopathology test com. 1979-85), AAAS, Am. Soc. Dermatopathology (sec., treas. 1985-89, pres.-elect 1989, pres. 1990), Am. Acad. Dermatology (chmn. coun. on clin. and lab. svcs., coun. sci. assembly 1987-91, bd. dirs. 1987-91, chmn. joint dermatopathology com.), Soc. Pediat. Dermatology (pres. 1981), Soc. Investigative Dermatology, Pacific Dermatol. Assn. (exec. com. 1979-89, sec.-treas. 1984-87, pres. 1988), Noah Worcester Dermatol. Soc. (publs. com. 1980, membership com. 1989-90), Colo. Dermatol. Soc. (pres. 1978), Am. Bd. Dermatology Inc. (chmn. part II test com. 1989—, exec. com. 1993—, v.p. 1994, pres.-elect 1995, pres. 1996, dir. Emeritus, cons. to bd. 1997—), Colo. Med. Soc., Denver Med. Soc., Denver Soc. Dermatopathology, Am. Dermatol. Assn., Women's Dermatologic Soc., So. Med. Assn., Internat. Soc. Pediat. Dermatology, Am. Contact Dermatitis Soc., Am. Soc. Dermatologic Surgery, Physicians Who Care, Am. Bd. Med. Specialties (del.), N.Y. Acad. Scis., Brit. Assn. Dermatologists (hon.), Brazilian Soc. Dermatology (hon.), U. Mo. Med. Alumni Orgn. (bd. govs. 1993—). Office: Dermatopathology Svc PO Box 6218 Denver CO 80206-0218

GOLLEHER, GEORGE, food company executive; b. Bethesda, Md., Mar. 16, 1948; s. George M. and Ruby Louise (Beecher) Golleher; 1 child, Carly Lynn. BA, Calif. State U., Fullerton, 1970. Supr. acctg. J.C. Penney, Buena Park, Calif., 1970-72; sys. auditor Mayfair Markets, Los Angeles, 1973, v.p., CFO, 1982-83; contr. Fazio's, Los Angeles, 1974-78; group contr. Fisher Foods, Ohio, 1978-79; v.p. fin. Stater Bros. Markets, Colton, Calif., 1979-82; sr. v.p., CFO Boys Markets Inc., Los Angeles, 1983-95; exec. v.p. The Yucaipa Companies, LLC, 1989—; CEO Ralph Grocery Co., Compton, Calif., 1995-99; pres., COO Fred Meyer Inc., Portland, Oreg., 1997-99; chmn. Furrs Supermarkets, Albuquerque, 2001; chmn., CEO Smart & Final, Inc., 2007—. Bd. dirs. Simon Worldwide, Inc., 1999—2006, Gen. Nutrition Centers Inc., 2003—07, Rite Aid Corp., 2002—, Linens N Things, 2006—08, Claire's Stores. Office: The Yucaipa Companies 9130 West Sunset Blvd Los Angeles CA 90069*

GOLOMB, BEATRICE ALEXANDRA, physician, medical researcher; b. Pasadena, Calif., May 16, 1959; d. Solomon W. Golomb; m. Terrence Joseph Sejnowski, Mar. 24, 1990. BS in Physics, U. So. Calif., 1979; PhD in Biology, U. Calif. at San Diego, 1988, MD, 1989. Lic. Calif., 1991, cert. Am. Bd. Internal Medicine, 1993. Technical aide A Jet Propulsion Lab., 1978, engr. I, 1979; postdoctoral fellow, computational neurobiology lab. Salk Inst., 1989—90; resident West LA VA Med. Ctr., 1990-93, chief med. resident, 1993-94, attending physician, emergency room, 1993—94; attending physician, divsn. gen. internal medicine VA San Diego Healthcare Sys., 1996—; Robert Wood Johnson clin. scholar UCLA, 1994—96; rsch. asst. prof. psychology U. So. Calif., 1995—98, rsch. assoc. prof., dept. psychology, Social Sci. Rsch. Inst., 1998—; asst. prof. medicine U. Calif., San Diego, 1998—2004, asst. prof. psychology, 2001—04, asst. prof. family and preventive medicine, 2002—04, assoc. prof. family and preventive medicine, 2004—, assoc. prof. medicine, divsn. gen. medicine, 2004—, dir. statin study rsch. group, 1999—. Health cons. RAND, Santa Monica, Calif., 1996—; mem. Stein Inst. for Rsch. on Aging, 2001—; scientific dir. Dept. VA Rsch. Adv. Com. on Gulf War Veterans Illnesses, 2002—03, chief scientist, 2003—05, mem., 2005—; mem. pharmacy and therapeutics com. West LA VA Med. Ctr., 1993—94, VA San Diego Med. Ctr., 2001—05, Robert Wood Johnson generalist phys. faculty scholar, 2003—07; mem. adv. bd. The Science Network, 2004—; expert panel participation in field; mem. briefings to govt. agencies; lectr. and presenter in field. Contbr. articles to profl. jours.; peer reviewer for numerous jours. Mem. Am. Soc. for Preventive Cardiology, Phi Kappa Phi.; fellow Am. Heart Assn. (assoc. fellow, Coun. on Epidemiology and Prevention, 1999, fellow 2000-) Office: U Calif San Diego Dept Medicine 0995 9500 Gilman Dr #0995 La Jolla CA 92093-0995

GOLOMB, SOLOMON WOLF, mathematician, electrical engineer, director, educator; b. Balt., May 31, 1932; s. Elhanan Hirsh and Minna (Nadel) G. AB, Johns Hopkins U., 1951; MA, Harvard U., 1953, PhD, 1957; postgrad., U. Oslo, 1955—56; DSc (hon.), Dubna Internat. U., Russia, 1995; DHL (hon.), Hebrew Union Coll., LA, 1996. Mem. faculty Boston U., 1954-55, Harvard U., 1954-55, UCLA, 1957-61, Calif. Inst. Tech., 1960-62; sr. rsch. engr. Jet Propulsion Lab., Pasadena, Calif., 1956-58, rsch. group supr., 1958-60, asst. chief telecom. rsch. sect., 1960-63; assoc. prof. U. So. Calif., LA, 1963-64, prof. elec. engring. and math., 1964—, vice provost for rsch., 1986-89, univ. prof., 1993—, dir. tech. Annenberg Ctr. for Comm., 1995-98, Viterbi prof. comm., 1997—. Cons. to govt. and industry. Author: Digital Communications with Space Applications, 1964, 81, Polyominoes, 1965, rev. edit., 1994, Shift Register Sequences, 1967, 82, Basic Concepts in Information Theory and Coding, 1994, Signal Design for Good Correlation, 2005; contbr. articles to profl. jours. Recipient Lomonosov medal Russian Acad. Sci., 1994, Disting. Alumnus award Johns Hopkins U., 2002. Fellow IEEE (Shannon award Info. Theory Soc. 1995, Hamming medal 2000), AAAS, Am. Acad. Arts and Scis.; mem. NAS, NAE, Internat. Sci. Radio Union, Russian Acad. Natural Scis. (fgn., Kapitsa medal 1995), Am. Math. Soc., Math. Assn. Am., Soc. Indsl. and Applied Math., Golden Key, Phi Beta Kappa, Sigma Xi, Pi Delta Epsilon, Eta Kappa Nu, Phi Kappa Phi. Office: U So Calif Univ Park Dept Elec Engring Eeb 504A Los Angeles CA 90089-2565 Home Phone: 818-790-1745. E-mail: milly@usc.edu.

GOLOMBEK, MATTHEW PHILIP, research scientist, planetary geologist; b. New Haven, Sept. 20, 1954; s. Martin I. and Sonia G.; m. Connie M. Morgan, Apr. 26, 1980; children: Sydney, Benjamin. AB in Geology with honors, Rutgers U., 1976; MS in Geology, U. Mass., 1978, PhD in Geology, 1981. Rsch. asst. in sedimentology Rutgers U., New Brunswick, NJ, 1976; tchg. asst. U. Mass., 1979, rsch. asst. in structural and planetary geology, 1976-81; vis. postdoctoral fellow Lunar and Planetary Inst., Houston, 1981-82, vis. scientist, 1982-83; rsch. scientist Jet Propulsion Lab. Calif. Inst. Tech., Pasadena, 1983—2000, Mars Pathfinder project scientist Jet Propulsion Lab., 1994-98, sr. rsch. scientist Jet Propulsion Lab., prin. scientist, 2000—. Lectr. U. Houston, Clear Lake City, 1983, Calif. State Poly. U., Pomona, 1986; Viking guest investigator Jet Propulsion Lab., 1977, US Geol. Survey, Astrogeology Br., Flagstaff, Ariz., 1978; mem. Mars Sci. Working Group, 1989-96, Mars Exploration Edn. Outreach Adv. Bd., 1994-98; chmn. Mars Pathfinder Project Sci. Group, 1994-98; mem. Am. Geophys. Union, Planetology Exec. Com., 1994-97; mem. assessment group Mars Exploration Program, 1999—, landing site scientist, 2000—, Mars Exploration Rover sci. ops. working group chair, 2002—; vis. scientist U. Colo., Boulder, 2000; vis. full prof. Inst. de Physique du Globe de Paris, 2001; spkr., lectr. in field. Planetology editor EOS, Transactions Am. Geophy. Union; assoc.

editor Tectonophysics, 1986; contbr. articles to profl. jour. Recipient Vinton Gwinn Meml. prize, Rutgers U., 1976, Laurels award for outstanding achievement in space, Aviation Week and Space Tech., 1997, award for excellence, Jet Propulsion Lab./Project Scientist for Mars Pathfinder Mission, 1998, Disting. Alumni award for Profl. Svc., U. Mass., 1998, Hall of Disting. Alumni award, Rutgers U. Alumni Fedn., 1998, Exceptional Sci. Achievement medal, NASA, 1998, others, Dr. Matt Golombek Day named in his honor, City of Hackensack, NJ, 1998, asteroid named Golombek in his honor, 1992; Schlumberger scholar, Rutgers U., 1975—76, numerous grants, 1983—. Fellow Geol. Soc. Am.; mem. Am. Geophy. Union. Office: Jet Propulsion Lab MS 183-501 4800 Oak Grove Dr Pasadena CA 91109-8001 Business E-Mail: mgolombek@jpl.nasa.gov.

GOLTZ, ROBERT WILLIAM, retired dermatologist; b. St. Paul, Sept. 21, 1923; s. Edward Victor and Clare (O'Neill) G.; m. Patricia Ann Sweeney, Sept. 27, 1945; children: Leni, Paul Robert. BS, U. Minn., 1943, MD, 1945. Diplomate: Am. Bd. Dermatology (pres. 1975-76). Intern Ancker Hosp., St. Paul, 1944-45; resident in dermatology Mpls. Gen. Hosp., 1945-46, 48-49, U. Minn. Hosp., 1949-50; practice medicine specializing in dermatology Mpls., 1950-65; clin. instr. U. Minn. Grad. Sch., 1950-58, clin. asst. prof., 1958-60, clin. assoc. prof., 1960-65, prof., head dept. dermatology, 1971-85; prof. medicine and dermatology U. Calif., San Diego, 1985—2004, emeritus prof., 2004—, acting chair divsn. dermatology, 1995-97; prof. dermatology, head div. dermatology U. Colo. Med. Sch., Denver, 1965-71; ret. Former mem. editl. bd. Archives of Dermatology; editor Dermatology Digest. Served from 1st lt. to capt., M.C. U.S. Army, 1946-48. Mem. Assn. Am. Physicians, Am. Dermatol. Assn. (dir. 1976-79, pres. 1985-86, Hon. 2009), Am. Soc. Dermatopathology (pres. 1981), Am. Dermatologic Soc. Allergy and Immunology (pres. 1981), AMA (chmn. sect. on dermatology 1973-75), Dermatology Found. (past dir.), Minn. Dermatol. Soc., Soc. Investigative Dermatology (pres. 1972-73, hon. 1988), Histochem. Soc., Am. Acad. Dermatology (pres. 1978-79, past dir.) (hon.), Brit. Assn. Dermatology (hon.), Chilean Dermatology Soc. (hon.), Colombian Dermatol. Soc. (corr. mem.), Can. Dermatol. Soc. (hon. mem.), German Dermatol. Soc. (hon.), Pacific Dermatol. Soc. (hon.-mem.), S. African Dermatol. Soc. (hon. mem.), N.Am. Clin. Dermatol. Soc., Assn. Profs. Dermatology (sec.-treas. 1970-72, pres. 1973-74), West Assn. Physicians. Home: 400 Prospect St Apt 233 La Jolla CA 92037-4708 Personal E-mail: rwgoltz@san.rr.com.

GOLUB, BEN, Internet company executive; BA, Princeton Univ.; MBA, Harvard Univ.; MPA, Kennedy Sch. Govt., Harvard Univ. Cert. CISSP. Mgmt. positions Avid Technology Inc., Sun Microsystems; sales & mktg. mgmt. positions VeriSign Inc., Mountain View, Calif., 1997—2001, sr. v.p., gen. mgr. security & payments div., 2001—02, sr. v.p. mktg. & corp. affairs, 2002—05; pres., CEO Plaxo Inc., Mountain View, Calif., 2005—. Office: Plaxo Inc 203 Ravendale Dr Mountain View CA 94043 Office Phone: 650-254-5400. Office Fax: 650-254-1435.

GOLUB, MIKE, professional sports team executive; m. Sam Golub. BA, Dartmouth Coll., 1983; MBA, Stanford U., 1988. Dir. mktg. Oakland-Alameda County Coliseum, 1988—91; mng. dir. events and attractions NBA, 1991—97; founding mem. Nike Sports Entertainment, 1996—99; v.p. mktg. Trakus Inc., Boston; exec. v.p. Memphis Grizzlies, 2000—05; sr. v.p. mktg. and bus. ops. NY Rangers, 2005—06; exec. v.p. bus. ops. Portland Trail Blazers, 2006—07, COO, 2007—. Office: Portland Trail Blazers Rose Garden One Center Ct Portland OR 97227

GOMES, WAYNE REGINALD, academic administrator; b. Modesto, Calif., Nov. 15, 1938; s. Frank C. and Mary (Rogers) G.; m. Carol L. Gerlach, Sept. 2, 1964 (deceased); children: John Charles, Regina Carol; m. Anne Freitas, Nov. 27, 2004. BS, Calif. Poly. State U., 1960; MS, Wash. State U., 1962; PhD, Purdue U., 1965. Asst. prof. dairy sci. Ohio State U., Columbus, 1965-69, assoc. prof. dairy sci., 1969-72, prof. dairy sci., 1972-81; prof., head dept. dairy sci. U. Ill., Urbana, 1981-85, prof., head dept. animal scis., 1985-89, acting dean Coll. Agr., 1988-89, dean, 1989-95; v.p. agr. and natural resources U. Calif. System, Oakland, 1995—2007. Fulbright prof. Zagreb U., Yugoslavia, 1974; vis. scholar Kyoto U., Japan, 1980; mem. bd. on agr. and natural resources NRC. Editor: The Testis, Vols. 1-4, 1970—77; contbr. over 100 articles to jours., chapters to books. Mem. Coun. for Agrl. Sci. and Tech., Am. Soc. of Animal Sci., Am. Dairy Sci. Assn., Soc. for Study of Reprodn., Endocrine Soc., others. Lodges: Rotary. Office: U Calif 1111 Franklin St Oakland CA 94607-5201 Home Phone: 510-841-3581; Office Phone: 510-986-0060. Business E-Mail: regmail@ucop.edu.

GOMEZ, LARRY, former prosecutor; US atty. US Dept. Justice, Albuquerque, 1993—, asst. US atty. N.Mex., acting US atty. N.Mex., 2007—08.

GOMEZ, LOUIS SALAZAR, college president; b. Santa Ana, Calif., Dec. 7, 1939; s. Louis Reza and Mary (Salazar) G.; m. Patricia Ann Aboytes, June 30, 1962; children: Louis Aboytes, Diana Maria, Ramon Reza. Student, Calif. State Poly. U., 1959-65; BA, Calif. State U., San Bernardino, 1971; MA, Calif. State U., 1975; EdD, U. So. Calif., LA, 1987. Cert. tchr., counselor, adminstr., Calif. Tchr., counselor San Bernardino City Schs., 1971-76; human rels. coord. San Bernardino Valley Coll., 1976-78, counselor, 1978-82, coord. of counseling, 1982-87; asst. dean student svcs. Crafton Hills Coll., Yucaipa, Calif., 1987-89, dean student svcs., 1989-90, acting pres., 1990-92, pres., 1992—. Lectr. Calif. State U., San Bernardino, 1976-81, mem. adv. bd., 1987-95. Bd. dirs. Redlands YMCA, 1995—; pres. San Bernardino Regional Emergency Tng. Ctr. Joint Power Authority, 1998—. Mem. San Bernardino Valley Coll. Faculty Assn. (treas. 1980-82), Faculty Assn. Calif. Community Colls., San Bernardino Community Coll. Dist. Mgmt. Assn., Kiwanis (pres. San Bernardino chpt. 1982). Democrat. Roman Catholic. Avocations: financial planning, photography, treasure hunting. Home: 10682 Berrywood Cir Yucaipa CA 92399-5924 Office: Crafton Hills Coll 11711 Sand Canyon Rd Yucaipa CA 92399-1742

GOMO, STEVEN J., technical communications product company executive; BSBA, Oreg. State U.; MBA, Santa Clara U. Numerous positions to gen. mgr. inkjet mfg. ops. Hewlett-Packard Co., 1974-98; sr. v.p., CFO Silicon Graphics Inc., Mountain View, Calif., 1998—. Bd. dirs. Hello Direct Inc.

GONICK, HARVEY CRAIG, nephrologist, educator; b. Winnipeg, Man., Can., Apr. 10, 1930; s. Joseph Wolfe and Rose (Chernick) G.; m. Gloria Granz, Dec. 16, 1967; children: Stefan, Teri, Julie, Suzanne. BS in Chemistry, UCLA, 1951; MD, U. Calif., San Francisco, 1955. Diplomate Am. Bd. Internal Medicine, Am. Bd. Nephrology. Intern Peter Bent Brigham Hosp., 1955-56; fellow in nephrology Mass. Meml. Hosp., 1956-57; fellow in nephrology, resident in internal medicine Wadsworth VA Hosp., Los Angeles, 1959-61, clin. investigator, 1961-64, chief metabolic balance unit, 1964-67, rsch. assoc. LA, 2002—; instr. medicine Sch. Medicine, UCLA, 1961-64, asst. prof., 1964-69, assoc. prof., 1969-72, adj. assoc. prof., 1972-76, adj. prof., 1976—2003, clin. prof., 2003—, assoc. chief div. nephrology, 1965-72, co-dir. Bone and Stone Clinic, 1972-76, coordinator postgrad. nephrology edn., 1975-78; mem. staff St. John's Hosp., Santa Monica, Calif., Century City Hosp., LA, med. dir. dialysis unit, 1972-79, chief medicine, 1978-79; mem. staff Cedars-Sinai Med. Ctr., LA, dir. trace element lab., 1979-96, clin. chief nephrology, 1983-85, coord. renal tng., dir. hypertension rsch., 1996—2003; practice medicine specializing in nephrology Los Angeles, 1972-94. Co-founder, med. dir. Berkeley East Dialysis Unit, Santa Monica, 1971-75; co-founder, cons. Kidney Dialysis Care Units Inc., Lynwood, Calif., 1971-78; co-dir. Osteoporosis Prevention and Treatment Ctr., Santa Monica, 1987-93; mem. numerous adv. coms. to state and fed. agys., 1969-83. Contbr. articles to profl. jours.; editor: Current Nephrology, 1977-96. Served to capt. M.C., USAF, 1957-59. Fellow Charles Nelson Fund, Kaiser Found., NIH; recipient Oliver P. Douglas Meml. award Los Angeles County Heart Assn., 1959, Vis. Scientist award Deutscher Academischer Austauschendienst, 1978. Fellow ACP; mem. AMA, AAAS, Internat. Soc. Nephrology (organizing com. internat. cong. 1984), Am. Soc. Nephrology, European Dialysis and Transplant Assn., Soc. Exptl. Biology and Medicine, Calif. Med. Assn., Los Angeles County Med. Assn., Nat. Kidney Found. (active ann. conf. 1963-65, sec. nat. med. adv. coun. 1969-70, regional rep. and legis. com. nat. med. adv. coun. 1970-73, grantee 1963), So. Calif. Kidney Found. (chmn. sci. adv. coun. 1968-70, co-chmn. legis. com. 1970-73, bd. dirs. 1974-83, honoree 1979), Am. Soc. Bone and Mineral Rsch., Am. Coll. Toxicology, Soc. Toxicology, Am. Heart Assn. (renal sect. of coun. on circulation), Am. Fedn. Clin. Rsch., Western Soc. Clin. Rsch., Western Assn. Physicians, Phi Beta Kappa, Sigma Xi, Alpha Omega Alpha, Phi Eta Sigma, Alpha Mu Gamma, Phi Lambda Upsilon. Avocation: tennis. Business E-Mail: hgonick@ucla.edu.

GONZALES, RICHARD L., protective services official; AA in Fire Sci. Tech., Red Rocks C.C., 1988; BS summa cum laude in Bus. Adminstrn., Regis U., 1991; MA, Harvard U., 1991; student, U. Colo. Firefighter Denver Fire Dept., 1972-75, mem. fire prevention bureau, dist. 5 roving officer, 1976-79, mem. training divsn., 1980-81, dist. roving officer firefighter, 1981-82, capt. firefighter pumper 2 and 27, 1982-85, asst. chief, 1985-87, chief fire dept., 1987—. Mem. Nat. Fire Protective Assn. Urban Fire Forum, Internat. Assn. Fire Chiefs, Metro Fire Chiefs Assn., Denver Metro Fire Chiefs Assn., Colo. State Fire Chiefs Assn., Urban Fire Forum, IAFF Local 858 Negotiating Team; bd. trustees Nat. Fire Protection Assn., 1992-95. Mem. adv. bd. U. Colo. Denver Sch. of Pub. Affairs, Red Rocks C.C., Denver Ptnrs., KAZY Denver Marathon; bd. trustees Nat. Multiple Sclerosis Soc.; bd. dirs. Rocky Mountain Poison Drug Found., Chic Chicana, Golden Gloves Charity. Recipient Outstanding Achievement award Hispanics of Colo., 1987; named Young Firefighter of the Yr., 1981. Office: Denver Fire Dept 745 W Colfax Ave Denver CO 80204-2612

GONZALES, RICHARD STEVEN, broadcast executive; b. San Diego, Apr. 25, 1954; s. Lawrence Avila and Catalina Victoria (Salvaterra) G.; m. Tara Norcross Siler, Oct. 12, 1991; 1 child, Diego Siler. BA in Psychology and Social Relations, Harvard U., 1977. Pub. affairs dir. KPFA-FM, Berkeley, Calif., 1979-85; frelance prod. KQED-TV, San Francisco, 1986; fgn. affairs corr., State Dept. Nat. Pub. Radio, Washington, 1986-90, White House corr., 1990-93, congl. corr., 1993-94, reporter, nat. affairs corr., for All Things Considered, Morning Edition and Weekend Edition San Francisco, 1995—. Documentary: Street Children in Maputo, 1988. Co-founder Familias Unidas, Richmond, Calif., 1980. Recipient Media award World Hunger Inc., N.Y.C., 1988, Thomas Starke award World Affairs Coun. No. Calif., San Francisco, 1984; John S. Knight fellow Stanford U., 1994-95. Office: Nat Pub Radio 2601 Mariposa St San Francisco CA 94110-1426

GONZALES, RON, mayor, former county supervisor; b. San Francisco, 1951; m. Alvina Gonzales; 3 children: Miranda, Rachel, Alejandra. BA in Community Studies, U. Calif., Santa Cruz. Formerly with Sunnyvale (Calif.) Sch. Dist., City of Santa Clara, Calif.; then human resource mgr. Hewlett-Packard Co.; market program mgmt. cons. state and local govts.; mem. city coun. City of Sunnyvale, 1979-87, mayor, 1982, 87; mem. bd. suprs. Santa Clara County, 1989-96; edn. program mgr. Hewlett Packard Co., 1996-98; mayor City of San Jose, Calif., 1999—2006. Bd. chair, 1993; bd. transit suprs. Santa Clara County, 1989—; bd. dirs. Joint Venture: Silicon Valley, The Role Model Program, Bay Area Biosci. Ctr., Am. Leadership Forum, Santa Clara County.

GONZALES, SARAH, women's organization director; b. 1976; Dir., Racial Justice Prog. YWCA. Mem. Ariz. Collegiate Leadership Conf. Mem. Jewish Cmty. Rels. Coun., Tunnel of Oppression, U. Ariz., Tucson Save Darfur Coalition. Named one of 40 Under 40, Tucson Bus. Edge, 2006. Office: YWCA 738 N 5th Ave Tucson AZ 85705 Office Phone: 520-884-7810. Office Fax: 520-884-5205.

GONZALES, STEPHANIE, state official; b. Santa Fe, Aug. 12, 1950; 1 child, Adan Gonzales. Degree, Loretto Acad. for Girls. Office mgr. Jerry Wood & Assocs., 1973-86; dep. sec. of state Santa Fe, 1987-90; sec. of state, 1991-99; state dir. rural devel. U.S. Dept. of Agriculture, Albuquerque, 1999—; state liaison dept. energy Los Alamos Eviron. Mgmt. Site. Bd. dirs. N.Mex. Pub. Employees Retirement, N.Mex. State Convassing Bd., N.Mex. Commn. Pub. Records. Mem. exec. bd. N.Mex. AIDS Svc.; mem. Commn. White House Fellowships. Mem. Nat. Assn. Secs. State, United League United Latin Am. Citizens (women's coun.), Nat. Assn. Latin Elected and Appointed Ofcls. Office: Los Alamos Nat Lab PO Box 1663 Los Alamos NM 87545

GONZALEZ, ADRIAN, professional baseball player; b. San Diego, May 8, 1982; s. David; m. Betsy Gonzalez. First baseman Tex. Rangers, 2004—05, San Diego Padres, 2006—. First baseman Venados de Mazatlan, Mexico; mem. Mex. nat. team World Baseball Classic, 2006, 09. Founder Adrian and Betsy Gonzalez Found. Recipient Gold Glove award, 2008; named to Nat. League All-Star Team, Maj. League Baseball, 2008. Achievements include leading the National League in: games played (162), 2008. Office: PETCO Pk 100 Park Blvd San Diego CA 92101*

GONZALEZ, ARTHUR PADILLA, artist, educator; b. Sacramento, July 22, 1954; s. John and Rita (Padilla) G.; m. Christine Carol Ciavarella, Feb. 11, 1988; stepchild, Nick Port. BA, Calif. State U., Sacramento, 1977, MA, 1979; MFA, U. Calif., Davis, 1981. Vis. artist La. State U., Baton Rouge, 1982-83, U. Ga., Athens, summer 1984, R.I. Sch. Design, Providence, 1985; asst. prof. U. Calif., Davis, 1985-86, Berkeley, 1987-88; vis. artist, instr. San Francisco Art Inst., 1990-91; assoc. prof. art Calif. Coll. Arts, Oakland, 1991—. Juror Sacramento Met. Arts Commn., 1994-95. One-person shows include Sharpe Gallery, N.Y.C., 1984, 85, 86, 88, Phyllis Kind Gallery, N.Y.C., 1995, John Elder Gallery, N.Y.C., 1999, 2002. Recipient awards Nat. Endowment for Arts, 1982, 84, 86, 90, Virginia Groot award, 1997. Democrat. Avocation: polynesian dance. Home: 1713 Versailles Ave Alameda CA 94501-1650 Office: Calif Coll Arts & Crafts 5212 Broadway Oakland CA 94618-1426 Office Phone: 510-594-3617. Business E-Mail: art@arthurgonzalez.com. E-mail: windeater@alamedanet.net.

GONZALEZ, IRMA ELSA, federal judge; b. Palo Alto, Calif., 1948; BA, Stanford U., 1970; JD, U. Ariz., 1973. Law clk. to Hon. William C. Frey US Dist. Ct. (Ariz. dist.), 1973-75; asst. U.S. atty. US Attys. Office Ariz., 1975-79, US Attys. Office (ctrl. dist.) Calif., 1979-81; trial atty. antitrust divsn. US Dept. Justice, 1979; assoc. Seltzer Caplan Wilkins & McMahon, San Diego, 1981-84; judge US Magistrate Ct. (so. dist.) Calif., 1984-91; ct. judge San Diego County Superior Ct., 1991-92; judge US Dist. Ct. (so. dist.) Calif., San Diego, 1992—, chief judge, 2005—. Adj. prof. U. San Diego, 1992; trustee Calif. Western Sch. Law; bd. visitors Sch. Law U. Ariz. Mem. Girl Scout Women's Adv. Cabinet. Mem. Lawyers' Club San Diego, Inns of Ct. Office: Edward J Schwartz US Courthouse 940 Front St Ste 5135 San Diego CA 92101-8911

GONZALEZ, MATT, lawyer; b. McAllen, Tex., 1965; s. Mateo and Oralia Gonzalez. BA in Polit. Theory and Comparative Lit., Columbia U., NYC, 1987; JD, Stanford U. Law Sch., Calif., 1990. Trial lawyer Office the Pub. Defender, San Francisco, 1991—2000; mem. San Francisco Bd. Supervisors, 2000—05, pres., 2003—05; ptnr., trial lawyer Gonzalez & Leigh LLP, San Francisco, 2005—. Lectr. New Coll. Calif., San Francisco Art Inst. Mayoral candidate Green Party, San Francisco, 2003; US vice presdl. candidate Ind. Party, 2008. Recipient Guardian award, In Def. of Animals, 2003, Bert Corona award, Calif. Mexican-American Polit. Assn., 2004; named Lawyer of Yr., San Francisco La Raza Lawyers Assn., 2000, Robert D. & Leslie-Kay Raven Lecture, U. Calif. Berkeley Sch. Law, 2004. Independent. Office: Gonzalez & Leigh LLP Two Shaw Alley San Francisco CA 94105 Office Phone: 415-512-2000. Office Fax: 415-512-2001.*

GONZÁLEZ-TRUJILLO, CÉSAR AUGUSTO, Chicano studies educator, writer; b. LA, Jan. 17, 1931; s. José Andalón and Camerina (Trujillo) González; m. Bette L. Beattie, Aug. 30, 1969. BA, Gonzaga U., 1953, MA, Licentiate in Philosophy, 1954; MST, Licentiate in Sacred Theology, U. Santa Clara, 1961; postgrad., UCLA, 1962-65. Tchr. Instituto Regional Mex., Chihuahua, Mexico, 1954-57; comty. devel. specialist Centro Laboral Méx., México D.F., Mexico, 1965-68; supr. ABC Headstart East LA, 1968-69; employment counselor Op. Svc. Employment Redevelopment, San Diego, 1969-70; prof., founding chair dept. Chicano studies San Diego Mesa Coll., 1970-99, prof. emeritus, 1999—. Founding chairperson Raza Consortium, San Diego, 1971-72; cons. Chicano Fedn. San Diego, Inc., 1987-89. Author poetry, short fiction and criticism, 1976—. Mem. Ednl. Issues Coordinating Com., LA, 1968-69; founding bd. dirs. Mex.-Am. Adv. Com. Bd. Edn., LA, 1969. Fulbright-Hays fellow, Peru, 1982, NEH fellow, 1984; recipient Cmty. Svc. award Chicano Fedn. San Diego Inc., 1982, Tchg. Excellence award Nat. Inst. Staff Orgnl. Devel., 1993, Outstanding Tchr. San Diego Mesa Coll., 1985, 95, Editor's Choice award Poet Mag., 1993, Cesar Chavez Social Justice award, 1994, Latina Latino Indigenous People Coalition award, 1995; named Outstanding Tchr. Scholar, Concilio Chicano Studies San Diego, Imperial Valley Baja, Calif., 1990; Spl. Congl. recognition Congressman Bob Filner, 1995; AVID Writer Yr. award San Diego Imperial Counties, 1997, Premio Aztla'n, 2000. Mem. Am. Fedn. Tchrs., Centro Cultural De La Raza (past bd. dirs.), Poets and Writers, Internat. Assn. Hispanicists. Democrat. Roman Catholic. Avocations: reading, travel. Office: San Diego Mesa Coll 7250 Mesa College Dr San Diego CA 92111-4902 Personal E-mail: cesargonzalez2@cox.net.

GOO, VALERIE M., lawyer; BA, U. Calif., LA, 1992, JD, 1996. Bar: Calif. 1996, US Dist. Ct. (ctrl. dist.) Calif., US Ct. Appeals (9th cir.). Sr. assoc. Pillsbury Winthrop Shaw Pittman, LA, 2005—06, ptnr., 2006, Orrick, Herrington & Sutcliffe, LA, 2006—. Mem.: State Bar of Calif. Office: Orrick Herrington & Sutcliffe LLP 777 S Figueroa St Ste 3200 Los Angeles CA 90017 Office Phone: 213-629-2020.

GOODACRE, CHARLES J., dean, educator; b. 1946; m. Ruth E. Goodacre. DDS, Loma Linda U., 1971; MSD, Ind. U., Indpls., 1974. Diplomate Am. Bd. Prosthodontics. Prof., chmn. dept. prosthodontics Sch. Dentistry Ind. U., Ind., 1974; prof. Loma Linda U., dean Sch. Dentistry. Contbr. articles to profl. jours.; co-author: (textbook) Johnston's Modern Practice in Fixed Prosthodontics (4th edit.); editor: Internat. Journal of Prosthodontics. Fellow: Acad. Prosthodontics, Am. Coll. Prosthodontics; mem.: Am. Acad. of Fixed Prosthodontics, Am. Bd. Prosthodontics (pres.). Avocations: woodworking, sports, Lionel trains, off-road motorcylcing. Office: Loma Linda Univ Loma Linda CA 92350 Business E-Mail: cgoodacre@llu.edu.

GOODALE, DORIS, state legislator; b. Tucson, Ariz., Mar. 8, 1949; m. William Goodale; 4 children. Attended, Phoenix Coll., Ariz. State U. With Mohave County Sheriff's Office, 1971—73; chief dep. probation officer & adminstr. Mohave County Probation Dept., 1977—87, asst. chief probation officer-Adult Svcs. Div., 1987—2006; mem. Dist. 3 Ariz. House of Reps., 2008—. Mem. Govs. Task Force on Marriage & Family, 1976—78; former mem. Performance Measures Com., Ednl. Sub-com. for Curriculum. Bd. mem. Kingman Elem.-Unified Sch. Dist., 1988—2006, Kingman Youth Football League, former pres.; bd. mem. Kingman Cmty. Methamphetamine Coalition, Kingman Partnership for Children With Spl. Needs; bd. mem. & publicity chmn. Kingman Cancer Care Unit; vice chmn. Mohave Substance Treatment-Edn. Prevention Partnership; mem. K-12 Sch. Dist.-Redistrict Commn., 2005, Kingman Drug Free Alliance, Kingman Parks & Recreation Commn., Kingman Hist. Preservation Commn.; former Sunday sch. tchr. Manzanita Bapt. Ch. Recipient Achievement award, Nat. Dist. Atty. Assn., 1973, Nat. Coun. Juvenile Ct. Judges, 1973, Nat. Conf. Criminal Justice, 1975, Juvenile Justice Mgmt. Inst. Achievement award, Nat. Coun. Juvenile & Family & Ct. Judges, 1979, Mohave County Women Making Hist.

award, 2006; named Citizen of Yr., Kingman C. of C., 1995. Mem.: Ariz. Sch. Bds. Assn. (named to All State Sch. Bd. 2005), Ariz. Chief Probation Officer Assn. (Supr. of Yr. 2000, "Round of Applause" Jud. Employee Recognition award 2005), Ariz. METH Cmty. Coalition-Kingman Chpt., Kingman Cmty. Vision Group, Kingman Rep. Women's Club (chmn. Ednl. Com.). Republican. Office: Capitol Complex 1700 W Washington Rm 310 Phoenix AZ 85007-2890 Office Phone: 602-926-5408. Office Fax: 602-417-3103. Business E-Mail: dgoodale@azleg.gov.*

GOODALL, JACKSON WALLACE, JR., restaurant company executive; b. San Diego, Oct. 29, 1938; s. Jackson Wallace and Evelyn Violet (Koski) G.; m. Mary Esther Buckley, June 22, 1958; children: Kathleen, Jeffery, Suzanne, Minette. BS, San Diego State U., 1960. With Foodmaker, Inc., San Diego, 1963—, pres., 1970—, CEO, 1979—, also chmn. bd. dirs. Founder, bd. dir. Grossmont Bank, La Mesa, Calif.; bd. dirs. Thrifty Drug Stores Inc., Van Camp Seafood Inc., Ralcorp.; owner, dir., bd. dirs. San Diego Padres Baseball Club. Bd. dirs. Greater San Diego Sports Assn.; mem. Pres.'s Coun. San Diego State U.; chmn. Child Abuse Prevention Found.; dir. San Diego Hall Champions. Recipient Golden Chain award, 1982, Silver Plate award Internat. Foodsvc. Mfg. Assn., 1985; named Disting. Alumni of Yr. San Diego State U., 1974, 89, Golden Chain Operator of Yr. Multi Unit Food Svc. Operators, 1988, State of Israel Man of Yr., 1987, Citizen of Yr. City Club of San Diego, 1992, Marketer of Yr. Acad. Mktg. Sci., 1992, Manchester Cmty. Svc. award, 1997; inducted into San Diego Bus. Hall of Fame, 1992. Mem. Am. Restaurant Assn., Fairbanks Ranch Country Club (founder), Univ. Club of San Diego, San Diego Intercollegiate Athletic Coun., Kadoo Club of N. Am., La Jolla Country Club. Republican.

GOODALL, LEONARD EDWIN, public administration educator; b. Warrensburg, Mo., Mar. 16, 1937; s. Leonard Burton and Eula (Johnson) G.; m. Lois Marie Stubblefield, Aug. 16, 1959; children: Karla, Karen, Greg. BA, Ctrl. Mo. State U., 1958; MA, U. Mo., 1960; PhD, U. Ill., 1962; AA (hon.), Schoolcraft Coll., 1977; DHL (hon.), Ctrl. Mo. State U., Warrensburg, 2000. Asst. prof. polit. sci., asst. dir. Bur. Govt. Rsch., Ariz. State U., Tempe, 1962-65, bur. dir., 1965-67; assoc. prof. polit. sci., assoc. dean faculties U. Ill. at Chgo. Circle, 1968-69, vice chancellor, 1969-71; chancellor U. Mich., Dearborn, 1971-79; pres. U. Nev., Las Vegas, 1979-85, prof. mgmt. and pub. administrn., 1985—2000. Cons. Ariz. Acad., Phoenix, 1964-67; dir. Peace Corps tng. program for Chile, 1965; vice chmn. bd. Comml. Bank of Nev., 1993-98; chmn. bd. Colonial Bank Nev., 1998—. Contbg. editor: Can. Moneysaver, 1997—; Author: The American Metropolis: Its Governments and Politics, 1968, rev. edit., 1975, Gearing Arizona's Communities to Orderly Growth, 1965, State Politics and Higher Education, 1976, When Colleges Lobby States, 1987, Managing Your TIAA-CREF Retirement Accounts, 1990, The World Wide Investor, 1991, Nevada Government and Politics, 1996, Reinventing the System, 2001; editor: Urban Politics in the Southwest, 1967. Mem. univ. exec. com. United Fund, 1966-67; v.p. Met. Fund, Inc.; mem. Mich. Gov.'s Commn. Long Range Planning, 1973-75, Tempe Planning and Zoning Commn., 1965-67, New Detroit Com., 1972-79; mem. Wayne County (Mich.) Planning Commn., 1973-79, vice chmn., 1976-79; mem. exec. bd. Clark County chpt. NCCJ, 1979-86; bd. dirs. Nev. Devel. Authority, 1980-86, Boulder Dam coun. Boy Scouts Am., 1980-89; bd. dirs. Nev. Power Co. Consumer Adv. Coun., 1984-90, chmn., 1986-89. Served with AUS, 1959. Kendrick C. Babcock fellow, 1961—62. Mem. Am. Polit. Sci. Assn., Am. Soc. Pub. Adminstrn. (chpt. pres. 1989-90), Western Govtl. Rsch. Assn. (exec. coun. 1966-68), Clark County Growth Task Force (chmn. 2004-05), Las Vegas Rotary Found. (pres. 2005-06), Dearborn C. of C. (dir. 1974-79), Rotary, Phi Sigma Epsilon, Phi Kappa Phi Found. (bd. dirs. 1994-96). Home: 6530 Darby Ave Las Vegas NV 89146-6518 Office: U Nev Dept Pub Adminstrn Las Vegas NV 89154 Personal E-mail: patgoodall@aol.com.

GOODBY, JEFFREY, advertising agency executive; m. Jan Goodby; 3 children. B in English, Harvard U., 1973. Former newspaper reporter, Boston; various positions J. Walter Thompson; with Ogilvy & Mather, San Francisco, 1979; co-founder, co-chmn., creative dir. Goodby, Silverstein & Ptnrs. (formerly Goodby, Berlin, & Silverstein), San Francisco, 1983—. Jury pres. Cannes Lions Internat. Advt. Festival, 2005—; jury head ADOI Advt. Awards, Indonesia, 2008. Work represented in permanent collections Mus. Modern Art, NY. Trustee Art Ctr. Coll. of Design, Pasadena, Calif.; bd. dirs. Salvador Dali Mus., St. Petersburg, Fla., San Francisco Mag. Named Creative Dir. of Yr., Adweek mag., 1990, 1992, 1994; named to Creative Hall of Fame, The One Club for Art & Copy, 2004. Office: Goodby Silverstein & Ptnrs 720 California St San Francisco CA 94108-2404 Office Phone: 415-392-0669. Office Fax: 415-788-4303.*

GOODCHILD, MICHAEL FRANK, geographer, educator; b. Feb. 24, 1944; married; 3 children. BA in Physics, Cambridge U., Eng., 1965; PhD in Geography, McMaster U., Ont., Can., 1969; DSc (hon.), Laval U., Can., 1999, Keele U., 2001, McMaster U., Ont., Can., 2004; LLD (hon.), Ryerson U., Toronto, Can., 2004. Asst. prof. U. Western Ont., 1969—71, assoc. prof., 1971—79, prof., 1979—89; prof. geography U. Calif., Santa Barbara, 1989—. Cons.; vis. prof. McGill U., 1972, U. Iowa, 1973, rsch. assoc., 74, vis. assoc. prof., 74; vis. prof. U. Calif., Santa Barbara, 1978, 79, 1988—89, chair dept. geography, 1998—2000, dir. Ctr. Spatially Integrated Social Sci., 1999—; chmn. dept. geography U. Western Ont., 1982—85, hon. prof., 1989—94; vis. prof. U. Auckland, 1986; vis. scholar Commonwealth Sci. and Indsl. Rsch. Orgn., Canberra, Australia, 1986; mem. adv. bd. Inst. Market and Social Analysis, Toronto, Canada, 1987—89; co-dir. Nat. Ctr. Geog. Info. and Analysis, 1988—91, dir., 1991—96, chair exec. com., 1997—; mem. sci. adv. bd. Internat. Cartographic Assn., 1990—; assoc. dir. Alexandria Digital Libr., 1994—; chair mapping sci. com. NRC, 1997—99; vis. prof. U. London Birkbeck Coll., 1997. Contbr. articles to profl. jours.; mem. adv. editl. bd.: Internat. Jour. Geog. Info. Systems, 1986—; editor: Geog. Analysis, 1987—90; mem. editl. bd.: Operational Geographer, 1989—97, Geog. Systems: The European Jour. Theoretical and Applied Geography, 1990—, Jour. Geog. Systems, 1998—, Cartography and Geog. Info. Systems, 1999—, Geoinformation Sci. Jour., 2005—, Profl. Geographer, 2005—, mem. editl. adv. bd.: Geog. Info. Systems, 1990—, GIS World, 1990—, Geog. Analysis, 1990—, assoc. editor: Annals of the Assn. of Am. Geographers, 1996—2000, editor methods, models and geog. info. scis.:, 2000—. Recipient Applied Geography Citation award, Assn. Am. Geographers, 1983, Award for Disting. Scholarship, 1996, Scholarly Distinction in Geography award, Can. Assn. Geographers, 1990, Award of Distinction for Exceptional Scholarly Contbns. to Cartography, Can. Cartographic Assn., 1999, Lifetime Achievement award, Environ. Systems Rsch. Inst., 2001, Founder's medal, Royal Geog. Soc., 2003; co-recipient Horwood Critique prize, Urban and Regional Info. Systems Assn., 1993, 1995, Gerald McCalden award, Australasian Urban and Regional Info. Systems Assn., 1994, Intergraph award, Am. Soc. Photogrammetry and Remote Sensing, 1996; named Educator of Yr., Univ. Consortium for Geog. Info. Sci., 2002; grantee Leave fellowship, Social Scis. and Humanities Rsch. Coun., 1986. Fellow: Royal Soc. Can. (fgn. fellow), Am. Acad. Arts & Scis.; mem.: NAS. Office: Dept Geography U Calif 5707 Ellison Hall Santa Barbara CA 93106-4060 E-mail: good@ncgia.ucsb.edu.

GOODE, BARRY PAUL, lawyer; b. NYC, Apr. 11, 1948; s. Hy and Charlotte (Langer) G.; m. Erica Tucker, Sept. 1, 1974; children: Adam, Aaron. AB magna cum laude, Kenyon Coll., 1969; JD cum laude, Harvard U., 1972. Bar: Mass. 1972, Calif. 1975, Hawaii 1995, U.S. Dist. Ct. Mass. 1972, U.S. Dist. Ct. (no. dist.) Calif. 1975, U.S. Dist. Ct. (ctrl. dist.) Calif. 1983, U.S. Dist. Ct. Hawaii 1995, U.S. Ct. Appeals (9th cir.) 1976, U.S. Ct. Appeals (6th cir.) 1999, U.S. Supreme Ct. 1986. Spl. asst. Sen Adlai E. Stevenson III, Washington, 1972-74; assoc. McCutchen, Doyle, Brown & Enersen, San Francisco, 1974-80, ptnr., 1980-2001; legal affairs sec. Gov. Gray Davis, 2001—. Co-author: Federal Litigation Guide, 1985. Advisor Gov.'s Com. to Review Water Law, San Francisco, 1979; bd. dirs. Stanford Pub. Interest Law Found., 1979-82; bd. dirs. Coro No. Calif., 1997—. Mem. San Francisco Bar Assn. (exec. com. environ. law sect. 1989-91), Am. Law Inst. Office: Gov Gray Davis State Capitol Sacramento CA 95814

GOODE, ERICA TUCKER, internist; b. Berkeley, Calif., Mar. 25, 1940; d. Howard Edwin and Mary Louise (Tucker) Sweeting; m. Bruce Tucker (div. 1971); m. Barry Paul Goode, Sept. 1, 1974; children: Adam Nathaniel, Aaron Benjamin. BS summa cum laude, U. Calif., Berkeley, 1962, MPH, 1967; MD, U. Calif., San Francisco, 1977. Diplomate Am. Bd. Internal Medicine. Chief dietitian Washington Hosp. Ctr., Washington, 1968; pub. health nutritionist Dept. Human Resources, Washington, 1969—73; intern Children's Hosp. (now Calif. Pacific Med. Ctr.), San Francisco, 1977—78, resident, 1978—80, chief med. resident internal medicine, 1979—80; pvt. practice internal medicine San Francisco, 1980—. Expert witness med.-legal issues, Calif., 1990—; lectr., tchr. med. house staff Calif. Pacific Med. Ctr. Hosp., 1982—; assoc. prof. medicine U. Calif., San Francisco, 1984—; apptd. mem. Calif. Commn. on Aging, 2003—. Contbr. articles to profl. publs. Co-chair Physicians for Clinton, No. Calif., 1992, 96 Mem. AMA, ACP, Calif. Med. Assn., Calif. Soc. Internal Medicine, San Francisco Med. Soc. (mem. editl. bd.), U. Calif. Alumni Assn. (del.), Alpha Omega Alpha (named Best Doctor's list 1996-). Office: CPMC Inst for Health & Healing Clinic 2300 California St Ste 200 San Francisco CA 94115-2754 Office Phone: 415-600-3503. Business E-Mail: goodee@sutterhealth.org.

GOODE, JOE, performing company executive; BA in theater arts, Va. Commonwealth U. Founder, artistic dir. Joe Goode Performance Group, San Francisco, 1986; prof. theater, dance and performance studies U. Calif., Berkeley. Co-founder, curator EDGE Festival, San Francisco, 1986; co-founder Parachute Fund, 1989. Choreographer The Ascension of Big Linda into the Skies of Montana, 1986 (Isadora Duncan dance award for outstanding achievement in performance, 1987), The Disaster Series, 1989 (Isadora Duncan dance awards for outstanding achievement choreography and in performance, 1990), Maverick Strain, 1996 (Nat. Endowment Arts award, 1996, Isadora Duncan dance awards for best commissioned score and best stage lighting, 1997), Deeply There (stories of a neighborhood), 1998 (Nat. Endowment Arts award, 1998, NY Dance and Performance award, 1999, Isadora Duncan dance award, 2000), Jane Eyre, 1999, Gender Heroes, 1999, What the Body Knows, 2001 (Isadora Duncan dance award, 2001), Transparent Body, 2002, Mythic, Montana, 2002, Folk, 2003, Grace, 2004, Hometown, 2005, Stay Together, 2006, Humansville, 2007, Wonderboy, 2008; author: (plays) Body Familiar, 2003; dir.: (Operas) Transformations, 2006. Recipient Artistic Excellence award, San Francisco Bus. Arts Coun., 1994, Outstanding Arts award, Amman Theater, 1997, Pres.'s award, Irvine Barclay Theatre, 1997, Heritage award, Calif. Dance Educators Assn., 2000; grantee Calif. Arts Coun., 1988—, Grants for the Arts, 1988—, Nat. Endowment Arts, 1990—, Dance USA, 1994, San Francisco Arts Commn., 1995—, NY Found. Arts, 1995, Arts Internat., 1997, USIA, 1997, Andrew W. Mellon Found., 1999, 2002, Creative Capital, 2000, Irvine Found., 2001; fellow Nat. Endowment Arts, 1985—89, James Irvine Found., 1998, John Simon Guggeneim Found., 2007, US Artists, 2008; Agnes Fourne fellowship, 1991. Office: Joe Goode Performance Group 1007 General Kennedy Ave Ste 209 San Francisco CA 94129 also: Dept Theater Dance and Performance Studies U Calif Berkeley 101 Dwinelle Annex Berkeley CA 94720-2560 Office Phone: 415-561-6565, 510-643-4341. Office Fax: 415-561-6562. E-mail: info@joegoode.org, joegoode@berkeley.edu.*

GOODING, CHARLES ARTHUR, radiologist, physician, educator; b. Cleve., Feb. 28, 1936; s. Joseph J. and Florence G. (Pitt) G.; m. Gretchen Wagner, June 19, 1961; children: Gunnar, Justin, Britta. BA, Western Res. U., 1957; MD, Ohio State U., 1961. Intern Ohio State U. Hosp., 1961-62; resident in radiology Peter Bent Brigham Hosp., Children's Hosp. Med. Center, both Boston, 1963-65; rsch. fellow radiology Harvard Med. Sch., Boston, 1962, tchg. fellow, 1965-66; Harvard Med. Sch. fellow Hosp. for Sick Children, London, Karolinska Hosp., Stockholm, 1966; faculty U. Calif. Med. Center, San Francisco, 1967—, prof. radiology and pediatrics, 1976—, exec. vice-chmn. dept. radiology, 1974—2001. Pres. Radiology Rsch. and Edn. Found., 1973-96, Radiology Outreach Found., 1988-2002, pres. emeritus 2002—; hon. mem. faculty Francesco Maroquin U. Sch. Medicine, Guatemala City. Contbr. chpts. to books.; Editor: Pediatric Radiology, 1973—96; editor: Diagnostic Radiology, 1972-92; contbr. articles to profl. jours. Capt. M.C. USAR, 1967-68. Recipient Outstanding Alumni award Brigham Women's Hosp. Harvard Med. Sch., 1994, Disting. Alumnus award Ohio State U., 1986, Case Western Res. U., 1999, Beclere medal Internat. Soc. Radiology, 1998; named to Disting. Alumni Hall of Fame Cleve. Heights H.S., 1999, Top Pediat. Radiologist San Francisco mag., 2001. Fellow Am. Coll. Radiology, Royal Coll. Radiologists London (hon.), Armenian Radiol. Soc. (hon.); mem. Am. Roentgen Ray Soc., Assn. Univ. Radiologists, European Soc. Pediat. Radiologists (hon.), Pacific Coast Pediat. Radiologists Assn. (past pres.), Radiol. Soc. N.Am., Polish Radiology Soc. (hon.), Hungarian Radiology Soc. (hon.), San Francisco Med. Soc., Soc. Pediat. Radiology (v.p. 1994, pres. 1997 pres. SPR rsch. and edn. found. 1993-96, chmn., bd. dirs. 1998), Rocky Mountain Mountain Radiol. Soc. (hon.), Australian Soc. for Pediatric Imaging (hon.), Chinese Radiol. Soc. (hon.), Swiss Radiol. Soc. (hon.), Malaysian Radiol. Soc. (hon.), Vietnamese Radiol. Soc. (hon.), Thailand Radiology Soc. (hon.), French Soc. Radiology (hon.), Indian Radiol. and Imaging Soc. (hon.), Radiol. Soc. Pakistan (hon.), Indonesian Radiol. Soc. (hon.), Mongolian Nat. Radiol. Assn. (hon.), Nepal Radiol. Soc. (hon.), Armenian Med. Diagnostic Assn. (hon.), Brazilian Coll. Radiology (hon.), Cuban Radiol. Soc. (hon.), Indonesian Pediatric Radiol. Soc. (hon.), Asian and Oceanean Radiol. Soc. (gold medal 2004, Project Home Hall of Fame, 2007). Office: U Calif Med Ctr Dept Radiology San Francisco CA 94143-0628 E-mail: charles.gooding@radiology.ucsf.edu.

GOODING, GRETCHEN ANN WAGNER, physician, educator; b. Columbus, Ohio, July 2, 1935; d. Edward Frederick and Margaret (List) Wagner; m. Charles A. Gooding, June 19, 1961; children: Gunnar Blaise, Justin Mathias, Britta Meghan. BA magna cum laude, Ohio Dominican U., 1957; MD cum laude, Ohio State U., 1961. Diplomate Am. Bd. Diagnostic Radiology. Intern Univ. Hosps., Columbus, 1961-62; rsch. fellow Boston City Hosp., 1962-63, Boston U., 1963-65; with dept. radiology U. Calif., San Francisco, 1975—, assoc. prof. in radiology, 1981-85, prof., vice chmn., 1986—2003; asst. chief radiology VA Med. Ctr., San Francisco, 1978-87, chief radiology, 1987—2003, chief ultrasonography, 1975—. Chair com. acad. pers. U. Calif., San Francisco, 1993-94, bd. dirs. commn. accreditation vascular labs., 1993-96. Co-editor Radiologic Clinics of N.Am., 1993—; mem. editl. bd. San Francisco Medicine, 1986—, Applied Radiology, 1987-89, Current Opinion in Radiology, 1992-93, The Radiologist, 1993—, Emergency Radiology, 1993-2003, Jour. Clin. Ultrasound, 1997—; guest editor Emergency Radiology, 1999; contbr. articles to profl. jours. Recipient Recognition award Inter Societal Commn. for Accreditation of Vascular Labs., 1997, Disting. Alumna award, Ohio State U. Coll. Medicine and Pub. Health, 2001, Alice Ettinger Disting. Achievement award, 2003; named Reviewer Extraordinaire, Jour. Ultrasound in Medicine, 2006. Fellow Am. Coll. Radiology (mem. commn. on ultrasound 1984-2000, chair stds. com. commn. on ultrasound 2004—, chmn. com. practice guidelines and tech. standards 2004—), Am. Inst. Ultrasound in Medicine (bd. govs. 1981-84, chair conv. program 1986-88, Presdl. Recognition award 1984), Am. Soc. Emergency Radiology, Soc. Radiologists U.S.; mem. AMA, San Francisco Med. Soc. (chmn. membership com. 1992-94, bd. dirs. 1996—), RSNA (course com. 1984-88, tech. exhibit com. 1992-96, mem. site med. advisor 2005-06), Bay Area Ultrasound Soc. (pres. 1979-80), Soc. Radiologists Ultrasound (chair membership com. 1991-93, chair corp. com. 1996-97), ARRS, AUR, CRS, Calif. Med. Assn., Am. Assn. Women Radiologists (pres. 1984-85, trustee 1991-94, Alice Ettinger Disting. Achievement award 2003), VA Chiefs of Radiology Assn. (pres.-elect, pres. 1994-95), San Francisco Radiol. Soc. (pres. 1990-91), Hungarian Radiol. Soc. (hon.), Pakistan Radiol. Soc. (hon.), Cuba Radiol. Soc. (hon.). Office: Dept Veteran Affairs Med Ctr Radiology Svc 4150 Clement St San Francisco CA 94121-1545 Home Phone: 415-388-0536.

GOODLAD, JOHN INKSTER, education educator, writer; b. North Vancouver, BC, Can., 1920; s. William James and Mary Goodlad; m. Evalene M. Pearson, 1945; children: Stephen John, Mary Paula. BA, U. B.C., 1945, MA, 1946; PhD, U. Chgo., 1949; DPS (hon.), Brigham Young U., 1995; LHD (hon.), Nat. Coll. Edn., 1967, U. Louisville, 1968, So. Ill. U., 1982, Bank Street Coll. Edn., 1984, Niagara U., 1989, SUNY Coll. Brockport, 1991, Miami U., 1991, Linfield Coll., 1993, W.Va. U., 1998; LLD (hon.), Kent State U., 1974, Pepperdine U., 1976, Simon Fraser U., 1983, U. Man., 1992; DEd (hon.), Eastern Mich. U., 1982, U. Victoria, 1998; LittD (hon.), Montclair State U., 1992; PedD (hon.), Doane Coll., 1995; LHD (hon.), U. Nebr., Lincoln, 1999, U. So. Maine, 2001. Cert. tchr. Vancouver Normal Sch., 1939. Tchr. Surrey Schs., B.C., 1939-41, prin., 1941-42; dir. edn. Provincial Sch. For Boys, B.C., 1942-46; cons. curriculum Atlanta Area Tchr. Edn. Service, 1947-49; assoc. prof. Emory U., 1949-50; prof., dir. div. tchr. edn. Agnes Scott Coll. and Emory U., 1950-56; prof., dir. U. Chgo. Center Tchr. Edn., 1956-60; prof., dir. Univ. Elem. Sch. UCLA, 1960-85, dean Grad. Sch. Edn., 1967-83; prof. U. Wash., Seattle, 1985-91; prof. emeritus, 1991—; dir. Ctr. for Ednl. Renewal U. Wash., Seattle, 1986-2000; pres. Inst. for Ednl. Inquiry, Seattle, 1992—. Chmn. Coun. on Coop. Tchr. Edn., Am. Coun. Edn., 1959-62; dir. rsch. Inst. for Devel. of Ednl. Activities, 1966-82; mem. governing bd. UNESCO Inst. for Edn., 1971-79. Author: (with others) The Elementary School, 1956, Educational Leadership and the Elementary School Principal, 1956, (with Robert H. Anderson) The Nongraded Elementary School, 1959, rev. edit., 1963, reprinted, 1987, (with others) Computers and Information Systems in Education, 1966, Looking Behind the Classroom Door, 1970, rev. edit., 1974, Toward a Mankind School, 1974, The Conventional and the Alternative in Education, 1975, Curriculum Inquiry: The Study of Curriculum Practice, 1979, Planning and Organizing for Teaching, 1963, School Curriculum Reform, 1964, The Changing School Curriculum, 1966, School, Curriculum and the Individual, 1966, The Dynamics of Educational Change, 1975, Facing the Future, 1976, What Schools Are For, 1979, A Place Called School, 1983, 2004, Teachers for Our Nation's Schools, 1990, Educational Renewal: Better Teachers, Better Schools, 1994, In Praise of Education, 1997, (with others) Education for Everyone: Agenda for Education in a Democracy, 2004, Romances with Schools: A Life of Education, 2004; author, editor: The Changing American School, 1966, (with Harold S. Shane) The Elementary School in the United States, 1973, (with M. Frances Klein and Jerrold M. Novotney) Early Schooling in the United States, 1973, (with Norma Feshback and Alvima Lombard) Early Schooling in England and Israel, 1973, (with Gary Fenstermacher) Individual Differences and the Common Curriculum, 1983, The Ecology of School Renewal, 1987, (with Kenneth A. Sirotnik) School-University Partnerships in Action, 1988, (with Pamela Keating) Access to Knowledge, 1990, (with others) The Moral Dimensions of Teaching, 1990, Places Where Teachers Are Taught, 1990, (with Thomas C. Lovitt) Integrating General and Special Education, 1992, (with Timothy J. McMannon) The Public Purpose of Education and Schooling, 1997, (with others) Developing Democratic Character in the Young, 2001, (with Timothy J. McMannon) The Teaching Career, 2004, (with Roger and Bonnie McDaniel) Education and the Making of a Democratic People, 2008; mem. bd. editors Sch. Rev, 1956-58, Jour. Tchr. Edn, 1958-60; contbg. editor: Progressive Edn, 1955-58; mem. editorial adv. bd. Child's World, 1952-80; chmn. editorial adv. bd. New Standard Ency, 1953-; chmn. ednl. adv. bd. Ency. Brit. Ednl. Corp, 1966-69; contbr. chpts. to books, articles to profl. jours. Recipient Disting. Svc. medal Tchrs. Coll., Columbia U., 1983, Outstanding Book award Am. Ednl. Rsch. Assn., 1985, Disting. Contbns. to Ednl. Rsch. award 1993; named Faculty Rsch. Lectr. U. Wash., 1987-88, faculty of High Distinction, UCLA, 1987, Edward C. Pomeroy award, Am. Assn. Coll. Tchr. Edn., 1995, Disting. Svc. award Coun. Chief State Sch. Officials, 1997, Harold W. McGraw, Jr. Prize in Edn., 1999, Edn. Commn. State James Bryant Conant award, 2000, Brock Internat. prize in edn., 2002, NY Acad. Edn. medal, 2003, Am. Edn. award Am. Assn. Sch. Adminstrs., 2004, Disting. Educator award Assn. Tchr. Educators, 2005. Fellow Internat. Inst. Arts and Letters; mem. Nat. Acad. Edn. (charter; sec.-treas.), Am. Ednl. Rsch. Assn. (past pres., award for Disting.

Contbns. to Ednl. Rsch. 1993), Nat. Soc. Coll. Tchrs. Edn. (past pres.), Nat. Soc. for Study of Edn. (dir.), Am. Assn. Colls. for Tchr. Edn. (pres. 1989-90). Office: Inst for Ednl Inquiry 124 E Edgar St Seattle WA 98102

GOODMAN, COREY SCOTT, neuroscientist, biotechnologist, educator; b. Chgo., June 29, 1951; s. Arnold Harold (dec.) and Florence (Friedman) G.; m. Marcia M. Barinaga, Dec. 8, 1984. BS in Biology, Stanford U., Calif., 1972; PhD in Neurobiology, U. Calif., Berkeley, 1977. Postdoctoral fellow U. Calif., San Diego, 1979; asst. prof. dept. biol. scis. Stanford U., 1979-82, assoc. prof., 1982-87; prof. neurobiology and genetics U. Calif., Berkeley, 1987—2005, co-founder Helen Wills Neurosci. Inst., 1997, Evan Rauch prof. neuroscience, 1999—2001; dir. Helen Wills Neurosci. Inst., 1999—2000; co-founder Exelixis, Inc., 1995, Renovis Inc., 2000, pres., CEO, 2001—07; adj. prof. neurobiology U. Calif., 2005—; pres. biotherapeutics & bioinnovation ctr. Pzifer, NYC, 2007—. Investigator Howard Hughes Med. Inst., 1988—2001; chair bd. life sci. NRC, 2001—06; mem. governing bd. emerging co. sect. Biotech. Industry Orgn., 2005—; mem. bd. Bay Bio, 2005—, Bay Area Sci. and Innovation Constorium, 2006—; mem. Calif. Coun. Sci. & Tech. Contbr. more than 200 articles to profl. jours. Pres. McKnight Found. Endowment Fund Neurosci., 2000—05, v.p., 2005—. Recipient Charles Judson Herrick award, 1982, Alan T. Waterman award Nat. Sci. Bd., 1983, Javits Neurosci. Investigator award NIH, 1985, 92, NIH Merit award, 1985, Found. IPSEN Neuronal Plasticity prize, 1996, J. Allyn Taylor Internat. prize in medicine, 1996, Gairdner Found. Internat. award for achievement in med. sci., 1997, Ameritec Found. Basic Rsch. Toward Cure Paralysis prize, 1997, Wakeman award for rsch. in neuroscis., 1998, March-Of-Dimes prize in Devel. Biology, 2001, Rsch. medal Reeve-Irvine, 2007. Fellow Am. Acad. Arts and Scis.; mem. NAS, Am. Philos. Soc. Office: Pfizer 235 E 42d St New York NY 10017

GOODMAN, JIM, former professional sports team executive; b. Blounstown, Fla. m. Jennie Goodman; children: Jeff, Nancy, Tyler. AA, Chipola Jr. Coll., Marianna, Fla., 1972; BS in Phys. Edn., U. Fla., Gainesville, 1974; MA in Edn. Adminstrn., U. North Ala., Florence, 1977. Football coach Vanguard HS, Ocala, Fla., 1974—75, U. North Ala. Lions, 1976—78; head football/baseball coach, athletic dir. Marion Mil. Inst. Jr. Coll. Tigers, Ga., 1979—80; outside linebackers coach USAF Acad. Falcons, 1981; head football coach, assoc. athletic dir. Valdosta State U. Blazers, Ga., 1982—84, athletic dir., 1985; recruiting coord., wide receivers coach U. Ark. Razorbacks, 1986—88; asst. athletic dir. U. Fla. Gators, 1989—90; assoc. athletic dir., kickers coach Clemson U. Tigers, SC, 1991—93; tight ends, spl. teams coach Rice U. Owls, Tex., 1994—97, wide receivers coach, 1997; area scout, South region Denver Broncos, 1998—2001, dir. coll. scouting, 2002—05, dir. player pers., 2006—07, v.p. football ops., player pers., 2008—09.*

GOODMAN, JOHN M., construction executive; b. Omaha, Apr. 5, 1947; BS in Acctg., Calif. State U., Long Beach, 1970; JD, Pepperdine U., 1974. CPA, Calif.; cert. real estate broker, Calif.; cert. ins. agt., Calif.; lic. contractor, Calif. CFO Lewis Homes Mgmt. Corp., Upland, Calif., 1978—92, sr. v.p., CEO, dir., 1992—. Office: Lewis Operating Corp 1156 N Mountain Ave PO Box 670 Upland CA 91785-0670

GOODMAN, JOSEPH WILFRED, electrical engineering educator; b. Boston, Feb. 8, 1936; s. Joseph and Doris (Ryan) G.; m. Hon Mai Lam, Dec. 5, 1962; 1 dau., Michele Ann. BA, Harvard U., 1958; MS in E.E., Stanford U., 1960, PhD, 1963; DSc (hon.), U. Ala., 1996. Postdoctoral fellow Norwegian Def. Rsch. Establishment, Oslo, 1962-63; rsch. assoc. Stanford U., 1963-67, asst. prof., 1967-69, assoc. prof., 1969-72, prof. elec. engring., 1972-99; vis. prof. Univ. Paris XI, Orsay, France, 1973-74; dir. Info. Sys. Lab. Elec. Engring. Stanford U., 1981-83, chmn. dept. of elec. engring., 1988-96, William E. Ayer prof. elec. engring., 1988-99, sr. assoc. dean engring., 1996-98, acting dean engring., 1999, prof. emeritus, 2000—. Cons. govt. and industry, 1965—; v.p. Internat. Comm. Optics, 1985-87, pres., 1988-90, past pres., 1991-93; founding chmn. bd. ONI Sys., Inc.; former chmn. bd. Nanoprecision Products Inc.; former bd. mem. E-TEK Dynamics. Author: Introduction to Fourier Optics, 1968, 3d edit., 2005, Statistical Optics, 1985, (with R. Gray) Fourier Transforms: An Introduction for Engineers; editor: International Trends in Optics, 1991, Speckle Phenomena in Optics, 2006; contbr. articles to profl. jours. Recipient F.E. Terman award Am. Soc. Engring. Edn., 1971, Frederic Ives Medal, 1990, Optical Soc. Am., Ester Hoffman Beller award Optical Soc. of Am., 1995. Fellow AAAS, Optical Soc. Am. (dir. 1977-83, editor jour. 1978-83, Max Born award 1983, Frederick Ives award 1990, Esther Hoffman Beller medal 1995, v.p. 1990, pres.-elect 1991, pres. 1992, past pres. 1993), IEEE (edn. medal 1987), Soc. Photo-optical Instrumentation Engrs. (bd. govs. 1979-82, 88-90, Dennis Gabor award 1987, Gold medal 2007), Am. Acad. Arts and Scis.; mem. NAE, Electromagnetics Acad. Home: 570 University Ter Los Altos CA 94022-3523 Office: Stanford U Dept Elec Engring Stanford CA 94305 Business E-Mail: goodman@ee.stanford.edu.

GOODMAN, MAX A., lawyer, educator; b. Chgo., May 24, 1924; s. Sam and Nettie (Abramowitz) G.; m. Marlyene Monkarsh, June 2, 1946; children: Jan M., Lauren A. Packard, Melanie Murez. AA, Herzl Jr. Coll., 1943; student, Northwestern U., 1946—47; JD, Loyola U., 1948; LLD (hon.), Southwestern U. Sch. Law, 2000. Bar: Calif. 1948; cert. family law specialist, 1980, 85, 90. Pvt. practice, LA, 1948-53; ptnr. Goodman, Hirschberg & King, LA, 1953-81; prof. Southwestern U. Sch. Law, LA, 1966—2006, prof. emeritus in residence, 2006—. Lectr. Calif. Continuing Edn. of the Bar, 1971—90. Contbr. articles to profl. jours. Served to cpl. U.S. Army, 1943-45. Mem. ABA (chmn. law sch. curriculum com. family law sect. 1987-88, family law sect. 1987-88, 97-98), State Bar Calif. (del. conf. dels. 1972, 80-87, 91, exec. com. family law sect. 1981-85), Los Angeles County Bar Assn. (chmn. family law sect. 1971-72, editor family law handbook 1974-89). Avocation: bridge. Office: Southwestern U Sch Law 3050 Wilshire Blvd Los Angeles CA 90010-1106 Office Phone: 213-738-6823. Business E-Mail: mgoodman@swlaw.edu.

GOODMAN, OSCAR BAYLIN, Mayor, Las Vegas, lawyer; b. Phila., July 26, 1939; s. A. Allen and (Baylin) Goodman; m. Carolyn Goldmark, June 6, 1962; children: Oscar B., Ross C., Eric A., Cara Lee. BA, Haverford Coll., 1961; JD, U. Pa., 1964. Bar: Nev. 1965, US Ct. Appeals. Chief dep. pub. defender Clark County, Nev., 1966—67; sr. ptnr. Goodman, Chesnoff and Keach (formerly Goodman, Stein & Chesnoff), Las Vegas, 1965—; mayor City of Las Vegas, 1999—. Adv. bd. Us. Conf. of Mayors. Guest appearance (films) Casino, 1995, (TV series) CSI: Crime Scene Investigation, 2004. Named one of Best Criminal Defense Attys., Las Vegas Review-Jour., 1999. Mem.: Nat. Assn. Criminal Def. Lawyers (pres. 1983). Democrat. Jewish. Office: City Hall 10th Fl 400 Stewart Ave Las Vegas NV 89101-2927 also: Goodman Chesnoff & Keach 520 S 4th St Las Vegas NV 89101-6524 Office Phone: 702-229-6241, 702-384-5563.*

GOODMAN, ROGER ELLIOT, state legislator, lawyer, state agency director; b. Providence, Feb. 4, 1961; s. Elliot Raymond and Norma (Bromberg) G.; m. Liv, 2 children. AB, Dartmouth Coll., 1983; JD, George Washington U., 1986; MPA, Harvard Univ., 1998. Bar: R.I. 1987, U.S. Dist. Ct. R.I. 1987, U.S. Ct. Appeals (1st cir.) 1987, U.S. Supreme Ct. 1990. Comml. litigation assoc. Tillinghast, Collins & Graham, Providence, 1986-88; staff atty., field coord. Dukakis for Pres., 1988; legis. dir., counsel U.S. Rep. Bob Wise, Washington, 1989-93; chief of staff U.S. Rep. Rick Boucher, Washington, 1993-95; mem. Dist. 45 Wash. House Reps., 2007—. Exec. dir. Sentencing Guidelines Commn., Olympia, Wash., 1998-2000. Mem. ABA, Fed. Bar Assn., R.I. Bar Assn. Democrat. Jewish. Avocation: adventure travel. Office: 320 O'Brien Bldg PO Box 40600 Olympia WA 98504-0600 Office Phone: 360-786-7878. Business E-Mail: goodman.roger@leg.wa.gov.

GOODMAN, SAM RICHARD, electronics executive; b. NYC, May 23, 1930; s. Morris and Virginia (Gross) G.; m. Beatrice Bettencourt, Sept. 15, 1957; children: Mark Stuart, Stephen Manuel, Christopher Bettencourt. BBA, CCNY, 1951; MBA, NYU, 1957, PhD, 1968. Chief acct. John C. Valentine Co., NYC, 1957-60; mgr. budgets and analysis Gen. Foods. Corp., White Plains, NY, 1960-63; budget dir. Crowell Collier Pub. Co., NYC, 1963-64; v.p., chief fin. officer Nestle Co., Inc., White Plains, 1964; chief fin. officer Aileen, Inc., N.Y.C., 1973-74, Ampex Corp., 1974-76; exec. v.p. fin. and adminstrn. Baker & Taylor Co. div. W.R. Grace Co., NYC, 1976-79, Magnuson Computer Systems, Inc., San Jose, Calif., 1979-81; v.p., chief fin. officer Datamac Computer Systems, Sunnyvale, Calif., 1981; pres. Nutritional Foods Inc., San Francisco, 1983-84; chmn., chief exec. officer CMX Corp., Santa Clara, Calif., 1984-88; dir., sr. v.p. Masstor Systems Corp., Santa Clara, 1988—; pvt. cons. Atherton, Calif., 1990—; sr. mgmt. cons. Durkee/Sharlit, 1991—; pres. Mayfair Packing Co., 1991—; mng. dir. Quincy Pacific Ptnrs., L.P., 1992—; pres., CEO Mayfair Packing Co., San Jose, Calif., 1991-94; pvt. cons. BMG Assocs., 1994—. Lectr. NYU Inst. Mgmt., 1965-67, U. San Francisco, 2006; asst. prof. mktg. Iona Coll. Grad. Sch. Adminstrn., 1967-69; prof. fin. and mktg. Pace U. Grad. Sch. Bus. Adminstrn., 1969-79, prof. Golden Gate U., 1974—. Author 7 books, including Controller's Handbook; contbr. articles to jours. Lt. (j.g.) USNR, 1951—55. Decorated Korean Occupation Svc. medal Armed Forces Svc., Nat. Def. Svc. medal. Mem. Fin. Execs. Inst., Nat. Assn. Accts., Am. Statis. Assn., Am. Econs. Assn., Planning Execs. Inst., Am. Arbitration Assn., Turnaround Mgmt. Assn. Home and Office: 60 Shearer Dr Atherton CA 94027-3957 Office Phone: 650-207-7411. Personal E-mail: bgoodman@cbnorcal.com.

GOODMAN, STUART B., medical educator; b. Toronto, May 15, 1951; married. BS, U. Toronto, 1973, MD, 1978; MS, Inst. Med. Sci./U. Toronto, 1982; PhD in Med. Sci., U. Lund, 1994. Diplomate Am. Bd. Orthopaedic Surgery. Intern Toronto Gen. Hosp., 1978-79; resident orthopaedic surgery U. Toronto, 1979-84; rsch. fellow Hosp. for Sick Children, Toronto, 1979-80; orthopaedic arthritis and trauma fellow Wellesley Hosp./Sunnybrook Med. Ctr., Toronto, 1984-85; acting asst. prof., attending orthopaedic surgeon Stanford U. and Med. Ctr., 1985, asst. prof., attending orthopaedic surgeon, 1985-92; chief of orthopaedic trauma, asst. dir. surg. arthritis Stanford U. Med. Ctr., 1986-90, assoc. faculty - biomechan. engring. program, 1990—, assoc. prof. with tenure, dept. function restoration, 1992-98; head Divns. of Orthopedic Surgery Stanford U. Sch. Medicine, 1994—, assoc. chmn. functional restoration, 1997—, prof. functional restoration, 1998—. Vis. prof., lectr. numerous regional, nat. and internat. orgns. Editl. bd. Orthopaedic Capsule and Comment, 1990-92, Jour. of Arthroplasty, The Joint Letter, Jour. Biomed. Material Rsch., Jour. Applied Biomaterials; reviewer for 20 jours. in field; contbr. articles to profl. jours. and publs. Fellow ACS, Am. Acad. Orthopaedic Surgeons; mem. Royal Coll. Physicians and Surgeons of Can., Acad. Orthopaedic Soc., Assn. Bone and Joint Surgery, Orthopaedic Trauma Assn., Knee Soc., Soc. for Biomaterials, Can. Orthopaedic Assn., Calif. Orthopaedic Assn., Calif. Med. Assn., Santa Clara Orthopaedic Assn., Santa Clara Med. Assn. Office: Stanford Med Ctr Divsn Ortho Surg Sch of Medicine R-144 Stanford CA 94305-5341

GOODSTEIN, DAVID LOUIS, physics professor; b. Bklyn., Apr. 5, 1939; s. Sam and Claire (Axel) G.; m. Judith R. Koral, June 30, 1960; children: Marcia, Mark. BS, Bklyn. Coll., 1960; PhD, U. Wash., 1965. Research instr. U. Wash., Seattle, 1965-66; research fellow Calif. Inst. Tech., Pasadena, 1966-67, asst. prof., 1968-71, asso. prof., 1971-76, prof., 1976—, vice-provost, 1987—2007, Frank J. Gilloon disting. teaching and svc. prof., 1995—. Vis. scientist Frascati Nat. Lab., Italy, 1971—. Author: States of Matters, 1975, (with J. Goodstein) Feynman's Lost Lecture, 1996, Out of Gas, 2004, Matter of Fact & Fraud, 2009; mem. editl. bd. Il Nuovo Cimento, 1987—; contbr. articles to profl. jours.; project dir., host physics TV course The Mechanical Universe. Bd. dirs. Calif. Coun. Sci. and Tech., 1989-2007, David and Lucille Packard Found., 1988—. NSF postdoctoral fellow, 1967-68; Sloan Found. fellow, 1969-71; recipient Oersted medal, 1999, John P. McGovern Sci. and Soc. award, 2000. Fellow AAAS; mem. Am. Phys. Soc., Am. Inst. Physics. Office: Calif Inst Tech Dept Physics Pasadena CA 91125-0001 Home: 430 South Parkwood Ave Pasadena CA 91107 Business E-Mail: dg@caltech.edu.

GOODWIN, ALFRED THEODORE, federal judge; b. Bellingham, Wash., June 29, 1923; s. Alonzo Theodore and Miriam Hazel (Williams) G.; m. Marjorie Elizabeth Major, Dec. 23, 1943 (div. 1948); 1 child, Michael Theodore; m. Mary Ellin Handelin, Dec. 23, 1949; children: Karl Alfred, Margaret Ellen, Sara Jane, James Paul. BA, U. Oreg., 1947; JD, 1951. Bar: Oreg. 1951. Newspaper reporter Eugene (Oreg.) Register-Guard, 1947—50; practiced in Eugene until, 1955; circuit judge Oreg. 2d. Jud. Dist., 1955—60; assoc. justice Oreg. Supreme Ct., 1960—69; judge US Dist. Ct. Oreg., 1969—71, US Ct. Appeals (9th cir.), Pasadena, Calif., 1971—88, chief judge, 1988—91, sr. judge, 1991—. Editor: Oreg. Law Rev., 1950—51. Adv. bd. Eugene Salvation Army, 1956—60; chmn., 1959; Bd. dirs. Central Lane YMCA, Eugene, 1956—60, Salem (Oreg.) Art Assn., 1960—69. Capt., inf. AUS, 1942—46, ETO. Mem.: ABA (ho. of dels. 1986—87), Am. Law Inst., Am. Judicature Soc., Order of Coif, Alpha Tau Omega, Sigma Delta Chi, Phi Delta Phi. Republican. Office: US Ct Appeals 9th Cir PO Box 91510 125 S Grand Ave Pasadena CA 91105-1621 Home Phone: 626-441-2797; Office Phone: 626-229-7100. E-mail: alfred_goodwin@ca9.uscourts.gov.

GOODWIN, ANNIE M., state agency administrator; b. Helena, Mont., 1958; BSN magna cum laude, Carroll Coll., Helena, Mont., 1981; JD magna cum laude, U. Mont., Missoula, 1984. Bar: Mont. 1984, US Dist. Ct. (dist. Mont.) 1984, US Ct. Fed. Claims 1990, US Dist. Ct. (dist. DC) 1991. Law clk. Mont. Supreme Ct., 1984; litig. atty. risk mgmt. tort def. divsn. Mont. Dept. Adminstrn.; chief legal counsel Mont. Dept. Commerce, 1988—2001; commr. Mont. Divsn. Banking & Fin. Instns., Helena, 2001—. Bd. dirs. Am. Lung Assn., 1988—91. Office: Mont Divsn Banking & Fin Instns PO Box 200546 Helena MT 59620 Office Phone: 406-841-2920. Office Fax: 406-841-2930. E-mail: angoodwin@mt.gov.

GOODWIN, BRUCE T., engineer; BS in Physics, City Coll. NY; MS in Aeronautical and Astronautical Engring., PhD in Aeronautical and Astronautical Engring., U. Ill. Staff mem. Los Alamos Nat. Lab.; with Lawrence Livermore Nat. Lab., 1985—, B Program/B Divsn. leader def. and nuclear tech., 1996—2001, assoc. dir. def. and nuclear tech., 2001—. Recipient Aerospace Laurels Honor, Aviation Week & Space Tech. Mag., 2000, Ernest Orlando Lawrence award, US Dept. Energy, 2002. Office: Lawrence Livermore Nat Lab 7000 E Ave Livermore CA 94550

GOODWIN, DAVID B., lawyer; AB, U. Calif., Santa Cruz, 1974; BA, Oxford U., 1976, MA, 1979; JD, Stanford U., 1982. Bar: Calif. Atty., shareholder Heller Ehrman LLP, San Francisco, 1986—. Office: Heller Ehrman LLP 333 Bush St San Francisco CA 94104 Office Phone: 415-775-6319. Fax: 415-772-6268. Business E-Mail: david.goodwin@hellerehrman.com.

GOODWIN, GINNIFER, actress; b. Memphis, May 22, 1978; d. Tim and Linda Goodwin. BFA in Acting, Boston U., 2001; studied, London Acad. Music and Dramatic Arts, Shakespeare Inst. Actress (plays) Joan of Arc, Hamlet, The Merchant of Venice, Dead End, As You Like It, (TV films) Porn 'n Chicken, 2002, (TV series) Ed, 2001—04, Robot Chicken, 2005—07, Big Love, 2006—, (films) Mona Lisa Smile, 2003, Win a Date with Tad Hamilton, 2004, Walk the Line, 2005, Love Comes to the Executioner, 2006, In the Land of Women, 2006, Day Zero, 2007, He's Just Not That Into You, 2009, (TV appearances) Law & Order, 1990. Recipient Acting Shakespeare Cert., Royal Acad. Dramatic Art, London, Excellence in Acting/Profl. Promise award, Betty Davis Found., 2001, MaxMara Face of the Future award, Women in Film, 2008. Office: c/o PMK/HBH Ste G910 700 San Vicente Blvd West Hollywood CA 90069

GOODWIN, MARTIN BRUNE, retired radiologist; b. Vancouver, BC, Can., Aug. 8, 1921; came to US, 1948; m. Cathy Dennison, Mar. 7, 1980; 1 child, Suzanne; stepchildren: Chuck Glikas, Dianna; 1 child from previous marriage, Nancijane Goodwin Hilling. BSA in Agriculture, U. BC, 1943, postgrad., 1943-44; MD, CM, McGill U. Med. Sch., Montreal, Can., 1948. Diplomate Am. Bd. Med. Examiners, lic. Med. Coun. Can.; cert. diagnostic and therapeutic radiology Am. Bd. Radiology; cert. Am. Bd. Nuclear Medicine. Intern Scott & White Hosp., Temple, Tex., 1948-49; fellow radiology Scott & White Clinic, 1949-52, mem. staff, 1952-53; instr. U. Tex., Galveston, 1952-53; radiologist Plains Regional Med. Ctr., Clovis, N.Mex., Portales, N.Mex., pres. med. staff; chief radiology De Baca Gen. Hosp., Ft. Sumner, N.Mex.; cons. Cannon AFB Hosp., Clovis; pvt. practice radiology Clovis, Portales, Ft. Sumner and Tucumcari, 1955—2005; ret., 2005. Adj. prof. health scis. Ea. N.Mex. U., 1976-77; adj. clin. prof. health scis. We. Mich. U., 1976-78 Apptd. N.Mex. Radiation Tech. Adv. Coun., N.Mex. Bd. Pub. Health; former chmn. N.Mex. Health and Social Svcs. Bd.; mem. Regional Health Planning Coun.; treas. Roosevelt County Rep. Ctrl. Com. Capt. U.S. Army M.C., 1953-55; Col. USAF M.C., 1975-79. Fellow AAAS, Am. Coll. Radiology, Am. Coll. Radiology (past councillor); mem. Am. Soc. Thoracic Radiologists (founder), Radiol. Soc. of N.Am. (past councillor), N.Mex. Med. Soc. (various coms., chmn. joint practice com., councillor bd. dirs.), N.Mex. Radiol. Soc. (past pres.), N.Mex. Thoracic Soc. (past pres.), N.Mex. Med. Review Assn. (bd. dirs. 1970-93), N.Mex. Med. Soc. Found. for Med. Care (bd. dirs. 1975—, former v.p., former treas.), County Med. Soc. (past pres., past v.p., past sec.), Clovis C. of C. (chmn. civic affairs com., bd. dirs.), Clovis Elks Lodge (past exalted ruler), Clovis Noonday Lions Club (past sec.), Republican. Presbyterian. Home: 505 E 18th St Portales NM 88130-9201 Home Fax: 505-356-5035.

GOOKIN, THOMAS ALLEN JAUDON, civil engineer; b. Tulsa, Okla., Aug. 5, 1951; s. William Scudder and Mildred (Hartman) G.; m. Sandra Jean Andrews, July 23, 1983. BS with distinction, Ariz. State U., 1975. Registered profl. engr., Calif., Ariz., Nev., land surveyor Ariz., hydrologist. Civil engr., treas. Gookin Engrs. Ltd, Scottsdale, Ariz., 1968—. V.p. instl. devel. Am. Inst. Hydrologists, 2006. Chmn. adv. com. Ariz. State Bd. Tech. Registration Engring., 1984—. Recipient Spl. Recognition award Ariz. State Bd. Tech. Registration Engring., 1990. Mem. NSPE, ASCE, Ariz. Soc. Profl. Engrs. (sec. Papago chpt. 1979-81, v.p. 1981-84, pres. 1984-85, named Young Engr. of Yr. 1979, Outstanding Engring. Project award 1988), Order Engr., Am. Inst. Hydrology (nat. v.p.), Ariz. Congress on Surveying and Mapping, Ariz. Water Works Assn., Tau Beta Pi, Delta Chi (Tempe chpt. treas. 1970-71, sec. 1970, v.p. 1971), Phi Kappa Delta (pres. 1971-73). Republican. Episcopalian. Achievements include co-author Globe Equity # 59 Call System. Avocations: disneyana, science fiction, computer gaming. Home: 10760 E Becker Ln Scottsdale AZ 85259-3868 Office: Gookin Engrs Ltd 4203 N Brown Ave Ste A Scottsdale AZ 85251-3946 Office Phone: 480-947-3741. Business E-Mail: water@gookin.biz.

GOOSBY, ERIC PAUL, epidemiologist; b. Aug. 28, 1952; MD, U. San Francisco, 1978. AIDS activity divsn. attending physician San Francisco Gen. Hosp., 1986, assoc. med. dir. AIDS Clinic, 1987; dir. HIV Svcs. US Pub. Health Svc., Health Resources and Svcs. Adminstrn., Washington, 1991—94; dir. Office HIV/AIDS Policy US Dept. Health and Human Services, Washington, 1994—2000; interim. dir. Nat. AIDS Policy Office, The White House, Washington, 1997, acting dep. dir., 2000; CEO, chief medical officer Pangaea Global AIDS Found., San Francisco, 2001—. Prof. clin. medicine U. Calif., San Francisco. Office: Pangaea Global AIDS Foundation 995 Market St Ste 200 San Francisco CA 94103*

GORDLEY, JAMES RUSSELL, law educator; b. 1946; BA, U. Chgo., 1967, MBA, 1968; JD, Harvard U., 1970. Fellow U. Florence Inst. Law, Italy, 1970-71; assoc. Foley, Hoag & Eliot, Boston, 1971-72; fellow comparative law Harvard U., Cambridge, Mass., 1973-78; acting prof. U. Calif., Berkeley, 1978-81, prof., 1981—,

Shannon Cecil Turner prof. jurisprudence, 1995—. Fellow Deutsche Forschungsgemeinschaft, 1983, sr. NATO fellow, 1991, Guggenheim fellow, 1995-96, Fulbright fellow, 1996. Fellow Am. Acad. Arts and Scis.

GORDLY, AVEL LOUISE, state legislator, political organization worker; b. Portland, Oreg., Feb. 13, 1947; d. Fay Lee and Beatrice Bernice (Coleman) G.; 1 child, Tyrone Wayne Waters. BS in Adminstrn. of Justice, Portland State U., 1974; Grad. John F. Kennedy Sch. Govt., Harvard U., 1995; grad., U. Oreg. Pacific Program, 1998. Phone co. clk. Pacific West Bell, Portland, 1966-70, mgmt. trainee, 1969-70; work release counselor Oreg. Corrections Divsn., Portland, 1974-78, parole and probation officer, 1974-78; dir. youth svcs. Urban League of Portland, 1979-83; dir. So. Africa program Am. Friends Svc. Com., Portland, 1983-89, assoc. exec. sec., dir. Pacific N.W. region, 1987-90; freelance writer Portland Observer, Portland, 1988-90; program dir. Portland House of Umoja, 1991; mem. Oreg. Ho. of Reps., Portland, 1991-96, mem. joint ways and means com., adv. mem. appropriations com., rules and reorgn. com., low income housing com., energy policy rev. com., others; mem. Oreg. Senate from 10th dist., Salem, 1997—; mem. crime and corrections com., trades econ. devel. com. Oreg. Senate, 1997, mem. joint ways and means com. on pub. safety, 1997, mem. joint ways and means com. on edn., 1999, emergency bd., co-chair, interim task force on parental and family abductions, 2003—04, mem. joint ways and means pub. safety com., 2005—, mem. joint ways and means edn. com., 2005—, chair, joint ways and means, full com., 2005. Mem. joint ways and means com. on edn., mem. gov. drug and violent crime policy bd., mem. Oreg. liquor control commn. task force, mem. sexual harrassement task force, mem. Hanford waste bd., mem. Gov.'s Commn. for Women, Gov.'s Drug and Violent Crime Policy Bd.; originator, producer, host Black Women's Forum, 1983-88; co-producer, rotating host N.E. Spectrum, 1983-88; assoc. prof. dept. black studies Portland State U., 2006—. Mem. corrections adv. com. Multnomah Cmty.; mem. adv. com. Oregonians Against Gun Violence; mem. Black Leadership Conf.; treas., bd. dirs. Black United Fund; co-founder, facilitator Unity Breakfast Com.; co-founder Sisterhood Luncheon; past project adv. bd. dirs. Nat. Orgn. Victims Assistance; past citizen chmn. Portland Police Bur.; past mem. coordinating com. Portland Future Focus Policy Com.; past coord. Cmty. Rescue Plan; past vice chmn. internat. affairs Black United Front; past sec. Urban League Portland, past vice chmn. and exec. com.; past adv. com. Black Ednl. Ctr.; past vice chmn. Desegregation Monitoring; also past adv. com., past chmn. curriculum com., founder African Am. Leg. Issues Roundtable; founder Black Women Gathering; other past orgn. coms.; elected state senate First African Am. Woman, 1996. Recipient Outstanding Cmty. Svc. award NAACP, 1986, Outstanding Women in Govt. award YWCA, 1991, Girl Scout-Cmty. Svc. award, 1991, N.W. Conf. of Black Studies-Outstanding Progressive Leadership in the African-Am. Cmty. award, 1986, Cmty. Svc. award Delta Sigma Theta, 1981, Joint Action in Cmty. Svc.-Vol. and Cmty. Svc. award, 1981, Quality of Life Photography award Pacific Power & Light Co., 1986, Am. Leadership Forum Sr. fellow, 1988, Equal Opportunity award, Urban League, 1996, Outstanding Alumni, 1996, PSU, Causa '98 En Defensa de la Comunidad award, 1997, Matrix award Assn. for Women in Comm., 1999, Pres.'s award Portland Oreg. Visitors Assn., 1999, Legacy award Black United Fund, 2000, Leadership award Albina Ministerial Alliance, 2000 Mem. NAACP. Avocations: reading, photography, walking. Home: 6805 NE Bradway St Portland OR 97213-5304

GORDON, BASIL, retired mathematics professor; b. Balt., Dec. 23, 1932; s. Basil and Helen (Williams) G. MA, Johns Hopkins, 1953; PhD, Calif. Inst. Tech., 1956. Instr. Calif. Inst. Tech., 1956-57; asst. prof. math. U. Calif. at Los Angeles, 1959-63, assoc. prof., 1963-67, prof., 1967-93; prof. emeritus, 1993—. Editor: Pacific Jour. Mathematics, 1969-70, 72-73, Jour. Combinatorial Theory, 1970-2002, Ramanujan Jour., 1997—; contbr. articles to profl. jours. Served with AUS, 1957-59. Alfred P. Sloan fellow, 1962-64 Mem. Am. Math. Soc., Math. Assn. Am., Pi Mu Epsilon. Achievements include research in number theory, combinatorics, group theory, and function theory. Home: 526 Palisades Ave Santa Monica CA 90402-2722 Office: 405 Hilgard Ave Los Angeles CA 90095-9000 Office Phone: 310-458-9730. Business E-Mail: bg@math.ucla.edu.

GORDON, DAVID ELIOT, lawyer; b. Santa Monica, Calif., Mar. 8, 1949; s. Sam and Dee G.; m. Mary Debora Lane, Mar. 5, 1978. BA, Harvard U., 1969, JD, 1972. Bar: Calif. 1972. Ptnr. O'Melveny & Myers, LA, 1980—. Adj. prof. Loyola Law Sch., 2000—. Founder, editor ERISA Litigation Reporter; contbr. articles on tax and employee benefits to profl. jours. Trustee Ctr. for Early Edn., 1997—. Fellow Los Angeles County Bar Found. (life, pres. 1984-85, bd. dirs. 1980-86); mem. ABA (employee benefits com. 1986—), Am. Coll. Tax Counsel, Los Angeles County Bar Assn. (tax sect., pres. 1990-91). Republican. Avocations: tennis, squash, racquetball. Office: O'Melveny & Myers 400 S Hope St Ste 1869 Los Angeles CA 90071-2899 Office Fax: 323-669-6407.

GORDON, JOHN CHARLES, forestry educator; b. Nampa, Idaho, June 10, 1939; s. John Nicholas and Ada Elizabeth (Scheuermann) G.; m. Helka Lehtinen, Aug. 6, 1964; 1 child, Sean Nicholas. BS, Iowa State U., Ames, 1961, PhD, 1966; postgrad., U. Helsinki, Finland, 1961-62; MA (hon.), Yale U., New Haven, Conn., 1984; LHD (hon.), Unity Coll., Maine, 2000. Instr. forestry Iowa State U., Ames, 1965-66; plant physiologist US Forest Service, Rhinelander, Wis., 1966-70; prof. forestry Iowa State U., Ames, 1970-77; prof., head dept. forest sci. Oreg. State U., Corvallis, 1977-83; prof., dean forestry and environ. studies Yale U., New Haven, 1983-92, 97-98, Pinchot prof. forestry and environ. studies, 1991—2001, acting dir. Inst. for Biospheric Studies, 1994-95, 96, Pinchot prof. emeritus, 2001—; founding ptnr. Interforest LLC, 1996—, Maximum Yields Assocs. LLC, 2007—; chmn., mem. exec. com. Candlewood Timber Group, 1999—. Chmn. Commn. on Rsch. and Resources Mgmt. in Nat. Pks., 1988—89; bd. dirs. Nat. Commn. on Sci. and Sustainable Forestry, 2000—, chmn., 2000—02; chmn. com. on forestry rsch. NAS, 1989—92; adj. prof. Portland State U., 2004—; lectr. in field. Editor: Symbiotic Nitrogen Fixation, 1983; author: Agroforestry Research, 1991, Environmental Leadership, 1993, Ecosystems, 1998, Forests to Fight Poverty, 1999, Forest Certification, 1999, Buy on the Upside: Stock Investing, 2005, Environmental Leadership Equals Essential Leadership, 2006, Eat Your Spinach: Spend Less and Save More, 2006, Planning Research, 2007; contbr. articles to profl. jours. Bd. dirs. Friends of Gray Towers, Milford, Pa., 1983-87, Yale U. Alumni Fund, 1985-92, Tropical Forest Found., 1991-94, Wintock Internat., 1993-95, Soc. for Protection NH Forests, 2001-05; vis. com. Harvard U., 1985-92; pres. C.V. Riley Found., NYC, 1985, 92-94, Conn. Fund for Environ., 1986-92; mem. rsch. adv. com. US AID, 1988-92; co-chmn. 7th Am. Forest Congress, 1994-97. Fulbright scholar, 1961, 84; hon. sr. fellow U. Glasgow, Scotland, 1975-76; Green vis. prof. U. BC, Vancouver, 1985; named Conservationist of the Yr., Pacific Rivers Coun., 1992; fellow Timothy Dwight Coll., Yale U., medal, U. Helsinki, 1993; disting. svc. award Am. Forests, 1996. Mem. Soc. Am. Foresters (Gifford Pinchot medal 2005), Am. Forestry Assn. (Disting. Svc. award 1996), Yale Club (NYC), Morys (New Haven), Cosmos Club (Washington), Sigma Xi, Phi Kappa Phi. Presbyterian. Avocations: hiking, fishing, writing short stories. Home: 28072 SW Morgan St Wilsonville OR 97070-6791 Office Phone: 503-956-3574. Personal E-mail: jgordon@iforest.com.

GORDON, JOSEPH HAROLD, lawyer; b. Tacoma, Mar. 31, 1909; s. Joseph H. and Mary (Obermiller) G.; m. Jane Wilson, Sept. 12, 1936 (dec.); children: Joseph H., Nancy Jane; m. Eileen (Rylander) Rademaker, Jan. 7, 1967 (dec. 2001). BA, Stanford U., 1931; LLB, JD, U. Wash., 1935. Bar: Wash. 1935. Sole practice, Tacoma; ptnr. Gordon & Gordon, Tacoma, 1935—50, Henderson, Carnahan, Thompson & Gordon, Tacoma, 1950—57, Carnahan, Gordon & Goodwin, Tacoma, 1957—70, Gordon, Thomas, Honeywell, Malanca, Peterson & Daheim, Tacoma, 1970—. Elder Presbyn. Ch. Mem.: ABA (ho. dels. 1951—, bd. govs. 1962—72, treas. 1965—72), Tacoma Bar Assn. (past pres.), Wash. State Bar Assn., Tacoma Golf and Country Club, Tacoma Club, Rotary. Office: Gordon Thomas Honeywell Malanca Peterson & Daheim PO Box 1157 2200 Wells Fargo Plz Tacoma WA 98401-1157 Office Phone: 253-620-6408. Personal E-mail: gordsr@gmail.com. Business E-Mail: gordsr@gth-law.com.

GORDON, JUDITH, communications consultant, writer; b. Long Beach, Calif. d. Irwin Ernest and Susan (Perlman) G.; m. Lawrence Banka, May 1, 1977. BA, Oakland U., 1966; MS in LS, Wayne State U., 1973. Researcher Detroit Inst. of Arts, 1968-69; libr. Detroit Pub. Libr., 1971-74; caseworker Wayne County Dept. Social Svcs., Detroit, 1974-77; advt. copywriter Hudson's Dept. Store, Detroit, 1979; mgr. The Poster Gallery, Detroit, 1980-81; mktg., corp. communications specialist Bank of Am., San Francisco, 1983-84, mgr., consumer pubs., 1984-86; prin. Active Voice, San Francisco, 1986—. Contbr. edit. The Artist's Mag., 1988-93; contbr. to book Flowers: Gary Bukovnik, Watercolors and Monotypes, Abrams, 1990. Vol. From the Heart, San Francisco, 1992, Bay Area Book Festival, San Francisco, 1990, 91, Aid & Comfort, San Francisco, 1987, Save Orch. Hall, Detroit, 1977-81, NOW sponsored abortion clinic project. Recipient Nat. award Merit. Soc. Consumer Affairs Profls. in Bus., 1986, Bay Area Best award Internat. Assn. Bus. Communicators, 1986, Internat. Galaxy awards, 1992, 95, 97, Internat. Mercury awards, 1995, Charles Schwab Excellence in Svc. award, 2000. Mem. AAUW, Nat. Writers Union, Editl. Freelancers Assn. Inc., Clarity, Achenbach Graphics Arts Coun., Women's Nat. Book Assn., Assn. Women in Comms., Fin. Women's Assn., Plain Lang. Assn., FIMA West (bd. dirs.), ZYZZYVA (bd. dirs.). Office: 899 Green St San Francisco CA 94133-3756 E-mail: activvduo@msn.com.

GORDON, KENNETH MARSHALL, state legislator; b. Detroit, Feb. 6, 1950; son of Harold Gordon & Marion G; married to Helen Shreves; children: Wendy & Ben. Colorado State Representative, 1993-2000, minority leader, 1999-2000, chairman, State Senate Judiciary Committee, 2001-2002, asst minority leader, 2003-04, Colorado House Representative; Colorado State Senator, District 35, 2000-, majority leader, currently, member, Exec Committee Legislature Coun, Legislature Coun, and Senate ServsComts, currently, Colorado State Senate, currently. Best of Denver-Pro Bono Atty of Year, Westword, 88; Most Promising Green Legislator Award, Clean Water Action, 94; Highest Rating in Colorado House, Colorado Sr Lobby. Democrat. Office: 200 E Colfax Denver CO 80203 Office Phone: 303-866-3341. E-mail: ken@kengordon.com.

GORDON, LARRY JEAN, sanitarian, environmental health consultant; b. Tipton, Okla., Oct. 16, 1926; s. Andrew J. and Deweylee (Stewart) G.; m. Nedra Callender, Aug. 26. 1950; children: Debra Gordon Dunlap, Kent, Gary. Student, U. Okla., 1943-44; BS, U. N.Mex., 1949, MS, 1951; DHL (hon.), U. N.Mex., Albuquerque, 2007; MPH, U. Mich., 1954. Diplomate laverde Am. Acad. Sanitarians, 2003, emeritus 2008. High sch. sci. tchr., N.Mex., 1949-50; various positions N.Mex. Dept. Health, 1950-55; commd. officer USPHS, 1957—, advanced through grades to Dir. Grade (Navy capt.), dir. Albuquerque Environ. Health Dept., 1955-68, 82-86; dir. Environ. Improvement Agy., Santa Fe, 1968-73; adminstr. for health and environ. programs N.Mex. HHS Dept., Santa Fe, 1976-78; dir. N.Mex. Sci. Lab. System, Albuquerque, 1973-76; dep. sec. N.Mex. Health and Environ. Dept., Santa Fe, 1978-82, sec., 1987-88; vis. prof. pub. adminstrn. U. N.Mex., Albuquerque, 1988—, adj. prof. polit. sci., 1997—, sr. fellow Inst. for Pub. Policy, 1997—. Chmn. N.Mex. Water Quality Commn., 1971-73, New Mex. Coal Surface Mining Commn., 1971-73 Asst. editor Jour. Environ. Health, 1975-78; cons. editor Environ. News Digest, 1970-82; editl. cons. Jour. Pub. Health Policy, 1980-96, Underwriters Labs., 1996; contbr. over 240 articles to profl. jours. With USN, 1944—46. Recipient Samuel J. Crumbine award for Outstanding Devel. of Comprehensive Program for Environ. Sanitation, 1959 and 65, Sanitarians Disting. Service award Internat. Assn. Milk, Food, and Environ. Sanitarians, 1962, Outstanding Contrbn. award N.Mex. Assn. Pub. Health Sanitarians, 1967, Boss of Yr. award Santa Fe chpt. Nat. Secs. Assn., 1970, Walter F. Snyder award For Achievement in Environ. Quality, 1978, Commendation for Leadership in Health Care N.Mex. Hosp. Assn., 1981, N.Mex. Outstanding Pub. Svc. award, 1988, Zimmerman award U. N.Mex. Alumni, 1993, L.A. County Breslow award L.A. County Dept. Health Svcs., 1994, Outstanding Leadership in Environ. Adminstrn. award Am. Soc. for Pub. Adminstrn., 1994. Hon. Doctor of Humane Letters award, U. New Mexico Bd. Regents, May 2007 Mem. APHA (exec. bd. 1975-82, pres. 1980-81, John J. Sippy Meml. award 1962, other coms., Sedgwick award 1987), Am. Acad. Sanitarians (founder, David Calvin Wagner Excellence award 1984), N.Mex. Pub. Health Assn. (past pres., Disting. Svc. award 1970, Spl. award, 1978, D.A. Larrazola award 1989), N.Mex. Environ. Health Assn., (past pres.), Am. Lung Assn. N.Mex. (bd. dirs. 1982-94, Clinton P. Anderson award for Oustanding Contbn. to Lung Health 1987), Nat. Accreditation Coun. Environ. Health Curricula, Nat. Audubon Soc. (pres. coun. 1982-86), U. Mich. Sch. Pub. Health Alumni Assn. (bd. govs. 1985-88, Outstanding Alumnus award 1995), Royal Soc. Promotion of Health, London (hon.), N.Mex. Soc. Pub. Adminstrn. (Disting. Pub. Adminstr. award 1996), Am. Acad. Sanitarians (diplomate emeritus), Delta Omega, Phi Kappa Phi, Phi Sigma. Independent. Avocations: fishing, travel, golf, genealogy. Home: 1674 Tierra Del Rio NW Albuquerque NM 87107-3259 Personal E-mail: 1016Larry@msn.com.

GORDON, LEONARD, social sciences educator; b. Detroit, Dec. 6, 1935; s. Abraham and Sarah (Rosen) G.; m. Rena Joyce Feigelman, Dec. 25, 1955 (dec. Nov. 24, 2005); children: Susan Melinda, Matthew Seth, Melissa Gail. BA, Wayne State U., 1957; MA, U. Mich., 1958; PhD, Wayne State U., 1966. Instr. Wayne State U., Detroit, 1960-62; rsch. dir. Jewish Cmty. Coun., Detroit, 1962-64; dir. Mich. area Am. Jewish Com., NYC, 1964-67; asst. prof. Ariz. State U., Tempe, 1967-70, assoc. prof., 1970-77, prof., 1977—, chmn. dept. sociology, 1981-90, assoc. dean for acad. programs Coll. Liberal Arts and Scis., 1990-2001, rsch. prof., 2001—02, prof. emeritus, 2002—, founding mem. emeritus coll. coun., 2005—; dean Ariz. State U. Emeritus Colls., 2007—. Cons. OEO, Maricopa County, Ariz., 1968, with Gdansk U., Polish and Am. Ctr. Dispute Resolution Labor Mgmt. Disputes, Poland Author: A City in Racial Crisis, 1971, Sociology and American Social Issues, 1978, (with A. Mayer) Urban Life and the Struggle To Be Human, 1979, (with R. Hardert, M. Laner and M. Reader) Confronting Social Problems, 1984, (with J. Hall and R. Melnick) Harmonizing Arizona's Ethnic and Cultural Diversity, 1992. Sec. Conf. on Religion and Race, Detroit, 1962-67; mem. exec. bd. dirs. Am. Jewish Com., Phoenix chpt., 1969-70. Grantee NSF, 1962, Rockefeller found., 1970, 84; Recipient James W. Creasman award for Lifetime Achievement, Ariz. State U., 2000. Fellow Am. Sociol. Assn. (chair task force on current knowledge on hate/bias acts on coll. and univ. campuses 2000—, chair ASU emeritus coll. policy com., 2005-) mem. AAUP, Pacific Sociol. Assn. (v.p. 1978-79, pres. 1980-81), Soc. Study Social Problems (chair C. Wright Mills award com. 1988, treas. 1989-96), Ariz. State U. Alumni Assn. (faculty dir. 1981-82, founding mem. emeritus coll. coun., 2005-), Emeritus Coll.(dean, 2007) Democrat. Jewish. Home: 13660 E Columbine Dr Scottsdale AZ 85259-3753 Office: Ariz State U Emeritus Coll Wilson Hall 101 Tempe AZ 85287-5203 Home Phone: 480-451-7899; Office Phone: 480-965-0002. Business E-Mail: len.gordon@asu.edu.

GORDON, MALCOLM STEPHEN, biology professor; b. Bklyn., Nov. 13, 1933; s. Abraham and Rose (Walters) G.; m. Diane M. Kestin, Apr. 16, 1959 (div. Sept. 1973); 1 child, Dana Malcolm; m. Marjorie J. Weinzweig, Jan. 28, 1976 (dec. Mar. 1990); m. Carol A. Cowen, July 19, 1992. BA with high honors, Cornell U., 1954; PhD, Yale U., 1958. Instr. UCLA, 1958-60, asst. prof., 1960-65, assoc. prof., 1965-68, prof. biology, 1968—, dir. Inst. Evolutionary and Environ. Biology, 1971-76, chmn. interdept. com. Environ. Sci. Engring. Program, 1984-88; asst. dir. rsch. Nat. Fisheries Ctr. and Aquarium, U.S. Dept. of Interior, Washington, 1968-69. Vis. prof. zoology Chinese U. Hong Kong, 1971-72; panel on marine biology, panel on oceanography Pres.'s Sci. Adv. Com., 1965-66; nat. adv com. R/V Alpha Helix, Scripps Inst. Oceanography, 1969-73; com. on Latimeria, NAS, 1969-72; mem. tech. adv. com. Santa Monica Bay Restoration Project, EPA, 1988-2006; tech. adv. group on milkfish reprodn. AID, 1984-92; chmn. Commn. on Comparative Physiology, Internat. Union Physiol. Sci., 1993-2009; co-founder Inst. of Environment, UCLA, 1997; vis. assoc. in bioengring. and aeronautics Calif. Inst. Tech., 2003-06. Author coll. textbooks, technical books; mem. editorial bd. Fish Physiol. Biochem. Jour., 1986-2008, Jour. Exptl. Zool., 1990-93; mem. joint mng. bd. Physiology Jour., 2007-; contbr. articles to profl. jours. Active cmty. orgns. on environ., civil liberties. NSF fellow Yale U., 1954-57, Fulbright fellow U.K., 1957-58, Guggenheim fellow Italy and Denmark, 1961-62; Sr. Queen's fellow in marine sci. Australia, 1976; Irving-Scholander Meml. lectr., U. Alaska-Fairbanks, 2000. Fellow AAAS; mem. Am. Physiol. Soc. (exec. com. pub. affairs 1989-92, internat. physiol. com. 2002-05), Soc. Integrative Comparative Biology (chmn. divsn. ecology 1979-80, chmn. divsn. comparative biochem. physiology 1988-89), Soc. Exptl. Biology, Internat. Union Physiol. Sci. (coun. mem. 2005—, treas. 2007—) Home: 2801 Glendower Ave Los Angeles CA 90027-1118 Office: UCLA Dept Ecology Evolutionary Biol PO Box 951606 Los Angeles CA 90095-1606 Office Phone: 310-825-4579. Business E-Mail: msgordon@ucla.edu.

GORDON, MILTON ANDREW, academic administrator; b. Chgo., May 25, 1935; s. Herrmann Andrew Gordon and Ossie Bell; m. Margaret Faulwell, July 18, 1987; children: Patrick Francis, Vincent Michael; 1 stepchild, Michael Faulwell. BS, Xavier U. La., New Orleans, 1957; MA, U. Detroit, 1960; PhD, Ill. Inst. Tech., 1968; postgrad., Harvard U., 1984. Teaching asst. U. Detroit, 1958-59; mathematician Lab. Applied Scis. U. Chgo., 1959-62; part-time tchr. Chgo. Pub. Sch. System, 1962-66; assoc. prof. math. Loyola U., Chgo., 1966-67; dir. Afro-Am. Studies Program Loyla U., Chgo., 1971-77; dean Coll. Arts and Scis., prof. math. Chgo. State U., 1978-86; v.p. acad. affairs, prof. math. Sonoma State U., Rohnert Park, Calif., 1986-90; pres., prof. math. Calif. State U., Fullerton, 1990—. Bd. dirs. Associated We. Univs., Inc.; hon. admissions counselor United States Naval Acad., 1979; mem. exec. coun. Calif. State U., 1990; rep. for Calif. univs.Am. Assn. State Colls. and Univs., 1992; commn. on leadership devel. Am. Coun. on Edn., 1992; nat. task force on gender equality Nat. Collegiate Athletic Assn., 1992-94, pres.'s commn., 1994—; commr. joint commn. on accoutability reporting project Am. Assn. of State Colls. and Univs./Nat. Assn. of State Univs. and Land Grant Colls., 1994—, Am. Assn. Applied Ethics. Contbr. articles to profl. jours. Chmn. Archdiocese of Chgo. Sch. Bd., 1978-79; bd. govs. Orange County Community Found., Costa Mesa, Calif., 1990—, NCCJ, 1991—; bd. dirs. United Way of Orange County, Irvine, Calif., 1991, Pacific Symphony Orch., Santa Ana, 1993—; bd. adv. St. Jude Med. Ctr., Fullerton, Calif., 1992, Partnership 2010, Orange County, 1994, Black Leadership in Orange County, 1995—; bd. dirs. Orange County Bus. Coun., 1996—. Recipient cert. of appreciation Community Ch. Santa Rosa, Calif., 1988, Tree of Life award Jewish Nat. Fund, 1994, Humanitarian of Yr. award North Orange County YMCA, 1995; named Adminstr. of Yr., Chgo. State U., 1979. Mem. Am.conf. Acad. Deans (chmn. bd. dirs. 1983-85), Am. Assn. Univ. Adminstrs. (bd. dirs. 1983-86), Calif. Coalition of Math., Sigma Xi, Phi Beta Delta. Roman Catholic. Avocations: photography, sports, walking, movies. Office: Calif State Univ 800 N State College Blvd PO Box 6810 Fullerton CA 92834-6810

GORDON, PHILLIP BRUCE, Mayor, Phoenix; b. Chgo., Apr. 18, 1951; s. Sid and Judy Gordon; m. Christa Severns; children: David, Jeff, Rachel, Jacob. BA in History Edn., U. Ariz.; JD cum laude, Ariz. State U. Chmn. Landiscor Aerial Photography Co.; atty. Pearlstein Law Firm; chief of staff for Mayor Rimsza, 1996; councilman Phoenix City Coun., 1997—2003; mayor City of Phoenix, 2004—. Founder, chmn. Slumlord Task Force; chmn. Ariz. Child Occupant Protection Task Force, Men's Anti-Violence Network; bd. dir. Voice for Crime Victims; mem Madison Sch. Bd. Bd. dir. Orpheum Theatre Found., Downtown YMCA, Phoenix (Ariz.) Ballet Co., Roosevelt Action Assn. Office: City Hall 200 W Washington St 11th Fl Phoenix AZ 85003-1611 Office Phone: 602-262-7111. Office Fax: 602-495-5583. Business E-Mail: mayor.gordon@phoenix.gov.

GORDON, ROBERT ALLEN, JR., food service executive, lawyer; b. Evanston, Ill., Sept. 14, 1951; s. Robert A. Sr. and Elizabeth (Bergman) G.; m. Ellen Slater Guba, Feb. 2, 1985; children: Robert A. III, Sarah Ellen. BA, Yale U., 1973; JD, U. Va., 1976. Bar: Calif. 1976, US Dist. Ct. (no. dist.) Calif. 1977, US Dist. Ct. (ea. & ctrl. districts) Calif. 1978, US Ct. Appeals (9th Cir.) 1978. Law clk. to Hon. James R. Browning US Ct. Appeals (9th Cir.), San Francisco, 1976-77; assoc. Pillsbury, Madison & Sutro, San Francisco, 1977-83, ptnr., 1984—99; dep. gen. counsel Safeway, Inc., Pleasanton, Calif., 1999—2000, sr. v.p., gen. counsel, sec., chief governance officer, 2000—. Mem. Order of Coif. Office: Safeway Inc 5918 Stoneridge Mall Rd Pleasanton CA 94588 E-mail: robert.gordon@safeway.com.*

GORDON, ROBERT EUGENE, lawyer; b. LA, Sept. 20, 1932; s. Harry Maurice and Minnie (Shaffer); 1 child, Victor Marten. BA, UCLA, 1954; LLB, U. Calif., Berkeley, 1959, JD, 1960; cert., U. Hamburg, Germany, 1960. Bar: Calif. 1960. Assoc. Lillick, Geary, McHose, Roethke & Myers, LA, 1960—64, Schoichet & Rifkind, Beverly Hills, Calif., 1964—67; ptnr. Baerwitz & Gordon, Beverly Hills, 1967—69, Ball, Hunt, Hart, Brown & Baerwitz, Beverly Hills, 1970—71; of counsel Jacobs, Sills & Coblentz, San Francisco, 1972—78; ptnr. Gordon & Hodge, San Francisco, 1978—81; pvt. practice San Francisco, 1981—89, Corte Madera, Calif., 1989—2002, Sausalito, Calif., 2002—. Adj. prof. entertainment law Hastings Coll. Law, San Francisco, 1990-91, U. Calif., Berkeley, 1992. Served to 1st lt. U.S. Army, 1954-56. Mem. ABA (forum com. on entertainment and sports law), LA Copyright Soc. (bd. trustees 1970-71), Copyright Soc. of USA. Avocations: bicycling, skiing. Home: 35 Elaine Ave Mill Valley CA 94941-1014 Office: One Harbor Dr Ste 106 Sausalito CA 94965 Office Phone: 415-331-0611. Business E-Mail: lawmuse@pacbell.net.

GORDON, STEPHEN MAURICE, manufacturing company executive, rancher; b. Chgo., Aug. 20, 1942; s. Milton A. and Elinor (Loeff) G.; m. Helene Lindow, Feb. 11, 1978 (div. Mar. 1998); 2 children: Hallie Lindow, Lacey Edison; m. Marilee Ann Enright, Mar. 21, 1998. Student, Middlebury Coll., 1960-61; BA, U. Chgo., 1964; JD, NYU, 1967; D.I.L., Cambridge U., Eng., 1968. Bar: N.Y. State 1968. Aide to Vice Pres. Hubert Humphrey, Democratic Nat. Com., Washington, 1968; assoc. firm Marshall, Bratter, Greene, Allison & Tucker, NYC, 1968-70; sr. rsch. assoc. Halle & Stieglitz, Inc., NYC, 1970-72, v.p., 1972-75, pres., 1975-79; pres., chief exec. officer Irvin Industries Inc., NYC, 1979-89; pres. Diamond G Ranch Inc., Dubois, Wyo. Chmn. bd. dirs. Vincennes Steel Corp., 1989—97; mem. vis. com. U. Chgo. Mem. Nat. Wildlife Art Mus. (dir., treas.), MacLean-Fogg (dir.), Am. Red Angus Assn., Young Pres.' Orgn., Beta Gamma Sigma, Psi Upsilon. Home: Diamond G Ranch Dunoir Rd Dubois WY 82513 Office: PO Box 1887 Wilson WY 83014

GORDON, WILLIAM BINGHAM (BING GORDON), venture capitalist, former software marketing executive; b. Detroit, Feb. 5, 1950; s. William Chalmers and Barbara (Bingham) G.; m Debra Radabaugh, Sept. 27, 1980; 1 child Chloe. BA in English, Yale U., New Haven, Conn., 1972; MBA, Stanford Grad. Sch. of Bus., Stanford, Calif., 1978. Actor Actors Equity, NYC, 1973; fisherman Astoria, Oreg., 1974-76; product mktg. Fairchild Test SYstems, San Jose, Calif., 1978-80; acct. exec. Ogilvy and Mather, San Francisco, 1980-81; acct. supr. Ketchum Communication, San Francisco, 1982; dir. mktg. Electronic Arts, Inc., San Mateo, Calif., 1982-83, v.p. mktg., 1984-86, v.p. GM Entertainment, 1987-89, sr. v.p. mktg. & planning, 1990—98, exec. v.p., chief creative officer, 1998—2008; ptnr. Kleiner Perkins Caufield & Byers, Menlo Park, Calif., 2008—. Bd. dirs., Amazon.com, Inc., 2003-; sec. Debra Radabaugh Assn., Menlo Park, Calif., 1984. Steering com., San Francisco Museum of Mdern Art Archtl. and Design Dept., 1978. Recipient All New England Lacrosse, ECAC, 1972. Avocations: ice hockey, computer games, skiing, travel, parenting. Office: Kleiner Perkins Caufield & Byers 2750 Sand Hill Rd Menlo Park CA 94025 E-mail: bingg@kpcb.com.

GORDY, BERRY, entrepreneur, film producer, recording industry executive; b. Detroit, Nov. 28, 1929; children from a previous marriage: Berry IV, Hazel Joy, Terry James, Kerry A., Sherry R., Kennedy W., Stefan K., Rhonda Ross-Kendrick. PhD in Music (hon.), Ea. Mich. U., 1971. Founder Motown Record Corp., 1961—; exec. prodr. motion pictures; chmn. bd. dirs. West Grand Media, 1998—; founder Jobete Music Co., Inc., 1997—. Dir.: (films) Mahogany, 1975; exec. prodr.: Lady Sings the Blues, 1972, Bingo Long Traveling All-Stars and Motor Kings, 1975, Berry Gordy's the Last Dragon, 1984; author: To Be Loved: The Music, the Magic, the Memories of Motown, 1994. Recipient Bus. Achievement award, Interracial Coun. for Bus. Opportunity, 1967, Golden Mike and MLK, Jr.'s Leadership award, NATRA, 1969, 2d Ann. Am. Music award for outstanding contbn. to music industry, 1975, Whitney M. Young Jr. award, L.A. Urban League, 1980, Trustees award, NARAS, 1991, 20th Century award, Black Radio Exclusive, 1993, Abe Olman Pub. award, Songwriters Hall of Fame, 1993, Livetime Achievement award, Black Bus. Assn., 1993, Generation award, Congl. Black Caucus Found., 1993, Am. Legend award, ASCAP Pop Music Awards, 1998, Lifetime Achievement award, NABOB, 1998, Legend award, BESLA, 1998, A.G. Gaston Lifetime Achievement award, Black Ent./Bank of Am., 2001, Wall St. Project Millennium award, Rainbow/Push, 2000, Legend award, Rainbow/Push Coalition, 2001, Candle award for Lifetime Achievement in Arts and Entertainment, Morehouse Coll., 2005; named star, Hollywood Walk of Fame, 1996; named to Minority Hall of Fame, Atlanta U. Sch. Bus. Adminstrn., 1981, Leading Entrepreneurs of Nation, Babson Coll., 1978, Rock and Roll Hall of Fame, 1988, Nat. Bus. Hall of Fame, Jr. Achievement, 1998; Gordon Grand fellow, Yale U., 1985. Mem.: NAACP, Acad. Motion Picture Arts and Scis., BMI, Dirs. Guild Am.

GOREN, EDWARD GERALD (ED GOREN), broadcast executive; b. Greensboro, NC, June 15, 1944; s. Herb and Betty Goren; m. Patti Goren; 1 child. B in Journalism and Polit. Sci., Syracuse U., 1966. Copy boy, news divsn. CBS, 1966—67, news writer, prodr., 1967—69, prodr., Newsnet, 1969—75, prodr., sports, 1975—91, sr. prodr., sports, 1991—94; exec. prodr. FOX Sports, 1994—, pres., 2000—. Named one of The Most Influential People in the World of Sports, Bus. Week, 2007, 2008; named to Power 100, The Sporting News. Office: FOX Sports 10201 W Pico Blvd FNC/Bldg 101 5th Fl Los Angeles CA 90035 Office Phone: 310-369-6000.

GOREN, HOWARD JOSEPH, biochemistry educator; b. Bialocerkwe, Ukraine, Apr. 9, 1941; came to Can., 1940's; s. Morris Mordechai and Bracha (Nissenbaum) G.; m. Frances Claire, Sept. 18, 1965; children: Robyn Pearl, Jeffrey Michael. BSc, U. Toronto, Ont., Can., 1964; PhD, SUNY, Buffalo, 1968. Postdoctoral fellow Weizman Inst, Rehovot, Israel, 1968-70; asst. prof. U. Calgary, Alta., Canada, 1970-75, assoc. prof. Alta., 1975-82, prof., 1982—86, prof. emeritus, 1986—, chmn. univ. biochemistry group, 1987—91. Vis. scientist NIH, Bethesda, Md., 1977-78; vis. prof. Harvard Med. Sch., Boston, 1984-85, 1999-2000, U. Calif., San Francisco, 1992-93. Asst. editor Molecular Pharmacology, 1974-77; contbr. articles to profl. jours. Mem. Am. Soc. Biochemistry and Molecular Biology, Am. Soc. Pharmacology and Exptl. Therapeutics, Can. Soc. Biochemistry, Molecular and Cellular Biology. Avocations: running, curling. Office: U Calgary 3330 Hospital Dr Calgary AB Canada T2N 4N1 E-mail: goren@ucalgary.ca.

GORENBERG, ALAN EUGENE, physician; b. Japan, Apr. 30, 1959; s. Daniel and Louise Gorenberg; m. Ladan Hariri. BS in Biology, U. Calif., Irvine, 1981; MD, Loma Linda U., 1986. Diplomate Am. Bd. Internal Medicine, Am. Bd. Allergy and Immunology. Pvt. practice, San Bernardino, Calif., 1991—, Victorville, Calif., 1991—; asst. clin. prof. medicine Loma Linda (Calif.) U. Sch. Medicine, 1996—, Western U. Sch. Medicine, 1997—. Office: 2130 N Arrowhead Ave Ste 101 San Bernardino CA 92405-4023 also: 12408 Hesperia Rd Ste 7 Victorville CA 92392-5839

GORES, THOMAS C., lawyer; b. Milw., Sept. 24, 1948; s. Kenneth W. and Carolyn (Camblin) G.; m. Ann P. Pacelli, June 13, 1970; children: Lauren, Jake, Kathryn. BA, U. Notre Dame, 1970, JD, 1973; LLM, U. Miami, 1977. Bar: Wash. 1973, U.S. Tax Ct. 1973. Assoc., then ptnr. Bogle & Gates, Seattle, 1973-78, ptnr., 1978-93, Gores & Blais, Seattle, 1993-2001, Perkins Coie LLP, 2001—. Fellow Am. Coll. Trust and Estate Counsel; mem. Wash. State Bar Assn., Seattle Estate Planning Coun. (pres.). Office: Perkins Coie LLP 1201 3rd Ave Ste 4800 Seattle WA 98101-3099 Office Phone: 425-635-1444. Business E-Mail: tgores@perkinscole.com.

GORES, TOM T., investment company executive; b. Nazareth, Israel, 1964; married; 3 children. BA, Mich. State U. Entrepreneur; founder, chmn., CEO Platinum Equity, LA, 1995—. Bd. dirs. St. Joseph's Hosp., LA, UCLA Med. Ctr. Named one of 400 Richest Ams., Forbes mag., 2006; named to several Forbes' World Billionaires lists. Office: Platinum Equity 360 N Crescent Dr South Bldg Beverly Hills CA 90210 Office Phone: 310-712-1850. Office Fax: 310-712-1848.

GORHAM, RAMSAY L., state legislator, political organization administrator; b. Rocky Mount, NC, July 11, 1951; BA, Converse Coll., SC. Artist; mem. N. Mex. Senate, Dist. 10, Sante Fe, 1996—; mem. edn. com., mem. rules com.; chmn. Republican Party N.Mex., 2003—. Republican. Office: State Capitol Santa Fe NM 87501

GORIN, SUSAN, Mayor, Santa Rosa, California; BA, Sonoma State U. Grad. Leadership Santa Rosa, Leadership Inst. Econ. and Ecology. Planning commr. City of Santa Rosa, councilwoman, 2006—08, mayor, 2008—. Exec. bd. mem. New Economy Working Solutions. Former bd. mem. Santa Rosa Sch. Bd., Santa Rosa Pub. Utilities Bd.; former chmn. Santa Rosa Bicycle and Pedestrian Adv. Com.; former co-chmn. Concerned Citizens for Santa Rosa; former v.p. Sonoma County Pub. Libr. Found.; former adv. bd. mem. Safe Havens for Youth. Mem.: Ct. Appointed Spl. Advocates (bd. mem. & former pres.), Sonoma County League Women Voters (former pres.). Office: 100 Santa Rosa Ave Santa Rosa CA 95404 Office Phone: 707-543-3010. E-mail: sgorin@srcity.org.*

GORMAN, JOSEPH GREGORY, JR., lawyer; b. Chgo., Sept. 27, 1939; s. Joseph Gregory and Genevieve C. (Smith) Gorman; m. Mary (Molly) O'Donovan, Mar. 23, 1968 (dec. Aug. 15, 2005); children: Jennifer Ann Gorman Patton, Joseph Gregory III. BA, UCLA, 1961, MBA, 1963, JD, 1966. Bar: U.S. Dist. Ct. (cen. dist.) Calif. 1967, U.S. Ct. Appeals (9th cir.) 1967, U.S. Tax Ct. Atty. Sheppard, Mullin, Richter & Hampton LLP, LA, 1966—. Chair death and gift tax com. LA County Bar Assn., chair probate & trust law sect., 1980-81; chair death and gift tax com. Calif. State Bar, 1976-77; co-founder U. So. Calif. Probate & Trust Conf., 1974—; adv. bd. U. Miami Heckerling Inst. Estate Planning, 1978—. Contbr. articles to profl. jours. Served with USAR, Calif. NG, 1962-68. Fellow Am. Coll. Trust and Estate Counsel, Academician, The Internat. Acad. of Estate and Trust Law. Clubs: Annandale Golf (Pasadena); Jonathan (Los Angeles). Republican. Roman Catholic. Office: Sheppard Mullin Richter & Hampton LLP 333 S Hope St Fl 48 Los Angeles CA 90071-1448 Office Phone: 213-617-4121. Business E-Mail: jgorman@sheppardmullin.com.

GORMAN, MAUREEN J., lawyer; b. Rockford, Ill., Dec. 17, 1955; d. John William and Joanne Mary (Ollman) G.; m. Alan O. Sykes, 1980. BA, Coll. William and Mary, 1978; JD, Yale U., 1981. Bar: DC 1983, Ill. 1987. Law clk. to Hon. Warren W. Eginton US Dist. Ct. Conn., 1981-82; assoc. Caplin & Drysdale, Wash., 1982-85; legis. atty. joint com. on taxation US Congress, Wash., 1985-86; assoc. Mayer, Brown & Platt, Chgo., 1986-88, ptnr., 1988, Mayer, Brown, Rowe & Maw LLP, Palo Alto, Calif. Mem. ABA (chairperson subcom. tech. corrections, employee benefits com., tax sect. 1987-91). Office: Mayer Brown Rowe & Maw LLP 2 Palo Alto Sq Ste 300 Palo Alto CA 94306 Office Phone: 650-331-2033. Business E-Mail: mgorman@mayerbrown.com.

GORMAN, MICHAEL JOSEPH, retired library director, educator; b. Witney, Oxfordshire, Eng., Mar. 6, 1941; came to U.S. 1977; s. Philip Denis and Alicia F. (Barrett) G.; m. Anne Gillett, Mar. 6, 1962 (div. 1992); children: Emma, Alice; m. Anne Christine Reuland, June 6, 2003. Student, Ealing Sch. Librarianship, 1964-66. Dir. gen. services dept. Univ. Library U. Ill., Urbana, 1977-88, acting univ. librarian, 1986-87; prof. library adminstrn. U. Ill., Urbana, 1977-88; vis. prof. U. Chgo. Library Sch., 1984, 86-88, U. Calif., Berkeley, 1989-91; dean libr. svcs. Calif. State U., Fresno, 1988—2007; ret., 2007. Vis. lectr. U. Ill. Grad. Sch. Library Sci., Urbana, 1974-75; bibliog. cons. Brit. Library Planning Secretariat, 1972-74; head cataloguing Brit. Nat. Bibliography 1969-72. Author: A Study of the Rules for Entry and Headings in the Anglo-American Cataloguing Rules, 1967, 68, Format for Machine Readable Cataloguing of Motion Pictures, 1973, Concise AACR2, 1980, 4th edit., 2004, Technical Services Today and Tomorrow,1990, 2nd edit., 1998, Future Libraries (with Walt Crawford) 1995, Our Singular Strengths: Meditations for Librarians, 1998, Our Enduring Values, 2000, The Enduring Library, 2002, Our Own Selves, 2005, others; editor: Anglo-American Cataloguing Rules, 2d edit., 1978, rev., 1988, Catalogue and Index, 1973, Non Solus, 1981, Crossroads, 1986, Convergence, 1990; contbr. articles to profl. jours., chpts. to books. Recipient Blackwell scholarship award, 1997. Fellow: Libr. Assn. (Eng.), Brit. Libr. Assn., Chartered Inst. Libr. and Info. Profls. U.K. (hon.); mem.: ALA (mem. coun. 1991—95, 2002—, mem. exec. bd. 2003—07, pres.-elect 2004—05, pres. 2005—06, Margaret Mann citation 1979, Melvil Dewey medal 1992, Highsmith award 2001), Libr. Info. and Tech. Assn. (mem.-at-large exec. bd. 1982—85, pres. 1999—2000). Home Phone: 559-436-0105.

GORMAN, PAMELA, state legislator; m. Larry Gorman; 1 child, Ryan. BA in Comm., Ariz. State U. Mem. Dist. 6 Ariz. House of Reps., 2005—07, Ariz. State Senate, 2007—, mem. rules com., appropriations com., natural resources, infrastructure & pub. debt com., majority whip leader. Usher Desert View Bible Ch., Phoenix; active Pure Heart Christian Fellowship. Republican. Office: Ariz State Senate Capitol Complex 1700 W Washington Rm 212 Phoenix AZ 85007 Office Phone: 602-926-6284. Office Fax: 602-417-3106. Business E-Mail: pgorman@azleg.gov.*

GORMAN, STEVE, musician; Formed band Mr. Crowe's Garden, 1980s, changed name to Black Crowes; albums include Shake Your Money Maker, 1990 (Album of Yr. Internat. Rock Awards 1991, double platinum record 1991), The Southern Harmony and Musical Companion, 1992, Amorica, 1994, Three Snakes and One Charm, 1996, Souled Out Live, 1998, By Your Side, 1999, Armorica, 2000, Lions, 2001, Live, 2002, Freak 'n' Roll...Into the Fog, 2006, Warpaint, 2008. Recipient (with Black Crowes) Grammy award nomination for Best New Artist; voted Best New Am. Band, Rolling Stone readers and critics polls; named Artist of Yr. Office: Def Am Records 3500 W Olive Ave Ste 1550 Burbank CA 91505-4628

GORNEY, RODERIC, psychiatrist, educator; b. Grand Rapids, Mich., Aug. 13, 1924; s. Abraham Jacob Gorney and Edelaine (Roden) Harburg; m. Carol Ann Sobel, Apr. 13, 1986. BS, Stanford U., 1948, MD, 1949; PhD in Psychoanalysis, So. Calif. Psychoanalytic Inst., 1977. Diplomate Am. Bd. Psychiatry and Neurology. Pvt. practice psychiatry, San Francisco, 1952-62; asst. prof. UCLA, 1962-71, assoc. prof., 1971-73, prof. psychiatry, 1980—, dir. psychosocial adaptation and the future program, 1971—85; psychoanalytic mem. emeritus New Ctr. Psychoanalysis, 2005—. Faculty So. Calif. Psychoanalytic Inst. Author: The Human Agenda, 1972. Served with USAF, 1943-46. Fellow AAAS, Acad. Psychoanalysis, Am. Psychoanalytic Assn., Internat. Psychoanalytic Assn., Am. Psychiatric Assn. (essay prize 1971), Group for Advancement of Psychiatry, New Ctr. for Psychoanalysis. Avocation: music. Office: Semel Inst Neurosci and Human Behavior 760 Westwood Plz Los Angeles CA 90095-8353 Office Phone: 310-476-3099, 310-472-7631. Business E-Mail: preadapt@ucla.edu.

GORONKIN, HERBERT, physicist; b. Pitts., Jan. 9, 1936; s. Sander (Tammie) and Mae (Shulman) G.; children: David, Jeffrey, Michael; m. Pamela Louise Cooper, Oct. 4, 1980; children: Rebecca Louise, Theresa Louise, James David. BA, Temple U., 1961, MA, 1962, PhD, 1973. Physicist Internat. Resistance Co., Phila., 1963-65; sr. rsch. physicist Honeywell Inc., Ft. Washington, Pa., 1965-66; sect. head Am. Electronic Labs., Colmar, Pa., 1966-69; project engr. GE, Syracuse, NY, 1969-75; mgr. semiconductor ops. Varian Assocs., Beverly, Mass., 1975-77; from mgr. high speed devices to chief scientist Phoenix corp. rsch. labs. Motorola Inc., Phoenix, 1977-88, mgr. to dir. phys. rsch. lab., 1988-99; v.p. phys. rsch. labs. Phys. Scis. Rsch. Labs., Phoenix, 1999—2003, dir. rsch. activities in molecular electronics, spintronics, biotechnology and nanosci.; pres. Tech. Acceleration Assoc., 2003—; venture ptnr. Lux Capital, 2003—. Chmn. Workshop on Compound Semiconductor Microwave Materials and Devices, 1984-86, Quantum Electronics, Quantum Functional Devices and Compound Semiconductor Devices, 1986, Advanced Hetrostructure Workshop, 1994; program chair Internat. Symposium on Compound Semiconductors, 1994, gen. chair, 1997; govering bd. Ctr. of Intergrated Nanosystems, 2003-, co-chmn. NanoBus. Alliance Tech. Adv. Bd., Venture Ptnr. Lux Capital, 2005. Guest editor MRS Bull. on Future Memories; contbr. articles to profl. jours., chpts. to books; patentee in field. Served with USAF, 1954-57. Recipient Motorola Disting. Innovator award, 1993, Motorola Master Innovator award, 1995, Motorola Dan Noble fellow, 1996; named IEEE Phoenix Sect. Sr. Engr. of Yr., 1993. Fellow IEEE (IEDM compound semiconductor tech. program com. 1983-86); mem. Am. Phys. Soc., Sigma Xi. Avocations: hiking, japanese, cooking. Home and Office: 8641 S Willow Dr Tempe AZ 85284-2473 E-mail: hgoronkin@cox.net.

GORSUCH, EDWARD LEE, former chancellor; Degree in Econ. and Cmty. Devel., U. Mo. Dir. Inst. Social and Econ. Rsch., 1976-94; dean Sch. Pub. Affairs U. Alaska, Anchorage, 1988-94, chancellor, 1994—2004. Bd. dirs. Commonwealth North; mem. adv. bd. Alaska Airlines Anchorage Cmty.; mem. civilian adv. bd. ALCOM; mem. Fiscal Policy Coun. Alaska, U.S. Artic Rsch. Com., U.S. MAB; dir. High Latitude Ecosystems. Mem., pres. Alaska Assn. Sch. Bds. Mem.: AAAS (pres. Alaska chpt.). Home Phone: 360-647-5233; Office Phone: 360-647-5233. Business E-Mail: lee.gorsuch@uaa.alaska.edu.

GORSUCH, NEIL MCGILL, federal judge, lawyer; b. Denver, Aug. 29, 1967; s. David Ronald Gorsuch and Anne McGill Burford; m. Marie Louise Burletson, June 22, 1996; children: Belinda Loveday, Emma Louise. BA with honors, Columbia U., NYC, 1988; JD cum laude, Harvard U., Cambridge, Mass., 1991; DPhil, Oxford U., Eng. Bar: NY 1992, Colo. 1994, DC 1997. Law clk. to Hon. David B. Sentelle US Ct. Appeals DC cir., 1991—92; law clk. to Justice Byron R. White & Justice Anthony M. Kennedy US Supreme Ct., DC, 1993—94; assoc. Kellogg, Huber, Hansen, Todd & Evans, DC, 1995—97, ptnr., 1998—2005; prin. dep. assoc. atty. gen., acting assoc. atty. gen. US Dept. Justice, DC, 2005—06; judge US Ct. Appeals 10th cir., Denver, 2006—; adj. prof. U. Colo. Law Sch., 2007—. Contbr. articles to profl. jours. Recipient Edmund J. Randolph award for Outstanding Svc., US Dept. Justice, 2006, Joseph Stevens Pub. Svc. award, Harry S. Truman Found., 2007; Marshall scholar, 1992—95, Harry S. Truman scholar, 1987—90. Mem.: Coun. Fgn. Rels., Trout Unltd., Phi Beta Kappa. Avocations: skiing, fly fishing, tennis. Office: US Ct Appeals 10th Cir Byron White Ct House 1823 Stout St Denver CO 80257

GORTON, SLADE (THOMAS SLADE GORTON III), lawyer, lobbyist, former senator; b. Chgo., Jan. 8, 1928; s. Thomas Slade and Ruth (Israel) Gorton; m. Sally Jean Clark, June 28, 1958; children: Tod, Sarah Jane, Rebecca Lynn. BA magna cum laude, Dartmouth Coll., 1950; LLB with honors, Columbia U., 1953. Bar: Wash. 1953. Assoc. law firm, Seattle, 1953—65; ptnr. law firm, 1965—69; atty. gen. State of Wash., Olympia, 1969—81; ptnr. Davis, Wright & Jones, Seattle, 1987—89; senator from Wash. US Senate, Washington, 1981—87, 1989—2001; of counsel K&L Gates, Seattle, Washington, DC, 2001—. Mem. Wash. Ho. of Reps., 1959—69, majority leader, 1967—69, US Senate budget com., appropriations com., commerce/sci. and transp. com., energy and natural resources com.,

1981—87, 1989—2001; chmn. commerce, sci. and transp. subcom. on aviation, com. on appropriations subcom. on interior; commr. The Nat. Commn. on Terrorist Attacks Upon the U.S. (The 9-11 Commn.), 2002—04, Nat. Commn. on War Powers, 2006—; bd. dirs. Microvision Inc., Redmond, chair, 2007—, Nat. Transp. Policy Project, Kochi, 2007—. Trustee, founding mem. Pacific Sci. Ctr., Seattle, 1977—78; mem. Pres.'s Consumer Adv. Coun., 1975—77, Wash. State Law and Justice Commn., 1969—80, chmn., 1969—76; mem. State Criminal Justice Tng. Commn., 1969—80, chmn., 1969—76. With US Army, 1946—47, 1st lt. USAF, 1953—56, col. (ret.) USAFR. Mem.: Nat. Assn. Attys. Gen. (pres. 1969—81, Wyman award 1980), Wash. Bar Assn., Bellevue Club, Seattle Tennis Club, Phi Beta Kappa, Phi Delta Phi. Office: K&L Gates 925 4th Ave Ste 2900 Seattle WA 98104-1158 also: 1601 K St, NW Washington DC 20006-1600 Office Phone: 206-370-8339, 202-661-3880. Office Fax: 206-623-7022, 202-331-1024. Business E-Mail: slade.gorton@klgates.com.

GOSINK, JOAN P., retired engineering educator; BS in Math., MIT, 1962; MS in Engring., Old Dominion U., 1973; PhD in Mech. Engring., U. Calif., Berkeley, 1979. Registered profl. hydrologist. NASA fellow Langley Rsch. Ctr., Hampton, Va., 1972—73; Fulbright-Hayes fellow U. Southampton, England, 1974—75; tchg. assoc. U. Calif., Berkeley, 1975—76; postdoctoral fellow Geophys. Inst., U. Alaska, 1979—81; asst. prof. geophysics U. Alaska, Fairbanks, 1981—86, geophysics coord. dept. geology and geophysics, 1986—88, assoc. prof. geophysics, 1986—91; program dir. chem. and thermal sys. NSF, 1990—91; prof., dir. divsn. engring. Colo. Sch. Mines, Golden, 1991—2003, prof. emerita. Mem. mech. engring. dept. adv. bd. Carnegie Mellon U., 1992—. Treas., bd. dirs. Women in Crisis: Counseling and Assistance, Fairbanks, 1985—87; mem. Internat. Women's Forum. Recipient N.Y. State Regents scholarship in sci. and engring., 1958, N.Y. State Regents scholarship, 1958, MIT scholarship, 1958—61, NASA fellowship, Langley Rsch. Ctr., 1972—73, Pacific Gas and Electric fellowship, 1976—78. Mem.: ASCE (rsch. com. of tech. coun. on cold regions rsch. 1986—), ASME (bd. on engring. edn. 1999—, com. on low temperature and Arctic regions heat transfer K-18 1991—, com. on govt. rels. 1992—96), Women in Engring. Programs Advocates Network, Am. Inst. Hydrology, Am. Soc. Engring. Edn. Office: Colo Sch of Mines Divsn Engring Golden CO 80401

GOSLIN, THOMAS B., career officer; BA in Polit. Sci., La. State U., 1970; grad., Officer Tng. Sch., 1970; student pilot tng., Columbus AFB, Miss., 1971-72; student, Squadron Officer Sch., 1974; MA in Guidance and Counseling, La. Tech U., 1975; student, Air Command and Staff Coll., 1975, Air War Coll., 1980, Armed Forces Staff Coll., 1981, Can. Nat. Def. Coll., 1988, Duke U., 1995. Commd. 2d lt. USAF, 1970, advanced through grades to lt. gen., 2002; forward air controller Tan Son Nhut Air Base, S. Vietnam, 1972-73; pilot, instr. pilot 71st Air Refueling Squadron, Barksdale AFB, La., 1973-76; air staff tng. officer, intelligence threat assessment Pentagon, Washington, 1976-77, various positions, 1993-94; pilot, instr. pilot, flight comdr. 62d Bomb Squadron, Barksdale AFB, 1977-80; stationed at Hdqs. USAF, Pentagon, Washington, 1981-84, 94-95, now dep. dir. programs, dep. chief staff plans and programs; fighter lead-in tng. Holloman AFB, N.Mex., 1984; pilot 162d Tactical Fighter Group Air N.G., Tucson, 1984; various comdr. assignments, 1984-93; asst. dir. ops. Hdqs. Air Combat Command, Langley AFB, Va., 1995-96; comdr. 509th Bomb Wing, Whiteman AFB, Mo., 1996—98; dep. dir. prog., dep. chief of staff for plans and programs HQ USAF, Washington, 1998—99; dir., ops. HQ US Space Command, Peterson AFB, Colo., 1999—2001; commander Space Warfare Ctr., Schriever AFB, Colo., 2001—02; dep. commander US Strategic Command, Offutt AFB, Nebr., 2002—. Decorated Legion of Merit, D.F.C. with oak leaf cluster, Air medal with seven oak leaf clusters, Rep. Vietnam Gallantry Cross.

GOSLING, JAMES, computer scientist, web programmer; BSc in Computer Sci., U. Calgary, Can., 1977; PhD in Computer Sci., Carnegie-Mellon U., 1983. With IBM TJ Watson Rsch. Ctr., Sun Microsystems, Inc., 1984—, lead engr. NeWS window sys., CTO, v.p., Sun fellow. Named officer, Order of Canada, 2007. Mem.: NAE (fgn. assoc.). Achievements include creating the Java (Object Oriented Programming) language. Office: Sun Microsystems Inc 4150 Network Cir Santa Clara CA 95054

GOSLING, JOHN THOMAS, space plasma physicist, researcher; b. Akron, Ohio, July 10, 1938; s. Arthur Warrington and Wilhelmina (Bell) G.; m. Marie Ann Turner, Dec. 21, 1963; children: Mark Raymond, Steven Arthur; m. Margaret Judith Hughes, Jan. 8, 1994. BS in Physics, Ohio U., 1960; PhD in Physics, U. Calif., Berkeley, 1965; postdoctoral studies, Los Alamos Nat. Lab., N.Mex., 1965-67. Staff mem. Nat. Ctr. Atmospheric Research, Boulder, Colo., 1967-75; staff mem., Space Plasma Physics Team Los Alamos Nat. Lab., 1975—2005, fellow; sr. rsch. assoc. Lab. Atmospheric & Space Physics U. Colo., Boulder, 2005—. Mem. Nat. Rsch. Council Com. on Solar-Terrestrial Rsch, 1994-97. Contbr. more than 400 articles to profl. jours. Recipient Tech. Achievement award Nat. Ctr. Atmospheric Research, Boulder, 1974, several Achievement Awards from NASA. Fellow Am. Geophys. Union (pres. space physics and aeronomy sect. 2000-02, John Adam Fleming medal, 2000, Parker Lecture 2004), fellow AAAS, Internat. Astron. Union. Democrat. Avocations: sports, hiking, music. Home: 790 Niwot Ridge Ln Lafayette CO 80026 Office: LASP 1234 Innovation Dr Boulder CO 80303 Business E-Mail: jack.gosling@lasp.colorado.edu.

GOSS, KENT, lawyer; BA in Economics, Occidental Coll., 1983; JD, U. Calif., 1987. Bar: Calif. 1987, US Dist. Ct. (so. dist.) Calif., US Dist. Ct. (ctrl. dist.) Calif., US Dist. Ct. (no. dist.) Calif., US Ct. Appeals (9th cir.). Ptnr. Pillsbury Winthrop Shaw Pittman, Orrick, Herrington & Sutcliffe LLP, LA, 2006—. Mem.: US Trademark Assn., ABA. Office: Orrick Herrington & Sutcliffe LLP 777 S Figueroa St Ste 3200 Los Angeles CA 90017 Office Phone: 213-612-2411.

GOSSARD, ARTHUR CHARLES, physicist, researcher; b. Ottawa, Ill., June 18, 1935; s. Arthur Paul and Mary Catherine (Lineberger) G.; m. Marsha Jean Palmer, Jan. 8, 1965; children: Girard Christopher, Elinore Suzanne. BA, Harvard U., 1956; PhD, U. Calif., Berkeley, 1960. Solid state physicist, disting. mem. tech. staff AT&T Bell Labs., Murray Hill, NJ, 1960-87; prof. materials and electrical and computer engring. U. Calif., Santa Barbara, 1987—. Author tech. papers magnetic resonance, magnetism, transition metals, molecular beam epitaxy, quantum structures, semiconductors. Recipient John Bardeen award TMS, 2005, Newcombe-Cleveland prize AAAS, 2006, 2007; sr. fellow Humboldt Found. Fellow IEEE, Am. Phys. Soc. (Oliver Buckley condensed matter physics prize 1984, James McGroddy prize for New Materials 2001); mem. NAS, Nat. Acad. Engring. Office: U Calif Materials Dept Santa Barbara CA 93106 Business E-Mail: gossard@engineering.ucsb.edu.

GOTH, HARVEY L., construction company executive; Former v.p. Blackfield Hawaii Corp. (subs. Pacific Enterprises); former pres. Malama Pacific Corp. (subs. Hawaiian Electric Industries); sr. v.p. acquisition and development Schuler Homes, Inc., Honolulu. Office: Schuler Homes Inc 828 4th St Mall Fl 4 Honolulu HI 96813-4321

GOTHOLD, STUART EUGENE, school system administrator, education educator; b. LA, Sept. 20, 1935; s. Hubert Eugene and Adelaide Louise (Erickson) G.; m. Jane Ruth Soderberg, July 15, 1955; children: Jon Ernest, Susan Louise, Eric Arthur, Ruth Ann. BA, Whittier Coll., Calif., 1956, MA in Edn., 1961, LLD (hon.), 1988; EdD, U. So. Calif., 1974. Tchr. grades 1-9 El Rancho Sch. Dist., Pico Rivera, Calif., 1956-61, prin. jr. h.s., 1961-66; curriculum cons. LA County Office Edn., 1966-70; asst. supt. South Whittier Sch. Dist., Calif., 1970-72, supt. Calif., 1972-77; asst. supt. LA County Office Edn., Downey, 1977-78, chief dep. supt., 1978-79, supt., 1979-94; clin. prof. emeritus U. So. Calif., LA, 1994—. Exec. dir. Edn. Insights, Detroit, 1990—; chmn., bd. dirs. Fedco Found.; co-chmn. LA Music Ctr. Edn. Coun. Author: (book) Inquiry, 1970, Decisions-A Health Edn. Curriculum, 1971. Recipient Alumni Merit award USC, 1993, Alumni Achievement award Whittier Coll., 1986; named Dist. Educator Calif. State U., 1993. Republican. Roman Catholic. Avocations: tennis, singing, photography, hiking. Home: 10121 Pounds Ave Whittier CA 90603-1649 Office: U So Calif WPH 902 C Los Angeles CA 90089-4039 Office Phone: 213-740-3451. Business E-Mail: gothold@usc.edu.

GOTO SABAS, JENNIFER, legislative staff member; b. Honolulu, Dec. 23, 1961; BA, U. Hawaii, 1983; JD, Georgetown U., 1986. Bar: Va. 1986. Law clerk, Office the Gen. Counsel NEA, 1985—86; legal rsch. and writing instr. Cath. U. Law Sch., 1986-87; legis. asst., Senator Daniel K. Inouye US Senate, Washington, 1987-90, dep. chief of staff, Senator Daniel K. Inouye, 1990-91, chief of staff to Senator Daniel K. Inouye Honolulu, 1993—. Adj. instr. legal rsch. and writing Am. U. Sch. of Law, 1988. Office: Dist Office Prince Kuhio Fed Bldg 300 Ala Moana Blvd Rm 7-212 Honolulu HI 96850-4975*

GOTTFRIED, IRA SIDNEY, management consulting executive; b. Bronx, NY, Jan. 4, 1932; s. Louis and Augusta (Champagne) G.; m. Judith Claire Rosenberg, Sept. 19, 1954; children: Richard Alan, Glenn Steven, David Aaron. BBA, CCNY, 1953; MBA, U. So. Calif., 1959. Lic. airline transport pilot. Sales mgr. Kleerpak Plastics, North Hollywood, Calif., 1956-57; head sys. and procedures Hughes Aircraft Co., Culver City, Calif., 1957-60; mgr. corp. bus. sys. The Aerospace Corp., El Segundo, Calif., 1960-61; dir. adminstrn. Eldon Industries, Inc., Hawthorne, Calif., 1962; mgr. info. sys. Litton Industries, Inc., Woodland Hills, Calif., 1963-64; exec. v.p. Norris & Gottfried, Inc., LA, 1964-69; pres. Gottfried Cons., Inc., LA, 1970-85; exec. ptnr. PriceWaterhouseCoopers, LLP, LA, 1985-88, ret., 1988. V.p. Cresap/Towers Perrin, 1988-90; pres., dir. Gottfried Cons. Internat. 1990—; vice chmn. ACME Inc., 1984-85; dir., mem. exec. com. Blue Cross of Calif., 1968-77. Contbr. articles to profl. jours. Bd. dirs. ARC, 1988-2003, Westside Amateur Radio Club, 1997-, Univ. Synagogue, 1986-92. With USNR, 1953-56. Recipient Pres.'s award United Hosp. Assn. Mem. Inst. Mgmt. Cons. (life), Assn. Info. Tech. Profls. (life), Alpha Phi Omega (life), Brentwood Country Club. Jewish. Avocations: radio, flying, model building. Home: 12118 La Casa Ln Los Angeles CA 90049-1530 Office Phone: 310-476-2124.

GOTTHOLD, WILLIAM EUGENE, emergency physician; b. Long Beach, Calif., Sept. 20, 1942; BA, Trinity U., 1964; MD, Tulane U., 1969. Cert. emergency medicine. Intern Letterman Army Med. Ctr., San Francisco, 1969-70, resident in gen. surgery, 1970-72; mem. staff Ctrl. Wash. Hosp., Wenatchee, 1978—; med. infomatics officers Wenatchee (Wash.) Valley Clinic. Mem. AMA, Am. Coll. Emergency Physicians, Wash. State Med. Assn., Am. Bd. Emergency Medicine (cert., sr. dir.). Office: Wenatchee Valley Med Ctr 820 N Chelan Ave Wenatchee WA 98801-2028 Office Phone: 509-663-8711. E-mail: wgotthold@wvclinic.com.

GOTTSCHLING, DANIEL E., molecular research biologist; Rsch. biologist U. Chgo.; now prin. investigator Fred Hutchinson Cancer Rsch. Ctr., Seattle. Recipient Molecular Biology award NAS, 1995. Office: Fred Hutchinson Cancer Rsch Ctr 1100 Fairview Ave N Seattle WA 98109-4417

GOUGH, DENIS IAN, geophysics educator; b. Port Elizabeth, Cape, South Africa, June 20, 1922; came to Can., 1966; s. Frederick William and Ivy Catherine (Hingle) G.; m. Winifred Irving Nelson, June 2, 1945; children— Catherine Veronica, Stephen William Cyprian B.Sc., Rhodes U., Grahamstown, Republic of South Africa, 1943, M.Sc., 1947, D.Sc. (hon.), 1990; PhD, U. Witwatersrand, Johannesburg, Republic of South Africa, 1953. Research officer Nat. Phys. Lab., Johannesburg, S. Africa, 1947, sr. research officer; lectr. Univ. Coll. Rhodesia, Salisbury, 1958, sr. lectr.; assoc. prof. geophysics Southwest Ctr. for Advanced Studies, Dallas, 1964-66; prof. geophysics U. Alta., Edmonton, Can., 1966-87, prof. emeritus, 1987—, dir. Inst. Earth and Planetary Physics, 1975-80. Contbr. numerous articles to profl. jours. Royal Soc. Can. fellow, 1972 Fellow Royal Astron. Soc. (Chapman medal 1988), Am. Geophys. Union; Geol. Assn. Can.; mem. Can. Geophys. Union (past pres., J. Tuzo Wilson medal 1983), Internat. Assn. Geomagnetism and Aeronomy (pres. 1983-87), S. African Geophys. Assn. (Rudolf Krahmann medal 1989). Avocations: reading, music, poetry. Office: Univ Alta Dept Physics Edmonton AB Canada T6G 2J1 E-mail: iangough@shaw.ca.

GOULD, DAVID, lawyer; b. LA, Feb. 19, 1940; s. Erwin and Beatrice (Altman) G.; m. Bonnie Becker, Feb. 12, 1967; children: Julie M., Michael. AB, U. Calif., LA, 1962; LLB, U. Calif., Berkeley, 1965. Bar: Calif. 1965, U.S. Dist. Ct. (cen., so., ea. and no. dists.) Calif. 1966, U.S. Ct. Appeals (9th cir.) 1967, U.S. Supreme Ct. 1995. Dep. atty. gen. Calif. Dept. of Justice, LA, 1965-68; assoc. Loeb & Loeb, LA, 1968-73, Danning, Gill, Gould, Diamond & Spector, LA, 1974-76, ptnr., 1976-92, McDermott, Will & Emery, LA, 1992—. Adj. assoc. prof. Southwestern U. Sch. of Law, L.A., 1978-80; adj. prof. Pepperdine U. Sch. of Law, Malibu, Calif., 1982. Co-author: Local Bankruptcy Practice Manual for the Central District of California, 2d edit., 1990—. Fellow: Am. Coll. Bankruptcy; mem.: L.A. Bankruptcy Forum (bd. trustees 1989, sec. 1990—, pres. 1993—94, lawyer rep. ctrl. dist. Calif. to 9th cir. jud. conf.), Calif. Bankruptcy Forum, L.A. County Bar Assn. (fed. cts. com. 1987—, treas. 1998—99, sec. 1999—), Calif. Bar Assn. (debtor/creditor rels. and bankruptcy com. 1984—87, chair 1987—88, advisor 1988—89, uniform comml. code com. 1988—92, bankruptcy cons. gorup bd. legal specialization 1989—93), ABA (bus. bankruptcy com. sect. on bus. law 1982—, vice chair rules subcom. 1986—92, chair 1992—). Avocation: trap and skeet shooting.

GOULD, MARTHA BERNICE, retired librarian; b. Claremont, NH, Oct. 8, 1931; d. Sigmund and Gertrude Heller; m. Arthur Gould, July 29, 1960; children: Leslie, Stephen. BA in Edn., U. Mich., Ann Arbor, 1953; MS in Libr. Sci., Simmons Coll., Boston, 1956; cert., U. Denver Libr. Sch., 1978. Childrens libr. NY Pub. Libr., 1956-58; adminstr. libr. svcs. act demonstration regional libr. project Pawhuska, Okla., 1958-59; cons. N.Mex. State Libr., 1959-60; children's libr. then sr. children's libr. LA Pub. Libr., 1960-72; acctg. dir. pub. svcs., reference libr. Nev. State Libr., 1972-74; pub. svcs. libr. Washoe County Libr., Nev., 1974-79, asst. county libr. Nev., 1979-84, county libr. Nev., 1984-94; ret., 1994. Cons. Nev. State Libr. and Archives, 1996—2003; part-time lectr. libr. adminstrn. U. Nev.; acting dir. Nev. Ctr. for the Book; vice-chair Nat. Commn. in Librs. and Info. Sci., 1993—2000, chair, 2000—03; mem. adv. coun. Nev. Coun. on Librs. and Literacy, 2001—05; mem. adv. bd. Fleischmann Planetarium, 1999—2003; intern advisor Nevada Newsmakers outreach program, 2007—. Co-editor: Nevada Women's History Project Annotated Bibliography, 1999; contbr. articles to jours. Exec. dir. Kids Voting/USA, Nev., 1996; treas. United Jewish Appeal, 1981; bd. dirs. Temple Sinai, Planned Parenthood, 1996-97, Truckee Meadows Habitat for Humanity, 1995-98; trustee RSVP, North Nevadans for ERA; No. Nev. chmn. Gov.'s Conf. on Libr., 1990; bd. dir. Campaign for Choice, No. Nev. Food Bank, Nev. Women's Fund (Hall of Fame award 1989); mem. No. Nev. NCCJ, Washoe County Quality Life Task Force, 1992—, Washoe County Elections Taskforce, 1999—; bd. dirs. KUNR Pub. Radio, 1999-00, chair bd. dirs., 2000-04; chair Sierra Nevada Cmty. Access TV; adv. bd. Partnership Librs. Washoe County; co-chair social studies curriculum adv. task force Washoe County Sch. Dist.; mem. Nev. Women's History Project Bd. 1997-99; chair Downtown River Corridor Com., 1995-97; vice chair Dem. Party Washoe County, 1998-00; v.p. Nev. Diabetes Assn. for Children and Adults, 1998-02, pres., 2002-04, mem. adv. bd., 2004-06, sec., 2007-08, mem. adv., 2008-; chair devel. com. Planned Parenthood, 2002-2007; bd. dir. Washoe Libr. Found., 2003-05; mem. adv. Adv. Coun. on Edn./to the Holocaust, 2000-; chair Washoe County Dem. Women's Club, 2003-05; coord. Diabetes Edn. Prevention Program, Nev., 2007; chair 2nd Century Endowment for Friends of Washoe County Libr., 2005—; mem. bd. Reno chpt. AAUW, 2006-2008, Nev. Women's History Project, 2007-. Recipient Nev. State Libr. Letter of Commendation, 1973, Washoe County Bd. Commrs. Resolution of Appreciation, 1978, ACLU of Nev. Civil Libertarian of Yr. 1988, Freedom's Sake award AAUW, 1989, Leadership in Literacy award Sierra chpt. Internat. Reading Assn., 1992, Woman of Distinction award 1992, Cornerstone award Sierra chpt. Assn. Fundraising Profls., 2003, Women Helping Women award Soroptimist Internat., 2005, Alumni Achievement award Simmmons Coll. Grad. Sch. Libr. and Info. Sci., 2006. Mem. ALA (bd. dirs., intellectual freedom roundtable 1977-79, intellectual freedom com. 1979-83, coun. 1983-86), ACLU (bd. dir. Civil Libertarian of Yr. Nev. chpt. 1988, chair gov.'s conf. for women 1989), Nev. Libr. Assn. (chmn. pub. info. com. 1972-73, intellectual freedom com. 1975-78, govt. rels. com. 1978-79, v.p., pres.-elect 1980, pres. 1981, Spl. Citation 1978, 87, Libr. of Yr. 1993). E-mail: mgould@unr.edu.

GOULD, RONALD M., state legislator; b. Orange County, Calif. m. Janice Gould; children: Ronald Jr., Robbie, Rachael. Small bus. owner; mem. Dist. 3 Ariz. State Senate, 2005—, chair transp. com., vice-chair judiciary com., K — 12 edn. com., fin. com. Republican. Office: Ariz House Reps Capitol Complex 1700 W Washington Rm 303 Phoenix AZ 85007 Fax: 602-417-3165. Business E-Mail: rgould@azleg.gov.*

GOULD, RONALD MURRAY, federal judge; b. St. Louis, Oct. 17, 1946; s. Harry H. and Sylvia C. (Sadofsky) Gould; m. Suzanne H. Goldblatt, Dec. 1, 1968; children: Daniel, Rebecca. BS in Econs., U. Pa., 1968; JD, U. Mich., 1973. Bar: Wash. 1975, US Dist. Ct. (we. dist.) Wash. 1976, US Ct. Appeals (9th cir.) 1980, US Supreme Ct. 1981, US Dist. Ct. (ea. dist.) Wash. 1982, US Ct. Appeals (fed. cir.) 1986. Law clk. to hon. Wade H. McCree Jr. US Ct. Appeals (6th cir.), Detroit, 1973—74; law clk. to hon. justice Potter Stewart US Supreme Ct., Washington, 1974—75; assoc. Perkins Coie, Seattle, 1975—80, ptnr., 1981—99; judge US Ct. Appeals (9th cir.), Seattle, 1999—. Adj. prof. U. Washington Law Sch., 1986—89. Editor-in-chief: Mich. Law Rev., 1972—73; editor: Washington Civil Procedure Deskbook, 1981. Exec. bd. chief Seattle coun. Boy Scouts Am., 1984—; bd. dirs. econ. devel. coun. Seattle and King County, 1991—94; citizens cabinet mem. Gov. Mike Lowry, Seattle, 1993—96; bd. trustees Bellevue CC, 1993—99; mem. cmty. rels. coun. Jewish Fedn. of Greater Seattle, 1985—88. Fellow: ABA (antitrust sect., litig. sect.); mem.: Am. Judicature Soc., King County Bar Assn. (Disting. Svc. award 1987), Wash. State Bar Assn. (bd. govs. 1988—91, pres. 1994—95), 9th Jud. Cir. Hist. Soc. (bd. dirs. 1994—), Supreme Ct. Hist. Soc. Jewish. Avocations: reading, chess. Office: US Courthouse 1200 6th Ave Fl 21 Seattle WA 98101-3123

GOULD, ROY WALTER, engineering educator; b. LA, Apr. 25, 1927; s. Roy Walter Gould and Rosamonde Belle (Stokes) Termain; m. Ethel Stratton, Aug. 23, 1952; children: Diana Stratton, Robert Clarke. BS, Calif. Inst. Tech., 1949, PhD, 1956; MS, Stanford U., 1950. With Calif. Inst. Tech., Pasadena, 1955—. exec. officer for applied physics, 1972-79, chmn. div. engring. and applied sci., 1979-84, Simon Ramo prof. engring., 1979-96, prof. emeritus, 1996—. Dir. div. controlled thermonuclear research U.S. Energy Research Devel. Agy., Washington, 1970-72. Contbr. articles to profl. jours. Served with USN, 1945-46. Fellow IEEE, Am. Phys. Soc. (James Clerk Maxwell prize in plasma physics 1994); mem. NAS, Am. Acad. Arts and Scis., Nat. Acad. Engring. Office: Calif Inst Tech Dept Engring Applied Sci Ms 128 95 Pasadena CA 91125-0001 Business E-Mail: rwgould@caltech.edu.

GOULD, WILLIAM BENJAMIN, IV, law educator; b. Boston, July 16, 1936; AB, U. R.I., 1958; LLB, Cornell U., 1961; postgrad., London Sch. Econs., 1962—63; LLD (hon.), U. R.I., 1986, D.C. Sch. Law, 1995, Stetson U., 1996, Capital U., 1997, Rutgers U., 1998. Bar: Mich. 1962. Asst. gen. counsel UAW, AFL-CIO, Detroit, 1961—62; atty. NLRB, Washington, 1963—65; assoc. Battle, Fowler, Stokes & Kheel, NYC, 1965—68; prof. Wayne State U., Detroit, 1968—71, Stanford U. Law Sch., 1972—, Charles A. Beardsley prof. law, 1984—2002, prof. emeritus, 2002—; William M. Ramsey Disting. Prof. Law Willamette Coll. Law, 2002—04; chmn. NLRB, 1994—98. Chmn. Coun. Adminstrv. Conf. U.S., Washington, 1994—95; vis.

prof. Harvard U., 1971—72; overseas fellow and vis. prof. Churchill Coll., Cambridge, England, 1975; vis. scholar U. Tokyo, 1975, 78; Fulbright-Hays Disting. lectr. Kyoto Am. Studies Summer Seminar; Charles A. Beardsley prof. Stanford Law Sch., 1984; vis. fellow Australian Nat. U. Faculty of Law, 1985; vis. prof. European U. Inst., Florence, Italy, 1988, U. Witwatersrand, Johannesburg, 1991, U. Hawaii Law Sch., 2005; lectr. Am. and fgn. indsl. rels., labor law U.S., Europe, Japan, S.E. Asia, Africa, Eastern Europe. Author: Black Workers in White Unions: Job Discrimination in the United States, 1977, A Primer on American Labor Law, 1982, Japan's Reshaping of American Labor Law, 1984, Strikes, Disputes and Arbitration Essay on Labor Law, 1985, Labor Relations in Professional Sports, 1986, Agenda for Reform: The Future of Employment Relationships and the Law, 1993, Labored Relations: Law, Politics and the NLRB- A Memoir, 2000, International Labor Standards: Globalization, trade and Public Policy, 2003, Diary of a Contraband: The Civil War Passage of a Black Sailor, 2002. Named one of The Most Influential Black Americans, Ebony mag., 1996—98; fellow, Rockefeller Found., 1975, Guggenheim, 1978. Mem.: ABA (sec. labor and employment law sect.), Internat. Soc. for Labor Law and Social Security (exec. com. U.S. nat. br.), Nat. Acad. Arbitrators. Office: Stanford Law School Crown Quadrangle 559 Nathan Abbot Way Stanford CA 94305-8610 Office Phone: 650-723-2111. E-mail: wbgould@stanford.edu.*

GOUNARES, ALEXANDER, computer software company executive; B in Sci. and Engring. cum laude, Princeton U., 1993. With Microsoft Corp., Redmond, Wash., 1993—, software developer, develop. mgr. Microsoft Office, develop. mgr., architect., acting gen. mgr. Tablet PC platform, tech. asst. to Bill Gates, corp. v.p. corp. strategy, corp. v.p. adCenter & commerce platforms. Office: Microsoft Corp 1 Microsoft Way Redmond WA 98052-6399

GOURLEY, RONALD ROBERT, architect, educator; b. St. Paul, Oct. 5, 1919; s. Robert Thomas and Eva Irene (Cardle) G.; m. Phyllis Mary McDonald, Apr. 10, 1950; children: Robert McDonald, Karen Ellen, Geoffrey James. BArch, U. Minn., 1943; MArch, Harvard U., 1948. Instr. architecture MIT, Cambridge, 1948-53; vis. prof. Royal Acad., Copenhagen, Denmark, 1952; prof. architecture Harvard U., 1953-70; ptnr., co-founder Sert, Jackson & Gourley, Cambridge, 1958-64, Integrated Design Svcs. Group, Cambridge, 1966-72; ptnr. Gourley/Richmond, 1972-76, Gourley, Richmond & Mitchell, 1976-82; tech. coord. Boston Archtl. Ctr., 1976-77; prof. architecture U. Ariz., Tucson, 1977-87, dean Coll. Architecture, 1977-87, pres. Architecture Lab., 1986-89, dean, prof. emeritus, 1990—, disting. vis. prof. architecture, 1990—; pvt. practice Cambridge, 1954-58, 64-66, Tucson and Chilmark, 1990—. Prin. works include U. N.H. Meml. Union Bldg., Harvard U. Married Student Housing (Nat. Honor award AIA 1965), Cunningham Found. Bldg., Radcliffe Coll. Faculty Housing (Nat. Honor award AIA 1973), Brookline (Mass.) Pub. Libr., Kingston Housing for Elderly, Wheaton Coll. Libr., Mass. Hosp Sch. Recreation Bldg. With AUS, 1944-46. Inducted to Hall of Fame, The Humboldt Complex, St. Paul, 1995. Fellow AIA; mem. Boston Archtl. Ctr. (hon.). Home: 2522 E 3rd St Tucson AZ 85716-4115 Office: U Ariz Coll Architecture Tucson AZ 85721-0001 also: 2522 E 3rd St Tucson AZ 85716-4115

GOUTERMAN, MARTIN PAUL, chemistry educator; b. Phila., Dec. 26, 1931; s. Bernard and Melba (Buxbaum) G.; 1 child, Mikaelin BlueSpruce. BA, U. Chgo., 1951, MS, 1955, PhD in Physics (NSF Predoctoral fellow), 1958. Faculty Harvard U., Cambridge, Mass., 1958-66, postdoctoral fellow to asst. prof. chemistry dept.; mem. faculty U. Wash., Seattle, 1966—, prof. chemistry, 1968-99, prof. emeritus, 2000—. Fellow Am. Inst. Physics; mem. Am. Chem. Soc., Sigma Xi. Achievements include research and publications in spectroscopy and quantum chemistry of porphyrins and their use as luminescence sensors for biomedical and aeronautical application, in particular pressure sensitive paint; developed BS degree program in biochemistry and a chemistry minors program. Office: U Wash Chemistry Box 351700 Seattle WA 98195-1700

GOUW, JULIA SURYAPRANATA, bank executive; b. Surabaya, Indonesia, Aug. 22, 1959; arrived in US, 1978; d. Moertopo and Indira (Koelani) Suryapranata; m. Ken Keng-Hok Gouw, June 1, 1981. BS with highest honors, U. Ill., 1981. CPA Ill. Acct. Texaco, Inc., LA, 1981—83; from asst. acct. to sr. audit mgr. KPMG Peat Marwick, 1983—89; v.p., contr. East West Bank, San Marino, Calif., 1989; exec. v.p., CFO East West Bancorp. Inc., 1994—, dir., 1997—. Mem. Alexis de Tocqueville Soc., United Way; bd. dirs. Huntington Meml. Hosp.; bd. visitors UCLA; bd. overseers LA Philharmonic. Recipient Women Making a Difference award, LA Bus. Jour., 2003; named Philanthropist of Yr., United Way's Women Leaders for Giving, Nat. Assn. Bus. Owners, 2003; named one of Top 25 Most Powerful Women in Banking, US Banker mag., 2003, 2005, 2006, 2007. Mem.: Calif. Soc. CPA's, Fin. Execs. Inst., Nat. Assn. Female Execs., Chinese Am. CPA's, Beta Alpha Psi. Home Phone: 626-793-2428; Office Phone: 626-583-3512, 626-583-3512. Office Fax: 626-799-2799. E-mail: jgouw@eastwestbank.com.

GOVE, WALTER R., sociology educator; b. June 8, 1938; married; 2 children. BS, SUNY, Syracuse, 1960; MA in Sociology, U. Wash., 1967, PhD in Sociology, 1968. From asst. prof. to assoc. prof. Vanderbilt U., Nashville, 1968-75, prof. sociology, 1975—, dir. grad. studies, 1985-86. Dir. grad tng. program NIMH, 1972-76; organizer confs., symposia in field; presenter in field. Author: (with Michael Geerken) At Home and at Work: The Family's Allocation of Labor, 1983; (with Michael Hughes) Household Crowding: Social and Structural Determinants of Its Effects, 1983; editor: Deviance and Mental Illness, 1982, co-editor: Labelling Deviant Behavior: Evaluating a Perspective, 1975, 2 edit., 1980, The Fundamental Connection Between Nature and Nurture, 1982, A Feminist Perspective in the Academy, 1983; adv. editor Social Forces, 1971-74; cons. editor Am. Jour. Sociology, 1974-76, Women and Politics, 1978-86; assoc. editor Social Sci. Rsch., 1974—, Social Psychology Quarterly, 1978-80, Jour. Health and Social Behavior, 1981-83, 1997-2003, Jour. Family Issues, 1984-92; contbr. articles to profl., non-profl. jours., book revs. Recipient Reuben Hill award Nat. Coun. Family Rels., 1979, Outstanding Grad. Tchr. award Vanderbilt U., 2001; grantee PHS, 1963-65, 71-76, 79-82, NSF, 1973-77, 93, Dept. Justice, 1984-85, Okla. Dept. Corrections, 1993-94, Ethel Mae Wilson Found., 1980-81, Shell Found., 1974, others. Fellow: AAAS; mem.: So. Sociol. Soc. (pres.-elect 1992—93, pres. 1993—94, exec. coun., program com. 1986), Am. Sociol. Assn. (liaison com. to AAAS 1990—94, Leo Reeder award for disting. svc. to med. sociology 2003), Am. Soc. Criminology, Sociology Rsch. Assn., Soc. Study of Social Problems (Outstanding Scholarship and Svc. to Psychiat. Sociology award 1989). Avocation: numerous first ascents as mountaineer, primarily in Alaska. Home: PO Box 1399 Boulder UT 84716 Home Phone: 435-335-7326. Business E-Mail: walter.r.gove@vanderbilt.edu.

GOVEDARE, PHILIP BAINBRIDGE, artist, educator; b. Yuba City, Calif., Oct. 5, 1954; s. Philip Wright and Virginia (Pease) G.; m. Christine Lambert; 1 child, Eloise. BFA, San Francisco Art Inst., 1980; MFA, Tyler Sch. of Art, Phila., 1984. Instr. Tyler Sch. of Art, Phila., 1985-88, asst. prof., 1988-91, Univ. of Wash., Seattle, 1991-96, assoc. prof., 1996—. Mem. program com. Sch. of Art Wash. U., 1993—; chmn. painting U. Wash.,1993-95. Represented by Francine Seders Gallery, Seattle. Recipient fellowship NEA, Washington, 1993; grantee Pa. Coun. on the Arts, Harrisburg, 1988, Pollock Krasner Found., N.Y.C., 1991. Home: 4702 35th Ave NE Seattle WA 98105-3004 Office: Univ Wash Sch Art M-10 Seattle WA 98103

GOWAN, DAVID, state legislator; b. Sept. 13, 1969; married; 2 children. BA in Edn., U. Ariz. Mem. Dist. 30 Ariz. House of Reps., 2008—, vice chair mil. affairs & pub. safety com., mem. govt. com. Co-founder, chmn. Cochise County Young Rep. League. Sunday sch. tchr. Mountain Vista Bapt. Ch. Republican. Office: Ariz House Reps Capitol Complex 1700 W Washington Rm 117 Phoenix AZ 85007 Office Fax: 602-926-3312, 602-417-3130. Business E-Mail: dgowan@azleg.gov.*

GOWDY, FRANKLIN BROCKWAY, lawyer; b. Burlington, Iowa, Dec. 27, 1945; s. Franklin Kamm and Dorothy Faye (Brockway) G.; m. Jennifer June McKenrick, Nov. 27, 1982; stepchildren: Jeffrey F. Hammond, Tracy Cullens, Jonathan R. Hammond, Julie E. Rawls. BA in Polit. Sci., Stanford U., 1967; JD, U. Calif., Berkeley, 1970. Bar: US Dist. Ct. (no. dist.) Calif. 1971, US Ct. Appeals (9th cir.) 1971, US Dist. Ct. (ea. dist.) Tex., 1971, US Supreme Ct. 1979, US Dist. Ct. (ctrl. dist.) Calif. 1984, US Ct Appeals (fed. cir) 2003. Assoc. Brobeck, Phleger & Harrison, San Francisco, 1971-78, ptnr., 1978—2003; mng. ptnr.-San Francisco Office Morgan, Lewis & Brockius LLP. Named Calif. Lawyer of Yr. for civil litigation, Calif. Lawyer mag., 2003, Calif. Lawyer of Yr. for law practice, 2004. Fellow Am. Coll. Trial Lawyers; mem. ABA, Calif. Bar Assn., San Francisco Bar Assn., Assn. Bus. Trial Lawyers (bd. govs.). Office: Morgan Lewis Bockius LLP Spear St Tower 1 Market Plz San Francisco CA 94105-1420 Office Phone: 415-442-1525. Office Fax: 415-442-1001. Business E-Mail: fgowdy@morganlewis.com.

GOWLER, VICKI SUE, editor-in-chief; b. Decatur, Ill., Apr. 16, 1951; d. Carroll Eugene and Audra Janet (Briggs) G. BS in Journalism, U. Ill., 1973. Reporter Iroquois County Daily Times, Watseka, Ill., 1973-75, Quincy (Ill.) Herald-Whig, 1975-78; from reporter to mng. editor Miami (Fla.) Herald, Stuart, Delray Beach, West Palm Beach, 1089-88; asst. news editor Knight-Ridder Washington Bur., 1988-93; exec. editor Duluth (Minn.) News-Tribune, Knight-Ridder newspaper, 1978—2001, editor and v.p., 1993—97, editor, 2001—; mng. editor Pioneer Press, Knight-Ridder newspaper, 1997—2001, editor, 2001—05; sr. v.p. and editor St. Paul Pioneer Press, Knight-Ridder newspaper, 2001—05; editor & v.p. Idaho Statesman, Boise, 2005—. Recipient numerous awards for journalistic works, including RFK award, state AP awards in all categories. Mem. Am. Soc. Newspaper Editors. Methodist. Avocations: reading, tennis, playing clarinet, travel, visiting with her family. Office: Idaho Statesman PO Box 40 Boise ID 83707 Office Phone: 208-377-6403. E-mail: vgowler@idahostatesman.com.

GOZANI, TSAHI, nuclear physicist; b. Tel Aviv, Nov. 25, 1934; came to U.S., 1965; s. Arieh and Rivcca Gozani; m. Adit Soffer, Oct. 14, 1958; children: Mor, Shai Nachum, Or Pinchas, Tal. BSc, Technion-Israel Inst. Tech., 1956, MSc, 1958; DSc, Swiss Fed. Inst. Tech., 1962. Registered profl. nuc. engr., Calif.; accredited nuc. material mgr. Rsch. physicist Israel Atomic Energy Commn., Beer-Sheva, 1962—65; rsch. assoc. nuc. engring. dept. Rensselaer Poly. Inst., Troy, NY, 1965—66; sr. staff scientist Gen.-Atomic & IRT, San Diego, 1966—70, 1971—75; prof. applied physics Tel Aviv U., 1971; chief scientist, divsn. mgr. SAIC, Palo Alto and Sunnyvale, Calif., 1975—84, v.p., chief scientist Sunnyvale, 1984—87, corp. v.p. Santa Clara, Calif., 1987—93, sr. v.p., 1993—97; pres., CEO Ancore Corp., Santa Clara, 1997—2002; pres. Rapiscan Sys. Neutronics and Advanced Tech. Corp., Santa Clara, 2002—07, CEO, pres. emeritus, chief scientist, 2007—. Lady Davis vis. prof. Technion-Israel Inst. Tech., 1983-84; bd. dirs. Radiation Sci. Inst., San Jose State U. Author: Active Non-Destructive Assay of Nuclear Materials, 1981; co-author: Handbook of Nuclear Safeguards Measurement Methods, 1983; contbr. articles to profl. jours., chapters to books. Recipient 1989 Laurel award Aviation Week Jour., R&D 100 award, 1988, Most Innovative New Products. Fellow Am. Nuc. Soc.; mem. Am. Phys. Soc., Inst. Nuc. Materials. Achievements include patents for explosive detection system, explosive detection system using an artificial neural system, multi sensor explosive detection system, composite cavity structure for an explosive detection system, apparatus and method for detecting contraband using fast neutron activation, contraband detection system using direct imaging pulsed fast neutrons; invention of method to measure nuclear reactor's reactivity. Office: Rapiscan Sys Neutronics and Advanced Tech Corp 520 Almanor Ave Sunnyvale CA 94085-3533 Business E-Mail: tgozani@rapiscansystems.com.

GOETZ, DENNIS, state legislator; Employee Burlington Northern Santa Fe RR; farm/ ranch Wibaux Co., Dawson Co.; mem. Dist. 38 Mont. House of Reps., 2008—. Democrat. Office: Montana House of Representatives PO Box 200400 Helena MT 59620-0400 Mailing: 1105 N River Ave Glendive MT 59330-1932 Home Phone: 406-365-5127; Office Phone: 406-444-4800. Office Fax: 406-444-4825. Business E-Mail: ddgetz@peoplepc.com.

GRABER, SUSAN P., federal judge; b. Oklahoma City, July 5, 1949; d. Julius A. and Bertha (Fenyves) Graber; m. William June, May 3, 1981; 1 child, Rachel June-Graber. BA, Wellesley Coll., 1969; JD, Yale U., 1972. Bar: N.Mex. 1972, Ohio 1977, Oreg. 1978. Asst. atty. gen. Bur. of Revenue, Santa Fe, 1972—74; assoc. Jones Gallegos Snead & Wertheim, Santa Fe, 1974—75, Taft Stettinius & Hollister, Cin., 1975—78; assoc., then ptnr. Stoel Rives Boley Jones & Grey, Portland, Oreg., 1978—88; judge pro tem Multonomah County Dist. Ct., 1983—88; arbitrator Oreg. Circuit Ct., 4th Jud. Dist., 1985—88; mediator US Dist. Ct., Dist. Oreg., 1986—88; judge, then presiding judge Oreg. Ct. Appeals, Salem, 1988—90; assoc. justice Oreg. Supreme Ct., Salem, 1990—98; judge US Ct. Appeals (9th cir.), Portland, 1998—. Mem. Gov.'s Adv. Coun. on Legal Svcs., 1979—88; mem. bd. visitors Sch. Law, U. Oreg., 1986—93; bd. dirs. US Dist. Ct. of Oreg. Hist. Soc., 1985—, Oreg. Law Found., 1990—91. Mem.: Am. Law Inst., ABA, Am. Inns of Ct. (master), Oreg. Appellate Judges Assn. (sec.-treas. 1990—91, vice chair 1991—92, chair 1992—93), Oreg. Jud. Conf. (edn. com. 1988—91, program chair 1990), Ninth Cir. Jud. Conf. (chair exec. com. 1987—88), Oreg. State Bar (jud. adminstrn. com. 1985—87, pro bono com. 1988—90), Phi Beta Kappa. Mailing: US Ct Appeals 9th Cir Pioneer Courthouse 555 SW Yamhill St Portland OR 97204

GRABER, WILLIAM RAYMOND, former pharmaceutical executive; b. Vancouver, Wash., Apr. 10, 1943; s. R. Archie and Josephine N. (Martin) G.; m. Mary Lynn McArthur, June 19, 1965; children: Kristine, Kathleen, Timothy. BA in Math., Wash. State U., 1965. Fin. mgr. GE, 1965-91; contr. The Mead Corp., Dayton, Ohio, 1991—99; CFO, sr. v.p. McKesson HBOC, San Francisco, 2000—03. Avocations: golf, jogging.

GRABINER, JUDITH VICTOR, mathematics professor; b. LA, Oct. 12, 1938; d. Alfred and Ruth (Tofield) Victor; m. Sandy Grabiner, June 14, 1964; children: David Joseph, Rebecca Gail. BS in Math. with honors, U. Chgo., 1960; MA in History of Sci., Radcliffe Grad. Sch., Cambridge, Mass., 1962; PhD in History of Sci., Harvard U., Cambridge, 1966. Instr. history of sci. Harvard U., Cambridge, 1966—69; fellow Am. Coun. Learned Soc., 1971—72; from asst. to prof. history Calif. State U., Dominguez Hills, Calif., 1972—85; prof. math. Pitzer Coll., Claremont, Calif., 1985—94, Flora Sanborn Pitzer prof. math., 1994—. Vis. prof. U. Calif., Santa Barbara, 1969—70, Calif. State U., LA, 1970—71; reviewer in field. Author: The Origins of Cauchy's Rigorous Calculus, 1981, The Calculus as Algebra, 1990; contbr. articles to profl. jours. Recipient Carl B. Allendoerfer award, Math. Mag., 1984, 1988, 1996, Lester R. Ford award, Am. Math. Monthly, 1984, 1998, 2005, Disting. Coll. or Univ. Tchg. award, So. Calif. sect. Math. Assn. Am., 2002, Deborah and Franklin Tepper Haimo award, Math. Assn. Am., 2003; fellow, NSF, 1981—82; Rsch. grant, 1979—81. Mem.: Sigma Xi, Phi Beta Kappa. Office: Pitzer Coll Claremont CA 91711 Office Phone: 909-621-8218.

GRABINER, SANDY, mathematics professor; b. NYC, Dec. 15, 1939; s. Morris and Anna (Present) G.; m. Judith Victor, June 14, 1964; children: David, Rebecca. BA, Rice U., 1960; AM, Harvard U., 1961, PhD, 1967. Instr. MIT, Cambridge, 1967-69; asst. prof. Claremont Grad. Sch., Calif., 1969-74; assoc. prof. math. Pomona Coll., Claremont, 1974-82, prof., 1982—. Editl. bd. Carus Monographs, 1990-93; contbr. articles to profl. jours. Mem. Math. Assn. Am. (program chmn. 1984-85), Am. Math. Soc., London Math. Soc., AAAS. Office: Pomona Coll Dept Maths 610 N College Ave Claremont CA 91711-6398 Office Phone: 909-621-8707.

GRABOWSKI, RICHARD JOSEPH, lawyer; b. LA, 1961; BA with gt. distinction, Calif. State U., Long Beach, 1983; JD, U. Calif., LA, 1986. Bar: Calif. 1986, admitted to practice: US Ct. of Appeals, Ninth Cir., US Dist. Courts, Northern, Southern, Eastern, Central Districts of Calif. Ptnr.-in-charge Irvine office Jones Day, Calif. Mem.: Orange County Bar Assn., Fed. Bar Assn., Assn. of Bus. Trial Lawyers (bd. dir.), Order of Coif. Office: Jones Day Ste 1100 3 Park Plz Irvine CA 92614-8505 Office Phone: 949-851-3939. Office Fax: 949-553-7539. Business E-Mail: rgrabowski@jonesday.com.

GRACE, JOHN ROSS, chemical engineering educator; b. London, Ont., Can., June 8, 1943; s. Archibald John and Mary Kathleen (Disney) G.; m. Sherrill Elizabeth Perley, Dec. 20, 1964; children: Elizabeth, Malcolm. BESc, U. Western Ont., 1965, DSc (hon.), 2003; PhD, Cambridge U., Eng., 1968. From asst. prof. to prof. chem. engring. McGill U., Montreal, Que., Canada, 1968-79; sr. rsch. engr. Surveyor Nenniger & Chenevert Inc., 1974-75; prof. chem. engring. U. B.C., Vancouver, Canada, 1979—, head dept. chem. engring., 1979-87, dean faculty grad. studies, 1990-96, prof. chem. and biol. engring., 2000—, Can. rsch. chair, 2001—; pres., CEO Membrane Reactor Techs. Ltd., 1998—2003. Cons. in field. Co-author: Bubbles, Drops and Particles, 1978; co-editor: Fluidization, 1980, Fluidization VI, 1989, Circulating Fluidized Beds, 1997, Circulating Fluidized Bed Technology VII, 2002; editor: Chem. Engring. Sci., 1984—90; contbr. articles to profl. jours. NRC sr. indsl. fellow; Athlone fellow; Can. Coun. Killam Rsch. fellow, 1999. Fellow Royal Soc. Can., Can. Acad. Engring., Chem. Inst. Can. (v.p. 1994-95, pres. 1995-96); mem. Can. Soc. Chem. Engring. (pres. 1989-90, Erco award, R.S. Jane award), Assn. Profl. Engrs. B.C., Instn. Chem. Engrs. Office: 2360 East Mall Vancouver BC Canada V6T 1Z3 E-mail: jgrace@chml.ubc.ca.

GRACE, SUE, state legislator; b. Milw., Jan. 31, 1958; m. Vincent Grace. BA, Marquette U. Mem. Ariz. Ho. of Reps., 1991-96; mktg. specialist; mem. Ariz. Senate, Phoenix, 1996—. Named Legis. of Yr., Mental Health Assn., 1991. Mem., Paradise Valley Chamber of Commerce, United Fund Council, Phoenix Mountaineers. Republican. Home: 5302 E Van Buren St Apt 2039 Phoenix AZ 85008-7972

GRADEL, JAMES D., lawyer; b. Toldedo, Sept. 1, 1954; BBA summa cum laude, U. Cin., 1975; JD with honors, Ohio State U., 1978. Bar: Wash. 1979. Ptnr., Fin. Inst. Practice Area Perkins Coie LLP, Seattle. Named a Wash. Super Lawyer, Washington Law & Politics. Mem.: King County Bar Assn., Wash. State Bar Assn., Beta Gamma Sigma. Office: Perkins Coie LLP 1201 Third Ave Ste 4800 Seattle WA 98101-3099 Office Phone: 206-359-8401. Office Fax: 206-359-9000. Business E-Mail: jgradel@perkinscoie.com.

GRAFE, WARREN BLAIR, broadcast executive; b. NYC, June 22, 1954; s. Warren Edward and Maree Lee Grafe; m. Pamela Arden Rearick, Mar. 8, 1980 (div. Nov. 1982). Student, Kendall Coll., 1974-75, U. Wis., Platteville, 1975-76; BA, Ind. U., 1979. Sales rep. Sta. WGTC-FM, Bloomington, Ind., 1979-84, account exec., coop. cord., 1980-84; nat. sales rep. Stas. WTTS-WGTC, Bloomington, 1984; sales rep. Sta. KLFF-KMZK, Phoenix, 1985; account exec. Rita Sanders Advt. and Pub. Rels. Agy., Tempe, Ariz., 1985, Am. Cable TV, Phoenix, 1985-86, Dimension Media Svcs., Phoenix, 1986-89, Greater Phoenix Interconnect, 1989-95, CableRep/Phoenix, 1995-99, CableRep/Ariz., Phoenix, 1999—2001; nat. sales mgr., rep. QWEST Choice TV and Cable Am. CableWest, Phoenix, 2001—06; nat. sales mgr. Qwest Choice TV, Phoenix, 2006—. Recipient Nat. Sales award, Cable TV Advt. Bur., 1986, 1987, 1991, 1994, 1996, 1998, $5 Million Career Sales award, 1997, $10 Million Career Sales award, 1999; named one of Cable's Best Top Ten Cable Advt. Sales Reps. in Country, Cable Avails, 1995; finalist Nat. Sales award, Cable TV Advt. Bur., 1995, 1999, CAB, 1995, 1999, 2000. Mem.: Mesa (Ariz.) C. of C., Chandler (Ariz.) C. of C., Tempe C. of C. Home: 9616 N 26th Pl Phoenix AZ 85028-4708 Office: CableWest 300 W Osborn 201 Phoenix AZ 85013 Office Phone: 602-274-0777 24. Business E-Mail: blair@cablewestaz.com.

GRAFF, CYNTHIA STAMPER, health facility administrator; b. Fairbanks, Alaska, May 22, 1953; d. Marshall Bernard and Nell

(Buntyn) Stamper; m. Grant H. Van de Walker, July 13, 1974 (div. 1980); m. Dennis Alan Graff, July 10, 1990 (div. 1996). BS in Fin., Calif. State U., Long Beach, 1975; LLB, York U., Toronto, 1985. Pres. MC Fin., Inc., Salt Lake City, 1976-82; founder, pres. The Road Butler, Toronto, 1985-86; house counsel Polyvoltec Inc., Toronto, 1986-87; v.p. Lindora Med. Clinics, Costa Mesa, Calif., 1988-91; pres. Lindora, Inc., Costa Mesa, 1992—. Mem. Am. Soc. Bariatric Physicians, Young Pres.'s Orgn. Republican. Avocations: golf, skiing, reading. Office: Lindora Med Clinics 3505 Cadillac Ave Ste N-2 Costa Mesa CA 92626-1466

GRAFF, JOAN MESSING, lawyer; BS, Cornell U.; JD, Columbia U., 1967. Bar: DC 1969, Calif. 1973. Atty. EEOC, 1967—70; vol. atty. Davis, Dunlap and Williams; co-founder, v.p. Equal Rights Advocates (ERA), 1974—81; exec. dir. Legal Aid Soc. of San Francisco-Employment Law Ctr. (LAS-ELC), 1981—. Mem.: State Bar Calif. (Loren Miller Legal Svcs. Award 2006). Office: Legal Aid Soc-ELC 600 Harrison St #120 San Francisco CA 94107 Office Phone: 415-864-8848. Office Fax: 415-864-8199.

GRAFF, PAT STUEVER, secondary school educator; b. Tulsa, Mar. 24, 1955; d. Joseph H., Sr. and Joann (Schneider) Stuever; m. Mark A. Rumsey; children: Earl, Jr., Jeremy. BS in Secondary Edn., Okla. State U., 1976; postgrad., U. N.M., 1976-87. Cert. tchr. lang. arts, social studies, journalism, French, N.Mex. Substitute tchr. Albuquerque Pub. Schs., 1976-78; tchr. Cleveland Mid. Sch., Albuquerque, 1978-86, La Cueva H.S., Albuquerque, 1986—, co-chair English dept., 1996—, chair sch. restructuring coun., 1999-2001. Adviser award winning lit. mag. El Tesoro, sch. newspapers The Edition, Huellas del Oso; instr. journalism workshops, N.Mex. Press Assn., Ind. U., Bloomington, Nat. Scholastic Press, Mpls., Kans. State U., Manhattan, Interscholastic Press League, Austin, Tex., St. Mary's U., San Antonio, Ala. Scholastic Press Assn., Wash.; keynote spkr. at numerous confs. in Ohio, Ind., Kans., S.C., Utah, La., Okla., Ala., N.Mex., Tex., Wash., Idaho, and N.Y.; reviewer of lang. and textbooks for several cos.; instr. Dial-A-Tchr., N.Mex., 1991-05; texbook evaluator Holt Pub., Inc., 1991; nat. bd. cert. tchr. adolescent/young adult English lang. arts, 2001—; mem. N.Mex. Network of Nat. Bd. Cert. Tchrs., 2002—, 2d v.p., 2003-; state bd. dirs. N.Mex. Coun. for the Social Studies, 1998-2006, chair state conf., 2001, state pres., 2002-03, state treas., 2003-06; comm. officer, sec. ABQ Tchrs. Fedn. 2003-05. Author: Journalism Text, 1983; contbg. author: Communication Skills Resource Text, 1987, Classroom Publishing/Literacy, 1992; contbr. articles to profl. jours. Troop leader Girl Scouts U.S., 1979—90, coord. various programs, asst. program com. chmn. Chaparral Coun., 1988—89, chmn. adult recognition task force, 1991—96, bd. dirs., 1991—98; active PTA Gov. Bent Elem. Sch., 1983—86, v.p., 1985—86, Osuna Elem. Sch., 1986—92, N.Mex. PTA, 1994—2000; pub. various children's lit. mags., 1987—; pub. parent's newsletter, 1986—; newsletter layout editor Albuquerque Youth Soccer Orgn., 1985—88; active YMCA youth and govt. model legis.; faculty advisor La Cueva del., 1986—, press corps advisor, 1987—2001, asst. state dir., 2001—; asst. den. leader Boy Scouts Am., 1987—88, den leader, 1988—91. Recipient Innovative Tchg. award Bus. Week mag., 1990, Svc. commendation Coll. Edn. Alumni Assn., Okla. State U., 1990, Alumni Recognition award, 1993, Mem. Yr. Svc. award Bernalillo County Coun. Internat. Reading Assn., Thanks to Tchrs. award Apple Computers, 1990, Spl. Recognition Albuquerque C. of C., 1992, Disting. Svc. award NCTE, 2002; named one of Gov.'s Outstanding Women in N.Mex., 2004; Spotlighted Mem. Phi Delta Kappa, 1990; Spl. Recognition Advisor Dow Jones Newspaper Fund, 1990; named Nat. H.S. Journalism Tchr. of Yr., 1995, Disting. Advisor, 1991, N.Mex. Pubs. Adviser of Yr., 1991, N.Mex. State Tchr. of Yr., 1993, USA Today All-Am. Tchr., 1999; finalist U.S. West Tchr. Yr. finalist, 1991, Nat. Tchr. of Yr., 1993, Am. Tchr. Awards, Disney, 1998; named to Nat. Tchr. Hall Fame, 2005; grantee Phi Delta Kappa 1989, 91, Geraldine R. Dodge Found., 1990, 92, 95-97, Learn and Serve Am., 1999. Mem.: AAUW (chpt. newsletter editor 1995—2001, local v.p. 1997—99, state program v.p. 1997—99, state media chair 2000—03), ASCD (editor newsletter 1991—92, focus on excellence awards com. 1992—94, state bd. dirs. 2002—, Focus on Excellence award 1990), Albuquerque (N.Mex.) Tchrs. Fedn. (PR and comms. officer 2003—05, sec. 2003—05), N Mex. Coun. for Social Studies (mem. bd. 1999—2002, state v.p. 2001—02, pres. 2002—03), N. Mex. World Class Tchr. Network (state vice-pres. 2002—), N.Mex. Goals 2000 (panel mem. 1994—97), Quill & Scroll (adv. La Cueva chpt. 1986—, judge nat. newspaper rating contest 1988—97), Albuquerque Press Women (v.p. 1994, pres. 1995, Communicator of Achievement award 1993), N.Mex. Press Women (state scholarship chair 1994, publicity chair 1995—96, state treas. 1996—98, state v.p. 1998—99), N.Mex. Scholastic Press Assn. (state v.p. 1985—89, coord. workshop 1986, editor newsletter 1986—89, asst. chair state conf. 1988, 1989, state bd. dirs. 1991—2000, state v.p. 1992—95), N.Mex. Coun. Tchrs. English (regional coord. Albuquerque 1983—86, chair state confs. 1985—87, editl. bd. N.Mex. English Jour. 1986—88, state pres. 1987—88, chair facilities for fall conf. 1988—93, chair English humanities expo com. 1988—99, adv. mgr. 1989—90, editor N.Mex. English Jour. 1999—2003, Svc. award 1989, Outstanding H.S. English Tchr. N.Mex. 1991), Journalism Edn. Assn. (judge nat. contests 1988—, mem. nat. cert. bd. 1989—99, presenter nat. convs. 1989—, cert. journalism educator 1990, nat. bd. 1991—2002, master 1991—), Nat. Fedn. Press Women, Nat. Sch. Pub. Rels. Assn. (issues seminar planning com. 1990, chair 1991, master journalism educator 1991—, nat. conf. chmn. 1997—99, Zia chpt., contest winner 1991—94, Pres.'s award 1993), Nat. Coun. Tchrs. English (nat. chair com. English Tchrs. and Pubs. 1988—91, chair English humanities expo com. 1990—99, standing com. affiliates 1991—94, nat. chair 1995—98, chair English humanities expo com. 2001—03, nat. exec. com. 2001—03, chmn. English humanities expo com. 2005—, nat. chair assembly for advisors of student pubs., regional rep. Tex., La., N.Mex., Disting. Svc. award 2002), Nat. Alliance High Schs. (tchr. rep. 1997—2000), Nat. Assn. Secondary Sch. Prins. (Breaking Ranks tchr. rep.), Phi Delta Kappa (pres. U. N.Mex. br. 2002—05), Delta Kappa Gamma (state profl. affairs com. chair 2003—07), Pi Lambda Theta (Ethel Mary Moore award Outstanding Educator 1993, Gov.'s Outstanding Women in N.Mex. 2004). Roman Catholic. Avocations: soccer, running, hiking, travel, skiing. Home: 8101 Krim Dr NE Albuquerque NM 87109-5223 Office: La Cueva H S 7801 Wilshire Ave NE Albuquerque NM 87122-2807 Office Phone: 505-823-2327. Personal E-mail: pgraff@aol.com.

GRAHAM, ANNA REGINA, pathologist, educator; b. Phila., Nov. 1, 1947; d. Eugene Nelson and Anna Beatrice (McGovern) Chadwick; m. Larry L. Graham, June 29, 1973; 1 child, Jason. BS in Chemistry, Ariz. State U., 1969, BS in Zoology, 1970; MD, U. Ariz., 1974. Diplomate Am. Bd. Pathology. With Coll. Medicine U. Ariz., Tucson, 1974—, asst. prof. pathology, 1978-84, assoc. prof. pathology, 1984-90, prof. pathology, 1990—. Fellow Am. Soc. Clin. Pathologists (bd. dirs. Chgo. chpt. 1993-2003, sec. 1995-99, v.p. 1999-2000, pres.-elect 2000-01, pres. 2001-02), Internat. Acad. Pathology, Am. Telemedicine Assn., Coll. Am. Pathologists; mem. AMA (alt. del. Chgo. chpt. 1992-99, del. Chgo. chpt. 1999-2004), Ariz. Soc. Pathologists (pres. Phoenix chpt. 1989-91), Ariz. Med. Assn. (treas. Phoenix chpt. 1995-97). Republican. Baptist. Avocations: motorcycles, piano, choir. Office: Ariz Health Scis Ctr Dept Pathology 1501 N Campbell Ave Tucson AZ 85724-5108 Office Phone: 520-626-6828. Business E-Mail: agraham@umcaz.edu.

GRAHAM, BILL, opera company director; Artistic dir. Spokane (Wash.) Opera, Spokane, Wash. Vet. dir. over 50 shows ranging from grand opera to musical theatre; active vocal coach.

GRAHAM, DENIS DAVID, marriage and family therapist, educational consultant; b. Santa Rosa, Calif., Oct. 21, 1941; s. Elbert Eldon and Mildred Bethana (Dyson) G.; m. Margaret Katherine Coughlan, Aug. 31, 1968; children: Kathleen Ann, Todd Cameron (dec.). BS in Edn., U. Nev., 1964, MEd, 1973, MA, 1982. Cert. for ednl. pers.; lic. marriage and family therapist, Nev. Tchr. vocat. bus. edn. Earl Wooster HS, Reno, 1964-66, chmn. dept. bus. edn., 1966-67; state supr. bus. and office edn. Nev. Dept. Edn., Carson City, 1967-70, adminstr. vocat. edn. field svcs., 1970-74, asst. dir., 1974-78, vocat. edn. cons., 1978-85; edn. curriculum specialist Washoe County Sch. Dist., Reno, 1985-89, curriculum coord., 1989-94, ret., 1994; pres. Midpoint Inc., 1995—. Marriage and family counselor Severance & Assocs., Carson City, 1983-85, Mountain Psychiat. Assocs., 1985-87; tng. and youth employment coun. S.W. Regional Lab. for Ednl. R&D, Los Alamitos, Calif., 1982, career edn. coun., 1980-81. Editor Coun. of Chief State Sch. Officers' Report: Staffing the Nation's Schools: A National Emergency, 1984; contbr. articles to profl. jours. Bd. dirs. U. Nev.-Reno Campus Christian Assn., 1988-90, 97-99; adv. com. Truckee Meadows C.C., Reno, 1988-94; mem. Gov.'s Crime Prevention Com., Carson City, 1979-83, Atty. Gen.'s Anti-Shoplifting Com., Carson City, 1974-78, Gov.'s Devel. Disabilities Planning Coun., Carson City, 1977-79; bd. dirs. Jr. Achievement No. Nev., 1989-92, sec., exec. com., 1990-91; bd. dirs. Friends of the Coll. of Edn., U. Nev., Reno, 1995-99. Recipient award for svc. Bus. Edn. Assn. No. Nev., 1973, Svc. award YMCA, 1962, 63, Helping Hand award Procter R. Hug HS, 1993-94. Mem. ACA, Am. Vocat. Assn., Nat. Assn. Vocat. Edn. Spl. Needs Pers. (Outstanding Svc. award Region V 1982), Am. Assn. Marriage and Family Therapy, Nev. Vocat. Assn. (Outstanding Svc. award 1991, Bill Trabert Meml. award Excellence in Occup. Edn. 1994), Internat. Assn. Marriage and Family Counselors, U. Nev. Reno Alumni Assn. (exec. com. 1971-75), Phi Delta Kappa, Phi Kappa Phi. Democrat. Methodist. Home: 3056 Bramble Dr Reno NV 89509-6901 Office: PO Box 33034 Reno NV 89533-3034 Personal E-mail: midpoint@charter.net.

GRAHAM, HOWARD HOLMES, winemaker, restaurant manager, small business owner, retired financial executive; b. Greensburg, Pa., Apr. 24, 1947; s. Howard B. and Dorothy (Holmes) G.; m. Roberta A. Grant, June 8, 1968 (div. Feb. 1984); m. Linda A. Cossarek, Mar. 14, 1987; children: Christina Ross, John Howard. BS, Carnegie Mellon U., 1968; MBA, U. Chgo., 1973. CPA, Ill. Various positions Zenith Electronics Corp., Glenview, Ill., 1973-81, dir. acctg., 1981-82, v.p. fin. svcs., 1982-87, v.p. fin., 1987-88; sr. v.p. fin. Wyse Tech. Inc., San Jose, Calif., 1988-90, Informix Corp., Menlo Park, Calif., 1990-96; sr. v.p. fin. and adminstrn., CFO, Siebel Sys., San Mateo, Calif., 1997—2000; founder, owner Graham Family Vineyard, 2001—; proprietor Lavanda Restaurant, Palo Alto, Calif., 2006—. Capt. U.S. Army, 1968-71, Vietnam. Decorated Bronze Star; recipient Elijah Watt Sells award Am. Inst. CPA's, 1982. Mem. La Rinconada Country Club, Beta Gamma Sigma. Office: Graham Family Vineyard 1300 Montgomery Rd Ste 2 Sebastopol CA 95472 Personal E-mail: hgraham@hgraham.com.

GRAHAM, JANET C., former state attorney general; b. Salt Lake City, 1949; BS in Psychology, Clark U., Worcester, Mass., 1973; MS in Psychology, U. Utah, 1977, JD, 1980. Bar: Utah. Ptnr. Jones, Waldo, Holbrook & McDonough, Salt Lake City, 1979—89; soliciter gen. Utah Atty. Gen.'s Office, Salt Lake City, 1989—93; atty. gen. State of Utah, 1993—2001. Adj. prof. law U. Utah Law Sch.; bar commr. Utah State Bar, 1991; master of bench Utah Inns Ct. VII; mem. Utah Commn. on Justice in 21st Century; bd. dirs. Jones, Waldo, Holbrook & McDonough; bd. trustees, pres. Coll. Law U. Utah. Fin. devel. chair YWCA; chair Ctrl. Bus. Improvement Dist.; mem. Salt Lake City Olympic Bid Com. 1988 Games. Named Woman Lawyer of Yr., Utah, 1987. Mem.: Women Lawyers Utah (co-founder, mem. exec. com.), Am. Arbitration Assn. (nat. panel arbitrators). Democrat.

GRAHAM, RONALD LEWIS, mathematician; b. Taft, Calif., Oct. 31, 1935; s. Leo Lewis and Margaret Jane (Anderson) G.; children: Cheryl, Marc. Student, U. Chgo., 1951-54; BS, U. Alaska, 1958; MA, U. Calif., Berkeley, 1961, PhD, 1962; LLD (hon.), Western Mich. U., 1984; DSc, St. Olaf Coll., 1985, U. Alaska, 1988. Mem. tech. staff Bell Labs., Murray Hill, N.J., 1962—, head dept. discrete math., 1968—, dir. Math. Scis. Rsch. Ctr., 1983—, adj. dir. rsch., info. scis. divsn., 1987-95; prof. Rutgers U., 1987—; chief scientist AT&T Labs. Rsch., Florham Park, N.J., 1996-98; Irwin and Joan Jacobs prof. computer and info. sci. U. Calif., San Diego, 1999—. Regents' prof. UCLA, 1975; vis. prof. computer sci. Stanford U., 1979, 81, Princeton (N.J.) U., 1987, 89. Author: Ramsey Theory, 1980, Concrete Mathematics, 1989, Erdös on Graphs, 1998. Served with USAF, 1955-59. Recipient Polya prize, 1975; Euler prize, 1993; named Scientist of Yr. World Book Encyclopedia, 1981; scholar Ford Found., 1958, Fairchild Found. Disting. scholar Calif. Inst. Tech., 1983; fellow NSF, 1961, Woodrow Wilson Found., 1962. Fellow AAAS, N.Y. Acad. Scis., Assn. Computing Machinery; mem. NAS (treas. 1996—), Am. Math. Soc. (pres. 1993-94, Lifetime Achievement award 2003), Math. Assn. Am. (pres. 2003—), Soc. Indsl. and Applied Math., Am. Acad. Arts and Scis., Internat. Jugglers Assn. (past pres.). Office: U Calif San Diego CSE La Jolla CA 92093-0114

GRAHAM, STEPHEN MICHAEL, lawyer; b. Houston, May 1, 1951; s. Frederick Mitchell and Lillian Louise (Miller) G.; m. Joanne Marie Sealock, Aug. 24, 1974; children: Aimee Elizabeth, Joseph Sealock, Jessica Anne. BS, Iowa State U., 1973; JD, Yale U., 1976. Bar: Wash. 1977. Assoc. Perkins Coie, Seattle, 1976-83, ptnr., 1983-2000, Orrick, Herrington & Sutcliffe LLP, Seattle, 2000—, practice leader corp. div. Bd. dirs. Wash. Spl. Olympics, Seattle, 1979—83, pres., 1982—83; trustee Friends of the Children of King County, 2002—; mem. Seattle Fair Campaign Practices Commn., 1982—88; trustee Cornish Coll. Arts, 1986—91, mem. exec. com., 1989—91; trustee Seattle Repertory Theatre, 1993—95, Seattle Children's Theatre, 1996—98, mem. exec. com., 1997—98; trustee Fred Hutchinson Cancer Rsch. Ctr., 1999—2005; bd. dirs., mem. exec. com. WSA, 2002—05; trustee Arboretum Found., 1994—96; mem. Seattle Bd. Ethics, 1982—88, chmn., 1983—88; mem. exec. com. Sch. Law Yale U., 1988—92, 1993—97; bd. dirs. Wash. Biotech. and Biomed. Assn., 1996—, mem. exec. com., 1997—. Mem.: ABA, Wash. State Bar Assn., Rainier Club, Wash. Athletic Club. Episcopalian. Office: Orrick Herrington & Sutcliffe Ste 900 719 Second Ave Seattle WA 98104-7063 Home Phone: 206-329-5242; Office Phone: 206-839-4320. Business E-Mail: sgraham@orrick.com.

GRAHAM, SUSAN LOIS, computer scientist, consultant; b. Cleve., Nov. 16, 1942; m., 1971 AB in Math., Harvard U., 1964; MS, Stanford U., 1966, PhD in Computer Sci., 1971. Assoc. rsch. scientist, adj. asst. prof. computer sci. Courant Inst. Math. Sci., NYU, 1969-71; asst. prof. computer sci. U. Calif., Berkeley, 1971-76, assoc. prof., 1976-81, prof. computer sci., 1981—2004, Chancellor's prof., 1997—2000, Pehong Chen disting. prof., 2001—06; Pehong Chen disting. prof. emeritus, 2006—; prof. U. Calif., 2004—; chief computer scientist NSF Nat. Partnership for Advanced Computational Infrastructure, 1997—2005; sr. scientist Lawrence Berkeley Nat. Lab., Calif., 1999—. Vis. scientist Stanford U., 1981; mem. adv. com. div. computer and computation rsch. NSF, 1987-92, mem. program sci. and tech. ctrs., 1987-91, Alan T. Waterman award com., 2001-04; mem. vis. com. elec. engring. and computer sci. MIT, 1989—; mem. vis. com. for engring. and applied sci. Calif. Inst. Tech., 1994-99; mem. vis. com. applied scis. Harvard U., 1995—; mem. commn. on phys. sci., math. and applications NRC, 1992-95; mem. Pres.'s Com. on Nat. Medal Sci., 1994-00; mem. Pres.'s Info. Tech. Adv. Com., 1997-03; bd. dirs. Harvard Alumni Assn., 1997-2000; mem. bd. overseers Harvard U., 2001-, pres., 2006-07; co-chair Nat. Rsch. Coun. Study Future Supercomputing, 2002-04. Co-editor: Comms. ACM, 1975—79; editor: ACM transactions on Programming Langs. and Systems, 1978—92. Mem. bd. trustees Calif. Performances, 2005-. NSF grantee. Fellow AAAS, Assn. for Computing Machinery, Am. Acad. Arts and Sci.; mem. IEEE, NAE. Office: U Calif-Berkeley Computer Sci Div EECS 771 Soda Hall 1776 Berkeley CA 94720-1776 Office Phone: 510-642-2059. Business E-Mail: graham@CS.Berkeley.edu.

GRAHAME, HEATHER H., lawyer; b. 1955; BA in Human Biology, Stanford U., 1978; JD, U. Oreg., 1984. Bar: Alaska 1984. Atty. Bogle & Gates PLLC, Anchorage; ptnr., co-chair, telecom. practice group Dorsey & Whitney LLP, Anchorage. Editor-in-chief Oreg. Law Rev., 1983—84. Pres. Alaska Dance Theatre, 2002—. Named Assoc. Mem. Yr., Alaska Telephone Assn., 1993. Mem.: ABA, Alaska Bar Assn., Federal Comm. Bar Assn. (Pacific NW chapt.). Achievements include Sixth place, US Cycling Team Time Trial Championships, 1988; Seventh place, Women's World Championship Sled Dog Race, 2002. Avocation: dog sledding. Office: Dorsey & Whitney LLP Ste 600 1031 W Fourth Ave Anchorage AK 99501-5907 Office Phone: 907-257-7822. Office Fax: 907-276-4152. Business E-Mail: grahame.heather@dorsey.com.

GRAINGER, JOHN R., medical association administrator; COO Laidlaw, 1997-99; pres., CEO Am. Med. Response, Aurora, Colo., 1999—. Office: Am Med Response Inc 6200 S Syracuse Way Ste 200 Greenwood Village CO 80111-4739

GRALOW, JULIE RUTH, physician; b. Sanford, Fla., Feb. 10, 1959; d. Richard Thomas and Ruth Haas Gralow; m. Hugh Willison Allen. BS, Stanford U., 1981; MD, U. So. Calif., 1988; residency, Brighman Women's, Harvard, 1991. Cert. internal medicine 1991, med. oncology 1995. Rsch. asst. Becton Dickinson Monoclonal Ctr., Mountain View, Calif., 1981—83, Stanford U. Sch. Medicine, 1983—84; rsch. fellow U. So. Calif. Sch. Medicine, 1985; acting instr. U. Wash., Fred Hutchinson Cancer Rsch. Ctr., Seattle, 1994—97, asst. prof., 1998—2002, assoc. prof. med. oncology, 2002—. Dir. breast cancer inst. U. Wash. and Fred Hutchinson Cancer Rsch. Inst., Seattle, 2003—; assoc. program head breast cancer Fred Hutchinson Cancer Rsch. Ctr., 2001—. Author: (jour. article) Jour. Immunology, 1984, New Eng. Jour. Medicine, 1984; co-author: Breast Fitness: An Optimal Exercise and Health Plan for Reducing Your Risk of Breast Cancer; contbr. several articles to profl. jours.; helped launch (traveling exhibit of art by women with breast cancer) Living Well With Cancer Series and Innervisions. Cons. program for appropriate tech. in health USAID Ukraine Breast Cancer Assistance Project, 1997—2000; co-chair breast cancer com. Southwest Oncology Group, 2000—; del. U. Wash. Ctr. for Women and Democracy, 2003; med. dir., team physician Team Survivor Northwest (exercise and fitness program for women cancer survivors). Recipient Career Devel. award, Am. Soc. Clin. Oncology, 1995—98, Clin. Career Devel. award, Am. Cancer Soc., 1995—98, Irving I. Lasky award, 1988, Janet M. Glasgow Achievement award, Am. Med. Women's Assn., 1988; U.S.C. Rsch. Fellowship, 1984—85, 1985—86. Mem.: Wash. State Med. Oncology Soc., Am. Soc. Breast Disease, Susan G. Komen Found. Breast Cancer Rsch., Nat. Alliance Breast Cancer Orgn., Puget Sound Oncology Group, Am. Assn. Cancer Rsch., Am. Soc. Clin. Oncology (Pub. Issues Com. 1999—, co-chair, Pub. Issues Com. 2000—02, liaison, Health Svcs. Rsch. Com. 2000—, chair, Patient Communication Com.), AMA. Office: (SCCA) Seattle Cancer Care Alliance 825 Eastlake Ave E PO Box 19023 Seattle WA 98109-1023 Office Phone: 206-288-7722.

GRANATO, CATHERINE (CAMMI GRANATO), former olympic athlete, sports association executive; b. Downers Grove, Ill., Mar. 25, 1971; d. Natalie and Don Granato; m. Ray Ferraro, Sept. 4, 2004; 1 child, Riley. B in Social Sci., Providence Coll., 1993; student, Concordia U., 1994-97. Center US Nat. Women's Hockey Team, 1992—2005. Radio broadcaster LA Kings, 1998—99; rinkside reporter NHL on NBC, 2005—06, feature reporter, 2007—; dir. devel. for women's hockey FASTHockey, Brookline, Mass., 2007—. Founder Golden Dreams for Children Found., 1999. Recipient Lester Patrick Award, 2007; named to Internat. Ice Hockey Fedn. Hall of Fame, 2008. Achievements include being a member of gold medal winning USA Women's Hockey Team, Nagano Olympic Games, 1998, silver medal team, Salt Lake City Olympic Games, 2002; being inducted into the US Hockey Hall of Fame, 2008.

GRANCHELLI, RALPH S., company executive; b. Framingham, Mass., Jan. 2, 1955; s. Ralph S. and Avon L. (Chadwick) G. ASEE, Wentworth Inst. Tech., Boston, 1975; postgrad., U. Mass., 1975-78. Nat. sales mgr. Teledyne Semiconductor Co., Mountain View, Calif., 1981-85; v.p. Elantec, Inc., Milpitas, Calif., 1985—.

GRAND, MARCIA, civic worker; b. NYC, Aug. 9, 1933; d. Irving and Dorothy (Miller) Kosta; m. Richard Grand, Jan. 27, 1952. Student, U. Ariz., 1950-52, 59-60. Docent, coord., docent trainer

Tucson Mus. Art, 1965-71, bd. dirs., 1972-79, chmn. edn. com., 1975-79; v.p., sec. Richard Grand Found., 1966-80, pres., 1980—. Bd. dirs., sec. U. Ariz. Found., 1979-80, v.p., 1986-87, chmn. exec. com., 1986-87; mem. spl. com. office of chair U. Ariz., 1987-92; bd. dirs. Tucson Airport Authority, Greenfield Schs., 1977-82; bd. fellows Ctr. Creative Photography, 1984-98, chmn., 1993-98, mem.-at-large, bd. dirs. Tucson Mus. Art League, 1977-78; bd. trustees San Francisco Art Inst., 1995-2003. Nominated for YWCA Woman on the Move award, 1982; recipient Cmty. Svc. award Mortar Bd., 1978, Disting. Citizen award U. Ariz. Coll. Fine Arts, 1979. Office: 6870 N Andrea Doria Dr Tucson AZ 85704 Personal E-mail: rg@rgrand.com.

GRAND, RICHARD D., lawyer; b. Danzig, Feb. 20, 1930; came to U.S., 1939, naturalized, 1944; s. Morris and Rena Grand; m. Marcia Kosta, Jan. 27, 1952. BA, NYU, 1951; JD, U. Ariz., Tucson, 1958. Bar: Ariz. 1958, Calif. 1973, U.S. Supreme Ct. 1973; cert. specialist in injury litigation Ariz. Bd. Legal Specialization. Dep. atty., Pima County, Ariz., 1958-59; pvt. practice trial law Tucson, 1959—; founder, 1st pres. Inner Circle Advocates, 1972-75; founder Richard Grand Found., 1966, now chmn.; hon. pres. Richard Grand Soc., 1997—. Contbr. articles to legal publs. Mem. bd. visitors law sch. Ariz. State U. Recipient citation of honor Lawyers Coop. Pub. Co., 1964, Profl. Achievement award U. Ariz., 2002. Fellow Am. Acad. Forensic Scis., Internat. Soc. Barristers; mem. Internat. Med. Soc. Paraplegia (assoc.), Am. Coll. Legal Medicine (assoc.), ABA, Pima County Bar Assn., Am. Bd. Trial Advs. (cert. in civil trial advocacy), Brit. Acad. Forensic Scis., Richard Grand Soc. (hon. pres.), Bohemian Club. Office: 6870 N Andrea Doria Dr Tucson AZ 85704 Office Phone: 520-622-8855. Business E-Mail: RG@rgrand.com.

GRANDIN, TEMPLE, industrial designer, science educator; b. Boston, Aug. 29, 1947; d. Richard McCurdy and Eustacia (Cutler) Grandin. BA in Psychology, Franklin Pierce Coll., 1970; MS in Animal Sci., Arizona State U., 1975; PhD in Animal Sci., U. Ill., Urbana, 1989; D (hon.), McGill U., 1999. Livestock editor Ariz. Farmer Ranchman, Phoenix, 1973-78; equipment designer Corral Industries, Phoenix, 1974-75; ind. cons. Grandin Livestock Systems, Urbana, 1975-90, Fort Collins, Colo., 1990—; lectr., prof. animal sci. dept. Colo. State U., Fort Collins, 1990—. Chmn. handing com. Livestock Conservation Inst., Madison, Wis., 1976—; surveyor USDA. Author: Emergence Labelled Autistic, 1986, Recommended Animal Handling Guidelines for Meat Packers, 1991, Livestock Handling and Transport, 1993, 3d edit., 2007, Thinking in Pictures, 1995, Genetics and the Behavior of Domestic Animals, 1998, Beef Cattle Behavior Handling and Facilities Design, 2000, Animals in Translation, 2005 (One of Top Sci. Books of Yr., 2005), Developing Talents, 2005, Unwritten Rules of Social Relationships, 2005, Humane Livestock Handling, 2008, Animals Make Us Human, 2009, New York Times and Canadian Best Seller, 2009; contbr. articles to profl. jours. Recipient Meritorious Svcs. award Livestock Conservation, Madison, Wis., 1986, Disting. Alumni award Franklin Pierce Coll., 1989, Industry Innovators award Meat Mktg. and Tech. Mag., 1994, Brownlee award for internat. leadership in sci. publ. promoting respect for animals Animal Welfare Found. of Canada, 1995, Harry Roswell award Scientists Ctr. for Animal Welfare, 1995, Humane Ethics in Action award Geraldine R. Dodge Found., 1998, Forbes award Nat. Meat Assn., 1998, Founders award Am. Soc. Prevention Cruelty Animals, 1999, Humane award Am. Vet. Med. Assn., 1999, Joseph Wood Krutch award, Humane Soc. of U.S., 2001, Knowlton Innovation award in Meat Mktg. and Tech. Mag., 2001, 2002, Animal Welfare award, Brit. Soc. Animal Sci. and Royal Soc. Prevention Cruelty to Animals, 2002, Pres.'s award, Nat. Inst. Animal Agr., 2004; named Woman of Yr. in Svc. to Agr. Progressive Farmer, 1999; named one of Processing Stars of 1990, Nat. Provisioner, 1990. Mem.: US Sec. of Health & Human Svcs. (Highest Recognition award 2007), Am. Soc. Agrl. Cons. (bd. dirs. 1981—83), Am. Registry Profl. Animal Scis., Am. Meat Inst. (supplier mem., Industry Advancement award 1995), Am. Soc. Agrl. Engrs., Am. Soc. Animal Sci. (Animal Mgmt. award 1995, Disting. Svc. award We. sect. 2003), Autism Soc. Am. (bd. dirs. 1988—, Trammel Crow award 1989, Founders award 2007). Republican. Episcopalian. Achievements include patents in field; design of stockyards and humane restraint equipment for major meat packing companies in the U.S., Canada and Australia; development of objective scoring system used for monitoring animal welfare in slaughter plants. Office: Colo State U Animal Sci Dept Fort Collins CO 80523-0001 Office Phone: 970-229-0703.

GRANEY, PAT, choreographer; Attended, Evergreen Coll. Founder, dir. Pat Graney Co., Seattle, 1990—; founder Keeping the Faith Prison Project, 1992. Choreographer Tattoo, 2000, The Vivian Girls, 2004, House of Mind, 2008. Recipient Golden Umbrella award, 2000, Alpert award for Dance, Herb Alpert Found., 2008; fellow US Artists, 2008. Office: Pat Graney Co Studio 11 1419 S Jackson St Seattle WA 98144 Office Phone: 206-329-3705. Office Fax: 206-329-3730. E-mail: staff@patgraney.org.*

GRANGER, CLIVE WILLIAM JOHN (SIR CLIVE GRANGER), retired economist; b. Swansea, Wales, Sept. 4, 1934; arrived in U.S., 1974; s. Edward John and Evelyn Agnes (Hessey) G.; m. Patricia Anne Loveland, May 14, 1960; children: Mark, Claire. BA, U. Nottingham, Eng., 1955, PhD in Stats., 1959, DSc, 1992; DSc (hon.), Carlos III, Madrid, 1997; D in Econs. (hon.), Stockholm Sch. Econs., 1998; DSc (hon.), Loughborough U., 2002. Lectr. in math. U. Nottingham, 1956—64, prof. stats., 1964—74; prof. econs. U. Calif., San Diego, 1976—2002, chancellor's assoc. chair, 1994—2002; ret., 2003. Author: Forecasting Stock Markets, 1970; editor: Commodity Markets, 1973. Decorated knight bachelor Royal Order Queen Elizabeth of Britain, 2005; fellow Harkness Fund, 1959-60, Econometric Soc., 1973, Guggenheim Found., 1988, recipient Nobel Prize in Econs., 2003. Fellow: Am. Econ. Soc. (Disting.), Am. Acad. Arts and Scis., Brit. Acad. (corr.); mem.: We. Econ. Assn. (pres. 2002—03), Econometric Soc. Avocations: hiking, swimming, travel, reading. Office: U Calif San Diego Econs Dept D-008 La Jolla CA 92093 Office Phone: 858-534-3856. Business E-Mail: cgranger@ucsd.edu.

GRANIRER, EDMOND ERNEST, mathematician, educator; b. Romania, 1935; s. Jacob G. MSc, Hebrew U., Jerusalem, 1959, PhD, 1962. Mem. faculty dept. math. U. Ill., 1962-64, Cornell U., 1964-65, U. B.C., Vancouver, Canada, 1965—66, 1967—, prof. math., 1970-97, prof. emeritus, 1997—; faculty U. Montreal, Canada, 1966-67. Contbr. articles to profl. jours. Grantee NSERC, 1996. Fellow Royal Soc. Can.; mem. Can. Math. Soc., Am. Math. Soc. Office: U BC Dept Math Vancouver BC Canada V6T 1Z2 Home Phone: 604-224-6785. Business E-Mail: granirer@math.ubc.ca.

GRANNEMAN, VERNON HENRY, lawyer; b. Chico, Calif., Aug. 2, 1953; s. Vern Henry and Mary Elizabeth (Riley) G.; m. Stephanie Sampson, Aug. 19, 1978; children: Kelly, Michael. BA, Santa Clara U., 1975, JD, 1978. Bar: Calif. 1978, U.S. Dist. Ct. (no. dist.) Calif. 1978, U.S. Dist. Ct. (cen. dist.) Calif. 1984, U.S. Dist. Ct. (so. and ea. dists.) Calif. 1985. Assoc. atty. Ruffo Ferrari & McNeil, San Jose, Calif., 1978-81, Pillsbury, Madison & Sutro (merger with Ruffo Ferrari & McNeil), San Jose, 1981-85, ptnr., 1986-96, O'Donnell, Rice, Davis, Alexander & Granneman, San Jose, 1996-97, Genesis Law Group, LLP, San Jose, 1997-99, Skjerven, Morrill, MacPherson LLP, San Jose, 1999—. Mem. ABA, Internat. Found. Employee Benefit Plans (arbitration com. 1991-94), Santa Clara County Bar, Santa Clara Univ. Law Alumni (bd. dirs. 1986-92). Democrat. Roman Catholic.

GRANOVETTER, MARK, sociology educator; b. Jersey City, Oct. 20, 1943; s. Sidney and Violet (Greenblatt) G.; m. Ellen Susan Greenebaum, June 14, 1970; 1 child, Sara. AB, Princeton U., NJ, 1965; MA, Harvard U., 1967, PhD, 1970; PhD (hon.), Stockholm U., 1996, Inst. Polit. Studies, Paris, 2006. Asst. prof. social rels. Johns Hopkins U., Balt., 1970-73; from asst. to assoc. prof., dir. undergraduate program in sociology Harvard U., Cambridge, Mass., 1973-77; from assoc. prof. to prof. sociology SUNY, Stony Brook, 1977-92, chair dept. sociology, 1989—92; prof. sociology Northwestern U., Evanston, Ill., 1992-95, chair dept. sociology, 2002—05; prof. sociology Stanford U., 1995—, Joan Butler Ford prof. sociology, 1997—. Mem. Inst. Advanced Study, Princeton, NJ, 1981—82; sci./technical adv. bd. Merchant Circle, Inc., Los Altos, Calif., Wisdom Ark, Inc., Mountain View, Calif., Spoke Software, Inc., San Mateo, Calif. Author: Getting A Job, 1974; series editor Cambridge U. Press, 1986—; contbr. articles to profl. jours. Faculty Devel. award, Woodrow Wilson Nat. Fellowship Found., 1980-81, Sci. Faculty Profl. Devel. award, Nat. Sci. Found., 1982-83; Ctr. for Advanced Study fellow, 1977, J.S. Guggenheim Found. fellow, 1981. Fellow: Am. Acad. Arts and Sciences, Am. Acad. Polit. and Social Sci.; mem.: John Hopkins U. Soc. Scholars, Sociological Rsch. Assn., European Assn. Evolutionary Polit. Economy, Soc. Advancement of Socio-Economics, Internat. Network for Social Network Analysis, Am. Sociological Assn. (Theory section prize 1985). Office: Dept Sociology Stanford U Stanford CA 94305-2047 Office Phone: 650-723-4664. Office Fax: 650-618-0301. E-mail: mgranovetter@stanford.edu.

GRANT, ALAN J., business executive, educator; b. Chgo., Dec. 18, 1925; s. Hugo Bernard and May (Gardner) G.; m. Margaret Stewart, Dec. 21, 1946; children: Pamela Rose, Deborah May, Bruce David. BSEE, Ill. Inst. Tech., 1946, MSEE, 1948; EdD, U. San Diego, 1992. Cert. instr. math. H.S. Calif., 2004. Instr. elec. engring. Ill. Inst. Tech., Chgo., 1946-49; with N.Am. Aviation, Inc. (Autonetics), Anaheim, Calif., 1949-64, v.p., gen. mgr. computer and data systems div., 1962-64; pres. Lockheed Electronics Co. div. Lockheed Aircraft Corp., Plainfield, N.J., 1965-69; also v.p. parent co.; exec. v.p. Aerojet-Gen. Corp., El Monte, Calif., 1970-74; chmn., pres. Wavecom Industries, Sunnyvale, Calif., 1974-78, Primark Corp., San Mateo, Calif., 1975-80; chmn., chief exec. officer Internat. Rotex, Inc., Reno, Nev., 1980-86; dir. UNC Resources Inc, Falls Church, Va., 1974-81; chmn. Atasi Corp., San Jose, Calif., 1982-85; gen. ptnr. EMC Venture Ptnrs., San Diego, 1984-86; pres. Grant Venture Mgmt. Co., Coronado, Calif., 1986-96; chmn. Am. Innovision, San Diego, 1986-92, SalePoint Systems Corp., San Diego, 1987-92. Adj. prof. managerial scis. U. Nev., Reno, 1979—84; mgmt. San Diego State U., 1986—90; pres. Corp. Mgmt. Assocs., 1996—; adj. prof., dir. Ctr. for Entrepreneurship, Calif. State U., Long Beach, 1999—2001; adj. prof. entrepreneurship Calif. State U., Hayward, 2001—03. Paul T. Babson prof. entrepreneurship Babson Coll., Babson Park, Mass., 1992-94. Mem. Am. Electronics Assn. (chmn. 1973, dir. 1970-74). Home: 4523 Calaveras Ave Fremont CA 94538-1121 Personal E-mail: agrant105@comcast.net.

GRANT, LEWIS O., agricultural products executive, meteorology educator; b. Washington, Pa., Mar. 29, 1923; s. Lewis F. and Rita J. (Jacqmain) G.; m. Patricia Jean Lovelock, July 23, 1949; children: Ann, Nancy, Brenda, Andrew, Laura. BS, U. Tulsa, Okla., 1947; MS, Calif. Inst. Tech., Pasadena, 1948. Meteorological cons. Water Resources Devel. Corp., Pasadena, Calif., 1948-54, Denver, 1948-54; rschr. and rsch. dir. Am. Inst. Aerological Rsch., Denver, 1954-59; asst. prof., assoc. prof., prof. atmospheric sci. dept. Colo. State U., Ft. Collins, 1959-93, emeritus prof., 1993—; pres. Piedmont Farms, Inc., Wellington, Colo., 1975-98; sr. cons. Grant Family Farms, Wellington, 1998—. Cons. Colo. Legis., Denver, 1971-73; bd. dirs. adv. com. Integrated Pest Mgmt. Contb. to profl. jours. Scout master, com. chmn. Boy Scouts of Am.; pres. Partner Communities, Ft. Collins, Colo., 1988; elder Presbyn. Ch., 1980—; 1st lt. U.S. Field Artillery and USAF, 1943-46., bd. dirs. Legacy Land Trust, 2004-, bd. mem., 2001-, co-agrl. adv. bd. Larma County, 1998-2004, 09-. Recipient Vincent J. Schaefer award Weather Modification Assn., 1991, Soil and Water Conservation award Ft. Collins Soil Conservation Dist., 1994. Fellow Am. Meterological Assn.; mem. NAS (sect. chmn. 1975-76, mem. climate com.), Organic Farming Rsch. Found. (bd. mem. 1995-2001). Republican. Presbyterian. Avocation: gardening. Office: Grant Family Farms 1020 W County Road 72 Wellington CO 80549-1912 also: Colo State U Dept Atmospheric Sci Fort Collins CO 80523-0001 Personal E-mail: lgrant3309@aol.com.

GRANT, PAUL, chemical engineer, real estate broker, lawyer; b. Patuxent River, Md., May 19, 1949; s. Ralph F. and Elizabeth (Payne) G. BS in Chem. Engring., Auburn U., Ala., 1971; MS in Chem. Engring., U. Md., College Park, 1975; Cert. Hungarian linguist, U.S. Army, 1972; JD U. Denver, 1995. Lic. real estate broker. Sales engr. Mixing Equipment Co., Rochester, N.Y., 1976-78; precious metals salesman James U. Blanchard & Co., New Orleans, 1979; owner, operator PK Grant & Co., Lakewood, Colo., 1979—; atty.; criminal def., comml., and civil litigator Denver, 1995—. Instr. Jr. Achievement Project Bus., Lakewood, Colo., 1984; state chmn. Libertarian Party, La., 1979, Libertarian Party candidate for gov. Colo., 1982, nat. chmn. Libertarian Party, 1983-85. Served with U.S. Army, 1971-74 Basketball scholar Pensacola Jr. Coll., Fla., 1967-69; named Nat. Merit scholar Auburn U., 1969-71; recipient Outstanding Translator award U.S. Army Def. Intelligence Agy., 1974 Office: Paul Grant PO Box 2720 Parker CO 80134-1422 Office Phone: 303-771-1908.

GRANT, RAYMOND THOMAS, arts administrator; b. Yonkers, NY, Nov. 1, 1957; s. Kieran J. and Rita B. (Benedek) G.; m. Susan Mary McLoughlin, Nov. 6, 1993; children: Kieran John, Stephen Thomas. B of Music Edn., U. Kans., 1980; MA in Arts Adminstrn., NYU, 1984. Cert. music edn. tchr. Intern John F. Kennedy Ctr. for the Performing Arts, Washington, 1980; band dir. Lawrence Pub. Schs., Kans., 1980—81; dir. spl. projects 92nd St. YM-YWHA, NYC, 1983—85; gen. mgr. Am. Symphony Orch., NYC, 1985—91; pres. Raymond T. Grant, Ltd., 1989—93; dir. Tisch Ctr. for the Arts of the 92d St. Y, NYC, 1991—92; mgr. program devel. performing arts and film The Disney Inst., Celebration, Fla., 1993—96; programming cons. Walt Disney Attractions, Inc., 1996—98; mng. dir. arts and culture Salt Lake Organizing Com. for Olympic Winter Games of 2002, 1998—2003; artistic dir. 2002 Cultural Olympiad; exec. dir. Sundance, 2003—05; dir. club ops. Promontory-Ranch Club, Park City, Utah, 2006—07, dir. programming, 2008—; dir. programming and guest experience Discovery Gateway, Salt Lake City, 2008—. Guest lectr., spkr. King's Coll., NYU, NYC, 1990, The Hartt Sch., U. Hartford, U. No. Iowa, Ind. U., 1997, The Sch. of Art Inst. Chgo., 1998, Va. Tech., 1998, U. Utah, 2000, U. Mainz, Germany, 2007; mem. cmty. rels. coun., Utah Valley State Coll.; mem. adv. com. Carnegie Hall Profl. Tng. Workshops, 1990-91; programming cons. Imperial Tombs of China Exhbn., Orlando Mus. Art, Fla., 1997—. Contbr. articles to Olympic Rev., Sports Jour., Arts Mgmt. Newsletter. Bd. dirs. North Fork Preservation Alliance, 2003-05, Kans. Alliance for Arts Edn., Lawrence, 1981, Concerts for Young People, Lawrence, 1981, Negro Spiritual Scholarship Found., Orlando, Fla., 1997-2001; mem. adv. bd. NY Youth Symphony, 1986; panel mem. presenting and commissioning program, challenge grant program NEA, 1993, site visitor presenting and commissioning program, 1994; mem. music orgn. panel divsn. cultural affairs Fla. Dept. State, 1994, 95, 96; facilitator, mem. panel Martin Luther King, Jr. Forum, Diocese of Orlando, Orlando Mus. Art, 1997, 98. Named to Peekskill HS Alumni Hall of Honor; Stella Wolcott Aten grantee U. Kans., 1978, Scholarship Found. grantee, NYC, 1980; Power Found. scholar U. Kans., 1979. Mem. Internat. Soc. Olympic Historians. Home: 2188 Wilson Ave Salt Lake City UT 84108-3022 Office Phone: 801-456-5437 ext. 113. Personal E-mail: raymondtgrant@comcast.net.

GRANT, WILLIAM WEST, III, banker; b. NYC, May 9, 1932; s. William West and Katherine O'Connor (Neelands) G.; m. Rhondda Lowery, Dec. 3, 1955. BA, Yale U., 1954; postgrad., NYU Grad. Sch. Bus., 1958, Columbia U. Grad. Sch. Bus., 1968, Harvard U. Grad. Sch. Bus., 1971. With Bankers Trust Co., NYC, 1954-58, br. credit adminstr., 1957-58; with Colo. Nat. Bank, Denver, 1958-93, pres., 1975-86, chmn. bd., 1986-93. Chmn. bd. Colo. Capital Advisors, 1989-94; mem. adv. bd. US Bancorp., Colo., 1993-99. Tsee Nat. Trust Hist. Preservation; trustee Rocky Mountain Nat. Park Assocs., Estes Pk., Midwest Rsch. Inst., Kansas City; mem. adv. bd. Rocky Mtn. Pub. Broadcasting Sys.; dir. Colo. Energy Sci. Ctr., Four Mile Hist. Pk. Mem.: Tsee Colo. Symphony Found., Denver Country Club. Episcopalian. Home: 545 Race St Denver CO 80206-4122 Office Phone: 303-321-1566. Business E-Mail: petergrant1155@comcast.net.

GRANTHAM, DONALD, computer company executive, former computer systems network executive; married; 2 children. Various leadership roles in sales, mktg. and ops. IBM, 1980—99, head server product mktg. Europe, Mid. East and Africa, head svcs. sales No. Europe; with Sun Microsystems, Inc., San Jose, Calif., 1999—2008, head worldwide sales ops., exec. v.p. services, exec. v.p. global sales & services mem. exec. mgmt. group, 2006—08; sr. v.p., chief sales officer Hewlett-Packard Co., Palo Alto, Calif., 2008—. Recipient Sun Leadership award, 2003. Office: Hewlett-Packard Co 3000 Hanover St Palo Alto CA 94304

GRANT-HERRIOT, LAURA, state legislator; 3 children. Degree in Tchg., Ea. Wash. U., Cheney. Served on Prescott Sch. Bd.; several years tchg. fifth-grade elem. Walla Walla, Wash.; employee family wheat farm; mem. Dist. 16 Wash. House of Reps., 2009—. Democrat. Office: 305 John L O'Brien Bldg PO Box 40600 Olympia WA 98504-0600 Office Phone: 360-786-7828. Business E-Mail: grant-herriot.laura@leg.wa.gov.

GRAUBART, JEFFREY LOWELL, lawyer; b. Chgo., Aug. 18, 1940; s. John H. and Florence R. G.; m. Mary Linda Carey, June 24, 1973; children: Joshua Gordon, Noah Carey. BS in Fin., U. Ill., 1962; JD, Northwestern U., Chgo., 1965. Bar: Ill. 1965, Calif. 1968, N.Y. 1980. Assoc. Curtis Friedman & Marks, Chgo., 1965-67, Capitol Records, Inc., Los Angeles, 1968-70; prin. Hadfield, Jorgensen, Graubart & Becker, San Francisco, 1970-81; counsel Frankfurt, Garbus, Klein & Selz, P.C., N.Y., 1981-85; prin. Strote, Graubart & Ashley, P.C., Beverly Hills, Calif. and NY, 1986-87; counsel Cohen & Luckenbacher, LA, 1988-90, Engel & Engel, LA, 1991-92; pvt. practice LA, 1992—. Sec. Paramount Growers, Inc., Delano, Calif., 1968-70; v.p., dir. London Internat. Artists, Ltd., Los Angeles, 1969-70, Jazz Images, Inc., N.Y.C., 1983-86; adj. prof. NYU, 1982-85; lectr. Columbia U. Sch. Law, N.Y.C., 1982-85, UCLA, 1988—, U. So. Calif., 1988—. Contbr. articles to profl. jours. and mags. Counsel San Francisco Jazz Found., 1980-81. Recipient Deems Taylor award ASCAP, 1981. Mem. NARAS (San Francisco chtp. legal counsel 1973-93, gov. 1973-85, gov. and legal counsel N.Y. chpt. 1982-85, gov. L.A. chpt. 1988-92), Calif. Copyright Conf. (dir. 1995—), Internat. Fedn. Festival Orgns. (dir. 1994—), Inter-Pacific Bar Assn., Beverly Hills Bar Assn. (chair internat. law sect. 1995—), Internat. Radio and TV Soc., Country Music Assn., Assn. of the Bar of the City of N.Y., Soc. Preservation of Film Music (trustee 1989—), v.p. 1991-94). Lodges: B'nai Brith (N.Y. and Los Angeles); Golden Gate (San Francisco) (v.p. 1974-75), Entertainment Industry Unit L.A. (founder, trustee 1988—). Office: 350 W Colorado BLVD STE 200 Pasadena CA 91105-1855

GRAVES, ANNA MARIE, lawyer; b. Arlington, Va., Sept. 26, 1959; d. George W. and Anna (Czikora) G. AB cum laude, Cornell U., 1981; JD, U. Va., 1985. Bar: Calif. 1985, U.S. Dist. Ct. (cen. dist.) Calif. 1986. Corp. assoc. Memel, Jacobs, Pierno, Gersh & Ellsworth, LA, 1985-87, Stroock & Stroock & Lavan, LA, 1987—96; ptnr., co-chmn. Restaurant Food & Beverage industry group Pillsbury Winthrop Shaw Pittman, LA, 1989—2001. Chmn. UCLA Extension Calif. Restaurant Industry Conf. Named a So. Calif. Super Lawyer, LA Mag., 2004. Mem. ABA, Beverly Hills Bar Assn., Calif. Women Lawyers. Democrat. Office: Pillsbury Winthrop Shaw Pittman 725 S Figueroa St Los Angeles CA 90017 Office Phone: 213-488-7164. Office Fax: 213-226-4017. Business E-Mail: anna.graves@pillsburylaw.com.

GRAVES, EARL WILLIAM, JR., journalist; b. Kodiak, Alaska, June 30, 1950; s. Earl William Graves, Sr. and Lola (Olson) Raab; m. Karin Ann Steichen, July 30, 1972; children: Emma, Mark, Max. BA in English with honors, U. Puget Sound, 1972; MA in English, Western Wash. State U., 1976. Tchr. English Naselle (Wash.) High Sch., 1972-74, Clatskanie (Oreg.) High Sch., 1975-77; police reporter Coeur d'Alene (Idaho) Press, 1978-79, city editor, 1980-82, mng. editor, 1983-84; sr. reporter Bulletin, Bend, Oreg., 1984-86; edn. reporter News and Observer, Raleigh, N.C., 1986-87; state edn.

reporter News and Observer/Raleigh Times, 1987-89; edn. reporter The Oregonian, Portland, 1990—. Author: Poisoned Apple, 1995. Recipient Outstanding Svc. award N.C. chpt. Phi Delta Kappa, 1988, Third Prize So. Journalism Feature Reporting award Inst. for So. Studies, 1989, N.C. Sch. Bell award N.C. Assn. Educators, 1989, Benjamin Fine award Nat. Assn. Secondary Sch. Prins., 1989, First Pl. Gen. News Reporting award N.C. Press Assn., 1990, First Pl. Edn. Reporting award Pacific Northwest Excellence in Journalism, Soc. Profl. Journalists, 1991, 92, 2001, Media award Assn. Retarded Children Oreg., 1992, Seconad Pl. Spot News Reporting award Best of West, 1992, Second Pl. Best Writing award Oreg. Newspaper Pubs. Assn., 1993, Excellence in Edn. award Oreg. Assn. Supervision and Cirriculum Devel., 1993; Nieman fellow Harvard U., 1998-99. Mem. Edn. Writers Assn. (pres., sec., bd. dirs. 1990—, Spl. Citation Nat. Awards for Edn. Reporting 1987, 91, Second Pl. Newspaper Series award 1989, Second Pl. Nat. Awards Edn. Reporting 1989). Democrat. Avocations: gardening, photography, outdoors, running, travel. Office: Oregonian 1320 SW Broadway Portland OR 97201-3499

GRAVES, KAREN LEE, counselor; b. Twin Falls, Idaho, Dec. 9, 1948; d. Isaac Mason and Agnes Popplewell; m. Frederick Ray Graves, Apr. 2, 1987 (dec. Dec. 2001). BA, Idaho State U., 1971; MEd, Coll. of Idaho, 1978. Cert. tchr. secondary edn., english 7-12, vocat. home econs. 7-12, pupil pers. svcs. K-12, Idaho. Tchr. Filer (Idaho) Sch. Dist., 1971-74, 76-80, Twin Falls (Idaho) Sch. Dist., 1974-76; counselor Mountain Home (Idaho) Sch. Dist., 1980—2004, dept. chairperson, dir., ret., 2004—. Mem.: Retired Eucators of Idaho-Local Organ. Avocations: painting ceramics, crafting, stamping, reading, crossword puzzles. Home: 944 Bitterroot Pl Twin Falls ID 83301

GRAVES, ROD, professional sports team executive; b. Houston; s. Jackie Graves; m. Dreama Graves; children: Brittany, Taylor, Joshua. B in Econs., Tex. Tech. U. Regional scout Phila. Stars, US Football League, 1982—83, asst. dir. player pers., 1983—84; regional scout Chgo. Bears, 1984—93, dir. coll. scouting, 1993—94, dir. player pers., 1994—96; asst. to the pres. Ariz. Cardinals, 1997—2002, v.p. football ops., gen. mgr., 2002—. Mem. NFL C.E.C. Working Group Com., NFL Coll. Adv. Com. Named one of 101 Most Influential Minorities in Sports, Sports Illus., 50 Most Powerful Blacks in Sports, Black Enterprise Mag. Mailing: Ariz Cardinals PO Box 888 Phoenix AZ 85001-0888*

GRAVITZ, HERBERT L., clinical psychologist, writer; b. Washington, Aug. 18, 1942; s. Phillip Benjamin and Sophie (Korin) G.; m. Leslie Ann Gravitz; children: Brian Eric, Aaron David, Jason Michael. BS, U. Md., 1964; MA, U. Tenn., Knoxville, 1966, PhD, 1969. Diplomate Am. Bd. Forensic Examiners, in psychotherapy Am. Acad. Experts in Traumatic Stress; lic. clin. psychologist; bd. cert. in illness trauma. Asst. dir. Counseling Ctr., U. Calif., Santa Barbara, 1972—79, counseling program dir., 1979-80, coord. tng., 1980-81; cons. psychologist Psychiat. Emergency Team, Santa Barbara, 1980-81, Sanctuary House, Inc., Santa Barbara, 1980-82; core faculty Suzanne Somers Inst., Palm Springs, Calif., 1989—93; pvt. practice Santa Barbara, 1979—. Asst. prof. psychology U. Windsor, Ont., Can., 1969-72. Author: Obsessive Compulsive Disorder: New Help for the Family, 1998, 2nd edit., 2005, Facing Adversity: Words that Heal, 2005, Mental Illness and the Family: Unlocking the Doors to Triumph, 2005; co-author: Recovery: A Guide for Adult Children of Alcoholics, 1985, Genesis: Recovery from Childhood Traumas, 1988. Fellow Am. Acad. Experts in Traumatic Stress; mem. Calif. State Psychol. Assn. Avocations: music, writing, meditation, stamps. Office: Ste 217 2020 Alameda Padre Serra Santa Barbara CA 93103-1756 Office Phone: 805-963-9309. Personal E-mail: gravitz@earthlink.net

GRAVLEE, GLENN P(AGE), anesthesiologist, educator, director; b. Birmingham, Ala., Aug. 15, 1950; BS in Medicine, Northwestern U., 1972, MD, 1974. Diplomate Am. Bd. Anesthesiology, Nat. Bd. Echocardiography. Intern Hartford Hosp., Conn., 1974—75; resident anesthesiology Mass. Gen. Hosp., Harvard Med. Sch., Boston, 1975—77, chief resident, cardiac anesthesia fellow, 1977—78, instr., 1978—79; from asst. prof. to prof. Wake Forest U., 1978—94; prof. Allegheny U. Health Scis., Pitts., 1994—99, chair, 1994—99; prof. dept. anesthesiology Coll. Med. and Pub. Health, Ohio State U., Columbus, 1999—, chmn. dept. anesthesiology Coll. Med. and Pub. Health, 1999—2002, vice chmn., 2002—06; prof. Health Scis. Ctr. U. Colo., 2006—, dir. edn. Dept. Anesthesiology Health Scis. Ctr., 2006—. Editor: Cardiopulmonary Bypass: Principles and Practice, 1994, 2000; co-editor: A Practical Approach to Cardiac Anesthesia, 2003, Year Book of Anesthesia, 2004; contbr. articles to profl. jours. Mem.: Am. Soc. Anesthesiologists, Internat. Anesthesiology Rsch. Soc., Soc. Cardiovasc. Anesthesiologists (pres. 2003—05), Am. Bd. Anesthesiologists (dir. 1999—). Office: Univ Colo Health Scis Ctr Dept Anesthesiology 4200 E 9th Ave B113 Denver CO 80262 Business E-Mail: glenn.gravlee@uchsc.edu.

GRAY, CAMPBELL, museum director; Degree in Art, Sydney Coll., Alexander Mackie Coll.; PhD in Art History, U. Sussex, Eng. Faculty mem., coord. postgraduate studies visual arts & art hist. U. Western Sydney; dir. Brigham Young U. Mus. Art, Provo, Utah, 1996—. Office: Mus Art Brigham Young U Provo UT 84602 Office Phone: 801-422-8257.

GRAY, CHARLES DALE (CHUCK GRAY), state legislator; b. Mesa, Ariz., Jan. 20, 1958; s. Dale Ivan and Janice Stewart Gray; m. Connie Ann Jones, May 10, 1980; children: Dallin Stephen, Miranda Nadene, Brandon Charles, Kindra Marie, Amber Lynn. Student, Mesa Cmty. Coll. Cert. police officer Ariz. Brick/block mason Dale Gray Corp., Mesa, 1979—90; officer, detective auto theft unit Mesa Police Dept., 1990—2000; mem. Ariz. House of Reps., Phoenix, 2003—06; mem. Dist. 19 Ariz. State Senate, 2006—, majority leader. Owner/operator www.Seatcovers.net, Ariz., 1997—. Missionary LDS Ch., Spain, 1977—79. Republican. Mem. Lds Ch. Office: Ariz State Senate Capitol Complex 1700 W Washington St Rm 212 Phoenix AZ 85007 Office Phone: 602-926-5288. Office Fax: 602-417-3161. Business E-Mail: cdgray@azleg.gov.*

GRAY, HARRY BARKUS, chemistry professor; b. Woodburn, Ky., Nov. 14, 1935; s. Barkus and Ruby (Hopper) Gray; m. Shirley Barnes, June 2, 1957; children: Victoria Lynn, Andrew Thomas, Noah Harry Barkus. BS, Western Ky. U., 1957; PhD, Northwestern U., 1960, DSc (hon.), 1984, U. Chgo., 1987, U. Rochester, 1987, U. Paul Sabatier, 1991, U. Göteborg, 1991, U. Firenze, 1993, Columbia U., 1994, Bowling Green State U., 1994, Ill. Wesleyan, 1995, Oberlin Coll., 1996, U. Ariz., 1997, Carleton U., 2001, U. SC, 2003, U. Copenhagen, 2003, U. Edinburgh, 2006. Postdoctoral fellow U. Copenhagen, 1960—61; faculty Columbia U., 1961—66, prof., 1965—66; prof. chemistry Calif. Inst. Tech., Pasadena, 1966—, now Arnold O. Beckman prof. chemistry and founding dir. Beckman Inst. Vis. prof. Rockefeller U., Harvard U., U. Iowa, Pa. State U., Yeshiva U., U. Copenhagen, U. Witwatersrand, Johannesburg, South Africa, U. Canterbury, Christchurch, New Zealand, U. Hong Kong; George Eastman prof. Oxford (Eng.) U., 1997—98; cons. govt., industry; Kistiakowsky lectr. Harvard U., 1999. Author: Electrons and Chemical Bonding, 1965, Molecular Orbital Theory, 1965, Ligand Substitution Processes, 1966, Basic Principles of Chemistry, 1967, Chemical Dynamics, 1968, Chemical Principles, 1970, Models in Chemical Science, 1971, Chemical Bonds, 1973, Chemical Structure and Bonding, 1980, Molecular Electronic Structures, 1980, Braving the Elements, 1995. Recipient Franklin Meml. award, Stanford U., 1967, Fresenius award, Phi Lambda Upsilon, 1970, Shoemaker award, U. Louisville, 1970, award for excellence in tchg., Mfg. Chemists Assn., 1972, Centenary medal, Royal Soc. Chemistry, 1985, Nat. medal of Sci., 1986, Alfred Bader Bioinorganic Chemistry award, 1990, Gold medal, Am. Inst. Chemists, 1990, Linderstrom-Lang prize, 1992, Priestly award, Dickinson Coll., 1991, Chandler medal, Columbia U., 1999, Harvey prize, Technion Israel Inst. Tech., 2000, Benjamin Franklin medal in Chemistry, Franklin Inst., 2004, Wolf prize in chemistry, Wolf Found., Israel, 2004; named Calif. Scientist of Yr., 1988, Achievement Rewards for Coll. Scis. Man of Sci., 1990; Guggenheim fellow, 1972—73, Phi Beta Kappa scholar, 1973—74. Fellow: AAAS; mem.: NAS (Nichols medal 2003, award in chem. scis. 2003), Royal Danish Acad. Scis. and Letters, Am. Philos. Soc., Royal Soc. (London), Royal Swedish Acad., Am. Chem. Soc. (award pure chemistry 1970, Harrison Howe award 1972, award inorganic chemistry 1978, Remsen Meml. award 1979, Tolman medal 1979, award for disting. svc. in advancement of inorganic chemistry 1984, Pauling medal 1986, Priestley medal 1991, Willard Gibbs medal 1992, Wolf prize for chemistry 2004, Benjamin Franklin medal in chemistry 2004, City of Florence prize in molecular scis. 2006), Phi Lambda Upsilon, Alpha Chi Sigma. Office: Calif Inst Tech 408 Beckman MC 127-72 1200 E California Blvd Pasadena CA 91125-0001

GRAY, JAMES N., computer scientist; BS in Math. and Engring., U. Calif., Berkeley, 1966, PhD in Computer sci., 1969; D of Natural Sci. (hon.), U. Stuttgart, Germany, 1990. Sys. rschr. Bell Labs, Whippany, NJ, 1966—67; rsch. asst., computer sci. U. Calif., Berkeley, Calif., 1967—69; ops. sys. rschr. T.J. Watson Rsch. Lab IBM, Yorktown Heights, NY, 1971—72; UNESCO expert Polytech. Inst., Bucharest, Romania, 1972; database rschr. IBM, San Jose, Calif., 1972—80; rschr. Tandem Computers, Cupertino, Calif., 1980—90; corp. cons. engr. Digital Equipment Corp., 1990—94; sr. rschr. Microsoft Corp., 1995—; founder, mgr., disting. engr. Scaleable Servers Rsch. Group Microsoft Bay Area Rsch. Ctr., San Francisco, 2000—; Missing since Jan. 28, 2007 after a weekend sailing trip to scatter mother's ashes in the waters off Northern Calif.; Coast Guard called off search on Feb. 1, 2007. Vis. scholar U. Calif., Berkeley; pres. Adv. Com. on Info. Tech.; mem. adv. bd. Sch. Engring., Stanford U. Editor: Morgan Kaufmann Data Management Series, Data Mining and Knowledge Discovery; moderator database sect. Computer Sci. Online Rsch. Repository; past editor in chief and endowment bd. VLDB Jour. Recipient A.M. Turing award Assn. Computer Machinery, 1998, Phi Beta Kappa, Sigma Chi. Fellow Assn. Computing Machinery; mem. NAE, NRC (mem. computer sci. and telecomm. bd.).

GRAY, JAN CHARLES, lawyer, business owner; b. Des Moines, June 15, 1947; s. Charles Donald and Mary C. Gray; 1 child, Charles Jan. BA in Econs., U. Calif., Berkeley, 1969; MBA, Pepperdine U., 1986; JD, Harvard U., 1972. Bar: Calif. 1972, D.C. 1974, Wyo. 1992. Law clk. Kindel & Anderson, LA, 1971-72; assoc. Halstead, Baker & Sterling, LA, 1972-75; sr. v.p., gen. counsel and sec. Ralphs Grocery Co., LA, 1975-97; pres. Am. Presidents Resorts, Custer, S.D., Casper/Glenrock, Wyo., 1983—; owner Big Bear (Calif.) Cabins-Lakeside, 1988—; pres. Mt. Rushmore Broadcasting, Inc., 1991—; owner Sta. KGOS/KERM, Torrington, Wyo., 1993—, Sta. KRAL/KIQZ, Rawlins, Wyo., 1993—, Sta. KZMX, Hot Springs, SD, 1993—, Sta. KFCR, Custer, SD, 1992—, Sta. KQLT-FM, Casper, Wyo., 1994—, Sta. KASS-FM, Casper, 1995—, Sta. KVOC-AM, Casper, 1997—, KAWK-FM, Rapid City, SD, 1997—, KHOC, Casper, Wyo., 1998—, KMLD, Casper, Mt. Rushmore Farms Horse Racing, 1999—. Judge pro tem L.A. Mcpl. Ct., 1977-85; instr. bus. UCLA, 1976-85, Pepperdine MBA Program, 1983-85; arbitrator Am. Arbitration Assn., 1977-97; media spokesman So. Calif. Grocers Assn., 1979-90, Calif. Grocers Assn., 1979-97, Calif. Retailers Assn., 1979-97; real estate broker, Calif., 1973—. Contbg. author: Life or Death, Who Controls?, 1976; contbr. articles to profl. jours. Trustee South Bay U. Coll. Law, 1978-79; mem. bd. visitors Southwestern U. Sch. Law, 1983—; mem. L.A. County Pvt. Industry Coun., 1982-96, exec. com. 1984-88, chmn. econ. devel. task force, 1986-89, chmn. mktg. com. 1991-93; mem. L.A. County Martin Luther King, Jr. Gen. Hosp. Authority, 1984—94; mem. L.A. County Aviation Commn, 1986-92, chmn., 1990-91; L.A. Police Crime Prevention Adv. Coun., 1986—97; Angelus Plaza Adv. Bd., 1983-85; bd. dirs. RecyCAL of So. Calif., 1983-89; trustee Santa Monica Hosp. Found., 1986-91, adv. bd., 1991—94; mem. L.A. County Dem. Cen. Com., 1980-90, L.A. City Employees' Retirement System Commn., 1993—; del. Dem. Nat. Conv., 1980. Recipient So. Calif. Grocers Assn. award for outstanding contbns. to food industry, 1982, appreciation award for No on 11 Campaign, Calif./Nev. Soft Drink Assn., 1983; Tyler Price Meml. award Mex.-Am. Grocers Assn., 1995, Radio Affiliate of Yr.-Classic Rock ABC, 1998. Mem.: ABA, Harvard Club of So. Calif., U. Calif. Alumni Assn., Town Hall L.A., Food Mktg. Inst. (govt. rels. com. 1977—97, chmn.lawyers, economists 1993—95, benefits coun. 1993—97), Calif. Retailers Assn. (supermarket com.), L.A. World Affairs Coun., L.A. Pub. Affairs Officers Assn., San Fernando Valley Bar Assn. (chmn. real property sect. 1975—77), L.A. County Bar Assn. (exec. com. corp. law depts. sect. 1979—2000, exec. com. barristers sect. 1974—75, exec. com. corp. law depts. sect. 1974—76, exec. com. barristers sect. 1979—81, chmn. 1989—90, trustee 1991—93, jud. evaluation com. 1993—96, nominating com. 1994), Calif. Bar Assn., Ephebian Soc. L.A., So. Calif. Bus. Assn. (bd. dirs. 1981—99, mem. exec. com. 1982—99, sec. 1986—91, chair 1991—98), Casper Country Club, L.A. Athletic Club, Phi Beta Kappa. Personal E-mail: jcg4321@aol.com.

GRAY, KARLA MARIE, retired state supreme court chief justice; b. Escanaba, Mich., May 10, 1947; BA, Western Mich. U., MA in African History; JD, Hastings Coll. of Law, San Francisco, 1976. Bar: Mont. 1976, Calif. 1977. Law clk. to Hon. W. D. Murray U.S. Dist. Ct., 1976-77; staff atty. Atlantic Richfield Co., 1977-81; pvt. practice law Butte, Mont., 1981-84; staff atty., legis. lobbyist Mont. Power Co., Butte, 1984-91; justice Mont. Supreme Ct., Helena, 1991-2000, chief justice, 2000—09. Mem. Mont. Supreme Ct. Gender Fairness Task Force. Fellow Am. Bar Found., Am. Judicature Soc., Internat. Women's Forum; mem. State Bar Mont., Silver Bow County Bar Assn. (past pres.), Nat. Assn. Women Judges. Avocations: travel, reading, piano, genealogy, cross country skiing.

GRAY, LINDA J., state legislator; b. St. Charles, Mo., June 23, 1949; life ptnr. Larry Gray; children: Larry Jr., Michelle. BS in Sociology, U. Northern Colo., 1971. Mem. Dist. 10 Ariz. House of Reps., 1996—2002, 2002—04, Ariz. State Senate, 2004—, chair pub. safety & human svcs. com., vice-chair edn. accountability & reform com. Mem. Washington Elem. Sch. Bd., 1994—98, Nat. Conf. State Legislators; mem. edn. com. Am. Legion Exchange Coun., 1998—; mem. Edn. Commn. of States, 2000—, mem. steering com., 2006. Ariz. dir. Nat. Found. Women Legislators; vol. Angel Tree Project. Recipient Making a Difference award, MADD. Mem.: Concerned Women for America, Am. Family Assn. Republican. Christian. Office: Ariz House Reps Capitol Complex 1700 W Washington Rm 309 Phoenix AZ 85007 Office Phone: 602-542-3376. Fax: 602-417-3253. Business E-Mail: lgray@azleg.gov.*

GRAY, MARVIN LEE, JR., lawyer; b. Pitts., May 9, 1945; s. Marvin L. and Frances (Stringfellow) G.; m. Jill Miller, Aug. 14, 1971; children: Elizabeth Ann, Carolyn Jill. AB, Princeton U., 1966; JD magna cum laude, Harvard U., 1969. Bar: Wash. 1973, U.S. Supreme Ct. 1977, Alaska 1984. Law clk. to judge U.S. Ct. Appeals, NYC, 1969-70; law clk. to justice U.S. Supreme Ct., Washington, 1970-71; asst. U.S. atty. U.S. Dept. Justice, Seattle, 1973-76; ptnr. Davis Wright Tremaine, Seattle, 1976—, mng. ptnr., 1985-88. Staff counsel Rockefeller Commn. on CIA Activities in U.S., Washington, 1974; lectr. trial practice U. Wash. Law Sch., Seattle, 1979-80. Lay reader Episcopal Ch. of Ascension, Seattle, 1982-94. Capt. USAF, 1971-73. Fellow Am. Coll. Trial Lawyers; mem. ABA, Am. Law Inst. Office: Davis Wright Tremaine 1201 3rd Ave Ste 2200 Seattle WA 98101-3045 Business E-Mail: montygray@dwt.com.

GRAY, PATRICIA JOYCE, retired legal association administrator; b. Carlsbad, N.Mex., Feb. 5, 1951; d. Owen Corbett and Bobby Jo (Jones) G.; m. Patrick A. Edwards, Oct. 29, 1981 (div. June 1990). Student, U. Nev., Las Vegas, 1974-77. Receptionist, clk. Nationwide Fin., Las Vegas, 1969-70; dep. clk. US Bankruptcy Ct. Dist. Nev., Las Vegas, 1970-74, chief dep. clk., 1974-75, chief clk., 1975-79, clk. ct., 1979—2007. Mem. bankruptcy work measurement subcom. of com. adminstrn. bankruptcy sys. Jud. Conf. US, 1989-91; mem. tng. edn. com. US Bankruptcy Cts. Adminstrv. Office US Cts., 1990-91; mem. Bankruptcy Work Measurement subcom. Clerk's adv. com. Adminstrv. Office US Cts., 1992-93, local rules subcom. Dist. Nev., 1991-2007. Mem. Space Facilities Ad Hoc Task Force Personnel Adminstrv. Office US Cts., 1994-95, 9th Cir. Task Force Race, Religious, Ethnic Fairness, 1994-97; mem. bd. dirs. Clark County, Nev. chpt. ARC, 1994-98; chair 9th cir. Bankruptcy Clerks Liaison Com., 2004-05. Mem.: Nat. Conf. Bankruptcy Clks. Republican. Avocations: reading, pottery, gardening.

GRAY, PAUL RUSSELL, academic administrator, electrical engineering educator; b. Jonesboro, Ark., Dec. 8, 1942; married; 2 children. BS in Elec. Engring., U. Ariz., 1963, MS in Elec. Engring., 1965, PhD in Elec. Engring., 1969. Vis. lectr. dept. elec. engring. and computer sci. U. Calif., Berkeley, 1971—72, asst. prof., 1972—74, assoc. prof., 1974—78, prof., 1978—, acting dir. Electronics Rsch. Lab., 1985—86, vice chmn. EECS Dept. for Computer Resources, 1988—90, chmn. Dept. Electrical Engring. and Computer Scis., 1990—93, dean Coll. Engring., 1996-2000, Roy W. Carson chair in engring., 1996, exec. vice chancellor, provost, 2000—06, Andrew S. Grove chair in electrical engring., 2000—. Mem. tech. staff Semiconductor Div. Fairchild Camera and Instrument Corp., 1969—71; project mgr. Telecommunications Filter Prog., Intel Corp., 1977—78; dir. CMOS Product Develop. Microlinear Corp., 1984—85. Coauthor: Analysis and Design of Analog Integrated Circuits; contbr. articles to profl. jours. Recipient Solid-State Circuits award IEEE, 1994. Fellow IEEE (Baker prize 1980, Morris N. Liebmann Meml. award 1983, Robert N. Noyce medal, 2008); mem. NAE (councillor 2008-). Office: U Calif Office Chancellor 200 California Hall Berkeley CA 94720-1502 Office Phone: 510-642-1961, 510-642-5179. Office Fax: 510-643-5499. E-mail: pgray@berkeley.edu.

GRAY, PHILIP HOWARD, former psychologist, writer, educator; b. Cape Rosier, Maine, July 4, 1926; s. Asa and Bernice (Lawrence) G.; m. Iris McKinney, Dec. 31, 1954; children: Cindelyn Gray Eberts, Howard. MA, U. Chgo., 1958; PhD, U. Wash., 1960. Asst. prof. dept. psychology Mont. State U., Bozeman, 1960—65, assoc. prof., 1965—75, prof., 1975—92; ret., 1992. Vis. prof. U. Man., Winnipeg, Can., 1968-70, U. N.H., 1965, U. Mont., 1967, 74, Tufts U., 1968, U. Conn., 1971; pres. Mont. Psychol. Assn., 1968-70 (helped write Mont. licensing law for psychologists); chmn. Mont. Bd. Psychologist Examiners, 1972-74; spkr. sci. and geneal. meetings on ancestry of U.S. presidents; presenter, instr. grad. course on serial killers and the psychopathology of murder; founder Badger Press of Mont., 1998. Organizer folk art exhbns. Mont. and Maine, 1972-79; author: The Comparative Analysis of Behavior, 1966, (with F.L. Ruch and N. Warren) Working with Psychology, 1963, A Directory of Eskimo Artists in Sculpture and Prints, 1974, The Science That Lost Its Mind, 1985, Penobscot Pioneers vol. 1, 1992, vol. 2, 1992, vol. 3, 1993, vol. 4, 1994, vol. 5, 1995, vol. 6, 1996, Mean Streets and Dark Deeds: The He-Man's Guide to Mysteries, 1998, Ghoulies and Ghosties and Long-leggety Beasties: Imprinting Theory Linking Serial Killers, Child Assassins, Molesters, Homosexuality, Feminism and Day Care, 1998, Egoteria of a Psychologist: Poetry, Letters, Memos from Nether Montana, 2001, Classic Inuit Artists: A Critique and Directory of 500 Eminent Artists in Sculpture and Prints, 2006; contbr. numerous articles on behavior to psychol. jours.; contbr. poetry to lit. jours; pub. military articles. With US Army, 1944—46. Decorated EAME medal Ctrl. Europe and Rhineland Campaigns, Victory medal WWII, Presdl. Unit citation, Ardennes-Alsace Army Occupation medal, Meritorious Unit Commendation; recipient numerous rsch. grants. Fellow: APA, AAAS, Internat. Soc. Rsch. on Aggression, Am. Psychol. Soc.; mem.: SAR (trustee 1989, v.p. Sourdough chpt. 1990, pres. 1991—2006, v.p. gen. intermountain dist. 1997—98, pres. state soc. 1998—99, trustee 2001—, v.p. gen. intermountain dist. 2003—04, 2007—08), NRA (life), Order of the Crown of Charlemagne, Gallatin County Geneal. Soc. (charter, pres. 1991—93), Nat. Geneal. Soc., 78th Divsn. Vets. Assn. (life), Vets. of the Battle of the Bulge WWII (life), New Eng. Hist. Geneal. Soc., Deer Isle-Stonington Hist. Soc., Flagon and Trencher, Order Descs. Colonial Physicians and Chirugiens, Internat. Soc. Human Ethology, Descs. Illegitimate Sons and Daus. of Kings of Britain, Bozeman Rifle and Pistol Club. Republican. Avocations: collecting folk art, first and signed editions of novels, pistol shooting. Home: 1207 S Black Ave Bozeman MT 59715-5633 E-mail: phgray1@mac.com.

GRAY, RICHARD MOSS, retired college president; b. Washington, Jan. 25, 1924; s. Wilbur Leslie and Betty Marie (Grey) G.; m. Catherine Claire Hammond, Oct. 17, 1943; children: Janice Lynn Gray Armstrong, Nancy Hammond Gray Schultz. BA, Bucknell U., 1942; MDiv summa cum laude, San Francisco Theol. Sem., 1961; PhD, U. Calif., Berkeley, 1972; doctorate degree (hon.), World Coll. West, 1988. Writer, creative dir. N.W. Ayer & Son, Phila., 1942-58; univ. pastor Portland State U., Oreg., 1961-68; founder, pres. World Coll. West, Petaluma, Calif., 1973-88, pres. emeritus, 1988—. Bd. dirs. World Centre, San Francisco, Life Plan Ctr.; founder Presidio World Coll., 1992—. Author poetry Advent, 1989. Bd. dirs. Citizens Found. Marin, San Rafael, Calif., 1988—, Marin Ednl. Found.; ruling elder Presbyn. Ch. U.S.A. Named Disting. Alumnus of Yr. San Francisco Theol. Sem., 1988, Marin Citizen of Yr. Citizens Found., 1988; recipient Svc. to Humanity award Bucknell U., 1992. Mem. Phi Beta Kappa. Avocations: song-writing, poetry.

GRAY, ROBERT MOLTEN, electrical engineering educator; b. San Diego, Nov. 1, 1943; s. Augustine Heard and Elizabeth DuBois (Jordan) G.; m. Arlene Frances Ericson; children: Timothy M., Lori A. BSEE, MSEE, MIT, 1966; PhD in Elec. Engring., U. So. Calif., LA, 1969. Elec. engr. US Naval Ordnance Lab., White Oak, Md., 1963-65, Jet Propulsion Lab., Pasadena, Calif., summers 1966, 67; lectr. U. So. Calif., 1969; asst. prof. elec. engring. Stanford U., 1969-75, assoc. prof., 1975-80, prof., 1980—, dir. Info. Systems Lab., 1984-87, vice chair dept. elec. engring., 1993—2005, Lucent Technologies prof. engring., 2004—. Author: Probability, Random Processes and Ergodic Properties, 1988, Source Coding Theory, 1990, Entropy and Information Theory, 1990; co-author: Random Processes, 1986, Vector Quantization and Signal Compression, 1992, Fourier Transforms, 1995; contbr. articles to profl. jours., chtps. to books. Fireman La Honda Vol. Fire Brigade, Calif., 1970-80, pres., 1971-72; coach Am. Youth Soccer Orgn., La Honda, 1971-78, commr., 1976-78. Japan Soc. for Promotion Sci. fellow, 1981, Guggenheim fellow, 1982, NATO/CNR fellow, 1990. Fellow IEEE (Centennial medal 1984, 3rd Millennium medal 2000, Jack S. Kilby Signal Processing medal, 2008), Inst. Math. Stats.; mem. Info. Theory Soc. IEEE (assoc. editor Trans. 1977-80, editor-in-chief 1980-83, paper prize 1976, Golden Jubilee award for technol. achievement 1998), Signal Processing Soc. IEEE (Sr. award 1983, Soc. award 1993, prog. co-chmn. 1997 Internat. Conf. on Image Processing, Tech. Achievement award 1998, Presdl. Mentoring award 2002, Disting. Alumni award U. SC 2003, Meritorious Svc. award 2006), NAE. Avocations: maritime and gilded age history, hiking, computers. Office: Stanford U Dept Elec Engring 161 Packard Bldg 350 Serra Mall Stanford CA 94305-9505 Office Phone: 650-723-4001. Office Fax: 650-723-8473. E-mail: rmgray@stanford.edu.

GRAY, THOMAS STEPHEN, writer; b. Burbank, Calif., Aug. 22, 1950; s. Thomas Edgar and Lily Irene (Ax) G.; m. Barbara Ellen Bronson, Aug. 27, 1977; children: Jonathan Thomas, Katherine Marie. BA, Stanford U., 1972; MA in English, UCLA, 1976. Tchg. assoc. UCLA, 1976-77; reporter LA Daily News, 1977-79, editl. writer, 1979-84, editl. page editor, 1984-95; sr. editor Investor's Bus. Daily, LA, 1995-98; v.p. and account group mgr. Investor Rels. Internat., 2003—; co-prin. Pontifex Mktg. and Comm., 2008—. Author: Teach Yourself Investing Online, 1999, Investing Online for Dummies-Quick Reference, 2000, Online Investing Bible, 2001; contbg. writer: Convergence: Mag. of Sci. and Engring., UC Santa Barbara. Recipient 1st Place award Editl. Writing Greater LA Press Club, 1988, Inland Daily Press Assn., 1993. Office Phone: 818-889-4799. Business E-Mail: tsgray@pontfexmarketing.com. E-mail: tsgray@sbcglobal.net.

GRAY, WILLIAM MASON, meteorologist, atmospheric science educator; b. Detroit, Oct. 9, 1929; BA, George Washington U., 1952; MS, U. Chgo., 1959, PhD, 1964. Rsch. asst. meteorologist U. Chgo., 1957-61; asst. meteorologist Colo. State U., Ft. Collins, 1961-64, from asst. to assoc. prof., 1964-74, prof. atmospheric scis., 1974—, sci. team prin. investigator. NSF Rsch. grantee, 1965-66, 70-71; Jule G. Charney award Am. Meteorol. Assn., 1994, Banner I. Miller award, 1994, Jack E. Cermak award, 1992, Neil Frank award Nat. Hurricane Conf., 1995, Man of Sci. award Colo. chpt. Achievement Reward Coll., 1995; named Person of Week ABC TV, 1995. Mem. Am. Meteorol. Assn. (Jule G. Charney Award, 1994). Office: Colo State U Dept Atmospheric Scis Fort Collins CO 80523-0001

GRAYBILL, DAVID WESLEY, chamber of commerce executive; b. Council Bluffs, Iowa, Apr. 8, 1949; s. John Donald and Dorothy Lorraine (King) G.; m. Kortney Loraine Steinbeck, Aug. 17, 1974; 1 child, Darcy Lorraine. BA in Journalism, U. Iowa, 1971; MA in Mgmt. and Leadership Studies, City U., 1999. Cert. econ. developer; cert. chamber exec. Adminstrv. asst. Iowa City C. of C., 1972-74; exec. v.p. Brighton (Colo.) C. of C., 1974-77; pres. Fremont (Nebr.) C. of C., 1977-83; pres., chief exec. officer Tacoma-Pierce County C. of C., 1983—. Pres. Nebr. C. of C. Execs., 1981-82; treas. NE Nebr. Econ. Devel. Dist., 1980-83. Presiding elder U. Pl. (Wash.) Cmty. of Christ; charter mem. Gov.'s Small Bus. Improvement Com., Wash., 1984—86. Recipient Barr Quality Mentor award, U. of Puget Sound, 2001, Leadership award, U. Wash., 2002. Mem. Am. Econ. Devel. Coun. (bd. dirs. 1985-87), Am. C. of C. (bd. dirs. 1990-94), Wash. C. of C. Execs. (pres. 1988-89, bd. dirs. 1988-90, 98-2002), Rotary (bd. dirs. Tacoma 1985-87). Office: Tacoma Pierce County C of C PO Box 1933 Tacoma WA 98401-1933

GRAYSMITH, ROBERT, political cartoonist, author; b. Pensacola, Fla., Sept. 17, 1942; s. Robert Gray and Frances Jane (Scott) Smith; m. Melanie Krakower, Oct. 15, 1975 (div. Sept. 1980); children: David Martin, Aaron Vincent, Margot Alexandra. BA, Calif. Coll. Arts and Crafts, 1965. Polit. cartoonist Oakland (Calif.) Tribune, 1964—65, Stockton (Calif.) Record, 1965—68, San Francisco Chronicle, 1968—83; author: Zodiac, 1986, Trailside, 1986, The Sleeping Lady, 1990, The Murder of Bob Crane, 1993, Unabomber: A Desire to Kill, 1997, The Bell-Tower, A True Detective Story of Gas-Lit San Francisco, 1999, Ghost Fleet, 1999, Zodiac Unmasked, 2002, Amerithrax: The Hunt for the Anthrax Killer, 2003, The Laughing Gorilla, 2008, (films) Auto-Focus, 2002, Zodiac, 2006; cons. Zodiac, Phoenix Pictures, 2004; illustrator: I Didn't Know What to Get You, 1993. Recipient 2d place Fgn. Press Awards 1973, World Population Contest 1976. Democrat. Presbyterian. Office: San Francisco Chronicle 901 Mission St San Francisco CA 94103-2905 Office Phone: 415-731-4069. Personal E-mail: robert_graysmith@yahoo.com.

GRAZER, BRIAN, film company executive; b. LA, July 12, 1951; m. Gigi Levangie, 1997 (separated); children: Patrick, Thomas. Grad., U. So. Calif., 1974. Co-founder, co-chair Imagine Films Entertainment, 1986—. Prodr.: (films) Night Shift, 1982, Splash, 1984, Real Genius, 1985, (with George Folsey Jr.) Spies Like Us, 1985, (with James Keach) Armed & Dangerous, 1986, (with David Valdes) Like Father, Like Son, 1987, Parenthood, 1989, (with Jim Abrahams) Cry Baby, 1990, (with Ivan Reitman) Kindergarten Cop, 1990, (with Ron Howard) Closet Land, 1991, (with Nicholas Clainos & Mario Kassar) The Doors, 1991, (with Raffaella DeLaurentiis) Backdraft, 1991, My Girl, 1991, (with Ron Howard) Far and Away, 1992, (with Warrington Hudlin) Boomerang, 1992, Housesitter, 1992, (with Sean Daniel) CB4, 1993, For Love or Money, 1993, (with Frederick Zollo) The Paper, 1994, My Girl 2, 1994, Greedy, 1994, The Cowboy Way, 1994, (with Ron Howard) Apollo 13, 1995 (Daryl F. Zanuck Motion Picture Prodr. of Yr. award, Academy Award nomination for best picture, 1996), Sgt. Bilko, 1996, Ransom, 1996, Bowfinger, 1999, Beyond the Mat, 1999, Curious George, 2000, Nutty Professor II: The Klumps, 2000, How the Grinch Stole Christmas, 2000, (with Ron Howard) A Beautiful Mind, 2001 (Academy Award, Best Picture, 2002), Undercover Brother, 2002, Blue Crush, 2002, 8 Mile, 2002, Intolerable Cruelty, 2003, The Cat in the Hat, 2003, The Missing, 2003, Friday Night Lights, 2004, Inside Deep Throat, 2005, Cinderella Man, 2005, Flightplan, 2005, Fun with Dick and Jane, 2005, Inside Man, 2006, The Da Vinci Code, 2006, American Gangster, 2007, Kids in America, 2008; (TV miniseries) From the Earth to the Moon, 1998 (Emmy Award, Outstanding Miniseries); exec. prodr.: (TV series) The PJs, 1999, Wonderland, 2000, The Beast, 2001, 24, 2001—, Miss Match, 2003—05, Arrested Development, 2003—05 (Emmy Award, Outstanding Comedy Series, 2004), The Big House, 2004, The Inside, 2005, Treasure Hunters, 2006, Shark, 2006—07, Bra Boys, 2007, Friday Night Lights, 2007; prodr.: (Broadway plays) Cry-Baby, 2008. Recipient David O. Selznick Lifetime Achievement award, Prodrs. Guild America, 2001, Milestone award, 2009, Lifetime Achievement award, ShoWest, 2003; named one of 50 Most Powerful People in Hollywood, Premiere mag., 2004—06, The World's Most Influential People, TIME mag., 2007, 100 Most Powerful Celebrities, Forbes-.com, 2007, 50 Smartest People in Hollywood, Entertainment Weekly, 2007. Office: Imagine Films Entertainment 9465 Wilshire Blvd Fl 7 Beverly Hills CA 90212-2606

GREAVER, HARRY, artist; b. LA, Oct. 30, 1929; s. Harry Jones and Lucy Catherine (Coons) G.; m. Hanne Synnestvedt Nielsen, Nov. 30, 1955; children: Peter, Paul, Lotte. BFA, U. Kans., Lawrence, 1951, MFA, 1952. Assoc. prof. art U. Maine, Orono, 1955—66; exec. dir. Kalamazoo Inst. Arts, 1966—78; dir. Greaver Gallery, Cannon Beach, Oreg., 1978—. Mem. visual com. Mich. Coun. Arts, 1976-78. One-man exhbns. include Baker U., Baldwin, Kans., 1955, U. Maine, Orono, 1958, 59, Pacific U., 1985; group exhbns. include U. Utah Mus. Fine Arts, 1972-73, Purdue U., 1977, Drawings, USA, St. Paul, 1963, San Diego Mus., 1971, Rathbun Gallery, Portland, Oreg., 1988; 10-yr. print retrospective Cannon Beach Arts Assn., 1989, 20-yr. retrospective, 1998, 25th and 30th Anniversary exhibit., 2008. Mem. adv. bd. Haystack Ctr. for the Arts, Cannon Beach, 1988-91. Recipient Purchase award Nat. Endowment Arts, 1971; grantee U. Maine, 1962-64. Address: PO Box 120 Cannon Beach OR 97110-0120

GREAVES, JAMES LOUIS, art conservator; b. Middletown, Conn., Jan. 25, 1943; s. Wellington North and Mabel (Frazer) G.; divorced; 1 child, Stephen Frazer. BS in Biology, Coll. William and Mary, 1965; MA in Art History, NYU; Diploma in Art Conservation, Inst. Fine Arts, 1970. Conservation intern Los Angeles County Mus., 1968-70, conservator, 1970, asst. head conservator, 1977-79, acting head conservator, 1979-81, sr. paintings conservator, 1981-85; owner, cons. Conservation Svcs., Santa Monica, Calif., 1985—. Chief conservator Detroit Inst. Arts, 1970-77; cons. conservator Art Gallery of Huntington Library, San Marino, Calif., 1979-91; part-time instr. art conservation for sr. and grad. level art historians, UCLA and Calif. State U., Fullerton, 1979-83. Fellow Internat. Inst. Conservation, Am. Inst. Conservation; mem. Western Assn. Art Conservators (past pres.).

GREAVES, ROGER F., health and medical products executive; b. 1937; BA, Calif. State U., Long Beach, 1962. With Allstate Ins. Co., Chgo. and Pasadena, Calif., 1962-68; various positions, then v.p. human resources Blue Cross So. Calif., 1968-82; pres., CEO Health Net, Inc., Woodland Hills, Calif., 1982—91, chmn. bd., 1989—; co-chmn bd., co-pres., co-CEO Health Systems Internat., Woodland Hills, 1991-95, non-exec. bd. dir., 1996—2004, non-exec. chmn., 2004—. Mem. Calif. Wellness Found. (bd. dirs.). Office: Health Net Life Insurance Co 21281 Burbank Blvd Woodland Hills CA 91367-6607

GREBER, ROBERT MARTIN, retired financial investments executive; b. Phila., Mar. 15, 1938; s. Joseph and Golda (Rubin) G.; m. Judith Ann Pearlstein, Dec. 23, 1962; children: Matthew, Jonathan. BS in Fin., Temple U., 1962; grad., Sch. Mgmt. and Strategic Studies, 1982-84. Account exec. Merrill Lynch, Phila., 1962-68; portfolio mgr. v.p. Afuture Funds Inc., Lima, Pa., 1968-70; instl. account exec. Merrill Lynch, Phila., 1970-75, officer, mgr.-v.p. Los Angeles, 1975-79; chief fin. officer Lucasfilm Ltd., Los Angeles, 1979-80, pres., CEO San Rafael, Calif., 1980-84, Diagnostic Networks, Inc., San Francisco, 1984-87; ptnr. Leon A. Farley Assocs., San Francisco, 1988-90; pres., COO, Pacific Stock Exch., San Francisco, 1990-95, chmn., CEO, 1996-99; ret., 1999. Bd. dirs. Bay View Capital Group. Bd. dirs. KQED Pub. Broadcasting Sys., San Francisco, 1983, chmn. bd., 1988; bd. dirs. Film Inst. No. Calif., Marin Symphony Orch., 1981-83, Sonic Solutions, 1993—; trustee Western Behavior Scis. Inst., La JOlla, 1982-89; vice chmn. Assn. Am. Pub. TV, 1992-94; trustee Beryl Buck Inst. for Edn., 1990-93. With Army NG, 1959-60.

GRECO, JOSEPH A., lawyer; b. Sacramento, May 12, 1957; s. Joseph A. Greco Sr. and Shirley M. Greco; m. Roslyn M. Moschan, Jan. 24, 1981; children: Jason A., Justin A. AB magna cum laude, Dartmouth Coll., 1979; JD, Stanford Law Sch., 1982. Bar: Calif. 1982. Assoc. Fenwick, Davis & West, Palo Alto, Calif., 1982—86, Skjerven, Morrill, MacPherson, Franklin & Friel, San Jose, Calif., 1986—89, ptnr., 1989—97; dir. Howard, Rice, Nemerovski, Canady, Falk & Rabkin, Palo Alto, 1997—2001; of counsel Skjerven Morrill LLP, San Jose, 2001—03; spl. counsel Townsend and Townsend and Crew LLP, Palo Alto, 2003—05, ptnr., 2006—. Author: (essay) The California Droit de Suite Law (Nathan Burkan Meml. Competition, Stanford Law Sch., First Prize award, 1982). Recipient Order of the Coif award, Stanford Law Sch., 1982, Rufus Choate scholar, Dartmouth Coll., 1976—79, Northern Calif. Super Lawyer award, Law & Politics Mag., 2005—07, 2009. Master: San Francisco Bay Area Intellectual Property Inn Ct.; mem.: ABA, Santa Clara County Bar Assn., Fed. Circuit Bar Assn., Phi Beta Kappa. Home: 1031 Estrellita Way Los Altos CA 94022 Office: Townsend and Townsend and Crew LLP 379 Lytton Ave Palo Alto CA 94301 Office Fax: 650-326-2422. Personal E-mail: jgreco57@yahoo.com. Business E-Mail: jagreco@townsend.com.

GREELY, HENRY T. (HANK), law educator; b. 1952; AB in Polit. Sci., Stanford U., 1974; JD, Yale U., 1977. Law clk. to Hon. John Minor Wisdom US Ct. Appeals 5th Cir., 1977—78; law clk. to Hon. Potter Stewart US Supreme Ct., 1978—79; spl. asst. to gen. counsel Deanne C. Siemer US Dept. Def., 1979; staff asst. to Sec. Energy Charles W. Duncan, Jr., 1979—81; assoc. Tuttle & Taylor, LA, 1981—84, ptnr., 1984—85; assoc. prof. Stanford Law Sch., 1985—92, prof., 1992—, C. Wendell and Edith M. Carlsmith prof. law, 2002—04, Deane F. and Kate Edelman Johnson prof. law, 2004—; dir. Stanford Program in Law, Sci. & Tech., 2000—01; co-dir. Stanford Program on Genomics, Ethics, and Soc., 1995—2000; dir. Stanford Ctr. for Law and Biosciences, Stanford Program on Stem Cells & Soc., 2005—. Mem. Calif. Adv. Com. on Human Cloning, 1999—, Calif. Adv. Com. on Human Stem Cell Rsch., 2005—. Office: Stanford Law Sch Crown Quadrangle 559 Nathan Abbott Way Stanford CA 94305-8610 Business E-Mail: hgreely@stanford.edu.

GREEN, CAROL H., consultant, retired lawyer, journalist, educator; b. Seattle, Feb. 18, 1944; BA in History/Journalism summa cum laude, La. Tech. U., 1965; MSL, Yale U., 1977; JD, U. Denver, 1979. Reporter Shreveport (La.) Times, 1965-66, Guam Daily News, 1966-67; city editor Pacific Jour., Agana, Guam, 1967-68, reporter, editl. writer, 1968-76, legal affairs reporter, 1977-79; asst. editor editl. page Denver Post, 1979-81, house counsel, 1980-83, labor rels. mgr., 1981-83; assoc. Holme Roberts & Owen, 1983-85; v.p. human resources and legal affairs Denver Post, 1985-87, mgr. circulation, 1988-90; gen. mgr. Distbn. Systems Am., Inc., 1990-92; dir. labor rels. Newsday, 1992-95, dir. comm. and labor rels., 1995—96; v.p. Weber Mgmt. Cons., 1996—98; v.p. human resources and labor rels. Denver Post, 1998—2000; v.p. human resources, labor rels. Denver Newspaper Agy., 2001—06, sr. v.p., labor rels. and legal affairs, 2006—08, labour rels. cons., 2009—. Vice chair bd. Colo. Bus. Health Forum, 1985; speaker for USIA, India, Egypt; mem. Mailers Tech. Adv. Com. to Postmaster Gen., 1991-92. Recipient McWilliams award for juvenile justice, Denver, 1971, award for interpretive reporting Denver Newspaper Guild, 1979. Mem.: ABA, Soc. Human Resources Mgmt., Colo. and Internat. Women's Forum, Denver Bar Assn. (co-chair jud. selection and benefits com. 1982—85, 2nd v.p. 1986), Newspaper Assn. Am. (mem. human resources and labor rels. com.), Colo. Bar Assn. (bd. govs. 1985—87, chair BAR-press com. 1980), Leadership Denver. Episcopalian.

GREEN, CORDELL, computer scientist, educator; b. Ft. Worth, Dec. 26, 1941; s. William and Rebecca (Glickman) Green; m. Christine Louise Ochs, June 21, 1979; children: Jeffrey Adam, Laura Leah. BSBA, Rice U., 1964, MS, 1965; PhD, Stanford U., 1969. Rsch. mathematician Artificial Intelligence Group Stanford Rsch. Inst., 1966—69; r & d program mgr. Info. Processing Techniques Office, ARPA, 1970—71; asst. prof. computer sci. Stanford U., 1971—78; cons. prof. computer sci., 1979—; chief scientist computer sci. dept. Sys. Control Inc., Palo Alto, Calif., 1979—81; dir., chief scientist Kestrel Inst., 1981—; cons. in field. Rschr. in field of computer sci. Contbr. articles to profl. jours.; mem. editl. bd. Jour. Cognitive Sci., 1977—80. Serve to capt. US Army, 1969—71. Air Force Office Sci. Rsch. grantee, 1978—83, NSF grantee, 1980—83, Rome Air Devel. Ctr. grantee, 1982—83. Mem.: Advanced Rsch. Projects Agy. (grantee 1973—83), Assn. for Computing Machinery (artificial intelligence area editor jour. 1972—79). Office: 1801 Page Mill Rd Palo Alto CA 94304-1216

GREEN, DAVID, nonprofit organization administrator; b. 1956; m. Tanya Shaffer; 1 child, Tavi. BA, U. Mich., 1978, MPH, 1982. With Seva Found. Aravind Eye Hosp., Madurai, India, 1983—2000, founder Aurolab, 1992; founder, CEO Project Impact, Inc., 2000—. Named MacArthur Fellow, John D. and Catherine T. MacArthur Found., 2004, Ashoka Fellow. Achievements include first to establish a non-profit manufacturing facility in a developing country which produces, manufactures and distributes affordable medical technologies. Office: Project Impact 1782 Fifth St Berkeley CA 94710 Office Phone: 510-981-1103. Office Fax: 313-668-6861.

GREEN, DAVID EDWARD, retired librarian, priest, translator; b. Adrian, Mich., June 22, 1937; s. Edward Robert Alexander and Fannie Amelia (Nadler) G.; m. Sharon Weiner, June 1, 1961; children: Alexis Ann, Philip DeWitt. BA, Harvard U., 1960; BD, Ch. Div. Sch. of Pacific, Berkeley, Calif., 1963; MLS, U. Calif., Berkeley, 1970. Ordained priest Episc. Ch., 1964. Assoc. librarian Grad. Theol. Union, Berkeley, 1970-82; libr. dir. Gen. Theol. Sem., NYC, 1982—2002. Translator many German theol. works. Mem. Am. Theol. Libr. Assn., N.Y. Area Theol. Libr. Assn., Beta Phi Mu. Avocation: English country dancing. Office: 6103 Harwood Ave Oakland CA 94618 E-mail: degreen@post.harvard.edu.

GREEN, DOLORES L., medical association administrator; Exec. dir. Riverside County Med. Assn., Calif., 1983—. CFO Calif. Found. Med. Care; CEO Inland Empire Found. Med. Care. Recipient Med. Exec. Achievement award, AMA, 2005. Office: Riverside County Med Assn 3993 Jurupa Ave Riverside CA 92506 Office Phone: 951-686-9049. Office Fax: 951-686-1692. Business E-Mail: dgreen@rcmanet.org.

GREEN, GWYN M., state legislator; b. New Orleans, Nov. 21; d. Edgar Joseph and Gwynith (Anderson) Druilhet; m. Daniel Arthur Green, Dec. 27, 1961; children: Laura, Kevin, Mark, Ben. BA in Social Sci., St. Mary's Coll., 1961; MSW with cert. in Gerontology, Denver U., 1984. Lic. clin. social worker. Intern, geriatric team Jefferson County Mental Health, Lakwood, Colo., 1983-84; social worker Rx Home Health Agy., Lakwood, 1984; adult foster care case worker Adams County Dept. Social Svcs., Commerce City, Colo., 1984-89; med. social worker Western Dialysis Ctr., Lakewood; gerontol. social worker, owner Svc. Options for Srs., Lakewood; councilwoman Golden City Coun., Colo.; mem. Dist. 23 Colo. House of Reps., Denver, 2004—. Mem. Nat. Assn. Social Workers. Democrat. Avocations: creative writing, painting, hiking, reading. Office: Colo State Capitol 200 E Colfax Denver CO 80203 Office Phone: 303-866-2951. Business E-Mail: gwynithgreen@yahoo.com.*

GREEN, HARRY WESTERN, II, geology and geophysics educator; s. Harry Buetel and Mabel (Hendrickson) G.; children from previous marriage: Mark, Stephen, Carolyn, Jennifer; m. Maria Manuela Marques Martins, May 15, 1975; children: Alice, Miguel, Maria. AB in Geology with honors, UCLA, 1963, MS in Geology and

Geophysics, 1967, PhD in Geology and Geophysics with distinction, 1968. Postdoctoral rsch. assoc. materials sci. Case Western Res. U., Cleve., 1968-70; asst. prof. geology U. Calif., Davis, 1970-74, assoc. prof., 1974-80, prof., 1980-92, chmn. dept., 1984-88, prof. geology and geophysics Riverside, 1993-99, disting. prof. geology and geophysics, 1999—, dir. Inst. Geophysics and Planetary Physics, 1993-95, 2001, dir. analytical electron microscopy facility, 1994—2000, vice chancellor for rsch., 1995-2000, dir. ctrl. facility advanced microscopy and microanalysis, 2000—, acting chair dept. earth sci., 2005, vice chair, 2005—. Exch. scientist U. Nantes, France, 1973, vis. prof., 1978-79; vis. prof. Monash U., Melbourne, Australia, 1984; specialist advisor World Bank Program, China U. of Geoscis., Wuhan, 1988; adj. sr. rsch. scientist Lamont-Doherty Earth Obs., Columbia U., 1989-95, Vetlesen vis. prof., 1991-92; expert advisor geophysics rev. panel NSF, 1991-94; co-founder Gordon Conf. on Rock Deformation, 1995, chmn. 2d conf., 1997; hon. faculty China U. Geoscis., Wuhan, 1998—; vis. scientist Carnegie Inst. Washington, 2000—, Abelson lectr., 2000, vis. rev. com., 2004; faculty rsch. lectr. U. Calif., Riverside, 2002-03; mem. facilities com. Consortium for Materials Properties Rsch. in Earth Scis., 2002-04, chmn. exec. com., 2004-07, vis. prof. Stanford U., 2007, Alan Cox fellow, 2007-. Contbr. articles to books and profl. jours. Grantee NSF, 1969—, Dept. Energy, 1988-94. Fellow AAAS, Mineral Soc. Am., Am. Geophys. Union (N.L. Bowen award 1994, Francis Birch lectr. 1995); Cosmos Club (Washington), Sigma Xi. Achievements include discovery and characterization of new mechanisms of deep earthquakes; discovery of exhumation of rocks from hundreds of km depth in subduction zones. Office: U Calif Earth Scis 900 University Ave Riverside CA 92521 Office Phone: 951-827-4505. Business E-Mail: harry.green@ucr.edu.

GREEN, JONATHAN WILLIAM, museum director, educator, artist, writer; b. Troy, NY, Sept. 26, 1939; s. Alan Singer and Frances (Katz) G.; m. Louise Lockshin, Sept. 16, 1962 (div. 1985); children: Raphael, Benjamin; m. Wendy Hughes Brown, Aug. 12, 1988. Student, MIT, 1958-60, Hebrew U., 1960-61; BA, Brandeis U., 1963, postgrad., 1964-67; MA, Harvard U., 1967. Photographer Jonathan Green, Photography, Boston, 1966-76, Ezra Stoller Assocs., Mamaroneck, N.Y., 1967-68; prof. MIT, Cambridge, Mass., 1968-76, dir. Creative Photography Lab, 1974-76; editor Aperture Books and Periodical, NYC, 1972-76; prof. Ohio State U., Columbus, 1976-90; dir. Univ. Gallery Fine Arts, Columbus, 1981-90; founding dir. Wexner Ctr. for the Arts, Columbus, 1981-90; dir. Calif. Mus. Photography U. Calif., Riverside, 1990—, exec. dir. ARTSblock, 2007—, prof., 1990—. Cons. Nat. Endowment for Arts, Washington, 1975-76, 85, 88, 94, Harry N. Abrams, Pubs., N.Y.C., 1982-84, Oxford U. Press, N.Y.C., 1977-82, Polaroid Corp., Cambridge, 1976; co-founder Visible Lang. Workshop, MIT Media Lab., 1973. Author: American Photography, 1984 (Nikon Book of Yr. award 1984, Benjamin Citation 1986), The Snapshot, 1974 (N.Y. Type Dirs. Club award 1974), Camera Work: A Critical Anthology, 1973 (Best Art Book award 1973), Continuous Replay: The Photographs of Arnie Zane, 1999 (Am. Assn.'s Mus.'s Publ. award 1999); editor, essayist Re-framing History in Jean Ruiter Photo Works, 1985-1995, 1996, The Garden of Earthly Delights: Photographs by Edward Weston and Robert Mapplethorpe, 1995, New Photographs by Pedro Meyer: Truths & Fictions, An Interactive CD-ROM, 1993, 5 Celebrations of Leslie J. Payne in Leslie Payne: Visions of Flight, 1991, Algorithms for Discovery, 1989, Pink Noise: Three Conversations concerning a Collaborative acoustic Installation with Philip Glass, Richard Serra, Kurt Munacsi, 1987, Rudolf Baranik Elegies: Sleep Napalm Night Sky, 1987, Straight Shooting in America, 1985, James Friedman: Rephotographing the History of the World in James Friedman, Color Photographs 1979-1982, 1982, Aperture in the 50's: The Word and the Way, in Afterimage, 1979, others; represented in permanent collections Mus. Fine Arts, Boston, Mus. Fine Art, Houston, Cleve. Mus. Art, Va. Mus. Fine Art, Richmond, Princeton U. Art Mus., Bell System Collection, Moderna Museet, Stockholm, Ctr. for Creative Photography, Tucson, De Saisset Art Gallery and Mus., Internat. Ctr. Photography, N.Y.C., MIT, Mpls. Inst. Arts; photographs pub.: American Images: New Work by Twenty Contemporary Photographers, 1979, Aperture, 1972, 73, 74, 25 Years of Record Houses, 1981, Architectural Record, Architecture and Urbanism, Progressive Architecture, A Field Guide to Modern American Architecture. Danforth fellow, 1963-67, NEA Photographer fellow, 1978, AT & T fellow, 1979. Office: UCR ARTSblock Downtown Hist Pedestrian Mall 3824 Main St Riverside CA 92501-3624 Office Phone: 951-827-5191. Office Fax: 951-827-4797. E-mail: jonathan.green@ucr.edu.

GREEN, JOSHUA, III, foundation administrator, retired bank executive; b. Seattle, June 30, 1936; s. Joshua, Jr. and Elaine (Brygger) G.; m. Pamela K. Pemberton, Nov. 1, 1974; children: Joshua IV, Jennifer Elaine, Paige Courtney. BA in English, Harvard U., 1958. With Peoples Nat. Bank Wash., Seattle, 1960-88, exec. v.p., 1972-75, pres., 1975—77, CEO, 1977-78, chmn. bd., 1979-88, US Bank Washington (merger PeoplesBank and Old Nat. Bank), 1988-96; chmn. Joshua Green Corp., Seattle, 1996—. Bd. dirs., chmn., CEO Far Bank Enterprises, Inc., Fourth Ave. Investments Co., Pacific Sci. Ctr., Joshua Green Corp., Safeco, Port Blakely Tree Farms, Rio Products Internat., Inc., Sage Mfg., U. Wash. Bus. Sch., U. Wash. Found., Va. Mason Hosp. Found., Va. Mason Hosp. Rsch.; dir. Pacific Sci. Ctr., Va. Mason Health Sys. Bd. dirs. Rhododendron Species Found.; trustee Downtown Seattle Assn., ArtsFund (formerly known as Corp. Coun. Arts). Mem. Univ. Club, Rainier Club, Seattle Tennis Club, Wash. Athletic Club. Home: 414 McGilvra Blvd E Seattle WA 98112-2308 Office: PO Box 21829 Seattle WA 98111-3829 also: Joshua Green Corporation PO Box 21829 Seattle WA 98111-3829 Personal E-mail: jiiigreen@aol.com.

GREEN, LYDA, state legislator; b. Livingston, Tex., Oct. 16, 1938; m to Curtis; children: Shelton, Kristie & Bradley. Member, Govs Coun on Disabilities, 91-94; member, Department of Education Special Education Regulations Task Force, 93-94; Alaska State Senator, District N, 1995-2002, vchairwoman, State Affairs Committee, currently, member, Finance & Resources Committees, currently, Alaska State Senate; Alaska State Senator, District G, 2003-.Teacher, West High Sch, 62-63; administration asst, Pan America Petroleum, 63-65; co-owner, Anchorage Racquet Club, 78-88; business owner & educator, The Study, formerly; adjunct instructor, Mat-Su Community Col, 91-93; instructor's asst, Univ Alaska, Anchorage, 91. Defender of Freedom Award, Nat Rifle Association; Legislator of Year, Alaska Farm Bureau, 96; 4-H Legislator Appreciation Award. Soroptimists; Palmer Pioneer Lions; Chamber of Commerce. Republican. Mailing: 600 E Railroad Ave Suite 1 Wasilla AK 99654 Fax: Off: 907-465-3805; Interim: 907-376-3157.

GREEN, MONICA H., history professor; BA, Barnard Coll., 1978; MA, Princeton U., 1981; PhD in History of Sci., Princeton U., NJ. Fellow U. N.C., Chapel Hill; assoc. prof. history Duke U.; prof. history Ariz. State U., Tempe, 2001—. Author: (essays) Women's Helathcare and the Medieval West: Texts and Contexts, 2000; contbr. articles; editor, translator: The Trotula: A Medieval Compendium of Women's Medicine, 2001. Fellow, NEH, Inst. Advanced Study, Princeton U., Nat. Humanities Ctr., John Simon Guggenheim Meml. Found., 2003. Office: Ariz State U Dept History PO Box 872501 Tempe AZ 85287-2501

GREEN, RICH, information technology executive; Mgr. software tools divsn. Sun Microsystems, Inc., Santa Clara, Calif., 1989, v.p., gen. mgr. Solaris products orgn., v.p., gen. mgr. Java orgn., exec. v.p. software, 2006—; exec. v.p. products Cassatt Corp., San Jose, Calif., 2004—06. Office: Sun Microsystems Inc 4150 Network Cir Santa Clara CA 95054 Office Phone: 650-960-1300.

GREEN, RICHARD E., real estate company executive; married; two children. BS in Acctg. and Fin., San Jose State U. With Price Waterhouse & Co., May Ctrs., Inc., 1968-80, exec. v.p.; co-pres. Westfield Group, LA, 1980—. Bd. dirs. UCLA Armand Hammer Mus. of Art and Cultural Ctr. Office: 11601 Wilshire Blvd Fl 12 Los Angeles CA 90025-1770

GREEN, RICHARD FREDERICK, astronomer; b. Omaha, Feb. 13, 1949; m. Joan Auerbach; children: Alexander Simon, Nathaniel Martin. AB in Astronomy magna cum laude, Harvard U., 1971; PhD in Astronomy, Calif. Inst. Tech., 1977. Physics lab instr. Harvard U., Cambridge, 1970-71; NSF trainee Calif. Inst. Tech., Pasadena, 1971-72, grad. teaching asst. in astronomy, 1972-74, grad. rsch. asst. in astronomy, 1974-77, rsch. fellow in astronomy, 1977-79; asst. astronomer Steward Observatory, U. Ariz., Tucson, 1979-83, Kitt Peak Nat. Observatory, Tucson, 1983-85, assoc. astronomer, 1986-90, astronomer, 1990—, dir., 1997—2005; acting dir. Nat. Optical Astronomy Observatories, Tucson, 1992-93, acting dep. dir., 1993-94, dep. dir., 1994-99; dir. Large Binocular Telescope Obs. U. Ariz., Tucson, 2005—. Rsch. asst. Smithsonian Astrophys. Observatory, 1970-71; adj. asst. prof. Steward Observatory, U. Ariz., 1983-85, adj. assoc. astronomer and prof., 1986-90, adj. astronomer, 1990—; mem. users' com. Internat. Ultraviolet Explorer Satellite, NASA, 1979-81, chair proposal rev. panel, 1986-88, 93, final sci. program com., 1993, mem. sci. team Far Ultraviolet Spectroscopic Explorer Satellite, 1981—, Space Telescope Imaging Spectrograph, 1982—, guest observer working group Extreme Ultraviolet Explorer Satellite, 1988-92, chair proposal rev. panel ROSAT Guest Observer Program, 1989, 92, ROSAT Users' Coms., 1990-93, chair HST Cycle 2 Porposal Rev. Panel, mem. time allocation com., 1991, STSDAS users' com., 1991-92, Hubble Space Telescope Program Rev., 1997; mem. panel ultraviolet and optical astronomy from space, astronomy survey com. Nat. Acad. Scis., 1989-90; mem. panel HST and Beyond AURA, 1994-95; mem. proposal rev. panels NSF, 1996-97; instrument scientist Gemini 8-m Telescopes Project, 1991-92; mem. U.S. Gemini sci. adv. com., Gemini (Internat.) sci. com. U.S. Gemini Project Office, 1991-93, acting U.S. Gemini Project scientist, 1992-93, mem. instrument forum, optical instrumentation sci. working group, chair multi-object spectrograph critical design rev., 1997. Nat. Merit scholar; Hon. scholar Harvard U. Mem. AAAS (astronomy divsn. nominating com. 1992, coun. astronomy rep. com. coun. affairs 1995-97), Am. Astronomical Soc., Internat. Astronomical Union, Astronomical Soc. of the Pacific, Phi Beta Kappa. Office: U Ariz Steward Obs PO Box 210065 933 N Cherry Ave Tucson AZ 85721 Office Phone: 520-626-7088.

GREEN, ROBERT LEONARD, hospital management company executive; b. LA, Mar. 20, 1931; s. Leonard H. and Helene (Rains) G.; m. Susan Wolf, June 9, 1957; children— Wendy, Julie BA, Stanford U., 1952, LL.B., 1956. C.P.A., Calif. Acct. John F. Grieder, San Francisco, 1957-59; assoc. Heller, Ehrman, White & McAuliffe, San Francisco, 1959-61; pres. Sutter Capital Co., San Francisco, 1961-69; chmn. bd. Community Psychiat. Ctrs., San Francisco, 1969-89, VIVRA, 1989-94, pres., 1989-92; chmn. Edn. Ptnrs., San Francisco, 1994-2000. Trustee Sta. KQED-Pub. TV, San Francisco, 1981-91, Mus. Modern Art, 1984-89, Mt. Zion Hosp., 1985-86. 1st lt. U.S. Army, 1954-56 Avocations: bicycling, golf. Office: 2601 Mariposa St San Francisco CA 94110-1426

GREEN, SETH, actor; b. Phila., Feb. 8, 1974; Actor: (TV series) Tales from the Darkside, 1984, Amazing Stories, 1985, Spensere: For Hire, 1985, The Facts of Life, 1979, Free Spirit, 1989, Mr. Belvedere, 1985, The Comic Strip, 1987, Action Family, 1987, Divided We Stand, 1988, The Wonder Years, 1988, Batman: The Animated Series, 1988, Life Goes On, 1989, It, 1990, Evening Shade, 1990, Beverly Hills, 90210, 1990, Our Shining Moment, 1991, The Day My Parents Ran Away, 1993, The Byrds of Paradise, 1994, Real Ghosts, 1995, Mad TV, 1995, Temporarily Yours, 1997, Buffy the Vampire Slayer, 1997, That '70s Show, 1998, Batman Beyond, 1999, (voice) Family Guy, 1999—, Whatever Happened to Robot Jones?, 2002, Greg the Bunny, 2002, Jimmy Kimmel Live, 2003, Punk'd, 2003, (voice) Robot Chicken, 2005—; (TV films) I Want to Go Home, 1985, The X-Files, 1993, SeaQuest DSV, 1993, Weird Science, 1994, Step by Step, 1991, Something So Right, 1996, Pearl, 1996, Mad About You, 1992, The Drew Carey Show, 1995, Cybil, 1995, Angel, 1991; (films) The Hotel New Hampshire, 1984, Billions for Boris, 1984, Charlie's Christmas Secret, 1985, Willy/Milly, 1986, Radio days, 1987, Can't Buy Me Love, 1987, Big Business, 1988, My Stepmother Is An Alien, 1988, Pump Up the Volume, 1990, Missing Parents, 1990, Good & Evil, 1991, Arcade, 1993, Airborne, 1993, Ticks, 1993, The Double O Kid, 1993, Notes from Underground, 1995, White Man's Burden, 1995, To Gillian on Her 37th Birthday, 1996, Boys Life 2, 1997, Austin Powers: International Man of Mystery, 1997, Nunzio's Second Cousin, 1997, Can't Hardly Wait, 1998, Enemy of the State, 1998, Stonebrook, 1999, Idle Hands, 1999, Austin Powers: The Spy Who Shagged Me, 1999, Diary of a Mad Freshman, 2000, The Trumpet of the Swan, 2001, The Attic Expeditions, 2001, Josie and the Pussycats, 2001, America's Sweetheart, 2001, Rat Race, 2001, Knockaround Guys, 2001, Rock Star 101, 2001, Austin Powers in Goldmember, 2002, Party Monster, 2003, The Italian Job, 2003, Scooby-Doo 2: Monsters Unleashed, 2004, Without a Paddle, 2004, (voice) Family Guy Presents Stewie Griffin: The Untold Story, 2005, The Best Man, 2005, Electric Apricot, 2006, Sex Drive, 2008. Office: United Talent Agy 9560 Wilshire Blvd Beverly Hills CA 90212

GREEN, WILLIAM L., lawyer; b. Syracuse, NY, Oct. 13, 1954; BA in Polit. Sci. cum laude, Middlebury Coll., 1976; JD magna cum laude, Boston Coll., 1980. Bar: Mass. 1980, NY 1981, Wash. 1986. Assoc. Quint, Marx, Chill & Greene, NY, 1980—82, Skadden, Arps, Slate, Meagher & Flom, NY, 1982—86; ptnr. real estate group Perkins Coie LLP, Seattle, 1986—. Limited Practice Bd. Wash. State Supreme Ct., 1993—2000; trustee Intiman Theatre Co., 1996—2002. Mem.: Wash. State Bar Assn. (Real Property, Probate & Trust Sect 1995—97), Mt. Baker Cmty. Club (pres. 1993—95). Office: Perkins Coie LLP 1201 Third Ave Ste 4800 Seattle WA 98101-9000 Office Phone: 206-359-8513. Office Fax: 206-359-9513. Business E-Mail: wgreen@perkinscoie.com.

GREEN, WILLIAM PORTER, lawyer; b. Jacksonville, Ill., Mar. 19, 1920; s. Hugh Parker and Clara Belle (Hopper) G.; m. Rose Marie Hall, Oct. 1, 1944; children: Hugh Michael, Robert Alan, Richard William. BA, Ill. Coll., 1941; JD, Northwestern U., Evanston, Ill., 1947. Bar: Ill. 1947, Calif. 1948, U.S. Dist. Ct. (so. dist.) Tex. 1986, U.S. Ct. Customs and Patent Appeals, U.S. Patent and Trademark Office 1948, U.S. Ct. Appeals (fed. cir.) 1982, U.S. Ct. Appeals (5th and 9th cir.), U.S. Supreme Ct. 1948, U.S. Dist. Ct. (cen. dist.) Calif. 1949, (so. dist.) Tex.1986. Pvt. practice, LA, 1947—; mem. Wills, Green & Mueth, LA, 1974-83; of counsel Nilsson, Robbins, Dalgarn, Berliner, Carson & Wurst, LA, 1984-91; of counsel Nilsson, Wurst & Green LA, 1992—. Del. Calif. State Bar Conv., 1982—, chmn., 1986. Bd. editors Ill. Law Rev., 1946; patentee in field. Mem. L.A. world Affairs Coun., 1975—; deacon local Presbyn. Ch., 1961-63. Mem. ABA, Calif. State Bar, Am. Intellectual Property Law Assn., L.A. Patent Law Assn. (past. sec.-treas., mem. bd. govs.), Lawyers Club L.A. (past treas., past sec., mem. bd. govs., pres. 1985-86), Los Angeles County Bar Assn. (trustee 1986-87), Am. Legion (past post comdr.), Northwestern U. Alumni Club So. Calif., Big Ten Club So. Calif., Town Hall Calif. Club, PGA West Golf Club (La Quinta, Calif.), Phi Beta Kappa, Phi Delta Phi, Phi Alpha. Republican. Home: 3570 Lombardy Rd Pasadena CA 91107-5627 Office: 707 Wilshire Blvd Ste 3200 Los Angeles CA 90017-3514 Home Phone: 760-777-1886; Office Phone: 213-362-9501. Personal E-mail: wpgreen@aol.com.

GREENBAUM, JAMES RICHARD, liquor distributing company executive, real estate developer; b. Cleve., July 3, 1933; s. Harold and Miriam (Lion) G.; m. Peggy Strauss, Jan. 29, 1955; children: Robert Strauss, James R., Clifford Harold. BA, Tulane U., 1955. V.p. Strauss Distbrs., Ark., 1961—. Bd. dirs. S&D Realty, Little Rock. Bd. dirs. Jewish Fedn. Palm Springs, Betty Ford Ctr., Rancho Mirage, Calif. Lt. U.S. Army, 1955-57. Mem. Beaver Creek Club (Colo.), Tamarisk Club (Rancho Mirage, Calif.), Country Club of Rockies (Vail, Colo.), Club at Morningside (Rancho Mirage), Tamarisk Country Club, Zeta Beta Tau. Jewish (past pres., bd. dirs. temple). Office: 4 Big Sioux RD Rancho Mirage CA 92270-2311

GREENBERG, BYRON STANLEY, newspaper and business executive, consultant; b. Bklyn., June 17, 1919; s. Albert and Bertha (Getleson) G.; m. Helena Marks, Feb. 10, 1946; children: David, Eric, Randy. Student, Bklyn. Coll., 1936-41. Circulation mgr. N.Y. Post, 1956-62, circulation dir., 1962-63, bus. mgr., 1963-72, gen. mgr., COO, 1973-79; sec., dir. N.Y. Post Corp., 1966-75, treas., dir., 1975-76, v.p., 1976-81. V.p., dir. Leisure Systems, Inc., 1978-80; pres., chief exec. officer, dir. Games Mgmt. Services, Inc., 1979-80 Bd. dirs. 92d St YMHA, 1970-71, Friars Nat. Found., 1981-82. Served with AUS, 1942-45. Mem. Friars Club. Home and Office: 2560 S Grade Rd Alpine CA 91901-3612 Home Phone: 619-445-8559. E-mail: slugger19@cox.net.

GREENBERG, DANIEL, electronics rental company executive; b. Mpls., May 14, 1941; s. Mayer and Ruth G.; m. Susan L. Steinhauser, Oct. 19, 1985. BA, Reed Coll., 1962; JD, U. Chgo., 1965. Staff atty. State of Calif. Dept. Water Resources, 1965-67; various positions, then pres., ceo Telecor, Inc., 1967-79; with Electro Rent Corp., Van Nuys, Calif., 1973—, chmn., chief exec. officer, 1979—. Former mem. U.S./Mex. Counsultive Group. Trustee Reed Coll., chmn., 2002--; trustee Nat. Pub. Radio Found.; former mem. visiting com. U. Chgo. Law Sch.; former mem. adv. com. Dept. Commerce, Fgn. Comml. Svc. Mem. Am. Bus. Conf. (charter, past bd. dirs.), Earthjustice(chmn. 1991-94), Bus. Execs. for Nat. Security. Office: Electro Rent Corp 6060 Sepulveda Blvd Van Nuys CA 91411-2512

GREENBERG, DAVID ETHAN, communications consultant; b. NYC, Oct. 8, 1949; s. Abraham M. and Norma B. (Jacovitz) G.; m. Kerri Shwayder, Apr. 24, 1983; children: Alison Leigh, Zachary Scott. BA cum laude, Columbia U., 1971; JD, Harvard U., 1975. Bar: Colo. 1975. Speechwriter Gov. Richard D. Lamm, Denver, 1977-78, legal counsel, 1978-79; dir. mktg. Colo. Ski Country U.S.A., Denver, 1979-82; founder and mng. ptnr. GBSM, Denver, 1982; sec. of bd. & founder Denver Sch. of Sci. and Tech., Denver. Adj. assoc. prof. U of Colo., Denver, 1984-89. Columnist, The Denver Post, 1985-88. Spl. asst. to adminstr. for communications EPA, Wash. 1989; pres. Children's Mus. Denver, 1988; vice chair Colo. Ocean Journey Aquarium, 1994—; mem. Colo. Commn. Higher Edn., 1993-2003, trustee Clayton Coll. Found. Nat. Merit Scholar, NYC, 1967, fellow White House, 1988-89. Office: Denver Sch of Sci and Tech 2000 Valentia St Denver CO 80238 Office Phone: 303-320-5570. Office Fax: 303-377-5101.

GREENBERG, E. PETER, microbiologist; BA in Biology, Western Wash. U., 1970; MS in Microbiology, U. Iowa, 1972; PhD in Microbiology, U. Mass., 1977. With Cornell U., U. Iowa, 1988—2004, Sheppard prof. molecular pathogenesis; chair dept. microbiology U. Wash. Sch. Med., 2005—07, prof. microbiology, 2007—. Sci. advisor Genelux, San Diego, 2007—; chief sci. officer Quorum Scis., 1998—2001. Editor: Jour. Bacteriology; assoc. editor Annual Reviews Microbiology. Mem.: Am. Acad. Microbiology, AAAS, NAS. Office: U Wash Sch Medicine Dept Microbiology 1705 NE Pacific St Box 357242 Rm K-359A Seattle WA 98195-7242 Office Phone: 206-616-2881. Business E-Mail: epgreen@u.washington.edu.

GREENBERG, EDWARD SEYMOUR, political science professor; b. Phila., July 1, 1942; s. Samuel and Yetta (Kaplan) G.; m. Martha Ann Baker, Dec. 24, 1964; children: Joshua, Nathaniel. BA, Miami U., Ohio, 1964, MA, 1965; PhD, U. Wis., 1969. Asst. prof. polit. sci. Stanford (Calif.) U., 1968-72; assoc. prof. Ind. U., Bloomington, 1972-73; prof. U. Colo., Boulder, 1973—, dir. research program polit. and econ. change Inst. Behavioral Sci., 1980—, chair dept. polit. sci., 1985-88. Author: Serving the Few, 1974, Understanding Modern Government, 1979, Capitalism and the American Political Ideal, 1985, The American Political System, 1989, Workplace Democracy, 1986 (Dean's Writing award Social Scis. 1987), The Struggle for Democracy, 1993, 8th edit., 2007, 4th brief edit., 2002, The American Democratic Republic, 2005, 2d edit., 2007; contbr. articles to profl. jours. Recipient fellowship In Recognition of Disting. Tchg., 1968, Jeffrey Pressman award Policy Studies Assn.; grantee Russell Sage Found., 1968, U. Wis., 1968, NSF, 1976, 82, 85, NIH, 1991-94, 96-2001. Mem.: Internat. Polit. Sci. Assn., Am. Polit. Sci. Assn.,

Western Polit. Sci. Assn. (mem. exec. bd. 1986—89). Avocations: reading, bicycling, travel, golf, skiing. Home: 755 11th St Boulder CO 80302-7512 Office: U Colo Inst Behavioral Sci PO Box 487 Boulder CO 80309-0487 Home Phone: 303-443-8517; Office Phone: 303-492-2141. Business E-Mail: edward.greenberg@colorado.edu.

GREENBERG, GORDON ALAN, lawyer; b. Chgo., July 2, 1954; s. Henry and Ruth (Bluestien) G.; m. Patricia L. Collins; children: Haley, Danielle. BA, U. Ill., 1976; JD with honors, Ill. Inst. Tech./Chgo.-Kent, 1980. Bar: Ill. 1980, U.S. Dist. Ct. (no. dist.) Ill. 1980, U.S. Ct. Appeals (7th cir.if. 1980, Calif. 1984, U.S. Ct. Appeals (9th cir.) 1984. Asst. state atty. Cook County, Chgo., 1980-83; spl. asst. U.S. atty. No. Dist. Ill., Chgo., 1982-83; asst. U.S. atty., chief Fin. Investigations Unit L.A. U.S. Atty. Office, 1983-89; ptnr. Sheppard, Mullin, Richter & Hampton, LA, 1989—; ptnr.-in-charge L.A. Office McDermott Will & Emery LLP, LA. Instr. U.S. Dept. Justice, 1985-89, lawyer rep. 9th cir., L.A., 1993-96. Contbr. articles profl. jours. Named one of top 50 trial lawyers in L.A., L.A. Bus. Jour. Mem. ABA, State Bar Assn. Calif., L.A. County Bar Assn. (chmn. White Collar Def. Com.). Office: McDermott Will & Emery 2049 Century Park E Fl 34 Los Angeles CA 90067-3101 Office Phone: 310-551-9398. Office Fax: 310-277-4730. Business E-Mail: ggreenberg@mwe.com.

GREENBERG, HARRY B., gastroenterologist, educator; b. NYC, May 30, 1944; BA, Dartmouth Coll., 1966; MD, Columbia U., 1970. Diplomate Am. Bd. Gastroenterology, Am. Bd. Internal Medicine. Intern then resident Bellevue Hosp., NYC, 1970—72; gastroenterology fellow Stanford U., Calif., 1974—76; assoc. prof. medicine, microbiology and immunology Sch. Medicine Stanford U. and VA Palo Alto Health Care Sys., 1983—85, chief div. gastroenterology, 1988—98, prof. medicine, microbiology and immunology, 1989—; assoc. chmn. acad. affairs dept. medicine Sch. Medicine Stanford U., 1995—98, acting chmn. acad. affairs dept. medicine Sch. Medicine, 1996, sr. assoc. dean rsch. Sch. Medicine, 1999—2000, Joseph D. Grant Endowed Professorship Sch. Medicine, 1999—; sr. v.p. R&D and chief sci. officer Aviron, Mt. View, Calif., 2000. Invited cons. PATH Diarrheal Program, Washington, 1985; vis. prof. Duke U., Durham, NC, 1991; vis. prof. div. gastroenterology Mass. Gen. Hosp., Boston, 1995; Wade Volwiler vis. prof. U. Wash., Seattle, 1997; mem. vaccines and related biol. products adv. com. USFDA, 1997—2000, cons., 2000, chmn. vaccines and related biol. products adv. com., 1999—2000; ACOS for rsch. VA Palo Alto Health Care Sys., 1997—2000, dir. GRECC search com., 1997—; chmn. sect. immunology and microbiology AGA Rsch. Coun., 1989—91; mem. steering and rev. com. DDW, viral sub-com. WHO, 1991—96; mem. task force on intestinal microecology and environment CCFA, 1993, mem. rsch. initiative panel, 94; invited chmn. Nat. Found. Ileitis and Colitis Rsch., 1987; mem. adv. bd. Inflammatory Bowel Disease Ctr. UCLA, 1988; mem. various coms. NIH; co-chair Stanford health care RVU and productivity com. U. Calif., San Francisco, 1997—98, mem. adv. bd. Liver Ctr., 1997—99; mem. adv. com. Virus Rsch. Ctr. Kon-Kuk U., 1998; mem. ad hoc com. HCV rsch. VA, 1998, mem. planning com. rsch. hepatitis C, 2001—; mem. mucosal immunity working group HIV Vaccine Trials Network, 2000—. Editor (assoc. editor): Virology, 1994—99; mem. editl. bd. Infection and Immunity, 1983—85, Molecular and Cellular Probes, 1986—91, Jour. Clin. Microbiology, 1988—99, Jour. Virology, 1989, mem. editl. com. Jour. Investigation, 1990—95, ad hoc reviewer in field. Mem. adv. coun. Textile Mus., 1994—96, trustee, 1997—99. With USPHS, 1972—83. Recipient Rsch. prize, We. Gut Club, 1992; Rufus Choate scholar, Dartmouth Coll., 1966. Mem.: ACP (fellow), Soc. Mucosal Immunology, We. Assn. Physicians, Am. Fedn. Clin. Rsch., Calif. Acad. Medicine, Am. Soc. Virology (co-chair med. virology club 1997, mem. membership nominating com. 1995), Am. Gastroent. Assn., Infectious Diseases Soc. Am. (fellow), Am. Soc. Microbiology (chmn. panel on rotavirus 1982), Palo Alto VA (mem. R&D com. 1985—88), Nat. Commn. on Digestive Diseases (mem. workshop on basic scis. rsch. related to digestive diseases 1977). Office: Div Gastroenterology and Hepatology Stanford U Sch Medicine 300 Pasteur Dr CCSR Bldg Rm 3115 Stanford CA 94305-5187

GREENBERG, LENORE, public relations professional; b. Flushing; d. Jack and Frances Orenstein. BA, Hofstra U.; MS, SUNY. Dir.pub. rels. Bloomingdale's, Short Hills, N.J., 1977-78; dir. comms. N.J. Sch. Bds. Assn., Trenton, 1978-82; dir pub. info. N.J. State Dept. Edn., Trenton, 1982-90; assoc. exec. dir. Nat. Sch. Pub. Rels. Assn., Arlington, Va., 1990-91; pres. Lenore Greenberg & Assocs., Inc., 1991—. Adj. prof. pub. rels. Rutgers U. Freelance feature writer N.Y. Times. Mem. bd. assocs. McCarter Theatre, Princeton, N.J.; mem. Franklin Twp. Zoning Bd. Adjustment; mem. Franklin Twp. Human Rels. Commn.; chair Somerset County LWV; instr. Bus. Vols. for the Arts. Recipient award Am. Soc. Assn. Execs., award Women in Comms., award Internat. Assn. Bus. Communicators; Gold Medallion awrd Nat. Sch. Pub. Rels. Assn. Mem. Pub. Rels. Soc. Am. (accredited; pres. N.J. State chpt., nat. nominating and accreditation coms., Silver Anvil award), Nat. Health/Edn. Consortium. Home and Office: 30971 Carrara Rd Laguna Niguel CA 92677-2757

GREENBERG, MYRON SILVER, lawyer; b. LA, Oct. 17, 1945; s. Earl W. and Geri (Silver) G.; m. Shlomit Gross; children: David, Amy, Sophie, Benjamin. BSBA, UCLA, 1967; JD, 1970. Bar: Calif., 1971, U.S. Dist. Ct. (middle dist.) Calif. 1971, U.S. Tax Ct. 1977; cert. splst. in taxation law bd. legal specialization State Bar Calif.; CPA, Calif. Staff acct. Touche Ross & Co., LA, 1970-71; assoc. Kaplan, Livingston, Goodwin, Berkowitz, & Selvin, Beverly Hills, Calif., 1971-74; ptnr. Steefel, Levitt, & Weiss, 1975—82, Myron S. Greenberg, a Profl. Corp., Larkspur, Calif., 1982—. Professorial lectr. tax. Golden Gate U.; instr. estate planning U. Calif., Berkeley, 1989-2003. Author: California Attorney's Guide to Professional Corporations, 1977, 79; bd. editors UCLA Law Rev., 1969-70. Mem. San Anselmo Planning Commn., 1976-77; mem. adv. bd. cert. program personal fin. planning U. Calif., Berkeley, 1991-2003; bd. dirs. Marin County Estate Planning Coun., 2001—06, pres., 2004. Mem.: ABA, AHA (bd. dirs. Marin county chpt. 1984—90, pres. 1988—89), Calif. Bd. Legal Specialization (mem. tax commn. 1998—2001, chmn. tax. commn. 2001, bd. dirs. 2003—07, chair bd. 2006—07), Real Estate Tax Inst. Calif. Cont. Edn. Bar (planning com.), Marin County (Calif.) Bar Assn. (bd. dirs. 1994—2007, pres. 1999), Larkspur C. of C. (bd. dirs. 1985—87). Democrat. Jewish. Office: # 205 700 Larkspur Landing Cir Larkspur CA 94939-1711 Office Phone: 415-461-5844. Business E-Mail: msg@eplaw.com.

GREENBERG, RICHARD, playwright; b. 1958; Author: (plays) The Dazzle, Everett Beekin, Hurrah at Last, Night and Her Stars, 1997, The Bloodletters, 1984, Vanishing Act, 1986, The Author's Voice, 1987, The Hunger Artist, 1987, The Maderati, 1987, Eastern Standard, 1988, Neptune's Hips, 1988, The American Plan, 1990, The Extra Man, 1991, Jenny Keeps Talking, 1992, Pal Joey, 1992, (on Broadway), 2008, Three Days of Rain, 1998 (Pulitzer prize for drama nominee, 1998), (on Broadway), 2006, Take Me Out, 2002 (Tony award, best play, 2003, Drama Desk award, outstanding new play, 2003, Pulitzer prize for drama nominee, 2003), The Dance of Death, 2003, The Violet Hour, 2003, A Naked Girl on the Appian Way, 2004, (on Broadway), 2005, Bal Masque, 2006, The House in Town, 2006, The Injured Party, 2008, (TV screenplay) Ask Me Again, 1989, Life Under Water, 1989. Recipient NY Drama Critics' Cir. award, Lucille Lortel award, Oppenheimer award, PEN/Laura Pels award. Office: c/o Creative Artists Agy Calif 9830 Wilshire Blvd Beverly Hills CA 90212

GREENBERGER, ELLEN, psychologist, educator; b. NYC, Nov. 19, 1935; d. Edward Michael and Vera (Brisk) Silver; m. Michael Burton, Aug. 26, 1979; children by previous marriage: Kari Edwards, David Silver. BA, Vassar Coll., 1956; MA, Harvard U., 1959, PhD, 1961. Instr. Wellesley (Mass.) Coll., 1961—67; sr. rsch. scientist Johns Hopkins U., Balt., 1967-76; prof. psychology and social behavior U. Calif., Irvine, 1976—. Author: (with others) When Teenagers Work, 1986; contbr. articles to profl. jours. USPHS fellow, 1956-59; Margaret Floy Washburn fellow, 1956-58; Ford Found. grantee, 1979-81; Spencer Found. grantee, 1979-81, 87, 88-91. Fellow Am. Psychol. Assn., Am. Psychol. Soc.; mem. Soc. Rsch. in Child Devel., Soc. Rsch. on Adolescent Devel. Office: U Calif 3340 Social Ecology II Irvine CA 92697-7085 Office Phone: 949-824-6328. Business E-Mail: egreenbe@uci.edu.

GREENBERGER, MARTIN, biotechnologist, information scientist, educator; b. Elizabeth, NJ, Nov. 30, 1931; s. David and Sidelle (Jonas) G.; m. Ellen Danica Silver, Feb. 2, 1959 (div. June 1974); children: Kari Edwards, David Silver; m. Liz Attardo, Dec. 11, 1982; children: Beth Jonit, Jonah Ben, Jilly Sal. Grad. with hons., USAF Officer Candidate Sch., 1953; AB, Harvard U., 1955, AM, 1956, PhD, 1958. Teaching fellow, resident adviser, staff mem. Computation Lab., Harvard U., Cambridge, 1954-58; mgr. applied sci. Cambridge IBM, 1956-58; asst. prof. mgmt. Mass. Inst. Tech., Cambridge, 1958-61, assoc. prof., 1961-67; prof., chmn. computer sci., dir. info. processing Johns Hopkins U., Balt., 1967-72; prof. math. scis., sr. research assoc. Center for Met. Planning and Research, 1972-75, prof. math. scis., 1978-82; IBM chair in tech. and info. systems UCLA Anderson Grad. Sch. Mgmt., 1982—; dir. UCLA Ctr. Digital Media, 1995-2000; pres. Council for Tech. and the Individual, 1985—; sr. fellow Milken Inst., 1999—. Mgr. systems program Electric Power Research Inst., Palo Alto, Calif., 1976-77; Isaac Taylor vis. prof. Technion-Israel Inst. Tech., Haifa, 1978-79; vis. prof. Internat. Energy Program, Grad. Sch. Bus., Stanford U., 1980, MIT Media Lab., 1988-89, Harvard U., 2001; computer sci. and engring. bd. NAS, 1970-72; chmn. COSATI rev. group NSF, 1971-72; evaluation com. Internat. Inst. for Applied Systems Analysis, Laxenburg, Austria, 1980; adv. panels, Office Tech. Assessment, GAO, U.S. Congress; adv. com. Getty Info. Inst.; cons. IBM, AT&T, CBS, Rand Corp., Morgan Guaranty, Arthur D. Little, TRW, Munger Tolles, Bolt, Beranek & Newman, Brookings Inst., Resources for Future, Electric Power Rsch. Inst., Atlantic Richfield, Rockwell Internat., Security Pacific Corp., John F. Kennedy Sch. of Govt. Harvard U., Bell Atlantic Corp., Sony Corp., Applied Minds, Mitchell Silberberg and Knupp, Am. Online, Kirkland and Ellis, Vertex Pharmaceuticals, Nat. Cancer Inst. Author: (with Orcutt, Korbel and Rivlin) Microanalysis of Socioeconomic Systems: A Simulation Study, 1961; (with Jones, Morris and Ness) On-Line Computation and Simulation: The OPS-3 System, 1965; (with Crenson and Crissey) Models in the Policy Process: Public Decision Making in the Computer Era, 1976; (with Brewer, Hogan and Russell) Caught Unawares: The Energy Decade in Retrospect, 1983; editor: Management and The Computer of the Future, 1962, republished as Computers and the World of the Future, 1964; Computers, Communications, and the Public Interest, 1971; (with Aronofsky, McKenney and Massy) Networks for Research and Education, 1973; Electronic Publishing Plus: Media for a Technological Future, 1985, Technologies for the 21st Century, Vol. 1, On Multimedia, 1990, Vol. 3, Multimedia in Review, 1992, Vol. 5, Content and Communication, 1994, Vol. 7, Scaling Up, 1996. Mem. overseers' vis. com. Harvard U., 1975-81; founder and mem. working groups Energy Modeling Forum, Stanford U., 1978-81; mem. adv. com. Nat. Center Analysis of Energy Systems Brookhaven Nat. Lab., 1976-80, chmn., 1977; mem. rev. com. Energy and Environment div. Lawrence Berkeley Lab., 1983, applied sci. div., 1986-88; chmn. forum on electronic pub. Washington program Annenberg, 1983-84; co-founder ICC Forum, 1985; chmn. CTI Roundtable Digital Media, 1990-99; chmn. CTI Roundtable Healthy Aging, 2006; trustee Educom, Princeton, N.J., 1969-73, chmn. council, 1969-70. With USAF, 1952-54, USAFR, 1954-60. Named a Disting. Grad. Officer Candidate Sch., USAF, 1953; NSF fellow, 1955-56; Guggenheim fellow U. Calif., Berkeley, 1965-66. Fellow: AAAS (v.p., chmn. sect. T 1973—75); mem.: Sigma Xi, Phi Beta Kappa. Office: UCLA Anderson Grad Sch Mgmt Los Angeles CA 90095-1481

GREENE, ALVIN, management consultant; b. Aug. 26, 1932; s. Samuel David and Yetta Kroff Greene; m. Louise Sokol, Nov. 11, 1977; children: Sharon, Aaron, Ami, Ann, Daniel. BA, Stanford U., 1954, MBA, 1959. Asst. to pres. Narmco Industries, Inc., San Diego, 1959—62; adminstrv. mgr., mgr. mktg. Whittaker Corp., LA, 1962—67; sr. v.p. Cordura Corp., LA, 1966—75; chmn. bd. Sharon-Sage, Inc., LA, 1975—79; exec. v.p., COO Republic Distbrs., Inc., Carson, Calif., 1979—81, also dir.; COO Memel, Jacobs & Ellsworth, 1981—87, 1987—; pres. SCI Cons., Inc. Bd. dirs. Sharon-Sage Inc., True Data Corp.; vis. prof. Am. Grad. Sch. Bus., Phoenix, 1977—81. Chmn. bd. commrs. Housing Authority City of L.A., 1983—88; tchr., mentor Anderson Grad. Sch. Bus., UCLA, 2002—; bd. dirs. Spl. Olympics, 2003; dir. Industry Coun., City of Hope. 1st lt. US Army, 1955—57. Mem.: Bradley Group, Safety Helmet Mfrs. Assn., Direct Mail Assn. Business E-Mail: sciconsultants@aol.com.

GREENE, DAVID LEE, physical anthropologist, educator; b. Denver, Aug. 23, 1938; s. Ralph Francis and Dorothy Elizabeth (Allen) G.; m. Kathleen Ann Kerger, Sept. 4, 1962; 1 son, Andrew David. BA, U. Colo., 1960, MA, 1962, PhD in Anthropology (NSF fellow). Asst. prof. anthropology and orthodontics SUNY, Buffalo, 1964-65; asst. prof., head dept. anthropology U. Wyo., 1965-67; asst. prof. U. Colo., Boulder, 1967-69, asso. prof., 1969-71, prof., 1971—, chmn. dept. anthropology, 1974-77, 81-83, 1990-91. Dir. NSF Summer Inst. in Anthropology, 1970-71; outside grad. examiner U. Toronto, 1974, field rsch. in Sudan, 1963-64, Micronesia, 1969, Brazil, 1986, 88. Author: Genetics, Dentition and Taxonomy, 1967, (with G.J. Armelagos) The Wadi Halfa Mesolithic Population, 1972; contbr. articles to profl. jours. NSF grantee, 1978-80 Fellow Am. Anthrop. Assn.; mem. Am. Assn. Phys. Anthropologists, AAAS, Sigma Xi. Office: U Colo Dept Anthropology Boulder CO 80309-0001

GREENE, DIANE B., information technology executive; b. Annapolis, Md. m. Mendel Rosenblum. BS in Mech. Engring., U. Calif., Berkeley; MS in Computer Sci. and Naval Architecture, MIT. Joined Sybase, 1986; various tech. leadership positions Tandem, Silicon Graphics Inc.; co-founder, CEO Vxtreme (sold to Microsoft Corp.), Palo Alto, Calif., 1995—98; co-founder, press CEO VMware, 1998—2004; pres., CEO VMware (sub. of EMC), 2004—08. Bd. dirs. Intiut Inc., 2006—, West Marine Inc., 2004—06. Named one of 50 Most Powerful People in Networking, Network World Mag., 2003, 50 Most Powerful Women in Bus., Fortune Mag., 2007. Mem.: MIT Corp., St. Francis Yacht Club. Avocation: sailing.

GREENE, ENID, former United States Representative from Utah; b. San Rafael, Calif., Oct. 5, 1958; m. Joe Waldholtz (div.). BS in Pol. Sci., U. Utah, 1980; JD, Brigham Young U., 1983. Caseworker, rsch. asst. to Rep. Dan Marriott, US Congress, 1980; atty. Ray, Quinney & Nebeker, 1983-90; dep. chief of staff to Gov. Norman H. Bangerter State of Utah, 1990-92; corp. counsel Novell, Inc., 1993-94; mem. US Congress from 2nd Utah Dist., Washington, 1995-97; atty. Smith & Glauser, Salt Lake City, 1998—; chair Utah Republican Party, 2007. Republican.*

GREENE, FRANK SULLIVAN, JR., investment company executive; b. Washington, Oct. 19, 1938; s. Frank S. Sr. and Irma O. Greene; m. Phyllis Davison, Jan. 1958 (dec. 1984); children: Angela, Frank. BS, Washington U., St. Louis, 1961; MS, Purdue U., 1962; PhD, U. Santa Clara, Calif., 1970. Part-time lectr. Washington U., Howard U., Am. U., 1959-65; pres., dir. Tech. Devel. Corp., Arlington, Tex., 1985-92; pres. Zero One Systems Inc. (formerly Tech. Devel. of Calif.), Santa Clara, Calif., 1971-87, Zero One Systems Group subs. Sterling Software Inc., 1987-89. Asst. chmn., lectr. Stanford U., 1972—74; mng. mem. New Vista Capital, LLC, Palo Alto, Calif., 1993—; pres. Networked Picture Sys. Inc., 1989—91, chmn., 1991—94; bd. dirs. Reach Comms., Compliance Coach. Author two indsl. textbooks; also articles; patentee in field. Bd. dirs. NCCJ, Santa Clara, 1980—2005, NAACP, San Jose chpt., 1986-89, Am. Musical Theatre of San Jose, 1995—2005; bd. regents Santa Clara U., 1983-90, trustee, 1990-2000; trustee emeritus, 2007-; mem. adv. bd. Urban League, Santa Clara County, 1986-89, East Side Union High Sch., 1985-88. Capt. USAF, 1961-65. Mem IEEE, IEEE Computer Soc. (governing bd. 1973-75), Assn. Black Mfrs. (bd. dirs. 1974-80), Am. Electric Assn. (indsl. adv. bd. 1975-76), Fairchild Rsch. and Devel. (tech. staff 1965-71), Bay Area Purchasing Coun. (bd. dirs. 1978-84), Security Affairs Support Assn. (bd. dirs. 1980-83), Sigma Xi, Eta Kappa Nu, Sigma Pi Phi. Office Phone: 650-714-3749. Business E-Mail: fgreene@nvcap.com.

GREENE, HERBERT BRUCE, lawyer, investor, entrepreneur; b. NYC, Apr. 13, 1934; s. Joseph Lester and Shirley (Kasen) G.; m. Judith Jean Metricks, Dec. 31, 1958; children: Pamela S., Scott L. AB, Harvard U., 1955; JD, Columbia U., 1958. Bar: N.Y. 1959, Conn. 1975. Asst. U.S. atty So. Dist. N.Y., Dept. Justice, NYC, 1958-61; assoc. Kaye, Scholer, Fierman, Hays & Handler, NYC, 1961-66; asst. to gen. counsel CIT Fin. Corp., NYC, 1966-67; group gen. counsel Xerox Corp., Rochester, NY, 1967-68, v.p. adminstrn., 1968-71; sr. v.p. Xerox Edn. Group, Stamford, Conn., 1971-75; v.p., gen. counsel, sec. Lone Star Industries, Inc., Greenwich, Conn., 1976-79, sr. v.p., asst. to chmn., 1979-82; chmn., CEO Earle and Greene & Co., Westport, 1982-96, Portland, Oreg., 1997—. Mem. Phi Delta Phi. Republican. Home and Office: Herbert B Greene & Co 4233 W Redondo Ave Portland OR 97239

GREENE, JOHN THOMAS, judge; b. Salt Lake City, Nov. 28, 1929; s. John Thomas and Mary Agnes (Hindley) G.; m. Dorothy Kay Buchanan, Mar. 31, 1955; children: Thomas Buchanan Greene, John Buchanan Greene, Mary Kay Greene Platt. BA in Polit. Sci., U. Utah, 1952, JD, 1955. Bar: Utah 1955, U.S. Dist. Ct. (10th cir.) 1955, U.S. Supreme Ct. 1966. Pvt. practice, Salt Lake City, 1955-57; asst. U.S. atty., 1957-59; ptnr. Marr, Wilkins & Cannon (and successor firms), Salt Lake City, 1959-75; ptnr., pres., chmn. bd. dirs. Greene, Callister & Nebeker, Salt Lake City, 1975-85; judge U.S. Dist. Ct., Salt Lake City, 1985—. Author: (manual) American Mining Law, 1960; contbr. articles to profl. jours. Chmn. Salt Lake City Cmty. Coun., 1970-75, Utah State Bldg. Authority, Salt Lake City, 1980-85; Regent Utah State Bd. Higher Edn., Salt Lake City, 1982-86. Recipient Order of Coif U. Utah, 1955, Merit of Honor award, 1994, Utah Fed. Bar Disting. Svc. award, 1997. Fellow ABA Found. (life); ABA ho. of dels. 1972-92, bd. govs. 1987-91; mem. Dist. Judges Assn. (pres. 10th cir. 1998-2000), Utah Bar Assn. (pres. 1971-72, Judge of Yr. award 1995), Am. Law Inst. (life, panelist and lectr. 1980-85, advisor 1986-98); Phi Beta Kappa. Mem. Lds Ch. Avocations: travel, reading, tennis. Office: US Dist Ct 350 S Main St Ste 447 Salt Lake City UT 84101-2180 Office Phone: 801-524-6180. Personal E-mail: JTGJR@hotmail.com. Business E-Mail: Thomas_Greene@utd.uscourts.gov.

GREENE, SHECKY, entertainer; b. Chgo., Apr. 8, 1926; s. Carl and Bessie (Harris) Greenfield; m. Nalani Kele, Dec. 6, 1972. Student public schs., Chgo. Entertainer in night clubs, 1947—, on TV, 1953—, also in movies, night club appearances at all major clubs throughout, U.S., 1947—, night club appearances, Las Vegas, 1953—; films include The Love Machine, 1970, Tony Rome, 1967; co-star: TV series Combat, 1956; host: TV series Johnny Carson and Merv Griffin TV shows; co-host: numerous TV guest appearances on talk, variety and game shows Mike Douglas TV show; author all materials and songs for appearances. Recipient Las Vegas Best Lounge Entertainer award, 1972, 1st Jimmy Durante award as best comedian Miami, Fla., 1975; named Comedy Performer of Yr. South Fla. Entertainment Writers Assn., 1978, Male Comedy Star of Yr. Las Vegas Acad. Variety and Cabaret Artists, 1977 Mem.: Las Vegas Country. Jewish. Home: 1642 S La Verne Way Palm Springs CA 92264-9296

GREENE, WARNER CRAIG, medical educator, administrator; b. Mexico, Mo., June 13, 1949; BA, Stanford U.; MD, PhD, Washington U. Sch. Medicine, St. Louis, 1977. Lic. physician Md., N.C., Calif., diplomate Am. Bd. Allergy and Immunology, Am. Bd. Internal Medicine. Intern, medicine Mass. Gen. Hosp., Boston, 1977—78, resident, allergy and immunology, 1978—79; investigator metabolism br. Nat. Cancer Inst., NIH, Bethesda, Md., 1979—83, sr. investigator metabolism br., 1983—86; investigator Howard Hughes Med. Inst., Chevy Chase, Md., 1987—92; prof. medicine Duke U. Sch. Medicine, Durham, NC, 1987—92; prof. medicine, microbiology and immunology U. Calif., San Francisco, 1992—, dir. & sr. investigator Gladstone

Inst. for Virology and Immunology, 1992—, co-dir., Gladstone Ctr. for AIDS Rsch., 1994—, Nick and Sue Hellmann Dist. Prof. Translational Medicine, 2006—. Cons. Merck Pharms., Whitehouse Station, NJ, Eli Lilly Inc., Indpls., Abbott Pharms., Abbott Park, Ill., Hoffman LaRoche, Nutley, NJ, Sagres Pharm., Alliance Pharms., Inc., San Diego, Pfizer, Inc., NYC; mem. Nat. Inst. Allergy and Infectious Diseases, AIDS Rsch. Rev. Com., 1988—90; co-chair Keystone AIDS Symposium, 1995; mem. postdoctoral fellowship rev. com. Pfizer, 1995—; mem. adv. bd. exec. com. Inst. Human Virology, 1999—; Syntex lectr. Laurentian Hormone Conf., 1987; Kroc vis. prof. rheumatology UCLA, 1989; Plenary lectr. Sandoz Symposium on Human Retroviruses, 1990; keynote address Calif. Acad. Scis., 1994; pres. Academic Alliance Found. Assoc. editor: Jour. of Acquired Immune Deficiency Syndromes, mem. editl. bd.: Cytokine, Growth Factors, 1987, Blood, others, 1987, assoc. editor: Jour. of Immunology, 1984—88; contbr. several articles to profl. jours. Recipient rsch. grants in field, Washington Acad. of Scis. Award in Biol. Scis., 1984; named one of 100 Most Cited Scientists, Inst. for Sci. Info., 1981—88. Fellow: AAAS, Am. Rheumatism Assn. (Young Investigator award 1988); mem.: ACP, Inst. Medicine, Assn. Am. Physicians, Calif. Acad. Medicine, Am. Soc. for Clin. Investigation (v.p. 1993—94), Am. Assn. Immunologists, Am. Fedn. for Clin. Rsch. (Outstanding Investigator award 1987), Alpha Omega Alpha, Sigma Xi. Achievements include research in basic scientific studies aimed at further understanding how HIV grows and interacts with its cellular host; biology of NF-kB, an inducible eukaryotic transcription factor that is capable of activating HIV replication. Office: Gladstone Inst Virology and Immunology 1650 Owens St San Francisco CA 94158-2261 Office Phone: 415-734-4805. Office Fax: 415-355-0153. E-mail: wgreene@gladstone.ucsf.edu.

GREENLAW, ROGER LEE, interior designer; b. New London, Conn., Oct. 12, 1936; s. Kenneth Nelson and Lyndell Lee (Stinson) Greenlaw; children: Carol Jennifer, Roger Lee. BFA, Syracuse U., 1958. Interior designer Cannell & Chaffin, 1958-59, William C. Wagner, Arch., LA, 1959-60, Gen. Fireproofing Co., LA, 1960-62, K-S Wilshire, Inc., LA, 1963-64; dir. interior design Calif. Desk Co., LA, 1967-67; sr. interior designer Bechtel Corp., LA, 1967-70; sr. interior designer, project mgr. Daniel, Mann, Johnson & Mendehall, LA, 1970-72, Morganelli-Heumann & Assocs., LA, 1972-73; owner, prin. Greenlaw Design Assocs., Glendale, Calif., 1973—96, Greenlaw Interior Planning & Design, 1996—. Lectr. UCLA; mem. adv. curriculum com. Mt. San Antonio Coll., Walnut, Calif., Fashion Inst. Design, LA; bd. dirs. Calif. Legis. Conf. Interior Design, treas., 1992—94, v.p., 1990—92, pres., 1994—98. Past scoutmaster Verdugo coun. Boy Scouts Am.; pres. bd. dirs. Unity Ch., La Crescenta, Calif., 1989—91. Mem.: ASID (treas. Pasadena chpt. 1983—84, 1st v.p. 1985, chmn. So. Calif. Regional Conf. 1985, pres. 1986—87, nat. dir. 1987—89, v.p., treas. 1992, pres. 1994—98, mem. nat. com. legis., chmn. stds. task force, mem. nat. com. jury catalog award, spkr. ho. dels., nat. bd. dirs., regional v.p., nat. chair ethics com., nat. exec. com., medallist award), Adm. Farragut Acad. Alumni Assn., Glendale C. of C. (bd. dirs. 1998), Kiwanis (bd. dirs.), Delta Upsilon. Republican. Home: 1145 W Bella Casa Dr Pueblo CO 81007-3104 Business E-Mail: greenlawdesign@msn.com.

GREENLEAF, JOHN EDWARD, human research consultant; b. Joliet, Ill., Sept. 18, 1932; s. John Simon and Julia Clara (Flint) G.; m. Carol Lou Johnson, Aug. 28, 1960. MA, N.Mex. Highlands U., 1956; BA in Phys. Edn., U. Ill., 1955, MS, 1962, PhD in Physiology, 1963. Tchg. asst. N.Mex. Highlands U., Las Vegas, 1955-56; engring. draftsman Allis-Chalmers Mfg. Co., Springfield, Ill., 1956-57; tchg. asst. in phys. edn. U. Ill., Urbana, 1957-58, rsch. asst. in phys. edn., 1958-59, tchg. asst. in human anatomy and physiology, 1959-62; summer fellow NSF, 1962; pre-doctoral fellow NIH, 1962-63; rsch. physiologist Life Scis. Directorate, NASA, Ames Rsch. Ctr., Moffett Field, Calif., 1963—66; rsch. physiologist Space Scis. directorate NASA/Ames Rsch. Ctr., Moffett Field, Calif., 1967—2002; postdoctoral fellowship Karolinska Inst., Stockholm, 1966-67. Adj. prof. biology dept. San Francisco State U., 1988-2002; adj. prof. dept. exercise sci. U. Calif., Davis, 1996-01; adj. prof. dept. human performance San Jose State U., 2002—; Japan Soc. for Promotion of Sci. vis. prof. Kyoto Prefectural U. Medicine, 1997; mem. internat. adv. bd. Medicina Sportiva. Mem. editorial bd. Jour. Applied Physiology, 1989-99, Med. Sci. Sports Exercise, 2000-02; contbr. articles to profl. jours. Pub. dir. N.Mex. Highlands U. Found., 1999—. Served with U.S. Army, 1952-53. Recipient Disting. Alumni award N.Mex. Highlands U., 1990, Disting. Alumni award dept. molecular and integrative physiology U. Ill., 1998, Am. Coll. Sports Medicine Citation award, 1999, Water and Medicine prize Internat. Cannes and Nestle Water Inst., 2003; exch. fellow NAS, 1973-74, 77, 89, NIH, 1980; named to Springfield (Ill.) H.S. Hall of Fame, 2005. Fellow AIAA (assoc.), Am. Coll. Sports Medicine (trustee 1984-87), Aerospace Med. Assn. (Harold Ellingson award 1981-82, Eric Liljencrantz award 1990), NASA Ames Assn. (assoc.); mem. Am. Physiol. Soc. (mem. com. on coms. 1984-87, long range planning com. 1987-90, internat. physiol. com. 1997-00, environ. and exercise physiology sect. Honor award, 2004), Polish Soc. Sports Medicine (hon.), Shooting Sports Rsch. Coun. (internat. shooters devel. fund 1984), Sigma Xi. Achievements include patents in field. Home: 12391 Farr Ranch Ct Saratoga CA 95070-6527 Office Phone: 408-867-5680.

GREENLICK, MERWYN RONALD, health services researcher; b. Detroit, Mar. 12, 1935; s. Emanuel and Fay Greenlick; m. Harriet Greenlick, Aug. 19, 1956; children: Phyllis, Michael; 1 child, Vicki. BS, Wayne State U., 1957; MS, U. Mich., 1961, PhD, 1967. Pharmacist, Detroit, 1957—60; spl. instr., instr. pharmacy adminstrn. Coll. Pharmacy Wayne State U., 1958—62; dir. of research n.w. region Kaiser-Permanente, Portland, Oreg., 1964—95; v.p. (rsch.) Kaiser Found. Hosp., 1981—95; sr. fellow Ctr. for Advanced Study in the Behavioral Sci., Stanford, Calif., 1995—96; adj. prof. sociology and social work Portland State U., 1965—; clin. prof. preventive medicine and pub. health Oreg. Health Sci. U., 1971—89, prof., acting chair preventive medicine and pub. health, 1990—93, prof., chair preventive medicine and pub. health, 1993—2000, emeritus prof., 2000—. Mem. Gov.'s Commn. on Health Care, 1988; cons. Gov.'s Health Manpower Coun.; mem. Oreg. State House of Reps., 2003—. Pres. Jewish Edn. Assn., Portland, 1976—78; bd. dirs. Washington County Cmty. Action Orgn., 1966—70; Jewish Fedn., 1975—79. Recipient USPHS trainee award, 1962—63, 1963—64. Fellow: APHA, Inst. Medicine NAS; mem.: AAAS, Oregon House of Rep. (mem. (HD33) 2003), N.W. Health Found. (bd. dir. 1997—), Assn. Health Svc. Rsch. (Disting. fellow, Pres.'s award 1995). Jewish. Home: 712 NW Spring Ave Portland OR 97229-6913 Office: Oreg Health Svcs U CB 669 3181 SW Sam Jackson Park Rd Portland OR 97201-3011

GREENSPAN, DEBORAH, dental educator; BDS, U. London, 1960, BDS, 1964; LDS, Royal Coll. Surgeons, Eng., 1964; ScD (hon.), Georgetown U., 1990; DSc, U. London, 1991; DDS, U. Sheffield, Eng., 2008; DSc, Kings Coll., London, 2007. Registered dental practioner, U.K.; diplomate Am. Bd. Oral Medicine. Vis. lectr. oral medicine U. Calif., San Francisco, 1976-83, asst. clin. prof., 1983-85, assoc. clin. prof., 1985-89, clin. prof., 1989-96, prof. clin. oral medicine, 1996—, interim chair dept. orofacial scis. Sch. Dentistry, 2004—05, interim chair dept. orofacial scis., 2004—07, chair orofacial scis., 2007—. Lectr. in oral biology, U. Calif., San Francisco, 1972, clin. dir. Oral AIDS Ctr., 1987—, active Sch. Dentistry coms. including admissions com., 1985—, chair task force on infection control, 1987—; cons. Joint FDI/WHO Working Group on AIDS, 1989—, EEC, 1990, WHO, 1990, 91, Dept. Health State Calif., 1991, others; ad hoc reviews Epidemiology and Disease Control Sect. Div. Rsch. Grants NIH, 1987—, Rsch. Am. Global Ambassador; mem. programs adv. com. Nat. Inst. Dental Rsch., 1989—, mem. spl. ad hoc tech. rev. panel, 1991, mem. panel Fed. Drug Adminstrn., 1991-94; other svc. to govtl. agys.; participant numerous sci. and profl. workshops, meetings, and continuing edn. courses, numerous radio, TV, and press interviews concerning AIDS and infection control in dentistry. Author: (with J.S. Greenspan, Pindborg, and Schiødt), AIDS and the Dental Team, 1986 (transl. German, French, Italian, Spanish, Japanese), AIDS and the Mouth, 1990, (with others) San Francisco General Hospital AIDS Knowledge Base, 1986, Dermatologic Clinics, 5th edit., 1987, Infectious Disease Clinics of North America, 2nd. edit., 1988, Oral Manifestations of AIDS, 1988, Contemporary Periodontics, 1989, Opportunistic Infections in AIDS Patients, 1990, AIDS Clinical Review, 1990, Oral Manifestations of Systemic Disease, 1990, others; mem. editl. bd. rev. Jour. Am. Coll. Dentists, 1991; mem. editl. bd. Oral Diseases, 1999; ad hoc referee Jour. Oral Pathology, 1983—, Cancer, 1985—, Jour. Acad. Gen. Dentistry, 1986—, European Jour. Cancer & Clin. Oncology, 1986, Archives of Dermatology, 1988—, Jour. AMA, 1988—, AIDS, 1991; contbr. numerous articles to profl. jours. Mem. dental subcom. of profl. edn. com. Calif. div. Am. Cancer Soc., 1982-90, profl. health care providers task force, 1991. Nat. Cancer Inst. fellow, 1978-79, Am. Coll. Dentists fellow, 1988; recipient Woman of Distinction award, London, 1986, Commendation cert. Asst. Sec. for Health, 1989; named Seymour J. Kreshover lectr. Nat. Inst. Dental Rsch., 1989, Hon. Lectr. United Med. and Dental Schs. of Guys and St. Thomas Hosps., U. London, 1991. Fellow AAAS, Royal Soc. Medicine, Royal Coll. Surgeons; mem. ADA (vis. lectr. speaker's bur. 1988—, cons. coun. on dental therapeutics 1988—, mem. coun. sci. affairs 1999—), Am. Assn. Dental Rsch. (session chair 1986-87, constitution com. 1988-91, chair 1990-91, pres. San Francisco sect. 1990—, treas. 1992—), Am. Acad. Oral Pathology, Am. Soc. Microbiology, Am. Assn. Women Dentists, Am. Acad. Oral Medicine, Am. Assn. Dental Schs., Internat. Assn. Dental Rsch. (pres. exptl. pathology group 1989-90, v.p. 2004-05, other coms. and offices), Internat. Assn. Oral Pathologists, Internat. Assn. for Dental Rsch. (v.p. 2005—), Internat. Dental Assn. for Dental Rsch. (pres., 2007-08), Calif. Dental Assn., San Francisco Dental Soc., Internat. AIDS Soc., Inst. of Medicine. Achievements include rsch. on oral candidiasis in HIV infection, on HIV-associated salivary gland disease, on oral hairy leukoplakia, and on the prevalence of HIV-associated gingivitis and periodontitis in HIV-infected patients. Office: U Calif Sch Dentistry Dept Orofacial Scis S 612 513 Parnassus Ave Box 0422 San Francisco CA 94143-0422

GREENSPAN, FRANCIS S., physician; b. Perth Amboy, NJ, Mar. 16, 1920; s. Philip and Francis (Davidson) G.; m. Bonnie Jean Fisher, Oct. 25, 1945; children: Richard L., Robert H., Susan L. BA, Cornell U., 1940, MD, 1943. Diplomate Am. Bd. Internal Medicine. Mem. endocrinology staff U. Calif.-San Francisco; chief endocrinology Stanford (Calif.) Hosp., 1949-59; chief thyroid clinic U. Calif. Med. Ctr., San Francisco, 1959—, now clin. prof. medicine and radiology; practice medicine specializing in endocrinology San Francisco; chief of staff U. Calif. Hosps. and Clinics, San Francisco, 1976-78. Editor: Textbook of Endocrinology; contbr. articles to med. jours. Served with USNR, 1944-45. Mem. San Francisco Med. Soc., Calif. Med. Assn., AMA, Endocrine Soc., Am. Thyroid Assn., Western Soc. Clin. Rsch., Western Assn. Physicians, Calif. Acad. Medicine. Office: U Calif Med Ctr Ste 553 400 Parnassus Ave San Francisco CA 94143-1222 Home Phone: 415-751-7570; Office Phone: 415-353-2350. Business E-Mail: frankg@medicine.ucsf.edu.

GREENSPAN, JOHN S., dental and medical educator, researcher, academic administrator; b. London, Jan. 7, 1938; came to U.S., 1976; s. Nathan and Jessie (Dion) G.; m. Deborah, Dec. 1962; children: Nicholas J., Louise C. BSC in Anatomy with 1st class honors, U. London, 1959, B in Dental Surgery, 1962, PhD in Exptl. Pathology, 1967; ScD (hon.), Georgetown U., 1990. Licentiate in dental surgery Royal Coll. of Surgeons of Eng. Asst. house surgeon in conservation and periodontology Royal Dental Hosp. London, 1962; asst. lectr. oral pathology Sch. of Dental Surgery Royal Dental Hosp. of London, U. London, 1963-65, lectr. oral pathology Sch. of Dental Surgery, 1965-68, sr. lectr. oral pathology Sch. of Dental Surgery, 1968-75; prof. oral biology and oral pathology Sch. of Dentisty, U. Calif., San Francisco, 1976—, vice chmn. dept. oral medicine and hosp. dentistry, 1977-82, chmn. div. oral biology, 1981-89, coord. basic scis., 1982-96; chmn. dept. stomatology Sch. of Dentistry, U. Calif., San Francisco, 1989—2000, dean rsch., 2001—; dir. AIDS Rsch. Inst. U. Calif., 2004—. Cons. oral pathology St. John's Hosp. and Inst. of Dermatology, London, 1973-76; cons. dental surgeon St. George's Hosp., 1972-76; prof. dept. pathology Sch. Medicine U. Calif., San Francisco, 1976—; dir. U. Calif. AIDS Specimen Bank, San Francisco, 1982—, U. Calif. Oral AIDS Ctr., San Francisco, 1987—; assoc. dir. dental clin. epidemiology program U. Calif., San Francisco, 1987-95; dir. U. Calif. AIDS Clin. Rsch. Ctr., San Francisco, 1992-2005; Burroughs Wellcome vis. prof. Royal Soc. Medicine, U.K., 1996-97; dir. UCSF Aids Rsch. Inst., 2004—; fellow Kings Coll., London, Eng., 2003; presenter, lectr. in field. Author: (with others) Opportunistic Infections in Patients with the Acquired Immunodeficiency Syndrome, 1989, Contemporary Periodontics, 1989, Gastroenterology Clinics of North America, 1988, Perspectives on Oral Manifestations of AIDS, 1988, AIDS: Pathogenesis and Treatment, 1988, others; contbr. articles to profl. jours.; editorial cons. Achives of Oral Biology, 1968—, Jour. of Calif. Dental Assn., 1980—; editoral adv. bd. Jour. of Dental Rsch., 1977—; editorial bd. AIDS Alert, 1987-89, Brit. Dental Jour., 1998—; sr. editor Oral Diseases, 1994-98. Rsch. grantee NIH-Nat. Inst. Dental Rsch., 1978-82, 86—, U. Calif. Task Force on AIDS, 1983—, rsch. com. Royal Dental Hosp., London, 1964-76, Med. Rsch. Coun. of U.K., 1974-77, chmn. U. Calif. San Francisco Acad. Senate, 1983-85; Nuffield dental scholar, 1958-59; fellow Am. Coll. Dentists, 1982—, AAAS, 1985—; recipient Seymour J. Kreshover Lecture award Nat. Inst. Dental Rsch., NIH, 1989, Rsch. in Oral Biology award Internat. Assn. Dental Rsch., 1992. Fellow: Royal Coll. Surgeons Faculty of Dental Surgery, Royal Coll. Pathologists; mem.: AAAS, ADA, Am. Assn. Pathologists, Calif. Soc. Oral Pathologists Histochem. Soc., Calif. Dental Assn., San Francisco Dental Soc., Internat. Assn. Oral Pathologists, Bay Area Tchrs. Oral Pathology, Am. Acad. Oral Pathology, Oral Pathology Soc. (U.K.), Pathological Soc. (U.K.), Royal Soc. Medicine (U.K.), Internat. Assn. Dental Rsch. (pres. 1996—97), Am. Assn. Dental Rsch. (pres. 1988—89), Inst. Medicine of Nat. Acad. Scis. Avocations: skiing, gardening, travel, wine. Office: U Calif PO Box 422 San Francisco CA 94143-0422 Office Phone: 415-476-2220. Business E-Mail: john.greenspan@ucsf.edu.

GREENSPAN, LOUISE CATHERINE, pediatrician; b. London, Apr. 19, 1969; 2 children. BA, Univ. Calif., Berkeley; MD, Cornell Univ., 1995. Cert. Am. Bd. Pediatrics, 1998, in pediatric endocrinology Am. Bd. Pediatrics, 2001. Resident in pediatrics Univ. Calif., San Francisco, 1995—98, fellow in pediatric endocrinology, 1998—2001; pediatric endocrinologist Permanente Med. Group, San Francisco, 1998—; asst. clin. prof. Univ. Calif., San Francisco, 2001. Mem.: Am. Acad. Pediatrics, Am. Diabetes Assn., Endocrine Soc., Lawson Wilkens Pediatric Endocrinology Soc. Office: Permanente Med Group 8th Fl N 2200 O'Farrell St San Francisco CA 94115 Office Phone: 415-833-4625.

GREENSTEIN, MARLA NAN, lawyer; b. Chgo., Jan. 20, 1957; d. Charles Allen and Lenore Greenstein. Cert., Oxford U., Eng., 1978; AB, Georgetown U., 1979; JD, Loyola U., 1982. Bar: Ill. 1982, Alaska 1997, U.S. Dist. Ct. (no. dist.) Ill. 1982, U.S. Ct. Appeals (7th cir.) 1983. Sr. staff atty. Am. Judicature Soc., Chgo., 1982-85, Alaska Jud. Council, Anchorage, 1985-89; exec. dir. Ala. Commn. Jud. Conduct, Anchorage, 1989—. Cons. Com. on Cts. and Justice, Chgo., 1985. Author: Handbook for Judicial Nominating Commissioners, 1984. Mem. ABA (chair lawyers conf. jud. divsn. 1996-97), Assn. Jud. Disciplinary Counsel (bd. dirs. 1992—), Am. Judicature Soc. (bd. dirs. 1992-97, exec. com. 1997—2003), Pi Sigma Alpha. Avocations: photography, drawing. Office: Commn Jud Conduct 1029 W 3rd Ave 550 Anchorage AK 99501-1944 E-mail: mgreenstein@acjc.state.ak.us.

GREENSTEIN, MARTIN RICHARD, lawyer; b. Boston, Dec. 29, 1944; s. Paul and Sarah Greenstein; m. Judith Stevens; children: Stacey, Marc, Seth, Andrew. BSEE magna cum laude, Tufts U., 1965; MSEE, Princeton U., 1966; JD with highest honors, John Marshall Law Sch., 1971. Bar: Ill. 1971, N.Y. 1982, Calif. 1982, U.S. Patent Office 1971, U.S. Supreme Ct. 1981. Mem. tech. staff Bell Telephone Labs., Naperville, Ill., 1965-70, mem. patent staff, 1970-71; assoc. firm Baker & McKenzie, Chgo., 1971-78, ptnr., 1978-89, Palo Alto, Calif., 1989-93, TechMark, Trademark and Intellectual Property Law, San Jose, Calif., 1993—. Instr. John Marshall Law Sch., Chgo., 1972-76 Editorial bd. The Trademark Reporter, 1976-92. Trustee Village of Lisle, 1980-83; bd. dirs. Ill. Software Assn. and Ctr., 1984-87 Mem. ABA, State Bar Calif., Internat. Trademark Assn., Am. Intellectual Property Law Assn., Tau Beta Pi, Eta Kappa Nu. Home: 1709 Whitham Ave Los Altos CA 94024 Office: TechMark 16th Fl 55 S Market St San Jose CA 95113-2327

GREENSTEIN, MERLE EDWARD, import/export company executive; b. Portland, Oreg., June 22, 1937; s. Sol and Tillie Germaine (Schnitzer) Greenstein; m. Nasi Jenab; children: Todd Aaron, Boback Emad, Lela Emad. BA, Reed Coll., 1959. Pres. Acme Trading and Supply Co., Portland, 1963—82; chmn. MMI Group, Portland, 1982—91, Internat. Devel. Assocs., Portland, 1991—, Kesef Devel., LLC. Com. mem. ISRI, Washington, 1987—89; dist. export coun. U.S. Dept. Commerce, 1980—; mem. 1st U.S. trade missions to Vietnam, 1996; Ariz. regional export coun. trade mission to Eastern Europe; bd. advisor Ruscan Diamond Internat., Toronto. Chmn. fin. Portland Opera, 1966; bd. dirs. Met. YMCA, 1964—67; active Internat. Sculpture Invitational Bd.; del. to China State of Oreg. Ofcl. Trade Mission, 1979; chmn. Western Internat. Trade Group, 1981—82; fin. chmn. Anne Frank exhibit, Portland; joint chmn. State of Oreg. Youth Legislature; joint chmn. bldg. campaign Oreg. Mus. Sci. and Industry; treas. ASC; bd. dirs. Waverly Children's Home; property task force com., mem. capital campaign cabinet Oreg. Food Bank; bd. dirs. Metro Family Svc.; mem. Oreg. Mentoring Group; fin. chmn. return of Anne Frank exhibit, 2002; mem. devel. com. Alzheimer's Assn.; mem. scholarship com. Iranian Am. Profl. Assn. Oreg.; mem. Oreg. Uniting Group Discussions; bd. dirs. Oreg. Jewish Cmty. Found.; fin. chmn. Oreg. Holocaust; mem. steering com. Camp Rosenbaum; v.p. Oreg.-Fujian (China) Sister State Assn.; mem. State of Oreg. Legis. Fujian Com.; com. chmn. Oreg. Fujian Joint Econ. Com.; bd. advisor Cypress Corp.; advisor UCSF Medical Fund Raise Com.; pres. Komak, Non-Profit Charity Corp.; med. advisor UCSF Fund Raising Com.; campaign chair United Jewish Appeal; mem. Am. Jewish Com.; bd. dirs. Jewish Welfare Fedn. Recipient Pres.'s E for Export, U.S. Dept. Commerce, 1969, Maurice D. Sussman Meml. award, 2007; named Citizen of the Week, City of Portland, 1953; scholar, U. Chgo. Law Sch., 1959. Mem.: City Club, Multnomah Athletic Club Portland, Rolls Royce Owners Club (London), Shriners, Masons. Avocations: skiing, antique autos, Arabian horses. Personal E-mail: merlenasi@yahoo.com, merlenasi@gmail.com.

GREENWALD, ARTHUR M., federal judge; b. 1936; BBA, UCLA; JD, Southwestern Sch. Law. Asst. U.S. atty. L.A., 1964-87; apptd. bankruptcy judge cen. dist. U.S. Dist. Ct. Calif., 1987. Mem. FBA, Am. Judicature Soc., Calif. Soc. CPAs, L.A. County Mus., KCET Pub. Broadcasting Sys. Office: 21041 Burbank Blvd Ste 324 Woodland Hills CA 91367-6606 Fax: 818-587-2949.

GREENWOOD, COLLETTE P., municipal official, finance officer; b. Summit, Ill. BA, Ea. Wash. U., 1980. With acctg. dept. Montgomerty Ward, Spokane, Wash., 1976-90; acctg. clk. water, hydro City of Spokane, 1979-93, budget acctg., 1993-96, dir. of office of mgmt. & bufget, 1996—. Recipient Class of 1998 award Leadership Spokane Spokane C. of C. Mem. Nat. Mgmt. Assn. (elected dir. 1999), Govt. Fin. Officers Assn., Wash. Fin. Officers Assn. Office: City Spokane 808 W Spokane Falls Blvd Spokane WA 99201-3333

GREENWOOD, M. R. C., biologist, nutrition educator, former academic administrator; b. Gainesville, Fla., Apr. 11, 1943; d. Stanley James and Mary Rita (Schmeltz) Cooke; m. (div. 1968); 1 child, James Robert. AB summa cum laude, Vassar Coll., 1968; PhD, Rockefeller U., 1973; LHD (hon.), Mt. St. Mary Coll., 1989. Rsch. assoc. Inst. of Human Nutrition, Columbia U., NYC, 1974-75, adj. asst. prof., 1975-76, asst. prof., 1976-78; assoc. prof. dept. biology Vassar Coll., Poughkeepsie, NY, 1978-81, prof. biology, 1981-86, dir. animal model, CORE Lab. of Obesity Rsch. Ctr., 1985-89, dir. undergrad. rsch. summer inst., 1986-88, dir. Howard Hughes biol.

scis. network program, 1988, chmn. of biology dept., John Guy Vassar prof. natural scis., 1986-89; prof. nutrition and internal medicine, dean grad. studies U. Calif., Davis, 1989-96, chancellor Santa Cruz, 1996—2004; provost, sr. v.p. academic affairs U. Calif. sys., 2004—05; prof. biology U. Calif., Santa Cruz, 2005—; prof. nutrition and internal medicine dept. nutrition U. Calif. Davis, 2005—. Mem. nutrition study sect. NIH, 1983-87; mem. NRC; assoc. dir. for sci. White House Office Sci. and Tech., 1993-95. Editor: Obesity, Vol. 4, 1983; contbr. over 250 articles and abstracts to profl. jours., 1974-89. Recipient Rsch. Career Devel. award NIH, 1978-83; Mellon scholar-in-residence St. Olaf Coll., Northfield, Minn., 1978; NY State Regents fellow, 1968. Mem. AAAS (pres. 1998-99), NRC (policy and global affairs divsn. chair 2004-), Inst. Medicine of Nat. Acad. Scis. (chair food and nutrition bd., diet and health subcom. 1986—), N.Am. Soc. Study of Obesity (pres. 1987-88), Am. Inst. Nutrition (BioServ 1982), Am. Physiol. Soc., The Harvey Soc., Am. Diabetes Assn., Am. Acad. Arts and Scis., Internat. Assn. Study of Obesity (treas. 1991—). Home: 5033 El Cemonte Ave Davis CA 95616 Office: U Calif Davis Meyer Hall Dept Nutrition 1 Shields Rd Davis CA 95616

GREENWOOD, RICHARD A., state legislator, protective services official; m. Dessa Rae Greenwood; 4 children. Attended, Miami Daded Jr. Coll.; BS in Criminal Justice, Weber State U.; grad., FBI Nat. Acad., 1992. Trooper Metro-Dade Police Dept., Miami, 1972-76; with Utah Hwy. Patrol, 1976—, trooper, 1976-86, sgt., accident reconstrn. specialist, adminstrv. asst. to supt., 1990-91, lt., comdr. protective svcs. at the state capitol, comdr. exec. protection, 1992, supt., 1993—; mem. Dist. 12 Utah House of Reps., 2007—. Republican. Office: W030 Capitol Complex Salt Lake City UT 84114 Office Phone: 801-538-1029. Office Fax: 801-538-1908. Business E-Mail: rgreenwood@utah.gov.*

GREER, HOWARD EARL, retired career officer; b. Tyler, Tex., May 1, 1921; s. Earl Abner and Ollie (Lightfoot) G.; m. Dale Price, Nov. 1, 1986; children— Margaret, Darby, David, Briand, Holly, Howard. Student, Tyler Jr. Coll., 1939-40; BS, U.S. Naval Acad., 1943; MBA, George Washington U., 1965. Commd. ensign U.S. Navy, 1943, advanced through grades to vice adm., 1975; comdr. Aircraft Carrier Hancock, 1967-69, Carrier Force, Vietnam, (4 tours), Naval Air Forces, U.S. Atlantic Fleet, Norfolk, Va., 1975-78. Mem. CEDAM Internat. Decorated D.S.M. (2), Legion of Merit (4), Knights of Malta Order St. John of Jerusalem. Mem. Assn. Naval Aviation, Golden Eagles (early pioneer naval aviators), Tailhook Assn., Naval Res. Assn., Lomas Santa Fe Country Club. Republican. Methodist. Home: 8539 Prestwick Dr La Jolla CA 92037-2025

GREER, JUDY EVANS, actress; b. Detroit, July 20, 1975; BFA in Theatre, DePaul U., Chgo., 1997. Actress (films) Stricken, 1998, Kissing a Fool, 1998, Desperate But Not Serious, 1999, The Reel, 1999, Jawbreaker, 1999, Three Kings, 1999, The Big Split, 1999, What Planet Are You From?, 2000, Sunset Strip, 2000, The Specials, 2000, What Women Want, 2000, Without Charlie, 2001, The Wedding Planner, 2001, Audit, 2001, The Cat Returns, 2002, Rules of Love, 2002, Adaptation, 2002, The Hebrew Hammer, 2003, I Love Your Work, 2003, 13 Going on 30, 2004 (nominated Choice Movie Sleazebag, Teen Choice Awards, 2004), The Village, 2004, The Last Shot, 2004, LolliLove, 2004, The Moguls, 2005, Cursed, 2005, The Great New Wonderful, 2005, In Memory of My Father, 2005, Elizabethtown, 2005, Full Disclosure, 2005, American Dreamz, 2006, The TV Set, 2006, The Key Man, 2007, The Go-Getter, 2007, The Grand, 2007, 27 Dresses, 2008, (TV series) Love & Money, 1999, Arrested Development, 2003—05, Love Monkey, 2006, Miss Guided, 2008—, (TV films) Silicon Follies, 2001, Other People's Business, 2003. Avocation: knitting. Office: c/o Principato Young Mgmt Ste 880 9465 Wilshire Blvd Beverly Hills CA 90212

GREER, MONTE ARNOLD, endocrinologist, educator; b. Portland, Oreg., Oct. 26, 1922; s. William Wallace and Rose (Rasmussen) G.; m. Peggy Johnson, Dec. 31, 1943; children: Susan Elizabeth, Richard Arnold. Student, Oreg. State U., 1940-43; AB, Stanford U., 1944, MD, 1947. Intern San Francisco Gen. Hosp., 1946—47; rsch. fellow endocrinology New England Med. Ctr., Boston, 1947—49; resident internal medicine Mass. Meml. Hosp., Boston, 1949—50; rsch. assoc. in endocrinology New England Med. Ctr. Hosp., 1950—51; sr. investigator, sr. asst. surgeon USPHS, Nat. Cancer Inst., NIH, Bethesda, Md., 1951—55; chief radioisotope unit D.C. Gen. Hosp., Washington, 1951—55; clin. asst. prof. medicine UCLA, 1955—56; chief radioisotope svc. VA Hosp., Long Beach, Calif., 1955—56; head div. endocrinology Oreg. Health & Sci. U. (formerly U. Oreg. Med. Sch.), Portland, 1956—80, assoc. prof., 1956—62, prof. medicine, 1962—, prof. physiology, 1992—, head divsn. endocrinology, metabolism and clin. nutrition, 1980—84, head sect. endocrinology, 1984—90. Author: (with H. Studer) The Regulation of Thyroid Function in Iodine Deficiency, 1968, (with P. Langer) Antithyroid Drugs and Naturally Occurring Goitrogens, 1977; editor: The Thyroid Gland, 1990, (with D.H. Solomon) The Thyroid, 1974; mem. editorial bd. Endocrinology, 1960-72, Neuroendocrinology, 1965-76, Endocrine Regulations, 1971—; contbr. articles to profl. jours. Mem. Thyroid Task Force NIH Com. for Evaluation of Endocrinology and Metabolic Diseases, 1977-80, Endocrinology Study Sect., NIH, 1977-80. Pharmacol. and Endocrinology fellowship study sect. NIH, 1968-72; recipient Oppenheimer award Endocrine Soc., 1958, Rsch. Career award NIH, 1962-81, Discovery award Med. Rsch. Found. Oreg., 1985, DeMolay Legion of Honor award, 1988. Mem. AAAS, Am. Fedn. for Clin. Rsch. (chmn. Western sect. 1958-59), Western Soc. for Clin. Rsch. (v.p. 1963-64, pres. 1967-68), Endocrine Soc. (mem. council 1965-68, v.p. 1976-77), Am. Thyroid Assn. (v.p., dir. 1974-77, pres. 1980, Disting. Service award 1985), Am. Soc. Clin. Investigation, Soc. Exptl. Biology and Medicine, Western Assn. Physicians (sec.-treas. 1974-77), Assn. Am. Physicians, Internat. Brain Rsch. Orgn., Internat. Soc. Neuroendocrinology, European Thyroid Assn., Japan Endocrine Soc. (hon.), Czechoslovak Endocrine Soc. (hon.), Rotary, Sigma Chi. Office: Oreg Health and Sci Univ Portland OR 97201

GREER, SANDRA CHARLENE, academic administrator, chemistry professor; d. Charles Williams and Louise (Childress) Thomason; m. William Louis Greer, 1968 (div. 1992); children: Andrew Sean, Michael Geoffrey. BS, Furman U., Greenville, SC, 1966; PhD, U. Chgo., 1969. Rsch. chemist Nat. Bur. Stds., Gaithersburg, Md., 1969—78; assoc. prof. U. Md., College Park, 1978—83, prof. chemistry and biochemistry Coll. Chem. and Life Scis., 1983—2008, prof. chemical and biomolecular engring. A. James Clark Sch. Engring., 1995—2008; program dir. NSF, Washington, 1985—86; provost, dean faculty, prof. chemistry Mills Coll., Oakland, Calif., 2008—. Contbr. articles to profl. jours. Mem. Com. Advancement Women Chem., Eugene, Oreg., 1998. Fellow AAAS, Am. Phys. Soc.; mem. AICE, Am. Chem. Soc., Assn. Women in Sci. Office: Mills Coll Mills Hall 5000 MacArthur Blvd Oakland CA 94613 Office Phone: 510-430-2096. Office Fax: 510-430-3119. E-mail: provost@mills.edu.

GREGG, CHARLES THORNTON, research and development company executive, molecular biologist, researcher; b. Billings, Mont., July 27, 1927; s. Charles Thornton and Gertrude (Hurst) G.; m. Elizabeth Whitaker, Dec. 20, 1947; children: Paul, Diane, Brian, Elaine. BS in Physics, Oreg. State U., 1952, MS in Organic Chemistry, 1955, PhD in Biochemistry, 1959. Postdoctoral fellow Nat. Cancer Inst., Johns Hopkins Sch. Med., Balt., 1959-63; mem. staff Los Alamos (N.Mex.) Nat. Lab., 1963-85; sr. scientist Mesa Diagnostics, Los Alamos, 1985-86; v.p. rsch. Los Alamos Diagnostics, 1986-90; pres. Innovative Surg. Tech. Inc., 1991—. Pres. Bethco, Inc., 1972—; vis. prof. The Free U., Berlin, 1973-74; cons. internat. tech. div. Los Alamos Nat. Lab., 1985-90. Author: Plague, 1978, The Virus of Love, 1983, Tarawa, 1985; patentee bacterial identification apparatus, safe surg. knife. Bd. dirs. Friends of Mesa Pub. Libr., Los Alamos, 1981-83, County Libr. Los Alamos, 1983-85, Los Alamos Arts Coun., 1985-87, bd. dir., Lukens Med. Corp., 1996-97. Served in U.S. Navy, 1944-46. Fellow AAAS; mem. Am. Soc. Biochemistry and Molecular Biology, Am. Soc. Microbiology, Sigma Xi, Sigma Pi Sigma, Phi Lambda Upsilon. Democrat. Unitarian Universalist. Avocation: hiking. Office: 190 Central Park Sq Los Alamos NM 87544-4001 Home Phone: 505-662-7429; Office Phone: 505-662-3240. Personal E-mail: cgregg3@yahoo.com. Business E-Mail: president@1stmedmart.com.

GREGOIRE, CHRISTINE O'GRADY, Governor of Washington, former state attorney general; b. Auburn, Wash., Mar. 24, 1947; m. Michael Gregoire; children: Courtney, Michelle. BA in Speech & Sociology, U. Wash., 1969; JD cum laude, Gonzaga U., 1977, LLD (hon.), 1995. Clerk, typist Wash. State Adult Probation/ Parole Office, Seattle, 1969; caseworker Wash. Dept. Social and Health Scis., Everett, 1974; asst. atty. gen. State of Wash., Spokane, 1977—81, sr. asst. atty. gen., 1981—82, dep. atty. gen. Olympia, 1982—88, atty. gen., 1992—2005, gov., 2005—; dir. Wash. State Dept. Ecology, 1988—92. Chair States/B.C. Oil Spill Task Force, 1989—92, Puget Sound Water Quality Authority, 1990—92, Nat. Com. State Environ. Dirs., 1991—92. Bd. dirs. Wash. State Dept. Ecology, 1988—92. Recipient Conservationist of Yr. award, Trout Unlimited/N.W. Steelhead & Salmon Coun., 1994, Gov.'s Child Abuse Prevention award, 1996, Myra Bradwell award, 1997, Wyman award, 1997—98, Bd. of Gov.'s award for professionalism, WSBA, 1997, Kick Butt award, The Tobacco Free Coalition of Pierce County, 1997, Wash. State Hosp. Assn. award, 1997, Citizen Activist award, Gleitsman Found., 1998, Woman of Achievement award, Assn. for Women in Comm. Matrix Table, 1999, Pub. Justice award, WSTLA, 1999, Excellence in Pub. Health award, Wash. State Assn. Local Pub. Health Ofcls., 1999, Women in Govt. award, Good Housekeeping, 1999, Spl. Recognition award, Wash. State Nurses Assn., 2000; named Woman of Yr., Am. Legion Aux., 1999; named one of 25 Most Influential Working Mothers, Working Mother mag., 2000. Mem.: Nat. Assn. Attys. Gen. (consumer protection and environment com., energy com., children and the law subcom., pres. 1999—2000). Democrat. Office: Office of Gov PO Box 40002 Olympia WA 98504 Office Phone: 360-753-6780. Office Fax: 360-753-4110.

GREGOR, DOROTHY DEBORAH, retired librarian; b. Dobbs Ferry, NY, Aug. 15, 1939; d. Richard Garrett Heckman and Marion Allen (Richmond) Stewart; m. A. James Gregor, June 22, 1963 (div. 1974). BA, Occidental Coll., 1961; MA, U. Hawaii, 1963; MLS, U. Tex., 1968; cert. in Library Mgmt., U. Calif., Berkeley, 1976. Reference libr. U. Calif., San Francisco, 1968-69; dept. libr. Pub. Health Libr. U. Calif., Berkeley, 1969-71, tech. services libr., 1973-76; reference libr. Hamilton Libr., Honolulu, 1971-72; head serials dept. U. Calif., Berkeley, 1976-80, assoc. univ. libr. tech. svcs. dept., 1980-84, univ. libr., 1992-94; chief Shared Cataloging div. Libr. of Congress, Washington, 1984-85; univ. libr. U. Calif.-San Diego, La Jolla, 1985-92, OCLC asst. to pres. for acad. and rsch. libr. rels., 1995—98; docent Asian Art Mus., San Francisco, 1997—, ret. Instr. sch. libr. and info. studies U. Calif., Berkeley, 1975, 76, 83; cons. Nat. Libr. of Medicine, Bethesda, Md., 1985, Ohio Bd. Regents, Columbus, 1987; trustee Online Computer Libr. Ctr., 1988-96; dir. Nat. Coordinating Com. on Japanese Libr. Resources, 1995-98; docent Asian Art Mus., San Francisco, 1997-. Mem.: ALA, Libr. Info. Tech. Assn., Program Com. Ctr. for Rsch. Libns. (bd. chair 1992—93, Hugh Atkinson award 1994). E-mail: dgregor@mcn.org.

GREGORIAN, LISA, broadcast executive; m. Fred Gregorian; 1 child. Grad., Emerson Coll., Boston. Joined Lorimar Telepictures (later acquired by Warner Bros.), 1986, dir. internat. home video & Caribbean TV, dir. internat. rsch. & pre-sale mktg., v.p. internat. mktg. & rsch.; sr. v.p. mktg. internat. TV distbn. Warner Bros. Entertainment, sr. v.p. TV creative svcs., 2003—05; exec. v.p. worldwide mktg. Warner Bros. TV Group, 2005—. Named a Studio Brand Builder, PROMAX, 2003; named one of The 100 Most Powerful Women in Entertainment, Hollywood Reporter, 2007. Office: Warner Bros TV Group 4000 Warner Blvd Burbank CA 91522

GREGORY, CALVIN, real estate investor; b. Bronx, NY, Jan. 11, 1942; s. Jacob and Ruth Gregory; m. Rachel Anna Carver, Feb. 14, 1970 (div. Apr. 1977); children: Debby Lynn, Trixy Sue; m. Carla Deane Deaver, June 30, 1979. AA, L.A. City Coll., 1962; BA, Calif. State U., LA, 1964; MDiv, Fuller Theol. Sem., 1968; M in Religious Edn., Southwestern Sem., Ft. Worth, 1969; PhD in Religion, Universal Life. Ch., Modesto, Calif., 1982; DDiv (hon.), Otay Mesa Coll., 1982. Ordained to ministry Am. Bapt. Conv., 1970; cert. notary pub., real estate lic., casualty lic. Calif. Youth minister First Bapt. Ch., Delano, Calif., 1964—65, 1969—70; youth dir. St. Luke's United Meth. Ch., Highland Park, Calif., 1969—70; tchr. polit. sci. Maranatha High Sch., Rosemead, Calif., 1969—70; aux. chaplain U.S. Air Force 750th Radar Squadron, Edwards AFB, Calif., 1970—72; pastor First Bapt. Ch., Boron, Calif., 1971—72; ins. agt. Prudential Ins. Co., Ventura, Calif., 1972—73, sales mgr., 1973—74; casualty ins. agt. Allstate Ins. Co., Thousand Oaks, Calif., 1974—75; pres. Ins. Agy. Placement Svcs., Thousand Oaks, Calif., 1975—; head youth minister Emanuel Presbyn. Ch., LA, 1973—74; owner, investor real estate, Wales, England, Canada, Australia. Counselor YMCA, Hollywood, Calif., 1964, Soul Clinic-Universal Life Ch. Inc., Modesto, Calif., 1982. Mem.: Life Underwriter Tng. Coun., Apt. Assn. L.A., Kiwanis (club spkr. 1971), X32 Club (Ventura, Calif.), Forensic Club (L.A.). Republican. Office: PO Box 4407 Thousand Oaks CA 91359-1407

GREGORY, HEROLD LA MAR, chemical company administrator; b. Farmington, Utah, Nov. 9, 1923; s. Elijah B. and Julia Ellen (Tree) G.; m. Mary Ethel Eccles, Aug. 15, 1951; children— Vicki McGregor, Walter E., Suellen Winegar. BA, U. Utah, 1949. Exec. dir. Utah Symphony, Salt Lake City, 1957-86; asst. to chmn. Huntsman Corp., 1986—. Pres. East German mission Ch. of Jesus Christ of Latter-day Saints, Berlin, 1953-57, mission sec., 1949-51; assoc. prof. arts adminstrn. U. Utah, 1976-85 Mem. Mormon Tabernacle Choir, 1978-85, adminstrv. asst. 1987—; mem. Utah Symohony Chorus, 1985—; sec. Utah Symphony Bd., 1957—, Tanner Gift of Music Trust, 1983—. With AUS, 1943-45. Office: 500 Huntsman Way Salt Lake City UT 84108-1235 Home: 2255 N Tuweap DR Unit 25 Saint George UT 84770-5300

GRESHAM, ZANE OLIVER, lawyer; b. Mobile, Ala., Dec. 16, 1948; S. Charles Brandon and Lillian Ann (Oliver) G. BA cum laude, Johns Hopkins U., 1970; JD magna cum laude, Northwestern U., 1973. Bar: Calif. 1973. Assoc. Morrison & Foerster, San Francisco, 1973-79, ptnr., 1980—, co-chair land use and environ. law group, 1987-97, co-chair airports and aviation law group, 1996—; chair Latin Am. Group, 1998—. Dir., v.p. (Latin Am.) Internat. Private Water Assn., 1999—; dir. Fromm Inst., 2000—. Cons. editor: Environ. Compliance and Litigation Strategy. Pres. San Francisco Forward, 1980-85; bd. dirs. Regional Inst. Bay Area, Richmond, Calif., 1989-95, Regional Parks Found., Oakland, Calif., 1992—, pres., 1995; spl. counsel Grace Cathedral, San Francisco, 1991—; dir., exec. v.p. Pan Am. Soc. Calif., 1995-97, pres. 1998-2006; vice chmn. Nat. Youth Sci. Found., 1997—; bd. dir. Found. San Francisco (Calif.) Archl. Heritage, 2004—08, Grail Gatheral, 2008-. Mem. State Bar Calif., Urban Land Inst., Lambda Alpha. Avocations: opera, sketching. Office: Morrison & Foerster 425 Market St Ste 3100 San Francisco CA 94105-2482 Office Phone: 415-268-7145. Business E-Mail: zgresham@mofo.com.

GRESSAK, ANTHONY RAYMOND, JR., sales executive; b. Honolulu, Jan. 22, 1947; s. Anthony Raymond and Anne Tavares (Ferreira) G.; m. Catherine Streb, Apr. 11, 1981; children: Danielle Kirsten, Anthony Raymond III, Christina Michelle. AA, Utah State U., 1967; postgrad., U.S. Army Inf. Officers Candidate Sch., 1968. Restaurant mgr. Ala Moana Hotel, Honolulu, 1970-72; gen. mgr. Fred Harvey, Inc., Ontario, Calif., 1972-73; regional mgr. So. Calif., 1972-73, regional mgr. tollway ops., 1973; divisional mgr. Normandy Lane, 1973; resident mgr. Royal Inns of Am., San Diego, 1974; food and beverage dir. Asso. Inns & Restaurant Co. of Am. (Aircoa), Big Sky, Mont., 1974-75; condominium mgr. Big Sky, 1975; asst. gen. mgr. Naples (Fla.) Bath and Tennis Club, 1975-76; food and beverage dir. Nat. Parks, Grand Canyon, Ariz., 1976-77; gen. mgr. Grand Canyon Nat. Park Lodges, 1977-79; divisional v.p. food services The Broadway, Carter Hawley Hale, Inc., Los Angeles, 1979-82; exec. v.p. Silco Corp., Los Angeles, 1982-84; mktg. mgr. Interstate Restaurant Supply, 1984-85; dir. mktg. and merchandising S.E. Rykoff & Co., Los Angeles, 1986-91; nat. accounts sales mgr. healthcare and hospitality Rykoff-Sexton, Inc., LA, 1991-93; v.p. distbr. sales The Cheesecake Factory Bakery Inc., Calabasas Hills, Calif., 1993—. Mem. edn. culinary steering com. LA Trade Tech. Coll. With U.S. Army, 1967-70. Decorated Silver Star, Bronze Star, Purple Heart; South Vietnamese Cross of Gallantry. Mem.: Internat. Foodservice Mfrs. Assn., Smithsonian Assocs., Nat. Restaurant Assn. (assoc.), Am. Culinary Fedn. (assoc. Presdl. Medallion award 1991), Calif. Restaurant Assn. (assoc.), Internat. Order DeMolay (life; chevalier). Roman Catholic. Home: 20301 Minnehaha St Chatsworth CA 91311-2540 Office: The Cheesecake Factory 26950 Agoura Rd Agoura Hills CA 91301-5335 Home Phone: 818-998-2563; Office Phone: 818-871-3000. Business E-Mail: tgressak@thecheesecakefactory.com.

GRETZKY, WAYNE DOUGLAS, professional hockey coach, retired professional hockey player; b. Brantford, Ont., Can., Jan. 26, 1961; s. Walter and Phyllis Gretzky; m. Janet Jones, July 16, 1988; children: Paulina, Ty Robert, Trevor Douglas, Tristan Wayne, Emma Marie. Center Peterborough Petes, Jr. Ont. Hockey Assn., 1977—78, Sault Ste. Marie Greyhounds, 1977—78, Indpls. Racers, World Hockey Assn., 1978, Edmonton Oilers, 1979—88, LA Kings, 1988—96, St. Louis Blues, 1996, NY Rangers, 1996—99, ret., 1999; investor Los Arcos Sports LLC / Phoenix Coyotes, 1999—; mng. ptnr., alt. gov. Phoenix Coyotes, 2000—, head coach, 2005—; exec. dir. Can. Nat Team, Olympic Games, Salt Lake City, 2002, Torino, Italy, 2006, Can. Nat Team, World Cup of Hockey, 2004. Recipient Hart Meml. Trophy, 1974—80, William Hanley Trophy, 1977—78, Lemms Family award, 1977—78, Lady Byng Meml. Trophy, 1979—80, 1990—91, 1991—92, 1993—94, Art Ross Meml. Trophy, NHL, 1981—87, 1989—90, 1990—91, 1993—94, Lester B. Pearson award, 1982, 1984—85, 1986—87, Emery Edge award, 1983—84, 1984—85, 1986—87, Conn Smythe Trophy, 1985, 1988, Lester Patrick Trophy, 1993—94; named Rookie of Yr., World Hockey Assn., 1978—79, Sportsman of Yr., Sports Illustrated, 1982, Sporting News NHL Player of Yr., 1980—81, 1986—87, Sporting News Man of Yr., 1981, Can. Athlete of Yr., 1985, Dodge Performer of Yr., 1984—85, 1986—87, All-Star Game MVP, 1983, 1989, 1999; named one of Most Influential People in the World of Sports, Bus. Week, 2008; named to NHL All-Star Team, 1980—94, 1997—99. Achievements include being the record holder for points, goals, assists, overtime assists and others; being a member of the Stanley Cup Champion Edmonton Oilers, 1984, 1985, 1987, 1988; being inducted into the Hockey Hall of Fame in 1999. Office: Phoenix Coyotes Hockey Club 6751 N Sunset Blvd, #200 Glendale AZ 85305

GREUEL, WENDY, councilwoman; m. Dean Schramm; 1 child, Thomas. Grad., UCLA. Mayor's liaison to City Coun. City of LA, 1983—93; field ops. officer, southern Calif. Sec. of Housing & Urban Development, 1993—97; with corporation affairs dept. Dreamworks SKG, 1997—2002; councilwoman, Dist. 2 LA City Coun., 2002—, pres. pro tempore. Mem. Calif. Film Commn. Bd. dir. LA's Best, Tree People, Shelter Partnership, Project Restore, Alternate Living for Aging, Enterprise Found., Glendale C. of C., Coro Found. Mem.: UCLA Alumni Assn. (v.p.). Office: City Hall 200 N Spring St Rm 475 Los Angeles CA 90012 Office Phone: 213-473-7002. Office Fax: 213-680-7895. Business E-Mail: councilmember.greuel@lacity.org.*

GREY, BRAD, film company executive; b. Bronx, NY, Dec. 29, 1957; m. Jill Grey; children: Sam, Max, Emily. Student, SUNY; BS in Comm. & Bus., U. Buffalo, 1979; LHD (hon.), SUNY, 2003. With Harvey & Corky Productions, Brillstein-Grey Entertainment, Beverly Hills, Calif., 1985—92, ptnr., 1992—96, chmn. CEO, 1996—2005; co-founder (with Jennifer Anniston and Brad Pitt) Plan B Entertainment, 2002; chmn., CEO Paramount Motion Pictures Group, Hollywood, Calif., 2005—. Bd. dirs UCLA Sch. Medicine, Project ALS, KCET LA Pub. TV, Dean's Coun., NYU Tisch Sch. Arts; bd. dirs. Environ. Media Assn., Comic Relief; bd. councilors U. So. Calif. Sch. Cinema. Exec. prodr.: (films) Opportunity Knocks, 1990; exec. prodr.: (films) The Celluloid Closet, 1995, Happy Gilmore, 1996, The Cable

Guy, 1996, Bulletproof, 1996, The Replacement Killers, 1998, The Wedding Singer, 1998, Dirty Work, 1998, What Planet Are You From?, 2000, Screwed, 2000, Scary Movie, 2000; prodr. (films) City by the Sea, 2002, View From the Top, 2003, Charlie and the Chocoloate Factory, 2005, The Departed, 2006, Running with Scissors, 2006, prodr., writer The Burning, 1981; exec. prodr.: (TV films) Don't Try This at Home!, 1990, Three Sisters Searching for a Cure, 2004, In Memoriam: New York City, 2002 (Pare Lorentz award, Internat. Documentary Assn., 2002); (TV series) The Boys, 1989, Good Sports, 1991, The Larry Sanders Show, 1992 (CableACE award, 1993, 1994, 1995, 1996), NewsRadio, 1995, Mr. Show, 1995, The Naked Truth, 1995, The Steve Harvey Show, 1996, The Dana Carvey Show, 1996, Just Shoot Me!, 1997, Alright Already, 1997, C-16: FBI, 1997, Politically Incorrect, 1997—98, 2000—01, Applewood 911, 1998, The Sopranos, 1999— (Golden Globe award for best dramatic series, TV Prodr. of Yr. award in Episodic, PGA Awards, 2000, 2005, Primetime Emmy for Outstanding Drama Series, Acad. TV Arts and Scis., 2004, 2007), Sammy, 2000, Pasadena, 2001, Real Time with Bill Maher, 2003, My Big Fat Greek Life, 2003, The Lyon's Den, 2003, Cracking Up, 2004, Married to the Kellys, 2003, Jake in Progress, 2005—. Recipient George Foster Peabody award (4 times); named one of 50 Most Powerful People in Hollywood, Premiere mag., 2005—06. Office: Paramount Studios 5555 Melrose Ave West Hollywood CA 90038

GREY, ROBERT DEAN, biology professor, former academic administrator; b. Liberal, Kans., Sept. 5, 1939; s. McHenry Wesley and Kathryn (Brown) G.; m. Alice Kathleen Archer, June 11, 1961; children: Erin Kathleen, Joel Michael. BA, Phillips U., 1961; PhD, Washington U., 1966. Asst. prof. Washington U., St. Louis, 1966-67; from asst. prof. to full prof. zoology U. Calif., Davis, 1967—, chmn. dept., 1979-83, dean biol. scis., 1985—, interim provost, 1993-95, provost, exec. vice chancellor, 1995—2001, sr. advisor to chancellor, 2001—02, provost, exec. vice chancellor emeritus, 2002—, exec. asst. to chancellor health affairs Riverside, 2005—07, acting chancellor, 2007—08. Author: (with others) A Laboratory Text for Developmental Biology, 1980; contbr. articles to profl. jours. Recipient Disting. Tchg. awrd Acad. Senate U. Calif., Davis, 1977, Magnar Ronning award for tchg. Associated Students U. Calif., Davis, 1978, Disting. Alumnus award Phillips U., 1991. Avocations: music, hiking, gardening. Business E-Mail: rdgrey@ucdavis.edu.

GREY, THOMAS C., law educator; b. 1941; BA, Stanford U., 1963, Oxford U., Eng., 1965; LLB, Yale U., 1968; LLD (hon.), Chgo.-Kent Law Sch., 1998. Bar: DC 1969. Law clk. to Hon. J. Skelly Wright US Ct. Appeals (DC cir.), 1968—69; law clk. to Hon. Thurgood Marshall US Supreme Ct., 1969—70; staff atty. Washington Rsch. Project, 1970—71; asst. prof. Stanford Law Sch., 1971—74, assoc. prof., 1974—78, prof., 1978—, Nelson Bowman Sweitzer and Marie B. Sweitzer prof. law, 1990—. Office: Stanford Law Sch Crown Quadrangle 559 Nathan Abbott Way Stanford CA 94305-8610 Office Phone: 650-723-3579. Business E-Mail: tgrey@law.stanford.edu.

GREYSON, CLIFFORD RUSSELL, internist; b. NYC, 1958; AB, Harvard Coll., 1980; MSEE, Stanford U., 1985, MD, 1987. Cert. internal medicine and cardiovascular diseases, critical care medicine. Resident in internal medicine Stanford U. Hosp., 1987-90, fellow in critical care, 1990-91; fellow in cardiovasc. disease U. Calif., San Francisco, 1991-95, faculty cardiology divsn., 1995-99, U. Colo. Health Scis. Ctr., Denver, 1999—. Co-dir. med. intensive care unit San Francisco VA Med. Ctr., 1998-99. Elected to city coun. Town of Woodside, Calif., 1995. Recipient Clinician Scientist award Am. Heart Assn., 1995-96, Clin. Investigator Devel. award NIH, 1996-01, R01 rsch. award NIH, 2003. Fellow Am. Coll. Cardiology; mem. ACP, Western Soc. Clin. Investigation. Office: Denver VA Med Ctr Cardiology 111B 1055 Clermont St Denver CO 80220-3808

GRIBBON, DEBORAH, museum director; b. Washington, June 11, 1948; d. Daniel M. Gribbon and Mary Jane Retzler Gribbon; m. Winston Alt; children: Sarah Alt, Jane Alt. PhD, Harvard U., 1982, MA, 1971; BA, Wellesley Coll., 1970. Tchg. fellow Dept. Fine Arts Harvard U., Cambridge, Mass., 1972—74; curator Isabella Steward Gardner Mus., Boston, 1976—84; asst. dir. curatorial affairs The J. Paul Getty Mus., LA, 1984—87; assoc. dir. curatorial affairs The J. Paul Getty Mus., LA, 1987—91, assoc. dir., chief curator, 1991—98, dep. dir., chief curator, 1998—2000, dir., 2000—04. Instr. Ext. Sch. Harvard U., Cambridge, 1982—84; v.p. J.Paul Getty Trust, LA, 2000—04; bd. dirs. Courtauld Inst. Art, London. Co-author: The J. Paul Getty Museum and Its Collections: A Museum for a New Century, 1997; author (book): Sculpture in the Isabella Stewart Gardner Museum, 1978; contbr. articles to profl. jours. Recipient Plogsterth Prize for Art History, Wellesley Coll., 1970; fellow Theodore Rousseau Fellowship for Mus. Studies, Harvard U., 1982. Mem.: Assn. Art Mus. Dirs., Internat. Women's Forum.

GRIECO, PAUL ANTHONY, chemistry professor; b. Framingham, Mass., Oct. 27, 1944; married; 4 children. BA, Boston U., 1966; MA, Columbia U., 1967, PhD in Organic Chemistry, 1970. NSF fellow Harvard U., 1970-71; from asst. prof. to prof. chemistry U. Pitts., 1971-80; prof. chemistry Ind. U., Bloomington, 1980-85, Earl Blough prof. chemistry, 1985—, chmn. dept., 1988-97; head of chemistry and biochemistry dept. Mont. State U., 1999—. William P. Timmie lectr. Emory U., 1977; Abbott lectr. Yale U., 1984; H.C. Brown lectr. Purdue U., 1984; Disting. lectr. U. Wyo., 1986; Conv. Intercantonale Romande pour L'Enseignement du Troisième Cycle en Chimie, Switzerland, 1987; Centennial lectr. Abbott Labs., Chgo., 1988; H. Martin Friedman lectr. Rutgers U., 1988; Centennial Anniversary lectr. 1st Internat. Conf. on Organic Chem. Nomenclature, Geneva, 1992. Fellow Alfred P. Sloan Found., 1974-76, Japan Soc. Promising Scientists, 1978-79; recipient Ernest Guenther award, 1982, NIH-Nat. Cancer Inst. Merit award, 1988. Mem. Am. Chem. Soc. (Akron sect. award 1982, Arthur C. Cope Scholar award 1990, award for creative work in synthetic organic chemistry 1991, lectr. French.-Am. socs. meeting in France 1992), Royal Soc. Chemistry, Chem. Soc. Japan, Swiss Chem. Soc. Achievements include rsch. in the devel. of new synthetic methods for constrn. of complex natural products. Office: Mont State U Dept Biochem & Chem 108 Gains Hl Bozeman MT 59717-0001

GRIEGO, LINDA, entrepreneur; b. Tucumcari, N.Mex., 1949; m. Ronald C. Peterson. BA in History, UCLA, 1975. Pres., CEO Griego Enterprises, Inc., 1985—; restaurant founder, mng. ptnr. Engine Co. No. 28, 1988—; dep. mayor for econ. devel. City of LA, 1991—93, candidate for mayor, 1993; pres., CEO Rebuild LA Inc., 1994—97; pres. Zapgo Entertainment Group LLC, 1997—99; interim pres. & CEO LA Cmty. Devel. Bank, 1999—2000. Mem. Am. Devel. Bank Cmty. Adjustment Com., 1995—2000; sr. fellow UCLA Sch. Pub. Policy, 1998—2000; bd. dirs. Fed. Res. Bank San Francisco, 1998—2003, Granite Construction Inc., 1999—, City Nat. Corp., 2006—, Southwest Water Co., 2001—06, 2006—, CBS Corp., 2007—. Bd. trustees Robert Wood Johnson Found., 1995—2003, 2005—, Cedars Sinai Med. Ctr., 2004—, David & Lucile Packard Found., 2006—.

GRIEP, DAVID MICHAEL, astronomical scientist, researcher; b. Mpls., Oct. 13, 1957; s. Richard Arthur Sr. and Carole Elaine (Bengal) G.; m. Carolina May Von Gnechten, Nov. 19, 1994. BS in Astrophysics, U. Minn. Inst. Tech., 1979; MS in Astronomy, U. Minn., 1981. Rsch. assoc. Inst. Astronomy U. Hawaii, Hilo, 1982—. Office: 640 N Aohoku Pl Hilo HI 96720-2700

GRIER, JAMES EDWARD, hotel executive, lawyer; b. Ottumwa, Iowa, Sept. 7, 1935; s. Edward J. and Corinne (Bailey) G.; m. Virginia Clinker, July 4, 1959; children: Michael, Susan, James, John, Thomas. BSc, U. Iowa, 1956, JD, 1959. Bar: Iowa 1959, Mo. 1959. Mng. ptnr. Hillix, Brewer, Hoffhaus & Grier, Kansas City, Mo., 1964-77, Grier & Swartzman, Kansas City, 1977-89; pres. Doubletree Hotels Corp., Phoenix, 1989-94; chmn. Sonoran Hotel Capital, Inc., Phoenix, 1994-96; mng. ptnr. Copa Investments, 1996—, Gainey Hotel Co., 1996—. Bd. dirs. Iowa Law Sch. Found., Iowa City, St. Joseph Healthcare Ariz., Phoenix, Homeward Bound, Phoenix. Home: 3500 E Lincoln Dr Phoenix AZ 85018-1010 Office: Gainey Hotel Co 7300 E Gainey Suites Dr Ste 169 Scottsdale AZ 85258-2061 Home Phone: 602-840-4979. Business E-Mail: jegrier@gaineysuiteshotel.com.

GRIEVE, ROBERT BURTON, parasitologist, educator; b. Torrington, Wyo., Oct. 27, 1951; s. Burton William and Eulah Ann (Scott) Grieve; m. Marcia Ann Mika, Jan. 16, 1982; children: Jonathon Robert, Megan Mika, Madeline Reno. BS in Microbiology, U. Wyo., 1973, MS in Microbiology, 1975; PhD in Parasitology, U. Fla., 1978. Postdoctoral assoc., then rsch. assoc. Cornell U., Ithaca, N.Y., 1978-81; asst. prof. U. Pa., Phila., 1981-84; assoc. prof. U. Wis., Madison, 1984-87, Colo. State U., Ft. Collins, 1987-90, prof. parasitology, 1990—; v.p. R & D, chief sci. officer, CEO Heska Corp., Ft. Collins, 1991—. Assoc. investigator USAF, Keesler AFB, Miss., 1979-84; adviser WHO, Geneva, 1984; cons. NIH, 1985, 88. Patentee heartworm diagnosis procedure; contbr. articles to profl. jours. Recipient Ralston Purina Small Animal Rsch. award, 1991. Mem. AAAS, Am. Soc. Parasitologists (editorial bd., Henry Baldwin Ward medal 1990, pres. 1996-97), Am. Soc. Tropical Medicine and Hygiene, Am. Assn. Immunologists (assoc. editor 1991-95), Am. Assn. Veterinary Parasitologists (chair nominating com. 1987-88), Sigma Xi, Alpha Zeta. Home: 38501 WCR21 Fort Collins CO 80524 Office: Heska Corp 3760 Rocky Mtn Ave Loveland CO 80538-7084

GRIFFEN, AGNES MARTHE, retired library administrator; b. Ft. Dauphin, Madagascar, Aug. 25, 1935; d. Frederick Stang and Alvilde Margrethe (Torvik) Hallanger; m. Thomas Michael Griffen (div. Nov. 1969); children: Shaun Helen Griffen D'Antoni, Christopher Patrick, Adam Andrew; m. John H.P. Hall, Aug. 26, 1980. BA cum laude in English, Pacific Luth. U., 1957; MLS, U. Wash., 1965; Urban Exec. cert., MIT, 1976; postgrad., Harvard U., 1993. Cert. librarian, Wash., Md., Ariz. Area children's libr. King County Libr. Sys., Seattle, 1965-68, coord. instl. librs., 1968-71, dep. libr. for staff and program devel., 1971-74; dep. libr. dir. Tucson Pub. Libr., 1974-80; dir. Montgomery County Dept. Pub. Librs., Rockville, Md., 1980-96; libr. dir. Tucson-Pima Pub. Libr., 1997—2003; ret., 2003. Lectr. Grad. Libr. Sch., U. Ariz., Tucson, 1976-77, 79; vis. lectr. Sch. Librarianship, U. Wash., Seattle, 1983. Contbr. articles to library periodicals and profl. jours. Active Md. Humanities Coun., Balt., 1986-92, Ariz. Humanities Coun., Phoenix, 1977-80; charter mem. Exec. Women's Coun. of So. Ariz., Tucson, 1979-80; mem. coun. Nat. Capital Area Pub. Access Network, 1992-94, pres. bd., 1993-94, Ariz. Statewide Libr. Devel. Commn., 2000-02' mem. adv. coun. to Ariz. State Libr., 1998--. Recipient Helping Hand award Md. Assn. of the Deaf, 1985, Cert. Recognition Montgomery County Hispanic Employees Assn., 1985; Henry scholar U. Washington Sch. Librarianship, 1965. Mem. ALA (exec. bd. 1989-93, divsn. pres. pub. libr. assn. bd. 1981-82, councilor-at-large 1972-76, 86-93, chmn. com. on program evaluation and support 1987-88, legis. com. 1998-2002), Ariz. State Libr. Assn. (legis. com. 1997--), Md. Libr. Assn. Democrat. Home: 1951 N El Moraga Dr Tucson AZ 85745-9070

GRIFFEY, KEN, JR., (GEORGE KENNETH GRIFFEY JR.), professional baseball player; b. Donora, Pa., Nov. 21, 1969; s. Ken and Bertie Griffey; m. Melissa Griffey; 1 adopted child, Tevin Kendall children: George Kenneth III, Taryn Kennedy. Outfielder Seattle Mariners, 1989—99, 2009—, Cin. Reds, 2000—08, Chgo. White Sox, 2008. Mem. US Team World Baseball Classic, 2006. Am. pub. diplomacy envoy US Dept. State, 2008—. Recipient Gold Glove award, 1990—99, Silver Slugger award, 1991, 1993—94, 1996—99; named All-Star Game MVP, 1992, Am. League MVP, 1997, Maj. League Player of Yr., 1997, Nat. League Comeback Player of Yr., 2005; named to Am. League All-Star Team, 1990—99, MLB All-Century Team, 1999, Nat. League All-Star Team, 2000, 2004, 2007, All-Time Rawlings Gold Glove Team, 2007. Achievements include leading the American League in: home runs (40), 1994, (56) 1997, (56) 1998, (48) 1999; runs scored (125), RBI (147), 1997; hitting his 600th career home run on June 9, 2008; becoming fifth all-time on the career home run list, 2008. Office: Seattle Mariners Safeco Field PO Box 4100 Seattle WA 98104*

GRIFFEY, LINDA BOYD, lawyer; b. Keokuk, Iowa, Aug. 6, 1949; d. Marshall Coulter and Geraldine Vivian (White) Boyd; m. John Jay Griffey, June 24, 1972. BS in Pharmacy, U. Iowa, 1972; JD, Duke U., 1980. Bar: Calif. 1980; lic. pharmacist, Iowa, N.C. Pharmacist Davenport (Iowa) Osteo. Hosp., 1972-75, Wagner Pharmacy, Clinton, Iowa, 1975-77, Durham (N.C.) County Gen. Hosp., 1977-80; assoc. O'Melveny & Myers, LA, 1980-88, ptnr., 1988—. Spkr., writer in field of employee benefits and exec. compensation; former pres. L.A. chpt. Western Pension and Benefits Conf., 1998-99. Active L.A. Philharm. Bus. & Profl. Assn.; bd. dirs. Hillsides Home for Children, Pasadena Playhouse. Mem. ABA (employee benefits com. tax sect.), Am. Law Inst., L.A. County Bar Assn. (former chair employee benefits com. 1994-95), L.A. Duke Bar Assn. (pres. 1987-90, 91-92), Rotary (L.A. chpt. bd. dirs. 1995-97). Avocations: golf, reading, swimming. Office: O'Melveny & Myers 400 S Hope St Los Angeles CA 90071-2899 E-mail: lgriffey@omm.com.

GRIFFIN, DOMINIC B., III, state agency administrator; s. Dominic B. Griffin Jr. and Margaret Robinson. With Bank of Hawaii, Hawaii, NY and Pacific Islands, Bank of Am., Malaysia and Hawaii; commr. divsn. fin. instns. Hawaii Dept. Commerce and Consumer Affairs, 2003—. Regulatory chmn. governing bd. Conf. State Bank Suprs. Office: Divsn Fin Instns Dept Commerce and Consumer Affairs PO Box 2054 Honolulu HI 96805 Office Phone: 808-586-2820. Office Fax: 808-586-2818. E-mail: dominic.b.griffin@dcca.hawaii.gov.

GRIFFIN, ELAINE B., educator; b. Westfield, NY; m. Ned Griffin; 3 adopted daughters: Vera, Marie, Marjeena. BA in Am. studies, Barnard Coll., 1969; MLS, U. Calif., Berkeley, 1971. Cert. tchr., Ariz. Head tchr. Akhiok Sch., Alaska, Chiniak Sch., Alaska. Recipient Coun. of Chief State Sch. Officers Tchr. of Yr. award, 1995. Office: Chiniak Sch PO Box 5529 Chiniak AK 99615-5529 Personal E-mail: egriffin@kodiak.k12.ak.us.

GRIFFIN, JEAN (ALVA JEAN GRIFFIN), entertainer; b. Detroit, June 1, 1931; d. Henry Bethel White and Ruth Madelyn (Gowen) Durham; m. Francis Jay Griffin, July 8, 1958 (dec.); stepchildren: Patra, Rodney; 1 adopted child, Donald; children: Rhonda Jean, Sherree Lee. Student, Anderson Coll., 1952-53; DD (hon.), Ministry of Salvation, Chula Vista, Calif., 1990, Ministry of Salvation, 1990. Ordained minister, 1990. Supr. Woolworth's, Detroit, 1945-46; operator, supr. Atlantic Bell Tel. Co., Detroit, 1947-51, Anderson, Ind., 1952-56; sec. to div. mgr. Food Basket-Lucky Stores, San Diego, 1957-58; owner, mgr. Jay's Country Boy Markets, Riverside, Calif., 1962-87; entertainer, prodr., dir., singer Mae West & Co., 1980—. Past owner The Final Touch, Colorado Springs; owner Omega Communique Co., 1997—; tchr. art Grant Sch., Riverside, 1964-65; tchr., adviser Mental Retarded Sch., Riverside, 1976-77; instr. Touch for Health Found., Pasadena, Calif., 1975-79; cons., hypnotist, nutritionist, Riverside, 1976-79; mem., tchr. Psi field parapsychology. Writer children's stories and short stories, author Santas Message For You, 2006. Mem. Rep. Presdl. Task Force, 1983. Recipient svc. award Rep. Presdl. Task Force, 1986. Mem. Parapsychology Assn. Riverside (pres. 1981-82). Mem. Ch. of Religious Science New Thought. Avocations: arts and crafts, photography, hiking, horseback riding, travel. Office Phone: 480-654-0387.

GRIFFIN, KEITH BROADWELL, retired economics professor; b. Colon, Panama, Nov. 6, 1938; came to U.S., 1988; s. Marcus Samuel Griffin and Elaine Ann (Broadwell) Fabick; m. Dixie Beth, Apr. 2, 1956; children: Janice, Kimberley. BA, Williams Coll., 1960, DLitt (hon.), 1980; PhB, Oxford U., Eng., 1962, PhD, 1965. Fellow and tutor in econs. Magdalen Coll. Oxford (Eng.) U., 1965-76, fellow Magdalen Coll., 1977-79, pres., 1979-88, hon. fellow, 1988; acting warden, dir. Queen Elizabeth House, Inst. Commonwealth Studies, 1973, 77-78, warden, dir., 1978-79; prof. U. Calif., Riverside, 1988—2004, chmn. dept. econs., 1988-93, Presdl. prof., 1988-90, Disting. prof., 1997—2004. Vis. prof. Inst. Econs. and Planning U. Chile, 1962-63, 64-65; chmn. bd. UN Rsch. Inst. for Social Devel., 1988-95, sr. cons., 1971-72; mem. UN com. for devel. planning, 1987-94; mem. coun. UN Univ., 1986-92, chmn. fin. and budget com., 1988-90; mem. Marshall Aid Commemoration Commn., 1984-88; mem. World Commn. on Culture and Devel., 1994-95; chief ILO Employment Adv. Mission to Ethiopia, 1982; econ. advisor Govt. of Bolivia, 1989-91; pres. Devel. Studies Assn., U.K., 1978-80; chief rural and urban employment policies br. ILO, 1975-76; cons. ILO on rural devel. in Ecuador, 1974; sr. adviser OECD Devel. Centre, Paris, 1986-91; adviser to Inter-Am. Com. for Alliance for Progress on copper expansion programme in Chile, 1968, to FAO/ICO/IBRD World Coffee Study in Guatemala, El Salvador and Colombia, 1967; rsch. advisor Pakistan Inst. Devel. Econs., Karachi, 1965, 70; expert on agrl. planning to Govt. of Algeria, acting chief FAO Mission, Algiers, 1963-64; cons. IBRD on land reform in Morocco, 1973; head UN Devel. Program Poverty Alleviation Mission to Mongolia, 1994; head ILO Social Policy Rev. Mission to Uzbekis, 1995; cons. on econ. reform in Vietnam, UNDP, 1997; head ILO Employment and Social Protection Mission to Kazakstan, 1997; head UNDP mission to Mongolia, 2001, Armenia, 2002; leader UNDP program evaluation team in China, 2004-05. Author: Underdevelopment in Spanish America, 1969, 2d edit., 1971, Spanish edit., 1972, The Green Revolution: An Economic Analysis, 1972, The Political Economy of Agrarian Change, 1974, 2d edit., 1979, Spanish edit., 1982, Hindi edit., 1983, Land Concentration and Rural Poverty, 1976, 2d edit., 1981, Spanish edit., 1983, International Inequality and National Poverty, 1978, Spanish edit., 1984, World Hunger and the World Economy, 1987, Alternative Strategies for Economic Development, 1989, 2d edit., 1999, Chinese edit., 1992, Studies in Globalization and Economic Transitions, 1996, Studies in Development Strategy and Systemic Transformation, 2000; co-author: Comercio Internacional y Politicas de Desarrollo Economico, 1967, Planning Development, 1970, Spanish edit., 1975, The Transition to Egalitarian Development, 1981, Globalization and the Developing World, 1992, Implementing a Human Development Strategy, 1994; editor: Financing Development in Latin America, 1971, Institutional Reform and Economic Development in the Chinese Countryside, 1984, The Economy of Ethiopia, 1992, Poverty and the Transition to a Market Economy in Mongolia, 1995, Social Policy and Economic Transformation in Uzbekistan, 1996, Economic Reform in Vietnam, 1998, Poverty Reduction in Mongolia, 2003; co-editor: Ensayos Sobre Planificacion, 1967, Growth and Inequality in Pakistan, 1972, The Economic Development of Bangladesh, 1974, Human Development and the International Development Strategy for the 1990s, 1990, The Distribution of Income in China, 1993, also numerous articles. Vis. fellow Oxford Ctr. Islamic Studies, 1998. Fellow: AAAS. Avocation: travel. Office: Univ Calif Dept Econs Riverside CA 92521-0001 Home: 24870 SW Mountain Rd West Linn OR 97068 Personal E-mail: keithdixiegriffin@verizon.net.

GRIFFITH, OSBIE HAYES, retired chemistry professor; b. Torrance, Calif., Sept. 14, 1938; s. Osbie and Mary Belle (Neathery) G.; m. Karen Hedberg; 2 sons BA, U. Calif.-Riverside, Riverside, 1960; PhD, Calif. Inst. Tech., 1964; postgrad., Stanford U., 1965. NAS-NRC postdoctoral Stanford (Calif.) U., 1965; asst. prof. chemistry U. Oreg., Eugene, 1966-69, assoc. prof., 1969-72; prof. chem. Inst. Molecular Biology, 1972—2003, prof. emeritus of chemistry, 2003—. Co-editor: Lipid-Protein Interactions, 1982; mem. edtl. bd. Biophysical Jour., 1974-78, Chemistry & Physics of Lipids, 1974-95, Microscopy and Microanalysis, 1995-2002; contbr. articles to profl. jours. Camille and Henry Dreyfus Found. scholar, 1970; Career Devel. award Nat. Cancer Inst., 1972-76; fellow Sloan Found., 1967-69, Guggenheim Found., 1972-76; Faculty Achievement award for Tchg. Excellence, Burlington No. Found., 1987, Dean's Devel. award, 1991, Creativity Ext. NSF, 1992, Outstanding Faculty award U. Oreg. Office of Multicultural Affairs, 2004. Mem. Am. Chem. Soc., Biophys. Soc., Microscopy Soc. Am. Home: 2550 Charnelton St Eugene OR 97405-3216 Office: Univ Oreg Dept Chemistry Eugene OR 97403 Business E-Mail: griffith@uoregon.edu.

GRIFFITH, YOLANDA EVETTE, professional basketball player; b. Chgo., Mar. 1, 1970; d. Harvey Griffith; 1 child, Candace. Student, Palm Beach Jr. Coll., Fla. Atlantic U. Player, Germany, 1993—97, Long Beach StingRays, ABL, 1997—98, Sacramento Monarchs, WNBA, 1999—. Mem. USA Basketball Women's Sr. Nat. Team, 1998, 99, 2000, 04. Named Defensive Player of Yr., ABL, 1998, WNBA, 1999, MVP, 1999, Newcomer of Yr., 1999; named to First Team All-ABL, 1998, First Team All-WNBA, 1999, WNBA Western Conf. All-Star Team, 1999—2001, 2003, 2005—07. Achievements include winning a Gold Medal at the 2000 Sydney Olympics. Avocations: softball, music. Office: Sacramento Monarchs One Sports Pkwy Sacramento CA 95834

GRIGG, NEIL S., civil engineering educator; Grad., U.S. Mil. Acad., 1961; MS in Civil Engring., Auburn U., 1965; PhD in Civil Engring., Colo. State U., 1969. Dir. Colo. Water Resources Rsch. Inst., Internat. Sch. Water Resources, Colo. State U., 1988-91; asst. sec. natural resources State of N.C., 1979-81, dir. environ. mgmt., 1980-81; dir. U. N.C. Water Resources Rsch. Inst., 1979-82; co-founder Sellards & Grigg, Inc., Denver; prof., head dept. civil engring. Colo. State U., Fort Collins, 1991—. Organizer confs.; advocate pub. works edn. and rsch.;mem. working groups Nat. Coun. on Pub. Works Improvement; mem. Edn. Found. Com. on Govt. Affairs, 1992 U.S.-Japan Infrastructure Delegation, Top Ten Selection Panel, Coun. on Internat. Collaboration; pres. Ft. Collins Water Bd., 1991—. Contbr. articles to profl. jours. Fellow ASCE (chair exec. com., water resources planning and mgmt. divsn. 1995, chmn. water pricing task com. 1990-92, founding chair WP&M Divsn. Urban Water Com. 1986-88, chair tech. coun. on rsch. 1983-85, chmn. urban water resources rsch. coun. 1978-79, nat. water policy com. 1981, chmn. nat. environ. systems policy com. 1983), Am. Pub. Works Assn. (bd. dirs., chair mgmt. practices evaluation com.), Am. Water Works Assn., Ft. Collins C. of C. (chmn. water com. 1989—). Office: Colo State U Dept Civil Engring Fort Collins CO 80523-0001

GRIGGS, GARY BRUCE, oceanographer, geologist, educator, director; b. Pasadena, Calif., Sept. 25, 1943; s. Dean Brayton and Barbara Jayne (Farmer) G.; children: Joel, Amy, Shannon, Callie, Cody. BA in Geology, U. Calif., Santa Barbara, 1965; PhD in Oceanography, Oreg. State U., 1968. Registered geologist, Calif.; cert. engr. geologist, Calif. Rsch. asst., NSF grad. fellow in oceanography Oreg. State U., 1965-68; from asst. prof. to prof. earth scis. U. Calif., Santa Cruz, 1969—; Fulbright fellow Inst. for Ocean & Fishing Rsch., Athens, Greece, 1974-75; oceanographer Joint U.S.A.-N.Z. Rsch. Program, 1980-81; chair earth scis. U. Calif., Santa Cruz, 1981-84, assoc. dean natural scis., 1992-95; dir. Inst. of Marine Scis., 1991—. Vis. prof. Semester at Sea program U. Pitts., 1984-96; guest lectr. World Explorer Cruises, 1987; chair marine coun. U. Calif., 1999—; bd. govs. Consortium for Oceanographic Rsch. and Edn., 1995—2006, bd. trustee, 2007-. Author: (with others) Geologic Hazards, Resources and Environmental Planning, 1983, Living with the California Coast, 1985, Coastal Protection Structures, 1986, California's Coastal Hazards, 1992, Formation, Evolution and Stability of Coastal Cliffs-Status and Trends, 2004, Living With Changing California Coast, 2005, The Santa Cruz Coast: Then and Now, 2006; mem. editl. bd. Jour. of Coastal Rsch.; contbr. numerous articles to profl. jours. Mem. Am. Geophys. Union, Am. Geol. Inst., Coastal Found. Achievements include research in coastal processes; coastal erosion and protection; coastal engineering and hazards; sediment yield, transport and dispersal; geologic hazards and land use. Office: U Calif Inst Marine Scis Santa Cruz CA 95064 Business E-Mail: griggs@pmc.ucsc.edu.

GRIGSBY, FREDERICK J., JR., human resources executive; BBA, Ctrl. State U.; grad. exec. program, U. Va. Various positions in human resources Westinghouse; v.p. human resources Thermo King Corp., 1995-98; v.p. human resources and adminstrn. Fluor Corp., Aliso Viejo, Calif., 1998—. Diversity bd. dirs. Westinghouse Savannah River Co. Bd. dirs. Exec. Leadership Found. Mem. Nat. Black MBA Assn., Ctrl. State Alumni Assn., Human Resources Mgmt. Soc. (human resources exec. coun.), Kappa Alpha Psi. Office: Fluor Corp One Enterprise Dr Aliso Viejo CA 92656-2606

GRIJALVA, RAUL, United States Representative from Arizona; b. Tucson, Feb. 19, 1948; m. Ramona F. Grijalva; children: Adelita, Raquel, Marisa. BA in Sociology, U. Ariz., 1988. Dir. El Pueblo Neighborhood Ctr.; asst. dean Hispanic student affairs U. Ariz.; mem. Pima County Bd. Suprs., 1989—2003, U.S. Congress from 7th Ariz. dist., 2003—; mem. Edn. and Workforce com., Resources com. and Small Bus. com. U.S. Ho. Reps. Democrat. Roman Catholic. Office: US Ho Reps 1440 Longworth Ho Office Bldg Washington DC 20515-0307

GRILL, LAWRENCE J., lawyer, accountant, bank executive; b. Chgo., Nov. 5, 1936; s. Samuel S. and Evelyn (Wollack) G.; m. Joan V. Krimston, Dec. 16, 1961; children: Steven Eric, Elizabeth Anne. BS with honors, U. Ill., 1958; postgrad., U. Chgo., 1959—60; LLB, Northwestern U., 1963. CPA Ill.; bar: Ill. 1963, Calif. 1965. Audit and tax mgr. Arthur Anderson & Co., Chgo., 1958-60; with firm Aaron, Aaron, Schimberg & Hess, Chgo., 1963-64, Gendel, Raskoff, Shapiro & Quittner, LA, 1964-66; sec., gen. counsel Traid Corp., LA, 1966-69; v.p., sec., gen. counsel Kaufman & Broad, Inc., LA, 1969-78; pres. Kaufman & Broad Asset Mgmt., dir. subs.; v.p., sec., gen. counsel AM Internat., Inc., Century City, Calif., 1979-82, dir. subs.; sr. v.p., group ops. officer, dir. subs. Wickes Cos., Inc., Santa Monica, Calif., 1982-85; acting CEO, COO, mem. exec. com. Barco of Calif., Gardena, 1985-86; pres. Lawrence J. Grill & Assocs., LA, 1985-94; pres., CEO Pan Am. Bank and United Pan Am. Fin. Corp., San Mateo, Calif., 1994-2000; also bd. dirs. Chmn., pres., CEO Universal Savs. Bank, Orange, Calif., 1988-90; cons. bd. dirs. World Trade Bank, N.A., 1992, Marathon Nat. Bank, 1992-93; spl. advisor to Fed. Home Loan Bank Bd. San Francisco, FDIC for Distressed Savs. Instns., 1986-88; arbitrator Am. Arbitration Assn. Served with AUS, 1958-59. Office: 1300 S El Camino Real San Mateo CA 94402-2963 Home: 70377 Tamarisk Ln Rancho Mirage CA 92270-2456 Personal E-mail: larg36@yahoo.com.

GRILLER, GORDON MOORE, legal association administrator, consultant; b. Sioux City, Iowa, Feb. 3, 1944; s. Joseph Edward and Arlene (Searles) G. m. Helen Mary Friederichs, aug. 20, 1966; children: Heather, Chad. BA in Political Sci., U. Minn., 1966, MA in Pub. Affairs, 1969. Mgmt. analyst Hennepin County Adminstr., Mpls., 1968-72; asst. court adminstr. Hennepin County Municipal Ct., Mpls., 1972-77, ct. adminstr., 1977-78; judicial dist. adminstr. 2nd Dist. Ct. Minn., St. Paul, 1978-87; ct. adminstr. Superior Ct. Ariz., Phoenix, 1987—2002, Trial Cts. in Maricopa County Ariz., Phoenix, 2002—03; v.p. Justice Practice Group, ACS, Inc. Bd. dirs. Nat. Conf. Metro Cts., 1999—. Vice-chmn. Bloomington Sch. Bd., Minn., 1981-87. Sgt. USAAF, 1968-74 Res. Recipient Warren E. Burger award Inst. Ct. Mgmt.,1988, Leadership Fellows award Bush Leadership Program, 1974. Mem. Nat. Assn. Trial Ct. Adminstrs.(pres. 1983-84), Ariz. Ct. Assn., Nat. Assn Ct. Mgmt. (award of merit), Am. Judicature Soc., (bd. dirs. 1997-2003). Lutheran. Avocations: running, scuba diving, kayaking, hiking. Home: 8507 E San Jacinto Dr Scottsdale AZ 85258-2576 Office: Ste 1750 101 N 1st Ave Phoenix AZ 85003

GRILLO-LÓPEZ, ANTONIO J., physician; b. Hato Rey, PR, Nov. 20, 1939; s. Antonio Grillo-Ramírez and Lolita López-Grillo; m. Maria S. Marxuach-Grillo, Nov. 7, 1964; children: Antonio G. Grillo, Miguel A. Grillo, Javier J. Grillo. BS, U. P.R., Rio Piedras, 1960; MD, U. P.R., San Juan, 1964. V.p. clin. rsch. Parke Davis, Ann Arbor, Mich., 1980—92; exec. med. dir. DuPont Merck Pharm., Wilmington, Del., 1987—92; chief med. officer IDEC Pharms., San Diego, 1992—2001; chmn. Neoplastic and Autoimmune Diseases Rsch. Inst., Rancho Santa Fe, Calif., 2001; consul., clin. rsch., regulatory strategy US Nat. Cancer Inst. Mem. sci. advisory bd. Conforma Therapeutics. Contbr. articles to profl. jours. Lt. comdr. USNR, 1974, 1965. Recipient Discovery Health Channel Med. Honors, 2004. Roman Catholic. Avocations: music, theater, opera, travel, cars.

GRIMES, DUANE D., state legislator; b. Spokane, Wash., Sept. 17, 1957; m. Connie Grimes; 3 children. Student, Colo. Aero. Tech.; BA, Bob Jones U., 1983, postgrad. Pilot, aircraft insp.; pers. officer Mont. Dept. Revenue; mem. Mont. Senate, Dist. 20, Helena, 1998—; mem. legis. adminstrn. com., mem. local govt. com. Mont. Senate, mem. pub. health, welfare/safety com., mem. judiciary com. Republican. Home: 4 Hole In The Wall Clancy MT 59634-9516

GRIMM, RUSS, professional football coach, retired professional football player; b. Scotsdale, Pa., May 2, 1959; children: Chad, Cody, Devin, Dylan. Grad., U. Pitts., 1981. Guard Washington Redskins, 1981—91, tight ends coach, 1992—96, offensive line coach, 1997—2000, Pitts. Steelers, 2000—04, offensive line coach/asst. head coach, 2004—07, Ariz. Cardinals, Tempe, 2007—. Named NFL All-Pro, AP, 1983—85; named to Nat. Football Conf. Pro Bowl Team, 1983—86. Achievements include being a member of 3 Super Bowl Championship teams with the Washington Redskins, 1983, 1988, 1992. Office: Ariz Cardinals 8701 S Hardy Dr Tempe AZ 85284*

GRIMSLEY, SEAN C., lawyer; BA with highest honors, U. Tex., 1994; JD summa cum laude, U. Mich., 2000. Law clk. U.S. Ct. Appeals (D.C. cir.), Washington, 2000—01; law clk. to Hon. Sandra Day O'Connor U.S. Supreme Ct., Washington, 2003—04; assoc. Bartlit Beck Herman Palenchar & Scott, Denver, 2004—. Office: Bartlit Beck Herman Palenchar & Scott 8th Fl 1899 Wynkoop St Denver CO 80202

GRIMWOOD, HELEN PERRY, lawyer; b. Phoenix, Aug. 9, 1953; BSBA magna cum laude, Univ. Ariz., 1973; JD magna cum laude, Ariz. State Univ., 1980. CPA Ariz., 1979. Law clerk Judge L. Ray Haire, Ariz. Ct. of Appeals, 1980—81, Judge William C. Canby Jr., U.S. Ct. of Appeals, Ninth Cir., 1981—82; judge pro tempore Ariz. Superior, Maricopa County, 1993—, Ariz Ct. of Appeals, 1998; ptnr. Grimwald Law Firm PLC, Phoenix. Recipient Friedman award for excellence in legal edn., Maricopa County Bar Assn., 1995, Justice Gordon award for pro bono svc., 1996, Solin award for outstanding leadership, Ariz. Women Lawyer's Assn.; named a Fellow, Am. Bar Found., 2000; named one of the Valley's Most Influential in Law, Bus. Journal, 2000. Mem.: Ariz. Women Lawyer's Assn. (pres. 1996—97), Nat. Conf. of Women's Bar Assn. (dir. 1977—), Maricopa County Bar Assn. (dir. 1992—96, chair, comml. litig. CLE Com. 1993—96), Ariz. State Bar Assn. (mem., bd. gov. 1997—, pres.-elect 2004—05, pres. 2005—06). Office: Grimwood Law Firm PLC Ste A 205 301 E Bethany Home Rd Phoenix AZ 85012-1269

GRINDAL, MARY ANN, former sales professional; b. Michigan City, Ind., Sept. 9, 1942; d. James Paxton and Helen Evelyn (Koivisto) Gleason; m. Bruce Theodore Grindal, June 12, 1965 (div. Sept. 1974); 1 child, Matthew Bruce. BSBA, Ind. U., 1965. Sec. African studies program Ind. U., Bloomington, 1965-66; rsch. aide Ghana, West Africa, 1966-68; exec. sec. divsn. biol. scis. Ind. U., Bloomington, 1968-69; office asst. Dean of Students office Middlebury (Vt.) Coll., 1969-70; exec. sec. Remo, Inc., North Hollywood, Calif., 1974-76; sec., asst. to product mgrs. in cosmetic and skin care Redken Labs., Canoga Park, Calif., 1976-79; various sec. and exec. sec. positions LA, 1979-81, 85-89; exec. sec. Sargent Industries, Burbank, Calif., 1981-85; sales asst. Chyron Graphics, Burbank, Calif., 1989-97; adminstrv. sec. divsn. instructional svcs. Burbank Unified Sch. Dist., 1998—. Author of poems and essays. Mem. U.S. Navy Meml. Found. Mem. DAR (chpt. registrar 1988-91, chpt. regent 1991-94, chpt. chmn. pub. rels. and pub. 1994-2001, chpt. chaplain 1994-2001, mem. spkrs. staff 1995-2001, state chmn. Am. Heritage 1994-96, state chmn. Calif. DAR scholarship com. 1996-98), Daus. of Union Vets. of Civil War, 1861-65, Inc., Ladies of the Grand Army of the Republic, Nat. Soc. Dames of the Ct. of Honor (state chaplain 1997-2001). Episcopalian. Avocations: travel, writing, genealogy.

GRINELL, SHEILA, museum director, consultant; b. NYC, July 15, 1945; d. Richard N. and Martha (Mimiless) G.; m. Thomas E. Johnson, July 15, 1980; 1 child, Michael; stepchildren: Kathleen, Thomas. BA, Radcliffe Coll., 1966; MA, U. Calif., Berkeley, 1968. Co-dir. exhibits and programs The Exploratorium, San Francisco, 1969-74; promotion dir. Kodansha Internat., Tokyo, 1974-77; traveling exhbn. coord. Assn. Sci. Tech. Ctrs., Washington, 1978-80, exec. dir., 1980-82, project dir. traveling exhbn. Chips and Changes, 1982-84; assoc. dir. N.Y. Hall of Sci., 1984-87; pres., CEO Ariz. Sci. Ctr., Phoenix, 1993—2004; principal Grinell, LLC. Cons. Optical Soc. Am., 1987, Nat. Sci. Ctr. Found., 1988, Interactive Video Sci. Consortium, 1988, Assn. Sci. Tech. Ctrs., 1988-89, Found. for Creative Am., 1989-90, Am. Assn. for World Health, 1990, Children's TV Workshop, 1991, Sciencenter, 1991, SciencePort, 1991, The Invention Factory, 1992, N.Y. Bot. Garden, 1992-93; Sonoran Desert Ctr., 2005-08, Tech. Mus. Innovation, 2006-07, Joyce Found., 2007—. Author: Light, Sight, Sound, Hearing: Exploratorium '74, 1974; editor A Stage for Science, 1979, A New Place for Learning Science: Starting and Running A Science Center, 1992, 2d edit., 2003, (with Mark St. John) Vision to Reality: Critical Dimensions in Science Center Development, Vol. I, 1993, II, 1994. Fulbright teaching asst., 1966; hon. Woodrow Wilson fellow, 1967 Fellow AAAS, ASTC; mem. Am. Assn. Mus., Phi Beta Kappa.

GRINNELL, ALAN DALE, neuroscientist, educator; b. Mpls., Nov. 11, 1936; s. John Erle and Swanhild Constance (Friswold) Grinnell; m. Verity Rich, Sept. 30, 1962 (div. 1975); m. Feelie Lee Grinnell, Dec. 23, 1996. BA, Harvard U., Cambridge, Mass., 1958, PhD, 1962. Jr. fellow Harvard U., 1959-62; rsch. assoc. biophysics dept. Univ. Coll. London, 1962-64; asst. rsch. zoologist UCLA, 1964-65, from asst. prof. to prof. dept. biology, 1965-78, prof. physiology, 1972—; dir. Jerry Lewis Neuromuscular Research Ctr. UCLA Sch. Medicine, 1978—2003; head Ahmanson Lab. Cellular Neurobiology UCLA Brain Research Inst, 1977—; dir. tng. grant in cellular neurobiology UCLA, 1968—2006, rsch. assoc. Fowler Mus. Cultural History, 1990—, chmn. dept. physiol. sci., 1997—2001. Author: Calcium and Ion Channel Modulation, 1988, Physiology of Excitable Cells, 1983, Regulation of Muscle Contraction, 1981, Introduction to Nervous Systems, 1977, others; contbr. editorial revs. to profl. jours., pub. houses, fed. granting agys. Guggenheim fellow, 1986; recipient Sr. Scientist award Alexander von Humboldt Stiftung, 1975, 79, Jacob Javits award NIH, 1986. Mem. AAAS (mem.-at-large neurosci. steering group 1998-2002), Muscular Dystrophy Assn. (mem. med. adv. com. LA chpt. 1980-92), Soc. for Neurosci. (councilor 1982-86), Am. Physiol. Soc. (mem. neurophysiol. steering com. 1981-84), Soc. Fellow, Phi Beta Kappa, Sigma Xi, others. Avocations: music, anthropology, archaeology, travel. Home: 510 E Rustic Rd Santa Monica CA 90402-1116 Office: UCLA Sch Medicine Dept Physiology Los Angeles CA 90095-0001 Office Phone: 310-825-4468. Business E-Mail: agrinnell@mednet.ucla.edu.

GRISEZ, JAMES LOUIS, physician, plastic surgeon; b. Modesto, Calif., Feb. 25, 1935; s. John Francis and Josephine Marie (Tournahu) G.; m. Diane Madeline Skidmore, Mar. 7, 1989; children: James, Stephen, Suzanne, Kathleen. MD, St. Louis Sch. Medicine, 1960. Diplomate Am. Bd. Plastic and Reconstructive Surgery. Intern D.C. Gen. Hosp., Washington, 1960-61; resident med. ctr. Georgetown U., Washington, 1961-64; resident plastic and reconstructive surgery ctr. St. Francis Meml. Hosp., San Francisco, 1964-66; military surgeon Brook Army Med Ctr., San Antonio, 1966, Second Gen. Hosp., Landstuhl, Germany, 1966-69; pvt. practice Napa, Calif., 1969-82, Salinas, Calif., 1982-90, Kailua-Kona, Hawaii, 1990-93, South Valley Plastic Surgery, Gilroy, Calif., 1993—2002; provl. staff French Hosp. San Luis Obispo, 2002—03; active staff Arroyo Grande Cmty. Hosp., 2003—. Active staff mem. St. Louise Regional Hosp.; chief of staff South Valley Hosp., Hazel Hawkins; chief staff St. Helena Hosp., 1977-78, exec. com. 1973-80; radio talk show host All About Plastic Surgery, sta. KRNY, 1986-88. Contbr. articles to med. jours. Mem. Am. Cancer Soc. (pres. 1988-90), Am. Soc. Plastic Surgeons, Calif. Soc. Plastic and Reconstructive Surgeons, Hawaii Plastic Surgery Soc. Home: 1595 Chesapeake Pl Arroyo Grande CA 93420 Office: 200 Station Way Ste B Arroyo Grande CA 93420-3348

GRITTON, EUGENE CHARLES, nuclear engineer, director; b. Santa Monica, Calif., Jan. 13, 1941; s. Everett Mason and Matilda Gritton; m. Gwendolyn O. Gritton; children: Dennis Mason, Kathleen Wanda. BS, UCLA, 1963, MS, 1965, PhD, 1966. Research engr., def. systems analyst RAND, Santa Monica, Calif., 1966-73, project leader advanced undersea tech. program, 1973-76, program dir. marine tech., 1974-76, program dir. applied sci. and tech., 1976-94, head dept. phys. scis., 1975-77, head engring. and applied scis. dept., 1977-86, RAND resident scholar for tech., 1990-93, dep. v.p. Nat. Security Rsch. Divsn., 1986-93, dep. v.p. Rsch. Ops. Group, 1986-90, dir. Acquisition and Tech. Policy Ctr., 1994—2004, acting dir. Nat Security Rsch. divsn., 1997—98, v.p. Nat Security Rsch. divsn., 2004—. Bd. dirs. Nat. Def. Rsch. Inst.; vis. lectr. dept. mech. engring. U. So. Calif., LA, 1967-72; vis. lectr. dept. energy and kinetics UCLA, 1971, 73; mem. Def. Sci. Bd. Study, 1996, 98. Recipient Engring. Alumnus of Yr. award UCLA Sch. Engring. and Applied Sci., 1985-86; AEC fellow, 1963, NSF Coop. Grad. fellow, 1964-66. Mem. Am. Nuclear Soc. (mem. exec. com. aerospace and hydrospace div. 1974-75), AIAA Office: Rand PO Box 2138 1776 Main St Santa Monica CA 90407-2138 Home: 4324 Promenade Way #315 Marina Del Rey CA 90292 Office Phone: 310-393-0411 ext. 6933. Business E-Mail: gene@rand.org.

GROBAN, JOSH, vocalist; b. LA, Feb. 27, 1981; Student, Interlochen Arts Acad. Performer Inauguration ceremonies of Gov. Joseph Graham 'Gray' Davis Jr., 1999; performer with Sarah Brightman in concert, Rotterdam, Netherlands, 2000; performer Closing ceremony of the 2002 Winter Olympics, Salt Lake City, 2002. Singer: (albums) Josh Gordon, 2001, Josh Groban in Concert (live), 2002, Closer, 2003, Live at the Greek, 2004, Awake, 2005, Noel, 2007, Awake Live, 2008; singer: (duet with Lara Fabian) (songs) For Always, 2001; singer: (duet with Charlotte Church) The Prayer, 2001; singer: (TV series) Ally McBeal, 2001, (TV spls.) A Home for the Holidays with Mariah Carey, 2001, Great Performances, 2003. Office: c/o Julie Colbert William Morris Agy 1 William Morris Place Beverly Hills CA 90212 also: Special Artists Agency 9465 Wilshire Blvd Ste 470 Beverly Hills CA 90212-2618

GROBE, CHARLES STEPHEN, lawyer, accountant; b. Columbus, Ohio, May 5, 1935; s. Harry A. and Bertha S. (Swartz) G.; m. Ila Silverman, Aug. 30, 1964; children— Eileen, Kenneth. BS, UCLA, 1957; JD, Stanford U., 1961. Bar: Calif. 1962; CPA, Calif. 1963. Tax acct., Beverly Hills, Calif., 1961—63; tax atty. LA, 1963—. Author: Guide to Investing Pension and Profit-Sharing Trust Funds, 1973, Guardianship, Conservatorship and Trusts on Behalf of Persons Who Are Mentally Retarded— An Assessment of Current Applicable Laws in the State of California, 1974, Using an Individual Retirement Savings Plan and the Related Rollover Provisions of the Pension Reform Act of 1974, 1975, Guide to Setting Up a Group Term Life Insurance Program Under IRC Section 79, 1976, Practical Estate Planning, 1988, Planning for Incapacity, 1989, Planning to Reduce the Generation Skipping Tax, 1989, Estate Planning Considerations for Community Property Interests, 1990, Legal and Tax Problems of Joint Tennancy as a Form of Ownership, 1990, The Tax Economics of Using the Generating Skipping Tax Exemptions, 1992, The Tax Economics of Gifting Property, 1992, Saving Estate Taxes with Life Insurance and a Life Insurance Trust, 1992, Family Wealth Transfer Planning, The Tax Economics of a Qualified Personal Residence Trust, also articles. Capt. US Army, 1957—64. Mem. ABA, State Bar Calif., L.A. County Bar Assn., Beverly Hills Bar Assn., Calif. Soc. CPAs. Office: 12110 Wilshire Blvd Los Angeles CA 90025-1104 Home: 172 S Woodburn Dr Los Angeles CA 90049-3041

GROBSTEIN, RUTH H., health facility administrator; 3 children. BA, NYU, 1945; PhD in Biology, Yale U., 1957; MD, UCLA, 1976. Post-doctoral fellow Yale Med. Sch., Calif., mem. staff microbiology Calif.; prin. investigator U. Calif., San Diego, asst. prof. radiation oncology San Francisco, 1980—83; divsn. head radiation oncology Scripps Clin., La Jolla, Calif. Dir. The Ida M. and Cecil H. Green Cancer Ctr. Grantee Atomic Energy Commn., 1966, Nadonal Inst. Health, 1966.

GROCE, AUGUSTUS BEN, paper company executive; BS in Pulp and Paper Tech., N.C. State U., 1963. Various mgmt. positions Boise Cascade Corp., Boise, Idaho, 1979-91, v.p. Maine opers., 1991-93, v.p. paper mfg., engring., transp. and procurement, 1993-94, sr. v.p. mfg. paper divsn., 1994-2000, sr. v.p., gen. mgr. paper divsn., 2000—. Office: Boise Cascade Corp 1111 W Jefferson St Boise ID 83728-0071

GRODSKY, GEROLD MORTON, biochemistry professor; b. St. Louis, Jan. 18, 1927; s. Louis and Goldie B.; m. Kayla Deane Wolfe, Dec. 6, 1952; children: Andrea, Jamie. BS, U. Ill., 1946, MS, 1947; PhD, U. Calif., Berkeley, 1954; postgrad., Cambridge U., Eng., 1954-55. Prof. biochemistry U. Calif., San Francisco, 1961-92, prof. emeritus (active status), 1992—, cons. to Diabetes Ctr., 1999—. Vis. prof. U. Geneva, 1968—69, U. Paris VII, 1989; Somogyi Meml. lectr., 72; Helen Martin lectr., 76; Herman Rosenthal lectr., 86; cons. in field; bd. dirs. Active Health Solutions, 2006—. Mem. editl. bd. Diabetes, 1965-73, 86-90, Am. Jour. Physiology, 1977-94, Diabetologia, 1990-92, Endocrinology, 1992-96; founding adv. editor: Diabetes Tech. and Therapy, 1998—2006; founding assoc. editor Diabetes Sci. and Tech., 2006—; contbr. chpts. to books; contbr. over 200 articles on diabetes and storage, secretion of insulin to profl. jours. Med. adv. bd. Juvenile Diabetes Found., 1974-77, 80-85; program dir. NIH Diabetic Animal Program, 1978-82, chmn. diabetes rsch. adv. bd. to Sec. Health, 1982-87. Lt. (s.g.) USNR, 1944-54. Recipient David Rumbough Internat. award Juvenile Diabetes Found., 1984, Williams-Levine award, 1990, Merit award NIH, 1987, Juvenile Diabetes Found. annual endowed Grodsky award, 1994—, Western Region Islet Study Group annual Gerold M. Grodsky Disting. Scientist award, 2004—. Career Achievement award, UCSF Diabetes Ctr.; named Grodsky Lectr. Diabetes Ctr. in his honor U. Calif., San Francisco, 2001; named one of 1000 most cited world scientists. Mem.: Am. Diabetes Assn. (rsch. bd. 1974—77, chmn. rsch. policy com. 1977, bd. dirs. Calif. chpt. 1989—91, nat. grant rev. com. 1992—96), Endocrine Soc., European Diabetes Assn., Am. Fedn. Clin. Rsch., Soc. Exptl. Biology, Am. Soc. Biol. Chemists, Internat. Diabetes Found., Meadowood Club, Harborpoint Club, Calif. Tennis Club. Office: U Calif Sch Medicine Diabetes Ctr PO Box 0540 San Francisco CA 94143-0001 Home: 501 Beale St Unit 21a San Francisco CA 94105-5024 E-mail: grodoskygm@aol.com.

GRODY, WAYNE WILLIAM, physician, educator; b. Syracuse, NY, Feb. 25, 1952; s. Robert Jerome and Florence Beatrice (Kashdan) G.; m. Gaylen Ducker, July 8, 1990. BA, Johns Hopkins U., 1974; MD, Baylor Coll. Medicine, 1977, PhD, 1981. Diplomate Am. Bd. Pathology, Am. Bd. Med. Genetics; lic. physician, Calif. Intern, resident UCLA Sch. Medicine, 1982-85, postdoctoral fellow, 1985-86, asst. prof., 1987-93, dir. DNA Diagnostic Lab., 1987—, assoc. prof., 1993-97, prof. depts. pathology and lab. medicine, pediat., human genetics, 1997—. Panelist Calif. Children's Svcs., 1987—, U.S. FDA, Washington, 1989—; DNA tech. com. Pacific Southwest Regional Genetics Network, Berkeley, Calif.; mem. task force genetic testing, NIH, 1987—; med., tech. cons., writer Warner Bros., NBC, Tri-Star, CBS, Twentieth Century Fox, Universal, others, 1987—; chair, molecular genetics com. Coll. Am. Pathologists, Assn. Molecular Pathology; chmn. genomic medicine adv. com. VA and others. Contbg. editor, film critic: MD Mag., 1981-91; assoc. editor Diagnostic Molecular Pathology, 1993—; contbr. articles to profl. jours., chpts. to books. Recipient best paper award L.A. Soc. Pathology, 1984, Joseph Kleiner Meml. award Am. Soc. Med. Technologists, 1990; Basil O'Connor scholar March of Dimes Birth Defects Found., 1989, Nakamura Lectureship Scripps Clinic, 1996, Moss Lectureship LSU, 1998, Stop Cancer Fdn. Rsch. award, 1998, Hill Lectureship Baylor Coll. Medicine, 2003; named One of Am.'s Top Doctors, 2001—. Mem. AAAS, AMA, Am. Soc. Clin. Pathology, Am. Soc. Human Genetics, Am. Coll. Med. Genetic(chair, bd. dirs. 2001-2006, pres. elect), Soc. Inherited Metabolic Disorders, Soc. Pediat. Rsch. Democrat. Jewish. Achievements include application of molecular biology to clinical diagnosis and genetic screening, molecular genetics research and AIDS and cancer research. Office: UCLA Sch Medicine Divsns Med Genetics and Molecular Pathology Los Angeles CA 90095-1732 Home Phone: 310-573-0268; Office Phone: 310-825-5648. Business E-Mail: wgrody@mednet.ucla.edu.

GROENING, MATTHEW (ABRAM), writer, cartoonist; b. Portland, Oreg., Feb. 15, 1954; s. Homer Philip and Margaret Ruth (Wiggum) Groening; m. Deborah Lee Caplan (div.); children: Homer, Abe. BA, Evergreen State Coll., 1977. Cartoonist Life in Hell weekly comic strip (syndicated by Acme Features Syndicate), Sheridan, Oreg., 1977—; creator, writer, cartoonist Simpson Shorts, The Tracey Ullman Show, 1987—; creator Akbar and Jeff; pres. Matt Groening Prodns., Inc., LA, 1988—; writer, story, prodr., exec. prodr., creator, developer The Simpsons, 1989—; writer, creator, exec. prodr., developer Futurama, 1999—; founder, pub. Bongo Comic Group, 1993—, Bongo Comics, 1995; exec. prodr. Olive, The Other Reindeer, 1999; writer, exec. prodr. Boo Boo Runs Wild. Author: Work is Hell, Love is Hell, School is Hell, The Big Book of Hell, The Huge Book of Hell, Love is Hell, Akbar & Jeff's Guide to Life, Binky's Guide to Love, The Simpsons: A Complete Guide to Our Favorite Family, The Simpsons Xmas Book, The Simpsons Rainy Day Fun Book, Making Faces With The Simpsons, Bart Simpson's Guide To Life, The Simpsons' Uncensored Family Album, Cartooning With The Simpsons, Simpsons Illustrated mag., Simpsons Comics Simps-O-Rama, Simpson Comics & Stories comic book, Simpsons Comics Extravaganza, Simpsons Comics Spectacular, Bartman: The Best of The Best; creater, developer, exec. prodr. The Simpsons Christmas Special, 1989, writer The Simpsons: Family Therapy, 1989, creater Bart vs the Space Mutants, 1991, original character designer The Simpsons Wrestling, 2001, creative consultant The Simpsons: Hit & Run, 2003, exec. prodr. The Simpsons: Bart's Nightmare, 1993, Bart Wars, the Simpsons Strike Back, 1999, writer, prodr. (films) The Simpsons Movie, 2007, voice of Arturo Olive, the Other Reindeer, 1999, voice of Dill Hair High, 2004, guest appearances The Tracey Ullman Show, 1988, Space Ghost Coast to Coast, 1996, The Big Breakfast, 2000, Great Performances, 2000, (voice) The Simpsons, 2004. Recipient The Simpsons, Emmy award for Outstanding Animated Program, 1990, 1991, 1995, 1997, 1998, 2000, 2001, 2003, Futurama, Emmy Award for Outstanding Animated Program, 2002; named New Pub. Yr., Diamond Distbn. Gem awards, 1993. Achievements include The expression "d'oh!" from The Simpsons was added to the Oxford English Dictionary in 2001. Office: The Simpsons c/o Twentieth Television Matt Groening's Office PO Box 900 Beverly Hills CA 90213 Address: Bongo Comics Group 1999 Avenue of Stars 15th Fl Los Angeles CA 90067 Office Phone: 310-788-1367. Office Fax: 310-788-1200.

GROFF, PETER, state legislator; b. Chgo., 1963; s. Regis F. and Ada L. Groff; m. Regina C. Groff; children: Malachi, Moriah. BA, U. Redlands, Calif., 1985; JD, U. Denver, 1992. Staff mem. Gov. Romer's Ombudsman Office, 1988—90; asst. Denver City Councilwoman Allegra Haynes, 1991—94; sr. asst. Mayor Webb, 1994—97; lectr. pub. policy dept. U. Denver; founder, exec. dir. U. Denver Ctr. African Am. Policy; pub. U. Denver Ascent Press; mem. Dist. 7 Colo. House of Reps., Denver, 2001—03; mem. Dist. 33 Colo. State Senate, Denver, 2003—, senate pres., 2009—. Dep. polit. dir. Roy Romer for Gov. Campaign, 1994; campaign mgr. City Coun. Pres. Allegra Haynes, 1999; v.p., region 12 Nat. Black Conf. State Legislature, 2001—, mem. exec. bd.; bd. dirs. Iliff Sch.; adj. prof. Luff Sch. Theology. Co-author: Standing in The Gap: Leadership for the 21st Century; editor: I Do Solemnly Swear, A Chronology of African American Politics and Public Policy, blackpolicy.org, ascentpress.org. Mem. Campbell AME Ch. Recipient Rising Star award Senator Gloria Tanner, 1997, People to Watch in the New Millennium award Denver Post, 1999, Chmn. award Urban League Met. Denver, 2000, Mountain award for govt. African Am. Leadership Inst., 2001, Families First award Denver County Dems., 2003; named Legislator of Yr. Colo. Progressive Coalition, 2001, Colo. Contractors Assn., 2006. Mem. Colo. Bar Assn., Colo. Golf Assn., Nat. Black Caucus State Legislators, Colo. Black Caucus State Legislators, US Midwest Legislature Leaders. Democrat. Methodist. Office: Colo State Capitol 200 E Colfax Rm 259 Denver CO 80203 Office Phone: 303-866-3342. Business E-Mail: peter.groff.senate@state.co.us.*

GROGAN, JAMES J., real estate company executive; Grad. cum laude, Coll. Holy Cross, 1976; grad., U. Cin., 1979. Mng. atty. Gallagher and Kennedy, Phoenix; sr. exec. v.p. UDC Homes; pres., CEO Samoth Capital Corp. and Samoth USA Inc., Scottsdale, Ariz., 1998—. Sterling Financial Corp., Scottsdale, Ariz. Bd. dirs. AMERCO. Bd. trustees Coll. of the Holy Cross. Office: Sterling Realty Group 7373 N Scottsdale Rd D210 Scottsdale AZ 85253-3559

GROGAN, VIRGINIA S., lawyer; b. Pasadena, Calif., Nov. 19, 1951; d. Bruce Mason and Helen Maude Gorsuch; m. Aug. 17, 1973 (div. June 1975); m. Allen R. Grogan, Jan. 10, 1982; children: Travis, Tess. BS, Occidental Coll., Eagle Rock, Calif., 1973; JD, U. So. Calif. Bar: Calif. 1979. Assoc. Latham & Watkins, LA, 1979-86, ptnr., 1987-97, chmn. assocs. com., 1995-97, mng. ptnr. Orange County Office Costa Mesa, Calif., 1997—. Mem. exec. roundtable U. Calif., Irvine, 1998—; mem. adv. com. Orange County Performing Arts, Costa Mesa, 1998—, Mem. ABA, Los Angeles County Bar Assn., Orange County Bar Assn. (judiciary com. 1998—), Legion Lex. Avocations: tennis, classical music. Office: Latham & Watkins 650 Town Center Dr Costa Mesa CA 92626-1989

GROHL, DAVE (DAVID ERIC GROHL), musician; b. Warren, OH, Jan. 14, 1969; s. James and Virginia Grohl; m. Jennifer Youngblood, 1993 (div. 1997); m. Jordyn Blum, Aug. 2, 2003; children: Violet Maye, Harper Willow. Drummer Scream, 1987—90, Nirvana, 1990—94; singer, guitarist Foo Fighters, 1995—. Drummer (albums with Scream) No More Censorship, 1988, Your Choice Live Series Vol.10, 1990, Fumble, 1993, (albums with Nirvana) Nevermind, 1991, In Utero, 1993, MTV Unplugged in New York, 1994, From the Muddy Banks of the Wishkah, 1996, singer, guitarist (albums with Foo Fighters) Foo Fighters, 1995, The Colour & the Shape, 1997, There is Nothing Left to Lose, 1999 (Grammy Award, Best Rock Album, 2001), One by One, 2002 (Grammy Award, Best Rock Album, 2004), In Your Honor, 2005, Echoes, Silence, Patience & Grace, 2007 (Grammy Award, Best Rock Album, 2008), with Foo Fighters (songs) Big Me, 1996 (MTV Music Video Award for Best Group Video, 1996), Learn to Fly, 1999 (Grammy Award, Best Music Video, Short Form, 2001, named one of VH1: 100 Greatest Videos, 2001), All My Life, 2002 (Grammy Award, Best Hard Rock Performance, 2003), The Pretender, 2007 (Grammy Award, Best Hard Rock Performance, 2008); actor: (films) Tenacious D: The Pick of Destiny, 2006. Achievements include Foo Fighters named one of 100 Greatest Rock Artists, VH1, 2000, 100 Sexiest Artists, VH1, 2002, Top Pop Artists of the Past 25 Yrs., 2004. Office: RCA Records 12720 Gateway Dr Seattle WA 98168 also: c/o Erin Culley-LaChapelle Creative Artists Agy 2000 Ave of the Stars Los Angeles CA 90067 Office Phone: 212-930-4000.

GROLLMAN, JULIUS HARRY, JR., cardiovascular and interventional radiologist; b. LA, Nov. 26, 1934; s. Julius Harry and Alice Carolyn (Greenlee) G.; m. Alexa Jule Silverman, May 20, 1959; children: Carolyn, David, Elizabeth. BA, Occidental Coll., 1956; MD, UCLA, 1960. Diplomate Am. Bd. Radiology. Intern L.A. VA Hosp., 1960-61; resident in radiology UCLA Med. Ctr., 1961-64; chief cardiovascular radiology Walter Reed Gen. Hosp., 1965-67; chief cardiovascular radiology Ctr. Health Svcs. UCLA, 1967-78; chief cardiovascular and interventional radiology Little Company of Mary Hosp., Torrance, Calif., 1978—2005, retired, 2005; clin. prof. radiol. sci. UCLA, 1978—. Contbr. over 150 articles to profl. jours., 9 chpts. to med. books. Fellow Soc. Cardiac Angiography and Interventions (trustee 1992-95), Am. Coll. Radiology, Coun. Cardiovascular Radiology, Am. Heart Assn., Soc. Cardiovascular and Interventional Radiology; mem. AMA, Am. Roentgen Ray Soc., Radiol. Soc. N.Am., Western Angiographic and Interventional Soc. (pres. 1976-77), N.Am. Soc. for Cardiac Imaging (pres. 1991-92). Republican. Presbyterian. Home: 211 S Guadalupe Ave Unit 3 Redondo Beach CA 90277 E-mail: grollmanj@mac.com.

GROSETA, ANDY (PETER ANDREW GROSETA), lobbyist; b. Cottonwood, Ariz., 1950; m. Mary Beth Groseta; children: Paul, Katy, Anna. BS in Agrl. Edn. & Animal Sci., U. Ariz., 1972, MS in Agrl. Edn., 1978. Mgr. Yolo Ranch, Inscription Canyon Ranch, Prescott, Ariz., 1989—93; farm and ranch appraiser, co-owner, ptnr. Hdqs. West, Ltd., Ariz.; chmn. fed. lands com. Nat. Cattlemen's Beef Assn., 2002—04, pres., 2008—. Past pres. Yavapai Cattle Growers Assn.; past chmn. Cath. Cmty. Found.; chmn. fed. lands. com. Ariz. Cattle Growers Assn.; dir. Pub. Lands Coun., Ariz., 1999—2007; chmn. U. Ariz. Yavapai County Cooperative Ext. Adv. Bd.; pres. sch. bd. Mingus Union HS; exec. com. Ariz. Cattle Growers Assn. Co-recipient Agriculturist of Yr., Ariz. State FFA, 2004. Office: Hdqs W Ltd PO BOX 1840 Cottonwood AZ 86326 Office Phone: 928-634-8110. Office Fax: 928-634-2113.

GROSS, ALLEN JEFFREY, lawyer; b. Wheeling, W.Va., May 2, 1948; s. Arthur and Bertyl (Kahn) G.; m. Carolyn McGuire, May 2, 1982; children: Alexander, Lindsay, Matthew. BS, Ohio State U., 1970; JD, Georgetown U., 1974. Bar: Pa. 1974, U.S. Dist. Ct. (ctrl. and we. dists.) Pa., Calif. 1989, U.S. Dist. Ct. (no., so. and ctrl. dists.) Calif. 1989, U.S. Ct. Appeals (3d and 6th cirs.). Ptnr. Morgan, Lewis & Bockius, Phila., 1974-89, Orrick, Herrington & Sutcliffe, LA, 1989-93; now with Mitchell, Silberberg & Knupp, LA. Mem. Corp. Counsel Inst. adv. bd. Georgetown U. Law Ctr; vice chair Georgetown Corp. Coun. Inst; co-chair Georgetown ELLI, 1993-. Author: Survey of Wrongful Discharge Cases in the United States, 1979, Employee Dismissal Laws, Forms, Procedures, 1986, 2d edit. 1992. Fellow Coll. Labor and Employment Lawyers Inc.; mem. ABA (chair trial advocacy supcom. 1989-93, employee rights and responsibilities com. 1991—, co-chair Nat. Advocacy Inst. 1992, com., Sect. Insts. Spl. Programs sub-com, gov. coun., 1998), L.A. County Bar Assn. Office: Mitchell Silberberg & Knupp 11377 W Olympic Blvd Los Angeles CA 90064-1625

GROSS, ARIELA JULIE, law educator; b. San Francisco, Sept. 22, 1965; d. David Jonathan and Shulamith Pia Gross; m. Jon Edward Goldman, Sept. 2, 1990; children: Raphaela, Sophia. BA in History and Literature, magna cum laude, Harvard U., 1987; JD, Stanford U., 1994, MA in History, 1991, PhD in History, 1996. Bar: Calif. 1995. Acting asst. prof. law Stanford Law Sch., 1996; vis. prof. law Tel Aviv U., 2006; asst. prof. law U. So. Calif. Law Sch., LA, 1996—98, assoc. prof. law, 1998—2001, prof. law and history, 2001—; vis. prof. Ecole des Hautes Etudes en Sciences Sociales, 2007—08. Co-dir. Ctr. for Law, History & Culture, USC, LA, 2004—06, 2006—07; juror Frederick Douglass Book prize Gilder Lehman Ctr., 2002—03; adv. bd. mem. Law & Hist. Rev., 2005—; adv. coun. mem. Lincoln Prize, Gettysburg, Pa., 2002—; presenter H.S. Teacher Workshops Ctr. for Constitutional Rights, 2003—05. Author: Double Character: Slavery & Mastery in the Antebellum Southern Courtroom, 2000 (Phi Kappa Phi award, 2001); contbr. articles to profl. jours. Grantee Fgn. Lang. Area Studies scholar, US Dept. Edn., 1993; Littleton-Griswold grant, Am. Hist. Assn., 1995, Zumberge Rsch. Innovation grant, U. S.C., 1997—98, Guggenheim fellow, 2003—, Huntington fellow, NEH, 2003—, Burkhardt fellow, Am. Coun. Learned Socs., 2003—. Mem.: Am. Hist. Assn. (Littleton-Griswold prize com. 2006—08), Law and Soc. Assn. (Willard Hurst prize com. 1999—), Am. Soc. Legal History (exec. com. 2001—03, bd. dirs. 2001—03, com. on future projects 2001—, chair subcom. on grad. students 2001, prog. com. ann. meeting 1998). Office: Univ Southern Calif Gould School of Law 699 Exposition Blvd 406 Los Angeles CA 90017 Office Phone: 213-740-4793. Office Fax: 213-740-5502. Business E-Mail: agross@law.usc.edu.

GROSS, BILL (WILLIAM H. GROSS), investment company executive, financial analyst; b. Middletown, Ohio, Apr. 13, 1944; m. Sue Gross; children: Jeff, Jennifer, Nick. BA in Psychology, Duke U., 1966; MBA in Fin., UCLA, 1971. Chartered Fin. Analyst. Investment analyst Pacific Mut. Life Ins. Co., Newport Beach, Calif., 1971-73, sr. analyst, 1973-76, asst. v.p., Fixed Income Securities, 1976-78, 2d v.p., Fixed Income Securities, 1978-80, v.p. Fixed Income Securities, 1980-82; from mng. dir. to chief investment officer Pacific Investment Mgmt. Co. (PIMCO) subs. Pacific Mut. Life Ins. Co., Newport Beach, Calif., 1982—. Regular panelist Wall Street Week with Louis Rukeyser TV program. Author: Everything You've Heard About Investing Is Wrong!, 1997, Bill Gross on Investing, 1998. Served tour of duty USN, Vietnam. Recipient Fixed Income Mgr. of the Year, Morningstar, 1998, 2000, 2007, Disting. Svc. award, Bond Market Assn., 2000; named one of Forbes' Richest Americans, 2006, The Top 25 Market Movers, US News & World Report, 2009. Mem. L.A. Soc. Fin. Analysts. Office: PIMCO 840 Newport Center Dr Newport Beach CA 92660-6310*

GROSS, DAVID JONATHAN, physicist; b. Washington, Feb. 19, 1941; s. Bertram M. and Nora (Faine) G.; m. Shulamith Toaff, Mar. 30, 1962; children: Ariela, Elisheva; m. Jacquelyn Savani, Aug. 12, 2001; Miranda Savani (stepdaughter). BSc, Hebrew U., Jerusalem, 1962; PhD, U. Calif., Berkeley, 1966; Doctorate (Docteur Honoris Causa) (hon.), U. Montpellier, 2000, Hebrew U., 2001. Harvard Soc. of Fellows jr. fellow Harvard U., 1966-69; asst. prof. physics Princeton U., 1969-71, assoc. prof., 1971-73, prof., 1973-86, Eugene Higgens prof. physics, 1986—95, Jones prof. physics, 1995—97, Jones prof. physics emeritus, 1997—; dir. U. Calif., Santa Barbara, Inst. for Theoretical Physics, Santa Barbara, Calif., 1997—; prof. U. Calif., Santa Barbara, Calif., 1997—, Gluck prof. theoretical physics, 2001—. Vis. prof. CERN, Geneva, 1968—69, Geneva, 1993, Ecole Normale Superioure, Paris, 1983, Paris, 1988—89, Hebrew U., Jerusalem, 1984, Lawrence Radiation Lab., Berkeley, Calif., 1992; invited lecturer for several universities; chair, evaluation com. Scuola Internazionale Superiore di Studi Avanzati, Italy, 1994—. Assoc. editor Nuclear Physics, 1972—. Dir. Jerusalem Winter Sch., 1999—. Recipient Alfred P. Sloan fellow, 1970-74, MacArthur Prize fellow, 1987, Dirac medal, 1988, Harvey prize, Technion-Israel Inst. Tech., 2000, Oscar Klein medal, Stockholm U., 2000, grande médaille, French Academy Sciences, 2004, Golden Plate award, Acad. Achievement, 2005; co-recipient High Energy and Particle Physics prize, European Physical Soc., 2003, Nobel Prize in Physics, 2004. Fellow AAAS, Am. Phys. Soc. (J. J. Sakurai prize 1986), Am. Acad. Arts and Scis.; mem. Nat. Acad. Scis. Research, numerous publs. in field; discovered asymptotic freedom, 1973; proposal of non-Abelian gauge theories of the strong interactions, 1973, heterotic string theory, 1984; discovery of (with H. David Politzer and Frank Wilczek) the asymptotic freedom in the theory of the strong interaction. Office: Kavli Inst for Theoretical Physics Univ Calif Santa Barbara Kohn Hall 1219 Santa Barbara CA 93106 Office Phone: 805-893-7337. Office Fax: 805-893-2431. Business E-Mail: gross@kitp.ucsb.edu.

GROSS, EDWARD, retired sociologist; b. Nagy Genez, Romania; s. Samuel and Dora (Levi) G.; m. Florence Rebecca Goldman, Feb. 18, 1943; children— David P., Deborah L., Teagardin. BA, U. B.C., Can., 1942; MA, U. Toronto, Ont., Can., 1945; PhD, U. Chgo., 1949; JD, U. Wash., 1991. Prof. Wash. State U., Pullman, Wash., 1947-51, 53-60; prof. U. Wash., Seattle, 1951-53, 65-89, prof. emeritus, 1990—; prof. sociology U. Minn., Mpls., 1960-65. Vis. prof. Australian Nat. U., Canberra, 1971, U. Queensland, U. New South Wales, Griffith U., Australia, 1977; invited lectr. Cen. China Poly. Inst., 1987; lectr. arts and sci. honor program U. Wash., 1998—; pres. resident coun. Ida Culver Broadview Ret. Facility, 2005-06. Author: Work and Society, 1958, Univ. Goals and Academic Power, 1968, Changes in Univ. Orgn., 1964-71, The End of a Golden Age: Higher Ed. in a Steady State, 1981, Embarrassment in Everyday Life, 1994; co-author (with A. Etzioni) Orgn. in Soc., 1985; contbg. author: Handbook of Sociology and Encyclopedia of Sociology, 2d edit.; former assoc.

editor Social Problems, Symbolic Interaction, Can. Jour. Sociology; contbr. articles to profl. jour. Trustee Temple Beth Am, Seattle, 1993-97. Fulbright scholar Australia, 1977, 87. Mem.: Wash. State Bar Assn., Am. Sociol. Assn. (emeritus), Pacific Sociol. Assn. (pres. 1971, coun. 1983—85). Office: U Wash Dept Sociology Seattle WA 98195-0001 Business E-Mail: egross@u.washington.edu.

GROSS, LARRY PAUL, communications educator; b. Washington, Nov. 22, 1942; s. Bertram Myron and Nora (Faine) G. BA, Brandeis U., 1964; PhD, Columbia U., 1968; MA (hon.), U. Pa., 1973. Asst. prof. U. Pa., Phila., 1968-73, assoc. prof., 1973-82, prof., 1982—, Sol Worth prof., 1998—, assoc. dean for grad. studies, 1989-93, chair faculty senate, 2000-01, dep. dean, 2001—03; prof., dir. Sch. Comm., U. So. Calif., 2003—. Author: Contested Closets: The Politics and Ethics of Outing, 1993; editor: Communications Technology and Social Policy, 1973, Between Men-Between Women book series, 1991—, Studying Visual Communication, 1981, Image Ethics, 1988, Studies in Visual Communications, 1977-85, On the Margins of Art Worlds, 1995, The Columbia Reader on Lesbians and Gay Men in Media, Society and Politics, 1999, Up From Invisibility: Lesbians, Gay Men and the Media in America, 2001; author, editor: Image Ethics in the Digital Age, 2003; assoc. editor Internat. Ency. Comm., 1989; contbr. articles to profl. jours. Chair Phila. Lesbian and Gay Task Force, 1981-2000; mem. Pa. Humanities Coun., 1985-90. Guggenheim fellow, 1998-99. Fellow Am. Anthrop. Assn. (co-chmn. rsch. group on homosexuality 1981-84); mem. Internat. Comm. Assn. (chair task force on diversity 1992—, lesbian and gay studies interest group 1993-96), Nat. Comm. Assn., Phi Beta Kappa, Sigma Xi. Home: 329 S Sycamore Los Angeles CA 90036 Office: U So Calif Annenberg Sch Los Angeles CA 90089 Home Phone: 310-306-9376; Office Phone: 213-740-3770. Business E-Mail: lpgross@usc.edu.

GROSS, LAWRENCE ALAN, lawyer; b. Phila., Oct. 1, 1952; s. Herbert and Rita Lila (Garelik) G.; m. Lynda Kinsfather, May 27, 1979; 1 child, Alyssa Rachel. AB with highest honor, U. Mich., 1973, AM in Philosophy, 1978, JD magna cum laude, 1979. Bar: Pa. 1979. Assoc. Blank, Rome, Comisky & McCauley, Phila., 1979-86; v.p., gen. counsel Sungard Data Systems Inc., Wayne, Pa., 1986—2006; exec. v.p. legal, interim gen. counsel KLA-Tencor Corp., San Jose, 2006—. Bd. dirs. Sungard Data Sytems Inc. and subs. Mem. ABA, Corp. Counsel Assn., Am. Soc. Corp. Secs., Pa. Bar Assn., Phila. Bar Assn., U. Mich. Alumni Assn.

GROSSER, BERNARD IRVING, psychiatrist, educator; b. Boston, Apr. 19, 1929; s. John and Katherine (Russman) G.; children: Steven, Mark, Minda; m. Karen Grosser. BA, U. Mass., Amherst, 1950; MS, U. Mich., Ann Arbor, 1953; MD, Case Western Res. U., Cleve., 1959. Diplomate Am. Bd. Psychiatry and Neurology. Intern U. Utah, 1959-60, resident in psychiatry, 1960-65; asst. prof. psychiatry U. Utah Sch. Medicine, Salt Lake City, 1967-71, assoc. prof., 1971-75, prof., 1975—, chmn. dept., 1978—2007. Mem. pre-clin. and clin. psychopharm. rev. com. NIMH, Washington, 1974-79, 80-84, mem. NIMH internat. sci. adv. bd., 1984-88; mem. merit rev. bd. VA, Washington, 1988-91; sr. sci. advisor Alcohol, Drug Abuse and Mental Health Adminstrn., Washington, 1987-88; ad hoc mem. Mental Health Clin. Rsch. Ctr. rev. com. NIMH, 1997, ad hoc mem. mental health clin. contracts rev. com., 1998, NIMH ad hoc mem. spl. emphasis panel, 2000-06; rev. panel R13, 2005, R03, 2006, Extramural LRP, 2008-09. Contbr. chpts. to books, articles to profl. jours. Capt. USAF, 1965-67. Grantee NIMH, 1959-84, FDA, 1985-88; recipient Exemplary psychiatrist award Nat. Alliance for Mentally Ill, 1997. Fellow Am. Psychiat. Assn. (disting. life); mem. Internat. Soc. Psychoneuroendocrinology (treas. 1974-88), Utah Psychiat. Assn. (pres. 1995-96), Psychiat. Rsch. Soc. (pres. 1986-87), Am. Coll. Neuropsychopharmacology, Soc. Neurosci., NY Acad. Scis., Collegium Internat. Neuro-psychopharmacologicum, Am. Assn. Psychiatry Dept. Chairmen (coun. 1997-2005, sec.-treas. 2005-06). Republican. Jewish. Home: 511 Perrys Hollow Rd Salt Lake City UT 84103-4245 Office: U Utah Sch Medicine Dept Psychiatry 50 N Medical Dr Salt Lake City UT 84132-0001 Office Phone: 801-581-4888. Business E-Mail: bernard.grosser@hsc.utah.edu.

GROSSER, T.J., not-for-profit fundraiser; b. Milw., Oct. 17, 1938; s. Owen Henry and Ethel Clare (Hathazy) G.; m. Mary Janet McClanahan, Apr. 3, 1976; children: Paul Howard, Julie Anne, Philip Owen, Peter John, Elizabeth Michelle. BA, U. Wis., 1958, MA, 1962, EdD, 1971; DD (hon.), Union Theol. Sem., Richmond, Va., 1972. Min. edn. Cross Luth. Ch., Milw., 1957-62; assoc. Christ Luth. Ch., Oshkosh, Wis., 1962-65; preacher/tchr. Trinity Luth. Ch., Santa Barbara, Calif., 1966-71; pres. Amigos de las Ams., Houston, 1972-79, Vols. in Internat. Svc. & Awareness, LA, 1980-84; v.p. Pacific Clinics, Pasadena, Calif., 1985-87; pres., CEO Children's Aid Internat., San Diego, 1987-97, Angelcare, 1998—. Bd. dirs. Am. Devel. Found., Washington, 1981-95; bd. dirs., pres. End Hunger Network, L.A., 1983-87; bd. dirs., v.p. Ind. Charities of Am., San Francisco, pres., 1988—; bd. dirs. Children's Charities Am.; advisor numerous internat. and religious agys. Contbr. 200 articles to profl. jours. Advisor African Refugee Ctr., L.A., 1989—; worker priest Hope Luth. Ch., Hollywood, Calif., 1983—. Named Educator of Yr. Am. Luth. Ch., Mpls., 1966, exec. of Yr. Coun. Internat. Vol. Orgn., Geneva, 1975, 76; recipient Papal medal Pope John Paul II, Rome, 1979. Mem. Fund Raising Execs., Rotary (Paul Harris fellow 1987). Democrat. Avocations: reading, speaking, travel, promoting internat. adoptions. Home: 1146 San Lori Ln El Cajon CA 92019 Office: Anglecare PO Box 600370 San Diego CA 92160-0370 Office Phone: 619-795-6234. E-mail: tjgrosser@angelcare.org.

GROSSMAN, ARTHUR R., science educator, researcher; BS with honors in Biology, Bklyn. Coll., NY, 1973; PhD, Ind. U., 1978. Postdoctoral fellow, dept. cell biology Rockefeller U., 1978—82; staff mem., dept. plant biology Carnegie Institution of Washington, 1982—. Asst. prof. by courtesy, dept. biology Stanford U., Calif., 1982—89, assoc. prof. by courtesy, dept. biology, 1989—2000, prof. by courtesy, dept. biology, 2000—; mem. sci. adv. bd. Wallenberg Consortium North, 2000—03; cons. Exelixis Pharm.; with Solazyme, 2004—, chmn. sci. adv. bd., chief of genetics. Mem. several editl. bds.; contbr. several articles to profl. jours.; ad hoc reviewer for NSF, USDA, NIH and Dept. Energy, 1982—2002. Recipient L. Whorley award in Biology, 1972, Darbaker prize for work on microalgae, Botanical Soc. America, 2002, Gilbert Morgan Smith medal, NAS, 2009; NSF Predoctoral Fellowship, 1974—79, Floyd Fellowship, 1977, NIH Postdoctoral Fellowship, 1979—81, Lady Davis Fellowship, 2001. Mem.: Am. Soc. Plant Physiologists, Phi Beta Kappa. Office: Carnegie Instituton Washington Dept Plant Biology 260 Panama St Stanford CA 94305 Address: Dept Biology Herrin Hall Stanford Stanford CA 94305 Office Phone: 650-325-1321 ext. 212. Office Fax: 650-325-6857. Business E-Mail: arthurg@stanford.edu.*

GROSSMAN, BONNIE, art gallery director; m. Sy Grossman. Former kindergarten teacher; founder The Ames Gallery, Berkeley, Calif., 1970—. Lectr. on Am. folk art and outsider art. Exec. prod., co-dir., prod. nine TV programs on Calif. artists; contbr. articles to profl. pubs. Avocations: cake sculpture, knitting. Office: The Ames Gallery 2661 Cedar St Berkeley CA 94708 Home Phone: 510-549-1055; Office Phone: 510-845-4949. Office Fax: 510-845-6219. E-mail: amesgal@comcast.net.

GROSSMAN, DAN, state senator; b. Denver, May 28, 1968; BA in Polit. Scis., U. Kans., 1990; JD, U. Denver, 1993. Atty., 1993—; sr. corp. counsel TeleTech Holdings, Inc., Colo.; state rep. Colo. Ho. of Reps., Denver, 1996—2002; minority caucus chmn., minority leader, 2000; state sen. dist. 32 Colo. State Senate, Denver, 2002, mem. agr., natural resources and energy and appropriations coms., and joint com. on legal svcs. Mem.: Temple Emanuel, Anti-Defamation League. Democrat. Jewish. Avocations: running, skiing, mountain biking. Office: State Capitol # 274 200 E Colfax Ave Denver CO 80203

GROSSMAN, ELMER ROY, pediatrician; b. LA, Jan. 30, 1929; s. Harry and Reta (Frankel) G.; m. Rosalind Nagin, June 24, 1951 (div. 1976); children: Deena, Marianna; m. Pamela Canfield Antoncich, July 29, 1976; stepchildren: Camilla Sutter, Michael A. Antoncich. AB, U. Calif.-Berkeley, 1949; MD, U. Calif. Sch. Medicine, San Francisco, 1953. Intern Orange County Gen. Hosp., Orange, Calif., 1953-54; resident U. Calif. Hosps., San Francisco, 1957-59; practice medicine specializing in pediatrics Berkeley Pediatric Med. Group, Calif., 1959-92. Assoc. clin. prof. health and med. scis. U. Calif., Berkeley, 1978-80; clin. prof. pediat. emeritus U. Calif. Sch. Medicine, San Francisco; chmn. dept. pediat. Alta Bates Hosp., Berkeley, 1972-74, chmn. infant care ethics com., 1984-90. Author: Everyday Pediatrics, 1993, Everyday Pediatrics for Parents, 1996; columnist The Everyday Pediatrician; contbr. articles to nat. mags. Mem. Berkeley Schs. Master Plan Com., 1966—68, Berkeley Schs. Child Care Com., 1968—70, Berkeley Cmty. Environ. Adv. Commn., 2000—02, Berkeley Cmty. Health Commn., 2002; pres. Temple Beth El, Berkeley, 1970—72. Served to capt USAF, 1954—56. Fellow Am. Acad. Pediatrics; mem. Alameda-Contra Costa Med. Assn., Physicians for Social Responsibility, Physicians for a Nat. Health Program. Democrat. Jewish. Avocations: wine making, gardening. Home and Office: 899 Euclid Ave Berkeley CA 94708-1305 Office Phone: 510-526-9614. Personal E-mail: elmer@grossmanfamily.com.

GROSSMAN, GEORGE STEFAN, library director, law educator; b. Poltar, Czechoslovakia, May 31, 1938; m. Suzi Herczeg, 1960; 1 child, Zoltan BA, U. Chgo., 1960; LL.B., Stanford U., 1966; MA in Library Sci., Brigham Young U., 1971. Bar: Calif. 1966, Minn. 1974. Tech. processes law librarian U. Pa., 1966-68; assoc. prof. law, law librarian U. Utah, 1968-70, prof., law librarian, 1970-73; prof., dir. law library U. Minn., 1973-79, Northwestern U., Chgo., 1979-93; prof., dir. law libr. U. Calif., Davis, 1993—. Cons. to univs. Author: Legal Research: Historical Foundations of the Electronic Age, 1994, The Spirit of American Law, 1999; contbr. articles to legal jours. Mem. Indian rights com. ACLU, 1973-92, pres. Utah affiliate, 1972-73, bd. dirs. Ill. affiliate, 1982-87. Mem. Am. Assn. Law Libraries, Internat. Assn. Law Libraries. Office: U Calif Sch Law Libr 400 Mrak Dr Davis CA 95616 Office Phone: 530-752-0548. Fax: 530-752-8766.

GROSSMAN, LAWRENCE MORTON, nuclear engineering educator; b. NYC, Aug. 2, 1922; married; 1 child. BChem Engring., CCNY, 1942, MSc (Standard Oil Co. Calif. fellow), 1944; PhD in Engring. Sci., U. Calif., Berkeley, 1948. Chem. engr. E.I. du Pont de Nemours & Co., Niagara Falls, N.Y., 1942-43; instr. mech. engring. U. Calif., Berkeley, 1944-46, lectr., 1946-48, asst. prof., 1948-54, assoc. prof. mech. engring., 1954-59, prof. nuclear energy, 1959—, chmn. dept. nuclear engring., 1969-74. Fulbright lectr. U. Delft, 1952-53; NSF Sr. research fellow Saclay Nuclear Research Center, France, 1961-62; NATO sr. fellow, 1974 Recipient Berkeley Citation, 1991. Mem. A.A.A.S., Am. Nuclear Soc. Office: U Calif Etcheverry Hl Berkeley CA 94720-0001 E-mail: grossman@nuc.berkeley.edu.

GROSSMAN, MARSHALL BRUCE, lawyer; b. Omaha, Mar. 24, 1939; s. Lee and Elsie (Stalmaster) G.; m. Marlene Belle Delson, Aug. 19, 1962; children: Rodger Seth, Leslie Erin. Student, U. Calif. at Los Angeles, 1957-59; BSL., LL.B., U. So. Calif., 1964. Bar: Calif. 1965. With Alschuler, Grossman, LA, 1965-67, ptnr., 1967—2007, Bingham McCutcheon LLP, LA, 2007—. Lectr. law U. So. Calif., Los Angeles, 1966-69; lectr., author on comml. litigation, 1968—; mem. Calif. Commn. Jud. Performance, 2001—, chmn., 2005—07. Mem. Calif. Coastal Commn., 1981-86; bd. dirs. Bet Tzedek Legal Services, 1986-2006, United Way, 1992-95, Jewish Big Brothers, 1995-, Amer. Jewish Com., 2000-. Mem. ABA, LA Bar Assn., Beverly Hills Bar Assn. (bd. govs. 1971-76), Barristers Bar Assn. (pres. 1972-73), Assn. Bus. Trial Attys. (bd. govs. 1974-75), LA Jewish Fedn. (chmn. commn. on law and legislation 1973-74, chmn. commn. on Soviet Jewry 1981, chmn. cmty. rels. com. 1984-86), Order of Coif, Tau Delta Phi, Phi Alpha Delta. Clubs: Mason. Office: Bingham McCutcheon LLP The Water Garden 1620 26th St Fourth Fl N Tower Santa Monica CA 90404-4060 Office Phone: 310-907-1000.

GROSSMAN, WILLIAM, medical researcher, educator; b. NYC, 1940; MD, Yale U., 1965. Intern Peter Bent Brigham Hosp., Boston, 1965-66, resident in medicine, 1968-69, rsch. fellow in cardiology, 1969-71; dir. cardiac catheterization labs. N.C. Meml. Hosp., Chapel Hill, 1971-75, Peter Bent Brigham Hosp., Boston, 1975-81; chief cardiovasc. divsn. Beth Israel Hosp., Boston, 1981-94; tchg. fellow in medicine Harvard U., Boston, 1968-71, assoc. prof., 1975-81, prof., 1981-84, Herman Dana prof. medicine, 1984-94; exec. dir. cardiovasc. rsch. Merck & Co., West Point, Pa., 1994-95, v.p., 1996-97; prof. medicine U. Calif., San Francisco, 1997—, chief cardiology, 1997—. Served as sr. asst. surgeon USPHS, 1966-68. Fellow Am. Coll. Cardiology, Am. Heart Assn., Assn. Am. Physicians, Am. Physiol. Soc., Am. Soc. Clin. Investigation. Office: UCSF Med Ctr Dept Cardiology Box 0124 San Francisco CA 94143-0124

GROSZ, PHILIP J., lawyer; b. Oshkosh, Wis., Feb. 1, 1952; s. Joseph Otto and Marjorie (Berkhoel) G.; m. Linda Marie Ondrejka, Dec. 29, 1973. BA with honors, U. Wis., 1973; JD, Yale Law Sch., 1977. Bar: Calif. Ptnr. Loeb & Loeb, LA, 1983-92, mng. ptnr., 1992-96. Founder, bd. dirs. Love is Feeding Everyone, L.A., 1983-94. Mem. Calif. Bar Assn. Democrat. Office: Loeb & Loeb 10100 Santa Monica Blvd Los Angeles CA 90067-4164

GROTH, ALEXANDER JACOB, political science professor; b. Warsaw, Mar. 7, 1932; came to U.S., 1947, naturalized, 1953; s. Jacob and Maria (Hazenfuss) Goldwasser; m. Marilyn Ann Wineburg, Dec. 15, 1961; children: Stevin James, Warren Adrian. BA magna cum laude, CCNY, 1954; MA, Columbia U., NYC, 1955, PhD, 1960. Instr. polit. sci. Trinity Coll., Hartford, Conn., 1957-58, CUNY, 1960-61; asst. prof. Harpur Coll., Binghamton, NY, 1961-62, U. Calif., Davis, 1962—, prof., 1971—. Author: Revolution and Elite Access, 1966, Comparative Politics, 1971, Major Ideologies, 1971, 2d rev. edit., 1983, People's Poland, 1972, Progress and Chaos, 1984, Lincoln: Authoritarian Savior, 1995, Democracies Against Hitler, 1999, Holocaust Voices, 2003; co-author: Contemporary Politics: Europe, 1976, Comparative Resource Allocation, 1984, Public Policy Across Nations, 1985; editor: Revolution and Political Change, 1996; mem. editl. bd. Political Crossroads, 1996-, The Jersualem Rev., 2007, Israel Jour. Fgn. Affairs; contbr. Encyclopedia Americana Annuals, Poland, 1965-2001, World Book Encyclopedia, 1999, The Encyclopedia of Political Revolutions, 1998, Yearbook of Internat. Communist Affairs, 1975-76; contbr. numerous articles to encys., scholarly jours. Recipient Ward medal dept. govt. CCNY, 1954, T. R. Dye award, 2000; grantee Am. Co. Learned Socs. and Social Sci. Research Council, 1965-66; nominee Panunzio award, U. Calif., Davis, 2004, 05. Mem. Western Polit. Sci. Assn., Policy Studies Assn., Far West Slavic Assn., Phi Beta Kappa. Republican. Avocations: baseball, writing, painting, travel, reading. Home: 1848 Rushmore Ln Davis CA 95616-6654 Office: U Calif Dept Polit Sci Davis CA 95616 Home Phone: 530-758-1429; Office Phone: 530-752-0966. Personal E-mail: marilynag@aol.com.

GROTZINGER, JOHN PETER, paleontologist, educator; BSc, Hobart Coll., 1979; MSc, U. Mont., 1981; PhD, Va. Poly. Inst. and State U., 1985. Postdoctoral rschr. Columbia U. Lamont-Doherty Geol. Obs., 1985—88; asst. prof. MIT, 1988—91, assoc. prof., 1991—95, prof., 1998—2005, Waldemar Lingren Disting. scholar, 1998—2001, Robert E. Shrock prof. geology, 2001—05; Fletcher Jones prof. geology dept. geol. and planetary scis. Calif. Inst. Tech., Pasadena, 2005—. Mem. geology and long term planning grps. Mars Exploration Rover mission, 2004. Contbr. articles to sci. jours.; co-author: Understanding Earth. Recipient Donath medal, Geol. Soc. Am., 1992, Henno Martin medal, Geol. Soc. Namibia, Jubilee medal, Geol. Soc. South Africa. Mem.: NAS (Charles Doolittle Walcott medal 2007). Office: Calif Inst Tech Dept Geol and Planetary Scis MC 170-25 1200 E California Blvd Pasadena CA 91125 Office Phone: 626-395-6785. E-mail: grotz@gps.caltech.edu.

GROUNDS, VERNON CARL, seminary administrator; b. Jersey City, July 19, 1914; s. John and Bertha Barbara (Heimburg) G.; m. Ann Barton, June 17, 1939; 1 child, Barbara Ann Grounds Owen. BA, Rutgers U., 1937; BD, Faith Theol. Sem., 1940; DD (hon.), Wheaton Coll., 1954; PhD, Drew U., 1960; LHD (hon.), Gordon Coll., 1977. Pastor Paterson (NJ) Gospel Tabernacle, 1935-45; dean, prof. theology Bapt. Bible Sem., Johnson City, 1945-51; dean Denver Conservative Bapt. Sem., 1951-55, pres., 1955-79, chancellor, 1979—. Author: Yes, But How?, Emotional Problems and the Gospel, Evangelicalism and Social Responsibility, The Reason for Our Hope, Revolution and the Christian Faith; contbg. editor Christianity Today, 1980—. Sec. Evang. Theol. Soc., Lynchburg, Va., 1963-76; bd. dirs. Radio Bible Class Ministries. Office: 6399 S Sante Fe Dr Littleton CO 80120 Home: 3455 S Corona St Apt 447 Englewood CO 80113-2878 Office Phone: 303-762-6890.

GROUSBECK, HAROLD IRVING, professional sports team owner, management educator; 1 child, Wycliffe. AB, Amherst Coll., 1956; MBA, Harvard Bus. Sch., 1960; LHD (hon.), Amherst Coll., 2000. Co-founder Continental Cablevision, 1963, pres., 1964—80, chmn. bd., 1980—85; lectr. Harvard U. Grad. Sch. Bus. Adminstrn., 1981—85; vis. lectr. Stanford U., Calif., 1985—86, lectr., 1986—96, consulting prof. mgmt., co-head Ctr. Entrepreneurial Studies, 1996—; mng. ptnr., mem. exec. com. Boston Celtics, 2002—. Bd. dirs. Asurion. Co-author: New Bus. Ventures and the Entrepreneur. Office: Stanford Grad Sch Bus Ctr Entrepreneurial Studies 518 Memorial Way Stanford CA 94305-5015 Office Phone: 650-723-7655. Office Fax: 650-725-7461. E-mail: grous@stanford.edu.

GROVE, ANDREW STEVEN, electronics executive; b. Budapest, Hungary, Sept. 2, 1936; m. Eva Kaston, 1958; 2 children. BS in Chemical Engring., CCNY, 1960; PhD, U. Calif., Berkeley, 1963; DSc (hon.), CCNY, 1985; DEng (hon.), Worcester Poly. Inst., 1989; LLD (hon.), Harvard U., 2000. With Fairchild Semiconductor, 1963—67, asst. dir. rsch. & devel., 1967—68; co-founder Intel Corp., Santa Clara, Calif., 1968, v.p., dir. ops., 1968—74, exec. v.p., 1975—76, COO, 1976—87, pres., 1979—97, CEO, 1987—98, chmn. bd., 1997—2005, sr. adviser, 2005—. Mem. bd. dirs. Intel Corp., 1974—; tchr. grad. course in semiconductor device physics U. Calif., Berkeley; lectr. Stanford Grad. Sch. of Bus. Author: Physics and Technology of Semiconductor Devices, 1967, High Output Management, 1983, One on One with Andy Grove, 1987, Only the Paranoid Survive: How To Exploit the Crisis Points That Challenge Every Company and Career, 1996, (autobiography) Swimming Across, 2001; co-author (with Robert A. Burgelman): Strategic Dynamics: Concepts and Cases, 2005, author of articles in Fortune, The Wall Street Journal, and The NY Times, weekly column on mgmt. carried by several newspapers, (column on mgmt.) Working Women. Patient advocate U. Calif., San Francisco, nat. chair of campaign; bd. dir. Prostrate Cancer Found.; active Grove Found. Recipient Am. Inst. Chemists medal, 1960, Merit cert., Franklin Inst., 1975, Townsend Harris medal, CCNY, 1980, Hall of Fame award, Information Industries Assn., 1984, Enterprise award, Bus. and Profl. Advt. Assn., 1987, George Washington award, Am. Hungarian Found., 1990, Achievement medal, Am. Electronics Assn., 1993, Heinz Family Tech. Found. award, 1995, John von Neumann medal, Am. Hungarian Assn., 1995, Steinman medal, CCNY, 1995, Internat. Achievement award, World Trade Club, 1997, Cinema Digital Technols. award, Internat. Film Festival, 1997, Cinema Digital Tech. award, Cannes Film Festival, 1997, Disting. Exec. of the Yr., Acad. of Mgmt., 1998, Lifetime Achievement award, Strategic Mgmt. Soc., 2001, Ernest C. Arbuckle award, Stanford U. Grad. Sch. Bus., 2004; named Exec. of Yr., U. Ariz., 1993, Citizen of Yr., World Forum Silicon Valley, 1993, Statesman of Yr., Harvard Bus. Sch., 1996, Tech. Leader of Yr., Industry Week, 1997, Man of Yr., Time mag., 1997, CEO of Yr., CEO mag., 1997, Distinguished Exec. of Yr., Acad. Mgmt., 1998, Most Influential Bus. Person in the Last Twenty-Five Yrs., Wharton Sch. Bus., 2004, Nightly Business Report, 2004, in honor of CCNY Grove School of Engring., 2005. Fellow: IEEE (Achievement award 1969, J.J. Ebers award 1974, Engring. Leadership Recognition award 1987, Computer Entrepreneur award 1997, Medal of Honor award 2000), Am. Acad. Arts and Scis.; mem.: NAE (award 1979). Achievements include patents in field. Office: Intel Corp 2200 Mission College Blvd Santa Clara CA 95052 Office Phone: 408-765-8080. Office Fax: 408-765-9904.

GROVE, STEVE, Internet company executive; b. Northfield, Minn., 1968; MA in Pub. Policy, Harvard U., 2006. Reporter Boston Globe, ABC News; dir. news and politics YouTube Inc., San Bruno, Calif., 2005—. Editor (blogs) Citizentube, 2007—. Office: YouTube Inc 1000 Cherry Ave San Bruno CA 94066*

GROVER, NEEL, Internet company executive; BA, U. Calif. Irvine; JD cum laude, U. San Diego. Sr. assoc. Brobeck, Phleger, & Phleger, Jones, Day, Reaves & Pogue; various positions including gen. mgr. ThinkTank Holdings; pres. BuyNetwork, 2003—; pres., COO Buy-.com, 2003—. Bd. dirs. TechSpace. Office: Buy dot com 85 Enterprise Ste 100 Aliso Viejo CA 92656 Office Phone: 949-389-2000. Office Fax: 949-389-2800.

GRUBB, EDGAR HAROLD, financial services industrial executive; b. Harrisburg, Pa., May 8, 1939; s. Harold E. and Ruth (Longenecker) G.; m. Patricia A. Kerwin, Dec. 14, 1963; children: Dennis, Lisa, Mary, Jennifer. BS, Pa. State U., 1961; MBA, Calif. State U., Fullerton, 1967. CPA, Calif. Cons. mgr., auditor Coopers & Lybrand, San Francisco and L.A., 19678-72; group contr. Crown Zellerbach Corp., San Francisco, 1972-75, gen. mgr. packaging papers, 1976-77, dir. planning, 1978-80, v.p. consumer, 1981-82, v.p., contr., 1983-84, sr. v.p., chief fin. officer, 1984-86, Lucky Stores, Inc., Dublin, Calif., 1986-89; sr. v.p. Transamerica Corp., 1989-93, CFO, 1993-99. Bd. dirs. Goodwill Industries of Alameda/Contra Costa/Solano Counties. Trustee Mills Coll., Oakland, Calif. Capt. USMC, 1961-65. Mem. AICPA, Calif. Soc. CPA's, Fin. Execs. Inst. Roman Catholic. Home: 41 Comistas Ct Walnut Creek CA 94598-4523 Office: Transamerica Corp 600 Montgomery St Ste 2300 San Francisco CA 94111-2770

GRUBBS, ROBERT HOWARD, chemistry professor; b. Calvert City, Ky., Feb. 27, 1942; s. Henry Howard and Faye (Atwood) G.; m. Helen Matilda O'Kane; children: Robert B., Brendan H., Kathleen M. BS, U. Fla., 1963, MS, 1965; PhD, Columbia U., 1968. NIH postdoctoral fellow Stanford U., Calif., 1968-69; asst. prof. Mich. State U., East Lansing, 1969-73, assoc. prof., 1973-78; prof. chemistry Calif. Inst. Tech., Pasadena, 1978—, Victor and Elizabeth Atkins prof., 1989. Contbr. articles to profl. publs.; patentee in field. Recipient award in organic synthesis Bristol Myers Squibb, 2004, Golden Plate award, Acad. Achievement, 2006; co-recipient Nobel Prize in Chemistry, 2005, Paul Karrer Gold medallion, 2005, August-Wilhelm-von-Hofmann-Denkmünze, 2005; fellow Sloan Found., 1974-76, Alexander von Humboldt Found., 1975; Dreyfus Found. scholar, 1975-78. Fellow Am. Acad. Arts and Scis.; mem. AAAS, NAS, Am. Chem. Soc. (Organic Chemistry award 1989, Polymer Chemistry award 1995, Benjamin Franklin medal in chemistry 2000, Herman F. Mark polymer chemistry award 2000, Herbert C. Brown award for creative rsch. in synthetic methods 2001, Arthur C. Cope award, 2002, Richard C. Tolman medal 2003, Tetrahedron prize 2003, Kirkwood medal New Haven sect. 2005). Democrat. Achievements include research in homogeneous or heterogeneous catalysis. Office: Divsn of Chemistry and Chemical Engring Calif Inst Tech Mail Code 164 30 Pasadena CA 91125 Business E-Mail: rhg@caltech.edu.

GRUBE, JAMES R., federal judge; b. 1942; BA, U. Santa Clara, 1964; JD, U. Calif., 1967. Asst. dist. atty. City and County of San Francisco, 1970-75; with Murray & Grube, Palo Alto, Calif., 1975-79, Campeau & Grube, San Jose, Calif., 1980-88; apptd. bankruptcy judge no. dist. U.S. Dist. Ct. Calif., 1988. With U.S. Army, 1968-69. Mem. ABA, Am. Bankruptcy Inst., Nat. Conf. Bankruptcy Judges, U.S. Dist. Ct. for State Bar of Calif., No. Dist. of Calif. Histo. Soc., Santa Clara County Bar Assn., Bay Area Bankruptcy Forum, Bench and Bar Hist. Soc. of Santa Clara County. Office: US Bankruptcy Ct Rm 3035 280 S 1st St San Jose CA 95113-3002

GRUBER, RONALD P., plastic surgeon, researcher; b. London, Apr. 13, 1941; came to U.S., 1946; s. Paul and Edith (Lieblein) G.; m. Gloria Lynn Rubel, June 4, 1967; children: Alicia, Brandon, April, Amanda. BA in Speech, U. Calif., Berkeley, 1962; MD, U. Calif. Sch. Medicine, San Francisco, 1966. Diplomate Am. Bd. Plastic Reconstructive Surgery. Intern Maimonides Med. Ctr., NYC, 1966-67; resident, gen. surgery Montefiore Med. Ctr., NYC, 1967-68; resident, surgery U. Calif., San Francisco, 1970-71, Stanford U. Med. Ctr., 1971-73, Bank of Am. Giannini fellow, dept. plastic surgery Calif., 1972—73, chief resident, plastic surgery, 1973-74, clin. instr., surgery Calif., 1974—96; NIH fellow Stanford U., 1971—72, clin. asst. prof. Calif., 1996—; chief, clin. and exptl. br., biphysics lab. Edgewood Arsenal Biophysics Lab., Md., 1968-70; clin. asst. prof. U. Calif., San Francisco, 2002—. Asst., neuropharmacological rsch., Langley Porter Inst., San Francisco, 1965-66, Moses Inst. Rsch., NYC, 1967-68; assoc. staff Alta Bates Hosp., Berkeley, 1974-, mem. med. edn. com. 1974-75, Children's Hosp., Oakland, Calif., 1974-92; active staff Summit Hosp., Oakland, Calif., 1974-, Oakland Hosp., Calif. 1974-; chief of plastic surgery, Providence Hosp., Oakland, 1978-84, 1988-90, mem. med. edn. com., 1974-76, ambulatory surgery com., 1978-84, exec. com. 1983-85, peer review com., 1988; mem. med. edn. com. Merritt Hosp., 1976-84; lectr. on maxillofacial trauma, U. Calif., Divsn. Emergency Medicine, 1977-83; adj. clin. faculty, Stanford U. Med. Ctr., 1996-; vis./traveling professorships U. So. Calif., 1994, U. Calif. San Diego, 1994, U. Tex. Houston, 1996, Brown U., 1998, 2001, U. Miami, 1998, Loma Linda U., 2001, U. Va., 2001, U. Cinn., 2001, John Hopkins U., 2001, Georgetown U., 2001, Wash. U., 2002, NY Soc. Plastic Surgery, 2002, St. Barnabas Med. Ctr., 2002; presenter in fields of plastic surgery rsch. and physics rsch. Editl. cons. Annals of Plastic Surgery, 1986-, Plastic & Reconstrucive Surgery, 1992-; Aesthetic Surgery Jour. 1996-; reg. editor Aesthetic Plastic Surgery Jour., 2000-; Rhinoplasty editor On-Line Plastic and Reconstructive Surgery Jour. 2001; co-author: Rhinoplasty: State of the Art, 1993; contbr. numerous articles to scientific jours., including Plastic & Reconstructive Surgery, Annals of Plastic Surgery, Clin. Plastic Surgery, others; co-author numerous videos; contbr. numerous chpts. to books. Major, U.S. Army, Edgewood Arsenal, Md., 1968-70. Maj. Oakland Army Base-Reserve Duty, 1970—72. Recipient Am. Cancer Soc. award, 1978, Hon. Thomas Jefferson Prof. Plastic Surgery, U. Va., 2001; named to Best Doctors in America, 1996, Best Plastic and Reconstructive Surgeons, 1999; named one of Top Doctors in the Bay Area, San Francisco Mag., 1999. Mem. AAAS, AMA, ACS, Royal Soc. Medicine, Psychonomic Soc., Am. Physicians Fellowship Inc., Internat. Coll. Surgeons (regent, Northern Calif. 1984, local host chmn. 1988, v.p., 1988), Am. Soc. Plastic and Reconstructive Surgeons(scientific program com. 1981, 1982, 1994-95, 1998 exhibits com. 1994, 1995, scientific exhibit/poster com. 1996, technical exhibits com. 1998, N.Y. Acad. Scis., Internat. Soc. Study of Time, Am. Soc. Aesthetic Plastic Surgery (traveling prof. 2001-03, scientific com., 1983, 1988, strategic planning com., 1986, chmn. audiovisual com., 1987-88, bd. dirs. ad hoc 1987-88, scholarship com., 1984-87, local arrangements com., 1988, ethics com. (western US) rep. 1990-93, scientific program com. 1994-95, 1998, 1999, technical exhibits com., 1998, edn. com., 1999, regional editor jour., Walter Scott Brown award, best video or film, 1983), Am. Soc. Maxillofacial Surgeons (traveling prof.), Am. Assn. Plastic Surgeons (by invitation), Am. Physics Soc., Calif. Med. Assn., Alameda Contra Costa County Med. Assn.(mediation com. 1976-, ethics com. 1990-96), Calif. Soc. Plastic Surgeons (Insurance mediation com., 1983, scientific com. 1982, chmn. scientific com., 1986, 1987, 1988, mktg. com. 1986, awards com. 1996, best overall paper award, Rhinoplasty Soc. (founding mem. 1995, sec. 1996, v.p., 1997, pres.-elect 1998, pres. 1999-2000, immediate past pres.), Assn. for the Advancement of Behavior Therapy, Assn. Military Surgeons of the US, Am. Burn Assn., Internat. Acad. Cosmetic Surgery, Am. Assn. Hand Surgery, Pan Pacific Surgical Assn., Am. Astron. Soc., Lipolysis Soc. N.Am., Northwestern Soc. Plastic & Reconstructive Surgery (hon. mem. by invitation), Plastic Surgery Edn. Found. (curriculum com., 1988, rsch. grant com, 1988, instructional course com. 1987, 1988, silicone rsch. com., 1992), Am. Cancer Soc. (bd. dirs. ad hoc 1981-84, Surgery Ctr. Oakland, Calif. bd. dirs. 1985-91). Achievements include development of the periareolar subpectoral augmentation mammaplasty; innovations include Gruber Open Rhinoplasty Retractor, 1996, Gruber Rhinoplasty Set, Nasal Tip Graft Sizes, 2001, Mucoperichondrial elevator/knife combination, 2002, Columella Retractor, 2002, Cartilage Carving Block, 2002; pioneer of the open rhinoplasty. Office: East Bay Aesthetic Plastic Surgery Ctr 3318 Elm St Oakland CA 94609 also: 911 Moraga Rd Ste 201 Lafayette CA 94549-4500 Office Phone: 510-654-9222. Office Fax: 510-654-2349. Business E-Mail: rgrubermd@pacbell.net.

GRUEL, STEVEN FRANCIS, lawyer; b. Savannah, Ga., Sept. 24, 1956; s. Virgil Lenard and Nancy Ann (Gruber) G. BA, U. Wis., Eau Claire, 1980; JD, U. Wis., Madison, 1985. Bar: Wis. 1985, US Dist. Ct. (we. dist. Wis.) 1985, US Dist. Ct. (no. dist. Calif.) 1988. Assoc. Lee, Johnson, Kilkelly & Nichol, Madison, 1985-87; trial atty. US Dept. Justice, San Francisco, 1987-88; spl. asst. criminal divsn. US Atty., San Francisco, 1988; asst. US atty. US Atty.'s Office No. Dist. Calif., San Francisco, chief Major Crimes Unit, 2002—05; pvt. practice San Francisco, 2005—. Vol. San Francisco Neighborhood Legal Assistance, 1988—. Recipient Atty. of Yr. award, Calif. Lawyer, 2005. Mem. ABA, Wis. Bar Assn. (active lawyers hotline 1985-87), U. Wis. Alumni Assn., U. Wis.-Eau Claire Alumni Assn. Democrat. Roman Catholic. Avocations: basketball, camping, reading history. Office: 655 Montgomery St Ste 1700 San Francisco CA 94122 Office Phone: 415-989-1253. Office Fax: 415-576-1442. E-mail: attystevengruel@sbcglobal.net.

GRUMBACH, MELVIN MALCOLM, pediatrician, educator; b. NYC, Dec. 21, 1925; s. Emanuel and Adele (Weil) G.; m. Madeleine F. Butt, Dec. 1, 1951; children: Ethan Malcolm, Kevin Lawrence, Anthony Havemeyer. Student, Columbia U., 1945, MD, 1948; DM honoris causa (hon.), U. Geneva, 1991; D honoris causa (hon.), U. René Descartes Paris V, 2000, U. Athens, 2008. Diplomate Am. Bd. Pediatrics, Am. Bd. Pediatric Endocrinology (com. mem. 1975-79). Resident in pediatrics Babies Hosp., Presbyn. Hosp., Columbia U. Med. Ctr., NYC, 1949-51; trainee Oak Ridge Inst. Nuc. Studies, 1952; postdoctoral fellow, asst. pediatrics Johns Hopkins Sch. Medicine, 1953-55; mem. faculty Columbia U. Coll. Physicians and Surgeons, NYC, 1955-65, from instr. to assoc. prof. pediatrics, 1961-65; from asst. to assoc. attending pediatrician Babies Hosp. and Vanderbilt Clin., Columbia-Presbyn. Med. Ctr., 1955-65, founding head postdoctoral tng. program pediat. endocrinology Pediat. Endocrine Divsn., 1955—65; dir. pediatric svc. U. Calif. Hosps., 1966-86; prof. pediatrics, chmn. dept. U. Calif. Sch. Medicine, San Francisco, 1966-86, first Edward B. Shaw prof. pediatrics, 1983-94, acting dir. Lab. Molecular Endocrinology, 1987-89, Edward B. Shaw prof. emeritus pediatrics (active), 1994—. Vis. prof. Vanderbilt U., 1961, Emory U., 1962, U. Western Ont., 1962, U. NC, 1963, 82, U. Rochester, 1972, UCLA, 1981, U. Tex., Dallas, 1983, Peking Union Med. Coll. and Hosp., 1986, U. Hong Kong, 1986; cons. Letterman Gen. Hosp., 1966-94, Children's Hosp., San Francisco, U.S. Naval Hosp., Oakland, Calif., 1966-94, HEW, NIH, 1961-, Nat. Bd. Med. Examiners, 1964-68; human embryology and devel. study sect. NIH, 1962-66, endocrinology study sect., 1967-71; bd. sci. counselors Nat. Inst. Child Health and Human Devel., 1971-75; gen. clin. rsch. ctrs. com., divsn. rsch. resources NIH, 1976-80, com. for rev. Clin. Ctr., 1984-85, IOM com. study AIDS rsch. program NIH, 1989-91, nat. adv. coun. Nat. Inst. Child Health and Human Devel., 1991-96; adv bd. Nat. Inst. Environ. Health Scis., 2007-; sci. adv. com., clin. rsch. adv. com. Nat. Found.-March of Dimes, 1969-94, chmn. clin. rsch. adv. com., 1974-82, Basil O'Connor starter scholar rsch. award comm., 1995-99, grant screening com., 2000-; awards com. Lita Annenberg Hazen Award for Excellence in Clin. Rsch., 1981-86; sci. adv. bd. Scripps Clinic and Rsch. Found., 1977-78, Princesse Marie Christine Found., Brussels, 1981-91, U. Mich. Ctr. for Human Growth and Devel., 1982-89, U. Colo. Health Scis. Barbara Davis Ctr., 1986-93, Rsch. Inst. Hosp. for Sick Children, Toronto, 1984-88, Children's Hosp. LA, 1987-92; sci. and med. adv. bd. Whittier Inst. Diabetes and Endocrinology, 1987-92; adv. bd. Nat. Pituitary Agy., 1965-69; sci. adv. com. Nat. Inst. Environ. Health Scis., 2007-; mem. NIH Evaluation of Endocrinology and Metabolic Diseases, 1977-79; Dean's bd. vis. Mt. Sinai Sch. Medicine, NYC, 1986-87; sci. adv. coun. Cin. Children's Hosp. Rsch. Found., 1997-98; pres. bd. trustees Internat. Pediat. Rsch. Found., Inc., 1984-89; sci. coun. Aid Pour la Recherche Medicale a l'enfance, Paris, 1981-89; com. future pub. health Inst. Medicine, 1986-87; del. to Chinese Acad. Med. Scis., 1986; lectr. in field; chmn. various confs. Assoc. editor, mem. editl. bd. Jour. Clin. Endocrinology Metabolism, 1957-70, 2006-; adv. editor Jour. Pediat., 1966-73, mem. editl. bd., 1973-79; assoc. editor Pediat. Rsch., 1970-84, Barnett Pediatrics, 14th-15th edits., Rudolph Pediatrics, 16th-22nd edits., Current Topics in Experimental Endocrinology, 1968-72; mem. internat. editl. bd. pediat. and pediatric surgery: Excerpta Medica, 1974-2000; mem. editl. bd. Biology of Reproduction, 1968-70, Endocrinologic Clinica Metabolism, 1981—, Pediat. in Rev., 1982-84, Jour. Endocrinol. Investigation, 1982-90, Endocrine Revs., 1984-88, Jour. Pediat. Endocrinology Metabolism, 1984—, Trends in Endocrinology, 1989—, Monographs on Endocrinology, Springer-Verlag, 1975-90, Clinical Pediat. Endocrinology, 1992—, Jour. Endocrine Genetics, 1999—, Internat. Jour. Pediat. Endocrinology, 2008-; contbr. articles to profl. jours. Capt. USAF, 1951—53. Postdoctoral fellow Nat. Found. Infantile Paralysis, 1953-55; recipient Joseph M. Smith prize Columbia U., 1962; Career Scientist award Health Research Coun. City N.Y., 1961-66; Silver medal Bicentennial Columbia Coll. Physicians and Surgeons, 1967, Gold medal, 1988; Clin. Endocrinology Trust medal (U.K.), 1985, Centennial Medallist award Babies Hosp., Columbia-Presbyn. Med. Ctr., 1987, Coll. de France medal, 1979, Winthrop award, Am. Fertility Soc., 1981; Sci. Patron, Liggins Inst. Faculty Med. Health Sci., U. Auckland, New Zealand, 2001—. Fellow: AAAS, NY Acad. Scis., Am. Acad. Pediats. (Bordon award 1971, Lifetime Achievement award 1996), Am. Acad. Arts and Scis.; mem.: Inst. Medicine NAS (mem. nominating com. 2007), Lawson Wilkins Pediat. Endocrine Soc., Am. Pediat. Soc. (pres.-elect 1988—89, pres. 1989—90, John Howland award 1997), Calif. Acad. Medicine, Western Assn. Physicians, Internat. Neuroendocrinology Soc., Internat. Endocrine Soc. (del. to ctrl. com. 1976—92, exec. com. 1984—92, hon. pres. 2000—04), Endocrine Soc. (coun. 1968—71, pres. elect 1980—81, coun. 1980—83, pres. 1981—82, Robert H. Williams Disting. Leadership award 1980, Fred Conrad Koch award 1992), Teratology Soc., Soc. Pediat. Rsch., Western Soc. Pediat. Rsch. (pres. 1978—79), Lawson Wilkins Pediat. Endocrine Soc. (pres. 1975—76, 1975—76, Inaugural Judson Van Wyk prize 2006), Harvey Soc., Am. Soc. Human Genetics, Assn. Am. Physicians, Am. Soc. Clin. Investigation, Assn. Med. Sch. Pediat. Dept. Chmn. (exec. coun. 1967—72, pres. 1973—75, task force on Pediat. Scientist Tng. Program 1984—91, chmn. selection com. 1986—91), Inst. Medicine Nat. Acad. Scis. (mem. pub. health com. 1985—87, mem. AIDS rsch. com. 1989—91, chmn. adolescent devel. and biology of puberty 1998—99, mem. com. on understanding the biology of sex and gender differences 2000—01), Soc. Française de Pediatrie (corr.), European Soc. Pediat. Endocrinology (corr.), Italian Soc. Pediat. Endocrinology & Diabetology (hon.), Israel Endocrine Soc. (hon.), Pacific Coast Fertility Soc. (hon.), Japanese Soc. Pediat. Endocrinology (hon.), Can. Soc. Endocrinology and Metabolism (hon.), Argentine Soc. Endocrinology and Metabolism (hon.), Johns Hopkins U. Soc. Scholars, U. Club NYC, Alpha Omega Alpha, Sigma Xi. Office: U Calif Sch Medicine Dept Pediatrics S672 San Francisco CA 94143-0434 Office Phone: 415-476-2244. Business E-Mail: grumbach@peds.ucsf.edu.

GRUNDFEST, JOSEPH ALEXANDER, law and business educator; b. NYC, Sept. 8, 1951; s. Michael A. and Esther Grundfest; m. Carol Chia-Ming Hsu, Aug. 6, 1978. Student MSc program in math. economics and econometrics, London Sch. Econometrics, 1971—72; BA, Yale U., 1973; JD, Stanford U., 1978, doctoral studies in Economics, 1975—78. Bar: Calif. 1978, DC 1979, US Supreme Ct. 1987. Economist, cons. Rand Corp., Santa Monica, Calif., 1973-78; rsch. assoc. The Brookings Instn., 1978—79; assoc. Wilmer, Cutler & Pickering, Washington, 1979-84; counsel, sr. economist legal and regulatory matters Coun. Econ. Advisers, Exec. Office of the Pres., Washington, 1984-85; commr. SEC, Washington, 1985-90; assoc. prof. law Stanford U. Law Sch., 1990—94, prof., 1994—97, William A. Franke prof. law & bus., 1997—, John M. Olin faculty fellow, 1991—92, Helen L. Crocker faculty scholar, 1996—97, dir. George R. Roberts Program in Law, Bus. and Corporate Governance, 1993—2002, co-dir. Program in Law, Economics and Bus., 2002—, co-dir. Rock Ctr. on Corp. Governance, 2006. Mem. legal adv. com. NY Stock Exch., 1993—96; nat. fellow Hoover Instn. Stanford U., 1992—93; bd. dirs. Oracle Corp., 2001—06. Recipient John Bingham Hurlbut Award for Excellence in Tchg., Stanford Law Sch., 1992, 2001. Fellow Coun. Fgn. Rels.; mem. ABA, Am. Law Inst., Am. Fin. Assn., Am. Economics Assn., Am. Law and Economics Assn. Avocations: swimming, jogging. Office: Stanford Law Sch Crown Quadrangle 559 Nathan Abbott Way Stanford CA 94305-8610 Office Phone: 650-723-0458. Business E-Mail: grundfest@stanford.edu.*

GRUSHOW, SANDY, broadcast executive; BA in Comm., UCLA, 1983. Former v.p. creative advtg. 20th Century Fox Film Corp.; sr. v.p. advtg. and promotion Fox Broadcasting Co., 1988—90, exec. v.p. programming and scheduling, 1990—91; exec. v.p. Fox Entertainment Group, 1991—92, pres., 1992—95, Tele-TV Media, 1995—97, Twentieth Century Fox TV, LA, 1997—99; chmn. Fox Entertainment Group, 1999—2004.

GUADARRAMA, BELINDA, computer company executive; B in Econs., Trinity U.; postgrad., U. Tex. Pres. CEO GC Micro Corp., 1986—. Chair NASA Minority Bus. Resource Adv. Com., 1997-99. Recipient Adminstrs. Excellence award U.S. Small Bus. Adminstrn., 1997; named 1 of 4 Women Who Could Be Pres., LLWV, San Francisco, 1998, U.S. Dept. Commerce NAt. Minority Female Entrepreneur of Yr., 1997. Mem. Hispanic Bus. CEO Roundtable, Calif. Hispanic C. of C. (Outstanding Bus. Mem. of Yr. award 1997). Office: GC Micro Corporation 3910 Cypress Dr Petaluma CA 94954-5694

GUALANDRIS, FABIO LUIGI, company executive; b. Bergamo, Lombardia, Italy, Mar. 9, 1959; s. Angelo and Lory (Bertozzi) G.; m. Lucia Riceputi, Sept. 23, 1986 (div. 1992); m. Paola Luisa Cagnoni, June 25, 1992. Dottore in Fiscia, U. Milan, Italy, 1983. Scientist Ctrl. R&D SGS-Thomson, Milan, 1984-87, engr. mgr., 1987-89, mfg. mgr., 1989-91, ops. mgr., 1991-96; automotive dir. STM, 1996-97; pres. and CEO Semitool, Inc., Kalispell, Mont., 1998—. Rschr. CNR, Milan, 1983. Patentee in field; contbr. articles to profl. jours. Mem. IEEE. Avocations: flute, horseback riding, climbing, gardening, photography. Home: Residenza Delle Botteghe 20090 Milano Segrate Italy Office: Semitool Inc 655 W Reserve Dr Kalispell MT 59901-2127

GUAY, GORDON HAY, federal agency administrator, marketing educator, consultant; b. Hong Kong, Aug. 1, 1948; came to U.S., 1956; s. Daniel Bock and Ping Gin (Ong) G. AA, Sacramento City Coll., 1974; BS, Calif. State U., Sacramento, 1976, MBA, 1977; postgrad., U. of the Pacific, 1978; PhD, U. So. Calif., 1981. Mgmt. assoc. U.S. Postal Svc., Sacramento, 1980-82, br. mgr., 1982-83, fin. mgr., 1983-84, mgr. quality control, 1984-86, mgr. tech. sales and svcs. divsn., 1986-91, dir. mktg. and comm., 1991-95, postmaster, 1996—. Prof. bus. adminstrn., mktg. and mgmt. Calif. State U., Sacramento, 1981-85; prof. mktg. Nat. U., San Diego, 1984-1994; pres. Gordon Guay and Assocs., Sacramento, 1979-84; cons. Mgmt. Cons. Assocs., Sacramento, 1977-79. Author: Marketing: Issues and Perspectives, 1983; also articles to profl. jours. With U.S. Army, 1968-70. Recipient Patriotic Svc. award U.S. Treasury Dept., San Francisco, 1985. Fellow Acad. Mktg. Sci.; mem. NEA, AAUP, Am. Mgmt. Assn., Am. Mktg. Assn. (Outstanding Mktg. Educator award 1989), Am. Soc. Pub. Adminstrn., Soc. Advancement Mgmt. (Outstanding Mem. 1976), Assn. MBA Execs. Democrat. Avocations: teaching, golf, tennis, fishing, camping. E-mail: erudite@juno.com.

GUBER, MYLES STUERT, surgeon; b. Denver, July 3, 1956; s. Frank Friday Guber and Celia Elsie Kramish; m. Deborah Ann Bishop, Aug. 25, 1996; children: Michael Albert, Samuel David, Halle Anderson. BS, Northwestern U., 1978, MD, 1980. Diplomate Am. Bd. Surgery, Am. Bd. Thoracic Surgery. Staff cardiac surgeon Porter Meml. Hosp., Denver, 1987—. Fellow: Am. Coll. Surgeons; mem.: Western Thoracic Surg. Assn., County Thoracic Surgeons. Jewish. Avocations: skiing, golf, climbing, basketball. Home: 355 Ash St Denver CO 80222 Office: Colo Cardiovascular Surg Assocs Ste 550 950 E Harvard Ave Denver CO 80210 Office Phone: 303-778-6527. Office Fax: 303-733-1288. Personal E-mail: mgube@aol.com.

GUBINS, SAMUEL, publishing executive; b. NYC, Nov. 10, 1942; s. Jack and Mae (Sorin) Gubins; m. Eleanor Bush, June 27, 1965; children: Sara Rebecca, Tamar Rachel. BA, Reed Coll., 1964; PhD, Johns Hopkins U., 1970. Asst. prof. economics Haverford Coll., Pa., 1968—74, v.p. fin. Pa., 1974—81; sr. v.p., treas. Acad. Nat. Sciences, Phila., 1981—85; treas. Am. Type Culture Collection, 1993—95; pres., editor-in-chief Annual Reviews Inc., Palo Alto, Calif., 1995—. Co-author: Macroeconomics, 1974; contbr. articles to profl. publications. Chmn. Pa. Humanities Coun., 1987—92. Fellow: Am. Acad. Arts and Sciences; mem.: Soc. Indsl. and Applied Math. (treas. 1982), Am. Econ. Assn. Home: 981 Terrace Dr Los Altos CA 94024-5938 Office: Annual Reviews Inc 4139 El Camino Real PO Box 10139 Palo Alto CA 94303-0139 Office Phone: 650-843-6645. Office Fax: 650-855-9815. E-mail: sgubins@annualreviews.org.

GUBLER, DUANE J., virologist, educator, researcher; b. Santa Clara, Utah, June 4, 1939; s. June and Thelma (Whipple) G.; m. Bobbie J. Carroll, Mar. 1, 1958; children: Justin Chase, Stuart Jefferson. BS, Utah State U., 1963; MS, U. Hawaii, 1965; ScD, Johns Hopkins U., 1969; AS, So. Utah State U., 1962, DSc (hon.), 1988. Asst. prof. pathobiology Sch. Hygiene Johns Hopkins U., Balt. and Calcutta, 1969-71; assoc. prof. tropical medicine Sch. Medicine U. Hawaii, Honolulu, 1971-75; head virology dept. Naval Med. Rsch. Unit Number 2, Jakarta, Indonesia, 1975-78; assoc. prof. entomology and microbiology U. Ill., Urbana, 1978-79; rsch. microbiologist divsn. vector-borne viral diseases Ctrs. for Disease Control and Prevention, Fort Collins, Colo., 1980-81, dir. San Juan (P.R.) Labs., 1981-89, dir. divsn. vector-borne infectious diseases Ft. Collins, Colo., 1989—2003; dir. Asia Pacific Inst. Tropical Medicine and Infectious Diseases, U. Hawaii, Honolulu, 2004—; prof., chair, dept. tropical medicine, med. microbiology, and pharm. U. Hawaii Sch. Medicine, 2004—; dir. Duke U. Nat. U. Singapore Grad. Med. Sch., 2007—. Cons. NRC, 1972, South Pacific Commn., 1972-76, WHO, Geneva, New Delhi and Manila, 1974—, AID, Washington, 1977—, Pan Am. Health Orgn., 1981—, Internat. Devel. Rsch. Ctr., Ottawa, Can., 1977—, Rockefeller Found., NYC, 1987—, US Dept. Defense, 1992-, Nat. Inst. of Allergy and Infectious Diseases, 2002-, numerous nat. ministries of health, 1972—; Bailey K. Ashford meml. lectr. U. P.R. Sch. Medicine, 1999; chmn. bd. coun. Pediat. Dengue Vaccine Initiative, 2002-; mem. sci. adv. bd. Novartis Inst. Tropical Diseases, 2003—, Hawaii BioTech., Inc., 2006-, Environ. Health Inst., Singapore, 2006-08; sci. advisor Inviragen Inc., 2006-, mem. Strategic and Tech. Adv. Group on Neglected Tropical Diseases, WHO, 2007-. Contbr. numerous articles to profl. jours. Lt. USN, 1975—77. Recipient Commendation medal, 1984, Outstanding Svc. medal, 1988, Honorary Dr. of Sci., Southern Utah State U., 1988, Meritorious Svc. medal, 1991, Outstanding Unit citation, 1995, 98, 2000, Outstanding Alumni award for sci. and rsch. Johns Hopkins U. Sch. Pub. Health, 1997, Chuck Alexander Operational award La. Mosquito Control Assn., 1998, Disting. Svc. award Dept. HHS, 1996, 2000, 01, 03, Charles Shepard award in Sci., Ctr. for Disease Control, 2001; selected as one of 90 Illustrious Alumni in celebration of U. Hawaii's 90th year, 1997, Woodward Lectr. award USN Preventive Medicine Unit, 2000. Fellow Infectious Disease Soc. Am., Am. Assn. for Advancement of Sci., Am. Soc. Tropical Medicine (Charles Franklin Craig lectr. 1988, pres.-elect 1998, pres. 2000), Am. Mosquito Control Assn., Entomol. Soc. Am. (highlights in med. entomology lecture 1979, 95), Soc. Vector Ecologists, Rotary (Rotarian of Yr. San Juan chpt. 1986, Meritorious Svc. award Rotary Found., Evanston, Ill. 1990, Svc. Above Self award Fort Collins Club 1999, Internat. Svc. Above Self award 2000); mem. AAAS. Office: U Hawaii Sch Medicine Kaka'ako Campus BSB 320 651 Ilalo St Honolulu HI 96813 Office Phone: 808-692-1606. Business E-Mail: dgubler@hawaii.edu.

GUERIN, CHARLES ALLAN, museum director, artist; b. San Francisco, Feb. 27, 1949; s. John Warren and Charlene (Roovaart) G.; m. Katherine Riccio. BFA, Northern Ill. U., 1971, MA in Painting, 1973, MFA in Printmaking, 1974. Co-dir. Guerin Design Group, Colorado Springs, Colo., 1972-77; dir., exhbns. Colorado Springs Fine Arts Ctr., 1977-80, curator, fine arts, 1980-86; dir. U. Wyo. Art Mus., Laramie, 1986—2000; exec. dir. U. Ariz. Mus. Art, 2001—. Author catalogues including various Colorado Springs Fine Arts Ctr. catalogues; contbg. author The Encyclopedia of Crafts, 1974; exhbns. include Purdue U. West Lafayette, Ind., 1974, 76, DePauw U., Greencastle, Ind., 1976, Colorado Springs Fine Arts Ctr., 1977, Mus. of Fine Arts, Santa Fe, N.Mex., 1978, Wis. State U., Platteville, 1972, Suburban Fine Arts Ctr., Highland Park, Ill., 1974, Colo. Woodworking Invitational, Silver Plume, 1977, Colo. Craft Invitational, Arvada, 1981, Leslie Levy Gallery, Scottsdale, Ariz., 1983, Robischon Gallery, Denver, 1983, Adams State Coll., Alamosa, Colo., 1984, U. Wyo. Art Mus., 1986—, Elaine Horwitch Gallery, Scottsdale, 1990, William Havu Gallery, Denver, 1999; represented in permanent collections Lloyds of London, Dallas, Art Inst. Chgo., Marriott Hotel, Albany, N.Y., Ill. State Mus., Springfield, U.S. West Corp., Denver, Thresholds, Chgo., others. Grantee Nat. Endowment for the Arts, Ill. Arts Council, 1973. Mem. Coll. Art Assn. Am., Am. Assn. Mus., Western Mus. Conf. Office: U Ariz Mus Art PO Box 210002 Tucson AZ 85721 Office Phone: 520-621-5676. Business E-Mail: caguerin@u.arizona.edu.

GUERRERO, VLADIMIR ALVINO, professional baseball player; b. Nizao Bani, Dominican Republic, Feb. 9, 1976; Outfielder Montreal Expos, 1996—2004, LA Angels of Anaheim (formerly Anaheim Angels), 2004—. Recipient Silver Slugger award, 1999—2000, 2002, 2004—07; named Am. League MVP, 2004; named to Nat. League All-Star Team, 1999—2002, Am. League All-Star Team, 2004—07. Achievements include leading the Nat. League in hits (206), 2002; led the Am. League in runs (124), 2004; won the 2007 Home Run Derby. Mailing: LA Angels of Anaheim 2000 Gene Autry Way Anaheim CA 92806

GUERTIN, TIMOTHY E., medical products executive; b. 1949; BS in Elec. Engring. & Computer Scis., U. Calif., Berkeley, 1971. With Singer Bus. Machines, Varian Med. Systems, Inc., Palo Alto, Calif., 1976—, gen. mgr. customer support, 1982—89, gen. mgr., pres. Oncology Systems, 1990—2005, corp. v.p., 1992—99, exec. v.p., 1999—2005, pres., COO, 2005—06, pres., CEO, 2006—. Chmn. bd. dirs., mem. Silicon Valley/No. Calif. Coun. Am. Electronics Assn.; bd. dirs. Diagnostic Imaging sect., chmn. Therapy Systems divsn. Nat. Elec. Mfrs. Assn.; mem. corp. coun. Am. Soc. Therapeutic Radiology and Oncology, Can. Assn. Radiation Oncologists; bd. dirs. Varian Med. Systems, Inc., 2005—. Served in USAR. Recipient AeA/Stanford Alumni of the Yr. award, 2008. Office: Varian Med Systems 3100 Hansen Way Palo Alto CA 94304 Office Phone: 650-493-4000. Office Fax: 650-842-5196.

GUEST, CHRISTOPHER, actor, director, screenwriter; b. NYC, Feb. 5, 1948; m. Jamie Lee Curtis, Dec. 18, 1984; 2 children. Grad., High Sch. Music and Art, NYC; student, Bard Coll., NYU. Appeared in Broadway plays Room Service (debut) 1970, Moonchildren, 1972; Off-Broadway plays include National Lampoon's Lemmings (also writer), 1973, East Lynne, 1975; actor: (films) The Hospital, 1971, The Hot Rock, 1972, Death Wish, 1974, The Fortune, 1975, La Honte de la Jungle, 1975, Girlfriends, 1978, The Last Word, 1979, The Long Riders, 1980, The Missing Link, 1980, Heartbeeps, 1981, Little Shop of Horrors, 1986, Beyond Therapy, 1987, The Princess Bride, 1987, Sticky Fingers, 1988, A Few Good Men, 1992, Small Soldiers (voice), 1998, Mrs. Henderson Presents, 2005; actor, writer & composer: This is Spinal Tap, 1984; actor, writer, dir., composer: Waiting for Guffman, 1996, Best in Show, 2000, A Mighty Wind, 2003, For Your Consideration, 2006; dir.: The Big Picture, 1989, Edwards & Hunt, 1997, Almost Heroes, 1998; actor: (TV films) It Happened One Christmas, 1977, Haywire, 1980, Million Dollar Infield, 1982, A Piano for Mrs. Cimino, 1982, Close Ties, 1983; dir. (TV films): Attack of the 50 ft. Woman, 1993, D.O.A., 1999; actor, writer & dir.: (TV series) Saturday Night Live with Howard Cosell, 1975, Saturday Night Live, 1984-85, Morton & Hayes, 1991; TV specials: The Lily Tomlin Special (also writer, Emmy award 1976), 1975, Billion Dollar Bubble, 1977, How to Survive the 70's and Maybe Even Bump into Happiness, 1978, Martin Short Concert for the North Americas, 1985, Billy Crystal-Don't Get me Started, 1986; albums: Six albums with National Lampoon, This is Spinal Tap, 1984, Break like the Wind (with Spinal Tap), 1992. Co-recipient Grammy award for Best Song (A Mighty Wind) Written for a Motion Picture, 2004. Office: 190 N Canon DR STE 302 Beverly Hills CA 90210-5314

GUGGENHEIMER, STEVE, computer software company executive; BS, Univ. Calif., Davis, 1987; M in engring. mgmt., Stanford Univ. Tech. positions Spectra-Physics Inc., 1988—93; product mgr. Windows products Microsoft Corp., Redmond, Wash., 1993—2000, mgmt. positions, small bus. & ops. divisions, 2000—05, gen. mgr. application platform & develop., 2005—08, corp. v.p. original equip. manufacturer div., 2008—. Contbr. articles to profl. jours. Achievements include patents in field. Office: Microsoft Corp 1 Microsoft Way Redmond WA 98052-6399

GUGGENHIME, RICHARD JOHNSON, lawyer; b. San Francisco, Mar. 6, 1940; s. Richard E. and Charlotte G.; m. Emlen Hall, June 5, 1965 (div.); children: Andrew, Lisa, Molly; m. Judith Perry Swift, Oct. 3, 1992. AB in Polit. Sci. with distinction, Stanford U., 1961; JD, Harvard U., 1964. Bar: Calif. 1965, U.S. Dist. Ct. (no. dist.) Calif. 1965, U.S. Ct. Appeals (9th cir.) 1965. Assoc. Heller, Ehrman, White & McAuliffe, San Francisco, 1965—71, ptnr., 1972—2005; of counsel Schiff Hardin, 2008—. Spl. asst. to U.S. Senator Hugh Scott, 1964. Mem. San Francisco Bd. Permit Appeals, 1978—86; bd. dirs. Marine World Africa USA, 1980—86; mem. San Francisco Fire Commn., 1986—88, Recreation and Parks Commn., 1989—92, 2003—04; chmn. bd. trustees San Francisco Univ. H.S., 1987—90; trustee St. Ignatius Prep. Sch., 1987—96; mem. San Francisco Airport Commn., 2006—. Mem.: Am. Coll. Probate Counsel, Mayacama Golf Club, Olympic Club (bd. dirs. 1999—2002, pres. 2002), Wine and Food Soc., Bohemian Club. Home: Apt 401 1000 Mason St San Francisco CA 94108 Office: Schiff Hardin LLP One Market St Spear Tower 32nd Fl San Francisco CA 94105 Office Phone: 415-901-8726. Business E-Mail: rguggenhime@schiffhardin.com.

GUGINO, CARLA, actress; b. Sarasota, Fla., Aug. 29, 1971; Studied acting, with Gene Bua. Appearances include (TV series) Falcon Crest, 1989-90, Spin City, 1996, Chicago Hope, 1999-2000, Karen Sisco, 2003-04, Threshold, 2005-06, Entourage, 2007-,(TV films) Murder Without Motive, 1992, A Private Matter, 1992, Motorcycle Gang, 1994, A Season for Miracles, 1999, Mermaid Chronicles Part 1: She Creature, 2002, (TV miniseries) The Buccaneers, 1995, (films) Troop Beverly Hills, 1989, Welcome Home, 1990, Son-in-Law, 1993, Miami Rhapsody, 1995, Homeward Bound II: Lost in San Francisco, 1996, Michael, 1996, Red Hot, 1996, The War at Home, 1996, Wedding Bell Blues, 1996, Lovelife, 1997, Snake Eyes, 1998, Spy Kids, 2001, Spy Kids 2: Island of Lost Dreams, 2002, The Singing Detective, 2003, Spy Kides 3-D: Game Over, 2003, Life Coach: The Movie, 2005, Sin City, 2005, Even Money, 2006, Night at the Museum, 2006, The Lookout, 2007, Rise: Blood Hunter, 2007, American Gangster, 2007, Righteous Kill, 2008, The Unborn, 2009, Sparks, 2009, Watchmen, 2009, Race to Witch Mountain, 2009; (broadway) After the Fall, 2004, (Theatre World award, 2005), Suddenly Last Summer, 2006. Avocations: yoga, travel. Office: c/o Untitled Entertainment 1801 Century Park E Ste 700 Los Angeles CA 90067

GUILBEAU, ERIC J., biomedical and electrical engineer, educator; b. Tullos, La., June 5, 1944; BS, La. Tech. U., 1967, MS, 1968, PhD in Chem. Engring., 1971. Rsch. assoc. chem. engring. La. Tech. U., 1971-72, rsch. assoc. biomed. engring., 1972-73, from asst. to assoc. prof., 1973-77; prof. chem. and biomed. engring. Ariz. State U., Tempe, 1973-77, assoc. prof., 1977-81, prof. chem. and biomed. engring., 1981—, dir. bioengring., 1990—. Affiliate med. staff St. Joseph's Hosp., Phoenix, 1977. M. AICE, Am. Chem. Soc., Internat. Soc. Study Oxygen Transport to Tissue, Biomed. Engring. Soc., Soc. Biomat. Achievements include research in biomedical engineering, development of transducers for measurement of cellular biological parameters, research in transport phenomena in physiological systems, investigation of myocardial protection techniques, development of pericardial substitutes. Office: Ariz State U Coll Engring ECG 202 Tempe AZ 85287

GUILD, CLARK JOSEPH, JR., lawyer; b. Yerington, Nev., May 14, 1921; s. Clark Joseph and Virginia Ellen (Carroll) G.; m. Elizabeth Ann Ashley, July 20, 1945 (div. 1977); children: Clark J. III, Jeffrey S., Daniel E. (dec.), Jann Cademartori. BA, U. Nev., 1943; JD, Georgetown U., 1948. Bar: Nev. 1948, D.C. 1948, U.S. Dist. Ct. (no. dist.) Nev. 1948, U.S. Ct. Appeals (D.C. cir.) 1948, U.S. Supreme Ct. 1959, U.S. Ct. Appeals (9th cir.) 1984. Ptnr. Guild, Hagen & Clark, Ltd., Reno, Nev., 1953-88, Guild, Russell, Gallgher & Fuller Ltd., Reno (formerly Guild, Hagen & Clark Ltd.), 1988—. Pres. YMCA, Reno, 1954, 64; regent U. Nev. System, 1972. Capt. inf. U.S. Army, 1942-46. Recipient Disting. Nevadan award U. Nev., 1989. Fellow Am. Coll. Trial Lawyers; mem. ABA, State Bar Nev., Clark County Bar Assn., Washoe County Bar Assn. (pres. 1959-60), Masons, Elks. Democrat. Episcopalian.

GUILES, EDWIN A., utilities company executive; With Sempra Energy, 1972—, various mgmt. positions, sr. v.p. energy supply, 1993-97; sr. v.p. Enova Corp.; pres. San Diego Gas and Electric, 1998-2000; group pres. Sempra Energy, 2000—. Chmn. San Diego Gas and Electric, So. Calif. Gas. Co., 2000—. Office: Sempra Energy 101 Ash St San Diego CA 92101-3017

GUILFORD, ANDREW JOHN, federal judge; b. Santa Monica, Calif., Nov. 28, 1950; s. Howard Owens and Elsie Jennette (Hargreaves) G.; m. Loreen Mary Gogain, Dec. 22, 1973; children: Colleen Catherine, Amanda Joy. AB summa cum laude, UCLA, 1972, JD, 1975. Bar: Calif. 1975, US Dist. Ct. (ctrl. dist.) Calif. 1976, US Ct. Appeals (9th cir.) 1976, US Supreme Ct. 1979, US Dist. Ct. (so. dist.) Calif. 1981, US Dist. Ct. (no. and ea. dists.) Calif. 1990. Assoc. Sheppard, Mullin, Richter & Hampton, L.A. and Orange County, Calif., 1975-82, ptnr. Orange County, 1983—2006; judge US Dist. Ct. (Ctrl. dist.) Calif., LA, 2006—. Lectr. The Rutter Group, Encino, Calif., 1983—, Continuing Edn. of the Bar, Berkeley, 1978—, Hastings Ctr. for Advocacy, San Francisco, 1988; judge pro tem, arbitrator Calif. Superior Ct., 1983-2006; mem. commn. future legal profession and state bar; mem. adv. task force on multi-juristictional practice, task force on self-represented litigants. Author UCLA Law Review, 1975. Mem. Amicus Publico, Santa Ana, Calif., 1986; bd. dirs. Pub. Law Ctr. Orange County, 1990-2006, pres., 2003-06; bd. dirs. Constl. Rights Found., 1990, Baroque Music Festival, 1992-96, NCCJ, 1995-99, UCLA Law Alumni Assn., 1992-95, Western Justice Ctr. Found., 2008-; dean adv. coun. Bren Sch. Law, UCI, 2007-; subdeacon, warden, del. Episcopal Ch. Recipient resolution of commendation Calif. State Senate and Assembly, Outstanding Svc. award Poverty Law Ctr., 1991, Bernard E. Witkin Amicus Curiae award Calif. Jud. Coun., Jurisprudence award Anti-Defamation League, J. Reuben Clark award, cert. of recognition US Congress, others; co-recipient President's Pro Bono award State Bar; Regents scholar U. Calif., Berkeley, 1968-72; named one of Calif.'s 100 Top Influential Attys., The Daily Jour., Bus. Litig. Trial Lawyer of Yr., Orange County Trial Lawyers Assn. Fellow Am. Coll. Trial Lawyers (named a Best Lawyer in Am.); mem. ABA, FBA (bd. dirs. 2001—), Assn. Bus. Trial Lawyers (founding officer Orange County chpt., pres. 2000-2001), Am. Arbitration Assn. (arbitrator large complex case program 1993-95), Calif. Bar Assn. (pres. 1999-2000, bd. govs. 1996-2000), Orange County Bar Assn. (bd. dirs. 1985-87, officer 1988-90, pres. 1991, chmn. bus. litigation sect. 1983, state bar conv. 1986, 87, law-motion com. 1982, standing com. trial ct. delay reduction 1987-93, Franklin G. West award 2003), 9th Cir. Jud. Conf. (rep. 1990-92, 99—2001), Phi Beta Kappa (sec.-treas. 1978-80, v.p. 1980-84), Pi Gamma Mu, Sigma Pi. Republican. Avocations: theater, photography, sports, gardening, poetry. Office: US Dist Ct 411 W 4th St Rm 10-D Santa Ana CA 92701-4516

GUILLEMIN, ROGER C.L., physiologist, academic administrator; b. Dijon, France, Jan. 11, 1924; arrived in U.S., 1953, naturalized, 1963; BA, U. Dijon, 1941, BSc, 1942; MD, Faculty of Medicine, Lyons, France, 1949; PhD, U. Montreal, 1953; PhD (hon.), U. Rochester, 1976, U. Chgo., 1977, Baylor Coll. Medicine, 1978, U. Ulm, Germany, 1978, U. Dijon, France, 1978, Free U. Brussels, 1979, U. Montreal, 1979, U. Man., Can, 1984, U. Turin, Italy, 1985, Kyung Hee U., Korea, 1986, U. Paris, Paris, 1986, U. Barcelona, Spain, 1988, U. Madrid, 1988, McGill U., Montreal, Can., 1988, U. Claude Bernard, Lyon, France, 1989, Laval U., Quebec, Can., 1990, PhD (hon.), 1996, Sherbrooke U., Quebec, 1997, U. Franche-Comté, France, 1999. Intern, resident, prosecutor of anatomy U. Hosps., Dijon, 1946—47; rsch. asst., assoc. dir., asst. prof. Inst. Exptl. Medicine and Surgery, U. Montreal, 1949—53; asst. prof. physiology Baylor Coll. Medicine, 1953-57, assoc. prof., 1957, prof., dir. labs. neuroendocrinology, 1963-70, adj. prof. physiology, 1970—; assoc. dir. dept. exptl. endocrinology Coll. de France (as joint appt. with Coll. Medicine Baylor U.), Paris, 1960-63; resident fellow, rsch. prof. chmn. labs. neuroendocrinology Salk Inst., La Jolla, Calif., 1970-89, adj. rsch. prof., 1970—, dean, 1972—73, 1976—77, disting. prof., 1989—, interim pres., 2007—09; disting. scientist Whittier Inst., 1989-97, med. and sci. dir., 1993-94; adj. prof. medicine U. Calif., San Diego, 1994—97. Cons. physiology VA Hosp., Houston, 1954—60, Houston, 1967—70; lectr. exptl. endocrinology dept. biology Rice U., Houston, 1958—60; cons. biochemistry MD Anderson Hosp. and Tumor Inst., Houston, 1967—70; dir. rsch. CNRS, Paris, 1963—68; bd. dirs. Sanofi, 1982—86, Erbamont, Nev., 1986—92, ICN Pharms., 1987—89, 1994—2001, Roussel-UCLAF, Hoechst, 1989—90, SPI Pharm., 1989—95, Whittier Inst. Diabetes Endocrinology, 1989—94, Prizm Pharm., 1992—98, Viratek, 1992—95, Jonas Salk Fedn., 1995—2005, Humetrix, 1999—, Ribapharm, 2001—02. Decorated chevalier Legion d'Honneur France, officer de la Légion d'Honneur French Republic; recipient Gold medal, 1st Internat. Congress Pharmacology, Stockholm, 1961, Saintour award for exptl. endocrinology, Coll. de France, Paris, 1961, Disting. Scientist award, Nat. Diabetes Rsch. Coalition, 1966, U.S. NIH lectureship, Bethesda, Md., 1973, La Madonnina award for medicine, The Carlo Erba Found., 1974, Gairdner Internat. award, 1974, Lasker award, Lasker Found., 1975, Dickson prize in medicine, 1976, Passano award sci., 1976, Schmitt medal neurosci., 1977, Nobel Prize in Medicine, The Nobel Found., 1977, Nat. Medal of Sci., Pres. of the U.S.A., 1977, Barren Gold medal, 1979, Dale medal, Soc. for Endocrinology, UK, 1980, Ellen Browning Scripps Soc. medal, Scripps Meml. Hosps. Found., 1988; scholar, John and Mary R. Markle Found., N.Y., 1952—56. Fellow: AAAS; mem.: NAS, Tex. Med. Ctr. Rsch. Soc. (pres. elect 1959, pres. 1960, hon. 1970), Assn. des Physiologistes, Am. Inst. Biol. Sci., Western Soc. Clin. Rsch., Internat. Soc. Neurosci. (charter), Acad. Royale de Medecine de Belgique, Acad. Sci., Academie Nat. de Medicine, French Acad. Scis., Am. Acad. Arts & Scis., Soc. Neuroscis., Internat. Soc. Rsch. Biology Reprodn., Internat. Brain Rsch. Orgn., Soc. Exptl. Biology and Medicine, Endocrine Soc. (coun. 1969—73, nominating com. 1974—75, pres. 1986), Assn. Am. Physicians, Am. Physiol. Soc., Soc. Francaise d'Endocrinologie (hon.; pres. 1982—83), Soc. de Biology Paris (hon.), Soc. Can. Biology (hon.), Internat. Soc. for Immunology of Reproduction (hon.), Howard Florey Inst. Exptl. Physiology and Medicine (hon.), Houston Philos. Soc. (hon.), Can. Soc. Endocrinology and Metabolism (hon.), Swedish Soc. Med. Sci. (hon.), Am. Peptide Soc. (hon.), Club of Rome. Office: The Salk Inst 10010 N Torrey Pines Rd La Jolla CA 92037-1099 Address: The Salk Inst PO Box 85800 San Diego CA 92186-5800 Business E-Mail: guillemin@salk.edu.*

GUILLERMO, TESSIE, foundation administrator; b. San Francisco; Grad., Calif. State U., Hayward, Gallup Leadership Inst. Founder, CEO Asian and Pacific Islander Am. Health Forum, 1987—2002; pres., CEO Community Tech. Found. of Calif., 2002—. Fellow Asian Pacific Am. Women's Leadership Inst., 1997; mem. President's Advisory Commn. on Asian Am. and Pacific Islanders, 2000; bd. mem. Catholic Healthcare W. Bd. dirs. Calif. Pan Ethnic Health Network; mem. Kaiser Arbitration Oversight Bd., Filipino Task Force on HIV/AIDS, Nat. Coalition of Asian Pacific Am.; bd. dirs. Calif. Endowment, 2003—; trustee Health Professions Edu. Found. Home: 425 Bush St Ste 300 San Francisco CA 94108-3721

GUINASSO, VICTOR, delivery service executive; BS, U. San Francisco, 1977. Exec. v.p., coo DHL Corp., 1982—99; pres. & CEO DHL Airways, Redwood City, Calif., 1999-2001, chmn., 2000-2001; pres., CEO DHL Worldwide Express Inc., San Francisco, 2001.

GUINN, KENNY C. (KENNETH CARROLL GUINN), former governor; b. Garland, Ark., Aug. 24, 1936; m. Dema Guinn, July 7, 1956; children: Jeff, Steve. BA, Calif. State U., Fresno, 1959, MA, 1965; EdD, Utah State U., 1970. Supt. Clark County Sch. Dist., 1969—78; v.p. adminstrn. Nev. Savs. and Loan Assn. (PriMerit Bank), 1978-80; pres., COO Nev. Savs. & Loan Assn. (PriMerit Bank), 1980-85, CEO, 1985-92; pres. Southwest Gas Corp., 1987-88, chmn., CEO, 1988-93; interim pres. U. Nev., Las Vegas, 1994—95; gov. State of Nev., Carson City, 1999—2007. Bd. dirs. MGM Mirage, 2007—. Republican.

GUINOUARD, DONALD EDGAR, psychologist; b. Bozeman, Mont., Mar. 31, 1929; s. Edgar Arthur and Venabell (Ford) G.; m. Irene M. Egeler, Mar. 30, 1951; children: Grant M., Philip A., Donna I. BS, Mont. State U., Bozeman, 1954; MS, Mont. State U., 1955; EdD, Wash. State U., Pullman, 1960; postdoctoral, Stanford U., 1965; grad., Indsl. Coll. of the Armed Forces, 1964, Air War Coll., 1976. Lic. psychologist, Ariz., counselor, Wash., Mont.; cert. secondary tchr. and sch. adminstr., Wash., Mont.; diplomate Am. Psychotherapy Assn., Am. Bd. Forensic Counselors, Am. Bd. Psychol. Specialities. Advanced through grades to col. USAFR, 1946-84, ret., 1984; dir. counseling Consol. Sch. Dist., Pullman, Wash., 1955-60; assoc. prof. Mont. State U., Bozeman, 1960-66; field selection officer Peace Corps, U.S., S.Am., 1962-68; prof. counseling, counseling psychologist Ariz. State U., Tempe, 1966-90; prof. emeritus, 1990; co-owner Forensic Cons. Assocs., Tempe, 1970—; pvt. practice, 1990—. Admissions liaison officer USAF Acad., Colo. Springs, 1967-84; assessment officer Fundamental Edn. Ctr. for the Devel. of the Latin American Community, Patzcuaro, Mex., 1963-64; expert witness on vocat. and psychol. disability for fed. and state cts. Contbr. articles to profl. jours. Mem. Ariz. Psychol. Assn., Am. Assn. Counseling & Devel., Reserve Officers Assn., Am. Psychotherapy Assn., Am. Coll. Forensic Examiners. Democrat. Methodist. Avocations: photography, woodworking, camping, fishing, silversmithing. Home and Office: 112 E Cairo Dr Tempe AZ 85282-3606 E-mail: donaldg516@aol.com.

GUIRE, RONALD W., electronics company executive; Exec. v.p., CFO, bd. dirs. Exar Corp., Fremont, Calif. Chmn. bd. dirs. XeTel Corp., Austin, Tex. Office: Exar Corp 48720 Kato Rd Fremont CA 94538

GULCHER, ROBERT HARRY, aerospace transportation executive; b. Columbus, Ohio, Aug. 26, 1925; s. Alban H. and Beatrice (Plohr) G.; m. Barbara Witherspoon, June, 1949 (div.); 1 child, Robert; m. Anne Cummings, Dec. 14, 1959 (dec.); children: Jeffrey, Donald; m. Suzanne K. Kane, Apr. 12,1969; children: Andrew, Kristin. BS, U.S. Marine Acad., 1945; B.E.E., Ohio State U., 1950. Third asst. engr. Am. Petroleum Transp. Co., NYC, 1945-46; engr. Capital Elevator & Mfg. Co., Columbus, Ohio, 1949-51, Columbus div. N. Am. Aviation, 1951-53, various mgmt. engring. positions, 1953-66; chief engr. Columbus div. Rockwell Internat., 1966-79, v.p. rsch. and engring. N.Am. aircraft ops. El Segundo, Calif., 1979-85, v.p. advanced programs N.Am. aircraft ops., 1985-87, v.p., program mgr. nat. aerospace plane, 1987-90, v.p. hypersonic programs Downey, Calif., 1990-91; retired, 1991; aerospace cons., 1992—. Trustee Little Company of Mary Hosp. Found., 1992—2005, chmn. bd. trustees, 1996-97; trustee coun. LCMH Hosp., 1997—2002, trustee emeritus, 2005; pres. St. Paul Lutheran Ch., 2004-07. Fellow AIAA, IEEE (sr. mem.); mem. Rotary Internat. (dir. cmty. svc. 2006—, Rotarian of Yr. 2006-07). Republican. Lutheran. E-mail: rgulcher@aol.com.

GUMP, BARRY HEMPHILL, chemistry and food science educator; b. Columbus, Ohio, Nov. 12, 1940; BS, Ohio State Univ., 1962; PhD, Univ. Calif., 1966. Rsch. assoc. Bureau Sci., Food & Drug Adminstrn., Washington, 1966-67; asst. prof. to assoc. prof. Calif. State Univ., 1967-74, prof. chemistry, 1974—, prof. enol., 1981—. Vis. scientist Bioorg. Standards Sec. Analysis Divsn., Nat. Inst. Sci. and Tech., 1974-76; Fulbright lectr. U. Repub. Montivideo, Uruguay, 1983; assoc. referee for sulfur dioxide in wine, AOAC, 1986. Mem. Am. Chem. Soc., Am. Soc. Enology and Viticulture. Achievements include research separation methods in chemistry, especially chromatographic methods; analytical methods development, trace components in foods and wine; characterization of grape juice concentrates. Office: Calif State U Fresno Dept Chemistry Fresno CA 93740-8034 E-mail: barryg@csufresno.edu.

GUMPEL, GLENN J., association executive; Pres. internat. and global bus. affairs Universal Studios Recreation Group, Universal City, Calif.; pres. Internat. Global Affairs; exec. v.p., chief adminstrv. officer MCA Recreation divsn. Universal Studios Recreation Group. Mem. Dirs. Guild Am. Office: Universal Studios Recreation Group Universal City Plaza LRW 11 Universal City CA 91608

GUND, GEORGE, III, financier, professional sports team executive; b. Cleve., May 7, 1937; s. George and Jessica (Roesler) G.; m. Mary Theo Feld, Aug. 13, 1966; children: George, Gregory. Student, Western Res. U., Menlo Sch. Bus., Calif. Engaged in personal investments, San Francisco, 1967—; cattle ranching Lee, Nev., 1967—; partner Calif. Seals, San Francisco, 1976-77; pres. Ohio Barons, Inc., Richfield, 1977-78; chmn. bd. Northstar Fin. Corp., Bloomington, Minn., from 1978; formerly chmn. bd. Minn. North Stars, Bloomington; chmn., co-owner San Jose Sharks, NHL, San Jose, CA, 1991—; co-owner Cleve. Cavaliers; film prodr. Caipirinha Prodns., San Francisco. Dir. Ameritrust Cleve.; vice-chmn. Gund Investment Corp., Princeton, N.J.; chmn. North Stars Met Center Mgmt. Corp., Bloomington; v.p. hockey Sun Valley Ice Skating, Inc., Idaho Chmn. San Francisco Internat. Film Festival, 1973—; mem. sponsors council Project for Population Action; adv. council Sierra Club Found.; mem. internat. council Mus. Modern Art, N.Y.C.; collectors com. Nat. Gallery Art; bd. dirs. Calif. Theatre Found., Bay Area Ednl. TV Assn., San Francisco Mus. Art, Cleve. Health Museum, George Gund Found., Cleve. Internat. Film Festival, Sun Valley Center Arts and Humanities, U. Nev. Reno Found., Sundance Inst. Served with USMCR, 1955-58. Mem.: Calif. Tennis (San Francisco), University (San Francisco), Olympic (San Francisco); Union (Cleve.), Cleve. Athletic (Cleve.), Kirkland Country (Cleve.), Rowfant (Cleve.); Ranier (Seattle). Office: 39 Mesa St Ste 300 San Francisco CA 94129-1019

GUNDERSEN, WAYNE CAMPBELL, energy executive, consultant; b. Elgin, Ill., May 27, 1936; s. LeRoy Arthur and Jean Ellen (Campbell) Gundersen; m. Gail Andrews, Mar. 21, 1959; children: Thomas Dexter, Lori Ann, Kathy Lee. BS, U. Nebr., 1959, MS, 1961. Advisor fgn. ops. Std. Oil Calif., San Francisco, 1974-76; asst. to v.p. Chevron Overseas Petroleum, San Francisco, 1976-80; dir. oil and gas Kaiser Aluminum & Chem. Corp., Oakland, Calif., 1980-81; v.p., gen. mgr. Kaiser Energy, Inc., Oakland, 1983-85, pres., 1985-87; v.p. Kaiser Aluminum and Chem. Corp., Oakland, 1983-87; pres. Kaiser Aluminum Exploration Co., Oakland, Kaiser Exploration and Mining Co., Oakland, 1985-87; cons. in oil and gas., 1987—; CEO, chmn. bd. dirs. Petroleum Synergy Group, Inc., 1988—. Mem. geology adv. bd. U. Nebr., Lincoln, 1984—87; mgr. Western Geothermal Ptnrs., LLC. Contbr. articles to profl. jours. Pres. Parents Club Foothill Sch., Walnut Creek, Calif., 1978—79. Named Man-of-Yr., New Orleans Jaycees, 1973; Sinclair fellow, 1960—61. Mem.: Am. Assn. Petroleum Geologists. Republican. Methodist. Office: The Petroleum Synergy Group 980 Caughlin Crossing Ste 102 Reno NV 89519-0660 Personal E-mail: renooilman@aol.com.

GUNDERSON, ROBERT VERNON, JR., lawyer; b. Memphis, Dec. 4, 1951; s. Robert V. and Suzanne (McCarthy) G.; m. Anne Durkheimer, May 15, 1982; children: Katherine Paige, Robert Graham. BA with distinction, U. Kans., 1973; MBA, U. Pa., 1974; MA, Stanford U., 1976; JD, U. Chgo., 1979. Bar: Calif. 1979, U.S. Dist. Ct. (no. dist.) Calif. 1979. Assoc. Cooley, Godward, San Francisco, 1979-84, Palo Alto, 1979—84, ptnr. San Francisco, 1984-88, Palo Alto, 1984—88, Brobeck, Phleger & Harrison, 1988-95, mem. exec. com., 1991-95, chmn. bus. and tech. practice, 1992-95; founder, ptnr. Gunderson Dettmer Stough Villeneuve Franklin & Hachigian, Menlo Park, 1995—. Panelist Venture Capital and Pub. Offering Negotiation, San Francisco and N.Y.C., 1981, 83, 85, 92, Practicing Law Inst., N.Y.C. and San Francisco, 1986; moderator, panelist Third Ann. Securities Law Inst., 1985; dir. Vitae Pharms., Ft. Washington, Pa., Theravance, Inc., South San Francisco, Inc.; sec. Dionex Corp., Sunnyvale, Calif., 1983-88, Southwall Techs., Inc., Palo Alto, 1985-88, Conductus, Inc., Sunnyvale, 1992-2001, Remedy Corp., Mountain View, Calif., 1995-97; vis. lectr. U. Santa Clara Law Sch., 1985, 89 Exec. editor U. Chgo. Law Rev., 1978-79; contbr. articles to profl. jours. Mem. ABA (bus. law sect., various coms.), State Bar Calif. (panelist continuing legal edn. 1984), San Francisco Bar Assn., Am. Fin. Assn., Wharton Club (San Francisco Bay area). Avocations: contemporary art, music, travel. Home: 243 Polhemus Ave Atherton CA 94027-5442 Office: Gunderson Dettmer Stough Villeneuve 1200 Seaport Blvd Redwood City CA 94063-5537 Home Phone: 650-327-9313; Office Phone: 650-321-2400.

GUNDY-BURLET, KAREN, research scientist; B in Engring., U. Calif., Berkeley; M in Aeronautical Engring., Stanford U., PhD. Rsch. scientist, computational fluid dynamics NASA Ames Rsch. Ctr., Moffett Field, Calif. Sponsor high sch. students Space Biology Program. Fellow Stanford U. Office: NASA Ames Rsch Ctr Moffett Field CA 94035

GUNN, GILES BUCKINGHAM, language, religios studies and global and international studies educator; b. Evanston, Ill., Jan. 9, 1938; s. Buckingham Willcox and Janet (Fargo) G.; m. Janet Mears Varner, Dec. 29, 1969 (div. July 1983); 1 child, Adam Buckingham; m. Deborah Rose Sills, July 9, 1983; 1 child, Abigail Rose. BA, Amherst Coll., 1959; student, Episc. Theol. Sch., Cambridge, Mass., 1959-60; MA, U. Chgo., 1963, PhD, 1967. Prof. religion and lit. U. Chgo., 1966-74; prof. religion and Am. studies U. N.C., Chapel Hill, 1974-85; prof. English and Religion U. Fla., 1984-85; prof. English U. Calif., Santa Barbara, 1985—, chmn. English dept., 1993-97, prof. global and internat. studies, 1998—, chmn. global studies, 2001—05, chmn. global and internat. studies, 2005—. Vis. asst. prof. religion Stanford U., Palo Alto, Calif., 1973; Benedict Disting. vis. prof. religion Carleton Coll., Northfield, Minn., 1977; William R. Kenan Disting. vis. prof. humanities Coll. William and Mary, Williamsburg, Va., 1983-84; Humanities Disting. vis. prof. U. Colo., 1989; Eric Yoegelin Disting. prof. Am. Studies, U. Munich, 1994-95; dir. NEH summer sems. for coll. and univ. tchrs., 1979, 81, 85, 94, for sch. tchrs., 1987, 88, 89, 91; cons. Libr. of Am. Author: F.O. Matthiessen, The Critical Achievement, 1975, The Interpretation of Otherness: Literature, Religion and the American Imagination, 1979, The Culture of Criticism and The Criticism of Culture, 1987, Thinking Across the American Grain: Ideology, Intellect, and the New Pragmatism, 1992, Beyond Solidarity: Pragmatism and Difference in a Globalised World, 2001; editor: Literature and Religion, 1971, Henry James, Senior: A Selection of His Writings, 1974, New World Metaphysics: Readings on the Religious Meaning of the American Experience, 1981, The Bible and American Arts and Letters, 1983, Church, State, and American Culture, 1984, Early American Writing, 1994, William James, Pragmatism and Other Writings, 2000, A Historical Guide to Herman Melville, 2005, War Narratives and American Culture, 2005; co-editor: Redrawing the Boundaries: The Transformation of English and American Literary Studies, 1992; contbr. numerous articles to profl. jours. Bd. dirs. Fund for Santa Barbara. Edward John Noble Leadership grantee, 1959-63; Amherst-Doshisha fellow, Kyoto, Japan, 1960-61, Kent fellow, Danforth Found., 1963-65, Guggenheim fellow, 1978-79, Nat. Endowment for Humanities fellow, 1990, U. Calif. Pres.'s Rsch. fellow, 1990; Phi Beta Kappa vis. scholar, 2000-01. Mem. MLA, Am. Acad. Religion (dir. research and pubs. 1974-77), Am. Studies Assn., Soc. Religion, Arts and Contemporary Culture, Soc. Am. Phil., Nat. Critics Book Circle. Democrat. Avocations: walking, motorcycling, travel. Office: U Calif Dept English Santa Barbara CA 93106 Home: 5488 Rincon Beach Park Dr Ventura CA 93001-9749

GUNSUL, BROOKS R. W., architect; b. Seattle, Aug. 7, 1928; s. Frank Justus and Phyllis (Webster) G.; m. Marilyn Thompson, Aug. 26, 1950; children: Robin, Karen, David, Jana. BS in Archtl. Engring., Wash. State U., 1952. Registered architect, Oreg., Wash., Ill., N.Y. Architect Stewart & Richardson architect, Portland, 1952-57, Scott & Payne, Portland, 1957-59, Wolff & Zimmer, 1959-65; ptnr. Wolff, Zimmer Gunsul. Frasca, Portland, 1966-77, Zimmer Gunsul Frasca, Portland, 1977—, Seattle, 1987—, LA, 1988—. Mem. adv. com. Wash. State U. Dept. Architecture, Pullman, 1983-93, found. adv. bd., 1994-96; dir., founder Architecture Found., Portland, 1980-88; trustee Wash. State U. Found. Contbr. articles to profl. jours. Chmn. adv. com. Oreg. Maritime Ctr. and Mus.; trustee Wash. State U. Found. With U.S. Army, 1946-47. Recipient Wash. State U. Achievement award, 1991. Fellow AIA (Firm of Yr. award 1991), Portland Yacht Club, Multnomah Athletic Club. Office: Zimmer Gunsul Frasca Partnership 320 SW Oak St Ste 500 Portland OR 97204-2737

GUNTHEROTH, WARREN GADEN, pediatrician, educator; b. Hominy, Okla., July 27, 1927; s. Harry William and Callie (Cornett) G.; m. Ethel Haglund, July 3, 1954; children: Kurt, Karl, Sten. MD, Harvard U., 1952. Diplomate: Am. Bd. Pediatrics, Am. Bd. Pediatric Cardiology, Nat. Bd. Med. Examiners. Intern Peter Bent Brigham Hosp., Boston, 1952-53; fellow in cardiology Children's Hosp., Boston, 1953-55, resident in pediatrics, 1955-56; rsch. fellow physiology and biophysics U. Wash. Med. Sch., Seattle, 1957-58, mem. faculty, 1958—, prof. pediatrics, 1969—, head divsn. pediatric cardiology, 1964-91. Author: Pediatric Electrocardiography, 1965, How to Read Pediatric ECGs, 1981, 4th edit., 2006, Crib Death (Sudden Infant Death Syndrome), 1982, 3d edit., 1995, Climbing With Sasha, a Washington Husky, 1995; also more than 300 articles; mem. editl. bd. Am. Heart Jour., 1977-80, Circulation, 1980-83, Am. Jour. Noninvasive Cardiology, 1985-94, Jour. Am. Coll. Cardiology, 1988-94, Am. Jour. Cardiology, Jour. Noninvasive Cardiology, 1996-00; sect. editor Practice of Pediatrics, 1979-87, Pediatric Cardiology, 2004-07. Served with USPHS, 1950-51. Spl. research fellow NIH, 1967. Mem. Soc. Pediatric Rsch., Biomed. Engring. Soc. (charter), Am. Heart Assn. (chmn. N.W. regional med. rsch. adv. com. 1978-80), Cardiovascular System Dynamics Soc. (charter), Am. Coll. Cardiology. Democrat. Home: 13201 42nd Ave NE Seattle WA 98125-4626 Office: U Wash Med Sch Dept Pediatrics PO Box 356320 Seattle WA 98195-6320 Office Phone: 206-543-3186. Business E-Mail: wgg@u.washington.edu.

GUO, SU, science educator; BS in Bioengring., Fudan U., 1991; PhD in Genetics and Devel., Cornell U., 1996. Postdoctoral fellow Harvard Med. Sch., 1996—97, Genentech, 1997—2000; asst. prof. biopharm. scis. U. Calif., San Francisco. Office: Sch Pharmacy 513 Parnassus Ave Box 0446 San Francisco CA 94143

GUPTA, ANJU, risk management consultant; b. Bangalore, India, Sept. 14, 1971; d. Dharam Singh and Neera Gupta; m. Parag Gupta. PhD, Stanford U., California, USA, 1997. Postdoctoral rsch. scholar Stanford U., Palo Alto, Calif., 1997—98; from sr. engr. to sr. dir. product mgmt. Risk Mgmt. Solutions Inc., Newark, Calif., 1998—2005, sr. dir. product mgmt., 2005—; product mgmt. weather risk Risk Link, 2001—02, 2002—05, sr. dir. product mktg., 2007—. Cons. Wharton team on NSF project, Palo Alto, 1996; mem. Curee, LA, 1998; mem. com. earthquake risk financing and transfer Earthquake Engring. Rsch. Inst., Oakland, Calif., 1999. Contbr. articles to profl. jours. Vol. for adult literacy, Mountain View, Calif., 1998; vol. for childhood literacy New Delhi, 1995—97. Mem.: Earthquake Engring. Rsch. Inst. Achievements include development of financial risk model for Central America; a standardized national earthquake loss estimation software tool, Hazards US (HAZUS); participation in project dealing with urban search and rescue requirements for responding to catastrophic disasters in the U.S; project to assess annualized losses from earthquakes in the U.S; project to validate and calibrate the HAZUS methodology. Office: Risk Mgmt Solutions Inc 7015 Gateway Blvd Newark CA 94560 Home: 660 Curtner Rd Fremont CA 94539 Personal E-mail: anjurisk@yahoo.com. E-mail: anju.gupta@rms.com.

GUPTA, ANOOP, computer software company executive; B in elec. engring., Indian Inst. Tech., Dehli, 1980; PhD in computer sci., Carnegie Mellon Univ., 1986. Mem. rsch. faculty Carnegie Mellon Univ., 1986—87; prof. computer sci. & elec. engring. Stanford Univ., 1987—97; leader collaboration & multimedia group Microsoft Corp., Redmond, Wash., 1997—2001, tech. asst. to Bill Gates, 2001—03, corp. v.p. unified comm. group, 2003—07, corp. v.p. Microsoft edn. products & solutions, tech. policy & strategy, 2007—. Co-author: Parallel Computer Architecture: A Hardware-Software Approach, 1998; contbr. articles to profl. jours. Recipient President's Gold Medal, Indian Inst. Tech., 1980, Presdl. Young Investigator award, Nat. Sci. Found., 1990; Robert N. Noyce Faculty Scholar Chair, Stanford Univ., 1993—94. Achievements include patents in field.

GUPTA, MADHU SUDAN, electrical engineering educator; b. Lucknow, India, June 13, 1945; came to U.S., 1966; s. Manohar Lal and Premvati Gupta; m. Vijaya Lakshmi Tayal, July 9, 1970; children: Jay Mohan, Vineet Mohan; m. Manorama Vyas, May 29, 1985. BS, Lucknow U., India, 1963; MS, Allahabad U., India, 1966, Fla. State U., 1967; MA, U. Mich., 1968, PhD, 1972. Registered profl. engr., Ont. Asst. prof. elec. engring. Queen's U., Kingston, Ont., Canada, 1972-73, MIT, Cambridge, 1973-78, assoc. prof. elec. engring., 1978-79, U. Ill., Chgo., 1979-84, prof. elec. engring., 1984-87, dir. grad. studies, 1980-83; vis. prof. elec. and computer engring. U. Calif., Santa Barbara, 1985-86; sr. staff engr. Hughes Aircraft Co., 1987-95; prof. elec. engring., chmn. dept. elec. engring. Fla. State U., Tallahassee, 1995-2000; prof. elec. engring., RF comm. sys. industry chair San Diego State U., 2000—; dir. Comm. Sys. and Signal Processing Inst., 2000—; adj. prof. elec. engring. U. Calif., San Diego, 2002—. Cons. Lincoln Lab. MIT, Lexington, 1976-79, Hughes Research Labs., Malibu, Calif., 1986-87. Editor: Electrical Noise, 1977, Teaching Engineering, 1987, Noise in Circuits and Systems, 1988; editor-in-chief IEEE Microwave and Guided Wave Letters, 1998-2000, IEEE Microwave Mag., 2003-05; contbr. articles to profl. jours. Lilly fellow, 1974-75. Fellow IEEE; mem. IEEE Microwave Soc. (vice chmn. 1984-85, chmn. 1986-87). Achievements include patents in field. Office: San Diego State U Dept Elec Engring 5500 Campanile Dr San Diego CA 92182-1309 Business E-Mail: mgupta@mail.sdsu.edu.

GURALNICK, MICHAEL J., medical research administrator; Dir. Child Devel. and Mental Retardation Ctr., U Wash., Seattle, 1986—. Office: Ctr Human Devel & Disability Box 357920 Seattle WA 98195-7920

GURFEIN, PETER J., lawyer; b. NYC, Sept. 13, 1948; m. Pamela Hedin, June 23, 1976; children: Diana, William, Eva. BA, NYU, 1969; JD, George Washington U., 1973. Bar: N.Y. 1976, U.S. Supreme Ct. 1976, US. Dist. Ct. (so. and ea. dists.) N.Y. 1976, U.S. Ct. Appeals (2d cir.) 1979, Internat. Ct. Trade 1979, U.S. Ct. Appeals (9th cir.) 1986, Calif. 1986, U.S Dist. Ct. (no., ea., so. and cen. dists.) Calif. 1987, D.C. 1993. Project dir. Commn. on Correctional Facilities and Scs. ABA, Washington, 1973-76; asst. dist. atty., spl. narcotics prosecutor Dist. Atty.'s Office N.Y. County, NYC, 1976-81; assoc. Zalkin, Rodin & Goodman, NYC, 1981-83, Moses & Singer, NYC, 1983-86; ptnr. Morrison & Foerster, San Francisco, 1986-92, Sonnenschein, Nath & Rosenthal, L.A. and San Francisco, 1993-2000, Akin, Gump, Strauss, Hauer & Feld, LLP, LA, 2001—. Editor-in-chief The Calif. Bankruptcy Jour., 1995-2000; contbr. articles to handbooks and profl. jours. Mem. Bar Assn. San Francisco (chmn. bankruptcy and comml. law sect. 1993), L.A. County Bar Assn.; dir.

L.A. Bankruptcy Forum, 1995—. Office: Akin Gump Strauss Hauer & Feld LLP Ste 2400 2029 Century Park E Los Angeles CA 90067 Office Phone: 310-229-1000. E-mail: pgurfein@akingump.com.

GURNEY, DANIEL SEXTON, race car manufacturing company and racing team executive; b. LI, NY, Apr. 13, 1931; s. John R. and Roma (Sexton) G.; m. Evi B., July 7, 1969; children: Justin B., Alexander R.; children by previous marriage: John, Lyndee, Danny, Jimmy. Grad., Menlo Jr. Coll., 1951. Profl. race car driver, 1955-70; pres., owner Dan Gurney's All Am. Racers, Inc. (doing bus. as): Dan Gurney Eagle Racing Cars, U.S.A., Santa Ana, Calif., 1964-65; mgr. Eagle Racing Team (Indpls. 500 winners 1968, 73, 75, U.S. Auto Club Nat. Championship winners 1968, 74), Formula A Championship winners 1968, 69); TV sports commentator. Mem. Automobile Competition Com. for U.S.A.; car owner, builder Fed Ex Championship Series, Santa Ana, Calif. Served with U.S. Army, 1952-54, Korea. Recipient numerous racing awards including GTO driving championship Internat. Motor Sports Assn. (driver Chris Cord), 1987, GTO Mfrs.' championship Internat. Motor Sports Assn. (mfr. Toyota), 1987, Norelco Cup championship (driver Willy T. Ribbs), 1987, IMSA Camel GTP championship, 1992, 93, IMSA mfrs. championship for Toyota, 1992, 93. Mem. Screen Actors Guild, AFTRA, U.S. Auto Club, Sports Car Club Am., U.S. C. of C., Championship Auto Racing Teams, Inc., Soc. Automotive Engrs., Fedn. Internationale de L'Automobile, Internat. Motor Sports Assn. Clubs: Balboa Bay, Eagle.

GURNIS, MICHAEL CHRISTOPHER, geological sciences educator; b. Boston, Oct. 22, 1959; s. George Albert and Barbara (Dempsey) G. BS, U. Ariz., 1982; PhD, Australian Nat. U., Canberra, 1987. Rsch. fellow in geophysics Calif. Inst. Tech., Pasadena, 1986-88, assoc. prof. geophysics, 1994-96; asst. prof. geol. scis. U. Mich., Ann Arbor, 1988-93, assoc. prof., 1993—2003; assoc. dir. Seismological Lab. Calif. Inst. Tech., Pasadena, 1995—, prof. geophysics, 1996—; dir. Computational Infrastructure for Geodynamics, 2004—; John and Hazel Smits prof. geophysics Caltech, 2005—. Recipient Presdl. Young Investigator award NSF, 1989, fellowship David and Lucile Packard Found., 1991. Fellow Am. Geophys. Union (Macelwance medal 1993), Geol. Soc. Am. (sr., Donath medal 1993). Achievements include research in the linkage of sedimentary rocks deposited in the interiors of continents to geodynamic processes within the earth; global dynamics, mantle convection, plate tectonics, sea level changes, evolution of mantle and crust; computational and visual fluid mechanics. Office: Calif Inst Tech Seismol Lab-252-21 Pasadena CA 91125-0001

GUST, ANNE BALDWIN, former retail apparel company executive; b. Grosse Pointe Farms, Mich., Mar. 15, 1958; d. Rockwell Thomas Jr. and Anne Elizabeth (Baldwin) G.; m. Jerry Brown, June 18, 2005 BA, Stanford U., 1980; JD, U. Mich., 1983. Bar: Calif. 1983, U.S. Dist. Ct. (no. dist.) Calif. 1983, U.S. Ct. Appeals (9th cir.) 1983. Assoc. Orrick, Herrington & Sutcliffe, San Francisco, 1983-86, Brobeck, Phleger & Harrison, San Francisco & Palo Alto, Calif., 1986—91; assoc. gen. counsel The Gap, Inc., San Francisco, 1991—94, sr. v.p., gen. counsel, 1994—98, exec. v.p., human resources, legal & corp. adminstrn., 1998—99, exec. v.p., human resources, legal, global compliance & corp. adminstrn., 1999—2000, exec. v.p., chief adminstrv. officer, 2000—05. Mem. bd. dirs., Jack in the Box Inc., 2003- Contbr. articles to labor trade jours. Mem. ABA (labor subcom.), Calif. Bar Assn.

GUSTAFSON, ALICE FAIRLEIGH, lawyer; b. Houston, Dec. 1, 1946; d. William H. and Mary Davis (McCord) Bell; m. Charles R. Gustafson, May 30, 1971. BA in Econs., Wellesley Coll., Mass., 1968; JD, U. Puget Sound, 1976. Bar: Wash. 1976. Various positions U.S. Dept. HEW, various locations, 1968-75; assoc. Graham & Dunn, Seattle, 1977-83, ptnr., 1983—. Bd. dirs. King County Am. Cancer Soc., Seattle, 1983-85, Women & Bus., Inc., Seattle, 1984-87; mem. nominating com. YWCA Seattle-King County, 1985-88. Mem. ABA, Wash. State Bar Assn. (chair Bench-Bar-Press com. 1988-90), Seattle-King County Bar Assn. (trustee young lawyers divsn. 1980-83, treas. 1985-87), N.W. Comm. Lawyers, Met. Seattle Urban League (bd. dirs. 1991-93). Avocations: sailing, bicycling, skiing. Home: PO Box 2127 Bothell WA 98041-2127

GUSTAVSON, CARRIE, museum director; BA magna cum laude, UCLA, 1974, MA summa cum laude, 1974; ABD with distinction, U. Toronto, 1979. Cert. in mus. studies Ariz. State U., 1991. Rschr., asst. prof. U. Tubingen, Germany, 1980—82, asst. dir., program dir., 1983—86; tech. editor Soil Sys., Inc., 1987—90; collections mgmt. staff The Heard Mus., Phoenix, 1990—91; dir. Bisbee Mining and Hist. Mus., Ariz., 1992—. Adj. faculty Cochise Coll., 2001—. Contbr. articles to profl. publs. Mem. Bisbee Unified Sch. Dist., 1997—2003; bd. dirs. Copper Queen Cmty. Hosp., 1996—2002, Chiricahua Cmty. Health Ctrs., 2002—. Mem.: Cochise County Mus. Assn. (founder 1999), Soc. Mining Engrs. (v.p., treas.), Mus. Assn. Ariz. (bd. dirs. 1994—, pres. 1998—99), Ariz. Hist. Soc., Am. Assn. for State and Local History, Am. Assn. Mus., Westerners Internat., Bisbee Rotary Club (v.p. 2005, pres. 2006, sec. 2007), Bus. and Profl. Women's Club (pres. 2003—, Woman of Achievement 1998), Rotary Club Internat. Office: Bisbee Mining & Hist Mus PO Box 14 Bisbee AZ 85603-0014 Office Phone: 520-432-7071. Business E-Mail: carrie@bisbeemuseum.org.

GUTHRIE, LAURA D., energy executive, human resources specialist; BS in Pers. Adminstrn. & Indsl. Rels., Oreg. State U. Various mgmt. positions Unocal Corp., BHP Petroleum; head human resources Input / Output, Splitrock Services; v.p. human resources Hercules Offshore Inc., 2007—08; sr. v.p. human resources Calpine Corp., San Jose, Calif., 2008—. Office: Calpine Corp 50 W San Fernando St San Jose CA 95113

GUTHRIE, SCOTT, computer software company executive; Grad. in computer sci., Duke Univ., 1997. Tech. mgmt. positions through gen. mgr., for develop. of Microsoft Visual Studio tools, ASP.NET, Silverlight & other developer products Microsoft Corp., Redmond, Wash., 1997—2008, corp. v.p., .NET Developer div., 2008—. Office: Microsoft Corp 1 Microsoft Way Redmond WA 98052-6399

GUTIERREZ, CARLOS G., chemistry professor; BS, UCLA; PhD in Synthetic Organic Chemistry, U. Calif., Davis, 1975. Prof. chemistry Calif. State U., LA, 1976—. Vis. scholar U. Calif., Berkeley, 1989—91. Recipient Presdl. Award for Excellence in Sci., Math. and Engring. Mentoring, 1996, Lifetime Achievement Award, AAAS, US Professors of Yr. Award for Outstanding Master's Universities and Colleges Prof., Carnegie Found. for Advancement of Tchg. and Coun. for Advancement and Support of Edn., 2005. Office: Calif State U 5151 State University Dr Los Angeles CA 90032 Office Phone: 323-343-2356. Office Fax: 323-343-6411. E-mail: cgutier@calstatela.edu.

GUTIERREZ, PHILIP S., federal judge; b. LA, 1959; BA, U. Notre Dame, 1981; JD, UCLA, 1984. Bar: Calif. 1985. Assoc. LaFollette, Johnson, DeHaas, Fesler & Ames, 1986, Kern & Wooley, 1986—88; mng. ptnr. Cotkin & Collins, 1988—97; LA County judge Superior Ct. Calif., 1997—2006; judge US Dist. Ct. (Ctrl. dist.) Calif., 2007—. Office: US Dist Ct 312 N Spring St Los Angeles CA 90012

GUTIERREZ, SIDNEY M., federal agency administrator; b. Albuquerque, June 27, 1957; BS in Aero. Engring., USAF Acad., 1973; MA in Mgmt., Webster U., 1977. Commd. 2d lt. USAF, advanced through grades to col., test pilot, ret.; dir. satellite ctr. Sandia Nat. Labs., Albuquerque, now dir., sys. assessment and rsch.; ret. space shuttle pilot and comdr. NASA, mem. aerospace safety adv. panel, 2000—03. Chmn. Goodwill Industries of N.Mex., N.Mex. Bd. regents N.Mex. Inst. Mining and Tech. Named one of 50 Most Important Hispanics in Govt., Edn., Hispanic Engineer and Info. Tech. mag., 2005. Office: Sandia Nat Labs PO Box 5800 Albuquerque NM 87185 E-mail: smgutie@sandi.gov.

GUTJAHR, ALLAN LEO, mathematics educator, researcher; b. Hosmer, SD, Mar. 20, 1938; s. Christian E. Gutjahr and Emma Preszler; m. Ellen Troxel, Nov. 21, 1959 (div. 1978); children: Kurt, Eric, Kristin; m. Margaret Rae Sjostedt, Aug. 15, 1981; children: Ted, Meghan. Student, Cen. Wash. Coll., 1958-59; BS in Math., U. Wash., 1962; MSE, Johns Hopkins U., 1963; PhD in Stats., Rutgers U., 1970. Tech. staff Bell Labs., Holmdel, N.J., 1962-71; prof. math. N.Mex. Tech. U., Socorro, 1971-99, prof. emeritus, 1999—, chmn. dept. math., 1985-88, assoc. v.p. acad. affairs, 1990-92, v.p. rsch. and econ. devel., 1992-97. Vis. rschr. Ecole Des Mines, Paris, 1978, U.S. Geol. Survey, Denver, 1978, Stanford U., fall 1989, U. Poly. Catalonia, Barcelona, fall 1997. Contbr. articles to profl. jours. Bd. dirs. V.I.A. With U.S. Army, 1956-58. Recipient Disting. Tchg. award N.Mex. Tech. U., 1987, Disting. Rsch. award Nimex Tech. U., 1999. Fellow Am. Geophys. Union; mem. Math. Assn. Am., Am. Statis. Assn., Internat. Assn. of Math. Geol., Sigma Xi. Avocations: reading, writing, jogging. Home: 445 Aquina Ct Belen NM 87002-6345

GUTSCHE, CARL DAVID, chemistry professor; b. LaGrange, Ill., Mar. 21, 1921; s. Frank Carl and Vera (Mutchler) G.; m. Alice Eugenia Carr, June 4, 1944; children: Clara Jean, Betha Lynn, Christopher Glenn. BA, Oberlin Coll., 1943. With Office Sci. Devel., USDA, 1943-44; instr. chemistry Washington U., St. Louis, 1947-48, asst. prof., 1948-51, assoc. prof., 1951-59, prof., 1959-89, prof. emeritus, 1989—, chmn. dept., 1970-76; Robert A. Welch prof. chemistry Tex. Christian U., Ft. Worth, 1989—2002; vis. scholar U. Ariz., Tucson, 2002—. Cons. in field; mem. adv. bd. Petroleum Rsch. Fund., 1971—74; chmn. medicinal chemistry study sect. NIH, 1978—81. Author: The Chemistry of Carbonyl Compounds, 1967, Carbocyclic Ring Expansion Reactions, 1968, Fundamentals of Organic Chemistry, 1975, Calixarenes, 1989, Calixarenes Revisiited, 1998, Calixarenes, 2nd edit., 2008; mem. adv. bd.: Jour. Organic Chemistry, 1979-83; mem. editorial bd.: Organic Preparations and Procedures Internat., 1968—, Jour. Inclusion Phenomena, 1993-2000; contbr. articles to profl. jours. Bd. dirs. St. Louis Conservatory and Schs. for Arts, 1978—82, Ft. Worth Chamber Music Soc., 1999—2002, Olympic Peninsula Festival Concerts, 2008—. Recipient Alumni award Washington U., 1977; Guggenheim fellow, 1981. Fellow AAAS; mem. Am. Chem. Soc. (chmn. St. Louis sect. 1959, mem. pub. com. 1974-77, com. on coms. 1977-80, com. on profl. tng. 1980-89, cons. to com. 1990-98, councilor and dir., St. Louis sect. award 1971, Midwest award 1988, Doherty award 1998, Izatt-Christensen award 2002), Chem. Soc. (London), AAUP, Phi Beta Kappa (mem. qualifications com. 1992—2003), Sigma Xi. Home: 9755 Shore Dr NE Indianola WA 98342-0009 Office Phone: 206-922-2648. Business E-Mail: d.gutsche@tcu.edu.

GUTSCHE, STEVEN LYLE, physicist; b. St. Paul, Nov. 10, 1946; s. Lyle David and Phyllis Jane (Stubstad) G.; divorced; children: Kristina, Angela; m. Marilyn D. Maloney, Oct. 4, 1980; children: Taylor Steven, Daniel Mark. BS, U. Colo., 1968; MS, U. Calif., Santa Barbara, 1970. Physicist USN Pacific Missile Range, Point Mugu, Calif., 1968-71; staff scientist Mission Rsch. Corp., Santa Barbara, 1971-76, group leader, 1977-79, div. leader, 1979—, v.p., 1987-89; pres., 1989—; also bd. dirs. Mission Rsch. Corp., Santa Barbara. Contbr. articles to tech. publs. Presbyterian. Avocations: collecting oriental rugs, soccer, running, reading. Office: Mission Rsch Corp 735 State St Santa Barbara CA 93101-3351

GUTSHALL, THOMAS L., clinical diagnostics company executive; b. Huntingdon, Pa., Feb. 24, 1938; s. Joseph Boyd and Katherine Pauline (Wear) G.; m. Jane Kipp Taylor, Aug. 22, 1959; children: Jennifer, Douglas, Jodi. BS ChemE, U. Del., 1960. Process engr. Union Carbide Corp., S. Charleston, W.Va., 1960-61, 63-69; mfg. supt. Mallinckrodt, Inc., St. Louis, 1969-72, plant mgr. Raleigh, N.C., 1972-75, v.p., gen. mgr. St. Louis, 1975-81; group v.p. Syntex Corp., Palo Alto, Calif., 1981-83, sr. v.p., 1985-86, exec. v.p., 1987—94; pres. Syva Co., Palo Alto, Calif., 1983-85; pres., Coo CV Therapeutics, Palo Alto, Calif., 1994—96; chmn., CEO Cepheid, Sunnyvale, Calif., 1996—. Chmn. City Team Ministries, San. Jose, Calif., 1984—. Served to 1st lt., U.S. Army, 1961-62. Mem. Inst. Chem. Engrs., Tau Beta Pi. Republican. Presbyterian. Home: 24968 Okeefe Ln Los Altos CA 94022-4612 Office: Cepheid 904 Caribbean Dr Sunnyvale CA 94089-1189

GUTTENBERG, DAVID, state legislator; b. NYC, May 26, 1951; m. Marilyn Guttenberg. Attended, Pa. Acad. Fine Arts, 1970. Major, Alaska Civil Airpatrol; auditor, Alaska Laborers Local 943, 1990-96, polit. dir., Fairbanks Ctrl. Labor Coun., 1990, 1992; legis. aide, 1991; legis. staff, Rep. Tom Moyer, 1999; fin. staff, Rep. John Davies, 1999-2002; chairman, Alaska State Democratic Party, formerly; Alaska State Representative, District 8, 2003-. Commr. Jennifer Dr Svc. Area, Chena Goldstream Fire and Rescue. Mem. bd. dirs. Borealis Cmty. Land Trust; mem. Alaska Laborers Polit. Edn. Com. Mem.: Assn. State Dem. Chairs (vice chair, Western Region). Democrat. Avocations: sculpting, painting, fly fishing, gardening. Office: Dist 8 1292 Sadler Way Ste 304 Fairbanks AK 99701 also: State Capitol Rm 418 Juneau AK 99801 Office Phone: 907-456-8172, 907-465-4457. Office Fax: 907-456-2490, 907-465-3519. Business E-Mail: Rep_David_Guttenberg@legis.state.ak.us.*

GUTTENBERG, STEVE, actor; b. Bklyn., Aug. 24, 1958; s. Jerome Stanley and Ann Iris (Newman) G. Student, Albany State U. Actor (films) The Chicken Chronicles, 1977, Something For Joey, 1977, Rollercoaster, 1977, The Boys From Brazil, 1979, Players, 1979, Can't Stop the Music, 1980, Diner, 1982, The Man Who Wasn't There, 1983, Police Academy, 1984, Police Academy II, 1985, Cocoon, 1985, Bad Medicine, 1985, Police Academy 3, 1986, Short Circuit, 1986, The Bedroom Window, 1987, (also assoc. prodr.) Police Academy IV: Citizens on Patrol, 1987, Three Men and A Baby, 1987, Amazon Women on the Moon, 1987, Surrender, 1987, High Spirits, 1988, Cocoon: The Return, 1988, Don't Her It's Me, 1990, Three Men and a Little Lady, 1990, Tower of Terror, 1997, Airborne, 1998, Love and Fear, 1999; actor, dir.: Love Off Limits, 1992; TV films: Something For Joey, 1976, To Race the Wind, 1980, Billy, 1976, Miracle On Ice, 1980, The Day After, 1984, The Magical World of Chuck Jones, 1992, It takes Two, 1995, Home for the Holidays, 1995, The Big Green, 1995, Zeus and Roxanne, 1997, Casper: The Beginning, 1997, (TV series) Billy, 1979, No Soap, Radio, 1982, Storytime, 1994; performer (TV series) Dancing with the Stars, 2008; stage: Broadway debut Prelude to a Kiss, 1991.

GUTTENTAG, LUCAS, advocate, lawyer; b. San Francisco, Mar. 12, 1951; s. Otto Ernst and Erika Guttentag. AB, U. Calif., Berkeley, 1973; JD, Harvard U., 1978. Bar: Calif. 1979, N.Y. 1988, U.S. Supreme Ct. 1982, U.S. Ct. Appeals (2d, 5th, D.C. cirs.) 1989, (9th cirs.) 1980, (6th cirs.) 1988, (4th cirs.) 1990, U.S. Dist. Ct. Calif. (ctrl. dist.) 1979, (no. dist.) 1990, (ea. dist.) 1992, N.Y. (so. dist., ea. dist., we. dist,) 1988. Law clk. to judge William Wayne Justice U.S. Dist. Ct. (ea. dist.) Tex., Tyler, 1978-79; staff atty. Ctr. for Law in the Pub. Interest, LA, 1979-83; clin. prof. Columbia U. Sch. Law, NYC, 1983-88; dir. immigrants rights project ACLU Nat. Hqrs., NYC and San Francisco, 1987—. Adj. prof. Columbia U. Law Sch., 1989-98, U. Calif. at Berkeley Law Sch., 1997-, Stanford Law Sch., 2004, 2007-. Co-author: Rights of Aliens and Refugees, 1990; contbr. books and TV shows, profl. law jours. Recipient Wasserman Excellence in Litigation award Am. Immigration Lawyers Assn., 1990, 91, 97, 2002, King Contbn. to Immigration Law award Nat. Immigration Project of NLG, 1991; named Calif. Lawyer of the Yr., Appellate, 2001; named one of Top 100 Lawyers in Calif. Daily Jour., 2007 Mem. ABA (co-chair labor law sect., immigration law com. 1991-94, coordinating com. immigration law 1995-98, named ABA Human Rights Jour. Hero, 2001), Am. Bar Found. (elec. fellow 2007) Office: ACLU Immigrants' Rights Project 39 Drumm St San Francisco CA 94111 Business E-Mail: lguttentag@aclu.org.

GUY, ARTHUR WILLIAM, electrical engineering educator, researcher; b. Helena, Mont., Dec. 10, 1928; s. Arthur Jack and Evelyn (Hebb) G.; m. Vivian Ruth Walker, June 12, 1952; children: William, Sandra, Fred, Arla. BSEE, U. Wash., 1955, MSEE, 1957, PhDEE, 1966. Rsch. asst. elec. engring. dept. U. Wash., Seattle, 1956-57; rsch. engr. Boeing Airplane Co., Seattle, 1957-63; cons. engr. rehab. medicine U. Wash., Seattle, 1963-65, rsch. engr. elec. engring. dept., 1964-66, prof. elec. engring. dept., rehab. medicine, 1966-83, prof., dir. bioelectromagnetics rsch. lab. Ctr. for Bioengineering, 1983-91, prof. emeritus, 1991—. Cons. Bioelectromagnetics Cons., Seattle, 1991-2000; telecomms. facilities adv. com. Seattle City Coun., 1991-92; Sci. Adv. Group on Wireless Tech., 1993-95; active Wireless Tech. Rsch., LLC, 1993-97. Contbr. articles to profl. jours. Mem. Electromagnetic Field Task Force State Dept. Health, Olympia, Wash., 1991-92. Sgt. USAF, 1947-52. Recipient Achievement award, Westinghouse Co., 1954, spl. award for the decade internat., Power Inst. for Med. and Biol. Rsch., 1980. Fellow AAAS, IEEE (life, vice chair SCC 28 stds. bd. 1989-94, mem. COMAR 1974-89, 92-98, chair COMAR 1987-89); mem. Nat. Coun. on Radiation Protection and Measurements (hon.), Bioelectromagnetic Soc. (charter mem., pres. 1984, d'Arsenval award 1987). Methodist. Home and Office: 18122 60th Pl NE Kenmore WA 98028-8901 Home Phone: 425-486-6439. Personal E-mail: gbemc@comcast.net.

GUY, MARY ELLEN JOHNSTON, political science professor; b. Carlinville, Ill., Dec. 2, 1947; d. Charles Oren and Marilyn Elinor (Denby) Johnston; divorced. BA cum laude, Jacksonville U., 1969; M of Rehab. Counseling, U. Fla., 1970; MA in Psychology, U. SC, 1976, PhD in Polit. Sci., 1981. Rehab. counselor Ga. Dept. Human Resources, Augusta, 1970-73; psychologist SC State Hosp., Columbia, 1973-80, quality assurance coord., 1980-82; prof. polit. sci. and pub. affairs U. Ala., Birmingham, 1982-97; Collins prof. pub. adminstrn. Fla. State U., 1997—2008; prof. U. Colo. Denver, 2008—. Adv. bd. Cooper Green Hosp., Birmingham, 1991-97. Author: Ethical Decision Making, 1990, From Organizational Decline, 1989, Professionals in Organizations, 1985, Emotional Labor: Putting the Service in Public Service, 2008; Editor: Women and Men of the States, 1992, Review of Public Personnel Administration, 2001-06. Mem. ASPA (Disting. Rsch. award 1992, Outstanding Paper award 1992, coun. mem. 1987-90, pres. 1997-98), So. Polit. Sci. Assn. (pres. 2001-02), Am. Polit. Sci. Assn., Women's Caucus in Polit. Sci./South (pres. 1990-92). Unitarian Universalist. Avocations: golf, dog breeding. Office: Univ Colo Denver Sch Pub Affairs 1380 Lawrence St Ste 500 Denver CO 80217-3364

GUY, RICHARD P., retired state supreme court justice; b. Coeur d'Alene, Idaho, Oct. 24, 1932; s. Richard H. and Charlotte M. Guy; m. Marilyn K. Guy, Nov. 16, 1963; children: Victoria, Heidi, Emily. JD, Gonzaga U., 1959. Bar: Wash. 1959, Hawaii 1988. Former judge Wash. Superior Ct., Spokane, from 1977; chief justice Wash. Supreme Ct., Olympia, 1998—2001; mediator, arbitrator Judicial Arbitration and Mediation Svc., 2001—. Capt. USAS. Recipient Herbert Harley Award, Am. Judicature Soc., Outstanding Judge Award, Wash. St. Bar Assn., Supreme Ct. Medal, Canada. Mem. Wash. State Bar, Spokane County Bar Assn. Roman Catholic. Office: Wash Supreme Ct Temple Justice PO Box 40929 Olympia WA 98504-0929 also: JAMS Seattle 600 University St Ste 1910 Seattle WA 98101

GUYARDO, PAUL, broadcast company executive; b. 1964; BS, MA, Northwestern U., Ill. With Lintas NY, Saatchi & Saatchi, Tracy-Locke/BBDO; product dir. Johnson & Johnson Co.; gen. mgr. AT&T Inc.; exec. v.p. TV and mktg. Home Shopping Network (now HSN), 1996—2004; sr. v.p., chief mktg. officer KMart Sears Holdings Corp., 2004—05; exec. v.p., chief mktg. officer Direct TV Inc., 2005—. Bd. dirs. DirectTV Inc., 2005—. Bd. dirs. Starbright Found., LA. Office: DirectTV Inc Corp Hdqs 2230 E Imperial Hwy El Segundo CA 90245 Office Phone: 310-535-5000.

GUYMON, GARY LEROY, civil engineering educator; b. Farmington, N.Mex., Nov. 5, 1935; s. Leland W. and Grace E. (Cumming) G.; m. Lucinda A. Kemmis, June 11, 1988; children by previous marriage: Gary Jr., Richard, Marisa, Michael. BS, U. Calif., Davis, 1966, MS,

1967, PhD, 1970. Asst. civil engr. Calif. Dept. Water Resources, LA, 1955-66; asst. rsch. engr. U. Calif., Davis, 1969-71; assoc. prof. U. Alaska, Fairbanks, 1971-74; prof. U. Calif., Irvine, 1974-94, chmn. dept. civil engring., 1984-88, prof. emeritus, 1994—. Mem. coordinating bd. U. Calif. Water Resources Ctr., Berkeley, 1985-89; del. Univs. Coun. on Water Resources, Carbondale, Ill., 1980-94. Author: Unsaturated Zone Hydrology, 1994; contbr. numerous articles to profl. jours.; assoc. editor Advances in Water Resources, Southampton, U.K., 1981-89. Fellow ASCE; mem. Am. Geophys. Union, U.S. Com. on Large Dams, Phi Beta Kappa, Tau Beta Pi, Chi Epsilon. Independent. Avocations: woodworking, physical fitness. Office Phone: 760-635-0233. Business E-Mail: gguymon@att.net.

GUYNES, DEMI See MOORE, DEMI

GUZE, PHYLLIS ARLENE, internist, educator, academic administrator; MD, U. So. Calif., 1971. Resident in internal medicine Harbor UCLA Med. Ctr., fellow; dean of edn. UCLA, 1991-95, prof. medicine, vice chair, 1985—; chief dept. medicine VA Greater LA Healthcare Systems, LA, 1985—. Contbr. numerous articles to profl. jours. Recipient Disting. Tchr. award in clin. scis. Assn. Am. Med. Colls., 1995, Sherman M. Melinkoff Faculty award UCLA Sch. Medicine, 1995, Luckman Disting. Tchg. award, 1996, Disting. Tchr. award Alpha Omega Alpha, 1995. Mem. ACP, Am. Bd. of Internal Medicine (cert. com.), Assn. of Program Dirs. in Internal Medicine, Assn. of VA Chiefs of Medicine. Office: VA Greater LA Healthcare Sys West LA 11301 Wilshire Blvd # Mc111 Los Angeles CA 90073-1003

GWALTNEY, LAMAR EDWARD, state senator; b. Osceola, Ark., Apr. 21, 1933; s. Louie Edward and Lillian (Ward) Gwaltney; m. Mary Gail Anderson, Apr. 1, 1956; children: Cindy, Tracy, Rebecca, Lamar. Student, N. Mex. State U. Pres. Lamar Liquors, Inc., 1958—81, Gail, Inc., 1966—, Andy, Inc., 1970—; mem. N. Mex. Senate, Las Cruces, 1975—84. With US Army, 1951—59. Democrat. Episcopalian. Office: PO Box PO Box 2078 Las Cruces NM 88004-2078

GWINN, MARY ANN, editor; d. Lawrence Baird and Frances Evelyn (Jones) Gwinn; m. Richard A. King, June 3, 1973 (div. Jan. 1981); m. Stephen E. Dunnington, June 10, 1990. BA in Psychology, Hendrix Coll., 1973; MEd in Spl. Edn., Ga. State U., 1975; MA in Journalism, U. Mo., 1979. Tchrs. aide DeKalb County Schs., Decatur, Ga., 1973—74, tchr., 1975—78; reporter Columbia (Mo.) Daily Tribune, 1979—83, Seattle Times, 1983—, internat. trade and workplace reporter, 1992—96, asst. city editor, 1996—98, book editor, 1998—. Instr. ext. divsn. U. Wash., Seattle, 1990; instr. journalism Seattle U., 1994. Bd. dir. Nat. Book Critics Cir. Recipient Edn. Reporting award, Charles Stewart Mott Found., 1980, Enterprising reporting award, C.B. Blethen Family, 1989, Pulitzer Prize for Nat. Reporting, 1990. Mem.: Newspaper Guild. Avocations: writing, gardening, reading, camping. Office: Seattle Times PO Box 70 Seattle WA 98111-0070

GWIRE, WILLIAM, lawyer; b. Hof, Germany, Nov. 27, 1946; BA, Boise State U., 1971; JD with high honors, Golden Gate U., 1974. Bar: Calif. 1974, US Dist. Ct. (no. dist. Calif.) 1974, US Dist. Ct. (so. dist. Calif.) 1984. Served in air rescue and recovery USAF, 1966—70. Named a Super Lawyer, No. Calif. Super Lawyers, 2005, 2006; named one of Top 100 Attys., Worth mag., 2005, 2006. Mem.: Assn. Profl. Responsibility Attys., Internat. Bar Assn., San Francisco Trial Lawyers Assn., ABA (mem. litig. sect.), State Bar Calif. (arbitrator, fee disputes 1991—), Bar Assn. San Francisco (arbitrator, fee disputes 1991—, mem. litig. sect.). Office: Gwire Law Offices Ste 1100 455 Market St Ste 2220 San Francisco CA 94105-2446 Office Phone: 415-296-8880. Office Fax: 415-296-8029. E-mail: gwire@gwirelaw.com.

GWOZDZ, KIM ELIZABETH, interior and furniture designer; b. Spokane, Wash., June 10, 1958; d. Myron Marcus and Marilyn Kay (Alsterlund) Westerkamp; children: Ryan Marcus, Lauren Taylor. Student, U. Florence, Italy, 1979; BFA in Graphic Design, Illustration and Art History, U. Ariz., 1980. Interior designer Pat Bacon & Assocs., 1983-88; prin, interior designer Kim E. Gwozdz/Provenance, Phoenix, 1988—. Prin., designer Marcus Taylor Furniture. Contbr. articles to profl. jours. Mem. Mt. Cavalry Luth. Ch., Phoenix, 1981-96, trustee, 1993-96; mem. Christ Luth. Ch., Phoenix, 1996-2002; Jr. League of Phoenix, 1989—, HIV/AIDS com., 1994-2000; mem. Orpheum Theater com., 1989-94, vice chmn., 1990-91, chmn., 1992-2002, Gift Mart com. Design Decorations, 1991-92, chmn., 1991, exec. com. Orpheum Theatre Found., 1989-91, bd. dirs., 1992—; active annual gala com. Am. Cancer Soc., 1993-94, 94-95, 95-96, 97-98, 98—, March of Dimes Gourmet Gala, 1991, 93, 95, 97; design affiliate Nat. Trust for Hist. Preservation, 1986—. Recipient 1st place award Ann. Wool Rug Design Competition, Edward Fields, Inc., 1989, 2d place award, 1990, 3d place award, 1991; Internat. Illumination design awards, 1998, Cutler award, 1998, Lumen award, 1998. Mem. Am. Soc. Interior Designers (assoc. Ariz. North chpt., significant interiors survery com. 1975-91, chmn. 1990-91, Phoenix Home and Garden com. 1989-90, Herberger Theatre com. 1989-91, awards com. 1989, 91, chmn. 1990, competitions com. 1991, 96, chmn. 1989-90, Rosson House Christmas chmn. 1986-91, hist. preservation chmn. 1988-91, directory chmn. Designers Market 1991, project designer, 1996, 97, mem. nominating com. 1991-92, 98, mktg. com. 1995, 3d place award Ariz. Norh 1987, 96, 2d place award 1987, 88, 92, 95, 1st place award Nat. 1989, 94, 95, 97). Republican. Lutheran. Avocations: art, gardening, cooking. Home: 4820 E Merrell St Phoenix AZ 85018 Office: 2415 E Camelback Rd Ste 700 Phoenix AZ 85016-4245 Home Phone: 602-944-8663; Office Phone: 602-912-8552.

GYANI, MOHAN, communications company executive; b. Goa, India, June 15, 1951; MBA with distinction, San Francisco State U., 1978. V.p., contr. Pacific Bell; v.p., treas. Pacific Telesis; CFO for internat. subs. AirTouch Comm., San Francisco, v.p. fin., treas., 1994-95, exec. v.p., CFO, 1995-99; exec. v.p., CFO wireless svcs. unit AT&T, Redmond, Wash., 2000, pres., CEO wireless svcs. unit, 2000—. Former lectr. San Francisco State U.; participant Pvt. Sector Coun.; bd. dirs. PCS Prime Co. Inc., Mannesman Arcor. Mem. exec. bd. Boy Scouts Am.

HAAG, JOSEPH F., lawyer; BS in Mech. Engring., Northwestern U., 1994; JD magna cum laude, U. Minn., 1997. Bar: Mass., Mich., US Patent and Trademark Office. Ptnr. Intellect Property Dept. Wilmer Cutler Pickering Hale and Dorr LLP, Boston & Palo Alto, 2001—. Mem.: Order of Coif. Office: Wilmer Cutler Pickering Hale and Dorr LLP 1117 California Ave Palo Alto CA 94304 also: Wilmer Cutler Pickering Hale and Dorr LLP 60 State St Boston MA 02109 Office Phone: 650-858-6032. Office Fax: 650-858-6100. E-mail: joseph.haag@wilmerhale.com.

HAAN, STEVEN WILLIAM, physics researcher; b. Denver, Nov. 21, 1951; BS in Math. and Physics with honors, Calvin Coll., 1973; PhD in Physics, U. Md., 1977. Rsch. assoc. Nat. Bur. Stds., Gaithersburg, Md., 1977-79; lectr., rsch. assoc. dept. chem. U. Calif., Berkeley, 1979-81; staff physicist X-Divsn. Lawrence Livermore (Calif.) Nat. Lab., 1981-85, assoc. divsn. leader X-Divsn., 1985—. Recipient Alan Berman Rsch. Publ. award Naval Rsch. Lab., 1994. Fellow Am. Phys. Soc. (Excellence in Plasma Physics Rsch. award 1995, Edward Teller medal 1995). Office: Lawrence Livermore Nat Lab PO Box 808 L-23 Livermore CA 94551-0808 Home: 1988 Pulsar Ave Livermore CA 94550-6362

HAARSAGER, DENNIS LEE, broadcast executive; b. Wadena, Minn., Apr. 18, 1947; s. Ralph Oliver and Doris Blanche (Johnson) Haarsager; m. Julie Carol Wince, July 16, 1966 (div. 1976); 1 child, Jennie Ella; m. Sandra Lynn Smith, Jan. 1, 1977; children: Anna Lynn, Andrew Lee. BS, U. S.D., 1972, MA, 1975. Dir. adminstrn. S.D. Pub. TV Network, Vermillion, 1972—75; state coord. pub. broadcasting Idaho State Bd. Edn., Boise, 1975—78; gen. mgr. KWSU Radio-Television Services, 1978—95; assoc. v.p., gen. mgr. ednl. & pub. media Wash. State U., Pullman, 1995—; chmn. Nat. Pub. Radio (NPR), Washington, 2007—08, interim CEO, 2008—09. Owner H2A Comm., Moscow, 1982—; pres. Wash. Ednl. Network, 1980—82, 1983—84; chmn. Sta. Resource Group, 1990—93; v.p. West Coast Pub. Radio, 1990—92, pres., 1994—96; sec. Pacific Mountain Network, 1990—92, v.p., 1994—95; nat. coord. TV Small Sta. Assn., 1995—97; bd. dirs. Nat. Pub. Radio (NPR), 2005—, Am. Pub. Television, 2008—. Author: (computer software) H2A Microwave Transmission Planner, 1983. Dir. Washington-Idaho Symphony, 1984—87; bd. trustees Nat. Pub. Radio Found., 2007—. With USAF, 1966—69. Avocations: computer programming, amateur radio. Office: Wash State U Box 642530 382 Murrow Veterans Way Pullman WA 99164-0001 also: Nat Pub Radio 635 Massachusetts Ave NW Washington DC 20001 E-mail: haarsager@wsu.edu.

HAAS, CHARLIE, screenwriter; b. Bklyn., Oct. 22, 1952; s. Philip and Eunice (Dillon) H.; m. Barbara K. Moran, Dec. 21, 1981. BA, U. Calif., Santa Cruz, 1984. Editorial dir. Warner Bros. Records, Burbank, Calif., 1974-76; contbg. editor New West Mag., Beverly Hills, Calif., 1976-80; freelance writer LA, 1976-80, Oakland, Calif., 1980—. Co-author: (movies) Over the Edge, 1979, Tex, 1982, Gremlins 2, 1990, Matinee, 1993, Runaway Daughters, 1994; contbr. articles to mags. Mem. Friends of Oakland Parks & Recreation, Friends of Oakland Pub. Libr. Avocations: fountain pens, mountain bikes.

HAAS, RAYMOND P., lawyer; b. Corpus Christi, Tex., Dec. 9, 1942; BA cum laude, Yale U., 1964, LLB, 1967. Bar: Calif. 1967. Law clk. to Hon. Roger J. Traynor Supreme Ct. of Calif., 1967-68; atty. Howard, Rice, Nemerovski, Canady, Falk & Rabkin, San Francisco. Trustee San Francisco U. High Sch., 1973-78, 85-88, chmn., 1973-76, treas., 1986-88; trustee Pacific Presbyn. Med. Ctr., 1979-91, vice chmn. 1986-91. Mem. ABA (forum com. on franchising, antitrust law sect., bus. law sect., internat. law sect., patent, copyright and trademarks sect., sci. and tech. sect.), State Bar Calif., Bar Assn. San Francisco (computer law sect.), Licensing Execs. Soc., Internat. Tech. Law Assn., Order of Coif. Office: Howard Rice Nemerovski Canady Falk & Rabkin 3 Embarcadero Ctr Ste 7 San Francisco CA 94111-4074 Office Phone: 415-399-3090.

HAAS, ROBERT DOUGLAS, retired apparel company executive; b. San Francisco, Apr. 3, 1942; s. Walter A. Haas Jr. and Evelyn (Danzig) Haas; m. Colleen Gershon, Jan. 27, 1974; 1 child, Elise Kimberly. BA, U. Calif., Berkeley, 1964; MBA, Harvard U., 1968. With Peace Corps, Ivory Coast, 1964-66; fellow The White House, Washington, 1968-69; assoc. McKinsey & Co., 1969-72; with Levi Strauss & Co., San Francisco, 1973—2008, sr. v.p. corp. planning and policy, 1978-80, pres. new bus. group, 1980, pres. operating groups, 1980-81, exec. v.p., COO, 1981-84, pres., CEO, 1984-89, CEO, 1989—99, chmn., 1989—2008, chmn. emeritus, 2008—. Pres. Levi Strauss Found.; mem. Global leadership team. Hon. dir. San Francisco AIDS Found.; trustee Ford Found.; bd. dirs. Bay Area Coun.; past bd. dirs. Am. Apparel Assn. Fellow White House fellow, 1968—69. Mem.: Meyer Freidman Inst. (bd. dirs.), Calif. Bus. Roundtable, Trilateral Commn., Coun. Fgn. Rels., Conf. Bd., Bay Area Com., Brookings Inst. (trustee), Phi Beta Kappa.

HABER, SCOTT R., lawyer; BA, Cornell U., 1980, MBA, 1983, JD magna cum laude, 1984. Bar: Calif. 1984. Law clk. Hon. Richard J. Cardamone, US Ct. of Appeals, Second Cir., 1984; joined Latham & Watkins, 1985—, now ptnr. San Francisco. Editor: Cornell Law Rev., 1984. Mem.: ABA, Calif. Bar Assn., Order of Coif. Office: Latham & Watkins Ste 2000 505 Montgomery St San Francisco CA 94111-2562 Business E-Mail: scott.haber@lw.com.

HACKEN, CARLA, film company executive; Talent agent Internat. Creative Mgmt.; exec. v.p. Fox 2000 Fox Filmed Entertainment, 1999—. Named one of The 100 Most Powerful Women in Entertainment, Hollywood Reporter, 2007. Office: Fox 2000 Fox Filmed Entertainment 10201 W Pico Blvd Los Angeles CA 90035

HACKER, THOMAS OWEN, architect; b. Dayton, Ohio, Nov. 4, 1941; s. Homer Owen and Lydia (McLean) H.; m. Margaret (Brooks) Stewart, Mar. 21, 1965; children: Jacob, Sarah, Alice. BA, U. Pa., 1964, MArch, 1967. Registered arch., Oreg.; registered Nat. Coun. Archtl. Registration Bds. Intern architect Office of Louis I. Kahn, Phila., 1964-70; mem. faculty architecture U. Pa., Phila., 1967-69, U. Oreg., Eugene, 1970-84; design prin. Thomas Hacker and Assocs. Architects P.C., Portland, Oreg., 1983—. Vis. profl. architecture, U. Oreg., 1985—. Prin. works include Biomed. Info. Comm. Ctr., Oreg. Health Scis. U., Sch. Nursing, Oreg. Health Scis. U., Portland Art Mus., High Desert Mus., Bend, Oreg.; designer crystal vase for Steuben Inc., Spokane Pub. Libr., Yellowstone Art Mus., Billings, Mont., Lewis & Clark Coll. Signature Project, Multnomah County Librs., Columbia Gorge Interpretive Ctr., Portland State U. Urban Ctr., Whitman Coll. Penrose Meml. Libr., Portland 1st Unitarian Ch., Bend Pub. Libr. Office: 34 NW 1st Ave Ste 406 Portland OR 97209-4017 Home: 2762 SW Montgomery Dr Portland OR 97201-1693

HACKETT, ROBERT JOHN, lawyer; b. NYC, Feb. 6, 1943; s. John P. and Marie S. (Starace) Hackett; m. Anita Carlile, Apr. 19, 1969; children: Robert John Hackett Jr., John Peter, Kathryn Marie. AB, Rutgers U., 1964; JD, Duke U., 1967. Bar: NY 1967, Ariz. 1972. Assoc. Milbank, Tweed, Hadley, McCloy, NYC, 1967—71; ptnr. Evans, Kitchel & Jenckes, Phoenix, 1971—89; dir. Fennemore Craig, Phoenix, 1989—2004, course dir. seminar on mergers and acquisitions, 1996, 1999; mem. Jennings, Strouss & Salmon, P.L.C., Phoenix, 2004—. Mem. editl. bd. Duke Law Jour., 1966—67. Former bd. dirs. Xavier Coll. Prep., mem. steering com. for Fine Arts Ctr. capital campaign. Mem.: ABA (com. on fed. securities regulation), Maricopa County Bar Assn., State Bar Ariz. (past chmn. securities regulation sect.), Assn. Corp. Growth (past bd. dirs., past pres. Ariz. chpt.), Phoenix Duke U. Law Alumni Club (past pres.), Pi Sigma Alpha. Republican. Roman Catholic. Home Phone: 602-254-8038. Business E-Mail: rhackett@jsslaw.com.

HACKWOOD, SUSAN, electrical and computer engineering educator; b. Liverpool, Eng., May 23, 1955; came to U.S., 1980; d. Alan and Margaret Hackwood. BS with honors, DeMonfort U., Eng., 1976; PhD in Solid State Ionics, DeMontfort U., Eng., 1979; PhD (hon.), Worcester Poly. Inst., 1993; DSc (hon.), DeMontfort U., 1993. Rsch. fellow DeMonfort U., Leicester, Eng., 1976-79; postdoctoral rsch. fellow AT&T Bell Labs., Homdel, N.J., 1980-81, mem. tech. staff, 1981-83, supr. robotics tech., 1983-84, dept. head robotics tech., 1984-85; prof. elec. and computer engring. U. Calif., Santa Barbara, 1985-89, dir. Ctr. Robotic Systems in Microelectronics, 1985-89, dean Bourns Coll. Engring. Riverside, 1990-95; exec. dir. Calif. Coun. on Scis. and Tech., Riverside, 1995—. Editor Jour. Robotic Systems, 1983, Recent Advances in Robotics, 1985; contbr. over 100 articles to tech. jours.; 7 patents in field. Fellow AAAS, IEEE (sr.). Office: 5262 King St Riverside CA 92506-1623

HADAS, ELIZABETH CHAMBERLAYNE, editor; b. Washington, May 12, 1946; d. Moses and Elizabeth (Chamberlayne) H.; m. Jeremy W. Heist, Jan. 25, 1970 (div. 1976); m. Peter Eller, Mar. 21, 1984 (div. 1998). AB, Radcliffe Coll., 1967; postgrad., Rutgers U., 1967—68; MA, Washington U., St. Louis, 1971. Editor U. N.Mex. Press, Albuquerque, 1971—85, dir., 1985—2000, spl. acquisitions editor, 2000—06. Bd. dirs. N.Mex. Humanities Coun., 2001—07. Bd. dirs. Anne Noggle Found. 2007-; Mem. Assn. Am. U. Presses (pres. 1992-93). Democrat. Home: 2900 10th St NW Albuquerque NM 87107-1111 E-mail: ehadas@unm.edu.

HADDA, JANET RUTH, language educator, lay psychoanalyst; b. Bradford, Eng., Dec. 23, 1945; arrived in US, 1948; d. George Manfred and Annemarie (Kohn) H.; m. Allan Joshua Tobin, Mar. 22, 1981; stepchildren: David, Adam. BS in Edn., U. Vt., 1966; MA, Cornell U., 1969; PhD, Columbia U., 1975. Rsch. psychoanalyst So. Calif. Psychoanalytic Inst., LA, 1988—, tng. and supervising analyst, 1995—, Inst. Contemporary Psychoanalysis, 1993—; prof. Yiddish emerita UCLA, 2004—. Author: Yankev Glatshteyn, 1980, Passionate Women, Passive Men: Suicide in Yiddish Literature, 1988, Isaac Bashevis Singer: A Life, 1997, with New Introduction, 2003; contbr. articles to profl. jours. Mem. MLA, Assn. Jewish Studies, Am. Psychoanalytic Assn., Inst. Contemporary Psychoanalysis, New Ctr. Psychoanalysis, Phi Beta Kappa.

HADDAD, EDWARD RAOUF, civil engineer, consultant; b. Mosul, Iraq, July 1, 1926; came to U.S., 1990. s. Raouf Sulaiman Haddad and Fadhila (Sulaiman) Shaya; m. Balquis Yousef Rassam, July 19, 1961; children: Reem, Raid. BSc, U. Baghdad, Iraq, 1949; postgrad., Colo. State U., 1966-67; PhD (hon.), 1995. Project engr., cons. Min. Pub. Works, Baghdad, 1949-63; arbitrator Engring. Soc. & Ct., Kuwait City, Kuwait, 1963-90; tech. advisor Royal Family, Kuwait, 1987-90; cons. pvt. practice Haddad Engring., Albuquerque, 1990-95; owner, pres. Overseas Contacts-Internat. Bus. and Consulting, Albuquerque, 1995—. Organizer reps abroad, Kuwait, 1990. Pres. Parents Assn., U. N.Mex., 1995. Recipient Hon. medal Pope Paul VI of Rome, 1973, Men of Achievement award Internat. Biog. Ctr., 1994. Mem. ASCE, NSPE, ABA (assoc.), Am. Arbitration Assn. (mem. adv. bd.), Sierra Cath. Internat. (trustee), Lions (bd. dirs. 1992), Inventors Club (bd. dirs. 1992), KC (chancellor 1992). Address: 1425 Monte Largo Dr NE Albuquerque NM 87112-6378 E-mail: edward.haddad@yahoo.com.

HADDON, HAROLD ALAN, lawyer; b. Flint, Mich., Dec. 2, 1940; s. Russell Daniel and Virginia Sibyl (Johnston) H.; m. Beverly Jean Reading, July 2, 1966. AB, Albion Coll., 1962; A.M., U. Mich., 1963; JD, Duke U., 1966. Bar: Colo. 1966, U.S. Dist. Ct. Colo. 1966, U.S. Ct. Appeals (10th cir.) 1966, U.S. Supreme Ct. 1977; cert. trial counsel U.S. Cts. Martial. Asso. firm Davis, Graham & Stubbs, Denver, 1966-70; chief trial dep. Colo. Pub. Defender, 1970-73; ptnr. Haddon, Morgan & Foreman, Denver, 1975—. Adj. prof. law in criminal trial advocacy U. Denver Sch. Law, 1972-73; spl. prosecutor Colo. State Grand Jury, 1976-78 Editor-in-chief Duke Law Jour., 1965-66. Sec. Nat. Multiple Sclerosis Soc., 1970-76; mem. Colo. U.S. Jud. Selection Com., 1977, 93; campaign mgr. U.S. Sen. Gary W. Hart, 1974-80; fin. chmn. Colo. Gov. Richard D. Lamm, 1978; nat. polit. coordinator Hart for Pres. campaign, 1987. Lt. comdr. USNR, 1968—. Fellow Am. Coll. Trial Lawyers, 1988; mem. Am., Colo., Denver bar assns., Nat. Assn. Criminal Def. Lawyers, Order of Coif, Phi Beta Kappa, ABA (commn. on complex fed. criminal cases, 1981-82, criminal justice standards com., 1991-92, 2002-). Democrat. Office: Haddon Morgan Mueller Jordan Mackey & Foreman PC 150 E 10th Ave Denver CO 80203 E-mail: hhaddon@hmflaw.com.

HADDON, SAM ELLIS, lawyer; b. West Monroe, La., June 19, 1937; s. James Charlie and Letha (Daughtry) H.; m. Betty G. Loyd, Dec. 22, 1958; children: Elizabeth Anne Haddon Alexander, Steven Craig Haddon, Allison Lee Haddon Conover. BS, Rice U., 1959; student, Border Patrol Acad., El Paso, Tex., 1959-60, Treasury Law Enforcement Sch., Washington, 1961; JD with honors, U. Mont., 1965. Bar: Mont. 1965, U.S. Ct. Appeals (9th cir.) 1966, U.S. Dist. Ct. Mont. 1966, U.S. Supreme Ct. 1975. Immigration patrol insp. U.S. Border Patrol, 1959-61; agt. Fed. Bur. Narcotics, 1961-62; rsch. asst. in law U. Mont., 1964-65; law clk. to judge U.S. Dist. Ct., 1965-66; assoc. Anderson, Symmes, Forbes, Peete and Brown, Billings, Mont., 1966-69; ptnr. Boone, Karlberg, and Haddon, Missoula, Mont., 1969—. Instr. U. Mont. Sch. Law, 1971-99; chmn. Mont. Supreme Ct. Commn. on Rules of Evidence, 1975—; mem. Mont. Supreme Ct. Comm. on Practice, 1986—, chmn., 1996—; judge pro tem Mont. Dist. Ct. 4th Jud. Dist., 1975; spl. master Mont. Supreme Ct., 1978; del. Jud. Conf. 9th Cir., 1975, rep., 1977-80. Editor-in-chief Mont. Law Rev., 1964-65. Fellow Am. Coll. Trial Lawyers; mem. ABA, Am. Acad. Appellate Lawyers, Am. Judicature Soc. (bd. dirs. 1976-79), Am. Bd. Trial Advocates, Am. Law Inst., Mont. Bar Assn. (chmn. sect. young lawyers 1967-68, exec. com. 1968-69), State Bar Mont. (trustee 1976-78), Western Mont. Bar Assn. Office: PO Box 1529 Great Falls MT 59401-1529

HADFIELD, GILLIAN KERELDENA, economist, law educator; b. Toronto, Ont., Can., July 14, 1961; came to U.S. 1983; s. Colin David and Audrey Joan (Williams) H. BA with hons., Queen's U., Kingston, Ont., 1983; JD, Stanford U., 1988, MA in Econs., 1988, PhD in Econs., 1990. Law clk. to chief judge U.S. Ct. Appeals, D.C. Cir., Washington, 1988-89; asst. prof. U. Calif., Berkeley, 1990—94; nat. fellow Hoover Inst., 1993—94; assoc. prof. Univ. Toronto, 1995—98, prof., 1999—2001; ptnr. Law & Econ. Associates, 1995—98; prof. N.Y. Univ., 1999—2001, Univ. So. Calif. Law Sch., 2001—; prin. Law & Econ. Consulting Group, 2001—; vis. prof. Univ. Calif. Hastings Coll. Law. Mem. bd. adv. Inst. Policy Analysis, Univ. Toronto, 1997—2001. Co-author: The Second Wave of Law and Economics, 1999; contbr. chapters to books, articles to prof. jour. Social Scis. & Humanities Rsch. Coun. of Can. doctoral fellow, 1984; Mellon Found. fellow, 1987; Sloan Found. fellow, 1989; Nathan Burkan Nat. 1st prize, ASCAP, 1988; senior Olin fellow Columbia Law Sch. 1998; Connaught fellow Univ. Toronto 1999; Olin fellow Cornell Law Sch. 1999-2000, Univ. So. Calif. Law Sch. 2001. Mem. Am. Econ. Assn., Am. Law & Econ. Assn. (dir. 1995-98), Canadian Law & Econ. Assn. (pres. 1999-2000), Am. Law & Society Assn., Internat. Soc. New Institutional Econ., Order of the Coif. Avocations: hiking, canoeing. Office: The Law Sch Univ So Calif Los Angeles CA 90089

HADFIELD, TOMI SENGER, hospital administrator; b. Ft. Lee, Va., Dec. 8, 1954; d. Joseph Anthony and Vesta Ilene (Murray) Senger; m. Hal Burton Hadfield, June 6, 1975; children: Bradie Suzanne, Michael Burton, Evan Scott. Cert. in bus., U. N.D., 1975; BA in Bus., U. Calif., Riverside, 1979; M in Health Adminstrn., Chapman Coll., 1989. Project mgr. Control Data Corp., Mpls., 1980-84; asst. hosp. adminstr. Riverside Gen. Hosp., 1987—. Membership campaign cabinet Arthritis Found., Riverside, 1988, YWCA, Riverside, 1988, United Way, Riverside, 1988-89. Fellow Nat. Assn. Pub. Hosps.; mem. Calif. Assn. Pub. Hosps., So. Calif. Healthcare Mktg. Assn., Jr. League Riverside (v.p.), Medi-Trans (bd. dirs.), Riverside C. of C. (v.p. 1989—), Women in Healthcare. Avocations: travel, skiing, volunteer. Home: 1395 Rimroad Riverside CA 92506-5558 Office: Riverside Gen Hosp 26520 Cactus Ave Moreno Valley CA 92555-3911

HADLEY, MARLIN LEROY, financial planner, consultant; b. Mankato, Kans., Jan. 5, 1931; s. Charles LeRoy and Lillian Fern (Dunn) H.; m. Clarissa Jane Payne, Sept. 17, 1949; children: Michael LeRoy, Steven Lee. BS, U. Denver, 1953; postgrad., Harvard U., 1966. Pres. Jewel Home Shopping Service div. Jewel Cos., Inc., Barrington, Ill., 1953-72; pres., chief exec. officer, dir. Beeline Fashions, Inc., Bensenville, Ill., 1972-82; chmn. bd. HAS Originals, Blairstown, NJ, 1984—; fin., bus. cons. Pres., dir. Beeline Real Estate Corp., Act II Jewelry, Inc., Home Galleries, Inc.; dir. Goulder Co., Inc., Climax Spltys., Inc. Mem.: Economics (Chgo.). Home and Office: 7062 W Arlington Dr Lakewood CO 80123

HADLEY, PAUL BURREST, JR., (TABBIT HADLEY), domestic engineer; b. Louisville, Apr. 26, 1955; s. Paul Burrest and Rose Mary (Ruckert) H. Grad. in Computer Ops. and Programming, No. Ky. Vocat. Sch., 1975. Floor mgr. reconciling dept. Cen. Trust Co., Cin., 1974-76; freelance photographer Ky., Ohio, Colo., 1975—; chef mgr. The Floradora, Telluride, Colo., 1978-96; domestic engr. Telluride Resort Accomodations, 1996—2001, The River Club, 2001—03, Telluride (Colo.) Svcs., 2003—. Pres. Tabbit Enterprises; freelance recipe writer, Telluride, 1978— Author poetry (Golden Poet award 1989, Silver Poet award 1990); actor: (plays) Of Mice and Men, The Exercise, Crawling Arnold, A Thousand Clowns, The Authentic Life of Billy The Kid, others. Actor The Plunge Players, Telluride; v.p. Telluride Coun. for Arts and Humanities, 1989. Mem. Plan Internat. USA, Christian Children's Fund. Avocations: mountain climbing, hiking, photography, travel. Home: PO Box 923 Telluride CO 81435-0923 Personal E-mail: tabhad@peoplepc.com.

HADLEY, WILLIAM MELVIN, retired dean; b. San Antonio, June 4, 1942; s. Arthur Roosevelt and Audrey Merle (Barrett) H.; m. Dorothy J. Hadley, Jan. 21, 1967 (div. July 1989); children: Heather Marie, William Arthur; m. Jane F. Walsh, Oct. 13, 1990. BS in Pharmacy, Purdue U., West Lafayette, Ind., 1967, MS in Pharmacology, 1971, PhD in Toxicology, 1972. Teaching and grad. asst. Purdue U., West Lafayette, 1967-72; asst. prof. U. N.Mex., Albuquerque, 1972-76, assoc. prof., 1976-82, prof., 1982—2002, asst. dean Coll. Pharmacy, 1984-86, acting dean Coll. Pharmacy, 1985, dean Coll. Pharmacy, 1986—2002; prof. and dean emeritus Coll. Pharmacy, 2002—. Vis. scientist Lovelace Inhalation Toxicology Inst., Albuquerque, 1981, adj. scientist, 1991-2002, sr. scientist, 2002—; adv. bd. Waste Edn. Rsch. Consortium, Las Cruces, N.Mex., 1989-2003; dirs. adv. com. Nat. Ctr. for Eviron. Health, CDC, 2002-04, mem. NIH Proposal Rev. Panels, Bethesda, Md., 1983-84; mem. Gov.'s PCB Expert Adv. Panel, Santa Fe, 1985-86; sci. adv. bd. Carlsbad Environ. Monitoring Ctr., 1992-97; sci. adv. com. S.W. Regional Spaceport, Las Cruces, 1992-94; bd. dirs. Ctr. Excellence Hazardous Materials Mgmt., Carlsbad, N.Mex., 2005—; cons. in field. Steering com. United Fund, U.N.Mex., 1987, key person, 1988—97. NIH grantee, 1974-80, 83-87; Bowl of Hygeia, N.Mex. Pharm. Assn., 1998. Mem. AAAS, Am. Pharm. Assn., Am. Assn. Colls. of Pharmacy, Soc. Toxicology (pres. Rocky Mt. chpt. 1990-91), Western Pharmacology Soc. Republican. Achievements include research in biotransformation of xenobiotics with emphasis on nasal tissue; effects of heavy metals on biotransformation with emphasis on cadmium; toxic effects of xenobiotics on the immune system. Office Phone: 623-465-1813. Personal E-mail: wmhadley@aol.com.

HAEGER, JOHN DENIS, academic administrator; BA, M, D, Loyola U., Chgo. Prof., history dept. Ctrl. Mich. U., chair, history dept., interim dean, coll. grad. studies, assoc. dean, coll. grad. studies, dean, coll. arts & sci., dir., grad. student affairs; provost, v.p. Towson U.; provost, academic student affairs divsn. Northern Ariz. U., pres., 2001—. Chair, coun. of presidents Big Sky Conf.; mem. Ariz. Bd. Edn., P-20 Coun.; mem., bd. dirs. Transitional Genomics Rsch. Inst.; commr. Western Interstate Commn. Higher Edn. Contbr. articles to jours. Former chair United Way, Northern Ariz. bd. Office: No AZ U S San Francisco St Flagstaff AZ 86011

HAERLE, PAUL RAYMOND, judge; b. Portland, Oreg., Jan. 10, 1932; s. George William and Grace (Soden) H.; m. Susan Ann Wagner, May 30, 1953 (div. Apr. 1973); children: Karen A. Haerle D'Or, David A.; m. Michele A. Monson, June 1, 1991. AB, Yale U., 1953; JD, U. Mich., 1956. Bar: Calif. 1956, U.S. Supreme Ct. 1962. Assoc. Thelen, Marrin, Johnson & Bridges, San Francisco, 1956-64, ptnr., 1965-67, 69-94, mng. ptnr., 1990-93; appointments sec. Office of Gov., State of Calif., Sacramento, 1967-69; assoc. justice Calif. Ct. Appeal (1st dist.), San Francisco, 1994—. Lawyer rep. 9th Cir. Jud. Conf., 1985-88. Editor-in-chief Mich. Law Rev., 1955-56 Presdl. elector, 1972; del. Rep. Nat. Conv., 1972; vice chmn. Calif. Rep. Com., 1973-75, chmn., 1975-77; mem. Rep. Nat. Com., 1975-77; chair applicants evaluation and nominating com. 2003-; trustee World Affairs Coun. No. Calif., 1997-2003; mem. adv. com. on internat. law U.S. Dept. State, 2002-06; regional panelist, White House Fellowship Program, 2008-. Fellow Am. Coll. Trial Lawyers; mem. Yale Club of San Francisco, Order of Coif. Avocations: tennis, travel, hiking. Office: Calif Ct Appeal 350 McAllister St San Francisco CA 94102-3600

HAFEMEISTER, DAVID WALTER, physicist; b. Chgo., July 1, 1934; s. Lester David and Alma Doris (Schmidt) H.; m. Gina Rohlander, June 10, 1961; children: Andrew, Jason, Heidi. MS in Physics, U. Ill., 1959, PhD in Physics, 1964. Asst. prof. physics Carnegie-Mellon U., Pitts., 1966-69; prof. physics Calif. Poly. State U., San Luis Obispo, 1969-2000; study dir. on arms control on beyond START NAS, Washington, 2000—02; chair external rev. com. Los Alamos Nonproliferation Divsn., 2003—06; sci. fellow Ctr. Internat. Security and Cooperation Stanford U., 2005—06; sr. tech. adv. Arms Control Assn., 2009. Sci. advisor Sen. John Glenn US Senate, Washington, 1975-77; spl. asst. to Under Sec. State Benson and Nye US State Dept., Washington, 1977-79; vis. scientist U. Groningen, The Netherlands, 1971, 80, Program Sci. Tech. in Internat. Security, MIT, Cambridge, 1983-84, Ctr. for Bldg. Scis. Lawrence Berkeley (Calif.) Lab., 1985-86, Office Strategic Nuc. Policy US Dept. State, 1987, Ctr. Internat. Security and Arms Control Stanford U., 1988; program on nuc. policy alternatives Princeton U., 1989; profl. staff Senate Fgn. Rels. Com., 1990-92; staff Senate Gov. Affairs Com., 1992-93, Sch. Pub. Affairs, U. Md., 1996; Foster fellow Office of Strategic Negotiations, US Arms Control and Disarmament Agy., 1997-98. Author: Physics of Societal Issues, 2007; co-author: Physics of Modern Architecture, 1983; co-editor: Energy Sources: Conservation and Renewables, 1985, Physics Sustainable Energy, 2008, Arms Control Verification, 1986, Nuclear Arms Technologies in the 1990s, 1988, Physics and Nuclear Arms Today, 1990, Physics of Sustainable Energy, 2008, Global Warming: Physics and Facts, 1991, Biological Effects of Low-Frequency Electromagnetic Fields, 1998. Fellow Am. Phys. Soc. (chmn. forum on physics and soc. 1985-86, chair panel on pub. affairs 1996, Leo Szilard award for Physics in the Pub. Interest 1996); mem. AAAS (congl. fellow 1975-76, arms control fellow 1987), Fedn. Am. Scientists, Arms Control Assn., Am. Inst. Physics (co-editor books). Home: 553 Serrano Dr San Luis Obispo CA 93405 Business E-Mail: dhafemei@calpoly.edu.

HAFEY, JOSEPH MICHAEL, health association executive; b. Annapolis, Md., June 25, 1943; s. Edward Earl Joseph and Verna (Hedlund) H.; m. Mary Kay Miller, Dec. 30, 1978; children: Erin Catherine, Ryan Michael. BA, Whittier Coll., 1965; MPA, UCLA, 1967. Sr. asst. health officer HHS, Washington, 1967-69; dir. govt. relations Alliance for Regional Community Health, St. Louis, 1969-71; exec. dir. Contra Costa Comprehensive Health Assn., Richmond, Calif., 1971-74, Bay Area Comprehensive Health Planning Coun., San Francisco, 1974-76, Western Ctr. for Health Planning, San Francisco, 1976-86, Western Consortium for Pub. Health, Berkeley, 1980-95; pres., CEO Pub. Health Inst. (formerly Calif. Pub. Health Found.), 1985—. Chmn. Contra Costa Pub. Health Adv. Body, Martinez, Calif., 1987-93; founder Calif. Coalition for Future of Pub. Health, Sacramento, 1988—; co-founder Calif. Healthy Cities Program, Berkeley, 1987—. Chmn. United Way Com. for the Uninsured, San Francisco, 1985-93; bd. dirs. Eugene O'Neill Found., 1980-89. With USPHS, 1967-69. Recipient fellowship WHO, Geneva, 1987. Mem. Am. Pub. Health Assn. (governing coun. 1984-87), Am. Health Planning Assn. bd. dirs., chmn. annual meeting 1982). Avocations: jogging, tennis, skiing, collecting political campaign buttons. Home: 1749 Toyon Rd Lafayette CA 94549-2111 Office: Pub Health Inst 555 12th St Oakland CA Office Phone: 510-285-5531. Business E-Mail: joehafey@phi.org.

HAFFNER, F. KINSEY, lawyer; b. San Francisco, Feb. 20, 1948; BA with distinction, Stanford U., 1971, JD, 1974. Bar: Calif. 1974, DC. Ptnr. Pillsbury, Madison & Sutro, San Jose & Palo Alto, Calif., 1980—2000; sr. v.p. & gen. counsel Converge Inc., 2001; ptnr. Pillsbury Winthrop LLP, NYC & Palo Alto, Calif., 2002—05; ptnr., co-chmn. Global Sourcing practice Pillsbury Winthrop Shaw Pittman, NYC & Palo Alto, Calif., 2005—. Office: Pillsbury Winthrop Shaw Pittman 1540 Broadway New York NY 10036 also: Pillsbury Winthrop Shaw Pittman 2475 Hanover St Palo Alto CA 94304-1114 Office Phone: 212-858-1747. Office Fax: 212-858-1500. Business E-Mail: kinsey.haffner@pillsburylaw.com.

HAFTER, ERVIN R., psychology educator; Prof. dept. psychology U. Calif., Berkeley. Office: U Calif Dept Psychology Berkeley CA 94720-0001

HAFTER, RUTH ANNE, library director, educator; b. NYC, Apr. 18, 1935; BA in History and Econs. cum laude, Brandeis U., 1956; cert. Bus. Adminstrn., Harvard-Radcliffe U., 1957; MLS, Columbia U., 1963; PhD in Libr. and Info. Studies, U. Calif., Berkeley, 1984. Supr. sch. librs. Halifax County, N.S., Can., 1965-66; asst. edn. libr. Harvard U., Cambridge, Mass., 1967-68; univ. libr. St. Mary's U., Halifax, N.S., Can., 1969-75; libr. dir. Sonoma State U., Rohnert Park, Calif., 1978-86, San Jose (Calif.) State U., 1986-91, prof. div. libr. and info. sci., 1987-99, prof. emeritus, 1999—. Instr. St. Mary's U., 1972-75, Sonoma State U., 1982-85, U. Calif., Berkeley, 1975-78, 85-86; cons. Ministry of State Urban Affairs, Can., 1975, Sonoma County Hist. Records, 1979-80; coord. Geysers Info. Project., 1980-81; project humanist Calif. Coun. for Humanities, 1981-83; dir. Indochinese Cultures project Nat. Endowment for Humanities, 1983-84, Videodisc Work Shop Calif. State U., 1987—, Online Pub. Catalog Implementation, 1989; pres. Beethoven Ctr. San Jose State U., 1987-88. Author: Academic Librarians and Cataloging Networks: Visibility, Quality and Professional Status, 1986, (with George Rawlyk) Acadian Education in Nova Scotia, 1970; contbr. articles to profl. jours. Mem. Mayor Feinstein's com. on Teaching of Holocaust, San Francisco, 1986, adv. com. Foothill Coll. Libr. Tech. Asst. Program, 1987—, San Jose Pub. Libr. Found., 1987—, bd. govs. 1987-89, exec. bd. Friends of San Jose Pub. Libr., 1989—, Calif. State Libr. Networking Task Force, 1989—, adv. bd. dirs. Frances Gullard Child Devel. Ctr., 1990—; pres. alumni bd. Sch. Libr. and Info. Sci, U. Calif., Berkeley, 1993-94. Inst. Ethnography grantee Dept. Edn., 1994-95. Mem. ALA (com. on accreditation, field site vis. bd. 1982—, libr. career resource network 1987—, program com. reference and adult svcs. div. 1989—), Coop. Libr. Agy. Systems and Svcs. (bd. govs. 1988—, acad. librs. rep.), Calif. Acad. and Rsch. Librs. (pres. 1983-84), Calif. Libr. Assn. (legis. network 1988—, chair continuing edn. com. 1997), North Bay Coop. Assn. (exec. com. 1984-85), Phi Beta Kappa, Phi Kappa Phi. Home: 177 19th St Apt 1E Oakland CA 94612-4653 E-mail: rhafter@earthlink.net.

HAGA, DAVID L., lawyer; BS, W.Va. U., 1958; LLB with high distinction, U. Ariz., 1965; LLM in Tax, NYU, 1967. Bar: Ariz. 1965, U.S. Dist. Ct. Ariz. 1965, U.S. Tax Ct. 1965, U.S. Ct. Appeals (9th cir.) 1965, U.S. Supreme Ct. 1965, cert.: Ariz. Bd. Legal Specialization (tax specialist). Law clk. to Hon. Jesse H. Udall Supreme Ct. State of Ariz., 1965—66; shareholder, atty. Gallagher & Kennedy, P.A., Phoenix, 1999—. Mem. com. exams. Ariz. Supreme Ct., 1987—94, chmn., 1993—94. Asst. editor: Ariz. Law Rev. Bd. dirs. Ariz. Found. Legal Svcs. and Edn., sec., 2002, treas., 2003; bd. visitors U. Ariz. Law Sch., 1998—2004. Mem.: ABA, Order of Coif, Ariz. Bar Assn. (mem. specialization com. 1983—87), Maricopa County Bar Assn., Ctrl. Ariz. Estate Planning Coun., State Bar Ariz. (mem. com. preparid and group legal svcs. 1974—76, mem. tax sect. 1974—, pres. 1981—82), Phoenix Country Club, Phi Delta Phi. Office: Gallagher and Kennedy PA 2575 E Camelback Rd Phoenix AZ 85016-9225 Office Phone: 602-530-8380. Business E-Mail: dlh@gknet.com.

HAGEDORN, ROBERT (BOB), JR, state legislator; b. Elizabeth City, NC, Feb. 16, 1952; son of Robert L Hagedorn & Lee M Bahlmann H; married 1975 to Ann Gardiner Stoddart, division; children: Robert G. Assistant government relations director, Metro Wastewater Reclamation District, Denver, 87-89; Colorado State Representative, District 42, 1992-2001, member, Bus Affairs & Labor & Local Govt Committees, 93-94, member, Health Environ, Welfare & Inst & State, Vet & Mil Affairs Committees, formerly, Colorado House Representative; member, Tax & Fiscal Policy Task Force, America Legislature Exchange Coun, currently; Colorado State Senator, District 29, 2001-, chairman Health & Human Servs Committee, currently, member, Transportation and Joint Computer Management Committees, currently, Colorado State Senator.Newspaper reporter, Aurora Sun, Colorado, 72-75; owner, Public Relations/Printing, Denver, Colorado, 75-79; col relations director, Peru State Col, Peru, Nebraska, 79-80; community relations director, Aurora Public Sch, Colorado, 80-83; accounting repr, Aspen Graphics, Denver, Colorado, 83-87; consultant, self-employed, Aurora, Colorado, 89-92; instructor political sci, Metrop State Col, Denver, Colorado, 90-. Bus Legislator of Year, Colorado Association Commerce & Indust, 95. Democratic Bus Coalition; Downtown Aurora Bus Association; Soc Prof Jounalists; Democratic Leadership Coun; Nat Conf State Legislators. Democrat. Presbyterian. Mailing: 200 E Colfax Rm 271 Denver CO 80203 E-mail: senbob@msn.com; bhagedor@sni.net.

HAGEN, DAVID WARNER, retired judge; b. 1931; BBA, U. Wis., 1956; LLB, U. San Francisco, 1959. Bar: Washoe County 1981, Nev. 1992. With Berkley, Randall & Harvey, Berkeley, Calif., 1960-62; pvt. practice Loyalton, Calif., 1962-63; with Guild, Busey & Guild (later Guild, Hagen and Clark Ltd. and Guild & Hagen Ltd.), Reno, 1963-93; judge US Dist. Ct. Nev., Reno, 1993—2005, chmn. 9th Cir. Art. III Judge's Edn. Com., 1998—2000; ret., 2005. Lectr U. Nev., 1968-72; acting dean Nev. Sch. of Law, 1981-83, adj. prof., 1981-87; mem. Nev. Bd. Bar Examiners, 1972-91, chmn., 1989-91; chmn. Nev. Continuing Legal Edn. Com., 1967-75; mem. Nev. Uniform Comml. Code Com. Sgt. USAF, 1949—52. Fellow Am. Coll. Trial Lawyers (state chmn. 1983-85); mem. Nev. Bar Assn., Calif. Bar Assn., Washoe County Bar Assn., Am. Bd. Trial Advocates (advocate), Nat. Maritime Hist. Soc., VFW, U.S. Sailing Assn. Office Phone: 775-848-2695. Personal E-mail: dwhadr@aol.com.

HAGEN, NICHOLAS STEWART, medical educator, consultant; b. Plentywood, Mont., Aug. 6, 1942; s. William Joseph and June Janette (Reuter) H.; m. Mary Louise Edvalson, July 26, 1969; children: Brian Geoffrey, Lisa Louise, Eric Christopher, Aaron Daniel, David Michael. BS in Chemistry, Ariz. State U., 1964; MBA in Internat. Bus., George Washington U., 1969; MD, U. Ariz., 1974. Lic. physician Ariz., Utah, Idaho.; diplomate Nat. Bd. Med. Examiners. Intern., resident Good Samaritan Hosp., Phoenix, 1974-75; pvt. practice Roy, Utah, 1975-77; dir. clin. rsch. Abbott Labs., North Chicago, Ill., 1977-84; v.p. med. affairs Rorer Group, Inc., Ft. Washington, Pa., 1984-88; clin. prof. Ariz. State U., Tempe, 1988-90. Pres. Southwestern Clin. Rsch., Tempe, 1987—, Travel Profl. Internat., Tempe, 1989-98; mem. Ariz. Bd. Med. Student Loans, 1998-2002. Author: Valproic Acid: A Review of Pharmacologic Properties and Clinical Use in Pharmacologic and Biochemical Properties of Drug Substances, 1979; contbr. articles to med. jours.; patentee in field. Bishop Ch. Jesus Christ of Latter-day Saints, Gurnee, Ill., 1981-84; various positions with local couns. Boy Scouts Am., 1988—; active Rep. campaigns, Mesa, Ariz., 1988—; 2d vice chmn. Maricopa County Rep. Assembly, 1997-99; dist. republican chmn., 1996-98; mem. governing bd. East Valley Inst. Tech., 1998-2003. Lt. comdr. USCG, 1965-69. Joan Mueller-Etter scholar Ariz. State U., 1960, Phelps-Dodge scholar Ariz. State U., 1961; NASA fellow Brigham Young U., 1964. Mem. Am. Coll. Sports Medicine, Eagle Forum, Nat. Right-to-Life Assn., Utah Hist. Soc., Nat. Geneal. Soc., Bucks County Geneal. Soc., Sons of Norway, Soc. Descendants Emigrants from Numedal, Hallingdal and Hedmark, Norway, Blue Key, Archons, Kappa Sigma (treas. Greater Phoenix alumni chpt. 1999—), Beta Beta Beta, Alpha Epsilon Delta, Phi Eta Sigma, Sophos. Republican. Mem. Lds Ch. Avocations: genealogy, swimming, stamp collecting/philately, medieval history, art collecting. Office: 9802 E Irwin Ave Mesa AZ 85209

HAGENBUCH, JOHN JACOB, investor; b. Park Forest, Ill., May 31, 1951; s. David Brown and Jean Iline (Reeves) H.; m. Kimberly A. Steel, Aug. 20, 2000; children: Henry, Hunter, Hilary, Sydney, John. AB magna cum laude, Princeton U., 1974; MBA, Stanford U., 1978. Assoc. Salomon Bros., NYC, 1978-80, v.p. San Francisco, 1980-85; gen. ptnr. Hellman & Friedman, 1985-93; chmn. M&H Realty Ptnrs., L.P., 1993—. Chmn. Onconome, Inc., 2005—. Mem. Burlingame Country Club, Pacific-Union Club, Calif. Tennis Club, Villa Taverna Club, Bohemian Club, Valley Club. Office: M&H Realty Ptnrs 425 California St San Francisco CA 94104

HAGER, MICHAEL W., museum director; m. Denise LeAnn Rikansrud; children: Amy, Brian. BA in Biology, Grinnell Coll.; PhD in Geology, U. Wyo. Asst. prof. geology Augustana Coll., 1973-78; dir. Mus. of the Rockies, Mont., 1978-89, Va. Mus. Natural History, Va., 1989-91; exec. dir. San Diego Natural History Mus., Calif., 1991—. Mus. cons. Exec. prodr. film Baja California, 2000. Bd. dirs. com. Balboa Pk., Cultural Partnership, Immigration Mus. New Ams.

Mem. Assn. Sci. Mus. Dirs. (past pres.). Office: San Diego Natural History Mus PO Box 121390 San Diego CA 92112-1390 Office Phone: 619-255-0216, 619-255-0216. Business E-Mail: mhager@sdnhm.org.

HAGGERTY, ANCER LEE, federal judge; b. 1944; BS, U. Oreg., 1967; JD, Hastings Coll. Law, 1973. Law clk. Metro. Pub. Defender, Portland, 1972, 73, staff atty., 1973-77; assoc. Souther, Spaulding, Kinzey, Williamson and Schwabe, 1977-82, Schwabe, Williamson & Wyatt, 1983-88; judge Multnomah County Dist. Ct., 1989-90, Multnomah County Cir. Ct., 1990-93; dist. judge US Ct. Appeals (9th cir.), Portland, Oreg., 1994—, chief judge, 2002—. Mem. Gov.'s task force evaln.Oreg. Liquor Control Commn., 1978, Jud. Conduct Com., 1989-92; coord. Multnomah County Bar Pro Bono program, 1983-88; mem. Oreg. State Bd. Bar Examiners, 1979-82. Coach, practice judge mock ct. team Jefferson H.S.; asst. coach Whitaker 7th and 8th grade Pop Warner football teams. 1st lt. USMC, 1967-70, Vietnam. Decorated Silver Star medal, Purple Heart; recipient award Alumni Assn. U. Oreg., Local Hero award Martin Luther King, Jr. Elem. Sch. Fifth Grade, 1993. Mem. ABA, Am. Bridge Assn., Oreg. State Bar Assn., Nat. Bar Assn., Lloyd Ctr. Racquet Club, Marine Corps League, Phoenix Bridge Club. Address: US District Ct Mark O Hatfield US Courthouse 1000 SW 3rd Ave Portland OR 97204-2902

HAGGIS, PAUL EDWARD, scriptwriter, television producer, television director; b. London, Ont., Can., Mar. 10, 1953; came to US, 1979; s. Edward H. and Mary Yvonne (Metcalf) H.; m. Diane Christine Gettas, Apr. 9, 1977-94; children: Alissa Sullivan, Lauren Kilvington, Katy Elizabeth; m. Deborah Rennard, Jun. 21, 1997; 1 child. Studied, Fanshawe Coll., London. Writer: (TV series) One Day at a Time, 1975, The Love Boat, 1977, Diff'rent Strokes, 1978, The Facts of Life, 1979, (also prodr. 1984-86), The Tracey Ullman Show, 1987, Thirtysomething, 1987 (Emmy award for Outstanding Drama Series, 1988), Walker, Texas Ranger, 1993 (also creator), (TV films) The Return of the Shaggy Dog, 1987, (films) The Last Kiss, 2006, Flags of Our Fathers, 2006, Casino Royale, 2006, Quantum of Solace, 2008; writer, dir.: (films) Red Hot, 1993; writer, exec. prodr.: (TV films) Due South, 1994, (TV series) Michael Hayes, 1997; writer, prodr.: (films) Million Dollar Baby, 2004; writer, exec. prodr., dir.: (TV series) EZ Streets, 1996-97, Family Law, 1999, (TV films) Ghost of a Chance, 1998; writer, prodr., dir.: (films) Crash, 2004 (Best Writer, Broadcast Film Critics Assn., 2006, Original Screenplay, British Acad. Film and TV Arts, 2006, Best First Feature, Independent Spirit award, 2006, Motion Picture of Yr. and Original Screenplay, Acad. Motion Picture Arts & Sciences, 2006); exec. prodr. (TV series) Crash, 2008. Trustee Found. for Religious Freedom; mem. adv. bd. Mus. Broadcasting; co-founder Artists for Peace and Justice, bd. dirs. Hollywood Edn. Lteracy Project, For the Arts for Every Child, Environmental Media Assn.; founding mem. Earth Comm. Office; mem. adv. bd. Ctr. Advancement Non-Violence; mem. Pres. Coun. Defenders of Wildlife. Office: Becsey Wisdom Kalajian Agency 849 S Wooster St Apt 7 Los Angeles CA 90035-1792

HAGMAN, CURT, state legislator; m. Grace Hagman; 2 children. BA, Calif. U. Commr. Parks Recreation, Chino Hills; mem. City Coun.; Mayor Chino Hills; founding mem. & chmn. Cmty. Volunteers; pres. Kiwanis Club, Chino Hills; bd. dirs. Chino Valley YMCA; chmn. Bernardino County Workforce Investment Bd.; mem. Calif. State Assembly, 2008—. Republican. Mailing: Diamond Bar Office 23355 E Golden Springs Dr Diamond Bar CA 91765 Office: Capitol Office PO Box 942849 Rm 4116 Sacramento CA 94249-0060 Office Phone: 909-860-5560, 916-319-2060. Office Fax: 909-860-5664, 916-319-2160.*

HAGOOD, RICHARD A., academic administrator, educator; b. Ontario, Oreg. m. Junella Hagood; children: Heidi, Holly, Lincoln. BA in History, Northwest Nazarene U.; MA, U. Oreg.; PhD in Educational Policy Studies, U. Ill. With Wash. State U., 1983—93, assoc. provost office of exec. v.p. and provost Pullman, 1990—93; pres. N.W. Nazarene U., 1993—. Spkr. in field. Mem. bd. dirs. Nampa Sch. Dist., US/Can. Coun. of Edn., Ch. Nazarene; mem. gen. bd. Ch. Nazarene, 1997—2001; mem. bd. dirs. Boise Airport Comm., Great Northwest Athletic Conf., United Way; chmn. bd. dirs. Mercy Med. Ctr. Office: NW Nazarene U 623 Holly St Nampa ID 83686

HAHN, ELLIOTT JULIUS, lawyer; b. San Francisco, Dec. 9, 1949; s. Leo Wolf and Sherry Marion (Portnoy) H.; m. Toby Rose Mallen; children: Kara Rebecca, Brittany Atira Mallen, Michael Mallen, Adam Mallen. BA cum laude, U. Pa., 1971, JD, 1974; LLM, Columbia U., 1980. Bar: N.J. 1974, Calif. 1976, D.C. 1978, U.S. Dist. Ct. N.J. 1974, U.S. Dist. Ct. (cen. dist.) Calif. 1976, U.S. Supreme Ct. 1980. Assoc. von Malitz, Derenberg, Kunin & Janssen, NYC, 1974-75; law clk. L.A. County Superior Ct., 1975-76; atty. Atlantic Richfield Co., LA, 1976-79; prof. Summer in Tokyo program Santa Clara Law Sch., 1981-83; assoc. prof. law Calif. Western Sch. Law, San Diego, 1980-85; atty. Morgan, Lewis & Bockius, LA, 1985-87; assoc. Whitman & Ransom, LA, 1987-88, ptnr., 1989-93, Sonnenschein Nath & Rosenthal, LA, 1993-97, Hahn & Bolson, LLP, 1997—. Vis. scholar Nihon U., Tokyo, 1982; vis. lectr. Internat. Christian U., Tokyo, 1982; adj. prof. law Southwestern U. Sch. Law, 1986-93, Pepperdine U. law Sch., 1986-93, U. So. Calif. Law Sch., 1997-98; lectr. U. Calif., Davis, Law Sch. Orientation in U.S.A. Law Program, 1994-97. Author: Japanese Business Law and the Legal System, 1984; contbr. chpt. on Japan to The World Legal Ency.; internat. law editor Calif. Bus. Law Reporter. Vice-chmn. San Diego Internat. Affairs Bd., 1981-85; bd. dirs. San Diego-Yokohama Sister City Soc., 1983-85, L.A.-Nagoya Sister City Soc., 1986-1996; mem. master planning com. City of Rancho Palos Verdes, Calif., 1989-91; advisor, exec. com. Calif. Internat. Law Sect., 1990-91, 95, appointee exec. com., 1991-94, vice-chmn., 1992-93, chair, 1993-94; appointee, trustee Palos Verdes Libr. Dist., 1993-94; bd. dirs. Internat. Student Ctr. UCLA, 1996-2004, pres., 2000-01; mem. Congress Fellows Ctr. Internat. Legal Studies, 2002-. Fellow Ctr. Internat. Legal Studies; mem. ABA, State Bar Calif., LA County Bar Assn. (bd. dirs. internat. sect., exec. com. Internat. Legal Sec. 1987—, sec. 1995-96, 2d v.p. 1996-97, 1st v.p. 1997-98, chmn. 1998-99, appointee Pacific rim com. 1990-98, chmn. 1991-92, 95-98, trustee 1997-98), Assn. Asian Studies, U. Pa. Alumni Club (pres. San Diego chpt. 1982, pres. coun. Phila. 1983), Anti Defamation League, Japanese-Am. Soc. (book rev. editor Seattle 1983-85). Jewish. Office: 21250 Hawthorne Blvd Ste 500 Torrance CA 90503 Home Phone: 310-377-4940; Office Phone: 310-792-7406. Business E-Mail: ehahn@hahnbolsonllp.com.

HAHN, ERWIN LOUIS, physicist, researcher; b. Sharon, Pa., June 9, 1921; s. Israel and Mary Hahn; m. Marian Ethel Failing, Apr. 8, 1944 (dec. Sept. 1978); children: David L., Deborah A., Katherine L.; m. Natalie Woodford Hodgson, Apr. 12, 1980. BS, Juniata Coll., 1943, D.Sc., 1966; MS, U. Ill., 1947, PhD, 1949; D.Sc., Purdue U., 1975, U. Stuttgart, Germany, 2001; DrRerNat, U. Stuttgart, 2001; DSc in Physics, U. Warwick, Eng., 2007. Asst. Purdue U., 1943-44; research assoc. U. Ill., 1950; NRC fellow Stanford, 1950-51, instr., 1951-52; research physicist Watson IBM Lab., NYC, 1952-55; assoc. Columbia U., 1952-55; faculty U. Calif., Berkeley, 1955—, prof. physics, 1961—, assoc. prof., then prof. Miller Inst. for Basic Rsch., 1958-59, 66-67, 85-86. Eastman vis. prof. Balliol Coll., Oxford, Eng., 1988-89; cons. Office Naval Rsch., Stanford, 1950-52, AEC, 1955—; spl. cons. USN, 1959; adv. panel mem. Nat. Bur. Stds., Radio Stds. div., 1961-64; mem. NAS/NRC com. on basic rsch.; advisor to U.S. Army Rsch. Office, 1967-69; faculty rsch. lectr. U. Calif., Berkeley, 1979. Author: (with T.P. Das) Nuclear Quadrupole Resonance Spectroscopy, 1958. Served with USNR, 1944-46. Fellow Guggenheim Found., 1961-62, 69-70, NSF, 1961-62; recipient prize Internat. Soc. Magnetic Resonance, 1971, Humboldt Found. award, 1977, 94, Alumni Achievement award Juniata Coll., 1986, citation U. Calif., Berkeley, 1991, Russell Varian prize Varian Corp., 2004; Wolf prize in physics, Wolf Found., Israel, 1984; named to Calif. Inventor Hall of Fame, 1984; vis. fellow Brasenose Coll., Oxford U., 1969-70, life hon. fellow, 1984—. Fellow AAAS, Internat. Soc. Electron Paramagnetic Resonance, Am. Phys. Soc. (past mem. exec. com. div. solid state physics, Oliver E. Buckley prize 1971), Soc. Magnetic Resonance in Medicine (hon.), Royal Soc. U.K. (London fgn. mem.); mem. NAS (co-recipient Comstock prize in electricity, magnetism and radiation 1993), French Acad. Sci. (fgn.), Acad. Arts and Scis., Slovenian Acad. Scis. and Arts (fgn.), Berkeley Fellows. Home: 69 Stevenson Ave Berkeley CA 94708-1732 Office: U Calif Dept Physics 257 Birge Berkeley CA 94720-0001

HAHN, HAROLD THOMAS, physical chemist, chemical engineer; b. NYC, May 31, 1924; s. Gustave Hahn and Lillie Martha (Thomas) H.; m. Bennie Joyce Turney, Sept. 5, 1948; children: Anita Karen, Beverly Sharon, Carol Linda, Harold Thomas Jr. Student, Hofstra U., 1941-43; BSChemE, Columbia U., 1943-44; PhD in Chemistry, U. Tex., 1950-53. Chem. engr. Manhattan Dist. U.S. Army, Los Alamos, N.Mex., 1945-47; chem. engr. U. Calif., Los Alamos, 1947-50; sr. scientist Gen. Electric Co., Hanford, Wash., 1953-58; sect. chief, chem. research dept. Phillips Petroleum Co., Idaho Falls, Idaho, 1958-64; sr. staff scientist Lockheed Missiles & Space Co., Palo Alto, Calif., 1964-92; private cons., 1992—. Contbr. articles to profl. jours. Pres. Edgemont Gardens PTA, Idaho Falls, 1963-64; commr. cub scout div. Stanford area council Boy Scouts Am., Palo Alto, 1973-76, also cubmaster pack 36, 1973-80, chmn. troops 36 and 37, 1975-77; mem. adminstrv. bd. Los Altos Meth. Ch. Served to col. U.S. Army, 1944-46, with res., 1946-84, col. res. ret. Humble Oil Co. fellow, 1952, Naval Bur. Ordnance fellow, 1953. Fellow Am. Inst. Chemists; mem. AIAA, Magnetics Soc. IEEE (life, elected sr. mem.), Calif. Acad. Scis., Internat. Platform Assn., Am. Chem. Soc., Sigma Xi, Phi Lambda Upsilon, Kappa Rho. Achievements include patents in field. Home and Office: 661 Teresi Ln Los Altos CA 94024-4162

HAHN, JANICE, councilwoman; children: Danny, Mark, Katy. Pub. affairs region mgr. Southern Calif. Edison; v.p. Prudential Securities In Pub. Fin.; dir. mktg. Alexander Haagen Co.; elected rep., Dist. 15 Charter Reform Commn., 1997—99; councilwoman, Dist. 15 LA City Coun., 2001—. Chairwoman South Bay Sch. to Career Alliance; pres., bd. dir. Harbor Area Gang Alternative Program. Harbour area mem. adv. bd. Habitat for Humanity; mem. Gardena Econ. Devel. Com.; bd. dir. South Bay Pvt. Industry Coun., Watts/Willowbrook Boys & Girls Clubs. Recipient Rosa Parks award, Southern Christian Leadership Conf., Bold Vision award, San Pedro C. of C., Pub. Svc. award, African Am. C. of C., Recognition award, Harbor Area Gang Alternative Program. Office: City Hall 200 N Spring St Rm 435 Los Angeles CA 90012 Office Phone: 213-473-7015. Office Fax: 213-626-5431. E-mail: councilmember.hahn@lacity.org.*

HAHN, JOSEPH, disc jockey, video director; b. Glendale, Calif., Mar. 15, 1977; m. Karen Benedit, 2005. Student, Art Ctr. Coll. Design, Pasadena, Calif. DJ, music video dir. Linkin Park, 1997—. Dir.: (films) The Seed, 2008; musician: (albums) Hybrid Theory, 2000, Meteora, 2003, Live in Texas, 2003, Minutes to Midnight, 2007, Road to Revolution Live at Milton Keynes, 2008, (songs) Crawling, 2000 (Grammy award for Best Hard Rock Performance, 2002), In the End, 2000 (MTV Video Music award for Best Rock Video, 2002), Somewhere I Belong, 2003 (MTV Video Music award for Best Rock Video, 2003), Breaking the Habit, 2003 (MTV Video Music award for Viewers' Choice, 2004), (with Jay-Z) Numb/Encore, 2004 (Grammy award for Best Rock/Sung Collaboration, 2006), What I've Done, 2007 (Top Modern Rock Track, Billboard Year-End Charts, 2007), Shadow of the Day, 2007 (MTV Video Music award for Best Rock Video, 2007). Recipient Best-Selling Rock Group award, World Music Awards, 2002, 2003, Favorite Alternative Artist award, Am. Music Awards, 2003, 2004, 2007, 2008; named Top Modern Rock Artist, Billboard Year-End Charts, 2001, 2004, 2007. Office: Linkin Park c/o Machine Shop Recordings PO Box 36915 Los Angeles CA 90036

HAIGHT, JAMES THERON, lawyer; b. Racine, Wis., Dec. 10, 1924; s. Walter Lyman and Geraldine (Foley) H.; m. Patricia Aloe, Apr. 26, 1952; children: Alberta, Barbara, Catherine, Dorothy, Elaine. Student, U. Nebr., 1943—44, U. Bordeaux, France, 1947; diplome d'Etudes, U. Paris, 1948; BA, U. Wis., 1950, LLB, 1951. Bar: D.C. 1952, U.S. Supreme Ct. 1955, Calif. 1968. Atty. Covington & Burling, Washington, 1951-56, Goodyear Tire & Rubber Co., Goodyear Internat. Corp., Akron, Ohio, 1956-61; gen. counsel, sec. George J. Meyer Mfg. Co., Milw., 1961-66; sr. v.p., sec., chief corp. counsel Thrifty Corp., LA, 1966-92, spl. counsel, 1992-96. Fellow: Am. Bar Found. (life); mem.: ABA (chmn. internat. law sect. 1974—75), Am. Soc. Corp. Secs., Pasadena Bar Assn., Calif. Bar Assn., Order of Coif. Home and Office: 1390 Ridge Way Pasadena CA 91106-4514

HAIGHT, WARREN GAZZAM, investor; b. Seattle, Sept. 7, 1929; s. Gilbert Pierce and Ruth (Gazzam) H.; m. Suzanne H., Sept. 1, 1951; children— Paula Lea, Ian Pierce; m. Ottina Mehau, June 25, 1985 AB in Econs, Stanford U., 1951. Asst. Treas. Hawaiian Pineapple Co., Honolulu, 1955-64; v.p., treas. Oceanic Properties, Inc., Honolulu, 1964-67, pres., dir., 1967-85, chmn., 1983-85; pres. Hawaii, Castle & Cooke Inc., 1983-85, Warren G. Haight & Assocs., 1985—; chmn. Molokai Ranch, Ltd., 1996—2002, Pacific Is. Resources, LLC, 2000—03. Bd. dirs. Round Hill Enterprises, Inc., Las Positas Land Co., Inc., Baldwin Pacific Properties, Inc., Hawaii Project Mgmt., Inc., Transamerica Realty Advisors, Inc., Queen Emma Corp., Queens Devel. Corp., Dole Corp., Standard Fruit and Steamship Co., Inc., Bumble Bee Seafoods, Inc. Mem. Transit Coalition, Honolulu, Gov.'s Com. on Econ. Futures; pres., bd. dirs. Land Use Rsch. Found. of Hawaii, Pacific Found. for Cancer Rsch., Hawaii Nature Ctr.; mem. policy adv. bd. for elderly affairs State of Hawaii; bd. dirs. Downtown Improvement Assn., Oahu Devel. Conf., Hawaii Island Econ. Devel. Bd., Econ. Devel. Corp. Honolulu, Intellect, Inc., Hawaii Resort Developers Conf., Homeless Solutions, Inc., Mutual Housing of Hawaii, Mediation Ctr. of the Pacific, Kailua Urban Design Task Force. Mem. Housing Coalition, Calif. Coastal Coun., Outrigger Canoe Club, Plaza Club, Pacific Club, Mid Pacific Country Club. Home: 319 Lala Pl Kailua HI 96734-3224 Office: 220 S King St Ste 1170 Honolulu HI 96813-4542 Office Phone: 808-523-8900. Personal E-mail: haighthawaii@aol.com.

HAILE, L. JOHN, JR., journalist, publishing executive; b. Cleveland, Tenn., Mar. 20, 1945; m. Gwen Marie, 1965; children: Philip Alan, John Christopher. BA, Vanderbilt U., Nashville, 1967; MS in Journalism, Boston U., 1969. Polit. reporter The Nashville Tennessean, 1966-79; dep. mng. editor The Orlando Sentinel, Fla., 1979-81, assoc. editor Fla., 1981-85, editor Fla., 1985—2000; founding ptnr., prin. Inside Out Media Ptnrs., 2000—. Juror Pulitzer Prize Com., 1992—93; former chair New Directions for News; sr. fellow The Media Ctr. at the Am. Press Inst., 2002—; cons. Tribune Co., 2001—, Media Gen., 2003, CCN, Trinidad, 2003, Denver Newspaper Agy., 2005. Bd. dirs. Mt. Evans Hospice. Nat. Endowment Humanities Profl. Journalism fellow, 1975-76 Home Phone: 303-489-2430; Office Phone: 303-679-3262. E-mail: johnhaile@aol.com.

HAILE, LAWRENCE BARCLAY, lawyer; b. Atlanta, Feb. 19, 1938; m. Ann Leon; children: Gretchen Vanderhoof, Eric McKenzie (dec.), Scott McAllister. BA in Econs, U. Tex., 1958, LLB, 1961. Bar: Tex. 1961, Calif. 1962. Law clk. to U.S. Judge Joseph M. Ingraham, Houston, 1961-62; pvt. practice San Francisco, 1962-67, LA, 1967—. Instr. UCLA Civil Trial Clinics, 1974, 76; lectr. law Calif. Continuing Edn. of Bar, 1973-74, 80-89; nat. panel arbitrators Am. Arbitration Assn., 1965—. Mem. editl. bd. Tex. Law Rev, 1960-61; contbr. articles profl. jours. Mem. State Bar Calif., Tex., U.S. Supreme Ct. Bar Assn., Internat. Assn. Property Ins. Counsel (founding mem., pres. 1980), Vintage Motorsports Coun. (past pres.), Phi Delta Phi, Delta Sigma Rho. Office: 26363 Silver Spur Rd Rancho Palos Verdes CA 90275 Office Phone: 310-378-0514. Personal E-mail: lhaile1938@aol.com.

HAILE, LISA A., lawyer; BA in Biology, Rollins Coll., 1982; PhD in Microbiology & Immunology, Georgetown U. Sch. Medicine, 1987; JD, Calif. Western Sch. Law, 1991. Bar: Calif. 1992, cert.: US Patent and Trademark Office. Postdoctoral fellow La Jolla Cancer Rsch. Found., NIH, 1987—89; ptnr. Gray, Cary, Ware, & Freidenrich, 1999—2004; ptnr., co-chmn. Life Sciences practice group DLA Piper, San Diego, 2005—. Adj. prof. patent law Calif. Western Sch. Law; bd. mem. BIOCOM Sci. and Tech. Com., 2004. Bd. mem. Am. Liver Found., Athena. Named one of Top 45 Attorneys Under 45, The Am. Lawyers, 2003. Mem.: ABA, Licensing Exec. Soc., Am. Intellectual Property Law Assn., Calif. Bar Assn., San Diego Bar Assn., San Diego Intellectual Property Law Assn. (pres. 1997—99), Ass. for Women in Sci. Office: DLA Piper 4365 Executive Dr San Diego CA 92121 Office Phone: 858-677-1456. Office Fax: 858-677-1401. Business E-Mail: lisa.haile@dlapiper.com.

HAINER, EUGENE, state librarian; Grad., U. Colo., Boulder; MLS, U. Tex., Austin. Tchr.; music instr.; libr. media specialist Poudre Sch. Dist., Fort Collins, Colo.; sch. libr. cons. Colo. State Libr., Denver, head libr. devel., 2000—05, state libr., 2005—. Office: Colorado State Library State Office Bldg Rm 309 201 E Colfax Ave Denver CO 80203-1799 Office Phone: 303-866-6733. Business E-Mail: hainerg@cde.state.co.us.

HAINES, JOHN MEADE, poet, translator, writer; b. 1924; Homesteader in Alaska, 1947-69; poet-in-residence U. Alaska, Anchorage, 1972-73; vis. prof. English U. Wash., Seattle, 1974; vis. lectr. U. Mont., Missoula, 1974-75; Guggenheim fellowship, 1984-85; disting. vis. lectr. U. Calif., Santa Cruz, 1986; writer-in-residence Montalvo Ctr. for the Arts, 1987-88, Djerassi Found., 1988; vis. prof. Ohio U., Athens, 1989-90. Vis. writer George Washington U., 1991-92; Elliston fellow in poetry U. Cin., 1992; chmn. creative arts Austin Peay State U., Clarksville, Tenn., 1993—; vis. lectr. Ann. Summer Wordsworth Conf., Grasmere, Eng., 1996; writer-in-residence Bellagio Ctr., Italy, 2000; poet-in-residence Bucknell U., 2001; guest poet Internat. Shakespeare Conf, Vladimir U., Russia, 2002; reader Libr. of Congress, 2005. Translator: El Amor Ascendia, 1967; author: Winter News: Poems, 1966, Suite for the Pied Piper, 1967, The Legend of Paper Plates, 1970, The Mirror, 1971, The Stone Harp, 1971, Twenty Poems, 1971, Leaves and Ashes: Poems, 1974, In Five Years Time, 1976; The Sun on Your Shoulder, 1976, Cicada, 1977, In a Dusty Light, 1977, Living Off the Country: Essays on Poetry and Place, 1981, Of Traps and Snares, 1981, Other Days, 1982, News from the Glacier: Selected Poems 1982, Forest Without Leaves, 1984, Stories We Listened To, 1986, The Stars, The Snow, The Fire, 1989, Meditation On a Skull Carved in Crystal, 1989, New Poems, 1980-88, 1990 (Western States Art Fedn. award, Lenore Marshall/Nation award, Poets prize 1990), (poetry) Rain Country, 1990, The Owl in the Mask of the Dreamer, Collected Poems, 1993, A Guide to the Four-Chambered Heart, 1996, At the End of this Summer, 1948-54, 1997, (essay) Fables and Distances, New and Selected Essays, 1996, For the Century's End, Poems 1990-1999, 2001, Of Your Passage, O Summer, Uncollected Poems from the 1960s, 2004, Wartime, A Late Memoir, 2004. Recipient Acad. award in Lit. Am. Acad. of Arts and Letters, 1995; 63d fellow Acad. Am. Poets, 1997; named Alaska Poet Laureate, 1969-73; Gugggenheim fellow, 1965-66, NEA fellow, 1967-68; Amy Lowell traveling scholar, 1976-77; No. Momentum scholar U. Alaska, 2003. Home: 717 Longstaff Missoula MT 59801-3605 Office Phone: 907-474-6612. Business E-Mail: ffjmh@uaf.edu.

HAINES, RICHARD FOSTER, retired psychologist; b. Seattle, May 19, 1937; s. Donald Hutchinson and Claudia May (Bennett) H.; m. Carol Taylor, June 17, 1961; children: Cynthia Lynn, Laura Anne. Student, U. Wash., 1955-57; BA, Pacific Luth. Coll., Tacoma, 1960; MA, Mich. State U., 1962, PhD, 1964. Predoctoral rsch. fellow NIH, 1964; Nat. Acad. Sci. postdoctoral resident rsch. assoc. Ames Rsch. Ctr./NASA, Moffett Field, Calif., 1964-67, rsch. scientist, 1967-86, chief of space human factors office, 1987-88, rsch. scientist Rsch. Inst. Advanced Computer Sci., 1988-90; assoc. prof. dept. psychology San Jose State U., 1988-89; computer scientist RECOM Techs., Inc., Moffett Field, Calif., 1993-2000, Raytheon Corp., 2000—01; ret., 2001. Rsch. cons. to NASA Foothill Coll.; cons. Stanford U. Sch. medicine, 1966-67, TRW-Systems Group, 1969-70; mem. adv. com. on vision NRC; founding mem. advanced tech. applications com. Calif. Coun. AIA and NASA, 1975-80; mem. adv. bd. Space Scis. Ctr.-Foothill Coll., 1976-78; bd. advisors Fund for UFO Rsch., Washington; chmn. bd. Novosibirsk Christian Pub.-Calif., 1993-2007;

chief scientist Nat. Aviation Reporting Ctr. on Anomalous Phenomena, 2001—. Author: UFO Phenomena and the Behavioral Scientist, 1979, Observing UFOs, 1980, Melbourne Episode: Case Study of a Missing Pilot, 1987, Advanced Aerial Devices Reported During the Korean War, 1990, Night Flying, 1992, Project Delta, 1994, Close Encounters of the Fifth Kind, 1999, Aviation Safety in America - A Previously Neglected Factor, 2000; mem. editl. and sci. bd. Jour. UFO Studies, Internat. UFO Reporter, Cuadernos de Ufologica; contbr. articles to profl. jours. Mem. Palo Alto (Calif.) Mayor's Com. on Youth Activities, 1967; chmn. adv. coun. Christian Cmty. Progress Corp., Menlo Park, Calif.; v.p., dir. Ctr. Counseling for Drug Abuse, Menlo Park; bd. dirs., chmn. sci. adv. team Threshold Found.; founding co-dir. Joint Am.-Soviet Aerial Anomaly Fedn., 1991—97. Named Alumnus of Yr., Pacific Luth. U., 1972 Fellow Aerospace Med. Assn. (assoc.); mem. Optical Soc. Am., Word to Russia (bd. dirs., 2008), Soc. for Sci. Exploration, Sigma Xi. Achievements include patents for device of advanced detection of glaucoma, optical projector of vision performance data for design engineers, visual simulator optical alignment device, grooming aid for use by astronauts in space.

HAIR, KITTIE ELLEN, retired secondary school educator; b. Denver, June 12, 1948; d. William Edward and Jacqueline Jean (Holt) H. BA, Brigham Young U., 1971; MA in Social History, U. Nev., Las Vegas, 1987, cert. paralegal, 1995. cert. tchr., Nev. Health educator Peace Corps, Totota, Liberia, 1971—72; tchr. Clark County Sch. Dist., Las Vegas, Nev., 1972—77, 1979—2007, chair dept. social studies, 1993—95, chair social studies dept., 2005—07; ret., 2007. Assessor Nat. Bd. Profl. Tchg. Stds. Missionary LDS Ch., Canada, 1977—79. Recipient Outstanding Faculty award U. Nev./Southland Corp., Las Vegas, 1991, State Champion Coach, Nev. HS, 2006; named Educator of Yr. Kiwanis Club, 1998-99. Mem.: Nev. HS Mock Trial Bd. (chmn. 2003—04, 2007—08), Phi Alpha Theta, Phi Kappa Phi. Democrat. Avocations: collecting western and Native American art, gardening, cooking. Office: Law Office Julie Mersch 701 S 7th St Las Vegas NV 89101-6907

HAISCH, BERNARD MICHAEL, astronomer, researcher; b. Stuttgart-Bad Canstatt, Federal Republic of Germany, Aug. 23, 1949; s. Friedrich Wilhelm and Gertrud Paula (Dammbacher) H.; m. Pamela S. Eakins, July 29, 1977 (div. 1986); children: Katherine Stuart, Christopher Taylor; m. Marsha A. Sims, Aug. 23, 1986. Student, St. Meinrad Coll., Ind., 1967-68; BS in Astrophysics, Ind. U., 1971; PhD in Astronomy, U. Wis., 1975. Rsch. assoc. Joint Inst. Lab. Astrophysics, U. Colo., 1975-77, 78-79; vis. scientist space rsch. lab. U. Utrecht, The Netherlands, 1977-78; rsch. scientist Lockheed Rsch. Lab., Palo Alto, Calif., 1979-83, staff scientist, 1983-99; dep. dir. Ctr. for EUV Astrophysics U. Calif., Berkeley, 1992-94; dir. Calif. Inst. Physics and Astrophysics, 1999—2002; chief sci. officer Many One Networks, Scotts Valley, Calif., 2002—; pres. Digital Universe Found., Scotts Valley, Calif., 2005—07. Guest investigator Internat. Ultraviolet Explorer, Einstein Obs., Exosat, ROSAT Obs., EUVE Obs., Astro-D (ASCA), X-Ray Timing Explorer, 1980—; vis. fellow Max Planck Inst. Extraterr. Physik, Garching, Germany, 1991-94. Author: The God Theory, 2006; editor-in-chief Jour. Sci. Exploration, 1988-99, Solar and Stellar Flares, 1989; sci. editor The Astrophys. Jour., 1993-2003; monograph The Many Faces of the Sun, 1999; mem. editl. bd. Solar Physics, 1992-95, Speculations in Sci. and Tech., 1995-99; contbr. articles to profl. jours. Fellow AIAA (assoc.), Royal Astron. Soc.; mem. Internat. Astron. Union, Am. Astron. Soc., European Astron. Soc., Sigma Xi, Phi Beta Kappa, Phi Kappa Phi. Avocations: skiing, song writing. Business E-Mail: haisch@calphysics.org.

HAKANSSON, NILS HEMMING, economist, educator; b. Marby, Sweden, June 2, 1937; came to U.S., 1956; s. Nils and Anna (Nilsson) H.; m. Joyce Beth Kates, Aug. 28, 1960; children— Carolyn Ann, Nils Alexander BS with honors, U. Oreg., 1958; MBA, UCLA, 1960, PhD, 1966; D. of Econs. (hon.), Stockholm Sch. Econs., 1984. C.P.A., Calif. Staff acct., cons. Arthur Young & Co., LA, 1960-63; asst. prof. UCLA, 1966-67, Yale U., New Haven, 1967-69; assoc. prof. U. Calif.-Berkeley, 1969-71, prof., 1971-77, Sylvan C. Coleman prof. fin. and acctg., 1977—2003, chmn. fin., 1976-79, 1997—2000. Cons. Rand Corp., Santa Monica, Calif., 1965-71, Bell Labs., Murray Hill, NJ, 1974, 79-81; chmn. bd. dirs. Anna och Nils Hakanssons Stiftelse; bd. dirs. Laudus Mut. Funds. Editorial cons. Acctg. Rev., 1977-80; cons. editor Jour. Acctg. and Econs., 1978-81; contbr. articles to profl. jours. Served with Royal Swedish Corps Engrs., 1956. Recipient Graham and Dodd award Fin. Analysts Fedn., 1976, 82; Ford Found. fellow UCLA, 1963-66; Hoover fellow U. New South Wales, 1975 Fellow Acctg. Rschrs. Internat. Assn.; mem. AICPA (hon. mem.), Fin. Economists Roundtable, Am. Fin. Assn., Western Fin. Assn. (pres. 1983-84), Am. Acctg. Assn., Soc. for Promotion Fin. Studies (founding). Office: U Calif Sch Bus Berkeley CA 94720-1900 Business E-Mail: hakansso@haas-berkeley.edu.

HAKKILA, EERO ARNOLD, retired nuclear safeguards technology chemist; b. Canterbury, Conn., Aug. 4, 1931; s. Jack and Ida Maria (Lillquist) H.; m. Margaret W. Hakkila; children: Jon Eric, Mark Douglas, Gregg Arnold. BS in Chemistry, Cen. Conn. State U., 1953; PhD in Analytical Chemistry, Ohio State U., 1957. Staff mem. Los Alamos (N.Mex.) Nat. Lab., 1957-78, assoc. group leader safeguard systems, 1978-80, dep. group leader, 1980-82, group leader, 1982-83, project mgr. internat. safeguards, 1983-87, program coord., 1987-95; ret., 1995. Editor: Nuclear Safeguards Analysis, 1978; contbr. numerous articles to profl. jours. Fellow Am. Inst. Chemists; mem. N.Mex. Inst. Chemists (pres. 1971-73), Am. Chem. Soc., Am. Nuclear Soc. (exec. com. fuel cycle and waste mgmt. div. 1984-86), Inst. Nuclear Materials Mgmt. Avocations: skiing, fishing, rockhounding, golf.

HALABY, NOELLE M., lawyer; BA, UCLA, 1993; JD, Southwestern Univ., 1996. Bar: Calif., US Dist. Ct. (ctrl. dist.) Calif., US Ct. Appeals (9th cir.), cert.: family law specialist, Calif. Ptnr. Moore, Halaby & Associates, Pasadena, Calif.; assoc. Lisa Helfend Meyer & Associates, Century City, Calif.; prin., family law private practice Glendale, Calif., 2003—. Family Law Judge Pro Tem LA Superior Ct., mediator, Family Law dept. Named a Rising Star, So. Calif. Super Lawyers, 2006. Mem.: State Bar Calif., LA County Bar Assn., Beverly Hills Bar Assn., Century City Bar Assn., Calif. Assn. Family Law Specialists, Woman Lawyers LA, Am. Bus. Women Assn. Office: Noelle M Halaby Ste 200 130 N Brand Blvd Glendale CA 91203 Office Phone: 818-502-3939. Office Fax: 818-502-3999. Business E-Mail: noelle@noellehalaby.com.

HALBACH, EDWARD CHRISTIAN, JR., law educator; b. Clinton, Iowa, Nov. 8, 1931; s. Edward Christian and Lewella (Sullivan) H.; m. Janet Elizabeth Bridges, July 25, 1953; children: Kristin Lynn, Edward Christian III, Kathleen Ann, Thomas Elliot, Elaine Diane. BA, U. Iowa, 1953, JD, 1958; LLM, Harvard U., 1959; LLD, U. Redlands, 1973. Assoc. prof. Sch. Law, U. Calif., Berkeley, 1959-62, prof., 1963—, dean, 1966-75. Co-author: Materials on Decedents' Estates and Trusts, 1965, 73, 81, 87, 93, 2000, 06, Materials on Future Interests, 1977, Death, Taxes and Family Property, 1977, California Will Drafting, 1965, 77, 92; author: Use of Trusts in Estate Planning, 1975, 81, 84, 86, 91, Fundamentals of Estate Planning, 1983, 86, 87, 89, 91, 93, 95, Summary of the Law of Trusts, 1990, 1998, 2004, 07, Principles and Techniques of Estate Planning, 1995; reporter Uniform Probate Code, 1969, Restatement 3d Trusts Prudent Investor Rule, 1992, Restatement of Law of Trusts, vols. 1 and 2, 2003, vol. 3, 2007; also articles. 1st lt. USAF, 1954-56. Mem. ABA (chmn. various coms. sect. individual rights and responsibilities and sect. real property probate and trust law, dir. probate and trust divsn., sect. chmn.), Iowa Bar Assn., Am. Law Inst. (reporter Restatement 3d Trusts, advisor Restatement 2d, 3d Property), Am. Acad. Polit. and Social Scis., Am. Bar Found., Am. Coll. Trust and Estate Counsel, Am. Coll. Tax Counsel, Internat. Acad. Estate and Trust Law (v.p., exec. com., pres.). Home: 679 San Luis Rd Berkeley CA 94707-1725 Office: U Calif Sch Law Boalt Hall Berkeley CA 94720 Personal E-mail: bubzed@comcast.net.

HALBERSTADTER, DAVID, lawyer; b. Elizabeth, NJ, Sept. 1, 1957; BA, Cornell U., 1979; JD magna cum laude, Georgetown U., 1982. Bar: Calif. 1982. Ptnr., co-chair entertainment and media practice Katten Muchin Rosenman LLP, L.A. Mem.: ABA, LA County Bar Assn., LA Copyright Soc. Office: Katten Muchin Rosenman LLP 2029 Century Park E STe 2600 Los Angeles CA 90067 Office Phone: 310-788-4408. Office Fax: 310-712-8481. E-mail: david.halberstadter@cattenlaw.com.

HALE, ALBERT A., state legislator; b. Klagetoh, Ariz. BS, Ariz. State U., Tempe, 1973; JD, U. N.Mex. Sch. Law, Albuquerque, 1977. Bar: N.Mex., US Fed. Ct. Pres. Navajo Nation, 1995—98, also asst. atty gen., spl. counsel; pvt. practice atty. St. Michaels, Ariz.; mem. Dist. 1 Ariz. State Senate, 2004—, mem. vets. & mil. affairs com., appropriations com., natural resources, infrastructure & pub. debt com. Chair Navajo Nation Water Rights Commn.; judge pro tempore Laguna Courts, N.Mex. Mem.: Navajo Nation Bar Assn., NM State Bar Assn. Democrat. Mailing: Ariz State Senate Capitol Complex 1700 W Washington Rm 313 Phoenix AZ 85007 Office Fax: 602-417-3160. Business E-Mail: ahale@azleg.gov.*

HALE, DAVID FREDRICK, biotechnology executive; b. Gadsden, Ala., Jan. 8, 1949; s. Millard and Mildred Earline (McElroy) Hale; m. Linda Carol Sadorski, Mar. 14, 1975; children: Shane Michael, Tara Renee, Erin Nicole, David Garrett. BA, Jacksonville State U. Dir. mktg. Ortho Pharm. Corp. divsn. Johnson & Johnson, Raritan, NJ, 1978—80; v.p. mktg. BBL Microbiology Sys. divsn. Becton Dickinson & Co., Cockeysville, Md., 1980—81, v.p., gen. mgr. BBL Microbiology Sys. divsn., 1981—82; sr. v.p. mktg. and bus. devel. Hybritech, Inc., San Diego, 1982, pres., 1983—86, CEO, 1986—87; pres., CEO, dir. Gensia Sicor, Inc., San Diego, 1987—97; pres., CEO Women First HealthCare, Inc., 1998—2000; pres., CEO, dir. Cancer-Vax Corp., Carlsbad, Calif., 2000—06; chmn. Hale BioPharms Ventures LLC, 2006—. Chmn. bd. Santarus, Inc., Somaxon Pharms., SkinMedica, Metabasis Therapeutics; bd. dirs. Verus Pharms., BIO, Children's Hosp., San Diego Econ. Devel. Corp., BIOCOM San Diego, Connatus Pharm., Neureles Inc.; co-founder, chmn. Connect. Mem.: Chief Exec.'s Orgn., World Pres.'s Orgn. Republican. Episcopalian. Home: PO Box 8925 17079 Circa del Sur Rancho Santa Fe CA 92067 Office: 1042 B W El Camino Rd Ste480 Encinitas CA 92024 Office Phone: 858-756-2480.

HALE, NATHAN ROBERT, architect; b. Battle Creek, Mich., July 20, 1944; s. Nathan Shirley and Gertrude Anges (Barnes) H.; m. CarolAnn Purrington, May 28, 1966; children: Marilyce, Maile, Martha. BA, Syracuse U., 1967, BArch, 1971. Dir. Archs. Hawaii, Honolulu, 1971—86, pres., 1986—, now vice chmn. Adj. prof., sch. arch. Univ. Hawaii. Served with AUS, 1968-70, Vietnam. Mem. AIA (bd. dirs. 1984, pres. 1992), Hawaii C. of C. (exec. com. 1994-99), Econ. Devel. Corp. Honolulu (chair 1993-96, bd. dirs. 1982—), Rotary Club (bd. dirs. 1986-88), Friends of Children's Advocacy Ctr. (pres. 1991, 93, bd. dirs., 1986—). Office: Architects Hawaii Ltd Pacific Tower 300 1001 Bishop St Honolulu HI 96813-3429 Office Fax: 808-521-3280. Business E-Mail: ahl@architects-hawaii.com.

HALE, PATRICIA S., state legislator; b. Durham, NC, Jan. 9, 1937; m. Tom Hale; 5 children. Degree in mktg., U. N.C.; degree in econs., U. Richmond. Dir. strategic initiatives Fluor Daniel Hanford; mem. Wash. Senate, Dist. 8, Olympia, 1994—; majority whip Wash. Senate, Olympia, 1997—, Rep. caucus chair, 1999—. Bd. Tri-Cities Cancer Ctr. Found., United Way, Tri-Cities Vis. and Conv. Bur.; dir. Tri-Cities Indsl. Devel. Coun., Mid-Columbia Reading Found.; chair Econ. Devel. Com.; co-chair Mission Impossible com., March of Dimes, Walk Am. 96; fundraising co-chair Boys and Girls Club; campaign chair Benton/Franklin United Way, 1997; vice chair Pvt. Industries Coun. Recipient Total Quality Achievement award Westinghouse Hanford Co., 1989, Nat. Mgmt. award Westinghouse Electric Corp., 1990, Toastmasters Internat. Commns. and Leadership award, 2000, Top Notch award, Rockwell Internat., 2002, Citizen of Yr. award, Washington Asssn. Realtors, 2002, Legis. of Yr., Wash. Coun. of Police and Sheriffs, 2003. Mem. Wash. State Hist. Soc. (bd. mem.), Kennewick C. of C. (former dir.), Pvt. Indsl. Coun. (past vice chair and econ. devel. com. chair 1997), Richland Club, Rotary Club. Republican. Roman Catholic. Office: 303 Legislative Bldg Olympia WA 98504-0001 E-mail: hale_pa@leg.wa.gov.

HALES, ALFRED WASHINGTON, mathematics professor, consultant; b. Pasadena, Calif., Nov. 30, 1938; s. Raleigh Stanton and Gwendolen (Washington) H.; m. Virginia Dart Greene, July 7, 1962; children— Andrew Stanton, Lisa Ruth, Katherine Washington BS, Calif. Inst. Tech., 1960, PhD, 1962. NSF postdoctoral fellow Cambridge U., Eng., 1962-63; Benjamin Peirce instr. Harvard U., 1963-66; faculty mem. UCLA, 1966-92, prof. math., 1973-92, prof. emeritus, 1992—; dir. IDA Ctr. Comm. Rsch., 1992—2003. Cons. Jet Propulsion Lab., La Canada, Calif., 1966-70, Inst. for Def. Analyses, Princeton, NJ. and LaJolla, Calif., 1964-65, 76, 79-92; vis. lectr. U. Wash., Seattle, 1970-71; vis. mem. U. Warwick Math. Inst., Coventry, Eng., 1977-78, Math. Sci. Rsch. Inst., Berkeley, 1986-87. Co-author: Shift Register Sequences, 1967, 82; contbr. articles to profl. jours. Bd. trustees Math. Sci. Rsch. Inst., Berkeley, 1995—99. Mem. Am. Math. Soc., Math. Assn. Am., Soc. Indsl. and Applied Math. (Polya prize in combinatorics 1972), Pasadena Badminton Club, Sigma Xi. Office: Ctr for Comm Rsch 4320 Westerra Ct San Diego CA 92121-1969 Home Phone: 858-454-8126; Office Phone: 858-622-5423. Business E-Mail: hales@ccrwest.org.

HALES, RALEIGH STANTON, JR., retired mathematics professor, academic administrator; b. Pasadena, Calif., Mar. 16, 1942; s. Raleigh Stanton and Gwendolen (Washington) Hales; m. Diane Cecilia Moore, July 8, 1967; children: Karen Gwen, Christopher Stanton. BA, Pomona Coll., 1964; MA, Harvard U., 1965, PhD, 1970. Tchg. fellow Harvard U., Cambridge, Mass., 1965—67; instr. math. Pomona Coll., Claremont, Calif., 1967—70, asst. prof., 1970—74, assoc. prof., 1974—85, prof., 1985—90, assoc. dean. coll., 1973—90; pres. Claremont Computations, 1983—90; prof. math. scis., v.p. acad. affairs Coll. Wooster, Ohio, 1990, pres., 1995—2007, pres. emeritus, 2007—; sr. cons. Academic Search, Inc., 2007—; with Claremont U. Consortium, Calif., 2008—. Cons. Calif. Divsn. Savs. and Loan, 1968—70, Econs. Rsch. Assocs., LA, 1969, Devel. Econs., LA, 1971, Fed. Home Loan Bank Bd., Washington, 1971—72. Author: computer software; contbr. articles to profl. jours.; patentee calculator. Trustee Polytech. Sch., Pasadena, Calif., 1973—79, Foothill Country Day Sch., Claremont, 1985—90, chmn., 1989—90; coun. Internat. Badminton Fedn., 1989—99; bd. dirs. U.S. Badminton Assn., 1967—73, 1978—89, pres., 1985—88; mem. exec. bd. U.S. Olympic Com., 1989—90. Named Wig Disting. prof., Pomona Coll., 1971. Mem.: Math. Assn. Am., Am. Math. Soc., Pasadena Badminton Club (pres. 1978—85). Republican. Episcopalian. Home: 3632 Incantare Ct Santa Rosa CA 95404 Business E-Mail: shales@wooster.edu.

HALES, ROBERT ERNEST, psychiatrist, educator; s. Herbert and Matilda Hales; m. Dianne Plucinnik, Dec. 24, 1977; 1 child, Julia. MD, George Wash. U., Washington, 1977. Diplomate Am. Bd. Psychiatry and Neurology, 1983. Chair,dept. psychiatry Calif. Pacific Med. Ctr., San Francisco, 1990—95; Joe P. Tupin prof., chair dept. psychiatry U. Calif.,Sch. Medicine, Sacramento, 1995—. Dep. editor: Jour. Neuropsychiatry and Clinical Neurosci., editor in chief: Am. Psychiat. Pub., Inc., 2001—. Mem. Am. Psychiat. Pub., Arlington, Va., 2001—07. Named Educator of Yr., Assn. Acad. Psychiatry, 2006. Fellow: Am. Psychiat. Assn. (chair sci. program com. 1984—88). Office: Univ Calif Davis 2230 Stockton Blvd Sacramento CA 95817 Office Fax: 916-734-3384. Business E-Mail: rehales@ucdavis.edu.

HALEY, GEORGE PATRICK, lawyer; b. Bad Axe, Mich., Sept. 23, 1948; s. Glen Kirk and Bernice (Cooper) H.; m. Theresa L. Thomas, Dec. 24, 1975. BS, U. Mich., 1970; MS, U. Calif., Berkeley, 1971; JD, Harvard U., 1974. Bar: Calif. 1974, U.S. Dist. Ct. (no. dist.) Calif. 1974, U.S. Dist. Ct. (ea. dist.) Calif. 1980. Assoc. Pillsbury Winthrop Shaw Pittman LLP, San Francisco, 1974-81, ptnr., 1982—. Prof. U. Shanghai, Shanghai-San Francisco Sister City Program, 1986-1989. Author numerous articles on uniform comml. code, project fin. Dir. Calif. Shakespeare Festival, Berkeley, 1986-93; dir. Nat. Writing Project, 1996—. Mem. ABA (chmn. com. 1976-93), Am. Coll. Comml. Fin. Lawyers, State Bar Calif. (chmn. fin. instns. com. 1980, comml. code com. 1988). Republican. Methodist. Avocations: tai chi chuan, golf, cooking. Home: 1825 Marin Ave Berkeley CA 94707-2414 Office Phone: 415-983-1272. Business E-Mail: george.haley@pillsburylaw.com.

HALKETT, ALAN NEILSON, lawyer; b. Chungking, China, Oct. 5, 1931; came to U.S., 1940; s. James and Evelyn Alexandrina (Neilson) H.; m. Mary Lou Hickey, July 30, 1955; children: Kent, James, Kate BS, UCLA, 1953, LL.B., 1961. Bar: Calif. 1962. Mem. firm Latham & Watkins, LA, 1961-95, mem. exec. com., 1968-72, chmn. litigation dept., 1980-86, chmn. succession com., 1986-87. State chmn. Am. Coll., Calif., 1992-94. Served to lt. USN, 1954-58 Fellow Am. Coll. Trial Lawyers; mem. Calif. Bar Assn., Nat. Arbitration Forum, Chancery Club, UCLA Law Alumni Assn. (pres. 1968), Order of Coif, Palos Verdes Country Club (Palos Verdes Estates, Calif.). Republican. Avocations: golf, old cars. Office: Latham Watkins 355 S Grand Ave Los Angeles CA 90071-1560 Personal E-mail: halkett6@aol.com.

HALKIN, HUBERT, mathematics professor, researcher; b. Liege, Belgium, June 5, 1936; came to U.S., 1960; s. Leon E. and Denise H.; m. Carolyn Mulliken, June 22, 1964 (div. 1971); children: Christopher, Sherrill-Anne; m. Katherine Hodges, Dec. 24, 1988 (div. 2001); m. Kathy Ziegler, Oct. 10, 2004. Ingenieur, U. Liège, 1960; PhD, Stanford U., 1963. Tech. staff Bell Telephone Labs., Whippany, NJ, 1963-65; assoc. prof. math. dept. U. Calif., San Diego, 1965-69, prof., 1969—, dept. chmn. San Diego, 1981-87. Editor Jour. Optimization Theory and Applications, 1968—, Revue Française d'Automatique de Recherche Operationnelle, 1973—. Guggenheim fellow, 1971-72. Mem.: Idyllwild, Club Aroma, Sierra Club. Office: U Calif San Diego Dept Math La Jolla CA 92093 Business E-Mail: hhalkin@ucsd.edu.

HALL, ANTHONY ELMITT, agriculturist, physiologist; b. Tickhill, Yorkshire, Eng., May 6, 1940; came to U.S., 1964; s. Elmitt and Mary Lisca (Schofield) H.; m. Bretta Reed, June 20, 1965; children: Kerry, Gina. Student, Harper Adams Agrl. Coll., Eng., 1958-60; student in agrl. engring., Essex Inst. Agrl. Engring., Eng., 1960-61; BS in Irrigation Sci., U. Calif., Davis, 1966, PhD in Plant Physiology, 1970. Farmer Dyon House, Austerfield, England, 1955-58; extension officer Ministry of Agr., Tanzania, 1961-63; research asst. U. Calif., Davis, 1964-70, asst. research scientist, 1971; research fellow Carnegie Inst., Stanford, Calif., 1970; prof. U. Calif., Riverside, 1971—2003, chmn. dept botany and plant scis., 1994—97, prof. emeritus, 2003. Adv. UN; cons. in field. Author: Crop Responses to Environment, 2001, Sahelian Droughts: A Partial Agronomic Solution, 2007; editor: Agriculture in Semi-Arid Environments, 1979, Stable Isotopes and Plant Carbon-Water Relations, 1993; contbr. articles to profl. jours. Recipient BIFAD chair's award for scientific excellence, 2000, USDA Sec.'s Honor award plant breeding rsch., 2001. Fellow: Crop Sci. Soc. Am., Am. Soc. Agronomy; mem.: Phi Kappa Phi, Phi Beta Kappa, Gamma Sigma Delta (Disting. Achievement in Agr. award of merit 1999), Alpha Zeta. Achievements include design (with others) of a steady state porometer for measuring stomatal conductance; research on the physiology and breeding of heat and chilling tolerant, pest resistant and drought adapted cowpea cultivars including developing cowpea varieties CB27 and Ein El Gazal; patents in field, no6,501,006 B1, 2002. Mailing: 2922 Lindsay Lane Quincy CA 95971 Home Phone: 530-283-3052; Office Phone: 951-236-1580. Business E-Mail: anthony.hall@ucr.edu.

HALL, BLAINE HILL, retired librarian; b. Wellsville, Utah, Dec. 12, 1932; s. James Owen and Agnes Effie (Hill) H.; m. Carol Stokes, 1959; children: Suzanne, Cheryl, Derek. BS, Brigham Young U., 1960, MA, 1965, MLS, 1971. Instr. English, Brigham Young U., Provo, Utah, 1963—72, humanities libr., 1972—96. Book reviewer

Am. Reference Book Ann., 1984-2000. Author: Collection Assessment Manual, 1985, Saul Bellow Bibliography, 1987, Jerzy Kosinski Bibliography, 1991, Jewish American Fiction Writers Bibliography, 1991, Conversations with Grace Paley, 1997; editor: Utah Libraries, 1972-77 (periodical award ALA 1977); contbr. articles to profl. jours. Bd. dirs. Orem (Utah) Pub. Libr., 1977-84; mem. Orem Media Rev. Commn., 1984-86; chmn. Utah Adv. Commn. on Librs., 1983-91. With U.S. Army, 1953-54, Korea. Mem. ALA (coun. 1988-92), Utah Libr. Assn. (pres. 1980-81, Disting. Svc. award 1989), Mountain Plains Libr. Assn. (bd. dirs. 1978-83, editor newsletter 1978-83, pres. 1994-96, grantee 1979, 80, Disting. Svc. award 1991), Phi Kappa Phi. Mem. Lds Ch. Avocations: writing, photography, carpentry, reading, genealogy. Home: 230 E 1910 S Orem UT 84058-8161 Personal E-mail: blainehall@comcast.net

HALL, CLARENCE ALBERT, JR., geologist, educator; b. LA, Jan. 5, 1930; s. Clarence Albert and Margaret Hall; children: Eric Robert, Kris Delorah. BS, Stanford U., 1952, MS, 1953, PhD, 1956. Instr. U. Oreg., Eugene, 1954-55; mem. faculty UCLA, 1956—, prof. geology, chmn. dept. geology, 1974-76, chmn. dept. geophysics and space physics, 1976, chmn. dept. earth and space scis., 1976-78, dean of phys. scis., 1983-94; dir. White Mountain Rsch. Sta. U. Calif. Systemwide, 1979-95. Contbr. articles to profl.jours.; editor Jour. Paleontology, 1971-71. Fulbright rsch. fellow in Italy, 1963-64, 70-71; recipient Dibblee medal, 1998. Fellow Geol. Soc. Am., Paleontol. Soc. Office: UCLA Dept Earth & Scis Los Angeles CA 90095-1567 Business E-Mail: hall@ess.ucla.edu.

HALL, CYNTHIA HOLCOMB, federal judge; b. LA, Feb. 19, 1929; d. Harold Romeyn and Mildred Gould Holcomb; m. John Harris Hall, June 6, 1970 (dec. Oct. 1980). AB, Stanford U., 1951, JD, 1954; LLM, NYU, 1960. Bar: Ariz. 1954, Calif. 1956. Law clk. to judge US Ct. Appeals (9th cir.), 1954—55; trial atty. tax divsn. Dept. Justice, 1960—64; atty.-adviser Office Tax Legis. Counsel, Treasury Dept., 1964—66; mem. firm Brawerman & Holcomb, Beverly Hills, Calif., 1966—72; judge US Tax Ct., Washington, 1972—81, US Dist. Ct. for Ctrl. Dist. Calif., LA, 1981—84, US Ct. Appeals (9th cir.), Pasadena, Calif., 1984—97, sr. judge, 1997—. Lt. (j.g.) USNR, 1951—53. Office: US Ct Appeals 9th Cir 125 S Grand Ave Pasadena CA 91105-1621

HALL, DAVID RAMSAY, architect; b. Lansing, Mich., Oct. 24, 1945; s. Harold Wendell and Sarah Katherine (Schlademan) H.; m. Catherine Anne Weeks, Dec. 23, 1967; children: Sarah Catherine, Rebecca Jane. BArch, Wash. State U., 1968. Registered architect, Wash. Designer, draftsman Earl Flansburgh & Assocs., Cambridge, Mass., 1968-70, NBBJ, Seattle, 1970, Mel Streeter & Assoc., Seattle, 1971-72; designer, ptnr. Henry Klein Partnership, Architects, Mt. Vernon, Wash., 1972—. Author, designer, contbr. articles to profl. publs. Commr. Dike Dist. # 19, Skagit County, Wash., 1984-95; mem. adv. bd. Wash. State U., Pullman, 1990-96; bd. dirs. Self Help Housing, Mt. Vernon, 1980-84. Recipient Prograssive Architecture Design award, 1972, Honor award Cedar Shake & Shingle, 1991, Am. Wood Coun., 1993, Sunset Mag. Western Home award, 1995. Mem. AIA (bd. dirs. N.W. chpt. 1985-88, Honor award Seattle chpt. 1991, N.W. chpt. 1991, 94, 96, 97, 98, Commendation award Seattle chpt. 1987). Avocations: painting, photography, hiking, gardening, fishing. Home: 5871 Farm To Market Rd Bow WA 98232-9254 Office: Henry Klein Partnership 314 Pine St Ste 205 Mount Vernon WA 98273-3852

HALL, DON ALAN, editor, writer; b. Indpls., Aug. 7, 1938; s. Oscar B. and Ruth Ann (Leak) H.; m. Roberta Louise Bash, Apr. 30, 1960; children: Alice Leigh, Nancy Elizabeth. BA, Ind. U., 1960, MA, 1968. News editor Rock Springs (Wyo.) Daily Rocket-Miner, 1960-63; mag. editor, picture editor Waukegan (Ill.) News-Sun, 1964-66; reporter, copy editor Salem (Oreg.) Capital Jour., 1966-70; freelance journalist Victoria, B.C., Canada, 1970-74; copy editor, sci. writer, music reviewer Corvallis (Oreg.) Gazette-Times, 1974-78, copy desk chief, 1978-82, news editor, 1983-84, author weekly opinion column, 1985-87; author weekly nature column for Oreg. newspapers, 1976-85; instr. dept. journalism Oreg. State U., 1984-87. Author: On Top Of Oregon, 1975, Bird in the Bush, 1986; editor Mammoth Trumpet, Center for the Study of the First Americans, 1991-2001. Recipient Westinghouse-AAAS sci. writing award, 1977 Home and Office: 620 NW Witham Dr Corvallis OR 97330-6535

HALL, GENE E., education educator; b. Rutland, Vt; BS, Castleton State Coll.; MS, PhD, Syracuse U. Faculty mem., project dir. nat. R&D Ctr. for Tchr. Edn. U. Tex., Austin, Tex., 1968—86; prof. ednl. leadership U. Fla., 1986—88; dean Coll. Edn. U. NC, 1988—93; prof. ednl. leadership U. No. Colo., Colo., 1993—98; dean Coll. Edn. U. Nev., Las Vegas, 1999—2004, prof., 2004—. Author (with S.M. Hord): Implementing Change: Patterns, Principles and Potholes, 2d edit., 2006; contbr. articles to profl. jours.; co-author (L.F. Quinn, D.M. Gollnick): The Joy of Teaching Making Difference in Student Learning. Office: Univ Nev Las Vegas 4505 Maryland Pkwy Las Vegas NV 89154 Office Phone: 702-895-3441. Business E-Mail: gene.hall@unlv.edu.

HALL, HARVEY L., Mayor, Bakersfield, California, medical transportation company executive; m. Lavonne Hall; children: Amy, Shelly, Paul, Rochelle. Attended, Bakersfield Cmty. Coll., San Francisco City Coll. Pres. & founder Hall Ambulance Svc., Inc., 1971—; mayor City of Bakersfield, Calif., 2001—. Adv. coun. mem. Mount Elgon Corp., 1999—. Bd. mem. Coalition to Protect and Preserve Private Property Rights, 1991—, African Am. Network, 1999—; pres., bd. mem. Kern County Law Enforcement Found., 1990—2000; bd. mem. Downtown Bus. Assn., 1992—2000, Bakersfield Coll. Found., 1994—2000, Bakersfield Firefighters' Burn Found., 1994—, MARE Adv. Bd., 1997—2002, Police Activities League, 1998—2000, Mexican Am. Opportunity Found., 1999—; hon. bd. mem. Police Activities League, 2000—; bd. mem. San Joaquin Valley Rail Com., 2001—, Hwy. 99 Task Force, 2002—; trustee Kern County Network for Children, 1995—2002, Kern Cmty. Coll. Dist., 1996—2000. Mem.: 15th Dist. Agr. Assn. (dir. 1998—2001), Boys and Girls Club of Bakersfield (pres. 1997—99). Office: 1600 Truxtun Ave Bakersfield CA 93301 also: Hall Ambulance Svc 1001 21st St Bakersfield CA 93301 Office Phone: 661-326-3770. Fax: 661-323-3780; Office Fax: 661-852-2035. E-mail: AdmMayor@bakersfieldcity.us.*

HALL, HENRY KINGSTON, JR., chemistry professor; b. NYC, Dec. 7, 1924; s. Henry Kingston and Agnes (Furrer) H.; m. Alene Winifred Brown, Mar. 9, 1951; children: Joan, Douglas, Lillian. BS, Poly. Inst. Bklyn., 1944; MS, Pa. State U., 1946; PhD, U. Ill., 1949. Sr. research chemist textile fibers dept. E.I. DuPont de Nemours & Co., Inc., Wilmington, Del., 1952-65, group leader central research dept., 1965-69; prof. chemistry U. Ariz., Tucson, 1969-96, chmn. dept., 1970-73, emeritus prof., 1996—. Cons. Eastman Kodak Co., Rochester, Ticona Corp., Summit, N.J.; vis. prof. Imperial Coll., London, 1976, Max Planck Inst. for Polymer Rsch., Mainz, Federal Republic of Germany, Jan.-June, 1988; sr. vis. fellow Japan Soc. for Promotion Sci., summer 1981 Contbr. articles profl. jours. Recipient Japan Award for Disting. Svc. in Advancement of Polymer Sci., Soc. Polymer Sci., 1996. Mem. Am. Chem. Soc. (PMSE divsn. award for industry-univ. coop. 1997, Award for Polymer Chemistry 1996, H.F. Mark award 2000). Achievements include research in mechanisms of organic reactions and synthesis of new high polymers. Office: U Ariz Dept Chem PO Box 210041 Tucson AZ 85721-0041 Office Phone: 520-621-6325. Business E-Mail: hkh@u.arizona.edu.

HALL, ISADORE, III, state legislator; b. Compton, Calif; BBA, U. Phoenix; MPA, Nat. Univ. Former bd. trustee and bd. trustee pres. Compton Unified Sch. Dist.; former mayor pro tem City of Compton, Calif.; former councilman Compton City Coun.; mem. Dist. 52 Calif. State Assembly, Calif., 2008—, asst. spkr. pro tempore Calif., 2008—. Democrat. Baptist . Office: PO Box 942849 Rm 6025 Sacramento CA 94249-0052 also: 2200 W Artesia Blvd Rn 210 Compton CA 90220*

HALL, JEROME WILLIAM, research engineering educator; b. Brunswick, Ga., Dec. 1, 1943; s. William L. and Frances K. H.; m. Loretta E. Hood, Aug. 28, 1965; children: Jennifer, Bridget, Bernadette. BS in Physics, Harvey Mudd Coll., Claremont, Calif., 1965; MS in Engring., U. Wash., 1968, PhDCE, 1969. Registered profl. engr., D.C., N.Mex., Va. Asst. prof. civil engring. U. Md., College Park, 1970-73, assoc. prof., 1973-77, U. N.Mex., Albuquerque, 1977-80, prof., 1980—, dir. bur. engring. research, 1981-88, asst. dean engring., 1985-88, chmn. dept. of civil engring., 1990-97. Cons. in field. Co-author: Fundamentals of Traffic Engineering, 2007; contbr. articles to profl. jours. Recipient Teetor award Soc. Automotive Engrs., 1975; Pub. Partnership award Alliance Transp. Rsch., 1997.; ITE Western District, Lifetime Achievement Award, 2006. Fellow Inst. Transp. Engrs. (pres. N.Mex. sect. 1985, pres. western dist. 1989, internat. bd. dir. 1993-95); mem. Transp. Rsch. Bd. (chmn. com. 1986-92, chmn. group coun. 1992-95, panel chmn. 1990-03), Am. Soc. Engring. Edn., Am. Rd. and Transp. Builders Assn. (pres. rsch. and edn. divsn. 2002-03, bd. dirs. 2003-05), Nat. Assn. County Engrs. Republican. Roman Catholic. Office: Dept Civil Engring MSC01 1070 UNM Albuquerque NM 87131 Business E-Mail: jerome@unm.edu.

HALL, JOHN LEWIS, physicist, researcher; b. Denver, Aug. 21, 1934; s. John Ernest and Elizabeth Rae (Long) H.; m. Marilyn Charlene Robinson, Mar. 1, 1958; children: Thomas Charles, Carolyn Gay, Jonathan Lawrence. BS in Physics, Carnegie Mellon U., Pitts., 1956, MS in Physics, 1958, PhD in Physics, 1961; PhD (hon.), U. Paris XIII, 1989; DSc (hon.), Carnegie Mellon U., Pitts., 2006. Postdoctoral rsch. assoc. Nat. Bur. Standards, Washington, 1961-62, physicist Boulder, Colo., 1962-75, sr. scientist, 1975—2004, sr. fellow, emeritus, 2005—. Lectr. U. Colo., Boulder, 1977-; cons. Los Alamos Sci. Labs., 1963-65; cons. numerous firms in laser industry, 1974—. Contbr. articles to profl. jours.; patentee in laser tech.; editor: Laser Spectroscopy 3, 1977. Recipient IR-100 award IR Mag., 1975, 77, Nat. Bur. Stds. Stratton award, 1971, E.U. Condon award, 1979, Gold medal Dept. Commerce, 1969, 74, 2002, Presdl. Meritorious Exec. award, 1980, 2002, Meritorious Alumnus award Carnegie Mellon U., 1985, Humboldt Sr. Scientist award Munich, 1989, A.V. Astin award NIST, 2000, Rabi award IEEE, 2004, Golden Plate award, Acad. Achievement, 2006; co-recipient Nobel Prize for Physics, 2005; named Knight French Legion Honor, 2004; Sherman Fairchild Disting. scholar Calif. Tech., 1992. Fellow Optical Soc. Am. (bd. dirs. 1980-82, Charles H. Townes award 1984, Frederic Ives medal 1991, Max Born award 2002), Am. Phys. Soc. (Davisson-Germer award 1988, Arthur L. Schawlow prize 1993); mem. NAS. Office: U Colo JILA Boulder CO 80309-0440 Office Phone: 303-492-7843. Business E-Mail: jhall@jila.colorado.edu.

HALL, LARRY DEAN, utilities executive, lawyer; b. Hastings, Nebr., Nov. 8, 1942; s. Willis E. and Stella W. (Eckoff) H.; m. Jeffe D. Bryant, July 5, 1985; children: Scott, Jeff, Mike, Bryan. BA in Bus., U. Nebr., Kearney; JD, U. Nebr. Bar: Nebr. 1967, Colo. 1981. Ptnr. Wright, Simmons, Hancock & Hall, Scottsbluff, Nebr., 1967-71; atty., asst. treas. KN Energy Inc., Hastings, 1971-73, dir. regulatory affairs, 1973-76, v.p. law divsn. Lakewood, Colo., 1976-82, sr. v.p., 1982-85, exec. v.p., 1985-88, pres., COO, 1988-94, pres., CEO, 1994—99, also bd. dirs., 1988-94, chmn., CEO, pres., 1996-99; mng. dir. CPS Investments, 1999—. Bd. dirs. Colo. Assn. Commerce and Industry, Gas Rsch. Inst., Colo. Alliance for Bus., MLA, Magnum Techs., Riverview Tech. Corp.; chmn. Natural Gas Coun., 1998, Ingaa, 1998. Bd. dirs. Boy Scouts Am., St. Mary's Hosp. Found., Western Slope Hospice; active Canyon View Vineyard Ch. Mem. ABA, Colo. Assn. Commerce and Industry (bd. dirs.), Interstate Natural Gas Assn. Am. (chmn. 1997), RTC (bd. dirs.), Nebr. Bar Assn., Colo. Bar Assn., Midwest Gas Assn. (chmn.). Avocations: skiing, golf, photography. Home: 329 Red Ridge Ct Grand Junction CO 81503 Office: CPS Investments LLC 1400 16th St Ste 400 Denver CO 80202

HALL, PAUL J., lawyer; b. San Diego, Jan. 13, 1951; AB with highest honors, U. Calif., Santa Cruz, 1972; postgrad, Yale U.; JD, U. Calif., Berkeley, 1975. Bar: Calif. 1975. Mem. Manatt, Phelps & Phillips, LA, 1975-94, Stein & Lubin LLP, San Francisco, 1995-98, Lillick & Charles LLP, San Francisco, 1998—. Bd. regents U. Calif., 1992-93, regent designate, 1991-92. Trustee U. Calif. Santa Cruz Found., 1986—. Mem. Calif. State Bar, Boalt Hall Alumni Assn. (bd. dirs. 1983-90, treas. 1985-86, sec. 1986-87, v.p. 1987-89, pres.-elect 1989-90, pres. 1990-91), U. Calif. Santa Cruz Alumni Assn. (bd. dirs. 1983-90, pres. 1986-90).

HALL, ROBERT EMMETT, JR., investment banker, realtor; b. Sioux City, Iowa, Apr. 28, 1936; s. Robert Emmett and Alvina (Faden) H.; m. De Phan. BA, U. S.D., 1958, MA, 1959; MBA, U. Santa Clara, 1976; grad., Am. Inst. Banking, Realtors Inst. Grad. asst. U. S.D., Vermillion, 1958-59; mgr. ins. dept., asst. mgr. installment loan dept. Northwestern Nat. Bank Sioux Falls, S.D., 1959-61, asst. cashier S.D., 1961-65; asst. mgr. Crocker Nat. Bank, San Francisco, 1965-67, loan officer, 1967-69, asst. v.p., asst. mgr. San Mateo (Calif.) br., 1969-72; v.p., western regional mgr. Internat. Investments & Realty, Inc., Washington, 1972—; owner Hall Enterprises Co., San Jose, Calif., 1976—; pres. Alamaden Oaks Realtors, Inc., 1976—. Instr. West Valley Coll., Saratoga, Calif., 1972-82, Grad. Sch. Bus., U. Santa Clara (Calif.), 1981-82, Evergreen Valley Coll., San Jose, Calif. Treas. Minnehaha Leukemia Soc., 1963, Lake County Heart Fund Assn., 1962, Minnehaha Young Rep. Club, 1963. Mem. Am. Inst. Banking, Calif. Assn. Realtors (vice chmn.), Alamaden Country Club, Elks, Rotary (past pres.), KC, Beta Theta Pi. Office: Hall Enterprises 100A Crown Blvd San Jose CA 95120-2903 Home: 6501 Crown Blvd Ste 100 San Jose CA 95120 E-mail: rehall5257@aol.com.

HALL, ROBERT ERNEST, economics professor; b. Palo Alto, Calif., Aug. 13, 1943; s. Victor Ernest and Frances Marie (Gould) H.; m. Susan E. Woodward; children: Christopher, Anne, Jonathan, Andrew. BA in Econs., U. Calif.-Berkeley, 1964; PhD in Econs., MIT, 1967. Asst. prof., acting assoc. prof. U. Calif., Berkeley, 1967-70; from assoc. prof. to prof. MIT, Cambridge, 1970-78; prof., sr. fellow Stanford U., Calif., 1978—, Robert and Carole McNeil joint prof. and sr. fellow, 1998. Dir. econ. fluctuation program Nat. Bur. Econ. Research, Cambridge, 1978—; adv. com. Congl. Budget Office, Washington, 1993—. Author: Macroeconomics, 1985, 7th rev. edit., 2006, Booms and Recessions in a Noisy Economy, 1990, The Rational Consumer: Theory and Evidence, 1990, Flat Tax, 1995, Economics, 1997, 4th rev. edit., 2007, Digital Dealing, 2001; editor: Inflation, 1983. NSF fellow, 1964, Ford Found. faculty rsch. fellow, 1969. Fellow: Soc. Labor Economists, Am. Acad. Arts and Scis., Econometric Soc.; mem.: NAS, Am. Statis Assn., Am. Econs. Assn. (Ely lectr. 2001, v.p. 2005—08, pres. 2009—). Democrat. Office: Stanford U Hoover Instn Stanford CA 94305 Office Phone: 650-723-2215. Business E-Mail: rehall@stanford.edu.

HALL, TENNIEBEE M., editor; b. Bakersfield, Calif., May 21, 1940; d. William Elmer and Lillian May (Otis) Hall; m. Harold Robert Hall, Feb. 20, 1965. BA in Edn., Fresno State Coll., 1962; AA, Bakersfield Coll., 1960. Cert. tchr., Calif. Tchr. Edison (Calif.) Sch. Dist., 1962-65; substitute tchr. Marin and Oakland Counties (Calif.), Berkeley, 1965-66; engring. asst. Pacific Coil Co., Inc., Bakersfield, 1974-81; editor United Ostomy Assn., Inc., Irvine, Calif., 1986-91. Co-author: Treating IBD, 1989, Current Therapy in Gastroenterology, 1989; author, designer: Volunteer Leadership Training Manuals, 1982-84; editor: Calif. Parliamentarian, 1999-2003, 04—; contbr. articles to Ostomy Quar., 1973-2005. Mem. Pacific Beach Town Coun., San Diego, 1977-2006; campaign worker Maureen O'Connor (1st woman mayor of city), San Diego, 1986; mem. Nat. Digestive Diseases Adv. Bd., NIH, Washington, 1986-91; mem. planning and devel. bd. Scripps Clinic and Rsch. Found. Inflammatory Bowel Disease Ctr., San Diego, 1993-2003; various vol. activities, 1966-74, 81-86. Recipient Outstanding Svc. award VA Vol. Svc., Bur. of Vets. Affairs, Washington, 1990. Mem. Nat. Assn. Parliamentarians, United Ostomy Assn. Inc. (regional program dir. 1980-84, pres. 1984-86, Sam Dubin award 1983, Industry Adv. award 1987), Crohn's and Colitis Found. Am. (nat. trustee 1986-95, nat. v.p. 1987-92). Avocations: travel, volunteerism. Home and Office: 8585 Via Mallorca Unit 7 La Jolla CA 92037-2585

HALL, WILLIAM E., engineering and construction company executive; b. Washington, Sept. 5, 1942; s. George W. and Jane F. (Brogger) H.; m. Lavinia Swift, Sept. 21, 1974; children: Deborah A., Douglas E., L. Jane, Elizabeth D. BSChemE, Va. Poly. Inst. and State U., 1963, MSChemE, 1964; postgrad., Stanford U., 1991. Process engr. Stone & Webster Engring. Co., Boston, 1967-70, project mgr. London, 1970-76, NYC, 1976-78, regional bus. devel. mgr. Houston, 1978-79; prin. project mgr. RM Parsons Co., Pasadena, Calif., 1979-81, sr. v.p., 1989-92; pres. Ralph M. Parsons Co., Pasadena, Calif., 1992—; prin. project mgr. Saudi Arabia Parsons Ltd., Yanbu, 1981-84, mng. dir., 1984-89. Bd. dirs. Proye Parsons, Caracas, Venezuela, Latisa; alt. dir. Constrn. Industry Inst., Austin, Tex., 1990-92, dir. 1992—. CHmn. Tournament of Life, Pasadena, 1990-92. Mem. Am. Inst. Chem. Engrs. Republican. Lutheran. Avocations: golf, bridge. Office: Ralph M Parsons Co 100 W Walnut St Pasadena CA 91124-0002 also: Parsons Energy & Chemicals Group Inc 5 E Greenway Plz Houston TX 77046-0500

HALL, ZACH WINTER, former scientist and research administrator; b. Atlanta, Sept. 15, 1937; s. Dixon Winter and Marjorie Elizabeth (Owens) H.; m. Anne Browning, June 1958 (div. Aug. 1960); m. Marion Nestle, Dec. 1973 (div. June 1985); m. Julie Ann Giacobassi, Nov. 9, 1987. BA, Yale U., 1958; PhD, Harvard U., 1966. Asst. prof., then assoc. prof. Harvard Med. Sch., Boston, 1968-76; prof. U. Calif., San Francisco, 1976-94; dir. Nat. Inst. Neurol. Disorders and Stroke, Bethesda, Md., 1994-97; assoc. dean for rsch. U. Calif., San Francisco, 1997-98, vice chancellor rsch., 1998-2000, exec. vice chancellor, 2000—01; pres., CEO EnVivo Pharms., Inc., 2001—02; sr. assoc. dean for rsch. Keck Sch. Medicine, U. So. Calif., 2002—05; pres. Calif. Inst. Regenerative Medicine, 2005—07. Med. Adv. Bd., Chevy Chase, Md., 1995-99, Howard Hughes Med. Inst.; Alexander Forbes lectr. Grass Found., 1994; David Nachmanson lectr. Weizmann Inst., Rehovath, Israel, 1996; adv. coun. RIKEN Inst., Tokyo, 2001-. Author, editor: Molecular Neurobiology, 1992; editor jour. Neuron, 1988-94. Recipient Purkynje medal for sci. achievement, Czech Acad. Sci., 2003. Fellow AAAS; mem. Am. Acad. Arts and Scis., Inst. Medicine. Home: PO Box 519 575 N Fall Creek Rd Wilson WY 83014-0519 Office Phone: 415-378-5359. Personal E-mail: zwhall@gmail.com.

HALLA, BRIAN L., electronics executive; b. Springfield, Ill., 1946; BSEE, U. Nebr., 1969. Applications engr. Control Data Corp., 1969—74; dir. mktg. Intel Corp., 1974—78; exec. v.p. LSI Logic, 1988—96; chmn. bd., pres., CEO Nat. Semiconductor Corp., Santa Clara, Calif., 1996—2006, chmn., CEO, 2006—. Bd. dir. Cisco Systems Inc., 2007—, Semiconductor Ind. Assn. Mem.: N.Y. Stock Exch. (adv. com.), Foveon Inc. (bd. dirs.), Tech. Network (bd. dirs.), Silicon Valley Mfg. Group, Semi-Conductor Indsl. Assn. (bd. dirs..). Office: Nat Semiconductor Corp 2900 Semiconductor Dr Santa Clara CA 95051-0695

HALLE, BRUCE T., automotive products company executive; b. Springfield, Mass., 1930; m. Diane Halle. Student, Ea. Mich. U., 1948-50, BBA, 1956, Phd (hon.). Various entry level positions including landscaping, janitor; founder, owner Discount Tire Co., Ann Arbor, 1960—, now CEO largest ind. tire dealer in N.Am. Scottsdale. Discount Tire Co. has 290 stores in 12 states. Supporter March of Dimes, Am. Heart Assn., Am. Cancer Soc., Am. Liver Found., ARC, Muscular Dystrophy Assn., Ariz. Boys and Girls Clubs, Ariz. Opera League, Phoenix Symphony, Crisis Nursery, Scottsdale Symphony and Children's Urban Survival Program, Phoenix; contbr. funds for new bldgs., Eastern Mich. U. With USMC, 1950-53. Named one of Top 200 Collectors, ARTnews mag., 2008; recipient Gold Plate award, Am. Acad. Achievement, 1994; hon. chmn. Muscular Dystrophy Assn. event, 1994; entrepreneurial fellow U. Ariz. Mem. Beta Gamma Sigma. Avocation: collecting Latin American art and contemporary sculpture.

HALLECK, CHARLES WHITE, lawyer, photographer, former judge; b. Rensselaer, Ind., July 6, 1929; s. Charles Abraham and Blanche (White) H.; m. Carolyn L. Wood, Dec. 23, 1950 (div. Oct. 1968); children: Holly Louise, Charles White, Todd Alexander, Heather Leigh, Heidi Lynne, William Hemsley, Hope Leslie; m. Jeanne Wahl, May 16, 1970. AB, Williams Coll., 1951; JD, George Washington U., 1957; LL.D. (hon.), St. Joseph's Coll., 1971; AA in Photography, Foothill Coll., Los Altos Hills, Calif., 1996. Asst. U.S. atty. for D.C., 1957-59; assoc. Hogan and Hartson, Washington, 1959-65; judge Superior Ct. D.C., 1965-77; mem. firm Lamb, Halleck & Keats, Washington, 1977-80; sole practice, 1980-86; photojournalist, 1986-99; fine art photographer, 1999—. Served with USNR, 1951-55; to lt. Res. (ret.). Mem. Beta Theta Pi, Phi Delta Phi.

HALLENBECK, HARRY C., architect; Dir. State of Calif., Sacramento, 1997; dir. planning and design svc. Vanir Constrn. Mgmt., Inc., Sacramento, 1997—. Recipient Edward C. Kemper award Archtl. Inst. Am., 1994. Office: Vanir Constrn Mgmt Inc 980 9th St Ste 900 Sacramento CA 95814-2725 also: 7485 Rush River Dr # 333 Sacramento CA 95831-5259

HALLER, EUGENE ERNEST, materials scientist, educator; b. Basel, Switzerland, Jan. 5, 1943; s. Eugene and Maria Anne Haller; m. Marianne Elisabeth Schlittler, May 26, 1973; children: Nicole Marianne, Isabelle Cathrine. Diploma in Physics, U. Basel, 1967, PhD in Physics, 1970. Postdoctoral asst. Lawrence Berkeley (Calif.) Nat. Lab., 1971—73, from staff scientist to sr. staff scientist, 1973—80, faculty sr. scientist, 1980—; assoc. prof. U. Calif., Berkeley, 1980-82, prof. materials sci., 1982—. Co-chmn. Materials Rsch. Soc. Symposia, Boston, 1982, 89, Internat. Conf. on Shallow Levels in Semiconductors, Berkeley, 1984, 94; chair 20th Internat. Conf. on Defects in Semiconds., 1999; adv. com. Paul Drude Inst., Berlin, 2001—; rev. com. instrument div. Brookhaven Nat. Lab., Upton, N.Y., 1987-93; mem. Japanese tech. panel on sensors NSF-Nat. Acad. Sci., Washington, 1988; vis. prof. Max-Planck-Inst. for Solid State Rsch., Stuttgart, 1986, Imperial Coll. Sci., Tech. and Medicine, London, 1991, German Aerospace Assn., Berlin, 1996; disting. prof. Keio u., Tokyo, 2004. Mem. editl. bd. Jour. Phys. and Chem. Solids, 1993—, Material Sci. Founds., 1998—; contbr. articles to profl. jours. U.S. Sr. scientist award Alexander von Humboldt Soc., Germany, 1986, Max-Planck Rsch. award, 1994; rsch. fellow Miller Inst. Basic Rsch., Berkeley, 1990, 2001. Fellow AAAS, Am. Phys. Soc. (James C. McGroddy prize in new materials 1999); mem. Materials Rsch. Soc. (David Turnbull Lectureship award 2005), Swiss Phys. Soc., Sigma Xi. Achievements include patents in surface passivation of semiconductors, synthesis of crystalline carbon nitride potentially a superhard material, and far infrared germanium laser. Office: U Calif Berkeley 328 Hearst Mining Meml Bldg Berkeley CA 94720-1760 Office Fax: 510-486-5530. Business E-Mail: eehaller@lbl.gov.

HALLERMAN, LISA, agent; Grad., U. Mich., 1990. Atty., NYC; TV asst. Internat. Creative Mgmt.; joined United Talent Agy., 1996, agent, 1998—2005, ptnr., 2005—08, Endeavor Agy., 2008—. Named one of The 100 Most Powerful Women in Entertainment, Hollywood Reporter, 2007. Office: Endeavor Agy LLC 9601 Wilshire Blvd 3rd Fl Beverly Hills CA 90210

HALLMAN, HUGH, Mayor, Tempe, Arizona; b. Tempe, Ariz. m. Susan Hallman; children: Louis, Eli, Marcus. BA in Economics and Polit. Sci., Claremont Men's Coll.; JD, U. Chgo. Former atty. Bain & Brown, Tempe; former prof. bus. law & econ. East Kazakhstan State Univ; former lectr. Ariz. State U., Kazakh-Am. Free U.; councilman Tempe City Coun., Ariz., 1998—2002; mayor City of Tempe, Ariz., 2004—. Author (book): (novels) How to Do Business in Kazakhstan, 1999. Mem. Tempe Aviation Com.; bd. mem. Airport Noise Abatement Com.; vol. East Valley Habitat for Humanity, Assistance for Independent Living, Tempe Cmty. Action Agy. Mailing: PO Box 5002 Tempe AZ 85280 Office: 31 E Fifth St Tempe AZ 85281 Office Phone: 480-350-8865, 480-967-2001. E-mail: hugh_hallman@tempe.gov.*

HALLMAN, MAX O., humanities and philosophy professor, director; b. Graniteville, SC, Feb. 21, 1952; s. Oneal and Naomi (Screws) Hallman; m. Gail Ann Davis Marconi, June 15, 1972 (div. July 21, 1975); m. Bobbie Ann Redd, June 28, 1978 (div. Oct. 7, 1998); children: Hannah, Dylan, Aliena Kyzer; m. Cheryl Louise Botts, July 11, 2007. BA, U. SC, Columbia, 1974, MA, 1976; PhD, Tulane U., New Orleans, 1985. Instr. philosophy Loyola U., New Orleans, 1983—85; prof. philosophy and humanities Merced Coll., Calif., 1986—, dir. honors program, 1987—, chair humanities divsn., 2006—08. Contbr. articles to profl. jours. Recipient Advisor Continued Excellence award, Phi Theta Kappa, 1997, 1999. Mem.: Am. Philos. Assn. D-Liberal. Avocations: record collecting, travel, poetry. Home: 2927 Santa Cruz Ave Merced CA 95340 Office: Merced Coll 3600 M St Merced CA 95348 Business E-Mail: hallman.m@mccd.edu.

HALLOCK, C. WILES, JR., athletic official; b. Denver, Feb. 17, 1918; s. Claude Wiles and Mary (Bassler) H.; m. Marjorie Louise Eldred, Mar. 23, 1944; children: Linda Eldred Hallock Rinne, Michael Eldred. AB, U. Denver, 1939. Sports info. dir. U. Wyo., 1949-60, track coach, 1952-56; sports info. dir. U. Calif., Berkeley, 1960-63; dir. pub. relations Nat. Collegiate Athletic Assn., 1963-68; dir. Nat. Collegiate Sports Services, 1967-68; commr. Western Athletic Conf., 1968-71; exec. dir. Pacific-8 Conf. (now Pacific-10 conf.), San Francisco and Walnut Creek, Calif., 1971-83; historian Pacific 10 Conf., 1983. Mem. Laramie (Wyo.) City Council, 1958-60. Served to lt. comdr. USNR, World War II. Decorated Air medal; mem. Nat. Football Found. and Hall of Fame Honors Ct. Mem. Nat. Collegiate Athletic Assn., Nat. Assn. Collegiate Dirs. Athletics (Corbett award 1983), Collegiate Commrs. Assn., Coll. Sports Info. Dirs. Am. (Arch Ward award 1963), Football Writers Assn. Am. (past dir.), U.S. Basketball Writers Assn., Lambda Chi Alpha. Presbyterian. Office: 800 S Broadway Walnut Creek CA 94596-5218 Home: 451 Sutcliffe PL Walnut Creek CA 94598-3923 E-mail: i4claude@aol.com.

HALLORAN, JEAN M., human resources specialist; b. NY; B in History, Princeton U.; MBA, Harvard U. Various positions in human resources, mfg., and strategic planning med. products group Hewlett-Packard, 1980—93, personnel mgr. measurement sys. orgn., 1993—97, dir. corp. edn. and devel., 1997—99; sr. v.p. human resources Agilent Technologies, Palo Alto, Calif., 1999—. Office: Agilent Technologies Inc 5301 Stevens Creek Blvd Santa Clara CA 95051-7201 Office Phone: 650-752-5633. Office Fax: 650-752-5633.

HALLORAN, PHILIP FRANCIS, nephrologist, immunologist; b. Hamilton, Ohio, June 14, 1944; MD, Univ. Toronto, 1968; PhD, Univ. London, Eng., 1978. Asst. prof. Univ. Toronto, 1975—80, assoc. prof., 1980—86, prof., 1986—87; dir., renal transplantation Toronto Gen. and Mount Sinai Hosp., 1975—87; staff phys. Tri-Hosp. Nephrology Svc., 1975—87; med. dir., HOPE program Univ. Alberta Hosp., 1987—99, dir., tissue typing lab., 1987—99, med. dir., transplantation programs, 1987—99; dir., divsn. nephrology, immunology Univ. Alberta, 1987—2003, prof., med. microbiology, immunology, 1987—, prof., dept. medicine, 1987—, Muttart chair, clin. molecular immunology & autoimmunity, 1993—; dir. Alberta Transplant Inst., 2002—. Vis. prof., immunology Hammersmith Hosp., Imperial Coll. Sch. Medicine, London, 2002. Recipient Medical award, Kidney Found. Can., 1991, Commemorative Medal, 1993, Medal of Excellence in Rsch., 2000, Disting. Scientist award, Can. Soc. Clin. Investigation, 2006; named Officer of the Order of Can., 2005; named one of Top 100 Physicians of Century in Alberta, 2005. Fellow: Acads. Arts, Humanities and Scis. Can., Royal Soc. Can., Royal Coll. Phys.and Surgeons of Can. (Medal in Medicine 1985); mem.: AAAS, Internat. Soc. Nephrology, Fedn. Am. Soc. Experimental Biology, Can. Inst. Academic Medicine, Can. Transplantation Soc. (pres. 1988—89, Lifetime Achievement award 2005), Can. Soc. Nephrology, Can. Soc. Immunology, Can. Med. Assn., Brit. Transplantation Soc., Brit. Soc. Immunology, Am. Soc. Transplant Surgeons, Am. Soc. Transplantation (Roche Ernest Hodge Disting. Achievement award 2007), Am. Soc. Clin. Investigation, Am. Assn. Immunologists, Alta. Med. Assn. Office: Nephrology & Transplantation Immunology Univ Alberta 250 Heritage Medical Research Centre Edmonton AB T6G 2S2 Canada Office Phone: 780-407-8880. Business E-Mail: phil.halloran@ualberta.ca.

HALLQUIST, JOHN O., engineering company executive; BS in Indsl. Engring. magna cum laude, Western Mich. U., 1970; MS in Engring. Mechanics, Mich. Technol. U., 1972, PhD in Mech. Engring. and Engring. Mechanics, 1974. With weapons lab. Lawrence Livermore Nat. Lab.; founder, pres. Livermore Software Tech. Corp., Calif., 1987. Recipient Dept. Energy award for Significant Contbns. to Nuc. Weapons Prog., 1986, Applied Mechanics Divsn. award, ASME, 2003. Mem.: NAE. Achievements include patents in field. Office: Livermore Software Tech Corp 7374 Las Positas Rd Livermore CA 94551 Business E-Mail: john@lstc.com.

HALM, HOWARD LEE, lawyer; b. Honolulu, July 17, 1942; s. Gilbert and Mary A.S. (Kim) H.; m. Margaret Kurashita Halm, Dec. 19, 1964; children: David Gilbert, Eric Charles, Marisa Karin. BA, UCLA, 1965; JD, U. San Diego, 1968. Bar: Calif. 1969, US Dist. Ct. (ctrl. dist.) Calif. 1969, US Ct. Appeals (9th cir.) 1969, US Dist. Ct. (we. and no. dist.) NY, US Dist. Ct. (ea., so. and no. dist.) Calif. Dep. atty. gen. State's Atty.'s Office, LA, 1969-75; ptnr. Breidenbach, Buckley, Huchting, Halm & Hamblet, LA, 1975—, Wilson, Elser, Moskowitz, Edelman & Dicker LLP, LA. Mediator, judge pro tem LA County Superior and Mcpl. Cts., 1979—90; lawyer rep. Ninth Cir. Judicial Conf. Capt. US Army, 1965—70. Recipient Commendation award City of Los Angeles, 1986, Napa Trailblazers award, 1998. Mem. ABA (pres. 1998-99, mem. Standing Com. on Profl. Liability 2002-05), Calif. Bar Assn. (various coms.), Los Angeles County Bar Assn. (various coms., chair jud. evaluation com. 1990), Def. Research Inst., Japanese Am. Bar Assn. (pres. 1985), Korean Am. Bar Assn. (pres. 1989), Korean Am. Coalition (chair 1997-99), Lawyers Liability Review (adv. bd. mem.), Fed. Bar Coun., Internat. Assn. Defense Counsel (IADC), Am. Bd. Trial Advocates, Asian Pacific Am. Bar Assn. of LA, Asian Pacific Am. Legal Ctr., Assn. So. Calif. Defense Counsel Trial Lawyers Assn. Avocation: golf. Office: Wilson Elser 555 S Flower St Ste 2900 Los Angeles CA 90071-2407 Office Phone: 213-624-3044 307. Office Fax: 213-624-8060. Business E-Mail: hylandt@wemed.com.

HALPERIN, ROBERT MILTON, retired electrical machinery company executive; b. Chgo., June 1, 1928; s. Herman and Edna Pearl (Rosenberg) H.; m. Ruth Levison, June 19, 1955; children: Mark, Margaret, Philip. Ph.B., U. Chgo., 1949; B.Mech. Engring., Cornell U., 1949; MBA, Harvard U., 1952. Locomotive prodn. engr. Electro-Motive divsn. Gen. Motors Corp., La Grange, Ill., 1949—50; trust rep. Bank of Am., San Francisco, 1954—56; adminstr. Dumont Corp., San Rafael, Calif., 1956—57; with Raychem Corp., 1957—94, pres., 1982—90, vice chmn. bd. dir. Menlo Park, Calif., 1990—94; chmn. bd. dir. Avis Tech., 1994—2004, Vitira Tech., Inc., 1994—2004; ret., 2004. Life trustee U. Chgo.; bd. dir. Harvard Bus. Sch. Pub. Co., Stanford U. Hosp. and Clinics; vice-chair, bd. dir. Stanford U. Hosp. and Clinics. Lt. USAF, 1952-53. Mem. Harvard Club of N.Y.C. Office: 2121 Sand Hill Rd Menlo Park CA 94025 E-mail: rmhalperin@sbcglobal.com.

HALPERN, BARRY DAVID, lawyer; b. Champaign, Ill., Feb. 25, 1949; s. I. L. and Trula M. Halpern; m. Cynthia Ann Zedler, Aug. 4, 1972; children: Amanda M., Trevor H. BA, U. Kans., 1971, JD, 1973. Bar: Kans. 1973, U.S. Dist. Ct. Kans. 1973, Fla. 1975, U.S. Supreme Ct. 1976, Ariz. 1978, U.S. Dist. Ct. Ariz. 1978, Colo. 1991. Ptnr. Snell & Wilmer, Phoenix, 1978—. Faculty Ariz. State U., 2002—03. Mem. Gov.'s Task Force Edn. Reform, 1991; judge pro tem Maricopa County Superior Ct.; bd. dirs. Crisis Nursery, Phoenix, 1987, Friends of Foster Children, Phoenix, 1987, Phoenix Symphony, Greater Phoenix Econ. Coun., 2003—, Combined Orgn. Met. Phoenix Arts and Scis., 1994—98, pres., 1996—97, mem. exec. com., 1998—2002. Mem.: ABA, Maricopa County Bar Assn. (chmn. med.-legal com. 1995—96), State Bar Colo., State Bar Kans., State Bar Fla., State Bar Ariz., Phoenix C. of C. (health care coun. 1993—96). Office: Snell & Wilmer 1 Arizona Ctr Phoenix AZ 85004-2202 Home Phone: 602-943-3384; Office Phone: 602-382-6345. Business E-Mail: bhalpern@swlaw.com.

HALPERN, MARTIN BRENT, physics professor; b. Newark, Aug. 26, 1939; s. Melvin M. and Blanche B. (Friedman) H.; m. Penelope J. Dutton, June 2, 1988; 1 child, Tamar Lillian. BSc, U. Ariz., 1960; PhD, Harvard U., 1964. Postdoctoral fellow CERN, Geneva, 1964—65, U. Calif., Berkeley, 1965—66, prof. physics, 1967—; postdoctoral fellow Inst. Advanced Study, Princeton, NJ, 1966—67. Office: U Calif 366 Le Conte Hall Berkeley CA 94720-7303

HALPRIN, ANNA SCHUMAN (MRS. LAWRENCE HALPRIN), dancer; b. Wilmette, Ill., July 13, 1920; d. Isadore and Ida (Schiff) Schuman; m. Lawrence Halprin, Sept. 19, 1940; children: Daria, Rana. Student, Bennington Summer Sch. Dance, 1938-39; BS in Dance, U. Wis., 1943; PhD in Human Services (hon.), Sierra U., Riverside, Calif., 1987; PhD (hon.), U. Wis., 1994, Santa Clara U., Calif.; student, Calif. Arts Coll., Calif., 2003; PhD (hon.), Art Inst. of San Francisco, Calif., 2003. Presenter opening invocation State of the World Forum by spl. invitation from Mikhail S. Gorbachev. Author: Moving Toward Life, Five Decades of Transformative Dance, Dance as a Healing Art, A Teachers' Guide and Support Manual for People with Cancer; dancer: at Kennedy Ctr., Washington, Yerba Buena Ctr. for Arts, San Francisco, Joyce Theatre, NYC, 2001—, d'Autumne Festival Paris, Pompidou Theatre, 2004, Cowell Theatre, Returning Home (1st prize Film Dance Festival N.Y.C., 2004), (film) Moving with the Earth Body, Learning Lessons in Life, Loss & Liberation, 2003, Intensive Care, Reflections on Death and Dying, 2003, Jewish Cmty. Ctr. Kinball Theatre, 2006, San Francisco, Jewish Cmty. Ctr., 2006, Art Contemporain Lyon Anna Halprin: The origines and performance, 2006, Dance, USA honour, 2006, 100 Irreplaceable dance treassures, 2002, Hist. Survey, Anna Halprins Work, others Bd. dirs. East West Holistic Healing Inst.; mem. Gov.'s Coun. on Phys. Fitness and Wellness. Recipient award Am. Dance Guild, 1980, Guggenheim award, 1970-71, Woman of Wisdom award Bay Area Profl. Women's Network, Tchr. of Yr. award Calif. Tchrs. Assn., 1988, Lifetime Achievement award in visual and performing arts San Francisco Bay Guardian newspaper, 1990, Women of Achievement, Vision and Excellence award, 1992, Lifetime Achievement award, Am. Dance Festival, 1997, Womens Hall of Fame, Marin, 1998, Cyril Magnin award, 1998, Body Wisdom, Internat. Somatic Congress, 1999, Shining Star award, Internat. Expressive Arts Therapy Assn., 2000, Lifetime Achievement award, Calif. arts coun., 2001, named: Am. 100 Irreplaceable Dance Treasures, Dance Heritage Coalition, 2003, Outstanding Leadership, Congress on Rsch.in dance, 2005, Lifetime Achievement award, Assn. Theatre Movement Educators, 2005, Pioneer award, Calif. Pacific Med. Ctr., 2007, Marin Arts Coun. award, Marin, 1993, Annual Dance Heritage award, 1989, Teacher of year, West Coast, 1988, Wisdom award, Profl. Womens Assn., 1987, Coalition dance award, San Francisco, 1985, Balasaraswati/Joy Ann Dewey Bieneke chair for disting. tchg. Am. Dance Festival, 1996, Lifetime Achievement in Modern Dance award Am. Dance Festival, 1997, Lifetime Achievement award Calif. Arts Coun., 2000, Lifetime Achievement award, Breast Cancer Watch, 2001, Dance Mag. N.Y.C. award, 2004; Person of Yr. in field of Dance award Ballet-ranz, Berlin; named to Isadora Duncan Hall of Fame, Bay Area Dance Coalition, 1986; Nat. Endowment Arts Choreographers grantee, 1976, NEA choreography grantee, 1977, San Francisco Found. grantee, 1981, Calif. Arts. Coun. grantee, 1990—; inductee Marin Women's Hall of Fame, 1998, lifetime achievement award Marin Arts Coun., Sustained Achieve. award Am. Theatre Edn. Assn., 2005, award Healing Arts Network, 2006, USA Artist Award, 2007. Fellow Am. Expressive Therapy Assn.; mem. Assn. Am. Dance, Conscientious Artists Am., San Francisco C. of C. Home and Office: 15 Ravine Way Kentfield CA 94904-2713 Home Phone: 415-461-5362; Office Phone: 415-461-5362. Personal E-mail: anna@annahalprin.org.

HALSTED, CHARLES HOPKINSON, internist; b. Cambridge, Mass., Oct. 2, 1936; s. James Addison and Isabella (Hopkinson) H.; m. June 7, 1959, (div. 1986); children: John, Michael, Ellen; m. Ann Wyant, Dec. 20, 1986. BA, Stanford U., 1958; MD, U. Rochester, 1962; post grad., Cleve. Metro Gen. Hosp., 1966, John Hopkins U., 1970. Diplomate Am. Bd. Internal Medicine. Asst. prof. John Hopkins U., Balt., 1971-74, U. Calif., Davis, 1974-76, assoc. prof., 1976-80, prof., 1980—, dir. div. clin. nutrition and metabolism, 1983—. Editor: Nutrition in Organ Failure, 1989; co-editor The Laboratory in Clinical Medicine, 1981; editor-in-chief Am. Jour. Clin. Nutrition, 1997—; contbr. articles to profl. jours. Surgeon USPHS, 1966-68. Fellow ACP, Am. Soc. Nutritional Scis.; mem. Am. Soc. Clin. Nutrition (pres. 1988-89), Am. Soc. Clin. Investigation, Am. Gastroentrological Assn., Am. Soc. for Study Liver Diseases, Western Assn. Physicians, Am. Bd. Nutrition (pres. 1990-91), Calif. Acad. Medicine, Am. Clinical and Climatological Assn. Office: U Calif Sch Medicine TB 156 Davis CA 95616

HALVER, JOHN EMIL, nutritional biochemist; b. Woodinville, Wash., Apr. 21, 1922; s. John Emil and Helen Henrietta (Hansen) Halver; m. Jane Loren, July 21, 1944; children: John Emil, Nancylee Halver Hadley, Janet Ann Halver Fix, Peter Loren, Deborah Kay Halver Hanson. BS, Wash. State U., 1944, MS in Organic Chemistry, 1948; PhD in Med. Biochemistry, U. Wash., 1953. Plant chemist Assoc. Frozen Foods, Kent, Wash., 1946-47; asst. chemist Purdue U., 1948—49; instr. U. Wash., Seattle, 1949—50, affiliate prof., 1960—75; prof. U. Wash. Sch. Fisheries, 1978—92; prof. emeritus U. Wash., 1992—. Condr. research on vitamin and amino acid requirements for fish; identified aflatoxin B1 as specific carcinogen for rainbow trout hematoma; identified vitamin C2 for fish; dir. Western Fish Nutrition Lab. U.S. Fish and Wildlife Service, Dept. Interior, Cook, Wash., 1950—75, sr. scientist, nutrition, Seattle, 1975—78; cons. FAO, UNDP, Internat. Union Nutrition Scientists, Nat. Fish Research Inst., Hungary, World Bank, Euroconsult, UNDP, IDRC; affiliate prof. prof. U. Oreg. Med. Sch., 1965—69; vis. prof. Marine Sci. Inst. U. Tex., Port Aransas; pres. Fisheries Devel. Technology, Inc., 1980—90, Halver Corp., 1978—. Lay leader Meth. Ch., 1965—70. Capt. US Army, World War II, col. USAR. Decorated Purple Heart, Bronze Star with oak leaf cluster, Meritorious Service Conduct medal. Fellow: Am. Inst. Nutrition, Am. Inst. Fishery Research Biologists; mem.: NAS, Hungarian Acad. Sci., World Aquaculture Soc., Am. Fishery Soc., Am. Chem. Soc., Am. Sci. Affiliation, Soc. Exptl. Biol. Medicine, Rotary, Alpha Chi Sigma, Pi Mu Epsilon, Phi Lambda Upsilon. Achievements include founder JE Halver Fellowship at University of Washington; founder JE Halver Lecture at Washington State University. Home: 16502 41st Ave NE Seattle WA 98155-5610 Office: U Wash Box 355100 Sch Fisheries and Aquatic Scis Seattle WA 98195-5100 Office Phone: 206-543-9619. Business E-Mail: halver@u.washington.edu.

HALVORSEN, CLAY A., lawyer, construction executive; BA in Econs., Calif. State U., 1982; JD, U. Southern Calif., 1985. Bar: Calif. Atty. Gibson, Dunn & Crutcher, 1985—95, ptnr., 1995—97; v.p., gen. counsel, sec. Standard Pacific Corp., Costa Mesa, Calif., 1998—2001, sr. v.p., gen. counsel, sec., 2001—04, exec. v.p., gen. counsel, sec., 2004—. Mem.: Calif. State Bar Assn. Office: Standard Pacific Corp 26 Technology Dr Irvine CA 92618-2301

HALVORSON, ARDELL DAVID, soil scientist, researcher; b. Rugby, ND, May 31, 1945; s. Albert F. and Karen Halvorson; m. Linda Halvorson; children: Renae, Rhonda. BS, N.D. State U., 1967; MS, Colo. State U., 1969, PhD, 1971. Soil scientist Agr. Rsch. Svc., USDA, Sidney, Mont., 1971-83, Akron, Colo., 1983-88, rsch. leader, 1988-94; lab. dir. USDA-Agr. Rsch. Svc., Mandan, N.D., 1994-97, soil scientist Ft. Collins, Colo., 1997—. Contbr. numerous articles to profl. publs. Fellow Am. Soc. Agronomy (assoc. editor 1983-87), Soil Sci. Soc. Am. (chmn. divsn. S-8 1989), Soil and Water Conservation Soc. (chpt. pres. 1991); mem. Crop Sci. Soc. Am. Office: USDA-ARS 2150 Centre Ave #D-100 Fort Collins CO 80526 Office Phone: 970-492-7230. Business E-Mail: ardell.halvorson@ars.usda.gov.

HALVORSON, FRANK ELSWORTH, sales executive; b. Stockton, Calif., Feb. 5, 1956; s. William Elsworth and Lorraine (Rogers) H.; m. Lori Thom, Sept. 30, 1980; children: Amanda Rose, Lauren Elizabeth. Student, U. the Pacific, 1979. Dist. mgr. Oldsmobile div. Gen. Motors, St. Louis, Fresno, Calif. and San Francisco, 1979-83; gen. mgr., v.p. Prospect Motors Inc., Jackson, Calif., 1983—, pres. County chmn. membership drive Boy Scouts Am., 1987. Mem. Soc. Sales Execs. (Gen. Motors Div.). Lodges: Rotary, Moose. Republican. Roman Catholic. Avocations: golf, fishing, hunting. Office: Prospect Motors Inc 645 Hwy 49 & 88 PO Box 1360 Jackson CA 95642-1360

HAMADA, DUANE TAKUMI, architect; b. Honolulu, Aug. 12, 1954; s. Robert Kensaku and Jean Hakue (Masutani) H.; m. Martha S.P. Lee, Dec. 22, 1991; children: Erin, Robyn, David. BFA in Environ. Design, U. Hawaii, 1977, BArch, 1979. Registered architect, Hawaii, Guam, Florida, Puerto Rico, Saipan. Intern Edward Sullam, FAIA & Assocs., Honolulu, 1979-80; assoc. Design Ptnrs., Inc., Honolulu, 1980-86; prin. AM Ptnrs., Inc., Honolulu, 1986-98, Design Ptnrs. Inc., Honolulu, 1998—. Chmn. 31st Ann. Cherry Blossom Festival Fashion Show, Honolulu, 1982, 32d Ann. Cherry Blossom Festival Cooking Show, 1983, mem. steering com., 1982, 83. Recipient Gold Key award for Excellence in Interior Design Am. Hotel and Motel Assn., 1990, Renaissance '90 Merit award Nat. Assn. Home Builder's Remodeler Coun., Merit award Honolulu mag., 1990, Cert. of Appreciation PACDIV USN, 1992, Gold Nugget award of Merit, 1997, Design Excellence Concept Design award USAF Hawaii, 2003, Pub. Govt. New Project award NAIOP, 2005 Mem. AIA (jury student awards 1997, 98, jury profl. awards 1999), Constrn. Specifications Inst., Nat. Coun. Archtl. Registration Bds., Colegio de Arcquitectos de P.R Avocations: astronomy, music. Office: Design Ptnrs Inc 1580 Makaloa St Ste 1100 Honolulu HI 96814-3240 Home Phone: 808-988-1753. E-mail: dhamada@hawaii.rr.com.

HAMADA, HAROLD SEICHI, civil engineer, educator; b. Honolulu, Nov. 1, 1935; s. Kihachi and Tsuruyo (Hamada) H.; m. Lucy Tachiko Igawa, Aug. 24, 1958; children: Kyle Hideo, LeeAnn Hiroko. BS, U. Hawaii, Manoa, 1957; MS, U. Ill., Urbana, 1958, PhD, 1962. Registered profl. engr, Hawaii. Project officer Air Force Weapons Lab., Kirtland AFB, N.Mex., 1962-65; engr. Lawrence Radiation Lab., Calif., 1965-67; prof. civil engring. U. Hawaii, Honolulu, 1967-90, interim chmn. civil engring., 1990-92, chmn. civil engring., 1992—95, prof. civil engring., 1995—2000, prof. emeritus, 2000; with KSF, Inc., Honolulu, 2000—. Served with USAF, 1962-65. Fellow ASCE (pres. Hawaii sect. 1974), Am. Concrete Inst., Structural Engrs. Assn. Hawaii (pres. elect 1989, pres. 1990, past pres. 1991), Hawaii Soc. Profl. Engrs. (Engr. of Yr. 1993), Sigma Xi. Home: 2084 Alaeloa St Honolulu HI 96821-1021 Office: KSF Inc Ste 300 615 Piikoi St Honolulu HI 96814 Office Phone: 808-593-0939 ext. 245. Personal E-mail: hamada2084@aol.com. Business E-Mail: haroldh@ksfinc.us.

HAMADA, RICK, electronics executive; BS in Fin., San Diego State U. Various positions including tech. specialist Hamilton/Avnet Electronics, 1983—94; v.p. mktg. Hall-Mark Computer Products (now Avnet Hall-Mark), 1994—97; exec. v.p. Avnet Computer (now Avnet Enterprise Solutions), 1998—99; corp. v.p. Avnet, Inc., 1999, sr. v.p., 2002—, COO; pres. Avnet Hall-Mark N.Am., 2000—02, Avnet Computer Mktg. (now Avnet Tech. Solutions), 2002. Named one of Top 25 Most Influential Execs. in Computer Industry, Computer Reseller News mag., 2002. Office: Avnet Inc 2211 S 47th St Phoenix AZ 85034-6403 Office Phone: 480-643-2000.

HAMAI, JAMES YUTAKA, manufacturing executive; b. Oct. 14, 1926; s. Seizo and May (Sata) H.; m. Dorothy K. Fukuda, Sept. 10, 1954; children: Wendy A. BS cum laude, U. So. Calif., 1952; MS, 1955; postgrad. bus. mgmt. program ind. exec., UCLA, 1962—64. Lectr. chem. engring. dept. U. So. Calif., LA, 1961—64; process engr., sr. process engr. Fluor Corp., LA, 1954—64; sr. project mgr. ctrl. rsch. dept. Monsanto Co., St. Louis, 1964—67, mgr. rsch., devel. and engring. graphic sys. dept., 1967—68; mgr. comml. devel. New Enterprise Divsn., 1968—69; exec. v.p., dir. Concrete Cutting Industries, Inc., LA, 1969—72; pres., dir. Concrete Cutting Internat. Inc., LA, 1972—78, chmn. bd., 1978—; pres., CEO, dir. Techno Enterprises U.S.A., Ltd., LA, 2000—04. Cons. Fluor Corp., Los Angeles, 1970-74; dir. Intech Systems Co., Ltd., Tokyo, Cutting Industries Co., Ltd., Tokyo; internat. bus. cons. Served with AUS, 1946-48. Mem. AIChE, Am. Mgmt. Assn., Tau Beta Pi, Phi Lambda Upsilon. Club: Rotary (gov. dist. 1982-83). Home: 6600 Via La Paloma Rancho Palos Verdes CA 90275-6449 Office: PO Box 6683 San Pedro CA 90734

HAMAMOTO, PATRICIA, school system administrator, educator; b. Honolulu, Sept. 30, 1944; BA in History, Calif. State Coll., Long Beach, 1967, profl. tchg. diploma, 1967; education administrator's cert., U. Hawaii M, 1985. Social studies tchr. Fountain Valley H.S., Calif., 1967—72; social studies tchr., dept. chair Iiima Intermediate Sch., Ewa Beach, Hawaii, 1976—81; tchg. grad. asst. geography dept. U. Hawaii at Manoa, 1981—83; tchr. guidance/math. Pearl City H.S., Hawaii, 1985; vice prin. Maui H.S., Kahlui, Hawaii, 1983—85, Nanakul H.S. and Intermediate Sch, Nanakuli, Hawaii, 1985—87; prin. Pearl City Highlands Elem. Sch, Hawaii, 1987—89; contract adminstrn. specialist II Office Personnel Svcs., Honolulu, 1989—91; prin. Likelike Elem., 1991—92, Pres. William McKinley H.S., Honolulu, 1992—99; dep. supt. Hawaii Dept. Edn., Honolulu, 1999—2001, interim supt., 2001; supt. of edn. Hawaii Dept Edn., Honolulu, 2001—. Co-chairperson Tchr. Edn. Coordinating Com., Venture Edn. Forum; mem. adv. coun. Univ. Hawaii Coll. Edn. Mem.: ASCD, Am. Assn. Sch. Adminstr., Assn. for Supervision and Curriculum Develop., Pacific Resources for Edn. and Learning, Coun. of Chief State Sch. Officers, Nat. Assn. Secondary Sch. Prins. Avocations: golf, reading, travel, walking. Home: 1767 Puowaina Dr Honolulu HI 96813 Office: Hawaii Dept Edn PO Box 2360 Honolulu HI 96804-2360 Home Phone: 808-536-0296; Office Phone: 808-586-3310. E-mail: patricia_hamamoto@notes.k12.hi.us.

HAMAN, RAYMOND WILLIAM, retired lawyer; b. St. Maries, Idaho, Jan. 22, 1927; s. William and Eva Kate (Colliver) H.; m. Phyllis Maxine Garrett, June 24, 1948; children: Lorinda Ann, Bradley Lawrence (dec.). Student, Whitman Coll., 1947-49; JD, Washington and Lee U., 1952. Bar: Wash., 1952, U.S. Dist. Ct. (we. dist.) Wash. 1952, U.S. Ct. Appeals (9th cir.), U.S. Supreme Ct. Assoc. Evans, McLaren, Lane, Powell & Beeks, Seattle, 1952-59, ptnr., 1959-66, Lane Powell, Seattle, 1966-89, 1989-91, of counsel, 1991-2001; ret. Legal counsel Gov. Daniel J. Evans, Olympia, Wash., 1965, 67; mem. statute Law Com., 1966-95, chmn. 1988-95. Trustee, past pres. Lighthouse for the Blind, Inc., Seattle, 1964—; mem. vestry St. Augustine's Episcopal Ch., 1999—2002; bd. dirs. Mercer Island (Wash.) Sch. Dist., 1967—72, Island County (Wash.) United Way, 1993—, pres., 1997—98. With USMC, 1945—46, PTO. Mem.: Wash. Bar Assn., Order of the Coif. Republican. Episcopalian. Home: PO Box 926 Langley WA 98260-0926 Office: Lane Powell PC 1420 5th Ave Ste 4100 Seattle WA 98101-2338

HAMBRICK, JOHN, state legislator; b. St. Paul, Minn., 1945; m. Nancy Hambrick; children: Laura, John. Cert. Fraud Examiner, U. Minn.; attended, Fed.Law Enforcement Tng. Ctr., Brunswick, Ga., Border Patrol Acad., Brownsville, Tex., Basic & Advanced Treas. Sch., Washington, DC. Ret. mem. Presdl. Protection Detail, US Secret Svc.; past chair Clark County Rep. Party; agent Immigration & Naturalization Svc.; ret. investigator Fed. Inspector's Gen. Office; chief investigator Nev. Bd. of Osteopathic Medicine; chair Nev. Juvenile Justice Commn.; mem. Dist. 2 Nev. State Assembly, 2008—. Recipient Worker's Compensation Fraud Taskforce Outstanding Team award, 1999, Vice President's Excellence award (Hammer award), 1999, Inspector General's Career Achievement award, 2000. Republican. Office: 401 South Carson St Room 3129 Carson City NV 89701 Home: 1930 Village Center Cir Suite 3-419 Las Vegas NV 89134-6245 Home Phone: 702-242-8580; Office Phone: 775-684-8827. Fax: 702-242-3406. Business E-Mail: jhambrick@asm.state.nv.us.

HAMBURGER, ROBERT N., pediatrician, educator, consultant; b. NYC, Jan. 26, 1923; s. Samuel B. and Harriet (Newfield) H.; m. Sonia Gross, Nov. 9, 1943; children: Hilary, Debre (dec.), Lisa. BA, U. NC, 1947; MD, Yale U., 1951. Diplomate Am. Bd. Pediatrics, Am. Bd. Allergy and Immunology. Instr., asst. clin. prof. sch. medicine Yale U., New Haven, 1951-60; assoc. prof. biology U. Calif. San Diego, La Jolla, 1960-64, assoc. prof. pediatrics, 1964-67, prof., 1967-90, prof. emeritus, 1990—, asst. dean sch. medicine, 1964-70, lab. dir., 1970-98, head fellows tng. program allergy and immunology divsn., 1970-90; pres., CEO RNA and Co., Inc., 1997—. Chmn., bd. dirs. BioVigilant Sys., Inc., 2002-; cons. various cos., Calif., Sweden, Switzerland, 1986—. Author 1 book; contbr. articles to profl. jours. Vol. physician, educator Children of the Californias, Calif. and Baja California, Mex., 1993—, Baker Sch. Free Clinic, 1999—. 1st lt. Air Corps, U.S. Army, 1943-45, PTO. Decorated Air medal with oak leaf clusters, Purple Heart; grantee NIH and USPHS, 1960-64, 64-84; Fulbright fellow, 1980, Disting. fellow Am. Coll. Allergy, Asthma, Immunology, 1986. Mem. U. Calif. San Diego Emeriti Assn. (pres. 1992-94). Achievements include patentee for allergy peptides, allergen detector, Pathogen Detector System and Methods. Avocations: flying, skiing, writing. Office: U Calif San Diego Revelle Coll Sch Medicine La Jolla CA 92093-0950 Office Phone: 858-534-7555. E-mail: rhamburger@ucsd.edu.

HAMEL, MICHAEL A., career officer; BS in Aero. Engring., USAF Acad., 1972; MBA, Calif. State U., Dominguez Hills, 1974; grad., Squadron Officer Sch., 1975, Air Command and Staff Coll., 1980. Commd. 2d lt. USAF, 1972, advanced through grades to Lt. Gen.; devel. planner Space and Missile Sys. Orgn., L.A. AFB, 1972-75; missile analyst fgn. tech. divsn. Lowry AFB, Colo., 1975-77; mission dir. Aerospace Data Facility, Buckley Air N.G. Base, Colo., 1975—79; air staff tng. officer Hdqs. USAf, Washington, 1979-80; project mgr., manned spaceflight engr. Office of Sec. of Air Force for Spl. Projects, L.A. AFB, 1980-86; staff exec. officer Hdqs. USAF, Washington, 1986-90; chief plans divsn. Hdqs. Air Force Space Command, Peterson AFB, Colo., 1991-94; comdr. 750th Space Group, Onizuka Air Sta., Calif., 1994-95; vice comdr. 21st Space Wing, Peterson AFB, 1995-96; mil. adviser to v.p. The White House, Washington, 1996-98; vice comdr. Space and Missile Sys. Ctr., L.A. AFB, 1998-99, comdr., 2005—; dir. requirements Air force Space Command HQ, Peterson AFB, Colo., 1999—; dir. space ops. and intergration HQ USAF, Pentagon, 2000—02; comdr. 14th AF Vanderberg AFB, Calif., 2002—05. Decorated Def. Superior Svc. medal, Disting. Svc. medal, Legion of Merit, Meritorious Svc. medal with 3 oak leaf clusters. Office: Space & Missile Ctr 2420 Vela Way Ste 1 Bldg 6 El Segundo CA 90245 Business E-Mail: michael.hamel@losangeles.af.mil.

HAMILL, PATRICK JAMES, physics professor, environmental scientist; b. Salt Lake City, Utah, Apr. 29, 1936; m. Elsa Gloria Li, Jan. 14, 1961. PhD, U. Ariz., Tucson, 1971. Prof., physics San Jose State U., Calif., 1980—. Mem. bd. dirs. Bay Area Environ. Rsch. Inst., Sonoma, Calif., 2000—. Recipient H. Julian Allen award, NASA Ames Rsch. Ctr., 1988. Mem.: Am. Inst. Physics. Office: San Jose State Univ 1 Washington Square San Jose CA 95192 Business E-Mail: hamill@wind.sjsu.edu.

HAMILTON, BEVERLY LANNQUIST, investment executive; b. Roxbury, Mass., Oct. 19, 1946; d. Arthur and Nancy Lannquist. BA cum laude, U. Mich., 1968; postgrad., NYU, 1969-70. V.p. Auerbach, Pollak & Richardson, NYC, 1972-75, Morgan Stanley & Co., NYC, 1975-80, United Techs., Hartford, Conn., 1980-87; dep. comptr. City of N.Y., 1987-91; pres., ret. ARCO Investment Mgmt Co, LA, 1991-2000. Bd. dirs. Oppenheimer Funds, Am. Fund's Emerging Markets Growth Fund; trustee The Calif. Endowment, Monterey Inst. Internat. Studies, Cmty. Hosp. Monterey, Middlebury Coll.; investment coms. U. Mich. Trustee Hartford Coll. for Women, 1981-87, Stanford Univ. Mgmt. Co., 1991-99; bd. dirs. Inst. for Living, 1983-87. Mem. NCCJ (bd. dirs. 1987-91). Address: 5485 Quail Meadows Dr Carmel CA 93923-7971

HAMILTON, DARDEN COLE, construction management company executive; b. Pitts., Nov. 28, 1956; s. Isaac Herman Hamilton and Grace Osborne (Fish) Thorp; m. Linda Susanne Moser, Aug. 7, 1976; children: Christopher Moser, Elijah Cole. BS in Aeronautics, St. Louis U., Cahokia, Ill., 1977; postgrad., Ariz. State U. Lic. pilot, airframe and power mechnic. Engr. McDonnell Douglas Aircraft Co., St. Louis, 1977-80; group leader, engring. Cessna Aircraft Co., Wichita, Kans., 1980-83, sr. flight test engr., 1983-85, Allied-Signal Aerospace (Honeywell) Co., Phoenix, 1986-92, flight test engr. specialist, 1992-98, prin. engr., 1988—2003; mem. Ariz. Senate, Dist. 16, Phoenix, 1998—2003; vice chair transp. com., mem. appropriations com. Ariz. Senate, Phoenix, 1999-2000, chmn. rules com., appropriations edn. sub-com., 2001—02, vice chmn. natural resources, agr. and environ. com., 2001—02, mem. commerce com., 2001—02; corp. pres. CANAMEX, Inc., 2003—05. Editor: Family Proponent Newsletter, 1994—98. Mem. Ariz. Gov.'s Constl. Commemoration Com., 1997—99; bd. dirs. Ariz. Ho. and Senate Chaplaincy, 1997—98, Crisis Pregnancy Ctr. of Greater Phoenix, 2003—; chmn. bd. advisors Ariz. Ho. and Senate Chaplaincy, 1998—2000; mem. resolutions com. Ariz. Gov.'s Mil. Base Retention Task Force, 1999—2003; chmn. domestic violence task force Ariz. Senate, 1999—2003; Desert Sky precinct committeeman Glendale Rep. Com.; vol. coord. legis. dist. 16 campaign John Shadegg for Congress, 1994—96; del. dist. 16 Ariz. Rep. Conv., 1995—98; mem. resolutions com. Ariz. Rep. Com.; mem. adult edn. dept. Rivers Cmty. Ch.; exec. v.p. Marketplace Resources, 2003—. Mem.: NRA (life cert. instr.), Am. Legis. Exch. Coun., Am. Helicopter Soc., Soc. Flight Test Engrs., Ariz. State Rifle and Pistol Assn. (life). Avocations: horses, target shooting, camping.

HAMILTON, FREDERIC CRAWFORD, oil company executive; b. Columbus, Ohio, Sept. 25, 1927; s. Ferris F. and Jean (Crawford) H.; m. Jane C. Murchison, Feb. 14, 1953; children: Christy, Frederic C., Crawford M., Thomas M. Grad., Lawrenceville Sch., 1945, Babson Coll., 1947. Pres. Hamilton Bros. Oil Co., Denver, 1957—, Hamilton Bros. Can. Gas Co., Ltd., Calgary, Alta., 1968—; chmn. bd. Hamilton Bros. Oil and Gas (Gt. Brit.), Ltd., London, Eng., 1964—, Hamilton Bros. Petroleum Corp., Denver; chmn., chief exec. officer, pres. Hamilton Oil Corp.; chief exec. ofcr. Denver Art Mus., Denver. Bd. dirs. Gates Learjet Corp., IntraWest Fin. Corp., U.S. Trust Co., Skandinaviska, Enskilda Banken Internat. Corp.; adv. bd. Volvo Internat. Served with USAAF, 1944-46. Mem. Am. Petroleum Inst. (bd. dirs.). Office: Hamilton Oil Corp 1560 Broadway Denver CO 80202-6000 also: Denver Art Museum 100 W 14th Ave Denver CO 80204

HAMILTON, HARRY LEMUEL, JR., academic administrator, science educator; b. Charleston, SC, May 26, 1938; s. Harry Lemuel and Velma Fern (Bell) H.; m. LaVerne McDaniel, June 26, 1965 (div. 1978); children: David M., Lisa L; m. Mary MacIntyre, May 10, 1997. BA in Physics, Beloit Coll., 1960; MS in Meteorology, U. Wis., 1962, PhD in Meteorology, 1965. Asst. prof. atmospheric sci. SUNY, Albany, 1965-71, assoc. prof., 1971-90, dir. ednl. opportunity program, 1968-71, chairperson atmospheric sci., 1976-83, dean undergrad. studies, assoc. v.p. acad. affairs, 1983-88; rsch. scientist GE, Schenectady, NY, 1973-75; sr. v.p., provost Chapman U., Orange, Calif., 1990-2000, prof. atmospheric sci., 2000—05, interim provost, exec. v.p., 2005—. Trustee Beloit (Wis.) Coll., 1972—, Newport Beach Pub. Libr., 2001—, pres., 2003--; bd. dirs. Albany Med. Ctr., 1988-90, Mohawk Hudson Cmty. Found., 1988-90; pres. Empire State Inst. for Performing Arts, Albany, 1986-90; bd. dirs. world affairs coun. Orange County, 1995-2003; treas. Arts Orange County, 1995-2000; bd. dirs. Discovery Sci. Ctr., 1998-2004. Mem. Am. Meteorol. Soc., Am. Assn. for Higher Edn. Office: Chapman U 1 University Dr Orange CA 92866-1005 Home Phone: 949-760-1918; Office Phone: 714-997-6826. Business E-Mail: hamilton@chapman.edu.

HAMILTON, JAMES WILLIAM, lawyer; b. Omaha, Sept. 6, 1932; s. James William and Mary (Morgans) H.; m. Carol Lorraine Kircher, July 10, 1954; children: Theodore, Evelyn, Bonnie. BA, Stanford U., 1954, LLB, 1959. Bar: Calif. 1960, D.C. 1983. Assoc. Paul, Hastings, Janofsky & Walker, LA, 1959-65, ptnr., 1965-93, sr. counsel, 1993—, ptnr. Costa Mesa, Calif., 1974-82, 85-93, Washington, 1982-85, of counsel, 1993—. Bd. dirs. Nat. Bank So. Calif., Newport Beach. Bd. dirs. Art Inst. So. Calif., Laguna Beach, Opportunity Internat., Chgo.; bd. visitors Stanford U. Law Sch., 1978-81, 96—. 1st lt. USAF, 1954-56. Mem. ABA, Los Angeles County Bar Assn. (chmn. corp. sect. 1973-74, editor bull. 1970-71), Orange County Bar Assn., Big Canyon Country Club (Newport Beach), Ironwood Country Club (Palm Desert, Calif.), Phi Gamma Delta. Republican. Presbyterian. Avocations: golf, skiing, swimming. Home: 895 Cliff Dr Laguna Beach CA 92651-1410 Office: Paul Hastings Janofsky & Walker 695 Town Center Dr Fl 17 Costa Mesa CA 92626-1924

HAMILTON, JOAN NICE, editor-in-chief; b. Chgo., 1948; d. William and Dorothy Nice. Grad., Pomona Coll., 1970. Former editor High Country News; editor Climbing Mag.; editor-in-chief Sierra Mag., San Francisco. Contbr. articles to Audubon, Defenders, Nat. Wildlife Mags. Office: Sierra Mag 85 2nd St San Francisco CA 94105-3459

HAMILTON, LAURELL KAYE, writer; b. Heber Springs, Ark., Feb. 19, 1963; m. Jonathon Green; 1 child. Degree in English and Biology, Ind. Wesleyan U., Marion. Author: (Anita Blake: Vampire Hunter series) Guilty Pleasures, 1993, The Laughing Corpse, 1994, Circus of the Damned, 1995, The Lunatic Cafe, 1996, Bloody Bones, 1996, The Killing Dance, 1997, Burnt Offerings, 1998, Blue Moon, 1998, Obsidian Butterfly, 2000, Narcissus in Chains, 2002, Cerulean Sins, 2003, Incubus Dreams, 2004 (Publishers Weekly bestseller), Micah, 2006, Danse Macabre, 2006, The Harlequin, 2007, Blood Noir, 2008, (Merry Gentry series) A Kiss of Shadows, 2001, A Caress of Twilight, 2002, Seduced By Moonlight, 2004, A Stroke of Midnight, 2005, Mistral's Kiss, 2006, A Lick of Frost, 2007, Swallowing Darkness, 2008 (Publishers Weekly bestseller), (Marvel Comics series) Laurell K. Hamilton's Anita Blake, Vampire Hunter: The First Death, 2008; contbr. short stories to anthologies. Office: c/o Author Mail Berkley Pub Penguin Group 375 Hudson New York NY 10014

HAMILTON, MARK R., academic administrator; m. Patty Hamilton; 4 children. BS, US Mil. Acad., 1967; MA in English Lit., Fla. State U., 1973; grad., Armed Forces Staff Coll., US Army War Coll. Comdr. Divsn. Artillery, Fort Richardson, 1988-90; chief staff Alaskan Command, Elmendorf AFB, 1992-93; dep. dir. force structure, resource and analysis Joint Staff, Washington, 1995-97; head recruiting US Army, Fort Knox, Ky., 1997-98; pres. U. Alaska, Fairbanks, 1998—. Mem. Denali Commn.; chair, bd. dirs. Alaska Aerospace Devel. Corp.; mem., bd. dirs. Alaska Air Group, Inc.; chair Alaska Distance Edn. Technology Consortium; co-chair Alaska State Com. on Rsch. Mem., bd. dirs. Alaska SeaLife Ctr.; mem. Morris Thompson Cultural Ctr. Bd. Decorated DSM US Army, Joint Disting. Svc. medal; named Person of Wk., Peter Jennings, ABC News; named one of 25 Most Powerful Alaskans for past 5 yrs., Alaskan Jour. Commerce. Office: U Alaska PO Box 755000 Fairbanks AK 99775-5000 Office Phone: 907-450-8000.

HAMILTON, PATRICIA ROSE, art dealer; b. Phila., Oct. 21, 1948; d. William Alexis and Lillian Marie (Sloan) Hamilton. BA, Temple U., Phila., 1970; MA, Rutgers U., New Brunswick, NJ, 1971. Sec. to curator Whitney Mus., NYC, 1971-73; sr. editor Art in Am., 1973; curator exhbns. Crispo Gallery, 1974-75; dir. Hamilton Gallery, 1976-84; artist's agt., 1984—2002; art dealer, 2002—. Democrat. Avocations: tennis, swimming, cooking. Home and Office: 6753 Milner Rd Los Angeles CA 90068-3214 Office Phone: 323-512-4737. Personal E-mail: hamiltonpatricia@sbcglobal.net.

HAMILTON, RITA, library director; BA in Libr. Sci., Western Mich. U., Kalamazoo, 1975; MLS, U. Ariz., Tucson, 1986. Libr. tech. asst. reference dept. Tucson Pub. Libr., 1979—84, adminstrv. asst., 1984—88, prin. cataloger tech. svcs. dept., 1988—89, cataloging mgr. tech. svcs. dept., 1989—91; tech. svcs. mgr. Pub. Libr. Nashville and Davidson County, 1991—95, asst. dir., 1995—2000; pub. svcs.

adminstr. Phoenix Pub. Libr., 2000—02; dir. Scottsdale Pub. Libr., Ariz., 2002—. Contbr. articles to profl. publs. Recipient Scottsdale City Mgr.'s Award of Excellence, 2006, Honor award, ALA/Internat. Interior Design Assn., 2006. Mem.: ALA, Ariz. State Libr. Assn. (pres. pub. libr. divsn. 2001—02, mem. libr. automation roundtable 1988—91), Maricopa County Libr. Coun. (v.p./pres.-elect 2003—04, pres. 2004—05), Urban Librs. Coun. (mem. forecasting strategy group 2003—, chair Highsmith/Urban Librs. Coun. award jury 2006—07), Pub. Libr. Assn. (chair cataloging needs of pub. librs. 1994—96, mem. evaluating electronic info. com. 1998—2002, mem. Charlie Robinson award jury 2001—02, mem. 1004 nat. conf. prog. com. 2002—04, mem. Highsmith award jury 2003, bd. dirs. 2003—06, mem. Highsmith award jury 2004, mem. 2006 nat. conf. prog. com. 2004—06), AMIGOS (bd. dirs. 2005—, mem. budget and fin. com. 2005—, sec. 2006—). Office: Scottsdale Pub Libr Sys 3839 N Drinkwater Blvd Scottsdale AZ 85251-4452 Office Phone: 480-312-7049. Office Fax: 480-312-7993. E-mail: rhamilton@scottsdaleaz.gov.

HAMILTON, RONALD RAY, minister; b. Evansville, Ind., May 6, 1932; s. Floyd Ray Hamilton and Ruby Dixon (Chism) Hahn; m. Norma Jean Robertson, Mar. 25, 1956; children: Ronnetta Jean, Andrea, Robert Rae. BA, U. Evansville, 1955; BD, Garrett Theol. Sem., 1958, MDiv, 1972; PhD, Oxford Grad. Sch., Eng., Dayton, Tenn., 1989. Ordained elder United Meth. Ch. Minister Scobey (Mont.) Meth. Ch., 1958-61, St. Andrew Meth. Ch., Littleton, Colo., 1961-67; sr. minister First Meth. Ch., Grand Junction, Colo., 1967-75, Christ United Meth. Ch., Salt Lake City, 1975-80, Littleton United Meth., 1980-86, U. Park United Meth., Denver, 1986-91, First United Meth. Ch., Sun City, Ariz., 1992-98; chaplain Banner Boswell Med. Ctr., Sun City, 1998—2009. Author: The Way to Success, 1972, The Greatest Prayer, 1983, A Chosen People, 1986; editor jour., 1978. Recipient Spl. award Mental Health Assn., Mesa County, Colo., 1974, Goodwill Rehab. Inc., 1975. Mem. Lions Club, Rotary Club, Civitan (chaplain 1964-67). Republican. Avocations: acting, directing, travel, chess. Home: 20846 N 107th Dr Sun City AZ 85373-2388

HAMILTON, SCOTT SCOVELL, professional figure skater, former Olympic athlete; b. Toledo, Aug. 28, 1958; adopted s. Ernest Scovell and Dorothy (McIntosh) H. m. Tracie Robinson, Nov. 12, 2002, 1 child. Grad. high sch., Bowling Green, Ohio, 1976; student, Metro State Coll., 1979. Nat. spokesman Discover Card youth programs, 1995—. Amateur competitive career includes Nat. Figure Skating Championships: jr. men's 1st pl., 1976, sr. men's 9th pl., 1977, 3d pl., 1978, 4th pl., 1979, 3d pl., 1980, 1st pl., 1981, 82, 83, 84, Mid-Western Figure Skating Championships: sr. men's 3d pl., 1977, 78, 79, Norton Skate Championships (now Skate Am.): men's divsn. 1st pl., 1979, 80, 81, 82, South Atlantic Figure Skating Championships: sr. men's divsn. 1st pl., 1980, Eastern Figure Skating Championships: sr. men's 1st pl., 1980, 81, 82, 83, 84, World Figure Skating Championships: men's divsn. 5th pl., 1980, 1st pl. 81, 82, 83, 84, Nat. Sports Festival Championships: 1st pl. men's divsn., 1981; Winter Olympics: men's divsn. 5th pl., Lake Placid, N.Y., 1980, 1st pl., Sarajevo, Yugoslavia, 1984, Nippon Hoso Kykai Figure Skating Championships, men's divsn. 1st pl., 1982, Golden Spin of Zagreb Championships, men's divsn. 1st pl., 1983; Profl. competitive career includes Nutrasweet/NBC-TV World Profl. Figure Skating Championships mens. divsn., 1st pl., 1984, 86, 2d pl., 85, 87, 88, 89, 91; World Challenge Championships/ABC-TV men's divsn., 2d pl., 1985, 1st pl., 1986; U.S. Open men's divsn. 1st pl., 1990, 2d pl., 1991, Diet Coke Profl. Skaters Championship men's divsn. 1st pl., 1992, Hershey's Kisses Pro-Am. Figure Skating Championships 2d Place Men's divsn. 1993, Sun Valley Men's Outdoor Championship 2d pl., 1994, The Gold Championship men's divsn. 1st pl., 1994, Can. Profl. Skating Championship men's divsn. 1st pl., 1994, Fox's Rock and Roll Skating Championship men's divsn. 1st pl., 1994; profl. performances include Nat. Arena Tour Ice Capades, 1984-85, 85-86, star Scott Hamilton's Am. Tour, 1986-87, 1990-91, co-star Concert On Ice, Harrah's Hotel, Lake Tahoe, Nev., 1987, spl. guest star Festival On Ice, Nat. Theatre Tour, 1987, star Discover Card Stars On Ice Nat. Arena Tour, 1987-88, 88-89, star Festival On Ice, Harrah's Hotel, 1988, guest star ABC-TV spl. Ice Capades With Kirk Cameron, 1988, A Very Special Christmas, ABC-TV, 1988, An Olympic, Calgary Christmas, ABC-TV, 1988, star and mus. comedy and acting debut Broadway On Ice, Harrah's Hotel and Nat. Theatre Tour, 1989; CBS-TV Sports Figure Skating Commentator 1984-91 various skating competitions and CBS-TV coverage Winter Olympics, Albertville, France, 1992, Lillehammer, Norway, 1994; star, dir., producer Scott Hamilton's Celebration On Ice, Sea World of Calif., 1988, Scott Hamilton's Time Traveler: An Odyssey On Ice, Sea World of Calif., 1989; host, guest star TV spl. A Salute To Dorothy Hamill, 1988; star, co-producer Discover Card Stars On Ice, Nat. Arena Tour, 1989-91; guest star CBS-TV spl. Disney's Christmas on Ice, 1990; co-producer, star Discover Card Stars on Ice Nat. Arena Tour, 1991-92; co-host, star HBO TV spl. Vail Skating Festival, 1992; co-prodr., star Discover Card Stars on Ice Nat. Arena Tour, 1992-93, 93-94, 94-95, Canadian Nat. Tour, 1995; guest TV spl. A Disney Christmas on Ice, 1992, CBS-TV spl. Disney on Ice, 1992, HBO-TV spl. Vail Skating Festival, 1993, Skates of Gold I, Boston, 1993, Skates of Gold II, Cin., 1994, CBS-TV Disney Fantasy on Ice, 1993, CBS-TV spl. Nancy Kerrigan & Friends, 1994, CBS-TV spl. Disney's Greatest Hits, 1994, CBS-TV spl. Dreams on Ice, 1995; creator original concepts in arena figure skating. Cons. Friends of Scott Hamilton Found. named in his honor to fundraise and benefit youth oriented causes throughout U.S., 1988, Scott Hamilton's Friends and Legends 1st Annual Celebrity Charity Golf Tournament, Ford's Colony, Williamsburg, Va., 1991; participant fund-raising Athletes for Reagan, March of Dimes, Am. Cancer Soc., Spl. Olympics, Starlight Found., United Way Adoption Home Socs., Make A Wish Found, Big Bros., 1984—, Athletes For Bush, Adult and Ped. AIDS Rsch., Edn. and Funding, 1988—, Homeless, 1989—, Great Am. Workout for Pres.'s Coun. Phys. Fitness & Sports, 1990, 92; nat. spokesman Discover Card youth programs, 1995—. Winner Olympic Gold medal, Sarajevo, 1984; U.S. Olympic Com. awards and honors include carrier Am. Flag in opening ceremonies Lake Placid, 1980, Figure Skating Athlete of Yr., 1981, 82, 83, 84, Athlete of Yr., 1981, Olympic Spirit award, 1987; recipient Olympia award Southland Corp., 1984, Achievement award March of Dimes, 1984, Colo. Athlete of Yr. award Denver Athletic Club, 1984, Most Courageous Athlete award Phila. Sportswriters Assn., 1985, Profl. Skater of Yr. award Am. Skating World mag., 1986, Jacques Favart award Internat. Skating Union, 1988, The Crown Royal Achievement award from House of Seagrams and Jimmy Heuga Ctr., 1991, Clairol's Personal Best award, 1991, Spirit of Giving award U.S. Figure Skating Assn., 1993, 9th Ann. Great Sports Legends award Nick Buonoconti Fund The Miami Project, 1994, Ritter F. Shumway award U.S. Figure Skating Assn., 1994; inducted U.S. Olympic Hall of Fame, 1990, World Figure Skating Hall of Fame, 1990; honoree nat. com. for adoption, 1992. Hon. mem. Phila. Skating Club, Humane Soc. Republican. Avocation: golf. Address: CBS Sports CBS Inc 7800 Beverly Blvd Los Angeles CA 90036-2188 Home: 2419 Hidden River Ln Franklin TN 37069-6933

HAMILTON, STEVEN C., lawyer; b. 1939; BS, Mont. State U., 1962; JD, UCLA, 1966. Pvt. practice, 1966-68; asst. gen. counsel Garrett Corp., LA, 1968-80, v.p., gen. counsel, 1980-88; v.p., legal and gen. counsel Alaska Airlines, Inc., Seattle, 1988—. Office: Alaska Airlines PO Box 68900 Seattle WA 98168-0900

HAMILTON, W. W., religious organization administrator; Gen. sec. Ch. of God in Christ, Memphis. Office: Church God in Christ Office Gen Sec 1620 Broadway Ave Seaside CA 93955-5121

HAMILTON, WARREN BELL, geologist, geophysicist, educator, researcher; b. LA, May 13, 1925; s. Errett Campbell and Erva Laura (Bell) Hamilton; m. Alicita Victoria Koenig, Dec. 23, 1947; children: Lawrence C., Kathryn E., James D. BA, UCLA, 1945, PhD, 1951; MS, U. So. Calif., 1949. Asst. prof. U. Okla., Norman, 1951-52; from geologist to sr. scientist U.S. Geol. Survey, Denver, 1952-95, Pecora fellow emeritus, 1995-96; Disting. sr. scientist Colo. Sch. Mines, Golden, 1996—. Sr. exch. scientist Acad. Scis., USSR, 1967; vis. prof. Scripps Inst. Oceanography, San Diego, 1968, 79, Calif. Inst. Tech., Pasadena, 1973, Yale U., New Haven, 1980, U. Amsterdam, 1981; mem. plate tectonics del. to China and Tibet, 79; disting. lectr. Am. Assn. Petroleum Geologists, 1983—84; nominator MacArthur Found., 1984—85; vis. scholar We. Mich. U., 1984; Wilbert disting. lectr. La. State U., 1985, adj. prof., 2000—02; regents lectr. U. Calif., Santa Barbara, 1986, San Diego, 90, UCLA, 1988; Hooker disting. lectr. McMaster U., 1990; Ketin lectr. Istanbul (Turkey) Tech. U., 1998; adj. prof. U. Wyo., 2000—; Allday lectr. U. Tex., Austin, 2002; Disting. Alumni lectr. UCLA, 2004. Author: Tectonics of the Indonesian Region, 1979, others, monographs; contbr. articles to profl. jours.; assoc. editor: Geology, 1973—82, Jour. Geophys. Rsch., 1974—76. With USN, 1943—46. Recipient Disting. Svc. medal, U.S. Dept. Interior, 1981. Fellow: Geol. Assn. Can., Geol. Soc. Am. (chmn. Cordilleran sect. 1987—88, councilor 1995—98, Penrose medal 1989, Structural Geology and Tectonics Career Achievement award 2007), Geol. Soc. London (hon.); mem.: NAS, Am. Geophys. Union, Colo. Sci. Soc. (hon.). Office: Colo Sch of Mines Dept of Geophysics Golden CO 80401 Business E-Mail: whamilto@mines.edu.

HAMLIN, HARRY ROBINSON, actor; b. Pasadena, Calif., Oct. 30, 1951; s. Chauncey Jerome and Bernice (Robinson) H.; c. 1 son, Dimitri Alexander (with Ursula Andress); m. Laura Johnson, 1985-89; m. Nicollette Sheridan, 1991-93; m. Lisa Rinna, Mar. 29, 1997; c. Delilah Belle and Amelia Gray BA, Yale U.; postgrad., Am. Conservatory Theatre, San Francisco. Performances include: (films) Movie Movie, 1979, Clash of The Titans, 1981, King of the Mountain, 1981, Making Love, 1982, Blue Skies Again, 1983, Maxie, 1985, Dinner At Eight, 1990, The Celluloid Closet, 1995, Badge of Betrayal, 1996; (TV mini-series) Studs Lonigan, Master of the Game, 1984, Space, 1985, Favorite Son, 1988, Night Sins, 1997, Strange Hearts, 2001, Perfume, 2001, Shoot or Be Shot, 2002, Strang Wilderness, 2008; (TV films) Laguna Heat, 1987, Deceptions, 1990, Deadly Intentions...Again?, 1991, Deliver Them From Evil: The Taking of Alta View, 1991, Save Me, 1992, Under Investigation, 1993, Poisoned by Love: The Kern County Murders, 1993, In the Best of Families: Marriage, Pride and Madness, 1994, Tom Clancy's Op Center, 1995, Her Deadly Rival, 1995, One Clean Move, 1996, Badge of Betrayal, 1996, Allie & Me, 1997, Night Sins, 1997, Stranger in Town, 1998, Frogs for Snakes, 1998, The Hunted, 1998, Like Father, Like Santa, 1998, Quarantine, 1999, Silent Predators, 1999; (TV series) L.A. Law, 1986-91, Movie Stars, 1999, Veronica Mars, 2004-06, Dancing with the Stars, 2006; (Broadway debut) Awake and Sing!, 1984, Chicago, 2007. ITT Fulbright grantee, 1977; Named Sexiest Man Alive People mag., 1987. Office: care Larry Taub Gersh Agency Inc 232 N Canon Dr Beverly Hills CA 90210-5302

HAMMANN, GREGG C., fitness equipment executive; b. Ft. Madison, Iowa, Mar. 3, 1963; s. Clifford Carl and Nancy Ann (Schruers) H.; m. Carol Craddock, June 20, 1987;children: Derek Henry, Grant Campbell. BBA, U. Iowa, 1985; MBA, U. Wis., 1997. Sales rep., unit mgr., then oral care brand project mgr. Procter & Gamble, Cin., 1985-91; dir. trade mktg. Rayovac Corp., Madison, 1991-92, pres., gen. mgr. of Can. Toronto, Ont., Can., 1992-94; v.p. mktg. and strategic planning, Famous Footwear, Madison, 1994-96; dir. strategic issues The Coca-Cola Co., Atlanta, 1996, v.p. fountain products divsn., 1997, v.p. nat. chain accounts, 1999; group v.p. bus. devel. McLeodUSA, 2000; sr. v.p., chief customer officer Levi Strauss & Co., 2001—03; pres, CEO The Nautilus Group Inc., 2003—. Active Big Bros./Big Sisters, 1995—, Give Kids the World, 1997—; bd. dirs. Edn. Found., Chgo., 1997—. Avocations: hiking, biking, tennis, golf, running.

HAMMAR, SHERREL LEYTON, medical educator; b. Caldwell, Idaho, May 21, 1931; m. Shirley; children: Kathryn M., David Jefferson. BA, Coll. Idaho, 1953; MD, U. Wash., 1957. Intern Mpls. Gen. Hosp., 1957-58; resident U. Wash., Seattle, 1958-60; instr. dept. pediat. U. Wash. Sch. Medicine, Seattle, 1962-64, asst. prof. dept. pediat., 1964-69, assoc. prof. dept. pediat., 1969-71, U. Hawaii, Honolulu, 1971-73; prof. U. Hawaii Sch. Medicine, Honolulu, 1973—2001; interim dean John A. Burns Sch. Medicine U. Hawaii, Honolulu, 1996-99, emeritus prof., 2001—. Chief adolscent clinic U. Wash., 1964-65, acting dir. clin. tng. unit devel. & mental health ctr., 1964, asst., 1965-71, acting dir. clin. tng. unit child devel. and mental retardation ctr., 1970-71; dir. ambulatory pediatric svcs., chief adolescent medicine Kauikeolani Children's Hosp., Honolulu, 1971-72, dir. med. svcs. and tng., 1972-73, chief pediat., 1973—, dir. pediatric med. edn., 1979—; chmn. dept. pediat. U. Hawaii, 1973-97, residency program dir., 1973-97; cons. in field. Contbr. articles to profl. jours. Fellow U. Wash., 1960-62. Fellow APHA, Am. Acad. Pediat. (com. youth 1967-73, 75-81, sect. adolescent health, exec. coun. 1978-80, com. early childhood, adoption and dependent care 1990-92, task force on AIDS 1990-92); mem. AMA (med. sch. sect.), Western Soc. Pediatric Rsch., Hawaii Med. Assn. (pres. 2003-04), Ambulatory Pediatric Assn., Seattle Pediatric Soc., Honolulu County Med. Soc., Alpha Omega Alpha. Personal E-mail: lerram@aol.com.

HAMMER, BONNIE, broadcast executive; b. 1950; m. Dale Huesner. BA in Edn., Boston U., 1971, MA in Media and New Tech., 1975. With WGBH, Boston; dir. devel. Dave Bell Associates, LA; programming exec. Lifetime Television Network; v.p. current programs USA Networks, NYC; sr. v.p. Sci-Fi programming and USA org. productions NBC Universal, 1998—99; exec. v.p., gen. mgr. Sci-Fi Channel (subsidiary of USA Networks), 1999, pres., 2001, USA Network, 2004—; pres., cable entertainment & cable studio NBC Universal, 2008—. Bd. dirs. ShopNBC, 2008—. Recipient Lillian Gish award, Women in Film; named one of The 100 Most Powerful Women in Entertainment, Hollywood Reporter, 2006, 2007.

HAMMER, CHARLES F., retired chemistry professor; b. Fremont, Ohio, July 22, 1933; m. Lois Reel, 1957; 1 child, Laurence N. BA, Bowling Green State U., Ohio, 1955; PhD in Organic Chemistry, U. Minn., Mpls., 1959. NIHPD fellow NMR and x-ray crystallography of steroids Brandeis U., 1961—63; from asst. prof. to assoc. prof. Georgetown U., 1963—82, prof. chemistry, 1982-95, emeritus prof., 1995—. Vis. prof. dept. hydrocarbon Chem. Sch. Eng. Kyoto Nat. U., Japan, 1971-72; vis. scholar dept. chem. U. Calif., Berkeley, 1978, Nat. Inst. Diabetes, Digestive & Kidney Disease NIH, 1986, Inst. Chemistry, Ljubjana, Slovenia, 1993, Nanjing U., 1994; pres. governing coun. Acad. Tech. and the Classics Charter Sch. 7-12, Santa Fe County, 2000—; bd. dirs. Hoya N.Mex. Schs. Chemobile, Santa Fe, N.Mex. Founder ATC Found., 2002, bd. dirs., 2004—; bd. mem. Santa Fe CC Training Ctr. Corp., 2005—. Recipient Alan Berman Rsch. Publication award NRL, 1987, USN & UR Bronze award, Newsweek Bronze award, 2007. Mem. AAAS, Am. Chem. Soc. (ChemTec Writing Team 1970-72, Am. Chem. Soc. award for creative invention 1990), Am. Soc. Mass Spectrometry, Soc. Appl. Spectros, Am. Soc. Testing & Materials, Sigma Xi. Achievements include research in chemistry and mechanisms of nitrogen heterocyclics and steroids; bromination-dehydrobromination reactions; structure elucidation of natural products by instrumental methods; complete structure by 2D-nuclear magnetic resonance; isotope ratio kinetics by mass spectrometry; computer software applications to spectrometric analysis; synthesis of plant growth hormones and antitumor agents. Office: Hoya/NMex Schs Chemobile 2017 Calle Lejano Santa Fe NM 87501-8747 Business E-Mail: cfhammer75@q.com.

HAMMER, SUSAN W., educational foundation executive, former mayor; b. Altadena, Calif., Dec. 21, 1938; d. James Nathan and Katrine (Krutzsch) Walker; m. Philip Hammer, Sept. 4, 1960; children: Philip, Hali, Matthew. BA in History, U. Calif., Berkeley, 1960. Svc. rep. Pacific Telephone Co., Berkeley, 1960-61; staff asst. Peace Corps, Washington, 1962-63; councilwoman City of San Jose, Calif., 1980-81, 83-90, spl. asst. to mayor Calif., 1981-82, vice mayor Calif., 1985-87, mayor Calif., 1991-99; CEO Synopsys Outreach Found. and Synopsys Silicon Valley Sci. and Tech. Championship, 1999—. Chair, pres. Adv. Com. on Trade Policy and Negotiations, 1994—. Bd. dirs. San Jose Mus. Art, 1971-90, pres., 1978-80; mem. governing bd. NCCJ, 1978—; mem. adv. bd. Cmty. Found. Santa Clara County, 1978—; mem. Santa Clara County Transp. Com., 1976-77, Santa Clara County Juvenile Justice Commn., 1980, Victim-Witness Adv. Bd., 1977-90, Children's Health Coun., San Jose, 1981-89, Santa Clara Valley Leadership Program, 1986-90, Childrens Shelter Project, 1991—, Am. Leadership Forum, 1992—; past chmn. parents adv. com. Trace Sch.; chair Pres.' Adv. Com. on Trade Policy and Negotiation; mem. San Jose Fine Arts Commn., 1980; v.p. Calif. Bd. Edn., 1999— Recipient Rosalie M. Stern Community Svc. award U. Calif., 1975, Disting. Citizen of San Jose award Exch. Club, 1979, Investment in Leadership award Coro Found., 1985, Tzedek award for honor, compassion and community svc. Temple Emanu-El, 1987, Recognition award YWCA, Santa Clara County, 1989, resolution of commendation Assn. for Responsible Alcohol Control, 1990, Woman of Achievement award The Women's Fund, 1990, Dox Quixote award Nat. Hispanic U., 1991, Friends of Bay Area Mcpl. Elections Com. award, 1991. Democrat.

HAMMERGREN, JOHN H., health products executive; BBA, U. Minn.; MBA, Xavier U. With Baxter Healthcare Corp./Am. Hosp. Corp. and Lyphomed Inc., 1981-91; pres. med./surgical divsn. Kendall Healthcare Products Co., Mansfield, Mass., 1991-96; corp. exec. v.p., pres., CEO supply mgmt. bus. McKesson HBOC, Inc., 1996-99; group pres. McKesson Health Systems, 1997—99; chief exec. officer supply chain mgmt. McKesson Corp. (formerly McKesson HBOC, Inc.), 1997—99, dir., 1999—, co-pres, co- CEO, 1999—2001, pres., CEO, 2001—, chmn. bd., 2002—. Dir. Nadro, S.A. de C.V., Mexico, Verispan LLC; bd. trustee Healthcare Leadership Coun. Recipient Cap Gemini Ernst & Young Leadership award for Global Integration, 2004, Warren Bennis award for Leadership, 2004. Office: McKesson Corp One Post St San Francisco CA 94104*

HAMMES, MICHAEL NOEL, automotive company executive; b. Evanston, Ill., Dec. 25, 1941; s. Ferdinand Edward and Winifred Hammes; m. Lenore Lynn Forbes, Jan. 3, 1964; children: Michael, Nicole, Karl, Erik, Heide. BS, Georgetown U., 1963; MS, NYU, 1965. Exec. dir. internat. bus. Ford Internat. Automotive Ops., Dearborn, Mich., 1975-78; pres. Ford Mex. SA, Mexico City, 1978-83; v.p. truck ops. Ford Europe, Warley, Essex, Eng., 1983-86; pres. internat. ops. Chrysler Corp., 1986-90; corp. vice chmn., pres. worldwide consumer product ops. Black & Decker Corp., 1990-93; chmn., CEO The Coleman Co., 1993-97; CEO Guide Corp., Anderson, Ind., 1998-2000; pres., CEO Sunrise Medical Inc., Carlsbad, Calif., 2000—. Bd. dirs., chmn. audit com. Sunrise Med. Inc., 1998—. Office: Sunrise Med Inc 2382 Faraday Ave Ste 200 Carlsbad CA 92008-7220

HAMMOND, CHARLES AINLEY, clergyman; b. Asheville, NC, Aug. 7, 1933; s. George Bradley and Eleanor Maria (Gantz) H.; m. Barbro Stigsdotter Laurell, July 16, 1960; children: Stig Bradley, Inga Allison. BA, Occidental Coll., Los Angeles, 1955; B.D., Princeton Theol. Sem., 1958; D.D., Missouri Valley Coll., 1981, Wabash Coll., 1982. Ordained to ministry United Presbyn. Ch., 1958; pastor chs. in Pa. and Calif., 1958-75; exec. presbyter Presbytery Wabash Valley, West Lafayette, Ind., 1975-87, Presbytery Phila., 1987-98; interim pastor Presbyn. Ch., New Providence, NJ, 1998-99, 1st Presbyn. Ch., Salt Lake City, 1999-2001, San Luis Obispo, Calif., 2002. Moderator 192d gen. assembly United Presbyn. Ch., 1980-81; chmn. Gen. Assembly Mission Coun., 1982-83. Author: Newtonian Polity in an Age of Relativity, 1977, Seven Deadly Sins of Dissent, 1979. Sec. Hallam (Pa.) Borough Planning Commn., 1962-64, Westchester Cmty. Plans, L.A., 1966-68, Pasadena (Calif.) Planning Commn., 1971-75; chmn. pvt. land use com., 1972-73, chmn. pub. land use com., 1973-74; mem. gen. assembly coun. Presbyn. Ch. (U.S.A.), 1983-91; bd. dirs. Met. Coun. Chs. of Phila., 1990-95; trustee Beaver Coll., 1991-99; gen. assembly Permanent Jud. Com., 1995-2001; mem. bd. corporators Pres. Min. Found. Recipient Disting. Alumnus award Princeton Theol. Sem., 1981. Mem. Assn. Presbyn. Ch. Educators, Friends of Old Pine (trustee). Republican. Presbyterian.

HAMMOND, GEORGE CHARLES, lawyer; b. Kenosha, Wis., Mar. 6, 1953; s. Eugene Raymond and Patricia Verda (Lawler) H.; m. Maria Elisabeth Hammond, Oct. 30, 1986; children: Sophie Claire, Anne Marie. BA, Dartmouth Coll., 1974; JD, U. Wis., 1985. Bar: Wis.

1985, N.Y. 1986, Calif. 2001. Assoc. Dewey Ballantine LLP, NYC, 1984-93, LeBoeuf, Lamb, Greene & MacRae, LLP, NYC, 1996-99, ptnr. San Francisco, 2000—05, Haarmann, Hemmelrath & Ptnr., Frankfurt, Germany, 1999. Author: Mark Twain's Visit to Heaven, 1999, The Senior Partner, 1999, Bob and Charlie, 1999, Conversations with Socrates, 1999, The Gospel According to Andrew, 1999, Even More Relativity, 1999, The Morning Light, 2000, Rational Idealism, 2005, Fragments, 2005, Innocence Abroad, 2005, The Nuclear Conspiracy, 2005; (computer program) Syndicator's Delight, 1984 Avocations: philosophy, literature, travel, art, golf. Office Phone: 925-258-8200.

HAMMOND, HARMONY, artist, educator; b. Chgo., Feb. 8, 1944; d. William Joseph and Harmony R. (Jensen) H.; m. Stephen Clover, May 1963 (div. 1970); 1 child, Tanya Hammond. BA, U. Minn., 1967. Prof. art dept. U. Ariz., Tucson, 1988—2005. Vis. artist Phila. Coll. Art, Rutgers U., Art Inst. Chgo., U. N.Mex., Tyler Sch. Fine Art, Santa Fe Art Inst., Anderson Ranch, Vt. Studio Ctr.; co-founder Heresies Mag., A.I.R. Gallery. Author: Wrappings: Essays on Feminism, Art and the Martial Arts, 1984, Lesbian Art in America: A Contemporary History, 2000; one-woman shows include A.I.R. Gallery, N.Y.C., 1973, 1982, 1984, Lerner-Heller Gallery, 1982, Matrix Gallery, Wadsworth Atheneum, Hartford, Conn., 1984, Luise Ross Gallery, N.Y.C., 1984, Bernice Steinbaum Gallery, N.Y.C., 1986, Trabia-MacAffe Gallery, N.Y.C., 1987, Etherton-Stern Gallery, Tucson, 1987, 1994, Linda Durham Gallery, Galisteo, N.Mex., 1988, Tucson Mus. Art, 1993, Linda Durham Gallery, Santa Fe, 1998, Site Santa Fe, 2002, Mus. Contemporary Art, Tucson, 2002, Dwight Hackett Projects, Santa Fe, 2004, Ctr. Contemporary Arts, Santa Fe, 2005, others, Represented in permanent collections Dwight Hackett Projects. Recipient award, Nat. Endowment of Arts-Sculpture, 1979, Nat. Endowment for Arts-Graphics, 1983; grantee, Pollock-Krasner Found., 1989, Guggenheim Found., 1991, Rockefeller Found. Bellagio, 1994, Adolph and Ester Gottlieb Found., 1995, Joan Mitchell Found., 1998, Andrea Frank Found., 2000; CAPS grantee, NY State Coun. of Arts-Sculpture, 1982. Mem. Coll. Art Assn. Avocation: Aikido.

HAMMOND, JUDY MCLAIN, business services executive; b. Downey, Calif., June 24, 1956; d. Ernest Richard and Bernice Elaine (Thompson) McLain; m. Dennis Francis Hammond, Aug. 15, 1981. BS in Mgmt., Pepperdine U., 1982; MBA magna cum laude, U. So. Calif., 1986. Br. mgr. Kelly Svcs., Encino, Calif., 1978-81; mktg. mgr. Payco Am. Corp., Encino, 1981-83, GC Svcs. Corp., Santa Ana, Calif., 1983—; pres. Resource Mgmt. Svcs. Inc., Norwalk, Calif., 1986—; founder CEO The Debt Marketplace, Inc, 1994—. Cons. in field. Author: Collect More From Collection Agencies. Mem.: LA Underwater Photographic Soc., Toastmasters. Avocations: scuba diving, underwater photography. Office: 10440 Pioneer Blvd Ste 2 Santa Fe Springs CA 90670-8235 Business E-Mail: judy.hammond@debtmarketplace.com.

HAMMOND, LARRY AUSTIN, lawyer; b. Wichita, Kans., Sept. 17, 1945; BA, U. Tex., 1967, JD, 1970. Bar: Calif. 1971, Ariz. 1975. Law clk. to Hon. Carl McGowan U.S. Ct. Appeals (D.C. cir.), Washington, 1970-71; law clk. to Hon. Hugo L. Black U.S. Supreme Ct., Washington, 1971, law clk. to Hon. Lewis F. Powell Jr., 1971-73; asst. spl. prosecutor Watergate spl. prosecution force U.S. Justice Dept., Washington, 1973-74, dep. asst. atty. gen. office legal counsel, 1977-80; mem. Osborn Maledon P.A., Phoenix, 1995—. Adj. prof. law Ariz. State U., 1977, 85—, U. Ariz., 1983, U. N.Mex., 1983. Editor-in-chief Tex. Law Rev., 1969-70. Mem. ABA, Am. Judicature Soc. (pres. 2003-05), Order of Coif. Office: Osborn Maledon PO Box 36379 Phoenix AZ 85067-6379 Office Phone: 602-640-9361. Business E-Mail: lhammond@omlaw.com.

HAMMOND, R. PHILIP, chemical engineer; b. Creston, Iowa, May 28, 1916; s. Robert Hugh and Helen Hammond; m. Amy L. Farmer, Feb. 28, 1941 (div. 1969); children: Allen L., David M., Jean Phyllis, Stanley W.; m. Vivienne Fox, 1972. BSChemE, U. So. Calif., 1938; PhD in Phys. and Inorganic Chemistry, U. Chgo., 1947. Registered profl. engr., Ill., Calif. Chief chemist Lindsay Chem. Co., West Chicago, Ill., 1938-46; group leader Los Alamos (N.Mex.) Sci. Lab., 1947-62, assoc. divsn. leader reactor devel. divsn., 1960-62; dir. nuc. desalination program Oak Ridge Nat. Lab., 1962-73; adj. prof. UCLA, 1972—80; head energy group R & D Assos. Corp., Santa Monica, Calif., 1973-83; desalination cons., 1987—; leader advanced sea water evaporator design Met. Water Dist. of So. Calif., LA, 1989-98. Contbr. to encyclopedias, articles to profl. jours. Mem. U.S. del. Conf. on Peaceful Uses Atomic Energy, Geneva, Switzerland, 1955, 65, 71, IAEA Panel on Desalination, Vienna, Austria, 1964, 65, 66, 71; mem. U.S. team to USSR on desalination, 1964. Naval Rsch. fellow, U. Chgo. Mem. Am. Nuc. Soc. (charter), Am. Chem. Soc., Am. Inst. Chem. Engrs., Sigma Xi, Phi Kappa Phi, Phi Lambda Upsilon. Achievements include patents for improved safety for high speed rail transport, for devices for preventing collisions at sea and for storing nuclear waste; origination of advanced concepts in sea water evaporator construction, and efficient coupling to nuclear energy sources; design (with others) of advanced reactor containment system capable of withstanding melt-down accidents with zero leakage, and of automotive engine using liquid air and liquid natural gas as fuel. Home and Office: 5370 Punta Alta 3A Unit 3A Laguna Hills CA 92637 Personal E-mail: hammondp@comline.com.

HAMNER, ROME, social services administrator; b. 1974; Grants mgr. Our Family Services, Inc. Co-founder Odaiko Sonora. Vol. grant reviewer Tucson Pima Arts Coun. Named one of 40 Under 40, Tucson Bus. Edge, 2006. Mem.: Arizona Commn. on Arts Roster of Artists, Southern Ariz. Alliance of Nonprofits, Japan Am. Soc. of Tucson (bd. dir.), OTO Dance Studios. Avocation: Taiko drumming. Office: c/o Tucson Pima Arts Council 10 E Broadway 106 Tucson AZ 85701

HAMREN, NANCY VAN BRASCH, office manager; b. LA, Feb. 2, 1947; d. Milton Carl and Winifred (Taylor) Van Brasch; m. Jerome Arthur Hamren, Feb. 14, 1981; children: Emily Allison, Meredith Ann. Student, Pasadena City Coll., 1964-65, San Francisco State Coll., 1966-67, U. Oreg., 1975-79. Bookkeeper/office mgr. Springfield Creamery, Eugene, Oreg., 1969—, also bd. dirs. Originator Nancy's Yogurt, Nancy's Cultured Dairy Products. Active Oreg. Shakespearean Festival, Ashland, 1986, Planned Parenthood, Sta. KLCC Radio; bd. dirs., treas. Willamette Valley Sustainable Food Alliance; pres. bd. dirs. Oreg. Dairy Industries; treas., bd. dir. Internat. Probiotics Assn. Mem.: Slow Food Movement, Oreg. Country Fair, Provender Alliance, Conservation Internat., Oreg. Pub. Broadcasting, Wilderness Soc., N.Am. Truffling Soc. Democrat. Avocations: gourmet cooking, gardening, walking, wine tasting, reading. Home: 1315 Ravenwood Dr Eugene OR 97401-1912 Office: Springfield Creamery 29440 Airport Rd Eugene OR 97402-9524 Office Phone: 541-689-2911.

HAN, BERNARD L., communications executive; BS, Cornell U., 1986, M in Engring., 1987, MBA, 1988. Various positions Am. Airlines, Northwest Airlines; v.p. fin. planning and analysis Am. West Airlines, 1996—98, sr. v.p. planning, 1998—2000, sr. v.p. mktg. and planning, 2000—01, exec. v.p., CFO, 2001—02, Northwest Airlines, Eagan, Minn., 2002—05, EchoStar Communications Corp., Englewood, Colo., 2006—. Office: EchoStar Communications Corp 9601 S Meridian Blvd Englewood CO 80112

HANABUSA, COLLEEN W., state legislator, lawyer; b. Honolulu, May 4, 1951; d. June and Isao Hanabusa. BA in Economics and Sociology, U. Hawaii, 1973, MA in Sociology, 1975; JD, U. Hawaii William S. Richardson Sch. Law, 1977. Legal rschr., Madison, Wis., 1978; pvt. practice atty., 1978—80, 1998—; ptnr. Koshiba & Young, 1980—90; atty. Sakurai & Sing, AAL, ALC, 1990—98; mem. Dist. 21 Hawaii State Senate, Honolulu, 1999—, v.p., 2001—02, majority leader, 2003—07, pres., 2007—. Del. Hawaii State Judicial Conf., 1991—93. Trustee St. Andrew's Primary Sch., 1984—87. Mem.: ABA, Hawaii State Bar Assn., Ikenobo Ikebana Soc. America. Democrat. Avocation: reading. Office: Hawaii State Capitol 415 S Beretania St Rm 409 Honolulu HI 96813-2407 Home: 92-1019 Koio Dr Apt J Kapolei HI 96707-4290 Office Phone: 808-586-7793. Office Fax: 808-586-7797. Business E-Mail: senhanabusa@capitol.hawaii.gov.*

HANAUER, JOE FRANKLIN, real estate company officer; b. Stuttgart, Fed. Republic Germany, July 8, 1937; came to U.S., 1938; s. Otto and Betty (Zurndorfer) H.; m. Jane Boyle, Oct. 20, 1972; children: Jill, Jason, Elizabeth. BS, Roosevelt U., 1963. Pres. Thorsen Realty, Oak Brook, Ill., 1974-80; sr. v.p. Coldwell Banker, Newport Beach, Calif., 1980-83, pres., 1984, chmn. bd., CEO, 1984-88; prin. Combined Investments LP, Laguna Beach, Calif., 1989—; chmn. bd. dirs. Grubb & Ellis Co., San Francisco, 1993-97. Bd. dirs. MAF Bancorp, Chgo.; chmn. bd. Move, Inc., Calamos Mutual Funds; chmn. policy adv. bd. Joint Ctr. for Housing Studies Harvard U., 1995-96. Bd. dirs. Chgo. Chamber Orch., 1976—; trustee Roosevelt U. Home: 105 S La Sensa Dr Laguna Beach CA 92651 Office: Combined Investments LP 1200 S Coast Hwy Ste 204 Laguna Beach CA 92651-2146

HANAWALT, PHILIP COURTLAND, biology professor, researcher; b. Akron, Ohio, Aug. 25, 1931; s. Joseph Donald and Lenore (Smith) H.; m. Joanna Thomas, Nov. 2, 1957 (div. Oct. 1977); children: David, Steven; m. Graciela Spivak, Sept. 10, 1978; children: Alex, Lisa. Student, Deep Springs Coll., 1949-50; BA, Oberlin Coll., 1954, ScD (hon.), 1997; MS, Yale U., 1955, PhD, 1959; doctorate honoris causa, U. Bio Bio, Concepcion, Chile, 2006. Postdoctoral fellow U. Copenhagen, Denmark, 1958-60, Calif. Inst. Tech., Pasadena, 1960-61; rsch. biophysicist, lectr. Stanford U., Calif., 1961-65, assoc. prof., 1965-70, prof., 1970—, Howard H. and Jessie T. Watkins univ. prof., 1997—2002, chmn. dept. biol. scis., 1982-89; faculty dept. dermatology Stanford Med. Sch., 1979—. Mem. Stanford Comprehensive Cancer Ctr.; mem. physiol. chemistry study sect. NIH, Bethesda, Md., 1966—70, mem. chem. pathology study sect., 1981—84; mem. sci. adv. com. Am. Cancer Soc., NYC, 1972—76, Coun. for Extramural Grants, 1998—2001; chmn. 2d ad hoc senate com. on professoriate Stanford U., 1988—90; mem. NSF fellowship rev. panel, 1985; mem. carcinogen identification com. Calif. EPA, 1995—98; mem. toxicology adv. com. Burroughs-Welcome Fund, 1995—2001, chmn., 1997—2000; mem. sci. adv. bd. Fogarty Internat. Ctr., NIH, 1995—99; chmn. Gordon Conf. on Mutagenesis, 1996, Gordon Conf. on Mammalian DNA Repair, 1999; mem. bd. on radiation effects rschr. NAS Commn. on Life Scis., 1996—98, 2005—; mem. internat. adv. bd. Chulabhorn Rsch. Inst., Bangkok; trustee Oberlin Coll., 1998—2007; lectr. Curie Inst., Paris, 2003; keynote lectr. for conf. on DNA repair & mutagenesis Am. Soc. Microbiology, 2004; pres., chair organizing com. 9th Internat. Conf. on Environ. Mutagens, San Francisco, 2005; vis. scholar Grad. Sch. Frontier Bioscis., Osaka U., Japan, 2007. Author: Molecular Photobiology, 1969; author, editor: DNA Repair: Techniques, 1981, 83, 88, Molecular Basis of Life, 1968, Chemical Basis of Life, 1973, Molecules to Living Cells, 1980; mng. editor DNA Repair Jour., 1982-93; sr. editor Jour. Cancer Rsch., 2003—; assoc. editor Jour. DNA Repair, Molecular Carcinogenesis, Environ. Health Perspectives, Mechanism of Aging and Development; bd. rev. editors Sci.; mem. editl. bd. Procs. of NAS, 2003—; contbr. more than 400 articles to profl. jours. Recipient Outstanding Investigator award Nat. Cancer Inst., 1987-2001, Excellence in Tchg. award No. Calif. Phi Beta Kappa, 1991, Environ. Mutagen Soc. Ann. Rsch. award, 1992, Peter and Helen Bing award for Disting. Tchg., 1992, Am. Soc. for Photobiology Rsch. award, 1996, Internat. Mutation Rsch. award, 1997, Ellison Found. Sr. scholar award, 2001-04, John B. Little award in radiation scis. Harvard Sch. Pub. Health, 2002; Hans Falk lectr. Nat. Inst. Environ. Health Scis., 1990, Severo Ochoa Meml. Hons. lectr. NYU, 1996, IBM-Princess Takamatsu lectr. Japan, 1999, Sonnebonn lectr. Ind. U., 2002; Fogarty sr. rsch. fellow, 1993. Fellow: AAAS, Am. Acad. Arts and Sciences, Am. Acad. Microbiology; mem.: NAS, European Molecular Biology Orgn. (fgn. assoc.), Radiation Rsch. Soc., Environ. Mutagen Soc. (pres. 1993—94, Student Mentoring award 2001), Am. Soc. Biochemistry and Molecular Biology, German DNA Repair Network (hon.), Biophys. Soc. (exec. bd. 1969—71), Genetics Soc., Am. Soc. for Photobiology, Am. Assn. Cancer Rsch. (bd. dirs. 1994—97). Achievements include co-discovery of DNA excision-repair and transcription-coupled DNA repair; research on the role of DNA changes in human genetic disease and aging. Office: Stanford U Dept Biol Herrin Biology Labs 371 Serra Mall Stanford CA 94305-5020 Office Phone: 650-723-2424. Business E-Mail: hanawalt@stanford.edu.

HANCOCK, ELLEN MARIE, communications executive; b. NYC, Apr. 15, 1943; d. Peter Joseph and Helen Gertrude (Houlihan) Mooney; m. W. Jason Hancock, Sept. 17, 1971. BA, Coll. New Rochelle, 1965; MA, Fordham U., 1966. With IBM, 1966—, programmer Armonk, NY, 1966-81, dir. comm. programming sect., comm. products divsn. Raleigh, NC, 1981-83, v.p. comm. programming sect., comm. products divsn., 1983-84, asst. group exec. systems devel. info. systems and storage group Armonk, NY, 1985, v.p. telecomm. systems comm. prodn. divsn., 1985-86, pres. comm. products divsn., 1986-88, v.p., gen. mgr. comm. sys. Somers, NY, 1988-91, v.p., gen. mgr. networking systems Staines, England, 1991-92, sr. v.p., 1992—95; exec. v.p., COO Nat. Semiconductor Corp., 1995—96; exec. v.p. R&D, chief tech. officer Apple Computer, Inc., Cupertino, Calif., 1996-97; pres. Exodus Comm., Inc., 1998—2000, CEO, 1998—2001, chmn., 2000—01; co-founder, pres., COO, CFO, sec., bd. dir. Acquicor Tech. Inc., Irvine, Calif., 2005—. Bd. dirs. Aetna, Inc., Colgate-Palmolive, Watchguard Technologies, Inc., Electronic Data Systems Corp., Inst. for Advanced Catholic Studies Trustee Marist Coll., Poughkeepsie, Santa Clara Univ. Council on Fgn. Rels., Pacific Council of Internat. Policy Roman Catholic. Office: Acquicor Tech Inc 4910 Birch St Ste 102 Newport Beach CA 92660

HANCOCK, JOHN WALKER, III, banker; b. Long Beach, Calif., Mar. 8, 1937; s. John Walker and Bernice H.; m. Elizabeth Hoien, June 20, 1959; children: Suzanne, Donna, Randy, David. BA in Econs, Stanford U., 1958, MBA, 1960. With Security Pacific Nat. Bank, LA, 1960-92, v.p., 1968-77, sr. v.p., 1977-84, exec. v.p., 1984-92; pres. Bancap Investment Group, Long Beach, Calif., 1992—. Bd. dirs. Harbor Bank; chmn. Meml. Med. Ctr.; pres. Port of Long Beach. Bd. dirs. Long Beach Symphony, Meml. Hosp., Long Beach City Coll. Found. Mem. Stanford U. Alumni Assn., Calif. Club (L.A.), Va. Country Club, Balboa Bay Club, Pacific Club, Bohemian Club, Thunderbird Country Club. Republican. Home: 258 Roycroft Ave Long Beach CA 90803-1717 Office: Bancap Investment Group 192 Marina Dr Long Beach CA 90803-4613

HANCOCK, LONI, state legislator; b. NYC; m. Tom Bates; 4 children. BA, Ithaca Coll., 1963; MA, Wright Inst., 1978. City councilwoman, Berkeley, 71-79, mayor, 86-94; advisor board, Working Assets, currently; regional repr, Secretary of United States Department Education, formerly; California State Aseemblywoman, District 14, 2003-08; mem. Dist. 9, Calif. State Senate, 2008-. Sierra Club; Nat Women's Polit Caucus. Democrat. Office: State Capitol PO Box 942849 Rm 3092 Sacramento CA 94249 also: Dist 9 1515 Clay St Ste 2202 Oakland CA 94612 Office Phone: 916-651-4009, 510-286-1333. Office Fax: 916-327-1997, 510-286-3885. Business E-Mail: senator.Hancock@sen.ca.gov.*

HANDEL, NEAL, plastic surgeon, researcher, educator; b. LA, Sept. 2, 1947; s. Max and Ruth H. BA, Columbia U., 1969; MD, Yale U., 1973. Diplomate Am. Bd. Plastic Surgery. Resident surgery UCLA Sch. Medicine, 1973—75; resident UCLA, 1975—76, Tulane U., New Orleans, 1976—78, U. Colo., Denver, 1978—; plastic and reconstructive surgeon The Breast Ctr., Van Nuys, Calif., 1982—99, assoc. med. dir., 1982—99; asst. clin. prof. Divsn. Plastic Surgery David Geffen Sch. Med., UCLA. Mem. adv. bd. Ctr. for Devel. Biology Calif. State U., Northridge, 1985—. Featured on Body Work series, Plastic Surgery Beverly Hills, The Learning Channel, 2005; contbr. articles to profl. jours. Rsch. grantee Am. Soc. Aesthetic Plastic Surgery, 1991. Fellow ACS; diplomat, Am. Bd. Plastic Surgery; mem. Am. Soc. Plastic and Reconstructive Surgery, Calif. Soc. Plastic and Reconstructive Surgeons, Am. Soc. Plastic Surgeons, Am. Soc. Aesthetic Plastic Surgery, Am. Assn. Plastic Surgeons. Office: Neal Handel Md 13400 Riverside Dr Ste 101 Sherman Oaks CA 91423-2513 Office Phone: 805-682-9100. Office Fax: 805-862-9101.

HANDELMAN, ALBERT G., lawyer; b. River Edge, NJ, Oct. 5, 1953; BS cum laude in Econs., U. Pa. Wharton Sch., 1975; JD, U. So. Calif., 1978. Bar: Calif. 1978, US Dist. Ct. (ctrl. and no. dists. Calif.) 1979, US Dist. Ct. (ea. dist. Calif.) 1989, cert.: State Bar Calif. Bd. Legal Specialization (estate planning, trust and probate law). Pvt. practice atty., Santa Rosa, Calif. Officer, dir. Redwood Empire Estate Planning Coun., 1992—96, pres., 1994—95; mem., founder Calif. Trust and Estate Counselors, LLP. Contbg. author, cons.: Calif. Wills and Trusts, 1991—; editor: Calif. Trusts and Estates Quarterly, 2001—04. Mem. profls. adv. grp. Cmty. Found. Sonoma County, 1995—, chmn., 1997—2001, bd. dirs., 2004—, chmn. bd. dirs., 2006—. Named one of Top 100 Attys., Worth mag., 2006. Fellow: Am. Coll. Trust and Estate Counsel; mem.: State Bar Calif. (mem. exec. com. Trusts and Estates Sect. 1998—2004), Sonoma County Bar Assn. Office: 420 Aviation Blvd Ste 203 Santa Rosa CA 95403 Office Phone: 707-521-2800. Office Fax: 707-521-2803. E-mail: aghlaw@sonic.net.

HANDLER, CAROLE ENID, lawyer, city planner; b. NYC, Dec. 23, 1945; d. Milton and Marion Winter (Kahn) Handler; m. Peter U. Schoenbach, May 30, 1965 (div. Sept. 1979); children: Alisa, Ilana. AB, Radcliffe Coll., 1957; MS, U. Pa., 1963, JD, 1975. Bar: Pa. 1975; Calif. 1987; U.S. Dist Ct. Ea. Pa. 1976, N.J. 1979, Ctrl. Calif. 1987, So. Calif. 1990, So. N.Y. 1990, No. Calif. 1991, Ea. Calif. 1993, Mid. & So. Fla. 1994; U.S. Ct. Appeals 3d cir. 1976, 9th cir. 1988, 2d cir. 1989, 11th cir. 1992; Pa. Supreme Ct.; U.S. Supreme Ct. Planner Boston Redevel. Authority, 1959-61; head gen. plans sect. Phila. City Planning Commn., 1963-66; cdnl. facilities planning cons. Phila. Sch. Dist., 1966-67, coordinator and dir. policy planning, 1967-69; instr. U. Sao Paulo, Rio de Janeiro, 1970-71, Cath. U., Rio de Janeiro, 1970-71; law clk. to Hon. Edmund B. Spaeth Jr. Pa. Superior Ct., Phila., 1975-76; assoc. Goodman & Ewing, Phila., 1976-78, Schnader, Harrison, Segal & Lewis, Phila., 1978—; sr. v.p., gen. counsel MGM/UA Distbn. Co., Los Angeles, 1985-87; ptnr. Le Boeuf, Lamb, Leiby & MacRae, LA, 1987-89, Proskauer Rose Goetz & Mendelsohn, LA, Alschuler Grossman Pines, LA, Kaye Scholer Fierman Hays & Handler, LA, 1997—2000, O'Donnell & Shaeffer, LA, 2000—04, Thelen Reid & Priest, LA, 2004—05, Foley & Lardner, LLP, Century City, Calif., 2005—. Adj. prof. Univ. So. Calif. Bd. dirs. St. Peter's Sch.; former bd. dirs. Soc. Hill Synagogue, LA Chamber Orch., 1990—, Public Counsel 1999-; exec. bd. Am. Jewish Congress 2004-; mem Bet Tzedek Legal Svcs. Named one of Top 50 Women Litigators in Calif., Daily Journal Extra, 2002—04. Mem. Phila. Vol. Lawyers for the Arts (v.p.), ABA, Fed. Bar Assn., Pa. Bar Assn., N.Y. Bar Assn., Beverly Hills Bar Assn., L.A. County Bar Assn. (chair antitrust sect. 1992-93), Assn. Bus. Trial Lawyers, Copyright Soc., Calif. Women's Law Ctr. Jewish.

HANDLER, JOEL F., law educator; b. 1932; AB, Princeton U., 1954; JD, Harvard U., 1957. Asst. prof. Vanderbilt U., 1961-62, U. Ill., 1962-64; prof. U. Wis., 1965-80, George A. Wiley prof., 1980-82; vilas rsch. prof., 1982-85; vis. prof. UCLA, 1984-85, prof., 1985—. Vis. prof. Stanford, 1969-70. Fellow John Simon Guggenheim, 1974-75, German Marshall Fund, 1978. Mem. Law and Soc. Assn., Nat. Res. Coun. Status of Black Am; fellow, Am. Acad. of Arts and Sci. Office: UCLA Law Sch 405 Hilgard Ave Los Angeles CA 90095-9000

HANDZLIK, JAN LAWRENCE, lawyer; b. NYC, Sept. 21, 1945; s. Felix Munso and Anna Jean Handzlik; m. Jennifer Maria Handzlik; children: Grant, Craig, Anna, Jacob, Magritte. BA, U. So. Calif., 1967; JD, UCLA, 1970. Bar: Calif. 1971, US Dist. Ct. (ctrl. dist.) Calif. 1971, US Ct. Appeals (9th cir.) 1971, US Supreme Ct. 1975, US Dist. Ct. (no. dist.) Calif. 1979, US Tax Ct. 1979, US Dist. Ct. (ea.

dist.) Calif. 1981, US Dist. Ct. (so. dist.) Calif. 1982, US Ct. Internat. Trade 1984, US Ct. Appeals (2d cir.) 1984, US Ct. Appeals (11th cir.) 2007. Law clk. to Hon. Francis C. Whelan, US Dist. Ct. (ctrl. dist.) Calif., LA, 1970-71; asst. US atty. fraud and spl. prosecutions section criminal divsn. US Dept. Justice, LA, 1971-76; assoc. Greenberg & Glusker, LA, 1976-78; ptnr., prin. Stilz, Boyd, Levine & Handzlik, P.C., LA, 1978-84; prin. Jan Lawrence Handzlik, P.C., LA, 1984-91; ptnr. Kirkland & Ellis, LLP, LA, 1991—2004, Howrey LLP, LA, 2004—. Counsel to Ind. Christopher Commn. Investigation regarding racism and brutality LA Police Dept., 1991; dep. gen. counsel to Ind. Webster Commn. Investigation LA Police Dept. response to urban disorders, 1992; mem. adv. com. Office LA County Dist. Atty., 1994—96; mem. standing com. on atty. discipline US Dist. Ct. (ctrl. dist.) Calif., 1997—2001; dep. gen. counsel Rampart ind. rev. panel investigation police corruption LA Police Commn., 2000; mem. blue ribbon rev. panel for investigation handling of Rampart corruption incident L.A. Police Dept., 2003—06. Mem. editl. adv. bd. DOJ Alert, 1994—95. Bd. dirs. Friends Child Advs., LA, 1987—91, Inner City Law Ctr., LA, 1995—2002. Fellow: Am. Bar Found.; mem.: FBA, ABA (mem. criminal justice sect. 1990—, chair west coast white collar crime com. 1996—98, vice chmn. nat. com. white collar crime 1998—2000, chair nat. com. white collar crime 2000—02, mem. criminal justice sect. governing coun. 2002—05, mem. task force on implementation of Sarbanes-Oxley Act of 2002 2002—, chair criminal justice sect. working group on atty.-client privilege 2003—04, mem. anti-terrorism and money laundering working group 2003—04, mem. ABA pres.'s task force on atty.-client privilege 2004—, mem. criminal justice standards com. 2006—), Bus. Crime Com., 2d Cir. Fed. Bar Coun., Internat. Bar Assn., Supreme Ct. Hist. Soc., LA County Bar Assn. (coms. on fed. cts. 1988—2001, chair criminal practice subcom. 1989—90, fed. appts. evaluation 1989—93, white collar crime com. 1991—97, exec. com. criminal justice sect. 1997—2002, fed. cts. coord. com. 2001—), State Bar Calif. (sects. on criminal law and litigation), The Calif. Club, Chancery Club of LA. Office: Howrey LLP Ste 1100 550 S Hope St Los Angeles CA 90071-2636 Home Phone: 310-546-3050; Office Phone: 213-892-1802. Office Fax: 213-402-8721. Business E-Mail: handzlikj@howrey.com.

HANE, LAURIE S., lawyer; BA summa cum laude, Knox Coll., 1981; JD, Northwestern U., 1984. Bar: Calif. 1984. Law clk. to Hon. Robert F. Peckham U.S. Dist. Ct., No. Dist. Calif., 1984—85; assoc. Morrison & Foerster LLP, 1985—91, ptnr., co-mng. ptnr. ops. Mem.: Phi Beta Kappa. Office: Morrison & Foerster LLP 425 Market St San Francisco CA 94105-2482 Office Phone: 415-268-7092. Office Fax: 415-268-7522. Business E-Mail: lhane@mofo.com.

HANES, JOHN GRIER, lawyer, state legislator; b. Cheyenne, Wyo., 1936; s. Harold H. and Mary Elizabeth H.; m. Liv Paul; children: Greg, Clint. BS in Bus. Adminstrn., U. Wyo., 1958, JD, 1960. Bar: Wyo. 1960, U.S. Ct. Appeals (10th cir.) 1960, U.S. Ct. Mil. Appeals, 1960, U.S. Supreme Ct. 1964. Dep. sec. of state State of Wyo., 1963-65; prin. Burke Woodard & Bishop, Cheyenne, 1965-90, of counsel, 1990—; atty. Wyo. Senate, 1967-71; mcpl. judge City of Cheyenne, 1970-73; mem. Burke, Woodard & O'Donnell, Cheyenne, until 1990; of counsel Woodard & White, P.C. and predecessor firms, Cheyenne, 1990—; mem. Wyo. Ho. of Reps., 1993-99, Wyo. Senate, 1999—2006. Chmn. Senate Jud. Com. Vol. Cheyenne Frontier Days; mem. Heels; Rep. precinct committeeman, 1976-94. With U.S. Army JAGC. Mem. C. of C., Rotary (pres. 1982-83, dist. gov. 1990-91), Sigma Nu. Avocations: sports, travel. Home: 848 Creighton St Cheyenne WY 82009-3231 Business E-Mail: jhanes@wyoming.com.

HANIFEN, RICHARD CHARLES PATRICK, bishop emeritus; b. Denver, Colo., June 15, 1931; s. Edward Anselm and Dorothy Elizabeth (Ranous) Hanifen. BS, Regis Coll., 1953; STB, Cath. U., 1959, MA, 1966; JCL, Pontifical Lateran U., Italy, 1968. Ordained priest Archdiocese of Denver, Colo., 1959; asst. pastor Cathedral Parish, Denver, 1959—66; sec. to archbishop Archdiocese Denver, 1968—69, chancellor, 1969—76, aux. bishop, 1974—83; ordained bishop, 1974; bishop Diocese of Colorado Springs, 1984—2003, bishop emeritus, 2003—. Roman Catholic. Office: 228 N Cascade Ave Colorado Springs CO 80903 Office Phone: 719-636-2345. Office Fax: 719-636-1216. E-mail: rhanifen@diocs.org.

HANKINS, ANTHONY P., chemicals executive; Various mgmt. positions in plastics, fibers and polyurethanes ICI, 1980—98; v.p. Asia Pacific for Polyurethanes bus. Huntsman Corp., 1998—2000, v.p. Ams. for Polyurethanes bus., 2000—01, global v.p. rigids divsn. Polyurethanes bus., 2002—03, pres. performance products, 2003—04, divsn. pres. polyurethanes, 2004—. Office: Huntsman Corp 500 Huntsman Way Salt Lake City UT 84108 Office Phone: 801-584-5700.

HANKS, STEPHEN GRANT, construction executive, lawyer; b. Rexburg, Idaho, June 7, 1950; s. Grant E. and Elaine (Stephens) H.; m. Debra Joan Dyrr, Aug. 6, 1975; children: Adrianne, Brandon, Tiffany, Lindsey. BS, Brigham Young U., 1974; MBA, U. Utah, 1975; JD, U. Idaho, 1978. Bar: Idaho 1978, U.S. Dist. Ct. Idaho 1978. Corp. atty. Morrison-Knudsen Co., Inc., Boise, Idaho, 1978-82, asst. gen. counsel, 1982-85, Morrison Knudsen Corp., Boise, 1985-86, assoc. gen. counsel, 1986-90, sec., assoc. gen. counsel, 1990—91, v.p., corp. sec., gen. counsel, 1991—92, sr. v.p., gen. counsel, 1992—95, exec. v.p., chief legal officer, 1995—2000; pres. Washington Group Internat. (formerly Morrison Knudsen Corp.), Boise, Idaho, 2000—01, pres., CEO, bd. dir., 2001—. Bd. dir. Danny Thompson Memorial Leukemia Found., Inc., U. Idaho President's Spl. Adv. Group; bd. dir., pres. Boise Pub. Schs. Edu. Found., Discovery Ctr. Idaho, Ore-Idaho Coun. of Boy Scouts of Am., St. Alphonsus Reg. Med. Ctr. Found.; adv. bd. U. Idaho Coll. Bus. and Econs., U. Idaho Found.; chmn. Character and Fitness Com. of Idaho State Bar. Mem. ABA, AICPA, Idaho Soc. CPAs. Home: 3130 Terra Dr Boise ID 83709-3860 Office: Washington Group International PO Box 73 720 Park Blvd Boise ID 83729-0073

HANKS, TOM, actor, film producer, director; b. Concord, Calif., July 9, 1956; m. Samantha Lewes, Jan. 24, 1978 (div. Mar. 19, 1987); children: Colin, Elizabeth; m. Rita Wilson, Apr. 30, 1988; children: Chester Marlon, Truman Theodore. Student, Calif. State U., Sacramento. Actor: (films) He Knows You're Alone, 1980, Splash, 1984, Bachelor Party, 1984, Volunteers, 1985, The Man with One Red Shoe, 1985, The Money Pit, 1986, Nothing in Common, 1986, Every Time We Say Goodbye, 1986, Dragnet, 1987, Big, 1988, Punchline, 1988, Turner and Hooch, 1989, The 'Burbs, 1989, Joe Versus the Volcano, 1990, The Bonfire of the Vanities, 1990, Radio Flyer, 1992, A League of Their Own, 1992, Sleepless in Seattle, 1993, Philadelphia, 1993 (Golden Globe for Best Actor - Drama 1994, Academy Award for Best Actor 1994), Forrest Gump, 1994 (Academy Award for Best Actor 1995), Apollo 13, 1995, Celluloid Closet, 1995, Toy Story (voice), 1995, Saving Private Ryan, 1998 (nominated Acad. awards), You've Got Mail, 1998, Toy Story 2 (voice), 1999, The Green Mile, 1999, Cast Away, 2000 (also prodr.) (Golden Globe for Best Actor 2001), Road to Perdition, 2002, Catch Me If You Can, 2002, The Ladykillers, 2004, The Terminal, 2004, The Polar Express, 2004 (also exec. prodr.), Da Vinci Code, 2006, Charlie Wilson's War, 2007 (also prodr.), The Great Buck Howard, 2008, Angels & Demons, 2009; actor, dir., writer (films) That Thing You Do!, 1996; prodr. (films) My Big Fat Greek Wedding, 2002, Connie and Carla, 2004, Neil Young: Heart of Gold, 2006, The Ant Bully, 2006; actor (TV movies) Mazes and Monsters, 1982, I Am Your Child, 1997, exec. prodr. We Stand Alone Together, 2001; actor (TV series) Bosom Buddies, 1980-82; exec. prodr. West Point, 2000, My Big Fat Greek Life, 2003; dir., prodr., writer (miniseries) From the Earth to the Moon, 1998 (Emmy award for best miniseries, 1999), Band of Brothers, 2001 (Emmy awards for best directing and best miniseries, 2002), exec. prodr. John Adams, 2008 (Primetime Emmy for Outstanding Miniseries, Acad. TV Arts and Scis., 2008, Best Mini-Series or Motion Picture Made for TV, Golden Globe award, Hollywood Fgn. Press Assn., 2009, David L. Wolper Prodr. of Yr. award in Long-Form TV, Prodrs. Guild America, 2009). Recipient Louella O. Parsons Awd., Hollywood Women's Press Club, 1994, Golden Globe award, 1995, People's Choice award, 1995, 99, Disting. Pub. Svc. award, USN, 1999, Life Achievement award, Am. Film Inst., 2002; named Man of the Yr., Harvard's Hasty Pudding Theater Club, 1995; named one of 50 Most Powerful People in Hollywood Premiere mag., 2004-06, 100 Most Powerful Celebrities, Forbes.com, 2007, The World's Most Influential People, 2009; inducted as an honorary mem., US Army Ranger Hall of Fame, 2006; honoree, Film Soc. Lincoln Ctr., 2009. Mem. Actors' Equity Assn., Screen Actors Guild, AFTRA., Am. Acad. Motion Picture Arts & Sciences (v.p., 2007-), Internat. Thespian Soc. Office: c/o Creative Artists Agy 2000 Ave of the Stars Los Angeles CA 90067*

HANLEY, FRANK LOUIS, surgeon, educator; b. Providence, May 19, 1952; BA, Brown U.; MD, Tufts U. Sch. Medicine, 1978. Diplomate Am. Bd. Surgery, Am. Bd. Thoracic Surgery. Resident, surgery U. Calif., San Francisco, 1978—81, resident, cardiothoracic surgery, 1986—88, fellow, 1981—84, prof., chief divsn. cardiothoracic surgery, 1993—2001; assoc. prof. Harvard Med. Sch., Boston Children's Hosp., 1989—92; prof., cardiothoracic surgery, dir. heart ctr. Stanford U. Med. Ctr., Calif., 2001—; svc. chief, pediatric cardiothoracic surgery Lucile Packard Children's Hosp. at Stanford, Calif., dir., Children's Heart Ctr. Calif., Lawrence Crowley, MD, Endowed Prof. in Child Health Calif., 2004—. Invited guest lectr. Editor: (books) Cardiac Surgery in the Neonate and Infant, Cardiac Surgery, Pediatric Cardiac Intensive Care, Infant-Annals of Thoracic Surgery; contbr. several articles to profl. pubs. Recipient Excellence in Tchg. Award, Dept. of Surgery, U. of California-San Francisco, 1992-1994, Outstanding Surg. Chief Resident Award, U. of California-San Francisco, 1986, Outstanding Resident Tchg. Award, 1986, Alpha Omega Alpha Med. Soc., 1986, Outstanding Graduating Studen in Surgery (Martin J Loeb Award), Tufts Sch. of Medicine, 1978. Mem. Am. Assn. for Thoracic Surgery (adv. editl. bd.), Am. Heart Assn., Congenital Heart Surgeons' Soc. Data Ctr., Soc. Thoracic Surgeons, Thoracic Surgery Dirs. Assn., Howard C. Naffziger Surgical Soc., Western Thoracic Surgical Assn., Alpha Omega Alpha. Office: Stanford U Sch Medicine Falk Cardiovasc Rsch Bldg 300 Pasteur Dr Falk CVRB MC 5407 Stanford CA 94305 Address: U Calif 505 Parnassus Ave S-549 San Francisco CA 94143 Office Phone: 650-724-2925, 650-723-0190. Office Fax: 415-476-9678, 650-725-0707. Business E-Mail: frank.hanley@stanford.edu, fhanley@stanford.edu.

HANLEY, HOWARD JAMES MASON, research scientist; b. Hove, Sussex, Aug. 19, 1937; arrived in U.S., 1962; s. Charles Edward Mason and Evelyn Agnes (Palmer) H.; m. Janet Mary Kettlewell, July 29, 1964; 1 child, Elizabeth Mary. BSc, London U., 1959, PhD, 1963. Rsch. assoc. Dept. Chemistry, Pa. State U., State College, 1963-65; phys. chemist Nat. Bur. of Stds., Boulder, 1965-83; fellow Nat. Inst. of Stds. and Tech., Boulder, 1983—. Adj. prof. Dept. Chem. Engring., U. Colo., 1974—, vis. prof. 1969; vis. rsch. fellow Australian Nat. U., 1973-74, 78-79, 87, 88, 92; vis. scientist Inst. Laue-Langevin, Grenoble, France, 1984, 85; fellow Wissenschaftskolleg zu Berlin, Berlin Inst. Advanced Studies, 1989-90; rsch. adv. com. Nat. Bur. Stds., 1980-83; Australian Nuclear Sci. and Tech. Orgn. vis. prof. Rsch. Sch. Chemistry, Australian Nat. U., 1998—. Author: Transport Phenomena in Fluids, 1969, Turner in Dorset, 1992; cons. editor Marcel Dekker Inc., N.Y., 1968—; editor NIST Jour. of Rsch., 1975-88; adv. editor Internat. Jour. of Thermophysics, 1981—; contbr. articles to profl. jours. Recipient Silver medal U.S. Dept. of Commerce, 1982, Gold medal, 1985; recipient Humboldt Rsch. prize, 1992. Fellow Royal Chem. Soc.; mem. ASME (com. thermophys. properties 1980-94, chmn. 1980-85), Internat. Union Pure and Applied Chemistry (transport properties com. 1976-88, com. on quantum fluids), MaryLeBone Cricket Club. Avocations: landscape art, literature, history, music, cricket. Office: 325 Broadway St Boulder CO 80305-3337 E-mail: howard.hanley@nist.gov.

HANNA, WILLIAM JOHNSON, electrical engineering educator; b. Longmont, Colo., Feb. 7, 1922; s. William Grant and Anna Christina (Johnson) H.; m. Katherine Fagan, Apr. 25, 1944 (dec. 1993); children: Daniel August, Paul William; m. Helen Yeager McCarty, Sept. 19, 1996. BSEE, U. Colo., 1943, MS, 1948, D in Elec. Engring., 1951. Registered profl. engr., Colo., Kans. Mem. faculty U. Colo., 1946-91, prof. elec. engring., 1962-91, prof. emeritus, 1991—; ret., 1991. Cons. in field; mem. Colo. Bd. Engring. Examiners, 1973-85; with Ponderosa Assocs., Lafayette, Colo. Author articles, reports. Served to 1st lt. AUS, 1943-46. Recipient Faculty Recognition award Students Assn. U. Colo., 1956, 61, Alfred J. Ryan award, 1978, Archimedes award Calif. Soc. Profl. Engrs., 1978, Outstanding Engring. Alumnus award U. Colo., 1983, Faculty Service award, 1983; named Colo. Engr. of Yr. Profl. Engrs. Colo., 1968; named to Hon. Order of Ky. Cols. Mem. IEEE, Am. Soc. Engring. Edn., Nat. Soc. Profl. Engrs. (pres. Colo. 1967-68), Nat. Coun. Engring. Examiners (pres. 1977-78, Disting. Svc. award with spl. commendation 1990), AIEE (chmn. Denver 1961-62) Clubs: Masons. Republican. Presbyterian. Home and Office: 27 Silver Spruce Nederland Star Rt Boulder CO 80302-9604 Office Phone: 307-666-8182.

HANNAFORD, PETER DOR, public relations executive, writer; b. Glendale, Calif., Sept. 21, 1932; s. Donald R. and Elinor (Nielsen) H.; m. Irene Dorothy Harville, Aug. 14, 1954; children: Richard H., Donald R. II. AB, U. Calif. V.p. Kennedy-Hannaford, Inc., San Francisco and Oakland, Calif., 1957-62, pres., 1962-67, Pettler & Hannaford, Inc., Oakland, Calif., 1967-69; v.p. Wilton, Coombs & Colnett, Inc., 1969-72; pres. Hannaford & Assoc., Oakland, Calif., 1973; asst. to Gov. of Calif., Calif.; dir. pub. affairs Gov. Office, Calif., 1974; chmn. bd. Hannaford Co., Inc. (formerly Deaver & Hannaford, Inc.), 1975-95; pub. Ferndale Enterprise, Calif., 1996-98; pres. Hannaford Enterprises Inc., 1998—; sr. counselor APCO Worldwide, 2001—; editl. pages editor Eureka Reporter, Calif., 2007—. Vice chmn. Calif. Gov. Consumer Fraud Task Force, 1972—73; bd. dirs. Eberle Comms. Group Inc. Author: The Reagans: A Political Portrait, 1983, Talking Back to the Media, 1986 (Japanese edit. 1990); co-author: Remembering Reagan, 1994, Recollections of Reagan, 1997, My Heart Goes Home: A Hudson Valley Memoir, 1997, The Quotable Ronald Reagan, 1998, The Essential George Washington, 1999, The Quotable Calvin Coolidge, 2000, Ronald Reagan and His Ranch, 2002. Mem. Alameda County Rep. Ctrl. Com., Rep. State Ctrl. Com. Calif., 1968-74, Commonwealth Fund's Commn. on Elderly People Living Alone, 1986-91; Rep. nominee for U.S. Congress, 1972; governing bd. Tahoe Regional Planning Agy., 1973-74; trustee White House Preservation Fund, 1981-89, pub. rels. adv. com. USIA, 1981-92; adv. com. Mt. Vernon 1991-96; fin. adv. commn. City of Eureka, Calif., 2007—. 1st lt. Signal Corps, U.S. Army, 1954-56. Shapiro fellow, George Washington U. Sch. Media and pub. affairs, 2002. Mem.: Author's Guild. Episcopalian. Personal E-mail: hannafordwashdc@aol.com.

HANNAH, DAVID H., metal products executive; BSBA, U. So. Calif. CPA. Mgr. audit divsn. Ernst & Whinney, LA, 1973-81; CFO Reliance Steel & Aluminum, LA, 1981-87, v.p., 1987-92, dir., exec. v.p., CFO, 1992-95, pres., 1995—2002, CEO, 1999—2007, chmn., CEO, 2007—. Office: Reliance Steel & Aluminum Ste 5100 350 S Grand Ave Los Angeles CA 90071 Office Phone: 213-687-7700. Office Fax: 213-687-8792.

HANNEMAN, LEROY C., JR., real estate executive; married; 2 children. BS in Constrn. Engring., Ariz. State U. Estimator Del Webb Corp., Sun City, 1972, v.p. housing, 1984, exec. v.p., 1996, pres., COO, Phoenix, 1998—2001, CEO, 1999—2001; co-founder, CEO Element Homes, 2003—. Office: Element Homes One Gateway 426 N 44th St Ste 204 Phoenix AZ 85008

HANNEMANN, MUFI, Mayor, Honolulu; b. Honolulu, July 16, 1954; s. Gustav and Faiaso Hannemann; m. Gail Hannemann. BA with honors, Harvard U. Former v.p. C. Brewer & Co.; White House fellow Assigned to V.P. George H.W. Bush, City Coun., Honolulu, 1995—2000; mayor City of Honolulu, 2005—. Mem. President's Coun. 21st Century Workforce, 2004, US Sec. Labor Adv. Comm. Apprenticeship, 2005, US Conf. Mayors Adv. Co.; chair Com. Tourism and Arts; former dir. Hawaii Dept. Bus., Econ. Develop. & Tourism, Hawaii Official Internat. Rels. Fulbright scholar, Victoria U., New Zealand. Office: Office of Mayor 530 S King St Honolulu HI 96813 Business E-Mail: mayor@honolulu.gov.*

HANNIGAN, ALYSON, actress; b. Washington, Mar. 24, 1974; m. Alexis Denisof, Oct. 11, 2003; 1 child, Satyana Denisof. Attended, Calif. State U. Actor: (films) Impure Thoughts, 1986, My Stepmother Is an Alien, 1988, Dead Man on Campus, 1998, American Pie, 1999, Boys and Girls, 2000, American Pie 2, 2001, Beyond the City Limits, 2001, American Wedding, 2003, (voice only) Farce of the Penguins, 2006, Date Movie, 2006; (TV films) Switched at Birth, 1991, The Stranger Beside Me, 1995, A Case for Life, 1996, For My Daughter's Honor, 1996, Hayley Wagner, Star, 1999; (TV series) Free Spirit, 1989—90, Buffy the Vampire Slayer, 1997—2003, How I Met Your Mother, 2005—, (TV appearances) Roseanne, 1988, Picket Fences, 1992, Almost Home, 1993, Touched by an Angel, 1994, The Torkelsons, 1991, 100 Deeds for Eddie McDowd, 1999—2000, The Wild Thornberrys, 2000, Angel (3 episodes), 2003, The 70's Show, 2004, (voice only) King of the Hill, 2004, Veronica Mars (3 episodes), 2005. Office: c/o Innovative Artists 1505 10th St Santa Monica CA 90401

HANRAHAN, PATRICK M., computer scientist; PhD, U. Wis., 1986. Canon USA prof. dept. computer scientist Stanford (Calif.) U. Fellow Am. Acad. Arts & Scis.; mem. NAE. Office: Stanford U Rm 3B Gates Computer Sci Bldf 370 Stanford CA 94305-4070

HANSCHEN, PETER WALTER, lawyer; b. San Francisco, July 7, 1945; s. Walter A. and Dorothy E. (Watkins) H.; m. Brenda C. Hanschen, Feb. 7, 1987. BA, San Francisco State U., 1967; JD, U. Calif.-Berkeley, 1971. Bar: Calif. 1972, U.S. Supreme Ct. 1985, U.S. Ct. Appeals D.C. Cir. 1975. Assoc. Lawler, Felix & Hall, LA, 1971-73; atty. Pacific Gas Transmission Co., San Francisco, 1973-76, Pacific Gas & Elec. Co., San Francisco, 1976-79; gen. counsel Pacific Gas Transmission, San Francisco, 1979-83; asst. gen. counsel Pacific Gas & Elec. Co., San Francisco, 1983-88; ptnr. Graham & James, San Francisco, 1988-99, Morrison & Foerster, San Francisco, 1999—. Arbitrator Am. Arbitration Assn., 2006. Mem. ABA, Assn., Fed. Energy Bar Assn., Counsel of Calif. Pub. Utilities. Avocations: golf, gardening, sports. Office: Morrison & Foerster LLP Ste 450 101 Ygnacio Valley Rd PO Box 8130 Walnut Creek CA 94563-8130 Office Phone: 925-295-3450. Personal E-mail: phanschen@mofo.com.

HANSELL, DEAN, lawyer; b. Bridgeport, Conn., Mar. 24, 1952; BA, Denison U., 1974; JD, Northwestern U., 1977. Bar: Ill. 1977, US Dist. Ct. (no. dist.) Ill. 1977, US Ct. Appeals (7th cir.) 1978, US Ct. Appeals (DC cir.) 1978, US Ct. Appeals (9th cir.) 1979, Calif. 1980, US Dist. Ct. (ctrl. dist.) Calif. 1981, US Dist. Ct. (so. dist.) Calif. 1989, US Supreme Ct. 1998, US Ct. Appeals (8th cir.) 2001. Asst. atty. gen. for environ. control State of Ill., Chgo., 1977-80; atty. FTC, LA, 1980-83; assoc. Donovan Leisure Newton & Irvine, LA, 1984-86; ptnr. Dewey & LeBoeuf, LA, 1986—2001, 2007—, co-mng. ptnr. LA office, 2001—07. Mem. Ill. Solar Resources Adv. Panel, 1978—80; adj. assoc. prof. Southwestern Univ. Sch. Law, LA, 1982—86; judge pro tem LA County Mcpl. Ct., 1987—97, LA County Superior Ct., 1989—2005; mem. adv. bd. Fayette Haywood Legal Svcs., Tenn., 1979—83, Nat. Inst. Citizen Edn. in Law, 1989—94, Asian Pacific Am. Legal Ctr., 1996—. Mem. editl. bd.: Los Angeles Lawyer Mag., 1995—2005, Internat. Reins. Dispute Reporter, 1996—2001; contbr. articles to profl. jours. V.p., commr. LA Bd. Police Commrs., 1997—2001, v.p., 2001; commr. LA Bd. Info. Tech., 2001—08, v.p., 2003—04, pres., 2004—; trustee Denison U., 2006—; dir. LA CC Found., 2007—; mem. adv. bd. UCLA Sch. Pub. Health; bd. dirs. Jewish Fedn. Coun. Met. LA Region, 1984—87, Project LEAP, Legal Elections All Precincts, Chgo., 1976—80, Martin Luther King Jr. Ctr. Nonviolence, LA, 1991—95, LA Pub. Libr. Found., 1997—2005. Mem.: ABA, Calif. Bar Assn., LA County Bar Assn. (mem. exec. com. antitrust sect. 1982—92, chair 1989—90), Phi Beta Kappa, Omicron

Delta Kappa. Office: Dewey & LeBoeuf Ste 2600 333 South Grand Ave Los Angeles CA 90071-1530 Home Phone: 323-931-4883; Office Phone: 213-621-6031. Office Fax: 213-621-6100. Business E-Mail: dhansell@dl.com.

HANSEN, ALEXANDER E., advertising agency executive; BA, Williams Coll.; MDiv, Princeton Theol. Seminary; studied, Cal State LA bus. program. CPA Lic., Calif. Fin. exec. with DS Waters of Am. LP, Groupe Danone, J. Walter Thompson; pres., CEO Bravant LLC, LA; fin. leadership (CFO) ptnr. Tatum CFO Ptnrs., LLP, LA; CFO Adchek, Ventura, Calif. Mem.: Calif. Soc. CPA, AICPA. Office: Tatum CFO Ptnrs LLP 11755 Wilshire Blvd Ste 1100 Los Angeles CA 90025

HANSEN, CHRISTOPHER W., trade association administrator; b. Boston, Dec. 7, 1948; m. Linda Hansen. BA in Polit. Sci., U. Denver; MA in Internat. Mgmt., Am. Grad. Sch. Internat. Mgmt. Mgr. legis. affairs Gen. Dynamics Corp., dir. Washington ops.; with The Boeing Co., 1986—93, v.p. cong. affairs, 1993—94, v.p. Washington office Washington, 1994—97, v.p. govt. rels. Chgo., 1997—99, sr. v.p. govt. rels., 1999—2001; sr. mng. fir for govt. rels. & advocacy AARP, Washington, 2002—03, group exec. officer state & nat. initiatives, 2003—07; pres, CEO AeA, Advancing the Bus. of Tech. (formerly Am. Electronics Assn.), Santa Clara, Calif., 2007—. Bd. dirs. Career Coll. Assn. Vol. Wolf Trap Found. Mem.: Career Coll. Assn., Nat. Bur. Asian Rsch., Nat. Aeronautics Assn., Pacific Basin Econ. Coun., US Coun. Internat. Bus. Office: AeA Advancing the Bus of Tech Ste 600 North Bldg 601 Pennsylvania Ave NW Washington DC 20004 also: 5201 Great America Pkwy Ste 520 Santa Clara CA 95054 Office Phone: 202-682-9110. Office Fax: 202-682-9111.

HANSEN, CURTIS LEROY, federal judge; b. 1933; BS, U. Iowa, 1956; JD, U. N.Mex., 1961. Bar: N.Mex. Law clk. to Hon. Irwin S. Moise N.Mex. Supreme Ct., 1961-62; ptnr. Snead & Hansen, Albuquerque, 1962-64, Civerolo, Hansen & Wolf, P.A., 1964—92; dist. judge U.S. Dist. Ct., N.Mex., 1992—2003, sr. dist. judge, 2003—. Mem. State Bar N.Mex., Albuquerque Bar Assn., Am. Coll. Trial Lawyers, Am. Bd. Trial Advocates, Albuquerque Country Club. Mailing: PO Box 669 Albuquerque NM 87103 Office: US Courthouse 421 Gold Ave SW 5th Fl Albuquerque NM 87102

HANSEN, H. REESE, law educator, former dean; b. Logan, Utah, Apr. 8, 1942; s. Howard F. and Loila Gayle (Reese) H.; m. Kathryn Traveller, June 8, 1962; children: Brian T., Mark T., Dale T., Curtis T. BS, Utah State U., 1964; JD, U. Utah, 1972. Bar: Utah, 1974. Atty. Strong, Poelman & Fox, Salt Lake City, 1972-74; from asst. prof. to assoc. prof. Brigham Young U., Provo, Utah, 1974-79, prof. law, 1979—, from asst. dean to assoc. dean, 1974-89, dean, 1989—2004. Commr. ex officio Utah State Bar, Salt Lake City, 1989-2004; commr. Nat. Conf. Commrs. on Uniform State Laws, 1988-95. Co-author: Idaho Probate System, 1977, Utah Probate System, 2nd edit., 2005, Cases and Text on Laws of Trusts, 7th edit., 2001; editor: Manual for Justices of Peace--Utah, 1978; contbr. articles to profl. jours. Mem. Lds Ch. Office: Brigham Young U 536 JRCB Provo UT 84602-1029 Home Phone: 801-375-1795; Office Phone: 801-422-3616.

HANSEN, JAMES LEE, sculptor; b. Tacoma, June 13, 1925; s. Hildreth Justine and Mary Elizabeth Hansen; m. Annabelle Hair, Aug. 31, 1946 (dec. Sept. 1993); children: Valinda Jean, Yauna Marie; m. Jane Lucas, May 13, 1994. Grad., Portland Art Mus. Sch. Faculty Oreg. State U., Corvallis, 1957-58, U. Calif., Berkeley, 1958, Portland (Oreg) State U., 1964-90. One-man shows include Fountain Gallery, Portland, 1966, 69, 77-81, U. Oreg. Art Mus., Eugene, 1970, Seligman (Seders Gallery), Seattle, 1970, Portland Art Mus., 1971, Cheney Cowles Meml. Mus., Spokane, Wash., 1972, Polly Freidlander Gallery, Seattle, 1973, 75-76, Smithsonian Instn., Washington, 1974, Hodges/Banks Gallery (now Linda Hodges Gallery), Seattle, 1983, Abanté Gallery, Portland, 1986, 88, 92, Maryhill Mus. of Art, Goldendale, Wash., 1997-98, Bryan Ohno Gallery, Seattle, 1997, 99, 2002, 04, Mus. Northwest Art, La Conner, Wash., 1999; exhibited in group shows at N.W. Ann. Painters and Sculptors, Seattle, 1952-73, Oreg. Ann. Painters and Sculptors, Portland Art Mus., 1952-75, Whitney Mus. Am. Art, NYC, 1953, Santa Barbara (Calif.) Mus. Art, 1959-60, Denver Art Mus., 1960, San Francisco Art Mus., 1960, Smithsonian Instn., Washington, 1974, Wash. State U., Pullman, 1975, Benton County Hist. Mus., 1998; represented in permanent collections Graphic Arts Ctr., State Capitol, Olympia, Wash., U. Oreg., Eugene, Salem (Oreg.) Civic Ctr., Clark Coll., Vancouver, Wash., Portland Art Mus., Transit Mall, Portland, Seattle Art Mus., Gresham Town Fair (Oreg.), Oreg. Health Scis. U., Portland, Vancouver Sculpture Park, others; represented by Hansen Studio, Battle Ground, Wash., Peter Bartlow Gallery, Chgo. Address: 28219 NE 63rd Ave Battle Ground WA 98604-7107 Office Phone: 360-687-4627. Business E-Mail: info@jamesleehansen.com.

HANSEN, JAMES VEAR, former congressman; b. Salt Lake City, Aug. 14, 1932; s. J. Vear and Sena H.; m. Ann Burgoyne, 1958; children: Susan, Joseph James, David Burgoyne, Paul William, Jennifer. BS, U. Utah, 1960. With Framington City Coun., 1960-72, Utah State Legis., 1972-80; mem. Utah Ho. of Reps., 1973-80; spkr. of the house U.S. Ho. of Reps., 1979-80; mem. U.S. Congress from 1st Utah dist., Washington, 1981—2002; mem. nat. security com., resource com. Pres. James V. Hansen Ins. Agy., Woodland Springs Devel. Co. Republican. Office: Ho of Reps 242 Cannon Ho Office Bldg Washington DC 20515-0001

HANSEN, JENNIE CHIN, association executive; Grad., Boston Coll., 1970; MSN, U. Calif.; Doctorate (hon.), Boston Coll., 2008. RN. Exec. dir. On Lok, Inc., 1980—2005; sr. fellow U. Calif. San Francisco Ctr. for the Health Professions; prof. nursing San Francisco State U. Commr. Medicare Payment Adv. Commn.; bd. dirs. Nat. Acad. Social Insurance, Robert Wood Johnson Exec. Nurse Fellows Prog., Lumetra, Calif. Regional Health Info. Orgn. Recipient Maxwell Pollack award for Productive Living, Gerontological Soc. America, 2002, Adminstr.'s Achievement award, Ctr. Medicare and Medicaid Services, 2005; named Woman of the Yr., Women's Healthcare Exec., 2000. Fellow: Am. Acad. Nursing; mem.: Am. Soc. on Aging (past pres.), AARP (pres. 2008—10). Office: AARP 601 E St NW Washington DC 20049*

HANSEN, LIBBY, broadcast executive; b. Dec. 9, 1971; m. Brett Hansen. Comml. real estate broker; with Brillstein-Grey; dir. devel. Burrow Owl Prodns. Touchstone TV; mgr. alternative series & spls. ABC, 2000—02, dir., 2002—03, exec. dir. alternative series & spls., 2003—04; v.p. alternative series & spls. NBC Universal's USA Network, 2004—06, NBC & USA Network, 2006—08; sr. v.p. alternative series & spls. NBC, 2008—. Achievements include working on reality shows such as The Bachelor, The Bachelorette, Extreme Makeover, Extreme Makeover: Home Edition, Wife Swap, Nashville Star and Made in the USA. Avocation: cooking. Office: NBC 3000 W Alameda Ave Burbank CA 91523

HANSEN, MARKA, retail executive; BA in Liberal Studies, Loyola Marymount U., LA. With Robinson's Dept. Stores, Calif.; mdse. mgr. Banana Republic women's divsn. Gap, Inc., San Francisco, 1987, v.p. men's merchandising Banana Republic, v.p. merchandising Internat. divsn., 1993—95, sr. v.p., 1995—2000, head human resources orgn., 2000—02, exec. v.p. Gap adult merchandising, 2002—03, pres. Banana Republic, 2003—07, pres. Gap No. Am., 2007—. Bd. mem. Gap Found. Office: Gap Inc 2 Folsom St San Francisco CA 94105 Office Phone: 650-952-4400.

HANSEN, MATILDA, former state legislator; b. Paullina, Iowa, Sept. 4, 1929; d. Arthur J. and Sada G. (Thompson) Henderson; m. Robert B. Michener, 1950 (div. 1963); children: Eric J., Douglas E.; m. Hugh G. Hansen (dec.). BA, U. Colo., 1963; MA, U. Wyo., 1970. Tchr. history Englewood (Colo.) Sr. H.S., 1963-65; dir. Albany County Adult Learning Ctr., Laramie, Wyo., 1966-78, Laramie Plains Civic Ctr., 1979-83; treas. Wyo. Territorial Prison Corp., Laramie, 1988-93, also bd. dirs. Bd. dirs. Wyo. Territorial Pk. Author: (textbooks) To Help Adults Learn, 1975, Let's Play Together, 1978, Clear Use of Power, A Slice of Wyoming Political History, 2002. Legislator Wyo. Ho. of Reps., Cheyenne, 1975-95, minority whip, 1987-88, asst. minority leader, 1991-92, 93-94; mem. mgmt. coun. Wyo. State Legislature, Cheyenne, 1983-84; chair Com. for Dem. Legislature, Cheyenne, 1990-94, Wyo. State Dems., 1995-99; clk. Wyo. Soc. of Friends meeting, 2003-. GE fellow in econs. for high sch. tchrs., 1963; named Pub. Citizen of Yr., Wyo. Assn. Social Workers, 1980-81. Mem. LWV Wyo. (v.p. 1966-68), LWV Laramie (bd. dirs. 1966-72, Nat. Conf. State Legislators (vice chair human resources 1983, nat. exec. com. 1990-94), Laramie Area C. of C., Laramie Women's Club, Faculty Women's Club. Democrat. Avocations: gardening, mountain climbing, quilting. Home and Office: 1306 E Kearney St Laramie WY 82070-4142

HANSEN, ROBERT CLINTON, electrical engineer, consultant; b. St. Louis, 1926; married, 1952; 2 children. BS, U. Mo., 1949, DEng (hon.), 1975; MS, U. Ill., 1950, PhD, 1955. Rsch. assoc. antenna lab. U. Ill., 1950-55; sr. staff engr. microwave lab. Hughes Aircraft Co., 1955-59; sr. staff engr. telecomm. lab. Space Technol. Labs., 1959-60; dir. test mission analysis office Aerospace Corp., Calif., 1960-67; head electronics divsn. KMS Technol. Ctr., 1967-71; pres., cons. R.C. Hansen, Inc., Tarzana, Calif., 1971—. Mem. commn. B Internat. Sci. Radio Union. Editor: Microwave Scanning Antennas, 1964—65, Significant Phased Array Papers, 1973, Geometric Theory of Diffraction, 1981, Moment Methods in Antennas and Scattering, 1990; author: Phased Array Antennas, 1998, Electrically Small, Superdirective and Superconducting Antennas, 2006. Recipient Disting. Alumnus award, U. Ill. Elec. Engring. Dept., 1981, Disting. Alumnus Svc. medal, 1986. Fellow: IEEE (pres. antennas and propagation soc. 1964, 1980), Inst. Elec. Engrs. (London), Aerospace & Electronic Sys. Soc. (Barry Carlton award 1991, AP Disting. Achievement award 1994, Electromagnetics award 2002); mem.: NAE, Am. Phys. Soc. Office: RC Hansen Inc PO Box 570215 Tarzana CA 91357

HANSEN, THOMAS CARTER, college athletics conference commissioner; b. Seattle, Nov. 30, 1937; s. Herbert and Marjorie Jean (Jordan) H.; m. Melva Marie Fuhr, Oct. 11, 1962; children: Sarah Marie Hansen Reeves, Bryan Thomas. BA, U. Wash., 1959. Reporter The Columbian, Vancouver, Wash., 1959-60; dir. pub. rels. Pacific-10 Conf., San Francisco, 1960-67, NCAA, Kansas City, Mo., 1967-71, asst. exec. dir., 1971-83; commr. Pacific-10 Conf., Walnut Creek, Calif., 1983—. Author: (chpt.) Administration for Athletic Programs, 1987. Mem. Kiwanis Club, Vancouver, 1959-60, San Francisco, 1960-67, Kansas City, 1967-83. Mem. Nat. Assn. Collegiate Dirs. of Athletics (exec. com. 1988-92, Adminstrv. Excellence award 1994), Collegiate Commrs. Assn. (pres. 1992, 93), Football Found. Hall of Fame (honors ct. 1994-01, Contbns. to Football award 2001). Republican. Lutheran. Avocations: golf, reading, music. Office: Pacific 10 Conf 1350 Treat Blvd Ste 500 Walnut Creek CA 94597-8853

HANSEN, THOMAS NANASTAD, hospital administrator, pediatrician; b. Neenah, Wis., Oct. 11, 1947; m. Cheryl Bailey, June 9, 1979; children: Elaine Christ, William Thomas. BS in Physics summa cum laude, Tex. Christian U., 1970; MD, Baylor Coll. Medicine, 1973. Diplomate Am. Bd. Pediatrics. Intern in pediatrics Baylor Coll. Medicine, Houston, 1973-74, resident in pediatrics, 1974-76, postdoctoral fellow in neonatal perinatal medicine, 1976-78; postdoctoral fellow in pediatric pulmonary disease U. Calif., San Francisco, 1978-81; asst. prof. pediatrics Baylor Coll. Medicine, 1978-84, assoc. prof. pediatrics, 1984-89; prof. pediatrics and cell biology Tex. Children's Hosp. Found., Houston, 1989-95; head sect. on neonatology Baylor Coll. of Medicine, 1987-95, vice-chmn. rsch. dept. pediatrics, 1994-95, dir. child health rsch. ctr., 1994-95, co-dir. ctr. for tng. in molecular medicine, 1994-95; chmn. pediat., CEO Children's Hosp., Columbus, Ohio, 1995—2005; pres., CEO Children's Hosp. and Regional Med. Ctr., Seattle, 2005—. Mem. exam com. Am. Bd. Pediatrics, 1982—, sub-bd. neonatal-perinatal medicine, 1992—, chmn. credentials com., 1993—, chmn.-elect sub-bd. neonaatal perinatal medicine, 1994. Contbr. numerous articles to profl. jours. Trustee Tex. Women's Hosp., 1988-91. Mem. Western Soc. for Pediatric Rsch., So. Soc. for Pediaatric Rsch., Soc. for Pediatric Rsch. (sec.-treas. 1986-91, chmn. student rsch. com. 1990—, trustee internat. chpt. 1992—), Am. Physiol. Soc., Am. Pediatric Soc., Am. Fedn. for Clin. Rsch., Am. Thoracic Soc., Am. Acad. of Pediatrics, N.Y. Acad. of Scis., Am. Soc. for Cell Biology, Assn. of Med. Sch. Pediatric Dept. Chmn., Sigma Xi. Office: Children's Hosp and Regional Med Ctr PO Box 5371 Seattle WA 98105-0371

HANSEN, WALTER EUGENE, insurance executive; b. Woodland, Wash., May 15, 1929; s. August Hans and Esther Johanna (Johnson) H.; m. Barbara Inez Cowart, Oct. 12, 1950; m. Donna Carol Phillips, Aug. 1, 1953; children: Larry, Lindsey, Monty, Gena, Martin, Lori, Bradley, Walter Eugene Jr. Grad. high sch. Farmer, logger, 1943-51; svc. mgr. Sears Roebuck & Co., L.A. and Portland, Oreg., 1951-57; agt. various ins. cos., 1957-63; dist. mgr. Bankers Life & Casualty Co., 1960-61; state mgr. Protective Security Life Ins. Co., 1963-65; regional mgr. Amn. Pacific Life Ins. Co., 1963-72; owner Pacific N.W. Ins. Svc., Portland, 1963—, Am. Pacific Svcs., Portland, 1970—, N. Fork Motors, Woodland, Wash., 1987—. Owner Nat. Rsch. Assocs., Seattle, 1968—, N. Fork Ranch, 1962—. Mem. editl.bd. Longview Daily News, 1999-00. Past Boy Scouts Am.; chmn. Community USA Bicentennial Commn., 1976; mem. Wash. State Centennial Com., 1989; commr. Woodland Recreation Dist., 2000-2002; mem. Woodland Urban Growth Com., 1999-2002; historian City Woodland Centennial, Wash., 2006. Mem. Internat. Platform Assn., Nat. Assn. Life Underwriters, Nat. Trust Hitoric Preservation, Libr. Congress, Wa. Trust Hist. Preservation, Accident and Health Underwriters Assn., Smithsonian Assocs., Navy League of U.S, Woodland Downtown Revitalazation, Inc. (historian, v.p., dir.), Woodland Planter Days, Inc. (treas.). Home: PO Box 2000 Woodland WA 98674-1900 Office Phone: 503-236-5236. Personal E-mail: weh.1@netzero.com.

HANSEN, WAYNE W., lawyer; b. Clintonville, Wis., June 7, 1942; s. William W. and Berniece M. (Kuehn) H.; m. Carolyn M. Lemke, Dec. 21, 1969; children: Drew D., Janna J. BBA, U. Wis., 1965, JD, 1967. Bar: Wis. 1967, U.S. Dist. Ct. (we. dist.) Wis. 1971, U.S. Ct. Appeals (7th cir.) 1972, U.S. Dist. Ct. (ea. dist.) Wis. 1975, Wash. 1979, U.S. Dist. Ct. (we. dist.) Wash. 1979, U.S. Ct. Appeals (9th cir.) 1982, U.S. Dist. Ct. (ea. dist.) Wash. 1986. Atty. NLRB, Mpls., 1967-70, Schmitt Nolan Hansen & Hartley, Merrill, Wis., 1970-79; ptnr. Lane Powell Spears Lubersky, Seattle, 1979-98; mng. ptnr. Seattle office Jackson Lewis LLP, 1998—. Contbg. author: Developing Labor Law, 1971, Doing Business in Washington State*Guide for Foreign Business, 1989. Office: Jackson Lewis LLP 600 University St Ste 2900 Seattle WA 98101-4174 Office Phone: 206-626-6400. Business E-Mail: hansenw@jackson.law.com.

HANSON, CURTIS, film director, scriptwriter; b. Reno, Mar. 24, 1945; Dir., screenwriter (film) Sweet Kill, 1972, The Bedroom Window, 1988; dir., co-producer (film) The Little Dragons, 1977; dir. (films) The Arousers, 1970, Losin' It, 1983, Bad Influence, 1990, The Hand That Rocks the Cradle, 1992, The River Wild, 1994; dir., prodr., screenwriter (films) L.A. Confidential, 1997; dir., prodr. (film) Wonder Boys, 1999, 8 mile, 2002, In Her Shoes, 2005, Lucky You, 2007; screenwriter: The Dunwich Horror, 1970, The Silent Partner, 1978, White Dog, 1982, Never Cry Wolf, 1983; actor (TV) Hitchcock: Shadow of a Genius, 1999; (film) Adaptation, 2002. Office: United Talent Agy 9560 Wilshire Blvd Fl 5 Beverly Hills CA 90212-2400

HANSON, GERALD WARNER, retired county official; b. Alexandria, Minn., Dec. 25, 1938; s. Lewis Lincoln and Dorothy Hazel (Warner) H.; m. Sandra June Wheeler, July 9, 1960; 1 child, Cynthia R. AA, San Bernardino Valley Coll., Calif., 1959; BA, Redlands U., Calif., 1979; MA, U. Redlands, 1981; EdD, Pepperdine U., 1995. Cert. advanced metrication specialist. Dep. sealer San Bernardino (Calif.) County, 1964-80, div. chief, 1980-85, dir. weights and measures, 1985-94; CATV cons. City of Redlands, 1996—2004, City of Yucaipa, 1998-99, ret., 1994. Substitute tchr. Redlands Unified Sch. Dist., 2003-04. Chmn. Redlands Rent Rev. Bd., 1985-99; bd. dirs. House Neighborly Svc., Redlands, 1972-73, Boys Club, Redlands, 1985-86; mem. Redlands Planning commn., 1990-98. With USN. Fellow U.S. Metric Assn. (treas. 1986-88, 92—); mem. NRA (benefactor, life), Nat. Conf. on Weights and Measures (life, asst. treas. 1986-94), Western Weights and Measures Assn. (life, pres. 1987-88), Calif. Assn. Weights and Measures Ofcls. (life, 1st v.p. 1987), Calif. Rifle and Pistol Assn. (life), Masons, Shriners, Kiwanis (treas. Redlands club 1983-95), Over the Hill Gang (San Bernardino, newsletter editor 1998-2000). Avocations: golf, digital photography, mechanics, microcomputers. Home: 225 E Palm Ave Redlands CA 92373-6131 Personal E-mail: doctorjer@hotmail.com.

HANSON, JANICE CRAWFORD, artist, financial analyst; b. Norwalk, Conn., Oct. 8, 1952; d. Arthur James and Jean Alice (MacKinnon) Crawford; m. Jeffrey Becker Hanson, May 29, 1976; children: Forrest James, Shane Crawford. BA, Wellesley Coll., 1974; MBA, U. Denver, 1979. CFA. Sec. to assoc. dean Yale Sch. of Music, New Haven, Conn., 1975-76; adminstrv. asst. to dir. of internships Inst. Policy Scis. Duke U., Durham, N.C., 1976-78; fiscal analyst Denver Water Bd., 1979-84; fin. analyst Englewood, Colo., 1984; part-time fin. analyst Jeffrey B. Hanson M.D., P.C., Granger, Ind., 1989-92; part-time watercolorist Englewood, Colo., 1989—. Exhibited in group shows at Watercolor West Exhbn., Riverside, Calif., 1995, 1999, Western Colo. Watercolor Soc., Grand Junction, Colo., 1994—96, 2000, 2004—09, Rocky Mountain Nat. Watermedia, Golden, Colo., 1996, 1998, 2002 (Betty Simpson award, 2002), 2006, Pikes Peak Watercolor Soc., Colorado Springs, Colo., 1997—2000, 2003 (Daler-Rowney award, 2000), Colorado Springs, 2003, Colo. Watercolor Soc., 1993—94, 1996—97, 2000, 2002, 2004—06, 2008—09, Am. Women Artists, Taos, N.Mex., 1999, Nat. Watercolor Soc., Brea, Calif., 2001, 2006, Nat. Watercolor Soc. Mems. Show, Sherman Oaks, Calif., 2000, 2008, Western Fedn. Watercolor Soc., 2002—03, 2005—06. Vol. Denver Dumb Friends League, 1986-88, Cherry Creek Schs., Englewood, Colo., 1992-2006. Recipient Best of Show awards Nat. Greeley Art Mart, 1994, Steamboat Springs Art Coun. Summer Art, 2003, others; Platinum award, Nat. Greeley Art Mart, 1995, Dean Witter award for originality Colo. Watercolor Soc. State Juried Exhbn., 1996, Exec. award, 2004; WinsorNewton Merchandise award Am. Women Artists, 1999; Am. Women Artists scholar, 1999. Mem.: Rocky Mountain Nat. Watermedia Soc. (signature mem.), Western Fedn. Watercolor Socs. (signature), Denver Soc. Security Analysts, Western Colo. Watercolor Soc. (signature), Colo. Watercolor Soc. (bd. mem. 2005, signature, treas. 2006—, Exec. award 2004), Watercolor West (juried assoc.), Assn. for Investment Mgmt. and Rsch., Nat. Watercolor Soc. (signature). Avocations: running, fiber arts, needlecrafts, photography.

HANSON, JOHN J., retired lawyer; b. Aurora, Nebr., Oct. 22, 1922; s. Peter E. and Hazel Marion (Lounsbury) H.; m. Elizabeth Anne Moss, July 1, 1973; children from their previous marriages— Mark, Eric, Gregory. AB, U. Denver, 1948; LL.B. cum laude, Harvard U., 1951. Bar: N.Y. bar 1952, Calif. bar 1955. Asso. firm Dewey, Ballantine, Bushby, Palmer & Wood, NYC, 1951-54; ptnr. firm Gibson, Dunn & Crutcher, LA, 1954—, mem. exec. com., 1978-87, adv. ptnr., 1991—2004, ret., 2004. Contbr. articles to profl. jours. Trustee Palos Verdes (Calif.) Sch. Dist., 1969-73. Served with U.S. Navy, 1942-45. Fellow Am. Coll. Trial Lawyers; mem. Am. Bar Assn., Los Angeles County Bar Assn. (chmn. antitrust sect. 1979-80), Bel Air Country Club. Home: 953 Linda Flora Dr Los Angeles CA 90049-1630 Office: Gibson Dunn & Crutcher 333 S Grand Ave Ste 4400 Los Angeles CA 90071-3197 Personal E-mail: jjhgolfer@gmail.com.

HANSON, JOHN NILS, industrial high technology manufacturing company executive; b. Berwyn, Ill., Jan. 22, 1942; s. Robert and Stephanie Ann (Kazluskas) H.; m. Stephanie Morgan, June 5, 1965; children: Laurel, Mark Nils. BS in Chem. Engring., MIT, 1964, MS in Nuclear Engring., 1965; PhD in Nuclear Sci. and Engring., Carnegie-Mellon U., 1969. Sr. scientist Bettis Atomic Power Labs., Westinghouse Electric Corp., West Mifflin, Pa., 1965-70; fellow White House, Washington, 1970-71; exec. asst. to U.S. Sec. Labor, Washington,

1971; asst. to gen. mgr. advanced test core Bettis Atomic Power Labs., Westinghouse Electric Corp., West Mifflin, Pa., 1971-73; asst. to pres. Gould Inc., Rolling Meadows, Ill., 1973-74, pres., gen. mgr. electric motor div. St. Louis, 1974-78, group v.p. elec. products Rolling Meadows, 1978-80; pres. Solar Turbines Internat., San Diego, 1980; v.p. Internat. Harvester, 1980-81, Caterpillar Tractor Co., Peoria, Ill., 1981—90; pres., COO Joy Technologies, 1990—94; pres. Joy Mining Machinery unit Harnischfeger Industries (renamed Joy Global Inc.), 1994—95; exec. v.p., COO Joy Global Inc., Milw., 1995—96, pres., COO, 1996—98, pres., CEO, 1998—2006, chmn., 2000—. Contbr. articles on indsl. tech. to profl. jours. Vice chmn. Friends of Scouting Fundraising-Boy Scouts Am., San Diego council, 1983—; mem. Judge Wallace Longrange planning com., 1983—, vice chmn. fin. adv. com., 1983—; mem. cabinet fund drive United Way, San Diego County Chpt., 1982—; mem. exec. fin. com. Pete Wilson for Senate campaign, San Diego, 1982; vice chmn. Children's Hosp. Research Ctr., 1983—; mem. vis. com. sponsored research MIT, Cambridge, 1978—; mem. Pvt. Industry Council, 1983. Mem. White House Fellows Assn., Greater San Diego C. of C. (bd. dirs.) Office: Joy Global PO Box 554 Milwaukee WI 53201

HANSON, LARRY KEITH, plastics company executive; b. Hawkins, Wis., Aug. 14, 1932; s. Harold and Clara Pauline (Lund) H.; m. Patricia Rosalie Sammarco, Aug. 6, 1955; children: Lawrence Keith, John Steven, James Paul. BS, U.S. Mcht. Marine Acad., 1955. Engr. Curtis-Wright Corp., Woodridge, N.J., 1955-58; sales engr. Gits Bros. Mfg. Co., Chgo., 1958-66, Aeroquip Corp., Burbank, Calif., 1966-70; exec. v.p. Furon Co., Laguna Niguel, Calif., 1970-97; mng. dir. Furon SA/NV subs. Furon Co., Kontich, Belgium, 1983-90; exec. v.p. Furon Co., Laguna Niguel, Calif., 1990-97; retired, 1997; cons. (part-time) Furon Co., Laguna Niguel, 1997—. Patentee in field. Mem. ASME, Soc. Automotive Engrs. Avocations: fly fishing, drawing, inventions.

HANSON, MARIAN W., state legislator; b. Santa Maria, Calif., Jan. 17, 1933; m. Darrel Hanson; 4 children. Rancher, Ashland, Mont.; mem. Mont. Ho. of Reps., Helena, 1983-2000, spkr. of ho. pro tem, 1993-97. County mem. Local Govt. Study Commn. Republican. Office: Mont Ho of Reps State Capitol Helena MT 59620 Home: PO Box 575 Ashland MT 59003-0575

HANSON, RICHARD E., retired paper company executive; BS in Indsl. Mgmt., U. Oreg., 1965. Joined Weyerhaeuser Co., Tacoma, 1969—, v.p., western timberlands, 1996—98, sr. v.p., timberlands, 1998—2002, exec. v.p., timberlands and international, 2002—03, exec. v.p., COO, 2003—08. Bd. dirs. Oreg. Forest Industries Coun., mem. operating com.; adv. com. Oreg. State U. Forest Rsch. Lab.; mem. exec. bd. World Forestry Ctr. Bd. trustees Oreg. Zoo, Pacific U.; mem. founder's cir. Stop Oreg. Litter & Vandalism.

HANSON, ROBERT DUANE, engineering educator; b. Albert Lea, Minn., July 27, 1935; s. James Edwin and Gertie Hanson; m. Kaye Lynn Nielsen, June 7, 1959; children: Craig Robert, Eric Neil. Student, St. Olaf Coll., Northfield, Minn., 1953-54; BSE, U. Minn., 1957, MS in Civil Engring., 1958; PhD, Calif. Inst. Tech., Pasadena, 1965. Registered profl. engr., Mich., N.D. Design engr. Pitts.-Des Moines Stel, Des Moines, 1958-59; asst. prof. U. N.D., Grand Forks, 1959-61; rsch. engr. Calif. Inst. Tech., 1965; asst. prof. U. Calif.-Davis, 1965-66; from asst. prof. to prof. civil engring. U. Mich., Ann Arbor, 1966—2001, prof. emeritus, 2001—, chmn. dept. civil engring., 1976-84; sr. earthquake engr. Fed. Emergency Mgmt. Agy., 1994-2000. Vis. prof., dir. Earthquake Engring. Rsch. Ctr., U. Calif., Berkeley, 1991; dir. BCS divsn. NSF, Washington, 1989-90; cons. NSF, 1979-88, 92-94; cons. Bechtel Corp., Ann Arbor, 1976-87, Sensei Engrs., Ann Arbor, 1977-90, Bldg. Seismic Safety Coun., 1988-94, Fed. Emergency Mgmt. Agy., 1992-94, 2000-05, applied tech. coun., 2005—. Contbr. articles to profl. jours. Recipient Reese Rsch. award ASCE, 1980; recipient Disting. Svc. award U. Mich., 1969; tchg. award Chi Epsilon, 1985, Attwood Engr. Excellence award, 1986. Fellow ASCE (life; com. chmn. 1975-94); mem. NAE, Earthquake Engring. Rsch. Inst. (hon., v.p. 1977-79, bd. dirs. 1976-79, 88-92, pres.-elect 1988, pres. 1989-91, past pres. 1991-92). Lutheran. Home: 2926 Saklan Indian Dr Walnut Creek CA 94595-3911 Home Phone: 925-946-9463. Personal E-mail: rdhanson2@aol.com.

HANSTEN, PHILIP DOUGLAS, pharmacist, educator; b. Chgo., Aug. 21, 1943; s. Herman Walter Hanstein and Alberta Cecile Hansten; m. Ruth Irene Bernhoft, June 28, 1986; children: Michelle Lynne Ingalsbe, Christopher Aaron, Martin Aaron, Matthew Scott Shirley, Kirk Lawrence Shirley. PharmD, U. Calif., San Francisco, 1968. Cert. in hospital pharmacy U. Calif., 1968. Rsch. assoc. Stanford U. Sch. Medicine, Palo Alto, Calif., 1972—74; prof. pharmacy Wash. State U., Pullman, 1974—86, U. Wash., Seattle, 1988—2003. Author: (book) Drug Interactions Analysis and Management, The Top 100 Drug Interactions. A Guide to Patient Management. Recipient Disting. Alumnus award, U. Calif., 1989, Gibaldi Excellence in Tchg. award, U. Wash., 1997. Liberal. Lutheran. Avocations: philosophy, photography, kayaking, accordion. Office: Univ Wash 1959 NE Pacific St Seattle WA 98195-7630 Business E-Mail: hansten@u.washington.edu.

HANUSHEK, ERIC ALAN, economics professor; b. Lakewood, Ohio, May 22, 1943; s. Vernon F. and Ruth (Hostetler) H.; m. Nancy L. Keleher, June 11, 1965 (div.); children: Eric Alan, Megan E.; m. Margaret E. Raymond, Oct. 10, 2003. BS, U.S. Air Force Acad., 1965; PhD in Econs., MIT, 1968. Sr. staff economist Coun. Econ. Advisers, Washington, 1971-72; assoc. prof. USAF Acad., Colo., 1972-73; sr. economist Cost of Living Coun., Washington, 1973-74; assoc. prof. econs. Yale U., New Haven, 1975-78; dir. pub. policy analysis U. Rochester, N.Y., 1978-83, prof. econs. and polit. sci. NY, 1978-2000, chmn. dept. econs. NY, 1982-87, 88-90, dir. W. Allen Wallis Inst. Polit. Economy NY, 1992-99; rsch. assoc. Nat. Bur. Econ. Rsch., 1996—; Hanna sr. fellow Hoover Instn. Stanford (Calif.) U., 2000—; sr. rsch. fellow Green Ctr. U. Tex., Dallas, 2000—; sr. fellow Stanford Inst. for Econ. Policy Rsch., 2003—. Dep. dir. Congl. Budget Office, Washington, 1984-85; mem. com. nat. stats. Nat. Rsch. Coun., 1992-98, adv. coun. on Edn. Statistics, 2002; cons. World Bank 1984-95, U.S. Com. on Civil Rights, 1986-89; chair exec. bd. Tex. Schs. Project, U. Tex., Dallas, 2003—; mem nat. bd. for edn. scis. U.S. Dept. Edn., 2005—; rsch. prof. IFO Inst. Econ. Rsch., U. Munich. Author: Education and Race, 1972, (with J. Jackson) Statistical Methods for Social Scientists 1977, (with C. Citro) Improving Information for Social Policy Decisions, 1991, (with R. Harbison) Education Performance of the Poor, 1992, Making Schools Work, 1994, (with J. Banks) Modern Political Economy, 1995, (with N. Maritato) Assessing Knowledge of Retirement Behavior, 1996, (with Dale W. Jorgenson) Improving America's Schools, 1996, (with Constance F. Citro) Assessing Policies for Retirement Income, 1997, The Economics of Schooling and School Quality, 2003, Courting Failure, 2006, (with Finis Welch) Handbook of Economics of Education, 2006. Served to capt. USAF, 1965-74. Disting. vis. fellow Hoover Instn., Stanford U., 1999-2000. Fellow Internat. Acad. Edn. (bd. dirs. 2002—), Nat. Acad. Edn., Soc. Labor Econs., Assn. Pub. Policy Analysis and Mgmt. (v.p. 1986-87, pres. 1988-89), Am. Econ. Assn., Econometric Soc., Soc. Labor Economists, Am. Edn. Fin. Assn. (bd. dirs. 2006—). Office Phone: 650-736-0942. Business E-Mail: hanushek@stanford.edu.

HAPKA, CATHERINE M., Internet company executive; BS, U. Minn.; MBA, U. Chgo. Gen. mgr. Gen. Electric, 1984-87, McKinsey and Co., Inc.; pres. Data Svcs., 1989-91; pres., COO Interprise, U.S. West Comms., 1991-94, exec. v.p., 1994-96; pres., CEO, chmn. and founder Rhythms NetConnections, Englewood, Colo., 1997—2001.

HARAD, GEORGE JAY, retired manufacturing executive; b. Newark, Apr. 24, 1944; m. Beverly Marcia Harad, June 12, 1966; children: Alyssa Dawn, Matthew Corde. BA, Franklin and Marshall Coll., 1965; MBA with high distinction, Harvard Bus. Sch., 1971. Staff cons. Boston Cons. Group, 1970-71; asst. to sr. v.p. housing Boise Cascade Corp., 1971, asst. to v.p. Palo Alto, Calif., 1971; fin. mgr. Boise Cascade Realty Group, Palo Alto, Calif., 1972-76; mgr. corp. devel. Boise Cascade Corp., Boise, Idaho, 1976—80, dir. retirement funds, risk mgmt., 1980—82, v.p., contr., 1982—84, sr. v.p., CFO, 1984—89, exec. v.p., CFO, 1989—90, exec. v.p. paper, 1990—91, pres., COO, 1991—94, pres., CEO, 1994—95, chmn., bd. dirs., 1995, CEO, chmn., 1995—2004; exec. chmn. OfficeMax Inc., Itasca, Ill., 2004—05, interim pres., CEO, 2005. Bd. govs. Nat. Coun. for Air and Stream Improvement Inc., 1994—2004; bd. dirs. US West, 1997—2000, Dial Corp., 2003—04, The Clorox Co., 2006—. Founder, pres. Boise Coun. for Gifted and Talented Students, 1977—79; bd. dirs. Boise Philharm. Assn., 1983—84; dir. bd. trustees Coll. Idaho, 1986—91. Recipient George F. Baker scholar, 1970—71; Grad. Prize fellow, Harvard Grad. Sch. Arts and Scis., 1965—69, Frederick Roe fellow, Harvard U. Sch. Bus., 1971. Mem.: NAM (bd. dirs), Am. Forest and Paper Assn. (bd. dirs., mem. exec. com. 1994—2004, chmn. 2004—05), Century Club (Boston), Arid Club, Crane Creek Country Club. Office: Harad Capital Mgmt 877 W Main St Ste 606 Boise ID 83702 Office Phone: 208-429-0606.

HARARI, ELI, computer company executive; BS in Physics with honors, Manchester Univ.; MA, Princeton Univ., PhD in Solid State Scis. Technical mgmt. positions Hughes Aircraft, Honeywell; co-founder, pres., CEO Wafer Scale Integration; founder, pres., CEO SanDisk Corp., Sunnyvale, Calif., 1988—2006, chmn., CEO, 2006—. Patentee in field. Office: SanDisk Corp 601 McCarthy Blvd Milpitas CA 95035

HARBAUGH, JIM (JAMES JOSEPH HARBAUGH), college football coach, retired professional football player; b. Toledo, Dec. 23, 1963; m. Miah Harbaugh (div.); children: Jay, James Jr., Grace; m. Sarah Feuerborn. BA in Comm., U. Mich., 1987. Quarterback Chgo. Bears, 1987-93, Indpls. Colts, 1994-98, Balt. Ravens, 1998-99, San Diego Chargers, 1999—2000, Carolina Panthers, 2001; offensive asst. Oakland Raiders, 2002—03; head football coach U. San Diego, 2004—06, Stanford U., 2006—. Named to Am. Football Conf. Pro Bowl Team, 1995; named NFL Comeback Player of Yr., 1995 Achievements include inducted into the Indpls. Colts Ring of Honor, 2005. Office: Stanford U Athletics Stanford CA 94305 E-mail: jharbaugh@stanford.edu.

HARBAUGH, JOHN WARVELLE, geologist, educator; b. Madison, Wis., Aug. 6, 1926; s. Marion Dwight and Marjorie (Warvelle) H.; m. Josephine Taylor, Nov. 24, 1951 (dec. Dec. 25, 1985); children: Robert, Dwight, Richard; m. Audrey Wegst, Oct. 21, 2000. BS, U. Kans., 1948, MS, 1950; PhD, U. Wis., 1955. Prodn. geologist Carter Oil Co., Tulsa, 1951-53; prof. geol. sci. Stanford U., Calif., 1955—99, prof. emeritus, 1999—. Mgr. Harbaugh Mineral Lands LLC. Author: (with G. Bonham Carter) Computer Simulation in Geology, 1970, (with D.M. Tezlaff) Simulating Clastic Sedimentation, 1989, (with P. Martinez) Simulating Nearshore Environments, 1993, (with R. Slingerland and K. Furlong) Simulating Clastic Sedimentary Basins, 1994, (with J.C. Davis and J. Wendebourg) Computing Risk for Oil Prospects: Principles and Programs, 1995, (with J. Wendebourg) Simulating Oil Entrapment in Clastic Sequences, 1997. Recipient Haworth Disting. Alumni award U. Kans., 1968, Krumbein medal Internat. Assn. Math. Geologists, 1986, U. Wis.-Madison Disting. Alumni award, 2003. Fellow Geol. Soc. Am.; mem. Am. Assn. Petroleum Geologists (Levorsen award 1970, Disting. Svc. award 1987, Disting. Edn. award Pacific sect. 1999, 2001). Independent. Home: 683 Salvatierra St Stanford CA 94305-8539 Office Phone: 650-723-3365. Business E-Mail: john.harbaugh@stanford.edu.

HARBERT, TED (EDWARD W. HARBERT III), broadcast executive; b. 1955; m. Susan Harbert; children: Emily, William. Degree in Comm., Boston U., 1977. Prodr. news dept. WHDH Radio, Boston, 1976—77; feature film coord. ABC Entertainment, 1977—79, feature film and late night programming supr., 1979, asst. to v.p. of program planning and scheduling, 1979—81, dir. program planning and scheduling, 1981—83, v.p. program planning and scheduling, 1983, v.p. of motion pictures, 1986—87, v.p. of motion pictures and scheduling, 1987—88, v.p. prime time, 1988—89, exec. v.p. prime time, 1989—93, pres., 1993—96, chmn., 1996—97; prodr. DreamWorks TV, 1997—99; pres. NBC Studios, 1999—2003; prodr. 20th Century Fox TV, 2003—04; pres., CEO E!Networks, 2004—06, Comcast Entertainment Group, 2006—. Mem. dean's adv. bd. U. So. Calif. Sch. of Theater, Film and TV; mem. TV adv. coun. U. So. Calif. Sch. of Cinema-TV; exec. com. Boston U. Sch. Comm.; bd. govs. UCLA Ctr. for Comm. Policy; bd. dirs. Friends of the LA Free Clinic. Recipient Disting. Alumni Award, Boston U., 1999.

HARDEN, CLINTON DEWEY, JR., state legislator; b. Belen, N.Mex., Apr. 12, 1947; s. Clinton Dewey and Doretha E. (Miller) H.; m. Kathrine H. Harden, Aug. 5, 1968; children: Danielle, Dionne, Dustin. BS in Bus. Mgmt., U. Utah, 1970; MBA, Ea. N.Mex. U., 1994. Bus. adminstr.; owner restaurant Twin Cronnie Enterprises, Clovis, N.Mex., 1978—; cabinet sec. Dept. Labor, Albuquerque, 1995—; account exec. Continental Ins., Salt Lake City, 1970-78; mem. Dist. 7 N.Mex. State Senate, 2003—. Chmn. Cabinet Coun. on State Pers., Santa Fe, 1995—. Mem. Sch.-to-Work Adv. Bd., Santa Fe, 1995—, Pardon and Parole Com., Santa Fe, 1995—, Human Resource Investment Coun., Santa Fe, 1995—, Gov.'s Com. for the Concerns of the Handicapped, 1998; pres. Clovis chpt. Amateur Athletic Union; mem., coach Clovis Girls Athletic Assn.; mem. Mayor's Coun. on Juvenile Crime, Clovis; mem. Children Youth and Families Interagy. Coord. Group, 1995—; bd. dirs. Interstate Conf. of Employment Security Agencies, 1995—; rep. Nat. Gov.'s Assn. Human Resources Coun., 1995—; lead sec. Workforce Devel. Reform, 1996—. Mem. Clovis C. of C. (v.p.). Republican. Methodist. Office: Labor Dept PO Box 1928 Albuquerque NM 87103-1928 also: 1348 CRH Clovis NM 88101 also: NM State Capitol Rm 414B Santa Fe NM 87503 Office Phone: 505-986-4369. E-mail: charden@theosogroup.com.*

HARDER, WENDY WETZEL, communications executive; b. Oceanside, Calif., Feb. 14, 1951; d. Burt Louis and Marjorie Jean (Evans) W.; m. Peter N. Harder, Dec. 1, 1984; 1 child, Jonathan Russell. AA, Palomar Coll., 1971; BA in Comm., U. So. Calif., 1973; MBA, Pepperdine U., 1988. Accredited Pub. Rels. Soc. Am. Pub. rels. dir. Orange County Cmty. Devel. Coun., Santa Ana, Calif., 1975-76; assoc. prodr. Sta. KOCE-TV, Huntington Beach, Calif., 1976-77, reporter, 1977-79, anchor, assoc. prodr., 1979-82; sr. adminstr. comm. Mission Viejo (Calif.) Co., 1983-84, mgr. corp. affairs, 1984-85, dir. corp. affairs, 1985-91, v.p. corp. affairs, 1991-93, v.p. mktg. and corp. comm., 1993-97; dir. cmty. rels. Soka Univ. Am., 1998—. 1st v.p. Aliso Viejo Cmty. Found., Calif., 1988-93, 03-04, pres., 1993-97, Saddleback Coll. Found., Mission Viejo, 1989-94; co-chmn. The Ctr. on Tour-Schs. Com., Orange County, Calif., 1989-92; v.p. Found. for Vocat. Visions, 1996-02, pres., 2000-03; bd. dirs. Dunaj Internat. Dance Ensemble, Orange County, 1985-00, Aliso Viejo C. of C., 2002-05, Mt. of Olives Found., 2003-07., Laguna Niguel C. of C., 2007-; den leader Pack 709 Cub Scouts, 2001-05; mem. troop com. 1602 Boy Scouts Am., 2005—, asst. scout master, 2006-. Recipient Golden Mike award, Radio & TV News Assn., 1981, Best Feature Release award, Orange County Press Club, 1983; co-recipient Golden Mike award, Radio & TV News Assn., 1979; named to, Palomar Coll. Alumni Hall of Fame. South Orange County C. of C., Anaheim/Orange County Conv. & Visitors Bur., Phi Beta Kappa, Phi Kappa Phi, Laguna Niguel C. of C. Republican. Lutheran. Avocations: folk dancing, reading. Office: Soka Univ Am 1 University Dr Aliso Viejo CA 92656 Office Phone: 949-480-4081. Business E-Mail: wwharder@soka.edu.

HARDESTY, JAMES W., state supreme court chief justice; b. Reno, Nov. 28, 1948; m. Sandy Hardesty, 1971; 2 children. BS in Acctg., U. Nevada, Reno, 1970; JD, U. Pacific McGeorge Sch. of Law, 1975. Bar: Nev. 1975, U.S. Dist. Ct. Nev. 1975, U.S. Tax Ct. 1976, U.S. Ct. of Appeals, Ninth Circuit 1980. Atty. priv. practice, 1978—80; prtnr. Breen, Young, Whitehead, Belding & Hardesty, 1980—84, Anderson, Pearl, Hardesty, Lyle and Murphy, 1991—95; judge Nev. Second Jud. Dist. Ct., 1999—2001, chief judge, 2001—04; justice Nev. Supreme Ct., 2005—, chief justice, 2009—. Prof. Nat. Jud. Coll., 2002—; former lecturer media law U. Nev. Donald Reynolds Sch. of Journalism; co-chair Nev. Supreme Ct. Task Force to Create Bus. Ct., 2000; mem. Nev. Supreme Ct. Task Force Multi-Jurisdictional Practice of Law, 2001, Nev. Supreme Ct. Commn. on Jud. Funding, 2003—, Nev. State Bd. of Ed., 1983—84. Mem.: ABA, Am. Inns of Ct., Assn. of Trial Lawyers of Am., Nev. Dist. Judges Assn. (bd. trustees pres. 2000, bd. trustees 2000—04), Washoe County Bar Assn. Office: Nev Supreme Ct 201 S Carson St Carson City NV 89701

HARDESTY, ROBERT ALAN, plastic surgeon; b. St. Helena, Calif., Apr. 24, 1953; m. Marti F. Baum; children: Ashley, Bradford, Chelsea. BA, Loma Linda U., 1974, MD, 1978. Diplomate Am. Bd. Surgery, Am. Bd. Plastic Surgery. Resident in gen. surgery Loma Linda (Calif.) U. Med. Ctr., 1979-83; resident in plastic surgery U. Pitts. Med. Ctr., 1984-86; fellow in craniofacial surgery Children's Hosp., Washington U., St. Louis, 1986-87; instr. dept. surgery, dept. emergency medicine Loma Linda U. Sch. Medicine, 1983-84; instr. in surgery, divsn. plastic and reconstructive surgery Washington U., 1986-87; asst. prof. dept. surgery, divsn. plastic and reconstructive surgery Loma Linda U. Sch. of Medicine, 1987-90; assoc. prof. dept. pediatrics Loma Linda U. Sch. Medicine, 1995—; prof. surgery, chief divsn. plastic/reconstructive surgery Loma Linda U. Sch. of Medicine, 1990—; prof. oral maxillofacial surgery and pediats. Sch. Dentistry Loma Linda U., 1995—, mem. numerous coms., 1987—; divsn. chief plastic & reconstructive surgery Loma Linda Med. Ctr. Apptd. to various hosps. including Loma Linda Community Hosp., 1987—, Jerry L. Pettis VA Med. Ctr., Loma Linda, 1987—, Riverside (Calif.) Gen. Hosp., 1987—, San Bernardino (Calif.) County Med. Ctr., 1990—; chmn. various symposiums; lectr., rschr. in field. Guest editor: Clinics in Plastic Surgery, 1993; mem. internat. editorial adv. bd. Jour. Reconstructive Microsurgery, 1990-91, 91-92, 92-93; contbr. articles to profl. jours., chpts. to books. Recipient Clin. Resident Competition Second Prize award Robert H. Ivy Soc. Plastic and Reconstructive Surgeons, 1986, First prize Ohio Valley Soc. Plastic Surgery, 1986, Second prize Pitts. Acad. Medicine, 1986, Traveling Fellow award Royal Coll. Surgeons, 1991-92; Rsch. grantee Valley Lab, 1988, Plastic Surgery Ednl. Found., Am. Soc. Aesthetic Plastic Surgery, 1988, 93, Maxillofacial Surgeons Found., 1992; grantee Loma Linda U. Med. Ctr., 1989, NIH, 1989-92, Am. Cleft Palate-Craniofacial Assn., 1991, The Aesthetic Soc., 1992, Nat. Inst. Dental Rsch., 1992; Craniofacial Seed grantee Loma Linda U., 1992. Fellow ACS; mem. AMA, AAAS, Am. Acad. Pediatrics (plastic surgery sect.), Am. Assn. Clin. Anatomists, Am. Assn. Pediatric Plastic Surgeons, Am. Burn Assn., Am. Cleft Palate-Craniofacial Assn., Am. Soc. Maxillofacial Surgeons, Am. Soc. Plastic and Reconstructive Surgeons, Internat. Confedn. Plastic, Reconstructive and Aesthetic Surgery, Pan-Pacific Surg. Assn., Tri-County Surg. Soc., Calif. Med. Assn., Calif. Soc. Plastic Surgeons, San Bernardino County Med. Soc., Aesthetic Surgery Edn. and Rsch. Found., Adventist Internat. Med. Soc., Assn. Acad. Chairmen of Plastic Surgery, Lipoplasty Soc. N.Am., Loma Linda Med.- Dental Soc., Walter E. Macpherson Soc., Plastic Surgery Rsch. Coun., Wound Healing Soc., Alpha Omega Alpha. Home: 1515 W Cypress Ave Redlands CA 92373-5614 Office: Loma Linda U Health Care Divsn Plastic Surgery 11370 Anderson St Ste 2100 Loma Linda CA 92354-3450

HARDIE, GEORGE GRAHAM, casino executive; b. Cleve., Aug. 19, 1933; s. William M. and Helen (Graham) H.; children: George Graham Jr., Jennifer. With sales dept. Hardie Bros., Pitts., later various mgmt. positions, operator dist. sales agys.; owner, driver, trainer, racer standardbred horses, 1963—; owner, mgr. Profile, Inc., Las Vegas, 1973—; founder, mng. ptnr. Bell Gardens Bicycle Club Casino, 1984-94; mayor City of Cathedral City, Calif., 1988-90, mayor pro tem, 1990-92; owner, mgr. Profile Comm. Inc., 1990—, Hardie's Korn Kettle Inc., 1990—, Hardie's Korn Kettle Gold, 2003; owner Las Vegas Hotel & Casino, Belize. Owner, mgr. investment and acquisitions co. Lodestar Internat. Inc. (formerly The Hardie Group), 1990—; owner Emerald Meadows Ranch, 1989—. Active cmty. and civic affairs. Recipient Congl. award, 1987; commendation L.A. County Suprs., 1987, L.A. County Office Dist. Atty., 1987; resolution Calif. Senate, 1987, cert. of recognition City of Bell Gardens, 1987; named Man of Yr. Variety Boys & Girls Club of the Desert, 1996.

Mem. Calif. Harness Drivers Guild (past pres.), Western Standardbred Assn. (past bd. dirs.), Golden State Greyhound Assn. (organizer, pres. 1973), Bell Gardens C. of C. (pres. 1986). Achievements include owner of largest casino in Central America. Office: Lodestar Internat Inc 1350 E Flamingo Rd # 347 Las Vegas NV 89119 Home Phone: 702-262-6773; Office Phone: 702-891-5252. E-mail: gghardie@aol.com.

HARDING, KAREN ELAINE, chemistry professor, department chairman; b. Atlanta, Sept. 5, 1949; d. Howard Everett and Ruth Evangeline (Lund) H.; m. Bruce Roy McDowell, Aug. 30, 1975. BS in Chemistry, U. Puget Sound, Tacoma, 1971; MS in Environ. Chemistry, U. Mich., 1972; postgrad., Evergreen State Coll., 1972-84, Yale U., 1986, Columbia U., 1991. Chemist Environ. Health Lab., Inc., Farmington, Mich., 1972—73, U. Mich. Med. Sch., Ann Arbor, 1973—75; instr. chemistry Schoolcraft Coll., Livonia, Mich., 1975—77; chair chemistry dept. Pierce Coll., Lakewood, Wash., 1977—. Adj. prof. U. Mich., Dearborn, 1974-77; instr. S.H. Alternative Learning Ctr., Tacoma, 1980-83, Elderhostel, Tacoma, 1985-89; mem. exec. com. Chemlinks project NSF. Mem. County Solid Waste Adv. Com., Tacoma, 1989—, Superfund Adv. Com., Tacoma, 1985-89, Sierra Club, Wash., 1989—; mem., past pres. Adv. Com. Nature Ctr., Tacoma, 1981-87. Faculty Enhancement grantee Pierce Coll., 1990; recipient Nat. Teaching Excellence award, 1991. Mem. NW Assn. for Environ. Studies (treas. 1985—), Am. Chem. Soc., Ft. Steilacoom Running Club (race dir. 1986—). Avocations: running, skiing, backpacking, bicycling, reading. Office: Pierce Coll 9401 Farwest Dr SW Lakewood WA 98498-1999 Business E-Mail: kharding@pierce.ctc.edu.

HARDISON, KADEEM, actor; b. NYC, July 24, 1965; m. Chante Moore (div.); 1 child. Actor: (TV series) ABC Afterschool Specials, 1981, The Cosby Show, 1984, Spenser: For Hire, 1987, A Different World, 1987—93 (NAACP Image award, 1991, 1992), Roc, 1992, Living Single, 1995, Touched by an Angel, 1997, Between Brothers, 1997, The Love Boat: The Next Wave, 1998, Fantasy Island, 1998, The Crow: Stairway to Heaven, 1998—99, Just Shoot Me, 2000, Static Shock, 2000—03, Livin' Large, 2002, Abby, 2003, One on One, 2005, Just for Kicks, 2006, My Name Is Earl, 2006, House, 2006, Girlfriends, 2007; (TV films) House of Dies Drear, 1984, Go Tell It on the Mountain, 1985, Dream Date, 1989, Words Up!, 1992, Fire & Ice, 2001, Red Skies, 2002, Life Is Not a Fairytale: The Fantasia Barrino Story, 2006 (NAACP Image award, 2007); (films) Rappin', 1985, Enemy Territory, 1987, School Daze, 1988, I'm Gonna Git You Sucka, 1988, Def by Temptation, 1990, White Men Can't Jump, 1992, Gunmen, 1994, Renaissance Man, 1994, Wes Craven's Vampire in Brooklyn, 1995, Panther, 1995, The Sixth Man, 1997, Drive, 1997, Blind Faith, 1998, Dancing in September, 2000, Thank Heaven, 2001, Thirty Years to Life, 2001, Instinct to Kill, 2001, Showtime, 2002, Face of Terror, 2003, Biker Boyz, 2003, Dunsmore, 2003, The Cassidy Kids, 2006, Love Hollywood Style, 2006; dir.: (TV series) A Different World, 1992—93; writer: TV series A Different World, 1992—93. Office: c/o Untitled Entertainment 1801 Century Park E Los Angeles CA 90067

HARDWICK, DAVID FRANCIS, pathologist; b. Vancouver, BC, Can., Jan. 24, 1934; s. Walter H. W. and Iris L. (Hyndman) H.; m. Margaret M. Lang, Aug. 22, 1956; children: Margaret F., Heather I., David J. MD, U. B.C., 1957, LLD (hon.), 2001. Intern Montreal (Que., Can.) Gen. Hosp., 1957-58; resident Vancouver Gen. Hosp., 1958-59, Children's Hosp., Los Angeles, 1959-62; research assoc. U. So. Calif., 1961-62; clin. instr. U. B.C., Vancouver, 1963-65, asst. prof. pathology, 1965-69, assoc. prof., 1969-74, prof., 1974—, head dept. pathology, 1976-90, assoc. dean rsch. and planning, 1990-96; dir. labs. Children's Hosp., Vancouver, 1969-92, Vancouver Gen. Hosp., 1976-90; chmn. M.A.C., Children's Hosp., 1970-87; interinstitutional planning U. B.C. Medicine, 1996-98, spl. advisor on planning, 1999—. Adj. prof. Chinese U. Hong Kong; mem. U. B.C. Senate, 1966-71. Author: Acid Base Balance and Blood Gas Studies, 1968, Intermediary Metabolism of Liver, 1971, Directing the Clinical Laboratory, 1990, Laboratory Supervision and Management, 2d edit., 2002; contbr. numerous articles to profl. publs. Bd. dirs. Children and Family Rsch. Inst., BC, 1998—, Women's Hosp. Found., 1997-2000, BC Transplant Found., 1993-2006. Recipient Queen's Centennial medal Govt. Can., 1978, U. B.C. Faculty Citation Teaching award, 1987, Wallace Wilson Leadership award, 1990, William Boyd Lectureship award Canadian Assn. Path, 1994, Sydney Israels Founders award B.C. Rsch. Inst. Children and Family, 1997, Univ. medal for Outstanding Svc., U. B.C., 1997; Sydney Farber lectr., Soc. Ped. Path., 1998, Excellence award Coll. Physicians & Surgeons, 2008, other awards. and honors Fellow Royal Coll. Physicians (Can.), Coll. Am. Pathologists; mem. Internat. Acad. Pathology (pres. 1996, v.p. N.Am. 1998—, Gold medal 2002, sec. 2006-), Can. Med. Assn., BC Assn. Lab. Medicine, BC Med. Assn., NY Acad. Sci., Soc. Pediat. Pathology, Internat. Acad. Pathology (sec. 2006-, Disting. Svc. award 1994, Gold Medal award 2004), US and Can. Acad. Pathology (Pres.'s award 2004), U BC Alumni (Lifetime Achievement award 2007), BC Transplant Found. (chmn. bd. 2000—06), Med. Student and Alumni Ctr. Soc. (chair 2001-05), Alpha Omega Alpha. Home: 727 W 23rd Ave Vancouver BC Canada V5Z 2A7 Office: U BC Dept Pathology 2211 Wesbrook Mall Vancouver BC Canada V6T 1W5 Business E-Mail: david.f.hardwick@ubc.ca.

HARDY, WALTER NEWBOLD, physics professor, researcher; b. Vancouver, BC, 1940; s. Walter Thomas and Julia Marguerite H.; m. Sheila Lorraine Hughes, July 10, 1959; children: Kevin James, Steven Wayne. BSc in Math and Physics with honors, U. B.C., 1961; PhD in Physics, Univ. B.C., 1965. Postdoctral fellow Centre d'Etudes Nucleaires de Saclay, France, 1964-66; mem. tech. staff N.Am. Rockwell, Thousand Oaks, Calif., 1966-71; assoc. prof. physics U. B.C., 1971-76, prof., 1976—. Vis. scientist Ecole Normale Superieure, Paris, 1980-81, 85, 95. Contbr. articles to sci. jours.; patentee precision microwave instrumentation. Recipient Stacie prize NRC of Can., 1978, Gold medal B.C. Sci. Coun., 1989, Killam prize Can. Coun., 1999, Fritz London Prize, 2002, Brockhouse Can. prize for interdisciplinary rsch. in sci. and engring, 2006; Rutherford Meml. scholar, 1964; Alfred P. Sloan fellow, 1972-74; Can. Coun. Rsch. fellow, 1984-86. Fellow Am. Phys. Soc.; mem. Can. Assn. Physicists (Herzberg medal 1978, gold medal for achievement in physics, 1993, Brockhouse medal 1999). Office: U BC Dept Physics Astronomy Vancouver BC Canada V6T 1Z1

HARE, JULIA, educational psychologist, author, consultant; b. Tulsa, Okla. m. Nathan Hare. BA in Music, Langston U., Okla., 1960; MA in Music Edn., Roosevelt U., Chgo., 1962; PhD in Edn., Calif. Coast U., Santa Ana, 1987. Elem. sch. tchr., Chgo.; dir. ednl. progs. Oakland Mus., Calif.; pub. rels. dir. local fed. housing prog. San Francisco; co-founder, nat. exec. dir. The Black Think Tank, San Francisco, 1979—. Numerous TV appearances including CNN & Co., C-SPAN, Tony Brown's Jour., Inside Edition; spkr. Congl. Black Caucus. Co-author (with husband): The Endangered Black Family, 1984, Bringing the Black Boy to Manhood: The Passage, 1985, Crisis in Black Sexual Politics, 1989, The Miseducation of the Black Child, 1991, How to Find and Keep a BMW (Black Man Working), 1995; contbr. articles to newspapers and mags.; spkr. in field. Recipient Abe Lincoln award for outstanding broadcasting, Carter G. Woodson Edn. award, Harambee award, Assn. Black Social Workers', Lifetime Achievement award, Internat. Black Writers & Artists Union, Presdl. citation, Nat. Assn. Equal Opportunity in Higher Edn.; named Educator of Yr., Washington DC Jr. C. of C., Scholar of Yr., Assn. African Historians; named one of 10 Most Influential African Americans in San Francisco Bay Area; named to Power 150, Ebony mag., 2008. Office: Black Think Tank 1801 Bush St San Francisco CA 94109 Office Phone: 415-929-0204.

HARGRAVE, SARAH QUESENBERRY, consulting company and training executive; d. Teddie W. Quesenberry and Lois Knight Quesenberry Stout. Student, Radford Coll., 1963-64, Va. Poly. Inst. and State U., 1964-67. Mgmt. trainee Thalhimer Bros. Dept. Store, Richmond, Va., 1967-68; Cen. Va. fashion and publicity dir. Sears Roebuck & Co., Richmond, 1968-73, nat. decorating sch. coord. Chgo., 1973-74, nat. dir. bus. and profl. women's programs, 1974-76; v.p., treas., program dir. Sears-Roebuck Found., Chgo., 1976-87, program mgr. corp. contbns. and memberships, 1981-84, dir. corp. mktg. and pub. affairs, 1984-87; v.p. personal fin. svcs. and mktg. Northern Trust Co., Chgo., 1987-89; pres. Hargrave Consulting, 1989—. Spkr., seminar leader in field. Bd. dirs. Am. Assembly Collegiate Schs. Bus., 1979-82, mem. vis. com., 1979-82, mem. fin. and audit com., 1980-82, mem. task force on doctoral supply and demand, 1980-82; mem. Com. for Equal Opportunity for Women, 1976-81; chmn., 1978-79, 80-81; mem. bus. adv. coun. Walter E. Heller Coll. Bus. Adminstrn., Roosevelt U., 1979-89; co-dir. Ill. Internat. Women's Yr. Ctr., 1975. Named Outstanding Young Women of Yr. Ill., 1976; named Women of Achievement State Street Bus. and Profl. Woman's Club, 1978 Mem. ASTD, Profl. Women's Network, Profl. Coaches and Mentors Assn. Home and Office: 396 Pine Hill Rd Ste 21 Mill Valley CA 94941 Personal E-mail: shargrave@earthlink.net.

HARGREAVES, GEORGE HENRY, civil and agricultural engineer, researcher; b. Chico, Calif., Apr. 2, 1916; s. Carey and Luella May (Raymond) H.; m. Elizabeth Ann Gardner, Aug. 9, 1941 (dec. Dec. 1947); 1 child, Margaret Ann Hargreaves Stolpmann; m. Sara Etna Romero, Jan 6, 1951; children: Mark Romero, Sonia Maria Hargreaves Hart, George Leo. BS in Soils, U. Calif., Berkeley, 1939; BSCE, U. Wyo., 1943. Civil engr. U.S. Bur. Reclamation, Sacramento, 1946-48; reclamation engr. U.S. Army C.E., Greece, 1948-49; engr. AID, Greece, Peru, Haiti, Philippines, Brazil and Colombia, 1950-68; chief civil engr. engring. br. Natural Resources divsn. Inter-Am. Geodetic Survey, Ft. Clayton, 1968-70; rsch. engr. in irrigation Utah State. U., Logan, 1970-86; rsch. Internat. Irrigation Ctr., 1980-86, rsch. prof. emeritus, 1986—. Author: World Water for Agriculture, 1977; co-author: Irrigation Fundamentals, 1998, Fundamentos Del Riego, 2000; contbr. numerous articles to profl. jours. Lt. (j.g.) USNR, 1943-46, PTO. Recipient Royce J. Tipton award, 1997. Fellow: ASCE; mem.: Internat. Commn. Irrigation and Drainage (chmn. U.S. Com. on crops and water use 1992—96, drainage and flood control 1999—2003, chmn. U.S. com. on history of irrigation), Am. Soc. Agrl. Engrs. (chmn. Rocky Mountain sect. 1974). Achievements include development of methodology used by the International Water Management Institute in the IWMI World Water and Climate Atlas, providing worldwide climate data and an index of rainfall adequacy for agricultural production. Home: 1660 E 1220 N Logan UT 84341-3040

HARGROVE, JAMES (JIM) E., state legislator; b. Portland, Oreg., Oct. 5, 1953; m to Laurie; children: Jimmy-Jack, Jewel & Daniel. Washington State Representative, District 24, 85-92; Washington State Senator, District 24, 93-, member, Trade, Econ Develop, Natural Resources, Judiciary & Human Serv Committees, currently, Washington State Senate.Forester, Olympic Peninsula, currently. Democrat. Christian. Office: State Senate 411 Legislative Bldg PO Box 40424 Olympia WA 98504 Address: 311 7th St PO Box 427 Hoquiam WA 98550 also: 630E E Front St Port Angeles WA 98362

HARGROVE, JOHN JAMES, bankruptcy judge; b. Bay Shore, NY, May 4, 1942; s. John A. and Cecelia L. Hargrove; m. Jane A Nagle, Oct. 21, 1967; children: David, Kristin, Kelly, Kathryn. BAin Polit. Sci., U. Notre Dame, 1964, JD, 1967. Bar: N.Y. 1968, Calif. 1971. Atty. Gant & Asaro, San Diego, 1972-76; ptnr. Weeks, Willis, Hoffman & Hargrove, San Diego, 1976-79, Strauss, Kissane, Davis & Hargrove, San Diego, 1979-83, Britton & Hargrove, San Diego, 1983-84; prin. John J. Hargrove & Assocs., San Diego, 1984-85; judge U.S. Bankruptcy Ct., San Diego, 1985—, chief bankruptcy judge. Adj. prof. Calif. Western Sch. Law, 1986. Coach University City Bobby Sox Softball Team; lector Our Mother of Confidence Roman Cath. Ch.; trustee U. Notre Dame, 1987-89. Lt. col. USMCR, 1968-90. Mem. U. Notre Dame Alumni Assn. (bd. dirs. 1985-89, pres. 1988-89). Republican. Avocations: basketball, softball, running. Office: US Bankruptcy Ct So Dist Calif 325 W F St San Diego CA 92101-6989 Fax: 619-557-6925.

HARITON, LORRAINE JILL, information technology executive; b. NYC, Nov. 7, 1954; d. Martin and Barbara (Jaffee) H.; m. Stephen Alan Weyl June 17, 1979; children: Eric, Laura. BS in Math Sci., Stanford U., 1976; MBA, Harvard U., 1982. Sales rep. IBM, NYC, 1977-80, regional rep. San Francisco, 1982-84, sales mgr. Oakland, Calif., 1984-86; mgr. pricing Rolm, Santa Clara, Calif., 1986-87, adminstrv. asst. to v.p. sales, 1987-88, br. mgr., 1988-90, product line mgr., 1990-92; dir. mktg. Verifone, Inc., Redwood City, Calif., 1992-93; v.p. mktg. Network Computing Devices, Mountain View, Calif., 1993—99; pres., CEO Beatnik Inc., San Mateo, Calif., 1999—2003, chmn., 2003—; pres., CEO Apptera, Inc., San Bruno, Calif., 2003—05. Business E-Mail: chariton@applera.com.

HARKER, CHRIS, state legislator; m. Georgia Harker, 1980; children: Ayla, Graham. Med. rschr. OHSU Physiology Dept., Div. Vascular Surgery; dir. Core Lab. OHSU Gen. Clinical Rsch. Ctr.; pres. & founder Cayuse, Inc; mem. Dist. 34 Oreg. House of Reps., 2008—. Democrat. Avocations: camping, fishing. Office: 900 Court St NE H-485 Salem OR 97301 also: PO Box 1368 Beaverton OR 97075 Office Phone: 503-986-1434. Business E-Mail: rep.chrisharker@state.or.us.

HARKEY, DIANE L., state legislator; m. Dan Harkey; 1 child, Jaclyn. BA in Economics, U. Calif., Irvine. Archtl. rev. bd. mem. County of Orange, 1987; mayor City of Dana Point, Dana Point; dir. San Joaquin Hills Transp. Corridor Agy.; mem. Dana Point City Coun., Dana Point; mem. Dist. 73 Calif. State Assembly, Calif., 2008—. Republican. Office: State Capital Room 4177 PO Box 942849 Sacramento CA 95814 also: 300 North Coast Hwy Oceanside CA 92054 Office Phone: 760-757-8084, 916-319-2073. Office Fax: 760-757-8087, 916-319-2173.*

HARKNESS, NANCY P., lawyer; b. 1959; BA in Econs., Cornell U., 1980; JD, Fordham U., 1985. Bar: NY, Calif. With Internat. Broadcasting, LA; cons. Olympic Regional Devel. Authority, Lake Placid; head bus. & legal affairs dept. Motown Record Co. LP, 1995—97; named v.p. bus. & legal affairs Universal Studios Consumer Products Group, 1997; sr. v.p. bus. affairs Digital Entertainment Network Inc.; sr. counsel Akin, Gump, Strauss, Hauer & Feld, LLP; of counsel Sonnenschein Nath & Rosenthal, LA. Office: Sonnenschein Nath Rosenthal 601 S Figueroa St Ste 2500 Los Angeles CA 90017-5709 Office Phone: 213-892-5151. Office Fax: 213-623-9924. Business E-Mail: nharkness@sonnenschein.com.

HARKONEN, WESLEY SCOTT, physician, pharmaceutical company executive; b. Mpls., Dec. 17, 1951; s. Wesley Sulo and Frances (Fedor) H.; children: Kirsten, Alan. BA summa cum laude, U. Minn., 1973, MD, 1977. Resident internal medicine U. Minn., Mpls., 1977-81; fellow allergy and immunology U. Calif., San Francisco, 1983-85, fellow clin. pharmacology, 1984-85; project dir. Xoma Corp., Berkeley, Calif., 1983-87; rsch. assoc. Stanford U., 1987-88; assoc. med. dir. Becton Dickinson, Mountain View, Calif., 1988-89; v.p. med. affairs Calif. Biotechnology, Mountain View, Calif., 1989-91; v.p. med. and regulatory affairs Univax Biologics, Rockville, Md., 1991-95; sr. v.p. devel. and ops. Connective Therapeutics, Palo Alto, Calif., 1995-99; pres., CEO, InterMune Pharms., Palo Alto, 1999—. Author: Traveling Well, 1984; contbr. articles to profl. jours. J. Thomas Livermore Rsch. award, U. Minn., 1977. Office: InterMune Pharms 3294 W Bayshore Rd Palo Alto CA 94303-4043

HARLAN, NANCY MARGARET, lawyer; b. Santa Monica, Calif., Sept. 10, 1946; d. William Galland and Betty M. (Miles) Plett; m. John Hammack, Dec. 1, 1979; children: Laryssa Maria Rebello, Leea Elyce. BS magna cum laude, Calif. State U., Hayward, 1972; JD, U. Calif., Berkeley, 1975. Bar: Calif. 1975, Fed. Bar, U.S. Dist. Ct. (ctrl. dist. 9th cir.) 1976. Assoc. Poindexter & Doutr+248, LA, 1975—80; residential counsel Coldwell Banker Residential Brokerage Co., Fountain Valley, Calif., 1980—81; sr. counsel for real estate subs. law dept. Pacific Lighting Corp., Santa Ana, Calif., 1981—87; sr. v.p., gen. counsel The Presley Cos., 1987—. Bd. dirs. La Casa; exec. v.p. student body U. Calif., Berkeley, 1974—75. Mem.: NAFE, ABA, Bus. and Profl. Women, L.A. Women Lawyers Assn., Orange County Women Lawyers Assn., Calif. Women Lawyers Assn., Orange County Bar Assn. (dir. corp. counsel sect. 1982—), L.A. County Bar Assn., State Bar Calif. Office: William Lyon Homes Inc 4490 Von Karman Ave Newport Beach CA 92660-2008

HARLAN, ROBERT DALE, library and information scientist, educator, academic administrator; b. Hastings, Nebr., Aug. 4, 1929; s. Hugh Allan and Madge Keister (Newmyer) H. BA, Hastings Coll., 1950; MA in Library Sci., U. Mich., 1956, MA, 1958, PhD, 1960. Head book order sect. Library U. Mich., Ann Arbor, 1956-58, lectr., 1960; asst. prof. Sch. Library Sci. U. So. Calif., Los. Angeles, 1960-63; asst. prof. library and info. studies U. Calif., Berkeley, 1963-70, assoc. prof., 1970-76, prof., 1976-94, prof. emeritus, 1994—; assoc. dean Sch. Library and Info. Studies, 1971-74, 77-82; acting dean Sch. Library and Info. Studies U. Calif., Berkeley, 1985-86. Vis. assoc. prof. Sch. Libr. Sci. UCLA, summer 1973; cons. NEH, Washington; proprietor Park Hills Press. Author: John Henry Nash, 1970, Bibliography of the Grabhorn and Grabhorn-Hoyem Presses, 1977, George L. Harding, 1978, The Colonial Printer: Two Views, 1978, Chapter Nine, 1982, William Doxey's Publishing Venture: At the Sign of the Lark, 1983, The Two Hundredth Book, 1993; chmn. edit. bd. catalogues and bibliographies series U. Calif. Press, 1982-99; contbr. numerous articles and revs. to profl. jours. Rackham pre-doctoral fellow, U. Mich., 1958-60, summer faculty fellow U. Calif., Berkeley, 1964; grantee Assn. Coll. and Research Libraries, 1960, 63. Mem. Will Cather Pioneer Meml. Soc., Fine Press Book Assn., Book of Calif. Club (bd. dirs. 1982-88, sec. bd. 1987-88, Lewis award 2004). Office: U Calif Sch Info 102 South Hall Berkeley CA 94720-4600 Office Phone: 415-642-4375. Business E-Mail: rharlan@sims.berkely.edu.

HARLIN, MARILYN MILER, marine botany educator, researcher, consultant; b. Oakland, Calif., May 30, 1934; d. George T. and Gertrude (Turula) Miler; m. John E. Harlin II, Oct. 25, 1955 (dec. Feb. 1966); children: John E. III, Andrea M. Harlin Cilento. AB, Stanford U., 1955, MA, 1956; PhD, U. Wash., 1971. Instr. Am. Coll. Switzerland and Leysin, 1964-66; asst. prof. Pacific Marine Sta., Dillon Beach, Calif., 1969; asst. prof. marine biology U. R.I., Kingston, 1971-75, assoc. prof., 1975-83, prof., 1983-2000, prof. emerita, 2000—, chair botany dept., chair dept. biol. scis. Guest scientist Atlantic Regional Lab., Halifax, N.S., Can., 1973-78; hon. vis.prof. LaTrobe U., Bundoora, Victoria, Australia, 1984; resource person R.I. Coastal Resource Mgmt. Coun., 1980-2000, R.I. Dept. Environ. Mgmt., 1980; cons. Applied Sci. Assocs., Narragansett, R.I., 1988-98, Western Australia Water Authority, Perth, 1994; rsch. assoc. U. Calif., Santa Cruz, 1993. Co-editor: Marine Ecology, 1976, Freshwater and Marine Plants of Rhode Island, 1988. Bd. dirs. Westminster Unitarian Ch., East Greenwich, R.I., 1987; bd. govs. Women's Ctr., Kingston, 1989-90. Grantee NOAA, 1975-81, Dept. Environ. Mgmt./EPA, 1989-91, U.S. Fish and Wildlife, 1995. Mem. Internat. Phycological Soc., Phycological Soc. Am. (editor newsletter 1982-84, editorial bd. 1988-90), Union Concerned Scientists (nat. adv. bd. 2004—), N.E. Algal Soc. (exec. com.), Sigma Xi (pres., sec. 1979-82). Avocations: yoga, hiking, reading, writing, gardening. Personal E-mail: mharlin@macforcego.com.*

HARMAN, JANE, United States Representative from California; b. NYC, June 28, 1945; d. A.N. and Lucille (Geier) Lakes; m. Sidney Harman, Aug. 30, 1980; children: Brian, Hilary, Daniel Geier, Justine Leigh. BA in Govt., Smith Coll., 1966; JD, Harvard U., 1968. Bar: DC 1969, US Ct. Appeals (DC cir.) 1972, US Supreme Ct. 1975. Spl. asst. Commn. Chs. on Internat. Affairs, Geneva, 1969-70; assoc. Surrey & Morse, Washington, 1970-72; chief legis. asst. senator John V. Tunney, Washington, 1972-73; chief counsel, staff dir. subcom. rep. citizen interests Com. on Judiciary, Washington, 1973-75, chief counsel, staff dir. subcom. constl. rights, 1975-77; dep. sec. to cabinet White House, Washington, 1977-78; spl. counsel Dept. Def., Washington, 1979; ptnr. Manatt, Phelps, Rothenberg & Tunney, Washington, 1979-82, Surrey & Morse, Washington, 1982-86; of counsel Jones, Day, Reavis & Pogue, Washington, 1987-92; mem. US Congress from 36th Calif. dist., 1992—98, 2000—, mem. homeland security com., mem. energy & commerce com., intelligence com., 2001—; mem. nat. security com., intelligence com. 103rd-105th Congresses. Adj. prof. Georgetown Law Ctr., 1974—75; mem. vis. com. Harvard Law Sch., 1976—82, Kennedy Sch. Govt., 1990—96; regents prof. UCLA, 1999; mem. New Dem. Coalition, Blue Dog Coalition, Congl. Fire Services Inst., Congl. Task Force Tobacco & Health, Women's Policy Inc.; former mem. Nat. Commn. on Terrorism, Joint 9/11 Inquiry. Vice-chmn. Ctr. for Nat. Policy, Washington, 1981—90; trustee Smith Coll.; counsel Dem. Platform Com., Washington, 1984; chmn. Dem. Nat. Com. Nat. Lawyers' Coun., Washington, 1986—90; bd. dirs. Planned Parenthood, LA, 1998—2000, Venice Family Clinic, Calif., 1998—2000. Mem.: Phi Beta Kappa. Democrat. Jewish. Office: US Ho Reps 2400 Rayburn Ho Office Bldg Washington DC 20515-0536 also: Dist Office Ste 3270 2321 Rosecrans Ave El Segundo CA 90245-4932

HARMAN, JENNIFER (JENNIFER HARMAN-TRANIELLO), professional poker player; b. Reno, Nevada, Nov. 29, 1964; m. Marco Traniello. BS in Biology, U. Nev., Reno. Profl. poker player World Series Poker Cir. Founder Creating Organ Donation Awareness. Achievements include invention of winning No Limit Deuce to Seven World Series Poker Bracelet, 2000; winning Texas Hold 'Em 5k World Series Poker Bracelet, 2002; total winnings over over 1.5 mil; generally considered to be the best female poker player in the world.

HARMON, ANGIE MICHELLE (ANGIE SEHORN), actress; b. Dallas, Aug. 10, 1972; d. Larry and Daphne Harmon; m. Jason Sehorn, June 9, 2001; children: Finley Faith, Avery Grace, Emery Hope. Actor: (TV series) Baywatch Nights, 1995-97, C-16: FBI, 1997-98, Law & Order, 1998-2001, Inconceivable, 2005, Women's Murder Club, 2007-2008, (TV films) Video Voyeur: The Susan Wilson Story, 2002, Sudden Fear, 2002, Living Proof, 2008, (films) Lawn Dogs, 1997, Good Advice, 2001, Agent Cody Banks, 2003, The Deal, 2005, Fun with Dick and Jane, 2005, End Game, 2006, Seraphim Falls, 2006. Office: c/o Creative Artists Agy 9830 Wilshire Blvd Beverly Hills CA 90212

HARMON, DANIEL PATRICK, classics educator; b. Chgo., May 3, 1938; s. Bernard Leonard and Dorothy Mildred (Lesser) H. AB, Loyola U., Chgo., 1962; MA, Northwestern U., 1965, PhD, 1968; postdgrad., Am. Sch. Classical Studies, Athens, Greece, 1975. Acting asst. prof. U. Wash., Seattle, 1967-68, asst. prof. classics, 1968-75, assoc. prof., 1975-76, assoc. prof. classics and comparative lit., 1976-84, prof. classics, 1984—2004, prof. emeritus, 2004—, chmn. classics, 1976-91; dir. U. Wash. Rome Ctr., 1992-2000. Contbr. articles and revs. to profl. jours. Mem. Am. Philol. Assn., Archaeol. Inst. Am., Société des Études Latines, County Louth (Ireland) Archaeol. and Hist. Soc., Classical Assn. Pacific Northwest (pres. 1974-75). Avocations: painting, photography, music. Home: 3149 NE 83rd St Seattle WA 98115-4751 Office: U Wash Dept Classics PO Box 353110 Seattle WA 98195-3110 Business E-Mail: dph@u.washington.edu.

HARNDEN, EDWIN A., lawyer; BA, Columbia U., NYC, 1969, JD, 1972. Mng. ptnr. Barran Liebman LLP, Portland, Oreg.; pres. Oreg. State Bar, 2001—02. Past pres. Profl. Liability Fund. Fellow: Am. Coll. of Labor and Employment Lawyers, Am. Bar Found. (life). Office: ODS Tower 601 SW 2d Ave Ste 2300 Portland OR 97204-3159 Home Phone: 503-292-6490; Office Phone: 503-276-2101. Business E-Mail: eharnden@barran.com.

HARNISH, JOHN J., manufacturing executive; Gen. mgr. Tractor & Equipment Co., Sidney, Mont., 1977-82, pres. Williston, N.D., 1982—, CEO, 1984—. Office: Tractor & Equipment Co 17025 W Valley Hwy Tukwila WA 98188-5519

HARP, JOHN G., state legislator; b. Vancouver, Wash., Sept. 26, 1952; m. Kathy Harp. Student, Missoula Bus. Coll. Contractor, bus. exec.; mem. Mont. Ho. of Reps., 1981-88, Mont. State Senate, 1988—, chair rules com., minority whip, 1993-94, majority leader, 1995. Mem. Evergreen Sch. Bd. Mem. Evergreen Lions Club. Republican. Home: 633 Sylvan Ct Kalispell MT 59901-5077

HARPEN, SHAWN M., lawyer; BA, U. Toledo, 1990, JD, 1998. Bar: Calif. Ptnr., bus. litigation McDermott Will & Emery, Irvine, Calif. Named a Rising Star, So. Calif. Super Lawyers, 2004—06. Mem.: ABA, Calif. Bar Assn., Fed. Bar Assn., LA County Bar Assn., Orange County Bar Assn., Order of the Coif. Office: McDermott Will & Emery Ste 500 18191 Von Karman Ave Irvine CA 92612 Office Phone: 949-757-6061. Office Fax: 949-851-9348. Business E-Mail: sharpen@mwe.com.

HARPENDING, HENRY COSAD, anthropologist, educator; b. Penn Yan, NY, Jan. 13, 1944; married, 1966; 2 children; married 1995; 1 child. AB, Hamilton Coll., 1964; MA, Harvard U., 1965, PhD in Anthropology, 1972. Asst. prof. anthropology Yale U., 1971-72; from asst. prof. to prof. anthropology U. N.Mex., 1972-85; prof. anthropology Pa. State U., 1986-97, U. Utah, 1997—. Mem. Nat. Acad. Sci., Am. Assn. Anthrop. Genetics, Human Behaviour Evolution Soc. Office: U Utah Dept Anthropology Stuart Salt Lake City UT 84112

HARPER, HILL (FRANK HARPER), actor; b. Iowa City, Iowa, May 17, 1966; BA cum laude, Brown Univ.; JD cum laude, Harvard Univ., MPA. Theater: Black Folk's Theater Co., Boston; Actor: (Films) Confessions of a Dog, 1993, Pumpkinhead II: Blood Wings, 1994, Drifting School, 1995, One Red Rose, 1995 (also writer), Get on the Bus, 1996, Hoover Park, 1997, Steel 1997, Hav Plenty, 1997, He Got Game, 1998, Park Day, 1998, The Nephew 1998, Beloved, 1998, Slaves of Hollywood, 1999, In Too Deep, 1999, Box Marley, 2000, The Skulls 2000, The Visit, 2000 (Best Actor, Method Fest, 2000), Higher Ed, 2001, Rockboy, 2002, The Badge, 2002, Love, Sex and Eating the Bones, 2003, Andre Royo's Big Scene, 2004, America Brown, 2004, My Purple Fur Coat, 2004, Constellation, 2005, Whitepaddy 2006, Max and Joshm 2006 (also writer), Premium, 2006, The Breed, 2006, 30 Days, 2006, TV movies: Zooman, 1995, Mama Flora's Family, 1998, Loving Jezebel, 1999, Lackawanna Blues, 2005; TV series: Holla, 2002, CSI: NY, 2004- (Outstanding Actor in a Drama Series, NAACP Image award, 2008, Best Actor in a Drama Series, NAACP Image award, 2009); Author: Letters to a Young Brother, 2006 (Best Debut Author, NAACP Image award, 2007). Recipient W.E.B. DuBois Scholar award, 13th Annual Inner City Awards; named one of Sexiest Men Alive, People Mag., 2004. Office: CSI: NY CBS TV City 7800 Beverly Blvd Los Angeles CA 90036

HARPER, JACK W., state legislator; b. Indpls., Sept. 9, 1967; m. Holly Harper, 1990; children: Jaclyn, Amanda. Small bus. and franchise owner, 1998—; mem. Dist. 4 Ariz. State Senate, 2003—, chair vets. & mil. affairs com., mem. appropriations com. Served with 1st inf. divsn. US Army, Germany, sgt. E-5 Ariz. Army Nat. Guard. Republican. Office: Ariz State Senate Capitol Complex 1700 W Washington Rm 301 Phoenix AZ 85007 Office Phone: 602-926-4178. Office Fax: 602-417-3154. Business E-Mail: jharper@azleg.gov.*

HARPER, JUDSON MORSE, retired university administrator, consultant, educator; b. Lincoln, Nebr., Aug. 25, 1936; s. Floyd Sprague and Eda Elizabeth (Kelley) H.; m. Patricia Ann Kennedy, June 15, 1958; children: Jayson K., Stuart H., Neal K. BS, Iowa State U., 1958, MS, 1960, PhD, 1963. Registered profl. engr., Minn. Instr. Iowa State U., Ames, 1958-63; dept. head Gen. Mills, Inc., Mpls., 1964-69, venture mgr., 1969-70; prof., dept. head agrl. and chem. engring. Colo. State U., Ft. Collins, 1970-82, v.p. rsch. and info. tech., 1982-2000, interim pres., 1989-90, spl. asst. to the pres., 2000—04. Cons. USAID, Washington, 1972-74, various comml. firms., 1975—; Lady Davis scholar Technion, Haifa, Israel, 1978-79. Author: Extrusion of Foods, 1982, Extrusion Cooking, 1989; editor newsletter Food, Pharm. & Bioengring. News, 1979-83, LEC Newsletter, 1976-89; contbr. articles to profl. publs.; patentee. Mem. sch. bd. St. Louis Park, Minn., 1968-70. Recipient Disting. Svc. award Colo. State U., 1977, Fulbright-Hayes scholar, 1978, Svc. award Centro de Investigaviones y Asistencia Technologica de Estado de Chihuahua, Chichuahua, Mex., 1980, Food Engring. award Dairy and Food Industry Supply Assn. and Am. Soc. Agrl. Engrs., 1983, Cert. of Merit, USDA Office Internat. Coop. and Devel., 1983, Cert. of Merit, Consejo Nacional de Ciencia y Technologie en Mexico, Mexico City, 1984, Profl. Achievement Citation Iowa State U., 1986, Cert. Appreciation Chinese Inst. of Food Tech., 1987, Charles Lory Pub. Svc. award, 1993, Hammer award The Nat. Performance Rev., 1994. Fellow: AAAS, Inst. Food Technologists (Internat. award 1990); mem.: Am. Soc. Engring. Edn. (com. chmn. 1976—77), Am. Chem. Soc., Am. Soc. Agrl. Engrs. (com. chmn. 1973—78, hon. engr. Rocky Mountain region), Am. Inst. Chem. Engring. (dir. 1981—84), Rotary Internat., Ind. Ind. United Meth. Ch. Home and Office: 1818 Westview Rd Fort Collins CO 80524-1891 Office Phone: 970-493-1191. Business E-Mail: judson.harper@colostate.edu.

HARPER, LYNN D., biologist; children: Travis, Christopher, MacKenzie. BA, MS in Cell and Molecular Biology, U. Bridgeport. Tech. writer, asst. mgr. Bionetics Corp., Washington, 1982—83; tech. dir. space sys. divsn. Gen. Electric Mgmt. and Tech. Svcs. Co., Washington, 1983—86; program mgr. advanced missions and spl. projects space life scis. divsn. NASA, 1986—89, dep. project mgr. Search Extraterrestrial Intelligence; chief advanced life support divsn. NASA Ames Rsch. Ctr., 1990—93, acting chief advanced life support divsn., 1993—94, sr. sys. engr. space scis. divsn., 1994—96, lead, integrative studies astrobiology, 1996—2000, lead astrobiology advanced concepts and technologies, 2000—05; lead integrative studies astrobiology space rsch., 2005—08. Contbr. scientific papers. Recipient Exceptional Leadership medal, NASA, 6 other achievement awards. Achievements include co-founding the science of Astrobiology, Space Portal, and RosettaSpace; significant contributions to in space experiments on Space Shuttle, Mir, Space Station, Stardust, Mars missions; contributor to human exploration of the solar system studies. Office: NASA Ames Rsch Ctr MS 555-3 Bldg 555 Rm 3 Moffett Field CA 94035

HARPER, ROBERT, actor; b. NYC, May 19, 1951; BA in English with high distinction, Rutgers U., 1974. Mem. repertory co. Arena Stage, Washington, 1974-76. Guest artist Rutgers U., New Brunswick, NJ, 1977, New Brunswick, 84. Actor: Long Wharf Theater, 1978, 1984, Theater for a New City, 1981; (Broadway plays) Once in a Lifetime, 1978, The Inspector General, 1978, The American Clock, 1980; (TV films) J. Edgar Hoover, The Wrong Man, Not Quite Human, Payoff, Running Mates, The Story of Bill W, Paper Angels, Ruby Ridge; (TV series) Newhart, Roseanne, Murphy Brown, Wiseguy, L.A. Law, NYPD Blue, Law and Order, Philly, Frank's Place, Commander-in-Chief; (films) Creepshow, 1982, Once Upon a Time in America, 1984, Amazing Grace and Chuck, 1987, Twins, 1989, Final Analysis, 1992, Deconstructing Harry, 1997, The Insider, 1999. Adviser charity events The Laugh Factory, Hollywood, 1981—. Recipient Kennedy Ctr. award, Am. Coll. Theater Festival, 1974; named commencement spkr., Rutgers U., 2007; Regents fellow, U. Calif., 1974. Mem.: SAG, ACLU (sponsor Garden Event 1994), MLA (spkr. conv. 1996), Actor's Equity Assn., Acad. TV Arts and Scis., Acad. Motion Picture Arts and Scis. Office: 8721 Santa Monica Blvd West Hollywood CA 90069-4507

HARPER, STEVEN V., state legislator; b. Tampa, Fla., Oct. 19, 1943; m. Sharron Harper; 4 children. BGS, U. Nebr., 1976. Commd. 2d lt. USAF, 1963, advanced through grades, 1993; Rep. rep. dist. 53 Oreg. Ho. of Reps., 1996-2000; Rep. senator dist. 30 Oreg. State Senate, 2000—. Mem. gen. govt. com. Oreg. Ho. of Reps. Mem. Rotary, C. of C. Baptist. Office: Oreg State Senate H-295 State Capitol Salem OR 97310 E-mail: harper.rep@state.or.us.

HARRELSON, WOODY, actor; b. Midland, Tex., July 23, 1961; s. Charles Voyde Harrelson & Diane Lou Oswald; m. Nancy Simon, June 29, 1985 (div. Jan. 20, 1986); m. Laura Louie, Dec. 28, 2008; children: Deni Montana, Zoe Giordano, Makani Ravello. BA in Theater Arts and English, Hanover Coll., Ind. Actor (TV series) Cheers, 1985-93 (Emmy nomination 1986, 87, 89, 91, Emmy award 1988); (TV movies) Bay Coven, 1987, Killer Instinct, 1988, Mother Goose Rock 'n' Rhyme, 1990; (films) Wildcats, 1986, Eye of the Demon, 1987, Cool Blue, 1990, Doc Hollywood, 1991, Ted and Venus, 1991, L.A. Story, 1991, White Men Can't Jump, 1992, Indecent Proposal, 1993, The Cowboy Way, 1994, I'll Do Anything, 1994, Natural Born Killers, 1994, The Sunchaser, 1996, The People vs. Larry Flynt, 1996, Kingpin, 1996, Wag the Dog, 1997, The Thin Red Line, 1998, The Hi-Lo Country, 1998, Edtv, 1999, Austin Powers: The Spy Who Shagged Me, 1999, Grass (voice), 1999, Play It to the Bone, 1999, American Saint, 2000, Scorched, 2002, Anger Management, 2003, She Hate Me, 2004, After the Sunset, 2004, North Country, 2005, The Prize Winner of Defiance, Ohio, 2005, A Prarie Home Companion, 2006, (voice) Free Jimmy, 2006, A Scanner Darkly, 2006, The Walker, 2007, No Country for Old Men, 2007 (Outstanding Performance by a Cast in a Motion Picture, SAG, 2008), The Grand, 2007, Battle in Seattle, 2007, Semi-Pro, 2008, Sleepwalking, 2008, Transsiberian, 2008, Seven Pounds, 2008; (TV appearances) Will & Grace, 2001; (TV host) Comedy Club All-Star IV, 1990; understudy Broadway prodn. Biloxi Blues; starred in Off-Broadway prodns. The Boys Next Door, 1987, The Zoo Story; actor, playwright Two on Two, Furthest From the Sun, 1993. Avocations: sports, writing, juggling, chess, playing guitar, Elvis Presley, playing piano. Office: c/o Ziffren Brittenham Branca Fischer Gilbert-Lurie 1801 Century Park West Los Angeles CA 90067-6406

HARRIGAN, ROSANNE CAROL, medical educator; b. Miami, Fla., Feb. 24, 1945; d. John H. and Rose (Hnatow) Harrigan; children: Dennis, Michael, John. BS, St. Xavier Coll., 1965; MSN, Ind. Univ., 1974, EdD in Nursing and Edn., 1979. Staff nurse, recovery rm. Mercy Hosp., Chgo., 1965, evening charge nurse, 1965—66; head nurse Chgo. State Hosp., 1966—67; nurse practitioner Health and Hosp. Corp. Marion County, Indpls., 1975—80; assoc. prof. Ind. U. Sch. Nursing, Indpls., 1978—82; nurse practitioner devel. follow up program Riley Hosp. for Children, Indpls., 1980—85; prof. Ind. U. Sch. Nursing, Indpls., 1982—85; chief nursing sect. Riley Hosp. Child Devel. Ctr., Indpls., 1982—85; chmn., prof. maternal child health Loyola U., Niehoff Sch. Nursing, Chgo., 1985—92; dean sch. nursing U. Hawaii, Honolulu, 1992—2002; nurse practitioner Waimanalo Health Ctr., Hawaii, 1998—2002; Frances A. Matsuda chair women's health John A. Burns Sch. Medicine U. Hawaii Manoa, Honolulu, 2000—05, chair faculty devel., 2002—, chair dept. Complementary and Alternative Medicine, 2002—, prof. pediat., 2003—. Lectr. Ind. U. Sch. Nursing, 1974-75, chmn. dept. pediat., family and women's health, 1980-85; adj. prof. of pediat. Ind. U. Sch. Med., 1982-85; editl. bd. Jour. Maternal Child Health Nursing, 1984-86, Jour. Perinatal Neo-natal, 1985—, Jour. Perinatology, 1989—, Loyola U. Press, 1988-92; adv. bd. Symposia Medicus, 1982-84, Proctor and Gamble Rsch. Adv. Com. Blue Ribbon Panel; sci. rev. panel NIH, 1985; mem. NIH nat. adv. coun. nursing rsch., 2000-; cons. in field. Contbr. articles to profl. journals. Bd. dir. March of Dimes Ctrl. Ind. Chpt., 1974-76, med. adv., 1979-85; med. and rsch. adv. March of Dimes Nat. Found., 1985—, chmn. Task Force on Rsch. Named Nat. Nurse of Yr. March of Dimes, 1983; faculty rsch. grantee Ind. U., 1978, Pediatric Pulmonary Nursing Tng. grant Am. Lung Assn., 1982-85, Attitudes, Interests, and Competence of Ob-Gyn. Nurses Rsch. grant Nurses Assn. Am. Coll. Ob-Gyn., 1986, Attitudes, Interests, and Priorities of Neo-natal Nurses Rsch. grant Nat. Assn. Neonatal Nurses, 1987, Biomedical Rsch. Support grant, 1988; Doctoral fellow Am. Lung Assn. Ind. Tng. Program, 1981-86. Mem. AAAS, ANA (Maternal Child Nurse of Yr. 1983), Assn. Women's Health, Obstetrical and Neonatal Nursing (chmn. com. on rsch. 1983-86), Am. Nurses Found., Nat. Assn. Neo-natal Nurses, Nat. Perinatal Assn. (bd. dir. 1978-85, rsch. com. 1986), Midwest Nursing Rsch. Soc. (theory devel. sect.), Ill. Nurses Assn. (commn. rsch. chmn. 1990-91), Ind. Nurses Assn., Hawaii Nurses Assn., Ind. Perinatal Assn. (pres. 1981-83), N.Y. Acad. Sci., Ind U. Alumni Assn. (Disting. Alumni 1985), Sigma Xi, Pi Lambda Theta, Sigma Theta Tau (chpt. pres. 1988-90). Home Phone: 808-728-2904. Business E-Mail: harrigan@hawaii.edu.

HARRINGTON, CHARLENE ANN, sociology and health policy educator; b. Concordia, Kans., Sept. 28, 1941; d. Lyman K. and Maxine (Boucher) Harrington; m. Ben Yerger, Aug. 28, 1976. BSN, U. Kans., Kansas City, 1963; MA in Cmty. Health, U. Wash., 1968; PhD in Sociology and Higher Edn., U. Calif., Berkeley, 1975. Staff nurse Good Samaritan Hosp., Portland, Oreg., 1963-64; sch. nurse U.S. Army Dependent Schs., Heilbronn, Germany, 1964-65; pub. health nurse Seattle King County and Group Health, Seattle, 1966-68; asst. prof., nursing program U. Kans., Kansas City, 1968-70; dep. dir., spl. asst. Calif. State Dept. Health, Sacramento, 1975-78; dir. Golden Empire Health Planning Agy., Sacramento, 1978-80; sr. rschr. Inst. for Health and Aging, U. Calif., San Francisco, 1980-83, asst. prof. Sch. Nursing, 1983-85, assoc. prof. dept. social and behavioral scis. Sch. Nursing, 1985-89, prof., vice chair dept. social and behavioral scis., 1989-93; chair dept. social and behavioral scis. U. Calif., San Francisco, 1994-96, prof. social and behavioral scis., 1997—. Assoc. dir. Inst. for Health and Aging, U. Calif., San Francisco, 1981-94; cons. Nat. Coalition for Nursing Home Reform, Washington, 1987—; com. on regulation nursing homes Inst. Medicine, 1984-86, com. on nursing staff, 1994-96. Author: Health Policy and Nursing, 3d edit., 2001; contbr. over 125 chpts. to books, articles to profl. jours. Fellow Am. Acad. Nursing (chair commn. on health policy 1991-93); mem. ANA, APHA, Nursing Econs. (bd. dirs. 1985-93), Inst. Medicine (com. nurse staffing 1995-96, roundtable of quality 1997-98, com. on quality in long-term care 1997—), Am. Sociol. Assn. (sect. coun. mem. 1992-94), Elected Inst. of Medicine (com. on longterm care quality 1998-2001, round table on quality 1997-98), Sigma Theta Tau. Democrat. Avocation: gardening. Office: U Calif Sch Nursing 3333 California St San Francisco CA 94143-0001

HARRINGTON, DANIEL WILLIAM, state legislator; b. Butte, Mont., Feb. 12, 1938; son of Bernard J Harrington & Nova M Maddock H; married 1962 to Patricia E Gallagher; children: three. President, Silver Bow Young Democratic, Montana, 1960-62; delegate, Montana Const Conv, 1971-72; chairman, Silver Bow Co Democratic Cent Committee, 1971-; director, Montana State Democratic Exec Committee, currently; Montana State Representative, District, 88, 1977-85, District 68, 1985-94, District 38, 1995-01, Majority Whip, 1983 & 95, Minority Whip, 1995-96, Montana House Representative; delegate, Democratic Nat Conv, 1980; chairman, Silver Bow Democratic Party, currently; Montana State Senator, District 19, 2001-05, District 38, 2005-, President Pro Tempore, Montana State Senate.Teacher, Sch District 1, Butte, Montana, 1961-. America & Montana Fedn Teachers; AFL-CIO. Democrat. Roman Catholic. Address: 1201 N Excelsior Butte MT 59701 Mailing: State Capitol PO Box 201706 Helena MT 59620 Home Phone: 406-782-0332; Office Phone: 406-723-4312; 406-496-2030. E-mail: house@state.mt.us.

HARRINGTON, PATTI, school system administrator; BA, MEd, Brigham Young U.; PhD in Ednl. Adminstrn., U. Utah. Prin. Provo HS, Utah; asst. supt. Provo; supt., 2001; assoc. supt. State of Utah, 2002—04, supt. of pub. instrn., 2004—. Recipient Secondary Sch. Prin. of Yr., 1997. Office: Utah Office of Edn 250 E 500 S PO Box 144200 Salt Lake City UT 84114-4200 Office Phone: 802-538-7500. Office Fax: 801-538-7768.

HARRINGTON, ROGER FULLER, electrical engineering educator, retired; b. Buffalo, Dec. 24, 1925; s. Henry Bassett and Emilie (Fuller) H.; m. Juanita L. Crawford, Aug. 7, 1954; m. Sandra, Judith, Alan, Laura. BS, Syracuse U., 1948, MS, 1950; PhD, Ohio State U., 1952. Instr. Syracuse U., NY, 1948-50, asst. prof. NY, 1952-56, assoc. prof. NY, 1956-60, prof. NY, 1960-94, dir. Electromagnetics Ctr. NY,

1982-94. Vis. prof. U. Ill., Urbana, 1959-60, U. Calif., Berkeley, 1964, E. China Normal U., 1983, Ecole Poly. Fédéral de Lausanne, Switzerland, 1991; guest prof. Tech. U. Denmark, Lyngby, 1969; cons. in field. Author: Introduction to EM Engineering, 1956, Time-Harmonic EM Fields, 1961, Field Computation by Moment Methods, 1968. Served with USN, 1944-46. Rsch. fellow Ohio State U., Columbus, 1950-52; Fulbright lectr., Denmark, eng., 1969; named Disting. Alumni Ohio State U., 1970; recipient Chancellor's Citation Syracuse U., 1984, URSI van der Pol Gold medal, 1996, jubilee medal Nicola Tesla Found., 1998. Mem. IEEE (Centennial medal 1984, Disting. Achievement award 1989, Electromagnetics award 2000, Third Millennium medal 2000), AAUP, Sigma Xi, Sigma Nu.

HARRIS, BARBARA S., publishing executive, editor-in-chief; BS in Phys. Edn., Fla. State U., 1978; Masters, N.E. Mo. State U. Editor-in-chief Weider Publ., Woodland Hill, Calif., 1987—2003; exec. v.p. Am. Media, Woodlands Hills, 2003—. Current advisor Calif. Gov.'s Coun. on Phys. Fitness and Sports; past chmn. bd. dirs. Am. Coun. on Exercise; mem. adv. bd. Fitness Cert. program U. Calif., LA; nat. women's wellness expert and presenter. Appearances on Oprah, Today Show, CNN, MSNBC, Access Hollywood, Entertainment Tonight. Achievements include climbing 20,000 foot mountain in the Bolivian Andes, Mt. Rainier and Mt Kilimanjaro. Avocations: running, weight training, kayaking, photography, rock climbing. Office: Am Media 21100 Erwin St Woodland Hills CA 91367-3712 Business E-Mail: bharris@weiderpub.com.

HARRIS, DALE RAY, lawyer, arbitrator, mediator; b. Crab Orchard, Ill., May 11, 1937; s. Ray B. and Aurelia M. (Davis) H.; m. Toni K. Shapkoff, June 26, 1960; children: Kristen Dee, Julie Diane. BA in Math., U. Colo., 1959; LLB, Harvard U., 1962. Bar: Colo. 1962, U.S. Dist. Ct. Colo. 1962, U.S. Ct. Appeals (10th cir.) 1962, U.S. Supreme Ct. 1981. Assoc. Davis, Graham & Stubbs, Denver, 1962-67, ptnr., 1967—2008, chmn. mgmt. com., 1982-85, sr. of counsel, 2008—. Spkr. instr. in field; civil litigation editl. adv. bd. Bradford Pub. Co., 2005—07. Mem. campaign cabinet Mile High United Way, 1986—87, chmn., atty. adv. com., 1988, sec., legal counsel, trustee, 1989—94, 1996—2001, mem. exec. com., 1989—2001, chmn. bd. trustees, 1996, 1997; trustee The Spaceship Earth Fund, 1986—89, Legal Aid Found. Colo., 1989—95, 2000—01; mem. devel. coun. U. Colo. Arts and Scis. dept., 1985—93; area chmn. law sch. fund Harvard U., 1978—81; bd. dirs. Colo. Jud. Inst., 1994—2003, vice chair, 1998; bd. dir. Colo. Lawyers Trust Account Found., 1996—2001; steering com. Youth-At-Work, 1994, School-To-Work, 1995; mem. jud. adv. coun. Colo. Supreme Ct., 2001—; bd. dirs. Rocky Mountain Arthritis Found., 2002—, Qualife Wellness Cmty., 2002—08, chmn. bd., 2009—; mem. cmty. leadership bd. Mile High Montessori Early Learning Ctr., 2006—. With reserves USAR, 1962—68. Recipient Williams award Rocky Mountain Arthritis Found., 1999. Fellow: Am. Coll. Trial Lawyers, Am. Bar Found. (Colo. state chmn. 1998—2005); mem.: ABA (antitrust and litigation sects.), Am. Arbitration Assn. (mem., comml. arbitration and mediation panels 2005—), Colo. Assn. Corp. Counsel (pres. 1973—74), Denver Bar Assn. (chmn. centennial com. 1990—91, bd. trustees 1992—95, pres. 1993—94, Merit award 1997), Colo. Bar Assn. (coun. corp. banking and bus. law sect. 1978—83, chmn. antitrust com. 1980—84, bd. govs. 1991—95, chmn. family violence task force 1996—2000, pres.-elect, co-chair multi-disciplinary practice task force 1999—2000, bd. govs. 1999—2002, pres. 2000—01, chmn. transitions com. 2001—03, chmn. profl. reform initiative task force 2001—, chmn. transitions com. 2006—), Colo. Bar Found. (award of merit 2002), Rotary (Denver), Colo. Forum, The Two Percent Club (exec. com. 1994—2007), Denver Law Club (pres. 1976—77, Lifetime Achievement award 1997), Citizens Against Amendment 12 Com. (exec. com. 1994), Phi Beta Kappa. Home: 2032 Bellaire St Denver CO 80207-3722 Office: Davis Graham & Stubbs 1550 17th St Ste 500 Denver CO 80202-1202 Home Phone: 303-377-8926; Office Phone: 303-892-9400. Business E-Mail: dale.harris@dgslaw.com.

HARRIS, DARRYL WAYNE, publishing executive; b. Emmett, Idaho, July 29, 1941; s. Reed Ingval and Evelyn Faye (Wengreen) H.; m. Christine Sorenson, Sept. 10, 1965; children: Charles Reed, Michael Wayne, Jason Darryl, Stephanie, Ryan Joseph. BA, Brigham Young U., 1966. Staff writer Deseret News, Salt Lake City, 1965, Post-Register, Idaho Falls, 1966-67; tech. editor Idaho Nuc. Corp., Idaho Falls, 1967-68; account exec. David W. Evans & Assocs. Advt., Salt Lake City, 1968-71; pres. Harris Pub., Inc., Idaho Falls, 1971—; pub. Potato Grower of Idaho mag., 1972—, SnoWest Mag., 1974—, Sugar Prodr. mag., 1974—, Blue Ribbon mag., 1987-90, Modstock mag., 1992—, SnowAction mag., 1987—2000, Western Guide to Snowmobiling, 1988—, Houseboat Mag., 1990—, Pontoon and Deck Boat Mag., 1995—, Mountain Turf mag., 2001—, Idaho Falls mag., 2001—, SnoWest Canada mag., 2001—, Today's Playground mag., 2001—, SkatePark Mag., 2001—, Sledheads Mag., 2001—, River Jet Mag., 2004—. Campaign mgr. George Hansen for Congress Com., 1974, 76; campaign chmn. Mel Richardson for Congress Com., 1986; 1st counselor to pres. Korean Mission, Ch. Jesus Christ of Latter-day Saints, Seoul, Korea, 1963, area pub. comm. dir., Ea. Idaho, 1976-86; pres. Korea Seoul Mission, 1997-2000; High Priest, LDS Ch., 1987-2002, Bishop BYU, Idaho 27th Ward, 2003—, high coun. Idaho Falls Ammon Stake, 1987-91, Ammon 8th Ward Bishopric, 1991-96; founder Blue Ribbon Coalition, 1987; v.p. Teton Peaks coun. Boy Scouts Am., 1987-92; publicity chmn. Upper Snake River Scout Encampment, 1988; founder, pres. Our Land Soc., 1989-92. Mem. Agr. Editors Assn., Internat. Snowmobile Industry Assn. (Best Overall Reporting journalism award 1979, 80), Western Publs. Assn., World Champion Cutter and Chariot Racing Assn. (historian 1966-80), Nat. Snowmobile Found. (founder 1988), Kappa Tau Alpha, Pres. Club (award 1978), Idaho Falls Kiwanis (Disting., pres. 1978). Office: Harris Pub Inc 360 B St Idaho Falls ID 83402

HARRIS, DAVID M., information technology executive; Grad. in Chem. Engring., Howard U., Washington; MS in Real Estate Devel. and Investment, NYU. Various mgmt. positions Pepsi-Cola, Ameritech; sr. dir. workplace resources advanced planning group Sun Microsystems, Inc., Santa Clara, Calif., 2000, sr. v.p. workplace resources, sr. v.p. global bus. svcs. Office: Sun Microsystems Inc 4150 Network Cir Santa Clara CA 95054 Office Phone: 650-960-1300.

HARRIS, DAVID THOMAS, immunology educator; b. Jonesboro, Ark, May 9, 1956; s. Marm Melton and Lucille Luretha (Buck) Harris; m. Francoise Jacqueline Besencon, June 24, 1989; children: Alexandre M., Stefanie L., Leticia M. BS in Biology, Math. and Psychology, Wake Forest U., 1978, MS, 1980, PhD in Microbiology and Immunology, 1982. Fellow Ludwig Inst. Cancer Rsch., Lausanne, Switzerland, 1982-85; rsch. asst. prof. U. NC, Chapel Hill, 1985-89; assoc. prof. U. Ariz., Tucson, 1989—2004, prof., 1996—. Cons. Teltech, Inc. Mpls., 1990—, Advanced Biosci. Resources, 1994-95; bd. sci. advisors Cryo-Cell Internat., 1992-95; bd. dir. Ageria, Inc., Tuscon; dir. Cord Blood Stem Cell Bank, 1992—; mem. Ariz. Cancer Ctr., Steele Meml. Children's Rsch. Ctr., Ariz. Arthritis Ctr. Program, sci. adv. bd. Cord Blood Registry, Inc., chief sci. div. Cord Blood Registry, Inc.; founder ImmuneRegen BioScis., Inc., 2002, Advanced Genetic Tools (Quregen, Inc.), 2004. Co-author chpts. to sci. books, articles to profls. jour.; reviewer sci. jour.; co-holder 9 scientific patents. Grantee numerous grants, 1988—. Mem. AAAS, Am. Assn. Immunologists, Reticuleondothelial Soc., Internat. Soc. Hematotherapy and Graft Engring., Internat. Soc. Devel. and Comparative Immunology, Scandanavian Soc. Immunology, Sigma Xi, Democrat. Church Of Christ. Avocations: tennis, hiking, jogging, skiing, travel. Office: Univ Ariz Dept Immunology POBox 245221 Tucson AZ 85724 Office Phone: 520-626-5127. Business E-Mail: davidh@U.Arizona.edu.

HARRIS, DAVID W., academic administrator; m. Linda Harris; two children. Grad., Ea. N.Mex. U., 1971. Trainee analyst Legis. Fin. Com., 1972; asst. fin. dir. State Hwy. Dept.; dir. property control divsn. Dept. Fin. and Adminstrn., sec. natural resources dept.; sec. fin. and adminstrn. N.Mex. Dept. Fin. and Adminstrn., 1995—2000; dep. chief of staff N.Mex State Govt., 2001—03; exec. dir. N.Mex Fin. Authority, 2003—04; exec. v.p. adminstrn. U. N.Mex., Albuquerque, 2004—, acting pres., 2006—07. Exec. officer State Bd. Fin.; mem. State Investment Coun., Pub. Sch. Capital Outlay Coun., N.Mex. Fin. Authority, N.Mex. Cmty. Assistance Coun. With USAF, Korea. Recipient N.Mex. Disting. Pub. Svc. award, 1997. Office: U New Mexico MSC05 3350 1 Univ of New Mexico Albuquerque NM 87131

HARRIS, DONALD J., economics educator; b. Jamaica; BA, London U., 1960; PhD, U. Calif., Berkeley, 1965. Asst. prof. econs. U. Ill., Urbana, 1965-67; assoc. prof. U. Wis., Madison, 1968-72; prof. Stanford (Calif.) U., 1972—. Econ. cons. UN, N.Y.C., 1966-67, Inter-Am. Devel. Bank, Washington, 1993-94; vis. fellow Cambridge (Eng.) U., 1966, 68, 77, 82, assoc. fellow Trinity Coll., 1982; disting. vis. prof. Yale U., New Haven, 1977-78; Fulbright scholar, Brazil, 1990-91, Mex., 1992. Author: Capital Accumulation and Income Distribution, 1978, Japanese ed., 1982, Spanish edit., 1984, Jamaica's Export Economy, 1997; mem. bd. editors Jour. Econ. Lit., 1979-84; contbr. articles to profl. jours. Ford Found. fellow, 1984-85. Mem. Am. Econ. Assn., Nat. Econ. Assn. Avocations: music, theater. Office: Stanford U Dept Econs Stanford CA 94305

HARRIS, DOUGLAS CLAY, retired newspaper executive; b. Owensboro, Ky., Oct. 9, 1939; s. Marvin Dudley and Elizabeth (Adelman) H. BS, Murray State U., 1961; MS, Ind. U., 1964, EdD, 1968; grad. advanced mgmt. program, Harvard U., 1987. Counselor, asst. to dean of students Ind. U., Bloomington, 1965-68; mgmt. appraisal specialist United Air Lines, Elk Grove Village, Ill., 1968-69; dir. manpower div. Computer Age Industries, Washington, 1969; area personnel dir. Peat Marwick Mitchell & Co., NYC, 1969-72; v.p. personnel Knight-Ridder, Inc., Miami, Fla., 1972-85, v.p., sec., 1986-98. Served to capt. U.S. Army, 1961-62. Republican. Home and Office: 218 Fairchild Dr Highlands Ranch CO 80126-4751 E-mail: drdoug.harris@comcast.net.

HARRIS, EDWARD DAY, JR., physician; b. Phila., July 7, 1937; children: Ned, Tom, Chandler. AB, Dartmouth Coll., 1958, grad. with honors, 1960; MD cum laude, Harvard U., 1962. Diplomate Am. Bd. Internal Medicine and Rheumatology (chmn. subsplty. bd. in rheumatology 1986-88). Intern Mass. Gen. Hosp., Boston, 1962-63, asst. resident, 1963-64, sr. resident, 1966-67, clin. research fellow arthritis unit, 1967-69; asst. prof. Harvard Med. Sch., Boston, 1970; from asst. prof. to prof. Dartmouth Med. Sch., Hanover, NH, 1970-83, Eugene W. Leonard prof., 1979-83, chief connective tissue disease sect., 1970-83; mem. staff Mary Hitchcock Meml. Hosp., 1970-83; chief med. service Middlesex Gen. U. Hosp., New Brunswick, NJ, 1983—; asst. prof. Harvard U. Med. Sch., Boston, 1970; prof., chmn. medicine U. Medicine and Dentistry N.J.-Rutgers U. Med. Sch., New Brunswick, 1983-88; Arthur L. Bloomfield prof. medicine Stanford U. Sch. Medicine, 1988-95, chmn. dept. medicine, 1988-95, George DeForest Barnett prof. medicine, 1988—2003, George DeForest Barnett prof. medicine emeritus, 2003—; acad. sec. to Stanford U., 2002—07. Chief med. svc. Stanford U. Hosp., 1988-95; dir. Ctr. for Musculoskeletal Diseases, Stanford, 1996-99, emeritus, 2003—; pres. med. staff, Stanford U. Hosp., 1997-99; med. dir. Internat. Med. Svc., 1997—2002. Master: ACP (gov. No. Calif. chpt. 2000—), Am. Coll. Rheumatism (numerous coms. 1967—, pres. 1985—86, Dist. Rheumatism award 2004); fellow: Royal Soc. Medicine; mem.: Alpha Omega Alpha (exec. sec. 1997—, editor The Pharos 1997—). Office: Alpha Omega Alpha 525 Middlefield Rd Ste 130 Menlo Park CA 94025 Office Phone: 650-320-9875. Business E-Mail: madera@stanford.edu.

HARRIS, EVA, molecular biology educator; b. NYC, Aug. 6, 1965; BA, Harvard U., 1987; PhD in Molecular and Cell Biology, U. Calif., Berkeley, 1993. Dir. applied molecular biology/appropriate technol. transfer program U. Calif., San Francisco, 1993—, asst. adj. prof., 1997-98, asst. prof. Sch. Pub. Health Berkeley, 1998—. John D. and Catherine T. MacArthur Found. fellow, 1997. Mem. AAAS, Am. Soc. Microbiology. Office: U Calif Sch Pub Health 239 Warren Hl Berkeley CA 94720-0001

HARRIS, FRED R., political scientist, educator, former United States Senator from Oklahoma; b. Walters, Okla., Nov. 13, 1930; s. Fred Byron and Alene (Person) Harris; m. LaDonna Crawford, Apr. 8, 1949 (div. 1981); children: Kathryn, Byron, Laura; m. Margaret S. Elliston, Sept. 5, 1982. BA, U. Okla., 1952, JD, 1954. Bar: Okla. 1954. Founder, sr. partner firm Harris, Newcombe, Redman & Doolin, Lawton, Okla., 1954-64; mem. Okla State Senate, 1956-64; US Senator from Okla., 1964-73; prof. polit. sci. U. N.Mex., Albuquerque, 1976—. Author: (book) Alarms and Hopes, 1969, Now is the Time, 1971, The State of the Cities: Report of the Commission on Cities in the 70's, 1972, Social Science and National Policy, The New Populism, 1973, Potomac Fever, 1977, America's Democracy, 1980, America's Democracy, 3d edit., 1985, Readings on the Body Politic, 1987, Deadlock or Decision, 1993, In Defense of Congress, 1994, Coyote Revenge, 1999, Easy Pickin's, 2001, Following the Harvest, 2004, The Baby Bust, 2006, Does People Do It?: A Memoir, 2008; co-author: America's Legislative Processes, 1983, Understanding American Government, 1988, Quiet Riots, 1988, America's Government, 1990, Locked in the Poor House, 1998. Mem. Nat. Adv. Commn. Civil Disorders, 1967—68; chmn. Dem. Nat. Com., 1969—70. Mem.: Order of Coif, Phi Beta Kappa. Office: U New Mexico Dept Polit Sci Albuquerque NM 87131-0001 Business E-Mail: fharris@unm.edu.

HARRIS, HOWARD JEFFREY, marketing executive; b. Denver, June 9, 1949; s. Gerald Victor and Leona Lee (Tepper) H.; m. Michele Whealen, Feb. 6, 1975; children: Kimberly, Valerie. BFA with honors, Kansas City Art Inst., 1973; M of Indsl. Design with honors, Pratt Inst., 1975; postgrad., Rochester Inst. Tech., 1977; cert. mktg. exec., U. Utah, 1987. Indsl. designer Kivett & Myers, Architects, 1970-71, United Rsch. Corp., Denver, 1971-72; indsl. designer, asst. to v.p., pres. JFN Assocs., NYC, 1972-73; dir. facility planning Abt & Assocs., Cambridge, Mass., 1973-74; pres., COO Eagle XM, Denver, 1974—; pres. EagleXm LLC, Denver, 2005—. Vol., past chmn. bd. dirs. Stepping Stones. Recipient Small Bus. Person of Yr. award for State of Colo., SBA, 1997. Mem. Indsl. Designers Soc. Am., Graphic Arts Tech. Found., Direct Mktg. Assn., Cable TV Adminstrn. and Mktg. Assn., Mail Advt. Assn., Am. Avt. Fedn., Nat. Assn. Print Leadership, Piams Trade Assn. (sec., treas.). Democrat. Jewish. Office: 5105 E 41st Ave Denver CO 80216-4420 Office Phone: 303-320-5411. Business E-Mail: hharris@eaglexm.com.

HARRIS, JACK F., police chief; b. 1950; m. Connie Harris. BA in Polit. Sci., Ariz. State U., 1977, grad. cert. pub. mgr. program; M in human resources, Ottawa U., 2000; grad., FBI Nat. Acad. Patrol officer Phoenix Police Dept., 1972, spl. investigations, undercover, vice and narcotics, 1981—84, sgt. patrol divsn., 1984—88, sgt. tng. acad. and street crimes, 1985—88, lt. patrol and motorcycle divsn., 1988—89, unit comdr. spl. assignments unit (SWAT team), 1989—95, city mgr. liaison, 1996—97, comdr. Desert Horizon Police Precinct, 1997—99, comdr. profl. standards divsn. (internal affairs), 1999—2000, asst. police chief North Divsn., 2000—04, interim police chief, 2004, chief of police, 2004—. Achievements include development of the first community policing station in the Palomino area of northeast Phoenix. Office: 620 W Washington St Phoenix AZ 85003 Office Phone: 602-262-7626. Business E-Mail: jack.harris@phoenix.gov.

HARRIS, JAY TERRENCE, communications educator; b. Washington, Dec. 3, 1948; s. Richard James and Margaret Estelle (Burr) H.; m. Eliza Melinda Dowell, June 14, 1969 (div.); 1 child, Taifa Akida; m. Anna Christine Harris, Oct. 25, 1980; children: Jamarah Kai, Shala Marie. BA, Lincoln U., 1970, LHD (hon.), 1988. Reporter Wilmington (Del.) News-Jour., 1970-73, spl. project editor, 1974-75; instr. journalism and urban affairs Medill Sch. Journalism, Northwestern U., Evanston, Ill., 1973-75, asst. prof., 1975-82, asst. dean, 1977-82; nat. corr. Gannett News Service, Washington, 1982-84, columnist Gannet newspapers and USA Today, 1984-85; exec. editor Phila. Daily News, 1985—88; v.p. Phila. Newspapers, Inc., 1987—94; chmn., pub. San Jose Mercury News, 1995—2001; Annenberg prof. journalism & comm. Annenberg Sch. for Comm., USC, 2001—. Asst. dir. Frank E. Gannett Urban Journalism Ctr., Northwestern U., 1977-82; founder, exec. dir. Consortium for Advancement of Minorities in Journalism Edn., Evanston, 1978-81; dir. Dow Jones Newspaper Fund, Princeton, N.J., 1980—; bd. visitors John S. Knight Profl. Journalism Fellowships, Palo Alto, Calif., 1982—; head Minorities and Communication Div. Assn. for Edn. in Journalism, 1982-83; journalist in residence Notre Dame, 2002-03; bd. mem. Deep River Assocs., 2002—. Author: (annual census) Minority Employment in Daily Newspapers, 1978-82; co-author series articles on drug trafficking in Wilmington, 1972 (Pub. Service awards AP Mng. Editors Assn. 1972, Greater Phila. chpt. Sigma Delta Chi 1973) Past mem. bd. advisors Sch. Journalism U. Mo. Frank E. Gannett Urban Journalism fellow, 1973-74; recipient Pub. Service award Greater Phila. chpt. Sigma Delta Chi, 1973; Pub. Service award AP Mng. Editors Assn., 1972; Spl. Citation Nat. Urban Coalition, 1979; Par Excellence Disting. Service in Journalism award Operation PUSH, 1984; Drum Maj. for Justice award Southern Christian Leadership Conf., 1985; Robert C. Maynard Fellow, 2001—. Mem. Am. Soc. Newspaper Editors (chmn. readership and rsch. com.), Women in Communication, Nat. Assn. Black Journalists, Omega Psi Phi Office: San Jose Mercury News 750 Ridder Park Dr San Jose CA 95190-0001

HARRIS, JEREMY, former mayor; b. Wilmington, Del., Dec. 7, 1950; s. Ann Harris; m. Ramona Sachiko Akui. BA, BS in Biology, U. Hawaii, 1972; MS in Population and Environ. Biology, U. Calif., Irvine, 1973. Lectr. oceanography, biology Kauai C.C.; marine advisor Sea Grant Program, U. Hawaii; del. Hawaii Constl. Conv., 1978; chmn. Kauai County Council, 1979—81; exec. asst. to mayor City and County of Honolulu, 1984—86, dep. mng. dir. of Honolulu, 1986-94, mng. dir., 1986—94, acting mayor, 1994, mayor, 1994—2004. Founder, chair Mayors' Asia-Pacific Environ. Summit, 1999; established Pacific Islands Environmental Symposium, China-US Conf. of Mayors and Bus. Leaders, Asia-Pacific Urban Tech. Inst. Am.-Nat. chair Japan-Am. Conf. of Mayors and C. of C. Presidents, 1996—. Recipient Keystone award, Am. Architectural Found., 2005. Mem.: Am. Planning Assn. (Disting. Leadership award 2002), Internat. Downtown Assn. (Merit award), Am. Soc. Pub. Adminstrn. (Pub. Adminstr. of Yr. 1993, 1994), Am. Inst. Archs. (hon.).

HARRIS, JOHN, state legislator; b. Glennallen, Alaska, Oct. 15, 1957; m. Nicole Harris; 1 child, John Paul. Attended, Spartan Sch. Aeronautics, Tulsa, Okla. City councilman, Valdez, Alaska, 90-98, mayor, 92-96; Alaska State Representative, District 35, 1999-2002, co-chmn, Community & Regional Affairs Committee, 99, member, Labor & Commerce, Resources, Admin Regulation Rev Committees & Special Committees on Oil & Gas & Fisheries, 99, Alaska House Representative; Alaska State Representative, District 12, 2003-, Speaker of House, 2005-08, Alaska House Representative. Owner, Valdez Indust Supply, currently; advisor board, Prince William Sound Community Col, currently. Bd. mem. Horizons Unlimited, Resource of Alaska, United Way; mem. Valdez C. of C., Delta C. of C., Glennallen C. of C., St. Frances Xavier Cath. Ch. Republican. Mailing: State Capitol Rm 208 Juneau AK 99801-1182 Office Phone: 907-465-4859, 907-465-3719. Fax: 907-465-3799; Office Fax: 907-465-3258. Business E-Mail: Rep_John_Coghill@legis.state.ak.us.*

HARRIS, JOHN J., food products executive; b. 1951; married; 3 children. BA, Calif. State U.; MBA, U. Calif., 1974. Mktg. mgmt. trainee Carnation Co., LA, 1974, v.p., gen. mgr. products divsn., 1987; v.p., gen. mgr. Friskies PetCare, 1991; sr. v.p. Nestlé S.A., Switzerland, 1997—99, pres. Friskies PetCare Co., 1999—2001, chief worldwide integration officer, 2001—02, CEO Nestlé Purina PetCare Europe, 2002—05, CEO Nestlé Purina PetCare Europe, Asia, Oceania, Africa, 2005—07, exec. v.p., 2007—, chmn. CEO Nestlé Waters, 2007—. Chmn. bd. dirs. Pet Food Inst., 1993. Named to Power 150, Ebony mag., 2008. Office: Nestle USA Inc 800 North Brand Blvd Glendale CA 91203

HARRIS, KAMALA D., prosecutor; b. Oakland, Calif., 1964; BA, Howard U., Washington, DC; JD, U. Calif. Bar: 1990. Dep. dist. atty. Office Dist. Atty., Alameda County, Calif., 1990—98, mng. atty. career criminal unit San Francisco, 1998—2000, head city atty.'s divsn. on families and children, 2000—04, dist. atty., 2004—. Co-chair Lawyers' Com. Civil Rights; pres. bd. dirs. Partners Ending Domestic Abuse; founder mentoring program San Francisco Mus. Modern Art; founder Coalition to End Exploitation of Kids. Recipient award, Crime Victims United, County Counsel Assn. Calif., Thurgood Marshall award, Nat. Black Prosecutors Assn., 2005; named Child Advocate of Yr., San Francisco Child Abuse Prevention Coun., 2004; named one of Top 20 Young Lawyers Calif., Daily Journal, 1998; named to Power 150, Ebony mag., 2008. Office: San Francisco Dist Attys Office 850 Bryant St Rm 322 San Francisco CA 94103

HARRIS, LARRY, professional basketball coach; s. Del Harris; children: Zachary, Janaya. Grad. in Math., Eastern N.Mex. U. Assoc. Electronic Data Systems; actuary Wyatt Corp., Dallas; scout/video coord. Milw. Bucks, 1988—96, dir. scouting, 1996—98, dir. player pers., 1998—2001, asst. gen. mgr., 2001—03, gen. mgr., 2003—08; asst. coach Golden State Warriors, 2008—. Office: Golden State Warriors 1011 Broadway Oakland CA 94607

HARRIS, LESLIE, think-tank executive, lawyer; BA, U. NC, Chapel Hill; JD cum laude, Georgetown U. Atty. pvt. practice, Washington; chief legis. counsel Washington nat. office ACLU; dir. pub. policy People for the Am. Way; founder, pres. Leslie Harris & Assocs.; pres., CEO Ctr. for Democracy & Tech., Washington. Spkr. in field. Contbr. articles to profl. jours. Mem.: ABA, Washington Women's Forum. Office: Ctr for Democracy & Tech 1634 I St NW #1100 Washington DC 20006 also: 55 New Montgomery St #513 San Francisco CA 94105 Office Phone: 202-637-9800. Office Fax: 202-637-0968.

HARRIS, MARK O., state legislator; b. Omaha, Nov. 26, 1950; m. Michele Harris. BS, U. Albuquerque, 1975. Mem. Wyo. Ho. Reps., Cheyenne, 1989-92, Wyo. Senate, Dist. 14, Cheyenne, 1992—; mem. appropriations com. Wyo. Senate, Cheyenne, mem. travel, recreation, wildlife, and cultural com., minority caucus chair, 1995-96. With USNR, 1971-73. Mem. U.S. Steelworkers Am., Nat. Eagle Scout Assn., N.Am. Hunting Club. Democrat. also: Wyo Senate State Capitol Cheyenne WY 82002-0001 Home: PO Box 296 Saint Stephens WY 82524-0296 E-mail: mharris@senate.wyoming.com.

HARRIS, MARK W., former mayor, lawyer; b. Evanston, Wyo., May 17, 1957; m. Diane Harris; children: Bryan, Cameron. BS, U. Wyo., 1979, JD, 1982. Bar: Wyo. 1982. Atty. Harris Law Firm PC, Evanston, Wyo.; city atty. Evanston, Wyo., 1983—87; spl. asst. atty. gen. Wyo.; ct. commr. and magistrate Uinta County Circuit Ct., Wyo., Third Jud. Dist. Ct., Wyo.; mayor City of Evanston, 2003—07. Adj. instr. We. Wyo. CC, Evanston. Past chmn. Evanston Urban Renewal Agency; past pres. Uinta Med. Found. Bd. Mem.: Wyo. State Bar (commr. 1994—97, sec., treas. 1997—2002, pres. 2004). Office: Harris Law Firm 927 Main St Evanston WY 82930-3440 Office Phone: 307-789-3210. Office Fax: 307-789-0410. E-mail: mayor@allwest.net.

HARRIS, PHILIP ROBERT, management and space psychologist; b. Bklyn., Jan. 22, 1926; s. Gordon Roger and Esther Elizabeth (Delahanty) H.; m. Dorothy Lipp, July 3, 1965 (dec. 1997); m. Janet Belport, Feb. 14, 2001. BBA, St. John's U., 1949; MS in Psychology, Fordham U., 1952, PhD, 1956; spl. student, NYU, 1948-49, Syracuse U., 1961. Lic. psychologist U. of State of N.Y., 1959, N.Y. Dir. guidance St. Francis Prep. Sch., NYC, 1952-56; dir. student personnel, v.p. St. Francis Coll., NYC, 1956-63; exec. dir. Assn. Human Emergency-Thomas Murray Tng. Program, 1964-66; vis. prof. Pa. State U., 1965-66; vis. prof., cons. Temple U.; sr. assoc. Leadership Resources Inc., 1966-69; v.p. Copley Internat. Corp., La Jolla, Calif., 1970-71; pres. Mgmt. and Orgn. Devel. Inc. (now Harris Internat. Ltd.), La Jolla, 1971—; edn. dir. Air/Space Am., 1988; sr. scientist Netrologic, Inc., La Jolla, Calif., 1990-93; prof. Calif. Sch. Internat. Mgmt., 2005—. Rsch. assoc. Calif. Space Inst., U. Calif., San Diego, 1984-90; adj. prof. Pepperdine U., U. No. Colo., Calif. Sch. Internat. Mgmt., 2005-07; acad. adv. Command Coll., Commn. on Peace Officers Stds. and Tng. State of Calif., Dept. Justice, 1986-94; past cons. Westinghouse, N.V. Philips, I.B.M., Computer Sci. Corp. Control Data, govt. agys.; chmn. bd. dirs. United Socs. in Space, Inc., 1993-97 Author, 48 vols. including: Effective Management of Change, 1976, Improving Management Communication Skills, 1978, Managing Cultural Differences, 1979, 7th edit., 2007, New Worlds, New Ways, New Management, 1983, Managing Cultural Synergy, 1982, Management in Transition, 1985, Living and Working in Space, 1992, 2d edit., 1996, High Performance Leadership, 2d edit., 1994, New Work Culture, 1998, Launch Out, 2003; co-author: Transcultural Leadership, 1993, Developing Global Organizations, 1993, 2d edit., 2001, Multicultural Management 2000, 1998, Multicultural Law Enforcement, 1995, 4th edit., 2007, Space Enterprise Living and Working Offworld in The 21st Century, 2008, Toward Human Emergence, 2008, Managing the Knowledge Culture, 2005; editor: Innovations in Global Consultation, 1980, Global Strategies in Human Resource Development, 1983; author (series) New Work Culture, 3 vols., 1994-98; co-editor Manging Cultural Differences Series Butterworth-Heinemann/Elsevier Sci., 1979-2007; mem. editl. bd. European Bus. Rev., 1996-2006; founding editor emeritus Space Governance Jour., 1993-98; contbr. 260 articles to profl. jours. V.p. Bklyn. Downtown Renewal Effort, 1957-59. Recipient Literati Club award for excellence, 2005; named to Gulf Pub. Author Hall of Fame, 1999; Fulbright prof. to India U.S. State Dept., 1962; NASA faculty fellow, 1984. Fellow AIAA (assoc.); mem. ASTD (Torch award 1975), Aviation Space Writers Assn. (journalism awards 1986, 88, 89, 93), World Bar Assn. (Space Humanitarian award1992), Nat. Space Soc., United Socs. in Space (dir. emeritus), Soc. for Human Performance in Extreme Environments, La Jolla Beach and Tennis Club. Independent. Home and Office: 2702 Costebelle Dr La Jolla CA 92037-3524 E-mail: philharris@aol.com.

HARRIS, RICHARD A., film editor; Works include: (films) Downhill Racer, 1969, Dusty and Sweets McGee, 1971, The Christian Licorice Store, 1971, The Candidate, 1972, Chandler, 1972, Catch My Soul, 1974, Smile, 1975, The Bad News Bears, 1976, Semi-Tough, 1977, The Bad News Bears Go To Japan, 1978, An Almost Perfect Affair, 1979, The Island, 1980, The Toy, 1982, The Survivors, 1983, Fletch, 1985, Tiger Town, 1985, The Golden Child, 1986, Wildcats, 1986, The Couch Trip, 1988, Fletch Lives, 1989, L.A. Story, 1991, The Bodyguard, 1992, Terminator 2: Judgement Day, 1991 (Acad. award nomination, Emmy nomination), True Lies, 1994 (Emmy nomination); (TV films) A Mother's Courage: The Mary Thomas Story, 1990, My Boyfriend's Back, 1990, Indictment: The McMartin Trial (Emmy award, Outstanding Individual Achievement in Editing for a Mini Series of a Spl. 1995, ADB Cable ACF award 1995); editor (films) Last Action Hero, 1993, Titanic, 1997. Address: 3001 Old Calzada Rd Santa Ynez CA 93460-9527

HARRIS, RICHARD EUGENE VASSAU, lawyer; b. Detroit, Mar. 16, 1945; s. Joseph and Helen Harris; m. Milagros A. Brito; children: Catherine, Byron. AB, Albion Coll., 1967; JD, Harvard U., 1970; postdoctoral, Inst. Advanced Legal Studies, London, 1970-71. Bar: Calif. 1972. Assoc. Orrick, Herrington, Rowley & Sutcliffe, San Francisco, 1972-77; ptnr. Orrick, Herrington & Sutcliffe, San Francisco, 1978-98; pvt. practice Richard E. V. Harris Law Office, Oakland, Calif., 1998—. Faculty Calif. Tax Policy Conf., 1987, 95; spkr. univ., govtl. and profl. groups. Knox fellow, Harvard U., 1970—71. Mem.: ABA (litig. sect. corp. counsel com., subcom. chmn. 1980—82, antitrust law sect. state action com. 1981—, vice chmn. 1982—83, vice chmn. govt. liability com. 1982—84, co-chmn. Nat. Insts. Antitrust Liability 1983, Boulder task force 1983—84, coun. urban state and local govt. sect. 1983—88, litig. sect. corp. counsel com., subcom. chmn. 1983—, co-chmn. Nat. Insts. Antitrust Liability 1985, bus. law sect., SEC investigation atty.-client privilege waiver task f 1988, profl. conduct com., tax sect., state and local taxes com. 1989—, tax litig. com. 1992—, conflicts of interest task force 1993—96, internat. com. 1994—, corp. counsel com. 1995—, conflicts of interest com. 1996—2000, ad hoc com. on ethics 2000, com. profl. conduct 2001—, Ctr. Profl. Responsibility, ABA Ethics 2000 adv. group), Bar Assn. San Francisco (ethics com. 1980—, state bar conf. del. 2003), Am. Law Inst. (cons. restatements of law unfair competition 1991—94, governing lawyers com. 1991—2000, torts com. 1993—, agy. com. 1996—2006, trusts com. 1996—). E-mail: richardevh@aol.com.

HARRIS, ROBERT ADRON, pharmacologist; b. El Paso, Tex., Nov. 23, 1945; s. James Buford and Maurine Harris; m. Diane Snell. BS in Chemistry, N.Mex. State U., 1967; MS in Chemistry, U. Ariz., 1970; PhD in Pharmacology, U. N.C., 1973. Postdoctoral fellow U. Calif., San Francisco, 1973-76; asst. prof. pharmacology Sch. Medicine U. Mo., Columbia, 1976-81, assoc. prof. pharmacology, 1981-83; rsch. pharmacologist Truman Meml. VA Hosp., Columbia, 1979-83; assoc. prof. pharmacology Sch. Medicine U. Colo., Denver, 1983-88, prof. pharmacology, 1988—, acting chmn. dept. pharmacology, 1989-90; assoc. rsch. career scientist VA Med. Ctr., Denver, 1983-88, rsch. career scientist, 1988—; faculty mem. Inst. Behavioral Genetics U. Colo., Boulder, 1992—. Sci. dir. VA Alcohol Rsch. Ctr., Denver, 1992—. Co-editor Internat. Rev. Neurobiology, 1992—; contbr. over 180 articles to sci. jours. Grantee VA Med. Ctr., 1979—, NIH, 1994—; recipient Merit award NIH, 1989—. Mem. AAAS, Am. Soc. Pharmacology and Exptl. Therapeutics, Soc. for Neurosci., Rsch. Soc. for Alcoholism (pres. 1993-95). Office: U Colo Health Scis Ctr 4200 E 9th Ave # 236 Denver CO 80220-3706

HARRIS, ROBERT M., college president; BA in Anthropology, U. Calif., Santa Barbara, 1970; MA with honors, U. Kans., 1973, PhD with honors, 1975. Life cert. cmty. coll. instr. spl. edn., counselor, supr., psychology instr., chief adminstr. Dir. Kansas state demographic studies U. Kans. Med. Ctr., United Way of Wyandotte County, 1973-75; sr. clin. rehab. psychologist Casa Colina Hosp. for Rehab. Medicine, Pomona, Calif., 1976, program mgr., 1976-77; dist. specialist programs for students devel. disabilities Chaffey C.C., Alta Loma, Calif., 1977-79, dist. dir. spl. edn., 1981, acting assoc. dean student svcs., 1981, acting supt., pres., 1985, v.p., bus. and student svcs., 1985-86, v.p. student svcs., 1981-87; pres. Sacramento City Coll., 1987—. Cons. and presenter in field. Contbr. articles to profl. publs. Bd. dirs. United Way, Sacramento, bd. chair 1998—. Named Affirmative Action Officer of Yr., 1980-81; doctoral fellow U. Kans., 1974-75; recipient various grants. Mem. Assn. of Calif. C.C. Adminstrs., Calif. C.C. Chief Student Svcs. Adminstrs. Assn. (v.p. southern sect.), Nat. Assn. of Student Pers. Adminstrs., Am. Psychol. Assn. (divsn. 22 rehab. psychology), Calif. Assn. of Post-Secondary Educators for the Disabled, Easter Seal Soc. of Superior Calif. (bd. dirs.). Office: Sacramento City Coll 3835 Freeport Blvd Sacramento CA 95822-1318

HARRIS, ROBERT NORMAN, advertising executive, educator; b. St. Paul, Feb. 11, 1920; s. Nathan and Esther (Roberts) H.; m. Paula Nidorf, May 2, 1992; children: Claudia, Robert Norman, Randolph B. BA, U. Minn., 1940. A founder Toni Co., div. Gillette Co., 1940-55; exec. v.p. Lee King & Ptnrs., Chgo., 1955-60, Allen B. Wrisley Co., Chgo., 1960-62, North Advt., Chgo., 1962-72; pres. Robert Piguet, Ltd., Chgo., 1972-73, Westbrook/Harris, Inc., Chgo., 1973-77; exec. v.p., gen. mgr. Creamer Inc., Chgo., 1977-81; pres. The Harris Creative Group, Inc., 1981—; prof. advt. and mass communications San Jose State U. (Calif.), 1983-92. Bd. dirs. KTEH Pub. Broadcasting Sys. Found., San Jose, 1987-99, CHM Villages Golf and Country Club CATV Sys., 1995-99. Mem. NATAS, Am. Mktg. Assn., Am. Advt. Fedn., Am. Assn. Advt. Agys., Sons in Retirement (bd. dirs. 1986-90). Office Phone: 310-474-0302. Personal E-mail: zugmir11@aol.com.

HARRIS, ROBERT W., lawyer; b. Hindsdale, Ill., Feb. 5, 1948; BA, U. Kans., 1970; JD, U. Denver, 1973. Bar: Colo. 1973. Formerly ptnr. Hall & Evans, Denver; pres., sr. ptnr. Harris, Karstaedt, Jamison & Powers, P.C., Englewood, Colo., 1995—. Mem. ABA. Office: Harris Karstaedt Jamison Powers Pc 188 Inverness Dr W Ste 300 Englewood CO 80112-5205

HARRIS, T. GEORGE, editor; b. Hillsdale, Ky., Oct. 4, 1924; s. Garland and Luna (Byrum) Harris; m. Sheila Hawkins, Oct. 31, 1952 (dec. Jan. 1977); children: Amos, Anne, Crane, Gardiner; m. Ann Rockefeller Roberts, Mar. 3, 1979 (div. Apr. 1993); children: Clare, Joseph, Mary Louise, Rachel Pierson; m. Jeannie Pinkerton, Sept. 12, 1998; 1 child, Arthur Joseph Clancy. Student, U. Ky., 1946; BA, Yale U., 1949. Reporter Clarksville (Tenn.) Leaf-Chronicle, 1942; corr. Time-Life, Dallas, Atlanta and Washington, 1949—55; Chgo. bur. chief Time-Life-Fortune, 1955-58, San Francisco bur. chief, 1960-62; sr. editor Look mag., 1962-68; editor in chief Psychology Today mag., 1969-76, 88-90, US, 1977; founding editor Am. Health mag., Behavior Today, AH Fitness Bull., Spirituality & Health, 1980-90; exec. editor Harvard Bus. Rev., Boston, 1992-93; cons. Beliefnet.com, 1993—, Procter & Gamble Creative Svcs. Group, 1993—; editor UCSD-Connect Hi-tech. Weekly Online, 2000—03. Sci. adv. ABC's 20/20 Program, Inst. Advancement of Health. Editor: WGBH TV Bodywatch on PBS; cons. editor Sci. & Spirit, Next, Runner, Somatics, Aware, Industry Week, Psychologia Contemporanea, Japans Man the Mystery, Modern Maturity, Psychologie Heute mags., Addison-Wesley Pub. Co., Abby Press of Benedictine Order, Age Wave, editor-in-residence UCSD Connect, columnist, cons. Beliefnet.com. Bd. dirs. Am. Health Found., Ch. Soc. for Coll. Work, Nat. Vol. Ctrs., Rockefeller Bros. Fund, Go Code Corp.; med. adv. com. YMCA; regent Cathedral of St. John the Divine, NYC. Staff sgt. US Army, WWII. Recipient Bronze Star for Heroism, Commissioned Battle Field for leadership under fire at Bostogne Belgium; Hall of Fame, U. Ky., 2008. Mem.: Time-Life Alumni, Century Assn., Yale Club N.Y.C., UCSD Faculty Club, La Jolla Beach and Tennis Club, Phi Beta Kappa. Episcopalian. Home and Office: 8115 Paseo Del Ocaso La Jolla CA 92037-3140 Office Phone: 858-459-5694. Office Fax: 858-459-0838. Personal E-mail: tgeorgeh@aol.com.

HARRIS, WALTER EDGAR, chemistry professor; b. Wetaskiwin, Alta., Can., June 9, 1915; s. William Ernest and Emma Moisie (Humbke) H.; m. Phyllis Pangburn, June 14, 1942; children: Margaret Anne, William Edgar. BS, U. Alta., 1938, MS, 1939; PhD, U. Minn., 1944; DSc (hon.), U. Waterloo, 1987, U. Alta., 1991. Research fellow U. Minn., 1943-46; prof. analytical chemistry U. Alta., Edmonton, 1946-80, chmn. dept. chemistry, 1974-79, chmn. Pres.'s Adv. Com. on Campus Revs., 1980-90. Author: (with H.W. Habgood) Programmed Temperature Gas Chromatography, 1965, (with B. Kratchovil) Chemical Separations and Measurements, 1974, Teaching Introductory Analytical Chemistry, 1974, An Introduction to Chemical Analysis, 1981, Risk Assessment, 1997, (with H.A. Laitinen) Chemical Analysis, 1975; contbr. numerous articles to profl. jours. Decorated Order of Can.; recipient Outstanding Achievement award U. Minn., 1973; Govt. Alta. Achievement award, 1974, Honor award U. Alta. Alumni, 2003. Fellow AAAS, Royal Soc. Can., Chem. Inst. Can. (hon., Fisher Sci. Lecture award 1969, Chem. Edn. award 1975, hon. fellow, 2001); mem. Am. Chem. Soc., Sigma Xi. Home: Ste 515 11148-84 Ave Edmonton AB Canada T6G 0V8 Office: U Alta Dept Chem Edmonton AB Canada T6G 2G2 Home Phone: 780-433-8220; Office Phone: 780-492-3252. Business E-Mail: Walter.Harris@ualberta.ca.

HARRISON, JOHN CONWAY, retired state supreme court justice; b. Grand Rapids, Minn., Apr. 28, 1913; s. Francis Randall and Ethlyn (Conway) H.; m. Ethel M. Strict; children: Nina Lyn, Robert Charles, Molly M., Frank R., Virginia Lee. LLD, George Washington U., 1940. Bar: Mont. 1947, U.S. Dist. Ct. 1947. County atty. Lewis and Clark County, Helena, Mont., 1934-60; justice Mont. Supreme Ct., Helena, 1961-98, ret., 1998. Pres. Mont. TB Assn., Helena, 1951-54, Am. Lung Assn., N.Y.C., 1972-73, Mont. coun. Boy Scouts Am., Great Falls, Mont., 1976-78. Col. U.S. Army Mem. ABA, Mont. Bar Assn., Kiwanis (pres. 1953), Sigma Chi. Home: 215 S Cooke St Helena MT 59601-5143 Office Phone: 404-442-5833.

HARRISON, MARK I., lawyer; b. Pitts., Oct. 17, 1934; s. Coleman and Myrtle (Seidenman) H.; m. Ellen R. Gier, June 15, 1958; children: Lisa, Jill. AB, Antioch Coll., Yellow Springs, Ohio, 1957; LLB, Harvard U., Cambridge, Mass., 1960. Bar: Ariz. 1961, Colo. 1991. Law clk. to justices Ariz. Supreme Ct., 1960-61; ptnr. Harrison, Harper, Christian & Dichter, Phoenix, 1966-93, Bryan Cave, LLP, Phoenix, 1993—2003, Osborn Maledon, P.A., Phoenix, 2004—. Adj. prof. U. Ariz. Coll. Law, 1995-97, Ariz. State Coll. Law, 2001—; nat. bd. visitors, 1996—; judge pro tem Ariz. Ct. Appeals, Maricopa County Superior Ct. Co-author: Arizona Appellate Practice, 1966; editl. bd. ABA/BNA Lawyers Manual on Profl. Conduct, 1983-86; contbr. articles to profl. jours. Chmn. Phoenix City bond Adv. Commn., 1976—79; pres. Valley Commerce Assn., 1978, Ariz. Friends of Talking Books, Inc., 2000—01; vice chmn. Maricopa County Dem. Cen. Com., 1967—68, Ariz. Dem. Com, 1969—70, legal counsel, 1970—72; del. Dem. Nat. Conv., 1968; bd. dir. Careers for Youth, 1963—67, pres., 1966—67; bd. dir. Planned Parenthood of Cen. and No. Ariz., 1992—98, pres., 1995; bd. dir. Ariz. Policy Forum, 2000—03. Recipient Peggy Goldwater award, Planned Parenthood, 2003, Planned Parenthood of Ctrl. and No. Ariz., 2003, Good Guys award, Ariz. Women's Polit. Caucus, 2004, Learned Hand Cmty. Svc. award, Am. Jewish Com., 2005, Disting. Hon. Alumni award, U. Ariz., Presdl. Commendation, Ariz. Attys. Criminal Justice, 2008. Fellow: Am. Acad. Appellate Lawyers (pres. 1993—94), Am. Bar Found.; mem.: ABA (standing com. profl. discipline 1976—84, chmn. 1982—84, chmn. com. pub. understanding law 1984—87, chmn. coord. com. on professionalism 1987—89, com. on women in the profession, 1996-98, ethics com. 1999—2002, commn. Brown v. Bd. of Edn. 2003—04, chmn. joint com. Code of Judicial Conduct 2003—07, Michael Franck Profl. Responsibility award 1996), Justice At Stake (bd. mem. 2008—), Justice for All (founding mem. 2005, pres. 2005—), Lawyers Com. for Civil Rights Under Law (bd. dirs.), Law Coll. Assn. U. Ariz. (bd. dir. 1999—2004, pres. 2002—03), Am. Law Inst. (lawyers com. for human rights nat. coun. 1995—), Harvard Law Sch. Assn. (nat. exec. coun. 1980—84), Ariz. Civil Liberties Union, Am. Judicature Soc. (exec. com. 1983—86, bd. dir. 1983—87), Western States Bar Conf. (pres. 1978—79), Nat. Conf. Bar Pres. (pres. 1976—77), Am. Inns of Ct. (master, pres. Sandra Day O'Connor chpt. 1993—94), Ariz. Bar Found. (pres. 1991, Walter E. Craig Disting. Svc. award 2002), State Bar Ariz. (bd. govs. 1971—77, pres. 1975—76), Am. Bd. Trial Advocates, Maricopa County Bar Assn. (pres. 1970), Assn. Profl. Responsibility Lawyers (pres. 1992—93). Office: Osborn Maledon PA 2929 N Central Ave Ste 2100 Phoenix AZ 85012 Office Phone: 602-640-9324. Personal E-mail: ellenmark1@cox.net. Business E-Mail: mharrison@omlaw.com.

HARRISON, NEDRA JOYCE, surgeon; b. Buffalo, Apr. 16, 1951; d. Herman Lloyde and Gertrude (Newsom) H. BS, Rosary Hill Coll., 1973; MD, SUNY, Buffalo, 1977. Diplomate Am. Bd. Surgery. Resident in surgery Millard Fillmore Hosps., Buffalo, 1977-82, mem. active attending staff in gen. surgery, 1983—2000; practice medicine specializing in gen. surgery Buffalo, 1982—2000; courtesy staff Scottsdale (Ariz.) Healthcare, 2000—. Cons. staff Bry-Lyn Hosp., 1986-89; provisional staff in gen. surgery St. Joseph Intercommunity Hosp., 1986-87, active staff, 1995-2000; courtesy staff Scottsdale (Ariz.) Healthcare, Shea, Ariz., 2001—, Osborn, Ariz., 2001— Chmn. United Thank Offering, Episcopal Ch., Buffalo, 1982; bd. dirs. Niagara Luth. Home, 1987-2000; mem. alumni bd. dirs. SUNY at Buffalo Sch. Medicine, 1986-92. Recipient Best Rsch. Paper in Gen. Surgery award Millard Fillmore Hosps., 1978, 81. Fellow ACS; mem. AMA, Am. Med. Women's Assn., Maricopa County Med. Soc., Christian Med. Soc., Delta Epsilon Sigma. Episcopalian. Office: 10210 N 92nd St Scottsdale AZ 85258 Office Phone: 480-551-2528.

HARRISON, WALTER ASHLEY, physicist, researcher; b. Flushing, NY, Apr. 26, 1930; s. Charles Allison and Gertrude (Ashley) H.; m. Lucille Prince Carley, July 17, 1954; children: Richard Knight, John Carley, William Ashley, Robert Walter. B. Engring. Physics, Cornell U., 1953; MS, U. Ill., 1954, PhD, 1956. Physicist Gen. Elec. Research Labs., Schenectady, 1956-65; prof. applied physics Stanford (Calif.) U., 1965-2001, prof. emeritus, 2001—, chmn. applied physics dept., 1989-93, prof. emeritus, 2001—. Scientific adv. bd. Max Planck Inst., Stuttgart, Germany, 1989-92. Author: Pseudopotentials in the Theory of Metals, 1966, Russian transl., 1968, Solid State Theory, 1970, Chinese transl., 1970, Polish transl., 1976, Electronic Structure and the Properties of Solids, 1980, Russian transl., 1983, Japanese transl., 1986, Elementary Electronic Structure, 1999, revised edit., 2004, Applied Quantum Mechanics, 2000; editor: the Fermi Surface, 1960, Proceedings of the International Conference on the Physics of Semiconductors, 1985, Proceedings of the International Conference on Materials and Mechanisms of High-Temperature Superconductivity, 1989. Guggenheim fellow, 1970-71; recipient von Humboldt sr. U.S. scientist award, 1981, 89, 94; vis. fellow Clare Hall, Cambridge U., 1970-71. Fellow Am. Phys. Soc.; mem. European Phys. Soc. Home: 817 San Francisco Ct Stanford CA 94305-1021 Office: Stanford U Dept Applied Physics Stanford CA 94305-4045 Home Phone: 650-857-0807; Office Phone: 650-723-4224. Business E-Mail: walt@stanford.edu.

HARRY, DEBORAH ANN, singer; b. Miami, Fla., July 11, 1945; d. Richard Smith and Catherine (Peters) H. AA, Centenary Coll., 1965. Singer, songwriter rock group Blondie, 1975-83. Albums include Blondie, 1976, Plastic Letters, 1977, Parallel Lines, 1978, Eat to the Beat, 1979, Autoamerican, 1979, The Best of Blondie, 1981, The Hunter, 1982; (solo) Koo Koo, 1981, Rockbird, 1981, Def, Dumb & Blond, 1989, Debravation, 1993, Blonde and Beyond, 1993, Jazz Passengers - In Love, 1994, Rapture, 1994, The Platinum Collection, 1994, Virtuosity, 1995, Los Fabulosos Caillacs-Rey Azucar, 1995, Blodie-Atomic, 1995, Rockbird, 1996, Der Einziger Weg, 1999, Necessary Evil, 2007; songs include Heart of Glass, 1978 (ASCAP award), Call Me, Tide is High, Rapture, 1980; film appearances include Union City Blues, 1980, Videodrome, Roadie, 1980, Hairspray, 1988, Tales From the Darkside: The Movie, 1990, Joe's Day, 1999, Zoo, 1999, Six Ways to Sunday, 1999, Ghost Light, 2000, Dueces Wild, 2000, Red Lipstick, 2000, The Fluffer, 2001, Deuces Wild, 2002, Spun, 2002, Try Seventeen, 2002, My Life Without Me, 2003, A Good Night to Die, 2003, The Tulse Luper Suitcases, Part 1, 2003, Honey Trap, 2005, Patch, 2005, I Remember You Now..., 2005, Full Grown Men, 2006, Anamoroh, 2007, Elegy, 2008; TV appearances include Saturday Night Live, The Muppet Show, Tales from the Darkside, Wiseguy; appeared on Broadway Teaneck Tanzi, The Venus Flytrap, 1983; (movie) Satisfaction, New York Stories, 1989, Wigstock: The Movie, 1995, Heavy, 1995, Copland, 1997. Recipient Gold, Silver and Platinum records; named to Rock and Roll Hall of Fame, 2006. Mem. ASCAP, AFTRA, Screen Actors Guild, Equity. Office: c/o Paradigm 16th Fl 360 Park Ave S New York NY 10010 also: c/o 10th St Entertainment Ste G410 700 San Vicente Blvd West Hollywood CA 90069 Office Phone: 212-897-6400. Office Fax: 212-764-8941.

HART, BROOK, lawyer; b. NYC, Aug. 24, 1941; s. Walter and Julie H.; divorced; children: Morgan M., Leilani L., Ashley I., Ariel I. BA, Johns Hopkins U., 1963; LLB, Columbia U., 1966. Bar: N.Y. 1966, U.S. Ct. Appeals (9th cir.) 1967, Hawaii 1968, U.S. Supreme Ct. 1972, Calif. 1973. Law clk. to chief judge U.S. Dist. Ct. Hawaii, 1966-67; chief pub. defender Legal Aid Soc. Hawaii, 1970—72; assoc. Greenstein and Cowan, Honolulu, 1968-70; co-founder, ptnr. Hart, Leavitt, Hall and Hunt, Honolulu, 1972-80, Hart and Wolff, Honolulu, 1980-96; sr. ptnr. Law Offices of Brook Hart; pvt. practice. Instr. course U. Hawaii, 1972-73, lectr. Sch. Law, 1974—; apptd. Nat. Commn. to Study Def. Svcs., 1974, Planning Group for U.S. Dist. Ct. Hawaii, 1975; spl. counsel City Coun. of City and County of Honolulu, 1976-77, spl. investigative counsel to trustee in bankruptcy THC Fin. Corp., 1977; mem. Jud. Coun. State of Hawaii com. on revision state penal codes, 1984—; lectr. schs., profl., civic groups; mem. com. to select Fed. Pub. Defender Dist. Hawaii, 1981, 95; guest commentator Court TV, 1995, 99, 2002, 03, 04; with faculty Hawaii Inst. Continuing Legal Edn., 1988, Hawaii Pub. Defender Advocacy Inst., 1993-. Contbr. chpts. to books, articles to profl. publs. Named Bencher, Am. Inn of Ct., Hawaii, 1982—. Fellow Am. Bd. Criminal Lawyers; mem. ABA, Hawaii Bar Assn., State Bar Calif., Am. Judicature Soc., Nat. Legal Aid and Defender Assn. (Reginald Herber Smith award Outstanding Pub. Defender in Nation, 1971), Nat. Assn. Criminal Def. Lawyers, Calif. Attys. for Criminal Justice. Office: Ste 610 Melim Bldg 333 Queen St Honolulu HI 96813-4726 Office Phone: 808-526-0811. Office Fax: 808-531-2677. E-mail: hartlaw@hawaii.rr.com.

HART, FREDERICK MICHAEL, law educator; b. Flushing, NY, Dec. 5, 1929; s. Frederick Joseph and Doris (Laurian) H.; m. Joan Marie Monaghan, Feb. 13, 1956; children: Joan Marie, Ellen, Christiane, F. Michael, Margaret, Andrew, Brigid, Patrick. BS, Georgetown U., 1951, JD, 1955; LL.M., N.Y. U., 1956; postgrad., U. Frankfurt, Germany, 1956-57. Lectr., dir. food law program N.Y. U., NYC, 1957-58, asst. prof., 1958-59; prof. law Albany Law Sch., Union U., 1959-61, Boston Coll., 1961-66, Law Sch., U. N.Mex., Albuquerque, 1966—, dean, 1971-79, acting dean, 1985-86; dir. Law Sch., U. N.Mex. (Indian Law Center), 1967-69; vis. prof. U. Calif., Davis, spring 1981. Pres., chmn. bd. trustees Law Sch. Admission Test Council, 1974-76 Author: Forms and Procedures Under the Uniform Commercial Code, 1963, Uniform Commercial Code Reporter-Digest, 1965, Handbook on Truth in Lending, 1969, Commercial Paper Under the U.C.C, 1972, Student Guide to Secured Transactions, 1985, Student Guide to Sales, 1987, (with Nathaliie Martial) Emanual Guide to Secured Transaction, 2006; editor: Am. Indian Law Newsletter, 1968-70. Served to lt. USAF, 1951-53. Mem. ABA (law sch. accreditation com. 1986-93, skills tng. com. 1995-98, nominating com. 1987), Order of Coif, Phi Delta Phi. Roman Catholic. Home: 1505 Cornell Dr NE Albuquerque NM 87106-3703 Office: U NMex Sch Law 1117 Stanford Dr NE Albuquerque NM 87131-1431 Office Phone: 505-277-4737. Business E-Mail: hart@law.unm.edu.

HART, GARY, former United States Senator from Colorado, lawyer; b. Ottawa, Kans., Nov. 28, 1936; m. Lee Ludwig, 1958; children: Andrea, John. BA, Bethany Nazarene Coll., Okla., 1958; BD, Yale Div. Sch., 1961; JD, Yale U., 1964; D.Phil. in Politics, Oxford U., 2001. Bar: Colo. 1964. Began career as atty. U.S. Dept. Justice, Washington; then spl. asst. to sec. U.S. Dept. Interior; practiced in Denver, 1967-70, 72-74; nat. campaign dir. Senator George McGovern Democratic Presdl. Campaign, 1970-72; U.S. senator from Colo., 1976-84; of counsel Davis, Graham & Stubbs, Denver, 1985; of counsel, strategic and legal advisor, internat. law Coudert Brothers, San Francisco, 1988—; co-chmn. US Commn. Nat. Security/21st Century Dept. of Def., 1998—2001. Founder, 1st chmn. Environ. Study Conf., 1975; congl. adviser Salt II Talks, 1977; adviser UN Spl. Session on Disarmament, 1978; chmn. Nat. Commn. on Air Quality, 1978-81; founder Congl. Mil. Reform Caucus, 1981 Author: Right From the Start, 1973, A New Democracy, 1983, America Can Win, 1986, The Strategies of Zeus, 1987, Russia Shakes the World, 1991, The Good Fight: The Education of an American Reformer, 1993, The Patriot, 1996, The Minuteman, 1998, Restoration of the Republic, 2002, The Shield & The Cloak, 2006; co-author: The Double Man, 1985. Student vol. John F. Kennedy Presdl. Campaign, 1960; vol. organizer Robert F. Kennedy Presdl. Campaign, 1968; bd. visitors U.S. Air Force Acad., 1975—, chmn., 1978-80; nat. co-chmn. Share Our Strength, 1985; candidate for Democratic presdl. nomination, 1983-84, 87-88.

HART, JOHN EDWARD, lawyer; b. Portland, Oreg., Nov. 21, 1946; s. Wilbur Elmore and Daisy Elizabeth (Bowen) H.; m. Bianca Mannheimer, Mar. 29, 1968 (div. 1985); children: Ashley Rebecca, Rachel Bianca, Eli Jacob; m. Serena Callahan, Nov. 9, 1991; 1 child, Katelyn Elizabeth. Student, Oreg. State U., 1965-66; BS, Portland State U., 1971; JD, Lewis and Clark Coll., 1974. Bar: Oreg. 1974, U.S. Dist. Ct. Oreg. 1974, U.S. Ct. Appeals (9th cir.) 1975. Ptnr. Schwabe, Williamson and Wyatt, Portland, 1973-92, Hoffman, Hart & Wagner, Portland, 1992—. Adj. faculty U. Oreg. Dental Sch., 1987—; legal cons. Oreg. Chpt. Obstetricians, Gynecologists, Portland, 1985—, Am. Cancer Soc. Mammography Project, 1987—. Contbr. articles to profl. jours. Co-chmn. Alameda Sch. Fair, Portland, 1983. With U.S. Army, 1967-68. Mem. ABA, Am. Coll. Trial Lawyers, Am. Bd. Trial Advocates (pres. 1995) Am., Inns of Ct., Oreg. State Bar Assn., Oreg. Assn. Def. Counsel (pres. 1989), Multnomah Athletic Club. Democrat. Presbyterian. Avocations: jogging, weightlifting, outdoor activities. Office: Hoffman Hart & Wagner 1000 SW Broadway Ste 2000 Portland OR 97205-3072

HART, JOHN H., communications engineer; BS, Univ. Ga. Former positions in network architecture/product devel. with Control Data Corp., South Ctrl. Bell, So. Bell.; v.p. engring. Vitalink Comm. Corp., 1982—90; v.p., chief tech. officer 3Com Corp., 1990—96, sr. v.p., chief tech. officer, 1996—2000, fellow, 2000—01. Bd. dir. Coherent Inc., PLX Technologies Inc., Clearspeed Technology PLC, Plantronics Inc. Mem. IEEE.

HART, JOSEPH HUBERT, bishop emeritus; b. Kansas City, Mo., Sept. 26, 1931; Attended, St. John Sem., Kansas City, St. Meinrad Sem., Indpls. Ordained priest Diocese of Kansas City - St. Joseph, Mo., 1956; ordained bishop, 1976; aux. bishop Diocese of Cheyenne, Wyo., 1976—78, bishop, 1978—2001, bishop emeritus, 2001—. Roman Catholic. Office: Diocese of Cheyenne 2121 Capitol Ave PO Box 1468 Cheyenne WY 82003-0426 Office Phone: 307-638-1530. Office Fax: 307-637-7936. E-mail: jhart@dioceseofcheyenne.org.

HART, MARY, television talk show host; b. Sioux Falls, SD, Nov. 8, 1951; m. Burt Sugarman, Apr. 8, 1989; 1 child. BA, Augustana College, 1972. Co-host, prodr. Danny's Day, Oklahoma City, Iowa; co-host PM Mag., LA, 1978, The Regis Philbin Show, NYC, 1981-92, Entertainment Tonight, Hollywood, 1982—; co-owner Customer's Last Stand. Host: Tournament of Roses Parade, Macy's Thankgiving Day Parade; other TV appearences include (miniseries) Hollywood Wives, 1985, Circus of the Stars, Good Morning America, Blossom, Coach; exec. prodr., host Mary Hart Presents: Love in the Public Eye, 1990, Mary Hart Presents: Power in the Public Eye, 1990; musical debut Dolly, ABC-TV; headliner, dancer, singer, Las Vegas debut Golden Nugget, 1988, Resorts Internat., Atlantic City; videos include: Shape Up with Mary Hart, 1989, Mary Hart: Fit and Firm, 1990. Office: Paramount Vantage 5555 Melrose Ave Los Angeles CA 90038-3989

HART, PHIL, state legislator; Structural engr.; mem. Dist. 3 Idaho House of Reps., Boise. Republican. Office: Dist Office PO Box 1988 Hayden ID 83835 also: Legis Services Office PO Box 83720 Boise ID 83720-0054 Office Phone: 208-772-2522. Office Fax: 208-772-1881.*

HARTENBACH, DAVID LAWRENCE, school system administrator; b. St. Louis, Dec. 6, 1934; s. Henry Charles and Loretta S. (Schwarz) H. BA, St. Louis U., 1958, MEd, 1960; EdD in Sacred Theology, U. No. Colo., 1981. Cert. adminstr., Colo. Adminstrv. intern St. Louis U. H.S., 1966-67, asst. prin., 1967-68; prin. Regis H.S. Archdiocese of Denver, 1968-70; prin. Benton Harbor (Mich.) H.S., 1970-72; prin. W.C. Hinkley H.S. Aurora (Colo.) Pub. Schs., 1972-77, exec. dir. H.S.'s, 1977-86, assoc. supt. instrn., 1986-89, assoc. supt. aux., 1989-93, supt. schs., 1993—. Mem. state com. Colo. North Ctrl. Assn., Greeley, 1976-83. Membership chmn. Centennial Dist. Unit PTA, Aurora, 1993—; mem. human rels. com. City of Aurora, 1978-84. Named Colo. Supt. of Yr., Nat. Sch. Bds. Assn., 1995; grantee Ford Found., 1965-66, Nat. Acad. Rsch. in Vocat. Edn., 1979. Mem. ASCD, Nat. Assn. Secondary Sch. Prins. (nat. com. large secondary schs. 1980-83, adminstrv. intern J. Lloyd Trump grantee 1966-67), Am. Assn. Sch. Adminstrs., Colo. Assn. Sch. Bds., Colo. Assn. Sch. Execs., Kiwanis (past pres. Centennial chpt.). Avocations: golf, fishing, sports, music. Office: Aurora Pub Schs 1085 Peoria St Aurora CO 80011-6203

HARTENSTEIN, EDDY W., publishing executive, former electronics executive; b. 1950; BS in Aerospace Engring. and Math., Calif. State Poly. U., 1972; MS in Applied Mechanics, Calif. Inst. Tech., 1974. Joined Hughes Electronics Corp., 1972, vice chmn.; pres. DirecTV, Inc. (formerly Hughes Electronics Corp.), 1990—2001, chmn., CEO, 2001—04, bd. dirs., 2003—04; chmn., CEO HD Ptnrs., Santa Monica, Calif.; pub. LA Times, 2008—. Bd. dirs. Thomson Multimedia, XM Satellite Radio, 2005—, Broadcom Corp., 2008—. Recipient Broadcasting and Cable Hall of Fame, 2002, Emmy award for lifetime achievement, 2007. Mem.: NAE, Consumer Electronics Assn. (bd. dirs.), Satellite Broadcasting and Comm. Assn. (SBCA). Office: LA Times 202 W 1st St Los Angeles CA 90012 Office Phone: 213-237-5000. Office Fax: 213-237-7679.

HARTER, CAROL CLANCEY, academic administrator, English language educator; m. Michael T. Harter, June 24, 1961; children: Michael R., Sean P. BA, SUNY, Binghamton, 1964, MA, 1967, PhD, 1970; LHD, Ohio U., 1989. Instr. SUNY, Binghamton, 1969-70; asst. prof. Ohio U., Athens, 1970-74, ombudsman, 1974-76, v.p., dean students, 1976-82, v.p. for adminstrn., assoc. prof., 1982-89; pres., prof. English SUNY, Geneseo, 1989-95; pres. U. Nev., Las Vegas, 1995—2006, pers. emerita, regents prof., 2006—; exec. dir. Black Mountain Inst. Co-author: (with James R. Thompson) John Irving, 1986, E.L. Doctorow, 1990; author dozens of presentations and news columns; contbr. articles to profl. jours. Bd. dirs., mem. exec. com. NCAA, 2000-05; mem. exec. com. Nev. Devel. Authority, 2001-06; bd. dirs. Nev. Test Site Devel. Corp., 2000—06 trustee Associated Western Univs., 2001-04. Office: U Nev Las Vegas Box 445085 4505 S Maryland Pkwy Las Vegas NV 89154-5085 Business E-Mail: carol.harter@unlv.edu. E-mail: harter@ccmail.nevada.edu.

HARTER, LAFAYETTE GEORGE, JR., retired economics professor; b. Des Moines, May 28, 1918; s. Lafayette George and Helen Elizabeth (Ives) H.; m. Charlotte Mary Toshach, Aug. 23, 1950; children— Lafayette George III, James Toshach, Charlotte Helen. BA in Bus. Adminstrn, Antioch Coll., 1941; MA in Econs, Stanford, 1948, PhD, 1960. Instr. Menlo Coll., Menlo Park, Calif., 1948-50; instr. Coll. of Marin, Kentfield, Calif., 1950-60; prof. econs. dept. Oreg. State U., 1960-85, prof. emeritus, 1985—, chmn. dept., 1967-71. Mem. panel arbitrators Fed. Mediation and Conciliation Svc., 1965-84, Oreg. Conciliation Svc., 1967-84; mem. Univ. Ctrs. for Rational Alternatives. Author: John R. Commons: His Assault on Laissez-faire, 1962, Labor in America, 1957, Economic Responses to a Changing World, 1972; editorial bd. Jour. Econ. Issues, 1981-84. Assoc. campaign chmn. Benton United Good Neighbor Fund, 1970-72, campaign chmn., v.p., 1972-73, pres., 1973-74, vice chmn.; pub. mem. Adv. Commn. on Unemployment Compensation, 1972, 73, chmn., 1974-78; Bd. dirs. Oreg. Coun. Econ. Edn., 1971-89; pub. mem. local profl. responsibilities Oreg. State Bar Assn., 1980-83; pub. mem. Oreg. Coun. on Ct. Procedures, 1985-93, bd. mem. Community Econs. of Corp., Community Econ. Stabilization Corp. Lt. comdr. USNR, 1941-46. Mem. AAUP, Am. Arbitration Assn. (pub. employment disputes panel 1970-92), Am. Western Econ. Assns., Indsl. Rels. Rsch. Assn., Am. Assn. for Evolutionary Econs., Oreg. State Employees Assn. (v.p. faculty chpt. 1972, pres. 1973), Am. Assn. Ret. Persons (pres. local chpt. 1992-93), Corvallis Retirement Village (fin. com., bd. dirs.). Democrat. Mem. United Ch. of Christ (moderator 1972, 73; mem. fin. com. Oreg. conf. 1974-82, dir. 1978-81, mem. personnel com. 1983-85). Home: 4123 SW Comus St Portland OR 97219

HARTKE, STEPHEN PAUL, composer, educator; b. Orange, NJ, July 6, 1952; s. George William Hartke, Jr. and Priscilla Nancy (Redfearn) Elfrey; m. Lisa Louise Stidham, Sept. 12, 1981; 1 child, Alexander Stidham. BA magna cum laude, Yale U., 1973; MA, U. Pa., 1976; PhD, U. Calif., Santa Barbara, 1982. Advt. mgr. Theodore Presser Co., Bryn Mawr, Pa., 1977-78; advt. and art dir. European Am. Music Corp., Clifton, NJ, 1978-79; ednl. dir. Carl Fischer Inc., NYC, 1980; Fulbright prof. composition U. São Paulo, Brazil, 1984-85; disting. prof. composition U. So. Calif. Thornton Sch. Music, LA, 1987—. Vis. composer Coll. Creative Studies U. Calif., Santa Barbara, 1981-83, 85-87; composer-in-residence LA Chamber Orch., 1988-92. Composer: Caoine, 1980, Sonata-Variations for violin and piano, 1984 (Kennedy Friedheim award 1985), Oh Them Rats Is Mean In My Kitchen, 1985, Pacific Rim for orch., 1988, The King of the Sun, 1988, Symphony Number 2, 1990, Concerto for violin and orch., 1992, Wulfstan aut the Millennium, 1995, The Ascent of the Equestrian in a Balloon, 1995, Sons of Noah, 1996, The Horse with the Lavender Eye, 1997, Piano Sonata, 1998, The Rose of the Winds, 1998, Tituli, 1999, Gradus, 1999, Cathedral in the Thrashing Rain, 2000, Concerto for Clarinet and Orchestra, 2001, Beyond Words, 2001, Symphony No. 3, 2003, Suite for Summer, 2004, Percolative Processes, 2005, Meanwhile, 2007, Precepts, 2007, A Brandenburg Autumn, 2007, (Operas) The Greater Good, 2006 (Charles Ives Opera prize, AAAL, 2008); recs. on CRI, New World Records, ECM EMI record labels. Recipient Acad. award, AAAL, 1993, Charles Ives Opera prize, 2008, Rome prize Am. Acad. in Rome, 1992, Stoeger award Lincoln Ctr. Chamber Music Soc., 1997; Composer-in-Residence grantee Nat. Endowment for Arts (1990, 91), Commn. grantee Koussevitzky Music Found., 1992, Fromm Found. Commn. grantee, 1994, Inst. for Am. Music Commn. grantee; Guggenheim fellow, 1997. Mem. Opera Am., Am. Mus. Ctr. Office: Dept Composition MUS 201 USC Thornton Sch Music Los Angeles CA 90089-0851 also: c/o 21C Media Group Ste 506 162 W 56th St New York NY 10019 Office Phone: 213-740-3125. E-mail: stephenhartke@earthlink.net.

HARTL, JOHN GEORGE, film critic; b. Wenatchee, Wash., June 28, 1945; s. David and Georgiann (MacLean) H. BA in Journalism, U. Wash., 1967. Film critic Seattle Times, 1966-2001; freelance writer Seattle, 2001—. Avocations: swimming, reading, camping. Office: Seattle Times PO Box 70 Fairview Ave N & John St Seattle WA 98111-0070 E-mail: johnhart.@yahoo.com.

HARTLEY, JAMES EDWARD, lawyer; b. Orange, NJ, Nov. 4, 1949; s. George and Carolyn (Stewart) H.; m. Judy Franklin, Mar. 1, 1986; 1 child, Jonathan. BA, U. Calif., Berkeley, 1971, JD, 1974. Bar: Colo. 1974, U.S. Dist. Ct. Colo. 1974, U.S. Ct. Appeals (10th cir.) 1975, U.S. Supreme Ct. 1981, U.S. Ct. Appeals (Fed. cir.) 1993. Assoc. Holland & Hart, Denver, 1974-80, ptnr., 1980—. Adj. prof. Denver U. Law Sch., 1985-86. Co-author: Private Litigation Under Section 7 of the Clayton Act: Law and Policy, 1989, Antitrust Pitfalls in Outpatient Services, 1992, Rule of Reason Monograph, 1999, State Antitrust Practice and Procedure, 1999; asst. editor: ABA Antitrust Law Jour., 1994-98. Mem. ABA (coun. antitrust law sect. 2003—06), Colo. Bar Assn., Denver Bar Assn., Order of Coif, Phi Beta Kappa (named one of Best Lawyers in Am. 2004-). Home: 2540 Briarwood Dr Boulder CO 80305-6804 Office: Holland & Hart LLP 555 17th St Ste 3200 Denver CO 80202-3950

HARTLEY, MARY, state legislator; b. Bronx, NY, Aug. 16, 1954; m. John Hartley; three children. Student, Air Force C.C. Mem. Ariz. Senate, Dist. 20, Phoenix, 1994—; mem. family svcs. com., mem. health com. Active Alhambra Elem. Sch. Dist. Governing Bd., DES Child Care Adv. Com., Ariz. State PTA, Kids Voting, Coalition for Tobacco Free Ariz. Recipient award of excellence All Ariz. Sch. Bd., 1995. Mem. MADD, Nat. Assn. for Partnership Edn. (award 1992), Sierra Club, Audubon Coun. Democrat.

HARTMAN, ROBERT LEROY, artist, educator; b. Sharon, Pa., Dec. 17, 1926; s. George Otto and Grace Arvada (Radabaugh) H.; m. Charlotte Ann Johnson, Dec. 30, 1951; children: Mark Allen, James Robert. BFA, U. Ariz., 1951, MA, 1952; postgrad., Colorado Springs Fine Arts Ctr., 1947, postgrad., 1951, Bklyn. Mus. Art Sch., 1953—54. Instr. architecture, allied arts Tex. Tech. Coll., 1955-58; asst. prof. art U. Nev., Reno, 1958-61; mem. faculty dept. art U. Calif., Berkeley, 1961—, prof., 1972-91, prof. emeritus, 1991—, chmn. dept., 1974-76. Mem. Inst. for Creative Arts, U. Calif., 1967-68. One-man shows include Bertha Schafer Gallery, N.Y.C., 1966, 69, 74, Santa Barbara Mus. Art, 1973, Cin. Art Acad., 1975, Hank Baum Gallery, San Francisco, 1973, 75, 78, San Jose Mus. Art, 1983, Bluxome Gallery, San Francisco, 1984, 86, U. Art Mus., Berkeley, 1986, Instituto D'Arte Dosso Dossi, Ferrara, Italy, 1989, Victor Fischer Galleries, San Francisco, 1991, Triangle Gallery, San Francisco, 1992, 93, 95, 97, 1999-2002, 04, 06, 08, Augusta State U., 1998, Mary Pauline Gallery, Augusta, Ga., 2001, Oakland Mus., 2002, Viewpoint Photographic Art Ctr., Sacramento, CAlif., 2006, Fla. Mus. of Photogrphic arts, Tampa, 2007; group exhbns. include Richmond Mus., 1966, Whitney Mus. Biennial, 1973, Oakland Mus., 1976, San

Francisco Arts Commn. Gallery, 1985 (award), Earthscape Expo '90 Photo Mus., Osaka, Japan, 1990, In Close Quarters, American Landscape Photography Since 1968, Princeton Art Mus., 1993, Facing Eden: 100 Years of Landscape Art in The Bay Area, de Young Mus., San Francisco, 1995, Colorado Springs Fine Arts Ctr., 1998; represented in permanent collections, Nat. Collections Fine Arts, Colorado Springs Fine Arts Ctr., Corcoran Gallery, Roswell Mus., Princeton Art Mus. U. Calif. humanities rsch. fellow, 1980. Office: U Calif Dept Art Berkeley CA 94720-0001

HARTMAN, SUSAN P(ATRICE), adult education administrator; Dir. adult edn. Front Range CC, Westminster, Colo., 1995—. Recipient Regional Person of Yr. award, 1992. Office: Cmty Learning Ctr Front Range Community Coll Westminster CO 80031

HARTMANN, DENNIS LEE, atmospheric science educator; b. Salem, Oreg., Apr. 23, 1949; s. Alfred R. and Angeline K. Hartmann. BS, U. Portland, 1971; PhD, Princeton U., 1975. Rsch. assoc. McGill U., Montreal, Que., Can., 1975-76; vis. scientist Nat. Ctr. Atmospheric Rsch., Boulder, Colo., 1976-77; asst. prof. U. Wash., Seattle, 1977-83, assoc. prof. atmospheric sci., 1983-88, prof. atmospheric sci., 1988—, chair dept. atmospheric sci., 2002—. Mem. MAP panel NRC, 1981-87; mem. steering com. GEWEX Sci., 1995—. Author: Global Physical Climatology, 1994; ssoc. editor Jour. Atmospheric Scis., 1983-93, Jour. Geophys. Rsch., 1985-88; mem. editl. bd., contbr. Atmospheric Physics; mem. bd. reviewing editors Sci., 2002—; contbr. articles to sci. jours. Recipient Editors award Am. Geophys. Union, 1994; Aldo Leopold Leadership fellow, 1999, Disting. Pub. Svc. award NASA, 2005. Fellow AAAS (chmn.-elect atmospheric and hydrospheric scis. sect. 1997—), Am. Geophys. Union; mem. Joint Inst. for Study of Atmosphere and Ocean (sr.), Am. Meteorol. Soc. (mem. com. upper atmosphere 1978-83, chmn. com. 1980-82, com. undergrad. awards 1983-85, com. climate variations, 1993—, Editors award 1993, 96, 98), NAS (space sci. bd. com. on earth scis. 1987-90, U.S. Toga panel 1990-95, climate rsch. com. 2001—, mem. bd. atmospheric scis. and climate 2006-). Office: U Wash PO Box 351640 Dept Atmospheric Scis Seattle WA 98195-1640 Office Phone: 206-543-7460. Business E-Mail: dennis@atmos.washington.edu.

HARTMANN, THOM, radio personality, political commentator, writer; b. Grand Rapids, Mich., May 7, 1951; m. Louise Hartmann; 3 children. Part-time news announcer WITL, Lansing, Mich., 1968; DJ, reporter, news anchor, program dir., 1968—78; radio talk show host KPOJ, Portland, Oreg., 2005—07; host Thom Hartmann Radio Program, Air America Radio Network, 2007—. Founder Mich. Healing Arts Ctr.; guest faculty mem. Goddard Coll., Vt. Author: ADD: A Different Perception, 1992, ADHD Secrets of Success: Coaching Yourself to Fulfillment in the Business World, 1994, Focus Your Energy: Hunting for Success in Business, 1994, ADD Success Stories: A Guide to Fulfillment for Families with Attention Deficit Disorder, 1995; co-author: Think Fast: The ADD Experience, 1996; author: Beyond ADD: Hunting for Reasons in the Past and Present, 1996, The Greatest Spiritual Secret of the Century, 2000, Thom Hartmann's Complete Guide to ADD, 2000; co-author: The Edison Gene: ADHD and the Gift of the Hunter Child, 2003; author: Unequal Protection: The Rise of Corporate Dominance and the Theft of Human Rights, 2004, The Prophet's Way: A Guide to Living in the Now, 2004, The Last Hours of Ancient Sunlight: Revised and Updated: The Fate of the World and What We Can Do Before It's Too Late, 2004, We the People: A Call to Take Back America, 2004, What Would Jefferson Do?: A Return to Democracy, 2004; co-author: Ultimate Sacrifice: John and Robert Kennedy, the Plan for a Coup in Cuba, and the Murder of JFK, 2005; author: Walking Your Blues Away: How to Heal the Mind and Create Emotional Well-Being, 2006, Screwed: The Undeclared War Against the Middle Class - And What We Can Do about It, 2006, Cracking the Code: How to Win Hearts, Change Minds, and Restore America's Original Vision, 2007. Co-founder New England Salem Children's Village, 1978, The Hunter Sch., 1997. Office: c/o KPOJ Radio 4949 SW Macadam Ave Portland OR 97239

HARTMANN, WILLIAM KENNETH, astronomy scientist; b. June 6, 1939; m. Gayle Harrison, Mar. 22, 1970; 1 child, Amy. BS in Physics, Pa. State U., 1961; MS in Geology, U. Ariz., 1965, PhD in Astronomy, 1966. Asst. prof. Lunar and Planetary Lab., U. Ariz., 1967-70; assoc. and sr. scientist IIT Research Inst., 1970-72; sr. scientist Planetary Sci. Inst., Sci. Applications Internat. Corp., Tucson, 1972-95, Planetary Sci. Inst., San Juan Rsch. Inst., 1995—. Co-investigator 1971 Mariner 9 Mars Mission, 1971-72, Mars Observer Mission, 1991, Mars Global Surveyor Mission, 1996-2003, Russian Mars 96 Mission; vis. assoc. prof. Inst. for Astronomy, U. Hawaii; affiliate faculty U. Hawaii at Hilo, 1990—, U. Ariz., 1993—; cons. Smithsonian Air and Space Mus., 1977; photog. cons. House Select Com. on Assassinations, 1978-79; mem. various coms. NASA, 1978—; co-organizer Kona Conf. on Origin of Moon, 1984; mem. com. on planetary exploration NRC, 1984-87. Author: Astronomy: The Cosmic Journey, 1978, last edit., 1993, Moons and Planets, 1972, 4th edit., 1999, Out of the Cradle, 1984, Cycles of Fire, 1987, The History of Earth, 1991, Traveler's Guide to Mars, 2003, (novels)Mars Underground, 1997, Cities of Gold, 2002; co-author: The Grand Tour: A Traveller's Guide to the Solar System, 1981, last edit., 1993; co-editor: Origin of the Moon, 1986, Desert Heart, 1989; prin. editor: In the Stream of Stars: The Soviet-American Space Art Book, 1990; also numerous tech. articles to sci. publs. Co-winner 1965-66 Ninninger Meteorite award, Runcorn-Florensky medal European Geophys. Soc., 2002; Asteroid 3341 named Hartmann in honor of his rsch. on solar system evolution; 1st recipient Carl Sagan medal Am. Astron. Soc., 1997. Fellow: AAAS. Office: 1700 E Fort Lowell RD STE 106 Tucson AZ 85719-2395

HARTNETT, JOSH, actor; b. San Francisco, July 21, 1978; s. Daniel and Molly Hartnett (Stepmother). Student, SUNY, Purchase. Actor: (films) Halloween: H2O, 1998, The Faculty, 1998, The Virgin Suicides, 1999, Here on Earth, 2000, Blow Dry, 2001, Member, 2001, Town & Country, 2001, Pearl Harbor, 2001, O, 2001, Black Hawk Down, 2001, The Same, 2001, 40 Days and 40 Nights, 2002, Hollywood Homicide, 2003, Wicker Park, 2004, Sin City, 2005, Mozart and the Whale, 2005, Lucky Number Slevin, 2006, The Black Dahlia, 2006, Resurrecting the Champ, 2007, 30 Days of Night, 2007, August, 2008; (TV films) Debutante, 1998; (TV series) Cracker, 1997—98. Named ShoWest Male Star of Tomorrow, 2002. Office: Petricola 9171 Wilshire Blvd Ste 390 Beverly Hills CA 90210-5515

HARTOG, JOHN A., lawyer; b. Scarsdale, NY, Jan. 27, 1952; BA cum laude, Pomona Coll., 1974; JD, U. Calif. Hastings Coll. Law, 1979; LLM in Taxation, Golden Gate U., 1984. Bar: Calif. 1979, US Tax Ct. 1984, US Ct. Appeals DC 1997, NY 2002, US Ct. Appeals (3rd cir.). Adj. prof. Golden Gate U. Sch. Tax. Contbr. articles to profl. publs.; co-author: California Trust Practice, 1996. Named one of Top 100 Attys., Worth mag., 2005—06. Fellow: Am. Coll. Trusts and Estates Counsel; mem.: Calif. Trust and Estate Counselors, State Bar Calif. (mem. trusts and estates law and taxation sects.), ABA (mem. taxation, real property, probate and trust law sects.), Alameda County Bar Assn. (chair estate planning com. of probate sect.). Office: John A Hertog Inc Bldg B Ste 250-B 4 Orinda Way Orinda CA 94563 Office Phone: 925-253-1717. Office Fax: 925-253-0334. E-mail: jahartog@calteclaw.com.

HARTSHORN, TERRY O., health facility administrator; b. 1944; Adminstrv. sec. Centinela Valley Hosp., Inglewood, Calif., 1965-68, adminstrv. asst., 1969; adminstr., cons. Community Health Svc., USPHS, LA, 1969-71; adminstr. Luth. Hosp. Soc. So. Calif., LA, 1971-73, Moore-White Med. Clinic, LA, 1973-76; chmn. Pacificare Health Systems, Inc., Cypress, Calif., 1977—, chmn., pres., CEO Burbank, Calif., 1993—; chmn. bd., pres., CEO UniHealth Am., Inc., Burbank, 1993—. Office: Pacificare Health 3120 Lake Center Dr Burbank CA 92704

HARTSOUGH, GAYLA ANNE KRAETSCH, management consultant; b. Lakewood, Ohio, Sept. 16, 1949; d. Vernon W. and Mildred E. (Austin) Kraetsch; m. James N. Heller, Aug. 20, 1972 (div. 1977); m. Jeffrey W. Hartsough, Mar. 12, 1983; 1 child, Jeffrey Hunter Kraetsch. BS, Northwestern U., Evanston, Ill., 1971; EdM, Tufts U., Medford, Mass., 1973; MEd, U. Va., Charlottesville, 1978; PhD, U. Va., 1978. Vol. VISTA, Tenn., 1970-71; asst. tchr. Perkins Sch. for the Blind, Watertown, Mass., 1971-72; resource tchr. Fairfax (Va.) County Pub. Schs., 1972-76; asst. dir. ctr. U. Va., Charlottesville, 1976-78; sr. program officer Acad. Edn. Devel., Washington, 1978-80; mng. cons. Cresap/Towers Perrin, Washington, LA, 1980-86; pres. KH Consulting Group, LA, 1986—. Former mem. nat. adv. coun. Sch. Comm. Northwestern U., Evanston, Ill., 1992—2005. Contbr. articles to profl. jours. Co-founder LA Higher Edn. Roundtable, 1987—94; mem. coun. of 100 Northwestern U., 1999—. Recipient Outstanding Women of Achievement award, Century City C. of C., 1991, Top 50 Women Sot award, LA, BTW. Mem.: Earth Protect Inc. (adv. bd. mem.), Orgn. Women Execs. Home: 15624 Royal Ridge Rd Sherman Oaks CA 91403-4207 Office: KH Consulting Group 1901 Ave Of Stars Ste 1900 Los Angeles CA 90067-6020 Office Phone: 310-203-5417. Office Fax: 310-203-5419. Personal E-mail: kheggak@aol.com.

HARTWELL, LELAND HARRISON (LEE HARTWELL), geneticist, educator; b. LA, Oct. 30, 1939; s. Majorie (Taylor) H.; m. Theresa Naujack. BS, Calif. Inst. Tech., 1961; PhD, MIT, 1964. Postdoctoral fellow Salk Inst., 1964-65; asst. prof. U. Calif., Irvine, 1965-67, assoc. prof., 1967-68, U. Washington, Seattle, 1968-73, prof. genome sciences, 1973—, adj. prof. of medicine, 2003; pres., dir. Fred Hutchison Cancer Rsch. Ctr., Seattle, 1997—. Named rsch. prof. of genetics Am. Cancer Soc., 1990; chmn. sci. adv. bd., Canary Fund. Recipient Eli Lilly award, 1973, NIH Merit award, 1990, GM Sloan award, 1991, Hoffman LaRoche Mattia award, 1991, Gairdner Found. Internat. award, 1992, Simon Shubitz award U. Chgo., 1992, Brandeis U. Rosenstiel award, 1993, Sloan Kettering Cancer Ctr. Katherine Berkan Judd award, 1994, Genetics Soc. of Am. medal, 1994, MGH Warren Triennial prize, 1995, Keith Porter award Am. Soc. Cell Biology, 1995, Carnegie Mellon Dickson award, 1996, Louisa Gross Horwitz prize Columbia U., 1995, Albert Lasker Basic Med. Rsch. award Albert and Mary Lasker Found., 1998, Brinker Internat. award for basic sci. Susan G. Komen Breast Cancer Found., 1998, Disting. Alumni award Calif. Inst. Tech., 1999, City of Medicine award, 1999, medal of honor Am. Cancer Soc., 1999, Léopold Giffuel prize Assn. pour la Recherche sur le Cancer, France, 2000, The Massry prize The Meira and Shaul G. Massry Found., Nobel prize in Physiology or Medicine, 2001, Wash. Medal of Merit, 2003; Guggenheim fellow, 1983-84; Am. Bus. Cancer Rsch. grantee, 1983—; Am. Cancer Soc. scholar; laureate Passano Found., 1996. Mem. NAS, AAAS, Am. Soc. Microbiology, Am. Soc. Cell Biology, Genetics Soc. Am. (pres. 1990). Office: Hutchinson Cancer Rsch Ctr D1-060 1100 Fairview Ave N PO Box 19024 Seattle WA 98109-1024

HARUTUNIAN, ALBERT T(HEODORE), III, judge; b. San Diego, May 15, 1955; s. Albert Theodore Jr. and Elsie Ruth H.; m. Rebecca Blair, 1999. BA, Claremont McKenna Coll., 1977; JD, U. Calif., Berkeley, 1980. Bar: Calif. 1980, U.S. Dist. Ct. (so. dist.) Calif. 1980, U.S. Ct. Apppeals (9th cir.) 1982, U.S. Supreme Ct. 1984. Law clk. to Hon. Howard B. Turrentine U.S. Dist. Ct., San Diego, 1980-81; assoc. Luce, Forward, Hamilton & Scripps, San Diego, 1982-87, ptnr., 1988-95; judge San Diego Mcpl. Ct., 1995-98, San Diego Superior Ct., 1998—. Spl. counsel standing com. on discipline U.S. Dist. Ct. Calif., San Diego, 1983-85; chmn. San Diego Bar Labor and Employment Sect., 1988-89; chmn. fed. cts. com. Calif. State Bar, 1989-90. Bd. dirs. ARC San Diego chpt., 1992-2002, Crime Victims Fund, 1995-97; bd. govs. Muscular Dystrophy Assn., San Diego, 1985; grad. LEAD Inc., San Diego, 1986; planning com. San Diego United Way, 1986-92. Named one of Outstanding Young Men of Am., 1983; recipient Outstanding Service award 9th Cir. Jud. Conf., 1986. Mem. ABA, Calif. State Bar Ct. (referee 1985-88), Am. Arbitration Assn. (arbitrator 1986-95), Calif. Judges Assn. (mem. criminal law and procedure com. 1997-2000), Boalt Hall Alumni Assn. (bd. dirs. 1994-97), Claremont McKenna Coll. Alumni Assn. (founding dir. San Diego chpt. 1984-2000), Rotary (bd. dirs. San Diego club 1995—). Republican. Avocations: music, golf. Office: San Diego Superior Ct PO Box 122724 San Diego CA 92112-2724

HARVEY, DONALD, artist, educator; b. Walthamston, Eng., June 14, 1930; s. Henry and Annie Dorothy (Sawell) H.; m. Elizabeth Clark, Aug. 9, 1952; children— Shan Mary, David Jonathan. Art tchrs. diploma, Brighton Coll. Art, 1951. Art master Ardwyn Grammar Sch., Wales, 1952-56; mem. faculty dept. art U. Victoria, B.C., Canada, 1961-95, now prof. emeritus painting. One man exhbns. include, Albert White Gallery, Toronto, 1968, retrospective, Art Gallery of Victoria, 1968; represented in permanent collections, Nat. Gallery Can., Montreal Mus. Contemporary Art, Albright-Knox Mus., Seattle Art Mus. Mem. accessions com. Art Gallery of Victoria, 1969-72. Can. Council fellow, 1966 Mem. Royal Can. Acad. of Arts (full academician), Can. Group Painters, Can. Painters and Etchers. Home: 1025 Joan Crescent Victoria BC Canada V8S 3L3 E-mail: doharvey@telus.net.

HARVEY, ELINOR B., child psychiatrist; b. Boston, Jan. 11, 1912; d. William and Florence (Maysles) H.; m. Donald K. Freedman, July 2, 1936; children: Peter, F. Kenneth. BS cum laude, Jackson Coll., 1933; MD, Tufts U., 1936. Diplomate Am. Bd. Psychiatry and Neurology, Nat. Bd. Med. Examiners. Intern New Eng. Hosp. Women and Children, Roxbury, Mass., 1936-37; resident Sea View Hosp., Staten Island, N.Y., 1937-39; adminstrv. and indsl. physician Assoc. Hosp. Svc. N.Y., 1939-41; house physician, resident Henry St. Settlement House, NYC, 1939-41; pvt. practice Arlington, Va., 1941-43; pvt. practice as pediatrician Newport News, Va., 1943-46; clinician Westchester County Health Dept., White Plains, N.Y., 1947; pediatrician Arrowhead Clinic, Duluth, Minn., 1947-48; resident in psychiatry VA Hosp., Palo Alto, Calif., 1949-52; resident in child psychiatry child guidance clinic Children's Hosp. San Francisco, 1952-53, fellow in child psychiatry, 1953-54; pvt. practice as child and family psychiatrist Berkeley, Calif., 1954-68, Juneau, Alaska, 1968-77. Instr. Am. Univ. Washington, 1941—43; clinician prenatal clinics Arlington County Health Dept., Arlington, 1941—43; clinician Planned Parenthood, Wash., 1941—43; mem. adv. bd. emergency maternal and infant care program C's. Bur., Wash., 1942—48; instr. pediatrics schs. nursing Buxton and Riverside Hosps., 1943—46; consult pediatrician Community Hosp. and Clin, Two Harbors, Minn., 1947—48; mem. courtesy staff Herrick Hosp., Berkeley, Calif., 1955—68, Bartlett Mem. Hosp., Juneau, 1968—77; consult. US Bur. Indian Affairs Dept. Educ., Alaska, 1968—76, Southeast Regional Mental Health Clin., Juneau, 1975—77, Mars & Kline Psychiat. Clin. and Hosp., Port-Au-Prince, Port-Au-Prince, Haiti, 1977—78, Navajo Area Indian Health Serv., Gallup, N.Mex., 1980—, Brookside Hosp., San Pablo, Calif., 1980—84, San Pablo, 1984—; instr. mental health and mental illness Alaska Homemaker-Home Health Aide Servs., Juneau C.C., 1968—77, 1984—99; coord. State Alaska Program Continuing Educ. Mental Health, 1974—76; clin. assoc. prof. dept. psychiat. and behavioral scis. Univ. Washington, 1976—77; vol. child and family psychiatrist Baptist Mission, Fermathe, Haiti, 1977—79; instr. child develop. Mars and Kline Pscychiat. Clin and Hosp., 1977—78; mem. hosp. staff Gallup (NM) Indian Med. Cent., 1980—; consult. Brazelton neonatal behavioral assessment Navajo Area Indian Health Serv., 1982—; consult. infant-parent program Brookside Hosp., 1984—; demonstrator Brazelton neonatal behavioral assessment scale Cent. Recursos Educatius Deficients Visuals Catalunya, Barcelona, 1992; active Child Protection Agency, Juneau; mem. planning bd. Coordinated Child Care Cent., Juneau; presenter in field. Author: (with others) Annual Progress in Child Psychiatry and Child Development, 10th ann. edit., 1977, Expanding Mental Health Intervention in Schools, Vol. I, 1985, Psychiatric House Calls, 1988, The Indian Health Service Primary Care Provider, 1991; contbr. articles to profl. jours. Mem. comprehensive health planning coun. City and Borough of Juneau. Grantee NIMH, 1958-63. Fellow Am. Psychiat. Assn. (life), Am. Acad. Child and Adolescent Psychiatry (life, mem. task force Am. Indian children); mem. No. Calif. Psychiat. Assn. (Outstanding Achievement award 1996), Internat. Assn. Child Psychiatry, World Fedn. Mental Health, Internat. Assn. Circumpolar Health, Soc. Reproductive and Infant Psychology, Phi Beta Kappa. Home: 4220 Viscount Cir Anchorage AK 99502-4282

HARVEY, JOSEPH PAUL, JR., orthopedist, educator; b. Youngstown, Ohio, Feb. 28, 1922; s. Joseph Paul and Mary Justinian (Collins) H.; m. Martha Elizabeth Toole, Apr. 12, 1958; children: Maryalice, Martha Jane, Frances Susan, Helen Lucy, Laura Andre. Student, Dartmouth Coll., 1939—42; MD, Harvard U., 1945. Diplomate Nat. Bd. Med. Examiners. Intern Peter Bent Brigham Hosp., Boston, 1945-46; resident Univ. Hosp., Cleve., 1951-53, Hosp. Spl. Surgery, NYC, 1953-54; instr. orthopedics Cornell Med. Coll., NYC, 1954-62; mem. faculty Sch. Medicine, U. So. Calif., Los Angeles, 1962-92; prof. orthopedic surgery U. So. Calif., 1966-92, prof. emeritus, 1992—; chmn. sect. orthopedics Keck Sch. Medicine, U. So. Calif., 1964-78. Dir. dept. orthopedics U. So. Calif.-LA County Med. Ctr., 1964-79, staff, 1979— Editor-in-chief: Contemporary Orthopedics, 1978-96. Served to capt. AUS, 1946-48. Exchange orthopedic fellow Royal Acad. Hosp., Upsala, Sweden, 1957. Fellow Western Orthop. Assn., Am. Acad. Orthop. Surgery, A.C.S., Am. Soc. Testing Materials; mem. AMA, Calif. Med. Assn., Los Angeles County Med. Assn., Am. Rheumatism Assn., Am. Orthop. Assn., Internat. Soc. Orthopedics and Traumatology. Home: 432 Arlington Dr Pasadena CA 91105-2850 Address: The Athenaeum 551 South Hill Ave Pasadena CA 91106 Business E-Mail: harvey@usc.edu.

HARVEY, KENT M., utilities executive; B in Econs., Stanford U., Calif., M in Engring. - Econ. Systems. Engr. PG&E Corp., San Francisco, 1982, various positions including corp. sec., dir. fin. analysis, dir. investor rels., v.p., and treas., sr. v.p., CFO, treas. Pacific Gas and Electric Co., sr. v.p., chief risk and audit officer, 2005—. Treas., trustee Am. Conservatory Theater; dir. North Bay Coun. Office: PG&E Corp One Market Spear Tower Ste 2400 San Francisco CA 94105-1126 Office Phone: 415-267-7070. Office Fax: 415-267-7268.

HARVEY, TED, state legislator; b. Las Vegas, N.Mex., July 23, 1949; m. Janie Harvey; children: Sean, Don. BS in Civil Engring., Colo. State U., Ft. Collins. Civil engr.; mem. Dist. 43 Colo. House of Reps., Denver, 1998—2006; mem. Dist. 30 Colo. State Senate, Denver, 2007—. Bd. dirs. Pueblo YMCA. Mem. Nat. Soc. Profl. Engrs., Pueblo C. of C. (past pres.). Republican. Roman Catholic. Office: Colo State Capitol 200 E Colfax Rm 271 Denver CO 80203 Office Phone: 303-866-4881. Business E-Mail: ted.harvey.senate@state.co.us.*

HARWOOD, IVAN RICHMOND, retired pediatric pulmonologist; b. Huntington, W.Va., July 3, 1939; BA, Dartmouth Coll., 1961; MD, U. W.Va., 1965. Diplomate Nat. Bd. Med. Examiners; lic. physician, Calif., Can.; cert. Am. Bd. Pediatrics. Intern in pediatrics U. W.Va. Hosp., Morgantown, 1965-66; resident in pediatrics Yale-New Haven (Conn.) Hosp., 1966-68, sr. resident outpatient dept., 1968-69; chief pediatrics USAF Hosp. 3646, Del Rio, Tex., 1968-70; asst. prof. pediatrics U. Calif. Med. Ctr., San Diego, 1971-78, chief pediatric pulmonary div., 1972-93, dir. pediatric intensive care unit, 1972-78, assoc. adj. prof. pediatrics, 1978-86, prof., 1987—. Mem. patient care rev. and numerous other coms. U. Calif. Med. Ctr., 1976—; co-dir. Cystic Fibrosis Ctr., San Diego, 1972-73, dir., 1973; mem. Cystic Fibrosis Young Adult Com., Atlanta, 1974-80, chmn., 1976-80, Cystic Fibrosis Ctr. Com., 1986-89, vice-chmn., 1990-94; mem. San Diego County Tuburculosis Control Bd., 1974-78; dir. Cystic Fibrosis Ctr. Children's Hosp. and Health Ctr., San Diego, 1995—; presenter, lectr. in field. Producer: (videos) Issues in Cystic Fibrosis Series; mem. rev. bd., CF Film, 1980; contbr. chpts. to books, and numerous articles to profl. jours. Mem. Air Quality Adv. Com., State of Calif., 1974-80; mem. Genetically Handicapped Persons Program Adv. Com., Calif., 1977-87; mem. adv. bd. Grossmont Coll. Inhalation Therapy Sch., San Diego, 1975-76; mem. inpatient adolscent adv. com., Mercy Hosp., 1982-85. U. Calif. fellow in pediatric cardiology, 1970-71; recipient 1st Prize Internat. Rehab. Film Library Competition, 1980. Mem. Calif. Med. Assn. (patient care audit com. 1975-78), Nat. Cystic Fibrosis Found. (mem. adv. com. 1976-80, planning ad hoc com. 1976-77, patient registry subcom. 1986-90), San Diego Found. for

Med. Care (major med. rev. com. 1978-84), San Diego Lung Assn. (pediatric com. 1976-80, chmn. Project Breath-Easy 1976-78). Home: PO Box 431 Jamul CA 91935-0431

HARWOOD, R.J., state legislator; m. Carole Harwood. Owner, janitorial & constrn. businesses; mem. Dist. 7 Idaho House of Reps., Boise, 2001—02, mem. Dist. 2, 2003—. Republican. Office: Dist Office 81527 Hwy 3 S Saint Maries ID 83861 also: Legis Services Office PO Box 83720 Boise ID 83720 Office Phone: 208-245-4446.*

HASELTINE, JAMES LEWIS, artist, consultant; b. Portland, Oreg., Nov. 7, 1924; s. William Ambrose and Clara Thusnelda (Scharpf) H.; m. Jane Winsberg, Nov. 14, 1948 (div. 1953); m. Margaret Ann Wilson, Aug. 15, 1955; children: Thomas, Jean, Kay, Suzanne, Angela. Student, Ark. State Coll., 1943—44, Reed Coll., 1946—47, Mus. Art Sch., 1947, student, 1949, Art Inst. Chgo., 1947—48, Bklyn. Mus. Sch., 1950—51. Dir. Salt Lake Art Ctr., Salt Lake City, 1961—67; exec. dir. Wash. State Arts Commn., Olympia, 1967—80, prof. art, 1950—. Vis. lectr. art history U. Utah, Salt Lake City, 1964-65; panel mem. Nat. Endowment for Arts, Washington, 1969-80; cons. in field. Author: 100 Years of Utah Painting, 1965 (Mormon History Assn. award 1965); paintings and prints represented in permanent collections Portland Art Mus., Oakland Art Mus., Mus. Art U. Oreg., Mus. Fine Arts U. Utah, Tacoma Art Mus., Willamette U., Salem, Oreg Mem. search com. for pres. Evergreen State Coll., Olympia, 1984; trustee Portland Art Mus., 1953-55. With U.S. Army, 1942-46, ETO. Mem. We. Assn. Art Mus. (pres. 1964-66), Artists Equity Assn. (nat. dir. 1955-58, chmn. Oreg. chpt. 1953-55), We. States Arts Found. (bd. dirs. 1975-77), Brit.-Am. Art Assn. (trustee 1980-84) Home and Office: 3820 Sunset Beach Dr NW Olympia WA 98502-3542

HASELTON, RICK THOMAS, lawyer; b. Albany, Oreg., Nov. 5, 1953; s. Shirley (Schantz) H. AB, Stanford U., 1976; JD, Yale U., 1979. Chair Oreg. State Bd. Bar Examiners, 1988-89, bd. dirs., 1986-88; mem. adv. com. on rules of practice 9th Cir. Ct., 1991-93. Law clk. U.S. Ct. Appeals (9th cir.) Oreg., Portland, 1979-80; from assoc. to ptnr. Lindsay, Hart, Neil & Weigler, Portland, 1979-93; sole practice Portland, 1993-94; assoc. judge Oreg. Ct. Appeals, Salem, 1994—. Chair Multnomah County Legal Aid, Portland, 1985-86, bd. dirs., 1982-87. Mem. ABA, Oreg. Bar Assn., ACLU (cooperating atty. 1982-94), Phi Beta Kappa. Jewish. Office: 300 Justice Blvd Salem OR 97310-0001

HASHE, JANIS HELENE, editor; d. James William and Arlene Florence (Houses) H. AA with honors, Cabrillo Coll., 1974; BA summa cum laude, San Francisco State, 1976; MA, San Jose State, 1982. Asst. editor Sunset Trade Publs., LA, 1988-89, assoc. editor, 1989-90; editor Western Grocery News, LA, 1990-95; sr. editor L.A. Parent Mag., Burbank, Calif., 1995—, nat. column editor. Author: (radio play) A Knot in the Heart, 1990; writer essays. Vol. Braille Inst., L.A., 1988—; block capt. Crime Watch Catalina, L.A., 1990-91. Scholar Am. Assn. U. Women, 1972. Mem. Nat. Writers Union, New One-Act Theatre Ensemble (artistic dir., 1985-88, pres., bd. dirs. 1995—). Democrat. Buddhist. Office: L A Parent Mag 443 Irving Dr Burbank CA 91504-2447

HASHIMOTO, CHRISTINE L., physician; b. Chgo., June 29, 1947; d. Shigeru and Kiyo (Sato) H. BA, Oberlin Coll., 1968; MD, Med. Coll. of Pa., 1973. Clin. instr. internal medicine, emergency medicine Med. Coll. and Hosp. of Pa., Phila., 1976-77; asst. prof. medicine Health Service Ctr. U. Colo., Denver, 1977-80, clin. asst. prof. medicine, 1980-87; staff physician emergency dept. St. Joseph Hosp., Denver, 1980-88, Rose Med. Ctr., Denver, 1988-91, Luth. Med. Ctr., Wheatridge, Colo., 1991—. Mem. Colo. Med. Soc., Denver Med. Soc., Am. Coll. Emergency Physicians. Office: Luth Med Ctr 8300 W 38th Ave Wheat Ridge CO 80033-6005

HASKAYNE, RICHARD FRANCIS, retired petroleum company executive; b. Calgary, Alta., Can., Dec. 18, 1934; s. Robert Stanley and Bertha (Hesketh) H.; m. Lee Mary Murray, 1958 (dec. 1993); m. Lois P. Heard, 1995. B Comm., U. Alta., 1956; postgrad., U. We. Ont., 1968, LLD, U. Calgary, U. Alta. Chartered acct., Alta. With Riddell, Stead & Co., chartered accts., Calgary, 1956—60; corp. acctg. supr. to v.p. fin. Hudson's Bay Oil & Gas Co., Ltd., Calgary, 1960—73; comptr. Can. Arctic Gas Study Ltd., 1973—75; sr. v.p. to pres. Hudson's Bay Oil & Gas Co. Ltd., Calgary, 1975—81; pres., CEO Home Oil Co., Ltd., Calgary, 1981—91; chmn. bd. NOVA Corp., Calgary, 1992—98; ret., 1998. Pres., CEO Interprovincial Pipe Line Co., 1987—91, Interhome Energy, 1989—91; bd. dirs. Fording Inc., chmn. bd., 2001—03; past chmn. bd. dirs. TransCanada Corp., 1998—2005; chmn. bd. TransAlta Corp., 1998—2005, TransCan Corp., 1998—2005, MacMillan Bloedel Ltd., 1996—99; dir. emeritus CIBC. Chmn. emeritus bd. govs. U. Calgary. Recipient award Officer Order of Can., 1997, Woodrow Wilson Corp. Citizenship award; named to Can. Bus. Hall of Fame, Calgary Bus. Hall of Fame, Petroleum Hall of Fame Fellow Fin. Execs. Inst., Inst. Corp. Dirs.; mem. Calgary Petroleum Club (past pres.), Calgary Golf and Country Club, Earl Grey Golf Club, Ranchmen's Club, U. Calgary Chancellor's Club, The York Club, Libr. Club, Commerce Club, Alta Inst. Chartered Accts., Kappa Sigma Office: 3845 Bankers Hall 855 2d St SW Calgary AB Canada T2P 4J8 Office Phone: 403-265-5931.

HASKELL, BARRY GEOFFRY, computer engineer, researcher; b. Lewiston, Maine, 1941; s. George Raymond and Dorothy H.; m. Ann Kantrow, Sept. 13, 1964; children: Paul Eric, Andrew. AA, Pasadena City Coll., 1962; BSEE, U. Calif., Berkeley, 1964, MSEE, 1965, PhD, 1968. Electronics engr. Lawrence Livermore Lab., Calif., 1965; rsch. asst. Electronics Rsch. Lab. U. Calif., Berkeley, 1965-68; mem. tech. staff AT&T Bell Labs., Holmdel, NJ, 1968-76, head radio comm. rsch. dept., 1976-83, visual comm. cons., 1984-86, head visual comm. rsch. dept., 1987-95; head image processing rsch. dept. AT&T Labs., Middletown, NJ, 1996-99; sr. scientist Apple Computer, Inc., Cupertino, Calif., 2002—. Adj. prof. Rutgers U., New Brunswick, NJ, 1976-79, CCNY, 1983-84, Columbia U., NYC, 1987, 93; negotiator Internat. Stds. Orgn., Am. Nat. Stds. Inst., Internat. Telecom. Union - Telecom Sector. Co-author: Image Transmission Tech., 1979, Digital Pictures, 1988, 2d edit., 1995, Digital Video—An Introduction to MPEG-2, 1996; contbr. articles to profl. jours.; patentee in field. Recipient Elec. Engring. Dept. Outstanding Alumnus award U. Calif., Berkeley, 1998; co-recipient Japan's Computer and Comm. prize, 1997, NJ Inventor Hall of Fame Inventor of Yr., 2000; AT&T fellow, 1998; picture coding symposium award for leadership, pioneering rsch., 2006. Fellow: IEEE (life), Phi Beta Kappa. Avocations: sailing, skiing, guitar playing. Office: Apple Computer 302-3KS 2 Infinite Loop Cupertino CA 95014

HASLAM, DENNIS V., lawyer, former professional sports team executive; b. Salt Lake City, Sept. 19, 1948; m. Deborah Haslam; children: Peter, Carter, Madeleine. BA magna cum laude in Hist., U. Utah, 1973, JD, 1976. Bar: Utah 1976, US Ct. Appeals (10th cir.) 1984, US Supreme Ct. 1985. Co-founder Winder & Haslam, Salt Lake City, 1983—97, of counsel; pres., COO sports and entertainment divsn. Larry Miller Group, 1997—2007; pres. Utah Jazz, Salt Lake City, 2000—07, cons. Adj. prof. U. Utah Coll. Law, 1994—96; chair Access to Justice Found. Active Utah Jud. Coun., Utah Sports Authority, 2002 Winter Olympics venues. Mem. Utah State Bar (chmn. character and fitness com. 1981-90, mem. ethics and discipline screening panel 1987-90, mem. admission rules com. 1989, bd. commrs. 1990-95, pres. 1995-96), Utah Bar Found. Office: Winder & Counsel PC 175 W 200 South Ste 4000 Salt Lake City UT 84101

HASLAM, GERALD WILLIAM, writer, educator; b. Bakersfield, Calif., Mar. 18, 1937; s. Fredrick Martin and Lorraine Hope (Johnson) H.; m. Janice Eileen Pettichord, July 1, 1961; children: Frederick W., Alexandra R., Garth C., Simone B., Carlos V. BA, San Francisco State U., 1963, MA, 1965; PhD, Union Grad. Sch., 1980. Instr. English San Francisco State U., San Francisco, 1966-67; asst. prof. English Sonoma State U., Rohnert Park, Calif., 1967-70, assoc. prof. English, 1970-74, prof. English, 1971-97, emeritus prof. English, 1997—; prof. Fromm Inst./U. San Francisco, 2001—. Adj. prof. Union Grad. Sch., Cin., 1984—, The Nat. Faculty, Atlanta, 1984—; prof. Oscher Lifelong Learning Inst., Sonoma State U., 2003—. Editor various anthologies; author various booklets, monographs, film scripts, (fiction) Okies: Selected Stories, 1973, Masks: A Novel, 1976, The Wages of Sin: Collected Stories, 1980, Hawk Flights: Visions of the West, 1983, Snapshots: Glimpses of the Other California, 1985, The Man Who Cultivated Fire and Other Stories, 1987, That Constant Coyote: California Stories, 1990, Condor Dreams and Other Fictions, 1994, The Great Tejon Club Jubilee, 1996, Manuel and the Madman, 1999, Straight White Male, 2000, Haslam's Valley, 2005, (fiction/nonfiction) Voices of a Place, 1987, Straight White Male 2008,Coming of Age in California, 1990, The Other California, 1990, The Great Central Valley: California's Heartland, 1993, Workin' Man Blues: Country Music in California, 1999, Coming of Age in California, 2d enlarged edit., 2000, Grace Period, 2006; contbg. writer West (LA Times' mag.). With U.S. Army, 1958-60. Creative Writing fellow Calif. Arts Coun., 1989; recipient Benjamin Franklin award, 1993, Bay Area Book Reviewers' Non-fiction award, 1994, Commonwealth Club medal for Calif., 1994, Merit award Assn. State & Local History, 1994, Commendation citation, 2001; Fulbright sr. lectr., 1986-87, Josephine Miles award, 1990, Ralph J. Gleason award, 2000, Carey McWilliams award, 2001, Western States Book Fiction award, 2001, Sequoia - Giant of the Valley award, 2003, Cert. of Commendation, Calif. Arts Coun., 2004, Delbert and Edith Wyler award, 2005, Josephine Miles award, 2006. Mem. Great Valley Ctr. (adv. bd.), Western Lit. Assn. (bd. dirs., past pres., Disting. Achievment award 1999, Delbert and Edith Wylder award 2005), Calif. Studies Assn. (steering com., founding mem.), Calif. Hist. Assn., Calif. Tchrs. Assn., San Francisco State U. Alumni Assn. (life), Union Inst. Alumni Assn., Multi-Ethnic Lit. of U.S. (founding mem.), Robinson Jeffers Assn. (founding mem.), Sierra Club, The Nature Conservancy, Calif. Trout (founding mem.), Tulare Basin Archeology Group, Defenders of Wildlife, Common Cause, Soc. of the Third Infantry Divsn., Yosemite Assn. (bd. dirs.). Roman Catholic. Avocations: bicycling, hiking, fishing. Office: PO Box 969 Penngrove CA 94951-0969 Office Phone: 707-792-2944. Personal E-mail: ghaslam@sonic.net.

HASLAM, ROBERT THOMAS, III, lawyer; b. Taunton, Mass., May 4, 1946; s. Robert Thomas and Marcella Neale (Compton) H.; children: Laurel Ashley, Julia Compton; m. Molly Haslam. BS Aeronautics and Astronautics, MIT, 1968; JD, Hastings Coll., 1976. Bar: Calif., 1976. Atty., ptnr. Heller, Ehrman, Menlo Park, Calif., 1976—. Capt. USAF 1969-73. Mem. ABA (co-chair litigation, intellectual property sect. 1993—). Avocations: tennis, soccer. Office: Heller Ehrman 275 Middlefield Rd Menlo Park CA 94025-3506 Home: 1410 Enchanted W San Mateo CA 94402 Office Phone: 650-324-7073.

HASLER, WILLIAM ALBERT, electronics executive; b. Los Angeles, Nov. 22, 1941; s. Albert Ernst and LaDella (Stewart) H.; m. Janet Louise Kindstrom, June 10, 1963; children— Claire, Laura, James BA, Pomona Coll., 1963; MBA, Harvard U., 1967. C.P.A., Calif. Ptnr. Peat, Marwick, Mitchell & Co., Los Angeles, 1972-76, ptnr.-in-charge, 1976-81, NYC, 1981-84; vice chmn., dir., mem. operating com. Peat, Marwick, Main & Co., San Francisco and NYC, 1984-91; dean Haas Sch. Bus., U. Calif., Berkeley, 1991-98; co-CEO Aphton Corp., Miami, 1998—2003, vice chmn., 2003; chmn. Solectron, 2003—. Mem. council KPMG Internat., 1985— Mem. editorial adv. bd. Jour. Accountancy Fellow Huntington Library, San Marino, Calif.; treas. Harvard U. Bus. Sch. Alumni Bd.; trustee Pomona Coll.; bd. dirs. Nat. Ctr. Fin. Services; mem. Pacific Basin Econ. Council Mem. Am. Inst. C.P.A.s, Calif. Soc. C.P.A.s, Calif. C. of C. Clubs: Calif. (Los Angeles); Union League (N.Y.C.); University (bd. dirs.); St. Francis Yacht. Avocations: sailing, skiing, diving. Office: Solectron 847 Gibraltar Dr Milpitas CA 95035

HASS, MARK, state legislator; b. Newport, RI, Dec. 10, 1956; m. Tamra Hass; 1 child, Isabelle. BS in Journalism, U. Oreg., 1978; M, Am. U., 1982. Reporter KNPT radio, Newport, Oreg., 1980—81, KVAL-TV, 1981—84, KATU-TV, Portland, Oreg., 1984—2000; mem. Oreg. House of Reps., 2000—07; former house dem. whip; journalist; prof.; real estate agt.; brand strategist Cappelli Miles; mem. Dist. 14 Oreg. State Senate, 2007—. Founder journalism scholarship fund Oreg. State Scholarship Commn., 1999—; trustee Tom Dargan Scholarship. Recipient numerous Emmy awards, Assoc. Press awards, Child Inc., 1999. Democrat. Presbyterian. Office: Oreg State Senate 900 Court St NE S-419 Salem OR 97301 Office Phone: 503-986-1714. E-mail: sen.markhass@state.or.us.*

HASS, ROBERT LOUIS, poet, literature educator; b. San Francisco, Calif., Mar. 1, 1941; m. Brenda Hillman, 1994; 1 stepchild, Louisa; children: Leif, Kristin, Luke. Grad., St. Mary's Coll., Moraga, Calif., 1963; MA in English, Stanford U., 1965, PhD in English, 1971. Asst. prof. SUNY, Buffalo, 1967—71; prof. English St. Mary's Coll., Moraga, Calif., 1971—89, U. Calif., Berkeley, 1989—; US Poet Laureate, 1995—97. Vis. lectr. U. Va., 1974, Goddard Coll., 1976, Columbia U., 1982, U. Calif., Berkeley, 1983; vis. faculty U. Iowa Writers' Workshop; poet-in-residence The Frost Pl., Franconia, NH, 1978; spkr. in field. Author: (books of poetry) Field Guide, 1973 (Yale Series of Younger Poets award, 1972), Praise, 1979 (William Carlos Williams award, 1979), Human Wishes, 1989, Sun Under Wood: New Poems, 1996 (Nat. Book Critics Cir. award, 1996), Time and Materials: Poems 1997-2005, 2007 (Nat. Book award for poetry, 2007, Pulitzer prize for poetry, 2008), (book of criticism) Twentieth Century Pleasures: Prose on Poetry, 1984 (Nat. Book Critics Cir. award, 1984); editor: Rock and Hawk: A Selection of Shorter Poems by Robinson Jeffers, 1987, The Essential Haiku: Versions of Basho, Buson and Issa, 1994; co-editor: The Pushcart Prize XII, 1987, Tomaz Salamum: Selected Poems, 1988, The Essential Neruda: Selected Poems, 2004; co-translator (with Czeslaw Milosz): (vols. of poetry) The Separate Notebooks, 1984, Unattainable Earth, 1986, Provinces, 1991, Facing the River: New Poems, 1995, Road-Side Dog, 1999, Treatise on Poetry, 2001, Second Space: New Poems, 2004; actor: (film) Wildflowers, 1999. Trustee Griffin Poetry Prize; co-founder River of Words (youth internat. poetry and art contest). Apptd. Poet Laureate of U.S., 1995-97; MacArthur "Genius" fellow; named Educator of the Yr., N.Am. Assn. on Environ. Edn., 1997, chancellor Acad. Am. Poets, 2000. Mem.: Acad. Am. Poets (chancellor). Office: U Calif 405 Wheeler Berkeley CA 94720 Office Phone: 510-642-2746. E-mail: bobhass@berkeley.edu.

HASSELBECK, MATT, professional football player; b. Westwood, Mass., Sept. 25, 1975; s. Don Hasselbeck; m. Sarah Hasselbeck, 2000; 2 children. Grad., Boston Coll. Quarterback Green Bay Packers, 1999—2001, Seattle Seahawks, 2001—. Named to Nat. Football Conf. Pro Bowl Team, NFL, 2003, 2005, 2007. Office: Seattle Seahawks Qwest Field 800 Occidental Ave S Seattle WA 98134

HASSON, KIRKE MICHAEL, lawyer; b. East St. Louis, Ill., Oct. 25, 1949; s. David S. and Audrey (Leber) Hasson. BA magna cum laude, Yale U., 1971; JD cum laude, Harvard U., 1974. Bar: Calif. 1974, U.S. Dist. Ct. (all dist. Calif.), US Ct. Appeals (2d, 5th, 9th cir.). Assoc. Pillsbury Winthrop Shaw Pittman LLP (formerly Pillsbury Winthrop LLP), San Francisco, 1974—81, ptnr., 1982—2007, ptnr., chmn. life sci. and tech. group, 2007—. Office: Pillsbury Winthrop Shaw Pittman LLP 50 Fremont St San Francisco CA 94105 Office Phone: 415-983-1077. Office Fax: 415-983-1200. E-mail: kirke.hasson@pillsburylaw.com.

HASSRICK, PETER HEYL, art historian, educator; b. Phila., Apr. 27, 1941; s. Royal Brown and E. Barbara (Morgan) H.; m. Elizabeth Drake, June 14, 1963; children: Philip Heyl, Charles Royal. Student, Harvard U., 1962; BA, U. Colo., 1963; MA, U. Denver, 1969. Tchr. Whiteman Sch., Steamboat Springs, Colo., 1963-67, also bd. dirs.; curator of collections Amon Carter Mus., Ft. Worth, 1969-75; dir. Buffalo Bill Hist. Ctr., Cody, Wyo., 1976-96, Georgia O'Keefe Mus., Santa Fe, 1996-97; dir., prof. art history Charles M. Russell Ctr. Study Art U. Okla., Norman, 1998—; dir., Inst. Western Am. Art Denver Mus. Art, 2005—. Author: Frederic Remington, 1973, The Way West, 1977, (with others) The Rocky Mountains, 1983, Treasures of the Old West, 1984, (with others) Frederic Remington, The Masterworks, 1988, (with others) Frontier America, 1988, Charles M. Russell, 1989, (with others) Frederic Remington: A Catalogue Raisonne, 1996, Georgie O'Keeffe Mus., 1997, (intro.) The American West: Out of Myth Into Reality, 2000, Unending Frontier: Art of the West, 2000, Remington and Russell, 2000, Alexander Phimister Proctor; Sculptor, 2004. Office: Denver Museum Art 100 West 14th Ave Pkwy Denver CO 80204

HASTINGS, DOC (RICHARD NORMAN HASTINGS), United States Representative from Washington; b. Spokane, Wash., Feb. 7, 1941; m. Claire Hastings; c. Kristen, Petrina, Colin. Student, Columbia Basin Coll., 1958—61, Ctrl. Wash. U., 1964. Mem. Wash. State Ho. Reps., 1979-87, asst. majority leader; pres. Columbia Basin Paper & Supply, 1983-94; mem. US Congress from 4th Wash. dist., 1995—, mem. rules com., chmn. rules and orgn. of the house, chmn. stds. ofcl. conduct com., 2005—, chair Congl. Nuc. Cleanup Caucus, asst. majority whip. Bd. dirs. Yakima Fed. Savings & Loan; chmn. Franklin County Rep. Com., 1974-78 Del. Rep. Nat. Conv., 1976—84. With USAR, 1963—69. Republican. Office: US House Reps 1203 Longworth House Office Bldg Washington DC 20515-0001 Office Phone: 202-225-5816.

HASTINGS, EDWARD WALTON, theater director; b. New Haven, Apr. 14, 1931; s. Edward Walton and Madeline (Cassidy) H. BA, Yale, 1952; postgrad., Royal Acad. Dramatic Art, London, 1953, Columbia U., 1955-56. Bd. dirs. Eugene O'Neill Found., 1993; guest instr. Shanghai Drama Inst., 1984. Dir. Australian premiere Hot L Baltimore, 1975, Shakespeare's People nat. tour, 1983, Nothing Sacred, Hong Kong, 1992, Come Back Little Sheba, Gogol Theater, Moscow, 1995, Dial M for Murder nat. tour, 1995, Beggars Opera, Santa Fe Opera, 2000, H.M.S. Pinafore, Santa Fe Opera, 2001, Italian Girl, 2005, Oliver!, St. Louis Mcpl. Opera, 2005, others; exec. dir. Am. Conservatory Theatre, San Francisco, 1965-80, artistic dir., 1986-92; freelance dir., 1980-86. Mem. Santa Fe Arts Commn. Served with U.S. Army, 1953-55. Recipient Tao House award, Eugene O'Neill Found. Mem. Coll. of Fellows of the Am. Theatre. Clubs: Elizabethan (New Haven). Office: Am Conservatory Theatre 30 Grant Ave San Francisco CA 94108-5800 Home: 945 Acequia Madre Santa Fe NM 87505

HASTINGS, L(OIS) JANE, architect, educator; b. Seattle, Mar. 3, 1928; d. Harry and Camille (Pugh) H.; m. Norman John Johnston, Nov. 22, 1969. B.Arch., U. Wash., Seattle, 1952, postgrad. in Urban Planning, 1958. Architect Boeing Airplane Co., Seattle, 1951-54; recreational dir. Germany, 1954-56; architect (various firms), Seattle, 1956-59, pvt. practice architecture, 1959-74; instr. archtl. drafting Seattle Community Coll., part-time 1969-80; owner/founder The Hastings Group Architects, Seattle, 1974—; lectr. design Coll. Architecture, U. Wash., 1975; incorporating mem. Architecta (P.S.), Seattle, 1980, pres., from 1980. Mem. adv. bd. U. Wash. YWCA, 1967—69; mem. Mayor's Com. on Archtl. Barriers for Handicapped, 1974—75; chmn. regional public adv. panel on archtl. and engring. services GSA, 1976; mem. citizens adv. com. Seattle Land Use Adminstrn. Task Force, 1979—; AWIU guest of Soviet Women's Con., 1983; spkr. Pacific Rim Forum, Hong Kong, 1987; guest China Internat. Conf. Ctr. for Sci. and Tech. of the China Assn. for Sci. and Tech., 1989; mem. adv. com. Coll. architecture and urban planning U. Wash., 1993; mem. accreditation team U. Oreg. Coll. Architecture, 1991, N.J. Inst. Tech. Sch. Architecture, 1992; juror Home of the Yr. ann. award AIA/Seattle Times, 1996; mem. architect selection com. Wash. State capital carillon project, Pratt Art Ctr. new bldg., 2001. Design juror for nat. and local competitions, including Red Cedar Shingle/AIA awards, 1977, Current Use Honor awards, AIA, 1980, Exhibit of Sch. Architecture award, 1981; Contbr. to: also spl. features newspapers, articles in profl. jours. Sunset mag. Mem. bd. Am. Women for Internat. Understanding, del. to, Egypt, Israel, USSR, 1971, Japan and Korea, 1979, USSR, 1983; mem. Landmarks Preservation Bd. City of Seattle, 1981-83; mem. Design Constrn. Rev. Bd. Seattle Sch. Dist., 1985-87; mem. mus. con. Mus. History and Industry, 1987—; leader People to

People del. women architects to China, 1990. Recipient AIA/The Seattle Times Home of Month Ann. award, 1968; Exhbn. award Seattle chpt. AIA, 1970; Environ. award Seattle-King County Bd. Realtors, 1970, 77,; AIA/House and Home/The American Home Merit award, 1971, Sp. Honor award Wash. Aggregates and Concrete Assn., 1993, Prize bridge Am. Inst. Steel Contrn., 1993; Honor award Seattle chpt. AIA, 1977, 83; Women Achievement award Past Pres. Assembly, 1983, Washington Women and Trading Cards, 1983; Nat. Endowment for Arts grantee, 1977, BRAVA award Women's U. Club Seattle, 2008; others; named to West Seattle High Sch. Hall of Fame, 1989, Woman of Achievement Matrix Table, 1994; named Woman of Distinction, Columbia River Girl Scout Coun., 1994. Fellow AIA (pres. Seattle chpt. 1975, pres. sr. coun. 1980, state exec. bd. 1975, N.W. regional dir. 1982-87, Seattle chpt. found. bd. 1985-87, Bursar Coll. Fellows 1989-90, Coll. of Fellows historian 1994—, internat. rels. com. 1988-92, vice chancellor 1991, chancellor 1992, Seattle chpt. medal 1995, Northwest & Pacific region Medal of Honor 2002, Leslie N. Boney Spirit of Fellowship award 2003, Richard Upjohn Fellows medal), Internat. Union Women Architects (v.p. 1969-79, sec. gen. 1985-89, del. UIA Congress, Montreal 1990), Am. Arbitration Assn. (arbitrator 1981—), Coun. of Design Professions, Assn. Women Contrs., Suppliers and Design Cons., Allied Arts Seattle, Fashion Group, Tau Sigma Delta, Alpha Rho Chi (medal).

HASTINGS, REED (WILMOT REED HASTINGS JR.), film rental company executive, former education association administrator; b. Boston, Oct. 8, 1960; married; 2 children. BA, Bowdoin Coll., Brunswick, Maine, 1983; MS in Computer Sci., Stanford U., Calif., 1988. High sch. math tchr. US Peace Corps, Swaziland, 1983—86; founder, CEO Pure Atria Software, 1991—97; CEO Tech. Network, 1998—99; co-founder, chmn., CEO Netflix, Inc., Los Gatos, Calif., 1998—, pres., 1998—. Bd. dirs. Microsoft Corp., 2007—. Pres. Calif. State Bd. Edn., 2000—04; founding mem. NewSchools.org, Aspire Pub. Schs., Pacific Collegiate Sch., EdVoice.net. Named a Maverick, Details mag., 2007; named one of World's 100 Most Influential People, Time mag., 2005. Office: Netflix Inc 100 Winchester Cir Los Gatos CA 95032 Office Phone: 408-540-3700. Office Fax: 408-540-3737.*

HATAMIYA, LON SHOSO, consultant, former state official; m. Nancy Hatamiya; 2 children. BS in Economics, Harvard U.; MBA in Internat. Bus. & Entrepreneurial Studies, UCLA; JD, UCLA Sch. of Law. Former atty. Procter & Gamble Co., Cincinnati, Ohio, Sony Corp., Tokyo; administrator Agricultural Mktg. Svc., USDA, 1993—97, Foreign Agricultural Svc., USDA, 1997—99; secy. Calif. Techn., Trade and Commerce Agy., 1999—2003; dir. LECG, 2004—. Mem. Calif. Rural Economic Develop. Infrastructure Panel; exec.-in-residence U. Calif. Grad. Sch. of Bus., Davis, 2004. Office: Lecg 2049 Century Park E Ste 2300 Los Angeles CA 90067-3125

HATCH, CHARLES R., dean; BS in Forest Mgmt., U. Mont., 1964; M in Forestry, Forest Mensuration, Oreg. State U., 1966; PhD in Forest Mensuration/Stats., U. Minn., 1971. Grad. asst. Oreg. State U. Sch. Forstry, Corvallis, 1965-66; instr. U. Minn. Sch. Forestry, St. Paul, 1967-71; asst. prof. dept. forestry So. Ill. U., Carbondale, 1971-73; assoc. prof. Coll. Forestry, Wildlife and Range Scis., U. Idaho, Moscow, Idaho, 1973-77, prof., 1977—, program dir. continuing edn. in forest ecology/silviculture, 1977-82, assoc. dean rsch., assoc. dir. forestry, wildlife, 1979-83, head dept. forest resources, 1987-89, assoc. dean rsch., internat. programs, dir. experiment sta., 1994-95; dean now U. Idaho, Coll. Natural Resources, Moscow, Idaho, 1995—. Forestry advisor U.S. AID, New Delhi, India, 1983-87; chief of party forestry planning and devel. project Winrock Internat., Islamabad, Pakistan, 1989-94. Contbr. articles to profl. jours. Recipient Outstanding Svc. to Am. Embassy Cmty. award Am. Amb. to Pakistan. Recipient Outstanding Svc. award to Am. Embassy Cmty., Islamabad, Pakistan, 1993, 94. Mem. Mont. Druids, Gamma Sigma Delta, Sigma Xi, Xi Sigma Pi. Office: U Idaho Coll Natural Resources Range Scis Moscow ID 83844-0001

HATCH, GEORGE CLINTON, television executive; b. Erie, Pa., Dec. 16, 1919; s. Charles Milton and Blanche (Beecher) Hatch; m. Wilda Gene Glasmann, Dec. 24, 1940; children: Michell Arnow, Diane Glasmann Orr, Jeffrey Beecher, Randall Clinton, Deepika Hatch Avanti. AB, Occidental Coll., 1940; MA in Econs., Claremont Coll., 1941; HHD (hon.), So. Utah U., 1988. Pres. Comms. Investment Corp., Salt Lake City, 1945-95; chmn. Double G Comm. Corp., Salt Lake City, 1956—; dir. Republic Pictures Corp., Los Angeles, 1971-94; pres. Sta. KVEL, Inc., 1978-94. Pres. Standard Corp., Ogden, 1993-98, Hatch Family LLC, 1998—; past mem. Salt Lake adv. bd. First Security Bank Utah; past chmn. Rocky Mountain Pub. Broadcasting Corp.; past chmn. bd. govs. Am. Info. Radio Network; past bd. govs. NBC-TV Affiliates. Past pres. Salt Lake Com. on Fgn. Relations; past mem. Utah Symphony Bd., Salt Lake City; past chmn. and mem. Utah State Bd. Regents, 1964-85. Recipient Svc. to Journalism award U. Utah, 1966, silver medal Salt Lake Advt. Club, 1969, Disting. Svc. award Utah Tech. U., 1984, Disting. Utahan Centennial Yr. award Margaret Thatcher U.K., Utah Festival, 1996. Mem. Nat. Assn. Broadcasters (past pres., radio bd. dirs., ambassador to Inter-Am. mtgs. in Latin Am. 1962), Utah Broadcasters Assn. (past pres., Mgmt. award 1964, Hall of Fame award 1981), Salt Lake City Advt. Club (silver medal 1969), Phi Beta Kappa, Phi Rho Pi (life). Democrat. Avocations: hiking, rock art. Office: Hatch Family LLC 1537 Chandler Dr Salt Lake City UT 84103-4220 Home Phone: 801-532-7963.

HATCH, ORRIN GRANT, United States Senator from Utah; b. Homestead Park, Pa., Mar. 22, 1934; s. Jesse and Helen (Kamm) H.; m. Elaine Hansen, Aug. 28, 1957; children: Brent, Marcia, Scott, Kimberly, Alysa, Jess. BS in History, Brigham Young U., 1959; JD, U. Pitts., 1962; LLD (hon.), U. Md., 1981; MS (hon.), Def. Intelligence Coll., 1982; LLD (hon.), Pepperdine U., 1990, So. Utah State U., 1990. Bar: Pa. 1962, Utah 1962. Ptnr. firm Thomson, Rhodes & Grigsby, Pitts., 1962-69, Hatch & Plumb, Salt Lake City, 1976; US Senator from Utah, 1977—. Mem. com. fin. US Senate, com. health, edn., labor, and pensions, com. judiciary, joint com. tax, select com. intelligence. Author: The Equal Rights Amendment: Myths and Realities, 1983, Understanding the Doctrines of Christ, 1995, Square Peg: Confessions of a Citizen Senator, 2003; contbr. articles to newspapers and profl. jours. Recipient Excellence in Public Svc. award Am. Acad. Pediatrics, 1988, Senator of Yr. award Nat. Multipule Sclerosis Soc., 1996, Lifetime Achievement award Asian Assn. Utah, 1998, Small Investor Empowerment award Nat. Assn. Real Estate Investment Trusts, 2001, Campbell award, Am. Soc. Law Enforcement Tng., 2002, Elmer P. Martin Public Svc. award Great Blacks in Wax Mus., 2003, Legis. of Yr. award biotechnology Industry Orgn., 2003, Nat. Leadership award, Coalition for Juvenile Justice, 2004. Mem. ABA., Nat. Bar Assn., Utah Bar Assn., Pa. Bar Assn., Am. Judicature Soc. Republican. Mem. Lds Ch. Avocations: golf, poetry, piano playing, composer lyrics. Office: US Senate 104 Hart Senate Office Bldg Washington DC 20510-0001 also: Federal Bldg Rm 8402 125 S State St Salt Lake City UT 84138-1191 Office Phone: 202-224-5251, 801-524-4380. Office Fax: 202-224-6331, 801-524-4379. E-mail: senator_hatch@hatch.senate.gov.*

HATELEY, J. MICHAEL, human resources executive; BA in Psychology, U. Calif. Mgr. human resources Monogram Industries, ITT; v.p. pres. human resources Mil. Aircraft, Elec., Aircraft Northrop Grumman, Inc., LA, 1976-99, corp. v.p. personnel, 1999; corp. v.p., chief human resourve Northrop Grumman Corp., LA, 2000—. Mem. human resources adv. coun. conf. bd. USC Marshall Sch. Bus., mem. corp. adv. bd. Bd. dirs. Ind. Colls. So. Calif. Office: Northrop Grumman Corp 1840 Century Park E Los Angeles CA 90067-2101 Office Phone: 310-553-6262.

HATFIELD, MARK ODOM, former senator; b. Dallas, Oreg., July 12, 1922; s. Charles Dolen and Dovie (Odom) H.; m. Antoinette Kuzmanich, July 8, 1958; children: Mark, Elizabeth, Theresa, Charles. AB, Willamette U., 1943; AM, Stanford U., 1948. Instr. Willamette U., 1949, dean students, assoc. prof. polit. sci., 1950-56; mem. Oreg. Ho. of Reps., 1951-55, Oreg. Senate, 1955-57; sec. State of Oreg., 1957-59, gov., 1959-67; U.S. senator from Oreg., 1967-97. Chmn. appropriations com., energy and natural resources com., rules and adminstrn. com., joint printing com., joint libr. com., select com. Indian Affairs, Republican Policy Com.; chmn. Appropriations subcom. on transp. & related agencies. Author: Not Quite So Simple, 1967, Conflict and Conscience, 1971, Between A Rock and A Hard Place, 1976; co-author: Amnesty: The Unsettled Question of Vietnam, 1976, Freeze! How You Can Help Prevent Nuclear War, 1982, The Causes of World Hunger, 1982; co-author: What About the Russians, 1984, Vice Presidents of the United States 1789-1993, 1997. Lt. (j.g.) USN, 1943-45, PTO. Recipient over 100 hon. degrees Republican. Baptist.

HATHAWAY, ANNE, actress; b. Bklyn., Nov. 12, 1982; d. Gerard Hathaway and Kate McCauley. Actor: (TV series) Get Real, 1999—2000; (films) The Princess Diaries, 2001, The Other Side of Heaven, 2001, (voice) The Cat Returns, 2002, Nicholas Nickleby, 2002, Ella Enchanted, 2004, The Princess Diaries 2: Royal Engagement, 2004, (voice) Hoodwinked, 2005, Havoc, 2005, Brokeback Mountain, 2005, The Devil Wears Prada, 2006, Becoming Jane, 2007, Get Smart, 2008, Rachel Getting Married, 2008 (Best Actress Nat. Bd. Review, 2008, 2008 Best Actress, Critics' Choice award, Broadcast Film Critics Assn., 2009), Passengers, 2008, Bride Wars, 2009. Recipient Women in Hollywood Tribute award, Elle Mag., 2008, Desert Palm Achievement award, Palm Springs Internat. Film Soc., 2009. Office: c/o Management 360 9111 Wilshire Blvd Beverly Hills CA 90210

HATHAWAY, PETER S., corporate financial executive; Auditor Arthur Anderson, LLP, 1979—91; contr. and fin. dir. BFI, 1991—95; chief acctg. officer Allied Waste Industries, Phoenix, 1995—2001, treas., 1996—97, v.p., 1996—2000, sr. v.p., fin., 2000—03, exec. v.p., CFO, 2003—. Office: Allied Waste Industries Inc 18500 N Allied Way Phoenix AZ 85054

HATLEN, JOEL S., electronics manufacturing executive; b. 1958; With Ernst & Young LLP; sr. tax acct., tax mgr., corp. contr., chief acctg. officer Data I/O Corp., Redmond, Wash., 1991, v.p. fin., CFO, 1998—. Office: 10525 Willows Rd NE Redmond WA 98052-2545

HATTER, TERRY JULIUS, JR., federal judge; b. Chgo., Mar. 11, 1933; AB, Wesleyan U., 1954; JD, U. Chgo., 1960. Bar: Ill. 1960, Calif. 1965, U.S. Dist. Ct. 1960, U.S. Ct. Appeals 1960. Adjudicator, Chgo., 1960-61; assoc. Harold M. Calhoun, Chgo., 1961-62; asst. pub. defender Cook County Chgo., 1961-62; asst. U.S. atty. No. Dist. Calif., San Francisco, 1962-66; chief counsel San Francisco Neighborhood Legal Assistance Found., 1966-67; regional legal svcs. dir. Exec. Office Pres. OEO, San Francisco, 1967-70; exec. dir. Western Ctr. Law and Poverty, LA, 1970-73; exec. asst. to mayor, dir. criminal justice planning LA, 1974-75; spl. asst. to mayor, dir. urban devel., 1975-77; judge Superior Ct. Calif., LA, 1977-80, U.S. Dist. Ct. (cen. dist.) Calif., LA, 1979-98, chief judge, 1998—. Lectr. Police Acad., San Francisco Police Dept., 1963-66, U. Calif., San Diego, 1970-71, Colo. Jud. Conf., 1973; assoc. clin. prof. law U. So. Calif. Law Ctr., L.A., 1970-74, mem. bd. councilors; prof. law Loyola U. Sch. Law, L.A., 1973-75; mem. faculty Nat. Coll. State Judiciary, Reno, 1974. V.p. Northbay Halfway House, 1964-65; vice chmn. Los Angeles Regional Criminal Justice Planning Bd., 1975-76; mem. Los Angeles Mayor's Cabinet Com. Econ. Devel., 1976-77, Mayor's Policy Com., 1973-77, chmn. housing econ. and community devel. com., City Los Angeles, 1975-77, chmn. housing and community devel. tech. com., 1975-77; vice chmn. Young Dems. Cook County, 1961-62; chmn. bd. Real Estate Coop; bd. dirs. Bay Area Social Planning Coun., Contra Costa, Black Law Center L.A., Nat. Fedn. Settlements & Neighborhood Ctrs., Edn. Fin. & Governance Reform Project, Mexican Am. Legal Def. & Ednl. Fund, Nat. Health Law Program, Nat. Sr. Citizens Law Ctr., Calif. Law Ctr., L.A. Regional Criminal Justice Planning Bd.; mem. exec. com. bd. dirs. Constl. Rights Found; trustee Wesleyan Univ. Meth. Ch.; mem. bd. visitors U. Chgo. Law Sch. Mem. NAACP (exec. com., bd. dirs. Richmond chpt.), Nat. Legal Aid & Defender Assn. (dir., vice chmn.), L.A. County Bar Assn. (exec. com.), Am. Judicature Soc., Charles Houston Law Club, Phi Delta Phi, Order Coif. Office: US Dist Ct 312 N Spring St Los Angeles CA 90012-4701

HATTERY, ROBERT RALPH, radiologist, educator; b. Phoenix, Dec. 15, 1939; s. Robert Ralph and Goldie M. H.; m. D. Diane Sittler, June 18, 1961; children: Angela, Michael. BA, Ind. U., Bloomington, 1961; MD, Ind. U., Indpls., 1964; cert. in diagnostic radiology, U. Minn. Mayo Grad. Sch. Medicine, Rochester, 1971. Diplomate Am. Bd. Radiology. Intern Parkland Meml. Hosp.-Southwestern Med. Sch., Dallas, 1964-65; fellow Mayo Clinic, Rochester, Minn., 1967-70, cons., 1970-81, chmn. dept. diagnostic radiology, 1981-86; instr. radiology Mayo Med. Sch., 1973-75, asst. prof. radiology, 1975-78, assoc. prof. radiology, 1978-82, prof. radiology, 1982—. Chair Mayo Group Practice Bd., 1991-93; chmn. bd. govs Mayo Clinic, Rochester, 1994-98; trustee Mayo Found., 1992-2002; trustee Am. Bd. Radiology. Author numerous jour. articles and abstracts, book chpts. Capt. USAF, 1965-67, Willford Hall Hosp., San Antonio. Fellow Am. Coll. Radiology; mem. Radiol. Soc. N.Am. (bd. dirs. 1999—), Am. Roentgen Ray Soc., Soc. Computed Body Tomography (pres. 1982-83), Soc. Genitourinary Radiography (pres. 1986-88), Am. Bd. Radiology (exec. dir.). Office: American Bd Radiology 5441 E Williams Blvd Tucson AZ 85711 Home Phone: 520-219-8599. Business E-Mail: rhattery@theabr.org.

HAUGEN, MARY MARGARET, state legislator; b. Camano Island, Wash., Jan. 14, 1941; d Melvin Harry Olsen & Alma Cora Huntington O; married 1990 to Basil Badley; children: Mary Elizabeth, Katherine, Richard & James, five grandchildren. Member, Stanwood Sch Bd, formerly; Washington State Representative, District 10, 82-92; Washington State Senator, District 10, 93-, chairman, Munic Research Coun & Transportation Committee, currently, member, Judiciary & State & Local Govt Committees, currently, Washington State Senate. Eastern Star; League Women Voters; Camano Island Chamber of Commerce; Stanwood & Camano Soroptomists. Democrat. Methodist. Address: 1268 N Olsen Rd Camano Island WA 98292 Mailing: 414 John A Cherberg Olympia WA 98504-0482 Fax: 360-786-1999. E-mail: haugen_ma@leg.wa.gov, mmhaugen@whidbey.net.

HAUGHTON, JAMES GRAY, health facility administrator, consultant; b. Panama City, Republic of Panama, Mar. 30, 1925; came to U.S., 1942, naturalized, 1953; s. Johnathan Antonio and Alice Eugeney (Gray) H.; m. Vivian Bruna Sodini, July 10, 1982; children: James Gray, Paula Yvette BA, Pacific Union Coll., 1947; MD, Loma Linda U., 1950; M.P.H., Columbia U., 1962; D.Sc. (hon.), U. of Health Scis., Chgo. Med. Sch., 1971. diplomate Am. Bd. Preventive Medicine. Intern Unity Hosp., Bklyn., 1949-50, fellow in abdominal surgery, 1950-54; resident in preventive medicine N.Y.C. Health Dept., 1960-63, exec. med. dir., 1964-66; first dep. N.Y.C. Health Svcs. Adminstrn., 1966-70; exec. dir. Health and Hosps. Governing Commn. Cook County, Ill., 1970-79; v.p. Drew Postgrad. Med. Sch., Los Angeles, 1980-83; dir. Houston Dept. Health and Human Services, 1983-87; med. dir. Martin. Luther King Jr./Charles Drew Med. Ctr., L.A. Dept. Health Svcs., 1987-93; assoc. dean Drew U., 1989-93. Prof. medicine Charles Drew U., 1987—, UCLA, 1987—; cons. AID Costa Rica Mission, 1982; adj. prof. adminstrv. scis. U. Tex. Health Sci. Ctr., Houston, 1984-87; mem. health svcs. com. Houston Red Cross, 1984-87; mem. Houston Mayor's Task Force on Aids, 1984-87; bd. dirs. Alan Gutmacher Rsch. Inst., 1985-91; AIDS cons. Regional Ministry Pub. Health, Santiago de Compostela, Spain, 1986; sr. investigator Digestive Diseases Ctr., L.A., 1987-91; AIDS med. adv. com. L.A. County Dept. Health Svcs., 1988-91, chair com. on access to health svcs., 1988-91, sr. health svcs. policy advisor, 1993-96, med. dir. pub. health programs and svcs., 1996-2004, emeritus, 2004-05, chair instnl. rev. bd., 1998-2005; mem. substance abuse coverage study com. Inst. Medicine NAS, 1988-90, study com. environ. justice, 1996-99; mem. Commn. Future Structure of VA Med. Care, 1990-91; com. study co-adminstrn. svc./rsch. programs of Alcohol, Drug Abuse and Mental Health Adminstrn. HHS, 1990-91; mem. nat. adv. com. AIDS Svcs. Program, Robert Wood Johnson Found., 1986-91, AIDS Prevention Program, 1987-91; mem. personal health svcs. planning com. L.A. County Dept. of Health Svcs., 1991-93; mem. AIDS adv. com. Alcohol, Drug Abuse, Mental Health Adminstrn., U.S. Dept. Health and Human Svcs., 1991-93, mem. study com. ethics of the business aspects of Healthcare, 1995-97, study com. ethical considerations in managed care, 1997-99, Woodstock Theological Ctr., Georgetown; mem. health info. sys. com. Local Health Officers, 1993-2001, co-chair personal health svcs. com., 1996-2001; bd. dirs. Preventive Med. Residence Adv. Com., State Calif. Preventive Med. Residency Prog., Calif. Conf. Local Health Officers; hosp. surveyor Consolidated Accreditation and Licensure Survey Program, Calif. Med. Assn./Joint Com. Accreditation Healthcare Orgn., 1992-96. Mem. editl. bd. Jour. Cmty. Health, 1990—, Jour. Pub. Health Policy, 1999—. Mem. Houston Clean City Commn., 1985-87. Lt. comdr. USN, 1956-58. Recipient Merit award N.Y.C. Pub. Health Assn., 1964, Humanitarian award Nat. Assn. of Health Svc. Execs., 1972, cert. meritorious svc. Health and Hosp. Governing Commn. Cook County, Ill., 1979, Merit award March of Dimes, 1987, Sanville lectureship U.C.L.A. Sch. of Pub. Health, 1992. Fellow Am. Coll. Preventive Medicine (v.p. 1976-78), Am. Pub. Health Assn. (governing council 1965-70, medicine/pub. health initiative, chair com. on pub. health edn. in medicine residencies 1994-97, managed care task force 1997—, Rosenhaus award 1974); mem. AMA, Inst. Medicine Nat. Acad. Scis., Tex. Med. Assn. (sexually transmitted diseases com. 1984-87), L.A. County Med. Assn., Calif. Med. Assn., Health Care Assn. So. Calif. (med. adv. com. 1995-99), L.A. Acad. Medicine. Democrat. Avocations: music, photography, swimming. Office: 313 N Figueroa St Ste 227 Los Angeles CA 90012-2602 Home: 8327 Mason Hill Rd Woodstock IL 60098 Home Phone: 815-337-0098; Office Phone: 815-337-0032. E-mail: james4g@sbcglobal.net.

HAUPT, RANDY LARRY, electrical engineering educator; b. Johnstown, Pa., Aug. 11, 1956; s. Howard and Anna Mae Haupt; m. Sue E. Slagle, Feb. 17, 1979; children: Bonny Ann, Amy Jean. BSEE, USAF Acad., 1978; MS in Engring. Mgmt., Western New Eng. Coll., 1981; MSEE, Northeastern U., 1983; PhD in Electrical Engring., U. Mich., 1987. Registered profl. engr., Colo. Commd. 2d lt. USAF, 1974, advanced through grades to lt. col., 1990, project engr. OTH-B Radar electronic systems divsn. Hanscom AFB, Mass., 1978-80, rsch. engr. in microwave antennas Rome Air Devel. Ctr., 1980-84; instr., then asst. prof. elec. engring. USAF Acad., Colo., 1987-91; dir. rsch. dept. elec. engring. USAF, Colo., 1990-91, chief comm. div. dept. elec. engring. Colo., 1991—; assoc. prof. USAF Acad., Colo., 1991-94, prof. Colo., 1994-97, dept. for ops. dept. elec. engring. Colo., 1995-97; prof., chair dept. elec. engring. U. Nev., Reno, 1997—. Vis. rsch. engr. Los Alamos Nat. Lab., 1992; presenter numerous papers and tech. reports in field. Author: (with others) Practical Genetic Algorithms, 1998; contbr. numerous articles to engring. jours. Nordic ski team coach USAF Acad., 1992-93. Recipient USAF Rsch. and Devel. award, 1983, 87, Frank J. Seiler award for rsch. excellence, 1990, 92, Founder's Gold medal, 1993, 6 Rome Air Devel. Ctr. Sci. Achievement awards; named Outstanding Mil. Educator in Electrical Engring., 1992, USAF Mil. Engr. of Yr., 1993, Fed. Engr. of Yr., Nat. Soc. Profl. Engrs., 1993; rsch. grantee Rome Air Devel. Ctr., 1988-90, Frank J. Seiler Rsch. Lab., 1990—, Cray Rsch., Inc., 1991-92, Phillips Lab., 1992—. Mem. IEEE (sr., student br. counselor 1988-90, reviewer Transactions on Antennas and Propagation 1984—), Am. Soc. for Engring. Edn. (reviewer), Applied Computational Electromagnetics Soc., Tau Beta Pi. Achievements include research in electromagnetics, scattering, antennas, electro-optics, numerical methods, chaos theory, radar, systems engineering, communications systems. Office: U Nev Dept Elec Engring 260 Reno NV 89557-0001

HAUPTMANN, RANDAL MARK, biotechnologist; b. Hot Springs, SD, July 6, 1956; s. Ivan Joy and Phyllis Maxine (Pierce) H.; m. Beverly Kay Suko, May 22, 1975; 1 child, Erich William. BS, S.D.

State U., 1979; MS, U. Ill., 1982, PhD, 1984. Postdoctoral rschr. Monsanto Corp. Rsch., St. Louis, 1984-86; vis. rsch. scientist U. Fla., Gainesville, 1986-88; asst. prof. No. Ill. U., DeKalb, 1988-90, dir. plant molecular biology ctr., 1989-90; sr. rsch. scientist Amoco Life Sci. Techs., Naperville, Ill., 1990-94; dir. advanced tech. Seminis Vegetable Seeds, Woodland, Calif., 1994-98; gen. mgr. Ball Helix, West Chicago, Ill., 1998—2003; pres. Varro Inc., Chgo.; head raw product rsch. Fresh Express, Salinas, Calif. Author: (with others) Methods in Molecular Biology, 1990; contbr. articles to profl. jours. Mem. Internat. Assn. Plant Tissue Culture, Internat. Soc. Plant Molecular Biology, Am. Soc. Plant Physiologists, Tissue Culture Assn. (Virginia Evans award 1982), Sigma Xi, Gamma Sigma Delta. Democrat. Office Phone: 831-772-6054. Business E-Mail: randalhauptmann@varroinc.com.

HAUSDORFER, GARY LEE, management consultant; b. Indpls., Mar. 26, 1946; s. Walter Edward and Virginia Lee (Bender) Hausdorfer; children: Lisa Ann Turner, Janet Lee Fortner. AA, Glendale Coll., 1966; BS, Calif. State U.-L.A., 1968. Rsch. officer Security Pacific Bank, LA, 1968-73; v.p., mgr. W. Ross Campbell Co., Irvine, Calif., 1973-81; sr. v.p. Weyerhaeuser Mortgage Co., Irvine, 1982-87; exec. v.p., ptnr. L.J. Melody & Co. of Calif., 1987-89; pres. Hausdorfer Co., 1989—, The Diamond Group, 1994—; chmn., CEO Cofiroute USA, 2003—. Councilman, City of San Juan Capistrano, 1978-94, mayor, 1980-81, 84-85, 88-90; chmn. Capistrano Valley Water Dist., 1980-81, San Juan Capistrano Redevel. Agy., 1983-84, 85-86, South Orange County Leadership Conf.; bd. dirs. Orange County Trans. Corridor Agy., Orange County Transit Dist.; chmn. Orange County Transp. Authority. Recipient cert. of commendation Orange County Bd. Suprs., 1981, congl. commendation, 1985, Theodore Roosevelt Conservation award Pres. Bush, 1990. Republican. Personal E-mail: ghausdorfer@cofiroutusa.com.

HAUSER, RAY LOUIS, engineer, researcher, entrepreneur; b. Litchfield, Ill., Apr. 16, 1927; s. A. Vernon and Grace (Gregg) H.; m. Consuelo Wright Minnich, Sept. 2, 1951; children: Beth, Cynthia, Dewi, Chris. BS, U. Ill., 1950; M in Engring., Yale U., 1952; PhD, U. Colo., 1957. Registered profl. engr., Colo., safety engr., Calif. Sr. project engr. Conn. Hard Rubber Co., New Haven, 1950-52; rsch. staff U. Colo., Boulder, 1954-57; material tech. staff Martin Co., Denver, 1957-61; owner, mgr. Hauser Labs., Boulder, 1961-89; materials/process cons., expert witness Ray Hauser Expertise, Boulder, 2000—. Bd. dirs. Surface Solutions Inc.; vis. lectr. U. Colo., Boulder, 1957-63. Pres. Boulder Civic Opera, 1971-72. Sgt. U.S. Army, 1952-54. Recipient U. Colo. medal, 1995, Gold medal Colo. Engring. Coun., 1999. Fellow AAAS, Soc. Plastics Engrs. (bd. dirs. 1959-62, 2004—); mem. AIChE, Rotary (bd. dirs. 1975-77). Home and Office: 5758 Rustic Knolls Dr Boulder CO 80301-3029

HAUSER, STEPHEN L., medical educator; SB, MIT, 1971; MD, Harvard Medical School, 1975. Postdoctoral fellow in immunology Harvard Med. Sch., 1980—83; postdoctoral fellow Institut Pasteur, Paris, 1983—86; chair, Robert A. Fishman dist. prof. neurology U. Calif., San Francisco, 1987—. Editor Harrison's Principle of Internal Medicine. Fellow American Academy of Arts and Sciences, American Associations of Physicians. Mem.: Institute of Medicine, 1999-. Office: U Calif San Francisco Dept Neurology PO Box 114 San Francisco CA 94143-0001

HAUSMAN, ARTHUR HERBERT, electronics company executive; b. Chgo., Nov. 24, 1923; s. Samuel Louis and Sarah (Elin) H.; m. Helen Mandelowitz, May 19, 1946; children: Susan Lois, Kenneth Louis, Catherine Ellen. BSEE, U. Tex., 1944; MS, Harvard U., 1948. Electronics engr. Engring. Rsch. Assocs., St. Paul, 1946-47; supervisory electronics scientist U.S. Dept. Def., Washington, 1948-60; now advisor, v.p., dir. rsch. Ampex Corp., Redwood City, Calif., 1960-63, v.p. ops., 1963-65, group v.p., 1965-67, exec. v.p., 1967-71, exec. v.p., pres., CEO, 1971-83, chmn. bd., 1981-87, chmn. bd. emeritus, 1987—. Chmn. tech. adv. com. computer peripherals Dept. Commerce, 1973-75; mem. Pres.'s Export Coun.; chmn. Subcom. on Export Adminstrn., 1984-88; bd. dirs. Lasercard Inc., Vista Advanced Tech. Group Inc., Calamp, Inc. Trustee United Bay Area Crusade.; mem. vis. com. dept. math. MIT; bd. dirs. Bay Area Coun. Served with USNR, 1944-54. Recipient Meritorious Civilian Svc. award Dept. Def. Mem. IEEE, Army Ordnance Assn. (dir. chpt. 1969-71), Am. Electronics Assn. (dir.), Cosmos Club.

HAUSSMANN, TRUDY DIANE, financial planner; b. St. Louis, May 5, 1965; d. Erich Alfred and Willy (Welboren) Haussmann; married; 4 children. BA in Internat. Econs., U. Calif., LA, 1988, BA in Polit. Sci., 1988. CFP; registered investment advisor, securities prin., life, disability and annuity insurance agent. Sr. fin. planner Lewis Wallensky Assocs., LA, 1985-89; owner, pres. Haussman Fin., Newport Beach, Calif., 1989—. Named one of The Top 100 Women Fin. Advisors, Barron's, 2008. Mem. MENSA, Internat. Assn. Fin. Planners (v.p. edn. Orange County chpt. 1993-94, v.p. conf. com. 1994-95), Inst. Cert. Fin. Planners, Aliso Viejo C. of C. (bd. dirs. 1991-93), South Orange County C. of C. (bd. dirs. 1990-93), Nat. Assn. Women Bus. Owners, Bus. and Profl. Women, Gamma Phi Beta Alumnae (alumni adv. 1991). Avocations: skiing, bicycling, reading, sailing, rollerblading. Office: Haussmann Fin Inc 4590 MacArthur Blvd Ste 390 Newport Beach CA 92660

HAVEKOST, DANIEL JOHN, architect; b. Fremont, Nebr., May 12, 1936; s. Alvin Deidrich and Magdalen (Osterman) H.; m. Patricia Jo Haney, June 6, 1959 (div. June 1983); children: Christopher, Karen; m. Sandra Schwendemann, Aug. 29, 1993 (div. Nov. 1999). Lic. architect, Colo., Calif., Tex., N.D.; cert. Nat. Council Archtl. Registration Bds. Designer Papachristou & Assoc., Denver, 1959-61; architect Anshen & Allen, San Francisco, 1961-62; assoc. Hornbein & White, Denver, 1962-63; ptnr. Papachristou & Havekost, Denver, 1963-64; prin. Havekost & Assocs., Denver, 1964-71; pres. HWH Assocs., Inc., Denver, 1971-91, Havekost & Lee Architects P.C., Denver, 1991-95, Havekost & Assoc., P.C., 1996—. Vis. lectr. U. Colo., Denver, 1969, 72, 82; sec., treas. Encore Devel. Corp., Denver, 1984-91. Prin. works include Havekost Residence (Western Mountain Region AIA award 1971), Reverend's Ridge (Western Mountain Region AIA award 1973), Grant Street Mansion (Colo. Soc. Archs. AIA award 1979), Encore Redevel. (AIA award 1985,86), Antlers Redevelopment, Vail, Colo., 2002. Bd. dirs. Denver Cmty. Design Ctr., 1968-72, Hist. Paramount Found., Denver, 1980-94, Hist. Denver, 1978-82; panel mem. Gen. Svcs. Adminstrn., Denver, 1978-79, mem. plan enforcement rev. and variation com., Denver, 1970-76. Served with USNR, 1954-62. Recipient Archtl. Excellence awards WOOD Inc., 1968-82, Honor award for Adaptive Re-use, Historic Denver, 1975, WOOD Design award Nat. Cattlemen's Hdqrs., 1982. Fellow AIA (pres. Denver chpt. 1978-81, chmn. Colo. chpt. govt. affairs com. 1984-91, pres. Colo. chpt. 1981-83, Colo. hist. preservation officer 1982—, recipient Fisher Traveling award of Colo. AIA Ednl. Fund 1988, excellence archtl. design award 1960). Avocations: skiing, tennis, drawing. Home: 1905 Sherman St Ste 345 Denver CO 80203-1164

HAVEL, RICHARD JOSEPH, physician, educator; b. Seattle, Feb. 20, 1925; s. Joseph and Anna (Fritz) Havel; m. Virginia Johnson, June 25, 1947; children: Christopher, Timothy, Peter, Julianne. BA, Reed Coll., 1946; MS, MD, U. Oreg., 1949. Intern Cornell U. Med. Coll., NYC, 1949—50, resident in medicine, 1950—53; clin. assoc. Nat. Heart Inst., NIH, 1953—54, rsch. assoc., 1954—56; faculty Sch. Medicine, U. Calif., San Francisco, 1956—, prof. medicine, 1964—; assoc. dir. Cardiovasc. Rsch. Inst., 1961—73, dir., 1973—92. Chief metabolism sect., dept. medicine Sch. Medicine, U. Calif., San Francisco, 1967—97; dir. Arteriosclerosis Specialized Ctr. Rsch., 1971—96; mem. bd. sci. counselors Nat. Heart, Lung and Blood Inst., 1976—80; chmn. food and nutrition bd. NRC, 1987—90; pres. Lipid Rsch., Inc., 1999—. Editor: Jour. Lipid Rsch., 1972—75; assoc. editor: Am. Jour. Clin. Nutrition, 1997—2007, mem. editl. bd.: Jour. Biol. Chemistry, 1981—85, Jour. Arteriosclerosis, 1980—; contbr. chapters to books, articles to profl. jours. Established investigator Am. Heart Assn., 1956—61, chmn. coun. on arteriosclerosis, 1977—79. With USPHS, 1951—53. Recipient Disting. Achievement award, Am. Heart Assn., 1993, Bristol-Myers award for nutrition rsch., 1989, Gold medal, Charles U. Med. Faculty, Prague, Czech Republic, 1996, Commemorative Gold medal, Charles U., Prague, Czech Republic, 2007. Fellow: AAAS (Theobald Smith award 1960), Am. Inst. Nutrition; mem.: NAS, Western Soc. Clin. Investigation (Mayo Soley award 1997), Am. Soc. for Clin. Investigation, Assn. Am. Physicians, Am. Soc. Clin. Nutrition (McCollum award 1993), Am. Acad. Arts and Scis., Inst. Medicine of NAS, Alpha Omega Alpha, Phi Beta Kappa. Office: U Calif San Francisco Cardiovascular Rsch In San Francisco CA 94143-0130 Home Phone: 415-461-8583. Business E-Mail: richard.havel@ucsf.edu.

HAVEL, RICHARD W., lawyer; b. Fairmont, Minn., Sept. 20, 1946; s. Thomas Earl and Elizabeth (Shiltz) H.; m. Arlene Havel, July 6, 1968; children: Stephanie, Derek. BA, Notre Dame U., 1968; JD, UCLA, 1971. Bar: Calif., U.S. Dist. Ct. (no., ea., cen. and so. dists.) Calif., U.S. Ct. Appeals (9th cir.). Atty. Shutan & Trost, LA, 1971—80, Sidley Austin LLP, LA, 1980—. Adj. prof. law Loyola Law Sch., 1975-80; bd. govs. Fin. Lawyers Conf., 1991-94, 95-98, officer, 1998-01; spkr., panelist Bankruptcy Litigation Inst., 1989-95, ALI-ABA, 1989, 90, 91; chmn. L.A. City Indsl. Devel. Authority, 1993-98, bd. dirs., 1998-00. Contbr. articles to profl. jours. Trustee Jonsson/UCLA Cancer Ctr., 1998-2007; bd. dirs. Dollars for Scholars, So. Calif. region, 1999-05. Fellow Am. Coll. Bankruptcy, 1997; mem. ABA, Calif. Bar Assn., L.A. County Bar Assn. (comml. law and bankruptcy sect. bankruptcy subcom. 1986-89, exec. com. 1987-90, lawyer assistance com. 1985-90), UCLA Law Alumni Assn. (trustee 1996—2001). Office: Sidley Austin LLP 555 W 5th St 40th Fl Los Angeles CA 90013-1010 Office Phone: 213-896-6017. Business E-Mail: rhavel@sidley.com.

HAVEMANN, MICHAEL R., legal administration; b. San Francisco, Aug. 31, 1944; BA in Polit. Sci., Brigham Young U., 1969, MPA, 1972. Coord. criminal justice planning City Mgr.'s Office City of Phoenix, 1972-74, asst. ct. adminstr. Mcpl. Ct., 1975-78, ct. adminstr., 1978-83; mgmt. asst. planning and rsch. bur. Phoenix Police Dept., 1974-75; ct. exec. State of Utah 4th Jud. Dist., 1983-92; ct. adminstr. Las Vegas Mcpl. Ct., 1992—. Mem. Ct. Exec. Devel. Program. Co-author: (study) Internal Audition in State Govt., 1972. Fellow Inst. Ct. Mgmt. (Nat. Ctr. State Cts.); mem. Nat. Assn. Ct. Mgmt. Office: Mcpl Ct City Las Vegas City Hall 400 Stewart Ave Las Vegas NV 89101-2927

HAVILAND, PETER L., lawyer; BA, Harvard U., 1977; JD, Stanford Law Sch., 1989. Bar: Calif. 1989. Law clk. to Hon. Warren Ferguson, US Ct. Appeals 9th Circuit; litig. ptnr. Kaye, Scholer, Fierman, Hays & Handler LLP; ptnr., nat., internat. comml. disputes Akin Gump Strauss Hauer & Feld LLP, LA. Assoc. editor Stanford Law Review. Bd. dirs. Constl. Rights Found., So. Christian Leadership Conf. Named one of Am. Top Black Lawyers, Black Enterprise Mag., 2003. Mem.: Black Entertainment and Sports Lawyers Assn., State Bar Calif. Office: Kaye Scholer LLP 1999 Avenue of the Stars Ste 1700 Los Angeles CA 90067 Office Phone: 310-229-1034. Business E-Mail: phaviland@akinggump.com, phaviland@kayescholer.com.

HAWK, TONY, professional skateboarder; b. San Diego, May 12, 1968; s. Frank and Nancy Hawk; m. Cindy Dunbar, 1990; 1 child, Riley; m. Erin Lee, Sept. 28, 1996; children: Spencer, Keegan; m. Lhotse Merriam, Jan. 12, 2006; 1 child, Kadence Clover. Profl. skateboarder, 1983—; founder Tony Hawk Found., Vista, Calif., 2002. Founder Tony Hawk's Demolition Radio, Sirus Satellite Radio. Actor: (films) Thrashin', 1986, Police Academy 4: Citizens on Patrol, 1987, Gleaming the Cube, 1989, xXx, 2002, Haggard: The Movie, 2003; (TV films) The Contest, 1989, Reunion X, 2004, (video) Destroying America, 2001, CKY 3, 2001, Dogwotn and Z-Boys, 2002, Lords of Dogtown, 2005, (guest appearances): (TV series) Arli$$, 1999; (TV series, voice) The Simpsons, 2003; (TV series) CSI: Miami, 2005; prodr.: (soundtrack for Tony Hawk's Underground) T.H.U.G. (MTV Music award, 2004); actor(guest appearances): (TV series) Extreme Home Makeover, 2005. Recipient 6 gold medals for skateboarding, ESPN X Games, 16 medals, No. 1 Vertical Skateboarder in the World, 1984—96, 4 time Favourite Male Athlete, Nickelodeon Kids Choice Awards, 3 time Male Athlete, Fox Teen Choice, Lifetime Achievement award, ESPN ESPY; named one of The Most Influential People in the World of Sports, Bus. Week, 2007, 2008. Achievements include first skateboarder in history to do "The 900" skateboarding trick; Video Game Series is the top selling sports video game franchise in history. Office: Tony Hawk Found 1611-A Melrose Dr 360 Vista CA 92081 Office Phone: 760-477-2479.

HAWKE, BERNARD RAY, planetary scientist, researcher; b. Louisville, Oct. 22, 1946; s. Arvil Abner and Elizabeth Ellen (Brown) H. BS in Geology, U. Ky., 1970, MS, 1974, Brown U., 1977, PhD in Planetary Geology, 1978. Geologist U.S. Geol. Survey, 1967-68; researcher U. Ky., 1972-74, Brown U., 1974-78; planetary scientist Hawaii Inst. Geophysics, U. Hawaii, Honolulu, 1978—; dir. NASA Pacific Regional Planetary Data Ctr., 1981—; prin. investigator NASA grants. Assoc. dir. Hawaii Space Grant Coll. Author papers in field. Served with USAR, 1970-72. Decorated Bronze Star Mem. Geochem. Soc., Meteoritical Soc., Am. Geophys. Union, Am. Chem. Soc., Geol. Soc. Am., Sigma Xi, Sigma Gamma Epsilon, Alpha Tau Omega. Republican. Office: U Hawaii SOEST Hawaiian Inst Geophysics Honolulu HI 96822

HAWKE, ROBERT FRANCIS, dentist; b. Pasadena, Calif., Oct. 26, 1946; s. George Herbert and Mildred Estelle (Wood) H.; m. Emily Sue Wilkins, Aug. 17, 1973; 1 child, Kristen. BA, U. Ariz., 1969; DDS, Baylor U., Dallas, 1973. Assoc. B.J. Barber, Tucson, 1976-78; ptnr. Barber-Hawke, P.C., Tucson, 1978-87; pvt. practice Tucson, 1987—. Bd. dirs., pres. Delta Dental Ariz., Phoenix, 1985-91. Mem. Tucson Bus. Alliance, 1981—, pres., 1983, 94, Comty. Auto Immune Deficiency Syndrome Adv. Coun., Tucson, 1987-90, Auto Immune Deficiency Syndrome Edn. Project, Tucson, 1988-90. Maj. U.S. Army. Fellow Am. Coll. Dentists, Internat. Coll. Dentists; mem. ADA (alt. del. 1988-92, del. 1994-2000, 14th dist. chmn. polit. action com. 1995-98), Ariz. State Dental Assn. (trustee 1988, v.p. 1991, pres.-elect 1992-93, pres. 1993-94, past pres. 1994-95, mem. legal liaison com. 1993-94, chmn. coun. on constitution and bylaws 1996-97, chmn. coun. on budget planning 1992-93, chmn. coun. on ins. 1998-2003, Svc. award 2002), So. Ariz. Dental Soc. (bd. dirs. 1983-89, pres. 1987-88), Pierre Fauchard Acad., Acad. Laser Dentistry, Acad. Gen. Dentistry, Tucson Advanced Cosmetic & Restorative Study Club, World Clin. Laser Inst., Give Kids a Smile Day (So. Ariz. chmn. 2003-04), Rotary (Paul Harris fellow), Beta Beta Beta. Republican. Evangelical. Avocations: golf, jogging, tennis, racquetball, reading. Home: 6745 E Tivani Dr Tucson AZ 85715-3348 Office: 1575 N Swan Rd Ste 200 Tucson AZ 85712-4068 Office Phone: 520-323-3842. Personal E-mail: hawkerobertf@qwestoffice.net.

HAWKER, CRAIG J., research scientist; BSc, U. Queensland, 1984; PhD, U. Cambridge, 1988. Postdoctoral fellow Cornell U., 1988—90; fellow U. Queensland, 1991—93; rsch. scientist IBM Almaden Rsch. Ctr., San Jose, 1993—. Mem. sci. adv. bd. SYMYX Techs., Microbar Techs., Warwick Effect Polymers; mem. adv. bd. Knowledge Found.; adj. prof. chemistry U. Queensland. Contbr. articles to profl. publs.; editor: Jour. Polymer Sci.; mem. editl. bd.: Internat. Jour. Polymeric Materials. Recipient ACS Arthur K. Doolittle award, 1997, IUPAC Young Scientists award, 2000, Carl S. Marvel Creative Polymer Chemistry award polymer chemistry divsn., Am. Chem. Soc., 2001, Coop. Rsch. award in Polymer Sci. & Engring. Eastman Kodak Co., 2003, award in Applied Polymer Sci., 2005; named one of Top 100 most cited chemists worldwide, 1992—2002. Achievements include patents in field; research in the interface between organic and polymer chemistry; the design, synthesis, and application of macromolecular structures in biotechnology, microelectronics, and surface science.

HAWKER, KENO, former mayor, trucking company executive; BA, Wis. State U.; MBA, U. Wis. Owner & pres. Hawker Trucks & Materials, Inc.; mem. coun. City of Mesa, Ariz., 1986—94, 1998—2000, vice mayor, 1990—92, mayor, 2000—08. Mem. U.S. Conf. Mayors, Ariz. League of Cities and Towns Bd., Williams Gateway Authority, Regional Public Transportation Authority, Regional Aviation System Policy Com., Ariz. Mcpl. Water Users Assn., Nat. League of Cities Transp. TEA 21 Reauthorization Task Force, Nat. League of Cities Transp. Infrastructure and Svcs. Steering Com., Nat. League of Cities, Maricopa Assn. Govt.'s, Mesa Chamber of Commerce, Valley Metro Rail Bd.; chair Maricopa Assn. Govt.'s Regional Coun., Regional Coun. Transp. Subcom.; pres. Ariz. Mcpl. Water Users Assn.; ex-officio mem. adv. bd. City of Mesa Econ. Develop. Mem.: Maricopa Assn. Govts. (treas.), Mesa HoHoKams, Mesa Baseline Rotary. Avocations: biking, hiking, climbing, rappelling, travel, rollerblading, owns his own palne and is a lic. pilot, dirt bike racing, river rafting, motorcycle riding. Office: Mesa City Plaza 20 E Main St Mesa AZ 85201 Address: Hawker Trucks and Materials Inc 315 S Morris Mesa AZ 85210

HAWKER, MIKE, state legislator; b. Manchester, Iowa, June 25, 1956; m to Carol Carlson. BA in Acctg., U. Northern Iowa, 1979, BA in Humanities, 1979. CPA. Alaska State Representative, District 32, 2002-. CPA, Price Waterhouse, 1974-91; Ptnr, Hawker & Raleigh, CPAs, 1991-95; Corp fin officer, 1995-97; Bus and acctg cons, 1997-2002. Dir. Abused Women's Aid in Crisis; trustee Alaska Aviation Heritage Mus. Sons of America Vets; Lions Club; Isaak Walton League (board director, formerly); NRA; Alaska Gun Collectors Association; Texas Gun Collectors Association; life mem. Alaska Territorial Calvery, Harley Davidson Owners Group. Republican. Office: State Capitol Rm 502 Juneau AK 99801-1182 also: Dist 32 716 W 4th Ave Ste 620 Anchorage AK 99501 Office Phone: 907-465-4949, 907-269-0244. Office Fax: 907-465-4979, 907-269-0248. Business E-Mail: representative_mike_hawker@legis.state.ak.us.*

HAWKINS, ALAN J., family life educator, researcher; b. Washington, July 8, 1955; s. Carl Stolworthy and Nelma Jean (Jones) H.; m. Lisa Anne Bolin, Feb. 18, 1977; children: Caitlin Anne, Brian Alan. BS, Brigham Young U., 1979, MS, 1984; PhD, Pa. State U., 1990. From personnel rsch. analyst to sr. compensation analyst BankAm. Corp., San Francisco, 1983-86; asst. prof. family scis. Brigham Young U., Provo, Utah, 1990—. Bd. dirs. Utah Coun. on Fam. Rels., 1992—. Assoc. editor Family Rels., 1992—, Family Perspective, 1990-93; reviewer Jour. Marriage & the Family, 1989—. Avocations: backpacking, basketball, racquetball. Office: Brigham Young U 1054 Kimball Tower Provo UT 84602

HAWKINS, BRIAN LEE, former educational association administrator; b. Lafayette, Ind., Aug. 5, 1948; s. Robert H. and Marjorie Joan (Bradley) H.; m. Lisa Ellen Herrick, Dec. 30, 1970; children: Timothy, Steven. BA, Mich. State U., 1970, MA, 1972; PhD, Purdue U., 1975. Asst. prof. U. Tex., San Antonio, 1975—76, asst. dean bus., 1976—81; assoc. v.p. academic affairs Drexel U., Phila., 1981—86, assoc. v.p. computing and telecom., 1984—86; v.p. Brown U., Providence, 1986, spl. asst. to pres., assoc. provost academic planning, 1990—92, v.p. academic planning and adminstrn., 1992—96, sr. v.p. academic planning and adminstrv. affairs, 1997—98; pres., CEO EDUCAUSE, Boulder, Colo., 1998—2007. Trustee EDUCOM, Washington, 1986-90, chmn. bd., 1989-90; trustee U. Richmond, 1999-2003; dir. Forum for Future of Higher Ed., 1999-, Am. Coun. Edn., 2005-. Author: Managerial Communications, 1981; editor: Managing & Organizing Information Resources on Campus, 1990, The Mirage of Continuity: Reconfiguring Academic Information Resources in the 21st Century, 1998; Tech. Everywhere, 2002. Bd. dirs. CAUSE, 1992-96. Office Phone: 303-939-0335. E-mail: hawkins@educause.edu.

HAWKINS, GREGORY J., consumer products company executive; BSBA, Oreg. State U. With J.C. Penney, GTE, Mitel Corp.; v.p. sales Ingram Micro., Inc., v.p. major accounts div. consumer markets, sr. v.p. global sales; CEO, chmn. Buy.com, 1999—2000; CEO BMS, Inc., 2001—04, bd. dirs., 2004—. Office: BMS Reimbursement Mgmt 2058 Mills Ave PMB 201 Claremont CA 91711

HAWKINS, JAMES VICTOR, former state official; b. Coeur d'Alene, Idaho, Sept. 28, 1936; s. William Stark and Agnes M. (Ramstedt) H.; m. Gail Ruth Guernsey, June 19, 1959; children—John William, Nancy Clare. BS, U. Idaho, 1959, D of Adminstrv. Sci., 1996; postgrad., Am. Savs. and Loan Inst., 1960-67, Pacific Coast Banking Sch., 1970—. Mgmt. trainee Gen. Telephone Co. of N.W., Coeur d'Alene, 1959-60; asst. mgr. First Fed. Savs. & Loan Assn., Coeur d'Alene, 1960-67; v.p., gen. mgr. Idaho S.W. Devel. Co., Boise, 1967-68; v.p., trust officer First Security Bank of Idaho, N.A., Boise, 1968-72; pres. Statewide Stores Inc., Boise, 1972-82; spl. projects adminstr. Lucky Stores Inc., 1982-84; pvt. practice fin. cons. Boise, 1984-87; dir. dept. commerce State of Idaho, Boise, 1987-96, ret., 1996; mng. ptnr. Hwy. 12 Ventures, 2000—. Bd. dirs. Blue Cross of Idaho, Early Childhood Devel., State of Idaho, Summit Securities, Old Standard Life, Old West Annuity and Life. Bd. dirs., chmn. adv. bd. Coll. Bus. and Econs. U. Idaho; bd. dirs. Idaho Total Quality Inst., Boise United Fund, Boise Art Assn.; pres. U. Idaho Found.; exec. bd. Coun. State Community Affairs Agys.; bd. dirs., pres. Nat. Assn. State Devel. Agys.; mem. Indsl. Devel. Rsch. Coun.; exec. com. Coun. State and Community Devel. Agys.; chmn. Idaho R.R. Adv. Coun. Named Outstanding Young Idahoan Idaho Jr. C. of C., 1967. Mem. Am. Inst. Banking, Boise C. of C., U. Idaho Alumni Assn. (mem. exec. bd.), Elks, Coeur d'Alene, Hayden Lake Country Club, Phi Gamma Delta. Episcopalian.

HAWKINS, JAMESETTA See JAMES, ETTA

HAWKINS, JASPER STILLWELL, JR., architect; b. Orange, NJ, Nov. 10, 1932; s. Jasper Stillwell and Bernice (Ake) H.; m. Patricia A. Mordigan, Mar. 22, 1980; children: William Raymond, John Stillwell, Karen Ann, Jasper Stillwell III. B.Arch., U. So. Calif., 1955. Registered architect, Calif., Ariz., N.Mex. Founder, prin. Hawkins & Lindsey & Assocs., LA, 1958-90, Hawkins Lindsey Wilson Assocs., L.A. and Phoenix, 1978-85; pres. Fletcher-Thompson Assocs., 1981-84; prin. Jasper Stillwell Hawkins, F.A.I.A., architect, Phoenix, 1990—. Bd. visitors Nat. Fire Acad., 1978-80; bd. dirs. Nat. Inst. Bldg. Scis., 1976-85, chmn. bd. dirs., 1981-83, consultative council, 1978—; mem. com. protection of archives and records centers GSA, 1975-77; mem. archtl. adv. panel Calif. State Bldg. Standards Commn., 1964-70; mem. U.S. del. to UN Econ. Commn. for Europe Working Party on Bldg., 1978-84; mem. U.S. presdl. del. to Honduran Presdl. Elections, 1985; mem. com. standards and evaluation Nat. Conf. States on Bldg. Codes and Standards, 1971-74; mem. Am. Arbitration Assn., 1992-2002; trustee Underwriter's Labs., 1984-2002, mem. nat. coun. Archtl. Registration Bds., 1971—; participant and speaker numerous confs. Contbr. articles to profl. jours.; maj. works include Valley Music Theatre, L.A., Houston Music Theatre, Sundome Theatre and R.H. Johnson Ctr., Sun City West, Ariz., Bell Recreation Ctr., Sun City, U. Calif. at Irvine Student Housing, Oxnard (Calif.) Fin. Ctr., condominium devels., Lakes Club, Sun City. Mem. Nev. Gov.'s Commn. Fire Safety Codes, 1980-81, Pres. Reagan's Commn. on Housing, 1981-82, City of Phoenix ACDC Task Force, 1985-86, ACDC Aesthetics Commn., 1986-89, City of Phoenix Camelback East Village Planning Com., 1983-89; mem. fire rsch. panel Nat. Bur. Stds., 1978-81; chmn. NAS fire assessment rev. com., 1987-88, com. on analytical methods for designing bldgs. for fire safety, 1977-78; chmn. bldg. seismic safety coun. ind. rev. panel San Francisco War Meml. Opera House, 1995; bd. dirs. Jazz in Ariz., 2004—. Recipient design awards from Ariz. Rock Products Assn., Theater Assn. Am., Nat. Food Facilities, House and Home Mag., Practical Builders Mag., Am. Builders Mag., Nat. Inst. of Bldg. Sci. Inst. award, 1995, others. Mem. AIA (mem. codes and stds. com. 1970—, chmn. 1970-73, nat. liaison commn. with Assoc. Gen. Contractors 1969-70, chmn. nat. fire safety task force 1972-74, chmn. Calif. coun. AIA state code com. 1964-68, chmn. nat. conf. industrialized constrn. 1969-70, nat. com. bldg. industry coordination 1969-70, nat. rep. to Internat. Conf. Bldg. Ofcls. 1969, state Calif. AIA codes com. 1960-70, chmn. 1965-70, nat. AIA codes and stds. com. 1970-80, chmn. 1970-74, nat. crisis adv. com. 1988-89, coll. of fellows 1976—), ASCE (task force bldg. codes 1971-74), ASTM, Nat. Fire Protection Assn. (com. bldg. heights and areas 1965-72, chmn. 1968-72, fire prevention code com. 1974-76, bd. dirs. 1985-93, chmn. nat. model codes coordinating com. 1983-86, stds. coun. 1996—, bldg. code task force 2000—), Nat. Fire Acad. (bd. regents 1980-83), Nat. Bur. Stds. Fire (rsch. adv. com. 1979-82), Nat. Acad. Forensic Engrs., Ariz. C. of C. (policy com. 1983-84), Ariz. Biltmore Village Estates Homeowners Assn. (pres. 1981-83), Phoenix C. of C. (chmn. Water task force 1982-83), So. Calif. Phoenix Alumni Club (chmn. scholar com. 1997—). Office: 5332 N 24th Pl 220 Phoenix AZ 85016

HAWKINS, JAY L., electronics executive; BSBA, Boise State U. With test dept. Micron Tech., Inc., various positions, test prodn. control mgr., mgr. test dept., dir. mfg., 1991-96, v.p. ops., 1996—. Office: PO Box 6 Boise ID 83707-0006

HAWKINS, JEFF, information technology company executive; b. LI, NY, June 1, 1957; BSEE, Cornell U., 1979; student, U. Calif., 1986—88. Key tech. positions Intel Corp., 1982; with GRiD Sys. Corp., 1982—92, v.p. rsch.; co-founder Palm Computing (sold to US Robotics in 1995, in 1997 sold to 3Com Corp., now palmOne Inc.), 1992, with, 1992—98; co-founder Handspring, Inc. (merged with Palm Hardware Group to create new co. palmOne, Inc., 2003, now called Palm. Inc., 2005), 1998, chief product officer, bd. mem., 1998—2003; CTO palmOne, Inc. (now called Palm, Inc.), Milpitas, Calif., 2003—; founder Redwood Neuroscience Inst., Menlo Park, Calif., 2002, exec dir, chmn.; co-founder Numenta, Inc., Menlo Park, Calif., 2005—. Mem. sci. bd. dirs. Cold Spring Harbor Labs; mem. adv. bd. Redwood Ctr. for Theoretical Neuroscience, U. Calif. Berkeley. Co-author (with Sandra Blakeslee): (non-fiction) On Intelligence, 2004 (Wired Mag RAVE award, 2005). Named one of Digital 50 with Donna Dubinsky, Time Mag., 1999; named to Innovators Hall of Fame with Donna Dubinsky. Mem.: NAE. Achievements include invention of architect for the original PalmPilot, 1994 and Treo smart phone, 2001; patents for nine various handheld devices and features; prin. architect and designer for GRiDPad (1989) and GRiD Convertible; Numenta Inc. is creating a new pattern recognition software called Hierarchical Temporal Memory modeled on the human brain's neocortex. Avocations: sailing, playing musical instruments. Office: Palm Inc 950 W Maude Ave Sunnyvale CA 94085 also: Numenta Inc 1010 El Camino Real Ste 380 Menlo Park CA 94025 Office Phone: 408-503-7000, 650-321-8282. Fax: 408-503-2750; Office Fax: 650-321-8585.

HAWKINS, MICHAEL DALY, federal judge; b. Winslow, Ariz., Feb. 12, 1945; s. William Bert and Patricia Agnes (Daly) H.; m. Phyllis A. Lewis, June 4, 1966; children: Aaron, Adam. BA, Ariz. State U., 1967, JD cum laude, 1970; LLM, U. Va., 1998. Bar: Ariz. 1970, US Ct. Mil. Appeals 1971, US Supreme Ct. 1974. Pvt. practice law, 1973—77; US atty. Dept. Justice, Phoenix, 1977—80; pvt. practice law, 1980—94; judge US Ct. Appeals (9th cir.), Phoenix, 1994—. Mem. Appellate Cts. Jud. Nominating Commn., 1985—89. Staff editor: Ariz. State U. Law Jour., 1968—70. Mem. Ariz. Lottery Commn., 1980—83, Commn. on Uniform State Laws, 1988—93. Capt. USMC, 1970—73. Recipient Alumni Achievement award, Ariz. State U., 1995. Mem.: ABA, Nat. Assn. Former U.S. Attys. (pres. 1989—90), Adminstrv. Conf. U.S. (pub. mem. 1985—94), Phoenix Trial Lawyers Assn., Ariz. Trial Lawyers Assn. (bd. dirs. 1976—77, state sec. 1976—77), State Bar of Ariz. (James Walsh Outstanding Jurist Award 2003), Maricopa County Bar Assn. (bd. dirs. 1975—77, 1981—89, pres. 1987—88). Office: US Ct Appeals 9th Cir Sandra Day O'Connor Cthse 401 W Washington St Ste 510 Phoenix AZ 85003-2151 Office Phone: 602-322-7310.

HAWKINS, OLIVER TAYLOR (TAYLOR HAWKINS), musician; b. Fort Worth, TX, Feb. 17, 1972; Band co-founder, drummer Sylvia; touring drummer for Alanis Morissette; drummer Foo Fighters, 1997—. Musician: (albums) The Colour & the Shape, 1997, There is Nothing Left to Lose, 1999 (Grammy, Best Rock Album, 2001), One by One, 2002 (Grammy, Best Rock Album, 2004), In Your Honor, 2005, Echoes, Silence, Patience & Grace, 2007 (Grammy, Best Rock Album, 2008), (songs) Learn to Fly, 1999 (Grammy, Best Short Music Video, 2001, VH1: 100 Greatest Videos, 2001), All My Life, 2002 (Grammy, Best Hard Rock Performance, 2003), The Pretender, 2007 (Grammy, Best Hard Rock Performance, 2008). Achievements include Foo Fighters named one of VH1: 100 Greatest Rock Artists, 2000, VH1: 100 Sexiest Artists, 2002, Top Pop Artists of the Past 25 Yrs., 2004. Office Phone: 212-930-4000.

HAWKINS, ROBERT B., think-tank executive; PhD, U Wash. Chmn. Adv. Commn. on Intergovt. Rels., Washington, 1982-93; dir. Am. pub. policy program Woodrow Wilson Internat. Ctr. for Scholars, Washington; pres., CEO Inst. for Contemporary Studies, Oakland, Calif. Tv co-host, That's Politics, 1987-91; radio California Political Review; Books American Federalism: A New Partnership for the Republic, Self-government by District: Myth and Reality. Office: Institute For Contemporary Studies 815 Harbour Way S Ste 17 Richmond CA 94804-3616

HAWKINS, TRIP, electronics executive; Chmn. bd. dirs., CEO 3DO, Redwood City, Calif. Office: The 3do Company 345 California St Ste 1150 San Francisco CA 94104-2664

HAWKS, BILL, state legislator, oil industry executive; b. Tulsa, Okla., Nov. 17, 1936; s. Jeff and Mary Blanche (Scrogham) H.; m. Jan G. Heibucher, Aug. 15, 1970; children: Brents, Christopher, James, Michael. BSBA, U. Denver, 1962. Cert. landman, airplane pilot. Landman Ozark Corp., Casper, Wyo., 1957-66; pvt. practice landman Casper, 1966-71; pres. Burton-Hawks Inc., Casper, from 1971; mem. Wyo. Senate, Dist. 29, Casper, 1994—. Mem. State of Wyo. Aero. Commn., 1987—. Bd. dirs. Natrona County Airport, Casper, 1980-85; mem. joint powers bd., Casper, 1984-85. Mem. Am. Assn. Petroleum Landmen, Wyo. Assn. Petroleum Landmen, Rocky Mountain Oil and Gas Assn., Aircraft Owners and Pilots Assn., Ind. Petroleum Assn. Am., Ind. Petroleum Assn. Mountain States, Petroleum Club (pres. Casper chpt. 1980-81). Clubs: Casper Country, Denver Country, PGA West (Palm Springs). Avocations: flying, fly tying and fishing, skiing, golf. Office: Burton Hawks Inc PO Box 359 Casper WY 82602-0359 Address: PO Box 1950 Casper WY 82602-1950

HAWLEY, PHILIP METSCHAN, retired retail executive, management consultant; b. Portland, Oreg., July 29, 1925; s. Willard P. and Dorothy (Metschan) H.; m. Mary Catherine Follen, May 31, 1947; children: Diane (Mrs. Robert Bruce Johnson), Willard, Philip Metschan Jr., John, Victor, Edward, Erin (Mrs. Kevin Przybocki), George. BS, U. Calif., Berkeley, 1946; grad. advanced mgmt. program, Harvard U., 1967. With Carter Hawley Hale Stores, Inc., LA, 1958-93, pres., 1972-83, chief exec. officer, 1977-93, chmn., 1983-93. Bd. dirs. Weyerhaeuser Co. Trustee Calif. Inst. Tech., U. Notre Dame; chmn. L.A. Energy Conservation Com., 1973-74. Decorated hon. comdr. Order Brit. Empire, knight comdr. Star Solidarity Republic Italy; recipient Award of Merit L.A. Jr. C. of C., 1974, Coro Pub. Affairs award, 1978, Medallion award Coll. William and Mary, 1983, Award of Excellence Sch. Bus. Adminstrn. U. So. Calif., 1987, Bus. Statesman of Yr. award Harvard Bus. Sch., 1989, 15th ann. Whitney M. Young Jr. award L.S. Urban League, 1988; named Calif. Industrialist of Yr. Calif. Mus. Sci. and Industry, 1975. Mem. Calif. Retailers Assn. (chmn. 1993-95, dir.), Beach Club, Calif. Club, L.A. Country Club, Bohemian Club, Pacific-Union Club, Newport Harbor Yacht Club, Multnomah Club, Links Club, Phi Beta Kappa, Beta Alpha Psi, Beta Gamma Sigma. Office: 800 W 6th St Ste 920 Los Angeles CA 90017

HAWLEY, ROBERT CROSS, lawyer; b. Douglas, Wyo., Aug. 7, 1920; s. Robert Daniel and Elsie Corienne (Cross) Hawley; m. Mary Elizabeth Hawley McClellan, Mar. 3, 1944; children: Robert Cross, Mary Virginia, Laurie McClellan. BA with honors, U. Colo., 1973; LLB, Harvard U., 1949, JD, 1989. Bar: Wyo. 1950, Colo. 1950, U.S. Dist. Ct. Colo. 1950, U.S. Dist. Ct. Wyo. 1954, U.S. Ct. Appeals (10th cir.) 1955, Tex. 1960, U.S. Ct. Appeals (5th cir.) 1960, U.S. Supreme Ct. 1960, U.S. Dist. Ct. (so. dist.) Tex. 1961, U.S. Ct. Appeals (D.C. cir.) 1961, U.S. Ct. Appeals (8th cir.) 1979, U.S. Ct. Appeals (11th cir.) 1981, U.S. Dist. Ct. (we. dist.) Tex. 1987. Assoc. Bannister Weller & Friedrich, Denver, 1949—50; sr. atty. Continental Oil Co., Denver, 1952—58, counsel Houston, 1959—62; ptnr., v.p. Ireland, Stapleton & Pryor, Denver, 1962—81; ptnr. Dechert Price & Rhoads, Denver, 1981—83, Hawley & VanderWerf, Denver, 1983—94; sole practice Denver, 1994—. Pres. Highland Minerals, Denver; bd. dirs. Bank of Denver; speaker oil and gas insts. Author (co-author): Landman's Handbook, Law of Federal Oil and Gas Leases, Problems of Surface Damages, Federal Oil and Gas Leases--The Sole Party in Interest Debacle; contbr. articles pub. to oil & gas profl. jour. Treas. Am. Cancer Soc., Denver, 1981—82; chmn. U. Colo. Devel. Found., 1960—61; sec. Rocky Mountain Arthritis Found., 1993—94, vice chmn. Colo., 1994—; mem. adv. bd. ARC, 1988—; chmn. 1st Annual Retarded Children Campaign, 1963; dir. East Seal Chpt., 1966—68; bd. dirs. Am. Cancer Soc., Denver, 1967—87, Rocky Mountain Arthritis Found., 1987—, Craig Hosp., 1964—68. Lt. col. US Army, Korean War. Recipient Alumni Recognition award, U. Colo., Boulder, 1958, Meritorious Svc. award, Monticello Coll., Godfrey, Ill., 1967, Humanitarian award, Arthritis Found., 1992, Honored Lawyer award, Law Club, 1993; scholar Sigma Alpha Epsilon scholar, 1941—43. Mem.: ABA, Wyo. Pioneer Assn., Rocky Mountain Petroleum Pioneers (pres. 1991—92), Rocky Mountain Oil and Gas Assn., Harvard Alumni Assn., Interstate Oil and Gas Compact Comn., Fed. Energy Bar Assn. (legal and lands com.), Wyo. Bar Assn., Tex. Bar Assn., Denver Bar Assn., Colo. Bar Assn. (bd. govs. 1999—), Associated Alumni U. Colo. (pres. and bd. dirs. 1956—57), Harvard Law Sch. Assn. Colo. (pres. 1980—81), Denver Assn. Oil and Gas Title Lawyers (pres. 1983—84), U. Colo. Alumni Club (Living Legend award), Mile High Club, Colo. Arlberg Club, Garden of the Gods Club (Colo. Springs), Univ. Club Denver, Gyro Club, Petroleum Club, Denver Country Club, Chevaliers du Tastevin, Denver (pres. 1958—59), Law Club, Denver Petroleum Club (pres. 1978—79). Republican. Episcopalian. Address: Unit 71 2552 E Alameda Ave Denver CO 80209-3322

HAY, HOWARD CLINTON, lawyer; b. Portland, Maine, Apr. 16, 1944; s. Willis and Ruth (Clark) H.; m. Carol Anne Newsome, Dec. 21, 1968; children: Mark, David, Scott. AB (with distinction), Duke U., 1966; JD magna cum laude, U. Mich., 1969. Bar: U.S. Supreme Ct. 1977, Calif. 1970. Law clerk U.S. Ct. Appeals, Boston, 1970; atty. NLRB; ptnr. Paul, Hastings, Janofsky & Walker, Costa Mesa, Calif., 1971—. Program chmn. Certificate in Employee Rels. Law; instr. U. S.C. Grad. Sch. Bus. Editor Mich. Law Review; contbr. articles to profl. jours. Mem. State Bar Calif. (exec. com. labor and employment sect.), Calif. Bar Assn. Office: Paul Hastings Janofsky & Walker 695 Town Center Dr Fl 17 Costa Mesa CA 92626-1924 Office Phone: 714-668-6266. E-mail: howardhay@paulhastings.com.

HAY, RICHARD LAURENCE, theater set designer; b. Wichita, Kans., May 28, 1929; s. Laurence Charles and Ruth Mary (Rhoades) H. BA, Stanford U., 1952, MA, 1955. Tech. dir., designer Oreg. Shakespeare Festival, Ashland, 1953-55, prin. scenic designer, 1970—; instr. drama Stanford U., Palo Alto, Calif., 1957-62, assoc. prof., 1965-69; assoc. artistic dir. for design Denver Ctr. Theater Co., 1984-91. Freelance scenic designer Guthrie Theater, Mpls., Am. Conservatory Theater, San Francisco, Mo. Repertory Theater, Kansas City, Mark Taper Forum, Los Angeles, Old Globe Theater, San Diego, Berkekey (Calif.) Repertory Theater, Eisenhower Theatre, others; theatre designer: Source and Space Theatres, Denver Ctr. Theatre Co., New Old Globe Theatre and Festival Stage, Old Globe Theatre, San Diego, Intiman Theatre, Seattle, Black Swan, Angus Bowmer Theatre, Elizabethan Stage, New Theatre, Oreg. Shakespeare Festival. Author: (with others) A Space for Magic: Stage Settings by Richard L. Hay, 1979; exhibitor Prague Quadriennial, 1987, 99, 2003, US Inst. Theatre Tech. Biennial Scenography Expn., 1984, 88, 90, 2006, Schneider Mus. of Art, 2001. Recipient Critics award Hollywood (Calif.) Drama-Logue, 1982, 85, 86, 89, Gov's. award for the Arts State of Oreg., 1989; Fulbright grantee, 1955. Fellow US Inst. Theatre Tech. (bd. dirs. 1994-97, Disting. Achievement award in scenic design 1998); mem. United Scenic Artists, League Hist. Am. Theaters. Democrat. Congregationalist. Avocation: book collecting. Home: 707 Liberty St Ashland OR 97520-3140 Office: Oreg Shakespeare Festival PO Box 158 Ashland OR 97520-0158 Home Phone: 541-482-8885; Office Phone: 541-482-2111. Business E-Mail: richardh@osfashland.org.

HAY, SYDNEY, public relations executive; m. Dan Hay; children: Andrew, Sarah. BS summa cum laude, Kansas Newman Coll. Former chmn. bd. govs. Ariz. Dept. Mines and Mineral Resources; exec. dir. AMIGOS (Arizona Mining and Industry Get Our Support). Radio talk show host; spkr. in field. Mem.: Ariz. Mining Assn. (pres.). Republican. Office: PO Box 17576 Munds Park AZ 86017 Office Phone: 928-286-1128.

HAYCOCK, KENNETH ROY, academic administrator, educator, consultant; b. Hamilton, Ont., Can., Feb. 15, 1948; s. Bruce Frederick T. and Doris Marion P. (Downham) H.; m. Sheila Tripp, Jan. 28, 1990. BA, U. Western Ont., 1968, diploma in edn., 1969; specialist cert., U. Toronto, Can., 1971; MEd, U. Ottawa, Can., 1973; AMLS, U. Mich., 1974; EdD, Brigham Young U., 1991; MBA, Royal Roads, 2004. Tchr., dept. head Glebe Collegiate Inst., Ottawa, 1969-70, Col. By Secondary Sch., Ottawa, 1970-72; cons. Wellington County Bd. Edn., Guelph, Ont., 1972-76; coord. libr. svcs., supr. instrn. Vancouver (B.C.) Sch. Bd., Canada, 1976-84, acting mgr., elem./secondary edn. Canada, 1984-85, dir. instrn., head program svcs., 1985-89, 91-92; prin. Waverley Elem. Sch., 1989-91; prof. Sch. Libr., Archival and Info. Studies U. B.C., Vancouver, 1992—2005, dir., 1992—2002; prof. Sch. Libr. and Info. Sci., dir. San Jose State U., 2005—. Instr. univs. and colls.; pres. Ken Haycock and Assocs., Inc. Editor Tchr. Libr., 1978-2004; contbr. articles to profl. jours. Trustee Guelph Pub. Libr., 1975-76; trustee West Vancouver Sch. Bd., 1993-99, chair, 1994-97, councilor Dist. of West Vancouver, 1999-2002; trustee West Vancouver Pub. Libr., 1999-2000. Recipient award Beta Phi Mu, 1976, Queen Elizabeth Silver Jubilee medal, 1977. Fellow: Can. Coll. Tchrs.; mem.: ASCD (urban curriculum leaders 1985—92, internat. panel 1990—94), ALA (life; coun. 1995—2003, exec. bd. 1999—2003, coun. 2004—07, Herbert and Virginia White Advocacy award 2001), Coun. for Can. Learning Resources (pres. 1995—98), Internat. Assn. Sch. Librarianship (dir. N.Am. 1993—95, exec. dir. 1995—2000, Ken Haycock Leadership Devel. award named in his honor 2001), B.C. Libr. Assn. (Ken Haycock Student Conf. award named in his honor 1999, Helen Gordon Stewart Outstanding Contbns. award 2005), Assn. for Libr. and Info. Sci. Edn. (sec. coun. dean and dirs. 1993—96, pres. 2005—06, Outstanding Svc. award 2008), Can. Libr. Assn. (life; pres. 1977—78, Outstanding Svc. award 1991, Ken Haycock award for promoting librarianship named in his honor 2005), Ont. Libr. Assn. (life), B.C. Tchr. Libr. Assn. (Ken Haycock Profl. Devel. award named in his honor 1984, Disting. Svc. award 1989), Can. Sch. Libr. Assn. (pres. 1974—75, Margaret B. Scott award of merit 1979, rsch. award 1984, Disting. Sch. Adminstr. award 1989, rsch. award 1995), Am. Assn. Sch. Librs. (pres. 1997—98, Baker and Taylor Disting. Svc. award 1996), Internat. Fedn. Libr. Assns. and Instns. (sect. on Edn. and Tng. 1997—2005, chair 1999—2001), Phi Delta Kappa (Young Leader in Edn. award). Office: San Jose State U One Washington Sq San Jose CA 95192-0029 Home and Office: 46 W Julian St Ste 229 San Jose CA 95110 Office Phone: 408-924-2491. Personal E-mail: ken@kenhaycock.com. Business E-Mail: khaycock@slis.sjsu.edu.

HAYDEN, CEDRIC L., former state legislator, dentist; b. Eugene, Oreg., Aug. 4, 1934; s. Jesse and Gwendolen (Lampshire) H.; m. Marilyn Adele Jaekel, Dec. 27, 1961; children: Jonathan, Christopher, Matthew, Daniel, Cedric Ross, Kaminda. BS, U. Oreg., 1957; DMD, Washington U., St. Louis, 1960; MPH, Loma Linda U., 1979. Dentist Antioch (Calif.) Dental Group, 1963-65; missionary Seventh Day Adventist Ch., Port of Spain, Trinidad, 1965-69; dentist Hayden Family Dentistry Group, Eugene, Oreg., 1970—; legislator Oreg. Ho. of Reps., Salem, 1985-97, chmn. house com. on transp., house com. on gen. govt., 1991-95, asst. majority leader, asst. caucus leader, 1991-95, mem. ways and means com., 2001—. Lt. (s.g.) USN, 1960-63. Fellow Am. Dental Soc. Anesthesiology. Avocations: skiing, hiking, camping, horseback riding, travel. E-mail: hayden.rep@state.or.us.

HAYDEN, JOHN OLIN, English literature educator, writer; b. LA, Dec. 18, 1932; s. John Ellsworth and Norah Elizabeth (Bussens) H.; m. Mary Kathleen Garland, Dec. 18, 1965; children— Michael, John, Mark, Ann BA, U. Calif.-Santa Barbara, 1958; MA, Columbia U., 1959, PhD, 1965. Asst. prof. U. Colo., Boulder, 1964-66; assoc. prof. English lit. U. Calif.-Davis, 1966-75, prof. English lit., 1975-94, prof. emeritus, 1994—. Author: Romantic Reviewers, 1969, Polestar of the Ancients, 1979, William Wordsworth and the Mind of Man, 1993, Why the Great Books are Great, 1998; editor: Sir Walter Scott, 1970, Wordsworth: The Poems, 1977, Wordsworth: The Prose, 1988, Wordsworth: Selected Poetry, 1994. Served with USAF, 1951-55 E. J. Noble Found. fellow Columbia U., N.Y.C., 1959-61; fellow NEH, 1971, Am. Council Learned Socs., 1984 Republican. Roman Catholic. Avocation: coin collecting/numismatics. Home: 25199 Carlsbad Ave Davis CA 95616-9434 Office: U Calif English Dept Davis CA 95616 E-mail: johayden@ucdavis.edu.

HAYDEN, RON L., library director; b. San Pedro, Calif., Dec. 24, 1948; s. Larnie Alphonsis and Myrtie Louise (Pilcher) H.; m. Marilee Ann Brubaker, May 30, 1971 (dec. June 1978); m. Susan Ann Huffman, Jan. 1, 1982. AA, Golden West Coll., 1969; BA, Long Beach State U., 1972; MLS, Fullerton U., 1974. Reference sr. libr. Huntington Beach (Calif.) Libr., 1975-79, pub. svc. libr., 1979-86, libr. dir., 1986—. Liason Libr. Patrons Assn., Huntington Beach, 1986—. Author: Collection Development Library Journal, 1979. Recipient Award of Excellence Calif. S.W. Recreation Park Conf., 1990. Mem. ALA (Libr. in Media award, Best of Show award 1990), Calif. Libr. Assn., Friends Libr., So. Calif. Tennis Assn., Rotary (bd. dirs., vocat. chmn. 1988—). Avocations: tennis, running, reading. Office: Huntington Beach Libr 7111 Talbert Ave Huntington Beach CA 92648-1232

HAYDEN, STEPHEN R., emergency physician, educator; b. Argentia, Newfoundland, Canada, July 7, 1961; 3 children. MD, Albany Med. Coll., NY, 1985. Diplomate in emergecy medicine Am. Bd. Emergency Medicine, 1994, in undersea and hyperbaric medicine Am. Bd. Preventive Medicine, 2004. Prof. emergency medicine U. Calif. San Diego Med. Ctr., 1993—, program dir. emergency medicine residency, 1998—; editor-in-chief Jour. Emergency Medicine, 2006—. Pres. Coun. Emergency Medicine Program Dirs., Lansing, Mich., 2003—05. Editor: (med. textbook) The 5 Minute Emergency Medicine Consult. Mem. at large Am. Acad. Emergency Medicine, Milw., 2005—08. Comdr. USN, 1985—89, NAS Fallon, Nev. Recipient Dir. of Yr., Am. Acad. Emergency Medicine, 2005, Nat. Tchg. award, Am. Coll. Emergency Physicians, 2001. Office: UCSD Medical Ctr 200 West Arbor Dr San Diego CA 92103 Office Fax: 619-543-7598. Business E-Mail: srh@ucsd.edu.

HAYDEN, WILLIAM ROBERT, lawyer; b. Chgo., May 22, 1947; s. Robert George and Dorothy (Honan) H.; m. Carol Ann Brock, Aug. 12, 1978; 1 child, Nathaniel. BA, Kans. State U., 1969; JD with honors, George Washington U., 1972. Bar: D.C. 73, U.S. Dist. Ct. D.C. 75, U.S. Ct. Appeals (D.C. cir.) 75, Ariz. 78, U.S. Dist. Ct. Ariz. 78, U.S. Ct. Appeals (9th cir.) 79, U.S. Ct. Appeals (10th cir.) 97, U.S. Ct. Appeals (11th cir.) 01, Colo. (U.S. Dist. Ct.) 2002. Mem. gen. counsel's staff NLRB, Washington, 1973-75; assoc. O'Donoghue and O'Donoghue, Washington, 1975-78, Snell and Wilmer, Phoenix, 1978-82, ptnr., 1982—. Contbg. editor: Developing Labor Law, 1974, Employment Discrimination Law, 1989. Mem. ABA (labor and employment law sect.), Nat. Panel, Am. Arbitration Assn. (employment dispute resolution), Ariz. Bar Assn. (exec. com., past chmn. labor and employment law sect. 1984-89, employment civil jury instructions com.), Maricopa County Bar Assn., D.C. Bar Assn., Ariz. C. of C. (employee rels. subcom.). Avocations: tennis, softball, skiing. Office: Snell & Wilmer 1 Arizona Ctr Phoenix AZ 85004 Office Phone: 602-382-6000. Business E-Mail: bhayden@swlaw.com.

HAYEK, CAROLYN JEAN, financial consultant, retired judge; b. Portland, Oreg., Aug. 17, 1948; d. Robert A. and Marion L. (DeKoning) H.; m. Steven M. Rosen, July 21, 1974; children: Jonathan David, Laura Elizabeth. BA in Psychology, Carleton Coll., 1970; JD, U. Chgo., 1973. Bar: Wash. 1973; cert. webmaster Lake Washington Tech. Coll., 2000. Assoc. Jones, Grey & Bayley, Seattle, 1973-77; pvt. practice Federal Way, Wash., 1977-82; judge Federal Way Dist. Ct., 1982-95; ret., 1995. Task force Alternatives for Wash., 1973-75; mem. Wash. State Ecol. Commn., 1975-77; columnist Tacoma News Tribune Hometown Sect., 1995-96; bus. law instr. Lake Washington Tech. Coll., 2000-01; exec. dir. People's Meml. Assn., Seattle, 2002-03; owner Hayek Svcs., 2003-. Bd. dirs. 1st Unitarian Ch., Seattle, 1986-89, vice-chair 1987-88, pres. 1988-89; ch. adminstr. Northlake Unitarian Universalist Ch.; treas. Eastshore Unitarian Universalist Ch. Women's Perspective, 2001-02; den leader Mt. Rainier coun. Boy Scouts Am., 1987-88, scouting coord., 1988-89; bd. dirs. Twin Lakes Elem. Sch. PTA; v.p. Friends of the Libr. Kirkland, 2000-05; mem. City of Kirkland Planning Commn., 2002—, chair, 2005—06; regional liaison Nat. Girls Collaboration Project, 2007-09. Recipient Women Helping Women award Fed. Way Soroptimist, 1991, Martin Luther King Day Humanitarian award King County, 1993, Recognition cert. City of Fed. Way Diversity Commn., 1995. Mem.: ABA, AAUW (pres. Federal Way br. 1978—80, chair state level conf. com. 1986—87, pres. Federal Way br. 1990—92, diversity com. 1991—98, state bd. 1995—97, co-pres. Kirkland-Redmond br. 1999—2000, co-v.p. Lake Washington br. 2001—03, Wash. State pres. 2004—06, dir. ESL project, nat. girls colaborative project, mem. nat. bylaws com.), Nat. Assn. Women Judges (dist. bd. dir. 1984—86, chmn. rules com. 1988—89, chmn. bylaws com. 1990—91, nat. bd. dir.), Elected Wash. Women (dir. 1983—87), King County Dist. Ct. Judges Assn. (treas. exec. com. 1990—93, chair and rules com. 1990—94), Wash. State Bar Assn., Wash. Women Lawyers, Plz. on State Owners Assn. (pres. 1997—99, bd. dir. 1997—2000, sec. 1999—2000, webmaster 2000—08), Eliot Inst. (bd. dir. 1996—2000, vice chair 1998—99, bd. chair 1999—2000, webmaster 1999—2002), Unitarian Universalist Women's Fedn. (chair bylaws com. 1996), Greater Federal Way C. of C. (dir. 1978—82, sec. 1980—81, v.p. 1981—82), Fed. Way Women's Network (bd. dir. 1984—91, pres. 1985, program co-chair 1989—91, bd. dir. 1995—97, co-editor newsletter), Wash. Women United (bd. dir. 1995—97), Rotary (Sunrise Fed. Way chpt.) (membership com. 1991—96, youth exch. officer 1994—95, comty. svc. chair, bd. dir.). Office Phone: 425-822-2794. Personal E-mail: hayekservices@aol.com.

HAYES, DOTTY (DOROTHY DAMON HAYES), computer software company executive; b. Concord, Mass., Dec. 10, 1950; d. Henry Orr and Luthena Pearl (Carpenter) Damon; m. Terry Nolan Hayes, Sept. 20, 1980; 1 child, Carolyn. BA, U. Mass., 1972, MBA, 1976; MS in Fin., Bentley Coll., 1986. Cert. Internal Auditor. Cost acct. Data Gen. Corp., Westboro, Mass., 1976-77, internal auditor, 1977-80, cost acct. supr., 1980; asst. to corp. controller Apollo Computer Inc., Chelmsford, Mass., 1980-82, controller tech. ops., 1982-83, dir. group ops., 1983-85, v.p., contr., 1985-89; with Hewlett-Packard Co., 1989—99; v.p., corp. contr. Agilent Technologies, 1999—2002, Intuit Inc., 2003—05, v.p. internal audit, 2005—. Bd. dirs. Range Fuels, Inc., 2008—, Addison Ave. Fed. Credit Union. Mem. chancellor's exec. com. U. Mass., Amherst, Mass., 1987—; bd. trustees Woodside Priory School, 1999-2006, Computer History Mus. Mem. Fin. Execs. Inst. Office: Intuit Inc 1401 N Shoreline Blvd Mountain View CA 94043

HAYES, EDWARD LEE, religious organization administrator; b. Modesto, Calif., Sept. 26, 1931; s. George Lester and Sylvia (Utzinger) H.; m. Marilyn Elizabeth Bjorklund, July 31, 1954; children: Carla Hayes Strickfaden, Darryl, Bryan. BA in Social Sci., Westmont Coll., 1953; ThM in Bibl. Studies, Dallas Theol. Sem., 1957; postgrad., Calif. State U., LA, 1962-65, Iliff Theol. Sem., Denver, 1962-65; PhD in Higher Edn. Adminstrn., U. Denver, 1966. Ordained to ministry Bapt. Ch., 1957. Min. to youth Reinhardt Bible Ch., Dallas, 1954-57; asst. prof. ch. edn. Biola U., La Mirada, Calif., 1957-60; min. edn. First Bapt. Ch., Montebello, Calif., 1958-61; prof., acad. dean Denver Sem., 1960-79, pres., 1993-97, pres. emeritus, 1997—; exec. dir. Mt. Hermon (Calif.) Assn., 1979-92. Cons. Scripture Press Pub. Co., 1963-73; lectr. in field. Author: Words To Live By, 1968, The Focused Life, 1986, The Church, 1999. Pres. PTA, Littleton, Colo., 1975-77; trustee Westmont Coll., Santa Barbera, 1973—. Grantee Lilly Found., Assn. Theol. Schs., 1968, Rsch. grantee Assn. Theol. Schs., 1976. Mem. Evang. Theol. Soc., Assn. Governing Bds. Republican. Avocations: art, horticulture, music, travel. Office: Denver Sem PO Box 10000 Denver CO 80250-9099

HAYES, JANET GRAY, retired management consultant, mayor; b. Rushville, Ind., July 12, 1926; d. John Paul and Lucile (Gray) Frazee; m. Kenneth Hayes, Mar. 20, 1950; children: Lindy, John, Katherine, Megan. AB, Ind. U., 1948; MA magna cum laude, U. Chgo., 1950. Psychiat. caseworker Jewish Family Svc. Agy., Chgo., 1950-52; vol. Denver Crippled Children's Service, 1954-55, Adult and Child Guidance Clinic, San Jose, Calif., 1958-59; mem. San Jose City Coun., 1971-75, vice mayor, 1973-75; mayor San Jose, 1975—82; co-chmn. com. urban econs. U.S. Conf. Mayors, 1976-78, co-chmn. task force on aging, mem. sci. and teck task force, 1976-80, bd. trustees, 1977-82; bd. dirs. League Calif. Cities, 1976-82, mem. property tax reform task force, 1976-82; chmn. State of Calif. Urban Devel. Adv. Com., 1976-77; mem. Calif. Commn. Fair Jud. Practices, 1976-82; client-community relations dir. Q. Tech., Santa Clara, Calif., 1983-85; bus. mgr. Kenneth Hayes MD, Inc., 1985-88; CEO Hayes House, Book Distbr., 1998—. Mem. Dem. Nat. Campaign Com., 1976; mem. Calif. Dem. Commn. Nat. Platform and Policy, 1976; del. Dem. Nat. Conv., 1980; bd. dirs. South San Francisco Bay Dischargers Authority; chmn. Santa Clara County Sanitation Dist.; mem. San Jose/Santa Clara Treatment Plant Adv. Bd.; chmn. Santa Clara Valley Employment and Tng. Bd. (CETA), League to Save Lake Tahoe adv. bd., 2000—; past mem. EPA Aircraft/Airport Noise Task Group; bd. dirs. Calif. Center Rsch. and Edn. in Govt, Alexian Bros. Hosp., 1983-92; bd. dirs., chmn. adv. council Public Tech. Inc.; mem. bd. League to Save Lake Tahoe, 1984-2000; pres. bd. trustees San Jose Mus. Art, 1987-89; founder, adv. bd. Calif. Bus. Bank, 1982-85; polit. advisor Citizens Against Airport Pollution, 2003—. AAUW Edn. Found. grantee. Mem. Assn. Bay Area Govts. (exec. com. 1971-74, regional housing subcom. 1973-74), LWC (pres. San Francisco Bay Area chpt. 1968-70, pres. local chpt. 1966-67), Mortar Bd., Phi Beta Kappa, Kappa Alpha Theta.

HAYES, JOHN A., packaging company executive; b. Wilmette, Ill., Dec. 2, 1965; BA in English and Econs., Colgate U., 1988; MBA in Fin. and Strategy, Northwestern U. V.p. mergers and acquisitions Lehman Brothers, Chgo.; sr. dir. corp. planning and devel. Ball Corp., Broomfield, Colo., v.p. corp. planning and devel., 2000—03, v.p. corp. strategy, mktg. and devel., 2003—05, exec. v.p. Ball Packaging Europe, v.p., 2005—06, pres. Ball Packaging Europe, v.p. to sr. v.p., 2006—08, exec. v.p., COO, 2008—. Office: Ball Corp 10 Longs Peak Dr Broomfield CO 80021 Office Phone: 303-469-3131. Office Fax: 303-460-2127.

HAYES, MARY ESHBAUGH, editor, writer; b. Rochester, NY, Sept. 27, 1928; d. William Paul and Eleanor Maude (Sievert) Eshbaugh; m. James Leon Hayes, Apr. 18, 1953; children: Pauli, Eli, Lauri Le June, Clayton, Merri Jess Bates. BA in English and Journalism, Syracuse U., NYC, 1950. With Livingston County Republican, Geneseo, NY, summers, 1947-50, mng. editor, 1949-50; reporter Aurora Advocate, Colo., 1950—52; reporter-photographer Aspen Times, Colo., 1952-53, columnist, 1956—, reporter, 1972-77, assoc. editor, 1977-89, editor-in-chief, 1989-92, contbg. editor, 1992—. Instr. Colo. Mountain Coll., 1979; Aspen corr. Reuters, 1997—. Author, editor: The Story of Aspen, 1996 (1st prize, 1996); contbg. editor: Destinations Mag., 1994—97, Aspen Mag., 1996—, Aspen Sojourner Mag., 2005—; editor: Aspen Pot Pourri, 1968 (1st prize, 1990), rev. edit., 2002 (1st prize, 2002). Recipient Living Landmark award, Aspen Hist. Soc., 2002. Mem.: Colo. Press Women's Assn. (writing award 1974—75, 1978—85, sweepstakes award for writing 1977—78, 1984—85, 1991—2003, 2d pl. award 1976, 1979, 1982—83, 1994—95, Woman of Achievement 1986), Nat. Fedn. Press Women (1st prize in writing and editing 1976—80, 1st prize in adv. photography 1998). Home: PO Box 497 Aspen CO 81612-0497 Office: Box E Aspen CO 81612 Personal E-mail: meh@sopris.net.

HAYES, ROBERT MAYO, dean, library and information scientist, educator; b. NYC, Dec. 3, 1926; s. Dudley Lyman and Myra Wilhelmina (Lane) H.; m. Alice Peters, Sept. 2, 1952; 1 son, Robert Dendrou. BA, UCLA, 1947, MA, 1949, PhD, 1952. Mathematician Nat. Bur. Standards, Washington and Los Angeles, 1949-52; mem. tech. staff Hughes Aircraft Co., 1952-54; head applications group Nat. Cash Register Co., 1954-55; head bus. systems group Magnavox Co., 1955- 60; pres. Advanced Information Systems, Inc., Los Angeles, 1960-64; v.p., sci. dir. Electrada Corp., Los Angeles, 1960-64; lectr. dept. math. UCLA, 1952-64, prof. library and info. sci., 1964-91, dean, 1974-89, dean emeritus, 1989—, dir. Inst. Libr. Rsch., 1965-70; prof. emeritus, 1991—. Vis. prof. U. NSW, 1979, 93, 2002, 03, Tskuba U., 1987, Nankai U., 1987, Loughborough U., 1989, Keio U., Japan, 1994, Khazar U., Azerbaijan, 1995; mem. adv. com. White House conf. Libr. and Info. Svcs., 1979; v.p. Becker & Hayes, Inc., 1969-73, 93-96; cons. On Line Computer Libr. Ctr., 1990-94; lectr. in field. Author: Strategic Management for Academic Libraries, 1993, Models for Library Management, Decision-Making and Planning, 2001; co-author: Introduction to Information Storage and Retrieval:Tools, Elements, Theory, 1963, Handbook of Data Processing for Libraries, 2d edit., 1974, Strategic Management for Public Libraries, 1996; U.S. regional editor: Problems in Info. Storage and Retrieval, 1959—63; editor: Info. Scis. Series, 1963—75; mem. editl. bd.: Libr. Info. Sci. Rsch., 1978—. Recipient Profl. Achievement award, UCLA Alumni Assn., Beta Phi Mu award, ALA, 1st Tezak award, U. Zagreb, 1990. Mem. ALA (pres. info. sci. and automation div. 1969), Am. Soc. Info. Sci. (pres. 1962-63, nat. lectr. 1968, Award of Merit 1993), Am. Math. Soc., Assn. for Computing Machinery (assoc. editor jour. 1959-69, nat. lectr. 1969), Cosmos Club, Phi Beta Kappa, Sigma Xi. Home: 3943 Woodfield Dr Sherman Oaks CA 91403-4239 Office: UCLA 405 Hilgard Ave Los Angeles CA 90095-9000 E-mail: rhayes@ucla.edu.

HAYES, SEAN (SEAN PATRICK HAYES), actor, comedian; b. Chgo., Ill., June 26, 1970; s. Ron and Mary Hayes. Attended, Ill. State Univ. Music dir. Pheasant Run Theatre, Chgo., comedian Second City Improvisational Comedy Group, stand-up comedian in clubs in LA and Chgo.; actor: (TV films) A & P, 1996; (films) Billy's Hollywood Kiss, 1998, Sin City Spectacular (Episode: Penn & Teller's Sin City Spectacular), 1999, Martin and Lewis, 2002, Pieces of April, 2003, Win a Date with Tad Hamilton!, 2004, The Bucket List, 2007, (voice) Igor, 2008, Soul Men, 2008; (TV series) Silk Stalkings (Episode: Services Rendered), 1996, Will & Grace, 1998—2006 (Emmy award for Outstanding Supporting Actor in a Comedy, 2000, Outstanding Performance by an Ensemble in a Comedy Series, Screen Actors Guild award, 2001, Outstanding Performance by a Male Actor in a Comedy Series, Screen Actors Guild award, 2002, 2003, 2006), Scrubs (Episode: My Super Ego), 2001; voice Buzz Lightyear of Star Command: The Adventure Begins, 2000, Cats & Dogs, 2001, The Cat in the Hat, 2003, host (TV series) Saturday Night Live, 2001; exec. prodr.: (TV series) Situation: Comedy, 2005. Office: c/o Principato Young Mgmt 9465 Wilshire Blvd Ste 880 Beverly Hills CA 90212

HAYES, STEVEN CHARLES, psychologist, educator; b. Aug. 12, 1948; s. Charles Aloysius and Ruth Esther (Dryer) Hayes; m. Angela Fe Butcher (div.); 1 child, Camille; m. Linda Jean Parrott (div.); children: Charles Frederick, Esther Marlena; m. Jacqueline Pistorello; 1 child, Steven Joseph. BA cum laude in Psychology, Loyola U., 1970; postgrad., Calif. State U., San Diego, 1971-72; MA in Clin. Psychology, W.Va. U., 1974, PhD, 1977. Lic. psychologist, N.C., Nev. Intern psychology Brown U. Sch. Medicine, Providence, 1975-76; asst. prof. U. N.C., Greensboro, 1976-82, assoc. prof., 1982-86; prof. U. Nev., Reno, 1986—, dir. clin. tng., 1994—. Found. prof. W.Va. U. Author: The Effects of Monthly Feedback, Rebate Billing and Consumer Directed Feedback on the Residential Consumption of Electricity, 1977; Abnormal Psychology, 1979; (with J.D. Cone) Environmental Problems/Behavioral Solutions, 1980; (with D.H. Barlow and R.O. Nelson) The Scientist Practitioner: Research and Accountability in Clinical and Educational Settings, 1984, (with R.O. Nelson) Conceptual Foundations of Behavioral Assessment, 1986, Rule-Governed Behavior, 1989, (with L.J. Hayes) Understanding Verbal Relations, 1992, (with others) Varieties of Scientific Contextualism, 1993, Behavior Analysis of Language and Cognition, 1994, Acceptance and Change, 1994, Scientific Standards of Psychological Practice, 1995, (with K. Strosahl and K.G. Wilson) Acceptance and Commitment Therapy, 1999, (with E. Heiby) Prescription Privileges for Psychologists, 1998, (with D.H. Barlow & R.O. Nelson-Gray) The Scientist-Practitioner: Research & Accountability in the Age of Managed Care, 1999, 2d edit., (with D. Barnes-Holmes and B. Roche) Relational Frame Theory, 2001, (with W. O'Donohue, D. Henderson, J. Fisher and L. Hayes) A History of the Behavior Therapies, 2001, (with N. Cummings, W. I'Donohue and V. Follette) Intergrated Behavioral Healthcare, (with E.T. O'Donohue and J.E. Fisher) Cognitive Behavior Therapy, 2003, (with V.M. Follette & M.M. Linehan) Mindfulness and Acceptance: Expanding the Cognitive Behavioral Tradition, 2004, (with R. Lappalainen, T. Lehtonen, S. Batten, E. Gifford, K. Wilson, N. Afari, and S.M. McCurry) Applying Acceptance and Commitment Therapy, 2004, (with K. Strosahl) A Practical Guide to Acceptance and Commitment Therapy, 2005, (with J. Dahl, K. Wilson, and C. Luciano) Acceptance and Commitment Therapy for Chronic Pain, 2005, (with S. Smith) Get Out of Your Mind and Into Your Life, 2005, (with D. Barnes-Holmes, F. Bond, and J. Austin) Acceptance and mindfulness at work: Acceptance and Commitment Therapy, Relational Frame Theory, and organizational behavior management, 2006, (with J. Luoma and R. Walser) Learning ACT, 2007; contbr. chpts. to books, articles to profl. jours.; editor APS Observer, 1988-89, The Scientist Practitioner, 1990-92; assoc. editor Jour. Applied Behavior Analysis, 1982-85; editl. bd. Behavioral Assessment, Behavior Modification, Jour. Cons. and Clin. Psychology, The Behavior Analyst, Behaviorism, Jour. Experimental Analysis of Behavior, The Psychological Record. Found. Inc. grantee, 1975; NIMH grantee, 1976-77; U. NC grantee, 1976-77, 77-78, 81-82, 82-83, NSF 1992, NIDA, 1994-2003, 2005—, NCI, 2000-02, Nat. Adv. Coun. on Drug Abuse, NIH, 2000-04, Clin. Trials Network Adv. Coun., NIDA, 2000-02, U. Nev. Found. grantee, 1992-94, 97—; named 30th highest impact psychologist in world Inst. Sci. Info, 1986-90; recipient Don F. Hake award APA, 2000, Rschr. of Yr. award U. and Cmty. Coll. Sys. of Nev. Regents, 2000, Disting. Alumni award W.Va. U., 2000, Rschr. of Yr. award U. Nev. Reno, 1997, Psychologist of Yr., Nev. Psychol. Assn., 2006, Impact of Sci. on App. award, Soc. for Advancement of Behavior Analysis, 2007. Fellow Assn. Psychol.Sci. (sec.-treas. 1988-89), Assn. Applied and Preventive Psychology (exec. com., mem.-at-large, bd. dirs., 1992-96, v.p. 1993, pres. 1994-96), Western Psychol. Assn.; mem. AAAS, Am. Psychol. Assn. (divsn. 25 student affairs coord., 1977, 78, continuing edn. chmn., 1980-82, program co-chmn., 1980-82, chmn. long-term planning com. 1982, mem.-at-large 1982-85, pres. 1987, council of reps., 1988-89, fellow divsn. 12, 24, and 25), Assn. Behavior Analysis, Assembly of Sci. and Applied Psychology (sec.-treas. 1987-88), Assn. Behavioral and Cognitive Therapy (student affairs coord. 1978, assoc. program chmn. 1979, program chmn. 1980, chmn. task force student involvement 1980-81, pres.-elect, 1996-97, pres. 1997-98, Lifetime Achievement award 2007), Assn. for Contextual Behavioral Sci. (pres.-elect 2007); Soc. Exptl. Analysis Behavior (sec. 1985, pres.-elect, 1996—, co-chmn. practice guidelines coalition 1997—, co-chair practice guidelines coalition 1996-2001), Southeastern Assn. for Behavior Analysis (sec. 1985-86), Sigma Xi. Democrat. Avocations: guitar, boating. Home: 933 Gear St Reno NV 89503-2729 Business E-Mail: hayes@unr.edu.

HAYFLICK, LEONARD, cell biologist, biogerontologist, microbiologist, educator, writer; b. Phila., May 20, 1928; s. Nathan Albert and Edna H.; m. Ruth Louise Heckler, Oct. 3, 1954; children: Joel, Deborah, Susan, Rachel, Anne. BA in Microbiology and Chemistry, U. Pa., 1951, MS in Med. Microbiology, 1953, PhD in Med. Microbiology and Chemistry, 1956. McLaughlin rsch. fellow in infection and immunity, dept. microbiology U. Tex. Med. Br., Galveston, Tex., 1956-58; assoc. mem. Wistar Inst. Anatomy and Biology, Phila., 1958-68; asst. prof. rsch. medicine U. Pa., Phila., 1966-68; prof. med. microbiology Stanford U. Sch. Medicine, Calif., 1968-76, senator-at-large, Basic Med. Scis., 1970-73, chmn. gen. rsch. support grant com., 1972-74; sr. rsch. cell biologist Children's Hosp., Oakland, Calif., 1976-81; prof. zoology, prof. microbiology and immunology U. Fla., Gainesville, 1981-87, dir. Ctr. for Gerontol. Studies, Coll. Liberal Arts and Scis., 1981-87; prof. anatomy U. Calif. Sch. Medicine, San Francisco, 1988—. Mem. subcom. on mycoplasmataceae Internat. Com. Bacteriol. Nomenclature, 1965-78; mem. steering com. cell and devel. biology film program MIT, 1970-73; chmn. Calif. State Com. Health White Ho. Conf. Aging, 1971-72, Calif. state rep., 1972; Nat. Cancer Planning Com. Nat. Cancer Inst., NIH, 1972; chmn., adult devel. and aging rsch. and tng. com. Nat. Inst. Child Health and Human Devel., NIH, 1972-73; non-resident fellow Inst. Higher Studies, Santa Barbara, Calif., 1973—; mem. Argonne Nat. Lab. rev. com. biol. and med. rsch. div. Argonne Nat. Lab., 1973-76; mem. rsch. adv. com. Tchrs. Ins. and Annuity Assn. Am.-Coll. Retirement Equities Funds, NYC, 1974-80; founding mem. Nat. Adv. Coun. on Aging, Nat. Inst. on Aging, NIH, Bethesda, Md., 1975; cons. Office of Dir. Nat. Cancer Inst., Bethesda, 1963-74; vis. scientist Ctr. for Aging Weizmann Inst. Sci., Rehovoth, Israel, 1980, 86; mem. adv. bd. Internat. Exchange Ctr. Gerontology, Fla. Univ. System, Tampa, 1982-86; mem. jury for Sandoz prize in gerontology and geriatrics, 1985-89; bd. dirs. Ctr. for Climacteric Studies, Inc., Gainesville, 1985-88; expert cons. various coms. US Congress, vis. prof. Oita Med. U., Japan, 1991-95, U. Parma, Italy, 1991, Kurume U. Med. Sch., Japan; lectr. in field. Author: How and Why We Age, 1996; editor: Biology of the Mycoplasmas, 1969, Handbook of the Biology of Aging, 1977; sr. editor Biol. Scis. Microfiche Collection Info. on Gerontology and Geriatric Medicine Univ. Microfilms Internat., Ann Arbor, Mich., 1984-98; editor-in-chief Exptl. Gerontology, 1984-98; asst. editor In Vitro jour. Tissue Culture Assn., 1969-75; editor biol. scis. sect. Jour. Gerontology, 1975-80; assoc. editor Cancer Rsch., 1972-80; mem. editorial bd. Jour. Bacteriology, 1964-72, Jour. Virology, 1967-70, Infection and Immunity jour., 1968-78, Exec. Health Report, 1970—, Mechanisms of Aging and Devel., 1972—, Gerontology and Geriatrics Edn., 1980—, A Revista Portuguesa de Medicina Geriatrica, 1987—; mem. adv. com. Bergey's Manual of Determinative Bacteriology, 1965-78; bd. dirs., mem. editorial bd. Bollettino Dell Instituto Sieroterapico Milanese, Archivo de Microbiologia ed Immunologia, Milan, Italy, 1968—; contbr. numerous articles in field to profl. jours. Staff sgt. US Army, 1946-48. Recipient Samuel Roberts Noble Found. Rsch. Recognition award, 1984; co-recipient Sandoz prize Internat. Assn. Gerontology, 1991, Biomed. Scis. & Aging award U. So. Calif., 1974, Rsch. Recognition award Samuel Roberts Noble Found., 1984; Karl-Forster lectr. Acad. Sci. and Lit., Mainz, Germany, 1983, Hoffman-LaRoche lectr. Waksman Inst. Microbiology Rutgers U., 1984, Wadworth Meml. Fund lectr. Rush-Presbyn.-St. Luke's Med. Ctr., Chgo., 1984, hon. lectr. Rosenfield Program Pub. Affairs Grinnell Coll., 1989, invited speaker Sandoz lectrs. in Gerontology, Basle, Switzerland, 1986, 92, numerous other lectureships U.S.A., Can. and Europe, 1970—, Career Devel. award Nat. Cancer Inst., NIH, 1962-70, Lifetime Achievement award Soc. In Vitro Biology, 1996, Van Wezel prize Euro. Soc. Animal Cell Technology, 1999, Lord Cohen of Birkinhead medal Brit. Soc. Rsch. on Aging, 1999, Life Extension prize, Regenerative Medicine Secretariat, 2001. Fellow AAAS, Gerontol Soc. Am. (program and awards com. 1972-77, chmn., exec. com. biol. scis. sect. 1972-74, com. on internat. rels. 1980-82, pub. policy com. 1980-82, pres. 1982-83, ann. Robert W. Kleemeier award 1972, Brookdale award 1980); mem. Am. Soc. for Microbiology, Tissue Culture Assn. (hon., trustee 1966-68, program com. 1970, mem. coun. 1972-74, v.p. 1974-76, pres. Calif. chpt. 1971-73), Soc. for Exptl. Biology and Medicine (councillor 1984-88), Assn. for Advancement of Aging Rsch. (adv. coun. 1970-71), Am. Aging Assn., Am. Cancer Soc. (virology and cell biology study sect. 1974-76), Internat. Assn. Microbiol. Standardization (sec. cell culture com. 1963-73, chmn. 1985—, mem. coun. 1987-89), Internat. Orgn. for Mycoplasmology (Presdl. award 1984), Am. Gerontol. Soc. (v.p., coun. 1972-74, 81-83, program com. 1977-79, bdu. dirs. 1981-83), Am. Fedn. Aging Rsch. (bd. dirs., exec. com., rsch. adv. com. 1981—, chmn. study sect. 1987—, v.p. 1988—, Leadership award 1983), Fedn. Am. Socs. for Exptl. Biology, Aging Prevention Rsch. Found. (sci. adv. bd. dirs.), Am. Assn. for Cancer Rsch., Am. Soc. Pathologists, Calif. Found. for Biomed. Rsch., Am. Longevity Assn. (sci. adv. bd. dirs. 1981—), Western Gerontology Assn. (coun. 1972-74, bd. dirs. 81-83), Internat. Assn. Gerontology (mem. Am. exec. com. 1972-75, treas., exec. com. 1985-89, co-recipient Sandoz award gerontology 1991), Found. on Gerontology (sci. adv. bd. 1985—), Soc. Medicine and Natural Sci., Ukrainian Acad. Med. Scis. (fgn., Academician 1991, 2005), French Biol. Soc. (fgn.), Euro. Soc. Animal Cell Tech. (Van Wezel prize), Brit. Soc. Rsch. on Aging (Lord Cohen of Burkinhead medal), France Soc. Biology. Achievements include prototype of inverted microscope acquisitioned by Smithsonian Natural Museum of American History in 2006. Office: U Calif 36991 Greencroft Close PO Box 89 The Sea Ranch CA 95497-0089 Business E-Mail: lenh38@aim.com.

HAYMET, ANTHONY DOUGLAS-JOHN, research scientist, chemistry educator; b. Sydney, Feb. 5, 1956; came to US, 1978; s. William Brian and Coral Elizabeth (Snaden) H.; m. Nan Christine Jackson, Nov. 21, 1984. BSc with honors, U. Sydney, 1977; PhD in Chemistry, U. Chgo., 1981; DSc, U. Sydney, 1997. Postdoctoral rsch. fellow Harvard U., Cambridge, Mass., 1981-83; asst. prof. chemistry U. Calif., Berkeley, 1983-88; assoc. prof. chemistry U. Utah, Salt Lake City, 1988-91, adj. prof. chemistry, 1991—95; prof. chemistry U. Sydney, Australia, 1991—98, vis. prof., 1998—99; dep. dir. physical sciences CAUT Ctr. Ednl. Software in Sci., Sydney, 1994—97; chmn. physical chemistry divsn. U. Houston, 1998—2001, founder Environ. Modeling Inst., 2000—02, disting. U. prof. chem., 1998—2002; hon. rsch. prof. chemistry U. Tasmania, 2002—06; dir. sci. & policy Australian Commonwealth Sci. & Indsl. Rsch. Orgn. (CSIRO), 2005—06, chief marine & atmospheric rsch., 2006; vice chancellor marine sciences U. Calif. San Diego, 2006—, dean Grad. Sch. Marine Sciences & dir. Scripps Instn. Oceanography, 2006—. Affiliate staff scientist Pacific N.W. Nat. Lab., 1996—2002; mem. faculty W.M. Keck Ctr. Computational Biology, Washington, 1998—2002; adv. bd. Environ. Inst. Houston, 2001—02; bd. dirs. Coop. Rsch. Ctr. Antarctic Climate & Ecosystems, Tasmania, 2003—06; mem. founding group Western Australia Marine Sci. Instn., 2005—06. Recipient Student Disting. Svc. award, U. Utah, 1990, Antarctic Svc. medal, US Dept. Navy & Nat. Sci. Found., 1994, Disting. Young Chemist award, Fedn. Asian Chem. Socs., 1997. Mem. Am. Chem. Soc., Am. Phys. Soc., AAAS, Royal Australia Chem. Inst. (Masson medal, 1977, Rennie medal, 1988). Avocations: running, cross country skiing, hiking. Office: U Calif San Diego #0210 9500 Gilman Dr La Jolla CA 92093-0210 Office Phone: 858-534-2827. Office Fax: 858-453-0167. E-mail: thaymet@ucsd.edu.

HAYN, CARL HUGO, physics professor, priest; b. LA, July 13, 1916; s. Hugo Sebastian and Mary Caroline (Schumann) H. AB, Gonzaga U., 1939, MA, 1940; Lic. in Sacred Theology, Alma Coll., Los Gatos, Calif., 1948; PhD, St. Louis U., 1955. Ordained priest Roman Cath. Ch., 1947. Tchr. Loyola H.S., LA, 1940-43; prof. physics Loyola U., LA, 1943-44, Santa Clara U., Calif., 1955—2007, emeritus prof. physics, 2007—. Mem. Am. Assn. Physics Tchrs. (past sec., pres.), Sigma Xi. Office: Santa Clara U 500 El Camino Real Santa Clara CA 95053-0001 Home Phone: 408-554-4124; Office Phone: 408-554-6956. E-mail: chayn@scu.edu.

HAYNES, CALEB VANCE, JR., geology and archaeology educator; b. Spokane, Wash., Feb. 29, 1928; m. Elizabeth Hamilton, Jan. 11, 1954 (dec. 2004); 1 child, Elizabeth Anne. Student, Johns Hopkins U., 1947-49; degree in geol. engring., Colo. Sch. Mines, 1956; PhD, U. Ariz., 1965. Mining geology cons., 1958-60; sr. project engr. Am. Inst. Research, Golden, Colo., 1956-60; sr. engr. Martin Co., Denver, 1960-62; geologist Nev. State Mus. Tule Springs Expedition, 1962-63; research asst. U. Ariz., Tucson, 1963-64, asst. prof. geology, 1965-68, prof. geoscis., anthropology, 1974-99, Regents prof., 1991-99, Regents prof. emeritus, 1999; assoc. prof. So. Meth. U., Dallas, 1968-73, prof., 1973-74. With USAF, 1951—54. Guggenheim fellow 1980-81, Smithsonian sr. post doctoral fellow, 1987; grantee NSF, Nat. Geographic Soc., others. Fellow: AAAS, Geol. Soc. Am. (Archaeol. Geology award 1984, Kirk Bryan award 2003); mem.: Soc. Am. Archaeology (Fryxell award 1978), Am. Quaternary Assn. (pres. 1976—78, Disting. Career award 2002), Nat. Acad. Sci., Sigma Xi. Office: U Ariz Dept Anthropology Tucson AZ 85721-0030

HAYNES, GARY ANTHONY, archaeologist; b. Long Beach, Calif., Sept. 30, 1948; s. Ellsworth Wallace and Martha Louise Haynes. BA, U. Md., 1970; MA, Cath. U. Am., 1978, PhD, 1981. Vis. asst. prof. anthropology Cath. U. Am., Washington, 1981; visiting prof. lectr. George Washington U., Washington, 1982; research assoc. anthropology dept. Smithsonian Inst., Washington, 1981-85; asst. prof. anthropology U. Nev., Reno, 1985-88, assoc. prof. anthropology, 1988-95, prof. anthropology, 1995—, chair dept., 1998—2004. Founder, vice-chmn. bd. Hwange Rsch. Trust, 1987—. Author: Mammoths, Mastodonts and Elephants, 1991, The Early Settlement of North America, 2002; editor: Mammoths and the Mammoth Fauna, 2000; contbr. articles to profl. jours. Active Scientist Exchange Acad. Scis. U.S. Nat. Research Council, 1987. Smithsonian Inst. fellow, 1980; grantee Nat. Geog. Soc., 1981-88, 91, Leakey Found., 1990, 91, IREX, 1995, Wenner-Gren Found., 2000; Fulbright sr. scholar Subsaharan Africa Rsch. Program, 1993. Mem. Soc. Am. Archaeology (Fryxell com. chmn. 1986-89), Am. Quaternary Assn., Zimbabwe Sci. Assn., Inqua Commn. on Palaeoecology and Human Evolution (pres. 2003—). Office: U Nev Dept Anthropology Reno NV 89557-0001

HAYNES, RAYMOND NEAL, JR., lawyer, state legislator; b. Merced, Calif., Aug. 26, 1954; s. Raymond Neal and Leona Faye (Ollar) H.; m. Diane Marie McDonald, Dec. 29, 1979 (div. May 1988); 1 child, Jennifer Marie; m. Pamela Davis, Sept. 9, 1989; children: Caitlin Joy, Sarah Elizabeth. BA, Calif. Luth. Coll., 1976; MPA, Ea. Ky. U., 1981; JD, U. So. Calif., 1980. Bar: Calif. 1980. Assoc. Best, Best and Krieger, Riverside, Calif., 1980-83; ptnr. Lawson and Hartnell, Redlands, Calif., 1983-88; pvt. practice Moreno Valley, Calif., 1988-92; assemblyman Calif. State Legis., Sacramento, 1992—; mem. CA State Senate, 1994—. Planning commr. City of Moreno Valley, 1985-86; dir. Youth Svc. Ctr., Riverside, 1984-86; treas. Citizens for Property Rights, Moreno Valley, 1986-90; chmn. Com. for No New Taxes, Moreno Valley, 1989-92. Republican. Office: CA State Senate Rm 2187 State Capitol Sacramento CA 95814

HAYNES, WILLIAM JAMES, II, lawyer; b. Waco, Tex., Mar. 30, 1958; s. William James and Caroline H.; m. Margaret Frances Campbell, 1982; 3 children. BA, Davidson Coll., 1980; JD, Harvard U., 1983; LLD (hon.), Stetson U., 1999. Bar: NC 1983, Ga. 1989, DC 1990. Law clk. to Hon. James B. McMillan US Dist. Ct. NC, Charlotte, 1983-84; assoc. Sutherland, Asbill & Brennan, Washington, 1989; spl. asst. to gen. counsel US Dept. Def., Washington, 1989-90, gen. counsel Dept. Army, 1990-93; ptnr. Jenner & Block LLP, Washington, 1993—96; v.p., assoc. gen. counsel Gen. Dynamics Corp., Falls Church, Va., 1996-98; gen. counsel Gen. Dynamics Marine Grp., 1997-98; ptnr. Jenner & Block LLP, Washington, 1999—2001; gen. counsel, dir. def. legal services agy. US Dept. Def., Washington, 2001—08; chief corp. counsel Chevron Corp., San Ramon, Calif., 2008—. Vol. Merry Corps Internat., Kazakhstan, 1999. Capt. US Army, 1984—89. Mem. ABA, NC Bar Assn., DC Bar Assn., Ga. Bar Assn. Presbyterian. Avocation: tennis. Office: Chevron Corp 6001 Bollinger Canyon Rd San Ramon CA 94583 Office Phone: 925-842-1298.

HAYO, GEORGE EDWARD, management consultant; b. LA, Nov. 2, 1934; s. George Edward Hayo Sr. and Esther Marie (Goodman) Arthur; m. Nixie Joanne Hunt, Aug. 4, 1956; children: Michael Edward, Kenneth Marvin, Michelle Virginia. BS in Applied Math., Calif. State U., 1960; MBA in Mgmt., U. Denver, 1968. Cert. mgmt. cons. Mathematician U.S. Naval Civil Engring. Lab., Port Hueneme, Calif., 1961-63; corp. systems planner No. Natural Gas Co., Omaha, 1963-66; asst. to pres. C.A. Norgren Co., Littleton, Colo., 1966-68; sr. staff cons. Emerson Electric, St. Louis, 1968-71; dir. adminstrn. Fisher Radio, NYC, 1971-72; v.p., dir. The Emerson Cons., NYC, 1973-87; pres. The Hayo Cons., Albuquerque, 1988—. Arbitrator Am. Arbitration Assn., N.Y., 1985—. Contbr. articles to profl. jours. Mem. Inst. Mgmt. Cons., Am. Inst. Plant Engrs., Am. Prodn. and Inventory Control Soc. Avocations: running, sailing, golf. Home and Office: The Hayo Cons 335 Pinon Creek Tr SE Albuquerque NM 87123-4123 Office Phone: 505-237-0313. Personal E-mail: hayocon@aol.com.

HAYS, GARRY D., academic administrator; Pres. US Internat U., San Diego, 1992—. Office: US Internat U Office Pres 10455 Pomerado Rd San Diego CA 92131-1717

HAYS, MARGUERITE THOMPSON, nuclear medicine physician, educator; b. Bloomington, Ind., Apr. 15, 1930; d. Stith and Louise (Faust) Thompson; m. David G. Hays, Feb. 4, 1950 (div. 1975); children: Dorothy Adele, Warren Stith Thompson, Thomas Glenn. AB cum laude, Radcliffe Coll., 1951; postgrad., Harvard U. Med. Sch., 1954; MD, UCLA, 1957; ScD (hon.), Ind. U., 1979. Diplomate Am. Bd. Internal Medicine, Am. Bd. Nuc. Medicine. Intern UCLA Sch. Medicine, 1957-58, resident, 1958-59, 61-62, USPHS postdoctoral trainee, 1959-61, USPHS postdoctoral fellow, 1963-64, asst. prof. medicine, 1964-68, SUNY-Buffalo, 1968-70, asst. prof. biophys. sci., 1968-74, assoc. prof. medicine, 1970-76, clin. assoc. prof. nuc. medicine, 1973-77; asst. chief nuc. medicine VA Med. Ctr., Wadsworth, Calif., 1967-68; chief nuc. medicine Buffalo VA Med. Ctr., 1968-74, assoc. chief of staff for rsch., 1971-74; dir. med. rsch. svc. VA Ctrl. Office, Washington, 1974-79, asst. chief med. dir. for R & D, 1979-81; chief of staff Martinez VA Med. Ctr., Calif., 1981-83; prof. radiology Sch. Medicine U. Calif., Davis, 1981-93, prof. medicine and surgery, 1983-91, assoc. dean, 1981; clin. prof. radiology Stanford U. Sch. Medicine, 1990—; assoc. chief of staff for rsch. Palo Alto (Calif.) VA Med. Ctr., 1983-97, staff physician, 1997-99, cons., 1999—2001. Vis. rsch. scientist Euratom, Italy, 1962-63; chmn. radiopharm. adv. com. FDA, 1974-77; co-chmn. biomedicine com. Pres.'s Fed. Coun. on Sci., Engring. and Tech., 1979-81; mem. rsch. restructuring adv. com. Va. R & D Office, 1995-96, chair task group to restructure R & D Career Devel. Program, 1996-97; chmn. coop. studies evaluation com., Med. Rsch. Svc., VA, 1990-93; mem. sci. rev. and evaluation bd. Health Svcs. Rsch. and Devel. Svc., VA, 1988-91, chmn. career devel. com., 1991-99, chmn. career devel. com. Rehab. Rsch. and Devel. Svc., 1997-2003. Rsch. grantee VA, 1968-2003. NIH grantee, 1964-71; recipient Exceptional Svc. award Sec. Vets. Affairs, 2000. Fellow ACP; mem. Soc. Nuc. Medicine (chmn. publs. com., trustee, v.p. 1983-84), Am. Thyroid Assn. (bd. dirs. 1993-96), Endocrine Soc. Home: 270 Campesino Ave Palo Alto CA 94306-2912 Office: 3801 Miranda Ave Palo Alto CA 94304-1207 E-mail: ritahays19@yahoo.com.

HAYS, PATRICK GREGORY, healthcare executive; b. Kansas City, Kans., Sept. 9, 1942; s. Vance Samuel and Mary Ellen (Crabbe) H.; m. Penelope Ann Hall, July 3, 1976; children: Julia L., Jennifer M., Emily J., Drew D. BS in Bus. Adminstrn, U. Tulsa, 1964; M.H.A., U. Minn., 1971; postgrad., U. Mich. Grad. Sch. Bus. Adminstrn., 1977. Mfg. analyst N.Am. Rockwell Corp., Tulsa, 1964-66; asst. adminstr., adminstr. for ops. Henry Ford Hosp., Detroit, 1971-75; exec. v.p. Meth. Med. Ctr. of Ill., Peoria, 1975-77; adminstr. Kaiser Found. Hosp., Los Angeles, 1977-80; pres. Sutter Community Hosps. and Sutter Health, Sacramento, 1980-95; pres., CEO Blue Cross Blue Shield Assn., Chgo., 1995—2000; faculty, School of Policy, Planning and Devel. U. So. Calif., Los Angeles. Trustee Cen. Area Teaching Hosps., Inc., L.A., 1977-79; mem. exec. com. St. Jude Children's Rsch. Hosp. Midwest Affilate, Peoria, 1975-77; past chmn. adv. bd. grad. program in health svcs. adminstrn. U. So. Calif., Sacramento; regent Am. Coll. Healthcare Execs., 1989-95, 90-96, founding pres. Sacramento Regional Purchasing Coun., bd. govs., 1998-02; mem. adv. bd. the Governance Inst.; mem. civil justice reform act com., U.S. Dist. Ct., Ea. Calif.; adj. faculty Ariz. State U.; bd. dirs. Trinity Health, Novi, Mich., chmn. HR and compensation com.; vice chmn. bd. dirs. Trinity Health, Novi, Mich., commr. accrediting commn. edn. in health adminstrn., adv. to mgmt. Contbr. articles on health services to publs. Mem. Pvt. Industry Coun., Sacramento Employment and Tng. Agy., 1984-85; bd. dirs. Consumer Credit Counselors Sacramento, 1984-87, Sacramento Area United Way, campaign chair, 1992-93; bd. dirs. Comstock Club, 1986-89; pres. Sacramento Camellia Festival Assn., 1987-88; chmn. Whitney M. Young Jr. Award, 1987; pres. Sacramento Regional Purchasing Coun., 1989-90. With U.S. Army, 1966-69. Decorated Army Commendation medal, cert. of appreciation Dept. Army; recipient Commendation resolution Calif. Senate, 1979, Whitney M. Young award Sacramento Urban League, 1983; named Chief Exec. Officer of Yr., Soc. for Healthcare Planning and Mktg. of Am. Hosp. Assn., 1991; USPHS fellow, 1969-71, Calif. Assn. Hosps. and Health Systems Walker fellow, 1989. Fellow Am. Coll. Healthcare Execs. (Calif. regent, Gold medal for career excellence 2003); mem. Calif. Assn. Hosps. and Health Systems (chmn. bd. dirs. 1991), Sacramento-Sierra Hosp. Assn. (exec. com., bd. dirs., pres. 1984), Royal Soc. Health (U.K.), Am. Mgmt. Assn. (Pres. Club), Hollywood C. of C. (revitalization com. 1979), Sacramento C. of C. (bd. dirs. 1982-85, 87-88), Vol. Hosps. Pacific (bd. dirs.), Rotary (bd. dirs. Sacramento 1987-89), Rotary Club (Las Vegas), Kappa Sigma (treas.). Presbyterian.

HAYS, RONALD JACKSON, career officer; b. Urania, La., Aug. 19, 1928; s. George Henry and Fannie Elizabeth (McCartney) H.; m. Jane M. Hughes, Jan. 29, 1951; children: Dennis, Michael, Jacquelyn. Student, Northwestern U., 1945-46; BS, U.S. Naval Acad., 1950; HHD (hon.), Northwestern State U. Commd. ensign U.S. Navy, 1950, advanced through grades to adm., 1983; destroyer officer Atlantic Fleet, 1950-51; attack pilot Pacific Fleet, 1953-56; exptl. test pilot Patuxent River, Md., 1956-59; exec. officer Attack Squadron 106, 1961-63; tng. officer Carrier Air Wing 4, 1963-65; comdr. All Weather Attack Squadron, Atlantic Fleet, 1965-67; air warfare officer 7th Fleet Staff, 1967-68; tactical aircraft plans officer Office Chief Naval Ops., 1969-71; comdg. officer Naval Sta., Roosevelt Roads, P.R., 1971-72; dir. Navy Planning and Programming, 1973-74; comdr. Carrier Group 4, Norfolk, Va., 1974-75; dir. Office of Program Appraisal, Sec. of Navy, Washington, 1975-78; dep. and chief staff, comdr. in chief U.S. Atlantic Fleet, Norfolk, Va., 1978-80; comdr. in chief U.S. Naval Force Europe, London, 1980-83; vice chief naval ops. Dept. Navy, Washington, 1983-85; comdr. in chief U.S. Pacific Command, Camp H.M. Smith, Hawaii, 1985-88; pres., chief exec. officer Pacific Internat. Ctr. for High Tech. Rsch., Honolulu, Hawaii, 1988-92; tech. cons., 1992—. Chmn. Pacific Aviation Mus Pearl Harbor Bd. Decorated D.S.M. with 3 gold stars, Silver Star with 2 gold stars, D.F.C. with silver star and gold star, Legion of Merit, Bronze Star with combat V, Air Medal with numeral 14 and gold numeral 3, Navy Commendation medal with gold star and combat V; recipient Disting. Eagle Scout award, 1987. Republican. Baptist. Home and Office: 869 Kamoi Pl Honolulu HI 96825-1318 Personal E-mail: rjhayshawaii@msn.com.

HAYUTIN, DAVID LIONEL, lawyer; b. Phoenix, Apr. 19, 1930; s. Henry and Eva (Gaines) H.; m. Lee June Rodgers, June 15, 1951. AB, U. So. Calif., 1952, JD, 1958. Bar: Calif. 1958. Assoc. Pillsbury Winthrop Shaw Pittman LLP and predecessor firms, LA, 1958-67, ptnr., 1967—. Author: Distributing Foreign Products in the United States, 1988, revised edit., 2000; assoc. editor So. Calif. Law Rev.; contbr. legal articles to profl. jours. Served to lt. (j.g.) USN, 1952-55. Mem. ABA, Internat. Bar Assn., Calif. Bar Assn., Maritime Law Assn.

Republican. Avocations: opera, golf. Office: Pillsbury Winthrop Shaw Pittman LLP 725 S Figueroa St Los Angeles CA 90017-5524 Office Phone: 213-488-7351. Business E-Mail: dhayutin@pillsburylaw.com.

HAYWARD, LANI, bank executive; 2 children. Grad., Univ. Ariz. Mgmt. positions through sr. v.p. mktg. Umpqua Bank, Portland, Oreg., 1998—2005, exec. v.p. creative strategy group, 2005—. Named Advt. Profl. of the Yr., Portland Advt. Fedn., 2006; named a Rising Star, Fin. Mktg. Mag., 2001; named one of 25 Most Powerful Women in Banking, US Banker mag., 2006. Office: Umpqua Holdings Corp Ste 1200 Umpqua Plz 1 SW Columbia Portland OR 97258

HAYWOOD, L. JULIAN, cardiologist, educator; b. Reidsville, NC, Apr. 13, 1927; s. Thomas Woodly and Louise Viola (Hayley) H.; m. Virginia Elizabeth Paige, Dec. 3, 1953; 1 child, Julian Anthony. BS, Hampton Inst., 1948; MD, Howard U., DC, 1952. Intern St. Mary's Hosp., Rochester, NY, 1952-53; resident L.A. County Hosp., 1956-58; fellow cardiology White Meml. Hosp., 1959-61; traveling fellow U. Oxford, England, 1963; instr. medicine Loma Linda (Calif.) U., 1960-61, asst. prof., 1961-73, assoc. clin. prof., 1973-82, clin. prof., 1982—; asst. prof. medicine U. So. Calif., 1963-67, assoc. prof., 1967-76, prof., 1976—; dir. EKG dept. L.A. County/U. So. Calif. Med. Ctr. Past dir. coronary care unit, physicians tng. program Regional Med. Programs L.A. County/U. So. Calif. Med. Ctr, 1970-75; cons. Los Angeles County Coroner, Indsl. Accident Bd. Calif., Health Care Tech. Divsn., USPHS, Nat. Heart and Lung Inst.; past mem. cardiology adv. com. divsn. heart and vascular diseases; bd. dirs., pres. Sickle Cell Diseases Found.; mem. Armed Forces Epidemiol. Bd., 1996-2006; active U. So. Calif. Salerni Collegium, 1997-98; bd. dirs. Charles Drew U. Medicine and Scis., 1999—. Contbr. articles profl. jours.; Mem. editorial bds.: Jour. Nat. Med. Assn. Past pres., hon. mem., bd. dirs. Am. Heart Assn. Greater L.A., 1989—. With M.C. USNR, 1954-56. Recipient award of merit L.A. County Heart Assn., 1968, 69, 73, 75, 78, 79, 95, Disting. Alumnus award Howard U. Sch. Medicine, 1982, Disting. Svc. award, 1996, Disting. Health Educator award, 2003, Louis B. Russel award Am. Heart Assn., 1988, Merit award, 1991, Heart of Gold award Am. Heart Assn./Greater L.A. Affiliate, 1989, Dedicated Svc. award, 1991, 93, Award of Achievement in Rsch., 1994, 20th Anniversary Founder's award Assn. Black Cardiologists, 1994, Cert. of Appreciation, Armed Forces Epidemiology Bd., 2001, Eagle Cert. of Excellence award Nat. Med. Fellowships, N.Y.C., 2004, Cert. of Appreciation, Office of Def., 2006, Disting. Svc. award Black History Month, LA County/U. So. Calif. Med. Ctr., 2007; J.B. Johnson Meml. lectr., 1975, 88; honoree Internal Medicine sect. Nat. Med. Assn., 1988; named Alumnus of Yr.-at-Large, Hampton U., 1993; nat. med. fellow Gala West 2004, 2004, Lifetime Achievement award Sickle Cell Diseases Found., 2007. Fellow ACP, AAAS (Disting. Svc. award 2007), L.A. Acad. Medicine, Am. Coll. Cardiology (Disting. Svc. award 2001, Cert. of Merit 2003, Cert. of Appreciation 2003), Am. Heart Assn. (coun. on clin. cardiology, coun. on atherosclerosis, exec. com. coun. on epidemiology, long range planning com., dir., past sec., v.p. Greater L.A. affiliate, pres.); mem. AMA, AAUP, Am. Fedn. Clin. Rsch., Western Soc. Clin. Investigation, Assn. Advancement Med. Instrumentation, Nat. Med. Assn. (Charles Drew Med. Soc.), N.Y. Acad. Scis., Hampton Inst. Alumni Assn. (past pres. L.A. chpt.), Med. Faculty Assn. U. So. Calif. Sch. Medicine (past pres.), Assn. Physicians L.A. County Hosp. (pres. 1991-2006), Western Assn. Physicians, Fedn. Am. Scientists, Assn. Black Cardiologists (Walter Booker Innovation award 1990), Assn. Minority Physicians (councilor, pres.-elect 1992-93, pres. 1993-94), Alpha Omega Alpha, Am. Coll. Physicians (Laureate award So. Calif. Region I 1997). Office: LACt USC Med Ctr 1200 N State St Rm 8305 Los Angeles CA 90033-1029 Office Phone: 323-226-7116. Business E-Mail: jhaywood@hsc.usc.edu.

HAYWORTH, J.D. (JOHN DAVID JR.), former congressman; b. High Point, NC, July 12, 1958; s. John David and Gladys Ethel (Hall) H.; m. Mary Denise Yancey, Feb. 25, 1989; children: Nicole Irene, Hannah Lynne, John Micah. BA in Speech and Polit. Sci., N.C. State U., 1980. Sports anchor, reporter Sta. WPTF-TV, Raleigh, N.C., 1980-81, Sta. WLWT-TV, Cin., 1986-87; sports anchor Sta. WYFF-TV (formerly Sta. WFBC-TV), Greenville, S.C., 1981-86, Sta. KTSP-TV, Phoenix, 1987-94; mem. US Congress from 5th Ariz. dist., Washington, 1995—2007, mem. ways and means com., mem. resources com., asst. whip. Co-author: (With Joseph J. Eule) Whatever It Takes: Illegal Immigration, Border Security, and the War on Terror, 2006 Dist. committeeman Ariz. Rep. Com., Scottsdale, 1988-89; bd. dirs. Am. Humanics Found., Ariz. State U., Tempe, 1991-92; chmn. Scout-A-Rama, Theodore Roosevelt coun. Boy Scouts Am., 1991-92. Recipient honor roll award Atlantic Coast Conf., 1977, Young Am. award Unharrie coun. Boy Scouts Am., 1979, Friend of Edn. award Sch. Dist. Greenville County, 1985, Sch. Bell/Friend of Edn. award S.C. Dept. Edn., 1985. Mem. Rotary (bd. dirs. Phoenix 1989-90). Republican. Baptist. Avocations: reading, running, bible study, public speaking, television trivia.

HAZARD, GEOFFREY CORNELL, JR., law educator; b. Cleve., Sept. 18, 1929; s. Geoffrey Cornell and Virginia (Perry) H.; m. Elizabeth O'Hara; children: James G., Katherine W., Robin P., Geoffrey Cornell III. BA, Swarthmore Coll., 1953, LLD (hon.), 1988; LLB, Columbia U., 1954; LLD (hon.), Gonzaga U., 1985, U. San Diego, 1985, Ill. Inst. Tech., 1990, Republica Italiana, 1998. Bar: Oreg. 1954, Calif. 1960, Conn. 1982, Pa. 1994. Assoc. Hart, Spencer, McCulloch, Rockwood & Davies, Portland, Oreg., 1954-57; exec. sec. Oreg. Legis. Interim Com. Jud. Adminstrn., 1957-58; assoc. prof. law, then prof. U. Calif., Berkeley, 1958-64; prof. law U. Chgo., 1964-71, Yale U., 1971-94, prof. mgmt., 1979-83, acting dean Sch. Orgn. and Mgmt., 1980-81, Sterling prof. law, 1986-94; trustee prof. U. Pa., Phila., 1994—; disting. prof. U. Calif. Law, Hastings, 2005—. Mem. Adminstrv. Conf. U.S., 1971-78; cons. jud. conf. U.S. com. on rules practice and procedure, 2004. Author: (Law text) Research in Civil Procedure, 1963, Ethics in the Practice of Law, 1978; author: (with D.W. Louisell, C. Tait, W. Fletcher) Pleading and Procedure, 1972; author: 9th rev. edit., 2005; author: (with M. Taruffo) (Law text) American Civil Procedure, 1994; author: (with S. Koniak, R. Cramton and G. Cohen) Law and Ethics of Lawyering, 4th edit., 2004; author: (with W.W. Hodes) Law of Lawyering 3d edit., 2000; author: (with F. James and J. Leubsdorf) Civil Procedure 5th rev.edit., 2001; author: (with A. Dondi) Legal Ethics: A Comparative Study, 2004; editor: (Law text) Law in a Changing America, 1968; editor: (with D. Rhode) Legal Profession: Responsibility and Regulation, 2006; contbr. articles to profl. jours. Served with USAF, 1948-49. Fellow Am. Bar Found. (exec. dir. 1964-70, rsch. award 1986); mem. ABA (cons. code jud. conduct 1970-72, reporter stds. jud. adminstrn. 1971-77, reporter model rules of profl. conduct 1978-83), Am. Law Inst. (reporter restatement of judgments 1973-81, dir. 1984-99, dir. emeritus, 1999-), Am. Acad. Arts and Scis., Am. Philos. Soc., Nat. Legal Aid and Defender Assn., Am. Judicature Soc., Selden Soc., Calif. State Bar, Phi Beta Kappa. Episcopalian. Avocations: tennis, history, golf. Home: 2263 California St San Francisco CA 94115

HAZARD, ROBERT CULVER, JR., retired hotel executive; b. Balt., Oct. 23, 1934; s. Robert Culver and Catherine B. H.; m. Mary Victoria Cranor, Jan. 2, 1981; children by previous marriage: Alicia W., Letitia A., Robert Culver, III, Thomas E.J., Anne. BA cum laude, Woodrow Wilson Sch., Princeton U., 1956; postgrad., Johns Hopkins U., U. Denver. Mktg. rep. IBM Corp., Denver, 1959-68; with Am. Express Co., 1968-74, v.p. exec. accounts, 1973-74; CEO Best Western Internat., 1974-80; CEO, retired chmn. Choice Hotels Internat., Silver Spring, Md., 1980-96; chmn. Creative Hotel Assocs., Rockville, Md., 1996—2007. Capt. USAF, 1956-59. Recipient Man of Yr. award Motel Brokers Assn. Am., 1976, Silver Plate award Hospitality mag., 1979, Albert E. Koehl award HSMA, 1992, Cecil B. Day Hospitality award AAHOA, 1993, Silver Plate award Lodging Hospitality Mag., 1995. Mem.: Am. Hotel and Lodging Assn. Personal E-mail: roberthazard@msn.com.

HAZEN, PAUL MANDEVILLE, private equity firm executive, retired bank executive; b. Lansing, Mich., Nov. 29, 1941; married; 2 children. BA, U. Ariz., 1963; MBA, U. Calif., Berkeley, 1964. Asst. mgr Security Pacific Bank, 1964-66; v.p. Union Bank, 1966-70; chmn. Wells Fargo Realty Advisors, 1970-76, exec. v.p., mgr. Real Estate Industries Group San Francisco, 1979-80, mem. exec. office Real Estate Industry Group, 1980, vice-chmn. Real Estate Industries Group, 1980-84, pres., COO Real Estate Industries Group, 1984—; pres., treas. Wells Fargo Mortgage & Equity Trust, San Francisco, 1977-84; exec. v.p. Wells Fargo & Co., San Francisco, 1978—81, vice chmn., 1981—84, pres., COO, 1984—95, CEO, 1995—97, chmn., CEO, 1997—98, chmn., 1998—2001, KKR Financial Holdings LLC (formerly Accel-Kohlbert, Kravis, Roberts and Co.), San Francisco, 2001—. Avocations: gin rummy, golf. Office: KKR Financial Holdings LLC 555 California St San Francisco CA 94108

HAZEWINKEL, VAN, manufacturing executive; b. LA, Oct. 2, 1943; s. Ben J. and Betty J. (Bishop) Hazewinkel; m. Linda Bennett Hazewinkel, Sept. 11, 1965; children: Van, Karey. BS, Calif. State U., Long Beach, 1967. With Daily Indsl. Tools Inc., Costa Mesa, Calif., 1959—, v.p., 1966—78, pres., 1978—. Founding mem. bd. dirs. Greater Irvine (Calif.) Indsl. League, 1970—73. Mem.: Soc. Mfg. Engrs. Office: 3197 Airport Loop Dr Ste D Costa Mesa CA 92626-3424 Office Phone: 714-540-6622.

HAZLETT, MARK A., lawyer; b. NYC, Aug. 18, 1948; BA, Stanford U., 1970, JD, 1973. Bar: Hawaii 1973. Ptnr. Cades Schutte LLP, Honolulu. Adv. com. to Commr. of Fin. Insts., 1984-86; adj. prof. law U. Hawaii Law Sch., 1995—2001. Co-editor: Hawaii Commercial Real Estate Manual, 1988; co-editor, co-author: Hawaii Real Estate Financing Manual, 1990, Hawaii Real Estate Law Manual, 1997. Mem. ABA, Hawaii State Bar Assn. (dir. fin. svcs. divsn. 1982-83, chmn. real property and fin. svcs. sect. 1984, bd. dirs. 1982-98), Waikiki Yacht Club (commodore 2007). Office: Cades Schutte LLP PO Box 939 1000 Bishop St Honolulu HI 96808 Office Phone: 808-521-9224.

HAZZARD, MARY ELIZABETH, nursing educator; b. Evansville, Ind., Mar. 2, 1941; d. John Waven and Lucille Elizabeth (Theobold) H.; 1 child, Mary Lucille. BSN, Nazareth Coll., 1963; AM, NYU, 1965, PhD, 1970; family nurse practitioner, U. Tenn., 1997. Cert. min.; cert. family nurse practitioner. Staff nurse Caldwell County War Meml. Hosp., Princeton, Ky., 1962, staff nurse supr., 1963, 65; asst. nurse St. Joseph's Hosp., Louisville, 1962-63; teaching fellow NYU, 1966, instr., 1966-68; nursing sister-in-charge Meru (Kenya) Dist. Hosp., 1966; asst. prof. U. Va. Sch. Nursing, Charlottesville, 1968-70, assoc. prof., 1970-74, dir. learning resources, 1971-74; assoc. prof. Sangamon State U., Springfield, Ill., 1974-79; prof. Western Ky. U., Bowling Green, 1979-99; prof. emeritus, 1998; prof. Nat. U., LaJolla, Calif., 1998—. Head dept. nursing Western Ky. U., Bowling Green, 1979-96; adj. assoc. prof. U. Ky., Lexington, 1983-94; curriculum cons. MacMurray Coll., Jacksonville, Ill., 1978, U. Louisville, 1981; pres. So. Coun. on Collegiate Edn. in Nursing, 1993-95; nurse practitioner Cmty. Health Care Plus, Brownsville, 1997-98, St. Vincent DePaul Med. Clin. Homeless, San Diego, 1998—. Author: Review of Med-Surg Nursing, 1976, Nursing Outline Series: Critical Care Nursing, 1978; also articles; mem. edit. rev. bd. Health Care for Women Internat., 1984—. Pres. So. Coun. on Collegiate Edn. in Nursing, 1993-95. Fellow Am. Acd. Nursing; mem. ANA, Ky. Nurses Assn. (pres. 1986-87), Ky. Assn. Baccalaureate and Higher Degree Programs (sec. 1986-87), Ky. Cols., Sigma Theta Tau, Pi Lambda Theta. Democrat. Roman Catholic. Office: Nat U 11255 N Torrey Pines Rd La Jolla CA 92037-1011 Office Phone: 858-642-8361. Business E-Mail: mhazzard@nu.edu.

HAZZARD, WILLIAM RUSSELL, geriatrician, educator; b. Ann Arbor, Mich., Sept. 5, 1936; s. Albert Sidney and Florence Bernice (Woolsey) Hazzard; m. Ellen Bennett Friedman, June 10, 1961; children: Susan Lovejoy Roque, Russell Holden, Rebecca Cornell Oliver, Daniel Bennett. AB, Cornell U., 1958, MD, 1962. Diplomate Am. Bd. Internal Medicine, Am. Bd. Geriatrics. Resident in internal medicine U. Wash. Sch. Med. and Affiliated Hosps., Seattle, 1966—67, fellow in endocrinology and metabolism, 1965—66, 1967—69; from instr. to prof. medicine U. Wash., Seattle, 1969—82, dir. Northwest Lipid Rsch. Clinic, 1972—78; investigator Howard Hughes Med. Inst., U. Wash., Seattle, 1972—80; chief divsn. gerontology and geriatric medicine, 1978—82; prof. medicine, assoc. dir. dept. medicine Johns Hopkins Med. Instns., Balt., 1982—86, dir. ctr. on aging, 1983—86; prof., chmn. dept. internal med. Bowman Gray Sch. Medicine of Wake Forest U., Winston-Salem, NC, 1986—98; dir. J. Paul Sticht Ctr. on Aging of Wake Forest U., Winston-Salem, NC, 1987—97; sr. adv. J. Paul Ctr. On Aging of Wake Forest U., 1998—; prof. medicine U. Wash., Seattle, 1999—; dir. geriatrics and extended care VA Puget Sound Health Care Sys., 1999—. Vis. lectr., hon. sr. registrar Oxford (Eng.) U., 1977—78, St. Thomas Sch. Medicine, London, 1977—78; dir. sect. gerontology and geriatric medicine VA Puget Sound Health Care Sys., Seattle, Tacoma, Wash., 1999—. Editor: Principles of Geriatric Medicine and Gerontology, 1984, 1989, 1993, 1999, 2003; contbr. over 200 articles to jours. in field. Lt. USNR, 1963—65. Fellow: ACP; mem.: Nat. Inst. on Aging (mem. nat. adv. coun. 1995—99, aging rev. com. 1990—94, Geriatric Medicine Acad. award 1980), Am. Clin. and Climatol. Assn., Assn. Am. Physicians, Am. Soc. Clin. Investigation (mem. emeritus), Am. Fedn. Biomed. Rsch. (mem. emeritus), Am. Heart Assn. (coun.on arterosclerosis), Gerontol. Soc. Am. (chmn. clin. med. sect. 1984), Am. Geriatrics Soc. (bd. dirs. 1988—94, pres. 1993), Inst. Medicine of NAS. Avocations: gardening, conservation and nature study, music, athletics. Home: 3515 E Conover Ct Seattle WA 98122-6426 Office: VA Puget Sound Health Care Sys Geriatric Extended Care 1660 S Columbian Way Seattle WA 98108-1532 E-mail: william.hazzard@med.va.gov.

HEALY, ALICE FENVESSY, psychology professor, researcher; b. Chgo., June 26, 1946; d. Stanley John and Doris (Goodman) Fenvessy; m. James Bruce Healy, May 9, 1970; 1 child, Charlotte Alexandra. AB summa cum laude, Vassar Coll., 1968; PhD, Rockefeller U., 1973. Asst. prof. psychology Yale U., New Haven, 1973-78, assoc. prof. psychology, 1978-81, U. Colo., Boulder, 1981-84, prof. psychology, 1984—, prof. of distinction, 2007—. Rsch. assoc. Haskins Labs., New Haven, 1976—80; com. mem. NIMH, Washington, 1979—81; co-investigator rsch. contract USAF U. Colo., 1985—86, prin. investigator rsch. contract U.S. Army Rsch. Inst., 1986—2007; prin. investigator rsch. contract Naval Tng. Sys. Ctr., 1993—94; rsch. grant prin. investigator U.S. Army Rsch. Office U. Colo., 1995—2002, 2005—; rsch. grant prin. investigator NASA, 1999—. Co-author: Cognitive Processes, 2d edit., 1986; editor: Memory and Cognition, 1986—89, Experimental Cognitive Psychology and its Applications, 2005; co-editor (with S. M. Kosslyn and R. M. Shiffrin): (Essays in Honor of William K. Estes) From Learning Processes to Cognitive Processes Vol I, 1992; co-editor: (with S.M. Kosslyn and R.M. Shiffrin) From Learning Theory to Connectionist Theory: Essays in Honor of William K. Estes, Vol. II, 1992; co-editor: (with L.E. Bourne Jr.) Learning and Memory of Knowledge and Skills: Durability and Specificity, 1995, Foreign Language Learning: Psycholinguistic Studies on Training and Retention, 1998; co-editor: (with R. W. Proctor) Experimental Psychology, 2003; assoc. editor: Jour. Exptl. Psychology, 1982—84; contbr. articles to profl. jours. and chpts. to books. Recipient Sabbatical award, James McKeen Cattell Fund, 1987—88; grantee, NSF, 1977—86, 2003—05, Spencer Found. Rsch., 1978—80. Fellow: AAAS (nominating com. 1988—91, chair nominating com. 1991, chair psychology sect. 1995—96), APA (chair membership com. 1992—93, exec. com. divsn. 3 2001—04, pres. 2004—05), Soc. Exptl. Psychologists (chair 2008—); mem.: Soc. for Applied Rsch. in Memory and Cognition, Cognitive Sci. Soc., Rocky Mountain Psychology Assn. (pres. 1994—95), Soc. Math. Psychology, Psychonomic Soc. (governing bd. 1987—92, publs. com. 1989—93), Univ. Club, Sigma Xi, Phi Beta Kappa. Avocation: French pastries. Home: 840 Cypress Dr Boulder CO 80303-2820 Office: U Colo Dept Psychology 345 UCB Boulder CO 80309-0345 Home Phone: 303-494-9222; Office Phone: 303-492-5032. Business E-Mail: healy@colorado.edu.

HEALY, SONYA AINSLIE, retired health facility administrator; b. Sudbury, Ont., Can., Apr. 7, 1937; arrived in U.S., 1949; d. Walter B. and Wilma A. Scott; m. Richard C. Healy, Jr., Dec. 16, 1961. Diploma, Good Samaritan Hosp., West Palm Beach, Fla., 1958; student, U. Mass., 1963—64, NYU, 1964—66; BS, Boston U., 1969, MS in Med.-Surg. Nursing, 1974. Various staff nursing, charge nurse positions, suprs., med.-surg. and obstet. nursing, 1958—69; chmn. jr.-sr. teaching team Sch. of Nursing Melrose (Mass.) Wakefield Hosp., 1969—73; asst. dir. nurses Boston State Hosp., 1973—74; asst. dir., DON Mt. Zion Hosp. and Med. Ctr., 1974—75; asst. dir. patient care svcs., DON St. Elizabeth's Hosp., Boston, 1975—80, St. Joseph's Hosp., Nashua, NH, 1980—82; adminstr. U. Calif. Med. Ctr., San Diego, 1982—91, corp. chief nursing officer, 1991, assoc. dir. hosp. and clinics, dir. patient care svcs., 1982—93; exec. mgmt. cons. Noyes & Assocs. Ltd., Bainbridge Island, Wash., 1993—. Mem. acad. affairs com., bd. trustees U. San Diego, clin. assoc., 1984—; mem. adj. faculty San Diego State U.; mem. clin. faculty UCLA Sch. of Nursing; presenter in field. Author: The 12-hour Shift: Is It Viable?-Nursing Outlook, 1984, (handbook) Human Resource Management Handbook, 1987, Human Resources Management Handbook, 1987, Nursing Economics, 1989; mem. editl. adv. bd. dirs. OR Nurse Today, 1989—96, editl. rev. Nursing Economics; contbr. articles to profl. jours. Mem.: San Diego Dirs. of Nurses (sec. 1982—83, pres. 1988—89), Calif. Soc. of Nursing Svc. Adminstrs. (task force on orgns. program com. 1984—85, bd. dirs. 1985—87, mem. com. 1987—88, long range planning com.), Mass. Soc. of Nursing Svcs. Adminstrs. (pres. 1977), Am. Orgn. Nurse Execs. (bd. dirs. 1990—92, by-laws com. 1990—92), Am. Soc. Nursing Svc. Adminstr. (nominations com. 1978, cert.), Sigma Theta Tau (Zeta Mu chpt.). Avocations: reading, golf.

HEALY, STEPHANIE LEMME, hospital organization administrator; b. 1972; Pres. Hosp. Coun. Southern Ariz. Mem. Southern Ariz. AIDS Found.; hostess Silver and Turquoise Ball; bd. mem. Juvenile Diabetes Rsch. Found.; bd. dir. Pledge-A-Job. Named one of 40 Under 40, Tucson Bus. Edge, 2006. Mem.: Pima Assn. (Governments Population Planning Com.), Ariz. Assn. for Econ. Devel., Armory Park Neighborhood Assn. Office: Southern Arizona Leadership Council 4400 E Broadway Ste 307 Tucson AZ 85711

HEAPHY, JANIS BESLER, retired publishing executive; b. Kalamazoo, Oct. 10, 1951; d. Elvin Julius and Margaret Louise (Throndike) Olson; m. Douglas R. Dern, Aug. 15, 1980 (div. Nov. 1985); m. Robert Thomas Heaphy, Feb. 11, 1989; 1 child, Tanner. BS, Miami U., 1973, MEd, 1976. Tchr. Edgewood Jr. HS, Seven Mile, Ohio, 1973—75; acct. exec. LA Times, 1976—79, sr. acct. exec., 1986—87, ea. mag. mgr., 1987—89, nat. advt. mgr., 1989—92, retail advt. mgr. then sr. v.p. advt./mktg., 1992—97; acct. exec. LA Mag., 1979—82; mgr. LA Omni Mag., 1982—86; pres., pub. Sacramento Bee, 1998—2008. Co-editor: Secrets of the Master Sellers, 1987. Bd. dirs. Sacramento Region Cmty. Found., Valley Vision, Sacramento; mem. Sacramento Host Com., Pride Industries Bd., Sacramento, Mountain Valley ch., Am. Leadership Forum Bd.; hon. chmn. Children's Receiving Home, Sacramento. Recipient Ruth Standish Baldwin award, Sacramento Urban League; named one of Women Who Mean Business, Sacramento Bus. Jour. Mem.: Calif. Newspaper Publishers Assn., Advt. Club LA. Avocations: home decorating, reading, swimming, music.

HEARST, JOHN EUGENE, retired chemistry professor, consultant, researcher; b. Vienna, July 2, 1935; came to U.S., 1938; s. Alphonse Bernard and Lily (Roger) Hirsch; m. Jean Carolyn Bankson, Aug. 30, 1958; children: David Paul, Leslie Jean. BE, Yale U., New Haven, Conn., 1957; PhD, Calif. Inst. Tech., Pasadena, 1961; DSc (hon.), Lehigh U., Bethlehem, Pa., 1992. Postdoctoral rschr. Dartmouth Coll., Hanover, NH, 1961-62; prof. chemistry U. Calif., Berkeley, 1962-95, prof. emeritus, 1996—, Miller rsch. prof., 1970-71; founder, dir. HRI Rsch. Inc., 1978—92; sr. rsch. scientist Lawrence Berkeley Lab., 1980-99, faculty chemist, 2000—, dir. divsn. chem. biodynamics, 1986-89; founder, sr. cons. Advanced Genetics Rsch., Inc., Oakland, Calif., 1981-84; founder, dir. Steritech Inc., Concord, Calif., 1992-96;

founder, dir., v.p. new sci. opportunities Cerus Corp., Concord, 1992—2004, cons., 2005—06; sci. adv. bd. Oncologics, Inc., 2007—08; hon. prof. Qingdao U., China, 2008—; sci. adv. bd. Aduro Biotech., Inc., Berkeley, 2008—. Disting. lectr. Purdue U., 1986; Merck Centennial lectr. Lehigh U., 1992, Robert A. Welch Found. lectr., 1992-93; adv. bd. Pharm. and Chem. Scis. Graduate Program Univ. of the Pacific, 2000—; cons. Codon, Inc., 1993-97; scientific adv. bd. Thomas McNerney & Ptnrs., 2003-07; mem. governing bd. dirs. Leonardo Internat. Soc. Arts, Sci. and Tech., 2007-09. Author: Contemporary Chemistry, 1976. editor: General Chemistry, 1974; exec. editor Nucleic Acids Rsch., 1990-93; inventor, patentee in field. Bd. dirs. U. No. Calif., 1993-95, dir. Disability Policy and Planning Inst., Berkeley, 2000-2002. Recipient Sci. Profl. Devel. award NSF, 1977-78, The Berkeley citation, 1999, Mortimer Bortin award for outstanding rsch. in bone marrow transplant, 2000, Tech Mus. Discover award, San Jose, 2001; John Simon Guggenheim fellow, 1968-69, European Molecular Orgn. sr. fellow, 1973-74. Fellow AAAS; mem. Am. Chem. Soc., Biophys. Soc., Am. Soc. Biol. Chemists, Am. Soc. for Photobiology (coun., pres. elect 1990-91, pres. 1991-92, Rsch. award 1994), Am. Phys. Soc. Home: 101 Southampton Ave Berkeley CA 94707-2036 Office: U Calif Dept Chemistry Berkeley CA 94720-1460 Office Phone: 510-407-4555. Business E-Mail: jehearst@berkeley.edu.

HEARST, WILLIAM RANDOLPH, III, lawyer, former newspaper publisher; b. Washington, June 18, 1949; s. William Randolph and Austine (McDonnell) Hearst; m. Margaret Kerr Crawford, Sept. 23, 1990; children: William, Adelaide, Caroline. AB, Harvard U., 1972. Reporter, asst. city editor San Francisco Examiner, 1972-76, publisher, 1984-96; editor Outside Mag., 1976-78; asst. mng. editor LA Herald Examiner, 1978-80; mgr. devel. Hearst Corp., 1980-82, dir., 1992—; v.p. Hearst Cable Comm. Divsn., 1982-84; dir. Hearst-Argyle TV; affiliated ptnr. Kleiner, Perkins, Caufield & Byers, Menlo Park, Calif., 1995—. Pres. William Randolph Hearst Found., 2003—; bd. dir. Akimbo, Applied Minds, Juniper Networks, Oblix, OnFiber, RGB Networks, FORA.tv, 2007—. Bd. trustees Grace Cathedral, San Francisco, Carnegie Inst. Washington, Math. Scis. Rsch. Inst. Named one of 400 Richest Ams., Forbes mag., 2006. Fellow: AAAS; mem.: Calif. Acad. Scis. (bd. trustees). Office: Kleiner Perkins Caufield & Byers 2750 Sand Hill Rd Menlo Park CA 94025 Office Phone: 650-233-2750. Office Fax: 650-233-0300.

HEATH, GEORGE ROSS, oceanographer; b. Adelaide, Australia, Mar. 10, 1939; s. Frederick John and Eleanora (Blackmore) H.; m. Lorna Margaret Sommerville, Oct. 5, 1972; children: Amanda Jo, Alisa Jeanne. BSc, Adelaide U., 1960, BSc with honors, 1961; PhD, U. Calif., 1968. Geologist S. Australian Geol. Survey, Adelaide, 1961-63; asst. prof. oceanography Oreg. State U., Corvallis, 1969-72, assoc. prof., 1972-75, prof., dean, 1978-84; assoc. prof. oceanography U. R.I., Narragansett, 1974-77, prof., 1977-78; dean U. Wash., Seattle, 1984-96, prof., 1984—2006, prof. emeritus, 2006—, dean emeritus, 1996—, chair, faculty senate, 2004—05; pres., exec. dir. Monterey Bay Aquarium Rsch. Inst., Moss Landing, Calif., 1996-97. Co-chmn. exec. com. oceans and atmosphere Nat. Assn. State Univs. and Land Grant Colls., 1992-93; chmn. legis. com. Commn. on Food, Environment and Renewable Resources, 1994-96; chmn. bd. ocean sci. and policy NRC, 1984-85; bd. govs. Joint Oceanographic Instns., Inc., 1978-96, chmn., 1982-84; v.p. sci. com. on oceanic rsch. of Internat. Coun. of Sci. Unions, 1984-90; chmn. performance assessment peer rev. panel Waste Isolation Pilot Plant, 1987-98; bd. dirs. Monterey Bay Aquarium Rsch. Inst.1987-; found. com. Coll. Marine Sci. and Fisheries, Sultan Qaboos U., Muscat, Sultanate of Oman, 1994—; adv. panel Odyssey, 1990-2001, bd. govs., 1999-2000; environ. analyst Sta. KIRO-TV, Seattle, 1993; bd. govs. Consortium for Oceanographic Rsch. & Edn., 1994-98, chmn., 1996-98; bd. govs. Seattle Aquarium Soc., 1998—; mem. Nat. Sea Grant rev. panel, 2001—, vice chmn., 2006—. Contbr. articles to profl. jours. Recipient Fulbright award, 1963, medal Seattle Aquarium Soc., 2006. Fellow AAAS, Geol. Soc. Am., Am. Geophys. Union; mem. Oceanography Soc. Home: 12513 237th Way NE Redmond WA 98053 Office: U Wash Sch Oceanography PO Box 357940 Seattle WA 98195-7940 Home Phone: 425-898-7388; Office Phone: 206-543-3153. Business E-Mail: rheath@u.washington.edu.

HEATH, JAMES R., chemistry educator; BSc, Baylor U., 1984; PhD in Chemistry, Rice U., 1988. Mem. technical staff IBM Watson Labs, Yorktown Heights, NY, 1991—94; with UCLA, 1994—, asst. prof. dept. chemistry, 1994—96, tenure prof., 1996, prof. molecular & med. pharmacology, 1997—; Elizabeth W. Gilloon prof. chemistry Calif. Inst. Tech., 2004—; dir. Nat. Ctr. Inst. NSB Cancer Ctr. Founder Calif. Nanosystems Inst., 2000, dir., 2000—03; co-dir., bd. dir. Crump Inst. for Molecular Imaging, 2003—. Contbr. articles to profl. jours. Miller Fellow, Univ. Calif. Berkeley, 1988-91, Packard fellow David and Lucile Packard Found., 1994-99, Alfred P. Sloan Fellow, 1997. Achievements include being the principal student involved in the Nobel Prize winning discovery of C60 and the fullerenes; being the co-creator of world's densest memory circuit in 2007. Office: Nanosystem Biology Cancer Ctr Caltech Chemistry 127-72 1200 E California Blvd Pasadena CA 91125 Office Phone: 310-825-2836. Office Fax: 626-395-2355. Business E-Mail: heath@caltech.edu.

HEATH, RICHARD RAYMOND, retired investment company executive; b. La Junta, Colo., June 22, 1929; s. Perry Stanford and Genevieve Anabelle (Whitney) H.; m. Arlene Newbrow, Nov. 3, 1961. BA in Econs., U. Colo., 1951, LLB, 1954. Bar: Colo. 1954, Calif. 1957, Ark. 1973. Mem. firm Neyhart & Grodin, San Francisco, 1957-66; dep. Peace Corps dir. Ivory Coast, 1966-68; dir., 1968-69; Peace Corps dir. Mali, 1969-72; dir. Ark. Dept. Fin. and Adminstrn.; also chief fiscal officer, commr. revenues State of Ark., mem. gov.'s cabinet, 1972-77; dir. San Francisco Internat. Airport, 1977-81; v.p., dir. mktg. AIS, Inc., 1981-84; exec. v.p., CFO United Bank, San Francisco, 1984-85; chmn., CEO Nat. Bus. Resources Inc., 1985-87; ptnr. Hakman & Co., Investment Bankers, 1987-2000; chmn., CEO Podarok Internat., Inc., 1993-96; chmn., pres. Heath Mgmt. Svcs., 1994-2000; chmn. Laser Design Internat., LLC, 1996—. Chmn., CEO 1st Calif. Bus. and Indsl. Devel. Corp., United Bus. Ventures; bd. dirs. V-Ray Imaging, Inc.; vice chmn. Multi-State Tax Commn., 1973-74, chmn., 1976-77, mem. exec. com., 1974-77; del. Conf. State Bar Dels. Bd. dirs., treas. San Francisco Midsummer Mozart Festival, 1986-92, chmn., 1999-2000; mem. nat. bd. dirs. Coalition for a Dem. Majority, 1973-76; chmn. bd. dirs. FORUM; mem. conservative caucus nat. Tax Limitation Com., 1980—; mem. rep. presdl. task force Rep. nat. Com., 1980-91. Mem. State Bar Calif., San Francisco Bar Assn. (past chmn. indsl. accident com.), San Francisco Lawyers Club, Am., Calif. trial lawyers assns., San Francisco Planning and Urban Renewal Assn., Nat. Parks Assn., Calif. Applicants Attys. Assn. (v.p.) Clubs: Little Rock Racquet, Little Rock Athletic, San Francisco Tennis (gov.), Rotary Internat., World Trade. Home: 1904 21st Ave E Seattle WA 98112-2906 Personal E-mail: dickheath@aol.com.

HEATH, S. ROLLIE, JR., state legislator; married. BS, U. Wis., 1959, LLM, 1961. With Armco Steel Co., 1961-73, Manville Corp., Denver, 1973—, sr. v.p., pres. internat. group, 1973-84; sr. v.p., pres. Manville Bldg. Materials Group, Denver, 1984-86; exec. v.p. Manville Corp., Denver, 1986—; mem. Dist. 18 Colo. State Senate, Denver, 2009—. Served to lt. col. USAR. Democrat. Office: Colo State Capitol 200 E Colfax Denver CO 80203 also: Manville Corp 717 17th St Denver CO 80202-3330 Office Phone: 303-866-4872. Business E-Mail: rollie.heath.senate@state.co.us.*

HEATHCOCK, CLAYTON HOWELL, chemistry educator, researcher; b. San Antonio, July 21, 1936; s. Clayton H. and Frances E. (Lay) H.; m. Mabel Ruth Sims, Sept. 6, 1957 (div. 1972); children: Cheryl Lynn, Barbara Sue, Steven Wayne, Rebecca Ann; m. Cheri R. Hadley, Nov. 28, 1980. BSc, Abilene Christian Coll., Tex., 1958; PhD, U. Colo., 1963. Supr. chem. analysis group Champion Paper and Fiber Co., Pasadena, Tex., 1958-60; asst. prof. chemistry U. Calif.-Berkeley, 1964-70, assoc. prof., 1970-75, prof., 1975—, Gilbert Newton Lewis prof., 2003—05, chmn., 1986-89, dean Coll. of Chemistry, 1999—2005; chief scientist Berkeley QB3 Calif. Inst. Quantitative Biosciences, 2005—. Chmn. Medicinal Chemistry Study Sect., NIH, Washington, 1981-83; mem. sci. adv. coun. Abbott Labs., 1986-97. Author: Introduction to Organic Chemistry, 1976; editor-in chief Organic Syntheses, 1985-86, Jour. Organic Chemistry, 1989-99; contbr. numerous articles to profl. jours. Recipient Alexander von Humboldt U.S. Scientist, 1978, Allan R. Day award, 1989, Prelog medal, 1991, Centenary medal Royal Soc. Chemistry, 1995. Mem. AAAS, Am. Acad. Arts and Scis., Am. Chem. Soc. (chmn. divsn. organic chemistry 1985, Ernest Guenther award 1986, award for creative work in synthetic organic chemistry 1990, A.C. Cope scholar 1990, H.C. Brown medal 2002, Paul Gassman award 2004), Nat. Acad. Scis., Royal Soc. Chemistry (Centenary medal 1995), Am. Soc. Pharmacology. Home: 5235 Alhambra Valley Rd Martinez CA 94553-9765 Office: U Calif QB3 Inst 3220 Berkeley CA 94720 Office Phone: 510-666-3316. Business E-Mail: heathcock@berkeley.edu.

HEBELER, HENRY KOESTER, retired electronics executive, aerospace engineer; b. St. Louis, Aug. 12, 1933; s. Henry and Viola O. (Koester) H.; m. Mirriam Robb, Aug. 12, 1978; children by previous marriage: Linda Ruth, Laura Ann. BS in Aero. Engring., MIT, 1956, MS, 1956, MBA, 1970. Gen. mgr. rsch./engring. Boeing Aerospace Co., Seattle, 1970-72, pres., 1980-85; v.p. bus. devel. The Boeing Co., Seattle, 1973-74, exec. coun. and corp. v.p. planning, 1988-89; pres. Boeing Engring. & Constrn. Co., Seattle, 1975-79, Boeing Electronics Co., Seattle, 1985-87. Bd. dirs. Microelectronics and Computer Tech. Corp.; mem. fusion panel Ho. of Reps., 1979-81, energy rsch. adv. bd. Dept. Energy, 1980-81, task force on internat. industry Def. Sci. Bd., 1982-84, adv. com. nat. strategic materials and minerals program U.S. Dept. Interior, 1986—. Author: Your Winning Retirement Plan, 2001, Getting Started in a Financially Secure Retirement, 2007. Bd. govs. Sloan Sch., MIT, 1980-84; bd. visitors Def. Systems Mgmt. Coll., Ft. Belvoir, Va. Recipient Mead prize for aero. engrs., 1956; Kuljian humanities award, 1954; Sperry Gyroscope fellow, 1956; Sloan fellow M.I.T., 1970 Mem. AIAA, Nat. Aeros. Assn., Assn. of U.S. Army, Armed Forces Comm. and Electronics Assn. (bd. dirs.), Aviation Hall of Fame, Ala. Space and Rocket Ctr. (sci. and adv. com. 1980-85), Nat. Space (bd. govs. 1980-85), Meridian Valley Country Club. Achievements include patents in field. Home and Office: 24600 140th Ave SE Kent WA 98042-5160

HEBERT, GUY, professional hockey player; b. Troy, NY, Jan. 7, 1967; m. Sarah Szalach, 1995; 1 child, Madeline. Goalie St. Louis, 1991-93, Mighty Ducks, Anaheim, Calif., 1993-99, Phoenix (Ariz.) Coyotes, 1999—. Avocations: fly fishing, deep sea fishing, basketball, golf.

HEBERT, WILLIAM N., lawyer; b. Iowa City, Iowa, Oct. 19, 1960; AB with distinction, Stanford Univ., 1983; JD, Boalt Law Sch., Univ. Calif., Berkeley, 1988. Bar: Calif. 1988, US Dist. Ct. (no., ctrl. & ea. Calif., Colo.), US Ct. Appeals, 9th cir. Ptnr., Global Litigation practice Coudert Bros. LLP, San Francisco. Mediator US Dist. Ct., no. Calif. dist. Contbr. articles to profl. jours. Mem.: Fed. Bar Assn. (mem. steering com., no. dist. Calif.). Office Phone: 415-267-6200. Office Fax: 415-977-6110. Business E-Mail: whebert@coudert.com.

HECHE, ANNE (ANNE CELESTE HECHE), actress; b. Aurora, Ohio, May 25, 1969; d. Donald Heche; m. Coley Laffoon, Sept. 1, 2001 (div. 2009); 1 child, Homer Heche Laffoon; 1 child, Atlas Heche Tupper. Actress: (films) An Ambush of Ghosts, 1993, The Adventures of Huck Finn, 1993, A Simple Twist of Fate, 1994, Milk Money, 1994, I'll Do Anything, 1994, The Wild Side, 1995, Pie in the Sky, 1995, Walking and Talking, 1996, The Juror, 1996, Volcano, 1997, Donnie Brasco, 1997, Wag the Dog, 1997, I Know What You Did Last Summer, 1997, Return to Paradise, 1998, Six Days Seven Nights, 1998, Psycho, 1998, The Third Miracle, 1999, Auggie Rose, 2000, Prozac Nation, 2001, John Q., 2002, Timepiece, 2003, Birth, 2004, Sexual Life, 2005, Suffering Man's Charity, 2007, What Love Is, 2007, Spread, 2009; (TV movies) O Pioneers!, 1992, Against the Wall, 1994, Girls in Prison, 1994, The Investigator, 1994, Kingfish: A Story of Huey P. Long, 1995, If These Walls Could Talk, 1996, Wild Side, 1996, SUBWAYStories: Tales from the Underground, 1997, One Kill, 2000, Gracie's Choice, 2004, Silver Bells, 2005, Fatal Desire, 2006; (TV series) Another World, 1987-91, Murphy Brown, 1991-92, Ally McBeal, 2001, Ellen, 1998, Everwood, 2004-05, Higglytown Heroes, 2005-06, Men in Trees, 2006-08; (stage) Getting Away with Murder, 1991-92; (Broadyway plays) Proof, 2002-03, Twentieth Century, 2004- (Tony nom. best actress in a play, 2004); actor, prodr. (TV movies) The Dead Will Tell, 2004; dir. (films) Reaching Normal, 2001; dir., writer (TV films) On the Edge; dir.(TV movies) If These Walls Could Talk 2, 2000; writer (short film) Stripping for Jesus, 1998; author: (autobiography) Call Me Crazy: A Memoir, 2001. Recipient Emmy award Another World; named one of the 50 Most Beautiful People in the World, People, 1998.

HECHT, FREDERICK, pediatrician, medical geneticist, writer, editor; b. Balt., July 11, 1930; s. Malcolm and Lucile Burger (Levy) H.; m. Irene Winchester Duckworth, Aug. 29, 1953 (div. 1977); children: Frederick Malcolm, Matthew Winchester, Maude Bancroft, Tobias Ochs; m. Barbara Kaiser McCaw, May 29, 1977; children: Kerrie Kristine, Brian Stuart. Student, U. Paris, 1950-51; BA with distinction, Dartmouth Coll., 1952; student, Boston U., 1955-56; MD with honors, U. Rochester, 1960. Lic. physician, Oreg., Ariz., Nev., Kans.; diplomate Am. Bd. Pediatrics, Am. Bd. Med. Genetics. Intern Strong Meml. Hosp., Rochester, NY, 1960-61, resident, 1961-62, U. Wash. Hosp., Seattle, 1962-64, asst. in pediat., med. genetics, 1962-64, instr. pediatrics, med. genetics, 1962-65; asst. in pediat. U. Rochester, 1960-62; prof. pediat. U. Oreg., Portland, 1965-78; founder, pres., dir. S.W. Biomed. Rsch. Inst., Scottsdale, Ariz., 1978-89; founder, pres. Hecht Assocs. Inc., Jacksonville, Fla., 1989—2004; prof. zoology Ariz. State U., Tempe, 1978-89; prof. ob-gyn. U. Nev., Reno and Las Vegas, 1983-89; dir. molecular medicine Children's Mercy Hosp., Kansas City, Mo., 1990-91; prof. medicine U. Mo., Kansas City, 1990-91; founder, dir. div. molecular medicine Children's Mercy Hosp., Kansas City, Mo., 1990-91. Vis. prof. cytogenetics and molecular genetics Adelaide Children's Hosp., North Adelaide, South Australia, 1992; prof. medicine Lab. de Génetique Moleculaire des Cancers Humains, l'Université de Nice, France, 1992-95; bd. dirs. Youth Law Ctr., San Francisco; prof. med. U. Mo., Kansas City, 1990-91. Author: Fragile Sites on Human Chromosomes, 1985; editor: Trends and Teaching in Medical Genetics, 1977; co-editor in chief: Webster's New World Medical Dictionary, 2000, 2003; mem. editl. bd. Am. Jour. Human Genetics, Cancer Genetics and Cytogenetics; chief editor MedTerms.com, 2000—04; assoc. chief editor MedicineNet.com, 1997—2004; contbr. over 600 articles to profl. jours. and over 200 articles to med. websites. Sgt. M.I. Corps, U.S. Army, 1952-55. NIH grantee, 1968-89, USPHS grantee, 1968-89; recipient Pediatric Rsch. award Ross Labs., 1970; Royal Soc. Medicine traveling fellow, London, 1971-73. Mem. Am. Pediatric Soc., Am. Soc. Human Genetics (bd. dirs.), Am. Acad. Pediatrics (charter mem. genetics sect. 1990), Soc. Pediatric Rsch., Western Soc. Pediatric Rsch. (bd. dirs.), Nat. Found. Jewish Genetic Diseases. Jewish. Avocations: gardening, writing, classical music, poetry. Office: 6945 E Montgomery Rd Scottsdale AZ 85262-3154 E-mail: TBHecht@aol.com.

HECHTER, MICHAEL NORMAN, sociologist; b. LA, Nov. 15, 1943; s. Oscar Milton and Gertrude (Horowitz) H.; children: Joshua Rachel, Eliana. AB, Columbia U., 1966, PhD, 1972. From asst. prof. to prof. U. Wash., Seattle, 1970-84; prof. sociology, dir. research group for instnl. analysis U. Ariz., Tucson, 1984—99; prof. sociology U. Wash., Seattle, 1999—2005; found. prof. global studies Ariz. State U., 2005—, interim dir. sch. global studies, 2007—. Univ. lectr., fellow New Coll., Oxford (Eng.) U., 1994-96; vis. prof. U. Bergen, Norway, 1984. Author: Internal Colonialism, 1975, Principles of Group Solidarity, 1987, Containing Nationalism, 2000; editor: The Microfoundations of Macrosociology, 1983, Social Institutions, 1989, The Origin of Values, 1993, Social Norms, 2001, Theories of Social Order, 2003. Fellow Russell Sage Found., 1988-89, Ctr. Advanced Study Behavioral Scis., 1990-91, Udall Ctr. for Studies in Pub. Policy. Fellow: Am. Acad. of Arts and Sci.; mem.: Am. Polit. Sci. Assn., Soc. for Comparative Rsch., Internat. Sociol. Assn., Sociol. Rsch. Assn., Am. Sociol. Assn. Office: School Global Studies Ariz State Univ Tempe AZ 85287 Home Phone: 206-217-0207; Office Phone: 480-727-0735. Business E-Mail: michael.hechter@asu.edu.

HECKER, PETER S., lawyer; b. NYC, Sept. 4, 1949; BA, Carleton Coll., 1970; JD, U. Calif., Berkeley, 1973. Bar: N.Y. 1974, Calif. 1975, Am. Bar. Assoc. Atty. Heller, Ehrman, White & McAuliffe, San Francisco, 1975—. Mem. ABA, Order of Coif, Phi Beta Kappa. Office: Heller Ehrman White & McAuliffe 333 Bush St San Francisco CA 94104-2806 Office Phone: 415-772-6080. E-mail: phecker@hewm.com.

HECKMANN, RICHARD J., sporting goods company executive; m. Mary Heckmann; 6 children. Attended, Univ. Hawaii, Small Co. Mgmt. Prog., Harvard Bus. Sch. Founder & chmn. Tower Scientific Corp., 1971—77; assoc. adminstr. SBA, Washington, 1978—79; founding shareholder Callaway Golf Inc.; owner & dir. Smith Goggles, Sun Valley, Idaho; founder & chmn. USFilter Inc., 1990—99; chmn. Vivendi Water, 1999—2001; dir. K2 Inc., Carlsbad, Calif., 1997—, chmn., 2000—, CEO, 2002—. Trustee Eisenhower Med. Ctr., Univ. Calif., Riverside; mem. Bus. Council Univ. Notre Dame Bus. Sch.

HECOX, MORRIS B., academic administrator; Grad., Colo. Coll., U. Colo. Law Sch. Lawyer, mining and natural resources law, Denver, NYC; pres., founder Cook Street Sch. of Fine Cooking, Denver, 1999—. Served in US Army. Office: Cook Street School of Fine Cooking 1937 Market St Denver CO 80202 Office Phone: 303-308-9300. Office Fax: 303-308-9400.

HEDBERG, STEVEN MICHAEL, lawyer; b. Coeur d'Alene, Idaho, Dec. 30, 1958; s. Robert J. and Helenmarie (Nielsen) H.; m. Mary P. Dever, July 10, 1982. BBA, cert. in fin. law, Portland State U., 1981; JD, Lewis and Clark Coll., 1984. Bar: Oreg. 1984, Wash., US Dist. Ct. Oreg. 1984, US Dist. Ct. (We. Dist.) Wash. 1985, US Dist. Ct. (Ea. Dist.) Wash. 1987. Assoc. Weaver & Layne, Portland, 1984-85, Miller, Nash, Wiener, Hager & Carlsen, Portland, 1985-88, ptnr., 1988-92, Perkins Coie LLP, Portland, Seattle, 1992—, mng. ptnr. Portland office. Bd. dir. Spl. Deliveries, 2000—02, Am. Red Cross, 1994—2000; pres. adv. coun. U. Portland, 2000—. Mem.: Wash. State Bar Assn., Oreg. Bar Assn., ABA.

HEDGES, JERRIS, medical educator, health services researcher; MS, MD. Chmn. dept. emergency medicine Oreg. Health & Scis. U., 1997—2005, vice-dean Sch. Medicine, 2005—. Editor: (med. jour.) Acad. Emergency Medicine, 1993—97; co-editor: (med. text) Clinical Procedures in Emergency Medicine, 4th edit. Mem.: Nat. Acad. Scis. Inst. of Medicine, Soc for Acad. Emergency Medicine. Achievements include research in the evaluation of Trauma System impact and effectiveness. Office: Oreg Health Scis U 3181 SW Sam Jackson Pk Rd Portland OR 97201-3098 Office Phone: 503-494-8220. Business E-Mail: hedgesj@ohsu.edu.

HEDICAN, BRET, professional hockey player; b. St. Paul, Minn., Aug. 10, 1970; m. Kristi Yamaguchi; children: Keara Kiyomi, Emma Yoshiko. Defenseman St. Louis Blues, 1991—94, Vancouver Canucks, 1994—99, Florida Panthers, 1999—2002, Carolina Hurricanes, 2002—08, Anaheim Ducks, 2008—. Achievements include being a member of Stanley Cup Champion Carolina Hurricanes, 2006. Office: Anaheim Ducks Honda Ctr 2695 E Katella Ave Anaheim CA 92806*

HEDRICK, BASIL CALVIN, state agency administrator, ethnohistorian, educator, museum and multicultural institutions consultant; b. Lewistown, Mo., Mar. 17, 1932; s. Truman Bloice and M. LaVeta (Stice) H.; m. Anne Kehoe, Jan. 19, 1957 (div. 1979); 1 dau., Anne Lanier Hedrick Caraker; m. Susan Elizabeth Pickel, Oct. 2, 1980. AB, Augustana Coll., Rock Island, Ill., 1956; MA, U. Fla., 1957; PhD, Inter-Am. U., Mex., 1965; cert., U. Vienna, Strobl, Austria, 1956.

Asst. prof., assoc. prof., prof. So. Ill. U., Carbondale, 1967-74, asst. dir. Univ. Mus., 1967-70, dir. Univ. Mus. and Art Galleries, 1970-77, dean internat. edn., 1972-74; asst. dir. Ill. Div. Mus., Springfield, 1977-80; prof. history U. Alaska, Fairbanks, 1980-88, dir. U. Alaska Mus., 1980-88, founder, dir. internat. affairs, 1985-87; founder, dir. Div. Mus., Archaeology and Publs. State of Mich., Lansing, 1988-91; multicultural cons., 1991—; dir. mktg., cons. Rosalie Whyel Mus. Doll Art, Bellevue, Wash., 1991—; cons. museums and cultural instns., 1995—. Fulbright sr. lectr., Brazil, 1972; mem. nat. register adv. panel, Ill., 1977-80; mem. Alaska Coun. on Arts, Anchorage, 1983-85; chmn. Fairbanks Hist. Preservation Commn., 1982-88; mem. Alaska Land Use Coun.; bd. dirs. Alaska Hist. Preservation Found., 1986-88; mem. Gov.'s Revitalization Task Force, Lansing, Mich., mem. ethnic coun., Mich., 1988-89; bd. dirs. East King County Visitors Bur., 1993-2000, officer, 1997-2000; officer, bd. dirs. Wash. Mus. Assn., 1993-2000. Author: (with others) A Bibliography of Nepal, 1973, (with Carroll L. Riley) The Journey of the Vaca Party, 1974, Documents Ancillary to the Vaca Journey, 1976, (with C.A. Letson) Once Was A Time, a Wery Good Time: An Inquiry into the Folklore of the Bahamas, 1975, (with J.E. Stephens) In the Days of Yesterday and in the Days of Today: An Overview of Bahamian Folkmusic, 1976, It's A Natural Fact: Obeah in the Bahamas, 1977, Contemporary Practices in Obeah in the Bahamas, 1981; compilations and collections, 1959-69; editor: (with J. Charles Kelley and Riley) The Classic Southwest: Readings in Archaeology, Ethnohistory and Ethnography, 1973, (with J. Charles Kelley and Riley) The Mesoamerican Southwest: Readings in Archaeloy, Ethnohistory and Ethnology, 1974, (with Riley) Across the Chichimec Sea, 1978, (with others) New Frontiers in the Archaeology and Ethnohistory of the Greater Southwest, 1980, Trans. of Ill. Acad. Sci., 1979-81, (with Susan Pickel-Hedrick) Ethel Washington: The Life and Times of an Eskimo Dollmaker, The Role of the Steamboat in the Founding and Development of Fairbanks, Alaska, 1986, (with Susan Savage) Steamboats on the Chena, 1988; co-editor: Led Zeppelin live, 1993, 94, 97, Beautiful Children, 1996; author and editor of various other publications; contbr. articles to profl. jours. Chmn. Goals for Carbondale, 1972; active various local state, nat. polit. campaigns. Mem. NMA (bd. dirs. 1989-91), Am. Assn. Mus. (leader accreditation teams 1977-93, sr. examiner), Ill. Archaeol. Soc. (pres. 1973-74), Mus. Alaska, Assn. Sci. Mus. Dirs., Midwest Mus. Conf. (treas. 1977-80), Western Mus. Assn., Wash. Mus. Assn. (bd. dirs. 1994-99, v.p. 1995-97, pres. 1997-99), BD Arts (bd. dirs. 1995-96), Phi Kappa Phi. E-mail: djangob@aol.com.

HEDRICK, JERRY LEO, biochemistry and biophysics educator; b. Knoxville, Iowa, Mar. 11, 1936; s. Harvard L. and Dorothy E. (Hardin) H.; m. Karel J. Harper, June 22, 1957; children: Michael L., Kerry L., Benjamin A., Kimberly L. BS, Iowa State U., 1958; PhD, U. Wis., 1961, postgrad., 1961-62, U. Wash., 1962-65. Asst. prof. U. Calif.-Davis, 1965-68, assoc. prof., 1968-74, chmn. dept., 1982-84, assoc. dean grad. studies, 1998—, prof. biochemistry, 1974—2003, rsch. prof., 2003—. Sabbatical leave Hakkaido U., Sapporo, Japan, 1985-86, 89, 96; U. Calif. exch. scientist, Hokkaido U., 1989; vis. sr. scientist Mitsubishi-Kasei Inst. of Life Scis., Machida, Japan, 1989. Recipient Guggenheim Found. award; John Simon Guggenheim fellow, Cambridge U., Eng., 1971-72, Disting. Grad. Mentoring award, U. Calif., Davis; grantee NIH, NSF, USDA, 1966—. Mem. AAAS, Am. Soc. Biol. Chemists, Am. Chem. Soc., Soc. Study Reprodn., Am. Soc. Cell Biology, Sigma Xi Home: 25280 Carlsbad Ave Davis CA 95616-9434 Office: U Calif Dept Animal Sci 1 Shields Ave Davis CA 95616-5200

HEEGER, ALAN JAY, physicist, educator; b. Sioux City, Iowa, Jan. 22, 1936; s. Peter J. and Alice (Minkin) Heeger; m. Ruthann Chudacoff, Aug. 11, 1957; children: Peter S., David J. BA with high distinction, U. Nebr., 1957; PhD in Physics, U. Calif., Berkeley, 1961; degree (hon.), U. Mons, Belgium, 1993; DTech (hon.), Linköping U., Sweden, 1996; PhD (hon.), Abo Akademie, Turku, Finland, 1998; DHL (hon.), U. Mass., 1999; DSc (hon.), U. Nebr., 1999, So. China U. Tech., Japan Adv. Inst. Sci. & Tech., Bar Ilan U., Israel, Trinity Coll., Dublin, 2005, U. Alicante, Spain, 2006. Asst. prof. U. Pa., Phila., 1962—64, assoc. prof., 1964—66, prof. physics, 1966—82, U. Calif., Santa Barbara, 1982—, dir. Inst. for Polymers and Organic Solids, 1983—2000; pres. UNIAX Corp., Santa Barbara, 1990—94, chief tech. officer, 1999—2002; chmn. CBritu, Inc., 2005—; dir. Heeger Ctr. Advanced Materials Gwangju Inst. Sci. and Technology, 2005; co-founder and chief scientist Konarka Tecnologies, Inc., Lowell, Mass., 2004—; founder, vice-chmn. CytomX, Inc., 2006. Dir. Lab. Rsch. on Structure of Matter U. Pa., 1974—81; acting vice provost for rsch. U. Pa., 1981—82; Morris Loeb lectr. Harvard U., 1973. Editor-in-chief Synthetic Metals jour., 1983—2000, contbr. sci. articles to profl. jours. Recipient John Scott medal, City of Phila., 1989, Oliver P. Buckley prize, 1983, Balzan prize, Balzan Found., Italy and Switzerland, 1995, Pres. medal, U. Pa., 2000, Nobel prize in Chemistry, 2000, Italgas prize, Eni, Inc., Italy, 2007; grantee, Govt.; fellow, Alfred P. Sloan, Guggenhaim. Fellow: Am. Physics Soc. (Buckley prize for solid state physics 1983); mem.: NAE, NAS, Korean Acad. Scis. (fgn.). Achievements include patents in field. Avocation: skiing. Office: U Calif Dept Physics Santa Barbara CA 93106 Business E-Mail: ajhe@physics.ucsb.edu.

HEEL, JOE, information technology executive; b. Germany; PhD in Computer Sci., MIT, Cambridge. Ptnr. High Tech Practice McKinsey and Co., head Miami office and pvt. equity practice; sr. exec. StorageTek; with Sun Microsystems, Inc., Santa Clara, Calif., 2005—, sr. v.p. global storage practice. Contbr. articles to profl. jours. Avocations: hiking, boating, bicycling, skiing. Office: Sun Microsystems Inc 4150 Network Cir Santa Clara CA 95054 Office Phone: 650-960-1300.

HEEN, WALTER MEHEULA, retired judge, former political party executive; b. Honolulu, Apr. 17, 1928; s. Norma K. Tada; 1 child, Cameron K. BA in Econs., U. Hawaii, 1953; JD, Georgetown U., 1955. Bar: Hawaii 1955, U.S. Dist. Ct. Hawaii 1955. Dep. corp. counsel, Honolulu, 1957-58; territorial ho. of reps., 1958-59; mem. State Ho. Reps., 1959-64; state senator, 1966-68; mem. Honolulu City Coun., 1969-72, chair, 1972-74; state dist. ct. judge, 1972-74; state cir. ct. judge, 1974-78; U.S. atty. U.S. Dist. Hawaii, 1978-80, U.S. dist. ct. judge, 1981; assoc. judge State Intermediate Ct. Appeals, 1982-94; ret., 1994. Past pres. Honolulu Hawaiian Civic Club; precinct club pres. Dem. Party, 1956-72, former chmn.; chmn. Hawaii Dem. Party, 1998-2001; vice chmn. Oahu Dem. County Com., 1956-62, chmn., 1962-64; del. State Dem. Party Conv., 1956-70; com. mem. Andy Anderson for Gov., 2002. Recipient Lei Hulu Mamo award, 1992; named Outstanding Young Man of the Yr., 1962. Mem. Native Hawaiian Bar Assn. (dir. 1994—). Avocations: photography, fishing, surfing, golf.

HEER, NICHOLAS LAWSON, language educator; b. Chapel Hill, NC, Feb. 8, 1928; s. Clarence and Jean Douglas (MacAlpine) H. BA, Yale U., New Haven, Conn., 1949; PhD, Princeton U., NJ, 1955. Transl. analyst Arabian Am. Oil Co., Saudi Arabia, 1955-57; asst. prof. Stanford U., Calif., 1959-62; vis. lectr. Yale U., New Haven, 1962-63; asst. prof. Harvard U., Cambridge, Mass., 1963-65; assoc. prof. U. Wash., Seattle, 1965-76, prof. Near Eastern langs. and civilization, 1976-90, prof. emeritus, 1990—; chmn. dept. Near Eastern langs. and civilization U. Wash, 1982-87. Middle East curator Hoover Instn., Stanford, Calif., 1958-62 Editor: Tirmidhi: Bayan al-Farq, 1958, Jami: Al-Durrah al-Fakhirah, 1981, Islamic Law and Jurisprudence: Studies in Honor of Farhat J. Ziadeh, 1990; translator: Jami: The Precious Pearl, 1979, (with Kenneth Honerkamp) Three Early Sufi Texts, 2003. Mem. Am. Oriental Soc., Middle East Studies Assn., Am. Assn. Tchrs. of Arabic (treas. 1964-76, pres. 1981, dir. 1982-84) Home: 1821 10th Ave E Seattle WA 98102-4214 Office: U Wash Dept Near Ea Langs & Civ PO Box 353120 Seattle WA 98195-3120 Personal E-mail: heer@eskimo.com. Business E-Mail: heer@u.washington.edu.

HEERE, KAREN R., astrophysicist; b. Teaneck, NJ, Apr. 9, 1944; d. Peter N. and Alice E. (Hall) H. BA summa cum laude, U. Pa., 1965; MA, U. Calif., Berkeley, 1968; PhD, U. Calif., Santa Cruz, 1976. Rsch. assoc. NRC NASA Ames Rsch. Ctr., Moffett Field, Calif., 1977—79; rsch. astronomer NASA Ames Rsch. Ctr., U. Calif., Santa Cruz, 1979—86, sr. analyst, 2004—; assoc. prof. San Francisco State U., 1986-87; scientist Sci. Applications Internat. Corp., Los Altos, Calif., 1974-76, 87-93; rsch. specialist Sterling Software, Redwood City, Calif., 1993-98; sr. scientist Raytheon, Moffett Field, 1998—2003, mgr. space and earth sci., 2001—03. Vis. scientist TATA Inst. for Fundamental Rsch., Bombay, 1984. Contbr. articles to profl. jours. Mem.: Am. Astron. Soc. Avocations: hiking, travel. Home: PO Box 2427 El Granada CA 94018-2427 Office: MS 210-8 NASA Ames Rsch Ctr Moffett Field CA 94035

HEFFRON, WARREN A., physician, educator; b. St. Louis, Nov. 7, 1936; s. Willard Page H. and Alma Alberta Revington; m. Rosalee Bowdish, June 10, 1961; children: Kimberly, Wanda, Kara, Arthur. AB, U. Mo., 1958, MD, 1962. Diplomate Am. Bd. Family Practice (pres. 1998—). Rotating intern U. Calif., Orange, 1962-63; physician Hosp. Castaner (P.R.), 1966-68; resident internal medicine U. N. Mex., Albuquerque, 1968-71, asst. prof., chief divsn., 1971-76; assoc. prof., asst. chair Family Cmty. and Emergency Medicine, Albuquerque, 1976-82; prof., chmn. Family Committee and Emergency Medicine, Albuquerque, 1982-93; chief med. staff U. N. Mex. Hosp., Albuquerque, 1993—. Bd. dirs. Am. Acad. Family Physicians, Am. Bd. Family Practice; dir. family Med. Residency Program, Albuquerque, 1971-82; vis. prof., cons. Dept. Cmty. Health, Punjab, India, Christian Med. Coll., Punjab U., Ludihiana; prof. Dept. Family and Cmty. Medicine, Albuquerque, 1993—; various internat. vis. professorships; internat. cons. family medicine residences in missionary settings. Contbr. numerous articles to profl. jours. Mem. free clinic Albuquerque Rescue Mission. Lt. comdr. USPHS, 1964-66. Named N. Mex. Family Physician of the Yr. 1990; recipient Recognition award Am. Med. Assn. Physicians, 1971, 74, 77, 80, 83, 86, 89, 92, 95, 98. Mem. N. Mex. Am. Acad. Family Physicians (pres. 1985, N. Mex. Family Dr. of Yr. award, chpt. svc. award 1988), Am. Bd. Family Practice (pres. 1998-99), N. Mex. Med. Soc. (pres. 1996-97, Robbins award Cmty. Svc. 1981), Soc. Tchrs. of Family Medicine (bd. dirs., treas. 1997, Smilkstein award 1998), Christian Med. and Dental Assn. (bd. dirs. 1998-06, pres. 2003-05, residency rev. com. for family practice 1999-05, Educator of Yr. award 2007), World Orgn. Family Drs. (pres. Ams. 2000-07). Methodist. Home: 2406 Ada Pl NE Albuquerque NM 87106-2550 Business E-Mail: wheffron@salud.unm.edu.

HEFLEBOWER, CHARLES R., career officer; b. Washington, Sept. 18, 1945; s. Roy Cleveland and Barbara (Koenig) H.; m. Susan Ann McAvoy, Mar. 9, 1974; children: Jennifer, Michael. BS in Aeroengring., USAF Acad., 1967; MA in Internat. Rels., U. Ark., 1973; student, Nat. War Coll., 1984-85. Commd. 2d lt. USAF, 1967, advanced through grades to maj. gen., 1994, dep. comdr. ops. 31st tactical fighter wing Homestead AFB, Ill., 1985-86, dir. spl. programs hdqs. tactical air command Langley AFB, Va., 1986-87, vice comdr. 388th tactical fighter wing Hill AFB, Utah, 1987-88, comdr. 388th tactical fighter wing, 1988-90, dep. bases and units hdqs. Washington, 1990-91, dir. assignments hdqs. Air Force mil. pers. ctr. Randolph AFB, Tex., 1991-92, dir. pers. programs hdqs. Washington, 1992-94, dir. programs/evaluation hdqs., 1994-95; comdr. 17th Air Force and comdr. Interim Combined Air Ops. Ctr., Sembach Air Base, Germany, 1995-96; asst. chief of staff Ops. and Ligistics Divsn., Supreme HQ Allied Powers Europe, Casteau, Belgium, 1996-98; vice comdr. HQ Pacific Air Forces, Hickam AFB, Hawaii, 1998-99; dep. comdr.-in-chief UN Command, 1999—. Dep. comdr. U.S. Forces Korea, 1999—; comdr. Air Component Command, Republic of Korea and U.S. Combined Forces Command, 1999—, 7th Air Force, Pacific Air Forces, Osan Air Base, South Korea, 1999— Office: PACAF 25 E St Ste 6214 Hickam AFB HI 96853-5420 also: APO AE 17 AF/CC 09142 Sembach Air Base Germany

HEFLEY, JOEL MAURICE, former congressman; s. J. Maurice and Etta A.; m. Lynn Christian, Aug. 25, 1961; children: Jana, Lori, Juli. BA, Okla. Baptist U., 1957; MS, Okla. State U., 1962. Exec. dir. Community Planning and Research, Colorado Springs, Colo., 1966-86; mem. Colo. State Ho. of Reps., 1977-78, Colo. State Senate, 1979-86, US Congress from 5th Colo. dist., 1987—2007; mem. armed svcs. com.; mem. natural resources com.; mem. small bus.-SBA com.; mem. nat. security com.; chmn. stds. ofcl. conduct com., 2001—05. Mem.: Rotary, Colorado Springs Country. Republican. Presbyterian.

HEFNER, HUGH MARSTON, editor-in-chief; b. Chgo., Apr. 9, 1926; s. Glenn L. and Grace (Swanson) H.; m. Mildred M. Williams, June 25, 1949 (div.); children: Christie A., David P.; m. Kimberley Conrad, July 1, 1989 (div.); children: Marston G., Cooper B. BS, U. Ill., 1949. Subscription promotion writer Esquire mag., 1951; promotion mgr. Pubs. Devel. Corp., 1952; circulation mgr. Children's Activities mag., 1953; chmn. bd. HMH Pub. Co. Inc. (now Playboy Enterprises, Inc.), 1953-88; editor-in-chief Playboy mag., 1953—; pres. Playboy Clubs Internat., Inc., 1959-86; editor, pub. VIP mag., 1963-75, Oui mag., 1972-81. Film appearances include History of the World, Part I, 1981, The Comeback Trail, 1982, Beverly Hills Cop II, 1987, The House Bunny, 2008, Miss March, 2009; TV series) The Girls Next Door, 2005-. Served with AUS, 1944-46. Recipient 1st Amendment Freedom award B'nai B'rith Anti-Defamation League, L.A., 1980, Internat. Pub. award Internat. Press Directory in London, 1997; named Man of Yr. Mag. Industry Newlsetter, 1967; named to Pub. Hall of Fame, 1989; honored with Hugh M. Hefner chair in study of Am. film U. So. Calif. Sch. Cinema/TV, 1996, Henry Johnson Fisher award, 2002. Mem.: N.Y. Friars Club (hon.). Office: Playboy Enterprises Inc 2706 Media Ctr Dr Los Angeles CA 90065-1733

HEFNER, JOHN, principal; Prin. Fruitvale Jr. HS. Recipient Blue Ribbon award US Dept. Edn., 1990-91. Office: Fruitvale Jr HS 2114 Calloway Dr Bakersfield CA 93312-2706

HEFTER, LEE, chef; Chef China Moon Cafe, San Francisco; sous chef Spago, Hollywood, Calif., exec. chef Beverly Hills, Calif.; chef Granita, LA; mng. ptnr., corp. chef Wolfgang Puck Fine Dining Grp., Wolfgang Puck Catering and Events. Recipient American Express Best Chef: California award, James Beard Found., 2005; named one of Best Young Chefs in Am., Restaurants & Instn., 1997, America's Best New Chefs, Food & Wine mag., 1998; nominee Rising Star, James Beard Found., 1997, Best Calif. Chef, 2003. Office: Spago 176 N Canon Dr Beverly Hills CA 90210 Office Phone: 310-385-0880.

HEGARTY, CHRISTOPHER JOSEPH, management and financial consultant; b. Jersey City; s. Michael John and Catherine Mary (Morrissey) H.; children: Mahren, Cahlil, Michael. PhD in Mgmt. Edn., Creative Devel. Inst. Internat., 1977; DD, Am. Inst. Theology, 1998. Investors exec., zone mgr. Investors Diversified Svcs., Mpls., 1960-65; pres. Hegarty & Co., NYC, 1965-67; founder, sr. v.p. Competitive Capital Corp., San Francisco, 1967-69; founder, pres. Charter St. Corp., San Francisco, 1969-71; pres. C.J. Hegarty & Co., Payson, Ariz., 1971—. Chmn. bd. dirs. Advanced Resources Mgmt.; faculty for continuing edn. U. So. Calif.; cons. SRI Internat.; founder, regent Coll. Fin. Planning; prin. Inst. Exceptional Performance, 1989; chmn. emeritus bd. govs. Nat. Ctr. for Fin. Edn.; spl. adv. Alternative Medicine.com., 1991—. Author: How To Manage Your Boss, 1980, Financial Planning for Chief Executives, 1983, Consistently Exceptional Leadership, 1989, Fiscal Fitness for Organizations, 1992, 7 Secrets of Exceptional Leadership, 1997, The Future Belongs to the Omnicompetent, 1997; co-author: Peak Performance for Executives and Professionals, 1983, Out of Harm's Way, 2001, Tyranny of the Familiar, 2002; contbg. editor Fin. Planning mag., 1973-77; mem. editl. bd. Health Consciousness mag., 1989, Alternative Medicine Mag., 1995; spl. advisor Future Medicine Pub., 1992—. Adv. bd. Small Bus. Coun. Am., 1982—; advisor Calif. Gov.'s Task Force for Emergencies, 1981-83; advisor Nat. Foun. Alternative Medicine, 2002; maj. Nat. Chaplains Corps, 1999; bishop Original Ch. of Apostles of Christ, 2002; chmn., bd. govs. Digest Fin. Planning, 1983—; pres., CEO Internat. Ctr. Life Improvement, 1987. Recipient Judge U.S. C. of C. Blue Chip Enterprise award, 1991, Top Preview Spkr. of Yr. award Internat. Platform Assn., 1972, Spl. award Sci. Found., 1977, Leadership and Comm. award Toastmasters Internat., 1978-79, Innovative Mktg. award Sales and Mktg. Assn., 1979, Outstanding Spkr. award Am. Soc. Tng. and Devel., 1980, Spkr. of Decade award Internat. Comm. Congress, 1980, Legion of Honor award Nat. Chaplains Assn., 1981, Leadership award UN, 1981, Excellence award Am. Film Guild; named Spkr. of Yr., Young Pres.'s Orgn., 1982. Mem. Nat. Spkrs. Assn. (founding dir., Continuare Professos Articulatus Excellence award 1977, named to Spkrs. Hall of Fame 1998), Am. Inst. Mgmt. (pres. coun. 1981—), Sales and Mktg. Execs. Internat., Internat. Assn. Fin. Planners (founder, nat. adv. bd., Spokesman of Yr. 1974), Commonwealth Club. Office: CJ Hegarty & Co 1116 S Elk Ridge Dr Ste A Payson AZ 85541 Home: 1116 S Elk Ridge Dr Payson AZ 85541 Office Phone: 800-247-4738. E-mail: hegarty@cutting-edge.com.

HEGARTY, GEORGE JOHN, university president, literature and language professor; b. Cape May, NJ, July 20, 1948; s. John Joseph and Gloria Anna (Bonelli) H.; m. Joy Elizabeth Schiller, June 9, 1979. Student, U. Fribourg, Switzerland, 1968-69; BA in English, LaSalle U., Phila., 1970; Cert., Coll. de la Pocatiere, Que., Can., 1970; postgrad., U. Dakar, Senegal, 1970, Case Western Res. U., 1973-74, U. N.H., 1976; MA in English, Drake U., 1977; cert., U. Iowa, 1977; ArtsD in English, Drake U., 1978; Cert., UCLA, 1979, U. Pa., 1981. Tchr. English, Peace Corps vol. College d'Enseignment General de Sedhiou, Senegal, 1970-71; tchr. English Belmore Boys' and Westfields High Schs., Sydney, 1972-73; teaching fellow in English Drake U., Des Moines, 1974-76; mem. faculty English Des Moines Area CC, 1976-80; assoc. prof. Am. lit. U. Yaounde, Cameroon, 1980-83; prof. Am. lit. and civilization Nat. U. Cote D'Ivoire, Abidjan, 1986-88; dir. ctr. for internat. programs and svcs. Drake U., Des Moines, 1983-91; prof. grad. program intercultural mgmt. SIT Grad. Inst., World Learning, Inc., Brattleboro, Vt., 1991—93; pres., prof. English, Teikyo Westmar U., Le Mars, Iowa, 1994-95; program dir. Am. degree program Taylor's U. Coll., Malaysia, 1996-97; provost, prof. English Teikyo Loretto Heights U., Denver, 1992-94, v.p. academic affairs, prof. English, 1997—2001, pres., prof. English, 2005—08; rector Webster U., Thailand, 2002—03; prof. Am. lit. & civilization U. Antananarivo, Madagascar, 2003—05; pres. Okinaga Found., 2006—08; prof. faculty lang. studies Teikyo U., Tokyo, 2009—. Acad. specialist USIA, 1983-84; workshop organizer/speaker Am. Field Svcs., 1986; cons. Coun. Internat. Ednl. Exch., 1986; evaluator Assn. des Univ. Partiellment Entierément de Langue Francais, 1987, Iowa Humanities Bd., 1990-91, USAID's Ctr. for Univ. Coop. and Devel., 1991; evaluator, consulate of Japan, Denver, 2000; Fulbright lectr., rschr. Am. Lit U., 2003-05; study leader Am. Mus. Natural History Expeditions, 2007—; cons. in field. Book reviewer African Book Pub. Record, Oxford, Eng., 1981-1996, African Studies Rev., 1990-1993; host, creator TV show Global Perspectives, 1989-91; exhibitor of African art, 1989—; contbr. articles to profl. jours. Commr. Des Moines Sister City Commn., 1984-87, 91; bd. dirs. Iowa Sister State Com., 1988-91; pres. Chautauqua Park Nat. Hist. Dist. Neighborhood Assn., 1991; bd. dirs. Melton Found., 1994-95; bd. mem., Douglas Soc. Denver Art Mus., 2008-. Drake U. fellow, 1971-72, 74-76; Nat. Endowment for Humanities grantee, 1981; Fulbright grantee, USIA, 1980-83, 86-88; Dept. of State grantee, 2003-05. Mem.: NAFSA: Assn. Internat. Educators (sectional chmn. region VI 1986—87, Vt. rep. 1992). Avocations: collecting tribal art, travel, swimming, writing. Personal E-mail: georgehegarty@aol.com.

HEGYVARY, SUE THOMAS, nursing school dean, educator, editor; b. Dry Ridge, Ky., Nov. 28, 1943; BSN, U. Ky., 1965; MN, Emory U., 1966; PhD in Sociology, Vanderbilt U., 1974. Asst. prof. nursing and sociology Rush U. Med. Coll., 1974, assoc. prof. med. nursing, chair dept., 1974-77, asst. prof. sociology, 1977-80; prof. nursing, assoc. v.p., assoc. dean Coll. Nursing Rush Presbyn. St. Luke's Med. Ctr., 1977—86; assoc. prof. sociology Rush U. Med. Coll., 1980—86; dean, prof. Sch. Nursing U. Wash., Seattle, 1986—98, adj. prof. Sch. Pub. Health and Cmty. Med. Mem. health care adv. com. Rep. Jennifer Dunn, 1993-96; vis. com. Bd. 50 Emory U. Sch. Nursing, Atlanta, 1990-92; mem. adv. panel outcomes rsch. Nat. Ctr. Nursing Rsch. NIH, 1990-91; external mem. Five Yr. Review com. Coll. Nursing U.

Ky., 1989-90; mem. govtl. affairs com. Am. Assn. Colls. Nursing, 1988-92; chair planning com. Wash. State Conf. Nursing Shortage, 1989; mem. Wash. State Commn. Nursing, 1989; mem. adv. com. Child Devel. & Mental Retardation Ctr. U. Wash., 1986—; mem. task force nursing shortage Seattle Area Hosp. Coun., 1987-88; vis. prof., ann. lectr. Sch. Nursing U. Va., Charlottesville, 1988; vis. prof. U. Oulu, Finland, 1985; site visitor accreditation schs. nursing Nat. League Nursing, 1977-80; cons. VA Hosp., Miami, Fla., 1968-69, Vanderbilt U., Nashville, 1971-72, Area Health Edn. Sys., Rockford, Ill., 1975, Western Interstate Commn. Higher Edn., Denver, 1975, Andrews U., Berrian Springs, Mich., 1976, dept. nursing studies Nat. Hosp. Inst., Utrecht, The Netherlands, 1976-80, Haukeland Sykehaus, Bergen, Norway, 1976-77, Sch. Nursing Marquette U., Milw., 1977, Wayne State U., Detroit, 1978, Cath. U. Leuven, Belgium, 1980, Walter Reed Army Med. Ctr., Washington, 1979-83, Dalhousie U. Sch. Nursing, Halifax, N.S., 1981, U. Minn., Mpls., 1988, U. Mo., Columbia, 1992. Editl. adv. bd. Nursing Policy Forum, 1995-96; editl. cons. Nursing Care Guide Pfizer Corp., 1993; editl. bd. Jour. Nursing & Health, 1993—, Nursing Adminstrn. Quarterly, 1988—; mem. manuscript review panel Jour. Nursing Quality Assurance, 1986—, Nursing Outlook, 1983—, Jour. Rsch. Nursing & Health, 1981—, Nursing Rsch., 1979-89; contbr. chpts. to books and articles to profl. jours. Mem. ANA, Am. Acad. Nursing, Sigma Theta Tau. Office: U Wash Sch Nursing BNHS PO Box 357266 Seattle WA 98195-7266

HEIDRICH, ROBERT WESLEY, lawyer; b. Chgo., Aug. 1, 1927; children: John G., Robert G., Kimberly L Student, U. Wis., 1944-45, 47-48; JD, DePaul U., 1951. Bar: Calif. 1974. Atty. Brunswick Corp., Chgo., 1953-60, 65-69; v.p. Brunswick AG (Switzerland), 1960-61; dir. Brunswick Internat. Fin. AG (Switzerland), 1962-65; sec., corp. counsel Nat. Can Corp., Chgo., 1969-73; v.p., sec., gen. counsel, dir. Rohr Industries, Inc., Chula Vista, Calif., 1973-79; corp. v.p., gen. counsel Holiday Inn Hotels, Memphis, 1979-85; counsel Kaiser Steel Corp., LaVerne, Calif., 1985-87, San Diego Real Estate Devel., 1987—. Bd. dir., Am. Internat. Sch. Zurich, 1964-65. Served with U.S. Army, 1945-47 Mem. Frederick Law Olmstead Soc. (founding pres. 1967-69). Home: 5157 Long Branch Ave Apt 4 San Diego CA 92107-2032 Office: O'Nido LLC PO Box 70075 San Diego CA 92167 Personal E-mail: derobdude@cox.net.

HEILBRON, DAVID MICHAEL, lawyer, arbitrator, mediator; b. San Francisco, Nov. 25, 1936; s. Louis H. and Delphine A. (Rosenblatt) H.; m. Nancy Ann Olsen, June 21, 1960; children: Lauren Ada, Sarah Ann, Ellen Selma. BS summa cum laude, U. Calif., Berkeley, 1958; AB first class, Oxford U., Eng., 1960; LL.B. magna cum laude, Harvard U., Cambridge, Mass., 1962. Bar: Calif. 1962, U.S. Dist. Ct. (no. dist.) Calif. 1963, U.S Ct. Appeals (9th cir.) 1963, U.S. Ct. Appeals (D.C. cir.) 1972, U.S. Ct. Appeals (8th cir.) 1985, U.S. Ct. Appeals (1st cir.) 1987, U.S. Ct. Appeals (10th cir.) 1988, U.S. Ct. Appeals (7th cir.) 1988, U.S. Ct. appeals (11th cir.) 1988, U.S. Dist. Ct. Nev. 1982, U.S. Dist. Ct. (cen. dist.) Calif. 1983, U.S. Supreme Ct. 1988, U.S. Ct. Appeals (3rd cir.) 1992, (6th cir.), 1995, U.S. Ct. Appeals (2d cir.) 1998, U.S. Ct. Appeals (5th cir.) 1998. Assoc. McCutchen, Doyle, Brown & Enersen, San Francisco, 1962-69, ptnr., 1969—, mng. ptnr., 1985-88. Vis. lectr. appellate advocacy U. Calif., Berkeley, 1981-82, 82-83. Bd. trustees Golden Gate U., 1993-97, vice chair, 1995-97; bd. dirs. San Francisco Jewish Cmty. Ctr., 1974—, Legal Aid Soc., 1974-78, Legal Assistance to Elderly, San Francisco, 1980, San Francisco Renaissance, 1982—; pres. San Francisco Sr. Ctr., 1972-75; co-chmn. San Francisco Lawyers' Com. for Urban Affairs, 1976. Rhodes scholar. Fellow Am. Bar Found.; mem. ABA, Am. Coll. Trial Lawyers, Am. Arbitration Assn. (bd. dirs. 1986-98, 2002--, adv. coun. No. Calif. chpt. 1982—, chmn. 1987, jud. coun. 1986-88, exec. bd. 1994-98, instr. and panelist arbitrator tng. programs), Am. Acad. Appellate Lawyers, State Bar Calif. (chmn. com. cts. 1982-83. bd. govs. 1983-85, mem. commn. on discovery 1984-86, pres. 1985-86), Calif. Acad. Appellate Lawyers, Coll. Comml. Arbitrators, Bar Assn. San Francisco (chmn. conf. dels. 1975-76, pres. 1980). Clubs: Calif. Tennis. Democrat. Office: Bingham McCutchen LLP 3 Embarcadero Ctr San Francisco CA 94111-4003 Office Phone: 415-393-2177. Business E-Mail: david.heilbron@comcast.net.

HEILES, CARL EUGENE, astronomer, educator; b. Toledo, Sept. 22, 1939; children: Tod Scott, Katrina Marie. B in Engring. Physics, Cornell U., 1962; PhD in Astronomy, Princeton U., 1966. Asst. prof., then assoc. prof. U. Calif., Berkeley, 1966-69, astronomy prof., 1970—; rsch. astronomer Arecibo (P.R.) Obs., 1969-70. Vis. fellow Joint Inst. for Lab. Astrophysics, Boulder, Colo., 1989-90. Recipient Dannie Heineman prize in astrophysics Am. Astron. Soc., 1989. Mem. NAS, Am. Acad. Scis., Calif. Acad. Scis. Office: U Calif Dept Astronomy Berkeley CA 94720-0001

HEIMANN, M.L. (DICK HEIMANN), auto dealership executive; BS in Biology and Langs., U. Colo. Dist. mgr. Chrysler Corp., 1967—70; pres., COO Lithia Motors Inc., Medford, Oreg. Mem.: Medford New Car Dealers Assn., Jeep Dealer Coun., Oregon Auto Dealers Assn. Office: Lithia Motors Inc 360 E Jackson St Medford OR 97501

HEIMBUCH, BABETTE E., bank executive; b. 1948; 2 children. BS in Math. summa cum laude, U. Calif., Santa Barbara, 1972. Sr. v.p., CFO FirstFed. Bank Calif., Santa Monica, 1982—85, exec. v.p., CFO, 1985—87, dir., 1986—, FirstFed. Fin. Corp., 1987—; sr. exec. v.p., CFO FirstFed. Fin. Corp. & FirstFed Bank Calif, 1987—88, pres., COO, 1989—97, CEO, 1997—, chmn., 2002—. Bd. dirs. Water Pik Technologies Inc., 2002—, Scape Industries. Chair bd. advisors Santa Monica-UCLA Med. Ctr.; fin. oversight com. Santa Monica/Malibu Unified Sch. Dist. Named one of 25 Women to Watch, US Banker Mag., 2003, 25 Most Powerful Women in Banking, 2007. Office: First Fed Bank Calif 401 Wilshire Blvd Santa Monica CA 90401-1416

HEIN, LEONARD WILLIAM, accounting educator; b. Forest Park, Ill., Feb. 17, 1916; s. Harry Christian and Clara Antoinette (Klein) H.; m. Akemi Kishi, Feb. 28, 1981. BSc, Loyola U., Chgo., 1952; MBA, U. Chgo., 1954; PhD (U. Calif. at Los Angeles Bus. Sch. Alumni Assn. fellow, Univ. fellow, Ford Found. fellow), U. Calif., LA, 1962. C.P.A., Ill. With San. Dist. Chgo., 1941-56; asst. prof. accounting Calif. State U. at Los Angeles, 1956-59, asso. prof. accounting, 1959-65, prof. accounting, 1965—, coordinator program bus. info. systems, 1956-73, asst. dean grad. studies, 1963-72. Mem. nat. panel arbitrators Am. Arbitration Assn., 1972— Author: Introduction to Electronic Data Processing for Business, 1961, Quantitative Approach to Managerial Decisions, 1967, Contemporary Accounting and the Computer, 1969, The British Companies Acts and the Practice of Accountancy, 1844-1962, 1978; Contbr. articles to profl. jours. Served with USNR, 1942-45. Mem. Am. Inst. C.P.A.'s, Am. Accounting Assn., Calif. Soc. C.P.A.'s, Beta Gamma Sigma, Beta Alpha Psi, Alpha Kappa Psi, Phi Kappa Phi.

HEINDL, CLIFFORD JOSEPH, physicist, researcher; b. Chgo., Feb. 4, 1926; s. Anton Thomas and Louise (Fiala) H. BS, Northwestern U., 1947, MS, 1948; AM, Columbia U., 1950, PhD, 1959. Sr. physicist Bendix Aviation Corp., Detroit, 1953-54; student rschr. Oak Ridge Nat. Lab., 1954-55; asst. sect. chief Babcock & Wilcox Co., Lynchburg, Va., 1956-58; rsch. group supr. Jet Propulsion Lab., Pasadena, Calif., 1959-65, mgr. rsch. and space sci., 1965—2005. Served with AUS, 1944-46. Mem. AIAA, Am. Nuclear Soc., Health Physics Soc., Planetary Soc., Am. Phys. Soc. Office: 4800 Oak Grove Dr Pasadena CA 91109-8001

HEINEMANN, STEPHEN F., molecular neurobiologist educator; BS, Calif. Inst. Tech., 1962; PhD, Harvard U., 1967; postgrad., MIT, Stanford U. Prof. molecular neurobiology lab. Salk Inst., 1989—, dir. molecular neurobiology lab., 1989-95, chmn. of the faculty, 1992-93. Adj. prof. U. Calif. Med. Sch., San Diego. Section editor: Jour. Neurosci. Molecular Neurosci.; mem. assoc. editl. bd. Current Opinion in Neurobiology, Proceedings of the Royal Soc. series B, Hippocampus, Cellular and Molecular Neurobiology, Receptors and Channels, Neuron, 1987-91, Jour. Neurosci., 1987-91. Recipient Disting. Achievement in Neurosci. Rsch. award Bristol-Myers Squibb, 1995; named Schmidt. Lectr. U. Pa., Feigen Lectr. Stanford U., Cooper Lectr., Flynn Lectr. Yale U. Mem. NAS (vice-chair com. IBRO), Inst. Medicine, Max-Planck Inst. (external mem.), Soc. Neurosci. (councilor 1992, Grass lectr.). Achievements include research in structure and function of brain receptors and their role in neurological disease and mental illness. Office: The Salk Inst PO Box 85800 San Diego CA 92186-5800

HEINEN, NANCY REGINA, lawyer, former computer company executive; b. 1956; m. Dennis Heinen. AB in Psychology and English cum laude, U. Calif., Berkeley, 1977, JD, 1982. Pvt. practice, San Francisco & Palo Alto; group counsel, asst. sec. Tandem Computers Inc., 1989—94; v.p., gen. counsel, sec. NeXT Software, Inc., 1994—97; sr. v.p., gen. counsel, sec. Apple Computer, Inc., Cupertino, Calif., 1997—2006.

HEINER, DENNIS GRANT, manufacturing executive; b. Ogden, Utah, Aug. 18, 1943; s. Grant and Mary (Stoker) H.; m. Margo Proctor, Dec. 17, 1970; children: Shalayna, Bryce James, Jillian, Brittany. BA, Weber State Coll., 1969; MBA, Brigham Young U., 1971; M in Mktg., Northwestern U., 1983; cert. strategic mktg. mgmt., Harvard U., 1985. V.p. mktg., gen. mgr. Sportplay, Inc., Salt Lake City, 1971-72; dir. mktg. adminstrn. and fin. Sno-Jet, Inc., Burlington, Vt., 1972-74; v.p. fin. Glastron Boat Co., Austin, Tex., 1974-78, v.p. fin. and adminstrn., 1978-79; v.p. fin. Delmar Window Coverings, Westminster, Calif., 1979-81, pres., 1981-84; pres. window coverings div. Beatrice Cos., Inc., Westminster, Calif., 1984-85; group v.p. U.S. Household Prducts div. Black & Decker, Shelton, Conn., 1985-86, exec. v.p., pres., 1986-92, exec. v.p., pres. security hardware group Anaheim, Calif., 1992—. Bd. dirs. Raytech Corp., Trumbull, Conn. Bd. dirs. Jr. Achievement, Austin, 1978-79. Mem. Young Pres.' Orgn. (So. Calif. and Fairchester chpts.). Republican. Mem. Lds Ch. Avocations: sports, running, piano.

HEINER, DOUGLAS CRAGUN, pediatrician, educator, immunologist, allergist; b. Salt Lake City, July 27, 1925; s. Spencer and Eva Lillian (Cragun) H.; m. Joy Luana Wiest, Jan. 8, 1946; children: Susan, Craig, Joseph, Marianne, James, David, Andrew, Carolee, Pauli. BS, Idaho State U., 1946; MD, U. Pa., 1950; PhD, McGill U., 1969. Intern Hosp. U. Pa., Phila., 1950-51; resident, fellow Children's Med. Ctr., Boston, 1953-56; asst. prof. pediat. U. Ark. Med. Ctr., Little Rock, 1956-60; assoc. prof. pediat. U. Utah Med. Ctr., Salt Lake City, 1960-66; fellow in immunology McGill U., Montreal, 1966-69; prof. pediat. Harbor-UCLA Med. Ctr., Torrance, Calif., 1969-94; disting. prof. pediat. UCLA Sch. Medicine, 1985-94, prof. emeritus, 1994—; med. specialist Russia Latter-day Saints Missions, 1997-99. Author: Allergies to Milk, 1980; mem. editl. bd. Jour. Allergy and Clin. Immunology, 1975-79, Allergy, 1981-88, Jour. Clin. Immunology, 1981-87, Pediat. Asthma, Allergy and Immunology, 1986-94; contbr. over 150 original articles to profl. jours., chpts. to books. Scoutmaster Boy Scouts Am., Salt Lake City, 1963; com. chmn. Rancho Palos Verdes, 1979-81; high coun. mem. LDS Ch., Rancho Palos Verdes, 1983-86. With U.S. Army, 1952-53, Korea. Recipient Disting. Alumnus award Idaho State U., 1987. Fellow: Am. Coll. Allergy, Asthma and Immunology (Disting.), Am. Acad. Allergy and Immunology (food allergy com. 1981—94), Am. Pediatric Soc.; mem.: Am. Acad. Pediat., Clin Immunology Soc., Am. Assn. Immunologists, Western Soc. for Pediatric Rsch. (Ross award 1961), Soc. for Pediatric Rsch. Republican. Avocations: gardening, tennis, fishing.

HEINKE, REX S., lawyer; b. Ill., 1950; s. William and Versa Heinke; m. Margaret Nagle, 1978; children: William, Meghan. BA, U. Witwatersrand, Johannesburg, Republic of South Africa, 1971; JD, U. Columbia, 1975. Bar: Calif. 1975. Ptnr. Gibson, Dunn & Crutcher, LA, 1983-99, Greines, Martin, Stein & Richland, 1999—2001, Akin, Gump, Strauss, Hauer & Feld, 2001—. Office: 2029 Century Park E Ste 2400 Los Angeles CA 90067 Office Phone: 310-229-1000. Business E-Mail: rheinke@akingump.com.

HEINRICH, CHRISTOPH, curator; b. Frankfurt, Germany, 1960; m. Kira van Lil. PhD, Ludwig-Maximilian U., Munich. Chief curator contemporary art, collection and exhibitions Hamburger Kunsthalle, Hamburg, Germany, 1995—2007; Polly and Mark Addison curator modern and contemporary art Denver Art Mus., 2007—. Curator (exhibitions) Andy Warhol: Photography, 1999, Mona Hatoum, 2004, Storytellers, 2005, Francis Bacon: The Portraits, 2005, Return to Space, 2005, Mahjong: Contemporary Chinese Art from the Sigg Collection, 2006, Daniel Richter: A Major Survey, 2007. Co-founder Young Friends of the Kunsthalle, Hamburg, Germany. Office: Denver Art Mus 100 W 14th Ave Pkwy Denver CO 80204

HEINRICH, DANIEL J., chemicals executive; b. Gridley, Calif. BBA, U. Calif., Berkeley, Calif.; MBA, Saint Mary's Coll. CPA. With Ford Fin. Svcs. Group; acct. Ernst and Young; sr. v.p., treas. Transamerica Fin. Corp., San Francisco; controller The Clorox Co., Oakland, Calif., 2001—03, sr. v.p., CFO, 2004—. Office: Clorox Co 1221 Broadway Oakland CA 94612-1888

HEINRICH, MARTIN T., United States Representative from New Mexico; b. Fallon, Nev., Oct. 17, 1971; m. Julie Heinrich; children: Carter, Micah. BSc in Engring., U. Mo., 1995; grad. courses cmty. and regional planning program, U. N.Mex. Small bus. owner pub. affairs consulting firm; exec. dir. Cottonwood Gulch Found.; natural resources trustee State of N.Mex.; mem. Albuquerque City Coun., 2003—07, pres., 2006; mem. US Congress From 1st N.Mex. Dist., 2009—. Bd. mem. Albuquerque Open Space Adv. Bd., New Mexico Wilderness Alliance, Southeast Heights Neighborhood Assn. Democrat. Lutheran. Office: US Congress 1505 Longworth House Office Bldg Washington DC 20515-3101 also: Dist Office 20 First Plz NW Ste 603 Albuquerque NM 87102 Office Phone: 202-225-6316, 505-346-6781. Office Fax: 202-225-4975, 505-346-6723.*

HEINZ, MATTHEW G., state legislator; b. Midland, Mich., June 6, 1977; BA in Chemistry, Albion Coll., Mich., 1999; MD, Wayne State U. Sch. Medicine, Detroit, 2003. Intern/resident U. Ariz.; mem. Dist. 29 Ariz. House of Reps., 2008—, mem. appropriations com., pub. employees, retirement & entitlement reform com. Mem.: AMA, Pima County Med. Soc., Ariz. Med. Assn., Phi Beta Kappa. Democrat. Home: Ariz House Reps Capitol Complex 1700 W Washington Rm 126 Phoenix AZ 85007 Office Phone: 602-926-3424. Office Fax: 602-417-3129. Business E-Mail: mheinz@azleg.gov.*

HEINZE, CHERYLL BOREN, state representative; b. Wewoka, Okla., Oct. 30, 1946; m. Harold Heinze. Diploma, East Ctrl. U.; BA, Alaska Pacific U. Art instr. UAA; co-owner His-N-Her Antiques; former dep. commr. natural resources; with Alaska Divsn. Tourism; mem. Alaska Ho. of Reps., 2002—; owner Adventure North Fishing & Guiding. Former pres. Anchorage Symphony League; bd. dirs. Breast Cancer Focus, Inc.; pres.'s steering com. Alaska Pacific U.; former rep. State C. of C., regional citizens adv. coun.; former bd. dirs. Pacific No. Acad., Anchorage Symphony Orch. Mem.: Alaska C. of C., Anchorage Women's Club. Republican. Avocations: music, art, poetry. Address: 1336 Staubbach Cir Anchorage AK 99508

HEIRD, JAMES C., agricultural studies educator; b. Blount County, Tenn. BS in Agr., U. Tenn., 1970, MS in Agr., 1971; PhD in Agr., Tex. Tech. U., 1978. Livestock and horse specialist N.C. State U., Raleigh, 1972-76; horse specialist Tex. Tech. U., Lubbock, 1976-86; tchg. coord. equine sci. program Colo. State U., Fort Collins, 1986-89, acting dean, Coll. Agrl. Scis., 1991-92, interim dean, Coll. Bus., 1993-94, assoc. dean/dir. acad. programs, Coll. Agrl. Scis., 1989—. Office: Colo State U Coll Agrl Scis Fort Collins CO 80523-0001

HEISER, JAMES S., manufacturing executive; b. 1956; BA in Econs., U. Va.; JD, Stanford U. Gen. counsel, v.p. Ducommun Inc., Carson, Calif., 1985—. Office: Ducommun Inc 23301 Wilmington Ave Carson CA 90745 Office Phone: 310-513-7280. E-mail: jheiser@ducommun.com.

HEITING, JAMES OTTO, lawyer; b. Chgo., Apr. 21, 1949; m. Cindy Heiting; 3 children. BS, Riverside Univ., 1971; JD, Western State Univ., 1975. Bar: Calif. 1976, U.S. Supreme Court and U.S. District Ct. 1977, Central Dist. of Calif., U.S. Dist. Ct., So. Dist. of Calif. 1982. Founder, partner Heiting & Irwin, 1976—. Mem. bd. dirs The Other Bar, 1998—2003, pres., chmn., 1991—93. Mem.: Calif. State Bar Assn. (v.p., treas. 2004—05, pres. 2005—06), Am. Soc. Law and Medicine, Am. Bar Assoc. Office: Heiting & Irwin 5885 Brocton Avenue Riverside CA 92506

HEITMAN, GREGORY ERWIN, state agency administrator; b. Lewiston, Idaho, June 7, 1947; s. Elmer William and Carmelita Rose Ann (Kinzer) H.; m. Phyllis Ann Pryor, Sept. 25, 1982. BS in Math., U. Idaho, 1969, MBA, 1971; student, Wash. State U., Pullman, 1965—67. Dir. student comm. Assoc. Students U. Idaho, Moscow, 1970—72, advisor, apt. mgr. dept. housing, 1971—72; traffic fatality analyst Idaho Dept. Transp., Boise, 1973—74; mgr. ops. Region IV Health & Welfare State of Idaho, Boise, 1974—78, supr. computer svcs., divsn. environ. in health and welfare, 1978—85; coord. field svcs., program dir. Idaho Bur. Vital Records and Health Stats., Boise, 1985—; acting dir. Idaho Ctr. for Health Stats., Boise, 1988—89, spl. asst. program and policy devel., 1989—. Mem. med. records adv. com. Boise State U., 1987—, cons., lectr. 1987—. Active various charitable orgns.; precinct committeeman Dem. of Latah County, 1972; election day coord. Ada County, 1986; vol. Am. Cancer Soc., 1990, Easter Seals, 1992, Arthritis Found., 1996. Mem. Assn. Vital Records and Health Stats., Idaho Pub. Employees Assn., Assn. Govt. Employees. Roman Catholic. Avocations: bowling, card collecting. Home: 1762 E Summerridge Dr Meridian ID 83642-5586 Office: Idaho Vital Stats PO Box 83720 Boise ID 83720-0036

HEJDUK, MILAN, professional hockey player; b. Usti-nad Labem, Czech Republic, Feb. 14, 1976; m. Zlatuse Hejduk; children: Marek, David. Right wing Colo. Avalanche, 1998—. Mem. Czech Nat. Hockey Team, Olympic Games, Nagano, Japan, 1998, Salt Lake City, 2002, Torino, Italy, 06, Czech Nat. Hockey Team, World Cup of Hockey, 2004. Recipient Maurice Richard Trophy, NHL, 2003; co-recipient Bud Light Plus/Minus Award, 2003; named to All-Rookie Team, 1999, Second All-Star Team, 2003, NHL All-Star Game, 2000, 2001, 2009. Achievements include being a member of gold medal winning Czech Republic Hockey Team, Nagano Olympics, 1998, bronze medal team, Torino Olympics, Italy, 2006; being a member of Stanley Cup Champion Colorado Avalanche, 2001. Office: Colo Avalanche Pepsi Ctr 1000 Chopper Cir Denver CO 80204*

HELFERT, ERICH ANTON, management consultant, writer, educator; b. Aussig/Elbe, Sudetenland, May 29, 1931; came to U.S., 1950; s. Julius and Anna Maria (Wilde) H.; m. Anne Langley, Jan. 1, 1983; children: Claire L., Amanda L. BS, U. Nev., 1954; MBA with distinction, Harvard U., 1956, DBA, 1958. Newspaper reporter, corr., Neuburg, Germany, 1948—52; rsch. asst. Harvard U., 1956-57; asst. prof. bus. policy San Francisco State U., 1958-59; asst. prof. fin. and control Grad. Sch. Bus. Adminstrn. Harvard U., 1959-65; internal cons., then asst. to pres., dir. corp. planning Crown Zellerbach Corp., San Francisco, 1965-78, asst. to chmn., dir. corp. planning, 1978-82, v.p. corp. planning, 1982-85; mgmt. cons. San Francisco, 1985—. Co-founding dir., chmn. Modernsoft, Inc.; mem. Dean's adv. coun. San Francisco State Bus. Sch., sch. fin. Golden Gate U.; bd. dirs., past chmn. and pres. Harvard U. Bus. Sch. No. Calif.; trustee Saybrook Inst. Author: Techniques of Financial Analysis, 1963, 11th edit., 2003, Valuation, 1966, Valley of the Shadow, 1997, (with others) Case Book on Finance, 1963, Controllership, 1965; contbr. articles to profl. jours. Exch. student fellow U.S. Inst. Internat. Edn., 1950, Ford Found. doctoral fellow, 1956. Mem. Assn. Corp. Growth (past pres., bd. dirs. San Francisco chpt.), Inst. Mgmt. Cons., Commonwealth Club, Forensic Expert Witness Assn., Phi Kappa Phi. Roman Catholic. Home: 111 St Matthews Ave No 307 San Mateo CA 94401-4519 Office Phone: 650-377-0540. E-mail: heleassoc@rcn.com.

HELINSKI, DONALD RAYMOND, biologist, educator; b. Balt., July 7, 1933; s. George L. and Marie M. (Naparstek) H.; m. Patricia G. Doherty, Mar. 4, 1962; children: Matthew T., Maureen G. BS, U. Md., 1954; PhD in Biochemistry, Western Res. U., 1960; postdoctoral fellow, Stanford U., 1960-62. Asst. prof. Princeton (N.J.) U., 1962-65; mem. faculty U. Calif., San Diego, 1965—, prof. biology, 1970—, chmn. dept., 1979-81, dir. Ctr. for Molecular Genetics, 1984-95, assoc. dean Natural Scis., 1994-97, prof. emeritus, 2006—. Mem. com. guidelines for recombinant DNA research NIH, 1975-78 Author papers in field. Mem. Am. Soc. Biol. Chemists, Am. Soc. Microbiology, AAAS, Am. Acad. of Arts and Scis., Am. Acad. Microbiology, Nat. Acad. Scis., European Molecular Biology Orgn. (assoc.). Office: Bonner Hall 9500 Gilman Dr La Jolla CA 92093-0322

HELLEBOID, OLIVIER, information technology executive; Degree in Engring., Ecole Nationale Superieure des Telecom. de Paris; MS, MIT. Participant in design and launch of data network for indsl. automation Telemecanique Electrique, Valbonne, France; with Hewlett-Packard, 1982—2002, mktg. mgmt. positions, gen. mgr. comml. svc. bus., v.p., gen. mgr. HP OpenView Software Bus. Unit; CEO, pres. Rainfinity; exec. v.p. corp. devel. BEA Systems, Inc., San Jose, Calif., 2002—. Office: BEA Systems Inc 2315 N First St San Jose CA 95131

HELLER, DEAN, United States Representative from Nevada, former state official; b. Castro Valley, Calif., May 10, 1960; m. Lynne Brombach, children: Hilary, Harrison, Andrew, Emmy. BS with honors, U. S. Calif., 1985. Stockbroker, broker, trader Pacific Stock Exch.; chief dep., Office of State Treas. State of Nev.; mem. Nev. State Assembly, 1990—94; sec. state State of Nev., Carson City, 1995—2006; mem. US Congress from 2nd Nev. dist., 2007—, mem. edn. & labor com., nat. resources com., small bus. com. Bd. dirs. Western Nev. Cmty. Coll. Found. Mem.: We. Nev. C C. Found., Boys & Girls Club We. Nev., N.Am. Securities Adminstrs. Assn. Republican. Mem. Lds Ch. Achievements include being the first secretary of state in the nation to demand a voter-verifiable paper audit trail printer on touchscreen voting machines. Avocation: stockcar racing. Office: 405 Idaho St Ste 214 Elko NV 89801 also: 125 Cannon House Office Bldg Washington DC 20515

HELLER, EDWARD P., III, lawyer; b. 1947; BS, Ill. Inst. Tech.; JD, Western State U. Bar: Calif. 1976. Patent counsel Seagate Technology, Inc., Scotts Valley, Calif. Office: 4585 Scotts Valley Dr Scotts Valley CA 95066-4517 also: PO Box Bldg 14 920 Disc Dr Scotts Valley CA 95066-4544

HELLER, PAUL MICHAEL, film company executive, producer; b. NYC, Sept. 25, 1927; s. Alex Gordon and Anna (Rappaport) H.; children: Michael Peter, Charles Paul. Student, Drexel Inst. Tech., 1944-45; BA, Hunter Coll., 1950. Freelance scenic designer, NYC, 1952-61; film producer, 1961—; instr. NYU, NYC, 1964-66; prodn. exec. Warner Bros., 1970-71; pres. Paul Heller Prodns. Inc., Beverly Hills, Calif., 1973—. Producer over 30 films including David and Lisa, 1962, Enter the Dragon, 1973, First Monday in October, 1981, Withnail and I, 1987, My Left Foot, 1989, The Lunatic, 1990, The Annihilation of Fish, 1999; mus. multi-media prodr. The Skirball Cultural Center Museum, 1997, The Hong Kong Museum of History, 2000. Founding mem. Com. 100, Am. Film Inst. Served with U.S. Army. Recipient spl. award Nat. Assn. Mental Health. Mem. Dirs. Guild Am., Screen Actors Guild, Actors Equity Assn., Acad. Motion Picture Arts and Scis., Brit. Acad. Film and TV Arts (bd. dirs.), Hearst Castle Preservation San Simeon (bd. dirs.), Lotos Club (N.Y.C.). Home and Office: 1666 N Beverly Dr Beverly Hills CA 90210-2316 E-mail: pheller@earthlink.net.

HELLER, PHILIP, lawyer; b. NYC, Aug. 12, 1952; s. Irving and Dolores (Soloff) Heller; married; children: Howard Philip, John Philip, Madison Irene Sarah. Attended, Harvard Coll.; BA summa cum laude, Boston U., 1976, JD, 1979. Bar: Mass. 1979, NY 1980, Calif. 1984, US Dist. Ct. Mass., US Dist. Ct. (ea. and so. dists.) NY, US Dist. Ct. (all dists.) Calif., US Ct. Appeals (1st, 2d and 9th cirs.) 1980, US Supreme Ct. 1983. Law clk. to Judge Cooper US Dist. Ct. NY, NYC, 1979; ptnr. Fagelbaum & Heller LLP, LA. Mem.: ABA (litigation sect), LA County Bar Assn., Calif. Bar Assn. Office: 2049 Century Park E Ste 4250 Los Angeles CA 90067-3168 Home Phone: 310-203-0677; Office Phone: 310-286-7666. Office Fax: 310-286-7086. Business E-Mail: ph@philipheller.com.

HELLER, ROBERT, financial executive, economist; b. Cologne, Germany, Jan. 8, 1940; m. Emily Mitchell, Dec. 5, 1970; children: Kimberly, Christopher. MA in Econs., U. Minn., 1962; PhD, U. Calif., Berkeley, 1965. Instr. U. Calif., Berkeley, 1965; assoc. prof. econs. UCLA, 1965-71; prof. U. Hawaii, Honolulu, 1971-74; chief fin. studies divsn. Internat. Monetary Fund, Washington, 1974-78; sr. v.p., dir. internat. econ. rsch. Bank of Am., San Francisco, 1978-86; mem., bd. govs. Fed. Res. System, Washington, 1986-89; exec. v.p. VISA Internat., San Francisco, 1989-91; pres., CEO VISA, U.S.A., San Francisco, 1991-93; exec. v.p. Fair, Isaac and Co., San Rafael, Calif., 1994-2001; chmn. Govs. Group, 2001—. Bd. dirs. Fair, Isaac and Co., Plus Sys. Inc., Interlink, Mcht. Bank Svcs. Corp., Bay Area Coun., San Francisco, Sonic Automotive, Bank of Marin, San Rafael, Calif., 2006—; bd. dirs., mem. adv. bd. BMW of N.Am., Inc.; vice-chmn. Fed. Fin. Instns. Exam. Coun., 1988-89; mem. Nat. Adv. Coun. Internat. Monetary and Fin. Policies, 1987-89, U.S. Coun. Internat. Bus., N.Y.C., 1979—; trustee World Affairs Coun., 1990-96; mem. adv. bd. Nat. Ctr. Fin. Svcs., U. Calif., Berkeley, 1984-90, Ctr. Fin. Sys. Rsch., Ariz. State U., Tempe, 1989, Inst. Internat. Edn., San Francisco, 1989; mem. Bay Area Internat. Forum, 1989, Bay Area Coun., 1992; dir. Am. Inst. Contemporary German Studies, Johns Hopkins U., Washington, 1989; dir. Wharton Fin. Instns. Ctr., U. Pa., 1989—2004. Author: International Trade, 1968, rev. edit. 1973, International Monetary Economics, 1974, The Economic System, 1972, Japanese Investment in the U.S., 1974; mem. editorial bd. Jour. Money, Credit and Banking, 1975-83, Internat. Trade Jour., 1985-88. Bd. dirs. Marin Gen. Hosp., 2001— Mem. Bankers Club of San Francisco, Royal Econ. Soc., Am. Econ. Assn., Western Econo. Assn. (exec. bd. 1977-81), San Francisco Yacht Club, Tiburon Peninsula Club. Avocations: sailing, skiing.

HELLER, THOMAS CHARLES, law educator; b. Phila., Feb. 27, 1944; married; 2 children. AB, Princeton U., 1965; LLB, Yale U., 1968. Bar: Wis. 1975. Atty. Cleary, Gottlieb, Steen & Hamilton, Brussels, 1968; fellow Internat. Legal Ctr., Bogota, Colombia, 1968—70; fellow law and modernization Yale Law Sch., 1970—71; asst. to assoc. prof. U. Wis., Madison, 1971—79; co-dir. Ctr. Pub. Representation, 1976—77; assoc. Yale Inst. Social Policy Studies, 1978—79; vis. assoc. prof. Stanford Law Sch., 1978—79, prof. law, 1979—96, Lewis Talbot and Nadine Hearn Shelton prof. internat. legal studies, 1996—, assoc. dean, 1997—2001. Vis. prof. Ctr. for Law and Econs. U. Miami, 1977—78; dir. overseas studies program Standford U., 1985—92, dep. dir. Internat. Studies Inst., 1989—92; fellow Humanities Rsch. Inst. U. Calif., Irvine, 1989; Jean Monnet vis. prof. European U. Inst., 1992—93, 1996—99; sr. fellow Standford U., 1993—; vis. prof. Ctr. for Law and Econs. Cath. U., Louvian, 1998. Office: Stanford Law Sch 559 Nathan Abbott Way Stanford CA 94305-8610 Office Phone: 650-723-7650. Business E-Mail: theller@stanford.edu.

HELLEWELL, PARLEY G., state legislator; b. Feb. 1, 1950; m. Marilyn Barlow. AA in Bus. Mgmt. and Mktg., Utah Valley C.C. Owner plumbing, heating, air and elec. svc. maintenance bus. PPM, Inc.; mem. Utah Senate, Dist. 15, Salt Lake City, 1998—; chair bus., labor and econ. devel. com; mem. judiciary com.; exec. office, criminal justice and legis. appropriation com. Republican. Home: 492 S 1000 W Orem UT 84058-5828 E-mail: parley@itsnet.com.

HELLIWELL, THOMAS MCCAFFREE, physicist, researcher; b. Mpls., June 8, 1936; s. George Plummer and Eleanor (McCaffree) H.; m. Bernadette Egan Busenberg, Aug. 9, 1997. BA, Pomona Coll., 1958; PhD, Calif. Inst. Tech., 1963. Asst. prof. physics Harvey Mudd Coll., Claremont, Calif., 1962-67, assoc. prof., 1967-73, prof., 1973—2005, prof. emeritus, 2005—, chmn. dept. physics, 1981-89, chair of faculty, 1990-93, Burton Bettingen prof. physics, 1990—2004, interim dean of faculty, 2004—05. Author: Introduction to Special Relativity, 1966; author papers in field of cosmology, gen. relativity and quantum theory. Sci. faculty fellow NSF, 1968. Mem.: AAAS, Am. Phys. Soc., Am. Assn. Physics Tchrs. Avocations: music, hiking. Office: Harvey Mudd Coll Dept Physics 301 Platt Blvd Claremont CA 91711-5901

HELLMAN, F(REDERICK) WARREN, investor; b. NYC, July 25, 1934; s. Marco F. and Ruth (Koshl) H.; m. Patricia Christina Sander, Oct. 5, 1955; children: Frances, Patricia, Marco Warren, Judith. BA, U. Calif., Berkeley, 1955; MBA, Harvard U., 1959. With Lehman Bros., NYC, 1959-84, ptnr., 1963-84; exec. mng. dir. Lehman Bros., Inc., NYC, 1970-73, pres., 1973-75; ptnr. Hellman Ferri Investment Assocs., 1981-89, Matrix Ptnrs., 1981—; chmn. Hellman & Friedman LLC, San Francisco. Bd. dirs. DN & E Walter, Hall Capital Advisors, LLC, Sugar Bowl Corp. Former chmn. The San Francisco Found., trustee; hon. trustee emeritus The Brookings Instn.; co-chair Calif. Commn. for Jobs and Econ. Growth; mem. Governor's Coun. Econ. Advisors, Com. on JOBS; mem. adv. bd. Walter A. Haas Sch. Bus., UC Berkeley; pres. Voice of Dance; bd. dirs. Bay Area Coun., San Francisco C. of C. Mem. Am. Acad. Arts and Scis. (award, 2005), Bond Club, Century Country Club, Pacific Union Club. Office: Hellman & Friedman LLC 1 Maritime Plz Fl 12 San Francisco CA 94111-3404

HELLON, MICHAEL THOMAS, tax specialist, political organization worker; b. Camden, NJ, June 24, 1942; s. James Bernard and Dena Louise (Blackburn) H.; m. (div.); 2 children. BS, Ariz. State U., 1972. Ins. investigator Equifax, Phoenix, 1968-69; exec. v.p. Phoenix Met. C. of C., 1969-76; exec. Londen Ins. Group, 1976-78; pres. Hellon and Assocs., Inc., 1978—. Small claims hearing officer Pima County Justice Ct., 1990—; mem. Pima County Bd. Adjustments, 1993-00, Pima County Merit Commn., 2000—, Ariz. Jud. Performance Rev. Commn., 2004-; Ariz Jud. Coun., 2008-;cochair Machine Proceding, Ariz, 2008; nat. def. exec. res. U.S. Dept. of Commerce, 1986-97; bd. dirs. Equity Benefit Life Ins. Co., Modern Income Life Ins. Co. of Mo., First Equity Security Life Ins. Co., Tucson Classics; mem. commn. jud. performance rev., Ariz., 2004—. Mem. Ariz. Occupl. Safety and Health Adv. Coun., 1972-76, mem. Speaker's Select Com. Auto Emissions, 1976; Phoenix Urban League, 1972-73, Area Manpower Planning coun., 1971-72, Phoenix Civic Plaza Dedication Com., 1972, Phoenix Air Quality Maintenance Taks Force, 1976; pres. Vis. Nurse Svc., 1978-79; Rep. precinct capt., 1973—; state campaign dir. Arizonans for Reagan Com., 1980; alt. del. Rep. Nat. Conv., 1980, 84, 88; mem. staff Reagan-Bush Nat. Conv., 1984; campaign mgr. for various candidates, 1972-82; mem. exec. com. Ariz. Rep. Party, 1989-90, chmn., 1997-99; mem. Rep. Nat. Com., 1992-04, mem. exec. com., 1997-04; bd. dirs. ATMA Tng. Found., 1981-84. Served with USAF, 1964-68. Decorated Bronze Star medal, Purple Heart; Recipient George Washington Honor medal Freedom's Found., 1964; commendation Fed. Bar Assn., 1973. Mem. U.S. C. of C. (pub. affairs com. western divsn. 1974-76), Inst. of Property Taxation, Internat. Assn. Assessing Officers, U.S. Dept. Commerce Exec. Res., Ariz. C. of C. Mgrs. Assn. (bd. m em. 1974-76), Tucson C. of C., Trunk 'N Tusk Club, Catalina Soccer Club (bd. dirs. 1984-88). Home: 1261 W Hopbush Way Tucson AZ 85704-2647

HELLOW, JOHN R., lawyer; b. Grosse Point City, Mich., Jan. 2, 1956; BA, Oakland Univ., 1977; MHCA, St. Louis Univ., 1981, JD cum laude, 1982. Bar: Calif. 1982. Ptnr., health care law Hooper Lundy & Bookman, LA. Symposium editor: St. Louis Health Law Rev., 1980—81; editor (note & comment): St. Louis Univ. Law Rev., 1980—81. Mem.: Am. Health Lawyers Assn., Health Fin. Mgmt. Assn. Office: Hooper Lundy & Bookman Ste 1600 1875 Century Park E Los Angeles CA 90067 Office Phone: 310-551-8111. Office Fax: 310-551-8181. Business E-Mail: jhellow@health-law.com.

HELLSTRÖM, INGEGERD, medical researcher; b. Stockholm; permanent resident, US, 1966, US citizen, 1996; m. Karl Erik Hellström; children: Katarina Elisabet, Per Erik. MD of Medicine, Karolinska Inst. Med. Sch., Stockholm, 1964, PhD of Medicine (Tumor Biology), 1966. Rsch. assoc. (docent), dept. Tumor Biology Karolinska Inst. Med. Sch., Stockholm, 1959-66, asst. prof. dept. tumor biology, 1966; asst. prof. microbiology U. Wash., Seattle, 1966—, rsch. assoc. prof. microbiology, 1969-72, prof. microbiology/immunology, 1972—85, adj. prof. pathology, 1972—85, affiliate prof. pathology, 1985—; mem. and program head, divsn. tumor immunology Fred Hutchinson Cancer Rsch. Ctr., Seattle, 1975—83; sr. scientist Oncogen, Seattle, 1983—85, lab. dir., 1985—86; v.p. Oncogen/Bristol-Myers Squibb, Seattle, 1986-90; v.p. immunological diseases Bristol-Myers Squibb Pharm. Rsch. Inst., Seattle, 1990—97; pron. investigator Pacific Northwest Rsch. Inst., Seattle, 1997—2004. Patents in the field: 17 US patents and 1 UK Patent; mem. editl. adv. bd., Jour. of Nat. Cancer Inst.; assoc. editor, Cancer Research, 1980-87, 1988-93, 1995-; mem. editl. bd., Anticancer Research; mem. gen. assembly, GM Cancer Rsch. Found.; mem. external adv. com, Specialized Ctr. for Cancer Rsch., U. Ill. at Chgo., Coll. Medicine, 1991-; contbr. to 450 sci. publs. Recipient Lucy Wortham James award, Ewing Soc., 1971, Matrix Table award, 1972, Pap award for Outstanding Contbn. Cancer Rsch., Papanicolaou Cancer Rsch. Inst., 1973, Am. Cancer Soc. Nat. award 1974, RNO (Knight of Northern Star, First Class Swedish Order of Merit), 1976, Humboldt award to Sr. US Sci., Humbolt Stiftung Bonn, W. Germany, 1980. Mem. AMA, Am. Assn. Immunologists, Am. Fedn. Clin. Rsch., Am. Assn. Cancer Rsch., Soc. Biol. Therapy. Office: Harborview Med Ctr Box 359939 325 Ninth Ave Seattle WA 98104-2499 Home Phone: 206-525-9968; Office Phone: 206-341-5908. Business E-Mail: ihellstr@u.washington.edu.

HELLSTRÖM, KARL ERIK, science educator, researcher; b. Stockholm; permanent resident, US, 1966, US Citizen, 1996; m. Ingegerd Hellström; children: Katarina Elisabet, Per Erik. Candidate of medicine, Karolinska Inst. Med. Sch., Stockholm, 1955, MD, PhD, Karolinska Inst. Med. Sch., Stockholm, 1964. Rsch. fellow, dept. histology Karolinska Inst. Med. Sch., Stockholm, 1953—57, rsch. assoc., dept. histology, 1957, docent in tumor biology, 1958—62, asst. prof., dept. tumor biology, 1962—66; investigator in cell biology funded by Swedish Medical Rsch. Coun, 1964—66; assoc. prof. pathology U. Wash. Sch. Medicine, Seattle, 1966—69, prof. pathology, 1969—83, adj. prof. microbiology and immunology, affiliate prof. pathology, 1984—; prin. investigator Pacific Northwest Rsch. Inst., Seattle, 1997—2004; mem. and head, program of tumor immunology Fred Hutchinson Cancer Rsch Ctr., Seattle, 1975—83; sr. scientist Oncogen, Seattle, 1983—85, lab. dir., 1985—86; v.p. Oncogen/Bristol-Myers, 1986—90; v.p. oncology drug discovery Bristol-Myers Squibb Pharm. Rsch. Inst., 1990—95, v.p. immunotherapeutics drug discovery, 1995—97. Bd. dirs. Seattle Genetics, Inc.; sci. adv. coun. Cancer Rsch. Inst. Inc. Editl. bd.: Cancer Immunology and Immunology; contbr. to 460 sci. publs. Assessor Anti-Cancer Coun., Victoria, BC, Canada; Can. reviewer Netherlands Cancer Found. Recipient Lucy Wortham James award, Ewing Soc., 1971, Parke Davis award in Exptl. Pathology, 1972, Pap award for Outstanding Contbn. in Cancer Rsch., Papanicolaou Cancer Rsch. Inst., Miami, Fla., 1973, Nat. award for Cancer Rsch., Am. Cancer Soc., 1974, RNO (Knight of the Northern Star, 1st Class, Swedish Order of Merit), 1976, Humboldt award to Sr. US Sci., Humboldt Stiftung, Bonn, Germany, 1980. Mem.: Clin. immunology Soc., Am. Assn. for Clin. Rsch., AAAS, Am. Assn. of Immunologists, Am. Assn. Exptl. Pathology, Am. Assn. for Cancer Rsch., NY Acad. Sciences, Sigma XI, The Sci. Rsch. Soc., Alpha Omega Alpha, U. Wash. Chap. Achievements include patents in field. Office: Harborview Med Ctr Box 359939 325 Ninth Ave Seattle WA 98104-2499 Office Phone: 206-341-5907. Business E-Mail: hellsk@u.washington.edu.

HELMBERGER, DONALD VINCENT, geophysical educator, researcher; b. Perham, Minn., Jan. 23, 1938; s. John David and Mary (Klein) H.; m. Florence Coles; 1 child, Genna; m. Annette Sellon; 1 child, Elliott. B in Geophysics, U. Minn., 1961; MS, U. Calif., San Diego, 1965, PhD, 1967; postdoctoral, MIT, 1968-69. Asst. prof. Princeton (N.J.) U., 1969-70, Calif. Inst. Tech., Pasadena, 1970-74, assoc. prof., 1974-79, prof. geophysics, 1979—, Smits Family prof. geophysics and planetary sci. Recipient medal, Seismological Soc. Am., 2002. Fellow Am. Geophysical Union (Inge Lehmann medalist, 1997); mem. NAS. Office: Calif Inst Tech Dept Geol & Planetary Sci Pasadena CA 91125-0001

HELMICK, D.O., protective services official; b. Tex. A in Police Sci., Yuba Coll., Calif.; BA, Golden Gate U.; grad., FBI Nat. Inst. State trooper Calif. Hwy. Patrol, Sacramento, 1969-75, liaison to legis., spl. rep., 1975-86, comdr. coastal divsn. San Luis Obispo, 1986-89, dep. commr. Sacramento, 1989-95, commr., 1995—. Office: Calif Highway Patrol PO Box 942898 Sacramento CA 94298-0001

HELOU, GEORGE, science administrator, educator; BS in Physics with High Distinction, tchg. diploma in sci. edn., Am. Univ. Beirut, 1975; MSc, Cornell U., 1977, PhD in Astrophysics and Radio Sci., 1980. With Cornell U., Arcetri Astrophysical Observatory; mem. faculty in Physics, Math and Astronomy Divsn. Calif. Inst. Tech., Pasadena, Calif., exec. dir., Infrared Processing and Analysis Ctr., with, 1983—; dir. NASA Herschel Sci. Ctr.; dep. dir. Spitzer Sci. Ctr. Lectr. in field; visiting positions at several European Universities, including Paris, Leiden and Florence; associated with Infrared Astronomical Satellite, 1983, Infrared Space Observatory, 1995—98, Spitzer Space Telescope, 2003. Contbr. articles to profl. jours. Recipient Philip K. prize for Academic Excellence, 1975, Arcetri Internat. Fellowship, 1980, Dudley award, 1982, NASA Exceptional Svc. medal, 1992, NASA Exceptional Achievement medal, 2001, NASA Pub. Svc. medal, 2004. Mem.: Internat. Astronomical Union, Am. Astronomical Soc. Office: Infrared Processing and Analysis Ctr Calif Inst Tech Mail Code 100-22 770 S Wilson Ave Pasadena CA 91125 Office Phone: 626-395-1919. Office Fax: 626-397-7018.

HELPER, LEE, strategic business marketing and marketing communications consultant; Pres., co-owner Bender/Helper Impact, LA, 1986—; pres. EMbizImpact, Inc.; founder, chmn. Channel Lab LLC. Office: Bender Helper Impact 11500 W Olympic Blvd Ste 655 Los Angeles CA 90064-1597 Office Phone: 310-473-4147. Office Fax: 310-478-4727. E-mail: Lee_Helper@embizimpact.com.

HELSELL, ROBERT M., construction executive; b. Seattle, Mar. 29, 1937; s. Frank P. and Ellen (Bringloe) H.; m. Linda M. Clark, Dec. 19, 1961; children— Kristina, Ingrid, Spencer, Alexa BA, Dartmouth Coll., 1959, M.B.E., 1960. C.P.A., Wash. With Haskins & Sells, 1961-64; treas. Cascade Natural Gas Co., 1964-68; successively sec.-treas., exec. v.p., pres. and chief exec. officer Howard S. Wright Constrn. Co., Seattle, 1974-84; pres., chief exec. officer Wright Schuchart, Inc., 1980-84, Sprague Resources Corp., 1984-89; vice chmn. bd. Schuchart & Assocs., 1980-87; pres., chief exec. officer Wilder Constrn. Co., Bellingham, Wash., 1989—. Dir. Ranier Bancorp. and Security Pacific Bank, Seafirst Corp., 1992. Bd. dirs. Virginia Mason Hosp., 1984-89, Lakeside Sch., 1969-73, 93—, Seattle Children's Home, 1968-77, pres., 1972-75, Corp. Council for Arts, 1981—, pres., 1984, chmn., 1985, Washington Roundtable, 1988—; trustee Seattle Art Mus., 1973-88, Western Washington U., 1994—; mem. men's adv. com. Children's Orthopedic Hosp., 1980-89, Western Found., 1992. Lt. comdr. USCG, 1961-68. Mem. Assoc. Gen. Contractors. Clubs: Univ., Rainier, Seattle Tennis, Seattle Yacht, Wash. Athletic (Seattle), Bellingham Yacht Club. Republican. Episcopalian. Office: Wilder Constrn Co 1525 E Marine View Dr Everett WA 98201-1927

HELTON, TODD, professional baseball player; b. Knoxville, Tenn., Aug. 20, 1973; m. Kristi Helton, Jan. 29. Student, U. Tenn. Player Colo. Rockies, 1997—. Recipient Nat. League Gold Glove Award, 2001, 2002, 2004; named to Nat. League All-Star Team, 2000—04. Achievements include led Nat. League in Hits (216), RBI's (147), and Batting Avg. (.372), 2000. Office: Colo Rockies 2001 Blake St Denver CO 80205-2008

HELWICK, CHRISTINE, lawyer; b. Orange, Calif., Jan. 6, 1947; d. Edward Everett and Ruth Evelyn (Seymour) Hailwood; children: Ted C., Dana J. BA, Stanford U., 1968; MA, Northwestern U., 1969; JD, U. Calif., San Francisco, 1973. Bar: Calif., U.S. Supreme Ct. U. S. Ct. Appeals (9th cir.), U.S. Dist. Ct. (no., ctrl., so. and ea. dist.) Calif. Tchr. history New Trier Twp. High Sch., Winnetka, Ill., 1968-69; sec. to the producer Flip Wilson Show, Burbank, Calif., 1970; assoc. Crosby, Heafey, Roach & May, Oakland, Calif., 1973-78; asst. counsel litigation U. Calif., Oakland, 1978-84, mng. univ. counsel, 1984-94, counsel Berkeley campus, 1989-94; gen. counsel, chief exec. systemwide legal office, and sec. for the institution Calif. State U. Sys., 1994—. Lectr. in field. Mem. instnl. rev. bd. Devel. Studies Ctr., Oakland, 1990—; mem. Alameda County Fee Arbitration Panel. Mem. Nat. Assn. Coll. and Univ. Attys. (bd. dirs. 1995-98, 2000-2004, pres. 2002-03), Nat. Assn. Coll. and Univ. Bus. Officers (bd. dirs. 2002—), State Bar Calif. (exec. com. 1980-83, Leadership Calif. 1998), dirs. 1977), Alameda County Bar Found. (adv. trustee 1988-90, bd. dirs. 1991), Order of Coif. Episcopalian. Office: Calif State U 401 Golden Shore 4th Fl Long Beach CA 90802-4275

HEMANN, RAYMOND GLENN, research company executive; b. Cleve., Jan. 24, 1933; s. Walter Harold and Marsha Mae (Colbert) H.; m. Lucile Tinnin Turnage, Feb. 1, 1958; children: James Edward, Carolyn Frances; m. Pamela Schaap Lehr, Dec. 18, 1987. BS, Fla. State U., 1957; postgrad., U.S. Naval Postgrad. Sch., 1963-64, U. Calif., LA, 1960—62; MS in Systems Engring., Calif. State U., Fullerton, 1970, MA in Econs., 1972; cert. in tech. mgmt., Calif. Inst. Tech., Pasadena, 1990. Comml., glider and pvt. pilot. Aero. engring. aide U.S. Navy, David Taylor Model Basin, Carderock, Md., 1956; analyst Fairchild Aerial Surveys, Tallahassee, 1957; research analyst Fla. Rd. Dept., Tallahassee, 1957-59; chief Autonetics divsn. N.Am. Aviation, Inc., Anaheim, Calif., 1959-69; v.p., dir. R.E. Manns Co., Wilmington, Calif., 1969-70; mgr. Avionics Design and Analysis Dept. Lockheed-Calif. Co., Burbank, 1970-72, mgr. Advanced Concepts divsn., 1976-82; gen. mgr. Western divsn. Arinc Research Corp., Santa Ana, 1972-76; dir. Future Requirements Rockwell Internat., 1982-85, dir. Threat Analysis, Corp. Offices, 1985-89; pres., CEO Advanced Systems Rsch., Inc., 1989—. Adj. sr. fellow Ctr. Strategic and Internat. Studies, Washington, 1987—; bd. dirs., mem. exec. com. Fla. State U. Rsch. Found., 1995-2003; bd. dirs. Assn. Mgmt. Svc. Inc., Numedeon, Inc., Am. Heart Assn., Pasadena Civic Auditorium Found. Inc., 2000-02; chmn. adv. coun. Coll. Engring. Fla. State U./Fla. A&M U., 1995—; cons. to dir. Ctrl. Intelligence, Nat. Intelligence Coun., Nat. Air Intelligence Ctr., Inst. Def. Analyses, Battelle Meml. Inst., Ctr. Strategic and Internat. Studies; sec., bd. dirs. Calif State U., Fullerton, Econs. Found.; mem. naval studies bd. panels, 1985—, chmn. indsl. panel Nat. Labs. Infrastructure Study, Office Sec. Def., 1995; chmn. indsl. panel Future Dirs. Mil. Aeronautics Study, 1996; asst. prof. ops. analysis dept. U.S. Naval Postgrad. Sch., Monterey, Calif., 1963-64, Monterey Peninsula Coll., 1963; instr. ops. analysis Calif. State U., Fullerton, 1964-67, instr. quantitative methods, 1969-72; program developer, instr. systems engring. indsl. rels. ctr. Calif. Inst. Tech., 1992-96; lectr. Brazilian Navy, 1980, U. Calif., Santa Barbara, 1980, Yale U., 1985, Princeton U., 1986, U.S. Naval Postgrad. Sch., 1986, Ministry of Def., Taiwan, Republic of China, 1990; Calif. Inst. Tech. Assocs., 1992—; mem. exec. forum Calif. Inst. Tech., 1991—. Contbr articles to profl. jours. and new media. Chmn. comdr.'s adv. bd. CAP, Calif. Wing; reader Recording for the Blind, 1989—; bd. dirs. Pasadena Civic Auditorium Found., 2000-02, Boy Scouts Am., 2971-79; bd. dirs., sec.-treas. Jr. All-Am. Football; trustee Art Ctr. Coll. Design, Pasadena, Calif., 2003—; chmn. mech. engring. adv. coun. Fla. A&M U./Fla. State U. Coll. Engring, Tallahassee; mem. dean's adv. coun. Coll. Engring. and Computers Scis. Calif. State U., Fullerton. Syde P. Deeb scholar, 1956; recipient honor awards Nat. Assn. Remotely Piloted Vehicles, 1975, 76, Grad Made Good Fla. State U., 2005; named to Hon. Order Ky. Cols., 1985; named One of Top 100 Grads, Calif. State U., Fullerton, 2007. Fellow AAAS, AIAA (assoc.); mem. IEEE (life), Ops. Rsch. Soc. Am., Air Force Assn., US Marines Meml. Club (life), N.Y. Acad. Scis., Assn. Old Crows., L.A. World Affairs Coun., Phi Kappa Tau (past pres.). Episcopalian. Office Phone: 626-564-8845.

HEMBREE, JAMES D., retired chemical company executive; b. Morris, Okla., Feb. 27, 1929; s. James D. and Mary Eleanor H.; m. Joyce Pickrell, Aug. 25, 1951; children: Victoria Lee Krivacs, Alex James, Kent Douglas. BSCh.E., Okla. State U., 1951; MSCh.E., U. Mich., 1952. Dir. mktg. inorganic chems. Dow Chem U.S.A., Midland, Mich., 1968-78, gen. mgr. designed products dept., 1976-78, v.p., 1978-80, group v.p., 1980-83; pres., chief exec. officer Dow Chem. Can., Sarnia, Ont., 1983-86; ret., 1986. Home and Office: 4620 Jupiter Dr Salt Lake City UT 84124-3900 Personal E-mail: jandj_84124@yahoo.com.

HEMINGER, STEVE, city official; b. Ohio; BA, Georgetown U., Washington; MA, U. Chgo. Staff asst. rep. Gregory W. Carman US Ho. Reps., Washington; office dir. San Francisco Bd. Supervisors; dir. dist. office Senator Quentin L. Kopp Calif. State Senate; v.p. transp. Bay Area Coun., San Francisco, 1990—93; mgr. legis./pub. affairs Met. Transp. Commn., San Francisco Bay area, 1993—99, dep. dir., 1999—2001, exec. dir., 2001—. Bd. dirs. Californians for Better Transp., 1991—2000, RIDES for Bay Area Commuters, 1992—95, San Francisco Parking & Traffic Commn., 1992—96; adv. coun. Bay Area Air Quality Mgmt. Dist., 1992—94; appt. mem. Nat. Surface Transp. Policy & Revenue Study Commn., 2006—; bd. trustees Mineta Transp. Inst., San Jose, Calif.; bd. dirs. Assn. Met. Planning Orgns., Internat. Bridge, Tunnel & Turnpike Assn. Office: MTC 101 Eighth St Oakland CA 94607 Office Phone: 510-817-5810. Business E-Mail: sheminger@mtc.ca.gov.*

HEMMINGER, PAMELA LYNN, lawyer; b. Chgo., June 29, 1949; d. Paul Willis and Lenore Adelaide (Hennig) H.; m. Robert Alan Miller, May 14, 1979; children: Kimberly Anne, Jeffrey Ryan, Eric Douglas. BA, Pomona Coll., 1971; JD, Pepperdine U., 1976. Tchr. Etiwanda (Calif.) Sch. dist., 1971-74; law clerk Gibson Dunn & Crutcher, Newport Beach, Calif., 1974-76, assoc. LA, 1976-84, ptnr., 1985—. Contbg. author Sexual Harassment, 1992, Employment Discrimination Law, 3d edit. and supplements, Employment Litigation, Calif. Practice Guide; contbr. articles to profl. jours. Mem. Comparable Worth Task Force Calif., Sacramento, 1984, Pepperdine U. Sch. of Law Bd. Visitors, 1990-2007, Calif. Law Revision Commn., 1998-99, 2005-; mem., bd. dirs. Dispute Resolution Svcs., 1998—. Named alumnus of yr. Pepperdine Sch. Law, 1996; listed in Best Lawyers in Am., 1998--. Mem. L.A. County Bar Assn. (chair, labor and employment sect. 1996-97), Calif. C. of C. (employment rels. com. 1984—). Republican. Lutheran. Office: Gibson Dunn & Crutcher Ste 4921 333 S Grand Ave Los Angeles CA 90071-3197

HEMMINGS, FREDERICK M., state legislator; b. Honolulu, Jan. 9, 1946; s. Fred and Lillian (Freitas) Hemmings; m. Lydia Hemmings; children: Heath, Meaghan, Gordon, Kaui. Small bus. owner, 1970—; mem. Hawaii House of Reps., 1984—90, majority fl. leader, 1989—90; mem. Dist. 25 Hawaii State Senate, 2000—, minority leader, 2006—. Bd. dirs. Denver Broncos NFL, 1984—. Author: Surfing, Hawaii's Gift to the World, 1977, The Soul of Surfing is Hawaiian, 1997; co-author: Illustrated Surfing Encyclopedia, 1979; appeared in nat. TV commercials for United Airlines, 1966, Kellogg's Cereal, 1967, Eastman Kodak Europe, 1970, columnist Honolulu Star Bulletin, 1966, prodr., host (Sta. KITV) Hawaii Sports Scene, 1972, commentator (Am. Broadcasting Co.) Wide World of Sports, 1970—75, 1978, (Columbia Broadcasting Sys.) Sports Spectacular, 1976—77, (Nat. Broadcasting Co.) Sports World, 1979—83, talk show host KGU Radio, 1991—92; contbg. editor: Honolulu Mag., 1991—92; co-host (Sta. 97.5 KHNR Radio) Equal Time with Fred Hemmings, 2004—06. Bd. dirs. Boys Club Honolulu, 1976—76, Hui Nalu O'Hawaii, 1976—79, State Legis. Leaders Found., 2009. Recipient Top Ten Businessmen's award, Honolulu Jr. C. of C., 1969, Lincoln Legacy award, Hawaii Rep. party, 2006; named Athlete of Yr., Honolulu Quarterback Club, 1964, Waterman of Yr., Surf Industry & Mfr. Assn., 2002, Legislator of Yr., Hawaii Med. Assn., 2005; named one of Top 50 Athletes of Hawaii for 20th Century, Sports Illustrated mag., 2000; named to Internat. Surfing Hall of Fame, 1991, Punahou Sch. Athletic Hall of Fame, 1994, Hawaii Sports Hall of Fame, 1999. Mem.: US Surfing Fedn. (hon. lifetime dir. 1987—), Assn. Surfing Profl.'s (bd. dir. 1985), Outrigger Canoe Club. Republican. Catholic. Mailing: 916 Aalapapa Dr Kailua HI 96734 also: State Capitol Rm 221 415 S Beretania St Honolulu HI 96813 also: 490 Paumakua Way Kailua HI 96734 Office Phone: 808-587-8388. Fax: 808-587-7240. Business E-Mail: senhemmings@Capitol.hawaii.gov.

HEMMINGSEN, BARBARA BRUFF, retired microbiologist; b. Whittier, Calif., Mar. 25, 1941; d. Stephen Cartland and Susanna Jane Bruff; m. Edvard Alfred Hemmingsen, Aug. 5, 1967; 1 child, Grete. BA, U. Calif., Berkeley, 1962, MA, 1964; PhD, U. Calif., San Diego, 1971. Lectr. San Diego State U., 1973-77, asst. prof., 1977-81, assoc. prof., 1981-88, prof., 1988—2004; ret., 2004. Vis. asst. prof. Aarhus U., Denmark, 1971—72; cons. AMBIS, Inc., San Diego, 1984—85, Woodward-Clyde Cons., 1985, 1987—91, Novatron, Inc., 2000—06. Author (with others): (book) Microbial Ecology, 1972; contbr. articles to profl. jours. Mem. Planned Parenthood, San Diego. Mem.: AAAS, Civil War Round Table, San Diego, San Diego Assn. Rational Inquiry (sec. 1998—2001, treas. 2002—), Am. Women Sci., Am. Soc. Microbiology, Daus. of Union Vets. of Civil War (patriotic instr. Nancy Lincoln Tent 2007—), Brit. Isles Geneal. Rsch. Assn. (sec. 2006—), Phi Beta Kappa (corr. sec. Nu chpt. Calif. 1994—2002, historian 2003—, past pres.), Sigma Xi. Democrat.

HEMP, RALPH CLYDE, retired reinsurance company executive, consultant, arbitrator, umpire; b. Fresno, Calif., Sept. 9, 1936; s. Ralph Edward and Mabel Alice (Knox) H.; m. Mary Ann Corley, Aug. 25, 1962; children— Ralph Kenneth, Laura Elizabeth BA, San Diego State U., 1961; JD, Western States U., Santa Ana, Calif., 1971. Office mgr. Crawford & Co., LA, 1961-67; regional claims mgr. Olympic Ins. Co., LA, 1968—76; sr. v.p. Leatherby Ins. Co., Fullerton, Calif., 1976—86; pres. North Am. Co., Greenwich, Conn., 1986—; chmn. Mt. Eagle Cos., Whitefish, Mont. Republican. Avocations: hunting, fishing, golf, skiing. Home and Office: Mt Eagle Cos PO Box 1971 Whitefish MT 59937-1971 Office Phone: 406-888-5025.

HEMRY, LARRY HAROLD, former federal agency official, writer, inventor; b. Seattle, Jan. 4, 1941; s. Harold Bernard and Florence Usborne (Achilles) H.; m. Nancy Kay Ballantyne, July 10, 1964 (div. Apr. 1976); children: Rachel Dalayne, Aaron Harold, Andrew LeRoy. BA, Seattle Pacific Coll., 1963; postgrad., Western Evang. Sem., Portland, Oreg., 1969-70. Ordained to ministry Free Meth. Ch., 1968. Clergyman Free Meth. Ch., Vancouver, B.C., Can., 1963-64, Mt. Vernon, Wash., 1968-69, Colton (Oreg.) Community Ch., 1969-71; edit clk. Moody Bible Inst., Chgo., 1964-66; pres., founder Bethel Enterprises, Colton, 1969-71; immigration insp. U.S. Immigration and Naturalization Svc., Sumas, Wash., 1972-96. Author, historian: Some Northwest Pioneer Families, 1969, The Hemry Family History Book, 1985; author: An Earnest Plea to Earnest Christians, 1969; contbr. articles to profl. publs.; patentee mech. nut cracker. Chmn. com. to establish and endow the James A. Hemry meml. scholarship fund Seattle Pacific U., 1975, L.H. Hemry scholarship fund, 2007. Fellow Seattle Pacific U. (Centurians Club); mem. The Nature Conservancy, The Sierra Club, The Audubon Soc. Avocations: camping, nature study, woodcarving. Home: PO Box 532 Sumas WA 98295-0532

HEMSTREET, MARK S., hotel executive; b. Portland, Oreg., Mar. 15, 1950; Pres. Shilo Inns, Shilo Mgmt. Co., Portland, 1974—. Office: Shilo Inns 11600 SW Shilo Ln Portland OR 97225-5919

HENDERSON, BRIAN EDMOND, dean, physician, educator; b. San Francisco, June 27, 1937; s. Edward O'Brien and Antoinette (Amstutz) H.; m. Judith Anne McDermott, Sept. 3, 1960; children: Sean, Maire, Sarah, Brian John, Michael. BA, U. Calif.-Berkeley, 1958; MD, U. Chgo., 1962. Resident Mass. Gen. Hosp., Boston, 1962-64; chief arbovirology Ctr. Disease Control, Atlanta, 1969-70; assoc. prof. pathology U. So. Calif., LA, 1970-74, prof. pathology, 1974-78, prof. preventive medicine, dept. chmn., 1978-88, dir. Kenneth Norris Jr. Comprehensive Cancer Ctr., 1983—93, rschr., 1994—96, prof. dept. preventative medicine, Kenneth T. Norris Chair in Cancer Prevention, 1996—, dir. Zilkha Neurogenetic Inst., 2002—, dean Keck Sch. Medicine, 2004—; pres. Salk Inst. Biol. Studies, La Jolla, Calif., 1993—94. Established LA Cancer Surveillance Program, U. So. Calif., 1972, Hawaii-LA Multiethnic Cohort, 1993; cons. WHO, South Pacific Commn., U.S.-Japan-Hawaii Cancer Program; mem. Charles S. Mott selection com. Gen. Motors Cancer Research Found., 1982-88; bd. councillors Nat. Cancer Inst., 1979-82; mem. sci. council Internat. Agy. for Rsch. on Cancer, 1982-86 Contbr. articles to profl. jours., chpts. to books; mem. editorial bd. Jour. Clin. Oncology; assoc. editor: Cancer Research. Served to lt. col. USPHS, 1964-69 Nat. Acad. Sci. disting. scholar to China, 1982; recipient Richard & Hinda Rosenthal Found. award, Am. Assn. Cancer Research, 1987, Rsch. Excellence in Cancer Epidemiology and Prevention Award, Am. Aead. Cancer Rsch., U. Chgo. Disting. Svc. Award, Presdl. Medallion., U. So. Calif., 1999. Fellow Los Angeles Acad. Medicine; mem. AAAS, NAS, Inst. Medicine, Infectious Disease Soc. Am., Am. Epidemiol. Soc., Alpha Omega Alpha. Democrat. Roman Catholic. Office: Keck School Medicine Comprehensive Cancer Ctr 1441 Eastlake Ave # 44 Los Angeles CA 90089-0112

HENDERSON, DOUGLAS JAMES, physicist, chemist, educator, researcher; b. Calgary, Alberta, Canada, July 28, 1934; arrived in U.S., 1956; s. Donald Ross and Evelyn Louise (Scott) Henderson; m. Rose-Marie Steen-Nielssen, Jan. 21, 1960; children: Barbara, Dianne, Sharon. BA in Math., U. B.C., Vancouver, 1956; PhD in Physics, U. Utah, 1961. Instr. dept. math. U. Utah, Salt Lake City, 1960-61; asst. prof. physics U. Idaho, Moscow, 1961-62, Ariz. State U., Tempe, 1962-64, assoc. prof., 1964-67, prof. physics, 1967-69; assoc. prof. physics U. Waterloo, Can., 1964-67, prof. applied math. and physics, 1967-69; rsch. sci. IBM Almaden Rsch. Ctr., San Jose, Calif., 1969-90, IBM Corp., Salt Lake City, 1990-92, Utah Supercomputing Inst., U. Utah, Salt Lake City, 1990-95; Manuel Sandoval Vallarta prof. physics U. Autonoma Metropolitana, Mexico, 1985—86, Juan de Oyarzabal prof. physics, 1993—95; prof. chemistry Brigham Young U., Provo, Utah, 1995—. Vis. sci. CSIRO Chem. Rsch. Labs., Melbourne, Australia, 1966—67, Inst. Phys. Chemistry, Polish Acad. Scis., 1973, Korea Advanced Inst. Sci., Seoul, 1974, Inst. Theoretical Physics, Ukranian Acad. Scis., 1989; vis. prof. physics Nat. U. La Plata, Argentina, 1973; sabbatical visitor IBM Watson Rsch. Ctr., Yorktown Heights, NY, 1973—74; mem. evaluation panel Commn. Human Resources, NRC, 1976; vis. prof. chemistry U. Utah, 1976, adj. prof. chemistry and math, 1990—, Henry Eyring lectr., 1994; Manuel Sandoval Vallarta Disting. vis. prof. physics U. Autonoma Met., Mexico, 1985, 88, Juan de Oyarzabal prof. physics, Mexico, 1993—95; vis. prof. chem. physics U. Pisa, Italy, 1989; vis. prof. Scoula Normale Superiore, Pisa, Italy, 1989; adj. prof. applied math. and physics U. Waterloo, 1969—85; mem. adv. bd. Chem. Abstracts Svc., 1981—83; vis. prof. chemistry, math, and physics U. Guelph, Canada, 1991; adj. prof. physics Utah State U., 1990—93; hon. prof. chemistry and math. U. Hong Kong, 1992—; hon. prof. molecular biophysics Rush Med. Sch., 2003—. Author: (book) Statistical Mechanics and Dynamics, 1964, Statistical Mechanics and Dynamics, 2d rev. edit., 1982, Stochastic Differential Equations in Science and Engineering, 2006; editor: Physical Chemistry - An Advanced Treatise, Vols. 1-15, 1966—75, Theoretical Chemistry-Advances and Perspectives, Vols. 1-5, 1975—81, Fundamentals of Inhomogeneous Fluids, 1992; editor: (assoc. editor) Jour. Chem. Physics, 1974—76; mem. editl. bd.:, 1990—92, bd. editors: Ultitas Mathematica, 1971—87, Jour. Phys. Chemistry, 1984—89, Jour. Chem. Phys., 1990—92, assoc. editor: Electrochimica Acta, 1991—99, Condensed Matter Physics, 2005—; contbr. articles to profl. jours. Vol. Loma Prieta Vol. Fire Dept., Los Gatos, Calif., 1983—89; missionary Ch. Jesus Christ Latter Day Saints, Africa, 1957—59. Recipient Johnathan Rodgers award, 1954, Bursary award, NRC of Can., 1956, Outstanding Rsch. Contbn. award, IBM, 1973, Outstanding Innovation award, 1987, Catedra Patrimoniales de Excelencia, Mex., 1993—95; fellow, Corning Glass Found., 1959, Alfred P. Sloan Found., 1964, 1966, Ian Potter Found., 1966, CSIRO Rsch., 1966, Guggenheim Found., 1997; scholar Univ. Great War, 1953, Daniel Buchanan, 1955, Burbridge, 1955. Fellow: Royal Soc. Chemistry, Am. Inst. Chemists, Inst. Physics, Am. Phys. Soc.; mem.: N.Y. Acad. Scis., Mex. Nat. Acad. Sci. (corr.), Math. Assn. Am., Am. Chem. Soc. (Joel Henry Hildebrand award 1999, Utah award 2005), Can. Assn. Physicists, Sigma Pi Sigma, Sigma Xi, Phi Kappa Phi. Democrat. Member Lds Ch. Achievements include statistical mechanics of liquids; co-developer first successful perturbation theory of liquids; statis. mechanics of surfaces and solid-fluid and liquid-vapor interfaces; structure and electronic properties of amorphous solids; theory of electric double layer; theory of selectivity and transport of ions in biological membranes. Office: Brigham Young U Dept Chemistry Provo UT 84602 Office Phone: 801-422-5934. Business E-Mail: doug@chem.byu.edu.

HENDERSON, FLORENCE, actress, singer; b. Dale, Ind., Feb. 14, 1934; d. Joseph and Elizabeth Elder H.; m. Ira Bernstein, Jan. 9, 1956 (div.); children: Barbara, Joey, Robert Norman, Elizabeth; m. John Kappas, Aug. 4, 1987. Attended, St. Francis Acad., Owensboro, Ky; studied at, Am. Acad. Dramatic Arts. Broadway and stage debut in Wish You Were Here, 1952; on tour in Oklahoma!, 1952-53, at N.Y.C. Ctr., 1953, Fanny, 1954, The Sound of Music, 1961, in revival of Annie Get Your Gun, 1974; appeared in The Great Waltz, Los Angeles Civic Light Opera Assn., 1953, on Broadway in The Girl Who Came to Supper, 1963, in revival of South Pacific, 1967, in revival The Sound of Music, Los Angeles Civic Light Opera Assn., 1978, Bells are Ringing, Los Angeles Civic Light Opera Assn., 1979; appeared in Oldsmobile indsl. shows, 1958-61; actress: (movies) Song of Norway, 1970, Shakes The Clown, 1991, Naked Gun 33 1/2: The Final Insult, 1994, The Brady Bunch Movie, 1995, Holy Man, 1998, Get Bruce, 1999, Venus & Vegas, 2007; appeared on TV in Sing Along, 1958, The Today Show, 1959-60, The Brady Bunch, 1969-74, The Brady Bunch Hour, 1977, The Brady Girls Get Married, 1981, A Very Brady Christmas, 1988, The Bradys, 1990, Fudge-A-Mania, 1995, (host) Bradymania, 1993; numerous other TV appearances include The Love Boat, 1976, 83, The Brady Brides, 1981, Hart to Hart, 1981, Fantasy Island, 1981, 83, Alice, 1983, Murder She Wrote, Dean Martin TV Series; hostess Country Kitchen; appeared in TV spl. Just a Regular Kid; guest appearances It's Garry Shandling's Show, Wil Shriner Show, Jay Leno Family Spl.; first female host of The Tonight Show; co-host: Later Today, 1999-2000; writings, A Little Cooking, A Little Talking, and A Whole Lotta Fun; films include: Speaking of Women's Health, Lifetime. Recipient Sarah Siddons award

HENDERSON, FRANK N., state legislator; b. Chgo., Dec. 6, 1922; m. Lillian; children: Deb, Steve, Jennifer, Tom, Jane. Attended, U. Idaho, 1943. Mayor City of Post Falls, Idaho; co. commr. Kootenal Co., Idaho; dir. mktg. Syntax Labs.; ret. pub., owner Post Falls Tribune Newspaper; mem. Dist. 5 Idaho House of Reps., Boise. Republican. Protestant. Office: Dist Office 362 S Ponderosa Loop Post Falls ID 83854 also: Legis Services Office PO Box 83270 Boise ID 83720-0054 Office Phone: 208-773-2269. Office Fax: 208-446-0673.*

HENDERSON, JAMES, JR., state legislator, political organization worker, consultant; b. Ganado, Ariz., May 16, 1942; m. Deborah Henderson; children: Valencia, Clarissa, Jaime Jamesina, Marcus. Cert. in career counseling, Utah State U., 1962. Employment svcs. mgr. Ariz. Dept. Econ. Security-Employment Svcs., Phoenix, 1968-74; vocat. devel. specialist Bur. Indian Affairs, Ft. Defiance, Ariz., 1974-77; dir. divsn. resources The Navajo Tribe, 1977-84, dir. office legis. affairs, 1986-90; senator State of Ariz., 1990-98; cons., 1998—. With U.S. Army, 1966-68. Decorated Purple Heart; recipient Feed My People Internat. award, 1990, Outstanding Svc. award Navajo Nat. Coun. Resolution, 1990, Chief Manuelito Appreciation award Navajo Tribal Coun. Democrat. Presbyterian. Avocations: boxing, football, wildlife, travel. Office: PO Box 4588 Window Rock AZ 86515-4588

HENDERSON, JOHN DREWS, architect; b. St. Louis, July 30, 1933; s. Russell Dewey and Hazel Agnes (Drews) H.; m. Barbara Lee Beckman, June 25, 1955; children: Susan Lee, John Beckman. BArch, U. Ill., 1956. Registered architect, Calif. With Delawie, Macy & Henderson, San Diego, Calif., 1966-77, Macy, Henderson & Cole, AIA, San Diego, 1977-86; pres. John D. Henderson, FAIA, 1986—. Mem. San Diego Hist. Sites Bd., 1972-78, Gaslamp Quarter Task Force, 1976-78, Gaslamp Quarter Coun., 1984-86; mem. City Mgr.'s Com. for Seismic Retrofit for Older Bldgs., 1986-92; mem. Hist. Am. Bldg. Survey, 1972078, chair, 1976-78; bd. dirs. Hist. Am. Bldgs. Survey Found., 1984-86; Calif. Hist. Bldgs. Code Safety Bd., 1976-96; apptd. by Gov. of Calif. to State Hist. Resources Commn., 1990-02, reapptd., 1994-98, 98-02, chmn. 1992-93, 2000-01, chmn. Calif. Heritage Fund com. 1993—2001; Calif. advisor Nat. Trust Hist. Preservation, 1975-78; bd. dirs. Gaslamp Quarter Found., 1984-86. Lt. USNR, 1956-59. With USN, 1956—59, with USNR, 1959—64. Recipient Hist. Preservation awards from City San Diego, San Diego Hist. Soc., San Diego chpt. and Calif. Coun. AIA, La Jolla Women's Club, Am. Assn. State and Local History, Am. Inst. Planners, Save Our Heritage Orgn., Rancho Santa Fe Assn., Calif. Preservation Found., Ctrl. City Assn., Gaslmp Quarter Assn. Fellow AIA (officer, dir. local chpt. 1969-73, chpt. pres. 1972, editor guidebooks 1970, 76, state bd. dirs. 1971-73, nat. hist. resources com. 1974-76, 78—, emeritus 2002, regional rep. 1976-78, mem. guidebook com., 2002); mem. San Diego Archtl. Found. (bd. dirs. 1984-86, 89-91, mid. 20th century modern com. 2004—), San Diego Hist. Soc. (officer, bd. dirs. 1975, pres. 1975), San Diego Geneal. Soc., San Diego History Campaign (exec. com. 1981-86), Clan Henderson Soc. Republican. Presbyterian. Office Phone: 858-272-0434. E-mail: jhende33@sbcglobal.net.

HENDERSON, PAUL, III, journalist, private investigator; b. Washington, Jan. 13, 1939; s. Paul and Doris Olive (Gale) Henderson; m. JoAnn Burnham, Sept. 10, 1964; children: Leslee, Jill, Polly Ann; m. Janet Marie Horne, Jan. 22, 1982; children: Peter Paul, Brady Thomas. Student, Wentworth Mil. Acad. Jr. Coll., Lexington, Mo., 1957—59, Creighton U., 1963, U. Nebr.-Omaha, 1964—67. Reporter Coun. Bluffs, Nonpareil, Iowa, 1962—66, Omaha World-Herald, 1966—67; investigative reporter Seattle Times, 1967—85; pvt. practice investigator Seattle, 1985. Featured investigator in (documentaries) Home Box Office Crime Documentary, 1986. Co-founder Seattle Forgotten Children's Fund, 1976. With US Army, 1959—62. Recipient 1st Place C.B. Blethen award, 1977, 1982, Pulitzer prize for spl. local reporting, 1982, 1st Place Roy W. Howard Pub. Svc. award, Scripps-Howard Found., 1982; named one of 50 Outstanding Achievers Am., Am. Acad. Achievement, 1982. Methodist. Office: PO Box 70 Seattle WA 98111-0070

HENDERSON, ROGENE FAULKNER, toxicologist, researcher; b. Breckenridge, Tex., July 13, 1933; d. Philander Molden and Lenoma (Rogers) F.; m. Thomas Richard Henderson II, May 30, 1957; children: Thomas Richard III, Edith Jeanette, Laura Lee. BSBA, Tex. Christian U., 1955; PhD, U. Tex., 1960. Diplomate Am. Bd. Toxicology. Research assoc. U. Ark. Sch. Med., Little Rock, 1960-67; from scientist to sr. scientist and group supr. chemistry and toxicology Lovelace Inhalation Toxicology Research Inst., Albuquerque, 1967—; deputy dir. Nat. Environ. Respiratory Ctr. Lovelace Respiratory Rsch. Inst., Albuquerque, 1998—. Mem. adv. com. Burroughs Wellcome Toxicology Scholar award, 1987-89, NIH toxicology study sect., 1982-86, Nat. Inst. Environ. Health Scis. adv. coun., 1992-95, EPA scientific adv. bd. environ. health commn., 1991-95; mem. bd. sci. counselors EPA, 2002—; mem. Com to Assess the Sci. Base for Tobacco Harm Reduction, adv. group Am. Cancer Soc.on Cancer and the Environment, 1999—, Health Effects Inst. Rsch. Com., 1997—; vice chmn. US Environ. protection Agy. Bd. of Sci. Counselors, 2001—; chmn. clean air sci. adv. com. U.S. EPA, 2004—. Assoc. editor Toxicology Applied Pharmacology, 1989-95, Jour. Exposure Analysis and Environ. Epidemiology, 1991-95; contbr. articles to profl. jours. Named Woman on the Move YWCA, Albuquerque, 1985; grantee NIH, 1958-60, 1960-62, 1986—. Mem. AAAS, NAS (com. toxicology 1985-98, chair 1992-98, 2005-2006, com. epidemiology of air pollution 1983-85, com. biol. markers 1986—, com. on risk assessment methodology 1989-92, bd. environ. studies and toxicology 1998-2004, com. health effects of trichlosoethylene), Am. Chem. Soc. (chmn. ctrl. N.Mex. sect. 1981), Soc. Toxicology (pres. Mountain-West Regional chpt. 1985-86, pres. inhalation specialty sect. 1989—), N.Y. Acad. Scis., Nat. Acad. (nat. assoc.) Presbyterian. Home: 5609 Don Felipe Ct SW Albuquerque NM 87105-6765 Office: Lovelace Respiratory Rsch Inst 2425 Ridgecrest Ave SE Albuquerque NM 87108 Office Phone: 505-348-9464. Business E-Mail: rhenders@lrri.org.

HENDERSON, THELTON EUGENE, federal judge; b. Shreveport, La., Nov. 28, 1933; s. Eugene M. and Wanzie (Roberts) H.; 1 son, Geoffrey A. BA, U. Calif.-, Berkeley, 1956, JD, 1962. Bar: Calif. 1962. Social case worker County of Los Angeles, 1958; jr. rsch. scientist Sys. Devel. Corp., Santa Monica, Calif., 1958—59; atty. U.S. Dept. Justice, 1962-63; assoc. firm FitzSimmons & Petris, 1964, assoc., 1964-66; directing atty. San Mateo County (Calif.) Legal Aid Soc., 1966-69; asst. dean Stanford (Calif.) U. Law Sch., 1968-76; ptnr. firm Rosen, Remcho & Henderson, San Francisco, 1977-80; judge U.S. Dist. Ct. (no. dist.) Calif., San Francisco, 1980-90, 98—, chief judge, 1990-97. Asso. prof. Sch. Law, Golden Gate U., San Francisco, 1978-80 Bd. mem. Rosenberg Found. Served with U.S. Army, 1956-58. Recipient Bernard Witkin Medal, State Bar of Calif., 2004, Pearlstein Civil Rights award, Anti-Defamation League. Bd. mem. Am. Inns of Ct. (Professionalism award, 9th cir., mem. exec. com. Edward J. McFetridge Inn of Ct.); mem. ABA, Am. Law Inst., Fed. Judges Assn., Nat. Bar Assn. (Disting. Svc. award), Charles Houston Law Assn. Office: US Dist Ct US Courthouse PO Box 36060 San Francisco CA 94102

HENDERSON, VICTOR WARREN, behavioral and geriatric neurologist, epidemiologist, researcher, educator; s. Philip and Jean (Edsel) H.; m. Barbara Curtiss; children: Gregory, Geoffrey, Stephanie, Nicole. BS, U. Ga., 1972; MD, Johns Hopkins U., 1976; MS, U. Wash., 1996. Diplomate Am. Bd. Psychiatry and Neurology, 1981, United Coun. Neurologic Subspecialties, 2006. Intern Duke U., Durham, NC, 1976—77; resident Washington U., St. Louis, 1977—80; fellow Boston U., 1980—81; asst. prof. neurology U. So. Calif., LA, 1981—86, assoc. prof. neurology, gerontology and psychology, 1986—93, prof. neurology, gerontology and psychology, 1993—2001, chief divsn. cognitive neurosci. & neurogerontology, 1989—2001, Kenneth and Bette Volk prof. neurology, 1999—2001; prof. geriat., neurology, pharmacology and epidemiology U. Ark. Med. Scis., Little Rock, 2001—04, vice chair dept. geriat., 2001—04; prof. health rsch. and policy and neurology and neurological scis. Stanford U., 2004—, dir. grad. program in epidemiology, 2004—. Dir. NIH Alzheimer's Disease Rsch. Ctr. Clin. Core, 1985—2001, Rural Aging and Memory Study, 2001—04; dir. neurobehavior Clinic/Bowles Ctr. for Alzheimer's and Related Diseases, 1988—2001; chair neurology dept. Los Angeles County/U. So. Calif. Med. Ctr., 1992—97; vis. scientist MIT, 1988—89; vis. prof. U. Melbourne, 2002; co-dir. State of Calif. Alzheimer's Disease Rsch. Ctr. U. So. Calif., 1999—2001, NIH Alzheimer's Disease Ctr., 2001—03; Kearney vis. prof. Mental Health Rsch. Inst. Victoria, Australia, 2002; prof. fellow dept. psychiatry U. Melbourne, 2003—; assoc. chief of staff geriat. and extended care Ctrl. Ark. Vets. Healthcare Sys., 2003—04; lectr. and spkr. in field. Author: (with others) Principles of Neurologic Diagnosis, 1985, Hormone Therapy and the Brain, 2000; mem. editl. bd. profl. jours.; contbr. articles to profl. jours. Recipient Simons Lecture, Alzheimer's Assn. (Boston chpt.), 1995, Solvay Lecture, British Menopause Soc., 1997, Rsch. award, Alzheimer's Assn. (LA chpt.), 1998, Faculty Recognition award, Phi Kappa Phi, 2001, Vis. Rsch. Scholars award, U. Melbourne Collaborative Research Program, 2002; grantee, Alzheimer's Assn., Calif. Dept. Health Svcs., Adminstrn. on Aging, NIH, French Found., 1984—. Fellow: Am. Acad. Neurology (chair, geriatric neurology sect. 2008—, Lawrence McHenry award 2007); mem.: Soc. Epidemiologic Rsch., N.Am. Menopause Soc. (trustee 2002—, pres. 2007—08), French Found. Alzheimer Rsch., Nat. Aphasia Assn., Internat. Menopause Soc. (treas., Coun. Affiliated Menopause Socs. 2008—), Soc. for Behavioral and Cognitive Neurology, Gerontol. Soc. Am., Am. Neurol. Assn. Office: Stanford U Sch Medicine 259 Campus Dr HRP Redwood Bldg Stanford CA 94305-5405

HENDREN, ROBERT LEE, JR., academic administrator; b. Reno, Oct. 10, 1925; s. Robert Lee and Aleen (Hill) H.; m. Merlyn Churchill, June 14, 1947; children: Robert Lee IV, Anne Aleen. BA magna cum laude, Coll. Idaho, LLD (hon.); postgrad., Army Univ. Ctr., Oahu, Hawaii. Owner, pres. Hendren's Inc., 1947—; pres. Albertson Coll. Idaho, Caldwell, 1987—. Bd. dirs. 1st Interstate Bank Idaho. Trustee Boise (Idaho) Ind. Sch. Dist., chmn. bd. trustees, 1966; chmn. bd. trustees Coll. Idaho, 1980-84; bd. dirs. Mountain View coun. Boy Scouts Am., Boise Retail Merchants, Boise Valley Indsl. Found., Boise Redevel. Agy., Ada County Marriage Counseling, Ada County Planning and Zoning Com.; chmn. bd. Blue Cross Idaho. Recipient Silver and Gold award U. Idaho, Nat. award Sigma Chi. Mem. Boise C. of C. (pres., bd. dirs.), Idaho Sch. Trustees Assn., Masons, KT, Shriners, Rotary (Paul Harris fellow). Home: 3504 Hillcrest Dr Boise ID 83705-4503 Office: Albertson Coll Idaho 2112 Cleveland Blvd Caldwell ID 83605-4432

HENDRICK, HAL WILMANS, human factors educator; b. Dallas, Mar. 11, 1933; s. Harold Eugene and Audrey Sarah (Wilmans) H.; m. Mary Francis Boyle; children: Hal L., David A., John A. (dec.), Jennifer G. BA, Ohio Wesleyan U., 1955; MS, Purdue U., 1961, PhD, 1966. Cert. profl. ergonomist; bd. cert. forensic examiner. Asst. prof. U. So. Calif., LA, assoc. prof., 1979-86; exec. dir. Inst. of Safety and Systems Mgmt., U. So. Calif., LA, 1986-87; prof., dean Coll. of System Sci., U. Denver, 1987-90; prof. U. So. Calif., 1986-95, prof. emeritus LA, 1995—; prin. Hendrick and Assocs., Greenwood Village, Colo., 1996—2004; pres. Found. for Profl. Ergonomics, Highlands Ranch, Colo., 2004—07. Pres. Bd. Cert. in Profl. Ergonomics, 1992-94. Author: Behavioral Research and Analysis, 1980, 2d edit., 1989, 3rd edit., 1990, Good Ergomomics is Good Economics, 1996, Macroergonomics: An Introduction to Work System Design, 2001, Human Factors Issues in Handgun Safety and Forensics, 2007; editor 11 books; contbr. articles to profl. jours. Lt. col. USAF, 1956-76. Fellow APA, Am. Psychol. Soc., Human Factors Ergonomics Soc. (pres. L.A. chpt. 1986-87, 95-96, pres. Rocky Mountain chpt. 1989-90, pres. 1995-96), Internat. Ergonomics Assn. (pres. Geneva 1990-94, sec. gen. 1987-89, exec. com. 1984—2000, U.S. rep. 1981-87); mem. Ergonomics Soc. (U.K.), Soc. for Indsl. and Orgnl. Psychology. Democrat. Avocations: travel, camping, hiking, reading, fishing. Home and Office: 2901 Fairway View Ct Castle Rock CO 80108 Office Phone: 303-929-9996. Personal E-mail: hhendrick@aol.com.

HENDRICK, IRVING GUILFORD, education educator; b. LA, Aug. 30, 1936; s. Guilford and Ingeborg Johanna (Eid) H.; m. Sandra Lee Scheer, Aug. 16, 1958 (dec. Aug. 1994); children: Julie Lynn, Maralene Ayn, Stephanie Lee; m. Linda DeSoucey Scott, 1996; stepchildren: Denise Levesque, Eve Scott. AB, Whittier Coll., 1958, MA, 1960; EdD with honors, UCLA, 1964. Asst. prof. edn. U. Mich., Flint, 1964-65, U. Calif., Riverside, 1965-69, assoc. prof. edn., 1969-75, prof. edn., 1975—, chair dept. edn., 1970-75, assoc. dean Sch. of Edn., 1975-83, dean Sch. of Edn., 1987-98, asst. vice chancellor of devel., 1998—, dean emeritus. Mem. com. on planning & budget U. Calif. Sys., 1985-87, vice-chair com. on planning & budget, 1986-87, chair subcom. on pvt. devel. activities, 1986-87, chair, 1987-88; mem. subject A com. U. Calif.-Riverside, 1966-68, vice-chair con. on ednl. policy, 1972-73, mem. com. on courses, 1969-71, chair, 1972-73, mem. com. on coms., 1973-74, mem. acad. planning com., 1973-75, chair acad. planning com., 1974-75, mem. budget com. resources sect., 1984-87, chair budget com. resources sect. 1984-87, mem. adv. com., 1974-75, 85-87, mem. highlander awards com., 1967-71, search com. for dean of grad. divsn., 1974, chair com. on faculty devel., 1977-78, learning handicapped credential programs, 1984—, chair exec. vice chancellor search com., 1985, acad. program planning rev. bd. sub-com. on organized rsch., 1986, pres.'s com. on profl. edn., 1988-89, pres.'s budget adv. com., 1987, chair adv. com. on instrnl. tech., 1994—; chancellor's rep. citizen's adv. com. Univ. Area Comty. Plan, Riverside, 1982-83; profl. day spkr. Internat. Sch. Theology, 1985; adv. com. assembly com. on econ. devel. and new techs. State of Calif., 1983-85; proposal reviewer intermediate sch. coll. readiness program Calif. State U., 1986; chair campaign com. to re-elect Dale Holmes County Supt. of Schs., Riverside County, 1990; cons. Riverside County Commn. on Future of Edn., 1993; mem. com. accreditation Calif. Commn. on Tchr. Credentialing, 1995-90, chair, co-chair, 1995-97; presenter papers at numerous profl. meetings. Author: Academic Revolution in California, 1968, Development of a School Integration Plan in Riverside, California: A Hisotry and Perspective, 1968, Public Policy Toward the Education of Non-white Minority Group Children in California, 1848-1970, 1975, The Education of Non-Whites in California, 1848-1970, 1977, California Educations, 1980; co-editor: (with Reginald L. Jones) Student Dissent in the Schools, 1972; contbr. articles to profl. jours.; contbr. book revs. to profl. jours. including History of Edn. Quar., Pacific Hist. Rev., Calif. History, So. Calif. Quar., Jour. Ednl. Adminstrn. and History. Mem. Am. Ednl. Rsch. Assn. (divsn. F editl. com. 1981-82, co-chair divsn. F program ann. program com. 1983-85, chair nominating com. divsn. F 1977, 79, sec. divsn. F 1976-78), Am. Hist. Assn. (Pacific Coast br.), Calif. Coun. on Edn. of Tchrs. (bd. dirs. 1989-93, chair programs com. fall 1991 conf.), Coun. for Exceptional Children (com. on history of individual differences 1985, cons. on oral history project, guest reviewer of manuscripts), History of Edn. Soc. (program com. 1986, nominating com. 1981-82), Nat. Soc. for Study of Edn. (com. on expansion of soc. activities 1972), Pacific Coast History of Edn. Soc. (program chair 1985), So. Assn. of Schs. and Colls. (sr. coll. commn., on-site visitation com. Walden U. 1980), Western Assn. Schs. and Colls. (sr. coll. commn., on-site visitation com. mem. various univs.), Phi Delta Kappa (historian, mem. exec. com. Riverside chpt. 1976-78). Democrat. Lutheran. Achievements include research in history of education, specifically the history of teacher education and education of minority groups, as well as extension of public school's mission to include responsibility for education and training of learning disabled and mentally retarded children. Office: U Calif Sch Edn Riverside CA 92521-0001 E-mail: irving.hendrick@ucr.edu.

HENDRICK, JAMES T., lawyer; b. Fostoria, Ohio, Mar. 21, 1942; BA with honors and distinction in econs., U. Ill., 1963; JD, Harvard U., 1967. Bar: Ill. 1967, Calif. 1970. Ptnr. Thelen, Reid & Priest (formerly known as Thelen, Marrin, Johnson & Bridges), San Francisco, 1978—. Lt. USN JAG, 1968-71. Mem. ABA. Office: Thelen Reid & Priest 101 2nd St Ste 1800 San Francisco CA 94105-3659 Office Phone: 415-371-1200.

HENDRICK, RONALD LYNN, controller; b. Pontiac, Mich., Mar. 2, 1946; s. James B. and Iva L. (Bostic) H.; m. Terri L. Kellstrom, Nov. 28, 1970; children: Brad, Scott, Tyler. BA in Acctg., Mich. State U., 1969; MBA in Fin., U. Colo., Boulder, 1972. CPA, Colo. Staff acct. Arthur Young & Co., Detroit, 1969-71; controller, treas. Myers and Co./Coors Packaging Co., Boulder, 1972-76; group v.p., treas. Coors Distbg. Co., Denver, 1976-83; v.p., treas. Life Care Svcs., Inc., Boulder, 1983-84; pres. Advantage Health Systems, Golden, Colo., 1984-87; dir. treasury mgmt. Adolph Coors Co., Golden, 1987-89, v.p., corp. contr., asst. sec., 1989—. Bd. dirs. World Trade Ctr. Mem. investment, audit and ops. coms. U. Colo. Found., Boulder, 1989—. With U.S. Army Res., 1969-75. Mem. AICPA, Nat. Assn. Accts., Nat. Investor Rels. Inst., Fin. Execs. Inst. Office: Heska Corp 1613 Prospect Pkwy Fort Collins CO 80525

HENDRICKSON, ANITA ELIZABETH, biology professor; b. LaCross, Wis., Feb. 20, 1936; d. Walter V. and Alno (Larkin) Schnell; m. Morris N. Hendrickson, June 8, 1957; children: Lisa, Karin, Gordon. BA, Pacific Luth. Coll., 1957; PhD, U. Wash., Seattle, 1964. Instr. anatomy Northwestern Med. Sch., Chgo., 1964-65; rsch. assoc. Children's Meml. Hosp., Chgo., 1964-65; rsch. instr. dept. biol. structure U. Wash., Seattle, 1965-67, instr. dept. ophthalmology, 1967-69, asst. prof. dept. ophthalmology, 1969-73; affiliate/assoc. prof. dept. ophthalmology Reg. Primate Ctr./U. Wash., 1972—, 1973-81; affiliate Child Devel. & Mental Retardation Ctr., U. Wash., 1975; prof. dept. opthalmology U. Wash., 1981-97, prof. dept. biol. structure, 1984—, chair dept. biol. structure, 1994—, adj. prof. ophthalmology, 1997—. Vis. assoc. prof. neuropathology Harvard Med. Sch., Boston, 1975-76; adj. assoc. prof. dept. psychology U. Wash., 1975-78; mem. NIH VisB study section, 1976-80. Editorial bd. Jour. of Neurosci., 1982-88, Investigative Ophthalmology, 1977-82, Vision Research, 1990-95; contbr. articles to profl. jours. Dolly Green rsch. grantee, 1981; named Alumnus of the Yr., Pacific Luth. U., 1982. Mem. AAAS, Am. Assn. Anatomists, Soc. for Neurosci. (mem. nat. coun. 1982-86), Internat. Soc. for Eye Rsch., Assn. for Rsch. in Vision and Ophthalmology (prog. chmn. 1983-84, trustee 1993—), Cajal Club. Home: 1029C NE 120th St Seattle WA 98125-5003 Office: U Washington Dept Biol Structure Box 357420 Seattle WA 98195-7420

HENDRICKSON, D. JOHN, lawyer; b. Berkeley, Calif., July 16, 1955; BA with distinction, Stanford U., 1977; JD cum laude, Pepperdine U., 1981. Bar: Calif. 1981, Tenn. 1996, US Ct. Appeals, 9th Cir., US Dist. Ct., Ctrl. Dist Calif., US Supreme Ct. Ptnr. Katten Muchin Zavis Rosenman, LA. Instr. Inst. of Advanced Advertising Studies; adj. assoc. prof. Southwestern U. Sch. Law. Mem.: State Bar Tenn., State Bar Calif. (mem. Bus. Law Sect.), LA County Bar Assn.

HENDRICKX, ANDREW GEORGE, research physiologist; b. Butler, Minn., July 14, 1933; BS in Biology, Concordia Coll., Minn., 1959; MS, Kans. State U., 1961, PhD in Zoology, 1963. Head sect. embryology S.W Found., San Antonio, 1964—68, assoc. scientist, chmn., 1969; assoc. rsch. physiologist Calif. Primate Rsch. Ctr., Davis, 1969—73, rsch. physiologist, 1973—, assoc. dir., 1978—97, dir., 1987—; prof. Sch. Medicine U. Calif.-Davis, 1971—; adviser WHO, 1977. Author: (book) Embryology of the Baboon, 1971; contbr. numerous articles to profl. jours. With US Army, 1953—55. Recipient Disting. Alumni award, Concordia Coll., 1977; NDEA scholar, 1959—62. Mem.: AAUP, Internat. Soc. Primatologists, Am. Assn. Anatomists, Am. Soc. Primatologists (pres. 1982—84), Teratology Soc. (sec. 1979—83, pres. 1987). Office: U Calif Calif Primate Rsch Ctr Davis CA 95616

HENDRIX, LAURIN, state legislator; b. June 8, 1959; married; 5 children. BS, U. Calif. Self employed Stradlings Fine Cabinetry; mem. Dist. 22 Ariz. House of Reps., 2008—. Republican. Office: Capitol Complex 1700 W Washington Rm 344 Phoenix AZ 85007-2890 Office Phone: 602-926-5735. Office Fax: 602-417-3122. Business E-Mail: lhendrix@azleg.gov.*

HENDRIX, LYNN PARKER, lawyer; b. McCook, Nebr., Apr. 24, 1951; s. Jack Hall and Betty Lee (Parker) H.; m. Theresa Louise Zabawa, June 19, 1976; children: Paige Ashley, Parker Jerome, Pierce Reid. BSEE, U. Nebr., 1973, JD with distinction, 1978. Bar: Nebr. 1978, U.S. Dist. Ct. Nebr. 1978, Colo. 1979, U.S. Dist. Ct. Colo. 1979, U.S. Ct. Appeals (10th cir.) 1993, Wyo. 1993, Mont. 1995, N.Y., 2000, U.S. Patent Office, 1994, U.S. Supreme Ct. 2004. Surveyor Nebr. Dept. Roads, McCook, 1973; constrn. adminstr. Commonwealth Electric Co., Lincoln, Nebr., 1974, cons. engr., 1975; instr. U. Nebr., Lincoln, 1974-75; law clk. Nebr. Atty.-Gen., Lincoln, 1976-77; assoc. Holme Roberts & Owen, LLP, Denver, 1978-83, ptnr., 1984—. Trustee, treas., v.p. Rocky Mountain Min. Law Found., pres., 2006—. Editor-in-chief Nebr. Law Rev., 1977-78, exec. editor, 1976-77; contbr. articles to profl. jours. Sec., bd. dirs. Girls Club Denver, 1984-90, Girls Inc. Metro Denver, 1992—, Remember Found., 2004 Named Adm., Nebr. Navy. Mem. ABA, Colo. Bar Assn., Mont. Bar Assn., Nebr. Bar Assn., Wyo. Bar Assn., N.Y. Bar Assn., S.E. Law Club (pres. 1990-91), Meridian Golf Club, Sigma Alpha Epsilon, Tau Beta Pi, Sigma Tau (pres.), Eta Kappa Nu. Home: 8125 S Glencoe Ct Centennial CO 80122-3876 Office: Holme Roberts & Owen LLP 1700 Lincoln St Ste 4100 Denver CO 80203-4541

HENEL, CAROLYN E., lawyer; BA, Yale U., 1992; JD, U. Va., 1996. Bar: Calif. 1996, cert.: State Bar Calif. Bd. Legal Specialization (estate planning, trust and probate law). Assoc. Crosby, Heafey, Roach

& May, 1996—2002; ptnr. Roisman Henel, LLP, Oakland, Calif., 2002—. Mem. profl. adv. com. East Bay Cmty. Found. Named a No. Calif. Super Lawyer, Law & Politics and San Francisco Mag., 2004, 2005, 2006; named one of Top 100 Attys., Worth mag., 2006. Mem.: ABA, East Bay Tax Club, Estate Planning Coun. East Bay, Alameda County Bar Assn. (chair estate planning com. 2005, 2006), East Bay Regional Pks. Found. (v.p. bd. dirs. 2006). Office: Roisman Henel LLP 1999 Harrison St Ste 1400 Oakland CA 94612 Office Phone: 510-466-6000. Office Fax: 510-466-6040. E-mail: ehenel@roismanhenel.com.

HENG, DONALD JAMES, JR., lawyer; b. Mpls., July 12, 1944; s. Donald James and Catharine Amelia (Strom) H.; m. Kathleen Ann Bailey, Sept. 2, 1967; 1 child, Francesca Remy BA cum laude, Yale U., 1967; JD magna cum laude, Minn., 1971. Bar: Calif. 1971, U.S. Dist. Ct. (no. dist.) Calif. 1971, U.S. Ct. Appeals (9th cir.) 1971. Assoc. Brobeck, Phleger & Harrison, San Francisco, 1971-73, ptnr., 1978-90; atty.-adviser Office Internat. Tax Counsel, Dept. Treasury, Washington, 1973-75; pvt. practice law San Francisco, 1990—. Lectr., writer on tax-related subjects Note and comment editor Minn. Law Rev., 1970-71 Co-recipient award for outstanding performance Am. Lawyer Mag., 1981; Fulbright scholar, Italy, 1967-68 Mem. ABA, Calif. Bar Assn., Oakland Mus. Assn. (pres. 1985-87, bd. dirs. 1983-89), Mus. Soc. San Francisco, Fine Arts Mus. (bd. dirs. 1989-90), Order Coif. Republican. Congregationalist.

HENGSTLER, GARY ARDELL, publisher, editor, lawyer; b. Wapakoneta, Ohio, Mar. 23, 1947; s. Luther C. and N. Delphine (Sims) H.; m. Linda K. Spreen, Mar. 8, 1969 (div. Aug. 1986); children: Dylan A., Joel S.; m. Laura M. Williams, Dec. 15, 1986. BS, Ball State U., 1969; JD, Cleve. State U., 1983. Bar: Ohio 1984, U.S. Dist. Ct. (no. dist.) Ohio 1984, Nev. 2005. Assoc. Blaszak, Schilling, Coey & Bennett, Elyria, Ohio, 1984-85; editor The Tex. Lawyer, Austin, 1985-86; news editor ABA Jour., Chgo., 1986-89, editor, pub., 1989-2000; dir. Donald W. Reynolds Nat. Ctr. Cts. & Media, Reno, 2000—. Contbr. articles to profl. jours. Home: 5055 Carnoustie Dr Reno NV 89502-9724 Office: Donald W Reynolds Nat Ctr Cts & Media U Nev Jud Coll Bldg 358 Reno NV 89557-0001 Home Phone: 775-856-3532; Office Phone: 775-327-8270. Office Fax: 775-327-2160. Business E-Mail: hengstler@unr.edu.

HENLEY, DALE C., grocery company executive; b. Mt. Vernon, Wash., 1946; V.p. Trillium Corp., Bellingham, Wash.; mng. ptnr. Metcalf, Hodges & Co., Bellingham; sr. v.p., CFO, Haggen Inc., Bellingham, 1984-96, pres., CEO, 1996—. Office: Haggen Inc 2211 Rimland Dr Bellingham WA 98226-5664 Fax: 360-650-8235.

HENLEY, DON, singer, drummer, songwriter; b. Linden, Tex., July 22, 1947; m. Sharon Summerall, May 20, 1995; 3 children. Founding mem., drummer Eagles, 1971—. Musician (with Eagles): (albums) Eagles, 1972, Desperado, 1973, On the Border, 1974, One These Nights, 1975, Hotel California, 1976 (VH1's 100 Greatest Albums, 2001), The Long Run, 1979, Eagles Live, 1980, Hell Freezes Over, 1994 (Am. Music award, Favorite Rock Album, 1996), Long Road Out of Eden, 2007, (songs) Take it Easy, Lyin' Eyes (Grammy award, Best Group Pop Vocal Performance, 1976), Hotel California (Grammy award, Record of Yr., 1978, VH1's 100 Greatest Rock Songs, 2000, Rolling Stone & MTV's 100 Greatest Pop Songs, 2000), New Kid in Town (Grammy award, Best Arrangement for Voices, 1978), Heartache Tonight (Grammy award, Best Group Rock Vocal Peformance, 1980), How Long (Grammy award, Best Group Vocal Country Performance, 2008); musician: (with Eagles) I Dreamed There Was No War, 2007 (Grammy award for Best Pop Instrumental Performance, 2009); musician: (solo) (albums) I Can't Stand Still, 1982, Building the Perfect Beast, 1985, The End of Innocence, 1989 (Grammy award, Best Male Rock Vocal Performance, 1990), Actual Miles: Henley's Greatest Hits, 1995, Inside Job, 2000, (songs) The Boys of Summer, 1985 (Grammy award, Best Male Rock Vocal Performance, 1986), Dirty Laundry, 1982. Mem. Active So. Poverty Law Ctr., Walden Woods Project. Recipient Favorite Rock Group award, Am. Music Awards, 1981, 1996, Favorite Adult Contemporary Artist award, 1996, Favorite Rock Album award, 1996; named MusiCares Person of Yr., 2007; named one of Greatest Artists of Rock & Roll, VH1, 1998, 100 Greatest Artists of All Time, Rolling Stone, 2004; named to Songwriters' Hall of Fame, 2000. Office: c/o Azoffmusic Mgmt 1100 Glendon Ave #2000 Los Angeles CA 90024*

HENLEY, ERNEST MARK, physics professor, retired dean; b. Frankfurt, Germany, June 10, 1924; came to U.S., 1939, naturalized, 1944; s. Fred S. and Josy (Dreyfuss) H.; m. Elaine Dimitman, Aug. 21, 1948; children: M. Bradford, Karen M. BEE, CCNY, 1944; PhD, U. Calif., Berkeley, 1952; DSc (hon.), Ohio State U., 2004, Justus Liebig U., Germany, 2005. Physicist Lawrence Radiation Lab., 1950-51; research assoc. physics dept. Stanford U., 1951-52; lectr. physics Columbia U., 1952-54; mem. faculty U. Wash., Seattle, 1954—, prof. physics, 1961-95; prof. emeritus, 1995—; chmn. dept. U. Wash., 1973-76, dean Coll. Arts and Scis., 1979-87, dir. Inst. for Nuclear Theory, 1990-91; assoc. dir. Inst. for Nuclear Theory U. Wash., 1991—2006. Chmn. Nuclear Sci. Adv. Com., 1986-89. Author: (with W. Thirring) Elementary Quantum Field Theory, 1962, (with H. Frauenfelder) Subatomic Physics, 1974, 3rd edit., 2007, Nuclear and Particle Physics, 1975; mng. editor Internat. Jour. Modern Physics, 1992-; contbr. articles to profl. jours. Bd. dirs. Pacific Sci. Ctr., 1984-87, Wash. Tech. Ctr., 1983-87; trustee Associated Univs., Inc., 1989—, chmn. bd., 1993-96. Recipient Sr. Alexander von Humboldt award, 1984, T.W. Bonner prize Am. Physics Soc., 1989, Townsend Harris medal CCNY, 1989; F.B. Jewett fellow, 1952-53, Sr. fellow NSF, 1958-59, Guggenheim fellow, 1967-68, Sr. fellow NATO, 1976-77. Fellow AAAS (chmn. physics sect. 1989-90), Am. Phys. Soc. (chmn. divsn. nuclear physics 1979-80, pres. 1992, sec. treas. NW sect. 1999-2005, chair NW sect. 2007-08, Disting. Svc. award 2004), Am. Acad. Arts and Scis. 2008; mem. NAS (chmn. physics sect. 1998-2001), Sigma Xi. Achievements include research in symmetries, nuclear reactions, weak interactions and high energy particle interactions. Office: Univ Wash Physics Dept PO Box 351560 Seattle WA 98195-1560 Office Phone: 206-543-2896. Business E-Mail: henley@phys.washington.edu.

HENLEY, JEFFREY O., computer software company executive; b. Phoenix, Nov. 6, 1948; s. Justin Oniel and Jane Ellen (Rice) H.; children: Amy, Julie, Todd. BA in Econs., U. Calif., Santa Barbara, 1966; MBA in Fin., UCLA, 1967. Cost acctg. supr. Hughes Aircraft Co., Culver City, Calif., 1967-70; divsn. contr. Tridair Industries, Redondo Beach, Calif., 1970-72; divsn. contr. internat. ops. Fairchild Camera & Instrument, Mountain View, Calif., 1972-75; dir. fin. Memorex Corp., Santa Clara, Calif., 1975-79; v.p., contr. Saga Corp, Menlo Park, Calif., 1979-86, exec. v.p., CFO, 1986-91, Pacific Holding Co., Menlo Park, Calif., 1986—91, Oracle Corp., Redwood City, Calif., 1991—2004, chmn., 2004—, mem. exec. mgmt. com. Bd. dirs. Oracle Corp., 1995—, CallWave, Inc., 2004—. Bd. dirs. Herbert Hoover Boys' & Girls' Club, Menlo Park, Calif., 1983, pres., 1984; chmn. Mid-Pacific Region Trustees for Boys & Girls Club of Am. Recipient Outstanding Alumnus award, UCLA, 2004. Mem. Fin. Exec. Inst., Sigma Phi Epsilon. Republican. Presbyterian. Avocations: golf, running. Office: Oracle Corp 500 Oracle Pky Redwood Shores CA 94065-1675

HENNENHOEFER, JAMES A., lawyer; b. St. Louis, July 19, 1941; BS, U. Mo., 1963; JD, Western State U., San Diego, 1970. Bar: Calif. 1971, US Dist. Ct. (so. dist. Calif.) 1971, US Supreme Ct. 1974. Atty. James A. Hennenhoefer, Inc., Vista, Calif., 1971—. Lectr. family law Calif. Continuing Edn. of the Bar, 1978—; judge pro tempore San Diego County Superior Ct., 1975—. Trustee San Diego County Law Libr., 1999—2002. Comdr. USNR. Recipient Norby Judiciary award, Best Family Law Atty., San Diego County, 1999. Mem.: Inns of Ct. (master 1998—2003), Am. Coll. Family Trial Lawyers, Internat. Acad. Matrimonial Lawyers (bd. govs. 1995—98, 2002—06), San Diego County Assn. Cert. Specialists, Am. Acad. Matrimonial Lawyers (chmn. mktg. com. 1990—98, pres. so. Calif. chpt. 1993—94, pres.-elect 2001—03, pres. 2003—05, So. Calif. Family Law Person of Yr. 1998), State Bar Calif. (chmn. exec. com. in family law sect. 1994—95, family law edn. chair 1991—93, chmn. coun. sect. chairs 1997), ABA (chmn. pub. rels. com. in family law sect. 1993—94), North San Diego County Bar Assn. (dir. 1984—87). Office: James A Hennenhoefer PC 316 S Melrose Dr Ste 200 Vista CA 92083-6618 Office Phone: 760-941-2260. Office Fax: 760-945-1805. E-mail: jahesq@aol.com.

HENNESSY, JOHN L., academic administrator; b. NYC, Sept. 22, 1952; m. Andrea Hennessy; children: Thomas, Christopher. B in Engring. in Elec. Engring., Villanova U., 1973; MS in Computer Sci., SUNY, Stony Brook, 1975, PhD in Computer Sci., 1977, DSc (hon.), 2001; DHL (hon.), Villanova U., 2001; doctorate (hon.), Universitat Politecnica de Catalunya, 2002, Ecole Polytechnique Federale de Lausanne, 2003. Asst. prof. elec. engring. Stanford U., Calif., 1977—83, assoc. prof. elec. engring., 1983—86, dir., computer rsch. lab., 1983—93, prof. elec. engring. and computer sci., 1986—, Willard and Inez Kerr Bell Endowed Prof. Elec. Engring. and Computer Sci., 1987—2001, chmn. dept. computer sci., 1994—96, dean Sch. Engring., 1996—99, provost, 1999—2000, pres., 2000—. Founder, chief scientist MIPS Computer Sys., 1984—92; chief arch. Silicon Graphics Computer Sys., 1992—98; founder MIPS Techs. (formerly MIPS Computer Sys.), 1998—; chmn. bd. dirs. T-span; mem. com. study internat. devels. in computer sci. and tech. NRC, 1988, mem. computer sci. and tech. bd., 1989—94, mem. com. study acad. careers for exptl. computer scientists, 1992—93, mem. status and direction of high performance computing and comm. initiative, 1995, mem. commn. phys. scis., math. and applications, 1998—99; mem. adv. com. computer and info. sci. and engring. NSF, 1992—96, chair oversight rev. of computer and info. sci. and engring. instnl. infrastructure program, 1992, mem. task force on future supercomputer ctrs. program, 95; tech. adv. bd. Microsoft Corp., 1992—96, Virtual Machine Works, 1995—96, Tensilica, 1998—99; strategic adv. bd. NetPower, 1992—95; mem. fellowship sel. com. Sloan Found., 1993—96; chmn. info. sci. and tech. Def. Advances Rsch. Projects Found., 1993—96, chair, 1994—95; mem. com. study investment strategy DARPA Def. Sci. Bd., 1998—99; mem. various conf. coms.; spkr. in field; bd. dirs. Alantec Corp., 1995—96, Cisco Systems, 2002—; chmn., bd. dirs. Atheros, 1998—. Co-author (with D.A. Patterson): Computer Organization and Design: The Hardware/Software Interface, 1993, Computer Organization and Design: The Hardware/Software Interface, 2d edit., 1998; co-author: Computer Architecture: A Quantitative Approach, 1990; contbr. articles to profl. jours. Recipient Disting. Alumnus award, SUNY, Stony Brook, 1991, John J. Gallen Memorial award, Villanova U., 1983, J. Stanley Morehouse Meml. award, 1997, Benjamin Garver Lamme medal, Am. Soc. Engring. Edn., 2000, Eckert-Mauchly award, ACM and IEEE Computer Soc., 2001, Seymour Cray Award, 2001; named Profl. Young Investigator, NSF, 1984. Fellow: IEEE (Emmanuel R. Piore award 1994, John Von Neumann medal 2000), Am. Acad. Arts and Scis., Assn. Computing Machinery; mem.: NAS, Royal Acad. Engring. Spain (corr.), Nat. Acad. Engring. (peer selection com. computer sci. and engring. 1996—99, chair 2000), Pi Mu Epsilon, Eta Kappa Nu, Tau Beta Pi. Office: Stanford U Office of the Provost Bldg 10 Stanford CA 94305-2061 Fax: 650-724-4062. E-mail: hennessy@stanford.edu.

HENNEY, CHRISTOPHER SCOT, immunologist; b. Sutton-Coldfield, Eng., Feb. 4, 1941; s. William Scot and Rhoda Agnes (Bateman) Henney; m. Janet Barnsley, June 20, 1964; children: James Scot, Samantha Jane. BS with honors, U. Birmingham, Eng., 1962, PhD in Exptl. Pathology, 1965, DSc. in Research Immunology (hon.), 1973. Immunologist WHO, Lausanne, Switzerland; assoc. prof. medicine and microbiology med. sch. Johns Hopkins U., Balt., 1978; prof. microbiology and immunology U. Wash., Seattle, 1978-81; head. basic immunology Fred Hutchinson Cancer Research Ctr., Seattle, 1978-81; co-founder, sci. dir., vice chmn. Immunex Corp., Seattle, 1981-89; co-founder, sci. dir., exec. v.p. ICOS Corp., Seattle, 1989—2000; CEO Dendreon Corp., Seattle, 1995—2003, chmn., 1995—2004, Structural Genomix Inc., Xcyte Therapier, Inc. Mem. Am. Assn. Immunology (sect. editor 1972-73), Reticuloendothelial Soc. (sect. editor 1978-79), Am. Cancer Soc. (chmn. immunology rev. com. 1982-83), NIH (mem. pathology study sect. 1978-82). Personal E-mail: chenney@comcast.net.

HENNION, REEVE LAWRENCE, communications executive; b. Ventura, Calif., Dec. 7, 1941; s. Tom Reeve and Evelyn Edna (Henry) H.; m. Carolyn Laird, Sept. 12, 1964; children: Jeffrey Reeve, Douglas Laird. BA, Stanford U., 1963, MA, 1965. Reporter Tulare (Calif.) Advance-Register, 1960-62; reporter UPI, San Francisco, 1963-66, mgr. Fresno, Calif., 1966-68, regional exec. Los Angeles, 1968-69, mgr. Honolulu, 1969-72, San Francisco, 1972-75, Calif. editor, 1975-77, gen. news editor, 1977-81, bus. mgr., 1981-83, v.p., gen. mgr. Pacific div., 1983-85; v.p., gen. mgr. Calif.-Oreg. Broadcasting, Inc., 1985-86; pres. Viatech Inc., 1986-92; propr. Buncom Ranch; pres. Keypoint Svcs. Internat., Inc., Medford, Oreg., 1992—2002; interim exec. dir. Rogue Valley Coun. of Govts., 1998. Editor: The Modoc Country, 1971, Buncom: Crossroads Station, 1995. Chmn. Calif. Freedom of Info. Com., 1983-84; chair Jackson County Planning Commn.; mayor of Buncom, Oreg.; pres. Buncom Hist. Soc.; active Rogue C.C. Found. Bd. Mem. Am. Planning Assn., Delta Kappa Epsilon. Home: 3232 Little Applegate Rd Jacksonville OR 97530-9303

HENRIKSEN, MELVIN, mathematician, educator; b. NYC, Feb. 23, 1927; s. Kaj and Helen (Kahn) Henriksen; m. Lillian Viola Hill, July 23, 1946 (div. 1964); children: Susan, Richard, Thomas; m. Louise Levitas, June 12, 1964 (dec. Oct. 1997). BS, Coll. City N.Y., 1948; MS, U. Wis., 1949, PhD in Math, 1951. Asst. math., then instr. extension div. U. Wis., 1948-51; asst. prof. U. Ala., 1951-52; from instr. to prof. math. Purdue U., 1952-65; prof. math., head dept. Case Inst. Tech., 1965-68; research assoc. U. Calif. at Berkeley, 1968-69; prof., chmn. math. dept. Harvey Mudd Coll., 1969-72, prof., 1972-97, prof. emeritus, 1997—. Mem. Inst. Advanced Study, Princeton, 1956-57, 63-64; vis. prof. Wayne State U., 1960-61; rsch. assoc. U. Man., Winnipeg, Can., 1975-76; vis. prof. Wesleyan U., Middletown, Conn., 1978-79, 82-83, 86-87, 93-94. Author: (with Milton Lees) Single Variable Calculus, 1970; assoc. editor: Algebra Universalis, 1993—2008, Topology Atlas, 1996-2002, Topological Commentary, 1996-2002; mem. editl. bd. Functiones et Approximatio Commentario Mathematici, 2001-06; author articles on algebra, rings of functions, gen. topology. Sloan fellow, 1956—58. Mem. Am. Math. Soc., Math. Assn. Am. (assoc. editor Am. Math. monthly 1988-91, assoc. editor Algebra Universalis 1993-2008). Office: Harvey Mudd Coll Math Dept Claremont CA 91711 Office Phone: 909-626-3676. Business E-Mail: henriksen@hmc.edu.

HENRIKSEN, THOMAS HOLLINGER, researcher; b. Detroit, Nov. 16, 1939; s. Paul and Irene (Hollinger) H.; m. Margaret Mary Mueller, Sept. 9, 1968; children— Heather Anne, Damien Paul Hollinger BA, Va. Mil. Inst., 1962; MA, Mich. State U., 1966, PhD, 1969. Asst. prof. SUNY, Plattsburgh, 1969-73, assoc. prof., 1973-79, prof., 1979-80; Peace fellow Hoover Instn. on War, Revolution and Peace Stanford (Calif.) U., 1979-80, research fellow, 1980-82, sr. research fellow, 1982-86, sr. fellow, 1986—, assoc. dir., 1983—2003, exec. sec. nat. fellows program, 1984—2003, mem. Pres.'s Commn. on White House fellows, 1987-93. Mem. U.S. Army Sci. Bd., 1984-90. Author: Mozambique: A History, 1978, Revolutiona and Counterrevolution: Mozambique's War of Independence, 1964-74, 1983, The New World Order: War, Peace and Military Preparedness, 1992, Clinton's Foreign Policy in Somalia, Bosnia, Haiti, and North Korea, 1996, Using Power and Diplomacy to Deal With Rogue States, 1999; co-author: The Struggle for Zimbabwe: Battle in the Bush, 1981, American Power After The Berlin Wall, 2007; contbg. author, editor: Soviet and Chinese Aid to African Nations, 1980; Communist Powers in Sub-Saharan Africa, 1981; assoc. editor Yearbook on Internat. Communist Affairs, 1982-91; contbg. author, editor: One Korea? Challenges and Prospects for Reunification, 1994. Trustee George C. Marshall Found., 1993—. Served to lt. U.S. Army, 1963-65 Home: 177 Lundy Ln Palo Alto CA 94306-4563 Office: Stanford U Hoover Instn Stanford CA 94305 Office Phone: 650-723-4255.

HENRIKSON, DONALD MERLE, forensic pathologist; b. Walla Walla, Wash., May 2, 1947; s. James Christan and Carol Jean (DuBois) H.; m. Eileen Ruth Mikita, Oct. 12, 1980. BA, Harvard U., 1969; MD, U. Calif., Davis, 1981. Diplomate Am. Bd. Pathology. Assoc. pathologist Lab. Medicine Cons., Inc., Auburn, Calif., 1986-87, FPMG, Inc., 1987-88; owner, pathologist FFPMG, 1989-94; assoc. pathologist NCFP, Inc., Sacramento, 1994—2002; pathologist Placer County Coroner's Office, Auburn, 2002—. Mem. med. staff Sierra Valley Dist. Hosp., Loyalton, Calif., 1992-95, Oroville Hosp. and Med. Ctr., 1986-95, Sierra Nev. Meml. Hosp., Grass Valley, Calif., 1986-94, Sutter Auburn Faith Hosp., 1986—; asst. clin. prof. U. Calif. Sch. of Medicine, Davis, 1994-2002. Mem. Placer County Child Death Rev. Team, Auburn, 1990—; mem., former chair Sacramento County Child Death Rev. Team, Sacramento, 1994-2001; mem. Nevada County Child Death Rev. Team, Nevada City, 1996—. Sgt. U.S. Army, 1969-71. Fellow Coll. of Am. Pathologists; mem. AMA, AAAS, Am. Acad. Forensic Scis., Am. Soc. for Clin. Pathology. Avocations: hiking, golf, piano. Office: Placer County Coroner Auburn Justice Ctr 2929 Richardson Dr Auburn CA 95603 Office Phone: 530-889-7807. Business E-Mail: dhenriks@placer.ca.gov.

HENRY, CHARLES L. (JERRY), manufacturing executive; b. Chattanooga, 1941; m. Kay Henry; 4 children. BS in Engring. Physics, U. Tenn., 1963. Process engr. DuPont Co., 1963, various positions, 1963-84, v.p. Wilmington, Del., 1984-86, group v.p., 1986-93, exec. v.p., CFO, 1993-96; chmn., pres., CEO Johns Manville Corp., Denver, 1996—. Office: Johns Manville Corp 717 17th St Denver CO 80202

HENRY, HAROLD M., obstetrician, gynecologist, maternal-fetal medicine; b. Shreveport, La., Aug. 25, 1954; MD, Mayo Med. Sch., 1980. Cert. Am. Bd. Ob-gyn., Maternal-Fetal Medicine. Intern, ob-gyn. Long Beach Meml. Hosp., 1980—81; resident King-Drew Med. Ctr., LA, 1982—86; fellow Cedar-Sinai Med. Ctr./UCLA, Calif., 1986—88; hosp. appointment Kaiser Permanente Med. Ctr., Calif.; clin. asst. prof. UCLA, Calif. Achievements include being the member of a California team of doctors that delivered the second set of octuplets ever born in the US in 2009. Office: Kaiser Permanente Med Ctr 9400 Rosecrans Ave Ste 4100 Bellflower CA 90706*

HENSLEY, WILLIAM LYNN (WILLIE HENSLEY), state senator, corporate executive; b. Kotzebue, Alaska, June 17, 1941; s. John and Priscilla Hensley; m. Abigale Ryan; children: Priscilla, Mary Lynn, James, Elizabeth. Student, U. Alaska, 1960-62; BA in Polit. Sci., George Washington U., 1966; postgrad., U. Alaska, spring 1966, LLD (hon.), 1980; postgrad., UCLA, fall 1968. Mem. Alaska Ho. of Reps., 1966-70; senator State of Alaska, 1970-74, 86-88; chmn. United Bank Alaska, Anchorage, 1976-86; pres. N.W. Alaska Native Assn. Devel. Corp., Kotzebue, 1976-94; pres., sr. v.p., dir., founder N.W. Alaska Native Assn. Regional Corp., Kotzebue, 1986-94; commr. Dept. Commerce and Econ. Devel. State of Alaska, 1994—. Pres. Alaska Village Electric Coop., 1967-71; chmn., chmn., bd. dirs. Tundra Times, 1979—. Chmn. Alaska Dem. Party, 1968, 84-86, Rural Affairs Commn., 1968-74, Capital Site Selection Com., 1975-76, Reapportionment Commn., 1985, nat. committeeman; bd. regents U. Alaska, 1985-87, bd. dirs. Northwest Regional Ednl. Lab., 1969-71; bd. dirs. Nat. Coun. on Indian Opportunity, 1968-70, Alascom, 1977—, Alaska Fedn. Natives, 1966-80, exec. dir., pres., co-chair; mem. Providence Hosp. Adv. Bd., 1979-87; mem. Clinton Transition Staff, Little Rock, 1992; dir. South-Ctrl. Red Cross, apptd. mem. Pacific regional com. Recipient Nat. Pub. Svc. award Rockefeller Found., 1980; named Citizen of Yr. Alaska Fedn. Natives, 1981. Home: 8299 Armetale Ln Fairfax Station VA 22039-3112 Office: Commerce and Econ Devel PO Box 110800 Juneau AK 99811-0800

HENSON, GLENDA MARIA, newswriter; b. Marion, NC, June 17, 1960; d. Douglas Bradley and Glenda June (Crouch) H. BA in English cum laude, Wake Forest U., 1982. Reporter Ark. Dem., Little Rock, 1982-84; bur. reporter Tampa Tribune, Crystal River, Fla., 1984;

statehouse reporter Ark. Gazette, Little Rock, 1984-87, bur. chief Washington, 1987-89; editl. writer Lexington (Ky.) Herald-Leader, 1989-94; editl. writer, columnist The Charlotte (N.C.) Observer, 1994-98; dep. editl. page editor Austin (Tex.) American-Statesman, 1998-2001, asst. mng. editor enterprise, 2001—04; dep. editl. page editor Sacramento Bee, Calif., 2004—. Lectr. journalism, Indonesia, 2001; juror Nat. Headliner Awards, 2002—04, ASNE Writing Awards, 2001—03, Nieman Fellowship Selection Com., 2004. Editor: Pulitzer Prize Series, 2005, Jefferson Fellowship of the East-West Center, 2007. Mem. Wake Forest Presdl. Scholarship Com., Ky., 1992, Wake Forest Bd. Visitors, 1995-99; Pulitzer Prize juror, 1994, 95, 99, 2000. Nieman fellow Harvard U., 1993-94, Found. Am. Comm. Econs. fellow, 1997; recipient Pulitzer prize, 1992, Walker Stone award Scripps Howard Found., 1992, Ky. Press Assn. award, 1992, N.C. Press Assn. award, 1995-96, Leadership award Duke U., 1995, Nat. Headliner award, 1996, Mary Morgan Hewitt award, 2007; named Wake Forest Woman of Yr., 1992 Mem. Soc. Profl. Journalists (Sigma Delta Chi award 1991, Green Eyeshade award Atlanta chpt. 1992), Nat. Conf. Editorial Writers, Investigative Reporters & Editors Assn., Am. Soc. Newspaper Editors, Omicron Delta Kappa. Avocations: skiing, bicycling, swimming, travel, rafting. Office: Sacramento Bee 2100 Q St Sacramento CA 95816 Home Phone: 916-254-7370; Office Phone: 916-321-1907. Business E-Mail: mhenson@sacbee.com.

HENSON, RAY DAVID, law educator, consultant; b. Johnston City, Ill., July 24, 1924; s. Ray David and Lucile (Bell) Henson. BS, U. Ill., 1947, JD, 1949. Bar: Ill. 1950, U.S. Supreme Ct. 1960. Assoc. CNA Fin. Corp., Chgo., 1952-70; prof. law Wayne State U., 1970-75, Hastings Sch. Law, U. Calif., San Francisco, 1975—95, prof. emeritus, 1995—. Author: Landmarks of Law, 1960, Secured Transactions, 1973, 2d edit., 1979, Documents of Title, 1983, 2d edit., 1990, The Law of Sales, 1985, others; editor: The Business Lawyer, 1967-68; contbr. numerous articles to law revs. Mem. legal adv. com. N.Y. Stock Exch., 1971-75. Served with USAAC, 1943-46. Mem. Am. Law Inst. (life), ABA (chmn. bus. law sect. 1969-70, adv. bd. jour. 1974-80, chmn. uniform comml. code com.), Ill. Bar Assn. (chmn. corp. banking and bus. law sect. 1963-65, chmn. uniform comml. code com.), Chgo. Bar Assn. (chmn. uniform comml. code com.). Home: 1400 Geary Blvd San Francisco CA 94109-6561 Office: U Calif Hastings Sch Law 200 Mcallister St San Francisco CA 94102-4707

HENSON, TARAJI PENDA, actress; b. Washington, Sept. 11, 1970; d. Boris and Bernice Henson; 1 child, Marcel. Grad., Howard U., Washington, DC, 1995. Actress (films) Streetwise, 1980, The Adventures of Rocky & Bullwinkle, 2000, All or Nothing, 2001, Baby Boy, 2001 (Spl. Mention award, Locarno Internat.Film Festival, 2001), Hair Show, 2004, Hustle & Flow, 2005 (Outstanding Performance by an Actress in a Supporting Role, Black Movie award, 2005, Best Supporting Actress, Black Reel award, 2006), Four Brothers, 2005, Something New, 2006, Smokin' Aces, 2006, Talk to Me, 2007 (Best Ensemble Cast, Gotham award, 2007), The Family That Preys, 2008, The Curious Case of Benjamin Button, 2008 (Best Supporting Actress, Austin Film Critics Assn., 2008, Outstanding Supporting Actress in a Motion Picture, NAACP Image award, 2009), Not Easily Broken, 2009, (TV series) Smart Guy, 1997—98, Holla, 2002, The Division, 2003—04, Boston Legal, 2007—08, Eli Stone, 2008, (TV films) Satan's School for Girls, 2000, Murder, She Wrote: The Last Free Man, 2001. Recipient Best Actress award, BET, 2006. Office: c/o Vincent Cirrincione Assocs 1516 N Fairfax Ave Los Angeles CA 90046

HENTZ, VINCENT R., surgeon; b. Jacksonville, Fla., Aug. 29, 1942; MD, U. Fla., 1968. Intern Stanford (Calif.) Hosp., 1968-69, resident in plastic surgery, 1969-74; chief hand divsn. Stanford U. Sch. Medicine; fellow in hand surgery Roosevelt Hosp., NYC, 1974-75; prof. functional restoration Stanford (Calif.) U. Office: Stanford U Sch Medicine 900 Welsh Rd # 15 Palo Alto CA 94305

HEPPE, KAROL VIRGINIA, lawyer, educator; b. Vinton, Iowa, Mar. 14, 1958; d. Robert Henry and Audry Virginia (Harper) Heppe. BA in Law and Society, U. Calif., Santa Barbara, 1982; JD, People's Coll. Law, 1989. Cmty. organizer Oreg. Fair Share, Eugene, 1983; law clk. Legal Aid Found. L.A., summer 1986; devel. dir. Ctrl. Am. Refugee Ctr., LA, 1987-89; exec. dir. Police Watch-Police Misconduct Lawyer Referral Svc., LA, 1989-94; instr. People's Coll. Law, LA, 1992-94; dir. alternative sentencing project Ctr. Juvenile and Criminal Justice, 1994-95; cons. Bay Area Police Watch, 1996; investigator Office Citizen Complaints City and County of San Francisco, 1998—. Vol. law clk. Legal Aid Found. L.A., 1984—86, Lane County Legal Aid Svc., Eugene, 1983. Editor: (newsletter) NLG Law Students Action, 1986, Ctrl. Am. Refugee Ctr., 1986—89, Prison Break, 1994. Mem. Coalition Human Immigrants Rights, 1991—92, So. Calif. Civil Rights Coalition, 1991—92; bd. dirs. Nat. Police Accountability Project Adv. Bd., 1999—2003, People's Coll. Law, 1985—90, Law Student Civil Rights Rsch. Coun., NYC, 1986. Scholar, Kramer Found., 1984—88, Law Students' Civil Rights Rsch. Coun., 1986, Davis-Putter Found., 1988, Assn. Cmty.-Based Edn. Prudential, 1988. Avocations: reading, gardening. Office Phone: 415-241-7728. Business E-Mail: karol_heppe@sfgov.org.

HEPPELL, JACQUES PHILIPPE, surgeon, educator; m. Odette Lise Chamberland, Oct. 9, 1952; children: Patrick Jacques, Catherine Anne, Simon Pierre. MD, U. Montreal, 1975. Prof. surgery residency progam U. Montreal, 1979; prof. surgery Mayo Clinic Coll. Medicine, Scottsdale, Ariz., 1994—. Fellowship, GI Rsch. and Colo. Rectal Surgery, Mayo Clinic, Rochester. Office: Mayo Clinic 5777 E Mayo Blvd Phoenix AZ 85054

HERB, EDMUND MICHAEL, optometrist, educator; b. Zanesville, Ohio, Oct. 9, 1942; s. Edmund G. and Barbara R. (Michael) H.; divorced; children: Sara, Andrew; m. Jeri Herb. OD, Ohio State U., 1966. Pvt. practice optometry, Buena Vista, Colo., 1966—; past prof. Timberline campus Colo. Mountain Coll.; past clin. instr. Ohio State U. Sch. Optometry. Mem. Am. Optometric Assn., Colo. Optometric Assn. Home: 16395 Mt Princeton Rd Buena Vista CO 81211-9505 Office: 115 N Tabor St Buena Vista CO 81211 Office Phone: 719-395-6356.

HERBERT, GARY RICHARD, Lieutenant Governor of Utah; b. American Fork, Utah, May 7, 1947; s. Duane and Carol Herbert; m. Jeanette Snelson; children: Nathan, Daniel, Bradley, Kimberli, Shannon, Heather. Lic. real estate broker 1969. Pres. Herbert & Associates Inc., Orem, Utah; county commr. State of UT, Salt Lake City, 1990—2004, lt. gov., 2005—. Pres. Utah State Assn. County Commrs. and Couns., 2000; chmn. Mountainland Assn. Govts., Utah County Coun. Govts., Utah Adv. Coun. on Intergovernmental Relations. Bd. dirs. Provo/Orem C. of C. Mem.: Utah Assn. Counties (v.p. 2002, pres. 2003), Utah Assn. Counties Insurance Mutal (past pres.), Utah Assn. Realtors (past pres.), Nat. Assn. Realtors (chmn. Local Fiscal Affairs Com. 1999). Republican. Avocations: golf, tennis. Office: Utah State Capitol Ste 325 PO Box 142325 Salt Lake City UT 84114 Office Phone: 801-538-1041. Office Fax: 801-538-1133. Business E-Mail: gherbert@utah.gov.

HERBERT, GAVIN SHEARER, health care products company executive; b. LA, Mar. 26, 1932; s. Gavin and Josephine (D'Vitha) H.; children by previous marriage Cynthia, Lauri, Gavin, Pam; 2d. m. Ninetta Flanagan, Sept. 6, 1986. BS, U. So. Calif., 1954. With Allergan, Inc., Irvine, Calif., 1950—, v.p., 1956-61, exec. v.p., pres., 1961-77, chmn. bd., CEO, 1977-91, chmn. bd., 1992-95, chmn. emeritus; pres. Eye and Skin Care Products Group Smith Kline Beckman Corp., 1981-89. Exec. v.p. Smith Kline Beckman Corp., 1986-89; bd. dirs. Allergan, Inc. Mem. adv. bd. Am. Acad. Ophthalmology Found. Mem. Rsch. to Prevent Blindness (bd. dirs.), Big Canyon Country Club, Newport Harbor Yacht Club, Pacific Club, Beta Theta Pi. Republican.

HERBERT, KATHY J., retail executive; MBA, Lake Forest Grad. Sch. Mgmt., 1985. Dir. personnel tng. Jewel-Osco divsn. Am. Stores Co., 1996—98, v.p. human resources, 1998—2001; exec. v.p. human resources Albertson's, Inc., Boise, 2001—. Bd. dirs. TYCO Healthcare, 2007—. Chair Jewel-Osco United Way Campaign; bd. dirs. Chgo. Sinfonietta, Kohl's Childrens Mus. Office: Albertsons Inc 250 Parkcenter Blvd PO Box 20 Boise ID 83706 Office Phone: 208-395-6200. Office Fax: 208-395-6349.

HERBIG, GEORGE HOWARD, astronomer, educator; b. Wheeling, W.Va., Jan. 2, 1920; s. George Albert and Glenna (Howard) H.; m. Delia Faye McMullin, Oct., 1943 (div. 1968); children: Marilyn, Lawrence, John, Robert; m. Hannelore Helene Tillmann, Sept. 3, 1968. AB, UCLA, 1943; PhD, U. Calif., Berkeley, 1948. From jr. astronomer to assoc. astronomer Lick Obs., U. Calif., Mt. Hamilton, 1948-60, astronomer, 1960-67; prof. astronomy U. Calif., Santa Cruz, 1967-87; astronomer Inst. for Astronomy, U. Hawaii, 1987—2001, emeritus, 2001—. Asst. dir. Lick Obs., 1960-63, acting dir., 1970-71. Editor: Non-Stable Stars, 1955, Spectroscopic Astrophysics, 1970; author over 230 sci. papers, articles, revs. Martin Kellogg fellow U. Calif., Berkeley, 1946-48, NRC fellow Pasadena and U. Chgo., 1948-49, Washington, 1948-49; recipient Medaille U. de Liège, Belgium, 1970, Catherine Wolfe Bruce Gold medal Astron. Soc. Pacific, 1980, Petrie prize and lecture Can. Astron. Soc., 1995. Fellow Am. Acad. Arts and Scis; mem. Nat. Acad. Scis., Internat. Astron. Union, Am. Astron. Soc. (Warner prize 1955, Henry Norris Russell lectr. 1975), Max Planck Inst. für Astronomie (fgn. sci. mem.), Soc. Royale des Scis. de Liège (corr.). Democrat. Office: U Hawaii Inst Astronomy 2680 Woodlawn Dr Honolulu HI 96822-1839

HERBST, DAVID W., lawyer; b. Pomona, Calif., June 17, 1952; BA magna cum laude, Pomona Coll., 1974; JD, Stanford U., 1977. Bar: Calif. 1977, U.S. Tax Ct. 1979. Ptnr. Manatt, Phelps & Phillips (formerly known as Wise & Shepard), Palo Alto, Calif., 1983—. Mem. ABA, State Bar Calif., Santa Clara County Bar Assn., Palo Alto Bar Assn. Office: Manatt Phelps & Phillips 1001 Page Mill Rd Bldg 2 Palo Alto CA 94304-1020

HERGER, WALTER WILLIAM, JR., United States Representative from California; b. Yuba City, Calif., May 20, 1945; m. Pamela Sargent; 9 children. Grad., Calif. State U. Sacramento, 1969. Owner Herger Gas Co., Inc., 1969—80, Herger Ranch, 1969—80; mem. Calif. State Assembly, 1980—86, US Congress from 2nd Calif. dist., 1987—; mem. ways and means com., trade subcom., income security/family support subcom., joint com. on taxation. Mem. Rural Health Care Coalition. Bd. mem. East Nicolaus HS, 1976—80, bd. trustees; bd. dirs. Big Brothers Big Sisters. Recipient Spirit of America award, US C. of C., 2000; named Outstanding Young Man of America, US Jaycees, 1979. Mem.: NRA, Sutter County Taxpayers Assn., Nat. Fedn. Ind. Businesses, Calif. C. of C., Calif. Cattleman's Assn., Yuba-Sutter Farm Bureau, Yuba-Sutter Sunrise Rotary, South Yuba Rotary. Republican. Mem. Lds Ch. Office: US Ho Reps 2268 Rayburn Ho Office Bldg Washington DC 20515-0502 Office Phone: 202-225-3076. Office Fax: 202-225-0852.

HERLINGER, DANIEL ROBERT, hospital administrator; b. Boskovice, Czechoslovakia, Oct. 27, 1946; arrived in U.S., 1950, naturalized, 1956; s. Rudolf and Ingeborg (Gessler) Herlinger; m. Susanne Reiter, June 1, 1969; children: Lisa, Rebecca, Joanna. BS, Loyola U., Chgo., 1968; MBA, George Washington U., 1971. Asst. adminstr. Michael Reese Hosp., Chgo., 1971—73; v.p. Mercy Hosp., Chgo., 1973—84; pres. St. John's Regional Med. Ctr., Oxnard, Calif., 1984—94, Mercy Healthcare Ventura County, 1994—96, CHW Ctrl. Coast, Santa Barbara, Calif., 1996—. Fellow: Am. Coll. Hosp. Adminstrs.; mem.: World Pres. Orgn., Rotary. Jewish. Home: 15 Camino Verde Santa Barbara CA 93103-2144 Office: CHW Central Coast 1600 Rose Ave Oxnard CA 93030-3722

HERMAN, DAVID JAY, orthodontist; b. Rome, NY, Oct. 4, 1954; s. Maurice Joseph and Bettina S. (Stiener) H.; m. Mary Beth Appleberry, Apr. 11, 1976; children: Jeremiah D., Kellin A. BA in Biology, San Jose State U., 1976; DDS, Emory U., 1981; MS in Orthodontics, U. N.C., 1992, MPH, 1992. Comdr. USPHS, 1981-97; advanced gen. practice resident Gallup (N. Mex.) Indian Med. Ctr., 1983-84; Navajo area dental br. chief Window Rock, Ariz., 1986-89; mem. grad. residency com. U. N.C., Chapel Hill, 1990-91; Navajo area orthodontic specialist Shiprock, N.Mex., 1992-97; clin. dir. Nizhoni Smiles Inc., 1997-99; pvt. practice Farmington, N.Mex., 1998—; pres. Four Corners Orthodontics, Inc., 1998—. Mem. health adv. bd. Navajo Reservation Headstart, 1986—89; health promotion/disease prevention cons. USPHS/Indian Health Svc. Navajo Area, Window Rock, 1986—89; cons. Ariz. IHS Periodontal Health Task Force, 1986—90. Asst. wrestling coach Winslow (Ariz.) H.S., 1984-86, Gallup High Sch., 1987-89, Chapel Hill H.S., 1991-92, Farmington H.S., 1992—, Aztec H.S., 1998-2000; mem. H.S. Youth Wrestling Program, 1992-2000; mem. corp. bd. San Juan Reg. Med. Ctr., 1996—. Recipient Healthy Mothers/Healthy Babies Disease Prevention award, 1988, USPHS Achievement medal, 1985, Headstart Achievement award, 1989, Ariz. Pub. Health Assn. Hon. award, 1989; Nat. Health Svc. Corp. scholar Emory U., 1977-81. Mem. ADA, Am. Assn. Orthodontists, Rocky Mountain Soc. Orthodontists, N.Mex. Soc. Orthodontists (pres. 1998-99), Northwestern N.Mex. Sco. Orthodontists (pres. 1999-00, v.p. 2008-09), Navajo Area Dental Soc. (pres. 1985), Am. Assn. Mil. Orthodontists (sec.reas. 1992, v.p. 1993-94, pres. 1995-97), Northwest N. Mex. Dontae Soc. (v.p. 2008-09). Avocations: wrestling, weightlifting, jogging, skiing, backpacking. Office Phone: 505-564-9000.

HERMAN, GEORGE ADAM, writer, literature educator; b. Norfolk, Va., Apr. 12, 1928; s. George Adam and Minerva Nevada (Thompson) H.; m. Patricia Lee Glazer, May 26, 1955 (div. 1989); children: Kurt, Erik, Karl, Lisa, Katherine, Christopher, Jena, Amanda; m. Patricia Jane Piper Dubay, Aug. 25, 1989; children: Lizette, Paul, Kirk, Victoria. PhB, Loyola Coll., 1950; MFA, Cath. U., 1954; cert. of fine arts, Boston Coll., 1953. Asst. prof. Clarke Coll., Dubuque, Iowa, 1955-60, Villanova (Pa.) U., 1960-63; asst. prof., playwright in residence Coll. St. Benedict, St. Joseph, Minn., 1963-65; chmn. theatre dept. Coll. Great Falls, Mont., 1965-67; media specialist Hawaii State Dept. Edn., Honolulu, 1967-75, staff specialist, 1975-83; sr. drama critic Honolulu Advertiser, 1975-80; artistic dir. Commedia Repertory Theatre, Honolulu, 1978-80; freelance writer, lectr., composer Portland, Oreg., 1983—. Author: (plays) Company of Wayward Saints, 1963 (McKnight Humanities award 1964), Mr. Highpockets, 1968, A Stone for Either Hand, 1969, Tenebrae, 1984, Nine Dragons, The Hidden Place, 2003, (novels) Carnival of Saints, 1994 (finalist Oreg. Book Awards 1994), A Comedy of Murders, 1994, Tears of the Madonna, 1995, The Florentine Mourners, 1999, The Toys of War, 2002, Little Rome, Iowa, 2003, Nine Dragons, 2003, Necromancer, 2004, The Arno Serpent, 2007; composer (ballets) The Dancing Princesses, Fraidy Cat. Pres. local chpt. Nat. Sch. Pub. Rels. Assn., Honolulu, 1981-83; bd. dirs. Honolulu Community Theatre, 1981-82, Hawaii State Theatre Coun., Honolulu, 1981. With U.S. Army, 1950-52. Recipient Hartke Playwrighting award Cath. U., 1954, Humanities award McKnight Found., 1963, Excellence award Am. Security Coun., 1967. Avocations: directing theatre, lecturing. Office Phone: 503-452-3701. Personal E-mail: gadamo@aol.com.

HERMAN, JAMES EDWARD, lawyer; b. Kansas City, July 14, 1945; s. Everton Paul and Virginia May (Hutchinson) Herman; m. Denise deBellefeuille. BA, U. Calif., Santa Barbara, 1971; JD, Calif. Western Law Sch., San Diego, 1975; LLM, NYU, 1976. Bar: Calif. 1976. Sr. fellow Criminal Law Edn. Rsch. Ctr. NYU, 1975—76; atty. Pub. Defender's Office, Riverside County, Calif., 1976—80, Defenders Inc., San Diego, 1979—80, Santa Barbara County Pub. Defenders Office, 1980—84; assoc. Cappello and Foley, Santa Barbara, 1984—; ptnr. Reicker, Prau, Pyle, McRoy & Herman LLP, Santa Barbara. Trustee Calif. Western Sch. Law; lectr. voir dire and dramatic arts techniques applied to trials various profl. orgns. Author: articles to profl. jours. Bd. dirs. Ensemble Theatre Project. Recipient Bernard E. Witkin Disting. Svc. Amicus Curiae award, Judicial Coun., State of Calif., 2003. Mem.: Calif. Attys. Criminal Justice, Assn. Trial Lawyers Am., State Bar Calif. (pres., bd. govs. 1999, pres. 2002—03), Santa Barbara County Bar Assn. (pres., past chair, bench/bar com.). Office: Reicker Pfau Pyle McRoy & Herman LLP 1421 State St Ste B PO Box 1470 Santa Barbara CA 93102-1470

HERMAN, JOAN ELIZABETH, retired health insurance company executive; b. NYC, June 2, 1953; d. Roland Barry and Grace Gales (Goldstein) Herman; m. Richard M. Rasiej, July 16, 1977. AB, Barnard Coll., 1975; MS, Yale U., New Haven, 1977. Actuarial student Met. Life Ins. Co., NYC, 1978-82; asst. actuary Phoenix Mut. Life Ins. Co., Hartford, Conn., 1982-83, assoc. actuary, dir. underwriting rsch., 1983-84, 2nd v.p., 1984-85, v.p., 1985-89, sr. v.p., 1989-98; pres. splty. bus. WellPoint Health Networks, Woodland Hills, Calif., 1998, grp. pres., 1999—2001, pres. splty., sr. and state sponsored progs. divsn., 2002—04; pres., CEO, splty. sr. and state sponsored bus. divsn. WellPoint, Inc., Indpls., 2004—08. Bd. dirs. PM Holdings, Inc., Phoenix Grp. Holdings, Inc., Phoenix Am. Life Ins. Co., Emprendimiento Compartido, S.A.; v.p. BC Life & Health Co., Profl. Claims Svcs. Inc., Proserv., MEDIX. Contbr. articles to profl. jours. Bd. dirs. Health Ins. Assn. Am., 2002—03; capt. fundraising team Greater Hartford Arts Coun., Hartford, 1986; bd. dirs. Children's Fund Conn., 1992—98, My Sister's Pl. Shelter, Hartford, 1989—94, Western Mass. Regional Nat. Conf. Conn., 1995—98, Greater Hartford Arts Coun., 1997—98, Hartford Ballet, 1989—95, corporator, 1995—98; bd. dirs. Leadership Greater Hartford, 1989—94, chmn. bd. dirs., 1993—94; bd. dirs. So. Calif. Leadership Network, 2003—, South Ctrl. Scholars Found., 2007—; mem. bd. founders Am. Leadership Forum Hartford, 1991—98; corporator Hartford Sem., 1994—98; bd. dirs. Hadassah, Glastonbury, Conn., Temple Beth Hillel, South Windsor, Conn., 1983—84. Fellow: Soc. Actuaries (chair health sect. coun. 1994—95); mem.: Ctr. Dance Assn. (bd. dirs. 2008—), Am. Leadership Forum, Am. Acad. Actuaries (bd. dirs. 1994—97). Jewish. Avocations: reading, swimming, bicycling, jogging, aerobic dancing, hiking. Personal E-mail: hermaj1@verizon.net.

HERMAN, STEPHEN CHARLES, lawyer; b. Johnson City, NY, Apr. 28, 1951; s. William Herman and Myrtle Stella (Clark) Keithline; m. Jeanne Ellen Nelson, Sept. 9, 1972; children: Neelie Kristine, Stefanie Anne, Christopher William. Student, Cedarville Coll., 1969-72; BA, Wright State U., 1973; JD, Ohio No. U., 1976. Bar: Mo. 1977, Ill. 1977, Tex. 2004; U.S. Dist. Ct. (ea. dist.) Mo. 1978, U.S. Dist. Ct. (no. dist.) Ill. 1979, U.S. Dist. Ct. (ea. dist) Mich. 1988, U.S. Dist. Ct. (so. dist.) Tex. 1997; U.S. Ct. Appeals (D.C. cir.) 1979, U.S. Ct. Appeals (7th cir.) 1979, U.S. Ct. Appeals (5th cir.) 1980, U.S. Ct. Appeals (10th cir.) 1992; U.S. Supreme Ct. 1986, U.S. Ct. Internat. Trade, 1998. Atty. Mo. Pacific Railroad Co., St. Louis, 1977-78; assoc. Belnap, McCarthy, Spencer, Sweeney & Harkaway, Chgo., 1978-82; ptnr. Belnap, Spencer & McFarland, Chgo., 1982-83, Belnap, Spencer, McFarland & Emrich, Chgo., 1983-84, Belnap, Spencer, McFarland, Emrich & Herman, Chgo., 1984-89, Belnap, Spencer, McFarland, Herman, 1990-96, McFarland & Herman, 1996-01; atty. Stephen C. Herman, P.C., Chgo., 2001—03, Waco, Tex., 2003—06, LA, 2006—. Mem. Mo. Bar Assn., Ill. State Bar Assn., Chgo. Bar Assn., Tex. Bar Assn., Assn. Transp. Law Profls., Transp. Lawyers Assn. Office: 10850 Wilshire Blvd Ste 402 Los Angeles CA 90024 Home Phone: 310-470-4426; Office Phone: 310-470-8454. Personal E-mail: schrmn@aol.com.

HERMANN, ALLEN MAX, physics professor; b. New Orleans, July 17, 1938; s. Edward Frederick and Miriam (Davidson) H.; m. Leonora Christopher, May 19, 1979; children: Miriam, Mary, Neil, Scott. BS with honors in Physics, Loyola U., New Orleans, 1960; MS in Physics, U. Notre Dame, 1962; PhD in Physics, Tex. A&M U., 1965. Sr. rsch. scientist Jet Propulsion Lab, Pasadena, Calif., 1965—67, tech. mgr., 1985—86; asst. prof. physics Tulane U., New Orleans, 1967—70, assoc. prof. physics, 1970—75, prof. physics, 1975—81; task mgr. Solar Energy Rsch. Inst., Golden, Colo., 1980—85; prof., chmn. dept. physics U. Ark., Fayetteville, 1986—89, Disting. prof., 1989; prof. dept. physics U. Colo., Boulder, 1990—2005, prof. emeritus, dept. physics, 2005—; vis. prof. dept. elec. and computer engrng. U. Ky., Lexington, 2005—07; dir. Ctr. Nanoscale Sci. and Engrng. U Ky., 2005—07; adj. prof. Coll. Music, U. Colorado, 2008—, prof. adj., 2008—. Cons. Jet Propulsion Lab., 1978-81, 86-87, NASA-Lewis Rsch. Ctr., Cleve., 1978-80, Cardiac Pacemakers

Inc., Mpls., 1976-79, Radiation Monitoring Devices, Newton, Mass., 1990-93, Superconducting Core Techs., Denver, 1989-95, Sumitomo Electric Industries, Osaka, Japan, 1991-98, MV Sys., Inc., Golden, 1999—. Founding co-editor Applied Physics Communication; editor: Applied Physics Book Series; contbr. numerous articles to profl. jours. Bd. dirs. Colo. Assn. Retarded Citizens, Denver, 1983-85. Recipient NASA Outstanding Achievement award 1970, 72, Disting. Scientist award Am. Assn. Physics Tchrs., 1987; named Hero, State of Ark., Ark. Times mag.; named Person of the Yr., Superconductivity Week, 1989; elected to Acad. Disting. Grads., Coll. Sci., Tex. A&M U., 1999. Fellow Am. Phys. Soc.; mem. IEEE (sr.). Home: 2704 Lookout View Dr Golden CO 80401-2520 Office: U Colo PO Box 390 Boulder CO 80309-0390 Business E-Mail: allen.hermann@colorado.edu.

HERMANN, ROBERT JOHN, lawyer; b. Chgo., Apr. 17, 1944; s. Jacob L. and Rose E. (McCrudden) H.; m. Lyn D. Johnson; children by a previous marriage: Kelly, Brenna, Richard, Edana. Student, U. Ill., 1962-65; BS, No. Ill. U., 1967; JD, DePaul U., 1970. Bar: Ill. 1970, U.S. Supreme Ct. 1988; CPA, Ill., Tex. Tax staff Deloitte Haskins & Sells, Chgo., 1968-81; dir. corp. tax Houston Natural Gas, 1981-82, v.p. corp. tax, 1982-85, Enron Corp., Houston, 1985-99, mng. dir., gen. tax counsel, 2000—02. Mem. The Desert Mountain Club. Home: 11157 E Mesquite Dr Scottsdale AZ 85262-3533 E-mail: wooosh@cox.net.

HERMLE, LYNNE C., lawyer; b. New Haven, 1956; BA magna cum laude, U. Calif. Santa Barbara, 1978; JD, U. Calif., Hastings Coll., 1981. Bar: Calif. 1981. In house atty. AT&T; ptnr. Orrick, Herrington & Sutcliffe LLP, Menlo Park, mem. exec. com. Faculty mem. Nat. Ins. Trial Advocacy; co-editor in chief Start-up & Emerging Cos. Strategist Newsletter; Early Neutral Evaluator No. Dist. Calif., Fed. Ct. Co-author: Sexual Harassment in Workplace: Guide Law, 1994; author: Fuller: Intolerable Burden on Employers?, 1995, EAPs: Expert Roundtable Problems, Solutions, 1991. Named one of Am.'s top 50 women litigators, Nat. Law Jour. Mem.: ABA-labor & employment sect., State Bar Calif. Office: Orrick Herrington & Sutcliffe LLP 1000 Marsh Rd Menlo Park CA 94025 Office Phone: 650-614-7422. Office Fax: 650-614-7401. Business E-Mail: lchermle@orrick.com.

HERMSEN, JAMES R., lawyer; b. Orange, Calif., Oct. 2, 1945; BA, U. Wash., 1967, JD, 1970. Bar: Wash. 1971, Oreg. 2004. Mem. Bogle & Gates, PLLC, Seattle, Dorsey & Whitney, Seattle, 2000—, ptnr., trial, regulatory, tech. group. Mem. Bur. of Competition Fed. Trade Commn., 1971-73. Mem. Seattle-King County Bar Assn., Wash. State Bar Assn., Phi Beta Kappa, Omicron Delta Epsilon, Phi Delta Phi. Office: Dorsey & Whitney 1420 5th Ave Ste 3400 Seattle WA 98101-4010 Office Phone: 206-903-8852. Office Fax: 206-903-8820. E-mail: hermsen.james@dorsey.com.

HERNANDEZ, AILEEN C(LARKE), urban consultant; b. Bklyn., May 23, 1926; d. Charles Henry and Ethel Louise (Hall) Clarke; divorced. AB in Sociology and Polit. Sci. magna cum laude, Howard U., 1947; MA in Pub. Adminstrn. with honors, Calif. State U., LA, 1961; LHD (hon.), So. Vt. Coll., 1979. From organizer to dir. edn. and pub. rels. Internat. Ladies' Garment Workers' Union, Calif., 1950-61; asst. chief Calif. div. Fair Employment Practices, 1962-65; appointed commr. U.S. EEOC, Washington, 1965-66; prin. Aileen C. Hernandez Assocs., San Francisco, 1966—. Rsch. asst. dept. govt. Howard U., 1948; specialist in labor edn., lectr. U.S. Dept. State, 1960; mem. internat. conf. on minorities and the metropolis Konrad Adenauer Found./U.S. Dept. State, 1975; mem. Nat. Commn. on Study of People's Republic of China, 1978, Nat. Commn. on Am. Fgn. Policy Towards South Africa, 1981; advisor BART impact study com. Nat. Acad. Engring.; commr. Bay Vision 2020, 1990-93; vice chair San Francisco 2000; lectr. polit. sci. U. Calif., Berkeley, UCLA, San Francisco State U. Columnist Washington Tribune, 1946-47; contbr. commn. report South Africa: Time Running Out, 1981. Coord. Senator Alan Cranston's campaign for State Controller of Calif., 1961; chair Working Assets Money Fund; co-chair Nat. Urban Coalition, bd. dirs. Death Penalty Focus; vice chair nat. adv. couns. ACLU; coord. San Francisco African Am. Agenda Coun.; mem. adv. bd. Program for Rsch. on Immigration Policy; mem. nat. adv. coun. Nat. Inst. for Women of Color; bd. dirs. Ctr. for Women Policy Studies; mem. Citizens Commn. on Civil Rights; treas. Eleanor R. Spikes Meml. Fund; active San Franciscans Seeking Consensus, 1982—; founding mem., chair Coalition for Econ. Equity; chair Sec's Adv. Com. on Rights and Responsibilities of Women; officer, bd. dirs. Mt. Zion Hosp.; bd. dirs. Westside Community Mental Health Ctr.; chair Calif. Coun. Humanities; founding mem. Nat. Women's Polit. Caucus, Black Women Organized for Action, Bay Area Black Women United, Nat. Hook-Up of Black Women; bd. dirs., project dir. Nat. Com. Against Discrimination in Housing; mem. housing com. Assn. Bay Area Govts.; chmn. Ctr. Common Good, Calif. Women's Agenda; bd. dirs. Wellesley Ctrs. for Rsch.; bd. Ctr. Govtl. Studies. Named Woman of Yr., Cmty. Rels. Conf. So. Calif. 1961, One of Ten Most Disting. Women in the San Francisco Bay Area, San Francisco Examiner, 1969, One of Ten Women Who Make a Difference, San Francisco LWV, 1985; recipient Disting. Postgrad. Achievement award Howard U., 1968, disting. svcs. to urban cmtys. award Nat. Urban Coalition, 1985, Bicentennial award Trinity Bapt. Ch., 1976, humanitarian svcs. award Glide Meml. United Meth. Ch., 1986, appreciation awards Nat. Inst. for Women of Color, 1987, Western Dist. Conf. of Nat. Assn. Negro Bus. and Profl. Women's Clubs, 1988, San Francisco Conv. and Visitors Bur., Parren J. Mitchell award San Francisco Black C. of C., 1985, Silver Spur award, Wise Woman award Ctr. for Women Policy Studies, Women of Achievement award, Vison and Excellence award, Earl Warren Civil Liberties award ACLU, 1989, others. Mem. NAACP (life), NOW (past nat. pres.), Ms. Found. for Women (bd. dirs.), Bay Area Urban League (past bd. dirs.), Urban Inst. (life trustee), Gamma Phi Delta (hon.), Alpha Kappa Alpha. Office: Aileen C Hernandez Assocs 818 47th Ave San Francisco CA 94121-3208 Home Phone: 415-221-4679. Personal E-mail: aileenfem@aol.com.

HERNANDEZ, ANTONIA, foundation administrator, lawyer; b. Torreon, Coahuila, Mexico, May 30, 1948; came to U.S., 1956; d. Manuel and Nicolasa (Martinez) H.; m. Michael Stern, Oct. 8, 1977; children: Benjamin, Marisa, Michael. BA, UCLA, 1971, JD, 1974. Bar: Calif. 1974, D.C. 1979. Staff atty. Los Angeles Ctr. Law and Justice, 1974-77; directing atty. Legal Aid Found., Lincoln Heights, Calif., 1977-78; staff counsel U.S. Senate Com. on the Judiciary, Washington, 1979-80; assoc. counsel Mexican Am. Legal Def. Ednl. Fund, Washington, 1981-83, employment program dir., 1983-84, exec. v.p., dep. gen. counsel Los Angeles, 1984-85, pres., gen. counsel, 1985—2004; pres., CEO Calif. Community Found., 2004—. Bd. dirs. Golden West Financial Corp., Automobile Club of So. Calif., Am. Charities. Contbr. articles to profl. jours. Active Inter-Am. Dialogue Aspen Inst., Nat. Com. Innovations in State and Local Govt., Nat. Endowment for Democracy, Pres.'s Commn. White House Fellowships; trustee Rockefeller Found. AAUW fellow, 1973-74. Mem. ABA, State Bar Calif., Washington D.C. Bar Assn., Mexican-Am. Roman Catholic. Avocations: gardening, outdoor sports. Office: Calif Community Found 445 S Figueroa St Los Angeles CA 90071

HERNANDEZ, ENRIQUE, JR., (RICK HERNANDEZ), security firm executive; b. LA, Nov. 2, 1955; m. Megan Beth McLeod, June 12, 1982; 5 children. AB cum laude, Harvard U., 1977, JD, 1980. Litigation atty. Brobeck, Phleger & Harrison, LA; chmn., CEO Inter-Con Security Systems Inc., 1984—; co-founder, principal ptnr. Interspan Communications. Bd. dir. McDonalds Corp., 1996—, Nordstrom Inc., 1997—, non-exec. chmn.; bd. dir. Tribune Co., 2001—, Wells Fargo & Co., 2003—; mem. US Nat. Infrastructure Advisory Com., 2002—. Mem., pres. Bd. LA Police Commn., 1993—95; chmn. bd. regents Loyola High Sch., LA; vice chmn., bd. dir. Children's Hosp., LA; bd. trustees U. Notre Dame, LA County Mus. Art; com. mem. Harvard Coll. Visiting Com., Harvard U. Resources Com. Office: Inter-con Security Systems Inc 210 South De Lacey Ave Pasadena CA 91105

HERNANDEZ, GARY A., lawyer; b. Merced, Calif., Feb. 15, 1959; s. Rosendo and Margaret (Salazar) Hernandez; m. Teri L. Bond, Sept. 9, 1989. AB, U. Calif., Berkeley, 1981; JD, U. Calif., Davis, 1984. Bar: Calif. 1985, DC 2006. Dep. city atty. City and County of San Francisco, 1988-90; dep. ins. commr. Calif. Dept. Ins., San Francisco, 1991—95; ptnr. Long & Levit, San Francisco, 1995-97, Sonnenschein Nath & Rosenthal, LLP, San Francisco, 1997—. Bd. dirs. Iteris Inc., 1999—. Co-author eBusiness and Insurance: A Legal Guide To Transacting Insurance and Other Business on the Internet, 2001; editor (newspaper) Perspectiva, 1984-88; mem. editl. bd. Calif. Ins. Law & Regulation Reporter, 1998—. Bd. dirs. Ins. Regulators Examiners' Soc. Found.; bd. trustees U. Calif. Merced Found.; mem. Calif. adv. bd. Trust for Pub. Lands. Mem. Internat. Assn. Ins. Receivers, City Club of San Francisco, Club Mercedes. Democrat. Roman Catholic. Office: Sonnenschein Nath & Rosenthal LLP 26th Fl 525 Market St San Francisco CA 94105 Home Phone: 415-819-4845; Office Phone: 415-882-2466.

HERNANDEZ, HEATHER MARIE, organist, music director; b. Kenosha, Wis., Apr. 16, 1975; d. Thomas Anthony and Shelia Kay Harrington; m. Robert Lewis Hernandez, Aug. 4, 2001. BA in Music, Bethany Coll., Lindsborg, Kans., 1997; MusM, U. Nebr., Lincoln, 1999, D in Musical Arts, 2005. Organist Grace Episcopal Ch., Muskogee, Okla., 1990—93, First Presbyn. Ch., McPherson, Kans., 1996—97; grad. tchg. asst. U. Nebr., Lincoln, 1997—99; asst. organist St. George's Anglican Ch., Paris, 2000—01; cathedral organ scholar St. Cecilia Cathedral, Omaha, 2001—04; dir. parish music Luth. Ch. the Master, Phoenix, 2004—; accompanist Phoenix Girls Chorus, 2005—. Counselor, choral music liaison Okla. Summer Arts Inst., Tahlequah, 1997; participant Internat. Organ and Clavichord Acad., Smarano, Italy, 1998; competitor Mikael Tariverdiev Internat. Organ Competition, Kaliningrad, Russia, 2003. Recipient 3d prize, 6e Concours Internat. d'Orgue de Lorraine, 2000, 1st prize, 71e Concours Internat. d'Orgue de l'U.F.A.M., 2001; grantee Verna Ross Orndorff Career Performance Grant, Sigma Alpha Iota, 2002; fellow Eva Christensen Fellowship, U. Nebr., 2004. Mem.: Am. Guild Organists (sec. 2004—07), Pi Kappa Lamba Nat. Music Honor Soc., Sigma Alpha Iota Internat. Music Frat. (mem. at large 2006, sec. 2007—09). Episcopalian. Home: 22218 N 32d Ave Phoenix AZ 85027 Office: Lutheran Church Of Master PO Box 84468 Phoenix AZ 85071-4468 Personal E-mail: hmharrington@hotmail.com. Business E-Mail: mastermusic@cox.net.

HERNANDEZ, JENNIFER LYNN, lawyer; b. San Francisco, Oct. 30, 1959; BA with honors, Harvard U., 1981; JD, Stanford U., 1984. Bar: Calif., DC. Former ptnr. Beveridge & Diamond, PC, San Francisco; ptnr., co-chair nat. environ. team Holland & Knight LLP, San Francisco, 2005—. Bd. trustees Presidio Trust, Presidio Nat. Park, San Francisco, 1999—; bd. mem. Calif. League of Conservation Voters, Natural Heritage Inst.; mem. Calif. exec. com. Nat. Brownfields Assn.; mem. Urban Land Inst.; bd. mem. Environ. Fin. Adv. Bd., US EPA; co-founder, first bd. chair, gen. counsel Landbank, Inc.; vis. lectr. environ. and land use law Stanford Law Sch., U. Calif., Calif. Environ. Law Inst. Author: A Practical Guide to the California Environmental Quality Act (Am. Planning Assn. Award), New Paradigm that Intersects Environmental and Inner-City Economic and Health Goals (Big Brain Award), A Practical Guide to Environmental Law for California Hospital and Healthcare Facilities; contbr. articles to law jours. Bd. mem. Ctr. Creative Land Recycling. Named a No. Calif. Super Lawyer; named one of The 50 Most Influential Minority Lawyers in America, Nat Law Jour., 2008; named to LawDragon 500. Mem.: Calif. State Bar Assn. Office: Holland & Knight LLP 50 California St, Ste 2800 San Francisco CA 94111 Office Phone: 415-743-6927. E-mail: jennifer.hernandez@hklaw.com.

HERNANDEZ, JO FARB, museum director, consultant; b. Chgo., Nov. 20, 1952; BA in Polit. Sci. & French with honors, U. Wis., 1974; MA in Folklore and mythology, UCLA, 1975; postgrad., U. Calif., Davis, 1978, U. Calif., Berkeley, 1978-79, 81. Registration Mus. Cultural History UCLA, 1974-75; Rockefeller fellow Dallas Mus. Fine Arts, 1976-77; asst. to dir. Triton Mus. Art, Santa Clara, Calif., 1977-78, dir., 1978-85; adj. prof. mus. studies John F. Kennedy U., San Francisco, 1978; grad. advisor arts adminstrn. San Jose (Calif.) State U., 1979-80; dir. Monterey (Calif.) Peninsula Mus. Art, 1985-93, cons. curator, 1994—2000; prin. Curatorial and Mus. Mgmt. Svcs., Watsonville, Calif., 1993—2000; dir. Natalie and James Thompson Art Gallery, San Jose State U., Calif., 2000—, Saving and Preserving Arts and Cultural Environ., 2006—. Panelist Creative Works Fund, 2001, 04; adj. prof. gallery mgmt. art dept. U. Calif., Santa Cruz, 1999—2000; dir. Thompson Gallery, San Jose State U., 2000—; lectr., panelist, juror, panelist in field USIA, Calif. Arts Coun., Calif. Confedn. for Arts, Am. Assn. Mus., Western Mus. Assn., Am. Folklore Soc., Calif. Folklore Soc., Internat. Coun. on Mus., others; vis. lectr. U. Wis., 1980, U. Chgo., 1981, Northwestern U., 1981, San Jose State U., 1985, UCLA, 1986, Am. Cultural Ctr., Jerusalem, 1989, Tel Aviv, 89, Binational Ctr., Lima, Peru, 1988, Daytona Beach Mus. Art, 1983, UCLA, 1986, Israel Mus., 1989, Mont. State U., 1991, Oakland Mus., 1996, High Mus. Art, Atlanta, 1997, Mus. Am. Folk Art, NY, 1998, San Francisco Mus. Modern Art, 1998, U. Calif., 1998, Grinnell Coll., Iowa, 1999, Arts Coun. Silicon Valley, 2000, U. Calif., Santa Cruz, 2000, ICOM, Barcelona, 2001, Intuit Gallery, Chgo., 2004, Chgo., 07; guest curator San Diego Mus. Art, 1995—98; bd. dirs. Saving and Preserving Art and Cultural Environ.; cons. in field. Author: (mus. catalogs) The Day of the Dead: Tradition and Change in Contemporary Mexico, 1979, Three from the Northern Island: Contemporary Sculpture from Hokkaido, 1984, Crime and Punishment: Reflections of Violence in Contemporary Art, 1984, The Quiet Eye: Pottery of Shoji Hamada and Bernard Leach, 1990, Alan Shepp: The Language of Stone, 1991, Wonderful Colors: The Paintings of August Francois Gay, 1993, Jeannette Maxfield Lewis: A Centennial Celebration, 1994, Armin Hansen, 1994, Jeremy Anderson: The Critical Link/A Quiet Revolution, 1995, A.G. Rizzoli: Architect of Magnificent Visions, 1997 (one of 10 Best Books in field Amazon.com), Misch Kohn: Beyond the Tradition, 1998, Fire and Flux: An Undaunted Vision/The Art of Charles Strong, 1998, Mel Ramos: The Galatea Series, 2000, Holly Lane: Small Miracles, 2001, Irvin Tepper: When Cups Speak/Life with the Cup, 2002, Marc D'Estout: Domestic Objects, 2003, Peter Shire: Go Beyond the Ordinary, 2004, Forms of Tradition in Contemporary Spain, 2005, Gerald Walburg, 2007; co-author: Sam Richardson: Color in Space, 2002; mem. editl. bd. Raw Vision Mag., 2001-; contbr. articles to profl. jours. Bd. dirs. Bobbie Wynn and Co. of San Jose, 1981-85, Santa Clara Arts and Hist. Consortium, 1985, Non-Profit Gallery Assn., 1979-83, v.p., 1979-80; mem. nat. adv. bd. The Fund for Folk Culture, Santa Fe, 1995-98; mem. founding and exec. bd. Alliance for Calif. Traditional Arts, 2002—; mem. founding internat. adv. bd. Friends of Fred Smith, 2002—. Recipient Golden Eagle award, Coun. Internat. Nontheatrical Events, 1992, Leader of Decade award, Arts Leadership Monterey Peninsula, 1992, merit award, N.Y. Book Show, 1997, Chgo. Folklore prize, U. Chgo./Am. Folklore Soc., 2006, Fulbright Sr. Scholar Rsch. award, 2008; Rsch. grantee, Calif. State U., 2001—03, Dean's grantee, 2001, 2005, Lottery Fund grantee, 2000, 2004, Sr. Fulbright Scholar, 2007—. Mem.: Nat. Coun. for Edn. in Ceramic Arts, Western Mus. Conf. (bd. dir., exec. com. 1989—91, program chair 1990), Am. Folklore Soc., Art Table, Calif. Assn. Mus. (bd. dirs. 1985—94, v.p. 1987—91, chair nominating com. 1988, chair ann. meeting 1990, chair nominating com. 1990, pres. 1991—92, chair nominating com. 1993), Am. Assn. Mus. (lectr. 1986, mus. assessment program surveyor 1990, nat. program com. 1992—93, mus. assessment program surveyor 1994), Phi Beta Kappa. Office: School Art and Design San Jose State U One Washington Square San Jose CA 95192-0089 Office Phone: 408-924-4328, 408-924-4328.

HERNANDEZ, ROBERT MICHAEL, state legislator, software engineer; b. Pueblo, Colo., Mar. 5, 1953; BS in Bus. Adminstrn., Regis U. Mem. Colo. Ho. of Reps., 1991-95, Colo. Senate, Dist. 34, Denver, 1995—; mem. agr., natural resources and energy com. Colo. State Senate, mem. bus. affairs and labor com., mem. joint legis. coun. Active Boulder County Com., 1971; treas. Denver Young Dems., 1984-85, pres., 1986-87. Mem. Comm. Workers Am. (area rep. 1973-81). Democrat. Office: State Capitol 200 E Colfax Ave Ste 274 Denver CO 80203-1716 Home: PO Box 140238 Denver CO 80214-0238 Fax: 303-866-4543/303-624-2020.

HERNÁNDEZ, SANDRA R., foundation administrator; BA in Psychology (hon.), Yale U.; grad., John F. Kennedy Sch. Govt., Harvard U.; MD, Tufts U.; PhD (hon.), Calif. Inst. Integral Studies. Dir. San Francisco Dept. Pub. Health, 1994—97; CEO, sec. bd. trustees San Francisco Found., 1997—; asst. clin. prof. U. Calif. San Francisco Sch. Medicine; clin. practice San Francisco Gen. Hosp. AIDS Clinic. Former mem. Pres. Clinton's Adv. Commn. on Consumer Protection and Quality in Healthcare Industry; mem. Pew Commn. on Environ. Health; mem. exec. session on philanthropy John F. Kennedy Sch. Govt., Harvard U.; mem. Am. Found. for AIDS Rsch.; trustee Western Asbestos Settlement Trust; co-chair Universal Healthcare Coun., 2006; mem. Inst. Medicine's Com. on Implementation of Antiviral Medication Strategies for an Influenza Pandemic, 2007—08. Bd. mem. Coun. of Founds., Lucile Packard Children's Hosp., 2003—, Corp. for Supportive Housing, Nat. Alliance for Hispanic Health; mem. Calif. Commn. for Jobs and Econ. Growth; ex-officio bd. mem. Latino Cmty. Found. Named Hispanic Bus. Women of Yr., Hispanic Bus. Mag., 2008.

HERNQUIST, LARS ERIC, astronomer, educator; b. Princeton, NJ, Dec. 14, 1954; s. Karl Gerhard and Thyra Hildegard (Josefson) H.; m. Dale Marie Clarke, Aug. 28, 1982; 1 child, Kirsten Marie. BA, Cornell U., 1977; PhD, Calif. Inst. Tech., 1985. Rsch. fellow U. Calif., Berkeley, 1985-87, Inst. for Advanced Study, Princeton, NJ, 1987-90, Princeton U., 1990-91; asst. prof. of astronomy Lick Obs. U. Calif., Santa Cruz, 1991—98; prof. astronomy Harvard-Smithsonian Ctr. Astrophysics, 1998—. Contbr. articles to profl. publs. Fellow NSF, 1979, Sloan Found., 1991. Fellow Am. Acad. Arts & Scis.; mem. Am. Astron. Soc., Am. Phys. Soc., Internat. Astron. Union, Phi Beta Kappa, Phi Kappa Phi. Office: Harvard-Smithsonian Ctr Astrophysics P-222--MS 51 60 Garden St Cambridge MA 02138 Office Phone: 617-496-4180. Business E-Mail: lhernquist@cfa.harvard.edu.

HERR, RICHARD, history professor; b. Guanajuato, Mexico, Apr. 7, 1922; s. Irving and Luella (Winship) H.; m. Elena Fernandez Mel, Mar. 2, 1946 (div. 1967); children: Charles Fernandez, Winship; m. Valerie J. Jackson, Aug. 29, 1968; children: Sarah, Jane. AB, Harvard U., 1943; PhD, U. Chgo., 1954; Doctorate (hon.), U. Alcalá de Henares, Spain, 2001. Instr. Yale U., 1952-57, asst. prof., 1957-59; assoc. prof. U. Calif., Berkeley, 1960-63, prof. history, 1963-91, prof. emeritus, 1991—, chancellor's fellow, 1987-90. Directeur d'études associé, sixième sect. Ecole Pratique des Hautes Etudes, Paris, 1973; dir. Madrid Study Ctr., U. Calif., 1975-77; chair Portuguese Studies Program, U. Calif., Berkeley, 1994-98, chair Spanish Studies Program, U. Calif. Berkeley, 2002-04; vis. life mem. Clare Hall, Cambridge, Eng., 1985—; vis. prof. U. Alcalá. Henares, Spain, 1991; bd. dirs. Internat. Inst. Found. in Spain, Boston, 1997-2000; fellow Ctr. for History of Freedom, Washington U., St. Louis, 1994. Author: The Eighteenth Century Revolution in Spain, 1958, Tocqueville and the Old Regime, 1962, An Historical Essay on Modern Spain, 1974, Rural Change and Royal Finances in Spain at the End of the Old Regime, 1989 (Leo Gershoy award Am. Hist. Assn. 1990); co-author: An American Family in the Mexican Revolution, 1999; editor: Memorias del cura liberal don Juan Antonio Posse, 1984; co-editor, contbr.: Ideas in History, 1965, Iberian Identity, 1989; editor, contbr.: The New Portugal: Democracy and Europe, 1993, Themes in Rural History of the Western World, 1993; asst. editor: Jour. Modern History, 1949-50; mem. editl. bd. French Historical Studies, 1966-69, Revista de Historia Economica, 1983-91. With AUS, 1943-45. Decorated Comendador of the Orden de Isabel la Católica (Spain); recipient Bronze medal Collège de France, Paris, The Berkeley citation U. Calif., 1991; Social Sci. Rsch. Coun. grantee, 1963-64; Guggenheim fellow, 1959-60, 84-85; NEH sr. fellow, 1968-69. Fellow Am. Acad. Arts and Scis.; mem. Am. Philos. Soc., Real Academia de la Historia Madrid (corr.), Soc. for Spanish and Portuguese Hist. Studies. Office: U Calif Dept History Berkeley CA 94720-2550 E-mail: rherr@berkeley.edu.

HERRERA, DENNIS J., lawyer; b. Bay Shore, NY, Nov. 6, 1962; m. Anne Herrera; 1 child, Declan. BA, Villanova U.; JD, George Washington U. Bar: Calif. 1989. City. atty. City of San Francisco, 2002—; ptnr. Kelly, Gill, Sherburne & Herrera, San Francisco; chief staff U.S. Maritime Adminstrn., Washington; pres. San Francisco Police Commn.; with San Francisco Pub. Transp. Commn. Chmn. San Francisco Ethics Commn. Office: City Hall Rm 234 1 Doctor Carlton B Goodlett Pl San Francisco CA 94102 Office Phone: 415-554-4748. Business E-Mail: cityattorney@ci.sf.ca.us.

HERRERA, JAIME, state legislator; BA in Comm., U. Wash., Seattle. Former legis. asst. Congresswoman Cathy McMorris-Rodgers, US House of Reps.; former intern (dir. of polit. affairs) The White House; former event coord. (co-chair) Victory 2004; former intern State Senator Joe Zarelli, Wash. State Senate; asst. minority fl. leader Wash. House of Reps., mem. Dist. 18, 2007—. Generational leadership, dir. devel. Youth Leadership Devel. Program. Vol. Ground Zero, 9/11, NYC, 2001, Starbucks children's literacy program. Republican. Office: 416 John L O'Brien Bldg PO Box 40600 Olympia WA 98504-0600 also: 109 SW 1st St Suite 262 Battle Ground WA 98604 Office Phone: 360-786-7850, 360-687-0489. Office Fax: 360-687-1271. Business E-Mail: herrera.jaime@leg.wa.gov.

HERRERA, LUIS, library director; m. Nancy C. Herrera. BS, U. Tex., El Paso; MLS, U. Ariz.; MPA, Calif. State U., Long Beach. Mid. sch. libr.; assoc. dir. Long Beach Pub. Libr., 1983—89; dep. dir. San Diego Pub. Libr., 1989—95; dir. info. svcs. City of Pasadena, Calif., 1995—2005; city libr. San Francisco Pub. Libr., 2005—. Chair ptnrs. in edn. adv. bd. Pasadena Unified Sch. Dist.; bd. dirs. El Centro de Acción Social; bd. mem. Pacific Oaks Coll., Pasadena, Bill and Melinda Gates Libr. Found. Recipient Future Urban Adminstr. award, Calif. State U., Long Beach. Mem.: ALA, REFORMA (Libr. of Yr. 1993), Calif. Libr. Assn. (pres. 1982—83), Pub. Libr. Assn. (pres. 2003—04). Office: San Francisco Pub Libr 100 Larkin St San Francisco CA 94102 Office Phone: 415-577-4236. Personal E-mail: lherrerasfpl@yahoo.com. Business E-Mail: citylibrarian@sfpl.org.

HERRERA, MARY E., Secretary of State, New Mexico; b. Aug. 27, 1956; children: Nathan, Monique. BBA, Coll. Santa Fe, 1996, MBA, 1999; cert. in Prog. Adminstrn. for Sr. Execs., Harvard U. John F. Kennedy Sch. Govt.; certs. in Labor, Employment and Benefits Law, Inst. Applied Mgmt. Clk. typist Bernalillo County, N.Mex., 1974, asst. comptr., 1989—95, dir. human resources, 1996—2000, county clk., 2001—06; sec. state State of N.Mex., Santa Fe, 2007—. Voting mem. N.Mex. Election Reform Task Force; chair State Dem. Women N.Mex. Mem.: Nat. Assn. Hispanic Ofcls. (treas.), Nat. Assn. Counties, Nat. Assn. Latino Elected and Appointed Ofcls. (bd. mem.). Democrat. Office: Office Sec State State Capitol North Annex Ste 300 Santa Fe NM 87503

HERRERA, ROSE A., councilwoman; 1 child, David. BS, MS, Santa Clara U. Race rels. edn. instr. US Air Force; founder, CEO Cinnamon Software; founder Involved Evergreen Cmty. Group; councilwoman, Dist. 8 San José City Coun., 2008—. With County Human Rels. Commn. Vol. Sunrise Retirement Cmty., cert. trainer family support svcs. Served in USAF, 1972—75. Office: San Jose City Coun 200 E Santa Clara St San Jose CA 95113 Office Phone: 408-535-4908. Office Fax: 408-292-6469. Business E-Mail: district8@sanjoseca.gov.*

HERRERA, SHIRLEY MAE, personnel and security executive; b. Lynn, Mass., Apr. 5, 1942; d. John Baptiste and Edith Mae Lagasse; m. Christian Yanez Herrera, Apr. 30, 1975; children: Karen, Gary, Ivan, Iwonne. AS in Bus., Burdette Bus. Coll., Lynn, 1960; student, Wright State U., 1975-78. Cert. facility security officer, med. asst. in pediatrics. Med. asst. Christian Y. Herrera, M.D., Stoneham, Mass., 1972-74; human resource adminstr. MTL Systems, Inc., Dayton, Ohio, 1976-79; dir. pers. and security Tracor GIE, Inc., Provo, Utah, 1979-95; health professions vol. PHS/IHS Hosp., Rosebud, SD, 2001—03. Cons. on family dynamics family enrichment program Hill AFB, Utah, 1980-82; cons. on health care memt. Guam 7th Day Adventist Clinic, 1983; cons. on basic life support and CPR, Projecto Corazon, Monterrey, Mex., 1987—; faculty mem. Inst. for Reality Therapy, 1991—. Contbg. editor Inside Tracor, 1991—. Chmn. women's aux. YMCA Counselling Svcs., Woburn, Mass., 1970; chmn. youth vols. ARC, Wright-Patterson AFB, Dayton, 1974-76; trustee Quail Valley Homeowner's Assn., Provo, 1988-89; rep. A Spl. Wish Found., Provo, 1989. Recipient James S. Cogswell award Def. Investigative Svc., Dept. Def., 1987. Mem. Inst. for Reality Therapy (cert.), Pers. Assn. Ctrl. Utah, Women in Mgmt. (coun. 1991-95), Nat. Classification Mgmt. Soc. (chairperson Intermountain chpt. 1992-94). Republican. Avocations: writing, skiing, reading. Home: 3824 Little Rock Ln Provo UT 84604-5234

HERRES, PHILLIP BENJAMIN, computer software executive; b. Spokane, Wash., Nov. 5, 1941; s. Benjamin Jacob and Ollie Lee (Bell) H.; m. Lorelei Norma Munroe, June 15, 1963; children: Michele Marie, Anthony Phillip, Jason Randall. BSEE, Gonzaga U., 1963; MBA, U. Oreg., 1965. Registered profl. engr., Calif. Engr. Pacific N.W. Bell, Portland, Oreg., 1965-66; chief engr. Electronic Splty., Portland, Oreg., 1966-71; dir. engring. Arcata Communications, Mountain View, Calif., 1971-73; engring. mgr. Clare-Pendar, Post Falls, Idaho, 1973-76; v.p. network systems Northern Telecom, Dallas, 1976-87; sr. v.p. engring. Avanti Communications, Newport, R.I., 1987-89; chief oper. officer Aldus Corp., Seattle, 1989-92; mgmt. cons. Mercer Island, Wash., 1993-94; pres. Evergreen Software Tools, Redmond, Wash., 1994-95; mgmt. cons. Herres Co., Mercer Island, Wash., 1995—; pres. ST Labs., Bellevue, Wash., 1997-98. 1st lt. U.S. Army, 1967-71. Mem. IEEE, Columbia Tower Club. Republican. Roman Catholic. Avocations: golf, scuba diving, target shooting, collections. Office: The Herres Co 8460 W Mercer Way Ste 244 Mercer Island WA 98040-5633 also: ST Labs 3535 128th Ave SE Bellevue WA 98006-1261

HERRIDGE, ELIZABETH, museum director; Mng. dir. Guggenheim Hermitage Mus., Las Vegas, 2003—. Office: Guggenheim Hermitage Mus 3355 Las Vegas Blvd S Las Vegas NV 89109 Office Phone: 702-414-2002. E-mail: eherridge@guggenheim.org.

HERRING, CHARLES DAVID, lawyer, educator; b. Muncie, Ind., Mar. 18, 1943; s. Morris and Margaret Helen Herring; children: David, Margaret, Christopher. BA, Ind. U., 1965, JD cum laude, 1968. Bar: Ind. 1968, US Dist. Ct. (so. dist.) Ind. 1971, Calif. 1971, US Dist. Ct. (so. dist.) Calif. 1971, US Ct. Appeals (9th cir.) 1984. Rsch. assoc. Ind. U., 1965—68; intern Office of Pros. Atty., Monroe County, Ind., 1967—68; ptnr. Herring & Stubel, San Diego, Herring, Stubel & Lehr, San Diego, Herring & Loftus, San Diego, 1972—2002; shareholder Herring & Herring, 2002—; pvt. practice San Diego, 1972—. Prof. law Western State U., 1972—91; judge pro tem San Diego Probate Ct., 1983—91, San Diego Superior Ct., 1983—94, mediator, 1974—; spkr. in field. Author: (with Jim Wade) California Cases on Professional Responsibility, 1976. Vice chmn. Valle de Oro Planning Com., Spring Valley, Calif., 1972-75; chmn. Valle de Oro Citizens Exec. Com. for Cmty. Planning, Spring Valley, 1975-78; mem. Coronado Cays Architecture Com.; chmn. bd. Operation Interdependence, 2007-. Served with US Army, 1965—72, served with USAR, 1972—80. Mem.: ABA (Best Brief award 1968), Conf. Spl. Ct. Judges, San Diego County Bar Assn., Calif. Bar Assn., Ind. Bar Assn., San Diego Lions Club (past pres., chmn. bd. 1989—2006), Order of Coif. Republican. Avocations: computers, boating, swimming, golf. Home: 4 Gingertree Ln Coronado CA 92118 Office: Herring & Herring, APC 1001 B Ave Ste 215 Coronado CA 92118 Office Phone: 619-437-9175. Business E-Mail: dherring@herringlaw.net.

HERRING, (WILLIAM) CONYERS, retired physicist, educator; b. Scotia, NY, Nov. 15, 1914; s. William Conyers and Mary (Joy) H.; m. Louise C. Preusch, Nov. 30, 1946; children— Lois Mary, Alan John, Brian Charles, Gordon Robert. AB, U. Kans., 1933; PhD, Princeton, 1937. NRC fellow Mass. Inst. Tech., 1937-39; instr. Princeton, 1939-40, U. Mo., 1940-41; mem. sci. staff Div. War Research, Columbia, 1941-45; prof. applied math. U. Tex., 1946; research physicist Bell Telephone Labs., Murray Hill, NJ, 1946-78; prof. applied physics Stanford (Calif.) U., 1978-81, prof. emeritus, 1981—. Mem. Inst. Advanced Study, 1952-53 Recipient Army-Navy Cert. of Appreciation, 1947; Distinguished Service citation U. Kans., 1973; J. Murray Luck award for excellence in sci. reviewing Nat. Acad. Scis., 1980; von Hippel award Materials Rsch. Soc., 1980, Wolf prize in physics, Wolf Found., Israel, 1985. Fellow Am. Phys. Soc. (Oliver E. Buckley solid state physics prize 1959), Am. Acad. Arts and Scis.; mem. AAAS, NAS, Am. Soc. Info. Scis. Home: 3945 Nelson Dr Palo Alto CA 94306-4524 Business E-Mail: conyers@stanford.edu.

HERRING, SUSAN WELLER, dental educator, anatomist; b. Pitts., Mar. 25, 1947; d. Sol W. and Miriam (Damick) Weller; m. Norman S. Wolf, May 27, 1995. BS in Zoology, U. Chgo., 1967, PhD in Anatomy, 1971. NIH postdoctoral fellow U. Ill., Chgo., 1971-72, from asst. prof. to prof. oral anatomy and anatomy, 1972-90; prof. orthodontics U. Wash., Seattle, 1990—. Vis. assoc. prof. biol. sci. U. Mich., Ann Arbor, 1981; cons. NIH study sect., Washington, D.C., 1987-89; sci. gov. Chgo. Acad. Sci., 1982-90; mem. pub. bd. Growth Pub. Inc., Bar Harbor, Maine, 1982—. Mem. editl. bd. Cells, Tissues, Organs, 1989-2004, Jour. Dental Rsch., 1995-98, 2003—, Jour. Morphology, 1997—, Integrative Biology 2000—;, Archives of Oral Biology, 2003-; contbr. articles to profl. jours. Predoctoral fellow NSF, 1967-71; rsch. grantee NIH, 1975-78, 81—, NSF, 1990-92, 94-95. Fellow AAAS; mem. Internat. Assn. Dental Rsch. (dir. craniofacial biology group 1994-95, v.p. 1995-96, pres.-elect 1996-97, pres. 1997-98, Craniofacial Biology Rsch. award 1999), Soc. Integrated Comp. Biol.(chmn. vertebrate zoology 1983-84, exec. com. 1986-88), Am. Soc. Biomechanics, Am. Assn. Anatomists (chmn. Basmajian com. 1988-90), Soc. Vertebrate Paleontology, Internat. Soc. Vertebrate morphology (convenor 4th congress 1994, pres. 1994-97), Sigma Xi. Avocation: violin. Office: U Wash Box 357446 Seattle WA 98195-7446 E-mail: herring@u.washington.edu.

HERRINGER, FRANK CASPER, retired diversified financial services company executive; b. NYC, Nov. 12, 1942; s. Casper Frank and Alice Virginia (McMullen) H.; m. Maryellen B. Cattani; children: William, Sarah, Julia. AB magna cum laude, Dartmouth Coll., Hanover, NH, 1964, MBA with highest distinction, 1965. Prin. Cresap, McCormick & Paget, Inc., NYC, 1965-71; staff asst. to Pres. of US, Washington, 1971-73; adminstr. U.S. Urban Mass Transp. Adminstrn., Washington, 1973-75; gen. mgr. San Francisco Bay Area Rapid Transit Dist., 1975-78; exec. v.p. Transam. Corp., San Francisco, 1979-86, pres., dir., 1986-99, CEO, 1991-99, chmn., 1996—; mem. exec. bd. AEGON N.V., 1999-2000; chmn. AEGON USA, 1999-2000. Bd. dirs. Amgen Corp., Charles Schwab & Co., Aegon USA, Calif. Pacific Med. Ctr., Cardax Pharmaceuticals, Inc. Mem. Cypress Point Club, San Francisco Golf Club, Nanea Golf Club, Olympic Club, Claremont Country Club, Pacific Union Club, Stock Farm Club, Phi Beta Kappa.

HERRINGER, MARYELLEN CATTANI, lawyer; b. Bakersfield, Calif., Dec. 1, 1943; d. Arnold Theodore and Corinne Marilyn (Kovacevich) C.; m. Frank C. Herringer; children: Sarah, Julia. AB, Vassar Coll., Poughkeepsie, NY, 1965; JD, U. Calif., Boalt Hill, 1968; Exec. Program, Stanford Grad. Sch. Bus., 1994. Assoc. Davis Polk & Wardwell, NYC, 1968-69, Orrick, Herrington & Sutcliffe, San Francisco, 1970-74, ptnr., 1975-81; v.p., gen. counsel Transamerica Corp., San Francisco, 1981-83, sr. v.p., gen. counsel, 1983-89; ptnr. Morrison & Foerster, San Francisco, 1989-91; sr. v.p. gen. counsel APL Ltd., Oakland, Calif., 1991-95, exec. v.p., gen. counsel, 1995-97; gen. counsel allied bus. Littler & Mendelson, San Francisco, 2000. Bd. dirs. ABM Industries Inc., PG&E Corp., Pacific Gas and Electric Co., Wachovia Corp. Author: Calif. Corp. Practice Guide, 1977, Corp. Counselors, 1982. Regent St. Mary's Coll., Moraga, Calif., 1986-, pres., 1990-92, trustee, 1990-99, chmn., 1993-95; trustee Vassar Coll., 1985-93, The Head-Royce Sch., 1993-02, Mills Coll., 1999-, The Benilde Religious & Charitable Trust, 1999-, Alameda County Med. Ctr. Hosp. Authority, 1998-02, U. Calif. Berkeley Art Mus., 2001-; bd. dirs. The Exploratorium, 1988-93. Mem. ABA, State Bar Calif. (chmn. bus. law sect. 1980-81), Bar Assn. San Francisco (co-chair com. on women 1989-91), Calif. Women Lawyers, San Francisco C. of C. (bd. dirs. 1987-91, gen. counsel 1990-91), Am. Corp. Counsel Assn. (bd. dirs. 1982-87), Women's Forum West (bd. dirs. 1984-87). Democrat. Roman Catholic. Personal E-mail: mherringer@aol.com.

HERRMANN, CHRISTIAN, JR., medical educator; b. Lansing, Mich., 1921; s. Christian and Agnes (Bauch) H. AB, U. Mich., 1942, MD, 1944. Diplomate Am. Bd. Psychiatry and Neurology. Intern Harper Hosp., Detroit, 1944-45; asst. resident medicine Henry Ford Hosp., Detroit, 1945-46; resident neurology Neurol. Inst., NYC, 1948-50, research asst. neurology, 1950-51, chief resident neurology, 1951-52, asst. neurology, 1950-51, 51-52, asst. attending, 1953-54; mem. faculty U. Calif. at Los Angeles Med. Sch., 1954—, prof. neurology, 1969-86, prof. neurology emeritus, 1986—, vice chmn. dept. Neurology, 1970-86. Vice chmn. Calif. chpt. Myasthenia Gravis Found., 1966—, chmn. med. adv. bd., 1968-72, pres. 1972-74, chmn. nat. med. adv. bd., 1983-85. Served as lt. (j.g.) M.C. USNR, 1946-48. USPHS research fellow neurology Columbia Coll. Phys. and Surg., 1952-54 Office: U Calif Dept Neurology Reed Neurol Research Ctr Los Angeles CA 90095-1769 Office Phone: 310-206-3380.

HERRON, J. JAY, lawyer; b. Lake City, Minn., 1954; Student, Calif. State U., Fullerton; BS, U. Calif., Berkeley, 1977; JD, Stanford U., 1980. Bar: Calif. 1980, US Dist. Ct. (ctrl. dist.) Calif. 1980. Ptnr. O'Melveny & Myers LLP, Newport Beach, Calif., 1990—. Lectr. Calif. Continuing Edn. of the Bar, 1990—. Mem.: Order of the Coif, Beta Alpha Psi, Phi Beta Kappa. Office: O'Melveny & Myers LLP 610 Newport Ctr Dr 17th Flr Newport Beach CA 92660 Office Phone: 949-823-6922. Office Fax: 949-823-6994. Business E-Mail: jherron@omm.com.

HERSCHENSOHN, BRUCE, film director, scriptwriter; b. Milw., Sept. 10, 1932; Student, LA. With art dept. RKO Pictures, 1953-55; dir., editor Gen. Dynamics Corp., 1955-56; dir., writer, editor Karma for Internat. Communications Found.; editor, co-dir. Friendship Seven for NASA; dir., editor Tall Man Five-Five for Gen. Dynamics Corp. and SAC; dir. motion picture and TV Service USIA, 1968-72, spl. cons. to dir., 1972—; staff asst. to Pres. U.S., 1972; dep. spl. asst. to Pres., 1973-74, mem. transition team, 1981; sr. fellow Claremont (Calif.) Inst., 1993; Rep. nominee U.S. Senate (Calif.), 1992. Tchr. U.S. fgn. policy Pepperdine U., 1998—; tchr. U. Md., 1972; spl. cons. to Rep. Nat. Conv., 72; polit. analyst KABC-TV and KABC Radio, 1978—91. Directed and wrote films for USIA, including Bridges of the Barrios, The Five Cities of June, The President, John F. Kennedy: Years of Lightning, Day of Drums, Eulogy to 5:02; recipient Acad. award for Czechoslovakia 1968 as best documentary short 1969; author: The Gods of Antenna, 1976; contbg. editor: Conservative Digest. Bd. govs. Charles Edison Meml. Youth Fund; Rep. nom. U.S. Senate, Calif., 1992. Served with USAF, 1951-52. Recipient Arthur S. Flemming award as 10 of 10 outstanding young men in fed govt., 1969, DSM, USIA, 1972, Ann. award, Coun. Against Communist Aggression, 1972; fellow, JFK Sch., Harvard U., 1996. Office: Pepperdine Univ 24255 Pacific Coast Hwy Malibu CA 90263

HERSCHER, PENNY, information technology executive; BA in Maths. with honors, Cambridge U., England. R&D engr. Tex. Instruments, England; mgr. Daisy Sys. Corp. ASIC Program; from v.p. mktg., gen. mgr. to dir. product mktg. Design Environ. Group Synopsys Inc.; pres., CEO Simplex Solutions Inc., 1996—2002; exec. v.p., chief mktg. officer Cadence Design Systems, 2002—04; pres., CEO FirstRain, San Mateo, Calif., 2004—. Bd. dirs. FirstRain, 2004—, Rambus Inc., 2006—, JDSU, 2008—. Office: FirstRain 1510 Fashion Island Blvd Ste 120 San Mateo CA 94404

HERSH, NEAL RAYMOND, lawyer; b. LA, July 12, 1951; BA, UCLA, 1973; JD, Southwestern U., 1976. Bar: Calif. 1976, US Dist. Ct. (Ctrl. Dist. Calif.) 1977, US Supreme Ct. 1982. Pres., bd. dir. Levitt & Quinn Family Law Center, Inc., LA; prin. atty. Am. Assn. Mediate Divorce; ptnr. Hersh, Mannis & Bogen, LLP, Beverly Hills, Calif. Spkr. in field; commentator AM LA KABC news radio, Hard Copy, Entertainment Tonight, Celebrity Justice, Burden of Proof, CNN, 2001, CNBC, 2001, Court TV, 2001. Contbr. articles to numerous profl. jours. Named a Super Lawyer, LA mag., 2003, 2004. Fellow: Internat. Acad. Matrimonial Lawyers, Am. Acad. Matrimonial Lawyers; mem.: State Bar Calif. (mem. family law sect.), ABA (mem. family law sect.), LA County Bar Assn. (mem. family law sect.), Beverly Hills Bar Assn. (chmn. 2001—02, mem. family law sect., mem. exec. com. family law sect. 1997—). Office: Hersh Mannis & Bogen LLP Ste 209 9150 Wilshire Blvd Beverly Hills CA 90212 Office Phone: 310-786-1910. Office Fax: 310-786-1917. E-mail: nhersh@hershmannis.com.

HERSH, SARAH A., legislative staff member; BA in polit. studies, Pitzer Coll., 2005. Dist. scheduler for Rep. Jerry McNerney US House of Reps., Washington, 2007—08, comm. dir. to Rep. Jerry McNerney, 2009—. Office: Office of Rep Jerry McNerney 312 Cannon House Office Bldg Washington DC 20515-0511 also: 5776 Stoneridge Mall Rd Ste 175 Pleasanton CA 94588-2836 Office Phone: 202-225-1947, 925-737-0727. Office Fax: 202-225-4060, 925-737-0734. E-mail: sarah.hersh@mail.house.gov.

HERSHBERGER, ROBERT GLEN, architect, educator; b. Pocatello, Idaho, Apr. 4, 1936; s. Vernon Elver and Edna Syvilla (Kinsley) H.; m. Deanna Marlene Van Dyke, Mar. 25, 1961; children: Vernon, Andrew. AB, Stanford U., 1958; BArch, U. Utah, 1959; MArch, U. Pa., 1961, PhD, 1969. Registered architect, Idaho, Ariz. Project architect Spencer & Lee, Architects, San Francisco, 1961-63; project designer GBQC Architects, Phila., 1967-69; asst. prof. Idaho State U., Pocatello, 1963-65; adj. asst. prof. Drexel U., Phila., 1967-69; practicing architect Archtl. & Planning Cons., Tempe, Ariz., 1969-87; prof. Sch. of Architecture Ariz. State U., Tempe, 1969-87, acting dir. Sch. Architecture, 1986-87, assoc. dean. Coll. of Architecture and Environ. Design, 1987; prof. U. Ariz. Coll. Arch., Tucson, 1988—2001, dean, 1988-96; ptnr. Hershberger and Nickels Archs./Planners, 1998—; prin. Hershberger Arch. and Planner, Payson, Ariz., 2002—. Chmn. Environ. Design Rsch. Assoc., Washington, 1976-79, chair Archs. in Edn. Com. AIA, Washington, 1983-85; v.p. Arch. Rsch. Ctrs. Consortium, 1994-96. Prin. works include Covenant Bapt. Ch. (AIA Excellence award), Urban Renewal Plan Downtown Tempe (AIA Citation), Hershberger residence (AIA honor 1990); author: Architectural Programming and Predesign Manager, 1999; Archtl. Programming in Architect's Handbook of Professional Practice, 2001, Handbook of Environmental Psychology, 2002. Bd. dirs. Rio Salado Found.; mem. Tempe Design Rev. Com., 1985-87, Tempe Elec. Adv. Com., 1982-85, Pocatello Planning Commn., 1962-65; mem. Tucson Planning Commn., 2000-02; mem. pub. arts com. U. Ariz., 1988-96, chmn., 1994-96, mem. campus design rev. adv. com., 1990-96, chmn., 1990-93; chair staff parish com. Catalina United Meth. Ch., 1995; bd. dirs. Catalina Day Care Ctr., 1990-93, So. Ariz. chpt. Make-A-Wish Found., 1995-96; mem. fin. com. Christ Ch. United Meth., 2000-01; mem. Payson Hist. Preservation Conservation Commn., 2003-2006; archtl. rev. com. Portal 4, Pine, Ariz., 2003-2006; chair Payson Design Rev., 2003-2006; chair staff parish rels. com. Payson United Meth. Ch., 2004-2006. Recipient Crescordia Environ. Excellence award Valley Forward Assn., 1986, Hon. Mention award Ariz. Hist. Mus. competition, 1985. Fellow AIA (pres. Rio Salado chpt. 1981, 74-88, bd. dirs. So. Ariz. chpt. 1988-96, pres., 1993, Gold medal adv. bd. 1992-95). Democrat. Methodist. Avocations: fly fishing, skiing, hunting, tennis, golf, photography. Office: PO Box 2266 Payson AZ 85547 Home: 204 N Forest Park Dr Payson AZ 85541 Office Phone: 928-970-9280. E-mail: hershberger@npgcable.com.

HERSHMAN, LYNN LESTER, artist; b. Cleve. 1 dau., Dawn. BS, Case-Western Res. U., 1963; MA, San Francisco State U., 1972. Prof. U. Calif., Davis, 1984—. Vis. prof. art U. Calif., Berkeley, Calif. Coll. Arts and Crafts, San Jose State U., 1974-78; assoc. project dir. Christo's Running Fence, 1973-76; founder, dir. Floating Mus.,

1975-79; ind. film/video producer and cons., 1979— Author works in field; one-man shows include Santa Barbara Mus. Art, 1970, Univ. Art Mus., Berkeley, Calif., 1972, Mills Coll., Oakland, Calif., 1973, William Sawyer Gallery, 1974, Nat. Galleries, Melbourne, Australia, 1976, Mandeville Art Gallery, U. Calif., San Diego, 1976, M.H. de Young Art Mus., 1978, Pallazo dei Diamonte, Ferrara, Italy, 1978, San Francisco Art Acad., 1980, Portland Center Visual Arts, 1980, New Mus., New Sch., N.Y.C., 1981, Inst. Contemporary Art, Phila., 1981, Anina Nosai Gallery, N.Y.C., 1981, Contemporary Art Center, Cin., 1982, Toronto, Los Angeles Contemporary Exhibits, 1986, Univ. Art Mus. Berkeley, 1987, Madison (Wis.) Art Ctr., 1987, Intersection for the Arts, San Francisco, Pacific Film Archive, A. Space, "Guerilla Tactics" Toronto, Can., Venice Bienalle Global Village; group exhbns. include Cleve. Art Mus., 1968, St. Paul Art Ctr., 1969, Richmond (Calif.) Art Ctr., 1970, 73, Galeria del Sol, Santa Barbara, Calif., 1971, San Francisco Art Inst., 1972, Richard Demarco Art Gallery, Edinburgh, Scotland, 1973, Laguna Beach (Calif.) Art Mus., 1973, Univ. Art Mus., Univ. Calif., Berkeley, 1974, Bronx (N.Y.) Mus., 1975, Linda Ferris Gallery, Seattle, 1975, Madenville Art Gallery, San Diego, Contemporary Arts Mus., Houston, 1977, New Orleans, 1977, Ga. Mus. Art, Athens, 1977, New Mus., N.Y., 1981, Calif. Coll. Arts and Crafts, 1981, San Francisco Mus. Modern Art, 1979, 80, 90, Art-Beaubourg, Paris, 1980, Ars Electronica, 1989, Am. Film Inst., 1989, Mus. Moving Image Internat. Ctr. for Photography, 1989, Kitchen Ctr. for Video-Music, N.Y., 1990, Robert Koch Gallery, San Francsico, 1990, Inst. Contemporary Art, London, 1990, Frankfurt (Germany) Art Fair, 1990, Inst. Conteporary Art, Boston, 1991, Oakland (Calif.) Mus., 1991, La Cite des Arts et des Nouvelles Technologies, Montreal, 1991, Richard F. Brush Art Gallery, Canton, N.Y., 1992, Jack Tilton Gallery, N.Y., 1992, Southeastern Ctr. for Contemporary Art, Winston-Salem, N.C., 1992, Bonner Kunstverein, Bonn, Germany, 1992, Chgo. Ave. Armory, 1992, Retrospective, Tribute, 1994, Nelson Gallery, Paris, 1994, Hess Collection, 1994. Bd. dirs. San Francisco Art Acad., Spectrum Found., Motion a Performance Collective. Western States Regional fellow (film/video), 1990; grantee Nat. Endowment for the Arts, (2) Art Matters Inc., San Francisco Found., N.Y. State Coun. for the Arts, Zellerbach Family Fund, Inter Arts of Marin, Gerbode Found., The Women's Project; recipient Dirs. Choice award San Francisco Internat. Film Festival, 1987, tribute 1987 Mill Valley Video Festial, Exptl. Video award 1988, 1st prize Montbelliard, France, 1990, 2d prize, Vigo, Spain, 1992, 1993 Ars Electronica, Austria, WRO Poland, Nat. Film Theatre, London, Gerber award Seattle Art Mus., 1994, ZKM/Siemans award, 1995, Golden Nica, Ars Electronica, 1999, Flintridge award Lifetime Achievement in the Arts, 1999. Mem. Assn. Art Pubs. (dir., Annie Gerber award 1995). Office: 1201 California St San Francisco CA 94109-5001

HERTEL, JOHN R., state legislator, farmer, rancher; b. Lewistown, Mont., May 9, 1940; m. Dixie Hertel. BS, Rocky Mountain Coll., 1962. Tchr. high sch., 1962-73; farmer-rancher, 1973—; mem. Mont. State Senate, 1992—, chair bus./industry com., vice chair bills and jours. com., mem. edn. and cultural resources com., hwys. and transp. com. Bd. dirs. Moore Farmers Oil Co., Norwest Bank. Bd. dirs. Moccasin Experiment Sta.; mem. Moore Sch. Bd., 1972-92, chair 8 yrs. Mem. Mont. Stockgrowers, Fergus County Livestock Assn. (bd. dirs.)., Fergus County Farm Bur. (bd. dirs.), Masons. Republican. Home: RR 1 Box 30 Moore MT 59464-9703

HERTZBERG, ROBERT M., former state legislator; m. Cynthia Telles; children: Daniel, David, Raymond. Graduated magna cum laude, U. Redlands, 1976; JD magna cum laude, U. Calif., 1979. Mem. Calif. State Assembly, 1996—, spkr., 2000—02, spkr. emeritus, 2002—. Chmn. Calif. Assembly Rules Com., 1998—. Mem. L.A. County Quality and Productivity Commn., Calif. State Bd. Pharmacy, 1984-88; chmn. Calif. Adv. Commn. on Youth, 1978-79, dean's coun. Hebrew Union Coll., 1991-95, v.p. Am. Jewish Com.; bd. dirs. CORO Assocs., Chinatown Svc. Ctr., Mulholland Tomorrow.; mem. exec. com. Jewish Cmty. Rels. Com. of Valley Alliance, state issues com. Valley Industry and Commerce Assn., Sherman Oaks Town Coun. Commerce Assn. Recipient Paul Harris fellow Rotary Found. Rotary Internat, Joe Farber Legis. award Peace Officers Rsch. Assn. Calif., Gold Key award L.A. Opportunities Industrialization ctr., PTA award 31st Dist. PTSA, Disting. Svc. award Planned Parenthood. Office: Calif State Assembly Van Nuys State Bldg 6150 Van Nuys Blvd Ste 305 Van Nuys CA 91401-3345 also: State Capitol Rm 319 Sacramento CA 95814

HERZ, LEONARD, financial consultant; b. Bronx, NY, June 25, 1931; s. Emanuel and Henrietta (Morris) H.; m. Sally Jampolsky, May 2, 1954 (dec. Apr. 1994); children: Michael, Hildee, Larry; m. Debra Brody, July 28, 1995. BBA, CCNY, 1952. C.P.A., N.Y. Auditor Lybrand Ross Bros., C.P.A.s, NYC, 1954-60; asst. controller Merritt Chapman Scott, NYC, 1960-66; treas. Baker Industries Inc., Parsippany, N.J., 1966-73; v.p. finance Del Labs. Inc., Farmingdale, N.Y., 1973-74; exec. v.p. Holmes Protection, Inc., NYC, 1974-82; fin. cons. L. Herz, Denver, 1982-87. Dir. Oliver Exterminating Corp., Am. Med. Alert Corp.; bd. dirs. Ctrl. Sta. Electric Protective Assn. With AUS, 1952-54. Mem. N.Y. State Soc. C.P.A.s, Am. Inst. C.P.A.s, Exec. Assn. Greater N.Y. (bd. dirs. 1988-90). Home and Office: 2400 Cherry Creek S DR Unit 312 Denver CO 80209-3255

HERZ, MICHAEL JOSEPH, marine environmental scientist; b. St. Paul, Aug. 12, 1936; s. Malvin E. and Josephine (Daneman) H.; m. Joan Klein Levy, Feb. 3, 1962 (div. 1982); children: David M., Daniel J., Ann K.; m. Naomi Brodie Schalit, Aug. 21, 1984 (div. 1996); children: Nathaniel B., Hallie R.; m. Kate Pearson Josephs, Sept. 27, 1998. BA, Reed Coll., 1958; MA, San Francisco State U., 1962; PhD, U. So. Calif., 1966. Program coord. postdoctoral tng. program U. Calif., San Francisco, 1969-73, asst. prof., 1969-73, assoc. prof. in residence, 1973-74; exec. dir., dir. water quality tng. program San Francisco Bay. chpt. Oceanic Soc., 1974-77; exec. v.p., co-dir. rsch. and policy Oceanic Soc., San Francisco, 1977-84; sr. rsch. scientist San Francisco State U., 1984-88; exec. dir. and baykeeper San Francisco BayKeeper, 1989-95; pvt. cons. Alna, Damariscotta, Maine, 1995—; postdoc. fellow UCLA Brain Rsch. Inst., 1966—68. Chmn. bd. govs. Tiburon Ctr. Environ. Studies, San Francisco State U., 1985-86; NRC com. mem. Effectiveness of Oil Spill Disperants, Washington, 1985-87, Risk Assessment Mgmt. Marine Systems, Washington, 1996-98; mem. com. on ocean disposal of radwaste Calif. Dept. Health, Sacramento, 1985-92; mem. tech. adv. com. Calif. Office of Oil Spill Prevention and Response, 1992-95; bd. dirs. Friends of the Earth, Washington, 1989—, chmn. bd. dirs., 1997-99, 2007-; bd. dirs. Oceanic Soc., 1984-89; chmn. bd. dirs. Aquatic Habitat Inst.; mem. Alaska Oil Spill Commn., 1989-90; mem. NRC com. Risk Assessment and Mgmt. of Marine Systems, Washington, 1996—. Author, co-editor: Memory Consolidation, 1972, Habituation I & II, 1973;co-author: Cruise Control: A Report on How Cruise Ships Affect the Marine Environment, 2002; editor: Protection and Restoration of Salmon Habitat, 2001; contbr. reports to profl. publs. Chmn. cmty. adv. bd. Sta. KQED (Pub. Broadcast Sys. affiliate), 1979—85; San Francisco citizens adv. com. San Francisco Bay Conservation and Devel. Commn., 1979—94, chmn., 1984; mem. tech. adv. com. San Francisco Bay Regional Water Quality Control Bd., Oakland, Calif., 1979—82, Assn. Bay Area Govts., Oakland, 1983—84; mem. Bay area adv. com. Sea Grant Marine Adv. Program, San Francisco, 1983—89; mem. com. Bur. Land Mgmt., Pacific States Regional Tech. Working Group, 1979—83; bd. dirs. Maine Initiatives, 1996—2000, Sheepscot Valley Conservation Assn., 1994—, pres., 1999—2004; bd. dirs. Citizens for a Better Environment, 1986—94, Oceanic Soc., 1984—89, Maine Rivers, 2002—, Friends of Maine Seabird Islands, 2004—07. With US Army, 1958—59. Predoctoral fellow NIMH, U. So. Calif., 1963-64, postdoctoral fellow NIMH, UCLA Brain Research Inst, 1966-68. Mem. AAAS, Calif. Acad. Scis., San Francisco Bay and Estuarine Assn. Office Phone: 207-563-5435. Business E-Mail: mherz@lincoln.midcoast.com.

HERZBERGER, EUGENE E., retired neurosurgeon; b. Sotchi, USSR, June 7, 1920; came to U.S., 1957, naturalized, 1964; s. Eugene S. and Mary P. H.; married; children— Henry, Monica MD, U. King Ferdinand I, Cluj, Rumania, 1947. Diplomate Am. Bd. Neurol. Surgery. Intern Univ. Hosp., Cluj, Rumania, 1946-47, resident in surgery, 1947-48; resident in neurosurgery Beilinson Hosp., Tel Aviv, 1949-53; chief neurosurgeon Tel Hashomer Govt. Hosp., Tel Aviv, 1953-57; research asst. Yale U., 1958-59; instr. neurosurgery Med. Coll. Ga., 1959-60; attending neurosurgeon St. Clare Hosp., Monroe, Wis., 1960-76, Mercy Hosp. and Finley Hosp., Dubuque, Iowa, 1976-94. Contbr. articles to med. jours. Mem. Am. Assn. Neurol. Surgeons, Iowa Midwest Neurosurg. Soc., Congress Neurol. Surgeons, Am. Acad. Neurology, Iowa State Med. Soc.

HERZLICH, HAROLD J., chemical engineer; b. Bklyn. m. Carol Ast; children: Amy, Adam. BSChemE, NYU, 1956; student, So. Conn. Coll., Quinnipiac Coll. Mem. prodn. squadron Goodyear Tire & Rubber Co., Akron, Ohio, 1956-57, mem. process devel., 1957-58; prodn. compounder Armstrong Rubber Co., New Haven, 1958-61, sr. compounder, 1961-62, divsn. compounder, 1962-65, mgr. pass tire comp. devel., 1965-66, mgr. auto tire comp. devel., 1966-68, mgr. pass car tire comp. devel., 1968-70, sr. rsch. chemist, 1970-73, mgr. compound rsch., 1973-75, mgr. compound devel., 1975-85, dir. tire engring., legal matters and product reliability, 1985-88, Pirelli Armstrong Tire Co., New Haven, 1988-90; consulting tire engr. Tire Engring., Chemistry and Safety, Las Vegas, 1990—. Pres. Elasphalt Corp.; chmn. Internat. Tire Conf.; speaker in field. Tech. editor Rubber and Plastics News. With USCG. Mem. ASTM (mem. E-40), Am. Chem. Soc. (chmn. rubber divsn. 1982—, chmn.-elect 1981, mem. membership com., mem. edn. com., mem. budget and fin. com., treas. rubber divsn. 1978-81, bus. mgr. rubber chemistry and tech., mem. divsn. chemistry and law, hon. life), Soc. Automotive Engrs., Acad. Forensics Sci. (engring. divsn.), Tire Soc., Conn. Rubber Group (edn. chmn., vice chmn., chmn. 1966, hon. life). Avocations: sports, travel. Home and Office: Tire Engring Chemistry & Safety 8908 Desert Mound Dr Las Vegas NV 89134-8801 E-mail: harherz@juno.com.

HESS, CHARLES EDWARD, environmental horticulture educator; b. Paterson, NJ, Dec. 20, 1931; s. Cornelius W. M. and Alice (Debruyn) H.; children: Mary, Carol, Nancy, John, Peter; m. Eva G. Carroad, Feb. 14, 1981. BS, Rutgers U., 1953; MS, Cornell U., 1954, PhD, 1957; DAgr (hon.), Purdue U., 1983; DSc (hon.), Delaware Valley Coll., Doylestown, Pa., 1992. From asst. prof. to prof. Purdue U., West Lafayette, Ind., 1958-65; rsch. prof., dept. chmn. Rutgers U., New Brunswick, NJ, 1966, assoc. dean, dir. NJ Agrl. Exptl. Sta., 1970, acting dean Coll. Agrl. and Environ. Sci., 1971, dean Cook Coll., 1972-75; assoc. dir. Calif. Agrl. Exptl. Sta., 1975-89; asst. sec. sci. and edn. USDA, Washington, 1989-91; dean Coll. Agrl. and Environ. Scis. U. Calif., Davis, 1975-89, prof. dept. environ. horticulture, 1975-94, prof. emeritus, 1994—, dir. internat. programs Coll. Agrl. and Environ. Scis., 1992-98, spl. asst. to provost, 1994—2003, spl. asst. to chancellor, 2003—04, chair, dept. Nutrition, 2007—. Cons. U.S. AID, 1965, Office Tech. Assessment, U.S. Congress, 1976-77, Nat. Rsch. Coun., 2005—; chmn. study team world food and nutrition study NAS, 1976; mem. Calif. State Bd. Food and Agr., 1984-89; mem. Nat. Sci. Bd., 1982-88, 92-98, vice-chmn., 1984-88; co-chmn. Joint Coun. USDA, 1987-91; mem. external adv. com. Western Ctr. for Agrl. Health and Safety, 2005—. Mem. West Lafayette Sch. Bd., 1963-65, sec., 1963, pres., 1964; mem. Gov.'s Commn. Blueprint for Agr., 1971-73; bd. dirs. Davis Sci. Ctr., 1992-94; trustee Internat. Svc. for Nat. Agrl. Rsch., The Hague, Netherlands, 1992-98, bd. chmn., 1995-96; chair adv. com. U. Calif. Davis Retiree Ctr., 2005—. Mem. U.S. EPA (mem. biotech. sci. adv. com. 1992-96), AAAS (chmn. agriculture sect. 1989-90), Am. Soc. Hort. Sci. (pres. 1973), Internat. Plant Propagators Soc. (pres. 1973), Agrl. Rsch. Inst., U. Calif. Davis Emerti Assn. (pres. 2004-06), Phi Beta Kappa, Sigma Xi, Alpha Zeta, Phi Kappa Phi, Gamma Sigma Delta (Disting. Achievement in Agr. award 2004). Office: U Calif Coll Agrl Environ Scis Dept Nutrition Davis CA 95616 Office Phone: 530-754-0671, 530-754-0159. Business E-Mail: cehess@ucdavis.edu.

HESS, JOHN WARREN, professional society administrator; b. Lancaster, Pa., May 6, 1947; s. John Warren and Barbara Kathryn (Spencer) H.; m. Letitia Jean Schrantz, Mar. 20, 1971; children: Nathan James, Joshua Kyle. BS in Geol. Scis., Pa. State U., 1969, PhD in Geology, 1974. Asst. rsch. prof. water resources ctr. Desert Rsch. Inst., Las Vegas, Nev., 1974-78, assoc. rsch. prof., 1978-86, rsch. prof., 1985—2001, dir. environ. isotope lab., 1981-87, dep. dir., 1987-89, exec. dir., 1989-2000, interim v.p. rsch., 1994-95, v.p. acad. affairs, 1995—2001, congrl. fellow, 2000—01; exec. dir. Geol. Soc. Am., Boulder, Colo., 2001—. Past chmn. bd. dirs. Karst Waters Inst., Charlestown, W.Va. Contbr. over 91 articles to profl. jours. Adult leader Boy Scouts Am., Las Vegas, 1978—2001, Boulder, Colo., 2002—, chmn. US Nat. Com. of Internat. Yr. of Planet Earth. Recipient Alumni Achievement award Coll. Earth and Mineral Scis., Pa. State U., 2004; Hon. Rsch. fellow U. Glasgow, Scotland, 1980-81; Centennial fellow Coll. Earth and Mineral Scis., Pa. State U. Fellow Geol. Soc. Am. (chair hydrogeology divsn., 1995-96), Nat. Speleological Soc.; mem. AAAS, Am. Geophys. Union, Internat. Assn. Hydrogeologists, Geochem. Soc. Office: Geol Soc Am 3300 Penrose Pl Boulder CO 80301 Home Phone: 303-666-8615; Office Phone: 303-357-1039. Business E-Mail: jhess@geosociety.org.

HESS, RICHARD NEAL, plastic surgeon; b. Phila., June 16, 1957; MD, U. Ariz., 1983. Chmn. plastic surgery Northwest Hosp., Tucson. Office: 1050 E River Ste 200 Tucson AZ 85718

HESSE, MARTHA O., gas industry executive; b. Hattiesburg, Miss., Aug. 14, 1942; d. John William and Geraldine Elaine (Ossian) H. BS, U. Iowa, 1964; postgrad., Northwestern U., 1972-76; MBA, U. Chgo., 1979. Rsch. analyst Blue Shield, 1964-66; dir. div. data mgmt. Am. Hosp. Assn., 1966-69; dir., COO SEI Info. Tech., Chgo., 1969-80; assoc. dep. sec. Dept. of Commerce, Washington, 1981-82; exec. dir. Pres.' Task Force on Mgmt. Reform, 1982; asst. sec. mgmt. and adminstrn. Dept. of Energy, Washington, 1982-86; chmn. FERC, Washington, 1986-89; sr. v.p. 1st Chgo. Corp., 1990; CEO Hesse Gas Co., Houston, 1990—2003. Bd. dirs. Mut. Trust Life, AMEC plc, Terra Industries, Enbridge Energy Prnrs., chmn. bd., 2007—. Home: 4171 Autumn Hills Dr Winnemucca NV 89445

HESSELINK, LAMBERTUS, electrical engineering and physics educator; b. Enschede, The Netherlands, Dec. 4, 1948; came to U.S., 1971; s. Lambertus and Wilhelmina (ten Tye) H. BSME, Twente Inst. Tech., Enschede, 1970, BS in Applied Physics, 1971, postgrad., 1974; MSME, Calif. Inst. Tech., 1972, PhD in Applied Mechs., Physics, 1977. Rsch. fellow Calif. Inst. Tech., Pasadena, 1977-78, instr. applied physics, 1978-80, sr. rsch. fellow fluid mechs., 1979-80; asst. prof. aeros. and astronautics Stanford (Calif.) U., 1980-85, asst. prof., 1985—, assoc. prof. elec. engring., 1980-85, asst. prof., 1985-90, prof. electrical engring. and aeronautics/astonautics, 1990—. Cons. Hughes Aircraft Corp., Culver City, Calif., 1978-79, MCC Corp., 1986-92; invited scientist mem. image processing work group for Hubble Space Telescope, 1990; assoc. editor Jour. Applied Sci. and Applied Optics, 1990; founder Siros Technologies, Inc.; cons. to industry and govt.; mem. scientific adv. bd. USAF, 1995—; founder Senvid, Inc. Patentee in field. Recipient Stheeman prize Twente Inst. Tech., 1970; Fulbright fellow 1971-74; Josephine de Karman fellow, 1974-75. Fellow SPIE, Optical Soc. Am.; mem. AIAA (Engr. of Yr. 1982), Soc. Photo-Optical Instrumentation Engrs. Optical Soc. Am., Am. Phys. Soc., Royal Dutch Acad. Arts and Scis. (corr.), Sigma Xi. Office: Stanford U Mail Code 4075 CISX Bldg Rm 325 Stanford CA 94305-4075 E-mail: bert@kaos.stanford.edu.

HESTER, NORMAN ERIC, chemical company technical executive, chemist; b. Niangua, Mo., Dec. 16, 1946; s Eric Ira and Norma Josephine (Wright) H.; m. Sylvie Jean Hunt, June 16, 1973; children: Jenay Aimee, Yvette Joy, Trinity Marie. AA, El Camino Coll., 1966; BS, Calif. State U., Long Beach, 1968; MS, U. Calif., Riverside, 1971, PhD, 1972. Postdoctoral rsch. chemist U. Calif. Air Pollution Ctr., Riverside, 1972-74; air quality chemist EPA, Las Vegas, Nev., 1974-77; program mgr. Rockwell Internat., Newbury Park, Calif., 1977-80; group head Occidental Petroleum Rsch. Ctr., Irvine, Calif., 1980-83; tech. dir. Truesdail Labs. Inc., Tustin, Calif., 1983—. Pvt. environ. cons., Mission Viejo, Calif., 1983. Contbr. articles to profl. jours. Mem. Am. Chem. Soc., Assn. Ofcl. Racing Chemists. Republican. Avocations: growing hybrid roses, hiking, travel. Office: Truesdail Labs Inc 14201 Franklin Ave Tustin CA 92780-7008 Home Phone: 949-581-7620; Office Phone: 714-730-6239. E-mail: norman@truesdail.com, normanhester@netscape.net.

HESTER, RANDOLPH THOMPSON, JR., landscape architect, educator; b. Danville, Va., Dec. 12, 1944; s. Randolph Thompson and Virginia (Green) H.; m. Marcia Jeanne McNally, Mar. 17, 1983; 1 child, Nathaniel Christopher. BA, N.C. State U., 1969, BS in Landscape Architecture, 1968; M in Landscape Architecture, Harvard U., 1969. Registered landscape architect, N.C. Prof. Pa. State U., State Coll., 1969-70, N.C. State U., Raleigh, 1970-80, city univ. coord., 1972-75; prof. U. Calif., Berkeley, 1981—, chmn. dept. landscape architecture, 1987-92; assoc. dir. Ctr. Environ. Design Rsch., Berkeley, 1982-85. Designer community devel. sect., Cambridge, Mass., 1969-72; vis. scholar Kyoto (Japan) U., 2000-01. Author: Rural Housing Site Planning, 1974 (award 1975), Neighborhood Space, 1975, (Am. Soc. Landscape Archs. Merit award 1986), Community Goal Setting, 1982, Planning Neighborhood Space with People, 1984, The Meaning of Gardens, 1990, Community Design Primer, 1990, Living Landscape, 1999, Democratic Design in the Pacific Rim, 1999, A Theory for Community Building, 1999 (in Chinese); founder planning process Goals for Raleigh, 1972-76 (All Am. City award 1976); designer urban wilderness Runyon Canyon, 1986 (Am. Soc. Landscape Arch. Honor award 1987), Big Wild Park, Big Sky Gateway, 1990-95; mem. editl. bd. Places mag., 1985—. Chmn. Five Points Citizens Adv., Coun., Raleigh, 1973, Georgetown-Roanoke Neighborhood Assn., Raleigh, 1979; councilman City of Raleigh, 1975-77; commr. Parks and Recreation Bd., Berkeley, 1982-86; bd. dirs. Ctr. for Environ. Change, 1985—; trustee Small Town Inst., 1988—; founder Spoonbill Action Vol. Echo (SAVE), 1997. Recipient Outstanding Extension Svc. award N.C. State U., 1974, Virginia Dare award City of Manteo, N.C., 1981. Mem. Am. Soc. Landscape Archs. (Nat. Merit award 1976, Nat. Honor award 1984, Honor award 1991, Coun. of Educators in Landscape Architecture, Nat. Outstanding Educator award 1995, numerous other awards). Democrat. Methodist. Avocations: painting, leaded glass, drawing, gardening. Office: U Calif Dept Landscape Architecture 202 Wurster Hall Berkeley CA 94720-2000

HETT, JOAN MARGARET, ecological consultant; b. Trail, BC, Can., Sept. 8, 1936; d. Gordon Stanley and Violet Thora (Thors) Hett. BSc, U. Victoria, B.C., Can., 1964; MS, U. Wis., Madison, 1967; PhD, U. Wis., 1969. Ecologist Eastern Deciduous Forest Biome, Oak Ridge Nat. Lab., 1969-72; coord. sites dir. Coniferous Forest Biome, Oreg. State U. Corvallis and U. Wash., Seattle, 1972-77; ecol. cons. Seattle, 1978-84; plant ecologist Seattle City Light, 1986-91, vegetation mgmt. mgr., 1991-2000, ecol. cons., 2000—. Contbr. articles to profl. jours.; rsch. in plant population dynamics, land use planning, and forest succession. Mem. Ecol. Soc. Am., Brit. Ecol. Soc., Am. Inst. Biol. Scis., Am. Forestry Assn., Sigma Xi. Personal E-mail: joanhett@comcast.net.

HEWES, JONATHAN WILLIAM, lawyer; b. Springfield, Ohio, Apr. 16, 1945; m. Ellin Leventhal, July 8, 1973; children: Hilary Ann, David Aaron. BA summa cum laude, Ohio U., 1967; JD, Harvard U., 1972. Bar: N.Mex. 1972, U.S. Dist. Ct. N.Mex. 1972, U.S. Supreme Ct. 1979, U. S. Ct. Appeals, tenth cir. Shareholder Rodey, Dickason, Sloan, Akin & Robb, P.A., Albuquerque, 1972—, also bd. dirs. Bd. dirs. Rio Grande Planned Parenthood, Albuquerque, 1985-91. With U.S. Army, 1968-70, Vietnam. Decorated Vietnam Honor medal, Republic of Vietnam, 1970, Bronze Star. Mem.: Am. Arbitration Assn. (nat. panel arbitators), Associated Contractors N. Mex., N. Mex. Supreme Ct. (code profl. conduct com.), Albuquerque Lawyers Club, Albuquerque Bar Assn., ABA, State Bar N. Mex. (qulaity life taskforce), N.Mex. Symphony Orchestra (bd. dirs. 1988—98, bd. trustees 1988—98, bd. adv. 1988—98), Tennis Club Albuquerque.

Avocations: tennis, gardening. Office: Rodey Dickason Sloan Akin & Robb PA 201 3rd St NW Ste 2200 Albuquerque NM 87102-3380 Office Phone: 505-765-5900. Office Fax: 505-768-7395. Business E-Mail: jhewes@rodey.com.

HEWETT, THOMAS AVERY, petroleum engineer, educator; b. Lansing, Mich., Apr. 23, 1944; s. Richard Eugene and Frances Marion (Perry) H.; m. Marilyn Roberta Lawley, July 11, 1970 (div. Mar. 1979); m. Evro Lynn Stylianides, Nov. 3, 1984 (div. Nov. 1992); m. Janet M. Bostrom, Mar. 17, 1994. BS, Mich. State U., 1966; MS, MIT, 1968, ME, 1969, PhD, 1970. Asst. prof. CUNY, 1970-75; rsch. scientist Union Carbide Corp., Tarrytown, N.Y., 1975-79; sr. engring. assoc. Chevron Oil Field Rsch. Co., Lahabra, Calif., 1979-91; prof. petroleum engring. dept. Stanford (Calif.) U., 1991—. Contbr. over 40 articles to profl. jours. Recipient Engring. Merit award Orange County Engring. Coun., 1991. Fellow Inst. for Advancement of Engring.; mem. AAAS, Soc. Petroleum Engrs. Achievements include two patents on solar heating; pioneering use of fractals in petroleum reservoir modeling. Office: Stanford U Dept Petroleum Engring Green Earth Scis Bldg Rm 096 Stanford CA 94305-2220

HEWITT, CONRAD W., former commissioner, accountant; b. Sheffield, Ill. BS in Finance, U. of Ill. at Urbana-Champaign, 1958. CPA. Joined Comml. Nation Bank, Peoria, Ill., 1958, Ernst & Ernst (now Ernst & Young), LA, 1962; mng. ptnr. Ernst & Young, Hawaii, 1972, mng. ptnr. Northwest, 1979, mng. ptnr. No. Calif. San Francisco, 1986—95; supt. of banks State of Calif., 1995—97; state commr. Calif. State Dept. Financial Inst., 1997—98. Bd. dir. N. Bay Bancorp, 1999—, Point W. Capital Corp., San Francisco, 2000, Varian Inc., 2003—, Spectrum Organic Prod., Inc., 2002—. Past pres. No. Calif. Boy Scouts Am.; mem. bus. advisory coun. U. of Ill. at Urbana-Champaign. Joined USAF, 1958—62. Mem.: Nat. Assn. Corp. Directors (founder, past pres.), AICPA. Republican. Office: Point West Capital Corporation 800 Powell St San Francisco CA 94108-2006

HEWITT, HUGH, editor, writer, radio talk show host; b. Warren, Ohio, Feb. 22, 1956; s. William Robert and Marguerite Jane (Rohl) Hewitt; m. Elizabeth Johnston Helmer; children: Diana Taussig, William Robert. BA in Govt., cum laude, Harvard U., 1978; JD, U. Mich. Law Sch., 1983. Bar: DC. Clk. to judge US Ct. Appeals (DC cir.), 1983-84; spl. asst. to atty. gen. US Dept. Justice, Washington, 1984-85; asst. counsel The White House, Washington, 1985-86; gen. counsel NEH, Washington, 1986, US Office Pers. Mgmt., Washington, 1986-88, dep. dir., 1988-89; exec. dir. Richard Nixon Libr. & Birthplace Found., Yorba Linda, Calif., 1989—90; ptnr. Pettis Tester Kruse & Krinsky, Irvine, Calif., 1989—93; weekly columnist Daily Standard, WORLD Mag.; exec. editor TownHall.com, 2006—. Prof. Chapman U. Sch. Law, Orange, Calif. Author: First Principles, 1987, Searching for God in America: The Companion Volume to the Acclaimed TV Series, 1996, The Embarrassed Believer, 1998, In, But Not Of: A Guide to Christian Ambition, 2003, If It's Not Close, They Can't Cheat: Crushing the Democrats in Every Election and Why Your Life Depends on It, 2004, Blog: Understanding the Information Reformation That's Changing Your World, 2005, Painting the Map Red: The Fight to Create a Permanent Republican Majority, 2006, A Guide to Christian Ambition: Using Career, Politics, and Culture to Influence the World, 2006, A Mormon in the White House?: 10 Things Every American Should Know about Mitt Romney, 2007; radio talk show host Sta. KFI-LA, 1990—95, The Hugh Hewitt Show, 2001—, co-host (pub. affairs prog.) Life & Times, Sta. KCET-LA, 1992—2001 (3 Emmy awards), host (PBS series) Searching for God in America, 1996, TV appearances include Dennis Miller Show, Hardball with Chris Matthews, Larry King Live, O'Reilly Factor, The Today Show, Colbert Report. Mem.: Washington Fed. City Club, LA Lincoln Club, NYC Harvard Club. Republican. Roman Catholic. Office: Hugh Hewitt Show PO Box 8672 Brea CA 92822 Business E-Mail: hhewitt@hughhewitt.com.*

HEWITT, JENNIFER LOVE, actress, singer; b. Waco, Tex., Feb. 21, 1979; d. Danny and Pat. Actor: (films) Munchie, 1992, Little Miss Millions, 1993, Sister Act 2: Back in the Habit, 1993, Little Miss Millions, 1993, House Arrest, 1996, Trojan War, 1997, I Know What You Did Last Summer, 1997, Can't Hardly Wait, 1998, Telling You, 1998, Zoomates (voice), 1998, I Still Know What You Did Last Summer, 1998, The Suburbans, 1999, Heartbreakers, 2001, The Devil and Daniel Webster, 2001, The Tuxedo, 2002, Garfield: The Movie, 2004, Garfield: A Tale of Two Kitties, 2006, (voice) Delgo, 2008, (TV series) Kids Inc., 1989-91, Shaky Ground, 1992, The Byrds of Paradise, 1994, McKenna, 1994-95, Party of Five, 1995-99, Ghost Whisperer, 2005-, (TV films) The Audrey Hepburn Story, 2000, 100 Greatest Love Songs, 2002, A Christmas Carol, 2004; actor, prodr.: (films) If Only, 2004, (TV series) Time of Your Life, 1999-2000; actor, co-exec. prodr.: (TV movies) The Audrey Hepburn Story, 2000, In the Game, 2004, A Christmas Carol, 2004, (voice) The Magic 7, 2006. Prodr. (films) One Night, 2002. Singer: (albums) Let's Go Bang, 1995, Jennifer Love Hewitt, 1996, Love Songs, 1998, BareNaked, 2002. Named one of The 100 Most Powerful Celebrities, Forbes.com, 2008. Office: William Morris Agy 151 S El Camino Dr Beverly Hills CA 90212-2775

HEWITT, KAREN PECKHAM, prosecutor; b. 1964; Grad., U. Calif. Berkeley, 1986; JD, U. San Diego Sch. Law, 1989. Lawyer McInnis, Fitzgerald, Rees, Sharkey, and McIntyre, San Diego, 1989—92; trial atty., litig. team leader, Constl. Spl. Torts Sect., Civil Divsn. US Dept. Justice, 1992—2000, asst. US atty. (so. dist) Calif., 2000—03, dep. chief civil divsn. (so. dist.) Calif, 2003—06, exec. asst. US atty. (so. dist.) Calif., 2006—07, interim US atty. (so. dist.) Calif. San Diego, 2007—. Office: US Atty's Office 880 Front St Rm 6293 San Diego CA 92101 Office Phone: 619-557-5610. Office Fax: 619-557-5782. E-mail: karen.hewitt@usdoj.gov.

HEWITT, MIKE, state legislator; m. Cory Hewitt; 2 children. Owner Hewitt Distributing; chmn. Walla Walla Planning Commn., Wash.; mem. Dist. 16 Wash. State Senate, Olympia, 2000—, Republican leader, 2005—. Mem. Walla Walla Adult Day Care Adv. Com., State Penitentiary Citizen Adv. Coun., Walla Walla Valley Med. Bd. Dirs. Mem. Walla Walla Rotary Club (pres. 1995), Elks, United Way, YMCA. Republican. Office: 314 Legislative Bldg PO Box 40416 Olympia WA 98504-0416 Office Phone: 360-786-7630. Office Fax: 360-786-1266.*

HEWLETT, CLOTHILDE, lawyer; BA with distinction, U. Calif., Berkeley, 1976, JD, 1979. Bar: Calif. 1980. Asst. dist. atty. City and County of San Francisco; police commr. San Francisco; Undersecretary of State and Consumer Svcs. Agency Calif., 1999; interim dir. Dept. Gen. Svcs. (DGS), 2002; ptnr. Preston Gates & Ellis LLP. Bd. dirs. Women's Found. Calif.; bd. trustees Calif. Sci. Ctr. Found. Mem.: Nat. Assn. Women Bus. Owners, Calif. Assn. Black Lawyers, Calif. Women's Leadership Forum. Office: Preston Gates & Ellis LLP Ste 1700 55 Second St San Francisco CA 94105-3493 Office Phone: 415-882-8026. Office Fax: 415-882-8220. E-mail: chewlett@prestongates.com.

HEWLETT, WALTER B., application developer; b. Washington, June 23, 1944; s. William Hewlett. BA in Physics, Harvard U., 1966; MA in Engring., Stanford U., 1968, MA in Ops. Rsch., 1973, PhD in Music, 1980. Founder, dir. Ctr. for Computer Assisted Rsch. in Humanities, Stanford U., 1984—; mem. Humanities and Sci. Council Stanford U., 1990—, adv. bd. mem. Inst. for Econ. Policy Rsch., 1990—, mem. Libraries and Academic Info. Resources Adv. Council, 1992—2000, former adv. bd. mem. Ctr. for Study of Language and Info., hon. co-chair Think Again fundraising tour, 2000—01, consulting prof., music dept. Bd. dirs. Hewlett-Packard, 1987—2002, Agilent, 1999—; chmn. bd. dirs. Vermont Telephone. Trustee, now chmn. William & Flora Hewlett Found., 1966—; trustee Stanford U., 2003—, William R. Hewlett Revocable Trust, Packard Humanities Inst., Stanford Theatre Found.; mem. bd. of overseers Harvard U., 1997—2003; bd. dirs. Public Policy Inst. of Calif., 1998—, Flora Family Found., 2005—. Office: William and Flora Hewlett Found 2121 Sand Hill Rd Menlo Park CA 94025

HEY, RICHARD NOBLE, marine geophysicist; b. Lebanon, Tenn., June 2, 1947; s. Richard and Miriam (Jennings) Hey; m. Donna Dale, 2003; 1 child, Dylan. BS, Calif. Inst. Tech., Pasadena, 1969; PhD, Princeton U., NJ, 1975. Rsch. assoc. U. Tex., Galveston, 1974-75; from asst. to geophysicist Hawaii Inst. Geophysics, Honolulu, 1975-80; from asst. to assoc. rsch. geophysicist Scripps Inst. Oceanography, La Jolla, Calif., 1981-86; prof. U. Hawaii, Honolulu, 1986—. Adj. lectr. Scripps Inst. Oceanography, La Jolla, 1983—90. Fellow: Am. Geophys. Union, Geol. Soc. Am.; mem.: AAAS. Office: U Hawaii at Manoa Inst Geophysics Planetology Honolulu HI 96822 Office Phone: 808-956-8972. Business E-Mail: hey@soest.hawaii.edu.

HEY, TONY, computer software company executive; B physics, Oxford Univ., D theoretical physics. Prof. computer sci. Sch. Electronics & Computer Sci., Southampton Univ., 1986—2005, head of sch., 1994—99; dir. U.K. eScience Initiative, 2001—05; corp. v.p. tech. computing to corp. v.p. external rsch. divsn. Microsoft Rsch. Microsoft Corp., Redmond, Wash., 2005—. Named Comdr. Order of the British Empire, 2005. Fellow: Royal Acad. Engring.; mem.: European Union Info. Soc. Tech. Adv. Group, Inst. Elec. & Electronic Engineers, Inst. Elec. Engineers, British Computing Soc. Office: Microsoft Corp 1 Microsoft Way Redmond WA 98052-6399

HEYDMAN, ABBY MARIA, academic administrator; b. Des Moines, June 1, 1943; d. Frederick Edward and Zeta Margaret (Harrington) Hitchcock; m. Frank J. Heydman, Dec. 20, 1967; 1 child, Amy Lee. BS, Duchesne Coll., 1967; MN, U. Wash., 1969; PhD, U. Calif., Berkeley, 1987. Registered nurse, Calif. Staff nurse Bergan Mercy Hosp., Omaha, 1964—65; student health nurse St. Joseph's Hosp., Omaha, 1965—66, instr. sch. nursing, 1966—68; staff nurse Ballard Community Hosp., Seattle, 1968—69; instr. Creighton U., Omaha, 1969—70, asst. prof., 1970—74, acting dean, 1971—72; chairperson nursing dept. St. Mary's Coll., Moraga, Calif., 1978—85; dean nursing program Samuel Merritt-Saint Mary's Coll., Oakland and Moraga, Calif., 1985—93; acad. dean Samuel Merritt Coll., Oakland, 1989—99, acad. v.p., provost, 1999—2002, spl. asst. to pres., 2002—04, prof. emeritus, 2004—; prof. St. Mary's Coll. of Calif., 2005—. Lectr. U. Calif., San Francisco, 1974-75. Contbr. articles to profl. jours. Chmn. Newman Hall Community Council, Berkeley, 1985-87; bd. dirs. Oakland YMCA, 1981-83. Mem.: ACAD, ANA, AAHE, Phi Kappa Delta, Sigma Theta Tau (pres.-elect 2001—03, pres. 2003—05, treas. 2005—). Roman Catholic. Avocations: swimming, writing, travel, reading. Home: 78629 Rainswept Way Palm Desert CA 92211 E-mail: aheydman@samuelmerritt.edu.

HEYLER, GROVER ROSS, retired lawyer; b. Manila, June 24, 1926; s. Grover Edwin and Esther Viola (Ross) H.; m. Caroline Yarbrough, Aug. 10, 1949; children: Richard Ross, Sue Louise, Randall Arthur BA, UCLA, 1949; LLB, U. Calif., Berkeley, 1952. Bar: Calif. 1953. Atty. Latham & Watkins, LA, 1952—93, chmn., corp. securities dept., 1967-89. Chmn. Nat. Alliance for Rsch. into Schizophrenia and Depression, NYC, 2002—04. Mem. Calif. Bar Assn. (com. on drafting Calif. corps. code 1971-75), Order of Coif, UCLA ALumni Assn. (bd. dirs. 1966-70, 1988-90), L.A. Country Club. Home: 491 Homewood Rd Los Angeles CA 90049-2713

HEYMAN, MELVIN BERNARD, pediatric gastroenterologist; b. San Francisco, Mar. 24, 1950; s. Vernon Otto and Eve Elsie Heyman; m. Jody Ellen Switky, May 8, 1988. BA in Econs., U. Calif., Berkeley, 1972; MD, UCLA, 1976, MPH in Nutrition, 1981. Diplomate in pediatrics and pediatric gastroenterology Am. Bd. Pediatrics. Intern, resident L.A. County-U. So. Calif. Med. Ctr., 1976-79; fellow UCLA, 1979-81; asst. prof. U. Calif., San Francisco, 1981-88, assoc. prof., 1988-94, prof., 1994—, chief pediatric gastroenterology, hepatology and nutrition, 1990—, dir. tng. program i pediatric gastroenterology and nutrition, 1997—, Anita Ow Wing endowed chair, 2006—. Mem. cons. staff San Francisco Gen. Hosp., Scenic Gen. Hosp., Modesto, Calif.; assoc. dir. Pediatric IBD Consortium 2000—. Contbr. articles to profl. jours. Chmn. sci. adv. com. San Francisco chpt. Crohn's and Colitis Found. Am., 1987-94, bd. dirs., 1986-03; mem. City and County San Francisco Task Force on Nutrition and Phys. Activity for Children, 2003-04; bd. dirs. Nat. PTA, 2005-07; chmn. bd. Inflammatory Bowel Diseas Summer Camp Found., 2005-. Recipient Investigator award, NIH-NIDDK, 2002—; rsch. grantee, Children's Liver Found., 1984—85, John Tung grantee, Am. Cancer Soc., 1985—89, NIH-NIDDK grantee, 1998—, UC Mexus project grantee. Mem.: Am. Bd. Pediatric Gastroenterology (chair sub-bd. 2000—01), Am. Gastroenterol. Assn., Am. Inst. Nutrition, Am. Acad. Pediat. (com. on nutrition 1999—2006, exec. com. sect. on pediat. gastroenterology and nutrition 1999—, chair 2005—), N.Am. Soc. Pediat. Gastro Nutrition (chair patient care com. 1997—2000). Avocations: skiing, swimming, hiking, tennis, biking. Office: U Calif Dept Pediat PO Box 0136 San Francisco CA 94143-0136 Office Phone: 415-476-5892. Business E-Mail: mheyman@peds.ucsf.edu.

HEYNEMAN, DONALD, parasitology and tropical medicine educator; b. San Francisco, Feb. 18, 1925; s. Paul and Amy Josephine (KLauber) H.; m. Louise Davidson Ross, June 18, 1971; children: Amy J., Lucy A., Andrew P., Jennifer K., Claudia G. AB magna cum laude, Harvard U., 1950; MA, Rice U., 1952, PhD, 1954. Instr. zoology UCLA, 1954-56, asst. prof., 1956-60; head dept. parasitology U.S. Navy Med. Research unit, Cairo, also co-dir. Malakal, Sudan, 1960-62; assoc. research parasitologist Hooper Found. U. Calif., San Francisco, 1962-64, assoc. prof., 1966-68, prof., 1968-91, prof. emeritus, 1991—, asst. dir. Hooper found., 1970-74, acting chmn. dept. internat. health, 1976-78, assoc. dean Sch. Pub. Health Berkeley and San Francisco, 1987-91, assoc. dean emeritus, 1991—, chmn. joint med. program, 1987-91, chmn. emeritus, 1991—. Research coordinator U. Calif. Internat. Ctr. Med. Research and Tng., Kuala Lumpur, Malaysia, 1964-66; cons. physiol. processes sect. NSF, 1966-91; environ. biology div. NIH, 1968-91; mem. tropical medicine and parasitology study sect. NIAID-NIH, 1973-76; mem. adv. sci. bd. Gorgas Meml. Inst., 1967-90; cons. WHO, 1967, mem. sci. tech. rev. com. on Leishmaniases, 1984; cons. UN Devel. Program, 1978-91, US-AID, others; panel reviewer Internat. Nomenclature of Diseases, 1984—; Am. cons. and U.S. prin. investigator U. Linkage Project, Egypt-U.S., 1984—; mem. Calif. Health Adv. Com., 1983—. Author: (with R. Boolootian) An Illustrated Laboratory Text in Zoology, 1962, An Illustrated Laboratory Text in Zoology, A Brief Version, 1977, International Dictionary Medicine and Biology, (with R. Goldsmith) Textbook of Tropical Medicine and Parasitology, 1989;co-author, contbg. editor Phytolacca dodecandra: Endod, 1984, Endod II, 1987; contbr. articles to jours., chpts. to books.; editorial cons. Am. Jour. Tropical Medicine and Hygiene, Jour. Parasitology, Jour. Exptl. Parasitology, Sci., 1968—, other jours. Served with AUS, 1943-46. NIH grantee, 1966-85. Mem. Am. Soc. Parasitologists (council 1970-74, pres. 1982-83), Am. Micros. Soc. (exec. com. 1971-75), Am. Soc. Tropical Medicine and Hygiene (councilor 1981-84), So. Calif. Parasitol. Soc. (pres. 1957-58), No. Calif. Parasitologists (sec.- treas. 1969-72, pres. 1977-78), Phi Beta Kappa. Home: 1400 Lake St San Francisco CA 94118-1036 Home Phone: 415-221-6886. Personal E-mail: dheyneman@attglobal.net.

HEYREND, ALYSON L., legislative staff member; BA in journalism, Utah State U., 1975; Master's degree in mktg. and comm., U. Utah, 2006. News reporter, weekend anchor, Salt Lake City; dir. devel. and comm. for Utah and Idaho chapts. The Nature Conservancy, nat. comm. staff, 1998; press sec. Jim Matheson for Congress, 2000; press sec. to Rep. Jim Matheson US House of Reps., Washington, 2001—. Office: Office of Rep Jim Matheson 1323 Longworth House Office Bldg Washington DC 20515-4402 also: 240 E Morris Ave #235 Salt Lake City UT 84115-3296 Office Phone: 202-225-3011, 435-636-3722. Office Fax: 202-225-5638, 435-636-1834. E-mail: alyson.heyrend@mail.house.gov.

HIBBS, LOYAL ROBERT, lawyer; b. Des Moines, Dec. 24, 1925; s. Loyal B. and Catharine (McClymond) H.; children: Timothy, Theodore, Howard, Dean. BA, U. Iowa, 1950, LLB, JD, 1952. Bar: Iowa 1952, Nev. 1958, U.S. Supreme Ct. 1971. Ptnr. Hibbs Law Offices, Reno, 1972—. Moderator radio, TV Town Hall Coffee Breaks, 1970-72; mem. Nev. State Bicycle Adv. Bd., 1996-2000, Reno Bicycle Coun., 1995-99; mem. Reno Parks, Recreation and Cmty. Svc. Commn., 1998-2007, chmn., 2001. Fellow Am. Bar Found. (Nev. chmn. 1989-94); mem. ABA (standing com. Lawyer Referral Svc. 1978-79, steering com. state dels. 1979-82, consortium on legal svcs. and the pub. 1979-82, Nev. State Bar del. to Ho. of Dels. 1978-82, 89-90, bd. govs. 1982-85, mem. legal tech. adv. coun. 1985-86, standing com. on nat. conf. groups 1985-91, chmn. sr. lawyers divsn. Nev. 1988—), Nat. Conf. Bar Pres.'s Iowa Bar Assn., Nev. Bar Assn. (bd. govs. 1968-78, pres. 1977-78), Washoe County Bar Assn. (pres. 1966-67), Nat. Jud. Coll. (bd. dirs. 1986-92, sec. 1988-92), Assn. Def. Counsel No. Calif., Assn. Def. Counsel Nev., Assn. Ski Def. Attys., Aircraft Owners and Pilots Assn. (legal svcs. plan 1991-2007), Washoe County Legal Aid Soc. (co-founder), Lawyer-Pilots Bar Assn. (chmn. Nev.), Greater Reno C. of C. (bd. dirs. 1968-72), Washoe County Golf Task Force, Phi Alpha Delta. Home: 3600 Salerno Dr Reno NV 89509 Office: 421 Court St Ste 100 Reno NV 89501-1793 Office Phone: 775-786-3737. Personal E-mail: loyalhibbs@aol.com.

HICKEL, WALTER JOSEPH, retired investment company executive, foundation administrator, former United States Secretary of the Interior; b. Claflin, Kans., Aug. 18, 1919; s. Robert A. and Emma (Zecha) H.; m. Janice Cannon, Sept. 22, 1941 (dec. Aug. 1943); 1 child, Theodore; m. Ermalee Strutz, Nov. 22, 1945; children: Ted, Robert, Walter Jr., Jack, Joseph, Karl. DEng (hon.), Stevens Inst. Tech., 1970, Mich. Tech. U., 1973; LLD (hon.), St. Mary of Plains Coll., 1970, St. Martin's Coll., 1971, U. Md., Adelphi U., 1971, U. San Diego, 1972, Rensselaer Poly. Inst., 1973, U. Alaska, 1976, Alaska Pacific U., 1991, Benedictine Coll., Kans., 2003; D in Pub. Adminstrn. (hon.), Willamette U., 1971. Founder Hickel Investment Co., Anchorage, 1947—2007; gov. State of Alaska, Alaska, 1966—68, 1990—94; sec. US Dept. Interior, 1969-70; founder Inst. of the North, 1995—; sec. gen. The No. Forum with Arctic and Sub-Arctic Regional Govts., 1994—. Nominated for pres. at Rep. Nat. Convention, 1968, del., 68, 72, 76; founder Commonwealth North, 1979—; co-founder Yukon Pacific Corp. Author: Who Owns America?, 1971, Crisis in the Commons: The Alaska Solution, 2002; contbr. articles to newspapers. Mem. Rep. Nat. Com., 1954-64; bd. dirs. Salk Inst., 1972-79, NASA Adv. Coun. Exploration Task Force, 1989-91; USAR amb. representing Alaska. Named Alaskan of Year, 1969, Man of Yr. Ripon Soc., 1970; recipient DeSmet medal Gonzaga U., 1969, Horatio Alger award, Am. Schools & Colleges Assn., 1972, Grand Cordon of the Order of Sacred Treasure award, His Imperial Majesty the Emperor of Japan, 1988. Mem. Pioneers of Alaska, Equestrian Order Holy Sepulchre, KC. Democrat. Roman Catholic. Office: PO Box 101700 Anchorage AK 99510-1700 Personal E-mail: wjhickel@gci.net.

HICKENLOOPER, JOHN W., Mayor, Denver; b. Feb. 7, 1952; m. Helen Thorpe; 1 child, Teddy. BA in English, Wesleyan U., 1974, MS in Geology, 1980. Exploration geologist Buckhorn Petroleum, Denver, 1981—86; founder The Wynkoop Brewing Co., 1988—98; mayor City and County of Denver, 2003—. Co-founder CultureHaus, Chinook Fund; bd. dirs. Colo. Bus. Com. for the Arts, Denver Metro Conv. and Visitors Bur., Denver Art Mus., Denver Civic Ventures, Volunteers for Outdoor Colo. Named one of Top Five Big City Mayors of America, TIME Mag., 2005, Top Pub. Officials of Yr., Governing Mag., 2005. Office: City and County Bldg 1437 Bannock St Ste 350 Denver CO 80202 Office Phone: 720-865-9000. Office Fax: 720-865-8787. Business E-Mail: MileHighMayor@ci.denver.co.us.*

HICKERSON, GLENN LINDSEY, leasing company executive; b. Burbank, Calif., Aug. 22, 1937; s. Ralph M. and Sarah Lawson (Lindsey) H.; m. Jane Fortune Arthur, Feb. 24, 1973 BA in Bus. Adminstrn., Claremont McKenna Coll., Calif., 1959; MBA, NYU, 1960. Exec. asst. Douglas Aircraft Co., Santa Monica, Calif., 1963; sec., treas. Douglas Fin. Corp., Long Beach, Calif., 1964—67, regional mgr. customer financing, 1967; exec. asst. to pres. Universal Airlines, Inc., Detroit, 1967—68, v.p., treas., asst. sec., 1968—69, pres., 1969-72; v.p., treas., asst. sec. Universal Aircraft Svc., Inc., Detroit, 1968-69, chmn. bd., 1969—72; v.p., treas. Universal Airlines Co., Detroit, 1968—69, pres., 1969—72; group v.p. Marriott Hotels, Inc., Washington, 1972—76; dir. sales Far East and Australia Lockheed Calif. Co., 1976—78, dir. mktg. Americas, 1978—79, dir. mktg. Internat., 1979—81, v.p., internat. sales, 1981—83; v.p. comml. mktg. internat. Douglas Aircraft Co., McDonnell Douglas Corp., 1983—89; mng. dir. GPA Asia Pacific, El Segundo, Calif., 1989—90; exec. v.p. GATX Air Group, San Francisco, 1990—95, pres., 1995—98, chmn. adv. bd., 1998—; pres. Hickerson Assocs., 1998—; chmn. SkyWorks Leasing, LLC, 2006—. Lt. (j.g.) USCGR, 1960—62. H.B. Earhart Found. fellow, 1962 Mem.: St. Francis Yacht Club, Pacific Union Club. Office: SkyWorks Leasing LLC 101 California St Ste 2800 San Francisco CA 94111 Office Phone: 415-568-4822. Business E-Mail: ghickerson@skyworksleasing.com.

HICKLIN, RONALD LEE, music production company executive; b. Burlington, Wash., Dec. 4, 1937; s. Wendell C. and Theodora (Van Voorhis) H.; children: Jennifer Lynn, Mark Allan; m. Trudi Takamatsu, Oct. 23, 1994. Student, U. Wash., 1956-57. Pres. S.A.T.B. Inc., LA, 1979-98, Killer Music, Inc., San Marino, Calif., 1982—2003, T.T. B.B., Inc., Hollywood, 1989—97. Ptnr. Killer Tracks, Primat Am., Hollywood, 1990-96. Lead tenor The Eligibles, 1958-62; vocal dir., singer Piece of Cake Inc., 1968-81; arranger, producer Calif. Raisin Adv. Bd., 1982 (recipient 2 Clios 1983); producer/co-writer Wheaties, 1983 (Clio award); producer/composer Gatorade, 1983; producer/performer Levi's 501 Blues, 1984. With USAF, 1959-65. Mem. NARAS (MVP award 1973, 75), AFTRA (nat. bd. dirs. 1970-85, local bd. dirs. 1968-85), Screen Actors Guild (nat. bd. dirs. 1975), Am. Fedn. Musicians, Hollywood C. of C. Avocations: golf, tennis, basketball. Home and Office: 1175 Arden Rd Pasadena CA 91106 E-mail: killermusic@sbcglobal.net.

HICKMAN, BERT GEORGE, JR., economist, educator; b. LA, Oct. 6, 1924; s. Bert George and Caroline E. (Douglas) H.; m. Edythe Anne Warshauer, Feb. 9, 1947; children: Wendy Elizabeth, Paul Lawrence, Alison Diane. BS, U. Calif.-Berkeley, 1947, PhD, 1951. Instr. Stanford U., 1949-51; research asso. Nat. Bur. Econ. Research, 1951-52; asst. prof. Northwestern, 1952-54; mem. sr. staff Council Econ. Advisers, 1954-56; research assoc. Brookings Instn., 1956-58, mem. sr. staff, 1958-66; prof. Stanford U., 1966-95, prof. emeritus, 1996—. Vis. prof. U. Calif. at Berkeley, 1960, London Grad. Sch. Bus Studies, 1972-73,. Inst. Advanced Studies, Vienna, Austria, 1974, 1975, Kyoto U., 1977; NSF fellow Netherlands Econometric Inst., Rotterdam, 1964-65; Ford Found. Faculty research fellow, 1968-69; mem. com. econ. stability Social Sci. Research Council, 1959-61, chmn., 1962-95; chmn. exec. com. Project Link, 1969—; chmn. Energy Modeling Forum working group on macroecon. impacts of energy shocks Stanford U., 1982-83; Am. coord. US-USSR program on econ.-math. macromodeling Am. Coun. Learned Socs., 1988-90. Author: Growth and Stability of the Postwar Economy, 1960, Investment Demand and U.S. Economic Growth, 1965, (with Robert M. Coen) An Annual Growth Model of the U.S. Economy, 1976; Editor: Quantitative Planning of Economic Policy, 1965, Econometric Models of Cyclical Behavior, 1972, Global International Economic Models, 1983, International Monetary Stabilization and the Foreign Debt Problem, 1984, International Productivity and Competitiveness, 1992; co-editor: Global Econometrics, 1983, Macroeconomic Impacts of Energy Shocks, 1987, Link Proceedings, 1991, 92, Studies in Applied Economics, Vol. 1, 1997; contbr. articles to profl. jours. Served with USNR, 1943-46. Vis. fellow Internat. Inst. Applied Systems Analysis, 1979, 80; resident fellow Rockefeller Found., 1989; named Hon. Prof. U. Vienna, Austria, 1985. Fellow Econometric Soc.; mem. Am. Econ. Assn. (chmn. census adv. com. 1968-71, tech. subcom. to rev. bus. cycle devels. 1962-68, nominating com. 1978-79, chmn. seminar on global modeling, conf. on econometrics and math. econs. 1975-83), Phi Beta Kappa, Phi Eta Sigma. Home: 620 Sand Hill Rd Apt 312G Palo Alto CA 94304 Office: Stanford U Dept Econs Stanford CA 94305 Business E-Mail: bhickman@stanford.edu.

HICKS, BETHANY GRIBBEN, judge, lawyer; b. NY, Sept. 8, 1951; d. Robert and DeSales Gribben; m. William A. Hicks III, May 21, 1982; children: Alexandra Elizabeth, Samantha Katherine. AB, Vassar Coll., Poughkeepsie, NY, 1973; MEd, Boston U., 1975; JD, Ariz. State U., Tempe, 1984. Bar: Ariz. 1984. Pvt. practice, Scottsdale and Paradise Valley, Ariz., 1984-91; law clk. to Hon. Kenneth L. Fields Maricopa County Superior Ct. S.E. dist., Mesa, 1991-93; commr., judge pro tem domestic rels. and juvenile depts. Maricopa County Superior Ct. Ctrl. and S.E. Dists., Phoenix and Mesa, Ariz., 1993-99; magistrate Town of Paradise Valley, Ariz., 1993-94; judge ctrl. dist. domestic rels. dept. Maricopa County Superior Ct., Phoenix, 1999-2000, presiding judge family ct. dept., 2000—02, judge SE dist. civil dept., 2002—04, judge ctrl. dist. criminal dept., 2004—07, judge ctrl. dist. civil dept., 2007—. Dean Ariz. Jud. Coll., 2005. Mem. Jr. League of Phoenix, 1984-91, City Scottsdale Jud. Adv. Bd., 2003-05; bd. dirs. Phoenix Children's Theatre, 1988-90; parliamentarian Girls Club of Scottsdale, Ariz., 1985-87, 89-90, bd. dirs., 1988-91; exec. bd., sec. All Saints' Episcopal Day Sch. Parents Assn., 1991-92, pres., 1993-94; active Nat. Charity League, 1995-99, Valley Leadership Class XIX, 1997-98; vol., Teach for Am., 1997-2001. Mem.: ABA, Nat. Assn. of Women Judges, Assn. Family Ct. Conciliators (bd. dirs. 2001—03), Ariz. Women Lawyers' Assn. (steering com. mem. 1998—2001, 2009—), Maricopa County Bar Assn., State Bar Ariz. Democrat. Episcopalian. Office: 101/201 W Jefferson Phoenix AZ 85003 Office Phone: 602-506-2139. Business E-Mail: bhicks@superiorcourt.maricopa.gov.

HICKS, CHRISTOPHER, music company executive; b. Richmond, Calif. Student, Howard U., 1989—93. Co-founder Ivory Coast Entertainment, 1994—96; founding ptnr. Noontime Entertainment, Atlanta, 1997—; v.p. urban A&R Warner/Chappell Music, Inc., 2004—07, sr. v.p. A&R & head of urban music, 2007—; sr. v.p. urban A&R Atlantic Records, 2007—. Office: Warner/Chappell Music Inc 10585 Santa Monica Blvd Los Angeles CA 90025-4950 also: Atlantic Records Urban A&R 75 Rockefeller Plz 17th Fl New York NY 10019

HICKS, DAVID EARL, writer; b. Indpls., Jan. 1, 1931; s. John Arthur and Marguerite (Barnes) H.; m. Shirlene Lavan Barlow, Jan. 22, 1958 (div. June 1973); children: Sharon Lynn, Brenda Kay; m. Margaret Leigh Payne, Feb. 17, 1977; children: David Bradley, Leslie Ann, Brian Patrick. Grad., Nat. Radio Inst., 1953; student, Purdue U., 1959-60, Miami-Dade C.C., 1971-72. Cert. advanced paramedic. Tech. writer, editor Howard W. Sams, Inc., Indpls., 1958-64; tech. writer Systems Engring. Labs, Inc., Ft. Lauderdale, Fla., 1964-67; publs. mgr. Novatronics, Inc., Pompano Beach, Fla., 1967-69; pres. Datatek, Inc., Ft. Lauderdale, 1969-71; tech. writer Systems Devel. Corp., Colorado Springs, Colo., 1973-74, Ford Aerospace Corp., Colorado Springs, 1974-76; pres. Nutronics Corp., Colorado Springs, 1982-87; tech. writer Digital Equipment Corp., Colorado Springs, 1978-88; pres. Innovation USA Mag., Colorado Springs, 1989; tech. cons., inventor pvt. practice, Colo. Springs, 1964-65, 75-92; novelist Colo. Springs, 1992—. Tech. cons. Japan Electronics, Tokyo, 1962-63, Nutronics Corp., Longmont, Colo., 1987, Gates Motor Corp., Kailua, Hawaii, 2000—. Author of eight tech. books (two made best seller list) including: Citizens Band Radio Handbook, 1961, Amateur Radio-VHF and Above, 1965, CB Radio Operating Procedures, 1976; contbr. articles to electronics jours.; inventor of new electric charging system, 1978, awarded U.S. patent, 1981; lectr. numerous sci. and invention seminars, 1978—. Communications officer CD, Indpls., 1962-63; judge sci. fair Pub. Sch. System, Colorado Springs, 1986-87. Served with USN, 1948. Recipient Red Cross Hall of Fame, Indpls., 1963; grantee U.S. Dept. of Energy, 1984; recipient Nat. Energy Resources Tech. Innovation award, 1989, Disting. Leadership award Am. Biog. Inst. 1990, cert. of merit Internat. Biog. Ctr., 1990 Mem. Soc. of Am. Inventors (bd. dirs., Pres. award 1989), Am. Radio Relay League, Author's Guild, Author's League of Am. Republican. Avocations: travel, camping, hiking, photography. Personal E-mail: hicksde@hotmail.com.

HICKS, WILLIAM ALBERT, III, lawyer; b. Welland, Ont., Can., Apr. 6, 1942; s. William Albert and June Gwendolyn (Birrell) H.; m. Bethany G. Galvin, May 21, 1982; children: James Christopher, Scott Kelly, Alexandra Elizabeth, Samantha Katherine. AB, Princeton U., 1964; LLB, Cornell U., 1967. Bar: N.Y. 1967, Ariz. 1972, U.S. Dist. Ct. Ariz. 1972. Assoc. Seward & Kissel, NYC, 1967-68, Snell & Wilmer LLP, Phoenix, 1972-75, ptnr., 1976—2007, Ballard Spahr Andrews & Ingersoll, LLP, Phoenix, 2007—. Instr. Ariz. State U., 1974-75. Mem. U.S. Olympic Fencing Squad, 1964; bd. adv. Casino USA, Inc., 1981-84; bd. dirs. Scottsdale Arts Ctr. Assn., 1984-88, v.p. devel. 1985-87; bd. dirs. Valley Leadership, Inc., 1987-91, sec., 1988-89, sec.-treas., 1989-90; bd. dirs. Scottsdale Cultural Coun., 1988-97, vice chmn., 1992-95, chmn., 1995-96; active The Luke's Men, 1992-2003, bd. dirs., 1993-97, 99-2002, sec., 1993-94, v.p. 1995-96, pres., 1996-97; adv. bd. Scottsdale Arts Ctr., 1988-91, chmn., 1988-90; bd. dirs., vice chmn. Ariz. Coun. on Econ. Edn., 1999-2000, chmn., 2000—. Capt. JAG Corps, USAF, 1968-72. Decorated DSM. Mem. ABA, Ariz. State Bar Assn., N.Y. State Bar Assn., Nat. Assn. Bond Lawyers (vice chmn. com. on fin. health care facilities 1982-83, chmn. com. on fin. health care facilities 1983-86, securities law and disclosure com. 1994-2000), Assn. for Govtl. Leasing and Fin., Princeton U. Alumni Assn. Ariz. (pres. 1978-81, 2003—, sec. 1981—2003), Paradise Valley (Ariz.) Country Club, Princeton Club N.Y. Office: Ballard Spahr Andrews & Ingersoll LLP 3300 Tower 18th Fl 3300 N Central Ave Phoenix AZ 85012 Office Phone: 602-798-5432. Business E-Mail: hicksw@ballardspahr.com.

HICKSON, ERNEST CHARLES, financial executive; b. LA, July 14, 1931; s. Russell Arthur and Marilyn Louise (Mambert) H.; m. Janice Beleal, Sept. 5, 1959; children: Arthur, Jennifer, Barton. BS, U. So. Calif., 1961; postgrad., UCLA Grad. Sch. of Bus. Admin., 1961-63. Lic. real estate broker Calif., 1956. Credit supr. ARCO (Richfield Oil), LA, 1955-60; asst. v.p. Union Bank L.A., 1960-64; v.p. County Nat. Bank (now Wells Fargo), Orange, Calif., 1964-67; v.p., sr. loan ofcr. City Bank, Honolulu, 1967-70; pres., CEO Shelter Corp. (merged with USF), 1968-72; exec. v.p., dir. U.S. Fin., Inc. NYSE, San Diego, 1970-73, pres., CEO USF Investors, 1971-73; exec. v.p. Sonnenblick Goldman, LA, 1973-76; pres., CEO First Hawaiian Devel., Honolulu, 1976-82; sr. ptnr. TMH Resources and affiliates, Laguna Niguel, Calif., 1982—. Expert witness in fin. Author: The Developers, 1978; editor: (newsletter) Financial Marketing, 1978-83. Staff sgt. USAF, 1951—54. Recipient Exec. award Grad. Sch. of Credit and Fin. Mgmt., Stanford U., 1964, Assocs. award The Nat. Inst. of Credit, UCLA, 1959. Mem. U. So. Calif. Assocs., U. So. Calif. Pres.'s Circle, Urban Land Inst., Town Hall, Salt Creek Club (charter), Pacific Club (Honolulu), Outrigger Canoe Club (Honolulu), Phi Gamma Delta. Avocations: tennis, walking, writing, swimming. Office Phone: 949-495-9400. Fax: 948-495-9458. Personal E-mail: ernesth541@aol.com.

HICKSON, ROBIN JULIAN, mining company executive; b. Irby, Eng., Feb. 27, 1944; s. William Kellett and Doris Matilda (Martin) H.; m. P. Anne Winn, Mar. 28, 1964; children: Richard, Sharon, Nicholas, Steven. BS in Mining Engring. with honors, U. London, 1965; MBA, Tulane U., 1990. Chartered engr., U.K. and Europe. Mining engr. N.J. Zinc Co., Austinville, 1965-70, divisional mgr. Jefferson City, Tenn., 1970-71; spl. project engr. Kerr McGee Corp., Grants, N.Mex., 1971-72; gen. mgr. Asarco, Inc., Vanadium, N.Mex., 1972-78, Gold Fields Mining Corp., Ortiz, N.Mex., 1978-83, Mesquite, Calif., 1982-86; v.p. Freeport Mining Co., New Orleans, 1986-91, Freeport Indonesia Inc., Irian Jaya, 1991-92; pres. Freeport Rsch. and Engring. Co., New Orleans, 1992-93; sr. v.p. Cyprus Climax Metals Co., Tempe, Ariz., 1993-94; pres. Cyprus Amax Engring. and Project Devel. Co., Tempe, 1994-99; exec. officer Cyprus Amax Minerals Co., 1994-99; sr. v.p. engring. and project mgmt. Kvaerner Metals, San Ramon, Calif., 2000—02; pres., COO Gabriel Resources Ltd., Toronto, Ont., Canada, 2002—03; prin., sr. v.p. McIntosh Engring., Tempe, 2003—08; sr. prin. Fantec Inc., Tempe, 2008—. Author (with others): Interfacing Technologies in Solution Mining, 1981, Mineral Processing: Plant Design, Control and Practice, 2002. Recipient Robert Earll McConnell award AIME, 1999. Mem. Instn. Mining and Metallurgy, Am. Inst. Mining and Metallurgy, Mining and Metall. Soc., N.Mex. Mining Assn. (bd. dirs. Santa Fe chpt. 1975-83), Calif. Mining Assn. (bd. dirs. Sacramento chpt. 1982-86), Beta Gamma Sigma. Episcopalian. Avocations: ornithology, travel. Home: 12246 S Honah Lee Ct Phoenix AZ 85044-3455 Office: Ste 101 1438 W Broadway Tempe AZ 85282 Home Phone: 480-598-9693; Office Phone: 480-831-0310 215. Business E-Mail: rjhickson@mcintoshengineering.com. E-mail: annerobin@worldnet.att.net.

HIERONYMUS, EDWARD WHITTLESEY, retired lawyer; b. Davenport, Iowa, June 13, 1943; BA cum laude, Knox Coll., 1965; JD with distinction, Duke U., 1968. Bar: Calif. 1969, Iowa 1968. Ptnr. O'Melveny & Myers, LA, 1974—96, of counsel, 1996—99, ret., 1999. Contbr. articles on law to profl. jours. Exec. sec. Los Angeles Com. Fgn. Relations, 1975-86. Served with Judge Adv. Gen. U.S. Army, 1965-74. Mem. ABA (award for profl. merit 1968), Calif. Bar Assn. (founding co-chair natural resources subsect., real property sect. 1986-88), Los Angeles County Bar Assn., Iowa Bar Assn. Office: O'Melveny & Myers 400 S Hope St Los Angeles CA 90071-2899

HIGASHIDA, RANDALL TAKEO, radiologist, neurosurgeon, medical educator; b. LA, Oct. 26, 1955; s. Henry and Alice Higashida; m. Jean Kim, May 17, 1986. BS, U. So. Calif., 1976; MD, Tulane U. Diplomate Am. Bd. Radiology. Intern Harbor UCLA Med. Ctr., 1980-81, resident in radiology, 1981-84, fellow in diagnostic/interventional neuroradiology, 1984-85; asst. prof. radiology UCLA Med. Ctr., 1985-86; assoc. prof. radiology U. Calif. San Francisco Med. Ctr., 1986-94, prof. radiology and neurosurgery, 1994—. Cons. Target Therapeutics Corp., Fremont, Calif., 1989-93, Interventional Therapeutics Corp., Fremont, 1986-93, Cordis Corp., Miami Lakes, Fla., 1993-96; mem. exec. com. stroke rsch. grants Abbott Labs., Chgo., 1994-96. Mem. editl. bd. Jour. Endovasc. Surgery, 1994-96, Jour. Minimally Invasive Neurosurgery, 1994-96; manuscript reviewer Am. Jour. Neuroradiology, 1992—. Recipient rsch. award Am. Heart Assn., Dallas, 1978-79. Mem. AMA, Am. Soc. Neuroradiology (sr. mem., exec. coun. joint section of cerebrovascular neurosurgery), Soc. Cardiovascular and Interventional Radiology, Am. Soc. Interventional and Therapeutic Neuroradiology (exec. com. 1994-96), Internat. Soc. Endovascular Surgery. Republican. Protestant. Avocations: hiking, tennis, biking, photography, travel. Office: UCSF Medical Ctr 505 Parnassus Ave # L352 San Francisco CA 94143-0001

HIGBY, LAWRENCE M., medical products executive; BS, U. Calif. Exec. v.p. mktg., chmn. Orange County edit. LA Times, Times Mirror Co., 1986—94; group v.p., pres. & COO 76 Products Co. Unocal Corp., 1994—97; pres., COO Apria Healthcare Group, Lake Forest, Calif., 1997—2002, pres., CEO, 2002—. Office: Apria Health 26220 Enterprise Ct Lake Forest CA 92630-8405 Office Phone: 949-639-2000. Office Fax: 949-587-9363.

HIGGINS, DANIEL B., lawyer; b. Willcox, Ariz., Oct. 14, 1948; BA with distinction, Stanford U., 1973; JD magna cum laude, U. Santa Clara, 1977. Bar: Calif. 1977. Atty. McCutchen, Doyle, Brown & Enersen, San Francisco; ptnr. Paul, Hastings, Janofsky & Walker LLP, San Francisco, mem. policy com., chmn. healthcare practice group. Comment editor: U. Santa Clara Law Rev., 1976-77; contbr. articles to profl. jours. Mem. ABA (mem. healthcare and antitrust sects.), Am. Acad. Healthcare Attys., Nat. Health Lawyers Assn., Healthcare Fin. Mgmt. Assn., Phi Beta Kappa. Office: Paul Hastings Janofsky & Walker LLP 55 Second St Twenty-Fourth Floor San Francisco CA 94105 Office Phone: 415-856-7052. Office Fax: 415-856-7152. Business E-Mail: danhiggins@paulhastings.com.

HIGGINS, ELFREDA, state legislator; m. Paul Higgins; children: Kim, Sonya, Mark. BA in Bus. Mgmt. Ret.; mem. Dist. 16 Idaho House of Reps., 2008—. Mem. Assistance League of Boise, 2000—, Ada County Open Space Task Force Adv. Com., Boise River Trail Coalition Steering Com., Garden City Arts Commn.; chmn. bd. dirs. Garden City Libr. Found.; co-chmn. Found. Ada/Canyon Trail Sys., Garden City Parks & Waterways Com.; vol. Garden City Police. Mem.: Zonta Internat., Soroptimist Internat., Exec. Women's Golf Assn. (mem. com.), Treasure Valley Welcome Club (pres.). Democrat. Office: Capitol Annex PO Box 83720 Boise ID 83720-0054 Office Phone: 208-334-2475. Office Fax: 208-334-2125. Business E-Mail: ehiggins@house.idaho.gov.*

HIGGINS, PATTI CAROLYN, political organization administrator; b. Fort Bragg, NC, Sept. 15, 1953; m. Patrick Higgins; children: Gavin, Rachel, Tara. B.Ed, U. Alaska, Anchorage, 1986. Hydrologic tech. US Geol. Survey; data tech. Genwest Systems; substitute tchr. Anchorage Sch. Dist., 1996; owner Patti Higgins & Assocs., Consulting & Web Design; realtor Prudential Vista; chairwomen Alaska Dem. Party, 2007—. Mem. Anchorage Sch. Bd., 1993—96, sec., 1994—95, treas., 1995—96; mem. Abbott Loop Cmty. Coun.; former co-chair Anchorage Dem. Democrat. Avocations: skiing, hockey, hiking, bowling, horseback riding. Office: Alaska Dem Party 2602 Fairbanks St Anchorage AK 99503-2428 Office Phone: 907-258-3050. Office Fax: 907-258-1626.*

HIGGINS, ROBERT (WALTER), career naval officer, physician; b. Uniontown, Wash., Nov. 9, 1934; s. Nelson Leigh and Abbie Elizabeth (Rowe) H.; m. Barbara Jean Wright, Aug. 19, 1956 (dec. Feb. 2002); m. Judith Ellen Glenn, Nov. 15, 2003; children: Fred, Colleen, Jay. BS in Pharmacy, Wash. State U., Pullman, 1957; MD, U. Wash., Seattle, 1965. Pharmacist Wenatchee (Wash.) Thrifty Drugs, 1957-59; owner Higgins Drug Store, Pullman, Wash., 1959-61; intern L.A. County Harbor Gen. Hosp., Torrance, 1965-66; commd. lt. USN, 1966; ships surgeon USS Tutuila, Vietnam, 1966-68; ptnr. Ludwick, Zook & Higgins Family Medicine, Wenatchee, 1968-72; commd. lt. comdr. USN, 1972, advanced through grades to rear adm., 1988; chmn. dept. family medicine Naval Hosp., Charleston, SC, 1972-78, Camp Pendleton, Calif., 1978-80, Bremerton, Wash., 1980-86, comdg. officer Camp Pendleton, 1986-87; med. officer USMC Washington, 1987-89; dep. surgeon gen. USN, 1989-93. Specialty advisor surgeon gen. USN, Washington, 1973-86. Contbg. author: Behavioral Disorders, 1984, 90; contbr. articles to profl. jours. Scoutmaster Boy Scouts Am., Charleston, 1974-78, Camp Pendleton, 1978-80; trustee Family Health Found. Am., Wash. State U. Found., 1992-98; bd. visitors Wash. State U. Coll. Pharmacy, 1998—2007, pres., 2002-05. Decorated Disting. Svc. medal, Legion of Merit, Meritorious Svc. medal, Navy Commendation medal; recipient Alumni Achievement award Wash. State. U., 1988, Disting. Alumnus award U. Wash. Sch. Medicine, 1996; bd. regents disting. alumnus award, Wash. State U., 2002, Outstanding Alumnus award Wash. State U. Coll. Pharmacy, 2009. Fellow: Am. Acad. Family Physicians (pres. 1984—85, alt. del. to AMA 1985—91, del. 1992—2000, John G. Walsh award 2001), Philippine Acad. Family Physicians (hon.); mem.: World Orgn. Family Medicine (v.p. 1986—95, pres.-elect 1995—98, pres. 1998—2001), Coll. Family Physicians Can. (hon.), Uniformed Svcs. Acad. Family Physicians (pres. 1974—76), Masons. Avocations: birdwatching, fly fishing, model airplanes, stamp collecting/philately, jogging. Home and Office: 2303 Highland Dr Anacortes WA 98221-3143 Personal E-mail: rhigginsmd@aol.com.

HIGGINS, RUTH ANN, social worker, family therapist; b. Rock Valley, Iowa, Sept. 23, 1944; d. Neal and Tillie (Feekes) Vonk; m. 1972 (div. Sept. 1986); children: Ashlie Kay, Steven Grant. BA, Northwestern Coll., 1966; MA, U. Colo., 1978; LCSW, U. Denver, 1983. Cert. profl. tchr., Colo., LCSW, Am. Bd. Social Work, 2004. Tchr. Adams County Dist. 12, Northglenn, Colo., 1967-69, Dept. Def., Clark AFB, The Philippines, 1969-70, Jefferson County Schs., Lakewood, Colo., 1970-75; social worker Boulder County Mental Health Ctr., Colo., 1977, Boulder Cmty. Counseling Ctr., 1979-81, Columbine Counseling Ctr., Broomfield, Colo., 1981—; sch. social worker Adams County Sch. Dist. 12, Northglenn, Colo., 1985—2005; clin. social worker Exempla Luth. Hospice Care, 2006—. Part time social worker Hospice of Metro Denver, 1984-85, Boulder Valley Pub. Schs., 1985, Lutheran Hospice Care, Wheatridge, Colo., 1985; bd. dirs. Health and Human Svcs. City and County Broomfield, Colo.

Author, editor: Nothing Could Stop the Rain, 1976. Counselor trainer for Up With People (Worldsmart), 1998-2000. Recipient Hon. Mention Counselor of Yr. award Colo. Sch. Counselors Assn., 1994; named finalist Alteria M. Bryant award Met. Denver Baha'i Ctr., 1996. Mem.: NASW (nat. bd. cert. diplomate in clin. social work 2004). Democrat. Avocations: stained glass, hiking, reading, music.

HIGGINS, WALTER M., III, retired electric power industry executive; b. 1945; BS in Nuclear Sci., U.S. Naval Acad., 1966; student, U.S. Nuclear Power Tng. Program, 1966-68, U. Idaho, 1979; MBA, George Washington U., 1975-77. Commd. USN, 1966, advanced through grades; nuclear engr. Charleston Navy Shipyard, until 1974; sr. nuclear engr. Bechtel Power Corp., Washington, 1975; with U.S. Nuclear Regulatory Commn., Washington, 1975-77; various mgmt. and exec. positions Portland (Oreg.) Gen. Electric Co., 1977-91; pres., COO Louisville Gas and Electric Co., 1991—93; chmn., pres. CEO Sierra Pacific, 1993—98, AGL Resources Inc., Atlanta, 1998—2000, Sierra Pacific Resources, Las Vegas, 2000—07, chmn., 2007—08.

HIGGINSON, JOHN, retired career officer; b. St. Louis, Oct. 24, 1932; s. John and Clara Elizabeth (Lindemann) H.; married; children: Robert, Mark, Patrick, Paul. BA, St. Mary's U., 1954; BS, Naval Postgrad. Sch., 1966; MS, George Washington U., 1968. Ensign USN, advanced through grades to Rear Adm., ret.; comdr. Helicopter Anti-submarine Squadron 2, 1973-74, Helicopter Anti-submarine Squadron 10, 1976-78, USS Inchon, 1979-80, Amphibious Squadron 7, 1981-83, Amphibious Group 3, 1985, Naval Surface Group, Long Beach, 1986, ret., 1990-92; pres. Long Beach C. of C. Prof. mgmt. Naval War Coll., Newport, R.I. Co-author: Sea and Air, The Marine Environment, 1968, 2nd. edit., 1973. Bd. dirs. United Way, LA, Long Beach Symphony, Long Beach Youth Activities, DARE, Inc., Leadership Long Beach, St. Mary's Med. Ctr.; trustee Long Beach City Coll. Found.; dir. Internat. City Theater, Arts Coun. for Long Beach; exec. bd. Long Beach coun. Boy Scouts of Am.; trustee The Pacific; exec. coun. Industry-Edn. Coun. Calif.; former chmn. LA Combined Fed. Campaign; pres., CEO Am. Gold Star Manor Charitable Trust, 1993-2008. Mem. Navy Helicopter Assn. (former pres.), Fed. Exec. Bd. (former chmn.), Rotary (commr. Calif., mem. Vets. Meml. Commn.), Housing Opportunities Program for Elderly, (pres., 2007-). Home: 5341 Las Lomas Park Estates Long Beach CA 90815

HIGHBERGER, WILLIAM FOSTER, lawyer; b. Suffern, NY, May 15, 1950; s. John Kistler and Helen Stewart (Foster) H.; m. Carolyn Barbara Kuhl, July 12, 1980; children: Helen Barbara, Anna Mary. AB, Princeton U.; JD, Columbia U. Bar: Calif. 1976, U.S. Dist. Ct. (cen. dist.) Calif. 1976, U.S. Ct. Appeals (2d cir.) 1976, U.S. Ct. Appeals (9th cir.) 1977, U.S. Dist. Ct. (so. and ea. dists.) Calif. 1979, U.S. Supreme Ct. 1980, D.C. 1981, U.S. Dist. Ct. (no. dist.) Calif. 1981, U.S. Dist. Ct. D.C. 1982, U.S. Ct. Appeals (D.C. cir.) 1982, U.S. Ct. Appeals (3d cir.) 1983, N.Y. 1984, U.S. Dist. Ct. (so. dist.) N.Y. 1984, U.S. Dist. Ct. (ea. dist.) N.Y. 1985. Law clk. to judge U.S. Ct. Appeals (2d cir.), Bridgeport, Conn., 1975-76; assoc. Gibson, Dunn & Crutcher, Washington and L.A., 1976-82, ptnr., 1983-98; judge L.A. Superior Ct., 1998—. Notes and comments editor Columbia U. Law Rev., 1974. Mem. Nature Conservatory, Calif., 1981—; active Pacific Palisades (Calif.) Presbhn. Ch., 1987—. James Kent scholar Columbia U., 1973. Fellow: Coll. Labor and Employment Lawyers; mem.: ABA (com. on individual rights and responsibilities in workplace, labor sec), Am. Employment Law Coun., Indsl. Rels. Rsch. Assn., Am. Law Inst., Los Angeles County Bar Assn., Univ. Cottage Club. Republican. Office: LA County Courthouse Dept 32 111 N Hill St Los Angeles CA 90012 Business E-Mail: whighber@lasc.co.la.ca.us.

HIGHT, B. BOYD, retired lawyer; b. Lumberton, NC, Feb. 15, 1939; s. B. Boyd and Mary Lou (Lennon) H.; m. Mary Kay Sweeney, Mar. 31, 1962; children: Kathryn, Kevin. BA, Duke U., 1960; LLB, Yale U., 1966; diploma in comparative law, U. Stockholm, 1967. Assoc. O'Melveny & Myers, Los Angeles, 1967-74, ptnr., 1974—79, 1981—84, 1989—2005; dep. asst. sec. trans. and telecommunications U.S. Dept. State, Washington, 1979-81; exec. v.p., gen. counsel Sante Fe Internat. Corp., Alhambra, Calif., 1985—89. Bd. dirs. Planned Parenthood L.A., 1986-95, pres., 1992-94; mem. bd. overseers Rand Ctr. Russian and Eurasian Studies, 1987-2000, chair, 1994-2000; trustee Am. U. Cairo, 1987—, chmn., 2004—, Autry Nat. Ctr., 2002—; bd. dirs. Calif. Supreme Ct. Hist. Soc., 1993-2001; bd. overseers The Huntington, 1996-2008. Mem. Coun. Fgn. Rels., Pacific Coun. on Internat. Policy, Calif. Club (pres. 2005-07), LA Country Club. Democrat. Office: O'Melveny & Myers 400 S Hope St Los Angeles CA 90071-2899

HIGHWATER, JAMAKE, writer, educator; s. Jamie and Amana (Bonneville) H.; adopted by Alexander and Marcia Marks. Doctorate (hon.), Minn. Coll. Art. and Design, 1986. Lectr. primal and 20th century culture various univs. in, U.S. and Can., 1970—; grad. lectr. NYU Continuing Edn., 1979-83. Asst. adj. prof. Grad. Sch. Architecture, Columbia U., 1983-84, UCLA Film and Entertainment Ext., 1998—; cons. N.Y. State Council on the Arts, 1975-85; founding mem. Indian Art Found., Santa Fe, 1980-87, Cultural Council, Am. Indian Community House, N.Y.C., 1976, pres., 1976-78; mem. task force on individual artist N.Y. State Council on Arts, 1981, mem. lit. panel, 1982-83; mem. lit. panel N.Y. Found. of the Arts, 1989-90, Mass. Artists Fellowship, 1990-91; adj. faculty Inst. Am. Indian Art, Santa Fe, 1979—; lectr. UCLA Entertainment and Performing Arts Dept., 1999—; cons. Myth Quest, PBS, 2000—. Host, narrator and writer of: TV series Native Land, 1986, The Primal Mind, Public Broadcasting Svc. Network, 1986 (best film yr. Nat. Ednl. Film Festival, 1986, Ace award Discovery Channel 1991); Author: Indian America: A Cultural and Travel Guide, 1975, Song From the Earth: American Indian Painting, 1976 (Anisfield-Wolf award in race relations 1980), Ritual of the Wind: No. American Indian Ceremonies, Music and Dances, 1977, Many Smokes, Many Moons, 1978 (Jane Addams Peace Book award), Dance: Rituals of Experience, 1978, The Sweet Grass Lives On: 50 Contemporary North American Indian Artists, 1980, Masterpieces of American Indian Painting, 2 vols., 1978-80, The Primal Mind: Vision and Reality in Indian America, 1981 (Virginia McCormick Scully Lit. award 1982), Native Land (based on PBS program), 1986, Shadow Show: An Autobiographical Insinuation, 1987, Myth and Sexuality, 1990, The World of 1492, 1992, The Language of Vision, 1994, The Mythology of Transgression, 1997,; novels Anpao: An American Indian Odyssey (Newbery Honor award 1978), 1977 (Named Best Book for Young Adults, ALA 1978), Journey to the Sky: Stephens and Catherwood's Rediscovery of the Maya World, 1978, The Sun, He Dies: The End of the Aztec World, 1980 (named Best Book for Young Adults, Sch. Library Jour. 1980), Legend Days (Notable Book, ALA 1985), The Ceremony of Innocence, (Best book for Young Adults, ALA) 1986, I Wear the Morning Star, 1986, Eyes of Darkness, (Notable Book, ALA) 1985, I Took the Fire: A Memoir, 1988, Kill Hole, 1992, Dark Legend, 1994, Rama, 1994 (Best Books for Young Adults N.Y. Pub. Libr.), (poetry) Moonsong Lullaby, 1981, Songs for the Seasons, 1995; (as J. Marks) Rock and Other Four Letter Words, 1968, Mick Jagger: The Singer Not the Song, 1973; contbr. critiques to various lit. jours.; classical music editor: Soho Weekly News, 1975-79; sr. editor: Fodor Travel Guides, 1970-75; contbg. editor: N.Y. Arts Jours, 1978-84, Indian Trader, 1977-80, Stereo Rev., 1972-79, Native Arts/West, 1980-81; nat. adv. bd. PEW Fellowships in the arts, 1991-92; mem. bd. Am. Poetry Ctr., 1991—; contbg. arts critic Christian Sci. Monitor, 1988-92; mem. adv. bd. Visions Mag., 1992—, The Highwater papers, N.Y. Pub. Libr. Mem. art task panel Pres.'s Commn. on Mental Health, 1977-78; gen. dir. S.W. Native Arts Festival, U.Tex., Houston, 1985-86; gen. dir. Festival Mythos, Phila., 1991; mem. adv. bd. Wheelwright Mus. Indian Art, 1980-82, Lame Deer Coll., 1981—; mem. nat. adv. bd. Native Am. Rights Fund, 1980-83; nat. adv. Joseph Campbell Libr./Archives, 1989—; creative adv. Griot: N.Y., Great Performances, PBS, Star Trek Voyager, Paramount Pictures, Brian Wilson Documentary, Don Was, BBC, Myth Quest, PBS, 13-part series. Named Hon. Citizen of Okla., 1977, New Mex., 1978. Mem. AFTRA, PEN (children's lit. com. Am. Ctr., 1990—, exec. bd. PEN Am. Ctr. 1983-86), Authors Guild, Dramatists Guild, Authors League. Office: Native Land Found 8491 W Sunset Blvd Los Angeles CA 90069-1911 E-mail: nativeland@earthlink.net.

HILBERT, ROBERT S(AUL), optical engineer; b. Washington, Apr. 29, 1941; s. Philip G. and Bessie (Friend) H.; m. Angela Cinel Ferreira, June 19, 1966; children: David M., Daniel S. BS in Optics, U. Rochester, 1962, MS in Optics, 1964. Optical design engr. Itek Corp., Lexington, Mass., 1963-65, supr. lens design sect., 1965-67, asst. mgr. optical engr. dept., 1967-69, mgr. optical engring. dept., 1969-74, dir. optics, 1974-75; v.p. engring. Optical Rsch. Assocs., Pasadena, Calif., 1975-84, sr. v.p., 1985-91, pres., COO, 1991—, pres., CEO, 2000—, chmn. bd., 2008—. Lectr. Northeastern U., Burlington, Mass., 1967-69; mem. trustees vis. com. Sch. Engring. and Applied Sci., U. Rochester, 1995-97. Mem. devel. bd. Coll. Optical Sci., U. Ariz., 2007—. Recipient Future Scientist of Am. award, 1957; Am. Optical Co. fellow U. Rochester, 1962. Fellow Soc. Photo-Optical Instrumentation Engrs. (chmn. fellows com. 1998); mem. Optical Soc. Am. (engring. coun. 1990-92, mem. Fraunhofer award com. 1997-98), Lens Design Tech. Group (chmn. 1975-77). Jewish. Achievements include 6 patents in lens systems. Avocations: reading, movies. Home: 863 San Vicente Rd Arcadia CA 91007 Office: Optical Rsch Assocs 3280 E Foothill Blvd Pasadena CA 91107-3103 Home Phone: 626-446-9942; Office Phone: 626-795-9101 306. Business E-Mail: bob@opticalres.com.

HILBRECHT, NORMAN TY, lawyer; b. San Diego, Feb. 11, 1933; s. Norman Titus and Elizabeth (Lair) H.; m. Mercedes L. Sharratt, Oct. 24, 1980. BA, Northwestern U., 1956; JD, Yale U., 1959. Bar: Nev. 1959, U.S. Supreme Ct. 1963, U.S. Ct. Appeals, (9th circuit), 1986. Assoc. counsel Union Pacific R.R., Las Vegas, 1962; ptnr. Hilbrecht & Jones, Las Vegas, 1962-69; pres. Hilbrecht, Jones, Schreck & Bernhard, 1969-83, Hilbrecht & Assocs, 1983—, Mobil Transport Corp., 1970-72; gen. counsel Bell United Ins. Co., 1986-94; mem. Nev. Assembly, 1966-72, minority leader, 1971-72; mem. Nev. Senate, 1974-78; legis. commn., 1977-78; mng. mem. Corp. Svcs. Group, 1998—; pres. Corp. Svcs. Co., 1998—, Nev. Incorporating Co., 1998—; mng. mem. Amcorp LLC., 1999—. Asst. lectr. bus. law U. Nev., Las Vegas, 1968-1969 Author: Nevada Motor Carrier Compendium, 1990, Nevada Corporation Handbook, 1999. Labor mgmt. com. NCCJ, 1963; mem. Clark County Dem. Ctrl. Com., Nev., 1959-80, 1st vice chmn., 1965-66; del. Western Regional Assembly on Ombudsman; chmn. Clark County Dem. Conv., 1966, Nev. Dem. Conv., 1966; pres. Clark County Legal Aid Soc., 1964, Nev. Legal Aid and Defender Assn., 1965-83; assoc. for justice Nat. Jud. Coll., 1993-2006; active United Way Leadership Coun., 1994-. Capt. AUS, 1952-67. Named Outstanding State Legislator Eagleton Inst. Politics, Rutgers U., 1969. Mem. ABA, Am. Assoc. for Justice, Am. Judicature Soc., Am. Acad. Polit. and Social Sci., State Bar Nev. (chmn. adminstrv. law com. 1991-94, chmn. sect. on adminstrv. law 1996), Nev. Trial Lawyers (state v.p. 1966), Supreme Ct. Hist. Soc., Am. Assn. Ret. Persons (state legis. com. 1991-94), Literary Soc. Las Vegas, Las Vegas Social Register, Rotary, Las Vegas Rotary Found. (pres. 2004-05, sr. mem. 2006-), German Am. Soc. Club, Nev. (founder 1971); U. Nev.-Las Vegas Found., Elks, Phi Beta Kappa, Delta Phi Epsilon, Theta Chi, Phi Delta Phi. Lutheran. Office: 723 S Casino Ctr Blvd Las Vegas NV 89101-6716 Office Phone: 702-384-1036. Business E-Mail: hilbrecht@lvcm.com, hilbrecht@hillbrechtandassociates.com.

HILDEBRAND, VERNA LEE, human ecology educator; b. Dodge City, Kans., Aug. 17, 1924; d. Carrell E. and Florence (Smyth) Butcher; m. John R. Hildebrand, June 23, 1946; children: Carol Ann, Steve Allen. BS, Kans. State U., 1945, MS, 1957; PhD, Tex. Women's U., 1970. Tchr. home econs. Dickinson County H.S., Chapman, Kans., 1945-46; tchr. early childhood Albany (Calif.) Pub. Schs., 1946-47; grad. asst. Inst. Child Welfare U. Calif., Berkeley, 1947-48; tchr. kindergarten Albany Pub. Schs., 1948-49; dietitian commons and hosp. U. Chgo., 1952-53; instr. Kans. State U., Manhattan, 1953-54, 59, Okla. State U., Stillwater, 1955-56; asst. prof. Tex. Tech U., Lubbock, 1962-67; from asst. prof. to prof. Mich. State U., East Lansing, 1967-97, prof. emeritus, 1997—. Legis. clk. Kans. Ho. of Reps., Topeka, 1955. Author: Introduction to Early Childhood Education, 1971, 6th edit., 1997, Guiding Young Children, 1975, 7th edit., 2004, Parenting and Teaching Young Children, 1981, 1990, 2000, Management of Child Development Centers, 1984, 6th edit., 2007, Parenting: Rewards and Responsibilities, 1994, 7th edit., 2004, Guilding Young Children, 8th edit., 2008, tchrs. annotated edit., 2003; co-author: China's Families: Experiment in Societal Change, 1985, Knowing and Serving Diverse Families, 1996, 3rd edit., 2007. Mem. Nat. Assn. for the Edn. Young Children (task force 1975-77), Am. Home Econs. Assn. (bd. dirs., Leader award 1990), Women in Internat. Devel., Nat. Assn. Early Childhood Tchr. Edn. (award for meritorious and profl. leadership 1995).

HILDEBRANDT, DARLENE MYERS, retired information scientist; b. Somerset, Pa., Dec. 18, 1944; d. Kenneth Geary and Julia (Klim) Myers; m. Peter Anton Hildebrandt, May 26, 1983; 1 child, Robin Adaire. BA, U. Calif., Riverside, 1969; MA, U. Wash., 1970. Info. specialist U. Wash. Acad. Computer Ctr., Seattle, 1970-73, library assoc., 1974-75, mgr. computing info. services adminstr., 1976-85, adminstr. computing info. services, 1986-91; head sci. librs. Wash. State U., Pullman, 1991-2000. Spl. librs. rep. Wash. State Adv. Coun. Librs., 1992-98; mem. Wash. State Librs. Database Selection Com., 1997—. Editor: (newsletter) Points Northwest (Elaine D. Kaskela award 1973, 75, Best ASIS 1974), Wash. State Tribal Librs. Info. Newsletter, 1998—; compiler and editor Computing Info. Directory, 1985-96. Recipient Civitan award, 1963. Mem. Am. Soc. for Info. Sci. (founding mem. Pacific Northwest chpt. 1971, chairperson 1975, 76, bd. dirs. 1980-83, chpt. award 1978). Office: Wash State U Owen Sci & Engring Libr Pullman WA 99164-0001

HILDNER, ERNEST GOTTHOLD, III, solar physicist, researcher, administrator; b. Jacksonville, Ill., Jan. 23, 1940; s. Ernest Gotthold Hildner Jr. and Jean (Johnston) Duffield; m. Sandra Whitney Shellworth, June 29, 1968; children: Cynthia Whitney, Andrew Duffield. BA in Physics and Astronomy, Wesleyan U., 1961; MA in Physics and Astronomy, U. Colo., 1964, PhD in Physics and Astronomy, 1971. Experiment scientist High Altitude Obs., Nat. Ctr. Atmospheric Rsch., Boulder, Colo., 1972-80, vis. scientist, 1985-86; chief solar physics br. NASA Marshall Space Flight Ctr., Huntsville, Ala., 1980-85; dir. Space Environment Ctr. NOAA Oceanic and Atmospheric Rsch. and Nat. Ctrs. Environ., Boulder, 1986—. Mem. com. on solar and space physics NRC, Washington, 1986-90; chmn. Com. on Space Environment Forecasting, fed. coord. for meteorology, Washington, 1988-97; co-chmn. com. space weather Office of Fed. Coord. for Meteorology, 1998—. Contbr. rsch. papers in solar and interplanetary physics, 1971—; co-inventor spectral slicing X-ray telescope with variable magnification. Mem. AAAS, Am. Geophys. Union (assoc. editor Geophys. Rsch. Letters 1983-85), Am. Astron. Soc. (councillor solar physics div. 1979-80), Internat. Astron. Union, Sigma Xi. Achievements include patent for Spectral Slicing X-Ray Telescope with Variable Magnification. Office: NOAA Space Environment Ctr 325 Broadway St Boulder CO 80305-3337

HILDRETH, RICHARD G., lawyer, educator; b. 1943; BS, U. Mich., 1965, JD, 1969; diploma in Law, Oxford U., 1969, U. Stockholm, 1973. Bar: Calif. 1969. Atty. Steinhart & Falconer, San Francisco, 1969—78; prof. Univ. Oreg. Sch. Law, 1978—; dir. Environ. & Natural Resources Ctr., Univ. Oreg., Ocean & Coastal Law Ctr, Univ. Oreg. Mem. editl. adv. bd. Coastal Mgmt., Ocean Development & Internat. Law. Co-author: Coastal & Ocean Law: Cases & Materials, Coastal & Ocean Mgmt. Law in a Nutshell, Ocean & Coastal Law. Office: Ocean and Coastal Law Center School of Law 1221 University of Oregon Eugene OR 97403-1221

HILDRETH, SUSAN, library director; BA cum laude, Syracuse U., NY; MLS, SUNY Albany; MBA, Rutgers U., NJ. Libr. Edison Twp. Libr., NJ, Yolo County Libr., Woodland, Calif.; libr. dir. Benicia Pub. Libr., Calif.; county libr. Auburn-Placer County Libr., Calif.; dep. dir. support services Sacramento Pub. Libr., Calif.; dep. dir., then city libr. San Francisco Pub. Libr., San Francisco; planning cons. libr. devel. svcs. bur. Calif. State Libr., state libr., 2004—09; CEO, city libr. Seattle Pub. Libr., 2009—. Mem.: ALA, Calif. Libr. Assn. (pres., treas.), Pub. Libr. Assn. (pres. 2006—07, mem. exec. com.). Office: Seattle Pub Libr 1000 Fourth Ave Seattle WA 98104 Office Phone: 916-654-0174, 206-386-4636. Office Fax: 916-654-0064. Business E-Mail: csl-adm@library.ca.gov.*

HILL, BOB (ROBERT G. HILL), former professional basketball coach; b. Columbus, Ohio, Nov. 24, 1948; s. Robert Calvin and Kathryn Francis (Near) H.; m. Pamela Jean Postle, Aug. 10, 1974; children: Cameron Sage, Christopher Postle, Casey Tyler. Grad., Bowling Green State U., Ohio. Minor league baseball player San Diego Padres orgn.; asst. coach Bowling Green State U., 1971—75, U. Pitts., 1975—77, U. Kans., 1977—85, NY Knicks, 1985—86, head coach, 1986—87; scout Charlotte Hornets, 1987—88; TV analyst NJ Nets, 1987—88; head coach Virtus Knorr, Bologna, Italy, 1988—89; asst. coach Ind. Pacers, 1990, head coach, 1990—93; asst. coach Orlando Magic, 1993—94; head coach San Antonio Spurs, 1994—96, Fordham U., 1999—2002; asst. coach Seattle SuperSonics, 2005—06, head coach, 2006—07. Author: Coaching for Success and Beyond, 2000.

HILL, BONNIE GUITON, consulting company executive; b. Springfield, Ill., Oct. 30, 1941; d. Henry Frank and Elizabeth (Newman) Brazelton; m. Walter Hill Jr.; 1 child, Nichele Monique. BA, Mills Coll., 1974; MS, Calif. State U., Hayward, 1975; EdD, U. Calif., Berkeley, 1985. Adminstr. asst. to pres.'s spl. asst. Mills Coll., Oakland, Calif., 1970-71, adminstrv. asst. to asst. v.p., 1972-73, student svcs. counselor, adv. to resuming students, 1973-74, asst. dean of students, interim dir. ethnic studies, lectr., 1975-76; exec. dir. Marcus A. Foster Ednl. Inst., Oakland, 1976-79; adminstrv. mgr. Kaiser Aluminum & Chem. Corp., Oakland, 1979-80; v.p., gen. mgr. Kaiser CTR Inc., Oakland, 1980-84; vice chair Postal Rate Commn., Washington, 1985-87; asst. sec. for vocat. and adult edn. Dept. Edn., Washington, 1987-89; sec. State and Consumer Svcs. Agy. State of Calif.; spl. adv. to Pres. for Consumer Affairs, dir. U.S. Office Consumer Affairs, 1989-90; pres., CEO Earth Conservation Corps, Washington, 1990-91; sec. State and Consumer Svcs. Industry, State of Calif., 1991-92; dean McIntire Sch. Commerce U. Va., Charlottesville, 1992-97; v.p. The Times Mirror Co., 1997-2000; pres. B. Hill Enterprises, LLC, 2001—; co-founder Iconblue, Inc., LA Times, 2001—. Sr. v.p. comm. and pub. affairs L.A. Times, 1998—2001; pres., CEO The Times Mirror Found., 1997—2001; bd. dirs. The Home Depot Co., AK Steele Corp., Yum Brands, Inc., Calif. Water Svc. Co. Office: B Hill Enterprises LLC Ste 600 5670 Wilshire Blvd Los Angeles CA 90036 Office Phone: 323-634-5312.

HILL, BOYD H., JR., medieval history educator; b. Dunedin Isles, Fla., Feb. 21, 1931; s. Boyd Howard and Minnie Cauthen (Buchanan) H.; m. Alette Louise Olin, Jan. 26, 1956; children: Boyd Buchanan, Michael Howard. AB, Duke U., 1953; MA, U. N.C., 1957, PhD, 1963; postgrad., UCLA, 1957-58. Instr. La. State U., Baton Rouge, 1962-64; asst. prof. medieval history U. Colo., Boulder, 1964-66, assoc. prof., 1967-71, prof., 1971—, chmn. dept. history, 1981-85, chmn. dept. classics., 1986-87; scholarship dir. Coll. Arts and Sci., U. Colo., Boulder, 1992-96. Vis. asst. prof. UCLA, 1966-67 Author: Medieval Monarchy in Action, 1972; editor: The Rise of the First Reich, 1969, The Western World, 1974; contbr. articles to profl. jours. Town trustee Jamestown, Colo., 1990-92. With U.S. Army, 1953-55. Wellcome Hist. Med. Library fellow, 1962; Am. Philos. Soc. grantee, 1968; Council Research and Creative Work U. Colo. grantee, 1980 Mem. Am. Hist. Assn. (councillor Pacific Coast br. 1971-74), Medieval Acad. Am. (councillor 1973-76), Rocky Mountain Medieval and Renaissance Assn. (pres. 1983), Phi Kappa Psi Democrat. Presbyterian. Home: 1433 Tulip St Longmont CO 80501-2423 Office: U Colo Campus Dept History PO Box 234 Boulder CO 80309-0234

HILL, DAVID, broadcast executive; b. Australia; V.p., sports Nine Network, Australia, 1977—88; head Eurosport, England, 1988—91, Sky Sports, England, 1991—93; pres. Fox Sports, Los Angeles, 1993—99, chmn., CEO, 1999—; CEO Fox Sports Network, 1996—;

chmn., CEO Fox TV Network, 1997—99; pres., entertainment group DirecTV, 2005—07. Named one of Most Influential People in the World of Sports, Bus. Week, 2007, 2008. Office: Fox Sports PO Box 900 Beverly Hills CA 90213-0900 also: 575 Amalfi Dr Pacific Palisades CA 90272-4504

HILL, DAVID ALLAN, electrical engineer; b. Cleve., Apr. 21, 1942; s. Martin D. and Geraldine S. (Yoder) H.; m. Elaine C. Dempsey, July 9, 1971. BSEE, Ohio U., 1964, MSEE, 1966; PhD in Elec. Engring., Ohio State U., 1970. Vis. fellow Coop. Inst. for Rsch. Environ. Sci., Boulder, Colo., 1970-71; rsch engr. Inst. for Telecommunication Scis., Boulder, 1971-82; sr. scientist Nat. Inst. Stds. and Tech., Boulder, 1982—. Adj. prof. U. Colo., Boulder, 1980-. Editor Geosci. and Remote Sensing Jour., 1980-84, Antennas and Propagation Jour., 1986-89; contbr. over 150 articles to profl. jours., chpts. to books. Recipient award for best paper Electromagnetic Compatability Jour., 1987, 2003. Fellow IEEE (life, chpt. chmn. 1975-76, editor 1986-89); mem. Electromagnetic Soc. (bd. dirs. 1980-86), Internat. Union Radio Sci. (nat. com. 1986-89), Colo. Mountain Club (Boulder), Sierra Club. Office: Nat Inst Stds & Tech 818-02 325 Broadway St Boulder CO 80305-3337 Office Phone: 303-497-3472. Business E-Mail: dhill@boulder.nist.gov.

HILL, EARL MCCOLL, lawyer; b. Bisbee, Ariz., June 12, 1926; s. Earl George and Jeanette (McColl) H.; m. Bea Dolan, Nov. 22, 1968 (dec. Aug. 1998); children: Arthur Charles, John Earl, Tamara Fegert. BA, U. Wash., 1960, JD, 1961. Bar: Nev. 1962, U.S. Ct. Claims 1978, U.S. Ct. Appeals (9th cir.) 1971, U.S. Supreme Ct. 1978. Law clk. Nev. Supreme Ct., Carson City, 1962; assoc. Gray, Horton & Hill, Reno, 1962-65, ptnr., 1965-73, Marshall Hill Cassas & de Lipkau (and predecessors), Reno, 1974—2005, Sherman & Howard, Denver, 1982-91; of counsel Parsons Behle & Latimer, Reno, 2006—. Judge pro tem Reno mcpl. ct., 1964—70; lectr. continuing legal edn.; mem. Nev. Commn. on Jud. Selection, 1977—84; trustee Rocky Mountain Mineral Law Found., 1976—, sec., 1987—88. Contbr. articles to profl. jours. Mem. ABA, State Bar Nev. (chmn. com on jud. adminstrn. 1971-77), Washoe County Bar Assn., Lawyer Pilots Bar Assn., Soc. Mining Law Antiquarians (sec.-treas. 1975-2005), Prospectors Club. Office: 50 W Liberty St Ste 750 Reno NV 89501 Office Phone: 775-323-1601. Business E-Mail: ehill@parsonsbehle.com.

HILL, G. RICHARD, lawyer; b. Chapel Hill, NC, Oct. 22, 1951; BA magna cum laude, U. Minn., 1973, MA, 1975; JD, Yale U., 1978. Bar: Wash. 1978. Atty. McCullough Hill, Seattle. Adj. prof. law U. Wash., 1987-88; co-founder Pacific Real Estate Inst. Editor: Regulatory Taking: The Limits of Land Use Controls. Mem. ABA (mem. urban, state and local govt. law sect., chair 1995-96, mem. exec. com. 1992-95, chmn. land use planning and zoning com. 1990-92, co-chmn. subcom. hazardous waste and mcpl. liability 1984-86, chmn. subcom. on land use litigation and damages 1986-88). Office: McCullough Hill 701 Fifth Ave 7220 Seattle WA 98104 Office Phone: 206-812-3388. Business E-Mail: rich@mhseattle.com.

HILL, HARRY DAVID, city official, human resources professional; b. Whittier, Calif., Oct. 29, 1944; s. Harry Boreman and Winifred Nell (Purvis) Hill; m. Linda Mae Price, Nov. 8, 1969; 1 child, Jon Ryan. AA, Los Angeles Harbor Coll., Wilmington, Calif., 1964; BA in Polit. Sci., UCLA, 1966; M of Pub. Adminstrn. in Human Resources, U. So. Calif., 1972. Personnel aide City of Anaheim, Calif., 1966-67, personnel analyst, 1967-71, sr. personnel analyst, 1971-75, personnel svcs. mgr., 1975-83, asst. human resources dir., 1983-88, asst. labor rels. dir., 1988-94, dir. human resources, 1994—2006; ret. Chmn. supervisory com. Anaheim Area Credit Union, 1981-89, bd. dirs., 1989-95. Pres. personnel and employee rels. dept. League of Calif. Cities, 2002—03; pres. Leadership Anaheim, 2003—04. Mem. So. Calif. Pub. Labor Coun. (treas. 1986-87, pres. 1988), Internat. Pers. Mgmt. Assn. (pres. western region 1983-84), So. Calif. Pers. Mgmt. Assn. (pres. 1978-79), CPS Human Resource Svcs. (bd. dirs. 1986-2001, chmn. bd. 2001-06), Orange County ARC (bd. dirs. 2003-, pres. 2007-). Democrat.

HILL, HENRY ALLEN, physicist, researcher; b. Port Arthur, Tex., Nov. 25, 1933; s. Douglas and Florence Hill. BS, U. Houston, 1953; MS, U. Minn., 1956, PhD, 1957; MA (hon.), Wesleyan U., 1966. Research asst. U. Houston, 1952-53; teaching asst. U. Minn., 1953-54, research asst., 1954-57; research assoc. Princeton U., 1957-58, instr., then asst. prof., 1958-64; assoc. prof. Wesleyan U., Middletown, Conn., 1964-66, prof. physics, 1966-74, chmn. dept., 1969-71; prof. physics U. Ariz., Tucson, 1966-95, prof. emeritus, 1995—. Chmn. bd. Zetetic Inst., 1992—; researcher on nuclear physics, relativity, astrophysics, and optics. Contbr. articles to profl. jours. Sloan fellow, 1966-68 Fellow Am. Phys. Soc.; mem. AAAS, SPIE, Am. Astron. Soc., Optical Soc. Am., Am. Geophys. Union. Office: Zetetic Inst 1665 E 18th St Ste 206 Tucson AZ 85719-6809

HILL, JANE H., anthropologist, educator; Anthropology faculty U. Ariz., Tucson, 1983—, regents prof. anthropology. Recipient Viking Fund Medal, Wenner-Gren Found. for Anthrop. Rsch., 2004. Mem.: AAAS, Soc. Study of Indigenous Languages of the Americas (pres.), Soc. Linguistic Anthropology (pres.), Am. Anthrop. Assn. (past pres.), Am. Assn. for Advancement of Sci. Office: Coll Social & Behavioral Sci 310 Haury Bldg PO Box 210028 Tucson AZ 85721-0028 Office Phone: 520-621-4735. Office Fax: 520-621-9424.

HILL, JERRY, state legislator; m. Sky Hill; 1 child. BA, U. Calif., Berkeley. Tchg. credentials San Francisco State U. Owner pool cleaning bus.; mem. San Mateo City Coun., 1991—98; mayor City of San Mateo, 1994; mem. San Mateo Co. Bd. Suprs., 1998—; mem. Dist. 19 Calif. State Assembly, 2008—. Democrat. Office: PO Box 942849 Rm 4146 Sacramento CA 94249-0019 also: 1528 S El Camino Real Ste 302 San Mateo CA 94402 Office Phone: 916-319-2019, 650-349-1900. Office Fax: 916-319-2119, 650-341-4676.*

HILL, LOUIS ALLEN, JR., retired dean, civil engineer, consultant; b. Okemah, Okla., May 18, 1927; s. Louis Allen and Gladys Adelia (Dietrich) Hill Wise; m. Jeanne Rose Murray, June 14, 1951; children: Dawn, David, Dixon. BA, Okla. State U., 1949, BSC.E., 1954, MSC.E., 1955; PhD, Case Inst. Tech., 1965. Registered profl. engr., Okla., Ariz. Engr. Lee Hendricks Engring., Tulsa, 1955-57, Hudgins, Thompson, Ball & Assocs., Oklahoma City, 1957-58; asst. prof. civil engring. Ariz. State U., 1958-66, assoc. prof., 1966-70, prof., 1970-74, chmn. dept. civil engring., 1974-81; dean Coll. Engring. U. Akron, 1981-88, assoc. v.p. rsch. and grad. studies, 1988. Chmn. Ohio Engring. Dean's Council, 1983-85; trustee Engring. Found. of Ohio, 1985-88; staff engr. Salt River Project, Ariz., 1962; cons. in field. Author: Fundamentals of Structures, 1975, Compendium of Structural Aids, 1975, Structured Programming in Fortran, 1981; contbr. numerous articles to profl. jours.; designer numerous bridges, hwys. Ch. leader-tchr. 1st Bapt. Ch., 1971-88, Scottsdale Presbyn. Ch., 1990—. Served to capt. C.E., U.S. Army, 1945-47, 51-53, The Philippines, Japan. Recipient Disting. award Akron Coun. Engring. and Sci. Socs., 1987, commendation Minorities in Mainstream Tech. Com., 1990, Disting. Svc. award U. Akron Coll. Engring., 1994; named Educator of Yr., Inroads N.E. Ohio, Inc., 1986, Sr. Svc. award Presbytery of Grand Canyon, 2001; Louis A. Hill Jr. Ann. Faculty award established and endowed in his honor Qua Tech., 1987, Louis A. Hill Jr. scholarship established in his honor Minorities in Mainstream Tech. Com., 2004, Mayor Plusquellic proclaimed April 23, 1997 as Dr. Louis A. Hill Day in City of Akron; fellow Continental Oil Co., 1955, faculty fellow NSF, 1963. Fellow ASCE (life); mem. NSPE (sec., profl. engr. in edn. 1986-88), Am. Soc. Enging. Edn. (life, Western Electric Fund award 1967), Sigma Xi, Tau Beta Pi, Omicron Delta Kappa. Republican. Home and Office: 3208 N 81st Pl Scottsdale AZ 85251-5800

HILL, MICHAEL J., film editor; Works include TV movies Berlin Tunnel 21, 1981, Cagney & Lacey, 1981, The First Time, 1982, Baby Sister, 1983, Obsessive Love, 1984, Combat High, 1986, (films with Daniel P. Hanley): (also with Robert J. Kern) Night Shift, 1982, Splash, 1984, Cocoon, 1985, Gung Ho, 1986, (also with Gregory Prange) Armed and Dangerous, 1986, Willow, 1988, Parenthood, 1989, Pet Sematary, 1989, Problem Child, 1990, Backdraft, 1991, Far and Away, 1992, The Paper, 1994, Apollo 13, 1995 (Acad. award for best film editing 1996), Ransom, 1996, EdTV, 1999, How the Grinch Stole Christmas, 2000, A Beautiful Mind, 2001. Office: Broder Kurland Webb Uffner 10250 Constellation Blvd Los Angeles CA 90067-6200

HILL, NED CROMAR, dean, finance educator, consultant; b. Salt Lake City, Dec. 18, 1945; s. Richard G. Sharp and Bettie (Cromar) Hill; m. Claralyn Martin, Nov. 26, 1968; children: Evan M., Jonathan C., Aaron R., Joseph B., Alison. Student, Brigham Young U., 1967; BS in chemistry, U. Utah, 1969; MS in chemistry, Cornell U., Ithaca, NY, 1971, PhD in fin., 1976. Cert. cash mgr. Asst. prof. fin. Cornell U., 1976-77, Ind. U., Bloomington, 1977-81, assoc. prof. fin., 1981-87; Joel C. Peterson prof. fin. Brigham Young U., Provo, Utah, 1987-96, asst. to pres., 1996-98, dean, Marriot Chair Bus. Mgmt., Marriott Sch. Mgmt., 1998—. Cons. Hill Fin. Assocs., Bloomington, 1978—; bd. dirs. Beneficial Life Ins. Co., Morgan Stanley Bank, Pete Suazo Bus. Ctr. Author: Essentials in Cash Management, 1984, Short-Term Financial Management, 1987; co-founder Jour. Cash Mgmt., 1981, EDI Forum: Jour. Electronic Commerce, 1987. Mem. Utah Info. Tech. Commn., 1993-97; stake pres. Ch. Jesus Christ of the Latter Day Saints, 1982-87, 2000—05; fin. v.p. Boy Scouts Hoosier Trails Council, Bloomington, 1980-86. With US Army, 1971—72. Named Outstanding Faculty Mem., Marriott Sch. Mgmt., Brigham Young U., 1992. Mem. Fin. Mgmt. Assn. (bd. dirs. 1986-88), Phi Beta Kappa, Phi Kappa Phi. Republican. Avocations: vocal music, birding. Office: Brigham Young U Marriott Sch of Mgmt 730 TNRB Provo UT 84602 Home Phone: 801-375-2417; Office Phone: 801-422-4122. Business E-Mail: ned_hill@byu.edu.

HILL, RICHARD ALLAN (RICK HILL), former congressman; b. Grand Rapids, Minn., Dec. 30, 1946; m. Betti Christie, June 10, 1983; children: Todd, Corey, Mike. BA in Econs. and Polit. Sci., St. Cloud State U., 1968; JD, Concord U. Sch. Law, 2005. Surety bonding businessman, owner InsureWest, 1968-90; real estate and investment ptnr., 1983—; committeeman Mont. State Rep. Party, 1990-94; legis. liaison to Gov. Marc Racicot State of Mont., Helena, 1993; mem. US Congress from Mont. dist., Washington, 1997-2001, mem. banking and fin. svcs. com., resources com., small bus. com. Fin. chair State Rep. Party, 1989-91, state chair, 1991-92. Bd. dirs. Mont. Sci. and Tech. Alliance, 1992, Blue Cross Blue Shield Mont., 2003-. Republican.

HILL, RICHARD S., manufacturing executive; BSE, U. Ill., 1974; MBA, Syracuse U., 1981. With GE, Motorola, Hughes Aircraft; v.p., gen. mgr. oscilloscope group Tektronix, Inc., 1990—91, pres., test & measurement group, 1991—93; CEO Novellus Systems, Inc., San Jose, Calif., 1993—, chmn., 1996—. Mem.: bd. dirs., Novellus Systems, Inc., 2003-. Office: Novellus Systems Inc 4000 N First St San Jose CA 95134

HILL, WILLIAM U., state supreme court justice, former state attorney general; b. Montgomery, Ala., 1948; BA, U. Wyo., 1970, JD, 1974. Bar: Wyo. 1974. Asst. atty. gen. State of Wyo., Cheyenne, Wyo., 1974—77; atty. priv. practice, Riverton, Wyo., 1977—80, Seattle, 1977—80; chief of staff, chief counsel Sen. Malcolm Wallop, Wash., DC, 1980—89; atty. priv. practice, Cheyenne, Wyo., 1989—91; asst. U.S. atty., 1991—95; atty. gen. State of Wyo., Cheyenne, Wyo., 1995—98; justice Wyo. Supreme Ct., Cheyenne, 1998—, chief justice, 2002—06. Mem.: Wyo. State Bar Assn. Office: Wyoming Supreme Court 2301 Capitol Ave Cheyenne WY 82001-3656

HILLE, BERTIL, physiology educator; b. New Haven, Oct. 10, 1940; s. C. Einar and Kirsti (Ore) H.; m. Merrill Burr, Nov. 21, 1964; children: Erik D., J. Trygve. BS, Yale U., 1962; PhD, Rockefeller U., 1967, PhD hon causa, 2008. H.H. Whitney fellow Cambridge U., 1967-68; asst. prof. U. Wash., Seattle, 1968-71, assoc. prof., 1971-74, prof. physiology, 1974—. Vis. prof. U. Saarland, Hamburg, Germany, 1975-76. Author: Ion Channels of Excitable Membranes, 3d edit., 2001; mem. edit. bd.: Jour. Gen. Physiology, 1971—, Am. Jour. Physiology, 1984—87, Jour. Neurosci., 1984—87, Neuron, 1987—, Curr. Opinion Neurobiol., 1990—99, Procs. of NAS, 1996—99; contbr. articles to profl. jours. Recipient Alexander von Humboldt Sr. Scientist award, 1975, Bristol-Myers Squibb award, 1990, (with Dr. Clay Armstrong) Louisa Gross Horowitz prize for biology or biochemistry Columbia U., 1996, (with Drs. Clay Armstrong and Roderick MacKinnon) Albert Lasker Basic Med. Rsch. award, 1999, Gairdner Found. Internat. award, 2001. Mem. NAS, Biophys. Soc. (K.S. Cole award 1975), Am. Acad. Arts and Sci., Inst. of Medicine, Soc. Neurosci. Home: 10630 Lakeside Ave NE Seattle WA 98125-6934 Office: U Wash Physiology & Biophysics Dept 1959 NE Pacific St HSB Rm G424 Box 357290 Seattle WA 98195-7290 E-mail: hille@u.washington.edu.

HILLER, DAVID DEAN, former publishing executive; b. Chgo., June 12, 1953; AB, Harvard U., 1975, JD, 1978. Bar: Ill. 1981. Law clk. to Hon. Judge Malcolm Wilkey US Ct. Appeals (DC Cir.), 1978-79; law clk. to Hon. Justice Potter Stewart US Supreme Ct., 1979-80; spl. asst. to Atty. Gen. William French Smith US Dept. Justice, 1981—82, assoc. dep. atty. gen., 1982—83; assoc. Sidley & Austin LLP, Chgo., 1983—86, ptnr., 1986; v.p., gen. counsel The Tribune Co., Chgo., 1988—93, sr. v.p., gen. counsel, 1993, sr. v.p. devel., 1993—2000, pres. interactive, 2000—04, sr. v.p. pub., 2003—04; pres., pub. Chgo. Tribune, 2004—06; pub., pres., CEO L.A. Times, 2006—08. Bd. dirs. CareerBuilder, Classified Ventures, CrossMedia Services. Editor Harvard Law Rev., 1977-78. Bd. trustees Roosevelt U., Chgo. Hist. Soc.; bd. dirs. Chgo. Tribune Found., McCormick Tribune Found. Mem. ABA, Chgo. Coun. Fgn. Rels, Econ. Club Chgo. (bd. dirs.).

HILLMAN, MARK D., state legislator; b. Burlington, Colo., May 24, 1967; Student, Colby C.C., Kans., 1985-86, Morgan C.C., Colo., 1991. Newspaper reporter, sports editor, 1986-94; freelance reporter, 1994—; farmer Dryland Wheat, 1994—; mem. Colo. Senate, Dist. 2, Denver, 1998—; mem. agr., natural resources and energy com.; vice-chair local govt. com.; mem. state, vets. and mil. affairs. Treas. Evang. Free Ch.; active Colo. Farm Bur., Heritage Found.; county chair Wayne Allard for Congress, 1990-94; vice-chair Kit Carson County Reps., 1993-94, chair, 1994-98; mem. Colo. Rep. Leadership Program, 1995-96. Republican. Office: State Capitol 200 E Colfax Ave Ste 346 Denver CO 80203-1716 E-mail: mhillman@sni.net.

HILLS, AUSTIN EDWARD, vineyard executive; b. San Francisco, Oct. 13, 1934; s. Leslie William and Ethel (Lee) H.; m. Erika Michaela Brunar, May 20, 1978; children: Austin, Justin. AB, Stanford U., 1957; MBA, Columbia U., 1959. Chmn. bd. dirs. Hills Bros. Coffee, Inc., San Francisco, 1976, Grgich Hills Estate, Rutherford, Calif., 1977—. Pres. Hills Vineyards, Inc., Rutherford, 1975-97; pres. Pacific Coast Coffee Assn., San Francisco, 1975-76, Hills Vineyard, Inc., 1999—. Pres. San Francisco Soc. for Prevention of Cruelty to Animals, 1972-78, No. Calif. Soc. for Prevention of Cruelty to Animals, 1972-78. With Air N.G. Mem. Am. Soc. Enologists. Libertarian. Office: 2546 Jackson St San Francisco CA 94115-1121

HILLS, REGINA J., journalist; b. Sault Sainte Marie, Mich., Dec. 24, 1953; d. Marvin Dan and Ardithanne (Tilly) H.; m. Vincent C. Stricherz, Feb. 25, 1984. BA, U. Nebr., 1976. Reporter UPI, Lincoln, Nebr., 1976-80, state editor, bur. mgr., 1981-82, New Orleans, 1982-84, Indpls., 1985-87; asst. city editor Seattle Post-Intelligencer, 1987-99, online prodr., 1999—2001, mng. prodr., 2001—06; web editor U. Wash., Seattle, 2006—07, assoc. dir., Web Comm., 2007—. Panelist TV interview show Face Nebr., 1978-81; vis. lectr. U. Nebr., Lincoln, 1978, 79, 80; columnist weekly feature Capitol News, Nebr. Press Assn., 1981-82. Mem.: U. Nebr. Alumni Assn., Zeta Tau Alpha. Office: Univ Wash Box 351210 Seattle WA 98195-1210 Office Phone: 206-543-2561. E-mail: ghills@u.washington.edu.

HILLYARD, IRA WILLIAM, retired pharmacologist, educator; b. Richmond, Utah, Mar. 23, 1924; s. Neal Jacobsen and Lucille (Duce) H.; m. Venice Lenore Williams, July 10, 1945 (dec.); children: Christine, Kevin, Eric; m. Norma Larsen, May 1, 1970. BS, Idaho State U., 1949; MS, U. Nebr., 1951; PhD, St. Louis U., 1957. Pharmacologist Mead Johnson Co., Evansville, Ind., 1957-59; sr. pharmacologist, sect. leader Warner-Lambert Research Inst., Morris Plains, NJ, 1959-69; assoc. prof. pharmacology Idaho State U. Coll. Pharmacy, Pocatello, 1969-73, 77-79, dean, 1979-87, prof. pharmacology, 1979-91, prof. emeritus, 1991—; ret., 1991. Dir. pharmacology and toxicology ICN Pharms., Irvine, Calif., 1973-77, cons., 1977-80; cons. Pennwalt Pharm. Co., Rochester, N.Y., 1978-83 Contbr. articles to profl. jours. Served with USN, 1943-45, 51-53. Decorated Purple Heart. Fellow Am. Found. Pharm. Edn.; mem. Western Pharmacology Soc., Am. Assn. Colls. Pharmacy, Am. Soc. Pharmacology and Exptl. Therapeutics, N.Y. Acad. Scis., Sigma Xi, Rho Chi, Phi Delta Chi. Lodges: Rotary. Home: 594 S 800 W Mapleton UT 84664-4313 Personal E-mail: ihnh@aol.com.

HILLYARD, LYLE WILLIAM, state legislator; b. Logan, Utah, Sept. 25, 1940; son of Alma Lowell Hillyard & Lucille Rosenbaum H; married 1964 to Alice Thorpe; children: Carrie, Lisa, Holly, Todd & Matthew. Chairman, Cache County Republican Committee, 70-76; Utah State Representative, District 58, 81-82, District 4, 82-84, Assistant Majority Whip, 82-84, Utah House Representative; Utah State Senator, District 25, 85-, Assistant Majority Whip, 95-98, Majority Leader, 99-2000, president, 2000, chairman, Exec Appropriations & Judiciary Standing Committees, 87-90, 2004-, member, Public Education Appropriations Committee, 87-90, 2006-, Revenue & Taxation Standing Committee, 89-90, 93, & 2004, Judiciary & Revenue & Taxation Standing Committees, currently, Utah State Senate.President, Hillyard, Anderson & Olsen Law Firm, currently; member exec board, Trapper's Trail Coun Boy Scouts, currently. Distinguished Serv Award, Logan Jaycees, 72. Cache Chamber of Commerce (president, formerly); America Trial Lawyers Association; USU Alumni; America, Utah & Cache Co Bar Asns. Republican. Mem Lds Church. Mailing: 595 S Riverwoods Pkwy Ste 100 Logan UT 84321 Home Phone: 435-753-0043; Office Phone: 435-752-2610. Office Fax: 435-753-8895. E-mail: lhillyard@utahsenate.org.

HILPERT, EDWARD THEODORE, JR., retired lawyer; b. Frazee, Minn., Apr. 29, 1928; s. Edward Theodore Sr. and Hulda Gertrude (Wilder) H.; m. Susan Hazelton, May 5, 1973. AB, U. Wash., Seattle, 1954, JD, 1956. Bar: Wash. 1956, US Dist. Ct. (we. dist.) Wash. 1956, US Tax Ct. 1959, US Ct. Appeals (9th cir.) 1959, US Supreme Ct. 1970. Law clk. to Hon. George H. Boldt U.S. Dist. Ct. (we. dist.) Wash., Tacoma, 1956—58; assoc. Ferguson & Burdell, Seattle, 1958—63, ptnr., 1963—91; sr. ptnr. Schwabe, Williamson, Ferguson & Burdell, Seattle, 1992—2003, ret., 2004. Exec. com. 9th cir. Jud. Conf., San Francisco, 1987—90. Judge pro tem Seattle Mcpl. Ct., 1971-80. Capt. USAR, 1946-49, 50-52, Korea. Mem.: ABA, Mensa, The Rainer Club, Seattle Tennis Club, Broadmoor Golf Club, Sea Pines Country Club. Republican. Lutheran. Office: Schwabe Williamson Ferguson & Burdell US Bank Ctr 1420 5th Ave Ste 3010 Seattle WA 98101-2393 Home: 26 Twin Pines Rd Hilton Head Island SC 29928 Home Phone: 843-671-5545; Office Phone: 206-622-1711. Personal E-mail: suehilpert@aol.com.

HILTON, (WILLIAM) BARRON, hotel executive; b. Dallas, Oct. 23, 1927; s. Conrad Hilton; 8 children. DHL, U. Houston, 1986. Founder, pres. San Diego Chargers, 1960—66; pres. Am. Football League; v.p. Hilton Hotels Corp., Beverly Hills, Calif., 1954, pres., CEO, 1966—96, chmn., 1979—2004, co-chmn., 2004—; chmn. Hilton Equipment Corp., Beverly Hills, Calif. Mem. gen. adminstrv. bd. Mfrs. Hanover Trust Co., NYC; bd. dirs. Conrad N. Hilton Found., So. Calif. Visitors Coun. and Exec. Coun. on Fgn. Diplomats. Recipient Am. Spirit award, Nat. Bus. Aircraft Assn., 1995, Chevalier of Confrerie de la Chaine Des Rotisseurs, Magestrial Knight, Sovereign Mil. Order Malta; named one of 400 Richest Ams., Forbes mag., 2006; named to, Culinary Inst. Am. Hall of Fame, 1986. Mem.: Peace Found. Coun., Conouistadares del Cielo. Office: Hilton Hotels Corp 9336 Civic Center Dr Beverly Hills CA 90210-3604

HILTZIK, MICHAEL, journalist; b. NYC, Nov. 9, 1952; s. Harold & Bernice (Rothman) Hiltzik; m. Deborah Ibert, 2 children, Andrew, David. BA English, Colgate U., 1973; MS Journalism, Columbia U. Grad Sch Journalism, 1974. Journalist Buffalo Courier-Express, Buffalo, 1974-78, bureau chief, 1976-78; staff writer Providence Journal-Bulletin, Providence, 1979-81; finan. writer L.A. Times, 1981-83, N.Y. fin. corr. NYC, 1982-88, Nairobi bur. chief Nairobi, Kenya, 1988-93, Moscow corr. Moscow, 1993-94, fin. staff writer/editor, columnist LA, 1994—2006. Author, non-fiction: A Death in Kenya, 1991, Dealers of Lightning: Xerox PARC and the Dawn of the Computer Age, 1999, The Plot Against Social Security: How the Bush Plan is Endangering Our Financial Future, 2005. Co-recipient Pulitzer prize for Beat Reporting, 1999, recipient, ABA Silver Gavel award, Overseas Press Club citation for coverage of E. Africa.

HIMES, DIANE ADELE, buyer, fundraiser, actress, lobbyist; b. San Francisco, Aug. 11, 1942; d. L. John and Mary Louise (Young) H. BA, San Francisco State U., 1964. Founding mem., actress South Coast Repertory Co., 1964—66; rep. west coast home furnishings Allied Stores, nationwide; gift buyer Jordan Marsh, Miami; buyer The Broadway Stores; west coast sales mgr. Xmas divsn. Vincent Lippe Corp., LA; midwest sales mgr. Vincent-Lippe Chgo. Actress Nine 'O Clock Players, 1995, short film The Traveling Companion, 1998. Statewide co-chair Californians Initiative No On #102, 1988; founding co-chair Life AIDS Lobby, 1985—88; mem. Beverly Hills rent control bd., 1984; co-chair Californians Against Proposition #64, 1986; co-chmn. Mcpl. Elections Com., LA; bd. dirs. L.A. Women's Shakespeare Group, 1992—94. Named Woman of Yr. of L.A., ACLU, 1987, Christopher Street West, 1988. Avocation: acting.

HINCH, A.J. (ANDREW JAY HINCH), professional baseball coach; b. Waverly, Iowa, May 15, 1974; m. Erin Hinch; 1 child, Hayley. B in Psychology, Stanford U., Calif. Catcher Oakland Athletics, 1998—2000, Kansas City Royals, 2001—02, Detroit Tigers, 2003, Phila. Phillies, 2004; farm dir. Ariz. Diamondbacks, 2005—06, dir. player devel., 2006—09, mgr., 2009—. Office: Ariz Diamondbacks Chase Field 401 E Jefferson St Phoenix AZ 85001*

HINCHEY, BRUCE ALAN, environmental engineering company executive, state legislator, state legislator; b. Kansas City, Mo., Jan. 24, 1949; s. Charles Emmet and Eddie Lee (Scott) H.; m. Karen Adele McLaughlin, Nov. 27, 1969 (div. Nov. 1983); children: Scott Alan, Traci Denise, Amanda Lee, Richard Austin; m. Karen Robitaille, Apr. 10, 1993. Student, U. Mo., Rolla, 1967-71. Source testing crew chief Ecology Audits, Inc., Dallas, 1971-76, lab. mgr. Casper, Wyo., 1976-78, mgr. ops. Dallas, 1978-79; v.p. Kumpe & Assoc. Engrs., Casper, 1979-81; pres. Western Environ. Svcs. and Testing, Inc., Casper, 1981—2002, Hawk Industries, Inc., 1993-2000; mem. Wyo. Senate, Dist. 27, Cheyenne, 1998—; pres. Petroleum Assn. Wyo., Casper, 2002—. Pres. Mining Assocs. Wyo., Cheyenne, 1986-87. Mem. Wyo. State Ho. of Reps., Cheyenne, 1989-99, spkr. of house, mgmt. coun., rules com., energy coun., select water com., sel. edn. com., active Natrona County Rep. precinct, Casper, 1986—, Am. Legis. Exch. Coun., 1989; chair Natrona County Rep. Party, 1988-89; mem. appropriations com. Wyo. Senate, 1999—. Mem. Am. Inst. Mining Engrs., Nat. Fedn. Ind. Bus. (Guardian award), Air Pollution Control Assn., Casper C. of C., Rotary, Shriners, Masons. Methodist. Office: Petroleum Assn Wyo 951 Werner Ct Ste 100 Casper WY 82601

HINCKLEY, ROBERT CRAIG, lawyer; b. Sept. 5, 1947; s. Marsden Donald and Doris Camille (Engelhardt) H. BS, U.S. Naval Acad., 1969; JD, Tulane U., 1976. Bar: La. 1976, Calif. 1977. Commd. navigator anti-submarine warfare officer USS Brinkley Bass, Long Beach, Calif., 1969—71; aide to dir. naval intelligence Pentagon, Washington, 1971—73; spl. asst. U.S. atty., legal officer Naval Air Sta., Alameda, Calif., 1976—79; with Lillick McHose & Charles, San Francisco, 1979—81, Jones, Walker, Waechter, Poitevent, Carrere & Denegre, New Orleans, 1981; v.p., gen. counsel, sec. NEC Electronics, Inc., Mountain View, Calif., 1981—87; sr. v.p., CFO Spectra Physics, San Jose, 1988—90; v.p. strategic programs, COO Xilinx, Inc., San Jose, 1991—99. Bd. dirs. Lexar Media. Bd. dirs. San Jose Symphony, 1995. Mem.: Xandex, Inc., Assn. Publicly Traded Cos. (bd. dirs. 1995—99). Home: 79 Crescent Drive Palo Alto CA 94301 Home Phone: 650-321-1179.

HIND, HARRY WILLIAM, pharmaceutical company executive; b. Berkeley, Calif., June 2, 1915; s. Harry Wyndham and B.J. (O'Connor) H.; m. Diana Vernon Miesse, Dec. 12, 1940; children: Leslie Vernon Hind Daniels, Gregory William. BS, U. Calif., Berkeley, 1939, LLD, 1968; DSc (hon.), U. Scis. Phila., 1982. Founder Barnes-Hind Pharms., Inc., Sunnyvale, Calif., 1939—. Pres. Hind Health Care, Inc. Contbr. articles to profl. jours.; designer ph meter and developer of ophthalmic solutions. Recipient Ebert award for pharm. rsch., 1948, Eye Rsch. Found. award, 1958, Helmholtz Ophthalmology award for rsch., 1968, Carbert award for sight conservation, 1973, Alumnus of Yr. award U. Calif. Sch. Pharmacy, 1965, Disting. Svc. award U. Calif. Proctor Found., 1985, Commendation by Resolution State of Calif., 1987, Pharmaceutical Achievements commendation State of Calif. Assembly, Hon. Recognition award Contact Lens Mfrs. Assn., 1990. Fellow AAAS; mem. Am. Pharm. Assn., Am. Optometric Assn. (Man of Yr. award Pharmacist's Planning Svc. 1987), Contact Lens Soc. Am. (Hall of Fame 1989), Am. Assn. Pharm. Scientists, Am. Chem. Soc., Calif. Pharm. Assn., NY Acad. Scis., Los Altos Country Club, Sigma Xi, Rho Chi, Phi Delta Chi.

HINERFELD, ROBERT ELLIOT, lawyer; b. NYC, May 29, 1934; s. Benjamin B. and Anne (Blitz) H.; m. Susan Hope Slocum, June 27, 1957; children: Daniel Slocum, Matthew Ben. AB, Harvard U., 1956, JD, 1959. Bar: Calif. 1960. Asst. U.S. atty So. Dist. Calif., 1960-62; assoc. Leonard Horwin, Beverly Hills, Calif., 1962-66; mem. Simon, Sheridan, Murphy, Thornton & Hinerfeld, LA, 1967-74, Murphy, Thornton, Hinerfeld & Cahill, 1975-83, Murphy, Thornton, Hinerfeld & Elson, 1983-85, Manatt, Phelps & Phillips LLP, 1985-2000, sr. of counsel, 2000—05; pvt. practice, 2005—; arbitrator bus. panel L.A. Superior Ct., 1979-82; assoc. ind. counsel (diGenova), 1993-95. Judge pro tempore Beverly Hills Mcpl. Ct., 1967-74; clin. lectr. U. So. Calif. Law Ctr., 1980-81, guest lectr., 1993-96; expert witness, 1988—, legal affairs on-air guest spkr. sta. KCRW-FM, Santa Monica, Calif., 1998-99. Contbr. articles to profl. jours. Trustee Westland Sch., LA, 1970—75, Pacific Hills Sch., 1971—72. Fellow: Am. Bar Found. (life); mem.: ABA (mem. Ctr. for Profl. Responsibility), Calif. Acad. Appellate Lawyers (membership com. 1983—88, 2d v.p. 1985—87, 1st v.p. 1987—88, pres. 1988—89), Am. Arbitration Assn. (arbitrator comml. panel 1966—, mem. large complex case panel 2003—), State Bar Calif. (mem. disciplinary investigation panel dist. 7 1977—80, hearing referee State Bar Ct. 1981—83, exec. com. litig. sect. 1983—85, referee rev. dept. 1984—87, civil litig. adv. group 1985—88, mem. Jud. Nominees Evaluation Commn. 2000—04, mem. com. on criminal law and procedure, chmn. spl. com. revision fed. criminal code), L.A. County Bar Assn. (spl. com. jud. evaluation 1978—82, arbitration com. 1981—83, spl. com. on appellate elections evaluation 1996—2000, settlement officer 2d appellate dist. appellate case project 1996—2005), Assn. Profl. Responsibility Lawyers, Harvard Club So. Calif. (dir. 1974—83, sec. 1978—80, mem. prize book com. 1992—94). Home and Office: 371 24th St Santa Monica CA 90402-2517 Home Phone: 310-394-4261; Office Phone: 310-394-4902. Personal E-mail: rhinerfeld@me.com.

HINES, JOHN J., state legislator; b. Gillette, Wyo., Mar. 3, 1936; son of John Dwight Hines & Annie McKenzie H; single. Attended, U. Wyo. Treas. Campbell Co. Fire Bd., 12 years; pres. Campbell Co. Predatory Bd, 1977-84; former pres. Campbell Co. Fair Bd; mem. District 31, Wyo. House of Reps., 1985-2002; mem. Dist. 23, Wyo. State Senate 2002-, Senate Vice Pres., 2005-06, Senate Majority Fl. Leader, 2007-08, Pres., 2009-; dir. Am. Sheep Producer Coun, 75-85; dir., Nat Wool Grower's, 1982-84, mem., Exec Com., 1983-84; rancher. Wyo. Woolgrowers (former pres.); Nat Woolgrowers; Nat & Wyo. Stockgrowers; Rotary; C of C; Wyo. Unity Group (former pres.); Am. Legion; life mem. Campbell Co & Wyo. Hist Soc; Nat Cattlemen Assn.; Co Fair Bd. Republican. Mailing: 714 W Echeta Rd Gillette WY 82716 Office: 213 State Capitol Bldg Cheyenne WY 82002 Home Phone: 307-682-3943; Office Phone: 307-777-7881. Office Fax: 307-777-5466; Home Fax: 307-682-3943. Business E-Mail: jhines@wyoming.com.*

HINKINS, DAVID P., state legislator; Mem. Dist. 27 Utah State Senate, 2008—. Republican. Office: W115 State Capitol Complex Salt Lake City UT 84114 Mailing: PO Box 485 Orangeville UT 84537 Home Phone: 435-348-5550; Office Phone: 801-538-1035, 435-748-2828. Fax: 435-748-2089; Office Fax: 801-326-1475. Business E-Mail: dhinkins@utahsenate.org.

HINKLE, CHARLES FREDERICK, lawyer, educator; b. Oregon City, Oreg., July 6, 1942; s. William Ralph and Ruth Barbara (Holcomb) H. BA, Stanford U., 1964; MDiv, Union Theol. Sem., NYC, 1968; JD, Yale U., 1971. Bar: Oreg. 1971; ordained to ministry United Ch. of Christ, 1974. Instr. English, Morehouse Coll., Atlanta, 1966-67; assoc. Stoel Rives LLP, Portland, Oreg., 1971-77, ptnr., 1977—. Adj. prof. Lewis and Clark Law Sch., Portland, 1978-2001; bd. govs. Oreg. State Bar, 1992-95. Oreg. pres. ACLU, Portland, 1976-80, nat. bd. dirs., 1979-85; bd. dirs. Kendall Cmty. Ctr., 1987-93, Youth Progress Assn., 1994-98, Portland Baroque Orch., 1999-2000; mem. pub. affairs com. Am. Cancer Soc., 1994-99; mem. Oreg. Gov.'s Task Force on Youth Suicide, 1996. Recipient Elliott Human Rights award Oreg. Edn. Assn., 1984, E.B. MacNaughton award ACLU Oreg., 1987, Wayne Morse award Dem. Com. Oreg., 1994, Tom McCall Freedom of Info. award Women in Comm., 1996, Civil Rights award Met. Human Rights Commn., 1996, Pub. Svc. award Oreg. State Bar, 1997. Fellow Am. Bar Found.; mem. ABA (ho. of dels. 1998-2000), FBA, Multnomah County Bar Assn., Am. Constn. Soc. (bd. dirs. 2005—),City Club Portland (pres. 1987-88). Democrat. Home: 14079 SE Fairoaks Way Milwaukie OR 97267-1017 Office: Stoel Rives 900 SW 5th Ave Ste 2600 Portland OR 97204-1268 Office Phone: 503-294-9266. Business E-Mail: cfhinkle@stoel.com.

HINKLE, GREG W., state legislator; b. Bellingham, Wash., Nov. 12, 1946; m. Gail Hinkle; 3 children. Attended, Skagit Valley Junior Coll., 1965; diploma, Harcourt Learning Direct, 2000. Postmaster USPS, 1989—91; self-employed custom woodworking, 1991—; chmn. Sanders Co. Planning Bd., 1997—2000; mem. Dist. 7 Mont. State Senate, 2008—. US Army Nat. Guard, 1966—72. Republican. Christian. Office: Montana Senate PO Box 200500 Helena MT 59620-0500 Mailing: 5 Gable Rd Thompson Falls MT 59873-8512 Home Phone: 406-827-4645; Office Phone: 406-444-4800. Office Fax: 406-444-4875.

HINMAN, FRANK, JR., urologist, educator; b. San Francisco, Oct. 2, 1915; s. Frank and Mittie (Fitzpatrick) H.; m. Marion Modesta Eaves, Dec. 3, 1948. AB with great distinction, Stanford U., 1937; MD, Johns Hopkins U., 1941. Diplomate Am. Bd. Urology (trustee 1979-85). Intern Johns Hopkins Hosp., 1941-42; resident Cin. Gen. Hosp., 1942-44, U. Calif. Hosp., 1945-47; pvt. practice San Francisco, 1947-85; assoc. clin. prof. urology U. Calif., San Francisco, 1954-62, clin. prof., 1962—; urologist-in-chief Children's Hosp., 1957-85. Adv. council Nat. Inst. Arthritis, Diabetes, Digestive and Kidney Diseases, 1983-86 Lt. USNR, 1944-46. Named Disting. Alumnus, Johns Hopkins U., 1995. Fellow ACS (regent 1972-80, vice-chmn. 1978-79, v.p. 1982-83), Royal Coll. Surgeons (hon., Eng.); mem. Am. Urol. Assn. (hon.), Am. Assn. Genito-Urinary Surgeons (hon., pres. 1981, Keyes medalist 1998), Clin. Soc. Genito-Urinary Surgeons (pres. 1979), Internat. Soc. Urol. (pres. Am. sect. 1980-84), Am. Assn. Clin. Urologists, Am. Fedn. Clin. Research, Soc. Pediatric Urology (founding mem., pres. 1971), Soc. Univ. Urologists (founding mem., pres. 1973), Am. Acad. Pediatrics (pres. urology sect. 1986), Urodynamics Soc. (founding mem., pres. 1980-82), Genito Urinary Reconstructive Soc. (founding mem.), Pan Pacific Surg. Assn. (v.p. 1980-83), Internat. Continence Soc., Brit. Assn. Urologic Surgeons (hon.) (St. Paul Medalist 1991), Soc. Française d'Urologie, Australasian Soc. Urologic Surgeons (hon.), Phi Beta Kappa, Alpha Omega Alpha. Clubs: Bohemian, St. Francis Yacht, San Francisco Yacht. Office: U Calif Med Ctr San Francisco CA 94143-0738 Home Phone: 415-673-5553; Office Phone: 415-476-1611. Business E-Mail: fhinman@urol.ucsf.edu.

HINMAN, HARVEY DEFOREST, lawyer; b. May 7, 1940; s. George Lyon and Barbara H.; m. Margaret (Snyder), June 23, 1962; children: George, Sarah, Marguerite. BA, Brown U., 1962; JD, Cornell U., 1965. Bar: Calif., 1966. Assoc. Pillsbury, Madison, and Sutro, San Francisco, 1965—72, ptnr., 1973—93; v.p., gen. counsel Chevron Corp., San Francisco, 1993—2002; of counsel Pillsbury, Winthrop, Shaw, Pittman LLP, San Francisco, 2003—. Bd. dirs. Big Sur Environ. Inst., 2004—, pres., 2004. Bd. dirs., sec. Holbrook Palmer Park Found., 1977—86; trustee Castillija Sch., 1988—89; bd. govs. Filoli Ctr., 1988—2008, pres., 1994—95; bd. dirs. Phillips Brooks Sch., 1978—84, pres., 1983—84. Fellow: Am. Bar Found.; mem.: Legal Aid Soc. (bd. dirs. 2004—07). Office: 50 Fremont St San Francisco CA 94105

HINSHAW, DAVID B., JR., radiologist; b. LA, Dec. 28, 1945; s. David B. Sr. and Mildred H. (Benjamin) H.; m. Marcia M. Johns, Aug. 7, 1966; children: Amy, John. BA in German and Pre Medicine, Loma Linda U., Riverside, Calif., 1967; MD, Loma Linda U., 1971. Diplomate Am. Bd. Radiology in diagnostic radiology and neuroradiology. Intern Loma Linda U. Med. Ctr., 1971-72, resident diagnostic radiology, 1972-74; neuroradiologist 2d Gen. Army Hosp., Landstuhl, Fed. Republic Germany, 1975-77; asst. prof. Loma Linda U. Sch. Medicine, 1975-80, assoc. prof., 1981-85, prof., 1986—, vice chmn. dept. radiation scis., 1988-90, chmn. dept. radiology, 1990—; pres. med. staff Loma Linda U. Med. Ctr., 1994-95; vice chair faculty practice plan Loma Linda U., 1995—. Dir. sect. magnetic resonance imaging, Loma Linda, 1983—; cons. U.S. Army Med. command, Europe, 1976-77, Jerry L. Pettis Meml. VA Hosp., 1980— Contbr. numerous articles to profl. jours., book chpts. in field of radiology. Maj. U.S. Army, 1975-77. Recipient Pres's. award Loma Linda U., 1971, Donald E. Grggs award Internal Med. Fellow Am. Coll. Radiology, Walter E. McPherson Soc. (Outstanding Faculty Research award 1987); mem. AMA (Physicians Recognition award 1980-83, 84—), Am. Soc. Neuroradiology (sr., program com. 1989, chmn. pub. rels. com. 1989-90), Western Neuroradiol. Soc., Radiol. Soc. N.Am., Calif. Med. Assn., San Bernadino County Med. Assn., Inland Radiol. Soc. (pres. 1989-90), Calif. Radiol. Soc., Assn. Univ. Radiologists, Soc. Magnetic Resonance Imaging, Soc. Magnetic Resonance in Medicine, Fedn. Western Socs. Neurol. Scis., Am. Roentgen Ray Soc., Am. Soc. Head and Neck Radiology, L.A. Radiol. Soc., Soc. Chmn. Acad. Radiology Depts., Alpha Omega Alpha (pres. Epsilon chpt. 1987). Republican. Seventh-day Adventist. Avocations: travel, electronics.

HINSHAW, MARK LARSON, architect, urban planner; b. Glendale, Calif., Aug. 17, 1947; s. Lerner Brady and Alice Elaine (Larson) H.; m. Caryl Ann Kunsemuller, Dec. 21, 1968 (div. 1982); 1 child, Erica; m. Marilyn Kay Smith, June 18, 1983 (div. 1997); children: Lindsay, Christopher. BArch magna cum laude, U. Okla., 1970; M in Urban Planning, CUNY, 1972. Registered arch., Wash. Sr. planner Planning Dept., Anchorage, 1976-77; project planner TRA, Seattle, 1977-82; urban designer City of Bellevue, Wash., 1982-90; ind. cons., 1991-97; dir. urban design LMN Archs., Seattle, 1997—. Arch.-in-the-sch. Seattle Sch. Dist., 1979. Columnist on architecture, urban design: Seattle Times, 1993—2004; author: Citistate Seattle: Shaping a Modern Metropolis, 1999—; contbg. editor: Landscape Architecture Mag.; contbr. articles to profl. jours. and books. Mem. Urban Beautification Commn., Anchorage, 1975, Design Jury, Hemet (Calif.) Civic Ctr. Competition, Seattle Design Commn., 1990-91; mem. Downtown Seattle Design Rev. Bd., 1996-. 1st lt. USAF, 1972-76. NEA grantee, 1975; recipient merit award for Hist. Preservation, City of Seattle, 1983. Fellow AIA (pres. Seattle chpt. 1992-93), Am. Inst. Cert. Planners (mem. nat. bd. 1994-98); mem. Am. Planning Assn. (sec. Wash. chpt. 1982, v.p. 1983-85, pres. 1987-89).

HINTON, JAMES H., healthcare services administrator; m. Carol Hinton; children: Rebecca, Robert. BA in Econs., U. N.Mex.; M in Healthcare Adminstrn., Ariz. State U. Pres., CEO Presbyn. Healthcare Svcs., Albuquerque.

HIPP, KENNETH BYRON, lawyer; b. Charlotte, NC, Aug. 4, 1945; s. Junius B. and Jeanne Carol (Gwaltney) H.; m. Ann Winfield Birmingham, Sept. 23, 1966; children: Kenneth Byron Jr., Andrew Clay. AB, Duke U., 1967; JD with high honors, U. N.C., Chapel Hill, 1971. Bar: N.C. 1971, Hawaii 1987, U.S. Dist. Ct. (no. dist.) Tex. 1978, U.S. Dist. Ct. Hawaii 1987, U.S. Ct. Appeals (2d, 4th and 5th cirs.) 1972, U.S. Ct. Appeals (9th cir.) 1976, U.S. Ct. Appeals (10th cir.) 1977, U.S. Supreme Ct. 1993. Assoc. Micronesian Claims Com., Saipan, Northern Mariana Islands, 1973-74; regional dir. Micronesian Claims Co., Palau, Western Caroline Islands, 1974-76; atty. enforcement litigation NLRB, Washington, 1971-73, 76-77, supr. atty. enforcement litigation, 1977, dep. asst. gen. counsel spl. litigation, 1977-78, dep. asst. gen. counsel appellate litigation, 1978-86, dep. asst. gen. counsel contempt litigation, 1986-87; ptnr. Goodsill Anderson Quinn & Stifel, Honolulu, 1987-95; mem. Nat. Mediation Bd., Washington, 1995-98, chmn., 1996-97; ptnr. Marr Hipp Jones & Pepper, Honolulu, 1998—; mediator, mem. Hawaii Appellate Conf. Program, 1999—. Bar examiner State of Hawaii, 1988-92; vis. assoc. prof. Law Sch., Boston Coll., 1983-84; adj. prof. Law Sch., Cath. U. Am., 1978-79, Law Ctr., Georgetown U., Washington, 1984-87; adj. prof. Grad. Sch. Bus. U. Hawaii, 1989-94. Mem. Hawaii State Bar Assn. (chair labor and employment law sect. 1990-91), Order of Coif. Presbyterian. Home: 314 Poipu Dr Honolulu HI 96825-2125 Office: Marr Hipp Jones Pepper Ste 1550 1001 Bishop St Pauahi Tower Honolulu HI 96813 E-mail: khipp@marrhipp.com.

HIRAI, KAZUO (KAZ), electronics executive; b. Tokyo, 1964; B in Liberal Arts, Internat. Christian Univ., Tokyo, 1984. With CBS/Sony Inc. (now Sony Music Entertainment Japan), 1984, Sony Music Japan, NYC; joined Sony Computer Entertainment Am., Inc., Foster City, Calif., 1995—, pres., 1996—2006, CEO, 2003—06, chmn., 2006—07; v.p. corp. exec. group Sony Computer Entertainment, Inc., Tokyo, 2006—07, pres., 2006—07, group COO, 2006—07, chmn., group chief exec., 2007—; pres. Sony Computer Entertainment Worldwide Studios, 2008—. Named Mogul in the Running, "New Establishment List", Vanity Fair, 2004; named one of Most Powerful Executives in the Business, Entertainment Weekly. Office Phone: 650-655-8000.

HIRANO, IRENE ANN YASUTAKE, museum director; b. LA, Oct. 7, 1948; d. Michael S. and Jean F. (Ogino) Yasutake; 1 child, Jennifer. BS in Pub. Adminstrn., U. So. Calif., 1970, MPA, 1972. Project adminstr. U. So. Calif., 1970-72; assoc. dir. Asian Women's Ctr., 1972-73; nat. project coord., Japanese site supr. Nat. Asian Am. Field Study, LA, 1973-75; cons. U.S. Dept. Health, Edn. and Welfare, Adminstn. on Aging, San Francisco, 1975; exec. dir. T.H.E. Clinic for Women, Inc., LA, 1975-88; exec. dir., pres. Japanese Am. Nat. Mus., LA, 1988—. Pres., CEO Nat. Ctr. for Preservation of Democracy, 2000-; lectr., spkr. in field. Mem. L.A. Ednl. Alliance for Restructuring Now, 1993—, Pres's. Com. on Arts & Humanities, 1994—, Commn. on Future of Smithsonian Inst., 1993—, L.A. Coalition, 1993—, accreditation commn., Am. Assn. Mus.; trustee Malborough Sch., 1993—; co-founder Leadership Edn. for Asian Pacifics, 1983, pres. 1983-86, v.p. 1986-90; pres., bd. dirs. Asian Pacific Am. Support Group, U. So. Calif., 1984-88; bd. dirs. Liberty Hill Found., 1984-88, community funding bd., 1981-84; trustee, chair Kresge Found., Troy, Mich.; chairperson Calif. Commn. on the Status of Women, 1981-82, commn. mem., 1976-83; adv. bd. on North Am. Diversity, Toyota; nat. bd. mem. Smithsonian Inst.; bd. mem. and sec.-treas. LA, Inc. Convention and Visitors Bur.; vice-chair Calif. Japanese Am. Cmty. Leadership Coun. Recipient Nat. Outstanding Asian/Pacific Islander award NEA, 1983, Outstanding Women of the '90's, Robinson's Corp., 1992, Outstanding Svc. award Nat. Women's Polit. Caucus,

1986, Nat. Inst. Women of Color, 1984, Outstanding Alumni award U. So. Calif., 1994, So. Calif. Hist. Soc. Cmty. award, 1995. Office: Japanese Am Nat Mus 369 E First St Los Angeles CA 90012-3901

HIRONO, MAZIE KEIKO, United States Representative from Hawaii, former lieutenant governor; b. Fukushima, Japan, Nov. 3, 1947; arrived in U.S., 1955, naturalized, 1959; m. Leighton Kim Oshima. BA, U. Hawaii, 1970; JD, Georgetown U., 1978. Dep. atty. gen., Honolulu, 1978-80; Shim, Tam, Kirimitsu & Naito, 1984-88; mem. Hawaii Ho. of Reps., Honolulu, 1980-94; lt. gov. State of Hawaii, 1994—2002; mem. US Congress from 2nd Hawaiian dist., 2007—. Bd. dirs. Nat. Asian Pacific Am. Bar Assn.; chair Hawaii Policy Group, Nat. Commn. on Tchg. and Ams. Future, Govs. Task Force on Sci. and Tech. Dep. chair Dem. Nat. Com., 1997; bd. dirs. Nuuanu YMCA, Honolulu, 1982—2004, Moiliili Cmty. Ctr., Honolulu, 1984—, Blood Bank of Hawaii. Mem. U.S. Supreme Ct. Bar, Hawaii Bar Assn., Phi Beta Kappa. Democrat. Office: 5104 Prince Kuhio Fed Bldg Honolulu HI 96850 also: 1229 Longworth House Office Bldg Washington DC 20515 E-mail: hirono@hawaii.rr.com.

HIRSCH, ANTHONY TERRY, physician; b. NYC, Jan. 29, 1940; s. Robert S. and Minna Hirsch; m. Barbara Hershan, July 8, 1961; children: Deborah, Kenneth, Steven. BS cum laude, Tufts U., 1961, MD, 1965. Diplomate Am. Bd. Pediatrics, Am. Bd. Allergy-Immunology. Pvt. practice pediatrics Children's Med. Group, LA, 1973-84; chair dept. pediatrics, dir. residency tng. program in pediatrics White Meml. Med. Ctr., LA, 1984—. Capt. USAF, 1969-71. Fellow Am. Acad. Pediatrics (chair access task force Calif. br., mem. nat. access task force, chair coun. on pediatric practice), Am. Acad. Allergy-Immunology. Avocation: sailing. Office: White Meml Med Ctr Dept Pediat 1701 Cesar Chavez Ave # 456 Los Angeles CA 90033-2410

HIRSCH, BARRY L., lawyer; b. Chgo., Nov. 11, 1933; Student, UCLA; LLB, U. So. Calif., 1957. Bar: Calif. 1957, N.Y. 1985. Ptnr. Armstrong, Hirsch, Jackoway, Tyerman & Wertheimer, LA. Mem.: L.A. Copyright Soc., Beverly Hills Bar Assn., L.A. County Bar Assn., State Bar Calif. Office: Armstrong Hirsch Jackoway Tyerman & Wertheimer 1888 Century Park E Los Angeles CA 90067-1702

HIRSCH, GILAH YELIN, artist, writer; b. Montreal, Que., Can., Aug. 24, 1944; came to U.S., 1963; d. Ezra and Shulamis (Borodensky) Y. BA, U. Calif., Berkeley, 1967; MFA, UCLA, 1970. Prof. art Calif. State U., Dominguez Hills, L.A., 1973—. Adj. prof. Internat. Coll., Guild Tutors, L.A., 1980-87, Union Grad. Sch., Cin., 1990 50 solo exhbns., mus. collections, 15 publs. Founding mem. Santa Monica Art Bank, Calif., 1983-85; bd. dir. Dorland Mountain Colony, Temecula, Calif., 1984-88 Recipient Disting. Artist award, Calif. State U., 1985, Found. Rsch. award, 1988—89, 1997—98, Creative Rsch. award, Sally Canova Rsch. Scholarship and Creative Activities awards program, 1997—99, 2003; named artist-in-residence, RIM Inst., Payson, Ariz., 1989—90, Tamarind Inst. Lithography, Albuquerque, 1973, Rockefeller Bellagio Ctr., Italy, 1992, Tyrone Guthrie Ctr. for Arts, Annamahkerrig, Ireland, 1993, Internat. Sympat., Slovakia, 2004, 2005; grantee, Nat. Endowment Arts, 1985, Class Found., 2003, Calif. State U., Dominguez Hills, 2005, Panavision Films, Inc., L.A., 2005, Takahashi Found., 2007; Dorland Mountain Colony fellow, 1981—84, 1983, 1984, 1992, 1995, 2003, fellow, Banff Ctr. for Arts Can., 1985, MacDowell Colony fellow, N.H., 1987, Calif. Communication Found. grant, 2007. Office: Calif State Univ Dominguez Hills 1000 E Victoria St Carson CA 90747-0001 Office Phone: 310-821-6848. Personal E-mail: gilah@linkline.com.

HIRSCH, HORST EBERHARD, metal products executive, consultant; b. Woelsendorf, Fed. Republic Germany, July 26, 1933; came to U.S., 1984; s. Albert and Emilie (Eberhardt) H.; m. Helga G. Gruber, May 2, 1961; children: Manon K., Fabiane M., Erin A. Diploma in chemistry, Tech. U. Karlsruhe, Fed. Republic Germany, 1959, D in Chem. Tech., 1961. Postdoctoral fellow NRC of Can., 1961-62; R & D engr., mgr. Cominco Ltd., Trail, B.C., Canada, 1962-84; pres., CEO Cominco Electronic Materials Inc., Spokane, Wash., 1984-88; pres. Johnson Matthey Electronics N.Am., Spokane, 1989-91, MSM (Metals and Semiconductor Materials), 1991—; vis. exec. IESC (Internat. Exec. Svc. Corps), 1992, field assoc., 1993—; co-founder, CM, HT Metals LLC, 2001—. Mem. bd. mgmt. B.C. Rsch. Coun., Vancouver, 1980-84; senate U. B.C., Vancouver, 1981-85; mem. adv. com. Wash. Tech. Ctr., 1992-94. Contbr. articles on chemistry and metallurgy to profl. publs., chpts. to books; patentee in field. Recipient Excellence in Innovation award Fed. Govt. Can., 1985. Mem. Soc. German Mining and Metall. Engrs. Lutheran. Avocations: reading, skiing, swimming, golf. Personal E-mail: zollegeg@aol.com.

HIRSCH, JORGE E., science educator; Licenciado, U. Buenos Aires, 1974; MS, U. Chgo., 1977, degree, 1980. Tchg. asst. U. of Buenos Aires, 1974—76; rsch. asst. U. of Chgo., James Franck Inst., 1977—80; post grad. rsch. physicist U. of Calif., Inst. of Theoretical Physics, 1980—82; asst. prof. U. of Calif., Dept. of Physics, 1983—85, assoc. prof., 1985—87, prof., 1987—. Recipient Pres. Young Investigators award, Nat. Sci. Found., 1985; Alfred P. Sloan fellowship, Alfred P. Sloan Found., 1984. Fellow: Am. Physical Soc. Achievements include research in condensed matter physics (theory), superconductivity, magnetism. Office: Dept of Physics 0319 U of Calif San Diego 9500 Gilman Dr La Jolla CA 92093

HIRSCH, JUDD, actor; b. NYC, Mar. 15, 1935; s. Joseph Sidney and Sally (Kitzis) H. BS in Physics, CCNY, 1960. Broadway appearances in Barefoot in the Park, 1966, Knock Knock, 1976 (Drama Desk award for best featured actor), Chapter Two, 1977-78, Talley's Folly, 1980 (Tony nomination), I'm Not Rappaport, 1985-86, (Tony award for best actor in play 1986, Outer Critics Circle award, 1986), Conversations with My Father, 1992 (Tony award for best actor in play 1992, Outer Critics Circle award, 1992), A Thousand Clowns, 1996, Art, 1998, I'm Not Rappaport, 2002, Sixteen Wounded, 2004; off-Broadway appearances in On the Necessity of Being Polygamous, 1963, Scuba Duba, 1967-69, King of the United States, 1972, Mystery Play, 1972, Hot L Baltimore, 1973, Prodigal, 1973, Knock Knock, 1975, Talley's Folly, 1979 (Obie award), The Seagull, 1983, I'm Not Rappaport, 1985, Below the Belt, 1996; regional appearances include Theater for Living Arts, Phila., Line of Least Existence, Harry Noon and Night, The Recruiting Officer, 1969-70, Annenberg Ctr., Phila., Hough in Blazes, 1971, Seattle Repertory, Conversations with My Father, 1991, Scarborough, Eng., 1994, London, 1995, Chapel Hill, NC, Death of a Salesman, 1994, Long Wharf Theater Robbers, 1995, Manitoba Theatre Ctr., Winnipeg and Royal Alexandra Theatre, Toronto, Death of A Salesman, 1997, Art, London, 1999, 2001; stock and tours A Thousand Clowns, Threepenny Opera, Fantastiks, Woodstock, NY, 1964, Peterpat, Houston and Ft. Worth, 1970, Harvey, Chgo., 1971, And Miss Reardon Drinks a Little, Palm Beach, Fla., 1972, I'm Not Rappaport, nat. tour, 1986-87, Conversations With My Father, Doolittle Theatre, LA, 1993, Art, nat. tour, 1999-2000; TV series include Delvecchio, 1976-77, Rhoda, 1977, Taxi, 1978-83 (Emmy award for best actor in a comedy series, 1981, 1983), Dear John (Golden Globe award 1988), 1988-92, George and Leo, 1997, Regular Joe, 2003, Numbers, 2004-05; TV movies include The Law, 1974, Fear on Trial, 1975, The Legend of Valentino, 1975, The Halloween That Almost Wasn't, 1979, Sooner or Later, 1979, Marriage Is Alive and Well, 1980, First Steps, 1985, Brotherly Love, 1985, The Great Escape-Untold Story, 1988, She Said No, 1990, Betrayal of Trust, 1993, Color of Justice, 1997, Rocky Marciano, 1999; films include King of the Gypsies, 1978, Ordinary People (nominated Acad. Award), 1980, Without a Trace, 1983, Teachers, 1984, The Goodbye People, 1984, Running on Empty, 1988, Independence Day, 1996, Man On the Moon, 1999, A Beautiful Mind, 2001, Zeyda and the Hitman, 2004; dir. Squaring the Circle, 1962, Not Enough Rope, 1973, Talley's Folly, 1981, Art, 2000-01. Mem. Acad. Motion Picture Arts and Scis., Acad. TV Arts and Scis., Actors Equity Assn., SAG, AFTRA, SSDC. Office: C/O NKSF 10100 Santa Monica Blvd #1300 Los Angeles CA 90067 also: Richard Feldstein 10100 Santa Monica Blvd Los Angeles CA 90067

HIRSCH, (WILLIAM) REECE, lawyer; b. Dallas, Jan. 4, 1960; BS, Northwestern U., Evanston, Ill., 1982; JD, U. So. Calif., 1990. Bar: Calif. 1990. Assoc. Davis Wright Tremaine LLP, San Francisco, 1994—98, ptnr., 1998—2002, Sonnenschein Nath & Rosenthal LLP, San Francisco, 2002—. Mem. editl. adv. bd. BNA's Health Law Reporter, Healthcare Informatics, TIPS on Managed Care. Mem.: ABA (mem. health law sect.), Healthcare Fin. Mgmt. Assn., Am. Health Lawyers Assn., Calif. Soc. Healthcare Attorneys. Office: Sonnenschein Nath & Rosenthal 525 Market St, 26th Fl San Francisco CA 94105 Office Phone: 415-882-0300. Office Fax: 415-543-5472. Business E-Mail: rhirsch@sonnenschein.com.

HIRSCH, STEVEN A., lawyer; b. Ariz., 1955; BA with distinction, U. Ariz., 1977, JD with high distinction, 1980. Bar: Ariz. 1980; cert. real estate specialist State Bar Ariz. Law clerk to Hon. James D. Hathaway Ariz. Ct. Appeals Divsn. 2, 1980-81; ptnr. Bryan Cave, Phoenix, Ariz. Editorial bd. Ariz. Bar Jour., 1986-89. Fellow Ariz. Bar Found. (bd. dirs. 1989-97, pres. 1995); mem. ABA (del. and dist. rep. young lawyers divsn. assembly 1990-92), Maricopa County Bar Assn. (bd. dirs. 1987-88), Order of Coif. Office: Bryan Cave 2 N Central Ave Ste 2200 Phoenix AZ 85004-4406

HIRSCHFELD, GERALD JOSEPH, cinematographer; b. NYC, Apr. 25, 1921; s. Ralph and Kate (Zirker) H.; m. Sarnell Ogus, June 5, 1945 (div. June 1972); children: Alec, Marc, Eric, Burt; m. Julia Warren Tucker, July 28, 1981. Student, Columbia U., 1938—40. Cinematic instr. New Inst. for Film, Bklyn., 1947-49; freelance dir. photography for TV and Film NYC, 1949-54; dir. photography, v.p. MPO Videotronics, Inc., NYC, 1954-72; free-lance dir. and cameraman, cinematographer NYC and Hollywood, Calif., 1972—. Cinema instr. Am. Film Inst., L.A., 1980, Tahoe Film and Video Workshop, Lake Tahoe, Nev., 1984, Washington Film and Video Assn., 1987; staff mem. Internat. Film and Video Workshops, Rockport, Maine, 1996-99, cinema instr. So. Oreg. U., 1998—. Cinematographer for films including: Young Frankenstein, My Favorite Year, Diary of a Mad Housewife, The Neon Empire (ACE award nomination 1990); author: Image Control, 1992 (Kraszna-Krausz Internat. Book award 1994). With Signal Corps, U.S. Army, 1941-45. Recipient Billy Bitzer award Internat. Photographers of the Motion Picture Industry, 1994, Lifetime Achievement award Ashland Ind. Film Festival, 2004. Mem. Internat. Photographer's Union, IATSE, Am. Soc. Cinematographers, Acad. Motion Picture Arts and Scis. Avocations: woodworking, miniaturist. Home: 826 Pavilion Pl Ashland OR 97520-9130 Fax: 541-488-8742. E-mail: gjhfilms@mind.net.

HIRSCHMAN, CHARLES, JR., sociologist, educator; b. Atlanta, Nov. 29, 1943; s. Charles Sr. and Mary Gertrude (Mullee) H.; m. Josephine Knight, Jan. 29, 1968; children: Andrew Charles, Sarah Lynn. BA, Miami U., Oxford, Ohio, 1965; MS, U. Wis., 1969, PhD, 1972. Vol. Peace Corps, Malaysia, 1965-67; prof. Duke U., Durham, NC, 1972-81, Cornell U., Ithaca, NY, 1981-87, U. Wash., Seattle, 1987—, chair dept. sociology, 1995-98, Boeing internat. prof., 1999—. Cons. Ford Found., Malaysia, 1974-75; chair social scis. and population study sect. NIH, Washington, 1987-91; vis. scholar Russell Sage Found., 1998-99. Author: Ethnic and Social Stratification in Peninsula Malaysia, 1975; editor: The Handbook of International Migration: The American Experience, 1999; contbr. articles to profl. jours. Fellow Ctr. Advanced Study in the Bahavioral Scis., Stanford, Calif., 1993-94. Fellow AAAS (chair sect. K on social, econs. and polit. scis. 2004-), Am. Acad. Arts and Scis.; mem. Assn. for Asian Studies (bd. dirs. 1987-90), Population Assn Am. (bd. dirs. 1992-94, v.p. 1997, pres. 2005). Office: U Wash Dept Sociology PO Box 353340 Seattle WA 98195-3340 Home Phone: 206-525-5324; Office Phone: 206-543-5035. Business E-Mail: charles@u.washington.edu.

HIRSCHMANN, JAMES WILLIAM, III, diversified financial services company executive; b. Phila., Oct. 10, 1960; s. James William Jr. and Elizabeth Jane (Murray) H.; m. Laura Anne Gumina, May 16, 1986; children: James William IV, Samantha Anne. BSBA, Widener U., Chester, Pa., 1982. Internal auditor Western Savs. Bank, Phila., 1981-82; cost analyst Berkey Film Processing (name now Qualex), Bensalem, Pa., 1982-83; account mgr. U.S. Lines, Cranford, N.J., 1983-84, dist. sales mgr., 1984-85, regional sales mgr., 1985-86; v.p. Atalanta/Sosnoff Capital, NYC, 1986-88; v.p., dir. mktg. Fin. Trust Co., Denver, 1988-89; with Western Asset Mgmt. Co., Pasadena, Calif., 1989—, pres., CEO, 1999—; pres., COO Legg Mason, Inc., Balt., 2006—07. Patentee recycling trash receptacle. Trustee Widener U. Mem. Assn. Investment Mgmt. Sales Execs., Investment Mgmt. Inst., Fellowship Christian Athletes, Manhattan Country Club. Republican. Roman Catholic. Avocations: basketball, running, tennis, travel, collectables. Office: Western Asset Mgmt Co 385 E Colorado Blvd Pasadena CA 91101

HIRSCHMANN, PETER, video game company executive; b. Aug. 24, 1971; married. With Amblin Entertainment; prodr. LucasArts, San Francisco, 2002—04, v.p. product devel., 2004—. Prodr.: (video games) The Lost World: Jurassic Park, 1997, Medal of Honor, 1999, Medal of Honor: Underground, 2000, Medal of Honor: Frontline, 2002, Medal of Honor: Allied Assault, 2002, Star Wars: Galaxies - An Empire Divided, 2003, Secret Weapons Over Normandy, 2003, Star Wars: Knights of the Old Republic II - The Sith Lords, 2004, Star Wars: Galaxies - Jump to Light Speed, 2004, Star Wars: Battlefront, 2004, Star Wars: Republic Commando, 2005, Star Wars: Galaxies - The Total Experience, 2005, Star Wars: Episode III - Revenge of the Sith, 2005, Star Wars: Battlefront II, 2005, LEGO Star Wars: The Video Game, 2005, Star Wars: Empire at War - Forces of Corruption, 2006, Star Wars: Empire at War, 2006, LEGO Star Wars II: The Original Trilogy, 2006; exec. prodr.: (video games) Mercenaries: Playground of Destruction, 2005. Office: LucasArts PO Box 29908 San Francisco CA 94129-0908

HIRSCHORN, MICHAEL W., television producer, entertainment company executive; b. Feb. 20, 1964; BA, Harvard U., 1986; MA in Comparative Lit., Columbia U. Features editor, columnist Esquire mag., 1990—94; exec. editor NY Mag., 1994—97; editor-in-chief Spin mag., 1997—99; co-chmn., co-founder Powerful Media; editor-in-chief Inside.com; sr. v.p. news and production VH1, 2001—06, exec. v.p. original programming and prodn., 2006—08; co-founder Ish Entertainment, 2008—. Contbr. Wall St. Jour., NY Times, New Republic, Slate; contbg. editor The Atlantic Monthly. Exec. prodr.: (documentaries) Freestyle: The Art of Rhyme, 2000, Inside Out: Trey and Dave Go to Africa, 2004, Ego Trip's Race-O-Rama, 2005, DMC: My Adoption Journey, 2006 (Emmy Award for Outstanding Arts & Culture Programming, 2007), The U.S. vs. John Lennon, 2006, The Last Days of Left Eye, 2007; (TV series) The Fabulous Life of, 2003, Being, 2003, Web Junk 20, 2006, World Series of Pop Culture, 2006, Shoot to Kill, 2008, Bridging the Gap, 2008, Celebracadabra, 2008, Celebrity Rehab with Dr. Drew, 2008. Office: c/o VH1 1515 Broadway New York NY 10036

HIRSHBERG, ERIC, advertising executive; BA, UCLA Coll. Fine Arts. Sr. v.p., creative dir. Fattal & Collins; mng. partner, exec. creative dir. Deutsch Inc., LA, 1997—2005, pres., chief creative officer, 2005—. Named Creative Leader of the Year, WSAAA, 2002; named a Leader of the Year, thinkLA, 2006; named to Advt. Hall of Achievement, Am. Advt. Fedn., 2007. Achievements include work for Coors Light named one of top five campaigns of the year by the Wall Street Journal. Office: Deutsch Inc 5454 Beethoven St Los Angeles CA 90066

HIRSHON, ROBERT EDWARD, lawyer; b. Portland, Maine, Apr. 2, 1948; s. Selvin and Gladys (Wein) H.; m. Roberta Lynn Miller, Aug. 16, 1969; children: Todd, Sara, Jason, Miriam. BA, U. Mich., 1970, JD, 1973. Bar: Maine 1973, U.S. Dist. Ct. Maine 1973, U.S. Ct. Appeals (1st cir.) 1977, U.S. Supreme Ct. 2000. Shareholder Drummond, Woodsum & MacMahon P.A., Portland, Maine, 1973—2003; CEO Tonkon Torp LLP, Portland, 2003—. Adj. prof. law U. Maine Law Sch. Contbr. articles to profl. jours. Chairperson Breakwater Sch Bd., Portland, 1978-85; mem. Zoning Bd. Appeals, Cape Elizabeth, Maine, 1983-90. Mem. ABA (mem. Ho. of Dels. 1992—, chair standing com. lawyers pub. svc. responsibility 1990-93, chair steering com. pro bono ctr. 1991-96, chair torts and ins. practice sect. 1996-97, chair standing com. on membership 1997-2000, pres. 2001-02), Maine Bar Assn. (pres. 1986, chair continuing legal edn. com. 1975-83), Cumberland County Bar Assn., Maine Bar Found. (pres. 1990), Multromah Bar Assn. Avocations: reading, tennis, skiing. Office: Tonkon Torp LLP 1600 Pioneer Tower 888 SW Fifth Ave Portland OR 97204 also: 2160 SW Main St Portland OR 97205-1122 Business E-Mail: bobh@tonkon.com.

HIRT, CYRIL WILLIAM, physicist; b. Flushing, NY, Dec. 20, 1936; s. Cyril W. and Margret E. (Plumb) H.; m. Virginia L. Warren, June 22, 1968; children: Heather, Amber. BS, U. Mich., 1958, MS, 1959, PhD, 1963. Staff scientist Los Alamos (N.Mex.) Nat. lab., 1963-72, group leader, 1973-80; chief scientist Sci. Applications Inc., La Jolla, Calif., 1972-73; founder, pres., chief scientist Flow Sci. Inc., Los Alamos, 1980—. Contbr. numerous articles to profl. jours. Avocations: cooking, reading, hiking, skiing. Office: Ste A 683 Harkle Rd Santa Fe NM 87505-4750

HISAKA, ERIC TORU, plastic surgeon; b. Stockton, Calif., 1951; MD, U. Calif., Davis, 1977. Plastic surgoen Valley Care Hosp., Pleasanton, Calif.; also with Tri Valley Surgical Ctr., Pleasanton, Calif. Office: 5720 Stoneridge Mall Rd Ste 130 Pleasanton CA 94588-2829 Fax: 925-463-0748.

HISCOX, FRANK S., lawyer; b. 1952; BA in English with honors, U. Calif., Santa Barbara, 1974; MA in English with honors, U. Calif., 1977; student, U. Tex., Austin; JD with honors, U. San Francisco, 1982. Bar: Calif. 1982. Ptnr., intellectual property and trademark, copyright, and brand mgmt. practice groups Dorsey & Whitney LLP, Palo Alto, Calif. Named one of Best Lawyers in Silicon Valley, 2000—02. Mem.: Santa Clara County Bar Assn., Silicon Valley Intellectual Property Assn., Internat. Trademark Assn. Office: Dorsey & Whitney LLP Ste 200 850 Hansen Way Palo Alto CA 94304-1017 Office Phone: 650-494-8700. Office Fax: 650-494-8771. Business E-Mail: hiscox.frank@dorsey.com.

HISERT, GEORGE ARTHUR, lawyer; b. Schenectady, NY, Sept. 18, 1944; BS summa cum laude, Brown U., 1966, MS, 1966; JD cum laude, U. Chgo., 1970. Bar: Calif. 1971. Law clk. to Hon. Sterry R. Waterman U.S. Ct. Appeals (2d cir.), 1970—71; ptnr. McCutchen, Doyle, Brown & Enersen, San Francisco, 1977—93, Brobeck, Phleger & Harrison, San Francisco, 1993—2003, Bingham McCutchen LLP, 2003—. Mem. editl. bd. Chgo. Law Rev., 1969-70. Mem. ABA (subcom. letter of credit, vice chair 2003-06, chair 2006—, subcom. secured trans. of uniform comml. code com. bus. law sect., subcom. on syndications and loan participations of comml fin. svc. com., liaison bus. law sect. to uniform comml. code permanent editl. bd. 1993-05), Internat. Bar Assn. (banking law com., bus. law sect.), State Bar Calif. (uniform comml. code com. bus. law sect., vice-chair 1992-93, chair 1993-94), Am. Coll. Comml. Fin. Lawyers, Order of Coif, Sigma Xi. Office: Bingham McCutchen LLP Three Embarcadero Ctr San Francisco CA 94111 Office Phone: 415-393-2577. Business E-Mail: george.hisert@bingham.com.

HISKEY, J. BRENT, metallurgical engineer, educator; b. Salina, Utah, Aug. 18, 1944; m. 1967; 2 children. BS, U. Utah, 1967, MS, 1971, PhD in Metallurgy, 1973. Rschr. Alcoa Labs, 1973-74; asst. prof. N. Mex. Inst. Mining & Tech., 1974-77; rsch. scientist US Steel Rsch. Labs, 1977-80; mgr. metallurgy rsch. Kennecott Copper Corp., 1980-84; dir. Ariz. Mining & Mineral Resources Rsch. Inst., 1985-96; prof. U. Ariz., 1984—, assoc. dean Coll. Engring. and Mines, 1999—; dir. Copper Rsch. Ctr., 1989-97. Lectr. Carnegie Mellon U., 1977-79; cons. E.I. du Pont de Nemours & Co., Inc., 1984—, Phelps Dodge, 1985—, Newcrest Gold Co., 1985-95, Kennecott Corp., 1985-96; chmn. Nat. Assn. Mineral Inst. Dirs., 1990-91, Cyrus AMAX Metals Corp., 1994—; bd. dirs. Am. Chemet Corp., 1993—. Recipient James Douglas Gold medal Am. Inst. Mech. Engrs., 1993. Mem. Nat. Acad. Engrs., Soc. Metallurgy Engrs. (Taggart award 1974), Soc. Mining Metallurgy & Exploration Inc. (chmn. mineral & metallurgy processing div. 1991-92, Milton E. Wadsworth award 2002), Sigma Xi. Home: 5540 E Silver Dust Pl Tucson AZ 85750-1083 Office: U Ariz Coll Engring Mines Dept Math Sci & Engring Tucson AZ 85721-0001 Fax: 520-621-8159. E-mail: jbh@engr.arizona.edu.

HITCHCOCK, FREDERICK E., JR., (FRITZ), automotive company executive; CEO, owner Hitchcock Automotive Resources, City of Industry, Calif., 1980—. Recipient All Star Dealer Award, Sports Illus., 1988, 1995, Quality Dealer Award, Time Mag., 1993. Mem.: State of Calif. New Motor Vechicle Bd. (pres.), NADFC (ambassador), NADA (chmn. Gov. Rel. Com.).

HITLIN, DAVID GEORGE, physicist, researcher; b. Bklyn., Apr. 15, 1942; s. Maxwell and Martha (Lipetz) H.; m. Joan R. Abramowitz, 1966 (div. 1981); m. Abigail R. Gumbiner, 1982 (div. 1998); m. Martha Mann Slagerman, 2000. BA, Columbia U., 1963, MA, 1965, PhD, 1968. Instr. Columbia U., NYC, 1967-69; rsch. assoc. Stanford (Calif.) Linear Accelerator Ctr., 1969-72, asst. prof., 1975-79, mem. program com., 1980-82; asst. prof. Stanford U., 1972-75; assoc. prof. physics Calif. Inst. Tech., Pasadena, 1979-85, prof., 1985—. Mem. adv. panel U.S. Dept. Energy Univ. Programs, 1983; mem. program com. Fermi Nat. Accelerator Lab., Batavia, Ill., 1983—87, Newman Lab., Cornell U., Ithaca, NY, 1986—88; mem. rev. com. U. Chgo., Argonne Nat. Lab., 1985—87; chmn. Stanford Linear Accelerator Ctr. Users Orgn., 1990—93; mem. program com. Brookhaven Nat. Lab., Upton, NY, 1992—95; spokesman BABAR Collaboration, 1994—2000; mem. high energy physics adv. panel DOE/NSF, 2001—04; mem. Univs. Rsch. Assn. Fermilab Bd. Overseers, 2003—06; mem. bd. Fermi Rsch. Alliance. Contbr. numerous articles to profl. jours. Fellow Am. Phys. Soc. Achievements include research in elementary particle physics. Office: Calif Inst Tech Dept Physics 356-48 Lauritsen Pasadena CA 91125-0001 Home Phone: 310-472-0700; Office Phone: 626-395-6694. Business E-Mail: hitlin@hep.caltech.edu.

HIXSON, HARRY F., JR., health products executive; BSChemE, Purdue U.; MBA, U. Chgo.; PhD in Phys. Biochemistry, Purdue U. Pres., COO Amgen, Inc., 1985—91; pres., CEO GeneSys Therapeutics, Inc., 1991—92; CEO, chmn. bd., pres. Elitra Pharms., Inc., San Diego, 1998—. Dir. Signal Pharms., Inc.

HLATKY, MARK ANDREW, cardiologist, researcher; b. Windber, Pa., June 4, 1950; s. George Andrew and Rose Annette (Gonnella) H.; m. Donna Marie Alvarado, May 12, 1984; 1 child, Nicholas Michael. BS in Physics, MIT, 1972; MD, U. Pa. Sch. Medicine, 1976. Diplomate Am. Bd. Internal Medicine, Am. Bd. Cardiovasc. Disease; lic. physician, Calif. Intern, resident internal medicine U. Ariz., Tucson, 1976-79; Robert Wood Johnson clin. scholar U. Calif., San Francisco, 1979-81; fellow in cardiology Duke U. Med. Ctr., Durham, NC, 1981-83, assoc. medicine, cardiovascular divsn., 1983—86, asst. prof. medicine, cardiovascular divsn., 1986—89; assoc. prof. health rsch. and policy and of medicine (cardiovascular medicine) Stanford U. Sch. Medicine, Calif., 1989-96, prof. health rsch. and policy and of medicine (cardiovascular medicine) Calif., 1996—, chair, dept. health rsch. and policy Calif., 1996—2003. Assoc. dir., Duke Databank for Cardiovascular Disease, Duke U. Med. Ctr., 1983-89, attending heart station, 1985-89, attending cardiac care unit 1986-89; attending approach to cardiology, Duke U. Preventative, 1983-85, attending cardiology consult svc., 1983-89, attending gen. med. svc., 1983-89; chief, divsn. health services rsch., Stanford U. Sch. Medicine, 1989-2001, dir., Health Services Rsch. Masters Degree Program 1989-; attending cardiovascular medicine svc., Stanford U. Med. Ctr., 1989-; co-dir., U. Calif. San Francisco-Stanford Evidence-based Practice Ctr., 1997-2002; co-dir., Donald W. Reynolds Cardiovascular Clin. Rsch. Ctr., 2000-01, dir., 2002-; dir., Stanford-Kaiser Cardiovascular Outcomes Rsch. Ctr., 2008-. Contbr. articles to profl. jours.; ad hoc reviewer Agy. for Health Care Policy and Rsch., AHA, NSF, Robert Wood Johnson Found., Doris Duke Found., mem. editl. bds. Jour. Am. Coll. Cardiology, 1995—97, 2002—, Am. Heart Jour., 1996—, Cardiac Electrophysiology Review, 1996—, Am. Jour. Medicine, 1997—, Jour. Invasive Cardiology, 1997—. Sloan Scholar. Fellow Am. Coll. Cardiology; mem. AAAS, Am Fedn. for Clin. Rsch.Am. Heart Assn. (fellow coun. on clin. cardiology), Internat. Soc. for Technology Assessment in Health Care, Assn. for Health Services Rsch., Soc. for Med. Decision-Making, Phi Beta Kappa. Achievements include research in outcomes after coronary surgery, coronary angioplasty, acute myocardial infarction, and cardiac arrhythmias. Home: 168 Rinconada Ave Palo Alto CA 94301-3725 Office: Stanford U Sch Medicine HRP Redwood Bldg Rm 150 Stanford CA 94305 Office Phone: 650-723-6426. E-mail: hlatky@stanford.edu.*

HLOBIK, LAWRENCE S., agricultural products executive; With fertilizer, chem., and agribus. industries, 27 yrs.; CEO Terra Nitrogen, Tulsa; sr. v.p. Terra Industries, Tulsa; pres. AgriBusiness Group J.R. Simplot Co., Boise, 1998—2002, CEO, dir. bd., 2002—. Vice-chmn. Fertilizer Inst., 2002—04, bd. chmn., 2004—; bd. dir. Phosphate and Potash Inst. Office: JR Simplot Co PO Box 27 Boise ID 83707 also: JR Simplot Co 999 Main St Ste 1300 Boise ID 83702 Office Phone: 208-336-2110. Office Fax: 208-389-7515.

HO, CHIH-MING, physicist, researcher; b. Chung King, China, Aug. 16, 1945; arrived in U.S., 1968; s. Shao-Nan and I-Chu Ho; m. Shirley T.S. Ho, Mar. 4, 1972; 1 child, Dean. BSME, Nat. Taiwan U., 1967; PhD, Johns Hopkins U., 1974. Assoc. rsch. scientist Johns Hopkins U., Balt., 1974-75; asst. prof. U. So. Calif., LA, 1976-81, assoc. prof., 1981-85, prof., 1985-91; assoc. vice-chancellor for rsch. UCLA, 2001—05, prof., 1991—, Ben Rich-Lockheed Martin prof., 1996—, dir. Ctr. for Cell Control, 2006—. Dir. Ctr. for Micro Sys., 1993—2000; cons. Flow Industries, Kent, 1982, Dynamics Tech., Torrance, Calif., 1977—87, Rockwell Internat., Canoga Park, Calif., 1980—83; dir. Inst. for Cell Mimetic Space Exploration, 2002—, Ctr. for Cell Control, 2006—; sci. advisor LNM, Inst. Mechanics, China; K.T. Lee hon. chair prof. Nat. Cheng Jung U.; Kuo-Nien hon. chair prof. Nat. Tsinghua U.; hon. prof. Inst. Mechanics, Chin. Acad. Scies., Nanjing U. Aeronautics and Astronautics, China. Contbr. articles to profl. jours.; patentee in field. Fellow AIAA, Am. Phys. Soc.; mem. Nat. Acad. Engring., Academia Sinica, Phi Beta Kappa, Tau Beta Pi, Sigma Xi, Phi Tau Phi. Achievements include research in micro-electro-mechanical systems, biomedical engineering, turbulence, aerodynamics, noise. Business E-Mail: chihming@ucla.edu.

HO, RALPH TINGHAN, radiologist; BS in Biochemistry, Cornell U., 1991; MD, Northwestern U. Intern, OB/GYN then resident, diagnostic radiology Wayne State U., 1995—2000; trauma radiology fellow U. Wash., 2000—01; asst. prof. trauma and body imaging U. Tenn., vascular and interventional radiology fellow, 2002—03; interventional radiologist Mid-South Imaging and Therapeutics, Memphis, 2003—. Mem. Asian Young Professionals Group. Mem.: AMA, Am. Coll. of Radiology, Soc. of Interventional Radiology, Am. Soc. of Emergency Radiology, Am. Roentgen Ray Soc.

HO, REGINALD CHI SHING, medical educator; b. Hong Kong, Mar. 30, 1932; came to U.S., 1940; s. Chow and Elizabeth (Wong) Ho; m. Sharilyn Dang, Nov. 14, 1964; children: Mark, Reginald, Gianna Masca, Timothy. Student, St. Louis U., 1954, MD, 1959. Diplomate Nat. Bd. Med. Examiners, Am. Bd. Internal Medicine. Rotating intern U. Cin. Hosps., 1959-60, resident in internal medicine, 1960-62; fellow in hematology and oncology Barnes Hosp./Washington U., St. Louis, 1962-63; assoc. clin. prof. medicine JAB Sch. Medicine U. Hawaii, Honolulu, 1972-77, clin. prof. medicine, 1977—; attending physician dept. hematology and oncology Straub Clinic and Hosp., Honolulu, 1973—. Prin. investigator Hawaii Cmty. Clin. Oncology Program, Honolulu, 1983-86; adj. prof. clin. sci. Cancer Rsch. Ctr. Hawaii, 1989—, mem. various coms. Contbr. articles to med. jours. Bd. dirs. Cath. Svcs. for Families, 1987-91. Mem. AMA, ACP, Am. Cancer Soc. (divsn. del. 1982-93, del. dir. 1983-92, exec. com. 1989-94, chair med. and sci. exec. com. 1991-92, v.p. 1991-92, pres. 1992-93, immediate past pres. 1993-94, bd. dirs. Hawaii divsn. 1968—, pres. 1976-77, chmn. bd. dirs. 1977-78, hon. life mem. 1989—, bd. dirs.), Hawaii Med. Assn. (Hawaii cancer commn. 1980-85, chair cancer com. 1981-90), Honolulu County Med. Assn. (del. to Hawaii Med. Assn. 1969-72), Exptl. Med. Care Rev. Orgn. (exec. com., chair ambulatory care edn. audit com. 1972), Alpha Omega Alpha. Roman Catholic. Avocation: tennis. Office: Straub Clinic Hosp 888 S King St Honolulu HI 96813-3083 Home Phone: 808-247-0638; Office Phone: 808-522-4000.

HO, ROZ, computer software company executive; B in Computer Sci., U. Calif., Berkeley. Software engr. Bank of America, 1984—86, Hewlett-Packard, 1986—91; product planning & program mgmt. positions Microsoft Corp., Redmond, Wash., 1991—2003, gen. mgr. Macintosh bus. unit, 2003—07, gen. mgr. entertainment & devices div. labs, 2007—08, corp. v.p. premium mobile experiences, 2008—. Office: Microsoft Corp 1 Microsoft Way Redmond WA 98052-6399

HOAG, JOHN ARTHUR, retired bank executive; b. Freeport, NY, Sept. 29, 1932; s. John Hoag and Viola (Babcock) Hobson; m. Jeanette Makaio, Dec. 5, 1959; children: Steve, Vanessa, Kanani. BS, U. Mo., 1955; grad., Pacific Coast Banking Sch., Wash., 1970; MBA, U. Hawaii, 1977. Account exec. Walston & Co., NYC, 1960; mgmt. trainee 1st Hawaiian Bank, Honolulu, 1960, br. mgr., Hilo, 1968, Island v.p., 1970-76, sr. v.p., mgr., 1976, exec. v.p. loan group, 1979, pres., 1989-94, also bd. dirs.; vice chmn. bd. dirs., 1994; retired 1st Hawaiian Bank, 1995; pres. 1st Hawaiian Inc., Honolulu, 1991-95, also bd. dirs.; vice chm. 1st Interstate Bank Hawaii, Honolulu, 1991—; vice chmn. of bd., 1994—; ret., 1995. Chmn. bd. Hawaii Reserves, Inc.; vice chmn. Pioneer Fed. Savs. Bank; bd. dirs. Castle Med. Ctr., BancWest Corp. Bd. regents Tokai Internat. Coll., 1992-95, U. Hawaii, 1995—; bd. dirs. Hawaii Med. Svc. Assn., 1981-93, Honolulu Polynesian Cultural Ctr, 1990-93, Kapiolani Med. Ctr. for Women and Children, Honolulu, 1989-95. Capt. USMC, 1955-60. Mem. Pres.' Club U. Hawaii, C. of C. of Hawaii (chmn. bd. 1992-93). Mem. Lds Ch. Office: PO Box 3200 999 Bishop St Honolulu HI 96847 also: 1st Hawaiian Bank PO Box 3200 Honolulu HI 96847-0001

HOAGLAND, ALBERT SMILEY, electrical engineer, researcher; b. Berkeley, Calif., Sept. 13, 1926; s. Dennis Robert and Jessie Agnes (Smiley) H.; m. Janine Maryse Simart, May 23, 1950; children: Catherine, Nicole, Richard. BS, U. Calif.-Berkeley, 1947, MS, 1948, PhD, 1954. Registered profl. engr., Calif. Asst. prof. elec. engring. U. Calif.-Berkeley, 1954-56; sr. engr. IBM, San Jose, Calif., 1956-59; mgr. engring sci. San Jose Research Lab., 1959-62; sr. tech. cons. IBM World Trade, The Hague, Holland, 1962-64; mgr. engring. sci. IBM Research Ctr., NYC, 1964-68, dir. tech. planning Research Div., 1968-71; corporate program coordinator IBM, Boulder, Colo., 1971-76; mgr. exploratory magnetic rec. San Jose Research Lab., 1976-82; tech. adv. Gen. Products Div., 1982-84; acting dir. Ctr. for Magnetic Recording Research, U. Calif. San Diego, 1983-84; prof. elec. engring., dir. Inst. Info. Storage Tech. Santa Clara U., Calif., 1984—2005; exec. dir. Magnetic Disk Heritage Ctr., 2005—. Lectr. computer design U. Calif. Berkeley, 1948-54, 56-62; adj. prof. U. Calif. San Diego, 1986; cons. State Calif., 1955-56, IBM, 1954-56, also numerous cons. in data storage industry, 1984—; chmn. Nat. Computer Conf. Bd., 1976-78; adj. prof. Harvey Mudd Coll. Author: Digital Magnetic Recording, 1963; co-author 2d edit., 1991, reprinted, 1998; contbr. articles on magnetic rec. and info. storage tech. to profl. publs.; patentee in field Chmn. adv. com. The Magnetic Rec. Conf., 1993—97; trustee Charles Babbage Inst.; regent Inst. Info. Mgmt., 1985—92; exec. dir. Magnetic Disk Heritage Ctr. at Santa Clara U., 2001—05. With USNR, 1943—46. Recipient outstanding paper award IEEE, 1965 Fellow IEEE (dir. 1974-77, Centennial medal 1984, 3d Millenium medal 2000), Am. Fedn. Info. Processing Socs. (dir. 1969-78, pres. 1978-80); mem. IEEE Computer Soc. (pres. 1971-73), Rsch. Soc. Am. (pres. Sequoia chpt. 1962-63), Phi Beta Kappa, Sigma Xi, Eta Kappa Nu, Tau Beta Pi. Clubs: Golden Bear. Home: 13834 Upper Hill Dr Saratoga CA 95070-5334 Office: care Computer History Mus 1401 N Shoreline Blvd Mountain View CA 94043 Personal E-mail: ahoagland@gmail.com. Business E-Mail: ahoagland@magneticdiskheritagecenter.org.

HOAGLAND, DONALD WRIGHT, lawyer; b. NYC, Aug. 16, 1921; s. Webster Comley and Irene (Wright) H.; m. Mary Tiedeman, May 14, 1949; children: Peter M., Mary C., Sara H., Ann W. BA, Yale U., 1942; LLB, Columbia U., 1948. Bar: N.Y. 1948, Colo. 1951. Assoc. firm Winthrop, Stimson, Putnam & Roberts, NYC, 1948-51; ptnr. Davis, Graham & Stubbs, Denver, 1951-63, 66-87, of counsel, 1987—; with AID, 1964-66, asst. adminstr. devel. finance and pvt. enterprise, 1965-66, cons. Indonesia, 1967-75. Lectr. U. Denver Sch. Law, 1971-75; chmn. bd. Bi-Nat. Devel. Corp., 1968-70; dir. Centennial Fund, Inc., 2d Centennial Fund, Inc., Gryphon Fund, Inc., 1959-63; mem. Colo. Supreme Ct. Grievance Com., 1992-98. Mem. Denver Planning Bd., 1955-61, 67-70, chmn., 1959-61; bd. dirs., v.p. Denver Art Mus., 1959-63, 72-76, 79-82; bd. dirs. Colo. Urban League, 1960-63, 66-72, chmn. bd., 1968-72; adv. bd. Vols. Tech. Assistance vice-chmn. bd. Denver chpt. ARC, 1959-61; bd. dirs. Legal Aid Soc. Colo., 1972-84, pres., 1975-79; trustee Phillips Exeter Acad., 1960-67, Colo. Rocky Mountain Sch., 1981-84, Am. U., Washington, 1982-85; chmn. bd. dirs. Legal Aid Found., Colo., 1983-87; bd. dirs. Colo. Bus. Coalition for Health, 1988-89, Colo. Found. for Ednl. Excellence, 1998-2004; exec. dir. Ctr. for Health Ethics and Policy U. Colo., Denver, 1987-91; chmn. Colo. Health Data Commn., 1986-88, Gov. Romer's panel health advisors, 1992-94, Social Sci. Found. Denver U., 1975-2007; active Caring for Colo. Found., 1999-2002, chmn., program com., 2003—; chmn. Colo. Pub. Health Edn. and Rsch. Adv. Com., 2002—; pres. Colo. Found. Pub. Health and Environment, 1995-98, bd. dirs., 1995-2005; ethics com. Nat. Jewish Med. and Rsch. Ctr., 1993-2005. With USNR, 1943-45. Decorated Air medal with oak leaf cluster. Mem. ABA, Colo. Bar Assn., Denver Bar Assn. Home: 355 Garfield St Denver CO 80206-4509 Office: Davis Graham & Stubbs 1550 17th St Ste 500 Denver CO 80202

HOAK, JONATHAN S., SR., lawyer; b. Eugene, Oreg., July 1949; BA, U. Colo., 1971; postgrad., Exeter U., Eng.; JD, Drake U., 1977. With Heritage Comms., Des Moines, 1971-74; assoc. Sidley & Austin, 1979-85, ptnr., 1985-90; gen. atty. fed. sys. divsn. AT&T, 1990-93; sr. v.p., gen. counsel NCR Corp., Dayton, Ohio, 1993—2006; v.p., chief ethics and compliance officer Hewlett-Packard Co., Palo Alto, Calif., 2006—. Bd. counselors Drake U. Law Sch., U. Dayton Sch. Law Adv. Coun. Mem. ABA, Fed. Cir. Bar Assn., Ohio Bar Assn. Office: HP 3000 Hanover St Palo Alto CA 94304-1185

HOBBS, GREGORY JAMES, JR., state supreme court justice; b. Gainesville, Fla., Dec. 15, 1944; s. Gregory J. Hobbs and Mary Ann (Rhodes) Frakes; m. Barbara Louise Hay, June 17, 1967; children: Daniel Gregory, Emily Mary Hobbs Wright. BA, U. Notre Dame, 1966; JD, U. Calif., Berkeley, 1971. Bar: Colo. 1971, Calif. 1972. Law clk. to Judge William E. Doyle 10th U.S. Cir. Ct. Appeals, Denver, 1971-72; assoc. Cooper, White & Cooper, San Francisco, 1972-73; enforcement atty. U.S. EPA, Denver, 1973-75; asst. atty. gen. State of Colo. Atty. Gen.'s Office, Denver, 1975-79; ptnr. Davis, Graham & Stubbs, Denver, 1979-92; shareholder Hobbs, Trout & Raley, P.C., Denver, 1992-96; justice Colo. Supreme Ct., Denver, 1996—. Counsel No. Colo. Water Conservancy, Loveland, Colo., 1979-96. Contbr. articles to profl. jours. Vol. Peace Corps-S.Am., Colombia, 1967-68; vice chair Colo. Air Quality Control Com., Denver, 1982-87; mem. ranch com. Philmont Scout Ranch, Boy Scouts Am., Cimarron, N.Mex., 1988-98; co-chair Eating Disorder Family Support Group, Denver, 1992—. Recipient award of merit Denver Area Coun. Boy Scouts, 1993, Pres. award Nat. Water Resources Assn., Washington, 1995. Fellow Am. Bar Found.; mem. ABA, Colo. Bar Assn., Denver Bar Assn. Avocations: backpacking, fishing, poetry. Office: Colo Supreme Ct 2 E 14th Ave Denver CO 80203-2115

HOBBS, JOHN NEIL, communications executive; Gen. mgr. corp. clients British Telecom, 1994—97, gen. mgr. global sales & svc., 1997—98; dir. transition and implementation Concert, 1998—99, pres. global accounts, 1999—2000; group v.p. global sales Level 3 Comm., Inc., 2000—06, pres. global network svcs., 2006—08, exec. v.p. sales and ops., 2008, exec. v.p. ops., 2008—. Office: Level 3 Comm, Inc 1025 Eldorado Blvd Broomfield CO 80021

HOCHSTETTLER, THOMAS JOHN, academic administrator, historian; b. Bryan, Ohio, July 23, 1947; s. Hugh Donavon and Martha Lucille Taylor Hochstettler; m. Marcia Della Glas, Jan. 4, 1975; children: William Cameron Glas-Hochstetler, Taylor David Glas-Hochstettler, Benjamin Joseph Glas-Hochstettler. BA, Earlham Coll., 1969; MA, U. Mich., 1970, PhD, 1978. From lectr. history to sr. planning assoc. Stanford (Calif.) U., 1978—86, sr. planning assoc. and staff economist, 1986—87; lectr. history Bowdoin Coll., Brunswick, Maine, 1987—92, dean planning and gen. adminstrn., 1987—92, acting treas., 1990—92; dir. planning U. Houston Sys., 1992—96; assoc. provost Rice U., Houston, 1996—2002, adj. asst. prof. history, 1998—2000; vis. prof. history Internat. U. Bremen, Freie Hansestadt Bremen, Germany, 1999—2002, v.p. academic affairs, 1999—2004; pres. Lewis & Clark Coll., Portland, Oreg., 2004—. Mem. bd. trustees New Eng. Regional Computing Consortium, 1987—92; mem. bd. dir. Oregon Independent Coll. Edn., 2004—, Oregon World Affairs Comm., 2006—, chair, 2008—. Moderator First Congl. Ch., Houston, 1992—94; bd. dirs. Midcoast Maine Red Cross, Brunswick, Maine, 1987—91, United Way of Midcoast Maine, Brunswick, 1987—92. Grantee, Deutsche Akademische Austauschdienst, 1975—76; fellow, Woodrow Wilson Found., 1969—70, Horace H. Rackham Doctoral fellowship, U. Mich., 1973—74, Stanford U. Dept. of History, 1978—80. Mem.: Rotary Club of Bremen Germany (youth svc. officer. mem., exec. com. 2000—04), Rotary Club Houston. Achievements include founding of International University Bremen, the first comprehensive private research university to be established on the European Continent following World War II. Office: Lewis & Clark College 0615 SW Palatine Hill Road Portland OR 97219-7899 Business E-Mail: pres@lclark.edu.

HOCHULI, EDWARD G., lawyer; b. Milw., Dec. 25, 1950; BA with honors, U. Tex., El Paso, 1972; JD with distinction, U. Ariz., 1976. Bar: Ariz. 1976, U.S. Dist. Ct. Ariz. 1977, U.S. Ct. Appeals (9th cir.) 1981. Law clerk to Hon. C.A. Muecke U.S. Dist. Ct. Ariz., Phoenix, 1976-78; mem. Jones, Teilborg, Sanders, Haga & Parks P.C., 1978-83; spl. asst. atty. gen. State of Ariz., 1979; ptnr. Jones, Skelton & Hochuli, Phoenix, 1983—; referee NFL, 1990—92, head referee, 1992—. Mem. ABA, Assn. Trial Lawyers Am., Ariz. Trial Lawyers Assn., State Bar Ariz., Ariz. Assn. Def. Counsel (bd. dirs. 1982—), Maricopa County Bar Assn., Def. Rsch. and Trial Lawyers Assn., NFL Referee Assn.(bd. dirs., 1995-, pres., 1999-2001) Achievements include referee, Super Bowl XXXII, XXXVIII. Office: Jones Skelton & Hochuli 2901 N Central Ave Ste 800 Phoenix AZ 85012-2798 E-mail: ehochuli@jshfirm.com.

HOCKETT, CHRISTOPHER BURCH, lawyer; b. Hutchinson, Kans., Sept. 6, 1959; s. George Rundell and Shirley Hockett. BA, William & Mary, 1981; JD, U. Va., 1985. Bar: Calif. 1985, US Dist. Ct. (no. dist.) Calif. 1985, US Dist. Ct. (cen. dist.) Calif. 1988, US Dist. Ct. Colo. 1997, US Ct. Appeals (9th Cir.) 1988, U.S. Ct. Appeals (10th Cir.) 1996, US Ct. Appeals (Fed. Cir.) 2000. Assoc. McCutchen, Doyle, Brown, & Enersen, San Francisco, 1985-92, ptnr., 1992—2001, Bingham McCutchen LLP, 2001—08, chmn. litig. practice group; ptnr. Davis Polk & Wardwell LLP, 2008—. Editl. chair The Antitrust Source on-line mag., www.antitrustsource.com. Author: (chpt.) State Antitrust Law Handbook, 1990, 2nd edit., 1999; assoc. editor Antitrust Mag., 1990-91. Bd. dirs. San Francisco Neighborhood Legal Assistance Found., 1992-99, Bay Area Legal Aid, 1999—. Mem. ABA (program officer sect. antitrust law 2007-09, council sect. of antitrust law, 1998-2001, 2004-07, vice chairperson antitrust law civil practice and procedure com. 1991-95, chairperson 1995-98, mem. task force on civil justice reform 1992-93), No. Calif. Assn. Bus. Trial Lawyers, Calif. Bar Assn. Bar Assn. San Francisco, Wildlife Conservation Soc. (bd. advisors), Barristers Club, Assn. Bus.

Trial Lawyers, WCS Global Conservation Coun., 2007- Avocations: running, golf. Office: Davis Polk & Wardwell LLP 1600 El Camino Real Menlo Park CA 94025 Office Phone: 650-758-2200. Business E-Mail: chris.hockett@dpw.com.

HOCKNEY, DAVID, artist; b. Bradford, Yorkshire, Eng., July 9, 1937; s. Kenneth and Laura Hockney. Attended, Bradford Coll. Art, 1953—57, Royal Coll. Art, London, 1959—62, degree (hon.), 1992, U. Aberdeen, 1988. Lectr. U. Iowa, 1964, U. Colo., 1965, U. Calif., Berkeley, 1967, UCLA, 1966, hon. chair of drawing, 1980. One-man shows include Kasmin Gallery, 1963-89, Mus. Modern Art, NYC, 1964, 68, Stedelijk Mus., Amsterdam, Netherlands, 1966, Whitechapel Gallery, London, 1970, Andre Emmerich Gallery, NYC, 1972-96, Musee des Arts Decoratifs, Paris, 1974, Museo Tamayo, Mexico City, 1984, LA Louver, Calif., 1986, 89, 95, 98, 05, 07, Nishimura Gallery, Tokyo, 1986, 89, 90, 94, Met. Mus. Art, 1988, L.A. County Mus. Art, 1988, 96, 2006, Tate Gallery, London, 1988, 92, 2007, Royal Acad. Arts, London, 1995, 99, 2002-07, Hamburger Kunsthalle, 1995, Nat. Mus. Am. Art, Washington, 1997, 98, Mus. Ludwig, Cologne, 1997, MFA, Boston, 1998, 2006, Centre Georges Pompidou, Paris, 1999, Musee Picasso, Paris, 1999, Mus. Contemporary Art, L.A., 2001, Kunst-Und Ausstellung Halle, Bonn, 2001, La. Mus Mod. Art, Copenhagen, 2001, Annely Juda Fine Art, London, 1997, 99, 2003, 06, Richard Gray Gallery, NY, 1992, 99, 02, 04, Nat. Portrait Gallery, London, 2003, 06, Whitney Biennial, NY, 2004, others; designer: Rake's Progress, Glyndebourne, Eng., 1975; sets for Magic Flute, Glyndebourne, 1978, Parade Triple Bill, Stravinsky Triple Bill, Met. Opera House, 1980-81, Tristan und Isolde, Los Angeles Music Ctr. Opera, 1987; Turandot, Lyric Opera, Chgo., 1992—, San Francisco Opera, 1993, Die Frau Ohne Schatten, Covent Garden, London, 1992, L.A. Music Ctr.Opera, 1993; author: David Hockney by David Hockney, 1976, David Hockney: Travels with Pen, Pencil and Ink, 1978, Paper Pools, 1980, David Hockney Photographs, 1982, Cameraworks, 1983, David Hockney: A Retrospective, 1988, Hockney Paints the Stage, 1983, That's the Way I See It, 1993, David Hockney's Dog Days, 1998, Hockney on Art, 1999, Secret Knowledge: Rediscovering the Lost Techniques of the Old Masters, 2001, Hockney's Portraits and People, 2003, Hockney's Pictures, 2004, David Hockney: Portraits, 2006; illustrator: Six Fairy Tales of the Brothers Grimm, 1969, The Blue Guitar, 1977, Hockney's Alphabet, 1991. Recipient Guinness award and 1st prize for etching, 1961, Gold medal Royal Coll. Art, 1962, Graphic prize Paris Biennale, 1963, 1st prize 8th Internat. Exhbn. Drawings Lugano, Italy, 1964, 1st prize John Moores Exhbn. Liverpool, Eng., 1967, German award of Excellence 1983, 1st prize Internat. Ctr. of Photography, NY, 1985, Kodak photography book award for Cameraworks, 1984, Praemium Imperiale Japan Art Assn., 1989, 5th Ann. Gov. Calif. Visual Arts award, 1994, Charles Wollaston award Royal Acad. Arts London, 1999; named Companion of Honour, Her Majesty, the Queen of Eng., 1997. Office: 7508 Santa Monica Blvd Los Angeles CA 90046-6407

HODGE, MARY ANN, state legislator; b. St. Francis, Kans., Dec. 17, 1946; d. JW and Albina Clark; m. Richard; children: Andrew, Jeffrey, Michael. B, U. No. Colo., Greeley. Elem. sch. tchr. Weld County Dist. 6, Greeley; tchr. Glenwood Preschool, Colo.; co-owner, mgr. Chieftain Motel, Douglas, Wyo.; office clk. Yellow Freight Systems, Aurora, Colo.; office mgr. Roadway Express, Aurora; corp. sec., treas. Loyd Hodge & Sons, Inc.; mem. Dist. 30 Colo. House of Reps., 2000—09; mem. Dist. 25 Colo. State Senate, Denver, 2009—. Democrat. Office: Colo State Capitol 200 E Colfax Rm 307 Denver CO 80203 Office Phone: 303-866-4855. Business E-Mail: mary.hodge.senate@state.co.us.*

HODGE, PHILIP GIBSON, JR., mechanical and aerospace engineering educator; b. New Haven, Nov. 9, 1920; s. Philip Gibson and Muriel (Miller) Hodge; m. Thea Drell, Jan. 3, 1943; children: Susan E., Philip T., Elizabeth M. AB, Antioch Coll., Yellow Springs, Ohio, 1943; PhD, Brown U., Providence, 1949. Rsch. asst. Brown U., 1947-49, asso., 1949; asst. prof. math. UCLA, 1949-53; assoc. prof. applied mechanics Poly. Inst. Bklyn., 1953-56, prof., 1956-57; prof. mechanics Ill. Inst. Tech., 1957-71, U. Minn., Mpls., 1971-91, prof. emeritus, 1991—. Russell Severance Springer vis. prof. U. Calif., 1976; vis. prof. emeritus Stanford U., 1993—; sec. U.S. nat. com. Theoretical and Applied Mechanics, 1982-2000. Author: 5 books, the most recent being Limit Analysis of Rotationally Symmetric Plates and Shells, 1963, Continuum Mechanics, 1971; also numerous rsch. articles in profl. jour.; tech. editor Jour. Applied Mechanics, 1971-76. Recipient Disting. Service award Am. Acad. Mechanics, 1984; Karman medal ASCE, 1985. NSF sr. postdoctoral fellow, 1963 Mem. NAE, ASME (hon., Worcester Reed Warner medal 1975, ASME medal 1987, Daniel C. Drucker medal 2000), Internat. Union Theoretical and Applied Mechanics (del. 1982-2000, asst. treas. 1984-92, mem. at large 2000-08). Home: 580 Arastradero Rd Apt 701 Palo Alto CA 94306-3948 E-mail: philip@kellys.org.

HODGES, JOSEPH GILLULY, JR., lawyer; b. Denver, Dec. 7, 1942; s. Joseph Gilluly Sr. and Elaine (Chanute) H.; m. Jean Todd Creamer, Aug. 7, 1971; children: Ashley E., Wendy C., Elaine V. BA, Lake Forest Coll., 1965; JD, U. Colo., 1968. Bar: Colo. 1968, U.S. Dist. Ct. Colo. 1969, U.S. Ct. Mil. Appeals 1969. Assoc. Hodges, Kerwin, Otten & Weeks, Denver, 1969-73, Davis, Graham & Stubbs, Denver, 1973-76, ptnr., 1976-86; pvt. practice, Denver, 1986—. Bd. dirs. Arapahoe Colo. Nat. Bank, Littleton, Colo., 1971-90, Cherry Creek Improvement Assn., Denver, 1979-91; bd. trustees Lake Forest (Ill.) Coll., 1977-87; pres. Colo. Arlberg Club, Winter Park, Colo., 1984-85; treas. St. Johns Episcopal Cathedral, Denver, 1981-96; chmn. bd. Spalding Cmty. Found., 1995—. Capt. USAR, 1969-74. Named Best Lawyers in Am., Woodward/White, N.Y.C., 1994-95. Fellow Am. Coll. Trust and Estate Counsel (state chmn. 1991-96); mem. ABA (chmn. probate divsn. G-2 Tech. 1990-95, coun. mem. real property, probate and trust law sect. 1996—), Am. Judicature Soc., Colo. Bar Assn. (chair probate coun. 1981-82), Denver Bar Assn., Denver Estate Planning Coun., Colo. Planned Giving Roundtable (bd. 1991-94), Rotary Club Denver, Kappa Sigma, Phi Alpha Delta. Republican. Avocations: skiing, hiking, fishing, photography, computers. Office: 3300 E 1st Ave Ste 600 Denver CO 80206-5809 Home: 2552 E Alameda Ave Unit 5 Denver CO 80209-3324

HODGKIN, JOHN E., pulmonologist; b. Portland, Oregon, Aug. 22, 1939; s. Williard E. and Dorothy (Rigsby) H.; m. Jeanie (Walker), Sept. 6, 1980; children: Steve, Kathryn, Carolyn, Jonathan, and Jamie. BS, Walla Walla Coll., Wash., 1960; MD, Loma Linda U., Calif., 1964. Fellow pulmonology Mayo Clinic, Rochester, Minn., 1970-72; chief pulmonary sect. Loma Linda U., Calif., 1974-80; clin. prof. medicine U. Calif., Davis, 1983—2006. Med. dir. respiratory care St. Helena Hosp., St. Helena, Calif., 1983-2006, med. dir. pulmonary rehab., 1983-2006, med. dir. ctr. for health promotion, 1983-96, asst. to pres., 1994-2006, med. dir. smoke-free life program, 2003—; med. dir. Adventist Health No. Calif., Roseville, Calif., 1995-98, Calif. Med. Found., 1995-98; med. dir. pulmonary rehab., St. Helena Hosp. Clearlake, Calif., 2003-, med. dir. hospitalist program, 2008-. Editor: Chronic Obstructive Pulmonary Disease: Current Concepts in Diagnosis and Comprehensive Care, 1979, Respiratory Care: A Guide to Clin. Practice, 1977, 4th rev. edit. 1997, Pulmonary Rehabilitation: Guidelines to Success, 1984, 4th rev. edit., 2009, Fundamentals of Lung and Heart Sounds, 1988, 3d rev. edit., 2004. Decorated bronze star U.S. Army, 1968, Outstanding Clinician of Yr., Calif. Thoracic Soc., 2009 Fellow Am. Assn. Cardiovas. and Pulmonary Rehab. (pres. 1995-96), Am. Coll. Chest Physicians, Am. Coll. Physicians, Am. Thoracic Soc., Nat. Assn. Med. Direction of Respiratory Care, Am. Assn. Respiratory Care. Avocations: tennis, softball, skiing. Home: PO Box 147 Lower Lake CA 95457 Personal E-mail: johnhodgkin@gmail.com.

HODGKINS, FRANCIS IRVING (BUTCH HODGKINS), retired county official; BS in Civil Engring. with honors, Calif. State U., Sacramento, 1972. Licensed civil engr. Mem. staff County of Sacramento, Calif., 1965-89, engr. tech. Calif., 1965-68; pvt. prac. Sacramento, 1972-74; chief engr. Sacramento Co. Sanitation Dist., 1974-89; Dep. dir. pub. works Sacramento County (Calif.), 1989-93; exec. dir. Flood Ctrl. Agy. Sacramento Area, 1993—2005, ret., 2005. Mem. Calif. Flood Plain Mgrs. Assn.

HOECKER, THOMAS RALPH, lawyer; b. Chicago Heights, Ill., Dec. 14, 1950; s. William H. and Norma M. (Wynkoop) H.; m. V. Sue Thornton, Aug. 28, 1971; children: Elizabeth T., Ellen T. BS, No. Ill. U., 1972; JD, U. Ill., 1975. Bar: Ill. 1975, Ariz. 1985. Assoc. Davis and Morgan, Peoria, Ill., 1975-80, ptnr., 1980-84; assoc. Snell and Wilmer, Phoenix, 1984-86, ptnr., 1987—. Mem. steering com. Western Pension Conf., Phoenix, 1986-92, pres., 1991-92. Fellow Am. Coll. Employee Benefits Coun. (charter), Ariz. Bar Found.; mem. ABA (chair tax sect. employee benefits com. 2002-03, co-chair legis. and adminstrv. subcom. of labor sect. employee benefits com. 1994-96), Ariz. Bar Assn., Ill. Bar Assn., Marciopa County Bar Assn., (mem. investment com. 1988-94). Avocation: fly fishing. Office: Snell Wilmer 1 Arizona Ctr Phoenix AZ 85004 Office Phone: 602-382-6361. Business E-Mail: thoecker@swlaw.com.

HOEFFLIN, STEVEN M., plastic surgeon; b. Seattle, Feb. 7, 1946; m. Linda Manus (div. 1976); 2 children; m. Pamela Wilson. BA in Biology, Calif. St. U., in Northridge, 1968; MD with honors, UCLA, 1972. Intern UCLA Med. Ctr., 1972—73, resident, 1973—77; asst. clinical prof. Divsn. of Plastic Surgery at UCLA Med. Ctr., 1979—89; chief of plastic surgery Brotman Med. Ctr., 1980—85, UCLA-Santa Monica Hosp. Med. Ctr., 1982—89; plastic surgeon Santa Monica (Calif.) Hosp.; assoc. clin. prof. UCLA; visiting prof. Internat. School of Aesthetic Plastic Surgery. Co-author: Ethnic Rhinoplasty, 1998; author: (Medical, nonfiction) The Beautiful Face: The First Mathematical Definition, Classification, and Creation of True Facial Beauty, 2000. Recipient Joel McCrea Achievement award, Am. Cinema awards, 1994, Golden Star Halo award, So. Calif. Motion Picture Coun. for outstanding achievement as a plastic surgeon and contribution in the entertainment industry, 1994, Michael Bolton Humanitarian award, 1995. Fellow: The Internat. Coll. Surgeons, Am.Coll. Surgeons; mem.: Am. Assn. Hand Surgery, Am. Burn Assn., LA County Med. Assn., Royal Soc. Medicine, Rhinoplasty Soc., Plastic Surgery Edn. Found., Bay Surg. Soc., Lipoplasty Soc., Am. Soc. Aesthetic Plastic Surgery, Am. Soc. Plastic Surgeons, LA Soc. Plastic Surgeons (pres.), Am. Bd. Plastic Surgery (diplomat), Alpha Omega Alpha. Achievements include being Michael Jackson's former plastic surgeon. Office: 1530 Arizona Ave Santa Monica CA 90404-1208

HOEHN, ROBERT J., plastic surgeon, educator; b. East St. Louis, Ill., 1929; children: Robert Anthony Till, Margaret Eve, David Ivan, Daniel Vincent; m. Nancy Ruth Vincent. MD, Washington U., St. Louis, 1956. Diplomate Am. Bd. Plastic Surgery. Intern Vancouver (B.C., Can.) Gen. Hosp., 1956-57; resident in internal medicine, 1957-58; resident McGill U., Montreal, Que., Can., 1960-61; assoc. prof. plastic surgery U. Colo., Denver, 1970—78, Columbia U., NYC, 1965—70; resident in gen. surgery Boston City Hosp., 1961-62; fellow in orthopaedic surgery, 1962; fellow in transplantation immunology Westminster Hosp., London, 1962-63; resident in plastic surgery N.Y. Hosp.-Cornell, 1963-65; clin. prof. plastic surgery U. Colo., 1978—2002; with Aurora Presbyn. Hosp., 1978—2002, Aurora Regional Med. Ctr., 1978—2002, Denver Children's Hosp., 1978—2002, Porter Meml. Hosp., 1978—2002, Swedish Hosp., 1978—2002; pvt. practice; ret., 2002. Fellow ACS; mem. AAPS, Am. Soc. Plastic Surgeons, Plastic Surgery Rsch. Coun. Home: 2601 S Quebec St Villa 3 Denver CO 80231-6039

HOEPPNER, DAVID WILLIAM, mechanical engineering educator; b. Waukesha, Wis., Dec. 17, 1935; s. William Frank and Lillian Hulda (Rosche) H.; m. Sue Ellen McFarlane, June 13, 1959; children: Laura Anne, Lynne Susan, Amy McFarlane. BME, Marquette U., 1958; MS, PhD, U. Wis., 1963. Asst. prof. metall. engring. U. Wis., Madison, 1963-64; rsch. metallurgist Battelle Meml. Inst., Columbus, 1964-69; group leader Lockheed Calif. Co., Burbank, 1969-74; prof. U. Mo., Columbia, 1974-78; Cockburn prof. U. Toronto, Ont., Canada, 1978-85; prof., chmn. dept. mech. engring. U. Utah, Salt Lake City, 1985-92, prof. mech. engring., 1992—. Cons. Rolls Royce, Derby, Eng., 1973-95, Pratt and Whitney of Can., Longueuil, Que., 1978-2003, Lockheed Aircraft (1976, 1985-2003), Boeing, 1992-95; pres. Faside Internat. Inc., Salt Lake City, 1978—. Author: (with Wallace) Case Studies in Aircraft Corrosion, 1986; editor: Effect of Environment and Complex Load History on Fatigue, 1970, Fracture Prevention, 1974, Fatigue of Weldments, 1977; co-editor: Fretting Fatigue, Current Technology and Practice, 2000, Fretting Fatigue, Advances in Basic Understanding and Applications, 2003. Internat. senator Jaycees, Santa Paula, Calif., 1973; mem. city planning commn., Santa Paula, 1972-74. Recipient Outstanding Sci. and Tech. Achievement medal, Gov. Utah, 2005; named to Wall Fame, Waukesha South H.S., 2006. Mem. AIAA, ASME, ASTM (chmn. subcom. 1969-79, co-editor fretting fatigue, 1999, 2003), Am. Soc. Metals, Am. Soc. Engring. Edn., Soc. Automotive Engrs., Sigma Xi. Avocations: gardening, reading, skiing, hiking. Office Phone: 801-581-3851.

HOFACKET, JEAN, library director; MLIS, Emporia State U., Kans. Dir. info. svcs. AIDS Info. Network, Phila.; dir. Found. Ctr., San Francisco; dep. county libr. Alameda County Libr., Fremont, Calif., 2000—05, interim county libr., 2005, county libr., 2005—. Bd. dirs. Alameda County Libr. Found. Contbr. articles to profl. jours. Named an Outstanding Libr. in Support of Lit., Calf. Libr. Assn., 2008. Office: Alameda County Libr 2450 Stevenson Blvd Fremont CA 94538 Office Phone: 510-745-1510. E-mail: jhofacket@aclibrary.org.*

HOFFELT, RICHARD H., lawyer; b. Sacramento, Nov. 17, 1930; m. Elie Hoffelt, 1957; 4 children. BSBA, U. Calif. Berkeley, 1952; JD, U. Calif. Berkeley, Boalt Hall, 1955. Bar: Calif. 1955, U.S. Supreme Ct. 1955, U.S. Ct. Appeals, Ninth Cir. 1955, U.S. Dist. Ct., Ea. Dist. Calif. 1955. With Wilke, Fleury, Hoffelt, Gould & Birney LLP, Sacramento, 1957—, of counsel; judge pro tempore Superior Ct. Sacramento, El Dorado, Solano, Yuba, Amador & Calaveras counties. Recipient Beacon Light Award, Mayor & Coun. City Sacramento. Mem.: Assn. Conflict Resolution, Assn. Attys. -Mediators (mem. & cert. by), Fed. Bar Assn., Am. Arbitration Assn. (panel of arbitrators), Sacramento County Bar Assn.-Health Care Law Sect. (Health Care & Law Award 1990), Calif. Soc. Health Care Attys., Nat. Health Lawyers Assn. (nat. arbitration forum, panel of arbitrators), ABA (Health Law Forum, Construction Law Sect., ho. of dels., ADR Sect.), Calif. Assn. Local Bar Assn. (exec. com.), Barristers Club (founding mem. & early pres.), Sacramento County Bar Assn. (pres. 1990, Lawyer of Yr. 1997), Shriners Hosp. Northern Calif. (chmn. bd. govs.), Phi Delta Phi. Achievements include development of Minority Hiring & Retention Program, while pres. of Sacramento County Bar Assn. Office: Wilke Fleury Hoffelt Gould & Birney LLP 400 Capitol Mall 22nd Floor Sacramento CA 95814 Office Phone: 916-441-2430. Office Fax: 916-442-6664. Business E-Mail: rhoffelt@wilkefleury.com.

HOFFENBERG, MARVIN, retired political science professor; b. Buffalo, July 7, 1914; s. Harry and Jennie Pearl (Weiss) H.; m. Betty Eising Stern, July 20, 1947; children: David A., Peter H. Student, St. Bonaventure Coll., 1934—35; BSc, Ohio State U., 1939, MA, 1940, postgrad., 1941. Asst. chief divsn. interindustry econs. Bur. Labor Statistics, Dept. Labor, 1941-52; cons. U.S. Mut. Security Agy., Europe, 1952, Statistik Sentralbyra, Govt. Norway, Oslo, 1954; economist RAND Corp., 1952—56; dir. rsch., econ. cons. dept. deVegh & Co., 1956—58; staff economist Com. Econ. Devel., 1958-60; project chmn. Rsch. Analysis Corp. (formerly Johns Hopkins U. Ops. Rsch.), 1960-63; dir. cost analysis dept. Aerospace Corp., 1963-65; rsch. economist Inst. Govt. and Pub. Affairs, UCLA, 1965-67, prof.-in-residence polit. sci., 1967-85, prof. emeritus, 1985—; dir. M.P.A. program, co-chmn. Interdepartmental Program in Comprehensive Health Planning UCLA, 1974-76. Author: (with Kenneth J. Arrow) A Time Series Analysis of Inter-Industry Demand, 1959; editor: (with Levine, Hardt and Kaplan) Mathematics and Computers in Soviet Economics, 1967; contbr. articles to profl. jours., chpts. to books. Mem. bd. advisers Sidney Stern Meml. Trust; foreman L.A. County Grand Jury, 1990-91; commr. L.A. County Economy and Efficiency Commn., 1991-92. C.C. Stillman scholar Ohio State U., 1940, U. fellow, 1941; Littauer fellow Harvard U., 1946; recipient Disting. Svc. award Coll. Adminstrv. Scis., Ohio State U., 1971. Mem.: AAAS (life fellow 1957), UCLA Hillel (trustee), Am. Jewish Com. Jewish. Home: 1365 Marinette Rd Pacific Palisades CA 90272 Business E-Mail: hoffen@ucla.edu.

HOFFLUND, PAUL, retired lawyer; b. San Diego, Mar. 27, 1928; s. John Leslie and Ethel Frances (Cline) H.; m. Anne Marie Thalman, Feb. 15, 1958; children: Mark, Sylvia. BA, Princeton U., NJ, 1950; JD, George Washington U., 1956. Bar: D.C. 1956, U.S. Dist. Ct. D.C. 1956, U.S. Ct. Appeals (D.C. cir.) 1956, Calif. 1957, U.S. Dist. Ct. (so. dist.) Calif. 1957, U.S. Ct. Mil. Appeals 1957, U.S. Ct. Claims 1958, U.S. Ct. Appeals (9th cir.) 1960, U.S. Supreme Ct. 1964, U.S. Tax Ct. 1989. Assoc. Wencke, Carlson & Kuykendall, San Diego, 1961-62; ptnr. Carlson, Kuykendall & Hofflund, San Diego, 1963-65, Carlson & Hofflund, San Diego, 1965-72; Christian Sci. practitioner San Diego, 1972-84; arbitrator Mcpl. Cts. and Superior Ct. of Calif., San Diego, 1984-99; pvt. practice San Diego, 1985—2007. Adj. prof. law Nat. U. Sch. Law, San Diego, 1985-94; judge pro tem Mcpl. Ct. South Bay Jud. Dist., 1990-99; disciplinary counsel to U.S. Tax Ct., 1989-2003; asst. U.S. atty. U.S. Dept. of Justice, L.A., 1959-60, asst. U.S. atty. in charge, San Diego, 1960-61, spl. hearing officer, San Diego, 1962-68; asst. corp. counsel Govt. of D.C., 1957-59. Author: (chpt. in book) Handbook on Criminal Procedure in the U.S. District Court, 1967; contbr. articles to profl. jours. Treas. Princeton Club of San Diego; v.p. Community Concert Assn., San Diego; pres. Sunland Home Found., San Diego, Trust for Christian Sci. Orgn., San Diego; chmn. bd. 8th Ch. of Christ, Scientist, San Diego; chmn. Christian Sci. Com. on Instnl. Work in Calif., 2004—07. With USN, 1950—53, comdr. JAGC USNR, 1953—72, ret., 1972. Mem. ABA, San Diego County Bar Assn. Phi Delta Phi. Democrat. Avocations: theater, classical music, bridge, fine art, biblical study. Home and Office: 6146 Syracuse Ln San Diego CA 92122-3301

HOFFMAN, ALICE, writer; b. NYC, Mar. 16, 1952; m. Tom Martin; children: Jake, Zack. BA, Adelphi U., NY, 1973; MA, Stanford U., Calif., 1975. Author: (novels) Property Of, 1977, The Drowning Season, 1979, Angel Landing, 1980, White Horses, 1982, Fortune's Daughter, 1985, Illumination Night, 1987, At Risk, 1988, Seventh Heaven, 1990, Turtle Moon, 1992, Second Nature, 1994, Practical Magic, 1996, Here on Earth, 1997, Local Girls, 1999, The River King, 2000, Blue Diary, 2001, The Probable Future, 2003, Blackbird House, 2004, The Ice Queen, 2005, Skylight Confessions, 2007, The Third Angel, 2008, (young adult novels) Aquamarine, 2001, Indigo, 2002, Green Angel, 2003;: The Foretelling, 2005, Incantation, 2006, (children's books) Fireflies: A Winter's Tale, 1999, Horsefly, 2000, Moondog, 2004. Mailing: c/o Julie Mancini Lyceum Agy 433 NW Fourth Ave 2nd Fl Portland OR 97209-3903

HOFFMAN, ALLAN SACHS, chemical engineer, educator; b. Chgo., Oct. 27, 1932; s. Saul A. and Frances E. (Sachs) H.; m. Susan Carol Freeman, July 29, 1962; children: David, Lisa. BSChemE, MIT, 1953, MSChemE, 1955, ScDChemE, 1957. Instr. chem. engring. MIT, Cambridge, 1954-56, asst. prof., 1958-60, assoc. prof., 1965-70; research engr. Calif. Research Corp., Richmond, 1960-63; asso. dir. research Amicon Corp., Cambridge, 1963-65; prof. bioengring. and chem. engring. U. Wash., Seattle, 1970—; asst. dir. Center for Bioengring., 1973-83. Cons. to various govtl., indsl. and acad. orgns., 1958—; UN adviser to Mexican govt., 1973-74. Author: (with W. Burlant) Block and Graft Copolymers, 1960; author numerous articles and book chpts. on chem. engring. and biomaterials; patentee in field Kimberly Clark fellow, 1954-55, Visking fellow, 1955-56, Fulbright fellow, 1957-58, Battelle fellow, 1970-72; Festschrift in honor of 60th birthday 8 issues of Jour. Biomaterials Sci., Polymer Edn., 1993. 94; recipient Founders award Controlled Release Soc., 2004. Mem. AIChE, NAE, Am. Chem. Soc., Am. Soc. Artificial Internal Organs, Internat. Soc. Artificial Internal Organs (trustee, bd. dirs. 1987-90), Soc. Biomaterials (pres. 1983-84, Clemson award biomaterial sci. lit.,

1985, Founder's award, 2000), Controlled Release Soc. (Excellence in Guiding Grad. Rsch. award 1989, 98, Founders award 2007), Japan Biomaterials Soc. (Biomaterials Sci. prize 1990, elected mem. 2005), Soc. Polymer Sci. Japan (Internat. award 2006). Office: U Wash Mail Box 355061 Seattle WA 98195-5061 Business E-Mail: hoffman@u.washington.edu.

HOFFMAN, DANIEL STEVEN, lawyer, educator; b. NYC, May 4, 1931; s. Lawrence Hoffman and Juliette (Marbes) Ostrov; m. Beverly Mae Swenson, Dec. 4, 1954; children: Lisa Hoffman Ciancio, Tracy Hoffman Cockriel, Robin Hoffman Black. BA, U. Colo., 1951; LLB, U. Denver, 1958. Bar: Colo. 1958. Assoc., then ptnr. Fugate, Mitchem, Hoffman, Denver, 1951—55; mgr. of safety City and County of Denver, 1963—65; ptnr. Kripke, Hoffman, Carrigan, Denver, 1965—70, Hoffman, McDermott, Hoffman, Denver, 1970—78; of counsel Hoffman & McDermott, Denver, 1978—84; mem. Holme Roberts & Owen, LLC, Denver, 1984—94; dean Coll. Law, U. Denver, 1978—84, dean emeritus, prof. emeritus, 1984—; ptnr. McKenna & Cuneo LLP, Denver, 1994—2000, Hoffman Reilly Pozner & Williamson LLP, 2000—. Chmn., mem. Merit Screening Com. for Bankruptcy Judges, Denver, 1979—84; chmn. subcom. Dist. Atty.'s Crime Adv. Commn., Denver, 1984—; chmn. Senator Wirth's jud. nomination rev. com., Cong. DeGette's jud. nomination rev. com.; mem. jud. ethics adv. com. Colo. Supreme Ct., 2004—. Contbr. chpts. to books Mem. Rocky Mountain region Anti-Defamation League, Denver, 1985; bd. dirs. Colo. chpt. Am. Jewish Com., 1985, Legal Ctr., Denver, 1985—; mem. adv. com. Samaritan Shelter, Denver, 1985; chmn. Rocky Flats Blue Ribbon Citizens Com., Denver, 1980-83; mem. bd. visitors J. Reuben Clark Law Sch. Brigham Young U., 1986-88. With USAF, 1951-55. Recipient Am. Jewish Com. Nat. Judge Learned Hand award, 1993, Humanitarian award Rocky Mountain chpt. Anti-Defamation League, 1984, Alumni of Yr. award U. Denver Coll. Law, 1997, Lifetime Achievement award Colo. Trial Lawyers Assn., 2001. Fellow: Am. Bar Found., Colo. Bar. Found., Am. Coll. Trial Lawyers (state chmn. 1975—76), Internat. Soc. Barristers; mem.: Am. Judicature Soc. (bd. dirs. 1977—81), Assn. Trial Lawyers Am. (nat. com. mem. 1962—63), Colo. Trial Lawyers Assn. (pres. 1961—62, Lifetime Achievement award 2001), Colo. Bar. Assn. (pres. 1976—77, Young Lawyer of Yr. award 1965), Order of Coif (hon.). Democrat. Jewish. Avocation: tennis. Office: Hoffman Reilly Pozner & Williamson LLP Kittredge Bldg 511 16th St Ste 700 Denver CO 80202-4248 Home Phone: 303-770-1223; Office Phone: 303-893-6100. Business E-Mail: dhoffman@hrpwlaw.com.

HOFFMAN, DARLEANE CHRISTIAN, chemistry professor; b. Terril, Iowa, Nov. 8, 1926; d. Carl Benjamin and Elverna (Kuhlman) Christian; m. Marvin Morrison Hoffman, Dec. 26, 1951; children: Maureane R., Daryl K. BS in Chemistry, Iowa State U., 1948, PhD in Nuclear Chemistry, 1951; Doctorate (hon.), Clark U., 2000, U. Bern, Switzerland, 2001. Chemist Oak Ridge Nat. Lab., Tenn., 1952—53; staff radiochemistry group Los Alamos Sci. Lab., N.Mex., 1953—71, assoc. leader chemistry-nuclear group, 1971—79, leader chem.-nuclear divsn., 1979—82, leader isotope and nuclear chem. divsn., 1982-84; prof. chemistry U. Calif., Berkeley, 1984—91, prof. emeritus, 1991—93, prof. grad. sch., 1993—; faculty sr. scientist Lawrence Berkeley Nat. Lab., 1984—; dir.'s fellow Los Alamos Nat. Lab., 1990—; dir. G.T. Seaborg Inst. Transactinium Sci. Lawrence Livermore Nat. Lab., 1991—96. Panel leader, spkr. women in sci. confs. NAS-NRC, 1975, 79, 83, 97, 2003, subcom. nuc. and radiochemistry, 1978—81, chmn. subcom. nuclear and radiochemistry, 1982—84, bd. radioactive waste mgmt., 1994—99; titular mem. commn. on radiochem. and nuc. techniques Internat. Union of Pure and Applied Chem., 1983—87, sec., 1985—87, chmn., 1987—91, assoc., 1991—93; energy rsch. adv. bd. cold fusion panel Dept. Energy, 1989—90, nuc. energy rsch. adv. com, 2000—01; conf. lectr. Welch Fedn., 1991, 97, lect. tour Tex. univs., 2000; separations subpanel separations tech. and transmutation systems panel NAS, 1992—94; steering com. Accel. Transmutation Waste Roadmapping Study, 1999; ANTT subcom. NERAC, 2002—07; mem. commn. on endpoints spent nuc. fuel and hi-level radioactive waste NAS-NRC Bd. Radioactive Waste Mgmt., 1994—99, NAS-NRC BRWM Joint US/Russian Commn., 2001—02; mem. US-Russian Joint Commn. Collaboration to Prevent Radiol. Terrorism, 2004—06; presenter, spkr., lectr. in field; pres. selection com. US nat. Medal Sci., 2007—. Author: The Transuranium People, 2000; contbr. articles to profl. jours. Recipient Alumni Citation of Merit, Coll. Scis. and Humanities, Iowa State U., 1978, Disting. Achievement award, Iowa State U., 1986, Berkeley Citation, U. Calif., 1996, US Nat. Medal Sci., 1997, Leonard A. Ford Lectureship, Mankato State U., 1998, Frontiers Sci. award, Soc. Cosmetic Chemists, 1998, John V. Atanasoff Rsch. and Discovery award, Iowa State U. Coll. Liberal Arts and Sci., 2007; named Japan Soc. Promotion Sci. lectr., 1987, Disting. Lectr., Inst. Phys. Rsch. and Tech., Ames Lab., 1998; named to Women in Tech. Internat. Hall of Fame, 2000; fellow, Guggenheim Found., Berkeley, 1978—79; Sr. Postdoc. fellow, NSF, Norway, 1964—65. Fellow: AAAS (coun. mem. 1995—97), Norwegian Acad. Sci. and Letters, Am. Acad. Arts and Scis., Am. Phys. Soc., Am. Inst. Chemists (pres. N.Mex. chpt. 1976—78); mem.: Radiochem. Soc. (Lifetime Achievement award 2003), Am. Chem. Soc. (John Dustin Clark award 1976, Nuc. Chemistry award 1983, Francis P. Garvan-John M. Olin medal 1990, Priestley medal 2000, Mosher award 2001), Japan Soc. Nuc. and Radiochems. (hon.; internat. mem. 2004), Sigma Xi (Procter prize for sci. achievement 2003), Alpha Chi Sigma (Hall of Fame 2002), Sigma Delta Epsilon, Pi Mu Epsilon, Iota Sigma Pi (nat. hon. mem. 1993), Phi Kappa Phi. Office: Lawrence Berkeley Nat Lab MS70R0319 NSD Berkeley CA 94720 Business E-Mail: dchoffman@lbl.gov.

HOFFMAN, DONALD DAVID, cognitive and computer science educator; b. San Antonio, Dec. 29, 1955; s. David Pollock and Loretta Virginia (Shoemaker) H.; m. Geralyn Mary Souza, Dec. 13, 1986; 1 child from previous marriage, Melissa Louise. BA, UCLA, 1978; PhD, MIT. MTS and project engr. Hughes Aircraft Co., El Segundo, Calif., 1978-83; rsch. scientist MIT Artificial Intelligence Lab, Cambridge, Mass., 1983; asst. prof. U. Calif., Irvine, 1983-86, assoc. prof., 1986-90, prof., 1990—. Cons. Fairchild Lab. for Artificial Intelligence, Palo Alto, Calif., 1984; panelist MIT Corp. vis. com., Cambridge, 1985, NSF, Washington, 1988; conf. host IEEE Conf. on Visual Motion, Irvine, 1989, Office of Naval Rsch. Conf. on Vision, Laguna Beach, Calif., 1992; vis. prof. Zentrum für Interdisziplinäre Forschung, Bielefeld, Germany, 1995-96, cons. Sextant Tech. Inc., Irvine, Calif., 2000-05. Author: Visual Intelligence, 1998; co-author: Observer Mechanics, 1989, Automotive Lighting and Human Vision, 2007; mem. editl. bd. Cognition, 1991-2002, Psychol. Rev., 1995-96; contbr. articles to profl. jours. Vol. tchr. Turtle Rock Elem. Sch., Irvine, 1988-90. Recipient Distinguished Scientific award, Am. Psychol. Assn., 1989, Troland Rsch. award US Nat. Acad. Scis., 1994; grantee NSF, 1984, 87, 2001. Mem.: Am. Psychol. Soc., Assn. for Sci. Study of Consciousness. Avocations: running, swimming, racket sports, ice skating. Office: U Calif Dept Cognitive Sci Irvine CA 92697-0001 Office Phone: 949-824-6795. Business E-Mail: ddhoff@uci.edu.

HOFFMAN, DONALD M., lawyer; BS, UCLA, 1957, LL.B., 1960. Bar: Calif. 1961. Pvt. practice, L.A. County, 1961—; ptnr. firm Greenwald, Hoffman, Meyer & Montes, 1964—. Pres. L.A. Estate Planning Council. Served to 2d lt. U.S. Army. Mem. Am., Los Angeles County bar assns., Phi Alpha Delta, Beta Gamma Sigma. Office: 500 N Brand Blvd Ste 920 Glendale CA 91203-1923 Office Phone: 818-507-8100. Business E-Mail: dmhoffman@ghmmlaw.com.

HOFFMAN, JERRY IRWIN, retired dental educator; b. Chgo., Nov. 20, 1935; s. Irwin and Luba Hoffman; m. Sharon Lynn Seaman, Aug. 25, 1963; children: Steven Abram, Rachel Irene. Student, DePaul U., 1953-56; BS in Biology and Chemistry, Roosevelt U., 1956; DDS, Loyola U., Chgo., 1960; M of Health Care Adminstrn., Baylor U., 1972. Certificate, General Practice Residency, U.S. Army, 1978. Commd. officer U.S. Army, 1960 (served to 1962, returned 1964), advanced through grades to col., 1978, hdqrs. rep. local dental tng. confs. Europe Garmisch, Fed. Republic Germany, 1965-67; cons. to Comdg. Gen. U.S. Army Med. Research and Devel. Command, Washington, 1972-76; cons. Office of Surgeon Gen. U.S. Army, Washington, 1972-76, liaison rep. to Nat. Adv. Council and Oral Biology and Medicine Study Sessions of the Nat. Inst. Dental Research and NIH, 1973-76, resident in Gen. Practice Residency, 1976-78; comdg. officer U.S. Army Dental Activity, Fort Monmouth, NJ, 1979-82; ret., 1982; pvt. practice dentistry Chgo., 1962-64; assoc. prof. operative dentistry Loyola U. Sch. Dentistry, Maywood, Ill., 1982-93, dir. gen. practice residency, 1982-85, coordinator extramural dental resources, 1983-85, assoc. dean for clin. affairs, 1985-93; dir. sci. programs Chgo. Dental Soc., 1993—2002, ret., 2002. Staff dentist Silas B. Hayes Army Hosp., Fort Ord, Calif., 1976-79, Patterson Army Hosp., Ft. Monmouth, 1979-82; lectr., presenter seminars in field. Contbr. articles to profl. jours. Decorated Legion of Merit, Meritorious Svc. Medal with oak leaf cluster. Fellow: Am. Coll. Dentists, Internat. Coll. Dentists, Odontographic Soc.; master: Acad. Gen. Dentistry; mem. ADA, Ill. Dental Soc., Chgo. Dental Soc., Am. Assn. Dental Schs., Am. Soc. Assn. Execs., Assn. Healthcare Execs., Profl. Conv. Mgmt. Assn., Omicron Kappa Upsilon. Personal E-mail: ddscds@aol.com.

HOFFMAN, JULIEN IVOR ELLIS, pediatrician, cardiologist, educator; b. Salisbury, So. Rhodesia, July 26, 1925; arrived in U.S., 1957, naturalized, 1967; s. Bernard Isaac and Minrose (Bermant) H.; m. Kathleen (Lewis), 1986; children: Anna, Daniel. BS, U. Witwaterstrand, Johannesburg, South Africa, 1944, BSc (hon.), 1945, MB, BCh, 1949, MD, 1970. Intern, resident internal medicine, South Africa, 1950-56; rsch. asst., postgrad. Med. Sch., London, 1956-57; fellow pediatric cardiology Boston Children's Hosp., 1957-59; fellow Cardiovasc. Rsch. Inst., San Francisco, 1959-60; asst. prof. pediat., internal medicine Albert Einstein Coll., NYC, 1962-66; assoc. prof. pediat. U. Calif., San Francisco, 1966-70, prof., 1970-94, prof. physiology, 1981-88, prof. emeritus, 1994—. Sr. mem. Cardiovasc. Rsch. Inst. U. Calif., San Francisco, 1966—; mem. bd. examiners, sub-bd. pediat. cardiology Am. Bd. Pediat., 1973—78, sub-bd. pediat. intensive care, 1985—87; chmn. Louis Katz Award Com., Basic Sci. Coun., Am. Heart Assn., 1973—74, George Brown Meml. lectr., 1977; George Alexander Gibson Meml. lectr. Royal Coll. Physicians (Edinburgh), 1978; Lilly lectr. Royal Coll. Physicians (London), 1981; Isaac Starr lectr. Cardiac Systems Dynamics Soc., England, 1982, John Keith lectr., 85; Disting. Physiology lectr. Am. Coll. Chest Physicians, 1985; Nadas lectr. Am. Heart Assn., 1987; 1st Donald C. Fyler lectr. Children's Hosp., Boston, 1990; 1st MacDonald Dick lectr. U. Mich., Ann Arbor; Kreidberg lectr. Med. Sch. Tufts U., 2004; Tabatznik lectr. Mt. Sinai Hosp., Balt., 2005. Co-editor: Rudolph's Pediatrics, 1982—96, Coronary Circulation, 1990, Recent Advances in the Coronary Circulation, 1993, Pediatric Cardiovascular Medicine, 2000. Recipient Bayer Cardiovasc. Mentor award, 1989. Fellow Royal Coll. Physicians; mem. World Congress Pediat. Cardiology and Cardiac Surgery (hon. joint pres. Paris 1993), Am. Physiol. Soc., Am. Pediatric Soc., Soc. Pediatric Rsch. Achievements include extensive research into congenital heart disease and coronary blood flow. Home: 925 Tiburon Blvd Belvedere Tiburon CA 94920-1525 Home Phone: 415-435-6941. Personal E-mail: jiehoffman@yahoo.com. Business E-Mail: julien.hoffman@ucsf.edu.

HOFFMAN, LOU, public relations executive, educator, writer; Pvt. practice Hoffman Agy., 1987—. Spkr., writer of pub. rels. in field. Contbr. columns in newspapers including MC mag.; appeared in BusinessWeek, The Wall Street Jour., other pub. rels. trade mags.

HOFFMAN, LYMAN F., state legislator; b. Bethel, Alaska, Feb. 13, 1950; m to Lillian; children: Trina & Douglas. Attended, U. Alaska, 1968—72, attended, 1973—74. City manager, Bethal, 77-85, Planning Commissioner, formerly; Alaska State Representative, District 25, 86-90, District 39, 93-94, member, Budget & Audit Committee, formerly, Alaska House Representative; Alaska State Senator, District M, 91-92, District T, 1994-2002, member, Community & Regional Affairs, Labor & Commerce & Legislature Committees, currently, member, Select Committee on Legislature Ethics, currently, Alaska State Senate; Alaska State Senator, District S, 2003-.Owner, North Star Gas, formerly; board member, Bethel Native Corp & Bethel Family Clinic, formerly; chairman, Bethel Prematernal Home, formerly, board director, currently; dep director, Yukon-Kuskokwim Health Corp, currently; owner, Twilight Travel Agency & Bethel Drilling & Welding, currently; Businessman & fisherman, currently. Democrat. Office: Dist S 716 W 4th Ave Ste 360 Anchorage AK 99501-2133 also: State Capitol Rm 518 Juneau AK 99801 Office Phone: 907-465-4453, 907-269-0269. Office Fax: 907-465-4523, 907-269-0270. Business E-Mail: Senator_Lyman_Hoffman@legis.state.ak.us.*

HOFFMAN, MARK FREDERICK, lawyer; b. Bellevue, Wash., Mar. 30, 1971; s. Frederick Joseph and Molly K. Hoffman; m. Elizabeth Briggs, Aug. 17, 1996. AB summa cum laude, Princeton U., 1993; JD cum laude, U. Mich., 1996. Bar: Wash. 1996. Assoc. Graham & James LLP, Seattle, 1996—2000; ptnr. Gray Cary Ware & Freidenrich, Seattle, 2000—04; ptnr., co-chmn. Pub. Co. & Corp. Governance practice group DLA Piper Rudnick Gray Cary, Seattle, 2005—. Contbr. articles to profl. jours. Named a Rising Star, Washington Law & Politics, 1999—2003, Super Lawyer, 2003. Mem. ABA, Wash. State Bar Assn., King County Bar Assn., Order of the Coif. Avocations: running, skiing, hiking, biking, reading. Office: DLA Piper Rudnick Gray Cary Suite 7000 701 Fifth Ave Seattle WA 98104 Office Phone: 206-839-4823. Office Fax: 206-839-4801. Business E-Mail: mark.hoffman@dlapiper.com.

HOFFMAN, MICHAEL JEROME, humanities educator; b. Phila., Mar. 13, 1939; s. Nathan P. and Sara (Perlman) H.; m. Margaret Boegeman, Dec. 27, 1988; children by previous marriage: Cynthia, Matthew. BA, U. Pa., 1959, MA, 1960, PhD, 1963. Instr. Washington Coll., Chestertown, Md., 1962-64; asst. prof. U. Pa., Phila., 1964-67; from asst. prof. to prof. U. Calif., Davis, 1967—2001, asst. vice chancellor acad. affairs, 1976-83, chmn. English dept., 1984-89, dir. Davis Humanities Inst., 1987-91, coord. writing programs, 1991-94, undergrad. coord., 1994-95, grad. advisor, 1995-98, dir. honors program, 1992-99. Chmn. joint projects steering com. U. Calif.-Calif. State U., 1976-87; chmn. adv. bd. Calif. Acad. Partnership Program, 1985-87; dir. Calif. Humanities Project, 1985-91. Author: The Development of Abstractionism in the Writings of Gertrude Stein, 1965, The Buddy System, 1971, The Subversive Vision, 1972, Gertrude Stein, 1976, Critical Essays on Gertrude Stein, 1986, Essentials of the Theory of Fiction, 1988, 2d rev. edit., 2005, Critical Essays on American Modernism, 1992. With USAR, 1957-61. Nat. Def. Edn. Act fellow U.S. Govt., 1959-62. Mem. Modern Lang. Assn. (Am. lit. group). Democrat. Jewish. Avocation: tennis. Home: 4417 San Marino Dr Davis CA 95618-5012 Office: Univ Calif Dept English Davis CA 95618 Business E-Mail: mjhoffman@ucdavis.edu.

HOFFMAN, PHILIP SEYMOUR, actor; b. Fairport, NY, July 23, 1967; 1 child. Grad., NYU, Tisch Sch. Drama. Co-artistic dir. LAByrinth Theater Co.; co-founder Cooper's Town Productions. Actor: (TV films) The Yearling, 1994; (TV miniseries) Empire Falls, 2005; (films) Triple Bogey on a Par Five Hole, 1991, My New Gun, 1992, Leap of Faith, 1992, Scent of a Woman, 1992, Szuler, 1992, My Boyfriend's Back, 1993, Money for Nothing, 1993, Joey Breaker, 1993, The Getaway, 1994, When a Man Loves a Woman, 1994, Nobody's Fool, 1994, The Fifteen Minute Hamlet, 1995, Hard Eight, 1997, Twister, 1996, Boogie Nights, 1997, Montana, 1998, Next Stop Wonderland, 1998, The Big Lebowski, 1998, Happiness, 1998, Patch Adams, 1998, Culture, 1998, Flawless, 1999, Magnolia, 1999, The Talented Mr. Ripley, 1999, State and Main, 2000, Almost Famous, 2000, Forest Hills Bob, 2001, Love Liza, 2002, Punch-Drunk Love, 2002, Red Dragon, 2002, 25th Hour, 2002, Owning Mahowny, 2003, Cold Mountain, 2003, Along Came Polly, 2004, Capote, 2005 (Best Actor, Nat. Bd. Review, 2005, Best Actor, Broadcast Film Critics Assn., 2005, Best Actor, Critics Choice award, 2005, Best Performance by an Actor in a Motion Picture-Drama, Hollywood Fgn. Press Assn. (Golden Globe award), 2006, Best Actor, Nat. Soc. Film Critics award, 2006, Outstanding Performance by a Male Actor in a Leading Role, Screen Actors Guild award, 2006, Actor in a Leading Role, British Acad. Film and TV Arts, 2006, Performance by an Actor in a Leading Role, Acad. Motion Picture Arts & Sciences, 2006, Best Male Lead, Independent Spirit award, 2006), Mission: Impossible III, 2006, Before the Devil Knows You're Dead, 2007, The Savages, 2007 (Ind. Spirit award for Best Male Lead, Film Ind., 2008), Charlie Wilson's War, 2007, Synecdoche, New York, 2008, Doubt, 2008; dir.: (plays) The Last Days of Judas Iscariot, 2005, The Little Flower of East Orange, 2008; actor: Jack Goes Boating, 2007. Recipient Best Actor, Boston Soc. of Film Critics award, 2005; named one of 100 Most Influential People, Time Mag., 2006. Office: Paradigm Talent Agy # 2500 10100 Santa Monica Los Angeles CA 90067-4003

HOFFMAN, REID, Internet company executive; b. Aug. 5, 1967; BS with Distinction in Symbolic Systems, Stanford Univ., 1990; M in Phil., Oxford Univ., London, 1993. Prin. investor Nanosolar, Inc.; angel investor Friendster, Inc., Aufklarung LLC, 2001—; with divsn. human interface design Apple Computers, Inc.; founder SocialNet; exec. v.p. PayPal Inc. (sold to eBay), 2001—02; founding CEO LinkedIn Corp., Mountain View, Calif., 2003—07, chmn. & pres., products, 2007—. Bd. dir. Jumpstart Tech., LLC, Six Apart, 2003—, Grassroots Enterprises, 2003—, Vendio, 2003—, Mozilla Corp., 2005—, Tagged, 2005—, Kiva.org, 2006—; mem. advisory bd. EZCab, WeAttract.com, Lulan LLC, 2003—, Ctr. for Citizen Media, 2006—. Mem. provost coun. Coll. Eight, U. Calif., San Francisco, 2006—. Named one of 50 Who Matter Now, CNNMoney.com Bus. 2.0, 2006. Office: LinkedIn Corp 2029 Stierlin Ct Mountain View CA 94043*

HOFFMAN, SHARON LYNN, adult education educator; b. Chgo. d. David P. and Florence Seaman; m. Jerry Irwin Hoffman, Aug. 25, 1963; children: Steven Abram, Rachel Irene. BA, Ind. U., 1961; M Adult Edn., Nat.-Louis Univ., 1992. High sch. English tchr. Chgo. Pub. Schs., 1961-64; tchr. Dept. of Def. Schs., Braconne, France, 1964-66; tchr. ESL Russian Inst., Garmisch, Fed. Republic Germany, 1966, 67; tchr. adult edn. Monterey Peninsula Unified Schs., Ft. Ord, Calif., 1977-79; tchr. ESL MAECOM, Monmouth County, NJ, 1979-80; lectr., tchr. adult edn. Truman Coll./Temple Shalom, Chgo.; tchr. homebound Fairfax County Pub. Schs., Fairfax, Va., 1976; entry operator Standard Rate & Data, Wilmette, Ill., 1986-87; rsch. editor, spl. projects editor Marquis Who's Who, Wilmette, 1987-92; mem. adj. faculty Nat.-Louis U., Evanston and Wheeling, Ill., 1993-99, tutor coord., then coord. learning specialist, 1993-99; pres. Cultural Transitions, Pebble Beach, Calif., 1992—. Mem.: TESOL, ASTD, Nat. Coun. Tchrs. English. Personal E-mail: culturaltrans1@aol.com.

HOFFMAN, THOMAS EDWARD, dermatologist; b. LA, Oct. 14, 1944; s. David Maurice and Ann (Corday) H.; m. Donna Madsen, 1973 (div. 1977); m. Linda L., Feb. 20, 1979; children: David, Jay. AB, U. So. Calif., 1966; MD, Tulane U., 1970. Intern U. So. Calif. USC Med. Ctr., 1970-71; residency dermatology Stanford (Calif.) U., 1973-76, fellow dermatopathology, 1973-74; dermatologist pvt. practice, Menlo Park, Calif., 1976—. Clin. assoc. prof. Stanford (Calif.) U., 1981-97, clin. prof. dermatology, 1997. With USPHS, 1971-73. Recipient Achievement award Tulane U., 1970. Fellow Am. Coll. Physicians, Am. Acad. Dermatology, Am. Soc. Dermatopathology, Am. Soc. Dermatologic Surgery, Am. Soc. Laser Medicine & Surgery, San Francisco Dermatologic Soc. (pres. 2000-01). Avocations: tennis, skiing. Office: Menlo Dermatology Med Group 888 Oak Grove Ave Menlo Park CA 94025-4432 Office Phone: 650-325-1511. Business E-Mail: mdmg@mdmg.com.

HOFFMAN, WAYNE MELVIN, retired airline official; b. Chgo., Mar. 9, 1923; s. Carl A. and Martha (Tamillo) H.; m. Laura Majewski, Jan. 26, 1946; children— Philip, Karen, Kristin. BA cum laude, U. Ill., 1943, JD with high honors, 1947. Bar: Ill. bar 1947, N.Y. bar 1958. Atty. I.C. R.R., 1948-52; with N.Y.C. R.R. Co., 1952-57, exec. asst. to pres., 1958-60, v.p. freight sales, 1960-61, v.p. sales, 1961-62, exec. v.p., 1962-67; chmn. bd. N.Y. Central Trans. Co., 1960-67, Flying Tiger Line, Inc. and Tiger Internat., Inc., 1967-86. Trustee McCallum Theatre, Palm Desert, Calif., Eisenhower Med. Ctr., Rancho Mirage, Calif. Served to capt. inf. AUS, World War II. Decorated Silver Star, Bronze Star with oak leaf cluster, Purple Heart with oak leaf cluster;

Fourragere (Belgium). Mem. Bohemian Club (San Francisco), Vintage Club (Indian Wells), Phi Beta Kappa. Home: 74-435 Palo Verde Dr Indian Wells CA 92210-7367 Office: 2450 Montecito Rd Ramona CA 92065-1644

HOFFMAN, WILLIAM YANES, plastic surgeon, educator; b. Rochester, NY, Feb. 25, 1952; MD, U. Rochester, 1977. Cert. Am. Bd. Surgery, 1985, Am. Bd. Plastic Surgery, 1987. Intern gen. surgery U. Calif. Affiliated Hosps., San Francisco, 1977—78, resident plastic surgery, 1978—80, 1981—83, resident craniofacial surgery, 1980—81, 1984—85; fellow NYU Med. Ctr., NYC, 1985—86; plastic surgeon, chief Divsn. Plastic and Reconstructive Surgery, dir. Plastic Surgery Residency Program U. Calif. San Francisco Med. Ctr.; also prof. plastic surgery U. Calif., San Francisco. Office: U Calif Med Ctr 350 Parnassus Ave, Ste 509 San Francisco CA 94143 also: 505 Parnassus Ave, Ste M-593 San Francisco CA 94143-0932 Office Phone: 415-353-4287. Office Fax: 415-353-4330. Business E-Mail: hoffmanw@surgery.ucsf.edu.

HOFFMANN, JON ARNOLD, retired aeronautical engineer; b. Wausau, Wis., Jan. 13, 1942; s. Arnold D. and Rita J. (Haas) H.; m. Carol R. Frye. BSME, U. Wis., 1964, MSME, 1966. Register profl. engr., Calif. Rsch. engr. Trane Co., 1966—68; prof. aerospace engring. Calif. Poly. State U., San Luis Obispo, 1968—2001, prof. emeritus, 2002. Research engr. Stanford U. NSF Program, 1970; research fellow Ames Research Ctr. Ctr. NASA/ASEE, 1974-75; tech. cons. NASA/AMES Research Ctr., 1977; design engr. Cal/ Poly ERDA contract, 1976-77; prin. investigator NASA-ARC Cooperative Agreement, 1983. Contbr. articles to profl. jours. Grantee NASA, NSF. Home and Office: 1044 Via Chula Robles Arroyo Grande CA 93420-4915 Business E-Mail: jhoffman@calpoly.edu.

HOFFMANN, MICHAEL R., dean, environmental science educator; b. Fond du Lac, Wis., 1946; BA, Northwestern U., 1968; PhD in Chemistry, Brown U., 1974. Mem. civil engring. faculty U. Minn.; postdoctoral scholar Calif. Inst. Tech., Pasadena, 1973—75, assoc. prof., 1980—85, prof. environ. engring., 1986—90, prof. environ. chemistry, 1990—96, James Irvine prof. environ. sci., 1996—, exec. officer for environ. engring. sci., 1996—2002, dean grad. studies, 2002—. Mem. sci. adv. bd. Max Planck Inst. for Chemistry, Mainz, Germany, vis. prof.; Barnett F. Dodge disting. lectr. in chem. engring. Yale U., New Haven, 2002; vis. prof. Swiss Fed. Tech. Inst., Zurich, Switzerland; disting. lectr. Hebrew U., Jerusalem, U. Buenos Aires, U. Sao Paulo, Sao Paulo, Brazil. Mem. editl. bd.: Environ. Sci. and Tech., Jour. Phys. Chemistry. Commr. So. Calif. Intercollegiate Athletic Conf. Recipient Alexander von Humboldt prize, 1991, E. Gordon Young award, Chem. Soc. Can., 1995, Am. Chem. Soc. award for creative advances in environ. sci. and tech., 2001. Office: Calif Inst Tech M/C 138-78 1200 E California Blvd Pasadena CA 91125 Office Phone: 626-395-4391. Office Fax: 626-395-2940. E-mail: mrh@caltech.edu.

HOFFMANN, WILLIAM FREDERICK, astronomer; b. Manchester, NH, Feb. 26, 1933; s. Maurice and Charlotte (Hibbs) H.; m. Silke Elisabeth Margaretha Schneider, June 5, 1965; children: Andrea Charlotte, Christopher James. AB in Physics, Bowdoin Coll., 1954; PhD in Physics, Princeton U., 1962. Instr. physics Princeton (N.J.) U., 1958-61; rsch. assoc. NASA-GISS, NYC, 1962, staff astronomer, 1965-73; instr. physics Yale U., New Haven, 1963-64; adj. assoc. prof. Columbia U., NYC, 1970-73; prof. astronomy U. Ariz., Tucson, 1973-98, prof. emeritus astronomy, 1998—. Editor: (with H.Y. Chiu) Gravitation & Relativity, 1964. Pres. Spuyten Duyvil Assn., N.Y.C., 1971. NSF fellow, 1954; Danforth fellow, 1954-58. Fellow AAAS, Am. Physics Soc.; mem. Am. Astron. Soc., Sigma Chi, Phi Beta Kappa. Home: 4225 E Kilmer St Tucson AZ 85711-2825 Office: U Ariz Steward Obs Tucson AZ 85721-0001

HOFFMEISTER, GERHART, German language educator; b. Giessen, Germany, Dec. 17, 1936; came to U.S., 1966, naturalized citizen, 1993; s. Johannes and Inge Caecilie (Johannsen) H.; m. Margaret von Poletika, May 28, 1966 (div. Dec. 1988); 1 child, George A. Degree, U. Bonn, Fed. Republic Germany, 1963, U. Cologne, 1966; PhD, U. Md., 1970. Student tchr. U. Cologne, 1964-66; instr. U. Md., 1966-70; asst. prof. U. Wis., Milw., 1970-74; assoc. prof. Wayne State U., Detroit, 1974-75, U. Calif., Santa Barbara, 1975-79, prof., 1979—2002, bd. dirs. Comparative Lit. program, 1991-97. Author: (with others) Germany 2,000 Years III, 1986; editor: Goethe in Italy, 1988, French Revolution, 1989, European Romanticism, 1989, Petrarca, 1997, Heine in Romania, 2002. Recipient award Am. Philos. Assn., 1974, Max Kade Found., 1986, 88. Mem. MLA, Pacific Ancient and Modern Lang. Assn., Am. Assn. Tchrs. German, Goethe Soc. N.Am. Avocations: tennis, swimming, gardening. Home: 117 Calle Alamo Santa Barbara CA 93105-2818 Office: Dept German U Calif Santa Barbara CA 93106 Home Phone: 805-682-1824. Personal E-mail: hoffmeis@verizon.net.

HOFMANN, ALAN FREDERICK, biomedical researcher, educator; b. Balt., May 17, 1931; s. Joseph Enoch and Nelda Rosina (Durr) Hofmann; m. Marta Gertrud Pettersson, Aug. 15, 1959 (div. 1976); children: Anthea Karin, Cecilia Rae; m. Helga Katharina Aicher, Nov. 3, 1978. BA with honors, Johns Hopkins U., 1951, MD with honors, 1955; MD, U. Lund, Sweden, 1965; MD (hon.), U. Bologna, Italy, 1988. Intern, resident dept. medicine Columbia Presbyn. Med. Ctr., NYC, 1955-57; clin. assoc. clin. ctr. Nat. Heart Inst., NIH, Bethesda, Md., 1957-59; postdoctoral fellow, dept. physiol. chemistry U. Lund, Sweden, 1959-62; asst. physician Hosp. Rockefeller U., NYC, 1962-64, assoc. physician, 1964-66; outpatient physician N.Y. Hosp., NYC, 1963-64; cons. in medicine, assoc. dir. gastroenterology unit Mayo Clinic, Rochester, Minn., 1966-77; prof. medicine, attending physician Med. Ctr. U. Calif., San Diego, 1977-98, emeritus prof., 1998—. Asst. prof. dept. medicine Rockefeller U., NYC, 1964—66; assoc. prof. medicine and biochemistry U. Minn. Mayo Grad. Sch., 1966—69, assoc. prof. medicine and physiology, 1969—70, prof., 1970—73, Mayo Med. Sch., 1973—77; cons. physiology Mayo Clinic, Rochester, 1975—77; adj. prof. pharmacy U. Calif., San Francisco, 1986—94; vis. prof. U. Mich., Ann Arbor, 1980—85. Contbr. articles to profl. jours., chapters to books. Recipient Travel award, Wellcome Trust, 1961—63, NSF, 1964, Sr. Scientist award, Humboldt Found., Fed. Rep. Germany, 1976, 1991, Disting. Achievement award, Modern Medicine mag., 1978, Chancellor's Rsch. Excellence award, U. Calif., 1986, Disting. Alumnus award, Mayo Found., 2001, Disting. Mentor award, Found. Digestive Health Nutrition, 2004; co-recipient Eppinger prize, Falk Found., 1976; Sr. fellow, NIH, 1986. Fellow: AAAS, Royal Soc. Medicine, Royal Coll. Physicians (hon.); mem.: Am. Gastroent. Assn. (Disting. Achievement award 1970, co-winner Beaumont prize 1979, Friedenwald medal 1994), Am. Physiol. Soc. (Horace Davenport medal 1996), Am. Liver Found., Serbian Soc. Medicine (hon.), Royal Flemish Acad. Medicine (hon.; fgn. corr. mem.), Chilean Soc. Gastroenterology (hon.), Soc. Gastrointestinal Radiology (hon.), Swedish Soc. Gastroenterology (hon.), Gastroent. Soc. Australia (hon.), Brit. Soc. Gastroenterology (hon.), German Soc. Digestive and Metabolic Disease (hon. Siegfried Thannhauser medal 1996), Assn. Am. Physicians, Am. Soc. Clin. Investigation, Am. Assn. Study Liver Disease (Disting. Achievement award 1997), Sigma Xi, Phi Beta Kappa, Omicron Delta Kappa, Alpha Omega Alpha. Achievements include description and modelling of the enterohepatic circulation of bile acids; clarification of the multiple physiological roles of bile acids; conjugated bile acid replacement therapy for bile acid deficiency in short bowel syndrome; discovery of new vertebrate bile acids; structure-function relationships of bile acids; therapeutic uses of bile acids in liver, biliary and intestinal disease. Home: 5870 Cactus Way La Jolla CA 92037-7069 Personal E-mail: hofmannaf@cs.com. Business E-Mail: ahofmann@ucsd.edu.

HOFMANN, JOHN RICHARD, JR., retired lawyer; b. Oakland, Calif., June 24, 1922; s. John Richard and Esther (Starkweather) H.; m. Mary Macdonough, Feb. 6, 1954; children: John Richard III, Gretchen Hofmann, Sarah Worthington Hack, Joan Macdonough Alexander. AB, U. Calif., Berkeley, 1943; JD, Harvard U., 1949. Bar: Calif. 1950. Assoc. Pillsbury, Madison & Sutro, San Francisco, 1949-58, ptnr., 1959-92, of counsel, 1992-96, ret., 1996—; exec. v.p. MPC Ins., Ltd., 1988-96. City atty. City of Belvedere, Calif., 1958. Mem. County of Marin (Calif.) Aviation Commn., 2001—05, chmn., 2003—05. Office: Pillsbury Winthrop Shaw Pittman LLP PO Box 7880 San Francisco CA 94120-7880 Office Phone: 415-983-1522.

HOFMANN, PAUL BERNARD, healthcare consultant; b. Portland, Oreg., July 6, 1941; s. Max and Consuelo Theresa (Bley) H.; m. Lois Bernstein, June 28, 1969; children: Julie, Jason. BS, U. Calif., Berkeley, 1963, MPH, 1965, DPH, 1994. Research assoc. in hosp. adminstrn. Lab. of Computer Sci., Mass. Gen. Hosp., Boston, 1966-68, asst. dir., 1968-69; asst. adminstr. San Antonio Community Hosp., Upland, Calif., 1969-70, assoc. adminstr., 1970-72; dep. dir. Stanford (Calif.) U. Hosp., 1972-74, dir., 1974-77; exec. dir. Emory U. Hosp., Atlanta, 1978-87; exec. v.p., chief ops. officer Alta Bates Corp., Emeryville, Calif., 1987-91, cons., 1991-92, Alexander & Alexander, San Francisco, 1992-94; disting. vis. scholar Stanford (Calif.) U. Ctr. for Biomed. Ethics, 1993-97; sr. fellow Stanford (Calif.) U. Hosp., 1993-94; sr. cons. strategic healthcare practice Alexander & Alexander Cons. Group, San Francisco, 1994-97; sr. v.p. strategic healthcare practice Aon Cons., San Francisco, 1997-99; pres. The Hofmann Healthcare Group, San Francisco, 2000-01; with Provenance Health Ptnrs., Moraga, Calif., 2001—05; pres. The Hofmann Healthcare Group, Moraga, Calif., 2005—. Instr. computer applications Harvard U., 1968-69; lectr. hosp. adminstrn. UCLA, 1970-72, Stanford U. Med. Sch., 1972-77; assoc. prof. Emory U. Sch. Medicine, Atlanta, 1978-87. Author: The Development and Application of Ethical Criteria for Use in Making Programmatic Resource Allocation Decisions in Hospitals, 1994; co-editor: Managing Ethically: A Guide for Executives, 2001, Mistakes in Healthcare Management: Identification, Prevention and Correction, 2005; contbr. articles to profl. jours Served with U.S. Army, 1959. Fellow Am. Coll. Hosp. Adminstrs. (recipient Robert S. Hudgens meml. award 1976); mem. Am. Hosp. Assn., U. Calif. Grad. Program in Health Mgmt. Alumni Assn. (Disting. Leadership award 2004). Office Phone: 925-247-9700. Business E-Mail: hofmann@hofmannhealthcare.com.

HOFMEISTER, SALLIE ANN, editor; b. New Hartford, NY, Aug. 8, 1957; d. John Walter and Sally Ann (Moyer) H. BS, Kans. State U., 1980. Writer Chem. Week, NYC, 1983-84; sr. staff writer Venture Mag., NYC, 1985-89; story editor N.Y. Times, NYC, 1989-91, dep. bus. editor, 1991-92, asst. bus. editor, 1993-95; staff writer bus. sect. L.A. Times, 1995—2006, dep. bus. editor, 2007—08, bus. editor, 2008—. Office: LA Times 202 W 1st St Los Angeles CA 90012-3601

HOFSETH, PAULINE C., realtor; m. Torulf Hofseth; 3 children. BS in Journalism, U. Md., Coll. Park. Grad. Realtor Inst., Cert. Residential Specialist, Accredited Buyer's Rep., cert. e-Pro. Comml. and residential property mgmt. real estate agent Prudential Jack White/Vista Real Estate, Anchorage, 1986—89, assoc. broker residential sales, 1989—. Mem. Alaska Bd. Realtors, Anchorage Bd. Realtors, Anchorage Multiple Listing System, Cert. Residential Coun., Real Estate Buyer's Agent Coun. Co-author: (books) How to Make Your Realtor Get You the Best Deal, Alaska Edition. Recipient Pres. award for sales achievement. Mem.: Real Estate Cyberspace Soc., Nat. Assn. Realtors. Office: Prudential Jack White/Vista Real Estate 3801 Centerpoint Dr Ste 200 Anchorage AK 99503 Home: 12431 Alpine Dr Anchorage AK 99516 Office Phone: 907-273-7274. Office Fax: 907-562-5485. Business E-Mail: pauline@PaulineHofseth.com.

HOGAN, CRAIG J., astronomer, educator; BA in Astronomy summa cum laude, Harvard Coll., 1976; PhD in Astronomy, U. Cambridge, 1980. Asst. prof., astronomer Steward Obs. U. Ariz., 1985-89, assoc. prof., astronomer, 1989-90; assoc. prof. astronomy and physics dept.s U. Wash., Seattle, 1990-93, prof. astronomy and physics dept., 1993—, chair astronomy dept., 1995-2000. Mem. ad hoc com. on funding of cosmology NSF, 1996, proposal rev. panel chair, 1998, com. of visitors divsn. astron. scis., 1999; mem. dark time telescope time allocation com. Kitt Peak Nat. Obs., 1992-95; sci. adv. com. Sloan Digital Sky Survey, 1994—, co-chair so. survey working group, 1994—, sci. dirs. adv. com., 1998—, adv. coun., 1998—, fundraising task force, 1998—; mem. program adv. com. Ctr. for Particle Astrophysics, 1995-2000; program organizer Inst. for Nuc. Theory, 1996; grad. program rev. com. physics dept. U. Calif. San Diego, 1996; mem. HDF archive panel Space Telescope Sci. Inst., 1996, cycle 7 TAC and panel chair, 1996; mem. proposal rev. panel NASA, 1998, mission definition team LISA, 1998—; bd. govs. Astrophys. Rsch. Consortium, 1998—; chair dean search com. UW Coll. Arts and Scis., 1998-99; panel on theory, computation and data exploration in astronomy and astrophysics Astronomy and Astrophysics Survey Com., NRC, 1999; lectr. in field; others. Recipient Humboldt Rsch. award Max Planck Inst. for Astrophysics, 1999—; Enrico Fermi fellow U. Chgo., 1980-81, NSF postdoctoral fellow, Cambridge, Eng., 1981-82, Bantrell prize fellow in theoretical astrophysics Calif. Inst. Tech., 1982-85, Alfred P. Sloan Found. fellow, 1986-91, vis. fellow Inst. Astronomy, Cambridge U., 1987, 89, 94; grantee NASA and NSF, 1987—, UW Royalty Rsch. Fund, 1992, Murdock Charitable Trust, 1996-98. Office: C319 Physics/Astronomy PO Box 351580 Seattle WA 98195-1580 Office Fax: 206-685-0403. E-mail: hogan@astro.washington.edu.

HOGAN, CURTIS JULE, labor union administrator, industrial relations specialist, consultant; b. Greeley, Kans., July 25, 1926; s. Charles Leo and Anna Malene (Rousselo) H.; m. Lois Jean Ecord, Apr. 23, 1955; children: Christopher James, Michael Sean, Patrick Marshall, Kathleen Marie, Kerry Joseph. BS in Indsl. Rels., Rockhurst Coll., 1950; postgrad., Georgetown U., 1955, U. Tehran, Iran, 1955-57. With Gt. Lakes Pipeline Co., Kansas City, Mo., 1950-55; with Internat. Fedn. Petroleum and Chem. Workers, Denver, 1955-85, gen. sec., 1973-85; pres. Internat. Labor Rels. Svcs., Inc., 1976—. Cons. in field; lectr. Rockhurst Coll., Kansas City, 1951-52. Contbr. articles to profl. publs. Served with U.S. Army, 1945-46. Mem. Internat. Indsl. Rels. Assn., Indsl. Rels. Rsch. Assn., Oil Chem. and Atomic Workers Internat. Union. Office: Internat Fed Petroleum Chem Workers 435 S Newport Way Denver CO 80224-1321

HOGAN, KATHLEEN, computer software company executive; m. Ron Hogan; 1 child, James. BA magna cum laude, Harvard Univ.; MBA, Stanford Univ. Develop. mgr., sr. tech. mktg. mgr. Oracle Corp.; ptnr. McKinsey & Co.; v.p. CPE & worldwide field ops. Microsoft Corp., Redmond, Wash., 2003—06, corp. v.p. worldwide customer svc., support & CPE, 2006—. Mem. Women in Mgmt. bd. Grad Sch. Bus., Stanford Univ. Office: Microsoft Corp 1 Microsoft Way Redmond WA 98052-6399

HOGAN, MICHAEL R(OBERT), judge; b. Oregon City, Oreg., Sept. 24, 1946; married; 3 children. AB, U. Oreg. Honors Coll., 1968; JD, Georgetown U., 1971. Bar: Oreg. 1971, U.S. Ct. Appeals (9th cir.) 1971. Law clk. to chief judge U.S. Dist. Ct. Oreg., Portland, 1971-72; assoc. Miller, Anderson, Nash, Yerke and Wiener, Portland, 1972-73; magistrate judge U.S. Dist. Ct. Oreg., Eugene, 1973-91, dist. judge, 1991—, chief judge, 1995—; bankduptcy judge U.S. Dist. Oreg., Eugene, 1973-80. Mem. ABA, Oreg. State Bar Assn. Office: US Courthouse 211 E 7th Ave Eugene OR 97401-2773

HOGAN, STEVEN L., lawyer; b. LA, Aug. 31, 1953; s. Kenneth Carlton Hogan and Ninon Michelle Kingsley; m. Debra Karen Garshfield, July 27, 1975; children: Rebecca Sarah, Cheryl Lee. AB magna cum laude, UCLA, 1975; JD, U. So. Calif., 1978. Bar: Calif. 1978, U.S. Ct. Appeals (9th cir.) 1979,U.S. Dist. Ct. (cen. dist.) Calif. 1979, U.S. Supreme Ct. 2000, U.S. Ct. Appeals (3d cir.) 2002, U.S. Dist. Ct. (so. dist., ea. dist., no. dist.) Calif. 1985. Assoc. Anderson, McPharlin & Conners, LA, 1978-80; ptnr. Bryan Cave, LA, 1980-95; shareholder Lurie, Zepeda, Schmalz & Hogan, Beverly Hills, Calif., 1995—. V.p. Beverly Hills Estate Planning Coun. Recipient Am. Jurisprudence award in bus. organs. and advanced constl. law; named a Super Lawyer of So. Calif. Mem. LA County Bar Assn., Order of Coif, Phi Beta Kappa, Phi Gamma Mu, Water Buffalo Club. Office: Lurie Zepeda Schmalz & Hogan 9107 Wilshire Blvd Ste 800 Beverly Hills CA 90210-5533 Office Phone: 310-274-8700. Business E-Mail: shogan@lurie-zepeda.com.

HOGANS, MACK L., paper company executive; BS in Forestry, U. Mich.; MS in Forest Resources, U. Wash. Forester, govt. affairs mgr. Weyerhaeuser Co., Tacoma, Wash., 1979-90, v.p. govt. affairs, 1990-95, sr. v.p. corp. affairs, 1995—. Chair Weyerhaeuser Co. Found.; bd. dirs. Wash. Coun. Internat. Trade. Bd. dirs. U. Puget Sound, Zion Preparatory Acad., Pub. Affairs Coun., Discovery Inst., Nature Conservancy. Office: Weyerhaeuser Co PO Box 9777 Federal Way WA 98063-9777

HOGARTY, CHARLES J., automotive executive; b. 1941; Pres. Keystone Automotive Industries, Inc., Pomona, Calif., 1987—, COO, 1987-97, CEO, 1997—, also bd. dirs. Mem. Aftermarket Body Parts Assn. (bd. dirs. 1984-93, pres. 1989, chmn. 1990). Office: Keystone Automotive Industry Inc 700 E Bonita Ave Pomona CA 91767

HOGLUND, RICHARD FRANK, research and technical executive; b. Chgo., Mar. 22, 1933; s. Reuben Ture and Margaret Mabel (Thayer) H.; m. Arlene Diana Bieniasz, Jan. 7, 1956 (dec. Mar. 1986); children: Terrence, David, Mark; m. Susan Annette Vee, Feb. 10, 1987. Student, Valparaiso U., 1949-51; BS in Mech. Engring, Northwestern U., 1954, MS in Mech. Engring. (Gen. Electric fellow), 1955, PhD (Royal Cabell fellow), 1960. Dept. head Ford Aeronutronic, 1960-63; assoc. prof. aerospace engring., lab. dir. Purdue U., 1963-69; prof. aerospace engring. Ga. Inst. Tech., 1969; chief scientist Atlantic Research Corp., 1969-72; head ocean monitoring and control, chief advanced concepts tech. Def. Advanced Research Research Projects Agy., 1972-75; staff scientist Phys. Dynamics, Inc., Arlington, Va., 1975-77; v.p. Ops. Research, Inc., Silver Spring, Md., 1977; dep. asst. sec. of navy for research and advanced tech. and concepts Dept. Navy, Washington, 1977-80; sr. v.p. ORI, Inc., Silver Spring, Md., 1980-89; exec. v.p. Arete Assocs., Arlington, Va., 1989-90; staff v.p. undersea warfare Gen. Dynamics Corps., 1990-92; cons., 1993—. Contbr. articles to profl. jours.; editor: Energy Sources and Energy Conversion, 1967. Recipient Def. Meritorious Civilian Service medal Dept. Def., 1975 Home and Office: 76000 Frank Sinatra Dr 697 Palm Desert CA 92211-5031

HOI, SAMUEL CHUEN-TSUNG, academic administrator; b. Hong Kong, Mar. 25, 1958; came to U.S., 1975; JD, Columbia U. Bar: N.Y. 1983. Dir.-Paris Campus Parsons Sch. Design, 1988—91; dean Corcoran Coll. Art & Design, Washington, 1991—2000; pres. Otis Coll. Art & Design, LA, 2000—. Mem., bd. dirs. Leadership Washington, 1996. Mem. Assn. Ind. Colls. of Art and Design, Nat. Assn. Schs. Art and Design (bd. dirs.). Office: Office of the President Otis Coll Art & Design 9045 Lincoln Blvd Los Angeles CA 90045

HOLBROOK, CONNIE C., lawyer; b. 1946; BA, Brigham Young U.; JD, U. Utah. Bar: 1974. Asst. sec. Mountain Fuel Supply Co., staff atty., v.p., sec.; sr. v.p. gen. counsel, corp. sec. Questar Corp., Salt Lake City, 1993—. Bd. dirs. United Way, Salt Lake City. Mem.: ABA, Am. Soc. Corp. Secs.

HOLBROOK, MEGHAN ZANOLLI, fundraiser, public relations specialist, political organization chairman; b. NYC, Oct. 12, 1949; m. James R. Holbrook. BS in English and Edn., U. Tenn., 1971, postgrad., 1978-83. Dir. ancillary svcs. Ridgeview Psychiat. Hosp., Oak Ridge, Tenn., 1971-83; therapist The Children's Ctr., Salt Lake City, 1985-86; mgr. corp. contbns. Sundance Inst. and Film Festival, Salt Lake City, 1989-91; fund raising and pub. rels. cons. Salt Lake City, 1992—. Fundraiser congl. campaign Wayne Owens, 1986, bus. liaison, 1986-88; fin. dir. gubernatorial campaign Ted Wilson, 1988, mayoral campaign Deedee Corradini, 1991; campaign mgr. gubernatorial campaign Stewart Hanson, 1991-92; del. Dem. Nat. Conv., 1996; chair Utah State Dem. Party, 1996—; mem. bd. dirs. Sundance Inst., 1989—, Inst. at Deer Valley, 1995—; mem. Utah Air Travel Commn., 1996—; mem. pres.'s adv. com. on arts Kennedy Ctr.,

Washington, 1996—. Mem. Assn. State Dem. Chairs (exec. com. 1998—). Home: 775 Hilltop Rd Salt Lake City UT 84103-3311 Office: 455 S 300 E Ste 102 Salt Lake City UT 84111-3222

HOLDEN, FREDERICK DOUGLASS, JR., lawyer; b. Stockton, Calif., Nov. 21, 1949; s. Frederick Douglass and Sarah Frances (Young) H.; m. Patricia Brierton, June 25, 1988; children: Elizabeth, Andrew. BA, U. Calif., Santa Barbara, 1971; JD, U. Calif., Davis, 1974. Bar: Calif. 1974, DC 1996, US Dist. Ct. (no., ctrl., ea. and so. dists.) Calif. 1974, US Ct. Appeals (9th cir.) 1974, US Ct. Appeals (fed. cir.) 2004, US Dist. Ct. DC 1996, US Supreme Ct. 2001. Assoc. Brobeck, Phleger & Harrison LLP, San Francisco, 1974-81, ptnr., 1981—2003; chair bench-bar liaison com. U.S. Bankruptcy Ct. No. Dist. Calif., 2001—02; ptnr. Orrick, Herrington & Sutcliffe, LLP, 2003—. Mem. faculty Practising Law Inst., 1990; spkr. Nat. Conf. Bankruptcy Judges, 1987, 91, Banking Law Inst., 1986, Calif. Continuing Legal Edn. of Bar, Calif., 1983-85, Calif. State Bar, 1993; bd. dirs. Bay Area Bankruptcy Forum. Mng. editor U. Calif. Davis Law Rev., 1974. Fellow Am. Coll. Bankruptcy; mem. ABA (bus. bankruptcy com., spkr. 1991, 95), Calif. Bar Assn. (commendation 1983), San Francisco Bar Assn. (cert. appreciation 1985, 88, 90, 95, chair 2004), Internat. Bar Assn., Turnaround Mgmt. Assn. (dir., sec. 1994-96), Am. Bankruptcy Inst., Marin Audubon Soc. (chair fin. and membership, bd. dirs. 2003-08), San Francisco Yacht Club, Sigma Pi (pres. 1970). Democrat. Avocations: triathlons, skiing, sailing, mountain climbing. Home: 140 Bella Vista Ave Belvedere CA 94920-2466 Office: Orrick Herrington & Sutcliffe LLP The Orrick Bldg 405 Howard St San Francisco CA 94105-2669 Home Phone: 415-435-2702; Office Phone: 415-773-5985. Business E-Mail: fholden@orrick.com.

HOLDEN, RIC R., state legislator, farmer, rancher; b. Spokane, Wash., Aug. 31, 1961; m. Jan Holden; 3 children. BA, Mont. State U., 1984. Farmer, rancher; ins. rep.; mem. Mont. Senate, Dist. 1, Helena, 1994—. Active Dawson County 4-H Clubs, ABC Baseball. Mem. Mont. Stock Growers Assn., Mont. Wool Growers Assn., NRA, Mont. Farm Bur., Dawnson County Livestock Prodn. Assn. Republican. Lutheran. Home: 164 Road 253 Glendive MT 59330-9438

HOLDEN, THOMAS E., Mayor, Oxnard, California; m. Lisa Knapp; children: Patrick, Jack, Nicholas. PhD, Southern Calif. Coll. Optometry, 1986. Pvt. practice Family Optometric Group, Oxnard, 1987—; councilman City of Oxnard, Calif., 1993—2002, mayor Calif., 2005—. Bd. mem. St. John's and Pleasant Valley Regional hosps. Liaison Ventura Coun. Governments, South Coast Area Transit, Ventura County Air Pollution Control Dist., Big Ind. Cities Excess Pool Joint Powers Authority; rep. Graffiti Task Force, Econ. Devel. Corp. Oxnard, Water Task Force, Downtown Improvement Task Force, Ormond Beach Property Oversight Ad Hoc Com., Channel Islands Harbor Task Force, Oxnard Plain/RiverPark Reclamation, Recharge Joint Power Authority. Named Disting. Citizen of Yr., Knights of Columbus. Mem.: Rotary Internat. (Paul Harris award), Tri-County Optometric Soc., St. John's Humanitarians, Boys and Girls Club Oxnard and Port Hueneme (former pres., Nat. Man & Youth award). Mailing: City Council Off 305 W Third St 4th Fl Oxnard CA 93030 Office Phone: 805-385-7430. E-mail: drtomholden@aol.com.*

HOLDER, HAROLD D., public health administrator, communications specialist, educator; b. Raleigh, NC, Aug. 9, 1939; AB in History and Journalism, Samford U., 1961; MA in Comm., Syracuse U., 1962, PhD, 1965. Dir. Comm. Rsch. Ctr., asst. prof. Dept. Journalism and Oral Comm. Baylor U., Tex., 1965-67; rsch. scientist divsn. rsch., dir. systems analysis and program evaluation N.C. Dept. Mental Health, Raleigh, 1967-69; assoc. prof., mem. grad. faculty dept. Sociology N.C. State U., Raleigh, 1967-75; site mgr. The Human Ecology Inst., Wellesley, Mass., 1973-75, sr. scientist Chapel Hill, N.C., 1977-87, dir., 1980-87; mgr. devel. City of Portsmouth, Va., 1975-76; lectr. dept. Health Adminstrn. Sch. Pub. Health U. N.C., Chapel Hill, 1980-86; dir. prevention rsch. ctr. Pacific Inst. Rsch. and Evaluation, Berkeley, Calif., 1987—; lectr. health edn. program Sch. Pub. Health U. Calif., Berkeley, 1987—. Vis. prof. Newhouse Comm. Ctr., 1966, U. N.C. Chapel Hill, 1979-80; guest lectr. Sch. Pub. Health U. Carolina, Chapel Hill, 1967-68, dept. Psychiatry, 1967-68; instr. advanced exec. systems N.C. Dept. Mental Health, 1967-69; program coord. John Ulmstead Disting. Lecture Series, 1970; ednl. evaluator Syracuse (N.Y.) Sch. Dist., 1971-73; trainer systems approaches and model bldg., dynamo computer simulation, United Meth. Ch., N.Y., 1972-73; sr. analyst Caseway, Inc., Brockton, Mass., 1977-78; mem. psycho-social internal review group Office Sci. Affairs Nat. Inst. Alcohol Abuse and Alcoholism, 1983-87, chmn. 1986-87; cons. Nat. Inst. Alcohol Abuse and Alcoholism, Washington, Tex. Ednl. Agy., Austin, Ctrl. Tex. Regional Edn. Ctr., James Connally Tech. Inst., Waco, Tex., Tech. Edn. Rsch. Ctr., Cambridge, Mass., U. N.C., Chapel Hill, N.C. Dept. Health, Child Advocacy Ctr., Durham, United Meth. Ch., N.Y.C., NIMH, Svcs. Integration Tech. Inst., Boston, Learning Inst. N.C; presenter, chairperson numerous confs. Editor: Advances in Substance Abuse: Behavioral and Biological Rsch., 1987; co-editor: Monitoring Child Service Agencies: A Guide for Child Advocacy Groups, 1974, Control Issues in Alcohol Prevention: State and Local Designs for the 80s, 1984, OSAP Prevention Monograph 4: Research, Action and the Community: Experiences in the Prevention of Alcohol and Other Drug Problems, 1990, Community Prevention Trials for Alcohol Problems: Methodological Issues, 1992; mem. editorial bd. Alcohol Health and Research World, 1990—; contbr. chpts. to books, articles to profl. jours. Bd. dirs. Ctrl. Tex. Rsch. Coun., 1965-67. Newhouse Rsch. fellow Syracuse U., 1961-65. Mem. APHA (alcohol and drug sect.), Am. Sociol. Assn., Am. Assn. Pub. Opinion Rsch.Nat. Soc. Study Comm., Nat. Assn. Pub. Health Policy (mem. alcohol policy com., sec./treas. 1985-86), Soc. Gen. Systems Rsch. (nat. coms. social systems, health systems), Rsch. Soc. Alcoholism (com. nat. advocacy), Soc. Health Svcs. Rsch. Office: Prevention Research Center 1995 University Ave Ste 450 Berkeley CA 94704-5315

HOLDER, HAROLD DOUGLAS, SR., investor, hotel executive; b. Anniston, Ala., June 25, 1931; s. William Chester and Lucile (Kadle) H.; m. Anna Maria Yaccarino, 1996; children: Debra Holder Carnaroli, Harold Douglas Jr., Charlie Kadle. Student, Anniston Bus. Coll., 1949, Jacksonville State U., 1954-57, Druitt Sch. Speech, 1962. Dept. mgr. Sears, Roebuck & Co., Anniston, 1954-57, merchandising mgr. Atlanta, 1957-59, dir. coll. recruiting, 1959-61, dir. exec. devel. program, 1961, asst. personnel dir., 1962-63, store mgr. Cocoa, Fla., 1965-67, Ocala, Fla., 1963-65, opers. zone mgr. Atlanta, 1967-68, asst. gen. mgr. mdse., 1968-69, sales promotion mgr. So. area, 1968; pres., bd. dirs. Cunningham Drug Stores, Inc., Detroit, 1969-70; v.p. Interstate Stores, 1971; pres., bd. dirs. Rahall Communications Corp., 1971-73; chmn. bd., chief exec. officer, dir. Am. Agronomics Corp., 1973-86; pres. Harold Holder Leasing; mng. dir. The Holder Group, Inc., 1987—. CEO, bd. dirs. Cutler Mfg. Corp., 1989-2000, Atlas Aircraft Corp., 1987-2000; mem. exec. com., bd. dirs. Coastland Corp., Fla., 1979-84; pres., bd. dirs. Golden Harvest, Inc., 1976-88; bd. dirs., treas. Dome Products, Inc., 1989-2000; CEO Casino Mgmt. Svcs. Internat., 1999—, Stockmen's Hotel & Casino, Red Garter Hotel & Casino, Comml. Hotel & Casino, Scoreboard Sports Lounge, The Holder Group Wigwam, LLC, 2005; chmn., CEO The Holder Hospitality Group, Inc.; CEO Silver Club Hotel & Casino, El Capitan Resort Casino, Sharkey's Nugget Casino, Sundance Casino, Model "T" Resort Casino, Charlie Holder's Casino, 2003-07, Fernley Truck-Inn and Casino, Joe's Tavern; chmn. New Dawn Resorts, Ltd., Accra, Ghana; chmn. The Holder Group Vending Co. Author: Don't Shoot, I'm Only a Trainee, 1975. Chmn., bd. dirs. Miracle, Inc., Brevard County; chmn. United Appeal, Ocala, Fla., 1964, Cocoa, Fla., 1966; bd. dirs. United Way Hillsborough County (Fla.); chmn. Heart Fund Drive, Ocala, 1964, Marion (Fla.) Com. of 100; bd. dirs. So. Coll. Placement Assn., Am. Acad. Achievement; bd. dirs. Marion chpt. ARC, Opera Arts Assn.; exec. com. Share, U. Fla.; bd. trustees U. Tampa; chmn. bd. trustees, trustee emeritus Eckerd Coll. With USMC, 1950-53. Recipient Disting. Svc. award, Marion County 4-H Club, 1965, Golden Plate award, 1983, Champion of Higher Edn. award, 1982, Fla. NAACP Humanitarian award, 1984, Patriotic Employer award, US Dept. Def, 2005, Employer of Yr. award, Nev. Disabled Veterans Large; named Harold D. Holder chair of Internat. Bus. and Fin., Eckerd Coll., Nev. Hotelier of the Yr., 2004. Mem.: Young Pres. Orgn. (past chmn. Fla. chpt.), C. of C. (chmn. beautification com., retail bus. com.), Chief Execs. Forum, Omicron Delta Kappa. Episcopalian. Office: The Holder Hospitality Group Inc 1040 Victorian Ave Sparks NV 89431-4923 Office Phone: 775-358-4771.

HOLDING, R(OBERT) EARL, oil industry executive; b. Salt Lake City, Utah; m. Carol Holding; 3 children. BA/BS, U. Utah. Pres., CEO Sinclair Oil Corp., Salt Lake City, 1976—. Owner Sun Valley Resort, Idaho, 1977—, Grand Am. Hotel, Salt Lake City. Named one of Forbes' Richest Americans, 1999—, World's Richest People, Forbes mag., 2002—. Avocation: skiing. Office: Sinclair Oil Corp PO Box 30825 Salt Lake City UT 84130

HOLLAND, DAVID K., treasurer; Grad., Brigham Young U.; MBA, San Jose State U. With Apple Computer; head capital markets sales team Paribas Capital Markets, NYC; joined Cisco Sys. Inc., San Jose, Calif., 1998, v.p., treas., 2000—, bd. dirs., 2006—. Bd. dirs. Motricity. Office: Cisco Systems, Inc 170 W Tasman Dr San Jose CA 95134

HOLLAND, GARY NORMAN, ophthalmologist, educator; b. Long Beach, Calif., July 30, 1953; s. Richard L. and Edith (Hewson) H. MD, UCLA, 1979. Diplomate Am. Bd. Ophthalmology, Nat. Bd. Med. Examiners; lic. MD, Calif., Ga. Intern in internal medicine UCLA, 1979-80; resident in ophthalmology Jules Stein Eye Inst., LA, 1980-83; fellowship in uveitis rsch. Proctor Found. U. Calif. San Francisco, 1983-84; cornea fellowship Emory U. Med. Sch., Atlanta, 1984-85; prof. ophthalmology Jules Stein Eye Inst. UCLA, 1985—. Assoc. editor Am. Jour. Ophthalmology, 1993—. Mem. Am. Uveitis Soc. Office: UCLA 100 Stein Plz Los Angeles CA 90095-7003

HOLLAND, H. RUSSEL, federal judge; b. 1936; m. Diane Holland; 3 children. BBA, U. Mich., 1958, LLB, 1961. With Alaska Ct. System, Anchorage, 1961, U.S. Atty.'s Office, Dept. Justice, Anchorage, 1963-65; assoc. Stevens & Savage, Anchorage, 1965-66; ptnr. Stevens, Savage, Holland, Erwin & Edwards, Anchorage, 1967-68; sole practice Anchorage, 1968-70; ptnr. Holland & Thornton, Anchorage, 1970-78, Holland, Thornton & Trefry, Anchorage, 1978, Holland & Trefry, Anchorage, 1978-84, Trefry & Brecht, Anchorage, 1984; judge U.S. Dist. Ct. Alaska, Anchorage, 1984—. Mem. ABA, Alaska Bar Assn., Anchorage Bar Assn. Office: US Dist Ct 222 W 7th Ave Unit 54 Anchorage AK 99513-7504

HOLLAND, JEFFREY R., religious organization administrator; b. St. George, Utah, Dec. 3, 1940; s. Frank D. and Alice (Bentley) H.; m. Patricia Terry, June 7, 1963; children: Matthew, Mary, David. BS, Brigham Young U., 1965, MA, 1966; PhD, Yale U., 1973. Dean religious instrn. Brigham Young U., 1974-76; commr. Latter Day Saints Ch. Ednl. System, 1976-80; pres. Brigham Young U., 1980-89; gen. authority, mem. 1st Quorum of the 70 LDS Ch., 1989-94; Apostle Quorum of the Twelve, 1994—. Former bd. dirs. Deseret News Pub. Co., Key Bank of Utah, Key Bancshares of Utah, Inc. Author: (books) However Long & Hard the Road, 1993, Christ & the New Covenant: The Messianic Message of the Book of Mormon, 1997, Shepherds, Why This Jubilee?, 2000, Of Souls, Symbols & Sacraments, 2001, Trusting Jesus, 2003; co-author (with Patricia T Holland): On Earth as It Is in Heaven, 1993. Mem. Am. Assn. Presidents of Ind. Colls. and Univs. (past pres.), Nat. Assn. Ind. Colls. and Univs. (former bd. dirs.), Am. Council Edn., Phi Kappa Phi. Office: LDS Church 47 E South Temple Salt Lake City UT 84150-1200

HOLLAND, MICHAEL JAMES, computer services administrator; b. NYC, Nov. 20, 1950; s. Robert Frederick and Virginia June (Wilcox) H.; Anita Garay, Jan. 5, 1981 (Aug. 1989); 1 child, Melanie. BA in Comparative Lit., Bklyn. Coll., 1972. Enlisted USN, 1975, advanced to CPO, 1989, field med. technician Okinawa, Japan, 1976-77, Camp Pendleton, Calif., 1978-79, clin. supr. naval hosp. Subic Bay, Philippines, 1979-81; dept. head Tng. Ctr. USMCR, Johnson City, Tenn., 1981-84, clin. supr. no. tng. area Okinawa, 1984-85, clin. supr. 3d marine air wing Camp Pendleton, 1985-88; cons. naval regional med. commd. USN, San Diego, 1988-90, system analyst naval med. info mgmt. ctr. detachment, 1990-92, computer svcs. adminstr. naval hosp. Guam, 1993-95, ret., 1995; svc. rep. AT&T West, 1997—2006. Mem. Fleet Res. Assn., Comm. Workers Am., Nat. City C. of C. (com. 1989-91). Home: 4375 46th St 7 San Diego CA 92115-4326 Home Phone: 619-584-2044.

HOLLAND, WAYNE, JR., political organization administrator; Staff rep. United Steel Workers, Utah and No. Nev.; regional organizer Rocky Mountain for John Kerry, 2004; chmn. Utah State Dem. Party, 2005—. Democrat. Office: Utah Dem Party 455 S 300 E Suite 301 Salt Lake City UT 84111 Office Phone: 801-328-1212. Office Fax: 801-328-1238. E-mail: wholland@utdemocrats.org.

HOLLANDER, DANIEL, gastroenterologist, educator; Student, UCLA, 1960; MD, Baylor U., 1964. Diplomate Am. Bd. Internal Medicine, Am. Bd. Gastroenterology. Intern Phila. Gen. Hosp., 1964-65; resident in internal medicine Med. Ctr., U. Kans., Kansas City, 1965-67; NIH rsch. fellow in gastroenterology U. Wash., Seattle, 1967-69; asst. prof. medicine Albany (N.Y.) Med. Coll., Union U., 1971-73, assoc. prof., 1973; assoc. prof. medicine, head div. gastroenterology Wayne State U., Detroit, 1973-77, prof. medicine, head div. gastroenterology, 1977—94, U. Calif., Irvine, 1978-94, prof. physiology and biophysics, 1981-94, assoc. dean for rsch. and program devel. Coll. Medicine, 1984-85, assoc. dean for acad. affairs, 1985-89, sr. assoc. dean for clin. affairs, 1989-91, chief gastroenterology Irvine Med. Ctr., 1979-94; exec. dean Sch. of Medicine U. Kans., Kansas City, 1994—96; chief med. officer Sierra Pacific Network, San Francisco, 1996-98; prof. medicine U. Calif., San Francisco, 1996-98; pres., CEO Harbor-UCLA Rsch. and Edn. Inst., 1998-2001; prof. medicine UCLA, 1998—, dir. scientific and med. initiatives and inflammatory bowel disease grants, the Broad Found., 2001—. Attending physician, attending gastroenterologist Albany Med. Ctr. Hosp., 1971-73; chief gastroenterology svc., attending physician Harper Hosp., Detroit, 1973-78; cons. in gastroenterology Children's, Detroit Gen. and VA hosps., 1973-78; chief gastroenterology VA Med. Ctr., Long Beach, Calif., 1978-80; chmn. Gastrointestinal Gerontology Rsch. Group, 1988-89; vis. scientist dept. molecular medicine U. Auckland, New Zealand, 1990-91; vis. prof., invited speaker numerous other univs., profl. meetings, confs. Author: (with G. Gitnick, N. Kaplowitz, I.M. Samloff, L.J. Schoenfield) Principles and Practice of Gastroenterology and Hepatology, 1988, (with A. Tarnawski) Gastic Cytoprotection—A Clinician's Guide, 1989, (with Porro G. Bianchi) Treatment of Digestive Disease with Sucralfate, 1989; mem. editl. bd., reviewer Can. Jour. Gastroenterology; contbr. numerous articles, revs. to profl. jours., book chpt. With USAF, 1969-71. Major USAF, 1969—71. Calif. Heart Assn. rsch. fellow, 1960; Fogarty Sr. Internat. fellow Oxford (Eng.) U., 1984-85; grantee NIH, Nat. Inst. on Aging, Nat. Insts. Arthritis, Metabolism and Digestive Diseases, Skillman Found., VA, Goldsmith Found., Internat. Pharm. Products. Mem. ACP (A. Blaine traveling scholar 1973), Am. Fedn. for Clin. Rsch. (pres. Midwestern sect. 1979-80), Am. Gastroent. Assn., Am. Physiol. Soc., Am. Soc. for Clin. Investigation, Orange County Gastroenterology Assn. (pres. 1986-87), Brit. Soc. Gastroenterology, European Assn. Gastroenterology, Western Assn. Physicians, Western Gut Club (pres. 1981-82), Alpha Omega Alpha. Office: The Eli and Edythe L Broad Found 10900 Wilshire Blvd 12th Fl Los Angeles CA 90024-6532

HOLLANDER, NANCY, lawyer; b. NYC, Mar. 10, 1944; BA with honors, U. Mich., 1965; JD magna cum laude, U. N.Mex., 1978. Bar: N.Mex. 1978, US Dist. Ct. (dist. N.Mex.) 1979, US Ct. Appeals (10th cir.) 1980, US Supreme Ct. 1982, US Ct. Appeals (4th cir.) 1984, US Ct. Appeals (9th cir.) 1986, US Dist. Ct. (we. dist. Tenn.) 1988, US Dist. Ct. (we. dist. Tex.) 1990, US Ct. Appeals (6th cir.) 1990, US Ct. Appeals (2nd cir.) 1991, US Ct. Appeals (8th cir.) 1992, So. Ute Tribal Ct., US Ct. Appeals (5th cir.) 1993, US Dist. Ct. (no. dist. Ill.) 1996, US Dist. Ct. (no. dist. Tex.) 2004. Editor, photographer Medalist Pubs., Chgo., 1968; freelance editor and photographer Chgo., 1969—71; exec. dir. N.Mex. Civil Liberties Union, 1971—75; asst. pub. defender N.Mex. State Pub. Defender Dept., 1978—79; atty. Freedman, Boyd, Daniels, Hollander, Goldberg & Ives, P.A., Albuquerque, 1980—, ptnr., 1983—. Adj. prof. law evidence/trial practice U. N.Mex. Sch. Law, Albuquerque, 1983—; bd. regents Nat. Criminal Def. Coll., 1985—; faculty mem. Gerry Spence's Trial Lawyers' Coll., 1994—98; prog. coord. Russian Jury Trial Project, 1995—97. Contbr. articles to profl. publs. Recipient Charlie Driscoll award, Dismas House, 1997, Henrietta Pettijohn award, N.Mex. Women's Bar Assn., 2000, Profl. Lawyer of Yr. award, N.Mex. Trial Lawyers Assn., 2006; named one of Top 50 Women Litigators, Nat. Law Jour., 2001. Fellow: Am. Coll. Trial Lawyers, Am. Bd. Criminal Lawyers; mem.: Internat. Criminal Bar (mem. governing coun. 2003), Internat. Criminal Def. Attys. Assn. (bd. dirs. 2002—), NACDL (pres. 1992—93), Am. Inn Ct. (barrister 1989—92), State Bar N.Mex. (criminal law sect.), Order of the Coif. Office: Freedman Boyd Daniels Hollander Goldberg & Ives PA 200 3rd St NW Ste 700 Albuquerque NM 87102 Office Phone: 505-842-9960. E-mail: nh@fbdlaw.com.

HOLLANDSWORTH, ROY, state legislator; Mem. Dist. 28 Mont. House of Reps., 2008—. Republican. Office: Montana House of Representatives PO Box 200400 Helena MT 59620-0400 Mailing: 1463 Prairie Dr Brady MT 59416-8928 Home Phone: 406-627-2446; Office Phone: 406-444-4800. Office Fax: 406-444-4825. Personal E-mail: hgrain@3riversdbs.net.

HOLLANDSWORTH, TODD MATHEW, professional baseball player; b. Dayton, Ohio, Apr. 20, 1973; Baseball player L.A. Dodgers, 1995—2000, Colo. Rockies, 2000—01, Tex. Rangers, 2002, Fla. Marlins, 2003, Chgo. Cubs, 2004—05, Atlanta Braves, 2005—. Named Nat. League Rookie of the Yr. Baseball Writer's Assn. of Am., 1996.

HÖLLDOBLER, BERTHOLD KARL, zoologist; b. Erling-Andechs, Germany, June 25, 1936; came to U.S., 1973; s. Karl and Maria (Russmann) H.; m. Friederike Probst, Feb. 9, 1980; children: Jakob, Stefan, Sebastian. Dr. rer. nat., U. Wurzburg, 1965; Dr. habil., U. Frankfurt a.M., 1969; D (hon.), U. Konstanz, 2000. Prof. zoology U. Frankfurt a.M., 1971-72; prof. biology Harvard U., Cambridge, Mass., 1973-90, Alexander Agassiz prof. zoology, 1982-90; prof. U. Wurzburg, Germany, 1989—. Adj. prof. U. Ariz., Tucson; rsch. assoc. Harvard U.; Andrew D. White prof. at large Cornell U., 2002—; Found. prof. Ariz. State U., Tempe, 2004—. Author: (with Edward O. Wilson) The Ants, 1990 (Pulitzer Prize for gen. non-fiction 1991), (with E.O. Wilson) Journey to the Arts, (Shortlisted for the Rhone-Poulenc Sci. Book prize, 1995, Phi Beta Kappa prize, 1995). John Simon Guggenheim fellow, 1980; recipient Sr. Scientist award Alexander von Humboldt Found., 1986-87, Gottfried Wilhelm Leibniz prize, 1989, Phi Beta Kappa prize (with E.O. Wilson) 1995, Karl Ritter von Frisch medal and Sci. prize, German Zool. Soc., 1996, Körber-prize for European Sci., 1996, Benjamin Franklin, Wilhelm v. Humboldt Prize of the German Amer. Acad. Coun. (GAAC), 1999, Werner Heisenberg medal Alexander v. Humboldt Found., Alfried Krupp Sci. prize, 2004, Treviranus medal Soc. German Biologists, 2006; named to Bavarian Maximilian Order, 2003. Fellow AAAS, Am. Animal Behavior Soc.; mem. Nat. Acad. of Sci. (fgn. mem.), Am. Acad. Sci., German Acad. der Naturforscher Leopoldina, Bayerische Acad. der Wissenschaften, Acad. Europaea, Berlin-Brandenburgische Acad., Am. Philos. Soc. (fgn. mem.), Bundesverdienstkrenz (Nat. Merit medal Germany 2000). Office: Sch Life Scis Ariz State U PO Box 874501 Tempe AZ 85287 Office Phone: 480-727-8415. Business E-Mail: bertholl@asu.edu.

HOLLEMAN, MARIAN ISABEL, librarian, educator; b. Toronto, Ont., Can., July 23, 1923; came to U.S., 1961; d. Arnott Martin and Etta Margaret (Freeman) P.; m. Willard Roy Holleman (dec. 1969). BA, U. Toronto, 1945, MLS, 1946, MA, 1948. Libr. Acad. Medicine, Toronto, 1947-61, UCLA Biomed. Libr., 1962-63, Bishop's Sch., La Jolla, Calif., 1963-66, San Diego Coll. for Women, 1966-73, U. San

Diego Copley Libr., 1973-88, libr. emeritus, 1988—; libr. James S. Copley Libr., La Jolla, 1989—. Pres. San Diego chpt. Spl. Librs. Assn., 1968, Toronto chpt., 1950's; conv. chmn. Med. Libr. Assn., Toronto, 1959. Editor Sci. Meetings jour., 1962; contbr. articles to profl. jours. Recipient Murray Gottlieb Essay prize Med. Libr. Assn., 1957, Twin award YWCA, San Diego, 1988. Avocations: gardening, needlepoint.

HOLLENDER, LARS GÖSTA, dental educator; b. Veinge, Sweden, Oct. 22, 1933; arrived in U.S., 1984; s. Gunnar Yngve and Astrid Margareta (Andersson) H.; m. Gunnel Charlotta Bergdahl, May 19, 1956 (div. 1975); children: Peter, Marie, Lena, Stefan; m. Sheridan Ellen Houston, Apr. 8, 1989; 1 child, Ashley Ellen. DDS, Sch. Dentistry, Malmö, Sweden, 1958, PhD, 1964. Diplomate Am. Bd. Oral and Maxillofacial Radiology. Assoc. prof. Sch. Dentistry, Malmö, 1964-68, prof., chair Göteborg, Sweden, 1969-87; prof., dir. U. Wash. Sch. Dentistry, Seattle, 1988—. Sec. gen. Internat. Assn. Dentomaxillofacial Radiology, 1974-85; vis. prof. UCLA Sch. Dentistry, 1980-82, U. Wash. Sch. Dentistry, 1984-87; sec./treas. Am. Bd. Oral and Maxillofacial Radiology, 1992-94, pres., 1995, councillor, 1996—. Editor-in-chief Odontologist Revy, 1964-69; contbr. over 100 chpts. to books and articles to profl. jours. Recipient Rsch. prize South Swedish Dental Soc., 1964, Rsch. prize Swedish Dental Assn., 1965, Elander Rsch. prize Gothenburg Dental Soc., 1976. Fellow Am. Acad. Oral and Maxillofacial Radiology (pres. 1997-98); mem. ADA (mem. review com. for OMFR commn. on dental accreditation 1999—), Internat. Assn. Dental and Maxillofacial Radiology (hon.), Australian Maxillofacial Radiology Soc. (hon.), Wash. State Dental Assn., King County Dental Assn. Avocations: reading, golf, cooking, travel, music. Office: Univ Wash Sch Dentistry PO Box 356370 Seattle WA 98195-6370 Office Phone: 206-543-0615. E-mail: larsholl@u.washington.edu.

HOLLERAN, JOHN W., lawyer; b. Poughkeepsie, NY, June 17, 1954; BA, Gonzaga U., 1976, JD, 1979. Bar: Wash. 1979, Idaho, 1980, Calif. 1987. Counsel Boise (Idaho) Cascade Corp., 1979-83, assoc. gen. counsel, 1983-91, v.p., gen. counsel, 1991-96, sr. v.p., gen. counsel, 1996—. Chmn. Fibre Box Assn. Legal adv. com., 1989-91; bd. advisors Gonzaga U. Sch. Law, 1991—; mem. Idaho Vol. Lawyers Program Policy Coun., 1991—. Mem. ABA, Wash. State Bar Assn., Boise Bar Assn., Idaho State Bar, State Bar Calif., Am. Corp. Counsel Assn. Office: Boise Cascade Corp PO Box 50 1111 W Jefferson St Boise ID 83728-0071

HOLLEY, RICK R., lumber company executive; BS in Acctg. and Bus. Adminstrn., San Jose State U. Fin. mgmt. positions GE, 1974—83; asst. v.p. corp. audit Burlington No. Inc., 1983—85; v.p., CFO Plum Creek Timber Co., Seattle, 1985—94, pres., CEO, 1994—. Dir., past chmn. Am. Forest & Paper Assn.; mem. bd. gov. Nat. Assn. REITs Inc.; bd. mem. Am. Forest Found., World Forestry Ctr., Blethen Corp. Bd. mem. Children's Hosp. Found., Seattle; mem. vis. com. Univ. Wash. Sch. Med. Office: Plum Creek Timber 999 Third Ave Ste 4300 Seattle WA 98104 Office Phone: 206-467-3600. Office Fax: 206-467-3795.

HOLLIDAY, MATT, professional baseball player; b. Stillwater, Okla., Jan. 15, 1980; s. Tom Holliday; m. Leslee Holliday; children: Jackson, Ethan. Outfielder Colo. Rockies, 2004—08, Oakland Athletics, 2008—. Recipient Silver Slugger award, 2006—08; named Nat. League Championship Series MVP, 2007; named to Nat. League All-Star Team, 2006—08. Achievements include leading the National League in: batting average (.340), hits (216), doubles (50), RBI (137), extra base hits (92), 2007. Office: Oakland Athletics McAfee Coliseum 7000 Coliseum Way Oakland CA 94621

HOLLIDAY, THOMAS EDGAR, lawyer; b. Ft. Hood, Tex., July 3, 1948; s. William Lamont and Eileen (Fiebig) H.; children: Devon M., Trey S. BA, Stanford U., 1971; JD, U. So. Calif., 1974. Bar: Calif. 1974. Assoc. Gibson, Dunn & Crutcher LLP, LA, 1974-81; ptnr. Gibson, Dunn & Crutcher, LA, 1981—. Editor: (book, desk edition) Antitrust and Trade Regulations. Trustee S.W. Mus., L.A., 1981-98, bd. pres., 1995-97; trustee Found. for People, L.A., 1985-90, Clarkson U., 2000—; mem. L.A. Police Dept. Meml. Found. Bd. Fellow Am. Coll. Trial Lawyers; mem. Fed. Bar Assn. (exec. com. L.A. chpt. 1990, pres. 1998). Avocation: art. Office: Gibson Dunn & Crutcher LLP 333 S Grand Ave Ste 4400 Los Angeles CA 90071-3197

HOLLIGER, FREDRIC LEE, oil industry executive; b. Kansas City, Mo., Feb. 4, 1948; s. Ronald and Margorie (Klein) H.; m. Susan Lynn Harris, Oct. 6, 1972; children: Meredith, Allison, Lauren. BS in Petroleum Engring., U. Mo., Rolla, 1970; postgrad., U. Mich., 1978. Petroleum engr. Transok Pipeline Co., Tulsa, 1971; reservoir engr. No. Natural Gas Co., Omaha, 1972-73, project mgr. Lyons, Kans., 1974-76, area mgr. Great Bend, Kans., 1977-79, gen. mgr. mktg. Omaha, 1980-83, v.p. gas supply, 1984-85, v.p. mktg., 1986, pres., COO, 1987-88; sr. v.p. Giant Industries, Scottsdale, Ariz., 1989, exec. v.p., COO, 1989—2002, chmn., CEO, 2002—06. Dir. Giant Industries. Mem. Nat. Petroleum Refining Assn. (dir. 1990—). Desert Highlands Golf Club.

HOLLINGER, WILLIAM R., construction executive; BS in Bus. Adminstrn. summa cum laude, Calif. State U., Northridge. CPA. Auditor Pricewaterhouse, LA, 1981-87; mgr. control eval., audit Kaufman & Broad Hom, 1987, v.p., contr. Mem. Am. Inst. CPA, Ca. Soc. CPA. Office: Kaufman & Broad Home 10990 Wilshire Blvd Fl 7 Los Angeles CA 90024-3913

HOLLINGSWORTH, BOBBY G., career officer; m. Sue Taylor; children: Marc, Eric. Grad., Naval Flight Sch., 1965; BS in Elec. Engring., La. State Univ. Commd. comdr. USMCR, 1961, advanced through grades to maj. gen., 1999, internat. comml. airline pilot, mem., pilot; flight line officer Marine Attack Squadron 331, Beaufort, SC; embarkation officer Marine Attack Squadron 223, Chu Lai, Vietnam; landing signal officer Marine Aircraft Group 12, Chu Lai; air liaison officer 3d Marine Divsn., Phu Bai, Vietnam; asst. air liaison officer 3d Divsn. Staff; combat tactics flight instr. Marine Tng. Squadron 103, Yuma, Ariz.; capt. Boeing 767 Trans World Airlines; asst. ops. officer Marine Fighter Squadron 112, Dallas; exec. officer Marine Aircraft Group 42, Alameda, Calif.; comdr. Marine Attack Squadron 133, Alameda; asst. chief of staff 4th Marine Aircraft Wing, New Orleans; chief of staff II Marine Expeditionary Brigade, Camp Lejeune, NC; commdg. gen. USMCR Support Command, Kans. City, Mo., Fourth Force Svc. Support Group, New Orleans; dep. comdr. Jt. Task Force, Saudi Arabia; vice comdr. Marine Forces Pacific, Camp Smith, Hawaii; exec. dir. Nat. Com. Employer Support of Guard and Res., 2001—; pilot A-4 Skyhawk Fleet Marine Force Marine Corps Air Sta., Beaufort, SC; with VMA 223, MAG 12, Marine Aircraft Wing, Chu Lai. Advisor to Asst. Sec. Def. Res. Affairs US Armed Forces, rep. Nat. Chair Dept. Def. Decorated Legion of Merit, Disting. Flying Cross, Def. Meritorious Svc. medal, Air Medal with numeral 5 Combat Action Ribbon, Presdl. Unit Citation with Bronze Star, Meritorious Unit Commendation, Select Marine Corps. Res. medal with Silver Star, Nat. Def. Medal with Bronze star, Armed Forces Expiditionary medal, Vietnam Svc. medal with two Bronze Stars, Navy and Marine Corps Overseas Svc. Ribbon with two Bronze Stars, Armed Forces Res. medal with hourglass Device, Rep. of Vietnam Unit Citation, Rep. Vietnam Campaing medal with 1960 Device. Home: PO Box 1257 Westcliffe CO 81252-1257 Home Phone: 314-503-4850; Office Phone: 703-862-1917. E-mail: bob.hollingsworth@osd.mil.

HOLLIS, RICHARD B., pharmaceutical executive; Student, St. Mary's Coll.; BA in Psych., San Francisco State U. Product sales position Baxter Travenol (now Baxter Internat.); positions up to divsn. mgr. Imed Corp. (acquired by Warner Lambert, now part of Pfizer Inc.); western bus. unit mgr. Genentech, Inc., 1986—89; gen. mgr., v.p. mktg. and sales Instromedix, 1989—91; COO Bioject Med., 1991—94; founder, chmn., CEO Hollis-Eden Pharms., San Diego, 1994—. Office: Hollis Eden Pharms Inc 4435 Eastgate Hall Ste 400 San Diego CA 92121 Office Phone: 858-587-9333.

HOLLOWAY, CHARLES ARTHUR, public and private management educator; b. Whittier, Calif., May 28, 1936; s. Heber H. and Theodosia S. (Stephens) H.; m. Christina Ahlm, July 11, 1959; children: Deborah, Susan, Stuart. BSEE with honors, U. Calif., Berkeley, 1959; MS, UCLA, 1963, PhD in Bus. Adminstrn. with distinction, 1969. Sr. engr. Bechtel Corp., San Francisco, 1964-65; tchg. fellow UCLA, 1965-66; asst. prof. to prof. Stanford (Calif.) U., 1968—, Herbert Hoover prof. pub. and pvt. mgmt., 1980-91, assoc. dean acad. affairs Grad. Sch. Bus., 1980-87, 90-91, Kleiner Perkins Caufield and Byers prof. mgmt., 1991—2004, Kleiner Perkins Caufield and Byers prof. mgmt. emeritus, 2004—. Bd. dir. SRI Internat.; co-chair Stanford Ctr. Entrepreneurial Studies. Author: Decision Making Under Uncertainty: Models and Choices, 1979, Perpetual Enterprise Machine: Seven Keys to Corporate Renewal, 1994. With USN, 1959-63. Fellow Ford Found., 1966-68. Mem. Inst. Mgmt. Sci., Ops. Rsch. Soc. Am., Stanford Integrated Mfg. Assn. (co-chair 1991-95). Home: 730 Santa Maria Ave Palo Alto CA 94305-8438 Office: Stanford U Grad Sch Bus Stanford CA 94305 Business E-Mail: holloway_chuck@gsb.stanford.edu.

HOLLOWAY, DAVID JAMES, political science educator; b. Dublin, Oct. 13, 1943; came to U.S., 1983; s. James Joseph and Gertrude Mary (Kennedy) H.; m. Arlene Jean Smith, June 12, 1976; children: James, Ivor. MA, PhD, Cambridge U., Eng., 1964. Asst. lectr. U. Lancaster, Eng., 1967-69; rsch. assoc. Inst. for Strategic Studies, London, 1969—70; lectr. U. Edinburgh, Scotland, 1970—84, reader, 1984—86; prof. Stanford (Calif.) U., 1986—, co-dir. Ctr. Internat. Security and Arms Control, 1991—97, Raymond A. Spruance prof. in internat. history, 1997—, assoc. dean humanities and scis., 1997—98, dir. Inst. for Internat. Studies, 1998—. Dir. internat. rels. program Stanford U., 1989-91. Author: The Soviet Union and the Arms Race, 1983, Stalin and the Bomb, 1994; co-author: (with S. Drell and P. Farley) The Reagan Strategic Defense Initiative, 1985. Bd. dirs. Ploughshares Found., San Francisco, 1989—. Mem. Am. Polit. Sci. Assn., Am. Assn. for the Advancement of Slavic Studies. Avocations: opera, reading. Home: 710 Torreya Ct Palo Alto CA 94303-4160 Office: Stanford U Inst Internat Studies Encina Hall Stanford CA 94305-6055

HOLLOWAY, JOSH, actor; b. San Jose, Calif., July 20, 1969; m. Yessica Holloway; 1 child, Java Kumala. Studied, Univ. Ga. Actor: (films) Cold Heart, 2001, Moving August, 2002, Mi Amigo, 2002, My Daughter's Tears, 2002, Sabretooth, 2002, Dr. Benny, 2003; (TV series) Lost, 2004— (Outstanding Performance by an Ensemble in a Drama Series, Screen Actors Guild award, 2006), NCIS, CSI. Named hottest hunk on TV, In Touch Weekly mag., 2006. Office: Rough Diamond Mgmt 1424 N Kings Rd West Hollywood CA 90069 Office Phone: 343-848-2900. Office Fax: 323-848-8142.

HOLM, JAMES A., state representative; b. Glendale, Calif., July 15, 1945; m. Marcia Holm; children: Denyse Holm Moberley, Tamara Zizzo, Greg, Shanon Sehnert, Sam Sehnert. Diploma, U. Alaska. CEO Holm Town Nursery, Inc.; mem. Alaska Ho. of Reps. Trustee Greater Fairbanks Meml. Hosp. Found., Alaska Farm Bur. Century Club; bd. dirs. Fairbanks Summer Arts Fest. Mem.: AFA, AUSA, Fairbanks C. of C., Assn. Landscape Contractors Am., Am. Nursery Landscape Assn., Fairbanks Concert Assn., Fairbanks Drama Assn., Fairbanks Symphony Assn., Rotary. Republican. Avocations: theater, music, fishing, reading, history. Office: Rm 110 State Capitol Juneau AK 99801-1182 Address: 1292 Sadler Way Ste 328 Fairbanks AK 99701-3173

HOLMAN, BILL, composer; b. Calif. Student, U. Colo., 1944—45, UCLA, 1947, Westlake Coll. Music, 1948—50. Mem. Lighthouse All Stars, 1950—51, Conte Candoli, 1955, Shelley Manne, 1955, Shorty Rogers, 1957. Recs. include Kenton Presents: The Bill Holman Octet, 1954, The Fabulous Bill Holman, 1957, In a Jazz Orbit, 1958, Jive for Five, 1958, Bill Holman's Great Big Band, 1960, The Bill Holman Band, 1988, A View From the Side (Grammy award for Best Instrumental Composition, 1996), Brilliant Corners, 1997, composer for various artists including Count Basie, Louis Bellson, Natalie Cole, Maynard Ferguson, Woody Herman, Stan Kanton, Peggy Lee, Carmen McRae, Diane Schuur, Sarah Vaughn, Joe Williams, Doc Severinsen, others. Recipient Grammy award for Best Instrumental Arrangement, 1987, 1997, Golden Score award, ASMAC, 2008; named Best Arranger, Jazz Times Readers Poll, 1990, 1995, 1998—99, Arranger of Yr., Downbeat Readers' Poll and Critics Poll, 1998—99; named to Rutgers Jazz Hall of Fame, 2006.

HOLMAN, HALSTED REID, physician, educator; b. Cleve., Jan. 17, 1925; s. Emile Frederic and Ann Peril (Purdy) H.; m. Barbara Marie Lucas, June 26, 1949 (div. July 9, 1982); children: Michael, Andrea, Alison; m. Diana Barbara Dutton, Aug. 10, 1985; 1 child, Geoffrey. Student, Stanford U., 1942-43, UCLA, 1943-44; MD, Yale U., 1949. Med. resident Montefiore Hosp., NYC, 1952-55; staff physician Rockefeller Inst., NYC, 1955-60; prof. medicine Stanford (Calif.) U., 1960—, chmn. dept. medicine, 1960-71, co-chief, divsn. family and cmty. medicine, 1987-2001, dir. clin. scholar program, 1969-97, dir. Multipurpose Arthritis Ctr., 1977-97, co-chief, divsn. immunology and rheumatology, 1997-2000, dir. Stanford Program for Mgmt. of Chronic Disease, 1997—2001; project dir. Santa Clara Coalition to Improve Care Chronic Disease, 2009—. Pres. Midpeninsula Health Svc., Palo Alto, Calif., 1975-80; mem. adv. bd. Calif Health Facilities Commn., Sacramento, 1978-81, Office Tech. Assessment, U.S. Congress, 1979-81, Inst. Advancement of Health, NYC, 1982-90; Guggenhime prof. medicine, 1960—; mem. steering com., Pacific Bus. Group on Health Breakthroughs in Chronic Care Program, 2005-; adv.commn. Santa Clara County, 2006-; mem. planning com., Assn. Am. Med. Coll. Calif. Academic Chronic Care Collaborative, 2007-. Author 2 books; assoc. editor Arthritis and Rheumatism, 1995-2000; co-editor Chronic Illness, 2004—; contbr. articles to profl. jours. Recipient Bauer Meml. award, Arthritis and Rheumatism Found., N.Y., 1964, John W. Gardner Vision award, Pathways Found., 2003. Master: Am. Coll. Rheumatology (Presdl. Gold medal 2001); fellow: AAAS (coun. 1974—79), ACP (Laureate award no. Calif. chpt. 1994, John Phillips Meml. award 2004); mem.: Improving Chronic Illness Care-R.W. Johnson Found. (Vision award 2001), Arthritis Found. (Hero Overcoming Arthritis 1998, Engalitcheff award 1999, McGuire Educator award 2000), Western Assn. Physicians (pres. 1966), Am. Soc. Clin. Investigation (pres. 1970), Assn. Am. Physicians. Democrat. Home: 747 Dolores St Stanford CA 94305-8427 Office: Stanford U Divsn Immunol and Rheumatol 1000 Welch Rd Ste 203 Palo Alto CA 94304-1808 Office Fax: 650-723-9656.

HOLMAN, J(OHN) LEONARD, retired manufacturing corporation executive; b. Moose Jaw, Sask., Can., Aug. 30, 1929; s. Charles Claude and Lillian Kathleen (Haw) H.; m. Julia Pauline Benfield, July 18, 1953; children: Nancy Jane, Sally Joan. BS in Civil Engring., U. Alta., 1953. Pres. Consolidated Concrete Ltd., Calgary, Alta., Canada, 1969-72; dir., pres. BACM Industries Ltd., Calgary, 1972-76; exec. v.p. Genstar Corp., Calgary, 1976-79, San Francisco, 1980-87, dir. several subs. cos.; pres., CEO CBR Cement Corp., San Mateo, Calif., 1986-88, chmn. bd., 1988-89, ret., 1990. Bd. dirs., officer several nat. trade assns. Mem. Assn. Profl. Engrs. Alta. (life), Calgary Exhbn. and Stampede (hon., life, dir.), Calgary Golf and Country Club. Home: 111 Country Club Estates 111-5555 Elbow Dr SW Calgary AB Canada T2V 1H7 Personal E-mail: johnlholman@shaw.ca.

HOLMAN, ROBERT ALAN, oceanography educator; s. Donald Morison and Frances Margaret Holman; m. Kathryn Anne Jung, Dec. 20, 1975; 1 child, Sean Fraser. BSc in Math. and Physics, Royal Mil. Coll. Can., 1972; PhD, Dalhousie U., Halifax, Nova Scotia, 1979. Prof. Oreg. State U., Corvallis, 1979—. Recipient Sec. Navy, Chief Naval Ops. Chair in Oceanography, US Navy, 2003—; named Disting. Prof., Oreg. State U. Found., 2006. Mem.: US Naval Inst., Am. Geophys. Union, Oceanography Soc. Achievements include development of Argus program. Office: Oreg State U COAS 104 Ocean Admin Bldg Corvallis OR 97331 Business E-Mail: holman@coas.oregonstate.edu.

HOLME, RICHARD PHILLIPS, lawyer; b. Denver, Nov. 6, 1941; s. Peter Hagner Jr. and Lena (Phillips) H.; m. Barbara June Friel, July 17, 1944; children: Daniel Friel, Robert Muir. BA, Williams Coll., Williamstown, Mass., 1963; JD, U. Colo., 1966. Bar: Colo. 1966, U.S. Dist. Ct. Colo. 1966, U.S. Ct. Claims 1990, U.S. Ct. Appeals (10th cir.) 1966, U.S. Ct. Appeals (1st cir.) 1980, U.S. Dist. Ct. D.C. 1988, U.S. Ct. Appeals (D.C. cir.) 1988, U.S. Ct. Appeals (4th cir.) 1989, U.S. Ct. Appeals (fed. cir.) 1995, U.S. Supreme Ct. 1975. Assoc. Davis, Graham & Stubbs, Denver, 1966-68, ptnr., 1972-87, 91—, mng. ptnr., D.C. office, 1987-91; dep. Denver Dist. Atty., 1969-71. Grievance com. Colo. Supreme Ct., Denver, 1979-85, civil rules com., 1994—, civil justice com., 1998—, nomination commn.2008-. Fellow Am. Bar Found.; mem. ABA, ABA Found., Colo. Bar Found., Colo. Bar Assn. (bd. govs. 1974-76, 85-87, 95-99, 2001-03), Denver Bar Assn. (trustee 1977-80, 1st v.p. 1997-98), Order of Coif. Presbyterian. Home: 3944 S Depew Way Denver CO 80235-3105 Office Phone: 303-892-9400.

HOLMES, DALLAS SCOTT, judge, educator; b. LA, Dec. 2, 1940; s. Donald Cherry and Hazel H. (Scott) Holmes; m. Patricia McMichael, Aug. 21, 1965; children: Mark Scott, Tobin John. AB cum laude, Pomona Coll., 1962; MS, London Sch. Econs., 1964; JD, U. Calif., Berkeley, 1967. Bar: Calif. 1968. Assoc. Best, Best & Krieger, Riverside, Calif., 1968—74, ptnr., 1974—96; Superior Ct. judge, 1996—2007; adj. prof. U. Calif., Riverside, 2008—. Exec. asst. to Assembly majority fl. leader Calif. State Legislature, Sacramento, 1969—70; asst. adj. prof., Grad. Sch. Mgmt. U. Calif., Riverside, 1977—88, adj. prof. dept. polit. sci., 2008; lectr. UCLA Ext., 1987—2002, jud. local govt. and univ. ext. groups; adj. prof. Hastings Coll. Law, U. Calif., San Francisco, 1990; mem. bd. govs. State Bar Calif., 1990—93, v.p., 1992—93; mem. Calif. Jud. Coun., 1995—96, chair task force jury sys. improvements, 1998—2003; chair Riverside Superior Ct. Jury Com., 1997—2003, 2005—07; lectr. dept. politics Pawana Coll., 2008. Contbr. articles on mass transit, assessment of farmland in Calif., exclusionary zoning and environ. law to profl. jours.; author: proposed tort reform initiative for Calif. physicians. Pres. Pomona Coll. Alumni Coun., 1973—74, Century Club, Riverside, 1974—76, Citizens Univ. Com., 1983—85, Downtown Riverside Assn., 1987—88, Torchbearers Pomona Coll., 1995—96; city atty. City of Corona, Calif., 1976—96; mem. bd. trustees U. Calif. Riverside Found., 1983—2006; chmn. legal affairs com. Assn. Calif. Water Agys., 1985—91. Named Man of Yr., Riverside Press-Enterprise, 1962, Young Man of Yr., Riverside Jr. C. of C., 1972. Mem.: Am. Judicature Soc. (jury ctr. adv. com.), Calif. State Bar Assn. (exec. com. pub. law sect. 1983—86), Riverside County Bar Assn. (pres. 1982), Riverside Rotary Club. Republican. Presbyterian.

HOLMES, FONTAYNE, retired library director; BA in History magna cum laude, UCLA, 1964, MLS, 1966. Std. tchg. credential with a specialization in jr. coll. tchg. UCLA, 1979. Sr. libr., head interlibrary loan and mgr. West LA Regional br. LA Pub. Libr., 1984—87, asst. dir. brs., 1988—98, dir. ctrl. libr., 1998—99, dir. libr. facilities divsn., 1999—2002, asst. city libr., 2002—04, city libr., 2004—08, South Pasadena Pub. Libr., 1987—88. Contbr. articles to profl. publs. Bd. dirs. Libr. Found. LA. Mem.: ALA (chair intellectual freedom roundtable nominating com. 1982, mem. pay equity com. 1986—87), Urban Librs. Coun. (SirsiDynix Urban Player award for Outstanding Libr. and Cmty. Leadership 2007), Calif. Libr. Assn. (chair intellectual freedom com. 1981, pres. young adult reviewers of So. Calif. 1978—80), Phi Beta Kappa.

HOLMES, GENTA HAWKINS, former diplomat; b. Anadarko, Okla., Sept. 3, 1940; BA, U. So. Calif., 1962. Jr. officer U.S. Embassy, Abidjan, Ivory Coast, 1964-66; with office spl. assistance to Sec. of State for Refugee Affairs, 1966-68; spl. asst., youth officer U.S. Embassy, Paris, 1968-71; with N.Y. regional office OEO, 1972-73; with office devel. fin., econ. bur. U.S. Dept. State, 1973-74; chief econ. and commercial sect. U.S. Embassy, Bahamas, 1974-77; congl. fellow Am. Polit. Sci. Assn., 1977-78; with bur. congl. rels. U.S. Dept. State, 1978-79; asst. adminstr. legis. affairs AID, 1979-82; mem. 25th Exec.

Seminar in Nat. and Internat. Affairs, 1982-83; mem. bd. examiners, 1983-84; dep. chief of mission U.S. Embassy, Lilongwe, Malawi, 1984-86, Port-au-Prince, Haiti, 1986-88, Pretoria, South Africa, 1988-90; U.S. amb. to Namibia, 1990-92; dir. gen. fgn. svc., dir. pers. U.S. Dept. State, Washington, 1992-95; diplomat in residence U. Calif., Davis, 1995-97; U.S. amb. to Australia, 1997—2000.

HOLMES, GREGG, communications executive; B in Advt., Texas Tech U. Various positions Times Mirror Cable Television, Ohio, 1981-86; v.p., gen. mgr. Cox Comm., Inc., Phoenix, 1986—. Bd. dirs. Greater Phoenix Econ. Coun. (pat chmn.), Valley of the Sun United Way, Met. Musical Theater; vice chmn. Phoenix Meml. Hosp.; mem. Phoenix Youth Edn. Commn. (past chmn.), United Way campaign cabinet. Mem. Greater Phoenix C. of C. (past chmn.), Greater Phoenix Leadership, Dean's Coun. 100 Ariz. State Univ.

HOLMES, IRVIN R., JR., marketing professional; V.p. mktg. Del Monte Foods, San Francisco, sr. v.p. mktg., 1999—. Office: Del Monte Foods 1 Market Plz San Francisco CA 94105-1420

HOLMES, KING KENNARD, medical educator; b. St. Paul, Sept. 1, 1937; AB, Harvard Coll., 1959; MD, Cornell U., 1963; PhD in Microbiology, U. Hawaii, 1967. Diplomate Am. Bd. Internal Medicine, infectious diseases. Resident U. Wash., Seattle, 1967-68, chief resident, 1968-69, from instr. to assoc. prof. medicine, 1969-78, vice chmn. dept. medicine, 1984-89, prof. medicine, 1978—, dir. Ctr. AIDS and Sexually Transmitted Diseases, 1989—. Head divsn. pulmonary diseases USPHS Hosp., Seattle, 1969-70, asst. chief dept. medicine, 1969-83, head divsn. infectious diseases, 1970-83; dir. Sexually Transmitted Disease Clinic, Harborview Med. Ctr., 1972-79, chief med., 1984-89; mem. numerous adv. coms. Nat. Inst. Allergy & Infectious Diseases, NIH, USPHS, WHO, NAS; prin. investigator NIH, Nat. Cancer Inst., Nat. Inst. Allergy & Infectious Diseases, Nat. Inst. Child Health & Human Devel., Ctrs. Disease Control, 1983—. With USN, 1965-67. Recipient Squibb award Infectious Disease Soc. Am., 1978, Thomas Parran award Am. Veneral Disease Assn., 1983. Fellow ACP, Royal Coll. Physicians Eng.; mem. AMA, Inst. Medicine-NAS, Assn. Am. Physicians, Am. Epidemiol. Soc., Am. Fedn. Clin. Rsch. Office: U Wash Str AIDS & STDs Harborview Med Ctr 325 9th Ave MS# 359931 Seattle WA 98104-2420 Fax: 206-731-3694.

HOLMES, LINDSEY S., state legislator; b. Anchorage, Oct. 16, 1973; BA, Middlebury Coll., Vt., 1995; MA, Stanford U., 1996; JD, U. Chgo., 2001. Alaska State Representative, District 26, 2007-; member, Admin Regulation Review, Legislature Ethics, Fisheries, Health and Soc Serv, Judiciary, Law Committees, 2007-, Alaska House Representative; pub member, Select Committee on Legislature Ethics, 2006.law clerk, Alaska Supreme Court; attorney, Ashburn & Masont; attorney, Heller Ehrman White & McAuliffe; project manager, Rise Alaska, LLC. Alaska Bar Assoc (2001-present); Young Women's Chrisitan Assoc (board member, 2002-present); The Nature Conservancy Alaska Chap (trustee, 2003-present); Anchorage Downtown Rotary Club (2003-present); Anchorage Concert Found (board member, 2004-present); Anchorage Chamber of Commerce (board member, 2005-06). Democrat. Episcopalian. Avocations: tennis, scuba diving, reading. Address: 4149 Hood Court Anchorage AK 99517 Office: Dist 26 716 W 4th Ave Ste 330 Anchorage AK 99501-2133 also: State Capitol Rm 405 Juneau AK 99801-1182 Home Phone: 907-258-5841; Office Phone: 907-465-4919, 907-269-0130. Office Fax: 907-465-2137, 907-269-0132. Business E-Mail: Rep_Lindsey_Holmes@legis.state.ak.us.

HOLMES, MICHAEL L., career officer; m. Viola Holmes; children: Jared, Justin, Michael Jason. Diploma in Math., Pembroke State U., 1972. Commd. ensign USN, 1973, advanced through ranks to rear adm.; various assignments to aircraft comdr. Patrol Squadron 24, Jacksonville; comdr. Patrol Wings, U.S. Pacific Fleet, Pearl Harbor, Hawaii.

HOLMGREN, JANET L., academic administrator; b. Chgo., Dec. 1, 1948; d. Kenneth William and Virginia Ann (Rensink) H.; m. Gordon A. McKay, Sept. 7, 1968 (div. 1990); children: Elizabeth Jane, Ellen Katherine. BA in English summa cum laude, Oakland U., Rochester, Mich., 1968; MA in Linguistics, Princeton U., 1971, PhD in Linguistics, 1974. Asst. prof. English studies Federal City Coll. (now U. DC), Washington, 1972-76; asst. prof. English U. Md., College Park, 1976-82, asst. to chancellor, 1982-88; assoc. provost Princeton U., NJ, 1988-90, vice-provost NJ, 1990-91; pres. Mills Coll., Oakland, Calif., 1991—. Mem. external adv. bd. English dept. Princeton U. Bay Area Biosci. Ctr. Author: (with Spencer Cosmos) The Story of English: Study Guide and Reader, 1986, Narration and Discourse in American Realistic Fiction, 1982; contbr. articles to profl. jours. Faculty rsch. grantee U. Md., 1978; fellow NEH, 1978, Princeton U., 1968-69, 70-72, NSF, 1969-70; recipient summer study aid Linguistic Soc. Am., Ohio State U., 1970. Mem. Assn. Ind. Caif. Colls. and Univs. (exec. com.), Nat. Assn. Ind. Colls. and Univs., Am. Coun. on Education (chair office of women in higher edn.), Calif. Acad. Sci. (coun.). Democrat. Episcopal. Avocations: travel, swimming, reading. Office: Mills Coll Office Pres 5000 Macarthur Blvd Oakland CA 94613-1301 Office Phone: 510-430-2094. Office Fax: 510-430-2256. E-mail: president@mills.edu.

HOLMGREN, MIKE (MICHAEL GEORGE HOLMGREN), professional football coach; b. San Francisco, June 15, 1948; m. Kathy Holmgren; children: Gretchen, Emily, Jenny and Calla (twins). BS in Bus. Fin., U. So. Calif., 1970. Coach Lincoln HS, San Francisco, 1971-72, Sacred Heart HS, 1972-74, Oakgrove HS, 1975-80; quarterbacks coach, offensive coord. San Francisco State U., 1981-82; quarterbacks coach Brigham Young U., 1982-85, San Francisco 49ers, 1985-89, offensive coord., 1989-92; head coach Green Bay Packers, 1992-98; gen. mgr. Seattle Seahawks, 1999—2002, head coach, exec. v.p. football ops., 1999—. Achievements include being a member of Super Bowl Championship winning: San Francisco 49ers, 1989, 1990, Green Bay Packers, 1997. Office: Seattle Seahawks 12 Seahawks Way Renton WA 98056-1572

HOLMQUEST, DONALD LEE, health organization director, nuclear medicine physician, lawyer, retired aerospace engineer; b. Dallas, Apr. 7, 1939; s. Sidney Browder and Lillie Mae (Waite) H.; m. Ann Nixon James, Oct. 24, 1972. BS in Elec. Engring., So. Meth. U., 1962; MD, Baylor U., 1967, PhD in Physiology, 1968; JD, U. Houston, 1980. Student engr. Ling-Temco-Vought, Dallas, 1958-61; electronics engr. Tex. Instruments, Inc., Dallas, 1962; intern Meth. Hosp., Houston, 1967-68; pilot tng. USAF, Williams AFB, Ariz., 1968-69; scientist-astronaut NASA, Houston, 1967-73; research assoc. MIT, 1968-70; asst. prof. radiology and physiology Baylor Coll. Medicine, 1970-73; dir. nuclear medicine Eisenhower Med. Ctr., Palm Desert, Calif., 1973-74; assoc. dean medicine, assoc. prof. Tex. A&M U., College Station, 1974-76; dir. nuclear medicine Navasota (Tex.) Med. Ctr., 1976-84, Med. Arts Hosp., Houston, 1977-85; ptnr. Wood Lucksinger & Epstein, Houston, 1980-91, Holmquest & Assocs., Houston, 1991—2004; v.p. legal affairs N.Am. Med. Mgmt., Inc., Nashville, 1995-96; practice leader profl. svcs. group McKesson Info. Solutions, San Francisco, 2002—06; CEO Calif. Regional Health Info. Orgn., San Francisco, 2006—. Asst. prof. internal medicine Baylor Coll. Medicine, Houston, 1999—. Contbr. articles to med. jours. Mem. Soc. Nuclear Medicine, Am. Coll. Nuclear Physicians, Tex. Bar Assn., Am. Fighter Pilots Assn., Sigma Xi, Alpha Omega Alpha, Sigma Tau. Home and Office: 205 Princeton Rd Menlo Park CA 94025-5217 Office Phone: 415-537-6939.

HOLO, SELMA REUBEN, museum director, educator; b. Chgo., May 21, 1943; d. Samuel and Ghita (Hurwitz) Reuben; children from previous marriage: Robert, Joshua; m. Fred Croton, June 18, 1989. BA, Northwestern U., 1965; MA, Hunter Coll., 1972; PhD, U. Calif., Santa Barbara, 1980; postgrad., Mus. Mgmt. Inst., 1985. Lectr. Art Ctr. Coll. of Design, Pasadena, Calif., 1973-77; curator of acquisitions Norton Simon Mus., Pasadena, 1977-81; dir. Fisher Gallery and mus. MA art history/mus. studies program U. So. Calif., LA, 1981—. Guest curator, cons. Getty Mus., Malibu, Calif., 1975-76, 81; guest curator Isetan Mus., Tokyo, 1982, cons. Nat. Mus. for Women in Arts, Washington, 1984; reviewer grants Inst. Mus. Svcs., Washington, 1986-87, Getty Grant Program, 1988-90; panel chmn. Internat. Com. on Exhbn. Exch., Washington, 1984; panelist NEA, Washington, 1985, 91-93, Idaho Commn. on the Arts; admission panel mem. Mus. Mgmt. Inst., 1990; hon. curator Tokyo Fuji Mus.; lectr. museology IVAM, Valencia, Spain, 1994, Complutense U. Masters in Museology, 1994, U. Castilla La Mancha in Museology, 1995; presenter Museo/Mus. Conf., Barcelona, Spain, 1996, Bilbao (Spain) Mus. Fine Arts Conf. on Mus. Edn., 1996; co-author survey com. mus. studies programs, 1986. Author: (catalogues) Goya: Los Disparates, 1976, Beyond the Prado: Musems & Identity in Democratic Sapin, 1999; co-author: La Tauromaquia: Goya, Picasso and the Bullfight, 1986; editor: Keepers of the Flame, The Unofficial Artists of Leningrad, 1990; guest editor New Observations, 1990; contbr. articles to profl. jours. and mag. Fellow La Napoule Art Found., 1988, Fulbright Found., 1994; Kress Found. grantee, N.Y., 1979, Internationes Fed. Republic of Germany grantee, 1985, 92; recipient Fuj Fine Art award, 1990, Sr. Rsch. Fulbright fellowship to Spain, 1994, award from program for cooperation between the program for the Ministry of Culture of Spain and N.Am. Univ. Mem. Am. Assn. Mus., Art Table. Office: U So Calif Fisher Gallery 823 Exposition Blvd Los Angeles CA 90089-0001

HOLSCHER, MARK CHARLES, lawyer; b. Inglewood, Calif., 1962; BS, U. Calif., Berkeley, 1985; JD, Boalt Hall Sch. Law, U. Calif., 1988. Bar: Calif. 1988, U.S. Dist. Ct. ctrl. dist.) Calif. 1988. Law clk. to Hon. William Keller U.S. Dist. Ct., (ctrl. dist.) Calif., LA, 1988—89; asst. U.S. atty. (ctrl. dist.) Calif. US Dept. Justice, LA, 1989—95, spl. atty. to US atty. gen. Washington, 1994—95; ptnr. O'Melveny & Myers LLP, LA, 1995—. Vice chair Nat. White Collar Crime Com., West Coast White Collar Crime Com. Named one of Top 45 Under 45, Am. Lawyer Mag., 2003; named to Chambers, Best Lawyers in Am., 2004—06. Mem.: ABA (vice chair Nat. White Collar Crime Com.), Phi Beta Kappa. Office: O'Melveny & Myers LLP 400 S Hope St Los Angeles CA 90071-2899 Office Phone: 213-430-6000. Office Fax: 213-430-6407. Business E-Mail: mholscher@omm.com.

HOLSTI, KALEVI JACQUE, political scientist, department chairman; b. Geneva, Apr. 25, 1935; s. Rudolf Woldemar and Liisa Anniki (Franssila) H.; children: Liisa, Matthew, Karina. BA, Stanford U., 1956, MA, 1958, PhD, 1961. Mem. faculty U. BC, Vancouver, Canada, 1961—, U. Killam prof. polit. sci. Canada, 1997—. Vis. prof. McGill U., Montreal, Can., 1972, Kyoto U., Japan, 1977, Hebrew U., Jerusalem, 1978, Internat. U. Japan, 1988, 92, 94; vis. fellow Australian Nat. U., 1983; cons. in field. Author: International Politics: A Framework for Analysis, 7th edit., 1994, Why Nations Realign, 1982, The Dividing Discipline: Hegemony and Pluralism in International Theory, 1985, Peace and War: International Order and Armed Conflict, 1648-1989, 1991, Change in the International System: Essays on the Theory and Practice of International Relations, 1991, The State, War, and the State of War, 1996, Taming the Sovereigns: Institutional Change in International Politics, 2004; Politica Mundial: Cambio y Conflicto: Ensayos escogidos de Kal Holsti, 2005. editor: Internat. Studies Quar., 1970-75; co-editor: Can. Jour. Polit. Sci., 1978-81. Recipient Killam Rsch. prize, 1992; Fulbright scholar, 1959-60; Can. Coun. leave fellow, 1967, 72, 78, Can. Coun. Killam Rsch. fellow, 1987-89. Fellow Royal Soc. Can.; mem. Internat. Studies Assn. (pres. 1986-87), Can. Polit. Sci. Assn. (pres. 1984-85), Finnish Acad. Scis. and Letters (fgn. mem.). Office: U BC Dept Polit Sci Vancouver BC Canada V6T 1Z1 Office Phone: 604-822-4537. Business E-Mail: holsti@interchange.ubc.ca.

HOLSTON, MICHAEL JOSEPH, lawyer, computer company executive; b. Sept. 28, 1962; BSME, U. Notre Dame, 1984; JD cum laude, Villanova U., 1987. Bar: Pa. 1987. Asst. US atty. (ea. dist.) Pa. US Dept. Justice, 1990—93; assoc. Drinker Biddle & Reath LLP, Phila., 1993—96, ptnr., 1996—2005; ptnr. litig. practice Morgan, Lewis & Bockius LLP, Phila., 2005—07; exec. v.p., gen. counsel, mem. exec. council Hewlett-Packard Co., Palo Alto, Calif., 2007—. Lectr. trial advocacy Villanova U. Sch. Law, Nat. Inst. Trial Attys. Bd. dirs. ECHOES Around the World; former bd. dirs. Bryn Mawr Fire Co. Fellow: Am. Coll. Trial Lawyers; mem.: Police Athletic League (former mem. bd. dirs.), Order of Coif. Office: Hewlett-Packard Co 3000 Hanover St Palo Alto CA 94304-1185*

HOLT, DENNIS F., media buying company executive; Student, U. So. Calif. Salesman RKO, LA; founder, pres., CEO, chmn. Western Internat. Media Corp., LA; chmn., CEO Patriot Comm., LA. Office: Patriot Comm LLC 10441 Jefferson Blvd Culver City CA 90232-3512

HOLT, WILLIAM E., lawyer, managing partner; b. Phila., Aug. 31, 1945; BBA, U. Iowa, 1967, JD with distinction, 1970. Bar: Iowa 1970, Wash. 1971. Law clk. to Hon. William T. Beeks U.S. Dist. Ct. (we. dist.) Wash., 1970-71; mem., chmn. Gordon, Thomas, Honeywell, Malanca, Peterson & Daheim, Tacoma, 1999, 2000, 2006, 2007. Adj. prof. U. Puget Sound Law Sch., 1974-75. Note editor Iowa Law Rev., 1969-70, author, Court-awarded Attorney Fees, Costs and Penathes for Wa. CLE Desk book. Mem. ABA, Wash. State Bar Assn. (exec. com. real property, probate and trust sect. 1987-89), Phi Delta Phi. Office: Gordon Thomas Honeywell Malanca Peterson & Daheim PO Box 1157 Ste 2100 Tacoma WA 98401-1157 Office Phone: 253-620-6412. E-mail: holtw@gth-law.com.

HOLTAN, RAMER B., JR., lawyer; b. Wilmington, Del., Oct. 20, 1944; AB, Harvard U., 1966; JD cum laude, U. Ill., 1972; postgrad., U. Freiburg, West Germany. Bar: Wash. 1973. Mem. Perkins Coie, Seattle. Articles editor U. Ill. Law Rev., 1971-72. Mem. Order of the Coif. Office: Perkins Coie 1201 3rd Ave Fl 40 Seattle WA 98101-3029 Home Phone: 206-232-3538; Office Phone: 206-359-8400. Business E-Mail: rholtan@perkinscoie.com. E-mail: rholtan@comcast.net.

HOLTE, DEBRA LEAH, investment company executive, financial analyst; b. Madison, Wis. BA, Concordia Coll., Moorhead, Minn., 1973. Chartered Fin. Analyst, Cert. Divorce Planner. Capital markets specialist 1st Bank Mpls., 1981-83; v.p. Allison-Williams Co., Mpls., 1983-86; exec. v.p. Hamil & Holte Inc., Denver, 1986-93; pres. Holte & Assocs., Denver, Taos, N.Mex., 1993—. Active Denver Jr. League, Western Pension Com., 1986—; bd. dirs. Denver Children's Home, 1987—, treas., 1987-91, chmn. fin. com., 1987-91, v.p., 1990—, chmn. nominating com., 1991—, pres.-elect, 1994-95, bd. pres., 1995—; adv. bd. Luth. Social Svcs., 1987; co-chair U.S. Ski Team Fundraiser; bd. dirs. Minn. Vocat. Edn. Fin., Mpls., 1984-86; bd. dirs. Colo. Ballet, 1988-93, chair nominating com., 1991-93, v.p., 1992-93, chmn. bd., 1993; mem. Fin. Analyst Nat. Task Force in Bondholder Rights, 1988-90; bd. dirs. Ctrl. City Opera Guild, 1994-95, Western Chamber Ballet, 1994-96, Taos Humane Soc., 1997—; social co-chmn. The Arapahoe Fox Hunt, 1993-94; bd. dirs., mem. steering com. Denver Dumb Friends League, 2001-, mem. exec. com., 2004-, mem. audit com., 2004-; mem. exec. com., chair devel. com. Dumb Friends League, 2005—. Mem. Fin. Analysts Fedn., Denver Soc. Security Analysts (bd. dirs. 1990-97, chair ethics and bylaws com. 1987—, chair edn. com. 1988, chair membership com. 1989, rec. sec. 1990, sec. 1991, treas. 1992, program chair 1993, pres. 1994-95, dir. 1995-96).

HOLTKAMP, JAMES ARNOLD, lawyer, educator; b. Albuquerque, Apr. 4, 1949; s. Clarence Jules and Karyl Irene (Roberts) H.; m. Marianne Coltrin, Dec. 28, 1973; children: Ariane, Brent William, Rachel, Allison, David Roberts. BA, Brigham Young U., 1972; JD, George Washington U., 1975. Bar: Utah 1976, U.S. Dist. Ct. Utah 1977, U.S. Ct. Appeals (10th cir.) 1979, Colo. 1995. Mem. staff U.S. Senate Watergate Com., Washington, 1974; atty.-advisor Dept. Transp., Washington, 1975; atty. Dept. Interior, Washington, 1975-77; assoc. Van Cott, Bagley, Cornwall & McCarthy, Salt Lake City, 1977-81, ptnr., 1981-89, Davis, Graham & Stubbs, Salt Lake City, 1989-92, Stoel Rives, Salt Lake City, 1992-97, LeBoeuf, Lamb, Greene & MacRae, Salt Lake City, 1997—2003, Holland & Hart, Salt Lake City, 2003—. Adj. prof., Law Sch. Brigham Young U., Provo, Utah, 1979—2002; adj. prof. Coll. Law U. Utah, 1995—. Co-author: Utah Environmental and Land Use Permits and Approvals Manual, 1981; contbr. articles to legal jours. Missionary LDS Ch., 1968-70; active Gt. Salt Lake coun. Boy Scouts Am., 1977—; trustee Coalition for Utah's Future, 1996-2001. Mem. ABA (vice-chmn. air quality commn. 1985-89), Utah State Bar (chmn. energy and natural resources sect. 1984-85, chmn. pub. utilities law com. 1990-93, energy and natural resources sect., Lawyer of Yr. award 1981, Disting. Svc. award 2002), Utah Mining Assn. (bd. dirs. 1999—), Rocky Mtn. Mineral Law Found. (pres. 2005-06), Utah Petroleum Assn., George Washington Law Assn. (nat. bd. dirs. 1999—). Home: 7990 Deer Creek Rd Salt Lake City UT 84121-5752 Office: Holland & Hart 60 E South Temple Ste 2000 Salt Lake City UT 84111-1031

HOLTZ, SARA, marketing consultant; b. LA, Aug. 7, 1951; BA, Yale U., 1972; JD, Harvard U., 1975. Bar: D.C. 1975, Calif. 1982. Assoc. Brownstein, Zeidman & Schomer, Washington, 1975-77; dep. asst. dir. FTC, Washington, 1977-82; divsn. counsel Clorox Co., Oakland, Calif., 1982-90; v.p., dep. gen. counsel Nestle U.S.A., Inc., San Francisco, 1990-94; prin. Client Focus, 1996—. Mem. Am. Corp. Counsel Assn. (bd. dirs. 1986-95, chmn. 1994-95). Office: 5320 Olive Tree Ct Granite Bay CA 95746-9484

HOLTZMAN, ROBERT ARTHUR, lawyer; b. LA, July 17, 1929; s. Ruben and Bertha (Dembowsky) H.; m. Barbara Polis, June 26, 1954 (dec. 1985); children: Melinda, Mark, Bradley; m. Liliane Gurwith Endlich, July 6, 1986. BA, UCLA, 1951; LLB, U. So. Calif., 1954. Bar: Calif. 1955, U.S. Dist. Ct. (ctrl. dist.) Calif. 1955, U.S. Ct. Appeals (9th cir.) 1958. Assoc. Gang, Tyre & Brown, LA, 1954, Loeb and Loeb, LA, 1956-63, ptnr., 1964-95, of counsel, 1996—. Judge pro tem Mcpl. Ct. L.A. Jud. Dist.; lectr. Calif. Continuing Edn. of Bar. Contbr. articles to legal publs. With U.S. Army, 1954-56. Mem. ABA (dispute resolution sect., vice-chmn. arbitration com.), Calif. Bar Assn. (chmn. com. on adminstrn. of justice 1984-85), L.A. County Bar Assn., Am. Arbitration Assn. (panel arbitrators 1974—, panel mediators 1992—, arbitrator large complex case program 1993—); fellow Coll. Comml. Arbitrators (charter) Office: Loeb & Loeb LLP 10100 Santa Monica Blvd Ste 2200 Los Angeles CA 90067-4164 Home Phone: 818-783-3901; Office Phone: 310-282-2280. Business E-Mail: rholtzman@loeb.com.

HOLZER, THOMAS E., physicist; PhD, U. Calif., San Diego, 1970. Sr. scientist High Altitude Obs., Nat. Ctr. for Atmospheric Rsch., Boulder, Colo., 1978—, dir., 1990-95. Fellow Am. Geophys. Union (James B. MacElwane award 1978); mem. Norwegian Acad. Sci. and Letters, Internat. Astron. Union, Am. Astron. Soc., Internat. Union of Radio Scis. Office: High Altitude Obs NCAR 3450 Mitchell Ln Boulder CO 80301-2260 E-mail: holzer@ucar.edu.

HOLZMAN, D. KEITH, management consultant, record company executive; b. NYC, Mar. 22, 1936; s. Jacob Easton and Minnette Cathryn (Sternberger) H.; m. Jo Susan Handelman, Nov. 16, 1971; children: Susanne Carla, Lucas Jon, Rebecca Leigh. BA, Oberlin Coll., Ohio, 1957; MFA, Boston U., 1959. Asst. to gen. mgr. and stage mgr. N.Y.C. Light Opera, 1959, 62-64; dir. prodn. Elektra Records, NYC, 1964-70; v.p. prodn. and mfg. Elektra/Asylum/Nonesuch Records, Los Angeles, 1970-81, sr. v.p. prodn. and mfg., 1981-84; pres. ROM Records, 1987—2000; producer, arts cons. Treasure Trove, Inc., 1984—2000; mng. dir. Discovery Records, Santa Monica, Calif., 1991-98; prin. Keith Holzman Solutions Unltd., 1998—. Pres. Treasure Trove Inc.; dir. Nonesuch Records, 1980-84; music supr. Witches of Eastwick, Warner Bros., LA, 1986; bd. dirs. Plumstead Theatre Soc., LA, 1985—, Early Music Acad., LA, 1983-86, Assn. Classical Music, NYC, 1983-86, Wizard Music. Author: The Complete Guide to Starting a Record Company, 2004, The Complete Guide to Starting a Record Company, 2nd Edition, 2007. Served with AUS, 1960-62. Mem. Audio Engring. Soc., Early Music Acad. (bd. dirs.) Nat. Acad. Rec. Arts and Scis., Assn. Classical Music (bd. dirs.), Plumstead Theatre Co. (bd. dirs.). Avocation: flying.

HOMLDAHL, TODD, computer software company executive; B in elec. engring., Stanford univ.; M in elec. engring., Stanford Univ. Gen. mgr. Xbox product group Microsoft Corp., Redmond, Wash., corp v.p. gaming & Xbox product group, 2004—.

HONDA, MICHAEL M. (MIKE HONDA), United States Representative from California; b. Walnut Creek, Calif., June 27, 1941; m. Jeanne Honda (dec. 2004); children: Mark, Michelle. BS in Biol. Sci., San Jose State U., 1968, BA in Spanish, 1968, MA in Edn., 1974. Assoc. rschr. Urban-Rural Sch. Devel. Prog. Stanford U., 1974—75; vice prin. Sylvandale Mid. Sch., 1975—78; prin. Hillsdale Elem. Sch./McKinley Elem. Sch., 1978—86; mem. Santa Clara County Bd. Suprs., 1990—96, Calif. State Assembly, 1996—2000, US Congress from 15th Calif. dist., 2001—, mem. appropriations com., edn. & related agencies com. Mem. San Jose Planning Commn., 1971, San Jose Unified Sch. Bd., 1981—90, New Dem. Coalition, San Jose Mayor's Gang Task Force, Dem. Homeland Security Task Force; vice chair Dem. Nat. Com.; chair South County Agrl. Preservation Task Force, 1995—96; founder, co-chair Wireless Task Force/Congl. Internet Caucus, 2001—; founding co-chair Congl. Ethiopia & Ethiopian-Am. Caucus, 2003—; chair Congl. Asian-Pacific Am. Caucus, 2003—; regional whip Dem. Caucus US Ho. of Reps., 2000—06, sr. whip, 2007—. Named High Tech Legislator Yr., Am. Electronics Assn. Democrat. Office: 1713 Longworth Ho Office Bldg Washington DC 20515-0515*

HONEGGER, GITTA, language educator; PhD in Theater, U. Vienna, Austria. Prof. dramaturgy and dramatic criticism Yale Sch. Drama, 1983—93; stage dir. Yale Repertory Theatre; chair dept. drama Cath. U. Am., Washington, 1993—2001; prof. theatre and English Ariz. State U., Tempe, Ariz., 2001—. Author: Thomas Bernhard: The Making of an Austrian, 2001 (Austrian Cultural Forum bi-annual book award), Thomas Bernhard: Was ist das für ein Narr, 2002; contbg. editor Yale Theater Mag. Fellow, John Simon Guggenheim Meml. Found., 2003—04. Office: Ariz State U Herberger Coll of the Arts Sch Theatre & Film PO Box 872002 Tempe AZ 85287-2002 Office Phone: 480-965-6084. Office Fax: 480-965-5351. E-mail: gitta.honegger@asu.edu.

HONEY, RICHARD CHURCHILL, retired electrical engineer; b. Portland, Oreg., Mar. 9, 1924; s. John Kohnen and Margaret Fargo (Larrison) H.; m. Helen Waugaman, June 8, 1952 (div. Feb. 1980; children: Leslie, Steven, Laura, Janine; m. Jo Anne Kipp, Jan. 11, 1993. BS, Calif. Inst. Tech., 1945; EE, Stanford U., 1950, PhD, 1953. Research asst. Stanford U., 1948-52; sr. research engr. microwave group Stanford Research Inst., 1952-60; tech. program coordinator Electromagnetic Techniques Lab., 1960-64, lab. dir., 1964-70, staff scientist, 1970-89, sr. prin. scientist, 1989—; 86. Dir. ILC Tech.; mem. Army Sci. Bd., 1978-84. Contbr. articles to books, encyc., profl. jours.; patentee in field. Served with USN, 1943-46. Fellow IEEE, Optical Soc. Am.; mem. Coyote Point Yacht Club, Sigma Xi. Office: SRI Internat 333 Ravenswood Ave Menlo Park CA 94025-3453 Personal E-mail: honeykip@sbcglobal.net.

HONEYCUTT, VAN B., retired computer services company executive; b. Va., 1945; BSBA, Franklin U., Columbus, Ohio, 1971; grad. from Exec. Program, Stanford U., Calif., 1984. With Computer Scis. Corp., El Segundo, Calif., 1975—, pres. credit svcs., 1983—87, corp. v.p., pres. Industry Svcs. Group, 1987—93, pres., COO, 1993—95, CEO, 1995—2007, chmn., 1995—2007. Bd. dirs. Beckman Coulter Inc., Tenet Healthcare Corp., 1999—2005; mem. Pres. Nat. Security Telecom. Adv. Com.

HONEYFORD, JIM, state legislator; b. Ontario, Oreg., Jan. 24, 1939; m to Jerri; children: four. City councilman, Sunnyside, Washington, formerly; Washington State Representative, District 15, 94-98; Washington State Senator, District 15, 99-, Republican Caucus Chairman, currently, Washington State Senate.Educator, formerly; board member, Sunnyside Develop Corp, Sunnyside Tennis Club, Sunnyside Youth Recreation Association & Habitat for Humanity, formerly; police officer, formerly; farmer, currently. Outstanding Legislator, Nat Fedn Independent Bus, 97-98. Republican. Christian Reformed. Mailing: 100 Flagstone Ln Sunnyside WA 98944-9431 Fax: 360-786-1066. E-mail: honeyfor_ji@leg.wa.gov.

HONEYSTEIN, KARL, lawyer, media specialist; b. NYC, Jan. 10, 1932; s. Herman and Claire (Rosen) H.; m. Buzz Halliday, Sept. 14, 1965 (div. Dec. 1978); 1 child, Gail; m. Shauna Wood Trabert, Jan. 24, 1995. BA, Yale U., New Haven, Conn., 1953; JD, Columbia U., NYC, 1959. Bar: NY 1959. Assoc. Greenbaum, Wolff & Ernst, NYC, 1959-62; v.p. Ashley Famous Agy., NYC, 1962-69, Internat. Famous Agy., NYC, 1969-71; exec. v.p. The Sy Fischer Co., NYC and L.A., 1971-80; exec. v.p., chief operating officer The Taft Entertainment Co., L.A., 1980-88; pres. K.H. Strategy Corp., L.A., 1988—. Dir. Rhythm & Hues, Inc.; lectr. law Bklyn. Law Sch., NYC, 1973-75; mem. adv. group Wood Warren, Investment Bankers. Served to lt. j.g. USNR, 1953-56 Mem.: Internat. Acad. TV Arts and Scis., Friars Club. Office Phone: 310-273-0696. Personal E-mail: khs1@prodigy.net.

HOOD, LEROY EDWARD, molecular biologist, educator; b. Missoula, Mont., Oct. 10, 1938; s. Thomas Edward and Myrtle Evylan (Wadsworth) H.; m. Valerie Anne Logan, Dec. 14, 1963; children: Eran William, Marqui Leigh Jennifer. BS, Calif. Inst. Tech., 1960; MD, Johns Hopkins U., 1964; PhD in Biochemistry, Calif. Inst. Tech., 1968. Med. officer USPHS, 1967-70, staff scientist Bethesda, Md., 1967-70; sr. investigator Nat. Cancer Inst., 1967-70; asst. prof. biology Calif. Inst. Tech., Pasadena, 1970-73, assoc. prof., 1973-75, prof., 1975-92, Bowles prof. biology, 1977-92, chmn. divsn. biology, 1980-89; founder to Gates prof. molecular biotechnology, chmn. bd. U. Wash. Sch. Medicine, Seattle, 1992—2000; co-founder, pres. Inst. Systems Biology, Seattle, 2000—. Dir. NSF Sci. and Tech. Ctr. for Molecular Biotechnology, 1989-2001. Author: (with others) Biochemistry, a Problems Approach, 1974, Molecular Biology of Eukaryotic Cells, 1975, Immunology, 1978, Essential Concepts of Immunology, 1978, The Code of Codes: Scientific and Social Issues in the Human Genome Project, 1992; co-editor: Advances in Immunology, 1987, Genetics: From Genes to Genomics, 1999. Co-recipient, Albert Lasker Basic Med. Rsch. award, 1987, recipient Scientist of Yr. award, 1993, R & D Mag., Kyoto Prize, 2002, Lemelson prize MIT, 2003, Assoc. for Molecular Biology award for excellence in molecular diagnostics, 2004; named to the Nat. Inventors Hall of Fame, 2007. Mem. NAS, NAE, Am. Assn. Immunologists, Am. Assn. Sci., Am. Acad. Arts and Scis., Sigma Xi, Am. Philos. Soc., Inst. Medicine, 2004. Achievements include invention of automated DNA sequencer technique. Avocations: photography, running, reading. Office: Inst for Systems Biology 1441 N 34th St Seattle WA 98103-8904 Office Phone: 206-732-1201. E-mail: lhood@systemsbiology.org.

HOOD, WILLIAM BOYD, JR., cardiologist, educator; b. Sylacauga, Ala., Mar. 25, 1932; s. William Boyd and Katherine Elizabeth (Anderson) H.; m. Katherine Candace Todd, May 5, 1972; 1 son, Jefferson Boyce. BS summa cum laude, Davidson Coll., 1954; MD, Harvard U., 1958. Intern Peter Bent Brigham Hosp., Boston, 1958-59, resident in internal medicine, 1959-60, 62-63; from asst. prof. to assoc. prof. medicine Harvard U., 1967-71; from assoc. prof. to prof. medicine Boston U., 1971-82; chief cardiology Boston City Hosp., 1973-82; prof. medicine U. Rochester (N.Y.), 1982-98; head cardiology unit Strong Meml. Hosp., Rochester, 1982-98; emeritus prof. medicine U. Rochester, 1998—. Cons. NIH, 1975—, NASA, 1994—; clin. prof. medicine U. Wash. Sch. Medicine, Seattle, 2000—. Mem. editorial bd. New Eng. Jour. Medicine, 1974-81, Circulation, 1980-83, Circulation Research, 1982-89, Jour. Clin. Investigation, 1984-89, Cochrane Collaboration Heart Group, 1997—; contbr. articles, revs. and editorials on cardiovascular physiology to profl. jours., chpts. to books. Served to capt. USAF, 1963-65. Research grantee NIH, 1971-98; grantee Am. Heart Assn., 1971-76. Fellow ACP; mem. Am. Soc. Clin. Investigation, Assn. Am. Physicians, Am. Heart Assn., Am. Physiol. Soc., Assn. Profs. Cardiology (past pres.), N.Y. Cardiol. Soc. (past pres.), Phi Beta Kappa, Alpha Omega Alpha. Achievements include studies on experimental and clinical myocardial ischemia and infarction, and congestive heart failure.

HOOK, RALPH CLIFFORD, JR., business educator; b. Kansas City, Mo., May 2, 1923; s. Ralph Clifford and Ruby (Swanson) H.; m. Joyce Fink, Jan. 20, 1946; children: Ralph Clifford III, John Gregory. BA, U. Mo., Columbia, 1947, MA, 1948; PhD, U. Tex., Austin, 1954. Instr. U. Mo., 1947-48; asst. prof. Tex. A&M U., 1948-51; lectr. U. Tex., 1951-52; co-owner, mgr. Hook Buick Co., also Hook Truck & Tractor Co., Lee's Summit, Mo., 1952-58; assoc. prof. U. Kansas City, 1953-58; dir. Bur. Bus. Rsch. and Svcs., Ariz. State U., 1958-66, prof. mktg., 1960-68; dean Coll. Bus. Adminstrn., U. Hawaii, 1968-74; prof. mktg. U. Hawaii, 1974-96, prof. mktg. emeritus, 1996—. Vis. Disting. prof. N.E. La. U., 1979; dir. Hook Bros. Corp. Author: (with others) The Management Primer, 1972, Life Style Marketing, 1979, Marketing Service, 1983; contbr. (with others) monograph series Western Bus. Roundup; founder, moderator Western Bus. Roundup radio series, 1958-68. 1st lt. F.A., AUS, 1943-46; col. Res. Recipient alumni citation of merit U. Mo. Coll. Bus. and Pub. Adminstrn., 1969; Disting. Svc. award Nat. Def. Transp. Assn., 1977, God and Svc. award United Meth. Ch./Boy Scouts Am., 1986, Hawaii Jefferson award, 2004; named to Faculty Hall Fame Ariz. State U. Coll. Bus. Assn., 1977, Hawaii Transp. Hall of Fame, 1986, Hawaii Bus. Hall of Fame, 2000; named Educator of Yr., Western Mktg. Educators' Assn., 1998. Fellow Internat. Coun. for Small Bus. (pres. 1963); mem. Am. Mktg. Assn. (v.p. 1965-67, pres. Ctrl. Ariz. chpt. 1960-61, pres. Honolulu chpt. 1991-92, Wayne A. Lemberg award for disting. svc. 1995), Western Assn. Collegiate Schs. Bus. (pres. 1972-73), Sales and Mktg. Execs. Internat. (life), Nat. Def. Transp. Assn. (life, Hawaii v.p. 1978-82), Pi Sigma Epsilon (v.p. for edn. programs 1990-94), Mu Kappa Tau (pres. 1996-98), Beta Gamma Sigma, Omicron Delta Kappa, Beta Theta Pi, Delta Sigma Pi (gold coun.). United Methodist. Office: U Hawaii Coll Bus Adminstrn 2404 Maile Way Bldg C Honolulu HI 96822-2223 Home: 428 Kawaihae St Apt 202 Honolulu HI 96825-1288 Home Phone: 808-395-9251.

HOOKER, ELAINE NORTON, news executive; b. Rockville Center, NY, Dec. 4, 1944; d. Henry Gaither and Ann Lou (Allen) Norton; m. Ronald Wayne Johnson (div.); m. Kenneth Ward Hooker Jr. (div.); children: Alisa, Miranda, Nora, Emily. Student, Wilson Coll., 1962-64, U. Hartford, 1965, Trinity Coll., 1974, Andover Newton Theol. Sch., 1988-89. Reporter, editor The Hartford (Conn.) Courant, 1969-74; newswoman AP, Hartford, 1974-75, Conn. news editor, 1975-79, western Mass. corr. Springfield, Mass., 1979-80, Mass. day news supr. Boston, 1981-84, Mass. news editor, 1984, Conn. bur. chief Hartford, 1984-88, dep. dir. corp. comm. NYC, 1990, gen. exec. newspaper membership, 1991-97, Oreg. bur. chief Portland, 1997—. Spkr. in field. Active various corns. at chs. in Concord, Mass., Hartford, Briarcliff, N.Y., Greenwich, Conn., N.Y.C. Recipient Sigma Delta Chi award, 1974. Mem. Soc. Profl. Journalists (mem. Freedom Info. coun. 1984-87), New Eng. Soc. Newspaper Editors (rep. Soviet journalists conf. 1985), Open Oreg. Office: AP 121 SW Salmon St Ste 1450 Portland OR 97204-2924

HOOKS, ROSIE LEE, museum director, actor, filmmaker; Attended, Miami Dade CC, U. Miami, U. Md., NUY Tisch Sch. Film and TV. Tchr./social worker's aid, career devel. specialist Dade County Bd. Pub. Instrn., Miami, 1967—70; regional reps. Univ. Rsch. Corp. and Edn. Projects, Inc., 1970—74; program coord. Smithsonian Instn., Washington, 1974—77; freelance actress, cons., 1977—83. Actor, adminstrv./tng. coord. DC Black Repertory Co., Washington, 1974—77; dir., Office Festivals and Gallery Theatre City LA Cultural Affairs Dept., 1990—2002, dir., Watts Towers Arts Ctr., 2002—; prodr. various arts festivals and theatre prodns. Actor: (film) The Bodyguard, 1992; (plays) A Change is Gonna Come, Poetry Cabaret, Misanthrope, One Thousand Cranes, Checkmates, Song of the Lusitanian Bogey, Men's Eden and others; filmmaker: A Special Friend of Mine; Festival of Philippine Arts and Culture; A Dozen Drums; LA Cuban Festival; Storytelling Time; Fertile Ground: Stories from the Watts Towers Arts Center and others. Recipient Rainbow award, LA Women's Theatre Festival, Cmty. Svc. award, Festival Philippine Arts and Culture, King Drew Med. Sch., 2006. Mem.: Engring. and Architects Assn., Am. Fedn. TV and Recording Artists, Actors Equity Assn., SAG. Achievements include development of Jazz Mentorship Program. Office: Watts Towers Arts Ctr 1727 E 107th St Los Angeles CA 90002 Office Phone: 213-485-1795. Business E-Mail: cadofgt@earthlink.net.

HOOLEY, DARLENE KAY OLSON, former United States Representative from Oregon; b. Williston, ND, Apr. 4, 1939; d. Clarence Alvin and Alyce (Rogers) Olsen; m. John Hooley, 1965 (div.); children: Chad, Erin. BS in Edn., Oreg. State U., Corvallis, 1961, postgraduate student, 1963-65, Portland State U., 1966-67. Tchr. Woodburn & Gervais Sch., Oreg., 1962-65, David Douglas Sch. Dist., Portland, Oreg., 1965-67, St. Mary's Acad., Portland, 1967-69; mem. City Coun., West Linn, Oreg., 1976-80, Oreg. State House Reps. from Dist. 27, 1980-87; commr. Clackamas County Bd., Oreg., 1987-96; mem. US Congress from 5th Oreg. dist., 1996—2009, mem. energy and commerce com., mem. budget com., mem. sci. and tech. com. Vice chair Oreg. Tourism Alliance, Portland, 1991; bd. dirs. Providence Med. Ctr., Portland, 1989, Cmty. Corrections Bd., Oregon City, 1990; acting chair Oreg. Trail Found. Bd., Oregon City, 1991; mem. Urban Growth Policy Adv. Com., Portland, 1991. Named Legislator of Yr. Oreg. Libr. Assn., 1985-86, Oreg. Solar Energy Assn., 1985; recipient Spl. Svc. award Clackamas City Coun. for Child Abuse Prevention, 1989. Mem. LWV, Oreg. Women's Polit. Caucus (Woman of Yr. 1988). Democrat. Lutheran.*

HOOPER, EDWIN BICKFORD, physicist; b. Bremerton, Wash., June 18, 1937; s. E.B. and Elizabeth (Patrick) H.; m. Virginia Hooper, Dec. 28, 1963; children: Edwin, Sarah, William. SB, MIT, 1959, PhD, 1965. Asst. prof. applied sci. Yale U., New Haven, 1966-70; physicist, dep. program leader FE Lawrence Livermore (Calif.) Nat. Lab., 1970—2003, flex term physicist, 2003—. Adv. com. Fusion Energy Burning Plasmic Program, 2003—; mem. program adv. com. Virtual Lab. Fusion Tech., 2002—06. Contbr. articles to profl. jours. Pres. Danville (Calif.) Assn., 1982-84; pres. Friends Iron Horse Trail, 1984-86; v.p. San Ramon Valley Edn. Found., 1989-90, chair sci. adv. com., 2005-; dir. Leadership, San Ramon Valley, 1990-92; mem. adv. com. East Bay Regional Pk., 2002—. Fellow Am. Phys. Soc. (bd. dirs. div. Plasma Physics 1990-91); mem. AIAA (sr.), AAAS. Office: Lawrence Livermore Nat Lab L-637 Livermore CA 94550-4436 Office Phone: 925-423-1409.

HOOPER, PATRIC, lawyer; b. Altoona, Pa., Dec. 22, 1948; AB, UCLA, 1970; JD, Univ. San Diego, 1973. Bar: Calif. 1973, US Ct. Appeals (5th, 6th, 7th, 8th, 9th, 10th, Fed., DC cir.), US Supreme Ct. Dep. atty. gen. Calif. Dept. Justice, 1974—76; founding ptnr., health care law Hooper Lundy & Bookman, LA, 1987—. Gen. counsel Nat. Assn. Psychiatric Treatment Centers for Children. Mem.: ABA (chmn. health law sect. fraud & abuse interest group), Am. Health Lawyers Assn., Healthcare Fin. Mgmt. Assn., Calif. Clinical Laboratory Assn., Calif. Soc. Healthcare Attys., LA County Bar Assn. Office: Hooper Lundy & Bookman Ste 1600 1875 Century Park E Los Angeles CA 90067 Office Phone: 310-551-8111, 310-551-8165. Office Fax: 310-551-8181. Business E-Mail: phooper@health-law.com.

HOOPER, ROGER FELLOWES, retired architect; b. Southampton, NY, Aug. 18, 1917; s. Roger Fellowes and Justine Van Rensselaer (Barber) H.; m. Patricia Bentley, Aug. 10, 1946; children: Judith Bayard Teresi, Rachel Bentley Zingg, Roger Fellowes III. AB, Harvard U., 1939, MArch, 1948. Ptnr. Malone & Hooper, San Francisco, 1949-60; ptnr., pres. Hooper Olmsted & Emmons, San Francisco, 1964-79; chmn. Hooper Olmsted & Hrovat, San Francisco, 1980-94, retired, 1994. Bd. mgr. Marin YMCA, San Rafael, Calif.; bd. dirs., pres. Marin Conservation League, San Rafael. Lt. comdr. USNR, 1941-45, WWII. Mem. AIA.

HOOPES, FARREL G., secondary school educator; Tchr. Star Valley H.S., Afton, Wyo. Recipient Tchr. Excellence award Internat. Tech. Edn. Assn., 1992. Office: Star Valley HS PO Box 8000 Afton WY 83110-8000

HOOPS, ALAN R., health care company executive; b. 1947; Asst. administr. Long Beach Mem. Hosp., 1973-77; v.p. PacifiCare Health Sys. Inc., Cypress, Calif., 1977-85, sec., from 1982, sr. v.p., 1985-86, COO, exec. v.p., 1986-93, CEO, pres., 1993—2000; chmn. Benu, Inc., San Mateo, Calif., 2000—. Office: Benu Inc 1 Waters Park Dr Ste 101 San Mateo CA 94403-1163

HOOVER, GARY LYNN, retired banker; b. Tipton, Ind., Oct. 20, 1937; s. Carmel Wayne and Virginia Ruth (Mitchell) H.; m. Virginia Maxine James Monet, May 8, 1965 (div. Apr. 1976); m. Laura E. Grigg West, June 25, 1988 (div. May 13, 2002); children: Devin Page, Melissa Virginia. BS, Purdue U., 1959. Nat. bank examiner Internat. Comptroller of the Currency, Washington, 1962-71; v.p. Am. Fletcher Nat. Bank, Indpls., 1971-81; credit examiner Internat. Farm Credit Adminstrn., Washington, 1981-84; v.p. Nat. Bank for Cooperatives, Englewood, Colo., 1984-95. Dir. Hoover Farms, Inc., Tipton, Ind.; pres. Hoover Fin. Assn., LLC, Highlands Ranch, Colo., 1995—; mem. U. Colo. Scholarship Fund, Boulder; assoc. prof. Ind. Ctrl. Coll., Indpls., 1972—73. Mem. pres. coun. Purdue U., West Lafayette, Ind., 1997—; mem. Vail Valley Found., Colo., 2001—. With US Army, 1961—66. Mem.: Ind. Bankers Assn. Colo. Republican. Avocations: reading, travel, cartography. Home: PO Box 6424 Vail CO 81658-6424

HOOVER, GEORGE SCHWEKE, architect; b. Chgo., July 1, 1935; s. George Milton and Antoinette (Schweke) H.; children: Sandra Jean, Ranya Sue; m. Mary Elizabeth Benoit, June 6, 1987. BArch., Cornell U., 1958. Registered architect, Colo., Calif., Tex., Minn., Ala., Tenn. Draftsman Holabird Root and Burgee, Chgo., 1957, Designer James Sudler Assocs., Denver, 1961-62; architect Ream, Quinn Assocs., Denver, 1962-65, Muchow Assocs., Denver, 1965-76; prin. Hoover Berg Desmond, Denver, 1976—. Tenured prof. arch. U. Colo. Coll. Arch. and Planning, chmn. dept. arch., 1997—; vis. lectr. U. N.Mex., Okla. State U., Harvard U., Miami U. Prin. works include Douglas County Adminstrn. Bldg., Light of the World Cath. Ch., U. Colo. Bldg., Denver, Denver Diagnostic and Reception Ctr., Labs for Atmospheric and Space Physics, U. Colo., Boulder, Colo. Acad. Master Plan, U. Ariz. Engring. Complex Master Plan, Multipurpose Arena, Nat. Western Stockshow, Nat. Wild Animal Rsch. Ctr., Colo. State U. Conf. Ctr., Storage Tech. Corp., Aerospace & Mech. Engring. Bldg. U. Ariz., Environ. and Natural Resources Bldg. U. Ariz., Master Plan Cummins Power Generation Group Hdqs., Fridley, Minn., Master Plan Fleetguard and Mfg. Plant, Cookeville, Tenn.; finalist Denver Cen. Libr. Competition, 1991; exhbn. Gund Hall Gallery, Grad. Sch. Design, Harvard U., 1986; mem. editl. bd. Avant Garde. Lt. (j.g.) USN, 1958-61. Recipient 1st Design award Progressive Arch., 1972, Citation, 1974, Design award, 1984, 87, Charles Goodwin Sands Medal for excellence in design Tau Beta Pi, Fed. Design Achievement award, 1984, Honor award Interfaith Forum on Religion, Art, and Arch., 1986, Tau Sigma Delta medal, 1991; named Outstanding Young Architect, Archtl. Record, 1974, Fellow AIA (steering com., Pitts. Corning award 1989, Nat. Honor award 1975, 83, 90, Firm of Yr. award Colo. chpt. 1991, Regional Firm of Yr. award 1992, Architect of Yr. award Colo. chpt. 1995), Nat. Acad. Design.; mem. Nat. Com. Design (steering com., chmn. awards task group 1989-92), Nat. Com. Archtl. Edn. (steering com. 1990-92). Episcopalian. also: U Colo 1250 14th St Denver CO 80202-1702 Office Phone: 303-556-5965. E-mail: hoover@ar7.com.

HOOVER, R. DAVID, packaging company executive; b. Straughn, Ind., June 21, 1945; BS, DePauw U., Greencastle, Ind., 1967; MBA, Indiana U., Bloomington, 1970; postgrad mgmt. program, Harvard U., 1988. Corp. fin. analyst Eli Lilly & Co., Indpls.; asst. to treas. Ball Corp., v.p., fin. & admin. agrl. sys. divsn., 1980—85, v.p., fin. & admin. aerospace sys. group, 1985—87, asst. treas., 1987—88, v.p. & treas., 1988—92, sr. v.p. & CFO, 1992—96, exec. v.p. & mem. bd. dirs., 1996—98, vice chmn. & CFO, 1998—2000, COO, 2000—01, CEO & pres., 2001—, chmn., 2002—. Bd. mem. Datum, Inc., Maxon

Corp. & Energizer Holdings; mem. bd. dirs. & former chmn. Can Manufacturers Inst. Bd. mem. Nat. Food Processors Assn., Boulder Cmty. Found., DePauw U. Bd. Visitors & Bd. Trustees, Indiana U., Kelley Sch. Bus., Dean's Adv. Coun. Office: 10 Longs Peak Dr Broomfield CO 80021-2510

HOOVER, ROBERT ALLAN, university president; b. Des Moines, May 9, 1941; s. Claude Edward and Anna Doris H.; m. Jeanne Mary Hoover, Feb. 22, 1968 (dec. 2005); m. Leslee Hoover, Aug. 20, 2006; children: Jennifer Jill Jacobs, Suzanne Hoover Ogden. BS, Ariz. State U., 1967, MA, 1969; PhD, U. Calif., Santa Barbara, 1973. Instr. polit. sci. Utah State U., Logan, 1971-73, asst. prof. polit. sci., 1973-79, assoc. prof. polit. sci., chair polit. sci. dept., 1979-84, prof. polit. sci., 1984-91, dean Coll. Humanities, Arts and Social Scis., 1984-91; v.p. for acad. affairs U. Nev., Reno, 1991-96; pres. U. Idaho, Moscow, 1996—2003, Albertson Coll. Idaho, Caldwell, 2003—. Author: The Politics of MX: A New Direction in Weapons Procurement?, 1982, The MX Controversy: A Guide to Issues and References, 1982, Arms Control: The Interwar Naval Limitation Agreements, 1980. Bd. dirs. St. Scholastica Acad., Canon City, Colo., 1989-95, pres. 1991-95, United Way, Reno, 1994-96, Channel 5, Reno, 1991-95; bd. visitors USAF U., 1997-2003, chair, 2002-03; mem. Idaho Gov.'s Coun. for Sci. Tech., 1991-2003; chair bd. dirs. Inland Northwest Rsch. Alliance, 1998-2003; mem. pres. coun., Nat. Assn. State Univs. and Land Grant Colls., 2001-03, chair eco-terrorism task force, 2002; bd. trustees Albertson Coll. Idaho; mem. visitors group, Utah State U., 2001-03. Recipient Tchr. the Yr., Humanities, Arts and Social Scis. Coll., Utah State U., 1983—84, Dist. VII Leadership award, Coun. Advancement and Support Edn., 2002, Top Mgr. the Yr., Sales and Mktg. Execs., Boise, 2003. Mem.: Coun. Ind. Coll. Avocations: reading, skiing, jogging, piano. Office: Albertson Coll 2112 Cleveland Blvd Caldwell ID 83605-9990 Business E-Mail: rhoover@albertson.edu.

HOPE, MIKE, state legislator; b. Cleve. m. Sarai Hope. BA in Sociology, John Carroll U., U. Heights, Ohio; M in Policy Studies, U. Wash., Seattle. Served several years as police officer & detective, Seattle; asst. rep. whip Wash. House of Reps., mem. Dist. 44, 2008—. Served reserves USMC, 1994—2001. Republican. Office: 439 John L O'brien Bldg PO Box 40600 Olympia WA 98504-0600 Office Phone: 360-786-7892. Business E-Mail: hope.mike@leg.wa.gov.

HOPFENBECK, GEORGE MARTIN, JR., lawyer; b. NYC, Mar. 1, 1929; s. George Martin and Margaret Spencer (Felt) H.; m. Ruth Elizabeth Allen, June 27, 1953; children: Ann Elizabeth, James Allen. BA, Williams Coll., 1951; JD, Yale U., 1954. Bar: Colo., 1955. Assoc. Davis, Graham & Stubbs and predecessor Lewis, Grant & Davis, Denver, 1954-59, ptnr., 1959-92, of counsel, 1993—. Bd. dirs. Am. Cancer Soc. Inc., Colo. divsn., Denver, 1966-90, chmn., 1975-77; bd. dirs. Colo. Regional Cancer Ctr. Inc., Denver, 1974-81, pres., 1975-77; bd. dirs. Am. Cancer Soc. Inc., Atlanta, 1984-90, Denver Parks and Recreation Found., 1966-75; bd. dirs. Boys and Girls Clubs of Metro Denver, Inc., 1993-2007, chmn., 1998-2000; mem. Colo. State Pers. Bd., Denver, 1971-75, chmn., 1971-72; mem. Denver Bd. Parks & Recreation, 1961-69; trustee Kent Sch. for Girls, Denver, 1970-73; chmn. campaign com. for Gov. Love, Colo., 1966, campaign com. for McKevitt for Congress, Denver, 1970. Recipient St. George medal Am. Cancer Soc., 1982. Mem. ABA, Colo. Bar Assn., Denver Country Club (bd. dirs. 1967-70, 2002-2005), University Club (Denver) (bd. dirs. 1973-82). Republican. Episcopalian. Home: 2552 E Alameda Ave # 75 Denver CO 80209

HOPKINS, BERNARD, professional boxer; b. Phila., Jan. 15, 1965; Profl. boxer, 1988—; ptnr. Golden Boy Promotions, 2004—; pres. Golden Boy Promotions East, 2004—. Winner vacant title vs. Wayne Powell by tech. knockout, middleweight divsn. US Boxing Assn., 1992, winner title def. vs. Gilbert Baptist by unanimous decision, middleweight divsn., 93, winner title def. vs. Roy Ritchie by tech. knockout, middleweight divsn., 93, winner title def. vs. Wendall Hall by tech. knockout, middleweight divsn., 93, winner title def. vs. Lupe Aquino by unanimous decision, middleweight divsn., 94; winner vacant world title vs. Segundo Mercado by tech. knockout, middleweight divsn. Internat. Boxing Fedn., 1995, winner world title def. vs. Steve Frank by tech. knockout, middleweight divsn., 96, winner world title def. vs. Joe Lipsey by tech. knockout, middleweight divsn., 96, winner world title def. vs. William Bo James by tech. knockout, middleweight divsn., 96, winner world title def. vs. John David Jackson by tech. knockout, middleweight divsn., 97, winner world title def. vs. Glengoffe Johnson by tech. knockout, middleweight divsn., 97, winner world title def. vs. Andrew Council unanimous decision, middleweight divsn., 97, winner world title def. vs. Simon Brown by tech. knockout, middleweight divsn., 98, winner world title def. vs. Robert Allen by unanimous decision, middleweight divsn., 99, winner world title def. vs. Antwun Echols by unanimous decision, middleweight divsn., 99, winner world title def. vs. Syd Vanderpool by unanimous decision, middleweight divsn., 2000, winner world title def. vs. Antwun Echols by tech. knockout, middleweight divsn., 00, winner world title def. vs. Keith Holmes by unanimous decision, middleweight divsn., 01; winner world title vs. Keith Holmes by unanimous decision, middleweight divsn. World Boxing Coun., 2001, winner world title def. vs. Felix Trinidad by tech. knockout, middleweight divsn., 01, Internat. Boxing Fedn., 2001; winner world title vs. Felix Trinidad by tech. knockout, middleweight divsn. World Boxing Assn., 2001; winner world title def. vs. Carl Daniels by tech. knockout, middleweight divsn. World Boxing Coun., 2002, Internat. Boxing Fedn., 2002, World Boxing Assn., 2002; winner world title def. vs. Morrade Hakkar by tech. knockout, middleweight divsn. World Boxing Coun., 2003, Internat. Boxing Fedn., 2003, World Boxing Assn., 2003; winner world title def. vs. William Joppy by unanimous decision, middleweight divsn. World Boxing Coun., 2003, Internat. Boxing Fedn., 2003, World Boxing Assn., 2003; winner world title def. vs. Robert Allen by unanimous decision, middleweight divsn. World Boxing Coun., 2004, Internat. Boxing Fedn., 2004, World Boxing Assn., 2004; winner world title def. vs. Oscar De Le Hoya by knockout, middleweight divsn. World Boxing Coun., 2005, Internat. Boxing Fedn., 2005, World Boxing Assn., 2005; winner world title vs. Oscar De Le Hoya by knockout, middleweight divsn. World Boxing Orgn., 2005; winner world title def. vs. Howard Eastman by unanimous decision, middleweight divsn. World Boxing Coun., 2005, Internat. Boxing Fedn., 2005, World Boxing Assn., 2005, World Boxing Orgn., 2005; winner title vs. Antonio Tarver, light heavyweight divsn. Nat. Boxing Assn., 2006, Internat. Boxing Orgn., 2006. Appt. Mayor's Drug and Alcohol Exec. Commn., Phila., 2006—. Named Fighter of Yr., The Ring Mag., 2001, World Boxing Hall of Fame, 2001. Office: Golden Boy Promotions Ste 350 626 Wilshire Blvd Los Angeles CA 90017

HOPKINS, CECILIA ANN, business educator; b. Havre, Mont., Feb. 17, 1922; d. Kost L. and Mary (Manaras) Sofos; m. Henry E. Hopkins, Sept. 7, 1944. BS, Mont. State Coll., 1944; MA, San Francisco State Coll., 1958; postgrad., Stanford U.; PhD, Calif. Western U., 1977. Bus. tchr. Havre (Mont.) H.S., Mateo, Calif., 1942-44; sec. George P. Gorham, Realtor, San Mateo, 1944-45; escrow sec. Fox & Cars, 1945-50; escrow officer Calif. Pacific Title Ins. Co., 1950-57; bus. tchr. Westmoor H.S., Daly City, Calif., 1958-59, Coll. of San Mateo, 1959-63, chmn. real estate-ins. dept., 1963-76, dir. divsn. bus., 1976-86, coord. real estate dept., 1986-91. Cons. to commr. Calif. Divsn. Real Estate, 1963-91, mem. periodic rev. exam. com.; chmn. C.C. Adv. Com., 1971-72, mem. com., 1975-91; projector direction Calif. State Chancellor's Career Awareness Consortium, mem. endowment fund adv. com., c.c. real estate edn. com., state c.c. adv. com.; mem. No. Calif. adv. bd. to Glendale Fed. Savs. and Loan Assn.; mem. bd. advisors San Mateo County Bd. Suprs., 1981-82; mem. real estate edn. and rsch. com. to Calif. Commr. Real Estate, 1983-90; mem. edn., membership, and profl. exch. coms. Am. chpt. Internat. Real Estate Fedn., 1985-92. Co-author: California Real Estate Principles; contbr. articles to profl. jours. Recipient Citizen of Day award KABL, Outstanding Contbns. award Redwood City-San Carlos-Belmont Bd. Realtors, Nat. Real Estate Educators Assn. award emeritus, 1993; named Woman of Achievement, San Mateo-Burlingame br. Soroptimist Internat., 1979. Mem. AAUW, Calif. Assn. Real Estate Tchrs. (state pres. 1964-65, life hon. dir. 1962—, Outstanding Real Estate Educator of Yr. 1978-79), Real Estate Cert. Inst. (Disting. Merit award 1982), Calif. Bus. Edn. Assn. (cert. of commendation 1979), San Francisco State Coll., Guidance and Counseling Alumni, Calif. Real Estate Educators' Assn. (dir. emeritus, hon. dir. 1990), Real Estate Nat. Educators Assn. (award emeritus for outstanding contbns. 1993), San Mateo-Burlingame Bd. Realtors (award emeritus Outstanding Contbrs. to Membership), Alpha Delta, Pi Lambda Theta, Delta Pi Epsilon (nat. dir. interchpt. rels. 1962-65, nat. historian 1966-67, nat. sec. 1968-69), Alpha Gamma Delta. Home: 300 31st Ave San Mateo CA 94403

HOPKINS, DONALD J., retired lawyer; b. Long Beach, Calif., Jan. 9, 1947; m. Ellen Colokathis, Aug. 29, 1970; children: Melanie J., Shannon R., Christopher S. AB, Stanford U., 1968; JD, Harvard U., 1971. Bar: Mass. 1971, Colo. 1974, U.S. Dist. Ct. Colo. 1974. Mem. firm Holme Roberts & Owen LLP, Denver, 1973—2004. Fellow: Am. Coll. Trust and Estate Counsel. Home: PO Box 190 9329 US Hwy 50 Howard CO 81233

HOPKINS, HENRY TYLER, museum director, art educator; b. Idaho Falls, Idaho, Aug. 14, 1928; s. Talcott Thompson and Zoe (Erbe) Hopkins; children: Victoria Anne, John Thomas, Christopher Tyler. BA, Sch. of Art Inst., Chgo., 1952, MA, 1955; postgrad., UCLA, 1957—60; PhD (hon.), Calif. Coll. Arts and Crafts, 1984, San Francisco Art Inst., 1986. Curator exhbns., publs. LA County Mus. of Art, 1960-68; lectr. art history UCLA Ext., 1960—68; dir. Ft. Worth Art Mus., 1968-74, San Francisco Mus. of Modern Art, 1974-86; chmn. art dept. UCLA, 1991-94, dir. F.S. Wight Gallery, 1991-95, dir. Armand Hammer Mus. Art and Cultural Ctr., 1994-99, prof. art, 1999—2002, prof. emeritus, 2002—. Instr. Tex. Christian U., Ft. Worth, 1968—74; dir. U.S. representation Venice Bienniel, Italy, 1970; dir. art presentation Festival of Two Worlds, Spoleto, Italy, 1970; co-commr. U.S. representation XVI Sao Paulo Biennale, Brazil, 1981; cons. NEA, mem. mus. panel, 1979—84, chmn., 1981; cons., mem. mus. panel NEH, 1976; archivist pers. archives Getty Rsch. Ctr., LA, 2005. Contbr. numerous articles to profl. jours. and mus. publs. With AUS, 1952—54. Decorated knight Order Leopold II, Belgium; recipient Spl. Internat. award, Art LA, 1992. Mem.: We. Assn. Art Museums (pres. 1977—78), Am. Assn. Museums, Coll. Art Assn., Assn. Art Mus. Dirs. (pres. 1985—86). Home: 939 1/2 Hilgard Ave Los Angeles CA 90024-3032 Office: UCLA Art Dept 405 Hilgard Ave Los Angeles CA 90095-9000 Office Phone: 310-206-7102. Personal E-mail: hthopkins@verizon.net. Business E-Mail: hhopkins@ucla.edu.

HOPKINS, MICHAEL, communications executive; b. 1968; married; 1 child. BS in Bus. Adminstrn., Calif. State U.; MBA, Anderson Sch., U. Calif., LA. Dir., Affiliate Sales, Pacific Northwest region Fox Cable Networks, Calif., 1997, dir., Affiliate Sales and Mktg., Fox Sports West, West 2 Calif., v.p., Affiliate Sales Calif., 1999, sr. v.p., Affiliate Sales Calif. Named one of 40 Executives Under 40, Multichannel News, 2006. Office: Fox Broadcasting Company 10201 W Pico Blvd Los Angeles CA 90035

HOPKINSON, SHIRLEY LOIS, library and information scientist, educator; b. Boone, Iowa, Aug. 25, 1924; d. Arthur Perry and Zora (Smith) Hopkinson. Student, Coe Coll., 1942—43; AB cum laude, U. Colo., 1945; BLS, U. Calif., 1949; MA, Claremont Grad. Sch., 1951; EdM, U. Okla., 1952, EdD, 1957. Tchr. pub. sch., Stigler, Okla., 1946—47; tchr. Palo Verde HS., Jr. Coll., Blythe, Calif., 1947—48; asst. libr. Modesto Jr. Coll., Calif., 1949—51; tchr., libr. Fresno, Calif., 1951—52, La Mesa, Calif., 1953—55; asst. prof. librarianship, instrnl. materials dir. Chaffey Coll., Ontario, Calif., 1955—59; asst. prof. librarianship San Jose State Coll., Calif., 1959—64, assoc. prof., 1964—69, prof., 1969—. Dir. NDEA Inst. Sch. Librs., 1966; mem. Santa Clara County Civil Svc. Bd. Examiners; owner Claremont House Publishers, 1975—. Author: Descriptive Cataloging of Library Materials, 1970, 1985, Instructional Materials for Teaching the Use of the Library, 1975, 1986; editor: Calif. Sch. Libraries, 1963—64; asst. editor Sch. Libr. Assn. of Calif. Bull., 1961—63, book reviewer profl. jours.; contbr. articles to profl. jours. Honnold Honor scholar, Claremont Grad. Sch., 1945—46. Mem.: LWV (bd. dirs. 1950—51, publs. chmn.), AAUW (dir. 1957—58), NEA, ALA, AAUP, Kappa Delta Pi, Alpha Beta Alpha, Calif. Tchrs. Assn., San Diego County Sch. Librs. Assn. (sec. 1954—55), Sch. Librs. Assn. Calif. (treas. No. sect. 1951—52, com. mem.), Audio-Visual Assn. Calif., Calif. Library Assn., Bus. Profl. Women's Club, Alpha Lambda Delta, Phi Beta Kappa (scholar 1944), Delta Kappa Gamma (sec. 1994—96, legis. liaison 1996—2002, corr. sec. 2002—), Phi Kappa Phi (disting. acad. achievement award 1981). Office: 1340 Pomeroy Ave Apt 408 Santa Clara CA 95051-3658

HOPP, RICHARD A., lawyer; b. Seattle, Dec. 11, 1946; BA, San Luis Rey Coll., 1969; JD, U. Wash., 1976. Bar: Wash. 1976. Mem. Stoel, Rives, Boley, Jones & Grey, Seattle; ptnr. Stoel Rives LLP, Seattle, 2000—. Chmn. Seattle Pension Roundtable, 1987—. Articles editor Washington Law Review, 1975-76. Mem. ABA, Wash. State Bar Assn. (bd. dirs. Seattle chpt., western pension conf. 1985-87, tax coun., taxation sect.), Seattle-King County. Office: Stoel Rives LLP 600 University St Ste 3600 Seattle WA 98101-4109

HOPP, TERRY A., computer company executive; BA in Bus. Adminstrn., Calif. State U., Fullerton. CPA, Calif. Audit ptnr. Earnst & Young LLP, 1981-98; v.p. fin. Western Digital Corp., Irvine, Calif., 1998, now sr. v.p., CFO, 1998—2001. Mem. AICPA. Office: Western Digital Corp 20511 Lake Forest Dr Lake Forest CA 92630-7741

HOPPENSTEADT, FRANK CHARLES, mathematician, educator, dean; b. Oak Park, Ill., Apr. 29, 1938; s. Frank Carl and Margaret Hoppensteadt; children: Charles, Matthew, Sarah. BA, Butler U., 1960; MS, U. Wis., 1962, PhD, 1965. Instr. math. U. Wis., Madison, 1965; asst. prof. math. Mich. State U., East Lansing, 1965-68, dean Coll. Natural Sci., 1986-95; dir. sys. sci. engr. rsch., prof. math. and elec. engring. Ariz. State U., Tempe, 1995—2004; assoc. prof. NYU-Courant, 1968-76, prof., 1976-79, sr. vice provost, rsch. prof., 2004—; prof. U. Utah, Salt Lake City, 1977-86, chmn. dept. math., 1982—85. Author: Mathematical Methods in Population Biology, 1982, An Introduction to Mathematics of Neurons, 1986, 2d edit., 1997, Mathematics in Medicine and the Life Sciences, 1991, Analysis and Simulation of Chaotic Systems, 2000, Weakly Connected Neural Networks, 1997, Modeling and Simulation in Mathematics and the Life Sciences, 2001, Random Perturbation Methods, 2002. Named Christiensen fellow, Oxford U., 1994. Fellow: AAAS; mem.: IEEE, Soc. Indsl. and Applied Maths., Am. Math. Soc. (chmn. applied math. com. 1976—80), Sigma Xi. Business E-Mail: frank.hoppensteadt@nyu.edu.

HOPPER, DENNIS, actor, writer, photographer, film director; b. Dodge City, Kans., May 17, 1936; s. Jay and Marjorie Hopper; m. Brooke Hayward, 1961 (div. 1969); 1 child, Marin; m. Michelle Phillips, Oct. 31, 1970 (div. Nov. 8, 1970); m. Doria Halprin, 1972 (div. 1976); 1 child: Ruthana; m. Katherine LaNasa, June 17, 1989 (div. April 1992); 1 child, Henry Lee.; m. Victoria Duffy, Apr. 13, 1996; 1 child. Student, San Diego pub. schs. Participated in 2002 Whitney Biennial. Appeared in films: Rebel Without a Cause, 1955, Jagged Edge, 1955, I Died A Thousand Times, 1955, Giant, 1956, The Steel Jungle, 1956, Story of Mankind, 1957, Gunfight at the O.K. Corral, 1957, From Hell to Texas, 1958, The Youngland, 1959, Key Witness, 1960, Night Tide, 1963, The Sons of Katie Elder, 1965, Queen of Blood, 1966, The Trip, 1967, Glory Stompers, 1967, Hang 'Em High, 1968, Cool Hand Luke, 1967, True Grit, 1969, Easy Rider, 1969, The Last Movie, 1971, Kid Blue, 1973, Hex, 1973, The Sky is Falling, 1975, James Dean-The First American Teenager, Mad Dog Morgan, 1976, Tracks, 1976, American Friend, 1978, Apocalypse Now, 1979, Wild Times, 1980, Out of the Blue, 1980, King of the Mountain, 1981, Renacer, 1981, Human Highway, 1981, Rumble Fish, 1983, The Osterman Weekend, 1983, Slagskämpen, 1984, My Science Project, 1985, O.C. & Stiggs, 1985, White Star, 1985, The Texas Chainsaw Massacre Part 2, 1986, Blue Velvet, 1986 (Montreal World Film Festival award 1986), Hoosiers, 1986 (Acad. award nomination 1987), River's Edge, 1987, Black Widow, 1987, Pick-up Artist, 1987, Straight to Hell, 1987, Riders of the Storm, 1988, Let it Rock, 1988, Blood Red, 1989, Flashback, 1990, Motion & Emotion, 1990, Chattahoochie, 1990, Superstar: Life and Times of Andy Warhol, 1990, Backtrack, 1991, Sunset Heat, 1991, Schneeweißrosenrot, 1991, Indian Runner, 1991, Hearts of Darkness, 1991, Paris Trout, 1991, Eye of the Storm, 1991, Super Mario Brothers, 1993, Boiling Point, 1993, True Romance, 1993, Red Rock West, 1993, Speed, 1994, Chasers, 1994, Waterworld, 1995, Search and Destroy, 1995, Carried Away, 1996, Last Days of Frankie the Fly, 1996, Cannes Man, 1996, Basquiat, 1996, Top of the World, 1997, Road Ends, 1997, Good Life, 1997, Star Truckers, 1997, Blackout, 1997, Tycus, 1998, Meet the Deedles, 1998, Sources, 1999, Lured Innocence, 1999, Justice, 1999, Jesus' Son, 1999, Bad City Blues, 1999, EdTV, 1999, Straight Shooter, 1999, Spreading Ground, 2000, Luck of the Draw, 2000, Held for Ransom, 2000, Choke, 2000, Ticker, 2001, Knockaround Guys, 2001, L.A.P.D.: To Protect and to Serve, 2001, Unspeakable, 2002, Leo, 2002, The Keeper, 2003, Out of Season, 2004, House of 9, 2004, Americano, 2005, The Crow: Wicked Prayer, 2005, Land of the Dead, 2005, (narrator) Inside Deep Throat, 2005, Sleepwalking, 2008, Elegy, 2008, Swing Vote, 2008, Palermo Shooting, 2008, Hell Ride, 2008; writer, dir. Easy Rider 1969 (Cannes Film Festival Best New Dir. award 1969), The Last Movie, 1971, Out of the Blue, 1980, Chasers, 1994, Colors, 1988, The Hot Spot, 1990, Paris Trout, 1991, Double Crossed, 1991, Sunset Heat, 1992, Nails, 1992; TV movies include The Heart of Justice, 1993, Samson and Delilah, 1996, Marlon Brando: The Wild One, 1996, The Last Days of Frankie the Fly, 1996, Jason and the Argonauts, 2000, Firestarter 2: Rekindled, 2002, The Piano Player, 2002, The Groovenians (voice), 2002, Suspense, 2003, Last Ride, 2004; TV series: Flatland, 2002, E-Ring, 2005-2006, Crash, 2008; exhibited photographs at Fort Worth Art Mus., Denver Art Mus., Wichita Art Mus., Cochran Art Mus., Spileto Mus., Parco Gallery, Tokyo, Osaka, Kumatomo, Japan; author: (photographic book) Out of the Sixties, 1986. Recipient Best Film award Venice Film Festival, 1971, Best Film award Cannes Film Festival, 1980. Office: c/o The Collective 9100 Wilshire Blvd Ste 700 W Beverly Hills CA 90212

HOPPING, WILLIAM RUSSELL, hospitality industry consultant, appraiser; b. Balt., May 3, 1947; s. Russell Leroy and Janet Louise (Cloud) H.; m. Catherine Wilson; 1 child, William Alexander. BS in Hotel Adminstrn., Cornell U., 1969; MBA, U. Denver, 1978. Mgr. Sylvania (Ohio) Country Club, 1972-77; sr. cons. Pannell Kerr Forster, Denver, 1978-82; cons. Ginther Wycoff Grp., Denver, 1982-85; pres. W.R. Hopping & Co., Inc., Denver, 1985—. Mem. adv. bd. travel and tourism dept. Arapahoe C.C., 1998. Vol., Big Bros., Inc., Denver, 1990-2000; chmn. adv. bd. U. Denver Profl. Career Devel. Prog., 1987-88, chmn. task force, Career and Placement Ctr., 1989; mem. City of Littleton Historic Preservation Bd., 2003—, chmn., 2007-. Capt. U.S. Army, 1970-76. Mem. Appraisal Inst., Internat. Soc. Hospitality Cons. (pres. 1990-91, chmn. 1991-93, chmn. emeritus, 1993—), Cornell Soc. Hotelmen (pres. Rocky Mountain chpt. 1984-85). Avocations: bicycling, skiing. Office: W R Hopping & Co Inc 5773 Shasta Cir Littleton CO 80123-2732

HORAK, JAN-CHRISTOPHER, filmmaker, educator, curator; b. Bad Münstereifel, Fed. Republic Germany, May 1, 1951; came to U.S., 1951; s. Jerome V. and Giselle (Offermanns) H.; m. Martha F. Schirn, May 17, 1988; 1 child, Gianna. BA, U. Del., 1973; MS, Boston U., 1975; PhD, Westfälische Wilhelms-U., Münster, Germany, 1984. Intern Internat. Mus. Photography, Rochester, NY, 1975-76, assoc. curator George Eastman House, 1984-87, curator film, 1987-90, sr. curator, 1990-94; asst. prof. film studies U. Rochester, 1985-90, assoc. prof., 1990-93, prof., 1994; dir. Münchner Filmmuseum, Munich, 1994-98; prof. Hochschule f. Fernsehen u. Film, 1995-98; dir. Universal Studies, Archives & Collections, 1998—2000; prof. UCLA, 1999—, acting dir. moving image archives studies, 2006—08, dir. film and TV archives, 2007—; curator Hollywood Entertainment

Mus., 2000—06. Panelist, chmn. film panel NY State Coun. Arts, NYC, 1986—89; cons. USIA, 1988—90; archivists' adv. bd. The Film Found., NYC, 1990—94; v.p., pres. Assn. Moving Image Archivists, 1991—93; exec. com. Internat. Fedn. Film Archives, 1993—95, Kuratorium Junger Deutscher Film, 1995—97; peer reviewer Inst. for Mus. and Libr. Svcs., 2004—05; bd. Assn. of Moving Image Archivists, 2007—. Author: Anti-Nazi Filme der Emigration, 1984, Fluchtpunkt Hollywood, 1986, The Dream Merchants, 1989, Lovers of Cinema: The First American Film Avant-Garde, 1995, Berge, Licht und Traum: Arnold Fanck und der deutsche Bergfilm, 1997, Making Images Move: Photography and Avant-Garde Cinema, 1997; editor: Film und Foto der 20er Jahre, 1979, Helmar Lerski, 1982; founding editor: The Moving Image, 2001—06; contbr. articles to profl. jours. Recipient Louis B. Mayer award Mayer Found., Am. Film Inst., 1975, Acad. Film Scholars award, 2007, Koracs Essay award, Soc. Cinema and Media Studies, 2007; Heinrich Herz Stiftung fellow, 1979-81. Mem.: Internat. Assn. Audio-Visual Media and History, Soc. Exile Studies, Soc. Cinema Studies. Avocations: travel, skiing, swimming. Office: 545 Sierra Vista Ave Pasadena CA 91107 Personal E-mail: jchrishorak@aol.com. Business E-Mail: jchorak@ucla.edu.

HORAN, JOHN J., pharmaceutical company executive; b. SI, NY, July 9, 1920; s. Michael T. and Alice (Kelly) H.; m. Julie Fitzgerald, Jan. 2, 1945; children: Mary Alice, Thomas, Jack, David. AB, Manhattan Coll., 1940; LL.B., Columbia, 1946. Bar: N.Y. bar 1946. With firm Nims, Verdi & Martin, NYC, 1946-52; atty. Merck & Co., Inc., 1952-55; counsel Merck & Co., Inc. (Merck Sharp & Dohme div.), 1955-57; dir. pub. relations Merck & Co., 1957-61, exec. dir. rsch. adminstrn., 1961-62, dir. corp. planning, 1962-63; exec. v.p. mktg. Merck Sharp & Dohme, 1963-67; exec. v.p., gen. mgr., 1967-69; pres., 1969-72; corp. sr. v.p., 1972-74; exec. v.p., 1974-75; pres., chief operating officer, 1975-76; chmn., chief exec. officer, 1976-85; vice chmn., 1985-86; also bd. dirs. Bd. dirs. Atrix Labs., Inc., Myriad Genetics, Inc., PathoGenesis Corp.; trustee Robert Wood Johnson Found. Ret. dir. Burlington Industries, GM, J.P. Morgan, Morgan Guaranty Trust, NCR Corp. Mem. Pharm. Mfrs. Assn. (chmn. bd. 1979-80). Office: Myriad Genetics Inc 320 Wakara Way Salt Lake City UT 84108

HORGAN, SANTIAGO, surgeon; b. Buenos Aires, Sept. 22, 1965; s. Federico Guillermo Horgan and Marta Josefina Benavides; m. Maria Natalia Presas, June 9, 1995. MD, U. Buenos Aires, Argentina, 1989. Diplomate Buenos Aires, Argentina, 1990. Asst. prof. anatomy Medicine U., Buenos Aires, 1987—89; resident in surgery Hosp. de Clinicas, U. Buenos Aires, Argentina, 1991—94, chief resident in surgery, 1994—95; acting instr. surgery U. Wash. Med. Ctr., Seattle, 1995—98, fellow laparoscopic surgery, 1995—96, fellow esophageal surgery, 1996—98; prof. surgery U. Buenos Aires, 1998—; asst. prof. surgery U. Ill., Chgo., 1999—2005, assoc. prof. surgery, 2005—06, chief minimally invasive surgery and robotic surgery, 1999—2006, co-dir. Swallowing Ctr.; dir. Minimally Invasive Bariatric Ctr., Chgo.; prof. clin. surgery U. Calif., San Diego, 2006—, dir. minimally invasive surgery, 2006—, dir. Ctr. for Treatment of Obesity, 2006—. Hon. prof. surgery U. Tucuman, Argentina, 2000—. Recipient Young Surgeon award, Surg. Soc. Alimentary Tract, 2001. Mem.: AMA, Chgo. Surg. Soc., Kansas City Surg. Soc., Warren H. Cole Soc., Chgo. Soc. Gastroenterology, Soc. Laparoendoscopic Surgeons, Ill. Surg. Soc., Henry N. Harkins Surg. Soc., Argentinian Assn. Surgery, Peruvian Colo-rectal Surg. Soc. (hon.), Guatemalan Surg. Soc. (hon.), Peruvian Surg. Soc. (hon.), Assn. Surg. Edn. (assoc.), Internat. Soc. for Diseases of the Esophagus (assoc.), Soc. Am. Gastrointestinal Endoscopic Surgeons (assoc. Rsch. Award 1999), Surg. Soc. Alimentary Tract (assoc.), Club Italo-Argentino du Chirurgia. Achievements include research and development of techniques of robotic surgery in U.S; research in surgery for morbid obesity. Office: U Calif San Diego Dept Surgery 200 W Arbor Dr San Diego CA 92103-8220 Office Phone: 619-543-6711. Office Fax: 619-543-5869. E-mail: shorgan@ucsd.edu.

HORN, ALAN F., film company executive; MBA with distinction, Harvard U. With Proctor & Gamble, Tandem Prodns., T.A.T. Comm., Embassy Comm., 1973—86; pres., COO 20th Century Fox Film Corp., 1986—87; co-founder, chmn., CEO Castle Rock Entertainment, Beverly Hills, 1987—99; pres., COO Warner Bros. Entertainment, Burbank, Calif., 1999—. Bd. dirs. Univision Comm. Bd. dirs. Natural Resources Def. Coun.; vice chmn., bd. trustees Autry Mus. Western Heritage, LA; mem. bd. assocs. Harvard Bus. Sch.; founding mem., bd. dirs. Environ. Media Assn. Capt. USAF. Recipient Milestone award, Producers Guild Am., 2008; named one of 50 Most Powerful People in Hollywood, Premiere mag., 2004—06, Top 200 Collectors, ARTnews mag., 2006—08. Mem.: Hollywood Radio and TV Soc., Am. Film Inst., Acad. TV Arts and Scis., Acad. Motion Picture Arts and Scis. Office: Warner Bros 4000 Warner Blvd Burbank CA 91522-0002 Office Phone: 818-954-6000.

HORN, CHRISTIAN FRIEDRICH, venture capital company executive; b. Dresden, Germany, Dec. 23, 1927; came to U.S., 1954, naturalized, 1959; s. Otto Hugo and Elsa H.; m. Christa Winkler, Feb. 13, 1954; 1 child, Sabrina. MS, Technische Hochschule, Dresden, 1951; PhD, Technische Hochschule, Aachen, Germany, 1958. Rsch. scientist German Acad. Sci., Berlin, 1951-53, Farbwerke Hoechst, Germany, 1953-54; rsch. mgr. Union Carbide, NYC, 1954-65; pres. Polymer Tech. Inc., NYC, 1965-74; v.p. W.R. Grace & Co., NYC, 1974-81, sr. v.p., 1981-95, also bd. dirs.; pres. Horn Venture Ptnrs. (formerly Grace Horn Ventures), Cupertino, Calif., 1983-2000, mng. ptnr., 1987-2000; pres. Horn Investment Corp., Saratoga, Calif., 1996-2000. Bd. dirs. Timothy's Coffees of the World. Patentee in field With German Army, 1944-45. Decorated Iron Cross. Lutheran. Office: 20705 Meadow Oak Rd Saratoga CA 95070-3016

HORN, JAMES A., state legislator; m. Joyce Horn; 2 children. BSME, U. Ill.; postgrad., So. Meth. U. Mgr. Def. and Space group Boeing Co.; mem. Wash. Senate, Dist. 41, Olympia, 1988—; spkr. pro tempore Wash. Legislature, Olympia, 1996, mem. state and local govt. com., mem. higher edn. com., mem. rules com., mem. transp. com., mem. joint legis. audit and rev. com., mem. joint legis. sys. com., mem. legis. transp. com., mem. organized crime adv. bd., mem. legis. evaluation and accountability program com., mem. legis. ethics bd., gov.'s ethics commn. Mem. Puget Sound Regional Coun., State Bldg. Code Coun.; Mcpl. Rsch. Coun., Pacific N.W. Econ. Regional Del. Coun.; past mayor Mercer Island, 1988-89; past mem. Mercer Island city Coun., King County Subregional Coun. and Puget Sound Coun. Govts.; bd. advisors Eastside Sexual Assault Ctr. for Children. Mem. VFW (past bd. trustees), Tech. Mktg. Soc. Am. (nat. v.p.), Kent Boeing Mgmt. Assn. (past chmn. civic affairs), Lions (Mercer Island). Republican. Office: 107 Irving Newhouse Ofc Olympia WA 98504-0001

HORN, SUSAN DADAKIS, statistician, educator; b. Cleve., Aug. 30, 1943; d. James Sophocles and Demeter (Zessis) Dadakis; m. Roger Alan Horn, July 24, 1965; children: Ceres, Corinne, Howard. BA, Cornell U., 1964; MS, Stanford U., 1966, PhD, 1968. Asst. prof. Johns Hopkins U., Balt., 1968-76, assoc. prof., 1976-86, prof. stats. and health svcs. rsch. methods, 1986-92; sr. scientist Intermountain Health Care, Salt Lake City, 1992-95; prof. dept. med. informatics Sch. Medicine U. Utah, Salt Lake City, 1992—; rsch. prof. U. Tex.-Houston Sch. Nursing, 1999—2001. Sr. scientist Inst. for Clin. Outcomes Rsch., Salt Lake City; vis. prof. Vanderbilt U. Sch. Nursing, Nashville, 2004—05. Fellow Am. Statist. Assn., Assn. for Health Svcs. Rsch.; mem. Acad. Health, Sigma Xi, Phi Beta Kappa, Phi Kappa Phi. Presbyterian. Avocations: tennis, swimming. Home: 1793 Fort Douglas Cir Salt Lake City UT 84103-4451 Office: Inst Clin Outcomes 699 E South Temple Salt Lake City UT 84102-1282 Office Phone: 801-466-5595 125. Business E-Mail: shorn@isisicor.com.

HORNBEIN, THOMAS FREDERIC, anesthesiologist; b. St. Louis, Nov. 6, 1930; s. Leonard and Rosalie (Bernstein) Hornbein; m. Gene Schwartz (div. 1968); children: Lia, Lynn, Cari, Andrea, Robert; m. Kathryn Mikesell, Dec. 24, 1971; 1 child, Melissa. BA, U. Colo.; MD, Wash. U. Diplomate Am. Bd. Anesthesiology. Intern King County Hosp., Seattle; resident in anesthesiology Wash. U., St. Louis, USPHS postdoctoral residency, instr. anesthesiology div., 1960—61; asst. prof. U. Wash., Seattle, 1963—67, assoc. prof., 1967—70, prof. anesthesiology, physiology and biophysics, 1970—2002, prof. emeritus, 2002—. Vice chmn. dept. anesthesiology U. Wash., Seattle, 1972—74, asst. chmn. rsch., 1974—77, chmn., 1979—93, rsch. affiliate Primate Ctr., 1980; bd. dirs. Colo. Ctr. for Alternative Medicine and Physiology, 2003—. Author: Everest the West Ridge, 1966 (rated #1 Outside Mag., 2003). Mem. bd. trustees Little Sch., Bellevue, Wash., 1982—89; bd. dirs. Colorado Ctr. Alt. Medicine and Physiology, 2003. Served to lt. comdr. USN, 1961—63. Recipient George Norlin award, U. Colo., Denver, 1970, Alumni Centennial Symposium award, 1975, Disting. Tchg. award, U. Wash., 1982. Fellow: AAAS; mem.: Inst. of Medicine, Soc. Acad. Anesthesia Chmn., Assn. Univ. Anesthetists (treas. 1969—72, pres. 1974—75), Am. Soc. Anesthesiologists (Rovenstine lectr. 1989), Am. Physiol. Soc. (editor 1967—73), Alpha Omega Alpha, Phi Beta Kappa. Avocation: mountain climbing. Office: U Wash Sch Medicine Dept Anesthesiology PO Box 356540 Seattle WA 98195-6540 Business E-Mail: hornbnt@u.washington.edu.

HORNE, TERRY, publishing executive; 4 children. BA, Wichita State U., 1975; MS, Okla. State U., 1982. V.p., chief ops. officer, pub. Clarksburg Pub. Co., W.Va., 1996—2000; v.p. & chief ops. officer Swift Newspapers, Reno, 2000—04; v.p. cmty. newspapers Ariz. Republic, 2004—07; pub. East Valley Tribune, Mesa, Ariz., 2007; pres. & pub. Orange County Register, Santa Ana, Calif., 2007—. Named Citizen of Yr., Clarksburg (W.Va.) Bd. Edn., 1998. Office: Freedom Communications 17666 Fitch Irvine CA 92614-6022 also: Orange County Register 625 N Grand Ave Santa Ana CA 92701 Office Phone: 714-796-7000. Office Fax: 714-796-3681.

HORNE, THOMAS CHARLES, school system administrator; b. Montreal, Que., Can., Mar. 28, 1945; s. George Marcus and Ludwika (Tom) H.; m. Martha Louise Presbry, June 25, 1972; children: Susan Christine, Mary Alice, David Charles, Mark Walter. BA magna cum laude, Harvard U., 1967, JD with honors, 1970. Bar: Mass. 1970, Ariz. 1972, U.S. Supreme Ct. 1974. Assoc. Donovan, Leisure, Newton & Irvine, NYC; sr. ptnr. Lewis & Roca, Phoenix; mng. ptnr. Horne, Duncan, Lorona & Slaton, Phoenix; legislature Ariz. Dept. Edn., Phoenix, 1996—2000, superintendent pub. instrn., 2003—. Mem. Paradise Valley Sch. Bd., Ariz., 1978—, pres., Ariz., 1981—83, Ariz., 1985—88, Ariz., 1990—91, Ariz., 1994; mem. Ariz. Ho. of Reps., 1997—2001; supt. of pub. instrn. Ariz. Dept. Edn., 2003—. Author: Arizona Construction Law, 1978. Chmn. Ariz. Air Pollution Control Hearing Bd., Phoenix, 1976—78. Mem. Ariz. Bar Assn. (former chmn. constrn. law com. litigation sect.). Republican. Jewish. Office: Ariz Dept Edn 1535 W Jefferson St Phoenix AZ 85007-4497 Office Phone: 602-542-5393.

HORNER, ALTHEA JANE, psychologist; b. Hartford, Conn., Jan. 13, 1926; d. Louis and Celia (Newmark) Greenwald; children: Martha Horner Hartley, Anne Horner Benck, David, Kenneth. BS in Psychology, U. Chgo., 1952; PhD in Clin. Psychology, U. So. Calif., U. Park, 1965. Lic. psychologist NY, Calif. Tchr. Pasadena (Calif.) City Coll., 1965-67; from asst. to assoc. prof. LA Coll. Optometry, 1967-70; supr. Psychology interns Pasadena Child Guidance Clinic, 1969-70; pvt. practice specializing in psychoanalysis and psychoanalytic psychotherapy NYC, 1970-83; supervising psychologist dept. psychiatry Beth Israel Med. Ctr., NYC, 1972-83, coord. group therapy tng., 1976-82, clinician in charge Brief Adaptation-Oriented Psychotherapy Rsch. Group, 1982-83; assoc. clin. prof. Mt. Sinai Sch. Medicine, NYC, 1977-91, adj. assoc. prof., 1991—; mem. faculty Nat. Psychol. Assn. for Psychoanalysis, NYC, 1982-83; sr. mem. faculty Wright Inst. LA Postgrad. Inst., 1983-85; pvt. practice LA, 1983—2004; clin. prof. dept. psychology UCLA, 1985-95; ret., 2004. Author: (with others) Treating the Neurotic Patient in Brief Psychotherapy, 1985, Object Relations and the Developing Ego in Therapy, 1979, rev. edit., 1984, Little Big Girl, 1982, Being and Loving, 1978, 3rd edit., 2005, Psychology for Living (with G. Forehand), 4th edit., 1977, The Wish for Power and the Fear of Having It, 1989, The Primacy of Structure, 1990, Psychoanalytic Object Relations Therapy, 1991, Working With the Core Relationship Problem in Psychotherapy, 1998, Chrysalis, 1999, Get Over It! Untie Your Relationship Knots and Move On, 2000, Dealing with Resistance in Psychotherapy, 2005; mem. editl. bd. Jour. Humanistic Psychology, 1986—, Am. Jour. Psychoanalysis; assoc. editor Jour. Am. Acad. of Psychoanalysis; contbr. articles to profl. jours Mem. APA, Am. Acad. Psychoanalysis (sci. assoc.), So. Calif. Psychoanalytic Soc. and Inst. (hon.). Personal E-mail: altheajane@earthlink.net.

HORNER, ANTHONY ADAM, pediatrician, educator; b. NYC, May 24, 1960; s. Harry and Joan Ruth (Frankel) H. BA in Biochemistry, U. Calif. San Diego, 1983; MD, St. Louis U., 1987. Diplomate Am. Bd. Pediatrics, Am. Bd. Allergy and Immunology. Resident in pediatrics UCLA Med. Ctr., 1990; fellow in pediatric immunology Boston Children's Hosp., 1994; assoc. prof. pediatrics med. sch. U. Calif. San Diego, San Diego, 1994—. Co-principle investigator Children's Asthma Mgmt. Program, San Diego, 1994-99. Fellow Am. Acad. Pediatrics, Am. Acad. Allergy and Immunology. Achievements include rsch. in the devel. of DNA-based vaccination strategies for the treatment of disease. Office: U Calif San Diego Med Sch 9500 Gilman Dr # Mc663 La Jolla CA 92093-5004 Office Phone: 858-534-5435. E-mail: ahorner@ucsd.edu.

HORNER, JOHN ROBERT, paleontologist, researcher, curator; b. Shelby, Mont., June 15, 1946; s. John Henry and Miriam Whitted (Stith) H.; m. Virginia Lee Seacotte, Mar. 30, 1972 (div. 1982); 1 child, Jason James; m. Joann Katherine Raffelson, Oct. 3, 1986 (div. 1994); m. Celeste Claire Roach, Jan. 21, 1995 (div. 2005). Studied geology and zoology, U. Mont., 1964—66, studied geology and zoology, 1968—72, DSc (hon.), 1986, Pa. State, 2006. Rsch. asst. dept. geology, asst. curator, paleontology, dept. geological sciences, Mus. of Natural History Princeton U., NJ, 1975-82; curator paleontology Mus. of the Rockies, Mont. State U., Bozeman, 1982—; Regents prof. paleontology Mont. State U., 2001—. Rsch. scientist Am. Mus. Nat. History, N.Y.C., 1980-82; lectr. in field; Sigma XI National lecturer, 1987-1989, Phi Beta Kappa Visiting Scholar, 1997-1998. Co-author: Maia: A Dinosaur Grows up, 1985, Digging Dinosaurs, 1988 (N.Y. Acad. Sci. award 1989), Digging Up Tyrannosaurus Rex, 1993, The Complete T-Rex, 1993, Dinosaur Lives, 1997, Dinosaurs Under the Big Sky, 2001; co-editor (profl. book) Dinosaur Eggs and Babies, 1994; served as tech. advisor (films) Jurassic Park, The Lost World (Jurassic Park II), and Jurassic Park III; contbr. articles to profl. jours. With USMC, 1966-68; Vietnam. MacArthur fellow, 1986; recipient Am. Acad. Achievement award, 1993, Journalism award, Am. Assn. Petroleum Geologists, 1994, Award for Outstanding Contribution to Pub. Understanding of Geology, Am. Geological Inst., 1995. Achievements include discovery of a new genus of duckbilled dinosaur, Maiasaura; accomplishments include: the theory of endothermic metabolism in dinosaur development, of parental nurture of new-born hatchlings, that Tyrannosaurus rex was a scavenger; excavator of the Egg Mountain cache of dinosaur nests. Home: 310 Hoffman Dr Bozeman MT 59715-5724 Office: Mus Of The Rockies Mont State U 600 W Kagy Blvd Bozeman MT 59717-2730 Business E-Mail: jhorner@montana.edu.

HORNGREN, CHARLES THOMAS, finance educator; b. Milw., Oct. 28, 1926; s. William Einar and Grace Kathryn (Manning) H.; m. Joan Estelle Knickelbine, Sept. 6, 1952; children: Scott, Mary, Susan, Catherine. BS, Marquette U., 1949, DBA (hon.), 1976; MBA, Harvard U., 1952; PhD, U. Chgo., 1955; LHD (hon.), DePaul U., 1985. CPA, Wis. Instr. U. Chgo., 1952-54, asst. prof., 1954-55, Marquette U., Milw., 1955-56; assoc. prof. U. Wis., Milw., 1956-59, U. Chgo., 1959-63, prof., 1963-65, Stanford U., Calif., 1965—. Bd. dir. ABM Industries, San Francisco. Co-author: Introduction to Management Accounting, 13th edit., 2005, Cost Accounting, 13th edit., 2009, Accounting, 7th edit., 2007, Financial Accounting, 7th edit., 2008; editor: Prentice Hall Acctg. Series. With US Army, 1944—46. Recipient Alumni Merit award Marquette U., 1973, Edmund W. Littlefield professorship Stanford U., 1973; named to Acctg. Hall of Fame, 1990. Mem. Am. Acctg. Assn. (dir. research 1964-66, pres. 1976-77, Outstanding Acctg. Educator award 1973), AICPAs (acctg. prins. bd. 1968-73, council 1978-81, Outstanding Educator award 1985), Calif. Soc. CPAs (Faculty Excellence award 1975, Disting. Prof. award 1983), Nat. Assn. Accts. (bd. regents 1981-84), Financial Acctg. Standards Bd. (adv. council 1975-79, trustee 1984-89). Home: 620 Sand Hill Rd # 407C Palo Alto CA 94304-2002

HORNICK, ROBERT NEWTON, lawyer, educator; b. Indpls., May 30, 1944; s. Newton and Julia V. (Rigan) H.; m. Charlene Cella, Sept. 21, 1973; 1 child, William Charles. BA, Amherst Coll., 1966; JD, Harvard U., 1970. Fellow Internat. Legal Ctr., Bandung, Indonesia, 1970-73; from assoc. to ptnr. Coudert Bros., NYC, 1973—96; ptnr. Morgan Lewis & Bockius LLP, NYC, 1996—2006; adj. prof. U. Ariz. Rogers Coll. Law, 2006—. Author: Introduction to Indonesian Law, 1973; contbr. articles to profl. jours. Mem. ABA, Assn. Bar of City of N.Y., Internat. Bar Assn., Am. Indonesian C. of C. (bd. dirs., v.p.). Clubs: Harvard (N.Y.C.). Republican. Lutheran. Avocation: reading.

HORNUNG, HANS GEORG, aeronautical engineering educator, science administrator; b. Jaffa, Israel, Dec. 26, 1934; came to U.S., 1987; m. Gretl Charlotte Frank, Jan. 29, 1960; children: Ingrid, Karl, Lisa, Jenny. BMechE with honors, U. Melbourne, Australia, 1960, M in Engring. Sci. with honors, 1962; PhD in Aeros., U. London, 1965. Rsch. scientist Aero. Rsch. Labs., Melbourne, 1962-67; lectr., sr. lectr. then reader Australian Nat. U., Canberra, 1967-80; dir. Inst. Exptl. Fluid Mechanics (DLR), Göttingen, Germany, 1980-87; dir. Grad. Aero. Labs. and Clarence Johnson prof. aero. Calif. Inst. Tech., Pasadena, 1987—2003, emeritus, 2005—. Mem. fluid dynamics panel Adv. Group. Aerospace R & D, 1983-88; mem. adv. com. Internat. Shock Tube Symposia, 1979-95; chmn. adv. com. von Kármán Inst. for Fluid Dynamics, 1984-85; mem. German del. Internat. Union Theoretical and Applied Mechanics, 1984-87; Lanchester Meml. lectr. Royal Aero. Soc., London, 1988; hon. prof. U. Göttingen; Prandtl mem. lectr. Ges. Angew. Math. and Mech., Vienna, 1988. Mem. editl. adv. bd. Experiments in Fluids jour., 1987—, Physics of Fluids, 1988-91, Ing. Archiv, 1989-96; contbr. numerous articles to profl. jours. Recipient von Karman award and medal for internat. coop. in aero. Internat. Coun. Aero. Scis.; Humboldt fellow Tech. U., Darmstadt, Germany, 1974-75. Fellow Royal Aero. Soc., Am. Inst. Aero. & Astronautics, AIAA (life), AAAS; mem. Nat. Acad. of Engring. (fgn. assoc.), Sci. mem. of bd. DLR Germany, Deutsche Gesellschaft für Luft-und Raumfahrt, Gesellschaft für angewandte Mathematik und Mechanik, Am. Phys. Soc., Royal Swedish Acad. Engring. Scis., Ludwig Prandtl Ring German Soc. Aerospace Sci. Achievements include making important contbns. in hypersonic flow theory, exptl. methods and results in real-gas flows, Mach reflection and three-dimensional separation. Office: Calif Inst Tech 1200 E California Blvd Pasadena CA 91125-0001 Business E-Mail: hans@galcit.caltech.edu.

HOROVITZ, ADAM KEEFE (ADROCK, KING AD-ROCK), musician; b. South Orange, NJ, Oct. 31, 1966; s. Israel and Doris Horovitz; m. Ione Skye, 1991 (div. 1999); m. Kathleen Hanna, 2006. Founder, mem. Young and the Useless, 1981—83; mem. The Beastie Boys, 1983—; co-founder, mem. BS2000; co-founder Grand Royal Record Label, 1992—2001. Owner Grand Royal, Grand Royal mag., 1984—. Albums include (with Beastie Boys) Licensed to Ill, 1986, Paul's Boutique, 1989, Check Your Head, 1992, 94, Ill Communication, 1994, Some Old Bullshit, 1994, In Sound from Way Out, 1996, Def & Dumb, 1996, Hello Nasty, 1998, To the 5 Boroughs, 2004, The Mix Up, 2007 (Grammy award, Best Pop Instrumental Album, 2008), (with BS2000) BS2000, 1996, Buddy, 2000, (singles) Jimmy James, 1992, Gratitude, 1992, So What'cha Want, 1992, Sabotage, 1994, Hey Ladies, 1997, Real Men Don't Floss Up, (with BS2000) Simply Mortified, 2001, (extended play singles) Pollywog Stew, 1982, Cooky Puss, 1983, Rock Hard, 1984, Tour Shot, 1994, Sure Shot, 1994, Get

It Together, 1994, Root Down, 1995, Aglio E Olio, 1995, (video) Skills to Pay the Bills, 1992, Hello Nasty, 1998, The Sounds of Science, 1999; rap artist Heart of Soul, 1988, Rap's Biggest Hits, 1990, Rap Rap Rap, 1996, Rap: Most Valuable Players, 1996; vocals Rap's Biggest Hits, 1990; prodr. Cb4, 1993, Rebirth of Cool (vol. 3), 1995, Music for Our Mother Ocean, 1996, Rap Rap Rap, 1996, Rap: Most Valuable Players, 1996; (films) Krush Groove, 1985, Tougher than Leather, 1987, Lost Angels, 1989, A Kiss Before Dying, 1991, Long Road Home 1991, Roadside Prophets, 1992, Cityscrapes, 1994, Crossroads, 2002, Godspeed, 2007. Office: care Grand Royal Capitol Records 1750 Vine St Los Angeles CA 90028-5209

HOROWITZ, BEN, health facility administrator; b. Bklyn., Mar. 19, 1914; s. Saul and Sonia (Meringoff) H.; m. Beverly Lichtman, Feb. 14, 1952; children: Zachary, Jody. BA, Bklyn. Coll., 1940; LLB, St. Lawrence U., 1940; postgrad., New Sch. Social Rsch., 1942. Bar: N.Y. 1941. Dir. N.Y. Fedn. Jewish Philanthropies, 1940-45; assoc., ea. regional dir. City of Hope, 1945-50, nat. exec. sec., 1950-53, exec. dir., 1953-85, gen. v.p., bd. dirs., 1985—, bd. dirs. nat. med. ctr., 1980—. Bd. dirs. Beckman Rsch. Inst., 1980—. Mem. Gov.'s Task Force on Flood Relief, 1969-74; bd. dirs., v.p. Hope for Hearing Found., UCLA, 1972-96; bd. dirs. Forte Found., 1987-92, Ch. Temple Housing Corp., 1988-93, Leo Baeck Temple, 1964-67, 86-89, Westwood Property Owners Assn., 1991—. Recipient Spirit of Life award, 1970, Gallery of Achievement award, 1974, Profl. of Yr. award So. Calif. chpt. Nat. Sco. Fundraisers, 1977; Ben Horowitz chair in rsch. established at City of Hope, 1981; city street named in his honor, 1986. Jewish. Formulated the role of City of Hope as pilot center in medicine, science and humanitarianism, 1959. Office: City of Hope 11645 Wilshire Blvd Los Angeles CA 90025-1708

HOROWITZ, MARK A., electrical engineering and computer science educator; BSEE, MSEE, MIT, 1978; PhD in Elec. Engring., Stanford U., 1984. Prof. Stanford U., Calif., 1984—, dir. Computer Systems Lab., Yahoo! Founders prof. elec. engring. and computer sci. Co-founder, dir. Rambus Inc., 1990—2005, v.p., 1990—94, chief scientist, 2005—. Contbr. articles to sci. jours. Recipient Presdl. Young Investigator award, 1985, Tech. Field award, IEEE Solid-State Circuits, 2006. Fellow: Am. Acad. Arts & Scis., Assn. Computing Machinery, IEEE (Donald O. Pederson award in Solid-State Circuits 2006); mem.: NAE. Office: Stanford U Computer Systems Lab Gates Computer Sci Bldg 353 Serra Mall Stanford CA 94305 Office Phone: 650-725-3707. Office Fax: 650-725-6949. E-mail: horowitz@ee.stanford.edu.

HORTA, SILVIO, scriptwriter; b. Miami, Fla., Aug. 14, 1974; Grad., NYU Film Sch., 1995. Writer: (films) Urban Legend, 1998; The Furies, 1999; writer (characters) Urban Legend: Final Cut, 2000; writer, exec. prodr.: (TV series) The Chronicle, 2001; Jake 2.0: The Tech, 2003; Jake 2.0, 2003; Ugly Betty, 2006— (NAACP Image award, Writing in a comedy series, 2007, co-recipient Writer's Guild Am. award, New Series, 2007). Mailing: Ugly Betty Raleigh Studios 5300 Melrose Ave Los Angeles CA 90038

HORTON, FRANK ELBA, academic administrator, geographer, educator; b. Chgo., Aug. 19, 1939; s. Elba Earl and Mae Pauline (Prohaska) H.; m. Nancy Yocom, Aug. 26, 1960; children: Kimberly, Pamela, Amy, Kelly. BA, Western Ill. U., 1963; MS, Northwestern U., 1964, PhD, 1966. Faculty U. Iowa, Iowa City, 1966-75, prof. geography, 1966-75; dir. Inst. Urban and Regional Research, 1968-72, dean advanced studies, 1972-75; v.p. acad. affairs, research So. Ill. U., Carbondale, 1975-80; prof. geography and urban affairs, chancellor U. Wis., Milw., 1980-85; prof. geography, pres. U. Okla., Norman, 1985-88; prof. geography, higher edn. adminstrn., pres. U. Toledo, 1988-98, pres. emeritus, 1999—; prin. Horton & Assocs., Denver, 1999—; interim pres. So. Ill. U., 2000; interim dean coll. biol. scis. U. Mo.-Kansas City, 2001—02, exec. cons. to provost, 2003—04. Mem. commn. on leadership devel. and acad. adminstrn. Am. Coun. on Edn., 1983-85; mem. presdl. adv. com. Assn. on Governing Bds., 1986-98; dir. 1st Wis. Nat. Bank of Milw., 1980-85, Liberty Nat. Bank, Oklahoma City, 1986-89, Trustcorp. Bank, 1989-90; bd. dirs. Interstate Bakeries, 1993-2007. Author, editor: (with B.J.L. Berry) Geographic Perspectives on Urban Systems - With Integrated Readings, 1970, Urban Environmental Management - Planning for Pollution Control, 1974; editor: (with B.J.L. Berry) Geographical Perspectives on Contemporary Urban Problems, 1973; editorial adv. bd.: (with B.J.L. Berry) Transportation, 1971-78. Co-chmn. Goals for Milw. 2000, 1981-85, Greater Milw. Com., 1980; mem. bus. devel. sub-com. Okla. Coun. Sci. and Tech., 1985-88; mem. Harry S. Truman Library Inst., 1985-88, William Rockhill Nelson Trust, 1985-88; bd. govs. Am. Heart Assn., Wis., 1980-85, Ohio Supercomputer Ctr., 1993-97; mem. exec. com. Okla. Acad. State Goals, 1986-88; trustee Toledo Symphony Orch., 1989-96, Toledo Hosp., 1989-97, Pub. Broadcasting Found. Northwest Ohio, 1989-93, Key Bank, 1990-2000, Ohio Aerospace Inst., 1990-97; chair Inter-Univ. Coun. Pres. of Ohio Public Univs., 1992-93; mem. exec. com. Com. of 100, Toledo, 1989-92. Served with AUS, 1957-60. Mem. AAAs (nat. coun. 1976-78), Assn. Governing Bds. (mem. presdl. adv. commn. 1986-95), Assn. Am. Geographers, nat. Assn. State Univs. and Land Grant Colls. (chair urban affairs div. 1983-85, chmn. Coun. of Pres. 1987-88, exec. com. 1983-88), Nat. Hwy. Rsch. Soc., Okla. Coun. on Sci. and Tech., MidAm. State Univs. Assn. (pres. 1987-88), Ohio Supercomputer Ctr. (bd. govs. 1993), Ohio Aerospace Inst. (trustee 1990—), Okla. Acad. State Goals (pres. 1987-88), Okla. State C. of C. and Industry (v.p. 1987-88), Toledo Area C. of C. (vice chmn. bd. dirs. 1991-93). Home: 288 River Ranch Cir Bayfield CO 81122-8774 Office Phone: 970-884-2102. Personal E-mail: fehorton@attglobal.net.

HORTON, GARY BRUCE, transportation company executive; b. Vallejo, Calif., Aug. 27, 1943; s. John Vernon and Della Leona (Shock) H.; m. Janice DeLoach, Oct. 31, 1987; children: Cody Jacob, Dillon Edward, Rocky. Student, Ea. Ariz. Coll., 1964-65, Ariz. State U., 1965-68. Cost acct. Motorola, Inc., Mesa, Ariz., 1968-69; acct. supr. Arcoa, Phoenix, 1969-70, fin. acctg. mgr., 1970-77; fin. mgr. U-Haul Internat., Phoenix, 1977-82, v.p. fin., 1987-90; treas. Amerco, Reno, Nev., 1982-89, v.p. fin., 1989—; asst. treas. U-Haul Can., Ltd., Burlington, Ont., 1982—; pres., chmn. Sierra Entertainment, Ltd., Reno, 1993—. Bd. dirs. Amerco Lease, Las Vegas, Nationwide Comml. Co., Phoenix, Ponderosa Ins., U-Haul Real Estate Co. Pres. bd. trustees Nev. Mus. Art. Republican. Lutheran. Avocations: fishing, camping, golf, racquetball, water-skiing. Home: 3425 Meridian Ln Reno NV 89509-3883 Office: Amerco 1325 Airmotive Way Ste 100 Reno NV 89502-3294

HORTON, JOEL D., state supreme court justice; b. Nampa, Idaho, 1959; m. Carolyn Minder. BA in Polit. Sci., U. Wash., Seattle, 1982; JD, U. Idaho Coll. Law, 1985. Atty., Lewiston, Idaho, 1985—86; dep. prosecuting atty Twin Falls, Idaho, 1986—88; criminal dep. Ada County Prosecutor's Office, Idaho, 1988—91, dep. atty. gen., 1991—92, dep. criminal prosecutor, 1992—94; magistrate, family judge Ada County, 1994—96; judge Idaho Dist. Ct., Idaho, 1996—2007; assoc. justice Idaho Supreme Court, 2007—. Office: Idaho Supreme Ct PO Box 83720 Boise ID 83720 Office Phone: 208-334-2246.

HORTON, ROBERT CARLTON, geologist; b. Tonopah, Nev., July 25, 1926; s. Frank Elijah and Eathel Margaret (Miller) H.; m. Beverly Jean Burhans, Dec. 5, 1952; children: Debra, Robin, Cindy. BS, U. Nev., 1949, DSc (hon.), 1985. Cert. geol. engr., 1966. Assoc. dir. Nev. Bur. Mines, Reno, 1956-66; cons. Reno, 1966-76; dir. geology divsn. Bendix Field Engring. Corp., Grand Junction, Colo., 1976-81; dir. U.S. Bur. Mines, Washington, 1981-87; dir. strategic materials rsch. U. Nev., Reno, 1987-90, assoc. dean MacKay Sch. Mines, 1989-90, assoc. dean emeritus, 1990—. Mem. Nev. Gov.'s Mining Adv. Com., 1966-72. Author: Barite Deposits of Nevada, 1962, Fluorspar Deposits of Nevada, 1963, History of Nevada Mining, 1963. Rep. candidate for Congress from Nev., 1958. Served to lt. USNR, 1944-46, 53-56, PTO. Kennecott scholar, 1948; named Engr. of Yr. Reno chpt., NSPE, 1967; recipient Outstanding Alumnus John Mackay medal, Mackay Sch. Mines, 1991. Mem. AIME (subsect. chmn. Reno 1962-63), Soc. Econ. Geologists, Mining and Metall. Soc. Am. Methodist.

HORTON, SUSAN PITTMAN, bank executive; d. Rosie Pittman; m. Stan Horton; 1 child, Alexandria Rose. BA in Bus. Adminstrn., Wash. State U., 1984. CPA. Ptnr. McFarland & Alton PS, 1989—99; pres., CEO Wheatland Bank, Spokane, Wash., 1999—, chmn., 2001—; ptnr. Deloitte and Touche, Seattle. Bd. mem. Downtown Spokane; active Hope House. Named one of 25 Most Powerful Women in Banking, US Banker, 2006, 2007. Mem.: Spokane Club. Avocations: barrel racing, quarter horses. Office: Wheatland Bank 222 North Wall St Spokane WA 99201

HORTON, WILLIAM RUSSELL, retired utilities executive; b. Toronto, Ont., Can., Aug. 25, 1931; s. Russell Burton and Freda Catherine (Middleton) H.; m. Dorothy Viva Rye, Nov. 27, 1954; children: William Russell, Robert Freeman, Douglas Lloyd, Ronald Edward. BS in Mining Engring., U. Toronto, 1955. Engr. Imperial Oil Ltd., Calgary and Camrose, Alta., Canada, 1955-56; engr., mgr. Black Sivalls & Bryson Ltd., Edmonton, Alta., 1956—65; v.p. Gamma Engring. Ltd., Edmonton, 1965-68; pres. Horton Engring. Ltd., Edmonton, 1968-2000, chmn., 2000—; mem. Alta. Pub. Utilities Bd., Edmonton, 1973-76, chmn., 1976-83; exec. v.p. Can. Utilities Ltd., Edmonton, 1984-90. Hon. mem. Can. Assn. Members Pub. Utility Tribunals. Mem. Assn. Profl. Engrs. Geologists and Geophysicists Alta. (life). Avocations: sports, music, reading. Home: 17490 Coral Beach Rd Winfield BC Canada V4V 1C1 Home Phone: 250-766-4013. Business E-Mail: wrhorton@cablelan.net, wrhorton@show.com.

HORVATH, DEBORA D., bank executive; b. 1955; 2 adopted children. Grad., Baldwin Wallace Coll., Ohio, 1984. Joined GE, 1979; v.p., CIO Great Northern Annuity, Seattle, 1993—95, sr. v.p., 1995—97; sr. v.p., chief info. officer, chief tech. officer GE Fin. Assurance, 1997—2000, sr. v.p., chief info. officer, eBus. leader, 2000—02; mem. GE Info. Mgmt. Coun.; exec. v.p., chief info. officer Washington Mutual, Inc., 2004—08. Involved with Woodland Park Zoo, Child Haven. Recipient CIO award, GE; named one of 25 Women to Watch, US Banker, 2006.*

HORWITZ, DAVID A., rheumatologist, educator; BA, U. Mich., 1958; MD, U. Chgo., 1962. Intern, resident Michael Reese Hosp., Chgo., 1966; rheumatology fellow Southwestern Med. Sch. U. Tex., 1969, instr. internal medicine Southwestern Med. Sch. Dallas, 1968-69; from asst. prof. to assoc. prof. medicine Sch. Medicine U. Va., Charlottesville, 1969-79, prof. medicine, 1979-80; prof. medicine and microbiology, chief divsn. rheumatology and immunology sect. Sch. Medicine U. So. Calif., LA, 1980—. Vis. prof. Clin. Rsch. Ctr., Harrow, Eng., 1976-77; vis. investigator Imperial Cancer Rsch. Fund, London, 1988-89; vis. scientist Nat. Inst. Arthritis, Musculoskeletal and Skin Diseases, NIH, Bethesda, Md., 2001-02. Contbr. more than 100 articles to profl. jours. Recipient James R. Klinnenberg award for rsch., Arthritis Found. Mem.: Am. Rheumatism Assn. (pres. 1985). Achievements include research in elucidation of lymphocytes, cytokines and immunologic circuits involved in the regulation of antibody production, characterization of pathologic abnormalities in immune regulation in subjects with Systemic Lupus Erythematosus; The generation of regulatory T cell subsets ex-vivo, and their potential for the treatment of autoimmune diseases and to prevent graft rejection. Office: Divsn Rheumatology And Immunology 2011 Zonal Ave # 711 Los Angeles CA 90089-0110 Home Phone: 310-459-6106; Office Phone: 323-442-1946. Business E-Mail: dhorwitz@usc.edu.

HORWITZ, RALPH IRVING, internist, epidemiologist, educator, former dean; b. Phila., June 25, 1947; s. Sidney and Sara (Altus) H.; m. Sarah McCue, Aug. 5, 1970; 1 child, Rebecca Margaret Taylor. BS, Albright Coll., 1969; MD, Pa. State U., 1973. Diplomate Am. Bd. Internal Medicine. Intern McGill U., Royal Victoria Hosp., Montreal, Que., Canada, 1973-75; postdoctoral tng. in epidemiology, clin. scholars program Yale U. Sch. Medicine, New Haven, 1975; sr. resident Harvard U., Mass. Gen. Hosp., Boston, 1977-78; co-dir. clin. scholars program Yale U. Sch. Medicine, New Haven, 1978—2003, asst. prof. medicine, 1978-82, assoc. prof. medicine and epidemiology, 1982-88, prof., 1988—2003, chief gen. internal medicine, 1982-94, vice chmn. internal medicine, 1993-94, chmn. internal medicine, 1994—2003, Harold H. Hines Jr. Prof. Medicine and Epidemiology, 1991—2003; chief Beeson Med. Svc. Yale-New Haven Hosp., 1993—2003; v.p. med. affairs Case Western Res. U., Cleveland, Ohio, 2003—06, dean sch. medicine, 2003—06; dir. Case Rsch. Inst., 2003—06; Arthur Bloomfield prof., chmn. dept. medicine Stanford U. Sch. Medicine, Calif., 2006—. Mem. nat. selection com. faculty scholar program Henry J. Kaiser Family Found., Menlo Park, Calif., 1987-90; mem. com. allocating resources in biomed. rsch. Inst. Medicine, Washington, 1988-89; mem. profl. standards rev. orgn., Woodbridge, Conn., 1980-82; editorial bd. The Lancet, 1991-96; past chmn. bd. dirs. Am. Bd. Internal Medicine. Contbr. over 200 articles to profl. jours. Trustee Am. Bd. Internal Medicine Found. Recipient Faculty Scholar award Kaiser Family Found., 1981-86 Fellow ACP, AAAS, Am. Coll. Epidemiology, Pa. State U. Alumni Assn.; mem. Am. Soc. Clin. Investigation, Assn. Am. Physicians, Am. Epidemiol. Soc., Inst. Medicine. Jewish. Office: Stanford Univ Sch Medicine 300 Pasteur Dr S-102 Stanford CA 94305 Office Phone: 650-736-1484. Business E-Mail: ralph.horwitz@stanford.edu.

HOSICK, HOWARD LAWRENCE, cell biology professor, academic administrator; b. Champaign, Ill., Nov. 1, 1943; s. Arthur Howard and Eunice Irma (Miller) H.; m. Cynthia Ann Jacobson, June 15, 1968; children: Steven Cameron, Anna Elise, Rachel Victoria. BA, U. Colo., 1965; PhD, U. Calif., Berkeley, 1970. Postdoctoral fellow Karolinska Inst., Stockholm, 1970-72; asst. research biochemist U. Calif., Berkeley, 1972-73; asst. prof. Wash. State U., Pullman, 1973-78, assoc. prof., 1978-83, prof. cell biology, 1983—, chmn. dept. zoology, 1983-87, chmn. dept. genetics and cell biology, 1987-91. Vis. scientist U. Reading, Eng., 1978, B.C. Cancer Ctr., Vancouver, 2003; disting. scientist Aichi Cancer Ctr., Nagoya, Japan, 1986; vis. scholar Cambridge U., 1994; rsch. com. Am. Heart Assn., 1989; grant rev. com. Nat. Cancer Inst., 1993-2000; chair, breast cancer rsch. program, U.S. Army Med. Rsch. Command. Rev. editor In Vitro Cellular and Molecular Biology, 1986—97; contbr. articles to profl. jours. Bd. govs. Internat. Assn. Breast Cancer Rsch., 1993-2000. Recipient H.S. Boyce award, 1981, Shell Faculty Devel. award, 1984, Cancer Rsch. awards Eagles Club, 1989-2004, G. and L. Pfeiffer Rsch. Found. award, 1992; fellow NIH, NSF, Am. Cancer Soc., Damon Runyan-Walter Winchell Cancer Fund, Fogarty Internat. Ctr., 1968-2004; grantee NIH, NSF, Am. Cancer Soc., Am. Inst. Cancer Rsch., Pfeiffer Found., 1973-2004, U.S. Army, Internat. Assn. for Cancer Rsch., 2002-. Mem. Am. Soc. Cell Biology, Tissue Culture Assn., Am. Assn. Cancer Research, Internat. Assn. Breast Cancer Research. Lodges: Rotary. Democrat. Buddhist. Avocations: running, woodworking, model aviation. Office: Wash State U Sch Biol Scis Pullman WA 99164-4234 Home: 800 SE Edge Knoll Dr Pullman WA 99163-2408 Home Phone: 509-332-8687. Business E-Mail: hosick@wsu.edu.

HOSIE, SPENCER, lawyer; b. Toronto, Ont., Can., Apr. 24, 1956; BA summa cum laude, U. Calif., Berkeley, 1978; JD, U. Calif., Davis, 1981. Bar: Calif. 1981, Alaska 1982. Law clk. to Hon. Edmond W. Burke, Chief Justice Alaska Supreme Ct., 1981—82; assoc. Heller, Ehrman, White & McAuliffe, San Francisco, 1982—85; ptnr. Hosie, Frost, Large & McArthur, San Francisco, 1985—99; founder, ptnr. Hosie McArthur, LLP, San Francisco, 1999—. Editor: U. Calif. Davis Law Rev., 1980—81; mem. editl. bd.: RICO Litig. Reporter, 1984—85. Named one of Top 25 Attys. Under 45 in Calif., Calif. Lawyer, 1993, Top 10 Trial Lawyers in Am., Nat. Law Jour., 2005. Mem.: Assn. Trial Lawyers of Am., Alaska Bar Assn., Anchorage Bar Assn., Bar Assn. San Francisco, Order of Coif. Office: Hosie McArthur LLP 1 Market Spear Tower 22nd Fl San Francisco CA 94105 Office Phone: 415-247-6000. Office Fax: 415-247-6001. E-mail: shosie@hosielaw.com.

HOSKINS, H. DUNBAR, ophthalmologist, medical association administrator; b. Va. married; 3 children. MD, Med. Coll. Va. Cert. Am. Bd. Opthalmology, 1970. Chief, ophthalmology Naval Hosp., RI, 1968; exec. v.p. Am. Acad. Ophthalmology, San Francisco, 1993—; and clin. prof. ophthalmology Univ. Calif. Sch. Med., San Francisco. Chmn. St. Mary's Hosp. Med. Ctr., San Francisco, Mercy Svcs. Corp.; founder, chmn. Medem Corp.; founding dir. Am. Glaucoma Soc.; founder, dir. Glaucoma Rsch. Found. Recipient Med. Exec. Achievement award, AMA, 2005. Mem.: Internat. Coun. Ophthalmology, Am. Glaucoma Soc., Pan Am. Assn. Ophthalmology (former sec-treas.), Am. Eye Study Club. Office: Am Acad of Ophthalmology PO Box 7424 San Francisco CA 94120-7424 Office Phone: 415-561-8500. Office Fax: 415-561-8533.

HOSSLER, DAVID JOSEPH, lawyer, educator; b. Mesa, Ariz., Oct. 18, 1940; s. Carl Joseph and Elizabeth Ruth (Bills) H.; m. Gretchen Anne, Mar. 2, 1945; 1 child, Devon Annagret. BA, U. Ariz., Tucson, 1969, JD, 1972. Bar: Ariz. 1972, US Dist. Ct. Ariz. 1972, US Supreme Ct. 1977. Legal intern to chmn. FCC, summer 1971; law clk. to chief justice Ariz. Supreme Ct., 1972-73; chief dep. county atty. Yuma County, Ariz., 1973-74; ptnr. Hunt, Grogan, Meerchaum & Hossler, Yuma, Ariz., 1974—. Instr. in law and banking, law and real estate Ariz. Western Coll.; instr. in bus. law, mktg., ethics Webster U.; instr. agrl. law U. Ariz.; co-chmn. fee arbitration com. Ariz. State Bar, 1990—; instr. employee/employer law U. Phoenix. Editor-in-chief Ariz. Adv., 1971-72. Precinct com. Yuma County Rep. Ctrl. Com., 1974-2000, vice chmn., 1982; chmn. region II Acad. Decathalon competition, 1989; bd. dirs. Yuma County Ednl. Found. (Hall of Fame 2000), Yuma County Assn. Behavior Health Svcs., pres., 1981; bd. dirs. Yuma Union H.S. Dist. Found.; coach Yuma HS mock ct. team, 1987-94; bd. dirs. friends of U. Med. Ctr., Am. Red Cross, former ATLA. With USN. Recipient Man and Boy award, Boys Clubs Am., 1979, Freedoms Found. award, Yuma chpt., 1988, Demolay Legion of Honor, 1991, Francis Woodward award, Ariz. Pub. Svc., 2000, named Vol. of Yr., Yuma County, 1981—82, Heart of Yuma award, 2000, voted Yuma's Best (atty.), 2001—02, 2002—03. Mem. Am. Judicature Soc., Yuma County Bar Assn. (pres. 1975-76), Navy League, VFW, Am. Legion, U. Ariz. Alumni Assn. (nat. bd. dirs., past pres., hon. bobcat 1996, Disting. Citizen award 1997), Rotary (pres. Yuma club 1987-88, dist. gov. rep. 1989, dist. gov. 1992-93, findings com. 1996, dist. found. chair 1996-2000, co-chmn. internat. membership retention 2000-01, RI past dir., 2004-06, John Van Houton Look Beyond Yourself award 1995, Roy Slayton Share Rotary Share People award 1996, Al Face You Are the Key award 1997, Ted Day Let Svc. Light the Way award 1998, Rotary Found. citation for meritorious svc., Rotary Internat. (bd. dirs. 2004-06, bd. dirs. Katrina relief, chmn. elect Past Officers Reunion Exec. Com.), Four Avenues of Svc. award, 2004, Internat. Svc. Above Self award, Cliff Doctorman Real Happiness is Helping Others award, Disting. Svc. award). Episcopalian (vestry 1978-82). Home: 2802 S Fern Dr Yuma AZ 85364-2919 Office: Hunt Grogan Meerchaum & Hossler 330 W 24th St Yuma AZ 85364-6455 Mailing: PO Box 2919 Yuma AZ 85366-2919 Home Phone: 928-344-0840; Office Phone: 928-920-7830 101. Personal E-mail: dhossler@mindspring.com.

HOSTLER, CHARLES WARREN, retired ambassador, international affairs consultant; b. Chgo., Dec. 12, 1919; s. Sidney Marvin and Catherine (Marshall) Hostler; m. Chin-Yeh Rose Hostler; 1 child, Charles Warren Jr. BA, U. Calif. at Los Angeles, LA, 1942; MA, Am. U., Beirut, Lebanon, 1955, Georgetown U., 1950, PhD, 1956. Commd. 2d lt. U.S. Air Force, 1942, advanced through grades to col., 1955; ret., 1963; dir. internat. ops. McDonnell Douglas Corp., Middle East, N.Africa, Beirut, 1965-67, mgr. internat. ops. Paris, 1963-65, mgr. internat. mktg., missiles and space, 1967-69; pres. Hostler Investment Co., Coronado, Calif., 1967—; chmn. bd. Irvine (Calif.) Nat. Bank, 1972-74; dir. Wynn's Internat., Inc., Fullerton, Calif., 1971-74; dep. asst. sec. for internat. commerce, dir. Bur. Internat. Commerce, U.S. Dept. Commerce, Washington, 1974-76; regional v.p. Mid-East and Africa, E-Systems Inc., Cairo, 1976-77; pres. Pacific SW Capital Corp., San Diego, 1977-89; ambassador U.S. Govt., Bahrain, 1989-93. Hon. consul gen. Kingdom of Bahrain,

1993—; adj. prof. polit. sci. San Diego State U., 1999—. Author: Turkism and the Soviets, 1957, The Turks of Central Asia, 1993, Soldier to Ambassador, 2004. Chmn. Calif. Contractors State Lic. Bd., 1973—79, San Diego County Local Agy. Formation Commn., 1979—89, Calif. State Park and Recreation Commn., 1983—89; pres. San Diego Consular Corps, 1996—98; chmn., bd. dirs. People-to-People Internat. Decorated Purple Heart, Legion of Merit, Legion of Honor (France); recipient decorations from 9 nations, Eisenhower Disting. Svc. award, Fgn. Affairs award for Pub. Svc., U.S. State Dept., Pub. Svc. award, U. Calif., L.A., 2005. Mem.: VFW (life), Coun. Am. Ambs., Mid. East Inst. (bd. govs. 1962—80, 1993—), Vets. of Office of Strategic Svcs., Mil. Order Purple Heart (life), Mil. Officers Assn. of Am. (life), Navy League (life). Office: 1101 First St # 302 Coronado CA 92118-1474 Personal E-mail: hostler@san.rr.com.

HOSTON, GERMAINE ANNETTE, political science professor; b. Trenton, NJ; d. Walter Lee and Veretta Louise H. AB in Politics summa cum laude, Princeton U., 1975; MA in Govt., Harvard U., 1978, PhD in Govt., 1981. Rsch. asst. Princeton U., NJ, 1973-75; tchg. asst. Harvard U., Cambridge, Mass., 1977-78; asst. prof. polit. sci. Johns Hopkins U., Balt., 1980-86, assoc. prof. polit. sci., 1986-92; prof. polit. sci. U. Calif., San Diego, 1992—, dir. Ctr. for Democratization and Econ. Devel., 1993-99; founder, pres. Inst. Trans Pacific Studies in Values, Culture and Politics, 1999—. Vis. prof. L'Ecole des Hautes Etudes en Sci. Sociales, Paris, 1986, Osaka City U., Japan, 1990, U. Tokyo, 1991; faculty advisor Chinese lang. program Johns Hopkins U., 1981-92, undergrad. ethics bd., 1980-83, pub. interest investment adv. com., 1982-85, undergrad. admissions com., 1983-84, 86-89, pres.'s human climate task force, 1987, dir. undergrad. program, 1987, 88-89, mem. com. undergrad. studies, 1987-91, organizer comparative politics colloquium, 1987-89, dept. colloquium, 1987-89, 91-92; Japanese studies program com. U. Calif., San Diego, 1992—, Chinese studies program, 1994—, field coord. comparative politics, 1994—95, dir. grad. studies comparative politics, 1997-98; bd. dir. Inst. East-West Security Studies, NYC, 1990-97; Am. adv. com. Japan Found., 1992—; edn. abroad program com. U. Calif., 1996—; adv. com. Calif. Ctr. Asia Soc.; mem. com. tech. comms. Inst. East West Security Studies, 1997—; participant numerous workshops and seminars; lectr. in field. Author: Marxism and the Crisis of Development in Prewar Japan: The Debate on Japanese Capitalism, 1986, The State, Identity, and the National Question in China and Japan, 1994, (with others) The Biographical Dictionary of Neo-Marxism, 1985, The Biographical Dictionary of Marxism, 1986, Culture and Identity: Japanese Intellectuals During the Interwar Years, 1990, The Routledge Dictionary of Twentieth-Century Political Thinkers, 1992; mem. editl. bd. Jour. Politics, 1997—2001; contbr. articles to profl. jours. Active Md. Food Com., 1983-92, program concepts subcom. CROSS ROADS Com., Diocese of Md., 1987-88, outreach com. St. David's Episcopal Ch., Balt., standing commn. human affairs Gen. Conv. of the Episcopal Ch., 1991-97; chair peace and justice commn. Episcopal Diocese Md., 1984-87, co-chair companion diocese com., 1987-92, chair CROSS ROADS program bd., 1988-92; exec. bd. dir. Balt. Clergy and Laity Concerned, 1985-86; alternate, regular lay del. 69th Gen. Conv. of The Episcopal Ch., Detroit, 1988; trustee Va. Theol. Sem., 1988-2000; lay del. 70th Gen. Conv. of The Episcopal Ch., Phoenix, Ariz., 1991; dep. Nat. Conv. Episcopal Ch., 1988-93. Am. Legion Aux. scholar, 1972, Am. Logistical Assn. scholar, 1972-76; fellow Harvard U., 1975-77, NSF, 1975-77; Lehman fellow Harvard U., 1978-79, Fgn. Lang. and Area Studies fellow, 1978-79; fellow Am. Assn. Univ. Women Ednl. Found., 1979-80; Fgn. Rsch. scholar U. Tokyo, 1979, 82, 84, 85, 86, 91; Travel grantee Assn. Asian Studies, Japan-U.S. Friendship Commn., 1981; Internat. fellow Internat. Fedn. Univ. Women, 1982, 83; Postdoctoral grantee Social Sci. Rsch. Coun., 1983; fellow NEH, 1983; Kenan Endowment grantee Johns Hopkins U., 1984-85; fellow Rockefeller Found. Internat. Rels., 1985-88; Travel grantee Assn. Asian Studies, 1991; grantee Japan-US Friendship Commn., 1997; rsch. grantee Acad. Senate Com. on Rsch., 1996. Mem. Asia Soc. (trustee 1994—2000), Am. Polit. Sci. Assn. (mem. coun. 1991-93, mem. com. on internat. polit. sci. 1997—2003, v.p. 1998—), Assn. Asian Studies (mem. N.E. Asia coun. 1992-95, vice-chair N.E. Asia coun. 1993—94, nominated editor Jour. Asian Studies 1994, mem. coun. on fgn. rels. 1990—), Internat. Platform Assn., Pacific Coun. on Internat. Policy, Women's Fgn. Policy Group. Democrat. Episcopalian. Avocations: reading, cooking, sailing, tennis, working out. Office: 50855 Washington St Ste C206 La Quinta CA 92253 Home Phone: 858-549-3189; Office Phone: 888-489-0882. Business E-Mail: ghoston@myesa.com.

HOTCHKISS, BILL, author, educator; b. New London, Conn., Oct. 17, 1936; s. William H. and Merle B. (Stambaugh) H. BA in English, U. Calif., Berkeley, 1959; MA in English, San Francisco State U., 1960; MFA in Creative Writing, U. Oreg., 1964, DA in English, 1971, PhD in English, 1974. Tchr. English Colfax H.S., 1960-62; instr. English Sierra Coll., Rocklin, Calif., 1963-79, 84-85, prof. English, 1988—; instr. English Shasta Coll., 1980-81, Rogue C.C., 1985-88, 90. Author: Last Bear McCain, 2004, (textbook) Tilting at Windmills, 1966; (novels) The Medicine Calf, 1981, reissue, 1987, Crow Warriors, 1981, Soldier Wolf, 1982, Ammahabas, 1983, Spirit Mountain, 1984, Mountain Lamb, 1985, People of the Sacred Oak, 1986, Fire Woman, 1987, Dance of the Coyote, To Fell the Giants, 1991, Sierra Santa Cruz, 1992, Yosemite, 1995, (poetry) Steepholow Poems, 1966, The Graces of Fire, 1974, Fever in the Earth, 1977, Climb To The High Country, 1978, Middle Fork Canyon, 1979, Great Upheaval, 1990, Who Drinks the Wine, 2000, I Hear the Coyote, 2003, others, (criticism) Jeffers: The Sivaistic Vision, 1975, Poet from the San Joaquin, 1978; author numerous poems; co-author: Shoshone Thunder, 1983, Pawnee Medicine, 1983, McLaffertys, 1986, Desert Moon, 1987; (handbook) Sancho's Guide to Uncommon Literacy, 1990, 3rd edit., 1995; editor: Sierra Jour., 1965-78, 88-90, 95-96, 2003, 06-07, 08-; editor, book designer, printer, publ. Blue Oak Press; book designer, text editor Castle Peak Edits., 1966—; co-editor: Perspectives on William Everson, 1992, William Everson's The Residual Years, 1997, The Integral Years, 2000, Jeffers, The Double Axe, 1977; typesetter, book design adv. Dustbooks, Quintessence, Story Line, Blue Oak Press, Castle Peak Edits.; contbr. to programmed instructional software, filmstrips. Home: 3460 Cedar Flat Rd Williams OR 97544-9605 Office: Sierra Coll NCC 250 Sierra College Dr Grass Valley CA 95945-5726

HOTCHKISS, HARLEY N., professional hockey team owner, oil industry executive; b. Tillsonburg, Ont., Can., 1927; m. Rebecca Hotchkiss; children: Paul, Brenda, John, Richard, Jeffrey. BS with high honours, Mich. State U., 1951, DSc (hon.), 2000; LLD (hon.), U. Calgary, 1996. Geologist Can. Superior Energy, 1951; with Petroleum and Natural Gas Dept. Can. Imperial Bank of Commerce, 1953; pres. Alcon Petroleum, 1959—67; pres., dir. Spartan Holdings Ltd.; co-owner Calgary Flames, 1980—, CEO, gov. Dir. Hockey Hall of Fame; chmn. bd. govs. NHL, 1995—2007; bd. dirs. Conwest Exploration Co. Ltd., Nova Corp., Alberta Energy Co., Landin Resources, Jascan Resources, TransCanada Pipelines, Telus Corp. Chmn. bd. trustees Alberta Heritage Found. for Med. Rsch.; past chmn. Foothills Hosp. Bd.; vol. United Way, Calgary Family Svc. Bur., Alberta Paraplegic Assn., Mich. State U. Found. Bd.; gov., chair Alberta Govs., Olympic Trust of Can. Served in Can. Merchant Marine, 1944—45. Decorated Officer Order of Can.; recipient Alberta Order of Excellence, 1998, Disting. Bus. Leader Award, 2006, Outstanding Alumni Award, Mich. State U., 1989, Disting. Hockey Alumnus Award, 1998; named to Can. Petroleum Hall of Fame, 2004. Mem.: Soc. of Petroleum Engrs., Am. Inst. of Metallurgical Engrs., Geological Assn. of Can., Am. Assn. of Geologists, Can. Soc. of Petroleum Geologists, Can. Inst. of Mining and Metallurgy and Petroleum, Geologists and Geophysicists of Alberta, Assn. of Profl. Engrs., Griffiths Island Club, Ranchmen's Club, Calgary Petroleum Club. Achievements include being inducted into the Hockey Hall of Fame, 2006. Office: Calgary Flames PO Box 1540 Stn M Calgary AB Canada T2P 3B9

HOTCHKISS, RALF DAVID, engineer, educator; b. Rockford, Ill., Dec. 6, 1947; s. Hilton Delos and Katherine Ruth (Huffer) H.; m. Deborah Kaplan, Sept. 25, 1977; 1 child, Desmond. BA, Oberlin Coll., 1969, DSc (hon.), 1991. Machinist trainee, engr. Woodward Gov. Co., Rockford, 1962-71; dir. Ctr. for Concerned Engring., Washington, 1971-80; engring. cons. Appropriate Tech. Internat., Washington, 1981-86; lectr., sr. rsch. scientist San Francisco State U., 1986—; chief engr. Whirlwind Wheelchair Internat., 1989—. Cons. disability advisors and wheelchair mfrs. throughout Third World, 1980—; trained wheelchair riders in more than 45 developing countries in manufacture of low cost, high tech. wheelchairs, 1980—; contractor in devel. of internat. wheelchair industry to U.S. AID, 1981—, UN, 1993—, Swedish Handicapped Internat. Aid, 1991—. Author: Independence Through Mobility, 1985, Movilidad Para La Independencia, 1989; (with others) What to Do With Your Bad Car (The Lemon Book), 1971. Bd. dirs. Advocates for Hwy. Safety, Washington, 1990—. Recipient MacArthur Found. award, 1989, Henry B. Betts award, 1994, Kilby award, 2003. Mem. Rehab. Engring. Soc. N.Am. (bd. dirs.), Hesperian Found. (bd. dirs.). Unitarian Universalist. Achievements include Hotchkiss wheelchairs have been exhibited at the San Francisco Mus. Modern Art. Avocations: photography, harmonica. Home: 6505 Farallon Way Oakland CA 94611-1201 Office: San Francisco State U Dept Engring 1600 Holloway Ave Dept Engring San Francisco CA 94132-1722 Office Phone: 415-338-6277. Personal E-mail: ralfh@sfsu.edu. Business E-Mail: ralf@whirlwindwheelchair.org.

HOUGH, JOHN DENNIS, public relations executive; BA, Gonzaga U., 1968. Chief of staff Office of Gov. Cecil Andrus, Boise, Idaho, 1974-77; dir. field offices U.S. Dept. of Interior, 1977-80; regional mgr. ITT Corp., Seattle, 1980-84; exec. v.p. First Interstate Bank, 1984-90; co-pres. Rockey Co., Inc., Seattle, CEO, 1998—. Home: 221 Yale Ave N Ste 530 Seattle WA 98109-5490

HOUGHTON, MICHAEL, geneticist; PhD, U. London, 1976. Sr. rsch. investigator human interferon genetics Searle Rsch. Labs., Buckinghamshire, England; with Chiron Corp., Emeryville, Calif., 1982—, dir. non-A non-B hepatitis rsch., v.p. hepatitis rsch. Contbr. articles to profl. jours. Recipient Karl Landsteiner Meml. award, Am. Assn. Blood Banks, 1992, Albert Lasker award Clin. Med. Rsch., 2000. Achievements include first to conduct work leading to the discovery of the virus that causes hepatitis C; development of screening methods that reduce the risk of blood transfusion-associated hepatitis in the U.S. from 30% in 1970 to virtually zero in 2000. Office: Chiron Corp 4560 Horton St Emeryville CA 94608

HOUK, BENJAMIN NOAH, performing company executive, choreographer; b. Seattle, Apr. 4, 1962; s. Robert Louis Houk and Marilyn Joan (Haugen) Sundin; m. Lauri-Michelle Rohde, July 11, 1991; children: Madeline, Katherine, Elizabeth, Michael, Alexandra;children from previous marriage: Marissa, Skylar. Studied dance, Amherst Ballet Acad., 1978, Jan Collum Sch. Ballet, 1979, Jo Emery Sch., 1979-80, N.Y. studios, 1980-83, Robert Joffrey Workshop, 1981, Am. Ballet Ctr., 1980-83, Pacific NW Ballet, 1983—; student, U. Wash., 1988—. Prin. dancer Pacific Northwest Ballet, Seattle, 1983—; asst. dir. Bravo Ballet Arts in Edn. Program, Seattle, 1993-96; soloist Pacific Northwest Ballet, Seattle, 1987—89, prin. dancer, 1989-96; M.C., coord. Joffrey, NYC, 1983; artistic dir., choreographer Nashville Ballet, 1996-99; artistic dir. Fort Worth Dallas Ballet, 1998—2001; dir. San Elijo Dance and Music Acad., San Marcos, Calif., 2001—. Guest artist guest artist Orange County Ballet, Ithaca, NY, 1981, Koslovs and Friends, San Francisco, 1985, Ballet Oreg., Portland, 1988, Ballet Chgo., 1989, Nev. Dance Theatre, Las Vegas, 1990, Tacoma Perf. Dance Co., 1980, Nevada Festival Ballet, 1993—94, Maui Ballet Co., 1994; grant panelist Nat. Endowment for the Arts, 1999; dance instr., lectr., 1984—. Dancer (ballets) Pacific Northwest Ballet include Romeo in The Tragedy of Romeo and Juliet, Sigfried in Swan Lake, Franz in Coppelia, The Prince in The Nutcracker, others include Albrecht in Giselle, Othello in The Moor's Pavane, choreographer Capriole Suite, 1988, By When, 1989, Shard, 1990, First Light, 1992, Schubert 2-4-5, 1994, Bete Noir, 1993, Across and Back, 1994, Nutcracker, 1995, Open Water, 1995, Aida, 1997, Passage, 1998, Swan Lake (after Petipa), 1998, Nutcracker, Calif. Ctr. for the Arts, Escondido, 1998, 2001, 2005—; TV appearance Disney Presents Bill Nye the Science Guy, 1994. Artistic dir. Benefit for the Homeless, Everett, Wash., 1990—91. Grantee Tacoma (Wash.) Arts Coun., 1986. Mem.: Am. Guild Mus. Artists. Avocations: reading, windsurfing, pottery, mountain climbing, painting. Office: 1635 Rancho Santa Fe Ste 203 San Marcos CA 92078 Office Phone: 760-410-1999.

HOUK, KENDALL NEWCOMB, chemistry professor; b. Nashville, Feb. 27, 1943; s. Charles H. and Janet Houk; 1 child, Kendall M.; m. Robin L. Garrell. AB, Harvard U., 1964, MS, 1966, PhD, 1968. Asst. prof. chemistry La. State U., Baton Rouge, 1968-72, assoc. prof., 1972-75, prof., 1975-80, U. Pitts., 1980-86, UCLA, 1986-91, chmn. dept. chemistry and biochemistry, 1991-94. Dir. chemistry divsn. NSF, 1988—90. Contbr. articles to profl. jours. Recipient Schrodinger medal World Assn. Theoretically Oriented Chemists, 1998. Fellow AAAS, Am. Acad. Arts and Scis.; mem. Internat. Acad. Quantum Molecular Sci., Am. Chem. Soc. (Cope Scholar award 1988, James Flack Norris award 1991, award for computers in chemistry and pharm. sci. 2003). Office: UCLA Dept Chemistry Biochemistry 405 Hilgard Ave Los Angeles CA 90095-9000 E-mail: houk@chem.ucla.edu.

HOULIHAN, PATRICK THOMAS, museum director; b. New Haven, June 22, 1942; s. John T. and Irene (Rourke) H.; m. Betsy Eliason, June 19, 1965; children: Mark T. and Michael D. (twins). BS, Georgetown U., 1964; MA, U. Minn., 1969; PhD, U. Wis., Milw., 1971. Asst. commr. N.Y. State Mus., Albany, 1980-81; dir. Heard Mus., Phoenix, 1972-80, S.W. Mus., LA, 1981-87, Millicent Rogers Mus., 1988-93; writer, rschr. Ugo Prodns., LA, 1993—2000; founding ptnr. Walkabout Books, LLC, 2000—. E-mail: houlihanpth@aol.com.

HOUSE, CECIL R., utilities executive; BS, U. Va., Charlottesville; JD, Harvard Law Sch.; MBA, Columbia U., NYC. Bar: NY, Va.; cert. purchasing mgr. Assoc. Debevoise & Plimpton; ptnr. McDermott, Will & Emery, NY; v.p., asst. gen. counsel Automatic Data Processing Inc., v.p. bus. devel.; v.p. supply chain mgmt. Pub. Svc. Electric & Gas Co., v.p. customer ops.; chief procurement officer, sr. v.p. safety and ops. support Edison Internat., 2006—, chief procurement officer, sr. v.p. safety and ops. support So. Calif. Edison subs., 2006—. Office: Edison Internat 2244 Walnut Grove Ave Rosemead CA 91770-3714

HOUSE, DAVID L., electronics components company executive; b. 1943; With Raytheon, 1965-69, Honeywell, 1969-72, Microdata, 1972-74; v.p., gen. mgr. Intel Corp., 1974-96; chmn., pres., CEO Bay Network Computers, Santa Clara, 1996; now sr. v.p. Intel Corp., 1996-98; pres. Nortel Network, Santa Clara, 1998-2000. Home: 25330 Via Pacifica Valencia CA 91355-2634

HOUSE, GEORGE MICHAEL, museum curator; b. Silver City, N.Mex., Apr. 2, 1955; s. William Winfrey House and Ruth Lestra (Williams) Billings; m. Maria Cedillo Enriquez, Dec. 24, 1983; children: Vanessa Yvette, Joshua Michael, Benjamin Alexander. BA in History and Social Sci., Western N.Mex. U., 1984, MA in History, 1985. With forest svc. USDA, Silver City, N.Mex., 1973, Kingston, N.Mex., 1976; museum curator N.Mex Mus. of Space History, Alamogordo, N.Mex., 1985—. Cons., instr., rschr., lectr. Space Ctr., Alamogordo, 1985—. Contbr. articles to publs. Sunday sch. tchr. Ch. of Christ, Bayard, N.Mex., 1976-85, Alamogordo, 1985—; juror Otero County Courthouse, Alamogordo, 1990. With USN, 1973-76. Dean Caulkins Meml. scholar Western N.Mex. U., 1983, Bd. of Regents scholar Western N.Mex., 1983. Mem. Pi Gamma Mu (Cert. of Merit 1984). Avocations: hunting, fishing, camping, sports, reading. Home: PO Box 382 Alamogordo NM 88311-0382 Office: NMex Mus Space History PO Box 5430 top NM Hwy 2001 Alamogordo NM 88311-5430 Business E-Mail: george.house@state.nm.us.

HOUSE, JOHN WILLIAM, otolaryngologist; b. LA, July 12, 1941; s. Howard and Helen House; m. Barbara Breithaupt, Mar. 28, 1993; children: Hans, Chris, Kurt, Steven, Kevin. BS, U. So. Calif., 1964, MD, 1967. Bd. cert. otolaryngologist Am. Bd. Otolaryngology - Head & Neck Surgery, 1974, bd. cert. neurologist 2004. Intern L.A. County-U. So. Calif. Med. Ctr., 1967-68; resident Glendale (Calif.) Adventist Hosp., 1971-72, L.A. County Med. Ctr., 1972-74; fellow Otologic Med. Group, LA, 1974, pvt. practice, 1975—; pres. House Ear Inst., LA, 1987—. Mem. editorial bd. Am. J. Otology, 1986—; contbr. articles to jours. in field. Admissions com. interviewer, U. So. Calif. Sch. Medicine, Los Angeles, 1976—; Capt. U.S. Army, 1969-71. Recipient Hocks Meml. award Am. Tinnitus Assn., 1988; named Tchr. of Yr., U. So. Calif. Family Practice Dept., 1987. Fellow Am. Acad. Otolaryngology/Head and Neck Surgery (bd. dirs. 2005-08); mem. AMA, Am. Neurotology Soc. (past resident, pres. 1998-99), Am. Otol. Soc., Triologic Soc. (asst. via pres.), Pan-Am. Assn. Otorhinolaryngology Broncho Esophagology, Jonathan Club (Los Angeles). Avocations: skiing, computers, running, swimming, travel. Office: House Ear Clinic Inc 2100 W 3rd St Fl 1 Los Angeles CA 90057-1922 Office Phone: 213-483-9930.

HOUSER, DOUGLAS GUY, lawyer; b. Oregon City, Oreg., July 11, 1935; s. Roy B. and Shirley (Knight) H.; m. Lucy Anne Latham, Sept. 1, 1961; children: Brooks Bonham, Bradley Knight, Anne Elizabeth. BA, Willamette U., 1957; JD, Stanford, 1960. Bar: Oreg. 1960. Practice in Portland, 1961—; ptnr. Bullivant, Houser Bailey PC, 1965—. Chmn. com. CLE Oreg. State Bar, 1969-70, chmn. com. jud. adminstrn., 1975, bd. bar examiners, 1970-72, mem. bd. bar govs., 1977-80, treas., 1979-80; judge protem Circuit Ct., 1973-77; gen. counsel NIKE, Inc., 1972-84, dir, 1972—; bd. overseers RAND Inst. for Civil Justice, 1998-2004; gen. counsel Soc. Registered Profl. Adjusters; former gen. counsel Pacific N.W. Life Ins. Co.; lectr. Contbr. articles to profl. publs. Legal adviser Portland Sch. Dist. 1 Race and Edn. Com., 1963-64; mem. Eagle bd. Columbia-Pacific coun. Boy Scouts Am., 1962-70; past v.p., treas., bd. dirs. Waverley Children's Home; life trustee Willamette U.; bd. visitors Stanford U. Sch. Law, 1978-80, 89-91, 96-98, 98-00; past chmn. Oreg. State Jud. Fitness Commn. Recipient Best Lawyers in Am., 2008; named one of, 2007, Four Outstanding Oreg. Commn. Litigators, Chambers USA. Fellow Am. Bar Found. (life), Am. Coll. Trial Lawyers, Internat. Acad. Trial Lawyers; mem. ABA (past chmn. tort and ins. practice sect.), Multnomah County Bar Assn. (chmn. com. continuing legal edn. 1977), Oreg. Assn. Def. Counsel (dir. 1972-76, pres. 1976-77), Def. Research Inst. (bd. dirs. 1990-97, sec.-treas. 1996-97), Fedn. Def. and Corp. Counsel (chmn. bd. dirs. 1991-92), Am. Judicature Soc. (bd. dirs. 1985-88), Internat. Assn. Def. Counsel, Stanford Law Soc. Oreg., pres. Am. Law Inst., Nat. Jud. Coll. (adv. coun. 1990—), Willamette U. Alumni Assn. (pres. 1972-74), Waverly Country Club, Arlington Club, Beta Theta Pi (trustee, Nat. Found.), Phi Delta Phi, Omicron Delta Kappa, Pi Gamma Mu. Office: Bullivant Houser Bailey PC Portland OR 97204-2089 Home: 11476 SW Riverwood Rd Portland OR 97219-8449 Home Phone: 503-636-1948; Office Phone: 503-228-6351. E-mail: doug.houser@bullivant.com.

HOUSHMANDZADEH, T.J. (TOURAJ HOUSHMANDZADEH), professional football player; b. Victorville, Calif., Sept. 26, 1977; m. Kaci Houshmandzadeh; 1 child, Karrington. Student, Cerritos Coll., Norwalk, Calif.; B in Phys. Edn., Oreg. State U., Corvallis. Wide receiver Cin. Bengals, 2001—09, Seattle Seahawks, 2009—. Named to Nat. Football Conf. Pro Bowl Team, NFL, 2007. Achievements include leading the NFL in: receptions, 2007. Avocations: basketball, pool, video games. Office: Seattle Seahawks 12 Seahawks Way Renton WA 98056*

HOUSTON, ELIZABETH REECE MANASCO, correctional education consultant; b. Birmingham, Ala., June 19, 1935; d. Reuben Cleveland and Beulah Elizabeth (Reece) Manasco; m. Joseph Brantley Houston; 1 child, Joseph Brantley Houston III. BS, U. Tex., 1956; MEd, Boston Coll., 1969. Cert. elem. tchr., Calif., cert. spl. edn. tchr., Calif., cert. community coll. instr., Calif.; cert. adminstr., Calif. Tchr., elem. Ridgefield (Conn.) Schs., 1962-63; staff, spl. edn. Sudbury (Mass.) Schs., 1965-68; staff intern Wayland (Mass.) High Sch., 1972; tchr., home bound Northampton (Mass.) Schs., 1972-73; program dir.

Jack Douglas Ctr., San Jose, Calif., 1974-76; tchr. specialist spl. edn., coord. classroom svcs., dir. alternative schs. Santa Clara County Office Edn., San Jose, Calif., 1976-94. Instr. San Jose State U., 1980—86, U. Calif., Santa Cruz, 1982—85, Santa Clara U., 1991—94; cons. Houston Rsch. Assocs., Saratoga, Calif., 1981—; mem. neighborhood accountability bd. County of Santa Clara Probation Dept., 2002—04. Author: (manual) Behavior Management for School Bus Drivers, 1980, Classroom Management, 1984, Synergistic Learning, 1986, Learning Disabilities in Psychology for Correctional Education, 1992. Recipient President's award Soc. Photo-Optical Instrumentation Engrs., 1979, Classroom Mgmt. Program award Sch. Bds. Assn., 1984, Svc. to Youth award, Juvenile Ct. Sch. Adminstrs. of Calif., 1989-94; grantee Santa Clara County Office Edn. Tchr. Advisor Program U.S. Sec. Edn., 1983-84. Home: 12150 Country Squire Ln Saratoga CA 95070-3444

HOUSTON, IVAN JAMES, insurance company executive; b. LA, June 15, 1925; s. Norman Oliver and Doris Talbot (Young) H.; m. Philippa Elizabeth Jones, July 15, 1946; children: Pamela, Kathleen, Ivan Abbott. BS, U. Calif., Berkeley, 1948; postgrad., U. Man., 1948-49; LLD, U. La Verne, 1993. With Golden State Mut. Life Ins. Co., LA, 1948—62, v.p., actuary, 1962-66, sr. v.p., actuary, 1966-70, pres., CEO, 1970-77, chmn., pres., 1977-80, chmn., CEO, 1980-90, chmn., 1990—2000. Bd. dirs. First Interstate Bank Calif., Pacific Telesis Corp., Family Savs., Kaiser Aluminum and Chem. Corp., Metro-Media, Broadway Fed. Savs. and Loan. Mem. L.A. World Affairs Coun., 1970—; chmn. ctrl. region United Way, Inc., L.A., 1973-75, mem. corp. bd. dirs., 1973-80, v.p., 1973-75; bd. dirs. M & M Assn., L.A. Urban League, pres., 1977-; bd. fellows Claremont U. Ctr., 1972-80; bd. regents Loyola Marymount U., 1972-75, 79-82; bd. visitors Anderson Grad. Sch. Mgmt., UCLA, 1990-93; pres. City of L.A. Human Rels. Commn., 1993-95, 99-2000; mem. United Way of L.A, Cath. Charities of L.A. With Inf. AUS, 1944-45. Decorated Purple Heart, Bronze Star; knight comdr. Order St. Gregory the Great. Fellow Life Office Mgmt. Inst.; mem. Am. Acad. Actuaries, Am. Internat. Actuarial Assn., L.A. Actuarial Club, Conf. Cons. Actuaries (assoc.), Am. Coun. Life Ins. (dir.), Life Office Mgmt. Assn. (dir., mem. exec. com. 1972-75, chmn. 1979), Mil. Order of Purple Heart, DAV (life), Calif. C. of C. (dir.), L.A. Area C. of C. (dir.), Town Hall, Calif. Club, Cosmos Club, Kappa Alpha Psi, Sigma Pi Phi. Roman Catholic. Home: 5111 S Holt Ave Los Angeles CA 90056-1117 Personal E-mail: ihouston@aol.com.

HOUSTON, JOSEPH BRANTLEY, JR., optical instrument company executive; b. Birmingham, Ala., June 15, 1934; s. Joseph Brantley and Inez (Graben) H.; m. Elizabeth Reece Manasco; 1 child, J. Brantley III. AB in Astronomy, U. Tex., Austin, 1956; MS, Northeastern U., Boston, 1969. Commd. 2d lt. C.E., US Army, 1956, advanced through grades to capt., 1968; optical engr. Perkin-Elmer, Wilton, Conn., 1961-64; mgr. massive optics, chief engr. underwater optical sys. Itek Corp., Lexington, Mass., 1964-71; asst. to pres. Kollmorgen E-O Divsn., Northampton, Mass., 1971-73; v.p. advanced devel. and spl. projects Itek Corp., Sunnyvale, Calif., 1973-81; founder Houston Rsch. Assocs., Saratoga, Calif., 1981—, Houston Tech. Internat., Inc., San Jose, Calif., 1991-97; founder, exec. dir. Forum for Mil. Applications of Directed Energy, Huntsville, Ala., 1989-96. Contbr. articles to profl. jours.; inventor. Recipient Outstanding Civilian Svc. medal U.S. Army, 1987. Fellow Internat. Soc. Optical Engring. (life; pres. 1977-78, advanced tech. advisor 1981-2004, Goddard award 1982); mem. Optical Soc. Am. (pres. New Eng. sect., chmn. Fabrication and Testing Tech. Group, editor Optical Workshop Notebook). Home and Office: 12150 Country Squire Ln Saratoga CA 95070-3444

HOUTSMA, PETER C., lawyer; b. Denver, 1951; BA in Polit. Sci. and Econs. magna cum laude, U. Colo., 1973; JD magna cum laude, Cornell U., 1976. Bar: Colo. 1976. Mem. Holland & Hart, Denver, 1976—. Mem. Am. Arbitration Assn. (panel arbitrators), Order of Coif, Phi Beta Kappa. Office: Holland & Hart PO Box 8749 Denver CO 80201-8749 Home Phone: 303-795-1715; Office Phone: 303-295-8259, 303-295-8000. Personal E-mail: phoutsma@hollandhart.com.

HOVANESSIAN, SHAHEN ALEXANDER, electrical engineer, educator, consultant; b. Tehran, Iran, Sept. 6, 1931; arrived in US, 1949; s. Alexander and Jenik (Thadeus) Hovanessian; m. Mary Mashourian Hovanessian, Sept. 17, 1960; children: Linda Larsen, Christina Tchaparian. BSEE, UCLA, 1954, MSME, 1955, PhDEE, 1958. Registered profl. engr., Calif. Research scientist Chevron Research Corp., La Habra, Calif., 1958-63; sr. scientist Hughes Aircraft Co., El Segundo, Calif., 1963-86; sr. tech. specialist Aerospace Corp., El Segundo, Calif., 1986-96; lectr. UCLA, 1962—96; cons. engr. LA, 1996—. Mem. adv. group for aerospace R & D NATO, 1985-87. Author: (with Louis A. Pipes) Matrix—Computer Methods in Engineering, 1969; Digital—Computer Methods in Engineering, 1969; Radar, Detection and Tracking Systems, 1973; Computational Mathematics in Engineering, 1976; Synthetic Array and Imaging Radars, 1980; Radar System Design and Analysis, 1984; Introduction to Sensor Systems, 1988; (with Khalil Seyrafi) Introduction to Electro-Optical Imaging and Tracking Systems, 1993; editor Computers and Elec. Engring., 1973-76. Fellow IEEE (U.S. del. Moscow 1973, disting. lectr.); mem. ASME, Sigma Xi, Tau Beta Pi. Democrat. Roman Catholic. Achievements include invention of radar computer. Avocations: investments, real estate. Home: 3039 Greentree Ct Los Angeles CA 90077-2020

HOVANNISIAN, RICHARD G., historian, educator; b. Tulare, Calif., Nov. 9, 1932; s. Kaspar and Siroon (Nalbandian) H.; m. Vartiter Kotcholosian, Mar. 2, 1957; children: Raffi, Armen, Ani, Garo. BA in History, U. Calif., Berkeley, 1954; cert. in Armenian, Coll. Arménien, Beirut, 1956; MA in History, U. Calif., Berkeley, 1958; PhD in History, UCLA, 1966; doctorate (hon.), Erevan State U., Armenia, 1994, Artsakh State U., 1997. cert. tchr., Calif. Tchr. Fresno (Calif.) City Schs., 1958-62; lectr. Armenian UCLA, 1962-69, prof. Armenian and Near Ea. history, 1969—; chair modern Armenian history Armenian Ednl. Found., 1987—; assoc. dir. G.E. von Grunebaum Ctr. Near Ea. Studies UCLA, 1979-95. Assoc. prof. history Mt. St. Mary's Coll., L.A., 1965-69; advisor Calif. Bd. Edn., Sacramento, 1984-85, 86-88; cons. on multicultural edn.; lectr. to univ. and cmty. groups and profl. confs. worldwide; mem. U.S.-USSR commns. Am. Coun. Learned Socs., 1985-91, U.S. project coord. for study contemporary ethnic processes in U.S. and USSR. Author: Armenia on the Road to Independence, 1967, 4th edit., 1984, The Republic of Armenia, vol. I, 1971, vol. II, 1982, vols. III-IV, 1996, The Armenian Holocaust, 1980, The Armenian Genocide in Perspective, 1986, The Armenian Genocide: History, Politics, Ethics, 1992, The Armenian People form Ancient to Modern Times, vol. I, The Dynastic Periods: From Antiquity to the Fourteenth Century, vol. II, Foreign Dominion to Statehood: The Fifteenth to Twentieth Century, 1997, Remembrance and Denial: The Case of the Armenian Genocide, 1998, Armenian Van Vaspurakan, 2000, Armenian Baghesh/Bitlis and Taron/Mush, 2001, Armenian Tsopk/Kharpert, 2002, Looking Backward, Moving Forward, Confronting the Armenian Genocide, 2003, Armenian Karin/Erzerum, 2003; author: (with others) Transcaucasia: Nationalism and Social Change, 1983, Le Crime de Silence: Le Génocide des Arméniens, 1984, A Crime of Silence, 1985, Toward the Understanding and Prevention of Genocide, 1984, Genocide: A Critical Bibliographic Review, 1988, Embracing the Other: Philosophical, Psychological, and Historical Perspectives on Altruism, 1992, Diasporas in World Politics, 1993, Genocide and Human Rights, 1993, Genocide: Conceptual and Historical Dimensions, 1994, The Legacy of History in Russia and the New States of Eurasia, 1994; editor: The Armenian Image in History and Literature, 1981, Islam's Understanding of Itself, 1983, Ethics in Islam, 1985, Poetry and Mysticism in Islam: The Heritage of Rumi, 1994, The Thousand and One Nights in Arabic Literature and Society, 1997, The Persian Presence in Islam, 1998, Religion and Culture in Medieval Islam, 1999, Enlightenment and Diaspora: The Armenian and Jewish Cases, 1999; chmn. editorial bd. Armenian Rev., Ararat, Haigazian Armenological Rev., Mitk, Human Rights Rev.: Jour. of Soc. for Armenian Studies; contbr. numerous articles to profl. jours. Calif. rep. Western Interstate Commn. for Higher Edn., 1978-94; bd. dirs. Facing History and Ourselves Found., Internat. Alert, Found. for Rsch. on Armenian Architecture, Internat. Inst. Holocaust and Genocide Studies, Armenian Nat. Inst., Ctr. for Comparative Genocide Studies, Sydney, Australia, Armenian Ctr. for Nat. and Internat. Studies, Armenia. Recipient Nat. Svc. award Armenian Nat. Com. of Am., 1978, Man of Yr. award Armenian Profl. soc., 1980, Citizen of Yr. award Armenian Am. Citizens League, 1981, Citizen of Yr. award United Armenian Cultural Assn. of Chgo., 1981, Recognition award Armenian Cultural Assn., Fresno, Calif., 1982, Man of Yr. award Rep. Assembly Armenian Ch. Am., 1983, Recognition award Armenian Ednl. Found., 1984, Mesrop Mashdots medal and citation Catholicos of Cilicia, Lebanon, 1984, Person of Yr. award Armenian Cultural Assns. Western U.S., 1985, Disting. Scholar award and medal Armenian Cultural Assns. U.S. and Can., 1986, Recognition Program award Armenian Assembly and Hamazkaine, Nor Seroont and Tekeyan Cultural Assns., 1987, Humanity award Facing History and Ourselves Found., 1988, Dadian award for advancement of Armenian culture Armenian Students Assn. Am., 1990, Disting. Svc. award Armenian Nat. Com. Western U.S., 1996, Disting. Achievement award Internat. Soc. for Traumatic Stress Studies, 1998, Movses Khorenatsi award and medal Republic Armenia, 1998, Pan-Kharpert Assn., 2000, St. Sahak-St. Mesrop Medal, Catholicos of all Armenians, 2001, Lifetime Achievement award, Armenian Ednl. Found., 2001, Commendation, U.S. Congress, 2001, Disting. Scholar award, Armenian Acad. Scis., Recognition award, Iranian Armenian Soc. L.A., 2003, also other citations and recognitions; grantee NEH, 1981-82, Calif. Coun. Humanities, 1985-86; Humanities Inst. fellow, 1972, Guggenheim fellow, 1974-75. Fellow Middle East Studies Assn. (mem. editorial bd.), Am. Assn. Advancement of Slavic Studies; mem. Armenian Acad. Sci. (academician), Am. Hist. Assn., Soc. for Armenian Studies (founder, pres. 1974-75, 90-92, book rev. editor jour., mem. editorial bd.), Oral History Assn., Nat. Assn. Armenian Studies (hon.), Armenian Ednl. Found. (hon.). Armenian Apostolic. Office: UCLA Dept History PO Box 951473 Los Angeles CA 90095-1473

HOVEN, BRIAN E., state legislator; b. Great Falls, Mont., Nov. 28, 1941; m. Barbara Hoven; children: Dale, Sean. BSE, Princeton U., 1963. Mfg. mgr. Proctor & Gamble, 1963—78; pres. Hoven Equipment Co., 1978—; mem. Dist. 24 Mont. House of Reps., 2008—. Specialist 5 USAR, 1965—75. Republican. Protestant. Office: Montana House of Representatives PO Box 200400 Helena MT 59620-0400 Mailing: 1501 Meadowlark Dr Great Falls MT 59404-3325 Home Phone: 406-761-8533; Office Phone: 406-444-4800. Office Fax: 406-444-4825.

HOWARD, CAROLE MARGARET MUNROE, retired public relations executive; b. Halifax, NS, Can., Mar. 5, 1945; came to the U.S., 1965; d. Frederick Craig and Dorothy Margaret (Crimes) Munroe; m. Robert William Howard, May 15, 1965. BA, U. Calif., Berkeley, 1967; MS, Pace U., 1978. Reporter Vancouver (Can.) Sun, 1965; editl. assoc. Pacific N.W. Bell, Seattle, 1967-70, employee info. supr., 1970-72, advt. supr., 1972, project mgr. EEO, 1972-73, mktg. mgr., 1973, info. mgr., 1974-75; dist. mgr. media rels. AT&T, NYC, 1975-77, dist. mgr. planning, 1977-78, dist. mgr. advt., 1978-80; media rels. mgr. Western Electric, NYC, 1980-83; divsn. mgr. regional pub. rels. AT&T Info. Sys., Morristown, N.J., 1983-85; v.p., pub. rels. and comm. policy The Reader's Digest Assn., Inc., Pleasantville, N.Y., 1985-95; ret., 1995. Faculty profl. pub. course Stanford U., summer, 1993-95; bd. dirs. Andrew Corp. Author: On Deadline: Managing Media Relations, 1985, 2d edit., 1994, 3rd edit., 2000; contbg. author: Communicators' Guide to Marketing, 1987, Experts in Action: Inside Public Relations, 2d edit., 1988, Travel Industry Marketing, 1990, The Business Speakers Almanac, 1994, Majoring in the Rest of your Life, 2000, Marketing Communications, 2002; newsletter editor Wash. State Rep. Ctrl. Com., 1973-74; contbg. editor Pub. Rels. Quar.; pres. The Reader's Digest Found.; adv. bd. Pub. Rels. News, Pub. Rels. Rev., Jour. Employee Comm. Mgmt., Ragan Pub. Rels. Jour. Corp. adv. bd. Caramoor Ctr. for Music and the Arts; bd. dirs. The Hundred Club of Westchester, Inc., The Lila Acheson Wallace Fund for Met. Mus. of Art, Madison Square Boy's and Girl's Club of N.Y.C. Mem. Women in Comm. (bd. dirs. Wash. state 1973), Internat. Assn. Bus. Communicators, Pub. Rels. Soc. Am., Nat. Press Women, Wash. Press Women (bd. dirs. 1972), Issues Mgmt. Assn., Pub. Rels. Seminar, Am. Cancer Soc., Arthur Page Soc., Wisemen, The Aspen Club, La Paloma Country Club, Gray Wolf Ski Club, Sr. Golfers Am., San Juan Outdoor Club, Pagosa Springs Arts Coun., Pi Beta Phi. Anglican. Home and Office: PO Box 5499 Pagosa Springs CO 81147-5499

HOWARD, CHRISTOPHER PHILIP, management consultant, investor; b. NYC, Aug. 6, 1947; s. Murray and Hope (McGurn) H.; m. Danina Mary Hill, June 29, 1987; children: Sean, Stephen, Coby, Katherine, Sara. BA in Econs., Stanford U., 1968; MBA, Santa Clara U., 1970. Cert. mgmt. acct., bus. counselor, mgmt. cons. Ernst & Ernst, CPAs, Phoenix, 1972-74; ops. mgr. Jensen Tools & Alloys Inc., Phoenix, 1974-77; CFO Pioneer Industries, Inc., Phoenix, 1977-80; sr. v.p. Health-Tech Mgmt., Inc., Phoenix, 1980-84; mng. prin. Howard and Assocs., Inc., Phoenix, 1984-87; consulting mgr. Grant Thornton, CPAs, Reno, 1987-89; mng. dir. Howard Consulting Group, Inc., Reno, 1989—2002; faculty mem. U. Nev., Reno, 1991—; CEO North Star Investors, Inc., 2002—. 1st lt. USAF, 1970-72. Mem.: Inst. Cert. Mgmt. Cons., Stanford U. Alumni Assn., Inst. Cert. Bus. Counselors, Inst. Cert. Mgmt. Accts. Episcopalian. Office: NorthStar Investors 661 Sierra Rose Dr Reno NV 89511 Home: 4920 Turning Leaf Way Reno NV 89515 Office Phone: 775-954-2020. Business E-Mail: chris@northstarinvestors.com.

HOWARD, DAVID E., artist; b. NYC, Jan. 25, 1952; s. John C. and Florence (Martino) H. Student, Ohio U., 1969-71; MFA, San Francisco Art Inst., 1974. Comml. photographer, Athens, Ohio, 1969-71; tchr. photography San Francisco Ctr. for Visual Studies, 1971-74, visual artist in photography, 1975—, dir., 1975—. Vis. instr. City Coll. San Francisco; grad. instr. San Francisco Art Inst. Author: Photography for Visual Communicators, (monographs) Realities, 1976, Perspectives, 1978, The Last Filipino Head Hunters, 2001, American Artist, 1990, Objective Reality of Illusionistic Perceptions, 1970, The Hidden World of the Naga, 2003, Sacred Journey: The Ganges to the Himalayas Taschen, 2004, The World of Tattoo, 2005; photography numerous periodicals including Village Voice, N.Y.C., San Francisco Chronicle, Artweek, N.Y. Art Revs., 1990, L.A. Reader, Tribal Arts mag., 1998, 2002, Filipinas, 1998, Patagonia Mag., 2002, Vogue, 2995, Esquire Tokyo, 2005; TV Documentary series; one-man shows include G. Ray Hawkins Gallery, LA, Calif., Images Gallery N.Y.C., U. Calif. Extension, John Bolles Gallery, San Francisco, Hirshhorn Mus., Smithsonian Instn., Washington, San Francisco Art Inst., Ohio U., Athens, Thomas J. Crowe Gallery, L.A., Madison (Wis.) Art Ctr., Lehigh U., Pa., Fourth Street Gallery, N.Y.C., Intersection Gallery, San Francisco, Third Eye Gallery, N.Y.C., Ctr. for Visual Studies, San Francisco, Hutchinson Community Coll., Kans., Hank Baum Gallery, San Francisco, Martin Webber Gallery, 1986, Marc Richards Gallery, L.A., 1987, E.Z.T.V., L.A., 1987, 88, G. Ray Hawkins Gallery, L.A., 1988, Fine Arts Mus. L.I., 1989, Phila. Mus. Art, 1990, San Jose, Calif., 2000; numerous group shows including Art Commn. Gallery, San Francisco, DeYoung Mus., San Francisco, Oakland (Calif.) Mus., Palace of Fine Arts, San Francisco, Camera Work, L.A., Erie (Pa.) Art Ctr., Vorpal Gallery, 1985, Cal. State U., 1988, San Francisco Pub. Libr., 1987, Video Refuses, 1986, Hadley Martin Gallery, San Francisco, 1987, Fine Art Mus. L.I., 1989, Chandler Gallery, Seattle, 1991; represented in collections Mus. Modern Art, N.Y.C., Oakland (Calif.) Mus., San Francisco Mus. Modern Art, City of San Francisco, De Saisset Art Gallery, Santa Clara, Calif., Whitney Mus. Am. Art, Hirshhorn Mus., Smithsonian Instn., Art Ctr., Waco, Tex., Memphis Brooks Mus., Memphis, Akron (Ohio) Art Mus., Am. Mus. Natural History, N.Y.C. Spl. Collections; pvt. collections; prodr. videotape New York's East Village Art Scene, 1985, California's Art Scene, 1986, others; prodr. exptl. films: Analysis of Realities, 1974, Levels of Consciousness, 1976, Levels of Reality; prodr., dir. Art Seen, TV comml. documentary series on contemporary art televised in N.Y.C., L.A., San Francisco, Miami, Fla., Portland, Oreg., New Orleans, San Francisco, aired PBS, 1994, T.V. show Keith Haring: Artist at Work, selected segments shown Whitney Mus., Hirschhorn-Smithsonian Instn.; internat. exhbns. 10th and 13th Internat. Exhbns. Contemporay Art, Royan, France, 34thand 41st Internat. Salons of Japan, Tokyo, and 5 cities, Mex. Exhbn., Ex Convento de Carman, Guadalajara, 31st Cork Film Festival, 1986, Chgo. Film Festival, 1986, 42nd San Francisco Internatl. Film Fest., 1999, Presidio Earth Days Fest., 1999; other mus., galleries, univs. in U.S. and Europe; produced and directed films New York's East Village Art Scene, 1985, California's Art Scen, Parts 1 & 2, Levels of consciousness, Levels of Reality; presenter weekly cable TV series; Blackstar syndicated photographer, N.Y.C.; video journalist Asia-Pacific Econ. Conf., 1996, (documentary) Bill Clinton Pres. U.S. and 15 other heads of states, Manila, Philippines, 1996. Recipient San Francisco Art Festival award.

HOWARD, GARY SCOTT, communications executive; b. Waukegan, Ill., Feb. 21, 1951; s. Clarence Turner Howard and Jan E. (Reimer) Searcy; m. Jacquelyn Jule Milne, Apr. 22, 1978; children: Gentry, Matthew, Chad. BS in Acctg., Colo. State U., 1973. Audit mgr. Arthur Andersen, Denver, 1973-80; v.p. Castle Pines Land Co., Denver, 1980-82; v.p. fin., treas., sec. The Sienna Co., Boulder, Colo., 1982-84; v.p., treas. United Cable TV, Denver, 1987-89; sr. v.p., treas. United Artists Entertainment Co., 1989, sr. v.p., chief adminstrv. officer, 1990—. Mem. Am. Inst. CPA's, Colo. Soc. CPA's. Roman Catholic. Avocations: hockey, sports.

HOWARD, H. TAYLOR, electrical engineer, educator; BS, Stanford U. Prof. dept. elec. engring. Stanford U., 1967—, prof. emeritus dept. elec. engring. Leader radio sci. team on NASA Galileo mission to Jupiter; chief scientist Chaparral Comm. Contbr. articles to profl. jours. Recipient medal for exceptional sci. achievement NASA, 1973. Fellow IEEE (life); mem. NAE, AAS, AGU, URSI, Satellite and Broadcasting and Comm. Assn. (chmn.). Achievements include research in radar astronomy, development of instrumentation and experimental techniques for planetary exploration, antennas, transmitters, and satellite communication. Office: 350 Serra Mall # 309 David Packard EE Bldg Stanford U Stanford CA 94305-9515 Fax: 650-723-9251. E-mail: hthoward@stanford.edu.

HOWARD, H. WILLIAM, information technology executive; BS in Sci. and Engring., Princeton U.; MBA, Stanford U. Sales and mgmt. positions IBM, Systems Industries, Inc., Memorex; former v.p. info. tech. Bechtel Group; former corp. v.p. info. tech., chief info. officer Inland Steel Industries, Inc., Chgo.; chief info. officer Sun Microsystems, Inc., Santa Clara, Calif., 1998—.

HOWARD, JAMES NEWTON, composer; b. LA, June 9, 1951; m. Rosanna Arquette, 1986 (div.); m. Sophie Howard. Prodr. for Valerie Carter, 1978; session musician with Fanny, 1974, Ringo Starr, 1974, Elton John, 1975-80, Neil Diamond, 1976, Harry Nilsson, 1976, Neil Sedaka, 1976, Yvonne Elliman, 1978, The Dudek-Finnigan-Kruger Band, 1980, Boz Scaggs, 1980, Melissa Manchester. Film scores include Wildcats, 1986, Head Office, 1986, Nobody's Fool, 1986, Never Too Young to Die, 1986, 8 Million Ways to Die, 1986, Tough Guys, 1986, Promised Land, 1987, Russkies, 1987, Campus Man, 1987, Off Limits, 1988, Everybody's All American, 1988, Tap, 1989, Major League, 1989, The Package, 1989, Coupe de Ville, 1990, Pretty Woman, 1990, Three Men and a Little Lady, 1990, Flatliners, 1990, Marked for Death, 1990, Dying Young, 1991, The Prince of Tides, 1991 (Academy award nomination best original score 1991), The Man in the Moon, 1991, King Ralph, 1991, Guilty by Suspicion, 1991, My Girl, 1991, Grand Canyon, 1991, American Heart, 1992, Glengarry Glen Ross, 1992, Diggstown, 1992, Night and the City, 1992, Falling Down, 1993, Dave, 1993, Alive, 1993, The Saint of Fort Washington, 1993, The Fugitive, 1993 (Academy award nomination best original score 1993), Intersection, 1994, Wyatt Earp, 1994, Outbreak, 1995, French Kiss, 1995 Waterworld, 1995, Restoration, 1995, Eye for an Eye, 1996, The Juror, 1996, Primal Fear, 1996, The Trigger Effect, 1996, Space Jam, 1996, Romy & Michele's High School Reunion, 1997, Father's Day, 1997, My Best Friend's Wedding, 1997, The Devil's Advocate, 1997, The Postman, 1997, A Perfect Murder, 1998, Wing Commander, 1999, Runaway Bride, 1999, Stir of Echoes, 1999,

The Sixth Sense, 1999, Mumford, 1999, Snow Falling on Cedars, 1999, Dinosaur, 2000, Unbreakable, 2000, Vertical Limit, 2000, Atlantis, 2001, America's Sweethearts, 2001, Signs, 2002, Unconditional Love, 2002, The Emperor's Club, 2000, Treasure Planet, 2002, Dreamcatcher, 2003, Peter Pan, 2003, Hidalgo, 2004, The Village, 2004, Collateral, 2004, Batman Begins, 2005, King Kong, 2005, Freedomland, 2006, RV, 2006, Lady in the Water, 2006, Blood Diamond, 2006, The Lookout, 2007, Michael Clayton, 2007, The Water Horse, 2007, I Am Legend, 2007, The Dark Knight, 2008 (Grammy award for Best Score Soundtrack, 2009), Defiance, 2008, Confessions of a Shopaholic, 2009, Duplicity, 2009; composer for songs including (from White Nights) Prove Me Wrong, 1985, (from Cobra) Hold On to Your Vision, 1986, (from Everybody's All American) Until Forever, 1988, (from Major League) Most of All You, 1989; music condr., arranger: (film) Nothing in Common, 1986; music prodr., composer: (film) Five Corners, 1987; music condr., composer: (film) Some Girls, 1988; orchestra condr.: (TV spl.) Elton John in Australia, 1987; TV scores include (TV movies) Go Toward the Light, 1988, The Image, 1990, Somebody Has to Shoot the Picture, 1990, Descending Angel, 1990, Revealing Evidence, 1990, A Private Matter, 1992, (TV spls.) The Visit, 1987, Bedtime Story, 1987, The Hit List, 1989, Alive-The Miracle of the Andes, 1993, (TV series) Men, 1989 (Emmy award nominaton 1989), You'll Love the Ride, 1991, Middle Ages, 1992, 2000 Malibu Road, 1992, ER, 1994, The Sentinel, 1996, From the Earth to the Moon, 1998, The Fugitive, 2000, Gideon's Crossing, 2000 (Emmy award for Oustanding Main Title Theme Music, 2001); recs. include James Newton Howard and Friends, 1984. Recipient Henry Mancini award, ASCAP, 2000. Office: The Gorfaine Schwartz Agency Inc 4111 W Alameda Ave Ste 509 Burbank CA 91505-4171

HOWARD, MARILYN, retired school system administrator; BA in Edn., U. Idaho, 1960, MSc in Edn., 1965; EdD, Brigham Young U., 1986; postgrad., Idaho State U. adj. faculty Idaho State U., U. Idaho. Tchr. jr. HS history and lang. arts, Lewiston, 1960; tchr. various elem. & secondary schs. Washington and Idaho; prin. Moscow West Park Elementary Sch., 1988—99; supervisor, devel. pre-school Moscow sch. dists., 1992—99; supt. pub. instrn. Idaho State Dept. Edn., Boise, Idaho, 1999—2006. Bd. dirs. State Bd. Edn., State Land Bd., Northwest Regional Edn. Lab. Named Outstanding Educator of Yr., Idaho State U. Chpt. Kappa Delta Pi, 2000, Idaho State U., Coll. Edn., 2000. Mem.: Internat. Reading Assn. (state coord. and state pres. (Idaho), mem. nat. rsch. and studies com.), Coun. Chief State Sch. Officers, Phi Delta Kappa. Office Phone: 208-332-6811.

HOWARD, MARK J., hospital administrator; BS in Health Scis., Brigham Young U.; MS in Hosp. Adminstrn., UCLA. Asst. adminstr. Utah Valley Hosp., Provo; adminstr. Am. Fork (Utah) Hosp.; exec. dir. Utah Valley Regional Med. Ctr., Orem Cmty. Hosp., Provo; adminstr. Utah Valley Regional Med. Ctr.; CEO IHC Hosps., Utah County, Ctrl. Utah, MountainView Hosp., Las Vegas. Adj. faculty Brigham Young U., Provo, U. Minn., Mpls. Active Boy Scouts Am., chmn. Bighorn dist. Named Citizen of Month Las Vegas. Fellow Am. Coll. of Heathcare Execs. (chmn. 1999—, bd. govs. 1991-95, regent for Utah 1986-91); mem. Utah Hosp. Assn. (past chair), Am. Hosp. Assn. (ho. of dels.), E-mail: mark.howard@columbia.net.

HOWARD, NANCY E., lawyer; b. Ft. Wayne, Ind., Aug. 13, 1951; BA, Stanford U., 1973, JD, 1977. Bar: Calif. 1977. Mem. Tuttle & Taylor, LA, 1977—. Contbr. articles to profl. jours. Mem. Order of Coif., Phi Beta Kappa.

HOWARD, ROBERT FRANKLIN, observatory administrator, astronomer; b. Delaware, Ohio, Dec. 30, 1932; s. David Dale and Clarine Edna (Morehouse) H.; m. Margaret Teresa Farnon, Oct. 4, 1958; children: Thomas Colin, Alan Robert, Moira Catharine BA, Ohio Wesleyan U., 1954; PhD, Princeton U., 1957. Carnegie fellow Mt. Wilson and Palomar Obs., Pasadena, Calif., 1957-59, staff mem., 1961-81; asst. prof. U. Mass., Amherst, 1959-61; asst. dir. for Mt. Wilson Mt. Wilson & Las Campanas Obs., Pasadena, 1981-84; dir. Nat. Solar Obs., Tucson, 1984-88, astronomer, 1988-98, astronomer emeritus, 1998—. Editor: Solar Magnetic Fields, 1971; editor: (jour.) Solar Physics, 1987-98; contbr. articles to profl. jours. Mem. Am. Astron. Soc. (Hale prize 2003), Internat. Astron. Union.

HOWARD, ROBERT STAPLES, newspaper publisher; b. Wheaton, Minn., Oct. 23, 1924; s. Earl Eaton and Helen Elizabeth (Staples) H.; m. Lillian Irene Crabtree, Sept. 2, 1945(dec.); children: Thomas, Andrea, William, David. Student, U. Minn., 1942, student, 1945. Pub. various daily, weekly newspapers, 1946-55; pub. Chester, Pa. Times, 1955-61; Pres. Howard Publs. (18 daily newspapers), 1961—2002. With AUS, 1942-43; 2d lt. USAAF, 1944-45. Home: PO Box 1337 Rancho Santa Fe CA 92067-1337 Office: 2525 Pio Pico Dr Ste 202 Carlsbad CA 92008

HOWARD, RON, film director; b. Duncan, Okla., Mar. 1, 1954; s. Rance and Jean Howard; m. Cheryl Alley, June 7, 1975; 4 children: Bryce, Jocelyn, Paige, Reed. Student, U. So. Calif., Los Angeles Valley Coll. Co-chmn. Imagine Films Entertainment, LA. Actor: (theatre) The Seven Year Itch, 1956, Hole in the Head, 1963; (TV series) The Andy Griffith Show, 1960-68, The Smith Family, 1971-72, Happy Days, 1974-80, Fonz and the Happy Days Gang (voice), 1980, Mork & Mindy, 1982-83, Laverne & Shirley, 1982-83, The Fonz Hour, 1982-83, Arrested Development (voice), 2003-; (TV films) A Boy Called Nuthin, 1967, Smoke, 1970, The Migrants, 1974, Locusts, 1974, Huckleberry Finn, 1975, I'm a Fool, 1976, Act of Love, 1980, Where Have All the Children Gone, 1980, Bitter Harvest, 1981, Fire on the Mountain, 1981, Return to Mayberry, 1986; (TV appearances) Dennis the Meance, 1959, 60, Johnny Ringo, 1959, The Twilight Zone, 1959, The DuPont Show with June Allyson, 1959, General Electric Theater, 1959, Insight, 1959, The New Breed, 1962, Route 66, 1962, The Eleventh Hour, 1963, The Great Adventure, 1964, Dr. Kildare, 1964, The Fugitive, 1964, The Big Valley, 1965, Gomer Pyle, U.S.M.C., 1966, I Spy, 1966, The Monroes, 1967, Mayberry R.F.D., 1968, The F.B.I., 1968, Lancer, 1968, Land of the Giants, 1969, Daniel Boone, 1969, Gunsmoke, 1969, Lassie, 1970, Love, American Style, 1972, The Bold Ones: The New Doctors, 1972, Bonanza, 1972, M*A*S*H, 1973, The Waltons, 1974, Laverne & Shirley, 1976, 79, Happy Days, 1983, 84, The Simpsons (voice), 1998, Frasier (voice), 1999; (films) The Journey, 1959, Door-to-Door Maniac, 1961, The Music Man, 1962, The Courtship of Eddie's Father, 1963, Village of the Giants, 1965, The Wild Country, 1971, American Graffiti, 1973, Happy Mother's Day, Love George, 1973, The Spikes Gang, 1974, Eat My Dust!, 1976, The Shootist, 1976, Grand Theft Auto, 1977, More American Graffiti, 1979, Osmosis Jones (voice), 2001; dir. (films) Deed of Daring-Do, 1969, Night Shift, 1982, Splash, 1984, Cocoon, 1985, Willow, 1988, Backdraft, 1991, The Paper, 1994, Apollo 13, 1995 (DGA award dir. achievement, 1996), Ransom, 1996, Da Vinci Code, 2006; dir., prodr. (films) Edtv, 1999, How the Grinch Stole Christmas, 2000, A Beautiful Mind, 2001 (Academy award best dir., 2002, Broadcast Film Critics Assoc. award best dir., 2002, DGA award dir. achievement, 2002), The Missing, 2003, Cinderella Man, 2005, Frost/Nixon, 2008, Angels & Demons, 2009; actor, dir., writer (films) Grand Theft Auto, 1977; dir., prodr., writer (films) Far and Away, 1992; dir., exec. prodr. (films) Gung Ho, 1986; dir., writer (films) Parenthood, 1989; exec. prodr. (films) Leo and Loree, 1980, No Man's Land, 1987, Vibes, 1988, Clean and Sober, 1988, The Burbs, 1989, Closet Land, 1991; prodr. (films) The Chamber, 1996, Inventing the Abbotts, 1997, Beyond the Mat, 1999, The Alamo, 2004, Inside Deep Throat, 2005, Curious George, 2006; dir. (TV films) Through the Magic Pyramid, 1981; dir., writer, (TV films) Cotton Candy, 1978; dir., prodr. (TV films) Skyward, 1980, No Greater Gift, 1985, Take Five, 1987; exec. prodr. (TV films) Skyward Christmas, 1981, When Your Lover Leaves, 1983, Into Thin Air, 1985, Student Affairs, 1999, Boarding School, 2002; prodr. Student Affairs, 1999; exec. prodr. (TV series) Maximum Security, 1984, Parenthood, 1990, Hiller and Diller, 1997, Sports Night, 1998-2000, Felicity, 1998-2002, The PJs, 1999-2001, Wonderland, 2000, The Beast, 2001, 24, 2001-, Arrested Development, 2003-, The Inside, 2005; prodr. (miniseries) From the Earth to the Moon, 1998 (Emmy award outstanding miniseries, 1998) Recipient Lifetime Achievement award in Directing, Palm Springs Internat. Film Soc., 2009, Milestone award, Prodrs. Guild America, 2009; named one of 50 Most Powerful People in Hollywood, Premiere mag., 2004—06, 100 Most Powerful Celebrities, Forbes.com, 2007. Mem. AFTRA, SAG, Acad. Motion Picture Arts and Scis. Office: Richard Lovett Creative Artists Agy 9830 Wilshire Blvd Beverly Hills CA 90212

HOWARD, RONALD A., systems engineer, educator; DSc in Elec. Engring., MIT, 1958. Prof. dept. mgmt. sci. and engring. Stanford U., 1965—. Founder, dir. Strategic Decisions Group; dir. Decisions and Ethics Ctr. Author: Dynamic Programming and Markov Processes, 1960, Dynamic Probabilistic Systems, 1971, Readings in Decision Analysis, 1977, READINGS on The Principles and Applications of Decision Analysis, 1984, Decision Analysis, 1996; contbr. numerous articles to profl. jours. Recipient Frank P. Ramsey medal, Operational Rsch. Soc. UK, 1986. Fellow IEEE, Informs; mem. NAE. Office: Dept Mgmt Sci and Engring Terman Engring Ctr Rm 420 Stanford U Stanford CA 94305-4026 Business E-Mail: rhoward@stanford.edu.

HOWARD, TONI, talent agency executive; m. David Yarnell. Sec. to Freddie Fields CMA, casting agent; ptnr. Stalmaster-Howard talent agy.; agent William Morris Agy., 1983—90; joined Internat. Creative Mgmt., 1990, exec. v.p. motion picture talent dept., 1992—99, 2007—, sr. v.p. motion picture dept. Named one of The 100 Most Powerful Women in Entertainment, Hollywood Reporter, 2005, 2006, 2007. Office: Internat Creative Mgmt 10250 Constellation Blvd Los Angeles CA 90067

HOWARD, WILLIAM GATES, JR., electronics company executive; b. Boston, Nov. 6, 1941; s. William Gates and Mary Louise (Creager) H.; m. Kathleen Louretta Shipp, June 4, 1983. BEE with distinction, Cornell U., 1964, MS, 1965; PhD, U. Calif.-Berkeley, 1967. Asst. prof. dept. elec. engring. and computer scis. U. Calif.-Berkeley, 1967-69; group ops. mgr. Motorola Semicondr. Group, Mesa, Ariz., 1969-76; v.p., dir. tech. and planning Motorola Semicondr. Sector, Phoenix, 1976-83; v.p., dir. R&D Motorola Inc., Schaumburg, Ill., 1983-87; sr. fellow Nat. Acad. Engring., Washington, 1987-91; chmn. bd. dirs. Thunderbird Technologies, Inc. Bd. dirs. Ramtron Internat Corp., Xilinx, Inc., Sandia Corp.; chmn. semicondr. tech. adv. com. US Dept. Commerce, 1978-83; chmn. adv. group on electron devices Dept. Def., 1982-99, mem. def. sci. bd., 1996—; mem. study com. on tech. and implications of VLSI, NAS, 1980; chmn. vis. com. on advanced tech. Nat. Inst. Stds. and Tech., 1988-92; chmn. Def. Sci. Bd. Task Force on Microelectronics Rsch. Facilities, 1991-92; mem. Sandia Pres. Adv. Coun., 1997-2000. Author: (with D.J. Hamilton) Basic Integrated Circuit Engineering, 1976, (with B. Guile) Profiting from Innovation, 1992; patentee (with J.B. Cecil) improved reference current source, ladder termination circuit, three terminal zener diode. Fellow AAAS, IEEE (vice chmn. circuits and systems soc. 1976-78); mem. Nat. Acad. of Engring., Sigma Xi, Phi Kappa Phi, Eta Kappa Nu, Tau Beta Pi. Office: 10642 E San Salvador Dr Scottsdale AZ 85258-6114

HOWARD, WILLIAM MATTHEW, arbitrator, lawyer, writer; b. Oak Park, Ill., Dec. 16, 1934; s. William and Martha Geraldine H.; children: Matthew William, Stephanie Sue. BSBA, U. Mo., 1956, JD, 1958; postgrad., U. Nice, 1976, U. London, 1977; PhD, Ariz. State U., 1995. Bar: Mo. 1958, U.S. Supreme Ct. 1986, cert.: Fla. Supreme Ct. (mediator and arbitrator). Jr. ptnr. Bryan Cave, St. Louis, 1958—66; gen. counsel, asst. to pres. U.S. Steel Co., Granite City, Ill., 1966—69; pres. Thomson Internat. Co., Thibodaux, La., 1969—70; founder, pres., chmn. bd. The Catalyst Group, Phoenix, 1970—97; dean, ctr. adminstr. The Union Inst., San Diego, 1997—99; pres. Dispute Solutions, Inc., Scottsdale, Ariz., 1999—. Mem. adj. faculty U. Mo., Columbia, 1956-58, St. Louis U., 1958-61, Ariz. State U., 1994-96, Ottawa U., 1994-96, Nova Southeastern U., 1996-97; chmn. unauthorized practice law com. Mo. Bar, St. Louis, 1964-65; chmn. bd. N.V. Vulcaansoord, Terborg, The Netherlands, 1975-78, E. Chalmers Holdings, Ltd., Glasgow, Scotland, 1977-78; exec. com. Chem. Bank, Irvine, Calif., 1985-90; vis. lectr. UCLA, 1987; arbitrator Am. Arbitration Assn., N.Y.C., 1987—, N.Y. Stock Exch., 1987—, Nt. Assn. Securities Dealers, Chgo., 1987—, Nat. Futures Assn., Chgo., 1988—, Am. Stock Exch., N.Y.C., 1988; hearing officer Mo. Dept. Natural Resources, Jefferson City, 1987-89, Internat. Ct. Arbitration, 1993—, Inter-Am. Comml. Arbitration Commn., 1993—; mem. Fla. Automobile Arbitration Bd., 1997-98; bd. dirs. Xeric Corp., Denver, Phoenix. Editor newsletter Extras, 1970—; exec. producer: (motion picture) Twice a Woman, 1979; contbr. numerous articles and revs. to various jours. Bd. dirs. U. Mo. Alumni Assn., 1986, Breckenridge (Colo.) Film Festival, 1989, Actors Theatre Phoenix, 1990; mem. club adv. bd. Phoenix Art Mus., 1990; dir. Scottsdale Cultural Coun., 1991. Mem. Am. Arbitration Assn. (regional adv. com.), Soc. Profls. in Dispute Resolution, Fla. Acad. Mediators, Nat. Inst. Dispute Resolution, Mensa, Order of Coif. Avocations: literature, travel, theater, visual arts, skiing. Office: PO Box 3438 Phoenix AZ 85030-3438 Personal E-mail: howardbill@msn.com.

HOWATT, SISTER HELEN CLARE, human services administrator, director, retired school librarian; b. San Francisco, Apr. 5, 1927; d. Edward Bell and Helen Margaret (Kenney) H. BA, Holy Names Coll., 1949; MS in Libr. Sci., U. So. Calif., 1972; cert. advanced studies, Our Lady of Lake U., 1966. Joined Order Sisters of the Holy Names, Roman Cath. Ch., 1945. Life tchg. credential, life spl. svcs. credential, prin. St. Monica Sch., Santa Monica, Calif., 1957-60, St. Mary Sch., LA, 1960-63; tchr. jr. high sch. St. Augustine Sch., Oakland, Calif., 1964-69; tchr. jr. high math St. Monica Sch., San Francisco, 1969-71, St. Cecilia Sch., San Francisco, 1971-77; libr. dir. Holy Names U., Oakland, Calif., 1977-94; Spanish instr. Collins Ctr. Sr. Svcs., 1994-99; acct. St. Monica Sch., San Francisco, 1999—2002; libr. St. Martin de Porres Sch., Oakland, 2003—04; tutor Aurora Sch., Oakland, Calif., 2004—. Contbr. math. curriculum San Francisco Unified Sch. Dist., Cum Notis Variorum, publ. Music Libr., U. Calif., Berkeley. Contbr. articles to profl. jours. Needlecraft instr. Mercy Retirement Ctr., 2005—. Grantee, NSF, 1966, NDEA, 1966. Mem. Cath. Libr. Assn. (chmn. No. Calif. elem. schs. 1971-72). Home and Office: 4660 Harbord Dr Oakland CA 94618-2211

HOWE, BILL, information technology executive; BS in Math., U. Waterloo; MBA, Harvard Bus. Sch. Mktg., gen. mgmt. Intel Corp., 1983—2003; pres. Intel Japan, 1998—2003; pres., CEO Azaire Networks, 2003—.

HOWE, CON EDWARD, city manager; b. St. Louis, Oct. 23, 1949; BA, Yale U., 1972; MA in City Planning, MIT, 1975. Exec. dir. Mass. Land Bank; with Gov.'s Office Mass.; dir. Manhattan Office N.Y. City Planning Dept., 1982-87, exec. dir., 1987-91; dir. planning City of L.A., 1992—. Mem. Am. Planning Assn., Urban Land Inst. Office: Planning Dept 200 N Spring St Rm 525 Los Angeles CA 90012 E-mail: chowe@planning.lacity.org.

HOWE, DANIEL WALKER, historian, educator; b. Ogden, Utah, Jan. 10, 1937; s. Maurice Langdon and Lucie (Walker) H.; m. Sandra Fay Shumway, Sept. 3, 1961; children: Rebecca, Christopher, Stephen. AB magna cum laude, Harvard U., 1959; MA, Oxford U., Eng., 1965; PhD, U. Calif., Berkeley, 1966. From instr. to assoc. prof. history Yale U., 1966-73; assoc. prof. history UCLA, 1973-77, prof., 1977-92, chmn. dept., 1983-87. Harmsworth vis. prof. Am. history, Oxford (Eng.) U., 1989-90, Rhodes prof. Am. history, 1992-2002; vis. prof. Yale U., 2001. Author: The Unitarian Conscience, 1970, The Political Culture of the American Whigs, 1979, Making the American Self, 1997, What Hath God Wrought: The Transformation of America, 1815-1848, 2007 (Pulitzer prize for history 2008). Served to lt. U.S. Army, 1959-60. Kent fellow Danforth Found., 1964-66; Charles Warren Center for Studies in Am. History fellow, 1970-71; NEH fellow, 1975-76; Guggenheim fellow, 1984-85; Huntington Libr. fellow, 1992, 94, 2002-03. Fellow: Royal Hist. Soc.; mem.: Am. Historian Laureate (Pulitzer prize 2008), Am. Hist. Assn., Soc. Historians Early Am. Rep. (pres. 2000—01), Soc. Am Historians, Oxford and Cambridge Club (London). Episcopalian. Home: 3814 Cody Rd Sherman Oaks CA 91403-5019 E-mail: howe@history.ucla.edu.

HOWE, WARREN BILLINGS, physician; b. Jackson Heights, NY, Oct. 25, 1940; s. John Hanna and Francelia (Rose) H.; m. Hedwig Neslanik, Aug. 7, 1971; children: Elizabeth Rose, Sarah Billings. BA, U. Rochester, 1962; MD, Washington U., St. Louis, 1965. Diplomate in family medicine and sports medicine Am. Bd. Family Practice, Nat. Bd. Med. Examiners. Intern Phila. Gen. Hosp., 1965-66; resident physician Highland Hosp./U. Rochester, 1969-71; family physician Family Medicine Clinic of Oak Harbor (Wash.), Inc., PS, 1971-92; student health physician, univ. team physician We. Wash. U., Bellingham, 1992—. Team physician Oak Harbor HS, 1972-92; head tournament physician Wash. State HS Wrestling Championships, Tacoma, 1989-2006; attending physician Seattle Goodwill Games, 1990; clin. asst. prof. U. Wash. Sch. Medicine, 1975-82; bd. dirs. Nat. Operating Com. on Stds. for Athletic Equipment. Contbr. articles to profl. jours. and chpts. to books; editl. bd. The Physician and Sports Medicine Jour., 1984—2005. Bd. dirs. Oak Harbor Sch. Dist. #201, 1975-87; chmn. Oak Harbor Citizen's Com. for Sch. Support, 1988-90. Lt. comdr. USN, 1966-69, Vietnam. Recipient Disting. Svc. award City of Oak Harbor, 1984; named to Nat. Wrestling Hall of Fame, 2003; Paul Harris fellowship Oak Harbor Rotary Club. Fellow: Am. Acad. Family Physicians, Am. Coll. Sports Medicine (chair membership com. 1986—95, Citation award 2005); mem.: Am. Coll. Health Assn., Am. Med. Soc. for Sports Medicine (Humanitarian award 2002), Wash. State Med. Assn. Episcopalian. Home: 4222 Northridge Way Bellingham WA 98226-7804 Office: WWU Student Health Ctr 2001 Bill McDonald Pkwy Bellingham WA 98225-9132 Office Phone: 360-650-3400.

HOWELL, HELEN, state agency administrator; b. Seattle; BA, Vassar Coll.; diploma in Legal Studies, Oxford U.; JD, Columbia U. Counsel to Sen. Patty Murray; spl. asst. to Pres. Bill Clinton; dep. staff sec. at the White House; v.p. public policy Planned Parenthood Fedn. Am.; dir. intergovernmental affairs for Gov. Gary Locke, 1999; dep. chief of staff for Gov. Gary Locke, 1999—2002; dir. Wash. State Dept. of Fin. Insts., 2002—05.

HOWELL, JAMES EDWIN, economist, educator; b. Sterling, Colo., Mar. 6, 1928; s. James William, Jr. and Lois (Brown) H.; m. Linda Leinbach, 1965; children: Kenneth E., William J., Jan E., Caitlyn B. BA, Fresno State Coll., 1950; MA, U. Ill., 1951, Yale U., 1953, PhD, 1955. Instr. econs. and stats. Yale U., 1954-56; mem. staff Ford Found., 1956-58, 62, cons., 1958-72; Theodore J. Kreps prof. econs. Stanford U., 1958—, asso. dean Grad. Sch. Bus., 1965-70; vis. prof. econs. London Bus. Sch., 1992. Dir. gen. Internat. Inst. Mgmt. and Adminstrn., Berlin, 1970-72; dir. Stanford-Insead Advanced Mgmt. Program, European Inst. Bus. Adminstrn., France, 1979-81; sometime prof., lectr. U. Hawaii, U. Calif.-Berkeley, Stanford in Vienna, U. Pa., Nat. U. Singapore, London Bus. Sch.; vis. prof. Humboldt U., Berlin, 1995; cons. U.S. and Europe; bd. dirs. Edn. Devel. Corp. Author/co-author: Higher Education for Business, 1959, European Economics-East and West, 1967, Mathematical Analysis for Business Decisions, 1963, 2d edit., 1971, (with G. L. Bach) Economics, 11th edit., 1987. Served with AUS, 1946-47. Ford Found. faculty fellow Harvard U., 1959-60; NSF sr. postdoctoral fellow London Sch. Econs., 1963-64; recipient Davis award for lifetime achievement Stanford U., 1996. Mem.: University Club (N.Y.C.). Office: Stanford U Grad Sch Bus Stanford CA 94305-5015

HOWELL, KEVIN L., hotel executive; V.p. Nat. 9 Inns, Salt Lake City, 1987—.

HOWELL, R. SCOTT, industry executive; CEO Nicholson Industries, Seattle. Office: Nicholson Industries 200 S Orcas St Seattle WA 98108-2441

HOWELL, SCOTT NEWELL, computer company executive, state legislator, state legislator; b. Provo, Utah, Sept. 28, 1953; s. Varon L. and Kathryn (Tuttle) H.; m. Linda Skanchy, Sept. 8, 1978; children:

Bryan, Bradley, Jason, Jeffrey. BA, U. Utah, 1978. With sales IBM Corp., mgr., global policy exec.; chair., Utah State Judicial Conduct Review Comm., 1990—; mem. Utah Senate, Salt Lake City, 1990—, minority leader, 1993—; mem. Nat. Conference State Legislators, 1992—. Mem. Utah info. tech. com. Utah Senate, transportation & environ. quality appropriations subcom., mem. state & local affairs standing com.; chmn. Nat. Acad. Fin., Salt Lake City, 1991-93. Bd. dirs. Utah Chpt. Nat. Children's Protection of Child Abuse, Salt Lake City, 1992-93, visually handicapped divsn. United Way, Salt Lake City, 1992-93; trustee Utah Symphony, 1994—. Mem., Nat. Academy of Finance (chair. 1990-92); Utah Info. Tech. Assoc., Intermountain Healthcare, State Legis. Leaders Found., Dem. Leadership Coun., Harvard Policy Group. Democrat. Mem. Lds Ch. Address: 319 State Capitol Salt Lake City UT 84114 Home: 5630 Lions Cross Cir Granite Bay CA 95746-9027

HOWELLS, R. TIM, professional sports team executive; m. Patty Howells; four children. Grad., U. Utah, 1968. With Howells, Inc., Salt Lake City, 1968-82, v.p., co-owner, pvt. investor, from 1982; gen. mgr. Utah Jazz NBA, 1989—. Office: Utah Jazz 301 W South Temple Salt Lake City UT 84101-1216

HOWLAND, BEN, men's college basketball coach; b. Lebanon, Oreg., May 28, 1957; m. Kim Zahnow; children: Meredith, Adam. BA in Phys. Edn., Weber St. U., 1979; MS in Adminstrn. and Phys. Edn., Gonazaga U., 1981. Basketball player Santa Barbara City Coll., 1976—78, Weber State U., 1978—80; profl. basketball player Uruguay, 1980; grad. asst. Gonzaga U., 1981—82; asst. coach U. Calif., Santa Barbara, 1982—94; head coach No. Ariz. U., 1994—99, U. Pitts., 1999—2003, UCLA, 2003—. Recipient Pitts. Tribune-Rev. City of Champions award, 2002, Dapper Dan award, honoring Pitts.'s Sportsman of Yr., 2003, Jim Phelan award, Coach of Yr., CollegeInsider.com, 2006; named Big Sky Conf. Coach of Yr., 1997, Nat. Coach Yr. (AP, Naismith, US Basketball Writers Assn., ESPN Mag., The Sporting News), 2002, US Basketball Writers Assn. Dist. Coach of Yr., 2002, Big East Coach of Yr., 2002, Basketball Am. Big East Coach of Yr., 2002, Basketball Times Big East Coach of Yr., 2002, Pac-10 Coach of Yr., 2006, Nat. Coach of Yr., Collegehoops.net, 2006, Dist. 15 Coach of Yr., Nat. Assn. Basketball Coaches, 2007; named to No. Ariz. U. Athletic Hall of Fame, 2004. Achievements include coaching five conference championship teams; leading UCLA to NCAA championship game, 2006. Office: UCLA Intcol Ath BOX 951639 175 Morgan Ctr Los Angeles CA 90095-1639 Office Phone: 310-206-6276. Office Fax: 310-206-3440. E-mail: bhowland@athletics.ucla.edu.

HOWRY, JOE R., newspaper editor; B in History and Polit. Sci., U. Mont. Various positions with newspapers in Mont.; sports writer to city editor Nev. State Jour. and Reno (Nev.) Evening Gazette; mng. editor Salem (Oreg.) Statesman-Jour., Ventura (Calif.) County Star, 1992—2004, v.p., editor, 2004—. Office: Ventura County Star PO Box 6006 Camarillo CA 93011-6006

HOXIE, JOEL P., lawyer; b. Waterloo, Iowa, Dec. 4, 1948; s. Wirt Pierce and Jeanne (Ogle) H.; m. Cynthia Ann Mast, Aug. 12, 1978; children: Robert Lewis, Laura Ann. AB, Princeton U., 1971; JD, U. Iowa, 1978. Atty. Snell & Wilmer, Phoenix, 1978—. Trustee Heard Mus., Phoenix, 1990-2004, pres. 1995-97, life trustee 2005; pres. Princeton Alumni Assn. No. Ariz., Phoenix, 1990-2003. Lt. USN, 1971-75. Mem. Nat. Bar Assn., Ariz. State Bar Assn., County Bar Assn., Securities Industry Assn. (legal and compliance divsn. 1992—), Phoenix Country Club (bd. dirs. 2001—, pres. 2006—). Methodist. Avocations: golf, tennis, swimming, hiking. Home: 5301 E Mariposa St Phoenix AZ 85018-3029 Office: Snell & Wilmer 1 Arizona Ctr Phoenix AZ 85004 Home Phone: 602-840-7752; Office Phone: 602-382-6264. Business E-Mail: jhoxie@swlaw.com.

HOXIE, TIMOTHY GORDON, lawyer; b. Concord, NH, Aug. 11, 1960; s. Gordon Goss and Betty (Moorhouse) H.; m. Cara Rubinstein, May 2, 1992. BA summa cum laude, Yale U., 1982; JD magna cum laude, Harvard U., 1985. Bar: Calif. 1985. Law clk. Hon. Anthony M. Kennedy, U.S. Ct. Appeals, 9th Cir., Sacramento, Calif., 1985-86; assoc. Heller Ehrman White & McAuliffe, San Francisco, 1986-91, ptnr., 1992—. Editor Harvard Law Rev., 1983-85. Mem. ABA (co-chair, state and local bar rels.com. sect. of bus. law), San Francisco Bar Assn., Calif. State Bar Assn. (bus. law sect., co-chmn. corp. com. bus. law sect. 1998-99, section chair, 2002-03). Office: Heller Ehrman LLP 333 Bush St San Francisco CA 94104-2806 Office Phone: 415-772-6052. Personal E-mail: tim.hoxie@hellerehrman.com.

HOYT, DAVID A., bank executive; Loan officer Union Bank, Calif.; vice chair real estate, capital markets, internat. Wells Fargo & Co., 1997—98, group exec. v.p. wholesale banking, 1998—. Mem. finl svcs. roundtable, mem. adv. coun. U. So. Calif. Lust Ctr. Real Estate. Mem.: Urban Land Inst. Office: Wells Fargo & Co 420 Montgomery St San Francisco CA 94163

HSI, DAVID CHING HENG, plant pathologist, geneticist, educator; b. Shanghai, May 17, 1928; came to US, 1948, naturalized, 1961. s. Yulin and Sue Jean (King) H.; m. Kathy S.W. Chiang, 1952; children: Andrew C., Steven D. BSA, St. John's U., Shanghai, 1948; MS, U. Ga., 1949; PhD, U. Minn., 1951. Grad. teaching asst. U. Minn., St. Paul, 1950; postdoctoral fellow US Cotton Field Sta., Sacaton, Ariz., 1951-52; mem. faculty N.Mex. State U., Las Cruces, 1952—, prof. plant pathology and genetics, 1968-92, prof. emeritus, 1992—. Cons. AID, Pakistan, 1970; coord. external evaluation panel Peanut Collaborative Rsch. Support Program, USA, West Africa, S.E. Asia, 1993-95; acad. exch. People's Republic China, 1978, 84, 85, Republic China, 1979, 81, 82, Brazil and Argentina, 1980, Australia, 1983, South Africa, 1981; judge sr. botany N.Mex. Sci. and Engring. Fair, 1979—2007; adj. prof. biology U. N.Mex., 1986—. Author rsch. papers in field; co-developer new crop cultivars. Past bd. dir., treas. Carver Pub. Libr., Clovis, N.Mex.; elder 1st Presbyn. Ch., Albuquerque, workship com. chmn., 1981-82, adult edn. com. chmn., 1988-91, pers. com., 1995-98; mem. nat. adv. coun. discipleship and worship Gen. Assembly United Presbyn. Ch. USA, 1978-81, mem. nat. theol. reflections working group, 1980-81, mem. ednl. and congl. nurture unit, 1991-93, N.Mex. Child Abuse Neglect Prevention Implementation Task Force, 1993-97; mem. bd. edn. Albuquerque Pub. Schs., 1982, sec. bd. edn., 1983, v.p., 1984; bd. dir. Mid. Rio Grande Coun. Govts., 1983, 84; chair Albuquerque Sisters Cities Bd., 1986-88; 1st v.p. Albuquerque Sister Cities Found., 1995-96, pres., 1996-98; chair Albuquerque Biopark Adv. Bd., 2003-05; mem. com. higher edn. Gen. Assembly The Presbyn. Ch. (USA), 1991-93, preparation ministry com., Presbytery Santa Fe, 1993-98, chair, 1996-97; co-chair N.Mex. Advocates for Children and Families, 1993-95, vice chair, 1995-98; bd. dir. Greater Albuquerque Vol. Adminstr., 1992-95, 97-99, Project Change, 1994-98, v.p., 1996-98; v.p. Albuquerque Edn. Retirees, 1995-96, pres., 1996-98; v.p. Edn. Success Alliance, 1996-98; trustee All Faiths Receiving Home, 1997-03; trustee, Sandia Prep Sch., 2001-03; bd. dir., v.p. Explora Sci. Ctr. and Children Mus. Albuquerque, 1998—, v.p., 2004, v.p. exec. com. 2004-06; dir. emeritus 2006-; v.p. The Friendship Force of N.Mex., 2001, pres., 2002. Recipient Disting. Rsch. award Coll. Agr. and Home Econs. N.Mex. State U., 1971, Disting. Svc. award, 1985, Albuquerque Human Rights awad, 1997; inducted into Sr. Citizen's Hall of Fame, 1993. Fellow AAAS (hon., coun. mem. 1998-2004, Southwestern and Rocky Mountain divsn., exec. com. 1993-95, pres.-elect 1995-96, pres. 96-97); mem. Internat. Soc. Plant Pathology, Am. Phytopath. Soc. (judge Internat. Sci. and Engring. Fair 1983), Nat. Sweet Potato Collaborators Group (chmn. sprout prodn. and root piece propagation com. 1982-84), Nat. Geog. Soc., Am. Peanut Rsch. and Edn. Soc. (chmn. site selection com. 1981, award com., pres.-elect 1981, pres. 1982), N.Mex. Acad. Sci. (chmn. com. 1980, pres. 1981, 82, treas. 1984-92, dir. emeritus 2007-; dist. scientist award 1984), Nat. Assn. Acad. Sci. (pres.-elect 1992-93, pres. 1993-94), N.Mex. Chinese Assn. (pres. 1983-84, 92-93, treas. 1985-86, past bd. dir.), Chinese Am. Citizens Alliance (v.p. Albuquerque lodge 1988-92, v.p. 2002-04, pres. 2004-07, Spirit of Am. award, 2007), Albuquerque Coun. for Internat. Visitors (v.p. 1988, pres. 1989-91), Sigma Xi (life, N.Mex. coord. centennial celebration, sr. editor commemorative pub. Frm Sundaggers to Space Exploration), Kiwanis Internat. (past pres. Clovis, past chmn. spl. program com., past bd. dir. Albuquerque). Home and Office: 2504 Griegos Pl NW Albuquerque NM 87107-2874

HSIEH, MARINA CING, lawyer, educator; b. Waco, Tex., Aug. 30, 1960; d. George S. C. and Rose S. C. (Pu) H. AB, Harvard U., 1982; JD, U. Calif., Berkeley, 1988. Bar: Pa., 1990; U.S. Ct. Appeals (3rd cir.) 1992; U.S. Supreme Ct. 1996. Staff Hon. Leo T. McCarthy, Lt. Gov., Calif., 1983-85; law clk. to Hon. Louis H. Pollak U.S. Dist. Ct., Phila., 1988-89; law clk. to Hon. John Paul Stevens U.S. Supreme Ct., Washington, 1989-90; asst. counsel NAACP Legal Defense and Ednl. Fund, Inc., NYC, 1990-93; acting law prof. U. Calif., Berkeley, 1993-99; asst. prof. law U. Md., Balt., 1999—2005; asst. dean academic and profl. devel. Santa Clara U. Sch. Law, Calif., 2005—. Lectr. Bar/Bri, 1996—. Author: (with others) Asian American Almanac, 1994. Mem. ACLU (bd. dirs. 1998—, v.p.), Alumni of Deep Springs and Telluride Assn. Office: Santa Clara Univ Law 500 El Camino Real Santa Clara CA 95052-0448 Home Phone: 925-551-8243; Office Phone: 408-554-2764. Business E-Mail: mhsieh@scu.edu.

HSIEH, MING, information technology executive; married; 2 children. BSEE, U. So. Calif., 1983, MSEE, 1984. Rsch. devel. engr. Internat. Rectifier, 1985—87; founder, v.p. AMAX Tech., 1987—90; founder Cogent, Inc., South Pasadena, Calif., 1990, pres., chmn., CEO, 1990—. Office: Cogent Inc 209 Fair Oaks Ave South Pasadena CA 91030

HSU, CHIEH SU, applied mechanics engineering educator, researcher; b. Soochow, Kiangsu, China, May 27, 1922; came to U.S., 1947. s. Chung yu and Yong Feng (Wu) H.; m. Helen Yung-Feng Tse, Mar. 28, 1953; children: Raymond Hwa-Chi, Katherine Hwa-Ling. BS, Nat. Inst. Tech., Chungking, China, 1945; MS, Stanford U., 1948, PhD, 1950. Project engr. IBM Corp., Poughkeepsie, NY, 1951-55; assoc. prof. U. Toledo, 1955-58, Univ Calif.-Berkeley, 1958-64, prof., 1964—, chmn. div. applied mechanics, 1969-70. Sci. adv. bd. Alexander von Humboldt Found. Fed. Republic Germany, Bonn, 1985—; US nat. com. theoretical and applied mechanics US Nat. Acad. Scis., 1985-90. Author: Cell-to-Cell Mapping, 1987; contbg. author: Thin-Shell Structures, 1974, Advances in Applied Mechanics, vol. 17, 1977; tech. editor Jour. Applied Mechanics, N.Y.C., 1976-82; assoc. editor profl. jours.; author of over 106 tech. papers. Recipient Alexander von Humboldt award Fed. Republic Germany, 1986; Guggenheim Found. fellow, 1964-65; Miller Rsch. prof., U. Calif., Berkeley, 1973-74. Fellow ASME (Centennial award 1980, N.O. Myklestad award 1995) Am. Acad. Mechanics; mem. Acoustical Soc. Am., Soc. Indsl. and Applied Math., U. S. Nat. Acad. Engring., Acad. Sinica, Sigma Xi. Office: U Calif Dept Mech Engring Berkeley CA 94720-1740

HSU-LI, MAGDALEN, singer, poet, painter; d. George Tze-Ching Li. BFA in Painting, Rhode Island Sch. of Design; attended, Cornish Coll. of Arts. Founder Chickpop Records, 1997—, Femme Vitale, Seattle Women's Music and Arts Coalition, 1997. Singer: (albums) Muscle and Bone, 1997, Evolution, 1998, Fire, 2001.

HU, CHENMING, engineering educator; b. Beijing, July 12, 1947; arrived in US, 1969; BS, Nat. Taiwan U., Taipei, 1968; MS, U. Calif., Berkeley, 1970, PhD, 1973. Asst. prof. elec. engring. MIT, 1973-76; prof. U. Calif., Berkeley, 1976—, Chancellor's prof., 1998-2000, Taiwan Semicondr. Mfg. Corp. Disting. prof. microelectronics, 2000—. Mgr. nonvolatile memory devel. Nat. Semicondr., Santa Clara, 1980—81; hon. prof. Beijing U., 1988, Tsing Hwa U., 1991, Chinese Acad. Sci., 1991; dir. Joint Svcs. Electronics Program, 1989—92, Indsl. Liaison Program, 1992—95; founder, chmn. Celestry Design Tech. Inc., 1995—2003; chief. tech. officer TSMC, 2001—04. Co-author: Solar Cells, 1983, Advanced MOS Device Physics, 1989, Nonvolatile Semiconductor Memory, 1991, MOSFET Modeling, 1999, Modern Semiconductor Devices, 2009; contbr. articles to profl. jours. Chmn. bd. dirs. E. Bay Chinese Sch., Oakland, Calif., 1989—91. Recipient Design News Excellence in Design award, 1992, Outstanding Inventor award, 1993, R & D 100 award, 1996, Monie Ferst award, Sigma Xi, 1998, W. Y. Pang Found. award for Rsch. Excellence, 1999, Disting. Tchg. award, U. Calif., Berkeley, 1997. Fellow: IEEE (editl. bd. Trans. Electronic Devices 1986—88, Jack Morton award 1997, Solid State Cirs. award 2002, Paul Rappaport award 2004, Jumichi Nishizawa award), Taiwan Academia Sinica, Inst. Physics (Junichi Nishizawa medal 2009); mem.: Chinese Acad. Sci., US Nat. Acad. Egring. Achievements include patents for solid state devices and technology. Office: U Calif Dept Elec Engring Computer Sci Berkeley CA 94720-0001

HU, EVELYN LYNN, electrical and computer engineering educator; b. NYC, May 15, 1947; d. David Hosheng and Carolyn Jui-chen (Hsu) H. BA in Physics, Barnard Coll., 1969; MA in Physics, Columbia U., 1971, PhD in Physics, 1975. Mem. tech. staff AT&T Bell Labs., Holmdel, N.J., 1975-81, supr. Murray Hill, N.J., 1981-84; prof. elec. and computer engring. U. Calif., Santa Barbara, 1985—; assoc. dir. Ctr. Robotic Systems in Microelectronics, 1985—. Mem. MIT vis. com. EECS, 1983—; mem. program com. Nat. Research and Resource Facility for Submicron Structures; mem. steering com. Internat. Symposium on Electron, Ion and Photon Beams; chmn. Gordon Conf. on Chemistry and Physics of Microstructures, 1986. Contbr. articles to profl. jours.; patentee in field. Mem. IEEE, Am. Phys. Soc., Am. Vacuum Soc., Phi Beta Kappa, Sigma Xi. Office: U Calif Ctr Quantized Elec Structures Santa Barbara CA 93106

HUANG, JEN-HSUN, electronics executive; b. Taiwan; m. Lori Huang; 2 children. BSEE, Oreg.State U., 1984; MSEE, Stanford U., Calif. Microprocessor designer Advanced Micro Devices; dir. coreware LSI Logic; co-founder, pres., CEO NVIDIA Corp., Santa Clara, Calif., 1993—. Trustee RAND Corp. Recipient Dr. Morris Chang Exemplary Leadership award, Fabless Semiconductor Assn., 2004, Daniel J. Epstein Engring. Mgmt. award, Univ. So. Calif. Mem.: Com. of 100. Office: NVIDIA Corp 2701 San Tomas Expy Santa Clara CA 95050

HUANG, JIA-SHENG JACK, optics scientist, researcher; arrived in US, 1993, naturalized, 2005; s. Chang-Sung Huang and Fang-Mei Lee; m. Ming Lee, Aug. 9, 1998; children: Ashley, Shannon. BS in Physics, Nat. Taiwan U., Taipei, 1988—92; MS in Materials Sci. & Engring., UCLA, 1993—96, PhD in Materials Sci. & Engring., 1993—97. Rsch. asst. Inst. Atomic & Molecular Scis., Academia Sinica, Taipei, 1992—93; summer internship Nat. Nano Device Lab, Hsinchu, Taiwan, 1995—96; mem. tech. staff Bell Labs, Lucent Techs., Orlando, Fla., 1997—2000; wafer fab R&D tech. mgr, scientist Ortel divsn. Emcore, Alhambra, Calif., 2000—. Reviewer in field. Contbr. articles to profl. jours. Recipient Agere Patent award, Agere Sys., 2002, 10 Yr. Anniversary award, Emcore Corp., 2007. Mem.: Huntington Tennis Club (Silver medal for tennis double 2007—). Achievements include discovery of ultra-fast silicide line formation; polarity effect of contact failure in a paired contact structure; asymmetrical electromigration critical current density effect in multilevel interconnects; electromigration induced step-like resistance change behavior in multilevel interconnects; rippled optical spectrum of ESD stressed lasers; patents for dopant activiation of heavily-doped semiconductor by high current densities; a method of improving electromigration in semiconductor device manufacturing processes. Avocations: tennis, violin, travel, painting, basketball. Office: Emcore Ortel Divsn 2015 W Chestnut St Alhambra CA 91803 Office Fax: 626-293-3423; Home Fax: 323-254-4845. Personal E-mail: jshuang6@yahoo.com. Business E-Mail: jshuang@emcore.com.

HUANG, KAI, computer game company executive; B, U. Calif., Berkeley. Cons. Anderson Consulting; co-founder, CEO Adux Software; co-founder, pres. RedOctane Inc., Sunnyvale, Calif., 1999—, CEO, 1999—2006. Named a Maverick, Details mag., 2008; named one of Top 50 Prodrs. in New Media, Prodrs. Guild America New Media Coun., 2006. Office: Redoctane Inc 444 Castro St Ste 140 Mountain View CA 94041-2073

HUANG, LINDA CHEN, plastic surgeon; b. Ithaca, NY, July 24, 1952; MD, Stanford U., 1979. Office: 1601 E 19th Ave Ste 3150 Denver CO 80218-1220 Office Phone: 303-831-8400.

HUANG, PAN MING, soil science educator; b. Pu-tse, Taiwan, Sept. 2, 1934; arrived in Can., 1965; s. Rong Yi and Koh (Chiu) H.; m. Yun Yin Lin, Dec. 26, 1964; children: Daniel Chian Yuan, Crystal Ling Hui. BSA, Nat. Chung Hsing U., Taichung, Taiwan, 1957; MSc, U. Man., Winnipeg, Can., 1962; PhD, U. Wis., Madison, 1966. Cert. prof. agrologist. Asst. prof. soil sci. U. Sask., Saskatoon, Canada, 1965-71, assoc. prof., 1971-78, prof., 1978—. Invited rsch. chair Nat. Taiwan U., 1996, 2003, 04; nat. vis. prof., head dept. soil sci. Nat. Chung Hsing U., 1975-76, chair. prof. soil chemistry, 2007-, Y.C. Tang chair prof., Zhejiang U., 2007-; mem. agr. adv. bd. Lewis Pubs., 1991—; hon. prof. Huazhong Agr. U., 1992—, Guanxi Agrl U., 1993—, Henan Agrl. U., 1996—, Langzhou U., 1999—; acad. advisor Chinese Acad. Scis., 1996—; hon. scientist Rural Adminstrn., Republic of Korea, 2004—06. Author: Soil Chemistry, 1991, Environmental Soil Chemistry and Its Impact on Agriculture and the Ecosystem, 2000; editor: 17 books; mem. editl. bd.: Chemosphere, 1987—97, Pedosphere, 1990—, Trends in Agr. Sci., 1991—95, Advances in Environ. Sci., 1993, Geodema, 1994—2007, Soil Sci. Plant Nutrition, 1998—2005, Water, Air, and Soil Pollution, 1998—2001, Humic Substances in the Environment, 1998—, spl. editor, mem. editl. bd.: Water Pollution Rsch. Jour. Can., 1983—89, 1991—93, Agro's Ann. Rev. Crop Ecology, 1995—, mem. editl. adv. bd.: Trends in Soil Sci., 1995—, lead series editor: Wiley-IUPAC, Biophysico-Chemical Processes in Environmental Systems, 2006—; contbr. over 300 articles to profl. jours., chapters to books. Bd. dirs. Saskatoon Chinese Mandarin Sch., 1977-79, Saskatoon Soc. for Study Chinese Culture, 1983—. 2d lt. Taiwan Mil. Tng. Corps, 1957-59. Recipient Soil Sci. Rsch. award, Soil Sci. Soc. Am., 2000; grantee, numerous agys., 1965—, UN Environment Program, Nat. Scis. & Engring. Rsch. Coun., Can. Fellow: AAAS, World Innovation Found., Am. Soc. Agronomy, Soil Sci. Soc. Am. (rep. Clay Minerals Soc. 1979—83, chmn. divsn. S-9 1983—84, bd. dirs. 1983—84, editor spl. pub. 1986, Internat. Soil Sci. award com. 1986—87, assoc. editor 1987—92, Marion L. and Christie M. Jackson Soil Sci. award com. 1990—92, rep. to Internat. Union Pure and Applied Chemistry 1990—2000, fellow com. 1992—94, chmn.-elect divsn. S-2 1993—94, chmn. 1994—95, past chmn. 1995—96, spl. awards com. 1995—96, chair nominations com. divsn. S-2 1995—96, bd. dirs. 1995—96, editor spl. pub. 1998, Soil Sci. Rsch. award 2000), Can. Soc. Soil Sci.; mem.: Can. Network Toxicology (team on metal speciation 1993—96), Internat. Humic Substances Soc. (leader Can. nat. chpt. 1992—2005), Internat. Union Pure & Applied Chemistry (assoc.; commn. environ. analytical chemistry 1993—95, titular mem. com. fundamental environ. chemistry 1995—97, 1999—2001, divsn. chemistry & environment 2001—05, titular mem. divsn. chemistry and environment 2006—), Internat. Assn. Study Clays (treas. 1993—2001), NY Acad. Scis., Am. Chem. Soc., Internat. Union Soil Sci. (chmn. working grp. MO 1990—2004, chmn. commn. 2.5 soil phys., chem., biol. interfacial reactions 2004—06), Sigma Xi. Avocations: music, reading. Home: 130 Mount Allison Cres Saskatoon SK Canada S7H 4A5 Office: U Sask Dept Soil Sci Campus Dr 51 Saskatoon SK Canada S7N 5A8 Office Phone: 306-966-6838. Business E-Mail: pmh936@mail.usask.ca.

HUANG, ROBERT T., electronics executive; BS in Elec. Engring., Kyushu U., Japan; MS, U. Rochester; MBA, MIT. Sales mgr. Advanced Micro Devices; founder Synnex Corp. (as Compac Microelectronics), 1980; pres., CEO Synnex Corp., Fremont, Calif., 1992—2008, pres., co-CEO, 2008, chmn., 2008—. Office: Synnex Corporation 44201 Nobel Dr Fremont CA 94538-3178

HUANG, WENDY WAN-JUOH, lawyer; b. Taipei, Taiwan, Aug. 3, 1966; came to the US, 1977; d. Tsung-Che and Sheree (Shen) H.; m. Kermit Marsh, July 6, 1996; children: Dermot, Connor, Morgan. BA, Cornell U., Ithaca, NY, 1988; JD, Boston U., 1992. Bar: Calif. 1993, DC 1994, NY 1994. Intern UN Com. on US-China Rels., NYC, 1986, Internat. Bus. Cons., Washington, 1987; asst. editor P.C. Mag., NYC, 1988-89; law clk. San Diego City Attys., Calif., 1990, US Atty.-So. Dist. NY, NYC, 1991, LA Dist. Attys., Calif., 1991; assoc. Law Firm of Kinkle, Rodiger & Spriggs, LA, 1992-94, Knapp, Marsh, Jones & Doran, LA, 1994-97, Burkley, Greenberg, Fields & Whitcombe, 1997—2000; chief gen. counsel Olen Cos., Newport Beach, Calif., 2000—05; exec. v.p., gen. counsel Crown Realty and Devel. Corp., Irvine, Calif., 2005—. Sec., chmn. Pacific Rim bd. govs. Calif. Chinese Bar Assn., LA, 1993—; judge pro tem, LA Superior Ct.; arbitrator LA County Bar Client Dispute Svcs.; legal cons. Sta. KPFK Radio, Voice of Am. Radio, Chinese Daily News. Writer, actress Words Across Cultures Theatre Co., LA, 1993; actress, dancer Bethune Theatre Danse, LA, 1993; editl. bd. LA Lawyer mag. Recipient Westinghouse Nat. Sci. Talent Search scholarship NSF, Washington, 1984; named a Superlawyer Rising Star, LA Mag., 2006. Mem. LA County Bar Inns of Ct., Orgn. Chinese Ams. (pres.), So. Calif. Chinese Lawyer Assn. (bd. mem.), Screen Actors Guild. Republican. Avocations: tennis, piano. Home: 8571 Edgemont Cir Westminster CA 92683-7216 Office: Crown Realty and Devel 18201 Von Karman Ave Ste 950 Irvine CA 92612 Office Phone: 949-567-5861. E-mail: whuang@crowndev.com.

HUBBARD, ARTHUR THORNTON, chemist, educator; b. Alameda, Calif., Sept. 17, 1941; s. John White and Ruth Frances (Gapen) H.; children: David A., Lynne F. BA, Westmont Coll., 1963; PhD, Calif. Inst. Tech., 1967. Prof. chemistry U. Hawaii, Honolulu, 1967-76, U. Calif., Santa Barbara, 1976-86; Ohio eminent scholar and prof. chemistry U. Cin., 1986-99, dir. Surface Ctr., 1986-99; dir. Santa Barbara Sci. Project, 1999—. Chmn. Ohio Sci. and Engring. Roundtable, 1990-95. Co-editor Jour. Colloid and Interface Sci., 1993—; series editor Interface Sci and Tech, 2001—; Surfactant Sci. Series; editor: Encyclopedia of Surface and Colloid Science. Mem. Am. Chem. Soc. (assoc. editor jour. Langmuir 1984-90, vice chair surface and colloid div. 1999, chair-elect 2000, chair 2001, Kendall award 1989), Electrochem. Soc. (David C. Grahame award 1993), Am. Phys. Soc. Office: Santa Barbara Sci Project PO Box 42530 Santa Barbara CA 93140-2530

HUBBARD, JOHN RANDOLPH, retired academic administrator, diplomat; b. Belton, Tex., Dec. 3, 1918; s. Louis Herman and Bertha (Altizer) H.; m. Lucille Luckett, Jan. 29, 1947 (div. Dec. 1983); children: Elisa, Melisse, Kristin. AB, U. Tex., 1938, A.M., 1939, PhD, 1950; L.H.D., Hebrew Union Coll., Los Angeles, 1971, Westminster Coll., Fulton, Mo., 1977; LL.D., Sch. of Ozarks, 1973, U. So. Calif., 1980. Pvt. sec. to ICC commr., 1939-41; teaching fellow U. Tex., 1946-48; vis. asst. prof. Brit. history La. State U., 1948; asst. prof. European history Tulane U., 1949-52, assoc. prof., 1953-58, prof., 1958-65; dean Newcomb Coll., 1953-65; vis. asst. prof. European history Yale, 1952-53; chief edn. adviser U.S. AID, India, 1965-69; v.p. for acad. affairs, provost U. So. Calif., Los Angeles, 1969-70, pres., 1970-80, pres. emeritus, 1980—, John R. Hubbard chair Brit. history, 1980—; US amb. to India, 1988-89. Vis. disting. prof. Nat. U. Taipei, Taiwan, 1981; co-chmn. Indo-U.S. Subcommn. on Edn. and Culture, 1982—. Contbr.: articles and revs. to Jour. Modern History; other ednl. jours. Mem. bd. Tulane-Lyceum Assn., 1953-65, Isidore Newman Sch., 1953-65; mem. Region 12 selection com. Woodrow Wilson Fellowship Program, also chmn., 1955-65; mem. bd. U.S. Edn. Found., India; mem. Indian adv. bd. Women's Coll. Faculty Exchange program; pres. bd. Am. Internat. Sch., New Delhi; mem. So. Calif. adv. bd. Inst. Internat. Edn.; trustee Scholarships for Children of Am. Mil. Personnel; bd. dirs. Community TV So. Calif., Los Angeles. Served as an aviator in USN, 1941-46; flight instr. and patrol plane comdr. Atlantic and Pacific fleets; lt. comdr. Res. Decorated D.F.C., Air medals (4); chevalier des Palmes Académiques; Stella della Solidarietá Italiana Italy; Order of Taj 3d degree Iran; recipient Disting. Services to Higher Edn. in U.S. award Tulane U., New Orleans, 1976; Air U. award, 1976; Disting. Alumnus award U. Tex., Austin, 1978, Alben W. Barkley medal for disitng. svc., 1989. Mem. Am., Miss. Valley hist. assns., So. Hist. Soc. (exec. council 1954-56), Anglo-Am. Hist. Soc., Assn. Ind. Calif. Colls. and Univs. (trustee), Am. Council Edn. (commn. on fed. relations 1975-77), Assn. Am. Univs. (council on fed. relations 1975-79), Orgn. Am. Historians, Conf. Brit. Studies, Am. Council Learned Socs., Phi Beta Kappa, Phi Delta Kappa, Alpha Kappa Psi, Delta Kappa Epsilon, Omicron Delta Kappa. Clubs: Royal Aero (London), Athenaeum (London); Los Angeles Country; California (Los Angeles); University (N.Y.C.); Cosmos (Washington). Office: U So Calif Dept History Los Angeles CA 90089-0001

HUBBARD, WILLIAM BOGEL, planetary sciences educator; b. Liberty, Tex., Nov. 14, 1940; s. William Bogel and Marie Hubbard; m. Jean North Gilliland, June 8, 1963; children: Lynne Marie, Laurie North. BA, Rice U., Houston, 1962; PhD, U. Calif., Berkeley, 1967. Rsch. fellow Calif. Inst. Tech., Pasadena, 1967-68; asst. prof. astronomy U. Tex., Austin, 1968-72; assoc. prof. planetary scis. U. Ariz., Tucson, 1972-75, dir. Lunar and Planetary Lab., 1977-81, prof., 1975—. Cons. Lawrence Livermore (Calif.) Nat. Lab., 1972-86, NASA, 1994—; prin. investigator NASA, 1974—, NSF, 1970, 79, 83, 86-93; exch. scientist USSR Nat. Acad. Sci., 1973, mem. com. div. for planetary scis., 1985-88; mem. com. on planetary and lunar exploration NRC, 2003—. Contbr. articles to profl. jours.; assoc. editor Icarus, 1980-2003; receiving editor New Astronomy, 2004-. Fellow AAAS, Japan Soc. for Promotion of Sci., Am. Geophys. Union; mem. Am. Astron. Soc. (Gerard P. Kuiper prize 2005), Internat. Astron. Union, Am. Hereford Assn., Nat. Cattlemen's Beef Assn., Sigma Xi. Democrat. Episcopalian. Home: 2618 E Devon St Tucson AZ 85716-5506 Office: U Ariz Lunar & Planetary Lab Tucson AZ 85721-0092

HUBBELL, FLOYD ALLAN, internist, educator; b. Waco, Tex., Nov. 13, 1948; s. F.E. and Margaret (Fraser) H.; m. Nancy Cooper, May 23, 1975; 1 child, Andrew Allan. BA, Baylor U., 1971, MD, 1974; MS in Pub. Health, UCLA, 1983. Diplomate Am. Bd. Internal Medicine. Intern, then resident Long Beach med. program U. Calif., Irvine, 1975-78, asst. prof. medicine, 1981-89, assoc. prof. medicine and social ecology, 1989-97, prof. medicine and social ecology, 1997—, dir. primary care internal medicine residency, 1992-97, chief divsn. gen. internal medicine and primary care, 1992—2002, dir. Ctr. for Health Policy and Rsch., 1993—2003, chair dept. medicine, 2001—08, sr. assoc. dean, academic affairs, 2008—. Contbr. articles to profl. jours. Fellow ACP; mem. APHA, Soc. Gen. Internal Medicine, Physicians for Social Responsibility, Assn. Profs. Medicine. Democrat. Avocations: reading, skiing, water sports. Office: U Calif 264 Irvine Hall 1001 Health Scis Rd Irvine CA 92697-395 E-mail: fahubbel@uci.edu.

HUBBELL, ROBERT B., lawyer; BA in English and Polit. Sci. magna cum laude, Loyola Marymount U., 1978; JD magna cum laude, Loyola Law Sch., 1981. Bar: Calif., Am. Bar. Assoc. Atty. Heller, Ehrman, White, & McAuliffe, LLP, 1991—, Firmwide Managing Shareholder. Pres. Legal Aid Foundation of Los Angeles, 2000—01. Office: Heller Ehrman White & McAuliffe 333 Bush St San Francisco CA 94104 Office Phone: 213-689-7563. Office Fax: 213-614-1868. E-mail: rhubbell@hewm.com.

HUBBS, DONALD HARVEY, foundation executive; b. Kingman, Ariz., Jan. 3, 1918; s. Wayne and Grace Lillian (Hoose) H.; m. Flora Vincent, June 14, 1945; children: Donald Jr., Susan Tyner, Diane Schultz, Wayne, David, Adrienne Busk. BA in Edn., Ariz. State U., 1940; JD, Southwestern U., 1956; LLD (hon.), Pepperdine U., 2005. CPA; bar: Calif. 1956. Acct. Wright and Hubbs, LA, 1945-67; pvt. practice atty. LA, 1956-81; pres., dir. Conrad N. Hilton Found., LA, 1981-98, chmn. bd., CEO, 1998—2005. Bd. dirs. TWA Airline, 1977, Vita Pakt Citrus Products Co.; regent Mt. St. Mary's Coll., 1983-98; bd. councilors U. So. Calif. Law Sch., 1992-99, Donald H. Hubbs Disting. Profs. Chair U. Houston. Hon. chief of the tribes of Kapatinga and Oku, Ghana; spkr. So. Govs. Conf., 1986. 1st lt. (inf.) U.S. Army. Decorated Purple Heart; recipient Anne Sullivan medal Perkins Sch. for the Blind, 1992, Humanitarian award Nat. Coun. Juvenile and Family Ct. Judges, 1994, Humanitarian award Family Violence Prevention Fund, 2000, Spirit of Helen Keller award Helen Keller Internat., 1995; World Vision Hubbs scholarship, 2005. Mem. State Bar of Calif., So. Calif. Assn. for Philanthropy (pres. 1985-86), Riviera Country Club, LA Country Club. Avocations: cattle ranching, hunting, fishing, golf. Home: 1658 San Onofre Dr Pacific Palisades CA 90272-2735

HUBER, ALYSON, state legislator; b. Fremont, Calif., Mar. 1, 1972; m. Tim Huber; 4 children. BS, Cornell U.; JD, Hastings Coll. of Law. Assoc. attorney Bartko Zankel; mem. Dist. 10 Calif. State Assembly, 2008—. Democrat. Office: PO Box 942849 Rm 5175 Sacramento CA 94249-0010 also: 218 W Pine St Lodi CA 95240 Office Phone: 916-319-2010, 209-333-5330. Office Fax: 916-319-2110, 209-333-5333.*

HUBERMAN, BERNARDO A., physicist; b. Buenos Aires, Nov. 7, 1943; arrived in U.S., 1966, naturalized, 1974; s. Leon and Sara Huberman; children: Lara M., Andrew D. PhD in Physics, U. Pa., 1971. Mem. rsch. staff Xerox Palo Rsch. Ctr., Calif., 1974-80, prin. scientist Calif., 1983-84, rsch. fellow Calif., 1985-2001; sr. fellow HP Lab., Palo Alto, 2001—, dir. info. dynamics lab., 2001—. Vis. scientist Inst. Laue-Langevin, Grenoble, France, 1976; cons. prof. Stanford U., Calif., 1981—; vis. prof. U. Paris, 1981, U. Copenhagen, 1993, European Sch. Bus., 1999. Author: The Laws of the Web, 2001; contbr. articles to profl. jours. Trustee Aspen Ctr. Physics, Colo., 1980—. Fellow: AAAS, Japan Soc. Promotion of Sci., Am. Phys. Soc. Office: HP Labs 1500 Page Hill Rd Palo Alto CA 94304 E-mail: huberman@hpl.hp.com.

HUBERT, HELEN BETTY, epidemiologist; b. NYC, Jan. 22, 1950; d. Leo and Ruth (Rosenbaum) H.; m. Carlos Barbaro Arostegui, Sept. 11, 1976 (div. May 1987); 1 child, Joshua Daniel Hubert. BA magna cum laude, Barnard Coll., 1970; MPH, Yale U., 1973, MPhil, 1976, PhD, 1978. Rsch. assoc. Yale U., New Haven, 1977-78; rsch. epidemiologist Nat. Heart, Lung and Blood Inst., Bethesda, Md., 1978-84; rsch. dir. Gen. Health, Inc., Washington, 1984-87; sr. rsch. scientist Stanford (Calif.) U., 1988—. Peer rev. Am. Jour. Epidemiology, Am. Jour. Pub. Health, Chest, Jour. AMA (JAMA), Archives Internal Medicine; contbr. articles to profl. jours., chpts. to books. NIH grantee, 1997—. Mem. Am. Coll. Epidemiology, Soc. Epidemiol. Rsch., Assn. Rheumatology Health Profls., Phi Beta Kappa, Sigma Xi (grant-in-aid for rsch. 1978). Home: 1043 Oakland Ave Menlo Park CA 94025-2205 Home Phone: 650-323-4744. Business E-Mail: hhubert@stanford.edu.

HUCK, LARRY RALPH, manufacturing executive, sales consultant; b. Yakima, Wash., Aug. 10, 1942; s. Frank Joseph and Helen Barbara (Swalley) H.; 1 child, Larry Ralph II. Student, Wash. Tech. Inst., 1965-66, Edmonds Coll., 1966-67, U. Wash., 1967-69, Seattle C.C., 1969-70. Salesman Kirby Co., Seattle, 1964-68, sales mgr., 1968-69; salesman Sanico Chem. Co., Seattle, 1968-69, Synkoloid Co., Seattle, 1970-71; tech. sales rep. Vis. Queen divsn. Ethyl Corp., Seattle, 1971-75; western sales mgr. B & K Films, Inc., Belmont, Calif., 1975-77; pres. N.W. Mfrs. Assocs., Inc., Bellevue, Wash., 1977-86, pres. combined sales group, 1984, 86-96; nat. sales mgr. Gazelle Inc., Tomah, Wis., 1979-81; dir. sales J.M.J. Mktg. E.Z. Frame divsn., 1984-85; nat. accounts mgr. Upnorth Plastics, St. Paul, 1984-87; gen. mgr. Otool Co., 1996-98; N.W. sales mgr. Roberts Consol. divsn. Q.E.P. Inc., 1998-2000; dist. sales mgr. State Indsl. Products, Cleve., 2000—. V.p. Bellevue Nat. Little League; basketball cord. Cath. Youth Orgn., Sacred Heart Ch.; head baseball coach Pierce Coll., Tacoma. With USMC, 1959-66. Mem. Nat. Coun. Salesmen's Orgns., Mfrs. Agts. Nat. Assn., Am. Hardware Mfrs. Assn., N.W. Mfrs. Assn. (pres.), Hardware Affiliated Reps., Inc., Door and Hardware Inst., Internat. Conf. Bldg. Ofcls., Am. Baseball Coaches Assn., Marine Corps. Assn., 1st Marine Divsn. Assn., 3d Marine Divsn. Assn. (life, v.p.). Roman Catholic. Office: 21212 Island Pkwy E Lake Tapps WA 98391 Personal E-mail: lrhuck1@comcast.net.

HUCKESTEIN, DIETER H., hotel company executive; Mgmt. Hilton Internat., Americana Hotels, Intercontinental Hotels; exec. v.p., pres. hotel ops. Hilton Hotels Corp., Beverly Hills, Calif., 1999—. Mem. USA Nat. Tourism Orgn. (bd. dirs.), Am. Hotel & Motel Assn. Ednl. Inst. (bd. dirs.), Travel Bus. Roundtable, World Tourism Orgn. Office: Hilton Hotels Corp 9336 Civic Center Dr Beverly Hills CA 90210-3604

HUDAK, EVIE, state legislator; m. Edward Hudak. Mem. Dist. 19 Colo. State Senate, 2008—. House dist. chmn. & precinct com. mem. Colo. Dem. Party. Mem. Colo. Sch. Fin. Project, Colo. State Accountability Network, Early Childhood State Sys. Team, Metro-North Chamber's Devel. Breakfasts, RTD Gold Line Issue-Focused Team, Jefferson County Pub. Sch. Coordinated Sch. Health Adv. Team, Colo. Edn. Network Steering Com. Mem.: Nat. Assn. of State Bd. Edn. (govt. affairs com.), League of Women Voters, Bus. & Profl. Women, Colo. PTA (dir. leadership & pub. policy, regional dir.), Jefferson County PTA (coun. bd. mem.), Colo. Civic Canopy. Democrat. Office: State House 200 E Colfax Denver CO 80203 Office Phone: 303-866-4840. Business E-Mail: senatorhudak@gmail.com.*

HUDDLE, FRANKLIN PIERCE, JR., diplomat; b. Providence, May 9, 1943; s. Franklin Pierce and Clare (Scott) H.; m. Chanya Sawangrot, May 13, 1988; 1 child, Pavarage. BA, Brown U., 1965; postgrad., Columbia U., 1965-66; MA, Harvard U., 1970, PhD, 1978. Coord. Arabic affairs Peace Corps, Bisbee, 1968-69; instr. Harvard U., Cambridge, Mass., 1970-74; with Dept. of State, Washington and abroad, 1975—2003, charge d'affaires Rangoon, Burma, 1990-94; dir. Pacific Island Affairs, 1994-96; consul gen. Bombay, 1996-99, Toronto, 1999—2001; amb. to Tajikistan, 2001—03. Author: Libyan Arabic, 1966; author, editor: Let's Go Europe, 1972; co-author: Nationalities of the USSR, 1975; photography shows in Thailand, Nepal and Washington, 1980, 81, 84; patentee rocket coatings, 1960. Recipient Rivkin award, Presdl. Meritorious award, Sec. of State Lifetime Achievement award; Ford Found. grantee; Wayland scholar. Mem. Phi Beta Kappa. Avocations: piano, chess, ice skating. E-mail: fphuddle@hotmail.com.

HUDNER, PHILIP, lawyer, rancher; b. San Jose, Calif., Feb. 24, 1931; s. Paul Joseph and Mary E. (Dooling) H.; m. Carla Raven, Aug. 6, 1966; children: Paul Theodor, Mary Carla. BA with great distinction, Stanford U., 1952, LL.B., 1955. Bar: Calif. 1955. Lawyer Pillsbury, Madison & Sutro, San Francisco, 1958—, ptnr., 1970-99, Botto Law Group, San Francisco, 1999—; rancher San Benito County, Calif., 1970—. Asst. editor: Stanford Law Rev., 1954-55; author articles on estate and trust law. Pres. Soc. Calif. Pioneers, 1976-78, Louise M. Davies Found., 2002—, Charles D. and Frances K. Field Fund, 2003—; sec.-treas. Drum Found., 2003—. Served with U.S. Army, 1956-58. Fellow Am. Bar Found.; mem. Internat. Acad. Estate and Trust Law (steering com. 1974-75, exec. coun. 1980-85), San Benito County Saddle Horse Assn., Order of Malta, Phi Beta Kappa, Pacific Union Club, Lagunitas Country Club, Frontier Boys, Bohemian Club, Rancheros Visitadores. Democrat. Roman Catholic. Office: Botto Law Group 180 Montgomery St Fl 16 San Francisco CA 94104-3104

HUDSON, ELIOT R., lawyer; b. Oakland, Calif., Apr. 22, 1950; s. Harter Glen and Alice Eliot Hudson; m. Susan K., Apr. 15, 1978 (div. 1998); 1 child, Christopher. BA in Econs., Polit. Sci., U. Calif., Davis, 1982; JD, U. Calif., San Francisco, 1985. Assoc. Dullicy, Casey, Schaeferh & Ceccotti, San Rafael, Calif., 1975-96, Kincaid, Gianunzio, Caudle & Hubert, Calif., 1977-82; ptnr. McNamara, Houston, Dodge, McClura & Ney, Walnut Creek, 1996-97; atty. sr. litig. coun. law divsn. Aon Corp., San Francisco, 1997—2004; ptnr. DLA Piper Rudrick Grey Cory LLP, 2004—. Asst. cubmaster, cubmaster, asst. scoutmaster, cub com. chmn., troop com. chmn. Boy Scouts Am. Mt. Diablo Silverado Coun., 1987—; dir. Buckelew Ho., San Anselmo, Calif., 1975-77. Republican. Presbyterian. E-mail: eliot.hudson@piperrudnick.com.

HUDSON, JERRY E., foundation administrator; b. Chattanooga, Mar. 3, 1938; s. Clarence E. and Laura (Campbell) H.; m. Myra Ann Jared, June 11, 1957; children: Judith, Laura, Janet, Angela. BA, David Lipscomb Coll., 1959; MA, Tulane U., 1961, PhD, 1965; LL.D. (hon.), Pepperdine U., 1983; D of Comm. (hon.), Tokyo Internat. U., 1997; LHD (hon.), U. Portland, 1997, Willamette U., 1997. Systems engr. IBM, Atlanta, 1961; prof. Coll. Arts and Scis., Pepperdine U., 1962-75; provost, dean Coll. Arts and Scis., Malibu Campus, Pepperdine U., 1971-75; pres. Hamline U., St. Paul, 1975-80, Willamette U., Salem, Oreg., 1980-97; exec. v.p. Collins Found., Portland, Oreg., 1997—2007. Dir. Portland Gen. Co., E.I.I.A., trustee Collins Foundation, 2007- Bd. dirs. PGE Found. Mem. Nat. Assn. Ind. Colls. (bd. dirs.), Phi Alpha Theta. Office: Collins Found 1618 SW 1st Ave Portland OR 97201-5752 Home: 2020 SW Market Street Dr Apt 402 Portland OR 97201-7719 Home Phone: 503-203-1132; Office Phone: 503-227-7171.

HUDSON, JOHN IRVIN, retired career officer; b. Louisville, Oct. 12, 1932; s. Irvin Hudson and Elizabeth (Reid) Hudson Hornbeck; m. Zetta Ann Yates, June 27, 1954; children: Reid Irvin, Lori Ann, John Yates, Clark Ray BS in Bus. Mgmt., Murray State U., 1971. Commd. 2nd lt. USMC, 1954, advanced through grades to lt. gen., 1987; comdg. officer Marine Fighter Attack Squadron 122, 1965—66; commdg. officer Marine Fighter/Attack Squadron 122, 1966—67; comdg. officer Marine Fighter Attack Squadron 115, Vietnam, 1968, Marine Corps Air Sta., Yuma, Ariz., 1977-80; asst. wing comdr. 2nd Marine Air Wing, Cherry Point, NC, 1980-81; comdg. gen. Landing Force Tng. Command/At.4th Marine Amphibious Brigade, Norfolk, Va., 1981-83, 3rd Marine Aircraft Wing, El Toro, Calif., 1985-87, First Marine Amphibious Force, Campen, Calif., 1986-87; dep. chief staff for manpower Hdqrs. USMC, Washington, 1987-89; dir. U.S. Marine Corps Edn. Ctr., Quantico, Va., 1983-85; ret. active duty Hdqrs. USMC, Washington, 1989. Apptd. to Ariz. State Transp. Bd., 1994-2000, chmn., 1999; apptd. commr. Ariz. Power Authority, 2000—, chmn., 2006-07; apptd. bd. dirs. Greater Yuma Port Authority, chmn., 2000-02; operating bd. dirs. Yuma Regional Med. Ctr., 2001—; chmn. 2008—09. Decorated DFC, DSM, Bronze Star, Air medals, Silver Hawk; flew 308 combat missions in Vietnam in F-4 Phantom; inductee Early and Pioneer Naval Aviators' Assn., 1998. Mem. VFW (life), Golden Eagles, Marine Corps Aviation Assn. (life), Marine Corps Assn. (life), Marine Corps Hist. Soc. (life), Order of Daedalians (life). Avocations: sports, sailing, hunting, fishing. Home: 12439 E Del Rico Yuma AZ 85367-7366

HUDSON, LEONARD DEAN, physician; b. Everett, Wash., May 7, 1938; s. Marshall W. and Blanche V. (Morgan) H.; children: Sean Marshall, Margaret Kahle, Sherry Elizabeth, Kevin Arthur. BS, Wash. State U., Pullman, 1960; MD, U. Wash., Seattle, 1964. Diplomate: Am. Bd. Internal Medicine (pulmonary disease). Intern Bellevue Hosp. Ctr., NYC, 1964-65; resident in internal medicine N.Y. Hosp., 1965-66, U. Wash. Hosps., 1968-69; chief resident Harborview Med. Ctr., Seattle; also instr. U. Wash. Med. Sch., 1967-70; Am. Thoracic Soc. fellow in pulmonary diseases U. Colo. Med. Ctr., 1970-71, instr., then asst. prof. medicine, 1971-73; mem. faculty U. Wash. Med. Ctr., 1973—, assoc. prof. medicine, 1976-82, prof., 1982—, head pulmonary critical care medicine divsn., 1985—2003; endowed chair in pulmonary disease rsch. U. Wash. Hosps., 1999—; chief pulmonary critical care medicine divsn., med. dir. MICU, Harborview Med. Ctr., 1976-86. Chmn. Tb adv. com. Wash. Dept. Social and Health Svcs. Author papers, revs. in field. With USPHS, 1966-68. Named Outstanding Resident, Harborview Med. Ctr. Fellow ACP, Am. Coll. Chest Physicians (state gov. 1980-87); mem. Am. Fedn. Clin. Rsch., Am. Thoracic Soc. (sec.-treas. 1983-84, v.p. 1993-94, pres.-elect 1994-95, pres. 1995-96), Western Soc. Clin. Rsch., Assn. Am.

Physicians, Wash. Lung. Assn. (dir., Vol. Hall of Fame 1977), Wash. Thoracic Soc., Seattle Flounders Soc., Phi Beta Kappa. Democrat. Office: Harborview Med Ctr Mailbox 359762 325 9th Ave Seattle WA 98104-2420

HUDSON, ORLANDO THILL, professional baseball player; b. Darlington, SC, Dec. 12, 1977; Grad., Spartanburg Meth. Jr. Coll., SC. Draft pick Toronto Blue Jays, 1997, second baseman, 2002—05, Ariz. Diamondbacks, 2005—08, LA Dodgers, 2009—. Recipient Gold Glove award, 2005—07; named to Nat. League All-Star Team, 2007. Office: LA Dodgers Dodger Stadium 1000 Elysian Pk Ave Los Angeles CA 90012*

HUDSON, PATRICK A., plastic surgeon; b. Blickling, Eng., July 4, 1948; came to U.S., 1974; MD, London U., 1972. Diplomate Am. Bd. Plastic Surgery. Intern St. Stephens-Hillingdon, London, 1972-73; resident Danbury Hosp., 1973-74, U. N.Mex. Hosp., Albuquerque, 1974-78, fellow in hand surgery, 1978; with Presbyn. Hosp., St. Joseph Hosp., Albuquerque; pvt. practice. Preceptor U. N.Mex. Author: Esthetics: Comprehensive Online Information About Cosmetic Plastic Surgery, 1996. Fellow ACS; mem. BMA, NMMS, Am. Assn. Hand Surgery, Am. Soc. Plastic and Reconstructive Surgeons. Office: 1101 Med Arts Ave Bldg 3 Ste 300 Albuquerque NM 87102 Fax: 505-242-0060. E-mail: doctor@phudson.com.

HUDSON, WILLIAM L., lawyer, electronics executive; Ptnr. Brobeck, Phleger & Harrison, LLP, 1984—97, Gibson Dunn & Crutcher, LLP, 1997—99; sr. v.p., gen. counsel, corp. sec. Seagate Tech., Scotts Valley, Calif., 2000—02, exec. v.p., gen. counsel, corp. sec., 2002—. Office: Seagate Tech 920 Disc Dr Scotts Valley CA 95066

HUERTA, DOLORES CLARA (DOLORES FERNÁNDEZ), labor union administrator; b. Dawson, N. Mex., Apr. 10, 1930; d. Juan and Alicia Fernández; m. Richard Chavez; 11 children D. in Edn., U. of Pacific's Delta Community Coll.; PhD (hon.), New Coll. San Francisco, 1990, San Francisco State U., 1993, SUNY at New Paltz, 1999, Calif. State U., Northridge, 2003, SUNY Sch. Law, 2004, Wayne State U., 2004. Tchr. Stockton Pub. Schs., 1950; co-founder, staff mem. Cmty. Svc. Orgn., Stockton, Calif., 1955—60, Agrl. Workers Assn., Delano, Calif., 1960—62, Nat. Farm Workers Assn., 1962—66; co-founder, v.p. United Farm Workers Union (UFW), Keene, Calif., 1966—99, v.p. emeritus, 1999—; sec.-treas. emeritus United Farm Workers Union, AFL-CIO (UFW). Co-founder, first v.p., bd. mem. Fund for the Feminist Majority; bd. dirs. People for the Am. Way; spkr. at colleges and organizations throughout the country in support of "La Causa"; tchr. cmty. organizing, U. So. Calif. Co-founder with Cesar Chavez Robert Kennedy Med. Plan, Juan De La Cruz Farm Workers Pension Fund, Farm Workers Credit Union, the first med. and pension plans and credit union in history of farm workers; formed with Cesar Chavez Nat. Farm Workers Svc. Ctr.; pres. Dolores Huerta Found. Recipient Outstanding Labor Leader award, Calif. State Senate, 1984, Martin Luther King award NAACP, Roger Baldwin Medal of Liberty award ACLU, 1993, Labor award Eugene V. Debs Found. Outstanding Am. award, 1993, Trumpeters award Consumers Union, Women First award YWCA, 1993, Ellis Island Medal of Freedom award, 1993, Eleanor Roosevelt award, 1999, Nation/Puffin award for Creative Citizenship, 2002; inductee Nat. Women's Hall of Fame, 1993; named one of three Women of the Year, Ms. Mag., 1998, 100 Most Important Women 20th Century, Ladies Home Journal; short-term appointment as regent, U. Calif., 2003. Office: PO Box 9189 Bakersfield CA 93389-9189

HUESO, BEN, councilman; m. Laura Hueso; 4 children. BA, UCLA. Councilman, Dist. 8 San Diego City Coun., 2006—, coun. pres., chair Rules, Open Govt. and Intergovernmental Rels. Com. Founder Comml. Dist. Revitalization Corp.; mem. Calif. Coastal Commn., 2007—. Mem. Otay Valley Regional Park Policy Com.; former mem. Police Chief's Adv. Com.; bd. mem. Sherman Heights Cmty. Ctr. Mem.: Inner City Bus. Assn. Office: 663 E San Ysidro Blvd San Diego CA 92173 also: 202 C St, 10th Fl San Diego CA 92101 Office Phone: 619-236-6688. Office Fax: 619-231-7918. E-mail: benhueso@sandiego.gov.*

HUESTON, JOHN CHARLES, lawyer; b. Queens, NY, 1964; m. Mabelle Drake; children: Tara, Ryan, Kinsale, Shea. BA magna cum laude, Dartmouth Coll., 1986; JD, Yale Law Sch., 1991. Law clk. to Hon. Frank M. Johnson US Ct. Appeals (11th cir.), Montgomery, Ala., 1991—92; pvt. practice O'Melveny & Myers, LLP, 1992—2004; asst. US atty. (ctrl. dist. Calif.) US Dept. Justice, LA, 2004—06, chief Orange County divsn.; ptnr. Irell & Manella, LLP, 2006—. Atty. Enron Task Force, 2004—; adj. prof. Chapman U. Sch. Law. Notes editor: Yale Law Jour. Named a Calif. Atty. of Yr., Calif. Lawyer mag., 2007; named one of Top 20 Under 40, LA Daily Jour., Calif.'s Top 100 Leading Lawyers, Daily Jour., 25 People Who Shaped the Face of Bus. in 2006, Fortune mag., Fab 50 Young Litigators, Am. Lawyer, 2007. Office: Irell & Manella LLP 840 Newport Ctr Dr Ste 400 Newport Beach CA 92660-6324 Office Phone: 949-760-5152. E-mail: john.hueston@usdoj.com, jhueston@irell.com.

HUFF, C(LARENCE) RONALD, sociologist, criminologist, educator; b. Covington, Ky., Nov. 10, 1945; s. Nathaniel Warren G. and Irene Opal (Mills) H.; m. Patricia Ann Plankenhorn, June 15, 1968; children: Tamara Lynn, Tiffany Dawn. BA, Capital U., 1968; MSW, U. Mich., 1970; PhD, Ohio State U., 1974. Social worker Franklin County Children's Svcs., Columbus, Ohio, 1968; social work intern Pontiac (Mich.) State Hosp. and Family Svc. Met. Detroit, 1969-70; dir. psychiat. social work Lima (Ohio) State Hosp., 1970-71; chief psychiat. social worker N.W. Cmty. Mental Health Ctr., Lima, 1971-72; grad. tchg. assoc. sociology Ohio State U., 1972-74; asst. prof. social ecology U. Calif., Irvine, 1974-76; asst. prof. sociology Purdue U., 1976-79; assoc. prof. pub. policy/mgmt. Ohio State U., Columbus, 1979-87, dir. Criminal Justice Rsch. Ctr., 1979-99, prof., 1987-99, prof. emeritus, 1999—, dir. John Glenn Sch. Pub. Affairs, 1994-99; dean Sch. Social Ecology U. Calif., Irvine, 1999—, prof. criminology, law and society, 1999—, prof. sociology, 2004—. Vis. prof. U. Hawaii, 1995; cons. Bur. Justice Stats., Nat. Inst. Justice, Nat. Inst. Corrections, Nat. Inst. Juvenile Justice and Delinquency Prevention, Loyola Law Sch., Nat. Youth Gang Ctr., U.S. Senate Jud. Com., NSF, FBI, ABA, Guggenheim Found., W.T. Grant Found., others; expert witness fed. and state cts. Author: Wrongful Conviction: International Perspectives on Miscarriages of Justice, 2008, Youth Violence: Prevention, Intervention, and Social Policy, 1999, Convicted But Innocent: Wrongful Conviction and Public Policy, 1996, (Outstanding Acad. Book award Am. Libr. Assn., 1996), The Gang Intervention Handbook, 1993, Gangs in America, 1990, 2d edit., 1996, 3rd edit., 2002, House Arrest and Correctional Policy: Doing Time at Home, 1988, The Mad, The Bad, and The Different: Essays in Honor of Simon Dinitz, 1981, Attorneys as Activists: Evaluating the American Bar Association's BASICS Program, 1979, Contemporary Corrections: Social Control and Conflict, 1977, Planning Correctional Reform, 1975, and others; mem. editl. bd. various jours.; contbr. articles to profl. jours., chpts. to books. Recipient Nat. Security award Mershon Found., 1980, prize New Eng. Sch. Law, 1981, Outstanding Tchg. award, 1985, Donald R. Cressey award Nat. Coun. on Crime and Delinquency, 1992, Paul Tappan award Western Soc. Criminology, 1993, Herbert Bloch award Am. Soc. Criminology, 1994; grantee ABA, 1974-77, Purdue U., 1978, U.S. Dept. Justice, 1978-79, 85-88, 91-95, Ohio Dept. Mental Health, 1982-83, 84-85, 85-87, Gov.'s Office Criminal Justice, 1985-88, 92-95, 98, Ohio Dept. Youth Svcs., 1989-90, Ohio State U./Ohio Bd. Regents, 1990-92. Fellow Western Soc. Criminology, Am. Soc. Criminology (exec. bd., pres.-elect 1999-2000, pres. 2000-01, Herbert Bloch award 1994); mem. Acad. Criminal Justice Scis., Nat. Coun. on Crime and Delinquency, Phi Kappa Phi, Phi Beta Delta. Office: U Calif Irvine Sch Social Ecology 300 Social Ecology I Irvine CA 92697-7050 Office Phone: 949-824-6094. Business E-Mail: rhuff@uci.edu.

HUFF, GARY D., lawyer; b. Seattle, May 9, 1950; BA cum laude, U. Wash., 1972, JD, 1975. Bar: Wash. 1975. Lawyer Karr Tuttle Campbell, Seattle, 1986—. Mem. ABA, Wash. State Bar Assn., Seattle-King County Bar Assn., Phi Beta Kappa. Office: Karr Tuttle & Campbell 1201 3rd Ave Ste 2900 Seattle WA 98101-3028

HUFF, MARILYN L., federal judge; b. 1951; BA, Calvin Coll., Grand Rapids, Mich., 1972; JD, U. Mich., 1976. Assoc. Gray, Cary, Ames & Frye, 1976-83, ptnr., 1983-91; judge U.S. Dist. Ct. (so. dist.) Calif., San Diego, 1991-98, chief judge, 1998—. Contbr. articles to profl. jours. Mem. adv. coun. Calif. LWV, 1987—, Am. Lung Assn.; bd. dirs. San Diego and Imperial Counties, 1989—; mem. LaJolla Presbyn. Ch. Named Legal Profl. of Yr. San Diego City Club and Jr. C. of C., 1990; recipient Superior Ct. Valuable Svc. award, 1982. Mem. ABA, San Diego Bar Found., San Diego Bar Assn. (bd. dirs. 1986-88, v.p. 1988, chmn. profl. edn. com. 1990, Svc. award to legal profession, 1989, Lawyer of Yr. 1990), Calif. State Bar Assn., Calif. Women Lawyers, Am. Bd. Trial Advs., Libel Def. Resource Ctr., Am. Inns of Ct. (master 1987—, exec. com. 1989—), Lawyers' Club San Diego (adv. bd. 1989-90, Belva Lockwood Svc. award 1987), Univ. Club, Aardvarks Lt. Office: US Dist Ct Courtroom 1 940 Front St San Diego CA 92101-8994

HUFFINGTON, ARIANNA, columnist, writer, editor; b. Athens, Greece, July 15, 1950; arrived in US, 1980; d. Constantine Stassinopoulos and Helen Georgiadis; m. Michael Huffington, Apr. 12, 1986 (div. 1997); children: Christina, Isabella. MA in Econ., Cambridge U., Eng., 1971. Syndicated columnist Tribune Media Svcs., 1995—; founder, editor-in-chief Huffington Post, 2005—. Author: The Female Woman, 1974, After Reason, 1978, Maria Callas: The Woman Behind the Legend, 1981, Picasso: Creator and Destroyer, 1988, The Gods of Greece, 1993, The Fourth Instinct, 1994, Greetings From the Lincoln Bedroom, 1998, How to Overthrow the Government, 2000, Pigs at the Trough: How Corporate Greed and Political Corruption are Undermining America, 2003, Fanatics and Fools: The Game Plan for Winning Back America, 2004, On Becoming Fearless:...in Love, Work, and Life, 2006, Right Is Wrong: How the Lunatic Fringe Hijacked America, Shredded the Constitution, and Made Us All Less Safe, 2008; guest appearances on Larry King Live, Oprah, Nightline, Inside Politics, Charlie Rose, Crossfire, Hardball, Good Morning America, Today Show, McLaughlin Group, and the O'Reilly Factor, co-host (nationally syndicated pub. radio prog.) Left, Right & Center. Bd. dirs. A Place Called Home, LA; bd. trustees Archer Sch. for Girls. Recipient Webby award, Internat. Acad. Digital Arts & Scis., 2006, Rave Renegade award, WIRED Mag., 2007; named one of The 100 Most Influential People in the World, TIME mag., 2006, 50 Who Matter Now, Business 2.0, 2007, The 50 Most Powerful Women in NYC, NY Post, 2007. Office: Arianna Online 1158 26th St PO Box 428 Santa Monica CA 90403 Business E-Mail: arianna@huffingtonpost.com.*

HUFFMAN, EDGAR JOSEPH, oil industry executive; b. Hartford City, Ind., Aug. 24, 1939; s. Floyd Edgar and Elizabeth Jean Huffman; m. Margaret Mary Brenet, May 3, 1980; children: Donovan L. Walker, Maryanne Ramiriz. BBA, Ind. Cen. U., 1961; MA, NYU, 1968. V.p. corp. profitability Valley Nat. Bank, Phoenix, 1978—82, v.p. corp. planning, 1982—85; v.p., chief exec. officer Visa Industries Ariz., Phoenix, 1985—95. Chmn. bd. dirs. Montessori Day Schs., Inc., Phoenix, 1981. Home: 1710 E Cinnabar Ave Phoenix AZ 85020-1915 E-mail: ehuffman@mdpsc.org.

HUFFMAN, JAMES LLOYD, dean, law educator; b. Ft. Benton, Mont., Mar. 25, 1945; s. Roy E. and Menga (Herzog) H.; m. Leslie M. Spencer, Sept. 11, 1956; children: Kurt Andrew, Erica Leigh, James Spencer, Claire Menga, Margaret Murray. Student, Stanford U., 1963-64; BS, Mont. State U., 1967; MA, Fletcher Sch. Law and Diplomacy, Tufts U., 1967-68; JD, U. Chgo., 1972. Bar: Mont., U.S. Ct. Appeals (Fed. cir.), U.S. Supreme Ct. Asst. prof., then assoc. prof. Lewis and Clark Law Sch., Portland, Oreg., 1973-78, prof. law, 1978—, assoc. dean, 1978-80, dir. natural resources law inst., 1976—93, dean, 1994—2006, Erskine Wood Sr. prof. law, 2001—. Vis. prof. Auckland U. (N.Z.), 1980-81, U. Oreg. Law Sch., 1988, U. Athens, 1988-89; mem. com. socioecon. effects of earthquake prediction Nat. Acad. Scis., 1977-80; adv. coun. Nat. Environ. Justice, 2003-05; chair Federalist Soc. Environ. Law Property Rights Practice Group, 2003-05. Author: The Allocation of Water to Instream Flows: A Comparative Study of Policy Making and Technical Information in the States of Colorado, Idaho, Montana and Washington, 1980, Government Liability and Disaster Mitigation: A Comparative Study, 1986; contbr. articles to profl. jours. Bd. mem. Bishop Street Funds. NSF grantee, 1976-77, 81-84; Office of Water Rsch. Dept. Interior grantee, 1978-80; Raymond fellow, 1973. Mem. Am. Soc. Legal History, Rocky Mountain Mineral Law Found. Home: 5340 SW Hewett Blvd Portland OR 97221-2254 Office: Lewis & Clark Sch Law Portland OR 97219 Office Phone: 503-768-6601. Business E-Mail: huffman@lclark.edu.

HUFFMAN, JAMES THOMAS WILLIAM, oil industry executive; b. Norman, Okla., Mar. 27, 1947; s. Thomas William and Dorlese M. (Hicks) H.; children: Laura Anne, Christopher James. BBA, Baylor U., 1970. CPA. Mgr. Arthur Andersen & Co., Houston, 1970-76; sr. mgr. Price, Waterhouse & Co., Denver, 1976-79; v.p. Credo Petroleum Corp., 1978-80, pres., 1980-81, chmn., chief exec. officer, 1981—, also dir. Dir. Huffman Heat Exchangers Inc.; dir. XF&R, Inc.; pres., dir. SECO Energy Corp.; pres., dir. United Oil Corp. Mem. AICPA, Tex., Colo. socs. CPAs, Petroleum Landman, Ind. Petroleum Assn. Am., Ind. Petroleum Assn. Mountain State, Petroleum Accts. Soc.

HUFSTEDLER, SETH MARTIN, lawyer; b. Dewar, Okla., Sept. 20, 1922; s. Seth Martin and Myrtle (Younts) H.; m. Shirley Ann Mount, Aug. 16, 1949; 1 child, Steven. BA magna cum laude, U. So. Calif., 1944; LL.B., Stanford U., 1949. Bar: Calif. 1950. Pvt. practice, LA; assoc. Lillick, Geary & McHose, 1950-51; with Charles E. Beardsley, 1951-53; ptnr. Beardsley, Hufstedler & Kemble, 1953-81, Hufstedler, Miller, Carlson & Beardsley, 1981-88, Hufstedler, Kaus & Ettinger, LA, 1988-94; Hufstedler & Kaus, 1994-95; sr. of counsel Morrison & Foerster LLP, 1995—. Mem. Calif. Jud. Coun., 1977—78. Legis. editor Stanford U. Law Rev., 1948—49. Sec. regional planning coun. United Way, 1971-75; co-chmn. Pub. Commn. County Govt., L.A., 1975-76, 89-92; trustee AEFC Pension Fund, 1978-82; mem. Calif Citizens Commn. on Tort Reform, 1976-77; bd. visitors Stanford Law Sch., chmn., 1972-73. Lt. (j.g.) USNR, 1943-46. Mem. ABA (chmn. action commn. to reduce ct costs and delay 1979-81, mem. coun. sr. bar div. 1986-89, chmn. 1987-88), Los Angeles County Bar Assn. (trustee 1963-65, 66-70, pres. 1969-70, Shattuck Price award 1976), State Bar Calif. (bd. govs. 1971-74, pres. 1973-74, Bernard Witkin medal 2002), Am. Judicature Soc., Am. Law Inst., Am. Coll. Trial Lawyers, Am. Bar Found. (bd. govs. 1975-86, pres. 1982-84), Chancery Club (pres. 1974-75), Order of Coif, Phi Beta Kappa, Phi Kappa Phi, Delta Tau Delta. Democrat. Office: Morrison & Foerster 555 W 5th St Ste 3500 Los Angeles CA 90013-1024 E-mail: sethhufs@mofo.com.

HUFSTEDLER, SHIRLEY MOUNT, lawyer, former United States Secretary of Education; b. Denver, Aug. 24, 1925; d. Earl Stanley and Eva (Von Behren) Mount; m. Seth Martin Hufstedler, Aug. 16, 1949; 1 son, Steven Mark. BBA, U. N.Mex., 1945, LLD (hon.), 1972; LLB, Stanford U., 1949; LLD (hon.), U. Wyo., 1970, Gonzaga U., 1970, Occidental Coll., 1971, Tufts U., 1974, U. So. Calif., 1976, Georgetown U., 1976, U. Pa., 1976, Columbia U., 1977, U. Mich., 1979, Yale U., 1981, Rutgers U., 1981, Claremont U. Ctr., 1981, Smith Coll., 1982, Syracuse U., 1983, Mt. Holyoke Coll., 1985; PHH (hon.), Hood Coll., 1981, Hebrew Union Coll., 1986, Tulane U., 1988. Bar: Calif. 1950. Mem. firm Beardsley, Hufstedler & Kemble, LA, 1951-61; practiced in LA, 1961; judge LA Superior Ct., 1961-66, Calif. Ct. Appeals (2nd dist.), 1966-68, US Ct. Appeals (9th cir.), 1968-79; sec. US Dept. Edn., 1979-81; ptnr. Hufstedler & Kaus, LA, 1981-95; sr. of counsel Morrison & Foerster LLP, LA, 1995—. Emeritus dir. Hewlett Packard Co., US West, Inc., Harman Internat. Industries. Mem. staff Stanford Law Rev, 1947-49; articles and book rev. editor, 1948-49. Trustee Calif. Inst. Tech., Occidental Coll., 1972-89, Aspen Inst., Colonial Williamsburg Found., 1976-93, Constl. Rights Found., 1978-80, Nat. Resources Def. Coun., 1983-85, Carnegie Endowment for Internat. Peace, 1983-94; bd. dirs. John T. and Catherine MacArthur Found., 1983—2002; chair U.S. Commn. on Immigration Reform, 1996-97. Named Woman of Yr. Ladies Home Jour., 1976; recipient UCLA medal, 1981, Lifetime Achievement award, The Am. Lawyer mag, 2007 Fellow Am. Acad. Arts and Scis.; mem. ABA (medal 1995), L.A. Bar Assn., Town Hall, Am. Law Inst. (coun. 1974-84), Am. Bar Found., Women Lawyers Assn. (pres. 1957-58), Am. Judicature Soc., Assn. of the Bar of City of N.Y., Coun. on Fgn. Rels. (emeritus), Order of Coif. Office: Morrison & Foerster LLP 555 W 5th St Ste 3500 Los Angeles CA 90013-1024 Home Phone: 818-790-1637; Office Phone: 213-892-5804. Business E-Mail: shirhufs@mofo.com.

HUG, PROCTER RALPH, JR., federal judge; b. Reno, Mar. 11, 1931; s. Procter Ralph and Margaret (Beverly) H.; m. Barbara Van Meter, Apr. 4, 1954; children: Cheryl Ann English, Procter J., Elyse Marie Pasha. BS, U. Nev., 1953; LLB, JD, Stanford U., 1958. Bar: Nev. 1958. Mem. Springer, McKissick & Hug, 1958—63, Woodburn, Wedge, Blakey, Folsom & Hug, Reno, 1963—77; judge US Ct. Appeals (9th cir.), Reno, 1977—2002, chief judge, 1996—2000, sr. judge, 2002—. Dep. atty. gen. State of Nev., 1971—76; v.p. dir. Nev. Tel. & Telegraph Co., 1958—77. Mem. bd. regents U. Nev., 1962—71, chmn., 1969—71; bd. visitors Stanford Law Sch.; mem. Nev. Humanities Commn., 1988—94; vol. civilian aid sect. U.S. Army, 1977. Lt. USNR, 1953—55. Recipient Outstanding Alumnus award, U. Nev., 1967, Disting. Nevadan citation, 1982; named Alumnus of Yr., U. Nev., 1988. Mem.: ABA (bd. govs. 1976—78), Stanford Law Soc. Nev. (past pres.), U. Nev. Alumni Assn. (past pres.), Nat. Assn. Coll. and Univ. Attys. (past mem. exec. bd.), Nat. Jud. Coll. (bd. dirs. 1977—78, 2001—06, chmn. 2004—06), Am. Judicature Soc. (bd. dirs. 1975—77). Office: US Ct Appeals 9th Cir US Courthouse Fed Bldg 400 S Virginia St Ste 708 Reno NV 89501-2181 Office Phone: 775-686-5949.

HUGHES, GETHIN B., bishop; b. Lampeter, Wales, Oct. 1, 1942; m. Lenore Hughes, 1968; 1 child, Margaret. BA with honors, Exeter U.; MDiv, Seabury-Western Sem., Evanston, Ill. Ordained priest, 1967; assoc. priest LA, 1968—73; vicar Prince of Peace Ch., Woodland Hills, Calif., 1973—75; canon missioner for stewardship & devel. Episcopal Diocese of LA, 1975—80; rector All Saints by-the-Sea, Santa Barbara, Calif., 1980—92; bishop Episcopal Diocese of San Diego, 1992—2005; interim dean St. Mark's Cathedral, Shreveport, La., 2007—. Office: Episcopal Diocese San Diego 2728 6th Ave San Diego CA 92103-6301

HUGHES, GREGORY, information technology executive; BS in Elec. Engring., MIT, MS in Elec. Engring. and Computer Sci.; MBA, Stanford Grad. Sch. Bus. Founder, CEO Granite Microsystems; ptnr. McKinsey & Co., 1993—2003; exec. v.p. global svcs. VERITAS Software Corp., Mountain View, Calif., 2003—. Office: VERITAS Software Corp 350 Ellis St Mountain View CA 94043

HUGHES, (ROBERT) JOHN, journalist, educator; b. Neath, Wales, Apr. 28, 1930; came to U.S., 1954; s. Evan John and Dellis May (Williams) H.; m. Vera Elizabeth Pockman (div. 1987); children: Wendy Elizabeth, Mark Evan; m. Peggy Janeane Jordan, 1988; 1 child, Evan Jordan. LLD (hon.), Colby Coll., 1978; HHD (hon.), So. Utah U., 1994; LHD (hon.), Salt Lake CC, 2007. Africa corr. Christian Sci. Monitor, 1955-61, Far East corr., 1964-70, editor Boston, 1970-79, columnist, 1985—, dir. radio broadcasting, 1987-89; pres. Hughes Newspapers, Orleans, Mass., 1977-85; assoc. dir. USIA, Washington, 1981-82; dir. Voice of Am., Washington, 1982; asst. sec. of state Dept. State, Washington, 1982-85; prof. comm. Brigham Young U., Provo, Utah, 1991—96, 2007—; editor Deseret News, Salt Lake City, 1997—2006. Pres., pub., editor Concord Comm., Rockland, Maine, 1989-91; chmn. Pres. Bush Commn. on U.S. Govt. Internat. Broadcasting, 1991, Presdl./Congressional Commn. Broadcasting to People's Republic China, 1992; asst. sec.-gen. UN, NYC,

1995. Author: The New Face of Africa, 1961, Indonesian Upheaval, 1967. Nieman fellow, Harvard U., 1961-62; recipient Pulitzer prize, 1967, Sigma Delta Chi, 1977. Mem. Am. Soc. Newspaper Editors (past pres.), Coun. Fgn. Rels., Overseas Press Club (Best Reporting from Overseas 1970). Office: Brigham Young Univ Dept Comm Provo UT 84602 Business E-Mail: john_hughes@byu.edu.

HUGHES, JOHN W., film producer, director, screenwriter; b. Lansing, Mich., Feb. 18, 1950; m. Nancy Ludwig; children: John III, James. With Needham Harper & Steers, Chgo.; copywriter, creative dir. Leo Burnett Co.; editor National Lampoon; founder, pres. Hughes Entertainment, 1985—. Screenwriter: National Lampoon's Class Reunion, 1982, National Lampoon's Vacation, 1983, Mr. Mom, 1983, Nate and Hayes, 1983, National Lampoon's European Vacation, 1985, (as Edmond Dantes), 101 Dalmations, 1996, Maid in Manhattan, 2002, Just Visiting, 2001; screenwriter, prodr.: Pretty in Pink, 1986, Some Kind of Wonderful, 1987, The Great Outdoors, 1988, National Lampoon's Christmas Vacation, 1989, Home Alone, 1990, Career Opportunities, 1990, Dutch, 1991, Home Alone 2: Lost in New York, 1992, Dennis the Menace, 1993, Baby's Day Out, 1994, Miracle on 34th Street, 1994, 101 Dalmations, 1996, Flubber, 1997, Home Alone 3, 1997, Reach the Rock, 1998; screenwriter, dir.: Sixteen Candles, 1984, Weird Science, 1985; screenwriter, dir., prodr.: The Breakfast Club, 1985, Ferris Bueller's Day Off, 1986, Planes, Trains and Automobiles, 1987, She's Having a Baby, 1988, Uncle Buck, 1989, Curly Sue, 1991; prodr.: Only the Lonely, 1991, NewPort South, 2001; TV writer: Home Alone 2, 2002, National Lampoon's American Adventure, 2000. Recipient Commitment to Chgo. award, 1990; named NATO/ShoWest Prodr. of Yr., 1990. also: c/o Michael Wimer Creative Artists Agy 9830 Wilshire Blvd Beverly Hills CA 90212-1804

HUGHES, LINDA J., newspaper publisher; b. Princeton, BC, Can., Sept. 27, 1950; d. Edward Rees and Madge Preston (Bryan) H.; m. George Fredrick Ward, Dec. 16, 1978; children: Sean Ward, Kate Ward. BA, Victoria U., Can., 1972; LittD (hon.), Athabasca U., 1997; diploma in journalism (hon.), Grant MacEwan C.C., Edmonton, Alta., Can., 1999; LLD (hon.), U. Alberta, 2003. With Edmonton Jour., Alta., Canada, 1976—, from reporter to asst. mng. editor Alta., 1984-87, editor Alta., 1987-92, pub. Alta., 1992—. Southam fellow U. Toronto, Ont., Can., 1977-78; recipient Disting. Citizen award Grant MacEwan C.C., 1999, Dist. Alumni award U. Victoria, 2000. Office: Edmonton Journal 10006 101st St PO Box 2421 Edmonton AB Canada T5J 2S6 E-mail: lhughes@thejournalcanwest.com.

HUGHES, LOUIS RALPH, information technology executive; b. Cleve., Feb. 10, 1949; s. Louis R. and Anna E. (Holland) H.; m. Candice A. Baranchik, May 20, 1972; children: Brian W., Brittany K. B of Mech. Engring., GM Inst., 1971; MBA, Harvard U., 1973. V.p. fin. GM Can., 1985-86, GM Europe, Switzerland, 1987-89; chmn., mng. dir. Adam. Opel, Germany, 1989-92; pres. GM Europe, 1992-94; exec.v.p. GM Corp., 1992—2000; pres. GM Internat., Switzerland, 1994-98; exec. v.p. new bus. strategies Gen. Motors Corp., Detroit, 1998—2000; pres., COO Lockheed Martin Corp., 2000; chmn. Maxager Technology, San Rafael, Calif., 2001—; chief of staff Afghanistan Reconstruction Group, 2004. Bd. dir. BT Group, ABB, Sulzer; mem. supervisory bd. Deutsche Bank AG, 1993—2000. Avocations: skiing, mountain climbing, antiques. Office: Maxager Technology Bd Directors 2173 E San Francisco Blvd San Rafael CA 94901

HUGHES, MARGARET EILEEN, law educator, retired dean; b. Saskatoon, Sask., Can., Jan. 22, 1943; d. E. Duncan and Eileen (Shaver) Farmer; m. James Roscoe Hughes, May 21, 1966; children: Shannon Margaret, Krista Lynn. BA, U. Sask., 1965, LLB, 1966; LLM, MSW, U. Mich., 1968. Asst. prof. law U. Windsor, Ont., Can., 1968-71, assoc. prof. law Ont., 1971-75; exec. interchange Dept. Justice, Ottawa, 1975-77, counsel, 1977-78; prof. law U. Sask., 1978-84; dean law U. Calgary, Alta., Canada, 1984-89, prof. Alta., 1989—, assoc. v.p. human resources Alta., 2001—05. Faculty sr. univ. adminstrs.'s course Centre Higher Edn., R & D, Banff, Can., 1990—; bd. dirs. Indsl. Rels. Rsch. Group; co-chair Annual Labour Arbitration Conf., 1990-2000. Contbr. articles to profl. jours. and chpts. to books. William Cooke fellow U. Mich. Faculty Law, 1966-68. Mem. Law Soc. Alta., Law Soc. Sask., Legal Edn. Soc. Alta. (bd. dirs. 1984-89), Law Soc. Alta. (legal edn. com. 1984-89), Can. Assn. Law Tchrs., Council Can. Law Deans (sec. 1986-87, chmn. 1987-88), Can. Inst. Resources Law (exec. com. 1984-89, bd. dirs. 1984-89), Can. Research Inst. for Law and Family (exec. com. 1986-88, bd. dirs. 1986-89, 97-2001). Avocations: swimming, skiing. Office: U Calgary Human Resources 2500 University Dr NW Calgary AB Canada T2N 1N4 E-mail: hughesm@ucalgary.com.

HUGHES, TERESA P., state legislator; b. NYC, Oct. 3, 1932; m. Frank E. Staggers; children: Vincent, Deidre. BA, Hunter Coll.; MA, NYU; PhD, Claremont Grad. Sch. Prof. edn. Calif. State U., LA; social worker; mem. Calif. Assembly, 1975-92, Calif. State Senate, Sacramento, 1993—. Bd. trustees L.A. County H.S. for Arts and Edn. Coun. Music Ctr., Calif. Founder Aware Women. Mem. Nat. Coalition 100 Black Women, Calif. State Employees Assn., Calif. Tchrs. Assn., Coalition Labor Union Women. Democrat. Office: Calif Senate 5114 State Capitol Rm 5050 Sacramento CA 95814 also: 1 W Manchester Blvd Ste 600 Inglewood CA 90301-1750

HUHS, JOHN I., lawyer; b. Galveston, Tex., Sept. 18, 1944; s. Roy E. and Martha Mae (Hansen) H.; m. Vivian C. Swindley, 1970 (div. 1978); m. Renee J. Stillings, 2005; 1 child John J. Huhsi II BA, U. Wash., 1966; MBA with honors, JD with honors, Stanford U., 1970. Bar: NY 1971, DC 1981. Internat. cons. Satra Cons. Corp., NYC, 1970—73; sr. staff White House Office Mgmt. & Budget Nat. Security, Internat. Affairs, Washington, 1973—76; ptnr. Pisar & Huhs, NYC, 1976—85; sr. v.p., gen. counsel Tendler, Beretz Assocs., Ltd., NYC, 1985-87; pvt. practice NYC, 1987-88; sr. ptnr., chmn. internat. practice Dewey & LeBoeuf, NYC, 1989—; founder Moscow office LeBoeuf, Lamb, Greene & MacRae LLP; founder Almaty office Dewey the Boeuf; prof. Stanford Law Sch., 2007—. Prin. Ctr. for Excellence in Govt., 1984—99. Contbr. articles on internat. law, bus. and fin. to profl. jours.; comment editor Stanford Law Rev., 1967-69. Mem. bd. visitors Stanford Law Sch., 1996-98, 2004-07. Mem.: ABA (chmn. com. on Soviet and Ea. European law 1982—85, chmn. com. internat. comml. trans. 1985—90, coun. sect. internat. law and practice 1988—92, ABA rep. to Union Internat. Advs. 1991—94), DC Bar Assn., NY State Bar Assn. (chmn. internat. investment devel. com. 1987—91), Assn. of Bar of City of NY (internat. trade com. 1987—89, com. Newly Ind. States of former Soviet Union 1989—2000), 175 E. 74th Corp. (pres.), U. Club NYC, Order of Coif. Office: Dewey & LeBoeuf LLP One Embarcadero Ctr San Francisco CA 94111-3619 Office Fax: 415-951-1180. Business E-Mail: jhuhs@dl.com.

HUIZAR, JOSE, councilman; b. Zacatecas, Mex. m. Richelle Rios; children: Emilia, Isabella. BA, U. Calif. Berkeley; MPA in Urban Planning, Princeton U.; JD, UCLA. Dep. city atty. real estate and environmental divsn. LA City Atty.'s Office; pres., mem. bd. edn. LA United Sch. Dist., 2001—05; councilman, Dist. 14 LA City Coun., 2005—. Trustee Princeton U. Named one of 25 figures in the LA Area that stand out for their potential to shape lives, LA Bus. Jour., 100 most influential Hispanics, Hispanic Bus. Mag. Office: City Hall 200 N Spring St Rm 425 Los Angeles CA 90012 Office Phone: 213-473-7014. Office Fax: 213-847-0680. Business E-Mail: councilmember.huizar@lacity.org.*

HULET, ERVIN KENNETH, retired nuclear chemist; b. Baker, Oreg., May 7, 1926; s. Frank E. and Marjorie (Suiter) H.; m. Betty Jo Gardner, Sept. 10, 1949 (dec. Jan. 1992); children: Carri, Randall Gardner. BS, Stanford U., 1949; PhD, U. Calif., Berkeley, 1953. AEC grad. student U. Calif. Radiation Lab., Berkeley, 1949-53; research chemist nuclear chemistry div. Lawrence Livermore Nat. Lab., Livermore, Calif., 1953-66, group leader, 1966-91, ret., active emeritus, 1991—. Achievements include discovery of divalent oxidation state in actinide elements; co-discovery of symmetric fission in actinides. Served with USNR, 1944-46. Fulbright scholar Norway; Welch Found. lectr., 1990; recipient Am. Chem. Soc. award for Nuc. Chemistry, 1994. Fellow AAAS, Am. Inst. Chemists (chmn. Golden Gate chpt. 1992); mem. Am. Chem. Soc. (chmn. divsn. nuclear chemistry and tech. 1987, award in nuclear chemistry 1994), Am. Phys. Soc. Achievements include co-discovery of Element 106; discovery of bimodel fission. Personal E-mail: ekhulet@comcast.net.

HULL, CORDELL WILLIAM, engineering, construction, and project management executive, investor; b. Dayton, Ohio, Sept. 12, 1933; s. Murel George and Julia (Barto) H.; m. Susan G. Ruder, May 10, 1958; children: Bradford W., Pamela H., Andrew R. B of Engring., U. Dayton, 1956; MS, MIT, 1957; JD, Harvard U., 1962; doctorate (hon.), Dominican U. Registered profl. engr., Mass.; bar: Ohio 1962; lic. contractor Calif. Atty. Taft, Stettinius & Hollister, Cin., 1962-64, C & I Girdler, Cin., 1964-66; gen. counsel, treas., pres. C&I Girdler, Internat., Brussels, 1966-70; v.p. Bechtel Overseas Corp., San Francisco, 1970-73; pres., dir. Am. Express Mcht. Bank, London, 1973-75; v.p., treas. Bechtel Corp. and Bechtel Power, San Francisco, 1975-80; pres. Bechtel Fin. Svcs., San Francisco, 1975-82; v.p., CFO Bechtel Group Inc., 1980-85; pres. Bechtel Power Corp., 1987-89, dir.; chmn. Bechtel Enterprises, 1990-95. Bd. dirs. Fremont Group, Inc., 1980—2006; mng. dir. Infrastruct World LLC; former chmn. audit commn. Gilead Scis., 2001—04; mem. Accenture Energy Adv. Bd.; mgr. HWC LLC; former chmn. adv. com. U.S. Eximbank; former mem. svcs. policy com. Office of U.S. Trade Rep. Former trustee Dominican Coll.; former bd. trustees U. Dayton. Menlo Country Club also: HWC LLC 400 Oyster Point Blvd Ste 540 South San Francisco CA 94080 Home Phone: 650-328-5356.

HULL, JANE DEE, former governor, state legislator; b. Kansas City, Mo., Aug. 8, 1935; d. Justin D. and Mildred (Swenson) Bowersock; m. Terrance Ward Hull, Feb. 12, 1954; children: Jeannette Shipley, Robin Hillebrand, Jeff, Mike. BS in elem. edn., U. Kans., 1957; postgrad. in polit. sci., Ariz. State U., postgrad. in econs., 1972-78; grad., Josephson Sch. of Ethics, 1993. Former state legislator Ariz. Ho. of Reps., Phoenix, 1979—93, spkr. pro tem, 1993, chmn. ethics com., chmn. econ. devel., 1993, mem. legis. coun., 1993, mem. gov.'s internat. trade and tourism adv. bd., 1993, mem. gov.'s strategic partnership for econ. devel., 1993, mem. gov.'s office of employement implementation task force, 1993, spkr. of house, 1989—93, house majority whip, 1987-88; former sec. of state State of Ariz., Phoenix, 1995—97, former gov., 1997—2003; pub. del. to the UN, 2004—05. Author (edited by Michael S. Josephson and Wes Hanson): The Power of Character; author: Character in Soc.: The Challenge of Pub. Svc.; contbr. opinion pieces to periodicals and newspapers. Mem. dean's coun. Ariz. State U., 1989—92; assoc. mem. Heard Mus. Guild; mem. Maricopa Med. Aux., Ariz. State Med. Aux., Valley Citizens League, Charter 100, Ariz. Women's Forum; hon. chmn. Race for the Cure; hon. bd. mem. Teach for Am.; assoc. mem. Cactus Wren Rep. Women; mem. Freedom Found., North Phoenix Rep. Women, 1970; Trunk 'N Tusk Legis. Liaison Ariz. Rep. Party, 1993; mem. Gov.'s Emergency Coun., Ariz. -Mex. Commn., Phoenix Commn. on Internat. Rels.; Ariz. chmn. George W. Bush for Pres., 2000; mem. Adv. Coun. Hist. Preservation; chmn. Western Gov.'s Assn., 2002, Border Gov.'s Assn., 2002; bd. dir. Morrison Inst. for Pub. Policy, Beatitudes D.O.A.R., 1992, Ariz. Town Hall, Ariz. Econs. Coun. Recipient Econ. Devel. award, Ariz. Innovation Network, 1993, Spl. Achievement award, Nat. Notary Assn., 1997, Appreciation award, No. Ariz. U. Sch. of Forestry students, 2000. Mem. Nat. Orgn. of Women Legislators, Am. Legis. Exch. Coun., Nat. Rep. Legislators Assn. (Nat. Legislator of Yr. award 1989), Soroptimists (hon.). Republican. Roman Catholic.

HULL, JOSEPH L., state legislator; b. Ogden, Utah, Dec. 18, 1945; m. Sandra Glanville. BA, Weber State Coll.; MEd, Utah State U. Educator Utah State U.; mem. Utah State Senate, 1992—, asst. minority whip, 1995-96; mem. Utah Ho. of Reps., 1986-92; educator Sanders Jr. High Sch. Mem. various coms. including edn. and human svcs. Democrat. Office: 5250 W 4000 S Hooper UT 84315-9613

HULL, MCALLISTER HOBART, JR., retired university administrator; b. Birmingham, Ala., Sept. 1, 1923; s. McAllister Hobart and Grace (Johnson) H.; m. Mary Muska, Mar. 23, 1946; children: John McAllister, Wendy Ann. BS with highest honors, Yale U., 1948, PhD in Physics, 1951. Tech. asst. Los Alamos (N.Mex.) Lab., 1944-46; from instr. to assoc. prof. physics Yale U., 1951-66; prof. physics, chmn. dept. Oreg. State U., 1966-69, SUNY, Buffalo, 1969-72, dean Grad. Sch., 1972-74, dean. grad. and profl. edn., 1974-77; provost U. N.Mex., 1977-85, counselor to pres., 1985-88, prof. emeritus physics, 1988—. Adviser to supt. schs., Hamden, Conn., 1958-65. Author: Rider of the Pale Horse: A Memoir of Los Alamos and Beyond, 2005, others; author papers, chpts. to books, articles in encys. Bd. dirs. Western N.Y. Reactor Facility, 1970-72; trustee N.E. Radio Obs. Corp., 1971-77; pres. Western Regional Sci. Labs., 1977; chmn. tech. adv. com. N.Mex. Energy Rsch. Inst., 1981-83, mem., 1983-88; co-chmn. Nat. Task Force on Edn1. Tech., 1984-86. Served with AUS, 1943-46. Faculty fellow Yale U., 1964-65. Fellow Am. Phys. Soc.; mem. Am. Assn. Physics Tchrs. (chmn. Oreg. sect. 1967-68). Business E-Mail: machull@unm.edu.

HULLINGHORST, DICKEY LEE, state legislator; b. Maywood, Nebr., July 27, 1943; m. Bob Hullinghorst; 1 child, Lara. BA in Sociology, U. Wyo., 1965. Dem. precinct com. mem. Boulder County-Colo. Dem. Party Exec. Com., 1970—2007; govt. affairs dir. Colo. Open Space Coun., 1979—80; sr. v.p. Herrick S. Roth Assocs., 1980—85; intergovernmental rels. dir. Boulder County, 1985—2007; mem. Dist. 10 Colo. House of Reps., Denver, 2008—. V.p. Colo. Women's Polit. Caucus, 1974—76; chmn. Boulder County Democrats, 1975—79; pres. Colo. Dem. Women's Polit. Action Com., 2000—02. Bd. dirs. Eco-Cycle, 1978—81, Colo. Mined Land Reclamation Bd., 1981—85, Met. Water Roundtable, 1984—86, Boulder County Resource Conservation Adv. Bd., 2002—05, PLAN Boulder County, 2004—07, Boulder & Broomfield County Mental Health Ctr., 2005—; adv. com. Boulder County Parks & Open Space, 1978—82; chmn. Colo. Front Range Project Steering Com., 1981—85; bd. dirs. & treas. Colo. Open Lands, 1984—94. Democrat. Episcopalian. Office: State House 200 E Colfax Denver CO 80203 Office Phone: 303-866-2915. Business E-Mail: dl.hullinghorst.house@state.co.us.*

HULME, PAUL G., chemicals executive; b. Eng. Grad. in Bus. Studies, U. Manchester, Eng. Chartered acct. Various positions in fin., acctg. and info. systems ICI; global ops. dir. polyurethanes Huntsman Corp., Salt Lake City, 1999—2000, v.p. performance chems., 2000—03, divsn. pres. advanced materials, 2003—06, divsn. pres. materials and effects, 2006—. Office: Huntsman Corp 500 Huntsman Way Salt Lake City UT 84108 Office Phone: 801-584-5700.

HUME, FREDERICK RAYMOND, electronics executive; b. LA, Feb. 23, 1943; s. Laurence Frederick and Willetta Fredericka (Balderson) H.; m. Betty Ruth Dudley, Mar. 30, 1963; children: Joy Anne Sprague, Frederick William III. Student, Calif. State U., Long Beach, 1960-61, Biola Coll., 1961-62. Test engr. Autoretics div. Rockwell, Anaheim, Calif., 1964-67, research engr., 1967-72; mgr. new products John Fluke Mfg. Co. Inc., Everett, Wash., 1972-76, div. gen. mgr., 1976-80, v.p., 1980-88; v.p., gen. mgr. Keithley Investments, Cleve., 1988—. Bd. dirs. Artech Corp., Seattle, 1985—. Author: Transactions of IEEE, 1973. Inventor radio frequency power testing equipment, broadband spectral intensity measurement system. Chmn. Wash. High Tech. Coordinating Bd., Seattle, 1983-87; co. chmn. Jr. Achievement, Seattle, 1984. Mem. Higher Edn. Fin. Assn. (bd. dirs. 1987—), Am. Electronics Assn. (bd. dirs. 1982-86), Nat. Acad. Sci. (panel mem. 1986—), Electronics Edn. Found. (bd. dirs. 1985—), Soc. Mfg. Engrs. (sr. mem. 1983—), Precision Measurements Assn. (pres. 1978-79). Avocation: literature. Office Phone: 425-367-6213. Business E-Mail: humef@dataio.com.

HUME, JAMES BORDEN, foundation administrator, director; b. Halifax, NS, Can., Nov. 6, 1950; s. Thomas White and Elizabeth Mae (Spears) Hume; m. Penelope Ann Morris, June 3, 1972; children: Kathryn Ann, David Stuart. BA, U. Calgary, Alta., Can., 1972. Chartered Acct. V.p. TIW Industries Ltd., Ottawa, Ont., Canada, 1978-80; pres. Hume Mgmt. Cons. Ltd., Calgary, 1980-85, Kanesco Holdings Ltd., Calgary, 1985—. Pres. The Kahanoff Found., 1984—; bd. dirs. Can. West Found., Ecotrust Can., Southwestern Resources Group, The Kahanoff Found., Calgary, Paget Resources. Fellow, Inst. Chartered Accts., 2002. Mem.: Can. Inst. Chartered Accts. Office: Kahanoff Found 101 6th Ave SW Ste 105 Calgary AB Canada T2P 5K7 Office Phone: 403-237-7896. Business E-Mail: info@kahanoff.com.

HUMES, JAMES CALHOUN, lawyer, communications consultant, writer, educator; b. Williamsport, Pa., Oct. 31, 1934; s. Samuel Hamilton and Elenor Kathryn (Graham) H.; m. Dianne Stuart, July 25, 1957; children: Mary Stuart Quillen, Rachel Bailey. Student, Hill Sch., Stowe Sch., Eng., Williams Coll., 1953-55; AB, George Washington U., 1959, JD, 1962. Bar: Pa. 1963. Mem. Pa. Ho. of Reps., Harrisburg, 1962-65; exec. dir. Phila. Bar Assn., 1967-69; presdl. asst. policy planning sect. White House, Washington, 1969-70; dir. Office Policy and Plans, U.S. Dept. State, Washington, 1970-72; presdl. asst. White House Staff, Washington; White House cons. to Pres. Ford, Washington, 1976-77; Woodrow Wilson fellow Smithsonian Instn., Washington, 1982-83; adj. prof. Williams Coll., 1986-87; prof. Colo. State U., Pueblo, 1997—2004; vis. fellow U. Denver, U. Colo., Colorado Springs. Mem. U.S. Commn. for UNESCO; adj. prof. U. Pa., 1985-99; editl. advisor Pres. Ford's memoirs A Time To Heal. Author: Sweet Dream, 1966, Instant Eloquence, 1973, Podium Humor, 1975, Roles Speakers Play, 1976, How to Get Invited to the White House, 1977, Winston Churchill: Speaker of the Century, 1980, Talk Your Way to the Top, 1980, Standing Ovation, 1988, Sir Winston Method, 1991, The Benjamin Franklin Factor, 1992, My Fellow Americans, 1992, Citizen Shakespeare, 1993, Wit and Wisdom of Churchill, 1994, Wit and Wisdom of Benjamin Franklin, 1995, Wit and Wisdom of Abraham Lincoln, 1996, Confessions of a White House Ghost Writer, 1997, Nixon's Ten Commandments of Statecraft, 1998, Eisenhower and Churchill: The Partnership that Saved the World, 2001, Speak Like Churchill Stand Like Lincoln, 2002, Which President Killed a Man, 2002, Winston Churchill, 2003, Wit & Wisdom of Ronald Reagan, 2007, Wit and Wisdom of FDR., 2008, Wit and Wisdom of William F Buckley Jr. Decorated Order of Brit. Empire. Fellow Royal Soc. of Art; mem. SAR, St. Nicholas Soc. NY, Soc. Pilgrims, Soc. Cin., Order of Magna Charta, Union League Club, Phila. Cricket Club, Brook Club (NY). Republican. Presbyterian. Home: 4404 Turnberry Cres Pueblo CO 81001-1162

HUMES, WILLIAM D., information technology executive; BA economics, UCLA. Sr. audit mgr. PriceWaterhouseCoopers; sr. dir. Ingram Micro, 1998—2002, corp. v.p., controller, 2002—04, sr. v.p., CFO, 2005—. Office: c/o Ingram Micro 1600 E St Andrew Place Santa Ana CA 92799

HUMETEWA, DIANE J., prosecutor; b. 1964; married. AA, Phoenix Coll.; BA, Ariz. State U., 1987; JD, Sandra Day O'Connor Coll. Law, 1993. Victim-witness advocates US Dept. Justice, 1986, counsel Office of Tribal Justice Washington, spl. asst. to asst. US atty., 1996—98, sr. litig. counsel, tribal liaison Phoenix, 2001—07, US atty. Dist. Ariz., 2007—; counsel US Senate Com. on Indian Affairs, 1993—96. Judge pro-tem Hopi Tribal Appellate Ct., 2002—; ad-hoc mem. US Sentencing Commn., Native Am. Subcommittee; adv. coun. Indian legal programs Sandra Day O'Connor Coll. Law, Ariz. State U. Bd. dirs. Morris K. Udall Found., 2006—. Recipient Dir.'s Award for Superior Performance, Exec. Office of US Atty., 1999. Mem.: Hopi Tribe. Office: US Attys Office 2 Renaissance Sq 40 N Central Ave, Ste 1200 Phoenix AZ 85004 Office Phone: 602-514-7500.

HUMMEL, JOHN, information technology executive; Head, info. sys. Specialty Labs. Inc., Santa Monica, Calif., Brim, Inc., Portland, Oreg., Health Svc. Pharmacy/Option Care, Vancouver, Wash.; dir., sys. integration Sutter Health, Sacramento, 1997—99, chief info. officer, 1999—2002, sr. v.p., info. tech., 2002—. Commnr. Certification Commn. for Healthcare Info. Tech. Office: SVP Info Tech Sutter Health 2200 River Plz Dr Sacramento CA 95833

HUMPHREY, CHARLES EDWARD, JR., lawyer; b. Detroit, Jan. 20, 1943; s. Charles Edward and Betty Jane (Bixby) H.; children: Jennifer Jane Castle, Jordan Susan Trigler. BBA, U. Mich., 1964, JD cum laude, 1968, MBA, 1968. Bar: Mich. 1968, Tex. 1971, Colo. 1982. Assoc. Evans & Luptak, 1968; atty., fin. adviser SEC, Washington, 1969-71; ptnr. Foreman & Dyess, Houston, 1971-81; pres. Ptnrs. Oil Co., Houston, 1981-82; ptnr. Kirkland & Ellis, Denver, 1982-87; pres. Addoms & Humphrey (a bus. devel. co.), 1986-88; of counsel Cohen, Brame & Smith, 1987—88; pres. Vector Video, Inc., 1987-89, Venture Capital Investments, 1989—. Chmn. Advanced Cable Systems, Inc., 1989-99; mng. ptnr. Signature Stes., 1989-98; founder Tournament of Champions of Poker, 1999, chmn., 1999-2001; founder, mng. ptnr. Team Pegasus, 1998-2001; author, webmaster www.gambling-law-us.com, 2003—. Bd. dirs. Houston Civil Liberties Union, 1973-77, treas., 1975-77; pres. Tex. Civil Liberties Union, 1978-79, Ctrl. City Opera House Assn., 1982-84. Mailing: 1755 Swadley St Lakewood CO 80215 Office Phone: 303-238-2037. E-mail: cehjr@umich.edu.

HUMPHREY, MARK A., oil industry executive; b. Ohio, Mar. 1952; BS in Elec. Engring., Case We. Res. U., Cleve., 1974; MBA, Northwestern U., Evanston, Ill., 1976. Analyst to positions of increasing responsibility in Corp. Comptroller's, Chevron Chem. and Chevron USA orgs. Chevron Corp., 1976—90, mgr. fin., Chevron Overseas Petroleum, UK ops., 1990—93, v.p. fin., P&M Coal Mining Co. Colo., 1993—96, mgr. fin. services ctr., gen. mgr. auditing, v.p. fin., Chevron Products Co., gen. mgr. fin., Shared Services, 1996—2004, v.p., comptroller, 2005—. Office: Chevron Corp Hdqs 6001 Bollinger Canyon Rd San Ramon CA 94583

HUMPHREY, PATRICK PAUL, pharmacologist; b. Pietersburg, South Africa, Jan. 28, 1946; s. Gordon William and Judith Suzanne (LeRoux) H.; m. Mary Frances Letford, Sept. 14, 1968; children: Patrick Tobias, Damian Paul, Joel Anthony. B Pharmacy with honors, U. London, 1968, PhD in Pharmacology, 1972. Qualified pharmacist. Lectr. physiology dept. St. Mary's Hosp. Med. Sch., London, 1971-72; rsch. leader dept. pharmacology Allen and Hanbury, Ware, Eng., 1972-80; head dept. pharmacology Glaxo Group Rsch. Ltd., Ware, 1980-83, dir. divsn. pharmacology, 1983-92; dir. Glaxo Inst. Applied Pharmacology, U. Cambridge, England, 1992—2001; hon. prof., 1994—2001; dir. Glaxo Wellcom Headache Rsch. Group, 1999—2001; exec. v.p. rsch. Theravance (formerly Advanced Medicine), South San Francisco, Calif., 2001—. Mem. com. for receptor nomenclature and drug classification Internat. Union Pharmacology, 1990-2002, mem. exec. com., 1998-2002; chmn. receptor nomenclature com. Serotonin Club, 1987-93. Co-editor: Serotonin: Actions, Receptors, Pathophysiology, 1989, Receptor Classification, 1997, The Triptans, 2001; editor Brit. Jour. Pharmacology, 1984-90; team leader drug discovery and devel. Anti-Migraine Drug Sumatriptan (trademarks Imitrex and Imigran), 1972-92. Recipient Mullard award Royal Soc., 1997, OBE award, 1999. Fellow Royal Pharm. Soc.; mem. Am. Gastroenterological Assn., Brit. Pharm. Soc., Soc. Neurosci., Internat. Headache Soc. Roman Catholic. Avocations: fishing, tennis, gardening, ornithology. Office: Theravance Inc 901 Gateway Blvd South San Francisco CA 94080 Office Phone: 650-808-3704. E-mail: phumphrey@theravance.com.

HUMPHREYS, MICHAEL HARRINGTON, internist, researcher; b. NYC, Aug. 27, 1938; s. Albert and G. Blanke; m. Sheila Morrin, Aug. 22, 1964; children: Benjamin Duane, Elizabeth Harrington. MD, Western Res. U., 1965. Diplomate Am. Bd. Internal Medicine, 1972. Prof. medicine U. Calif., San Francisco, 1989—. Chief divsn. nephrology San Francisco Gen. Hosp., 1973—. Contbr. articles to profl. jours., books. Mem. med. adv. bd. Nat. Kidney Found. No. Calif., Foster City, Calif., 1980—98; bd. dirs. San Francisco Gen. Hosp. Found., 2001—01. Lt. comdr. USN, 1971—73. Mem.: APA, Western Assn. Physicians, Am. Soc. Hypertension, Am. Soc. Nephrology, Am. Clin. and Climatological Assn. Office: U Calif San Francisco Gen Hosp Box 1341 San Francisco CA 94143-1341 Home Phone: (510) 654-2835; Office Phone: (415) 502-3834. Office Fax: (415) 282-8182. Business E-Mail: mhumphreys@medsfgh.ucsf.edu.

HUMPHREYS, ROBERT LEE, advertising executive; b. Burbank, Calif., Dec. 30, 1924; s. Robert E. and Nancy Lucille (Gum) H.; m. Marie Dorthea Wilkinson, May 10, 1951; children: Dina Lizette, Gia Monique Thompson. BS in Mktg., UCLA, 1947. Merchandising rep. Life mag., LA, 1947-48; promotion mgr. Fortune mag., NYC, 1948-49; copywriter BBDO, LA, 1950-51; account exec. KNBC-TV, LA, 1951-52; v.p., account group mgr. Foote, Cone & Belding, LA, 1952-62; CEO, chmn. emeritus Western divsn. Grey Advt., Inc., LA, 1962-2000, dir., 1963-92; pres. Humphreys Seminars, LA, 2000—. Dir. William O'Neil Fund, Beverly Hills, Calif. Featured guest on Corp. Viewpoint, PBS, 1978. Founding pres. UCLA Chancellor's Assocs., 1967—; founding chmn. Motorcycle Safety Coun., 1966; founding vice chmn. UCLA Found., 1967—; mem. president's circle Los Angeles County Mus. Art, 1983—; bd. dirs. Advt. Industry Emergency Fund, Banning Park Mus., 1991-96. Mem. Am. Advt. Fedn. (bd. dirs. 1982-92), World Affairs Coun., Hollywood Radio and TV Soc. (bd. dirs. 1976-82), L.A. Advt. Club (bd. dirs. 1974-76), Sierra Club (life), Bel Air Bay Club, Phi Gamma Delta. Home and Office: 528 Palisades Dr Pacific Palisades CA 90272-2844

HUNDLEY, NORRIS CECIL, JR., historian, educator; b. Houston, Oct. 26, 1935; s. Norris Cecil and Helen Marie (Mundine) H.; m. Carol Marie Beckquist, June 8, 1957; children: Wendy Michelle Hundley Harris, Jacqueline Marie Hundley Reid. AA, Mt. San Antonio Coll., 1956; AB, Whittier Coll., 1958; PhD (Univ. fellow), UCLA, 1963. Instr. U. Houston, 1963-64; asst. prof. Am. history UCLA, 1964-69, assoc. prof., 1969-73, prof., 1973-94, prof. emeritus, 1994—, chmn. exec. com. Inst. Am. Cultures, 1976-93, chmn. univ. program on Mex., 1981-94, acting dir. Latin Am. Ctr., 1989-90, dir. Latin Am. Ctr., 1990-94. Exec. com. U. Calif. Consortium on Mex. and the U.S., 1981-86; adv. com. Calif. water atlas project Calif. Office Planning and Research, 1977-79 Author: Dividing the Waters: A Century of Controversy Between the United States and Mexico, 1966, Water and the West: The Colorado River Compact and the Politics of Water in the American West, 1975, 2nd edit., 2009, The Great Thirst: Californians and Water 1770s-1990s, 1992, Las aquas divididas: Un siglo de controversia entre México y Estados Unidos, 2000, The Great Thirst: Californians and Water-A History, 2001; co-author: The Calif. Water Atlas, 1979; co-author: California: History of a Remarkable State, 1982; editor: The American Indian, 1974, The Chicano, 1975, The Asian American, 1976; co-editor: The American West: Frontier and Region, 1969, Golden State Series, 1978-2002; mng. editor Pacific Hist. Rev., 1968-97; mem. editl. bd. Jour. San Diego History, 1970-79, Calif. Hist. Soc., 1980-89; contbr. articles to profl. jours. Bd. dirs. John and LaRee Caughey Found., 1983-2000, Henry J. Bruman Ednl. Found., 1983-2003, Forest History Soc., 1987-93. Recipient award of merit Calif. Hist. Soc., 1979; Am. Philos. Soc. grantee, 1964, 71, Ford Found. grantee, 1968-69, U. Calif. Water Resources Ctr. grantee, 1969-72, 91, 2000, Sourisseau Acad. grantee, 1972, NEH grantee, 1983-89, Hewlett Found. grantee, 1986-89, U. Calif. Regents faculty fellow in humanities, 1975, Guggenheim fellow, 1978-79, Hist. Soc. So. Calif. fellow, 1996—; Whitsett lectr., 2000. Mem. Am. Hist. Assn. (exec. coun. Pacific Coast br. 1968-97, v.p. 1993-94, pres. 1994-95), Western History Assn. (coun. 1985-88, 93-97, pres. 1994-95, Winther award 1973, 79), Orgn. Am. Historians. Office: UCLA Dept History Los Angeles CA 90095-1473

HUNNICUTT, RICK, state legislator; b. Cheyenne, Wyo., Apr. 14, 1948; m. Linda Hunnicutt; 2 children. BS in Zoology, U. Wis., 1971; MS in Spl. Edn. & Vocat. Rehab, U. Tenn., 1975. Mem. Dist. 5 Wyo. State Senate, 2009—. Republican. Office: 213 State Capitol Bldg Cheyenne WY 82002 also: PO Box 2656 Cheyenne WY 82003 Office Phone: 307-777-7881. Office Fax: 307-777-5466. Business E-Mail: rhunnicutt@wyoming.com.

HUNSBERGER, CHARLES WESLEY, library director; b. Elkhart, Ind., Sept. 25, 1929; s. Charles August and Emma Edna (Zimmerman) H.; m. Hilda Carol Showalter, July 3, 1949 (div.); children: Jonathan Wesley, Jerald Wayne, Jane Wannette. BA, Bethel Coll., Mishawaka, Ind., 1952; MLS, Ind. U., 1967. Mem. Ft. Wayne (Ind.) Libr. Staff, 1960-62; dir. Columbia (Ind.) City Libr., 1962-64, Monroe County Libr., Bloomington, Ind., 1964-71, Clark County Libr. Dist., Las Vegas, Nev., 1971-93. Owner Las Vegas Libr. Cons. Svcs., 1993—, Las Vegas, Nev. cons. sch., pub. librs., 1968-70; lectr. libr. schs. Ind. U., 1970-71, U. Ariz., 1974, U. Nev., Reno, 1976; mem. Nev. Coun. on Librs., 1973-81, chmn., 1980-81. Mem. Calif. Libr. Assn., Ala., Nev. Libr. Assn. (named Libr. of Yr. 1988), Internat. Assn. of Met. City Librs. (sec./treas., 1992-95), Rotary (pres. 1979-80, Las Vegas-Paradise chpt.). Democrat. Home: 9545 Passa Tempo Dr Reno NV 89511-9447

HUNSUCKER, (CARL) WAYNE, architectural firm executive, educator; b. Morganton, NC, Feb. 16, 1945; s. Earnest Howard and Reba (Laughridge) H.; m. Edith Mabel Whittaker Guisto, May 23, 1990; children: Wendy Edith Guisto, Bret Thomas Guisto. Student, Old Dominion Coll.; BFA, Coll. William and Mary, 1968; BArch with Distinction, U. Ariz., 1975. Lic. architect, Calif., Nev., Idaho, Oreg., Wash., Ariz.; cert. Nat. Coun. Archtl. Registration Bds. Archtl. draftsman Woodmoor Corp., Colorado Springs, Colo., 1971-72; architect-in-training James Gresham & Assocs., Tuscon, 1975-76; prin., pres. Hummel Hunsucker Archs., Boise, Idaho, 1976—, prin.-in-charge office ops. Spokane, Wash., 1998—. Part-time draftsperson Forrest Coile & Assocs., Newport News, Va., 1959-63; asst. instr. U. Ariz. Prin. works include U.S. Courthouse and Fed. Office Bldg., Boise, Idaho, Earl F. Chandler Bldg., Boise, Benton County Jud. Facility, San Francisco, Orchard Pl. Office Complex, Boise, 1st Security Bank addition and remodel, Nampa Main Br., Blue Cross Idaho, Idaho N.G. Armory Annex, Boise, various bldgs. Mt. Home AFB (Citation and Design awards Dept. Air Force), Mountain Home Town Jr. High Sch. addition; co-author: (text books) Architectural Drafting, 1976, Neighborhood Planning - Case Study of the Sam Hughes Neighborhood. Bd. dirs. Ada County Hist. Soc., 1989-90, Boise; mem. Lincoln Day Banquet Com., Boise, 1984-86; mem. licensing bd. Idaho Outfitters and Guides, 1996—; bd. mem. Bldg. Owners and Mgrs. Assn., Boise chpt., 1998. 1st lt. U.S. Army, 1969-71, Vietnam. Recipient Citation award USAF, Best Stand Alone Bldg. award TAC Air Force, 1984, Henry Adams Fund for Excellence award. Mem. AIA (state pres. 1990, pres. ctrl. sect. Idaho chpt. 1988, Silver medal 1976), Nat. Coun. Archtl. Registration Bds. Avocations: bird hunting, fishing, boating. Office: Hummel Architects PA 2785 N Bogus Basin Rd Boise ID 83702-0911

HUNT, BRIAN L., program manager; MA, Cambridge U.; ScM, PhD, Brown U. Acting program mgr. Northrop Grumman Corp., Hawthorne, Calif., England, 1967-79; tech. mgr. Northrop Corp., 1979-90, 92-97; chmn. aerospace engring. U. Md., 1990-92; program mgr. F/A 18A/B/C/D Northrop Grumman Corp., 1997-98, v.p. engring. and tech. air combat sys. El Segundo, Calif., 1998-2000. Recipient AIAA Aircraft Design award, 1996. Office: Northrop Grumman 1 Hornet Way El Segundo CA 90245-2804

HUNT, DAVID G., state legislator, coalition executive; b. Port Angeles, Wash., Nov. 10, 1967; s. Harley D. and Karin V. Hunt; m. Tonia M. Moore, Dec. 14, 1970; children: Andrew, Emily. BA in Polit. Sci./Am. Govt., Columbia U., 1990. Cmty. rep. to US Congresswoman Louise Slaughter, Rochester, NY, 1990-96; field dir. Oregonians for Quality Healthcare, Portland, 1996-97; dist. dir. US Congresswoman Darlene Hooley, Salem, Oreg., 1997-99, US Congressman Brian Baird, Vancouver, Wash., 1999-2001; exec. dir. Columbia River Channel Coalition, Portland, Oreg., 2001—; mem. Dist. 40 Oreg. House of Reps., 2002—, house majority leader, 2006—, spkr. of house, 2009—. Vice chair Oreg. City Sch. Bd., 1999—2002; nat. pres. Am. Bapt. Ch., 2002—03. Mem. Rotary. Democrat. Baptist. Home: 16655 SE Kingsridge Ct Milwaukie OR 97267 Office: Oreg House of Reps 900 Court St NE, 269 Salem OR 97301 also: Oreg House of Reps 900 Court St NE, H-295 Salem OR 97301 Mailing: PO Box 67190 Portland OR 97267 Office Phone: 503-986-1200, 503-986-1440. Business E-Mail: rep.davehunt@state.or.us.*

HUNT, GORDON, lawyer; b. LA, Oct. 26, 1934; s. Howard Wilson and Esther Nita (Dempsey) H. BA in Polit. Sci, UCLA, 1956; JD, U. So. Calif., 1959. Bar: Calif. 1960. Law clk. Appellate Dept., Superior Ct. LA County, 1959-60; mem. firm Behymer & Hoffman, LA, 1960-65; partner firm Behymer, Hoffman & Hunt, LA, 1965-68; ptnr. firm Munns, Kofford, Hoffman, Hunt & Throckmorton, Pasadena, 1969—90; mem. Hunt, Ortman, Blasco Palffy and Rossell Inc., Pasadena, 1990—2007, Hunt, Ortman, Palffy, Nieves, Lubka, Darling and Mah, Inc., Pasadena, 2007—. Lectr. UCLA, various yrs.; chmn. legal adv. com. Assoc. Gen. Contractors Calif., 1985; arbitrator LA Superior Ct., State of Calif. Author: Construction Surety and Bonding Handbook; co-author: California Construction Law, 16th edit.; contbr. numerous articles to legal jours. Named a Super Lawyer in Constrn. Law, 2004—09. Mem. ABA, Calif. Bar Assn. (del. Conv. 1964-69), LA County Bar Assn. (chmn. real property sect. 1975-76, co-chmn. continuing edn. bar com. 1969-71, Outstanding Real Estate Lawyer award 2000, Outstanding Achievement in Constrn. Law 2004, named one of Best Lawyers in Am., 2006-09), Am. Arbitration Assn. (arbitrator, mediator). Office: 301 N Lake Ave Fl 7 Pasadena CA 91101-4108 Office Phone: 626-440-5200. Business E-Mail: hunt@huntortmann.com.

HUNT, H(AROLD) KEITH, retired business management educator, marketing consultant; b. Apr. 16, 1938; married; 8 children. BS in Mktg. and Mgmt., U. Utah, 1961, MBA, 1962; PhD in Mktg., Northwestern U., 1972. Instr. Imperial Valley Coll., El Centro, Calif., 1962-64; teaching asst. Northwestern U., 1964-66, instr., 1966-67; asst. prof. bus. adminstrn. and journalism U. Iowa, 1967-73; cons., staff mem. Office Policy Planning and Evaluation, FTC, Washington, 1973-74; assoc. prof. bus. adminstrn. U. Wyo., Laramie, 1974-75; assoc. prof. bus. mgmt. Brigham Young U., Provo, Utah, 1975-78, prof., 1978—2005. Participant, chmn. various workshops, seminars, meetings; research expert, cons., expert witness on consumer research FTC, 1974-81; cons., expert witness div. drug advt. FDA, 1975-82; cons., adv. on consumer research Consumer and Corp. Affairs Can., 1978-82. Editor: Advances in Consumer Research, vol. 5, 1977; co-editor conf. proc. (with Frances Magrabi) Interdisciplinary Consumer Research, 1980, (with Ralph Day) Consumer Satisfaction/Dissatisfaction and Complaining Behavior, 8 vols., 1975-85, Jour. 1988-2005 Elected to Orem City Coun., Utah, 1986-93. Recipient Maeser Research award Brigham Young U., 1981; scholar-in-residence adv. dept. U. Ill., 1979; vis. research scholar Coll. Home Econs., U. Ala., 1980; vis. research scholar dept. mktg. and transp. U. Tenn., 1981; NSF grantee, 1975-77 Mem. Assn. Consumer Research (pres. 1979, exec. sec. 1983-2000, 1st Disting. Svc. award 1989), Am. Acad. Advt. (pres. 1982-83, exec. sec. 1983-86, elected fellow 1987), Am. Mktg. Assn., Soc. Consumer Psychology, Am. Council on Consumer Interests, Beta Gamma Sigma, Kappa Tau Alpha, Omicron Delta Epsilon, Phi Kappa Phi Home: 835 E High Country Dr Orem UT 84097-2370

HUNT, HELEN (HELEN ELIZABETH HUNT), actress; b. LA, June 15, 1963; d. Gordon Hunt; m. Hank Azaria July 17, 1999 (div. Dec. 18, 2000); 1 child Makena' Lei Gordon Carnahan with Matthew Carnahan. Attended, UCLA. TV guest appearances include Amy Prentiss, 1974, The Swiss Family Robinson, 1975-76, The Fitzpatricks, 1977, The Bionic Women, 1978, Weekend, Mary Tyler Moore Show, 1977, Family, 1976, 1980, Facts of Life, 1980, Knots Landing, 1980, 1981, Darkroom, 1981, Gimmie a Break!, 1982, It Takes Two, 1982, Highway to Heaven, 1985, St. Elsewhere (several episodes between 1984-86), The Hitchiker, 1987, China Beach, 1990, The Trials of Rosie O'Neill, 1990, My Life and Times, 1991, Friends, 1995; TV movies include Pioneer Woman, 1973, All Together Now, 1975, Death Scream, 1975, Having Babies, 1976, The Spell, 1977, Transplant, 1979, Angel Dusted, 1981, I Think I'm Having a Baby, 1981, The Best Little Girl in the World, 1981, The Miracle of Cathy Miller, 1981, Child Bride of Short Creek, 1981, Desperate Lives, 1982, Quarterback Princess, 1983, Bill: On His Own, 1983, Choices of the Heart, 1983, Sweet Revenge, 1984, Shooter, 1988, American Playhouse: Land of Little Rain, 1989, Incident at Dark River, 1989, Into the Badlands, 1991, Murder In New Hampshire: The Pamela Wojas Smart Story, 1991, In the Company of Darkness, 1993, Twelfth Night, or What You Will, 1998, Empire Falls, 2005; TV series Mad About You, 1992-99 (also prodr. 3 episodes, dir. 5 episodes)(Emmy nomination, Lead Actress - Comedy, 1993, 94, Golden Globe award for Best Actress, musical or comedy, 1994, 95, Emmy award for Best Leading Actress in a Comedy series, 1996); films include Rollercoaster, 1977, Girls Just Want To Have Fun, 1985, Waiting to Act, 1985, Trancers, 1985, Empire, 1985, Peggy Sue Got Married, 1986, Project X, 1987, Stealing Home, 1988, Miles From Home, 1988, The Frog Prince, 1988, Next Of Kin, 1989, Trancers II, 1991, The Waterdance, 1992, Only You, 1992, Bob Roberts, 1992, Mr. Saturday Night, 1992, Trancers III, 1992, Sexual Healing, 1993, Kiss of Death, 1995, Twister, 1996, As Good As It Gets, 1997 (Acad. award Best Actress in a Leading Role 1997), Twister: Ride It Out, 1998, Dr. T and the Women, 2000, Pay It Forward, 2000, Cast Away, 2000, What Women Want, 2000, Curse of the Jade Scorpion, 2001, A Good Women, 2004, Bobby, 2006, Then She Found Me, 2007 (also prodr., writer, dir.); plays include: Life (X)3, 2003; (voice) Galtar and the Golden Lance, 1985, The Nativity, 1986, The Easter Story, 1989, Captain Planet and the Planeteers, 1990, The Simpsons, 1998. Named one of 50 Most Beautiful People, People Mag., 1998.

HUNT, JAMES L., lawyer; b. Chgo., Oct. 20, 1942; BA magna cum laude, DePauw U., 1964; JD, Northwestern U., 1967. Bar: Calif. 1967. Atty. McCutchen, Doyle, Brown & Enersen, San Francisco, 1967, ptnr., chmn. firm, 1988—91, 1999—2001, chmn. litig. dept., 1991—95; ptnr. Bingham McCutchen LLP, San Francisco, 2001—, chmn. litig. practice group. Atty. rep. 9th Cir. Jud. Conf., 1991-94; bd. dirs. The Lurie Co.; trustee The Lurie Found. Assoc. editor: Northwestern U. Law Rev., 1966-67. Bd. dirs. San Francisco Giants; bd. visitors Northwestern U. Law Sch., 1989—. Named a No. Calif. Super Lawyer, Law & Politics & SF Mag., 2004. Mem. Am. Coll. Trial Lawyers, Phi Beta Kappa, Order Coif. Office: Bingham McCutchen LLP 3 Embarcadero Ctr Ste 18000 San Francisco CA 94111-4003 Office Phone: 415-393-2212. Business E-Mail: james.hunt@bingham.com.

HUNT, LORRAINE T., former lieutenant governor; b. Niagara Falls, NY, Mar. 11, 1939; Student, Westlake Coll. Music. Former pres., CEO Perri Inc.; founder, also bd. dirs. Continental Nat. Bank; lt. gov. State of Nev., 1998—2007; pres. Nev. State Senate, 1999—2007. Bd. dirs. First Security Bank Nev.; chmn. bd. trustees Las Vegas Convention and Visitors Authority; former commr. and vice chair Nev. Commn. on Tourism; dir. Nev. Hotel/Motel Assn.; vice chmn. Nev. Motion Picture Found., Nev. Motion Picture Commn. Commr. Clark county Commn., 1995-99; mem. cmty. bd. Wells Fargo Bank Recipient Govs. award for excellence in bus., 1987, First Enterprise award, 1993, First Lifetime Achievement award, Govs. Conf. on Tourism, 1993; named U.S. Small Bus. Adv. of the Yr., 1989, Nev. Restauranteur of Yr., 1992, Rep. Woman of Yr., 1996, Woman of Yr., Nev. Ballet Theater, 1998. Republican.

HUNT, ROGER LEE, federal judge; b. Overton, Nev., Apr. 29, 1942; s. Ferlin Hansen and Verda (Peterson) H.; m. Mauna Sue Hawkes, July 20, 1965; children: Roger Todd (dec.), Rachelle, Kristina, Tyler, Melanee, Ryan. Student, Coll. So. Utah, 1960-61; BA, Brigham Young U., 1966; JD, George Washington U., 1970. Bar: Nev. 1970, U.S. Dist. Ct. Nev. 1970, U.S. Supreme Ct. 1977, U.S. Ct. Appeals 1980. Dep. dist. atty. Clark County Dist. Atty.'s Office, Las Vegas, Nev., 1971; assoc. Rose & Norwood, Las Vegas, 1971-73; sr.

ptnr. Edwards, Hunt, Hale & Hansen, Las Vegas, 1973-92; magistrate judge US Dist. Ct. Nev., Las Vegas, 1992, judge, 2000—. Office: US Dist Ct 333 Las Vegas Blvd Ste 6018 Las Vegas NV 89101-5814

HUNT, SHARON ANN, cardiologist; b. Cleve., Oct. 2, 1946; MD, Stanford Univ. Sch. Med., 1972. Cert. Cardiovascular Medicine, Heart, Lung Transplantation Am. Bd. Internal Medicine, Internal Medicine Am. Bd. Internal Medicine. Intern Stanford Univ., med. dir., heart transplant program, and prof., medicine. Recipient Wyeth Senior Achievement award in Clin. Transplantation, Am. Soc. Transplantation, 2007. Office: Cardiovascular Medicine CVRB H2146 MC 5246 300 Pasteur Dr Stanford CA 94305 Office Phone: 650-498-6605. Office Fax: 650-725-1599.

HUNT, WILLIAM EDWARD, SR., lawyer, retired state supreme court justice; b. Feb. 28, 1923; BA, U. Mont., LLB, 1955. Bar: Mont. 1955, US Dist. Ct., Mont. 1956, US Supreme Ct. Atty. Liberty County, Chester, Mont., 1957—70; dir. Mont. Aeronautics Commn., 1970—75; judge Mont. First Worker Compensation Ct., 1975-81; justice Mont. Supreme Ct., Helena, 1985—2000; of counsel Hunt Law Firm, Helena, 2000—. Contbr. articles to law jours. Trustee Mont. Legal Svc., 1968—71. Capt. US Army, 1947—65. Mem.: Mont. Legal Found. (dir. 2003—). Office: Hunt Law Firm 310 E Broadway St Helena MT 59601-4237 Office Phone: 406-442-8552. Office Fax: 406-495-1660.

HUNT-COFFEY, NANCY, library director; b. Glendale, Calif. BA in English Lit., Occidental Coll., LA; MLS, PhD student, UCLA. Tech. cons. Glendale CC, Calif.; with LNX team Glendale Pub. Libr., 1992, mgr. LNX cmty. info. utility, exec. analyst/automation svcs. coord., asst. dir., dir., 2004—. Ex officio bd. mem. Assocs. of Brand Libr. and Arts Ctr.; bd. dirs. Friends of Glendale Pub. Libr. Contbr. articles to profl. publs. Office: Glendale Pub Libr 222 E Harvard St Glendale CA 91205 Office Phone: 818-548-2030. Office Fax: 818-548-7225. E-mail: nhunt-coffey@ci.glendale.ca.us.

HUNTEN, DONALD MOUNT, planetary scientist, educator; b. Montreal, Can., Mar. 1, 1925; came to U.S., 1963, naturalized, 1979; s. Kenneth William and Winnifred Binnmore (Mount) H.; m. Isobel Ann Rubenstein, Dec. 28, 1949 (div. Apr. 1995); children: Keith Atherton, Mark Ross; m. Ann Louise Sprague, May 21, 1995. B.Sc., U. Western Ont., 1946; PhD, McGill U., 1950. From research asso. to prof. physics U. Sask. (Can.), Saskatoon, 1950-63; physicist Kitt Peak Nat. Obs., Tucson, 1963-77; sci. adv. to asso. adminstr. for space sci. NASA, Washington, 1976-77; prof. planetary scis. U. Ariz., Tucson, 1977-88, Regents prof., 1988—. Cons. NASA, 1964—. Author: Introduction to Electronics, 1964; (with J.W. Chamberlain) Theory of Planetary Atmospheres, 1987; contbr. articles to profl. jours. Recipient Pub. Svc. medal NASA, 1977, 85,96, medal for exceptional sci. achievement, 1980, Space Sci. award Com. on Space Rsch., 2000. Mem.: AAAS, Can. Assn. Physicists (editor 1961—63), Royal Soc. Can., Nat. Acad. Scis., Internat. Assn. Geomagnetism and Aeronomy, Internat. Union Geodesy and Geophysics, Internat. Astron. Union, Am. Astron. Soc. (chmn. divsn. planetary scis. 1977), Am. Geophys. Union (John Adam Fleming medal 1998), Am. Phys. Soc., Cosmos Club (Washington), Explorers Club. Home: 3445 W Foxes Den Dr Tucson AZ 85745-5102 Office: U Ariz Dept Planetary Scis Tucson AZ 85721-0001 Business E-Mail: dhunten@lpl.arizona.edu.

HUNTER, CHUCK, state legislator; married; 4 children. EdM. Small bus. owner; mem. Dist. 79 Mont. House of Reps., 2008—. Democrat. Office: Montana House of Representatives PO Box 200400 Helena MT 59620-0400 Mailing: 717 Dearborn Ave Helena MT 59601-2712 Home Phone: 406-449-2327; Office Phone: 406-444-4800. Office Fax: 406-444-4825. Business E-Mail: chunter717@bresnan.net.

HUNTER, DUNCAN DUANE, United States Representative from California, military officer; b. San Diego, Dec. 7, 1976; s. Duncan Lee and Lynne (Layh) Hunter; m. Margaret Hunter; children: Duncan, Elizabeth, Sarah. BBA, San Diego State U., 2001; grad., USMC Officer Candidate Sch., 2002. Former bus. analyst, San Diego; lt. USMCR, 2002, lt. 1st Marine Divsn. Iraq, 2003, lt. Battery A, 1st Battalion, 11th Marines Fallujah, Iraq, 2004, promoted to capt., 2006, active duty Afghanistan, 2007; mem. US Congress from 52nd Calif. Dist., 2009—. Republican. Baptist. Office: US Congress 1429 Longworth House Office Bldg Washington DC 20515 also: 1870 Cordell Ct Ste 206 El Cajon CA 92020 Office Phone: 202-225-5672, 619-448-5201. Office Fax: 202-225-0235, 619-449-2251.*

HUNTER, DUNCAN LEE, retired United States Representative from California; b. Riverside, Calif., May 31, 1948; m. Lynne Layh, 1973; children: Robert Samuel, Duncan Duane. Attended, U. Calif., Santa Barbara, U. Mt., 1966—67; BSL, Western State U., 1968, JD, 1976. Bar: Calif. 1976. Pvt. practice, San Diego; mem. US Congress from 42nd Calif. Dist., 1981—83, US Congress from 45th Calif. Dist., 1983—93, US Congress from 52nd Calif. Dist., 1993—2009, chmn. armed services com., 2003—07. Mem. Congressional Jobs and Fair Trade Caucus; co-chair Congressional Task Force on Bowhunting, Nat. Security Caucus. With U.S. Army, 1969-71, South Vietnam. Decorated Air medal, bronze star. Mem. Navy League. Republican. Baptist.*

HUNTER, FORREST WALKER, lawyer; b. Arlington, Va., Jan. 25, 1950; s. Dallas Walker and Ann Arsell (Wheat) H.; m. Susan Gladys Zsamer, June 8, 1974; children: Andrew Chastain, Alison Christian. BA, U. Va., 1972; JD, Emory U., 1975. Bar: Ga. Idaho, 1975, U.S. Dist. Ct. (no. dist.) Ga. 1978, U.S. Ct. Appeals (5th cir.) 1978, U.S. Ct. Appeals (11th cir.) 1981, U.S. Dist. Ct. (mid. dist.) Ga. 1982, U.S. Dist. Ct. (so. dist.) Ga. 1983, U.S. Ct. Appeals (6th cir.) 1988, U.S. Dist. Ct. (we. dist.) Mich. 1994, U.S. Ct. Appeals (7th cir.) 1996, U.S. Dist. Ct. (ea. dist.) Tex. 1999, U.S. Dist. Ct. (no. dist.) Ind. 2002, US Supreme Ct., 2006, US Dist. Ct. Id., 2009. Atty. Office Chief Counsel IRS, Dept. Treasury, Washington, 1975-77, sr. atty. Office. Regional Counsel Atlanta, 1977-81; assoc. Jones, Bird & Howell and Alston & Bird, Atlanta, 1981-85; ptnr., labor, employment litig. Alston & Bird LLP, Atlanta, 1985—2008; of counsel Perkins Coie LLP, 2008—. Named one of Legal Elite, Ga. Trend, 2004, Super Lawyers, Atlanta Mag., 2008. Mem. Am. Health Lawyers Assn., Ga. Acad. Hosp. Attys., Atlanta Bar Assn., U. Va. Alumni Assn., Emory U. Alumni Assn. Office: Perkins Coie LLP 1111 W Jefferson St Ste 500 Boise ID 83702-5391 Office Phone: 208-343-3434. Business E-Mail: fhunter@pekinscoie.com.

HUNTER, LARRY DEAN, lawyer, broadcast executive; b. Leon, Iowa, Apr. 10, 1950; s. Doyle J. and Dorothy B. (Grey) H.; m. Rita K. Barker, Jan. 24, 1971; children: Nathan (dec.), Allison. BS with high distinction, U. Iowa, Iowa City, 1971; AM, U. Mich., Ann Arbor, 1974, JD magna cum laude, 1974, CPhil in Econs., 1975. Bar: Va. 1975, Mich. 1978, Calif. 1992. Assoc. McGuire, Woods & Battle, Richmond, Va., 1975-77; asst. counsel, internat. counsel Clark Equipment Co., Buchanan, Mich., 1977-80; ptnr. Honigman, Miller, Schwartz & Cohn, Detroit, 1980-93; asst. gen. counsel Hughes Electronics Corp., LA, 1993-98, corp. v.p., 1998—2001, sr. v.p., gen. counsel El Segundo, Calif., 2002—03, DIRECTV, Inc., El Segundo, Calif., 1996-98; chmn., pres. DIRECTV Japan Mgmt., Inc., Tokyo, 1998-2000; exec. v.p., gen. counsel, sec. DIRECTV Group, El Segundo, Calif., 2004—. Mem. faculty Wayne State U. Law Sch., Detroit, 1987-89. Mem. Order of Coif. Home: 1101 S Catalina Ave Redondo Beach CA 90277 Office: The DIRECTV Group Inc 2230 E Imperial Hwy El Segundo CA 90245 Office Phone: 310-964-0723. E-mail: larry.hunter@directv.com.

HUNTER, MILTON, construction company executive, retired career military officer; b. Houston, May 1, 1943; married; 2 children. BS in Archtl. Engring., Wash. State U., 1967; M in Engring., U. Wash., 1978; grad. Exec. Devel. Program, U. Va., 1988; postgrad., Tex. A&M U., 1990, Harvard U., 1994; DSc (hon.), N.J. Inst. Tech., 1997. Registered profl. engr., D.C. Commd. 2d lt. U.S. Army, 1967, advanced through grades to maj. gen.; instr. Tactical Bridging br., dept. applied engring. U.S. Army Engr. Sch., Ft. Belvoir, Va.; comdr. and dist. engr. Seattle Dist. U.S. Army CE, comdg. gen., divsn. engr. South Pacific, San Francisco, chief of staff Washington, comdg. gen., divsn. engr. North Atlantic divsn. N.Y., condg. gen., divsn. engr. North Atlantic divsn. Washington, 1997-2000, dep. chief of engineers., dep. comdr., 2000—01; sr. v.p. infrastructure and tech. group Parsons Corp., Pasadena, Calif., 2002—. Decorated Legion of Merit (2), Bronze Star medal, DSM, others; recipient Disting. Alumni award Wash. State U., 1991; named to Outstanding Young of Am., 1979. Fellow Soc. Am. Mil. Engrs.; mem. Army Engr. Regtl. Assn., Assn. U.S. Army, Tau Beta Pi. Office: Parsons Corp 100 W Walnut St Pasadena CA 91124

HUNTER, PATRICIA RAE (TRICIA HUNTER), state official; b. Appleton, Minn., June 15, 1952; d. Harlan Ottowa and Clara Elizabeth (Tryhus) Hunter; m. Clark Waldon Crabbe, May 28, 1978 (dissolved July 1994); 1 child, Marcantonio Samantha. AS in Nursing, Good Samaritan Hosp., Phoenix, 1974; BSN, U. San Diego, 1981; MSN, UCLA, 1985. RN, cert. oper. rm. nurse. Surg. svcs. educator Stanford (Calif.) Hosp., 1983-85; oper. rm. supr. Alexian Bros., San Jose, Calif., 1985-86; dir. surg. svcs. Cmty. Hosp. Chula Vista, Calif., 1986-89; mem. Calif. State Assembly, San Diego, 1989-92; spl. asst. Gov. Wilson Office Statewide Health Planning and Devel., Sacramento, 1993-94; commr. Calif. Med. Assistance Commn., Sacramento, 1994—98, sr. v.p., mng. dir., 1998—2002, The Flannery Group, San Diego, 1997—2002; prin., owner Govt. Rels. Group, Inc., 2004—. Cons. hosp., Monterey, Calif., 1984—, Summit Schs., Ontario, Calif., 1992—93. Mem. adv. bd. Alzheimers Assn., San Diego, 1990—92, Arthritis Found., 1990—92; pres. Calif. Rep. League, 1995—97; bd. dir. Am. Nurses Found., 2007—. Recipient Alice Pauly award, Nat. Women Polit. Caucus San Diego, 1991; named Rookie Legislator of the Yr., Calif. Psychol. Assn., 1990, Legislator of the Yr., Calif. Nurse Practitioners Assn., 1992. Mem.: NWPC, ANA (v.p. 1982—85), Bus. and Profl. Orgn., Assn. Oper. Rm. Nurses, Rotary (bd. dir. 1993—94), Sigma Theta Tau (Leadership award 1991). Republican. Lutheran. Home: 3260 E Fox Run Way San Diego CA 92111-7723 Office: Govt Rels Group Inc 1121 L St Ste 409 Sacramento CA 95814 Office Phone: 916-447-7821. Business E-Mail: grg@govrelationsgroup.com.

HUNTER, TONY (ANTHONY REX), molecular biologist, educator; b. Ashford, Kent, Eng., Aug. 23, 1943; arrived in U.S., 1971; s. Ranulph Rex and Nellie Ruby Elsie (Hitchcock) H.; m. Philippa Charlotte Marrack, July 19, 1969 (div. 1974); m. Jennifer Ann Maureen Price, June 8, 1992; children: Sean Alexander Brocas, James Samuel Alan. BA, U. Cambridge, Eng., 1965, MA, 1966. Rsch. fellow Christ's Coll., U. Cambridge, 1968-71, 73-75; rsch. assoc. Salk Inst., San Diego, 1971-73, asst. prof., 1975-78, assoc. prof., 1978-82, prof., 1982—, Am. Cancer Soc. rsch. prof., 1992—. Adj. prof. biology U. Calif. San Diego, La Jolla, 1982—. Contbr. articles to sci. jours. Recipient award, Am. Bus. Found. Cancer Rsch., 1988, Katharine Berkan Judd award, Meml. Sloan-Kettering Cancer Ctr., 1992, Internat. award, Gairdner Found., 1994, Hopkins Meml. award, 1994, Mott prize, GM Cancer Rsch. Found., 1994, Feodor Lynen medal, 1999, J. Allyn Taylor Internat. prize in medicine, John P. Roberts Rsch. Inst. and C.H. Stiller Meml. Found., 2000, Keio Med. Sci. prize, Keio U. Med. Sci. Fund, Tokyo, 2001, Sergio Lombroso award in cancer rsch., Weizmann Inst. Sci., 2003, City of Medicine award, Durham Health Ptnrs., 2003, Medal of Honor, Am. Cancer Soc., 2004, Kirk A. Landon prize, Am. Assn. Cancer Rsch., 2004, Prince of Asturias award for sci. and tech. rsch., 2004, Louisa Gross Horwitz prize, Columbia U., 2004, Wolf Found. prize, Israel, 2005, Daniel Nathans Meml. award, Van Andel Inst., 2005, Herbert Taylor award, Am. Soc. Biochemistry and Molecular Biology, 2007, Pasarow award Cancer, Robert J. and Claire Pasarow Found., 2006, Clifford prize for cancer rsch., Inst. Med. Vet. Sci., Adelaide. Fellow Am. Acad. Arts and Scis., Royal Soc. London, Royal Soc. Arts, Mfrs. and Commerce; mem. NAS, European Molecular Biology Orgn. (assoc.), Inst. Medicine, Am. Philos. Soc. Avocations: white water rafting, desert camping. Home: 4578 Vista de la Patria Del Mar CA 92014-4150 Office: Salk Inst Biol Studies Molecular-Cell Biology Lab 10010 N Torrey Pines Rd La Jolla CA 92037-1099 Office Phone: 858-453-4100 1385.

HUNTER, TORII KEDAR, professional baseball player; b. Pine Bluff, Ark., July 18, 1975; m. Katrina Hall; children: Torii Jr., Monshadrik. Outfielder Minn. Twins, 1997—2007, LA Angels of Anaheim, 2008—. Mem. South squad Jr. Olympics, 1992. Recipient Gold Glove award, 2001—08, Carl R. Pohlad award, 2004; named Gatorade Ark. Player of Yr., 1993; named to Am. League All-Star Team, 2002, 2007. Mailing: c/o LA Angels of Anaheim Angel Stadium 2000 Gene Autry Way Anaheim CA 92806

HUNTER, WILLIAM DENNIS, lawyer; b. Boise, Idaho, June 26, 1943; s. William Gregory and Lorene (Persilla) H.; m. Jane Emily Porter, Apr. 30, 1966; children: Keith Alan, Elise Aubrey. BA, Stanford U., 1965; JD, U. Calif., San Francisco, 1973. Bar: Calif. 1973, U.S. Dist. Ct. (no. dist.) Calif. 1974, U.S. Ct. Appeals (9th cir.) 1974, U.S. Supreme Ct. 1996. Assoc. Pettit & Martin, San Francisco, 1973-79, ptnr., 1980-92, counsel, 1993-95, Collette & Erickson LLP, San Francisco, 1995-2000; regional counsel The Nature Conservancy, San Francisco, 2000—. Bd. dirs. City Celebration, Inc., San Francisco, 1984-91, pres., 1989-91. Recipient Service award Calif. Nature Conservancy, 1987. Mem. ABA, Calif. State Bar Assn., San Francisco Bar Assn., Nat. Assn. Installation Devel. (regional dir. 1993-2000), Order of coif. Democrat.

HUNTER-BOWINGTON, DOROTHY DIANA, educator, consultant; b. Chgo., Dec. 21, 1930; d. William Paul and Dorothy (Proud) Hunter; m. James Paul Gingrich, July 31, 1948; children: James Gingrich, Mark Gingrich, Chris Gingrich, Suzanne Black, Margaret Gingrich, Eric Gingrich, John Gingrich; m. Howard F. Bowington, Feb. 14, 1975. AA, Am. River Coll., 1967; BA, Calif. State U.-Sacramento, 1969, postgrad., 1969—74, Calif. State U.-Chico, 1969—73; MAVE, Calif. State Consortium, 1975. Cert. in adminstrn., secondary home econs. for mentally retarded, specialist for learning handicapped and resource specialist Calif. Vocat. specialist for spl. needs students Grand Union HS Dist., North Highlands, Calif., 1969—2006; asst. prof. vocat edn. Calif. State Consortium, 1977—2006; ret., 2006. Cons. spl. needs workshop State Calif.; mem. ednl. adv. com. for spl. needs students Calif. State U.; chmn. pro tem Calif. Assn. Vocat. Edn.-Nat. Priority Students, 1982—83; cons. vocat. edn. hanicapped students Ctr. Equity Cons., 1983—84. Author: job-seeking curriculum, 1975, health handbook adopted by L.A. Cmty. Colls., 1976. Mem. Calif. Gov.'s Com. for Hired the Handicapped, Goldl Country Hire the Handicapped Com., Sacramento, 1982—83. Named Vocat. Trainer of Yr., Sacramento C. of C., 1978, Sacramento Tch. of Yr., 1983; grantee, Calif. Dept. Edn., 1980—91, vocat. coord. grant, 1986—. Mem.: Coun. Exceptional Children, Am. Vocat. Assn. for Spl. Needs Students, Calif. Assn. Vocat. Edn. (pres.-elect), Am. Vocat. Assn.

HUNTERTON, C. STANLEY, lawyer; BA, Syracuse U., NY, 1970, JD, 1974. Bar: Nev. Spl. atty. Organized Crine and Racketeering Sect. U.S. Dept. Justice, Detroit, 1975—78, Las Vegas, 1978—84; dep. chief counsel Pres.'s Commn. Organized Crime, 1984—85; atty. Hunterton and Assocs. Law Firm, 1986—2002; sr. v.p., gen. counsel, corp. sec. Sierra Pacific Resources, Reno, 2002—. Spl. counsel Ethics Rev. Bd. City Las Vegas; mem. election practice com. State Bar Nev. Named to Best Lawyers in Am., Bus. Litig., 2005—06. Master: Nev. Am. Inns Ct.; fellow: ACTL; mem.: State Bar Assn. Nev. (mem. standing com. judicial ethics and election practice), Clark County Bar Assn. Avocations: tennis, golf. Office: Sierra Pacific Resources 6100 Neil Rd Reno NV 89511

HUNTHAUSEN, RAYMOND GERHARDT, archbishop emeritus; b. Anaconda, Mont., Aug. 21, 1921; s. Anthony Gerhardt and Edna (Tuchacherer) Hunthausen. AB, Carroll Coll., 1943, St. Edward's Sem., 1946; MS, Notre Dame U., 1953; LLD, DePaul U., 1960; postgrad., St. Louis U., Cath. U., Fordham U. Ordained priest Diocese of Helena, Mont., 1946; instr. chemistry Carroll Coll., 1946-57, football, basketball coach, 1953-57, pres., 1957-62; ordained bishop, 1962; bishop Diocese of Helena, Mont., 1962-75; archbishop Archdiocese of Seattle, 1975-91, archbishop emeritus, 1991—. Recipient Thomas Merton award, 1982, Martin Luther King Jr. award, Fellowship of Reconciliation, 1987. Mem. American Chem. Soc. Office: Chancery Office 710 9th Ave Seattle WA 98104-2017

HUNTLEY, JAMES ROBERT, government official, international affairs scholar; b. Tacoma, July 27, 1923; s. Wells and Laura H.; m. Colleen Grounds Smith, May 27, 1967; children by previous marriage: Mark, David, Tziviah, Jean. BA in Econs., Sociology magna cum laude, U. Wash., 1948, postgrad., 1951; MA in Internat. Rels., Harvard U., 1956. Cons. Wash. Parks Recreation Commn., Olympia, 1949-51; exch. of persons officer U.S. Fgn. Svc., Frankfurt, Nuremberg, Germany, 1952-54; dir. cultural ctr. USIA, Hof/Saale, Germany, 1954-55; USIA postgrad. scholar Harvard U., 1955-56; asst. to Pres.'s coord. for Hungarian relief Washington, 1956; European regional affairs officer USIA, Washington, 1956-58; dep. pub. affairs officer U.S. Mission to European Cmtys., Brussels, 1958-60; mem. U.S. Del. to Atlantic Congress, London, 1959; sec. organizing com. Atlantic Inst., Brussels and Milan, 1960, exec. officer and co-founder Paris, 1960-63; dir. Atlantic Inst. (N.Am. Office), Washington, 1963-65; founder, sec. Com. Atlantic Studies, 1963-65; sec. edn. com. NATO Parliamentarians Conf., Brussels, 1960-64; program assoc., internat. affairs divsn. Ford Found., NYC, 1965-67; sec. gen. Coun. Atlantic Colls., London, 1967-68; ind. writer, cons., lectr., internat. affairs Guildford, England, 1968-74; founder, sec. Assn. Mid-Atlantic Clubs, 1970-74; founder, sec. gen. Standing Conf. Atlantic Orgns., 1972-74; rsch. fellow, sr. advisor to pres. on internat. affairs Battelle Meml. Inst., Seattle, 1974-83; pres., CEO Atlantic Coun. of U.S., Washington, 1983-85; ind. cons., author internat. affairs. European corr., environ. affairs Saturday Rev./World, 1972-74; Corrs. World Wide, London, 1970-74; European corr. Non-Profit Report, 1970-74. Author: The NATO Story, 1965; (with W.R. Burgess) Europe and America - The Next Ten Years, 1970, Man's Environment and the Atlantic Alliance, 1972, Uniting the Democracies, 1980, Pax Democratica—A Strategy for the 21st Century, 1998, 2d edit., 2001, An Architect of Democracy: Building a Mosaic of Peace, 2006; contbr. articles to profl. jours. Bd. dirs. Internat. Standing Conf. Phlanthropy, 1969-74, Assn. to Unite Democracies, 1976-94, Seattle Com. Fgn. Rels., 1975-78, World Affairs Coun. Seattle, 1975-83, adv. bd. 1986-95, Bainbridge Island Land Trust, 1994-97; founding chmn. Coms. for a Cmty. of Democracies, 1979-92; co-founder 21st Century Found., 1987-91; mem. adv. bd. 21st Century Trust, London, 1988—; co-founder Next Century Initiative, 1992-95, New Century Initiative, 1996-99, pres. 1996-98; co-founder, v.p. Coun. for Cmty. of Democracies, 1999—2007. Carnegie fellow U. Wash., 1949-51; recipient Disting. Eagle Scout award 1995; named Kappa Sigma Man of Yr., 1999. Mem. Rainier Club (Seattle), DACOR (Washington). Home and Office: 1213 Towne Rd Sequim WA 98382-8849 Business E-Mail: huntleypax@olypen.com.

HUNTSBERRY, FREDERICK D., film company executive; Bachelor's degree, Boston U. Mgr., mergers and acquistions Europe Gen. Electric, 1985—97; v.p. TV bus. devel. Universal Pictures Corp., 1997—98; sr. v.p., CFO Universal Studios TV and Networks Group, 1998—2001, Universal Studios, 2001—02; exec. v.p., CFO Vivendi Universal Entertainment, 2002—04; exec v.p. NBC Universal TV Distbn., 2004—06; interim pres., CEO Paramount Pictures Corp., 2005, COO, 2006—. Office: Paramount Pictures Corp 5555 Melrose Ave West Hollywood CA 90038

HUNTSMAN, JON MEADE, SR., chemicals company executive; b. Blackfoot, Idaho, May 21, 1937; s. A. Blaine and Kathleen (Robison) Huntsman; m. Karen Haight; children: Jon Jr., Peter R., Christina K., Kathleen A., David H., Paul C., James H., Jennifer, Mark H. BS, U. Pa., Phila., 1959; MBA, U. So. Calif., LA, 1970. With Olson Bros, Inc., North Hollywood, Calif., 1961; assoc. adminstr. social &

rehabilitation svc. US Dept. Health Edn. & Welfare, 1970—71, spl. asst. to the pres., 1971-72; with Huntsman Container Corp., Salt Lake City, 1972-83, Huntsman Chem. Corp, Salt Lake City, 1982—; CEO Huntsman Corp., Salt Lake City, 1996-2000, chmn., 2000—. Bd. mem. Chem. Mfrs. Assn., Am. Plastics Coun. Author: Winners Never Cheat: Everyday Values We Learned as Children (But May Have Forgotten), 2005. Bd. mem. ARC, Wharton Sch. U. Pa., Primary Children's Med. Ctr. Found.; Pres. mission LDS Ch., Washington, 1980-83; founder, chmn. Huntsman Cancer Inst. Recipient Spoon award, U. Pa., 1959, Internat. Balfour award, 1959, Leader Yr. award, Utah Young Republicans, 1978; named Top Chem. Ind. CEO, 1994, Humanitarian of Yr., Larry King, 2002; named an Hon. Citizen, Republic of Armenia; named one of The 50 Most Generous Philanthropists, BusinessWeek, 2005, Forbes' Richest Americans, 2006. Republican. Office: Huntsman Corp 500 Huntsman Way Salt Lake City UT 84108-1235 Office Phone: 801-532-5200.

HUNTSMAN, JON MEADE, JR., Governor of Utah, former federal agency administrator; b. Palo Alto, Calif., Mar. 26, 1960; s. Jon Meade and Karen (Haight) H.; m. Mary Katherine Cooper, Nov. 18, 1983; children: Mary Anne, Abigail, Elizabeth, Jon III. AB, U. Pa., 1987. Spl. asst. to chmn. Rep. Nat. Com., Washington, 1982; staff asst. The White House, Washington, 1983; state dir. UT Reagan-Bush campaign, Salt Lake City, 1984; v.p., dir. Huntsman Pacific Chem. Corp., Taipei, Taiwan, 1987-88; dep. asst. sec. Internat. Trade Administrn., Washington, 1989-90; dep. asst. sec. for E. Asia and Pacific Affairs US Dept. Commerce, Washington, 1990-91; US amb. to Singapore US Dept. State, 1992—93; dep. US Trade Rep. & US Trade Amb. Office US Trade Rep., Exec. Office of the Pres., Washington, 2001—03; chmn., CEO Huntsman Family Holdings Co. LLC, 2003—04; gov. State of UT, Salt Lake City, 2005—. Chmn. U.S.-China Comml. Commn. Groups, Washington, 1990-91, U.S.-Mongolia Trade Facilitation Group, 1990-91; exec. sec. U.S.-Thailand Joint Comml. Commn., 1990-91, U.S. Pacific Islands Joint Comml. Commn., 1990-91; pres., CEO Huntsman Cancer Found., 1995-2001. State dir. Utah Reagan-Bush campaign, Salt Lake City, 1984; chmn. Utah Reagan-Bush Inaugural Com., Salt Lake City, 1985; nat. del. Rep. Conv., 1984, 86. Mem. Internat. Club Washington, Asia Soc. Republican. Mem. Lds Ch. Office: Office of Gov UT E Office Bldg Ste E220 PO Box 142220 Salt Lake City UT 84114 Office Phone: 801-538-1000. Office Fax: 801-538-1528.

HUNTSMAN, LEE L., former academic administrator, director; BSc in Elec. Engring., Stanford U., 1963; PhD in Biomedical Engring., U. Pa., 1968. Dir. ctr. for bioengineering U. Wash., 1980—96, assoc. dean for sci. affairs, sch. of medicine, 1993—96, provost, v.p. acad. affairs Seattle, 1997—2002, interim pres., 2002—03, pres., 2003—04, pres. emeritus, 2004—. Mem. Whitaker Found. Governing Com., 1994—98; chmn. Working Gorup on Rev. of Bioengineering and Tech. Instrumentation Develop. Rsch. for the Ctro for Sci. Rev of the NIH, 1998. Fellow: Am. Ins. of Med. and Biol. Engring., Am. Assn. for the Advancement of Sci.

HUNTSMAN, PETER R., chemicals executive; Grad., U. Utah, Salt Lake City. Pres. Olympus Oil Corp., 1986; v.p. to sr. v.p., gen. mgr. Huntsman Polypropylene Corp., 1987—94; sr. v.p. Huntsman Chem. Corp., Huntsman Packaging Corp.; pres., COO Huntsman Corp., 1994—2000, pres., CEO, dir., 2000—. Office: Huntsman Corp 500 Huntsman Way Salt Lake City UT 84108 Office Phone: 801-584-5700.

HUNTWORK, JAMES RODEN, lawyer; b. Milw., May 6, 1948; s. Daniel Lawrence and Gladys (Roden) H.; m. Patience Tipton Huntwork, July 7, 1972; children: Andrew Stuart, Sarah Noel. BA with distinction, Shimer Coll., 1968; JD, Yale Law Sch., 1972; MA Econs., Yale U., 1973. Bar: Mass. 1972, Ariz. 1977. Atty. Sullivan & Worcester, Boston, 1972-77, Jennings, Strouss & Salmon, Phoenix, 1977-91, Fennemore Craig, Phoenix, 1992-98, Salmon, Lewis & Weldon, Phoenix, Ariz., 1998—. Dir. exec. com. Phoenix Econ. Growth Corp., 1987-91; state ballot security chmn. Ariz. Rep. Party, Phoenix, 1992-2006; originator The Comml. Law Project for Ukraine, 1991—; mem. Ariz. Ind. Redistricting Commn., 2000-. Co-recipient Judge Learned Hand Human Rels. award Am. Jewish Com., 1992. Mem. ABA, Ariz. Bar Assn., Maricopa County Bar Assn., Phoenix C. of C. (N.Am. Free Trade Task Force 1991-95). Republican. Office: Ste 200 2850 E Camelback Rd Phoenix AZ 85016-4316 Office Phone: 602-801-9077. Business E-Mail: jrh@slwplc.com. E-mail: jrh@huntwork.net.

HUPPENTHAL, JOHN, state legislator; b. Michigan City, Ind., Mar. 3, 1954; m. Jennifer Huppenthal; children: Morgan, Brooke. BS in Engring., North Ariz. U.; MS in Bus. Adminstrn., Ariz. State U. Mem. Chandler City Coun., Ariz., 1984—92; mem. Dist. 6 Ariz. State Senate, 1993—2001, mem., 2001—03, mem. Dist. 20, 2004—, chair edn. accountability & reform com., vice chair judiciary com. Mem.: Chandler Hist. Soc., Chandler C. of C. Republican. Roman Catholic. Office: Ariz State Senate Capitol Complex 1700 W Washington Rm 300 Phoenix AZ 85007 Office Phone: 602-926-5261. Office Fax: 602-417-3257. Business E-Mail: jhuppent@azleg.gov.*

HURD, GALE ANNE, film producer; b. LA, Oct. 25, 1955; d. Frank E. and Lolita (Espiau) Hurd; m. James Cameron, 1985 (div. 1989); m. Brian DePalma, July 20, 1991 (div.); 1 child; m. Jonathan Hensleigh, June 19, 1995. Degree in econs. and communications, Stanford U., 1977. Dir. mktg. and publicity, co-prodr. New World Pictures, LA, 1977-82; pres., prodr. Pacific Western Prodns., LA, 1982—. Owner Vertical Wine Bistro, Pasadena, Calif. Prodr.: (films) The Terminator, 1984 (Grand Prix Avoiriaz Film Festival award), Aliens 1986 (nominated for 7 Acad. awards, recipient Best Sound Effects Editing award, Best Visual Effects award Acad. Picture Arts & Scis.), Alien Nation (Saturn award for best sci. fiction film), The Abyss, 1989 (nominated for 4 Acad. awards, Best Visual Effects award), The Waterdance, 1991 (2 TFP Spirit awards, 2 Sundance Film Festival awards), Cast a Deadly Spell, 1991 (Emmy award), Raising Cain, 1992, No Escape, 1994, Safe Passage (Beatrice Wood award for Creative Achievement), 1994, The Ghost and the Darkness,(Acad. award) 1996, The Relic, 1996, Going West in America, 1996, Dante's Peak, 1997, Virus, 1997, Dead Man on Campus, 1997, Armageddon, 1998, Dick, 1999, Clockstoppers 2002, The Hulk, 2003 (TV series) Adventure, Inc., 2002, Punisher, 2004, Aeon Flux, 2005, (TV pilot) Coven, 2004; exec. prodr.: (films) Switchback, 1997, Tremors, 1990, Downtown, 1990, Terminator 2, 1991 (winner 3 Acad. awards), Witch Hunt, 1994, Sugartime, 1995, Terminator 3, 2004, Punisher, 2004, The Incredible Hulk 2008, Punisher: War Zone, 2008; creative cons. (TV program) Alien Nation, 1989-90. Juror Focus Student Film Awards, 1989, 90; chmn. Nicholl Fellowship Acad. Motion Picture Arts & Scis., 1989—; mem. Show Coalition, 1988—; mem. Hollywood (Calif.) Women's Polit. Com., 1987—; mem. U.S. Film Festival Juror; bd. dirs. IFP/West, Artists Rights Found.; trustee Am. Film Inst.; bd. dirs. L.A. Internat. Film Festival, Coral Reef Rsch. Found., Ams. for a Safe Future; mentor Peter Stark Motion Picture Producing Program, Sch. of Cinema-TV, U. of So. Calif., Women in Film Mentor Program. Recipient Spl. Merit award Nat. Assn. Theater Owners, 1986, Stanford-La Entrepreneur of Yr. award Bus. Sch. Alumni L.A., 1990, Fla. Film Festival award, 1994, Women in Film Crystal award, 1998, Ind. Vision award Temucala Film Festival, 2001, Nat. Bd. Rev. Prodr.'s award, 2004, Global Green Millennium award, 2004, Israel Film Festival Visionary award, 2004, Saturn awards, Donald Reed award, 2004, PGA Charles Fitz Simons award, 2007, NYWIFT Loreen Arbus award, 2007; named Prodr. of Yr., Stunt Awards, 2003. Mem. AMPAS (prodr.'s br. exec. com. 1990—, chair festival grants com.), Am. Film Inst. (trustee 1989—), Americans for a Safe Future (bd. dirs. 1993—), Prodr.'s Guild Am. (bd. dirs.), Women in Film (bd. dirs. 1989-90, 2000—03), Inst. for Rsch. on Women and Gender (nat. adv. panel 1997-2000), Feminist Majority, The Ocean Consrvancy (bd. dirs. 2001—, Heal the Bay (adv. bd.), Reef Check Internat. (adv. bd.), Seakeepers Soc., Mulholland Tomorrow, The Trusteeship (bd. dirs. 2006-), Explorers Club (N.Y.C.), Jamestowne Soc., Nat. Soc. DAR, Waterkeeper Alliance (bd. dirs. 2007-), Phi Beta Kappa. Avocations: scuba diving, paso fino horses. Office: Valhalla Motion Pictures 3201 Cahvenga Blvd W Los Angeles CA 90068

HURD, MARK VINCENT, computer company executive; b. NYC, Jan. 1, 1957; m. Paula Hurd; 2 children. BBA, Baylor U., Waco, Tex., 1979. With NCR Corp., 1980—2005; sr. v.p. Teradata Solutions Group (divsn. NCR Corp.), 1998—2000; COO Teradata (divsn. NCR Corp.), 2000—02; exec. v.p. NCR Corp., 2000—01, co-pres. Dayton, Ohio, 2001—02, COO, 2002—03, CEO, 2003—05; pres., CEO Hewlett-Packard Co., Palo Alto, Calif., 2005—06, chmn., pres., CEO, 2006—. Bd. dirs. Hewlett-Packard Co., 2005—, News Corp., 2008—. Co-author (with Lars Nyberg): The Value Factor: How Global Leaders Use Information. Bd. visitors Fuqua Sch. Bus. Duke U.; bd. trustees, Dayton Area Chap. Am. Red Cross. Named one of 50 Who Matter Now, CNNMoney.com Bus. 2.0, 2006, 2007, 25 Most Powerful People in Bus., Fortune Mag., 2007. Avocation: tennis. Office: Hewlett Packard Co 3000 Hanover St Palo Alto CA 94304-1185 Office Phone: 650-857-1501. Office Fax: 650-857-5518.*

HURDLE, CLINT (CLINTON MERRICK HURDLE), professional baseball manager, former professional baseball player; b. Big Rapids, Mich., July 30, 1957; m. Karla Hurdle; children: Madison Reilly, Christian Merrick; 1 child, Ashley. Outfielder Kansas City Royals, 1977—81, Cin. Reds, 1982, NY Mets, 1983, 1985, 1987, St. Louis Cardinals, 1986; mgr. NY Mets Minor League Sys., 1988—93, Colo. Rockies, 2002—, various positions, 1994—2001. Named a Coach, Nat. League All-Star Game, 2004. Office: c/o Colo Rockies 2001 Blake St Denver CO 80205

HURLBERT, ROGER WILLIAM, information technology executive; b. San Francisco, Feb. 18, 1941; s. William G. and Mary (Greene) H.; m. Karen C. Haslag, Nov. 6, 1982; children: Sage, Mica, Chula, Monk, Morris, Cassie, Bella. BS in Community Devel., So. Ill. U., 1965. Newspaper editor and reporter various, San Francisco Bay Area, 1958-62; pvt. practice investigation Ill., 1963-65; advisor San Francisco Planning Urban Rsch. Assn., 1969-87; pres. Sage Info. Svcs., Glen Ellen, Calif., 1988—. Compiler U.S. Land Data Base, 1972—. Pres. Haight-Ashbury Neighborhood Coun., San Francisco, 1959-61. With U.S. Army, 1966-68, Vietnam. Recipient Cert. of Merit, San Francisco Coun. Dist. Mchts. Assn., 1972. Mem. Real Estate Info. Profls. Assn. (sec. 1998-03), Direct Mktg. Assn., Mail Advt. Svc. Assn. Internat., League of Men Voters (v.p. 1959—), Internat. Assn. of Assessing Officials. Democrat. Office: Sage Info Svcs 13606 Arnold Dr PO Box 1832 Glen Ellen CA 95442-1832

HURLEY, BRUCE PALMER, artist; b. Tacoma, May 9, 1944; s. Gerald Baynton and Donna Ray (Whealey) H.; m. Ivy Jane Partridge; 1 child, Paul George. BS in Edn., Oreg. Coll. Edn., 1968. Cert. secondary edn. tchr. One-man shows include Goldberg's, 1966, Hillsboro Pub. Libr., 1969, 1971, Valley Art Assn., Forest Grove, 1971, 1974, Portland (Oreg.) Habilitation Ctr., 2004, exhibited in group shows at Portland Art Mus., 1970, Northwest Artist Workshop, 1979, Sun Bird Gallery, 1986, Sunriver Juried Show, 1986, 1992, Beaverton Arts Showcase, 1990, 1991, 1992, 1993, 1994, 1996, 1997, 1998 (1st place watercolor), 2003, Represented in permanent collections Oreg. Coll., Oriental Medicine, David Wheeler, Washington, Libr. of Am. Psychiat. Assn., Schools Med. Plz., Tigard, Oreg., Atty. Mark Olson, N.Y.C., Nicholas S. Law, Cambridge, Eng., Washington County Pub. Svc. Bldg., Hillsboro, Oreg., Portland Habilitation Ctr., Tuality Cmty. Hosp., Hillsboro, Oreg., others; author: Planet Ploob Vacation, 1992, Divine Soliloquy, 1994; inventor, poet, philosopher, cartoonist, numerous paintings, drawings and sculptures. Mem. Portland Art Mus. Recipient Cmty. Svc. award Beaverton Arts Commn., 1993, Royal Patronage award Hutt River, Australia, 1995. Mem. Theosophical Soc.(life) Mem. Soc. Of Friends. Avocations: musicology, camping, raw foods, naturopathy, mysticism. Home: 251 NW Bailey St Hillsboro OR 97124-2903

HURLEY, CHAD MEREDITH, Internet company executive; b. Jan. 24, 1977; s. Donald and JoAnn; m. Kathy Clark; 2 children. BFA, Ind. U. Pa., 1999. First user-interface designer PayPal Inc., 1999—2002; design cons. several tech. companies, 2002—05; co-founder, CEO YouTube Inc. (sold to Google in 2006), 2005—. Design cons.: (films) Thank You for Smoking, 2005. Recipient Vanguard award, Prodrs. Guild of America, 2008; named (with Steve Chen) Webby Person of Yr., 2007; named one of 50 Who Matter Now, CNNMoney.com Bus. 2.0, 2006, The World's Most Influential People, TIME mag., 2007, 25 Most Influential People in Web Music, Powergeek 25, 2007, 50 Most Important People on the Web, PC World, 2007. Fellow: World Tech. Network ((with Steve Chen) World Tech. award-Entertainment 2006). Achievements include logo design for PayPal.

HURLEY, ELIZABETH (LIZ HURLEY), actress, model; b. Hampshire, Eng., June 10, 1965; m. Arun Nayar, Mar. 2, 2007; 1 child, Damian Charles. Student, London Studio Ctr. Head devel. Simian Films, London and L.A., 1994—; model, cosmetic rep. Estee Lauder. Actress (films) Die Tote Stadt, 1987, Rowing with the Wind, 1988, Bloody Atlantic, 1991, The Orchid House, 1991, Passenger 57, 1992, El Largo Invierno, 1992, Beyond Bedlam, 1993, Goldeneye, 1995, Mad Dogs and Englishmen, 1995, Dangerous Ground, 1997, Austin Powers: International Man of Mystery, 1997, Permanent Midnight, 1998, Edtv, 1999, My Favorite Martian, 1999, Austin Powers: The Spy Who Shagged Me, 1999, The Weight of Water, 2000, Bedazzled, 2000, Double Whammy, 2001, Serving Sarah, 2002; (TV movies) Act of Will, 1989, Death Has A Bad Reputation, 1990, The Orchid House, 1991, Sharpe's Eneny, 1994, The Shamrock Conspiracy, 1995, Samson and Delilah, 1996, Harrison Cry of the City, 1996; (TV series) Aria, 1987, Inspector Morse, 1988, Cristabel, 1989, Rumpole and the Barrow Boy, 1989, The Young Indiana Jones Chronicles, 1992, Sharpe II, 1995; host (TV spl.) The World of James Bond, 1995; actor, exec. prodr. (films) Method, 2004; prodr. (films) Extreme Measures, 1996, Mickey Blue Eyes, 1999.

HURLEY, FRANCIS T., archbishop emeritus; b. San Francisco, Jan. 12, 1927; Grad., St. Patrick Sem., Menlo Park, Calif., Cath. U. Am. Ordained priest Archdiocese of San Francisco, 1951; with Nat. Cath. Welfare Conf., Washington, asst. sec., 1958—68; assoc. sec. Nat. Cath. Welfare Conf. (now U.S. Cath. Conf.), 1968—70; ordained bishop, 1970; aux. bishop Diocese of Juneau, Alaska, 1970—71, bishop, 1971—76; archbishop Archdiocese of Anchorage, 1976—2001, archbishop emeritus, 2001—. Roman Catholic.

HURST, DEBORAH, pediatric hematologist; b. Washington, May 9, 1946; d. Willard and Frances (Wilson) H.; m. Stephen Mershon Senter, June 14, 1970; children: Carlin, Daniel. BA, Harvard U., 1968; MD, Med. Coll. Pa., 1974. Diplomate Nat. Bd. Med. Examiners, Am. Bd. Pediatrics, Am. Bd. Pediatric Hematology-Oncology. Intern Bellevue Hosp., NYU Hosp., NYC, 1974-75, resident in pediatrics, 1975-76; ambulatory pediatric fellow Bellevue Hosp., NYC, 1976-77; hematology, oncology fellow Bellevue Hosp., Columbia U., NYC, 1977-80; assoc. hematologist Childrens Hosp. Oakland, Calif., 1980-92; asst. clin. prof. U. Calif. San Francisco Med. Ctr., 1992—2004; med. dir. Bayer Corp., Berkeley, Calif., 1992-98; sr. dir. clin. devel. Chiron Corp., Emeryville, Calif., 1998—2006; sr. director bio-oncology devel. Genentech, Inc., South San Francisco, Calif., 2006—. Hematology cons. Assn. Asian/Pacific Community Health Orgns., Oakland; dir. Satellite Hematology Clinic/Valley Childrens Hosp., Fresno, Calif., 1984-92; cons. state dept. epidemiology Calif. State Dept. Health, Berkeley, 1992; chelation cons. lead poisoning program Childrens Hosp., Oakland, 1986-92. Contbr. articles to profl. jours. Vol. cons. lead poisoning State Dept. Epidemiology and Toxicology, Berkeley, 1986-92. Fellow Am. Acad. Pediatrics; mem. Am. Soc. Hematology, Am. Soc. Gene Therapy, Am. Soc. Clin. Oncology, Am. Soc. Pediat. Hematology/Oncology. Office: Genentech Inc 1 DNA Way South San Francisco CA 94080-4990 Personal E-mail: hurst.deborah@gene.com.

HURT, WILLIAM, actor; b. Washington, Mar. 20, 1950; s. Henry Luce III (Stepfather) and Claire; m. Mary Beth Supinger, 1971 (div. 1981); m. Heidi Henderson, Mar. 5, 1989 (div. 1992); children: Sam, William Jr.; children: Alexander Devon, Jeanne. BA in Drama, Tufts U., 1972; student, Juilliard Sch.; ArtsD (hon.), U. Arts, 2006. Joined Oreg. Shakespeare Festival, 1975; performed regularly with Ashland Shakespeare Festival, Oreg.; joined Circle Repertory Theatre, NYC, 1977. Actor: (theatre) including Henry V, 1977, My Life, 1977, Ulysses in Traction, Lulu, 1978, Fifth of July, 1978, Hamlet, 1979, Mary Stuart, 1979, Childe Byron, 1981, The Diviners, 1981, The Great Grandson of Jedediah kohler, 1982, Richard II, 1982, A Midsummer Night's Dream, 1982, Hurlyburly, 1984, Joan of Arc at the Stake, 1985, Love Letters, 1989, Beside Herself, 1989, Ivanov, 1991, (films) Altered States, 1980, Eyewitness, 1981, Body Heat, 1981, The Big Chill, 1983, Gorky Park, 1983, Kiss of the Spider Woman, 1985 (Best Actor Award, Cannes Film Festival, 1985, Acad. Award for best actor, 1986), Children of a Lesser God, 1986 (Acad. Award nomination for best actor, 1987), Broadcast News, 1987 (Acad. Award nomination for best actor, 1988), A Time of Destiny, 1988, The Accidental Tourist, 1988, I Love You To Death, 1990, Marilyn Hotchkiss' Ballroom Dancing and Charm School (voice), 1990, Alice, 1990, The Doctor, 1991, Until the End of the World, 1991, The Plague, 1992, Mr. Wonderful, 1993, Trial by Jury, 1994, Second Best, 1994, Secrets Shared with a Stranger, 1994, Smoke, 1995, Michael, 1996, Jane Eyre, 1996, A Couch in New York, 1996, Loved, 1997, Dark City, 1998, Lost in Space, 1998, One True Thing, 1998, The Big Brass Ring, 1999, Sunshine, 1999, Do Not Disturb, 1999, The 4th Floor, 1999, The Simian Line, 2000, Artificial Intelligence: AI, 2001, The Contaminated Man, 2001, Rare Birds, 2001, Changing Lanes, 2002, Nearest to Heaven, 2002, Tuck Everlasting, 2002, The Tulse Luper Suitcases: The Moab Story, 2003, The Blue Butterfly, 2004, The Village, 2004, A History of Violence, 2005 (Best Supporting Actor, NY Film Critics Circle, 2005), Neverwas, 2005, Syriana, 2005, The Legend of the Sasquatch (voice), 2006, Beautiful Ohio, 2006, The Good Shepherd, 2006, Mr. Brooks, 2007, Into the Wild, 2007, Noise, 2007, Yellow Handkerchief, 2008, Vantage Point, 2008, The Incredible Hulk, 2008, (TV films) Verna: USO Girl, 1978, All the Way Home, 1981, The Miracle Maker (voice), 2000, The Flamingo Rising, 2001, Master Spy: The Robert Hanssen Story, 2002, Frankenstein, 2004, Hunt for Justice, 2005, (TV miniseries) The Best of Families, 1977, Dune 2000, (TV series) Riviere-des-Jeremie, 2001. Recipient 1st Spencer Tracy Award for outstanding screen performances and profl. achievement, UCLA, 1988. Office: c/o Creative Artists Agy 2000 Ave of the Stars Los Angeles CA 90067

HURT, WILLIAM HOLMAN, investment management company executive; b. LA, Mar. 29, 1927; s. Holman G. and Mary E. (Ortloff) H.; m. Sheridan Ann Stephens, Aug. 10, 1950 (div. May. 1970); children: Kelley Anne Hurt Purnell, Kathleen Constance, Courtney Diana Hurt MacMillan; m. Sarah Sherman, May 28, 1970. BS magna cum laude, U. So. Calif., 1949; MBA, Harvard U., 1951. With Dean Witter & Co., Los Angeles, 1951-71, ptnr., 1959, sr. v.p., 1968-70, exec. v.p., dir., mem. exec. com., dir. mktg. and rsch., 1969-71; chmn. exec. com. Capital Rsch. Co., 1972-77; chief exec. office Capital Group, Inc., LA, 1978-82; chmn. Capital Strategy Rsch., Inc., 1982—. Adv. com. Coldwell Banker Funds, 1978-99. Mem. bd. councilors Grad. Sch. Bus., U. So. Calif., L.A., 1978-88, vis. com., 1990-96; bd. dirs. L.A. Children's Hosp., 1985—. Served with USNR, 1945-46. Mem. Calif. Club, L.A. Athletic Club, N.Y. Athletic Club, Phi Kappa Phi, Beta Gamma Sigma, Kappa Alpha. Republican.

HURWITZ, ANDREW D., state supreme court justice; AB in Pub. and Internat. Affairs, Princeton U., 1968; JD, Yale U., 1972. Bar: Conn. 1973, Ariz. 1974, U.S. Dist. Ct. Ariz. 1975, U.S. Ct. Appeals (9th cir.) 1975, U.S. Supreme Ct. 1976, U.S. Dist. Ct. Conn. 1977, U.S. Ct. Appeals (2d cir.) 1977, U.S. Tax Ct. 1987, U.S. Ct. Appeals (7th cir.) 1987. Law clk. to Hon. Jon O. Newman U.S. Dist. Ct. Conn., 1972; law clk. to Hon. J. Joseph Smith U.S. Ct. Appeals, 1972—73; law clk. to Hon. Potter Stewart U.S. Supreme Ct., 1973—74; with Meyer Hendricks et. al., 1974—80, 1984—95, 1983—95, Osborn Maledon, 1995—2003; assoc. justice Ariz. State Supreme Ct., Phoenix, 2003—. Chief of staff Ariz. Gov. Bruce Babbitt, 1980—83, Ariz. Gov. Rose Mofford, 1988; mem. Ariz. Bd. of Regents, 1988—96, pres., 1992—93; co-chair of transition team Ariz. Gov. Janet Napolitano, 2002; vis. prof. law, civil procedure Ariz. State U., 1994—95, disting. vis. from practice, 2001, adjunct prof. law, ethics, supreme ct. litigation, legislative process, civil procedure, 1977—80, 1988, 2002. Mem. bd. dirs. Ariz. Ctr. for Law in Public Interest, 1986—88, Children's Action Alliance, 1999—2003, sec., 2002—03; chair City of Phoenix Neighborhood Improvement Com., 1986—88, City of Phoenix Street Environment Com., 1989—90. Mem.: State Bar of Ariz. (Com. on Rules of Professional Conduct 1985—90, Examination & Bar Review Com. 1986—87), Phi Beta Kappa. Office: Ariz State Supreme Ct Adminstrv Office Cts 1501 W Washington Phoenix AZ 85007 Office Phone: 602-542-4532.

HURWITZ, LAWRENCE NEAL, investment banking company executive; b. Austin, Tex., Mar. 21, 1939; s. John and Sarah Ruth (Blumenthal) H.; m. Kathleen O'Day, Feb., 1977 (div. Dec. 1985); 1 child, Kimberlee Colleen; m. Mynette Lee, Nov., 1989 (div. Jan. 1996); 1 child, Jonathan Lee. Student, U. Tex., 1957-59; MBA with distinction, Harvard U., 1961. With rsch. dept. Harvard U., 1961-62; asst. to v.p. Atlantic Rsch. Corp., 1962-65; comptr. TelAutograph Corp., 1965; dir. Gen. Artists Corp., 1965-69; pres. Sprayregen & Co., NYC, 1969-83; chmn. Country Junction, Inc., 1969-82; mktg. dir. Beneflex, Inc., 1985-86; v.p. Tech. Liberation Capital, Inc., Houston, 1986-89, Amex Systems, Houston, 1986-89; v.p., chief fin. officer Intile Designs, Inc., Houston, 1989-94; pres. Lawrence Fin. Ptnrs., LA, 1990—; dir. Kings Rd Entertain Pacific Coast Apparel Max Studios. Vice chmn., mem. exec. com. Empire Life Ins. Co. Am.; dir., mem. exec. com. Old Town Corp., Stratton Group Ltd., Sayre & Fisher Co., Tech. Tape, Inc., DFI Communications Inc., Columbia Gen. Corp., Cal. Data Systems Corp.; bd. dirs. Leon Max Inc., Pacific Coast Apparel, Air Motive Holdings Inc., Indsl. Electronic Hardware Corp., Bloomfield Bldg. Industries, Inc., Apollo Industries, Inc., Aberdeen Petroleum Corp., Investors Book Club, Inc., Ling Fund, Am. Land Co., Terrific Nutrient & Chem. Corp., N. Lake Corp., Datatronics, Inc., Merada Industries, Inc., AK Electric Corp., Aerocon, Inc., Hallmark Communications, Inc., Detroit Gray Iron & Steel Foundries, Inc., Fin. Tech., Inc., Wid's Films & Film Folks, Investors Preferred Life Ins. Co., Langdon Group, Inc., Essex Systems Corp., Chelsea Nat. Bank, Newport Chem. Industries, Inc. Editor: How to Invest in Letter Stock, 1970, Spin-Offs and Shells, 1970. Mem. Harvard Bus. Sch. Club, Comml. Fin. Assn., Am. Cash Flow Assn. (pres. L.A. chpt.), Harvard Club (v.p. Orange County). Jewish. Office: 11661 San Vicente Blvd Ste 408 Los Angeles CA 90049-5112

HUSAR, LINDA S., lawyer; b. Chgo., Sept. 12, 1955; BS summa cum laude, Boston U., 1977; JD magna cum laude, Loyola Law Sch., 1980. Bar: Calif. 1980, US Dist. Ct. (no., ea., so., and ctrl. dists.) Calif. 1981, US Ct. Appeals (9th cir.) 1981. Ptnr., labor & employment dept. Thelen Reid & Priest LLP, LA. Mem.: LA County Bar Assn. (Labor Law Sect.), ABA (Labor Law Sect.), Calif. State Bar. Office: Thelen Reid & Priest LLP 333 S Hope St Ste 2900 Los Angeles CA 90071-3048 Office Phone: 213-576-8017. Office Fax: 213-687-1817. Business E-Mail: lshusar@thelenreid.com.

HUSBAND, JOHN MICHAEL, lawyer; b. Elyria, Ohio, Apr. 7, 1952; s. Clint F. and Emma Husband; m. Jan Lee Umbenhour, Sept. 15, 1975; children: Heather, John. BS, Ohio State U., 1974; JD, U. Toledo, 1977. Law clk. to US Ct. Appeals (10th cir.), 1977—78; ptnr. Holland & Hart, Denver, 1978—, chair labor and employment law dept., 1991—96, mem. mgmt. com. Counsel Western Gov.'s Office, Denver, 1984. Editor: The Colorado Lawyer, Employment and Labor Rev., 1984—; co-editor: Colo. Employment Law Letter, —. Bd. dirs. Colo. Safety Assn., 1984—, sec., treas., 1988—; bd. dirs. Denver Four Mile House, Town of Bow Mar, 1987—90; bd. govs. U. Toledo Coll. Law. Named Best of the Bar for labor and employment law, Denver Bus. jour; named to Elyria Sports Hall of Fame, 1997, Best Lawyers in Am., Euromoney Guide to the World's Leading Labour and Employment Lawyers; fellow Coll. Labor and Employment Lawyers. Mem.: ABA (labor law sect., individual rights and responsibilities com., co-chair pub. subcom. individual rights and responsibilities com. 1998—2003, co-chair complex and class litigation subcom.), Denver Bar Assn., Colo. Bar Assn. (labor sect.), Ohio Bar Assn., Nat. Inst. Trial Advocate, Assn. Trial Lawyers Am., Denver Leadership Assn. Home: 5280 Ridge Trl Littleton CO 80123-1410 Office: Holland & Hart LLP PO Box 8749 555 17th St Ste 2900 Denver CO 80202-3979 Office Phone: 303-295-8228. E-mail: jhusband@hollandhart.com.

HUSKEY, HARRY DOUGLAS, information and computer science educator; b. Whittier, NC, Jan. 19, 1916; s. Cornelius and Myrtle (Cunningham) H.; m. Velma Elizabeth Roeth, Jan. 2, 1939 (dec. Jan. 1991); children: Carolyn, Roxanne, Harry Douglas, Linda; m. Nancy Grindstaff, Sept. 10, 1994. BS, U. Idaho, 1937; student, Ohio U., 1937—38; MA, Ohio State U., 1940, PhD, 1943. Temp. prin. sci. officer Nat. Phys. Labs., England, 1947; head machine devel. lab. Nat. Bur. Stds., 1948; asst. dir. Inst. Numerical Analysis, 1948-54; assoc. dir. computation lab. Wayne U., Detroit, 1952-53; assoc. prof. U. Calif., Berkeley, 1954-58, prof., 1958-68, vice chmn. elec. engring., 1965-66, prof. info. and computer sci. Santa Cruz, 1968-85, prof. emeritus, 1985—, dir. Computer Ctr., 1968-77, chmn. bd. info. sci., 1976-79, 82-83. Vis. prof. Indian Inst. Tech., Kanpur; (Indo-Am. program), 1963-64, 71, Delhi U., 1971; cons. computer divsn. Bendix, 1954-63; vis. prof. MIT, 1966; mem. computer sci. panel NSF, Naval Rsch. Adv. Com.; cons. on computers for developing countries UN, 1969-71; chmn. com. to advise Brazil on computer sci. edn. NAS, 1970-72; project coord. UNESCO/Burma contract, 1973-79; mem. adv. com. on use microcomputers in developing countries NRC, 1983-85. Co-editor: Computer Handbook, 1962. Recipient Disting. Alumni award Idaho State U., 1978, Pioneer award Nat. Computer Conf., 1978, IEEE Computer Soc., 1982; named U.S. sr.scientist award Fulbright-Alexander von Humboldt Found., Mathematisches Institut der Tech. U. Munich, 1974-75, 25th Ann. medal ENIAC; named to U. Idaho Alumni Hall of Fame, 1989. Fellow AAAS, IEEE (edit. bd., editor-in-chief computer group 1965-71, Centennial award 1984), Brit. Computer Soc.Computer Soc. India; mem. Am. Math. Soc., Math. Assn. Am., Assn. Computing Machinery (pres. 1960-62), Am. Fedn. Info. Processing Socs. (governing bd. 1961-63), Sigma Xi. Achievements include designing SWAC computer, Bendix G-15 and G-20 computers. Office: U Calif Computer & Info Sci Santa Cruz CA 95064 Home: 518 Summit Glen Ct Spartanburg SC 29307 Personal E-mail: harryhuskey@yahoo.com.

HUSTON, ANJELICA, actress; b. Santa Monica, Calif., July 8, 1951; d. John and Enrica Huston; m. Robert Graham, May 23, 1992 (dec. Dec. 27, 2008) Student, Loft Studio. Stage appearances include Hamlet, Roundhouse Theatre, London, Tamara, Il Vittorale Theatre, L.A.; actress: (films) A Walk with Love and Death, 1969, Hamlet, 1969, Sinful Davey, 1969, Swashbuckler, 1976, The Last Tycoon, 1976, The Postman Always Rings Twice, 1981, Rose for Emily, 1982, This is Spinal Tap, 1984, The Ice Pirates, 1984, Prizzi's Honor, 1985 (Academy award for Best Supporting Actress 1985, N.Y.Film Critics award 1985, L.A. Film Critics award 1985), Captain Eo, 1986, Gardens of Stone, 1987, The Dead, 1987 (Best Actress award Ind. Filmakers 1987), Mr. North, 1988, A Handfull of Dust, 1988, Witches, 1989, Crimes and Misdemeanors, 1989, Enemies, A Love Story, 1989, The Grifters, 1990, The Addams Family, 1991, The Player, 1992, Addams Family Values, 1993, Manhattan Murder Mystery, 1993, The Crossing Guard, 1995, The Perez Family, 1995, Buffalo '66, 1997, Phoenix, 1998, Ever After, 1998, The Golden Bowl, 2000, The Man From Elysian Fields, 2000, The Royal Tenenbaums, 2001, Blood Work, 2002, (voice only) Barbie as Rapunzel, 2002, Daddy Day Care, 2003, (voice only) Kaena: The Prophecy, 2003, The Life Aquatic with Steve Zissou, 2004, These Foolish Things, 2006, Art School Confidential, 2006, Material Girls, 2006, Seraphim Falls, 2006, The Darjeeling Limited, 2007, Martian Child, 2007, Choke, 2008; actor, dir, prodr.: (films) Agnes Browne, 1999; actor: (TV films) The Cowboy and the Ballerina, 1984, Family Pictures, 1993, And The Band Played On, 1993, Buffalo Girls, 1995, The Kentucky Derby, 2002, Iron Jawed Angels, 2004 (Golden Globe award for best supporting actress series, miniseries or TV movie, 2005), Covert One: The Hades Factor, 2006; (TV mini-series) Lonesome Dove, 1989, The Mists of Aalon, 2001; (TV appearances) Laverne & Shirley, 1976, Inside the Actors Studio, 1994, Huff, 2006, Medium, 2008; dir.: (films) Bastard Out of Carolina, 1996; (TV films) Riding the Bus with My Sister, 2005 Recipient Excellence award, Locarno Film Festival, 2008. Office: Internat Creative Mgmt c/o Toni Howard 8942 Wilshire Blvd Beverly Hills CA 90211-1934

HUSTON, DARREN, computer software company executive; married; 2 children. BS in econ., Trent Univ.; M in econ., Univ. BC; MBA with honors, Harvard Univ., 1994; grad., United World Coll., Trieste, Italy. Econ. adv. Govt. of Canada; cons. McKinsey & Co., 1994—98; v.p. retail strategy & new bus. Starbucks Coffee Co., 1998—2000, sr. v.p. acquisitions alliances & new product develop., 2000—03; corp. v.p. small & mid-market solutions & partners Microsoft Corp., Redmond, Wash., 2003—05, corp. v.p., pres. & CEO Microsoft Japan, 2005—. Office: Microsoft Corp 1 Microsoft Way Redmond WA 98052-6399

HUSTON, JOHN CHARLES, law educator; b. Chgo., Mar. 21, 1927; s. Albert Allison and Lillian Helen (Sullivan) H.; m. Joan Frances Mooney, Aug. 1, 1952; children: Mark Allison, Philip John, Paul Francis James; m. Inger Margareta Westerman, May 4, 1979 (dec. 2003); m. Heather Van Nuys, June 24, 2007. AB, U. Wash., 1950, JD, 1952; LLM, NYU, 1955. Bar: Wash. 1952, NY 1964, US Dist. Ct. (we. dist.) Wash. 1953, US Ct. Appeals (9th cir.) 1953, US Tax Ct. 1977, US Supreme Ct. 1993. Assoc. Kahin, Carmody & Horswill, Seattle, 1952—53; tchg. fellow NYU Law Sch., 1953—54; asst. prof. NYU, 1954—57; asst. co-dir. U. Ankara Legal Rsch. Inst., Turkey, 1954—55; asst. prof. Syracuse U., NY, 1957—60, assoc. prof., 1960—65, prof., 1965—67; prof., assoc. dean U. Wash., Seattle, 1967—73, prof. law, 1973—96, prof. emeritus, 1996—. Of counsel Carney, Badley, Smith & Spellman, Seattle, 1987—2002, Smith McKenzie Rothwell & Barlow, P.S., Seattle, 2002—07, Smith Law Partnership, Seattle, 2007—; vis. prof. U. Stockholm, 1986, U. Bergen, 1989, Bond U., Australia, 1991. Author: (with Redden) The Mining Law of Turkey, 1956, The Petroleum Law of Turkey, 1956, (with Mucklestone and Cross) Community Property: General Considerations, 1971, (with Price and Treacy) 4th edit., 1994, (with Sullivan and others) Administration of Criminal Justice, 166, 2d edit., 1969, (with Miyatake and Way) Japanese International Taxation, 1983, supplements through 1997, (with Cross and Shields) Community Property Desk Book, 1977, 2d edit., 1989, supplement, 1997, (with Williams) Permanent Establishment, 1993. With USNR, 1945-46; capt. USAFR. Mem.: ABA, Internat. Fiscal Assn. (past regional v.p., past mem. coun.), Japanese Am. Soc. Legal Studies, King County Bar Assn., Wash. State Bar Assn. (chmn. tax sect. 1984—85), Am. Coll. Trust and Estate Coun. Office: Second & Seneca Bldg Ste 1800 Seattle WA 98101 Personal E-mail: jc.huston@comcast.net.

HUTCHENS, TYRA THORNTON, pathologist, educator; b. Newberg, Oreg., Nov. 29, 1921; s. Fred George and Bessie (Adams) H.; m. Betty Lou Gardner, June 7, 1942; children: Tyra Richard, Robert Jay, Rebecca (Mrs. Mark Pearsall). BS, U. Oreg., 1943, MD, 1945. Diplomate: Am. Bd. Pathology, Am. Bd. Nuclear Medicine. Intern Minn. Gen. Hosp., Mpls., 1945—46; AEC postdoctoral research fellow Reed Coll., Med. Sch. U. Oreg., 1948—50; NIH postdoctoral research fellow Med. Sch. U. Oreg., 1951—53; mem. faculty Oreg. Health Scis. U., 1953—, prof., chmn. dept. clin. pathology, 1962—87, prof. emeritus, 1987—, prof. radiotherapy, 1963—71, allied health edn. coord., 1969—77. Vis. lectr. radiobiology Reed Coll., 1955, 56 Contbr. articles to profl. jours. Mem. adv. bd. Oreg. Regional Med. Program, 1968-75; mem. statuatory radiation adv. com. Oreg. Bd. Health, 1957-69, chmn., 1967-69; founding trustee Am. Bd. Nuc. Medicine, 1971-77, 82-84, sec., 1973-75, 84-85; voting rep. Am. Bd. Med. Specialties, 1973-78, chmn. com. long range planning, 1976-78; mem. sci. adv. bd. Armed Forces Inst. Pathology, 1978-83; chmn. Portland Com. on Fgn. Affairs, 1990-91. Lt. (j.g.) M.C., USNR, 1946-48. Charter mem. Acad. Clin. Lab. Physicians and Scientists, Soc. Nuc. Medicine (de Hevesey Nuc. Medicine Pioneer award 1995), Am. Coll. Nuc. Physicians; mem. AMA, Oreg. Pathologists Assn. (pres. 1968), Pacific N.W. Soc. Nuc. Medicine (pres. 1958), Coll. Am. Pathologists (bd. govs. 1967-74, pres. 1977-79, chmn. commn. on internat. affairs 1979-83, chmn. planning com. 1987 World Congress Pathology), Am. Soc. Clin. Pathologists (bd. registry med. technologists 1967-71), World Assn. of Socs. of Pathology (bur. of pathology 1981-87, 89-93, v.p. 1985-87, pres. 1989-91, chmn. commn. on world stds. 1981-86, Gold Headed Cane award 1995), World Pathology Found. (pres. 1987-89, trustee 1989-91), Assn. Clin. Pathologists (hon.), Italian Soc. Lab. Medicine (hon.), Phi Beta Kappa, Sigma Xi, Alpha Omega Alpha. Achievements include research radioactive carbon tracer studies of lipid metabolism, nuclear medicine techniques. Home: 17480 Holy Names Dr 413 Lake Oswego OR 97034 Personal E-mail: tyhutch@comcast.net.

HUTCHESON, JERRY DEE, manufacturing company executive; b. Oct. 31, 1932; s. Radford Andrew and Ethel Mae (Boulware) H.; m. Lynda Lou Weber, Mar. 6, 1953; children: Gerald Dan, Lisa Marie, Vicki Lynn. BS in Physics, Ea. N.Mex. U., 1965; postgrad., Temple U., 1962, U. N.Mex., 1965. Registered profl. engr., Calif. Rsch. engr. RCA, 1959—62; sect. head Motorola, 1962—63; rsch. physicist Dikewood Corp., 1963—66; sr. mem. tech. staff Signetics Corp., 1966—69; engring. mgr. Litton Sys., Sunnyvale, Calif., 1969—70, Fairchild Semiconductor, Mountain View, Calif., 1971; equipment engr., group mgr. Teledyne Semiconductor, Mountain View, 1971—74; dir. engring. DCA Reliability Labs., Sunnyvale, 1974—75; founder, prin. Tech. Ventures, San Jose, Calif., 1975—; CEO VLSI Rsch., Inc., San Jose, 1981—, chmn., 2004—. Contbr. articles to profl. jours. Dem. precinct committeeman, Albuquerque, 1964—66. With USAF, 1951—55. Mem.: NSPE, Am. Soc. Test Engrs., Soc. Photo-Optical Instrumentation Engrs., Semiconductor Equipment and Materials Inst., Calif. Soc. Profl. Engrs., Profl. Engrs. Pvt. Practice, Masons. Presbyterian. Office: VSLI Rsch 2880 Lakeside Dr 350 Santa Clara CA 95054-2822 Office Phone: 408-453-8844.

HUTCHESON, MARK ANDREW, lawyer; b. Phila., Mar. 29, 1942; s. John R. and Mary Helen (Willis) H.; m. Julie A. Olander, June 13, 1964; children: Kirsten Elizabeth, Mark Andrew II, Megan Ann. BA, U. Puget Sound, 1964; LLB, U. Wash., 1967. Bar: Wash. 1967, U.S. Dist. Ct. (we. and ea. dists.) Wash., U.S. Ct. Appeals (9th cir.), U.S. Supreme Ct. Staff counsel Com. on Commerce U.S. Senate, Washington, 1967-68; assoc. Davis Wright Tremaine, Seattle, 1968-72; ptnr. Davis, Wright Tremaine, Seattle, 1973—; mng. ptnr., chief exec. officer Davis Wright Tremaine, Seattle, 1989-94; chmn. Davis, Wright Tremaine, Seattle, 1994—. Mem., co-founder labor law com. Nat. Banking Industry, 1984—. Co-author: Employer's Guide to Strike Planning and Prevention, 1986; contbr. articles to profl. jours. Chmn., trustee Virginia Mason Hosp., Seattle, 1980-2003, Overlake Sch., Redmond, Wash., 1984-89, Epiphany Sch., Seattle, 1982-84, Legal Aid for Wash. Fund, 1991-2003; bd. dirs. Vis. Nurse Svcs., Seattle-King County, 1985-88; trustee Pacific N.W. Ballet, 1991-99, Pacific N.W. Assn. Ind. Schs., 1996-98. Nelson T. Hartson scholar U. Wash., 1966; Deerfield fellow Heritage Found., Deerfield, Mass., 1963. Mem. ABA (health care forum, employment law sect.), Seattle-King County Bar Assn. (employment law sect.), Am. Acad. Hosp. Attys., Am. Hosp. Assn. (labor rels. adv. com. 1978—), Coll. Labor and Employment Lawyers, Greater Seattle C. of C. (bd. dirs. 1991-94), Rainier Club, Seattle Tennis Club, Univ. Club, Order of Coif. Episcopalian. Avocations: sailing, tennis, skiing, reading, travel. Office: Davis Wright Tremaine 1201 3rd Ave Ste 2200 Seattle WA 98101-3045 Office Phone: 206-628-7678, 206-757-8065. Business E-Mail: markhutcheson@dwt.com.

HUTCHESON, S. DOUGLAS, telecommunications industry executive; BSME, Calif. State Polytechnic Univ.; MBA, Univ. Calif., Irvine. Mgmt. positions Solar Turbines Inc.; v.p. mktg. QUALCOMM, 1995—98; v.p. bus. develop. Leap Wireless Internat., San Diego, 1998—99, sr. v.p. bus. develop., 1999—2000, sr. v.p. product develop. & strategic planning, 2000—02, sr. v.p., CFO, 2002—05, pres., CFO, 2005, pres., CEO, 2005—, interim CFO, 2007. Mem.: Beta Gamma Sigma. Office: Leap Wireless Internat 10307 Pacific Ctr Ct San Diego CA 92121

HUTCHINGS, JOHN BARRIE, astronomer, researcher; b. Johannesburg, July 18, 1941; arrived in Can., 1967; BSc, Witwatersrand U., Johannesburg, 1962, MSc, 1964; PhD, U. Cambridge, Eng., 1967. Rsch. scientist Dominion Astrophysics Obs., NRC Can., Victoria, B.C., Canada, 1967—. Author numerous rsch. papers and revs., 1964—. Recipient Gold medal Sci. Coun. B.C., 1983, Royal Jubilee medal, 2002. Fellow Royal Soc. Can.; mem. Internat. Astron. Union, Am. Astron. Soc., Can. Astron. Soc. (Beals award 1982). Office: Dominion Astrophysics Obs 5071 W Saanich Rd Victoria BC Canada V9E 2E7 Home Phone: 250-656-5457; Office Phone: 250-363-0018. E-mail: john.hutchings@nrc.ca.

HUTCHISON, JAMES E., chemistry educator; Prof. dept. chemistry U. Oreg., Eugene. Chemistry grantee Camille and Henry Dreyfus Found., 1994. Office: U Oreg Dept Chemistry Eugene OR 97403

HUTTON, CAROLE LEIGH, not-for-profit executive, former newspaper editor; b. Framingham, Mass., Aug. 23, 1956; d. James and Norma Inez (Vitali) Hamilton; m. Tom Huff. B Journalism, Mich. State U., 1978. Editor Natick Sun, Mass., 1978—79; reporter, city editor, mng. editor Hammond Times, Ind., 1979—87; dir. publs. CNA Ins. Cos., Chgo., 1987—88; day city editor, accent editor Detroit News, 1988—90; city editor Detroit Free Press, 1992—95, dep. mng. editor for news, 1995—96, mng. editor, 1996—2002, exec. editor, 2002—03, pub., editor, 2004—05; v.p. news Knight Ridder Newspapers, 2005—07; v.p., exec. editor San Jose Mercury News, Calif., 2007—08; pres., CEO United Way Silicon Valley, 2008—. Tutor Detroit Pub. HS, 1994—94. Recipient Local News Coverage award, Hoosier State Press Assn., 1982; named one of 100 Most Influential Women in S.W. Mich., Crain's Detroit Bus. Mem.: AP Mng. Editors, Mich. AP Editors Assn. (pres., bd. dirs. 2000—), Am. Soc. Newspaper Editors, IAP Mng. Editors. Office: United Way Silicon Valley 1400 Parkmoor Ave Ste 250 San Jose CA 95126-3735

HUTTON, FIONA S., communications executive; Strategic planning coun. Gov. Pete Wilson, 1994-96; with Stoorza, Ziegaus and Metzger; v.p. corp. comm. Cadiz, Inc., Santa Monica, Calif. Mem. Pub. Rels. Soc. Am. Office: Ste 4250 777 S Figueroa St Los Angeles CA 90017-5860

HUTTON, PAUL ANDREW, historian, educator, writer; b. Frankfurt, Germany, Oct. 23, 1949; s. Paul Andrew and Louise Katherine (Johnson) Hutton; m. Vicki Lynne Bauer, 1972 (div. 1985); 1 child, Laura; m. Lynn Terri Brittner, Dec. 31, 1988 (div. 1996); children: Lorena, Paul; m. Tracy Lee Cogdill, Aug. 7, 2001. BA, Ind. U., 1972, MA, 1974, PhD, 1981. Editorial asst. Jour. Am. History, Bloomington, Ind., 1973-77; instr. history Utah State U., Logan, 1977-80, asst. prof., 1980-84, U. N.Mex., Albuquerque, 1984-86, assoc. prof., 1986-96; prof. U. N. Mex., Albuquerque, 1996—2006, disting. prof., 2006—. Author: Phil Sheridan and His Army, 1985; editor: Custer and His Times, 1981, Ten Days on the Plains, 1985, Soldiers West, 1987, The Custer Reader, 1992, Frontier and Region, 1997, (series) Eyewitness to the Civil War, 1991—93; writer, co-prodr. (TV series) Frontier: The Decisive Battls, 2000, Boone & Crockett: The Hunter Heroes, 2001, Carson and Cody: The Hunter Heroes, 2003, Eighty Acres of Hell, 2006, Investigating History, 2004—05; writer, co-prodr.: (films) Daniel Boone and the Westward Movement, 2002; The Wilderness Road: Spirit of a Nation, 2004; assoc. editor: Western Hist. Quar., 1977—84; editor: N.Mex Hist. Rev., 1985—91. Active Little Bighorn Battlefield Indian Meml. Adv. Com., Nat. Park Svc., 1994—2002. Recipient Evans Biography award, Brigham Young U., 1986, Paladin award, Mont. Hist. Soc., 1991, Western Heritage award, Nat. Cowboy Hall of Fame, 1996, 1999, 2003, 2005, 2008; Mead Disting. Rsch. fellow, Huntington Libr., 1988. Mem.: Writers Guild Am. West, Western Writers Am. (exec. bd. 1997—99, pres. 2002—04, exec. dir. 2007—, Spur award 1985, Pres. award 1998, Stirrup award 2000, Spur award 2002, 2004, Stirrup award 2004, Spur award 2006), Soc. Mil. History, Western Hist. Assn. (hon. life mem. 2006, exec. dir.

1990—2006, Billington award 2007), Orgn. Am. Historians (Ray A. Billington award 1986). Office: U NMex MSC06 3760 Dept History Albuquerque NM 87131-0001 Business E-Mail: hutton@unm.edu.

HUYNH, MY HANG VO, energetic materials chemist; b. Saigon, Vietnam, May 30, 1962; arrived in US, 1985; d. Louis V. Huynh and Ngoc Thom T. Huynh-Dang; BA in Math. with honors, SUNY, Geneseo, 1991, BS with honors in Chemistry, 1991; PhD, SUNY, Buffalo, 1998. Postdoctoral rsch. assoc. U. NC, Chapel Hill, 1998—2000; postdoctoral fellow Los Alamos Nat. Lab., N.Mex., 2000—02, rschrs. synthetic organic and inorganic chemist divsn., dynamic and energetic materials divsn., DE-1, High Explosive and Sci. Tech. Group, 2002—. Featured in 26 nat. and 13 internat. media appearances; contbr. articles to profl. jours. and patents. Recipient Found. Presdl. Scholarship award, SUNY, Geneseo, 1989—90, Outstanding Adult Student award, 1991—92, Postdoctoral Disting. Performance award, 2002, Dept. Chemistry Supplemental award, SUNY, Buffalo, 1992—93, Mattern-Tyler award, SUNY. Buffalo, 1995—96, Excellence in Tchg. award, 1996—97, R&D 100 award, Los Alamos Nat. Lab., 2005, 2006, Individual Disting. Licensing award, 2005, Individual Disting. Performance award, 2005, Health and Safety award, Nat. Registry Environ. Profls., 2006, Ernest Orlando Lawrence award in Chemistry, Dept. Energy, 2006, Internat. Medal of Honor, 2007, Best-in-Class Pollution Prevention award, Dept. Energy and Nat. Nuc. Security Assn., 2007, Alumni Assoc. award, U. NY, Geneseo, 2008, Best-in-class Polution Prevention award, Nat. Nuc. Security Assn., 2008, 2007, LA Nat. Lab., 2007, Polution Prevention LANL ward, 2007; named a MacArthur Fellow, John D. and Catherine T. MacArthur Found., 2007; named one of Outstanding Scientists of 21st Century, 2004, 2006, 2000 Outstanding Scientists of the 21st Century, 2005; fellow, Los Alamos Nat. Lab., 2001—; Found. Presdl. scholar Co-curricular activities, SUNY, Geneseo, 1989—90, Paul R. Neureiter scholar, 1990—91, Gordon M. Harris Chemistry fellow, SUNY, Buffalo, 1992—95. Mem.: ACS, Pi Mu Epsilon. Buddhist. Achievements include patents in field; discovery of green primary explosives; high-temperature secondary explosives, carbon nanomaterials, nitrogen-rich carbon nitride anano-materials, and metallic nano-foams. Personal E-mail: osmium2003@yahoo.com. Business E-Mail: mhuynh@los-alamos.net.

HWANG, CHUN, cardiologist; b. South Korea, June 10, 1955; Grad., U. Brasilia, Brazil, 1976—82, U. Hosp., Brasilila, 1983—84. Cert. Am. Bd. Internal Medicine, subspecialty cardiovasc. disease, clinical cardiac electrophysiology. Intern straight medicine King-Drew LA County Med. Ctr., 1987—88, resident jr. asst., 1988—89, resident sr. asst., 1989—90; fellow King-Drew/UCLA Hypertension Rsch. Ctr., LA, 1985—87; fellow cardiology & electrophysiology Cedars-Sinai Med. Ctr./UCLA, LA, 1990—93; cardiologist Ctrl. Utah Clinic, Provo; asst. prof. medicine UCLA. Mem.: Utah Med. Assn., Am. Coll. Cardiology, Electrophysiology Soc., North Am. Soc. Pacing and Electrophysiology, Am. Heart Assn. Office: Central Utah Clinic Heart Ctr 1055 N 500 W Ste 100 Provo UT 84604 Office Phone: 801-373-4366. Office Fax: 801-429-8191.

HWANG, CORDELIA JONG, retired chemist; b. NYC, July 14, 1942; d. Goddard and Lilly (Fung) Jong; m. Warren C. Hwang, Mar. 29, 1969; 1 child, Kevin. BA, Barnard Coll., 1964; MS, SUNY, Stony Brook, 1969. Rsch. asst. Columbia U., NYC, 1964-66; analytical chemist Veritron West, Inc., Chatsworth, Calif., 1969-70; asst. lab. dir., chief chemist Pomeroy, Johnston & Bailey Environ. Engrs., Pasadena, Calif., 1970-76; chemist Met. Water Dist. So. Calif., LA, 1976-79, rsch. chemist, 1980-91, sr. chemist, 1992—2000, sr. rsch. chemist, 2001—05. Mem. Joint Task Group on Instrumental Identification of Taste and Odor Compounds, 1983-85, Joint Task Group on Nitrosamines, 2004; instr. Citrus Coll., 1974-76; chmn. Joint Task Group on Disinfection by-products: chlorine, 1990. Mem. AAUW (chmn. edn. found. Palos Verdes Peninsula br. 2005—08), Am. Chem. Soc., Am. Water Works Assn. (life).

HWANG, JOHN DZEN, information systems educator; b. Shanghai, Sept. 8, 1941; came to U.S., 1956; s. John Ding and Sylvia H.; m. Gloria Hoi-Hoon Lum, June 17, 1967; children: John Dar, Andrew Cherng, Audrey Ming. BSEE, U. Calif., Berkeley, 1964; MA, Oreg. State U., 1966, PhD, 1968. Ops. rschr. Army Weapons Command, Rock Island, Ill., 1970-71; program mgr. Army Air Mobility R&D Lab., Moffett Field, Calif., 1971-75; divsn. chief Def. Comm. Agy., Arlington, Va., 1975-82; assoc. dir. Fed. Emergency Mgmt. Agy., Washington, 1982-96; gen. mgr. Info. Tech. Agy. City of L.A., 1996-99; prof. dept. info. sys. Calif. State U., Long Beach, 1999—. Editor: Analytical Concepts of Command and Control, 1976. Capt. U.S. Army, 1968-70. Univ. fellow Dept. Def., Harvard Bus. Sch., Boston, 1981. Home: 2157 Moreno Dr Los Angeles CA 90039-3061 E-mail: jdhwang@csulb.edu.

HYBL, WILLIAM JOSEPH, lawyer, foundation administrator; b. Des Moines, July 16, 1942; s. Joseph A. and Geraldine (Evans) H.; m. Kathleen (Horrigan), June 6, 1967; children: William J. Jr., Kyle Horrigan. BA, Colo. Coll., 1964; JD, U. Colo., 1967. Bar: Colo. 1967. Asst. dist. atty. 4th Jud. Dist. El Paso and Teller Counties, 1970—72; pres., dir. Garden City Co.; chmn., CEO, trustee El Pomar Found., Colorado Springs, Colo., 1973—; vice chmn. Broadmoor Hotel, Inc., 1987—; pres. emeritus U.S. Olympic Com., 1991—92, pres., 1996—2000; chmn. and CEO U.S. Olympic Found., 2002—; vice chmn. IFES, 2009—. Dir. USAA, San Antonio, Guest Svcs. Fairfax, Va., First Bank Holding Co., Lakewood, Colo.; mem. Colo. Ho. of Reps., 1972-73; spl. counsel The White House, Washington, 1981; U.S. Rep. to 56th Gen. Assembly of UN, 2001-02; bd. dirs. Vail Valley Found. Pres. Air Force Acad. Found.; sec., vice chmn., US Advisory Commn. on Pub. Diplomacy, 1990-97, chmn., 2008-; civilian aide emeritus to sec. of army, 1986—; bd. trustees Colo. Coll. Capt. US Army. 1967-69. Republican. Office Phone: 719-577-5712. Business E-Mail: wjhybl@elpomar.org.

HYMAN, MILTON BERNARD, lawyer; b. LA, Nov. 19, 1941; s. Herbert and Lillian (Rakowitz) Hyman; m. Sheila Goldman, July 4, 1965; children: Lauren Davida, Micah Howard. BA in Econs. with highest honors, UCLA, 1963; JD magna cum laude, Harvard U., 1966. Bar: Calif. 1967. Assoc. Irell & Manella LLP, LA, 1970-73, ptnr., 1973—. Co-author: Partnerships and Associations: A Policy Critique of the Morrisey Regulations, 1976, Consolidated Returns: Summary of Tax Considerations in Acquisition of Common Parent of Subsidiary Member of Affiliated Group, 1980, Tax Aspects of Corporate Debt Exchanges, Recapitalization and Discharges, 1982, Tax Strategies for Leveraged Buyouts and Other Corporate Acquisitions, 1986, Preservation and Use of Net Operating Losses and Other Tax Attributes in a Consolidated Return Context, rev. edit., 1992, Collier on Bankruptcy Taxation, 1992, Real Estate Workouts and Bankruptcies, 1993, Current Corporate Bankruptcy Tax Issues, 1993, Tax Strategies for Corporate Acquisitions, Dispositions, Financing, Joint Ventures, Reorganizations, and Restructurings, 1995; author: A Transactional Encounter with the Partnership Rules of Subchapter K: The Effects of the Tax Reform Act of 1984, 1984, Net Operating Losses and Other Tax Attributed of Corporate Clients, 1987. Past pres., bd. dirs. Sinai Temple, West Los Angeles, Calif. Capt. JAGC, U.S. Army, 1967-70. Sheldon traveling fellow Harvard U., 1966-67. Mem. ABA (chmn. com. affiliated and related corps. 1981-83, chmn. corp. tax com. 1999-2000), Calif. State Bar Assn., Am. Law Inst. (fed. income tax project tax adv. group 1976—), Masons, Phi Beta Kappa. Jewish. Office: Irell & Manella LLP Ste 900 1800 Avenue Of The Stars Los Angeles CA 90067-4276

HYMAN, URSULA H., lawyer; BA, Immaculate Heart Coll., 1973; MEd, Loyola Marymount Coll., 1977; JD, U. So. Calif., 1983. Bar: Calif. 1983. With Latham & Watkins, LA, 1983—, ptnr., 1990—. Founding mem. ad hoc com. Chpt. 9 Reform. Bd. dirs. Calif. Philharmonic. Named LA Super Lawyers, LA Mag., 2004, 2005, 2006. Mem.: ABA, L.A. Women's Lawyers Assns., Nat. Assn. Bond Lawyers, L.A. County Bar Assn., State Bar Calif., Order of the Coif. Office: Latham Watkins 355 S Grand Ave Los Angeles CA 90071-1560 Office Phone: 213-485-1234. Business E-Mail: ursula.hyman@lw.com.

IACOCCA, LEE (LIDO ANTHONY), venture capitalist, retired automotive executive; b. Allentown, Pa., Oct. 15, 1924; s. Nicola and Antoinette (Perrotto) I.; m. Mary McCleary, Sept. 29, 1956 (dec. May 16, 1983), children: Kathryn Lisa Hentz, Lia Antoinette Nagy; m. Peggy Johnson, Apr. 17, 1986 (annulled 1987); m. Darrien Earle, March 30, 1991 (div. 1994) BS, Lehigh U., 1945; ME, Princeton U., 1946. With Ford Motor Co., Dearborn, Mich., 1946-78, successively mem. field sales staff, various merchandising and tng. activities, asst. dirs. sales mgr. Phila., dist. sales mgr. Washington, 1946-56, truck mktg. mgr. div. office, 1956-57, car mktg. mgr., 1957-60, vehicle market mgr., 1960, v.p., gen. mgr., 1960-65, v.p. car & truck group, 1965-69, exec. v.p., 1967-69, pres., 1970-78; pres., COO Chrysler Corp., Highland Park, Mich., 1978-79, chmn., CEO, 1979-93; prin. Iacocca Partners, 1994—; pres. Lee Iacocca & Associates, Inc.; founder EV Global Motors, 1999—, Olivio Premium Products, 2000—. Co-author: (with William Novak) Iacocca: An Autobiography, 1984, (with Sonny Kleinfeld) Talking Straight, 1988, (with Catherine Whitney) Where Have All the Leaders Gone?, 2007; actor (TV appearances) Miami Vice, 1986 Chmn. The Statue of Liberty-Ellis Island Found., 1982; founder, The Iacocca Found., 1984-Wallace Meml. fellow Princeton U. Mem. NAE, Tau Beta Pi. Clubs: Detroit Athletic. Office: Lee A Iacocca 16760 Schoenborn St North Hills CA 91343-6108 also: Iacocca Foundation 17 Arlington St 4th Fl Boston MA 02116

IAMELE, RICHARD THOMAS, retired law librarian; b. Newark, Jan. 29, 1942; BA, Loyola U., LA, 1963; MSLS, U. So. Calif., 1967; JD, Southwestern U., LA, 1976. Bar: Calif. 1977. Cataloger U. So. Calif., LA, 1967-71; asst. cataloger L.A. County Law Libr., 1971-77, asst. ref. libr., 1977-78, asst. libr., 1978-80, libr. dir., 1980—2005; ret., 2005. Mem. ABA, Am. Assn. Law Librs., Calif. Libr. Assn., So. Calif. Assn. Law Librs., Coun. Calif. County Law Librs. (pres. 1981-82, 88-90). Office Phone: 213-629-3531.

IAPALUCCI, SAMUEL H., financial executive; b. Cresson, Pa., July 19, 1952; s. Anthony F. and Dorthy (Quartz) I.; m. Berniece Reichert, June 5, 1976; children: Amanda Berniece, Cara Elizabeth. BS, St. Francis Coll., Loretto, Pa., 1974; MBA, Duquesne U., 1980. CPA, Pa. Audit sr. Coopers & Lybrand, Pitts., 1974-76; asst. v.p. Equibank, N.A., Pitts., 1976-78; with Allegheny Internat., Inc., Pitts., 1978-91, v.p., treas., 1987-90, v.p., CFO, 1990, cons., 1990-91; v.p., CFO OHM Corp., Findlay, Ohio, 1991—; CFO CH2M Hill Companies, Greenwood Village, CO, sr. v.p., CFO, sec. Mem. AICPA, Pa. Inst. CPAs, Fin. Execs. Inst., Findlay Country Club. Avocations: golf, tennis, reading.

IBARRA, IRENE M., foundation administrator; b. 1952; m. Armando Quiroz. JD, U. Wash.; MPA, U. Denver, MS in Social Work in Community Svcs. & Social Planning; sr. exec. program, Harvard U. Dep. mgr. Dept. of Social Services City of Denver, 1984—87; former exec. dir. Dept. Health & Human Services State of Colo., 1987—91; atty., corp. & bus. law Hillis, Clark, Martin and Peterson, Seattle; COO Alameda Alliance of Health, 1996—98; CEO Alameda Alliance for Health, 1998—2003; dir. LA Health Action, 2003—05; exec. v.p. Calif. Endowment, 2005—06; pres., CEO The Colorado Trust, Denver, 2006—. Mem. Calif. Performance Review Commn. Trustee Blue Shield of Calif. Found., Casey Family Programs, 2003—. Office: The Colorado Trust 1600 Sherman St Denver CO 80203 E-mail: irene@coloradotrust.org.

ICE, JOYCE, museum director; PhD in Anthropology and Folklore, U. Tex. Austin. Folklorist Del. County Hist. Assn., Delhi, NY; asst. dir. Mus. Internat. Folk Art, Santa Fe, 1990, dir., 1999—. Mgr. devel. of programming Milner Plaza; involved in devel. and planning Santa Fe Internat. Folk Art Market; panelist Nat. Endowments; mem. state art councils, N.Mex., Colo., NY. Bd. mem. Fund for Folk Culture. Mem.: AAM/Internat. Coun. Museums (nat. bd. mem.). Office: Mus Internat Folk Art PO Box 2087 Santa Fe NM 87504-2087 Office Phone: 505-476-1200. Office Fax: 505-476-1300. Business E-Mail: joyce.ice@state.nm.us.

ICE CUBE, (O'SHEA JACKSON), rap artist, actor; b. LA, June 15, 1969; s. Hosea and "Moms" Doris Jackson.; m. Kim Jackson, 1992; 4 children. Attended, Phoenix Inst. Tech. Founder Lynch Mob Records, LA. Founder Cubevision Prodn. Co. Albums: (with NWA) Straight Outta Compton, 1989, (solo) Amerikkka's Most Wanted, 1990, Kill At Will, Death Certificate, 1991, The Predator, 1992, Lethal Injection, 1993, War & Peace, Vol. 1, 1998, War & Peace, Vol. 2, 2000, Laugh Now, Cry Later, 2006; Actor (films) Boyz n the Hood, 1991, Trespass, 1992, Higher Learning, 1995, Anaconda, 1997, I Got the Hook Up, 1998, Three Kings, 1999, Ghosts of Mars, 2001, Barbershop, 2002, Torque, 2004, xXx: State of the Union, 2005, First Sunday, 2008; actor, screenwriter (films) The Glass Shield, 1995; actor, prodr. (films)All About the Benjamins, 2002, Friday After Next, 2002, Barbershop 2: Back in Business, 2004, Are We There Yet?, 2005, Are We Done Yet, 2007, The Longshots, 2008; actor, exec. prodr. (films) Friday, 1995, Dangerous Ground, 1997, The Players Club, 1998, Next Friday, 2000, Barbershop 2: Back in Business, 2005; exec. prodr. (films) Beauty Shop, 2005. Office: Priority Records 6430 W Sunset Blvd Los Angeles CA 90028-7901

ICE-T, (TRACY MARROW), rap artist, actor; b. Newark, Feb. 16, 1958; m. Nicole Austin, 2004; children: Tracy Marrow Jr., Letesha Marrow. Albums: Rhyme Pays, 1987, O.G. Original Gangster, 1991, (with King Tee) Havin' a T Party, 1991, Body Count, 1992, Home Invasion, 1993, The Classic Collection, 1993, (with Body Count) Born Dead, 1994, 7th Deadly Sin, 1999, Greatest Hits: The Evidence, 2001, Gang Culture, 2004, Gangsta Rap, 2006; actor: (films) Breakin', 1984, Breakin' 2, 1984, New Jack City, 1991, Ricochet, 1991, Trespass, 1992, Why Colors?, 1992, Surviving the Game, 1994, Tank Girl, 1995, Johnny Mnemonic, 1995, Mean Guns, 1997, The Deli, 1997, Beyond Utopia, 1997, Crazy Six, 1998, Final Voyage, 1999, Corrupt, 1999, The Wrecking Crew, 1999, Sonic Impact, 1999, The Heist, 1999, Frezno Smooth, 1999, Urban Menace, 1999, Stealth Fighter, 1999, Corrupt, 1999, Guardian, 2000, Gangland, 2000, Luck of the Draw, 2000, The Alternates, 2000, Stranded, 2001, Kept, 2001, Crime Partners, 2001, 3000 miles to Graceland, 2001, Point Doom, 2001, Deadly Rhapsody, 2001, 'R Xmas, 2001, Ticker, 2001, Out Kold, 2001, Ablaze, 2001, On the Edge, 2002, Tracks, 2002, (TV films) Exiled, 1998, The Disciples, 2000, (TV Series) Players, 1997-98, Law and Order: Special Victims Unit, 2000-; author: The Iceberg/Freedom of Speech, Just Watch What You Say, 1989, The Ice Opinion, 1994. Office: Priority Records 6430 W Sunset Blvd Los Angeles CA 90028-7901

IDEKER, TREY, computational and molecular biologist; b. Memphis, June 24, 1972; s. Raymond Edwin Ideker, Mary Lou Ideker; m. Kristyn Gray. BS in Elec. Engring. and Computer Sci., MIT, 1994, MS in Elec. Engring. and Computer Sci., 1995; PhD in Molecular Biotechnology, U. Wash., 2001. Rsch. scientist Loral Infrared and Imaging Sys., Lexington, Mass., 1991—95; database cons. Klinikum Rechts der Isar, Munich, 1995—96; rsch. fellow Whitehead Inst., Cambridge, 2001—03; asst. prof. to assoc. prof. dept. bioengineering U. Calif., San Diego, 2003—. Cons. Genstruct, Cambridge, 2001—, Pfizer, Cambridge, 2001—. Fellow, Achievement Rewards for Coll. Scientists, 1996—98. Mem.: Internat. Soc. for Computational Biology. Achievements include pioneering research in the nascent field of systems biology; invention of methods for modeling cellular systems and circuitry. Avocations: running, piano, guitar, scuba diving, travel. Office: U Calif San Diego Bioengring 9500 Gilman Dr La Jolla CA 92093-0412 E-mail: trey@bioeng.ucsd.edu.

IDLE, ERIC, actor, scriptwriter, film producer, lyricist; b. South Shields, Eng., Mar. 29, 1943; Pres. The Cambridge Footlights, 1964-65. TV shows include The Frost Report, Monty Python's Flying Circus, 1969-74, Rutland Weekend TV, 1975, Suddenly Susan, 1999-2000; films include And Now For Something Completely Different, 1971, Monty Python and the Holy Grail, 1975, The Rutles, 1978, Monty Python's Life of Brian, 1979, Monty Python Live at the Hollywood Bowl, 1982, Monty Python's The Meaning of Life, 1983, Yellowbeard, 1983, National Lampoon's European Vacation, 1985, Transformers: The Movie, 1986, The Adventures of Baron Munchausen, 1988, Nuns on the Run, 1990, Too Much Sun, 1991, Mom and Dad Save the World, 1993, Splitting Heirs, 1993, Casper, 1995, The Wind in the Willows, 1996, Burn Hollywood Burn, 1998, Dudley Do-Right, 1999, South Park: Bigger, Longer and Uncut (voice), 1999; writer (broadway plays): Spamalot, 2005 (Drama Desk award, outstanding lyrics, 2005, Grammy award, Best Musical Show Album, 2006); author The Greedy Bastard Diary: A Comic Tour of America, 2005. Office: Grant & Tani Inc 9100 Wilshire Blvd Ste 1000 Beverly Hills CA 90212-3415 also: William Morris 151 S El Camino Dr Beverly Hills CA 90212-2704

IERARDI, STEPHEN JOHN, physician; b. Honolulu, July 5, 1960; s. Ernest John and Robert Ann (Hackett) I.; m. Erica Ewing, May 28, 1989; children: Daphne Alexandra, Weston Eric. BA in Biology, Williams Coll., 1982; MD, U. Rochester, 1986. Diplomate Am. Bd. Family Physicians. Intern U. Calif. at Irvine Med. Ctr., Orange, 1986-87, resident, 1987-89, chief resident, 1988-89; physician Laguna Hills, Calif., 1989—; med. dir. Lake Forest Nursing Ctr., 1993-96. Chief of medicine Saddleback Meml. Med. Ctr., Laguna Hills, 1996, chmn. family practice, 1994-96. Recipient UCI Care awards Univ. Calif. at Irvine Med. Ctr., 1986-89. Fellow Am. Acad. Family Physicians, AMA (Physician Recognition award 1996); mem. Am. Acad. Family Physicians, Calif. Acad. Family Physicians. Avocations: surfing, sailing, windsurfing, skiing, travel. Home: 13 Pacifico Laguna Hills CA 92677-4242 Office: Saddleback Family Medicine 24411 Health Center Dr Laguna Hills CA 92653-3633

IGE, DAVID Y., state legislator; b. Honolulu, Jan. 15, 1957; m to Dawn; children: Lauren, Amy & Matthew. Hawaii State Representative, 43rd District, 1986-93, chairman, Education Committee, formerly, Hawaii House Representative; member, Honolulu Financial Center Task Force, Task Force on Hawaiian Serv, Comn to Commemorate the 90th Anniversary of Okinawan Immigration, currently; Hawaii State Senator, 17th District, 1995-2002, 16th District, 2003-, chairman, Intergovt Affairs Committee, currently, vice chairman, Media, Arts, Sci, and Technology Committee, currently, Hawaii State Senate.Bd director, Pacific Space Center, currently; senior administrator, GTE-Hawaiian Telephone Co, currently; electronics engr/analyst, Pacific Analysis Corp, currently. Inst Electrical & Electronic Engr; Pearl City Community Association; Newtown Estates Community Association. Democrat. Mailing: Hawaii State Capitol 415 S Beretania St Rm 215 Honolulu HI 96813 also: PO Box 2999 Aiea HI 96701 Fax: 808-586-6231. E-mail: sendige@capitol.hawaii.gov.

IGE, MARSHALL, state legislator; b. Honolulu, Sept. 10, 1954; Student, Windward C.C., Kaneohe, 1974; B in Edn., U. Hawaii, Manoa, 1978. Mem. Hawaii Ho. of Reps., Honolulu, 1978-96, asst. majority floor leader, chair youth and elderly affairs com., 1982, vice spkr. of house, liaison to spkr., mem. house fin. com., 1984, asst. majority floor leader, 1986, 88, 90; mem. Hawaii Senate, Honolulu, 1996—, co-chair com. on govt. ops. and housing, 1996, mem. ways and means com., mem. edn. com., 1996, vice chair com. on labor and environ., 1998, mem. econ. devel. com., mem. ways and means com., 1998. Office: State Capitol 415 S Beretania St Honolulu HI 96813-2407

IGER, BOB (ROBERT ALLEN IGER), entertainment company executive; b. NYC, Feb. 10, 1951; s. Arthur and Mimi Iger; m. Willow Bay, Oct. 7, 1995; children: Max, William;children from previous marriage: Kate, Amanda. BA magna cum laude, Ithaca Coll., 1973. Studio supr. ABC-TV, 1974—76; various positions ABC-TV Sports, 1976—85; v.p. prog. planning, devel. ABC Sports, 1985—87, v.p. prog. planning & acquisition, 1987—88; exec. v.p. ABC TV Network Grp., 1988—89, pres., 1992—94, ABC Entertainment, 1989—92; exec. v.p. Capital Cities/ABC Inc., NYC, 1993—94, pres., COO,

1994—96; pres. ABC, Inc., NYC, 1996—99; chmn. ABC Grp., 1999—2000; pres. Walt Disney Internat., 1999—2000; pres., COO The Walt Disney Co., Burbank, Calif., 2000—05, pres., CEO, 2005—. Bd. dirs. The Walt Disney Co., 2000—, Hulu, 2009—, Lincoln Ctr. Performing Arts, NYC; bd. trustees Am. Film Inst. Bd., Mus. TV and Radio, Ithaca Coll. Trustee Ithaca Coll. Recipient Trustee award, Nat. Acad. TV Arts & Scis., 2005; named one of 50 Who Matter Now, CNNMoney.com Bus. 2.0, 2006, 25 Most Powerful People in Bus., Fortune Mag., 2007. Office: The Walt Disney Co 500 S Buena Vista St Burbank CA 91521-0001*

IGINLA, JAROME, professional hockey player; b. Edmonton, Alta., Can., July 1, 1977; Right wing Calgary Flames, 1996—, capt., 2003—. Mem. Team Canada, Olympic Games, Salt Lake City, 2002, Torino, Italy, 06, Team Canada, World Cup of Hockey, 2004; player NHL All-Star Game, 2002—04. Recipient Maurice Rocket Richard Trophy, NHL, 2002, Art Ross Trophy, 2002, Lester B. Pearson Award, 2002, King Clancy Meml. Trophy, 2004, Espy Award for Best NHL Player, 2002, 2004, NHL All-Star Game, 2002—04; co-recipient Maurice Rocket Richard Trophy, NHL, 2004; named to All-Rookie Team, 1997, First All-Star Team, 2002, 2008, NHL All-Star Game, 2008, 2009. Achievements include being a member of gold medal Canadian Hockey team, Salt Lake City Olympic Games, 2002; being a member of World Cup Champion Team Canada, 2004; becoming the Calgary Flames career goal-scoring leader, 2008. Office: Calgary Flames PO Box 1540 Stn M Calgary AB T2P 3B9 Canada*

IGLESIAS, DAVID CLAUDIO, former prosecutor; b. Jan. 1958; m. Cynthia J. Iglesias; 4 children. BA, Wheaton Coll., 1980; JD, U. N.Mex. Asst. atty. gen. N.Mex Atty. Gen. Office; asst. city atty. City of Albuquerque, 1991—94; spl. asst. to sec. transp. White Ho. Fellowship, 1995; chief counsel N.Mex Risk Mgmt. Legal Office, 1995—98; gen. counsel N.Mex Taxation and Revenue Dept., 1998—2001; assoc. Walz and Assoc., Albuquerque; US atty. N.Mex US Dept. Justice, 2001—06. Comdr. JAGC USNR.

IGLESIAS, DON, school system administrator; BA, Univ. Calif., Berkeley; MA, Univ. So. Calif. Tchr., sch. counselor, asst. principal Berryessa Sch. Dist., San Jose, Calif.; principal, dir. curriculum, asst. supt. Santa Cruz City Sch. Dist.; dep. supt. San Jose Unified School Dist., supt., 2004—. Office: San Jose Unified School District Office of the Superintendent 855 Lenzen Ave San Jose CA 95126

IGLESIAS, ENRIQUE (ENRIQUE MIGUEL IGLESIAS PREYSLER), singer; b. Madrid, May 8, 1975; arrived in US, 1983; s. Julio Iglesias and Isabel Preysler. Attended, U. Miami. Singer: (albums) Enrique Iglesias, 1995 (Grammy award for Best Latin Pop Performance, 1997), Version en Italiano, 1996, Master Pistas, 1997, Vivir, 1997, Canta Em Portugues, 1998, Cosas del Amor, 1998, Enrique Iglesias, 1998, Enrique, 1999, Escape, 2001, Quizás, 2002, Seven, 2003, Insomniac, 2007, 95/08 Exitos, 2008, Greatest Hits, 2008; actor: (films) Once Upon a Time in Mexico, 2003. Recipient Favorite Latin Artist Performance award, Am. Music Awards, 1999, Favorite Latin Artist award, 2001, 2002, 2003, 2008, Favorite Latino Artist award, Blockbuster Awards, 2000, Most Fashionable Male Artist award, VH1/Vogue Fashion Awards, 2000, Best-Selling Pop Male Artist, World Music Awards, 2002, Best-Selling Latin Male Artist, 2002; named Top Hot Latin Tracks Artist, Billboard, 1997, Top Latin 50 Artists, 1997, Top Latin Pop Album Artist, 1997, 1999, Top Hot Latin Pop Tracks Artist, 1997, Top Hot Latin Tracks Artist, 1999. Office: c/o The Firm 9465 Wilshire Blvd 6th Fl Beverly Hills CA 90212-2605

IGNARRO, LOUIS J., pharmacology educator; b. Bklyn., May 31, 1941; m. Sharon Elizabeth Williams, July 1997; 1 child from previous marriage. BA in Pharmacy, Columbia U., 1962; PhD in Pharmacology, U. Minn., 1966; degrees (hon.), U. Madrid, Lund U., U. Gent, U. NC. Postdoctoral rsch., Lab. Chem. Pharmacology Nat. Heart, Lung and Blood Inst., NIH; head, biochem, anti-inflammatory program Geigy Pharmaceuticals, 1968—73; asst. prof., pharmacology Tulane Univ. Sch. Medicine, New Orleans, 1973—79, prof., pharmacology, 1979—85; prof. dept. molecular and med. pharmacology UCLA Sch. Medicine, 1985—. Contbr. articles to profl. jours. Recipient Edward G. Schlieder Found. award, 1973, Merck Rsch. award, 1974, Rsch. Career Devel. award, USPHS, 1975—80, Nobel prize in physiology or medicine, 1998; fellow postdoctoral, NIH, 1966—68. Mem.: NAS, Alpha Omega Alpha (hon.). Achievements include research in biochemical, physiological, and pathophysioilogical roles of nitric oxide and cyclic GMP in mammalian cell function; the transcriptional, translational and catalytic regulation of constitutive and inducible nitric oxide synthases; the role of other biochemical pathways in the regulation of biosynthesis and metabolism of nitric oxide; the biochemical and chemical mechanisms by which nitric oxide elicits cytotoxic effects on invading target cells and microorganisms; the role of nitric oxide as a neurotransmitter in non-adrenergic non-cholinergic neurons innervating various issues. Office: UCLA Sch Medicine Dept Molecular & Med Pharmacology 23-315 Chs 10833 Leconte Ave Los Angeles CA 90095-1735

IGO, GEORGE JEROME, physics professor; b. Greeley, Colo., Sept. 2, 1925; s. Henry J. and Ida J. (Danielsen) I.; m. Nancy Tebow, May 12, 1953; children: Saffron, Peter Alexander. AB, Harvard Coll., 1949; MS, U. Calif., Berkeley, 1951, Phd, 1953. Postdoctoral Yale Univ., 1954, Brook Haven Nat. Lab., Upton, NY, 1955-57; instr. Stanford Univ., Palo Alto, Calif., 1957-59; guest prof. Univ. Heidelberg, Germany, 1960; staff mem. Lawrence Berkeley (Calif.) Lab., 1961-66, Los Alamos (N.Mex.) Nat. Lab., 1966-68; prof. UCLA, 1969—. With U.S. Army, 1944-46. Recipient Fulbright Travel award, 1960, Saclay, France, 1970, Sr. Scientist award Alexander von Humboldt Found., 1991, 95. Fellow: Am. Phys. Soc. Office: UCLA Dept Physics 405 Hilgard Ave Los Angeles CA 90095-9000 Office Phone: 213-825-1306. Business E-Mail: igo@physics.ucla.edu.

IHARA, LES, JR., state legislator; b. Honolulu, Apr. 19, 1951; son of Les Seichi Ihara & Shirley Sonoda I; single. Deleg & vice president, Hawaii State Const Conv, 78; member, Hawaii State Democratic Cent Committee, 80-86; chairman, Oahu Democratic Committee, Hawaii, 82-84, 90-94; delegate, Democratic Nat Conv, 84; Hawaii State Representative, 26th District, 1986-92, 19th District, 1993-94, Majority Floor Leader, 1993-94, Hawaii House Representative; Hawaii State Senator, 10th District, 1995-2002, 9th District, 2003-, vice chairman, Human Serv Committee, currently, Labor Committee, currently, Hawaii State Senate.Community developer, resource coordinator & communications director, formerly. Kaimuki Bus & Prof Association; Alabama Wai Moiliili McCully Neighbors; Friends for Diamond Head (director, 87-); Lions; Kapahulu Chiho Jinkai; Kaimuki-Waialae YMCA; Waikiki Residents Association; Kapahulu Bus Association. Democrat. Mailing: 1139 9th Ave #1204 Honolulu HI 96816 also: Hawaii State Senate 415 S Beretania St Rm 220 Honolulu HI 96813 Office Phone: 808-586-6250. Fax: 808-586-6251. E-mail: senihara@capitol.hawaii.gov.

IHRIG, JUDSON LA MOURE, chemist; b. Santa Maria, Calif., Nov. 5, 1925; s. Harry Karl and Luella (LaMoure) I.; m. Gwendolyn Adele Montz, July 22, 1950; children: Kristin, Neil Marshall. BS, Haverford Coll., 1949; MA, Princeton U., 1951, PhD, 1952. Asst. prof. chemistry U. Hawaii, 1952-58, assoc. prof., 1958-72, prof., 1972-94, dir. honors program, 1958-64, 87-95, dir. liberal studies program, 1973-79, chmn. chemistry dept., 1981-86, prof. emeritus, 1994—. Cons. chemistry local firms. Author publs. in field. Served with AUS, 1945-46. Mem. Am. Chem. Soc., Phi Beta Kappa, Sigma Xi. Home: 386 Wailupe Cir Honolulu HI 96821-1525 Office: U Hawaii 2545 The Mall Honolulu HI 96822-2233 Office Phone: 808-956-4590.

IKEDA, CLYDE JUNICHI, plastic and reconstructive surgeon; b. Kobe, Japan, 1951; s. Paul Tamotsu and Kazu Ikeda. BA, SUNY, Binghamton, 1973; MD, N.Y. Med. Coll., Valhalla, 1979. Resident St. Vincent Hosp., NYC, 1979-83, Francis Meml. Hosp., San Francisco, 1983-86; med. dir. Burn Ctr. St. Francis Meml. Hosp., San Francisco, 1992—2001, med. examiner, 1993—, med. dir. Wound Healing Ctr., 1994—2001; dir. Hosp. de la Familie, 2000—06, v.p., med. dir., 2006—. Asst. clin. prof. plastic surgery U. Calif., San Francisco, 1998-2003, assoc. clin. prof. plastic surgery, 2003—; adj. clin. prof. surgery Stanford Sch. Medicine, 2004—. Recipient Edward Weisband Disting. Alumni award, Binghamton U., 2003, medal of honor, Alumni Assn. N.Y. Med. Coll., 2004, Outstanding Physician award, Med. Bd. Calif., 2007. Fellow ACS. Office: 1199 Bush St Ste 640 San Francisco CA 94109-5977

ILETT, FRANK, JR., trucking executive, educator; b. Ontario, Oreg., June 21, 1940; s. Frank Kent and Lela Alice (Siver) I.; m. Donna L. Andlovec, Apr. 3, 1971; children: James Frank, Jordan Lee. BA, U. Wash., 1962; MBA, U. Chgo., 1969. CPA Idaho, Ill., Wash. Acct. Ernst & Young, Boise, Cleve., Spokane, 1962-69, mgr. Boise, 1970-72, regional mgr. San Francisco, 1972-73; treas. Interstate Mack, Inc., Boise, 1973-81, pres., CEO, 1981-82; pres. Interstate NationLease, Inc., Boise, 1975-81, Contract Carriers, Inc., Boise, 1983-89, Ilett Transp. Co., Boise, 1985-90; chmn. Carriers/West, Inc., Salem, Oreg., 1986-89; CFO, White GMC Trucks, 1988-92; v.p., CFO, May Trucking Co., Payette, Idaho, 1992-94; acct., mng. ptnr. F. Ilett, PLLC, Boise, 1994—. Spl. lectr. Boise State U., 1964-67, 94—, St. Mary's Grad. Sch., Moraga, Calif., 1989-92; cons. Calif. Hosp. Commn., 1973, Idaho Hosp. Assn., 1974; chmn. Mack Truck Western Region Distbr. Coun., 1979-82; nat. distbr. adv. com. Mack Trucks, Inc., 1980-82; dir. stds. enforcement Idaho State Bd. Accountancy, 1983-84; contr. Idaho Stampede, 2002—. Contbr. articles to profl. jours. Recipient Outstanding Prof. award KPMG, 2003, 05; named Arthur Andersen Outstanding Acctg. Prof., 1996, 2001 Mem.: Inst. Mgmt. Accts., SAR, Gen. Soc. Mayflower Descs., Crane Creek Country Club, Shriners, Masons, Alpha Kappa Psi (Outstanding Bus. Prof. award 1997, named Disting. Faculty Mem., Coll. Bus. 2002). Episcopalian. Home: 1701 Harrison Blvd Boise ID 83702-1015 Office: 1910 University Dr Boise ID 83725 Home Phone: 208-389-4624; Office Phone: 208-426-2568. Business E-Mail: filett@boisestate.edu.

ILL, CHARLES, III, information technology executive; BS in Mech. Engring., Lehigh U., MBA in Fin. Sales and mktg. IBM, 1978—2003, former v.p. worldwide software geo. sales, mktg. and tech. team; exec. v.p. worldwide sales BEA Systems, Inc., San Jose, Calif., 2003—. Office: BEA Systems Inc 2315 N First St San Jose CA 95131

ILLSTON, SUSAN Y., federal judge; b. 1948; BA, Duke U., 1970; JD, Stanford U., 1973. Ptnr. Cotchett, Illston & Pitre, San Francisco, 1973-95; judge U.S. Dist. Ct. (no. dist.) Calif., San Francisco, 1995—. Author: Insurance Coverage in a Toxic Tort Case, A Guide to Toxic Torts, 1987, California Complex Litigation Manual, 1990. Active Legal Aid Soc. San Mateo County, Svc. League San Mateo County. Recipient Appreciation for Vol. Svcs. cert. No. Dist. Calif. Fed. Practice Program, 1989, Svc. and Appreciation cert. 1992. Mem. ABA, ATLA, Assn. Bus. Trial Lawyers, San Mateo County Bar Assn. (Eleanor Falvey award 1994), State Bar Calif. (mem. jud. coun., mem. ethics com. 1975-79, mem. com. on women in law 1985-87, mem. jud. nominees evaluation commn. 1988, mem. exec. com. on litigation 1990-93), Calif. Women Lawyers, Calif. Trial Lawyers Assn., Trial Lawyers for Pub. Justice. Office: US Dist Ct No Dist Calif PO Box 36060 450 Golden Gate Ave San Francisco CA 94102-3661

IMBER, RICHARD JOSEPH, physician, dermatologist; b. Darby, Pa., Apr. 9, 1944; s. Joseph and Geraldine (Frances) I.; m. Helen Lee Stick, Nov. 18, 1971. BS, U. Dayton, 1966; MD, Temple U., 1970. Diplomate Am. Bd. Dermatology. Intern Denver Presbyn. Med. Ctr., 1970-71; resident dept. dermatology U. Colo. Health Sci. Ctr., 1971-74; chief of dermatology USAF Acad., Colorado Springs, 1974-76; sr. staff dermatologist Colo. Permanente Med. Group, Denver, 1976-83; dermatologist Denver Skin Clinic, 1983—. Asst. clin. prof. dermatology U. Colo. Med. Sch., Denver, 1974—. Contbr. articles to profl. jours. Maj. USAF, 1974-76. Fellow Am. Acad. Dermatology; mem. Pacific Dermatologic Assn., Colo. Med. Soc., Denver Med. Soc., Colo. Dermatologic Soc. (sec.-treas. 1980, v.p. 1981, pres. 1982). Avocation: scuba diving. Home: 4020 S Bellaire St Englewood CO 80110-5028 Office: Denver Skin Clinic 2200 E 18th Ave Denver CO 80206-1205

IMBROGNO, CYNTHIA, judge; b. 1948; BA, Ind. U., Pa., 1970; JD cum laude, Gonzaga U., 1979. Law clk. to Hon. Justin L. Quackenbush U.S. Dist. Ct. (Wash. ea. dist.), 9th circuit, 1980-83; law clk. Wash. State Ct. of Appeals, 1984; civil rights staff atty. Ea. Dist. of Wash., 1984-85, complex litigation staff atty., 1986-88; with Preston, Thorgrimson, Shidler, Gates & Ellis, 1988-90, Perkins Coie, 1990-91; magistrate judge U.S. Dist. Ct. (Wash. ea. dist.), 9th circuit, Spokane, 1991—. Office: 740 US Courthouse 920 W Riverside Ave Spokane WA 99201-1010

IMHOFF, WALTER FRANCIS, retired investment banker; b. Denver, Aug. 7, 1931; s. Walter Peter and Frances Marie (Barkhausen) I.; m. Georgia Ruth Stewart, June 16, 1973; children: Stacy, Randy, Theresa, Michael, Robert. BSBA, Regis U., Denver, 1955; D Pub. Svc. (hon.), Regis U., 1991. Asst. v.p. Coughlin & Co., Denver, 1955-60; pres., chief exec. officer Hanifen, Imhoff Inc., Denver, 1960-2000; mng. dir. Stifel, Nicolaus & Co., 2000—07. Guest lectr. U. Colo., 1976 Trustee Regis Coll., 1975—95, treas., 1976—79, vice chmn., 1981, chmn., 1982—89, life trustee, 1998—; bd. dirs. NCCJ, 1980—89, chmn., 1986—89, life trustee, 1998—; bd. dirs. Arapahoe Libr. Found., 1990—94, Channel 6 Ednl. TV, treas., 1996—97, vice chmn., 1997—98, chmn., 1998—99; bd. dirs. Highland Hills Found., 1993—, Denver Area coun. Boy Scouts Am., 1986—, v.p., 1989—2003; bd. dirs. St. Joseph's Hosp., mem. exec. com., 1991, vice chmn., 1994, chmn., 1995—98; bd. dirs. Kempe Children's Found., 1992—2009, chmn., 1994—97; bd. dirs. 9 Who Care, 1998—2006, Caring for Colo., 2001—08; chmn. Colo. Concern, 1988—2007, St. Joseph Hosp. Found., 2004—07; chmn. exec. com. 2% Club, 2000—; trustee Irish Cmty. Ctr., 2001. Named Outstanding Alumnus Regis Coll., 1970 Mem. Bond Club Denver (pres. 1965), Colo. Mcpl. Bond Dealers Assn. (pres. 1973), Mid-Continent Securities Industry Assn. (dir. 1972-75), Securities Industry Assn. (chmn. S.W. region 1991-95, dir. 1993-96), Nat. Assn. Security Dealers, Pub. Securities Assn. (dir. 1972-75), Denver C. of C. (bd. dirs. 1986-91, treas. 1989-91), Rose Hosp. Found., Centennial C. of C. (vice chmn.), NCCJ, Alpha Kappa Psi, Alpha Sigma Nu. (Daniel Ritchie Ethics Bus. award 2008) Clubs: Denver (pres. 1981-82). Republican. Roman Catholic. Home: 10432 E Ida Pl Greenwood Village CO 80111-3753

IMLE, JOHN F., JR., oil company executive; b. San Antonio; Degree in Mech. and Petroleum Engring., Tex. A&M, 1963. Registered petroleum engr., Calif. and Alaska. Engr. trainee Unocal, Houston, 1963-65, various positions Alaska, 1968-72, with divsn. internat. oil and gas West Africa and N. Sea, 1972-77, project mgr. Heather field Eng., 1974, dist. mgr. ops. Aberdeen, Scotland, 1977, resident mgr. Netherland's ops., 1980, pres. internat. divsn. internat. oil and gas, 1983, sr. v.p. energy resources, 1988; also bd. dirs. Unocal Corp., exec. v.p. energy resources, 1992, pres., 1994—; asst. Nev. Beech. Served mil., 1965-68. Mem. Am. Assn., Petroleum Geologists, Independent Petroleum Assn., Soc. Petroleum Engrs.

IMMERGUT, KARIN J., prosecutor; b. Bklyn. BA, Amherst Coll., 1982; JD, U. Calif., Berkeley, 1987. Bar: Calif. 1987, Vt. 1995, Oreg. 1996. Asst. US atty. Central. Dist., Calif., 1988—94; atty. Gravel & Shea, Burlington, Vt., 1994—96, Covington & Burling, Washington, 1987—89; assoc. independent counsel Office Independent Counsel, Washington, 1998; dep. dist. atty. Portland, Oreg., 1996—98; asst. US atty. dist. Oreg. US Dept. Justice, 1998—2001, US atty. dist. Oreg. Oreg., 2003—. Office: US Attys Office Mark O Hatfield US Courthouse 1000 SW Third Ave Ste 600 Portland OR 97204-2902 Office Phone: 503-727-1000.

IMPERIOLI, MICHAEL, actor; b. Mt. Vernon, NY, Jan. 1, 1966; m. Victoria Chlebowski, 1995; children: Vadim, David 1 stepchild, Isabella. Co-founder, co-artistic dir. Studio Dante, NYC, 2003—. Actor: (films) Alexa, 1988, Lean on Me, 1989, Goodfellas, 1990, Jungle Fever, 1991, Malcolm X, 1992, Fathers & Sons, 1992, Night We Never Met, 1993, Household Saints, 1993, Joey Breaker, 1993, Men Lie, 1994, Amateur, 1994, Postcards from America, 1994, Scenes From a New World, 1994, Hand Gun, 1994, Bad Boys, 1995, The Basketball Diaries, 1995, Clockers, 1995, Flirt, 1995, Dead Presidents, 1995, The Addiction, 1995, Trouble, 1995, I Shot Andy Warhol, 1996, Girls Town, 1996, Girl 6, 1996, Sweet Nothing, 1996, Tree's Lounge, 1996, Last Man Standing, 1996, Blixa Bargeld Stole My Cowboy Boots, 1996, Under the Bridge, 1997, Office Killer, 1997, The Deli, 1997, A River Made to Drown In, 1997, On the Run, 1999, Summer of Sam, 1999, Auto Motives, 2000, Love in the Time of Money, 2002, Stuey, 2003, My Baby's Daddy, 2004, (voice only) Shark Tale, 2004, The Inner Life of Martin Frost, 2007, The Lovebirds, 2007, The Higher Force, 2008; (TV films) Firehouse, 1997, Witness to the Mob, 1998, Disappearing Act, 2000, Hamlet, 2000, The Five People You Meet in Heaven, 2004, Mitch Albom's For One More Day, 2007; (TV series) The Sopranos, 1999—2007 (Emmy award Outstanding Supporting Actor in a Drama Series, 2004, Outstanding Performance by an Ensemble in a Drama Series, SAG, 2008), Life on Mars, 2008—09, (TV appearances) Law & Order, 2005, 2006, (voice only) The Simpsons, 2006,: (plays) Aven' U Boys, Displaced Persons, Half Deserted Street, The Writing on the Wall, Little Blood Brother, Late Fragment, 2005, Chicken, 2007; actor, exec. prodr., writer: films Summer of Sam, 1999. Office: c/o The Endeavor Agy 10th Fl 9601 Wilshire Blvd Beverly Hills CA 90212

IMWINKELRIED, EDWARD JOHN, law educator; b. San Francisco, Sept. 19, 1946; s. John Joseph and Enes Rose (Gianelli) I.; m. Cynthia Marie Clark, Dec. 30, 1978; children— Marie Elise, Kenneth West BA, U. San Francisco, 1967, JD, 1969. Bar: Calif. 1970, Mo. 1984, U.S. Supreme Ct. 1974. Prof. law U. San Diego, 1974-79; prof. law Washington U., St. Louis, 1979-85, Edward L. Barrett jr. prof. law, 2004—; prof. law U. Calif.-Davis, 1985—. Disting. faculty mem. Nat. Coll. Dist. Attys., Houston, 1978— Author: Evidentiary Foundations, 1980, 7th rev. edit., 2008, Uncharged Misconduct Evidence, 1984, rev. edit., 1999, The New Wigmore: Evidentiary Privileges, 2002; co-author: McCormick, Evidence, 6th edit., 2006, Materials for Study of Evidence, 1983, 6th edit., 2007, Scientific Evidence, 1986, 4th edit., 2007, Pretrial Discovery: Strategy and Tactics, 1986, rev. edit., 2004, Courtroom Criminal Evidence, 1987, 4th edit., 2005, California Evidentiary Foundations, 1988, 3d edit., 2000, Dynamics of Trial Practice, 1989, 3d edit., 2002, Exculpatory Evidence, 1990, 3d edit., 2004, Florida Evidentiary Foundations, 1991, 2d edit., 1997, Illinois Evidentiary Foundations, 1991, 2d edit., 1997, Texas Evidentiary Foundations, 1992, 3d edit., 2005, New York Evidentiary Foundations, 1993, 2d edit., 1997, Evidentiary Distinctions, 1993, Colorado Evidentiary Foundations, 1997; contbg. editor Champion pub. Assn. Criminal Def. Lawyers, 1983, Criminal Law Bull. Mem. Am. Acad. Forensic Sci., ABA (continuing edn. com. 1983-84), Am. Assn. Law Schs. (chmn. evidence sect. 1983) Democrat. Roman Catholic. Avocation: jogging. Home: 2204 Shenandoah Pl Davis CA 95616-6603 Office: U Calif Law Sch Davis CA 95616 Office Phone: 530-752-0727. Business E-Mail: ejimwinkelried@ucdavis.edu.

INAN, UMRAN SAVAS, electrical engineering educator, researcher; b. Erzincan, Turkey, Dec. 28, 1950; came to U.S., 1973; s. Mustafa and Ayse Hayriye (Basgoze) I.; m. Elif Basgoze, Sept. 3, 1973; children: Ayse, Ali. BSEE, Mid. East Tech. U., Ankara, Turkey, 1972, MSEE, 1973; PhD in Elec. Engring., Stanford, 1977. Rsch. affiliate Stanford (Calif.) U. Elec. Engring. Dept., 1977-78, acting asst. prof., 1978-80, 81-82, asst. prof., 1982-85, assoc. prof., 1985-91, prof., 1991—; acting asst. prof. Bogazici U. Elec. Engring. Dept., Istanbul, Turkey, 1980-81. Cons. Lockheed Palo Alto (Calif.) Rsch. Lab., 1989—. Contbr. over 95 articles to profl. jours. Mem. IEEE, Internat. Union Radio Sci., Am. Geophys. Union, The Electromagnetics Soc., Sigma Xi. Achievements include development of the first quantitative model of energetic electron precipitation induced by electromagnetic waves from lightning; discovery of ionospheric heating and ionization by lightning radiation; research includes ionospheric effects of lightning discharges, remote sensing, wave particle interaction. Home: 935 Mears Ct Palo Alto CA 94305-1041 Office: Star Lab Elec Engring Dept Packard Bldg # 355 Stanford CA 94305-9515

INFANTE, EDWARD A., federal judge; b. 1940; AB, Boston Coll., 1962; JD, Boston U., 1965. Law clk. to Hon. Edward McEntree 1st cir. U.S. Ct. Appeals; fed. pub. defender so. dist. U.S. Dist. Ct. Calif., 1970; bus. litigation and white collar criminal def. Pedersen, Flowers & Infante, San Diego, 1971-72; ptnr. bus. litigation Schall, Boudreau & Gore, San Diego, 1986-88; apptd. magistrate judge no. dist. U.S. Dist. Ct. Calif., 1990. Adj. prof. Santa Clara U. Sch. Law, 1990—. With USN, 1966-69, USNR, 1980-90. Mem. Nat. Magistrate Judges Assn. (treas. 1979, v.p. 1980, pres. 1981). Office: 4198 US Courthouse 280 S 1st St San Jose CA 95113-3002

INGELS, MARTY, agent, broadcast executive; b. Bklyn., Mar. 9, 1936; s. Jacob and Minnie (Crown) Ingerman; m. Jean Maire Frassinelli, Aug. 3, 1960 (div. 1969); m. Shirley Jones, 1977. Founder Ingels Inc., 1975—; formed Stoneypoint Prodns., 1981; TV and motion picture producer U.S. and Abroad; mgr. of Shirley Jones. Star: Dickens and Fenster series, ABC-TV, 1964; co-star: Pruitts of Southampton, 1968-69; films include Armored Command, 1962, Horizontal Lieutenant, 1965, Busy Body, 1967, Ladies Man, 1966, If It's Tuesday This Must Be Belgium, 1970, Wild and Wonderful, 1965, Guide for a Married Man, 1968; numerous TV appearances. Active various charity drives. Achievements include Owning the world's largest celebrity brokerage service, 1974; widely noted as the Henry Kissinger of Madison Avenue. Office: Network Prodns 4531 Noeline Way Encino CA 91436

INGERSOLL, ANDREW PERRY, planetary science educator; b. Chgo., Jan. 2, 1940; s. Jeremiah Crary and Minneola (Perry) I.; m. Sarah Morin, Aug. 27, 1961; children: Jeremiah, Ruth Ingersoll Wood, Marion Ingersoll Quinones, Minneola, George. BA, Amherst Coll., 1960; PhD, Harvard U., 1966. Rsch. fellow Harvard U., Cambridge, Mass., 1965-66; asst. prof. planetary sci. Calif. Inst. Tech., Pasadena, 1966-71, assoc. prof., 1971-76, prof., 1976—2003, Earle C. Anthony prof. planetary sci., 2003—. Mem. staff summer study program Woods Hole (Mass.) Oceanographic Inst., 1965, 70-73, 76, 80, 92; prin. investigator Pioneer Saturn Infrared Radiometer Team, NASA; mem. Voyager Imaging Team, NASA, Cassini Imaging Team; interdisciplinary scientist, Mars Global Surveyor Project, Galileo Project, NASA. Bd. trustees Poly. Sch., Pasadena. Fellow AAAS, Am. Geophys. Union, Am. Acad. Arts and Scis.; mem. Am. Astron. Soc. (vice-chmn. divsn. planetary sci. 1988-89, chmn. 1989-90, Gerard P. Kuiper prize 2007). Office: Calif Inst Tech Dept Planetary Sci 150 21 Pasadena CA 91125-0001 Home Phone: 626-564-0245; Office Phone: 626-395-6167. Business E-Mail: api@gps.caltech.edu.

INGERSOLL, RAYMOND VAIL, geologist, educator; b. NYC, June 17, 1947; s. Raymond Crary and Eleanor McLure (Jones) Ingersoll; m. Mary Martha Amadeo-Holl, July 8, 1972 (dec. Aug. 8, 2005). AB, Harvard U., 1969; MS, Stanford U., 1974, PhD, 1976. Tchr. Putney Sch., Vt., 1969—72; asst. prof. U. N.Mex., Albuquerque, 1976—80, assoc. prof., 1980—82; adj. assoc. prof. UCLA, 1982—85, prof., 1985—. Assoc. editor Jour. Sedimentary Petrology, Geol. Soc. America Bulletin, Internat. Geology Rev. Contbr. articles to profl. jours. Fellow: Geol. Soc. Am. (chair, sed. geol. div. 2000—01); mem.: N.Mex. Geol. Soc., Soc. Econ. Paleontologists and Mineralogists (pres. Pacific sect. 1987, 2009), Internat. Assn. Sedimentologists, Am. Geophys. Union, Sigma Xi. Office: Univ Calif Dept Earth And Scis Los Angeles CA 90095-1567 Business E-Mail: ringer@ess.ucla.edu.

INGLE, CRESS STUART, state legislator; divorced; children: Jennifer & Laura. New Mexico State Senator, District 27, currently, Minority Floor Leader, currently, member, Conserv, Indian & Cult Affairs, Committees Committee, formerly, member, Finance & Public Affairs Committee, currently, New Mexico State Senate.Farming, currently. Republican. Address: 2106 W University Portales NM 88130 Mailing: State Capitol Rm 109 Santa Fe NM 87503

INGLE, JAMES CHESNEY, JR., geology educator; b. LA, Nov. 6, 1935; s. James Chesney and Florence Adelaide (Geldart) I.; m. Fredricka Ann Bornholdt, June 14, 1958; 1 child, Douglas James BS in Geology, U. So. Calif., 1959, MS in Geology, 1962, PhD in Geology, 1966. Registered geologist, Calif. Research assoc. Univ. So. Calif., 1961-65; vis. scholar Tohoku U., Sendai, Japan, 1966-67; asst., assoc. to full prof. Stanford U., Calif., 1968—, W.M. Keck prof. earth scis., 1984—, chmn. dept. geology, 1982-86. Co-chief scientist Leg 31 Deep Sea Drilling Project, 1973, co-chief scientist Leg 128 Ocean Drilling Program, 1989; geologist U.S. Geol. Survey W.A.E, 1978-81 Author: Movement of Beach Sand, 1966; contbr. articles to profl. jours. Recipient W.A. Tarr award Sigma Gamma Epsilon, 1958; named Disting. lectr. Am. Assn. Petroleum Geologists, 1986-87, Joint Oceanographic Institutions, 1991; A.I. Leverson award Am. Assn. Petroleum Geologists, 1988. Fellow Geol. Soc. Am., Calif. Acad. Scis.; mem. Cushman Found. (bd. dirs. 1984-91), Soc. Profl. Paleontologists and Mineralogists (Pacific sect. 1958—, pres. 1993-94), Am. Geophys. Union. E-mail: ingle@pangea.stanford.edu.

INGLE, M(ORTON) BLAKEMAN, chemicals executive; b. Carlsbad, N.Mex., Apr. 25, 1942; s. Morton Blakeman and Bette Ruth Ingle; m. Connie Sue Cochran; children: David, Glenn. BS in Biology and Chemistry, Ft. Lewis Coll., 1964; MS in Microbiology and Biochemistry, Colo. State U., 1966, PhD in Microbiology and Biochemistry, 1968. Corp. staff v.p. R&D Internat. Minerals & Chem., Northbrook, Ill., 1980, v.p. R&D, 1980-85, v.p., chief tech. officer, 1985-87, sr. v.p., chief adminstrv. and tech. officer, 1987-88; sr. v.p., pres. Pitman-Moore, Inc., Lake Forest, Ill., 1988-89, exec. v.p., pres., 1989-90; pres., chief oper. officer IMCERA Group Inc., Northbrook, 1990-91, pres., chief exec. officer, 1991-92. Editor sci. jour., 1974-79; contbr. numerous articles to profl. jours., book chpts. Bd. dirs. United Way Lake County, Glen Oaks, Ill., 1992. Recipient Disting. Achievement award Coll. Vet. Medicine and Biomed. Sci., Colo. State U. Fellow Am. Acad. Microbiology; mem. Am. Soc. for Microbiology, Japan Am. Soc., Brit. N.Am. Com., Northwestern U. Assocs.

INGRAM, CECIL D., accountant, state legislator; b. Blackfoot, Idaho, Dec. 27, 1932; s. Orval Otto and Mary Marjorie (Evans) I.; m. Lois Ann Glenn, Dec. 28, 1952; children: Cynthia, William, Christopher. BBA, U. Oreg., 1962. Contr. transp. & distbn. divsn. Boise (Idaho) Cascade Corp., 1962-91; mem. Idaho Senate, Dist. 16, Boise, 1993—. Capt. U.S. Army, 1953-58, Korea. Mem. Masons, Mountain States Tumor Inst., Golf for Charity, Morrison Ctr., W Idaho Fair Bd., Salvation Army, United Way, Recreation Unlimited, Junior Achievement, Idaho Education Alliance for Science. Republican. Baptist. Home: 7025 El Caballo Dr Boise ID 83704-7320 Office: State Capitol PO Box 83720 Boise ID 83720-3720

INGRAM, DOUGLAS STEPHEN, lawyer; b. Aug. 31, 1962; BS magna cum laude, Ariz. State U., 1985; JD summa cum laude, U. Ariz., 1988. Bar: Calif. 1988. Atty. Gibson, Dunn & Crutcher, 1988—96; assoc. gen. counsel, asst. sec. Allergen, Inc., Irvine, Calif., 1998—2000, exec. v.p., gen. counsel, sec., 2000—. Mem.: ABA, Am. Soc. Corp. Secretaries, Am. Corp. Counsel Assn., State Bar Calif., Orange County Bar Assn., Order of Coif. Office: Allergan Inc 2525 Dupont Dr PO Box 19534 Irvine CA 92623-9534 Office Phone: 714-246-4535. Office Fax: 714-246-4971. E-mail: ingram_doug@allergan.com.

INGWERSON, DONALD W., educational administrator; Supt. schools Jefferson County, Louisville, LA County Office Edn., Downey, Calif., 1994—2001; dir. west coast field ops. Cmty. Tng. and Assistance Ctr., Calif., 2001—. Recipient Nat. McGraw-Hill Prize in Edn., 1996; named Nat. Supt. of Yr., Am. Assn. Sch. Administrators, 1992; named an Outstanding Exec. in N.Am., Exec. 100.

INKELES, ALEX, sociology educator; b. Bklyn., Mar. 4, 1920; s. Meyer and Ray (Gewer) K.; m. Bernadette Mary Kane, Jan. 31, 1942; 1 child, Ann Elizabeth BA, Cornell U., 1941; postgrad., Washington Sch. Psychiatry, 1943-46; MA, Cornell U., 1946; PhD, Columbia U., 1949; AM (hon.), Harvard U., 1957; student, Boston Psychoanalytic Inst., 1957-59; prof. (hon.), Faculdade Candido Mendez, Rio de Janerio, 1969, Faculdade Candido Mendez, 2002. Social sci. research analyst Dept. State and OSS, 1942-46; cons. program evaluation br., internat. broadcasting div. Dept. State, 1949-51; instr. social relations Harvard U., Cambridge, Mass., 1948, lectr., 1948-57, prof. sociology, 1957-71, dir. studies social rels. Russian Rsch. Ctr., dir. studies social aspects econ. devel. Ctr. Internat. Affairs, 1963-71, rsch. assoc., 1971-79; Margaret Jacks prof. edn., prof. sociology Stanford U., Calif., 1971-78, prof. sociology, 1978-90; sr. fellow Hoover Inst., 1978—; prof. emeritus, 1990—. Mem. exec. com. behavioral sci. div. NRC, 1968-75; lectr. Nihon U., Japan, 1985. Author: Public Opinion in Soviet Russia, 1950 (Kappa Tau Alpha award 1950, Grant Squires prize Columbia 1955); with R. Bauer, C. Kluckhohn) How the Soviet System Works, 1956, (with R. Bauer) The Soviet Citizen, 1959, Soviet Society (edited with H.K. Geiger), 1961, What is Sociology?, 1964, Readings on Modern Sociology, 1965, Social Change in Soviet Russia, 1968, (with D.H. Smith) Becoming Modern, 1974 (Hadley Cantril award 1974), Exploring Individual Modernity, 1983; editor: (with Masamichi Sasaki) Comparing Nations and Cultures, 1996, National Character: A Psychosocial Perspective, 1997, One World Emerging? Convergence and Divergence in Industrial Societies, 1998; editor-in-chief Ann. Rev. Sociology, 1971-79; editl. cons. Internat. Rev. Cross Cultural Studies; editl. bd. Ethos, Jour. Soc. Psychol. Anthropology, 1978; editor Founds. Modern Sociology Series; adv. editor in sociology to Little, Brown & Co.; contbr. articles to profl. jours. Recipient Cooley Mead award for Disting. Contbn. in Social Psychology, 1982; fellow Ctr. Advanced Study Behavioral Sci., 1955, Founds. Fund Research Psychiatry, 1957-60, Social Scis. Research Council, 1959, Russell Sage Found., 1966, 85, Fulbright Found., 1977, Guggenheim Found., 1978, Bernard van Leer Jerusalem Found., 1979, Rockefeller Found., 1982, Eisenhower Assn., Taiwan, 1984; NAS Disting. Scholar Exchange, China, 1983; grantee Internat. Rsch. and Exchs. Bd., 1989, NSF, 1989. Fellow AAAS (co-chmn. western ctr. 1984-87, chmn. Talcott Parsons award com. 1988-93), Am. Philos. Soc., APA; mem. NIMH, Nat. Inst. Aging (monitoring com. health retirement survey 1990—), Nat. Acad. Scis. (corr. human rights com. 1986-88, mem. com. on scholarly comms. with People's Republic of China, chmn. panel on social sci. and humanities, NRC panel on issues in democratization 1991-92), Am. Sociol. Soc. (coun. 1961-664, v.p. 1975-76), Ea. Sociol. Soc. (pres. 1961-62), World Assn. Pub. Opinion Rsch., Am. Assn. Pub. Opinion Rsch., Inter-Am. Soc. Psychology, Sociol. Rsch. Assn. (exec. com. 1975-79, pres. 1979), Soc. for Study Social Problems. Home: 1001 Hamilton Ave Palo Alto CA 94301-2215 Office: Stanford U Hoover Instn Stanford CA 94305 Home Phone: 650-327-4197; Office Phone: 650-723-4856. Business E-Mail: inkeles@hoover.stanford.edu.

INLOW, RUSH OSBORNE, chemist; b. Seattle, July 10, 1944; s. Edgar Burke and Marigale (Osborne) I.; m. Gloria Elisa Duran, June 7, 1980. BS, U. Wash., 1966; PhD, Vanderbilt U., 1975. Chemist, sect. chief U.S. Dept. Energy, Argonne, Ill., 1975-78, chief nuclear safeguards br. Cruise missile sys. Ops. Office Albuquerque, 1983-84; program mgr. Navy strategic sys., 1984-85; dir. weapon programs divsn., 1985-88; dir. prodn. ops. divsn., 1988-90; asst. mgr. safeguards and security, 1990-94; asst. mgr. nat. def. programs, 1994-96; dep. mgr., 1996-2000; prin. mem. tech. staff Sandia Nat. Labs., 2000—. Apptd. Fed. Sr. Exec. Svc., 1985. Served with USN, 1966-71. Tenn. Eastman fellow, 1974-75; recipient Pres. Meritorious Exec. awrd The White House, Pres. Clinton, 1994. Mem. Am. Chem. Soc., Sigma Xi. Republican. Episcopalian. Home Phone: 505-797-8375. Business E-Mail: roinlow@sandia.gov.

INMAN, WILLIAM PETER, lawyer; b. Cleve., June 29, 1936; s. James B. and Lillian (Frances) I.; m. Judith A. Clay, Feb. 5, 1994; children: William Peter, Elizabeth, David. Student, Miami U., 1954-55; BA, Ohio State U., 1958; JD, Case Western Res. U., 1960, MBA, 1966. Bar: Ohio 1960, Tex. 1985. Tax accountant U.S. Steel Corp., Cleve., 1960-63; asso. trust counsel Central Nat. Bank of Cleve., 1963-66; atty. Sherwin-Williams Co., Cleve., 1966-67, tax counsel, 1967, mgr. tax dept., 1967-68, corporate dir. taxes, 1968-69, asst. sec., dir. taxes, 1969-71, sec., dir. taxes, 1971-75, v.p., sec., asst. treas., 1975-78, v.p., treas., chief fin. officer, 1978-80; v.p. fin., chief fin. officer RTE Corp., Waukesha, Wis., 1980-83; fin. cons. Houston, 1983-85; corp. sec., gen. counsel Mera Bank, Phoenix, 1985-88; gen. counsel CADTEL Sys. Inc., Phoenix, 1988-95, Ariz. Bus. Assocs., L.L.C., Phoenix, 1995—. Mem. Greater Cleve. Growth Assn., 1969-80; Trustee Ohio Pub. Expenditure Council, 1969-80, v.p., 1970-73, pres., 1973-75, chmn. bd., 1975-77. Mem. Am. Soc. Corp. Secs., Fin. Execs. Inst., Cleve. Treasurers Club, N.A.M., Ohio Mfrs. Assn., Am., Ohio, Greater Cleve., Tex., Maricopa County, Ariz. bar assns., Estate Planning Council of Cleve., Tax Execs. Inst., Phi Delta Phi, Beta Gamma Sigma, Beta Alpha Psi. Home and Office: 5702 E Sylvia St Scottsdale AZ 85254-4364

INOCENCIO, E. BING, college president; came to U.S., 1979; Grad. journalism, Ateneo De Manila U.; MS in Mktg. and Advt., U. Ill.; MA in Bus. and Applied Econs., U. Pa., PhD in Econs. and Comm. Assoc. dean bus., math. and tech. C.C. of Balt.; instructional dean humanities and social scis. Inst. at Montgomery Coll., Takoma Park, Md.; dean instrn. and acad. svcs. Cumberland County Coll., Vineland, N.J.; assoc. provost acad. adminstrn. N.Y.C. Tech. Coll. CUNY; pres. L.A. Pierce Coll., 1996-99, Am. Intercontinental U., LA, 1999—. Fulbright scholar U. Ill.; fellowship Ford Found. Wharton Sch., Harvard Bus. Sch, Kellogg fellow, 1991; named One of Rising Stars in cmty. leadership League for Innovation in the C.C., 1993. Office: 12655 W Jefferson Blvd Los Angeles CA 90066-7008

INOUYE, DANIEL KEN, United States Senator from Hawaii; b. Honolulu, Sept. 7, 1924; s. Hyotaro and Kame Imananga; m. Margaret Shinobu Awamura, June 12, 1949 (dec. 1998); 1 child, Daniel Ken; m. Irene Y. Hirano, May 24, 2008 AB in Govt. & Economics, U. Hawaii, 1950; JD, George Washington U., 1952. Bar: Hawaii 1953. Dep. pub. prosecutor, Honolulu, 1953-54; pvt. practice, 1954—; mem. Hawaii Territorial Ho. of Reps., 1954-58, Hawaii Territorial Senate, 1958-59, US Congress from Hawaii-at-Large Dist., 1959—63; US Senator from Hawaii, 1963—; mem. US Senate Armed Services Com., 1963—71; sec. US Senate Dem. Conf., 1978-88; chmn. US Senate Select Com. on Intelligence, 1976—79, US Senate Select Com. on Indian Affairs, 1987—95, 2001, 2001—03; mem. US Senate Select Com. on Presdl. Campaign Activities, 1973-74; ranking mem. subcom. budget authorizations US Senate Select Com. on Intelligence, 1979-84; chmn. US Senate Select Com. on Secret Mil. Assistance to Iran & Nicaraguan Opposition, 1987; mem. US Senate Commerce, Sci. & Transp. Com., chmn., 2007—09, US Senate Appropriations Com., 2009—; mem. US Senate Indian Affairs Com., US Senate Rules & Adminstrn. Com. Mem. Senate Watergate Com., 1973-74; sr. counselor Kissinger Commn., 1984; chmn. Senate Dem. Ctrl. Am. Study Group, 1984. Co-author (with Lawrence Elliott): Journey to Washington, 1967. Active YMCA, Boy Scouts Am. Keynoter; temporary chmn. Dem. Nat. Conv., 1968, rules com. chmn., 1980, co-chmn. conv., 1984. Pvt. to capt. AUS, 1943-47. Decorated Medal of Honor, D.S.C., Bronze Star, Purple Heart with cluster; decorated Grand Cordon of the Order of the Rising Sun, Govt. Japan, 2000; named 1 of 10 Outstanding Young Men of Yr. U.S. Jr. C. of C., 1960; recipient Splendid Am. award Thomas A. Dooley Found., 1967 Golden Plate award Am. Acad. Achievement, 1968, Spirit of Hope award USO, 1999, Advocacy Conf. Congl. award Nat. Breast Cancer Coalition, 2002, Friend of Coast award Am. Coastal Coalition, 2002, Doughboy award U.S. Army, 2002, Sonny Montgomery award Nat. Guard Bur., 2003, Congressional Am. Spirit Medallion Nat. D-Day Mus., 2004, Leadership award Nat. Marine Sanctuary Found., 2005, Lifetime Achievement award Air Force Assn., 2005, Bryce Harlow award Bryce Harlow Found., 2006; Daniel K. Inouye Bldg. of Walter Reed Army Inst. Rsch., Naval Med. Rsch. Ctr., Bethesda, Md. dedicated in his honor, 2001; Hart-Dole-Inouye Fed. Ctr., Battle Creek, Mich. named in his honor, 2003. Mem. Disabled Am. Veterans (past comdr. Hawaii), Honolulu C. of C., Am. Legion (Nat. Comdr.'s award 1973); Clubs: Lion. (Hawaii), 442d Veterans (Hawaii). Democrat. Methodist. Home: 469 Ena Rd Honolulu HI 96815-1749 Office: US Senate 722 Hart Senate Bldg Washington DC 20510-0001 also: Prince Kuhio Fed Bldg Rm 7-212 300 Ala Moana Blvd Honolulu HI 96850-4975 Office Phone: 202-224-3934, 808-541-2542. Office Fax: 202-224-6747, 808-541-2549.*

INOUYE, LORRAINE R., state legislator; b. Hilo, Hawaii, June 22, 1940; m. Vernon Inouye; children: Ronald Jitchaku, Jay Kitchaku, Marcia Johansen. Mgr. Orchid Island Hotel, 1967-75; sales mgr. Hilo Hawaiian Hotel, Hilo and Kona Lagoon Hotels, 1975-86; pres. Aloha Blooms, Inc., 1998—; mem. Hawaii Senate, Dist. 1, Honolulu, 1998—; chair econ. devel. com. Hawaii Senate, Honolulu, mem. commerce and consumer protection com., mem. transp. and intergovtl. affairs com. Mayor County of Hawaii, 1990-92; mem. Hawaii County Coun., 1984-90, Hawaii County Planning Commn., 1974-79; dir. Girl Scout Coun. Hawaii, 1995X; charter mem. Ho'okumu, North Hawaii Cmty. Hosp., 1991X. Mem. Rotary Club of Hilo. Democrat. Office: State Capitol 415 S Beretania St Rm 201 Honolulu HI 96813-2407

INOUYE, MICHAEL K., medical products company executive; BS, U. Calif., Davis; MBA, Calif. State Poly. U. With Am. Home Products; to sr. dir. mktg. planning, sr. regional dir. field sales Merch and Co., Inc., 1980-94; v.p. sales and mktg. InSite Vision, 1991-95; v.p. sales and mgr. Gilead Scis., Inc., Foster City, Calif., 1995-2000, sr. v.p. sales and mktg., 2000.

INOUYE, WAYNE RYO, computer company executive; b. Yuba City, Calif., Aug. 25, 1952; m. Shannon Inouye; children: Lauren, Josh. Student in Biology, U. Calif. Berkeley, 1971—72. Founder No. Calif. Mktg., 1978; with Good Guys, 1986—95, head audio merchandising, 1986; mgr. Computer-Retailing Divsn. Best Buy, 1995—2001; pres., CEO eMachines, Inc. (acquired by Gateway, Inc.), Irvine, Calif., 2001—04, Gateway Inc., Irvine, Calif., 2004—06, advisor, 2006. Avocations: guitar, golf.

INSLEE, JAY ROBERT, United States Representative from Washington; b. Seattle, Feb. 9, 1951; s. Frank and Adele Inslee; m. Trudi Anne Inslee, Aug. 27, 1972; children: Jack, Connor, Joe. BA in Econs., U. Wash., Seattle, 1973; JD magna cum laude, Willamette U. Sch. Law, Salem, Oreg., 1976. Atty. Peters, Fowler & Inslee, Selah, Wash., 1976-92; mem. Wash. State House Reps. from 14th dist., 1988-92, US Congress from 4th Wash. dist., 1993-95; atty. Gordon, Thomas, Honeywell, Malanca, Peterson and Daheim, Seattle, 1995-96; regional dir. region 10 US Dept. Health and Human Svcs., Seattle, 1997-98; mem. US Congress from 1st Wash. dist., 1999—, mem. energy and commerce com., mem. resources com. Charter mem. Hoopaholics, 1988—. Democrat. Office: US House Reps 403 Cannon Ho Office Bldg Washington DC 20515-4701 Office Phone: 202-225-6311.

INSOGNA, ANTHONY M., lawyer; b. Bklyn., Sept. 5, 1967; BS in Organic Chemistry, NYU, 1989, MS in Bio-organic Chemistry, 1990; JD, Fordham Univ., 1994. Admitted to practice: US Patent and Trademark Office 1991, bar: NY 1995, DC 1996, Calif., US Ct. Appeals (fed. cir.), US Supreme Ct., US Dist. Ct. (so. dist.), Calif. Researcher, chemistry departments Columbia Univ. and NYU; law clk., biotechnology group Pennie & Edmonds LLP; now ptnr.-in-charge San Diego office Jones Day. Mem. selection com. 2006 UCSD Chancellor's Assoc. Annual Faculty Excellence Awards, 2006. Named one of Top 20 Under 40 attorneys in Calif., Daily Jour., 2005; named to the list of 2006 So. Calif. Super Lawyers, Law & Politics, 2006. Mem.: ABA, NY Intellectual Property Law Assn., NY State Bar Assn., Am. Chem. Soc., Sigma Xi. Office: Jones Day 12265 El Camino Real Ste 200 San Diego CA 92130-4096 Office Phone: 858-314-1130. Office Fax: 858-314-1150. Business E-Mail: aminsogna@jonesday.com.

INTRILIGATOR, DEVRIE SHAPIRO, physicist; b. NYC; d. Carl and Lillian Shapiro; m. Michael Intriligator; children: Kenneth, James, William, Robert. BS in Physics, MIT, 1962, MS, 1964; PhD in Planetary and Space Physics, UCLA, 1967. NRC-NASA rsch. assoc. NASA, Ames, Calif., 1967—69; rsch. fellow in physics Calif. Inst. Tech., Pasadena, 1969—72, vis. assoc., 1972—73; asst. prof. U. So. Calif., 1972—80; mem. Space Scis. Ctr., 1978—83; sr. rsch. physicist Carmel Rsch. Ctr., Santa Monica, Calif., 1979—; dir. Space Plasma Lab., 1980—. Cons. NASA, NOAA, Jet Propulsion Lab.; chmn. NAS-NRC com. on solar-terrestrial rsch., 1983-86, exec. com. bd. atmospheric sci. and climate, 1983-86, geophysics study com., 1983-86; U.S. nat. rep. Sci. Com. on Solar-Terrestrial Physics, 1983-86; mem. adv. com. NSF Divsn. Atmospheric Sci. Co-editor: Exploration of the Outer Solar System, 1976; contbr. articles to profl. jours. Recipient 3 Achievement awards NASA, Calif. Resolution of Commendation, 1982. Mem.: AAAS, Am. Geophys. Union, Am. Phys. Soc., Cosmos Club. Achievements include being a participant Pioneer 10/11 missions to outer planets; Pioneer Venus Orbiter, Pioneers 6, 7, 8 and 9 heliocentric missions. Home: 140 Foxtail Dr Santa Monica CA 90402-2048 Office: Carmel Rsch Ctr PO Box 1732 Santa Monica CA 90406-1732

INTRILIGATOR, MICHAEL DAVID, economist, educator; b. NYC, Feb. 5, 1938; s. Allan and Sally Intriligator; m. Devrie Shapiro; children: Kenneth, James, William, Robert. SB in Econs., MIT, 1959; MA, Yale U., 1960; PhD, MIT, 1963. Asst. prof. econs. UCLA, 1963—66, assoc. prof., 1968—72, prof., 1972—, prof. dept. polit. sci., 1981—, prof. dept. policy studies, 1994—, dir. Ctr. Internat. and Strategic Affairs, 1982—92, 2000—02; dir. Jacob Marschak Interdisciplinary Coll., 1977—; dir. Burkle Ctr. Internat. Rels., 2000—02. Cons. Inst. Def. Analysis, 1974—77, ACDA, 1968, Rand Corp., 1962—65; sr. fellow Milken Inst., 1998—. Author: Mathematical Optimization and Economic Theory, 1971; author: (with Ronald Bodkin and Cheng Hsiao) Econometric Models, Techniques, and Applications, 1996; author: (with others) A Forecasting and Policy Simulation Model of the Health Care Sector, 1979; mem. adv. editl. bd.: Math. Social Scis., 1983—; editor (assoc. editor): Jour. Optimization Theory and Applications, 1979—91, Conflict Mgmt. and Peace Sci., 1980—; co-editor: (series) Handbook sin Economics, 1980—, Advanced Textbooks in Economics, 1972—; editor (with Kenneth J. Arrow): (book) Handbook of Mathematical Economics, 3 vols., 1981—85; editor: (with Zvi Griliches) Handbook of Econometrics, 3 vols., 1983—86; editor: (with B. Brodie and R. Kolkowicz) National Security and International Stability, 1983; editor: (with H. A. Jacobsen) East-West Conflict: Elite Perceptions and Political Opinions, 1988; editor: numerous others; contbr. articles to profl. jours. Recipient Disting. Tchg. award, UCLA, 1966, Warren C. Scoville Disting. Tchg. award, 1976, 1979, 1982, 1984; fellow Woodrow Wilson, 1959—60, MIT, 1960—61, Ford, 1967—68. Fellow: AAAS, Econometric Soc.; mem.: We. Econ. Assn. Internat. (pres. 2008), Russian Acad. Sci., Coun. Fgn. Rels., Internat. Inst. Strategic Studies. Office: UCLA Dept Econs Los Angeles CA 90095-1477 Office Phone: 310-825-4144. Business E-Mail: intriligator@econ.ucla.edu.

INVERSO, MARLENE JOY, optometrist; b. LA, May 10, 1942; d. Elmer Encel Wood and Sally Marie (Sample) Hirons; m. John S. Inverso, Dec. 16, 1962; 1 child, Christopher Edward. BA, Calif. State U., Northridge, 1964; MS, SUNY, Potsdam, 1975; OD, Pacific U., 1981. Cert. doctor optometry, Wash., Oreg. English tchr. Chatsworth (Calif.) High Sch., 1964-68, Nelson A. Boylen Second Sch., Toronto, Ont., Can., 1968-70, Gouverneur (N.Y.) Jr.-Sr. High Sch., 1970-74, 76-77; reading resource room tchr. Parishville (N.Y.) Hopkinton Sch., 1974-75; optometrist and vision therapist Am. Family Vision Clinics, Olympia, Wash., 1982—. Coord. Lng. Disability Clin. SUNY, summers, 1975-77; mem. adv. com. Sunshine House St. Peter Hosp., Olympia, 1984-86, Pacific U. Coll. Optometry, Forest Grove, Oreg. 1986. Contbr. articles to profl. jours. Mem. Altrusa Svc. Club, Olympia, 1982-86; tchr. Ch. Living Water, Olympia, 1983-88, Olympia-Lacey Ch. of God, 1989—, sec. women's bd., 1990; bd. advisors Crisis Pregnancy Ctr., Olympia, 1987-89; den mother Cub Scouts Am. Pack 202, Lacey, Wash., 1987-88; vol. World Vision Countertop ptnr., 1986-97. Fellow Coll. Optometrists in Optometric Devel.; mem. Am. Optometric Assn. (sec. 1983-84), Assn. Children and Adults with Learning Disabilities, Optometric Extension Program, Sigma Xi, Beta Sigma Kappa. Home: 4336 Libby Rd NE Olympia WA 98506-2555 Office Phone: 360-491-2121.

IONTA, ROBERT W., federal judge, lawyer; Part-time magistrate judge for N.Mex., U.S. Magistrate Ct., Gallup, 1985—. Office: 300 W Hill Ave Gallup NM 87301-6364

IOVINE, JIMMY, recording industry executive; b. Bklyn., Mar. 11, 1953; s. Jimmy Iovine Sr.; m. Vicki Iovine; 4 children. Former engr. The Record Plant, NYC, 1973; ind. prodr., co-head Interscope Records, 1991—; chmn. Interscope Geffen A&M Records, Santa Monica, Calif. Prodr.: (albums) Patti Smith's Easter, 1978, Tom Petty's Damn the Torpedoes, 1979, Tom Petty's Hard Promises, 1981, Tom Petty's Long After Dark, 1982, Stevie Nicks' Bella Donna, 1981, Stevie Nicks' The Wild Heart, 1983, Stevie Nicks' Rock A Little, 1985, Pretenders' Get Close, 1986, U2's Rattle & Hum, 1989, Whitney Houston's I Will Always Love You, 1992, Dire Straits' Sultans of Swing, 1998, Gwen Stefani's Love.Angel.Music.Baby, 2004; (films) 8 Mile, 2002, Get Rich or Die Tryin', 2005; (TV series) Cane, 2007. Office: Interscope Geffen A&M Records 2220 Colorado Ave Santa Monica CA 90404 Office Phone: 310-865-1000. Office Fax: 310-865-7096.

IPSEN, GRANT RUEL, state legislator, insurance and investments professional; b. Malad, Idaho, Nov. 6, 1932; s. Nephi Ruel and Ada (Hughes) I.; m. Edna Wayne Hughes, July 27, 1956; children: Edna Gaye, LeAnn, Garin Grant, Shawna Lee, Wayne Ruel. BA, Brigham Young U., 1961. CPA, CLU, ChFC. Acct. Ernst & Ernst, Boise, Idaho, 1961-64; sales dept. Mut. of N.Y., Boise, 1964—93; mem. Idaho Senate, Dist. 17, Boise, 1992—2002; ret. Mut. of N.Y. Active Boy Scouts Am., 1945—; co-convener Boise Religious Freedom Com., 1991-94. With U.S. Army, 1956-58. Named Agt. of Yr., Boise Assn. Life Underwriters, 1978, Man of Yr., Mut. of N.Y., 1982. Mem. Million Dollar Round Table (life), Brigham Young Univ. Alumni (bd. dirs. 1987-93). Republican. Mem. Lds Ch. Avocations: reading, outdoor recreation, hiking, travel.

IRANI, RAY R., oil, gas and chemical company executive; b. Beirut, Jan. 15, 1935; came to U.S., 1953, naturalized, 1956; s. Rida and Naz I.; children: Glenn R., Lillian M., Martin R. BS in Chemistry, Am. U. Beirut, 1953; PhD in Phys. Chemistry, U. So. Calif., 1957. Rsch. scientist, then sr. rsch. scientist Monsanto Co., 1957-67; assoc. dir. new products, then dir. research Diamond Shamrock Corp., 1967-73; with Olin Corp., 1973-83, pres. chems. group, 1978-80, corp. pres., dir. Stamford, Conn., 1980-83, COO, 1981-83; chmn. Occidental Petroleum Corp. subs. Occidental Chem. Corp., Dallas, 1983-94; CEO Occidental Petroleum Corp., subs. Occidental Chem. Corp., Dallas, 1983-91; chmn. Can. Occidental Petroleum Corp. Ltd., Calgary, 1987-99; exec. v.p. Occidental Petroleum Corp., LA, 1983-84, pres., COO, 1984-91, pres., 1991—96, chmn., CEO, 1991—2005, chmn., pres., CEO, 2005—. Bd. dirs. Am. Petroleum Inst., KB Home Corp. 1992-2007, TCW Group, Wynn Resorts Ltd. Author: Particle Size; also author papers in field; numerous patents in field. Co-chmn. Am. U. Beirut; trustee U. So. Calif., St. John's Hosp.; bd. govs. Los Angeles Town Hall, Los Angeles World Affairs Coun.; adv. bd. Rand Ctr. Mid. East Pub. Policy. Mem. Nat. Petroleum Coun., Am. Inst. Chemists, Am. Chem. Soc., Sci. Rsch. Soc. Am., Indsl. Rsch. Inst., The Conf. Bd., The CEO Roundtable, Am. Petroleum Inst. (bd. dirs.), Am. Chem. Soc., Nat. Assn. Mfrs., Nat. Com. US-China Rels., Sigma Xi, US-Saudi Arabian Bus. Coun. Office: Occidental Petroleum Corp 10889 Wilshire Blvd Los Angeles CA 90024-4201

IREDALE, NANCY LOUISE, lawyer; BS summa cum laude, Georgetown U., 1969; JD, Yale U., 1972. Bar: D.C. 1973, Calif. 1977. Tax counsel to Senator William Brock Senate Fin. Com., 1976; ptnr. Paul Hastings, Janofsky & Walker, LA. Named one of Top 100 LA County Super Lawyers, Law & Politics Media, 2004, Top 50 Female Super Lawyers, Super Lawyers Tax, 2006. Fellow: Am. Coll. Tax Counsel; mem. Yale Law Sch. Assn. (exec. com. 1982-85), Phi Beta Kappa, Phi Beta Kappa Alumni (councilor alpha assoc.). Office: Paul Hastings Janofsky & Walker LLP 515 S Flower St Fl 25 Los Angeles CA 90071-2228 Office Phone: 213-683-6232. Office Fax: 213-627-0705. Business E-Mail: nancyiredale@paulhastings.com.

IRELAND, FAITH, retired state supreme court justice, lawyer; b. Seattle, 1942; d. Carl and Janice Enyeart; m. Chuck Norem. BA, U. Wash.; JD, Willamette U., 1969; M in Taxation with honors, Golden Gate U. Past assoc. McCune, Godfrey and Emerick, Seattle; pvt. practice Pioneer Square, Wash., 1974; judge King County Superior Ct., 1984—98; justice Wash. Supreme Ct., 1998—2005; atty. private practice, 2005—. Past dean Washington Jud. Coll.; past mem. Bd. Ct. Edn. Served on numerous civic and charitable bds.; past pro-bono atty. Georgetown Dental Clin.; past bd. dirs. Puget Sound Big Sisters, Inc.; founding mem. Wing Luke Asian Mus., 1967—, past pres., past bd. dirs.; bd. dirs. Youth and Fitness Found., 1998. Recipient Disting. Svc. award, Nat. Leadership Inst. Jud. Edn., 1998; named Judge of Yr., Washington State Trial Lawyer's Assn., Man of Yr. for efforts in founding Wing Luke Asian Mus. Mem.: Superior Ct. Judges Assn. (past bd. dirs., pres. 1996—97, vice chair bd. dirs. jud. adminstrn. 1996—98), Wash. State Trial Lawyer's Assn. (past chair bd. dirs.), Washington Women Lawyer's (founding mem., Pres.'s award, Vanguard award), Rotary (bd. dirs. Seattle No. 4 1998), Rainer Valley Hist. Soc. (life; founding mem.).

IRELAND, KATHY, actress, apparel designer; b. Glendale, Calif., Mar. 20, 1963; d. John and Barbara Ireland; m. Greg Olsen, 1988; children: Erik, Lily, Chloe. CEO, chief designer Kathy Ireland Worldwide. Designer Kathy Ireland Brand began 2000, appearances in Sports Illustrated's Ann. Swimsuit Issues, 25th Anniversary Show Swimsuit Edit., Kathy Ireland LPGA Championship, ESPN, 2001; films include: Alien from L.A., 1988, Necessary Roughness, 1991, Mom and Dad Save the World, 1992, National Lampoon's Loaded Weapon I, 1993, The Player, Mr. Destiny, Amore, Backfire; TV films include Beauty and the Bandit, 1994, Danger Island, 1994, Miami Hustle, 1995, Gridlock, 1996, Once Upon A Christmas, 2000, Twice Upon A Christmas, 2001; TV appearances include: Down the Shore, The Edge, Tales from the Crypt, Without a Clue, Grand, Charles in Charge, Perry Mason, Boy Meets World, Melrose Place, The Watcher, Deadly Games, Sabrina the Teenage Witch, Suddenly Susan, Gun, Cosby, Touched by an Angel, Pensacola, For Your Love, Strong Medicine. Recipient Entrepreneur of Yr., 2001, Mother of Yr., 2004, Received Good Housekeeping Seal, 2004, Bus. Owner of Yr., 2004, Entrepreneural Champian award, 2005. Office: Kathy Ireland Worldwide 15th Fl 10900 Wilshire BlvdLos Angeles CA 90024-4341 Office Phone: 310-557-2700.

IRIBE, P. CHRISMAN, utilities executive; BA in Econs., George Washington U., postgrad. Energy economist, policy analyst Exec. Office of the President; various positions predecessor agys. U.S. Dept. Energy; officer Am. Gas Assn.; sr. v.p. ANR Pipeline Co. Coastal Corp.; sr. v.p. PG&E Corp., U.S. Gen., 1998—. Office: PG&E Generating Co One Market Plz Spear Tower 32400 San Francisco CA 94105

IRMAS, AUDREY MENEIN, not-for-profit developer; m. Sydney Milton Irmas Jr., June 26, 1949 (dec.); children: Deborah, Robert, Matthew. Co-founding trustee Audrey & Sydney Irmas Charitable Found., 1983—, projects include Audrey & Sydney Irmas Campus of the Wilshire Blvd. Temple, Audrey & Sydney Irmas LA Youth Ctr., many others; bd. trustees Mus. Contemporary Art, LA, 1992—, past pres., chmn.; trustee Hirshhorn Mus. and Sculpture Garden, Washington; bd. govs. ctr curator studies Bard Coll., NY. Named one of Top 200 Collectors, ARTnews mag., 2004. Avocation: Collector contemporary art, photography. Office: Audrey & Sydney Irmas Charitable Found Ste 364 16830 Ventura Blvd Encino CA 91436-2797 Office Phone: 818-382-3313. Office Fax: 818-382-3315.

IRVING, PAUL HOWARD, lawyer; BFA with highest honors, NYU, 1975; JD, Loyola Marymount U., LA, 1980. Bar: Calif. 1980, US Dist. Ct. (ctrl. dist.). Chief exec., mng. ptnr. Manatt, Phelps & Phillips, LLP, LA, 1999—2006, chmn., 2007—. Adj. prof. Loyola Law Sch., 1980—85; exec. com. mem. Anti-Defamation League Pacific S.W. Region; bd. dirs. Chanin Capital Ptnrs., Prospect Fin. Advs., LLC; spkr. in field. Mem. nat. coun. Human Rights First; bd. dirs. Operation Hope; nat. co-chair Hope Coalition Am.; mem. bd. trustees and exec. com. New Rds. Sch. Named Mgr. of Yr., LA Daily Jour. and San Francisco Daily Jour., 2002; named one of Top 25 Up-and-Coming Legal Stars in Calif., 1993. Mem.: Calif. Bar Assn. Office: Manatt Phelps & Phillips LLP 11355 W Olympic Blvd Los Angeles CA 90064-1614 Office Phone: 310-312-4196. Office Fax: 310-312-4224. E-mail: pirving@manatt.com.

IRWIN, JAY R., federal judge; Apptd. part-time magistrate judge U.S. Dist. Ct. Ariz. Office: 888 W 16th St Yuma AZ 85364-4542

IRWIN, MICHAEL RAY, psychology professor, researcher; b. Casper, Wyo., May 25, 1954; s. Donald Charles and Carolyn Irwin; m. Jennifer Len Pike, Dec. 30, 1988. AB in Biophysics, magna cum laude, U. Pa., 1976; student, U. Colo. Sch. Medicine; MD, U. Calif., San Diego, 1981. Lic. Calif., diplomate Am. Bd. Psychiatry. Intern internal medicine U. Calif., San Diego, 1981—82, resident psychiatry LA, 1982—85, asst. prof. psychiatry San Diego, 1985—91, assoc. prof., 1991—95, prof., 1995—2001, dir. Psychopharmacology Rsch. Fellowship Training Prog., 1991—2001; Norman Cousins prof., chair psychoneuroimmunology UCLA Semel Inst. Neurosoci. & Human Behavior, 2001—, dir. Cousins Ctr. for Psychoneuroimmunology, 2001—; disting. prof. psychiatry and biobehavioral scis. UCLA David Geffen Sch. Medicine, 2001—. Chief resident Clin. Rsch. Ctr. on Schizophrenia, VA Med. Ctr., LA, 1984—85; assoc. dir. Clin. Ctr. Rsch. on Alcoholism, VA Med. Ctr., San Diego, 1985—91, staff psychiatrist, 1985—2001; assoc. med. dir. Scripps McDonald Ctr. Alcohol & Drug Treatment, 1992—97; mem. mental health, AIDS, and immunology II review panel Nat. Inst. Mental Health, Bethesda, Md., 1995—98; mem. adv. coun. Nat. Ctr. Complementary & Alternative Medicine, Washington, 2001—05. Cons. editor Annals of Behavioral Medicine, 1993—98, mem. editl. bd. Psychosomatic Medicine, 1995—, Brain, Behavior and Immunity, 1995—, Sleep, 2006—, assoc. editor Psychosomatic Medicine, 1998—2001, Brain, Behavior and Immunity, 2002—; contbr. articles to profl. jours., chapters to books. Recipient Faculty Rsch. Mentor award, UCLA Sch. Medicine, 2005; grantee NIH; fellow NSF, 1974, Boettcher Found., 1977. Fellow: Am. Psychiatric Assn., Soc. Behavioral Medicine, Acad. Behavioral Medicine Rsch. (pres. 2002—04); mem.: ACP (Laughlin Fellow 1985), Am. Psychosomatic Soc. (adv. coun. 2001—04, Early Career award 1995), Pschoneuroimmunology Rsch. Soc. (pres. 1999—2001, Norman Cousins Rsch. award 2007). Office: Cousins Ctr Psychoneuroimmunology 300 UCLA Med Plz Ste 3109 Los Angeles CA 90095 Office Phone: 310-825-8281. Office Fax: 310-794-9247. E-mail: mirwin1@ucla.edu.*

IRWIN, PHILIP DONNAN, lawyer; b. Madison, Wis., Sept. 6, 1933; s. Constant Louis and Isabel Dorothy (Elfving) I.; m. Sandra L. McMahan, Sept. 14, 1985; children: Jane Donnan, James Haycraft, Victoria Wisnom, Philip Donnan Jr. BA, U. Wyo., 1954; LLB, Stanford U., 1957. Bar: Wyo. 1957, Calif. 1958. Assoc. O'Melveny & Myers, LA, 1957-65, ptnr., 1965-2000, of counsel, 2000—. Mem. planning com. Inst. Fed. Taxation of U. So. Calif. Law Ctr., 1976—, chairperson, 1995-98; spkr. legal seminars. Contbr. articles legal jours. Trustee Mackenzie Found., Los Angeles, 1969—. Recipient Dana Latham Meml. Lifetime Achievement award, LA County Bar Assn. (Taxation Sect.), 2002. Mem.: Calif. Club (L.A.). Republican. Episcopalian. Office: O'Melveny & Myers 400 S Hope St Rm 1835 Los Angeles CA 90071-2899 Office Phone: 213-430-6467. Business E-Mail: pirwin@omm.com.

IRWIN, R. ROBERT, lawyer; b. Denver, July 27, 1933; s. Royal Robert and Mildred Mary (Wilson) Irwin; m. Sue Ann Scott, Dec. 16, 1956; children: Lori, Stacy, Kristi, Amy. Student, U. Colo., 1951-54; BS in Law, U. Denver, 1955, LLB, 1957. Bar: Colo. 1957, Wyo. 1967. Asst. atty. gen. State of Colo., 1958-66; asst. divsn. atty. Mobil Oil Corp., Casper, Wyo., 1966-70; prin. atty. No. Natural Gas Co., Omaha, 1970-72; sr. atty., asst. sec. Coastal Oil & Gas Corp., Denver, 1972-83; ptnr. Baker & Hostetler, 1983-87; pvt. practice Denver, 1987—. Mem.: Rocky Mountain Oil and Gas Assn., Colo. Bar Assn., Denver Law Club. Republican. Office: 650 S Alton Way Apt 4D Denver CO 80247-1669 Office Phone: 303-344-8074. Business E-Mail: rrisas@msn.com.

IRWIN, WILLIAM RANKIN, retired lawyer; b. Springfield, Ill., Feb. 26, 1940; s. William Ross and Helen Katherine (O'Brien) I.; m. Alyce-Kaye Moffett, Oct. 1969 (div.); children: Elizabeth, Stephanie; m. Brenda L. Reinertson, Oct. 1, 1983; children: Matthew, Cydney. BA with honors, U. Ill., 1962; LLB with honors, U. Calif., Berkeley, 1965. Bar: Calif. 1966. Asst. Adminstrv. Office of the Cts., San Francisco, 1965-66; assoc. atty., ptnr. Brobeck, Phleger & Harrison, San Francisco, 1966-99. Mem. ABA (litigation sect., com. on ins. coverage), Calif. Bar Assn., Bar Assn. of San Francisco, Order of Coif, Phi Delta Phi. Avocations: sailing, travel, reading.

ISAAK, CHRIS, popular musician, singer, songwriter, actor; b. Stockton, Calif., June 26, 1956; Attended, U. Pacific, 1980. Formed band, Silvertone, 1981—; recording artist Warner Bros., 1985—. Actor, films Married to the Mob, 1988, Silence of the Lambs, 1991, Twin Peaks: Fire Walk With Me, 1992, Little Buddha, 1994, The Informers, 2009; contbr. feature film soundtracks Blue Velvet, 1986, Wild at Heart, 1991, A Perfect World, 1993, Tin Cup, 1996, Beautiful Girls, 1996; albums: Silvertone, 1985, Chris Isaak, 1987, Heart Shaped World, 1989, San Francisco Days, 1993; #1 hit Wicked Game, 1991, Forever Blue, 1995; amateur boxer, 1976-80. Office: Warner Records 3300 Warner Blvd Burbank CA 91505-4632

ISAKI, LUCY POWER SLYNGSTAD, lawyer; b. Jersey City, Oct. 21, 1945; d. Charles Edward and Ann Mary (Power) Slyngstad; m. Paul S. Isaki, Aug. 26, 1967. BA summa cum laude, Seattle U., 1973; JD cum laude, U. Puget Sound, 1977. Bar: Wash. 1977. Case worker San Joaquin County Welfare, Stockton, Calif., 1968-70, Alameda County Welfare, Oakland, Calif., 1971-73; legal intern King County Prosecutor's Office, 1976-77; law clk. to hon. Justice Hamilton Wash. Supreme Ct., 1977-78; ptnr. Bogle & Gates, Seattle, 1978—99; sr. asst. atty. gen. State of Wash., 1999—2006; mem. exec. team for Atty. Gen. Gregoire, Seattle, 2001—04; Wash. sr. asst. dir., legal counsel, risk mgmt. contracts divsn. Office Fin. Mgmt., State of Wash., 2006—, state risk mgr., 2007—. Cons. Region X, HHS, 1975; chair task force alternative dispute resolution Atty. Gen. Gregoire, 1993—94; mem. sentencing guidelines commn. State of Wash., 2006—. Bd. dirs. King County Family Svcs., Seattle, 1982—84, Wash. State Coun. Crime and Delinquency, 1981, Northwest Kidney Ctr., 2001—, vice chair, 2003—05, chair, 2005—07; treas. Mother's Against Violence Am., 1994; pres. Kinnear Vistas Homeowners' Assn., 2003—05; trustee Ea. Wash. U., 1984—96, Legal Found., Wash., 1992—95, sec. bd. dirs. Wash., 1993, v.p. bd. dirs. Wash., 1994, pres. Wash., 1995; chmn. law sch. bd. visitors Seattle U., 1984—96; trustee U. Puget Sound, 1985—, Seattle Youth Symphony, 1995. Recipient Disting. Law Grad., U. Puget Sound, 1984, Majis award, Seattle U., 1997; Dean's scholar, U. Puget Sound, 1976—77. Mem.: ABA (ho. dels. 1995—97), King County Bar Assn. (sec. 1986—87, trustee 1987—90, treas. 1995—97, 1st v.p. 1998, pres. 1999—2000, chair govt. lawyers sect. 2004—06), Wash. State Bar Assn., Wash. Women Lawyers (pres. Seattle-King County chpt. 1982, v.p. 1984), U. Puget Sound Law Alumni Soc. (pres. 1979). Democrat. Office: Office of Fin Mgmt PO Box 41027 Olympia WA 98504-1027 Office Phone: 360-902-3058. E-mail: lucy.isaki@ofm.wa.gov.

ISEMAN, MICHAEL DEE, medical educator; b. St. Paul, Mar. 3, 1939; s. Manuel Wessel and Eileen Catherine (Croghan) I.; m. Joan Marie Christensen, Aug. 31, 1963; children: Thomas Michael, Matthew Charles. BA in History, Princeton U., 1961; MD, Columbia U.,

1965. Intern, jr. resident in medicine Columbia Svc., Bellevue Hosp., NYC, 1965-67; sr. resident in medicine Columbia Svc., Harlem Hosp., NYC, 1969-70; fellow pulmonary medicine Harlem Hosp., NYC, 1970-72; assoc. dir. pulmonary svc. Denver Gen. Hosp., 1972-82; chief clin. mycobacteriology svc. Nat. Jewish Med. and Rsch. Ctr., Denver, 1982—2004. Asst. prof. medicine U. Colo. Sch. Medicine, Denver, 1973-79, assoc. prof. medicine, 1979-89, prof., 1989—. Author: A Clinician's Guide to Tuberculosis, 1999; assoc. editor Am. Rev. Respiratory Diseases, N.Y., 1984-89; editor-in-chief Internat. Jour. Tuberculosis and Lung Disease, 1997-2003. Pres. Am. Lung Assn. Colo., Denver, 1982-83; alumni trustee Princeton U., 1981-85. Lt. comdr. USN, 1967-69. Prin. investigator devel. and evaluation of drugs for treatment of mycobacterium avium in AIDS, NIH, 1984-1992. Fellow ACP, Am. Coll. Chest Physicians; mem. Am. Thoracic Soc. (v.p. 1983-84). Presbyterian. Avocations: rowing, skiing, tennis, photography, history. Office: Nat Jewish Med and Rsch Ctr 1400 Jackson St Denver CO 80206-2762 Business E-Mail: isemanm@njc.org.

ISENBERG, SHERWIN JAY, pediatric ophthalmologist; b. Chgo., Feb. 1, 1948; MD, UCLA, 1973. Cert. Am. Bd. Ophthalmology, 1978. Intern LA County Univ. So. Calif. Med. Ctr., 1973—74; resident in ophthalmology Chgo. Med. Ctr., Univ. Ill., 1974—77, Children's Hosp., Nat. Med. Ctr., Washington, 1977—78; prof. of surgery, chief ophthalmology div. Harbor UCLA Med. Ctr., physician, pediatric ophthalmology & strabismus. Contbr. articles to profl. jours. Office: Harbor UCLA Med Ctr 21840 Normandie Ave Torrance CA 90502 Office Phone: 310-794-9770.

ISENBERG, WALTER L., recreational facility executive; Grad., Cornell U. Exec. v.p. ops., founder Sage Hospitality Resources, L.P., Denver; exec. v.p., COO, founder Sage Hospitality Resources LLC, Denver. Office: Sage Hospitality Resources LLC 1512 Larimer St Ste 800 Denver CO 80202-1623

ISERSON, KENNETH VICTOR, bioethicist, writer, medical educator; b. Washington, Apr. 8, 1949; s. Isadore I. and Edith (Swedlow) I.; m. Mary Lou Sherk, June 16, 1973. BS, U. Md., 1971, MD, 1975; MBA, U. Phoenix, 1987. Diplomate Am. Bd. Emergency Medicine, Nat. Bd. Med. Examiners; cert. in Thanatology: Death, Dying and Bereavement, Assn. Death, Dying and Counseling, 2003. Intern surgery Mayo Clinic, Rochester, Minn., 1975; resident emergency medicine Cin. Gen. Hosp., 1976-78; capt. USAF, 1978-80; chmn. emergency dept. Tex. A&M Coll. Medicine, Temple, 1980-81; asst. prof. surgery U. Ariz. Coll. Medicine, Tucson, 1981-84, residency dir. emergency medicine, 1981-91, assoc. prof. surgery, 1984-92; dir. Ariz. Bioethics Program U. Ariz., Tucson, 1991—2008, prof. surgery, 1992—2001; prof. emergency medicine U. Ariz. Coll. Medicine, Tucson, 2001—08, prof. emeritus emergency medicine, 2008—; supervisory med. officer Disaster Med. Assistance Team AZ-1 Dept. Health and Human Svcs., 2002—; chief med. officer Project Hope Carribean, 2009. Pres. Iserson Assocs. Ltd., Tucson, 1984—; vis. scholar Ctr. Clin. Med. Ethics U. Chgo., Pritzker Sch. Medicine, 1990-91. Author: Iserson's Getting Into a Residency: A Guide for Medical Students, 1988, 7th edit., 2006, Death to Dust: What Happens to Dead Bodies?, 1994, 2nd edit., 2001, Non-Standard Medical Electives in the U.S. and Canada, 1997, 2nd edit., 1998, Get Into Medical School! A Guide for the Perplexed, 1997, 2nd. edit., 2004, Grave Words: Notifying Survivors About Sudden Unexpected Death, 1999, (video and slide sets) The Gravest Words, 2000, Demon Doctors: Physicians as Serial Killers, 2002; sr. editor: Ethics in Emergency Medicine, 1986, 2nd edit., 1995; mem. editl. bd. Cambridge Quar., 1991—, Jour. Emergency Medicine, 1985—; contbr. sci. articles to profl. jours. Med. dir. So. Ariz. Rescue Assn., Pima County, 1983—. Fellow Am. Coll. Emergency Physicians (life): mem. AMA, Med. Soc. US and Mex. (treas. 2002-03, v.p. 2003-04, pres. 2004-06), Soc. Acad. Emergency Medicine (pres. 1984-85), Wilderness Med. Soc. (bd. dir. 1987-91). E-mail: kvi@u.arizona.edu.

ISGAR, JIM, state legislator; m. Brenda Isgar; 5 children. BA in Acctg., Ft. Lewis Coll., Durango, Colo., 1973. Farmer, 1976—; pres. HH Ditch, Co., 1978—; CPA Brock, Cordle & Associates, Longmont, Colo.; mem. Dist. 6 Colo. State Senate, Denver, 2001—. Bd dirs. Southwestern Colo. Agr. Trade and Devel. Ctr., Farmers Home Adminstrn., La Plata County Cattlemen, La Plata County Farm Bur., La Plata Water Conservancy; pres., dist. bd. dirs. La Plata Conservancy; mem. Colo. Bd. Agr., pres. bd. dirs., 1993, chmn. audit com.; bd. liaison Colo. Commn Higher Edn. Mem.: Colo. Soc. CPA's, La Plata County Cattlemen's Assn. Democrat. Methodist. Office: 200 E Colfax Rm 332 Denver CO 80203 Office Phone: 303-866-4884.*

ISH, DANIEL RUSSELL, law educator, academic administrator; b. Loon Lake, Sask., Can., Aug. 28, 1946; s. Leme Jay and Obeline Delia (Sicotte) I.; m. Diane Maureen Cote, Sept. 2, 1967 (div. 1970); m. Bonnie Jeanne Bolger, Dec. 22, 1970; children: Jason Bolger, Rachel Bolger. LLB, BA, U. Sask., 1970; LLM, Osgoode Hall Law Sch., Toronto, Ont., Can., 1974. Bar: Alta. 1971, Sask. 1979; called to Queen's Counsel, 1991. Lawyer H. Lloyd MacKay, Banff, Alta., Canada, 1970-71; asst. prof. law McGill U., Montreal, Que., Canada, 1972-75; assoc. prof. U. Sask., Saskatoon, 1975-80, prof. law, 1980—, asst. dean law, 1977-78, dean, 1982—88, 1996—97, 2002—04; dir. Ctr. for Study of Coops., 1989-95; chief adjudicators Indian Residential Schs., Canada, 2007—. Author: The Taxation of Canadian Co-operatives, 1975, The Law of Canadian Co-operatives, 1981, Co-operatives in Principle and Practice, 1992, Legal Responsibilities of Directors and Officers in Canadian Cooperation, 1996. Pres. Univ. Credit Union, Saskatoon, 1979-80. Fulbright fellow, Stanford U., 1995—96. Mem. Law Found. Sask. (trustee 1982-88, 2002—), Law Soc. Sask. (bencher 1982-88, 2002—). Avocations: skiing, running. Office: U Sask Coll Law Saskatoon SK Canada S7N 5A6 Office Phone: 306-966-5870. Business E-Mail: dan.ish@usask.ca.

ISHAM, MARK, composer, jazz musician; b. NYC, Sept. 7, 1951; s. Howard Fuller and Patricia (Hammond) I.; m. Donna Linson, Feb. 24, 1990. Film scores include: Never Cry Wolf, 1983, Mrs. Soffel, 1984, The Times of Harvey Milk, 1984, Country, 1984, Trouble in Mind, 1985, The Hitcher, 1986, Made in Heaven, 1987, The Moderns, 1988, The Beast, 1988, Everybody Wins, 1990, Love at Large, 1990, Reversal of Fortune, 1990, Mortal Thoughts, 1991, Crooked Hearts, 1991, Point Break, 1991, Little Man Tate, 1991, Billy Bathgate, 1991, Cool World, 1992, A Midnight Clear, 1992, Of Mice and Men, 1992, The Public Eye, 1992, A River Runs Through It, 1992, Sketch Artist, 1992, Nowhere to Run, 1993, Fire in the Sky, 1993, Made in America, 1993, Short Cuts, 1993, Hidden Hawaii, 1994, Romeo is Bleeding, 1994, The Getaway, 1994, Quiz Show, 1994, Mrs. Parker and the Vicious Circle, 1994, Nell, 1994, Losing Isiah, 1995, The Net, 1995, Home for the Holidays, 1995, Last Dance, 1996, Gotti, 1996, Fly Away Home, 1996, Night Falls on Manhattan, 1997, Afterglow, 1997, The Education of Little Tree, 1997, Kiss the Girls, 1997, Blade, 1998 (ASCAP award, 1999), The Gingerbread Man, 1998, At First Sight, 1999, Free Money, 1999, October Sky, 1999, Body Shots, 1999, Galapagos, 1999, Varsity Blues, 1999, Rules of Engagement, 2000, Save the Last Dance, 2001, Hardball, 2001, Don't Say a Word, 2001, Life as a House, 2001, The Majestic, 2001, Impostor, 2002, Moonlight Mile, 2002, Highwaymen, 2003, The Cooler, 2003, Spartan, 2004, Miracle, 2004, Twisted, 2004, Crash, 2004, Racing Stripes, 2005, Kicking & Screaming, 2005, In Her Shoes, 2005, Running Scared, 2006, Eight Below, 2006 (ASCAP award, 2007), The Black Dahlia, 2006, Invincible, 2006, Bobby, 2006, Gracie, 2007, Next, 2007, Reservation Road, 2007, Pride & Glory, 2008, TV themes include: Chicago Hope,: EZ Streets (Emmy award, 1997), recs. include: (solo) Vapor Drawings, 1983,: Castalia, 1988, Tibet, 1989, Mark Isham, 1991, Blue Sun, 1995, (with Charles Jankel): Charles Jankel, (with Tom Fogerty): Deal It Out, (with America): View From the Ground, (with Van Morrison): Live at the Belfast Opera House,: Into the Music, Inarticulate Speech of the Heart, Common One, Beautiful Vision, (with Art Lande): Story of Baku,: Eccentricities of Earl Dant, Rubisa Patrol, Desert Marauders, We Begin, (with Group 87): Group 87,: A Career in Dada Processing, (with the Rolling Stones): Voodoo Lounge, (with Bruce Springsteen): Human Touch, (with Willie Nelson): Across the Borderline, (with Toots Thielmans): Toots, Film Music. Recipient Henry Mancini award, ASCAP, 2006. Office: Earle Tones Music Inc 23679 Calabasas Rd #522 Calabasas CA 91302

ISHII, ANTHONY W., judge; b. Santa Ana, Calif., 1946; AS, Reedley Jr. Coll., 1966; PharmD, U. Pacific, 1970; JD, U. Calif., Berkeley, 1973. Dep. city atty. City Atty.'s Office, Sacramento, 1975; dep. pub. defender County of Fresno, 1979; pvt. practice Fresno, 1979—83; justice ct. judge Parlier-Selma Judicial Dist., Fresno, Calif., 1983—93; mcpl. ct. judge Central Valley Mcpl. Ct., Fresno, Calif., 1994—97; judge U.S. Dist. Ct. (ea. dist.) Calif., 1997—. Office: Fed Bldg, Rm 3654 US Courthouse 1130 O St Fresno CA 93721-2201

ISHII, CLYDE HIDEO, plastic surgeon; b. Lihue, Hawaii, Mar. 29, 1952; MD, Jefferson Med. Coll., 1978. Diplomate Am. Bd. Surgery, Am. Bd. Plastic Surgery. Past chief plastic surgery Queens Med. Ctr., Honolulu, asst. chief of surgery; chief plastic surgery Shriners Hosp., Honolulu, 1993—. Office: 1329 Lusitana St Ste 304 Honolulu HI 96813-2412

ISHIMARU, AKIRA, electrical engineering educator; b. Fukuoka, Japan, Mar. 16, 1928; came to U.S., 1952; s. Shigezo and Yumi I.; m. Yuko Kaneda, Nov. 21, 1956; children: John, Jane, James, Joyce. BSEE, U. Tokyo, 1951; PhD, U. Wash., 1958. Registered profl. engr., Wash. Engr. Electro-Tech. Lab, Tokyo, 1951-52; tech. staff Bell Telephone Lab, Holmdel, NJ, 1956; asst. prof. U. Wash., Seattle, 1958-61, assoc. prof., 1961-65, prof. elec. engring., 1965-98, prof. emeritus, 1998—. Vis. assoc. prof. U. Calif., Berkeley, 1963-64; cons. Jet Propulsion Lab., Pasadena, Calif., 1964—, The Boeing Co., Seattle, 1984—. Author: Wave Propagation & Scattering in Random Media, 1978, Electromagnetic Wave Propagation, Radiation and Scattering, 1991; editor: Radio Science, 1982; founding editor Waves in Random and Complex Media, U.K., 1990. Recipient Faculty Achievement award Burlington Resources, 1990; Boeing Martin professorship, 1993. Fellow IEEE (editl. bd., Region VI Achievement award 1968, Centennial medal 1984, Antennas and Propagation Disting. Achievement award 1995, Heinrich Hertz medal 1999), IEEE Geosci. and Remote Sensing (Disting. Achievement award 1998, Third Millennium medal 2000), Acoustical Soc. Am., Optical Soc. Am. (assoc. editor jour. 1983), Inst. Physics U.K. (chartered physicist); mem. NAE, Internat. Union Radio Sci. (chmn. commn. B, John Howard Dellinger Gold medal 1999). Home: 2913 165th Pl NE Bellevue WA 98008-2137 Office: U Wash Dept Elec Enging PO Box 352500 Seattle WA 98195-2500 Home Phone: 425-885-0018; Office Phone: 206-543-2169. Business E-Mail: ishimaru@u.washington.edu.

ISIDORI, JOE, chef; s. Arthur Isidori. Grad., Culinary Inst. America, Hyde Park, NY. Chef de cuisine Nemo Restaurant Group, Miami Beach; corp. exec. chef Trump Gold Mgmt.; personal chef, family chef Donald Trump; v.p. food & beverage, exec. chef Mar-a-Lago Club, Palm Beach, 2006, Trump Internat. Hotel & Tower Las Vegas, 2008—. Exec. chef Donald & Melania Trump wedding, 2005; host chef Rising Stars Galas, 2008. Recipient 3 Five Star Diamond awards, Am. Acad. Hospitality Scis.; named one of Las Vegas' Rising Stars, StarChefs.com, 2008. Office: Trump Internat Hotel & Tower 2000 Fashion Show Dr Las Vegas NV 89109

ISLAMBOULY, HAGAR ABDEL-HAMID, consul general; b. Cairo, Jan. 5, 1947; d. Abdel Hamid and Souad (ElSherif) I.; m. Mohamed Adel Ezzat, Jan. 22, 1970. Diploma, Am. Coll. Girls, Cairo, 1964; BSc in Polit. Sci., Cairo U., 1969. With state info. svc. Ministry Information, Cario, 1970-74; with the cabinet of the ofcl. spokesman Ministry Fgn. Affairs Diplomatic Inst., Cairo, 1974; mem. internal. orgn. dept. Ministry Fgn. Affairs, Cairo, 1975-76; second sec. Embassy of Egypt, Madrid, 1976-80; with cabinet of the asst. minister of fgn. affairs for legal internat. orgns. affairs Ministry Fgn. Affairs, Cairo, 1980-81, mem. cabinet of the head of Egyptian mechanism for negotiation with Israel, 1981-84; counselor Egyptian Embassy, Bonn, Germany, 1984-88; dep. dir. Israeli affairs dept. Ministry Fgn. Affairs, Cairo, 1988-90, dep. dir. internat. orgns. dept., 1990-91, dir. environ. affairs dept., 1991-93, dir. internat. environ. affairs dept., 1991-95, dir. internat. economic affairs dept., 1993-95; consul gen., chief of mission Egyptian Consulate, San Francisco, 1995—. Attended UN Conf. for Environ. and Devel., Rio De Janeiro, 1992, Middle East/North Africa Economic Summit, UN Gen. Assembly, UN Agencies and UN Environ. Programs, UN Conf. Trade and Devel., UN Conf. on Population and Devel., 1991-95; attended Morocco Conf. Internat. Trade for Gen. Agreements of Tarrifs and Trade, Uruguay, 1994; mem. Egyptian Gen. Com. assigned to prepare for the Peace Conf. in the Middle East, Ministry Fgn. Affairs, 1990-95; head of the Egyptian delegation to the working group of environ.-multi lateral track of the Peace Conf. in the Middle East, Ministry Fgn. Affairs, 1991-95. Contbr. articles to profl. jours. Active environ. groups in Egypt; mem. regional organization and related com., summits Islamic Conf. Orgn., Arab League, Orgn. African Unity, 1993-95. Recipient The Order of Civil Merit, King of Spain, 1980, Order of Civil Merit, Pres. Germany, 1988. Mem. World State Forum (coord. Middle East affairs 1996—), World Trade Club, UN, San Francisco Consular Corps., World Affairs Coun., San Francisco Ladies of Consular Corps, Commonwealth Club. Islamic. Avocations: reading, classical music, jogging. Office: Egyptian Consulate 3001 Pacific Ave San Francisco CA 94115-1099 Fax: 415-346-9480.

ISMAIL, ALEXANDRE, diversified technology and manufacturing company executive; BA in Fin., Dauphine U., Paris; MBA, HEC Sch. Mgmt., Jouy-en-Josas, France. Joined Honeywell Internat. Inc., 1999, various positions Honeywell Turbo Technologies divsn., including worldwide dir. mktg./bus. devel., v.p. Europe/Mid. East/Africa (EMEA) sales/customer mgmt., v.p., gen. mgr. EMEA & India, then pres. global passenger vehicles, 2006—08, pres. Honeywell Turbo Technologies, 2008—09, pres., CEO Honeywell Transp. Systems, 2009—. Office: Honeywell Internat Inc Worldwide Hdqs 23326 Hawthorne Blvd Ste 200 Torrance CA 90505 Office Phone: 310-791-9101. Office Fax: 310-791-9122.*

ISRAEL, ALLEN D., lawyer; b. Seattle, Nov. 28, 1946; m. Nettie Israel. BSME, U. Wash., 1968, MBA, 1971, JD, 1978. Bar: Wash. 1978. Ptnr. Foster Pepper PLLC, Seattle, 1978—. Office: Foster Pepper PLLC 1111 3rd Ave Ste 3400 Seattle WA 98101-3299 Office Phone: 206-447-8911. Business E-Mail: IsraA@Foster.com.

ISRAEL, DAVID, journalist, scriptwriter, film producer; b. NYC, Mar. 17, 1951; s. Hyman and Edith Oringer I.; m. Lindy De Koven, Aug. 8, 1987. BS in Journalism, Northwestern U., 1973. Reporter Chgo. Daily News, 1973-75; columnist Washington Star, 1975-78, Chgo. Tribune, 1978-81, L.A. Herald Examiner, 1981-84; chmn., pres. Big Prodn., Inc., LA; prod., writer OCC Prodn., LA, 1985-88; exec. prodr., writer Lorimar TV, LA, 1988-92, Paramount Pictures, Hollywood, Calif., 1992-93; writer, exec. prodr. Stephen J. Cannell Prod., Inc., Hollywood, 1993-95. Dir. office of Pres., Los Angeles Olympic Organizing Com., 1984; exec. prodr. House of Frankenstein, NBC, Universal, 1997, exec. prodr. Mutiny, NBC, 1999, Y2K, NBC, 1999, Tremors, SciFi, 2002-03. Supervising prodr., writer: A Comedy Salute to Baseball, NBC, 1985; supervising prodr., writer: Fast Copy, NBC, 1985-86; co-creator, supervising prodr.: Crimes of the Century, 1987-88; co-exec. prodr., writer: Midnight Caller, NBC, Lorimar TV, 1988-91, The Untouchables, Paramount TV, 1992-93; exec. prodr., writer: Jake Lassiter: Justice on the Bayou, NBC, Stephen J. Cannell Prodn., 1995; exec. prodr., writer: Pandora's Clock, NBC, Citadel Entertainment, 1996; consulting prodr., writer, Turks, CBS Studios, USA, 1998-99; coord. prodr. Monday Night Football, ABC Sports, 2000-01. Commr. LA Meml. Coliseum Commn., 2005—, v.p., 2007—; bd. dirs. Calif. Govs. and First Lady's Conf. on Women and Families, Calif. Sci. Ctr., 2004—, Calif. State Alliance, 2004—06, exec. com., 2004—06. Mem. AFTRA, Writers Guild Am., Chgo. Athletic Assn., Beverly Hills Tennis Club. Office: c/o Bob Broder & Chris Von Goetz ICM 10250 Constellation Blvd Los Angeles CA 90067

ISRAEL, JOAN, social worker; b. Bklyn., July 19, 1943; d. Joseph Israel and Irene (Solon) Kansey; 1 child, Ariel Naomi Janesh. BA, Bklyn. Coll., 1965; MSW, U. Mich., 1974. Lic. clin. social worker, Nev. Social worker Alameda County Welfare Dept., Oakland, Calif., 1965-72; group therapist Pacific Ctr. for Human Growth, Berkeley, Calif., 1975-77; individual and group therapist, bd. dir. Bi-Ctr., San Francisco, 1976-78; clin. social worker, supr. Audrey L. Smith Devel. Ctr., San Francisco, 1977-78; psychiat. social worker South Nev. Adult Mental Health Dept., Las Vegas, 1978-84, part-time clin. social worker, 1988—; pvt. practice clin. social worker Las Vegas, 1984—. Contbr. articles to profl. jours. Organizer Drug/Alcohol Abuse Task Force, Las Vegas, 1983-84, Task Force on AIDS, Las Vegas, 1985-86. Mem. NASW (chair nominating com. 1978-80, 82-84, sec. 1984-86, chair com. on inquiry 1988—, legis. chair 1982-84, diplomate clin. social work), Sierra Club. Democrat. Jewish. Avocations: hiking, singing, opera, dance. Office: Ste 120 7200 Cathedral Rock Dr Las Vegas NV 89128 Home Phone: 702-656-9921; Office Phone: 702-804-6686. Personal E-mail: joanofisrael@aol.com. E-mail: israeljoan@wgbtv.com.

ISRAEL, RICHARD STANLEY, investment banker; b. Oakland, Calif., Sept. 27, 1931; s. Sybil Noble, July 29, 1962; children: Richard Lee, Lynne, Lawrence. BA, MA, U. Calif., Berkeley, 1953. Copy editor San Francisco Chronicle, 1953-59; publicist CBS TV Network, LA, 1959-62; sr. v.p. Rogers & Cowan, Beverly Hills, Calif., 1962-69, Cantor, Fitzgerald, Beverly Hills, Calif., 1969-73; pres. Sponsored Cons. Svcs., LA, 1973—; managing ptnr. Mason, Israel & Ptnrs., Beverly Hills, Calif. Bd. dirs. Hurst Labeling Sys.; founding mem. dean's adv. bd. UCLA Extension. Pres. North Beverly Dr. Homeowners Assn., Beverly Hills, 1986-88; v.p. Temple Emanuel, Beverly Hills, 1988-93, L.A. chpt. Juvenile Diabetes Found. Internat. 1987—. With U.S. Army, 1956-58. Recipient Alumni citation U. Calif. Alumni Assn., Berkeley, 1984. Mem. L.A. Venture Assn. (pres. 1987), Assn. for Corp. Growth (pres. bd. dirs. L.A. chpt.). Democrat. Avocations: volleyball, travel. Office: Mason Israel & Ptnrs 8929 Wilshire Blvd Ste 214 Beverly Hills CA 90211-1951 Office Phone: 310-208-1234. Business E-Mail: dick@masonisrael.com.

ISRAEL, WERNER, physicist, educator; b. Berlin, Oct. 4, 1931; s. Arthur and Marie (Kappauf) I.; m. Inge Margulies, Jan. 26, 1958; children: Mark Abraham, Pia Lee. BSc, U. Cape Town, 1951, MSc, 1954; PhD, Trinity Coll., Dublin, 1960; DSc (hon.), Queen's U., Kingston, Ont., 1987; Docteur honoris causa, U. Francois Rabelais, France, 1994; DSc (hon.), U. Victoria, B.C., Can., 1999. Asst. prof. physics U. Alta., Canada, 1958-68, prof., 1968-85, Univ. prof., 1985-96; adj. prof. dept. physics and astronomy U. Victoria, Canada, 1996—; hon. prof. dept. physics and astronomy U. B.C., Canada. Sherman Fairchild disting. scholar Calif. Inst. Tech., 1974-75; vis. prof. Dublin Inst. Advanced Studies, 1966-68, U. Cambridge, 1975-76, Institut Henri Poincare, 1976-77, U. Berne, 1980, Kyoto U., 1986, 98; vis. fellow Gonville and Caius Coll., Cambridge, 1985; fellow Can. Inst. for Advanced Rsch., 1986—. Editor: Relativity, Astrophysics and Cosmology, 1973; co-editor: General Relativity, An Einstein Centenary Survey, 1979, 300 Years of Gravitation, 1987. Decorated officer Order of Can.; recipient Izaak Walton Killiam Meml. prize, 1984, Medal in math. physics, Ctr. Rsch. Math./Can. Assn. Physicists, 1995, Tomalla Found. for Gravitational Rsch. prize, 1996. Fellow Royal Soc. Can., Royal Soc. (London); mem. Can. Assn. Physicists (medal of Achievement in Physics 1981), Internat. Soc. Gen. Relativity and Gravitation (pres. 1997-2001). Jewish. Office: U Victoria Dept Physics Astronomy Victoria BC Canada V8W 3P6 Business E-Mail: israel@uvic.ca.

ISSA, DARRELL E., United States Representative from California; b. Cleve., Nov. 1, 1953; AA, Kent State U., Ohio, 1976; BA in Bus., Siena Heights U., Adrian, Mich., 1976. Founder, CEO Directed Electronics, Vista, Calif., 1982—99; mem. US Congress from 49th (formerly 48th) Calif. dist., 2000—, mem. judiciary com., oversight & govt. reform com., permanent select com. on intelligence. Co-chair Calif. Civic Rights Initiative, 1996, US-Philippines Caucus; former dir. Bus.-Industry Polit. Action Com. Bd. trustees Siena Heights U.

Served with US Army, 1970—80. Recipient Ellis Island Medal of Honor; named Entrepreneur of Yr., Inc. mag., 1994, Angel of Yr., North County Solutions for Change, 2004. Mem.: Consumer Electronics Assn. (past chair), Electronics Industries Assn. (past bd. gov.'s), San Diego County C. of C., San Diego Econ. Devel. Assn. Republican. Office: 211 Cannon House Office Bldg Washington DC 20515-0549

ISSEL, DANIEL PAUL, sports team executive, former professional basketball coach; b. Batavia, IL, Oct. 25, 1948; m. Cheri Issel; children: Sheridan, Scott. Student, U. Ky. Basketball player Ky. Cols., 1970-75, Denver Nuggets, 1975-85; broadcast analyst U. Ky., 1987-88; color analyst, mgr. player edn. and career enhancement programs Denver Nuggets, 1988-92, head coach, 1992-94, gen. mgr., 1998-99, pres., head coach, 1999—. Prin. Courtland Farms Horse Racing. Office: Denver Nuggets 1000 Chopper Cir Denver CO 80204-5809

ISTEL, JACQUES ANDRE, Mayor, Felicity, California; b. Paris, Jan. 28, 1929; came to US, 1940, naturalized, 1951; s. Andre and Yvonne Mathilde Cremieux I.; m. Felicia Juliana Lee, June 14, 1973; 1 dau. by previous marriage, Claudia Yvonne. AB, Princeton U., NJ, 1949. Stock analyst Andre Istel & Co., NYC, 1950, 55; pres. Parachutes Inc., Orange, Mass., 1957-87, Intramgmt. Inc., NYC, 1962-80; chmn. Pilot Knob Corp., 1982—; mayor Town of Felicity, Calif., 1986—; curator Ctrl. Point for Memories, Calif., 1992—. Pres. VI World Parachuting Championships, 1962; capt. U.S. Parachuting team, 1956, master of sports, USSR, 1956, capt., team leader, 1958; chmn. Mass. Parachuting Commn., 1961-62; life hon. pres. Internat. Parachuting Commn., Fedn. Aero. Internat., 1965-; chmn. Hall of Fame of Parachuting, 1973—, Imp. Co. water commn. 1997—; founder Nat. Collegiate Parachuting League, 1957, World Commemorative Ctr., 1993; co-leader Nat. Geog. Soc. Vilcabamba Expdn., 1964. Author: Coe the Good Dragon at the Center of the World, 1985, Coe le Bon Dragon au Centre du Monde, 1985; editor in granite Museum Walls, 2001—; contbr. articles to encys., profl. jours.; patentee in field. Trustee Inst. for Man and Sci., 1975-82; bd. dirs. Marine Corps Scholarship Found., 1975-85; founder Mus. History Granite, 2005—. Served with USMC, 1952-54; lt. col. Res. Recipient Leo Stevens award, 1958, Diplome Paul Tissandier, 1969, Air and Space medal, 2003, Official Citation, Mass. State Senate, 2007, Lifetime Achievement award, US Parachute Assn., 2009; decorated chevalier de la Legion D'Honneur; named Hon. Citizen Yuma, Ariz., 2007; world record holder for parachuting, 1961, Hon. Golden Knight, US Army, 2009. Mem. Nat. Aero. Assn. (bd. dirs. 1965-68), Fedn. Internat. des Centres (pres. 1990—), Cercle de l'Union Interalliée (Paris), Marine Corps Res. Officers Assn., DAV (life), Racquet and Tennis Club (NYC), Princeton Club (NYC). Home: Northview Felicity CA 92283 also: 10 rue Galilée 75116 Paris France Office: 1 Center Of The World Plz Felicity CA 92283-7777 Office Phone: 760-572-0100. Personal E-mail: ctrworld@aol.com.

ITABASHI, HIDEO HENRY, coroner, pathologist, educator, consultant; b. LA, July 7, 1926; s. Masakichi and Mitsuko (Kobayashi) I.; m. Yoko Osawa, Feb. 3, 1952; children: Mark Masa, Helen Yoko. AB, Boston U., 1949, MD, 1954; postgrad., Yale U., 1949—50. Diplomate in neuropathology Am. Bd. Pathology. Intern U. Mich. Hosp., Ann Arbor, 1954-55, resident in neurology, 1955-58; assoc. rsch. neurologist U. Calif., San Francisco, 1958-60, asst. clin. prof., 1964-65; asst. neuropathologist Langley Porter Neuropsychiat. Inst., San Francisco, 1960-65; cons. Neuropathologist San Francisco Gen. Hosp., 1964-65; assoc. prof. neurology, pathology U. Mich. Med. Sch., Ann Arbor, 1968-71; prof.-in-residence pathology and neurology UCLA, 1975-93, prof. emeritus, 1993—, acting vice chair dept. pathology Sch. Medicine; acting chair pathology Harbor-UCLA Med. Ctr., 1990-91; cons. neuropathology dept., chief med. examiner-coroner Los Angeles County, 1977—. Cons. VA Hosp., Sepulveda, Calif., 1977-92; spl. fellow in neuropathology Nat. Inst. Neurol. Diseases and Blindness, 1958-60. Contbr. numerous articles on neurol. disorders to med jours. Fellow Am Acad. Forensic Scis.; mem. Am. Assn. Neuropathologists (sr.), Am. Acad. Neurology (sr.). Office: County LA Dept Coroner 1104 N Mission Rd Los Angeles CA 90033 Home Phone: 310-377-0664.

ITANO, HARVEY AKIO, biochemistry educator; b. Sacramento, Nov. 3, 1920; s. Masao and Sumako (Nakahara) I.; m. Rose Nakako Sakemi, Nov. 5, 1949; children: Wayne Masao, Glenn Harvey, David George. BS, U. Calif., Berkeley, 1942; MD, St. Louis U., 1945; PhD, Calif. Inst. Tech., 1950; DSc (hon.), St. Louis U., 1987. Intern City of Detroit Receiving Hosp., 1945-46; commd. officer USPHS, Bethesda, Md., 1950-70, advanced through grades to chief, sect. on chem. genetics, Nat. Inst. Arthritis and Metabolic Diseases, NIH, 1962-70, mem. hematology study sect., NIH, 1959-63, research fellow then sr. research fellow, Calif. Inst. Tech. Pasadena, 1950-54; prof. Dept. Pathology U. Calif. San Diego, La Jolla, 1970-88, prof. emeritus, 1988—. Vis. prof. Osaka (Japan) U., 1961-62, U. Chgo., 1965, U. Calif., San Francsico, 1967; cons. sickle cell anemia, mem. hematology study sect. 1953-63, various sickle cell anemia rev. coms., 1970-81, NIH, Bethesda. Editor: (with Linus Pauling) Molecular Structure and Biological Specificity, 1957; contbr. articles to profl. jours. George Minot lectr., AMA, 1955; Japan Soc. for Promotion of Sci. fellow, Okayama U., 1983-84. Mem. NAS, Am. Acad. Arts and Scis., Am. Chem. Soc. (Eli Lilly award in Biol. Chemistry 1954), Am. Soc. Biochemistry and Molecular Biology, Am. Soc. Hematology, Internat. Soc. Hematology, Phi Beta Kappa, Sigma Xi, Alpha Omega Alpha. Office: U Calif Dept Pathology 9500 Gilman Dr La Jolla CA 92093-0612

ITO, HIROSHI, chemist, researcher; Rsch. scientist Almaden Rsch. Ctr. IBM, San Jose, Calif. Recipient award Coop. Rsch. in Polymer Sci. and Engring., Am. Chem. Soc., 1992, award Soc. of Polymer Sci. (Japan), 1990, Photopolymer Sci. and Tech. award Tech. Assn. Photopolymer Japan, 1997, Kosar Meml. award Soc. Imaging Sci. Tech., 1999. Office: IBM Almaden Rsch Ctr 650 Harry Rd San Jose CA 95120-6099

ITO, LANCE ALLAN, judge; b. LA, Aug. 2, 1950; s. Jim and Toshi Ito; m. Margaret York. BA cum laude, UCLA, 1972; JD, U. Calif., Berkeley, 1975. Bar: Calif. 1976. Civil atty., 1975—77; dep. dist. atty. gang unit, complaints divsn., organized crime unit LA County Dist. Attys. Office, 1977—87; judge LA County Mcpl. Ct., 1987—89, Superior Ct. Calif., LA County, 1989—. Vice chair Calif. Task Force on Youth Gang Violence, 1986, 89, Calif. Task Force on Victims Rights, 1988. Named Trial Judge of Yr., LA County Bar Assn., 1992. Mem.: Japanese-Am. Bar Assn., LA County Bar Assn., Calif. Judges Assn. (bd. dirs., mem. Calif. coun. on criminal justice). Democrat. Office: Criminal Cts Bldg 210 W Temple St Los Angeles CA 90012-3210

ITOH, TATSUO, engineering educator; b. Tokyo, May 5, 1940; BS, Yokohama Nat. U., Japan, 1964, MS, 1966; PhD, U. Ill., 1969. Registered profl. engr., Tex. Rsch. assoc. U. Ill., Urbana, 1969-71, rsch. asst. prof., 1971-76; sr. rsch. engr. Stanford Rsch. Inst., Menlo Park, Calif., 1976-77; assoc. prof. U. Ky., Lexington, 1977-78, U. Tex., Austin, 1978-81, prof., 1981-90, Hayden Head prof., 1983-90; prof.and TRW endowed chair UCLA, 1991—. Guest rschr. AEG-Telefunken, Ulm, Fed. Republic of Germany, 1979; vis. prof. Def. Acad. Japan, 1991, U. Leeds, Eng., 1994—; hon. vis. prof. Nanjing Inst. Tech., China; hon. prof. Beijing Aeronautical and Astron. U., China, 1995—; adj. rsch. officer Comms. Rsch. Lab., Ministry of Post and Telecom., Japan, 1994; cons. Tex. Instruments, Dallas, 1979, Hughes Aircraft. Editor (guest): Transactions, 1991. Recipient Engring. Found. faculty awards, 1980-81, Billy and Claude Hocott Disting. Rsch. award, 1988, Disting. Alumnus award U. Ill., 1990, Shida award Min. of Post and Telecom., Japan, 1998, Japan Microwave prize Asia-Pacific Microwave Conf., 1998. Fellow IEEE (Millennium medal 2000, MTT Disting. Microwave Educator award 2000), Nat. Acad. Engring.; mem. Microwave Theory and Techniques Soc. (hon. life; editor 1983-85, pres. 1990, jour. editor Microwave and Guided Wave Letters 1991-94), Internat. Sci. Radio Union (chmn. USNC commn. D 1988-90, chmn. commn. D 1993-96, long range planning com. 1996—), Inst. Electronics and Comm. Engrs., Nat. Acad. Engring. Achievements include invention of the millimeter-wave line; quasi-optical mixer; non-contact ID; high power photo detector. Office: UCLA Dept Elec Engring Los Angeles CA 90095-0001 Home: 12 Eastfield Dr Rolling Hills CA 90274-5226 Office Phone: 310-206-4820. Business E-Mail: itoh@ee.ucla.edu.

IVE, JONATHAN, information technology executive, product designer; b. London, 1967; Studies design and art, Northumbria U., Eng., 1985; BA, Doctorate, Newcastle Polytechnic. Ptnr. Tangerine, London, 1989—92; with Apple Computer, Inc., Cupertino, Calif., 1992—, head, design team, 1996—, sr. v.p. indsl. design apple computers, 1998—. Work widely exhibited in Europe, N.Am. and Asia, forming permanent collections at many museums. Recipient Designer of Yr. prize, Design Mus. London, 2003, Product Designer of Yr. award, BluePrint Magazine, 2004, President's award for Outstanding Contribution to the Industry, Design and Art Direction Awards, 2005; named as having the greatest impact on popular culture, BBC poll, 2002, New Media Hero, British Interactive Media Assn., 2003, Most Admired in the Creative Industries, Creative Review Peer Poll, 2003, No. 1 on the list. British Culture's Top 50 Movers and Shakers, BBC 3, 2004, Comdr. of the Most Excellent Order of the British Empire (CBE), 2005; named one of Best and Brightest, Esquire, 2002, Details, 2002, 25 Masters of Innovation, BusinessWeek, 2006. Fellow: Royal Soc. Arts (Inaugural medal for Design Achievement 1999, awarded title of Royal Designer for Industry 2003). Lead designer of the following launches: iMac, 1998; Apple iBook, the 22" Cinema Display, PowerMac G4 Tower and iSub, 1999; Apple G4 Cube, 2000; Titanium PowerBook G4 and iPod portable MP3 Player, 2001; sunflower-inspired iMac with 15" and 17" floating screens, 2002; eMac, 2002; Apple 12" PowerBook and 17" Powerbook, 1" thick and 6.8 lbs, world's slimmest and lightest 17" notebook computer, 2003, iMac G5, 2004, iPod Shuffle, 2005, Mac Mini, 2005, iPhone, 2007. Office: Apple Computer Inc 1 Infinite Loop Cupertino CA 95014 Office Fax: 408-974-2113.

IVERSON, PETER JAMES, historian, educator; b. Whittier, Calif., Apr. 4, 1944; s. William James and Adelaide Veronica (Schmitt) I.; m. Kaaren Teresa Gonsoulin, Mar. 7, 1983; children: Erika, Jens, Tim, Scott. BA in History, Carleton Coll., 1967; MA in History, U. Wis., 1969, PhD in History, 1975. Vis. asst. prof. Ariz. State U., Tempe, Ariz., 1975-76; from asst. prof to prof. U. Wyo., Laramie, Wyo., 1976-86; coord. divsn. social and behavioral scis. Ariz. State U., Phoenix, 1986-88, prof. history Tempe, Ariz., 1988—, regents prof. history, 2000—. Panelist, reviewer Nat. Endowment Humanities, Washington, 1986—; vis. prof. Carleton Coll., 1991. Author: The Navajos: A Critical Bibliography, 1976, The Navajo Nation, 1981, Carlos Montezuma, 1982, The Navajos, 1990, When Indians Became Cowboys: Native Peoples and Cattle Ranching in the American West, 1994, Barry Goldwater: Native Arizonan, 1997, We Are Still Here: American Indians in the 20th Century, 1998, Riders of the West: Portraits From Indian Rodeo, 1999, Diné: A History of the Navajos, 2002; co-editor: Indians in American History, 1998; editor: The Plains Indians of the 20th Century, 1985, For Our Navajo People: Din+248 Letters, Speeches, and Petitions, 1900-1960, 2002; co-editor: Major Problems in American Indian History, 1994, 2d edit., 2001; assoc. editor The Historian, 1990-95; editl. bd. Pacific Hist. Rev., 1986-88, Jour. Ariz. History, 1987-89, Social Sci. Jour., 1988-96, Montana: The Magazine of Western History, 1993—, Western Historical Quarterly, 2000-02. Acting dir. McNickle Ctr. for History of Am. Indian, Newberry Libr., 1994-95, mem. adv. bd., 1993-2003; bd. dir. Ariz. Humanities Coun., 1993-99; chmn. Wyo. Coun. Humanities, 1981-82; mem. Heard Mus., Phoenix, 1986—, Desert Bot. Garden, Phoenix, 1986—. Recipient Chief Manuelito Appreciation award Navajo Nation, 1984, Disting. Achievement award Carleton Coll. Alumni Assn., 1992, Lifetime Achievement award Am. Indian Hist. Assn., 1999, Him-Dak Eco-Mus. Svc. award Ak-Chin Indian Cmty., 2001, We. Writers Am. Spur award, 2002, Outstanding Doctoral Mentor award ASU Grad. Coll., 2002, Outstanding rsch. award ASU Alumni Assn., 2005; fellow Newberry Libr., Chgo., 1973-74, NEH, 1982-83, 99-2000, Kellogg Found., Battle Creek, Mich., 1982-85, Guggenheim Found., 1999-2000; Disting. Pub. scholar, Ariz. Humanities Coun., 1999. Mem.: Am. Soc. Ethnohistory (coun. 1991—93, chmn. program com. 1994, chmn. prize com. 1987), We. Social Sci. Assn. (pres. 1988—89), Orgn. Am. Historians, We. History Assn. (chmn. prize com. 1991, co-chmn. program com. 1995, coun. 1995—98, pres. elect 2003—04, pres. 2004—05). Office: Ariz State U Dept History Tempe AZ 85287-4302 Business E-Mail: piverson@asu.edu.

IVEY, THOMAS J., lawyer; b. Leeds, Yorkshire, UK, 1967; BA cum laude, UCLA, 1989; JD, U. Calif. Boalt Hall Sch. Law, 1992. Bar: Calif. 1993. Ptnr. Skadden. Co-chair PLI's seminar on Vulture Capital and Corporate Restructuring, 2002, PLI's seminar on Current Trends in Convertible Debt, 2003; guest lectr. UC Berkeley's Sch. Law. Contbr. article to firm website. Bd. mem. Bus. United in Investing, Lending and Devel. Office: Skadden 525 U Ave Ste 1100 Palo Alto CA 94301 Office Phone: 650-470-4522. Office Fax: 888-329-3302. Business E-Mail: tivey@skadden.com.

IWAN, WILFRED DEAN, mechanical engineer, educator; b. Pasadena, Calif., May 21, 1935; s. Wilfred August and Dorothy Anna Sarah (Glass) I.; m. Alta Joan Gish, Sept. 13, 1957; children: William Douglas, Robert Dean, Stephen Bruce. BS, Calif. Inst. Tech., 1957, MS, 1958, PhD, 1961. Asst. and assoc. prof. mechanics U.S. Air Force Acad., 1961-64; asst., assoc. and prof. applied mechanics Calif. Inst. Tech., 1964—; dir. Earthquake Engring. Rsch. Lab., 1993—, 1993—; pres. Calif. Univs. for Rsch. in Earthquake Engring., 1988-91. Chmn. Calif. Seismic Safety Commn., 1986-88, 92-94; cons. to industry; prin. investigator on various federally sponsored rsch. projects; mem. NRC Bd. on Natural Disasters, 1992—, chmn., 1996—, mem. com. on hazard mitigation engring., 1992-95, chmn., 1992-95. Assoc. editor Jour. Applied Mechanics, ASME, 1982-89; mem. editorial bd. Internat. Jour. Soil Dynamics and Earthquake Engring., 1981-93, Internat. Jour. Probabilistic Engring. Mechanics, 1985—; contbg. editor Internat. Jour. Nonlinear Mechanics, 1996—; contbr. articles to profl. jours. Active Lake Ave Congregational Ch., Pasadena. Capt. USAF, 1961-64. Fellow ASME; mem. ASCE (Nathan M. Newmark medal 1997), Earthquake Engring. Rsch. Inst. Rsch. in vibration dynamics, earthquake engring. Office: Calif Inst Tech Mail Code 104 # 44 Pasadena CA 91125-0001

IWASE, RANDALL YOSHIO, state legislator; b. Honolulu, Dec. 1, 1947; s. Bruce S. and Ruby N. (Hamasaki) Hamada; m. Jan W. Amemiya, Jan. 8, 1977; 3 children. BA, U. Fla., 1971; JD, U. San Francisco, 1974. Dep. atty. gen. Dept. of Atty. Gen., Honolulu, 1974-85; city coun. mem. Honolulu City Coun., 1986-88; exec. dir. Aloha Tower Devel. Corp., Honolulu, 1988-90; state senator Hawaii St. Senate, Honolulu, 1990-2000; atty. Dwyer, Imanaka, Schraff, Honolulu, 1991—. Mem. Japanese Am. Citizens League, Honolulu, 1990—; bd. dirs. Nanakuli (Hawaii) Neighborhood Housing Svc., 1990—, West Oahu YMCA, Mililani, Hawaii, 1990—. Mem. Hawaii State Bar Assn., Phi Beta Kappa, Phi Kappa Phi. Democrat. Avocations: reading, tennis. Office: Hawaii State Senate 415 S Beretania St Rm 222 Honolulu HI 96813-2407

IZATT, REED M., chemistry researcher; b. Logan, Utah, Oct. 10, 1926; s. Alexander Spowart Jr. and Marian (McNeil) I.; m. Helen Felix, Aug. 10, 1949 (dec. July 1998); children: Susan Marie Foster, Linda Jean, Neil Ernest, Ted Alexander, Steven Reed, Anne Marie; m. Virginia Bills Christensen, Oct. 24, 1998 (dec. November 2007); step-children: Mark, Larry, Blake, Scott, Holly; m. Janet Spilbury Bradshaw Sep. 5, 2008, Step-children: Karen, Brian, Tracy, Keith, Marie, Charles, Daniel. BS, Utah State U., 1951; PhD, Pa. State U., 1954; postgrad., Carnegie Mellon U., 1954-56. Dir. grad. and undergrad. student rsch. Brigham Young U., Provo, Utah, 1956—. Vis. prof. U. Utah, Salt Lake City, 1972, U. Calif., San Diego, 1977. Contbr. articles to profl. jours. and books. Recipient Karl G. Maeser Rsch. and Creative Arts award, 1967, NIH Career Devel. award, 1967-72, Huffman award, 1983, Utah Gov.'s medal for Sci., 1990, Alumni Achievement award, Utah State U., 2001. Fellow: AAAS; mem.: Internat. Symposium on Macrocyclic Chemistry (mem. internat. adv. com.), Calorimetry Conf. (bd. dirs. 1973—76), Utah Acad. Scis., Arts and Letters (Gardner prize 1983), Am. Chem. Soc. (chmn. Salt Lake sect. 1965, councilor Salt Lake and ctrl. Utah sects. 1966—72, mem. local sect. activities com. 1966—72, Separations Sci. and Tech. award 1996), Phi Kappa Phi, Sigma Xi (pres. Brigham Young U chpt. 1980—82). Office: Brigham Young U Dept Chem & Biochem C100 Benson Sci Bldg Provo UT 84602-5700

JABARA, MICHAEL DEAN, real estate developer, former technology entrepreneur; b. Sioux Falls, SD, Oct. 26, 1952; s. James M. and Jean Marie (Swiden) J.; m. Gundula Beate Dietz, Aug. 26, 1984; children: James Michael, Jenna Mariel. Student, Mich. Tech. U., 1970-72; BSBA, U. Calif., Berkeley, 1974; MBA, Pepperdine U., 1979. Mgr. original Sprint project team So. Pacific Communications Corp., 1976-78; network product mgr. ROLM Corp., 1978-81; cons. McGraw Hill Co., Hamburg and London, 1982—83; founder and CEO Friend Techs. Inc. (merger VoiceCom Sys., Inc., now Premiere Techs., Inc.), San Francisco, 1984—88; pres. VoiceCom Ventures, San Francisco, 1988-93; mng. dir. Telecom, EMS Group Ltd., London, 1993-95; owner Red Rock Ptnrs., Ltd., Las Vegas, Nev., 1993—; chmn. bd. and COO Bingo Card Minder Corp., Stateline, Nev., 1996; owner TOIR LLC, Glenbrook, 1998-99, NewHoldings, Ltd., Las Vegas, 2000—; dir. Bus. Devel. Kummer Kaempfer Bonner & Renshaw, Las Vegas, 2002—05; co-owner Highrise Ptnrs. Ltd., Las Vegas, 2004—05; prin. and owner Summit Realty, Utah, 2005—, Brian Head, LLC, Utah, 2005—; pres., CEO Altitude Devel. Co., Las Vegas, 2006—. Registered rep., sr. advisor Silver Pacific Advisors, LLC, 2004—08; trustee Nev. Devel. Authority, 2002—05. Patentee in field. Bd. dirs. Tahoe-Douglas C. of C.; chmn. Tahoe Citizens Com., 1995-2000. Mem.: Mich. Tech Alumni Assn., U. Calif. Berkeley Bus. Alumni, Pepperdine Bus. Alumni, Las Vegas Jaguar Club. Avocations: classic cars, flying, sailing. Office: Summit at Brian Head LLC 4750 W Flamingo Rd Ste A Las Vegas NV 89103 Office Phone: 702-696-9001. Business E-Mail: mjabara@altitudedevelopment.com.

JABLONS, DAVID M., surgeon, educator; BA in Lit., Yale U., 1979; MD, Albany Med. Coll., 1984. Resident Tufts-New England Med. Ctr., Boston; surg. oncology fellow Nat. Cancer Inst., NIH, Bethesda, Md.; fellow cardiothoracic surgery Cornell Med. Ctr., Meml.-Sloan Kettering Med. Ctr., NYC; head divsn. thoracic surgery Naval Med. Ctr., Oakland, Calif., 1993—; asst. clin. prof. surgery U. Calif. San Francisco Med. Ctr., 1994-95; asst. prof. surgery U. Calif. San Francisco/Mt. Zion Med. Ctr., 1995—, chief-sect. thoracic surgery, 1997—. Contbr. articles to profl. jours. Mem. ACS, Soc. Thoracic Surgeons, Am. Assn. for Cancer Rsch., Soc. Surg. Oncology. Office: UCSF Mt Zion Med Ctr San Francisco CA 94143-0001 also: # 4 1600 Divisadero St San Francisco CA 94115-3010 Fax: 415-353-9525. E-mail: jablonsd@surgery.ucsf.edu.

JABS, REINY, state legislator, farmer, rancher; b. Hardin, Mont., May 4, 1929; m. Monte Lee Jabs. BS in Agr./Edn., Mont. State U., 1951. Tchr. pub. schs., 1954-65; farmer, rancher, 1956-96; mem. Mont. State Senate, 1994—, chair agr., livestock and irrigation com.; mem. judiciary com., mem. hwys. and transp. com. Past bd. dirs. Big Horn County FHA; mem. Hardin Sch. Bd., 1972-78; trustee Big Horn County Electric Coop.; bd. dirs. REA, 1980-94. Served with USAF, 1951-53. Mem. Luth. Laymen's League, C. of C., Soil Conservation Assn. Republican. Home: 736 W Division St Hardin MT 59034-2012

JACKMAN, HUGH, actor; b. Sydney, NSW, Australia, Oct. 12, 1968; s. Chris Jackman; m. Deborra-Lee Furness, Apr. 11, 1996; adopted children: Oscar Maximilian, Ava Eliot. BA in Journalism, U. of Technology, Sydney; student, Actor's Ctr., Sydney; grad., Western Australian Acad. Performing Arts, Perth, 1994. Co-founder Seed Prodns., LA, Australia. Actor: (TV series) Correlli, 1995, Snowy River: The McGregor Saga, 1993, Halifax f.p: Afraid of the Dark, 1998, Oklahoma!, 1999; (films) Hey Mr. Producer, 1998, Paperback Hero, 1999, Erskineville Kings, 1999, X-Men, 2000, Someone Like You, 2001, Swordfish, 2001, Kate & Leopold, 2001, Standing Room Only, 2002, X2, 2003, Van Helsing, 2004, The Fountain, 2006, X-Men: The Last Stand, 2006, Scoop, 2006, The Prestige, 2006, (voice) Flushed Away, 2006, Happy Feet, 2006, Uncle Jonny, 2008, Deception, 2008, Australia, 2008, X-Men Origins: Wolverine, 2009, (Broadway debut) The Boy from Oz, 2003— (Tony award best actor in a musical, 2004, Drama Desk award best actor in a musical, 2004), (other stage appearances) Beauty and the Beast, Oklahoma!, Carousel, 2002; host Tony Awards, 2003, 2004, 2005 (Emmy award, outstanding individual performance in a variety or musical program, 2005), The Oscars, 2009. Named Sexiest Man Alive, People mag., 2008. Office: c/o Seed Prodns Bldg 52 105 10201 West Pico Blvd Los Angeles CA 90035

JACKMAN, ROBERT ALAN, retail executive; b. NYC, Mar. 22, 1939; s. Joseph and Kate Queenie (Silverman) J.; m. Lois Wiederschall, June 10, 1962; children: Jennifer Sharon, Deborah Lynn. BS, U. Bridgeport, 1961. Dir. sales Mattel Inc., Hawthorne, Calif., 1963-75; sr. v.p. mktg. and sales Tyco Industries Inc., Moorestown, NJ, 1975-78; gen. mgr. Aurora Products Inc., Stamford, Conn., 1978-80; ptnr. Scott Lancaster Jackman Mills Atha, Westport, Conn., 1980-83; pres., CEO Leisure Dynamics Inc. divsn. Coleco Industries, Westport, 1983-86; with Oak Tree Publs., San Diego, 1983-87; exec. v.p. Coleco Industries Inc., West Hartford, Conn., 1986-88; gen. mgr. Tomy Am., Inc., Southport, Conn., 1988-90, also bd. dirs.; owner Yes I Can, 1990—. Cons. Harvard U. Bus. Sch. Club, N.Y.C., 1984. Patentee in field. With USAR, 1961—62. Recipient Disting. Alumni award U. Bridgeport (Conn.), 1986. Mem. U. Bridgeport Mktg. Coun., Mission Hills Country Club (Rancho Mirage, Calif.). Avocations: tennis, music, reading. Home: 8 Via Elegante Rancho Mirage CA 92270-1969 Office: 35 325 Date Palm Dr Ste 131 Cathedral City CA 92234-7031 E-mail: bob@yesican.com.

JACKMAN, STEVEN H., lawyer, electronics executive; Bar: Fla. V.p., corp. counsel Sanmina-SCI, San Jose, Calif. Office: Sanmina-SCI Corp 2700 N First St San Jose CA 95134 Office Phone: 408-964-3630. Office Fax: 408-964-3636. E-mail: steven.jackman@sanmina-sci.com.

JACKSON, ALAN JAY, prosecutor; b. 1965; Grad., U. Tex., Austin; law degree, Pepperdine U., Malibu, Calif. Bar: Calif. 1994, US Dist. Ct. (ctrl. dist. Calif.) 1994. Dep. dist. atty. hardcore gang unit LA County Dist. Atty.'s Office, dep. dist. atty. major crimes divsn. Faculty mem. prosecuting gang violence Ernest F. Hollings Nat. Advocacy Ctr., Columbia, SC. Office: LA County Dist Attys Office 210 W Temple St Ste 18000 Los Angeles CA 90012 Office Phone: 213-974-3800.

JACKSON, ALLEN KEITH, retired museum administrator; b. Rocky Ford, Colo., July 22, 1932; s. Monford L. and Leliah Jean (Hipp) Jackson; m. Barbara May Hollard, June 13, 1954; children: Cary Vincent, Deborah Kay, Edward Keith, Fredrick James. BA, U. Denver, 1954; postgrad., Cambridge U., Eng., 1955; Th.M. (Elizabeth Iliff Warren fellow), Iliff Sch. Theology, 1958; PhD, Emory U., 1960. Instr. sociology Emory U., 1958-60; chaplain, asst. prof. religion and sociology Morningside Coll., Sioux City, Iowa, 1960-62, dean coll., 1962-67; pres. Huntingdon Coll., Montgomery, Ala., 1968-93; dir. Idaho Mus. Natural History, Idaho State U., Pocatello, 1993—98; exec. dir. Nat. Heritage Ctr., 1998—2002; ret., 2002—. Past pres. Montgomery Area United Appeal. Fulbright scholar, Cambridge U., 1955, honor fellow, Emory U., 1960. Mem.: Ala. Coun. Advancement Pvt. Colls. (pres. 1975—81), Ala. Assn. Ind. Colls. and Univs. (pres. 1969—71), Rotary, Phi Kappa Phi, Beta Theta Pi, Omicron Delta Kappa, Phi Beta Kappa. Home: 440 University Dr Pocatello ID 83201

JACKSON, CURTIS JAMES See FIFTY CENT

JACKSON, CYNTHIA L., lawyer; b. Houston, May 6, 1954; BA, Stanford U., 1976; JD, U. Tex., 1979. Bar: Tex. 1979, Calif. 1980. Mem. Heller, Ehrman, White & McAuliffe, Palo Alto, Calif., 1983—99, Baker & McKenzie, Palo Alto, 1999—. Mem. ABA. Office: Baker & McKenzie 660 Hansen Way Palo Alto CA 94304-1044 Office Phone: 650-856-5572.

JACKSON, DILLON EDWARD, lawyer; b. Washington, Apr. 18, 1945; s. Paul David and Virginia (Dillon) J.; children: David I., Anne E.; m. Misha Halvarsson, Aug. 19, 1989. BA, Middlebury Coll., Vt., 1967; JD, U. Wash., 1970. Bar: Wash. 1970, U.S. Dist. Ct. (we. and ea. dists.) Wash. 1970, U.S. Ct. Appeals (9th cir.) 1970, U.S. Dist. Ct. Ariz. 1991. Assoc. Kleist & Helmick, Seattle, 1971-73, Powell Livengood & Silvernale, Kirkland, Wash., 1973-75; ptnr. Keller Jacobsen Jackson & Snodgrass, Bellevue, Wash., 1975-85, Hatch & Leslie, Seattle, 1985-91, Foster Pepper & Shefelman, Seattle, 1991—. Chairperson creditor rights and bankruptcy dept. Am. Bankruptcy Bd. Cert.; bd. mem. Consumer Credit Counseling, Seattle, 1975-79; chmn. publs. com. Am. Bankruptcy Inst., bd. mem., 1999—. Co-author: Commercial Law Desk Book, 1995; contbg. author: Advance Chapter 11 Bankruptcy Practice, 1989-95. Pres. Dox Coop., Seattle, 1989-91. Fellow Am. Coll. Bankruptcy (co-founder, mem. copyright com.); mem. ABA, Wash. State Trial Lawyers Assn., Wash. State Bar Assn. (creditor-debtor sect., chairperson 1984-88), Continuing Legal Edn. Bd. (chairperson 1991-92). Office: Foster Pepper & Shefelman PLLC 1111 3rd Ave Ste 3400 Seattle WA 98101-3299

JACKSON, DYLAN E., lawyer; b. Eugene, Oreg., June 7, 1970; BA, Univ. Wash., 1996; JD, Univ. Montana, 1996. Bar: Mont. 1996, US Dist. Ct., Dist. Montana 1997, Wash. 1999, US Dist. Ct., Western Dist. Wash. 2000. Assoc. atty., civil litig. Wilson Smith Cochran Dickerson, Seattle. Contbr. articles to numerous profl. jours. Named Wash. Rising Star, SuperLawyer Mag., 2006. Mem.: State Bar Assn. Montana, Cascade Co. Young Lawyers Div. (v.p. 1997—99), Cascade Co. Bar Assn. Office: Wilson Smith Cochran Dickerson 1700 1215 Fourth Ave Seattle WA 98161

JACKSON, HANNAH BETH, former state legislator; BA, Scripps Coll.; JD, Boston U. Atty. Santa Barbara (Calif.) County Dist. Atty. Office; pvt. practice; assembly mem. Calif. State, Santa Barbara. Chair State Commn. Status of Women; appointee Blue Ribbon Commn. Child Support Devel. and Enforcement; task force Family Equity, State Senate. Home: PO Box 92010 Santa Barbara CA 93190-2010 Fax: 805-564-1651.

JACKSON, HARRY ANDREW, artist; b. Chgo., Apr. 18, 1924; s. Harry Shapiro and Ellen Grace Jackson; m. Theodora Rehard DuBois, 1946 (div.); m. Grace Hartigan, 1948 (div.); m. Claire Rodgers, 1950 (dec.); m. Joan Hunt, 1951 (div.); m. Sarah Mason, Sept. 10, 1962 (div.); children: Matthew, Molly; m. Tina Lear, Aug. 11, 1973 (div.); children: Jesse, Luke, Chloe. Diploma, H.S., 1945; LLD (hon.), U. Wyo., 1986. Founder fine art foundry, Camaiore, Italy, 1964—, Harry Jackson Studios, Italy, 1965—; CEO Harry Jackson Studios (formerly Wyo. Foundry Studios, Inc.), Cody, Wyo., 1971—; founder Western Arts Found., 1974—; foundry ptnr. Jackson-Mariani Fine Art Foundry, Camaiore, Italy, 1985-98; founder Harry Jackson Art Mus., Cody, Wyo., 1994. Author: Lost Wax Bronze Casting, 1972, New York School Abstract Expressionists, 2000; one man exhbns. include Ninth St. Show, N.Y.C., 1951, Tibor de Nagy Gallery, N.Y.C., 1952, 53, Martha Jackson Gallery, N.Y.C., 1956, M. Knoedler & Co., N.Y.C., 1960, Amon Carter Mus., Fort Worth, 1961, 68, Kennedy Galleries, N.Y.C., 1964, 68, Smithsonian Instn., Washington, 1964, Whitney Gallery Western Art, Cody, 1964, 81, Mont. Hist. Soc., 1964, NAD, 1965, 68, Nat. Cowboy Hall of Fame, Oklahoma City, 1966, XVII Mostra Internazionale d'Arte, Premio del Fiorino, Florence, Italy, 1966, Pennational Artists Ann., Pa., 1967, Mostra de Arte Moderna, Convento di S. Lazzaro, Camaiore, 1968, Am. Artists Profl. League, N.Y., 1968, Cowboy Artists Am., 1971-76, S.W. Mus., L.A., 1979, Smith Gallery, N.Y.C., 1981, 85, Buffalo Bill Hist. Ctr., 1981, Palm Springs Desert Mus., 1981, Mpls. Inst. Art, 1982, Camaiore, Italy, 1985, Met. Mus. Art, N.Y.C., 1987; represented in permanent collections Met. Mus. Art, NAD, Nat. Mus. Am. Art, Nat. Portrait Gallery, Washington, Her Majesty Queen Elizabeth II, Sandringam Castle, Eng., Am. Mus. of Gt. Britain, Bath, Eng., U.S. State Dept., Washington, Lyndon Baines Johnson Meml. Libr., Austin, Tex., Ronald Reagan Meml. Libr., Santa Barbara, Calif., Whitney Gallery Western Art, Plains Indian Mus., Buffalo Bill Hist. Ctr., Cody, Wyo., Wadsworth Atheneum, Hartford, Conn., Alberta Glenbow Mus., Calgary, Can., Univ. So. Calif., Stanford (Calif.) Univ., Love Libr. Univ. Nebr., Lincoln, Portsmouth (R.I.) Abbey, S.W. Mus., Gene Autrey Mus., L.A., Nat. Cowboy Hall of Fame, Oklahoma City, Gilcrease Mus., Tulsa, Fort Pitts Mus., Pitts., Amon Carter Mus., Pro Rodeo Cowboy Hall of Fame, Colorado Springs, Colo., Eiteljorg Mus., Indpls., Shelburne (Vt.) Mus., Columbus (Ga.) Mus. Arts & Scis., Oreg. Hist. Soc., Portland, Salt Lake City Art Ctr., Norfolk (Nebr.) Arts Ctr., Aspen (Colo.) Art Mus., Woolaroc Mus., Bartlesville, Okla., U. Wyo. Art Mus., Laramie, Mont. Hist. Soc., Helena, Norton Mus., Shreveport, La., Columbia U., N.Y.C., Trout Gallery Dickinson Coll., Carlisle, Pa., Ctrl. Wyo. Coll., Riverton, N.W. C.C., Powell, Wyo., Baylor Sch., Chattanooga, Orme Sch., Mayer, Ariz., others; commd. works include (sculpture) William R. Coe Commn., 1959, 60, Fort Pitt Mus., 1964, 73, Plains Indian Mus., Cody, Wyo., Ctrl. Wyo. Coll., Riverton, 1978, 81, Piazza della Chiesa, Capezzano, Pianore, Italy, 1985, Great Western Savs. & Loan, Santa Barbara, Calif., 1985, John Wayne monumental sculpture Beverly Hills, Calif, 1981, 84, (portrait busts) Met. Mus. Trustees, C. Douglas Dillon, 1985, 87, (portrait) "John Wayne" TIME cover, Aug. 8, 1969 (Nat. Best Cover Art award Am. Inst. Graphic Arts 1969), (paintings) Whitney Gallery Western Art, Cody, 1960, 66, (mural) R.K. Mellon. Served with USMC, 1942-45. Decorated Purple Heart with gold star; recipient Gold medal NAD, 1968; grantee Fulbright, 1954, Italian Govt., 1956, 57. Fellow NAD (academician), RISD, Nat. Acad. Western Art, Nat. Sculpture Soc., Am. Artists League; mem. Bohemian Club (San Francisco). Office: PO Box 2836 Cody WY 82414-2836 also: Via Monteggiori 55040 Camaiore Lucca Italy Office Phone: 307-587-5508. Office Fax: 307-587-6362. Business E-Mail: lora@harryjackson.net. E-mail: harry@harryjackson.net.

JACKSON, HUNTER, health products executive; PhD in Psychobiology, Yale U., New Haven; postgrad. dept. neurosurgery, U. Va. Assoc. prof. dept. anatomy U. Utah, Salt Lake City; CEO, chmn. bd., founder NPS Pharms., Inc., Salt Lake City, 1986—, pres., 1994—.

JACKSON, JACK C., state legislator, rancher; b. Leupp, Ariz., Sept. 14, 1933; m. Eloise Jackson. Student, No. Ariz. U. Rancher; educator; mem. Ariz. Ho. of Reps., 1985-98, Ariz. Senate, Dist. 3, Phoenix, 1998—. Active Window Rock (Ariz.) Sch. Bd.; past pres. N.A.C. of Navajoland. With Nat. Guard. Mem. All Indian Rodeo Cowboy Assn. (past pres.). Democrat. Address: PO Box 4 Window Rock AZ 86515-0004 E-mail: jjackson@azleg.state.az.us.

JACKSON, JAMES F., nuclear engineer, educator; b. Ogden, Utah, Aug. 15, 1939; s. Allyn Boyd and Virginia (Dixon) J.; m. Joan Borger, Aug. 25, 1960; children: James D., Bret A., Tracy L., Wendy L. BS, U. Utah, Salt Lake City, 1961; MS, MIT, Cambridge, 1962; PhD, UCLA, 1969. Rsch. engr. Atomics Internat., LA, 1962066; nuclear engr. Argonne Nat. Lab., Idaho Falls, Idaho, 1969-72, group leader Argonne, Ill., 1972-74; assoc. prof. Brigham Young U., Provo, Utah, 1974-76, adj. prof., 1998—; cons. Los Alamos Nat. Lab., N.Mex., 1974-76, group/div. leader N.Mex., 1976-82, dep. assoc. dir. N.Mex., 1979-81, div. leader N.Mex., 1983-84, assoc. dir. N.Mex., 1984-86, dep. dir. N.Mex., 1986-98, staff mem. N.Mex., 1998-99, cons. N.Mex., 1999—2006, Atomic Safety and Licensing Bd. Panel, US Nuc. Regulatory Commn., 2006—. Contbr. articles to jours. in field. Mem. atomic safety and licensing bd. panel US Nuc. Regulatory Commn., 2006-. Recipient E.O. Lawrence award Dept. Energy, Washington, 1983. Mem. NAE, Am. Nuclear Soc. (safety div. 1967—, exec. com. 1977-80), Tau Beta Pi. Republican. Mem. Lds Ch. Avocations: history, motorsports, photography. Home: 536 Sheffield Dr Provo UT 84604-5666

JACKSON, JAMES T., career officer; b. Ft. Knox, Ky. BS in Aerospace Engring., Kent State U.; MA in Personnel Mgmt. and Adminstrn., Ctrl. Mich. U.; grad., Army Command Gen. Staff Coll., Army War Coll. Commd. 2d lt. U.S. Army, advanced through grades to brig. gen., early assignments include co. comdr., asst. divsn. comdr., S-3 (air) 2d bn., S-3 (ops.) 1st bn.; ops. officer, then asst. chief of staff 1st corps support command; S-4 logistics, S-3 ops., then exec. officer 3d brigade, 82d airborne divsn.; G-3 ops. 7th Infantry divsn.; strategic planner U.S. Spl. Ops. Command, exec. officer to comdr.-in-chief; asst. divsn. comdr. 7th Infantry divsn., U.S. Army. Decorated Legion of Merit with oak leaf custer, bronze star, Def. Meritorious Svc. medal with oak leaf cluster, Meritorious Svc. medal with 3 oak leaf clusters, others. Achievements include being a master parachutist.

JACKSON, JANET, singer, dancer; b. Gary, Ind., May 16, 1966; d. Joseph and Katherine J.; m. James DeBarge, Sept. 7, 1984 (annulled Nov. 18, 1985), m. René Elizondo, March 31, 1991 (div. March 13, 2000). Singer: (Albums) Janet Jackson, 1982, Dream Street, 1984, Control, 1986, Rhythm Nation 1814, 1991, janet, 1993, Design of a Decade: 1986-1996, 1995, The Velvet Rope, 1997, All For You, 2001 (Grammy award, Best Dance Recording, 2002), Damita Jo, 2004, 20 Y.O., 2006, Dedication, 2008, Discipline, 2008; actress (TV series) Good Times, 1977-1979, A New Kind of Family, 1979, Diff'rent Strokes, 1981-1982, 1984, Fame, 1984-1985; (films) Poetic Justice, 1993 (Academy award nomination Best Original Song 1993), Nutty Professor II: The Klumps, 2000, Why Did I Get Married?, 2007 (Outstanding Supporting Actress in a Motion Picture, NAACP Image award, 2008). Recipient 6 Am. Music awards, 1987, 1988, 1991, 5 Grammy nominations, MTV Video Vanguard award, 1990, Grammy award, Best R&B song 1994 for "That's the Way Love Goes" with Terry Lewis and James Harris III, Vanguard award, Gay and Lesbian Alliance Against Defamation, 2008; MTV Best Female Video for "If", named one of 50 Most Influential African-Americans, Ebony Mag. 2004.

JACKSON, JEANNE PELLEGREN, apparel executive, former investment company executive; b. Denver, Aug. 10, 1951; d. John James and Barbara (Grove) Pellegren; m. Douglas Emmett Jackson, Nov. 23, 1984; children: Lindsay, Craig. BS in Fin., U. Colo., 1974; MBA, Harvard Bus. Sch., 1978. Buyer, mgr. Bullocks Dept. Stores, LA, 1978-85; v.p. merchandise mgr. to sr. v.p. direct mail pvt. brands Saks Fifth Ave., NYC, 1985-89; sr. v.p. merchandising Walt Disney Attractions, Orlando, 1989-92; exec. v.p. merchandising Victoria's Secret, Columbus, Ohio, 1992-95; pres., CEO Banana Republic, 1996-2000; CEO Gap, Inc. Direct, 1998—2000, Wal-Mart.com, 2000—02; founder, CEO MSP Capital, 2003—09; pres. Direct to Consumer NIKE, Inc., Beaverton, Oreg., 2009—. Instr. mktg. U. So. Calif., L.A., 1979-81; adv. bd. Navy Exch., Norfolk, Va., 1991—; bd. dirs. McDonald's Corp., 1999-, NIKE, Inc., 2001-, Nordstrom, Inc., 2002-, Williams-Sonoma Inc., 2003-, Harrah's Entertainment, Inc., 2008- Bd. dirs. Orlando Mus. Art, 1990-92; bd. advisors Harvard Grad. Sch. Bus. Republican. Avocations: skiing, tennis. Office: NIKE Inc One Bowerman Dr Beaverton OR 97005*

JACKSON, JOHN JAY, clergyman; b. Chula Vista, Calif., July 13, 1961; s. E. Marvin and Mildred L. Jackson; m. Pamela Harrison, Aug. 18, 1979; children: Jennifer, Dena, Rachel, Joshua. BA in Religion, Chapman U., 1981; MA in Theology, Fuller Theol. Sem., 1983; MA in Ednl. Adminstrn., U. Calif., Santa Barbara, 1984, PhD in Ednl. Adminstrn., 1986. Youth dir. First Bapt. Ch., Buena Park, Calif., 1979-81; min. of youth Oxnard (Calif.) First Bapt., 1981-83, min. of edn., 1983-84, assoc. pastor, 1984-87, sr. pastor, 1988-92; exec. min. Am.-Bapt. Chs. Pacific S.W., Covina, Calif., 1993-97; pastor Carson Valley Christian Ctr., Minden, Nev., 1997—. Bd. dirs. Am. Bapt. Homes of the West, Oakland, Calif., 1993-97, Atherton Bapt. Homes, 1993-97; chair integration adv. com. Oxnard Sch. Dist., 1990-92. Recipient Disting. Svc. award Oxnard Sch. Dist., 1992. Mem. Christian Mgmt. Assn., Oxnard C. of C. (leadership com. 1991, chair edn. com. 1988-90). Office: Carson Valley Christian Center 1095 Stephanie Way Minden NV 89423-8897

JACKSON, JOSHUA CARTER, actor; b. Vancouver, BC, Can., June 11, 1978; s. John and Fiona Jackson. Actor: (films) Crooked Hearts, 1991, The Mighty Ducks, 1992, Digger, 1993, D2: The Mighty Ducks, 1994, Andre, 1994, Magic in the Water, 1995, D3: The Mighty Ducks, 1996, Scream 2, 1997, The Battery, 1998, Apt Pupil, 1998, Urban Legend, 1998, Cruel Intentions, 1999, The Skulls, 2000, Gossip, 2000, The Safety of Objects, 2001, The Laramie Project, 2002, Lone Star State of Mind, 2002, I Love Your Work, 2003, (voice) Racing Stripes, 2005, Americano, 2005, Cursed, 2005, Aurora Borealis, 2005 (Best Actor, Jury award, 2005), The Shadow Dancer, 2005, Bobby, 2006 (Best Ensemble Cast, Hollywood Film award, 2006), Battle in Seattle, 2007, Shutter, 2008; (TV films) Payoff, 1991, Robin of Locksley, 1996, Ronnie & Julie, 1997, On the Edge on Innocence, 1997, Capitol Law, 2006; (TV series) Dawson's Creek, 1998—2003 (TV - Choice Actor, Teen Choice award, 1999, 2000, 2001). Recipient Superstar of Tomorrow - Male, Young Hollywood Awards, 2000. Avocation: harmonica. Office: c/o Water Street Mgmt 1099 S Orange Grove Ave Los Angeles CA 90019

JACKSON, KENNETH ARTHUR, physicist, researcher; b. Connaught, Ont., Can., Oct. 23, 1930; s. Arthur and Susanna (Vatcher) J.; m. Jacqueline Della Olyan, June 20, 1952 (div.); children: Stacy Margaret, Meredith Suzanne, Stuart Keith; m. Camilla M. Maruszewski, June 21, 1980 (div.); m. Gina Kritchevsky, April 30, 2005. BS, U. Toronto, 1952, MS, 1953; PhD, Harvard U., 1956. Postdoctoral fellow Harvard U., Cambridge, Mass., 1956-58, asst. prof. metallurgy, 1958-62; mem. tech. staff Bell Labs., Murray Hill, NJ, 1962-67, head material physics research dept., 1967-81, head optical materials research dept., 1981-89; prof. materials sci. and engring. U. Ariz., 1989—2003, prof. emeritus, 2004—. Lectr. Welch. Found., 1970, 85; mem. research adv. panel Air Force Office Sci. Research, 1976-82, space application bd. Nat. Acad. Sci., 1974-82. Editor-in-chief Optical Materials, 1999-2003; contbr. articles to profl. jours.; patentee in field. Recipient Mathewson Gold medal AIME, 1966, Crystal growth award AACG, 1993, Frank prize IOCG, 1998, TMS Chalmers award, 2003. Fellow AAAS, The Metall. Soc.-AIME, Am. Phys. Soc.; mem. NAE, Internat. Orgn. Crystal Growth (treas. 1978-86, Frank prize 1998), Am. Assn. Crystal Growth (pres. 1968-75, coun., award 1993), Materials Rsch. Soc. (v.p. 1975-77, pres. 1977-78, coun.), Am. Soc. Metals, Engring. Coun. for Profl. Devel. (mem. coun.), Fedn. Materials Soc. (trustee), Nat. Acad. Engring. E-mail: kaj@aml.arizona.edu.

JACKSON, KINGSBURY TEMPLE, educational and financial consultant; b. Newton, Mass., May 15, 1917; s. Ralph Temple and Elizabeth Mesarole (Rhodes) J.; m. June Stewart Cooper, July 29, 1950 (dec. Feb. 1976). BS, MIT, 1940; postgrad., NYU, 1949—51; MS, U. Ala., 1964, U. So. Calif., 1969, Pepperdine U., 1975. Registered profl. engr., Calif., Ala.; lic. and bonded tax preparer, IRS and Calif. Commd. 2d lt. U.S. Army, 1940, advanced through grades to lt. col., 1961, ret., 1965; comdr. U.S. Army Depot, also Camp Mercer, Republic of Korea, 1957-58; project officer, indsl. project dir. U.S. Army Saturn Space Vehicle Program and Pershing Missile Sys., 1959-61; dir. U.S. Army Missile Command Engring. Documentation Ctr., Redstone Arsenal, Ala., 1962-63; program coordinator NATO-Hawk Missile System, 1963-65; prin. contracting officer, chief European procurement U.S. Army Ordnance, 1964-65; lectr. mgmt. and engring. Grad. Sch., U. So. Calif., LA, 1965-69; contractual rels. supr. L.A. Bd. Edn., 1969-82; pres. Contract Consultants, LA, 1982—, K.T. Jackson, Gen. Contractors, LA, 1991—. Author: Engineering Documentation Systems Development: Department of Defense and NASA, 1963, Aerospace Propellants and Chemicals: The Manager's Approach, 1968. V.p., mem. bd. dirs. Kingsbury Properties Ltd.; corp. sec., bd. dirs. The Concert Singers, Inc. Mem.: Am. Soc. Automotive Engrs. (rep. to Aerospace gen. stds. divsn. 1962—65), Am. Ordinance Assn. (mem. exec. bd. prodn. technique divsn.,Army rep.to engring. doc. sect. 1962—65), Am. Soc. Mil. Comptrs., Am. Soc. Indsl. Engrs., Nat. Space Soc., Aircraft Owners and Pilots Assn., Calif. Assn. Bus. Ofcls., Ret. Officers Assn. (life), Internat. Assn. Sch. Bus. Ofcls. (emeritus), The Concert Singers Inc., The Planetary Soc., A&E Flying Club, MIT Club (So. and No. Calif.). Home: Ste C302 3400 Paul Sweet Rd Santa Cruz CA 95065-1541 Office: Contract Cons PO Box 402 Capitola CA 95010-0402 Office Phone: 831-464-1547. E-mail: kingtempj@sbcglobal.net.

JACKSON, LAUREN, professional basketball player; b. Australia, May 11, 1981; d. Gary and Maree Jackson. Player Seattle Storm, 2001—. Mem. Gems team Jr. World Championships, 1997, WNBL Championship team, 2000; mem. Australian Nat. Team Sydney Olympics, 2000, Athens Olympics, 2004. Recipient Silver medal, Sydney Olympics, 2000, ESPY award, Best WNBA Player, ESPN, 2004, 2005, 2008; named WNBA MVP, 2003, 2007, WNBA Defensive Player of Yr., 2007; named a Peak Performer, WNBA, 2003, 2007; named to WNBA Western Conf. All-Star Team, 2001—03, 2005—07, All-WNBA First Team, 2003, 2005, 2006, WNBA All-Defensive Team, 2007. Achievements include being selected first in the 2001 WNBA draft. Office: Seattle Storm 351 Elliott Ave W Ste 500 Seattle WA 98119

JACKSON, O'SHEA See ICE CUBE

JACKSON, PHILIP DOUGLAS, professional basketball coach; b. Deer Lodge, Mont., Sept. 17, 1945; m. June; 5 children. Grad., U. ND, 1967. Player NY Knicks, 1967-78, NJ Nets, 1978-80, asst. coach, 1980-82; head coach Continental Basketball Assn. Albany Patroons, 1982-87; asst. coach Chgo. Bulls, 1987-89, head coach, 1989-98, LA Lakers, 1999—2004, 2005—. Co-author (with Hugh Delehanty): Sacred Hoops: Spiritual Lessons of a Hardwood Warrior, 1996; co-author: (with Charley Rosen) More Than A Game, 2002; author: The Last Season: A Team in Search of Its Soul, 2004. Named NBA Coach of Yr., 1996; named one of NBA Ten Greatest Coaches, 1997; named to Naismith Meml. Basketball Hall of Fame, 2007. Achievements include winning NBA Championships as a member of the Knicks, 1970, 73; led the Bulls to NBA Championships as head coach, 1991, 92, 93, 96, 97, 98; led the Lakers to NBA Championships as head coach, 2000, 01, 02; best winning percentage as an NBA head coach in regular season and playoffs. Office: LA Lakers Staples Ctr 1111 S Figueroa St Los Angeles CA 90015

JACKSON, PHILLIP ELLIS, marketing executive, writer; b. Kansas City, Mo., June 4, 1952; s. Phillip Anthony and Lois Irene (Seward) J.; m. Dawn Mutolo Jackson, Aug. 9, 1975; 1 child, Emily Mutolo. AA, Mohawk Valley C.C., 1972; BA magna cum laude in Liberal Arts, SUNY, Albany, 1974; MA in Internat. Rels., SUNY, 1975; PhD in Polit. Sci., U. Chgo., 1981. Speech writer; speech writer, issue com. chmn. Steve Bartlett Congl. Campaign, 1982; sr. v.p. pub. affairs Greater Dallas C. of C., 1982-93; exec. dir. Dallas United, 1984-93; dir. Tex. office Cassidy & Assocs., Dallas, 1993-95; v.p. Signal Sites, Dallas, 1995—. Author fiction. Cons. Dallas Charter Rev. Com., 1989; dir. City of Dallas, Dallas C. of C. N.Am. Free Trade Agreement Labor Secretariat Task Force, 1991-93. Recipient Citizens award Chgo. Police Dept., 1978, Presdl. citations Pvt. Sector Initiatives, 1985, 86, 89.

JACKSON, RANDY, music producer, television personality, musician; b. Baton Rouge, June 23, 1956; s. Herman and Julia Jackson; m. Elizabeth Jackson (div. 1990); 1 child, Taylor; m. Erika Riker, 1995; children: Zoe, Jordan. BA in Music, So. U., 1979. Bass player Journey, 1983—87; v.p. A&R Columbia Records; sr. v.p. A&R MCA Records. Talent judge (TV series) American Idol, 2002—; prodr.: (albums) Truth About Cats & Dogs soundtrack, 1996, First Wives Club soundtrack, 1996, (various artists) Eddie Money, Trisha Covington, Richard Marx, Rahsaan Patterson, Gladys Knight, Jesse Powell, many others; musician (bass player): (instrn. video) Randy Jackson: Mastering the Groove, 1992, albums, Journey, Patti LaBelle, Michael Bolton, Bon Jovi, Mariah Carey, Tracy Chapman, Cher, Kelly Clarkson, Celine Deon, Bob Dylan, Aretha Franklin, Keeny G, Herbie Hancock, Whitney Houston, Billy Idol, Elton John, Madonna, others; co-writer: songs My Saving Grace (from Mariah Carey album "Charmbracelet", 2003, Irresistible (from Mariah Carey album "Charmbracelet", 2003; solo albums include Randy Jackson's Music Club, Vol. 1, 2008. Home: 700 N San Vicente Blvd Ste G910 West Hollywood CA 90069-5061

JACKSON, RICHARD BROOKE, judge; b. Bozeman, Mont., Mar. 5, 1947; s. William T. and Myra (McHugh) J.; m. Elizabeth Ciner, Sept. 19, 1971; children: Jeffrey, Brett, Jennifer. AB magna cum laude, Dartmouth Coll., 1969; JD cum laude, Harvard U., 1972. Bar: Colo. 1972, U.S. Dist. Ct. Colo. 1972, D.C. 1980, U.S. Dist. Ct. D.C. 1980,U.S. Ct. Appeals (10th cir.) 1972, U.S. Ct. Appeals (D.C. cir.) 1980, U.S. Supreme Ct. 1980. Assoc. Holland & Hart, Denver, 1972-78, ptnr. Denver and Washington, 1978-98; dist. ct. judge Jefferson County, Golden, Colo., 1998—. Instr. in trial practice U. Colo. Law Sch., Boulder, 1984-85, 87, 88, 89, 91, 98, Nat. Inst. Trial Advocacy, 1986, 87, 90, 91, 98. Co-author: Manual for Complex Insurance Coverage Litigation, 1993; editor: A Better New Hampshire, 1968; contbr. articles to profl. jours. Fellow Am. Coll. Trial Lawyers; mem. ABA (former co-chair ins. coverage com. sect. of litigation), Colo. Bar Assn., Denver Bar Assn. Democrat. Avocations: running, golf, reading, travel, languages. Home: 5355 Yellowstone St Bow Mar CO 80123-1423 Office: Dist Ct Jefferson Cty 100 Jefferson County Pkwy Golden CO 80401-6000 E-mail: rbrooke.jackson@judicial.state.co.us.

JACKSON, RICHARD JOSEPH, epidemiologist, educator, pediatrician, preventive medicine physician; b. Newark, Oct. 23, 1945; s. Robert Joseph Jackson and Dorothy C. (Devine) Connolly; m. Joan M. Guilford, June 21, 1975; children: Brendan, Devin, Galen. AB in Biology, St. Peter's Coll., Jersey City, 1969; M in Med. Sci., Rutgers U., 1971; MD, U. Calif. San Francisco, San Francisco, 1973; MPH in Epidemiology, U. Calif. Berkeley, Berkeley, 1979. Diplomate Am. Bd. Pediatrics, Am. Bd. Preventive Medicine; lic. physician, Calif. Intern, resident U. Calif., San Francisco, 1973-74, 77-78, resident San Francisco Gen. Hosp., 1974-75; officer Epidemic Intelligence Svc. U.S. Pub. Health Svc., Albany, N.Y., 1975-77; spl. epidemiologist World Health Orgn., Bihar State, India, 1976; med. officer Epidemiol. Studies Sect. Calif. State Dept. Health Svcs., Berkeley, 1979-88, acting chief Office Environ. Health Hazard Aassessment Sacramento, 1988-90, chief hazard identification and risk assessment br. Berkeley, 1990-91; chief hazard identification and risk assessment br. office environ. health hazard assessment Calif. EPA, Berkeley, 1991-92; chief divsn. communicable disease control Calif. State Dept. Health Svcs., 1992-94; dir. Nat. Ctr. Environ. Health, Ctrs. Disease Control and Prevention, Atlanta, 1994—2003; sr. advisor to dir. Ctr. Disease Control, Atlanta, 2003—04; state pub. health officer State of Calif., Sacremento, 2004—. Adj. lectr. U. Calif. San Francisco, 1980—, asst. clin. prof., 1986—; adj. prof. Emory U. Rollins Sch. Pub. Health, 1998—. Lt. comdr. USPHS, 1975-77. Office: Ca Dept Of Health Services PO Box 997413 Sacramento CA 95899-7413 Home Phone: 925-837-7890. E-mail: RJJackson@cdc.gov, rjackso6@dhs.ca.gov.

JACKSON, RUSSELL M., food service executive; BA, San Jose State U.; MBA, St. Mary's Coll.; M in Human Resources and Orgnl. Devel., U. San Francisco. Joined Pacific Gas and Electric Co. (PG&E), 1980, asst. to pres. and CEO, 1997—98, v.p. customer svc., 1998—99, v.p. human resources, 1999—2004, sr. v.p. human resources, 2004—08, PG&E Corp., 2004—08, Safeway Inc., Pleasanton, Calif., 2008—. Mem. Pub. Utilities Employer's Inst., Western States Labor Mgmt. Pub. Affairs Com., Calif. Pub. Utilities Commn.'s Calif. Utility Diversity Coun. Office: Safeway Inc 5918 Stoneridge Mall Rd Pleasanton CA 94588

JACKSON, RUTH MOORE, university librarian; b. Potecasi, NC, Sept. 27, 1938; d. Jesse Thomas and Ruth Estelle (Futrell) Moore; m. Roderick Earle Jackson, Aug. 14, 1965; 1 child, Eric Roderick. BS in Bus., Hampton Inst., 1960; MSLS, Atlanta U., 1965; PhD in Libr. and Info. Sci., Ind. U., 1976. Asst. edn. libr. Va. State U., Petersburg, Va., 1965-66, head reference dept., 1966-67, asst. prof., 1976-77, assoc. prof., program coord., 1977-84, interim dept. chair, 1978-79; teaching fellow Ind. U., Bloomington, Ind., 1968, vis. lectr., 1971-72; asst. dir. librs. U. N. Fla., Jacksonville, 1984-88; dean univ. librs. W.Va. U., Morgantown, W.Va., 1988—99, asst. to provost libr. outreach programs, 1999—2002; dean librs Wichita State U.; univ. libr. U. Calif., Riverside, 2002—. Pers. cons. Va. State U., 1980; archival cons. N.C. Ctrl. U., Durham, N.C., 1984-85; automation cons. W.Va. Acad. Libr. Consortium, 1991—; co-prin. investigator State-Wide Electronic Libr. Network (Project Infomine), 1994-98. Editor: W.Va. U. Press, 1990—; contbr. to books. Active Big Brother/Big Sister of Am., Jacksonville, Fla., 1985-88; den leader Boy Scouts of Am., Petersburg, Va., 1976-78. U.S. Office Edn. fellow, 1968-71, Rsch. fellow So. Fellowships Found., 1973-74; recipient Outstanding Alumni award Hampton Inst., 1980, Non-Italian Woman of Yr. award, 1992, Disting. West Virginian award Gov. W.Va., 1992; named Designated Hon. Tuskegee Airman, 2008. Mem. NAFE (named Hon. Tuskegee Airman), ALA, Southeastern Libr. Assn. (mem. standing com.), Assn. Coll. and Rsch. Librs. (mem. standing com., mem. Fla. chpt.), W.Va. Libr. Assn., Libr. Info. Tech. Assn., Coalition for Networked Info., Coun. of State Univ. Librs. (founding mem.), Alpha Kappa Alpha. Democrat. Roman Catholic. Avocations: walking, sightseeing, collecting rare coins and artifacts. Home: 5535 Via San Jacinto Riverside CA 92506-3652 Office: U Calif Rivera Libr, 1st Fl 900 University Ave Riverside CA 92521 Office Phone: 951-827-3221. E-mail: ruth.jackson@ucr.edu.

JACKSON, VICTORIA LYNN, actress, comedienne; b. Miami, Fla., Aug. 2, 1959; d. James McCaslin and Marlene Esther (Blackstad) J.; m. Nisan Mark Eventoff, Aug. 5, 1984; 1 child, Scarlet Elizabeth. Student, Fla. Bible Coll., 1976-77, Furman U., 1977-79, Auburn U., 1979-80. Actress Summerfest/Town & Gown, Birmingham, Ala., 1980; stand-up comedienne Variety Arts Ctr., LA, 1982-83, Tonight Show with Jonny Carson, NBC, LA, 1983; actress-comedienne The Half Hour Comedy Hour, Dick Clark, LA, 1983; comedienne Bizarre/John Beiner, Toronto, Can., 1983; actress commls. LA, 1983—; comedienne Bob Monkhouse Show, London, 1983; actress-comedienne Saturday Night Live, NBC, NYC, 1986—. Actress series Half Nelson, NBC, L.A., pilot Walter Fox, L.A. Actress (films) Stoogemania, Double Exposure, The Pick Up Artist, 1986, Baby Boom, 1987, Couch Trip, 1987, Dream a Lil Dream, 1988, Casual Sex, 1988, UHF with Weird Al, 1989, Family Business, 1990, I Love You to Death, 1990. Mem. ASCAP, SAF, AFTRA. Baptist. Avocations: motherhood, photography, gymnastics.

JACOB, DIANNE, county official; m. Paul, 1961; 1 son, Tom. Tchr. East County; mem. Jamul/Dulzura Sch. Bd.; supr. dist. 2 San Diego County Bd. Suprs., 1992—. Co-chmn. Criminal Justice Coun.; mem. San Diego (Calif.) Planning Commn., chmn.; pres. Calif. State Sch. Bds.; adv. bd. Mothers Against Drunk Driving; bd. dir. East County Econ. Devel. Coun. Recipient Alumna of Yr. award San Diego State U. Coll. Edn., 1993, Women Who Mean Bus. award San Diego Bus. Jour., 1995, Legislator of Yr. award Indsl. Environ. Assn., 1995, Most Accessible Politician award Forum Publs., award of excellence Endangered Habitats League, 1999, Legislator of Yr. award Calif. Narcotics Assn., 1998, Legislator of Yr. award Border Solution Task Force, 1998, Legislator of Yr. award San Diego Mchts. Assn., 2000, Ofcl. of Yr., San Diego Domestic Violence Coun., 2000, Legis. of Yr. award Indsl. Environ. Assn., 2000, Legis. of Yr. award Bldg. Owners and Mgrs. Assn., 2001, Headliner of Yr. award San Diego Press Club, 2002. Avocation: golf. Office: Office County Supr County Adminstrn Ctr 1600 Pacific Hwy Ste 335 San Diego CA 92101-2470

JACOB, STANLEY WALLACE, surgeon, educator; b. Phila., 1924; s. Abraham and Belle (Shulman) J.; m. Marilyn Peters; 1 son, Stephen; m. Beverly Swarts; children: Jeffrey, Darren, Robert; m. Gail Brandis; 1 dau., Elyse. BA, Ohio State U., Columbus, 1945; MD cum laude, Ohio State U. Med. Sch., Columbus, 1948. Diplomate Am. Bd. Surgery. Intern Beth Israel Hosp., Boston, 1948-49, resident surgery, 1949-52, 54-56; chief resident surg. svc. Harvard Med. Sch., 1956-57, instr., 1958-59; assoc. vis. surgeon Boston City Hosp., 1958-59; Kemper Found. rsch. scholar ACS, 1957-60; asst. prof. surgery U. Oreg. Med. Sch., Portland, 1959-66, assoc. prof., 1966—; Gerlinger prof. surgery Oreg. Health Scis. U., 1981—. Author: Structure and Function in Man, 5th edit, 1982, Laboratory Guide for Structure and Function in Man, 1982, Dimethyl Sulfoxide Basic Concepts, 1971, Biological Actions of DMSO, 1975, Elements of Anatomy and Physiology, 1989; contbr.: Ency. Britanica. Served to capt. M.C. AUS, 1952-54; col. Res. ret. Recipient Gov.'s award Outstanding N.W. Scientist, 1965; 1st pl. German Sci. award, 1960; Markle scholar med. scis., 1960. Mem. Phi Beta Kappa, Sigma Xi, Alpha Omega Alpha. Achievements include co-discovery of therapeutic usefulness of dimethyl sulfoxide and MSM. Home: 1055 SW Westwood Ct Portland OR 97239-2708 Office: Oreg Health Scis U Dept Surgery 3181 SW Sam Jackson Park Rd Portland OR 97239 Home Phone: 503-244-2124; Office Phone: 503-494-8474. Business E-Mail: jacobs@ohsu.edu.

JACOBS, CHARLOTTE DE CROES, oncologist, educator; b. Oak Ridge, Tenn., Jan. 27, 1946; BA, U. Rochester, 1968; MD, Washington U., St. Louis, 1972. Diplomate Am. Bd. Internal Medicine, Am. Bd. Med. Oncology, Nat. Bd. Med. Examiners. Intern, jr. resident dept. medicine Washington U. Sch. Medicine, St. Louis, 1972—74; sr. resident dept. medicine U. Calif., San Francisco, 1974—75; postdoctoral fellow divsn. oncology Stanford (Calif.) U. Med. Sch., 1975—77, acting asst. prof. oncology, 1977-80, asst. prof. medicine and oncology, 1980-86, assoc. prof. clin. medicine, 1986-92, assoc. prof. medicine and oncology, 1992-96, prof., 1996—, sr. assoc. dean. edn. and student affairs, 1990-97, acting dir. Clin. Cancer Ctr., 1994-97; dir. Oncology Day Care Ctr. Stanford Med. Ctr., 1977-90, dir. Clin. Cancer Ctr., 1997—2001. Bd. dirs. Nat. Comprehensive Cancer Network, Rockledge, Pa., 1994-2001. Recipient presdl. citation Am. Soc. for Head and Neck Surgery, 1990, Aphrodite Hofsomner award Washington U., 1993. Mem. AMA, Am. Soc. Clin. Oncology (bd. dirs. 1992-95), Am. Assn. for Cancer Rsch. Office: Clin Cancer Ctr Rm 2241 875 Blake Wilbur Dr Stanford CA 94305-5826 Office Phone: 650-725-8738. Business E-Mail: cjacobs@stanford.edu.

JACOBS, DEBORAH L., foundation administrator, former library director; b. LA, Feb. 28, 1952; d. Morton Daniel and Adrienne (Rimmel) Jacobs; m. Brian Brogan, Mar. 29, 1982 (div. 1985); 1 child, Jacob. BA in Govt., Mills Coll., Oakland, Calif., 1974; MLS, U. Oreg., 1975. Children's libr. Deschutes Libr., Bend, Oreg., 1976-77; extension svcs. libr. Sacramento City Libr., 1977-78; libr., libr. dir. Corvallis-Benton Pub. Libr., Oreg., 1978-97; city libr. Seattle Pub. Libr., 1997—2008; dir. Global Librs. Initiative Bill & Melinda Gates Found., 2008—. Treas. Freedom to Read Found., Chgo., 1994—98. Chair Commn. Children & Families, Corvallis, 1992—97; bd. dirs. Boys & Girls Club, Corvallis, 1993—97; sec. bd. dirs. da Vinci Days, Corvallis, 1993—97. Named Libr. of Yr., Libr. Jour., 1995, Pub. Employee of Yr., King Couny Mcpl. League (Seattle), 1999, Leader of Yr., City of Seattle Mgmt. Assn., 1999; named one of Top 25 Most Influential People, Seattle Mag., 2004. Mem.: ALA (co-chair presdl. initiative 1997—99, v.p. Leroy-Merritt Fund, Intellectual Freedom Champion award 1995), Internat. Network Pub. Librs., Wash. Libr. Assn., Wash. State Women's Forum, Oreg. Libr. Assn. (pres. 1992—93), Rotary. Democrat. Jewish. Avocations: baking, gardening, running, pottery. Office: Bill and Melinda Gates Found PO Box 23350 Seattle WA 98102 Office Phone: 206-709-3100.*

JACOBS, DONALD PAUL, architect; b. Cleve., Aug. 8, 1942; s. Joseph W. and Minnie Mae (Grieger) J.; m. Sharon Daugherty, Apr. 14, 1963 (dec. Feb. 1992); m. Julie Brinkerhoff, Apr. 24, 1993. BS, U. Cin., 1967. Registered architect, Calif., Tex., Ariz., Nev., Ga., Fla., Colo., Hawaii, N.C., Ill. Draftsman, intern Skidmore, Owings & Merrill, San Francisco, 1967-70; pvt. practice architecture Sea Ranch, 1970-86, chmn. design com., 1975-79; prin. Dorius Archs., Corona del Mar, Calif., 1986-94; pres. JZMK Ptnrs., Irvine, Calif., 1994—. Bd. dirs. Homeaid Am. Prin. works represented to numerous newspapers and magazines. Co-chair Project Playhouse, Homeaid, 1993-95. Mem. AIA (chmn. nat. housing com. 1996, awards 1973-74, 77-78, Bay Area Honor Design Excellence award 1974, Homes for Better Living Merit award 1976, Housing Merit award 1978), Sr. Housing Coun. (bd. dirs. Orange County chpt. 1993-94). Democrat. Avocations: tennis, skiing, hiking. Home: 309 Poppy Ave Corona Del Mar CA 92625-3024 Home Phone: 949-644-7919.

JACOBS, GARY N., lawyer, hotel executive; b. NYC, July 12, 1945; m. Robin Jacobs; children: Melissa, Matthew. BA summa cum laude, Brandeis U., 1966; student, London Sch. Econs.; LLB, Yale U., 1969. Bar: NY 1970, Calif. 1972. Law clk. to Hon. Wilfred Feinberg US Ct. Appeals (2nd cir.), 1969—70; assoc. to ptnr. Wyman, Bautzer, Christensen, Kuchel & Silbert, LA, 1971—88; sr. ptnr. Christensen, Miller, Fink, Jacobs, Glaser, Weil & Shapiro, LLP, LA, 1988—2000, of counsel, 2000—; exec. v.p., gen. counsel MGM Mirage, Las Vegas, 2000—, sec., 2002—. Vis. lectr. UCLA Law Sch., 1982; dir., mem. exec. com. The InterGroup Corp., LA. Bd. govs. Am. Jewish Com.; bd. overseers Brandeis U. Grad. Sch. Internat. Econs. and Fin.; bd. dirs. Nev. Ballet Theatre, Nev. Cancer Inst.; mem. exec. com. Las Vegas Performing Arts Ctr. Mem.: Order of Coif, Phi Beta Kappa. Office: MGM Mirage 3600 Las Vegas Blvd S Las Vegas NV 89109 also: Christensen Miller Fink Jacobs Glaser Weil & Shapiro LLP 10250 Constellation Blvd 19th Fl Los Angeles CA 90067 Office Phone: 702-693-7120. Office Fax: 702-693-8626. E-mail: gary_jacobs@mgmmirage.com.

JACOBS, IRWIN MARK, communications executive; b. New Bedford, Mass., Oct. 18, 1933; m. Joan Jacobs; 4 children. BS in Elec. Engring., Cornell U., 1956; MS in Elec. Engring. and Computer Sci., MIT, 1957, ScD in Elec. Engring. and Computer Sci., 1959; D (hon.), Technion U., 2000, U. Penn., 2002. Rsch. asst. elec. engring. MIT, Cambridge, Mass., 1958-59, from asst. to assoc. prof., 1959-66; from assoc. to prof. computer sci. and engring. U. Calif., San Diego, 1966-72; co-founder, pres., chmn., CEO Linkabit Corp. (now M/A-COM Linkabit), 1969—85; co-founder, chmn. bd. dirs. Qualcomm Inc., San Diego, 1985—2009, CEO, 1985—2005. Cons. Applied Rsch. Lab. Sylvania Elect. Products, Inc., 1959—, Lincoln Lab. MIT, 1961—62, Indsl. Tchg. Mpls. Honeywell, Inc., 1963, Bolt Beranek & Newman, Inc., 1965; NASA resident rsch. fellow Jet Propulsion Lab., 1964—65; chmn. sci. adv. group Def. Comm. Agy. and Engring. Adv. Coun. U. Calif.; mem. Coun. on Competitveness; mem. pub. awareness engring. com. Nat. Acad. Engring.; bd. dirs. Bldg. Engring. and Sci. Talent; vis. com. MIT Lab. for Info. and Decision Sys., Calif. Coun. on Sci. and Tech.; past chmn. U. Calif. Pres. Engring. Adv. Coun. Author: Principles of Communication Engineering, 1965. Recipient Biannual award for outstanding contbn. to aerospace comm., Am. Inst. Aeronautics and Astronautics (AIAA), 1980, elected to, Nat. Acad. Engring., 1982, Disting. Cmty. Svc. award, Anti-Defamation League of B'nai B'rith, 1984, Excel award, Am. Electronics Assn., 1989, Entrepreneur Yr. award, Inst. Am. Entrepreneurs, 1992, San Diego Bus. Leader Yr. award, San Diego Venture Group, 1993, Inventing America's Future award, AEA, 1993, Internat. Citizens award, World Affairs Coun. of San Diego, 1993, Nat. Tech. medal, U.S. Dept. Commerce Tech. Adminstrn., 1994, Albert Einstein award, Am. Soc. Technion, 1996, Person Yr. award, RCR, 1996, Medal Achievement award, Am. Electronics Assn. (AEA), 1998, Ernst & Young Leadership award for Global Integration, Computerworld Smithsonian Award Program, 1999, Golden State award, Bd. Dirs. Calif. Coun. for Internat. Trade, 2000, Dir. Yr. award for Enhancement of Econ. Values, Corp. Dir. Forum, 2000, Scientist Yr. award, Achievement Rewards for Coll. Scientists (ARCS), 2000, Bower award in Bus. Leadership, Franklin Inst., 2001, Innovation award in Comm., The Economist, 2002, Internat. Engring. Consortium Fellow award, 2002, Dr. Morris Chang Exemplary Leadership award, The Fabless Semiconductor Assn. (FSA), 2003; named Cornell's Entrepreneur, 1994, Entrepreneur Yr., Master Entrepreneur category, RCR, 1996, inductee for significant contbn. to advancement of wireless, Radio Comm. Report (RCR) Wireless Hall Fame, 2000; named one of Forbes' Richest Americans, 2006; fellow, Am. Acad. Arts and Sci., 2001. Fellow: IEEE (Alexander Graham Bell medal 1995, IEEE/RSE Wolfson James Clark Maxwell award 2007); mem.: NAE (chair 2008—), Assn. Computing Machinery, Tau Beta Pi (Disting. Alumnus award 2003), Eta Kappa Nu (Eminent Mem. award 2003), Sigma Alpha Mu, Phi Kappa Phi, Sigma Xi. Achievements include patents for several CDMA patents. Office: Qualcomm Inc 5775 Morehouse Dr San Diego CA 92121-1714 also: 10185 Mckellar Ct San Diego CA 92121-4233*

JACOBS, KENT FREDERICK, dermatologist; b. El Paso, Tex., Feb. 13, 1938; s. Carl Frederick and Mercedes D. (Johns) J.; m. Sallie Ritter, Apr. 13, 1971. BS, N.Mex. State U., 1960; MD, Northwestern U., 1964; postgrad., U. Colo., 1967-70. Dir. service unit USPHS, Laguna, N.Mex., 1966-67; pvt. practice specializing in dermatology Las Cruces, N.Mex., 1970—. Cons. U.S. Army, San Francisco, 1968-70, cons. NIH, Washington, 1983, Holloman AFB, 1972-77; research assoc. VA Hosp., Denver, 1969-70; preceptor U. Tex., Galveston, 1976-77; mem. clin. staff Tex. Tech U., Lubbock, 1977—; asst. clin. prof. U. N.Mex., Albuquerque, 1972—; bd. dirs. First Security Corp. of N.Mex. Author: Breckkan, 1996; contbr. articles to profl. jours. and popular mags. Trustee Mus. N.Mex. Found., 1987-99, mem. bd. regents, 1987-99, pres., 1989-91, 95-99; bd. dirs. Dona Ana Arts Coun., 1992-93, Border Book Festival, 1996—, N.Mex. State U. Found., 1993—. Invitational scholar Oreg. Primate Ctr., 1968; Acad. Dermatology Found. fellow, 1969; named Disting. Alumnus N.Mex. State U., 1985. Fellow Am. Acad. Dermatology, Royal Soc. Medicine, Soc. Investigative Dermatology; mem. AMA, Fedn. State Med. Bds. (bd. dirs. 1984-86), N.Mex. Med. Soc., N.Mex. Bd. Med. Examiners (pres. 1983-84, N.Mex. State U. Alumni Assn. (bd. dirs. 1975-79), Mil Gracias Club (pres. 1972-74) Pres.'s Assocs., Univ. Ambs., Rotary, Phi Beta Kappa, Beta Beta Beta. Democrat. Presbyterian. Home: 3610 Southwind Rd Las Cruces NM 88005-5556

JACOBS, MARIAN, advertising executive; b. Stockton, Calif., Sept. 11, 1927; d. Paul and Rose (Sallah) J. AA, Stockton Coll. With Bottarini Advt., Stockton, 1948-50; pvt. practice Stockton, 1950-64; with Olympius Advt., Stockton, 1964-78; pvt. practice Stockton, 1978—. Pres. Stockton Advt. Club, 1954, Venture Club, Stockton, 1955; founder Stockton Advt. and Mktg. Club, 1981. Founder Stockton Arts Comms., 1976; co-founder Sunflower Entertainment for Institutionalized, 1976, Women Execs., Stockton, 1978; founding dir. Pixie Woods, Stockton; bd. dir. Goodwill Industries, St. Mary's Dining Room, Alan Short Gallery; mem. Calif. Coun. for the Humanities, 1994-95. Recipient Woman of Achievement award, San Joaquin County Women's Coun., Stockton, 1976, Achievement award, San Joaquin Delta Coll., Stockton, 1978, Friend of Edn. award, Calif. Tchrs. Assn., Stockton, 1988, Stanley McCaffrey Disting. Svc. award, U. of the Pacific, Stockton, 1988, Athena award for business-woman of Yr., Greater Stockton C. of C., 1989, Role Model award, Tierra del Oro Girl Scouts U.S., 1989, Heart of Gold award, Dameron Hosp. Found., 2000, Bravo award, Stockton Civic Theater; named Stocktonian of Yr., Stockton Bd. Realtors, 1978, Outstanding Citizen, Calif. State Senate and Assembly, 1978, Woman of Yr., State of Calif. Assembly, 2002, Woman of Achievement, Kaiser-Permanente Women's Wellness Conf., 2002, Disting. Alumni Vol., U. of the Pacific, 2003, Marian Jacobs Lit. Forum Stockton Arts Commn. established in her honor; Paul Harris fellow, Rotary Club, 1994. Republican. Roman Catholic. Avocations: art, photography. Home and Office: 4350 Mallard Creek Cir Stockton CA 95207-5205

JACOBS, PAUL ALAN, lawyer; b. Boston, June 5, 1940; s. Samuel and Sarah (Rodman) J.; m. Carole Ruth Greenstein, Aug. 28, 1962; children: Steven N., Cheryl R., David F., Craig A. BA in Econs. magna cum laude, Tufts U., 1960; JD magna cum laude, U. Denver, 1968. Bar: Colo. 1968, U.S. Dist. Ct. Colo. 1968. Pers. officer First Nat. Bank Denver, 1964-68; assoc. Holme Roberts & Owen, Denver, 1968-73, sr. ptnr., 1973-93; exec. v.p., gen. counsel Colo. Rockies profl. baseball orgn., Denver, 1991-95; ptnr. Jacobs Chase Frick Kleinkopf & Kelley, Denver, 1995—. Bd. dirs. Anti-Defamation League B'nai B'rith, Denver, 1987-95, Colo. Sports Hall of Fame, 2000—, Am. Jewish Com., 2002-. Served to 1st lt. USAF, 1960-63. Recipient Outstanding Alumni award, U. Denver Sturm Coll. Law, 2004. Mem. ABA, Denver Bar Assn., Colo. Bar Assn. Jewish. Avocations: skiing, golf. Home: 4041 S Narcissus Way Denver CO 80237-2025 Office: Independence Plz 1050 17th St Ste 1500 Denver CO 80265-2078 Business E-Mail: pjacobs@jcfkk.com.

JACOBS, PAUL E., communications company executive; b. 1962; s. Irwin Mark and Joan Jacobs; m. Stacy Jacobs; 3 children. BS, U. Calif., Berkeley, 1984, MS, 1986, PhD in Elec. Engring, 1989. Engring. positions QUALCOMM Inc., 1990—95, v.p. & gen. mgr. handset & integrated circuit divsn., 1995, sr. v.p., 1996, pres. QCP, 1997, exec. v.p., 2000—05, group pres. QWI, 2001, mem. exec. com., 1992—, CEO, 2005—09, chmn., CEO, 2009—. Bd. dirs. Qualcomm Inc., 2005—. Bd. mem. Mus. Contemporary Art, San Diego, Salk Inst. Biol. Studies; mem. adv. bd. U. Calif., Berkeley, Coll. Engring.; chmn. adv. bd. U. Calif., San Diego, Jacobs Sch. Engring. Named one of 50 Who Matter Now, CNNMoney.com Bus. 2.0, 2006, 2007. Mem.: Phi Beta Kappa, Eta Kappa Nu, Tau Beta Pi. Office: QUALCOMM Inc 5775 Morehouse Dr San Diego CA 92121*

JACOBS, PETER ALAN, artist, educator; b. NYC, Jan. 31, 1939; s. Peter A. and Elsie Katherine (Hirchi) J.; m. Nanci Gardner, Apr. 1, 1961; children: Christopher P.D., Cathi Jacobs. BS, SUNY, New Paltz, 1960, MS, 1962; EdD, Vanderbilt U., 1965. Assoc. prof. art SUNY, New Paltz, 1961-62; prof. art and dept. chair U. Wis., Whitewater, 1965-70, No. Ariz. U., Flagstaff, 1970-74, Ctrl. Mich. U., Mt. Pleasant, 1975-76, Colo. State U., Ft. Collins, 1976-86, prof. and art dept. chair, emeritus, 1988—; vis. prof. and dept. head U. Wyo., Laramie, 1986—87; vis. prof. Guangxi Normal U., China, 2001. Founder, 1st pres. Nat. Coun. Art Adminstrs., 1972; pres. The Douglas Soc., Native Arts Dept.; pres. Denver Art Mus., 1994-95, bd. dirs., 1993—; mem. Semester at Sea faculty U. Pitts., 1998; vis. prof. Guangxi Normal U., Guilin, China, 2001; mediation officer Colo. State U. One-man shows include over 70 in 14 states including Nicolaysen Art Mus., Casper, Wyo., 1991, one-man shows include Wyo. State Mus., Cheyenne, 1991, Julliet Denious Gallery, Carnegie Ctr. for Arts, Dodge City, Kans., 1990, Banares Hindu U., Varanasi, India, Gallery Bog, Boulder, Colo., Scottsdale Fine Arts Ctr., Ariz., Port Huron Mus. of Art, Mich., Ohio State U., Northwestern U., Evanston, Ill., exhibitions include, Italy, India, Poland, Germany, Can., Bulgaria, numerous juried exhbns. Bd. dirs. Nightwalker Enterprises, Ft. Collins, Colo., 1985—, One-West Contemporary Art Ctr., Ft. Collins, 1979-86, Artists' Adv. Com., 1994-95, No. Colo. Intertribal Pow-wow Assn. Fulbright scholar, India, 1981-82; Named: Art Educator of Yr. - Higher Edn., Colo. Art Edn. Assoc., 2007, Art Educator of Yr. - Pacific Region, Nat. Art Edn. Assoc., 2008. Mem. Coll. Art Assn., Native Am. Art Study Assn., Artist Adv. Coun. One-West Contemporary Art Ctr. Lutheran. Avocation: canoeing. Office: Colo State U Dept Art Fort Collins CO 80523-0001 Office Phone: 970-491-5895. Business E-Mail: peter.jacobs@colostate.edu.

JACOBS, RALPH, JR., artist; b. El Centro, Calif., May 22, 1940; s. Ralph and Julia Vahe (Kirkorian) J. Paintings appeared in: Prize Winning Art (3 awards), 1964, 65, 66, and New Woman Mag., 1975; one man shows and exhbns. Villa Montalvo, Calif., Stanford Rsch. Inst., Calif., Fresno Art Ctr., Calif., de Young Meml. Mus., Calif., Rosicrucian Mus., Calif., Cunningham Meml. Gallery, Calif., 40th Ann. Nat. Art Exhibit, Utah, Nat. Exhbn. Coun. of Am. Artists Socs., N.Y.C., Am. Artists Profl. League Show, Armenian Allied Arts, Calif., Monterey Peninsula Mus. Art, Calif. Recipient 1st place award Statewide Ann. Santa Cruz Art League Gallery, 1963, 64; 2d place award Soc. We. Artists Ann. M.H. de Young Mus., 1964; A.E. Klumpkey Meml. award, 1965. Address: PO Box 5906 Carmel CA 93921-5906

JACOBS, ROBERT COOPER, political scientist, consultant; b. NYC, Jan. 23, 1939; s. Max and Paula (Glotzer) J.; m. Barbara Linda Lax (div.); children: Michael, Deborah; m. Mollie Jenks Edson (div.); children: Elliot, Madeleine, Eleanor. AB, CCNY, 1959; AM, Columbia U., 1961, PhD, 1970. Instr. Colby Coll., Waterville, Maine, 1965-68, asst. prof., 1968-70; from asst. prof. to prof. Cen. Wash. U., Ellensburg, 1970—, dir. law and justice, 1974-88, prof., 1982—2002, prof. emeritus, 2002—. Vis. prof. criminal justice Temple U., 1988-89. Contbr. articles to profl. jours. and encyclopedias. Mem. Kittitas County Juvenile Accountability Bd., Ellensburg, 1975-79; trustee Ellensburg Pub. Libr., 1994—, chmn., 1996, 2000; mem. Wash. State Pistol Team. N.Y. State Regents scholar, 1955-59; State of N.Y. teaching fellow, 1962-63. Mem. Am. Polit. Sci. Assn., Wash. Assn. Criminal Justice Educators (past pres.), Supreme Ct. Hist. Soc. Democrat. Avocations: computers, hiking, target shooting. Home: 209 East 18th Ellensburg WA 98926 Office Phone: 509-963-2375. Business E-Mail: jacobsr@cwu.edu.

JACOBS, SETH ALAN, lawyer; b. Englewood, NJ, Aug. 1, 1956; s. Robert and Shirley Ann (Levine) J.; m. Julie Ann Stern, Aug. 12, 1979; children: Jessica Lynn, Elizabeth Rose, Samuel Adam. BA, U. Rochester, 1978; JD, Case Western Res. U., 1981. Bar: Ohio 1981, U.S. Dist. Ct. (no. dist.) Ohio 1981, Mich. 1985, Calif. 1988, Tex. 1990. Assoc. Buckingham, Doolittle & Burroughs, Akron, Ohio, 1981-84, Dykema, Gossett, Spencer, Goodnow & Trigg, Detroit, 1984-87; v.p., gen. counsel Travelers Health Network, Dallas, 1987-94; dep. gen. counsel The Metra Health Companies, Vienna, Va., 1994—95; asst. gen. counsel UnitedHealth Group, 1995—96; sr. v.p., gen. counsel Blue Shield of Calif., San Francisco, 1996—. Rep. human studies com. Cleve. VA Hosp., 1981. Mem. Nat. Assn. Managed Care Regulators, Nat. Health Lawyers Assn., Group Health Assn. Am. (chmn. legal affairs work group). Office: Blue Shield of California 50 Beale St San Francisco CA 94105*

JACOBSEN, JEFFREY SCOTT, environmental scientist; BS in Soil Sci., Calif. Polytech. State U., San Luis Obispo, 1979; MS in Agronomy, Colo. State U., 1982; PhD in Soil Sci. Fertility and Plant Nutrition, Okla. State U., 1985. Rsch asst. dept. agronomy Colo. State U., Fort Collins, 1979-82, technician dept. agronomy, 1982; tchg. asst. dept. agronomy Okla. State U., Stillwater, 1982-86; from asst. prof. to assoc. prof, soil scientist Mont. State U., Bozeman, 1986—, interim head dept. plant, soil and environ. scis., 1994-98, dept. head land resources environ. sci., 1998—. Recipient CIBA-GEIGY award in Agronomy Am. Soc. of Agronomy, 1994. Fellow Am. Soc. Agronomy. Office: Montana State U Dept of Agriculture 202 Linfield Hall PO Box 172860 Bozeman MT 59717-0001

JACOBSEN, KEN, state legislator; b. Dannebrog, Nebr. m to Rachel; children: Sonja & Kiri. Washington State Representative, District 46, 83-96, chairman, Higher Education Committee, formerly, Washington House Representative; Washington State Senator, District 46, 97-, vice chairman, Majority Caucus, 99-, member, Environ Quality & Water Resource, Higher Education & Transportation Committees, chairman, Natural Resources, Parks & Recreation Committee, currently, Washington State Senate; member, Joint Pension & Policy Committee, currently.Director, Puget Consumers Co-op, currently; coun, United Way Early Childhood Hearing Impaired Prog, currently; member, America Indian Endowment Committee, currently; member, Ravenna & Thornton Creek Alliance, currently. Lake City Chamber of Commerce; DAV; Decatur Elementary Sch PTA; Seattle Audubon Soc (board, currently); North Seattle Community Col Found; Dollars for Scholars; Friends of Univ Washington Library; Citizen Scholarship Found America. Democrat. Address: Seattle WA Mailing: State Senate 427 John A Cherberg Bldg PO Box 40446 Olympia WA 98504-0482 Office Phone: 206-348-6570. Fax: 360-786-1999. E-mail: jacobsen_ke@leg.wa.gov.

JACOBSEN, RICHARD T., mechanical engineering educator; b. Pocatello, Idaho, Nov. 12, 1941; s. Thorleif (dec.), and Edith Emily (Gladwin) J. dec.); m. Vicki Belle Hopkins, July 16, 1959 (div. Mar. 1973); children: Pamela Sue, Richard T, Eric Ernest; m. Bonnie Lee Stewart, Oct. 19, 1973; 1 child, Jay Michael; stepchild: Erik David Lustig. BSME, U. Idaho, 1963, MSME, 1965; PhD in Engring. Sci., Wash. State U., 1972. Registered profl. engr., Idaho. From instr. to prof. emeritus U. Idaho, 1964—2006, prof. emeritus, 2006—, chmn. dept. mech. engring., 1980-85, assoc. dean engring., 1985-90, assoc. dir. Ctr. for Applied Thermodynamic Studies, 1975-86, dir., 1986-99, 2005—06, dean engring., 1990-99; chief scientist Idaho Nat. Engring. Environ. Lab. Bechtel BWXT Idaho LLC, 1999—2005, from dep. lab. dir. to assoc. lab. dir. Idaho Nat. Engring. Environ. Lab., 1999—2005; prof., dean engring. Idaho State U., 2006—. Guest rschr. Nat. Inst. Standards Tech., 1979, 86, 99; mem. annex 18 thermophys. properties environ. acceptable refrigerants com. Internat. Energy Agy., 1991-98; mem. nat. adv. coun. Fed. Lab. Consortium for Tech. Transfer, 2002—; mem. adv. coun Idaho State U. Coll. Engring., 2000-05; instl. rev. bd. protection human subjects in rsch. Idaho Nat. Engring. Environ. Lab., 2000-05, chmn., 2001-05 Author: International Union of Pure and Applied Chemistry, Nitrogen-International Thermodynamic Tables of the Fluid State-6, 1979; Oxygen-International Thermodynamic Tables of the Fluid State-9, 1987, Ethylene-International Thermodynamic Tables of the Fluid State-10, 1988, ASHRAE Thermodynamic Properties of Refrigerants (2 vols.), 1986, (monograph series) Thermodynamic Properties of Cryogenic Fluids, 1997; numerous chpts. in books and handbooks, reports on thermodynamic properties of fluids, 1971-; contbr. articles to profl. jours. Recipient Outstanding Engr. award Idaho State U., 2002; NSF sci. faculty fellow, 1968-69; NSF rsch. and travel grantee, 1976-83; Nat. Inst. Stds. and Tech. grantee, 1974-91, 95-98, 2006, Gas Rsch. Inst. grantee, 1986-91, 1992-98, Dept. Energy grantee, 1991-95. Fellow ASME (faculty advisor 1972-75, 78-84, chmn. region VIII dept. heads com. 1983-85, honors and awards chmn. 1985-91, K-7 tech. com. thermophys. properties 1985—, chmn. 1986-89, 92-95, 2001-04, rsch. tech. com. on water and steam in thermal power systems, 1988—, gen. awards com. 1985-91, chmn. 1988-91, com. on honors 1988-99, vice chmn. 1995-99, mem. bd. on profl. practice and ethics, 1991-2004, v.p. profl. practice 1998-2001, v.p. rsch. 2004-05, v.p. fin. ops. 2005-07, chair bd. rsch. and tech. devel. 2007—, Inland Empire Sect. Engr. of Yr. award 1999, Dedicated Svc. award 2003); mem. N.W. Coll. and Univ. Assn. for Sci. (bd. dirs. 1990-93), NSPE (Excellence in Engring. Educator award Idaho chpt. 2007), Am. Soc. Engring. Edn., Am. Nuc. Soc., Idaho Rsch. Found. (bd. dirs. 1991-99, 2000-06), Soc. Automotive Engrs. (Ralph R. Teetor Edn. award, Detroit 1968), Bonneville County Hist. Soc. (trustee 2001—), ASHRAE (co-recipient Best Tech. Paper award 1984), Sigma Xi, Tau Beta Pi, Phi Kappa Phi (Disting. Faculty award 1989). Office: Coll of Engring 921 S 8th Ave Stop 8060 Pocatello ID 83209-8060 Home Phone: 208-233-4095. Business E-Mail: jacorich@isu.edu.

JACOBSON, EUGENE DONALD, medical educator, academic administrator, researcher; b. Bridgeport, Conn., Feb. 19, 1930; s. Morris and Mary (Mendelsohn) J.; m. Laura Kathryn Osborn, June 9, 1973; children from previous marriage: Laura Ellen, Susan Ruth, Morris David, Daniel Frederick, Miriam Louise. BA, Wesleyan U., 1951; MD, U. Vt., 1955; MS, SUNY, Syracuse, 1960; DM (hon.), Jagiellonian U., 1996. Assoc. prof. UCLA Sch. Medicine, 1965-66; prof., chmn. U. Okla. Sch. Medicine, Oklahoma City, 1966-71, U. Tex. Med. Sch., Houston, 1971-77; vice dean Coll. Medicine U. Cin., 1977-85; dean Sch. Medicine, U. Kans., Kansas City, 1985-88; dean Sch. Medicine U. Colo., Denver, 1988-90, prof., 1990-99, prof. emeritus, 1999—, acting head divsn. gastroenterology, 1994. Cons. NIH, Bethesda, Md., 1968-72, mem. nat. digestive adv. bd., 1985-87; chmn. Nat. Commn., U.S. Congress, Washington, 1977-79; cons. Upjohn Co., Kalamazoo, 1970-87, G. D. Searle and Co., Chgo., 1984-85. Contbr. 320 articles to profl. jours. Served to maj. U.S. Army, 1956-64. NIH Rsch. grantee, 1967-97. Fellow ACP; mem. AMA (ho. of dels. 1991—2004), Am. Soc. Clin. Investigation, Assn. Am. Physicians, Am. Physiol. Soc., Am. Gastroenterol. Assn. (pres. 1989-90, Friedenwald medal 1998), Am. Digestive Health Found. (bd. dirs., vice chair 1995-98).

JACOBSON, FRANK JOEL, cultural organization administrator; b. Phila., Sept. 14, 1948; s. Leonard and June Anette (Groff) J.; m. Stephanie Lou Savage, July 5, 1970; children: Aaron Jeffery, Adam Michael, Ashley Celeste. BA, U. Wis., 1970; MFA, Boston U., 1973. Mng. dir. Mont. Repertory Theater, Missoula, Mo., 1973-75; asst. prof. drama U. Mont., Missoula, 1973-75; program dir. Western States Arts Found., Denver, 1975-77, dir. programs, 1977-78, gen. mgr. budget/planning, 1978-79; exec. dir. Arvada (Colo.) Ctr. for the Arts & Humanities, 1979-85; dir. theatres and arenas City & County of Denver, 1985-87; pres., CEO Scottsdale (Ariz.) Cultural Coun., 1987—. Bd. dirs. Met. Denver Arts Alliance, pres., 1979-85, Rocky Mountain Arts Consortium, pres., 1979-80. Contbr. articles to profl. jours. Mem. panel theater program Nat. Endowment for the Arts, Washington, 1990-92; bd. dirs. Scottsdale Focus, 1988-93, 93-97, Arizonans for Cultural Devel., 1992-97; bd. dirs. Scottsdale Edn. Found., 1994-99, chmn., 1994-96; bd. dirs. Scottsdale Convention and Visitors Bur., 2001—. Mem.: Assn. for Performing Arts Presenters (bd. dirs. 1984—87), Rocky Mountain Theatre Assn. (bd. dirs., pres. 1976—78), Mont. State Theatre Assn. (bd. dirs., pres. 1974—75), Am. Theatre Assn. (bd. dirs. 1976—78), Scottsdale C. of C. (bd. dirs. 2001—). Office: Scottsdale Cultural Council 7380 E 2nd St Scottsdale AZ 85251-5604

JACOBSON, GARY CHARLES, political science professor; b. Orange, Calif., July 7, 1944; s. Charles William and Ruth Hope (Brown) J.; m. Martha Ellen Blake, June 2, 1979. AB in Polit. Sci., Stanford U., 1966; MPhil, Yale U., 1969, PhD in Polit. Sci., 1972. From instr. to assoc. prof. Trinity Coll., Hartford, Conn., 1970-79; from assoc. prof. to prof. polit. sci. U. Calif., San Diego, 1979—; Woodrow Wilson fellow, 1969. Author: Money in Congressional Elections, 1980, (with Samuel Kernell) Strategy and Choice in Congressional Elections, 1981, The Politics of Congressional Elections, 1983, 87, 91, 97, 2000, 2004, The Electoral Origins of Divided Governments, 1990, The Logic of American Politics (with Samuel Kernell), 2000, 2003, 2006,2007, A Divider, Not a Uniter: George W. Bush and the American People, 2006. Grantee NSF, 1980-82. Mem. Am. Acad. Arts and Scis., Am. Polit. Sci. Assn. (Gladys E. Kammerer award 1981), Western Polit. Sci. Assn., Midwest Polit. Sci. Assn., So. Polit. Sci. Assn. Office: U Calif San Diego Dept Polit Sci # 0521 La Jolla CA 92093

JACOBSON, JON L., law educator; BA, Univ. Iowa, 1961, JD, 1963. Bar: Calif. 1964. Atty. Bronson Bronson & McKinnon, San Francisco, 1963—67; Bigelow Fellow Univ. Chgo., 1967—68; Bernard B. Kliks prof. emeritus U. Oreg. Sch. Law, founding dir. Ocean & Coastal Law Ctr. Stockton chair internat. law U.S. Naval War Coll., Newport, RI, 1982—83. Editor (in chief): Ocean Development & Internat. Law, 1990—99. Fulbright Found. scholar, Scandinavian Inst. Maritime Law, U. Oslo, 1976, 1984. Office: University of Oregon School of Law 1515 Agate St Eugene OR 97403 Office Phone: 541-346-3852.

JACOBSON, MICHAEL R., lawyer, Internet company executive; b. 1954; BA in Econs. magna cum laude, Harvard U., 1975; JD, Stanford U., 1981. Bar: Calif. 1981. Ptnr. Cooley Godward LLP; v.p. legal affairs to sr. v.p., gen. counsel, sec. eBay Inc., San Jose, Calif., 1998—. Mem.: Phi Beta Kappa. Office: eBay Inc 2145 Hamilton Ave San Jose CA 95125-5905 Office Phone: 408-558-7400. Office Fax: 408-558-7514.

JACOBSON, NINA R., film producer, former company executive; b. 1965; life ptnr.; 2 children. AB, Brown Univ., 1987. Doc. rschr. Arnold Shapiro Prodns.; story analyst Disney Sunday Movie, 1987; dir. develop. Silver Pictures; head develop. McDonald/Parkes Prodn.; sr. v.p. prodn. Universal Pictures, 1994—95; sr. film exec. DreamWorks SKG, 1995—98; exec. v.p. prodn. Walt Disney Pictures/Hollywood Pictures, 1998; co-pres. Buena Vista Motion Pictures Group (divsn. The Walt Disney Co.), Burbank, Calif., 1999—2000, pres., 2000—06; prodr. DreamWorks Studios, 2006—. Recipient Crystal award, Women in Film, 2003; named one of 100 Most Powerful Women in Entertainment, Hollywood Reporter, 2004, 2005, 100 Most Powerful Women in World, Forbes mag., 2005, 50 Most Powerful People in Hollywood, Premiere mag., 2004—06. Office: DreamWorks Studios 1000 Flower St Glendale CA 91201

JACOBSON, PHILLIP LEE, architect, educator; b. Santa Monica, Calif., Aug. 27, 1928; s. Allen Wilhelm and Greta Percy (Rohde) J.; m. Effie Laurel Galbraith, Nov. 6, 1954; children: Rolf Wilhelm, Christina Lee, Erik Mackenzie. B. Archtl. Engring. with honors, Wash. State U., 1952; postgrad. (Fulbright scholar), U. Liverpool, Eng., 1952-53; M.Arch., Finnish Inst. Tech., Helsinki, 1969. Field supr. Gerald C. Field Architect, 1950; designer, draftsman John Maloney Architect, 1951, 53-55; designer, project mgr. Young, Richardson, Carleton & Detlie Architects, 1955-56; designer, project architect

John Carl Warnecke Architect, San Francisco, 1956-58; ptnr., design dir. TRA, Seattle, 1958-92; prof. architecture and urban design and planning Coll. Architecture and Urban Planning, U. Wash., Seattle, 1962—2000. Author: Housing and Industrialization in Finland, 1969, The Evolving Architectural Design Process, 1969; contbr. articles to profl. jours.; major archtl. works include Aerospace Research Lab., U. Wash., Seattle, 1969, McCarty Residence Hall, 1960, Highway Adminstrn. Bldg., Olympia, Wash., 1970, Sea-Tac Internat. Airport, 1972, Issaquah (Wash.) High Sch., 1962, State Office Bldg. 2, Olympia, 1976, Sealaska Corporate Hdqrs. Bldg., Juneau, Alaska, 1977, Group Health Hosp., Seattle, 1973, Metro Shelter Program, Seattle, 1977, N.W. Trek Wildlife Preserve, 1976, Rocky Reach/Rock Island Recreation Plan, 1974, master plan mouth of Columbia River, 1976, U. Wash. Biol. Sci. Bldg., 1981, Wegner Hall, Wash. State U., 1982, Wash. Conv. Ctr., 1988, King County Aquatics Ctr., 1990, Albuquerque Airport, 1989, U. Wash. Health Scis. H Wing, 1993, Elegant Explorations The Designs of Phillip Jacobson, 2007. Mem. Seattle Planning and Redevel. Council, 1959-69, v.p., 1966-67; mem. Seattle Landmark Preservation Bd., 1976-81; trustee Pilchuck Sch., 1982-2001, Northwest Trek Found., 1987-94, AIA/Seattle Archtl. Found., 1986-92. With U.S. Army, 1946-47. Fulbright-Hays Sr. Rsch. fellow Finland, 1968-69; named to Order of White Rose Govt. of Finland, 1985; recipient Silver plaque Finnish Soc. Architects, 1992; recipient Alumni Achievement award Wash. State U., 2009, numerous design awards. Fellow AIA (pres. Wash. state Council 1965, dir. Seattle chpt. 1970-73, sr. council 1970—, Seattle chpt. medal 1994); mem. Am. Inst. Cert. Planners, Phi Kappa Phi, Tau Beta Pi, Tau Sigma Delta, Scarab, Sigma Tau (outstanding alumnus 1967). Office: U Wash PO Box 355720 Seattle WA 98195-5720

JACOBSON, RAYMOND EARL, electronics executive; b. St. Paul, May 25, 1922; s. Albert H. and Gertrude W. (Anderson) J.; m. div. 1986; children: Michael David, Karl Raymond, Christopher Eric. BE with high honors, prize for excellence in mech. engring., Yale U., New Haven, Conn., 1944; MBA with distinction, Harvard U., Cambridge, Mass., 1948; BA in Econ. and Politics (Rhodes Scholar), Oxford U., 1950, MA, 1954. Asst. to gen. mgr. Polytech Rsch and Devel. Co., Inc., Bklyn., 1951-55; sales mgr. Curtiss-Wright Electronics Divsn., Carlstadt, NJ, 1955-57; dir. mktg. TRW Computers Co., LA, 1957—60; v.p. ops. Electro-Sci. Investors, Dallas, 1960-63; pres. Whitehall Electronics, Inc., Dallas, 1961-63; chmn. bd. Gen. Electronic Control, Inc., Mpls., 1961-63, Staco, Inc., Dayton, Ohio, 1961-63; pres. Maxson Electronics Corp., Gt. River, NY, 1963-64, Jacobson Assocs., San Jose, Calif., 1964-67; co-founder, pres., chmn., CEO Anderson Jacobson, Inc., San Jose, Calif., 1967-88. Chmn. Anderson Jacobson, SA, Paris, 1974-88, Anderson Jacobson, Ltd., London, 1975-88, Anderson Jacobson Can., Ltd./Ltée, Toronto, 1975-85, Anderson Jacobson, GmbH, Cologne, 1978-83, CXR Corp., San Jose, 1988-94; bd. dirs. Tamar Electronics, Inc., LA, Rawco Instruments, Inc., Dallas, 1960-63, Micro Radionics, Inc., LA, 1964-67, ComputerMan USA, Inc., Reno, 1997—; lectr. engring., UCLA, 1958-60, lectr. bus. adminstrn. U. Calif. Berkeley, 1965-66; mem. underwriting Lloyd's London, 1975-96. Eagle Scout Boy Scouts Am., 1935, committeeman, 1968-80. Lt. (j.g.) USNR, 1943-46, radar maintenance officer, USS Puget Sound. Mem. Assn. Am. Rhodes Scholars, Oxford Soc., Brasenose Soc., Yale Club, Yale Class 1944 (exec. com.), Harvard Bus. Sch. Assn., Sigma Xi, Tau Beta Pi, Courtside Tennis Club, Seascape Swim and Racquet Club. Republican. Lutheran. Home and Office: 543 Elk River Ct Reno NV 89511 Office Phone: 775-851-3796.

JACOBSON, SIDNEY, editor; b. NYC, Oct. 20, 1929; s. Reuben and Beatrice (Edelman) J.; m. Ruth Allison, July 4, 1957 (div. Feb. 1975); children: Seth, Kathy Battat; m. Maggi Silverstein, Feb. 26, 1975 (dec.); m. Shure Lifton, Nov. 6, 2007. BA, NYU, 1950. Exec. editor Harvey Comics, NYC, 1952-83, Marvel Comics, NYC, 1983-89; v.p., editor-in-chief Harvey Comics Entertainment, LA, 1989—. Author: Streets of Gold, 1985, Another Time, 1989, Pistol: The Story of Pete Reiser, 2004, The 9/11 Report: A Graphic Adaptation, 2006 (Libr. Jour. Fall Editors' Pick, 2006), After 9/11: The War on Terror, 2008, Che: A Graphic Biography, 2009, Vlad: The Man Who Was Dracula, 2009; writer (comic books) Captain Israel, 1972, The Black Comic Book, 1973, (TV animation series) Johnny Cypher in Dimension Zero, 1975, (TV series) Felix the Cat, 1982, (monthly) You Can't Do That in Comics, 1986; lyricist various popular songs. Mem. Am. Soc. Composers, Authors and Pubs., Am. Guild Authors and Composers, Authors Guild. Home: 6333 West 6 St Los Angeles CA 90048 Personal E-mail: sidjacobson2@aol.com.

JACOBUS, ARTHUR, dance company administrator; BBA, Columbia Coll.; Artist's diploma, Academia di Musica, Italy; M in Arts Adminstrn., Golden Gate U., MBA; M in Human Resources Mgmt., Pepperdine U.; grad. exec. mgmt. program, U. Wash.; grad. strategic perspectives program, Harvard U. Founder, dir. NATO Internat. Band, Naples, 1973-79; pres., gen. mgr. Oakland Symphony, 1979-84; pres., chief exec. officer Pacific N.W. Ballet, Seattle, 1984-93; exec. dir. San Francisco Ballet, 1993—. Mem. Dance/USA.

JACOBY, IRVING, physician; b. NYC, Sept. 30, 1947; s. Philip Aaron and Sylvia Jacoby; m. Sara Kay Vartanian; children: James Tyler, Kathryn Aaryn. BS magna cum laude, U. Miami, Coral Gables, Fla., 1969; MD, Johns Hopkins U., 1973. Diplomate Am. Bd. Internal Medicine, Am. Bd. Infectious Diseases, Am. Bd. Emergency Medicine, Am. Bd. Preventive Medicine (undersea and hyperbaric medicine). Intern Boston City Hosp., 1973-74, resident in medicine, 1974-75, chief resident, 1978-79; resident in medicine Peter Bent Brigham Hosp., Boston, 1975-76, fellow in infectious diseases, 1976-78; asst. dir. emergency med. svcs. U. Mass. Med. Ctr., Worcester, 1979-84; asst. dir. dept. emergency med. San Diego (Calif.) Med. Ctr. U. Calif., 1984—, assoc. prof. med. surgery San Diego (Calif.) Med. Ctr., 1988-94, hosp. dir. for emergency preparedness and response San Diego (Calif.) Med. Ctr., 2003—, prof. med. surgery San Diego (Calif.) Med. Ctr., 1994—, disaster control officer San Diego (Calif.) Med. Ctr., 1985—. Assoc. dir. Hyperbaric Med. Ctr., 1985—; vis. physician, cons. infectious diseases Soroka Med. Ctr., Ben Gurion U., Beer-Sheva, Israel, 1980; flight physician New Eng. Life Flight, Worcester, 1982-84, Life Flight Aeromed. Program U. Calif., 1984-87. Sect. editor for disaster medicine Jour. Emergency Medicine, 1996—; assoc. editor Undersea and Hyperbaric Medicine, 1996-2002. Comdr. Disaster Med. Assistance Team CA-4, 1991-. Fellow ACP, Am. Coll. Emergency Physicians; mem. Am. Soc. Microbiology, Infectious Diseases Soc. Am., Nat. Assn. Disaster Med. Assistance Teams (vice chair 1999, chmn. 2000-01), Soc. Acad. Emergency Medicine, Undersea and Hyperbaric Med. Soc., World Assn. for Disaster and Emergency Medicine, Disaster Emergency Response Assn., Johns Hopkins Med. and Surg. Assn., Iron Arrow Leadership Soc., Omicron Delta Kappa, Phi Kappa Phi, Alpha Epsilon Delta, Phi Eta Sigma. Office: U Calif Med Ctr 200 W Arbor Dr San Diego CA 92103-8676 Office Phone: 619-543-6216.

JADVAR, HOSSEIN, nuclear radiologist, biomedical engineer; b. Tehran, Iran, Apr. 6, 1961; arrived in U.S., 1978, naturalized, 1995; s. Ramezan Ali and Fatemeh (Afzal) Jadvar; m. Mojgan Maher, 1995; children: Donya S., Delara A. BS, Iowa State U., Ames, 1982; MS, U. Wis., Madison, 1984, U. Mich., Ann Arbor, 1986, PhD, 1988; MD, U. Chgo., 1993; MPH, Harvard U., Boston, 2005; MBA, U. So. Calif., LA, 2007; student, U. Cambridge, Eng., 2007, U. Oxford, 2008. Diplomate Am. Bd. Nuc. Medicine, Bd. Nuc. Cardiology. Rsch. asst. dept. human oncology U. Wis., Madison, 1983-84; rsch. asst. dept. elec. engring. U. Mich., Ann Arbor, 1984-88; sr. rsch. engr. Arzco Med. Electronics, Inc., Chgo., 1988-89; sr. rsch. assoc. Pritzker Inst., Ill. Inst. Tech., Chgo., 1989-92; med. intern U. Calif., San Francisco, 1993-94; resident in radiology Stanford (Calif.) U., 1994-96, resident in nuclear medicine, 1996-98, chief resident in nucelar medicine, 1997-98; clin. fellow in radiology (positron emission tomography) Harvard Med. Sch., Boston, 1998-99; asst. prof. radiology and biomed. engring. U. So. Calif., LA, 1999—2005, assoc. prof. radiology and biomed. engring., 2005—, dir. rsch. radiology, 2006—. Reviewer study sect. small bus innovative rsch. program NIH, 1989, med. imaging, 2005—; vis. assoc. bioengring. Calif. Inst. Tech., Pasadena, 2001—; fellow clin. effectiveness program Sch. Pub. Health Harvard U., Boston, 2003; mem. radioactive drug rsch. com. FDA, 2003—; faculty fellow Ctr. Excellence in Rsch. U. So. Calif., 2007—. Author (with J.A. Parker): Clinical PET and PET-CT, 2005; mem. editl. bd. Clin. Nuc. Medicine, 2007—; asst. editor sect. nuc. medicine and molecular imaging: Am. Jour. Roentgenology, 2008—; contbr. chapters to books, articles to profl. jours. Recipient Resident Rsch. award, NIH, 1994; grantee, Am. Cancer Soc., The Wright Found., NIH/Nat. Cancer Inst. Fellow: Am. Coll. Nuc. Medicine (faculty New Orleans 2000, faculty Tampa 2001, faculty Scottsdale 2002, faculty San Antonio 2006, sci. sessions chmn. 2008, bd. reps.), Am. Coll. Nuc. Physicians (bd. regents); mem.: IEEE (sr.), Soc. Molecular Imaging, LA Radiol. Soc. (faculty 2002, pres. nuc. medicine sect. 2007—), Calif. Med. Assn. (nuc. med. sci. com. 2002—05), Computers in Cardiology (local organizing com. 1990), Acad. Molecular Imaging (mem. editl. bd. Molecular Imaging and Biology 2004—), Soc. Nuc. Medicine, PET Ctr.Excellence (mem. editl. bd. Jour. Nuc. Medicine 2006—, bd. dirs. 2008—, mem. pub. and govt. rels. com., pres., Pacific SW Chpt. 2009—, Tetalman Young Investigator award 2000, seed grant award 2000), Radiol. Soc. N.Am. (Resident Rsch. award 1997, seed grant award 2002), Eta Kappa Nu, Sigma Xi, Tau Beta Pi. Achievements include patents for esophgeal catheters and method and apparatus for detection of posterior ischemia. Office: U So Calif Divsn Nuc Medicine Dept Radiology Keck Sch Medicine 2250 Alcazar St CSC Ste 102 Los Angeles CA 90033 Business E-Mail: jadvar@usc.edu.

JAFEK, BRUCE WILLIAM, otolaryngologist, educator; b. Berwyn, Ill., Mar. 4, 1941; s. Robert William and Viola Mabel (Newstrom) J.; m. Mary Bell Kirkpatrick, Sept. 1, 1962; children: Lynette A., Robert K., Timothy B., Britta C., Kayla E., Kristen M. BS, Coe Coll., 1962; postgrad., U. Omaha, 1962; MD, UCLA, 1966; postgrad., Oxford U., 2002—03. Instr. dept. otology/laryngology Johns Hopkins Sch. Medicine, Balt., 1971-73; asst. prof. dept. otolaryngology U. Pa. Med. Sch., Phila., 1973-76; prof., dept. chmn. dept. otolaryngology/head and neck surgery U. Colo. Med. Sch., Denver, 1976-98, prof., 1998—. With USPHS, 1971—73. Recipient Fowler award Triologic Soc., 1983, Cottle award Am. Rhinol. Soc., 1991. Mem. Triologic Soc. (west region v.p. 1999), Am. Acad. Otolaryngology/Head and Neck Surgery. Republican. Mem. Lds Ch. Office: U Colo Health Sci Ctr 4200 E 9th Ave # B-205 Denver CO 80220-3706 Home Phone: 303-795-9584; Office Phone: 303-315-7988. Business E-Mail: bruce.jafek@uchsc.edu.

JAFFA, HARRY VICTOR, political philosophy educator emeritus; b. NYC, Oct. 7, 1918; s. Arthur Sol and Frances (Landau) J.; m. Marjorie Etta Butler, Apr. 25, 1942; children: Donald Alan, Philip Bertran, Karen Louise Jaffa McGoldrick. BA, Yale U., 1939; PhD summa cum laude, New Sch. for Social Rsch., 1951; LLD (hon.), Marietta Coll., 1979, Ripon Coll., 1987. Instr. Queens Coll., CCNY, New Sch. for Social Rsch., 1945-49, U. Chgo., 1949-51, Ohio State U., 1951-64; faculty Claremont (Calif.) McKenna Coll. and Claremont Grad. Sch., 1964-89, Henry Salvatori Rsch. prof. polit. philosophy, 1971-89, prof. emeritus, 1989—; disting. fellow The Claremont Inst., 1989—. Author: Thomism and Aristotelianism: A Study of the Commentary by Thomas Aquinas on the Nicomachean Ethics, 1952, Crisis of the House Divided: An Interpretation of the Issues in the Lincoln-Douglas Debates, 1959, Equality and Liberty, 1965, The Conditions of Freedom, 1975, How to Think About the American Revolution, 1978, American Conservatism and the American Founding, 1984, Original Intent and the Framers of the Constitution: A Disputed Question, 1994, Storm Over the Constitution, 1999, A New Birth of Freedom: Abraham Lincoln and the Coming of the Civil War, 2000; (with Allan Bloom) Shakespeare's Politics, 1964; contbg. author: Shakespeare As Political Thinker, 1981; editor, contbg. author: Statesmanship: Essays in Honor of Sir Winston Churchill, 1982; general editor: Studies in Statesmanship; co-editor: (with Robert Johannsen) In the Name of the People: Speeches and Writings of Lincoln and Douglas in the Ohio Campaign of 1859, 1959. Organizer/dir. Bicycle Racing Program at Claremont Coll., 1976—. Fellow Ford, Rockefeller, Guggenheim, and Earhart founds. Fellow The Claremont Inst. Study of Statesmanship & Political Philosophy (disting.); mem. Am. Polit. Sci. Assn. Republican. Jewish. Avocation: bicycling. Home: 549 W Baughman Ave Claremont CA 91711-3733 Office: Claremont Inst 937 W Foothill Blvd Claremont CA 91711 Office Phone: 909-621-6825.

JAFFE, CHARLES J., allergist; b. Phila., Feb. 3, 1946; MD, Duke U., 1971, PhD, 1972. Allergist Scripps Meml. Hosp., Encinitas, Calif. Prof. allergy and immunology U. Calif., San Diego. Mem. Am. Coll. Allergy Asthma and Immunology (chair computer sect.), Am. Acad. Allergy Asthma and Immunology (chair med. informatics), Am. Med. Informatics Assn. (chmn. clin. info. syss.).

JAFFE, EDWARD A., lawyer; b. Chgo., Sept. 17, 1945; s. Julius C. and Esther R. (Cohen) J.; m. Marlene E. Epstein, June 16, 1968; children: Kimberly A., Jonathan S. BA, Drake Univ., 1967; JD cum laude, Northwestern Univ., 1970. Bar: Ill. 1970, Hawaii 1971, U.S. Dist. Ct. Hawaii 1971, U.S. Ct. Appeals (9th cir.) 1972, (2d cir.) 1979, U.S. Supreme Ct. 1984. Assoc. Cades, Schutte, Fleming & Wright, Honolulu, 1970-75, ptnr., 1976-88; sr. ptnr. Torkildson, Katz, Fonseca, Jaffe, Moore & Hetherington, Honolulu, 1988—. Facualty Nat. Inst. Trail Advocacy, Honolulu, 1985—, Univ. Hawaii Col. Continuing Edn., Honolulu, 1973—; arbitrator Am. Arbitration Assn., Honolulu, 1973—, Ct. Annexed Arbitration Program, Honolulu, 1987—. Pres. Temple Emanu-El, Honolulu, 1989-91, bd. trustees, 1980-93. Office: Torkildson Katz Fonseca Jaffe Moore Hetherington Amfac Bldg 700 Bishop St Fl 15 Honolulu HI 96813-4187

JAFFE, F. FILMORE, lawyer, retired judge; b. Chgo., May 4, 1918; s. Jacob Isadore and Goldie (Rabinowitz) J.; m. Mary Main, Nov. 7, 1942; children: Jo Anne, Jay. Student, Southwestern U., 1936-39; JD, Pacific Coast U., 1940. Bar: Calif. 1945, U.S. Supreme Ct. 1964. Practiced law, Los Angeles, 1945-91; ptnr. Bernard & Jaffe, Los Angeles, 1947-74, Jaffe & Jaffe, Los Angeles, 1975-91; apptd. referee Superior Ct. of Los Angeles County, 1991-97, apptd. judge pro tem, 1991-97; ret., 1997; atty. in pvt. practice LA, 1997—. Mem. L.A. Traffic Commn., 1947-48; arbitrator Am. Arbitration Assn., 1968-91; chmn. pro bono com. Superior Ct. Calif., County of Los Angeles, 1980-86; lectr. on paternity; chair family law indigent paternity panel L.A. County Supr. Ct., 2001—. Served to capt. inf. AUS, 1942-45. Decorated Purple Heart, Croix de Guerre with Silver Star, Bronze Star with oak leaf cluster; honored Human Rights Commn. Los Angeles, Los Angeles County Bd. Suprs.; recipient Pro Bono award State Bar Calif., commendation State Bar Calif., 1983, Spencer Brandeis award LA County Bar, 2007, 08. Mem.: ABA, Beverly Hills Bar Assn., US Supreme Ct. Bar Assn., LA Criminal Ct. Bar Assn. (charter mem.), Los Angeles County Bar (honored by family law sect. 1983), Shriners, Masons. Office: 433 N Camden Dr Ste 400 Beverly Hills CA 90210-4408 Home Phone: 310-553-3350; Office Phone: 310-859-8921. Personal E-mail: filmorejaffe@sbcglobal.net.

JAFFE, ROBERT BENTON, obstetrician, gynecologist, endocrinologist; b. Detroit, Feb. 18, 1933; s. Jacob and Shirley (Robins) J.; m. Evelyn Grossman, Aug. 29, 1954; children: Glenn, Terri. MS, U. Colo., 1966; MD, U. Mich., 1957. Intern U. Colo. Med. Ctr., Denver, 1957-58, resident, 1959-63; asst. prof. Ob-Gyn. U. Mich. Med. Ctr., 1964-68, assoc. prof., 1968-72, prof., 1972-74, dir. steroid rsch. unit, 1964-74; prof. U. Calif., San Francisco, 1974—, chmn. dept. ob-gyn and reproductive scis., 1974-96, dir. reproductive endocrinology ctr., ctr. reproductive scis., 1977-2000. Mem. nat. adv. council, mem. human embryology and devel. and reproductive biology study sect. Nat. Inst. Child Health and Human Devel.; bd. dirs. Population Resource Center. Author: Reproductive Endocrinology: Physiology, Pathophysiology and Clinical Management, 1978, 4th edit., 1999, Prolactin, 1981, The Peripartal Period, 1985; contbr. numerous articles to profl. jours.; mem. editorial bd. Jour. Clin. Endocrinology and Metabolism, 1971-75, Fertility and Sterility, 1972-78; editor-in-chief Obstetric and Gynecologic Survey, 1991—. Josiah Macy Found. faculty fellow, 1967-70, 81; USPHS postdoctoral fellow, 1958-59, 63-64; Rockefeller Found. grantee, 1974-78; Andrew Mellon Found. grantee, 1978-81 Mem. Endocrine Soc. (coun. 1985-86, sec.-treas. 1994-99), Soc. Gynecologic Investigation (pres. 1975-76, Pres.'s Disting. Scientist award 1993, Pres.'s Mentorship award 2000), Perinatal Rsch. Soc. (pres. 1973-74), Am. Coll. Obstetricians and Gynecologists (awards), Assn. Am. Physicians, Inst. Medicine Nat. Acad. Scis., Royal Coll. Obstetricians and Gynaecologists, The Hormone Found. (pres. 1999—). Democrat. Jewish. Home: 90 Mt Tiburon Rd Belvedere Tiburon CA 94920-1512 Office: U Calif Med Sch OB Gyn & Reproductive Sci San Francisco CA 94143-0556

JAFFE, ROBERT STANLEY, lawyer; b. Walla Walla, Wash., May 16, 1946; BA, U. Wash., 1968, JD, 1972. Bar: Wash. 1972. Ptnr. Kirkpatrick & Lockhart Preston Gates Ellis LLP, 1972—86, Preston Gates & Ellis, L.L.P., Seattle, 1986—. Mem. ABA (mem. corp., banking and bus. law sect., mem. small bus. com. 1982-92), Order of Coif. Office: Preston K & L Gates 925 4th Ave Ste 2900 Seattle WA 98104-1158

JAFFE, SETH ROTH, lawyer, retail executive; b. NYC, Mar. 8, 1957; s. Harold and Ruth Jaffe; m. Merrie Fanshel, Oct. 20, 1991. AB, Brown U., 1977; JD, U. Mich., 1980. Bar: Calif. 1980, U.S. Dist. Ct. (no. dist.) Calif., U.S. Ct. Appeals (9th cir.). Assoc. McCutchen, Doyle, Brown & Enersen, San Francisco, 1980-84; chief gen. counsel Levi Strauss & Co., San Francisco, 1984—99; sr. v.p., gen. counsel CareThere, Inc., 2000—01; v.p., dep. gen. counsel Williams-Sonoma, Inc., San Francisco, 2002—03, sr. v.p., gen. counsel, sec., 2003—. Office: Williams Sonoma Inc 3250 Van Ness Ave San Francisco CA 94109 Office Phone: 415-421-7900.

JAFFER, ADRIAN MICHAEL, physician; b. Cape Town, S. Africa, Aug. 24, 1943; came to U.S., 1969; s. George Daniel Jaffer and Theresa (Kourie) Binsted; children: Brendan, Terence. MBChB, U. Cape Town Med. Sch., 1966. Diplomate Am. Coll. Physicians. Intern Loyola Univ. Hosp., Maywood, Ill., 1969-70; resident Northwestern U., Chgo., 1970-72; fellow Harvard U., Boston, 1972-73, Scapps Clinic & Rsch., LaJolla, Calif., 1973-75, Northwestern U., Chgo., 1975-76; pvt. practice LaJolla, 1976—. Assoc. clin. prof. U. Calif. San Diego, LaJolla, 1976—. Contbr. articles to profl. jours. Mem. AMA, Am. Coll. Rheumotology, Am. Acad. Allergy. Home: 9850 Genesee Ave Ste 810 La Jolla CA 92037-1219

JAGLOM, HENRY DAVID, actor, director, writer; b. London, Jan. 26, 1943; s. Simon M. and Marie (Stadthagen) J. Pres. Rainbow Film Co., Los Angeles, Jagfilms, Inc., Los Angeles, Rainbow Releasing, Los Angeles. Writer, dir. (films) A Safe Place, 1971 (selected for N.Y. Film Festival 1971), Tracks (selected for Cannes Film Festival 1976), Sitting Ducks, 1980 (selected for Cannes Film Festival), Can She Bake a Cherry Pie?, 1983 (selected for Berlin Film Festival 1983); actor, writer, dir. (films) Always (But Not Forever), 1985, Someone to Love, 1987 (selected for Cannes Film Festival), New Year's Day, 1989 (selected for Venice Film Festival 1989), Eating (selected for Deauville Film Festival 1990), Venice/Venice, 1991 (selected for AFI/L.A. Film Festival), BabyFever, 1993, Last Summer in The Hamptons, 1995 (selected for London Film Festival, AFI/L.A. Film Festival), Déjà Vu, 1998, Festival in Cannes, 2002; presenter Hearts and Minds, 1973 (Acad. award best documentary 1973); writer, dir.: Going Shopping, 2005, Hollywood Dreams, 2006. Office: Rainbow Film Co 9165 W Sunset Blvd West Hollywood CA 90069-3129 Office Phone: 310-271-0202. Business E-Mail: therainbowfilmco@aol.com.

JAGODA, BARRY LIONEL, communications executive, writer; b. Youngstown, Ohio, Feb. 5, 1944; s. Saul S. and Anne (Fradin) Jagoda; m. Karen Bernhardt, 1980. BA, U. Tex., 1966; MS, Columbia U., 1967. Writer, editor NBC News, Washington, 1967-69, NYC; prodr. CBS News, NYC, 1969-75; ptnr. Houston, Ritz, Cohen, Jagoda, NYC, 1975; TV advisor Jimmy Carter presdl. campaign, 1976; spl. asst. Pres., Washington, 1977-79, cons., 1979-80; pres. Am. Info. Exch., 1980—; dir. news and pub. affairs George Washington U., 1983-87; v.p. Stackig, Sanderson and White Advt. and Pub. Rels., 1988-93,

Shandwick Pub. Affairs, Washington, 1993-97, IMPAC Corp., 1997-2001; writer Washington Times, 2001—03; dir. comms. U. Calif., San Diego, 2003—. Recipient Emmy award as producer CBS news special, Watergate 1974. Chmn. bd. dirs. Friends of Raoul Wallenberg Found., 1989-96. Ford Found. fellow, 1967 Mem. Nat. Bus. Travel Assn., Sigma Delta Chi. Home: 9302 La Jolla Farms Rd La Jolla CA 92037-2901 Office: Univ Calif 9500 Gilman Dr San Diego CA 92093-0938 Business E-Mail: bjagoda@ucsd.edu.

JAHN, CHERI, state legislator; b. Sterling, Colo., Jan. 12, 1953; Colorado State Representative, District 24, Colorado, 2000-, Speaker Pro Tempore, currently, chairwoman, House Servs Committee, member, Finance and Judiciary Committees, currently. Colorado House Representative; citizens advisor board, Jeffco DA Off, currently; member, Strategic Planning Coun Jeffco Schs, advisor bd/accountability, currently.Owner, small business, currently. Democrat. Mailing: 200 E Colfax Room 307 Denver CO 80203 Office Phone: 303-866-5522. E-mail: cheri.jahn.house@state.co.us.

JAHN, PAUL E., lawyer; b. Manhasset, NY, 1963; AB in Rhetoric, U. Calif., Berkeley, 1986; JD, U. Calif., 1993. Bar: Calif. 1993. Extern to Hon. Robert F. Peckham U.S. Dist. Ct., No. Dist. Calif., law clk. to Hon. Claudia Wilken, 1995—96; ptnr. Morrison & Foerster LLP, San Francisco, co-chmn. tech. transaction group. Office: Morrison & Foerster LLP 425 Market St San Francisco CA 94105-2482 Office Phone: 415-268-6387. Office Fax: 415-268-7522. Business E-Mail: pjahn@mofo.com.

JAKUBOWSKY, FRANK RAYMOND, religious writer; b. Belfield, ND, Oct. 11, 1931; s. William and Catherine (O'bach) J. Student, U. N.D., 1950—52. Chemist Sherwin-Williams Paint Co., Emeryville, Calif., 1958—85; pres. Bold Books, Oakland, Calif., 1978—. Editor Spiritfest, Berkeley, Calif., 1997—. Author: Creation, 1978, Jesus Was a Leo, 1979, The Psychological Patterns of Jesus Christ, 1982, The Creative Theory of the Universe, 1983, Caldecott, 1985, Frank on a Farm, 1988, Lake Merritt, 1988, Thank God, I Am Alive, 1989, Whitman Revisted, 1989, Spiritual Symbols for the Astrology of the Soul, 1990, This New World; Birth: Sept. 8, 1958, 1990, Perceptive Types, 1993, Father Figure Frank's Stories, 1996, Inspiration Stories, 1998, Universal Mind, 1998, Big Bang Goes Puff, 1999, My Inspirational Stories, 2004, Oakland's Lake Merritt, 2004. Pfc. U.S. Army, 1952-54. Mem. Urantia Fellowship, Inst. Noetic Scis., Nat. Coun. Geocosmic Rsch. Roman Catholic. Avocation: writing songs for children on fraimba. Home: 1565 Madison St Apt 308 Oakland CA 94612-4511 Business E-Mail: boldbooks@sbcglobal.net.

JALALI, BEHNAZ, psychiatrist, educator; b. Mashad, Iran, Jan. 26, 1944; came to U.S., 1968; d. Badiolah and Bahieh (Shahidi) Samimy; m. Mehrdad Jalali, Sept. 18, 1968. MD, Tehran U., Iran, 1968. Rotating intern Burlington County Meml. Hosp., Mt. Holly, NJ, 1968—69; resident in psychiatry U. Md. Hosp., Balt., 1970—73; asst. prof. psychiatry dept. psychiatry Sch. Medicine Rutgers U., Piscataway, NJ, 1973—76, Yale U., New Haven, 1976—81, assoc. clin. prof. psychiatry, 1981—85; assoc. clin. prof. psychiatry dept. psychiatry UCLA, 1985—94, clin. prof. psychiatry dept. psychiatry Sch. Medicine, 1994—. Dir. psychotherapy Sch. Medicine Rutgers U., Piscataway, 1973-76; dir. family therapy unit dept. psychiatry Yale U., New Haven, 1976-85; chief clin. med. svcs. Mental Health Clinic, 1987-96; coord. med. student edn. in psychiatry West LA VA Hosp., 1985—2000; dir. family therapy clinic W.Va. VA Hosp., 1991—, co-dir. Schozophrenia Clinic, Mental Health Clinic, West LA VA Med. Ctr., 1996—; med. dir. Mental Health Clinic, West LA VA Med. Ctr., 2004-08; dir. recovery program West LA VA Med. Ctr., 2008-. Author: (with others) Ethnicity and Family Therapy, 1982, Clinical Guidlines in Cross-Cultural Mental Health, 1988; contbr. articles to profl. jours. Fellow Am. Psychiatric Assn., Am. Orthopsychiatry Assn., Am. Assn. Social Psychiatry; mem. Am. Family Therapy Assn., So. Calif. Psychiatric Assn. (chair com. for women 1992), World Fedn. Mental Health. Avocations: photography, hiking, cinema, painting. Home: 1203 Roberto Ln Los Angeles CA 90077-2304 Office: UCLA Dept Psychiatry West LA VA Med Ctr B116aa Los Angeles CA 90073-1003 Office Phone: 310-268-4651. Business E-Mail: behnaz.jalali@med.va.gov.

JAMES, BRUCE RICHARD, publishing executive; b. Cleve., Oct. 19, 1942; s. George R. and Dorothy B. (Watson) J.; m. Jo Ann Osborn, Feb. 5, 1966 (div. Feb. 1982); children: Michael, Jeffrey, Stephen; m. Nora Ellen Thomas, May 11, 1985. BS, Rochester Inst. Tech., NY, 1964; degree (hon.), Nev. Sys. Higher Edn., 2006. V.p. Keller-Crescent Co., Evansville, Ind., 1964-70, Cardinal Co., San Francisco, 1970-73; pres., CEO Uniplan Corp., San Francisco, 1973-83, Electrographic Corp., San Francisco, 1983-93, Nev. New-Tech, Inc., Incline Village, Nev., 1993—; chmn., CEO Barclays Law Pubs., San Francisco, 1986-94. Mem. dean's adv. coun. U. Nev. Las Vegas, Boyd Sch. Law, 1999-2002; bd. dirs. BIPAC, Washington, 1999-2002; chmn. bd. dirs. Polish-Am. Print Co., Warsaw, 1990-93; pres. Printing Industries Calif., 1989-91; pub. printer, CEO US Govt. Printing Office, 2002-07; mem. Nat. Digital Strategy Adv. Bd., 2004-07; dir. Associated Governing Bds. Univs. and Colls., 2006-2008, Davidson Acad. Nev., 2006-; commr. Northwest Commn. Colls. and Univs., 2006-; regent Nat. Libr. Medicine, 2007—; chmn. Nev. Sage Commn. Candidate US Senate, 1997-98; chmn. emeritus bd. trustees Rochester Inst. Tech., 1993—, Sierra Nev. Coll., Incline Village, 1997-2005; mem. Bd. Equalization, Reno, 1995-97; trustee U. Nev. Desert Rsch. Inst., 1999-2002; dir. Nev. Test Site Devel. Corp., 1999-2002, Western Folklife Ctr., Elko, Nev., 1999-2002; bd. dirs. Cmty. Found. Western Nev., 1999-2002; fin. chmn. Nev. Rep. Party, 2000-02. Commencement spkr. Rochester Inst. Tech., 1998, named Alumnus of Yr., 1997; recipient Silver Beaver award Boys Scouts Am., 1992; Civilian Exec. of Yr. US Govt., 2006. Mem.: Confrerie De La Chaine Des Rotisseurs, Internat. Wine and Food Soc., No. Nev. Network, Cosmos Club (Washington), Genesse Valley Club (Rochester NY). Republican. Episcopalian. Office Phone: 775-831-9499.

JAMES, CHARLES ALBERT, lawyer, oil industry executive; b. Newark, May 2, 1954; s. Charles Albert and Mary Letitia (Baskerville) J.; 1 child, Kathryn E. BA, Wesleyan U., Middletown, Conn., 1976; JD, George Washington U., Washington, 1979. Bar: D.C. 1979. Atty. FTC, Washington, 1979—85; assoc./ptnr. Jones, Day, Reavis & Pogue, Washington, 1986—91; dep. asst. atty. gen. US Dept. Justice, Washington, 1991, acting asst. atty. gen., 1991—93, asst. atty. gen. Antitrust Divsn., 2001—02; ptnr. Jones, Day, Reavis & Pogue, Washington, 1993—2001; v.p., gen. counsel Chevron Corp., San Ramon, Calif., 2002—09, exec. v.p., gen. counsel, 2009—. Recipient Chmn.'s award FTC, 1985, Edmund Randolph award Dept. Justice, 1992. Mem. ABA (sect. of bus. law chmn. com. 1999), Fed. Bar Assn. (chmn. antitrust com. 1990), U.S. C. of C. (mem. antitrust coun. 1993—), Psi Upsilon. Republican. Office: Office Gen Coun Chevron Corp 6001 Bollinger Canyon Rd San Ramon CA 94583 Home Phone: 925-743-4011; Office Phone: 925-842-3232. Personal E-mail: cjae@chevron.com.*

JAMES, CHARLES E., JR., lawyer; b. Pontiac, Mich., Sept. 19, 1948; BA, Occidental Coll., 1970; JD with high distinction, U. Ariz. Bar: Ariz. 1973. Ptnr. Gust Rosenfeld, Phoenix, 1979—86, Chapman and Cutler, Phoenix, 1986—92, Snell & Wilmer, Phoenix, 1992—99, Squire, Sanders and Dempsey LLP, Phoenix, 2000—. Mem. ABA, Nat. Assn. Bond Lawyers. Office: Squire Sanders & Dempsey LLP 40 N Central Ave Ste 2700 Phoenix AZ 85004-4498 Office Phone: 602-528-4000. E-mail: cjames@ssd.com.

JAMES, ETTA (JAMESETTA HAWKINS), recording artist; b. LA, Jan. 25, 1938; d. Dorothy Leatherwood Hawkins; m. Artis Dee Mills, May 20, 1969; children: Donto, Sametto. Blues singer Johnny Otis, LA, 1954, Bihari Bros. Record Co., LA, 1954, Leonard Chess Record Co., LA, 1960, Warner Bros., LA, 1978, Fantasy Record, LA, 1985, Island Record, LA, 1988. Record Albums include Respect Yourself, 1997, Love's Been Rough on Me, 1997, Come A Little Closer. The Essential Etta, 1993, Etta James Rocks the House, Etta, Red Hot'n Live, Her Greatest Sides, Vol. 1, Live, 1994, Mystery Lady: Songs of Billie Holliday, 1994 (Grammy award 1994), R&B Dynamite, 1987, reissue, 1991, The Right Time, 1992, Rocks the House, 1992, The Second Time Around, 1989, Seven Year Itch, 1988, Sticking to My Guns, 1990, The Sweetest Peaches, 1989, The Sweetest Peaches: Part One, 1989, The Sweetest Peaches: Part Two, 1989, Tell Mama, 1988, These Foolish Things: The Classic Balladry of Etta James, 1995, Time After Time, (with Eddie Cleanhead Vinson) Blues in the Night, Lane Supper Club, 1986, Blues in the Night, Vol. 2, 1987, Twelve Songs of X-mas, 1988, Life, Love & the Blues, 1988, Heart of a Woman, 1999, 20th Century Master: The Best of Etta James, 1999, Platinum Series, 2000, The Chess Box, 2000, Matriarch of the Blues, 2000, Etta James, 2001, Love Songs, 2001, Blue Gardenia, 2001, Blowin' in the Wind, 2002, Live and Ready, 2002, Burnin' Down the House, 2002, Let's Roll, 2003, Rock Me Baby, 2004, Live in New York, 2005. Recipient Lifetime Achievement award Rigby & Blues Assn., 1989, Living Legends award KJLH, 1989, Image award NAACP, 1990 W.C. Handy award, 1989, Blue Soc. Hall of Fame award, 1991; 5th Handy Blues award, 1993, 94, Soul of Am. Music award, 1992; 8 Grammy nominations, Beyond War award, Best Song, 1984; inducted into Rock & Roll Hall of Fame, 1993; sang opening ceremony of 1984 Olympics. Office: Etta James Enterprises 16409 Sally Ln Riverside CA 92504-5629

JAMES, GEORGE BARKER, II, financial executive; b. Haverhill, Mass., May 25, 1937; s. Paul Withington and Ruth (Burns) J.; m. Beverly A. Burch, Sept. 22, 1962; children: Alexander, Christopher, Geoffrey, Matthew. AB, Harvard U., 1959; MBA, Stanford U., 1962. Fiscal dir. E.G. & G. Inc., Bedford, Mass., 1963-67; fin. exec. Am. Brands Inc., NYC, 1967-69; v.p. Pepsico, Inc., NYC, 1969-72; sr. v.p., chief fin. officer Arcata Corp., Menlo Park, Calif., 1972-82; exec. v.p. Crown Zellerbach Corp., San Francisco, 1982-85; sr. v.p., chief fin. officer Levi Strauss & Co., San Francisco, 1985-98; sr. ptnr. Pacific States Investors Group LLC, 2002—. Bd. dirs. Pacific States Industries, Inc., Callious Software Inc. Author: Industrial Development in the Ohio Valley, 1962. Mem. Andover Town Com., Mass., 1965-67; mem. Select Congl. Com. on World Hunger; mem. adv. coun. Calif. State Employees Pension Fund; chmn. bd. dirs. Towle Trust Fund; trustee Nat. Corp. Fund for the Dance, chmn. Cate Sch., Levi Strauss Found., Stern Grove Festival Assn., Zellerbach Family Fund, San Francisco Ballet Assn., Com. for Econ. Devel.; bd. dirs. Stanford U. Hosp., Calif. Pacific Med. Ctr.; dir. KQED Pub. Broadcasting; chmn. World Affairs Coun.; mem. San Francisco Com. on Fgn. Rels.; overseer Hoover Instn., Standford U.; trustee Grace Cathedral, San Francisco. With US Army, 1960-61. Mem. Pacific Union Club, Bohemian Club, Menlo Circus Club, Harvard Club, N.Y. Athletic Club. Home: 207 Walnut St San Francisco CA 94118-2012

JAMES, HELEN ANN, plastic surgeon; b. Palmerston North, New Zealand, May 5, 1940; came to U.S., 1977; d. George Headley and Betty Beatrice (McDonald) J.; married (dec. Apr. 1993). MB, ChB, U. Otago, Dunedin, New Zealand, 1964; Fellow, Royal Coll. Surgeons, London, England, 1972. Diplomate Am. Bd. Plastic Surgery. Internship Palmerston North Hosp., New Zealand, 1965-66; residency plastic surgery Brdg Earn Hosp., Perthshire, England, 1973-74, St. Lukes Hosp., Bradford, England, 1975-77; fellow plastic surgery Mount Sinai Med. Ctr., Miami Beach, 1977-79; residency plastic surgery N.C. Meml. Med. Ctr., Chapel Hill, 1979-81; St. Joseph Hosp., Bellingham, Wash.; pvt. practice Bellingham, Wash. Mem. AMA, Am. Soc. Plastic and Reconstructive Surgeons, Am. Soc. Aesthetic Plastic Surgeons, Wash. State Med. Assn. Avocations: tennis, birdwatching, bicycling. Office: 3001 Squalicum Pkwy Ste 5 Bellingham WA 98225-1950

JAMES, JEANNETTE ADELINE, state legislator, accountant, small business owner; b. Maquoketa, Iowa, Nov. 19, 1929; d. Forest Claude and Winona Adeline (Meyers) Nims; m. James Arthur James, Feb. 16, 1948; children: James Arthur Jr., Jeannette, Alice Marie. Student, Merritt Davis Sch. Commerce, Salem, Oreg., 1956-57, U. Alaska, 1976—77. Payroll supr. Gen. Foods Corp., Woodburn, Oreg., 1956-66; cost acctg., inventory control clk. Pacific Fence & Wire Co., Portland, Oreg., 1966-67, office mgr., 1968-69; substitute rural carrier U.S. Post Office, Woodburn, 1967-68; owner, mgr., acct. and tax preparer James Bus. Svc., Goldendale, Wash., 1969-75, Anchorage, 1975-77, Fairbanks, Alaska, 1977—83, North Pole, Alaska, 1983—; co-owner, mgr. Jolly Acres Motel, North Pole, 1987—; mem. Alaska Ho. of Reps., Juneau, 1993—2003; chmn. House State Affairs, 1995-2000, jud. com., 1998—2002; vice chmn. Legis. Coun., 1995-96; chmn. joint com. Adminstrv. Regulation Rev., 1997-98, ho. majority leader, 2001—02. Instr. workshop Comm. Dynamics, 1988; railroad advisor to Gov. Murkowski, 2003-. Vice chmn. Klickitat County Dems., Goldendale, 1970-74; bd. dirs. Mus. and Art Inst., Anchorage, 1976-80; pres. Anchorage Internat. Art Inst., 1976-78; chmn. platting bd. Fairbanks North Star Borough, 1980-84, mem. Planning Commn., 1984-87; treas., vice chmn. 18th Dist. Reps., North Pole, Alaska, 1984-92; mem. City of North Pole Econ. Devel. Com., 1992-93; mem. Rep. State Ctrl. Com., 2004—. Recipient Defender of Freedom award, NRA, 1994, Friend of Municipalities award, Alaska Mcpl. League, 1996, Courage in Preserving Equal Access award, Alaska chpt. Safari Club Internat., 2000, Cmty. Svc. award, Arctic Alliance for People, 2001; named Legislator of Yr., Alaska Farm Bur., 1994, Alaska Outdoor Coun., 2000, Juneau Empire, 2002, Guardian of Small Bus., Nat. Fedn. Ind. Bus., 1998, Friend of Psycology, 2001. Mem. Internat. Tng. in Comm. (Alaska State winner speech contest 1981, 86), North Pole C. of C., Emblem Club, Rotary (treas. North Pole 1990, v.p. membership 2004-05, pres. 2006—), Eagles, Women of Moose Presbyterian. Avocations: bowling, dolls, children. Home: 3068 Badger Rd North Pole AK 99705-6117 Home Phone: 907-488-9093; Office Phone: 907-488-9339. Personal E-mail: jamesjeannette@gci.net, usually@acsalaska.net.

JAMES, MARK A., lawyer, former state legislator; b. Eugene, Oreg., Oct. 9, 1959; m. Lori M. James; children: Anne A., John S. BS, Lewis and Clark Coll., 1982; JD, U. Ariz., 1985. Bar: U.S. Dist. Ct. Nev., U.S. Dist. Ct. (so. dist.) Tex., U.S. Ct. Appeals (9th and 5th cirs.). Senate judiciary intern Senator Paul Laxalt, Nev., 1981; former mem. Nev. Senate, Dist. 8, Carson City; former Las Vegas County commr.; founder James, Driggs, & Walch; pvt. practice, 2000; of counsel Bullivant Houser Bailey PC. Apptd. Nat. Conf. Commissioners Uniform State Law, Nat. Conf. State Legislators law and justice sect., criminal justice sect., Coun. State Govts. West Trade and Transp. Com., We. Water Policy Com. Articles editor Ariz. Law Rev. Active Clark County Pub. Edn. Found., Boys and Girls Clubs; mem. statewide adv. coun. Water Resources Rsch. of the Desert; bd. dirs. Aquavision, chair water law forum, 1992; bd. dirs. Las Vegas Valley Water Dist., So. Nev. Water Authority, So. Nev. Regional Planning Coalition, Met. Police Dept. Fiscal Affairs Com., Nat. Multiple Sclerosis Soc., Clark County Pub. Edn. Found., statewide adv. coun. water resources rsch. Desert Rsch. Inst., Nev. Earthquake Safety Coun., Family and Child Treatment SW Nev. Named one of Top 40 Lawyers Under 40, Las Vegas Bus. Press, 1994. Mem. ABA, State Bar Nev., State Bar Tex., Nev. Water Resources Assn. Republican. also: Nev State Legis Bldg 401 S Carson St Rm 240 Carson City NV 89701-4747 Office: Bullivant Houser Bailey PC 3980 Howard Hughes Pwy Ste 550 Las Vegas NV 89109 Office Phone: 702-650-6565 708. Office Fax: 702-650-2995. E-mail: mark.james@bullivant.com.

JAMES, PHYLLIS A., lawyer; b. L.I., NY, Mar. 23, 1952; BA magna cum laude in Am. hist. and lit., Harvard U., 1974, JD, 1977. Bar: Calif. 1978, Mich., Fed. Dist. Ct. Calif., US Ct. Appeals (9th cir.). Jud. law clerk Hon. Theodore R. Newman Jr. DC Ct. Appeals, 1977—78; mem. Pillsbury Madison & Sutro, San Francisco, 1979—94; corp. counsel City of Detroit Law Dept., 1994—2001; sr. v.p. and sr. counsel MGM Mirage, Las Vegas, Nev., 2001—. Pursuant State Mich. Trial Ct. Assessment Commn., 1997—98. Recipient Capt. Jonathan Fay prize. Mem.: Mich. Bar Assn., Calif. Bar Assn., Phi Bet Kappa. Office: MGM Mirage 3600 Las Vegas Blvd S Las Vegas NV 89109 Office Phone: 702-693-7590. Office Fax: 702-693-7591. Business E-Mail: phyllis_james@mgmmirage.com.

JAMES, THOMAS LARRY, chemistry professor; b. North Platte, Nebr., Sept. 8, 1944; s. James Jennings and Guinevere (Richards) J.; m. Olga Schmidlin; children: Marc, Tristan. BS, U. N.M., 1965; PhD, U. Wis., 1969. Research chemist Celanese Chem. Co., Corpus Christi, Tex., 1969-71; NIH post-doctorate fellow U. Pa., Phila., 1971-73; prof. chem., pharmaceutical chemistry and radiology U. Calif., San Francisco, 1973—, chair dept. pharm. chemistry, 1995—, dir. Magnetic Resonance Lab., 1975. Author: NMR in Biochemistry, 1975; editor: Biomedical NMR, 1984, Methods in Enzymology, 1989, 5th edit., 2005; mem. edit. bd. Jour. Magnetic Resonance, Jour. Biomolecular NMR, Magnetic Resonance Imaging; editor FEBS Letters; contbr. articles to profl. jours. Mem. Internat. Soc. Magnetic Resonance, Am. Biophys. Soc., Am. Chem. Soc., Am. Biochem. Soc., Soc. Magnetic Resonance in Medicine, Phi Beta Kappa, Phi Kappa Phi, Kappa Mu Epsilon. Mem. Cmty. Of Christ. Avocations: skiing, kayaking, travel, photography. Office: UCSF MC2280 600 16th St San Francisco CA 94158-2517 Business E-Mail: james@picasso.ucsf.edu.

JAMESON, ANTONY, aerospace engineering educator; b. Gillingham, Kent, Eng., 1934; BA, Cambridge U., Eng., MA in Engring. with honors, 1958, PhD, 1963; docteur honoris causa (hon.), U. Pierre et Marie Curie, Paris VI, 2001, Uppsala U., 2002. Rsch. fellow Trinity Hall, Cambridge, England, 1960—63; economist Trades Union Congress, London, 1964-65; chief mathematician missile divsn. Hawker Siddeley Dynamics, Coventry, England, 1965-66; staff engr. Grumman Aerospace Corp., Bethpage, NY, 1966-72; sr. rsch. scientist Courant Inst. Math. Scis., NYU, NYC, 1972-74, prof. computer sci., 1974-80; prof. mech. & aerospace engring. Princeton U., NJ, 1980-82, James S. McDonnell Disting. U. prof. aerospace engring., 1982-96, prof. emeritus NJ, 1996—, dir. program in applied and computational math. NJ, 1986-88; Thomas V. Jones prof. engring. Stanford U., Calif., 1997—. Contbr. articles to profl. jours., chpts. to books. Served to 2nd Lt. British Army, 1953—55. Open scholar Trinity Hall, Cambridge, 1955, Hon. fellow, 1990; Alfred P. Sloan Fgn. Post-Doctoral fellow MIT, 1962; named Hon. Prof., Northwestern Polytech. U., Xian, China, 1986, W.R. Sears Disting. lectr. Cornell U., 1992; recipient NASA medal Exceptional Sci. Achievement, 1980, Spirit of St. Louis medal ASME, 1995, Theodorsen Lectureship award, ICASE NASA Langley, 1996, Fluid Dynamics award, US-ACM, 2005. Fellow AIAA (Fluid Dynamics award 1993, Elmer A. Sperry award 2006), Royal Soc. London, Royal Aeronautical Soc. (Gold medal 1988), Royal Acad. Engring.; Nat. Acad. Engring. (fng. assoc. 1997). Achievements include development of flo codes used in aerospace industry. Office: Dept Aeronautics & Astronautics Stanford Univ Durand Bldg Room 381 Stanford CA 94305-1928 Office Phone: 650-725-6208. Office Fax: 650-725-1685. E-mail: jameson@baboon.stanford.edu.

JAMIESON, JAMES BRADSHAW, foundation administrator; b. LA, June 10, 1931; s. Charles Cameron and Ruth (Bradshaw) J.; m. Perry McNaughton, Dec. 27, 1959; children: Jeffrey McNaughton, Dalton Charles. AA, Citrus Coll., 1950; BA, Claremont Men's Coll., 1955; MA, Claremont Grad. Sch., 1958; PhD, Brown U., 1966. Assoc. prof. polit. studies Pitzer Coll., Claremont Grad. Sch., 1968-75; rsch. polit. scientist UCLA, 1972-73; v.p. devel. Pitzer Coll., 1968-72, v.p., 1973-78, prof. polit. studies, 1975-83, exec. v.p., 1979-83, acting pres., 1978-79; prof. govt. Claremont Grad. Sch., 1975-87; v.p. rsch. Claremont McKenna Coll., 1983-87; exec. dir. Found. Performing Art Ctr., San Luis Obispo, Calif., 1987-96; pres. SLO Capers, San Luis Obispo, Calif., 1997—. Commr. Calif. Postsecondary Edn. Commn., Sacramento, 1987-92; dir. Global Village, Seattle, 1989-95; resident cons. Centennial Celebration Calif. Politech. State U., Obispo, Calif., 2000-02. Contbr. articles to profl. jours. Staff, sec. Ctrl. Coast Performing Arts Ctr. Commn., San Luis Obispo, 1993-95. Sgt. USAF, 1950-52. Fellow Brown U., 1960, 63, tchg. fellow, 1962, fellow Resources for the Future, 1964; rsch. grantee U.S. Dept. Interior, 1972-73; recipient Cal. Poly U. Pres. Arts award, 1999; Lifetime Achievement award Citrus Coll., 2005. Mem. Santa Lucia Flyfishers (bd. dirs. 1988-2001), Trout Unltd. (bd. dirs. Calif. coun. 1989-94, bd. dirs. nat. bd. 1986-90), Marine's Meml. Club. Avocations: fly fishing, tennis, auto restoration. Office: SLO Capers PO Box 12843 San Luis Obispo CA 93406-2843

JAMIESON, STUART WILLIAM, surgeon, educator; b. Bulawayo, Rhodesia, July 30, 1947; came to U.S., 1977; MB, BS, U. London, 1971. Intern St. Mary's Hosp., London, 1971; resident St. Mary's Hosp., Northwick Park Hosp., Brompton Hosp., London, 1972-77; asst. prof. Stanford U., Calif., 1980-83, assoc. prof. Calif., 1983-86; prof., head cardiac surgery U. Minn., Mpls., 1986-89, U. Calif., San Diego, 1989—. Dir. Minn. Heart and Lung Inst., Mpls., 1986-89; pres. Calif. Heart and Lung Inst., San Diego, 1991-95. Co-author: Heart and Heart-Lung Transplantation, 1989; editor: Heart Surgery, 1987; contbr. over 600 papers to med. jours. Recipient Brit. Heart Found. Fellowship award, 1978, Irvine H. Page award Am. Heart Found., 1979, Silver medal Danish Surg. Soc., 1986. Fellow ACS, Royal Coll. Surgeons, Royal Soc. Medicine, Am. Coll. Chest Physicians, Am. Coll. Cardiology; mem. Royal Coll. Physicians (licentiate), Internat. Soc. for Heart Transplantation (pres. 1986-88), Calif. Heart and Lung Inst. (pres. 1991—), Internat. Soc. Cardiothoracic Surgery (pres. 2003-.). Office: U Calif Divsn Cardiothoracic Surgery 200 W Arbor Dr San Diego CA 92103-8892 Office Phone: 619-543-7777. E-mail: sjamieson@ucsd.edu.

JAMIN, MATTHEW DANIEL, lawyer, judge; b. New Brunswick, NJ, Nov. 29, 1947; s. Matthew Bernard and Frances Marie (Newburg) J.; m. Christine Frances Bjorkman, June 28, 1969; children: Rebecca, Erica. BA, Colgate U., 1969; JD, Harvard U., 1974. Bar: Alaska 1974, U.S. Dist. Ct. Alaska 1974, U.S. Ct. Appeals (9th cir.) 1980. Staff atty. Alaska Legal Svcs., Anchorage, 1974-75, supervising atty. Kodiak, Alaska, 1975-81; contract atty. Pub. Defender's Office State of Alaska, Kodiak, 1976-82; prin. Matthew D. Jamin, Atty., Kodiak, 1982; ptnr. Jamin & Bolger, Kodiak, 1982-85, Jamin, Ebell, Bolger & Gentry, Kodiak, 1985-97; part-time magistrate judge U.S. Cts., Kodiak, 1984—; shareholder Jamin, Ebell, Schmitt & Mason, Kodiak, 1998—2005, Jamin Schmitt St. John, St. John, 2006—. Part-time instr. U. Alaska Kodiak Coll., 1975—; active Theshold Svcs., Inc., Kodiak, 1985—, pres., 1985-92, 95-96, 99-2000. Mem. Alaska Bar Assn. (Professionalism award 1988), Kodiak Bar Assn. Office: US Dist Ct 323 Carolyn Ave Kodiak AK 99615-6348 Office Phone: 907-486-6024. Business E-Mail: matt@jesmkod.com.

JAMISON, DANIEL OLIVER, lawyer; b. Fresno, Calif., Nov. 28, 1952; s. Oliver Morton and Margaret (Ratcliffe) J.; m. Debra Suzanne Parent, May 23, 1981; 1 child, Holly Elizabeth. Student, Claremont Men's Coll., 1970—72; BA in Philosophy, U. Calif., Berkeley, 1974; JD, U. Calif., Davis, 1977. Bar: Calif. 1977, U.S. Dist. Ct. (ea. dist.) Calif. 1977, U.S. Dist. Ct. (no. dist.) Calif. 1982, U.S. Ct. Appeals (9th cir.) 1987. Law clk. to judge M.D. Crocker U.S. Dist. Ct. (ea. dist.) Calif., Fresno, 1977—78; assoc. Stammer, McKnight, Barnum & Bailey, Fresno, 1978—83, ptnr., 1983—95; shareholder Sagaser, Franson, Jamison & Jones (formerly Sagaser, Hansen, Franson & Jamison), 1995—99; pvt. practice Law Offices of Daniel O. Jamison, P.C., Fresno, 1999—2005; preferred shareholder Dowling, Aaron & Keeler, Inc., 2005—, co-chair, Litig. Dept., 2008—09. Vol. atty. Calif. H.S., Fresno, 1983-87, 89-94; mem. Assocs. of Valley Children's Hosp., Fresno, 1980-81; co-chmn. Fresno County Law Day, 1995-96; panelist for CEB Selected Issues in Employment Discrimination and Wrongful Discharge Litigation; panelist on indigent care Calif. Soc. for Healthcare Attys.; panelist Lorman Edn. Svcs. on Health Care Corp. and Physician Compliance Programs in Calif., Bulldog Found., Calif. State U., Fresno; mem. San Joaquin River Pky Conservation Trust. Mem. ABA, Am. Arbitration Assn. (panel of neutrals, panel mem. comml. arbitration), Fresno County Superior Ct. Panel Neutral Evaluators, Fed. Bar Assn., Fresno County Bar Assn. (spkr.), East Dist. Hist. Soc. (charter mem.), 9th Jud. Cir. Hist. Soc., Calif. Soc. for Healthcare Attys., Am. Health Lawyers Assn. (panelist Alt. Dispute Resolution credentialing and peer rev., teleconf. ADR in credentialing and peer review). Republican. Avocations: golf, aerobics. Office Phone: 559-432-4500. Business E-Mail: djamison@daklaw.com.

JAMISON, DEAN TECUMSEH, economist; b. Springfield, Mo., Oct. 10, 1943; s. Marshall Verdine and Mary Dell (Temple) J.; m. Joanne Leslie, Sept. 14, 1971 (div. 1995); children: Julian C., Eliot A., Leslie S.; m. Kin Bing Wu, Jan. 19, 1997. AB in Philosophy, Stanford U., 1966, MS in Engring. Sci., 1967; PhD in Econs., Harvard U., 1970. Asst. prof. grad. sch. bus. Stanford U., Palo Alto, Calif., 1970-73; economist World Bank, Washington, 1976-88, dir., 1992-93, advisor, 1993-98; dir. Ctr. for Pacific Rim Studies UCLA, 1993-2000, prof. Sch. Pub. Health, Grad. Sch. Edn. and Info. Studies, 1988—2006; dir. econs. adv. svc. WHO, Geneva, 1998-2000; fellow Fogarty Internat. Ctr., NIH, 2002—06; prof. U. Calif, San Francisco, 2006—. Chmn. ad hoc com. on health R&D for developing countries WHO, Geneva, 1996-97; trustee Drug Strategies, 1994—; chmn. bd. on global health Inst. Medicine NAS, 2000-05; vis. prof. Harvard U., 2006—; chmn. expert group econs., fin., and impact Malaria control programs WHO, 2006—. Author: Farmer Education and Farm Efficiency, 1982, (with L. J. Lau) Disease Control Priorities in Developing Countries, 2006, World Bank World Development Report 1993: Investing in Health, 1993, WHO World Health Report 1999: Making a Difference, 1999; cons. editor AERA Ency. Rsch., 6th edit., 1992. Fellow Woodrow Wilson Found., 1967, NSF, 1968, Bill and Melinda Gates Found. fellow, 2001. Mem. Inst. Medicine Nat. Acad. Scis. Avocation: tennis. Office: UCSF Global Health Sci 50 Beale St 12th Fl San Francisco CA 94105 Business E-Mail: djamison@globalhealth.ucsf.edu.

JAMISON, HARRISON CLYDE, retired oil company executive; b. St. Louis, Jan. 15, 1925; s. William Clyde and Katherine Maurice (Fitzgerald) J.; m. Beverly Joy Johnson, June 26, 1946; children: Susan, David, Leslie, Daniel, Dale, Nancy, Sara BA cum laude, UCLA. Geologist Richfield Oil Corp., Bakersfield, Calif., 1950-52, Olympia, Wash., 1952-55, LA, 1955-60, regional exploration supr., 1961-65; Alaska dist. mgr. Atlantic Richfield Co., Anchorage, 1966-69, Alaska coord. Dallas, 1969-70; mgr. govt. rels. Alyeska Pipeline Svc. Co., 1971-72; chief geologist ARCO Oil & Gas Co., Dallas, 1973-80, v.p. dist. mgr. Denver, 1981; pres. ARCO Exploration Co., Dallas, 1981-85; sr. v.p. Atlantic Richfield Co., LA, 1981-85. Contbr. articles to profl. jours. Former bd. dirs. Tex. Rsch. League, Austin, Dallas Citizens Coun., Mex. Am. Legal Def. and Edn. Fund, Resolution Seismic Svcs. Inc., Wilmington, Del., ARCO Alaska Inc., Thomas Wilson Dibblee Jr. Geol. Found., Hospice of Bend. Fellow Geol. Soc. Am. (former chmn. bd. dirs., trustees GSA Found. 1986-88); mem. Am. Assn. Petroleum Geologists. Home and Office: 37615 S Stoney Cliff Ct Tucson AZ 85739-1412

JAMPOLIS, MELINA BETH, internist, physician nutrition specialist; b. Chgo., Ill., Apr. 8, 1970; BA, Tufts Univ.; MD, Tufts Sch. Med., 1996. Intern, internal medicine Santa Clara Valley Med. Ctr., San Jose, Calif., 1996—97, resident, 1997—99; private practice internist San Francisco, Burlingame; founder, pres. Amarna Medical Ctr., San Francisco. Lectr. throughout the country on nutrition for weight loss and optimal health; lauched own line protein bars, 2007. Host (10 episode diet program, Discovery Network, FIT TV) Fit TV Diet Doctor, 2005; author: The No-Time-to-Lose-Diet, 2007, Busy Person's Guide to Permanent Weight Loss, 2008; mem. adv. bd., regular contbr. vivmag.com, interviewed by USA Weekend, First for Women, Women's World, Alternative Medicine Mag., Women's Health, San Francisco Mag., Quick and Simple Mag., and more on nutrition and weight loss related topics, guest appearances Regis and Kelly, View from the Bay, NBC-11, & KRON-4. Mem.: Am. Coll. Physicians, Am. Coll. Sports Med., No. Am. Assn. Study Obesity. Achievements include being one of only 200 physician nutrition specialist in the country. Address: 3580 California St Ste 201 San Francisco CA 94118-1717 Office Phone: 415-885-6474. E-mail: info@amarnamedical.com.

JANAIRO, ALTHEA RAE DUHINIO See CARRERE, TIA

JANDA, KIM D., chemist, educator; b. Cleve., Aug. 23, 1958; married; children: Nikole, Christopher. BS, U. Southern Fla., 1980; MS, U. Ariz., 1983, PhD, 1984. Adj. asst. mem. dept. molecular biology Rsch. Inst. Scripps Clinic, La Jolla, Calif., 1987-88, asst. prof. dept. molecular biology, 1989-90, assoc. prof. dept. molecular biology and chem., 1991-92, assoc. prof., 1993—. Cons. Procter and Gamble, Unilever Rsch., Inc.; sci. adv. bd. mem. Catalytic Antibodies, Inc., Found. CombiChem.; lectr. in field. Contbr. numerous articles to profl. jours. Named Scholar Athlete of Yr. U. South Fla., 1979-80; recipient Alfred P. Sloan fellowship, 1993-95, NIH First award, 1990-95, Carl S. Marvel fellowship U. Ariz., 1984; numerous other grants. Fellow Am. Inst. Chemists; mem. Am. Chem. Soc. (Arhtur C. Cope Scholar Award, 1999), Themis Honor Soc., Sigma Phi Epsilon. Office: The Scripps Rsch Inst 10550 N Torrey Pines Rd La Jolla CA 92037-1000

JANES, RAENA, private school educator; b. 1973; m. Craig Janes; children: Chloe, Cole. Founder, superintendent La Paloma Acad., 2002—. Founder Grace Chapel Early Edn. Ctr. Recipient Excellence in Special Edn. Cmty. award, Ariz. Dept. Edn.; named one of 40 Under 40, Tucson Bus. Edge, 2006. Mem.: Nat. Assn. Edn. Young Children, Jr. League of Tucson. Office: La Paloma Academy Midtown 2151 N Palo Verde Blvd Tucson AZ 85716-2920 Office Phone: 520-733-7373.

JANES, ROBERT ROY, museum director, archaeologist, editor, consultant; b. Rochester, Minn., Apr. 23, 1948; m. Priscilla Bickel; children: Erica Helen, Peter Bickel. Student, Lawrence U., 1966—68, BA in Anthropology cum laude, 1970; student, U. of the Ams., Mexico City, 1968, U. Calif., Berkeley, 1968—69; PhD in Archaeology, U. Calgary, Alta., Can., 1976. Postdoctoral fellow Arctic Inst. N.Am., U. Calgary, 1981-82; founding dir. Prince of Wales No. Heritage Centre, Yellowknife, N.W.T., 1976-86, project dir. Dealy Island Archaeol. and Conservation Project, 1977-82; founding exec. dir. Sci. Inst. of N.W.T.; sci. advisor Govt. of N.W.T., Yellowknife, 1986-89; exec. dir., pres., CEO Glenbow Mus. Art Gallery Libr. and Archives, Calgary, 1989-2000; fellow Glenbow-Alta. Inst., 2000—. Mus./heritage cons., 2000—; adj. prof. archaeology U. Calgary, 1990—. Author: Preserving Diversity-Ethnoarchaeological Perspectives on Culture Change in the Western Canadian Subarctic, 1991, Museums and the Paradox of Change, 1995, 2d edit., 1997, Looking Reality in the Eye: Museums and Social Responsibility, 2005, (with Gerald Conaty) Museum Management and Marketing, 2007; (with Richard Sandell) The Arctic Institute of North America Technical Paper No. 28, 1983; editor-in-chief Jour. Mus. Mgmt. and Curatorship, 2003—; contbr. articles to profl. jours. Mem. First Nations/CMA Task Force on Mus. and First Peoples, 1989-92, Banff, Kootenay and Yoho Nat. Pks. Devel. Adv. Bd.; nat. adv. bd. Ctr. for Cultural Mgmt., U. Waterloo; chair bd. dirs. Friends of Banff Nat. Park, 2003-05; vice-chair, chair bd. dirs. Biosphere Inst. of Bow Valley, 2003—. Recipient Nat. Parks Centennial award Environ. Can., 1985, Can. Studies Writing award Assn. Can. Studies, 1989, Disting. Alumni award Alumni Assn. of U. Calgary, 1989, L.R. Briggs Disting. Achievement award Lawrence U., 1991, Queen Elizabeth II Golden Jubilee Commemorative medal 2003; Can. Coun. doctoral fellow, 1973-76; rsch. grantee Govt. of Can., 1974, Social Scis. and Humanities Rsch. Coun. Can., 1988-89. Fellow Arctic Inst. N.Am. (bd. dirs. 1983-90, vice chmn. bd. 1985-89, hon. rsch. assoc. 1983-84, chmn. priorities and planning com. 1983-84, exec. com. 1984-86, assoc. editor Arctic jour. 1987-97), Can. Mus. Assn. (hon. life, cert. accreditation 1982, Outstanding award in Mus. Mgmt., Outstanding Achievement award for publ. 1996), Am. Anthrop. Assn. (fgn.); mem. Can. Archaeol. Assn. (v.p. 1980-82, pres. 1984-86, co-chmn. fed. heritage policy com. 1986-88), Can. Art Mus. Dirs. Orgn. (mem.-at-large bd. dirs. 1992-95), Alta. Mus. Assn. (moderator seminars 1990, Merit award 1992, Merit award for Museums and the Paradox of Change 1996), Assn. Cultural Execs. (bd. dirs. 1999-2002, ACE award for Can. Cultural Mgmt. 1998), Sigma Xi. Home: 104 Prendergast Pl Canmore AB Canada T1W 2N5

JANIS, CONRAD, actor, musician, art dealer; b. NYC, Feb. 11, 1923; s. Sidney and Harriet J.; children: Christopher, Carin; m. Maria Grimm, Nov. 30, 1987. Appeared in numerous Broadway plays including Junior Miss, 1942, Dark of the Moon, 1945, The Next Half Hour, 1945, The Brass Ring, 1951 (World Theater award), Time Out for Ginger, 1952, Visit to a Small Planet, 1957, Sunday in New York, 1961, Marathon '33, 1963, The Front Page, 1969, Same Time Next Year, 1975-76; films include Snafu, 1945, Margie, 1946, That Hagen Girl, 1947, Let's Rock, 1958, Airport '75, The Duchess and the Dirtwater Fox, 1976, The Buddy Holly Story, 1977, Roseland, 1977, Oh, God! Book II, 1979, Nothing in Common, 1987, Sonny Boy, 1987, Mr. Saturday Night, 1992, The Gods Must Be Crazy III, 1992; star, dir. The Feminine Touch, 1995, The Cable Guy, 1995, Addams Family Reunion, 1998; actor, dir. The November Conspiracy, 1996, actor, dir., prodr., editor Bad Blood, 2006; appeared in over 350 major network TV shows including Suspense, 1950, Philco Play House, 1951, Studio One, 1952, Armstrong Circle Theater, 1953, Highway to Heaven, 1986, Golden Girls, 1987, 89, Murder, She Wrote, 1988, 91, Baywatch, 1996, The New Rockford Files, 1997, Frasier, 1997, 2000, 02,03-05,(recurring role), Diagnosis Murder, 1998, (recurring role) Family Law, 1999-2000; numerous TV movies including Miracle on 34th Street, 1973, The Virginia Hill Story, 1974, The Magnificent Magnet of Santa Mesa, 1977, The Gossip Columnist, 1984, The Red Light Sting, 1984, Asimov's Probe, 1987, Caddie Woodlawn, 1988, Time After Time, 2002; TV series include I Bonino, Quark, Mork and Mindy, 1978-82; spokesperson TV series on modern art, Appreciating Art, 1991; leader jazz group, 1951—; TV appearances with Johnny Carson, Dinah Shore, Mike Douglas, The Late Show with Ross Schaeffer, David Letterman Show, spls. include Burt Convy, Juke Box Hits, Jerry Lewis Telethons, others; appeared in major jazz clubs throughout US, jazz festivals, Monterey, Calif., Palm Springs, Calif., Sacramento, L.A. Classic and many others, concerts at N.Y. Carnegie Hall, Town Hall, Phila. Acad. Music, Nugget Jazz Festival, Playboy Jazz Festival, 1997, others; jazz trombonist with various artists including Roy Eldredge, Coleman Hawkins, Buddy Rich, Bobby Hackett, Hot Lips Page, Wild Bill Davison; leader Beverly Hills Unlisted Jazz Band, 1978- (subject of PBS spl. titled That's A Plenty 1981), The Tuxedo Junction, (PBS spl.) This Joint is Jumpin, 1997; writer, producer, star: (with others) (video spl.) This Joint Is Jumpin', 1997, numerous recs. for many jazz labels; co-owner. Sidney Janis Gallery, N.Y.C.; co-founder with Maria Grimm, prodr. Golden Era Pictures (co. now titled MiraCon Pictures), 1988—, ConMar Prodns. LLC, 2005. Recipient Theatre World award, 1952; named to Playboy Jazz Poll, 1960, 61; Silver Theatre award, 1950 Mem. SAG, AFTRA, Acad. Motion Picture Arts and Scis., Actors Equity Assn., Am. Fedn. Musicians, Nautico Club (Bilbao, Spain), Bohemian Club (San Francisco). Home Phone: 310-273-4062; Office Phone: 310-820-9225. Fax: (310) 273-0180. E-mail: traid43@aol.com.

JANKURA, DONALD EUGENE, hotel executive, educator; b. Bridgeport, Conn., Dec. 20, 1929; s. Stephen and Susan (Dirga) J.; m. Elizabeth Deborah Joynt, June 20, 1952; children: Donald Eugene Jr., Stephen J., Daria E., Diane E., Lynn M. BA in Hotel Adminstrn., Mich. State U., 1951. Asst. sales mgr. Pick Fort Shelby Hotel, Detroit, 1951-53; steward Dearborn Inn and Colonial Homes, Dearborn, Mich., 1953-54, sales mgr., 1954-60, resident mgr., 1960-62; gen. mgr. Stouffer's Northland Inn, Southfield, Mich., 1962-64; staff adviser Stouffer Motor Inns, Cleve., 1964-66, v.p., 1966-68, Assoc. Inns & Restaurants Co. Am., Denver, 1968-76, exec. v.p., 1976-81, sr. v.p., 1981-91; pres. Waverly Hospitality Assocs., Parker, Colo., 1991-94. Dir. Sch. Hotel and Restaurant Mgmt. U. Denver, 1988-91; disting. spl. lectr. hospitality U. New Haven, Conn.; pres. Am. Hotel Assn. Directory Corp., 1986; guest lectr. Mich. State U., 1964, Fla. Internat. U., 1968, Cornell U., 1983, Denver U., 1986-87; mem. industry adv. bd. U. Denver, Mich. State U.; mem. adv. bd. Acad. Travel and Tourism-Nat. Acad. found., Denver, 1991-99, chmn. 1998; commr. Accreditation Commn. Programs in Hospitality Adminstrn., 1995-99. Commr. Commn. on Accreditation for Hospitality Mgmt., 1994—; pres. Evergreen Homeowner's Assn., 1994-99; mem. USAF Innkeeper Evaluation Team, 1993, 95. Named to Hall of Fame Colo. Hotel and Lodging Assn., 1992, Mich. State U. Sch. Hospitality Bus., 1995, Wall of Fame, 1995; named Alumnus of Yr., Mich. State U. Hotel Sch., 1986. Mem. Am. Hotel and Motel Assn. (dir. 1978-80, vice chmn. industry adv. coun. 1980-81, sec.-treas. 1985, v.p. 1986, pres. 1987—, chmn. host com. 1994, Ednl. Inst. Emeritus award 1995), Colo./Wyo. Hotel and Motel Assn. (dir., bd. dirs. 1984—, Disting. Svc. award 1983), Pres.'s Club, Masons, Phi Kappa Tau. Episcopalian. Avocations: gardening, sailing, cooking, woodworking. Home and Office: 10052 Boca Cir Parker CO 80134-3588

JANNUZI, BUELL T., astronomer; m. Alison Lowell Jannuzi; 2 children. AB in Astronomy & Astrophysics, Harvard Coll., 1984; PhD in Astronomy & Astrophysics, U. Ariz., 1990. Mem. Inst. Advanced Study, Princeton, NJ, 1990—95; mem. sci. staff Nat. Optical Astronomy Obs., Tucson, 1995, co-prin. investigator Deep Wide-Field Survey; acting dir. Kitt Peak Nat. Obs., Tucson, 2005—07, dir., 2007—. Mem. US Gemini Sci. Adv. Com., 1995—2000, Gemini Sci. Com., 1996—2000, Space Infrared Telescope Facility User's Panel, 1998—; coord. Rsch. Experience for Undergraduates prog. Kitt Peak Nat. Obs., 1997—2000. Contbr. articles to sci. jours. Office: NOAO 950 N Cherry Ave Tucson AZ 85719 Office Phone: 520-318-8283. E-mail: jannuzi@noao.edu.

JANOLLARI, DAVID, television broadcasting executive, cable and television producer; With Nederlander TV Prodn., NY; dir. comedy devel. Fox Broadcasting; v.p. comedy devel. Warner Bros. TV Network, 1991—93, sr. v.p. comedy devel., 1993—95, exec. v.p. creative affairs, 1995—97, pres. entertainment, 2004—; co-founder, pres. Greenblatt Janollari Studio, 1997—2004. Exec. prodr.: (TV series) The Hughleys, 1998—2002, To Have & to Hold, 1998, Maggie Winters, 1998—99; exec. prodr.: (TV series) OH Grow Up, 1999; exec. prodr.: (TV series) Heat Vision and Jack, 1999, Chicks, 1999, The Chronicle, 2001—02, One on One, 2001—, Definitely Maybe, 2001; exec. prodr.: (TV series) Six Feet Under, 2001—; exec. prodr.: (TV series) American Family, 2002—04, Platinum, 2003, Eve, 2003—. Office: WB Network 4000 Warner Blvd Burbank CA 91522

JANSEN, ALLAN W., lawyer; b. Oak Park, Ill., July 22, 1948; BS in Aerospace Engring., U. Ill., 1971; JD, John Marshall Law Sch., 1978. Bar: Calif. 1978, U.S. Dist. Ct. (cen. dist.) Calif. 1978, U.S. Ct. Appeals (9th cir.) 1978, U.S. Patent Office, U.S. Ct. Appeals (fed. cir.) 1986. Ptnr. Lyon & Lyon, LA, 1986—. Mem. editorial bd. John Marshall Jour. Practice & Procedure, 1977-78. Mem. ABA, Am. Intellectual Property Law Assn., State Bar Calif., L.A. County Bar Assn., L.A. Intellectual Property Law Assn., Phi Delta Phi. Office: Lyon Lyon 2029 Century Park E Los Angeles CA 90067-2901

JANSEN, KATHLEEN MARY, retired librarian; b. San Francisco, Oct. 24, 1951; d. Wilfred Hugh and Margaret (Jack) Craig; m. Robert Lawrence Jansen, Oct. 8, 1978; children: Heather Margaret, Sarah Elizabeth. AA, Allan Hancock Coll., 1971; BA, U. Calif.-Riverside, 1973; MLS, San Jose State U., 1976. Children's libr. Ottumwa Pub. Libr., Iowa, 1977; reference libr. Lake County Libr., Lakeport, Calif., 1977—79, county libr., 1979—2009, ret., 2009. Deacon Kelseyville Presbyn. Ch., Calif., 1984—87, 2001—. Mem.: Calif. County Libr. Assn. Democrat. Office Phone: 707-263-8816. E-mail: kathyj@co.lake.ca.us.

JANSEN, ROBERT BRUCE, consulting civil engineer; b. Spokane, Wash., Dec. 14, 1922; s. George Martin and Pearl Margaret (Kent) Jansen; m. Barbara Mae Courtney, Sept. 18, 1943. BSCE, U. Denver, 1949; MSCE, U. So. Calif., LA, 1955. Registered profl. engr., Calif., Wash. Chief Calif. Div. Dam Safety, Sacramento, 1965-68; chief of ops. Calif. Dept. Water Resources, Sacramento, 1968-71, dep. dir., 1971-75, chief design and constrn., 1975-77; asst. commr. US Bur. Reclamation, Denver, 1977-80; cons. civil engr., 1980—. Cons. TVA, Chattanooga, 1981—2003, So. Calif. Edison Co., Rosemead, 1982—2002, Pacific Gas and Electric, San Francisco, 1982—93, Hydro-Quebec, Montreal, 1986—98, Ala. Power Co., Birmingham, 1986—2006, Ga. Power Co., 1989—94. Author: Dams and Public Safety, 1983; editor: Safety of Existing Dams, 1983; co-author: Development of Dam Engineering in the United States, 1988; editor, co-author: Advanced Dam Engineering for Design, Construction, and Rehabilitation, 1988. Mem. US Soc. on Dams (chmn.1979-81), ASCE, NAE (elected). Home and Office: 509 Briar Rd Bellingham WA 98225-7811

JANSON, RICHARD ANTHONY, plastic surgeon; b. Passaic, NJ, Nov. 30, 1945; m. Mary Ann Janson, 1971; children: Sarah, Matthew. BA, Rice U., 1967; MD, Med. Coll. Wis., 1971. Diplomate Am. Bd. Plastic Surgery. Intern St. Joseph Hosp., Denver, 1971-72, resident in gen. surgery, 1972-76; resident in plastic surgery U. Tex. Med. Branch, Galveston, 1976-79; pvt. practice Grand Junction, Colo., 1979—. Fellow ACS, Am. Soc. Plastic & Reconstructive Surgeons; mem. Colo. Soc. Plastic & Reconstructive Surgeons. Office: 1120 Wellington Ave Grand Junction CO 81501-6129 Office Phone: 970-243-6200.

JAOUDI, MARIA M., religious studies and humanities educator; BA in Philosophy summa cum laude, Bloomfield Coll., 1974; MA in Asian Studies summa cum laude, Seton Hall U., 1984; PhD in Hist. Theology, Fordham U., 1992. Tchg. asst. Bloomfield Coll., 1975; asst. prof. Seton Hall U., 1987—89; prof. world religions, culture, film Calif. State U., Sacramento, 1996—. Adj. lectr. Pace U., 1989-91; pres. N.Am. Conf. on Christianity and Ecology, 1985-88; chair document com. N.Am. Conf. on Christianity and Ecology/UN, fall 1987; lectr. in field of world religions and ecology. Author: Christian and Islamic Spirituality, 1993, Christian Mysticism West and East: What the Masters Teach Us, 1998; contbr. articles to profl. jours., chpts. to books. Office Phone: 916-278-7483. E-mail: jaoudim@csus.edu.

JAOUEN, RICHARD MATTHIE, plastic surgeon; MD, U. Autonoma de Guadalajara, Jalisco, Mexico, 1975. Intern St. Joseph Hosp., Denver, 1976-77, surgeon, 1977-81; plastic surgeon Ind. U. Med. Sch., Indpls., 1981-83, North Colo. Med. Ctr., Greeley, Colo., 1983—.

JARAMILLO, ALBA, community educator; b. Mex., 1980; Rschr., cmty. educator Southern Ariz. Ctr. Against Sexual Assault, Tucson. Mem. Tucson Youth Take Back the Night; dir., coordinator cmty. com., V-Day Tucson: The Vagina Monologues; bd. dirs. Borderlands Theatre Co. Named one of 40 Under 40, Tucson Bus. Edge, 2006. Office: Southern Arizona Center Against Sexual Assault 1600 N Country Club Tucson AZ 85716 Office Phone: 520-327-1171. Office Fax: 520-327-2992.

JARC, FRANK ROBERT, retail executive; b. Waukegan, Ill., Apr. 4, 1942; s. Frank Joseph and Edith Gertrude (Cankar) J.; m. MeRandy Jarc; 1 dau., Jennifer. BS in Indsl. Engring, U. Mich., 1964; MBA, Harvard U., 1967. Mgmt. trainee Mich. Bell Telephone Co., 1964; with regulatory proceedings dept. United Airlines, Chgo., 1966; fin. analyst Ford Motor Co., Dearborn, Mich., 1967, Freeport Minerals Co., NYC, 1972-73; Fin. analyst Esmark, Inc., Chgo., 1973; controller subs. Swift Grocery Products Co., Chgo., 1973-75; fin. v.p. subs. Estech, Inc., Chgo., 1975-77; v.p. consumer products subs. Estech Gen. Chem. Co., Agrl. Chems. Corp., Chgo., 1977-80; exec. v.p., chief fin. officer Wilson Foods, Oklahoma City, 1980-87; sr. v.p., chief fin. officer United Airlines, Chgo., 1987; exec. v.p., chief fin. officer R.R. Donnelley Co., Chgo., 1987-95; exec. v.p., CFO Viking Office Products, LA, 1996-99; sr. v.p. corp. devel. Office Depot, 1999—. Chmn. audit com. Brady Corp., 2000—. Bd. mgrs. YMCA. Capt. USAF, 1967-71. Mem. Evans Scholarship Alumni Assn., Chgo. Club, Execs. Club Chgo., Chgo. Commonwealth Club, Econ. Club. Home: 501 Oakwood # 3E Lake Forest IL 60045 Office: Office Depot 3366 E Willow St Signal Hill CA 90755-2311

JARDETZKY, OLEG, retired medical educator, researcher; b. Yugoslavia, Feb. 11, 1929; came to U.S., 1949, naturalized, 1955; s. Wenceslas Sigismund and Tatiana (Taranovsky) J.; m. Erika Albensberg, July 21, 1975; children by previous marriage: Alexander, Theodore, Paul. BA, Macalester Coll., 1950, D.Sc. (hon.), 1974; MD, U. Minn., 1954, PhD (Am. Heart Assn. fellow), 1956; postgrad., U. Cambridge, Eng., 1965-66; LL.D. (hon.), Calif. Western U., 1978; MD (hon.), U. Graz, Austria, 1994; Doctorate (hon.), U. Aix-Marseille II, 1998. Rsch. fellow U. Minn., 1954-56; NRC fellow Calif. Inst. Tech., 1956-57; assoc. Harvard U., 1957-59, asst. prof. pharmacology, 1959-66; dir. biophysics and pharmacology Merck & Co., 1966-68, exec. dir., 1968-69; prof. Stanford U., 1969—2006, prof. emeritus, 2006—, dir. Stanford Magnetic Resonance Lab., 1975-97, dir. NMR Ctr. Sch. Medicine, 1983-84, dir. emeritus, 1998—. Vis. fellow Merton Coll., Oxford (Eng.) U., 1976; cons., vis. prof., lectr. in field; chmn. Internat. Coun. on Magnetic Resonance in Biology, 1972-74; dir. Internat Sch. on Magnetic Resonance in Biology, 1993—; mem. adv. bd. Ettore Majorana, 2006—; chmn. biotech. panel World Fedn. Scientists, 1998-2003. Contbr. articles to profl. jours.; mem. editorial bd. Jour. Theoretical Biology, 1961-88, Molecular Pharmacology, 1965-75, Jour. Medicinal Chemsitry, 1970-78, Biochimica Biophypica Acta, 1970-86, Revs. on Bioenergetics, 1972-89, Biomembrane Revs., 1972-80, Jour. Magnetic Resonance in Biology and Medicine, 1986—2000, Jour. Magnetic Resonance, 1993—2000. Recipient Career Devel. award USPHS, 1959-66, Kaiser award, 1973, Von Humboldt award, 1977, Pauling medal, 1984, Grand Gold Honor insignia, Austria, 1993, Founder's Gold medal Internat. Coun. Magnetic Resonance in Biology, 1994, Prix Marianne Dessewffy Internat. Conf. of Genealogy and Heraldry, 1998; grantee NSF, 1957-2001, NIH, 1957-2006; travel fellow Am. Physiol. Soc., 1959. Fellow AAAS; mem. Am. Chem. Soc., Am. Soc. Biol. Chemistry and Molecular Biology, Biophys. Soc., Assn. Advanced Tech. in Biomed. Scis. (pres. 1981-88), Internat. Soc. Magnetic Resonance (chmn. divns. of biology and Medicine 1986-89), Phi Beta Kappa, Sigma Xi, Alpha Omega Alpha. Home: 950 Casanueva Pl Stanford CA 94305-1068 Office: Stanford U CCSR 269 Campus Dr Rm 4155 Stanford CA 94305-5174 Office Phone: 650-723-6153. Business E-Mail: jardetzky@stanford.edu.

JARVEY, PAULETTE SUE, publishing executive; b. Camp LeJuene, NC, Aug. 10, 1945; d. Charles O. and Reva Wanda (Shirley) McCord; m. John M. Jarvey, Aug. 22, 1964; children: Shawn M., J. Adam. Student, Portland Community Coll., Oreg., 1973. Teller new accounts Bank of Am., Anaheim, Calif., 1964-68; owner The Dough Nut, Canby, Oreg., 1971-85, P.J. Promotions, Canby, 1972-85; pres. Hot Off the Press, Inc., Canby, 1980—. Founder N.W. Assn. Book Pubs., Portland, 1983. Author: You Can Dough It, 1980, Let's Dough It Again, 1982, Dough Art Lumpies, 1983, Dough It For Christmas, 1983, Decorative Dough, 1984. Mem. Soc. Craft Designers. Democrat. Avocations: white-water rafting, reading. Office: Hot Off Press Inc 1250 NW 3rd Ave Canby OR 97013-3499

JARVIK, GAIL PAIRITZ, medical geneticist; b. Evanston, Ill., Feb. 8, 1959; d. Lawrence Alan and Lenore Mae P.; m. Jeffrey Gil Jarvik, Aug. 22, 1992. PhD in Human Genetics, U. Mich., 1986; MD, U. Iowa, 1987. Sr. rsch. fellow U. Wash., Seattle, 1992-95, asst. prof. medicine, divsn. med. genetics, 1995-2000, assoc. prof., 2000—. Affiliate mem. Fred Hutchinson Cancer Rsch. Ctr., Seattle, 1994—. Contbr. to profl. jours. Howard Hughes Rsch. fellow, 1992-95; Pew scholar, 1997—. Mem. Am. Soc. Human Genetics, Internat. Genetic Epidemiology Soc.

JARVIS, DONALD BERTRAM, judge; b. Newark, Dec. 14, 1928; s. Benjamin and Esther (Golden) J.; m. Rosalind C. Chodorcove, June 13, 1954; children: Nancie, Brian, Joanne. BA, Rutgers U., 1949; JD, Stanford U., 1952. Bar: Calif. 1953. Law clk. to justice John W. Shenk Calif. Supreme Ct., 1953-54; assoc. Erskine, Erskine & Tulley, 1955, Aaron N. Cohen, 1955-56; law clk. Dist. Ct. Appeal, 1956; assoc. Carl Hoppe, 1956-57; adminstrv. law judge Calif. Pub. Utilities Commn., San Francisco, 1957-91, U.S. Dept. of Labor, San Francisco, 1992—. Mem. exec. com. Nat. Conf. Adminstrv. Law Judges, 1986-88, sec. 1988-89, vice-chair, 1990-91, chair-elect, 1991-92, chair 1992-93; pres. Calif. Adminstrv. Law Judges Coun., 1978-84; mem. faculty Nat. Jud. Coll., U. Nev., 1977, 78, 80; mem. U.S. Bd. of Alien Labor Cert. Appeals, 1995—. Chmn. pack Boy Scouts Am., 1967-69, chmn. troop 1972; class chmn. Stanford Law Sch. Fund, 1959, mem. nat. com., 1963-65; dir. Forest Hill Assn., 1970-71; patron San Francisco Opera. Served to col. USAF Res., 1949-79. Decorated Legion of Merit. Mem. ABA (mem. ho. of dels. 1993-99, vice chair jud. divsn. 1997-98, chair elect 1998-99, chair 1999-2000), State Bar Calif., Bar Assn. San Francisco, Calif. Conf. Pub. Utility Counsel (pres. 1980-81), Air Force Assn., Res. Officers Assn., Ret. Officers Assn., San Francisco Gem and Mineral Soc., Stanford Alumni Assn., Rutgers Alumni Assn., Phi Beta Kappa (pres. No. Calif. 1973-74), Tau Kappa Alpha, Pi Alpha Theta, Phi Alpha Delta. Home: 530 Dewey Blvd San Francisco CA 94116-1427 Office: 50 Fremont St San Francisco CA 94105-2230

JARVIS, PETER R., lawyer; b. NYC, July 19, 1950; BA in Econs. magna cum laude, Harvard U., 1972; MA in Econs., Yale U., 1976, JD, 1976. Bar: Oreg. 1976, U.S. Dist. Ct. Oreg. 1976, U.S. Ct. Appeals (9th cir.) 1977, Wash. 1983, U.S. Dist. Ct. (we. dist.) Wash. 1983, U.S. Dist. Ct. (ea. dist.) Wash. 1985, U.S. Tax Ct. 1991. Assoc. Stoel Rives LLP, Portland, Oreg., 1976—82, ptnr., 1982—2003; ptnr.-in-charge, Portland, legal ethics, risk mgmt. Hinshaw & Culbertson LLP, Portland, Oreg., 2003—. Editor, author: (with others) The Ethical Oregon Lawyer, 2006; spkr. on legal ethics issues. Mem. ALI (Harrison Tweed Spl. Merit award 1993), Oreg. State Bar (former mem. legal ethics com., Pres.'s Membership Svcs. award 1991), Wash. State Bar (mem. profl. conduct com.), Assn. Profl. Responsibility Lawyers (bd. dir., 1999-,pres. 2005), Phi Beta Kappa. Office: Hinshaw & Culbertson LLP Ste 1250 1000 SW Broadway Portland OR 97205-3000 Office Phone: 503-243-3243. Office Fax: 503-243-3240. Business E-Mail: pjarvis@hinshawlaw.com.

JARVIS, RICHARD D., state legislator; b. Boise, Idaho; m. Mary Jarvis; 6 children. BA in Bus. Mgmt., Brigham Young U., 1974. Mem. Dist. 21 Idaho House of Reps., 2008—. Mem.: Ore-Ida Life Underwriters Assn, Southern Idaho Estate Planning Assn., Boy Scouts of America, Rotary Club Internat. Republican. Mem. Lds Ch. Office: Capitol Annex PO Box 83720 Boise ID 83720-0054 also: 5875 S Linder Rd Meridian ID 83642 Office Phone: 208-334-2475, 208-466-1234. Office Fax: 208-334-2125, 208-465-0125. Business E-Mail: rjarvis@house.idaho.gov.*

JARVIS, SCOTT, state agency administrator; Legal counsel Office of State Treas., Wash.; spl. policy and enforcement adminstr. Wash. State Dept. Fin. Instns., dir., 2005—; dep. commr. consumer protection Office of Ins. Commr., Wash., 2001. Office: Wash State Dept Fin Instns PO Box 41200 Olympia WA 98504-1200 Office Phone: 360-902-8707. Office Fax: 360-753-6070. E-mail: sjarvis@dfi.wa.gov.

JAVEY, ALI, engineering educator; b. 1980; BS in Chemistry, Old Dominion U., Norfolk, Va., 2001; PhD in Phys. Chemistry, Stanford U., 2005. Jr. fellow Harvard Soc. Fellows, Harvard U., 2005—06; asst. prof., elec. engring. and computer sciences U. Calif., Berkeley, 2006—; faculty prin. investigator, materials sciences divsn. Lawrence Berkeley Nat. Lab., 2006—; co-dir. Berkeley Sensor and Actuator Ctr., 2008—. Faculty affiliations, nanoscale sci. & engring. grad. group U. Calif., Berkeley, 2006—, faculty affiliations, applied sci. & tech. grad. program, 2007—; invited lectr. in field. Contbr. articles to peer-reviewed journals; jour. reviewer for several peer-reviewed publications; co-editor: Carbon Nanotube Electronics, 2009. Recipient Materials Rsch. Soc. Grad. Student Gold award, 2004, NSF Career award, 2008, NAS award for Initiatives in Rsch., 2009; Peter Verhofstadt Fellowship, Semiconductor Rsch. Corp., 2003—05. Achievements include patents pending in field. Office: EECS Dept U Calif 506 Cory Hall #1770 Berkeley CA 94720-1770 Office Phone: 510-643-7263. Business E-Mail: ajavey@eecs.berkeley.edu.*

JAY, CHRISTOPHER EDWARD, stockbroker; b. Walla Walla, Wash., May 2, 1949; s. Orville Elmo and Juanita Hope (Beckius) J.; m. Mardra Marguerite Jones, July 25, 1981; children: Pohaku Kepano, Hope Lauren, Christopher James. BS, Lewis and Clark Coll., 1972; MA, U. Nev., 1975. 1st v.p. Merrill Lynch & Co., Anchorage, 1975—. Dist. chair Rep. Cen. Com., Anchorage, 1980-81; bd. trustees Lewis and Clark Coll., Portland, Oreg., 1988—; bd. dirs. Anchorage Mus. History and Art Found., 1988-90, KSKA Pub. Radio, Anchorage, 1991-93, Alaska Pub. Broadcasting Inc., Anchorage, Providence Hosp. Found., Anchorage; bd. dirs., treas. Anchorage Symphony Orch.; active 1st Presbyn. Ch., Anchorage, apptd. by Anchorage mayor to sit on the Investment Adv. Bd. for the Mcpl. of Anchorage Endowment Fund, 2003 Named one of nation's top brokers Registered Rep. mag., 1995, 1998 Broker Hall of Fame, Rsch. Mag., 1998; recipient Disting. Alumni award Lewis and Clark Coll., 1996. Mem. Rotary (pres. Anchorage chpt. 1989-90, Paul Harris fellow 1989, co-chmn. dist. conv. 1997, elected del. to Nat. Rep. Conv. 2000, elected aternate to Nat. Rep. Convention), elected alternate Rep. Nat. Conv. Mpls. St. Paul 2008. Republican. Presbyterian. Avocations: reading, walking, travel, civic activities. Home: 11060 Hideaway Lake Dr Anchorage AK 99507-6141 Office: Merrill Lynch & Co 3601 C St Fl 14 Anchorage AK 99503-5925

JAY, DAVID JAKUBOWICZ, management consultant; b. Dec. 7, 1925; came to U.S., 1938, naturalized, 1944. s. Mendel and Gladys Gitta (Zalc) Jakubowicz; m. Shirley Anne Shapiro, Sept. 7, 1947; children: Melvin Maurice, Evelyn Deborah. BS, Wayne State U., 1948; MS, U. Mich., 1949, postgrad., 1956-57, U. Cin., 1951-53, MIT, 1957. Registered profl. engr., Calif., Mich., Ohio. Supr. manmade diamonds GE Corp., Detroit, 1951-56; instr. U. Detroit, 1948-51; asst. to v.p. engring. Ford Motor Co., Dearborn, Mich., 1956-63; project mgr. Apollo environ. control radiators N.Am. Rockwell, Downey, Calif., 1963-68; staff to v.p. corp. planning Aerospace Corp., El Segundo, Calif., 1968-70; founder, pres. PBM Sys. Inc., 1970-83; pres. Cal-Best Hydrofarms Coop., Los Alamitos, 1972-77, Inkmarks Corp., 1989—95. Cons. in field. Patentee in air supported ground vehicle, others. Pres. Cmty. Design Corp., Los Alamitos, 1971-75; bronze life master Am. Contract Bridge League. With USNR, 1944-46. Fellow Inst. Advancement Engring.; mem. Art Stamp and Stencil Dealers Assn. (pres. 1993-95), Inst. Mgmt. Sci. (chmn. 1961-62), Western Greenhouse Vegetable Growers Assn. (sec.-treas. 1972-75), Tau Beta Pi. Jewish. Home: 13441 Roane Santa Ana CA 92705-2271 Office: 137 W Bristol Ln Orange CA 92865 Business E-Mail: djay@biznetsyscorp.com.

JAY, LEE P. (LESLIE JAY), lawyer; b. Phila., 1941; AB, Princeton U., 1963; JD, Harvard U., 1966. Bar: Calif. 1966. Ptnr. Orrick, Herrington & Sutcliffe LLP, San Francisco, chmn. corp. dept., 1987—98, mng. ptnr.-all transactional practice groups, 1998—2000, mem. exec. com. Mem.: ABA (sect. corp., bus. & banking, sect. pub. utility law), State Bar Calif. Office: Orrick Herrington & Sutcliffe LLP The Orrick Building 405 Howard St San Francisco CA 94105 Office Phone: 415-773-5703. Office Fax: 415-773-5759. Business E-Mail: ljay@orrick.com.

JEANLOZ, RAYMOND, geophysics educator; b. Winchester, Mass., Aug. 18, 1952; BA, Amherst Coll, 1975; PhD in Geology and Geophysics, Calif. Inst. Tech., 1979. Asst. prof. Harvard U., 1979-81; from asst. prof. to assoc. prof. U. Calif., Berkeley, 1982-85, prof., 1985—. Exec. dir. Miller Inst. for Basic Rsch. in Sci., 1998-2003; chair bd. on earth scis. and resources NRC, 1999-2003; chair internat. security and arms control NAS Com, 2004-. Editor Ann. Rev. Earth and Planetary Sci., 1996—. Recipient Mineral. Soc. Am. award, 1988, life fellow, 1988; MacArthur grantee, 1988. Fellow AAAS, Am. Geophysics Union (J.B. Macelwane award 1984); mem. NAS, Am. Acad. Arts and Scis. Office: U Calif Dept Earth & Planetary Sci Berkeley CA 94720-4767

JEFF, GLORIA JEAN, city official; b. Detroit, Apr. 8, 1952; d. D. Lee and Harriette Virginia (Davis) J. BSE in Civil Engring., U. Mich., 1974, MSE, 1976, M in Urban Planning, 1976; cert. program in Urban Transp., Carnegie Mellon U., 1979; cert. program sr. mgrs. in govt., Harvard U., 1994. Prin. planner, program analyst, equipment engr. Southeastern Mich. Transp. Authority, 1976-81; divsn. adminstr., multi-regional planning divsn. Mich. Dept. Transp., 1981-83, divsn. adminstr., urban transp. planning divsn., 1983-85, asst. dep. dir. Bur. of Transp. Planning, 1985-90, dep. dir. Bur. Transp. Planning, 1990-93; assoc. adminstr. for policy Fed. Hwy. Adminstrn., U.S. Dept. Transp., Washington, 1993-97, acting adminstr., 1997—2000, dep. adminstr., 1997—2000; transp. programs mgr. Atlantic Dist. Parsons, Brinckerhoff, Quade & Douglas, 2000—03; dir. Mich. Dept. Transp., 2003—06; gen. mgr. Transp. Dept. City of LA, 2006—. Adj. prof. Coll. Architecture and Urban Planing U. Mich., Ann Arbor, 1988—; chair standing com. on planning Mississippi Valley Conf. State Hwys. and Transp. Ofcls., 1987-89, vice chair strategic issues com., 1990-94; mem. Transp. Rsch. Bd., 1989—; adv. bd. U. Mich. Coll. Engring., 1995—, U. Calif., Davis, 1995—. Bd. dirs. Capitol chpt. Child and Family Svcs. of Mich. Inc., 1990-93, chair long-range planning com., 1991-93, sec. bd. dirs., 1993. Recipient Young Engr. of Yr. award Detroit chpt. Soc. Women Engrs., 1979, Young Engr. of Yr. award Detroit chpt. NSPE, 1979, Disting. Alumni award U. Mich., 1991, 92, Regional Amb. award S.E. Mich. Assn. Govts., 1993, Adminstrs. award for superior achievement FHWA, 1996, Trailblazer award Garrett A. Morgan Soc., A.D. Gaither Leadership award FHWA 2004. Mem. Am. Assn. Hwy. and Transp. Ofcls. (mem. modal adv. tech. com. 1988-91, mem. econ. expansion and devel. com. 1990-91, vice chair intermodal issues com. 1990-93), Am. Planning Assn. (v.p. for programs Planning and the Black Cmty. divsn. 1990-92, mem. nat. membership com. 1990-92, chair transp. planning divsn. 1994—, pres. Mich. chpt. 1990-91), Am. Inst. Cert. Planners, U. Mich. Alumni Assn. (bd. dirs. 1985-90, v.p. 1995—), U. Mich. Coll. Architecture Alumni Soc., Delta Sigma Theta, others. Office: LA Dept Transp 100 S Main St 10th Fl Los Angeles CA 90012

JEFF, SANDRA D., state legislator; Consultant; mem. Dist. 5 N. Mex. House of Reps., 2009—. Democrat. Home: PO Box 631 Crownpoint NM 87313 Office: House of Representatives State Capitol Rm 205A Santa Fe NM 87503 Home Phone: 505-786-4994; Office Phone: 505-986-4243.

JEFFREY, JOHN ORVAL, Internet company executive, lawyer; b. Portsmouth, Va., Aug. 6, 1963; s. Orval L. and Mary L. (Coakley) J.; m. Jaimi Jeffrey, children: Logan, Emilie BA, U. Dayton, Ohio, 1985; diploma internat. legal studies, U. San Diego, Paris, 1987; JD, Southwestern U., LA, 1988. Bar: Calif. 1988, U.S. Dist. Ct. (cen. dist., US 9th cir.) Calif. 1988. Assoc. Shield & Smith, LA, 1988—90, Hewitt, Kaldor & Prout, LA, 1990-93; mgr. bus. & legal affairs fx subs. Fox TV, 1993—95; v.p. bus. & legal affairs, gen. counsel TCI Interactive, 1995—97; sr. counsel, dir. bus. and legal affairs Discovery Comms., 1997—99; exec. v.p. corp. strategy gen. counsel Live365.com, 1999—2003; gen. counsel, bd. sec. ICANN (Internet Corp. for Assigned Names & Numbers), 2003—. Mem. ABA (internat. law sect., litigation sect., entertainment/sports law sect.), Los Angeles County Bar Assn., Phi Alpha Delta, Alpha Nu Omega. Democrat. Avocations: tennis, golf, running. Office: ICANN 4676 Admiralty Way Ste 330 Marina Del Rey CA 90292 Office Phone: 310-301-5834. Personal E-mail: jj@ptbreak.net. Business E-Mail: jj@icann.org.

JEFFRIES, ROBIN, computer engineer; BA in Math. summa cum laude, U. Iowa, 1969; MA in Quantitative Psychology, U. Colo., 1977, PhD in Quantitative Psychology, 1978. Rsch. assoc. U. Colo., Boulder, Carnegie-Mellon U., 1983-93; mem. tech. staff Hewlett Packard Labs.; disting. engr. Sun Microsystems, Palo Alto, Calif., 1993—.

JEFFRIES, RUSSELL MORDEN, communications company official; b. Carmel, Calif., July 15, 1935; s. Herman M. and Louise (Morden) J.; m. Barbara Jean Borcovich, Nov. 24, 1962; 1 child, Lynne Louise. AA, Hartnell Coll., 1971. Sr. communications technician AT&T, Salinas, Calif., 1955-91. Mayor City of Salinas, 1987-91. Pres. El Gabilan Sch. PTA, Salinas, 1971-74, Salinas Valley Council PTA, 1975-76; mem. Salinas City Sch. Bd., 1975-81; mem. Salinas City Council, 1981-87; bd. dirs. Community Hosp. Salinas Found., 1987—, Salinas-Kushikino Sister City, 1987—, pres. 1992-93, John

Steinbeck Ctr. Found., 1987-96, Food Bank for Monterey County, 1992-96; hon. bd. dirs. Monterey Film Festival, 1987-96, Calif. Rodeo Assn., 1987; mem. ctrl. bd. Calif. Regional Water Quality, 1992—; commr. Moss Landing Harbor, 1996. Recipient hon. service award PTA, Salinas, 1976; cert. of appreciation Calif. Dept. Edn., 1980, Salinas City Sch. Dist., 1981, Calif. Sch. Bds. Assn., 1981, Steinbeck Kiwanis, Salinas, 1987; named hon. mem. Filipino community Salinas Valley, 1988. Mem. Salinas C. of C., Native Sons Golden West, K.C. Republican. Roman Catholic. Avocations: fishing, hunting, bowling, golf. Home: 204 E Curtis St Salinas CA 93906-2804

JELLEN, EDWARD D., federal bankruptcy judge; b. 1946; BA, U. Calif., Berkeley, 1967; JD, U. Calif., 1971. With legal dept. Bank of Am., 1972-78; with Jellen & Holman, 1978-82, Jellen & Assocs., 1982-87; apptd. bankruptcy judge no. dist. U.S. Dist. Ct. Calif., 1987, apptd. chief judge, 1997. Office: 1300 Clay St Rm 215 Oakland CA 94612-1425

JELLIFFE, ROGER WOODHAM, cardiologist, pharmacologist; b. Cleve., Feb. 18, 1929; s. Russell Wesley and Rowena (Woodham) J.; m. Joyce Miller, June 12, 1954; children: Susan, Amy, Elizabeth, Peter. BA, Harvard U., 1950; MD, Columbia U., 1954. Diplomate Am. Bd. Internal Medicine, Am. Bd. Cardiovascular Disease. Intern Univ. Hosps., Cleve., 1954-56; also jr. asst. resident in medicine; Nat. Found. Infantile Paralysis exptl. medicine fellow Case Western Res. U., Cleve., 1956-58; staff physician in medicine VA Hosp., Cleve., 1958-60, resident in medicine, 1960-61; instr. medicine U. So. Calif. Sch. Medicine, LA, 1961-63, asst. prof., 1963-67, assoc. prof., 1967-76, prof. medicine, 1976—. Developer Lab. Applied Pharmacokinetics, 1973—, The USC*PACK Computer Programs, 1973—; cons. Dynamic Scis., Inc., Van Nuys, Calif., 1976-93, Simes S.P.A., Milan, 1979-97, IVAC Corp., San Diego, 1983-88, Bionica, Sydney, Australia, 1987-94. Author: Fundamentals of Electrocardiography, 1990; co-author: (with V. Sergienko, R. Jelliffe, J. Bondareva) Applied Pharmacokinetics-Basic Foundations and Clinical Implementations, 2003; cons. editor Am. Jour. Medicine, 1972-78, Current Prescribing, 1974-79, Am. Jour. Physiology, 1984-91, Computers in Biology and Medicine, 1994—, Therapeutic Drug Monitoring, 1995—; contbr. articles to profl. jours.; patentee in field. Advanced Rsch. fellow L.A. County Heart Assn., 1961-64; recipient Rsch. Achievement award Clin. Scis. Am. Assn. Pharm. Scis., 1997. Fellow ACP, Am. Coll. Med. Informatics, Am. Coll. Clin. Pharmacology, Am. Heart Assn. Coun. on Clin. Cardiology; mem. Am. Soc. Clin. Pharmacology and Therapeutics (chmn. pharmacometric sect. 1995-97), Am. Fedn. Clin. Rsch. Achievements include research on optimal mgmt. of drug therapy; development of computer programs for optimal mgmt. of drug therapy; population pharmacokinetic modeling; development of intelligent infusion devices; supercomputer resources for parametric and nonparametric population modeling; software for "multiple model" design of drug dosage regimens. Office: 2250 Alcazar St Rm CSC-134-B Los Angeles CA 90089-0107 Home Phone: 626-792-5313; Office Phone: 323-442-1300. Business E-Mail: jelliffe@usc.edu.

JELLINEK, ROGER, editor; b. Mexico City, Jan. 16, 1938; came to U.S., 1961; s. Frank Louis Mark and Marguerite Lilla Donne (Lewis) J.; m. Margherita DiCenzo, Dec. 22, 1963 (div. 1984); children: Andrew Mark, Claire; m. Eden-Lee Murray, 1984; 1 child, Everett Peter Murray. Student, Bryanston Sch., Dorset, Eng., 1951—56; MA, Cambridge U., Eng., 1961. Assoc. editor Random House, 1963-64; editor Walker & Co., NYC, 1964—65, NY Times Book Rev., NYC, 1966—70, dep. editor, 1970—73; editor-in-chief Times Books, Quadrangle/NY Times Book Co., NYC, 1974—78, sr. editor, 1978—81, editor Lamont newsletter and yearbook Palisades, 1981—91; pres. Clairemark, Ltd., 1981—, Jellinek & Murray Lit. Agy. Editor Atlantic Realm Project, 1983-93; editl. dir. Inner Ocean Pub., 2000-03; pub. Hawaii map series. Pres. ArtMaps Ltd., 1996—; program chair Hawaii Book and Music Festival, 2006. With Royal Marines, 1956-57; 2d lt. Brit. Intelligence Corps, 1957-58. Mellon fellow Yale U., 1961-63. Home: 47-722 Hui Kelu St Apt 4 Kaneohe HI 96744-4557 Office Phone: 808-521-4057.

JEMELIAN, JOHN NAZAR, management consultant; b. NYC, May 10, 1933; s. Nazar and Angel (Jizmejian) Jemelian; m. Rose Melkonian, Nov. 22, 1958; children: Sheri, Lori, Brian, Joni. BS, U. So. Calif., 1956. CPA Calif., 1961. Mgr. audit staff Price Waterhouse & Co., LA, 1958-64; treas. The Akron, LA, 1964-82, v.p. fin., 1976, exec. v.p., 1977-82; v.p., gen. mgr., dir. Acromil Corp., City of Industry, Calif., 1982-85; sr. v.p. fin. and adminstrn., CFO, sec., treas. World Vision Inc., 1985-98; pres. Claremont Facilities Corp., 1990—2006, Pasadena Resources Corp., 1990-94. Dir. D.I. Engring., Inc.; fin. advisor African Enterprises, 1966—68. Bd. dirs. Pasadena Christian Sch., 1965—67, 1969—70, treas., 1965—67; chmn. bd. Donor Automation, 1975—2001; trustee Haigazian Coll., Beirut, 1974—78; deacon Lake Ave. Congl. Ch., 1964—68, trustee, 1970—73, chmn. bd. trustees, 1972—73, chmn. ch. com., 1974; chmn. bd. Media Ministries, Inc., 1975—95; trustee Narramore Christian Found., 1976—93, Met. Ministries, 1979—80; chmn. Christian Bus. Men's Com., 1979—81, 1986—87, Sahag Mesrob Armenian Christian Sch., 1980—85; deacon, elder Ch. on the Way, 1980—95; chmn. bd. dirs. Armenian Gospel Mission, 1999—; bd. dirs. Forest Home Christian Conf. Ctr., 1972—75, 1978—81, 1984—88, 1992—95, 2001—04. With F.A. US Army. Named Boss of Yr. Beverly Hills chpt., Nat. Secs. Assn., 1970. Mem.: AICPA, Retail Contr. Assn. (dir. 1973—74), Calif. Soc. CPA, Toastmasters-Windjammers LA (pres. 1963), LA Athletic Club, Beta Gamma Sigma, Beta Alpha Psi, Delta Sigma Pi. Home: 261 Sharon Rd Arcadia CA 91007-8044

JENDEN, DONALD JAMES, pharmacologist, educator; b. Horsham, Sussex, Eng., Sept. 1, 1926; came to U.S., 1950, naturalized, 1958; s. William Herbert and Kathleen Mary (Harris) J.; m. Jean Ickeringill, Nov. 18, 1950; children: Tricia Jenden Billes, Peter Donald, Beverly Jean Jenden Riedlinger. BSc in Physiology with 1st class honours, Kings Coll. London, 1947; MB, BS with honours, U. London, 1950; PhD in Pharm. Chemistry (hon.), U. Uppsala, Sweden, 1980. Demonstrator pharmacology U. London, 1948-49; lectr. pharmacology U. Calif.-San Francisco, 1950-51, asst. prof. pharmacology, 1952-53; mem. faculty UCLA, 1953, assoc. prof., 1956-60, prof. pharmacology, 1960—, prof. pharmacology and biomath., 1967—, chmn. dept. pharmacology, 1968-89. Wellcome vis. prof. U. Ala., Birmingham, 1984; mem. brain research inst. UCLA, 1961—. Contbr. articles in field. Served to lt. comdr. M.C., USNR, 1954-58. USPHS Postdoctoral fellow, 1951-53, NSF Sr. Postdoctoral fellow; hon. research assoc. Univ. Coll., London, 1961-62; Fulbright Short-Term Sr. Scholar award, Australia, 1983; recipient Univ. Gold medal U. London, 1950. Fellow Am. Coll. Neuropsychopharmacology; mem. AAAS, Am. Soc. Pharmacology and Exptl. Therapeutics, Am. Physiol. Soc., Physiol. Soc. (London), Soc. Neurosci., Western Pharmacology Soc. (pres. 1970), Assn. for Med. Sch. Pharmacology, Am. Soc. Neurochemistry. Home: 650 W Evergreen Farm Way Apt 6046 Sequim WA 98382-5090 Business E-Mail: jenden@ucla.edu.

JENES, THEODORE GEORGE, JR., retired military officer; b. Portland, Oreg., Feb. 21, 1930; s. Theodore George and Mable Marie (Moon) Jenes; m. Beverly Lorraine Knutson, Jan. 29, 1953; children: Ted, Mark. BS, U. Ga., 1956; MS, Auburn U., 1969; grad., Army Command and Gen. Staff Coll., Armed Forces Staff Coll., Air War Coll.; LLD (hon.), U. Akron, 1986. Enlisted U.S. Army, 1951, commd. 2d lt., 1953, advanced through grades to lt. gen., 1984, various assignments, 1953—75, combat duty Vietnam, 1965—66; comdr. 3d Brigade, 2d Inf. Divsn., Republic of Korea, 1975—76, 172d Inf. Brigade, Ft. Richardson, Alaska, 1978—81; dep. commdg. gen. U.S. Army Tng. Ctr., Ft. Dix, NJ, 1976—78; comdr. 4th Inf. Divsn., Ft. Carson, Colo., 1982—84; dep. commdg. gen. U.S. Army Combined Arms Combat Devel. Activity, Ft. Leavenworth, Kans., 1981—82; commdg. gen. 3d U.S. Army, Ft. McPherson, Ga., 1984—87; comdr. U.S. Army Forces Ctrl. Command, Ft. McPherson, Ga., 1984—87; dep. commdg. gen. hdqrs. U.S. Army Forces Command, Ft. McPherson, 1984—87, ret., 1987; cons. Burdeshaw and Assocs., 1987—88; gen. mgr. Seattle Tennis Club, 1988—94. Decorated D.S.M., Legion of Merit, Bronze Star, Meritorious Sevc. medal, Air medal, Army Commendation medal, Vietnamese Cross of Gallantry with Silver Star, Combat Infantry Badge. Mem.: Am. Hellenic Ednl. Progressive Assn., Assn. U.S. Army, Rotary. Methodist. Avocations: reading Biblical and military history, golf. Home: 809 169th Pl SW Lynnwood WA 98037-3307 Home Phone: 425-742-8207. Personal E-mail: tedbevjen2@comcast.net.

JENKINS, BRUCE STERLING, federal judge; b. Salt Lake City, May 27, 1927; s. Joseph and Bessie Pearl (Iverson) J.; m. Margaret Watkins, Sept. 19, 1952; children— Judith Margaret, David Bruce, Michael Glen, Carol Alice. BA with high honors, U. Utah, 1949, LLB, JD, U. Utah, 1952. Bar: Utah 1952, U.S. Dist. Ct. 1952, U.S. Supreme Ct. 1962, U.S. Circuit Ct. Appeals 1962. Pvt. practice, Salt Lake City, 1952-59; assoc. firm George McMillan, 1959-65; asst. atty. gen. State of Utah, 1952; dep. county atty. Salt Lake County, 1954-58; bankruptcy judge U.S. Dist. Ct., Utah, 1965-78, judge Utah, 1978—, chief judge Utah, 1984-93. Adj. prof. U. Utah, 1987-88, 95-99. Research, publs. in field; contbr. essays to Law jours.; bd. editors: Utah Law Rev, 1951-52. Mem. Utah Senate, 1959-65, minority leader, 1963, pres. senate, 1965, vice chmn. commn. on orgn. exec. br. of Utah Govt., 1965-66; Mem. adv. com. Utah Tech. Coll., 1967-72; mem. instl. council Utah State U., 1976. Served with USN, 1945-46. Named Alumnus of Yr. award Coll. Law Univ. Utah, 1985; recipient Admiration and Appreciation award Utah State Bar, 1995, Lifetime Svc. award, 2006, Emeritus Merit of Honor award U. Utah Alumni Assn., 1997. Fellow Am. Bar Found.; mem. ABA, Am. Inn Ct., Utah State Bar Assn. (Judge of Yr. 1993), Salt Lake County Bar Assn., Fed. Bar Assn. (Disting. Jud. Svc. awrd Utah chpt. 1993), Order of Coif, Phi Beta Kappa, Phi Kappa Phi, Phi Eta Sigma, Phi Sigma Alpha, Tau Kappa Alpha. Democrat. Mem. Lds Ch. Office: US Dist Ct 462 US Courthouse 350 S Main St Salt Lake City UT 84101-2106

JENKINS, DARRELL LEE, librarian; b. Roswell, N.Mex., Aug. 12, 1949; s. Lindon C. and Joyce (King) J.; m. Susan Jenkins. BA, Ea. N.Mex. U., 1971; MLS, U. Okla., 1972; MA, N.Mex. State U., 1976. Asst. edn., psychology, gift libr. N.Mex. State U., Las Cruces, 1972—73, edn. psychology libr., 1973—74, asst. reference libr., 1974—75, asst. catalog libr., 1975—76, asst. serials libr., 1976—77, acting head reference dept., 1977; adminstrv. svcs. libr. So. Ill. U., Carbondale, 1977—82, dir. libr. svcs., 1982—91, head social scis. divsn., 1992—2001. Cons. U.S. Naval Base, So. Ill. U., Groton, Conn., 1985-91; chmn. bd. dirs. CEC Comm., Inc., 1997-99. Author: Specialty Positions in ARL Libraries, 1982; co-author: Library Development and Fund Raising Capabilities, 1988; contbr. articles to profl. jours. Mem. ALA (chmn. libr. orgn. mgmt. sect. 1985-86), Am. Soc Info. Sci., Assn. Christian Librs., Ill. Libr. Computer System Orgn. (pres. 1985-86), Phi Kappa Phi, Beta Phi Mu, Phi Alpha Theta (Outstanding Libr. award 2002). Republican. Mem. Ch. Assembly God. Avocations: tennis, swimming, bicycling.

JENKINS, EVERETT WILBUR, JR., lawyer, writer, historian; b. Oklahoma City, Nov. 28, 1953; s. Everett Wilbur and Lillie Bell (Ingram) J.; m. Monica Lynn Endsley, June 3, 1978 (div. Aug. 13, 2003); children: Ryan, Camille, Jennifer, Cristina. BA cum laude, Amherst Coll., 1975; JD, U. Calif., Berkeley, 1978. Bar: Calif. 1979. Dep. county counsel Contra Costa County, Martinez, Calif., 1980—81; dep. city atty. City of Richmond, Calif., 1981—84; bd. atty. West County Agy., Richmond, 1981-90; asst. city atty. City of Richmond, 1984—2004; authority atty. West Contra Costa Solid Waste Mgmt. Authority, Richmond, 1985—87, 1988—91; interim city atty. City of Richmond, 2004—05, sr. asst. city atty., 2005—. Legal rep. tech. adv. com. Contra Costa County Solid Waste Commn., Martinez, Calif., 1986-87, pub. mem., 1987-88; adv. atty. West Contra Costa Transp. Adv. Com., San Pablo, 1991-2005; bd. atty. Richmond Housing Authority, 1992-99; bd. dirs. Contra Costa Co. Hazardous Materials Commn., Martinez, 1987-88. Author: Pan-African Chronology, 1996, Pan-African Chronology II, 1998, Pan-African Chronology III, 2001, The Muslim Diaspora, 1999, The Muslim Diaspora, vol. 2, 2000, The Creation, 2003. Bd. dirs. YMCA of the East Bay, Oakland, 1996—; bd. dirs. West Contra Costa YMCA, Richmond, 1987—, chair program com., 1991-92, vice chair bd. dirs. 1992-96, chair bd. dirs., 1996-98, chair cmty. gifts campaign, 1992-94 (named Rita Davis Vol. of the Yr., 1993); umpire Little League Baseball, 1997—, ASA Softball, 1997—. Mem. ABA, State Bar Calif. (exec. bd. pub. law sect. exec. com. 1987-91, editor Pub. Law News 1988-91, liaison to bd. govs. 1991-92), Continuing Edn. Bar (joint adv. com. 1993-96), Contra Costa County Bar Assn., Charles Houston Bar Assn., Nat. Assn. Sports Officials. Independent. Office: City Atty's Office 1401 Marina Way South Richmond CA 94804-1654 Office Phone: 510-620-6509.

JENKINS, JAMES C., lawyer; b. Logan, Utah, July 16, 1948; BA in Fin., U. Utah, 1972; JD, Gonzaga U., 1976. Bar: Utah 1976, U.S. Dist. Ct. Utah 1976, U.S. Ct. Appeals (10th cir.) 1992, U.S. Tax Ct. 1985, U.S. Supreme Ct. 1981. Ptnr. Olson & Hoggan, P.C., Logan, Utah; Rich county atty., 1978-81; Cache county dep. atty., 1981-95; gen. counsel Bear Lake Spl. Svcs. Dist., Rich County, Utah, 1978-2001. Instr. Utah State U., 1976; trustee Utah Bankruptcy Ct., 1977-80. Chair jud. conduct commn. Utah Jud. Coun., 1996-97, mem. jud. performance and evaluation com., mem. adv. bd. Utah State Crime Lab. Mem. ABA (trial practice com., litig. sect. 1986-95), Utah State Bar Assn. (pres.-elect 1997-98, pres. 1998-99, law benefit com. 1978-80, law day com. 1989-90, ethics and discipline com. 1992-93, exec. com., litig. com. 1993-95, bd. commrs. 1993-96), Utah Statewide Assn. Pros., Cache County Bar Assn. (sec.-treas. 1978-81) Office: Olson & Hoggan PC PO Box 525 130 S Main St Ste 200 Logan UT 84321-5387

JENKINS, MAYNARD L., JR., automotive executive; With Orchard Supply Hardware, pres., CEO, 1986-97; chmn., CEO CSK Auto Corp., Phoenix, 1997—2007.

JENKINS, SCOTT K., state legislator; b. Ogden, Oreg., Apr. 13, 1950; m. Becky Jenkins. Sales Mountain States Supply, 1977—82, Hajoca Corp, 1982—87; pres. & owner Great Western Supply, Inc., 1987—; mem. Plain City Coun., 1979—87; mayor Plain City, Utah, 1990—93; mem. Dist. 20 Utah State Senate, 2001—, Majority Whip. Republican. Mormon. Mailing: 4385 W 1975 N Plain City UT 84404 Office: W115 Capitol Complex Salt Lake City UT 84114 Home Phone: 801-731-5120; Office Phone: 801-621-5412, 801-538-1035. Office Fax: 801-326-1475. E-mail: sjenkins@utahsenate.org.*

JENKINS, SPEIGHT, opera company director, writer; b. Dallas, Jan. 31, 1937; s. Speight and Sara (Baird) J.; m. Linda Ann Sands, Sept. 6, 1966; children: Linda Leonie, Speight. BA, U. Tex.-Austin, 1957; LL.B., Columbia U., 1961; DMus (hon.), U. Puget Sound, 1992; HHD, Seattle U., 1992. News and reports editor Opera News, NYC, 1967-73; music critic NY Post, NYC, 1973-81; TV host Live from the Met, Met. Opera, NYC, 1981-83; gen. dir. Seattle Opera, 1983—. Classical music editor Record World, NYC, 1973—81; contbg. editor Ovation Mag., NYC, 1980—87. Served to capt. U.S. Army, 1961-66. Recipient Emmy award for Met. Opera telecast La Boheme TV Acad. Arts and Scis., 1982 Mem. Phi Beta Kappa Assocs. Presbyterian. Office: Seattle Opera PO Box 9248 Seattle WA 98109-0248 Office Phone: 206-389-7600.

JENKINS, TAMARA, scriptwriter, film director; b. Phila., May 2, 1962; m. Jim Taylor, 2002. Theater dir. The New Group; spl. film dir. Scenarios. Dir.: (films) Fugitive Love, 1991, Choices: The Good, The Bad, The Ugly, 2004; writer, dir. (films) Family Remains, 1993 (Spl. Jury prize for Excellence in Short Filmmaking, Sundance Film Festival, 1994), Slums of Beverly Hills, 1998, The Savages, 2007 (Best Original Screenplay, San Francisco Film Critics Cir., 2007, Best Screenplay, LA Film Critics Assn., 2007, Best Screenplay, Flanders Internat. Film Festival, 2007, Ind. Spirit award for Best Screenplay, Film Ind., 2008), actress Cheap Flight, 1996, Happy Accidents, 2000, Love in the Time of Money, 2002. Office: c/o Fox Searchlight 10201 W Pico Blvd Bldg 38 Los Angeles CA 90035

JENNERICH, EDWARD JOHN, academic administrator, dean; b. Bklyn., Oct. 22, 1945; s. William James and Anna Johanna (Whicker) J.; m. Elaine Zaremba, May 27, 1972; children— Ethan Edward, Emily Elaine BA, Trenton State Coll., 1967; MSL.S., Drexel U., 1970; PhD, U. Pitts., 1974. Cert. tchr., learning resources specialist. Tchr. U.S. history Rahway High Sch., NJ, 1967-70; librarian Westinghouse High Sch., Pitts. Pub. Sch., 1970-74; adminstrv. intern U. Pitts, 1973; chmn. dept. library sci. Baylor U., Waco, Tex., 1974-83; dean Sch. Library Sci. So. Conn. State U., New Haven, 1983-84; v.p. acad. affairs Va. Intermont Coll., Bristol, 1984-87; grad. dean Seattle U., 1987-89; assoc. provost for acad. adminstrn., dean Grad. Sch., 1989-97; pres. Knowledge N.W. Inc., 1997—. Mem. rev. panel Fulbright Adminstrv. Exch., 1983-86. Co-author: University Administration in Great Britain, 1983, The Reference Interview as a Creative Art, 1987, 2d edit., 1997; contbr. articles to profl. jours. Bd. dirs. Waco Girls Club, Tex., 1977-83 Mem. ALA (office for libr. pers. resources 1980-82), Am. Assn. Univ. Adminstrs. (bd. dirs. 1980-82, 83-86, 89-93, 94—, v.p. 1996—, exec. com. 1982-87, chmn. overseas liaison com. 1982-87, Eileen Tosney Adminstrv. Excellence award 1985), Assn. for Coll. and Rsch. Librs. (exec. bd. dirs. 1984-88), Queen City Yacht Club (rear commodore 2007-08), Queen City Yacht Club (vice commodore 2008-), Phi Delta Kappa. Republican. Episcopalian. Avocations: model building, reading, travel, sports, sailing. Home: 6935 NE 164th St Kenmore WA 98028-4282 E-mail: jennerich@mindspring.com.

JENNETT, SHIRLEY SHIMMICK, health facility administrator; b. Jennings, Kans., May 1, 1937; d. William and Mabel C. (Mowry) Shimmick; m. Nelson K. Jennett, Aug. 20, 1960 (div. 1972); children: Jon W., Cheryl L.; m. Albert J. Kukral, Apr. 16, 1977 (div. 1990) Diploma, Rsch. Hosp. Sch. Nursing, Kansas City, Mo., 1958. RN, Mo., Colo., Tex., Ill. Staff nurse, head nurse Rsch. Hosp., 1958-60; head nurse Penrose Hosp., Colorado Springs, Colo., 1960-62, Hotel Dieu Hosp., El Paso, Tex., 1962-63; staff nurse Oak Park (Ill.) Hosp., 1963-64, NcNeal Hosp., Berwyn, Ill., 1964-65, St. Anthony Hosp., Denver, 1968-69; staff nurse, head nurse, nurse recruiter Luth. Hosp., Wheat Ridge, Colo., 1969-79; owner, mgr. Med. Placement Svcs., Lakewood, Colo., 1980-84; vol., primary care nurse, admissions coord., team mgr. Hospice of Metro Denver, 1984-88, dir. patient and family svcs., 1988, exec. dir., 1988-94; pres., profl. geriatric care mgr. Care Mgmt. & Resources, Inc., Denver, 1996—. Mem. NAFE, Nat. Women Bus. Owners Assn., Nat. Hospice Orgn. (bd. dirs. 1992-95, coun. former bd. mems. 1995—), Nat. Orgn. Profl. Geriatric Care Mgrs., Denver Bus. Women's Network. Mem. Ch. of Religious Sci. Avocations: reading, walking, golf. Office: Care Mgmt & Resources Inc 900 S Dexter St Denver CO 80246 Home Phone: 303-757-6988; Office Phone: 303-639-5455. Business E-Mail: shirleyj@denvercmr.com.

JENNINGS, MARIANNE MOODY, lawyer, educator; b. Sept. 11, 1953; d. James L. and Jennie (Ure) Moody; m. Terry H. Jennings, Nov. 5, 1976; children: Sarah Anne, Claire Elizabeth. BS in Fin., Brigham Young U., 1974, JD, 1977. Bar: Ariz. 1977, U.S. Dist. Ct. Ariz. 1977. Law clk. Fed. Pub. Defender, Las Vegas, 1975; U.S. atty. Las Vegas, 1976, Udall, Shumway, Bentley, Allen & Lyons, Mesa, Ariz., 1976; from asst. prof. bus. law to assoc. prof. Ariz. State U., Tempe, 1977-83, prof., 1983—, assoc. dean, 1986-88. Columnist Tribune newspapers. Author: Business Strategy for the Political Arena, 1984, Real Estate Law, 6th edit., 2000, Business: Its Legal, Ethical and Global Environment, 5th edit., 2000, Avoiding and Surviving Lawsuits: An Executive Guide to Legal Strategy, 1988, N.Y. Times MBA Pocket Scenes: Corporate Boards, 2000. Bd. dirs. Ariz. Pub. Svc., Inc., 1987-2000. Named Outstanding Undergrad. Bus. Prof., Ariz. State U., 1980, 85, 2000; recipient Burlington No. Found. Tchg. Excellence award, 1986; Dean's Coun. of 100 scholar, 1996—. Mem. Ariz. Bar Assn., Am. Bus. Law Assn., Pacific S.W. Bus. Law Assn. Mem. Lds Ch. Office: Ariz State U c/o M Jennings Coll Bus Tempe AZ 85287 E-mail: marianne.jennings@asu.edu.

JENNINGS, PAUL CHRISTIAN, civil engineering educator, academic administrator; b. Brigham City, Utah, May 21, 1936; s. Robert Webb and Elva S. (Simonsen) J.; m. Millicent Marie Bachman, Aug. 28, 1981; m. Barbara Elaine Morgan, Sept. 3, 1960 (div. 1981); children: Kathryn Diane, Margaret Ann. BSCE, Colo. State U., 1958; MSCE, Calif. Inst. Tech., 1960, PhD, 1963. From prof. civil engring., applied mechanics to prof. emeritus Calif. Inst. Tech., Pasadena, 1966—2002, acting v.p. bus. and fin., 1995, 1998—99, prof. emeritus, 2002—, provost, 2004—07, 1989—95. Cons. in field. Author: (with others) Earthquake Design Criteria. Contbr. numerous articles to profl. jours. 1st lt. USAF, 1963-66. Recipient Honor Alumnus award Colo. State U., 1992, Achievement in Academia award Coll. Engring., 1992; Erskine fellow U. Canterbury, New Zealand, 1970, 85. Fellow AAAS, New Zealand Soc. Earthquake Engring.; mem. ASCE (Walter Huber award 1973, Newmark medal 1992), Seismol. Soc. Am. (pres. 1980), Earthquake Engring. Rsch. Inst. (pres. 1981-83), Athenaeum Club. Avocations: fly fishing, hiking. Home: 640 S Grand Ave Pasadena CA 91105-2423 Office: Calif Inst Tech Mail Code 206-31 Pasadena CA 91125-0001 Business E-Mail: pcjenn@caltech.edu.

JENNINGS, TIMOTHY ZEPH, state legislator; b. Roswell, NM, Sept. 4, 1950; s. James T. and Frances Schultz Jennings; m. Patricia K. Jennings; 5 children. BSBA, Creighton U., 1972. Rancher, 1974—; businessman; commr. Chaves County, Roswell, N.Mex., 1975—78; mem. Dist. 32 N.Mex. State Senate, 1978—, majority whip, 1992—96, pres. pro tempore. Democrat. Roman Catholic. Office: Dist 32 PO Box 1797 Roswell NM 88202 also: State Capitol Rm 105 Santa Fe NM 87503 Office Phone: 505-623-8331, 505-986-4733. Business E-Mail: tjennings@state.nm.us.*

JENSEN, ARTHUR ROBERT, psychologist, educator; b. San Diego, Aug. 24, 1923; s. Arthur Alfred and Linda (Schachtmayer) J.; m. Barbara Jane DeLarme, May 6, 1960; 1 child, Roberta Ann. BA, U. Calif., Berkeley, 1945; PhD, Columbia U., 1956. Asst. med. psychology U. Md., 1955-56; research fellowInst. Psychiatry U. London, 1956-58; prof. ednl. psychology U. Calif., Berkeley, 1958-94; prof. emeritus, 1994—. Author: Genetics and Education, 1972, Educability and Group Differences, 1973, Educational Differences, 1973, Bias in Mental Testing, 1979, Straight Talk about Mental Tests, 1981, The g Factor, 1998, Clocking the Mind: Mental Chronometry and Individual Differences, 2005; contbr. to profl. jours., books. Guggenheim fellow, 1964-65, fellow Ctr. Advanced Study Behavioral Scis., 1966-67 Fellow AAAS, Am. Psychol. Assn., The Galton Inst., Am. Psychol. Soc.; mem. Psychonomic Soc., Am. Soc. Human Genetics, Soc. for Social Biology, Behavior Genetics Assn., Psychometric Soc., Sigma Xi. Office: U Calif Sch Edn Berkeley CA 94720-0001

JENSEN, D. LOWELL, federal judge; b. Brigham, Utah, June 3, 1928; s. Wendell and Elnora (Hatch) J.; m. Barbara Cowin, Apr. 20, 1951; children: Peter, Marcia, Thomas. AB in Econs, U. Calif.-Berkeley, 1949, LL.B., 1952. Bar: Calif. 1952. Dep. dist. atty., Alameda County, 1955-66; asst. dist. atty., 1966-69; dist. atty., 1969-81; asst. atty. gen. criminal divsn. US Dept. Justice, Washington, 1981-83, assoc. atty. gen., 1983-85, dep. atty. gen., 1985-86; judge US Dist. Ct. (no. dist.) Calif., Oakland, 1986—97, sr. judge, 1997—. Mem. Calif. Coun. on Criminal Justice, 1974—81, US Jud. Panel on Multidistrict Litig., 2000—. Served with U.S. Army, 1952-54. Fellow Am. Coll. Trial Lawyers; mem. Nat. Dist. Atty.'s Assn. (victim/witness commn. 1974-81), Calif. Dist. Atty.'s Assn. (past pres.), Boalt Hall Alumni Assn. (past pres.) Office: US Dist Ct 1301 Clay St Rm 490C Oakland CA 94612-5217

JENSEN, DENNIS LOWELL, lawyer; b. Erie, Pa., July 5, 1951; s. Lowell and Roberta (Umbaugh) J. Student, Cornell Coll., 1969-70; BA, Macalester Coll., 1973; JD, U.Houston, 1977. Bar: Tex. 1977, U.S. Dist. Ct. (so. dist.) Tex. 1978, Calif. 1981. Sole practice, Houston, 1977-78; asst. housing coordinator Santa Ana Housing Authority, Calif., 1979; polit. cons. Huntington Beach, Calif., 1980-81; legis. analyst Tosco Corp., Los Angeles, 1981-82; polit. cons. Lynn Wessell Co., 1982-83, George Young & Assocs., 1983-84; legis. aide Los Angeles City Councilman Ernani Bernardi, 1984-86; dep. atty. Los Angeles City Atty.'s Office, 1986-95; pvt. practice Huntington Beach, 1995—. Lectr. in field. Contbr. articles to profl. jours. Campaign mgr. for Congressman Tom Kindness, Hamilton, Ohio, 1978, Initiative to Abolish Inheritance Tax, Bakersfield, Calif., 1980; alumni admissions rep. Macalester Coll., 1984; mem. bd. dirs. Adult Day Svc. Orange County, 1998-2004; instr. Calif. State U. Fullerton Extended Edn. programs gerontology and geriatric care mgmt., 1999-2006. Mem. Am. Assn. Polit. Cons., Nat. Acad. Elder Law Attys., Orange County Bar Assn. (chmn. elder law sect. 2004), Order of Barons, Phi Delta Phi. Republican. Home: 18801 Gregory Ln Huntington Beach CA 92646-1921 Office: Dennis L Jensen Atty at Law 18377 Beach Blvd Ste 212 Huntington Beach CA 92648-1349 Office Phone: 714-843-0450.

JENSEN, HANNE MARGRETE, pathologist, educator; b. Copenhagen, Dec. 9, 1935; came to US, 1957; d. Niels Peter Evald and Else Signe Agnete (Rasmussen) Damgaard; m. July 21, 1957 (div. Apr. 1987); children: Peter Albert, Dorte Marie, Gordon Kristian, Sabrina Elisabeth. Student, U. Copenhagen, 1954—57; MD, U. Wash., 1961. Resident and fellow in pathology U. Wash., Seattle, 1963-68; asst. prof. dept. pathology U. Calif. Sch. Medicine, Davis, 1969-79, assoc. prof., 1979—2001, dir. transfusion svc., 1973—, prof., 2001—. McFarlane prof. exptl. medicine U. Glasgow, Scotland, 1983. Fellow Pacific Coast Ob-Gyn. Soc., Coll. Am. Pathologists; mem. No. Calif. Soc. for Electron Microscopy, U.S. and Can. Acad. Pathology, Am. Cancer Soc., Am. Soc. Clin. Pathologists, AAAS, Am. Assn. Blood Banks, Calif. Blood Bank Sys., People to People Internat., Internat. Platform Assn. Office: U Calif Sch Medicine Dept Pathology Davis CA 95616 Office Phone: 530-752-7229. Business E-Mail: hmjensen@ucdavis.edu.

JENSEN, HENRIK WANN, computer graphics designer, educator; MSEE, Tech. U., Denmark, 1993, PhD in Computer Sci., 1996. Unix networking specialist Image Scandinavia ApS, 1995—96; rsch. scientist Mental Images, 1996—98; postdoctoral assoc. MIT, Cambridge, 1998—99; rsch. assoc. Stanford U., Calif., 1999—2002; asst. prof. U. Calif. San Diego, 2002—04, assoc. prof., 2004—. Cons. Pixar Animation Studios, 2001. Contbr. articles to profl. pubis.; author: Realistic Image Synthesis using Photon Mapping, 2001. Recipient Acad. award, Tech. Achievement, Acad. Motion Picture Arts and Scis., 2004; named one of 10 Brilliant, Popular Sci. mag., 2004; grantee Sloan Found. fellowship, 2004. Mem.: Assn. Computing Machinery Spl. Interest Grp. on Graphics and Interactive Techniques. Avocations: cooking, bicycling, scuba diving, swimming. Office: Computer Graphics Lab U Calif San Diego CSE 4116 9500 Gilman Dr La Jolla CA 92093-0404 E-mail: henrik@cs.ucsd.edu.

JENSEN, J. ALAN, lawyer; b. Cedar Falls, Iowa, July 27, 1938; BA, Carleton Coll., 1960; LLB, U. Mich., 1963; LLM in Taxation, NYU, 1967. Bar: Minn. 1963, Calif. 1968, Oreg. 1972. Ptnr. Holland & Knight, LLP, Portland, Oreg. Asst. prof. Lewis and Clark Law Sch., 1970—73, assoc. prof., 1973—74, prof. law, 1974—76, adj. prof. law, 1977, 89, 1999—2001. Mem. planned giving com. Oreg. Humane Soc.; gen. counsel Portland Marathon; bd. dirs., treas. Sister City Assn. Ulsan, Republic of Korea. Named one of Top 100 Attys., Worth mag., 2006. Fellow: Am. Coll. Trust and Estate Counsel; mem.: Oreg. State Bar Assn., Estate Planning Coun. Portland, Calif. State Bar Assn., ABA (mem. tax sect., mem. estate and gift tax com., mem. partnership com., chair subcommittee on life ins.). Office: Holland & Knight LLP 2300 US Bancorp Tower 111 SW 5th Ave Portland OR 97204 Office Phone: 503-243-5867. E-mail: alan.jensen@hklaw.com.

JENSEN, JACK MICHAEL, publishing executive; b. Salt Lake City, June 5, 1951; s. W. Donald and Catherine Ann (Hearley) J.; m. Cathleen Ann O'Brien, Sept. 15, 1985; children: Grace Ann, Ned Michael. BA, Ft. Wright Coll. of the Holy Names, 1974. Bookseller Dayton Hudson, 1972-76; salesman Chronicle Books, San Francisco, 1976-82, mktg. dir., 1983-86, gen. mgr., 1987-89, pub., 1989—, pres., 1996—. Mem. faculty Stanford Pub. Course, 1988-89.

JENSEN, MICHAEL ALLEN, engineering educator; b. Fullerton, Calif., Mar. 27, 1966; s. Paul Allen and Dorothy Carolyn Jensen; m. Angela Evans, June 28, 1991; children: Kamber Nicole, Paige Natalie, Matthew Allen, Andrew Michael. BSEE, Brigham Young U., 1990, MSEE, 1991; PhD, U. Calif., Los Angeles, 1994. Asst. prof. Brigham Young U., Provo, Utah, 1994—2000; v.p. AJ Design Group, Inc., Provo, Utah, 1999—; sr. scientist Wavetronix, LLC, Lindon, Utah, 2000—; assoc. prof. Brigham Young U., 2000—05; pres. RFWare, LLC, Springville, Utah, 2004—; prof. Brigham Young U., 2005—, chair, dept. elec. and computer engring., 2006—. Bd. mem. Wavetronix, LLC, Lindon, 2000—. Contbr. articles to profl. jours., chapters to books. Recipient Karl G. Maeser Rsch. and Creative Arts award, Brigham Young U., 2005, Cert. of Achievement, NASA, 1994; Rsch. award, NSF, 1999—, US Dept. Def., 2000—. Fellow: IEEE (adminstrv. com. mem. 2005—07). Lds Ch. Achievements include patents for radar technology for traffic monitoring; patents pending for multi-antenna communications technology; research in multi-antenna communications systems. Office: Brigham Young U 459 Clyde Bldg Provo UT 84602

JENSEN, RANDY, principal; Tchr. William Thomas Middle Sch., American Falls, Idaho, adminstr., prin. Recipient Idaho Middle Level Prin. of Yr., 2004, Nat. Middle Level Prin. of Yr., Nat. Assn. Secondary Sch. Principals, 2005. Office: William Thomas Middle School 827 Fort Hall Ave American Falls ID 83211 Office Phone: 208-226-5203.

JENSEN, RICHARD DENNIS, librarian; b. Payson, Utah, Oct. 20, 1944; s. Ruel Whiting and Ethel Josepha (Otte) J.; m. Maxine Swasey, Apr. 21, 1966; children: Shaun, Craig, Todd, Jana, Brad, Kristine, April, Lynne. BS in Zoology, Brigham Young U., 1971, MLS, 1976. From asst. sci. libr. to pub. svc. coord. Brigham Young U., Provo, Utah, 1971—2001, reference svc. coord., 2001—03, life sci. libr., 2003—, chair dept. sci./maps, 2004—. Co-author: Agricultural and Animal Sciences Journals and Serials: An Analytical Guide, 1986, (indexes) Great Basin Naturalist, 50 Year Index, 1991, BYU Geology Studies, Cumulative Index, vol. 1-37, 1954-1991, 1992. Mem. Lds Ch. Avocations: farming, sports, camping. Office: Brigham Young U Libr Sci & Maps Dept 2324 HBLL Provo UT 84602-2734 Home Phone: 801-375-1253; Office Phone: 801-422-6012. Business E-Mail: Richard_Jensen@byu.edu.

JENSEN, ROBERT TRYGVE, retired lawyer; b. Chgo., Sept. 16, 1922; s. James T. and Else (Uhlich) J.; m. Marjorie Rae Montgomery, Oct. 3, 1959 (div. June 1973); children: Robert Trygve, James Thomas, John Michael; m. Barbara Mae Wilson, Aug. 5, 1974. Student, U. N.C., 1943; LL.B., JD, BS, Northwestern U., 1949; LL.M., U. So. Calif., 1955. Bar: Calif. 1950. Asst. counsel Douglas Aircraft Co., Inc., 1950-52, 58-60, counsel El Segundo div., 1952-58; gen. counsel Aerospace Corp., El Segundo, 1960-84, asst. sec., 1961-67, sec., 1967-85. Founding mem. World Assn. Lawyers of World Peace Through Law Center. Served with AUS, 1942-46, PTO. Mem. Alpha Delta Phi, Phi Delta Phi. Fax: 310-475-0445. E-mail: rtjsr@aol.com.

JENSEN, RODNEY H., hotel executive; V.p. Nat. 9 Inns, Salt Lake City, 1985—.

JENSON, BOB, state legislator; b. Omaha, May 11, 1931; m to Evelyn; children: four, ten grandchildren. Oregon State Representative, District 57, formerly, member, Education & Children & Families Committees, formerly, District 57, 1999-2002, member, Education, Ways & Means Committees, Natural Resources Subcomt & Joint Subcomt on Species Recovery & Stream Restoration, currently, Oregon House Representative; Oregon State Representative, District 58, 2003-.Instr, formerly. Republican. Mailing: 2126 NW Despain Ave Pendleton OR 97801 Office: 900 Court St NE H-481 Salem OR 97301 Office Phone: 503-986-1458, 541-276-5821. Business E-Mail: rep.bobjenson@state.or.us. E-mail: jenson.rep@state.or.us.

JERGESON, GREG, Public Service Commissioner, Montana; b. Havre, Mont., Dec. 29, 1950; m. Barb Jergeson; 2 children. BA in Polit. Sci., U. Mont., 1974. Farmer, rancher, 1969-95; mem. Mont. Senate, Dist. 46, Helena, 1975—81, 1987—2003; asst. minority leader Mont. Senate, 1979-80, majority leader, 1993-94; dir. grants & bus.-indsl. linkages Mont. State Univ. Northern Found., Havre, 1995—2003; commr. Mont. Pub. Svc. Commn., Helena, 2003—. Mem. Mont. Bd. Investments, 1981-85; mem. Blaine County Planning Bd., 1983—; Blaine County Dem. State Committeeman, 1972-74; chair Mont. delegation Dem. Nat. Conv., 1984. Mem. Mont. Farmers Union, North Ctrl. Stockgrowers Assn., Chinook Lions Swim Team, Chinook Men's Bowling League, Eagles. Democrat. Roman Catholic. Home: PO Box 1568 Chinook MT 59523-1568 Office: Montana Public Service Comm PO Box 202601 Helena MT 59620-2601

JERRYTONE, SAMUEL JOSEPH, financial property broker; b. Pittston, Pa., Mar. 21, 1947; s. Sebastian and Susan Teresa (Chiampi) J.; children: Sandra, Cheryl, Samuel, Sebastian Assoc. in Bus., Scranton Lackawanna Jr. Coll., Pa., 1966. Mgr. House of Jerrytone Beauty Salon, West Pittston, Pa., 1967—68; regional sales dir. United Republic Life Ins., Harrisburg, Pa., 1970—76; night instr. Wilkes-Barre Vo-Tech H.S., Pa., 1976—78; spl. sales agt. Franklin Life Ins. Co., Wilkes-Barre, 1978—80; instr. Jerrytone Beauty Sch., Pittston, 1968—69, supr., 1969—95, pres., CEO, 1975, Jerrytone Tng. Ctrs., Pittston, 1989, Las Vegas, 1989; fin. broker Exec. Bus. Mgmt. and Property Svcs., Las Vegas, 2001—. Prof. sch. evaluator Nat. Accrediting Com. Arts and Scis., 1974-95; mem. adv. craft com. Wilkes-Barre Vo-Tech H.S., 1988 Mem. com. Rep. Presdl. Task Force, Washington, 1984, mem. parish coun. Guardian Angel Cathedral, Las Vegas, 1997 Mem. Pa. Hairdressers Assn., Nat. Accrediting Com. Cosmetology, Am. Coun. Cosmetology Educators, Masons (3d degree award 1983, 32d degree award Lodge Coun. chpt. consistory 1984), Shriners (Irem temple) Roman Catholic. Avocations: reading, golf, bowling, music, video filming. Personal E-mail: samuellv@embarqmail.com.

JESSOR, RICHARD, psychologist, educator, director; b. Bklyn., Nov. 24, 1924; s. Thomas and Clara (Merkin) J.; m. Shirley Glasser, Sept. 27, 1948 (div. 1982); children: Kim, Tom; m. Jane Ava Menken, Nov. 13, 1992. Student, CCNY, 1941-43; BA, Yale U., 1946; MA, Columbia U., 1947; PhD, Ohio State U., 1951. Intern, clin. psychology trainee VA, Ohio State U., Columbus, 1947-50; asst. prof. psychology U. Colo., Boulder, 1951-56, assoc. prof., 1956-61, prof., 1961—, disting. prof. behavioral sci., 2005—, dir. rsch. program problem behavior Inst. Behavioral Sci., 1966-97, dir. Inst. Behavioral Sci., 1980—2001, dir. health and soc. program Inst. Behavioral Sci., 2001—. Dir. MacArthur Found. Rsch. Network on Successful Adolescent Devel. Among Youth in High Risk Settings, 1987-96; cons. Nat. Inst. on Drug Abuse, 1975-76, Nat. Inst. on Alcohol Abuse and Alcoholism, 1976-80, WHO, Geneva, 1976-80; cons. in field. Author: (with T.D. Graves, R.C. Hanson & S.L. Jessor) Society, Personality, and Deviant Behavior: A Study of a Tri-Ethnic Community, 1968, (with S.L. Jessor) Problem Behavior and Psychosocial Development: A Longitudinal Study of Youth, 1977, (with J.E. Donovan and F. Costa) Beyond Adolescence: Problem Behavior and Young Adult Development, 1991; co-editor: Contemporary Approaches to Cognition, 1957, Cognition, Personality and Clinical Psychology, 1967, Ethnography and Human Development: Context and Meaning in Social Inquiry, 1996; editor: New Perspectives on Adolescent Risk Behavior, 1998, Perspectives on Behavioral Science: the Colorado Lectures, 1991; cons. editor Jour. Cons. and Clin. Psychology, 1975-77, Cmty. Mental Health Jour., 1974-78, Alcohol Health and Rsch. World, 1981-90, Alcohol, Drugs and Driving, 1985-92, Adolescent Medicine: State of the Art Revs., 1989—; mem. editl. bd. Prevention Sci., 1999—; cons. editor Sociometry, 1964-66, assoc. editor, 1966-69; contbr. articles to profl. jours. Served with USMC, 1943-46, PTO. Decorated Purple Heart; Social Sci. Rsch. Coun. pre-doctoral fellow Ohio State and Yale U., 1950-51; Social Sci. Rsch. Coun. fellow Ohio State U., 1954, Social Sci. Rsch. Coun. postdoctoral fellow U. Calif.-Berkeley, 1956-57, NIMH spl. rsch. fellow Harvard-Florence Rsch. Project, Italy, 1965-66, Ctr. for Advanced Study in the Behavioral Scis. fellow Stanford U., 1995-96; recipient Faculty Rsch. Lectureship award U. Colo., 1981-82; Gallagher lectr. Soc. Adolescent Medicine, 1987, Outstanding Achievement in Adolescent Medicine award, 2005; named Highly Cited Rsch. in Social Scis., Inst. for Sci. Inf., 2003. Fellow APA, Am. Psychol. Soc. (charter fellow); mem. Soc. for Psychol. Study of Social Issues, Soc. for Study of Social Problems. Avocations: mountain climbing, running marathons. Home: 1303 Marshall St Boulder CO 80302-5803 Office: U Colo Inst Behavioral Sci Cb 483 Boulder CO 80309-0001 Home Phone: 303-440-4024; Office Phone: 303-492-8148. Business E-Mail: jessor@colorado.edu.

JESTE, DILIP VISHWANATH, psychiatrist, researcher; b. Pimpalagaon, India, Dec. 23, 1944; came to U.S., 1974; naturalized Feb., 1980; m. Sonali D. Jeste, Dec. 5, 1971; children: Shafali, Neelum. B in Medicine & Surgery, U. Poona, India, 1966; D. Psychiat. Medicine, Coll. Physicians and Surgeons, 1970; MD, U. Bombay, 1970. Cer. Am. Bd. Psychiatry and Neurology, 1979; lic. physician, D.C., Md., Calif. Hon. asst. prof. KEM Hosp., G.S. Med. Coll., Bombay, 1971-74; staff psychiatrist St. Elizabeth's Hosp., Washington, 1977-82, chief movement disorder unit, 1982-86; clin. assoc. prof. psychiatry Walter Reed Med. Ctr., Bethesda, Md., 1981-84; assoc. clin. prof. psychiatry and neurology George Washington U., Washington, 1984-86; prof. psychiatry and neurosciences U. Calif., San Diego, 1986—; chief psychiatry svc. San Diego VA Med. Ctr., San Diego, 1989-92; dir. geriatric psychiatry clin rsch ctr. U. Calif. and VA Med. Ctr., San Diego, 1992—, disting. prof. psychiatry and neurosciences, chief, geriatric psychiatry divsn., dir. Sam and Rose Stein Inst. for Rsch. on Aging. Vis. scientist dept. neuropathology Armed Forces Inst. of Pathology, Washington, 1984-86; co-dir. Med. Students' Psychiatry Clerkship Program, 1987-91; ad-hoc mem. Vets. Adminstrn. Neurobiology Grant Rev. Bd., 1984—; participant numerous meeting and confs.; lectr. in field. Co-author: Understanding and Treating Tardive Dyskinesia, 1982; editor: Neuropsychiatric Movement Disorders, 1984, Neurpsychiatric Dementias, 1986, Psychosis and Depression in the Elderly, 1988; editor-in-chief: Am. Jour. Geriatric Psychiatry; contbr. articles to numerous profl. jours, reviewer numerous profl. jours. Mem. Acad. Geriatric Resource Com., U. Calif., 1986-87, mem. com. on joint doctoral program in clin. psychology, 1986-87, mgmt. com. faculty compensation fund com., 1988-89, chmn. Psychiat. Undergrad. Edn. Com., 1987. Recipient Merit award NIMH, 1988, Disting. Svc. commendation, Am. Legion, VA and Rehab. Commn., Calif., 1991, Disting. Investigator award, Nat. Alliance Rsch in Schizophrenia and Affective Disorders, 2002, Committed Svc. to Aging Population award, San Diego County Med. Soc., 2002, C. Charles Burlingame award, Inst. Living, Hartford, 2003, Asian Heritage award, Asia Jour. Culture and Commerce, 2004, Internat. Psychogeriatric Assn. award, 2005, Recovery Rsch. Inspiration award, Nat. Alliance on Mental Illness, San Diego chapt., 2006; named one of World's Most Cited Authors, Inst. Sci. Info., 2002; recipient numerous grants in field. Fellow Indian Psychiatric Soc. (recipient Sandoz award 1973), Am. Psychiatric Assn. (disting. fellow; co-chmn. Tardive Dyskinesia task force 1984-92; Rsch. award, 2005, George Tarjan award, 2006), Am. Coll. Neuropsychopharm. (co-chmn. fin. com. 1988-89), San Diego Soc. Psychiatric Physicians,; mem. NIH (nat. adv. mental health coun., 2006), Inst. Medicine of NAS, Soc. for Neurosci., Internat. Brain Rsch. Orgn., Soc. Biolog. Psychiatry (A.E. Bennett Neuropsychiatric Rsch. award 1981), Am. Acad. Neurology, Am. Geriatrics Soc., Calif. Psychiatric Soc., Am. Assn. Geriatric Psychiatry (pres., 1998-99, prs. edn. and rsch found., 1999-2000; Sr. Investigator award, 1996), West Coast Coll. Biolog. Psychiatry (pres., 1999-2000; Warren B. Smith award, 2004), Assn. Scientists of Indian Origin in Am. (pres. neurosci. chpt. 1988-89, named Outstanding Neuroscientist 1988, Disting. Physician Tchr./Rschr. award, 2004), Internat. Coll. Geriatric Psychoneuropharmacology (founding pres., 2001-03), Collegium Internationale Neuro-psychopharmacologicum, Am. Coll. Psychiatrists (Geriatric Rsch. award, 2005). Avocations: tennis, reading. Office: VA San Diego Healthcare System Psychiatry Svc 116A-1 3350 La Jolla Village Dr # 16A San Diego CA 92161-0002 also: Dept Psychiatry 0603 Univ Calif San Diego La Jolla CA 92093-0603 E-mail: djeste@ucsd.edu.*

JETT, STEPHEN CLINTON, geography and textiles educator, researcher; b. Cleve., Oct. 12, 1938; s. Richard Scudder Jett and Miriam Ida (Horn) Greene; m. Mary Frances Manak, Aug. 7, 1971 (div. 1977); 1 child, Jennifer Frances Jett; m. Lisa Sue Roberts, June 17, 1995. AB, Princeton U., 1960; postgrad., U. Ariz., 1962—63; PhD, Johns Hopkins U., 1964. Instr. geography Ohio State U., Columbus, 1963-64; asst. prof. geography U. Calif., Davis, 1964-72, assoc. prof., 1972-79, prof., 1979—2000, prof. textiles and clothing, 1996—2000, prof. emeritus geography, textiles and clothing, 2000—, chmn. geography dept., 1978-82, 87-89. Author: Navajo Wildlands, 1967 (1 of 50 Books of Yr., Am. Inst. Graphic Arts 1967, 1 of 20 Merit Award Books, Western Book Pubs. Assn. 1969), House of Three Turkeys, 1977, Navajo Architecture, 1981 (1 of Outstanding Acad. Books, Choice mag. ALA 1981), Navajo Placenames and Trails of the Canyon de Chelly System, Arizona, 2001, France, 2004; (monograph) Tourism in the Navajo Country, 1966; editor jour. Pre-Columbiana; curator textile exhbns.; contbr. numerous articles to profl. jours. and chpts. to books. Mem. Hist. and Landmarks Commn., Davis, 1969-73; vice chmn. Gen. Plan Noise Element Study Com., Davis, 1974-76, chmn. ad hoc citizens noise com., 1997-98; mem. exec. coun. Univ. Farms Unit Number 1 Neighborhood Assn., Davis, 1987-90. Fellow: Am. Geog. Soc., Explorers Club; mem.: AAAS, Found. Rsch. Ancient Maritime Explorations (bd. dirs. 2002—, treas. 2006—), Inst. for Study of Am. Cultures (bd. dirs. 1996—), Epigraphic Soc. (bd. dirs. 1996—, v.p. 2005—), Soc. Am. Archaeology, Assn. Am. Geographers (chair Am. Indian splty. group 1989—91). Avocations: travel, photography, textiles and other ethnographic arts, French language and culture. E-mail: scjett@hotmail.com.

JEUB, MICHAEL LEONARD, financial consultant; b. Mpls., Mar. 2, 1943; s. Leonard M. and Florence J.; m. Alice Ann Linden (div. 1980); children: Christopher Michael, Annette Michelle; m. Julia Jean Stephenson, Feb. 4, 1983; children: Michael Leonard Jr., Robert. BS in Acctg., Calif. State Poly. U., 1966. CPA, Tex., Calif. Staff acct. Ernst & Whinney, LA, 1966-70; CFO Internat. Clin. Lab., Inc., Nashville, 1970-85, pres. east, 1985-88; pres. August Enterprises, 1988-91; pres., COO, CFO MICA, San Diego, 1991-93; exec. v.p., CFO, treas. Nat. Health Labs., Inc., 1993-94; sr. v.p., CFO Jenny Craig Internat., 1994-2000; fin. cons. La Jolla, Calif., 2000—01; ptnr. Tatum CFO, 2000—; CFO The Immune Response Corp., San Diego, 2002—03, Road Runner Sparts, 2005—. Office: 5549 Copley Dr San Diego CA 92111 Home: 5526 Caminito Exquisito San Diego CA 92130-2822 Personal E-mail: MikeJeub@aol.com.

JEWEL, (JEWEL KILCHER), folk singer, songwriter; b. Payson, Utah, May 23, 1974; d. Lenedra Carroll and Atz Kilcher; m. Ty Murray, Aug. 7, 2008. Grad., Interlochen Arts Acad., Mich., 1992. Co-founder/owner Magic Lantern Entertainment, 2002—. Musician: (albums) Pieces of You, 1995, Spirit, 1998, Joy: A Holiday Collection, 1999, This Way, 2001, 0304, 2003, Goodbye Alice in Wonderland, 2006, Perfectly Clear, 2008, (singles) Woman to Woman, 1994, For the Last Time, 1995, Who Will Save Your Soul, 1996, (performs on soundtracks) I Shot Andy Warhol, 1996, The Craft, 1996, Phenomenon, 1996, Wizard of Oz in Concert: Dreams Come True, 1996, Batman & Robin, 1997, Ride with the Devil, 1999, Life or Something Like It, 2002, Sweet Home Alabama, 2002; actor: (films) Ride With the Devil, 1999, (TV appearances) The Lyon's Den, 2003, Las Vegas, 2006; author: (book of poetry) A Night Without Armor, 1998, (memoir) Chasing Down the Dawn, 2000. Co-founder Higher Ground for Humanity, 1998—. Recipient Am. Music Award for Favorite Pop/Rock New Artist, 1997. Office: c/o Azoffmusic Mgmt 1100 Glendon Ave Ste 2000 Los Angeles CA 90024

JEWELL, MARK LAURENCE, plastic surgeon; b. Kansas City, Mo., Oct. 26, 1947; s. James Lemley and Martha (Bullock) Jewell; m. Mary Rita Lind, Nov. 30, 1975; children: Mark II, James, Hillary. BS in Zoology, U. Kans., 1969, MD, 1973; postgrad., UCLA, 1977, U. Tenn., 1979. Cert. Am. Bd. Plastic Surgery, 1981. Resident in surgery UCLA, 1973—76; fellow, burn surgery U. So. Calif., LA, 1976—77; resident, plastic surgery U. Tenn., Chattanooga, 1977—79; practice medicine specializing in plastic surgery Eugene, Oreg., 1979—; plastic surgeon Inamed Aesthetics; asst. clin. prof. plastic surgery Oreg. Health Sci. U., Portland. Pres. Aesthetic Surgery Jour.; contbr. articles to profl. jours. Lt. USNR, 1970—79. Recipient Rsch. award, Am. Soc. Clin. Pathologists, 1972, U. Kans. Sch. Medicine, 1973; Joyce Kaye Lectureship, 1998—2004. Mem.: Nat. Endowment for Plastic Surgery (gov.), Aesthetic Soc. Edn. and Rsch. Found. (treas.), Oreg. Soc. Plastic Surgery, Am. Soc. for Aesthetic Plastic Surgery (pres. 2005—06, Tiffany award 2003), Am. Med. Joggers Soc., Lane County Med. Soc., Oreg. Med. Assn., Am. Soc. Plastic Surgeons (former mem. bd. dirs.). Episcopalian. Avocations: helicopter skiing, marathons, art, cooking, computers. Office: 630 E 13th Ave Eugene OR 97401-3625 Office Phone: 541-683-3234. Office Fax: 541-683-8610. E-mail: mljmd@teleport.com.

JHA, RAJESH K., computer software company executive; BS in Computer Sci., Indian Inst. Tech., Madras, 1984—88; MS in Computer Sci., U. Mass. Amherst, 1988—90. Software design engr. Microsoft Corp., Redmond, Wash., 1990, with consumer divsn., dir. devel., gen. mgr. Microsoft Office InfoPath, 2003, corp. v.p. Microsoft Office Live, 2004—. Office: Microsoft Corp One Microsoft Way Redmond WA 98052-6399

JIAMBALVO, JAMES, dean; BS, U. Ill., 1970, MAS, 1973; PhD in Acctg., Ohio State U., 1977. Auditor Haskins & Sells, 1970—72; mem. faculty U. Wash. Bus. Sch., Seattle, 1977—, chmn. dept. acctg., 1992—96, faculty dir. e-business, 2000—03, Pricewaterhouse Coopers and Alumni Prof. in Acctg., 1995—, dean, 2005—. Mem. editl. bd. Jour. Mgmt. Acctg. Rsch., 1989—, Contemporary Acctg. Rsch., 1989—; assoc. editor The Acctg. Rev. Author: (textbook) Managerial Accounting. Recipient Andrew V. Smith Award for Svc. to Sch. Bus., Wash. U., 2000, Lex N. Gamble award excellence in field e-commerce. Office: UW Business School Mackenzie Hall Box 353200 Seattle WA 98195-3200 Office Phone: 206-543-4750. Office Fax: 206-685-9392.

JIANG, WILLIAM YUYING, business educator, consultant, researcher; b. Hengyang, Hunan Province, China, Jan. 18, 1955; s. Rongguang Jiang and Hongkang Lei; m. Leslie Rongqui Yi, Sept. 5, 1988; children: Cosmo Yi, Cordelia Yi. BA in English, Hunan Normal U., Changsha, China, 1981; MA in English Lexicology, Xiamen U., China, 1984; MA in Comparative Lit., U. Ill., 1985, MS, 1986; MPhil in Bus., PhD in Bus., Columbia U., 1991. Asst. prof. San Jose State U., 1991—94, assoc. prof., 1994—97, prof., 1997—. Mng. dir. JS Cresvale Securities (US) Inc., Cupertino, Calif., 1999—2001; chancellor First Light Acad., Centreville, Va., 2002—. Translator: (novel) The Egoist, To Kill a Mockingbird; contbr. articles to profl. jours. Recipient Acad. Rsch. award, Chinese NSF, 1997, 2000; scholar, Pres. Fellowship, 1984—86, Columbia U., 1987, 1988, 1989, 1990; Marjorie Hope Nicolson scholar, 1987, Provost's Internat. scholar, San Jose State U., 2003. Mem.: Internat. Mgmt. Assn. Human Resource (chmn. mgmt. divsn. 1995—96), The Asian Am. Mfg. Assn., Chinese Economist Soc., Monte Jade Soc. Sci. and Tech., Indsl. Rels. Rsch. Assn., The Am. Econ. Assn., Assn. Chinese Profs. U.S. (dir. bd. 2001—03, dir. mem. 2001—03), Acad. Mgmt. (participation com. chair 1999—2002). Avocations: skiing, travel, foreign languages learning, reading. Home: 19901 La Mar Dr Cupertino CA 95014-3377 Office: San Jose State Univ One Washington Sq San Jose CA 95192-0070 Office Phone: 408-924-3551. Personal E-mail: jiang.w11@gmail.com. Business E-Mail: william.jiang@sjsu.edu.

JIN, DEBORAH, physicist, educator; b. 1968; AB, Princeton U., 1990; PhD in Physics, U. Chgo., 1995. NRC rsch. assoc. Nat. Inst. of Standards and Tech., Boulder, Colo., 1995—97, physicist, commerce dept., 1997—; fellow, JILA, adjoint prof., physics dept. U. Colo., Boulder, 1997—. Recipient Pres. Early Career for Sci. and Engr., 2000, Maria Goeppert-Mayer prize, Am. Phys. Soc., 2002, Svc. to America medal for the Sci. and the Environment, Partnership for Pub. Svc., 2004, Benjamin Franklin medal in Physics, Franklin Inst., 2008; named Rsch. Leader of Yr. within the "Scientific American 50", Scientific American, 2004; fellow MacArthur Found., 2003. Fellow: Am. Acad. Arts & Scis.; mem.: NAS (award for initiatives in rsch. 2002). Achievements include creation of the first Fermi condensate on Dec. 16, 2003 with research team. Office: Univ Colo JILA 440 UCB Boulder CO 80309-0440 Office Phone: 303-492-0256. Office Fax: 303-492-5235, 303-492-8994. Business E-Mail: jin@jilau1.colorado.edu.

JIRAUCH, CHARLES W., lawyer; b. St. Louis, Apr. 27, 1944; m. Sally J. Costello, 1968 (div. Mar. 1977); m. Dana K. Bowen, 1980; children: Melissa, Mathew, Kathleen. BSEE, Washington U., 1966; JD, Georgetown U., 1970; diploma in European Union Comml. Law, U. Eng. and Wales, 2008. Bar: Ill. 1971, Ariz. 1975, Nev. 1991, Calif. 1993, Colo. 1993, U.S. Patent Office 1970, U.S. Supreme Ct. 1978. Examiner US Patent Office, 1968—70; atty. Leydig, Voit & Mayer, Chgo., 1970-71, McDermott, Will & Emery, Chgo., 1971-75, Streich Lang, Phoenix, 1975-2000, Quarles & Brady LLP, Phoenix, 2000—. Bd. dirs. Valley Big Bros./Big Sisters, 1980-86, pres. bd. dirs., 1985-86; pres., bd. dirs. Valley Big Bros./Big Sisters Found., 1988-92; mem. Gov.'s Coun. on Workforce Policy, 2004; mem. bd. advisors to dean Ariz. State U. Sch. Engring., 1998-; bd. dirs., mem. exec. com., gen. counsel, v.p., pres. Ariz. Bus. and Edn. Coalition, 2002-2008, mem. Ariz. Dem. Coun., 2002-. Named one of Best Lawyers in Am., Intellectual Property Litig., 2005—09, SW Super Lawyers, 2007—09. Fellow Internat. Bar Assn.; mem. ABA, Fed. Cir. Bar Assn., Calif. Bar Assn., Ariz. Bar Assn. and Found., Maricopa County Bar Assn. (tech. law sect. bd. dirs. 2000-04, chmn. 2003-04), Am. Judicature Soc., Am. Intellectual Property Law Assn. and Found., Ariz. Civil Liberties Union, Am. Electronic Assn. (exec. com. Ariz. chpt. 1999-2003), Ariz. Tech. Coun. (bd. dirs. 2000-08, chair workforce devel. com. 2001-06, mem. emeritus bd. dirs. 2008-), Ariz. Tech. Coun. Found. (bd. dirs. 2008-, pres. 2008-), Ariz. C. of C. (edn. and tech. comms. 2002—), Ariz. Tech. Investment Forum (mem. screening com., 2007-), Rodel Found. (adv. com. mem., 2006-), Ariz. Bd. Regents & Dept. Edn. (adv. com., 2006-). Democrat. Roman Catholic. Office: Quarles & Brady LLP 2 N Central Ave Phoenix AZ 85004-2345 Office Phone: 602-229-5503. Office Fax: 602-420-5103. Business E-Mail: cjirauch@quarles.com.

JOAQUIN, LINTON, lawyer; b. 1950; JD, Univ. Calif., Berkeley. Bar: Calif. 1977. Atty. United Farm Workers, People's Coll., LA; exec. dir. Central Am. Refugee Ctr., Calif.; litigation dir. Nat. Immigration Law Ctr., LA, 1990—2004, exec. dir., 2004—. Adj. faculty Southwestern Univ. Sch. Law, 1991—96, Univ. So. Calif. Law Sch., 1997. Recipient Carol King award, Nat. Immigration Project, Nat. Lawyers Guild. Mem.: Am. Immigration Lawyers Assn. (Jack Wasserman award). Office: National Immigration Law Center Suite 2850 3435 Wilshire Blvd Los Angeles CA 90010 Office Phone: 213-639-3900.

JOBS, STEVE (STEVEN PAUL JOBS), computer company executive; b. Feb. 24, 1955; s. Paul J. and Clara J. (Hagopian) Jobs; m. Laurene Powell, Mar. 18, 1991; 4 children; 1 child, Lisa Brennan-Jobs. Student, Reed Coll. With Hewlett-Packard, Palo Alto, Calif.; designer video games Atari Inc., 1974; co-founder Apple Computer Inc., Cupertino, Calif., 1976, chmn. bd., 1976—85, interim CEO, 1997; CEO Apple Inc. (formerly Apple Computer Inc.), Cupertino, Calif., 1998—; pres. NeXT Computer, Redwood City, Calif., 1985—97; CEO NeXT Computer (acquired by Apple Computer Inc.), 1985—97; co-founder Pixar Animation Studios Inc., Emeryville, Calif., 1986, chmn., CEO, 1986—. Founder Steven P. Jobs Found., 1987—88; bd. dirs. Apple Inc. (formerly Apple Computer Inc.), 1997—, The Walt Disney Co., 2006—. Exec. prodr.: (films) Toy Story, 1995. Recipient Nat. Medal Tech., The White House, 1985, Jefferson award for Pub. Svc., 1987, Entrepreneur of the Decade award, Inc. Mag., 1989, The Steve Jobs Award, WIRED Rave award, 2006; named one of The 50 Most Powerful People in Hollywood, Premiere mag., 2002—06, The 100 Most Influential People in the World, TIME mag., 2005—08, The 50 Who Matter Now, CNNMoney.com Bus. 2.0, 2006, 2007, The 25 Most Influential People in Web Music, Powergeek 25, 2007, The 50 Most Important People on the Web, PC World, 2007, The 25 Most Powerful People in Bus., Fortune mag., 2007, The Global Elite, Newsweek mag., 2008, The Top 25 Market Movers, US News & World Report, 2009; named to The Calif. Hall of Fame, 2007. Achievements include co-designer (with Stephan Wozniak) Apple I Computer; development of Apple II Computer, 1977, Apple III, 1980, Apple Lisa, 1983, Macintosh, 1984; iMac, 1998; iPod portable music player in 2001, iTunes, 2002, iTunes Music Store, 2003, iPhone, 2007, MacBook Air, 2008; Apple Computer Inc. celebrated 30th birthday on April 1, 2006. Address: Apple Inc 1 Infinite Loop Cupertino CA 95014 Office Phone: 510-752-3000, 408-996-1010. Office Fax: 510-752-3151, 408-974-2113.*

JOCHIM, MICHAEL ALLAN, archaeologist; b. St. Louis, May 31, 1945; s. Kenneth Erwin and Jean MacKenzie (Keith) J.; m. Amy Martha Waugh, Aug. 12, 1967; children: Michael Waugh, Katherine Elizabeth. BS, U. Mich., 1967, MA, 1971, PhD, 1975. Lectr. anthropology U. Calif., Santa Barbara, 1975-77, asst. prof., 1979-81, assoc. prof., 1981-87, prof., 1987—, dept. chmn., 1987-92; asst. prof. Queens Coll. CUNY, Flushing, 1977-79. Mem. archaeology rev. panel NSF, Washington, 1988-90. Author: Hunter-Gatherer Subsistence and Settlement, 1976, Strategies for Survival, 1981, A Hunter-Gatherer Landscape, 1998; editor (series) Interdisciplinary Contributions to Archaeology, 1987—; editor Am. Antiquity, 2004-2007. Chmn. Community Adv. Com. for Spl. Edn., Santa Barbara County, 1980-82. Grantee NEH, 1976, NSF, 1980, 81, 83, 89, 91, 94, 2002, Nat. Geog. Soc., 1987, 97, Wenner-Gren, 1999. Fellow Am. Anthrop. Assn.; mem. Soc. for Am. Archaeology, Sigma Xi. Office: U Calif Dept Anthropology Santa Barbara CA 93106 Home Phone: 805-964-3667; Office Phone: 805-893-4396. Business E-Mail: jochim@anth.ucsb.edu.

JOE, PASKVAN, state legislator; b. Fairbanks, Alaska, May 19, 1952; m. Barbara Joe; children: Nicole, Chelsea, Tom, Ryan. BA in Polit. Sci., U. Alaska, Fairbanks, 1975; JD, U. Pugent Sound Sch. Law, 1981. Intern Alaska Ct. Appeals, 1981; atty. various law firms; mem. Alaska State Senate from Dist. E, 2008—. Former team mgr. & coach Fairbank Amateur Hockey Assn.; adv. Fairbanks North Star Youth Ct.; former bd. mem. Yukon Quest; mem. fin. com. Cath. Bishop Northern Alaska. Mem.: Sunrise Rotary, U. Alaska Fairbanks Face Off Club (life). Democrat. Catholic. Office: State Capitol Terry Miller Bldg Ste 111 Rm 7 Juneau AK 99801-1182 Office Phone: 907-465-4648, 907-465-3709. Office Fax: 907-465-2864, 907-465-4714. Business E-Mail: Senator_Joe_Paskvan@legis.state.ak.us.

JOHANSEN, JUDITH A., lawyer; b. Colo. Springs, Colo., June 17, 1958; d. John Carlo and Joan Elizabeth (Bischof) B.; m. Kirk Johansen, May 16, 1992. BA in Polit. Sci., Colo. State U., 1980; JD, Lewis & Clark Law Sch., 1983. Bar: Oreg. 1983, Washington 1986, U.S. Dist. Ct. Oreg. 1989, U.S. Ct. Appeals (9th cir. 1983). Staff counsel Pub. Power Coun., Portland, Oreg., 1983-86; assoc. Gordon, Thames, Honeywell, Tacoma, Wash., 1986-89, ptnr. Seattle, Wash., 1989-91; sr. policy advisor U.S. Dept. Energy, Bonneville Power Admin., Portland, Oreg., 1992-93, dir. fish and wildlife, 1993-94, v.p. generation supply, 1994-96; v.p. bus. devel. Avista Energy, WA Water Power, 1996-98; adminstr. and CEO Bonneville Power Adminstr., Dept. of Energy, Portland, OR, 1998—. Mem. editorial bd. Nat. Resource & Environ. Mag., 1992—. Contbr. articles to profl. jours. Mem. ABA, (vice chair 1989-91, chair 1992—). Democrat. Avocations: skiing, gardening, cooking, travel, fishing. Office: Bonneville Power Adminstrn Dept Energy PO Box 3621 Portland OR 97208-3621

JOHANSEN, KYLE, state legislator; b. Ketchikan, Alaska, July 13, 1967; m. Michelle Johansen; children: Jacie, Makena, Shelbi. BA in Elem. Edn., Wash. State U., 1992. Legis. aide, Alaska State Legislature, 1994-2000; Alaska State Representative, District 1, 2007-, currently majority leader; chair, Transportation, vice chairman, Fisheries, member, State Affairs, Econ Develop, Trade and Tourism Committees, 2007-08, Alaska House Representative. owner, Johansen Consult company. Republican. Avocations: Sport Fishing, motorcycling, Classic Literature, basketball, architecture. Address: PO Box 5963 Ketchikan AK 99901 Office: State Capital Rm 204 Juneau AK 99801 Home Phone: 907-617-5537; Office Phone: 907-465-3424. Fax: 907-465-3793. Business E-Mail: kylejo@gci.net. E-mail: Representative_Kyle_Johansen@legis.state.ak.us.*

JOHANSON, DONALD CARL, physical anthropologist; b. Chgo., June 28, 1943; s. Carl Torsten and Sally Eugenia (Johnson) Johanson; 1 child, Tesfaye Meles. BA, U. Ill., 1966; MA, U. Chgo., 1970, PhD, 1974; DSc (hon.), John Carroll U., University Heights, Ohio, 1979, Coll. of Wooster, Ohio, 1985. Mem. dept. phys. anthropology Cleve. Mus. Natural History, 1972-81, curator, 1974-81; pres. Inst. Human Origins, Berkeley, Calif., 1981-97, dir. Tempe, Ariz., 1997—. Prof. anthropology Stanford U., 1983-89, Ariz. State U., 1997, Virginia M. Ullman chair human origins, 2000; adj. prof. Case Western Res. U., 1978-81, Kent State U., 1978-81. Co-author: (with M.A. Edey) Lucy: The Beginnings of Humankind, 1981 (Am. Book award 1982), Blueprints: Solving the Mystery of Evolution, 1989, (with James Shreeve) Lucy's Child: Discovering a Human Ancestor, 1989, (with Kevin O'Farrell) Journey from the Dawn: Life with the World's First Family, 1990, (with Lenora Johanson and Blake Edgar) Ancestors: In Search of Human Origins, 1994, (with Blake Edgar) From Lucy to Language, 1997, 2d edit., 2006, (with Giancarlo Ligabue) Ecce Homo, 1999, (with W.H. Kimbel and Y. Rak) The Skull of Australopithecus afarensis, 2004; host PBS Natures Series; prodr. (film) Lucy in Disguise, 1982; host, narrator NOVA series In Search of Human Origins, 1994 (Emmy nomination 1995); contbr. numerous articles to profl. jours. Recipient Jared Potter Kirtland award for outstanding sci. achievement Cleve. Mus. Natural History, 1979, Profl. Achievement award U. Chgo., 1980, Gold Mercury Internat. ad personem award Ethiopia, 1982, Humanist Laureate award Acad. of Humanism, 1983, Disting. Svc. award Am. Humanist Assn., 1983, San Francisco Exploratorium award, 1986, Internat. Premio Fregene award, 1987, Alumni Achievement award U. Ill., 1995, Anthropology Media award Am. Anthropol. Assn., 1999, Webby award for best sci. web site, 2002; named Endowed Chair Virginia Ullman Chair in Human Origins, Webby award Internat. Acad. Digital Arts and Scis., 2002; grantee Wenner-Gren Found., NSF, Nat. Geog. Soc., L.S.B. Leakey Found., Cleve. Found., George Gund Found., Roush Found. Fellow AAAS, Calif. Acad. Scis., Rochester (NY) Mus., Royal Geog. Soc.; mem. Am. Assn. Phys. Anthropologists, Internat. Assn. Dental Rsch., Internat. Assn. Human Biologists, Am. Assn. Africanist Archaeologists, Soc. Vertebrate Paleontology, Soc. Study of Human Biology, Societe de l'Anthropologie de Paris, Centro Studi Ricerche Ligabue (Venice), Founders' Coun., Chgo. Field Mus. Natural History (hon.), Accademia Fisiocritici (hon., Sienna), Assn. Internationale pour l'etude de Paleontologie Humaine, Mus. Nat. d'Histoire Naturelle de Paris (corr.), Explorers Club (hon. dir.), Nat. Ctr. Sci. Edn. (supporting scientist). Office: Inst Human Origins Ariz State U PO Box 874101 Tempe AZ 85287-4101 Office Phone: 480-727-6578. Business E-Mail: johanson.iho@asu.edu.

JOHANSSON, VOLEEN, gun shop ownner; b. 1971; d. Mary and Michael Johansson; m. Vincent Vorhees; children: Jennifer, Charles, Bobby. BA, Temple U., 1993, MA, 1995. Gun handler Phila. Police Dept., 1995—97; asst. mgr. Wal Mart Weapons Dept., 1998—2001; weapons expert Las Cruces Police Dept., 2003—; head weapons dept. Meriks Gun Shop, Las Cruces, N.Mex., 2003—07, v.p., 2007—. Weapons trainer Mo's Gun & Boat Show, Phila., 1991—94. Author: Explaining Guns to your Children, 2004. Office: Meriks Gun Shop 630 King James Ave Las Cruces NM 88007

JOHJIMA, KENJI, professional baseball player; b. Sasebo, Japan, June 8, 1976; m. Maki Johjima; children: Yuta, Miu. Catcher Daiei Hawks, 1994—2005, Seattle Mariners, 2006—. Mem. Japanese nat. team World Baseball Classic, 2009. Recipient Japan League Gold Glove award, 1999—2005; named MVP, Pacific League, 2003; named to Japan League All-Star Team, 2000—04. Achievements include first Japanese catcher to start Major League Baseball game, 2006. Office: Seattle Mariners Safeco Field PO Box 4100 Seattle WA 98194*

JOHNS, CHRISTOPHER P., utilities executive; B in Acctg., U. Notre Dame, Ind., 1982. CPA Calif., Fla. Ptnr., assoc. nat. dir. Pub. Utilities KPMG Peat Marwick LLP; v.p., contr. Pacific Gas & Electric Co. PG&E Corp., San Francisco, 1996—97, v.p., 1997—2001, contr., 1997—2005, sr. v.p., 2001—, CFO, 2005—, treas., 2005—, sr. v.p., treas. Pacific Gas & Electric Co. Bd. trustees San Francisco Ballet. Mem.: Fin. Execs. Inst. Office: PG&E Corp One Market Spear Tower Ste 2400 San Francisco CA 94105-1126 Office Phone: 415-267-7070. Office Fax: 415-267-7268.

JOHNSEN, EUGENE CARLYLE, mathematician, educator; b. Mpls., Jan. 27, 1932; s. Bernhardt Thorwald and Esther Elvira (Eklund) J.; m. Marjorie Marie Wacklin, Aug. 31, 1957. BChem, U. Minn., 1954; PhD, Ohio State U., 1961. NAS/NRC Rsch. Assoc. Nat. Bur. Stds., Washington, 1962-63; lectr. math. U. Calif., Santa Barbara, 1963-64, asst. prof., 1964-68, assoc. prof., 1968-74, prof., 1974-94, prof. emeritus, 1994—, dir. summer sessions, 1981-94, 94-97, cons. rschr., 1994—. Vis. lectr. in math. U. Mich., Ann Arbor, 1968-69; vis. scholar in sociology Harvard U., Cambridge, Mass., 1984-85; mathematician Sperry Rand, St. Paul, 1956, 57; instr. chem. and math. U. Minn., 1956-57; instr. math. Ohio State U., Columbus, 1962; organizer and co-organizer of math. social sci. confs.; reviewer NSF. Contbr. numerous articles to profl. jours.; referee numerous profl. jours.; mem. editl. bd. Jour. Math. Sociology. Mem. Los Angeles County Mus. Art, 1985—, L.A. Music Ctr. Opera League, 1986—; mem. Santa Barbara C. of C./U. Calif. Santa Barbara Bus. Adv. Com., 1979-84. Grantee USAFOSR, NSF, Dept. Edn.; Fulbright travel award fellow U. Tübingen, 1969; fellow NSF, 1959. Mem. AAAS, Am. Math. Soc., Math. Assn. Am., Am. Statis. Assn., Soc. Indsl. and Applied Math., Internat. Network for Social Network Analysis, Am. Sociol. Assn. (acting chair, then chair math. sociology sect. 1995-97), U. Calif. Santa Barbara Faculty Club, Channel City Club, Am.-Scandinavian Found. (bd. dirs. Santa Barbara chpt. 2005—), Sons of Norway (pres. Ivar Aasen Lodge 1999-2001, 03—), Phi Beta Kappa, Sigma Xi, Phi Lambda Upsilon, Pi Mu Epsilon, Alpha Chi Sigma. Avocations: music, opera, tennis, travel. Home: 1603 Paterna Rd Santa Barbara CA 93103-1826 Office: U Calif Dept Math Santa Barbara CA 93106-3080 Business E-Mail: johnsen@math.ucsb.edu.

JOHNSEN, KEN C., steel products company executive; b. 1958; BA in Fin., Utah State U.; JD, Yale U. Assoc. Parr Waddoups Brown Gee & Loveless, 1986-91; mgr. spl. projects Geneva Steel Holdings Corp., Vineyard, Utah, 1991, v.p., gen. counsel, 1991-97, sec., 1992—, exec. v.p., gen. counsel, 1997—, also bd. dirs., dir., pres. and ceo, 2001—05; bd. mem. Amerityre Corp., Boulder City, Nev., 2005—. Mem. bd. dir. Joy Global, Inc., Milw. Mem. AISI (com. mem.). Office: Amerityre Corp 1501 Industrial Rd Boulder City NV 89005 Office Phone: 800-808-1268. Office Fax: 801-227-9090.

JOHNSON, ALAN BOND, federal judge; b. 1939; BA, Vanderbilt U., 1961; JD, U. Wyo., 1964. Pvt. practice law, Cheyenne, Wyo., 1968-71; assoc. Hanes, Carmichael, Johnson, Gage & Speight P.C., Cheyenne, 1971-74; judge Wyo. Dist. Ct., 1974-85, U.S. Dist. Ct. Wyo., 1986-92, chief judge, 1992—99. Part-time fed. magistrate U.S. Dist. Ct. Wyo., 1971-74; substitute judge Mcpl. Ct., Cheyenne, 1973-74. Served to capt. USAF, 1964-67, to col. Wyo. Air N.G., 1973-90. Mem. ABA, Fed. Judges Assn. (bd. dirs. 2003—), Wyo. State Bar, Laramie County Bar Assn. (sec.-treas. 1968-70), Wyo. Jud. Conf. (sec. 1977-78, chmn. 1979), Wyo. Jud. Council. Office: US Dist Ct O'Mahoney Fed Ctr 2120 Capitol Ave Ste 2242 Cheyenne WY 82001-3666 Office Phone: 307-433-2170. Business E-Mail: wyodudgeabj@wyd.uscourts.gov.

JOHNSON, ALEXANDER CHARLES, lawyer, electrical engineer; b. Richmond, Va., Aug. 1, 1948; BSEE, The Citadel, 1970; MSEE, Purdue U., 1974; JD cum laude, Brigham Young U., 1978. Bar: Oreg. 1978, U.S. Patent and Trademark Office 1979, U.S. Ct. Appeals (8th, 9th and Fed. cirs.) 1984. From assoc. to ptnr. Klarquist, Sparkman, Campbell, Leigh & Whinston, Portland, Oreg., 1978-86; prin. Marger, Johnson, & McCollom, P.C., Portland, 1986—. Author: IP Protection in Semiconductor Industry, 1989. Capt. USAF, 1975, USAFR, 1975-83. Mem. ABA (intellectual property sect.), Am. Intellectual Property Law Assn., Oreg. Bar Assn., Order of Barristers, Tau Beta Pi. Home: 210 SW Morrison St Ste 400 Portland OR 97204-3189

JOHNSON, ARTHUR WILLIAM, JR., retired research scientist; b. Steubenville, Ohio, Jan. 8, 1949; s. Arthur William and Carol (Gilcrest) J. BMus, U. So. Calif., 1973. Lectr. Griffith Obs. and Planetarium, 1969-73; planetarium writer, lectr. Mt. San Antonio Coll. Planetarium, Walnut, Calif., 1970-73; dir. Fleischmann Planetarium U. Nev., Reno, 1973-2001; ret., 2001. Apptd. Nev. state coord. NSTA/NASA Space Sci. Student Involvement Program, 1994. Writer, prodr. films (with Donald G. Potter) Beautiful Nevada, 1978, Riches: The Story of Nevada Mining, 1984. Organist, choirmaster Trinity Episcopal Ch., Reno, 1980—; bd. dirs. Reno Chamber Orch. Assn., 1981-87, 1st v.p., 1984-85. Nev. Humanities Com., Inc. grantee, 1979-83; Chautauqua scholar, 2007. Mem. Am. Guild Organists (dean No. Nev. chpt. 1984-85, 96-99, 2002-05), Assn. Anglican Musicians, Internat. Planetarium Soc., Cinema 360 (treas. 1985-90, pres. 1990-98), Pacific Planetarium Assn. (pres. 1980), Lions (pres. Reno Host Club 1991-92), Large Format Cinema Assn. (v.p. 1996-99), Nev. Opera Assn. (bd. mem. 2008-). Republican. Episcopalian. Office Phone: 775-322-9001. Business E-Mail: arthurj@unr.edu.

JOHNSON, AUSTON GILBERT, III, auditor; m. Mary Bosworth; 3 children. BS, Utah State U., 1976. CPA, Utah. Auditor State of Utah, Salt Lake City, 1996—. Mem. acctg. adv. bd. U. Utah Sch. Acctg., 1993; mem. sch. accountancy adv. coun. Utah State U., 1994—. With USN, 1969-73. Mem. AICPA (Outstanding Discussion Leader 1993), Utah Assn. CPAs (vice-chmn. state and local govt. com. 1987-88). Office: Office Utah State Auditor Utah State Capitol Complex East Office Bldg Ste 310 Salt Lake City UT 84114-2310 E-mail: austonjohnson@utah.gov.

JOHNSON, BRAD, former state official; b. Lake Forest, Ill., Mar. 6, 1952; s. Kenneth A. and Claire Rabe Johnson; m. Lisa Storey. Dist. rep. to Representative Ron Marlenee US Congress, 1983—84; mgr. Gallatin County Fairgrounds, 1985—89; sec. state State of Mont., Helena, 2005—09. Co-chmn. Young Voters for the Pres. (Nixon), Ill., 1972; volunteer John Connally for Pres, Tex., 1980. Mem.: Mont. Rep. Party (exec. bd. 1984—89, 2003—). Republican.*

JOHNSON, BRENDA L., university librarian; MLS, Rutgers U. Reference libr. Rutgers U., 1979, head interlibrary loan svcs. and NJ reference svcs.; libr. U. Mich., Ann Arbor, 1985—, assoc. univ. libr., 1997—2008, interim co-univ. libr., 2006—07; univ. libr. U. Calif., Santa Barbara, 2008—. Office: Library U Calif Santa Barbara CA 93106-9010 Office Phone: 805-893-3256. E-mail: bjohnson@library.ucsb.edu.

JOHNSON, BRUCE EDWARD HUMBLE, lawyer; b. Columbus, Ohio, Jan. 22, 1950; s. Hugo Edward and M. Alice (Humble) J.; children: Marta Noble, Winslow Collins, Russell Scott. AB, Harvard U., 1972; JD, Yale U., 1977; MA, U. Cambridge, Eng., 1978. Bar: Wash. 1977, Calif. 1992. Atty. Davis Wright Tremaine LLP, Seattle, 1977—. Mem. oversight com. King County Gov. Access Channel, 1996—2001. Co-author: Advertising and Commerical Speech, A First Amendment Guide, 2d edit., 2004. Bd. dirs. Seattle Repertory Theatre, 1993—, pres., 1999-2001, chair, 2004-06; bd. dirs. Huntington's Dis. Soc. of Am., N.W. chpt., 2001-06; mem. Nat. Coun. for Am. Theatre, 2005—. Mem. ABA (tort and ins. practice sect., media law and defamation torts com. chair 1999-2000). Office: Davis Wright Tremaine LLP 1201 3d Ave Ste 2200 Seattle WA 98101-3045 Office Phone: 206-628-7683, 206-757-8069. Business E-Mail: brucejohnson@dwt.com.

JOHNSON, CAGE SAUL, hematologist, educator; b. New Orleans, Mar. 31, 1941; s. Cage Spooner and Esther Georgianna (Saul) J.; m. Shirley Lee O'Neal, Feb. 22, 1968; children: Stephanie, Michelle. Student, Creighton U., 1958-61, MD, 1965. Cert. Am. Bd. Internal Medicine, 1972, Am. Bd. Hematology, 1974. Intern U. Cin., 1965-66, resident, 1966-67, U. So. Calif., 1969-71, instr. LA, 1971-74, asst. prof., 1974-80, assoc. prof., 1980-88, dir. Comprehensive Sickle Cell Ctr., 1991—, prof., 1988—. Chmn. adv. com. Calif. Dept. Health Svcs., Sacramento, 1977—; dir. Hemoglobinopathy Lab., L.A., 1976—; bd. dirs. Sicke Cell Self-Help Assn., L.A., 1982-86, Team HEAL, 2002-. Contbr. numerous articles to profl. jours. Dir. Sickle Cell Disease Rsch. Found., L.A., 1986-94; active Nat. Med. Fellowships, Inc., Chgo., 1979—; chmn. rev. com. NIH, Washington, 1986-91; chmn. adv. com., 1995-97, mem. adv. coun., 1997-2002. Major U.S. Army, 1967-69, Vietnam. Fellow N.Y. Acad. Scis., Am. Coll. Angiology; mem. Am. Soc. Hematology, Am. Fedn. Clin. Rsch., Western Soc. Clin. Investigation, Internat. Soc. Biorheology, E.E. Just Soc. (sec.-treas. 1985-93, pres. 1994-95, sec. 1996—). Avocation: restoring antique automobiles. Office: 2025 Zonal Ave Rm R304 Los Angeles CA 90089-0110 Office Phone: 323-442-1259.

JOHNSON, CANDICE ELAINE BROWN, pediatrician, educator; b. Cin., Mar. 21, 1946; d. Paul Preston and Naomi Elizabeth Brown; m. Thomas Raymond Johnson, June 30, 1973; children: Andrea Eleanor, Erik Albert. BS, U. Mich., 1968; PhD Microbiology, Case Western Reserve U., 1973, MD, 1976. Diplomate Am. Bd. Pediat., 1981. Intern, resident in pediat. Rainbow Babies and Children's Hosp./Met. Gen. Hosp., Cleve., 1976-78; fellow in ambulatory pediatrics Met. Gen. Hosp., 1978-79; asst. prof. pediat. Case Western Res. U., Cleve., 1980-90, assoc. prof., 1990-97; prof. pediat. U. Colo., Denver, 1997—; pediatrician Children's Hosp., Denver, 1997—. Mem. rev. panel NIH, Washington, 1993; faculty sen. Case Western Res. U., 1988-91; mem. spkrs. bur. Merck, GlaxoSmithKline, Abbott Labs. Contbr. articles profl. jours. Mem. Am. Acad. Pediat., Pediat. Infectious Disease Soc., Infectious Disease Soc. Am., Soc. for Pediat. Rsch., So. Utah Wilderness Alliance, Sierra Club. Home: 2290 Locust St Denver CO 80207-3943

JOHNSON, CAROL ANN, editor; b. Seattle, Aug. 19, 1941; d. Jack Rutherford and Marian Frances (Cole) Schisler; m. Gary L. Johnson, Sept. 8, 1962; children: Deborah Carol Johnson Erickson, Barbara Ann Johnson Lilland. Grad., Bethany Coll. of Missions, Mpls., 1962. Typesetter Bethany Printing Div., Mpls., 1960-69; librarian Bethany Coll. of Missions, Mpls., 1969-79; editl. dir. Bethany House Pubs., Mpls., 1980-98, v.p. editl., 1998—. Avocations: reading, sewing, tennis, bicycling, cooking, hiking. E-mail: carol.johnson@bethanyhouse.com.

JOHNSON, CHALMERS, educational association administrator, retired political science professor; b. Ariz., 1931; m. Sharon K. Johnson. BA in Economics, U. Calif., Berkeley, MA in Polit. Sci., PhD in Polit. Sci., U. Calif., Berkeley. Prof. polit. sci. U. Calif., Berkeley, 1962—88, U. Calif. San Diego, La Jolla, 1988—92, prof. emeritus; co-founder, pres. Japan Policy Rsch. Inst., San Francisco, 1994—. Author: Peasant Nationalism and Communist Power, Revolutionary Change, MITI and the Japanese Miracle, An Instance of Treason, Blowback: The Costs and Consequences of American Empire, 2000 (Am. Book award, 2001), Sorrows of Empire: Militarism, Secrecy, and the End of the Republic, 2004; chmn. academic adv. com.: (documentaries) The Pacific Century, 1992; contbr. articles to profl. jours. Served with USN, 1953, Korea. Recipient Local Author Lifetime Achievement award, San Diego Pub. Libr., 2004; fellow, Ford Found., Social Sci. Rsch. Coun., Guggenheim Found. Mem.: Am. Acad. Arts and Scis. Office: Japan Policy Rsch Inst Univ San Francisco Ctr the Pacific Rim 2130 Fulton St LM280 San Francisco CA 94117-1080 Business E-Mail: chaljohnson@jpri.org.*

JOHNSON, CHANNING D., lawyer; BA in Econ., Stanford U., 1972; JD, Harvard U., 1975. Bar: Calif. 1978, US. Dist. Ct., Central Dist. Calif. 1978. Ptnr. Akin Gump Strauss Hauer & Feld LLP, LA. Mem. Pasadena Planning Commn., 1982—86, Calif. State Bar Judicial Nominees and Evaluation Commn., 1992—94. Named one of Am. Top Black Lawyers, Black Enterprise Mag., 2003. Mem.: State Bar Calif. (mem. bus. law section). Office: Akin Gump Strauss Hauer & Feld LLP 2029 Century Pk E Ste 2400 Los Angeles CA 90067-3012 Office Phone: 310-229-1075. Business E-Mail: cjohnson@akingump.com.

JOHNSON, CHARLES BARTLETT, corporate financial executive; b. Montclair, NJ, Jan. 6, 1933; s. Rupert Harris and Florence (Endler) J.; m. Ann Demarest Lutes, Mar. 26, 1955; children: Charles E., Holly, Sarah, Gregory, William, Jennifer, Mary (dec.). BA, Yale U., 1954. With R.H. Johnson & Co., NYC, 1954-55; pres. Franklin Distbrs., Inc., 1957-97; chmn. Franklin Resources, Inc., 1969—, CEO, 1969—2004. Bd. dirs. various Franklin and Templeton Mut. Funds; bd. govs. Investment Co. Inst., 1973-88. Trustee Crystal Springs Uplands Sch., 1984-92; bd. dirs. Peninsula Cmty. Found., 1986-96, San Francisco Symphony, 1984-2002; bd. overseers Hoover Instn., 1993—. 1st lt. US Army, 1955—57. Mem. Nat. Assn. Securities Dirs. (bd. govs. 1990-92, 95-96, chmn. 1992), Commonwealth Club of Calif. (bd. dirs. 1995-97). Office: Franklin Resources Inc One Franklin Pkwy San Mateo CA 94403-1906

JOHNSON, CHARLES N., elementary school educator; Tchr., vice prin. Morgan (Utah) Middle Sch.; prin. Clinton (Utah) Elem., 1997-99, Burton Elem., Kaysville, Utah, 1999—. Recipient Tchr. Excellence award Internat. Tech. Edn. Assn., 1992. Office: Burton Elem 827 E 200 S Kaysville UT 84037-2299

JOHNSON, CHARLES WILLIAM, state supreme court justice; b. Tacoma, Mar. 16, 1951; m. Dana Johnson. BA in Economics, U. Wash., 1974; JD, U. Puget Sound, 1976. Bar: Wash. 1977. Former atty. priv. practice; justice Wash. Supreme Ct., 1991—, assoc. chief justice. Adjunct prof. Seattle U. Law Sch., 1977—91; co-chair Wash. State Minority and Justice Commn., Equal Civil Justice Funding Task Force. Mem. bd. dirs. Wash. Assn. Children and Parents; mem. vis. com. U. Wash. Sch. Social Work; bd. visitors Seattle U. Sch. Law; liaison ltd. practice bd., co-chair BJA subcom. on juc. svcs.; mem. Am. Inns of Ct., World Affairs Coun. Pierce County. Mem. Wash. State Bar Assn., Tacoma-Pierce County Bar Assn. (Liberty Bell award young lawyers sect. 1994). Avocations: sailing, downhill skiing, bicycling. Office: Wash State Supreme Ct PO Box 40929 Olympia WA 98504-0929

JOHNSON, CHRISTOPHER D., lawyer; b. Little Rock, 1952; BA magna cum laude, Princeton U., 1974; JD, U. Va., 1977. Bar: Ariz. 1977, registered: US Dist. Ct., Ariz. 1977, US Ct. Appeals (9th cir.) 1978. Ptnr. Squire, Sanders & Dempsey LLP, Phoenix, chmn., Corp. Fin. Practice Group. Contbr. articles to profl. jours.; spkr. in field. Bd. dir. Enterprise Network, Ariz. Tech. Incubator. Mem.: Ariz. Software & Internet Assn., State Bar Ariz. (exec. coun. mem. 1979—95, chmn. Securities Regulation Sect. 1994—95), Order of Coif. Office: Squire Sanders & Dempsey LLP Two Renaissance Sq 40 N Central Ave Ste 2700 Phoenix AZ 85004-4498 Office Phone: 602-528-4046. Office Fax: 602-253-8129. Business E-Mail: cjohnson@ssd.com.

JOHNSON, CONOR DEANE, mechanical engineer; b. Charlottesville, Va., Apr. 20, 1943; s. Randolph Holaday and Louise Anna (Deane) J.; m. Laura Teague Rogers, Dec. 20, 1966; children: William Drake, Catherine Teague. BS in Engring. Mechanics, Va. Poly. Inst., 1965; MS, Clemson U., 1967, PhD in Engring. Mechanics, 1969. Registered profl. engr., Calif. With Anamet Labs., Inc., 1973-82, sr. structural analyst Dayton, Ohio, 1973-75, prin. engr. San Carlos, Calif., 1975-81, v.p., 1981-82; program mgr. Aerospace Structures Info. and Analysis Ctr., 1975-82; co-founder, pres. CSA Engring., Inc., Mountain View, Calif., 1982—. Tech. dir. damping conf., exec. com. N.Am. Conf. on Smart Materials and Structures. Contbr. articles to profl. jours.; patentee in field. Capt. USAF, 1969-73 Mem. AIAA (structural dynamics tech. com.), ASME (adaptive structures tech. com., structures and materials award 1981), N.Am. Smart Structures and Materials Conf. (mem. exec. com., tech. chmn. Damping confs. 1991, 93, 95, 96), Gourmet Cooking Club, Sigma Xi. Methodist. Home: 3408 Beresford Ave Belmont CA 94002-1302 Office: CSA Engring Inc 2565 Leghorn St Mountain View CA 94043-1613 Home Phone: 650-591-1595; Office Phone: 650-210-9000. Business E-Mail: cjohnson@csaengineering.com.

JOHNSON, DARRYL NORMAN, former ambassador; b. Chgo., 1938; m. Kathleen Dessa Forance; 3 children. BA cum laude in English lit., U. Wash., 1960; grad. work in English lit., U. Minn., 1961, Princeton U., 1962. With Boeing Co., Seattle, 1962; vol. Peace Corps, Thailand, 1963—65; US Fgn. Svc. Officer, 1965—2005; ConGen Mumbai, 1966—67; Chinese language training, 1968—69; ConGen Hong Kong, 1969—73; Russian language training, 1973—74; US Embassy Moscow, 1974—77; Dept. of State, Officer-in-Charge Yugoslav Affairs, 1977—79; Officer-in-Charge PRC affairs, 1979—81; Pearson Fellow Office Sen. Clairborne Pell, 1981—82; special asst. Under Sec. Pol. affairs, 1982—84; Counselor for pol. affairs US Embassy Beijing, 1984—87; Dep. Chief of Mission US Embassy Warsaw, 1988—91; US Amb. to Lithuania, 1991—94; Dep. Coord. for asst. to former Soviet Union, 1994—96; Dir. Am. Inst. in Taiwan, 1996—99; pol. adv. to Chief of Naval Ops., 1999—2000; Dep. Asst. Sec. State for East Asian and Pacific Affairs, 2000—01; US Amb. to Thailand, 2001—04; US Charge d'Affairs Philippines, 2005; aux. prof. internat. studies U. of Washington, Seattle, 2005—. Office: U Washington Jackson Sch Internat Studies Seattle WA 98195 Personal E-mail: johnsondarryln@netscape.net.

JOHNSON, DAVID D., lawyer, game company executive; b. Sioux City, Iowa, Aug. 17, 1951; BA in Polit. Sci., U. Nev., 1975; JD, Creighton U., 1978. Chief dep. atty. gen. Gaming Divsn. Nev. Atty. Gen. Office, 1985—87; ptnr. Schreck, Jones, Bernhard, Woloson & Godfrey, 1987—95; sr. v.p., gen. counsel, sec. Alliance Gaming Corp., 1995—2000; gen. counsel Anchor Gaming, 2000—01; ptnr. Bernhard, Bradley & Johnson, Las Vegas, 2001—03; sr. v.p., gen. counsel, sec. Internat. Game Tech., Reno, 2003—. Office: International Game Tech 9295 Prototype Dr Reno NV 89521

JOHNSON, DAVID J., educational association administrator; b. 1946; Pres., CEO Cal Gas Corp., 1984-87; pres., COO, dir. Dillingham Holdings, San Francisco, 1986-88; gen. ptnr. Hellman & Friedman, San Francisco, 1989-91; pres., CEO, chmn. bd. Red Lion Hotels, 1991-96; CEO, chmn. bd. KinderCare Learning Ctrs., Inc., Portland, 1997—. Office: Kindercare Learning Centers Inc 650 NE Holladay St #1400 Portland OR 97232

JOHNSON, DAVID J., JR., lawyer; b. Huntington, NY, 1956; BA, U. Va., 1979, JD, MBA, U. Va., 1985. Bar: Calif. 1985, US Dist. Ct., Ctrl. Dist. Calif. 1985, DC 2006, NY 2006. Ptnr. corp./securities O'Melveny & Myers LLP, LA, co-head capital market group, ptnr. NYC. Office: O'Melveny & Myers LLP Times Square Tower 7 Times Sq New York NY 10036 also: O'Melveny & Myers LLP 1999 Avenue of the Stars Los Angeles CA 90067 Office Phone: 212-326-2000. Office Fax: 212-326-2601. Business E-Mail: djohnson@omm.com.

JOHNSON, DEBORAH LORRAINE, not-for-profit executive, consultant; b. Chgo., Dec. 13, 1952; d. Everett A. Johnson and Marion O. Wilson. PhD, Stanford U., Palo Alto, Calif., 1995. Cons., dir. internat. children's program Feed the Children, Oklahoma City, 2003—06; cons. Dramatic Results, Long Beach, Calif., 2000—06; CEO Give a Child Life, 2007—. Cons. Project STEPS, North Hollywood, Calif., 1999—; cons. early edn. dept. L.A. Unified Sch. Dist.

JOHNSON, DOUGLAS L., lawyer; BA, U. Southern Calif., 1996; JD, U. of Pacific, 2000. Bar: Calif., US Dist. Ct. Ctrl. & Ea. Calif., US Ct. Appeals Ninth Cir. Sr. assoc., entertainment law & bus. litigation Johnson & Rishwain LLP, Beverly Hills, Calif. Named a Rising Star, So. Calif. Super Lawyers, 2006. Mem.: ABA, Assn. Trial Lawyers

Am., Consumer Attorneys Assn. LA. Office: Johnson & Rishwain LLP Ste 200 430 N Canon Dr Beverly Hills CA 90210 Office Phone: 310-975-1080. Office Fax: 310-975-1095. Business E-Mail: djohnson@jrllp.com.

JOHNSON, DWAYNE DOUGLAS (THE ROCK), actor, former professional wrestler; b. Hayward, Calif., May 2, 1972; s. Rocky and Ata Johnson; m. Dany Garcia, May 3, 1997 (div. May 2008); 1 child, Simone Alexandra. BA in criminology & physiology, U. Miami, 1995. Profl. wrestler, 1996—2004. Actor: (films) The Mummy Returns, 2001, The Scorpion King, 2002, The Rundown, 2003, Walking Tall, 2004, Be Cool, 2005, Doom, 2005, Southland Tales, 2006, Gridiron Gang, 2006, The Game Plan, 2007, Get Smart, 2008, Race to Witch Mountain, 2009; wrestler (TV series) WWF Superstars of Wrestling, 1996, WWF Monday Night Raw, 1996—97, Sunday Night Heat, 1998—2004, Raw is War, 1997—2004, WWF Smackdown, 1999—2002, TV appearances include That 70s Show, 1999, The Net, 1999, Star Trek: Voyager, 2000. Achievements include 7 time World Wrestling Fedn. champion. Office: c/o Darren Statt United Talent Agy 9560 Wilshire Blvd #500 Beverly Hills CA 90212

JOHNSON, E. ERIC, insurance company executive; b. Chgo., Feb. 7, 1927; s. Edwin Eric and Xenia Alice (Waisanen) J.; m. Elizabeth Dewar Brass, Sept. 3, 1949; children: Christal L. Johnson Neal, Craig R. BA, Stanford U., 1948. Dir. group annuities Equitable Life Assurance Soc., San Francisco, 1950-54, div. mgr. LA, 1955-59; v.p. Johnson & Higgins of Calif., LA, 1960-67, dir., 1968-87, chmn., 1986-87, TBG Fin., LA, 1988—. Bd. dirs. Am. Mutual Fund; exec. v.p. Johnson & Higgins, N.Y.C., 1984-87, Law Environ. Group, Showscan Corp. Bd. dirs. Sta. KCET, pub. TV, L.A., chmn., 1992-94; mem. adv. bd. UCLA Med. Ctr., chmn. 1995-97; bd. dirs. Jonsson Comprehensive Cancer Ctr., UCLA, Stanford U. Grad Sch. Bus.; trustee Nuclear Decommissioning Trust, Calif. Health Ctr. Found., 2006—, Calif. State Dept. Mental Hygiene, Calif. Coun. for Econ. Edn., William H. Parker Police Found., 1992—. Mem. Calif. Club, L.A. Country Club, Vintage Club, Links Club N.Y.C., Beach Club, So. Calif. Tennis Assn. (v.p.). Avocations: golf, tennis, contemporary art, spectator sports. Office: Mullin TBG 2029 Century Park E Los Angeles CA 90067-2901

JOHNSON, EARL, JR., judge, author; b. Watertown, SD, June 10, 1933; s. Earl Jerome and Doris Melissa (Schwartz) J.; m. Barbara Claire Yanow, Oct. 11, 1970; children: Kelly Ann, Earl Eric, Agaam Yanovitch. BA in Econs., Northwestern U., 1955, LL.M., 1961; JD, U. Chgo., 1960. Bar: Ill. 1960, US Ct. Appeals (9th cir.) 1964, DC 1965, US Supreme Ct. 1966, Calif. 1972. Trial atty., organized crime sect. Dept. Justice, Washington, Miami, Fla. and Las Vegas, Nev., 1961-64; dep. dir. Neighborhood Legal Svc. Project, 1964-65, OEO Legal Svc. Program, 1965-66, dir., 1966-68; vis. scholar Ctr. for Study of Law and Soc. U. Calif., Berkeley, 1968-69; assoc. prof. U. So. Calif. Law Ctr., LA, 1969-75, dir. clin. programs, 1970-73, prof. law, 1976-82, dir. Program Study Dispute Resolution Policy, Social Sci. Rsch. Inst., 1975-82; assoc. justice Calif. Ct. Appeal, 1982—; co-dir. Access to Justice Project European U. Inst., 1975-79. Vis. scholar Inst. Comparative Law, U. Florence, Italy, 1973, 75; Robert H. Jackson lectr. Nat. Jud. Coll., 1980; adv. panel Legal Svc. Corp., 1976-80; legis. impact panel Nat. Acad. Sci., 1977-80; faculty Asian Workshop on Legal Svcs. to Poor, 1974; mem. Internat. Legal Ctr., Legal Svcs. in Developing Countries, 1972-75; founder, bd. mem. Action for Legal Rights, 1971-74; pres., trustee Western Ctr. on Law and Poverty, 1972-73, 76-80; v.p., chmn. exec. com. Calif. Rural Legal Assistance Corp., 1973-74; exec. com. Nat. Sr. Citizens Law Ctr., 1980-82; sec. Nat. Resource Ctr. for Consumers of Legal Svc., 1974-82; chair Nat. Equal Justice Libr. Com., 1989-92; pres., Consortium for Nat. Equal Justice Libr., Inc., 1992-95, bd. dir., 1995—; chair Calif. Access to Justice Working Group, 1993-96; mem. Calif. Commn. on Access to Justice, 1997—2004, co-chmn., 2002-03; spl. advisor Presdl. Commn. on Access to Justice, 2005-06. Author: Justice and Reform: The Formative Years of the Am. Legal Svc. Program, 1974, 2d edit., 1978, Toward Equal Justice: A Comparative Study of Legal Aid in Modern Soc., 1975, Outside the Courts: A Survey of Diversion Alternatives in Civil Cases, 1977, Dispute Processing Strategies, 1978, Dispute Resolution in Am., 1985, Calif. Trial Guide, 8 vols., 1986, Tex. Trial Guide, 6 vols., 1989, NY Trial Guide, 5 vols., 1990, Fla. Civil Trial Guide, 5 vols., 1990, Ill. Civil Trial Guide, 5 vols., 1991, Fed. Trial Guide, 5 vols., 1992, Ind. Civil Trial Guide, 5 vols., 1992, Calif. Family Law Trial Guide, 5 vols., 1992, Pa. Civil Trial Guide, 5 vols., 1992, Mich. Trial Guide, 5 vols., 1993, NC Civil Trial Guide, 5 vols., 1993, Calif. Criminal Trial Guide, 3 vols., 1994, Murder on Appeal (as Holmes Marshall), 2001, The Firenze Faction (as Gideon Black), 2004; editor U. Chgo. Law Rev, 1960; mem. editl. bd. Jour. Law and Social Inquiry, 1987-2001; contbr. articles to books and periodicals. Bd. dir. Beverly Hills Bar Found., 1972-73, Nat. Legal Aid and Defenders Assn., 1987-91; trustee LA Legal Aid Found., 1969-71; mem. LA County Regional Planning Commn., 1980-81; bd. visitors U. San Diego Law Sch., 1983-86. Served with USNR, 1955-58. Recipient Dart award for acad. innovation U. So. Calif., 1971, Loren Miller Legal Svc. award Calif. State Bar, 1977, Appellate Justice of the Yr. award LA Trial Lawyers Assn., 1989, Outstanding Jud. Achievement award Calif. Trial Lawyers Assn., 1991, Legal Svc. Pioneer award LA Legal Aid Found., 1999, Appelate Judge of the Yr. award, Consumer Attorneys of Calif., 2003, Aranda Access to Justice award Calif. Jud. Coun. Judges Assn. Bar Assn., 2004, Beacon of Justice award LA County Law Libr., 2006, Outstanding Jurist award LA County Bar Assn., 2007; named So. Calif. Citizen of Week, 1978; Ford Found. fellow, 1960; Dept. State lectr., 1975; grantee Ford Found., Russell Sage Found., Law Enforcement Assistance Adminstrn., NSF. Fellow Am. Bar Found. (rsch. adv. com. 1996-2001, chair 1999-2002); mem. ABA (com. chmn. 1972-75, spl. com. resolution minor disputes 1976-83, coun. sect. of individual rights and responsibilities 1990-91, consortium on legal svc. and the pub. 1991-94, standing com. on legal aid and indigant defendants 2007-), Calif. Bar Assn., LA Bar Assn. (neighborhood justice ctr. com. 1976-81, Outstanding Jurist award 2007), Law and Soc. Assn., Nat. Legal Aid and Defender's Assn. (bd. dir. 1968-74), Am. Acad. Polit. and Social Sci., Calif. Judges Assn. (appellate cts. com. 1983-87, 98-99, ethics com. 1985-89), Internat. Assn. Procedural Law, Internat. Legal Aid Group, Order of Coif. Democrat. Office: Ct Appeals Calif 2d Appellate Dist 300 S Spring St Los Angeles CA 90013-1230 E-mail: justej@aol.com.

JOHNSON, EARVIN See JOHNSON, MAGIC

JOHNSON, EDWARD ARNOLD, ecologist, educator; b. Long Branch, NJ, Aug. 24, 1943; s. Arnold Alfred and Dorthy (Grunander) J.; m. Susan Jean Bagley (div. 1988); 1 child, Joanne Sonia; m. Kiyoko Miyanishi, 1994. BSc, U. Wis., 1968; MSc, U. N.H., 1972; PhD, U. Sask., 1977. Asst. prof. biol. scis. U. Calgary, Alta., Canada, 1979-87, assoc. prof. biol. scis. Alta., 1987-93, prof. biol. scis. Alta., 1993—, dir. Kananaskis Field Stas. Alta., 1992—2006, G-8 Legancy chair in wildlife ecology Alta., 2003—, dir. biosci. inst., 2007—. Mem. editl. bd. Jour. Vegetation Sci., 1990-97; editor Ecology, 1993-96; assoc. editor Can. Jour. Forest Rsch., 1992-2002; editor-in-chief Ecol. Soc. Am. Bull., 2004—; contbr. articles to profl. jours. Mem. Internat. Assn. for Vegetation Sci. (sec. N.Am. sect. 1988-90), Brit. Ecol. Soc., Ecol. Soc. Am. (William S. Cooper award 1986), Wis. Acad. Sci., Arts and Letters, Sigma Xi. Achievements include research on plant population dynamics, on forest fire behavior and ecological effects, on ecological mechanics, aerodynamics and small particle dispersal models and on ecological effects of natural disturbances. Office: U Calgary Dept Biol Scis Calgary AB Canada T2N 1N4 Home Phone: 403-282-4911; Office Phone: 403-220-7635. Business E-Mail: johnsone@ucalgary.ca.

JOHNSON, ERIC B., police chief; b. Feb. 1967; 4 children. Patrol officer Santa Fe Police Dept., 1987—92, detective, 1992—2001, sergeant Spl. Investigations Sect., 2001—03, dep. police chief, 2003—06, police chief, 2006—. Office: Chief of Police City of Santa Fe PO Box 909 Santa Fe NM 87504-0909 Office Phone: 505-955-5010. Office Fax: 505-955-5052. E-mail: ebjohnson@ci.santa-fenm.gov.

JOHNSON, GARY EARL, former governor; b. Minot, ND, Jan. 1, 1953; s. Earl W. and Lorraine B. (Bostow) Johnson; m. Dee Simms, Nov. 27, 1976 (dec. Dec. 22, 2006); children: Sean, Erik. BA in Polit. Sch., U. N.Mex., 1975. Pres., CEO Big J Enterprises, Albuquerque, 1976—94; gov. State of N.Mex., 1995—2003. Bd. dirs. Entrepreneurship Studies at U. N.Mex., 1993-95, Students for Sensible Drug Policy. Named to list of Big 50 Remodelers in the USA, 1987; named Entrepreneur of Yr., 1995. Mem. LWV, C. of C. Albuquerque (bd. dirs. 1993-95). Republican. Lutheran. Achievements include Mt. Everest summit, 2003. Avocations: rock-climbing, mountain climbing, skiing, flying, triathlete.

JOHNSON, GORDON JAMES, performing company executive, conductor; b. St. Paul, 1949; BS, Bemidji State U., 1971; MS, Northwestern U., 1977; D in Mus. Arts, U. Oreg.; studied with Leonard Bernstein, Erich Leinsdorf, Herbert Blomstedt. Music dir., condr. Great Falls (Mont.) Symphony Assn., 1981—, Glacier Orch. and Chorale, Mont., 1982-97; artistic dir., condr. Flathead Music Festival, Mont., 1987-96; music dir., condr. Mesa (Ariz.) Symphony Orch., 1997—2005. Grad. tchg. fellow U. Oreg, 1979—81; artist in residence Condr's Guild Inst., W.Va. U., 1984; condr. Spokane Symphony at The Festival at Sandpoint; guest condr. St. Paul Chamber Orch., 1971, Spokane Symphony, 1983, 86, Dubuque Symphony, Iowa, 1985, Charlotte Symphony, NC, 1985, Lethbridge Symphony, Alberta, Canada, 1986, Cheyenne Symphony, Wyo., 1986, West Shore Symphony, Mich., 1988, Bozeman Symphony, Mont., 1989, Kumamoto Symphony, Kyshu, Japan, 1991, Kankakee Symphony, Ill., 1993, Toulon Symphonies, France, 1994, Guam Symphony, 1995, Tokyo Lumiere Orch., 1995, Fort Collins Symphony, Colo., 1995, Wilmslow Symphony Orch., England, 1997; guest ballet condr. Alberta Ballet, 1986, Oakland Ballet, Calif., 1988, Eugene Ballet, Oreg., 1993, David Taylor Ballet, Colo., Colo., 1994, St. Petersburg Ballet, Russia, 1995, Western Ballet Theater, Oreg., 1996; spkr. regional conf. Am. Symphony Orch. League, 1987, spkr. nat. conf., 88; mem. adj. faculty U. Great Falls, 1981—, U. Mont., 1996—; lectr. U. Guam, 1995; condr. seminars L.A. Philharmonic Inst., 1983, Condr.'s Guild Inst., 1984, Festival at Sandpoint, Condr.'s Program, 1986, Am. Symphony Orch. League's Am. Condr.'s Program, N.Y. Philharmonic, 1987, Condr.'s Guild "Bruckner Seminar", Chgo. Symphony Orch., 1989, Carnegie Hall Tng. Program for Condrs., Cleve. Orch., 1993. Named to Highland Park High Sch. Hall of Fame, St. Paul, 1997; Philharmonic Condr.'s scholar St. Paul Chamber Orch., 1971, L.A. Philharmonic Inst. fellow, 1983. Mem.: ASCAP. Office: Great Falls Symphony Assn PO Box 1078 Great Falls MT 59403-1078 Office Phone: 406-453-4102. E-mail: gordon@gfsymphony.org.

JOHNSON, GREGORY EUGENE, diversified financial services company executive; b. Orange, NJ, June 28, 1961; BBA, Washington and Lee U., 1983. CPA. Sr. acct. Coopers & Lybrand, 1983—86; with Franklin Resources Inc., San Mateo, Calif., 1986—, co-pres., 1999—2003, pres., co-CEO, 2003—04, pres., CEO, 2005—. Bd. dirs. Franklin Resources Inc., 2007—. Office: Franklin Resources Inc 1 Franklin Pky Bldg 970 1st Fl San Mateo CA 94403*

JOHNSON, JAMES ARNOLD, venture capitalist; b. Detroit, June 15, 1939; s. Waylon Z. and Elsie Jean (Peuser) J.; 1 child, Stephanie Louise. BA, Stanford U., 1961; MBA, U. Chgo., 1968. CPA, Calif. Asst. cashier internat. banking First Nat. Bank of Chgo., 1965-68; ptnr.-in-charge mgmt. cons. Peat, Marwick, Mitchell & Co., Honolulu, 1968-79, ptnr.-in-charge small bsu. svcs., 1977-80; pres. Johnson Internat., Inc., Incline Village, Nev., 1980—, BioEngring. Applications, Inc., Honolulu, 1981-90; gen. ptnr. numerous investment partnerships; CFO TransData Internat., Inc., 1995-2000, Ad Express Can. Inc., 1996-99; pres., CFO Board Vantage, Inc., 2001—03. Served to lt. USNR, 1962-65. Mem. AICPA, Calif. Soc. CPAs, Home: 685 Wilson Way Incline Village NV 89451-8832 Office: PO Box 5131 Incline Village NV 89450-5131 E-mail: tahoejj@aol.com.

JOHNSON, JAMES MARTIN, state supreme court justice, lawyer; b. Seattle; married; 2 children. BA in Economics, Harvard U., 1967; JD, U. Wash., 1970. Bar: Wash. 1970, U.S. Supreme Ct., Wash. Supreme Ct., Fed. Ct. of Appeals Eighth Circuit, Fed. Ct. of Appeals Ninth Circuit, Fed. Ct. of Appeals D.C. Circuit. Counsel Wash. Legislative Joint Com. on Banking Insurance & Transportation, 1970—71; chief atty. for fisheries/game div. Wash. State, 1973—83; chief special litigation div., sr. asst. atty. gen. fish & wildlife div. Wash. Atty. Gen. Office, 1983—93; atty. priv. practice, 1993—2004; justice Wash. Supreme Ct., 2005—. Lt., chief administrative services Ninth Infantry Div. US Army, 1971—73. Avocations: scuba diving, sailing, fishing, hunting, opera. Office: Wash Supreme Ct 415 12th Ave SW PO Box 40929 Olympia WA 98504-0929

JOHNSON, JEFFREY M., private equity company executive, former publishing executive; b. July 23, 1959; married; 3 children. BS in Accountancy, U. Ill.; M in Ops. Mgmt., U. Chgo. With KPMG Peat Marwick, 1981—84; mem. corp. office staff The Tribune Co., Chgo., 1984—86; various ops. positions Chgo. Tribune, 1986—92; v.p., dir. ops. Orlando Sentinel, 1992—98; exec. v.p., gen. mgr. & COO Landoll Inc., 1998—2000, pres., CEO, 2000; sr. v.p., gen. mgr. L.A. Times, 2000—05, exec. v.p., gen. mgr., 2005, pub., pres., CEO, 2005—06; prin. current media interests Yucaipa Cos. LLC, 2007—. Bd. dirs. YMCA of Met. LA, United Way of Greater LA, Orange County Performing Arts Ctr. Co-recipient Tribune Mgmt. Award, 1992. Office: Yucaipa Cos LLC 9130 W Sunset Blvd Los Angeles CA 90069 Office Phone: 310-789-7200. Office Fax: 310-228-2873.

JOHNSON, JOHN MALCOLM, JR., reporter; b. Calif., July 1, 1947; s. John Malcolm and Nadine Johnson; m. Peggy Ann Hinton, May 19, 1973; 1 child, Dylan Kenneth. Degree, Whittier Coll., 1967, U. Calif., Riverside, Calif., 1970. Reporter Ventura (Calif.) Star Free Press, 1975—78, Fresno (Calif.) Bee, 1978—81, Sacramento (Calif.) Bee, 1981—82, McClatchy News, Washington, 1982—88; sci. reporter LA (Calif.) Times, 1988—. Author (with Ronald Soble): Blood Brothers, 1994. Mem.: PEN USA. Office: Sci and Medicine Dept Los Angeles Times 202 W 1st St Los Angeles CA 90012 E-mail: john.johnson@latimes.com.

JOHNSON, JOHN PHILIP, geneticist, researcher; b. Wabash, Ind., June 6, 1949; s. Melvin Leroy and Cleo Pauline (Aldrich) J.; m. Sheryl Kay Kennedy, June 3, 1978; children: Craig Eric, Lindsay Sara. BS, U. Mich., 1971, MD, 1975. Diplomate Am. Bd. Pediatrics, Am. Bd. Med. Genetics. Intern, 2d-yr. resident Children's Hosp. Los Angeles, 1975-77; 3d yr. resident in pediatrics U. Utah, Salt Lake City, 1977-78, fellow in genetics, 1980-82, asst. prof. pediatrics, 1982-85; pediatrician Family Health Program, Salt Lake City, 1978-80; assoc. dir. med. genetics, attending/active staff physician Children's Hosp. Oakland, Calif., 1985-92; dir. med. genetics, attending/active staff physician Children's Hosp., Oakland, 1992-94; dir. med. genetics Shodair Children's Hosp., Helena, Mont., 1994—, active mem. staff, 1994—. Clinic physician Utah State Tng. Sch., American Fork, 1982-85; attending and staff physician Primary Children's Med. Ctr., Salt Lake City, 1978-80; pres., bd. dirs. Mtn. States Genetics Found., 2001-07, Principle Investigator Mountain States Regional Collaborative Ctr., 2004-. Assoc. editor Am. Jour. Med. Genetics, 1995-97; contbr. articles to med. jours. Mem. govs. adv. bd. Fetal Alcohol Spectrum Disorder, 2001—; bd. mem. Parents Let's Unite for Kids, Helena, Mont. Recipient William J. Branstrom award U. Mich., 1967. Fellow Am. Acad. Pediatrics; mem. Am. Soc. Human Genetics Avocations: skiing, hiking, camping, piano, jazz. Office: Shodair Childrens Hosp PO Box 5539 Helena MT 59604-5539 Home: 700 Saddle dr Helena MT 59601-5625 Office Phone: 406-444-7530. Business E-Mail: jjohnson@shodair.org.

JOHNSON, JON L., advertising executive; Chmn., CEO, dir. Publicis, Salt Lake City. Home: 10 W Broadway Ste 500 Salt Lake City UT 84101-2099

JOHNSON, JONATHAN EDWIN, II, lawyer; b. Whittier, Calif., May 1, 1936; s. Roger Edwin and Louise (Thompson) J.; m. Clare Hardy, June 23, 1963 (dec. 1995); children: Jonathan III, Hardy, Benjamin, Adam, Rufus, Bradford, Roger, Ralph; m. Garnet Kalsched, June 17, 2000. BChemE, Cornell U., 1959, MBA, 1960; JD with honors, George Washington U., 1963. Bar: Calif. 1964; cert. specialist family law, Calif. Assoc. Tuttle & Taylor, LA., 1963-65; pvt. practice LA, 1965-67; ptnr. Johnson & Jarvis, LA, 1967-68, Johnson, Poulson & Coons, LA, 1968—. Instr. paralegal probate U. West L.A. Sch. Law, 1974; mem. clergy adv. com. to supt. edn., City of L.A., 1978-81. Named Outstanding Lawyer, J. Reuben Clark Law Soc.-L.A. Chpt., 2000, a So. Calif. Super Lawyer(Family Law), 2004—09. Fellow Am. Acad. Matrimonial Lawyers (counsel So. Calif. chpt. 1998-99); mem. Calif. State Bar Assn. (legis. com. family law sect. 1978-88, chmn. 1980), Beverly Hills Bar Assn. (exec. com. family law sect. 1977-82, 86-88, 91—, chmn. 2003-2004), Inter-stake Bus. and Profl. Assn. L.A. (pres. 1974), Cornell Club of So. Calif. (pres. 1966-68), Order of Coif, Sigma Chi, Phi Delta Phi. Mem. Lds Ch. Home: 1094 Acanto Pl Los Angeles CA 90049-1604 Office: Johnson Poulson & Coons 1900 Avenue of the Stars Ste 1900 Los Angeles CA 90067 Office Phone: 310-475-0611.

JOHNSON, KENNETH BJORN, botanist, plant pathologist, educator; BS in Plant Health Tech. with high distinction, U. Minn., 1979, PhD in Plant Pathology, 1986; MS in Plant Pathology, Oreg. State U., 1986. Extension intern Plant Disease Clinic dept. plant pathology U. Minn., St. Paul, 1979, lab., field rsch. asst. dept. plant pathology, 1979-80, grad. rsch. asst. dept. plant pathology, 1983-86, rsch. assoc. dept. plant pathology, 1986-88, lectr. dept. plant pathology, 1987-88; grad. rsch. asst. dept. botany and plant pathology Oreg. State U., Corvallis, 1980-83, asst. prof. dept. botany and plant pathology, 1988-93, assoc. prof., 1993—, instr. plant disease mgmt., 1992, 96. Mem. Am. Phytopathol. Soc. (disease losses com. 1988-92, chair 1990-91, epidemiology com. 1988-93, chair 1991-92, adhoc com. plant pathology 2000: directions for plant pathology in the next century, 1993, Ciba Geigy award 1996), Internat. Soc. for Plant Pathology (epidemiology com. 1989-94, chair epidemiology symposium 1998 congress), Phi Kappa Phi, Gamma Sigma Delta, Sigma Xi. Office: Oreg State U Dept Botany & Plant Pathol 2082 Cordley Hall Corvallis OR 97331-8530

JOHNSON, KENNETH F., lawyer; b. Ft. Bragg, Calif., June 10, 1938; s. Frank W. and Gertrude Johnson; m. Jane Perry Drennan, June 11, 1961; children: Erik, Mark. BSCE, U. Calif., Berkeley, 1962; JD, U. Calif., Hastings, 1969. Bar: Calif. 1970. Atty. Crosby Heafey Roach & May PC, Oakland, Calif., 1969—2003; of counsel Reed-Smith LLP, Oakland, 2003—. Note and comment editor: Hastings Law Jour., 1968-69. Officer USNR, 1962—66. Scholar U. Calif. Hastings, 1967-68, 68-69. Mem. Calif. Bar Assn., Alameda County Bar Assn., Contra Costa County Bar Assn., Bar Assn. San Francisco, Assn. Bus. Trial Lawyers Assn., Order of Coif. Office: Reed Smith LLP 1999 Harrison St Fl 24 Oakland CA 94612-3520 Office Phone: 510-466-6724.

JOHNSON, KEVIN, information technology executive, former computer software company executive; married; 2 children. BBA, N.Mex. State U. Software developer, systems programmer petroleum and fin. services industries, 1981; with systems integration and consulting bus. units IBM Corp., 1986—92; gen. mgr., enterprise services Microsoft Corp., Redmond, Wash., 1992, v.p., product support svcs., mem. sr. leadership team and bus. leadership team, sr. v.p., Microsoft Americas, group v.p., worldwide sales, 2003—05, co-pres., platforms products & svcs. divsn., 2005—07, pres., platforms & services divsn., 2007—08; CEO Juniper Networks, Inc., Sunnyvale, Calif., 2008—. Founding mem. bd. dirs. NPower; bd. advisor, Western region Catalyst. Avocations: running, skiing, golf, roadie for son's rock 'n' roll band. Office: Juniper Networks Inc 1194 N Mathilda Ave Sunnyvale CA 94089

JOHNSON, KEVIN MAURICE, Mayor, Sacramento, retired professional basketball player; b. Sacramento, Calif., Mar. 4, 1966; BA in Polit. Sci., U. Calif., 1987; grad., Harvard Divinity Sch. Summer

Leadership Inst., 2000. Guard Cleve. Cavaliers, 1987—88, Phoenix Suns, 1988—98, 2000; ret., 2000; studio commentator The NBA on NBC, 2000—01; pres., CEO The Kevin Johnson Corp.; mayor City of Sacramento, Calif., 2009—. Mem. Dream Team II, 1994; bd. dirs. LISC Nat., Calif. Charter Sch. Assn., U. Calif. Berkeley Found.; nat. adv. coun. Inst. Govtl. Studies; adv. bd. summer leadership inst. Harvard Divinity Sch. Founder, CEO St. HOPE, 1989—2008, St. HOPE Pub. Schs. Recipient Gold Medal, FIBA World Championship, 1994, John Wooden Lifetime Achievement award, 411th Point of Light, Pres. George Bush, J. Walter Kennedy Citizenship award, NBA, Good Morning Am. award, Sports Illustrated, Most Caring American award, Caring Inst.; named NBA Most Improved Player, 1989; named one of 15 Greatest Men on Earth, McCall's Mag.; named to All-NBA 2d team, 1989—91, 1994, NBA All Star Team, 1990, 1991, 1994, All-NBA 3d team, 1992, World Sports Humanitarian Hall of Fame, Pac-10 Hall of Fame. Democrat. Office: New City Hall 5th Fl Mail Code 09100 915 I St Sacramento CA 95814 Office Phone: 916-808-5300. Office Fax: 916-264-7680. E-mail: KJohnson@cityofsacramento.org.*

JOHNSON, LAWRENCE M., retired bank executive; b. 1940; Student, U. Hawaii. With Bank of Hawaii, Honolulu, 1963-2000, exec. v.p., 1980-84, vice chmn., 1984-89, pres., 1989-2000, now chmn. bd., CEO, until 2000, ret., 2000. Address: Ste # 230 130 Merchant St Honolulu HI 96813 Office Phone: 808-537-8200.

JOHNSON, LAYMON, JR., management analyst; b. Jackson, Miss., Sept. 1, 1948; s. Laymon and Bertha (Yarbrough) Johnson; m. Charlene J. Johnson, Nov. 13, 1982. B in Tech., U. Dayton, 1970; MS in Sys. Mgmt., U. So. Calif., 1978. Mem. tech. staff Rockwell Internat., Canoga Park, Calif., 1975-77; sr. dynamics engr. Gen. Dynamics, Pomona, Calif., 1978-83; fin. sys. specialist Northrop Corp., Pico Rivera, Calif., 1983-90; utility budget analyst dept. water and power City of LA, 1991—97; mgmt. analyst LA Police Dept., 1997—. Lt. comdr. USNR, 1970—92. Mem.: Internat. Assn. Crime Analysts, Inst. Safety and Sys. Mgmt. Triumvirate, Internat. Assn. Law Enforcement Intelligence Analysts, Vietnam Vets. Am., Los Angeles County Mus. Art, Am. Philatelic Soc., Trojan Club, Am. Legion, Tau Alpha Pi. Roman Catholic.

JOHNSON, LIANE, political organization administrator; b. Browning, Mont. m. Jerry Johnson. Attended, Blackfeet CC, Mont. State U.-No. (formerly No. Mont. Coll.). Owner Liane Johnson Farms; chmn. Mont. Rep. Party, 2008—. With Women Involved in Farm Econs., Montana Cattlewomen; bd. dirs. Glacier Cmty. Healthcare Ctr. Republican. Office: Mont Rep Party PO Box 848 Cut Bank MT 59427 E-mail: lsjohnson1958@gmail.com.*

JOHNSON, LINDA SUE, academic administrator, state agency administrator, state legislator; b. Ft. Worth, Dec. 4, 1950; d. William Jr. and Helen Adelene (Loya) McCormick; m. Jerry Eugene Johnson, May 24, 1974 (div. 1984); children: Jeremy Scott, Nicholas Adam, Jennifer Leigh. BA in Biology, U. Tex., 1972; ADN, Shoreline C.C., Seattle, 1986; M in Healthcare Adminstrn., U. Wash., 1988. RN, Washington. Physician's asst. Children's Med. Ctr., Austin, Tex., 1973; collections corr. Sears Roebuck & Co., Seattle, 1973-77; nurse Northwest Hosp., Seattle, 1985-88; intern Univ. Hosp., Seattle, 1987-88; clin. mgr. ops. Evergreen Urgent Care Ctr., Woodinville, Wash., 1988-90; dir. med. staff Evergreen Hosp. Med. Ctr., Kirkland, Wash., 1990-94; mem. Wash. Ho. Reps., Olympia, 1993-95; immunization program mgr. Wash. Dept. Health, Olympia, 1995—98; dir. prof. svs. Ctrl. Oreg. Dist. Hosp., 1998—2000; assoc. provost Cascades campus Oreg. State U., 2000—03. Trustee, pres. Trustees Assn. Tech. and Community Colls., Olympia, 1990-92; trustee Shoreline C.C., 1987-92; active PTA. Mem. Am. Coll. Healthcare Execs., Wash. State Nurses Assn. (legis. com. 1991-93). Democrat.

JOHNSON, MAGIC (EARVIN JOHNSON JR.), professional sports team and development company executive, retired professional basketball player; b. Lansing, Mich., Aug. 14, 1959; s. Earvin and Christine Johnson; m. Earleatha "Cookie" Kelly, Sept. 1991; children: Earvin III, Elisa; 1 child, Andre. Student, Mich. State U., 1976-79. Guard LA Lakers, 1979—91, 1996, head coach, 1994, v.p., co-owner, 1994—; sportscaster NBC-TV, 1993-94; chmn., CEO Johnson Devel. Corp., 1993—; chmn. Magic Johnson Entertainment, Magic Johnson Productions & Magic Johnson Enterprises, 1997—; studio analyst Turner Sports, 2001—08; co-chmn. exec. steering com. for diversity NASCAR, 2004—; studio analyst ESPN, ABC Sports, 2008—. Author: (autobiography) Magic, 1983, What You Can Do to Avoid AIDS, 1992, 32 Ways to Be a Champion in Business, 2008; co-author: (with Roy S. Johnson) Magic's Touch, 1989, (with William Novack) My Life, 1992 Founder, Magic Johnson Found., 1991- Recipient All-Around Contributions to Team Success award, IBM, 1984, Schick Pivotal Player award, 1984, J. Walter Kennedy Citizenship award, NBA, 1992, AdColor award, 2008; named Most Outstanding Player, NCAA Divsn. I Tournament, 1979, NBA Finals MVP, 1980, 1982, 1987, NBA MVP, 1987, 1989, 1990, NBA All-Star Game MVP, 1990, 1992, Player of Yr., Sporting News, 1987; named one of The 50 Greatest Players in NBA History, 1996, The Most Influential Black Americans, Ebony mag., 2006, The Most Influential People in the World of Sports, Bus. Week, 2007, 2008; named to All-NBA first team, 1983—91, All-NBA Second Team, 1982, NBA All-Rookie Team, 1980, NBA All-Star Team, 1980, 1982—92, Mich. State U. Athletics Hall of Fame, 1992, Naismith Meml. Basketball Hall of Fame, 2002, The Power 150, Ebony mag., 2008. Achievements include being mem. of NCAA Championship Team, 1979, NBA Championship Team, 1980, 82, 85, 87, 88, US Olympic Basketball gold medal winning team, 1992; chosen first overall in 1979 NBA Draft; holder of career record for highest assists-per-game avg. (11.2), career playoff record for most assists (2346), NBA Finals single-series record for highest assists-per-game avg. (14.0), 1985, NBA Finals single-series highest assists-per-game avg. by a rookie (8.7), 1980, NBA Finals single-game record for most points by rookie (42), 1980. Office: Johnson Devel Corp & Magic Johnson Found 9100 Wilshire Blvd Beverly Hills CA 90212-3415

JOHNSON, MARK ANDREW, lawyer; b. Plainville, Kans., Feb. 27, 1959; s. Delton Lee and Margaret Ellen (McCracken) J. BA in Chemistry, Reed Coll., 1982; JD, U. Calif., Berkeley, 1987. Bar: Oreg. 1987, U.S. Supreme Ct. 1991. Jud. clk. U.S. Dist. Ct. Oreg., Portland, 1987-88, Oreg. Ct. of Appeals, Salem, 1988-89; assoc. Gevurtz, Menashe, Larson, Kurshner & Yates, PC, Portland, 1989-93; ptnr. Findling & Johnson LLP, Portland, 1993-99; of counsel Bennett Hartman Morris & Kaplan, LLP and predecessor, Portland, 1999—. Mem. ABA, Nat. Lesbian and Gay Law Assn. (co-chmn. 1994-95), Oreg. Gay and Lesbian Law Assn. (co-chair 1990-92), Oreg. State Bar (pres. 1998-99). Office: Mark Johnson 516 SE Morrison St Ste 1200 Portland OR 97214-2390 E-mail: johnsonm@bennetthartman.com.

JOHNSON, MARK BERNARR, preventive medicine physician; b. Addis Ababa, Ethiopia, June 10, 1953; MD, Loma Linda U., 1980. Diplomate Am. Bd. Preventive Medicine. Intern (rotation) White Meml. Med. Ctr., LA, 1980-81; resident in preventive medicine Johns Hopkins U., Balt., 1984-86; clin. assoc. prof. U. Colo. Health Sci. Ctr., 1986—2005. Fellow Am. Coll. Preventive Medicine; mem. AMA, APHA. Office: Jefferson County Dept Health & Environment 1801 19th St Dept Health& Golden CO 80401-1709 Office Phone: 303-271-5700. Personal E-mail: mbjohnsonmd@comcast.net. Business E-Mail: mjohnson@jeffco.us.

JOHNSON, MAURICE VERNER, JR., agricultural research and development executive; b. Duluth, Minn., Sept. 13, 1925; s. Maurice Verner Sr. and Elvira Marie (Westberg) J.; m. Darlene Ruth Durand, June 23, 1944; children: Susan Kay, Steven Dale. BS, U. Calif., 1953. Registered profl. engr. From research engr. to dir. research and devel. Sunkist Growers, Ontario, Calif., 1953-84, v.p. research and devel., 1984-90, ret., 1990—. V.p., dir. Calif. Citrus Quality Council, Claremont. Contbr. articles to profl. pubs.; patentee in field. Sgt. U.S. Army, 1944-46, ETO. Fellow Am. Soc. Agrl. Engrs. (dir. 1969-70); mem. ASME, Am. Inst. Indsl. Engrs., Am. Assn. Advancement Sci., Nat. Soc. Profl. Engrs., Tau Beta Pi. Republican. Avocation: golf.

JOHNSON, MICAH WILLIAM, television newscaster, director; s. William T. and Joann K. (Pierce) J. Student, Indiana U. Pa., 1981-84; AA in Law Enforcement Tech., Rio Solado Coll., 1999. Announcer WLEM-AM/WQKY-FM, Emporium, Pa., 1978-81; news dir., anchorman WIUP-TV, Indiana, Pa., 1981-84; anchorman, reporter WSEE-TV, Erie, Pa., 1984-85; anchorman, mng. editor WVVA-TV, Bluefield, W.Va., 1985-86; news dir., anchorman WKYN-TV, St. Mary's, Pa., 1986-87; anchorman television and radio news Cable News Network, Atlanta, 1987-89; anchorman, corr. NBC-TV News, Washington, 1989-90; sr. producer radio & TV U.S. Senate, Washington, 1990; anchorman, news dir. Sta. KTSM-TV-AM-FM, El Paso, Tex., 1990-93, Sta. WTOV-TV, Steubenville, Ohio, 1993-94; dir. news Sta. WBRE-TV, Wilkes-Barre, Pa., 1994-96; news dir. Sta. WPXI-TV, Pitts., 1996-97; dir. news and prodn. WVIT-TV Paramount Pictures, Hartford, Conn., 1997—; pres., CEO Mediastars Internat., 2001—; v.p. news ops. Meredith Corp., 2001—05; pres. Washington News Network, 2005—. Talk show host Sta. KTSM Newsradio, El Paso, 1990-93; adj. prof. Dekalb Coll., Clarkston, Ga., 1987-89; guest lectr. Ariz. State U., 2000—; bd. dirs. Conn. Assoc. Press. Vol. fireman Morris Twp. Fire Co., Morrisdale, Pa., 1980—, Erie Emergency Med. Svcs., 1984-85; dir. choir Morrisdale United Meth. Ch., 1982-87; bd. dirs. El Paso Humane Soc., El Paso Zool. Soc.; mem. adv. bd. Salvation Army. With Pa. N.G., 1981—. ROTC Pa. Army Nat. Guard. Recipient Presdl. Citation for Cmty. Svc., 1992, Best of the Best award/Cmty. Svc. Nat. Assn. Broadcasters, 1992, AP award, 1985, 86, 87, 90, 91, 92, 93, 94, 95, 96, 97, 98, Nat. Pianist award Am. Coll. Musicians, 1973-79, Ind. U. Disting. Alumni award, 1990, Gold medal award Internat. Radio Festival N.Y, 1990, Gavel award State Bar of Tex., 1992, Tex. Gov.'s award/Cmty. Svc., 1992, Outstanding Contbn. to Law Enforcement award combined law enforcement assns. of Tex., 1991-92, Spl. Recognition award U.S. Marshal's Svc., 1992, Pub. Safety award Pa. Gov., 1996; nominee Emmy award for Best Newscast, 1994, 95, 96, 97, 2004 nominee Emmy award for Outstanding News Operation, 2004; recipient Emmy award for Best Newscast, 1997. Mem. NATAS (bd. govs.), Nat. Press Club, Radio-TV News Dirs. Assn. (Overall Excellence in News award), Conn. Assoc. Press Bd. Dirs. (v.p.), Nat. Radio Broadcasters Assn., El Paso Police Officers Assn. (hon.), White House Corrs. Assn., Radio/TV Galleries, US Senate, House Reps., Nat. Wildlife Fedn. (bd. dirs. Ind. U. mag.), El Paso Humane Soc. (bd. dirs.), El Paso Zool Soc. (bd. dirs.) Nat. Press Club, Frat. Order Police, El Paso Downtown Lions Club, Masons. Methodist. Avocations: fishing, travel, piano, shark diving. Office: Entegy Group Exec Office Cir 7418 E Helm Dr Ste 220 Scottsdale AZ 85260 Office Phone: 602-999-8838. Business E-Mail: ceo@mediastars.tv.

JOHNSON, MICHAEL, councilman; With Phoenix Police Dept., 1974—95, ret. homicide investigator, former cmty. liaison; pres. & CEO Nkoski Inc.; councilman, Dist. 8 Phoenix City Coun., 2002—. Chmn. Downtown & Aviation City Coun. Com.; mem. Econ., Commerce & Sustainability, Pub. Safety, Veterans, Census Coms. Mem. South Mountain Village Planning Com., Rio Salado Adv. Com., Ariz. Super Bowl Com., 2008, City of Phoenix Fin. Com., Downtown Phoenix Partnership, Regional Pub. Transp. Authority Fin. Com., Ariz. Fiesta Bowl Com., Phoenix Globe Trade Initiative Com., Gov. African Am. Adv. Coun., Ariz. Atty. Gen. African Am. Adv. Bd.; treas. Regional Pub. Transp. Authority Bd.; bd. dirs. Young Arts Ariz., Phoenix Symphony. Recipient Pres. award, Nat. Coun. Negro Women, Inc., Visitor Industry Champion award, Greater Phoenix Conv. & Visitors Bur., Dreamer award, Downtown Phoenix Partnership, Achievement award, Ariz. Black Law Enforcement Employees, Cmty. Commitment award, Make A Difference Found., Cmty. award, Phoenix Met. Alumnae Chpt. Delta Sigma Theta Sorority, Rev. Leon H. Sullivan Exemplary Alumni award, Ariz. OIC, Polit. Achievement award, 100 Black Men of Phoenix, Inc., Spirit of Commitment award, Ebony House, Cmty. Recognition award, Southwest Prostate Cancer Found., Outstanding Svc. award, Peace Fest, Appreciation award, US Indian Am. C. of C., Achievement award, South Phoenix Rising Neighborhood Assn., Appreciation award, Phoenix Job Corps, Chinese Sch. Chinese Evang. Free Ch., Phoenix Sister Cities, Positive Image award, Mahogany Page Mag., Cert. Spl. Congl. Recognition, Congressman Bob Filner; named Detective of Yr., 1992. Mem.: Women in Mcpl. Govt., Phoenix Law Enforcement Assn., Nat. Forum Black Pub. Adminstrs. (gen. mgr., Nat. Leadership award), Nat. Black Caucus Local Elected Officials (2nd v.p.), Nat. Black Police Assn. (gen. mgr.), Nat. League Cities (bd. dirs., Human Devel. Policy Com., First Tier Suburbs Coun., Immigration Task Force), Phoenix OIC, Mentoring African Am. for Leadership, Phoenix Urban League, NAACP (Outstanding Leadership in Politics award), African Am. Strategic Leadership Group (chmn.), William H. Patterson Elks Lodge, Combined Fraternal Org. South Phoenix. Office: 200 W Washington St 11th Fl Phoenix AZ 85003 Office Phone: 602-262-7493. Office Fax: 602-495-0587. Business E-Mail: council.district.8@phoenix.gov.*

JOHNSON, MICHAEL, principal; b. Vail, Colo. s. Paul and Sally Johnson; m. Courtney Johnson, 2004. BA, JD, Yale U.; MEd, Harvard U. Tchr. Teach for America Greenville HS, Miss.; prin. Joan Farley Acad., Denver, 2003; dir. Mapleton Expeditionary Sch. Arts (MESA), Thornton, 2005—. Co-founder New Leaders for New Schs.; edn. advisor Barack Obama Presdl. Campaign, 2008. Author: In the Deep Heart's Core, 2002. Office: Mapleton Expeditionary Sch Arts 8990 York St Thornton CO 80229 Office Phone: 303-853-1270. E-mail: johnstonm@mapleton.us.*

JOHNSON, MIKKEL BORLAUG, physicist; b. Waynesboro, Va., Jan. 2, 1943; s. Wallace A. and Anne D. (Davies) J.; m. Lynne McFadden, June 14, 1966; children: Kara Marit, Krista Lynne. BS, Va. Poly. Inst., 1966; MS, Carnegie Mellon U., 1968, PhD, 1970. Rsch. assoc. Cornell U., Ithaca, NY, 1970-72; staff mem., fellow Los Alamos (N.Mex.) Nat. Lab., 1972—. Vis. prof. SUNY, Stony Brook, 1981-82, Carnegie Mellon U., 1997-98. Editor: Relativistic Dynamics and Quark-Nuclear Physics, 1986, Nuclear and Particle Physics on the Light Cone, 1989, LAMPF Workshop on (Pi,K) Physics, 1991; assoc. editor Nuclear Physics, 1975-97. Lab. fellow Los Alamos Nat. Lab, 1991; recipient Humboldt award for Sr. U.S. Scientist, Humboldt Found., 1986. Fellow Am. Phys. Soc. Home: 118 Piedra Loop Los Alamos NM 87544-3828 Office: Los Alamos Nat Lab P divsn Ms H846 Los Alamos NM 87545-0001 E-mail: mbjohnson@lanl.gov.

JOHNSON, MILDRED I., retired business educator; b. Oakland, Iowa, Feb. 27, 1924; d. Roy McKinley and Erna Emma (Klopping) F.; m. Robert Douglas Johnson, July 14, 1945; children: Douglas Wells, Lynn Anne. BS, Colo. State U., 1965, MS in Bus. Adminstr., 1968. Instr. Colo. State U., Fort Collins, 1967-78, asst. prof., 1979-82, lectr., 1983-85, asst. prof. emeritus, 1985. Cons. numerous firms and orgns. including Bell Telephone Labs., Murray Hill, NJ, 1983-85, Houghton Mifflin Co., Allyn and Bacon, Scott Foresman and Co., Boston, 1985, We. Temporary Svcs., Ft. Collins, 1982, Colo. Pub. Health Assn., Denver, 1983, Poudre R-1 Schs., Ft. Collins, 1983-84, Colo. Vocat. Edn. Assn., Denver, 1977, Colo. Civil Svc. Assn., Ft. Collins C. of C. Co-producer: (videotape) Computer Text Analysis, 1983, (film) Administrative Office Mng. and Bus. Tech. Edn., 1980; co-author: Business Report Computer Manual, 1983; contbr. articles to profl. jours.; speaker in field. Vol. Salvation Army, Ft. Collins, 1981-86, Girl Scouts U.S.A., Arvada, Colo., 1961, 4-H Clubs, Ft. Collins, 1965, March of Dimes, Denver, Boy Scouts Am., Denver, 1957-60, ARC, Denver, 1951, Am. Cancer Soc., Ft. Collins; bd. dirs. 1st Presbyn. Ch. Found., Ft. Collins, 1990-97, v.p., 1992-93, pres., 1993-95; pres. Kimberling Charitable Trust, 1993-2005; bd. dirs., com. chmn. Ft. Collins Audubon Soc., 1982-85; com. mem. United Way, Ft. Collins, 1977-84; rec. sec. Ft. Collins Symphony Guild, 1988-89, 2d v.p., bd. dirs., 1989-93, 1st v.p., 1994-96, pres. 1996-98; trustee Ft. Collins Symphony Assn., 1992-96, bd. dirs., 1993-96; patron Ft. Collins Symphony, 1979-80, 2006, 2007, Lincoln Ctr. Performing Arts, 1979-80, 92, 93, Gardens on Spring Creek 1979, 1992-93, 2005-07, Ft. Collins. Mem. Assn. for Bus. Comms., Colo. State U. Alumni Assn., Colo. State U. Faculty Club (bd. dirs., pres. 1979-83), Quota Internat. Ft. Collins Club (sec. 1981, bd. dirs. 1981-86, cons. 1983-84, dist. 9 sec., treas. 1982), Questers Internat. (pres. 2001, bd. dirs., treas. Ft. Collins club 1991-92), Ft. Collins Breakfast Spkrs. Com. Rotary (chmn. bull. com. 1992-94, chmn. club svc. com., chmn. club commn. com. 1992-95, pres.-elect 1995-96, pres. 1996-97, chmn. and pres. Ft. Collins Breakfast Rotary Charitable Found., 1995-98, Paul Harris fellow), Phi Omega Pi, Beta Epsilon, Delta Pi Epsilon (sec. 1983-85, bd. dirs. 1983-85), Beta Gamma Sigma, Colo. State U., Phi Kappa Phi (historian 1974, treas. 1975, sec. 1976, 77, v.p. 1978, pres.-elect 1979, pres. 1980, bd. dirs. 1974-80, regional v.p. 1983-89, nat. regent 1989-92, nat. found. trustee 1983-92, nat. dir. 1983-92, nat. v.p. Phi Kappa Phi Found. 1986-89, spkr.). Republican. Presbyterian. Home: 1330 Calabasas Ct Fort Collins CO 80525-2886

JOHNSON, NOBLE MARSHALL, research scientist; b. San Francisco, Feb. 23, 1945; BSEE cum laude, U. Calif., Davis, 1967, MSEE, 1970; PhD, Princeton U., 1974. Rsch. staff SRI Internat., Menlo Park, Calif., 1974—76; from rsch. staff to sr. rsch. staff Xerox Palo Alto Rsch. Ctr., Palo Alto, 1976—87, prin. scientist Electronic Materials lab., 1987—; mgr. Optoelectronic Materials and Devices, 1999—. Vis. lectr. Princeton (NJ) U., 1986, U. Erlangen-Nürnberg, Germany, 1988; presenter in field. Co-editor 5 books; contbr. over 330 articles to profl. jours.; patentee in field. Recipient Disting. Sr. U.S. Scientist award Alexander von Humboldt Found., Germany, 1987; Nat. Def. Grad. fellow, Princeton U., 1969-72. Fellow Am. Phys. Soc., IEEE; mem. Sigma Xi. Office: Palo Alto Rsch Ctr Electronic Materials Devices Lab 3333 Coyote Hill Rd Palo Alto CA 94304-1314 Business E-Mail: njohnson@parc.com.

JOHNSON, NOEL LARS, biomedical engineer; b. Palo Alto, Calif., Nov. 11, 1957; s. LeRoy Franklin and Margaret Louise (Lindsley) J.; children: Margaret Elizabeth, Kent Daniel. BSEE, U. Calif., Berkeley, 1979; M of Engring., U. Va., 1982, PhD, 1990. Mgr. R & D Hosp. Products divsn. Abbott Labs., Mountain View, Calif., 1986-99; founder HealtheTech., Inc., 1999—2004; pres., CEO NovaShunt, Inc., Saratoga, Calif., 2004—; CEO NovaShunt, AG, Zurich, 2006—. Contbr. articles to profl. jours. Fellowship NIH 1980-85; rsch. grantee Abbott Labs. 1989. Mem. IEEE, Biomed. Engring. Soc., Delta Chi (founder, 1st pres. chpt. U. Calif. at Berkeley). Achievements include invention of metabolic monitor, patented automated drug delivery system, pharmacokinetic drug infusion, and critical care disposables.

JOHNSON, NORM, state legislator; b. Toppenish, Wash. 5 children. Attended, Wash. State Coll. (U.), Pullman; BA in Edn., Adminstr. credentials, Ctrl. Wash. U., Ellensburg; MA in Counseling & Guidance, Fort Wright Coll. of Holy Names (Heritage U.), Toppenish, Wash. Tchr. & counselor Mabton Sch. Dist.; tchr., counselor & vice prin. Toppenish Jr. High Sch.; prin. Eagle High Sch., Toppenish, Wash.; ret., 1997; former councilman Mabton Town Coun.; former acting mayor City of Mabton; served several years as councilman Toppenish City Coun.; former mayor City of Toppenish; councilman Yakima City Coun., 2005—08; mem. Dist. 14 Wash. House of Reps., 2008—. Formerly with US Army. Republican. Office: 414 John L O'Brien Bldg PO Box 40600 Olympia WA 98504-0600 Office Phone: 360-786-7810. Business E-Mail: johnson.norm@leg.wa.gov.

JOHNSON, PAUL E., astronomer, educator; BS in Physics, Davidson Coll., 1973; MS in Astronomy, U. Wash., 1977, PhD in Astronomy, 1979. NASA-NRC resident rsch. assoc. Jet Propulsion Lab., Pasadena, Calif., 1979-80; sr. rsch. fellow U.K. Infrared Telescope Project Royal Obs., Edinburgh, Scotland, 1980-81; asst. prof. dept. physics and astronomy U. Wyo., Laramie, 1981-86, assoc. prof. dept. physics and astronomy, 1986-93, prof., chair dept. physics and astronomy, 1993—. Prof. invitée U. Paul Sabatier, Toulouse, France, 1994; assoc. dir. rsch. CNRS Obs. Midi-Pyrénées, Toulouse, 1994; dir. Wyo. Infrared Obs., 1999—. Contbr. articles to profl. jours. Grantee NASA, NSF, USAF, U.S. Dept. Edn., 1981—. Achievements include research on detection of individual selected bacteria with a CCD flow cytometer; management of the design and fabrication of CCD cameras using 7 different visible CCDS and 1 infrared CCD; design and fabrication of 2 optical and 2 infrared polarimeters, large-beam mid-infrared photometer, 2 high-throughput visible CCD spectrophotometers. Office: Dept Physics and Astronomy U Wyo Laramie WY 82071-3905 E-mail: pjohnson@uwyo.edu.

JOHNSON, RAMEY KAYES, community health nurse; b. Chgo., Oct. 11, 1946; d. Henry Vincent and Louise (Waskom) Kayes; m. Walter E. Johnson, Aug. 6, 1967; children: Gretchen, Roger, Aniela. Diploma, Presbyn. Hosp., Denver, 1968; BSN, Metro State Coll., Denver, 1989; MSN, U. Colo., 1993. CCNP. Staff nurse, CCU Luth. Med. Ctr., Wheatridge, Colo., homecare/hospice nurse; home care discharge planner Columbia Health Care System; surveyor Colo. Dept. Pub. Health & Environment, 2001—02; mem. Colo. State Ho. of Reps., 2002—. Mem. Health Edn. Environment Com., Agriculture, Livestock, & Natural Resources Com., Health Care Task Force. Scholar, Friends of Nursing. Home: 675 Estes St Lakewood CO 80215-5412

JOHNSON, RANDY (RANDALL DAVID JOHNSON), professional baseball player; b. Walnut Creek, Calif., Sept. 10, 1963; s. Bud and Carol Johnson; m. Lisa Johnson, 1993; children: Sammantha, Tanner, Willow, Alexandria; 1 child, Heather. Attended, U. Southern Calif. Pitcher Montreal Expos, 1988—89, Seattle Mariners, 1990—98, Houston Astros, 1998, Ariz. Diamondbacks, Phoenix, 1999—2004, 2007—08, NY Yankees, 2005—06, San Francisco Giants, 2008—. Recipient Am. League Cy Young award, 1995, Nat. League Cy Young award, 1999—2002, Nat. League Babe Ruth award, 2001; named Pitcher of Yr., Sporting News, 1995, Maj. League World Series Co-MVP, 2001, Sportsman of Yr., Sports Illustrated, 2001; named to Am. League All-Star Team, 1990, 1993—95, 1997, Nat. League All-Star Team, 1999—2002, 2004. Achievements include pitched a no-hitter vs. Detroit Tigers, 1990; becoming the first pitcher since Nolan Ryan to lead the National League in ERA and strikeouts in the same year, 1999; becoming the first pitcher since Mickey Lolich to win three games in the same World Series, 2001; being a member of the World Series Champion Arizona Diamondbacks, 2001; pitching a perfect game vs. Atlanta Braves, 2004; holding the Major League Baseball record for career strikeouts by a left-handed pitcher; being ranked 2nd for career strikeouts. Office: San Francisco Giants AT&T Pk 24 Wilie Mays Plz San Francisco CA 94107*

JOHNSON, REVERDY, lawyer; b. NYC, Aug. 24, 1937; s. Reverdy and Reva (Payne) J.; children: Deborah Ghiselin, Reverdy Payne. AB cum laude, Harvard U., Cambridge, Mass., 1960, LLB, 1963. Bar: Fla. 1963, Calif. 1964, N.Mex. 1997. Assoc. Brobeck, Phleger & Harrison, San Francisco, 1963-66; from assoc. to ptnr. Pettit & Martin, San Francisco, 1966-95; of counsel Steinhart & Falconer LLP, San Francisco, 1995-97, Scheuer Yost & Patterson, Sante Fe, N.Mex., 1996—, Fenwick and West, LLP, Mountain View, Calif., 1999—2003, Office Roverdy Scheuer, Pope Valley, Calif., 2006—. Co-owner Johnson Turnbull Vineyards, Napa Valley, Calif., 1977-93; tech. adv. com., com. open space lands Calif. Joint Legislature, 1968-69, chmn., 1969-70; owner Red Hawk Vineyards, Napa Valley, 2005-. Mem. Napa County Housing Commn., 2007—; bd. dirs. Planning and Conservation League, 1966—72, League to Save Lake Tahoe, 1972—77, Found. for San Francisco's Archtl. Heritage, 1975—84, San Francisco Devel. Found., 1986—96, Santa Fe Shakespeare Co., 2001—03, pres., 2002—03. Mem. Napa Valley Vintners Assn. (bd. dir. 1985-88, v.p. 1987, pres. 1988), Am. Coll. Real Estate Lawyers, Lambda Alpha Soc. Office: Scheuer Yost & Patterson 125 Lincoln Ave Ste 223 Santa Fe NM POBox 145,6027 PopeValley Rd Pope Valley CA 94567 Office Phone: 707-965-3430.

JOHNSON, ROBERT BRUCE, hydrologist; b. 1944; MS, U. Ariz., 1980, BS, 1968. Hydrologist W.S. Gookin & Assocs., Scottsdale, Ariz., 1972-75; hydrologist II City of Tucson, 1975-78, chief hydrologist, 1978-97, lead adminstr., 1997-98, asst. dir., 1998—. Office: City Tucson PO Box 27210 Tucson AZ 85726-7210

JOHNSON, ROBERT D., aerospace transportation executive; m. DeDe Johnson; 3 children. Grad., Miami U., Oxford, Ohio. Pres., mng. dir. GE Aircraft Engines, Singapore, 1983—93; v.p., gen. mgr., mfg. and svcs. AAR Corp., Chicago, 1993—94; v.p., gen. mgr., global repair and overhaul operations AlliedSignal Aerospace, Phoenix, 1994—96, v.p., gen. mgr., aerospace svcs., 1996—97, pres., CEO, mktg., electronic and avionics systems, 1997—99, pres., CEO, mktg., sales, & svcs., 1997—99, pres., CEO, 1999—2001, Honeywell Aerospace, Phoenix, 2001—04, chmn., 2005—. Bd. trustee Embry-Riddle Aeronautical U., 2002, Ariz. State U. Pres. Club; bd. Aviation Safety Alliance, Entrada Software. Bd. dirs. Scottsdale Home Nat. Bank, The Zanesville, Ohio. Mem.: Aerospace Inductries Assn. (exec. com.), Devel. and Flight Safety Edu. Com., U. Ariz. (adv. bd.), Miami U. of Ohio (adv. bd.), Conquistadores Del Cielo.

JOHNSON, RON, computer company executive; b. Minn., 1958; BA in Economics, Stanford U., 1980; MBA, Harvard U., 1984. Buying and inventory mgr. Mervyn (divsn. of Target Corp.), 1980—84; mgmt. exec. positions Target Corp., 1984—2000; sr. v.p. retail ops. Apple Inc. (formerly Apple Computer Inc.), Cupertino, Calif., 2000—. Office: Apple Inc 1 Infinite Loop Cupertino CA 95014 Office Phone: 408-996-1010.*

JOHNSON, ROY RAGNAR, electrical engineer, researcher; b. Chgo., Jan. 23, 1932; s. Ragnar Anders and Ann Viktoria (Lundquist) J.; m. Martha Ann Mattson, June 21, 1963; children: Linnea Marit, Kaisa Ann. BSEE, U. Minn., 1954, MS, 1956, PhD, 1959. Rsch. fellow U. Minn., 1957-59; from rsch. engr. to sr. basic rsch. scientist Boeing Sci. Rsch. Labs., Seattle, 1959-72; prin. scientist KMS Fusion, Inc., Ann Arbor, Mich., 1972-74, dir. fusion expts., 1974-78, tech. dir., 1978-91, dept. head for fusion and plasmas, 1985-88; tech. dir. Innovation Assocs., Inc., Ann Arbor, 1992; Inertial Confinement Fusion classification/records mgr. Lawrence Livermore (Calif.) Nat. Lab., 1992—; scientist Nat. Ignition Facility, 2001—. Vis. lectr. U. Wash., Seattle, 1959-60; vis. scientist Royal Inst. Tech., Stockholm, 1963-64; cons. Dept. Edn., Washington, 1995, 98, 2000, 03, 04, 05. Author: Nonlinear Effects in Plasmas, 1969, Plasma Physics, 1977, Inertial Confinement Fusion, 1992; contbr. articles to profl. jours.; patentee in field. Bd. advisors Rose-Hulman Inst. Tech., 1982-. Decorated chevalier Order of St. George; comdr. Order of Holy Cross of Jerusalem. Fellow: Am. Phys. Soc.; mem.: AIAA, AAAS, IEEE (life), N.Y. Acad. Scis., Nuc. Plasma Scis. Soc. of IEEE (exec. com. 1972—75), Swedish Am. Hist. Soc., Am. Swedish Inst., Swedish Coun. Am., Commonwealth Club Calif., Torpar Riddar Orden, Vasa Order Am. (past chmn. Svea lodge), Gamma Alpha, Eta Kappa Nu. Lutheran. Home: PO Box 166 Livermore CA 94551-0166 Office: Livermore Nat Lab PO Box 808 Livermore CA 94551-0808 Business E-Mail: johnson3@llnl.gov.

JOHNSON, RUPERT HARRIS, JR., diversified financial services company executive; married. BA, Washington and Lee U., 1962. With Franklin Resources, Inc., San Mateo, Calif., 1965—; sr. v.p., asst. sec. Franklin Templeton Distbrs., Inc.; pres. Franklin Advisers, Inc.; exec. v.p., chief investment officer, dir. Franklin Resources, Inc., San Mateo, Calif., vice-chmn. Mem. exec. com., bd. govs. Investment Co. Inst.; trustee Santa Clara U., Washington and Lee U.; chmn. bd. dirs. Franklin Mgmt., Inc.; exec. v.p., sr. investment officer Franklin Trust Co.; dir. various Franklin Templeton funds; portfolio mgr. Franklin DynaTech Fund. With USMC, 1962-65. Named one of Forbes' Richest Americans, 1999—, World's Richest People, Forbes mag., 2001—. Mem. Nat. Assn. Securities Dealers (dist. conduct com.). Office: Franklin Resources Inc One Franklin Pkwy San Mateo CA 94403-1906

JOHNSON, STEPHEN CHARLES, exercise physiology and sport science educator; b. Vancouver, Wash., Sept. 15, 1950; s. Russell Cahrles and Jeanne (Stephens) J.; m. Marianne Griffith, Dec. 27, 1971 (div. 1978); m. Kristine McTavish, June 26, 1994. BS in Biology, U. Utah, 1976, PhD in Exercise Physiology, 1985. Vis. asst. prof. dept. exercise and sport sci. U. Utah, Salt Lake City, 1985-87, asst. prof. dept. exercise and sport sci., 1987-91, assoc. prof., 1991—, adj. assoc. prof. dept. bioengring., 1996—. Adj. assoc. prof. dept. bioengring. U. Utah, 1996—; adj. asst. prof. div. foods and nutrition U. Utah, 1987-98, dir. Human Performance Rsch. Lab., 1987—; dir. physiology U.S. Ski Team, Park City, Utah, 1987-90; dir. sport sci. U.S. Skiing, 1991-97; cons. to Health Rider, Inc., Salt Lake City, 1995—, Vetta Sports, Inc., Park City, 1995-96, Orthopedic Splty. Hosp., Salt Lake City, 1994—, Utah Sports Found., 1988-91; cons. cardiac rehab. Holy Cross Hosp., Salt Lake City, 1985-90; dir. project triad U.S.a. Cycling, 1998—; dir. rsch. and edn. Orthop. Specialty Hosp., 1998—. Author: Coaches Guide to Diet and Weight Control, 1990; contbr. over 100 articles and abstracts to profl. jours. Mem. Utah Gov.'s Coun. on Health and Phys. Fitness, Salt Lake City, 1986-88, chmn. sport medicine, 1988; mem. Mayor's Bicycle Com., Salt Lake City, 1986-89. Grantee Purdue Frederick Co., 1988, U.S. Olympic Com., 1990, 98, HealthRider, Inc., 1994, 95, Nat. Operating Com. on Stds. in Athletic Equipment 1994-95, U.S. Ski Team Found., 1992, 93, 94, others; named U.S. Cycling Fedn. Masters Athlete of Yr., 1989; recipient Outstanding Contbn. to Fitness award Utah Gov. Coun. on Phys. Fitness, 1988. Mem. Am. Coll. Sports Medicine, AAHPERD (chmn. sports medicine S.W. dist.), AAAS, AAUP. Democrat. Avocations: skiing, bicycling, hiking. Office: U Utah Dept Exercise & Sport Sci 230 Hper Salt Lake City UT 84112-1184 Home: 14300 Timber Trl Larkspur CO 80118-6537

JOHNSON, STEPHEN L., lawyer, transportation executive; BA, Calif. State Univ., Sacramento; MBA, JD, Univ. Calif., Berkeley. Assoc. Bogle & Gates, Seattle; legal & mgmt. positions through sr. v.p. & gen. counsel GPA Group plc, 1989—94; legal mgmt. positions through sr. v.p. legal & exec. v.p. corp. America West Holdings Corp., 1995—2003; co-founder, ptnr. Indigo Partners LLC, Phoenix, 2003—09; exec. v.p. corp., gen. counsel US Airways Group Inc., Tempe, Ariz., 2009—. Office: US Airways 111 W Rio Salado Pkwy Tempe AZ 85281*

JOHNSON, STEPHEN PATRICK HOWARD, lawyer; b. Holmfirth, England, Feb. 23, 1957; came to U.S., 1982; s. Herbert Edward Johnson; 1 child, Graham Johnson. BA in genetics, Cambridge U., Eng., 1978, MA (hon.), 1993; solicitors final exam. with honors, Coll. of Law, London, 1980; JD with high honors, Ill. Inst. Tech., 1984. Bar: Ill. 1984, N.Y. 1991, Calif. 2002; solicitor Supreme Ct. Eng. 1982. Solicitor, trainee Bird & Bird, London, 1980-82; assoc. Kirkland & Ellis, Chgo., 1982-88, ptnr., 1988-90, NYC, 1990—2003, ptnr., mem. mgmt. San Francisco, 2003—. Contbr. chpt. to book. Office: Kirkland & Ellis LLP 555 California St San Francisco CA 94104 Office Phone: 415-439-1439. Office Fax: 415-439-1500. Business E-Mail: sjohnson@kirkland.com.

JOHNSON, STEPHEN WALTER, veterinarian; b. Columbus, Ohio, Apr. 21, 1960; s. Walter Eugene and Annemarie J.; m. Lynette Sue Johnson, Jan. 25, 1986. BS, Colo. State U., 1982, DVM, 1986. Hosp. owner and dir. Allard Animal Hosp., Loveland, Colo., 1986—92; state rep., 1997—2002; mem. state senate Dist. 15, 2003—. State rep. Dist. 49 Colo. Gen. Assembly, Denver, 1997—; chmn. Larimer County Colo. Planning Commn., Ft. Collins, 1987-96; pres. United Way of Loveland/Berthoud, 1994-95; bd. dirs. Loveland C. of C., 1991-94. Republican. Baptist. Avocations: stamp collecting/philately, hockey, current events.

JOHNSON, SUZANNE NORA, retired diversified financial services company executive, lawyer; b. Chgo., June 14, 1957; married. BA magna cum laude, U. So. Calif., 1979; JD, Harvard U. Bar: Calif. 1983. Law clk. to Hon. Francis Murnaghan US Ct. Appeals (4th Cir.), Balt.; atty. Simpson Thacher & Bartlett, 1980—84; with Goldman Sachs Group, NYC, 1985—2007, ptnr., 1992—2007, sr. dir., 2007—. Bd. dirs. Intuit Inc., 2007—, Visa Inc., 2007—, Pfizer Inc., 2007—, Am. Internat. Group, Inc. (AIG), 2008—, Am. Red Cross. Trustee Brookings Institution, Carnegie Institution, RAND Health, TechnoServe, Univ. So. Calif.; bd. dirs. Children Now, Markle Found., 2006—, Am. Red Cross; mem. adv. bd. of councilors Harvard Med. Sch. Named one of The World's 100 Most Powerful Women, Forbes mag., 2006. Avocations: fly fishing, kayaking.

JOHNSON, THOMAS FLOYD, former academic administrator, educator; b. Detroit, June 1, 1943; s. Edward Eugene and Adella Madeline (Norton) J.; m. Michele Elizabeth Myers, Mar. 26, 1965; children: Jason, Amy, Sarah. BPh, Wayne State U., 1965; BD, Fuller Theol. Sem., 1968; ThM, Princeton Sem., 1969; PhD, Duke U., 1979. Pastor Presbyn. Ch. U.S.A., Pa., Mich., 1969-76; asst. prof. U. Sioux Falls, S.D., 1978-83; acad. dean Sioux Falls (S.D.) Coll., 1981-83, pres., 1988-97; prof. N.Am. Baptist Sem., Sioux Falls, 1983-88; dean George Fox Evang. Sem., Portland, Oreg., 1997—2001; interim pres. George Fox U., Newberg, 1997-98, prof. bibl. theol., 1997—. Contbr. 9 articles to Internat. Standard Bible Ency., 1988; author: 1, 2, and 3 John New International Biblical Commentary, 1993. Bd. dirs. Children's Home Soc. S.D., Sioux Falls, 1980-86, S.D. Symphony Orch., 1988-92, Carroll Inst., 1989-93, Coalition Christian Colls. and Univs., 1992-97. Mem. Am. Bapt. Assn. Colls. and Univs. (pres. 1992-94), Soc. Bibl. Lit., Sioux Falls C. of C. (bd. dirs. 1992-95), Rotary (bd. dirs. Downtown Club 1991-95, pres. 1993-94). Office: George Fox Univ 414 N Meridian St Newberg OR 97132 Office Phone: 503-554-2663. Personal E-mail: tmj365@yahoo.com.

JOHNSON, VICTORIA L., library director; married; 2 children. B in Speech Comm., U. Southern Calif., MLS. Libr. positions City of Pasadena, 1986—95; dir. librs. Sunnyvale Pub. Libr. and Sunnyvale Ctr. for Innovation, Invention and Ideas, 1995—2004; dir. libr. services San Mateo County Libr., 2004—. Adj. faculty mem., grad. sch. edn. and info. services UCLA; bd. trustee Online Computer Libr. Ctr., Inc. (OCLC), Dublin, 2004—. Office: San Mateo County Libr 125 Lessingia Ct San Mateo CA 94402 Address: Online Computer Libr Ctr Inc -OCLC 6565 Kilgour Pl Dublin OH 43017-3395 Office Phone: 650-312-5258. Business E-Mail: johnson@smcl.org.

JOHNSON, WAYNE HAROLD, state legislator; b. El Paso, Tex., May 2, 1942; s. Earl Harold and Cathryn Louise (Greeno) J.; m. Patricia Ann Froedge, June 15, 1973; children: Meredith Jessica (dec.), Alexandra Noëlle Victoria. BS in History, Utah State U., 1968; MPA, U. Colo., 1970; MLS, U. Okla., 1972. Circulation libr. Utah State U., Logan, 1968, adminstrv. asst. libr., 1969; with rsch. dept. Okla. Mgmt. and Engring. Cons., Norman, 1972; chief adminstrv. svcs. Wyo. State Libr., Cheyenne, 1973-76, chief bus. officer libr. archives and hist. dept., 1976-78, state libr., 1978-89; county grants mgr. Laramie County, Wyo., 1989—2002; mem. Dist. 9 Wyo. House of Reps., 1993—2004; mem. Dist. 6 Wyo. State Senate, 2005—. Cons. in field. Trustee Bibliog. Ctr. for Rsch., Denver, pres., 1983-84; active Cheyenne dist. Longs Park coun. Boy Scouts Am., 1982-86; active Cheyenne Frontier Days, 1975-2008, Leadership Wyo., 2006; admissions and allocation com. United Way, 1991-94. With USCG, 1960—64. Mem. Aircraft Owners and Pilots Assn., Cheyenne C. of C. (chmn. transp. com. 1982, 83, mil. affairs com. 1994—), Am. Legion, Masons (Grand Lodge libr. 2001-, master Cheyenne Lodge No. 1, 2005-06), Kiwanis (bd. dirs. 1986-87), Cheyenne Frontier Days, No. Colo. Yacht Club, Cheyenne LEADS. Republican. Presbyterian. Office: Legislative Service Office 213 Capitol Building Cheyenne WY 82002 Home Phone: 307-635-2181; Office Phone: 307-777-7881. Office Fax: 307-777-5466; Home Fax: 307-635-2181. Personal E-mail: wajohnsons16@yahoo.com.*

JOHNSON, WENDY S., women's healthcare company executive; BS in Microbiology, U. Md.; MS in Clin. Microbiology, Hahnemann Med. Sch.; MBA, Loyola U., Balt. Asst. dir. Ctr. for Devices and Radiol. Health, FDA, 1976-86; internat. affairs adminstr. Coralab Rsch., 1986-88; mgr. bus. devel. Synbiotics Corp., 1988-90; v.p. bus. devel. and regulatory affairs Cytel Corp., 1990-94; v.p. corp. devel. and ops. Prizm Pharms. (now Selective Genetics Inc.), 1994-98; v.p. bus. devel. Women First HealthCare, Inc., San Diego, 1998—.

JOHNSON, WILLIAM LEWIS, materials scientist, educator; b. Bowling Green, Ohio, July 26, 1948; s. Melvin Carl and Martha Maxine (Roller) J.; m. Rachel Marie Newman, Jan. 21, 1984. BA in Physics, Hamilton Coll., 1970; PhD in Applied Physics, Calif. Inst. Tech., 1974. Mem. staff IBM Thomas J. Watson Rsch. Ctr., Yorktown Heights, NY, 1975-77; asst. prof. materials sci. Calif. Inst. Tech., Pasadena, 1977-80, assoc. prof., 1980-84, prof., 1984—, Ruben and Donna Mettler Prof. materials sci., 1989—. Cons., GM Rsch., Warren, Mich., 1983—, Amorphous Techs. Internat., Laguna,Calif., 1992—. Co-author: Glassy Metals I, 1981, Properties of Amorphous Metals, 1983, Physical Metallurgy, 1983, ASM Metals Handbook-Metallic Glasses, 1990. US Steel fellow, 1971; Alexander von Humboldt fellow, 1988; recipient William-Hume-Rothery award Metals Soc., 1996. Mem. AAAS, Metals Soc. AIME, Am. Phys. Soc., Materials Rsch. Soc. (Medal award 1998), NAE, NAS, Phi Beta Kappa, Sigma Xi. Lutheran. Office: Materials Sci Dept Calif Inst Tech MC 138-78 1200 California Blvd Pasadena CA 91125 Office Phone: 626-395-4433. E-mail: wlj@caltech.edu.

JOHNSON, WILLIAM POTTER, publishing executive, director; b. Peoria, Ill., May 4, 1935; s. William Zweigle and Helen Marr (Potter) J.; m. Pauline Ruth Rowe, May 18, 1968; children: Darragh Elizabeth, William Potter. AB, U. Mich., 1957. Gen. mgr. Bureau County Rep., Inc., Princeton, Ill., 1961-72; pres. Johnson Newspapers, Inc., Sebastopol, Calif., 1972-75, Evergreen, Colo., 1974-86, Canyon Commons Investment, Evergreen, 1974—, Johnson Media, Inc., Granby, Colo., 1987—. Author: How the Michigan Betas Built a $1,000,000 Chapter House in the '80s. Alt. del. Rep. Nat. Conv., 1968. Lt. USNR, 1958-61. Mem.: Vero Beach Yacht Club, Beta Theta Pi.

JOHNSON, WILLIAM STANLEY, metal distribution company executive; b. Elmhurst, Ill., May 11, 1957; s. Raymond J. and Nancy A. (Zinns) J.; m. Lisa Ann Grundy, July 14, 1990; 1 child, William Chase. BS in Bus. and Acctg., Ind. U., 1979; MBA in Fin., Mercer U., 1986. CPA, Calif.; CFP. Auditor, sr. auditor Ernst & Young, CPA's, Indpls., 1979-80; various fin. and acctg. positions Am. Hosp. Supply Co., Evanston, Ill., 1980-86; v.p. fin., dir. acctg. Abbey Med./Beaverbrook Group, Costa Mesa, Calif., 1987-91; corp. fin. mgr. Severin Group, Irvine, Calif., 1991-94; corp. contr., CFO, Earle M. Jorgensen Co., Brea, Calif., 1994—. Mem. adj. faculty U. Phoenix, Fountain Valley, Calif., 1998—. Mem. FEI, AICPA, Calif. Soc. CPA's. Home: 744 Via Lido Soud Newport Beach CA 92663-5558

JOHNSTON, ANN, Mayor, Stockton, California; BA in Social Sciences, San Francisco State U., 1964, cert. in Secondary Teaching, 1965. Pres. & mgr. The Ballooney, Inc., Stockton, 1981—; councilwoman City of Stockton, 1995—2002, mayor, 2009—. English tchr. Peace Corps, Iran, 1965—67, Weaver Sch., Merced, Calif., 1968—70; owner & ptnr. Allied Industrial Gas & Welding Supply, Calif., 1977—89. Chmn. Stockton Women's Network, 1987—, pres., 1990; bd. mem. Lodi Unified Sch. Dist. Bd. of Edn., 1979—92, Workforce Investment Bd., 1995—, CSUS Stanislaus Site Authority, 1999—2002, Greater Stockton C. of C., 1994—97. Recipient Small Bus. Person of Yr. award, Greater Stockton C. of C., 1993, Athena award, 1999, Action on Behalf of Children award, San Joaquin Family Resource & Referral Ctr., 1997, Women in Bus. Adv. of Yr. award, US Small Bus. Adminstrn., 2003, Susan B. Anthony Woman of Achievement award, San Joaquin County Commn. on Status of Women, 2004. Mem.: Stockton Women's Network, League of Women Voters, Harry S. Truman Club of Stockton, Downtown Rotary Club of Stockton. Office: 425 N El Dorado St Stockton CA 95202 Office Phone: 209-937-8244. Business E-Mail: mayor@ci.stockton.ca.us.*

JOHNSTON, BERNARD FOX, foundation executive, writer; b. Taft, Calif., Nov. 19, 1934; s. Bernard Lowe and Georgia Victoria (Fox) Johnston; m. Audrey Rhoades, June 9, 1956 (div. Sept. 1963); 1 child, Sheldon Bernard. BA in Creative Arts, San Francisco State U., 1957, MA in World Lit., 1959. Lectr. philosophy Coll. Marin,

Kentfield, Calif., 1957—58; lectr. humanities San Francisco State U., 1957—58, 1967—68; instr. English Contra Costa Coll., San Pablo, Calif., 1958—63, Knowles Found. philosophy fellow, 1962; fellow Syracuse U., 1964—66; freelance writer Piedmont, Calif., 1968—77; pres. Cinema Repertory, Inc., Point Richmond, Calif., 1978—89; pres., exec. dir. Athena Found., Tiburon, Calif., 1990—, Incline Village, Nev., 1990—. CEO Athena Found., Inc., 1997, Mahler Festival, U. Colo., Boulder, 1998; guest lectr. Sierra Nev. Coll., 2005; lectr. in field. Author: (screenplays) Point Exeter, 1979, Ascent Allowed, 1988 (award); author, editor: Issues in Education: An Anthology of Controversy, 1964, The Literature of Learning, 1971; musician: (resident pianist) Tahoe-Chrysler Corp., 1988, (festival pianist) Lake Tahoe Internat. Film Festival, 1998, (featured pianist) Lake Tahoe Hebrew Assn. Concert, 2001, Tahoe Forest Hosp. benefit, Lake Tahoe, Lake Tahoe Wildlife Benefit, 2003, Lake Tahoe Summer Music Series, 2000, Thunderbird Lodge, 2003 (North Tahoe Jury Arts award, 2004), Roseville Art Exhibit, 2004, Athena Reform Syllabus, 2006 (Smallwood Family Found. award, 2007), (piano soloist) Sierra Nevada Coll. Presdl. Dinner, 2000, (albums) Time Remembered; musical dir. (albums) Time Remembered; musician: (pianist) San Francisco State U. Athletic Awards Ceremony, 2001, Squaw Creek Resort, Lake Tahoe Forest Benefit, concert; contbr. articles pub. to profl. jour.; exec. prodr.: (TV series) The Heroes of Time; (documentaries) The Shudder of Awe. Recipient Bell-Brook Talent TV award, 1950, TV Arts award, Kirsch Found., 2001; Arts grantee, Silicon Valley Cmty. Found., 1998, Athena Reform Ednl. Project, 2005, Smallwood Family Fedn. grantee, 2006, Smallwood Family Renewal grantee, 2008. Mem.: Calif. Assn. Scholars, Nat. Assn. Scholars, Assn. Lit. Scholars and Critics, Wilson Ctr. Assocs., Coun. Basic Edn., Writers Guild Am., Dirs. Guild Am., San Francisco State Alumni Assn., Donner Land Trust, Smithsonian Instn., Commonwealth Club Calif. Avocations: classical music, backpacking, softball. Office: 845 Southwood Blvd Ste 50 Incline Village NV 89451-9463 Personal E-mail: athenaprods@peoplepc.com.

JOHNSTON, BRUCE FOSTER, economics professor; b. Lincoln, Nebr., Sept. 24, 1919; s. Homer Klotz and Ethel Matilda (Hockett) J.; m. Harriet L. Pollins, Mar. 31, 1944; children— Bruce C., Patricia C. BA, Cornell U., 1941; MA, Stanford U., 1950, PhD, 1953. Agrl. mktg. adminstr. Dept. Agr., 1941-42; chief food br. econ. and sci. sect. SCAP, Tokyo, 1945-48; agrl. economist Food and Agr. div. U.S. Mission to NATO and European Regional Orgn., Paris, 1952-54; assoc. prof. econs., assoc. economist Food Research Inst., Stanford U., Calif., 1954-59, prof. econs., economist Calif., 1959—. Cons. World Bank, FAO, others Author: (with Tomich and Kilby) Transforming Agrarian Economies: Opportunities Seized, Opportunities Missed, 1995, (with Clark) Redesigning Rural Development: A Strategic Perspective, 1982, (with Anthony, Jones and Uchendu) Agricultural Change in Tropical Africa, 1979, (with Kilby) Agriculture and Structural Transformation: Economic Strategies in Late-Developing Countries, 1975; co-editor:, contbr.: (with Ohkawa and Kaneda) Agriculture and Economic Growth: Japan's Experience, 1969. Guggenheim fellow, 1962, Internat. Inst. Applied Systems Analysis fellow, 1978-79, Adminstr.'s fellow AID, 1991. Fellow Am. Agrl. Econs. Assn.; mem. Am. Econ. Assn., African Studies Assn., Phi Beta Kappa, Phi Kappa Phi Office: Stanford U Food Rsch Inst Stanford CA 94305 E-mail: bfjohn@stanford.edu.

JOHNSTON, JAMES R., lawyer; b. Seattle, Aug. 19, 1953; BS magna cum laude, U. Wash., 1975, JS, 1978. Bar: Wash. 1978, US Ct. Appeals (9 Cir.), US Dist. Ct. (We. Dist.) Wash., Us Dist. Ct. (Ea. Dist.) Wash., US Tax Ct., Yakama Tribal Ct. Asst. atty. gen., Natural Resources Divsn. State of Wash., 1978—83; assoc. Bogle & Gates, PLLC, 1983—87, ptnr., 1988—97, chmn., Forest Resources Practices Group, 1994—97; ptnr., Envirn./Natural Resources/Land Use Practice Area Perkins Coie LLP, Seattle. Trustee Wash. Rsch. Coun. Mem.: Soc. Am. Foresters, ABA (vice chmn. forest resources com., Environ., Energy & Resources Sect. 1994—), Wash. State Bar Assn.

JOHNSTON, LAWRENCE R. (LARRY JOHNSTON), retired food products executive; b. Corning, NY, Aug. 29, 1948; married; 3 children. BA in Bus. Adminstrn., Stetson U., Deland, FL, 1972. Merchandising mgr. GE Appliances; region mgr. GE; gen. mgr. Eastern Sales & Distbn. Opers., GE Appliances; pres. Internat. GE Puerto Rico; gen. mgr. Domestic Sales Opers., GE; v.p. sales & distbn. GE Appliances, 1989—97; corp. v.p. GE Co., 1989—97, sr. v.p., 1999—2001; pres., CEO GE Med. Sys., Europe, Paris, 1997—99, GE Appliances, 1999—2001; chmn. bd., pres., CEO Albertson's, Inc., 2001—06. Bd. dirs. GE Co., 1989—2001, The Home Dept, Inc., 2004—07; chmn. GE's European Exec. Coun., 1998—99; bd. mem. Food Mktg. Inst., Washington, CIES World Food Forum, Paris.

JOHNSTON, NORMAN JOHN, retired architecture educator; b. Seattle, Dec. 3, 1918; s. Jay and Helen May (Shultis) J.; m. Lois Jane Hastings, Nov. 22, 1969. BA, U. Wash.-Seattle, 1942; B.Arch., U. Oreg., 1949; M. in Urban Planning, U. Pa.-Phila., 1959, PhD, 1964. Registered architect, Wash. City planner Seattle City Planning Commn., 1951-55; asst. prof. arch. U. Oreg.-Eugene, 1956-58; assoc. prof. architecture and urban planning U. Wash.-Seattle, 1960-64, prof., 1964-85, prof. emeritus, 1985—, assoc. dean, 1964-76, 79-84, chmn. dept. architecture, 1984-85. Mem. nat. exams. com. Nat. Coun. Archtl. Registration Bds., Washington, 1970-81, 88-99; vis. prof. Tokyo Inst. Tech., 1991, 98; Fulbright prof. Istanbul Tech. U., 1968-69; mem. Wash. State Archtl. Registration Bd., 1989-2000, chmn., 1988-89. Author: Cities in the Round, 1983, Washington's Audacious State Capitol and its Builders, 1988 (Gov.'s Book award 1984, 89), The College of Architecture and Urban Planning, 75 Years at the University of Washington: A Personal View, 1991, The Fountain and the Mountain - The University of Washington Campus, 1895-1995, 1995-2003, National Guide Series: The University of Washington, 2001; editor: NCARB Architectural Registration Handbook, 1980; contbr. articles to profl. jours. Mem. King County Policy Devel. Commn., Seattle, 1970-76; mem. Capitol campus design adv. com. State of Wash., Olympia, 1982-2000, chmn., 1980-88, 96; trustee Mus. History and Industry, 1997-2000. Recipient Wash. Disting. Citizen award, 1987, Barney award AIA Coll. of Fellows, 2003. Fellow AIA (pres. Seattle chpt. 1981, AIA medal Seattle chpt. 1991, Wash. Coun. medal 1997); mem. Phi Beta Kappa, Sigma Chi, Tau Sigma Delta. Presbyterian. Home: 900 University St Apt Au Seattle WA 98101-1778 Office: U Wash C Built Environments PO Box 355726 Seattle WA 98195-5726 E-mail: njjo@u.washington.edu.

JOHNSTON, PATRICK, state senator; b. San Francisco, Sept. 3, 1946; m. Margaret Mary Nevin. BA in Philosophy, St. Patrick's Coll. Mem. Calif. State Assembly, 1981-90, Calif. State Senate, 1991—, chair appropriations com., 1991—, mem. natural resources and wildlife com., 1991, mem. energy, utilities and comms. com., mem. ins. com., mem. agr. and water resources com., mem. local govt. com. Democrat. Office: State Capitol Rm 5066 Sacramento CA 95814 also: 1020 N St Ste 504 Sacramento CA 95814-5624 also: 31 E Channel St Ste 440 Stockton CA 95202-2314 E-mail: Senator.Johnston@sen.ca.gov.

JOHNSTON, RICHARD BOLES, JR., pediatrician, educator, biomedical researcher; b. Atlanta, Aug. 23, 1935; s. Richard Boles and Jane (Dillon) Johnston; m. Mary Anne Claiborne, Aug. 13, 1960; children: Richard B. III, S. Claiborne, Kristin M. BA, Vanderbilt U., 1957, MD, 1961; MS (hon.), U. Pa., 1986. Diplomate Am. Bd. Pediat., Am. Bd. Pediat. Infectious Disease. Resident in pediat. Vanderbilt U., 1961-63, Harvard U., 1963-64, fellow pediat. immunology, 1967-70; asst. prof., assoc. prof. depts. pediat. and microbiology U. Ala. Med. Ctr., Birmingham, 1970-76; vis. assoc. prof. Rockefeller U., NYC, 1976-77, vis. prof., 1983-84; prof. pediat. U. Colo. Sch. Medicine, Denver, 1977-86; chmn. dept. pediat. Nat. Jewish Ctr. Immunology and Respiratory Medicine, Denver, 1977-86, U. Pa. Sch. Medicine, Phila., 1986-90, Wm. H. Bennett prof. pediat., 1986-92; physician-in-chief Children's Hosp. of Phila., 1986—90; med. dir. March of Dimes Birth Defects Found., White Plains, NY, 1992-98. Adj. prof. pediat., chief sec. pediat. immunology Yale U. Sch. Medicine, 1992—98; prof. pediat. Sch. Medicine U. Colo., Denver, 1999—, assoc. dean rsch. devel., 2001—; trustee Internat. Pediat. Rsch. Found., 1983—87, 1995—98, chmn., 1984—87, 1997—98; chmn. adv. bd. for vaccines and related biols. FDA, Bethesda, Md., 1990—93, chmn. com. vaccine safety, Inst. Medicine, 1992—93, chmn. com. new rsch. in vaccines, 1993—94, chmn. forum vaccine safety, 1995—98, chmn. com. asthma and indoor air, 1998—99, bd. health promotion disease prevention, 1994—2001, chmn. com. rsch. in multiple sclerosis, 1999—2001, chmn. com. health implications of perchlorate, 2003—05, chmn. com. tng. physicians for pub. health careers, 2006—07; exec. v.p. acad. affairs Nat. Jewish Med. & Rsch. Ctr., 2004—07, v.p. rsch. affairs, 2007—08. Mem. editl. bd. 7 profl. jours., 1978—; contbr. 270 scholarly publs.; editor Current Opinion in Pediatrics, 1997—. Capt. M.C., U.S. Army, 1964-66. Faculty scholar Josiah Macy Jr. Found., 1976-77; recipient Commr. citation and Wiley medal FDA, 1994, John Howland medal, Am. Pediat Soc., 2008, Disting. Alumnus Vanderbilt Sch. Med., 2008. Fellow AAAS; mem. Inst. Medicine NAS, Am. Soc. Clin. Investigation, Am. Pediat. Soc. (pres. 1996-97), Assn. Am. Physicians, Soc. Pediat. Rsch. (pres. 1980-81). Office: Univ Colo Denver Sch Medicine Dean's Office C-290 13001 E 17th Pl Aurora CO 80045 Office Phone: 303-724-5365. Business E-Mail: richard.johnston@ucdenver.edu.

JOHNSTON, RICHARD C., newspaper editor; BS, Portland State U., 1965. Reporter The Oregonian, Portland, 1965-66, asst. city editor, 1966-79, Washington corr., 1979-82, asst. mng. editor, 1982-94, asst. to the editor, 1994—. Office: The Oregonian 1320 SW Broadway Portland OR 97201-3499

JOHNSTON, ROBERT JAKE, federal magistrate judge; b. Denver, Sept. 30, 1947; m. Julie Ann Black; children: Jennifer, Robert, Jr., Michelle. BS, Brigham Young U., 1973; JD, U. Pacific, 1977. Bar: Nev. 1977, U.S. Dist. Ct. Nev. 1978, U.S. Ct. Appeals (9th cir.) 1984. Law clk. to Hon. Merlyn Hoyt Nev. 7th Judicial Dist., Ely, 1977-78; dist. atty. White Pine County, Ely, 1979-82; pvt. practice Johnston & Fairman, Ely, 1979-82; deputy dist. atty. Office Clark County Dist. Atty., Las Vegas, Nev., 1983-84; asst. U.S. atty. Office U.S. Atty., Las Vegas, 1984-87, chief civil div., 1986-87; U.S. magistrate judge U.S. Dist. Ct., Las Vegas, 1987—. Dir. Boy Scouts Am. Boulder Dam Area Coun., Las Vegas. With U.S. Army, 1967-70. Mem. Nev. Bar Assn., Clark County Bar Assn., Ct. Adminstrn. and Case Mgmt. Com., Fed. Bar Assn., Fed. Magistrate Judges Assn. (dir. 1990-92), Las Vegas Track Club, 9th Jud. Cir. Hist. Soc., Southwest Oral History Soc. Office: US Dist Ct Ste 3005 333 Las Vegas Blvd S Las Vegas NV 89101

JOHNSTON, VIRGINIA EVELYN, retired editor; b. Spokane, Wash., Apr. 26, 1933; d. Edwin and Emma Lucile (Munroe) Rowe; m. Alan Paul Beckley, Dec. 26, 1974; children: Chris, Denise, Rex. Student, Portland C.C., 1964, Portland State U., 1966, 78-79. Proofreader the Oregonian, Portland, 1960—62, teletypesetter operator, 1962—66, operator Photon 200, 1966—68, copy editor, asst. women's editor, 1968—80, spl. sects. editor, 1981—83, editor FOOD day, 1982—2001; ret., 2002. Pres. Matrix Assocs., Inc., Portland, 1975—, chmn. bd., 1979—; past pres. Bones & Brew, Inc. Editor Principles of Computer Systems for Newspaper Mgmt., 1975-76. Cons. Portland Sch. Dist. No. 1, 1978, Dem. Party Oreg., 1969. Democrat. Home: 4140 NE 137th Ave Portland OR 97230-2624 Home Phone: 503-256-5084. E-mail: ginger1933@comcast.net.

JOHNSTON, WILLIAM FREDERICK, emergency services administrator; b. Oakridge, Tenn., Mar. 4, 1945; s. Leonard E. and Helene C. (Spicker) J.; m. Kathleen Jo Hotaling, Nov. 17, 1988; 1 child, Lindsey Anne. BS, U. Wash., 1969, MS, 1971, MD, 1974, MBA, 1998. Diplomate Am. Bd. Emergency Medicine. Med. intern U. Wash. Affiliated Hosps., Seattle, 1974-75; emergency medicine resident Valley Med. Ctr. Fresno/U. Calif. San Francisco, Fresno, 1975-77; pres., CEO N.W. Emergency Physicians, Seattle, 1977-81; med. dir. emergency svcs. N.W. Hosp., Seattle, 1977—. Bd. dirs. First Choice Health Plan, Inc., First Choice Health Network, Inc., Washington Casualty Co., N.W. Healthcare Ins. Svcs. Contbr. articles to med. jours. Fellow Am. Coll. Emergency Physicians (bd. dirs. Washington chpt. 2005-). Avocations: skiing, hiking, kayaking. Home: 4731 Beach Dr SW Seattle WA 98116-4340 Office: N W Hosp 1550 N 115th St Seattle WA 98133-8498 Office Phone: 206-999-1772. Personal E-mail: billj@nwlink.com.

JOHNSTONE, IAIN MURRAY, statistician, educator, consultant; b. Melbourne, Victoria, Australia, Dec. 10, 1956; s. Samuel Thomas Murray and Pamela Beatrice (Kriegel) J. BS with honors, Australian Nat. U., Canberra, 1978, MS, 1979; PhD, Cornell U., 1981. Asst. prof. stats. Stanford U., Calif., 1981—85, assoc prof. stats., 1986—92, assoc. prof. biostatis., 1987—92, prof. stats., biostats., 1992—, dept. chmn., 1994—97, sr. assoc. dean natural scis., 2003—05, vice dean acad. planning Sch. Humanities and Scis., 2005—08. Contbr. articles to profl. jours. Bd. dirs. Bd. on Math. Scis. and its Applications, Washington, 1999—2002; pres. Inst. Math. Stats., 2001—02. Recipient Presdl. Young Investigator award, NSF, 1985—91; Alfred P. Sloan Rsch. fellow, Sloan Found., 1988—90, Guggenheim fellow, John Simon Guggenheim Found., 1997—98. Fellow: AAAS; mem.: NAS, Math. & Phys. Scis. Adv. Com. (chair 2008—), Nat. Sci. Found. (dir.).

JOHNSTONE, KATHRYN I., lawyer; BS cum laude, Walla Walla Coll., 1979; MBA cum laude, Golden Gate U., 1983; JD cum laude, Harvard U., 1986. CPA Calif., 1981; bar: Calif. 1986. CPA KPMG Peat, Marwick's L.A. tax dept.; ptnr. Morrison & Foerster LLP, co-chmn. fin. group. Mem.: Fin. Lawyers Conf., State Bar Calif. (bus. law sect.), ABA (bus. law sect.), State Bar Calif. (Uniform Comml. Code Com. 1994—97). Office: Morrison Foerster LLP 555 W 5th St Ste 3500 Los Angeles CA 90013 Office Phone: 213-892-5200. Office Fax: 213-892-5454. Business E-Mail: kjohnstone@mofo.com.

JOINER, CHARLIE (CHARLES JOINER JR.), professional football coach, retired professional football player; b. Many, La., Oct. 14, 1947; m. Dianne Joiner; children: Jynaya, Kori. Grad., Grambling State U., 1969. Wide receiver Houston Oilers, 1969-72, Cin. Bengals, 1972—75, San Diego Chargers, 1976-86, wide receivers coach, 1987—91, Buffalo Bills, 1992—2000, Kansas City Chiefs, 2001—07, San Diego Chargers, 2008—. Named NFL All-Pro, 1980; named to Am. Football Conf. Pro Bowl Team, 1976, 1979, 1980, La. Hall of Fame, 1990, San Diego Chargers Hall of Fame, 1993, Pro Football Hall of Fame, 1996. Office: San Diego Chargers PO Box 609609 San Diego CA 92160-9609

JOKINEN, OLLI, professional hockey player; b. Kuopio, Finland, Dec. 5, 1978; m. Katerina Jokinen. Center LA Kings, 1998—99, NY Islanders, 1999—2000, Fla. Panthers, 2000—08, capt., 2003—08; center Phoenix Coyotes, 2008—09, Calgary Flames, 2009—. Mem. Finnish Olympic Hockey Team, Salt Lake City, 2002, Torino, Italy, 06. Named to NHL All-Star Game, 2003. Office: Calgary Flames PO Box 1540 Stn M Calgary AB T2P 3B9 Canada*

JOLLES, BERNARD, lawyer; b. NYC, Oct. 5, 1928; s. Harry and Dora (Hirschorn) J.; m. Lenore Madison Jolles, Oct. 11, 1953 (div. Jan. 1984); children: Abbe, Jacqueline, Caroline. BA, N.Y.U., 1951; LLB, Lewis & Clark Coll., 1961. Bar: Oreg. 1963, U.S. Dist. Ct. Oreg. 1964, U.S. Dist. Ct. (no. dist.) Miss. 1968, U.S. Ct. Appeals (9th cir.) 1965, U.S. Supreme Ct. 1979. Assoc. Anderson Franklin Jones & Olsen, Portland, Oreg., 1963-68; ptnr. Franklin Olsen Bennett & Desbarsay, Portland, Oreg., 1968-79, Jolles, Sokol & Bernstein and successor firms, Portland, Oreg., 1979—. Jolles Bernstein & Garone and predecessor firms Jolles Sokol & Bernstein, Portland, Oreg., 1979—, Law Offices of Bernard Jolles, Portland, Oreg., 2007—. Editor: Damages, 1974. Bd. dirs. ACLU, Portland, Oreg., 1975—. Fellow Am. Coll. Trial Lawyers; mem. Oreg. State Bar Assn. (pres. 1986-87), Am. Inns of Ct. (sr. barrister 1985—). Avocations: cooking, reading. Office: Jolles & Bernstein 721 SW Oak St Fl 2 Portland OR 97205-3712 Office Phone: 503-228-6474. E-mail: bj@bernardjolles.com.

JOLLEY, R. GARDNER, lawyer; b. Salt Lake City, May 12, 1944; s. Reuben G. and Varno J.; m. Sharon Lea Thomas, Aug. 21, 1965; children— Christopher Gardner and Jennifer Lea. B.S. in Econs., U. Utah, 1966; J.D., U. Calif.-Berkeley, 1969. Bar: Calif. 1970, Nev. 1970, U.S. Dist. Ct. Nev. 1970. Law clk. to presiding justice Nev. Supreme Ct., 1969-70; assoc. Wiener, Goldwater and Galatz, Las Vegas, 1970-73; ptnr. Jolley, Urga, Wirth & Woodbury, Las Vegas, Nev., 1974—; lectr. new law clks. for Nev. judges, 1973-74; instr. Clark County Community Coll., 1975-77; instr. Nev. Continuing Legal Edn., 1983. Bd. dirs. Catholic Community Services, 1973-80; bd. govs. Easter Seal Soc., 1977-78. Mem. Nev. State Bar Assn. (bd. govs. 1976-86, pres. 1985-86), ABA (Nev. rep. to Ho. Dels. 1986-88), Assn. Trial Lawyers Am., Nev. Trial Lawyers Assn.

JOLLIMORE, TROY, philosophy professor, poet; Student in Philosophy, Dalhousie U., Halifax, Nova Scotia; BA, U. King's Coll.; PhD, Princeton U., 1999. Former asst. prof. dept. Philosophy Georgetown U.; former assoc. prof., dept. Philosophy U. Cal. Davis; external faculty fell., Humanities Ctr. Stanford U., 2006—. Author: (book of poetry) Tom Thomson in Purgatory, 2006 (Nat. Book Critics Circle award for Poetry, 2006); contbr. articles to numerous profl. jours. Office: Stanford Humanities Ctr Stanford U 424 Santa Teresa Street Stanford CA 94305-4015 E-mail: tjollimore@csuchico.edu.

JONAITIS, ALDONA CLAIRE, museum director, art historian; b. NYC, Nov. 27, 1948; d. Thomas and Demie (Genaitis) J. BA, SUNY, Stony Brook, 1969; MA, Columbia U., 1972, PhD, 1977. Lectr. to prof. art SUNY, Stony Brook, 1973—89, Chair art dept., 1983-85, assoc. provost, 1985-86, vice provost undergrad. studies, 1986-89; v.p. for pub. programs Am. Mus. Natural History, NYC, 1989-93; dir. U. Alaska Mus. of North, Fairbanks, 1993—; prof. anthropology U. Alaska, Fairbanks, 1993—. Adj. prof. art history and archeology Columbia U., 1990—93; vis. disting. prof. Am. art history Stanford U., 2002. Author: From the Land of the Totem Poles, 1988; editor, author: Chiefly Feasts: The Enduring Kwakiutl Potlatch, 1991; editor: A Wealth of Thought: Franz Boas on Native American Art History, 1995, Looking North: Art from the University of Alaska Museum, 1998, The Yuquot Whaler's Shrine, 1999. Mem. Am. Assn. Mus. (bd. dirs. 1999-2002), Am. Assn. Mus./ICOM (bd. dirs. 2000-2003), Native Am. Art Studies Assn. (bd. dirs. 1985-95). Office: U Alaska Mus PO Box 756960 Fairbanks AK 99775-6960 Office Phone: 907-474-6939. Office Fax: 907-474-5469. E-mail: ffaj@naf.edu.

JONAS, CHRIS, composer; BA, Oberlin Coll., 1988; MA, Wesleyan U., 1999; Cert. in multimedia digital design, NYU, 2001. Co-leader, composer amitosis, 2001—03, BING; cur., dir. installation and performance arts Ctr. Contemporary Arts, Santa Fe, 2002—03; freelance graphic designer and composer Santa Fe, 2004—; co-founder Santa Fe Beehive, 2004, Littleglobe Productions, Inc., Santa Fe, 2005—; adj. faculty creative music program Coll. Santa Fe, 2005—. Performer: (albums) Child King Dictator Fool, 1997, The Sun Spits Cherries, 1999, Ensembles Unsynchronized, 2000, The Vermillion, 2001, Galore, 2004; composer: (documentary) Drought in New Mexico, 2003; composer, performer: music for silent films, 2001—, La Reina Roja, 2004—, NIGHT, 2004, In Situ, 2007, Memorylines, 2007. Fellow US Artists, 2008. Office: Littleglobe Inc 223 N Guadalupe #427 Santa Fe NM 87501 Office Phone: 505-989-1437. E-mail: chris@littleglobe.org.

JONAS, JOSEPH ADAM, singer; b. Casa Grande, Ariz., Aug. 15, 1989; Mem. Jonas Brothers, 2005—. Performer: (Broadway plays) La Bohème, 2002—03; singer: (albums) It's About Time, 2006, Jonas Brothers, 2007, Camp Rock soundtrack, 2008, A Little Bit Longer, 2008; actor: (TV films) Camp Rock, 2008; (TV series) J.O.N.A.S.!, 2008; performer: (TV series) Jonas Brothers: Living the Dream, 2008. Recipient Favorite Music Group award, Nickelodeon Kid's Choice Awards, 2008, 6 Teen Choice awards (with Jonas Brothers), 2008, Breakthrough Artist award, Am. Music Awards, 2008. Office: Jonas Brothers c/o Hollywood Records 500 S Buena Vista St Burbank CA 91521

JONAS, KEVIN (PAUL KEVIN JONAS II), singer; b. Teaneck, NJ, Nov. 5, 1987; Mem. Jonas Brothers, 2005—. Singer: (albums) It's About Time, 2006, Jonas Brothers, 2007, Camp Rock soundtrack, 2008, A Little Bit Longer, 2008; actor: (TV films) Camp Rock, 2008; performer: (TV series) J.O.N.A.S.!, 2008, Jonas Brothers: Living the Dream, 2008. Recipient Favorite Music Group award, Nickelodeon Kids' Choice Awards, 2008, 6 Teen Choice awards (with Jonas Brothers), 2008, Breakthrough Artist award, Am. Music Awards, 2008. Office: Jonas Brothers c/o Hollywood Records 500 S Buena Vista St Burbank CA 91521

JONASSEN, JAMES O., architect; b. Aberdeen, Wash., July 23, 1940; s. James E. and Marjorie E. (Smith) J.; m. Patricia E. Glen, June 9, 1958 (div. Oct. 1975); m. Marilyn Joan Kampa, June 11, 1977; children: Christian A., Steven E. BArch, U. Wash., 1964; MS in Architecture, Columbia U., 1965. Registered architect Ala., Alaska, Ariz., Calif., Colo., Fla., Ga., Idaho, Ill., Kans., La., Minn., Mo., Mont., Nebr., Nev., N.Mex., N.C., N.C., Ohio, Okla., Oreg., S.D., Tex. Wash., Utah., Wis., D.C., Del. Mass. Miss., N.H., N.Y., R.I., Vt., P.R., British Columbia, Can. Designer NBBJ Group, Seattle, 1965-70, ptnr., 1970—; CEO NBBJ West, 1983-96, mng. ptnr., 1997—. Bd. dirs. Health Insights Found; assoc. prof. Sch. Architecture U. Hawaii. Prin works include Bettelle Meml. Lab., Richland, Wash., 1965 (lab of yr. award 1968), Heath Profl. Bldg., 1970, Children's Orthopedic Hosp., Seattle, 1972 (AIA Honor award 1976), St. Mary's Hosp., Surg. Pavilion, Rochester, Minn., 1982, St. Vincent Med. Office Bldg., Portland, Oreg., 1983, Scottsdale Meml. Hosp. N., Ariz., 1984, Seattle VA Hosp., 1985, Stanford U. Hosp., 1986, St. Joseph Host. Med. Ctr., 1988, Providence Med./ Ctr., Seattle, 1990 (AIA Merit award), David Grant Med. Ctr., Fairfield, Calif., 1986 (USAF Honor award 1989, Spl. citation DOD 1988, Type i Honor award USAF 1989, Excellence in Design award DOD 1991), Alaska Native Med. Ctr., 1997, Kangbuk Med. Ctr., Seoul, Korea, 1998, Capital Coast Health Med. Ctr., Wellington, New Zealand, 2000. Bd. dirs. Sch. Zone Inst., 1990—94, Health Facilities Rsch. and Edn. Project, 1991—98, Swedish Med. Ctr. Found., 1993—2003; pres.bd. Architecture and Children project, 1990; mem. vis. com. U. Washington Sch. Medicine, 2001—; mem. bd. dirs. Seattle Architectural Found, 1986, 2000—05. Recipient Seattle Newsmaker Tomorrow award, Time Mag., 1978, Modern Health Care award, Swedish Med. Ctr., 1997—2000, Seattle Archtl. Found. Bd., 2000—; fellow fellow, Naramore Found., 1969; scholar Columbia U. scholar, 1964. Fellow AIA (chmn. steering com. 1983-85, nat. com. architecture for health, mem. Nat. Life Cycle Task Force 1977, bd. dirs. Seattle chpt. 1985-87, Modern Healthcare award 1998); mem. Sr. Coun. Archs. (pres. 1999, 2000), Wash. Athletic Club, Columbia Tower Club, Rotary. Office: NBBJ 223 Yale Ave N Seattle WA 98109 Business E-Mail: jjonassen@nbbj.com.

JONES, ALLAN, medical research organization executive; BS in Biology, Duke Univ.; PhD in Genetics and Develop. Biology, Washington Univ. Sch. Medicine. Post-doctoral tng. U. Pa.; various scientific and mgmt. positions Avitech Diagnostics, Rosetta Inpharmatics, Merck and Co.; with Allen Inst. for Brain Sci., Seattle, 2003—, dir., Allen Brain Atlas project, 2004—06, chief scientific officer, 2006—. Office: Allen Inst for Brain Sci 551 N 34th St Seattle WA 98103 Office Fax: 206-548-7000.

JONES, BILL, former state official, rancher; b. Coalinga, Calif., Dec. 20, 1949; s. C.W. and Cora Jones; m. Maurine Abramson, Aug. 29, 1971; children: Wendy, Andrea. BS in Agribus. and Plant Sci., Calif. State U., Fresno, 1971. Ptnr. ranch, nr. Firebaugh, Calif.; mem. Calif. Assembly, Sacramento, 1983—, Rep. leader, 1991—; Sec. of State State of California, 1994—2003. Former chmn. Fresno County Rep. Cen. Com. Named Outstanding Young Farmer, Fresno C. of C. Mem. Fresno County and City C. of C. (past bd. dirs.). Republican. Methodist. Avocations: horseback riding, golf, flying, travel.

JONES, CHARLES E., retired state supreme court chief justice; b. June 12, 1935; BA, Brigham Young U., 1959; JD, Stanford U., 1962. Bar: Calif. 1963, Ariz. 1964, US Dist. Ct. Ariz. 1964, US Ct. Appeals (9th cir.) 1963, US Ct. Appeals (10th cir.) 1974, US Supreme Ct. 1979. Law clk. to Hon. Richard H. Chambers U.S. Ct. Appeals (9th cir.), 1962-63; assoc., ptnr. Jennings, Strouss & Salmon, Phoenix, 1963-96; apptd. justice Ariz. Supreme Ct., Phoenix, 1996, vice chief justice, 1997—2002, chief justice, 2002—05; ret., 2005—. Bd. visitors Brigham Young U. Law Sch., 1973-81, chmn., 1978-81, Univ. Arizona Coll. Law, 2003—. Named Avocat du Consulat-Gen. de France, 1981—; Alumni Dist. Svc. award Brigham Young U., 1982; recipient Aaron Feuerstein award U. Ariz., 1998, Pub. Svc. award Ariz. Alumni Assn., 2005, Career Achievement award State Bar Ariz., 2005, Chapman award Ariz. League of Women Voters, 2005, Pub. Svc. award, U. Ariz. Fellow Am. Bar Found., Ariz. Bar Found.; mem. ABA, State Bar Ariz. (Career award, 2005), Fed. Bar Assn. (pres. Ariz. chpt. 1971-73), J. Reuben Clark Law Soc. (nat. chmn. 1994-97), Maricopa County Bar Assn., Am. Coll. Labor and Employment Lawyers (former dir.), Pi Sigma Alpha. Office: Phoenix Sch Law 4041 N Central Ave Phoenix AZ 85012 Home Phone: 602-952-0993.

JONES, CHARLES IRVING, bishop; b. El Paso, Tex., Sept. 13, 1943; s. Charles I. Jr. and Helen A. (Heyward) J.; m. Ashby MacArthur, June 18, 1966; children: Charles I. IV, Courtney M., Frederic M., Keith A. BS, The Citadel, 1965; MBA, U. N.C., 1966; MDiv, U. of the South, 1977, DD, 1989. CPA. Pub. acctg. D.E. Gatewood and Co., Winston-Salem, NC, 1966-72; dir. devel. Chatham (Va.) Hall, 1972-74; instr. acctg. U. of the South, Sewanee, Tenn., 1974-77; coll. chaplain Western Ky. U., Bowling Green, 1977-81; vicar Trinity Episcopal Ch., Russelville, Ky., 1977-85; archdeacon Diocese of Ky., Louisville, 1981-86; bishop Episcopal Diocese of Mont., Helena, 1986-2001. Bd. dirs. New Directions Ministries, Inc., N.Y.C.; mem. standing com. Joint Commn. on Chs. in Small Communities, 1988-91, Program, Budget and Fin., 1991-94; v.p. province VI Episcopal Ch., 1991-94, mem. Presiding Bishop's Coun. Advice, 1991-94. Author: Mission Strategy in the 21st Century, 1989, Total Ministry: A Practical Approach, 1993; bd. editors Grass Roots, Luling, Tex., 1985-90; contbr. articles to profl. jours. Founder Concerned Citizens for Children, Russelville, 1981; bd. dirs. St. Peter's Hosp., Helena, 1986-2001; bd. dirs. Christian Ministry in Nat. Parks, 1992—2001. With USMCR, 1961-65. Mem. AICPA, Mont. Soc. CPAs. Episcopalian. Avocations: running, flying, writing, skiing. Office: PO Box 4926 Helena MT 59604 Office Phone: 406-442-0345. E-mail: bpci@aol.com.

JONES, CHRIS, computer software company executive; B in Math. and Computational Scis., Stanford U. Joined Microsoft Corp., Redmond, Wash., 1991, gen. mgr., group program mgr. Internet Explorer, corp. v.p. Windows Client group, corp. v.p. Core Operating System Divsn., corp. v.p. Windows Client Core Devel., corp. v.p. Windows Live Experience Program Mgmt. Office: Microsoft Corp One Microsoft Way Redmond WA 98052-6399

JONES, CLARIS EUGENE, JR., botanist, educator; b. Columbus, Ohio, Dec. 15, 1942; s. Claris Eugene and Clara Elizabeth (Elliott) J.; m. Teresa Diane Wagner, June 26, 1966; children: Douglas Eugene, Philip Charles, Elizabeth Lynne. BS, Ohio U., 1964; PhD, Ind. U., 1969. Asst. prof. botany Calif. State U., Fullerton, 1969-73, assoc. prof., 1973-77, prof. botany, 1977—, chmn. dept. biol. sci., 1989—2004, dir. Fullerton Arboretum, 1970-80, dir. Faye MacFadden Herbarium, 1969—; disting. faculty mem. Sch. Natural Sci. and Math., 1999—. Author: A Dictionary of Botany, 1980; editor: Handbook of Experimental Pollination Biology, 1983; contbr. articles to profl. jours. Mem. Am. Inst. Biol. Sci., AAAS, Bot. Soc. Am., Internat. Assn. Plant Taxonomy, Am. Soc. Plant Taxonomists, Soc. Study Evolution, Systematics Assn., Ecol. Soc. Am., Calif. Bot. Soc., Sigma Xi Methodist. Office: 800 N State College Blvd Fullerton CA 92834-6850 Office Phone: 714-278-3548. Business E-Mail: cejones@fullerton.edu.

JONES, CRAIG ROBERT, financial executive; b. Long Branch, NJ, Apr. 5, 1946; s. Donald Robert and Ruth Budd (Thompson) J.; m. Tamara Edith Jamet, May 25, 1982; children: Alex, Nick. BA, Rutgers U., 1974. CPA. Sr. mgr. Price Waterhouse, Phila., 1974-83; contr. Ultrasystems, Inc., Irvine, Calif., 1983-85; dir. corp. acctg. Fluor Corp., Irvine, 1985-86; v.p., chief fin. officer Hollywood Park Cos., Inglewood, 1986-89, Electro Rent Corp., Van Nuys, 1989—. With USN, 1968-72, Viet Nam. Mem. AICPA, Fin. Execs. Inst., Assn. Corp. Growth. Avocations: sailing, skiing, chess, travel. Home: 2021 Jamestown Way Oxnard CA 93035-3747

JONES, DAVE, state legislator; b. Phila., Jan. 4, 1962; m Kim; children: Isabelle, William. Grad., DePauw U., Greencastle, Ind.; JD, Harvard U. Councilman, Sacramento City Coun., 1999-2004, California State Assemblyman, District 9, 2005-; chairman, Judiciary; member, Health, Public Employ, Retirement & Soc Sec, Revenue & Taxation, Ways & Means comts, currently. Legal Serv North California, Legal Aid Atty, formerly; Counsel to United States Atty General, formerly. White House Fellowship. 1995. Democrat. Office: Dist 9 915 L St Ste 110 Sacramento CA 95814 Office Phone: 916-324-4676. Office Fax: 916-327-3338. Business E-Mail: Assemblymember.jones@assembly.ca.gov.

JONES, DAVID MILTON, economist, educator; b. Newton, Iowa, June 22, 1938; s. Charles Raymond and Mary Evelyn (Corrough) J.; m. Becky Ann Jones Strait, Aug. 4, 1962; children: David, Jennifer, Stephen. BA with honors, Coe Coll., 1960; MA, U. Pa., 1961, PhD, 1969. Economist Fed. Res. Bank N.Y., NYC, 1963-68; v.p., fin. economist Irving Trust Co., NYC, 1968-72; vice-chmn., chief economist, bd. dirs. Aubrey G. Lanston & Co., Inc., NYC, 1972-2000; owner DMJ Advisors LLC, Denver, 2000—, Crystal Lake Resort, Pine, Colo. Advisor panel Fed. Res. Bank N.Y., 1982-93, cons. bd. govs., 1996—; mem. bd. vis. U. Pa.; former dir. pub. interest Suffolk County Savs. and Loan, Centereach, N.Y.; bd. dirs. Aubrey G. Lanston & Co., Inc., Coe Coll., Union Theol. Sem.; lectr. CFA security analysts seminar, Northwestern U.; chmn. bd. Investors' Security Trust Co., Ft. Myers, Fla., 2004—; adj. prof. econs., fin. Fla. Gulf Coast U., 2007-. Author: Fed Watching and Interest Rate Projections: A Practical Guide, 1986, The Politics of Money: The Fed under Alan Greenspan, 1991, The Buck Starts Here: How the Federal Reserve Can Make or Break Your Financial Future, 1995, Unlocking the Secrets of the Fed: How Monetary Policy Affects the Economy and Your Wealth Creation Potential, 2002. Chmn. fin. and investment com. United Ch. Bd. for World Ministries, N.Y.C., 1975-86; mem. bond com. Twp. of Montclair, 1982-83. Woodrow Wilson Found. fellow, 1960; NDEA fellow, 1960 Mem. Nat. Assn. Bus. Economists, Econ. Club of N.Y., Nat. Econ. Club (bd. dirs.). Home: 29200 Crystal Lake Rd Pine CO 80470-8807 Personal E-mail: dmj@allabouttrust.com.

JONES, DAVID ROBERT, retired zoology educator; arrived in Can., 1969; s. William Arnold and Gladys Margery Jones; m. Valerie Iris Gibson, Sept. 15, 1962; children: Melanie Ann, Vivienne Samantha. BSc, Southampton U., 1962; PhD, U. East Anglia, Norwich, Eng., 1965. Rsch. fellow U. East Anglia, 1965-66; lectr. zoology U. Bristol, 1966-69; prof. zoology U. BC, Vancouver, Canada, 1969—, Disting. U. scholar, 2004—, Killam Univ. prof., 2005—06, prof. emeritus, 2006—. Lectr. in field. Contbr. numerous articles to profl. jours. Decorated Order of Can.; recipient Killam Rsch. prize, 1993, Murry A. Newman award significant achievement aquatic rsch., Vancouver Pub. Aquarium and Marine Scis. Ctr., 2004; fellow, Killam Found., Can., 1973, 1989; scholar, Peter Wall Inst. Advanced Studies, Vancouver, 2002. Fellow Royal Soc. Can. (Flavelle medal 2000); mem. Soc. Exptl. Biology, Am. Physiol. Soc. (Scholander Lecture 2006, Krogh Lecture 2007), Can. Zool. Soc. (Fry medal 1992). Avocations: opera, music, theater, English cathedrals. Office: Zoology Animal Care U BC 6199 S Campus Rd Vancouver BC Canada V6T 1W5 Office Phone: 604-822-2180. Business E-Mail: jones@zoology.ubc.ca.

JONES, DONNA MARILYN, state agency administrator, former legislator; b. Brush, Colo., Jan. 14, 1939; d. Virgil Dale and Margaret Elizabeth (McDaniel) Wolfe; m. Donald Eugene Jones, June 9, 1956; children: Dawn Richter, Lisa Shira, Stuart. Student, Treasure Valley Community Coll., 1981-82; grad., Realtors Inst. Cert. residential specialist. Co-owner Parts, Inc., Payette, Idaho, 1967-79; dept. mgr., buyer Lloyd's Dept. Store, Payette, Idaho, 1979-80; sales assoc. Idaho-Oreg. Realty, Payette, Idaho, 1981-82; mem. dist. 13 Idaho Ho. of Reps., Boise, 1987-90, mem. dist. 10, 1990-94, mem. dist. 9, 1995-98; assoc. broker Classic Properties Inc., Payette, 1983-91; owner, broker ERA Preferred Properities Inc., 1991-98; mem. dist. 9 Idaho Ho. of Reps., 1992-98. Co-chmn. Apple Blossom Parade, 1982; mem. Payette Civic League, 1968-84, pres. 1972; mem. Payette County Planning and Zoning Commn., 1985-88, vice-chmn. 1987; field coordinator Idaho Rep. Party Second Congl. Dist., 1986; mem. Payette County Rep. Cen. Com. 1978—; precinct II com. person, 1978-79, state committeewoman, 1980-84, chmn. 1984-87; outstanding county chmn. region III Idaho Rep. Party Regional Hall of Fame, 1985-86; mem. Payette County Rep. Women's Fedn., 1988—, bd. dirs., 1990-92; mem. Idaho Hispanic Commn., 1989-92, Idaho State Permanent Bldg. Adv. Coun., 1990-98; bd. dirs. Payette Edn. Found., 1993-96, Western Treasure Valley Cultural Ctr., 1993-96; nat. bd. dirs. Am. Legis. Exchange Coun., 1993-98; mem. legis. adv. coun. Idaho Housing Agy., 1992-97; committeeperson Payette County Cen.; chmn. Ways and Means Idaho House of Reps., 1993-97, House Revenue & Taxation Com., 1997-98; mem. Multi-State Tax Compact, 1997-98; Idaho chmn. Am. Legis. Exchange Coun., 1991-95; exec. dir. Idaho Real Estate Commn., 1998—. Recipient White Rose award Idaho March of Dimes, 1988; named Payette/Washington County Realtor of Yr., 1987. Mem. Idaho Assn. Realtors (legis. com. 1984-87, chmn. 1986, realtors active in politics com. 1982-98, polit. action com. 1986, polit. affairs com. 1986-88, chmn. 1987, bd. dirs. 1984-88), Payette/Washington County Bd. Realtors (v.p. 1981, state dir. 1984-88, bd. dirs 1983-88, sec. 1983), Bus. and Profl. Women (Woman of Progress award 1988, 90, treas. 1988), Payette C. of C., Fruitland C. of C., Wiesr C. of C. Republican. Avocations: reading, interior decorating. Home: 1911 1st Ave S Payette ID 83661-3003 Office: Idaho Real Estate Commn 633 N 4th St Boise ID 83720-0001

JONES, DOUGLAS RAYMOND, farming executive, state legislator; b. Twin Falls, Idaho, Mar. 24, 1949; s. Leslie Raymond and Charlotte Jones; m. Mary Elizabeth Morris, June 11, 1972; children: Jennifer, Heather, Douglas Jr. BS in Agr., U. Idaho, 1972. V.p. Leslie R. Jones, Inc., Twin Falls, 1972-86, pres., 1986—; rep. Idaho Ho. of Reps., Boise, 1985—, chmn. agrl. affairs com., 1997—. Chmn. edn. com. Nat. Conf. State Legislators, 1994-95, mem. exec. com., 1995-98. Mem. Gov.'s Task Force on Agr., Boise, 1979-80; mem. exec. com. Agrl. Cons. Coun., U. Idaho, Moscow, 1984-96; pres. Twin Falls County Farm Bur., 1980-82; bd. dirs. young farmers Idaho Farm Bur., Boise, 1978-80; troop fin. chmn. Boy Scouts Am., Twin Falls, 1972-94; v.p. Twin Falls Zoning and Planning Bd., 1984-85; mem. Nat. Edn. Goals Panel, 1994—; mem. adv. bd. for standards for excellence in edn. project Coun. for Basic Edn., 1995-97. Recipient Golden Apple award Idaho Edn. Assn., 1988, Terry Reilly Dedication to Young Children with Disabilities award Assn. for Early Childhood Learning, 1989, Friends of Coops. award, Idaho Coop. Coun., 1992. Mem. Twin Falls C. of C. (chmn. agrl. com. 1982-85), Rotary (Blue Lakes chpt.), Alpha Zeta. Republican. Avocation: flying. Office: Leslie R Jones Inc 3653 Highway 93 Twin Falls ID 83301-0237

JONES, EDDIE, architect; m. Lisa Johnson. Founder, prin. Jones Studio Inc., Phoenix, 1979—. Prin. works include Halas Residence, 1985, Ariz. Cardinals Tng. Facility, 1988, Karsten Golf Course Clubhouse, 1994, Japan Eco House, 1996, Walner Residence, 1997, Ariz. State U. Soccer & Softball Stadiums, 1999, Johnson Carlier Office Bldg., 2000, House of 5 Dreams, 2004. Co-recipient Melvin R. Lohmann medal, Okla. State U., 2004. Mem.: AIA. Office: Jones Studio Inc 4450 N 12th St Ste 104 Phoenix AZ 85014 Office Phone: 602-264-2941. Office Fax: 602-264-3440.

JONES, EDWARD GEORGE, neuroscientist, educator; b. Upper Hutt, Wellington, NZ, Mar. 26, 1939; came to U.S., 1972; s. Frank Ian and Theresa Agnes (Riordan) J.; m. Elizabeth Suzanne Oldham, Apr. 27, 1963; children: Philippa Emilie, Christopher Edward. MD, U. Otago, Dunedin, New Zealand, 1962; PhD, U. Oxford, Eng., 1968. Med. and surg. intern Tauranga Hosp., New Zealand, 1963; demonstrator to assoc. prof. dept. anatomy U. Otago Med. Sch., Dunedin, New Zealand, 1964-72; Nuffield Dominions demonstrator and lectr. Balliol Coll., U. of Oxford, England, 1964-72; assoc. prof. to prof., dept. anatomy and neurobiology Washington U. Sch. Medicine, St. Louis, 1972-84, George H. and Ethel Ronzini Bishop scholar, 1981-84, dir. divsn. exptl. neurology, 1981-84; prof. and chmn. dept. anatomy and neurobiology U. Calif., Irvine, 1984-98, dir. Ctr. Neurosci. Davis, 1998—, prof. psychiatry, 1998—, Disting. prof. psychiatry, 2003—. Cons. NIH, 1972—; dir. Neural Systems Lab., Frontier Rsch. Program in Neural Mechanisms of Mind and Behavior, Riken, Japan, 1988-96; vis. sr. rsch. fellow St. John's Coll. at U. Oxford, Eng., 1989-90. Author: The Thalamus, 1984, 2d edit. 2005; co-author: Thalamus, 1997, The Thalamus and Basal Telencephalon, 1982; co-editor: (book series) Cerebral Cortex, 1984-2001; author, reviewer numerous sci. and hist. articles, chpts. in books, 1964—. Mem. Pres.'s Adv. Bd. Calif. State U., Long Beach, 1986-90. Recipient Rolleston Meml. prize, U. Oxford, 1970, Lashley award, Am. Philos. Soc., 2001; named one of 100 most cited biol. scientists, Sci. Citation Index, 1982, 151 Thompson scientific highly cited scientist database, 2001; grantee rsch. grantee, NIH, 1971—. Fellow: AAAS; mem.: NAS, Anat. Soc. Gt. Britain and Ireland (Symington Meml. prize 1968), Am. Assn. Anatomists (Cajal medal 1999, Henry Gray award 2001), Soc. Neurosci. (com. chair 1978—81, 1988—89, pres.-elect 1997—98, pres. 1998—99). Democrat. Avocations: reading, writing, carpentry. Office: U Calif Ctr Neurosci 1544 Newton Ct Davis CA 95616-4859

JONES, EDWARD LOUIS, historian, educator; b. Georgetown, Tex., Jan. 15, 1922; s. Henry Horace and Elizabeth (Steen) Jones; m. Dorothy M. Showers, Mar. 1, 1952 (div. Sept. 1963); children: Cynthia, Frances, Edward Lawrence; m. Lynn Ann McGreevy, Oct. 7, 1963; children: Christopher Louis, Teresa Lynne. BA in Philosophy, U. Wash., 1952, BA in Far East, 1952, BA in Speech, 1955, postgrad., 1952—54; JD, Gonzaga U., 1967. Social worker Los Angeles Pub. Assistance, 1956-57; producer, dir. Little Theatre, Hollywood, Calif. and Seattle, 1956-60; research analyst, cons. to Office of Atty. Gen., Olympia and Seattle, Wash., 1963-66; coordinator of counseling SOIC, Seattle, 1966-68; lectr., advisor, asst. to dean U. Wash., Seattle, 1968—. Instr. Gonzaga U., Spokane, Wash., 1961—62, Seattle CC, 1967—68; dir. drama workshop Driftwood Players, Edmonds, Wash., 1975—76. Author: Black Zeus, 1972, Profiles in African Heritage, 1972, Tutankhamon: Son of the Sun, King of Upper and Lower Egypt, 1978, Black Orators' Workbook, 1982, The Black Diaspora: Colonization of Colored People, 1988, From Rulers of the World to Slavery, 1990, President Zachary Taylor and Senator Hamlin: Union or Death, 1991, Why Colored Americans Need an Abraham Lincoln in 1992, Forty Acres and a Mule: The Rape of Colored Americans, 1994, Mister Moon Goes to Japan, a children's story, 2001, Black Zeus II, 2005; editor, pub.: various jours. V.p. Wash. Com. Consumer Interests, Seattle, 1966—68. Served to 2d lt. US Army, 1940—45. Recipient Appreciation award, Office Minority Affairs, 1987, Fla. chpt. Nat. Bar Assn., 1990, Acad. Excellence award, Nat. Soc. Black Engrs., 1987; Frederick Douglass scholar, Nat. Coun. Black Studies, 1985, 1986. Mem.: Western Polit. Sci. Assn., Nat. Acad. Advising Assn. (bd. dirs. 1979—82, editor Jour. 1981—, award for Excellence 1985), Am. Acad. Polit. and Social Sci., Nat. Assn. Student Pers. Adminstrs., Smithsonian Inst. (assoc.). Democrat. Baptist. Avocations: travel, research, chess. Office: U Wash Ethnic Cultural Ctr Seattle WA 98195-0001 Office Phone: 206-524-7627, 206-524-9604.

JONES, GEOFFREY MELVILL, physiology research educator; b. Cambridge, Eng., Jan. 14, 1923; s. Benett and Dorothy Laxton (Jotham) J.; m. Jenny Marigold Burnaby, June 21, 1953; children: Katharine, Francis, Andrew, Dorothy. BA, Cambridge U., 1944, MA, 1947, MB, BCh, 1949. House surgeon Middlesex Hosp., London, 1949-50; sr. house surgeon Addenbrookes Hosp., Cambridge, England, 1950-51; sci. med. officer Royal Air Force Inst. Aviation

Medicine, Farnborough, England, 1951-55; sci. officer Med. Rsch. Coun., England, 1955-61; assoc. prof. physiology, dir. aviation med. rsch. unit McGill U., Montreal, Que., Canada, 1961-68, prof., dir., 1968-88, Hosmer rsch. prof., 1978-91, emeritus prof. physiology, 1991—. Rsch. prof. clin. neuroscis. U. Calgary, Alta., Can., 1991—, Coll. France, 1979, 95; vis. prof. Stanford U., 1971-72. Author: (with another) mammalian Vestibular Physiology, 1979; editor: (with another) Adaptive Mechanisms in Gaze Control, 1985; contbr. numerous articles to profl. jours. Served to squadron leader Royal Air Force, 1951-55. Sr. rsch. assoc. Nat. Acad. Sci., 1971-72; recipient Skylab Achievement award NASA, 1974, 1st recipient Dohlman medal Dohlman Soc. Toronto U., 1987, Quinquennial Gold medal Barany Soc. Internat., 1988, Ashton Graybiel award U.S. Naval Aerospace Labs., 1989, Wilbur Franks Annual award Can. Soc. Aerospace Medicine, Buchanan-Barbour award Royal Aeronautical Soc., 1991, Mc Laughlin Medal, 1991, Royal Soc. Can. Fellow Can. Aeronautics and Space Inst., Aerospace Med. Assn. (Harry Armstrong award 1968, Arnold D. Tuttle award 1971), Royal Soc. Can. (McLaughlin medal 1991), Royal Soc. London, Royal Aeronautical Soc. London (Stewart Meml. award 1989, Buchanan Barbour award 1990); mem. U.K. Physiol. Soc., Can. Physiol. Soc., Can. Soc. Aerospace Med. Soc., Internat. Collegium Otolaryngology, Soc. Neurosci. Avocations: tennis, sailing, outdoor activities, reading, piano and violin playing/composition. Office: U Calgary Dept Clin Neuroscis 3330 Hospital Dr NW Calgary AB Canada T2N 4N1

JONES, GEORGIA ANN, publisher; b. Ogden, Utah, July 6, 1946; d. Sam Oliveto and Edythe June Murphy; m. Lowell David Jones; children: Lowell Scott, Curtis Todd. Sculptor, 1964-78; journalist, 1968-80; appraiser real property Profl. Real Estate Appraisal, San Carlos, Calif., 1980-95; online columnist, 1995-97; editor Ladybug-Flights Mag., 1997—; pub. LadybugPress, Sonora, 1996—; prin., owner IA Connections Network, 2001—05; pres. NewVoices, Inc., Sonora, 2005—, CEO, 2005—; v.p. Ctrl. Sierra Arts Coun., 2008. Leader workshops for writers, 1994—; founder, prodr. internat radio stas. Ladybughive, 1998—. Teen Talk Network, 1999—, Moose Meals, 2001—; v.p. Ctrl. Sierra Arts Coun., 2008. Author: A Garden of Weedin', 1997, Write What You Know: A Writer's Adventure, 1998, In Line at the Lost and Found, 2000, The Real Dirt on the American Dream: Home Ownership and Democracy, 2000, Isabelle's Appetite, 2008, Maple Memories, 2008; author, playwright, The Porters, 1979, A Stitch in Time, 1995, The Usual Suspects, 1995; editor, pub.: Women on a Wire, 1996, vol. 2, 2001, Memorable Seasons, 2009. Spkr. Jubillenium Interfaith Conf. for World Peace, 1999. Mem. Internat. Forum of Lit. and Culture (bd. dirs., U.S. chpt., Pave Peace keynote spkr. internat. congress 1999). Achievements include patents for Scruples-tag, 1980. Avocations: drawing, designing and building homes, landscape gardening. Office: 16964 Columbia River Dr Sonora CA 95370 Office Phone: 209-694-8340. Personal E-mail: georgiaj@ia-connections.com. Business E-Mail: georgia@ladybugbooks.com.

JONES, GLENN ROBERT, cable systems executive; b. Jackson Center, Pa., Mar. 2, 1930; BS in Econs., Allegheny Coll.; JD, U. Colo.; diploma exec. program, Stanford U.; LHD (hon.), Allegheny Coll. CEO, chmn. Jones Intercable Inc., Englewood, Colo. Author: (poetry) Briefcase Poetry of Yankee Jones, vol. I, 1978, vol. II, 1981, vol. III, 1985, Jones: Dictionary of Cable Television Terminology, 1973, 2d edit., 1976, 3d edit., 1987. Mem. World Future Soc., Nat. Cable TV Assn. Office: Jones Internat Ltd 9697 E Mineral Ave Englewood CO 80112-3408

JONES, GRANT RICHARD, landscape architect; b. Seattle, Aug. 29, 1938; s. Victor Noble and Iona Belle (Thomas) J.; m. Ilze Grinbergs, 1965 (div. 1983); 1 child, Kaija. Student in liberal arts, Colo. Coll., 1956-58; BArch, U. Wash., 1962; M in Landscape Arch., Harvard U., 1966, postgrad. (Frederick Sheldon fellow), 1967-68. Draftsman Jones Lovegren Helms & Archs., Seattle, 1958-59; designer Landscape Archs., Seattle, 1961-65, state conservation planner Honolulu, 1968-69; rsch. assoc. landscape architecture rsch. office Harvard U., 1966-67; prin. Archs. and Landscape Archs., Ltd., Seattle, 1969—. Instr., vis. critic U. Oregon, U. Washington, U. Calif. at Berkeley, CSN Calpoly, U. Va., Harvard U.; lectr. and spkr. in field 30 univs., U.S.; chmn. landscape archtl. registration bd., State of Wash., 1974-79; mem. coun. Harvard U. Grad. Sch. Design, 1978-82, 91-96; vis. com. Harvard U. Grad. Sch., 1993—; bd. visitors U. Oregon Sch. Arch. and Allied Artists; bd. dirs. Scenic Am., Stewardship Ptnrs., Landscape Arch. Found. Author: The Nooksack Plan: An Approach to the Investigation and Evaluation of a River System, 1973; (with B. Gray and J. Burnham) A Method for the Quantification of Aesthetic Values for Environmental Decision Making, 1975, Design as Ecogram, 1975; (with J. Coe and D. Paulson) Woodland Park Zoo: Long Range Plan, Development Guidelines and Exhibit Scenarios, 1976, Landscape Assessment...Where Logic and Feelings Meet, 1978, Design Principles for Presentation of Animals and Nature, 1982, What Are Zoos?, 1984, An Arboretum on a Landfill, 1984, Beyond Landscape Immersion to Cultural Resonance, 1989, Some Thoughts on Power and Influence, 1993; prin. works include Nooksack River Plan, Bellingham, Wash.; Yakima (Wash.) River Regional Greenway, Union Bay Teaching and Research Arboretum, U. Wash., Seattle, Newhalem Campground, North Cascades Nat. Park, Woodland Park Zool. Gardens, Seattle, Washington Park Arboretum, U. Wash., Seattle, zoo master plans for Kansas City, Roanoke, Va., Detroit and Honolulu, Dallas Arboretum and Bot. Garden, Dublin and Fota, Ireland, 2005, Thai Elephant Forest at Woodland Park Zoo, Singapore Bot. Gardens, Paris Pike Hist. Hwy, Denver Commons Park, others. Recipient Nat. award Am. Zoo Assn., 1981-84. Fellow Am. Soc. Landscape Architects (chmn. Wash. chpt. 1972-73, trustee 1979—, v.p., 1988-90, Merit award in community design 1972, Honor award in regional planning 1974, Merit award in regional planning 1977, Merit award in park planning 1977, Merit award in instnl. planning 1977, Pres.'s award of excellence 1980, merit awards in landscape planning), Nature Conservancy, Am. Hort. Soc., Am. Assn. Bot. Gardens and Arboreta, Audobon, Sierrra Club, Phi Gamma Delta, Diet, Rainier Club. Office: Jones & Jones Archs and Landscape Archs Ltd 105 S Main St Ste 300 Seattle WA 98104-2578

JONES, H(AROLD) GILBERT, JR., lawyer; b. Fargo, ND, Nov. 2, 1927; s. Harold Gilbert and Charlotte Viola (Chambers) J.; m. Julie Squier, Feb. 15, 1964; children: Lenna Lettice Mills Jones Carroll, Thomas Squier, Christopher Lee. B of Engring., Yale U., 1947; postgrad., Mich. U., 1948-49; JD, UCLA, 1956. Bar: Calif. 1957. Mem., ptnr. Overton, Lyman & Prince, LA, 1956—61; founding ptnr. Bonne, Jones, Bridges, Mueller & O'Keefe, LA, 1961—89, of counsel, 1990—92, Lewis, Brisbois, Bisgaard & Smith, 1992—; pvt. practice, 2001—. Bd. dirs. Wilshire YMCA, 1969-75. With U.S. Army, 1950-52. Fellow Am. Coll. Trial Lawyers, Am. Bd. Trial Advs. (nat. pres. 1988-89, nat. exec. com. 1990, 92, 96, nat. bd. dirs. 1977—, pres. L.A. chpt. 1980, Calif. Trial Lawyer of Yr. 1999), Internat. Acad. Trial Lawyers: mem. ABA, Calif. Bar Assn., Los Angeles County Bar Assn. (past. chmn. legal-med. rels. com.), Orange County Bar Assn., So. Calif. Assn. Def. Counsel, Jonathan Club, Transpacific Yacht Club (commodore 1996-98), Newport Harbor Yacht Club (commodore 1998), Cruising Club Am., L.A. Yacht Club (Blue Water Cruising award, 1985), Univ. Athletic Club. Home: 818 Harbor Island Dr Newport Beach CA 92660-7228 Office: 650 Town Center Dr Ste 1400 Costa Mesa CA 92626-7020 Home Phone: 949-673-3645; Office Phone: 714-668-5516. Personal E-mail: hg5150@aol.com. Business E-Mail: gjones@lbbslaw.com.

JONES, J. SORTON, lawyer; b. Llandudno, Wales, 1941; BSc, U. St. Andrews, Scotland, 1964; JD, U. Calif., Berkeley, 1973. Bar: Calif. 1973, N.Y. 1975; Registered Civil Engr. Calif. 1969. Mem. Carroll, Burdick & McDonough, San Francisco, 1994—; ptnr. Squires, Sanders & Dempsey LLP, San Francisco. Fellow Chartered Inst. of Arbitrators London; mem. ABA (internat. law sect.), Corp. Counsel Com., Am. Arbitration Assn., Inst. Civil Engrs. London (assoc.).

JONES, JAMES THOMAS, state supreme court justice, former state attorney general; b. Twin Falls, Idaho, May 13, 1942; s. Henry C. and Eunice Jones; m. Mary Kelleen Florence, Aug. 12, 1994; 1 child, Katherine A. Montgomery. Studied, Idaho State U., 1960—61; BA, U. Oreg., 1964; JD, Northwestern U., 1967. Bar: Idaho 1967. Legis. asst. to U.S. Senator, Washington, 1970-72; law practice Jerome, Idaho, 1973-82; atty. gen. State of Idaho, Boise, 1983—91; pvt. practice law Boise, 1991—2005; justice Idaho Supreme Ct., Boise, 2005—. Capt. US Army, 1967—69, Vietnam. Decorated Bronze Star, Air medal with 4 oak leaf clusters, Cross of Gallantry (Vietnam), Army Commendation medal. Mem.: Idaho Bar Assn., VFW, Am. Legion. Lutheran. Office: Idaho Supreme Ct PO Box 83720 Boise ID 83720-0101 Office Phone: 208-334-3186.

JONES, JAN LAVERTY, former mayor; B, Stanford U. Dir. human resources S.M.C. Restaurants, Menlo Park, Calif., 1972-74; dir. R & D Thriftmart Corp., 1976-85; CEO Jan-Mar Corp., 1985-89; mayor City of Las Vegas, 1991-99. Former pres. Fletcher Jones Mgmt. Group; bd. dirs. Bank of Am., Nev., Desert Springs Hosp., Pub. Edn. Found. Founder, chair Mayor's Com. for a Better Cmty.; adv. bd. U. Nev. Las Vegas Law Sch., Nathan Adelson Hospice, Lied Discovery Mus., Shade Tree Shelter for Homeless Women and Children. E-mail: mayor-jjjones@ci.las-vegas.nv.us.

JONES, JEFFREY W., retail executive; Grad. summa cum laude, Mercyhurst Coll. CPA. Sr. acct. Arthur Anderson & Co., 1984-88; v.p., contr., treas. Dairy Mart Convenience Stores, Inc., 1988-94; v.p., contr., mktg. Clark Refining and Mktg. Inc., 1994-98; treas., CFO Lids Corp., Boston, 1998—99; exec. v.p., CFO Clark Retail Group, Inc., Oak Brook, Ill., 1999—2003; sr. v.p., CFO Vail Resorts Devel. Co., Colo., 2003, Vail Resorts Inc., Colo., 2003—. Office: Vail Resorts Inc PO Box 7 Vail CO 81658

JONES, JERVE MALDWYN, construction company executive; b. LA, Sept. 21, 1918; s. Oliver Cromwell and Zola (Hill) J.; m. Alice Castle Holcomb, Apr. 12, 1942; children— Jay Gregory, Janey Lee Matt, Joel Kevin BS in Civil Engring., U. So. Calif., 1939. Registered profl. engr., Calif. Stress analyst Northrop Aircraft, L.A., 1940-43; ptnr. Jones Bros. Constrn. Co., Beverly Hills, Calif., 1946-56; pres., chief exec. officer Peck/Jones Constrn. Corp. (formerly Jones Bros. Constrn. Co.), Beverly Hills, Calif., 1956—. Cons. Jerve M. Jones Assocs., Beverly Hills, 1970—; chmn. exec. com. Jones Constrn. Mgmt., Beverly Hills, 1983— Bd. dirs. Huntington Library, San Marino, Calif., 1984—, Pepperdine U., Malibu, Calif., Boy Scouts Am., L.A., Santa Monica Hosp. Found., YMCA Met. L.A.; chmn. L.A. Music Ctr., United Fund Campaign; life mem. Town Hall Calif., L.A., adv. bd. UCLA Med. Ctr.; mem. State Calif. Strong Motion Instrumentation Program, Dept. Mines and Geology. With USNR, 1943-46, PTO Recipient Civil Engring. Alumnus of Yr. award U. So. Calif., 1985, Bronze Hat award United Contractors Assn., 1985, Disting. Scout award, 1989. Mem. Constrn. Mgmt. Assn. Am. (nat. pres. 1984, Founders award 1985), Archtl. Guild, Archimedes Circle, Constrn. Industry Commn. (chmn. 1980-84), Assoc. Gen. Contractors Am., Los Angeles Area C. of C. (dir.) Clubs: Los Angeles Country, California. Lodges: Rotary (dir. 1962-68). Republican. Episcopalian. Avocations: yachting; skiing; fly fishing. Office: Peck Jones Construction 2049 Century Park E Ste 2300 Los Angeles CA 90067-3125

JONES, JEWEL, social services administrator; b. Oklahoma City, Dec. 7, 1941; d. Joseph Samuel and Jewell (Hathyel) Fisher; m. Maurice Jones, July 17, 1976; children: Anthony, Carmen. BA in Sociology, Langston U., Okla., 1962; MA in Pub. Adminstrn., U. Alaska, Anchorage, 1974. Tchr. Seidman Sch., LA, 1962; correctional oifcer State of Calif. Dept. Corrections, Corona, 1963-65; probation officer County of San Bernardino, Calif., 1965-67; dep. exec. dir. Cmty. Action Agy., Anchorage, 1967-70; social svcs. dir. City of Anchorage, 1970-87; social svcs. mgr. Municipality of Anchorage, 1987-2000, dir. health & human svcs., 2000—. Chmn. bd. Alaska Housing Fin. Corp., Anchorage, 1995—; pres. Anchorage KidsPlace Project, 1994-95; chair Alaskan of the Yr. Scholarship Com., 1985—; chmn. bd. Janet Helen Tolan Gamble and Toby Gamble Ednl. Trust, 1998—. Mem. adv. bd. Salvation Army, Anchorage, 1982-87, Alaska R.R., Anchorage, 1990—; trustee United Way of Anchorage, 1990-97; bd. dirs Alaska Ctr. for Performing Arts, 1987-97. Recipient Pres.'s award Alaska Black Caucus, 1984, Employment of Handicapped award Mayor of Anchorage, 1979, Execs. in Profile award Region X Blacks in Govt. award, 1998. Mem. NAACP (Harambe award 1973), Alaska Black Leadership Conf. (Cmty. Svc. award 1979-80), Links Inc., Quota Club Intenrat., Valli Vue Homeowners Assn. (v.p.), Zeta Phi Beta. Democrat. Avocations: cooking, reading, gardening. Office: Municipality Anchorage PO Box 196650 Anchorage AK 99519-6650

JONES, JOEL MACKEY, academic administrator; b. Millersburg, Ohio, Aug. 11, 1937; s. Theodore R. and Edna Mae (Mackey) Jones; children: Carolyn Mae, Jocelyn Corinne. BA, Yale U., 1960; MA, Miami U., Oxford, Ohio, 1962; PhD, U. N.Mex., 1966. Dir. Am. studies U. Md., Balt., 1966-69; chmn. Am. studies U. N.Mex., Albuquerque, 1969-73, asst. v.p. acad. affairs, 1973-77, dean faculties, assoc. provost, prof. Am. studies, 1977-85, v.p. adminstrn., 1985-88; pres. Ft. Lewis Coll., Durango, Colo., 1988-99, pres. emeritus, 1999—; interim supr. of schs. Durango Pub. Schs., 1999; interim pres. Salisbury State U., 1999—2000. Bd. dirs. 1st Nat. Bank; pres. Durango Sch. Bd., 2001-2006. Contbr. numerous essays, articles and chpts. to books. Founder Rio Grande Nature Preserve Soc., Albuquerque, 1974—; bd. dirs., mem. exec. com. United Way, Albuquerque, 1980-83; na. bd. cons. NEH, 1978—; bd. dirs. Mercy Hosp., 1990-94; mem. ACE Commn. on Leadership. Farwell scholar Yale U., New Haven, 1960; sr. fellow NEH, 1972; adminstrv. fellow Am. Coun. Edn., Washington, 1972-73. Mem. Am. Studies Assn., Am. Assn. Higher Edn., Am. Assn. State Colls. and Univs. (chair com. on cultural diversity, Colo. state rep. 1994—).

JONES, JOHN STANLEY, urban development executive; b. Scranton, Pa., Mar. 25, 1947; BA, SUNY, Stony Brook, 1968; MS, U. Ariz., 1977. Prin. planner Pima County, Tucson, 1979-84; planning cons. pvt. practice, Tucson, 1984-89; dir. devel. svcs. ctr. City of Tucson, 1989-90, dir. devel. svcs. dept., 1990-93, acting water dir., 1993-94, dir. spl. projects, 1995-99; dir. Rio Nuevo Devel. Project, Tucson, 1999—. Recipient Local Official award, Nat. Assn. Homebuilders, 1995. Mem. Am. Planning Assn., Am. Inst. Cert. Planners. E-mail: jjones1@ci.tucson.az.us.

JONES, JOHN WESLEY, entrepreneur; b. Wenatchee, Wash., Nov. 15, 1942; s. Richard F. and Hazel F. (Hendrix) J.; m. Melissa L. Meyer, June 22, 1968 (div. 1982); children: John E., Jennifer L.; m. Deborah G. Matthews, Apr. 24, 1993. BA in Bus./Econs., Western Wash. U., Bellingham, 1966. Trainee Jones Bldg., Seattle, 1967-69, mgr., 1969-78; owner/mgr. N.W. Inboards, Bellevue, Wash., 1974-78, Jones Bldg., Seattle, 1978-86; pvt. investor Bellevue, 1987—; owner/mgr. J. Jones Enterprises, 1994—. Trustee BOMA Health & Welfare Trust, 1982-86, chmn. 1986; mem. Seattle Fire Code Adv. Bd., 1979-86. With USMCR, 1966-72. Mem. Seattle Bldg. Owners Mgrs. Assn. (trustee 1979-86), Bldg. Owners Mgrs. Internat., N.W. Marine Trade Assn., Am. Assn. Individual Investors, Composite Fabricators Assn., Soc. Naval Architects Marine Engrs., Boat US, Seattle Yacht Club, NRA, Internat. Show Car Assn., Nat. Street Rod Assn., Specialty Equipment Mktg. Assn. Republican. Avocations: boating, water-skiing, skiing, automobiles, photography. Home and Office: PO Box 2088 Port Townsend WA 98368

JONES, JOIE PIERCE, acoustician, writer, educator; b. Brownwood, Tex., Mar. 4, 1941; s. Aubrey M. and Mildred K. (Pierce) J.; m. Kay Becknell, June 12, 1965. BA, U. Tex., 1963, MA, 1965; PhD, Brown U., 1970. Sr. scientist Bolt Beranek & Newman, Inc., Cambridge, Mass., 1970-75; assoc. prof., dir. ultrasonics rsch. lab. Case Western Res. U. Sch. Medicine, Cleve., 1975-77; prof., chief med. imaging, dir. grad. studies, dept. radiol. scis. U. Calif., Irvine, 1977—. Cons. acoustics; pres. Computer Sci. Systems, 1978—; founding gen. ptnr. Of Food and Wine, 1982—, Meditherm Assocs., Ltd., 1983-85, Spar Techs., 1987-90, Surgisonics Inc., 1991—, Dermasonics, Inc., 2002-; proposal reviewer NSF/NIH, 1974—; appointee sci. and tech. adv. com. Pres. Carter, 1977-81, United Nat. Environ. Com., 2008-. Author: Acoustical Imaging, 1995, Acoustics and Society: Applications of Ultrasound in Medicine, 1972; co-author (with Z.H. Cho, M. Singh): Foundations of Medical Imaging, 1993; mem. editl. bd. Ultrasound in Medicine and Biology, 1976—; contbr. more than 300 articles to profl. jours. Active vol. local govt. Jr. fellow, U Tex., Austin, 1961—63. Fellow Am. Inst. Ultrasound in Medicine, IEEE, Acoustical Soc. Am., Am. Phys. Soc.; mem. Calif. Wine and Food Soc., Phi Beta Kappa. Democrat. Achievements include more than 50 patents in field. Home: 2094 San Remo Dr Laguna Beach CA 92651-2628 Office: U Calif Dept Radiol Sci Irvine CA 92697-5000 Home Phone: 949-494-6687; Office Phone: 949-824-6147. Business E-Mail: jpjones@uci.edu.

JONES, JULIUS ANDRE MAURICE, professional football player; b. Big Stone Gap, Va., Aug. 14, 1981; BA in Sociology, U. Notre Dame, So. Bend, Ind., 2003. Running back Dallas Cowboys, 2004—08, Seattle Seahawks, 2008—. Recipient All-American Honors, NCAA, 2003. Achievements include ranking in top four among University of Notre Dame Fighting Irish running backs for rushing attempts; holds school records for kick return yards and kickoff return yards. Office: Seattle Seahawks 800 Occidental Ave S Ste 200 Seattle WA 98134

JONES, KATHRYN CHERIE, pastor; b. Breckenridge, Tex., Nov. 26, 1955; d. Austin Thomas and Margaret May (Mohr) J. BA, U. Calif., San Diego, 1977; MDiv, Fuller Theol. Sem., 1982. Assoc. pastor La Jolla (Calif.) United Meth. Ch., 1982-84; pastor in charge Dominguez United Meth. Ch., Long Beach, Calif., 1984-88, San Marcos (Calif.) United Meth. Ch., 1988-90, Atascadero United Methodist Church, 2003—; dir. The Walk to Emmaus, Upper Rm. Ministries, Nashville, 1990-98, Resource Initiatives & Interpretation, Upper Rm. Ministries, Nashville, 1998—. Coord. chaplains Pacific Hosp., Long Beach, 1986-88. Bd. dirs. So. Calif. Walk to Emmaus Cmty., L.A., 1987-88, San Diego chpt., 1988-90; vol. victim advicacy groups, including You Have the Power, Forever Group. Mem. Christian Assn. Psychol. Studies, Evangs. for Social Action. Democrat. Office: Atascadero UMC PO Box 2037 11605 El Camino Real Atascadero CA 93423-2037 Office Phone: 805-466-2566. Office Fax: 805-466-2563.

JONES, KENNETH LYONS, pediatrician, birth defects researcher; b. Phila., Dec. 10, 1939; MD, Hahnemann U., 1966. Cert. Pediat., 1971. Intern pediat. Phila. Gen. Hosp., 1966—67; resident Children's Orthop. Hosp., U. Wash., Seattle, 1967—69, resident pediat., 1971—72; staff mem. Children's Hosp. U. Calif. San Diego, chief Divsn. Dysmorphology/Teratology, Dept. Pediat., founder, med. dir. Calif. Teratogen Info. Svc. (CTIS), prof. pediat. Co-chair Sci. Working Group on Diagnostic Guidelines for Fetal Alcohol Syndrome Disorder, Nat. Ctr. Birth Defects & Devel. Disabilities. Contbr. articles to med. jours. Recipient March of Dimes/Colonel Harland Sanders Award, 2007; named one of Am.'s Top Doctors, Castle Connolly Medical Ltd., 2002; Hartwell Biomedical Rsch. Award, 2008. Mem.: Teratology Soc. (pres. 2004—05), Western Soc. Pediat. Rsch. (past pres.). Achievements include being one of two doctors who identified fetal alcohol syndrome (FAS), 1973. Office: 9500 Gilman Dr # 0828 La Jolla CA 92093-0828 also: U Calif San Diego 200 W Arbor Dr San Diego CA 92103 Office Phone: 619-294-6460, 858-246-0047. Office Fax: 858-246-0014. E-mail: klyons@ucsd.edu.

JONES, L. Q. See MCQUEEN, JUSTICE

JONES, LEONADE DIANE, media publishing company executive; b. Bethesda, Md., Nov. 27, 1947; d. Leon Adger and Landonia Randolph Jones. BA with distinction, Simmons Coll., 1969; JD, MBA, Stanford U., 1973. Bar: Calif. 1973, DC 1979. Summer assoc. Davis Polk & Wardwell, NYC, 1972; securities analyst Capital Rsch. Co., LA, 1973-75; asst. treas. Washington Post Co., 1975-79, 86-87, treas., 1987-96; dir. fin. svcs. Post-Newsweek Stas., Inc., Washington, 1979-84, v.p. bus. affairs, 1984-86; ind. mgmt. cons., pvt. equity investor, 1997-99, 2001—; CFO, sec. VentureThink, LLC, 1999-2001; exec. v.p., CFO Versura, Inc., 2000-01. Bd. ind. chmn. Am.

Balanced Fund, Inc., Income Fund Am., Inc.; bd. dirs. Fundamental Investors, Growth Fund Am., Inc., The New Economy Fund, Small-cap World Fund, Inc.; mem. investment mgmt. subcom. of benefit plans com. Am. Stores Co., 1992—99; mem. investment adv. com. NY State Tchrs. Retirement Sys., 1999—; mem. investment mgmt. subcom. Albertson's Inc., 1999—2007. Bd. dirs. The Women's Found., 2000—03, Access Group, Inc., 2005—. Recipient Candace award for bus., 1992, Serwa award, 1993; named to D.C. Women's Hall of Fame, 1992. Mem.: DC Bar Assn., Calif. Bar Assn., Nat. Bar Assn., Stanford U. Bus. Sch. Alumni Assn. (bd. dirs. 1986—88, pres. Washington-Balt. chpts. 1984—85). Personal E-mail: leonade@att.net.

JONES, LIAL A., museum director; BA, U. Del., 1979; attended, Mus. Mgmt. Inst., U. Calif., Berkeley, 1996. Asst. dir. Del. Art Mus., Wilmington, 1979, dep. dir., CEO; dir. Crocker Art Mus., Sacramento, 1999—. Recipient Art Educator of Yr., Art Educators of Del., 1993, Paul Getty Trust Scholarship, 1996. Office: Crocker Art Mus 216 O St Sacramento CA 95814 E-mail: ljones@cityofsacramento.org.

JONES, LORIN V., state senator; b. St. George, Utah, Jan. 28, 1929; m. Ferral Leavitt. Student, Dixie Coll.; BEE, San Bernardino Valley Coll. Formerly oper. engr. and mgr. electric utility; mem. Utah State Senate, 1996—, chair edn. com., mem. energy, natural resources and agr. com., co-chair commerce and revenue appropriations com. Bd. dirs. Rural Water Assn. Utah; dir. tng. Western Sys. Coordinating Coun. Mem. Nat. Assn. Power Engrs., Am. Power Dispatchers Assn., St. George Rotary Club, Cinder Valley Lions Club. Republican. Home: 177 E Center St Veyo UT 84782-4040

JONES, M. DOUGLAS, JR., pediatrician, educator; b. San Antonio, Apr. 22, 1943; BA, Rice U., 1964; MD, U. Tex., 1968. Diplomate Am. Bd. Pediat. Intern U. Colo. Sch. Medicine, Denver, 1968-69, resident, 1969-71, fellow neonatal-perinatal medicine, 1973-75, prof. pediatrics, 1990—; faculty John Hopkins U. Sch. Medicine, 1977—90; dir. neonatal Intensive care John Hopkins Hosp. Mem. Am. Bd. Pediat., Am. Acad. Pediat., Am. Pediat. Soc., Soc. for Pediat. Rsch. Office: Children's Hospital Mail Stop 8402 PO Box 6508 Education 2 S Room 4304 13121 E 17th Ave Aurora CO 80045 Office Phone: 303-724-2851. Office Fax: 303-777-7323. Business E-Mail: jones.doug@fchden.org.

JONES, MICHAEL T., real estate development executive; Exec. v.p. ops., Pres. Hawaii divsn. Schuler Homes Inc., Honolulu, 1998—. Office: Schuler Homes Inc 828 4th St Mall Fl 4 Honolulu HI 96813-4321

JONES, MILTON BENNION, retired agronomist; b. Cedar City, Utah, Jan. 15, 1926; s. William Lunt and Claire (Bennion) Jones; m. Grace Elaine Guymon, Sept. 8, 1951; children: Milton B., Jr., Richard W., Jo Layne, Tamera, Sherilee, Karolyn. BS, Utah State U., 1951; PhD, Ohio State U., 1955. Successively jr. agronomist, asst. agronomist, assoc. agronomist, agronomist, lectr. emeritus U. Calif., Hopland, Davis, 1955—91; ret., 1991. Cons. IRI Rsch. Inst., Campinas, Brazil, 1963—65, CSIRO, Australia, 1974, BLM, Ukiah, Calif., 1970—77, Sulphur Inst., Washington, 1967—88, AID U., Evora, Portugal, 1984, Basque Govt., Bilbao, Spain, 1987, MAF, Invernay, New Zealand, 1990. Contbr. articles to profl. jours. Humanitarian mission, Scotland, 1991—93, Georgia, 1997—2000; mem. sch. bd. Ukiah Elem. Sch. Dist., 1962—63; scout leader local chpt. Boy Scouts Am., Ukiah, 1962—70. With USN, 1944—47. Fellow: Soil Sci. Soc., Agronomy Soc. Office: U Calif 4070 University Rd Hopland CA 95449-9717 Home: 1501 East 1500 N Provo UT 84604 Personal E-mail: gracegjones@yahoo.com, miltongrace@gmail.com.

JONES, MILTON WAKEFIELD, publisher; b. Burbank, Calif., Apr. 18, 1930; s. Franklin M. and Lydia (Sinclair) J.; m. Rita Strong, May 4, 1959; 1 son, Franklin Wayne. AA, Santa Monica City Coll., 1950; BS, U. So. Calif., 1952. V.p. mktg. Sav-Ink Co., Newport Beach, Calif., 1956-58; account exec. KDES-Radio, Palm Springs, Calif., 1958-60; pres. Milton W. Jones Advt. & Pub. Rels. Agy., Palm Springs, 1960—, Desert Publs., Inc., Palm Springs, 1965—, Riverside Color Press, Inc., Palm Springs, Olman Travel Svc., Palm Springs, 1979-84. Pres. Franklin Comms. (Sta. KPSL-Radio), 1987-98, Airport Displays Ltd., 1972—; vice chmn. Palm Springs Savings Bank, 1981-96; bd. dirs., treas. Canyon Nat. Bank. Pub. Palm Springs Life Mag., 1965—, Wheeler Bus. Letter, Palm Springs, 1969-77, San Francisco mag., 1973-79, Guest Life, Orange County, N.Mex., Carmel/Monterey, St. Petersburg/Clearwater, Vancouver, Can., El Paso, Houston, 1978—, Orange County mag., 1987-89, McCallum Theatre Program, 1989—, Ofcl. Guide to Houston, 1993, El Paso Guest Life, 1993, Pebble Beach, The Magazine, 2002. Pub. Record newspaper, 1996-2006, Official Guide to Ontario, 2001-06, Official Guide to Galveston Island, 2003-05, Official Guide to Newport Beach, 2007. Mem. Desert Press Club (pres. 1965). Home: 422 N Farrell Dr Palm Springs CA 92262-6559 also: 206 Abalone Ave Newport Beach CA 92662-1304 Office: 303 N Indian Canyon Dr Palm Springs CA 92262-6015 E-mail: milt@palmspringslife.com.

JONES, NAPOLEON A., JR., federal judge; b. 1940; BA, San Diego State U., 1962, MSW, 1967; JD, U. San Diego, 1971. Legal intern, staff atty. Calif. Rural Legal Assistance, Modesto, Calif., 1971-73; staff atty. Defenders, Inc., San Diego, 1973-75; ptnr. Jones, Cazares, Adler & Lopez, San Diego, 1975-77; judge San Diego Mcpl. Ct., 1977-82, San Diego Superior Ct., 1982-94, US Dist. Ct. (so. dist.) Calif., San Diego, 1994—2007, sr. judge, 2007—. Mem. San Diego County Indigent Def. Policy Bd. Bd. visitors Sch. Social Work San Diego State U.; active Valencia Park Elem. Sch. Mem. San Diego County Bar Assn., Earl B. Gilliam Bar Assn., San Diego Bar Found., Nat. Bar Assn., Calif. Bar Assn., Calif. Black Attys. Assn., Nat. Assn. Women Judges, Masons, Sigma Pi Phi, Kappa Alpha Psi. Office: US Dist Ct So Dist Calif US Courthouse 940 Front St Ste 2125 San Diego CA 92101-8912*

JONES, NATHANIEL B., JR., bishop; Bishop Ch. of God in Christ, Barstow, Calif. Founder, adminstr., prin. Barstow Ch. of God in Christ Christian Day Sch. Office: Ch God in Christ 1375 Sage Dr Barstow CA 92311-2446

JONES, ORLO DOW, retired lawyer, retired pharmaceutical executive; b. Logan, Utah, June 10, 1938; s. Orlo Elijah and Joyce (Lewis) Jones; m. Ilarene Balls, July 9, 1958; children: Monica, Orlo Courtney. BS, Utah State U., 1960; LL.B., U. Calif., Berkeley, 1963. Bar: Calif. 1964. Atty. Carlson, Collins & Bold, Richmond, Calif., 1968-69, AT&T, San Francisco, 1969-71, Longs Drug Stores, Inc., Walnut Creek, Calif., 1971-76, sec., gen. counsel, 1976—, v.p., 1979-87, sr. v.p., 1987—. Lectr. comml. leases Continuing Edn. Bar U. Ext., U. Calif., Berkeley. Served to capt. JAGC US Army, 1964—68. Republican. Mem. Lds Ch. Home: 156 Santiago Dr Danville CA 94526-1941

JONES, PAMELA S., realestate development executive; Sr. v.p. fin., CFO, bd. dirs. Schuler Homes Inc., Honolulu, 1996—. Office: Schuler Homes Inc 828 4th St Mall Fl 4 Honolulu HI 96813-4321

JONES, PETER ANTHONY, medical research administrator; b. Cape Town, South Africa, Jan. 21, 1947; naturalized citizen U.S. married; 3 children. BSc with 1st class honors, U. Coll. Rhodesia, 1969; PhD, U. London, 1973. NIH tng. fellow divsn. hematology-oncology Children's Hosp. of L.A., 1973-75; dir. basic rsch. and dir. Urol. Cancer Lab. U. So. Calif., LA, 1984-93, assoc. dean for acad. and sci. affairs Sch. Medicine, 1991-94, interim chmn. dept. molecular microbiology and immunology, dir. Comprehensive Cancer Ctr., 1993—. Mem. integration panel breast cancer program U.S. Army Med. Rsch. and Devel. Command to date; mem. cancer5 ctr. support rev. com. Nat. Cancer Inst., 1988-92; mem. Bladder Cancer Working Group of the Organ Sys. Program, 1986-89; mem. cellular biology and physiology study sect. NIH, 1984-87, mem. chem. pathology, spl. study sect., 1985, ad hoc mem. cellular physiology rev. group, 1983, ad hoc mem. pathology B study sect., 1981, mem. spl. study sect. tumor promoters, 1982. Assoc. editor Cancer Rsch., 1983—, Molecular Carcinogenesis, 1987—, Carcinogenesis, 1990-93, Invasion and Metastasis, 1982—. Cancer Assn. Rhodesia Jr. Rsch. fellow, 1969-70, U. Rhodesia Postgrad. fellow, 1971; rsch. grantee Am. Cancer Soc., 1977-78, 78-79, 79-82, Nat. Cancer Assn. South Africa, Nat. Inst. Gen. Med. Scis., 1982-85, Nat. Cancer Inst., 1978-89, 82-89, 89—. Mem. AAAS, Am. Soc. Biochemistry and Molecular Biology, Am. Assn. for Cancer Rsch. (pubs. com., bd. dirs. 1989-92, program com. 1988, chmn. biology sect. 1989, chmn. local arrangements com. ann. meeting 1986), Am. Urol. Assn. (affiliate), DNA Methylation Soc., Soc. for Basic Urol. Rsch. Achievements include research in DNA methylation and cell differentiation; molecular biology of cancer. Office: Norris Comprehen Cancer Ctr 1441 Eastlake Ave Los Angeles CA 90089-9181

JONES, PETER F., lawyer; b. Hanover, NH, Jan. 3, 1944; s. J. Franklin Jr. and Elizabeth Anne (Dunning) J.; m. Anne Meyer, Apr. 17, 1971; children: David, Philip. BA, Ripon Coll., 1967; JD, U. Denver, 1970. Bar: Colo. 1971, U.S. Dist. Ct. Colo. 1971. Assoc. Duane O. Littell, Denver, 1971-76, Hall & Evans, Denver, 1976-78, ptnr., 1978—. Office: Hall And Evans 1125 17th St Ste 600 Denver CO 80202-2052

JONES, QUINCY, producer, composer, arranger, conductor, trumpeter; b. Chgo., Mar. 14, 1933; s. Quincy Delight and Sarah J.; children: Kidada, Rashida, Jolie, Martina-Lisa, Quincy III, Rachelle, Kenya. Student, Seattle U., Berklee Coll. Music; studied with Nadia Boulanger; student, Boston Conservatory; degree (hon.), Berklee Coll. Music, 1983, Howard U., 1985, Seattle U., 1990, Wesleyan U., 1991, Loyola U., 1992, Brandeis U., 1992, Clark U., 1993. Head Quincy Jones Entertainment. Trumpeter, arranger Lionel Hampton Orch., 1950-53; arranger for orchs., singers including Frank Sinatra, Dinah Washington, Count Basie, Sarah Vaughan, Peggy Lee, USA For Africa; organizer, trumpeter Dizzy Gillespie Orch. for Dept. of State tour of Near East, Mid. East, S.Am., 1956; music dir. Barchlay Disques, Paris; leader own orch. European tour, concerts, TV, radio, 1960; music dir., Mercury Records, 1961, v.p., 1964; composer: background scores The Boy in the Tree, 1964; condr. (film music) The Pawnbroker, Mirage, The Slender Thread, 1965, Walk Don't Run, Made in Paris, 1966, Banning (Acad. awd. nom. best song 1967), The Deadly Affair, Enter Laughing, In Cold Blood (Acad. awd. nom. best score 1967), In the Heat of the Night, 1967, For the Love of Ivy (Acad. awd. nom. best song 1968), The Split, Mirage, A Dandy in Aspic, The Hell with Heroes, Jigsaw, 1968, Bob and Carol and Ted and Alice, Cactus Flower, John and Mary, The Italian Job, The Lost Man, MacKenna's Gold, 1969, Eggs, Of Men and Demons, The Out-Of-Towners, Up Your Teddy Bear, The Last of the Mobile Hotshots, They Call Me Mr. Tibbs, 1970, The Anderson Tapes, Brother John, Honky, 1971, Come Back Charleston Blue, The Hot Rock, 1972, The New Centurions, 1972, The Getaway, 1972, Mother, Jugs, and Speed, 1976, The Wiz, 1978, (also co-producer) The Color Purple (Acad. awd. noms., best picture, best song 1985), Fever Pitch, (exec. music producer) The Slugger's Wife, 1985, Listen Up: The Lives of Quincy Jones, 1990; composer, actor (film) Blues for Trumpet and Koto, Life Goes On; rec. artist numerous platinum albums including Body Heat, 1974, Mellow Madness, 1975, I Heard That, 1976, The Dude, 1981, Back on the Block, 1989, Snackwater Jack, 1991; producer videotape Portrait of An Album: Frank Sinatra with Quincy Jones and Orchestra, 1986 (platinum); producer recordings Michael Jackson's Off the Wall, 1980, Thriller, 1982 (world's best selling record), Bad; producer (with Steven Spielberg) The E.T. Storybook, (TV series) Fresh Prince of Bel Air, 1990—; composer (television) Hey Landlord, 1966-67, Ironside, 1967-75, The Bill Cosby Show, 1969-71, The New Bill Cosby Show, 1972-73, Sanford and Son, 1972-77, Sanford Arms, 1977, The Cosby Show, 1984-92, The Oprah Winfrey Show, 1989—; mini-series Roots (Emmy awd., best music composition, 1977), 1977; founder Vibe Magazine, 1992, exec. prodr. A Call for Reunion concert Lincoln Meml. for Clinton Inauguration, 1993. Recipient 76 Grammy nominations, 26 Grammy awards, numerous Readers Poll awards Downbeat Mag., Trendsetters awards Billboard Mag., Golden Note award ASCAP, 1982, Image award NAACP, 1974, 80, 81, 83, 90, 91, Hollywood Walk of Fame, 1980, Man of the Yr. award City of Hope, 1982, Whitney Young Jr. award Urban League, 1986, Humanitarian of Yr. award T.J. Martell Found., 1986, Lifetime Achievement award Nat. Acad. Songwriters, 1989, Grammy Living Legend award, 1990, Grammy award for Best Jazz instrumental, individual or group 1994 for "Miles and Quincy Live at Montreux", Scopus award Hebrew U., 1991, Spirit of Liberty award People for the Am. Way, 1992, Ivor Novello Spl. Internat. award, Brit. Acad. Composers & Songwriters, 2007; named Entrepreneur of the Yr. USA Today/Fin. News Network, 1991; film biography: Listen Up: The Lives of Quincy Jones, 1990; Named one of 100 Most Influential Black Americans Ebony mag., 2006; named to Power 150 Ebony mag., 2008; named to Calif. Hall of Fame, 2008. Office: Quincy Jones Music 6671 W Sunset Blvd Ste 1574a Los Angeles CA 90028-7123

JONES, RICHARD HUNN, biostatistician, researcher, educator; b. Ridley Twp., Pa., Oct. 31, 1934; s. Harold Lytton and Julia (Hunn) J.; m. Lois June Christian, Nov. 14, 1953 (div. Feb. 1980); children: Autumn Lynne Brandes, Monica Cecile McNulty; m. Julie Ann Marshall, July 18, 1981; children: Earl Richard Marshall, Kathryn Marie Marshall. BS, Pa. State U., 1956, MS, 1957; PhD, Brown U., 1961. Asst. prof. Johns Hopkins U., Balt., 1962-66, assoc. prof., 1966-68; prof. U. Hawaii, Honolulu, 1968-75; prof. biostats. U. Colo., Denver, 1975—2005, prof. emeritus, 2005—. Cons. Patrick AFB, Fla., 1962-66, Tripler Army Hosp., Honolulu, 1969-73, Nat. Bur. Standards, Boulder, Colo., 1979-85, Synergen, Boulder, 1988-93. Author: Longitudinal Data with Serial Correlation, 1993; contbr. over 130 articles to profl. jours. Fellow Am. Statis. Assn. Democrat. Avocations: running, biking, swimming. Personal E-mail: richardhunnjames@mns.com.

JONES, RICHARD K., information technology executive; Student in Computer sci., U. of Waterloo, Ontario, Can. Sr. cons. ptnr. JNL EFT Cons. Inc.; pres. & CEO Bethany Computer Sys. Inc.; dir. computing and comm. & CTO Technicolor Inc.; joined Countrywide Financial Corp., Calabasas, Calif., 1995—, sr. v.p., infrastructure, IT divsn., exec. v.p. of enterprise arch., IT, sr. mng. dir. & chief info. officer; exec. v.p., chief info. officer Fiserv, Inc., 2008—. Office: Fiserv, Inc PO Box 979 Brookfield WI 53008-0979

JONES, RICHARD MICHAEL, lawyer; b. Chgo., Jan. 16, 1952; s. Richard Anthony and Shirley Mae (Wilhelm) J.; m. Catherine Leona Ford, May 25, 1974. BS, U. Ill., 1974; JD, Harvard U., 1977. Bar: Colo. 1977, U.S. Dist. Ct. Colo. 1977. Assoc. Davis, Graham & Stubbs, Denver, 1977-81; corp. counsel Tosco Corp., Denver, 1981-82; asst. gen. counsel Anschutz Corp., Denver, 1982-88, gen. counsel, v.p., 1989—. Mem. ABA, Colo. Bar Assn., Denver Bar Assn. Office: Anschutz Corp 555 17th St Ste 2400 Denver CO 80202-3987

JONES, ROBERT EDWARD, federal judge; b. Portland, Oreg., July 5, 1927; s. Howard C. and Leita (Hendricks) J.; m. Pearl F. Jensen, May 29, 1948; children: Jeffrey Scott, Julie Lynn BA, U. Hawaii, 1949; JD, Lewis and Clark Coll., 1953, LHD (hon.), 1995; LLD (hon.), City U., Seattle, 1984. Bar: Oreg. Trial atty., Portland, Oreg., 1953-63; judge Oreg. Circuit Ct., Portland, 1963-83; justice Oreg. Supreme Ct., Salem, 1983-90; judge U.S. Dist. Ct. Oreg., Portland, 1990—. Mem. faculty Nat. Jud. Coll., Am. Acad. Jud. Edn., ABA Appellate Judges Seminars; former mem. Oreg. Evidence Revision Commn., Oreg. Ho. of Reps.; former chmn. Oreg. Commn. Prison Terms and Parole Stds.; adj. prof. Northwestern Sch. Law, Lewis and Clark Coll., 1963—, Willamette Law Sch., 1988-90. Author: Rutter Group Practice Guide Federal Civil Trials and Evidence, 1999—. Mem. bd. overseers Lewis and Clark Coll., mem. bd. visitors to Northwestern Sch. Law. Served to capt. JAGC, USNR. Recipient merit award Multnomah Bar Assn., 1979; Citizen award NCCJ, Legal Citizen of the Yr. award Law Related Edn. Project, 1988; Service to Mankind award Sertoma Club Oreg.; James Madison award Sigma Delta Chi; named Disting. Grad., Northwestern Sch. Law; Outstanding Profl. Achievement Alumnus award, U.S. Merchant Marine Acad., 1998; Judge Robert E. Jones Oreg. Justice award, Am. Judicature Soc., 1999, Lifetime Commitment to Jury Trial Sys. award Am. Bd. Trial Advs., 2004. Mem. Am. Judicature Soc. (bd. dirs. 1997-2001), State Bar Oreg. (past chmn. Continuing Legal Edn.), Oreg. Circuit Judges Assn. (pres. 1967-1968), Oreg. Trial Lawyers Assn. (pres. 1959, chair 9th cir. edn. com. 1996-97). Office: US Dist Ct House 1000 SW 3rd Ave Ste 1007 Portland OR 97204-2944 Home Phone: 503-636-2810; Office Phone: 503-326-8340. Business E-Mail: robert_jones@ord.uscourts.gov.

JONES, RONALD H., computer information systems executive; b. San Diego, Feb. 11, 1938; s. Henry G. and Geneva H. J.; m. Carol Sue Carmichael, Dec. 9, 1967. BS, San Diego State Coll., 1959, MS, 1961. Project mgr. UNIVAC, San Diego, 1961-67, Computer Scis. Corp., San Diego, 1967-75; v.p. Interactive, Inc., San Diego, 1975-92; owner Consulting Co., San Diego, 1992—; ind. cons., programmer various mfg. & distbg. cos., San Diego, 1992—. Contbr. articles to profl. jours; tech. advisor to Internat. Spectrum Mag. Advisor San Diego State Univ.; Conservation. Vol., 1979-. Mem. AARP, Am. Prodn. and Inventory Control Soc., Assn. for Computing Machinery, Calpirg and Ucan. Presbyterian. Avocations: golf, tennis, fishing. Home and Office: 2484 Pine St San Diego CA 92103-1042 also: Ron Jones Cons PO Box 370083 San Diego CA 92137-0083 Office Fax: 619-543-0619.

JONES, RUSSELL L., state legislator; b. San Diego, May 11, 1948; m. Janet Francis Jones, Jan. 13, 1968; children: Shelley, Eric. EdB, U. Ariz.; degree in Bus. Adminstrn., San Diego State U. Lic. US customhouse broker, Ariz. ins. broker, Ariz. notary pub. Mem. Dist. 24 Ariz. House of Reps., 2004—, vice chair natural resources & rural affairs com. Chmn. Ariz. Internat. Devel. Authority; past chmn. bd. dirs. Greater Yuma Econ. Devel. Corp. Bd. dirs. Yuma Cmty. Food Bank, Yuma Cmty. Found.; v.p. bd. dirs. Ariz. Cmty. Found.; past bd. dirs. Yuma Regional Hosp. Found., Cmty. Concert Assn., Yuma Orchestra Assn., Yuma Fine Arts Assn. Served with 82nd Airborne Divsn. US Army, 1970—72. Mem.: San Luis C. of C., Nat. Customhouse Brokers Freight Forwarders Assn., San Diego Customs Brokers Assn., Border Brokers Assn., Caballeros de Yuma, San Luis Frontera Rotary Club. Republican. Office: Ariz House Reps Capitol Complex 1700 W Washington Rm 345 Phoenix AZ 85007 Office Phone: 602-926-3002. Office Fax: 602-417-3124. Business E-Mail: rjones@azleg.gov.*

JONES, SARA SUE FISHER, librarian; b. Rupert, Idaho, May 2, 1962; d. Richard Sherman and Dana Louise Fisher; m. Martin R. Jones, Jan. 7, 1984; children: Russel, Elaine. BA in Comms., Boise State U., 1983; MLS, Syracuse U., 1999; postgrad., U. North Tex. Libr. dir. Stanley (Idaho) Cmty. Libr., 1984-86; English tchr. Minidoka County Schs., Rupert, Idaho, 1986-88; children's librarian Elko (Nev.) County Libr., 1988-95, libr. dir., 1995-2000; state libr., divsn. adminstr. Nev. State Libr. and Archives, 2000—. Commr. State Nev. Commn. on Ednl. Tech. Elko County Libr. Bd. scholar, 1997-99; IMLS scholar Mem. Nev. Libr. Assn. (pres. 2000—, pub. trustee, chair, Dorothy McAlindin award 1995, scholar 1997-98), Nev. Libr. Orgn. (chair N.E. dist.), Philanthropic Edn. Orgn., Soroptimist Internat. (pres. 1995-96). Avocations: reading, camping, golf. Office: 100 N Stewart St Carson City NV 89701

JONES, SHIRLEY, actress, singer; b. Smithtown, Pa., Mar. 31, 1934; d. Paul and Marjorie (Williams) J.; m. Jack Cassidy, Aug. 5, 1956 (div. 1975); children: Shaun, Patrick, Ryan; m. Marty Ingels, 1977. Grad. high sch., 1952; student, Pitts. Playhouse. Appeared with chorus South Pacific, 1953, in Broadway prodn. Me and Juliet, 1954; other state appearences include The Beggar's Opera, 1957, The Red Mill, 1958, Maggie Flynn, 1968, On a Clear Day, 1975, Show Boat, 1976, Bitter Suite, 1983; films include role of Laurey in Oklahoma, 1954, later stage tour Paris and Rome, sponsorship U.S. Dept. State, Carousel, 1956, April Love, 1957, Never Steal Anything Small, 1959, Bobbikins, 1959, Elmer Gantry, 1960 (Acad. Best Supporting Actress award 1961), Pepe, 1960, The Two Rode Together, 1961, The Music

Man, 1962, The Courtship of Eddie's Father, 1963, A Ticklish Affair, 1963, Bedtime Story, 1964, The Secret of My Success, 1965, Fluffy, 1965, The Happy Ending, 1969, The Cheyenne Social Club, 1970, Beyond the Poseidon Adventure, 1979, Tank, 1984, There Were Times, Dear, 1985; night club tour with husband, 1958, later TV and summer stock; star TV series The Partridge Family, 1970-74, Shirley, 1979; guest star: TV series McMillan, 1976; starred with Patrick Cassidy (Broadway): 42nd Street; Silent Night, Lonely Night, 1969, But I Don't Want To Get Married!, 1970, The Girls of Huntington House, 1973, The Family Nobody Wanted, 1975, The Lives of Jenny Dolan, 1975, Winner Take All, 1975, Yesterday's Child, 1977, Evening in Byzantium, 1978, Who'll Save Our Children, 1978, A Last Cry for Help, 1979, The Children Of An Lac, 1980, Inmates: A Love Story, 1981, There Were Times Dear, 1987, Carousel, 2005; one-woman concert: TV series Shirley Jones' America 1981; author: Shirley and Marty: An Unlikely Love Story, 1990. Nat. chairwoman Leukemia Found. Named Mother of Yr. by Women's Found., 1978. Office Phone: 818-728-9505. Business E-Mail: martyingels@msn.com.

JONES, STEPHEN B., academic administrator; m. Judy Jones; 2 children. BS, SUNY, Syracuse, PhD in Resources Mgmt. Dir. Ala. Coop. Ext. Sys., 1997—2001; vice chancellor ext. and engagement, prof. Coll. Nat. Resources NC State U., 2001—04; chancellor U. Alaska, Fairbanks, 2004—. Office: University of Alaska Chancellor's Office PO Box 757500 Fairbanks AK 99775

JONES, THORNTON KEITH, chemist, researcher; b. Brawley, Calif., Dec. 17, 1923; s. Alfred George and Madge Jones; m. Evalee Vestal, July 4, 1965; children: Brian Keith, Donna Eileen. BS, U. Calif., Berkeley, 1949, postgrad., 1951-52. Research chemist Griffin Chem. Co., Richmond, Calif., 1949-55; western product devel. and improvement mgr. Nopco Chem. Co., Richmond, Calif., 1955; research chemist Chevron Research Co., Richmond, 1956-65, research chemist in spl. products research and devel., 1965-1982; product quality mgr. Chevron USA, Inc., San Francisco, 1982-87, ret. Vol. fireman and officer, Terra Linda, Calif., 1957-64; mem. adv. com. Terra Linda Dixie Elem. Sch. Dist., 1960-64. Served with Signal Corps, U.S. Army, 1943-46. Mem. Am. Chem. Soc., Forest Products Research Soc., Am. Wood Preservers Assn., Alpha Chi Sigma. Republican. Presbyterian. Achievements include patents in field. Avocations: music, gardening.

JONES, SIR TOM (THOMAS JONES WOODWARD), singer; b. Pontypridd, Wales, June 7, 1940; s. Thomas and Freda (Jones) Woodward; m. Melinda Trenchard, 1956; 1 son, Mark. Student, Treforrest Secondary Modern Sch. Bricklayer, factory and constrn. laborer. Pub. singing debut at age 3 in village stores of Wales; sang in local pubs; changed name to Tom Jones, 1963; organized backup group the Playboys to sing in London clubs; first hit record was It's Not Unusual, 1964; appeared on Brit. radio and TV; toured U.S. in 1965, 68; appeared on Ed Sullivan Show; star of TV show This is Tom Jones, 1969-71; regular appearances in nightclubs, concert halls and on TV; songs recorded include What's New Pussycat, 1965, Thunderball, 1965, Green Green Grass of Home, 1966, Delilah, 1968, Love Me Tonight, 1969, Can't Stop Loving You, 1970, She's A Lady, 1971, Letter to Lucille, 1973, Say You'll Stay Until Tomorrow, 1976; albums Darlin, 1981, Move Closer, 1989, Carrying A Torch, 1990 (includes collaborations with Van Morrison); sang score for mus. play Matador; hit single A Boy From Nowhere, 1987, Kiss (in collaboration with Art of Noise), 1988, The Complete Tom Jones, 1993, Reload, 1999 (multi-platinum worldwide), Best of Tom Jones, 2000; film appearances include Mars Attacks, 1996, Agnes Brown, 1999, The Emperor's New Groove, 2000; TV appearances include Here, There and Everywhere: a Concert for Linda, 1999, Jerry Springer on Sunday, 1999, An Audience with Tom Jones, 2000, Millenium Celebrations at the White House, 2000, Queen's Jubilee Concert, 2002; TV series The Morecambe & Wise Show, The Sonny and Cher Show, (voice) The Simpsons, The Fresh Prince of Bel-Air, Russell Gilbert Live, The Panel, 20/20. Recipient Grammy award as Best New Artist, 1965, Brit. Best Male Vocalist award, 2003, Brit. Outstanding Contbn. award, 2003, Order Brit. Empire (OBE), 2006. Office: Tom Jones Enterprises 1801 Avenue Of The Stars Ste 200 Los Angeles CA 90067-5904

JONES, VAUGHAN FREDERICK RANDAL, mathematician, educator; b. Gisborne, New Zealand, Dec. 31, 1952; m. Martha Weare Myers, Apr. 7, 1979; children: Bethany Martha, Ian Randal, Alice Collins. BSc, U. Auckland, New Zealand, 1972, MSc with first class honors, 1973; DSc in Math., Ecoles Mathematiques, Geneva, 1979; DSc (hon.), U. Auckland, 1992, U. Wales, 1993. Asst. lectr. U. Auckland, New Zealand, 1974, now disting. alumni prof.; asst. U. Geneva, 1975—80; E.R. Hedrick asst. prof. math. UCLA, 1980—81; asst. prof. U. Pa., Phila., 1981—84, assoc. prof., 1984—85; prof. math. U. Calif., Berkeley, 1985—. Vis. lectr. U. Pa., Phila., 1981—82; dir. New Zealand Math. Rsch. Inst. Recipient F W W Rhodes Meml. Scholarship, Swiss Govt. Scholarship, 1973, Vacheron Constantin Prize, 1980, Guggenhein fellowship, 1986, Fields medal Internat. Congress, Kyoto, Japan, 1990, New Zealand Govt. Sci. medal, 1991, Onsager medal, Trondheim U., 2000. Fellow: Royal Soc.; mem.: Norwegian Royal Soc. Letters & Scis., U.S. Nat. Acad. Scis., London Math. Soc. (hon.), Am. Acad. Arts & Scis. Achievements include index theorem for von Neumann algebras; discovery of a new polynomial invariant for knots which led to surprising connections between apparently quite different areas of mathematics. Office: U Calif Berkeley Dept Math 970 Evans Hall Berkeley CA 94720-3841 Office Phone: 510-642-6550, 510-642-4196. E-mail: vfr@math.berkeley.edu.

JONES, WARREN EUGENE, state supreme court justice; b. Montpelier, Idaho, Oct. 19, 1943; m. Karen Jones; 2 stepchildren. BA magna cum laude, Albertson Coll. Idaho, Caldwell, 1965; JD, U. Chgo., 1968. Bar: Idaho 1968. Law clk. for Chief Justice Joseph J. McFadden Idaho Supreme Ct., Boise, 1968—70, justice, 2007—; atty. to sr. litigator Eberle Berlin, Kading, Turnbow, McKlveen and Jones, Boise, 1970—2007. Mem.: ABA, Assn. Def. Trial Attys., Idaho Assn. Def. Counsel, Def. Rsch. Inst., Am. Bd. Trial Advs., Boise Bar Assn. Office: Idaho Supreme Ct PO Box 83720 Boise ID 83720-0101*

JONES, WES, architect; b. 1958; Disting. cadet, US Mil. Acad., West Point, NY, 1978; AB with highest honors in Architecture, U. Calif., Berkeley, 1980; MArch with distinction, Harvard U., 1983. Lic. Calif., NY. With ELS Design Group, Berkeley, Calif., 1980—83, Eisenman/Robertson, Archs., NYC, 1983—87; design ptnr. Holt Hinshaw Pfau Jones, San Francisco, 1987—93; prin. Jones, Ptnrs.: Architecture, LA and San Francisco, 1993—. Vis. prof. Harvard U. Sch. Architecture, Princeton U., NJ, Ill. Inst. Tech., Columbia U., NYC, UCLA, Ohio State U.; studio tchr. So. Calif. Inst. Architecture. Recipient Rome prize, Architecture, Architecture award, AAAL, 2007. Mem.: Phi Beta Kappa. Office: Jones Ptnrs Architecture 141 Nevada St El Segundo CA 90245 Office Phone: 310-414-0761. Office Fax: 310-414-0765. E-mail: info@jonespartners.com.

JONES, WILLIAM ALLEN, retired lawyer; b. Phila., Dec. 13, 1941; s. Roland Emmett and Gloria J. (Miller); m. Margaret Smith, Sept. 24, 1965 (div. 1972); m. Dorothea S. Whitson, June 15, 1973 (div. 2007); children: Darlene, Rebecca, Gloria, David. BA, Temple U., 1967; MBA, JD, Harvard U., 1972. Bar: Calif. 1974. Atty. Walt Disney Prodns., Burbank, Calif., 1973-77, treas., 1977-81; atty. Wyman Bautzer et al, LA, 1981-83, MGM/UA Entertainment Co., Culver City, 1983, v.p., gen. counsel, 1983-86; sr. v.p., corp. gen. counsel, sec. MGM/UA Communications Co., Culver City, Calif., 1986-91; exec. v.p., gen. counsel, sec. Metro-Goldwyn-Mayer Inc., Santa Monica, Calif., 1991-95, exec. v.p. corp. affairs, 1995-97, sr. exec. v.p., 1997—2005. Bus. mgr. L.A. Bar Jour., 1974-75; bd. dirs. The Nostalgia Network Inc.; mem. bd. of govs. Inst. for Corp. Counsel, 1990-93. Charter mem. L.A. Philharm. Men's Com., 1974-80; trustee Marlborough Sch., 1988-93, Flintridge Preparatory Sch., 1993-96. With USAF, 1960-64. President's scholar Temple U., 1972 Mem. Harvard Bus. Sch. Assn. So. Calif. (bd. dirs. 1985-88). Home: 1557 Colina Dr Glendale CA 91208-2412

JONSEN, ALBERT R(UPERT), medical ethics educator; b. San Francisco, Apr. 4, 1931; s. Albert R. and Helen (Sweigert) Jonsen; m. Mary Elizabeth Carolan. BA, Gonzaga U., 1955, MA, 1956; STM, U. Santa Clara, 1963; PhD, Yale U., 1967. Mem. S.J., 1949—76; ordained priest Roman Cath. Ch.; instr. philosophy Loyola U., LA, 1956—59; asst. in instrn. Yale Div. Sch., 1966—67; asst. prof. theology and philosophy U. San Francisco, 1967—72, pres., 1969—72; prof. med. ethics Sch. Medicine, U. Calif.-San Francisco, 1972—87; adj. assoc. prof. dept. community medicine and internat. health Sch. Medicine, Georgetown U., 1977; prof. med. ethics, chmn. dept. med. history and ethics Sch. Medicine U. Wash., Seattle, 1987—99, prof. emeritus; faculty Fromm Inst. for Life-Long Learning, U. San Francisco, 2000—; co-dir. and sr. ethics scholar in residence, Program in Medicine and Human Values, Calif. Pacific Med. Ctr., San Francisco, 2004—. Vis. prof. Yale U., 1999—2000; mem. artificial heart assessment panel Nat. Heart and Lung Inst., 1972—73, 1984—86; mem. Am. Bd. Med. Spltys., 1978—81; cons. Am. Bd. Internal Medicine, 1978—82, ACOG, 1983—88; mem. Pres.'s Commn. for Study of Ethical Problems in Medicine, 1979—82, Nat. Commn. for Protection Human Subjects of Biomed. and Behavioral Rsch., HEW, 1974—78, Nat. Bd. Med. Examiners, 1985—87, Commn. on AIDS Rsch., NRC, 1986—92, Panel on Social Impact of AIDS (chmn.), 1989—91; chmn. nat. adv. bd. Ethics and Reprodn., 1991—96; mem. ethics adv. bd. GERON Corp., 2000—; vis. prof. Stanford U. Sch. Medicine, 2002, U. Va. Law Sch., 2002; vis. prof. dept. surgery U. Calif., San Francisco, 2004. Author: Responsibility in Modern Religious Ethics, 1968, Patterns of Moral Responsibility, 1969, Christian Decision and Action, 1970, Ethics of Newborn Intensive Care, 1976, Clin. Ethics, 1982, 6th edit., 2005, The Abuse of Casuistry: A History of Moral Reasoning, 1987, The New Medicine and the Old Ethics, 1990, The Social Impact of AIDS in the United States, 1993, Bioethics, 1997, The Birth of Bioethics, 1998, A Short History of Medical Ethics, 2000, Bioethics Beyond the Headlines, 2005; mem. editl. bd. Jour. Philosophy and Medicine, Jour. Clin. Ethics. Bd. trustees Inst. Ednl. Mgmt., Harvard U., 1971—74, Ploughshares Found., 1980—84; mem. San Francisco Crime Com., 1969—71; bd. dirs. Found. Critical Care Medicine, 1983—86, Sierra Health Found., 1987—. Fellow, Guggenheim, 1995—96. Fellow: The Hastings Ctr.; mem.: Am. Osler Soc. (McGovern award 1986), Am. Coll. Cardiology (Convocation Medal 1996), Am. Soc. for Bioethics and Humanities (Lifetime Achievement award 1999), Blue Cross and Blue Shield Assn. (tech. assessment program 1985—2003, med. adv. panel), Instituto de Bioetica (Madrid), Inst. Medicine (com. human values 1973, coun. 1983—85, 1990—92), Soc. Christian Ethics, Am. Soc. Law and Medicine (bd. dirs. 1986—88), Soc. Health and Human Values (pres. 1986—87). Home: 1333 Jones St # 502 San Francisco CA 94109 E-mail: arjonsen@aol.com.

JONSEN, ERIC RICHARD, lawyer; b. San Francisco, June 5, 1958; s. Richard William and Ann Margaret (Parsons) J.; m. Ida-Marie, May 8, 1982; children: Kaitlyn, Jeremy, Michelle. BA, Hartwick Coll., 1980; JD, U. Colo., 1985. Bar: Colo., N.Y., U.S. Dist. Ct. Colo., U.S. Ct. Appeals (10th cir., Fed. cir.), U.S. Ct. Appeals (fed. cir.). Assoc. William P. DeMoulin, Denver, 1986-88, Fairfield & Woods, Denver, 1988—91; ptnr. Ciancio & Jonsen PC, Denver, 1994—2001, Jonsen & Assoc. LLC, Broomfield, Colo., 2001—. Bd. dirs. Broomfield Blast Soccer Club, 2000—. Mem. ABA, Colo. Bar Assn., Rotary (pres. Broomfield Crossings 2000—). Home Phone: 303-465-6002; Office Phone: 303-991-5970. E-mail: erjonsen@jonsen.net.

JORDAHL, PATRICIA ANN, music educator, theater director; b. Clarkfield, Minn., June 1, 1951; d. Robert Stanley and Norma Burnette Shefveland; m. Owen Warren Jordahl, June 11, 1977; children: Melody Ann, Matthew Owen. BA, Luther Coll., Decorah, Iowa, 1969—73; MA, Western N.Mex U., Silver City, N. Mex, 1987—90. Cert. Cmty. Coll. Lifetime Tchr. Ariz., 1993. K-12 music tchr. Hubbard Cmty. Schools, Hubbard, Iowa, 1973—77; pvt. music tchr. Self-employed, Iowa Falls, Iowa, 1977—85; k-12 music tchr. Thatcher Cmty. Schools, Thatcher, Ariz., 1986—93; music/music theatre prof. Ea. Ariz. Coll., Thatcher, Ariz., 1993—. Music tech. chair/bd. of directors Ariz. Music Educator's Assn., Phoenix, 1995—99; music dept. chair Ea. Ariz. Coll., Thatcher, Ariz., 2001—08, chair fine arts divsn., 2008—. Recipient Kennedy Ctr. award for excellence in theater edn., Am. Coll. Theater Festival, 2005. Mem.: Am. Choral Dir. Assn. (assoc.), Music Educator Nat. Conf. (assoc.), Ariz. Music Educator Assn. (assoc.; sec. 1999—2001, O.M. Hartsell Excellence in Tchg. award 1998). Conservative. Meth. Avocations: travel, music, swimming, reading, theater. Office: Eastern Arizona Coll 615 North Stadium Ave Thatcher AZ 85552 Business E-Mail: trish.jordahl@eac.edu.

JORDAN, AMOS AZARIAH, JR., foreign affairs educator, retired military officer; b. Twin Falls, Idaho, Feb. 11, 1922; s. Amos Azariah and Olive (Fisher) J.; m. MarDeane Carver, June 5, 1946; children: Peggy Jordan Hughes, Diana Jordan Paxton, Keith, David, Linda Jordan Mabey, Kent. BS, US Mil. Acad., 1946; BA, Oxford U., Eng., 1950, MA, 1955; PhD, Columbia U., NYC, 1961. Commd. 2d lt. US Army, 1946, advanced through grades to brig. gen., 1972; instr. US Mil. Acad., 1950-53, prof. social scis., 1955-72; arty. battery comdr. US Army, Republic of Korea, 1954-55; asst. S-3 7th Divsn. Arty. Korea, 1955; adviser econ. and fiscal policy US Econ. Mission to Korea, 1955; ret. US Army, 1972; dir. Aspen Inst., 1972-74; prin. dep. asst. sec. for internat. security affairs Dept. Def., Washington, 1974-76; dep. undersec. and acting undersec. for security assistance Dept. State, Washington, 1976-77; with Ctr. for Strategic and Internat. Studies, Washington, 1977-94, pres, chief exec. officer, 1983-88, vice chmn., 1988-94, pres. Pacific Forum Honolulu, 1990-94, sr. adviser, 1994—; counselor Pacific Forum, CSIS, 1994—. Mem. staff Pres.'s Com. to Study Fgn. Assistance Program, 1959; staff dir. Adv. Com. to Sec. Def. on Non-Mil. Instrn., 1962; spl. polit. advisor to U.S. amb. to India, 1963-64; cons. NSC, 1979; mem. Nat. Com. on Security and Econ. Assistance, 1983; Henry Kissinger rsch. chair in nat. security policy CSIS, 1988-92; mem. Pres.'s Intelligence Oversight Bd., 1989-93; internat. co-chmn. Coun. on Sec. Coop. in the Asia Pacific, 1993-96, chmn. U.S. com., 1993-98; co-chmn. Korean-Am. Wisemen Coun., 1991-98; Asia area adminstr. Latter Day Saint Charities, 1998-99; spl. asst. to pres. Brigham Young U., Hawaii, 2001-02; bd. dirs. Pacific Forum, Ctr. for Strategic and Internat. Studies, Jackson Hole Ctr. for Global Affairs. Author: Foreign Aid and the Defense of Southeast Asia, 1962, Issues of National Security in the 1970's, 1967; co-author: American National Security Policy and Process, 1981, 6th edit., 2009; contbr. chpts. to books and articles to profl. jours. Decorated D.S.M., Legion of Merit with oak leaf cluster, Disting. Civilian Svc. medal Dept. Def. Mem.: Assn. Am. Rhodes Scholars. Office: Pacific Forum CSIS Pauahi Tower 1001 Bishop St Ste 1150 Honolulu HI 96813-3407 Office Phone: 808-521-6745.

JORDAN, GLENN, film, television and theater director; b. San Antonio, Apr. 5, 1936; BA, Harvard U., 1957; postgrad., Yale U. Sch. Drama, 1957—58. Dir. regional and stock theatre, including Cafe La Mama, late 1950s; N.Y. directorial debut with Another Evening With Harry Stoones, 1961; other plays include A Taste of Honey, 1968; Rosencrantz and Guildenstern Are Dead, 1969, A Streetcar Named Desire at Cin. Playhouse in the Park, 1973, All My Sons at Huntington Hartford Theatre, 1975; founder, N.Y. TV Theater, 1965, dir. various plays, including Paradise Lost and Hogan's Goat; dir. mini-series Benjamin Franklin, CBS, 1974 (Emmy award 1975, Peabody award); Family, ABC-TV series, 1976-77, including segment Rights of Friendship (Dirs. Guild Am. award); numerous TV plays for public TV, including Eccentricities of a Nightingale, 1976; The Displaced Person, 1976; TV movies including Shell Game, 1975, One Of My Wives Is Missing, 1975, Delta County U.S.A, 1977, In The Matter of Karen Ann Quinlan, 1977, Sunshine Christmas, 1977, Les Miserables, 1978, Son-Rise, A Miracle of Love, 1979, The Family Man, 1979, The Women's Room, 1980, Lois Gibbs and the Love Canal, 1982, Heartsounds, 1984 (Peabody award), Toughlove, 1985, Dress Gray, 1986, Something in Common, 1986, Promise, 1986 (2 Emmy awards for producing, directing, Peabody award, Golden Globe award), Echoes in the Darkness, 1987, Jesse, 1988, Home Fires Burning, 1988, Challenger, 1989, The Boys, 1990, Sarah Plain and Tall, 1990, Aftermath, 1990, O Pioneers!, 1991, Barbarians at the Gate, 1992 (Emmy award Outstanding Made for TV Movie, 1993, Golden Globe award, Best Mini-series or movie made for TV, 1994), To Dance with the White Dog, 1994, Jane's House, 1994, My Brother's Keeper, 1994, A Streetcar Named Desire, 1995, Jake's Women (Neil Simon), 1996, After Jimmy, 1996, Mary and Tim, 1996, A Christmas Memory, 1997, The Long Way Home, 1998, Legalese, 1998, Night Ride Home, 1999, Winter's End: Sarah Plain & Tall III, 1999, Midwives, 2000, Lucy, 2003; dir: feature film Only When I Laugh (Neil Simon), 1981, The Buddy System, 1983, Mass Appeal, 1984. Recipient Emmy awards for N.Y. TV Theater Plays, 1970, Actors Choice award, 1970. also: 9401 Wilshire Blvd Ste 700 Beverly Hills CA 90212-2920

JORDAN, JEFF, Internet company executive; BA in Polit. Sci. and Psychology, Amherst Coll.; MBA, Stanford U. From mgr. strategic planning Consumer Products Divsn. to CEO The Disney Store Worldwide The Walt Disney Corp.; exec. v.p., CFO Hollywood Entertainment; pres. website; sr. v.p. eBay U.S. eBay Inc., San Jose, Calif., gen. mgr. eBay U.S., sr. v.p. U.S. Bus., 2000—05; pres. PayPal Inc. (subs. eBay Inc.), 2005—. Office: PayPal Inc eBay Inc 2145 Hamilton Ave San Jose CA 95125

JORDAN, JEFFREY GUY, marketing professional, consultant; b. Oshkosh, Wis., May 21, 1950; s. Berwin Russell and Delores Suzanne (Tomlitz) J. BS, U. Wis., Oshkosh, 1973; postgrad., UCLA, 1978. Analyst corp. planning and rsch. May Co. Dept. Store, LA, 1973-77; dir. mktg. svcs. DJMC Advt., LA, 1977-80; dir. mktg. Wienerschnitzel, Internat., Newport Beach, Calif., 1980-84, York Steakhouse Restaurants (Gen. Mills), Columbus, Ohio, 1984-85, Paragon Restaurant Group, San Diego, 1985-87; v.p. mktg. Paragon Steakhouse Restaurants, Inc., San Diego, 1987-94; owner, pres. Mindset Rsch., 1994—. Cons., presenter U.S. Internat. U., San Diego, 1989. Mem. Conv. and Visitors Bur., San Diego; vol. Boys' Club of Am., Oshkosh, 1973-74; fundraising coord. Am. Cancer Soc., L.A., 1976. Mem. Am. Mktg. Assn. (treas., bd. dirs. 1996-97), Qualitative Rsch. Cons. Assn., Multi Unit Foodservice Operators Assn., San Diego Advt. Assn. (creative exec. 1986-88), San Diego C. of C. Republican. Lutheran. Avocations: sports, travel, photography. Office Phone: 858-484-2307.

JORDAN, LAMONT, professional football player; b. Forestville, Md., Nov. 11, 1978; s. Marie. B in Comm., U. Md., College Park, 2001. Running back NY Jets, 2001—05, Oakland Raiders, 2005—08, New Eng. Patriots, 2008, Denver Broncos, 2009—. Office: Denver Broncos 13655 Broncos Pky Englewood CO 80112*

JORDAN, MARTHA B., lawyer; m. David Lee; children: Stacy, Kristen. BS, Pa. State U., 1976; MBA, U. Cin., 1978; JD, U. Calif., Berkeley, 1983. Bar: Calif. 1983. With Latham & Watkins, LLP, LA, 1983—90, ptnr., 1990—98, 2005—, mng. ptnr., 1998—2004. Named Top US Lawyer, Law Dragon 500, 2005, 2006; named one of Calif.'s Top 100 Most Influential Lawyers, Calif. Law Bus., 1999. Office: Latham Watkins 355 S Grand Ave Los Angeles CA 90071-1560 Home Phone: 213-891-8716; Office Phone: 213-485-1234.

JORDAN, ROBERT LEON, lawyer, educator; b. Reading, Pa., Feb. 27, 1928; s. Anthony and Carmela (Votto) J.; m. Evelyn Allen Willard, Feb. 15, 1958 (dec. Nov. 1996); children: John Willard, David Anthony BA, Pa. State U., 1948; LLB, Harvard U., 1951. Bar: NY 1952. Assoc. White & Case, NYC, 1953-59; prof. law UCLA, 1959-70, 75-91, prof. law emeritus, 1991—, assoc. dean Sch. Law, 1968-69. Vis. prof. law Cornell U., Ithaca, N.Y., 1962-63; co-reporter Uniform Consumer Credit Code, 1964-70, Uniform Comml. Code Articles 3, 4, 4A, 1985-90; Fulbright lectr. U. Pisa, Italy, 1967-68 Co-author: (with W.D. Warren) Commercial Law, 1983, 5th edit., 2000, Bankruptcy, 1985, 5th edit., 1999. Lt. USAF, 1951—53. Office: UCLA Sch Law 405 Hilgard Ave Los Angeles CA 90095-9000

JORDAN, STEPHEN M., academic administrator; m. Ruth Kinnie; 3 children. BA in Polit. Sci., U. No. Colo., 1971; MPA in Fin. Adminstrn., U. Colo., Denver, 1979, PhD in Pub. Adminstrn./Policy Analysis, 1990. Vice chancellor for budgets and facilities U. Colo. Health Scis. Ctr., 1985—, asst. sec. bd. regents, 1985—; dep. exec. dir. fin. and planning, Bd. Regents Ariz. State U., 1989—; exec. dir. Kans. Bd. Regents, 1994—; pres. Ea. Wash. U., Cheney, 1998—2005. Met. State Coll. of Denver, 2005—. Mem. edn. subcom. Inland N.W. Tech. Edn. Ctr.; mem. commn. on internat. edn. Am. Coun. of Edn.; mem. com. on econ. and workforce devel. Am. Assn. State Colls. and Univs.; mem. Nat. Collaborative Adv. Group, N.W. Commn. on Colls. and Univs. Bd. dirs. Wash. Tech. Ctr., Wash. State Inst. for Pub. Policy, Coun. of Presidents; mem. exec. bd. Spokane Alliance Med. Rsch., 2003, Providence Health Svcs. Ea. Wash., Wash. Campus Compact, Air Edn. and Tng. Command, Health Industry Devel. Group, Higher Edn. Leadership Group. Mem. NCAA (mem. presdl. adv. group), Spokane Area C. of C. (bd. dirs. 2000 exec. com. 2004), Phi Kappa Phi. Office: Metropolitan State Coll of Denver PO Box 173362 Denver CO 80217-3362 Office Phone: 303-556-2070.

JORDAN, THOMAS HILLMAN, geophysicist, educator; b. Coco Solo, CZ, Republic of Panama, Oct. 8, 1948; s. Clarence Eugene and Beulah J.; m. Margaret Jordan; 1 child, Alexandra Elyse. BS, Calif. Inst. Tech., 1969, MS in Geophysics, 1970, PhD in Geophysics and Applied Math., 1972. Asst. prof. Princeton U., NJ, 1972-75, Scripps Instn. of Oceanography, U. Calif. San Diego, La Jolla, 1975-77, assoc. prof., 1977-82, prof., 1982-84; Robert R. Shrock prof. earth and planetary sciences MIT, Cambridge, 1984-85, head, earth, atmospheric and planetary sciences dept., 1988—98; W.M. Keck prof. geophysics, Coll. of Letters, Arts, and Sciences, dept. earth sciences U. So. Calif., LA, 2000—; scientific dir. So. Calif. Earthquake Ctr., 2000—. Contbr. over 140 articles to profl. jours. Fellow AAAS, Am. Geophys. Union (James B. Macelwane award 1983, George P. Woolard award 1998); mem. NAS (councilor, 2006-), Am. Philosophical Soc. Office: Dept Earth Scis U So Calif Los Angeles CA 90089-0740 Address: So Calif Earthquake Ctr U So Calif 3651 Trousdale Pkwy Ste 169 Los Angeles CA 90089-0742 Office Phone: 213-740-5843. Office Fax: 213-740-0011. E-mail: tjordan@usc.edu.

JORGENSEN, BLAKE J., former Internet company executive; b. 1959; m. Debra Jorgensen. BA with honors, Stanford U., 1982; MBA, Harvard U. Mgmt. cons. MAC Group/Gemini Consulting, Marakon Assocs.; mng. dir., prin. Corp. Fin. Dept. Montgomery Securities, 1996—98; co-founder Thomas Weisel Ptnrs., San Francisco, 1998, ptnr., dir. pvt. placements, 1998—2002, co-dir. investment banking, COO, mem. exec. com., 2002—07; CFO Yahoo! Inc., Sunnyvale, Calif., 2007—09. Former chmn. Empower Am.; founder, pres. Montgomery Sports (now Tailwind Sports). Bd. mem. Mus. Modern Art, NYC, San Francisco Mus. Modern Art, Stanford Endowment Mgmt. Com. Mem.: US Ski & Snowboard Found. (former chmn.), USA Cycling Devel. Found. (former bd. mem.).*

JORGENSEN, PAUL J., research company executive; b. Midway, Utah, Sept. 1, 1930; s. Joseph and Alice P. Jorgensen; m. Ardelle M. Bloom, Sept. 11, 1959; children: Paula, Mark, Janet, LaDell, Brett, Scott. Student, U. Utah, 1948-50, PhD, 1960; BS, Brigham Young U., 1954. Scientist Gen. Electric Co., Schenectady, N.Y., 1960-68; mgr. ceramics group Stanford Research Inst., Menlo Park, Calif., 1968-74, dir. materials research ctr., 1974-76; exec. dir. phys. sci. div. SRI Internat., Menlo Park, 1976-77, v.p. phys. and life sci. div., 1977-80, sr. v.p. scis. group, 1980-88, exec. v.p., COO, 1988-94, also bd. dirs., exec. v.p., 1994—. Cons. GTE, 1971-82; mem. com. high temperature chemistry NRC, 1972-75, nat. materials adv. bd., 1982-85; mem. Internat. Panel of Advisors on Tech., Singapore Inst. Stds. & Indsl. Rsch. Contbr. articles to profl. jours.; patentee in field. Served with U.S. Army, 1954-56. Recipient IR-100, Indsl. Research Mag., 1967. Fellow Am. Ceramic Soc. (chmn. basic sci. div. 1975). Republican. Mem. Lds Ch. Office: SRI Internat 333 Ravenswood Ave Menlo Park CA 94025-3453 E-mail: paul.jorgensen@sri.com.

JORGENSEN, PETER M., state legislator; b. Berkeley, Calif., June 22, 1935; m to Jean Jorgensen; children: Arne, Heidi, Kari & Paul. BS in Civil Engring., Bucknell U. Wyoming State Representative, District 16, 2002-, member, appropriations comt, Western Legislature Conf fiscal affairs.Highway engr. United States Bureau Public Lands, 1957-65; Resident engr, Tippers Asset, McCartny & Stratton, 1965-67; sole proprietor, Peter Jorgensen, Cons Engr, 1967-70; President, Jorgensen Eng and Land Surveyors, PC, 1974-2001; Cons. director, Jorgensen Assocs, PC, 2001-02. Democrat. Unitarian. Mailing: PO Box 9550 Jackson WY 83002-9550 Office Phone: 307-733-5150. Office Fax: 307-733-5187. Business E-Mail: pjorgensen@jorgensenassociates.com.

JOSEFF, JOAN CASTLE, manufacturing executive; b. Alta., Can., Aug. 12, 1922; naturalized U.S. citizen, 1945; d. Edgar W. and Lottie (Coates) Castle; BA in Psychology, UCLA; widowed; 1 child, Jeffrey Rene. With Joseff-Hollywood, jewelry manufacture and rental and aircraft components and missiles, Burbank, Calif., 1939—, chmn. bd., pres., sec.-treas. TV appearances include CBS This Morning, Australia This Morning, Am. Movie Channel. Active Burbank Salary Task Force, 1979—, LA County Earthquake Fact-Finding Commn., 1981—; bd. dirs. San Fernando Valley area chpt. Am. Cancer Soc., treas., Genesis Energy Systems, Inc., 1993—; mem. Rep. Cen. Com.; del. Rep. Nat. Conv., 1980, 84, 88, 92, 96, 2000; active Beautiful People Award Com. Honoring John Wayne Cancer Clinic; appointed by Gov. Wilson to Barber and Cosmotology Bd; appointed br Pres. Clinton to Selective Svc. System. Recipient Women in Achievement award Soroptimist Internat., 1988, Rep. Congl. Com. award, 2004, Bus. Woman of Yr. award Nat. Rep. Congl. Com., 2004. Mem. Women of Motion Picture Industry (hon. life), Nat. Fedn. Rep. Women (bd. dir., Caring for Am. award 1986), Calif. Rep. Women (bd. dir., treas. 1986-90), North Hollywood Rep. Women (pres. 1981-82, parliamentarian), Toluca Lake Property Owners Assn. (treas. 1992-), Nat. Fedn. of Rep (voting mem., program chair, 1994—, bylaws chair 1998—), Calif. Fedn. of Rep. Women (chaplain, Americanism chmn. so. div., regent chmn. Women of Achievement award 1988), L.A. County Fedn. of Rep. Women (scholarship chmn.), St. Joseph Hosp. (oral history 2006), NFRW Conv. (chmn., Gala 2040 Mems., 2007). Home: 10060 Toluca Lake Ave Toluca Lake CA 91602-2924 Office: 129 E Providencia Ave Burbank CA 91502-1922 Office Phone: 323-849-2306. Personal E-mail: joseff-hollywood@sbcglobal.net.

JOSELYN, JO ANN, space scientist; b. St. Francis, Kans., Oct. 5, 1943; d. James Jacob and Josephine Felzien (Firkins) Cram. BS in Applied Math., U. Colo., 1965, MS in Astro Geophysics, 1967, PhD in Astro Geophysics, 1978. Research asst. NASA-Manned Space Ctr., Houston, 1966; physicist NOAA-Space Environ. Lab., Boulder, Colo., 1967-78; space scientist NOAA-Space Environ. Ctr., Boulder, 1978-99; chief Geospace Branch, 1992-95; sec.-gen. Internat. Union Geodesy and Geophysics, 1999—2007; sec. sigma xi chpt. U. Colo., 2007—; with Share-A-Gift Inc.; bd. sec. Boulder Coun. Internat. Visitors, 2008—. U.S. del. study group 6 Consultive Com. for Ionospheric Radio, 1981, 83; mem. com. on data mgmt. and computation NASA Space Sci. Bd., 1988. Mem. U. Colo. Grad. Sch. Alumni Coun., 1986-90, U. Colo. Engring. Devel. Coun., 1991-99, U. Colo. Adv. Coun. for the Women in Engring. Program, 1992-98, Grad. Sch. Adv. Coun.; bd. trustees U. Colo. Found., 2002-06. Recipient unit citation NOAA, 1971, 80, 85, 86, sustained superior performance award 1985, 87-90, 92, 94; group achievement award NASA, 1983, Disting. Engring. Alumnus award U. Colo., 1987, Dir.'s award Space Environ. Lab., 1991, 95, Pacesetter award Boulder County, 1994, Sec. Commerce award for Customer Svc. Excellence, 1994, George Norlin award U. Colo. Alumni Assn., 2000; elected to U. Colo. Disting. Alumni Gallery, 1995; named Woman of Achievement, Zonta Club, Boulder, 1996; named to Colo. Women's Hall of Fame, 2002; fellow Sci. and Tech. Agy. Japan, 1990-91. Mem. AAAS, AAUW, PEO, Am. Women in Sci., Am. Geophys. Union, Union Radio Sci. Internat. (commns. G and H, membership chair of commn. H 1993-96), Internat. Assn. Geomagnetism and Aeronomy (co-chair Divsn. V on observatories, instruments, indices and data 1991-95, sec.-gen. 1995-99), Internat. Astron. Union (commns. 10 and 49), Rotary Internat., Ikebana Internat., Sigma Xi, Tau Beta Pi, Sigma Tau. Republican. Methodist.

JOSEPH, ALLAN JAY, lawyer; b. Chgo., Feb. 4, 1938; s. George S. and Emily (Miller) Cohen; m. Phyllis L. Freedman, Sept. 1, 1958; children— Elizabeth, Susan, Katherine. BBA, U. Wis., Madison, 1959; JD cum laude, 1962. Bar: Wis. bar 1962, Calif. bar 1964. Ptnr. Pettit & Martin, San Francisco, 1965-80; ptnr., co-chmn., govt. contracts practice group Rogers, Joseph, O'Donnell & Phillips, San Francisco, 1981—. Editor: (prof. journal) Wis. Law Rev., author articles law jours. Served to capt. JACG AUS, 1962-65. Am. Bar Found. fellow, 1978— Mem.ABA (treas. 2002-05, nat. chmn. pub. contract law sect. 1977-78, ho. of dels. 1980-84, 1995—, bd. govs. 1995-98, chair fin. com. 1997-98), FBA, Am. Bar Retirement Assn. (trustee 1984-92, pres. 1989-90), State Bar Calif., Nat. Contract Mgmt. Assn., Order of Coif. Home: 2461 Washington St San Francisco CA 94115-1816 Office: 311 California St Fl 10 San Francisco CA 94104-2614

JOSEPH, ANNE M., lawyer, educator; BA, Williams Coll., 1992; M.Phil., Cambridge Univ., 1995; JD, Yale Univ., 2000; PhD, Harvard Univ., 2002. Law clk. U.S. Ct. Appeals (D.C. Cir.), Washington, 2000—01; atty. U.S. Dept. Just. Civil Div., Washington, 2001—03; law clk. to Ruth Bader Ginsburg U.S. Supreme Ct., Washington, 2003—04; asst. prof. Law Sch. U. Calif., Berkeley, 2004—. Contbr. articles to prof. jour. Office: Univ Calif Berkeley Law Sch 433 North Addition Berkeley CA 94720-7200

JOSEPH, GEORGE, insurance company executive; b. 1921; BS, Harvard U., 1949. CLU, CPCU. Sys. analyst, salesman Occidental Ins., 1949—54; ins. agy. owner, 1954—62; founder, chmn. Mercury Gen. Corp., LA, 1961—, CEO, 1961—2007. B-17 navigator USAAF, WWII. Named one of 400 Richest Ams., Forbes mag., 2006. Office: Mercury Ins Grp 4484 Wilshire Blvd Los Angeles CA 90010

JOSEPH, GREGORY NELSON, media critic, writer, actor, advocate; b. Kansas City, Mo., Aug. 25, 1946; s. Theodore Leopold and Marcella Kathryn (Nelson) J.; m. Mary Martha Stahler, July 21, 1973; children: John, Jacqueline, Caroline. AA, Met. C.C., Kansas City, 1967; BA with honors, U. Mo., Kansas City, 1969. Intern, cub reporter Kansas City Star-Times, 1965-67; feature writer, asst. city editor The Pasadena (Calif.) Union, 1971-73; investigative reporter The Pasadena Star-News, 1973-75; bus. writer The Riverside (Calif.) Press Enterprise, 1975-76; reporter, consumer writer, feature writer, TV critic The San Diego Tribune, 1976-90; TV columnist The Ariz. Republic, Phoenix, 1990-94; writer, media critic, advocate, 1994—; profl. actor, 1997—; mem. Ariz. Film and Media Coalition, 2004—07. Recipient various writing awards Copley Newspapers, Pasadena and San Diego, 1971-73, 83, Pub. Awareness award San Diego Psychiat. Physicians, cert. of appreciation Epilepsy Soc. San Diego County, 1989. Mem.: NATAS-Rocky Mt. Region (bd. govs. 1990—92), SAG (Ariz. br. coun. 2004—07, nat. performers with disabilities com.), Phi Kappa Phi. Independent. Roman Catholic. Avocations: reading, writing about Hollywood history, politics, current events and the disabled. Home: 4864 W Alice Ave Glendale AZ 85302-5107 Office: Ford-Robert Black Agy 4032 N Miller Rd Ste 104 Scottsdale AZ 85251 Office Phone: 480-966-2537.

JOSEPH, MICHAEL THOMAS, broadcast consultant; b. Youngstown, Ohio, Nov. 23, 1927; s. Thomas A. and Martha (McCarius) J.; m. Eva Ursula Boerger, June 21, 1952. BA, Case Western Res. U., 1949. Program dir. Fetzer Broadcasting, Grand Rapids, Mich., 1952-55; nat. program dir. Founders Corp., NYC, 1955-57; program cons. to ABC, CBS, NBC, Capital Cities, Entercom, Cox, Greater Media, Gannett, Tribune, Telemundo, N.Y. Times, 1958—; v.p. radio Capital Cities, NYC, 1959—60; v.p. owned radio stas. NBC, NYC, 1963—65. Mem. Internat. Radio and TV Soc., Nat. Assn. Broadcasters

JOSEPHSON, NANCY, talent agency executive; d. Marvin J.; m. Larry Sanitsky; 3 children. BA in Economics, Brown U., 1980; JD, Harvard Law Sch., 1982. Atty. Loeb & Loeb, NY, 1982-86, Internat. Creative Mgmt., Beverly Hills, 1986, head N.Y. TV dept.; various positions as an agent, 1979-87; head TV lit. dept. Internat. Creative Mgmt., LA, 1991—95, exec. vp. TV, 1995—2006, co-pres., 1998—2006; ptnr. The Endeavor Agy., Beverly Hills, Calif., 2006—. Developer (TV shows) Friends, Nash Bridges, Caroline in the City, The Simpsons. Named one of top twenty-five most important women in entertainment Hollywood's Reporter, 2005, The 100 Most Powerful Women in Entertainment, 2006, 2007. Mem.: Hollywood Radio & Television Soc. (pres.). Office: The Endeavor Agy 9601 Wilshire Blvd 10th Fl Beverly Hills CA 90212

JOSEPHSON, RICHARD CARL, lawyer; b. Washington, Nov. 20, 1947; s. Horace Richard and Margaret Louise (Loeffler) J.; m. Jean Carol Attridge, Aug. 1, 1970; children: Lee Margaret, Amy Dorothy. AB, Case Western Res. U., 1969; JD, Coll. of William and Mary, 1972. Bar: Oreg. 1973. Law clk. Hon. John D. Butzner, Jr., U.S. Ct. Appeals, 4th Cir., Richmond, Va., 1972-73; mem. Stoel Rives LLP, Portland, Oreg., 1973—2006; v.p., gen. counsel Schnitzer Steel Industries, Inc., Portland, Oreg., 2006—. Bd. dirs. Tucker-Maxon Oral Sch., Portland, 1987-2006, Vis. Nurse Assn., Portland, 1978-89, Healthlink, Portland, 1984-89, St. Mary's Acad., Portland, 1998-2001, Portland Arena Mgmt., LLC, 2006-07. 1st lt. U.S. Army, 1973-79. Fellow Am. Coll. Bankruptcy, Am. Coll. Comml. Fin. Lawyers; mem. ABA, Am. Bankruptcy Inst., Oreg. Bar Assn. (chmn. debtor-creditor sect. 1980-81). Avocations: skiing, white-water rafting, running, bicycling, theater. Office: Schnitzer Steel Industries Inc 3200 NW Yeon Ave Portland OR 97210 Office Phone: 503-224-9900. Office Fax: 503-299-2277. Business E-Mail: rjosephson@schn.com.

JOSHI, CHANDRASHEKHAR JANARDAN, physics educator; b. Wai, India, July 22, 1953; came to U.S., 1981; s. Janardan Digambar and Ramabai (Kirpekar) J.; m. Asha Bhatt, Jan. 18, 1982. BS, London U., 1974; PhD, Hull U., UK, 1978. Research assoc. Nat. Research Council, Can., 1978-81; research engr. UCLA, 1981-83, adj. assoc. prof., 1983-86, assoc. prof.-in-residence, 1986-87, assoc. prof., 1987-88, prof. elec. engring., 1988—. Cons. Lawrence Livermore (Calif.) Nat. Lab., 1984, Los Alamos (N.Mex.) Nat. Lab., 1985—. Editor: Laser Acceleration of Particles, 1985, Advanced Acceleration Concepts, 1989; contbr. articles ot profl. jours. Grantee NSF, U.S. Dept. Energy; recipient Queen Mary Prize, Inst. Nuclear Engring., 1974. Mem. AAAS, IEEE, Am. Phys. Soc. (award for excellence in plasma rsch. 1996), N.Y. Acad. Scis. Avocation: travel. Office: UCLA 405 Hilgard Ave Los Angeles CA 90095-9000

JOSHI, VYOMESH I., computer company executive; MSEE, Ohio State U. Rsch. and devel. engring. Hewlett-Packard Co., Palo Alto, Calif., 1980—84, project mgr., 1984—89, sect. mgr., 1989—94, ops. mgr., San Diego Imaging Operation, 1994—95, digital copier bus., 1995—97, gen. mgr., 1997—99, v.p., gen. mgr., 1999—2002, exec. v.p. imaging & printing grp., 2002—, exec. v.p. imaging & personal systems grp., 2005. Mem. bd. dirs. Yahoo!, Inc., Sunnyvale, Calif., 2005—. Office: Hewlett-Packard Co 3000 Hanover Rd Palo Alto CA 94304*

JOSLIN, ANN, state librarian; With Idaho State Libr., Boise, 1979—, assoc. state libr., state libr., 2005—. Mem.: Idaho Libr. Assn. (officer, Libr. of Yr. award 1992, 2003). Office: Idaho Commn for Libraries 325 W State St Boise ID 83702 Office Phone: 208-334-2150. Office Fax: 208-334-4016. Business E-Mail: ann.joslin@libraries.idaho.gov.

JOSS, ROBERT L., dean; m. Betty Badger Joss; children: Randall, Jennifer Joss Bradley. BA in Economics, magna cum laude, U. Wash., 1963; MBA, Stanford U., 1967, PhD, 1970. Fellow The White House, Washington; dep. to asst. sec. for econ. policy US Treas. Dept., Washington, 1968—71; asst. v.p. Wells Fargo Bank, San Francisco, 1971—72, v.p., 1972—75, sr. v.p., 1975—81, exec. v.p., 1981—86, vice chmn., 1986—93, bd. dirs., 1999—; CEO, mng. dir. Westpac Banking Corp., Australia, 1993—99; Philip H. Knight prof. and dean Stanford Grad. Sch. Bus., 1999—. Bd. dirs. Student Loan Mktg. Assn., 1990—93, Bus. Coun. Australia, 1998—99, Shanghai Comml. Bank, Hong Kong, 1978—93, 2002—, Agilent Tech. Inc., 2003—, Epiphany Inc., Makena Capital; chmn. Australian Bankers Assn., 1997—99. Co-author (with Frank Blount): (book) Managing in Australia, 1999. Office: Stanford U Stanford Grad Sch Bus 518 Memorial Way Stanford CA 94305-5015 Office Phone: 650-723-3951. E-mail: joss_robert@gsb.stanford.edu.

JOULE, REGGIE, state legislator; b. Nome, Alaska, July 14, 1952; m to Linda; children: Lovisa, Reggie III, Angela, Dawn & Puyuk. Attended, U. Alaska, Fairbanks, 1970—72. Alaska State Representative, District 40, 1996-. Member, NW Arctic Borough Sch District, 1990-93. Mem. bd. dirs. NANA Regional Corp. Ext. adv. coun. mem. Boys and Girls club; mem. Alaska Human Resource Investment Coun.; vice chair Interim Commn. on Children & Youth; mem. adv. bd. Kotzebue Local Fish and Game. Alaska Association Sch Bds (board member, formerly). Democrat. Office: State Capitol Rm 421 Juneau AK 99801-1182 Office Phone: 907-465-4833. Office Fax: 907-465-4586. Business E-Mail: Rep_Reggie_Joule@legis.state.ak.us.*

JOURNEL, ANDRÉ G., petroleum engineering educator; BS in Mining Engring., Ecole Nat. Superieure Mines, Nancy, France, 1967; DSc in Econ. Geology, U. Nancy, 1974, DSc in Applied Math., 1977. Mining project engr. Ctr. Morphologie Math., 1969-73; maitre rsch. Ctr. Geostatisque Paris Sch. Mines, 1973-78; vis. assoc. prof. applied earth scis. Stanford (Calif.) U., 1978-79, assoc. prof. applied earth scis., 1979-86, chmn. applied earth scis., 1986-92, prof. applied earth scis., 1987-92, Donald and Donald M. Steel prof. earth scis., 1994, prof. petroleum engring. and geol. and environ. scis., 1992—, dir. Ctr. for Reservoir Forecasting, 1986—. Cons., spkr. in field; mem. sci. com. Geostats. Congress, 1980—. Assoc. editor Math. Geology, 1989-95. Recipient Krumbein medal Math. Geology, 1989, Anthony F. Lucas Gold medal Soc. Profl. Engrs., 1998. Mem. N.Am. Coun. on Geostats. (founder), NAE. Achievements include research in modeling of spatially heterogeneous media accounting for information of diverse sources, scales and accuracies. Office: Stanford U Dept Petroleum Engring Green Earth Scis Bldg 098 Stanford CA 94305-2220

JOVANOVIC, LOIS, medical researcher; b. Mpls. BS in Biology, Columbia U., 1969; B in Hebrew Lit., Jewish Theol. Seminary, 1968, M in Hebrew Lit., 1970; MD, Albert Einstein Coll. Medicine, 1973. Intern and resident NY Hosp. Cornell U. Med. Coll., 1973—76; fellow in endocrinology and metabolism Cornell U. Med. Coll., 1976—78, instr., asst to assoc. prof., 1978—86; asst. attending physician NY Hosp., 1978—85; asst. adj. prof. and physician Rockefeller U. and Rockefeller U. Hosp., 1979—85; assoc. adj. prof. U. Calif., Irvine, 1986—88; sr. scientist Sansum Med. Rsch. Found., 1985—96; dir. and chief sci. officer Sansum Diabetes Rsch. Inst., 1996—; clin. assoc. prof medicine U. SC- LA Med. Ctr., 1986—89, prof., 1989—; rsch. biologist U. Calif., Santa Barbara, 1990—. Author numerous books and articles on diabetes and women's health. Fellow: NY Acad. Medicine, Am. Coll. Endocrinology, Am. Coll. Nutrition, ACP. Office: Sansum Diabetes Rsch Inst 2219 Bath St Santa Barbara CA 93105

JOVANOVSKI, ED, professional hockey player; b. Windsor, Ont., Can., June 26, 1976; m. Kirstin Jovanovski; children: Kylie, Kyra. Defenseman Fla. Panthers, 1995—98, Vancouver Canucks, 1998—2006, Phoenix Coyotes, 2006—. Mem. Can. World Cup Team, 1996, 2004, Can. Olympic Hockey Team, Salt Lake City, 2002. Named to NHL All-Rookie Team, 1996, NHL All-Star Game, 2001—03, 2007, 2008. Achievements include being a member of gold medal Canadian Hockey team, Salt Lake City Olympic Games, 2002; being a member of World Cup Champion Team Canada, 2004. Office: Phoenix Coyotes 6751 N White Out Way Ste E200 Glendale AZ 85305-3158

JOY, BILL (WILLIAM NELSON JOY), venture capitalist, former computer software company executive; b. Detroit, Nov. 8, 1954; s. William C. Joy; m. Sara Joy; 4 children. BSEE, U. Mich., 1975; MSEE and Computer Sci., U. Calif. Berkeley, 1982; PhD in Engring. (hon.), U. Mich. Co-founder Sun Microsystems Inc., Mountain View, Calif., 1982, v.p. rsch., 1996—98, chief scientist, 1998—2003; co-founder HighBar Ventures, 2003; ptnr. Kleiner Perkins Caulfield & Byers, Menlo Park, Calif., 2005—. Bd. dirs. SpikeSource Inc., Redwood City, Calif., 2005—. Recipient Grace Murray Hopper award, Assn. for Computing Machinery, 1986, Lifetime Achievement Award, USENIX Assoc., 1993. Mem. NAE, Am. Acad. Arts & Sciences; bd. trustees, Aspen Inst.; co-chmn., Presidential Info. Tech. Adv. Com., 1997. Prin. designer University of California (Berkeley) version of UNIX operating system; co-designer Java technology, SPARC microprocessor architecture; key designer Sun Technologies including Solaris and chip architectures and pipelines; installed the first city-wide WiFi network, 1995; several patents in the field. Office: Kleiner Perkins Caulfield & Byers 2750 Sand Hill Rd Menlo Park CA 94025 Business E-Mail: billj@kpcb.com.

JOY, EDWARD BENNETT, electrical engineer, educator, consultant; b. Troy, NY, Nov. 15, 1941; s. Herman Johnson and Elizabeth (Bennett) J.; m. Patricia Marie Huddleston, Aug. 27, 1966; children: Frederick Huddleston, Rebecca Elizabeth. BEE, Ga. Inst. Tech., 1963, MSEE, 1967, PhD in Elec. Engring., 1970. Asst. prof. elec. engring. Ga. Inst. Tech., Atlanta, 1970-75, assoc. prof., 1975-80, prof., 1980-98, prof. emeritus, 1998—; pres. Joy Engring. Co., Boulder, Colo., 1981—. Cons. in field. Contbr. articles to profl. jours. Lt. USNR, 1963—65, Vietnam. Recipient Continuing Edn. award, Ga. Tech., 1997. Fellow IEEE (life), Fellow Antenna Measurements Techniques Assn. (Disting. Achievement award 1999). Republican. Presbyterian. Achievements include patents in field. Avocations: amateur radio, electronics, hiking. Home and Office: 1450 Rembrandt Rd Boulder CO 80302-9478 Home Phone: 303-545-5566; Office Phone: 303-545-5566. Business E-Mail: ed.joy@gatech.edu.

JOYCE, GERALD FRANCIS, biochemist, educator; b. Manhattan, Kans., Nov. 28, 1956; BA, U. Chgo., 1978; MD, PhD, U. Calif., San Diego, 1984. Postdoctoral fellow The Salk Inst., 1985-88, sr. rsch. assoc., 1988-89; clin. instr. dept. neurosci. U. Calif., San Diego, 1987—; asst. prof. dept. chemistry and molecular biology The Scripps Rsch. Inst., La Jolla, Calif., 1989-92, faculty grad. program in macromolecular and cellular structure and chemistry, 1989—, faculty grad. program in chemistry, 1990—, assoc. prof. dept. chemistry and molecular biology, 1992-96, prof. depts. chemistry & molecular biology, 1996—. Mem. exobiology discipline working group NASA, 1990—; investigator NASA Specialized Ctr. for Rsch. and Tng. in Exobiology, 1992—; sci. adv. bd. Ribozyme Pharms., Inc., Boulder, Colo., 1991—; admissions com. grad. program in chemistry The Scripps Rsch. Inst., 1991—, admissions com. grad. program in macromolecular and cellular structure and chemistry, 1994—; lectr. in field. Assoc. editor: Chemistry & Biology; contbr. articles to profl. jours. Recipient Pfizer award in Enzyme Chemistry Am. Chem. Soc., 1995, NAS award in Molecular Biology, 1994; Merck, Sharp & Dohme fellow Life Scis. Rsch. Found., 1985-88. Office: The Scripps Rsch Inst 10550 N Torrey Pines Rd La Jolla CA 92037-1000

JOYCE, ROSEMARY ALEXANDRIA, anthropology educator, department chairman; b. Lackawanna, NY, Apr. 7, 1956; d. Thomas Robert and Joanne Hannah (Poth) J.; m. Russell Nicholas Sheptak, Jan. 7, 1984. BA, Cornell U., 1978; PhD, U. Ill., 1985. Instr. Jackson (Mich.) Community Coll., 1983; lectr. U. Ill., Urbana, 1984-85; asst. curator Peabody Mus., Harvard U., Cambridge, Mass., 1985-86, asst. dir., 1986-89; asst. prof. anthropology Harvard U., Cambridge, Mass., 1989-91, assoc. prof. anthropology, 1991-94, U. Calif., Berkeley, 1994—2001, prof., 2001—, chair, 2006—. Author: Cerro Palenque, 1991, Encounters with the Americas, 1995, Gender and Power in Prehispanic Mesoamerica, 2001, The Languages of Archeology, 2002, Embodied Lives, 2003, Ancient Bodies, Ancient Lives, 2008; editor: Maya History, 1993, Women in Prehistory, 1997, Social Patterns in Preclassic Mesoamerica, 1999, Beyond Kinship, 2000, Mesoamerican Archeology, 2003; contbr. articles to profl. jours. NEH grantee, 1985, 86, NSF grantee, 1989, 98, 2001, Famsi grantee, 1996, Heinz Found., Wenner-Gren Found. grantee, 1997; Fulbright fellow, 1981-82, Fulbright Sr. Specialist, 2007. Mem. Soc. for Am. Archaeology, Am. Anthropol. Assn., Archeol. Inst. Am. Office: U Calif Anthropology Dept 232 Kroeber Hall # 3710 Berkeley CA 94720-3710 Business E-Mail: rajoyce@berkeley.edu.

JOYCE, STEPHEN MICHAEL, lawyer; b. LA, Mar. 19, 1945; s. John Rowland and Elizabeth Rose (Rahe) J.; m. Bernadette Anne Novey, Aug. 18, 1973; children: Natalie Elizabeth, Vanessa Anne. BS, Calif. State U., Los Angeles, 1970; JD, U. LaVerne, 1976. Bar: Calif. 1976, U.S. Dist. Ct. (cen. dist.) Calif. 1977, U.S. Ct. Claims 1981. Pvt. practice, Beverly Hills, Calif., 1976-93; ptnr. Gold & Joyce, Beverly Hills, 1982-84. Personal atty. to Stevie Wonder and various other celebrities, 1977—. Contbr. articles to profl. jours. Served to pvt. USAR, 1963-69. Mem.: ABA, San Fernando Valley Bar Assn., Consumer Atty. of So. Calif. Assn., Beverly Hills Bar Assn., L.A. County Bar Assn., Calif. Bar Assn., Calabasas Tennis & Swim Club. Democrat. Roman Catholic. Avocation: long distance running. Home: 4724 Barcelona Ct Calabasas CA 91302-1403 Office: 15260 Ventura Blvd Ste 640 Sherman Oaks CA 91403-5340 Office Phone: 818-906-1500. Personal E-mail: sjoycelaw@aol.com.

JOYNER, JEFFREY K., lawyer; b. Lawton, Okla., May 27, 1967; BA, George Washington Univ., 1989; JD cum laude, Southwestern Univ., 1995. Bar: Calif. 1995, US Dist. Ct. Ctrl., So. & No. Calif. Assoc. Baker & Hostetler, 1994—99; ptnr., intellectual property & entertainment law practice Keats McFarland & Wilson LLP, Beverly Hills, Calif., 1999—. Contbr. articles to law jours.; editor: Southwestern Univ. Law Rev., 1994—95. Recipient Am. Jurisprudence Book award; named a Rising Star, So. Calif. Super Lawyers, 2004—06; named one of America's Premier Lawyers, Forbes mag., 2006. Mem.: State Bar Calif., Beverly Hills Bar Assn., Internat. Anti-Counterfeiting Assn. Home: Keats McFarland & Wilson LLP 9720 Wilshire Blvd Beverly Hills CA 90212 Office Phone: 310-777-3725. Office Fax: 310-860-0363. Business E-Mail: jjoyner@kmwlaw.com.

JU, JIANN-WEN (WOODY JU), mechanics educator, researcher; b. Taiwan, 1958; s. Jiang and Kwai J.; m. Mali J., 1985; children: Derek, Tiffany. BS, Nat. (Taipei) Taiwan U., 1980; MS, U. Calif., Berkeley, 1983, PhD, 1986. Registered profl. engr., Calif., Ariz. Teaching asst. U. Calif., Berkeley, 1983-84, rsch. asst., 1984-86, lectr., 1986, postdoctoral rsch. engr., 1986-87; asst. prof. Princeton (NJ) U., 1987-93; assoc. prof. UCLA, 1993-98, prof., 1998—, chmn., 1999—2002, chmn., structural engr., 2001—. Cons. Air Force Engring. and Svcs. Ctr., Panama City, Fla., 1990—, Titan R&T, Chatsworth, Calif., Kasdan and Simonds, Irvine, Calif., Karagozian and Case, LA, Miller Law, Irvine, Calif.; rev. panel NSF, Washington, 1991—; conf. co-chair 7th World Congress Computational Mechanics, LA, 2006; sci. program com. 9th Nat. Congress Computational Mechanics, San Francisco, 2007; chmn., organizer of 40 symposia; lectr., presenter in field. Author, editor: Damage Mechanics in Engineering Materials, 1990, Recent Advances in Damage Mechanics and Plasticity, 1992, Damage Mechanics and Localization, 1992, Homogenization and Constitutive Modeling, 1993, Micromechanics and Inelasticity of Metal Matrix Composites, 1994, Damage Mechanics in Composites, 1994, Numerical Methods in Structural Mechanics, 1995, Damage Mechanics in Engineering Materials, 1998; mem. editl. bd. Internat. Jour. Damage Mechanics, 1992; editor: Internat. Jour. Damage Mechanics, 2006; contbr. articles to profl. jours. Fed. and indsl. rsch. grantee U.S. Govt., U.S. cos., Japanese cos., 1987—; recipient Presdl. Young Investigator award NSF, 1991. Fellow: ASME (com. mem. 1989—, assoc. editor Jour. Engring. Materials Tech., Jour. Applied Mechanics 1995—), ASCE (control group 1989-93, Walter L. Huber Civil Engring. Rsch. prize 1997), US Assn. Computational Mechanics (at-large mem., exec. com. 2006-); mem: Am. Acad. Mechanics, Am. Concrete Inst. (chmn. com. 446 fracture mechanics 2004—), Soc. Engring. Sci., Internat. Assn. Computational Mechanics. Office: UCLA Dept Civil Engring 5731 Boelter Hall Los Angeles CA 90095-1593 Business E-Mail: juj@ucla.edu.

JUDD, BRUCE DIVEN, architect; b. Pasadena, Calif., Sept. 28, 1947; s. David Lockhart and Martha Leah (Brown) J.; m. Diane Reinbolt, Feb. 4, 1976 (div. Oct. 1985); 1 child, Ian David. BArch, U. Calif., Berkeley, 1970, MArch, 1971. Registered arch., Calif., Nev.; cert. Nat. Coun. Archtl. Registration Bds. Designer Ribera and Sue Landscape Archs., Oakland, Calif., 1968-70, Page Clowdsley & Baleix, San Francisco, 1971-75; v.p. Charles Hall Page Assocs., San Francisco, 1975-80; prin. Archtl. Resources Group, San Francisco, 1980—. Mem. adv. bd. fed. rehab. guidelines program Nat. Inst. Bldg. Scis., HUD, 1979-80; mem. city-wide survey planning com. City of Oakland, Calif., 1979-80; cons. Nat. Main St. Program, Washington. Bd. dirs., co-founder Oakland Heritage Alliance, 1980-85; mem. Calif. Hist. Resources Commn., 1982-86, chmn., 1983-85; bd. dirs. Preservation Action, Washington, 1982-85, 90—, Friends of Terra Cotta, 1981-86, Berkeley Archtl. Heritage Assn., 1993—; mem. bd. advisors Nat. Trust for Hist. Preservation, Washington, 1981-90, advisor emeritus, 1990—; bd. trustees Calif. Preservation Found., San Francisco, 1985—, v.p., 1990-92, trustee, 1990—; active Calif. State Hist. Bldg. Safety Bd., 1991-93, also others. Recipient Excellence Honor award State of Calif., Excellence award in archtl. conservation, Spl. Restoration award Sunset Mag.; named Preservationist of Yr., Calif. Preservation Found., 1993. Fellow AIA (preservation officer No. Calif. chpt. 1978-81, hist. resources com. Calif. coun. 1979-80, nat. hist. resources com. 1981—, chmn. 1981-82); mem. Internat. Assn. for Preservation Tech. (bd. dirs. 1983-85), Park Hills Homes Assn. (chmn. archtl. com. 1992—), U.S./Internat. Coun. Monuments and Sites. Office: Archtl Resources Group Pier 9 The Embarcadero San Francisco CA 94111

JUDD, DENNIS L., lawyer; b. Provo, Utah, June 27, 1954; s. Derrel Wesley and Leila (Lundquist) J.; m. Carol Lynne Chilberg, May 6, 1977; children: Lynne Marie, Amy Jo, Tiffany Ann, Andrew, Jacquelyn Nicole. BA in Polit. Sci. summa cum laude, Brigham Young U., 1978, JD, 1981. Bar: Utah 1981, U.S. Dist. Ct. Utah 1981. Assoc. Nielson & Senior, Salt Lake City and Vernal, Utah, 1981-83; dep. county atty. Uintah County, Vernal, 1982-84; ptnr. Bennett & Judd, Vernal, 1983-88; county atty. Daggett County, Utah, 1985-89, 91-99, 2000—07; pvt. practice Vernal, 1988—; prosecutor City of Naples, Naples, 1996-99; legal counsel Uintah County Sch. Dist., 1996—2006; city atty. Naples City, Utah, 1999—, Vernal City, Utah, 2000—; atty. City of Vernal, 2000—; legal counsel Flaming Gorge Spl. Transp. Dist., 2006—, Uintah County Econ. Devel. Dist., 2007—. Mem. governing bd. Uintah Basin applied Tech. Ctr., 1991-95, v.p., 1993-94, pres., 1994-95. Chmn. bd. adjustment Zoning and Planning Bd., Naples, 1982-91, 94—99; mem. Naples City Coun., 1982-91; mayor pro tem City of Naples, 1983-91; legis. v.p. Naples PTA, 1988-90; sec. Friends of Utah Field House of Natural History, 2000—; v.p. Uintah Dist. PTA Coun., 1990-92; mem. resolution com. Utah League Cities and Towns, 1985-86, small cities com., 1985-86; trustee Uintah Sch. Dist. Found., 1988-97, 2005-, vice chmn., 1991-93; mem. Uintah County Sch. Dist. Bd. Edn., 1991-95, v.p., 1991-92, pres., 1992-95; chmn. Uintah County Rep. Conv., 1998. Hinkley scholar Brigham Young U., 1977; named Oustanding County Atty. Utah, 2003. Mem. Uintah Schs. Found. (bd. trustees, 2005-), Utah Bar Assn., Uintah Basin Bar Assn., Statewide Assn. Prosecutors, Vernal C. of C. Republican. Mem. Lds Ch. Avocations: hunting, photography, lapidary. Home: 1555 S 460 E Naples UT 84078 Office: 497 S Vernal Ave Vernal UT 84078 Office Phone: 435-789-7038. Personal E-mail: judd@easilink.com.

JUDD, JAMES THURSTON, savings and loan executive; b. Hurricane, Utah, Dec. 13, 1938; s. Finley MacFarland and Bessie (Thurston) J.; m. Janis Anderson, July 15, 1960; children: Juliet, Brian. BS, Utah State U., 1961; postgrad., Los Angeles State U., 1962-63, U. Detroit, 1963-64. Cert. flight instr. Fin. analyst automotive assembly div. Ford Motor Co., Detroit, 1961-64; sales mgr. Xerox Corp., Rocester, N.Y., 1966-75; loan mgr. Golden West Fin. Corp. Savs. and Loan, Oakland, Calif., 1975—, now sr. exec. v.p.; pres. World Savings and Loan Co. (formerly Golden West Fin. Corp. Savings and Loan), Oakland, Calif. Pres. Judd Ranch. Chmn. northbay Bringing Entertainment To The Elderly, Saratoga, Calif., 1972—; chmn. Beef for the Poor, Oakland, 1983-87. Mem. Nat. Assn. Real Estate Appraisers, Calif. Assn. Real Estate, Exptl. Aircraft Assn., Simga Nu. Republican. Mem. Lds Ch. Avocations: fly fishing, skiing, golf. Home: 3284 Blackhawk Meadow Dr Danville CA 94506-5804 Office: World Savings Loan 1901 Harrison St Fl 17 Oakland CA 94612-3588

JUDD, JOEL STANTON, state legislator, lawyer; b. Denver, Sept. 10, 1951; s. E. James and Eleanore Judd. BA, New Coll., 1973; JD, U. Denver, 1976. Bar: Colo. 1976, U.S. Dist. Ct. Colo. 1976, U.S. Ct. Appeals (10th cir.) 1976, U.S. Supreme Ct. 1980. Assoc. Feder & Morris, Denver, 1976-77, Reckseen & Lau, Northglenn, Colo., 1977-82; pvt. practice atty. Denver, 1982—; mem. Dist. 5 Colo. House of Reps., Denver, 2003—, chmn. fin. com. Mem. Colo. Bar Assn., Denver Bar Assn. (chair intraprofl. com. 1985-90), Colo. Trial Lawyers Assn., Allied Jewish Fedn. (chair young profls. div. 1984-86, chair Denver Jewish cmty. Israel Independence Day celebration 1987), Optimists (pres. 1980-83). Democrat. Avocations: skiing, river rafting. Office: 2222 S Albion St #100 Denver CO 80222-4928 also: Colo State Capitol 200 E Colfax Denver CO 80203 Office Phone: 303-866-2925. Business E-Mail: joeljudd@quesyoffice.net, repjoeljudd@joeljudd.com.*

JUDD, LEWIS LUND, psychiatrist, educator; b. LA, Feb. 10, 1930; s. George E. and Emmeline (Lund) J.; BS, U. Utah, 1954; M.D. cum laude, UCLA, 1956; m. Patricia Ann Hoffman, Jan. 26, 1974; children by previous marriage: Allison Clark, Catherine Anne, Stephanie. Intern, UCLA Sch. Medicine, 1958-59, resident in psychiatry, 1959-60, 62-64, fellow in child psychiatry, 1964-65, asst. prof. depts. psychiatry and psychology, 1965-70, dir. edn., child and adolescent psychiatry dept. psychiatry, 1968; asso. prof. psychiatry U. Calif. at San Diego, La Jolla, 1970, vice chmn., dir. clin. programs dept. psychiatry, 1970-73, dir. drug abuse programs, 1970-73, prof., from 1973, acting chmn. dept., 1974, co-chmn., 1975-77, chmn., 1977—; dir. NIMH, 1988—; chief psychiat. service San Diego VA Hosp., La Jolla, 1972-77; chief psychiat. service U. Calif. Med. Center, San Diego, from 1982, pres. med. staff, chmn. exec. com., from 1982; mem. adv. com. on evaluation drug abuse programs County of San Diego, 1970-73; chmn. clin. projects rev. com. NIMH, 1975-79; guest faculty San Diego Psychoanalytic Inst. Served to capt., M.C., USAF, 1960-62. Fellow Am. Psychiat. Assn.; mem. Soc. Neuroscis., Psychiat. Research Soc., Assn. Acad. Psychiatry, Soc. Research in Child Devel., Am. Coll. Neuropsychopharmacology, So. Calif., San Diego psychiat. socs., Am. Assn. Chmn. Depts. Psychiatry, Alpha Omega Alpha. Contbr. articles to med. jours. Home: 1367 Via Alta Del Mar CA 92014-2546

JUDD, O'DEAN P., physicist; b. Austin, Minn., May 26, 1937; MS in Physics, UCLA, 1961, PhD in Physics, 1968. Staff physicist and project dir. Hughes Rsch. Lab., Malibu, Calif., 1959-67; postdoctoral fellow UCLA Dept. Physics, 1968-69; researcher Hughes Rsch. Lab., Malibu, Calif., 1969-72; researcher, group leader Los Alamos (N.Mex.) Nat. Lab., 1972-82, chief scientist for def. rsch. and applications, 1981-87, energy and environ. chief scientist, lab. fellow, 1990-93, ind. tech. advisor and cons., 1995—; chief scientist Strategic Def. Initiative Orgn., Washington, 1987-90; nat. intelligence officer for sci. and tech. Nat. Intelligence Coun., Washington, 1993-94. Mem. numerous govt. coms. related to sci. and tech., def. and nat. security policy; adj. prof. physics U. N.Mex., Albuquerque; mem. sci. adv. bd. USAF, 1999-2003. Patentee in sci. and tech.; contbr. numerous articles to sci. and def.-related jours. Fellow IEEE, AAAS, Los Alamos Nat. Lab. Inst. Advanced Engring.; mem. Am. Phys. Soc. Office: Los Alamos Nat Lab B241 Los Alamos NM 87544-2648

JUDGE, MIKE, animator; b. Guayaquil, Ecuador, Oct. 17, 1962; m. Francesca Morocco, 1989; 2 children. BA in Phys. Sci., U. Calif., San Diego, 1985. Writer, dir., prodr. (TV series) Beavis and Butt-head, 1993-1997, King of the Hill, 1997—, Monsignor Martinez, 2000; (films) Beavis and Butt-head Do America, 1996, Office Space, 1999; actor (films) Inbred Jed (voice), 1991, King of the Hill (voice), 1997—, Mene Tekel (voice), 1997, Spy Kids, 2001, Spy Kids 2:Island of Lost Dreams, 2002, Serving Sara, 2002, Spy Kids 3-D:Game Over, 2003.

JUDSON, C(HARLES) JAMES (JIM JUDSON), lawyer; b. Oregon City, Oreg., Oct. 24, 1944; s. Charles James and Barbara (Busch) Judson; m. Diana L. Gerlach, Sept. 11, 1965; children: Kevin, Nicole. BA cum laude, Stanford U., 1966, LLB with honors, 1969. Bar: Wash. 1969, U.S. Tax Ct. 1970, DC 1981. Ptnr. Davis Wright Tremaine, Seattle, 1969—. Bd. dirs. Port Blakely Tree Farms, Garrett and Ring, Joshua Green Corp., Lumera, Sonata Capital, Airbiquity, Welco Lumber; spkr. in field. Author: State Taxation of Financial Intitutions, 1981; contbr. articles to profl. jours. Trustee Wash. State Internat. Trade Fair, Seattle, 1981—86; mem. Assn. Wash. Bus. Tax Com., 1978—, Seattle Tax Group, 1983—; chmn. lawyers divsn. United Way, Seattle, 1986, 1987, chmn. commerce and industry divsn., 1989—91; chmn. Bus. Tax Coalition, Seattle, 1987; bd. dirs. Pacific N.W. Ballet, Pacific Sci. Ctr., Olympic Pk. Inst., 1988—, Yosemite Nat. Insts., 1993—; advisor Wash. State Dept. Revenue; tax advisor Wash. State House Reps. Dem. Caucus. Fellow: Am. Coll. Tax Counsel; mem.: ABA (chmn. com. fin. orgns. tax sect. 1978—82, chmn. excise tax com. 1983—90, interorganization coordination com. 1985—, chmn. environ. tax com. 1991—), Seattle-King County Bar Assn. (mem. tax sect. 1973—86), Wash. State Bar Assn. (chmn. tax sect. 1984—86, chmn. western region IRS/bar liaison com. 1987—88, mem. rules com. 1991—), Seattle C. of C. (mem. tax. com. 1982—), Broadmoor Golf Club (Seattle), Wash. Athletic Club (Seattle) (bd. dirs. 2006—). Avocations: skiing, golf, basketball, woodworking, hiking. Office: Davis Wright Tremaine 2600 Century Sq 1501 4th Ave Seattle WA 98101-1688 Office Phone: 206-628-7686. Business E-Mail: jimjudson@dwt.com.

JULANDER, PAULA FOIL, retired foundation administrator; b. Charlotte, NC, Jan. 21, 1939; d. Paul Baxter and Esther Irene (Earnhardt) Foil; m. Roydon Odell Julander, Dec. 21, 1985; 1 child, Julie McMahan Shipman. Diploma, Presbyn. Sch. Nursing, Charlotte, NC, 1960; BS magna cum laude, U. Utah, 1984; MS in Nursing Adminstrn., Brigham Young U., 1990. RN, Utah. Nurse various positions, Fla. and S.C., 1960-66; co-founder Am. Laser Corp., 1970-79; tchg. asst. U. Utah, Salt Lake City; exec. dir. Utah Nurses Assn., 1987—89; mem. Utah Ho. of Reps., Salt Lake City, 1989-92; Dem. nominee lt. gov. State of Utah, 1992; minority whip Utah State Senate, Dist. 1, Salt Lake City, 1998—2000; health care/polit. cons. Salt Lake City, 1992—98. Mem. adj. faculty Brigham Young U. Coll. Nursing, 1987—95; bd. dirs. Block Fin. Svcs.; mem. Utah state exec. bd U.S. West Comm., 1993—96; bd. regents Calif. Luth. U., 1994—97; 2003 trustee KUED TV, 2000—03; trustee Intermountain Health Care Hosps., 2000—. Co-author (cookbook): Utah State Fare, 1995. Pres. Utah Nurses Found., 1986—88; mem. Nat. Conf. of State Legis. Com. on Families and Children, 1999—2001, The Coun. of State Govt. Com. on Health and Aging, 1999—2001, Women's Polit.Caucus, Statewide Abortion Task Force, 1990; bd. dirs. Cmty. Nursing Svc. Home Health Plus, 1992—94; mem. Planned Parenthood Assn. Utah, 1994—2001, Utahns for Choice, 1995—2002; trustee Westminster Coll., 1994—2002, HCA-St. Mark's Hosp., 1994—95; elected sen. State of Utah, 1998—2005; hon. chair Komem Race for Cure, 2007. Recipient Utah pub. health hero award, 2000, Legislator of Yr. awrd, YWCA, 2001, Jacquelyn Erbin MD award, Planned Parenthood Action Coun., 2002, Disting. Alumni award, Coll. Nursing, U. Utah, 2002, Legislator of Yr. award, Nat. Assn. Social Workers, 2002, Eleanor Roosevelt award, Utah State Dem. Com., 2004, Women's Achievement award, Utah Commn. for Women and Families, 2005, Lucy Beth Rampton award, Utah Women's Dem. Club, 2005, Outstanding Achievement award in Govt. and Polit. Svc., YWCA, 2005, Honored Alumni award, Brigham Young U. Coll.

Nursing, 2005; honored by, Govt. Commn. on Women and Families, 2005. Mem.: ANA, Women in Govt. (chair 2004), Nat Orgn. Women Legislators, Utah Nurses Assn. (legis. rep. 1987—88, Lifetime Achievement award), Phi Kappa Phi (Susan Young Gates award 1991), Sigma Theta Tau. Home: 476 B St Salt Lake City UT 84103-2544 Personal E-mail: paula@ulcu.com, ladyjulander@gmail.com.

JULIAN, PAUL C., health products executive; BS, Salem State Coll., Mass., 1978. Corp. officer Owens & Minor; sales mgr. to grp. v.p., COO Stuart Med., Inc.; dist. mgr. Ivac Corp.; dist. regional mgr. U.S. Surg.; exec. v.p. health systems McKesson Corp., San Francisco, 1996—97, pres. med.-surgical bus., 1997—2000, pres. distbn., retail automation, pharmacy outsourcing and svcs. for payors, 2000—04, grp. pres., 2004—. Bd. mem. GS1 US, NADRO, Parata Systems. Mem.: Internat. Fedn. Pharm. Wholesalers (chmn. bd.), Healthcare Distbn. Mgmt. Assn. (bd. mem.). Office: McKesson Corpn One Post St San Francisco CA 94104

JULIEN, ROBERT MICHAEL, anesthesiologist, writer; b. Port Townsend, Wash., Mar. 24, 1942; s. Frank Felton and Mary Grace (Powers) J.; m. Judith Dianne DeChenne, Feb. 26, 1963; children: Robert Michael, Scott M. BS in Pharmacy, U. Wash., 1965, MS in Pharmacology, 1968, PhD, 1970; MD, U. Calif.-Irvine, 1977. Intern Good Samaritan Hosp., Portland, Oreg., 1977—78; resident Oreg. Health Scis. U., 1978—80; asst. prof. pharmacology U. Calif.-Irvine, 1970—74, asst. clin. prof., 1974—77; assoc. prof. anesthesiology and pharmacology U. Oreg., Portland, 1980—83; staff anesthesiologist St. Vincent Hosp., Portland, 1983—2005. Author: Primer of Drug Action, 1975, 11th edit., 2008, Understanding Anesthesiology, 1984, Drugs and the Body, 1987. Recipient Svc. award Am. Epilepsy Soc., 1975. Mem. Am. Soc. Anesthesiologists, Am. Assn. Pharmacology and Exptl. Therapeutics, Soc. Neurosci., Oreg. Med. Assn., Western Pharmacology Soc. Roman Catholic. Home: 23 Becket St Lake Oswego OR 97035 Office Phone: 503-636-3180. Business E-Mail: drsjulien@comcast.net.

JULIUS, DAVID, biochemist; BS in Life Scis., MIT, 1977; PhD in Biochemistry, U. Calif., Berkeley, 1984. Undergraduate rsch. asst., dept. biology MIT, 1975—77; post-doctoral fellow Inst. Cancer Rsch., Columbia U., NY, 1984—89; asst. prof., dept. cellular & molecular pharmacology U. Calif., San Francisco, 1989—96, assoc. prof., dept. cellular & molecular pharmacology, 1996—99, prof. dept. cellular and molecular pharmacology, 1999—2006, prof., chair, dept. physiology, 2006—. Vis. rsch. assoc., dept. biochemistry U. Bordeaux, France, 1976; mem. sci. adv. bd. Senomyx, Inc., Hydra Biosciences, Inc. Contbr. several articles to peer-reviewed jours. Recipient March of Dimes Basil O'Connor Rsch. award, 1990, PEW Scholars award in Biomedical Sciences, 1990, Scholar award, McKnight Neuroscience Found., 1990, Investigator award, 1997, Presdl. Young Investigator award, NSF, 1990, Syntex prize in Receptor Pharmacology, 1997, First-Perl Neuroscience prize, UNC, 2000; co-recipient Julius Axelrod prize, Soc. for Neuroscience, 2007; Eloranta Rsch. Fellow, MIT, 1976, Jane Coffin Childs Postdoctoral Fellow, 1984. Mem.: NAS. Office: UCSF Genentech Hall Rm N-276E 600 16th St Mail Code 2140 San Francisco CA 94158-2517 Office Phone: 415-476-0431. Office Fax: 415-502-8644. Business E-Mail: julius@cmp.ucsf.edu.

JUMONVILLE, FELIX JOSEPH, JR., physical education educator, real estate company officer; b. Crowley, La., Nov. 20, 1920; s. Felix Joseph and Mabel (Rogers) J.; m. Mary Louise Hoke, Jan. 11, 1952; children: Carol, Susan. BS, La. State U., 1942; MS, U. So. Calif., 1948, EdD, 1952. Assoc. prof. phys. edn. L.A. State Coll., 1948-60; prof. phys. edn. Calif. State U., Northridge, 1960-87, emeritus prof. phys. edn., 1987—. Owner Felix Jumonville Realty, Northridge, 1974-82, Big Valley Realty, Inc., 1982-83, Century 21 Lamb Realtors, 1983-86, Cardinal Realtors, 1986-87; varsity track and cross-country head coach LA State Coll., 1952-60, Calif. State U., Northridge, 1960-71. With USCGR, 1942—46. Recipient U.S. Commendation medal; named to, Baton Rouge H.S. Hall of Fame. Mem.: Assn. Calif. State Univ. Profs., Pi Tau Pi, Kappa Sigma, Phi Epsilon Kappa. Home: 18427 Vincennes #36 Northridge CA 91325

JUNE, ROY ETHIEL, lawyer; b. Forsyth, Mont., Aug. 12, 1922; s. Charles E. and Elizabeth F. (Newnes) J.; m. Laura Brautigam, June 20, 1949; children: Patricia June, Richard Tyler. BA, U. Mont., 1948, BA in Law, 1951, LLB, 1952. Bar: Mont. 1952, Calif. 1961. Sole practice, Billings, Mont., 1952-57; atty. Sanders and June, 1953-57; real estate developer Orange County, Calif., 1957-61; ptnr. Dugan, Tobias, Tornay & June, Costa Mesa, Calif., 1961-62; city prosecutor Costa Mesa, 1962-63; asst. city atty., 1963-67; city atty., 1967-78; sole practice, 1962—. Atty., founder, dir. Citizens Bank of Costa Mesa, 1972-92; atty. Costa Mesa Hist. Soc., Costa Mesa Playhouse Patron's Assn., Red Barons Orange County, Costa Mesa Meml. Hosp. Aux., Harbor Key, Child Guidance Ctr. Orange County, Fairview State Hosp. Therapeutic Pool Vols., Inc. Active Eagle Scout evaluation team Harbor Area Boy Scouts Am., YMCA; atty. United Fund/Cmty. Chest Costa Mesa and Newport Beach; bd. dirs. Boys' Club Harbor Area, Mardan Ctr. Ednl. Therapy, United Cerebral Palsy Found., Orange County; docent Palm Springs Mus., 1996—. With USAF, WWII. Decorated Air medal with oak leaf cluster, DFC. Mem. Calif. Bar Assn., Costa Mesa C. of C. (bd. dirs.), Masons, Scottish Rite, Shriners, Santa Ana Country, Amigos Viejos, Los Fiestadores, Palm Springs Calif. Air Mus. (docent). Business E-Mail: RoyJune655@cs.com.

JUNG, DAVID JOSEPH, law educator; b. St. Louis, Aug. 19, 1953; s. Joseph Henry and Leona Louise Jung; m. Jennifer Beryl Hammett, Oct. 15, 1951; children: David O'Grady Hammett, Brennan Joseph Hammett. BA, Harvard U., 1975; JD, U Calif., Berkeley, 1980. Lectr. in law U. Calif., Berkeley, 1980-82, from asst prof. to assoc. prof. Hastings Coll. Law San Francisco, 1982-88, prof., 1988—; dir. Ctr. State and Local Govt. Law, San Francisco, 2003—. Vis. prof. U. Hamburg, Germany, 1992, U. Iowa, Iowa City, 1993—; dir. Pub. Law Rsch. Inst., 1994—. Co-author: Remedies: Public and Private, 2d edit., 1996; contbr. articles to profl. jours. Bd. dirs. San Francisco Neighborhood Legal Aid, 1983, North of Market Child Car Ctr., 1984-86; sec. El Cerrito Youth Baseball, 1997-99, pres., 1999-2000. Recipient U.S. Law Week award U.S. Law Week, 1980, 1066 Found. award 1066 Found., 1986. Mem. Am. Assn. Law Schs. (remedies section, exec. com. 1991-92). Office: U Calif Hastings Coll Law 200 Mcallister St San Francisco CA 94102-4707

JUNG, MICHAEL ERNEST, chemistry educator; b. New Orleans, May 14, 1947; s. Albert J. and Helen N. Jung; m. Alice M. Smith. BA, Rice U., 1969; PhD, Columbia U., 1973. Postdoctoral assoc. Eidgenossische Tech. Hochschule, Zurich, 1973-74; mem. faculty UCLA, LA, 1974—, prof. chemistry, 1983—. Contbr. acticles to profl. jours. Recipient Disting. Reaching award UCLA, 1978, Gold Shield Faculty prize, 1986—; ARthur C. Cope scholar Am. Chem. Soc., 1995, Fulbright-Hays rsch. scholar, Paris, 1980-81; Tchr.-Scholar grantee Camille and Henry Dreyfus Found., 1978-83; rsch. fellow Alfred p. Sloan Found., 1979-81. Mem. Am. Chem. Soc., Royal Chem. Soc.; mem. AAAS, UCLA Cancer Ctr. Office: UCLA Dept Chemistry & Biochemistry 405 Hilgard Ave Los Angeles CA 90095-9000

JUNGERMAN, JOHN ALBERT, physics professor; b. Modesto, Calif., Dec. 28, 1921; s. Albert Augustus and Freda (Durst) J.; m. Nancy Lee Kidwell, Oct. 23, 1948; children: Mark, Eric, Roger, Anne. AB, U. Calif., Berkeley, 1943, PhD, 1949. Research physicist Manhattan Project, Oak Ridge, Tenn. and Berkeley, 1944-45, Los Alamos, N.Mex., 1945-46, Lawrence Berkeley Lab., Berkeley, 1946-49, 50-51; asst. prof. physics U. Calif., Davis, 1951, prof. physics, 1960-91, prof. emeritus, 1991, founding dir. Crocker Nuclear Lab., 1965-80, chmn. physics dept., 1981-82, 83-87; assoc. mem. faculty Starr King Sch. for Ministry, Berkeley, Calif., 1992-93. Vis. prof. U. Grenoble, France, 1972; prin. investigator nuclear physics Atomic Energy Commn., U. Calif., Davis, 1956-71; cons. OAS U. Chile, Santiago, 1982, OAS, 1971, Internat. Atomic Energy Agy., 1982. Author: Nuclear Arms Race: Technology and Society, 1986, 2d edit., 1990, World in Process, 2000. Organizer, instr. Davis Summer Insts. on Nuclear Age Edn. for Secondary Sch. Instrs., 1986-93. NSF Nuclear Physics grantee, 1971-73, NSF Sci. Edn. grantee, 1990-93. Fellow Am. Physical Soc.; mem. Am. Solar Soc., Sigma Xi. Democrat. Avocations: piano, sailing, bicycling, painting. Office: U Calif Dept Physics Davis CA 95616 E-mail: jajungerman@ucdavis.edu.

JUNGERS, FRANCIS, oil consultant; b. July 12, 1926; s. Frank Nicholas and Elizabeth (Becker) J.; children: Gary M., Randall O. BSME, U. Wash., 1947; student, Advanced Mgmt. Program, Harvard U., 1967. With Arabian Am. Oil Co., 1947-78, chmn. bd., chief exec. officer, 1973-78. Bd. dirs. Donaldson Lufkin & Jenrette, Thermo Electron, The AES Corp., Esco, Thermo Ekotek Corp., Statia. Trustee Am. U., Cairo; bd. overseers Oreg. Health Scis. With USN, 1944-46. Mem. Waverly Golf Club, Multnomah Athletic Club, Athletic Club of Bend. Republican. Roman Catholic. Office: 822 NW Murray Blvd Ste 242 Portland OR 97229-5868

JUO, JAMES, lawyer; b. Peekskill, NY, Nov. 10, 1967; BSEE, Clarkson Univ., 1989; JD, George Washington Univ., 1993. Bar: Va. 1993, Calif. 1997, US Dist Ct. No. & Ctrl. Calif., US Ct. Appeals Fourth & Fed. Cir., registered: US Patent & Trademark Office. Patent examiner U.S. Patent & Trademark Office, 1989—90; ptnr. patent, trademark, copyright litigation practice Fulwider Patton LLP, LA. Named Rising Star, So. Calif. Super Lawyers, 2006. Mem.: Am. Intellectual Property Law Assn., So. Calif. Chinese Lawyers Assn. Office: Fulwider Patton LLP 10 th Fl Howard Hughes Ctr 6060 Center Dr Los Angeles CA 90045 Office Phone: 310-824-5555. Office Fax: 310-824-9696.

JURY, MEREDITH A., federal judge; Apptd. bankruptcy judge cen. dist. U.S. Dist. Ct. Calif., 1997. Office: 3420 12th St Riverside CA 92501-3801

JUSTER, KENNETH IAN, lawyer; b. NYC, Nov. 24, 1954; s. Howard H. and Muriel (Uchitelle) J. BA, Harvard U., 1976, MA in Pub. Policy, 1980, JD, 1980. Bar: DC and US Dist. Ct. DC 1981, US Ct. Appeals (DC cir.) 1982, US Ct. Internat. Trade 1984, US Ct. Appeals (Fed. cir.) 1985, US Supreme Ct. 1985. Staff Nat. Security Coun., 1978; law clk. to judge US Ct. Appeals (2d cir.), Brattleboro, Vt., 1980—81; assoc. Arnold and Porter, Washington, 1981—87, ptnr., 1988—89; dep., sr. adviser to the dep. Sec. of State, Washington, 1989—92; acting counselor US Dept. State, Washington, 1992—93; ptnr. Arnold and Porter, Washington, 1993—97, sr. ptnr., 1998—2001; under sec. export admin. US Dept. Commerce, Washington, 2001—02, under sec. industry & security, 2002—05; exec. v.p. law, policy and corp. strategy Salesforce.com, San Francisco, 2005—; mem. US Adv. Com. for Trade Policy and Negotiations, 2007—. Faculty Internat. Law Inst., 1987-89, 93-95; vis. fellow Coun. Fgn. Rels., Washington, 1993; mem. adv. com. Harvard Weatherhead Ctr. Internat. Affairs, 2008-; trustee Asia Found. 2009-; counsellor Am. Soc. Internat. Law, 2009-; bd. dirs. US-India Bus. Coun., US-Panama Bus. Coun. Editor Harvard U. Internat. Law Jour., 1979-80; contbg. articles to profl. jours. Recipient Sec. of State's Disting. Svc. award and Medal, 1993, US-Panama Bus. Coun. Friendship award, 2002, 2004, US-India Bus. Coun. Blackwill award, 2004, Pres. of Panama's Vasco Nunez de Balboa en el Grado de Gran Cruz decoration and medal, 2004, Sec. of Commerce's William C. Redfield award and medal, 2005, Pres. of Germany's Officer's Cross of Order of Merit, 2006, Scarsdale High Sch.'s Disting. Alumni award, 2007. Mem. ABA (internat. law sect., chair internat. investment and devel. com. 1994-96, coun. mem. 1996-99, chair tech. legal assistance bd. 2000-01, coun. mem. 2003-04), DC Bar Assn. (internat. law sect., mem. faculty continuing legal edn. program 1987-89), Am. Coun. on Germany, Coun. on Fgn. Rels., French-Am. Found., Pacific Coun. on Internat. Policy, World Affairs Coun., US, Phi Beta Kappa. Office: Salesforce.com Ste 300 One Market Plaza San Francisco CA 94105 Office Phone: 415-536-8004. Business E-Mail: kjuster@salesforce.com.

JUSTICE, RICHARD J., computer company executive; married; 3 children. BSME, U. Santa Clara, 1971; MBA, Stanford U., 1974. Former mem. sales orgn. Hewlett Packard; sr. v.p. Ams. Cisco Systems, Inc., San Jose, Calif., 1996—2000, sr. v.p. worldwide field ops., 2000—06; sr. v.p. worldwide ops. & bus. develop. Cisco Systems, Inc., San Jose, Calif., 2006—07; exec. v.p. worldwide ops. & bus. develop. Cisco Systems, Inc., San Jose, Calif., 2007—. Bd. regents U. Santa Clara. Avocation: golf. Office: Cisco Systems Inc 170 W Tasman Dr San Jose CA 95134

JUSTICE, WILLIAM J., bishop; b. Lawrence, Mass., May 8, 1942; MA, MDiv, St. Patrick Sem.; M in Applied Spirituality, Univ. San Francisco. Ordained priest Archdiocese of San Francisco, 1968; parochial vicar St. John the Evangelist, All Souls & St. Paul parishes, 1968—79; dir. Office for Permanent Diaconate Archdiocese of San Francisco, 1979—81, sec. of Pastoral Ministry, 1981—85; pastor St. Peter parish, 1985—91, All Souls parish, 1991—2003, Mission Dolores parish, 2003—07; vicar for Clergy Archdiocese of San Francisco, 2007—; ordained bishop, 2008; aux. bishop Archdiocese of San Francisco, 2008—. Roman Catholic. Office: Archdiocese of San Francisco 1 Peter Yorke Way San Francisco CA 94109-6602 Office Phone: 415-614-5500. Office Fax: 415-565-3617.

JUSTICE-MOORE, KATHLEEN E., lawyer; m. Steven Moore. JD, Vanderbilt U. Sch. of Law, 1991. Atty., employment law and litigation, Calif., 1991—2001; rsch. dir. Gordon & Betty Moore Found., 2001—03, trustee, 2003—. Mem. Los Altos Hills Public Ed. Comm., 2004—. Avocations: scuba diving, snorkeling, kayaking, hiking, skiing. Office: Los Altos Hills Public Ed Comm 26379 Fremont Rd Los Altos CA 94022

JUVET, RICHARD SPALDING, JR., chemistry professor; b. LA, Aug. 8, 1930; s. Richard Spalding and Marion Elizabeth (Dalton) J.; m. Martha Joy Myers, Jan. 29, 1955 (div. Nov. 1978); children: Victoria, David, Stephen, Richard P.; m. Evelyn Raeburn Elthon, July 1, 1984. BS, UCLA, 1952, PhD, 1955. Rsch. chemist Dupont, 1955; instr. U. Ill., 1955-57, asst. prof., 1957-61, assoc. prof., 1961-70; prof. analytical chemistry Ariz. State U., Tempe, 1970-95, prof. emeritus, 1995—. Founding mem. Emeritus Coll., Ariz. State U., Tempe, 2005—; vis. prof. UCLA, 1960, U. Cambridge, Eng., 1964-65, Nat. Taiwan U., 1968, Ecole Polytechnique, France, 1976-77, U. Vienna, Austria, 1989-90; air pollution chemistry and physics adv. com. EPA, HEW, 1969-72; adv. panel on advanced chem. alarm tech., devel. and engrng. directorate, def. sys. divsn. Edgewood Arsenal, 1975; adv. panel on postdoctoral associateships NAS-NRC, 1991-94; mem. George C. Marshall Inst., 1998—. Author: Gas-Liquid Chromatography, Theory and Practice, 1962, Russian edit., 1966; editl. advisor Jour. Chromatographic Sci., 1969-85, Jour. Gas Chromatography, 1963-68, Analytica Chimica Acta, 1972-74, Analytical Chemistry, 1974-77; biennial reviewer for gas chromatography lit. Analytical Chemistry, 1962-76. Deacon Presbyn. Ch., 1960—, ruling elder, 1972—, commr. Grand Canyon Presbytery, 1974-76; moderator, communion com. Valley Presbyn. Ch., Scottsdale, Ariz., 1999-2001. NSF sr. postdoctoral fellow, 1964-65; recipient Sci. Exch. Agreement award to Czechoslovakia, Hungary, Romania and Yugoslavia, 1977. Fellow Am. Inst. Chemists; mem. AAAS, Am. Chem. Soc. (nat. chmn. divsn. analytical chemistry 1972-73, nat. sec.-treas. 1969-71, divsn. com. on chem. edn., subcom. on grad. edn. 1988—, councilor 1978-89, coun. com. analytical reagents 1985-95, co-author Reagent Chemicals, 7th edit. 1986, 8th edit. 1993, 9th edit. 2000, chmn. U. Ill. sect. 1968-69, sec. 1962-63, directorate divsn. officers' caucus 1987-90), Internat. Union Pure and Applied Chemistry, Internat. Platform Assn., Am. Radio Relay League (Amateur-Extra lic.), Sigma Xi, Phi Lambda Upsilon, Alpha Chi Sigma (faculty adv. U. Ill. 1958-64, Ariz. State U. 1975-95, profl. rep.-at-large 1989-94, chmn. expansion com. 1990-92, nat. v.p. grand collegiate alchemist 1994-96, trustee ednl. found. 1994-2004). Achievements include research on gas and liquid chromatography, instrumental analysis, computer interfacing, plasma desorption mass spectroscopy. Home: 4821 E Calle Tuberia Phoenix AZ 85018-2932 Office: Ariz State U Dept Chem and Biochem Tempe AZ 85287-1604 Personal E-mail: rsjuvet@juno.com.

KABACK, MICHAEL, medical educator; b. Phila., Sept. 1, 1938; BA, Haverford Coll., Pa., 1959; MD, U. Pa., Phila., 1963. Diplomate Am. Bd. Med. Genetics, Am. Bd. Pediatrics. Intern Johns Hopkins Hosp., Balt., 1963—64, resident pediatrics, 1966—68; fellow molecular biology and genetics NIH, Bethesda, Md., 1964—66; mem. staff Children's Hosp., San Diego; prof. pediatrics and reproductive medicine U. Calif., San Diego. Recipient William Allan Meml. award, Am. Soc. Human Genetics, 1993, Harland Sanders award, March of Dimes, 2000. Fellow: AAAS; mem.: Inst. of Medicine-Nat. Acad. Scis., AMA, Soc. for Pediatric Rsch., Am. Soc. Human Genetics, Am. Coll. Med. Genetics, Am. Pediatric Soc., Am. Acad. Pediatrics. Home Phone: 858-259-6801; Office Phone: 858-822-6400. Business E-Mail: mkaback@ucsd.edu.

KADIN, HEATHER, broadcast executive; b. Aug. 7, 1972; Grad., U. Mich., 1994. Asst. to prodr. Lynda Obst; asst. to Kevin Misher TriStar and Universal Pictures; asst. to dir. Tom Shadyac; devel. exec. to Tom Shadyac; with longform dept. ABC, with drama dept.; v.p. drama devel. Warner Bros. TV, Burbank, Calif. Achievements include working on the TV shows Alias, Lost, Grey's Anatomy, Desperate Housewives, The Closer, Invasion, Traveler, Supernatural and Studio 60 on the Sunset Strip.

KADISH, SANFORD HAROLD, law educator; b. NYC, Sept. 7, 1921; s. Samuel J. and Frances R. (Klein) K.; m. June Kurtin, Sept. 29, 1942; children: Joshua, Peter. B Social Scis, CCNY, 1942; LLB, Columbia U., 1948; JD (hon.), U. Cologne, 1983; LLD (hon.), CUNY, 1985, Southwestern U., 1993. Bar: N.Y. 1948, Utah 1954. Pvt. practice law, NYC, 1948-51; prof. law U. Utah, 1951-60, U. Mich., 1961-64, U. Calif., Berkeley, 1964-91, dean Law Sch., 1975-82, Morrison prof., 1973-91, prof. emeritus, 1991—. Fulbright lectr. Melbourne (Australia) U., 1956; vis. prof. Harvard U., 1960-61, Freiburg U., 1967; lectr. Salzburg Seminar Am. Studies, 1965; Fulbright vis. lectr. Kyoto (Japan) U., 1975; vis. fellow Inst. Criminology, Cambridge (Eng.) U., 1968. Author: (with M.R. Kadish) Discretion to Disobey— A Study of Lawful Departures from Legal Rules, 1973, (with Schulhofer) Criminal Law and Its Processes, 8th edit., 2007, Blame and Punishment—Essays in the Criminal Law, 1987; editor-in-chief Ency. Crime and Justice, 1983; contbr. articles to profl. jours. Reporter Calif. Legis. Penal Code Project, 1964-68; pub. mem. Wage Stblzn. Bd., region XII, 1951-53; cons. Pres.'s Commn. Adminstrn. of Justice, 1966; mem. Calif. Coun. Criminal Justice, 1968-69. Lt. USNR, 1943-46. Fellow, Ctr. Advanced Study Behavioral Scis., 1967—68, Guggenheim fellow, Oxford U., 1974—75, vis. fellow, All Souls Coll. Oxford U., 1983. Fellow AAAS (v.p. 1984-86), Brit. Acad. (corr.); mem. AAUP (nat. pres. 1970-72), Am. Assn. Law Schs. (exec. com. 1960, pres. 1982), Order of Coif (exec. com. 1966-67, 74-75), Phi Beta Kappa. Home: 774 Hilldale Ave Berkeley CA 94708-1318 E-mail: shk@law.berkeley.edu.

KADO, CLARENCE ISAO, molecular biologist; b. Santa Rosa, Calif., June 10, 1936; s. James Y. and Chiyoko K.; m. Barbara M. Kawahara, June 30, 1963; children: Deborah, Diana M. B.Sc., U. Calif., Berkeley, 1959, PhD, 1964. Rsch. asst. Virus Lab., U. Calif., Berkeley, 1960-64, NIH postdoctoral fellow, 1964-67, asst. rsch. biochemist, 1967-68; asst. prof. plant pathology U. Calif., Davis, 1968-72, assoc. prof., 1972-76, prof., 1976—. Dir. Fallen Leaf Lake Confs., 1985—. Author: (textbook) Principles and Techniques in Plant Virology, 1972; editor: (novels) Molecular Mechanisms of Bacterial Virulence, 1994, Horizontal Gene Transfer, 1998, 2d edit., 2002; editor: (assoc. editor) Virology, 1970—73, (Jours.) Jour. Bacteriology, 1987—93, Molecular Microbiology, 1989—. Recipient Bronze medal for virus rsch., WHO, 1968; grantee, NIH, 1968—2001, Am. Cancer Soc., 1969—73, 1980—82, SEA, 1979—85, CRGO, 1985—99; fellow Sr. fellow, NATO, 1974—75. Fellow: Am. Acad. Microbiology (U.S. Presdl. Sci. award), Am. Phytopath. Soc.; mem.: Internat. Soc. Molecular Plant-Microbe Interactions, Am. Soc. Biochemistry and

Molecular Biology, Am. Soc. Microbiology, N.Y. Acad. Scis., AAAS, Fly Fishers Davis (dir, past pres.), Fly Fishers, Sigma Xi. Office: U Calif Davis Crown Gall Group One Shields Ave Davis CA 95616

KADONAGA, JAMES TAKURO, biochemist; b. Ft. Bragg, NC, Aug. 24, 1958; s. Tadashi and Alice Ayako K.; m. Anne Kadonaga, Sept. 15, 1984; children: William, Natalie. SB, MIT, 1980; AM, Harvard U., 1982, PhD, 1984. Fellow U. Calif., Berkeley, 1984-88, asst. prof. molecular biology San Diego, 1988-92, assoc. prof., 1992-94, prof., 1994—2008, vice chmn., 2000—03, chmn. Molecular Biology, 2003—07, disting. prof., 2008—. Mem. editl. bd. Molecular Cell Jour., 1997—, Genes and Devel. Jour., 1994-2007, Molecular and Cellular Biology, 1993-2001, Protein Expression and Purification, 1990—, Pub. Libr. of Sci., 2005—; contbr. articles to profl. jours. Recipient Biochemistry grant award Eli Lilly, 1989-91, Am. Inst. of Chemists/MIT award, 1980, prize Alpha Chi Sigma/MIT, 1980; named to Hall of Fame, East Side Union H.S. Dist., San Jose, Calif., 1991; DuPont fellow Harvard U., 1983-84, Miller fellow, 1984-86, sr. fellow Am. Cancer Soc. (Calif. divsn.), 1986-87, Presdl. Faculty fellow Pres. George Bush, 1992-97; Lucille P. Markey scholar, 1987-93. Fellow AAAS, Am. Acad. Microbiology; mem. Am. Chem. Soc., Am. Soc. Microbiology. Office: U Calif San Diego 2212B Pacific Hall 9500 Gilman Dr La Jolla CA 92093-0347 Office Phone: 858-534-4608.

KADUSHIN, KAREN DONNA, dean; b. LA, Sept. 3, 1943; BA in Dance, UCLA, 1964; JD, Golden Gate U., 1977. Bar: Calif. 1977, U.S. Dist. Ct. (no. dist.) Calif. 1977. Mem. adj. faculty law Golden Gate U. and U. San Francisco, 1977-84; assoc. Law Offices Diana Richmond, San Francisco, 1978-80; ptnr. Richmond & Kadushin, San Francisco, 1981-83; prin. Kadushin Law Offices, San Francisco, 1983-88; ptnr. Kadushin-Fancher-Wickland, San Francisco, 1989-94; dean Monterey Coll. Law, Monterey, Calif., 1995—2003. Judge pro tem settlement confs. dept. domestic rels. San Francisco Superior Ct., 1985-95; bd. dirs. Lawyers Mut. Ins. Co. Author: California Practice Guide: Law Practice Management, 1992—. Bd. dirs. Legal Assistance for Elderly, San Francisco, 1983, San Francisco Neighborhood Legal Assistance Found., 1984. Mem. Calif. Women Lawyers, Bar Assn. San Francisco (bd. dirs. 1985-86, pres. 1993, Merit award 1980, 90), Barristers Club (pres. 1982), Monterey County Women Lawyers (treas. 1999-2000, pres. 2001). Office: Monterey College Of Law 100 Colonel Durham St Seaside CA 93955-7300 Fax: 831-373-0143. E-mail: kdkdean@montereylaw.edu.

KAESZ, HERBERT DAVID, chemistry educator; b. Alexandria, Egypt, Jan. 4, 1933; BA, NYU, 1954; MA, Harvard U., 1956, PhD, 1959. Prof. inorganic chemistry UCLA, LA. Mem. Am. Chem. Soc. Office: UCLA Chem & Biochem Dept 1505 B Molecular Sci Bldg Los Angeles CA 90095-0001

KAFADAR, CHARLES BELL, mechanical engineer, engineering executive; b. Evanston, Ill., Oct. 13, 1945; s. Ahmed Dogan and Maryanna (Bell) K.; m. Ursula Lutz, Nov. 27, 1964; children: Kimberly, Paul. BS, MS, Purdue U., 1966, PhD in Aerospace and Mech. Sci., 1970. Rsch. fellow, lectr. Princeton (N.J.) U., 1970-73; mem. tech. staff TRW Systems Group, Redondo Beach, Calif., 1973-76; pres., chief oper. officer OEA, Inc., Denver, 1976—. Co-author: Continuum Physics, Vol. II, 1975, Vol. III, 1976; contbr. articles to profl. jours. Mem. vis. com. to math. dept. Colo. Sch. Mines, Golden, 1989—. NSF fellow, 1968-69; Phillips fellow, 1966-67. Mem. Sigma Pi Sigma, Tau Beta Pi, Sigma Gamma Tau. Achievements include expansion of everyday use of high-reliability pyrotechnic items for commercial and government applications.

KAFENTZIS, JOHN CHARLES, journalist, educator; b. Butte, Mont., Aug. 18, 1953; s. Christian and Betty Ann (Gaston) K.; m. Teresa Marie Nokleby, June 5, 1976; children: Kathryn Anne, Christian John. BA in Journalism, U. Mont., 1975; MA in Communication and Leadership studies, Gonzaga U., 2007. Reporter The Missoulian, Missoula, Mont., 1974-76, The Hardin (Mont.) Herald, 1976, The Spokesman-Rev., Spokane, Wash., 1976-80, copy editor, 1980-83, chief copy desk, 1983-89, news editor, 1989-94, news designer, 1994—2003, design editor, 2003—04. Adj. faculty Ea. Wash. U., Cheney, 1982—2007, Whitworth Coll., 1998, Gonzaga U. 2004-07, journalism instr., 2007-. Greek Orthodox. Avocation: swimming. Office: Gonzaga Univ 502 East Boone Ave Spokane WA 99258 Business E-Mail: kafentzis@gonzaga.edu.

KAGAN, ROBERT ALLEN, law educator; b. Newark, June 13, 1938; s. George and Sylvia K. AB, Harvard U., 1959; LLB, Columbia U., 1962; PhD, Yale U., 1974. Now prof. polit. sci. and law U. Calif., Berkeley. Office: U Calif Sch Law Boalt Hall Berkeley CA 94720

KAGAN, STEPHEN BRUCE (SANDY KAGAN), corporate financial executive; b. Elizabeth, NJ, Apr. 27, 1944; s. Herman and Ida (Nadel) K.; m. Susan D. Kaltman, July 3, 1966; children: Sheryl, Rachel BS in Econs., U. Pa., 1966; MBA in Fin., Bernard Baruch Coll., 1969. Chartered fin. analyst. CPA security analyst Merrill Lynch Pierce Fenner & Smith, NYC, 1966-68; dir. rsch. Deutschmann & Co., NYC, 1968-70; v.p. Equity Sponsors, Inc., NYC, 1970-72; v.p., investment counselor Daniel H. Renberg & Assocs., Inc., LA, 1972—78; CFO, COO Carlson Travel Network, Van Nuys, Calif., 1978—95; rep. Excel Telecomms., Van Nuys, Calif., 1995—2000; sr. CFO, ptnr. Tatum LLC, San Marcos, Calif., 2000—. Vice pres. bd. Temple Beth Hillel, North Hollywood, Calif., 1976-83 Mem. Inst. Cert. Fin. Analysts, Beta Gamma Sigma Avocations: golf, skiing, poker, travel. Home and Office: Tatum LLC 941 Bridgeport Ct San Marcos CA 92078

KAGIWADA, REYNOLD SHIGERU, electronics executive; b. LA, July 8, 1938; s. Harry Yoshifusa and Helen Kinue (Imura) K.; children: Julia, Conan. BS in Physics, UCLA, 1960, MS in Physics, 1962, PhD in Physics, 1966. Asst. prof. in residence physics UCLA, 1966-69; asst. prof. physics U. So. Calif., 1969-72; mem. tech. staff TRW (now NGST), Redondo Beach, Calif., 1972-75, scientist, sect. head, 1975-77, sr. scientist, dept. mgr., 1977-83, lab. mgr., 1984-87, project mgr., 1987-88, MIMIC chief scientist, 1988-89, asst. program mgr., 1989-90, advanced technology mgr., 1990—2001, dir. advanced electronics, 2002—. Presenter in field. Contbr. articles to profl. jours. Recipient Gold Medal award TRW, 1985, Ramo Tech. award, 1985, Transfer award, IEEE MTT-S N. Walter Cox award, 1997. Fellow IEEE (v.p. IEEE MTT-S adminstrn. com. 1991, pres. 1992, Disting. Svc. award 2001); mem. Assn. Old Crows, Sigma Xi, Sigma Pi Sigma. Achievements include patents for solid state devices. Home: 3117 Malcolm Ave Los Angeles CA 90034-3406 Office: NGST Bldg M5 Rm 1492 One Space Park Bldg Redondo Beach CA 90278 Personal E-mail: reynold.kagiwada@ngst.com.

KAHANE, JEFFREY, conductor, pianist, music director; b. LA, Sept. 12, 1956; BMus, San Francisco Conservatory, 1977. Prof. piano Eastman Sch. Music, 1988-95; music dir. Santa Rosa (Calif.) Symphony, 1995—2005, LA Chamber Orch., 1996—, Green Music Festival, 2001, Colo. Symphony Orch., 2005—. Office: Colo Symphony Assn Boettcher Concert Hall Denver Performing Arts 1000 14th St #15 Denver CO 80202-2333 E-mail: artistsny@imgworld.com.

KAHN, BRUCE S., obstetrician, gynecologist; BS, U. Calif., Irvine, 1984; MS, Georgetown U., Washington, 1986, MD, 1990. Diplomate in F.A.C.O.G. Am. Bd. Ob-gyn., 1999. Dir., chronic pelvic pain clinic Naval Med. Ctr., San Diego, 1996—98; dir. ambulatory gynecology, hillcrest U. Calif., San Diego, 1998—99; dir. grad. med. edn. Scripps Clinic Med. Group, La Jolla, Calif., 2001—; chmn. grad. med. edn. Scripps Meml. Hosp., La Jolla, 2008—. Lcdr USN, 1996—98, San Diego. Recipient Resident Tchg. award, Abington Meml. Hosp., 1994—95, Naval Med. Ctr. Scripps Clinic, 2001. Fellow: Am. Coll. Ob-gyn. Office: Scripps Clinic Medical Group 3811 Valley Center Dr S99 San Diego CA 92130 Office Fax: 858-764-9097. Business E-Mail: bkahn@scrippsclinic.com.

KAHN, EDWIN SAM, lawyer; b. NYC, Jan. 22, 1938; m. Cynthia Chutter, May 30, 1966; children: David, Jonathan, Jennifer. BA, U. Colo., 1958; JD, Harvard U., 1965. Bar: Colo. 1965, U.S. Dist. Ct. (Colo.) 1965, U.S. Ct. Appeals (10th cir.) 1965, U.S. Supreme Ct. 1968. Assoc. Holland & Hart, Denver, 1965-70, ptnr., 1970-77; ptnr., shareholder Kelly Garnsey Hubbell, Denver, 1978—. Spl. coun. Colo. Ctr. Law and Policies, 2004—. 1st lt. USAF, 1959-62. Fellow Am. Coll. Trial Lawyers; mem. Denver Bar Assn. (pres. 1984-85). Home: 2345 Leyden St Denver CO 80207-3441 Office: Kelly Haglund Garnsey & Kahn LLC 1441 18th St Ste 300 Denver CO 80202-1255 E-mail: ekahn77@msn.com.

KAHN, FREDRICK HENRY, retired internist; b. LA, Aug. 26, 1925; s. Julius and Josephine Leone (Langdon) K.; m. Barbara Ruth Visscher, Feb. 14, 1952; children: Susan, Kathryn, William. AB, Stanford U., 1947, MD, 1951. Diplomate Am. Bd. Internal Medicine. Rotating intern San Francisco Gen. Hosp., 1950-51, fellow pathology, 1951-52; resident medicine Los Angeles VA Hosp., 1954-57, sr. resident, 1956-57; asst. clin. prof. medicine UCLA Sch. Medicine, 1957—2005; attending physician Cedars Sinai Med. Ctr., LA, 1957-96, attending physician emeritus, 1996—2007; attending physician UCLA, 1957-95; ret. Med. advisor Vis. Nurse Assn., Los Angeles, 1957-87. Contbr. articles to med. jours.; inventor blow-through high altitude chamber; promoter iodine method of personal water disinfection for travelers and hikers. Served with USNR, 1943-46; lt. (M.C.), USNR, 1952-54. Fellow ACP; mem. AMA, Microscope Soc. So. Calif, Am. Handel Soc., Sierra Club. Mailing: 3309 Corinth Ave Los Angeles CA 90066-1312 Personal E-mail: fredandbarbara@ca.rr.com, fredkahn@verizon.net.

KAHN, STEVEN EMANUEL, medical educator; b. Durban, South Africa, July 28, 1955; m. Stephanie Berk Kahn; 2 children. MB, ChB, U. Cape Town, South Africa, 1978. Diplomate Am. Bd. Internal Medicine. Intern depts. ob-gyn and medicine Somerset Hosp., Cape Town, South Africa, 1979; resident dept. ob-gyn 2 Mil. Hosp., Wynberg, South Africa, 1980, resident and coord. dept. ob-gyn, 1981; resident dept. medicine divsn. endocrinology Groote Schuur Hosp., Cape Town, 1982; rsch. fellow diabetes and endocrine rsch. group U. Cape Town, 1983; resident dept. medicine Albert Einstein Med. Ctr., Phila., 1983—86; sr. rsch. fellow divsn. metabolism, endocrinology and nutrition U. Wash. Sch. of Medicine, VA Med. Ctr., Seattle, 1986—88; assoc. investigator, staff physician divsn. endocrinology and metabolism VA Med. Ctr., Seattle, 1988—91, rsch. assoc., staff physician divsn. endocrinology and metabolism, 1991—95; acting instr. divsn. metabolism, endocrinology and nutrition U. Wash. Sch. Medicine, Seattle, 1988—92, asst. prof. divsn. metabolism, endocrinology and nutrition, 1992—95, assoc. prof. divsn. metabolism, endocrinology and nutrition, 1995—2001, prof. divsn. metabolism, endocrinology and nutrition, 2001—; dir. R&D VA Puget Sound Health Care Sys., 2001—. Prizer vis. prof. Case Western Res. U., 1999. Mem. editl. bd.: Jour. Clin. Endocrinology and Metabolism, 1995—98, Diabetes Care, 1997—99; contbr. articles to profl. jours. Recipient Career Devel. award, Juvenile Diabetes Found., 1988, NIH, 1999, Feasibility award, Dana Found., 1989, Clin. Investigator award, NIH, 1991, New Investigator award, Diabetes Rsch. Coun., 1992—94, rsch. award, NIH, 1997, Novartis Young Investigator award in diabetes rsch., 2001; named Assoc. Investigator, Dept. VA, 1988, Rsch. Assoc., 1991; scholar Amelia Schenkman, 1973—75. Mem.: ACP, Gen. Med. Coun. (U.K.), Western Soc. Clin. Investigation (councillor 1998—), Endocrine Soc., Am. Soc. for Clin. Investigation, Am. Fedn. Clin. Rsch. (chair program com. for metabolism 1994, 1996, councillor western sect. 1994—96, pres.-elect western sect. 1996, pres. western sect. 1997, nat. councillor 1996), Am. Diabetes Assn. (bd. dirs. Wash. affiliate 1993—94, exec. bd. dirs. 1994—98, rsch. grant rev. panel 1994—97, rsch. award 1996, mentor award 1999). Office: VA Puget Sound Health Cr Dept Medicine 151 1660 S Columbian Way Seattle WA 98108-1532

KAHN, STEVEN MICHAEL, astrophysicist, educator; b. NYC, Nov. 23, 1954; s. George Arthur and Muriel Vera (Gross) K.; m. Susan Marlene Sacks, July 16, 1978; 1 child, Isaac Alden. AB, Columbia U, 1975; PhD, U. Calif., Berkeley, 1980. Postdoctoral fellow Smithsonian Astrophys. Obs., Cambridge, Mass., 1980-82; asst. prof. physics Columbia U., NYC, 1982-84; from asst. prof. to assoc. prof. physics U. Calif., Berkeley, 1984-90, assoc. prof. astronomy, 1989-90, prof. physics and astronomy, 1990—. Assoc. dir. Space Scis. Lab., U. Calif., Berkeley, 1986—. Contbr. articles to profl. jours. Recipient Earl C. Anthony fellowship, U. Calif., Berkeley, 1976, Andrew R. Michelson award, Columbia U., 1975.

KAHN, TIMOTHY F., food products company executive; b. 1954; grad., MBA, Dartmouth Coll. With PepsiCo., Inc., sr. v.p., fin. and devel. restaurant svcs. group; v.p. fin. and administrn., CFO Dreyer's Grand Ice Cream, Inc., Oakland, Calif., 1998—. Office: Dreyer's Grand Ice Cream Inc 5929 College Ave Oakland CA 94618

KAHNE, STEPHEN JAMES, systems engineering educator, engineering company executive, academic administrator; b. NYC, Apr. 5, 1937; s. Arnold W. and Janet (Weatherlow) Kahne; m. Irena Nowacka, Dec. 11, 1970; children: Christopher, Kasia. BEE, Cornell U., Ithaca, NY, 1960; MS, U. Ill., Urbana-Champaign, 1961, PhD, 1963. Asst. prof. elec. engring. U. Minn., Mpls., 1966-69, assoc. prof., 1969-76; dir. Hybrid Computer Lab., 1968-76; founder, dir., cons. InterDesign Inc., Mpls., 1968-76; prof. dept. sys. engring. Case Western Res. U., Cleve., 1976-83, chmn. dept., 1976-80; dir. divsn. elec., computer and sys. engring. NSF, Washington, 1980-82; prof. Poly Inst. N.Y., 1983-85, dean engring., 1983-84; pres. Oreg. Grad. Ctr., Beaverton, 1985-86, prof. dept. applied physics and elec. engring., 1985-89; chief engr. civil systems divsn. MITRE Corp., McLean, Va., 1989-90, chief scientist Washington Group, 1990-91, cons. engr. Ctr. for Advanced Aviation Sys. Devel., 1991-94; exec. dir., CEO Triangle Coalition for Sci. and Tech. Edn., 1994; chancellor, v.p. Embry-Riddle Aeronautical U., Prescott, Ariz., 1995-97, prof. engring., 1995—2009; emeritus prof. engring., 2009—. Cons. in field; exchange scientist NAS, 1968, 75 Contbr. articles to sci. jours. Active Mpls. Citizens League, 1968-75; regent L.I. Coll. Hosp., Bklyn., 1984-85; trustee Yavapai Regional Med. Ctr., 1999-2004; chmn. Beaverton Sister Cities Found., 1986-89; ct. appointed spl. adv. Superior Ct. Ariz., 2005—; bd. dirs. West Yavapai Guidance Clinic, 2005-, No. Ariz. Regional Behavioral Health Authority, 2006-, Am. Mensa, 2008-. Served with USAF, 1963-66. Recipient Amicus Poloniae award POLAND Mag., 1975, John A. Curtis award Am. Soc. Engring. Edn., Outstanding Svc. award Internat. Fedn. Automatic Control, 1990; Case Centennial scholar, 1980. Fellow: AAAS, IEEE (life; editor Transactions on Automatic Control 1975—79, mem. editl. bd. Spectrum 1979—82, pres. Control Sys. Soc. 1981, bd. dirs. 1982—86, v.p. tech. activities 1984—85, Centennial medal 1984, Disting Mem. award 1983, Richard Emberson award 1991, Disting. Lectr. 1998—2000), Internat. Fedn. Automatic Control (hon. editor 1975—81, dep. chmn. mng. bd. publs. 1976—87, v.p. 1987—90, pres.-elect 1990—93, pres. 1993—96, adv. 1999—, chmn. 1999—, mem. publs. mgmt. bd., Found. trustee); mem.: Eta Kappa Nu. Office: Embry Riddle Aero U 3700 Willow Creek Rd Prescott AZ 86301-3721 Office Phone: 928-777-3779. Personal E-mail: s.kahne@ieee.org.

KAIGLER, DENISE M., marketing executive; b. Huntington, W.Va., 1962; d. Diane Moore; m. Joseph Kaigler; children: Danielle, Joseph Jr. BA in Journalism, Emerson Coll., 1985; LHD (hon.), We. New England Coll., 2006. Freelance reporter WILD radio, Boston; reporter WLTZ-TV, Columbus, Ga., WHDH-TV, Boston; dir. comm. Boys & Girls Clubs of Boston, 1989—91; media rels. specialist Reebok Internat. Ltd., 1991—92, sr. media rels. specialist, 1992—94, mgr. corp. comm., 1994—97, dir. global pub. rels., 1997—99; dir. corp. comm. & entertainment mktg. The Rockport Co., 1998—99; sr. dir. global comm. Reebok Internat. Ltd., Canton, Mass., 2000—01, v.p. global comm. & talent rels., 2001—04, sr. v.p. corp. rels., chief corp. comm. officer, 2004—06, sr. v.p. global pub. rels. and comm., 2006—07, head global corp. comm. & corp. citizenship, 2007—08; v.p. mktg. & corp. affairs Nintendo of Am. Inc, Redmond, Wash., 2008—. Recipient Exceptional Women in Bus. award, Magic 106.7, 2005, Acad. Women Achievers award, YWCA, Mary Eliza Mahoney award, Dimrock Cmty. Health Ctr., Alumni Achievement award, Emerson Coll.; named a Woman Worth Watching, Profiles in Diversity Jour., 2006; named one of The 25 Most Influential Black Women in Bus., The Network Jour. mag., 2004, Six Women to Watch, Boston Women's Bus., 2005. Mem.: Boston Assn. of Black Communicators, Pub. Rels. Soc. Am. Office: Nintendo of Am Inc 4820 150th Ave NE Redmond WA 98052

KAIL, KONRAD, physician; b. Iowa City, July 7, 1949; s. Joseph Andrew Kail and Jean Lucille (Peterson) Tienan; m. Jane Marie Petersen, Jan. 5, 1973. BS in Biology, U. Houston, 1974; BS in Medicine, Baylor Coll. Medicine, 1976; ND, Nat. Coll. Naturopathic, Medicine, 1983; DACNFM, Am. Coll. Naturopathic Family, Medicine, 1995. Lic. naturopathic physician. Cardiac-catherization technician St. Luke's/Tex. Children's Hosp., Houston, 1972-75; physician's asst. various clinics, Silver City, N.Mex., 1976-80; dir. Naturopathic Wheeling and Healing Around Country Bike Tour, 1983-84; chmn. bd. dirs. U.S. Complementary Health, Inc., Phoenix, 1995—; bd. dirs., co-founder, mem. faculty S.W. Coll. of Naturopathic Medicine, Phoenix, 1996—; pvt. practice Ariz. Advanced Medicine, Phoenix, 1990—; dir. rsch. and devel. Western Rsch. Labs., 2002—07. Cons. Ins. Cos., Nutrient Supplement Cos., Govt. Agys., 1985—; mem. adv. bd. NIH Nat. Ctr. for Complementary and Alternative Medicine, 1999-2003; bd. med. examiners Ariz. Naturopathic Physicians, 2001-2008. Co-author: Allergy Free, an Alternative Medicine Definitive Guide; editor: Alternative Medicine, 1994; contbr. articles to profl. jours. Mem. adv. bd. Inst. for Natural Medicine. With USN Res., 1971-76. Recipient Tyler Pioneer award, 2001, In Office Rsch. award, AAWP, 2006. Fellow Am. Assn. Naturopathic Physicians (chmn. sci. affil. 1986-97, pres. 1992-94, Physician of Yr. 1997), Am. Coll. Naturopathic Family Practice (chmn., pres. 1995—). Green Party. Avocations: ultimate frisbee, bicycling, skiing, golf. Office: Ariz Advanced Medicine 7425 E Shea Blvd Ste 106 Scottsdale AZ 85260 Office Phone: 480-905-9200. E-mail: kkail@cox.net.

KAILATH, THOMAS, electrical engineer, educator; b. Poona, India, June 7, 1935; arrived in US, 1957, naturalized, 1976; s. Mamman and Kunjamma (George) Kailath; m. Sarah Jacob, June 11, 1962; children: Ann, Paul, Priya, Ryan. BE, U. Poona, 1956; SM, MIT, 1959, ScD, 1961; Dr. Tek (hon.), Linkoping U., Sweden, 1990; D honoris causa (hon.), Strathclyde U., Scotland, 1992; D (hon.), U. Carlos III, Madrid, 1999; D honoris causa (hon.), U. Bordeaux, France, 2003, Viswesaraya Tech. U., India, 2009. Comm. rschr. Jet Propulsion Labs., Pasadena, Calif., 1961-62; mem. faculty Stanford U., Calif., 1963—, prof. elec. engring., 1968—, Hitachi Am. prof. engring., 1988—2001, Hitachi Am. prof. emeritus, 2001—; dir. Info. Systems Lab., 1971-81, assoc. chmn. dept., 1981-87. Vis. prof., cons. univs., industry, govt. Author: Linear Systems, 1980, Least-Squares Estimation, 2nd edit, 1981, Linear Estimation, 2000; mem. editl. bd. various jours.; contbr. articles to profl. jours. Recipient Edn. award Am. Control Coun., 1986, Tech. Achievement and Soc. awards Signal Processing Soc. IEEE, 1989, 91, Donald G. Fink Prize award, 1996, Shannon award, 2000; Sr. Vinton Hayes fellow MIT, 1992, Guggenheim fellow, 1970, Churchill fellow, 1977, Michael fellow Weizmann Inst., Israel, 1984, Royal Soc. guest rsch. fellow, 1989, Alexander Humboldt fellow, 2003; named to Silcon Valley Engring. Hall of Fame, 2006, Padma Bhushan award, Govt. of India. Fellow: IEEE (life Edn. medal 1995, Jack S. Kilby medal 2006, Medal of Honor 2007, Padma Bhushan, India), Am. Acad. Arts and Scis., Inst. Math. Stats.; mem.: NAS, Royal Spanish Acad. Engring., Third World Acad. Scis., Soc. Indsl. and Applied Math., Am. Math. Soc., Indian Nat. Acad. Engring., Sigma Xi. Office: Info Systems Lab Stanford U 350 Serra Mall Packard Bldg 276 Stanford CA 94305-9510 Business E-Mail: kailath@stanford.edu.

KAISER, GLEN DAVID, construction company executive; s. David and Margaret Jane (Frye) K.; m. Pamela Blyo Barris, Sept. 7, 1972 (div. 1974); m. Pamela Blyo Barris, Nov. 7, 1976; children: Barris David, Katrina Tara. BS in Civil Engring., Stanford U., 1974, MS in Constrn. Mgmt., 1975. Registered profl. engr., Nev., Calif. Constrn. engr. Kaiser Engrs., Oakland, Calif., 1975-79; project coord. Corrao

Constrn., Reno, 1979-81; chief estimator Marnell Corrao Assocs., Las Vegas, Nev., 1981-82, exec. v.p., 1982-91, pres., 1991—. Bd. dirs. Pop Warner, Las Vegas, 1991-93, Las Vegas Symphony, 1992-93. Mem. Associated Gen. Contractors (2d v.p. 1992, sec.-treas. 1993), United Builders and Contractors (v.p. 1998, pres. 2001), Appaloosa Horse Club, Sigma Chi Alumni Assn., Stanford U. Alumni Assn. Roman Catholic. Avocations: skiing, horseback riding, golf. E-mail: gkaiser@marnellcorrao.com.

KALB, BENJAMIN STUART, television producer, director; b. LA, Mar. 17, 1948; s. Marcus and Charlotte K. BS in Journalism, U. Oreg., 1969. Sportswriter Honolulu Advertiser, 1971-76. Traveled with tennis profl. Ilie Nastase; contbr. articles N.Y. Times, Sport Mag. and Tennis U.S.A., 1976; editor Racquetball Illustrated, 1978-82; segment producer PM Mag. and Hollywood Close-Up, 1983-86; exec. producer Ben Kalb Prodns., 1986—; instr. sports in soc. U. Hawaii, 1974-75. Prodr. (video) The Natural Way to Meet the Right Person, 1987; prodr., dir. (video) Casting Call: Director's Choice, 1987, The Natural Way to Meet the Right Person (Best Home Videos of Yr. L.A. Times), (TV pilot and home video) Bizarro, 1988, (infomercial) How To Start Your Own Million Dollar Business, 1990, The Nucelle Promise, 1993-94, Koolatron Companion, 1997, Radiant Health, 1999, Facial Toner, 1999, AbTronic Fitness Sys., 2000; prodr.-dir. (infomercials) Banamex USA Credit Card, 1995, Slimaster Exerciser, 1996, Koolatron Companion, 1997, Yonex Golf, 1998, Toski's Touch, 2001, Beon Computer, 2001, Buffalo Milke, 2001, Restform Airbed, 2002, Abs & More, 2002, Chef O'Matic, 2003, Smoke Free, 2004, Restform Airbed II, 2004, Dyna Trainer, 2004, VetForm Sauma Belt, 2005, Vibroachor Belt, 2006, Total Sauma, 2006, Air-O-Dry, 2006, Magic Recliner, 2006, Steam-O-Bely, 2007, Hair Grow Plus, 2007, Primer Grw Comb, 2008, Contoma Jeans, 2008, Bona Tese Slim Come, 2008; segment dir. (home video) Movie Magic, 1990, (TV show) Totally Hidden Video; writer-segment dir. (home video) Making of The American Dream Calendar Girl, 1991; prodr., host (cable TV show) Delicious Sports, 1987-88; segment dir. Totally Hidden Video (Fox TV Network), 1991-92; prodr., dir. short feature films Love Match, 1995, The Last Great Infomercial, 2005; contbr. articles to mags. and newspapers. Served with Hawaii Army N.G., 1970-75. Named Outstanding Male Grad. in Journalism, U. Oreg., 1969. Mem. Sigma Delta Chi (chpt. pres. 1968). Democrat. Jewish. Office: 5045 Rogers Ste 7 Las Vegas NV 89118 also: 5340 South Proctor St Las Vegas NV 89118 Office Phone: 702-871-8787. Personal E-mail: bkalbprod@earthlink.net.

KALET, IRA JOSEPH, medical computer scientist; b. Stamford, Conn., Apr. 27, 1944; s. Bernard and Miriam Kalet; m. Teresa Lynn Kalet, Apr. 7, 1973; children: Nathan, Alan, Brian. AB in Physics, Cornell U., 1965; MA in Physics, Princeton U., 1967, PhD in Theoretical Physics, 1968. Rsch. assoc. physics U. Wash., Seattle, 1968-69; asst. prof. Sonoma State Coll., Rohnert Park, Calif., 1969-70; lectr. math. edn. U. Pa., Phila., 1974-75; sr. fellow med. physics U. Wash., Seattle, 1978-80, rsch. assoc., 1980-82, asst. prof. radiation oncology, 1982-88, adj. asst. prof. computer sci., 1982-88, assoc. prof. radiation oncology, 1988—2004, adj. assoc. prof. computer sci., bioengring./biol. structure, 1988—2004, prof. radiation oncology, prof. med. edn. and biomedical informatics, adj. prof. computer sci., 2004—. Mem. adv. bd. program in health info. mgmt. U. Wash., Seattle, 1993—; ad hoc grant reviewer NIH, Bethesda, Md., 1987—; Dozor vis. prof. Ben Gurion U., Israel, 1996; Disting. lectr. computer sci. Dalhousie U., N.S., Can., 2002. Assoc. editor Computerized Med. Imaging and Graphics, 1988—; contbr. articles to profl. jours. Recipient Nat. Rsch. Svc. award NIH, U. Wash., 1978-80, Best Paper award Am. Assn. Med. Sys. and Informatics, 1985, Biomed. and Health Informatics Excellence in Tchg. award U. Wsh., 2003; rsch. grantee NIH, U. Wash., 1984—. Mem. Assn. Computing Machinery, Am. Assn. Physicists in Medicine, Am. Assn. Artificial Intelligence, Am. Assn. Physics Tchrs. Jewish. Achievements include breakthroughs in design of software for radiation treatment planning for cancer; prodn. of the first commercially available three-dimensional radiation treatment planning software. Office: U Wash Radiation Oncology Dept PO Box 356043 Seattle WA 98195-6043

KALETA, PAUL J., lawyer, utilities executive; b. Queens, NY, Aug. 18, 1955; AB in Philosophy and English cum laude, Hamilton Coll., 1978; JD cum laude, Georgetown U., 1981. Bar: DC 1982, NY 1993, US Supreme Ct. 1987. Assoc. Skadden, Arps, Slate, Meagher & Flom, Washington, 1982—84; ptnr. Swidler & Berlin, Washington, 1985-91; v.p., gen. counsel Niagara Mohawk Power Corp., Syracuse, NY, 1991-98; v.p., gen. counsel, sec. Koch Industries, Inc., Wichita, Kans., 1998—2005; sr. v.p., gen. counsel, corp. sec. Sierra Pacific Resources, Reno, 2006—. Vice chmn. Utility Law Commn. Mem. ABA, NY State Bar Assn. Office: Sierra Pacific Resources 6100 Neil Rd Reno NV 89511

KALINA, ROBERT EDWARD, ophthalmologist, educator; b. New Prague, Minn., Nov. 13, 1936; s. Edward Robert and Grace Susan (Hess) K.; m. Janet Jessie Larsen, July 18, 1959; children: Paul Edward, Lynne Janet. BA magna cum laude, U. Minn., 1957, BS, MD, U. Minn., 1960. Diplomate Am. Bd. Ophthalmology (dir. 1981-89). Intern U. Oreg. Med. Sch. Hosp., Portland, 1960-61, resident in ophthalmology, 1961-62, 63-66; asst. in retina surgery Children's Hosp., San Francisco, 1966-67; Nat. Inst. Neurol. Diseases and Blindness Spl. fellow Mass. Eye and Ear Infirmary, Boston, 1967; instr. ophthalmology U. Wash., 1967-69, asst. prof., 1969-71, acting chmn. dept. ophthalmology, 1970-71, assoc. prof., 1971-72, chmn. dept. ophthalmology, 1971-96, prof., 1972—. Mem. staffs Univ. Hosp., Harborview Hosp., Children's Hosp., Seattle; cons. VA Hosp., Seattle, Madigan Hosp., Tacoma; assoc. head divsn. ophthalmology dept. surgery Children's Hosp., Seattle, 1975-86; pres. U. Wash. Physicians, 1990-93. Contbg. author: Introduction to Clinical Pediatrics, 1972, Ophthalmology Study Guide for Medical Students, 1975; contbr. numerous articles to profl. publs. Served to capt., M.C. USAF, 1962-63. Recipient Outstanding Achievement award, Nat. Eye Inst., 2003. Fellow ACS, Am. Acad. Ophthalmology (Sr. Honor award 1989); mem., Assn. Univ. Profs. Ophthalmology (pres. 1983-84, exec. v.p. 1989-94), Assn. Rsch. in Vision and Ophthalmology, Pacific Coast Oto-Ophthalmol. Soc. (councilor 1972-74), King County Med. Soc., Wash. State Acad. Ophthalmology, Phi Beta Kappa. Office: U Wash Dept Ophthalmology Box 356485 1959 NE Pacific St Seattle WA 98195-0001

KALLAHER, MICHAEL JOSEPH, mathematics professor; b. Cin., Sept. 4, 1940; s. Martin Henry and Lou Will (Huff) K.; m. Donalyn May Laraway, Aug. 17, 1963; children: Jay, Michael, Christopher, Daniel, Raymond. BS, Xavier U., 1961; MS, Syracuse U., 1963, PhD, 1967. Postdoctoral fellow U. Man., Winnipeg, Can., 1967-69; from asst. prof. prof. math. Wash. State U., Pullman, 1969—, assoc. dean scis., 1979-84, acting dean scis., 1982, chmn. math dept., 1984-92; vis. prof. Auckland U., New Zealand, 1988. Author: Affine Planes with Transitive Collineation Groups; contbg. editor Finite Geometries, 1982; contbr. articles to profl. jours. Grantee NSF; Fulbright Research scholar, Kaiserslautern, Fed. Republic Germany, 1975-76. Fellow Inst. Combinatories and Its Application (founding); mem. Am. Math. Soc., Math. Assn. Am., N.Y. Acad. of Scis., Assn. of Research Profs. (pres. 1986-87), Sigma Xi. Home: 235 NW Joe St Pullman WA 99163-3410 Office: Wash State U Dept Of Math Pullman WA 99163 Business E-Mail: mkallaher@pullman.com.

KALLENBERG, JOHN KENNETH, retired librarian; b. Anderson, Ind., June 10, 1942; s. Herbert A. and Helen S. K.; m. Ruth Barrett, Aug. 19, 1965; children: Jennifer Anne, Gregory John. AB, Ind. U., 1964, M.L.S., 1969. With Fresno County Library, Fresno, Calif., 1965-70, dir., 1976—2003; librarian Fig Garden Pub. Library br., 1968-70; asst. dir. Santa Barbara Pub. Library, Calif., 1970-76; ret. Mem. Calif. Libr. Svcs. bd., 1990—99, v.p., 1992—95, pres., 1996—98; mem. Libr. of Calif. Bd., 1999—2003, pres., 2003; Beth Ann Harnish lectr. com., 1988—91; mem. adv. bd. Pacific S.W. Regional Med. Libr., 1999—2008; mem. Heartland Regional Libr. Network Bd., 2000—04; bd. mem. Fresno County Retired Employees Assn., 2006—. Mem. editl. bd.: Past and Present, Fresno City and County Hist. Soc., 1980—2007. Mem.: ALA, Fresno County Employees Retirement Assn. (mem. bd. 2006—), William Saroyan Soc. (bd. dirs. 1984—, chmn. 2004—), Am. Soc. Pub. Adminstrn., Libr. Adminstrn. and Mgmt. Assn., Calif. Libr. Authority for Sys. and Svcs. (chmn. authority adv. com. 1978—80), Calif. County Librs. Assn. (pres. 1977), Calif. Libr. Assn. (councilor 1976—77, v.p., pres. 1987), Pub. Libr. Assn., Kiwanis (pres. Fresno 1981—82, lt. gov. divsn. 5 1991—92, co-editor Cal-Nev-Ha News 1993—94, 1995—96, bd. dirs. 1999—2001, 2002—04, editor Kiwaniscape 2004—05, co-editor 2005—06, 2006—08). Presbyterian. E-mail: jkk59@cvip.net.

KALLGREN, EDWARD EUGENE, lawyer; b. San Francisco, May 22, 1928; s. Edward H. and Florence E. (Campbell) K.; m. Joyce Elaine Kislitzin, Feb. 8, 1953; children: Virginia K. Pegley, Charles Edward. AB, U. Calif., Berkeley, 1951, JD, 1954. Bar: Calif. Assoc., ptnr. Brobeck, Phleger & Harrison LLP, San Francisco, 1954-93, of counsel, 1993—2003. Bd. dirs. Olivet Meml. Park, Colma, Calif., 1970-98, pres., 1991-98; chair, pres. Five Bridges Found., 1998—; mem. Berkeley City Council, 1971-75; bd. dirs., v.p./treas. Planned Parenthood Alameda/San Francisco, 1984-89. Served to sgt. USMC, 1945-48. Mem. ABA (ho. of dels. 1985-2000, state del. 1997-98, coun. sr. law divsn. 1996-2001, chair 1999-2000), State Bar of Calif. (bd. govs. 1989-92, v.p. 1991-92), Found. of State Bar Calif. (bd. dirs. 1993-98, v.p., 1994-96, chair fellows soc. 1996-98), Bar Assn. San Francisco (pres. 1988, bd. dirs.), San Francisco Lawyers Com. Urban Affairs (co-chair 1983-85), Lawyers Com. Civil Rights Under Law (trustee 1985—), The TenBroek Soc. (chair bd. dirs. 1992-95). Democrat.

KALLSHIAN, JAN, electronics manufacturing company executive; b. 1954; CPA. With Coopers & Lybrand; cons., CFO Datamarine Internat., Inc., Mountlake, Wash., 1995, CFO, 1997—. Office: 7030 220th SW Mountlake Terrace WA 98043

KALLSTROM, D. WARD, lawyer; b. Dec. 3, 1949; BA summa cum laude, U. Calif., Santa Barbara, 1972; JD, Duke U., 1977. Bar: Calif., admitted to practice: US Supreme Ct., US Ct. Appeals (9th Cir.), US Ct. Appeals (10th Cir.), US Dist. Ct. (Ariz.), US Dist. Ct. (No. Dist.) Calif., US Dist. Ct. (So. Dist.) Calif., US Dist. Ct. (Ctrl. Dist.) Calif., US Dist. Ct. (Ea. Dist.) Calif., US Dist. Ct. (Colo.). Ptnr., Labor and Employment Law Practice Group Morgan, Lewis & Bockius LLP, San Francisco. Editl. bd. Duke Law Jour. Fellow: Coll. Labor & Employment Lawyers, Am. Coll. Employee Benefits Counsel; mem.: Western Pension and Benefits Conf., Internat. Found. Employee Benefit Plans, ABA, Am. Employment Law Coun. Office: Morgan Lewis & Bockius LLP One Market Spear Street Tower San Francisco CA 94105 Office Phone: 415-442-1308. Office Fax: 415-442-1001. E-mail: dwkallstrom@morganlewis.com.

KALMAR, CARLOS, conductor, music director; b. Uruguay, 1958; m. Britta Kalmar; children: Svenja, Katja. Condr. Vienna Volksoper, Vienna, 1987; music dir. Hamburg Symphony, 1987—91, Stuttgart Philharmonic, 1991—95, Anhaltisches Theater Dessau and Philharmonie Dessau, 1996—2000, Vienna Niederosterreichisches Tonkunstlevorchester, Vienna, 2000—03, Oreg. Symphony, 2003—. Prin. condr. Grant Park Music Festival, Chgo.; guest condr. numerous symphonies and orch., guest appearance. Avocations: hiking, cooking. Office: Oregon Symphony 921 SW Washington Ste 200 Portland OR 97205

KALRA, ASH, councilman; BA in Comm., U. Calif., Santa Barbara, 1991—93; JD, Georgetown U., 1993—96. Atty. Santa Clara County Pub. Defender's Office, 1997—2008; instr. San José State U.; prof. Lincoln Law Sch. San José; councilman, Dist. 2 San José City Coun., 2008—. Chairperson San José Planning Commn., 2006—08. Vol. Habitat for Humanity; mem. bd. dirs. Fresh Lifelines for Youth. Mem.: Hayes Neighborhood Assn., Santa Teresa Foothills Neighborhood Assn. (mem. bd. dirs.), South Asian Bar Assn. (mem. bd. dirs.), Asian Law Alliance (mem. bd. dirs.), Santa Clara County Bar Assn. (mem. bd. dirs.), San José Rotary Club. Office: San Jose City Coun 200 E Santa Clara St San Jose CA 95113 Office Phone: 408-535-4902. Business E-Mail: ash.kalra@sanjoseca.gov.*

KALTENBACH, C(ARL) COLIN, dean, educator; b. Buffalo, Wyo., Mar. 22, 1939; s. Carl H. and Mary Colleen (McKeag) K.; m. Ruth Helene Johnson, Aug. 22, 1964; children: James Earl, John Edward. BSc, U. Wyo., 1961; MSc, U. Nebr., 1963; PhD, U. Ill., 1967. Postdoctoral fellow U. Melbourne, Australia, 1967-69; from asst. prof. to prof. U. Wyo., Laramie, 1969-89, assoc. dean, dir. Agrl. Expt. Sta., 1980-89; vice dean, dir. Agrl. Expt. Sta. U. Ariz., Tucson, 1989—2007, 2008—, dean, dir. Agrl. Expt. Sta., 2007—08. Contbr. 200 articles to profl. publs. Named Outstanding Alumnus Coll. Agriculture U. Wyo., 1991; named to USDA Hall Fame, 2005. Mem. Nat. Assn. State Univs. and Land Grant Colls. (mem. policy bd. dirs. 2002-05), Soc. for Study Reprodn. (treas. 1979-82), Am. Soc. Animal Sci., Civitan (officer 1972-85), Agrl. Experiment State Dirs. (chair 1996-97). Office: U Ariz Coll Agr and Life Scis Tucson AZ 85721-0001 E-mail: kltnbch@ag.arizona.edu.

KALYVAS, JAMES R., lawyer; b. Milw., Dec. 5, 1956; BA, Oakland U., 1977; JD, U. Mich., 1981. Bar: Calif. 1981, U.S. Dist. Ct., Ctrl. Dist. Calif. 1981, U.S. Dist. Ct., So. Dist. Calif. 1981. Ptnr. Foley & Lardner LLP, LA, chmn. e-bus. & info. tech. practice group. Co-author: Software Agreements Line By Line, 2004. Mem.: Healthcare Info. & Mgmt. Soc. Office: Foley & Lardner LLP 2029 Century Park E Ste 3500 Los Angeles CA 90067-3000 Office Phone: 310-975-7740. Office Fax: 310-557-8475. Business E-Mail: jkalyvas@foley.com.

KAMANGAR, SALAR, information technology executive; BS in Biol. Scis. with honors, Stanford U., 1999. Joined Google Inc., Mountain View, Calif., 1999, founding mem. production team, v.p. product mgmt., 2005, v.p., web applications, 2007—. Co-founder PARSA Cmty. Found. Achievements include created the Goggle's first business plan and was responsible for its legal and finance functions. Office: Google Inc 1600 Amphitheatre Pkwy Mountain View CA 94043 Office Phone: 650-253-0000. Office Fax: 650-253-0001.

KAMEMOTO, FRED ISAMU, retired zoologist; b. Honolulu, Mar. 8, 1928; s. Shuichi and Matsu (Murase) K.; m. Alice Takeyo Asayama, July 20, 1963; children: Kenneth, Garett, Janice. Student, U. Hawaii, 1946-48; AB, George Washington U., 1950, MS, 1951; PhD, Purdue U., 1954. Research assoc., acting instr. Wash. State U., 1957-59; asst. prof. zoology U. Mo., 1959-62; asst. prof. U. Hawaii, Honolulu, 1962-64, assoc. prof., 1964-69, prof. zoology, 1969-94, prof. emeritus, 1995—, chmn. dept., 1964-65, 71-80, 81-90, dir. biology program, 1992-94. Vis. rsch. scholar Ocean Rsch. Inst., U. Tokyo, Biol. Lab., Fukuoka U., 1968-69; vis. prof. Coll. Agr. and Vet. Medicine, Nihon U., Tokyo, summer 1973, 1979; vis. scholar dept. biology Conn. Wesleyan U., 1975-76; sr. scientist dept. fisheries Nihon U., Tokyo, 1986; vis. fgn. rschr. Tropical Biosphere Rsch. Ctr. U. of Ryukyus Okinawa, Japan, 1994. Contbr. articles to profl. jours. Chmn. Hawaii State Natural Areas Reserve System Commn., 1985-88. Served with AUS, 1954-57. NSF grantee, 1960-79; National Oceanic and Atmospheric Administration grantee, 1985-89. Fellow AAAS; mem. Sigma Xi. Buddhist. Home: 3664 Waaloa Way Honolulu HI 96822-1151 Office: U Hawaii Dept Zoology Honolulu HI 96822

KAMIL, ELAINE SCHEINER, pediatric nephrologist, educator; b. Cleve., Jan. 26, 1947; d. James Frank and Maud Lily (Severn) Scheiner; m. Ivan Jeffery Kamil, Aug. 29, 1970; children: Jeremy, Adam, Megan. BS magna cum laude, U. Pitts., 1969, MD, 1973. Diplomate Am. Bd. Pediat., Am. Bd. Pediatric Nephrology. Intern in pediat. Children's Hosp. Pitts., 1973-74, resident in pediat., 1974-76; clin. fellow in pediatric nephrology Sch. Medicine, UCLA, 1976-79, acting asst. prof. pediat., 1979-80, asst. clin. prof. pediat., 1988-91, assoc. clin. prof. pediat., 1991-97, clin. prof. pediat., 1997—; rsch. fellow in nephrology Harbor-UCLA Med. Ctr., Torrance, Calif., 1980-82; med. dir. The Children's Clinic of Long Beach, Calif., 1984-87; med. dir. pediat. nurse practitioner program Calif. State U., Long Beach, 1984-87; assoc. dir. pediatric nephrology and transplant immunology Cedars-Sinai Med. Ctr., LA, 1990—2001, clin. dir. pediatric nephrology, 2001—. Adj. asst. prof. pediat. Harbor-UCLA, Torrance, Calif., 1983-87, UCLA, 1987-88; cons. in pediatric nephrology Hawthorne Cmty. Med. Group, Calif., 1981-2000. Author chpts. to books; contbr. articles to profl. jours. Pres.-elect med. adv. bd. Nat. Kidney Found. So. Calif., 2000-02, pres. med. adv. bd., 2002-04. Recipient Vol. Svc. award Nat. Kidney Found., 1998. Mem. AAUW, Am. Soc. Nephrology, Am. Soc. Pediatric Nephrology (co-chair workforce com. 2003-05, chair 2006—, mem. coun. 2006—), Internat. Soc. Nephrology, Internat. Soc. Pediatric Nephrology, So. Calif. Pediatric Nephrology Assn. (chair steering com. 1998—), Nat. Kidney Found. So. Calif. (med. adv. bd. 1987-96, rsch. com. 1987-90, chmn. pub. info. med. adv. bd. 1988-92, handbook com. 1988, co-chair med. adv. bd. cmty. svcs. com. 1992-93, chair-elect patient svcs. and cmty. edn. com. 1993-94, chair patients svcs. and cmty. edn. com. 1994-95, kidney camp summer vol. physician 1988-91, 93, 94, 97, 99-2005, Arthur Gordon award 1991, Exceptional Svc. award 1992, Exceptional Leadership and Support award 1995, Sprit of Nephrology award, 2007; bd. dirs. 1995-96, 2002—), Alpha Omega Alpha, Phi Beta Kappa. Office: Cedars Sinai Med Ctr 1165 WT 8700 Beverly Blvd Los Angeles CA 90048-1865 Home Phone: 310-202-1307; Office Phone: 310-423-4747. Business E-Mail: elaine.kamil@cshs.org.

KAMIL, MICHAEL, education educator; BA, Tulane U., 1964; MA, U. Wis., 1967, PhD, 1969. Faculty assoc. U. Tex., 1969—71; faculty assoc., dir. Reading Clini Ariz. State U., 1971—72; asst. prof. psychology U. Minn., Duluth, 1972—74; asst. prof. edn., dir. Reading Clinic Purdue U., West Lafayette, Ind., 1978—80; asst. prof. edn. U. Ill., Chgo., 1980—89; assoc. prof. ednl. theory and practice Ohio State U., 1990—92, prof. ednl. theory and practice, 1992—96; prof. edn. Stanford (Calif.) U., 1997—. Vis. prof. ednl. theory and practice Ohio State U., 1989—90; mem. Rand Reading Study Group, 2000—, Nat. Inst. Child Health and Devel. Nat. Reading Panel, 1998—2000; chair tech. com. Nat. Reading Conf., 1998—2001; mem. nat. lit. panel Ctr. Applied Linguistics and SRI, 2002—04; chair reading framework com. Nat. Assessment Edn. Progress, 2003—04; chair nat. adv. bd. Pacific Resources Edn. and Learning, Honolulu, 2004—05; mem. adv. coun. advancing adolescent lit. Carnegie Corp., 2004—. Co-author: Methods of Literacy Research: The Methodology Chapters From the Handbook of Reading Research, Volume III, 2002 (Ed Fry Book award, 2004); editor: Successful Reading Instruction, 2002, Professional Development for Teaching Reading, 2004, Multidisciplinary Perspectives on Literary Research 2nd edit., 2005, Teaching and Learning Vocabulary, 2005; mem. editl. adv. bd.: Jour. Literacy Rsch., 1996—, Jour. Ednl. Psychology, —, Reading Rsch. Quarterly, Lit. Tchg. and Learning. Mem.: APA, Nat. Reading Conf. (Albert J. Kingston award 1989, Oscar B. Causey award 2006), Nat. Conf. Rsch. in Lang. and Lit., Internat. Reading Assn. (Milton Jacobson Readability Rsch. award 1983), Am. Ednl. Rsch. Assn., Sigma Xi. Office: Stanford U Sch Edn 485 Lasuen Mall Stanford CA 94305-3096

KAMINS, EDWARD, electronics executive; 2 children. BSEE with honors, Stevens Inst. Tech., Hoboken, NJ; MBA in Mktg., C.W. Post Ctr., LI U. Various positions up to v.p. channels Digital Equipment Corp.; sr. v.p. bus. devel. Avnet Computer Mktg. Avnet, Inc., 1996—99, sr. v.p., 1999—, pres. Avnet Applied Computing, 1999—2003, chief info. officer, 2003—05, chief operational excellence officer, 2005—08. Bd. dirs. InterDigital Comm. Corp, 2003—, Calence, LLC, 2006—. Bd. dirs. Lupus Found. of Am. Recipient Altruism award, Lupus Found. of Am., 2002. Office: Avnet Inc 2211 S 47th St Phoenix AZ 85034-6403 Office Phone: 480-643-2000.

KAMINS, PHILIP E., diversified manufacturing company executive; b. 1936; Salesman H. Muehlstein, 1957-62; founder Kamco Plastics Inc., Sun Valley, Calif., 1965-71; pres., CEO PMC Inc., Sun Valley, Calif., 1971—, also bd. dirs. Office: PMC Inc 12243 Branford St Sun Valley CA 91352-1010

KAMINSKI, JANUSZ ZYGMUNT, cinematographer; b. Ziembice, Poland, June 27, 1959; arrived in U.S., 1981; s. Marian Kaminski and Jadwiga Celner; m. Holly Hunter, May 20, 1995 (div. Dec. 21, 2001). BA in Cinematography, Columbia Coll., 1987; MA, Am. Film Inst. Mem. jury Berlin Internat. Film Festival, 2006. Cinematographer: (films) The Terror Within II, 1990, The Rain Killer, 1990, Grim Prairie Tales: Hit the Trail... to Terror, 1990, Pyrates, 1991, Killer Instinct, 1991, Cool as Ice, 1991, Mad Dog Coll, 1992, Trouble Bound, 1993, Schindler's List, 1993 (Best Cinematography, Acad. award, 1994, Best Cinematographer, NY Film Critics Cir. Awards, 1993, Best Cinematography, Boston Soc. Film Critics, 1993), Little Giants, 1994, How to Make an American Quilt, 1995, Jerry Maguire, 1996, The Lost World: Jurassic Park, 1997, Amistad, 1997 (Outstanding Cinematography, Golden Satellite Award, 1998), Artificial Intelligence: AI, 2001, Jumbo Girl, 2004, Munich, 2005, The Diving Bell and the Butterfly, 2007 (Technical Grand Prize, Cannes Film Festival, 2007, Best Cinematography, Boston Soc. Film Critics, 2007, Ind. Spirit award for Best Cinematography, Film Ind., 2008); (TV films) Wildflower, 1991, Class of '61, 1993; dir. photography (films) The Adventures of Huck Finn, 1993, Tall Tale, 1995, Saving Private Ryan, 1998 (Best Cinematography, Online Film Critics Soc. Awards, 1999, Best Cinematography, Acad. award, 1999, Best Cinematography, Boston Soc. Film Critics, 1998), Minority Report, 2002, Catch Me If You Can, 2002, The Terminal, 2004, War of the Worlds, 2005, Mission Zero, 2007; dir.: Lost Souls, 2000; dir. photography, dir. (films) Hania, 2007.

KAMINSKY, GLENN FRANCIS, business owner, retired protective services official; b. Passaic, NJ, Apr. 29, 1934; s. Francis Gustave and Leona Regina (Tubach) K.; m. Janet Lindesay Strachan (div. June 1985); childrenn: Lindesay Anne, Jon Francis; m. Melanie Sue Rhamey, Mar. 11, 1989. BS in Police Sci., San Jose Coll., Calif., 1958; MS in Adminstrn., San Jose State U., 1975. Cert. tchr., Alaska, N.Y., Calif., Colo., Fla., N.Mex., Oreg., Wyo., Va., Oreg., also others. Police officer San Jose Police Dept., 1957-65, sgt., 1965-75, lt., 1975-81; dep. chief Boulder (Colo.) Police Dept., 1981-92; ret. Pres. Kaminsky & Assocs., Inc., Longmont, Colo. 1981—. Author, editor: (textbook) The Field Training Concept in Criminal Justice Agencies, 2000; contbr. articles to profl. jours. Exec. dir. Nat. Assn. Field Tng. Officers Assn., 1993-2000. Sgt. U.S. Army, 1957-61, Korea. Recipinet Lifetime Achievement award Am. Soc. L.E. Trainers, 2000. Mem. Police Mgmt. Assn. (sec. 1983-88), Calif. Assn. Police Tng. Officers, Internat. Assn. Women Police, Calif. Assn. Adminstrn. of Justice Educators, Internat. Assn. Chiefs of Police (use of deadly force com.). Republican. Episcopalian. Avocations: bowling, softball, art collecting. Home and Office: 8965 Sage Valley Rd Longmont CO 80503-8885 E-mail: kaminskygf@msn.com.

KAMIONKOWSKI, MARC PAUL, astrophysicist, educator; b. Cleve., July 27, 1965; s. Mario David and Lelia (Sircovich) K. BA, Washington U., St. Louis, 1987; PhD, U. Chgo., 1991. Mem. Inst. Advanced Study, Princeton, NJ, 1991-94; asst. prof. Columbia U., NYC, 1994—99; prof. theoretical physics and astrophysics Calif. Inst. Tech., Pasadena, 1999—, Robinson prof. theoretical physics and astrophysics, 2006—. Contbr. articles to profl. jours. Recipient Ernest Orlando Lawrence award in Physics, Dept. Energy, 2007. Mem. Am. Phys. Soc., Am. Astron. Soc. (Helen B. Warner prize 1998). Office: Calif Inst Tech Mail Code 130-33 Pasadena CA 91125 Office Phone: 626-395-2563. Office Fax: 626-796-5675. E-mail: kamion@tapir.caltech.edu.

KAMM, BARBARA B., bank executive; BA in Comm., Stanford U.; M of Internat. Mgmt., Am. Grad. Sch. Internat. Mgmt. Exec. v.p., group mgr. So. Calif. Tech. and Life Scis. teams and Entertainment; chief adminstrv. officer Silicon Valley Bank, Santa Clara, Calif., 1996-98, exec. v.p., strategic products & svcs., 1998—. Chmn. adv. bd. UCI ACCELERATE Tech. SBDC. Bd. dirs. So. Calif. Entrepreneurship Acad., Orange County United Way. Office: Silicon Valley Bank Corp Hdqrs 3003 Tasman Dr Santa Clara CA 95054-1191

KAN, YUET WAI, hematologist, educator; b. Hong Kong, China, June 11, 1936; arrived in US, 1960; s. Tong-Po and Lai-Wan (Li) Kan; m. Alvera Lorraine Limauro, May 10, 1964; children: Susan Jennifer, Deborah Ann. BS, MB, U. Hong Kong, China, 1958, DSc, 1980, DSc (hon.), 1987, Chinese U., Hong Kong, 1981; MD (hon.), U. Cagliari, Sardinia, Italy, 1981; degree (hon.), Open U. Hong Kong. Investigator Howard Hughes Med. Inst., San Francisco, 1976—2003; prof. lab. medicine U. Calif., San Francisco, 1977—, Louis K. Diamond prof. hematology, 1991—. Mem. Nat. Inst. Diabetes Digestive Kidney Dieseases adv. coun. NIH, 1991—95; trustee Croucher Found., Hong Kong, 1992—, chmn., 1997—; mem. bd. adjudicators The Shaw prize, Hong Kong, 2005—, chmn. selection com., life sci. and medicine, 2005—. Contbr. chapters to books, over 250 articles to med. jours. Recipient Dameshek award, Am. Soc. Hematology, 1980, George Thorn award, Howard Hughes Med. Inst., 1980, Gairdner Found. Internat. award, 1984, Allan award, Am. Soc. Human Genetics, 1984, Lita Annenberg Hazen award for Excellence in Clin. Rsch., 1984, Waterford award, 1987, ACP's award, 1988, Genetic Rsch. award, Sanremo Internat., 1989, Warren Alpert Found. prize, 1989, Albert Lasker Clin. Med. Rsch. award, 1991, Christopher Columbus Discovery award, 1992, City of Medicine award, 1992, Excellence 200 award, 1993, Helmut Horten Rsch. award, 1995, Shaw prize, Shaw Found., Hong Kong, 2004. Fellow: AAAS, Am. Acad. Arts and Scis., Third World Acad. Scis., Royal Soc. (London), Royal Coll. Physicians (London); mem.: NAS, Acad. Sinica Taiwan, Soc. Chinese Bioscientists in Am. (pres. 1998—99), Am. Soc. Hematology (pres. 1990), Assn. Am. Physicians, Chinese Acad. Scis. (fgn. mem.). Office: U Calif 513 Parnassus Ave HSW 901 San Francisco CA 94143-0793 Office Phone: 415-476-5841. Business E-Mail: yw.kan@ucsf.edu.

KANAMORI, HIROO, geophysicist, professor emeritus; b. Tokyo, Oct. 17, 1936; BS in Physics, Tokyo U., 1959, MS in Geophysics, 1961, PhD in Geophysics, 1964. Rsch. assoc., Geophysics Inst. U. Tokyo, 1962—66, assoc. prof., Earthquake Rsch. Inst., 1966—70, prof., Earthquake Rsch. Inst., 1970-72; rsch. fellow Calif. Inst. Tech., Pasadena, 1965—66, prof., 1972-89, John E. and Hazel S. prof. geophysics, 1989—2005, John E. and Hazel S. prof. geophysics emeritus, 2005—, dir. Seismological Lab. Vis. prof. MIT, 1969—70; chmn., com. on seismology NRC, NAS, 1986—89; invited eminent scientist of Japan Soc. for Promotion of Sci. Award for Eminent Scientists Disaster Prevention Rsch. Inst., Kyoto U., 2005—06; vis. prof. Nagoya U., 2006—. Contbr. articles to profl. publications, scientific papers. Recipient Arthur L. Day prize and lectureship NAS, 1993; California Scientist of the Year, Calif. Museum of Science and Industry, 1993, Asahi prize, Asahi Shimbun, 1994, Japan Acad. prize, 2004, Person of Cultural Merit award, Japan, 2006, Kyoto prize, Basic Scis. Category, Earth and Planetary Scis., Astronomy and Astrophysics, Inamori Found., 2007. Fellow Am. Geophys. Union (Walter H. Bucher medal 1996); mem. Seismol. Soc. Am. (pres. 1985-86, Harry Fielding Reid medal, 1992), Seimol. Soc. Japan., Earthquake Engring. Rsch. Inst., Am. Acad. Arts & Scis. one of the world's best earthquake scientists. Office: Calif Inst Tech Seismological Lab So Mudd Bldg Rm 361 1200 E California Blvd MS 252-21 Pasadena CA 91125 Office Phone: 626-395-6914. Office Fax: 626-564-0715. Business E-Mail: hiroo@gps.caltech.edu.

KANE, ALAN HENRY, lawyer; b. Seattle, Nov. 7, 1940; s. Henry and Alice (Harbak) K.; m. Martha Dressler, June 25, 1966 (dec.); children: Karen, Graham, Amy. BA in Law, U. Wash., 1963, JD, 1965. Bar: Wash. 1965. Ptnr. Sax & Maciver, Seattle, 1966-84, Kirkpatrick Lockhart Preston Gales & Ellis, LLP, Seattle, 1985—. Fellow Am. Coll. Trusts and Estates Counsel (Wash. State chair 1985-88). Avocations: boating, water-skiing, fishing, skiing. Office: 925 Fourth Ave Ste 2900 Seattle WA 98104-1158 Office Phone: 206-623-7580. Business E-Mail: alan.kane@klgates.com.

KANE, CHRISTOPHER, lawyer; b. LA, Aug. 4, 1944; s. William Jerome and Mary Katherine Kane; m. Kathryn Ann Lalley, June 27, 1970; children: Kevin Jerome, Ryan Robert, Matthew Christopher, Molly Kathryn. BA in Polit. Sci., Seattle U., 1966; JD, Georgetown U., 1969. Bar: Wash. 1969, U.S. Ct. Mil. Appeals 1969, U.S. Dist. Ct. (we. dist.) Wash. 1973, U.S. Dist. Ct. (ea. dist.) Wash. 1975, U.S. Ct. Appeals (9th cir.) 1976, U.S. Ct. Appeals (10th cir.) 1977; cert. internat. arbitrator. Legis. aide to Henry M. Jackson U.S. Senate, Washington, 1968-69; assoc. Ferguson & Burdell, Seattle, 1973-79, ptnr., 1979-95; prin. Law Offices Christopher Kane, Seattle, 1995-96; chmn. bd., pres. Lawyer Selection Advisors, Seattle, 1996-97; of counsel Foster, Pepper & Shelfelman, Seattle, 1998-2000; orgnl. deve. cons. Reid & Assocs., Inc. and Baldwin Resource Group, Seattle and Bellevue, Wash., 2001—. Adj. prof. European single market law and bus. Seattle U., 1994-95; instr. law and civil procedure Edmonds (Wash.) C.C., 2001—. Contbr. articles to profl. jours. Capt. USAR, 1969-73. Mem. ABA (sects. of corp. law, internat. law and practice, antitrust), Wash. State Bar Assn. (chmn. antitrust sect. 1986-87), Rotary (vice chmn. internat. students com. 1992), Seattle Tennis Club. Roman Catholic. Avocations: skiing, tennis, jogging, writing. Office: Foster Pepper & Shefelman 1111 Third Ave Bldg Ste 3400 Seattle WA 98101 E-mail: kanelaw@home.com.

KANE, JACQUELINE P., chemical company executive; BS in Mgmt., DePaul U.; Grad., Exec. Program, U. Mich. With Continental Ill. Bank, 1978—88; sr. v.p. human resources capital raising and global capial markets group Bank of Am.; dir. exec. leadership devel., dir. strategic change The Hewlett-Packard Co., 2000—03; v.p. human resources The Clorox. Co., Oakland, Calif., 2004—05, sr. v.p. human resources & corp. affairs, 2005—. Bd. dirs. Comerica Inc., 2008—. Bd. trustees Oakland Mus. Calif. Office: The Clorox Co 1221 Broadway Oakland CA 94612-1888 Office Phone: 510-271-7000. Office Fax: 510-832-1463.

KANE, JOHN LAWRENCE, JR., judge; b. Tucumcari, N.Mex., Feb. 14, 1937; s. John Lawrence and Dorothy Helen (Bottler) K.; m. Stephanie Jane Shafer, Oct. 5, 1993; children: Molly Francis, Meghan, Sally, John Pattison. BA, U. Colo., 1958; JD, U. Denver, 1961, LL.D. (hon), 1997. Bar: Colo. 1961. Dep. dist. atty., Adams County, Colo., 1961-62; assoc. firm Gaunt, Byrne & Dirrim, 1961-63; ptnr. firm Andrews and Kane, Denver, 1964; pub. defender Adams County, 1965-67; dep. dir. eastern region of India Peace Corps, 1967-69; with firm Holme Roberts & Owen, 1970-77, ptnr., 1972-77; judge U.S. Dist. Ct. Colo., Denver, 1978-88, U.S. sr. dist. judge, 1988—. Adj. prof. law U. Denver, U. Colo., 1996—; vis. lectr. Trinity Coll., Dublin, Ireland, winter 1989; adj. prof. U. Colo., 1996, philosophy, 2003. Contbr. articles to profl. jours. Recipient St. Thomas More award Cath. Lawyers Guild, 1983, U.S. Info. Agy. Outstanding Svc. award, 1985, Outstanding Alumnus award U. Denver, 1987, Lifetime Jud. Achievement award Nat. Assn. Criminal Def. Lawyers, 1987, Civil Rights award B'nai B'rith, 1988, Justice Gerald Le Dain award Drug Policy Found., 2000. Fellow Internat. Acad. Trial Lawyers, Am. Bd. Trial Advs. (hon.). Roman Catholic. Office: US Dist Ct US Courthouse 901 19th St Denver CO 80294-1929 Office Phone: 303-844-6118. Business E-Mail: John_L_Kane@cod.uscourts.gov.

KANE, MARY KAY, academic administrator, law educator; b. Detroit, Nov. 14, 1946; d. John Francis and Frances (Roberts) K.; m. Ronan Eugene Degnan, Feb. 3, 1987 (dec. Oct. 1987). BA cum laude, U. Mich., 1968, JD cum laude, 1971. Bar: Mich. 1971. Rsch. assoc., co-dir. NSF project on privacy, confidentiality and social sci. rsch. data sch. law U. Mich., 1971-72, Harvard U., 1972-74; asst. prof. law SUNY, Buffalo, 1974-77; mem. faculty Hastings Coll. Law U. Calif., San Francisco, 1977—, prof. law, 1979—, assoc. acad. dean, 1981-83, acting acad. dean, 1987-88, acad. dean., 1990-93, dean, 1993—2006, chancellor, 2001—06, John D. Digardi Disting. Prof. Law. Vis. prof. law U. Mich., 1981, U. Utah, 1983, U. Calif., Berkeley, 1983-84, sch. law U. Tex., 1989; cons. Mead Data Control, Inc., 1971, 74, Inst. on Consumer Justice, U. Mich. Sch. Law, 1972, U.S. Privacy Protection Study Commn., 1975-76; lectr. pretrial mgmt. devices U.S. magistrates for 6th and 11th cirs. Fed. Jud. Ctr., 1983; Siebenthaler lectr. Samuel P. Chase Coll. Law, U. North Ky., 1987; reporter ad hoc com. on asbestos litigation U.S. Jud. Conf., 1990-91, mem. standing com. on practice and procedure, 2001—; mem. 9th Cir. Adv. Com. on Rules Practice and Internal Oper. Procedures, 1993-96; spkr. in field. Author: Civil Procedure in a Nutshell, 1979, 5th edit., 2003, Sum and Substance on Remedies, 1981; co-prodr.(with C. Wright and A. Miller): Pocket Supplements to Federal Practice and Procedure, 1975—; co-author (with C. Wright and A. Miller): Federal Practice and Procedure, vol. 7, 3d edit., 2001, 10, 10A and 10B, 3d edit., 1998, vols. 7-7C, 2d edit., 1986, vols. 6-6A, 2d edit., 1990, vols. 11-11A, 2d edit., 1995, vols. 7A-B, 3d edit., 2005; co-author: (with J. Friedenthal and A. Miller) Hornbook on Civil Procedure, 4th edit., 2005; co-author: (with C. Wright) Hornbook on the Law of Federal Courts, 2002, Federal Practice Deskbook, 2002; mem. law sch. divsn. West. Adv. Editl. Bd., 1986—; contbr. articles to profl. jours. Mem. standing com. on rules of practice and procedure U.S. Jud. Conf., 2000—. Mem. ABA (mem. bar admissions com. 1995-2000, mem. coun. sect. legal edn. and admission to bar 2004—), Assn. Am. Law Schs. (com. on prelegal edn. statement 1982, chair sect. remedies 1982, panelist sect. on prelegal edn. 1983, exec. com. sect. on civil procedure 1983, 86, panelist sect. on tchg. methods 1984, spkr. new tchrs. conf. 1986, 89, 90, chair sect. on civil procedure 1987, spkr. sects. civil procedure and conflicts 1987, 91, chair planning com. for 1988 Tchg. Conf. in Civil Procedure 1987-88, nominating com. 1988, profl. devel. com. 1988-91, planning com. for workshop in conflicts 1988, planning com. for 1990 Conf. on Clin. Legal Edn. 1989, chair profl. devel. com. 1989-91, exec. com. 1991-93, 2000-02, pres.-elect 2000, pres. 2001), Am. Law Inst. (co-reporter complex litigation project 1988-93, coun. 1998—), ABA/Assn. Am. Law Schs. Commn. on Financing Legal Edn., State Bar Mich. Home: 8 Admiral Dr Ste 421 Emeryville CA 94608-1567 Office: U Calif Hastings Coll Law 200 McAllister St San Francisco CA 94102-4707 Office Phone: 415-565-4777. E-mail: kanem@uchastings.edu.

KANE, THOMAS JAY, III, surgeon, educator; b. Merced, Calif., Sept. 2, 1951; s. Thomas J., Jr. and Kathryn (Hassler) Kane; m. Marle Rose Van Emmerik, Oct. 10, 1987; children: Thomas Keola, Travis Reid, Samantha Marie. BA in History, U. Santa Clara, 1973; MD, U. Calif., Davis, 1977. Diplomate Am. Bd. Orthopaedic Surgery. Intern U. Calif. Davis Sacramento Med. Ctr., 1977-78, resident in surgery, 1978-81; resident in orthopaedic surgery U. Hawaii, 1987-91; fellowship adult joint reconstruction U. SC, Rancho Los Amigos Med. Ctr., 1991-92; ptnr. Orthop. Assocs. Hawaii, Inc., Honolulu, 1992—; asst. prof. surgery U. Hawaii, Honolulu, 1993—, chief divsn. implant surgery, 1993—, asst. chief orthopedics, 2003—04; dir. joint reconstruction Inst. Pacific, 2008—. Contbr. articles to profl. jours. Mem.: AMA, Am. Coll. Sports Medicine, Western Orthop. Assn., Am. Acad. Orthop. Surgery, Hawaii Orthop. Assn. (v.p. 2003—04, pres. 2004—), Hawaii Med. Assn., Am. Assn. Hip and Knee Surgeons, Phi Kappa Phi, Alpha Omega Alpha. Avocations: tennis, golf, skiing, music, surfing. Office: Orthopaedic Svcs Co LLP 1380 Lusitana St Ste 608 Honolulu HI 96813-2442 Office Phone: 808-521-8124. Personal E-mail: tkaneiii@yahoo.com.

KANE, THOMAS REIF, engineering educator; b. Vienna, Mar. 23, 1924; came to U.S., 1938, naturalized, 1943; Ernest Kanitz and Gertrude (Reif) K.; m. Ann Elizabeth Andrews, June 4, 1951; children: Linda Ann, Jeffrey Thomas. BS, Columbia U., 1950, MS, 1952, PhD, 1953; D Tech. Scis. (hon.), Tech. U. Vienna, Austria, 1990. Asst. prof., assoc. prof. U. Pa., Phila., 1953-61; prof. Sch. Engring. Stanford U., Calif., 1961-93, prof. emeritus, 1993—. Cons. NASA, Harley-Davidson Motor Co., AMF, Lockheed Missiles and Space Co., Vertol Aircraft Corp., Martin Marietta Co., Kellet Aircraft Co. Author: (vol. 1) Analytical Elements of Mechanics, 1959, (vol. 2), 1961, Dynamics, 1972, Spacecraft Dynamics, 1983; Dynamics: Theory and Applications, 1985; contbr. over 150 articles to profl. jours. Served with U.S. Army, 1943-45, PTO. Recipient Alexander von Humboldt prize, 1988. Fellow Am. Astron. Soc. (Dirk Brouwer award 1983); mem. ASME (hon.), Sigma Xi, Tau Beta Pi. Office: Stanford University Dept Mechanical Engring Stanford CA 94305

KANES, WILLIAM HENRY, geology educator, research center administrator; b. NYC, Oct. 15, 1934; married. BS in Geol. Engring., CCNY, 1956; MS in Geology, W.Va. U., 1958, PhD in Geology, 1965. Sr. rsch. geologist Esso Prodn. Co., Houston Rsch. Co., 1964-65; sr. exploration geologist, head New Concepts Group Esso Stds., Libya, 1966-67, frontier exploration geologist, administr. Frontier Area Group, 1967-69; asst. prof. geology W.Va. U., Morgantown, 1970-71; assoc. prof. geology U. S.C., Columbia, 1971-74, prof. geology, dir. Earth Scis. and Resources Inst., 1975-95, Disting. prof. earth resources, chair Rsch. and Devel. Found., 1984-97, disting. prof. emeritus, 1998; prof. civil and environ. engring. U. Utah, 1994-96, dir. Earth Scis. and Resources Inst., 1994-96, dir. Energy and Geoscis. Inst., rsch. prof., civil and environ. engr., 1996-99; pres. W.H. Kanes & Assocs., 2000—. NSF Resident Rsch. prof. Acad. Sci. Rsch. and Tech., Cairo, 1976-77; hon. professorial fellow Univ. Coll. Aberystyth U. Wales, 1979-83, Univ. Coll. Swansea U. Wales, 1985-88, U. Bristol, U.K., 1986-89; hon. mem. Acad. Engring., Republic of Kazakhstan, 1994; academician Internat. Acad. Mineral Resources, Russia; vis. professorial fellow Univ. Coll. Swansea, 1977-83; vis. prof. Postgrad. Rsch. Inst. Sedimentology, U. Reading, U.K., 1989-92; co-dir. Earth Resources Inst. Univ. Coll. Swansea, U. Wales, U.K., 1980-86; advisor Atomic Energy Establishment, Egypt, 1974-77, Nat. Oil Co., Libya, 1975-78, U.S. Pres., exec. br. Energy Problems and Controls, 1977-78, Nuclear Materials Corp., Egypt, 1977-81; mem. tech. adv. task force Fed. Power Commn. Contbr. numerous articles, papers to profl. publs. 1st lt. C.E., U.S. Army, 1955, 58-59. Recipient Disting. Svc. award U. S.C. Ednl. Found., 1985; grantee NSF, 1971-81, U.S. Dept. Interior, 1972-74, others. Fellow AAAS, Geol. Soc. Am.; mem. Am. Assn. Petroleum Geologists (cert., chmn. rsch. symposium 1976, acad. affairs com. 1973-76, acad. liaison com. 1976—, rsch. com. on pub. affairs 1975—), Am. Geophys. Union, Sigma Xi.

KANG, ALVIN, bank executive; Field agent trainee IRS, LA; ptnr. KPMG LLP, Ernst & Young LLP; COO, CFO Broadway Fed. Bank; CFO Broadway Fin. Corp., Nara Bancorp, Inc., 2005—. Fin. officer, first lt. US Army, Fort Meade U.S. Army Base Md. Office: Nara Bancorp Inc 3731 Wilshire Blvd Ste 1000 Los Angeles CA 90010 Office Phone: 213-639-1700. Office Fax: 213-235-3033.

KANG, SUKHEE, Mayor, Irvine, California; b. South Korea; m. Joanne Kang; children: Angie, Alan. Graduated, Korea U., Seoul, 1977. Former sales & customer svc. rep. Circuit City, Inc.; appointed mem. Calif. Workforce Investment Bd.; fin. commr. City of Irvine, councilman, 2004—05, 2006—07, mayor pro tem., 2005—06, mayor, 2008—. Chmn. Orange County Korean Am. Coalition; pres. Korean Am. Scholarship Found., Western Region; exec. steering com. League of Calif. Cities Orange County Divsn.; bd mem. Orange County Great Park Bd.; bd. mem. Orange County Sanitation Dist. Bd., Transp. Corridor Agy. Bd., Orange County Transp. Authority Measure M Super Com., Calif. Water Quality Control, Santa Ana Region. Recipient Cmty. Leadership award, Orange County Asian Pacific Islanders Heritage Coun. Achievements include being first Korean-American mayor of major US city. Mailing: 1 Civic Center Plaza PO Box 19575 Irvine CA 92623-9575 Office Phone: 949-724-6000. Business E-Mail: sukheekang@ci.irvine.ca.us.*

KANG, SUNG-MO (STEVE KANG), electrical engineering educator; b. Seoul, Korea, Feb. 25, 1945; came to U.S., 1969; s. Chang-Shik and Kyung-Ja (Lee) K.; m. Myoung-A Cha, June 10, 1972; children: Jennifer, Jeffrey. BSEE, Fairleigh Dickinson U., 1970; MSEE, SUNY, Buffalo, 1972; PhD in Elec. Engring., U. Calif., Berkeley, 1975. Asst. prof. Rutgers U., Piscataway, NJ, 1975-77; mem. tech. staff AT&T Bell Labs., Murray Hill, NJ, 1977-82, supr., 1982-85; prof. U. Ill., Urbana, 1985-2000, head dept. electrical and computer engring., 1995-2000, assoc. Ctr. for Advanced Study, 1991-92, assoc. dir. microelectronics lab., 1988-95; univ. scholar U. Ill., Urbana, 1995-96. Dir. Ctr. for ASIC R&D, dean sch. engring. U. Calif., Santa Cruz, 2001—; pres. Silicon Valley Engring. Coun., 2002-03. Author 9 books; contbr. over 350 papers to internat. jours. and confs.; 12 patents. Recipient Meritorious Svc. award Cirs. and Sys. Soc., 1994, Humboldt Rsch. award for Sr. U.S. Scientists, 1996, Grad. Teaching award IEEE, 1996, IEEE CAS Soc. Tech. Achievement award, 1997, KBS award in Sci. and Tech., 1998, SRC Tech. Excellence award,

1999, Alumnus award U. Calif., Berkeley, 2001. Fellow AAAS, ACM, IEEE (various offices in Circuits and Systems Soc. including pres. 1991, founding editor-in-chief Trans. on VSLI systems, Disting. lectr. 1994-97, 2003-, Darlington award, SRC Inventor Recognition award 1993, 96, 99, 2001, 02, Meritorious Svc. award Compuer Soc. 1990, CAS Soc. Golden Jubilee medal 1999, Millennium medal 2000, Mac Van Valkenburg award, 2005, Chang-Lin Tien Edn. Leadership award 2007), Nat. Acad. Engring. of Korea (fgn. mem.). Presbyterian. Avocations: tennis, travel. Office: U Calif Baskin Sch Engring Santa Cruz CA 95064 Home Phone: 831-421-9330; Office Phone: 831-459-2158. E-mail: kang@soe.ucsc.edu.

KANNER, EDWIN BENJAMIN, electrical manufacturing company executive; b. NYC, July 2, 1922; s. Charles and Grace (Edelson) K.; m. S. Barbara Penenberg, Aug. 3, 1944; children: Jaimie Sue, Richard, Keith. BBA, CCNY, 1943; MBA, Harvard U., 1947. Asst. West Coast mgr. Fairchild Publs., NYC and L.A., 1948-50; gen. mgr. Dible Enterprises, LA, 1951-53; sales mgr., gen. mgr., prs. Western Insulated Wire Co. div. Teledyne, LA, 1954-68; pres. Carol Cable Co. West div. Avnet, LA, 1969-79; exec. v.p., COO Avnet Inc., NYC, 1980-83; pres. Pacific Electricord and Am. Ins. Wire Co., L.A., also Providence, 1948—. Lt. USNR, 1943—47, PTO. Office: Pacific Electricord 3780 Kilroy Airport Way Ste 400 Long Beach CA 90806-2498

KANNO, BRIAN M., state legislator, volunteer; b. Honolulu, Oct. 23, 1961; s. Toshio and Kimiko (Takahashi) K. BA in Econs., Yale U., 1983. Group asst. N.W. Ayer, NYC, 1983-84; adminstrv. asst. Benton & Bowles, NYC, 1984-85; account exec. Ogilvy & Mather Hawaii, Honolulu, 1985-87, Starr Seigle McCombs, Honolulu, 1987; campaign office mgr. Patsy T. Mink campaign com., Honolulu, 1988, 90; legis. asst. Rep. Patsy T. Mink, U.S. Ho. of Reps., Washington, 1990-91; advt. mgr. Servco Pacific Inc., Honolulu, 1988-90; youth vol. coord. Boys & Girls Club Waianae, 1991-92; mem. Hawaii Senate, Dist. 20, Honolulu, 1992—. Father facilitator Parents and Children Together (PACT), 2000—. Mem. Yale Club of Hawaii (treas. 1987-90, bd. dirs. 1987—). Office: Hawaii State Capitol 415 S Beretania St Rm 202 Honolulu HI 96813-2407

KANOFF, MARY ELLEN, lawyer; m. Chris Kanoff. BA in Econs., U. Calif., Berkeley, 1978, JD, 1984. Large systems mktg. rep. IBM, 1978—81; with Latham & Watkins, LA, 1984—, ptnr., 1991—. Bd. trustees St. Matthews Sch., Pacific Palisades, Calif., St. John's Hosp., Santa Monica, Calif.; bd. dirs. Chrysalis. Recipient Founders Spirit of Chrysalis award; named one of Top 25 Lawyers in Calif. under 45, Calif. Law Bus., 1993, Up and Coming Bus. Persons in So. Calif., L.A. Bus. Jour., 1997. Mem.: ABA (bus. law and entertainment law sects.), L.A. County Bar Assn., Calif. Bar Assn. Office: Latham Watkins 355 S Grand Ave Los Angeles CA 90071-1560 Home Phone: 310-459-9082; Office Phone: 213-891-8728.

KANT, ROBERT S., lawyer; b. Little Rock, Sept. 25, 1944; BA, Univ. Pa., 1966; JD, Villanova Univ., 1970. Bar: Pa. 1970, Ariz. 1978. Shareholder, corporate and securities, bd. dir. Greenberg Traurig LLP, Phoenix. Named one of Best of the Bar in Corp. Law, Phoenix Bus. Jour., 2003, Best of Bar in Securities Law, 2004. Mem.: State Bar Ariz. (small bus. capital formation, chmn., securities sect. 1987—88). Office: Greenberg Traurig LLP Ste 700 2375 E Camelback Rd Phoenix AZ 85016 Office Phone: 602-445-8302. Office Fax: 602-445-8100. Business E-Mail: kantr@gtlaw.com.

KANTER, STEPHEN, lawyer, educator, dean; b. Cin., June 30, 1946; s. Aaron J. and Edythe (Kasfir) K.; m. Dory Jean Poduska, June 24, 1972; children: Jordan Alexander, Laura Elizabeth. BS in Math., MIT, 1968; JD, Yale U., 1971. Spl. asst. Portland (Oreg.) City Commr., 1971-72; from staff atty. to asst. dir. Met. Pub. Defender, Portland, 1972-77; prof. law Lewis and Clark Law Sch., Portland, 1977—, assoc. dean, 1980-81, acting dean, 1981-82, dean, 1986-94. Fulbright prof. law Nanjing (China) U., 1984-85, U. Athens (Greece) Faculty of Law, 1993; bd. dirs. Northwest Regional China Coun., 1996-00, pres.- elect, 1997-98, pres., 1998-99; exec. com. Owen M. Panner Am. Inns of Ct., pres., 1994-95; mem. judicial selection com. U.S. Dist. Ct. Oreg., 1993; cons. on drafting and implementation of Kazakhstan Constn., 1992, 94, cons. on Sch. Police funciton, Portland Sch. Dist. Author: The Bear and the Blackberry, 1999; contbr. articles to profl. jours. Mem. bd. overseers World Affairs Coun. Oreg., Portland, 1986-89; mem. Oreg. Criminal Justice Coun., Salem, 1987-92, Oreg. Bicentennial Commn., Portland, 1986-89; pres. Portland Baseball Group, 2000—. Named One of 10 Gt. Portlanders, Willamette Week newspaper, 1980; recipient E.B. MacNaughton Civil Liberties award, 1991. Fellow Am. Bar Found. (life); mem. ACLU (bd. dirs. Oreg. chpt. 1976-82, pres. 1979-81, lawyers com. 1976-2003), Oreg. State Bar Assn., Am. Law Inst. (ex-officio 1986-94), Fulbright Assn. (bd. dirs. 1987-93, exec. com. 1989-93). Home: 3142 SW Fairview Blvd Portland OR 97205-1831 Office: Lewis & Clark Law Sch 10015 SW Terwilliger Blvd Portland OR 97219-7768 Office Phone: 503-768-6757. Business E-Mail: kanter@lclark.edu.

KANTOR, SUSAN, marketing executive; BA, U. Md. Coll. Park. V.p. advt., promotion Paramount TV; exec. v.p. USA Networks/Studios USA, NY; sr. v.p. mktg. Universal TV Worldwide; v.p., creative dir. VH1/MTV Networks, NYC; sr. v.p. mktg., creative Twentieth Century Fox TV, Inc., 2003—06; sr. v.p. mktg. Warner Bros. Domestic TV Distbr., Telepictures Prodns., Burbank, Calif., 2006—. Named an Entertainment Marketer of the Yr., Advt. Age mag., 2007. Office: Warner Bros Hdqs Bridge Bldg 156 S #5074 4000 Warner Blvd Burbank CA 91522 Office Phone: 818-954-6000. Office Fax: 212-954-7667.

KAPLAN, BARRY MARTIN, lawyer; b. NYC, Nov. 9, 1950; s. Stanley Seymour and Lillian (Schner) K.; m. Erica Green, July 26, 1981; children: Matthew Aaron, Elizabeth Rose, Andrew Nathan. BA, Colgate U., 1973; JD cum laude, U. Mich., 1976. Bar: Mich. 1976, Wash., 1978, U.S. Dist. (ea. dist.) Mich. 1976, U.S. Dist. Ct. (we. dist.) Wash. 1978, U.S. Dist. Ct. (ea. dist.) Wash. 1986, U.S. Tax Ct. 1983, U.S. Ct. Appeals (9th cir.) 1990. Law clk. to Hon. Charles W. Joiner U.S. Dist. Ct. (ea. dist.) Mich., Detroit, 1976-78; assoc. Perkins Coie, Seattle, 1978-85, ptnr., 1985—2005, Wilson Sonsini Goodrich & Rosati, Seattle, 2005—. Adj. prof. securities regulation U. Wash. Sch. Law; spkr. in field. Author: Washington Corporate Law, Corporations and LLCs, 2000; contbr. articles to legal jours. and procs. Mem. ABA (litigation sect., securities litigation com., bus. law sect., bus. and corp. litigation com., subcom. chmn. on control transactions 1993), Wash. State Bar Assn. (CLE spkr., bus. law sect., securities com., subcom. chair on dir.'s liability 1993), Wash. Athletic Club, Rainier Club. Home Phone: 206-324-0321; Office Phone: 206-883-2538. Business E-Mail: bkaplan@wsgr.com.

KAPLAN, GARY, executive recruiter; b. Phila., Aug. 14, 1939; s. Morris and Minnie (Leve) K.; m. Linda Ann Wilson, May 30, 1968; children: Michael Warren, Marc Jonathan, Jeffrey Russell Wilson. BA in Polit. Sci., Pa. State U., 1961. Tchr. biology N.E. High Sch., Phila., 1962-63; coll. employment rep. Bell Telephone Labs., Murray Hill, NJ, 1966-67; supr. recruitment and placement Unisys, Blue Bell, Pa., 1967-69; pres. Electronic Systems Personnel, Phila., 1969-70; staff selection rep. Booz, Allen & Hamilton, NYC, 1970-72; mgr. exec. recruitment M&T Chems., Rahway, NJ, 1972-74; dir. exec. recruitment IU Internat. Mgmt. Corp., Phila., 1974-78; v.p. personnel Crocker Bank, Los Angeles, 1978-79; mng. v.p. ptnr. western region Korn-Ferry Internat., Los Angeles, 1979-85; pres. Gary Kaplan & Assocs., Pasadena, Calif., 1985—. Bd. dirs. Greater L.A. Zoo Assn., Mgmt. columnist, Radio and Records newspaper, 1984-85; former bd. dirs. Pa. State U. Alumni Coun. & Coll. Liberal Arts Alumni Soc. Vis. Nurs Assn., La.; ptnrs. in Care fdn. Home Pharmacy Calif. The Wellness Cmty., Calif. Exec. Recruiters Assn.; alumni soc. mem. The Wellness Cmty., Calif. Exec. Recruiters Assn., Pa. State U. Indsl./Orgn. Psychology Adv. Alumni fellow Pa. State U., 1998. Mem. World at Work, Human Resources Mgmt., Mount Nittany Soc. Pa. State U., Pa. State U. Alumni Soc. Office: Gary Kaplan & Assocs 201 S Lake Ave Ste 804 Pasadena CA 91101-3018 Office Phone: 626-796-8100.

KAPLAN, GEORGE WILLARD, urologist; b. Brownsville, Tex., Aug. 24, 1935; s. Hyman J. and Lillian (Bennett) Kaplan; m. Susan Gail Solof, Dec. 17, 1961; children: Paula, Elizabeth, Julie, Alan. BA, U. Tex., Austin, 1955; MD, Northwestern U., Evanston, Ill., 1959, MS, 1966. Diplomate Am. Bd. Urology, 1971; cert. sub-splty. in pediat. urology, 2008. Intern Charity Hosp. of La. at New Orleans, 1959-60; resident Northwestern U., 1963-68, instr. Med. Sch. Chgo., 1968-69; clin. prof. U. Calif., San Diego, 1970—, chief pediatric urology, 1970—98. Trustee Children's Hosp. and Health Ctr., San Diego, 1978-90, Am. Bd. Urology, Bingham Farms, Mich., 1991-96; del. Am. Bd. Med. Specialties, Evanston, Ill., 1992-96. Author: Genitourinary Problems in Pediatrics; asst. editor Jour. Urology, Balt., 1982-89, 98-2002; assoc. editor Child Nephrology and Urology, Milan, Italy, 1988-94; contbr. articles to profl. publs. Pres. med. staff Children's Hosp., San Diego, 1980-82. Lt. USN, 1960-63. Recipient Joseph Capps prize Inst. of Medicine, 1967. Fellow ACS (pres. San Diego chpt. 1980-82), Am. Acad. Pediat. (chmn. sect. on urology 1986, Urology medal 2007); mem. AMA, Soc. for Pediatric Urology (pres. 1993), Am. Urol. Assn., Soc. Internat. Urologie, Soc. Univ. Urologists, Am. Assn. Genito-Urin. Surgeons. Independent. Jewish. Avocation: rare books. Office: 7930 Frost St Ste 300 San Diego CA 92123-2740 Business E-Mail: gkaplan@chsd.org.

KAPLAN, ISAAC RAYMOND, chemistry professor; b. Baranowicze, Poland, July 10, 1929; came to U.S., 1957; s. Morris and Anny (Chait) K.; m. Helen Fagot, Sept. 4, 1955; children: Debora, David Joel. BS, Canterbury U., Christchurch, New Zealand, 1951, MS, 1953; PhD, U. So. Calif., 1961. Rsch. scientist Commonwealth Sci. and Indsl. Rsch. Orgn., Sydney, Australia, 1953-57; postdoctoral fellow Calif. Inst. Tech., Pasadena, 1961-62; guest lectr. Hebrew U., Jerusalem, 1962-65; assoc. prof. UCLA, 1965-69, prof., 1969-93, prof. emeritus, 1993—. Contbr. over 300 articles to profl. jours. Guggenheim Found. fellow, Sydney, 1970-71. Fellow: AAAS, Geol. Soc. Am., Am. Inst. Chemists; mem.: Am. Assn. Petroleum Geologists (Pres. award 2002), Geochem. Soc. (Alfred Treibs medal 1993), Geophys. Union, Am. Chem. Soc., Russian Acad. Natural Sci. (fgn.) (Kapitsa medal 1998). Office: U Calif ESS Dept Plaza Circle Dr Los Angeles CA 90095

KAPLAN, JERRY (S. JERROLD KAPLAN), former electronics company executive; B in History and Philosophy of Sci., U. Chgo.; D in Computer and Info. Sci., U. Pa. Prin. technologist Lotus Devel. Corp.; co-founder, chmn. GO Corp.; co-founder, CEO ONSALE, Inc., Menlo Park, Calif., 1994—2000; CEO Egghead.com (merged with ONSALE, Inc.), Menlo Park, 2000. Author: Startup-A Silicon Valley Adventure, 1995.

KAPLAN, MARK S., healthcare educator; BA in Sociology, U. Miami, Coral Gables, 1975; MSW, Ariz. State U., Tempe, 1977; MPH in Behavioral Sciences, U. Calif., Berkeley, 1978, DPH in Behavioral Sciences, 1984. Cons. Ariz. Dept. Health Svcs., Divsn. Behavioral Health Sciences, 1976—77; rsch. specialist, mental health and social welfare rsch. group U. Calif., Sch. Social Welfare, Berkeley, 1979—85; asst. prof., dept. sch. and cmty. health U. Oreg., 1985—87; prof., cmty. health-urban & pub. affairs Portland State U., Oreg.; cons., Making Risky Decisions Eugene Rsch. Inst., Oreg., 1988; postdoctoral fellow Inst. for Health Promotion and Disease Prevention Rsch., Dept. Preventative Medicine, U. So. Calif., 1988—90; asst. prof., Sch. Social Work U. Ill., Urbana-Champaign, 1990—97, chair, mental health specialization, Sch. Social Work, 1992—97; assoc. prof., Sch. Cmty. Health, Coll. Urban and Pub. Affairs Portland State U., Oreg., 1997—2003, prof., Sch. Cmty. Health, Coll. Urban and Pub. Affairs Oreg., 2003—. Adj. assoc. prof., psychiatry Oreg. Health Sciences U., 1999—; mem. NIMH/NIH Spl. Emphasis Panel, 2004; vis. prof., dept. epidemiology & cmty. medicine U. Ottawa, 2004; contbr. to state and fed. suicide prevention initiatives; participated on review panels for the NIH, Canadian Social Sci. and Humanities Rsch. Coun. & Coun. for Internat. Exchange of Scholars.; mem. scientific adv. coun. Suicide Prevention Action Network (SPAN USA). Editl. bd. mem., book review editor Internat. Jour. Men's Health, 2002—, peer reviewer for several profl. jours. Recipient US Pub. Health Svc. Nat. Rsch. award, 1977—81, AAAS (Pacific Divsn.) award for Excellence for the best paper presented at the 65th Ann. Mtg. on the program sect. L, History of Sci., 1984; fellow NIMH Summer Rsch. Inst. in Geriatric Psychiatry, 1999; Nat. Inst. Alcohol Abuse and Alcoholism Pre-Doctoral Rsch. Traineeship, 1977—79, J. William Fulbright Scholar to Can., 2004. Mem.: Am. Assn. Suicidology (mem. strategic planning com. 1998—, serves on Coun. Delegates). Office: Portland State U Sch Cmty Health-SCH PO Box 751 Office 450J URBN Portland OR 97207-0751 Office Phone: 503-725-8588. Office Fax: 503-725-5100. Business E-Mail: kaplanm@pdx.edu.

KAPLAN, MARK VINCENT, lawyer; b. Oct. 30, 1947; m. Cynthia Lang, Oct. 3, 1982 (div.); m. Carolyn Kozuch, Oct. 9, 1988. BA, U. Ill.; JD, Southwestern U., Calif. Ptnr. Kaplan & Simon, Los Angeles; div. atty. representing Paul Abdul, Chris Judd, Kevin Federline and others. Office: Kaplan & Simon 2049 Century Park E #2660 Los Angeles CA 90067 Office Phone: 310-227-9009. Fax: 310-552-1970. E-mail: mkaplan@kaplansimonlaw.com.

KAPLAN, ROBERT DAVID, lawyer; b. Ossining, NY, July 9, 1939; s. Bernard I. and Helen Rosemarie (Gardner) K. AB, Brown U., 1961; LLM, JD, U. Wash., 1969. Bar: Wash. 1969, U.S. Dist. Ct. (we. dist.) Wash. 1969, U.S. Ct. Appeals (9th cir.) 1969. Ptnr. Bogle & Gates, Seattle, 1969—99; ptnr., chmn., Iraq practice Dorsey & Whitney LLP, Seattle, 1999—. Contbr. articles to law rev. Lt. USN, 1961-66. Named a Wash. Super Lawyer, Wash. Law & Politics Mag. Mem. ABA, Wash. State Bar Assn., U. Wash. Sch. Law Alumni Assn. (bd. dirs. 1975-85). Office: Dorsey & Whitney LLP Ste 3400 US Bank Ctr 1420 Fifth Ave Seattle WA 98101-4010 Office Phone: 206-903-8810. Office Fax: 206-903-8820. Business E-Mail: kaplan.robert@dorsey.com.

KAPLAN, ROBERT MALCOLM, health researcher, educator; b. San Diego, Oct. 26, 1947; s. Oscar Joel and Rose (Zankan) K.; children: Cameron Maxwell, Seth William AB in Psychology, San Diego State U., 1969; MA, U. Calif., Riverside, 1970, PhD, 1972. Lic. psychologist Calif., cert. Calif. Bd. Med. Quality Assurance. Tchg. asst. dept. psychology U. Calif., Riverside, 1969—72; sr. rsch. assoc. Am. Inst. for Rsch., Palo Alto, Calif., 1972-73; from asst. prof. to prof. U. Calif., San Diego, 1973—2004, chief health care svcs. divsn., 1989—96, chmn. health care svcs. divsn., 1997—2004, prof. dept. family and preventive medicine, 2004; from asst. prof. to prof. psychology San Diego State U., 1974-88, dir., Ctr. Behavioral Medicine; prof. medicine U. Calif., LA, 2004—. Mem. health svcs. rsch. study sect. Nat. Ctr. Health Svcs. Rsch., 1981-85, 88-92, VA Sci. Rev. and Evaluations Bd. Health Svcs., 1989-91, chair 1991-92; cons., lectr. in field. Faculty fellow San Diego State U., 1977, epidemiology fellow Am. Heart Assn., 1983; recipient Career Rsch. Devel. award NIH, 1981-86, Alumni and Assocs. Disting. Faculty award San Diego State U., 1982, Exceptional Merit Svc. award, 1984. Fellow APA (bd. dirs., Outstanding Sci. Achievement award health psychology divsn. 1987, 2001, pres. 1992-93); mem. AAAS (exec. com. Pacific divsn. 1978-82), Soc. Behavioral Medicine (bd. dirs., pres. 1996-97, pres. elect 2001—, editor-in-chief Annals of Behavioral Medicine, 2000-05, Health Psychology, 2005—), Inst. Medicine NAS. Office: UCLA Dept Health Svcs CHS-31-293C PO Box 951772 Los Angeles CA 90095-1772 Office Phone: 310-825-7652. Office Fax: 310-825-3317. Business E-Mail: rmkaplan@ucsd.edu.*

KAPLAN, SELNA L., medical educator; BA in Zoology cum laude, Bklyn. Coll., 1948; MA in Anatomy, Washington U., St. Louis, 1950, PhD in Anatomy, 1953, MD, 1955. Intern Bellevue Hosp., NYC, 1955—56; sr. resident Kings County Hosp., Bklyn., 1956—58; fellow in pediat. endocrinolgy, 1958—61; instr. Columbia U., NYC, 1961—66; asst. prof. pediatrics U. Calif., San Francisco, 1966—68, assoc. prof. pediatrics, 1968—74, prof. pediatrics, 1974—2001, dir. divsn. of pediatric endocrinology, 1966—2001, assoc. prof. pediatric clin. rsch. ctr., 1985—96, ret., 2001, recalled pediatric clin. rsch. ctr., 2002—. Med. dir. Bay Area chpt. Human Growth Found., 1967—98. Contbr. articles to profl. jours. Recipient Rsch. Career Devel. award, NIH, 1961—71, Myrtle Wreath award, Hadassah, San Francisco, 1972. Fellow: Am. Acad. Pediatrics, N.Y. Acad. Scis.; mem.: Women in Endocrinology, Am. Assn. Physicians, Internat. Neuroendocrine Soc., Lawson Wilkins Pediatric Endocrine Soc., European Soc. Pediatric Endocrinology, Soc. Study Reprodn., Am. Pediatric Soc., Western Soc. Pediatric Rsch., Soc. Pediatric Rsch., Endocrine Soc. (Ayerst award 1987, Koch award 1992), Sigma Xi. Home Phone: 415-661-7494. Office Fax: 415-476-8214. Business E-Mail: skaplan@peds.ucsf.edu.

KAPLOWITZ, NEIL, gastroenterologist, educator; b. NYC, Mar. 16, 1943; s. Louis and Henrietta (Schall) K.; m. Fattaneh E. Enayat; children: Hillary C., Gregory D., Daria. BS, NYU, 1964, MD, 1967. Diplomate Nat. Bd. Med. Examiners; diplomate in internal medicine and gatroenterology Am. Bd. Internal Medicine. Intern, resident Bellevue Hosp., 1967-69; resident Albert Einstein Med. Ctr., 1969-70; asst. res. phys. Rockefeller Univ. Hosp., 1970-71; fellowship Cornell U. Coll. Medicine, 1970-72; guest investigator Rockefeller U., NYC, 1970-71; instr. in med. Cornell Univ. Med. Coll., 1971-72; asst. prof. Cornell U. Med. Coll., NYC, 1972-73, UCLA Sch. Medicine, 1975-77; chief hepatology Wadsworth VA Hosp., Los Angeles, 1975-79; dir. UCLA Wadsworth Gastroenterology/Hepatology Fellshp. Tng. Prog., 1980-84; chief gastroenterology/hepatology section Wadsworth VA Hosp., Los Angeles, 1980-89; assoc. prof. UCLA Sch. Medicine, 1977-82, prof., 1982-90, U. So. Calif. Sch. Medicine, LA, 1990—, chief div. gastrointestinal and liver diseases, 1990—; chief gastroenterology Wadsworth VA Hosp., LA, 1980-90; prof. molecular pharmacology & toxicology USC Sch. of Pharmacy, 1992—; prof. physiology USC Sch. Med., 1993—; dir. USC Liver Diseases Rsch. Ctr. (NIDDK Digestive Disease Core Ctr. Grant), 1994—. Affiliated investigator Ctr. for Ulcer Rsch., 1978-89, coord. for liver disease UCLA Affiliated Hosps., 1975-89, coord. gastroenterology/hepatology, UCLA Sch. Medicine, 1981-84; vice chair for rsch., bd. dirs., chmn. sci. adv. coun. Am. Liver Found., 1994-96. Editor: Liver and Biliary Diseases, 1992, Drug Induced Liver Dieseases, 2002; assoc. editor: Hepatology, 1985-90, Am. Jour. Physiology, 1991—; contbr. over 150 articles to profl. publs. Lt. comdr. USN, 1973-75. Recipient Western Gastroenterology Rsch. prize Western Gut Club, 1986, Tchr. of Yr., Wadsworth VA, 1977-78, NIH Merit awd. 1992, William S. Middleton awd., 1993, Solomon A. Berson Med. Alumni Achievement awd. in clin. sci., NYU Sch. Med., 1994. Fellow Am. Coll. Gastroenterology; mem. Assn. Am. Physicians, Am. Soc. Clin. Investigation, Western Soc. Clin. Investigation (pres. 1985-86), Am. Fedn. for Clin. Rsch., Am. Assn. for Study of Liver Disease, So. Calif. Gastroenterology Soc., So. Calif. Liver Rsch. Forum (founder), Am. Gastroenterology Soc., Am. Soc. for Pharmacology and Experimental Therapeutics, Internat. Biliary Assn., Internat. Assn. for Study of Liver Disease, Soc. for Exptl. Biology and Medicine, Am. Physiol. Soc., Western Assn. Physicians, Rsch. Soc. on Alcoholism, European Assn. for Study of Liver, Phi Beta Kappa, Alpha Omega Alpha. Achievements include research in regulation and role of hepatic glutathione in detoxification; transport of glutathione and organic anions; identification and characterization of cytosol proteins in liver which bind and transport bile acids, organic anions and tocopherol; mechanisms of cell death due to drugs and toxins; redox regulation of suceptibility to hepatotoxicity; role of endoplasmic stress in alcohol liver injury; role of the innate immune system in drug hepatotoxicity. Home Phone: 323-667-0371; Office Phone: 323-442-5576. E-mail: kaplowit@usc.edu.

KAPOR, MITCHELL DAVID, application developer, foundation administrator; b. Bklyn., Nov. 1, 1950; s. Jesse and Phoebe L. (Wagner) K.; m. Judith M. Vecchione, June 4, 1972 (div. 1979); m. Ellen M. Poss, Aug. 7, 1983 (div. 1998); m. Freada Klein, June 19, 1999. BA, Yale U., 1971; MA, Campus-Free Coll. (now Beacon Coll.), Boston, 1978; postgrad., Sloan Sch. Mgmt., MIT, 1979; DHL (hon.), Boston U., 1985, Mass. Sch. Profl. Psychology, 1990; DSc (hon.), Suffolk U., 1988, U. Mass., 1996. Disc. jockey WHCN-FM, Hartford, Conn.; tchr., transcendental mediation in Cambridge, Mass, and Fairfield, Iowa; entry-level computer designer Cambridge, Mass.;

freelance cons., 1978-80; product mgr. Personal Software, Inc., Sunnyvale, Calif., 1980; founder Lotus Devel. Corp., Cambridge, Mass., 1982, dir., 1982—87, pres. Cambridge, Mass., 1982-84, CEO, chmn., 1984-86; chmn., CEO ON Tech. Inc., Cambridge, Mass., 1987-90; co-founder Electronic Frontier Found., Inc., Cambridge, Mass., 1990, chmn., 1990-94, chmn., pres., 1994-99; ptnr. ACCEL Ptnrs., Palo Alto, Calif., 1999—2001; pres. Kapor Enterprises Inc., 1985—; pres., chair Open Source Applications Found., San Francisco, 2001—; founding chair Mozilla Found., 2003—. Chmn. Mass. Commn. Computer Tech. and Law, 1992, 93, 2003—; mem., computer sci. and tech. bd. Nat. Rsch. Coun.; mem. adv. coun. Nat. Info. Infrastructure; adj. prof., Media Lab MIT, 1994—96; founding investor UUNET and Real Networks; chmn. bd. Linden Rsch.; bd. dir. Groove Networks; lectr. and co-taught, Open Source Development and Distribution of Information U. Calif. Berkeley, 2005—. Writer of articles, columns, & op-ed pieces on information infrastructure policy, intellectual property issues & antitrust to Scientific American, NY Times, Forbes, Tricycle: The Buddhist Review & Communications (Assn. Computing Machinery). Trustee Kapor Family Found., 1984—98, Level Playing Field Inst., San Francisco; founder, dir. Mitchell Kapor Found., 1997—. Recipient Fellow award, Computer History Mus., 1996. Jewish. Achievements include founder of Lotus Development Corporation and designer with other of Lotus 1-2-3 in 1983. Office: Mitchell Kapor Found 543 Howard St Ste 500 San Francisco CA 94105 Office Phone: 415-946-3016. Business E-Mail: mitch@kapor.com.

KAPPLER, JOHN W., microbiology educator; m. Philippa Marrack, 1974; children: Kate, Jim. BS in Chemistry, Lehigh U.; PhD in bioChemistry, Brandeis U. Postdoctoral work with Richard Dutton U. of Calif. San Diego; faculty U. Rochester Medical Sch.; prof. microbiology and immunology U. Colo., Denver; investigator Marrack and Kappler Rsch. Lab. Howard Hughes Med. Inst. Recipient Wellcome Found. Prize, Royal Society, Paul Ehrlich and Ludwig Darmstädter award, Paul Erhlich Found., Louisa Gross Horwitz prize, Columbia U., 1994. Mem.: Academy of Sciences. Office: Howard Hughes Med Inst H1400 Jackson St 5th fl Goodman Bldg Denver CO 80206

KAPPY, MICHAEL STEVEN, pediatrics educator; b. Bklyn., Feb. 8, 1940; s. Jack and Lilyan (Banchefsky) K.; m. Peggy Markson; children: Douglas Bruce, Gregory Louis. BA, Johns Hopkins U., 1961; MD, PhD, U. Wis., 1967. Asst. prof. U. Ariz. Med. Sch., Tucson, 1975-78; fellow pediatric endocrinology Johns Hopkins Hosp., Balt., 1978-80; assoc. prof. U. Fla. Med. Sch., Gainesville, 1980-85; clin. prof. U. Ariz. Med. Sch., Tucson, 1985-94; med. dir. Children's Health Ctr., Phoenix, 1985-94; prof. pediatrics U. Colo. Health Sci. Ctr., Denver, 1994—; chief pediatric endocrinology The Children's Hosp., Denver, 1994—. Editor: (jour.) Today's Child, 1985, Advances in Pediatrics, 2004, (book) Wilkins-The Diagnosis and Treatment of Endocrine Disorders in Childhood and Adolescence, 1994, Principles and Practice of Pediatric Endocrinology, 2005. Med. advisor Am. Diabetes Assn., Phoenix, 1985-94; bd. dirs. Ronald McDonald House, Phoenix, 1987-94. Named Tchr. of Yr., St. Joseph's Hosp., Phoenix, 1993, Disting. Alumni award, Johns Hopkins U., 1994, Med. Alumnus award, U. Wis., 2004. Mem. Assn. Pediatric Program Dirs. (pres. 1992-94), Soc. for Pediatric Rsch., Endocrine Soc., Am. Acad. Pediatrics, Physicians for Social Responsibility, Alpha Omega Alpha. Avocations: photography, cooking, four-wheel drive touring. Home: 460 S Marion Pkwy Apt 1706c Denver CO 80209-5547 Office: Childrens Hosp 13 23 E 16th Ave B-265 Aurora CO 80045

KAPTEYN, HENRY CORNELIUS, physics professor, engineering educator; b. Oak Lawn, Ill., Jan. 21, 1963; m. Margaret Mary Murnane, 1988. BS, Harvey Mudd Coll., 1982; MA, Princeton U., 1984; PhD, U. Calif., Berkeley, 1989. Postdoctoral rschr. U. Calif., 1989-90; asst. prof. physics Wash. State U., Pullman, 1990-95, assoc. prof., 1995, U. Mich., Ann Arbor, 1996-99; prof. JILA, U. Colo., Boulder, 1999—. Contbr. articles to profl. jours. Regents fellow U. Calif., 1985, Sloan rsch. fellow, 1995. Fellow Optical Soc. Am. (Adolph Lomb medal 1993), Am. Phys. Soc.; mem. IEEE, Soc. Photo-Optical Instrumentation Engrs. (scholar 1988). Office: JILA Univ Colo Boulder CO 80309-0440 Home Phone: 303-449-5060. E-mail: kapteyn@jila.colorado.edu.

KAPUR, AMIT, former Internet company executive; b. 1981; BS in Mech. Engring. & Advanced Thermal Sciences, Stanford U., Palo Alto, Calif., 2003. With strategic planning and bus. devel. group NBC-Universal; bus. developer MySpace, Beverly Hills, Calif., 2005—06, v.p. bus. devel., 2006—08, COO, 2008—09. Achievements include development of business relationships and deals between Myspace and Google, Skype, and Sony BMG.*

KAPUR, KAILASH CHANDER, industrial engineering educator; b. Rawalpindi, Pakistan, Aug. 17, 1941; s. Gobind Ram and Vidya Vanti (Khanna) K.; m. Geraldine Palmer, May 15, 1969; children: Anjali Joy, Jay Palmer. BS, Delhi U., India, 1963; M of Tech., Indian Inst. Tech., Kharagpur, 1965; MS, U. Calif., Berkeley, 1968, PhD, 1969. Registered profl. engr., Mich. Sr. rsch. engr. Gen. Motors Rsch. Labs., Mich., 1969-70; sr. reliability engr. TACOM, U.S. Army, Mich., 1978-79; mem. faculty Wayne State U., Detroit, 1970-89, assoc. prof. indsl. engring. and ops., 1973-79, prof., 1979-89; prof., dir. Sch. Indsl. Engring. U. Okla., Norman, 1989-92; dir., indsl. engring. U. Wash., Seattle, 1992—. Vis. prof. U. Waterloo, Can., 1977-78; vis. scholar Ford Motor Co., Mich., summer 1973. Author: Reliability in Engineering Design, 1977; contbr. articles to profl. jours. Grantee GM, 1974-77, U.S. Army, 1978-79, U.S. Dept. Transp., 1980-82. Fellow: Inst. Indsl. Engrs., Am. Soc. Quality; mem.: Ops. Rsch. Soc. Am. (sr.). Home: 4484 E Mercer Way Mercer Island WA 98040-3828 Office: U Wash PO Box 352650 Seattle WA 98195-2650 Office Phone: 206-543-4604. Personal E-mail: kalkapur@hotmail.com, kkapur@comcast.net. Business E-Mail: kkapur@u.washington.edu.

KAR, SAIBAL, cardiologist; b. Sept. 15, 1960; MD, Nil Ratan Sircar Med. Coll., Calcutta, 1986. Cert. internal medicine 1998, cardiovasc. disease 2000, interventional cardiology 2001. Resident in medicine Postgrad. Inst. Med. Edn. and Rsch., Chandigarh, India, fellow in cardiology, asst. prof.; fellow in interventional cardiology Epworth Hosp., Melbourne, Australia; resident in medicine West LA Veterans Adminstrn. Hosp.; fellow in cardiology Cedars-Sinai Med. Ctr., fellow in interventional cardiology, interventional cardiologist dept. medicine, dir. interventional cardiac rsch.; asst. prof. David Geffen Sch. Medicine, UCLA. Mem. sic. adv. com. World Congress Heart Failure. Fellow: Am. Heart Assn., Am. Coll. Cardiology; mem.: Cardiology Soc. India, AMA, Am. Coll. Physicians, Soc. Coronary Angiography and Intervention, Am. Heart Assn., Am. Coll. Cardiology. Home: 2783 Hollyview Ct Los Angeles CA 90068 Office: Cedars-Sinai Med Ctr 8700 Beverly Blvd Los Angeles CA 90048

KARABEL, JEROME BERNARD, sociologist, educator; b. Phila., May 20, 1950; s. Henry Leon and Dorothy (Forstein) K.; m. Kristin Luker, Nov. 11, 1984; children: Alexander, Sonya. BA, Harvard U., 1972, PhD, 1977; postgrad., Nuffield Coll., Oxford, Eng., 1972-73, Ecole Pratique des Hautes Etudes, Paris, 1974-75. Sr. research assoc. Huron Inst., Cambridge, Mass., 1977-84; asst. prof. sociology U. Calif., Berkeley, 1984-86, assoc. prof., 1986-93, prof., 1993—. Author: The Chosen: The Hidden History of Admission and Exclusion at Harvard, Yale, and Princeton, 2005; co-author: (with Steven Brint) The Diverted Dream: Community Colleges and the Promise of Educational Opportunity in America, 1900-1985, 1989 Co-author and co-editor: (with A.H. Halsey) Power and Ideology in Education, 1977; sr. editor: Theory and Society, 1978-96; corr. editor: Theory and Soc., 1996-; assoc. editor: Sociology of Edn., 1982-85; contbr. articles to profl. jours., mags. and newspapers. Recipient Outstanding Book award Am. Ednl. Rsch. Assn., 1991, Sr. Scholar award for Rsch. and Publs., Am. Assn. Community & Jr. Colls., 1991, Nat. Jewish Book award Am. Jewish history, 2006, Max Weber award Am. Sociol. Assn., 2006, Willard Waller award, 2006, Disting. Scholarship award Pacific Sociol. Assn, 2007, grantee Nat. Inst. Edn., 1977-81, NSF, 1972-75, 81-87, Ford Found., 1981-83, 97-04; fellow Inst. Advanced Study, 1993-94. Mem. AAUP, Am. Sociol. Assn. (coun. mem. soc. edn. sect. 1984-87, Disting. Scholarly Book award, 2007), Phi Beta Kappa. Home: 3015 Benvenue Ave Berkeley CA 94705-2509 Office: U Calif Dept Sociology 436 Barrows Hall Berkeley CA 94720 Business E-Mail: karabel@berkeley.edu.

KARÁDY, GEORGE GYÖRGY, electrical engineering educator, consultant; b. Budapest, Hungary, Aug. 17, 1930; arrived in U.S., 1976; s. Gyozo and Anna (Szamek) K.; 1 child, Gyuri. MSEE, Tech. U. Budapest, 1952, DEng, 1960, D (hon.), 1996. Registered profl. engr., NY, NJ, Que. From instr. to assoc. prof., docent Tech. U. Budapest, Hungary, 1952—66; lectr. U. Baghdad, Iraq, 1966—68, U. Salford, England, 1968—69; program mgr. Hydro Quebec Inst. of Rsch., Canada, 1969—76; chief elec. cons. engr. Ebasco Svcs., NYC, 1976—86; prof. Salt River Project Chair Ariz. State U., Tempe, 1986—. Adj. prof. McGill U., Montreal, 1972—76, Poly. Inst. NY, 1980—86; lectr. U. Montreal, 1970—76. Author: Operation of Electric Appliances and Network (in Hungarian), 1964; (with others) Advances in Electronics and Electron Physics, 1976; co-author: Electric Power Systems, Vol. V (in Hungarian), 1963, Electrical Power Systems and Networks (in Hungarian), 1964, Electrical Energy Conversion and Transport, 2005; contbr. articles to profl. jours. Fellow IEEE (paper award 1982, working group achievement award 1986); mem. U.S. Nat. Com. of Internat. Conf. of Large Elec. Network (sec.-treas. 1978-94), Princeton Ski Club (bd. dirs. 1977-86). Avocations: skiing, sailing, tennis, opera. Home: 11836 N 134th Way Scottsdale AZ 85259-3642 Office: Ariz State U Ira Fulton Sch Engring Dept Elec Engring Tempe AZ 85287-5706 Office Phone: 480-965-6569. Business E-Mail: karady@asu.edu.

KARALIS, JOHN PETER, computer company executive, lawyer; b. Mpls., July 6, 1938; s. Peter John and Vivian Karalis; m. Mary Curtis, Sept. 7, 1963; children: Amy Curtis, Theodore Curtis. BA, U. Minn., 1960, JD, 1963. Bar: Minn. 1963, Mass. 1972, Ariz. 1983, N.Y. 1986, Pa. 1986. Pvt. practice, Mpls., 1963-70; assoc. gen. counsel Honeywell Inc., Mpls., 1970-83, v.p., 1982-83; pvt. practice Phoenix, 1983-85; sr. v.p., gen. counsel Sperry Corp., NYC, 1985-87; v.p. gen. counsel Apple Computer Inc., Cupertino, Calif., 1987-89; of counsel Brown and Bain, Phoenix, 1989-92; sr. v.p. corp. devel. Tektronix, Inc., Portland, 1992-98; ret. Mem. bd. advisors Ctr. for Study of Law, Sci. and Tech., Ariz. State U. Coll. Law, Tempe, 1983-89, 2000—, adj. prof., 1990-91. Author: International Joint Ventures, A Practical Guide, 1992. Recipient Disting. Achievement award Ariz. State U., Tempe, 1985. Mem. Met. Club (N.Y.C.).

KARCHMER, SCOTT D., lawyer; b. Nov. 30, 1967; AB, Princeton U., 1990; JD, Boston Coll. Law Sch., 1994. Bar: Mass. 1994, Calif. 1997. Ptnr. Morgan, Lewis, San Francisco. Mem.: Lawyers' Com. Civil Rights, San Francisco Bay Area (dir.), State Bar Calif. (mem. bus. law sect.), ABA. Office: Morgan Lewis One Market Spear St Tower San Francisco CA 94105 Office Phone: 415-442-1091. Office Fax: 415-442-1001. Business E-Mail: skarchmer@morganlewis.com.

KARDASHIAN, KIM (KIMBERLY NOEL KARDASHIAN), apparel retailer, television personality; b. L.A., Oct. 21, 1980; d. Robert Kardashian and Kris Jenner, Bruce Jenner (Stepfather); m. Damon Thomas, Jan. 22, 2000 (div. 2004). Closet designer; fashion stylist to the stars; co-owner Dash clothing store, Calabasas, Calif., 2006—; owner Kimsaprincess Productions LLC. Stars in (TV series) Keeping Up with the Kardashians, 2007—, featured in Beyond the Break, 2006, (video) Workout with Kim Kardashian, 2008, (music video) Fall Out Boy, actress (films) Disaster Movie, 2008; performer: (TV series) Dancing with the Stars, 2008. Office: c/o Cindy Guagenti BWR Public Relations 9100 Wilshire Blvd 6th Fl Beverly Hills CA 90212 Office Phone: 310-248-6118.

KAREL, STEVEN, lawyer; b. 1950; BS, Stanford U.; JD, Harvard U. V.p., gen. counsel Robert Half Internat. Inc., Menlo Pk., Calif., 1989—, sec., 1993—. Office: Robert Half International Inc 2884 Sand Hill Rd Menlo Park CA 94025 Office Phone: 650-234-6000.

KARGES, WILLIAM A., III, food company executive; b. Newport Beach, Calif., Feb. 11, 1963; divorced; one child. AA, Marymount Palos Verdes Coll.; restaurant mgmt. courses, UCLA. Co-founder Jones Hollywood, 1994; ptnr. Johnnie's N.Y. Cafe Pizzeria, 1984, Rix, Santa Monica, 1997; owner Blueberry, 1999; founder Voda, Santa Monica. Conceived food and decor concepts for Johnnie's N.Y., Rix, Blueberry and Voda restaurants; food and operating sys. design; former ptnr. in Jones Hollywood. Recipient Best Pizza in L.A. award, 1995, Top Bang for the Buck for Johnnie's, Zagat Survey, 1996-98; Coming Into Focus award, Buzz mag., 1997. Office: Progressive Pizza 515 S Flower St Los Angeles CA 90071-2201

KARI, DAVEN MICHAEL, English and religious studies professor; b. Hot Springs, SD, Sept. 24, 1953; s. John Nelson and Corinna Nicolls (Morse) K.; m. Priya Perianayakam, Apr. 4, 1988; children: David Prem, Daniel Michael, Dante Gabriel. BA in English, Bibl. Studies, History, Fresno Pacific Coll., 1975, BA in Music, 1977; MA in English, Baylor U., 1983; MA, PhD in English, Purdue U., 1985-86; MDiv, PhD, So. Bapt. Theol. Sem., 1988-91. Lic. to ministry So. Bapt. Ch., 1971, ordained to ministry, 1996. Photography studio technician Johnson's Studio, Manteca, Calif., 1975-77; grad. teaching asst. Baylor U., Waco, Tex., 1978-79; minister of music Calvary Bapt. Ch., West Lafayette, Ind., 1984-85; grad. teaching asst. Purdue U., West Lafayette, Ind., 1979-85; lectr. in English Jefferson C.C., Louisville, 1987-90, Spalding U., Louisville, 1986-90, U. Louisville, 1986-90; asst. prof. English Mo. Bapt. Coll., St. Louis, 1991; assoc. prof. English Calif. Bapt. Coll., Riverside, 1991-93, assoc. prof. English, dir., Christian Ministry and Fine Arts, 1993-98; prof. Christian Studies and English Calif. Baptist U., 1998; acad. dean Washington Bible Coll., Lanham, Md., 1998-2000; adminstr., min. Bapt. Christian Sch., Hemet, Calif., 2000—01; freelance writer, 2001—02; assoc. prof. English Vanguard U. So. Calif., 2002—06, prof. English, 2006—. Author: T. S. Eliot's Dramatic Pilgrimage, 1990, Bibliography of Sources in Christianity and the Arts, 1995; co-editor: Baptist Reflections on Christianity and the Arts: Learning from Beauty, 1997, Contemporary Authors, 1997. Founder, co-dir. local Boys Brigade, Linden, Calif., 1969-71; asst. pastor Linden (Calif.) First Bapt. Ch., 1971; chair transp. com. Calvary Bapt. Ch., West Lafayette, 1982-83, dir. singles ministry, 1983-85; moderator Scholar's Bowl Quiz Contest, Riverside, 1993-94; min. First Bapt. Ch. Hemet, 2000-01. Recipient Lit. Criticism award Purdue U., 1983; named to Outstanding Young Men Am., 1985; named Faculty Mem. of Yr., Calif. Bapt. Coll., 1993; named to Contemporary Authors, 1997. Mem. Am. Acad. Religion, Conf. on Christianity and Lit., Evang. Theol. Soc. Democrat. Baptist. Avocations: poetry, stained glass windows, sculpture, photography, painting, music.

KARI, DONALD G., lawyer; b. Hood River, Oreg., Jan. 25, 1946; BS in Engring., with great distinction, Stanford U., 1967, MBA, JD, 1972. Bar: Wash. 1972, US Ct. Appeals (9th Cir.), US Dist. Ct. (We. Dist.) Wash. Ptnr., Energy & Utilities Practice Area Perkins Coie LLP, Bellevue, Wash. Mem.: Tau Beta Pi. Office: Perkins Coie LLP The PSE Bldg 10885 NE Fourth St Ste 700 Bellevue WA 98004-5579 Office Phone: 425-635-1406. Office Fax: 425-635-2400. Business E-Mail: dkari@perkinscoie.com.

KARI, ROSS, insurance company executive; BA in Math., U. Oreg., 1980, MBA in. Fin., 1983. Analyst in fin. Wells Fargo, 1983, v.p., 1987, sr. v.p. fin. and planning, gen. auditor, exec. v.p., 1995, head fin., mgr. controller's divsn./corp. tax., 1997, CFO, v.p., 1998—2001; CFO myCFO; exec. v.p., COO Fed. Home Loan Bank of San Francisco, 2002—07; exec. v.p., CFO Safeco Corp., Seattle, 2006—. Office: Safeco Corp Safeco Plz 4333 Brooklyn Ave Seattle WA 98185

KARIM, JAWED, Internet company executive, application developer; b. East Germany, May 1979; s. Naimul and Christine Karim. BS in Computer Sci., Univ. Ill. at Urbana-Champaign, 2004; MS in Computer Sci., Stanford Univ., 2005—. Student rschr. Univ. Minn. Supercomputing Inst., 1997, Nat. Ctr. Supercomputing Applications, 1998—99; intern, advanced graphics divsn. Silicon Graphics Inc; intern, internet sys., tech. divsn. IBM, 1999; staff tech. architecture team PayPal (an eBay Co.), 2000—05; co-founder YouTube, Inc. (sold to Google in 2006), San Meteo, Calif., 2005, advisor, 2005; limited ptnr. Sequoia Capital; co-founder Youniversity Ventures. Contbr. articles to numerous profl. jours.

KARKOSCHKA, ERICH, planetary science researcher, writer; b. Stuttgart, Federal Republic of Germany, Nov. 6, 1955; came to U.S., 1983; s. Erhard Karkoschka and Rothraut Leiter. Diploma in math., U. Stuttgart, 1981; PhD, U. Ariz., 1990. Wissenschaftlicher Mitarbeiter U. Stuttgart, 1982; rsch. assoc. U. Ariz., Tucson, 1992—2003, sr. staff scientist, 2003—. Group leader Internat. Workshop Astronomy, Europe, 1981-89. Author: The Observer's Sky Atlas, 1990, German edit., 1988, Japanese edit., 1991, Czech edit., 1995, Drehbare Welt-Sternkarte, 1990; co-author: Das Himmelsjahr, 1982—. Recipient 2d European prize European Philips Contest for Young Scientists and Inventors, 1973. Avocations: playing violin in symphony orchestra, playing organ, amateur astronomy, worldwide travel. Office: Univ Ariz Lunar & Planetary Lab Tucson AZ 85721-0001 Business E-Mail: erich@lpl.arizona.edu.

KARL, DAVID MICHAEL, oceanographer, educator; b. May 9, 1950; BA magna cum laude, SUNY, Buffalo, 1971; MS, Fla. State U., 1974; PhD, U. Calif., San Diego, 1978. Rsch. asst. dept. oceanography Fla. State U., Tallahassee, 1972—73; rsch. asst. food chain rsch. group Scripps Instn. Oceanography, La Jolla, Calif., 1974—78; asst. prof. oceanography U. Hawaii, Honolulu, 1978—81, assoc. prof. oceanography, 1981—87, chmn. oceanic biology rsch. divsn., 1986—90, prof. oceanography Sch. Ocean and Earth Sci. and Tech., 1987—, chmn. biol. oceanography divsn. Sch. Ocean and Earth Sci. and Tech., 1990—91. Rsch. oceanographer Palmer Sta. Antarctica U.S. Antarctic Program, rsch. biologist Ross Ice Shelf Project; participant exptl. microbial ecology course Marine Biol. Lab., Woods Hole, Mass., 1974; participant Scandinavian summer sch. for microbial ecology U. Aarhus, Denmark, 1976; mem. grad. faculty oceanography U. Hawaii, Honolulu, 1978—, mem. grad. faculty marine biology, 1991—; mem. affiliate faculty Bermuda Biol. Sta. for Rsch., Ferry Reach, 1995—; mem. adv. com. for ocean scis. NSF, 1984—87, mem. global ocean flux subcom. on transformations in ocean interior, 1986—88; mem. subcom. on so. ocean process studies U.S.-Joint Global Ocean Flux Study, 1990—92; mem. adv. com. Office Polar Programs NSF, 1994—97; mem. search com. for dir. Hawaii Inst. Marine Biology, 1996—; co-chair NSF-Sponsored Workshop on Lake Vostok, Antarctica, 1998; mem. dir. search com. Inst. for Astronomy, 1999—2000. Mem. editl. bd.: Applied and Environ. Microbiology, 1980—82, 1983—85, 1985—88, 1989—94, Microbial Ecology, 1990—92, Ecosystems, 1999—2001, Biogeosciences, 2004—, guest editor: Deep-Sea Rsch., Rsch. on Antarctic Coastal Ecosystem Rates, 1991; editor: Microbiology of Deep-Sea Hydrothermal Vents, 1995; editl. advisor: Aquatic Microbial Ecology, 1995—96, guest editor: Deep-Sea Rsch., Oceanic Time-Series, 1996, subject editor: Aquatic Microbial Ecology, 1997—. Recipient Presdl. Young Investigator award, NSF, 1984—89, A. G. Huntsman Medal, Bedford Inst. of Oceanography, 2001, Investigator in Marine Sci. award, Gordon and Betty Moore Found., 2004, Henry Bryant Bigelow Medal, Woods Hole Oceanog. Instn., 2004, David Packard Medal, Monterey Bay Aquarium Rsch. Inst., 2005. Fellow: Am. Geophys. Union (mem. exec. com. ocean scis. sect. 1996—98, mem. ad hoc com. on recognizing and encouraging the contbns. of biol. 1998—2000); mem.: NAS, Am. Soc. Limnology and Oceanography (mem. com. on edn. and human resources 1993—98, mem. selection com. Lifetime Achievement Award 1994, chairperson pub. policy com. 1998—, G. Evelyn Hutchinson Medal 1998), Am. Soc. for Microbiol. (v.p. Hawaii br. 1981—82, chmn.-elect divsn. aquatic and terrestrial microbiology 1984—85, mem. ann. meeting planning com. 1985—86, chmn. divsn. aquatic and terrestrial microbiology 1985—86), Oceanography Soc. (mem. membership com. 1996—99, coun. mem. 2000—), Hawaii Acad. Sci., Sigma Xi (councilor Hawaii br. 1991—92, mem. exec.

com. Hawaii chpt. 1991—92). Office: U Hawaii Sch Ocean and Earth Sci and Tech 1000 Pope Rd MSB 629 Honolulu HI 96822 Home: 2360 Halekoa Dr Honolulu HI 96821-1038

KARL, GEORGE, professional basketball coach; b. Penn Hills, Pa., May 12, 1951; children: Kelei Ryanne, Coby Joseph, Kaci Grace. Grad., U. NC, 1973. Draft pick NY Knicks, 1973; guard San Antonio Spurs, 1973-78, asst. coach, head scout, 1978-80; head coach Continental Basketball Assn. Mont. Golden Nuggets, 1980-83; dir. player acquisition Cleve. Cavaliers, 1983-84, head coach, 1984-86, Golden State Warriors, Oakland, Calif., 1986—88, Albany Patrons, NY, 1988—89, 1990—91, Real Madrid, Spain, 1991-92, Seattle SuperSonics, 1991—98, Milw. Bucks, 1998—2003, Denver Nuggets, 2005—; NBA analyst ESPN. Head coach USA Basketball Team Internat. Basketball Fedn. World Basketball Championships, Indpls., 2002. Named Coach of Yr., Continental Basketball Assn., 1981, 83, 91. Achievements include winning over 800 NBA games as head coach. Office: Denver Nuggets 1000 Chopper Cir Denver CO 80204

KARLAN, BETH YOUNG, obstrician-gynecologist; b. NYC, May 8, 1957; MD, Harvard Med. Sch. and Harvard-Mass. Inst. Tech. Program in Health Scis. and Tech., 1982. Diplomate Am. Bd. Ob.-Gyn., Gynecologic Oncology. Intern Yale-New Haven Hosp., 1982-83, resident in ob-gyn., 1983-86; fellow molecular biology Yale U. Sch. Medicine; fellow gynecologic oncology UCLA Sch. Medicine, 1987-89, assoc. prof., 1995—; obstetrian-gynecologist UCLA Med. Ctr., LA, St. Josephs Med. Ctr., Burbank, Calif., Cedars-Sinai Med. Ctr., LA, 1987—, dir., Women's Cancer Rsch. Inst., dir., divsn. gynecologic-oncology, dir., Gilda Radner Cancer Detection Program; prof., ob-gyn., Geffen Sch. Medicine UCLA. Spkr. in field. Contbr. several articles to profl. jours. Named one of America's Top Doctors in Cancer; awarded grants from Dept. Def., NIH and Ahmanson Found. Mem. AMA, Am. Coll. Ob-Gyn., Am. Assn. for Cancer Rsch., Am. Soc. of Clin. Oncology, Soc. Gynecol. Oncologists, Internat. Gynecologic Cancer Soc., Soc. for Gynecologic Investigation, ACS. Office: Cedars Sinai Med Ctr 8700 Beverly Blvd Ste 290-W Los Angeles CA 90048 Office Phone: 310-855-3302. Office Fax: 310-423-9753. Business E-Mail: karlanb@cshs.org.

KARLAN, PAMELA SUSAN, law educator; b. 1959; BA in History magna cum laude, Yale U., 1980, MA in History, 1984, JD, 1984. Bar: US Supreme Ct., US Dist. Ct. So. Dist. NY, US Ct. Appeals 4th, 5th, 8th, 9th, and 11th Circuits. Law clk. to Judge Abraham D. Sofaer US Dist. Ct. So. Dist. NY, 1984—85; law clk. to Justice Harry A. Blackman US Supreme Ct., 1985—86; asst. counsel NAACP Legal Def. and Ednl. Fund, Inc., 1986—88; assoc. prof. law U. Va. Sch. Law, 1988—93, prof., 1993—98, Roy L. and Rosamond Woodruff Morgan rsch. prof., 1994—98; prof. law Stanford Law Sch., 1998—99, Kenneth and Harle Montgomery prof. pub. interest law, 1999—, academic assoc. dean, 1999—2000. Lectr. FBI Nat. Acad., 1990—2001; commr. Calif. Fair Polit. Practice Commn., 2003; vis. prof. Yale Law Sch., 1992, NYU Sch. Law, 1993, Harvard Law Sch., 1994—95, Stanford Law Sch., 1996, U. Va. Law Sch., 2002. Fellow: Am. Acad. Arts & Scis.; mem.: Am. Law Inst. Office: Stanford Law Sch Crown Quadrangle 559 Nathan Abbott Way Stanford CA 94305-8610 Office Phone: 650-725-4851. Office Fax: 650-725-0253. Business E-Mail: karlan@stanford.edu.

KARLEN, PETER HURD, lawyer, writer; b. NYC, Feb. 22, 1949; s. S. H. and Jean Karlen; m. Lynette Ann Thwaites, Dec. 22, 1978. BA in History, U. Calif., Berkeley, 1971; JD, U. Calif., Hastings, 1974; MS in Law and Soc., U. Denver, 1976. Bar: Calif. 1974, Hawaii 1989, Colo. 1991, U.S. Dist. Ct. (so. dist.) Calif. 1976, U.S. Dist. Ct. (no. dist.) Calif. 1983, U.S. Dist. Ct. (Hawaii) 1989, U.S. Supreme Ct. 1990. Assoc. Sankary & Sankary, San Diego, 1976; teaching fellow Coll. of Law U. Denver, 1974-75; lectr. Sch. of Law U. Warwick, United Kingdom, 1976-78; pvt. practice La Jolla, Calif., 1979-86; prin. Peter H. Karlen, P.C., La Jolla, 1986—. Adj. prof. U. San Diego Sch. of Law, 1979-84; mem. adj. faculty Western State U. Coll. of Law, San Diego, 1976, 79-80, 88, 92. Contbg. editor Artweek, 1979-95, Art Calendar, 1989-96, Art Cellar Exch. mag., 1989-92; mem. editl. bd. Copyright World, 1988—, IP World, 1997—; contbr. numerous articles to profl. jours. Mem. Am. Soc. for Aesthetics, Brit. Soc. Aesthetics. Office: 1205 Prospect St Ste 400 La Jolla CA 92037-3613

KARLGAARD, RICH, publishing executive; b. Bismarck, ND; married; 2 children. BA in Polit. Sci., Stanford U., Calif. Co-founder, editor Upside mag., 1989—92, Forbes ASAP, 1992—98; pub. Forbes mag., NYC, 1998—. Co-founder Churchill Club (nonprofit); co-founder, bd. dir. garage.com, 1977—. Contbr. columns to Wall Street Journal. Named Entrepreneur of Yr., Ernst & Young, 1997; named to Elite 100 in computer/comm. industries, Upside mag., 1998. Office: Forbes 60 5th Ave New York NY 10011-8882 also: Forbes 555 Airport Blvd 5th Fl Burlingame CA 94010 Office Phone: 650-558-4810. Office Fax: 212-620-2245. E-mail: publisher@forbes.com.

KARLIN, MICHAEL JONATHAN ABRAHAM, lawyer; b. London, Aug. 27, 1952; came to U.S., 1980; s. Eli Karlin and Miriam (Stahl) Henderson; m. Fiona Jane Wilson, July 20, 1973; children: Laura, Toby. BA with Hons., Cambridge U., Eng., 1973, MA, 1977. Bar: Calif. 1980, U.S. Dist. Ct. (cen. dist.) Calif. 1980, U.S. Tax. Ct. 1981; solicitor, Eng. and Wales 1977. Asst. solicitor D.J. Freeman & Co., London, 1975-80; assoc. Gelles, Singer & Johnson, LA, 1980-83, Morgan, Lewis & Bockius LLP, LA, 1983-88, ptnr., 1988—97, KPMG LLP, 1998—2000. Contbr. articles to profl jours., 1980—. Mem. ABA (tax sect. com. on U.S. Activities of Foreigners and Tax Treaties 2004, chmn. task force new and temporary immigrants 2004), Calif. State Bar Assn., L.A. County Bar Assn. (chmn. fgn. tax law com. taxation sect. 1989-90). Office: Karlin & Peebles LLP 8383 Wilshire Blvd #649 Beverly Hills CA 90211 Office Phone: 310-274-5275. Business E-Mail: mjkarlin@karlinpeebles.com.

KARLINSKY, SIMON, language educator, writer; b. Harbin, Manchuria, Sept. 22, 1924; arrived in U.S., 1938, naturalized, 1944; s. Aron and Sophie (Levitin) Karlinsky; m. Peter Carleton, Oct. 2008. BA, U. Calif., Berkeley, 1960, PhD, 1964; MA, Harvard U., 1961. Conf. interpreter, music student Europe, 1947-57; tchg. fellow Harvard U., Cambridge, Mass., 1960-61; asst. prof. Slavic langs. and lits. U. Calif., Berkeley, 1963-65, prof., 1967-91, prof. emeritus, 1991—, chmn. dept., 1967-69. Vis. assoc. prof. Harvard U., 1966. Author: Marina Cvetaeva: Her Life and Her Art, 1966, The Sexual Labyrinth of Nikolai Gogol, 1976, 2d edit., 1992, Russian Drama from Its Beginnings to the Age of Pushkin, 1985, Marina Tsvetaeva: The Woman, Her World and Her Poetry, 1986, 2d edit., 1988, Italian edit., 1989, Spanish edit., 1990, Japanese edit., 1991; editor: The Bitter Air of Exile, 1977; editor, annotator: Anton Chekhov's Life and Thought, 1974, 2d edit., 1997, The Nabokov-Wilson Letters, 1979, 2d edit., 2001, French edit., 1988, German edit., 1995, Japanese edit., 2002; co-editor: Language, Literature, Linguistics, 1987, O RUS! Studia literaria slavica in honorem Hugh McLean, 1995; contbr. articles to profl. jours. Guggenheim fellow, 1969—70, 1977—78. Mem.: Phi Beta Kappa.

KARLSTROM, PAUL JOHNSON, art historian; b. Seattle, Jan. 22, 1941; s. Paul Isadore and Eleanor (Johnson) K.; m. Ann Heath, Dec. 29, 1964; 1 child, Clea Heath. BA in English Lit, Stanford U., 1964; MA, UCLA, 1969, PhD, 1973. Asst. curator Grunwald Ctr. for Graphic Arts UCLA, 1967-70; Samuel H. Kress fellow Nat. Gallery Art, Washington, 1970-71; instr. Calif. State U., Northridge, 1972-73; West Coast regional dir. Archives Am. Art, Smithsonian Instn. at De Young Mus., San Francisco, 1973-91, Huntington Libr., San Marino, Calif., 1991—2003. Guest curator Hirshhorn Mus., Washington, 1977; writer, curator art and cultural history, 2003-. Author: Louis M. Eilshemius, 1978, Los Angeles in the 1940s-Post Modernism and the Visual Arts, 1987, The Visionary Art of James M. Washington, Jr., 1989, Turning the Tide: Early Los Angeles Modernists, 1920-1956, 1990; editor: On the Edge of America: California Modernist Art, 1900-1950, 1996; contbg. author: Diego Rivera: Art and Revolution, 1999, Reading California, 2000, Over the Line: The Art and Life of Jacob Lawrence, 2000, Eros in the Studio in Art and the Performance of Memory: Text and Image, 2005; prodr. (video) David Hockney, 1984, 1993, George Tsutakawa in Japan, 1988, Richard Shaw, 1998, co-editor, project dir. Calif. Asian Am. Artist Biog. Survey; contbr. articles to profl. jours.; author: Raimonds Staprans: Art of Tranquility and Turbulence, 2005. Mem. adv. bd. Humanities West, Jacob Lawrence Catalogue Raisonné Project; former bd. dirs. S.W. Art History Coun., Bay Area Video Coalition; sec. Va. Steele Scott Found; v.p. Noah Purifoy Found. E-mail: pkarlstrom@sbcglobal.net.

KARLTON, LAWRENCE K., federal judge; b. Bklyn., May 28, 1935; s. Aaron Katz and Sylvia (Meltzer) K.; m. Mychelle Stiebel, Sept. 7, 1958 (dec.); m. Sue Gouge, May 22, 1999. Student, Washington Sq. Coll., 1952-54; LL.B., Columbia U., 1958. Bar: Fla. 1958, Calif. 1962. Acting legal officer Sacramento Army Depot, Dept. Army, Sacramento, 1958-60, civilian legal officer, 1960-62; individual practice law Sacramento, 1962-64; mem. firm Abbott, Karlton & White, 1964, Karlton & Blease, 1964-71, Karlton, Blease & Vanderlaan, 1971-76; judge Calif. Superior Ct. for Sacramento County, 1976-79, U.S. Dist. Ct. (ea. dist.) Calif., Sacramento, 1979-83; formerly chief judge U.S. Dist. Ct., Sacramento, 1983-90, chief judge emeritus, 1990-2000, sr. judge, 2000—. Co-chmn. Central Calif. council B'nai B'rith Anit-Defamation League Commn., 1964-65; treas. Sacramento Jewish Community Relations Council, chmn., 1967-68; chmn. Vol. Lawyers Commn. Sacramento Valley ACLU, 1964-76. Mem. Am. Bar Assn., Sacramento County Bar Assn., Calif. Bar Assn., Fed. Bar Assn., Fed. Judges Assn., 9th Cir. Judges Assn. Clubs: B'nai B'rith (past pres.). Office: US Dist Ct 501 I St Sacramento CA 95814-7300

KARNAS, FRED G., JR., poverty and homeless specialist; b. Olean, NY, Sept. 9, 1948; BCP, U. Va., 1971; MSW, Va. Commonwealth U., 1980; PhD, Va. Tech. U., 1984. Gen. program dir. Cmty. Coun., Phoenix, 1983-87; exec. dir. Cmty. Housing Partnership, Phoenix, 1987-89, Ctrl. Fla. Coalition for the Homeless, Orlando, Fla., 1989-91, Nat. Coalition for the Homeless, Washington, 1991-95; with HUD, Washington, 1995-2000, dep. asst. sec., 1997-2000; cons. on homelessness, AIDS, housing policies, 2000—; pres. Ariz. Family Housing Fund, Phoenix, 2002—03; policy advisor Gov. of Ariz., 2003—06; sr. dir. Fannie Mae Found., Washington, 2006—07; dir. Ariz. Dept. Housing, 2007—. Office: 1110 W Washington St Ste 310 Phoenix AZ 85007 E-mail: fkarnas1@msn.com.

KARNI, SHLOMO, retired engineering and religious studies professor; b. Lódz, Poland, June 23, 1932; came to U.S., 1956; BSEE cum laude, Technion, Israel, 1956; M of Engring., Yale U., 1957; PhD, U. Ill., Urbana, 1960. Asst. prof. U. Ill., Urbana, 1960-61, U. N.Mex., Albuquerque, 1961—64, assoc. prof., 1964—67, prof., 1967-99, Gardner-Zemke prof., 1993—96, prof. emeritus, 1999—. Vis. prof. U. Hawaii, 1969, Tel Aviv U., 1970, Technion, 1977; cons. Dept. Energy, Westinghouse Corp., USAF, Los Alamos Nat. Labs., Burnell Electronics, DOE, major pub. houses, 1962—; vis. mem. Acad. Hebrew Lang., Jerusalem, 1970-71. Author 8 engring. and Hebrew lang. textbooks, more than 90 papers in profl. jours.; editor or assoc. editor several IEEE publs. Fellow IEEE (life). Office: U NMex Dept Elect & Computer Engring Albuquerque NM 87131-0001 Office Phone: 505-277-1436. E-mail: karni@eceunm.edu.

KARP, RICHARD MANNING, computer science educator; b. Boston, Jan. 3, 1935; s. Abraham Louis and Rose (Nanes) Karp; m. Diana Leigh Grand; 1 child, Jeremy Alexander. AB, Harvard U., 1955, SM, 1956, PhD in Applied Math., 1959; DSc (hon.), U. Pa., 1986, Technion, 1989, U. Mass., 1990, Georgetown U., 1992, U. Ctrl. Fla., 2000. Rsch. staff mem. IBM Watson Rsch. Ctr., Yorktown Heights, NY, 1959—68; visiting assoc. prof. elec. engring. U. Mich., Ann Arbor, 1964—65; prof. computer sci., indsl. engring., ops. rsch. U. Calif., Berkeley, 1968—96, assoc. chmn. elec. engring., computer sci., 1973—75, prof. math., 1980—95, univ. prof., elec. engring. and computer sci., 1999—; co-chmn. program in computational complexity Math. Sci. Rsch. Inst., Berkeley, Calif., 1985—86; rsch. scientist Internat. Computer Sci. Inst., Berkeley, Calif., 1988—96, sr. rsch. scientist, 1996—; prof. computer sci. U. Wash., Seattle, 1995—99, adj. prof. molecular biotech., 1996—2000; Hewlett-Packard vis. prof. Math Sci. Rsch. Inst., Berkeley, 1999—2000. Bd. govs. Weizmann Inst. Soc.; adv. bd. Computer Profns. for Social Responsibility; faculty rsch. lectr., Berkeley, 1981—82; Miller rsch. prof., Berkeley, 1980—81. Contbr. articles to profl. jours. Recipient Fulkerson prize in Discrete Math., Am. Math. Soc., 1979, Lanchester prize in Ops. Rsch., Inst. for Ops. Rsch. and the Mgmt. Sciences, 1977, ORSA/TIS von Neumann Theory prize, 1990, Babbage prize, 1995, Nat. medal of Sci. award, NSF, 1996, Harvey prize, 1998, Benjamin Franklin medal in Computer and Cognitive Sci., Franklin Inst., 2004, Kyoto prize for Lifetime Achievement in Advanced Technology, Inamori Found., 2008; fellow Einstein, Technion, 1983, Lady Davis, 1983. Fellow: Assn. Computing Machinery (Turing award 1985), AAAS, Am. Acad. Arts and Scis.; mem.: NAS, NAE, Am. Philos. Soc., Inst. Combinatorics and Applications. Office: U Calif Computer Sci Divsn 387 Soda Hall # 1776 Berkeley CA 94720 E-mail: karp@icsi.berkeley.edu.

KARPELES, DAVID, museum director; b. Santa Barbara, Calif., Jan. 26, 1936; s. Leon and Betty (Friedman) Karpeles; m. Marsha Mirsky, June 29, 1958; children: Mark, Leslie, Cheryl, Jason. BS, U. Minn., 1956, postgrad., 1956-59; MA, San Diego State U., 1962; postgrad., U. Calif., Santa Barbara, 1965-69; PhD, Atlantic Internat. U., 2003. Founder Karpeles Manuscript Libr. Mus., Montecito, Calif., 1983—, dir., founder Santa Barbara, Calif., 1988—, NYC, 1990—, Tacoma, 1991—, Jacksonville, Fla., 1992—, Duluth, Minn., 1993—, Charleston, SC, 1995—, Buffalo, 1995—, Newburgh, NY, 1999—, Shreveport, 2004—. Dir. 202 mini-museums throughout U.S. and Can.; established the 1st cultural literacy program, presented to schs. by respective mus. staffs, 1993—; tchg. fellow Buffalo State U., 2001—. Creator program to provide ownership of homes to low-income families, 1981. Recipient Affordable Housing Competition award, Gov. Edmund G. Brown Jr., State of Calif. Dept. Housing and Cmty. Devel., 1981, Disting. Alumni award, U. Minn., 1996; named commencement spkr. to graduating class, 1996, hon. inductee, Acad. Sci. and Engring., U. Minn., 2002. Jewish. Home: 465 Hot Springs Rd Santa Barbara CA 93108-2029 E-mail: kmuseumsb@aol.com.

KARPLUS, PAUL ANDREW, biochemistry educator; b. Oakland, Calif., Sept. 25, 1957; s. Robert and Elizabeth Jane (Frazier) K.; m. Karen Elisabeth Andersen, July 26, 1980; children: Elisabeth Marie, Christina Jane, Timothy Robert. Student, U. Calif., Berkeley, 1974-76; BS in Biochemistry with highest honors, U. Calif., Davis, 1978. Postdoctoral rsch. assoc. Inst. Organic Chemistry and Biochemistry, U. Freiburg, Federal Republic of Germany, 1984-88; asst. prof. biochemistry, molecular and cell biology Cornell U., Ithaca, NY, 1988-93; assoc. prof. biochemistry, molecular and cell biology, 1993-98. Assoc. prof. dept. biochemistry and biophysics Oreg. State U., Corvallis, 1998-99, prof., 1999—. Recipient Nat. Rsch. Svc. award NIH-NIGMS, 1979, Pfizer award in enzyme chemistry Am. Chem. Soc., 1996, Milton Harris award for basic rsch., 2001; Alexander von Humboldt fellow, 1984-85, 90, Guggenheim fellow, 1996-97. Mem. Phi Kappa Phi. Home Phone: 541-758-6567; Office Phone: 541-737-3200. E-mail: karplusp@science.oregonstate.edu.

KARPMAN, HAROLD LEW, cardiologist, educator, writer; b. Belvedere, Calif., Aug. 23, 1927; s. Samuel and Dora (Kastleman) K.; m. Molinda Karpman. Student, UCLA, 1945-46; BA, U. Calif., Berkeley, 1950; MD, U. Calif., San Francisco, 1954. Diplomate Am. Bd. Internal Medicine. Rotating intern L.A. County Gen. Hosp., LA, 1954-55; cardiovascular trainee Nat. Heart Inst., LA, 1957-58; asst. resident Beth Israel Hosp., Boston, 1955-57; fellow Wyley Winsor Rsch. Found., LA, 1958-59; pvt. practice Beverly Hills, Calif., 1958—; clin. instr. medicine U. So. Calif., LA, 1958-64, asst. clin. prof., 1964-71, assoc. clin. prof., 1971-72; assoc. clin. prof. medicine David Soffen Sch. Medicine, UCLA, 1972—92, clin. prof. medicine, 1992—, attending physician. Bd. govs. Cedars-Sinai Med. Ctr., L.A., 1958-, UCLA Med. Ctr., 1958-04, Brotman Med. Ctr., 1958-04, Culver City, Calif.; founder, chmn., CEO Cardiovasc. Rsch. Found. Southern Calif., 2007-; examiner in cardiovascular diseases Calif. Indsl. Accident Commn., Calif. Dept. Vocat. Rehab.; founder, bd. dirs., chmn. bd. Cardio-Dynamics Labs., Inc., 1969-82; gen. ptnr. Camden Med. Bldg., L.A., 1970-86; bd. dirs. Mcht. Bank Calif.; bd. dirs. med. rsch. Faberge, Inc., N.Y.C., 1980-84; cardiovascular cons. Delta Air Lines, 1992-94; founder, bd. dirs., chmn. bd., chief med. officer CORDA Med. Care, Inc., 1995-2000; chmn., founder, dir. Integrated Diagnostic Ctrs., Inc., 2000-07. Author: Your Second Life, 1979, Preventing Silent Heart Disease, 1989; assoc. editor Internal Medicine Alert, 1992—; contbr. numerous articles to med. jours. Fellow ACP, Am. Coll. Cardiology, Am. Coll. Chest Physicians, Internat. Cardiovascular Soc., Am. Coll. Angiology, Internat. Coll. Angiology, Am. Thermographic Soc. (charter, pres. 1971-72), Am. Acad. Thermology; mem. AMA, Calif. Med. Assn., L.A. Med. Assn., Nat. Cardiovascular Network (exec. com., bd. dirs. 1994-98), Western Cardiovascular Network (chmn., med. dir. 1993-96), Am. Soc. Internal Medicine, Am. Heart Assn., Calif. Heart Assn., L.A. County Heart Assn. Office: 414 N Camden Dr 1100 Beverly Hills CA 90210-4532 Office Phone: 310-278-3400.

KARR, JAMES RICHARD, ecologist, educator, research director; b. Shelby, Ohio, Dec. 26, 1943; s. Rodney Joll and Marjorie Ladonna (Copeland) K.; m. Kathleen Ann Reynolds, Mar. 23, 1963 (div. Nov. 1982); children: Elizabeth Ann, Eric Leigh; m. Helen Marie Herbst Serrano, Dec. 22, 1984. BS, Iowa State U., 1965; MS, U. Ill., 1967, PhD, 1970. Fellow in biology Princeton (NJ) U., 1970-71, Smithsonian Tropical Rsch. Inst., Balboa, Panama, 1971-72, dep. dir., 1984-87, acting dir., 1987-88; asst. prof. biology Purdue U., Lafayette, Ind., 1972-75; assoc. prof. U. Ill., Urbana, 1975-80, prof., 1980-84; Harold H. Bailey prof. biology Va. Poly. Inst. and State U., Blacksburg, 1988-91; prof. zoology, fisheries, environ. health, civil engring. and pub. affairs U. Wash., Seattle, 1991—2006, dir. Inst. Environ. Studies, 1991-95, prof. emeritus, 2006—. Cons. on water resources EPA, 1978—, OAS, Washington, 1980, South Fla. Water Mgmt. Dist., West Palm Beach, 1989-2002, 2006—07; cons., gen. counsel Fla. Dept. Environ. Protection, 2002-03, 2004—06. Recipient Carl R. Sullivan Fishery Conservation award, Am. Fisheries Soc., 2004, Environ. Stewardship award, N.Am. Benthological Soc., 2005; grantee, EPA, 1972—85, 1993—2000, U.S. Forest Svc., 1980—81, 1990—91, U.S. Fish and Wildlife Svc., 1979—82, NSF, 1982—84, 1997—2000, TVA, 1990—93, Dept. Energy, 1995—2002. Fellow: AAAS, Am. Ornithologists Union; mem.: N.Am. Ornithological Soc. Achievements include development of Index of Biotic Integrity, now used in North and South America, Asia, Australia, and Europe to assess directly the quality of water resources. Home: 190 Cascadia Loop Sequim WA 98382 Home Phone: 360-681-3163. Personal E-mail: jrkarr@u.washington.edu.

KARRAS, ALEX, actor, retired professional football player; b. Gary, Ind., July 15, 1935; m. Susan Clark Player Detroit Lions, 1958-71; host NFL Monday Night Football Preview WLS-TV, Chgo. Former commentator Monday Night Football, ABC-TV; numerous TV appearances including Tonight Show, TV movies: Paper Lion, The 500 lb. Jerk, Mad Bull, Mighty Moose & The Quarterback Kid, Babe, 1975, Mulligan's Stew, 1977, Centennial, 1978, Jimmy B. and Andre, 1979, Alcatraz: The Whole Shocking Story, When Fame Ran Out, 1980, Maid in America, 1982, Fudge-A-Mania, 1994; star TV series Webster, ABC-TV, 1983-86; films include: Blazing Saddles, 1974, Win, Place or Steal, 1977, FM, 1978, Nobody's Perfect, 1981, Victor, Victoria, 1982, Porky's, 1982, Against All Odds, 1984; author: (with Herb Gluck) Even Big Guys Cry, 1977, Alex Karras: My Life in Football, 1979, Tuesday Night Football, 1991. Named All-Pro, 1960, 61, 63, 65; recipient Outland Trophy, 1957, 79. Office: Ste 308 13400 Riverside Dr Sherman Oaks CA 91423-2541

KARSH, PHILIP HOWARD, retired advertising executive; b. Salt Lake City, Sept. 19, 1935; s. Sol and Ruth (Marks) K.; m. Carol Hyman, July 3, 1962 (div. Sept. 1973); children: Michael David, Jill Ann; m. Linda Love, Sept. 7, 1984. BA, U. Colo., 1957. Account exec. Ted Levy/Richard Lane & Co., Denver, 1957-59; v.p. Jerome/Philip Advt., Denver, 1959—62, pres., 1962-65; v.p. Frye Sills

Advt., Denver, 1965—77; pres. Karsh & Hagan Advt. Inc., Denver, 1977-85, chmn., 1985-97; ret., 1998. Trustee Nat. Jewish Med. and Rsch. Ctr., Denver, 1963—, chmn. 1991-95, Kern Rsch. Found., Denver, 1984—, Mile High United Way, Denver, 1986-92; mem. Denver Metro Conv. and Visitors Bur., 1994—, chmn., 1997. Named to Colo. Tourism Hall of Fame, 2004. Mem. Worldwide Ptnrs. (internat. chmn. 1986-87), Denver Advt. Fedn. (bd. dirs. 1968-69, 87-88), Colo. Hist. Soc. (trustee 1998—, chair 2003-06). Democrat. Jewish. Avocations: skiing, travel, golf. Home: 11704 W Auburn Dr Denver CO 80228-4758 Personal E-mail: philkarsh@comcast.net.

KARSON, BURTON LEWIS, musician, educator; b. LA, Nov. 10, 1934; s. Harry L. and Cecilia K. BA, U. So. Calif., 1956, MA, 1959, DMA, 1964. Instr. music Univ. Coll., U. So. Calif., Los Angeles, 1958-59, univ. chapel organist, 1960-61; instr. music Glendale (Calif.) Coll., 1960-65; asst. prof. music Calif. State U., Fullerton, 1965-69, assoc. prof., 1969-74, prof., 1974-97, prof. emeritus, 1997—; writer, critic Los Angeles Times, 1966-71. Founder, condr., artistic dir., Baroque Music Festival, Corona del Mar, Calif., 1980—; concert preview lectr. Los Angeles Philharm. Orch., Carmel Bach Festival, Pacific Symphony, Pacific Chorale, Philharmonic Soc. Orange County, others; editor: Festival Essays for Pauline Alderman, Brigham Young Univ. Press, 1976; contbr. articles to profl. jours. including Mus. Quar. Musician, choirmaster St. Joachim Ch., Costa Mesa, Calif., 1974—82, St. Michael and All Angels Episc. Ch., Corona del Mar, Calif., 1982—2000, organist-choirmaster emeritus, 2000—; choral condr. Luth. Chorale L.A., 1979—83. Mem. Am. Musicol. Soc., Am. Guild Organists, Phi Mu Alpha Sinfonia (province gov. 1976-81, chair nat. com.), Pi Kappa Lambda, Orange County Performing Arts Ctr. (bd. dirs. Founder Plus), Philharmonic Soc. Orange County (bd. dirs.). Achievements include profl. rsch. on music history and criticism in early Calif., German, Czech and English Baroque, cantatas and concertos; conductor first American performances. Home: 404 De Sola Terr Corona Del Mar CA 92625-2650

KARST, KENNETH LESLIE, law educator; b. LA, June 26, 1929; s. Harry Everett and Sydnie Pauline (Bush) K.; m. Smiley Cook, Aug. 12, 1950; children— Kenneth Robert, Richard Eugene, Leslie Jeanne, Laura Smiley AB, UCLA, 1950; LL.B., Harvard U., 1953. Bar: Calif. 1954, U.S. Dist. Ct. (cen. dist.) Calif. 1954, U.S. Ct. Appeals (9th cir.) 1954, U.S. Supreme Ct. 1970. Assoc. Latham & Watkins, Los Angeles, 1954, 56-57; teaching fellow law Harvard U. Law Sch., 1957-58; asst. prof. Ohio State U. Coll. Law, Columbus, 1958-60, assoc. prof., 1960-62, prof., 1962-65; prof. law UCLA, 1965-90, David G. Price and Dallas P. Price prof. law, 1990—. Author: (with Harold W. Horowitz) Law, Lawyers and Social Change, 1969, (with Keith S. Rosenn) Law and Development in Latin America, 1975, Belonging to America: Equal Citizenship and the Constitution, 1989, Law's Promise, Law's Expression: Visions of Power in the Politics of Gender, Race, and Religion, 1993; assoc. editor Ency. of Am. Constn., 1986, co-editor-in-chief, 2d edit., 2000; contbr. articles to profl. jours. Served to 1st lt. JAGC, USAF, 1954-56. Law faculty fellow Ford Found., 1962-63. Fellow Am. Acad. Arts and Scis.; mem. State Bar Calif. Office: UCLA Law Sch PO Box 951476 Los Angeles CA 90095-1476 Business E-Mail: karst@law.ucla.edu.

KARTHA, KUTTY KRISHNAN, plant pathologist; b. Shertallai, India, Aug. 9, 1941; married, 1972; 2 children. BSc, Saugar U., India, 1962; MSc, Jawaharal Nehru Agrl. U., India, 1965; PhD in Plant Pathology, India Agrl. Rsch. Inst., 1969. Fellow Nat. Inst. Agrl. Rsch., France, 1970-72; vis. scientist Prairie Regional Lab., NRC, Saskatoon, Canada, 1973-74; asst. rsch. officer Plant Biotech. Inst., Saskatoon, 1974-76, assoc. rsch. officer, 1976-81, head cell tech. sect., 1985-87; sr. rsch. officer Plant Biotech. Inst., NRC, Saskatoon, 1981, group leader cereal biotech., 1985-93, acting rsch. dir., 1993-95, dir. gen., 1995—2007; ret., 2007. Adj. prof. U. Sask., Saskatoon, 1987—; mem. Can. Agrl. Rsch. Coun., 1990-94. Editor Jour. Plant Physiology, 1987, Cyropreservation Plant Cells and Organs, 1985. Recipient George M. Darrow award Am. Soc. Hort. Sci., 1981, C.J. Bishop award Can. Soc. Hort. Sci., 1992, Excellence in Rsch. award Treasury Bd. Can., 1992, Commemorative medal for 125th anniversary of Confedn. Can., 1992, Queen Elizabeth II Golden Jubilee medal, 2002, Gold Medal award Profl. Inst. Pub. Svc. Can., 2004. Mem. Internat. Assn. Plant Tissue Culture (nat. corr. 1982-86), Can. Soc. Plant Physiologists, Can. Phytopath. Soc. Achievements include research in plant biotechnology, cryopreservation of plant cells and organs, plant tissue culture.

KASSON, JAMES MATTHEWS, electronics executive; b. Muncie, Ind., Mar. 19, 1943; s. Robert Edwin and Mary Louise K.; m. Betty Roseman, Aug. 14, 1976. BSE.E., Stanford U., 1964; MSE.E., U. Ill., 1965. Engring. mgr. Santa Rita Tech., Santa Clara, Calif., 1963-69; engring. sect. mgr. Hewlett-Packard, Palo Alto, Calif., 1969-73; v.p. research and devel. ROLM Corp., Santa Clara, 1973-88; fellow IBM Corp., San Jose, Calif., 1988-95; v.p. engring. Echelon Corp., Palo Alto, Calif., 1995-98, CIO, 1998-2000. Patentee in field. Trustee Choate Rosemary Hall, Wallingford, Conn., 1990-96, Ctr. Photog. Art, Carmel, Calif., 2001-03, Monterey (Calif.) Mus. Art, 2005— Mem. IEEE (citation for contbn. 1981). Home: 33732 E Carmel Valley Rd Carmel Valley CA 93924 Personal E-mail: jim@kasson.com.

KASTAMA, JIM, state legislator; b. Bellingham, Wash., Oct. 5, 1959; m to Barbara; children: Isaac, Anna Laura, Sarah & Rachel. Washington State Representative, District 25, 96-2001, asst ranking minority member, Children & Family Serv, Judiciary & Technology, Telecommunications & Energy Committees, formerly, Washington House Representative; Washington State Senator, District 25, 2001-.Bus sales & management, formerly. Eastern Pierce Co Chamber of Commerce; Children's Rights Coun. Democrat. Address: 107 W Stewart St Ste E Puyallup WA 98371 Office: State Senate 402 John A Cherberg Bldg, PO Box 40425 Olympia WA 98504 Office Phone: 360-786-7968. E-mail: kastama_ja@leg.wa.gov.

KASTEN, KARL ALBERT, artist, printmaker, educator; b. San Francisco, Mar. 5, 1916; s. Ferdin and Barbara Anna Kasten; m. Georgette Gautier, Mar. 29, 1958; children: Ross, Lee, Beatrix, Joell, Cho-An. MA, U. Calif., 1939; postgrad., U. Iowa, 1949; student, Hans Hofmann Sch. Fine Arts, 1951. Instr. Calif. Sch. Fine Arts, 1941, U. Mich., 1946-47; asst. prof. art San Francisco State U., 1947-50; prof. U. Calif., Berkeley, 1950-83. Bibliography appears in Etching (Edmonston), 1973, Collage and Assemblage (Meilach and Ten Hoor), 1973, Modern Woodcut Techniques (Kuroski), 1977, California Style (McClelland and Last), 1985, Art in the San Francisco Bay Area (Albright), 1985, Breaking Type: The Art of Karl Kasten (Landauer), 1999, The Stamp of Impulse, Abstract Expressionist Prints (David Acton), 2001; group shows include San Francisco Mus. Art, 1939, Chgo. Art Inst., 1946, Whitney Mus., 1952, Sao Paolo Internat. Biennials, 1955, 61, Achenbach Found., 1976, World Print III Traveling Exhbn., 1980-83, Gallery Sho, Tokyo, 1994, Inst. Franco-Americain, Rennes, 1995, Calif. Heritage Gallery, 1999, Robert Green Fine Arts Gallery, 2002; patentee etching press. Capt. U.S. Army, 1942-46. Decorated 4 battle stars; fellow Creative Arts Inst., 1964, 71, Tamarind Lithography Artist Fellowship, 1968, Regents Humanities, 1977. Mem. Berkeley Art Ctr. Assn. (bd. dirs. 1987-92), Calif. Soc. Printmakers (Disting. Artist award 1997), Univ. Faculty Club, Univ. Arts Club. Home: 1884 San Lorenzo Ave Berkeley CA 94707-1841 Office: Univ Calif Berkeley Art Dept Berkeley CA 94707

KASTENBERG, WILLIAM EDWARD, engineering professor, former academic administrator; b. NYC, June 25, 1939; s. Murray and Lillian Kastenberg; m. Berna R. Miller, Aug. 18, 1963; children: Andrew, Joshua, Lillian; m. Gloria Hauser, May 3, 1992. BS, UCLA, 1962, MS, 1963; PhD, U. Calif., Berkeley, 1966. Asst. prof. Sch. Engring. and Applied Sci. UCLA, 1966-71, assoc. prof., 1971-75, assoc. dean Sch. Engring. and Applied Sci., 1981-85, chmn. mech. aerospace and nuc. engring., 1985-88, prof. mech., aerospace and nuc. engring. dept., 1975-94; sr. fellow U.S. NRC, Washington, 1979-80; prof. nuc. engring. dept. U. Calif., Berkeley, 1995—2007, chmn. nuc. engring. dept., 1995-2000, Chancellor's prof., 1996—99, Daniel Tellep disting. prof. engring., 1999—2009, prof. emeritus, 2008—. Guest scientist Karlsruhe Nuc. Rsch., Germany, 1972—73; mem. Nat. Rsch. Com. Reactor Safety, 1985—86; chmn. peer rev. com. U.S. NRC, Washington, 1987—88; mem. adv. com. nuc. facility safety Dept. of Energy, 1988—92; mem. adv. com. Diablo Canyon Nuc. Power Plant, 1999—2000; dir. risk and sys. analysis control toxics program UCLA, 1989—95, chmn. Ctr. Clean Tech., 1992—94; project dir. Ctr. Nuc. and Toxic Waste Mgmt. U. Calif., Berkley, 1995—2000; facilitator Emotional Body Enlightenment, 2006—; mem., bd. dirs. Project Theohumanity. Contbr. articles to profl. jours. Recipient Disting. Tchg. award, Am. Soc. Engring. Edn., 1973. Fellow: AAAS, Am. Nuc. Soc. (chmn. nuc. safety 1984—85, Arthur Holly Compton award); mem.: NAE. Office: Univ Calif Nuc Engring Dept 4155 Etcheverry Hall Berkeley CA 94720-1731 Office Phone: 510-643-0574. Personal E-mail: billkastenberg@mac.com. Business E-Mail: kastenbe@nuc.berkeley.edu.

KATAYAMA, ROBERT NOBUICHI, retired lawyer; b. Honolulu, Oct. 11, 1924; s. Sanji Katayama; married; children: Alice A. Katayama Jenkins, Robert Nobuichi Jenkins, Kent J. Jenkins, Susan H. Ono, Carole Y. Kaneshiro, Wendy L. Lee. BA, U. Hawaii, 1950; LLB, Yale U., New Haven, Conn., 1955; grad., Command and Gen. Staff Coll., 1964; LLM, George Washington U., Washington, DC, 1967; grad., Indsl. Coll. Armed Forces, 1971. Commd. 1st lt. JAGC U.S. Army, 1958, advanced through grades to col., 1973, ret., 1973; gen. counsel Overseas Mdse. Inspection Co., San Francisco, 1956-58, Army Contract Adjustment Bd., Washington, 1964-68; prof. law JAG Sch. U. Va., 1968—70; from assoc. to ptnr. Baker & McKenzie, Chgo., Tokyo and San Francisco, 1973-85; ptnr. Seki & Jarvis, San Francisco and San Jose, 1985-86, Nutter, McClennen & Fish, San Francisco, 1986-88; spl. counsel, sr. advisor Crosby, Heafey, Roach & May, Oakland, Calif., 1988; ptnr. Carlsmith Ball, Honolulu, 1988-95, counsel, 1994—2004, ret., 2004. Chmn., CEO Kapolei People's Inc. dba Kapolei Golf Course, Honolulu, 1996—99; pres. Kapolei Holding Corp., 1998—. Trustee Nat. Japanese Am. Meml. Found., 1995—97, gov., 1997—; mem. Hawaii Adv. Coun. to Japanese Am. Nat. Mus., 2001—03; bd. dirs. Japanese Cultural Ctr. Hawaii, 1997—98, bd. govs., 1998—. Recipient Disting. Alumni award, U. Hawaii, Honolulu, 2001; named Real Dean, 1950. Mem.: ABA, Ill. Bar Assn., 442d Regimental Combat Team Found. (trustee 1993—2004, pres. 1999—2002), Hawaii Army Mus. Soc. (trustee 2001—), Military Officers Assn. Am., Japanese Am. Soc. Legal Studies, Nat. Japanese Am. Hist. Soc. (legal officer 1984—89), Japan Am. Soc. Hawaii, Hawaii Bar Assn., Calif. Bar Assn., Oahu AJA Vets. Coun. (pres. 1997), Japanese C. of C. of No. Calif. (bd. dirs. 1987—89), 442d Vets. Club (legal advisor 1994—95, pres.-elect 1996, pres. 1997—98, legal advisor 2000—05, 1st v.p. 2006—08). Democrat. Buddhist. Home: 4389 Malia St Apt 553 Honolulu HI 96821 Personal E-mail: bobkata@earthlink.net.

KATCHER, JONATHON A., lawyer; b. Detroit, Oct. 2, 1954; BGS with distinction, Univ. Mich., 1976; JD, Lewis & Clark Coll., Portland, 1981. Asst. public defender State of Alaska, Anchorage, 1981—84; Supervising atty. Protection and Advocacy for Developmentally Disabled (PADD), Anchorage, 1984—85; Barrister I Alaska Inns of Court, Anchorage, 1993—2003; spec. edn. hearing officer State of Alaska, Dept. of Edn., 1990—. Mem.: ABA, Alaska Bar Assn. (pres. 2005—06). Office: Pope & Katcher Ste 220 421 W First Ave Anchorage AK 99501 Office Phone: 907-272-8577.

KATHREN, RONALD LAURENCE, health physicist; b. Windsor, Ont., Can., June 6, 1937; s. Ben and Sally (Forman) Kathren; m. Susan Ruth Krafft, Dec. 24, 1964; children: SallyBeth, Daniel, Elana(dec.). BS, UCLA, 1957; MSc, U. Pitts., 1962. Registered profl. engr., Calif.; diplomate Am. Bd. Health Physics. Health physicist Lawrence Radiation Lab. U. Calif., Livermore, 1962—67; mgr. external dose evaluation Battelle Pacific Northwest Labs., Richland, Wash., 1967—70, sr. rsch. scientist, 1970—72, staff scientist, program mgr., 1978—89; dir. US Transuranium and Uranium Registries Hanford Environ. Health Found., 1989—92; prof., dir. US Transuranium and Uranium Registries, Wash. State U., 1992—99, prof. emeritus, 1999—. US expert Internat. Atomic Energy Agy., Caracas, Venezuela, 1977; affiliate assoc. prof. U. Wash., 1978—94, program coord. radiol. scis., 1980—82, 1986—88, prof., 1994; cons. adv. com. Reactor Safeguards, Washington, 1979—89, Nuc. Waste, 1988—94; mem. adv. com. Richland City Schs., 1985—87; bd. dirs. Mid-Columbia Symphony, 1987—92; chmn. Nat. Coun. Radiation Protection and Measurements Sci. Com. Collective Dose, 1991—95; cons. Com. Environ. Radioactivity, 2005—. Author: Ionizing Radiation: Tumorigenic and Tumoricidal Effects, 1983, Radioactivity in the Environment, 1984, Radiation Protection, 1985, The Plutonium Story, 1994; co-editor (with others): Health Physics: A Backward Glance, 1980, Computer Applications in Health Physics, 1984, Environmental Health Physics, 1993, Radiation Protection Dosimetry, 1990—, Internat. Jour. Low Level Radiation, 2002—; contbr. numerous articles to profl. jours., tech. reports, chapters to books. Trustee Richland Pub. Libr. Found., 2003—04, 2008—, pres., 2004—08, Herbert M. Parker Found., 1987—, Master Gardner Found., 2004—06, Richland Players, 2007—09, Nev. Test Site Hist. Found., 2008—. Recipient Arthur Humm award, Nat. Registry Radiation Protection Technologists, 1988, Centennial Hartman Orator medal, 1995. Fellow: Health Physics Soc. (life; pres. Columbia chpt. 1971, dir. 1973—76, pres. 1989—90, Elda E. Anderson award 1977, Founders award 1985, Disting. Sci. Achievement award 2003, G. William Morgan Lectr. award 2006); mem.: NAS (com. on film badge dosimetry in atmospheric nuclear tests 1989, subcom. health effect depleted uranium 2005), Nat. Coun. Examiners Engring. and Surveying Com. on Exams. Profl. Engrs., Am. Acad. Environ. Engrs., Am. Bd. Health Physics (bd. dirs. 1982—84, sec.-treas. 1984), Am. Acad. Health Physics (bd. dirs. 1984—86, pres. 1993—96), Am. Assn. Physicists Medicine. Home: 137 Spring St Richland WA 99354-1651 Office: Wash State Univ 137 Spring Richland WA 99354-1641 Office Phone: 509-375-5643. Personal E-mail: kathren@bmi.net. Business E-Mail: rkathren@tricity.wsu.edu.

KATZ, CHARLES J., JR., lawyer; b. San Antonio, Mar. 25, 1948; AB, Stanford U., 1969; MA, N.Y.U., 1973; JD, U. Tex., 1976. Book review editor Tex. Law Review, 1975-76; mem. Perkins Coie, Seattle, 1982. Mem. Order of the Coif. Office: Perkins Coie 1201 3rd Ave Fl 40 Seattle WA 98101-3029

KATZ, DARYL A., pharmaceutical executive, entrepreneur, professional sports team executive; married; 2 children. BA, JD, U. Alberta. Chmn. Katz Group Inc., Edmonton, 1990—. Owner Edmonton Oilers, 2008—. Hon. adv. bd. mem. Anything Is Possible Tour. Mem.: Can. Coun. Chief Execs. Office: Katz Group of Companies Suite 1702 Bell Tower 10104-103rd Ave Edmonton AB Canada T5J 0H8 Office Phone: 780-990-0505. Office Fax: 780-702-0647.

KATZ, JASON LAWRENCE, lawyer, insurance executive; b. Chgo., Sept. 28, 1947; s. Irving and Goldie (Medress) K.; 2 children. B.A., Northeastern Ill. U., 1969; J.D., DePaul U., 1973. Bar: Calif. 1976, Ariz. 1973, U.S. Ct. Appeals (9th cir.) 1976. pvt. practice, Scottsdale, Ariz., 1973-76; v.p., corp. counsel Mission Ins. Group, Inc., Los Angeles, 1976-84; exec. v.p., gen. counsel Farmers Group, Inc., Los Angeles, 1984—, bd. dirs., 1986—; v.p., bd. dirs. Calif. Def. Counsel, 1986-88. Mem. Calif. Bar Assn. (exec. bd. ins. law subcom. 1991-94), Los Angeles County Bar Assn. (mem. exec. bd. corp. law sect. 1993-94), Conf. Ins. Counsel (v.p., pres. L.A. chpt. 1981-82), Assn. Calif. Tort Reform (bd. dirs. 1990-94), The Ins. Coun. So. Calif. (City of Hope chpt. 1991-94). Office: Farmers Group Inc 4680 Wilshire Blvd Los Angeles CA 90010-3807

KATZ, JOSEPH, aerospace engineer, educator; b. Budapest, Hungary, Apr. 10, 1947; BS, MS, Technion Israel Inst. Tech., Haifa, PhD, 1976. Rsch. assoc. NASA Ames, Moffett Field, Calif., 1978—80, 1984—86; prof. mech. engring. Technicu, Haifa, Ill., 1980—84; prof. San Diego State U., 1986—, chair, aerospace engring. dept., 1996—. Author: (books) various titles. Capt. Paratroops, 1966—69. Mem.: Soc. Automotive Engring., Aerospace Industries Assn. Am. (assoc.). Office: San Diego State Univ Aerospace Engring San Diego CA 92182

KATZ, RANDY H., electrical engineering, computer sciences educator; b. Aug. 19, 1955; AB, Cornell U., 1976; MS, U. Calif., Berkeley, 1978, PhD, 1980. With U. Wis., Madison; program mgr. Computing Sys. Tech. Office Def. Advanced Rsch. Projects Agy., office dep. dir.; with U. Calif., Berkeley, 1983-93, 94—, prof., chairperson dept. elec. engring. and computer sci., 1996—. Participant U.S. v.p. Al Gore's Nat. Performance Rev.; presenter sci. confs. Author: Contemporary Logic Design, 1993; contbr. articles to profl. publs. Mem. NAE. Office: Univ Calif Computer Sci Div 637 Soda Hall Berkeley CA 94720-0001 also: Univ Calif Adminstrv Office Cory Hall 1770 Rm 231 Berkeley CA 94720-0001 Office Phone: 510-642-8778, 510-642-4013. E-mail: randy@cs.berkeley.edu.

KATZ, ROGER, pediatrician, allergist, immunologist, educator; b. Menominee, Mich., Feb. 23, 1938; s. Peter W. and Mae C. (Chudacoff) Katz; children: Carl, Gary, Robyn. BS, U. Wis., 1960; MD, U. Louisville, 1965. Diplomate Am. Bd. Allergy and Immunology, Am. Bd. Pediatric Allergy, Am. Bd. Pediat. Clin. prof. pediat. UCLA, 1978—. Spkr. in field; expert legal evaluator. Author and editor sci. books and manuscripts. Maj. U.S. Army, 1970-72. Named One of Best Drs. in Am., 1996, 97, 2001, 02, 05. Fellow Am. Acad. Allergy, Asthma and Immunology, Am. Coll. Allergy, Asthma and Immunology (bd. regents 1990-93), Am. Acad. Pediat., Am. Coll. Chest Physicians, Joint Coun. Allergy, Asthma and Immunology (pres. 1986-90). Office: UCLA Med Ctr 11500 W Olympic Blvd #63 Los Angeles CA 90064 Office Phone: 310-393-1550.

KATZ, RONALD LEWIS, physician, educator; b. Bklyn., Apr. 22, 1932; s. Joseph and Belle (Charnis) K.; children: Richard Ian, Laura Susan, Margaret Karen. BA, U. Wis.-Madison, 1952; MD, Boston U., 1956; postgrad. in Pharmacology (NIH fellow), Coll. Physicians and Surgeons, Columbia U., 1959-60; postgrad. (John Simon Guggenheim fellow), Royal Postgrad. Med. Sch., U. London, 1968-69. Intern USPHS Hosp., SI, 1956-57; resident Columbia-Presbyn. Med. Center, 1957-60; asst. prof. anesthesiology Coll. Physicians and Surgeons, Columbia U., 1960-66, assoc. prof., 1966-70, prof., 1970-73; prof., chmn. dept. anesthesiology UCLA, 1973-90, prof. anesthesiology, 1990-94, chief staff Med. Ctr., 1984-86; prof., chmn. dept. anesthesiology U. So. Calif., LA, 1995—2000, prof., 1995—. Cons. NIH, FDA, numerous state agys. Author, editor: Muscle Relaxants, 1975; Contbr. numerous articles to profl. jours.; Mem. editorial bd.: Handbook of Anesthesiology, 1972—, Progress in Anesthesiology, 1973—; editor in chief Seminars in Anesthesia, 1982—. Mem. Am. Soc. Anesthesiologists, Am. Physiol. Soc., Am. Soc. Pharmacology and Exptl. Therapeutics, N.Y. Acad. Medicine; Faculty Anaesthetists of Royal Coll. Surgeons of Eng. Achievements include inventor peripheral nerve stimulator. Home: 2910 Neilson Way Apt 407 Santa Monica CA 90405-5323 Office: Harbor UCLA 1000 W Carson St Anesthesiology Box 10 Torrance CA 90509

KATZ, TONNIE, newspaper editor; BA, Barnard Coll., 1966; MSc, Columbia U., 1967. Editor, reporter newspapers including The Quincy Patriot Ledger, Boston Herald Am., Boston Globe; Sunday/projects editor Newsday; mng. editor Balt. News Am., 1983-86, The Sun, San Bernardino, Calif., 1986-88; asst. mng. editor for news The Orange County Register, Santa Ana, Calif., 1988-89, mng. editor, 1989-92, editor, v.p., 1992-98, editor, sr. v.p., 1998—2003. Office: Orange County Register 625 N Grand Ave Santa Ana CA 92701-4347

KATZ, TREUMAN P., health facility administrator; b. 1942; m. Sue Ellen Katz. Pres., CEO Children's Hosp. and Regional Med. Ctr., Seattle, 1979—2005, pres. emeritus, 2005—. Office: Children's Hosp and Regional Med Ctr 4800 Sand Point Way NE Seattle WA 98106

KATZ, VERA, former mayor, college administrator, state legislator; b. Dusseldorf, Germany, Aug. 3, 1933; came to U.S., 1940; d. Lazar Pistrak and Raissa Goodman; m. Mel Katz (div. 1985); 1 child, Jesse. BA, Bklyn. Coll., 1955, postgrad., 1955-57; PhD (hon.), Lewis & Clark Coll., Portland State U., Oreg. Market research analyst TIMEX,

B.T. Babbitt, NYC, 1957-62; mem. Oreg. Ho. of Reps., Salem, 1985—91; former dir. devel. Portland Community Coll.; mayor City of Portland, Oreg., 1992—2004. Mem. Gov.'s Council on Alcohol and Drug Abuse Programs, Oreg. Legis., Salem, 1985—; mem. adv. com. Gov.'s Council on Health, Fitness and Sports, Oreg. Legis., 1985—; mem. Gov.'s Commn. on Sch. Funding Reform; mem. Carnegie task Force on Teaching as Profession, Washington, 1985-87; vice-chair assembly Nat. Conf. State Legis., Denver, 1986—2003. Recipient Abigail Scott Duniway award Women in Communications, Inc., Portland, 1985, Jeanette Rankin First Woman award Oreg. Women's Polit. Caucus, Portland, 1985, Leadership award The Neighborhood newspaper Portland, 1985, Woman of Achievement award Commn. for Women, 1985, Outstanding Legis. Advocacy award Oreg. Primary Care Assn., 1985, Service to Portland Pub. Sch. Children award Portland Pub. Schs., 1985, Visionary Leadership award, 1998, Legal Citizen of Yr. award, 2002. Fellow Am. Leadership Forum (founder Oreg. chpt.); mem. Dem. Legis. Leaders Assn., Nat. Bd. for Profl. Teaching Standards. Democrat. Jewish. Avocations: camping, jogging, dance. Office: Office of the Mayor City Hall 1221 SW 4th Ave Rm 340 Portland OR 97204-1995

KATZEN, MOLLIE, writer; b. Rochester, NY, Oct. 13, 1950; d. Leon and Betty (Heller) K.; m. Jeffrey David Black, June 26, 1983 (div. Oct. 1985); 1 child, Samuel Katzen Black; m. Carl Shames, Dec. 12, 1986. BFA, San Francisco Art Inst., 1972. Author, illustrator: Mossewood Cookbook, 1977, Enchanted Broccoli Forest, 1982, Still Life with Menu, 1988, Molly Katzen's Still Life Sampler, 1993, Pretend Soup & Other Real Recipes: A Cookbook for Preschoolers & Up, 1994, Enchanted Broccoli Forest, 1995, Moosewood Cookbook Classics: Miniature Edition, 1996. Recipient Graphic Arts award Arnot Art Gallery, 1976, Cert. of Commendation, Calif. State Assembly, 1989. Jewish. Avocations: classical pianist, painter. Office: care Ten Speed Press PO Box 7123 Berkeley CA 94707-0123

KATZENBERG, JEFFREY, film company executive; b. NYC, Dec. 21, 1950; m. Marilyn Siegel, 1975; children: Laura, David. Asst. to chmn., chief exec. officer Paramount Pictures, NYC, 1975-77, exec. dir. mktg., 1977; v.p. programming Paramount TV, 1977-78; v.p., feature prodn. Paramount Pictures, 1978-80, sr. v.p., prodn. motion picture divsn., 1980—82, pres. prodn., motion pictures & TV, 1982—84; chmn. Walt Disney Studios, Burbank, Calif., 1984—94; co-founder (with Steven Spielberg & David Geffen), ptnr. Dream-Works SKG, Universal City, Calif., 1994—; CEO DreamWorks Animation, Inc., Glendale, Calif., 1994—. Chmn. Motion Picture and TV Fund; bd. dirs. Found. Motion Picture Pioneers; co-chmn. creative rights com. Directors Guild Am.; co-chmn. com. on profl. status of writers Writers Guild Am. Co-prodr.: Nightmare Before Christmas, 1993, exec. prodr.: Prince of Egypt, 1998, Road to El Dorado, 2000, Chicken Run, 2000, Joseph: King of Dreams, 2000, Shrek 2, 2004, Shark Take, 2004; prodr.: (films) Shrek, 2001, Spirit: Stallion of the Cimarron, 2002, Sinbad: Legend of the Seven Seas, 2003; exec. prodr.: (TV series) Father of the Pride, 2003, The Contender, 2005—. Bd. dirs. AIDS Project LA, Michael J. Fox Found. Parkinson's Rsch., Simon Wiesenthal Ctr., Calif. Inst. Arts, Cedars-Sinai Med. Ctr., Geffen Playhouse, Am. Mus. of Moving Image. Recipient Norma Zarky Humanitarian award, Women in Film, 2008; named one of 50 Most Powerful People in Hollywood, Premiere mag., 2005—06, 50 Smartest People in Hollywood, Entertainment Weekly, 2007. Office: Dreamworks SKG 1000 Flower St Glendale CA 91201-7500

KATZENSTEIN, ANDREW M., lawyer; b. Pa., Oct. 13, 1957; BA magna cum laude, U. Mich., 1979, JD cum laude, 1982; LLM in Taxation, U. San Diego, 1985. Bar: Calif. 1982, NY 1990, US Tax Ct. Ptnr. Katten, Muchin & Rosenman, LLP, LA. Tchr. estate tax UCLA Law Sch.; tchr. estate planning Golden Gate U. Grad. Tax Prog. Contbr. articles to profl. publs. Named a So. Calif. Super Lawyer, LA Mag. and So. Calif. Super Lawyers mag., 2004, 2005, 2006; named one of Top 100 Wealth Advs. in N.Am., Citywealth, 2006, Top 100 Attys., Worth mag., 2006. Mem.: Am. Coll. Trust and Estate Counsel, Am. Com. for Weizmann Inst. of Sci., LA County Bar Assn., Beverly Hills Bar Assn., Cure Diabetes Now. Office: Katten Muchin Rosenman Ste 2600 2029 Century Park E Los Angeles CA 90067-3012 also: Ste 450 260 Sheridan Ave Palo Alto CA 94306-2047 Office Phone: 310-788-4540. Office Fax: 310-712-8420. E-mail: andrew.katzenstein@kattenlaw.com.

KAUCHICH, JOHN STEVEN, oil and gas company executive; b. Rock Springs, Wyo., Feb. 1, 1943; s. Steve and Pauline (Martelok) K.; m. Georgia Rae Malicoat, Aug. 24, 1968; children: Bryan, Paul, Janet. BSEE, U. Wyo., 1965, MS in Indsl. Mgmt., Stats., 1967. Registered profl. engr., Wyo., Utah, Colo. Measurement and control engr. supr. Mountain Fuel Supply, Rock Springs, 1972-73, measurement and communication engr. supr., 1973-76, tech. services mgr., 1976, asst. gen. mgr. transmission, 1976-83, gen. mgr. transmission, 1983-84; gen. mgr. ops. Mountain Fuel Resources, Rock Springs, 1984-87, Questar Pipeline Co., Rock Springs, 1984—97; mgr. Questar Info-Comm Inc., Rock Springs, 1997—99; CEO Questar Baseline Ind., Rock Springs, 1998—99; ret., 1999. Bd. dirs. Am. Nat. Bank, Rock Springs, 1982—. Mem. operating com. S.W. Wyo. Indsl. Assn., Rock Springs;, Rock Springs Jaycees (v.p. 1970, pres. 1971-73), Rock Springs C. of C., Rock Springs Planning Zoning Comm. (vice-chmn. 1973-75), Rock Springs Housing Corp. (pres., bd. dirs., 1973-76), trustee Meml. Hosp. Sweetwater County; bd. dirs. Wyo. Community Devel. Authority, Casper, 1988-96. Mem. Wyo. Engring. Soc., Pacific Coast Gas Assn., U. Wyo. Alumni Assn. (life), Petroleum Assn. Wyo. (exec. com.), Rocky Mountain Oil & Gas Assn. Lodges: Elks. Home: 2036 Carson St Rock Springs WY 82901-6746

KAUFFMAN, GEORGE BERNARD, chemistry professor; b. Phila., Sept. 4, 1930; s. Philip Joseph and Laura (Fisher) K.; m. Ingeborg Salomon, June 5, 1952 (div. Dec. 1969); children: Ruth Deborah (Mrs. Martin H. Bryskier), Judith Miriam (Mrs. Mario L. Reposo); m. Laurie Marks Papazian, Dec. 21, 1969; stepchildren: Stanley Robert Papazian, Teresa Lynn Papazian Baron, Mary Ellen Papazian. BA with honors, U. Pa., 1951; PhD, U. Fla., 1956. Grad. asst. U. Fla., 1951-55; rsch. participant Oak Ridge Nat. Lab., 1955; instr. U. Tex., Austin, 1955-56; rsch. chemist Humble Oil & Refining Co., Baytown, Tex., 1956, GE, Cin., 1957, 59; asst. prof. chemistry Calif. State U., Fresno, 1956-61, assoc. prof., 1961-66, prof., 1966—. Guest lectr. coop. lecture tours Am. Chem. Soc., 1971; vis. scholar U. Calif., Berkeley, 1976, U. Puget Sound, 1978; dir. undergrad. rsch. participation program NSF, 1972. Author: Alfred Werner-Founder of Coordination Chemistry, 1966, Classics in Coordination Chemistry, Part I, 1968, Part II, 1976, Part III, 1978, Werner Centennial, 1967, Teaching the History of Chemistry, 1971, Coordination Chemistry: Its History through the Time of Werner, 1977, Inorganic Coordination Compounds, 1981, The Central Science: Essays on the Uses of Chemistry, 1984, Frederick Soddy (1877-1956): Early Pioneer in Radiochemistry, 1986, Aleksandr Porfirevich Borodin: A Chemists's Biography, 1988, Coordination Chemistry: A Century of Progress, 1994, Classics in Coordination Chemistry, 1995, Metal and Nonmetal Biguanide Complexes, 1999; contbr. articles to profl. jours.; contbg. editor: Jour. Coll. Sci. Tchg., 1973—, The Hexagon, 1980—. Polyhedron, 1983—85, Industrial Chemist, 1985—88, Jour. Chem. Edn., 1987—. Today's Chemist, 1989—91, The Chemical Intelligencer, 1994—2000, Today's Chemist at Work, 1995—, Chemical Heritage, 1996—, The Chemical Educator, 1998—, Chem. 13 News, 1998—, Pathways of Science, 2007—; guest editor: Coordination Chemistry Centennial Symposium (C3S) issue, Polyhedron, 1994; editor tape lecture series: Am. Chem. Soc., 1975—81. Named Outstanding Prof., Calif. State U. and Colls. Sys., 1973; recipient Exceptional Merit Svc. award, 1984, Meritorious Performance and Profl. Promise award, 1986-87, 88-89, Coll. Chemistry Tchr. Excellence award Mfg. Chemists Assn., 1976, Chugaev medal, 1976, Kurnakov medal, 1990, Chernyaev medal, 1991, USSR Acad. Sci., George C. Pimentel award in chem. edn. Am. Chem. Soc., 1993, Dexter award in history of chemistry, 1978, Marc-Auguste Pictet medal Soc. Physique et d'Histoire Naturelle de Genève, 1992, Pres.'s medal of Distinction, Calif. State U., Fresno, 1994, Rsch. award at an Undergraduate Instn., Am. Chem. Soc., 2000, Laudatory Decree Inst. History of Sci. and Tech. Russian Acad. Sci., 2000; Rsch. Corp. grantee, 1956-57, 57-59, 59-61, Am. Chem. Soc. Petroleum Rsch. Fund grantee, 1963-64, 69-70, NSF grantee, 1960-61, 63-64, 67-69, 76-77, NEH grantee, 1982-83; John Simon Guggenheim Meml. Found. fellow, 1972-73, grantee, 1975; Strindberg fellow Swedish Inst., Stockholm, 1983. Fellow: AAAS; mem.: Mensa, Am. Chem. Soc. (chmn. divsn. history of chemistry 1969, mem. exec. com. 1970, councilor 1976—78, George C. Pimentel award in chem. edn. 1993, Helen M. Free Pub. Outreach award 2002), Soc. History Alchemy and Chemistry, History of Sci. Soc., Assn. Univ. Pa. Chemists, AAUP, Gamma Sigma Epsilon, Alpha Chi Sigma, Phi Kappa Phi, Phi Lambda Upsilon, Sigma Xi. Home: 1609 E Quincy Ave Fresno CA 93720-2309 Office: Calif State U Dept Chemistry Fresno CA 93740-8034 Home Phone: 559-323-9123; Office Phone: 559-323-9123. Business E-Mail: georgek@csufresno.edu.

KAUFMAN, CHARLIE, scriptwriter; b. NY, Nov. 1958; m. Denise Kaufman. Student, Boston U., NYU. With circulation dept. Star Tribune, Mpls.; writer, 1991—. Author: (TV series) Get a Life, 1990, The Trouble with Larry, 1993, Ned and Stacey, 1995, The Dana Carvey Show, 1996, (screenplays) Being John Malkovich, 1999, Human Nature, 2001, Confessions of a Dangerous Mind, 2002, Adaptation, 2002, Eternal Sunshine of the Spotless Mind, 2004 (DC Film Critics award for best picture, 2004, DC Film Critics award for best original screenplay, 2004, Writers Guild of Am. award for best original screenplay, 2005, Academy award for best original screenplay, 2005), Synecdoche, New York, 2008 (Ind. Spirit award for Best First Feature, Film Ind., 2009); prodr.: (TV series) Ned and Stacey, 1995, Misery Loves Company, 1995; (films) Being John Malkovich, 1999, Human Nature, 2001, Adaptation, 2002; writer, prodr., dir. (films) Synecdoche, New York, 2008. Recipient L.A. Film Critics Assn. award, 1999, Boston Soc. Film Critics award, 1999, 2002, Toronto Film Critics Assn. award, 1999, 2002, San Diego Film Critics Soc. award, 1999, 2002, Saturn award, Acad. Sci. Fiction, Fantasy & Horror Films, 2000, BAFTA Film award, 2000, 2003, Chgo. Film Critics Assn. award, 2000, 2003, Ind. Spirit award, 2000, Nat. Soc. Film Critics award, 2000, Sierra award, Las Vegas Film Critics Soc., 2000, Online Film Critics Soc. award, 2000, 2003, ALFS award, London Critics Cir. award, 2001, Santa Fe Film Critics Cir. award, 2000, Nebula award, Sci. Fiction and Fantasy Writers Am., 2001, Nat. Bd. Rev. award, 2002, N.Y. Film Critics Cir. award, 2002, Southeastern Film Critics Assn. award, 2002, High Hopes award, Munich Film Festival, 2002, Fla. Film Critics Cir. award, 2003, Golden Satellite award, 2003, Broadcast Film Critics Assn. award, 2003; nominee Golden Globe award, 2000, 2003, Acad. award, 2000, 2003. Office: 9560 Wilshire Blcd 5th Fl Beverly Hills CA 90212

KAUFMAN, CHRISTOPHER LEE, lawyer; b. Chgo., Mar. 17, 1945; s. Charles R. and Violet-Page (Koteen) K.; m. Carlyn A. Clement, Jan. 25, 1986; children: Charles Alexander, Caroline Clement. BA, Amherst Coll., 1967; JD, Harvard U., 1970. Bar: Ill. 1970, Calif. 1972. Law clk. to judge U.S. Ct. Appeals (2d cir.), NYC, 1970-71; from assoc. to ptnr. Heller, Ehrman, White and McAuliffe, San Francisco, Palo Alto, Calif., 1974-90; ptnr. Latham & Watkins, Menlo Park, Calif., 1990—. Editor: Harvard Law Review., 1968-70. Mem. ABA (com. on negotiated acquisitions, com. on fed. regulation of securities). Office: Latham & Watkins LLP 140 Scott Dr Menlo Park CA 94025-1008 Business E-Mail: christopher.kaufman@lw.com.

KAUFMAN, DAVID GRAHAM, construction executive; b. North Canton, Ohio, Mar. 20, 1937; s. DeVere and Josephine Grace (Graham) Kaufman; m. Carol Jean Monzione, Oct. 5, 1957 (div. Aug. 1980); children: Gregory Allan, Christopher Patrick. Student, Kent State U., Ohio, 1956; grad., Internat. Corr. Schs., Scranton, Pa., 1965, NY Inst. Photography, NYC, 1983, Calif. Coast U., 1983—86. Cert. constrn. insp., constrn. project mgr., asbestos insp., lead insp., lead risk assessor, asbestos project designer, lock-out/tag-out, environ. insp., environ. specialist, environ. mgr., EPA cert. lead insp. and risk assessor, cert. concrete constrn. spl. inspector Am. Concrete Inst., cert. field testing technician Am. Concrete Inst., constrn. cons., environ. cons., concrete testing technician Am. Concrete Inst. Machinist apprentice Hoover Co., North Canton, Ohio, 1955-57; draftsman-designer Goodyear Aircraft Corp., Akron, Ohio, 1957-60, Boeing Co., Seattle, 1960-61; designer Berger Industries, Seattle, 1961-62, Puget Sound Bridge & Drydock, Seattle, 1963, C.M. Lovsted, Seattle, 1963-64, Tracy, Brunstrom & Dudley, Seattle, 1964, Rubens & Pratt Engrs., Seattle, 1965-66; founder, owner Profl. Drafting Svcs., Seattle, 1965, Profl. Take-Off Svcs., Seattle, 1966, Profl. Representation Svcs., Seattle, 1967; pres. Kaufman Inc., Seattle, 1967-83, Kaufman-Alaska Inc., Juneau, 1975-83, Kaufman-Alaska Constructors, Inc., Juneau, 1975-83; constrn. mgr. U. Alaska, 1979-84; constrn. cons. Alaskan Native and Eskimo Village Corps., 1984—; prin. Kaufman S.W. Assocs., N.Mex., 1984—, Graham Internat., 1992—, Parsons-Brinckernoff, Los Alamos, 2000—. Trustee advisor Kaufman Internat., Kaufman Group, Kaufman Enterprises. Mem.: Internat. Code Coun., Am. Welding Inst., Am. Concrete Inst., Am. Contractors Inst., Prodrs. Coun. Alaska, Prodrs. Coun. Hawaii, Prodrs. Coun. Idaho, Prodrs. Coun. Wash., Prodrs. Coun. Oreg., Associated Gen. Contractors Seattle Constrn. Coun., Internat. Conf. Bldgs. Ofcls., Assn. Constrn. Insps., Constrn. Specifications Inst., Environ. Assessment Assn., Portland C. of C., Toastmasters (past gov.), Nat. Eagle Scout Assn., Elks, Lions. Republican. Roman Catholic. Office: PO Box 458 Haines AK 99827-0458 also: PO Box 1781 Santa Fe NM 87504 Home: 505 Oppenheimer # 409 Los Alamos NM 87544

KAUFMAN, HAROLD RICHARD, mechanical engineer, physics educator; b. Audubon, Iowa, Nov. 24, 1926; s. Walter Richard and Hazel (Steere) K.; m. Elinor Mae Wheat, June 25, 1948; children: Brian, Karin, Bruce, Cynthia. Student, Evanston C.C., 1947-49; BSM.E., Northwestern U., 1951; PhD, Colo. State U., 1971. Researcher in aerospace propulsion NACA, Cleve., 1951-58; mgr. space propulsion research NASA, Cleve., 1958-74; prof. physics and mech. engring. Colo. State U., Ft. Collins, 1974-84, prof. emeritus, 1984—, chmn. dept. physics, 1979-84; pres. Kaufman & Robinson, Inc., Ft. Collins, 1984—; v.p. R&D Commonwealth Sci. Corp., Alexandria, Va., 1984-96. Pioneer in field of electron bombardment ion thruster, 1960; cons. ion source design and applications. Contbr. over 150 publs. and 35 patents in field. Served with USNR, 1944-46. Recipient NASA medal for exceptional sci. achievement, 1971. Fellow Am. Vacuum Soc. (Albert Nerken award 1991), AIAA (assoc. fellow, James H. Wyld Propulsion award 1969), Electric Rocket Propulsion Soc. (Outstanding Achievement in Electric Propulsion medal 2005); mem. Tau Beta Pi, Pi Tau Sigma. Office: Kaufman & Robinson Inc 1306 Blue Spruce Dr Ste A Fort Collins CO 80524-2067

KAUFMAN, IRVING, retired engineering educator; b. Geinsheim, Germany, Jan. 11, 1925; came to US., 1938, naturalized, 1945; s. Albert and Hedwig Kaufmann; m. Ruby Lee Dordek, Sept. 10, 1950; children— Eve Deborah, Sharon Anne, Julie Ellen. BE, Vanderbilt U., 1945; MS, U. Ill., 1949, PhD, 1957. Engr. RCA Victor, Indpls., Ind. and Camden, NJ, 1945-48; instr., research assoc. U. Ill., Urbana, 1949-56; sr. mem. tech. staff Ramo-Wooldridge & Space Tech. Labs., Calif., 1957-64; prof. engring. Ariz. State U., 1965-94, ret., 1994; founder, dir. Solid State Research Lab., 1968-78. Collaborator Los Alamos Nat. Lab., 1989, 91; vis. scientist Consiglio Nazionale delle Ricerche, Italy, 1973-74; vis. prof. U. Auckland, N.Z., 1974; liaison scientist U.S. Office Naval Rsch., London, 1978-80; lectr. and cons. elec. engring. Contbr. articles to profl. jours. and encys.; patentee in field. Recipient Disting. Research award Ariz. State U. Grad. Coll., 1986-87; Sr. Fulbright research fellow Italy, 1964-65, 73-74, Am. Soc. for Engring. Edn./Naval Rsch. Lab. fellow, 1988. Fellow IEEE (life, Phoenix sect. leadership award 1994); mem. Electromagnetics Acad., Gold Key (hon.), Sigma Xi, Tau Beta Pi, Eta Kappa Nu, Pi Mu Epsilon. Jewish.

KAUFMAN, JULIAN MORTIMER, broadcasting company executive, consultant; b. Detroit, Apr. 3, 1918; s. Anton and Fannie (Newman) K.; m. Katherine LaVerne Likins, May 6, 1942; children: Nikki, Keith Anthony. Grad., H.S., Newark. Pub. Elizabeth (N.J.) Sunday Sun, Inc., 1937-39; account exec. Tolle Advt. Agy., San Diego, 1947-49; pub. Tucson Shopper, 1948-50; account exec. ABC, San Francisco, 1949-50; mgr. Sta. KPHO-TV, Phoenix, 1950-52; gen. mgr., v.p. Bay City TV Corp., San Diego, 1952-95; v.p. Jai Alai Films, Inc., San Diego, 1961—; TV cons. Julian Kaufman, Inc., San Diego, 1985—. Dir. Spanish Internat. Broadcasting, Inc., L.A.; chmn. bd. dirs. Bay City TV Inc. Contbr. articles to profl. jours.; prodr. (TV show) Pick a Winner. Mem. Gov.'s adv. bd. Mental Health Assn., 1958—; bd. dirs. Francis Parker Sch., San Diego BBB, 1979-84, San Diego Conv. and Visitors Bur., World Affairs Coun., Pala Indian Mission. Served with USAAF, 1942-46. Recipient Peabody award, 1975, Emmy award, 1980. Mem. San Diego C. of C., Advt. and Sales Club, San Diego Press Club, Univ. Club (San Diego), Sigma Delta Chi. Republican. Home: 3125 Montesano Rd Escondido CA 92029-7302 Office: 7677 Ronsen Rd Ste 210 San Diego CA 92111-1538 Home Phone: 760-745-0258. E-mail: consultingjmk@aol.com, janoskj66@aol.com.

KAUFMAN, ROBERT, lawyer; b. NYC, July 15, 1937; BA, UCLA, 1959; JD, Southwestern Univ., 1963. Bar: Calif. 1964, US Ct. Appeals, Ninth Circuit 1975. Referee State Bar Cts. Calif., 1969—84; family law mediator LA Superior Ct., 1981—2000; family law atty. Kaufman, Young, Spiegel, Robinson & Kenerson, LLP, LA. Asst. prof. law Pepperdine U., Malibu, Calif., 1988—96; spkr. in field. Contbr. articles to numerous profl. jours. Mem.: ABA (Professionalism Committee of the Family Law Section 1993), Assn. Trial Lawyers in Am., Orange Co. Bar Assn., California State Bar Assn. (family law and litig. svcs. 1975—), LA Co. Bar Assn. (exec. com., Family Law Section 1992—93, judicial liaison com. 1992—93), Beverly Hills Bar Assn. Office: Kaufman Young Spiegel Robinson and Kenerson Ste 300 301 N Canon Dr Beverly Hills CA 90210-4724 Office Phone: 310-887-5100.

KAUFMAN, ROGER WAYNE, retired judge; b. Elizabeth, NJ, Aug. 27, 1938; s. Albert Henry and Selma Bernice (Cloner) K.; m. Lou Jan Erwin, Apr. 20, 1968; children: David Michael, Erin Anne. BA, Cornell U., 1960; JD, Harvard U., 1963. Bar: Ariz. 1964, U.S. Dist. Ct. Ariz. 1964, U.S. Ct. Appeals (9th cir.) 1965, U.S. Supreme Ct. 1971. Assoc. Lewis and Roca, Phoenix, 1963-68, ptnr., 1968-93; judge pro tem Superior Ct. State of Ariz. for Maricopa County, Phoenix, 1977-80; judge Maricopa County Superior Ct., Phoenix, 1993—, also chmn. alternative dispute resolution com., 1993-95, presiding judge Civil Dept., 1995-98, presiding judge Criminal Dept., 1998-2000. Chmn. Civil Jury Instrns. Com., 1993-96, Com. on Superior Ct.; mem. Ariz. Jud. Coun. Author: Arizona Courtroom Handbook, 1967, 70, Consent Manual, 1979. Mem. bd. visitors Ariz. State U. Law Sch., Tempe, 1979-85; bd. dirs. Bapt. Hosp. Found., Phoenix, 1980-83, Am. Cancer Soc., Phoenix, 1985-90. Mem. ABA, Ariz. Bar Assn. (bd. govs. 1979-81), Am. Judicature Soc., Ariz. Judges Assn. (sec., v.p., pres. 1995-96). Democrat. Home: 5188 Haystack Ct Park City UT 84098-7562

KAUFMAN, SANFORD PAUL, lawyer; b. NYC, Jan. 4, 1928; s. Max and Rose (Kornitzky) K.; m. Bernice R. Sulkis, June 17, 1956; children: Leslie Keith, Brad Leigh, Rona Sheryl, Jeffrey Scott, Adam Ira. BBA in Acctg., CCNY, 1948; LLB, NYU, 1952, LLM in Taxation, 1957. Bar: NY 1953, Calif. 1962. With firm Garey & Garey, NYC, 1953-55; asst. gen. counsel Olympic Radio & TV, L.I. City, NY, 1961-63; sec., gen. counsel Tel-Autograph Corp., LA, 1961-63; asst. gen. counsel Nat. Gen. Corp., LA, 1963-74; sec., gen. counsel Familian Corp., LA, 1974-77; pvt. practice Torrance, Calif., 1977—. Bd. dirs. Temple Ner Tamid, S. Bay, Calif. Mem. Am. Soc. Corp. Secs., Los Angeles County Bar Assn., Beverly Hills Bus. Men's Assn., K.P. Club (past chancellor). Home: 28412 Golden Meadow Dr Rancho Palos Verdes CA 90275-2926 Office: 23505 Crenshaw Blvd Ste 246 Torrance CA 90505-5223 Office Phone: 310-534-5901.

KAUPINS, GUNDARS EGONS, education educator; b. Mpls., Dec. 29, 1956; s. Alfreds and Skaidrite Kaupins; m. Debra Ann Queen, 1998; children: Amanda, Kyle. BA, Wartburg Coll., 1979; MBA, U. No. Iowa, 1981; PhD, U. Iowa, 1986. Sr. prof. in human resources. Grad. asst. U. No. Iowa, Cedar Falls, 1979-81, U. Iowa, Iowa City, 1981-86; prof. Boise State U., Idaho, 1986—, chair mgmt. dept.,

2007—. Cons. in field. Contbr. articles to profl. jours. Recipient rsch. grants Boise State U., 1987-2008, Ponder scholarship U. Iowa, 1983-85; named Adv. of the Yr., Boise State U., 1989; John Elorriaga fellow, 2005-. Mem. Soc. for Human Resource Mgmt. (faculty advisor 1986—). Avocations: racewalking, golf, racquetball, tennis, skiing. Home: 8475 W Beachside Ct Boise ID 83714 Office: Boise State U Dept Mgmt Boise ID 83725-0001 Office Phone: 208-426-4014. Business E-Mail: gkaupins@boisestate.edu.

KAVANAGH, JOHN, state legislator; m. Linda Kavanagh; children: Jonathan, Nicholas. BA in Liberal Arts, NYU; MA in Govt., St. John's U., Queens, NY; PhD in Criminal Justice, Rutgers U., NJ. Police officer NY Port Authority, NJ Police Dept.; instr. Ariz. State U.; criminal justice prof., dir. adminstrn. of justice studies & forensic sci. program Scottsdale Cmty. Coll., Ariz.; mem. Dist. 8 Ariz. House of Reps., 2007—, chair appropriations com. Former town coun. mem., Lafayette, NJ, Fountain Hills, Ariz. Mem.: Friends of C. of C., Hist. Soc., Civic Assn., Am. Legion, Fountain Hills Rep. Club. Republican. Office: Ariz House Reps Capitol Complex 1700 W Washington Rm 114 Phoenix AZ 85007 Office Phone: 480-837-5612, 602-926-5170. Office Fax: 602-417-3108. Business E-Mail: jkavanagh@azleg.gov. E-mail: drjohnkavanagh@ cox.net.*

KAVANAUGH, MICHAEL C., environmental engineer; V.p. Malcolm Pirnie, Inc., Oakland, Calif., 1997—. Mem. NAE. Office: Malcolm Pirnie Inc Ste 1180 2000 Powell St Emeryville CA 94608-1856

KAVLI, FRED, retired manufacturing and engineering executive, physicist; b. Norway, Aug. 20, 1927; came to U.S., 1956; Grad. in physics, Norwegian Inst. Tech., 1955. Founder, CEO, sole shareholder automotive and aerospace sensor engrng.-mfg. Kavlico Corp., Moorpark, Calif., 1958—2000; ret. Bd. dirs. The Found. for Santa Barbara City Coll.; trustee Found. for U. Calif., Santa Barbara; founder, chmn. The Kavli Found./The Kavli Operating Inst.; benefactor The Kavli Insts. (in neuroscience) at Columbia U., Yale U., UC San Diego, Norwegian U. Sci. & Tech; (in astrosci.) Stanford U. Chgo., MIT, Peking U., U. Cambridge; (in nanosci.) Harvard U., Caltech, Cornell U., Delft U. Tech.; (in theoretical physics) UC Santa Barbara, Chinese Acad. Sci; 2000 - mem. Pres. Bd. sci. and innovation, U. Calif.; endowed several chairs, one in engrng. at the U. Calif., Santa Barbara, another chair in Optoelectronics and Sensors, U. Calif., Irvine, in Nano-systems Sciences at UCLA, and Cosmology, Calif. Inst. Tech. Recipient Royal Norwegian Order of Merit for Outstanding Svc., 2005; named Disting. Grand Patron, Alliance of the Arts, 1998, Disting. Grand Patron of the Alliance for the Arts, in honor of the Fred Kavli Theatre for Performing Arts at the Thousand Oak Civic Arts Plaza, Scientific American 50: Policy Leader Yr., 2005. Fellow: Am. Acad. Arts & Sciences; mem.: Norwegian Acad. Technological Scis., US President's Coun. Advisors on Sci. and Tech. (PCAST). Achievements include patents in field. Office Fax: 805-988-4800.

KAWACHIKA, JAMES AKIO, lawyer; b. Honolulu, Dec. 5, 1947; s. Shinichi and Tsuyuko (Murashige) K.; m. Karen Keiko Takahashi, Sept. 1, 1973; 1 child, Robyn Mari. BA, U. Hawaii, Honolulu, 1969; JD, U. Calif., Berkeley, 1973. Bar: Hawaii 1973, U.S. Dist. Ct. Hawaii 1973, U.S. Ct. Appeals (9th cir.) 1974, U.S. Supreme Ct. 1992. Dep. atty. gen. Office of Atty. Gen. State of Hawaii, Honolulu, 1973-74; assoc. Padgett, Greeley & Marumoto, Honolulu, 1974-75, Law Office of Frank D. Padgett, Honolulu, 1975-77, Kobayashi, Watanabe, Sugita & Kawashima, Honolulu, 1977-82; ptnr. Carlsmith, Wichman, Case, Mukai & Ichiki, Honolulu, 1982-86, Bays, Deaver, Hiatt, Kawachika & Lezak, Honolulu, 1986-95; propr. Law Offices of James A. Kawachika, Honolulu, 1996—2002; ptnr. Reinwald, O'Connor & Playdon LLP, Honolulu, 2002—. Mem. Hawaii Bd. of Bar Examiners, Honolulu; arbitrator Cir. Ct. Arbitration Program State of Hawaii, Honolulu, 1986— Chmn. disciplinary bd. Hawaii Supreme Ct., 1991-97; adv. com. civil justice reform act 1990 US Dist. Ct., 1991—; bd. dir. Hawaii Justice Found., 2004—, pres., 2007—. Mem. ABA (ho. of dels., standing com. ethics and profl. responsibility, 2004-07), Am. Judicature Soc. (bd. dirs. Hawaii chpt. 2003-), Hawaii State Bar Assn. (bd. dirs. 1975-76, young lawyers sect. 1983-84, 92-93, treas. 1987-88, v.p./pres.-elect 1997-98, pres. 1998-99), 9th Cir. Jud. Conf. (lawyer rep. Honolulu chpt. 1988-90), Legal Aid Soc. Hawaii (bd. dirs. 2005—08). Avocations: running, tennis, skiing. Office: Pacific Guardian Ctr Makai Tower 733 Bishop St 24th Flr Honolulu HI 96813-4070 Home Phone: 808-373-1608; Office Phone: 808-524-8350. Business E-Mail: jak@roplaw.com.

KAWAMOTO, CALVIN KAZUO, state legislator; b. Pepeekeo, Hawaii, Apr. 14, 1940; m. Carolyn Kawamoto; children: Walter, Nina. BA, U. Hawaii, 1963; postgrad., No. Mich. U.; D, Oreg. State U. Mem. Hawaii Senate, Dist. 18, Honolulu, 1994—; chair transp. and mil. affairs, govt. ops. Hawaii Senate, Honolulu, 1996—, mem. ways and means com., mem. econ. devel. com., 1994—, sen. mil. liaison, 1994—, mem. edn. com., agrl. com., labor com., majority fl. leader. Exec. dir. Waipahu Cmty. Found.; dir. Waipahu Bus. Assn., Wahiawa Hosp. Bd., Rural Oahu Family Bd., Waianae Coast Comprehensive Ctr., Am. Box Car Racing Internat.; mem. Pearl City H.S., Manana Elem. PTA, Kanoelani Elem. PTA, Aiea/Pearl City Bus. Assn., Waipahu H.S.; mem. mgmt. coun. Waipahu H.S. Budget Com.; exec. dir. Waipahu Cmty. Adult Day Health Ctr. and Youth Ctr.; exec. dir., v.p. Waipahu Cmty. Found. With USAF. Recipient award Waipahu Pride, Eagle Scout, 1958; decorated Disting. Flying Cross, thirteen air medals. Mem. VFW (judge advocate). Democrat. Office: State Capitol 415 S Beretania St Honolulu HI 96813-2407

KAWAMOTO, HENRY KATSUMI, JR., plastic surgeon; b. Long Beach, Calif., Jan. 19, 1937; AA, East LA Coll., 1956; DDS, U. So. Calif., 1960, MD, 1964. Cert. Am. Bd. Surgery, 1972, Am. Bd. Plastic Surgery, 1976. Intern U. Calif. Hosp., LA, 1964—65; resident gen. surgery Columbia Presbyn. Med. Ctr., NYC, 1965—71; resident plastic surgery Inst. Reconstructive Plastic Surgery, NYU, 1971—73; fellow crano-facial surgery Dr. Paul Tessier, L' Hôpital Foch and Clinique Belvédère, Paris, 1973—74; joined UCLA Craniofacial Clinic, 1975, dir., chief pediatric plastic surgery emeritus; clin. prof. plastic and reconstructive surgery UCLA, LA; chief plastic surgery So. Calif. Sys. Clinics (formerly Sepulveda VA Hosp.). Spkr. in field. Contbr. articles to med. jours. Fellow: ACS; mem.: AMA, Childrens Craniofacial Assn. (med. adv. bd.), Am. Bd. Plastic Surgery (mem. Com. on Credential and Requirements, Com. on Rectification, chmn. Com. on Rectification), Am. Soc. Plastic and Reconstructive Surgeons (past historian and chmn. bd. trustees), Internat. Soc. Craniofacial Surgeons (founding mem., councilor), Am. Cleft Palate Assn., So. Calif. State Dental Assn., LA County Med. Assn., Calif. Soc. Plastic Surgeons, Am. Soc. Craniofacial Surgeons (founding mem.), Am. Soc. Maxillofacial Surgeons (past pres.), Am. Assn. Plastic Surgeons (Membership Com.). Office: 1301 20th St Ste 460 Santa Monica CA 90404-2054 Office Phone: 310-829-0391.

KAWAMURA, GEORGINA K., state treasurer, finance company executive; b. Lanai City, Hawaii, Sept. 19, 1952; m. Gary Kawamura, 1973; children: Bryan, Jon. AA in Acctg., Maui CC. Clk. to office mgr., budget dir. Maui (Hawaii) County Mayor's Office, 1987—88; planner Castle and Cooke Resorts, Lanai, Hawaii, 1998—2002; dir. fin. Dept. Budget and Fin., Hawaii, 2002—. Avocations: hula, reading. Office: Dept Budget and Fin PO Box 150 Honolulu HI 96810-0150

KAWASAKI, GUY, venture capitalist, investment banker, entrepreneur; b. Honolulu, Hawaii, 1954; m. Beth Kawasaki; 4 children. BA in Psychology, Stanford U., 1976; MBA, UCLA, 1979; attended, U Calif. Davis Sch. Law, 1977, Billy Graham Sch. Envangelism, 1990; PhD (hon.), Babson Coll., 2003. V.p. mktg. Nova Stylings, Inc., LA, 1977—83; dir. mktg. Eduware Services (acquired by Peachtree Software), Agoura Hills, Calif., 1983; software evangelist, dir. software product mgmt. Apple Computer, Inc., Cupertino, Calif., 1983—87, chief envangelist, 1995—97; CEO ACIUS, Cupertino, Calif., 1987—89, Fog City Software, 1993—95; ind. author, spkr., Forbes columnist, 1989—93; mng. dir. Garage Tech. Ventures, Palo Alto, Calif., 1997—. Bd. dir. Razz, FilmLoop, BitPass; advisor Kaboodle, Coghead, Simply Hired, TripWire. Frequent appearances on TV and radio including CNBC Power Lunch, CNN and Bloomberg; author: Hindsights: The Wisdom and Breakthroughs of Remarkable People, The Macintosh Way, How To Drive Your Competition Crazy, Selling the Dream, Rules for Revolutionaries: The Capitalist Manifesto for Creating and Marketing New Products and Services, The Art of the Start: The Time-Tested, Battle-Hardened Guide for Anyone Starting Anything; maintains blog website blog-.guykawasaki.com, columnist Entrepreneur mag. Former bd. dir. Stanford Alumni Assn.; bd. dir. Hawaiian Island Ministry; bd. trustee Bowman Internat. Sch. Named to Technorati 100. Office: Garage Technology Ventures 360 Bryant St Ste 100 Palo Alto CA 94301-1474 Office Phone: 650-354-1854. E-mail: kawasaki@garage.com.

KAY, ALAN C., computer scientist, nonprofit organization executive; b. Springfield, Mass., May 17, 1940; m. Bonnie MacBird. BS in Math., Molecular Biology, U. Colo., 1966; MSEE with distinction, U. Utah, 1968, PhD in Computer Sci. with distinction, 1969; PhD (hon.), Kungl Tekniska Hoegskolan, Stockholm, Ga. Inst. Tech., 2005; LHD (hon.), Columbia Coll., Chgo., 2005. Researcher Stanford Artificial Intelligence Lab., 1969—71, instr., 1970; group leader, principal scientist, Xerox Fellow Xerox Palo Alto Rsch. Ctr., Calif., 1971—81; chief scientist Atari, 1981—84; fellow Apple Computer, Brentwood, Calif., 1984-96; computer tchr. Open School, West Hollywood; fellow Walt Disney Imagineering, 1997—2001, v.p., rsch. & devel., 1996—2001; sr. fellow Hewlett-Packard Labs., 2002—05; adj. prof. computer sci. UCLA Henry Samueli Sch. Engrng. and Applied Sci., 2002—; vis. prof. Kyoto U., Japan; pres., founder Viewpoints Rsch. Inst., Glendale, Calif., 2001—. Recipient Turing award, Assn. for Computing Machinery, 2003, Systems Software award, Edn. award, Assn. for Computing Machinery SIGCSE, Outstanding Contributions to Computer Sci. Edn., J-D Warnier Prix d'Informatique, NEC Computers & Communications Found. prize, Funai prize, Lewis Branscomb Tech. award, Fellow award, Computer History Mus., 1999; co-recipient Kyoto prize for Advanced Tech., Inamori Found., 2004. Fellow AAAS, NAE (co-recipient, Charles Stark Draper prize, 2004), Royal Soc. Arts; named to Computer History Mus. Achievements include invention of Dynabook; creator of Smalltalk, the first complete dynamic object-oriented programming (OOP) language; created an early model of the laptop computer and contributed. to the development of graphical user interfaces, Ethernet, laser printing, and the "client-server" and peer-peer networking model. Avocations: keyboards, guitar, pipe organist. Office: Viewpoints Rsch Inst 1209 Grand Central Ave Glendale CA 91201 Office Phone: 818-332-3000. Office Fax: 818-244-9761.

KAY, CYRIL MAX, biochemist, educator; b. Calgary, Alta., Can., Oct. 3, 1931; s. Louis and Fanny (Pearlmutter) K.; m. Faye Bloomenthal, Dec. 30, 1953; children: Lewis Edward, Lisa Franci. B.Sc. in Biochemistry with honors (J.W. McConnell Meml. scholar), McGill U., 1952; PhD in Biochemistry (Life Ins. Med. Research Fund fellow), Harvard U., 1956; postgrad., Cambridge U., Eng., 1956-57. Phys. biochemist Eli Lilly & Co., Indpls., 1957-58; asst. prof. biochemistry U. Alta., Edmonton, 1958-61, assoc. prof., 1961-67, prof., 1967—, co-dir. Med. Rsch. Coun. Group on Protein Structure and Function, 1974-95, mem. protein engrng. network Centre of Excellence, 1990—, chmn. internat. rsch. adv. com. to protein engrng. network Centre of Excellence, 2000—; v.p. rsch. Alta. Cancer Bd., 1999—. Med. Rsch. Coun. vis. scientist in biophysics Weizmann Inst., Israel, 1969-70, summer vis. prof. biophysics, 1975, summer vis. prof. chem. physics, 1977, 80; mem. biochemistry grants com. Med. Research Council, 1970-73; mem. Med. Rsch. Coun. Can., 1982-88; Can. rep. Pan Am. Assn. Biochem. Socs., 1971-76; mem. exec. planning com. XI Internat. Congress Biochemistry, Toronto, Ont., Can., 1979; mem. med. adv. bd. Gairdner Found. for Internat. awards in Med. Sci., 1980-89; chmn. Internat. Scientific adv. com. on protein engrng., 2000—. Contbr. numerous articles to profl. publs.; asso. editor Can. Jour. Biochemistry, 1968-82; editor-in-chief Pan Am. Assn. Biochem. Socs. Revista, 1971-76. Recipient Ayerst award in biochemistry Can. Biochem. Soc., 1970, Disting. Scientist award U. Alta. Med. Sch., 1988, Outstanding Contbn. to Alta. Sci. and Tech. Cmty. award, 2006. Fellow NY Acad. Scis., Royal Soc. Can.; mem. Order of Can. (decorated mem. 1995, officer 2006), Can. Biochem. Soc. (coun. 1971—, v.p. 1976-77, pres. 1978-79). Home: 9408-143d St Edmonton AB Canada T5R 0P7 Office: U Alta Dept Biochemistry Med Scis Bldg Edmonton AB Canada T6G 2H7 Office Phone: 780-492-4549. Business E-Mail: ckay@ualberta.ca.

KAY, HERMA HILL, law educator; b. Orangeburg, SC, Aug. 18, 1934; d. Charles Esdorn and Herma Lee (Crawford) Hill. BA, So. Meth. U., 1956; JD, U. Chgo., 1959. Bar: Calif. 1960, U.S. Supreme Ct. 1978. Law clk. to Hon. Roger Traynor Calif. Supreme Ct., 1959-60; from asst. prof. to assoc. prof. law U. Calif., Berkeley, 1960-62, prof., 1963, dir. family law project, 1964-67, Jennings prof., 1987-96, dean, 1992-2000, Armstrong prof., 1996—; co-reporter uniform marriage and div. act Nat. Conf. Commrs. on Uniform State Laws, 1968-70. Vis. prof. U. Manchester, England, 1972, Harvard U., 1976; mem. Gov.'s Commn. Family, 1966. Author (with D. Currie, L. Kramer and K. Roosevelt): Conflict of Laws: Cases, Comments, Questions, 7th edit., 2006; author: (with Martha S. West) Sex-Based Discrimination: Text, Cases and Materials, 6th edit., 2005; contbr. articles to profl. jours. Trustee Russell Sage Found., NY, 1972—87, chmn. bd. trustees NY, 1980—84; trustee, bd. dirs. Equal Rights Advs., Calif., 1987—88, chmn. Calif., 1976—83; pres. bd. dirs. Rosenberg Found., Calif., 1987—88, bd. dirs. Calif., 1978—. Recipient Rsch. award, Am. Bar Found., 1990, Margaret Brent award, ABA Commn. Women in Profession, 1992, Marshall-Wythe medal, 1995; fellow, Ctr. Advanced Study Behavioral Sci., Palo Alto, Calif., 1963. Mem.: ABA (sect. legal edn. and admissions to bar coun. 1992—99, sec. 1999—2001), Order of Coif (nat. pres. 1983—85), Am. Philos. Soc., Am. Acad. Arts and Scis., Assn. Am. Law Schs. (exec. com. 1986—87, pres.-elect 1988, pres. 1989, past pres. 1990), Am. Law Inst. (mem. coun. 1985—), Calif. Women Lawyers (bd. govs. 1975—77), Bar U.S. Supreme Ct., Calif. Bar Assn. Democrat. Office: U Calif Law Sch Boalt Hall Berkeley CA 94720-7200 Home Phone: 415-391-5158; Office Phone: 510-643-2671. Business E-Mail: hkay@law.berkeley.edu.

KAY, KENNETH JEFFREY, hotel executive; b. LA, Apr. 2, 1955; s. Morton M. and Beverly J. Kay. BS in Acctg., U. So. Calif., 1978, MBA in Fin., 1980. CPA, Calif. Staff acct. in charge Price Waterhouse and Co. (now PriceWaterhouse Coopers LLC), Century City, Calif., 1980-82; mgr. acctg. TRW-Fujitsu Co., LA, 1982-83; corp. controller Ameron Internat., Pasadena, Calif., 1983-88, sr. v.p. fin. and adminstrn., CFO, 1990-92, group v.p., 1992-94; pres., CEO, dir. Bishop, Inc., Westlake Village, Calif., 1988-90; sr. v.p. fin. and adminstrn., CFO Systemed, Inc., Torrance, Calif., 1994-96; sr. v.p., CFO Playmates Inc., Costa Mesa, Calif., 1997; exec. v.p., CFO Universal Studios Consumer Products Group, Universal City, Calif., 1998-99; v.p., CFO Dole Food Co., Inc., Westlake Village, Calif., 1999—2002; sr. exec. v.p., CFO CB Richard Ellis Group, Inc., LA, 2002—. Chmn. supervisory com. Ameron Fed. Credit Union, South Gate, Calif., 1986. Bd. govs. Cedars-Sinai Med. Ctr.; mem. exec. com. Friends for Life, LA; mem. bd. dirs. Paralysis Project Am.; mem. bd. advisors U. So. Calif. Leven Sch. Acctg. Mem. AICPA, Am. Mgmt. Assn., Calif. Soc. CPAs, Assn. for Strategic Planning, Fin. Execs. Inst. Office: Las Vegas Sands Corp 3355 Las Vegas Blvd Las Vegas NV 89109*

KAY, MARK ALLAN, medical educator; BS in Phys. Sciences, Mich. State U., 1980; PhD in Develop. Genetics, Case Western Reserve U., 1986, MD, 1987. Diplomate Am. Bd. Pediat., Am. Bd. Med. Genetics in Clin. Biochemical Genetics and clin. genetics. Intern. resident, dept. pediat. Baylor Coll. Medicine, Houston, 1987—90, clin. fellow, med. genetics, 1990—93; acting asst. prof., dept. medicine U. Wash., 1993, asst. prof., dept medicine, investor. Molecular Medicine Ctr., 1993—94, adj. asst. prof., dept. pediat., 1994, adj. asst. prof., dept. biochemistry, 1995, adj. asst. prof., dept. pathology, 1995, assoc. prof. medicine with adjuncts in pediat., biochemistry and pathology, 1997—98; assoc. prof., dept. pediat. and genetics Stanford U. Sch. Medicine, 1998, dir., program in human gene therapy, 1998—, prof., dept. pediat. and genetics, 2001—. Invited spkr. in field; mem. scientific review bd. Nat. Gene Vector Lab., 1996—; ad-hoc reviewer NIH, 1997—2000; mem. scientific planning bd. German-Am. Frontiers of Sci. sponsored by Nat. Acad. Sci., 1997—98; NIH Study Sect. mem.-med. biochemistry, 2000—04; mem. com. on gene therapy for genetic diseases European Soc. for Gene Therapy, 2000—01; chair, organizing com. Gordon Conf. on Viral Vectors for Gene Therapy, 2003—04; co-founder, chief scientific advisor Avocel, 2003—. Mem. editl. bd. Gene Therapy, 1995—, Human Gene Therapy, 1995—, assoc. editor, 2000—, mem. editl. bd. Molecular Therapy, 1999—2003; contbr. several articles to profl. jours. Recipient Arthur F. Hughes Meml. award for Outstanding Rsch. in Develop. Biology, 1986, Upjohn Achievement award-Excellence in Clin. Pharmacology, 1987, Henry Christian award for Excellence in Rsch., Am. Fedn. for Clin. Rsch., 1992, Student award for best paper in category of post-doctoral-basic sciences, Am. Soc. Human Genetics, 1992, E. Mead Johnson award for Pediat. Researcher of the Yr., 2000, Nat. Hemophilia Found. Researcher of the Yr., 2000. Mem.: Am. Soc. for Clin. Investigation, Am. Soc. Microbiology, Am. Soc. Gene Therapy (bd. dirs. 1997—2000, founding bd. dirs. 1997—2000, chair. com. on genetic diseases 2001—03, v.p. 2003—04, pres.-elect 2004—05), Western Soc. for Clin. Investigation, AAAS, Am. Acad. Pediat., Am. Soc. Human Genetics, Japanese Soc. Inherited Metabolic Disease (hon.), Phi Kappa Phi. Office: Dept Pediat and Genetics Stanford U Sch Medicine 300 Pasteur Dr Rm G-305A Stanford CA 94305-5208 Office Phone: 650-498-6531. Office Fax: 650-498-6540. Business E-Mail: markay@stanford.edu.*

KAY, PAUL DE YOUNG, linguist; b. NYC, Nov. 7, 1934; s. William de Young and Alice Sarah Kay; m. Patricia Boehm, Feb. 13, 1934; children: Yvette, Suzanne de Young. BA in Econs., Tulane U., 1955; PhD in Anthropology, Harvard U., 1963. Asst. prof. MIT, Cambridge, 1964-65; assoc. prof., prof. Dept. Anthropology U. Calif., Berkeley, 1966-83, prof. Dept. Linguistics, 1983—, chmn. dept., 1986-91. Author: Words and the Grammar of Context, 1997; editor: Explorations in Mathematical Anthropology, 1971; co-author: Basic Color Terms, 1969; contbr. articles to Lang., Linguistic Inquiry, Foundations of Language, Linguistics and Philosophy, Lang. and Soc., Am. Anthropologist, Current Anthropology, Jour. of Linguistic Anthropology Grammars, Psychol. Scis., Procs. Nat. Acad. Sci., Cognition, others. Fellow Ctr. Advanced Study in Behavioral Scis., Stanford, Calif., 1965-66, Guggenheim Found., U. Hawaii, Oahu, 1972-73. Mem.: NAS, Am. Psychol. Soc., Soc. for Linguistic Anthropology (pres. 1988—89), Am. Anthrop. Assn., Linguistic Soc. Am. Office: Internat Computer Sci Inst 1947 Center St Ste 600 Berkeley CA 94704-1198 Office Phone: 510-666-2885. Business E-Mail: paulkay@berkeley.edu.

KAYE, JHANI, radio station executive, television producer and director; b. Maywood, Calif., June 18, 1949; s. Jimmie Eccak and Betty Jo (Holland) Kazaroff. BA, UCLA, 1971. Music dir. Sta. KFXM, San Bernardino, Calif., 1969-73; announcer Stas. KUTE-FM/KKDJ-FM, LA, 1972-74; asst. program dir. Sta. KROQ, LA, 1973-74, Sta. WCFL, Chgo., 1980-82, Sta. KFI, LA, 1982; program dir. Sta. KINT-FM, El Paso, Tex., 1975-80; sta. mgr., program dir. Sta. KOST-FM, LA, 1982-99; program dir. Sta. KBIG-FM, Glendale, Calif., 1999—2003, sta. mgr., 1999—2003. Dir. adult contemporary programming Clear Channel Radio, 1999—; owner Los Feliz Post Prodn. Video Svcs.; on-air host Radio Medium, radio program. Appeared in TV series Falcon Crest, 1985, Drew Carey Show, 1998; dir. TV commls., 1986—; voice-over motion picture The Couch Trip, 1987; dir., video editor Dick Clark TV Commls. Recipient Marconi Radio awards Nat. Assn. Broadcasters, 1990, 91. Office: Sta KBIG-FM 3400 West Olive Ave Ste 550 Burbank CA 91505 Office Phone: 818-566-4722. E-mail: jhanikaye@clearchannel.com.

KAYE, PETER FREDERIC, columnist; b. Chgo., Mar. 8, 1928; s. Ralph A. and Sara Corson (Philipson) K.; m. Martha Louise Wood, Mar. 20, 1955; children: Loren, Terry, Adam. BA in Govt., Pomona Coll., 1949. Reporter Alhambra (Calif.) Post-Advocate, 1950-53;

reporter, editorial writer, polit. writer The San Diego Union, 1953-68; news and pub. affairs dir. KPBS-TV, San Diego State Coll., 1968-72; corr., producer Nat. Pub. Affairs Ctr. for TV, Washington, 1972-74; comm. dir. So. Calif. First Nat. Bank, San Diego, 1974-75; press sec. The Pres. Ford Com., Washington, 1975-76; mgr. Copley Videotex, San Diego, 1982-84; assoc. editor The San Diego Union, 1976-94; edtl. dir. KNSD, San Diego, 1996-99. Freelance TV producer programs KPBS, PBS, BBC; San Diego corr. Newsweek, 1968-71, McGraw-Hill, 1959-67; lectr. comm. U. Calif., San Diego, 1971; copywriter Washburn-Justice Advt., San Diego, 1959-70. Producer 10 TV programs including including Jacob Bronowski: Life and Legacy, Twenty-Five Years of Presidency, The Presidency, The Press and the People. Press asst. Eisenhower-Nixon Campaign, L.A., 1952; asst. press sec. Richard Nixon Presdl. Campaign, Washington, 1960; dir. Pete Wilson for Mayor Campaign, San Diego, 1971; comm. dir. Flournoy for Gov. Campaign, Beverly Hills, Calif., 1974. With U.S. Mcht. Marines, 1945, U.S. Army, 1950-52. Jefferson fellow East-West Ctr., Honolulu, 1987; recipient Golden Mike awards So. Calif. TV News Dirs. Assn., 1969, 70, 71, Best Pub. Affairs Program award Nat. Ednl. TV, 1970, Best Local TV Series award Radio-TV Mirror, 1971, Nat. Emmy award Spl. Events Reporter, Watergate Coverage, 1973-74, Best Editorial awards Copley Newspapers Ring of Truth, 1979, Sigma Delta Chi, 1985, Calif. Newspaper Pubs. Assn., 1985; San Diego Emmy awards, 1985, 87, 91. Mem. NATAS, State Bar Calif. (bd. govs. 1991-97, v.p. 1993-94, 96-97), Sigma Delta Chi. Independent. Home: 240 Ocean View Ave Del Mar CA 92014-3322

KAYLAN, HOWARD LAWRENCE, musical entertainer, screenwriter, composer; b. NYC, June 22, 1947; s. Sidney and Sally Joyce (Berlin) Kaylan; m. Mary Melita Pepper, June 10, 1967 (div. Sept. 1971); 1 child, Emily Anne; m. Susan Karen Olsen, Apr. 18, 1982 (div. June 1996); 1 child, Alexandra Leigh. Student, UCLA; PhD in Philosophy, Am. Coll. Metaphys. Theology, St. Paul, Minn., 2000. Lead singer and founder rock group The Turtles, LA, 1965—; lead singer rock group Mothers of Invention, 1970-72, Flo and Eddie, 1972-83; radio, TV, recording entertainer various broadcast organizations, LA, 1972—; screenwriter Larry Gelbart, Carl Gotleib prodns., 1979-85; prodr. children's records Kidstuff Records, Hollywood, Fla., 1980-83; singer, prodr. rock band Flo and Eddie, LA, 1976-83; singer, prodr. The Turtles (reunion of original band), 1980—; actor, TV and film Screen Actors Guild, 1983—. Background vocalist various albums for numerous performers; syndicated talk show host Unistar Radio Network, 1989—; radio personality Sta. WXRK-FM, NYC, 1990—91, KLOU, St. Louis, 1993, WGRR, Cin., 1995—97. Author: Hi Bob, 1995, The Energy Pals, 1995; contbr. articles to profl. jours.; screenwriter (films) Death Masque, 1985, My Dinner With Jimi, 2003; actor: (films) 200 Motels, 1971, Get Crazy, 1985, General Hospital, Suddenly Susan, 1999, Riding the Bullet, 2004; performer: at White House, 1970; exec. prodr.(radio): Down Eerie Street, 1998; singer: numerous top ten hit songs with Turtles, Bruce Springstein, The Ramones, Duran Duran, T. Rex, John Lennon and others; singer: (commls.) Chevrolet, Pepsi, Bruger King and NFL, 1970— (awards); singer: (albums) Dust Bunnies, 2005. Recipient 10 Gold and Platinum LP album awards while lead singer, 1995—, Fine Arts award, Bank of Am., 1965, Spl. award, Billboard Mag., 1992, Best Script award, Slam Dunk Film Festival, 2003, Bubblegum award, 2003. Mem.: AGVA, AFRTA, Am. Fedn. Musicians, Screen Actors Guild. Personal E-mail: kaylan@howardkaylan.com. E-mail: hkaylan@theturtles.com.

KAYS, WILLIAM MORROW, academic administrator, mechanical engineer; b. Norfolk, Va., July 29, 1920; s. Herbert Emery and Margaret (Fechteler) K.; m. Alma Campbell, Sept. 14, 1947 (dec. June 1982); children: Nancy, Leslie, Margaret, Elizabeth.; m. Judith Scholtz, July 17, 1983. AB, Stanford U., 1942, MS, 1947, PhD in Mech. Engring., 1951. Asst. prof. mech. engring. Stanford U., 1951-54, assoc. prof., 1954-57, prof., 1957-90, prof. emeritus, 1990—, chmn. dept. mech. engring, 1961-72, dean engring., 1972-84. Dir. Acurex Corp., Alcohol Energy Systems; cons. to numerous firms. Author: Compact Heat Exchangers, 1964, 93, Convective Heat and Mass Transfer, 1966, 80. Hon. editorial adv. bd.: Internat. Jour. Heat and Mass Transfer. Served with U.S. Army, 1942-46. Fulbright fellow, 1959-60; NSF sr. postdoctoral fellow, 1966-67 Fellow ASME (Heat Transfer Divsn. Meml. award 1965, Max Jacob award 1992); mem. Am. Soc. Engring. Edn., Nat. Acad. Engring. Office: Stanford U Dept Mech Engring Stanford CA 94305

KAYTON, MYRON, engineering company executive; b. NYC, Apr. 26, 1934; s. Albert Louis and Rae K.; m. Paula Erde, Sept. 5, 1954; children: Elizabeth Kayton Kerns, Susan Kayton Barclay. BS, The Cooper Union, 1955; MS, Harvard U., 1956; PhD, MIT, 1960. Registered engr., Calif. Sect. head Litton Industries, Woodland Hills, Calif., 1960-65; dep. mgr. NASA, Houston, 1965-69; mem. sr. staff TRW, Inc., Redondo Beach, Calif., 1969-81; consulting engr. Kayton Engring. Co., Inc., Santa Monica, Calif., 1981—. Chmn. bd. dir. WINCON Conf., L.A., 1985-92; founding dir. Caltech-MIT Enterprise Forum, Pasadena, Calif., 1984—; dir. Electronic Convs., Inc., 2000-01; tchr. tech. courses UCLA Extension, 1969-88. Author: Avionic Navigation Systems, 1966, 2d edit., 1997, Navigation: Land, Sea, Air and Space, 1990; contbr. articles to profl. jours Founding dir. UCLA Friends of Humanities, 1971-75; West coast chmn. Cooper Union Fund Campaign, 1989-93. Fellow NSF, Washington, 1956-57, 58-60; recipient Gano Dunn medal The Cooper Union, N.Y.C., 1975. Fellow IEEE (life; nominating com. 1999-2001, corp. bd. dirs. 1996-97, pres. aerospace 1993-94, exec. v.p. aerospace 1991-92, v.p. tech. ops. 1988-90, nat. bd. govs. 1983—2000, vice-chmn. L.A. coun. 1983-84, avionics editor Aerospace Transactions 2002—06, M.B. Carlton award 1988, Disting. lectr., Millennium medal 2000); mem. ASME, Harvard Grad. Soc. (coun. mem. chmn. nominating com. 1988-91, Inst. Navigation (Kerschner award 2006), Soc. Automotive Engr., Harvard Club So. Calif. (pres. 1979-80), MIT Club (L.A.). Avocations: tennis, history, languages, flying. Office: Kayton Engring Co PO Box 802 Santa Monica CA 90406-0802 Office Phone: 310-393-1819.

KAZAN, LAINIE (LAINIE LEVINE), singer, actress; b. Bklyn., May 15, 1942; BA, Hofstra U. Appeared in: (films) Romance of a Horsethief, 1971, One From the Heart, 1981, My Favorite Year, 1982, Lust in the Dust, 1984, The Journey of Natty Gann, 1985, Harry and the Henderson's, 1986, Delta Force, 1986, Medium Rare, 1987, Beaches, 1988, Eternity, 1989, Out of the Dark, 1989, Earthday Birthday, 1990, 29th Street, 1991, I Don't Buy Kisses Anymore, 1992, The Cemetery Club, 1993, Movies Money Murder, 1996, Love is All There Is, 1996, The Associate, 1996, Allie & Me, 1997, Permanent Midnight, 1998, The Big Hit, 1998, The Unknown Cyclist, 1998, Kimberly, 1999, What's Cooking?, 2000, If You Only Knew, 2000, Bruno, 2000, The Crew, 2000, My Big Fat Greek Wedding, 2002, (singing voice) Eigh Crazy Nights, 2002, A Good Night to Die, 2003, Gigli, 2003, Red Riding Hood, 2004, Whiskey School, 2005, Beau Jest, 2008; (TV films) A Love Affair: The Eleanor and Lou Gehrig Story, 1978, A Cry for Love, 1980, Sunset Limousine, 1983, Obsessive Love, 1984, The Jerk, Too, 1984, (voice) Hagar the Horrible, 1989, Prince for a Day, 1995, Safety Patrol, 1998, Tempted, 2003, The Engagement Ring, 2005; (TV series) The Paper Chase, 1985-86, Karen's Song, 1987, St. Elsewhere, 1987-88, Amazing Stories, Pat Sajak Show, The Famous Teddy Z, The Nanny, Aunt Freida, My Big Fat Greek Life, 2003, In the Motherhood, 2007; (Broadway plays) The Happiest Girl in the World, 1961, Bravo Giovanni, 1962, My Favorite Year, 1992, The Government Inspector, 1994; cast mem., understudy for Barbra Streisand in Funny Girl, 1964; singer (albums) Body & Soul, 1995, In the Groove, 1998. Nominated Ace award, Golden Globe; recipient Woman of Yr. award, B'Nai Brith, Israeli Peace award, 1990. Mem. Actors Studio. Office: 9903 Santa Monica Blvd Ste 283 Beverly Hills CA 90212

KAZANJIAN, PHILLIP CARL, lawyer, educator; b. Visalia, Calif., May 15, 1945; s. John Casey and Sat-ten Arlene K.; m. Wendy Coffelt, Feb. 5, 1972; 1 child, John. BA with honors, U. So. Calif., 1967; JD with honors, Lincoln U., 1973. Bar: Calif. 1979, US Dist. Ct. (ctrl. dist.) Calif. 1980, US Tax Ct. 1980, US Ct. Appeals (9th cir.) 1980, US Mil. Ct. Appeals 1980, US Supreme ct. 1983. Ptnr. Brakefield & Kazanjian, Glendale, Calif., 1981-87; sr. ptnr. Kazanjian & Martinetti, Glendale, Calif., 1987—2005, of counsel, 2005—. Judge pro tem LA County Superior Ct., 1993—; instr. US Naval Acad., Annapolis, Md., 1981; asst. prof. Glendale CC, 1997-. Author: The Circuit Governor, 1972; editor-in-chief Lincoln Law Rev., 1973. Mem. Calif. Atty. Gen.'s Adv. Commn. on Cmty.-Police Rels., 1973; bd. dirs. LA County Naval Meml. Found., Inc. 1981-85, ARC, 1998-2003, Glendale CC Found., 1997—; pres., bd. trustees Glendale CC Dist., 1981-97, LA World Affairs Coun., Town Hall Calif.; vice chmn. bd. govs. Calif. Maritime Acad., 1986-94. Capt. USNR, 1969-99. Decorated Navy Commendation medal, Navy Achievement medal, knight Order of Knights Templar, 1990; recipient Patrick Henry medal Am. Legion, 1963, Congl. Record tribute U.S. Ho. of Reps., 1974, Centurion award Chief of Naval Ops., 1978; commendatory resolutions Mayor of L.A., L.A. City Coun., L.A. County Bd. Suprs., Calif. State Assembly and Senate, and Govt. of Calif., 1982, 2003, Justice award Calif. Law Student Assn., 1973. Mem. ABA (Gold Key 1972), Calif. Bar Assn., LA County Bar Assn., Am. Judicature Soc., ATLA, Glendale C. of C. (bd. dirs., Patriot Yr. 1986), Res. Officers Assn. (nat. judge adv., award 1981), Naval Res. Assn. (nat. adv. com.), US Naval Inst., Interallied Confedn. Res. Officers (internat. chmn. 1987-94), Explorers Club, Commonwealth of Calif. Club. Republican. Episcopalian. Office: Kazanjian & Martinetti 520 E Wilson Ave Ste 250 Glendale CA 91206-4346 Office Phone: 818-241-1011.

KAZEMI, HOSSEIN, petroleum engineer; BS in Petroleum Engring., U. Tex., 1961, PhD in Petroleum Engring., 1963. Rsch. scientist Sinclair Oil Corp./Atlantic Richfield Co., Tulsa, Dallas, 1963-69; adv. rsch. scientist Petroleum Tech. Ctr., Marathon, Littleton, Colo., 1969-74, sr. rsch. scientist, 1974-79, sr. tech. cons., 1979-81, mgr. engring., 1981-86, mgr. reservoir mgmt., 1986-88, assoc. dir., 1988-94, mgr. product tech., 1994-96, mgr. reservoir tech., 1997-99, exec. tech. fellow, 1999—. Adj. prof. Colo. Sch. Mines, Golden, 1981—; lectr., speaker in field. Contbr. articles to profl. jours. Mem. Soc. Petroleum Engrs. AIME (hon., disting., Henry Mattson tech. svc. award 1980, John Franklin Carll award 1987, Disting. Svc. award 1991, DeGolyer Disting. Svc. award 1995), Nat. Acad. Engring.

KAZI, SUMAYA, entrepreneur; b. 1982; B in Mktg. & Strategic Planning, U. Calif. Berkeley. Co-founder & exec. dir. The Cultural-Connect, San Francisco; mktg. mgr. Sun Microsystems Global Comm. Group. Young Entrepreneur mentor BUILD, Oakland, Calif. Named one of Best Entrepreneurs Under 25, BusinessWeek, 2006. Mem.: Young Professionals Internat. Network (World Affairs Coun.).

KEANE, DOUGLAS, chef; b. Mich., May 5, 1971; s. Noel Patrick Keane, Kathryn Keane. BS in Hotel Adminstrn., Cornell U., Ithica, NY, 1993. Chef, sous chef Four Seasons, NYC; chef Lespinasse, NYC; chef, exec. chef Jardiniere, San Francisco; sous chef Restaurant Gary Danko, San Francisco; co-owner, exec. chef Market, St. Helena, Calif., 2003—, Cyrus, Healdsburg, Calif., 2005—. Asst. chef (TV series) Cooking with Claudine. Recipient 2007 5 Diamond award for Cyrus Restaurant, AAA; named Rising Star Chef, San Francisco Chronicle, 2002, Best Chef: Pacific, James Beard Found., 2009; named one of America's Best New Chefs, Food and Wine Mag., 2006. Office: Cyrus 29 North St Healdsburg CA 95448 Office Phone: 707-433-3311.*

KEARNEY, JOSEPH LAURENCE, retired athletic conference administrator; b. Pitts., Apr. 28, 1927; s. Joseph L. and Iva M. (Nikirk) K.; m. Dorothea Hurst, May 13, 1950; children: Jan Marie, Kevin Robert, Erin Lynn, Shawn Alane, Robin James. BA, Seattle Pacific U., 1952, LLD, 1979; MA, San Jose State U., 1964; EdD, U. Wash., 1970. Tchr., coach Paradise (Calif.) H.S., 1952-53; asst. basketball coach U. Wash., 1953-54, athletic dir., assoc. dir., 1964-76; coach, tchr. Sunnyside (Wash.) H.S., 1954-57; prin., coach Onalaska (Wash.) H.S., 1957-61; prin. Tumwater (Wash.) H.S., 1961-63; asst. dir. Wash. H.S. Activities Assn., 1963-64; athletic dir. intercollegiate athletics Mich. State U., East Lansing, 1976-80, Ariz. State U., Tempe, 1980; commr. Western Athletic Conf., Denver, 1980-95; ret., 1995. Hon. chmn. Holiday Bowl, 1994, commr. emeritus, 1994. Pres. Cmty. Devel. Assn., 1957-61; bd. dirs. U.S. Olympic Com., 1985-94, chmn. games preparation com., 1985-2001. With USN, 1945—47. Recipient Disting. Svc. award Mich. Assn. Professions, 1979, Citation for Disting. Svc. Colo. Sports Hall of Fame, U.S. Olympic Com. Order of Olympic Shield, 1996. Mem. Nat. Football Found. (ct. of honors com., Western Regional Leadership award 1999), NCAA, Nat. Assn. Collegiate Dirs. Athletics (Corbett award 1991, Adminstr. Excellence award), Collegiate Commrs. Assn. (pres., award of Merit 1998), Am. Football Assn. (Commrs. award 1996, Athletic Dir.'s award 1998). Home: 2810 W Magee Rd Tucson AZ 85742-1500 Personal E-mail: josephlkea@earthlink.net, josephlkea@comcast.net.

KEARNS, DAVID RICHARD, chemistry professor; b. Urbana, Ill., Mar. 20, 1935; s. Clyde W. and Camille V. (French) K.; m. Alice Chen, July 5, 1958; children: Jennifer, Michael. BS in Chem. Engring., U. Ill., 1956; PhD., U. Calif., Berkeley, 1960. USAF doctoral fellow U. Chgo., 1960-61, MIT, Cambridge, 1961-62; asst. prof. chemistry U. Calif., Riverside, 1962-63, assoc. prof., 1964-67, prof., 1968-75, San Diego, 1975—. Assoc. editor Molecular Photochemistry, 1969-75, Photochemistry and Photobiology, 1971-75. Chem. Revs., 1974; assoc. editor Biopolymers, 1975-78, editorial bd., 1978-95. Sloan Found. fellow, 1965-67; Guggenheim fellow, 1969-70. Mem. Am. Chem. Soc. (Calif. sect. award 1973), Am. Phys. Soc., Am. Soc. Photobiology. Home: 8422 Sugarman Dr La Jolla CA 92037-2225 Office: U Calif San Diego Dept Chemistry La Jolla CA 92093 Office Phone: 858-534-2760. Business E-Mail: drk@chem.ucsd.edu.

KEASLING, JAY D., chemistry professor, research scientist; b. 1964; BSc in Chemistry and Biology, U. Nebraska, 1986; MSc in Chemical Engring., U. Michigan, 1988, PhD in Chemical Engring., 1991; post-doctorate in Biochemistry, Stanford U., 1992. Rsch. asst. Dept. Chemical Engring., U. Mich., 1986—91; post-doctoral rsch. assoc. Dept. Biochemistry, Stanford U., 1991—92; asst. prof. chemical engring. U. Calif.-Berkeley, 1992—98, assoc. prof. chemical engring., 1998—2001, vice-chmn. Dept. Chemical Engring., 1999—2000; dir. U. Calif. BioSTAR Program, 2000—; exec. com. mem. UC BioSTAR Program, 2000—; prof. chemical engring. U. Calif.-Berkeley, 2001—, Hubbard Howe Jr. Disting. prof. biochemical engring.; CEO Joint BioEnergy Inst., 2008—. Contbr. scientific papers to profl. jours. Recipient CAREER award, Nat. Sci. Found., 1995, AIChE award for Chemical Engring. Excellence in Academic Teaching, 1999, Scientist of Yr. award, Discover mag., 2006; fellow Chevron Young Faculty Fellowship, 1995, American Inst. of Med. and Biological Engring., 2000. Mem.: American Inst. of Med. and Biological Engring., American Soc. for Microbiology, American Inst. of Chemical Engrs., American Chemical Soc. Achievements include patents in field of "Reductive dehalogenation of organic halides in contaminated groundwater." US Patent No. 6,150,157 (1995). Office: Dept of Chemical Engring U California Berkeley CA 94720 also: Joint BioEnergy Institute 1 Cyclotron Rd MS: 978-4121 Berkeley CA 94720 Office Phone: 510-642-4862. Office Fax: 510-643-1228. E-mail: keasling@berkeley.edu, JDKeasling@lbl.gov.*

KEATING, DAVID, photographer; b. Rye, NY, Sept. 5, 1962; BA in Philosophy, Yale U., 1985; MA in Studio Art with distinction, U. N.Mex., 1991; student, Calif. Inst. Arts, Santa Clarita, 1992; MFA in Studio Art with distinction, U. N.Mex., 1994. Solo exhbns. include U. N.Mex., 1990 (traveled to Pace U., N.Y.C., Nat. Coun. Alcoholism Conf. of Affiliates, Nashville), 91, Calif. Inst. Arts, 1992, Graham Gallery, Albuquerque, 1994, Univ. Art Mus. Downtown, Albuquerque, 1995-96, George Eastman House, Rochester, N.Y., 1997, others; group exhbns. include Raw Space Gallery, Albuquerque, 1990, Betty Rymer Gallery, Sch. Art Inst. Chgo., 1991, 92, Randolph St. Gallery, Chgo., 1992, Atlanta Gallery Photography, 1992, San Jose (Calif.) Inst. Contemporary Art, 1992, Univ. Art Mus., Albuquerque, 1993, Ctr. African Am. History and Culture, Smithsonian Instn., Washington, 1994-95, Mus. Photographic Arts, San Diego, 1996-97, SF Camerawork, San Francisco, 1993, 98, others; represented in pub. collections, including Univ. Art Mus., Albuquerque; subject of various articles and catalogs, 1992—. NEA Visual Artists fellow in photography, 1994, Van Deren Coke fellow, U. N.Mex., 1991; recipient award Photographers and Friends United Against AIDS/Art Matters Inc., 1992. Home: 433 Ash St Ne Albuquerque NM 87106-4557

KEATING, EUGENE KNEELAND, animal scientist, educator; b. Liberal, Kans., Feb. 15, 1928; s. Arthur Hitch and Nilie Charlotte (Kneeland) K.; m. Iris Louise Myers, Aug. 12, 1951; children—Denise Keating Schnagl, Kimberly Alan. BS, Kans. State U., 1953, MS, 1954; PhD, U. Ariz., 1964. Owner, mgr. ranch, Kans., 1954—; instr., farm mgr. Midwestern U., Wichita Falls, Tex., 1957-60; rsch. asst. U. Ariz., Tucson, 1960-64; prof. animal sci. Calif. State Poly. U., Pomona, 1964-98, prof. emeritus, 1998—, chmn. dept., 1971-78. Contbr. articles to profl. jours. Bd. dirs. Los Angeles County Jr. Livestock Fair, 1971-79, chmn., 1975. With USAAF, 1946-49. Recipient Farm Bur. Century award, 2000. Fellow: Am. Inst. Chemists; mem.: NRA Whittington Ctr. Founders Club, NRA (benefactor), Brit. Soc. Animal Prodn., Am. Soc. Lab. Animal Sci., Coun. for Agrl. Sci. and Tech. (life), Am. Soc. Animal Sci. (life), Nat. Intercollegiate Rodeo Assn. (West Coast regional faculty dir. 1972—76), Western Heritage Ctr., Rep. Nat. Com. (life), Calif Rifle and Pistol Assn. (Gold Eagle), Am. Legion, Block and Bridle Club, Santa Fe Trail and Gun Club (life), Ind. Order Foresters, Sigma Xi, Alpha Zeta, Gamma Sigma Delta, Phi Lambda Upsilon. Presbyterian. Mailing: PO Box 1920 Veradale WA 99037 Office Phone: 509-893-3804.

KEATING, THOMAS FRANCIS, state legislator; b. Langdon, ND, Nov. 26, 1928; s. Thomas Delbert and Olive Mary (Bear) K.; m. Anna Louise Walsh, Aug. 22, 1953; children: Thomas J., Patrick, Michael, Kathryn, Terence. Student, Eastern Mont. Coll., 1951; BA in Bus. Adminstrn., U. Portland, 1953. Landman Mobil Oil Corp., Billings, Mont., 1954-61, Okla. City, 1961-66, Burlington No. R.R., Billings, 1966-67; Mont., landman Billings, 1967-81; mem. Mont. Senate, 1981—. Served with USAF, 1946-49. Mem. Am. Assn. Petroleum Landmen (pres. dir. 1971-73, Mont. chpt. pres. 1969), Ind. Petroleum Assn., Billings C. of C. Republican. Roman Catholic. Home: PO Box 20522 Billings MT 59104-0522

KEATING, TIMOTHY J., career military officer; b. Dayton, Ohio, Nov. 5, 1949; m. Wanda Lee Doerkson; children Daniel, Julie. Grad., U.S. Naval Acad., 1971; completed flight tng., 1973. Commd. ensign USN, 1971; advanced through grades to adm., 2004; duty USS Mason (DD-852); ordered to VA-82 deploying USS Nimitz (CVN-68); reported to VA-122 NAS Lemoore, Calif., 1978; staff LSO with comdr. carrier air wing fifteen USS Kitty Hawk, We. Pacific, Indian Ocean; adminstrv. officer, ops. officer, maint. officer VA-94 USS Enterprise, We. pacific, 1982-84; aide, flat lt. to Comdr. in Chief U.S. Pacific Cmd., 1984-87; comdr. VFA-87, deployed with CVW-8 USS Theodore Roosevelt North Atlantic and Mediterranean, 1987; head aviation LCDR/jr. officer assignments br. Naval Mil. Pers. Command, Washington; dep.comdr. carrier air wing seventeen combat. ops. Desert Storm USS Saratoga, 1991; CNO fellow strategic studies group Newport, R.I.; temp. duty with joint task force S.W. Asia Riyadh, Saudi Arabia; comdr. Naval Strike Warfare Ctr., 1994—95; dep. comdr. carrier air wing nine USS Nimitz Arabian Gulf; dir. aviation officer distbn. divsn. naval mil. personnel cmd., 1995—96; comdr. Battle Force 7th Fleet (carrier group 5, carrier strike force) USN, 1998—2000, dep. chief naval ops., (plans policy & ops.), 2000—02; comdr. US Naval Forces Ctrl. Command, US Fifth Fleet, 2002—03; dir. The Joint Staff, The Pentagon, Washington, 2003—04; comdr. N.Am. Aerospace Def. Command (NORAD), Peterson AFB, Colo., 2004—07, US No. Command, 2004—07, US Pacific Command, Honolulu, 2007—. Decorated Def. Disting. Svc. Medal with Oak Leaf Cluster, Disting. Svc. Medal with Gold Star, Legion of Merit with three Gold Stars, Def. Meritorious Svc. Medal, Meritorious Svc. Medal with Gold Star, Air Medals (3), Navy Commendation Medal with two Gold Stars Office: US Pacific Command/JO1PA PO Box 64031 Camp H M Smith HI 96861

KEATINGE, ROBERT REED, lawyer; b. Berkeley, Calif., Apr. 22, 1948; s. Gerald Robert and Elizabeth Jean (Benedict) Keatinge; m. Katherine Lou Carr, Feb. 1, 1969 (div. Dec. 1981); 1 child, Michael Towne; m. Cornelia Elizabeth Wyma, Aug. 21, 1982 (div. Jan. 2007); 1 child, Courteney Elizabeth. BA, U. Colo., 1970; JD, U. Denver, 1973, LLM, 1982. Bar: Colo. 1974, US Dist. Ct. Colo. 1974, US Ct. Appeals (10th cir.) 1977, US Tax Ct. 1980. Ptnr. Kubie & Keatinge, Denver, 1974-76; pvt. practice Denver, 1976; assoc. Richard Young, Denver, 1977-86; counsel Durham & Assoc. PC, Denver, 1986-89, Durham & Baron, Denver, 1989-90; project editor taxation Shepard's/McGraw-Hill, Colorado Springs, Colo., 1990-96; of counsel Holland & Hart, LLP, Denver, 1992—. Lectr. law U. Denver, 1982—92, adj. prof., 1983—94, 2005—; vis. assoc. prof. law Suffolk U. Law Sch., Boston, 2007—08; prof. Suffolk U. and Eötvöshorand U. LLM in US Law for Internat. Bus. Lawyers, Budapest, Hungary, 2008; spkr. in field. Author, cons. (CD-ROM) Entity Expert, 1996; co-author: Ribstein and Keatinge on Limited Liability Companies, 1992, 2d edit., 2004, Keatinge and Conaway on Choice of Business Entity, with ann. revisions, 2006—; contbr. articles to profl. jours. and treatises. Recipient Law Week award, U. Denver Bur. Nat. Affairs, 1974, Mertin I. Hubar award, Am. bar Assn. Bus. Law Sect. Com. on LLCs and Partnerships, 2008. Fellow: Am. Coll. Tax Counsel; mem.: ABA (chmn. subcom. ltd. liability cos. of com. on partnerships 1990—95, ABA adviser to Uniform Ltd. Liability Co. Act 1995, chmn. com. on taxation 1995—99, mem. ho. of dels. 1996—2002, ABA/Nat. Conf. Commrs. on Uniform State Laws joint editl. bd. on uninc 1996—, editl. bd. ABA/BNA Lawyer's Manual on Professional Conduct 1998—2002, chmn. com. on partnerships 2000—04, ABA adviser to Revision of Uniform Ltd. Partnership Act 2001), Am. Law Inst., Denver Bar Assn., Colo. Bar Assn. (taxation sect. exec. coun. 1988—94, sec.-treas. 1991—92, chmn. 1993—94, bd. govs. 1996—2004, bus. law sect. sec.-treas. 2001—03, vice chair 2003—05, chmn. 2005—07, ethics com., corp. code revision com., co-chmn. ltd. liability co. revision com.). Office Phone: 303-295-8595. Business E-Mail: rkeatinge@hollandhart.com.

KEATON, DIANE, actress; b. Santa Ana, Calif., Jan. 5, 1946; d. Jack and Dorothy Hall. Student, Neighborhood Playhouse, NYC, 1968. Appeared on NY stage in Hair, 1968, Play It Again Sam, 1969, The Primary English Class, 1976; actress: (films) Lovers and Other Strangers, 1970, Play It Again Sam, 1972, The Godfather, 1972, Sleeper, 1973, The Godfather Part II, 1974, Love and Death, 1975, I Will, I Will...For Now, 1975, Harry and Walter Go To New York, 1976, Annie Hall, 1977 (Best Actress Acad. award 1978, Brit. Acad. Best Actress award 1978, NY Film Critics Circle award 1978, Nat. Soc. Film Critics award 1978), Looking for Mr. Goodbar, 1977, Interiors, 1978, Manhattan, 1979, Reds, 1981 (Acad. award nominee), Shoot the Moon, 1982, Little Drummer Girl, 1984, Mrs. Soffel, 1984, Crimes of the Heart, 1986, Radio Days, 1987, Baby Boom, 1987, The Good Mother, 1988, The Lemon Sisters, 1990, The Godfather Part III, 1990, Father of the Bride, 1991, Manhattan Murder Mystery, 1993, Look Who's Talking Now, 1993 (voice), Father of the Bride 2, 1995, Marvin's Room, 1996, First Wives Club, 1996, The Only Thrill, 1997, The Other Sister, 1999, Hanging Up, 2000, Town and Country, 2001, Plan B, 2001, Something's Gotta Give, 2003 (Golden Globe for best actress in a musical or comedy, 2004, Acad. Award nomination for best actress, 2004, Screen Actors Guild Award nomination for best actress, 2004), The Family Stone, 2005, Smother, 2007, Mama's Boy, 2007, Because I Said So, 2007, Mad Money, 2008; (TV films) Running Mates, 1992, Amelia Earhart, 1994, Sister Mary Explains It All, 2001; actor, prodr: (TV films) Crossed Over, 2002, On Thin Ice, 2003, Surrender, Dorothy, 2005; dir. film: Heaven, 1987, Wildflower, 1991, Unstrung Heroes, 1995; exec. prodr.: (TV series) Pasadena, 2001; accomplished artist and singer; author book of photographs: Reservations, 1980; editor: (with Marvin Heiferman) Still Life, 1983, Mr. Salesman, 1994; prodr.: The Lemon Sisters, 1990; exec. prodr.: Northern Lights (TV), 1997. Recipient Golden Globe award, 1978, Trustees award, Internat. Ctr. Photography, 2008. Office: c/o Endeavor Agy 9601 Wilshire Blvd Beverly Hills CA 90212

KEATOR, CAROL LYNNE, library director; b. Annapolis, Md., Aug. 9, 1945; d. Lyle H. and Juanita F (Waits) K. BA, Syracuse U., 1967; MS, Simmons Coll., 1968. Librarian Bristol (Conn.) Pub. Sch.s, 1968-69, MIT, Cambridge, 1969-72, Santa Barbara (Calif.) Pub. Library, 1972-77, br. supr., 1977-81, prin. librarian, 1981-88, library dir., 1988—. Mem. ALA, Calif. Libr. Assn., Pub. Libr. Assn. Unitarian Universalist. Office: Santa Barbara Pub Libr 40 E Anapamu St Santa Barbara CA 93101-2722

KEDES, LAURENCE HERBERT, biochemistry professor, physician, researcher; b. Hartford, Conn., July 19, 1937; s. Sammuel Ely and Rosalyn (Epstein) K.; m. Shirley Beck, June 15, 1958; children: Dean Hamilton, Maureen Jennifer, Todd Russell. Student, Wesleyan U., 1955-58; BS with distinction, Stanford U., 1961, MD, 1962. Intern Presbyn. U. Hosp., Pitts., 1962-63, asst. resident, 1963-64; rsch. assoc. lab. biochemistry Nat. Cancer Inst. Peterson, 1964-66; sr. asst. med. resident Peter Bent Brigham Hosp., Boston, 1966-67; surgeon US-PHS, 1964-66; postdoctoral fellow dept. biology MIT, 1967-68; jr. assoc. in medicine and hematology assoc. Peter Bent Brigham Hosp., Boston, 1967-69; rsch. trainee in embryology Marine Biol. Lab., Woods Hole, Mass., 1969; instr. biology MIT, Boston, 1969-70; asst., assoc. then prof. medicine Stanford U., 1970-89, dir. admissions med. sch., 1978-81; William M. Keck prof. biochemistry and medicine U. So. Calif. Keck Sch. Medicine, LA, 1989—, dir. Inst. Genetic Medicine, 1989—, chair biochemistry, 1989—2002. Staff physician VA, 1970-92; vis. scientist Lab. Molecular Embryology, Naples, Italy, 1969-70, Dept. Animal Genetics, U. Edinburgh, 1970, Imperial Cancer Rsch. Fund, London, 1976-77; instr. embryology Marine Biol. Lab., Woods Hole, 1976; investigator Howard Hughes Med. Inst., 1974-82; founder, dir. IntelliCorp., Mountain View, Calif., 1980-90, chmn., 1982-86. Mem. editorial bd. Jour. Biol. Chemistry, 1982-88, Molecular and Cellular Biology, 1982-89, Jour. Applied Molecular Biology, 1982-85, Oxford Surveys on Eukaryotic Genes, 1983-94, Trends in Genetics, 1984-88; assoc. editor Jour. Molecular Evolution, 1982-90; cons. editor Circulation Rsch., 1994-99. Mem. fellowship award com. Am. Cancer Soc., 1978-81; co-principle investigator BIONET, 1984-89; mem. rsch. com. Am. Heart Assn., 1987; mem. sci. adv. bd. Muscular Dystrophy Assn., 1988-93. Fellow Med. Found. Boston, 1967-69, John Simon Guggenheim Found. fellow, 1976-77; Leukemia Soc. Am. scholar, 1969-74. Mem. Western Soc. for Clin. Rsch., Am. Soc. Clin. Investigation, Assn. Am. Psysicians, Am. Soc. Microbiology, Am. Soc. Biochemistry and Molecular Biology, Internat. Soc. Devel. Biology, Alpha Omega Alpha.

KEEFE, MAUREEN RUTH, dean; b. Madison, Wis., Oct. 30, 1947; m. Michael Gaviglio; children: Erin, Ryan. BSN, U. Mich., 1970; MS, U. Colo., 1974, PhD, 1984, postgrad., 1985. Cert. PNP. Pub. health nurse Washtenaw County Health Dept., Ann Arbor, 1971-73; PNP Denver (Colo.) Health and Hosps., 1974-75, Univ. Hosp., Denver, 1978-85; instr. dept. psychology Univ. Colo., Denver, 1985-86; v.p. nursing The Children's Hosp., Denver, 1985—; assoc. dir. Kempe Rsch. Ctr., Denver, 1985—; asst. prof. Univ. Colo., Sch. Nursing, Denver, 1985-90, assoc. prof., 1990—; dean Coll. Nursing Med. U. S.C., Charleston, U. Utah, Salt Lake City. Cons. Emergent Tech. Corp., Boca Raton, Fla., 1985; vis. prof. Children's Hosp., Columbus, Ohio, 1990; mem. Nat. Adv. Bd. for Clin. Trials of the Preterm; mem. adv. bd. Johnson & Johnson Pediat. Inst. Co-author: A Primary Care Process Measure: The Nurse Practitioner Rating Form, 1981. Troop leader Brownies, Denver, 1983-84; bd. mem. Step Families Assn. Denver, 1984-85, pres., 1985. Recipient Book of Yr. award Am. Jour. Nursing, 1981, First award NIH/NCNR, 1987; named People to Watch, Denver Mag., 1988. Mem.: Western Inst. Nursing (exec. com. 1992—), Nat. Assn. Pediatric Nurse Assocs. and Practitioners (co-chair Internat. Yr. of the Child 1979), Sigma Theta Tau (perinatal grant selection com./Mead Johnson 1991, internat. rsch. com. 1992—, Alpha Kappa chpt. rsch. com. 1984—85, 1991—92, v.p. 1985—87, pres. 1988—90, bd. dirs. 2000—, Rsch. Excellence award 1988). Office: U Utah Coll Nursing Deans Office 10 S 2800 E Front Salt Lake City UT 84112-5880

KEEGAN, JANE ANN, insurance executive, consultant; b. Watertown, NY, Sept. 1, 1950; d. Richard Isidor and Kathleen (McKinley) K. BA cum laude, SUNY, Potsdam, 1972; MBA in Risk Mgmt., Golden State U., 1986. CPCU. Comml. lines mgr. Lithgow & Rayhill, San Francisco, 1977-80; risk mgmt. account coord. Dinner Levison Co., San Francisco, 1980-83; ins. cons. San Francisco, 1983-84; account mgr. Rollins Burdick Hunter, San Francisco, 1984-85; account exec. Jardine Ins. Brokers, San Francisco, 1985-86; ins. cons. San Francisco, 1986-87; ins. adminstr. Port of Oakland, 1987—, risk mgr., 1989—, mgr. accts. payable, 1996—. Vol. San Francisco Ballet vol. orgn., 1981-96, Bay Area Bus., Govt. ARC disaster conf. steering com., 1987-88, 89, 90, 91-92; mem. Nob Hill Neighbors Assn., 1982—, City of Oakland Emergency Mgmt. Bd., 1990—. Mem. Safety Mgmt. Soc., CPCU Soc. (spl. events chairperson 1982-84, continuing profl. devel. program award 1985, 88, chair loss prevention), Calif. Assn. of Port Authorities (ins. chair 1998—), Risk and Ins. Mgr. Soc. (dep., sec. 1990—, dir. legis. 1993, dir. conf.). Democrat. Roman Catholic. Home: 17 Calafia Ct San Rafael CA 94903-2464 Office Phone: 510-627-1535. Business E-Mail: jkeegan@portoakland.com.

KEEGAN, JOHN CHARLES, former mayor, retired military officer, former state legislator; b. Tempe, Ariz., Feb. 21, 1952; s. William Edward and Lucille (Reay) K.; m. Lisa Graham, Dec. 18, 1995; children: Katherine, Mark, John II, Annie, Justin BS in Engring., Ariz. State U., 1975; MS in Geography and Urban Planning, Western Pacific U., 1990. Registered profl. engr., Az., Tex., Utah, Nev.; registered land surveyor, Ariz. Pres. Accels/Keegan Consulting Engrs., Peoria, Ariz., 1987—; mem. Ariz. Ho. Reps., Phoenix, 1991-95; mayor City of Peoria, Ariz., 1997—2007. Commr. Planning and Zoning Commn., Peoria, 1989-91; mem. criminal justice task force Am. Legis. Exch. Coun., 1991-96. Mem. selection com. Valley Leadership, Phoenix, 1988; chmn. Vision 2020 Com., Peoria, 1990-91. 1st lt. U.S. Army, 1975-79, comdr. USNR, 1988-2000. Recipient Silver Beaver award, Nat. Coun. Boy Scouts of Am., 2005. Mem. Ariz. Soc. Profl. Engrs. (pres. 1990-91, Young Engr. of Yr. award 1980, Disting. Svc. award 1991). Republican. Episcopalian. Avocations: sailing, scuba diving, flying.

KEEGAN, JOHN E., lawyer; b. Spokane, Wash., Apr. 29, 1943; BA, Gonzaga U., 1965; LLB, Harvard U., 1968. Bar: Wash. 1968, U.S. Ct. Appeals (9th cir.) 1976, U.S. Supreme Ct. Gen. counsel Dept. Housing and Urban Devel., Washington, 1968-70; instr. in bus. sch. and inst. environ. studies U. Wash., 1973-76, instr. land use and environ. law, 1976-78; now ptnr. Davis, Wright & Tremaine, Seattle. Author: (novels) Clearwater Summer, 1994, Piper, 2001, A Good Divorce, 2003. Office: Davis Wright Tremaine Ste 2200 1201 Third Ave Seattle WA 98101-3045 Office Phone: 206-628-7688, 206-987-7040. Business E-Mail: johnkeegan@dwt.com.

KEEGAN, LISA GRAHAM, state agency administrator; m. John Keegan; 5 children. BS in Linguistics, Stanford U.; MS in Comm. Disorders, Ariz. State U., 1983. Mem. Ariz. Ho. of Reps., 1991-95, chair edn. com., joint legis. budget com., 1993-94; state supt. of pub. instrn. Dept. of Edn., State of Ariz., Phoenix, 1994—2001; CEO Edn. Leaders Coun., Washington, 2001—.

KEELER, THEODORE EDWIN, retired economics professor; b. Enid, Okla., Mar. 25, 1945; s. Clinton Clarence and Lorene Adda Keeler; m. Marjorie Ann Nathanson, Aug. 29, 1982; 1 child, Daniel C. BA, Reed Coll., 1967; S.M., MIT, 1969, PhD, 1971. Asst. prof. econs. U. Calif.-Berkeley, 1971-77, assoc. prof., 1977-83, prof., 1983—2006; prof. emeritus econs., 2006—. Key faculty Robert Wood Johnson Postdoctoral Fellows Program, 1993-01. Author: Railroads, Freight, and Public Policy, 1983; co-author: Regulating The Automobile, 1986; also articles; editor: Research in Transportation Economics, vol. I, 1983, vol. II, 1985. Grantee NSF, 1973-75, 80-82, dept. transp. program, 1988-90, 93-94, NIH, 1990-91, Nat. Inst. on Aging, 1995-96; prin. investigator Sloan Found., 1975-80, Robert Wood Johnson Found., 1996-99; sr. fellow, vis. scholar Brookings Instn., Washington, 1980-82; co-prin. investigator Tobacco Tax Project Calif. Tobacco-Related Disease Fund, 1990-94, 99-2000 Democrat. Office: U Calif Dept Econs Berkeley CA 94720-3880

KEENAN, EDWARD L., linguist, educator; b. Somerset, Pa., Dec. 10, 1937; m. Carol Archie; 1 child, David. BA in Philosophy and Religion, Swarthmore Coll., 1959; diploma in lit., U. Paris, Sorbonne, 1961, cert. in French lit., 1962; MA in Linguistics, George Washington U., 1966; PhD in Linguistics, U. Pa., 1969. Sr. fellow King's Coll., Cambridge, England, 1970—74; vis. prof. U. Amsterdam, Netherlands, 1977, U. Tel Aviv, 1978—79; fellow Max Planck Inst. for Psycholinguistics, Nijmegen, Netherlands, 1984—85; Fulbright scholar U. Antananarivo, Madagascar, 1995; prof. linguistics UCLA, 1974—. Co-author: Boolean Semantics for Natural Language, 1985, Bare Grammar: A Study of Language Invariants, 2003, Universal Grammar: 15 Essays, 1987; mem. adv. editl. bd.: Lang. Rsch., 1985—, consulting editor: Jour. Semantics, 1987—, Jour. Lang. and Computation, 1997—. Grantee, NSF, 2000—01, Binational Sci. Found., 2000, 2002. Mem.: AAAS, ACLU, Linguistic Soc. Am., Am. Math. Soc. Green Party. Achievements include discovery of accessiblity hierarchy in syntactic typology; conservativity constraint on natural language quantification. Avocation: poetry. Office: UCLA Dept Linguistics 3125 Campbell Hall UCLA 405 Hilgard Ave Los Angeles CA 90094 Office Phone: 310-991-7967. Business E-Mail: edward.keenum1@gmail.com.

KEENAN, MIKE (MICHEAL EDWARD KEENAN), professional hockey coach, former professional sports team executive; b. Bowmanville, Ont., Can., Oct. 21, 1949; m. Nola Keenan; 1 child, Gayla. Student, St. Lawrence U., NYC. Hockey player St. Lawrence U. Skating Saints, 1969—72, U. Toronto, 1972—73, Roanoke Valley Rebels, Va., 1973-74, Whitby Warriors, 1976—77; coach Peterborough Petes, Ont. Hockey League, 1979-80; head coach Can. Nat. Jr. Team, 1980, Rochester Ams., Am. Hockey League, NY, 1980-83, Toronto Hockey Team, Can. Collegiate League, Ont., 1983-84, Phila. Flyers, 1984-88, Chgo. Blackhawks, 1988-92, gen. mgr., 1990-92; head coach NY Rangers, 1993-94; head coach, gen. mgr. St. Louis Blues, 1994-96; head coach Vancouver Canucks, 1998-99, Boston Bruins, 2000—01, Fla. Panthers, 2001—03, gen. mgr., 2004—06; head coach Calgary Flames, 2007—. Named MVP, Roanoke Valley Rebels, So. Hockey League, 1974; winning coach World Amateur Hockey Championships, 1980, Calder Cup Championship, 1982-83, Can. Collegiate Championship, U. Toronto, 1983-84, Stanley Cup Championship, 1994, Can. Cup Championship, 1987, 91; recipient Jack Adams award as NHL Coach of Yr., 1985; Coach of Yr. award Sporting News, 1985, Hockey News, 1985; Coach, NHL All-Star team 1985-86, 1987-88, 1992-93; Coach, Canadian Nat. Team, 1993. Achievements include being the coach of Stanley Cup Champion NY Rangers, 1994. Office: Calgary Flames PO Box 1540 Stn M Calgary AB Canada T2P 3B9

KEENAN, THOMAS J., chemicals executive; V.p., gen. mgr. Olefins and Polyolefins Mobil Chem. Co.; with Huntsman Corp., Salt Lake City, 1994—, sr. v.p. Hunstman Chem. Co. LLC, 1998—2000, pres. North Am. Petrochemicals and Polymers, 2000—03, divsn. pres. pigments, 2003—. Office: Huntsman Corp 500 Huntsman Way Salt Lake City UT 84108 Office Phone: 801-584-5700.

KEEVIL, NORMAN B., mining executive; b. Cambridge, Mass., Feb. 28, 1938; s. Norman Bell and Verna Ruth (Bond) Keevil; m. Joan E. MacDonald, Dec. 1990; children: Scott, Laura, Jill, Norman Bell III. BA in Sci., U. Toronto, Ont., Can., 1959; PhD, U. Calif., Berkeley, 1964; LLD (hon.), U. BC, 1993. V.p. exploration Teck Corp., Vancouver, B.C., Canada, 1962-68, exec. v.p., 1968-81, pres., CEO, 1981-89, chmn., pres., CEO, 1989-94, pres., CEO, 1994-2000, CEO, 2000—; chmn. Teck Cominco Ltd., Vancouver, 2001—. Named Mining Man of Yr., No. Miner, 1979; named to Can. Mining Hall of Fame, 2004. Mem.: Soc. Exploration Geophysicists, Prospectors and Developers Assn. (Disting. Svc. award 1990, Viola R. MacMillan Developer's award 1997), Can. Inst. Mining and Metallurgy (Selwyn G. Blaylock medal 1990, Inco medal 1999), Royal & Ancient Golf Club (St. Andrews, Scotland), Shaughnessy Golf and Country Club, Vancouver Club. Office: Teck Cominco Ltd 200 Burrard St # 700 Vancouver BC Canada V6C 3L9 Office Phone: 604-687-1117.

KEFALAS, JOHN MICHAEL, state legislator; m. Beth Kefalas; 2 children. B, Colo. State U., Ft. Collins; MA, Fairleigh Dickinson U., NJ. Advocate, cmty. devel. coord. Catholic Charities; counselor Larimer County, Colo.; advisor Project Self-Sufficiency of Loveland-Ft. Collins, Colo.; tchr. Poudre Sch. Dist., Colo.; dir. Colo. Progressive Coalition's Tax Fairness Project; mem. Dist. 52 Colo. House of Reps., Denver, 2007—. Vol. Peace Corps. Mem. Witness for Peace, Schools for Chiapas, The Compassionate Listening Project, Colo. Housing Investment Fund Coalition, Affordable Housing Coalition Larimer County; No. Colo. Cross-Disabilities Coalition, Ft. Collins Area Interfaith Coun., Older Am. Coalition, Ft. Collins Housing Authority, Colo. Women's Lobby, Colo. Consumer Health Initiative, Martinez Pk. Neighborhood Assn., Colo. Children's Campaign, Colo. Fiscal Policy Inst. Democrat. Office: Colo State Capitol 200 E Colfax Denver CO 80203 Office Phone: 303-866-4569. Business E-Mail: john.kefalas.house@state.co.us.*

KEGLEY, JACQUELYN ANN, philosophy educator; b. Conneaut, Ohio, July 18, 1938; d. Steven Paul and Gertrude Evelyn (Frank) Kovacevic; m. Charles William Kegley, June 12, 1964; children: Jacquelyn Ann, Stephen Lincoln Luther. BA cum laude, Allegheny Coll., 1960; MA summa cum laude, Rice U., 1964; PhD, Columbia U., 1971. Asst. prof. philosophy Calif. State U., Bakersfield, 1973-77, assoc. prof., 1977-81, prof., 1981—, chair dept. philosophy and religious studies. Vis. prof. U. Philippines, Quezon City, 1966-68; grant project dir. Calif. Coun. Humanities, 1977, project dir. 1980, 82; mem. work group on ethics Am. Colls. of Nursing, Washington, 1984-86; mem. Am. Bd. Forensic Examiners; chair acad. senate Calif. State U., 2000-03, exec. com., 2003-04, chair fiscal and gov. affairs com. Author: Introduction to Logic, 1978, Genuine Individuals and Genuine Communities, 1997, Royce in Focus, 2008; editor: Humanistic Delivery of Services to Families, 1982, Education for the Handicapped, 1982, Genetic Knowledge, 1998; mem. editl. bd. Jour. Philosophy in Lit., 1979-84; contbr. articles to profl. jours. Edit. bd. Libr. Living Philosophers; active CSU Acad. Senate, 1999—; Bd. dirs. Bakersfield Mental Health Assn., 1982—84, Citizens for Betterment of Community. Recipinet Golden Roadrunner award Bakersfield Cmty., 1991, Wang Family Excellence award, 2000, Soc. Advancement Am. Philosophy Herbert Schneider award, 2006. Mem. Philosophy of Sci. Assn., Soc. Advancement Am. Philos. Soc. (chmn. Pacific divsn. 1979-83, 2005—, nat. exec. com. 1974-79, 2003-, v.p. 2008-), Philosophy Soc., Soc. Interdisciplinary Study of Mind, Am. Philos. Assn. (bd. mem. 1999-2003, chair com. on tchg.), Dorian Soc., Phi Beta Kappa. Democrat. Lutheran. Avocations: music, tennis. Home: 7312 Kroll Way Bakersfield CA 93309-2336 Office: Calif State U Dept Philosophy Bakersfield CA 93311 Office Phone: 661-654-2249. Business E-Mail: jkegley@csub.edu.

KEHOE, CHRISTINE T., state legislator; b. Troy, NY, Oct. 3, 1950; life ptnr. Julie Warren. BA, SUNY, Albany, 1972. Editor San Diego Gayzette, 1984—86; dir. San Diego AIDS Assistance Fund, 1987—88; exec. dir. Hillcrest Bus. Assn., 1988—89; aide San Diego City Coun., 1989—92, councilwoman, 1993—2000; cmty. devel. specialist San Diego, 1992—93; mem. city mgr.'s office Econ. Devel., 1993; candidate Calif. Dist. 49 U.S. Congress, 1998; mem. Dist. 76 Calif. State Assembly, 2000—04; mem. Dist. 39 Calif. State Senate, 2005—. Mem. arts, entertainment, sports, tourism and Internet media com.; mem. housing and cmty. devel. com.; mem. pub. employees, retirement and social security com.; mem. transp. com.; mem. water, parks, and wildlife com.; mem. VA com.; chair select com. on park and river restoration, 2001—; chair pub. safety and neighborhood svcs. com., 1995—96; legis. aide State of Calif., 1992; coun. rep. City of San Diego, 1989—92; campaign coord. San Diegans for Neil

Good, 1987, San Diego Says No on 64, 1986. Mem.: NOW, Calif. Elected Women's Assn. for Edn. and Rsch. (bd. dirs.), Calif. Women in Govt., Nat. Women's Polit. Caucus, San Diego Assn. Govt., San Diego Small Bus. Adv. Bd., San Diego Cen. Dem. Com. (mem. San Diego City Coun. 1993—2000, chair subcom. on econ. prosperity 1998), Calif. Women in Edn., Uptown Dem. Club, Sierra Club, San Diego Dem. Club. Democrat. Office: Dist 39 2445 5th Ave Ste 200 San Diego CA 92101 also: State Capitol Rm 5050 Sacramento CA 94248 Office Phone: 619-645-3133. Office Fax: 619-645-3144. Business E-Mail: Senator.Kehoe@sen.ca.gov.

KEIL, KLAUS, geology educator, consultant; b. Hamburg, Germany, Nov. 15, 1934; s. Walter and Elsbeth K.; m. Rosemarie, Mar. 30, 1961; children: Kathrin R., Mark K.; m. Linde, Jan. 28, 1984. MS, Schiller U., Jena, Germany, 1958; PhD, Gutenberg U., Mainz, Fed. Republic Germany, 1961; D (hon.), Friedrich-Schiller U., Jena, Germany, 2002; DSc (hon.), U. N.Mex., 2003. Rsch. assoc. Mineral. Inst., Jena, 1958-60, Max Planck-Inst. Chemistry, Mainz, 1961, U. Calif., San Diego, 1961-63; rsch. scientist Ames Rsch. Ctr. NASA, Moffett Field, Calif., 1963-68; prof. geology, dir. Inst. Meteoritics, U. N.Mex., Albuquerque, 1968-90; pres., prof. U. N.Mex., 1985-90, chmn. dept. geology Albuquerque, 1986-89; prof. geology U. Hawaii, Honolulu, 1990—, rsch. prof., head planetary geoscis. div., 1990-93, dir. Hawaii Inst. Geophysics and Planetology, 1994—2003, interim dean Sch. Ocean Earth Sci. and Tech., 2003—06, prof., 2006—; cons. Sandia Labs., others. Contbr. over 600 articles to sci. jours. Recipient Apollo Achievement award, NASA, 1970, Exceptional Sci. Achievement medal, 1983, George P. Merrill award, NAS, 1970, Leonard medal, Meteoritical Soc., 1988, Zimmerman award, U. N.Mex., 1988, J. Lawrence Smith medal, NAS, 2006, others; named new extraterrestrial mineral Keilite named after him. Fellow Meteoritical Soc., AAAS, Mineral. Soc. Am., Am. Geophys. Union, German Mineral. Soc., Microbeam Analysis Soc. (Pres.'s Sci. award 2002), others. Office: U Hawaii at Manoa Hawaii Inst Geophys & Planetology Honolulu HI 96822 Office Phone: 808-956-7755. Business E-Mail: keil@hawaii.edu.

KEIL, STEPHEN LESLEY, astrophysicist; b. Billings, Mont., Feb. 21, 1947; s. Nolan F. and Billy Lou (Benjamin) K.; m. Alice Ann Orient, June 18, 1972; children: Pamela Lynn, Wesley Forrester. BS in Physics, Univ. Calif., Berkeley, 1969; PhD in Astronomy, Boston U., 1975. Teaching fellow Boston (Mass.) Univ., 1969-74; postdoctoral fellow Univ. Colo., Sunspot, N.Mex., 1975-76; rsch. fellow, applied math. dept. Univ. Sydney, Australia, 1976-78; NRC fellow Sacramento Peak Obs., Sunspot, 1978-80, rsch. scientist, 1980-83; chief, solar rsch. USAF Solar Rsch. Br., Sunspot, 1983-99; dir. Nat. Solar Observatory, Sunspot, 1999—. Mem. Nat. Solar Obs. adv. com., Tucson, 1983-89; prin. investigator USAF Solar Mass Ejection Imager, 1996-99; project dir. Advanced Tech. Solar Telescope, 2000—. Editor: (workshop proceedings) Small-Scale Dynamical Processes in Quiet Stellar Atmospheres, 1984; co-editor: (workshop proceedings) Solar Drivers of Interplanetary and Terrestial Disturbances, Innovative Telescopes and Instrumentation for Solar Astrophysics, SPIE 4853, 2003. Mayor Sacramento Peak Community, Sunspot, 1990-91, treas., 1981-87. Maj. USAF, 1980-85. Named Company Grade Officer of Yr., USAF, 1984, Officer of the Yr., Geophysics Lab., Boston, 1983. Mem. Internat. Astron. Union, Am. Astron. Soc., Am. Phys. Soc., Calif. Scholarship Fedn. (life). Achievements include first to make an accurate determination of the height variation of convective penetration in the solar atmosphere. Home: 3015 Corona Loop Sunspot NM 88349 Office: National Solar Observatory PO Box 62 Sunspot NM 88349-0062 Business E-Mail: skeil@nso.edu.

KEILIS-BOROK, VLADIMIR ISAACKOVICH, geophysicist, b. Moscow, July 31, 1921; s. Isaack and Kseniya (Ruvimova) Keilis-B.; m. Ludmila Malinovskaya, Oct. 6, 1956; 1 child by previous marriage, Irina. Geophysicist, Coll. Geol. Prospecting, Mocow, 1943; Ph.D., Acad. Sci. USSR, 1948, D.Sc. (hon.), prof., 1953. Research fellow Earth Physics Inst., Acad. Scis. USSR, Moscow, 1943-49, sr. research fellow, 1949-60, chair dept. computational geophysics, 1970—89, founder, co-dir., Abdus Salam Internat. Ctr. for Thepretical Physics, 1985-, founder, dir., Internat. Inst. for Earthquake Prediction Theory & Mathematical Geophysics, Russian Acad. Scis., 1989-98, rsch.group leader, 1998-, prof. earth & planetary scis., 1999-2002, prof-in-residence, UCLA, 2002-; Author/co-author numerous books and articles in field; Mem. AAAS (fgn. hon.), 1969, U.S. Nat. Acad. Scis. (fgn. assoc.), 1971, Russaian Acad. Scis., 1988, Austrian Acad. Scis., 1992, Pontifical Acad. Scis, 1994, Acadeia Eurpaea, 1999. Office: IGPP UCLA Box 951567 Los Angeles CA 90095 also: Earth Physics Acad Scis USSR 10 B Gruzinskaya 123810 Moscow Russia E-mail: vkb@ess.ucla.edu.

KEIM, MICHAEL RAY, dentist; b. Sabetha, Kans., June 8, 1951; s. Milton Leroy and Dorothy Juanita (Stover) K.; m. Christine Anne Lorenzen, Nov. 20, 1971; children: Michael Scott, Dawn Marie, Erik Alan. Student, U. Utah, Salt Lake City, 1969-72; DDS, Creighton U., Omaha, 1976. Pvt. practice, Casper, Wyo., 1976—. Mem. vertical math. com. Natrona County Sch. Dist., 1997-2000; mem. Coll. Nat. Finals Rodeo Com., 2002—; equality of care advising mem. State or Wyo., 2007—. Mem. organizing bd. dirs. Ctrl. Wyo. Soccer Assn., 1976-77; mem. Casper Mountain Ski Patrol, Nat. Ski Patrol Sys., 1980-2000, 2005—, Big Horn Ski Patrol, 2001-05, avalanche and ski mountaineering advisor No. Divsn. Region III, 1992-96, outdoor emergency care instr. trainer, 1996-99, 1st asst. patrol dir., 1996-98, patrol dir., 1998-99; bd. dirs., dep. commr. for fast pitch Wyo. Amateur Softball Assn., 1980-84; bd. dirs. Ctrl. Wyo. Softball Assn., 1980-84; head coach Big Horn Mountain Ski Team, 2002-05; pres. Wyo. Spl. Smiles Found., 1995-96; mem. organizing com. Prevent Abuse & Neglect thru Dental Awareness Coalition, Wyo., 1996; mem. adv. com. Natrona County Headstart, 1985—; mem. City of Casper Leisure Svc. Adv. Com., 2002—, vice chair, 2007—. Recipient Purple Merit Star for Saving a Life, 1992, Hixon award, 2002, Lusche Fellow award, 2008. Master: Acad. Gen. Dentistry; mem.: ADA, Internat. Coll. Dentistry, Wyo. Donated Dental Svcs. (organizing bd. dirs. 1994, pres. 1995—96, Outstanding Vol. Dentist 2007), Wyo. Dental Hist. Assn. (bd. dirs. 1989—95), Ctrl. Wyo. Dental Assn. (sec.-treas. 1981—82, pres. 1982—83, sec.-treas. 2002—03, pres. 2003—04), Wyo. Dental Polit. Action Com. (sec.-treas. 1985—97), Wyo. Dental Assn. (chmn. conv. 1987—, bd. dirs. 1992—97, chmn. conv. 1993, v.p. 1993—94, ADA alt. del. 1994—95, pres.-elect 1994—95, pres. 1995—96, editor 1997—, chmn. conv. 1999), Wyo. Acad. Gen. Dentistry (sec.-treas. 1980—82, pres. 1982—87, del. 2007—), Pierre Fauchard Acad., Fedn. Dentaire Internat., Am. Acad. Cosmetic Dentistry, Acad. Computerized Dentistry, Creighton Club (pres. 1982—84), Kiwanis (bd. dirs. 1986—96, v.p. Casper club 1988—89, pres.-elect 1989—90, internat. del. 1989—91, pres. 1990—91, chmn. internat. rels. com. 1992—99, Rocky Mountain dist. lt. gov.-elect divsn. 1 1997—98, lt. gov. divsn. 1 1998—99, Hixon award 2002). Methodist. Avocations: hunting, skiing, sports, woodworking, photography. Office: 1749 S Boxelder St Casper WY 82604-3538 Home: 3524 Aspen Ln Casper WY 82604-4571 Office Phone: 307-234-6358. Personal E-mail: mogul_mike@msn.com.

KEIM, WAYNE FRANKLIN, retired agronomist, geneticist; b. Ithaca, NY, May 14, 1923; s. Franklin David and Alice Mary (Voigt) K.; m. Ellen Joyce Neumann, Sept. 6, 1947; children: Kathryn Louise Keim Logsdon, David Wayne, Julie Anne Keim Hughes. BS with distinction, U. Nebr., 1947; MS, Cornell U., 1949, PhD, 1952. Instr., then asst. prof. Iowa State U., Ames, 1952-56; from asst. prof. to prof. Purdue U., West Lafayette, Ind., 1956-75; vis. prof., NSF sci. faculty fellow U. Lund, (Sweden), 1962-63; vis. prof. Colo. State U., Fort Collins, 1971-72, prof. dept. agronomy, 1975-92, chmn. dept., 1975-85. Recipient Best Tchr. award Sch. Agr., Purdue U., 1965, 68, Purdue Agronomy Legend. Fellow AAAS, Am. Soc. Agronomy (Agronomic Edn. award 1971, Agronomic Svc. award 1991), Fellow Crop Sci. Soc. Am. (pres. 1983-84); mem. Am. Inst. Biol. Sci. Home: 1441 Meeker Dr Fort Collins CO 80524-4311 Office: Colo State U Dept Soil Crop Scis Fort Collins CO 80523

KEIR, GERALD JANES, banker; b. Ludlow, Mass., Aug. 22, 1943; s. Alexander J. and Evelyn M. (Buckley) K.; m. Karen Mary Devine, July 22, 1972; children: Matthew J., Katherine B., Megan E. BA, Mich. State U., 1964, MA, 1966. Reporter Honolulu Advertiser, 1968-74, city editor, 1974-86, mng. editor, 1986-89, editor, 1989-95; exec. v.p. corp. comms. First Hawaiian Bank, Honolulu, 1995—. Co-author: Advanced Reporting: Beyond News Events, 1985, Advanced Reporting: Discovering Patterns in News Events, 1997. Bd. dirs. First Hawaiian Found., Salvation Army Bd. Hawaii, East-West Ctr. Found. Recipient Nat. Reporting award Am. Polit. Sci. Assn., 1971, Benjamin Fine Nat. award Am. Assn. Secondary Sch. Prins., 1981; John Ben Snow fellow, 1983, NEH fellow, 1973. Mem. Social Sci. Assn., Honolulu Cmty.-Media Coun. Office Phone: 808-525-7086. Business E-Mail: gerry.keir@fhwn.com.

KEITH, TOBY (TOBY KEITH COVEL), country singer, songwriter, producer; b. Clinton, Okla., July 8, 1961; s. H.K. and Joan Covel; m. Tricia Keith, Mar. 24, 1984; children: Shelly Reeve, Krystal, Stelen Keith Covel. Worked in oil industry; former band mem. The Easy Money Band; played defensive end Okla. City Drillers, minor league, semi-pro football team; football player Okla. Outlaws, US Football League (USFL) team; signed with Mercury Records, Nashville, 1984—99, DreamWorks, Nashville, 1999; founder Show Dog Nashville Records, 2005—. Singer: (albums) Toby Keith, 1993, Christmas to Christmas, 1995, Boomtown, 1995, Blue Moon, 1996, Dream Walkin', 1997, Greatest Hits, Vol. 1, 1998, How Do You Like Me Now?, 1999 (Album Yr., Acad. Country Music Awards, 2000), Pull My Chain, 2001, Unleased, 2002 (Favorite Country Album, Am. Music Awards, 2003), 20th Century Masters-The Millennium, 2003, Shock 'n Y'all, 2003 (Album Yr., Acad. Country Music Awards, 2003, Best Country Album, Am. Music Awards, 2004), Greatest Hits 2, 2004, Honkytonk University, 2005, White Trash with Money, 2006, Big Dog Daddy, 2007, A Classic Christmas, 2007, Love Me If You Can, 2007, That Don't Make Me a Bad Guy, 2008, (songs) Should've Been A Cowboy, 1993 (Most Played Song of Decade in the 90's, Billboard), How Do You Like Me Now?, 2000 (Named Most Played Song of 2000, Billboard), Whiskey Girl, 2003 (Hottest Video of Yr., Country Music TV Music Awards, 2005), As Good As I Once Was, 2005 (Music Video of Yr., Country Music Assn., 2005); actor: (films) Broken Bridges, 2006; writer, prodr., actor: Beer for My Horses, 2008 (Tex Ritter award, Acad. Country Music, 2009). Recipient Country Album Artist of Yr., Country Music Assn., 2005; named Entertainer of Yr., Acad. Country Music Awards, 2002, 2003, Top Male Vocalist, 2000, 2003, Favorite Male Country Artist, Am. Music Awards, 2004, 2006, Country Artist of Yr., Billboard Music Awards, 2005. Achievements include invited by George W. Bush to adddress at MacDill Air Force Base in Tampa, Fla., site of US Cent. Command and headquarters of Gen. Tommy Franks; a super-patriotic response to Sept. 11th that became one of country's most highly charged political statements; songwriting, 12 of his 16 #1 hits have been self-penned; radio airplay, 8 Billboard country #1's and eight R&R country #1's from his DreamWorks Records alone; sales of more than $13.5 million. Avocations: hunting, fishing, golf, collecting baseball cards and memorabilia.

KEKER, JOHN WATKINS, lawyer; b. Winston-Salem, NC, Jan. 4, 1944; s. Samuel J. and Lucy Hearn (Spinks) K.; m. Christina Snowden Day, Sept. 11, 1965; children: Adam, Nathan. AB cum laude, Princeton U., 1965; LLB, Yale U., 1970. Bar: Calif. 1971, US Dist. Ct. (all dists. Calif.) 1971, US Ct. Appeals (9th cir.) 1971, US Supreme Ct. 1974. Law clk. to chief justice Earl Warren US Supreme Ct., Washington, 1970-71; staff atty. Natural Resources Def. Coun., Washington, 1971, Office Fed. Pub. Defender, San Francisco, 1971-73; ptnr. Keker & Van Nest and predecessor firms, San Francisco, 1973—. Assoc. counsel Iran/Contra Investigation, Washington, 1987—. Co-author: Effective Direct and Cross Examination, 1986; contbr. articles to profl. jours. Chmn. bd. Bay Area Water Quality Control, Oakland, Calif., 1980-82; v.p. San Francisco Fire Commn., 1988; pres. San Francisco Police Commn., 1990-91, 96-97. Served to 1st lt. USMC, 1965—67, Vietnam. Recipient Significant Contbn. to Criminal Justice award, Calif. Attys. for Criminal Justice, 1996; named Best Lawyer in Bay Area, San Francisco Chronicle, 2003; named one of 100 Most Influential Lawyers, Nat. Law Jour., 2006; named to Litig. Hall of Fame, Calif. State Bar, 2002. Fellow: Am. Bar Found., Am. Bd. Trial Advs., Internat. Acad. Trial Lawyers, Am. Coll. Trial Lawyers. Office: Keker & Van Nest 710 Sansome St San Francisco CA 94111 Office Phone: 415-391-5400.

KELLEHER, ROBERT JOSEPH, judge; b. NYC, Mar. 5, 1913; s. Frank and Mary (Donovan) K.; m. Gracyn W. Wheeler, Aug. 14, 1940; children: R. Jeffrey, Karen Kathleen Kelleher King. AB, Williams Coll., 1935; LL.B., Harvard U., 1938. Bar: N.Y. 1939, Calif. 1942, U.S. Supreme Ct 1954. Atty. War Dept., 1941-42; asst. U.S. atty. So. Dist. Calif., 1948-50; pvt. practice Beverly Hills, 1951-71; U.S. dist. judge, 1971-83; sr. judge U.S. Dist. Ct. 9th Cir., 1983—. Mem. So. Calif. Com. Olympic Games, 1964; capt. U.S. Davis Cup Team, 1962-63; treas. Youth Tennis Found. So. Calif., 1961-64. Served to USNR, 1942-45. Recipient Bicentennial Medal award Williams Coll., 2001; enshrined in Internat. Tennis Hall of Fame, 2000. Mem. So. Calif. Tennis Assn. (v.p. 1958-64, pres. 1983-85), U.S. Lawn Tennis Assn. (pres. 1967-68), Internat. Lawn Tennis Club U.S.A., Gt. Britain, France, Can., Mex., Australia, India, Israel, Japan, All Eng. Lawn Tennis and Croquet (Wimbledon), Harvard Club (N.Y./So. Calif.), Williams Club (N.Y.), L.A. Country Club, Delta Kappa Epsilon. Office: US Dist Ct 255 E Temple St Ste 1434 Los Angeles CA 90012-3334 Office Phone: 213-894-5255.

KELLER, EDWARD LOWELL, electrical engineer, educator; b. Rapid City, SD, Mar. 6, 1939; s. Earl Lowell and E. Blanche (Oldfield) K.; m. Carole Lynne Craig, Sept. 1, 1963; children: Edward Lowell, Craig, Morgan. BS, U.S. Naval Acad., 1961; PhD, Johns Hopkins U., 1971. Mem. faculty U. Calif., Berkeley, 1971—, assoc. prof. elec. engring., 1977-79, prof., 1979-94, prof. emeritus, 1994—; assoc. dir. Smith Kettlewell Eye Rsch. Inst., San Francisco, 1998—; chmn. bioengring. program U. Calif., Berkeley and San Francisco, 1989; chmn. engring. sci. program Coll. of Engring. U. C., Berkeley, 1991-94. Contbr. articles to sci. jours. Served with USN, 1961-65. Sr. Von Humboldt fellow, 1977-78 Fellow IEEE; mem. AAAS, Assn. for Rsch. in Vision and Ophthalmology, Soc. for Neurosci., Internat. Neural Network Soc. Achievements include rsch. on oculomotor system and math. modelling of nervous system. Office: Smith-Kettlewell Eye Rsch Inst 2318 Fillmore St San Francisco CA 94115-1813 Business E-Mail: elk@ski.org.

KELLER, GLEN ELVEN, JR., lawyer; b. Longmont, Colo., Dec. 21, 1938; s. Glenn Elven and Elsie Mildred (Hogsett) K.; m. Elizabeth Ann Kauffman, Aug. 14, 1960; children: Patricia Carol, Michael Ashby. BS in Bus., U. Colo., 1960; JD, U. Denver, 1964. Bar: Colo. 1964, U.S. Dist. Ct. Colo. 1964, U.S. Ct. Appeals (10th cir.) 1982. Assoc. Phelps, Hall & Keller and predecessor, Denver, 1964-67, ptnr., 1967-73; asst. atty. gen. State of Colo., Denver, 1973-74; judge U.S. Bankruptcy Ct., Dist. Colo., 1974-82; ptnr. Davis, Graham & Stubbs LLP, Denver, 1982—2004, sr. counsel, 2004—. Lectr. law U. Denver, 1977-87; adj. prof., 1987-98, Frank E. Rickston Jr. adj. prof. law, 1998-2003; ct. adminstrn. com. Jud. Conf. US; fin. com. sch. constrn. Colo. Lawyers' Com., 1997-2000, exec. com., 1999-2000, chmn. task force on sch. discipline, 1999-2000; bd. dirs. Western Stock Show Assoc., 1985-; adj. instr. law U. Colo., 2003. Mem. Colo. Bd. Health, 1968-74, pres., 1970-74; pres., dir. The Westernaires, Golden, Colo., 1983-, Jefferson County R-1 Sch. Bd., 1984-89; dir. Jefferson County Sch. Fin. Corp., 1992—. Named Colo. Horse Person of Yr., Colo. Horse Coun., 1999, Best Lawyers in Am., 1995-. Fellow Am. Coll. Bankruptcy; mem ABA, Colo. Bar Assn., Denver Bar Assn., Nat. Conf. Bankruptcy Judges, Law Club. Republican. Office: Davis Graham & Stubbs LLP 1550 17th St Ste 500 Denver CO 80202-1202

KELLER, HUBERT, chef, restaurant owner; b. France; Student, Ecole Hoteliere, Strasbourg, France. Apprentice Auberge de L'Ill, Illhaeusern; formerly mem. staff Mermoz cruise ship, Domaine de Chateauneuf, Nans les Pins, France; former chef saucier Moulin de Mougins; formerly mem. staff Hotel Negresco, Nice, France, Hotel Prieure, Saumur; former chef La Cuisine du Soleil, São Paulo, Sutter 500, San Francisco; co-owner, chef Fleur de Lys Restaurant, San Francisco, 1986—; owner, chef Burger Bar, Las Vegas, St. Louis. Author: The Cuisine of Hubert Keller; contbr. Eat More, Weigh Less (Dean Ornish); host (TV series) Secrets of a Chef. Named Am. Express Best Chef, Calif., James Beard Found., 1997; nominee All-Clad Metalcrafters Outstanding Chef award, 2001. Office: Fleur de Lys 777 Sutter St San Francisco CA 94109

KELLER, JACK, agricultural engineering educator, consultant; b. Roanoke, Va., Jan. 5, 1928; s. Eugene and Clara (Lauber) Keller; m. Sara Altick, June 4, 1954; children: Andrew A., Jeffery S., Judith. BSCE, U. Colo., 1953; MS in Irrigation Engring., Colo. State U., 1955; PhD in Agrl. Engring., Utah State U., 1967. Registered profl. engr., Utah, Calif. Work unit engr. USDA Soil Conservation Svc., Victor, Colo., 1953; sales engr. So. Irrigation Co., Memphis, 1955-56; chief irrigation engr. W.R. Ames Co., San Jose, Calif., 1956-60; prof. Utah State U., Logan, 1960-88, dept. chmn., 1979-85, project mgr., 1978-88; pres., founder Keller-Bliesner Engring. Co., Logan, 1962—, CEO, 1989—. Co-dir. U.S. AID Water Mgmt. Synthesis Project, Logan, 1978—88, team leader tech. assistance teams, worldwide, 1980—98; chmn. Conservation Verification Cons. IID/MWD Conservation Agreement, Imperial, Calif., 1992—; sr. policy advisor to Egyptian Ministry Pub. Works and Water Resources U.S. AID WRSR Activity, 1995—98; sr. rsch. assoc. Internat. Water Mgmt. Inst., 1995—2000; sr. adv. agrl. water use efficiency program CALFED, 1999—2005; sr. irrigation policy advisor, bd. dirs. Internat. Devel. Enterprises, 2000—; team leader Project Advisor Cons. Navajo Indian Irrigation Project, 2001—03; chair water mgmt. sci. bd., mem. ind. sci. bd. Calif. Bay-Delta Authority, 2003—. Co-author: Trickle Irrigation Design, 1974, Sprinkle and Trickle Irrigation, 1990; contbr. NRC com. Soil and Water Rsch. Priorities for Devel. Countries, Washington, 1988; chmn. Red River Chloride Control Panel, Tulsa, 1988. With USN, 1945—47, PTO, sgt. USAF, 1951—53. Named Engr. of Yr., Utah Joint Engring. Coun., 1988. Fellow: ASCE (Royce J. Tipton award 2006), Am. Soc. Agrl. Engrs. (award for advancement of surface irrigation 2002); mem.: NAE, The Irrigation Assn. (Man of Yr. 1972), Internat. Commn. Irrigation and Drainage. Mem. Bahai Ch. Achievements include patents in field. Avocations: hiking, gardening, fishing. Home: 35 River Park Dr Logan UT 84321-4345 Office: Keller-Bliesner Engring 78 E Center St Logan UT 84321-4619 Business E-Mail: jkeller@kelbli.com.

KELLER, JENNIFER L., lawyer; b. Ft. Wayne, Ind., Feb. 26, 1953; BA, U. Calif., Berkeley, 1975; JD, U. Calif., Hastings Coll. Law, 1978. Bar: Calif. 1978, U.S. Dist. Ct., Ctrl. and So. Dists., Calif., U.S. Ct. Appeals, 9th Cir. 1984, U.S Dist. Ct., No. and Ea. Dists., Calif. 1997, U.S. Dist. Ct., Ariz. 1998, U.S. Supreme Ct. 1999, cert.: specialist in criminal law. Sr. rsch. atty. Ct. Appeals, 4th Dist., Div. 3, 1986—89; sr. dep. pub. defender Orange County Pub. Defender's Office; pvt. practice Law Offices of Jennifer L. Keller, 1992—. Bd. dir. Pub. Law Ctr. Orange County, 1995—2000; lawyer rep. 9th Cir. Jud. Conf., 1996—99; lectr. Calif. Pub. Defenders Assn., Continuing Edn. of the Bar, 1996. Mem. Hastings Constl. Law Quarterly, 1976—77. Bd. visitors Chapman U. Sch. Law, 1995—2003, Dean's Coun., 2004—. Recipient Wiley Manuel award for Pro Bono Svc., State Bar Calif., 1998, Lawyer of Yr., Constl. Rights Found. Orange County, 1983, Criminal Defense Trial Lawyer Yr., Orange County Trial Lawyers Assn., 2000, Jurisprudence Award, Anti-Defamation League of Orange County & Long Branch, 2001; named Atty. of Yr., Orange County Women Lawyers, 2003, Pub. Law Ctr. Orange County, 1996; named one of 100 Most Influential Lawyers in Calif., Calif. Law Bus., 2001, California's 30 Top Women Litigators, 2002, Top 100 Lawyers in Calif., LA Daily Jour., 2007, Calif.'s Top Women Litigators, LA Mag., 2007, Top 50 Women Superlawyer, So. Calif. Superlawyers, Top 50 Orange County Superlawyers, 2004—08. Mem.: Orange County Trial Lawyers Assn. (named Criminal Def. Atty. of Yr. 2000), Calif. Attys. for Criminal Justice (bd. govs. 1992—93, lectr.), State Bar Calif. (commr., Bd. Legal Specializtion, Criminal Law Advisory

Comn. 1990—92, vice-chair, Bd. Legal Specializtion, Criminal Law Advisory Comn. 1992—93, chair, Bd. Legal Specializtion, Criminal Law Advisory Comn. 1993—94, convention lectr., White Collar Crime 1994, commr. Bd. Legal Specialization 2002—05), Orange County Bar Assn. (bd. dir. 1991—93, officer 1993—97, pres. 1996, lectr., State Bar of Calif. President's Pro Bono Svc. award for Dist. 8), Orange County Women Lawyers (life; bd. dirs. 1984—86, Atty. of Yr. 2003). Office: 18500 Von Karman Ave Ste 560 Irvine CA 92612-1043 Office Phone: 949-476-8700. Office Fax: 949-476-0900. E-mail: jkeller@prodigy.net.

KELLER, JOHN FRANCIS, retired food products executive, mayor; b. Mt. Horeb, Wis., Feb. 5, 1925; s. Frank S. and Elizabeth K. (Meier) K.; m. Barbara D. Mabbott, Feb. 18, 1950; children: Thomas, Patricia, Daniel, David, John. BBA in Acctg., U. Wis., Madison, 1949; MBA, U. Chgo., 1963; grad., Stanford U. Sch. Bus., 1978. CPA, Wis., Ill. Acct. Bank of Am., 1949-51; mgr. statis. control and gen. accounting Miller Brewing Co., Milw., 1951—58; contr. Maremont Corp., 1958-68, Heublein, Inc., 1968-84; v.p. fin. Hamm's Brewing Co., 1968-70; v.p. fin., dir. United Vintners, Inc., San Francisco, 1970-80, chmn. bd., CEO, dir., 1980-84; group v.p. Heublein Wines Group, 1980-84; pres. ISC Wines of Calif., 1983-85; adminstrv. dir. Winegrowers of Calif. (a Calif. state mktg. order for wineries and grape growers), 1985-87; mgmt. cons. J.F. Keller & Assocs., 1985—2000. Lectr., assoc. prof. Calif. State U./Hayward Grad. Sch. Bus. and Econs., 1978-82; adj. prof. Golden Gate U. Grad. Sch. Bus., 1983-86, lectr., instr. Coll. San Mateo, 1990; bd. dirs. Servicor, Inc., Duckhorn Vineyards, Fife and Horn Vineyards. Active Boy Scouts Am., 1952—58; dir. Serra H.S. Bd., 1979—82; bd. dirs. U. Wis. Found., 1986—92, Seton Health Svcs. Found., 1988—2002, chmn., 1994—96; bd. dirs. Seton Med. Ctr., 1989—96; sec.-treas. St. Bartholomew Cath. Ch., 1992—94; bd. dirs. Cath. Health Care West, 1996—2001, fin. and investment com.; pres. bd. dirs. Alemany Scholarship Found., 1983—95; bd. dirs. Peace and Justice Task Force Commn., 1986—92; dir. St. Vincent de Paul-San Meteo County, 1997—; bd. dirs. Big Bros., San Francisco, 1971—75, Hill High St., St. Paul, 1969—70, Lesley Found., 1983—85; vol. Internat. Exec. Svc. Corp., 1995—2000; councilman City of Hillsborough, Calif., 1982—91, mayor, 1988—90; mem. parish coun. St. Lamberts Cath. Ch., 1966—68; pres. parish coun. St. Bartholomew Cath. Ch., 1970—; mem. Pastoral Planning Commn., San Francisco, 1994—95; trustee St. Patrick's Sem., 1994—2006, investment advisor, 1990—2008. 2d lt. 82d Airborne divsn. AUS, 1944—46, ETO, with USAR, 1946—52. Decorated Knight of Magistral Grace in Obedience, Order of Malta, Knight of Grand Cross, Equestrian Order of the Holy Sepulchre of Jerusalem; recipient Disting. Bus. Alumnus award, U. Wis. Sch. Bus., 1990, St. Louise de Marillas award, Daughters of Charity. Mem.: VFW, AICPA, Ill. Soc. CPAs, Nat. Assn. Accts., Calif. Soc. CPAs, Wis. Soc. CPAs, Fin. Execs. Inst., Junipero Serra Internat. (pres. San Mateo chpt. 1992—94, treas. Legatus chpt., San Francisco 1999—2005), Am. Legion, Peninsula Golf and Country Club, World Trade Club, Commonwealth Club, Phi Kappa Alpha (past treas., bd. dirs.). Republican. Roman Catholic. Home and Office: 785 Tournament Dr Hillsborough CA 94010-7423 Personal E-mail: jf.keller@comcast.net.

KELLER, JOSEPH BISHOP, mathematician, educator; b. Paterson, NJ, July 31, 1923; s. Isaac and Sally (Bishop) Keller; m. Evelyn Fox, Aug. 29, 1963 (div. Nov. 17, 1976); children: Jeffrey M., Sarah N. BA, NYU, 1943, MS, 1946, PhD, 1948. Prof. math. Courant Inst. Math. Scis., NYU, 1948—79; chmn. dept. math. Univ. Coll. Arts and Scis. and Grad. Sch. Engring. and Sci., 1967—73; prof. math. and mech. engring. Stanford U., 1979—93, prof. emeritus, 1993—. Hon. prof. math. scis. Cambridge U., 1990—; rsch. assoc. Woods Hole Oceanographic Instn., 1965—; Gibbs lectr. Am. Math. Soc., 1977; von Neumann lectr. Soc. Indsl. and Applied Math., 1983; Rouse Ball lectr. U. Cambridge, Eng., 1993. Contbr. articles to profl. jours. Recipient von Karman prize, Soc. Indsl. and Applied Math., 1979, Eringen medal, Soc. Engring. Scis., 1981, Timoshenko medal, ASME, 1984, U.S. Nat. medal of Sci., 1988, NAS award in Applied Math. and Numerical Analysis, 1995, Frederic Esser Nemmers prize in math., Northwestern U., Evanston, Ill., 1996, Wolf prize in math., Wolf Found., Israel, 1997, Lagrange prize, Internat. Coun. for Indsl. and Applied Math., 2006. Mem.: NAS, Soc. Indsl. and Applied Math., Am. Phys. Soc., Am. Math. Soc., Am. Acad. Arts and Scis., Royal Soc. (fgn.), London Math. Soc. (hon.). Home: 820 Sonoma Ter Stanford CA 94305-1072 Office: Stanford U Dept Math Stanford CA 94305-2125

KELLER, KAREN A., library director; BA with honors, Mich. State U., East Lansing; MLS, U. Mich., Ann Arbor. Cert. libr.'s permanent profl. cert. Libr. Mich. Positions including head adult svcs. and asst. dir. Brighton Dist. Libr., Mich.; dep. dir. Anchorage Mcpl. Librs., 2006, acting mcpl. libr., 2006—07, dir., exec. sec./tech. advisor libr. adv. bd., 2007—. Mem.: ALA, Alaska Libr. Assn., Pacific NW Libr. Assn., Pub. Libr. Assn. Office: Anchorage Mcpl Librs ZJ Loussac Pub Libr 3600 Denali St Anchorage AK 99503 Office Phone: 907-343-2892. E-mail: KellerKA@muni.org.

KELLER, LARRY ALAN, water transportation executive; b. San Pedro, Calif., Mar. 2, 1945; married; 3 children. BA in Anthropology, San Francisco State U. Various mgmt. positions Maersk Inc; COO Port of L.A., 1996-97, exec. dir., 1997—. Bd. dirs. Alameda Corridor Transp. Authority. Mem. Am. Assn. Port Authorities (bd. dirs.), Calif. Assn. Port Authorities (pres., 2001-02, bd. dirs.), Steamship Assn. So. Calif. (past sec.-treas., v.p., pres., chmn.), L.A. Area C. of C. (bd. dirs.), Alameda Corridor Transp. Authority (bd. dirs.), Danish-Am. C. of C., Internat. Assn. Ports and Harbors (bd. dirs.), Harbor Assn. Industry and Commerce (bd. dirs.). Office: Harbor Dept Port of Los Angeles 425 S Palos Verdes St San Pedro CA 90731-3309

KELLER, MARYANNE (MOE KELLER), state legislator; b. Buffalo, Feb. 19, 1949; d. William and Virginia Moslow; m. Stephen M Keller; children: Amy, Timothy. BS, Buffalo State U., 1971; MA, Canisius Coll., Buffalo, 1972. Tchr. of the deaf, interpreter Jefferson County and Denver Pub. Schs.; councilwoman City of Wheat Ridge, 1983—89; mem. Dist. 24 Colo. House of Reps., Denver, 1992—2001; mem. Dist. 20 Colo. State Senate, Denver, 2003—. Mem. West Chamber Edn. Task Force. Mem. Girl Scouts America, Parent Teachers Assn., Wheat Ridge Carnation Festival, Clear Creek Watershed Forum, Nat. Assn. Sch. Bds. Adv. Com. Recipient Disting. Legislator award Social Legislature Com., 1993, Nat. Alliance Mentally Ill, 1997, EPA award, Colo. Assn. Art Edn., 1993, Outstanding Achievement award EPA, 1994; named Legislator of Yr. Kempe Children's Found, 1994, Colo. Assn. Edn. Young Children, 1995, Cmty. Centered Bd. for Disabled, 1998, United Vet Assn., 1998 Democrat. Roman Catholic. Office: Colo State Capitol 200 E Colfax Denver CO 80203 Office Phone: 303-866-2585. Business E-Mail: moe.keller.senate@state.co.us.*

KELLER, MICHAEL ALAN, librarian, musicologist; b. Sterling, Colo., Apr. 5, 1945; s. Ephraim Richard and Mary Patricia (Warren) K.; m. Constance A. Kyle, Sept. 3, 1967 (div. Aug. 1979); children: Kristen J., Paul B.; m. Carol Lawrence, Oct. 6, 1979; children: Laura W., Martha M. BA, Hamilton Coll., 1967; MA, SUNY, Buffalo, 1970, postgrad., 1970-91; MLS, SUNY, Geneseo, 1972. Asst. libr. for reference and cataloging SUNY Music Libr., Buffalo, 1970-73; acting undergrad. libr. Cornell U., Ithaca, NY, 1976, music libr., sr. lectr., 1973-81; head music libr. U. Calif., Berkeley, 1981-86; assoc. univ. libr. for collection devel. Yale U., 1986-93; director Stanford U. Librs., Calif., 1993-94, univ. libr., dir. acad. info. resources Calif., 1994—; pub. HighWire Press, Stanford, 1995—, Stanford U. Press, 2000—. Mem. Nat. Digital Libr. Fedn., 1993—2005, chair exec. com., 2002—; mem. Bibliog Commn., Repertoire Internat. de la Presse Mus. de XIXve Siecle, 1981—84; chmn. music program com. Rsch. Librs. Group, 1982—86; reviewer NEH, 1982—88, panelist, 1979—95; chmn. Assoc. Music Librs. Group, Joint Com. Retrospective Conversion in Music, 1989—93; mem. collection mgmt. devel. com. Rsch. Librs. Group, 1986—91, chmn., 1989—91, mem. program adv. com., 1991—93; dir. Berkeley Italian Renaissance Project, 1985—95, Digital Libr. Fedn., 1994—; mem. bd. overseers Stanford U. Press, 1997—; mem. gov. com. Stanford-Japan Ctr. Rsch.; mem. adv. bd. Ebrary, Inc., 1999—; bd. dirs. Alibris Inc., 1999—; dir. Long Now Fedn., 1999—; trustee Hamilton Coll., 2001—05; mem. info. tech. adv. group New Libr. of Alexandria, Egypt, 2001—; mem. adv. bd. Groxis, Inc.; trustee Cisco Learning Inst., 2004—; chair adv. bd. rsch. libr. Los Alamos Nat. Lab., 2005—; vis. prof. Grad. Sch. Nat. Acad. Sci., China; cons. in field. Author: MSS on Microfilm in Music Libr. at SUNYAB, 1971, (with Duckles) Music Reference and Rsch. Materials: an annotated bibliography, 1988, 94; contbr. articles to profl. jours. Firefighter, rescue squad mem. Cuyuga Heights Vol. Fire Co., N.Y., 1980-81; bd. dirs. Long Now Found., 1998—; bd. trustees, Hamilton Coll., 2001-05; adv. bd. Digital Libr., Nat. Libr. China, 2005—, Global Edn. and Learning Cmty. Recipient spl. commendation Nat. Music Clubs, 1978, Berkeley Bronze medal U. Calif.-Berkeley, 1983, Deems Taylor award ASCAP, 1988; NDEA Title IV fellow SUNY-Buffalo, 1967-70, Pierson Coll., Yale U., Stanford U., 1994-95, World Econ. Forum, 2000, 01; Cornell Coll. Arts and Scis. rsch. grantee, 1973-81, U. Calif.-Berkeley humanities rsch. grantee, 1983-84, Coun. on Libr. Resources grantee, 1984, 93-99, Libr. Assn. U. Calif. grantee, 1985-86, NEH grantee, 1986; recipient various grants NSF, 1999—, State Libr. Calif., Mellon Found. Mem. ALA, AAUP, Music Libr. Assn. (bd. dirs. 1975-77, fin. com. 1982-83, editl. com. index and bibliography series 1981-85), Internat. Assn. Music Librs., Am. Musicol. Soc. (com. on automated bibliography 1982-83, coun. 1986-88), Conn. Acad. Arts and Scis. (bd. dirs.), Ctr. Rsch. Librs. (adv. com. 1988-90), Conn. Ctr. for Book (bd. dirs.), Book Club of Calif., Bohemian Club, San Francisco. Home: 809 San Francisco Ter Stanford CA 94305-1070 Office: Stanford U Cecil Green Libr Stanford CA 94305-6004 E-mail: michael.keller@stanford.edu.

KELLER, PETER CHARLES, museum director, mineralogist; b. Allentown, Pa., Aug. 16, 1947; s. Charles Donald and Barbara Jean (Miller) Keller; children: Bret Charles, Elizabeth Austin. BA, George Washington U., 1972; MA, U. Tex., 1974, PhD, 1977. Grad. gemologist 1980. Curator minerology L.A. County Mus., 1976—80; dir. edn. Gemological Inst. Am., Santa Monica, 1980—84; lectr. geology U. So. Calif., LA, 1980—87; assoc. dirs. L.A. County Mus. Natural History, 1987—91; exec. dir. Bowers Mus. of Cultural Art, Santa Ana, 1991—. Assoc. editor: Gems and Gemology; contbr. articles in field to profl. jours. Trustee Natural History Mus. Found., 1980—84; treas. Mineral Mus. Adv. Coun., 1984. Fellow: Explorers Club, Leakey Found.; mem.: Mineral Soc. Gt. Britain, Geol. Soc. Am., Internat. Mineral Assn. (U.S. rep. for mus.), Gemol. Assn. Gt. Britain, Mineral soc. Am., Am. Assn. Mus., Internat. Commn. Mus., Phi Kappa Phi, Sigma Xi. Office: Bowers Mus Cultural Art 2002 N Main St Santa Ana CA 92706-2731

KELLER, RACHAEL See ANDERSON, RACHAEL

KELLER, RICHARD ALLEN, chemist; b. Pitts., Nov. 28, 1934; BS, Allegheny Coll., 1956; PhD in Phys. Chemistry, U. Calif., Berkeley, 1961. Asst. prof. chemistry U. Oreg., Eugene, 1959-63; staff mem. Divsn. Phys. Chemistry Nat. Bur. Stds., 1963-76; staff mem. chemistry Los Alamos (N.Mex.) Nat. Labs., 1976—, fellow, 1983—. Recipient Lester W. Strock award Soc. for Applied Spectroscopy, 1996, ACS divsn. of analytical chemistry award for Spectrochemical Analysis, 1993. Mem. Am. Chem. Soc., Soc. of Flourescence. Office: Los Alamos Nat Lab Biosci Divsn Ms M888 Los Alamos NM 87545-0001

KELLER, ROBERTA LYNN, physician, researcher; d. William and Shirley Streifer; m. Bruce Adam Keller, May 18, 2000. MD, U. Calif., San Francisco, 1993. Cert. in neonatal-perinatal medicine Am. Bd. Pediat., 2003. Asst. prof. clin. pediat. U. Calif., San Francisco, 2005—.

KELLER, THOMAS A., chef; Chef, owner The French Laundry, Yountville, Calif., 1994—, Bouchon, Yountville, Calif., 1998—, Bouchon Bakery, Yountville, Calif., Bouchon, Las Vegas, 2004—, Per Se, NYC, 2004—. Spokesperson Calif. Milk Adv. Bd., 1997—98. Author: The French Laundry Cookbook (Cookbook of the Year, Internat. Assn. Culinary Professionals, 1999, Versailles Cookbook award, 1999). Recipient Ivy award, Restaurants & Instns., 1996, Robert Mondavi Culinary award of excellence, 1997, Wedgewood award, World Master Culinary Arts, 2001, Illy Best New Restaurant award, James Beard found., 2005, Outstanding Restaurant award, 2006, 2008 Am.'s Top Restaurant award for Per Se, Zagat Survey; named Best Am. Chef: Calif., James Beard Found., 1996, Outstanding Chef Am., 1997, Outstanding Restaurateur, 2007, Best Chef, San Francisco Focus, 1997, Chef of Yr., Bon Appétit, 1998, Ams. Best Chef, Time Mag., 2001, Best Wine Dir., San Francisco Mag., 2002, Best Chef, Readers' Digest, 2004; named one of America's Best New Chefs, Food & Wine mag., 1988. Mem.: Relais & Chateaux: Relais Gourmands, Traditions & Qualité. Office: 6640 Washington St Yountville CA 94599 also: Per Se Ten Columbus Cir at 60th St New York NY 10019 Office Phone: 707-944-2330.

KELLER, WES, state legislator; b. Mpls., Minn., Apr. 24, 1946; m. Gayle Keller; children: Matt, April, Zack. BS, U. Wis., Superior, 1986. Adminstr. & dir. Alaska Teamsters Training Ctr., Ship Creek, 1987—90; oilfield hand Schlumberger Oilfield Svcs., 1991—92; bldg. contractor First Am. Title, 1992—99; chief of staff Senator Fred Dyson, 1999—2007; mem. Alaska House of Reps from Dist. 14, 2007—. Pilot Alaska Air Nat. Guard USAF, 1971—75. Mem.: Pacific Northwest Econ. Region, Edn. Tech. Partnership. Republican. Office: State Capitol Terry Miller Bldg Ste 111 Rm 13 Juneau AK 99801-1182 Mailing: 600 E Railroad Ave Ste 1 Wasilla AK 99654 Office Phone: 907-465-4648, 907-465-2186, 907-373-1842. Office Fax: 907-465-2864, 907-373-4729. Business E-Mail: Representative_Wes_Keller@legis.state.ak.us.

KELLER, WILLIAM D., federal judge; b. 1934; BS, U. Calif., Berkeley, 1956; LLB, UCLA, 1960. Asst. U.S. atty. U.S. Dist. Ct. (so. dist.) Calif., 1961-64; assoc. Dryden, Harrington, Horgan & Swartz, Calif., 1964-72; U.S. atty. U.S. Dist. Ct. (cen. dist.) Calif., Los Angeles, 1972-77; ptnr. Rosenfeld, Meyer & Susman, 1977-78; solo practice, 1978-81; ptnr. Mahm & Cazier, 1981-84; judge U.S. Dist. Ct. (cen. dist.) Calif., Los Angeles, 1984—; sr. judge LA, 1999—; ptnr. Rosenfeld, Meyer & Susman, Calif., 1977-78; pvt. practice law Calif., 1978-81; ptnr. Hahn & Cazier, Calif., 1981-84. Office: William D Keller 312 N Spring St Ste 1624 Los Angeles CA 90012-2483

KELLEY, DAVID E., producer, writer; b. Waterville, Maine, Apr. 4, 1956; m. Michelle Pfeiffer, Nov. 13, 1993; 1 adopted child, Claudia Rose 1 child, Jack Henry. BA, Princeton U., 1979; JD, Boston U., 1983. CEO David E. Kelley Prodns., Inc., LA. Writer, story editor, exec. story editor, supervising prodr., exec. prodr. L.A. Law (Emmy award for Outstanding Drama Series 1989, 90, Emmy award for outstanding writing in a drama series 1990); writer, exec. prodr. Picket Fences (Emmy award for outstanding drama series 1993, 94), Chicago Hope, 1994-2000, The Practice, 1997—2004 (Golden Globe award for best TV drama 1998, Emmy award for outstanding drama series, 1998, 99), Ally McBeal, 1997-2002 (Golden Globe winner, Emmy award for best TV series-musical or comedy 1997, 98, Emmy award for outstanding comedy series 1999), Snoops, 1999-2000, Boston Public, 2000—04, Girl's Club, 2002, The Brotherhood of Poland, New Hampshire, 2003, Boston Legal, 2004-, The Law Firm, 2005, The Wedding Bells, 2007. Office: David E Kelly Prodns care 20th Century Fox 10201 W Pico Blvd Bldg 80 Los Angeles CA 90064-2606 also: William Morris Agency One William Morris Pl Beverly Hills CA 90212

KELLEY, DAVID G., state senator; b. Riverside County, Calif. m. Brigitte Kelley; 4 children. Grad., Calif. State Poly. U., San Luis Obispo. Served with USAF, Korea. With Peace Corps, India, 1968, 70-71; citrus rancher Hemet area, Calif.; mem. Calif. Assembly, 1978-92, Calif. State Senate, 1992—, vice chmn. agr. and water resources com., 1992—2000, chmn. select com. on So. Claif. Water Dists. Active Riverside County Farm Bur., 1955—, pat v.p. and pres.; bd. dirs. Calif. Farm Bur. Fedn.; bd. dirs. Hemet-San Jacinto Basin Resource Conservation Dist.; co-chair Assemly Ethics Com. Mem. Western Growers Assn., Farm Bur., Century Club of Riverside County (past pres.), Hemet-San Jacinto Noon Exch. Club, Lincoln Club of Coachella Valley. Republican. Lutheran. Address: 73-710 Fred Waring Dr 108 Palm Desert CA 92260

KELLEY, DAVID M., mechanical engineer, educator; BS in Elec. Engring., Carnegie Mellon U., 1973; MS in Product Design, Stanford U., 1978. Elec. engring. Boeing, Nat. Cash Register; assoc. prof. mech. engring. Stanford U., Calif., 1978, prof. Calif.; founder IDEO Product Devel., Palo Alto, Calif., 1978—, Onset, 1984—. Faculty mem. Ctr. for Work, Tech. & Orgn. Named one of 100 Most Powerful Men in Silicon Valley, San Jose Mercury News, one of 21 Most Important People of the 21st Century, Esquire mag. Mem. ASME, IEEE, NAE, Indsl. Designers Soc. Am. Office: Stanford U Dept Mech Engring Bldg 530 Stanford CA 94305-3030 E-mail: dkelley@ideo.com.

KELLEY, MICHAEL A., state agency administrator; BA in Econs., Calif. State U., Sacramento, MPA. Dir. Dept. Consumer Affairs, Calif., 1987—91; divsn. chief Dept. Motor Vehicles, Calif., 1991—95; dep. commr. Dept. Ins., Calif., 1995—99, chief dep. commr. Calif., 1999—2000; prin. prog. budget analyst Dept. Fin., Calif., 2000—02, chief performance rev. Calif., 2002—04; chief fin. and adminstrv. officer for sec. Bus., Transp. and Housing Agy., Calif., 2004—06; acting commr. Calif. Dept. Fin. Instns., 2006, commr., 2006—. Office: Calif Dept Fin Instns 1810 13th St Sacramento CA 95814 Office Phone: 916-322-5967. Office Fax: 916-445-7643.

KELLEY, MICHAEL JOHN, newspaper editor; b. Kansas City, Mo., July 5, 1942; s. Robert Francis and Grace Lauretta (Schofield) Kelley; 1 child, Anne Schofield. BA, Rockhurst Coll., 1964. Reporter, polit. writer Kansas City Star & Times, 1960-69; asst. Sen. Thomas F. Eagleton, Washington, 1969-76; pres. Swensen's Midwest, Inc., Kansas City, 1976-80; exec. asst. Ctrl. States Pension Fund, Chgo., 1981-83, 85-87; asst. mng. editor Kansas City Times, 1984; editor The Daily Southtown, Chgo., 1987-97; mng. editor Las Vegas (Nev.) Sun, 1997—. Office: Las Vegas Sun 2275 Corporate Cir Henderson NV 89074

KELLEY, RICHARD ROY, hotel executive; b. Honolulu, Dec. 28, 1933; s. Roy Cecil and Estelle Louise (Foote) K.; m. Jane Zieber, June 21, 1955 (dec. 1978); children: Elizabeth, Kathryn, Charles, Linda J., Mary Colleen; m. Linda Van Gilder, June 23, 1979; children: Christopher Van Gilder, Anne Marie. BA, Stanford U., 1955; MD, Harvard U., 1960. Pathologist Queen's Med. Ctr., Honolulu, 1962-70, Kapiolani Maternity Hosp., Honolulu, 1961-70; asst. prof. pathology John A. Burns Med. Sch., U. Hawaii, Honolulu, 1968-70; chmn. bd. Outrigger Enterprises, Honolulu. Bd. dirs. First Hawaiian Bank, Outrigger Internat. Travel, Inc. Former trustee, past chmn. Punahou Sch.; dean's adv. bd. Travel Industry Mgmt. Sch., U. Hawaii; former vice-dean Ednl. Inst. AH & MA Pres.'s Acad. Bd. Regents; former chmn. bd. councilors Hawaii Pacific divsn. Am. Cancer Soc., past chmn. commn. on performance stds. State of Hawaii; trustee Kent-Denver Sch., U. Denver, 2003, Colo. Neurol. Inst., 2005-. Named Marketer of Yr., Am. Mktg. Assn., 1985, Communicator of Yr., Internat. Bus. Communicators, 1987, Salesperson of Yr., Sales & Mktg. Execs. Honolulu, 1995; named to Hawaii Bus. Hall of Fame, 1993; recipient Hope award Multiple Sclerosis Soc., 1995, Ihe award Hawaii Army Mus. Soc., 2000, Lifetime Achievement award Nat. Assn. Indsl. and Office Properties, 2003, Legacy in Tourism award U. Hawaii Sch. Travel Industry Mgmt., 2004, Kama'aina of Yr., Hist. Hawaii Found., 2007. Mem.: World Travel and Tourism Coun., World Pres.'s Orgn., Pacific Asia Travel Assn., Japan Hawaii Econ. Coun., Chief Execs. Orgn., Hawaii Visitors Bur. (bd. dirs., chmn. 1991—92). Office: Outrigger Hotels & Resorts 2375 Kuhio Ave Honolulu HI 96815-2992 Office Phone: 808-921-6610. Business E-Mail: richard.kelley@outrigger.com.

KELLEY, TROY XAVIER, state legislator, lawyer; b. LA, Aug. 16, 1964; s. Harold Lloyd and Carol Ann (DeSapio) K.; m. to Diane, 2 children. BA, U. Calif., Berkeley, 1986; JD, SUNY, Buffalo, 1989, MBA, 1990. Bar: Calif. 1990, D.C., 1991, U.S. Ct. Appeals for Armed Forces, 1995, U.S. Supreme Ct. 1995, N.Y. 1996. Law clk. 1st Am. Fin. Corp., Santa Ana, Calif., summer 1987, 88, U.S. Atty.'s Office, U.S. Dept. Justice, we. dist. N.Y., Buffalo, 1988-89; atty., fin. advisor U.S. SEC, Washington, 1990-91; atty. San Diego, 1991-93; sr. v.p., gen. counsel First Am. Title Ins. Co., Glendale, Calif.; mem. Dist. 28 Wash. House Reps., 2007—. Editor-in-chief In the Pub. Interest law jour., 1988-89. Mgr. elderly companionship project East Bay United Way, Berkeley, 1982-84. Capt. U.S. Army Res., 1994—. Chancellor's scholar U. Calif., Berkeley, 1983; mem. Jessup Moot Ct. Bd./Team, Buffalo, 1987-89. Mem. ABA, Phi Delta Phi. Democrat. Avocations: travel, tennis, photography. Mailing: Ste 207 7406 27th St W University Place WA 98466 Office Phone: 253-534-3216. Business E-Mail: kelley.troy@leg.wa.gov.

KELLISON, CRAIG M., federal judge; b. 1950; BS, U. Nev., 1972; JD, Gonzaga U., 1976. Law clk. to Hon. Bruce Thompson U.S. Dist. Ct. Nev., 1976; with Office of U.S. Atty., Nev., 1976-78; apptd. magistrate judge ea. dist. U.S. Dist. Ct. Calif., 1988. Instr. law Lassen Coll., 1988-94. Mem. Calif. State Bar, Nev. State Bar, Oreg. State Bar, Lassen County Bar Assn., Washoe County Bar Assn. Office: PO Box 1238 Susanville CA 96130-1238 Fax: 916-257-2021.

KELLMAN, BARNET KRAMER, film, stage and television director; b. NYC, Nov. 9, 1947; s. Joseph A.G. and Verona D. (Kramer) K.; m. Nancy Mette, 1982; children: Katherine Mette, Eliza Mette, Michael Mette. BA, Colgate U., 1969; postgrad., Yale U., 1970; PhD, Union Grad. Sch., 1972. Dir. plays, TV and film prodns. Tchr., guest dir. N.C. Sch. Arts, 1973-80, CCNY, 1975-76, grad. film div. Columbia U., 1984-87. Dir.: (feature films) Key Exchange, 1985, Straight Talk, 1992, Stinkers, 1997, Mary and Rhoda, 2000; dir. 6 seasons Eugene O'Neill Theatre Ctr.; assoc. artistic dir. Williamstown Theatre Festival, 1974, 75; dir.: (off-Broadway plays) Key Exchange, 1981, Breakfast with Les and Bess, 1982, The Good Parts, 1982, Danny and the Deep Blue Sea, 1984, The Loman Family Picnic, 1989, Defiled, 2000; dir. (TV series) Gemini Showtime, 1981, All is Forgiven, 1986, My Sister Sam, 1987, Designing Women, 1987, E.R., 1996; prodr., dir.: (TV series) Murphy Brown, 1989-92 (Dir.'s Guild award 1990, Outstanding Dir. in Comedy Series Emmy award 1992); co-exec. prodr., dir.: (TV series) Mad About You, 1992-93, Good Advice, 1992-93, (TV pilot) The Second Half, 1993, Thunder Alley, 1994; exec. prodr., dir.: (TV series) Something Wilder, 1994, (TV pilots) Hope and Gloria, 1995, Bless This House, 1995, If Not For You, 1995, Suddenly Susan, 1996, Life with Roger, 1996, For Your Love, 1998, Felicity, 1999, Once and Again, 2000, Ally McBeal, 2000. Danforth fellow, 1969-72; Thomas J. Watson fellow, 1969-71 Mem. AEA, SAG, Dirs. Guild Am., Soc. Stage Dirs. and Choreographers (bd. dirs. 1984-86), New Dramatists (bd. dirs.). Jewish.

KELLNER, JAMIE, broadcast executive; With CBS, 1969; former v.p. first-run programming, devel., sales Viacom Enterprises; pres. Orion Entertainment Group, 1979—86; pres., CEO Fox Broadcasting Co., LA, 1986—93; CEO, pres. WBTV Network, Burbank, Calif.

KELLNER, RICHARD GEORGE, mathematician, computer scientist; b. Cleve, July 10, 1943; s. George Ernst and Wanda Julia (Lapinski) K.; m. Charlene Ann Zajc, June 26, 1965; children: Michael Richard, David George. BS, Case Inst. Tech., 1965; MS, Stanford U., 1968, PhD, 1969. Staff mem. Los Alamos Sci. Lab., N.Mex., 1969—79, Los Alamos Nat. Lab., 1983—88; co-owner, dir. software devel. KMP Computer Systems, Inc., Los Alamos, 1979—84; mgr. spl. projects KMP Computer Systems divsn. 1st Data Resources, Inc., Los Alamos, 1986—87, with microcomputer divsn., 1988. Owner CompuSpeed, 1986—; co-owner Computer-Aided Communications, 1982-84; v.p., COO, bd. dir. Applied Computing Systems Inc., 1988-2003; cons., 1979—; owner Sys. Automation Tech., 2003-4; pres., Autonomous Innovations, Inc., 2004-; CEO Innovative Autonomous Sys., LLC, 2005—. Recipient Commendation award for outstanding support of operation Desert Storm. Mem. IEEE, Assn. Computing Machinery, Math. Assn. Am., Soc. Indsl. and Applied Math., Am. Math. Soc. Home: 8 Lookout Ln Santa Fe NM 87506-8258

KELLOGG, KENYON P., lawyer; b. Dubuque, Iowa, Aug. 5, 1946; s. Kenyon P. and Maleta (Fleege) K.; m. Carolyn Jo Dick, July 18, 1970; children: Andrew P., Kenyon P., Jonathan P. BSBA summa cum laude, Creighton U., 1968; JD cum laude, U. Mich., 1971. Bar: U.S. Dist. Ct. (we. dist.) Wash. 1971, U.S. Tax Ct. 1980; CPA, Wash. With Arthur Andersen & Co., Omaha and Detroit, 1968-71; assoc. Lane Powell Spears Lubersky, Seattle, 1971-78, ptnr., 1978—. Bd. regents Seattle U., 1989—, dean's coun. Alber's Sch. Bus. and Econs., 1992—; mem. nat. alumni bd. Creighton U., 1995—; trustee Naval Undersea Mus. Found., 1995—; mem. FALES com. USN Acad., 1995—. Capt. USAR, 1968-77. Mem. AICPAs, Wash. Soc. CPAs, Seattle Rotary, Seattle Yacht Club (trustee), Cruising Club of Am., Naval Acad. Sailing Squadron. Avocations: sailing, skiing. Office: Lane Powell Spears Lubersky 1420 5th Ave Ste 4100 Seattle WA 98101-2338

KELLY, ARTHUR PAUL, physician; b. Asheville, NC, Nov. 23, 1938; s. Joseph Paul and Amanda Lee (Walker) Kelly; m. Beverly Gayle Baker, June 25, 1966; children: Traci Allyce, Kara Gisele. BA, Brown U., 1960; MD, Howard U., 1965. Intern Harper Hosp., Detroit, 1965-66; resident in dermatology Henry Ford Hosp., Detroit, 1968-71; instr. in dermatology Brown U., Providence, 1971-73; asst. prof. internal medicine Charles R. Drew U. Medicine and Sci., Los Angeles, 1973-77, prof. LA, 1983; chief div. dermatology King.-Drew Med. Ctr., LA, 1976—, interim chmn. dept. internal medicine, 1985-86, vice chmn., 1987-91, chmn., 1992-95; assoc. prof. medicine U. So. Calif., LA, 1977-80; prof. UCLA, 1995—. Contbr. articles to profl jours, chapters to books; editor-in-chief: Jour. Nat. Med. Assn., 1997—2004. Served to capt US Army, 1966—68, Vietnam. Recipient Act-So award, NAACP, 1983. Fellow: Am Acad Dermatology; mem.: Am Dermatology Asn (vpres 1997—98, pres 1998—99), Asn Profs Dermatology (pres-elect 1996—98, pres 1998—2000), Nat Med Asn (chmn sect dermatology 1978—80, Oustanding Minority Dermatology Fellow 1972), Metropolitan LA Dermatology Soc (vpres 1986—87, pres 1987—88). Democrat. Avocations: travel, tennis. Office: King/Harbor Med Ctr 12021 S Wilmington Ave Los Angeles CA 90059-3019 Office Phone: 310-668-4571. Business E-Mail: apkelly@cdrewu.edu. E-mail: apaulkelly@cdrewu.edu.

KELLY, BOB, computer software company executive; MA in English Lit., PhD in English Lit., U. Dallas. With Windows NT Server 3.51 mktg. team Microsoft Corp., Redmond, Wash., team lead Windows NT Server 3.51, group mgr. Windows NT Server, Windows 2000 Server mktg., mgr. Infrastructure Server mktg. team, info. tech. profl. team, bus. value mktg. team, gen. mgr. Windows Server Product Mgmt. team, 2002, gen. mgr. Infrastructure Server mktg. org., corp. v.p. Infrastructure Server Mktg., 2007—. Office: Microsoft Corp One Microsoft Way Redmond WA 98052-6399

KELLY, DANIEL GRADY, JR., lawyer; b. Yonkers, NY, July 15, 1951; s. Daniel Grady and Helene (Coyne) K.; m. Annette Susan Wheeler, May 8, 1976; children— Elizabeth Anne, Brigid Claire, Cynthia Logan. Grad., Choate Sch., Wallingford, Conn., 1969; BA magna cum laude, Yale U., 1973; JD, Columbia U., 1976. Bar: N.Y. 1977, U.S. Dist. Ct. (so. and ea. dists.) N.Y. 1977, Calif. 1986, U.S. Dist. Ct. (cen. dist.) Calif. 1987. Law clk. to judge U.S. Ct. Appeals (2d cir.), NYC, 1976-77; assoc. Davis Polk & Wardwell, NYC, 1977-83; sr. v.p. Lehman Bros., NYC, 1983-85; sr. v.p., gen. counsel Kaufman & Broad, Inc., LA, 1985-87; ptnr. Manatt, Phelps, Rothenberg & Phillips, LA, 1987-90, Sidley & Austin, LA and NY, 1990-99, Davis Polk & Wardwell, NYC and Menlo Park, Calif., 1999—. Mem. editl. bd. Columbia Law Rev., 1975-76. Office: Davis Polk & Wardwell 1600 El Camino Real Menlo Park CA 94025-4119 Office Phone: 650-752-2001. E-mail: dankelly@dpw.com.

KELLY, HENRY ANSGAR, language educator; b. Fonda, Iowa, June 6, 1934; s. Harry Francis and Inez Ingeborg (Anderson) K.; m. Marea Tancred, June 18, 1968; children— Sarah Marea, Dominic Tancred. AB, St. Louis U., 1959, A.M., Ph.L., St. Louis U., 1961; PhD, Harvard U., 1965. From asst. prof. English to prof. emeritus U. Calif., LA, 1967—2004, prof. emeritus, 2004—, dir. Ctr. for Medieval and Renaissance Studies, 1998—2003. Author: The Devil, Demonology and Witchcraft, 1968, 74, Divine Providence in the England of Shakespeare's Histories, 1970, Love and Marriage in the Age of Chaucer, 1975, The Matrimonial Trials of Henry VIII, 1976, Canon Law and the Archpriest of Hita, 1984, The Devil at Baptism, 1985, Chaucer and the Cult of St. Valentine, 1986, Tragedy and Comedy from Dante to Pseudo-Dante, 1989, Ideas and Forms of Tragedy from Aristotle to the Middle Ages, 1993, Chaucerian Tragedy, 1997, Inquisitions and Other Trial Procedures in the Medieval West, 2001, Satan: A Biography, 2006; co-editor Viator 1970-90, editor, 2003—. Jr. fellow Harvard Soc. of Fellows, 1964—67. Fellow Guggenheim fellow, 1971—72, Nat. Endowment Humanities, 1980—81, 1996—97. Fellow Medieval Acad. Am.; mem. Medieval Assn. of Pacific (pres. 1988-90). Roman Catholic. Home: 1123 Kagawa St Pacific Palisades CA 90272-3838 Office: UCLA Dept English 405 Hilgard Ave Los Angeles CA 90095-9000 Office Phone: 310-825-7486. E-mail: kelly@humnet.ucla.edu.

KELLY, J. MICHAEL, lawyer; b. Hattiesburg, Miss., Dec. 5, 1943; BA, Emory U., 1966; LLB, U. Va., 1969. Bar: Ga. 1969, U.S. Supreme Ct. 1978, D.C. 1980, Utah 1982, Calif. 1988. Law clerk to Judge Griffin B. Bell (5th cir.) US Ct. Appeals, Atlanta, 1969-70; ptnr. Alston & Bird (formerly Alston, Miller & Gaines), Atlanta, 1970-77, 81-82; counselor to atty. gen. US Dept. Justice, Washington, 1977-79; counselor to sec. US Dept. Energy, Washington, 1979-81; ptnr., shareholder, dir. Ray, Quinney & Nebeker, Salt Lake City, 1982-87; ptnr. Cooley Godward Kronish LLP, San Francisco, 1987—. Mem. Omicron Delta Kappa, Phi Alpha Delta. Democrat. Office: Cooley Godward Kronish LLP 101 California St 5th Fl San Francisco CA 94111-5800 Home Phone: 415-999-4446; Office Phone: 415-693-2076. Business E-Mail: kellyjm@cooley.com.

KELLY, JAMES ANTHONY, priest; b. Worcester, Mass., Apr. 22, 1949; s. James and Elisabeth (Allen) K. BA in Philosophy and Govt., Harvard Coll., 1971; PhD in Philosophy, CUNY, 1979; postgrad., Pontifical U. of Holy Cross, Rome, 2005—. ordained priest Roman Cath. Ch., 1982. Dir. Riverside Study Ctr., NYC, 1977-79; procurator Prelature of Opus Dei, Rome, 1984-88, vicar USA region New Rochelle, NY, 1988-98; work with vicar of Opus Dei, 1998—2002; work with Del. Vicar of Opus Dei in Calif., 2002—. Avocations: philosophy, jazz, literature. Home and Office: 765 14th Ave San Francisco CA 94118-3558 Office Phone: 415-386-0431. Personal E-mail: msgr.james.kelly@gmail.com.

KELLY, JAMES J., dean, social work educator; BS, Edinboro State U., 1970; MSW, U. Tenn., 1972; PhD, Brandeis U., 1975. Lic. clin. social worker. Clin. fellow in psychiatry UCLA, 1979; instr. San Diego State U., U. Hawaii; dir. dept. social work, prof. Calif. State U., Long Beach, dean Sch. Health and Human Svcs., prof. social work LA, 1997—. Mem. cmty. adv. bd. coun. County Dept. Children's Svcs.; mem. bd. govs. Sr. Care Action Network Health Plan. Named U.S. Social Worker of the Yr. NASW; recipient Merit award, 1981. Mem. Nat. Assn. Deans and Dirs. Schs. Social Work (pres.), Calif. Assn. Deans and Dirs. Schs. Social Work (pres.). Office: Calif State U 5151 State University Dr Los Angeles CA 90032-4226 Fax: 323-343-5598. E-mail: jkelly@calstatela.edu.

KELLY, JAMES S., personal care industry executive; BBA in Acctg., U. San Diego. CPA. Audit mgr. KPMG Peat Marwick LLP; contr. Jenny Craig Internat., 1989—, v.p., 1992—, CFO, 1999—, treas. Fax: 858-812-2718; 858-812-2713.

KELLY, JOHN F., air transportation executive; b. Tacoma; Degree in Bus. Adminstrn., U. Puget Sound. Various positions Continental Airliens, Seattle, Houston, L.A.; asst. v.p. sales Alaska Airlines, 1976-78; staff v.p. sales, 1978; v.p. mktg., 1981-87; COO; pres., CEO, 1995—, Horizon Air Industries Inc. subs. Alaska Air Group, 1987-94; chmn.; chmn., pres., CEO Alaska Air Group, Seattle, 1995—. Bd. trustees Seattle Repertory Theatre; mem. bus. adv. com. Northwestern U. Transp. Ctr.; bd. dirs. Wash. Roundtable; chmn. bd. vis. Sch. Bus. U. Puget Sound, mentor bus. leadership program. Office: Alaska Air Group 19300 Pacific Hwy S Seattle WA 98188

KELLY, JOHN J., lawyer, former prosecutor; US atty. N.Mex. US Dept. Justice, Albuquerque, 1993—2000; Southwest Border Repr US Dept Justice, N.Mex., 1998—2000; lawyer Modrall, Sperling, Roehl, Harris & Sisk, Albuquerque, 2001—. Office: Modrall Sperling Roehl Harris & Sisk PO Box 2168 500 4th St NW Albuquerque NM 87103 E-mail: jjk@modrall.com.

KELLY, KEVIN, editor; b. Penn State, Pa., Apr. 27, 1952; s. Joseph John and Patricia Kelly; m. Gia-Miin Fuh, Jan. 2, 1987; children: Kaileen, Ting, Tywen. Freelance photographer, 1971-80; editor, pub. Walking! Jour., Athens, Ga., 1982-84, Whole Earth Rev., Sausalito, Calif., 1984-90; exec. editor Wired Mag., San Francisco, 1992-98; chmn. All Species Found., 2001—. Editor: Signal, 1988; author: Out of Control, 1994, New Rules for the New Economy, 1998, Asia Grace, 2002, Cool Tools, 2003, True Films, 2004; pub. Cool Tools website. Recipient Gen. Excellence Nat. Mag. Award, 1993, 96. Mem.: Long Bets Found. (pres. 2002—). Avocation: beekeeping. Home and Office: 149 Amapola Ave Pacifica CA 94044-3102 Office Phone: 650-355-7676. E-mail: kk@kk.org.

KELLY, KEVIN FRANCIS, lawyer; b. New Orleans, Apr. 27, 1949; s. Frank J. and Dorothy P. (Paige) K.; m. Jean A. Friedhoff, Dec. 27, 1969; children: Bryan F., Eric W. BA, Gonzaga U., 1970; JD, U. Calif. Berkeley, 1973. Bar: Wash. 1973. Law clk. to Hon. Eugene A. Wright U.S. Ct. Appeals, 9th Cir., Seattle, 1973-74; assoc. Davis, Wright, Todd, Riese & Jones, Seattle, 1974-76; ptnr. Wickwire, Goldmark & Schorr, Seattle, 1976-88, Heller, Ehrman, White & McAuliffe, Seattle, 1988—. Bd. dirs. Big Bros. King County, Seattle, 1985-95, v.p., 1991, pres., 1992; bd. trustees Legal Found. Wash., Seattle, 1994-97, pres., 1997. Mem. Wash. Biotechnology and Biomedical Assn. (bd. dirs. 1996—), Wash. Soc. Hosp. Lawyers, Order of Coif. Avocation: bicycling. Home: 4040 55th Ave NE Seattle WA 98105-4957

KELLY, MINKA, actress; b. LA, June 24, 1980; d. Rick Dufay and Maureen Kelly. Actress (guest appearance TV series) Cracking Up, 2004, Drake & Josh, 2004, American Dreams, 2005, What I Like About You, 2005, (films) Devil's Highway, 2005, The Pumpkin Karver, 2006, State's Evidence, 2006, The Kingdom, 2007, (TV series) Friday Night Lights, 2006—. Office: c/o Management 360 9111 Wilshire Blvd Beverly Hills CA 90210

KELLY, PAUL JOSEPH, JR., federal judge; b. Freeport, NY, Dec. 6, 1940; s. Paul J. and Jacqueline M. (Nolan) Kelly; m. Ruth Ellen Dowling, June 27, 1964; children: Johanna, Paul Edwin, Thomas Martin, Christopher Mark, Heather Marie. BBA, U. Notre Dame, 1963; JD, Fordham U., 1967. Bar: N.Mex. 1967. Law clk. Cravath, Swaine & Moore, NYC, 1964—67; assoc. firm Hinkle, Cox, Eaton, Coffield & Hensley, Roswell, N.Mex., 1967—71, ptnr., 1971—92; judge US Ct. Appeals (10th cir.), Santa Fe, 1992—. Mem. N.Mex. Bd. Bar Examiners, 1982—85, N.Mex. Ho. of Reps., 1976—81, chmn. consumer and pub. affairs com., mem. judiciary com.; mem. N.Mex. Pub. Defender Bd., US Jud. Conf. Com. on the Jud. Br., 1994—99, US Jud. Conf. Civil Rules Adv. Com., 2002—07; chair 10th Cir. Rules com., 10th Cir. Uniform Criminal Jury Instrn. Com. Bd. visitors Fordham U. Sch. Law, 1992—2006; pres. Oliver Seth Inn of Ct., 1993—, Roswell Drug Abuse Com, 1970—71; mem. Appellate Judges Nominating Commn., 1989—92, Eastern N.Mex. State Fair Bd., 1978—83; pres. Chaves County Young Reps., 1971—72; vice chmn. N.Mex. Young Reps., 1969—71, treas., 1968—69; pres. parish coun. Roman Cath. Ch., 1971—76; bd. dirs. Zia coun. Girl Scouts Am., Roswell Girls Club, Chaves County Mental Health Assn., 1974—77, Santa Fe Orch., 1992—93, Roswell Symphony Orch. Soc., 1969—82, treas., 1970—73, pres., 1973—75. Mem.: State Bar N.Mex. (v.p. young lawyers sect. 1969, mem. continuing legal edn. com. 1970—73, co-chmn. ins. sub-com. 1972—73, mem. Bench-Bar com. 1994—), Fed. Bar Assn. Office: US Court Appeals 10th Circuit Federal Courthouse PO Box 10113 Santa Fe NM 87504-6113 Office Phone: 505-988-6541.

KELLY, REGIS BAKER, biochemistry and biophysics educator; b. Edinburgh, May 26, 1940; m. Rae L. Burke, 1992; children: Gordon, Alison, Colin. BSc, U. Edinburgh, 1961; PhD, Calif. Inst. Tech., 1967. Instr. neurobiology Harvard Med. Sch., Boston, 1969-71; from asst. prof. to prof. biochem. and biophysics U. Calif., San Francisco, 1971—, chair dept. biochemistry and biophysics, 1995—. Dir. cell biology program U. Calif., 1988-95, dir. Hormone Rsch. Inst., 1992—; adv. panelist Nat. Engring. Inst.; mem. study sect. NIH; vis. prof. MIT, Cambridge, 1986—. Helen Hay Whitney Found. fellow, 1967-70, Multiple Sclerosis Soc. fellow, 1970-71. Mem. Soc. Neurosci., Am. Soc. Biol. Chem., Am. Soc. Cell Biology. Office: Univ Calif Dept Biochem & Biophysics PO Box 534 San Francisco CA 94143-0001

KELLY, SEAN, entrepreneur; b. 1983; Attended, Johns Hopkins U.; grad., Columbia U. Personal trainer & fitness cons.; rsch. assoc. NYU Hosp. for Joint Disease; co-founder Fit Fuel, Gardena, Calif., 2004—. Co-author: HealthPundits.com. Named one of Best Entrepreneurs Under 25, BusinessWeek, 2006. Office: Fit Fuel Llc 71 Spectrum Blvd Las Vegas NV 89101-4838 E-mail: sean@fitfuel.com.

KELLY, THOMAS J., sports association executive; b. Madison, Wis. m. Carole Duh. BA in Journalism, U. Wis., 1974. Photographer Madison's daily newspapers; sports editor weekly newspaper; pub. rels. dir. midwestern ski resort, 1977; asst. nat. nordic dir. U.S. Ski Assn., 1988-95; dir. comms. U.S. Skiing, 1988—, dir. ops., 1995-96; v.p. pub. rels. U.S. Ski and Snowboard Assn. (formerly U.S. Skiing), 1996—. Mem. bd. dirs. Ski Utah. Mem. Rotary. Office: US Ski Snowboard Assn PO Box 100 Park City UT 84060-0100

KELLY, TIMOTHY DONAHUE, former state legislator; b. Sacramento, Aug. 15, 1944; m. Lisa Nelson, Jan. 1, 1994; children: Ingrid Brose, Theodore Ambrose. Former legis. aide to Calif. and Nev. Legislatures; mortgage banker; mem. Alaska Ho. of Reps., 1976—78, Alaska Senate, 1978—2001, senate pres., 1989—90. With USMCR, Alaska Air NG. Alaska Domestic Emergency Ribbon. Presidential Achievement Award, 82. Alaska Hist Soc; America Association Ret Persons; Kenai Sportfishing Association; Marine Corps League; Sons of Norway; America Legion; Association United States Army; Elks. Republican. Office: State Capitol Juneau AK 99801-1182

KELM, BONNIE G., art museum director, appraiser, educator, consultant; b. Bklyn., Mar. 29, 1947; d. Julius and Anita (Baron) Steiman; m. William G. Malis; 1 child, Michael Darren. BS in Art Edn., Buffalo State U., 1968; MA in Art History, Bowling Green State U., Ohio, 1975; PhD in Arts Adminstrn., Ohio State U., 1987. Cert. uniform standards of profl. appraisal practice NYU, 2004. Art tchr. Toledo Pub. Schs., 1968—71; ednl. cons. Columbus (Ohio) Mus. Art, 1976—81; prof. art Franklin U., Columbus, 1976—88; legis. coord. Ohio Ho. of Reps., Columbus, 1977; pres. bd. trustees Columbus Inst. for Contemporary Art, 1977—81; tech. asst. cons. Ohio Arts Coun., Columbus, 1984—88; dir. Bunte Gallery Franklin U., Columbus, 1978—88; dir. art mus. Miami U., Oxford, Ohio, 1988—96, assoc. prof., 1988—96; dir. Muscarelle Mus. of Art Coll. William and Mary, Williamsburg, Va., 1996—2002, assoc. prof. art and art history, 1996—2002; dir. Univ. Art Mus. U. Calif., Santa Barbara, 2002—06. Adj. prof. dept. art history U. Art Mus. U. Calif., Santa Barbara; grant panelist Ohio Arts Coun., Columbus, 1985—87, Columbus, 1991—95, 2006—; art book reviewer William C. Brown Pub., Madison, Wis., 1985—92; mem. acquisitions adv. bd. Martin Luther

King Ctr., Columbus, 1987—88; field reviewer Inst. Mus. Svcs., Washington, 1990—; chair grant panel Art in Pub. Places, 1992—95; trustee Ohio Mus. Assn., 1993—96; adv. bd. Women Beyond Borders, 2004—; state apptd. mem. adv. com. Ohio Percent for Art, 1994—96; spkr., presenter in field. Author, editor (mus. catalogues) Connections, 1985, Into the Mainstream: Contemporary Folk Art, 1991, Testimony of Images: PreColumbian Art, 1992, Collecting by Design: The Allen Collection, 1994, Photographs by Barbara Hershey: A Retrospective, 1995, Georgia O'Keeffe in Williamsburg, 2001; contbr. chpt. to books, articles to profl. jours. Founding mem., mem. adv. coun. Columbus Cultural Arts Ctr., 1977-81; coord., curator Cultural Exch. Program, Honolulu-Columbus, 1980; mem. acad. women achievers YWCA, 1991—; mem. adv. bd. Women beyond Borders, 2004—, Exploring Solutions Past: The Maya Forest Alliance, 2006-. Recipient Marantz Disting. Scholar award Ohio State U., 1995, Gelpe award YWCA, 1987, Cultural Advancement of City of Columbus award, The Columbus Dispatch, 1984, Disting. Svc. award, Columbus Art League, 1984, Critic's Choice award Found. for Cmty. of Artists, N.Y., 1981; Fulbright scholar USIA, 1988 (The Netherlands); NEH fellow East-West Ctr., Honolulu, 1991. Mem. Am. Assn. Mus. (advocacy task force, surveyor mus. assessment program 1996—, nat. program com. 2001), Assn. Coll. and Univ. Mus. and Galleries (bd. dirs. 1998-2006), Western Mus. Assn., Fulbright Assn., Coll. Art Assn. (session chair, mus. com. 2004-07), Internat. Coun. Mus., Calif. Assn. Mus., Internat. Soc. Appraisers. Office Phone: 805-815-5198. Business E-Mail: bgkelm@wavecable.com.

KELMAN, MARK GREGORY, law educator; b. NYC, Aug. 20, 1951; s. Kurt and Sylvia (Etman) Kelman; m. Ann Barbara Richman, Aug. 26, 1979; 1 child, Nicholas. BA in Social Studies, magna cum laude, Harvard U., 1972, JD magna cum laude, 1976. Bar: NY 1977. Cons., dir. criminal justice projects Fund for the City of NY, 1976—77; mem. faculty Stanford Law Sch., 1977—, prof. Calif., 1982—, William Nelson Cromwell prof., 1996—, academic coordinator, 1994—96, academic assoc. dean., 1999—2001, vice dean, 2004—. Author: A Guide to Critical Legal Studies, 1987, Strategy or Principle? The Choice Between Regulation and Taxation, 1999; co-author (with Gillian Lester): Jumping the Queue: An Inquiry into the Legal Treatment of Students with Learning Disabilities, 1997; author: (novels) What Followed Was Pure Lesley, 1973. Fellow: Am. Acad. Arts and Sciences. Office: Stanford Law Sch Crown Quadrangle 559 Nathan Abbott Way Stanford CA 94305-8610 Office Phone: 650-723-4069. E-mail: mkelman@stanford.edu.

KELSO, J(OHN) CLARK, law educator, consultant; b. Indpls., Aug. 26, 1959; s. Charles D. and Margaret Jane (Tandy) K.; m. Kari C. Kernan. Dec. 17, 1988. BA, U. Ill., 1980; JD, Columbia U., NYC, 1983. Bar: N.Y. 1985. Clk. to Judge Kennedy U.S. Ct. Appeals (9th cir.), Sacramento, 1983-84; asst. dir. Ctr. for Advanced Study U. of the Pacific, Sacramento, 1984-85; assoc. Kaye, Scholer, Fierman, Hays & Handler, NYC, 1985-86; asst. prof. law McGeorge Sch. Law, U. of the Pacific, Sacramento, 1986-89, assoc. prof. law, 1990, dir., capital ctr. govt. law & policy; and chief info. officer State of Calif., 2002—. Cre. legal cons. Kaye, Scholer, Fierman, Hays & Handler, L.A., 1986—. Author: (coursebook) Studying Law: An Introduction to legal Research, 1990; contbr. articles to profl. jours. Recipient Bernard E. Witkin Amicus Curiae award, Calif. Judicial Coun., 1998; named one of the 25 Top Chief Info. Officers in the public sector, Govt. Tech., 2004, Premier 100 IT Leaders, Computerworld, 2007. Mem. ABA (vice chair com. on comml. torts, torts and ins. practice sect.). Avocations: opera, piano, tennis, gardening, home remodeling. Office: U of the Pacific McGeorge Sch of Law 3200 5th Ave Sacramento CA 95817-2705

KELTON, ARTHUR MARVIN, JR., real estate developer; b. Bennington, Vt., Sept. 12, 1939; s. Arthur Marvin and Lorraine (Millington) K.; m. Elaine White, Nov. 1, 1986; 1 child, Ashley. BA, Dartmouth Coll., 1961; postgrad., U. Vt., 1963. Ptnr. Kelton and Assocs., Vail, Colo., 1966—77; pres. Kelton, Garton and Assocs. Inc., Vail, 1977—84, Kelton, Garton, Kendall, Vail, 1984—93, Christopher, Denton, Kelton, Kendall, Vail, 1993—2001, Kelton & Kendall, Vail, 2001—. Head agt. Dartmouth Alumni Fund, Hanover, NH, 1985-90, class pres., 1990-96; active Dartmouth Alumni Coun., 1996—, Eagle Valley Land Trust, 2001-; pres. Vail Valley Med. Ctr. Found., 1991—; bd. overseers Hanover Inn, 2002—, Dartmouth Real Estate Coun., 2003—; gov. bd. Vail Valley Med. Ctr., 2006—. Republican. Congregationalist. Avocations: skiing, golf, wingshooting. Home: 1034 Homestake Cir Vail CO 81657-5111 Office: Kelton & Kendall 225 Wall St Ste 200 Vail CO 81657-3615 Home Phone: 970-476-5411; Office Phone: 970-476-7995. E-mail: akjr@vail.net.

KEMMERLY, JACK DALE, retired state official; b. El Dorado, Kans., Sept. 17, 1936; s. Arthur Allen and Eythel Louise (Throckmorton) K.; m. Frances Cecile Gregorio, June 22, 1958; children: Jack Dale Jr., Kathleen Frances, Grant Lee. BA, San Jose State U., 1962; cert. in real estate, UCLA, 1970; MPA, Golden Gate U., 1973; cert. labor-mgmt. rels., U. Calif., Davis, 1978; cert. orgnl. change, Stanford U., 1985. Right of way agt. Calif. Div. Hwys., Marysville, 1962-71; adminstrv. officer Calif. Dept. Transp., Sacramento, 1971-82, dist. dir. Redding, 1982-83, chief aeros. Sacramento, 1984-94; mgmt. cons. U.S. Dept. Transp., Riyadh, Saudi Arabia, 1983-84. Chmn. tech. adv. com. on aeronautics Calif. Transp. Commn. Bd. dirs. Yuba-Sutter Campfire Girls, 1972-73. With USN, 1954-57. Recipient superior accomplishment award Calif. Dept. Transp., 1981. Mem. Nat. Assn. State Aviation Ofcls. (nat. pres. 1989—), Am. Assn. State Hwy. and Transp. Ofcls. (aviation com. 1985-94), Calif. Assn. Aerospace Educators (adv. bd. 1984—), Calif. Assn. Airport Execs., Calif. Aviation Coun., Aircraft Owners and Pilots Assn. (dir. regional reps.), Elks (exalted ruler Marysville, Calif. 1974-75). Republican. Roman Catholic. Avocations: non-partisan political activities, reading, flying. Office: 1285 Charlotte Ave Yuba City CA 95991-2803 Office Phone: 530-674-3694. Personal E-mail: jdkemmerly@sbcglobal.net.

KEMMIS, DANIEL ORRA, cultural organization administrator, author; b. Fairview, Mont., Dec. 5, 1945; s. Orra Raymond and Lilly Samantha (Shidler) K.; m. Jean Larson; children: Abraham, Samuel, Deva, John. BA, Harvard U., 1968; JD, U. Mont., 1978. Bar: Mont. 1978. State rep. Mont. Ho. of Reps., Helena, 1975-84, minority leader, 1981-82, Speaker of House, 1983-84; ptnr. Morrison, Jonkel, Kemmis & Rossbach, Missoula, 1978-80, Jonkel & Kemmis, 1981-84; mayor City of Missoula, Mont., 1990-96; dir. Ctr. Rocky Mountain West Univ. Mont., Missoula, 1996—. Cons. No. Lights Inst., Missoula, Mont., 1985-89; Kennedy fellow Inst. Politics Harvard U., 1998. Author: Community and the Politics of Place, 1990, The Good City and the Good life, 1995, This Sovereign Land, 2001; contbr. articles to profl. jours. Candidate for chief justice Mont. Supreme Ct.; mem. Am. Planning Assn. Growing Smart Initiative; former mem. adv. bd. and bd. dirs. Nat. Civic League, 1990-93; mem. adv. bd. Pew Partnership for Civic Change, 1991-97, Brookings Instn. Ctr. Urban and Met. Policy; chmn. leadership tng. coun. Nat. League Cities, 1992-94; bd. dirs. Redefining Progress, Charles F. Kettering Found., N.W. Area Found., Inst. for Environ. and Natural Resources U. Wyo., Bolle Ctr. for People and Forests, U. Mont., Missoula Redevelopment Agency; fellow Dallas Inst.for Humanities and Culture 1991-98; presdl. appt. Am. Heritage Rivers Commn., 1998. Inst. Politics fellow Kennedy Sch. Govt., Harvard LU., 1998; named Disting. Young Alumnus U. Mont., 1981, 100 Visionaries, Utne Reader, 1995; recipient Charles Frankel prize NEH, 1997, Disting. Achievement award, Soc. for Conservation Biology, 1997, Wallace Stegner award, Ctr. Am. West, 1998. Democrat. Home: 521 Hartman St Apt 10 Missoula MT 59802-4771 Office: U Mont Milw Sta 2nd Fl Ctr Rocky Mountain W Missoula MT 59812-3096

KEMP, ALSON REMINGTON, JR., lawyer, retired educator; b. Rossville, Ga., July 3, 1941; s. Alson R. Dorothy (Walters) K.; m. Martha Gudenrath, Aug. 7, 1967; children: Alson Remington, Colin T. BS, U. Tenn., 1962; JD, U. Cin., 1965. Bar: Tenn. 1965, Ohio 1965, Calif. 1970, US Dist. Ct. (no. and ctrl. dists.) Calif. 1971, US Ct. Appeals (9th cir.) 1971, US Ct. Appeals (DC cir.) 1982. Asst. prof. Hancock Coll., Santa Maria, Calif., 1966-68; asst. prof. U. Tenn., Chattanooga, 1969; mem. Morgan & Garner, Chattanooga, 1968-70, Pillsbury, Madison & Sutro, San Francisco, 1970-75, ptnr., 1975-99; pvt. practice Healdsburg, Calif., 1999—. Dir. Green Diamond Resource Co.; dir Smith Bros. Holding Co., 2001—, vice chair, 2001—03, chair, 2003—05; bd. dirs. No. Sonoma County Healthcare Found. Capt. USAF, 1965—68. Grantee Benwood Found., 1962-65. Fellow: Am. Coll. Trial Lawyers; mem.: Calif. Bar Assn. Republican. Home and Office: 22190 Puccioni Rd Healdsburg CA 95448 Office Phone: 707-433-1199. Personal E-mail: arkemp@gmail.com.

KEMP, JOHN DANIEL, biochemist, educator; b. Mpls., Jan. 20, 1940; s. Dean Dudley and Catherine Georgie (Treleven) K.; children: Todd, Christine, Laura. BA in chemistry, UCLA, 1962, PhD, 1965. NIH postdoctoral fellow U. Wash., Seattle, 1965-68; prof. plant pathology U. Wis., Madison, 1968-81; assoc. dir. Agrigenetics Advanced Research Labs., Madison, 1981-85; prof., dir. plant genetic engring. lab. N.Mex. State U., Las Cruces, 1985—. Author papers on plant molecular genetics. Grantee NSF; grantee Dept. Agr. Mem. Sigma Xi Office: N Mex State U Plant Genetic Engring Lab PO Box 3GL Las Cruces NM 88004-0003

KENDALL, JOHN WALKER, JR., internist, researcher, dean; b. Bellingham, Wash., Mar. 19, 1929; s. John Walker and Mathilda (Hansen) K.; m. Elizabeth Helen Meece, Mar. 19, 1954; children: John, Katherine, Victoria. BA, Yale Coll., 1952; MD, U. Wash., 1956. Intern, resident in internal medicine Vanderbilt U. Hosp., Nashville, 1956-59, fellow in endocrinology, 1959-60, U. Oreg. Med. Sch., Portland, 1960-62; asst. prof. medicine Oreg. Health Scis. U., Portland, 1962-66, assoc. prof. medicine, 1966-71, prof. medicine, 1971—, head divsn. metabolism, 1971-80; dean Oreg. Health Scis. U. Sch. Medicine, Portland, 1983—92; assoc. chief staff-rsch. VA Med. Ctr., Portland, 1971-83, dep. chief of staff, 1993, VA disting. physician, 1993-96, acad. affiliates officer, 1997—, grad. med. edn. adv. com., 2001—04. Cons. Med. Rsch. Found. Oreg., Portland, 1975-83; sec. Oreg. Found. Med. Excellence, Portland, 1984-89, pres., 1989-91; grad. med. edn. adv. com. Dept. Vets. Affairs, 2001—05; commn. mem. VA Cares, 2003-04; mem. VA Blue Ribbon Com. on Grad. Med. Edn., 2006—. Lt. comdr. M.C., USN, 1962-64 Recipient Outstanding Physician award Found. Med. Excellence, 1995. Mem. AMA (governing coun. med. sch. sect. 1989-93, chair 1991-92, alt. del. 1992-93, Oreg. del. 1994-98, rep. Coun. Grad. Med. Edn. 1993-94), Assn. Am. Physicians, Am. Soc. Clin. Investigation, Am. Fedn. Clin. Rsch., We. Soc. Clin. Rsch. (councillor 1972-75), Endocrine Soc., Multnomah County Med. Soc. (treas. 1989, pres. 1991), Med. Rsch. Found. (Mentor award 1992), Royal Soc. Medicine (endocrinology sect. coun. 1999—2004). Presbyterian. Home: 3131 SW Evergreen Ln Portland OR 97205-5816 Office: Oreg Health Scis U Sch Medicine L-607 3181 SW Sam Jackson Park Rd Portland OR 97239

KENDALL-MILLER, HEATHER, lawyer; b. Seward, Alaska; m. Lloyd Miller. BA in History magna cum laude, U. Alaska, Fairbanks, 1988; MA JD, Harvard U. Law Sch., Cambridge, Mass., 1991. Law clk., Justice Jay Rabinowitz Alaska Supreme Ct., 1991; staff atty. Alaska Legal Services Corp., 1992—94; legis. rschr. Sonosky, Chambers, Sasche & Miller, Anchorage, Washington; sr. staff atty. Native Am. Rights Fund, Anchorage. Mem. com. on fairness and access to the jud. sys. Alaska Supreme Ct., 1997. Mem. honoring nations adv. bd. Ford Found.; bd. mem. Alaska Conservation Found.; tribal mem. Dena'ina Athabascan, Dillingham, Alaska. Skadden fellow, 1992—94. Mem.: Alaska Bar Assn. (chair, Indian law sect. 1996—97). Office: Native Am Rights Fund 801 B St Ste 401 Anchorage AK 99501 Office Phone: 907-276-0680. Office Fax: 907-276-2466.*

KENDLER, HOWARD H(ARVARD), psychologist, educator; b. NYC, June 9, 1919; s. Harry H. and Sylvia (Rosenberg) K.; m. Tracy Seedman, Sept. 20, 1941 (dec. July 2001); children: Joel Harlan, Kenneth Seedman. AB, Bklyn. Coll., 1940; MA, U. Iowa, 1941, PhD, 1943. Instr. U. Iowa, 1943; rsch. psychologist OSRD, 1944; asst. prof. U. Colo., 1946-48; assoc. prof. NYU, 1948-51, prof., 1951-63; chmn. dept. Univ. Coll., 1951-61; prof. U. Calif., Santa Barbara, 1963-89, prof. emeritus, 1989—, chmn. dept. psychology, 1965-66. Project dir. Office Naval Rsch., 1950-68; prin. investigator NSF, 1953-65, USAAF, 1951-53; mem. adv. panel psychobiology NSF, 1960-62; tng. com. Nat. Inst. Child Health and Human Devel., 1963-66; cons. Dept. Def., Smithsonian Instn., 1959-60, Human Resources Rsch. Office, George Washington U., 1960; vis. prof. U. Calif., Berkeley, 1960-61, Hebrew U., Jerusalem, 1974-75, Tel Aviv U., 1990; chief clin. psychologist Walter Reed Gen. Hosp., 1945-46. Author: Basic Psychology, 1963, 3d edit., 1974, Psychology: A Science in Conflict, 1981, Historical Foundations of Modern Psychology, 1987, Amoral Thoughts About Morality: The Intersection of Science, Psychology, and Ethics, 2000, 2nd edit., 2008; co-author: Basic Psychology: Brief Edition, 1970; co-editor: Essays in Neobehaviorism: A Memorial Volume to Kenneth W. Spence; assoc. editor: Jour. Exptl. Psychology, 1963-65; contbr. to profl. jours., chpts. to books. Served as 1st lt. AUS. Fellow Ctr. for Advanced Studies in Behaviorial Scis., Stanford, Calif., 1969-70; NSF grantee, 1954-76. Mem. Am. Psychol. Assn. (pres. divsn. exptl. psychology 1964-65, pres. divsn. gen. psychology 1967-68), Western Psychol. Assn. (pres. 1970-71), Soc. Exptl. Psychologists (exec. com. 1971-73), Psychonomic Soc. (governing bd. 1963-69, chmn. 1968-69), Sigma Xi. Home and Office: 300 Hot Springs Rd Santa Barbara CA 93108 E-mail: kendler@psych.ucsb.edu.

KENDRICK, BUDD LEROY, psychologist; b. Pocatello, Idaho, Apr. 19, 1944; s. Oscar Fredrick Kendrick and Miriam Stuart (Thorn) Stewart; m. Sue Lorraine Allen, Nov. 11, 1966; children: Aaron Matthew and Edgar Seth; m. Beverly Ann Dockter, Dec. 26, 1978; children: Cassandra Rachelle, Angela Priscilla. BA, Idaho State U., Pocatello, 1967, MEd, 1969, EdD, 1974. Lic. psychologist, lic. clin. profl. counselor Mont., Idaho; cert. health svc. provider in psychology, nat. cert. counselor; cert. clin. mental health counselor; nat. bd. cert. fellow hypnotherapist; cert. profl. qualification in psychology, critical incident stress mgmt. provider, Red Cross disaster mental health svc. provider; cert. supr. Idaho Profl. Counselors and Marriage and Family Therapists. Tchr. psychology Pocatello H.S., 1967-69; dir. counseling svcs. Midwestern Coll., Denison, Iowa, 1969-70; rehab. counselor Idaho Divsn. of Vocat. Rehab., Pocatello, 1970-73; counselor (doctoral internship) Counseling Ctr., Idaho State U., Pocatello, 1973-74; rehab. counselor Idaho Divsn. of Vocat. Rehab., Pocatello, 1974-75; chief of psychology Mental Health and Devel. Disabilities Program, Boise, Idaho, 1975—; pvt. practice psychology Boise, 1977—. Vice-chmn. Idaho State Counselor Licensing Bd., 1982-84, chmn. 1984-85, sec. 1985-86; sec., treas. Nat. Bd. Cert. Counselors Inc., Alexandria, Va., 1986-93; mem. licensure com. Idaho Pers. and Guidance Assn., 1975-78, chmn. 1977-78, rep. Am. Pers. and Guidance Assn. Licensure Network, 1977-78; allied clin. staff Intermountain Hosp., Boise, 1983-93, Northwest Passages Adolescent Hosp., Boise, 1986-93, Saint Alphonsus Regional Med. Ctr., Boise, 1986-93; designated examiner and dispositioner involuntary commitments, conservatorships and guardianships State of Idaho, 1981—; cons. Idaho Pers. Commn., 1982—; grad. sch. lectr. Idaho State U., 1975; grad. sch. faculty affiliate, Coll. of Idaho, Caldwell, 1981-86; presenter concerning counselor credentialing issues, 1981-86; treas. Idaho Mental Health Assn., 1980-81; mem. Idaho Psychology, Social Work reclassification task force, 1990-91; mem. Idaho Assn. Counseling and Devel. Legis. Task Force for Third Party Benefits for Lic. Profl. Counselors, 1990. Editor: Directory of the Idaho Psychol. Assn., 1983; author numerous articles on hypnosis, counseling and profl. credentialing. Mem. adv. bd. Trio (Upward Bound, Talent Search, Head Start), Idaho State U. 1975-76; mem. Human Rights Com., Idaho State Sch. and Hosp., 1977; mem. adv. com. Nat. Bd. Cert. Counselors and WHO Internat. Global Counseling Survey, Surrey, Eng., 2005. Recipient Disting. Svc. award Idaho Pers. & Guidance Assn., 1978, Profl. Achievement award Idaho State U., 1987, Spl. Recognition award Idaho Assn. for Counseling and Devel., 1989, Lawrence Schumacher Meml. Employee of Yr. award State of Idaho, 1995, Disting. Grad. award Idaho State U., 2001, Friend of Rsch. and Assessment for Counseling, Inc. Fellow Am. Coll. Advanced Practice Psychologists (founding mem. Idaho chpt.), Idaho Psychol. Assn. (sec. 1982-84); mem. SCV, Idaho Mental Health Counselors Assn. (charter), Idaho Counseling Assn. (leadership coun. 1977-78), ACA (pub. policy and legis. com., mem.-at-large 1992-94, chair nat. licensure subcom. 1992-94), Am. Mental Health Counselors Assn., APA (divsn. 17 counseling psychology, divsn. 30 psychol. hypnosis), Chi Sigma Iota, Idaho Hist. Soc. (cert. Idaho pioneer desc.), Stuart-Mosby Hist. Soc., Kappa Delta Pi, Honor Soc. Edn., Ancora Impara Hon. Soc. (co-founder, v.p.). Avocations: sword collecting, genealogy, history, collecting autographed celebrity photographs. Office Phone: 208-334-0906, 208-334-0900. Personal E-mail: psy108@cableone.net.

KENDRICK, KATHERINE, lawyer; b. SC; BA, U. Calif., Berkeley; JD, Columbia U., 1986. Assoc. Latham & Watkins, Los Angeles; with legal dept. Walt Disney Studios, 1989—96; v.p. European legal affairs Walt Disney Co.; gen. counsel DreamWorks Animation SKG, Inc., 1996—2004, bd. dirs., gen. counsel, 2004—. Bd. mem. Next Generation Coun., Motion Picture and Television Fund; adv. bd. LA Sports and Entertainment Commn., Kernochan Ctr. Law, Media and Arts, Columbia U. Sch. Law, Western Region Bd. US Ski and Snowboard Assn. Office: DreamWorks SKG 1000 Flower St Glendale CA 91201

KENDRICK, WILLIAM BRYCE, biologist, consultant, editor, writer; b. Liverpool, Lancashire, Eng., Dec. 3, 1933; arrived in Can., 1958; s. William and Lillian Maud (Latham) K.; m. Laureen Anne Carscadden, Dec. 14, 1978; children: Clinton, Kelly. BSc with honors, U. Liverpool, 1955, PhD, 1958, DSc, 1980. Postdoctoral fellow NRC, Ottawa, Ont., Canada, 1958-59; rsch. scientist Agr. Can., Ottawa, 1959-65; asst. prof. U. Waterloo, Ont., 1965-66, assoc. prof. Ont., 1966-71, prof. Ont., 1971-94, disting. prof. emeritus Ont., 1994—, assoc. dean Ont., 1985-93. Adj. prof. U. Victoria, B.C., 1994—; propr. Mycologue Pub. and Cons., Ltd.; tech. adv. Aerobiology Lab. Assocs., Dulles, Va.; cons. in field. Author: The Fifth Kingdom, 1985, 2d rev. and enlarged edit., 1991, 3rd edit., 2001, CD Rom version 5.3, 2008, A Young Person's Guide To The Fungi, 1986; co-author: Genera of Hyphomycetes, 1980, An Evolutionary Survey of Fungi, Algae and Plants, 1992, (CD Rom) Seashore Life of British Columbia, 2007; editor: Taxonomy of Fungi Imperfecti, The Whole Fungus, Biology of Conidial Fungi; contbr. articles to profl. jours. Guggenheim fellow, 1979-80. Fellow Royal Soc. Can.; mem. Acad. Sci. (hon. sec. 1984-91), Mycol. Soc. Am. (Disting. Mycologist award 1995), Brit. Mycol. Soc. (centenary fellow 1996), Can. Bot. Assn. (Lawson medal 2001). Mem. Green Party. Avocations: reading, music, walking, photography, rowing, writing. Home and Office: 8727 Lochside Dr Sidney BC Canada V8L 1M8 Office Phone: 250-655-5051. Personal E-mail: mycologue@gmail.com. E-mail: bryce@mycolog.com.

KENISON, LYNN T., chemist; b. Provo, Utah, Feb. 20, 1943; s. John Silves and Grace (Thacker) Kenison; m. Daralyn Wold, June 10, 1969; children: Marlene, Mark, Evan, Guy, Amy, Suzanne. BS in Chemistry, Brigham Young U., 1968, MS in Chemistry, 1971. Tchr. Weber County Sch. Dist., Ogden, Utah, 1968-69; bench chemist Salt Lake City/County Health Dept., 1971-74; chemist U.S. Dept. Labor, OSHA Salt Lake Tech. Ctr., 1974—, bench chemist, 1974-77, supr., br. chief, 1977-84, sr. chemist, 1984—. Tech. writer OSHA; safety officer OSHA Tech. Ctr., 2002—. Editor: Review Methods and Analytical Papers Before Publication, 1984—; tech. writer:. Scouting coord. Boy Scouts Am., cub master, 2005—, cubmaster local pk., 1990—94, unit commr. scouting, 1995—97; vol. spkr. in local pub. schs., 1988—2003; councilman City of West Bountiful, Utah, 1980—83, 1985—89; missionary LDS Ch., 1962—64. Mem.: Fed. Exec. Assn. (Disting. Svc. award, Jr. award for Outstanding Fed. and Cmty. Svc. 1980), Am. Indsl. Hygiene Assn., Toastmasters Internat. (treas. Salt Lake City chpt. 1987—91). Avocation: woodworking. Home: 1745 N 600 W West Bountiful UT 84087-1150 Office: US Dept of Labor OSHA Salt Lake Tech Ctr 8660 S Sandy Pkwy Sandy UT 84070

KENNARD, JOYCE L., state supreme court justice; b. Bandung, West Java, Indonesia, May 6, 1941; AA, Pasadena City Coll., 1970, U. So. Calif., 1970, BA in German magna cum laude, 1971, MPA, JD, U.

So. Calif., 1974, LLD (hon.), 2007; JD (hon.), Pepperdine Sch. Law, 1989; LLD (hon.), Calif. Western Sch. Law, 1990, Southwestern U. Sch. Law, 1991, Whittier Law Sch., 1994, Northwestern Sch. Law, Lewis and Clark Coll., 1997, Lincoln Law Sch., 1997, San Joaquin Coll. Law, 2004. Dep. atty. gen., LA, 1975—79; sr. atty. State Ct. Appeals, LA, 1979—86; judge LA County Mcpl. Ct., 1986—87; assoc. justice pro tempore State Ct. Appeal (divsn. three), LA, 1987; judge LA County Superior Ct., 1987—88; assoc. justice State Ct. Appeals (divsn. five), LA, 1988—89, Calif. Supreme Ct., San Francisco, 1989—. Chair appellate adv. com. Calif. Jud. Coun., 1996—. Recipient Contbg. Progress of Dignity and Self-Esteem Among Amputees award, Sacramento Women Amputees Group, 1990, Lifetime Achievement award, Ind. Living Ctr. So. Calif., 1990, award, Gov.'s Hall of Fame for People with Disabilities, 1990, San Fernando Valley Bar, 1990, Asian/Pacific Women's Network, LA, 1991, YWCA, LA, 1991, Ernestine Stahlhut award, Women Lawyers' Assn. of LA, 1990, Justice of Yr. 1991 award, Calif. Trial Lawyers Assn., 1992 Chinese-Am. Pioneers So. Calif. Judiciary award, Chinese Hist. Soc. of So. Calif., First Ann. Women of 90's award, Robinson's Dep. Store, LA, 1992, First Ann. Netherlands-Am. Heritage award, Netherlands-Am. Arts and Cultural Found., 1992, Atty. Gen. award, Asian and Pacific Islander Employee Adv. Com., Atty. Gen.'s Office, 1992, award, ABA Task Force on Opportunities for Minorities in Jud. Adminstrn. Divsn. and Commn. on Opportunities for Minorities in Profession, 1992, Marin Women's Hall of Fame, 1997, San Francisco Women Lawyers Alliance, 1997, Asian Pacific Am. Legal Ctr. So. Calif., LA, 1997, Coun. Asian Pacific Islanders Together Active Leadership (C.A.P.I.T.A.L), 1997, Margaret Brent Women Lawyers of Achievement award, ABA, 1993, Trailblazer award, Nat. Asian Pacific Am. Bar Assn. (NAPABA), 1994, Founders award, Nat. Asian Pacific Am. Law Students Assn. (NAPALSA), 1994, Access award, LA County Commn. Disabilities, 1994, St. Thomas More Medallion award, St. Thomas More Law Honor Soc. and Loyola Law Sch., 1995, Spirit Excellence award, ABA's Commn. on Opportunities for Minorities in the Profession, 1996, Accompanying award, Asian Bar Assn. Sacramento, Legal Impact award, Asian Law Alliance, San Jose, Calif., 2000, First Justice Rose Bird Meml. award, Calif. Women Lawyers San Francisco, 2001, Pub. Svc. award, Asian Pacific Am. Bar Assn., 2001, Jud. Coun.'s award, San Francisco, 2004, Achieve with Inspiration and Courage award, Orgn. Chinese Ams., San Mateo, Calif., 2005, Cert. Spl. Congl. Recognition, Congressman Tom Lantos, 2005, Cert. of Recognition, Spkr. pro Tempore Leland Y. Yee Calif. State Assembly, 2005, Cert. of Commendation, Bd. Suprs. San Mateo County, 2005, Lifetime Achievement award, Japanese Am. Bar. Assn. LA, 2006, Alumni Merit award, U. So. Calif. Sch. Policy, Planning and Devel., 2006. Mem.: Alpha Gamma Sigma Soc., Alpha Mu Gamma, Phi Kappa Phi, Phi Beta Kappa. Office: Calif Supreme Ct 350 McAllister St San Francisco CA 94102-4783

KENNARD, LYDIA H., former airport terminal executive; b. 1954; BA, Stanford U., 1975; MS, MIT, 1979; JD, Harvard U., 1979. Former pres./prin.-in-charge KDG Devel. Constrn. Consulting, LA; former mem. L.A. Planning Commn.; dep. exec. dir. design and constrn. L.A. World Airports, 1994-99, interim exec. dir., 1999-2000, exec. dir., 1999—2003, 2005—07; chmn. KDG Develop. & Constrn. Cons., LA, 2003—05. Mem. Calif. Air Resources Bd., 2004-; bd. dir. IndyMac Bank; bd. trustees, The RAND Corp., 2002-05, 2007-, dir. URS Corp. Intermec, Inc. Active UniHealth Found. Bd.; past mem. Calif. Med. Ctr. Found. Bd., Equal Opportunity Adv. Coun. So. Calif. Edison. Named Woman of Yr. L.A. chpt. Women's Trans. Seminar, 1995, Civic Leader of Yr. Nat. Assn. Women Bus. Owners-L.A., 2000.

KENNEDY, BRIAN T., think-tank executive; Grad. in Polit. Sci. and History, Claremont McKenna Coll. With Claremont Inst., Sacramento, 1989—, v.p., now pres., dir. Ballistic Missile Defense project, former dir. Golden State Ctr. for Policy Studies. Pub. Claremont Review of Books; contbr. articles to profl. jours. Conservative. Office: Claremont Inst 937 W Foothill Blvd, Ste E Claremont CA 91711 Office Phone: 909-621-6825. E-mail: BKennedy@claremont.org.*

KENNEDY, CARY, state treasurer; b. Norwalk, Conn., June 28, 1968; d. J. Wade and Joycee Portnoy Kennedy; m. Saurabh Mangalik; children: David Kadin, Kyra Kennedy. BA, St. Lawrence U., 1990; MPA, Columbia U., 1993; JD, U. Denver, 1995. Budget officer for Gov. Roy Romer Office State Planning and Budgeting, Colo., 1995—98; fiscal analyst Colo. Dept. Health Care Policy and Financing, Children's Basic Health Plan, 1998—99; with Educare Colo. (now Qualistar), 2000—02, Colo. Children's Campaign; policy dir. for House Speaker Andrew Romanoff, 2004—05; state treas. State of Colo., 2007—. Guest lectr. U. Denver Coll. Law, U. Colo. Grad. Sch. Pub. Affairs, Bighom Ctr. Pub. Policy; treas. Coffman's Adv. Com. on Constl. Reform. Vol. guardian ad-litem atty. Children's Legal Clinic (now Rocky Mountain Children's Law Ctr.); bd. dirs. Paddington Station Preschool. Office: Office of Treas 140 State Capitol Denver CO 80203 Office Phone: 303-866-2441. Office Fax: 303-866-2123. E-mail: treasurer.kennedy@state.co.us.

KENNEDY, DAVID MICHAEL, historian, educator; b. Seattle, July 22, 1941; s. Albert John and Mary Ellen Kennedy; m. Judith Ann Osborne, Mar. 14, 1970; children: Ben Caufield, Elizabeth Margaret, Thomas Osborne. BA, Stanford U., 1963; MA, Yale U., 1964, PhD, 1968; MA, Oxford U., 1995; D (hon.), LaTrobe U., 2001. From asst. prof. history to prof. Stanford U., Calif., 1967—80, prof., 1980—, chmn. program in internat. relations, 1977—80, assoc. dean Sch. Humanities and Scis., 1981—85, William Robertson Coe prof. history and Am. studies, 1987—93, Donald J. McLachlan prof. history, 1993—, chair, history dept., 1990—94. Vis. prof. U. Florence, Italy, 1976—77; lectr. Internat. Comms. Agy., 1976—77; vis. prof. Am. history Oxford U., 1995—96, Tanner lectr., 2003; co-dir. Bill Lane Ctr. Study of the North Am. West, 2005—. Author: Birth Control in America: The Career of Margaret Sanger, 1970 (Bancroft prize, John Gilmary Shea prize), Over Here: The First World War and American Society, 1980, Freedom from Fear: The American People in Depression and War, 1929-1945, 1999 (Pulitzer prize, 2000, Francis Parkman prize, 2000, Ambassador's prize, 2000, Calif. Gold medal for lit., 2000); author: (with Thomas A. Bailey and Lizabeth Cohen) The American Pageant: A History of the Republic, 13th edit., 2006; co-editor: Power and Responsibility: Case Studies in American Leadership, 1986; mem. adv. bd. (TV program) The American Experience, Sta. WGBH, 1986—92. Mem. planning group Am. Issues Forum, 1974—75; bd. dirs. CORO Found., 1981—87, Environ. Traveling Companions, 1986—, Stanford U. Bookstore, 1994—2003, The Pulitzer Prizes, 2002—. Recipient Richard W. Lyman award, Stanford U. Alumni Assn., 1989, Laurance and Naomi Carpenter Hoagland prize for Undergraduate Teaching, Stanford U., 2005, Wilbur Lucius Cross Medal, Yale U., 2008; fellow, Am. Coun. Learned Socs., 1971—72, John Simon Guggenheim Meml. Found., 1975—76, Ctr. for Advanced Study in Behavioral Scis., 1986—87, Stanford Humanities Ctr., 1989—90. Fellow: Am. Philos. Soc., Am. Acad. Arts and Scis.; mem.: Soc. Am. Historians, Orgn. Am. Historians (Disting. Svc. award 2007), Am. Hist. Assn. Democrat. Roman Catholic. Office: Stanford U Dept History Stanford CA 94305 Office Phone: 650-723-0351. Business E-Mail: dmk@stanford.edu.

KENNEDY, DEBRA JOYCE, marketing professional; b. July 9, 1955; d. John Nathan and Drea Hannah (Lancaster) Ward; m. John William Kennedy, Sept. 3, 1977 (div.); children: Drea, Noelle. BS in Comm., Calif. State Poly. U., 1977; MA in Orgnl. Mgmt., U. Phoenix, 2003. Pub. rels. coord. Whittier (Calif.) Hosp., 1978—79, pub. rels. mgr., 1980; pub. rels. dir. San Clemente (Calif.) Hosp., 1979—80; dir. pub. rels. Garfield Med. Ctr., Monterey Park, Calif., 1980—82; dir. mktg. and cmty. rels. Charter Oak Hosp., Covina, 1983—85; mktg. dir. CPC Horizon Hosp., Pomona, 1985—89; dir. mktg. Sierra Royale Hosp., Azusa, 1989—90; mktg. rep. PacifiCare, Cypress, 1990—92; regional medicare mgr. Health Net, Woodland Hills, Calif., 1992—95; dist. sales mgr. Kaiser Permanente Health Plan, Pasadena, Calif., 1995—. Contbr. articles to profl. jours. Mem.: Healthcare Pub. Rels. and Mktg. Assn., Healthcare Mktg. Assn., Am. Soc. Hosp. Pub. Rels., Covina and Covina West C. of C., Soroptimists, West Covina Jaycees. Republican. Methodist. Personal E-mail: djkennedy0709@verizon.net.

KENNEDY, DENNIS L., lawyer; b. Tacoma, Oct. 28, 1950; BA, U. Wash., 1972, JD, 1975. Bar: Nev. 1975. Ptnr. Lionel Sawyer & Collins, Las Vegas, Nev., 1979—. Bd. editors Washington Law Review, 1974-75. Fellow Am. Coll. Trial Lawyers; mem. ABA (administrv. law sect., antitrust law sect., forum com. health law 1980—), Am. Acad. Hosp. Attys., Am. Soc. Law and Medicine, Internat. Assn. Gaming Attys., Nat. Health Lawyers Assn., State Bar Nev. (mem. disciplinary comm. 1988—), Office: Lionel Sawyer & Collins Bank Am Plz 300 S 4th St Ste 1700 Las Vegas NV 89101-6053

KENNEDY, DONALD, environmental scientist, educator, editor; b. NYC, Aug. 18, 1931; s. William Dorsey and Barbara (Bean) Kennedy; children: Laura Page, Julia Hale stepchildren: Cameron Rachel, Jamie Christopher. AB, Harvard U., 1952, AM, 1954, PhD, 1956; DSc (hon.), Columbia U., Williams Coll., U. Mich., U. Ariz., U. Rochester, Reed Coll., Whitman Coll., Coll. William & Mary. Mem. faculty Stanford U., 1960-77, prof. biol. scis., 1965-77, chmn. dept., 1965-72, sr. cons. sci. and tech. policy Exec. Office of Pres., 1976, commr. FDA, 1977-79, provost, 1979-80, pres., 1980-92, prof. emeritus, Bing prof. environ. sci., 1992—. Bd. overseers Harvard U., 1970—76; bd. dirs. Health Effects Inst., Nat. Commn. Pub. Svc., Carnegie Commn. Sci., Tech. and Govt. Author: Academic Duty, 1997; mem. editl. bd. Jour. Neurophysiology, 1969—75, Science, 1973—77; editor-in-chief: Science, 2000—08; contbr. articles to profl. jours. Bd. dirs. Carnegie Endowment Internat. Peace, David & Lucile Packard Found. Fellow: AAAS, Am. Acad. Arts and Scis.; mem.: NAS, Am. Philos. Soc. Office: Stanford Univ Inst Internat Studies Encina Hall 401 Stanford CA 94305-6055 Home Phone: 650-326-9009; Office Phone: 650-725-2745. Business E-Mail: kennedyd@stanford.edu.

KENNEDY, GEORGE HUNT, chemistry educator; b. Seattle, Apr. 24, 1936; s. George Francis and Frances (Huse) K.; m. Kay Rife, Sept. 1, 1961; children: Joseph, Jill. BS in Chemistry, U. Oreg., 1959; MS in Chemistry, Oreg. State U., 1962, PhD in Phys. Chemistry, 1966. Chemist Borden Chem. Co., Springfield, Oreg., 1957-58; rsch. chemist Chevron Rsch. Corp., Richmond, Calif., 1961-62; prof. chemistry Colo. Sch. Mines, Golden, 1965—. Pres. faculty senate Colo. Sch. Mines, 1992-93. Contbr. articles to profl. jours. With USNR, 1954-62. Recipient Outstanding Tchr. award Amoco Found., 1992. Mem. Am. Chem. Soc., Internat. Oceanographic Found., Sigma Xi, Phi Lambda Upsilon. Democrat. Avocations: fishing, hunting, mountain climbing, travel. Office: Colo Sch Mines Dept Chemistry Golden CO 80401

KENNEDY, GEORGE WENDELL, prosecutor; b. Altadena, Calif., Aug. 5, 1945; s. Ernest Campbell Kennedy and Mildred (Onstott) Stuckey; m. Janet Lynn Stites, Aug. 3, 1978; children: Campbell, Britton. BA, Claremont Men's Coll., 1968; postgrad., Monterey Inst. Fgn. Studies, 1968; JD, U. So. Calif., 1971; postgrad., Nat. Coll. Dist. Attys., 1974, F.B.I. Nat. Law Inst., 1989. Bar: Calif. 1972, U.S. Dist. Ct. (no. dist.) Calif. 1972, U.S. Ct. Appeals (9th cir.) 1972. Dep. dist. atty. Santa Clara County, San Jose, Calif., 1972-87, asst. dist. atty., 1987-88, chief asst. dist. atty., 1988-90, dist. atty., 1990—. Author: California Criminal Law Practice and Procedure, 1986. Active NAACP, 1989—, police chiefs' assn. Santa Clara County, San Jose, 1990—; chair domestic violence coun. Santa Clara County, San Jose, 1990-92; bd. dirs. Salvation Army, 1993. Recipient commendation Child Advocates of Santa Clara & San Mateo Counties, 1991, Santa Clara County Bd. Suprs., 1992, Valley Med. Ctr. Found., 1992, 93; elected Ofcl. of Yr. award Am. Electronics Assn., 1998. Mem. Nat. Dist. Attys. Assn., Calif. Dist. Attys. Assn. (bd. dirs. 1988-90, officer 1993-97, pres. 1997-98), Santa Clara County Bar Assn., Rotary Club. Avocation: sailing. Office: 70 W Hedding St 5th Flr West Wing San Jose CA 95110

KENNEDY, JAMES WAITE, management consultant, writer; b. Belding, Mich., Sept. 23, 1937; s. Lloyd Weston and Lois (Waite) K.; m. Anna Everest; children: David, Sarah, Polly, Leif, Damian. BA, Stanford U., 1959; P.MD, Harvard Bus. Sch., 1969. With Foote, Cone & Belding, San Francisco and Chgo., 1959-66, Gen. Foods Corp., White Plains, N.Y., 1966-79; dir. human resources J. Walter Thompson Co., NYC, 1979-83; pres. Mgmt. Team Cons., Inc., San Rafael, Calif., 1983—. Author: Getting Behind the Resume, Interviewing Today's Candidates, 1987. Mem. Instrnl. Sys. Assn., Theta Delta Chi. Office: Mgmt Team Cons Inc 1010 B St Ste 403 San Rafael CA 94901-2921

KENNEDY, KEVIN CURTIS, sports commentator, former professional baseball team manager; b. May 26, 1954; Student, San Diego State U.; BA, Cal. State U. Minor league baseball player, 1976-83; minor league mgr. L.A. Dodgers orgn., 1984-91; dir. minor league ops. Montreal Expos, 1991-92, coach, 1992; mgr. Texas Rangers, 1993-94, Boston Red Sox, 1994-97; baseball analyst Fox Sports TV, radio. Author: Twice Around the Bases: The Thinking Fan's Inside Look at Baseball, 2005. Pioneer League Mgr. Yr., 1985, Pacific Coast league Mgr. Yr., 1990.

KENNEDY, LYDIA, human resources specialist; b. 1971; BA in Psychology, U. Ariz.; M in Ednl. Leadership, No. Ariz. U., Tucson. Worked in Human Resources dept. Ariz. Daily Star, Tucson Citizen, Tucson Newspaper; tng. mgr. Casino, Sun/Casino Del Sol; dir., Human Resources dept. Buffalo Exch., Tucson, 2002—. Eller Assoc. U. Ariz. Eller Coll. of Bus. and Pub. Policy. Mem. League of United Latin Am. Citizens, 1993—; mentor Wakefield Mid. Sch.; mem., Women's Leadership Conf. Com. YWCA; mem. Ariz. Compensation survey adv. steering com., Newman Cath. Cmty. Ctr. Named one of 40 Under 40, Tucson Bus. Edge, 2006. Mem.: Am. Soc. Tng. and Devel., Soc. Human Resources Mgmt., Knights of Columbus. Office: Buffalo Exchange PO Box 40488 Tucson AZ 85717 Office Phone: 520-622-2711. Office Fax: 520-622-7015.

KENNEDY, MARJORIE ELLEN, librarian; b. Dauphin, Man., Can., Sept. 14, 1946; d. Stanley Harrison and Ivy Marietta (Stevens) May; m. Michael P.J. Kennedy, Apr. 3, 1980. BA, U. Sask., Regina, 1972; BLS, U. Alta., Edmonton, 1974; BEd, U. Regina, 1981. Profl. A cert. edn., Sask. Elem. sch. tchr. Indian Head (Sask) Pub. Sch., 1965-66, Elgin Sch., Weyburn, Sask., 1967-68; tchr., libr. Ctrl. Sch., Prince Albert, Sask., 1970-71; elem. sch. tchr. Vincent Massey Sch., Prince Albert, 1969-70, 72-73; children's libr. J.S. Wood br. Saskatoon (Sask.) Pub. Libr., 1974-77, asst. coord. children's svcs., 1977-79; programme head, instr. libr. tech. SIAST-Kelsey Campus, Saskatoon, 1979—. Presenter workshops on reference materials for elem. sch. librs., storytelling and libr. programming for children, 1980—; vol. dir. Children's Lit. Workshops, Sask. Libr. Assn., 1979-80; mem. organizing com. Sask. Libr. Week, Saskatoon, 1988. Mem. Vanscoy (Sask.) and Dist. Agr. Soc., 1983-95. Named to Libr. Edn. Honor Roll ALA, 1987. Mem. Can. Libr. Assn. (instl. rep. 1984—), Sask. Libr. Assn. (insl. rep. 1984—, mem. children's sect. 1982-83), Sask. Assn. Libr. Techs. (instl. rep. 1984—), Can. Club (bd. mem. 1981-84). Mem. United Ch. Can. Avocations: antique doll restoration, antiques, gardening. Office: SIAST Kelsey Campus Box 1520 Libr Info Tech Program Saskatoon SK Canada S7K 3R5 Office Phone: 306-659-3850. E-mail: Kennedy@siast.sk.ca.

KENNEDY, PARKER S., finance company executive; b. Orange, Calif. m. Sherry Kennedy; children: Donald, Katie. AB in Econs., U. So. Calif., LA, 1970; JD, U. Calif., Hastings, 1973. Assoc. Levinson & Lieberman, Beverly Hills, Calif.; sr. v.p. First Am. Title Co. of LA; various positions including v.p.-nat. sales dir. First Am., 1977—84; dir. First Am. Title, 1981—, exec. v.p., 1984-89, pres., 1989—99, chmn., 2003—; exec. v.p. First Am. Corp., 1986-93, dir., 1987—, pres., 1993—2003, chmn., CEO, 2003—. Bd. dir. Ellie Mae. Bd. dir. Fletcher Jones Found., Orange County Council, Boy Scouts of Am., Bowers Mus. Named one of Best Performing Bosses, Forbes Mag., 2003. Mem. Calif. Bar Assn., Am. Land Title Assn. (past pres.) Office: First Am Corp One First American Way Santa Ana CA 92707

KENNEDY, RAOUL DION, lawyer; b. San Jose, Calif., Feb. 6, 1944; s. Ralph and Maxine (Schoemake) Kennedy; m. Patricia Ann Bilbrey, Feb. 11, 1967 (dec. 2005); m. Martha Shaw Nolte, Oct. 18, 2006. BA, U. Pacific, 1964; JD, U. Calif., Berkeley, 1967. Bar: Calif. 1967, U.S. Supreme Ct. 1970. Assoc. Hagar, Crosby Heafey, Roach & May, Oakland, Calif., 1969-96, Morrison & Foerster, San Francisco, 1996-99; ptnr. Skadden, Arps, Slate, Meagher & Flom LLP, San Francisco, Calif., 1999—. Co-author: California Expert Witness Guide, 1983, 2d edit., 1991. Fellow Am. Coll. Trial Lawyers, Internat. Soc. of Barristers; mem. Am. Bd. Trial Advocates, Internat. Acad. of Trial Lawyers, Am. Acad. Appellate Lawyers, Calif. Acad. Appellate Lawyers (pres. 1983-84). Home: 1701 Gough St San Francisco CA 94109-4419 Office: Skadden Arps Slate Meagher & Flom LLP Four Embarcadero Ctr San Francisco CA 94111 Office Phone: 415-984-6450. Business E-Mail: rkennedy@skadden.com.

KENNEDY, RICHARD JEROME, writer; b. Jefferson City, Mo., Dec. 23, 1932; s. Donald and Mary Louise (O'Keefe) K.; m. Lillian Elsie Nance, Aug. 3, 1960; children: Joseph Troy, Matthew Cook. BS, Portland State U., 1958. Author: (novel) Amy's Eye, 1985 (Internat. Rattenfanger Lit. prize, Fed. Republic Germany 1988), also 18 children's books including Richard Kennedy: Collected Stories, 1988 and 3 musicals, including adaptation of H.C. Andersen's The Snow Queen; inclusion of stories in: The Oxford Book of Modern Fairy Tales, 1993, The Oxford Book of Children's Stories, 1993. With USAF, 1951-54. Home and Office: 415 W Olive St Newport OR 97365-3716

KENNEDY, THOMAS J., lawyer; b. Milw., July 29, 1947; s. Frank Philip and June Marian (Smith) K.; m. Cathy Ann Cohen, Nov. 24, 1978; children: Abby, Sarah. BA, U. Wis., 1969, JD cum laude, 1972. Bar: Wis. 1972, U.S. Dist. Ct. (ea. and we. dists.) Wis. 1972, Ariz. 1981, U.S. Dist. Ct. Ariz. 1981, U.S. Ct. Appeals (7th cir.) 1980, U.S. Ct. Appeals (9th cir.) 1981, U.S. Ct. Appeals (D.C. cir.) 1983, U.S. Supreme Ct. 1984, U.S. Ct. Appeals (11th cir.) 1986, US Ct. Appeals (5th cir.). Assoc. Goldberg, Previant, Milw., 1972-79, Brynelson, Herrick, Madison, Wis., 1979-81; ptnr. Snell & Wilmer, Phoenix, 1981-93, Lewis and Roca, Phoenix, 1993-96, Ryley, Carlock and Applewhite, Phoenix, 1996-99, Gallagher & Kennedy, 1999—2000, Sherman & Howard, 2000—. Contbg. editor The Developing Labor Laws, 2d, 3d edits., The Fair Labor Standards Act. Mem. ABA, Ariz. State Bar, State Bar Wis., Maricopa County Bar Assn. Avocations: tennis, reading, hiking. Office Phone: 602-636-2015. Business E-Mail: tkennedy@sah.com.

KENNEDY, W(ILBERT) KEITH, JR., retired electronics executive, transportation executive; b. Phoenix, Sept. 19, 1943; BSEE, MS, Cornell U., 1966, PhD, 1968. Researcher microwave solid-state devices Cornell U. and RCA Rsch. Labs., Princeton, NJ, 1964-68; researcher, leader devel. team thin-film fabrication facility Watkins-Johnson Co., Palo Alto, Calif., 1968-71, head R & D devel. dept., 1971-74, solid state div. mgr., 1974-78, also v.p., 1977, devices group v.p., 1978-86, v.p. shareowner rels. and planning coord., 1986-88, co. pres., chief exec. officer, 1988—2000; vice chmn. CNF, San Mateo, Calif., 2002—04; chmn. Con-Way, Inc., San Mateo, Calif., 2004—. Contbr. articles to profl. jours. and procs. Patentee microwave power generator. Bd. dir. & past chmn. Joint Venture: Silicon Valley Network Mem. IEEE (sr.); mem. Group Electronic Devices of IEEE, Group Microwave Theory and Techs. of IEEE, Calif. C. of C. (bd. dirs.), Phi Eta Sigma, Eta Kappa Nu, Tau Beta Phi, Phi Kappa Phi, Sigma Xi. Office: Con-way Inc 2855 Campus Dr Ste 300 San Mateo CA 94403-2512

KENNEL, CHARLES FREDERICK, atmospheric physics professor, academic administrator, government official; b. Cambridge, Mass., Aug. 20, 1939; s. Archie Clarence and Elizabeth Ann (Fitzpatrick) K.; m. Ellen Lehman; children: Matthew Bochner, Sarah Alexandra. AB, Harvard U., 1959; PhD in Astrophys. Scis., Princeton U., 1964; DSc (hon.), U. Ala., Huntsville, 2003. Prin. rsch. scientist Avco-Everett Rsch. Lab., Mass., 1960-61, 64-67; vis. scientist Internat. Ctr. Theoretical Physics, Trieste, Italy, 1965; faculty UCLA,

1967-71, prof. physics, 1971-98, chmn. dept., 1983-86, exec. vice-chancellor, 1996-98; mem. Inst. Geophysics and Planetary Physics, 1972-98, acting assoc. dir. inst., 1976-77; space sci. bd. NRC, 1977-80, chmn. com. space physics, 1977-80; Fairchild prof. Calif. Inst. Tech., 1987; assoc. adminstr. NASA, Washington, 1994-96; vice-chancellor, dir. Scripps Inst. Oceanography U. Calif.-San Diego, La Jolla, 1998—2006, founding dir. environment and sustainablility initiative, 2005—, disting. prof. atmospheric scis., 2006—. Space and earth scis. adv. com. NASA, 1986—89, adv. coun., 1998—2006, chmn., 2001—05; fusion policy adv. com. DOE, 1990; founding chmn. Partnership for the Observation of the Global Oceans, 1999—2002; bd. physics and astronomy NRC, 1987—94, chmn. plasma sci., 1990, chmn., 1992—94, chmn. fusion sci. adv. com., 1998—2001, chmn. com. on global change rsch., 1999—2002, co-chair Beyond Einstein Program adv. com., 2006—07, chmn., space studies bd., 2008—; Fulbright lectr., Brazil; visitor U.S.-USSR Acads. Exch., 1988—90; disting. vis. prof. U. Alaska, 1988—93; mem. Pew Oceans Commn., 2000—03; vis. scholar U. Cambridge, England, 2007, Christ Coll., Cambridge, 2007; cons. in field; chmn. Calif. Coun. Sci. and Tech., 2007—. Co-author: Matter in Motion, The Spirit and Evolution of Physics, 1977; co-editor: Solar System Plasma Physics, 1978. Bd. dirs. L.A. Jr. Ballet Co., 1977-83, pres., 1979-80; bd. dirs. Inst. for Theoretical Physics, Santa Barbara, Calif., 1986-90, San Diego Nat. History Mus., 1998-2002, Calif. Climate Action Registry, 2002-05; founding chmn. Calif. Ocean Sci. Trust, 2002-06. Nat. scholar Harvard U., 1959, W.C. Peyton Advanced fellow, 1962-63, NSF postdoctoral fellow, 1965-66, Sloan fellow, 1968-70, Fulbright scholar, 1985, Guggenheim fellow, 1987; recipient Aurelio Peccei prize Acad. Lincei, 1995, Hannes Alfven prize European Geophys. Soc., 1998, Disting. Svc. medal NASA, 1996, Disting. Pub. Svc. medal NASA, 2006; named CP Snow Lectr., U. Cambridge, 2007. Fellow: AAAS, Am. Phys. Soc. (pres. divsn. plasma physics 1989, James Clerk Maxwell prize 1997), Am. Geophys. Union; mem.: NAS, Am. Philos. Soc., Calif. Coun. on Sci. and Tech., Internat. Acad. Astronautics, Am. Acad. Arts and Scis. Office: U Calif San Diego SIO/DO 9500 Gilman Dr La Jolla CA 92093-0210 Business E-Mail: ckennel@ucsd.edu.

KENNELLY, DENNIS L., lawyer; b. Jersey City, July 23, 1948; s. Lawrence William and Florence (Taylor) Kennelly; m. Anne Marie Gilles, Jan. 14, 1978; children: Margaret Anne, Maureen Elizabeth. AB cum laude, Coll. of Holy Cross, 1970; JD, Duke U., 1973. Bar: Iowa 1973, Hawaii 1974, Calif. 1975, US Supreme Ct. 1997. Labor rels. mgr., counsel San Francisco Newspaper Agy. (Chronicle/Examiner), 1976—79; dir. employee rels., labor counsel Peninsula Times Tribune, Palo Alto, 1979—85; prin. Dennis L. Kennelly Law Office, Menlo Park, 1985—. Lt. JAGC USNR, 1973—76. Republican. Roman Catholic. Avocations: golf, sports, basketball. Office: 1030 Curtis St Ste 200 Menlo Park CA 94025-4501 Office Phone: 650-853-1291. E-mail: secretarymim@aol.com.

KENNEY, BELINDA JILL FORSEMAN, information technology executive; b. Oak Ridge, Tenn., Dec. 18, 1955; d. Jack Woodrow and Betty Jean Forseman; m. Ronald Gene Kenney, Feb. 23, 1985; 1 child, Brandon. BS, U. Tenn., Knoxville, 1977, postgrad., 1977—78; JD, U. Colo. Law Sch., 2008; MBA, Emory U., Atlanta, 2000. Sales rep. Xerox Corp., Nashville, 1978—82, maj. account sales mgr., 1982—83, region sales ops. mgr. St. Louis, 1984—86, dist. sales mgr. Overland Park, Kans., 1987—89, dist. mgr. San Antonio, 1989—95, v.p. Houston, 1995—97, v.p., region gen. mgr. Bus. Svcs. Atlanta, 1998—99, sr. v.p. region mgr. NASG, 2000—01; corp. officer, chief mktg. officer Storage Tech Corp., 2001—04; corp. officer, exec. v.p. sales and mktg. SpectraLink Corp., Boulder, Colo., 2004—07. Exec. in residence Leeds Sch. Bus. U. Colo. Patron M.D. Anderson Cancer Ctr.; vol. ARC, Disaster Assistance Call Ctr.; mem. Emergency Family Assistance Assn. Guild, live auction chairperson; vol. The Gathering Place; bd. dirs. Wise Women's Coun., Women's Vision Found., Foothills United Way Boulder, United Way Found. Mem.: Colo. Women's Bar Assn., Foothills Mensa. Lutheran. Avocations: jogging, reading, tennis, health and fitness. Office: 5755 Central Ave Boulder CO 80301 Office Phone: 303-249-8733.

KENNEY, RICHARD LAURENCE, poet, English language educator; b. Glens Falls, NY, Aug. 10, 1948; s. Laurence Augustine and Martha (Clare) K.; m. Mary Frances Hedberg, July 4, 1982; children: Hollis, Will. BA, Dartmouth Coll., 1970. Poet, 1970—; prof. U. Wash., Seattle, 1986—. Author: (poetry) The Evolution of the Flightless Bird, 1984, Orrery, 1985, The Invention of the Zero, 1993. Recipient Yale Series of Younger Poets prize Yale U. Press, 1983, Rome prize Am. Acad. and Inst. Arts and Letters, 1986, Lannan Literary award, 1994; Guggenheim Found. fellow, 1984; John D. and Catherine MacArthur Found. fellow, 1987-92. Office: U Wash Dept English Seattle WA 98195-0001

KENNEY, THOMAS FREDERICK, retired broadcast executive; b. Dearborn, Mich., Sept. 25, 1941; s. Charles B. and Grace M. (Wilson) K.; m. Beth H. Rockwood, Aug. 22, 1964; children: Sean, Blair. BS, Mich. State U., 1964. Program mgr. Sta. WMBD-TV, Peoria, Ill., 1969-71; exec. producer Sta. WJZ-TV, Balt., 1971-73; program mgr. Sta. KFMB-TV, San Diego, 1973-75; program mgr., then dir. broadcasting ops. Sta. KHOU-TV, Houston, 1975-79; v.p., gen. mgr. KHOU-TV, 1979-84, Sta. WROC-TV, Rochester, NY, 1984-90; owner Santa Fe Wireless, Inc., Gainesville, Fla., 1990—99; regional mgr. Trader Pub. Co., Phoenix, 1999—2007. Freelance TV cons., Houston, 1984. Home: 1858 E Campbell Ave Gilbert AZ 85234-8228 Personal E-mail: thoskenney@gmail.com.

KENNEY, WILLIAM JOHN, JR., real estate developer; b. Huntington Park, Calif., Mar. 9, 1949; s. William John, Sr. and Dorothy Marie (Smith) Kenney; m. Susan Louise Wattson, Sept. 26, 1987. BS in Econs., Calif. State U., Fullerton, 1970, BBA, 1971. Lic. real estate broker Calif., Ariz., cert. leasing specialist. Leasing agt. John S. Griffith, Irvine, Calif., 1972-78, dir. leasing, 1978-84; v.p. leasing John S. Griffith (name now Donahue Schriber), Newport Beach, Calif., 1984-85, sr. v.p., 1986-91, sr. v.p. devel., 1991-95; founder Kenney Co., Newport Beach, 1995—. Spkr. in field. Bd. dirs. Riverside (Calif.) YMCA, 1989—92, Promontary Bay Cmty. Assn. Recipient Cert. Appreciation, Hemet C. of C., Riverside Bd. Realtors, Hemet Valley Kiwanis, Riverside Kiwanis. Mem.: Newport Harbor Bd. Realtors (cert. Appreciation), Calif. Bus. Properties Assn. (dir. 1976—96, chmn. 1988—89), Internat. Coun. Shopping Ctrs. (assoc.; chair govt. affairs com. 1994—98), Balboa Yacht Club (sec. 2003, bd. dirs. 2004—), Frank Miller Club (life). Avocations: surfing, fishing, skiing. Office: The Kenney Co 824 Harbor Island Dr Newport Beach CA 92660-7228 Office Phone: 949-675-7038.

KENNICUTT, ROBERT CHARLES, JR., astronomer; b. Balt., Sept. 4, 1951; s. Robert Charles and Joyce Ann K.; m. Norma Graceila Crosa Kennicutt, Feb. 17, 1976 (div. Jan. 18, 1996); 1 child, Laura. BS in Physics, Rensselaer Polytech. Inst., Troy, NY, 1973; MS in Astronomy, PhD in Astronomy, U. Wash., Seattle, 1978. Carnegie fellow Hale Observatories, Pasadena, Calif., 1978-80; asst. prof. astronomy U. Minn., Mpls., 1980-85, assoc. prof. astronomy, 1985-88; assoc. prof., astronomer U. Ariz., Tucson, 1988-92, prof., astronomy, 1992—; Beatrice Tinsley Centennial prof. U. Tex., Austin, 1994; Plumian prof. astronomy and exptl. philosophy U. Cambridge, England, 2005—; profl. fellow Churchill Coll., 2007—. V.p. AAS, Washington, 1998-01; com. on Astronomy and Astrophysics Nat. Rsch. Coun., Washington, 1998-2001; Space Telescope Sci. Inst. coun., AURA, Washington, 2000-2004; next generation space telescope interim sci. working group, NASA, Washington, 2000-01, adv. com., chmn. 1996-99; vis. com. chmn. NOAO Observatories, AURA, Washington, 1996-2000; vis. com. European Southern Observatory, Garching bei Munich, Germany, 1997-2003, Gemini Obs., AURA, 2003—. Author: Galaxies: Interactions and Induced Star Formation, 1998; editor-in-chief The Astrophys. Jour., 1999-2006. Named Alfred P. Aloan fellowship 1983-87, Beatrice M. Tinsley Centennial professorship, U. Tex. at Austin, 1994, Carnegie fellowship Carnegie Instn. Washington, 1978-80, Blaauw Prof. U. Groningen, 2001. Fellow Am. Acad. Arts and Scis.; mem. NAS, Am. Astron. Soc. (v.p. 1998-01, Heinmen prize, 2007), Internat. Astron. Union, Astron. Soc. of the Pacific. Office: Steward Observatory U Arizona Tucson AZ 85721 Fax: 520-621-1532. E-mail: rkennicutt@as.arizona.edu.

KENNY, GEORGE EDWARD, pathobiology educator; b. Dickinson, ND, Sept. 23, 1930; s. Frank S. and Anna M. (Kelsch) K.; m. Mary Elisabeth Pearson, Aug. 23, 1958; children: Francis, Michael, Beth, Maureen, John, Edward. BS, Fordham U., 1952; MS, U. N.D., 1957; PhD, U. Minn., 1961. Rsch. instr. pathobiology U. Wash., Seattle, 1961-63, asst. prof., 1963-67, assoc. prof., 1967-70, 1970-71, prof., 1971—2003, emeritus prof., 2003—08, prof. global health, 2008—, chair dept. pathobiology, 1970-91. Contbr. articles to Jour. Immunology, Annals N.Y. Acad. Sci., Jour. Clin. Microbiology, Infection Immunity, Antimicrobiol Agents Chemotherapy; contbr. 185 papers and articles to profl. jours. Chair Archdiocescan Edn. Bd., Seattle, 1978-81; treas. Seattle Youth Symphony, 1996-2003; mem. bd. trustees Holy Names Acad., 1997-2006. With US Army, 1953-55. Recipient Kimble Methodology award APHA, 1971, Disting. Alumnus award U. N.D., 1983. Fellow Infectious Diseases Soc. Am., Am. Acad. Microbiology; mem. Am. Soc. Microbiology, Internat. Orgn. for Mycoplasmology (treas.). Achievements include patent for antigen for Trachoma LGV and non-gonococcal urethritis. Home: 1504 37th Ave Seattle WA 98122-3470 Office: Univ Wash Dept Global Health Box 357230 Seattle WA 98185-7230 Business E-Mail: kennyg@u.washington.edu.

KENOI, WILLIAM P., Mayor, Hilo, Hawaii; b. Kalapana, Hawaii; s. Pilipo and Nancy Jo (McCammon); m. Takako Culhane; children: Liam Pilipo Yutaka, Justin Kalapana Takashi, Angeline Mahinalani Kumiko. Attended, Hawaii Cmty. Coll., U. Hawaii, Hilo, 1989—90; grad., U. Mass., Amherst, 1990—93; JD, U. Hawaii William S. Richardson Sch. Law, Manoa, 1993—96. Bar: Hawaii. Congl. intern to US Senator Daniel K. Inouye, Washington, 1992; legis. aide State Senate & State House, Hawaii; dep. pub. defender Dist., Family, & Felony Trial Div., Hawaii; exec. asst. to Mayor Harry Kim, 2001; mayor City of Hilo, 2008—. Tchr. Adminstrn. Justice Hawaii Cmty. Coll. Bd. mem. Hawaii Justice Found., Hawaii Island United Way; vol. Legal Aid Soc. Hawaii, Native Hawaiian Legal Corp., Sierra Club Legal Defense Fund. Named one of 25 People Who Will Help Shape Hawaii, Hawaii Bus. Mag., 2007. Mem.: Hawaii State Bar Assn., UMASS Polit. Sci. Honor Soc. Mailing: 25 Aupuni St Hilo HI 96720 Office: 891 Ululani St Hilo HI 96720 Office Phone: 808-961-8211, 808-329-5226. Office Fax: 808-961-6553, 808-326-5663.*

KENT, ERNIE, men's college basketball coach; b. Jan. 22, 1955; m. Dianna Kent; children: Marcus, Jordan, McKenzie. BA in Cmty. Svc. and Pub. Affairs, U. Oreg., 1977. Freshman coach U. Oreg., 1977, 1979; head coach O'Hara Cath. Sch., Eugene, Oreg., 1979, al-Khaleeg Club, Sayhat, Saudi Arabia, 1980—87, St. Mary's Coll., Moraga, Calif., 1991—97, U. Oreg., 1997—; asst. coach Colo. State U., 1988—89, Stanford U., 1990—91. Asst. coach USA Basketball 21-and-Under Nat. Team Summer Games, Japan, 2001; head coach USA Basketball Jr. Nat. Team Internat. Basketball Fedn. World Championships, 2003, Global Games (gold medal), 2003; bd. dirs. Nat. Assn. Basketball Coaches; bd. govs. Wooden Award. Recipient Hope award, Nat. Multiple Sclerosis Soc., Oreg. chpt., 2004; named Pacific-10 Coach of Yr., 2002, Dist. Coach of Yr., Nat. Assn. Basketball Coaches, 2002, US Basketball Writers Assn., 2002, Basketball Times, 2002. Office: Mens Basketball Casanova Athletic Ctr 8835 University of Oreg Eugene OR 97403-8835 Office Phone: 541-346-0490. E-mail: ekent@uoregon.edu.

KENYON, CYNTHIA J., medical researcher; BS in Chemistry and Biochemistry, U. Ga., 1976; PhD, MIT, 1981. Post-doctoral fellow Med. Rsch. Coun. Lab. Molecular Biology, Cambridge, England; prof. U. Calif., San Francisco, 1986—, Herbert Boyer Disting. prof. biochemistry and biophysics. Co-founder Elixir Pharmaceuticals, Inc., Cambridge, Mass. Contbr. articles to profl. jours. Mem.: AAAS, NAS, Inst. Medicine, 2004. Achievements include suppressing a single gene in Caenorhabditis elegans worms-nematodes and doubling their normal life span; in recent research and a few more changes, their lifespan was expanded sixfold. Office: U Calif San Francisco, Genentech Hall 600 16th St Box 2200 San Francisco CA 94143-2200 Office Phone: 415-476-9250, 415-476-9864. Office Fax: 415-514-4147. E-mail: ckenyon@biochem.ucsf.edu.

KEOUGH, SHAWN, state legislator; b. Pompton Plains, NJ, 1959; m to Mike; children: two. Idaho State Senator, District 1, 96-, member, agriculture affairs, com & human resources & education comts, formerly, member, health & welfare, transp comts, currently, vice chairman, fin comt, currently, co-chmn, Joint Legislature Oversight Commerce, Idaho State Senate.Public relations, currently. Republican. Protestant. Address: Sandpoint ID Mailing: State Capitol Bldg PO Box 83720 Boise ID 83720-0081 also: PO Box 101 Sandpoint ID 83864 Home Phone: 208-263-1839; Office Phone: 208-332-1000. Fax: 208-334-5397. E-mail: skeough@senate.state.id.us, skeough@iglide.net.

KERCHNER, CHARLES TAYLOR, educator; b. Chgo., Feb. 18, 1940; s. Charles W. and Dorothy (Taylor) Kerchner; m. Leanne Bauman, Sept. 4, 1962; children: Paige, Charles Arthur. BS, U. Ill., 1962, MBA, 1964; PhD, Northwestern U., 1976. Reporter, news editor, asst. to gen. mgr. St. Petersburg Times, Fla., 1964-71; assoc. dir. Ill. Bd. Higher Edn., Chgo., 1971-73; dir. fed. projects City Colls. of Chgo., 1973; grad. fellow, project dir., asst. prof. Northwestern U., Evanston, Ill., 1974-76; prof. Claremont (Calif.) Grad. U., 1976—, holder endowed chair, directed ednl. leadership program, 1994—99. Co-author: The Changing Idea of a Teachers Union, 1988, A Union of Professionals, 1993, United Mind Workers, 1997, Learning from LA: Institutional Change in American Public Education, 2008; editor, contbr.: The Politics of Choice and Excellence, 1989; co-editor (contbr.): The Transformation of Great American School Districts, 2008; contbr. articles to profl. jours. Grantee Nat. Inst. Edn., Stuart Found., Carnegie Corp. N.Y., Annenberg Found., others. Mem. Am. Ednl. Rsch. Assn., Indsl. Rels. Rsch. Assn., Politics of Edn. Assn. Democrat. Presbyterian. Avocations: photography, scuba diving. Office: The Claremont Grad U 150 E 10th St Claremont CA 91711-5909 Office Phone: 909-607-9146. E-mail: charles.kerchner@cgu.edu.

KEREN, KINNERET, biophysicist; b. Jerusalem; PhD in Physics, Technion Israel Inst. Tech. Postdoctoral rschr. Theriot Lab., Dept. Biochemistry Stanford U. Contbr. articles to profl. jour. Named one of Top 100 Young Innovators, MIT Tech. Review, 2004. Office: Stanford U Dept Biochemistry Stanford CA 94305 Business E-Mail: kinneret@stanford.edu.

KERKORIAN, KIRK, investor, former motion picture company executive, consultant; b. Fresno, Calif., June 6, 1917; s. Ahron and Lily Kerkorian; m. Hilda Schmidt, Jan. 24, 1942 (div. Sept. 27, 1951); m. Jean Maree Hardy, Dec. 5, 1954 (div. 1983); children: Tracy, Linda; m. Lisa Bonder, Aug. 13, 1998 (div. 1999). Comml. airline pilot, from 1940; founder LA Air Svc. (later Trans Internat. Airlines Corp.), 1948, Internat. Leisure Corp., 1968; co-chmn., pres., CEO Tracinda Corp., 1969—; controlling stockholder Western Airlines, 1970; CEO Metro-Goldwyn-Mayer, Inc., Culver City, Calif., 1973-74, chmn. exec. com., vice-chmn. bd., 1974-79, dir., 1996—; controlling stockholder MGM/UA Comm. Co. Served as capt. Transport Command RAF, 1942—44. Named one of 50 Most Generous Philanthropists, Fortune Mag., 2005, World's Richest People, Forbes Mag., 1999—, Forbes 400, 1999—, Forbes Richest Americans, 2006. Office: Tracinda Corp 150 Rodeo Dr, Ste 250 Beverly Hills CA 90212

KERMAN, JOSEPH WILFRED, musicologist, critic; b. London, Apr. 3, 1924; U.S. citizen; married, 1946; 3 children. PhD in Music, Princeton U., 1951. Instr. music Princeton U., 1948-49; dir. grad. studies Westminster Choir Coll., 1949-51, from asst. prof. to assoc. prof., 1951-60, chmn. dept., 1961-64, 91-93; prof. music U. Calif., Berkeley, 1960-94, Jerry and Evelyn Hemmings Chambers prof. music, 1985-87, prof. emeritus, 1994—; C.E. Norton prof. poetry Harvard U., 1997. Heather prof. music Oxford U., 1972-74. Author: Opera as Drama, 1956, rev. edit., 1989, The Elizabethan Madrigal, 1962, The Beethoven, Quartets, 1967, The Masses and Motets of William Byrd, 1981, Contemplating Music, 1985, Write All These Down, 1994, Concerto Conversations, 1999, The Art of Fugue, 2005; (with others) History of Art and Music, 1968, Listen, 1972, 8th edit., 2003, The New Grove Beethoven, 1983; editor: Beethoven: Autograph Miscellany, 1970, Music at the Turn of the Century, 1970; co-editor Jour. 19th Century Music U. Calif., 1977-88; contbr. essays and revs. to Hudson Rev., N.Y. Rev. Recipient Nat. Inst. Arts and Letters award, 1956, Kinkeldey award Am. Musicol. Soc., 1970, 81, Deems Taylor award ASCAP, 1981, 95; Guggenheim fellow, 1960, Fulbright fellow, 1967, NEH fellow, 1982. Fellow Am. Philosophical Soc., Am. Acad. Arts and Scis., Brit. Acad. (corr.), Royal Musical Assn. (hon. fgn.), Am. Musicol. Soc. (hon.). Office: U Calif Berkeley Dept Music Berkeley CA 94720-1200 E-mail: josephkerman@comcast.net.

KERN, BRAD D., lawyer; s. Frank B. Kern and Donna Jacard. BA, U. Calif., Berkeley, 1995; JD, UCLA, 1999. Extern to Chief Justice Ronald M. George Supreme Ct. Calif., San Francisco, 1997; assoc. Shearman & Sterling, San Francisco, 1999—. Contbr. articles to profl. jours. Mem.: ABA, Calif. Bar Assn. Office: Shearman & Sterling 525 Market St Ste 1500 San Francisco CA 94105 Office Phone: 415-616-1100.

KERN, DONALD MICHAEL, internist; b. Belleville, Ill., Nov. 21, 1951; s. Donald Milton and Dolores Olivia (Rust) K. BS in Biology, Tulane U., 1973; MD magna cum laude, U. Brussels, 1983. ECFMG cert.; lic. Calif. Intern in surgery Berkshire Med. Ctr., Pittsfield, Mass., 1983-84; intern in psychiatry Tufts New England Med. Ctr., Boston, 1984-85; resident in internal medicine Kaiser Found. Hosp., San Francisco, 1985-87; with assoc. staff internal medicine Kaiser Permanente Med. Group, Inc., San Francisco, 1987-89; assoc. investigator AIDS Clin. Trial Unit Kaiser Permanente Med. Ctr., Stanford U., Nat. Inst. Allergy & Infectious Disease, San Francisco, 1988-90; mem. staff internal medicine Kaiser Permanente Med. Group, South San Francisco, 1989-96; mem. staff Desert Med. Group, Palm Springs, Calif., 1996—, assoc. med. dir., 2002—. Democrat. Roman Catholic. Avocations: theater, ballet, travel, antiques. Office: Desert Medical Group 275 N El Cielo Rd Palm Springs CA 92262

KERN, IRVING JOHN, retired food company executive; b. NYC, Feb. 10, 1914; s. John and Minnie (Weitzner) Kleinberger; m. Beatrice Rubenfeld, June 22, 1941; children John Alan, Arthur Harry, Robert Michael. BS, NYU, 1934, student Grad. Sch. Art and Sci., 1960-65; DHL, Mercy Coll., Dobbs Ferry, NY, 1980. Asst. buyer Bloomingdale's Dept. Store, NYC, 1934-40; with Dellwood Foods, Inc., Yonkers, NY, 1945-82, pres., 1966-77, chmn. and chief exec. officer, 1977-82. Dir. Scarsdale Nat. Bank; adj. prof. polit. sci., San Diego State U., 1989-95. Mem. County Mental Health Svcs. Bd. of Westchester County, 1954-59; mem. bd. dirs., sec. Westchester County Assn., 1950-57, 76-80; exec. bd. Westchester County Better Bus. Bur., 1970-73; bd. dirs. Westchester Coalition, 1972-80, Westchester Minority Bus. Assistance Orgn., 1973-75, Milk Industry Found., 1976-82, Nat. Dairy Coun., 1979-81; bd. dirs., vice chmn. Westchester Pvt. Industry Coun., 1979-82; mil. adv. coun. Ctr. for Def. Info., 1986-97. Lt. col. AUS, 1940-45. Decorated Bronze Star. Mem. N.Y. Milk Bottlers Fedn. (pres., dir.), Met. Dairy Inst. (exec. v.p., dir.), Phi Beta Kappa, Tau Epsilon Phi.

KERN, JEROME H., consulting firm executive; b. NYC, June 1, 1937; s. Michael and Rebecca (Saltzman) Kern; m. Mary Rossick; children: Jonathan, Peter. AB, Columbia U., 1957; LLB cum laude, NYU, 1960. Law clk. to justice US Ct. Appeals (2d cir.), NYC, 1960-61; assoc. Simpson Thacher & Bartlett, 1961-63; ptnr. Wachtell, Lipton, Rosen, Katz & Kern, 1963-68; sr. and mng. ptnr. (investment banking) J.H. Kern & Co., 1971-76; ptnr. Greenbaum, Wolff & Ernst, 1977-82, Olwine, Connelly, Chase, O'Donnell & Weyher, 1982-86; sr. ptnr., mem. exec. com. Shea & Gould, 1986-91; pvt. practice Law Offices of Jerome H. Kern, 1992; ptnr. Baker and Botts, 1992—98;

vice chmn., bd. dirs. TeleCommunications, Inc., Denver, 1998-99; chmn., CEO On Command Corp., 2000—01; pres. Kern Consulting, LLC, 2001—; founder, CEO Symphony Media Sys.; founder, mng. ptnr. Enki Strategic Advisors, LLC, 2007—. Adj. asst. prof. law NYU, 1964—71; bd. dirs. Playboy Enterprises, Inc., 2002—, interim non-exec. chmn., 2008—. Mng. editor NYU Law Rev., 1959—60. Bd. trustees NYU Law Ctr. Found., 1998—; bd. trustee City Meals-On-Wheels, NYC, 1990—2005; bd. dirs. Vol. of Am. (Colo. Chap.), 2001—03; chmn. Inst. Children's Mental Disorders; co-chmn. bd. trustees Colo. Symphony Found., 2001—05. Root-Tilden scholar, NYU, 1957—60. Mem.: ABA, Assn. Bar City NY, NY State Bar Assn. Office: Enki Strategic Advisors PO Box 102050 Denver CO 80250 Office Phone: 720-208-0808. Business E-Mail: jkern@kernconsulting.com.*

KERN, JOHN MCDOUGALL, lawyer; b. Omaha, Nov. 28, 1946; m. Susan McDougall Kern, Oct. 15, 1977. BA, Creighton U., 1970; JD cum laude, George Washington U., 1973. Bar: DC 1973, Calif. 1980, US Dist. Ct. DC 1974, US Dist Ct. ND Calif. 1980, US Dist. Ct. C.D. Calif. 1996, US Ct. Appeals (D.C. Cir.) 1974, US Ct. Appeals (9th Cir.) 1978. Asst. US atty. criminal divsn. Office of US Atty. DC, Washington, 1973-78; asst. US atty. civil divsn. Office US Atty. N. D. Calif., San Francisco, 1978-82; v.p., dir. Crosby, Heafey, Roach & May P.C., San Francisco, Oakland, LA, 1982—2002, Carlson, Calladine & Peterson, LLC, San Francisco, 2003—04. Faculty Nat. Inst. Trial Advocacy, 1987—; spkr., lectr. in field. Contbr. abstracts, book chpt., articles to profl. jours. Fellow: Am. Coll. Trial Lawyers; mem.: Am. Inn of Ct., Am. Bd. Trial Advs. (adv.). Address: 80 Maywood Dr San Francisco CA 94127 Office Phone: 415-682-7374. Personal E-mail: jmckern@gmail.com.

KERN, MICHAEL J., chemicals executive; Mgr. oxides and olefins Texaco Chem. Co., 1988—89, mgr. PO/MTBE project, 1989—92, plant mgr. Port Neches facility, 1992—93, area mgr. Jefferson County Ops., 1993—95; sr. v.p. mfg. Huntsman Corp., Salt Lake City, 1995—2001, sr. v.p. environ., health & safety, 2001—. Office: Hunstman Corp 500 Huntsman Way Salt Lake City UT 84108 Office Phone: 801-584-5700.

KERNS, JOANNA DE VARONA, actress, writer, director; b. San Francisco, Feb. 12, 1953; d. David Thomas and Martha Louise (Smith) de V.; m. Richard Martin Kerns, Dec. 11, 1976 (div. Dec. 1986); 1 child, Ashley Cooper. Student, NYU, 1970-71. TV series include The Four Seasons, 1984, Growing Pains; TV movies includes A Wedding On Waltons Mountain, 1982, V, 1983, Stormin' Home, 1985, The Return of Marcus Welby, M.D., 1984, The Rape of Richard Beck, 1985, Mother's Day On Waltons Mountain, 1982, A Bunny's Tale, 1985, Robin Cook's Mortal Fear, 1994, Whose Daughter is She?, 1995, No One Could Protect Her, 1995, See Jane Run, 1995, Terror In the Family, 1996; movies include Cross My Heart, 1986, Mother Knows Best, 1997, Sisters and Other Strangers, 1997, Emma's Wish, 1998, Girl Interrupted, 1999. Democrat.

KERR, ANDREW (ANDY KERR), state legislator; b. Aug. 30, 1954; m. Tammy Kerr; children: Braden, Kennedy. BA in Geography, U. Colo., MA in Info. and Learning Technologies. Lic. in adminstrv. leadership and policy studies U. Colo. Tchr., curriculum specialist Jefferson County Pub. Schools, Colo.; mem. Dist. 26 Colo. House of Reps., Denver, 2006—, asst. majority leader. Mem. Green Mountain Civic Assn. (bd. mem.), Dunstan Found. (past pres.), Colo. Edn. Assn. Fund for Children and Pub. Edn. (bd. mem.). Democrat. Office: 200 E Colfax Denver CO 80203 Office Phone: 303-866-2923. Business E-Mail: andy.kerr.house@state.co.us.*

KERR, ANDREW W., aerodynamics researcher; b. NYC, Feb. 15, 1941; BSE in Aero. Engring., Princeton U., 1962; MSAE, U. So. Calif., 1965. With Lockheed-Calif. Co., 1963-75, group engr. rotary-wing aero/propulsion, acting mgr., rotary-wing flight scis.; chief Advanced Sys. Rsch. Office U.S. Army Aviation and Troop Command, Moffett Field, Calif., dir. aeroflightdynamics directorate, 1986—. Contbr. articles to profl. jours. Fellow Am. Helicopter Soc. (hon., mem. aerodynamics and handling qualities tech. com.); mem. Am. Inst. Aero. and Astronaut. (sr., V/STOL com.) Office: US Army Aviation Missile Command Aeroflightdynamics Directorate MS 219-3 Ames Rsch Ctr Moffett Field CA 94035-1000

KERR, DEREK J., transportation executive; BS in Aero. Engring., U. Mich., MBA. Various fin. positions Northwest Airlines; sr. dir., fin. planning Am. West Holdings, 1996—98, v.p., fin. planning and analysis, 1998—2002, sr. v.p., fin. planning and analysis, 2002; sr. v.p., CFO Am. West Holdings (now US Airways Group), 2002—09; exec. v.p., CFO US Airways Group, Tempe, Ariz., 2009—. Office: US Airways Group 111 Rio Salado Pkwy Tempe AZ 85281

KERR, FREDERICK HOHMANN, retired health facility and academic administrator; b. Pitts., July 11, 1936; s. Nathan Frederick and Laura Marie (Hohmann) K.; m. Ethyl Nylene Bashline, 1960 (div. 1969); m. Phyllis Jensen, Aug. 21, 1970, 1 child, Linda Jean. BA, Pa. State U., 1958; MPA, U. Pitts., 1961; LLD (hon.), Luth. Coll. Health Professions, Ft. Wayne, Ind., 1996. Exec. sec. Pa. Economy League Fayette County Br., Uniontown, Pa., 1959, Armstrong County Br., Kittanning, Pa., 1959—62; exec. sec. Woodbury Tax Rsch. Conf., Sioux City, Iowa, 1962—65; dir. pub. svc. City of Sioux City, 1965—66; from asst. administr. to assoc. administr. St. Luke's Regional Med. Ctr., Sioux City, 1966—71; administr., CEO Meml. Hosp. of Michigan City, Inc., 1971—75; pres., CEO St. Luke's Hosp., Maumee, Ohio, 1975—86, Luth. Hosp. Ind., Luth. Coll. Health Professions, Ft. Wayne, 1986—95; v.p. for devel. Quorum Health Resources, Inc., Brentwood, Tenn., 1995—2001. Dir. Ohio Hosp. Ins. Co., Columbus, treas. 1981-84. Trustee Ohio Hosp. Assn., Columbus, 1983—85; dir. Siouxland United Way, 1968—71, Ft. Wayne Pub. TV, 1990—94, United Way Allen County, Ft. Wayne, 1990—; trustee Northwest Med. Ctr., Oro Valley, 2004—; mem. Iowa Intergovtl. Rels. Com., Des Moines, 1964—67; mem. Rancho Vistoso Adv. Bd. N.W. Med. Ctr., Tucson, 2002—05. Mem.: ASPA (life; nat. coun. 1966—69), Am. Protestant Health Assn. (vice chmn. 1988—90). Avocations: wine appreciation, writing. Business E-Mail: fhkerr@earthlink.net.

KERR, JAMES (JIM KERR), state legislator; Mem. Dist. 28 Colo. House of Reps., Denver, 2004—. Republican. Office: Colo State Capitol 200 E Colfax Denver CO 80203 Office Phone: 303-866-2939. Business E-Mail: james.kerr.house@state.co.us.*

KERR, STEVE (STEPHEN DOUGLAS KERR), professional sports team executive, retired professional basketball player; b. Beirut, Sept. 27, 1965; m. Margot Kerr; children: Nicholas, Matthew, Madeleine. Grad., U. Ariz. Guard Cleve. Cavaliers, 1989—92, Chgo. Bulls, 1993—98, San Antonio Spurs, 1998—2001, 2002—03, Portland Trail Blazers, 2001—02; NBA analyst Tuner Network TV, 2003—07; pres. basketball ops., gen. mgr. Phoenix Suns, 2007—. Mem. NBA championship team Chicago Bulls, 1996-98; participant NBA All-Star Weekend,1994, 95, 96, 97. Named to NBA All-Interview Second Team, 1997-98, 98-99. Winner AT&T Shootout NBA All-Star Weekend, Cleve., 1997. Office: Phoenix Suns 201 E Jefferson St Phoenix AZ 85004

KERRICH, ROBERT, geologist, educator; b. Dec. 15, 1948; BSc, U. Birmingham, 1971; MSc, Imperial Coll., London, 1972, PhD, 1975; DSc, U. Saskatchewan, 1996. NATO postdoctoral fellow U. Western Ontario, 1975—77, asst. prof., dept. geology, 1977—80, assoc. prof., dept. geology, 1980—86, prof., dept. geology, 1986—87; George J. McLeod chair, dept. geological sciences U. Saskatchewan, 1987—. Contbr. chapters to books; author book; contbr. to peer-reviewed papers. Fellow: Royal Soc. Can.; mem.: Am. Geophysical Union (Willet G. Miller medal 1999), Geological Soc. London, Geological Soc. Am., Geological Soc. Can. (W.H. Gross medal 1988), Mineralogical Assn. Canada, Canadian Inst. Mining and Metallurgy. Office: Rm 246 Dept Geological Sciences U Saskatchewan 114 Science Pl Saskatoon SK S7N 5E2 Canada Office Phone: 306-966-5719. Office Fax: 306-966-8593. Business E-Mail: robert.kerrich@usask.ca.

KERRICK, DAVID ELLSWORTH, lawyer; b. Caldwell, Idaho, Jan. 15, 1951; s. Charles Ellsworth and Patria (Olesen) K.; m. Juneal Casper, May 24, 1980; children: Peter Ellsworth, Beth Anne, George Ellis, Katherine Leigh. Student, Coll. of Idaho, 1969—71; BA, U. Wash., 1972; JD, U. Idaho, 1980. Bar: Idaho 1980, U.S. Dist. Ct. Idaho 1980, U.S. Ct. Appeals (9th cir.) 1981. Mem. Idaho Senate, 1990-96, majority caucus chmn., 1992-94, majority leader, 1994-96. Mem. S.W. Idaho Estate Planning Coun. Mem. ABA, ATLA, Idaho Bar Assn. (3d dist. pres. 1985-86), Idaho Trial Lawyers Assn., Canyon County Lawyers Assn. (pres. 1985), Elks. Republican. Presbyterian. Avocations: skiing, photography. Office: PO Box 44 Caldwell ID 83606-0044 Home Phone: 208-454-3373; Office Phone: 208-459-4574.

KERSCHNER, LEE R(ONALD), academic administrator, political scientist, educator; b. May 31, 1931; m. Helga Koller, June 22, 1958; children: David, Gabriel, Riza. BA in Polit. Sci. (Univ. fellow), Rutgers U., New Brunswick, 1953; MA in Internat. Relations (Univ. fellow), Johns Hopkins U., Paul H. Nitze Sch. Advanced Internat. Studies, 1958; PhD in Polit. Sci. (Univ. fellow), Georgetown U., 1964. From instr. to prof. polit. sci. Calif. State U., Fullerton, 1961-69, prof., 1988—; state univ. dean Calif. State Univs. and Colls. Hdqrs., Long Beach, 1969-71, asst. exec. vice chancellor, 1971-76, vice chancellor for adminstrv. affairs, 1976-77, vice chancellor acad. affairs, 1987-92; exec. dir. Colo. Commn. on Higher Edn., Denver, 1977-83, Nat. Assn. Trade and Tech. Schs., 1983-85, Calif. Commn. on Master Plan for Higher Edn., 1985-87; interim pres. Calif. State U., Stanislaus, 1992-94, spl. asst. to the chancellor, 1994-97; exec. vice chancellor Minn. State Colls. and Univs., St. Paul, 1996-97; vice chancellor emeritus Calif. State U., 1997—; presdl. advisor Calif. Maritime Acad. Mem. Calif. Student Aid Commn., 1993-96; cons. in field. Mem. exec. com. Am. Jewish Com., Denver, 1978-83; internat. bd. dirs. Amigos de las Americas, 1982-88 (chmn. 1985-87); chair Blue Ribbon Comm., Univ. Park and Rsch. Ctr., Chula Vista, Calif. Served with USAF, 1954-58; col. Res., ret. Home: PO Box 748 Weimar CA 95736-0748 Personal E-mail: lkconslt@pacbell.net.

KERSELS, MARTIN, conceptual artist; b. LA, 1960; BA in art, UCLA, 1984, MFA, 1995. Founding mem. SHRIMPS performance collaborative; co-dir. Program in Art Calif. Inst. Arts, Valencia. Represented in permanent collections Mus. Contemporary Art, San Diego, LA County Mus. Art, Mus. Contemporary Art, LA, Ctr. Georges Pompidou, Paris, solo performances, Sweaters, UCLA Fine Arts Prodns., 1984, Sweaters (part B), Backlot Threatre, Hollywood, 1987, The Shape of Pools Today, Wallenboyd Threatre, LA, 1987, Pools, Kid Aileck Gallery, Tokyo, 1989, Breath, Odyssey Theatre and Powerhouse Theatre, LA, 1989, Measured Tale, LA Contemporary Exhibitions, 1990, Weight, 1992, one-man shows include, Madison Art Ctr., Wis., 1997, Dan Bernier Gallery, LA, 1998, 1999, Kunsthalle Bern, Switzerland, 2000, Galerie Georges-Phillippe & Nathalie Vallois, Paris, 1999, 2002, 2005, ACME., LA, 2001, 2002, 2003, 2006, 2008, Tang Mus. Art, Saratoga Springs, NY, 2007, Santa Monica Mus. Art, 2008, exhibited in group shows at Ten LA Artists, Stephen Wirtz Gallery, San Francisco, 1997, Whitney Biennial, Whitney Mus. Am. Art, NYC, 1997, W-139, Amsterdam, 1998, EXTRAetORDINAIRE, Le Printemps de Cahors, Paris, 1999, Made in California, LA County Mus. Art, 2000, Majestic Sprawl: Some LA Photography, Pasadena Mus. Calif. Art, 2002, 100 Artists See God, Independent Curators Internat., NYC, 2004, Dionysiac, Pompidou Ctr., Paris, 2005, Conduct: Art in Tumultuous Times, Orange County Mus. Art, Calif., 2008. Grantee City of LA Cultural Affairs Dept., 1996; fellow Found. Contemporary Performance Arts, 1999, John Simon Guggenheim Meml. Found., 2008. Office: Calif Inst Arts Program in Art 24700 McBean Pkwy Valencia CA 91355 also: c/o ACME Spaces 1 and 2 6159 Wilshire Blvd Los Angeles CA 90048

KERTH, LEROY T., physics professor; b. Visalia, Calif., Nov. 23, 1928; s. Lewis John and Frances (Niccolls) K.; m. Ruth Lorraine Littlefield, Nov. 19, 1950; children: Norman Lewis, Randall Thomas, Christine Jane, Bradley Niccolls. AB in Physics, U. Calif., Berkeley, 1950, PhD, 1957. Mem. staff Lawrence Berkeley Lab, U. Calif., Berkeley, 1950-59, sr. scientist, 1959-61; assoc. prof. physics U. Calif., Berkeley, 1961-65, prof., 1965-93, prof. emeritus, 1993—, assoc. dean Coll. Letters and Scis., 1966-70, spl. asst. to chancellor, 1970-71, assoc. dir. for info. and computing scis. div., 1983-87, assoc. lab. dir. for gen. scis., Lawrence Berkeley Lab., 1987-89, assoc. lab. dir. sci. and tech. resources, Lawrence Berkeley Lab., 1990-92. Fellow Am. Phys. Soc. Home: 5 Los Conejos Orinda CA 94563-2214 Office: U Calif Lawrence Berkeley Lab Berkeley CA 94720-0001

KERTTULA, BETH, state legislator; b. Guthrie, Okla., Jan. 8, 1956; m to Jim Powell. BA, Stanford U., 1974—78; JD, U. Santa Clara, 1978—81. Law clerk, Alaska Court Syst, 79; clerk, Chief Judge Alaska Court of Appeals, 81-82; Assistant Atty General, Commerical, Natural Resources, Oil, Gas & Mining Sections, 90-98; Alaska State Representative, District 3, 99-, member, Special Committee Econ Develop & Tourism, Judiciary & State Affairs Committees, 99-, currently minority leader, Alaska House Representative. Bd governors, Alaska Bar Association, 92-97, president, 96-97; chairwoman, Coastal States Organization Legal Coun, 93. Coauth, Alaska Outer Continental Shelf Oil and Gas Lease Sale Review and Coastal Management, 93. Alaska Native Sisterhood Camp 2; Alaska Women's Polit Caucus; Alaska Legal Serv Pro Bono Prog; Big Brothers/Big Sisters Juneau (president, formerly). Democrat. Avocations: reading, skiing, kayaking. Office: State Capitol Rm 404 Juneau AK 99801-1182 Office Phone: 907-465-4766. Office Fax: 907-465-4748. Business E-Mail: representative_beth_kerttula@legis.ak.us.*

KERTZMAN, MITCHELL E., former software company executive, venture capitalist; LHD (hon.), U. Mass., Lowell. Founder Computer Solutions, 1974; founder, CEO Powersoft Corp. (merged with Sybase, Inc.), 1993—95; chmn. bd. dirs., CEO Sybase, Inc., Emeryville, Calif., 1995-98; pres., CEO Liberate Techs., Redwood Shores, Calif., 1998—2003; ptnr., mng. dir. Hummer Winblad Venture Partners, San Francisco, 2003—. Bd. dirs. Sybase, Inc., Shiva Corp., CNET, Interconnect Syss., Inc., Bridgestream, Sapias, Five9, ActiveGrid, Palamida, Akimbi Sys. Founder, former chmn. Mass. Inst. New Commonwealth; mem. N.Y. State Commn. Indsl. Competitiveness, chair task force indsl. policy. Recipient Inc. Mag. and Ernst & Young's New England Entrepreneur of Yr. award, 1993, Disting. Achievement award Tech. Unit New England B'nai B'rith, 1993. Mem.: Mass. Software Coun. (pres. 1994—96), Am. Electronics Assn. (chmn. 1990). Office: Hummer Winblad Venture Partners 1 Lombard St Ste 300 San Francisco CA 94111-1130 Office Phone: 415-979-9600. Office Fax: 415-979-9601. E-mail: mkertzman@humwin.com.

KERWIN, WILLIAM JAMES, electrical engineering educator, consultant; b. Portage, Wis., Sept. 27, 1922; s. James William and Nina Elizabeth Kerwin; m. Madolyn Lee Lyons, Aug. 31, 1947; children: Dorothy E., Deborah K., David W. BS, U Redlands, 1948; MS, Stanford U., 1954, PhD, 1967. Aero. research scientist NACA, Moffett Field, Calif., 1948-59; chief measurements research br. NASA, Moffett Field, Calif., 1959-62, chief space tech. br., 1962-64, chief electronics research br., 1964-70; head electronics dept. Stanford Linear Accelerator Ctr., 1962; prof. elec. engring. U. Ariz., Tucson, 1969-85, prof. emeritus, 1986—. Cons. Power Electronics, 1980—. Author: (with others) Active Filters, 1970, Handbook Measurement Science, 1982, Instrumentation and Control, 1990, Handbook of Electrical Engineering, 1993, 97, 2006; contbr. articles to profl. jours.; patentee in field. Served to capt. USAAF, 1942-46. Recipient Invention NASA, 1969, 70; recipient fellow NASA, 1966-67 Fellow IEEE (Centennial medal 1984) Home: 1981 W Shalimar Way Tucson AZ 85704-1250 Office: U Ariz Dept Elec And Computer Engring Tucson AZ 85721-0001 Office Phone: 520-297-8529.

KESHISHIAN, ALEEN NICOLE, talent agent; b. Feb. 3, 1968; Grad., Harvard U. Casting asst.; talent agent Internat. Creative Mgmt., NYC; mgr. Artists Mgmt. Group, 1999—2002; mgr., co-head talent dept. the Firm, LA, 2002—05; ptnr. Brillstein-Grey Entertainment, Beverly Hills, Calif., 2005—. Exec. prodr.: (films) Haven, 2004; prodr.: (TV series) Freddie, 2005—06. Named one of Next Generation Young Executives to Watch, The Hollywood Reporter, 2000, The 100 Most Powerful Women in Entertainment, Hollywood Reporter, 2007. Office: Brillstein-Grey Entertainment 9150 Wilshire Blvd Ste 350 Beverly Hills CA 90212

KESSEL, BRINA, ornithologist, educator, researcher; b. Ithaca, NY, Nov. 20, 1925; d. Marcel and Quinta (Cattell) K.; m. Raymond B. Roof, June 19, 1957 (dec. 1968). BS, Cornell U., 1947, PhD, 1951; MS, U. Wis., Madison, 1949. Student asst. Patuxent Rsch. Refuge, 1946; student tchg. asst. Cornell U., 1945-47, grad. asst., 1947-48, 49-51; asst. Wis. Alumni Rsch. Found., 1948—49; instr. biol. sci. U. Alaska, summer 1951, asst. prof. biol. sci., 1951-54, assoc. prof. zoology, 1954-59, prof. zoology, 1959-96, head dept. biol. scis., 1957-66, dean Coll. Biol. Scis. and Renewable Resources, 1961-72, curator terrestrial vertebrate mus. collections, 1972-90, curator ornithology collection, 1990-95, adminstrv. assoc. for acad. programs, grad. and undergrad., dir. acad. advising, office of chancellor, 1973-80, sr. scientist, 1996-99, prof. emeritus, dean emeritus, curator emeritus, 1999—. Project dir. U. Alaska ecol. investigations for AEC Project Chariot, 1959—63; ornithol. investigations N.W. Alaska pipeline, 1976—81, Susitna Hydroelectric Project, 1980—83. Author books; contbr. articles to profl. jours. Recipient Outstanding Contbn. award Alaska Bird Conf.; U. Alaska with ann. award Brina Kessel Medal for Excellence in Sci. named in her honor; swale pond at Creamer's Field Migratory Waterfowl Refuge in Fairbanks named in her honor. Fellow AAAS, Am. Ornithologists' Union (v.p. 1977, pres.-elect 1990-92, pres. 1992-94), Arctic Inst. N.Am.; mem. Wilson Ornithol. Soc., Cooper Ornithol. Soc., Soc. Northwestern Vertebrate Biology, Pacific Seabird Group, Arctic Audubon Soc. (hon.), Assn. Field Ornithologists, Sigma Xi (pres. U. Alaska 1957), Phi Kappa Phi, Sigma Delta Epsilon. Achievements include research in European Starling in North America; biogeography, seasonality, and biology of birds in Alaska. Office: U Alaska Mus of the North PO Box 80211 Fairbanks AK 99708-0211 Business E-Mail: ffbxk@uaf.edu.

KESSELHAUT, ARTHUR MELVYN, financial consultant; b. Newark, May 18, 1935; s. Harry and Rela (Wolk) K.; m. Nancy Slater, June 17, 1956; children— Stuart Lee, Amy Beth. BS in Bus. Adminstrn, Syracuse U., NY, 1958; postgrad., NYU. With Coopers & Lybrand, NYC, 1958-64; treas., chief fin. officer and sr. v.p. Anchor Group, Elizabeth, N.J., 1964-79; treas., sr. v.p. also Anchor Capital Fund, Anchor Daily Income Fund, Inc., Anchor Growth Fund, Inc., Anchor Income Fund, Inc., Anchor Spectrum Fund, Inc., Fundamental Investors, Inc., Westminster Fund, Washington Nat. Fund, Inc., Anchor Pension Mgmt. Co.; sr. v.p. corp. devel. USLIFE Corp., NYC, 1979-82, exec. v.p.; chief operating officer, 1982-86; pres., chief exec. officer, dir. USLIFE Equity Sales Corp, 1985-86; exec. v.p. Pacific Mut. Life Ins. Co., Newport Beach, Calif., 1986-92; chmn., CEO, bd. dirs. Pacific Equities Network, Newport Beach, Calif., 1992-93; chmn., CEO Resource Network, San Juan Capistrano, 1993—. Bd. dirs. Mut. Svc. Corp., United Planners Group, So. Calif. Entrepreneurship Acad. Commr. econ. devel., City of Dana Point, Calif. With U.S. Army, 1958-60. Home: 34300 Lantern Bay Dr Villa 69 Dana Point CA 92629

KESSELMAN, DAVID W., lawyer; b. Van Nuys, Calif., Jan. 20, 1973; BA, Univ. Calif., Irvine, 1994; MA, London Sch. Econ., 1995; JD, Univ. Calif., Davis, 1999. Bar: Calif. 1999, US Dist. Ct. Ctrl. Calif. Assoc., comml. litigation Blecher & Collins, LA, 2000—. Named a Rising Star, So. Calif. Super Lawyers, 2005—06. Mem.: ABA, State Bar Calif., LA County Bar Assn., Assn. Bus. Trial Lawyers. Office: Blecher & Collins 17th Fl 515 S Figueroa St Los Angeles CA 90071 Office Phone: 213-622-4222. Office Fax: 213-622-1656. Business E-Mail: dkesselman@blechercollins.com.

KESSELMAN, JONATHAN RHYS, economics professor, public policy researcher; b. Columbus, Ohio, Mar. 17, 1946; s. Louis C. and Jennie K.; m. Sheila Kaplan, Mar. 12, 1973; 1 child, Maresa. BA with honors, Oberlin Coll., 1968; PhD in Econs., MIT, 1972. Asst. prof. econs. U. B.C., Vancouver, Canada, 1972-76, assoc. prof., 1976-81, prof., 1981—2003, dir. Ctr. for Rsch. on Econ. and Social Policy, 1992—2003; prof. pub. policy Simon Fraser U., Vancouver, 2004—, Can. rsch. chair in pub. fin., 2004—. Rsch. assoc. Inst. for Rsch. on Poverty, Madison, Wis., 1974-75; vis. scholar Delhi Sch. Econs., New Delhi, 1978-79; cons. econs., 1973—; prin. investigator Equality, Security and Cmty. Rsch. Project, 1998-2004. Author: Financing Canadian Unemployment Insurance, 1983, Rate Structure and Personal Taxation, 1990, General Payroll Taxes, 1997, Tax Design for a Northern Tiger, 2004; co-editor: Dimensions of Inequality in Canada, 2006; Taxing Couples: Is Income Splitting Fair?, 2008; mem. editl. bd. Can. Pub. Policy, 1997—, Can. Tax Jour., 1999—; contbr. numerous articles on taxation, income security, employment policy to profl. jours. Bd. dirs. Tibetan Refugee Aid Soc., Vancouver, 1980-82; mem. adv. panel Can. Ministry Employment and Immigration, Ottawa, Ont., 1982-83; mem. B.C. Econ. Policy Inst., 1983-86; trustee pension plan U. B.C., 1988-90; chmn. Musqueam Indian Band Taxation Adv. Coun., 1992-96, mem., 1996-98; mem. B.C. Premier's Forum on New Opportunities for Working and Living, 1994-95; mem. compliance adv. com. Revenue Can. Taxation, 1997-99. Sr. scholar Oberlin Coll., 1967-68; NSF fellow, 1968-70; grantee U.S. Dept. Labor, 1971-72; leave fellow Can. Coun., (locat.) New Delhi, 1978-79; grantee Social Sci. and Humanities Rsch. Coun. Can., 1983-84, 90—; vis. fellow Australian Nat. U., Canberra, 1985; professorial fellow in econ. policy Res. Bank of Australia, 1985; recipient Doug Purvis award, Can. Econ. Assn., 1998, 2007. Mem. Am. Econ. Assn., Can. Econs. Assn., Can. Tax Found. (Douglas Sherbaniuk award 2002). Office: Simon Fraser U Graduate Pub Policy Program 515 W Hastings St Vancouver BC Canada V6B 5K3

KESSLER, DAVID AARON, dean, medical educator, former federal agency administrator; b. NYC, May 31, 1951; m. Paulette Kessler; children: Elise, Benjamin. BA, Amherst Coll., 1973; JD, U. Chgo., 1978; MD, Harvard U., 1979. Cert. Advanced Profl. Cert. NYU Grad. Sch. Bus. Adminstrn., 1986. Intern in pediatrics Johns Hopkins Hosp., 1979—80, resident in pediatrics, 1980—82; spl. asst. to pres. Montefiore Med. Ctr., NYC, 1982—84; med. dir. Hosp. of Albert Einstein Coll. Medicine, NYC, 1984—90; tchg. appts. dept. pediatrics and dept. epidemiology and social medicine; instr. food and drug law Columbia U., NYC, 1986—90; commr. FDA Dept. Health and Human Svcs., Rockville, Md., 1990—97; dean, prof. pediatrics, internal medicine and pub. health Yale U. Med. Sch., 1997—2003; dean, vice chancellor med. affairs, prof. pediatrics U. Calif. San Francisco Sch. Medicine, 2003—; attending pediatrician Children's Hosp. Cons. US Senate Labor and Human Resources Com., 1981—84; bd. dirs. Doctors of the World; bd. dirs. Nat. Ctr. for Addiction and Substance Abuse Columbia U.; mem. White House Commn. on Presdl. Scholars. Author: A Question of Intent, 2001, numerous articles in med. jours. Chmn. bd. dirs. Elizabeth Glaser Pediatric AIDS Found.; bd. dirs. Henry J. Kaiser Family Found. Recipient Medal of Honor, Am. Cancer Soc., 1996, Pub. Welfare Medal, NAS, 2001, Nat. Pub. Affairs Spl. Recognition Award, Am. Heart Assn., Sheldon W. Andelson Pub. Policy Achievement Award, Am. Fedn. AIDS Rsch., Pub. Svc. Award, Am. Acad. Pediatrics, Franklin Delano Roosevelt Leadership Award, March of Dimes. Fellow: Am. Acad. Arts and Scis.; mem.: Inst. Medicine. Office: U Calif San Francisco Sch Medicine Dean's Office 513 Parnassus Ave San Francisco CA 94143-0410 Office Phone: 203-785-4672, 415-476-2342. Office Fax: 415-476-0689. Business E-Mail: kesslerd@medsch.ucsf.edu.

KESSLER, JOHN OTTO, physicist, researcher; b. Vienna, Nov. 26, 1928; arrived in U.S., 1940, naturalized, 1946; s. Jacques and Alice Blanca (Neuhut) K.; m. Eva M. Bondy, Sept. 9, 1950; children: Helen J., Steven J. AB, Columbia U., 1949, PhD, 1953. With RCA Corp., Princeton, NJ, 1952-66, sr. mem. tech. staff, 1964-66, mgr. grad. recruiting, 1964-66; prof. physics U. Ariz., Tucson, 1966-93, prof. emeritus, 1994—. Vis. rsch. assoc. Princeton U., 1962-64; sr. vis. fellow, vis. prof. physics U. Leeds, Eng., 1972-73, sr. vis. fellow, 1990-91; vis. prof. Technische Hogeschool Delft, Netherlands, spring 1979; Fulbright fellow dept. applied math. and theoretical physics Cambridge U., Eng., 1983-84. Contbr. articles to profl. jours. Fellow: AAAS; mem.: Am. Phys. Soc. Achievements include patentee in field; research in low Reynolds number fluid mechanics; mechanisms of bacterial propulsion, interaction and formation of coherent swarms, leading to microturbulence; bioconvection and consumption patterns of micro-organism populations; locomotion, transport of metabolites, and signalling; complementary aspects of mobility of microorganisms; measurement of probability densities for swimming velocity of algae and bacteria; relationship of interorganism signalling, quorum sensing, and exchange of metabolites to individual and collective motility in Bacillus subtilis and the Volvocales. Home: 2740 E Camino La Zorrela Tucson AZ 85718-3126 Office: U Ariz Physics Dept Bldg 81 Tucson AZ 85721-0001 Home Phone: 520-299-6522; Office Phone: 520-621-2797. Business E-Mail: kessler@physics.arizona.edu.

KESSLER, KEITH LEON, lawyer; b. Seattle, July 18, 1947; s. Robert Lawrence and Priscilla Ellen (Allbee) K.; m. Lynn Elizabeth Eisen, Dec. 24, 1980; children: William Moore, Christopher Moore, Bradley Moore, Jamie Kessler. BA in Philosophy, U. Wash., 1969, JD, 1972. Bar: Wash. 1972, U.S. Dist. Ct. (we. dist.) Wash. 1973, U.S. Dist. Ct. (ea. dist. 1992); U.S. Ct. Appeals (9th cir.) 1973, U.S. Supreme Ct. 1975. Law clk. to Hon. Robert Finley Wash. Supreme Ct., Olympia, Wash., 1972-73; ptnr. Kessler, Tegland & Urmston, Seattle, 1973-75, Kessler & Urmston, Seattle, 1975-76, Kessler, Urmston & Sever, Seattle, 1976-77, Kessler & Sever, Seattle, 1977-79; assoc. Stritmatter & Stritmatter, Hoquiam, Wash., 1980-83; ptnr. Stritmatter, Kessler & McCauley, Hoquiam, Wash., 1983-93, Stritmatter Kessler, Hoquiam, Wash., 1993-97, Stritmatter, Kessler, Whelan, Withey, Hoquiam, Wash., 1997—2006, Stritmatter, Kessler, Whelan, Colvccio, Hoquiam/Seattle, Wash., 2006—. Chmn. LAW PAC, Seattle, 1991-93; mem. pattern jury instrns. com. Wash. Supreme Ct., 2000—, vice chair, bd. trustees Evergreen State Coll., 2008-. Editor: Trial Evidence, 1996, author: (with others) Motor Vehicle Accident Litigation Desk Book, 1988, 1995, 97; contbr. chpt. to book. Pres. Kairos Ctr., Aberdeen, Wash., 1984-86; co-founder Grays Harbor Support Group; bd. dir. Wash. State Head Injury Found., Bellevue, Wash., 1993-96. Recipient Founders award Wash. State Head Injury Found., 1990, Silver award United Way, 1992 Fellow Am. Coll. Trial Lawyers; mem. Am. Bd. Trial Advocates, (pres. Wash. chpt. 1997), Wash. State Trial Lawyers Assn. (pres. 1990-91, named trial lawyer of yr., 1994), Damage Attys. Round Table (pres. 2002-03), Wash. Trial Attys. Political Forum (chmn. 1993-95), Wash. Def. Trial Lawyers (named Outstanding Plaintiff Trial Lawyer 2002), Trial Lawyers for Public Justice. Office: Stritmatter Kessler Whelan Withey 413 8th St Hoquiam WA 98550-3607 Office Phone: 360-533-2710. Business E-Mail: keith@skwwc.com.

KESSLER, LYNN ELIZABETH, state legislator; b. Seattle, Feb. 26, 1941; d. John Mathew and Kathryn Eisen; m. Keith L. Kessler, Dec. 24, 1980; children: William John Moore, Christopher Scott Moore, Bradley Jerome Moore, Jamie. Attended, Seattle U., 1958-59. Legal sec. Davis, Wright, Todd, Reise & Jones; office mgr. Atomic Press, Kairos; program mgr. No. Life Ins.; co-owner Blacktop Pavers; mem. Dist. 24 Wash. House of Reps., Olympia, 1993—, majority leader. Mem. Centrum Adv. Com., Wash. State Arts Commn.; co-chair Wash. State Heritage Coun. Exec. dir. United Way Grays Harbor, 1984-92; mem. adv. coun. Head Start, 1986-89, Cervical Cancer Awareness Task Force, 1990-91; vocat. adv. coun. Hoquiam HS; strategic planning com. Grays Harbor Cmty. Hosp., 1991-92, Grays Harbor Food Bank Com., 1991-92, Grays Harbor Dem. Ctrl. Com.; vice-chair Grays Harbor County Shorelines Mgmt. Bd., 1988-90; chair Disability Awareness Com., 1988-90, Youth 2000 Com., 1990-91; pres. Teenage Pregnancy, Parenting and Prevention Adv. Coun., 1989-91; v.p. Grays Harbor Econ. Devel. Coun., 1990-; trustee Grays Harbor Coll., 1991-2001, Aberdeen YMCA, 1991—. Mem. Aberdeen Rotary (pres. 1993-94). Democrat. Office: Dist Office 535 E 1st St Port Angeles WA 98362 also: Wash House of Reps 339A Legislative Bldg PO Box 40600 Olympia WA 98504-0600 Office Phone: 360-457-2520, 360-786-7904. Business E-Mail: kessler.lynn@leg.wa.gov.*

KESSLER, ROBERT ALLEN, retired data processing executive; b. NYC, Feb. 2, 1940; s. Henry and Caroline Catherine (Axinger) K.; m. Marie Therese Anton, Mar. 17, 1967; children: Susanne, Mark. BA in Math., CUNY, 1961; postgrad., UCLA, 1963-64. EDP analyst Boeing Aircraft, Seattle, 1961-62; computer specialist System Devel. Corp., Santa Monica, Calif., 1962-66; mem. tech. staff Computer Scis. Corp., El Segundo, Calif., 1966-67, sr. mem. tech. staff, 1971-72, computer scientist, 1974-81; systems mgr. Xerox Data Systems, LA, 1967-71; prin. scientist Digital Resources, Algiers, Algeria, 1972-74; sr. systems cons. Atlantic Richfield, LA, 1981-94; computer cons. Pfizer Health Solutions, Santa Monica, Calif., 1994—2004; ret., 2005. Mem. Big. Bros. L.A., 1962-66; precinct capt. Goldwater for Pres., Santa Monica, 1964; mem. L.A. Conservancy, 1987. Mem. Assn. Computing Machinery. Avocations: racquetball, theater. Home: 6138 W 75th Pl Los Angeles CA 90045-1634 Office Phone: 310-500-7629. Personal E-mail: bob.kessler@excite.com. Business E-Mail: kesslb1@yahoo.com.

KESTER, KENNETH, state legislator; b. Lamar, Colo., Mar. 16, 1936; County commr.; mem. Dist. 47 Colo. House of Reps., Denver, 1999—2002; mem. Dist. 2 Colo. State Senate, Denver, 2003—. Republican. Roman Catholic. Office: Colo State Capitol 200 E Colfax Denver CO 80203 Office Phone: 303-866-4877. Business E-Mail: ken.kester.senate@state.co.us.*

KESTER, RANDALL BLAIR, lawyer; b. Vale, Oreg., Oct. 20, 1916; s. Bruce R. and Mabel M. (Judd) K.; m. Rachael L. Woodhouse, Oct. 20, 1940; children: Laura, Sylvia, Lynne. AB, Willamette U., 1937; JD, Columbia U., 1940. Bar: Oreg. 1940, U.S. Dist. Ct. Oreg. 1940, U.S. Ct. Appeals (9th cir.) 1941, U.S. Supreme Ct. 1960. Assoc., then partner firm Maguire, Shields, Morrison & Bailey, Portland, 1940-57; justice Oreg. Supreme Ct., Salem, 1957-58; partner Maguire, Shields, Morrison, Bailey & Kester, 1958-66, Maguire, Kester & Cosgrave, 1966-71, Cosgrave & Kester, Portland, 1972-78, Cosgrave, Kester, Crowe, Gidley & Lagesen, Portland, 1978-89, Cosgrave, Vergeer & Kester, Portland, 1989—. Instr. Northwestern Coll. Law, 1947-56; gen. solicitor northwestern dist. U.P. R.R., 1958-79; sr. counsel UPRR Co., 1979-81 Co-author: The First Duty: History of the U.S. District Court of Oregon, 1993; contbr. articles to profl. jours. Past v.p. Portland area coun. Boy Scouts Am.; past pres. Mountain Rescue and Safety Coun. Oreg.; past trustee Willamette U.; past bd. dirs. Oreg. Symphony Soc., Oreg. Mus. Sci. and Industry, Oreg. Ind. Colls. Found., United Way; mem. Portland Com. on Fgn. Rels. Recipient Silver Beaver award Boy Scouts Am., 1956, alumni citation Willamette U., 1987. Fellow Am. Acad. Appellate Lawyers; mem. ABA, Am. Bar Found. (life), Multnomah Bar Assn. (past pres. 1956, Professionalism award 1991), Oreg. State Bar (treas. 1965-66, Disting. Svc. award pub. utility sect. 1991), Am. Law Inst. (life), Nat. Ski Patrol, Mt. Hood Ski Patrol (past pres.), Mazamas (past pres., climbing chmn.), Wy'east Climbers, Portland C. of C. (pres. 1973, chmn. bd. 1974), U.S. Dist. Ct. Oreg. Hist. Soc. (past pres, bd. dirs., Lifetime Svc. award) Oreg. Ethics Commons (co-founder, sec.), Phi Delta Phi, Beta Theta Pi, Tau Kappa Alpha. Clubs: Arlington (Portland), City (Portland) (v.p. 1978-80, pres. 1986-87), University (Portland), Multnomah Athletic (Portland). Democrat. Unitarian Universalist. Office: Cosgrave Vergeer & Kester LLP 805 SW Broadway 8th Fl Portland OR 97205 Home Phone: 503-644-8970; Office Phone: 503-323-9000. Business E-Mail: rkester@cvk-law.com.

KETCHUM, ROBERT GLENN, photographer, print maker; b. LA, Dec. 1, 1947; s. Jack Burson and Virginia (Moorhead) K. BA. cum laude, UCLA, 1970; MFA, Calif. Inst. Arts, 1974; MS (hon.), Brooks Inst. Photography, 1995. Founder, tchr. photography workshops Sun Valley Center for Arts and Humanities, 1971-73; tchr. photography Calif. Inst. Arts, 1975; curator photography Nat. Park Found., Washington, 1979-95. Trustee L.A. Ctr. Photog. Studies, 1975-81, pres., 1979-81, v.p., 1981, 96—, bd. dirs.; bd. of councillors Am. Land Conservancy, 1993—; bd. trustees Alaska Conservation Found., 1994—, bd. dirs. Advocacy Arts Found., 1996—; bd. dirs. Earth Comm. Office, 1997—, Internat. Photography Coun.; co-chair west coast coun. Aperture Found., 1996—. Author: The Hudson River and the Highlands; The Photographs of Robert Glenn Ketchum, 1985, The Tongass: Alaska's Vanishing Rain Forest, 1987, Overlooked in America: The Success and Failure of Federal Land Management, 1991, The Legacy of Wildness: A 25 Year Retrospective, 1994, Northwest Passage, 1996; author and contbg. photographer: American Photographers and the National Parks, 1981; project dir. and contbg. photographer Presidio Gateways, 1994, Threads of Light: Chinese Embroidery From Suzhou and the Photography of Robert Glenn Ketchum, Rivers of Life: Southwest Alaska, The Last Great Salmon Fishery; one-man shows include Akron Art Mus., Ohio, 1985, 89, Santa Barbara Mus. Art, Calif., 1985, Chrysler Mus., Va., 1986, N.Y. Hist. Soc., 1987, The Hudson River Mus., N.Y., 1987, Pentax Forum Gallery, Tokyo, 1988, Fine Art Mus. of the South, Fla., 1990, Nat. Mus. Brazil, Rio de Janeiro, 1992, Am. House, Heidelburg, Germany, 1992, The Huntington Libr. and Art Collections, 1993, The Nat. Acad. Sci., 1994, Cleve. Mus. Art, 1996, Ga. Mus. Art, 1996-97, George Eastman House/Internat. Mus. Photography, 1997, Internat. Photography Hall of Fame Mus., 1997; group shows include Mpls. Inst. of Arts, 1978, White House, Washington, 1979, Friends of Photography, Calif., 1980, Nat. Mus. Am. Art, Washington, 1986, Internat. Photokina, Fed. Republic of Germany, 1986, San Francisco Mus. Art, 1987, Nat. Mus. Am. Art, 1991-94, Honolulu Acad. of the Arts, 1994, Stanford U. Art Mus., 1996, Amon Carter Mus., Ft. Worth, 1997, UCLA Fowler Mus., 1999. Recipient Ansel Adams award for conservation photography Sierra Club, 1989, UN award for outstanding environ. achievement, 1991, award of excellence for profl. achievement UCLA Alumni Assn., 1993, Chevron-Times Mirror Mag. Conservation award, 1994, Frank and Josephine Duveneck Humanitarian award, 2000, Photographer of Yr., 2001; rsch. grantee Ciba-Geigy, 1979, Nat. Park Found., 1978, 79, grantee Lila Acheson Wallace Fund, 1983, 85, 86, McIntosh Found., 1986-87, Akron Art Mus., 1987. Fellow The Explorer's Club; mem. Jonathan Club (resident artist), Phi Delta Theta. Home and Office: 696 Stone Canyon Rd Los Angeles CA 90077-2925 E-mail: peace2rth@aol.com.

KETTELL, RUSSELL WILLARD, former bank executive; b. Boston, Feb. 2, 1944; s. Prescott Lowell and Wilhelmina (Schurrman) K.; m. Carol Bailey, Oct. 27, 1973; 1 son, Alexander. BA in Econs., Middlebury Coll.; MBA, U. Chgo. Treas. Golden West Fin. Corp., Oakland, Calif., 1976—84, 1995—2002, 2004—, sr. v.p., 1980—84, exec. v.p., 1984—89, sr. exec. v.p., 1989—93, pres., 1993—2006, CFO, 1999—2006.

KEVORKIAN, JIRAIR, aeronautics and astronautics engineering educator; b. Jerusalem, May 14, 1933; came to U.S., 1952; s. Leon and Araxie (Kalemkerian) K.; m. Seta Tabourian, Mar. 8, 1980. BS, Ga. Inst. Tech., 1955, MS, 1956; PhD, Calif. Inst. Tech., 1961. Aerodynamicist Convair, Ft. Worth, 1956-57; rsch. fellow Calif. Inst. Tech., Pasadena, 1961-64; asst. prof. U. Wash., Seattle, 1964-66, assoc. prof., 1966-71, prof. applied math., aeros. and astronautics, 1971—2002, prof. emeritus, 2002—, acting chmn. applied math., 1986-87, 88-90. Vis. prof. U. Paris, 1971-72; Fulbright-Hayes vis. lectr., 1975-76. Author: Partial Differential Equations, 1990; co-author: Perturbation Methods in Applied Mathematics, 1981, Multiple Scale and Singular Perturbation Methods, 1996. Home: 3730 W Commodore Way Seattle WA 98199-1104 Office: U Wash Dept Applied Math PO Box 352420 Seattle WA 98195-2420 Business E-Mail: kevork@amath.washington.edu.

KEYES, CHERYL L., musician, educator; life ptnr. Abdoulaye N'Gom. BME, Xavier U., New Orleans; MME, PhD, Ind. U., Bloomington. Founder, CEO Cangom Publishing, LA, 2002—, Keycan Records, LA, 2008—; assoc. prof. ethnomusicology UCLA. Musical-artistic. dir. Lady Jazz concert series, Blues in the Summertime Instrumental Women Project. Author: Rap Music and Street Consciousness, 2004 (CHOICE Outstanding Academic Title, 2004); musician: (albums) Let Me Take You There, 2008 (NAACP Image award for Outstanding World Music Album, 2009). Mem.: Internat. Assn. for the Study of Popular Music, US chapt. (pres. 2008—09). Office: Keycan Records 914 Westwood Blvd #579 Los Angeles CA 90024 also: UCLA Herb Alpert Sch Music 2539 Shoenberg Music Bldg Box 951657 Los Angeles CA 90095-1657 Office Phone: 310-749-5733. E-mail: cherylkeyes@keycan.com, clkeyes@ucla.edu.*

KEYES, SAUNDRA ELISE, newspaper editor; b. Salt Lake City, June 28, 1945; d. Vernon Harrison and Mildred K.; m. William J. Ivey, June 13, 1969 (div. 1976). BA, U. Utah, 1966; MA, Ind. U., 1969, PhD, 1976. Tchr. Salt Lake City Pub. Schs., 1966-67; asst. prof. Fisk U., Nashville, 1971-76; reporter, city editor The Tennessean, Nashville, 1976-83; staff writer The Courier-Jour., Louisville, 1983-84; dep. mng. editor Orlando (Fla.) Sentinel, 1985-88; mng. editor Phila. Daily News, 1988-90; exec. editor, sr. v.p. Press-Telegram, Long Beach, Calif., 1991-93; mng. editor The Miami Herald, 1993-96, Contra Costa Times, 1996—2000; editor Honolulu Advertiser, 2000—. Ford Found. fellow, 1978. Mem.: Am. Soc. Newspaper Editors (pres. accrediting coun. on edn. in journalism and mass comm. 2004—). Office: Honolulu Advertiser 605 Kapiolani Blvd PO Box 3110 Honolulu HI 96802

KEYS, ALICIA (ALICIA AUGELLO COOK), singer; b. NYC, Jan. 25, 1981; d. Craig Cook and Terri Augello. Student, Columbia U. Singer: (albums) Songs in A Minor, 2001 (Video Music Award, 2 Billboard Awards, 2 Am. Music Awards, 2 NAACP Image Awards, 3 Soul Train awards, 2 World Music Awards, ECCHO award, Best R&B Album, Grammy Awards, 2001, Choice Album, Teen Choice awards, 2002), The Diary of Alicia Keys, 2003 (Grammy award, Best R&B Album, 2005), Unplugged, 2005, As I Am, 2007 (NAACP Image award for Outstanding Album, 2008, Favorite Pop Album and Favorite R&B Album, Am. Music Awards, 2008), (songs) Fallin', 2001 (Best Female R&B Vocal Performance, Best R&B Song, Song of Yr., Grammy Awards, 2001), If I Ain't Got You, 2003 (MTV Video Music award, Best R&B Video, 2004, R&B/Hip-Hop Singles of Yr., R&B/Hip-Hop Airplay Single of Yr., Billboard Music Awards, 2004, Grammy award, Best Female R&B Vocal Performance, 2005, Outstanding Song, Outstanding Music Video, NAACP Image Awards, 2005), You Don't Know My Name, 2003 (Grammy award, Best R&B Song, 2005), Karma, 2005 (MTV Video Music award, Best R&B Video, 2005), Unbreakable, 2005 (NAACP Image award for Best Video, 2006), No One, 2007 (Best R&B Song, Best Female R&B Vocal Performance, Grammy Awards, 2008), Like You'll Never See Me Again, 2007 (NAACP Image awards for Outstanding Music Video & Outstanding Song, 2008), Superwoman, 2007 (Grammy award for Best Female R&B Vocal Performance, 2009), (with Usher) My Boo, 2004 (Grammy award, Best Duo R&B Vocal Performance, 2005); composer: (films) Hollywood Homicide, Dr. Dolittle 2, Ali; actor: (films) Smokin' Aces, 2006, The Nanny Diaries, 2007, The Secret Life of Bees, 2008, (TV guest appearances) The Cosby Show, 1985, Saturday Night Live, 2001, Charmed, 2001, Tonight Show with Jay Leno, 2001, American Dreams, 2003, Oprah Winfrey Show, 2004; author: Tears for Water: Songbook of Poems and Lyrics, 2004. Co-founder, global amb. Keep a Child Alive. Recipient Grammy award for Best New Artist, 2001, Best New Artist award, Black Entertainment TV (BET) Awards, 2002, Top Female Artist, Top New Artist & Top Albums Artist, Billboard R&B/Hip-Hop Awards, 2002, Choice Singer Songwriter award, Teen Choice Awards, 2002, Favorite Female Artist-Soul/Rhythm & Blues Music, Am. Music Awards, 2004, Outstanding Female Artist, NAACP Image Awards, 2004, NAACP Image awards, 2006, 2008, Best Female R&B Artist, World Music Awards, 2004, 2008, Favorite R&B Song, People's Choice Awards, 2009; named Favorite Female Singer, 2005; named one of The 50 Most Influential African-Americans, Ebony Mag., 2004, The 100 Most Influential People in the World, TIME mag., 2005, The 100

Most Powerful Celebrities, Forbes.com, 2008. Office: c/o Jeff Robinson MBK Entertainment 240 W 35th St Fl 18 New York NY 10001 also: c/o David Wirtschafter William Morris Agy 1 William Morris Pl Beverly Hills CA 90212*

KEYS, SCOTT, bank executive; BS in Acctg., Loyola Marymount U. CPA. With Ernst & Young, Columbus, Ohio, 1986—2002, ptnr., 1999—2002, ptnr. in charge Ohio Valley Banking Practice; exec. v.p., CFO IndyMac Bank, Pasadena, Calif., 2002—. Mailing: IndyMac Bank PO Box 7137 Pasadena CA 91101 Office: Indymac Bancorp Inc 15260 Ventura Blvd Ste 1700 Sherman Oaks CA 91403-5349 Office Phone: 626-535-5901. Office Fax: 626-535-8203.

KEYT, DAVID, philosophy and classics educator; b. Indpls., Feb. 22, 1930; s. Herbert Coe and Hazel Marguerite (Sissman) K.; m. Christine Harwood (Mullikin) June 25, 1975; children by previous marriage: Sarah, Aaron. AB, Kenyon Coll., 1951; MA, Cornell U., 1953, PhD, 1955. Instr. dept. philosophy U. Wash., Seattle, 1957—60, asst. prof., 1960—64, assoc. prof., 1964—69, prof., 1969—, chmn. dept. philosophy, 1971-78, acting chmn. dept. philosophy, 1967—68, 1970, 1986, 1994. Vis. asst. prof. dept. philosophy UCLA, 1962-63; vis. assoc. prof. Cornell U., 1968-69; mem. Inst. for Advanced Study, 1983-84; vis. prof. U. Hong Kong, autumn 1987, Princeton U., autumn 1988, U. Calif., Irvine, autumn 1990; vis. scholar Social Philosophy and Policy Ctr., Bowling Green State U., autumn, 2001. Co-editor: (with Fred D. Miller, Jr.) A Companion to Aristotle's Politics, 1991, (with Fred D. Miller, Jr.) Freedom, Reason and the Polis: Essays in Ancient Greek Political Theory, 2007; Author: Aristotle Politics, Books V, VI, 1999; contbr. articles in field to profl. jours. With US Army, 1955—57. Inst. for Rsch. in the Humanities fellow U. Wis., 1966-67; Ctr. for Hellenic Studies fellow, 1974-75. Mem. Am. Philos. Assn., Soc. Ancient Greek Philosophy. Home: 12032 36th Ave NE Seattle WA 98125-5637 Office: U Wash Box 353350 Dept Philosophy Seattle WA 98195-3350 Business E-Mail: keyt@u.washington.edu.

KHAKI, JAWAD, computer software company executive; b. Tanzania; m. Kaniz Khaki; children: Atequah, Asiya, Ali. B in Computer Engring., City Univ. London. Hardware, firmware, and OS software developer GEC Computers, Ltd., England; developer UNIX OS software ATT Bell Labs.; software design engr. networking bus. unit Microsoft Corp., Redmond, Wash., 1989, corp. v.p. Windows networking and comm., 2000, corp. v.p. Windows Hardware Ecosystem, 2006—08. Pres., founding dir. cmty. orgn., King County, Wash.; active leader, tchr. cmty. weekend programs for children and youth, King County, Wash. Recipient Walter Cronkite Faith and Freedom award, Interfaith Alliance Found., 2003. Office: Microsoft Corp One Microsoft Way Redmond WA 98052-6399

KHALIL, MOHAMMAD ASLAM KHAN, environmental science, engineering and physics educator; b. Jhansi, India, Jan. 7, 1950; came to U.S., 1963; s. M. Ahsan Khan and Aleem-Un-Nisa K.; m. Giti Ara Eshraghi, June 1973; children: Kathayoon Azra, Kaviyaan Aslam. BS in Physics, U. Minn., BA in Math. and Psychology, 1970; MS in Physics, Va. Polytechnic Inst., 1972; PhD in Physics, U. Tex., 1976; MS in Environ. Sci., Oreg. Grad. Ctr., Beaverton, 1979; PhD in Eviron. Sci., Oreg. Grad. Ctr., 1979. Tchg. asst. dept. physics Va. Polytechnic Inst. and State U., 1970-71; grad. asst. dept. math. and physics U. Tex., Austin, 1971-72, tchg. asst. dept. physics, 1972-73, 76, rsch. scientist asst. Ctr. for Particle Theory, 1972-76; instr. dept. physics Pacific U., Forest Grove, Oreg., 1978; rsch. asst. dept. environ. sci. Oreg. Grad. Ctr., Beaverton, 1977-79, asst. prof. dept. environ. sci., 1980-82, assoc. prof. dept. environ. sci., 1982-84, prof. dept. chem., biol. and environ. sci., 1984-86, prof. Inst. Atmospheric Sci., 1986-90, prof. dept. environ. sci. and engring., dir. Global Change Rsch. Ctr., 1990-95; prof. dept. physics Portland (Oreg.) State U., 1995—, chmn. dept., 2004—05, dir. environ. sci. and resources program, 2005—. Owner Andarz Co., Portland, 1981—. Editor: Chemosphere: Global Change Science, 1990-05; mem. editl. bd. Handbook of Environ. Chemistry, Environ. Sci. and Pollution Rsch. Internat., Atmospheric Environment; contbr. some 200 articles to profl. jours. Recipient Oustanding Scientist award, Oreg. Acad. Sci., 2004, World's Most Cited Authors award, ICI, Branford Prince Miller award, Portland State U., 2006; grantee, NSF, EPA, Dept. Energy, NASA. Mem. Am. Phys. Soc., Am. Chem. Soc., Am. Geophys. Union, Sigma Xi. Avocations: marathon runner, bicycling. Office: Portland State U Dept Physics PO Box 751 Portland OR 97207-0751 also: Andarz Co 9961 NW Kaiser Rd Portland OR 97231-2701 Office Phone: 503-725-8396. E-mail: khalilm@pdx.edu.

KHAN, AMMAN A., lawyer; b. Hyderabad, India, May 11, 1968; married; 2 children. BA with distinction, McGill Univ., 1990; LLB cum laude, Univ. Ottawa, 1993; LLM, UCLA, 1994. Bar: Ontario 1997, Calif. 1998, US Dist. Ct. So. & Ctrl. Calif. Judicial clk. Fed. Ct. Canada, 1994—95; asst. prof. law Univ. Ottawa, 1995—96; sr. assoc., bus. litigation Christensen, Glaser, Fink, Jacobs, Weil & Shapiro, LA. Editor (assoc.): Ottawa Law Rev. Recipient J.S.D. Tory award for legal writing, 1992; named a Rising Star, So. Calif. Super Lawyers, 2006. Mem.: State Bar Calif., Law Soc. Upper Canada. Office: Christensen Glaser Fink Jacobs Weil & Shapiro 19th Fl 10250 Constellation Blvd Los Angeles CA 90067 Office Phone: 310-556-7865. Office Fax: 310-556-2920. Business E-Mail: akhan@chrisglase.com.

KHAN, CHAKA (YVETTE MARIE STEVENS), singer; b. Great Lakes, IL, Mar. 23, 1953; m. Hassan Khan, 1970 (div. 1971); m. Richard Holland, 1974 (div. 1980); m. Doug Rasheed, 2001; children: Damien Holland, Milini. D (hon.), Berklee Coll. Music, 2004. Singer musical group Rufus, 1972-76; solo performer Warner Bros. Records, 1978—96. Founder, chmn. Chaka Khan Found., Beverly Hills, Calif., 1999—; founder EarthSong Entertainment, Beverly Hills, Calif. Singer (with Rufus) (albums) Rufus, 1973, Rags to Rufus, 1974, Rufusized, 1974, Rufus Featuring Chaka Khan, 1975, Ask Rufus, 1977, Masterjam, 1979, Camouflage, 1981, Stompin' At the Savoy, 1983, (solo albums) Chaka, 1979, Naughty, 1980, Whatcha' Gonna Do For Me, 1981, Echoes of an Era, 1982, Chaka Khan, 1983 (Grammy award for Best Female R&B Vocal Performance, 1983), I Feel For You, 1984 (Grammy award for Best Female Vocal R&B Performance, 1984), Destiny, 1986, CK, 1989, Life is a Dance, 1989, The Woman I Am, 1992 (Grammy award for Best Female R&B Vocal Performance, 1992), Vol. 1: Epiphany: The Best of Chaka Kahn, 1996, Come 2 My House, 1998, Chaka Khan Live, 2003, ClassiKhan, 2004, Funk This, 2007 (Grammy award for Best R&B Album, 2008); singer (songs) Tell Me Something Good (Grammy award for Best Group R&B Performance, 1974), I'm Every Woman, 1978, Be Bop Medley (Grammy award for Best Vocal Arrangement, 1983), Reading Rainbow TV theme song, 1983, Ain't Nobody (Grammy award for Best Group Vocal R&B Performance, 1983), I'll Be Good to You (Grammy award for Best Vocal Duo, 1990), What's Going On, 2001 (Grammy award for Best Traditional R&B Vocal Performance, 2002), Disrespectful (Grammy award for Best Deuo R&B Performance with Vocals, 2008); appearances include (films) The Blues Brothers, 1980 (TV series) Hunter, 1984, New York Undercover, 1994, The Good News, 1997, Living Single, 1993, Malcolm & Eddie, 1996, Globehunters, 2000 (stage) Mama, I Want to Sing, 1995, Signed, Sealed, Delivered, 2002; author (autobiography) Chaka! Through the Fire, 2003. Recipient 8 Grammy awards, Diamond Life award, Internat. Assn. African Am. Music, 1992, Lena Horne Career Achievement award, Soul Train Lady of Soul Awards, 1998, Lifetime Achievement award, Music of Black Origin (MOBO) Awards, 2002, Emerging Artist & Tech. in Music, 2002, World Music Awards, 2003, Black Entertainment TV (BET), 2006, Beverly Hills C.A.R.E.S. award, 2004, Woman of Yr. award, I'm Every Woman Conf., 2004, Humanitarian award, Chaka Khan Found., 2004; named one of 200 Extraordinary Women Who've Changed the World, Essence mag., 1995, 100 Greatest Women of Rock 'N Roll, VH1, 1999. Office: Chaka Khan Found E Tower Ste 515 9100 Wilshire Blvd Beverly Hills CA 90212 also: c/o Jeff Frasco Creative Artists Agy 2000 Ave of the Stars Los Angeles CA 90067

KHAN, MOHAMMAD ASAD, geophysics educator, retired minister, former senator of Pakistan; b. Aima, Lahore, Pakistan, Aug. 13, 1940; came to U.S., 1964; s. Ghulam Qadir and Hajira (Karim) K.; m. Tahera Pathan, Jan. 4, 1974; 1 dau., Shehzi Samira. BS, U. Punjab, Lahore, Pakistan, 1957, MS, 1963; postgrad., Harvard U., 1964-65; PhD (East West Center scholar), U. Hawaii, 1967. Lectr. in geophysics U. Punjab, India, 1963-64; asst. prof. geophysics and geodesy U. Hawaii, 1967-71, assoc. prof., 1971-74, prof., 1974-96, prof. emeritus, 1996—; chmn. internat. advisors, 1987—. NSF and NASA fellow Summer Inst. Dynamical Astronomy at MIT, Cambridge, Mass., 1968—69; leader Am. Asian Studies and Contemporary Social Problems Seminar Series, Honolulu, 1968—69; sr. vis. scientist geodynamics Goddard Space Flight Ctr. NASA, Greenbelt, Md., 1972—74; sr. resident assoc. NAS, 1972—74; diplomatic minister/adviser Resource Survey and Devel. Pakistan, 1974—76; sr. scientist Computer Scis. Corp., Silver Spring, Md., 1974—76, sr. cons., 1976—77; minister of petroleum and natural resources Govt. of Pakistan, 1983—86; cabinet mem. Econ. Coord. Com. Cabinet Govt. of Pakistan, 1983—86, Nat. Econ. Council Govt. of Pakistan, 1984—86; chmn. Hydrocarbon Devel. Inst., Pakistan, 1984—86, Attock Oil Refinery, 1984—86; senator Govt. of Pakistan, 1984—86. Contbr. articles to profl. publs. Chmn. East and West: A Perspective for the 80's; mem. Hawaii Environ. Council, 1979-83, chmn. exec. com., 1979-83, vice chmn., 1981-83; chmn. Pakistan Relief Fund, Honolulu, 1971. Recipient Gold medal Rawalpindi Union of Journalists, 1985, Pakistan Engring. Coun., 1985, Pakistan Assn. of Minorities, 1984, 85, Disting. Alumnus award for pofl. excellence and leadership U. Hawaii, 1995. Fellow Explorers Club; mem. Geol. Soc. U. Punjab (pres. 1962-63), Am. Geophys. Union, Pakistan Assn. Advancement Sci., Am. Geol. Inst., Am. Geophys. Union, East West Ctr. Alumni Assn. (dir. 1976-80), Internat. Alumni of East West Ctr. (exec. com., chmn. 1977-80, Disting. Alumnus award for Outstanding Career Achievements and Leadership 1984). Achievements include research in geophysics, geodetic and oceanographic applications of satellites, geodynamics, planetary interiors, global tectonics, global correlations, core-mantle boundary problems, equilibrium figures, gravity, isostasy, satellite altimetry, geodesy, earth models, geophysical exploration, ocean dynamics. Office: U Hawaii-Hawaii Inst Geophysics Planetology Post 602 Honolulu HI 96822-2219

KHANDHERIA, BIJOY K., cardiologist; b. India, May 11, 1956; MS, U. Baroda, Vadodara, Gujarat, India; MD, 1979. Cert. Internal Medicine, 1997. Resident in internal medicine Shree Sayaji Gen. Hosp., India, St. Agnes Med. Ctr., Hahnemann U., Phila.; fellow in cardiovascular diseases Mayo Grad. Sch. Medicine, Rochester, Minn.; mem. divsn. cardiovascular diseases Mayo Clinic, Scottsdale, Ariz., chair cardiovascular diseases, prof. medicine. Office: Mayo Clinic 13400 E Shea Blvd Scottsdale AZ 85259 E-mail: khandheria@mayo.edu.

KHANG, CHULSOON, economics professor; b. Kaesong City, Republic of Korea, May 10, 1935; s. Woon-sung and Ji-chung (Lim) K.; m. Yee Yu Lau, Sept. 15, 1959; children: Kenneth, Maurice. BA in Econs., Mich. State U., 1959; MA in Econs., U. Minn., 1962, PhD in Econs., 1965. Asst. prof. econs. San Diego State U., 1963-66, U. Oreg., Eugene, 1966-69, assoc. prof., 1969-73, prof., 1973-97, prof. emeritus, 1997—. Vis. prof., rsch. grantee U. New South Wales, Australia, 1972-73; vis. prof., Fulbright fellow Hanguk U. Fgn. Studies, Seoul, Korea, 1979; vis. prof. U. Hawaii, Honolulu, 1989. Referee Am. Econ. Rev., Jour. Internat. Econs., Rev. Econ. Studies, Jour. Fin., Jour. Polit. Econs., Jour. Banking and Fin., Jour. Econs. and Bus., Internat. Econ. Rev.; contbr. articles to profl. jours. Mem. Eugene Area Korean Assn. (past pres.), Am. Econ. Assn. Republican. Home: 224 Edgewood Dr Port Ludlow WA 98365-9225 Office: U Oreg Dept Econs Eugene OR 97403 Personal E-mail: yeeyuchul@gmail.com.

KHOSLA, CHAITAN S., chemical engineer; BTech, Indian Inst. of Tech., Mumbai, 1985; PhD, Calif. Inst. Tech., 1990; postdoctoral work, John Innes Ctr., U.K., 1990—91. Prof. chem. engring, chemistry and biochemistry Stanford Univ., and Wells H. Rauser and Harold M. Petiprin prof., sch. of engring. Recipient Dreyfus new Investigator award, 1991, Young Investigator award, NSF, 1994—99, Allan P. Colburn award, 1997, ACS Lilly award in Biological Chemistry, 1999, Alan T. Waterman award, NSF, 1999, ACS Pure Chemistry award, 2000, Disting. Alumni award, Calif. Inst. Tech., 2000. Fellow: Am. Acad. Arts & Scis. Achievements include being credited with pathbreaking work on erythromycin biosynthesis and elucidating molecular mechanisms. Office: Stanford Dept Chemical Engring Keck Science Bldg Rm 389 381 North-South Mall Stanford CA 94305-5025 Business E-Mail: ck@chemeng.stanford.edu.

KHOSLA, VINOD, investment company executive; b. New Delhi, Jan. 28, 1955; married; 4 children. BSEE, Indian Inst. Tech., New Delhi, 1976; M in Biomed. Engring., Carnegie Mellon U., 1978; MBA, Stanford U., 1980. Co-founder Daisy Sys.; co-founding CEO Sun Microsystems, 1982—86; gen. ptnr. Kleiner, Perkins, Canfield and Byers, Menlo Park, Calif., 1986—; founder Khosla Ventures, 2004—. Bd. dirs. Asera, Centrata, Infinera, Juniper Networks, 1996—2004, QWEST Comms., 1998—2005, Nanotectonica, Redback, Zambeel, Zaplet, eASIC Corp., 2004—. Named one of 50 Who Matter Now, CNNMoney.com Bus. 2.0, 2006. Office: Khosla Ventures 3000 Sand Hill Rd Ste 3-170 Menlo Park CA 94025-7137

KHOSROWSHAHI, DARA, travel company executive; b. Tehran, Iran, May 28, 1969; married; 2 children. BS in Engring., Brown U., Providence, 1991. With Allen & Co. LLC, 1991—95, v.p., 1995—98; v.p. strategic planning IAC, 1998—99, pres. USA Networks Interactive, 1999—2000, exec. v.p., ops. and strategic planning, 2000—02, exec. v.p., CFO, 2002—04, CEO IAC Travel, 2004—05; pres., CEO Expedia, Inc., Bellevue, Wash., 2005—. Bd. dirs. Expedia, Inc., 2005—. Office: Expedia Inc 3150 139th Ave SE Bellevue WA 98005 Office Phone: 425-679-7200, 800-397-3342.

KICANAS, GERALD FREDERICK, bishop; b. Chgo., Aug. 18, 1941; STL, U. of St. Mary of the Lake, 1967, MEd, 1970; MA, Loyola Univ., Chgo., 1973, PhD, 1977. Ordained priest Archdiocese of Chgo., 1967; ordained bishop, 1995; aux. bishop Archdiocese of Chgo., 1995—2001; coadjutor bishop Diocese of Tucson, Ariz., 2001—02, bishop, 2003—. Roman Catholic. Office: Diocese of Tucson 192 S Stone Ave Tucson AZ 85701 Office Phone: 520-792-3410. Office Fax: 520-792-3410.

KIDD, DON, state legislator, bank executive; b. Crowell, Tex., Oct. 10, 1937; m. Sarrah D. Kidd; children: Vickye Faulk, Rena Shuller, Dion Kidd-Johnson. Student, San Angelo State Coll., 1961-63, So. Meth. U., 1972. Pres., CEO Western Commerce Bank, Carlsbad, N.Mex., 1973—; mem. N.Mex. Senate, Dist. 34, Santa Fe, 1992—. Pres., CEO Western Bank Alamorgordo, Western Bank Clovis; pres. Western Bancshares of Carlsbad, Inc., Western Commerce Bancshares of Clovis, Inc., Western Data Svcs., Inc.; bd. dirs. Bank of the S.W. N.Mex. state sen. dist. 34, 1993—; bd. dirs. N.Mex. Ednl. Assistance Found., Carlsbad Literacy Program; bd. dirs., past pres. Carlsbad Dept. Devel.; bd. dirs., past chmn. Western States Sch. Banking, U. N.Mex., 1978-84, Guadalupe Med. Ctr., 1988-91; mem., past pres. Eddy County Sheriff's Posse; past pres. Eddy County United Way, N.Mex. State U. Bd. Regents, 1985-91. Mem. Am. Bankers Assn., N.Mex. Bankers Assn. (past pres.), Carlsbad C. of C. (bd. dirs. 1979-83, past pres.). Republican. Avocation: reading. Office: Western Commerce Bank PO Box 1358 Carlsbad NM 88221-1358 also: N Mex Senate State Capitol Rm 423 Santa Fe NM 87503-0001

KIDDER, RAY EDWARD, physicist, consultant; b. NYC, Nov. 12, 1923; s. Harry Alvin and Laura Augusta (Wagner) K.; m. Marcia Loring Sprague, June 12, 1947 (div. Aug. 1975); children: Sandra Laura, David Ray, Matthew Sprague. BS, Ohio State U., 1947, MS, 1948, PhD, 1950. Physicist Calif. Rsch. Corp., La Habra, 1950-56, Lawrence Livermore Nat. Lab., Livermore, Calif., 1956—. Mem. adv. bd. Inst. for Quantum Optics, Garching, Germany, 1976-90; bd. editors Nuc. Fusion IAEA, Vienna, 1979-84; cons. Sci. Applications Internat. Corp., San Diego, 1991-94; mem. hon. adv. bd. Inst. for Advanced Physics Studies, La Jolla, Calif., 1991—. Contbr. chpts. to books. With USN, 1944-46. Recipient Humboldt award Alexander von Humboldt Found., 1988. Fellow Am. Phys. Soc. (Szilard award 1993); mem. AAAS, Sigma Xi. Achievements include research in physics of nuclear weapons, inertial confinement fusion, megagauss magnetic fields, laser isotope enrichment, containment of low-yield nuclear explosions. Home: 637 E Angela St Pleasanton CA 94566-7413 Office: Lawrence Livermore Nat Lab PO Box 808 Livermore CA 94551-0808

KIDDOO, ROBERT JAMES, engineering service company executive; b. Kansas City, Mo., July 8, 1936; s. Robert Leroy and Margaret Ella (Wolford) K.; m. Patricia Anne Wakefield, Apr. 17, 1957; children: Robert Michael, Stacey Margaret Kiddoo. BSBA, UCLA, 1960; MSBA, Calif. State U., Northridge, 1969; MBA, U. So. Calif., 1972, DBA, 1978. Cert. mgmt. acct. Asst. v.p., nat. divsn. loan officer Crocker-Citizen's Nat. Bank, LA, 1958—69; v.p., CFO, dir. corp. sec. Kirk-Mayer, Inc., LA, 1969—87; prof. emeritus acctg. and info. sys. Calif. State U., Northridge, 1970—2005; region adminstr. mgr. CDI Corp.-West, Chatsworth, Calif., 1990; exec. v.p. Kirk-Mayer, Inc., LA, 1990—92; pres. Creative Software Designs, Inc., Northridge, Calif., 1995—2002. Asst. v.p. financial affairs, univ. contr. Calif. State U., Northridge, 1997-2000. With U.S. Army, 1955-56. Mem. Mensa, Ltd., Beta Gamma Sigma, Beta Alpha Psi. Office: Calif State Univ Acctg And Is Northridge CA 91330-8372

KIDWELL, WAYNE L., retired state supreme court justice; b. Council, Idaho, 1938; m. Shari Linn; children: Vaughn, Blair. BA, JD, U. Idaho. Bar: Idaho 1964, Hawaii, former U.S. Trust Territories. Past atty. law firms, Idaho and Hawaii; past pvt. practice Idaho and Hawaii; atty. gen. State of Idaho, 1975—80; past majority leader Idaho Senate; past prosecuting atty. Ada County, Idaho; assoc. dep. atty. gen. Pres. Reagan adminstrn., liason Dept. Justice U.S. Govt., 1982—90; past atty. gen. Republic of Marshall Islands, 1994—98; justice Idaho Supreme Ct., 1998—2005. Photographer pvt. shows; one-man shows include galleries in Hawaii. Active numerous civic and profl. orgns. Served USMCR, U.S. Army Mil. Police Corps.

KIEFFER, GEORGE DAVID, lawyer; b. NYC, Nov. 17, 1947; m. Judith Kieffer; 2 children. BA in history, U. Calif., Santa Barbara, 1969; JD, UCLA, 1973. Bar: Calif. 1973. Extern to Hon. David L. Bazelon US Ct. Appeals DC Cir., 1972; joined Manatt, Phelps & Phillips, LA, 1973, ptnr., bd. dirs., co-chair govt. divsn. Mem. transition team Gov. Arnold Schwarzenegger; chair Mayor's Council of Econ. Advisors, Mayor's LA Econ. Impact Task Force, City of LA Charter Reform Commn. Author: (book) The Strategy of Meetings, 1988. Former bd. dirs. Constl. Rights Found.; former chmn. bd. dirs. Ctr. for the Study of Dem. Institutions; former mem., vice chair bd. dirs. LA Urban League, bd. dirs. Automotive Training Ctr.; active Citizens Adv. Coun. on Corporations, 1975—82, Commn. for the Rev. of the Master Plan for Higher Edn. in Calif., 1985—87; trustee, chmn. U. Calif. Santa Barbara Found., 1972—82; bd. regents U. Calif., 1979—80; bd. governors Calif. Cmty. Colleges, 1981—87, pres., 1984—85; mem. exec. com., chair bd. dirs. LA C. of C.; bd. dirs. Calif. C. of C., chair edn. com.; mem. mus. coun. Mus. Contemporary Art, LA; mem bd. dirs., exec. com. Ctrl. City Assn. LA. Recipient Social Responsibility Award, LA Urban League, 1999; named one of 100 Most Influential Lawyers in Calif., Calif. Law Bus., 2000. Mem.: LA County Bar Assn. Avocations: writing and performing music, tennis, golf, basketball. Office: Manatt Phelps & Phillips 11355 W Olympic Blvd Los Angeles CA 90064 Office Phone: 310-312-4146.

KIEHN, MOGENS HANS, aviation engineer, consultant; b. Copenhagen, July 30, 1918; came to U.S., 1957; s. Hans-Christian and Lydia-Thea-Constans (Theill) K.; children: Marianne, Hans. BS, ME, PE, Tech. Engring., Copenhagen, 1940; MS, Copenhagen, 1940; degree in Army Intelligence, Def. Indsl. Security Inst., 1972. Registered profl. engr., Ariz., also chemical engineer. Pres. Hamo Engring., Copenhagen, 1939-47, Evanston, Ill., 1958—70; engr. Sundstrand, Rockford, Ill., 1957-58; pres. Kiehn Internat. Engring. Co., Phoenix,

1970—, owner, 1970—, Processing Co. Inc.; chmn. ETO Internat. Engring., Phoenix, 1970—, pres., 1970—. Tech. engring. cons. Scandinavian Airlines, Sundstrand Engring., McDonnell Douglas, Ford, GM, Chrysler, Honeywell, Motorola, Gen. Electric, Hughes Aircraft; chmn. bd. Internat. Tech. Engring. With Finnish Army, 1939, Danish Underground, 1940-45, Morocco French Fgn. Legion, 1948-54, Vietnam. Mem. AIII, NSPE, Soc. Illuminating Engrs., Nat. Geog. Soc., Am. Fedn. Police, East Africa Wildlife Soc., Interpol Intelligence and Organized Crime Orgn., Adventures Club Denmarkk, Honors Club, Am. Inst. of Aeronautics and Astronautics., St. Joseph's Legacy Club., St. Joseph's Indian Sch. Achievements include patents for rehab. hosp. lighting for highmast, drafting machine, tooling machinery, parts for aircraft, garbage and pollution machine, optical coupler. Home: 4435 N 78th St Apt 248a Scottsdale AZ 85251-2562 Office Phone: 480-990-1846.

KIEKHOFER, WILLIAM HENRY, lawyer; b. Madison, Wis., June 19, 1952; s. William and Emily (Graham) K.; m. Leslie A. Cohen., Jan. 27, 1956; children: Allison Laura, Phoebe Leigh, Rachel Elizabeth. BA, U. Wis., 1976; JD, U. So. Calif., 1980. Assoc. Sidley & Austin, LA, 1980-82, Fried & King, LA, 1982-83, McKenna Conner & Cuneo, LA, 1983-90; ptnr. Kelley Drye & Warren LLP, LA, 1990—2001, Mayer, Brown, Rowe & Maw LLP, LA, 2001—. Office: Kelly Drye Warren 101 Park Ave New York NY 10178-0062

KIEL, JEFF E., former publishing executive; b. 1959; m. Gayle Kiel; children: Ryan, Alexa. BS, U. Fla., 1981. CPA. Acct. Ernst & Young, 1981—87, Kauffman, Rossin & Co., 1987; with Miami Herald, 1988—2002, v.p. fin., CFO, 1999—2002; v.p. advt. San Jose Mercury News, Calif., 2002—07, pub. Calif., 2007—08. E-mail: jkiel@mercurynews.com.

KIELY, W. LEO, III, (LEO KIELY), retired brewery company executive; b. Jan. 16, 1947; AB in Econ. summa cum laude, Harvard U., 1969; MBA, U. Pa., 1971. Brand asst., asst. brand mgr. Procter & Gamble, Cin., 1971—73; from bus. mgr. to v.p. mktg. Wilson Sporting Goods Co., Chgo., 1973—79; pres. Ventura (Calif.) Coastal Corp., 1979—82; v.p. brand mgmt. Frito-Lay, Inc., 1982—83, v.p. mktg., 1983—84, v.p. sales & mktg., 1984—89, sr. v.p. field ops., 1989—90, v.p., gen. mgr. central div., 1990—91, pres., central div., 1991—93; pres., COO Coors Brewing Co., Golden, Colo., 1993—2000, pres., CEO, 2000—05, Adolph Coors Co., 2002—05, Molson Coors Brewing Co., Golden, Colo., 2005—08; CEO Miller-Coors (joint venture), Chgo., 2008—. Bd. dirs. Molson Coors Brewing Co. (formerly Coors Brewing Co.), 1998—2008, SEI Ctr. for Advanced Studies Bd. Wharton Sch. Fin., Phila., Nat. Assn. Manufacturers, Washington. Trustee Boys & Girls Clubs Am.; bd. dirs. Met. State Coll. Denver Found. Bd., Denver Ctr. for Performing Arts; chmn. Mile High United Way Denver. Mem.: Nat. Assn. Mfrs. (bd. dirs.).

KIENITZ, LADONNA TRAPP, lawyer, librarian, municipal official; b. Bay City, Mich. d. Orlin D. and Mary (Stanford) Trapp; m. John Kienitz, Feb. 9, 1951 (div. Dec. 1974); children: John, Jim, Rebecca, Mary, Timothy, David. BA, Westmar Coll., 1951; MA in Libr. Sci., Dominican U., River Forest, Ill., 1970; M Mgmt., Northwestern U., 1984; JD, Western State U., Fullerton, Calif., 1995; LLM in Taxation, U. San Diego, 2004. Head libr. Woodlands Acad., Lake Forest, Ill., 1973-77; project officer North Suburban Libr. Sys., Wheeling, Ill., 1977-78; libr. dir. Lincolnwood Pub. Libr. Dist., Ill., 1978—86; city libr. City of Newport Beach, Calif., 1986—2002, dir. cmty. svcs. Calif., 1994—2002; adj. prof. Chapman U. Sch., Orange, 2003—; tax atty. Tustin Law Offices, 2005—. Mem.: ALA, ABA, US Tax Ct. Bar, US Supreme Ct. Bar, Pub. Libr. Assn. (pres. 1995—96), State Bar Calif., Orange County Bar Assn. Office Phone: 949-300-6951. Business E-Mail: ladonnakienitz@taxsolutionsite.com.

KIERNAN, DONALD E., telecommunications industry executive; BS, Boston Coll., 1962; MBA, Fla. State U., 1970. Ptnr. Ernst. & Young, 1966-90; sr. v.p. fin., treas. SBC Comm. Inc., San Antonio, 1990-93, CFO, 1993—99, sr. v.p., CFO, 1999—2001; dir. Viad Corp., 2001—04. Bd. dirs. Viad Corp., 2001—04, Seagate Tech., 2003—, Health Mgmt. Assocs. Inc, LaBranche & Co., Inc. With USN, 1963—66. Office: Seagate Tech 920 Disc Dr Scotts Valley CA 95066-4544

KIESLER, CHARLES ADOLPHUS, psychologist, academic administrator; b. St. Louis, Aug. 14, 1934; m. Teru Morton, Feb. 28, 1987; 1 child, Hugo; children from previous marriage: Tina, Thomas, Eric, Kevin. BA, Mich. State U., 1958, MA, 1960; PhD (NIMH fellow), Stanford U., 1963; D (hon.), Lucian Blaga U., Romania, 1995. Asst. prof. psychology Ohio State U., Columbus, 1963-64, Yale U., New Haven, 1964-66, assoc. prof., 1966-70; prof., chmn. psychology U. Kans., Lawrence, 1970-75; exec. officer Am. Psychol. Assn., Washington, 1975-79; Walter Van Dyke Bingham prof. psychology Carnegie Mellon U., Pitts., 1979-85, head psychology, 1980-83, acting dean, 1981-82, dean Coll. Humanities and Social Scis., 1983-85; provost Vanderbilt U., 1985-92; chancellor U. Mo., Columbia, 1992-96, Weil Disting. prof. health svcs. mgmt., 1996-98; prof., sr. advisor San Diego State U., 1998-99. Pres., CEO, Virtual Univ. Internat., 1996-97. Author: (with B.E. Collins and N. Miller) Attitude Change: A Critical Analysis of Theoretical Approaches, 1969, (with S.B. Kiesler) Conformity, 1969, The Psychology of Commitment: Experiments Linking Behavior to Belief, 1971, (with N. Cummings and G. VandenBos) Psychology and National Health Insurance: A Sourcebook, 1979, (with A.E. Sibulkin) Mental Hospitalization: Myths and Facts About a National Crisis, 1987, (with C. Simpkins) The Unnoticed Majority: Psychiatric inpatient care in general hospitals, 1993. Served with Security Service USAF, 1952-56. Recipient Disting. Alumnus award Mich. State U., 1987, Gunnar Myrdal award for Evaluation Practice Am. Evaluation Assn., 1989. Fellow AAAS, APA (Distng. Contbr. to Rsch. in Pub. Policy award 1989), Am. Psychol. Soc. (founding past pres. 1988-90); mem. AAUP, Inst. of Medicine of Nat. Acad. Scis., Sigma Xi, Psi Chi, Phi Kappa Phi. E-mail: ckiesler@san.rr.com.

KIEU, QUYNH DINH, pediatrician, not-for-profit developer; b. Hanoi, Vietnam, Mar. 18, 1950; m. Chan Kieu. MD, U. Saigon, Vietnam, 1975. Intern U. Calif., Irvine, Orange, 1976—77, resident, 1977—78, fellow, 1978—79, asst. clin. prof. pediat., 1985—; pvt. practice, 1979—; founder, pres. Project Vietnam, 1996—. Recipient Woman of Yr. award, Calif. Assembly's 69th Dist., 2004. Mem.: AMA Found. (Pride in Profession award 2004), Healthcare Found. Orange County (bd. dirs.), Vietnamese Med. Assn., Am. Acad. Pediat. Office: Project Vietnam 11100 Warner Ave Ste 116 Fountain Valley CA 92708-7500 Office Phone: 714-641-0850. Business E-Mail: qkieu@aap.org.

KILBOURN, LEE FERRIS, architect, specfications writer; b. LA, Mar. 9, 1936; s. Lewis Whitman and Kathryn Mae (Lee) K.; m. Joan Priscilla Payne, June 11, 1961; children: Laurie Jane, Ellen Mae. BS in Gen. Sci., Oreg. State U., 1963; BS in Architecture, U. Oreg., 1965. Registered architect, Oreg. Specifier Wolff Zimmer Assocs., Portland, Oreg., 1965-75; specifier, assoc. Wolff Zimmer Gunsul Frasca, Portland, 1975-77, Zimmer Gunsul Frasca Partnership, Portland, 1977-81, specifier, assoc. ptnr., 1981—. Jr. warden, then sr. warden St. Stephen's Episcopal Parish, Portland. With U.S. Army, 1959-60. Fellow AIA (mem. master spec. rev. com. 1976-78, mem. documents com. 1981-89), Constrn. Specifications Inst. (mem. participating tech. documents com. 1976-78, cert. com. 1980-82, Al Hansen Meml. award Portland chpt. 1987, Frank Stanton Meml. award N.W. region 1987, chpt. pres. 1979-80); mem. Internat. Conf. Bldg. Ofcls. Home: 3178 SW Fairmount Blvd Portland OR 97201-1468 Office: Zimmer Gunsul Frasca Partnership 320 SW Oak St Ste 500 Portland OR 97204-2737

KILCHER, JEWEL **See JEWEL**

KILEY, ANNE CAMPBELL, lawyer; b. Kalamazoo, July 2, 1964; d. James Francis and Mary Catherine (Brooks) Campbell; m. Jeffrey Thomas Kiley, Apr. 15, 1996. BA with high honors in Econs., U. Mich., 1986, JD cum laude, 1989. Bar: Calif. 1990. Assoc. O'Melveny and Myers, LA, 1989-91; ptnr. Trope and Trope, LA, 1991—. Vis. clinical prof. law U. So. Calif. Law Sch., 2003, 07; bd. mem. Levitt & Quinn. Named a So. Calif. Super Lawyer, LA Times mag., 2005—07. Mem. L.A. County Bar Assn., Order of the Coif. Office: Trope and Trope 12121 Wilshire Blvd Ste 801 Los Angeles CA 90025-1123 E-mail: Kiley@tropeandtrope.com.

KILLEEN, MICHAEL JOHN, lawyer; b. Washington, Oct. 5, 1949; s. James Robert and Georgia Winston (Hartwell) K.; m. Therese Ann Goeden, Oct. 6, 1984; children: John Patrick, Katherine Therese, Mary Clare, James Philip. BA, Gonzaga U., 1971, JD magna cum laude, 1977. Bar: Wash. 1977, U.S. Dist. Ct. (we. dist.) Wash. 1979, U.S. Ct. Appeals (9th cir.) 1984, U.S. Supreme Ct. 1990. Jud. clk. Wash. State Ct. Appeals, Tacoma, 1977—79; assoc. Davis Wright Tremaine LLP, Seattle, 1979—85, ptnr., 1985—. Bd. dirs. Seattle Goodwill, 1987—, sec., 1998-2002. Author: Guide to Strike Planning, 1985, Newsroom Legal Guidebook, 1996, Employment in Washington, 1984—. Mem. bd. advisors Gonzaga Law Sch., Spokane, Wash., 1988—, pres., 1992-96. Recipient Freedom's Light award Wash. Newspaper Pub. Assn., 1999, Disting. Alumni award Gonzaga U., 2002, Willard J. Wright award, 2009. Mem. ABA, Wash. State Bar Assn., King County Bar Assn. (treas. 1987-89, Pres. award 1989). Republican. Roman Catholic. Office Phone: 206-622-3150. Business E-Mail: mikekilleen@dwt.com.

KILLEEN, TIMOTHY LAURENCE, aerospace scientist, science administrator; b. Cardiff, Wales, Jan. 21, 1952; came to US, 1978; married. BS with 1st class honors in Physics, Univ. Coll., London, 1972, PhD in Atomic and Molecular Physics, 1975. Rsch. asst. Univ. Coll., London, 1975—78; postdoctoral scholar U. Mich., Ann Arbor, 1978-79, asst. rsch. scientist, 1979-84, assoc. rsch. scientist, 1984-87, assoc. prof. atmospheric, oceanic and space scis., 1987-90, prof. atmospheric, oceanic and space scis., 1990-2000, dir. Space Physics Rsch. Lab., 1993—98, assoc. v.p. rsch., 1997—2000; dir. Nat. Ctr. Atmospheric Rsch., Boulder, Colo., 2000—, sr. scientist high altitude obs., 2000—. Vis. scientist Nat. Ctr. Atmospheric Rsch., 1983, 85, 86, 87 summers, affiliate scientist, 1988-92; adj. prof. U. Mich., 2000-; cons. Rockwell Internat., Westinghouse GE Corp, 1989-92, PRC, Inc., NASA Hdqs., NSF, Taiwanese Space Prog.; referee for: Jour. Geophys. Rsch., Geophys. Rsch. Letters, NASA proposals, Applied Optics, Space Sci. Instrumentation, Phys. Scripta, Annales Geophysicae, Planetary and Space Scis, Radio Sci., AFOSR proposals, NSCF proposals, Cambridge U. Press, Am. Meteorol. Soc., NRC Can.; co-dir. Rsch. Experiences for Undergraduates Site at U. Mich., 1986; mem. US Nat. Com. Solar Terrestrial Energy Prog., prog. rev. com. for NSF CFS and UAF programs, 1989, 90; chmn. prog. rev. com. for the NSF Aeronomy prog., 1986-88, 89; mem. COSPAR Commn. C task force on the CIRA-86 model atmosphere, vice chmn. COSPAR Commn. C.; chmn. NSF CEDAR prog. sci. steering com., 1988-91; prin. investigator on projects for NASA, NSF, Phillip's Lab.; presenter in field. Contbr. articles to profl. jours.; assoc. editor Jour. Geophys. Rsch. (Space Physics), 1987-92; editor-in-chief Jour. Atmospheric and Solar-Terrestrial Physics 1997; presenter papers at over 200 sci. meetings, confs., symposiums. Mem. U. Mich. Civil Liberties Bd., 1990-93, chmn. 1992-93; mem. U. Mich. faculty grievance bd. Mem. AAAS (sci. prog. com., 2003-), AAUP, NAE, Am. Geophys. Union (solar-planetary rels. exec. com., meetings com., fed. budget rev. com., pub. affairs com., chmn. solar-planetary rels. prog. com. fall 1987; convenor and presider for spl. sci. sessions at nat. meetings, convenor of Chapman conf. on the lower thermosphere and upper mesosphere 1992, nominations com. 2002-, pres-elect 2004, pres. 2006-), Inst. Physics, Eng., Am. Meteorol. Soc. Office: Nat Ctr Atmospheric Rsch PO Box 3000 Boulder CO 80307-3000 Office Phone: 303-497-1111. E-mail: kileen@ucar.edu.

KILLIAN, GEORGE ERNEST, retired educational association administrator; b. Valley Stream, NY, Apr. 6, 1924; s. George and Reina (Moeller) K.; m. Janice E. Bachert, May 26, 1951 (dec.); children: Susan E., Sandra J.; m. Marilyn R. Killian, Sept. 1, 1984 BS in Edn., Ohio No. U., 1949; EdM, U. Buffalo, 1954; PhD in Phys. Scis., Ohio Northern U., 1989; PhD (hon.), U.S. Sports Acad., 1998, Yeungam U., Korea, 2003, Sch. Physical Edn., Wroclaw, Poland, 2006. Tchr.-coach Wharton (Ohio) High Sch., 1949-51; insp. USN, Buffalo, 1951-54; dir. athletics Erie County (N.Y.) Tech. Inst., Buffalo, 1954-69, asst. prof. health, phys. edn., recreation, 1954-60, asso. prof., 1960-62, prof., 1962-69; exec. dir. Nat. Jr. Coll. Athletic Assn., Colorado Springs, Colo., 1969—2005; ret., 2005. Editor: Juco Rev., 1960—. Served with AUS, 1943-45. Recipient Bd. Trustees award Hudson Valley C. of C., 1969, Erie County Tech. Inst., 1969, Service award Ohio No. U. Alumni, 1972, Service award Lysle Rishel Post, Am. Legion, 1982; named to Ohio No. U. Hall of Fame, 1979, Olympic Order, IOC, 1996, Women's Basketball Hall of Fame, 2000. Mem. Internat. Fedn. U. Students (pres.), U.S. Olympic Com. (dir.), Internat. Olympic Com., Am. Legion, Internat. Basketball Fedn. (pres. 1990-98), Internat. U. Sports Fedn. (1st v.p. 1995, pres. 2000), Masons, Rotary, Phi Delta Kappa, Delta Sigma Phi. Home: 325 Rangely Dr Colorado Springs CO 80921-2655 Personal E-mail: gkillian7@adelphia.net.

KILLIAN, RICHARD M., library director; b. Buffalo, Jan. 13, 1942; m. Nancy Killian; children from previous marriage: Tessa, Lee Ann. BA, SUNY, Buffalo, 1964; MA, Western Mich. U., 1965; grad. advanced mgmt. library adminstrn., Miami U., Oxford, Ohio, 1981; grad. library adminstrn. devel. program, U. Md., 1985. Various positions Buffalo and Erie County Pub. Libraries, 1963-74, asst. dep. dir., personnel officer, 1979-80; dir. Town of Tonawanda (N.Y.) Pub. Library, 1974-78; asst. city librarian, dir. pub. svcs. Denver Pub. Library, 1978-79; exec. dir. Nioga Library System, Buffalo, 1980-87; library dir. Sacramento (Calif.) Pub. Library, 1987—. Mem. ALA, Calif. Library Assn., Rotary. Office: Sacramento Pub Libr Adminstrn Ctr 828 I St Sacramento CA 95814-2589 Home: PO Box 342 The Sea Ranch CA 95497-0342

KILLINGER, KERRY KENT, retired bank executive; b. Des Moines, June 6, 1949; m. Linda Killinger BBA, U. Iowa, 1970, MBA, 1971. Exec. v.p. Murphey Favre, Inc., Spokane, 1976-82; exec. v.p. fin. mgmt., investor rels., corp. mktg. Wash. Mutual, Seattle, 1983-86; sr. exec. v.p., 1986-88; pres. Wash. Mutual Savs. Bank, Seattle, 1988—2005, CEO, 1990—2005, chmn. bd., 1991—2005; chmn., CEO Washington Mutual, Inc., Seattle, 2005—08, CEO, 2008. Mem. Thrift Inst. Adv. Coun. to Fed. Res. bd., 1992—94, NY Stock Exch. Listed Co. Adv. Com.; bd. dirs. Washington Mutual, Inc., 1988—2008, Simpson Investment Co, 1997—, Safeco Corp., 2003—, Green Diamond Resource Co. Bd. dirs. Fed. Home Loan Bank of Seattle, 1995—, Seattle Repertory Theatre, 1990—, Washington Roundtable, 1990—, Downtown Seattle Assn., 1991, Leadership Tomorrow, Seattle Found., 1992—, Com. to Encourage Corp. Philanthropy; mem. Alliance for Edn., 1992—, chair, 1994-96, co-chmn. AIDS Walk-a-thon, Seattle, 1990; chair Partnership for Learning, 1997. Recipient Banker of Yr. award, Am. Banker mag, 2001. Fellow Life Mgmt. Inst.; mem. Soc. Fin. Analysts, Greater Seattle C. of C. (bd. dirs. 1992—), Rotary.

KILLMAR, LAWRENCE E., animal park curator; BSBA, Calif. Coast Univ., 1995, postgrad., 1996—. directed transp. four So. White Rhino from San Diego Zoo and Wild Animal Park to Can., 1974, to Europe, 1977; participant Gian Eland capture, Senegal, West Afirca, 1979; accompanied four Asiatic Lions to Jerusalem Zoo, 1984, others; facilitator Feline Immunodeficiency Viruses Workshop for Cheetahs, Escondido, 1995, others. Park keeper to curatorial field supr. San Diego (Calif.) Wild Animal Park, 1970-80, curator of mammals, 1982-91, gen. curator/mammal and bird collections, 1991-92, gen. curator/mammal, bird and reptile collections, 1992—. Contbr. articles to profl. jours. Fellow Am. Assn. Zoos, Parks, Aquariums; mem. Wildlife Conservation Mgmt. Com./Am. Zool. Assn., Am. Zoo and Aquarium Assn. (bd. regents 1996). Office: San Diego Wild Animal Park 15500 San Pasqual Valley Rd Escondido CA 92027-7017

KILPATRICK, FRANK STANTON, marketing executive; b. San Jose, Calif., Dec. 2, 1950; s. Frank George and Marian (Polk) K. Student, U. Wis., 1968—71; AB in Polit. Sci., U. Calif., Berkeley, 1975, postgrad., 1976. Writer, advt. sales rep., Midwest regional mgr., mktg. mgr. 13-30 Corp. (Whittle Comm.), 1970—74; with Grey Advt., 1977; mktg. mgr. East/West Network, 1978—79; mktg. dir. Calif. Bus. mag., LA, 1979—81; v.p. mktg. Harlequin Mags., 1981; gen. mgr. new venture devel. Knapp Comm. Corp., 1981—84; gen. ptnr. Pacific Cellular, 1982—86, Calif. Coast Comm., 1981—84; dir., pres. Pasadena Media Inc., 1984—85; mgmt. cons. Kilpatrick & Assocs., LA, 1984—97. Lectr. entrepreneur program U. So. Calif. Sch. Bus. Adminstrn., 1984-85, UCLA Extension, 1989-94; pres. Capital Equity Group, 1986-87, Healthcare Comm. Group, 1998—. Vol. counselor 1736 Teen Crisis Ctr., Hermosa Beach, Calif., 1989-90. Mem. L.A. Advt. Club (Belding award 1980), Direct Mktg. Club So. Calif., World Affairs Coun., Town Hall Calif., U. Calif. Alumni Assn., Stanford Grad. Bus. Sch. Alumni Assn. (sec. 1985-86, v.p. events 1986-87, dir. 1987-90, pres. 1990-92), L.A. Venture Assn. (charter mem.). Office: 909 N Sepulveda Blvd 5th fl El Segundo CA 90245 Office Phone: 310-606-5700. E-mail: fkilpatrick@hcg.com.

KILPATRICK, JOHN AARON, construction and development company executive; b. Norfolk, Va., Jan. 7, 1954; s. Marion Calvin and Maude Elaine (Simms) K.; m. Lynnda Christina Peterson, Aug. 19, 1978; children: Lynnda Madonna, Jonathan Simms, Richard Marion, William Valien. B.S., U. S.C., 1976, M.B.A., 1981, PhD, 2002. Bus. mgr. J. Allen Shumaker Builders, Columbia, S.C., 1979-81; stockbroker Dean Witter Reynolds, Columbia, 1981-83; teaching assoc. U. S.C., Columbia, 1982-83; v.p., co-owner Carolina Microsystems, Columbia, 1983; controller Shumaker Bldrs., Columbia, 1985-87; v.p., gen. mgr. Sand Creek Properties, Columbia, 1987-88; pres. The Kilpatrick Co., 1987-90; adj. prof. Webster U., Columbia, 1986-90; asst. sr. v.p. rsch., U.S.C, 1990-94, lectr., Moore Sch. Bus., 1992-98; admin. S.C. Supercomputer Network, 1994-96; exec. dir., Acad. Coalition Intelligent Mfg., 1994-1995; pres., Greenfield Advisors 1998—. editor: Ctrl. Puget Sound Real Estate Rsch. Report; Author; Financing Development and Construction in the 90's, 1991, utstanding Home Construction, 1995, Subdivision Development, 1998. fellow Am. Real Estate Soc.; mem. Am. Real Estate Urban Econ. Assn., Am. Econ. Assn., Am. Fin. Assn., ABA (Assoc.), Appraisal Inst, Royal Inst. Chartered Surveyors (U.K.), Real Estate Counseling Group Am., Internat. Code Coun., Wash. Athletic Club, Ranier Club, Rotary Club, Omicron Delta Kappa, Phi Delta Theta. Episcopalian. Home: 5561 248th Pl Se Issaquah WA 98029-7619 Office: Greenfield Advt LLC Ste 650 2601 4th Ave Seattle WA 98121 Office Phone: 206-623-2935.

KIM, EDWARD WILLIAM, ophthalmic surgeon; b. Seoul, Korea, Nov. 25, 1949; came to U.S., 1957; s. Shoon Kul and Pok Chu (Kim) K.; m. Carole Sachi Takemoto, July 24, 1976; children: Brian, Ashley. BA, Occidental Coll., Los Angeles, 1971; postgrad., Calif. Inst. Tech., 1971; MD, U. Calif., San Francisco, 1975; MPH, U. Calif., Berkeley, 1975. Diplomate Nat. Bd. Med. Examiners, Am. Bd. Ophthalmology. Resident in ophthalmology Harvard U.-Mass. Eye and Ear Infirmary, Boston, 1977-79; clin. fellow in ophthalmology Harvard U., 1977-79, clin. fellow in retina, 1980; practice medicine in ophthalmic surgery Laguna Hills, San Clemente, Calif., 1980—. Vol. ophthalmologist Eye Care Inc., Ecole St. Vincent's, Haiti, 1980, Liga, Mex., 1989, Tonga, 1997; chief staff, South Coast Med. Ctr., 1988-89; assoc. clin. prof. dept. ophthalmology, U. Calif., Irvine. Founding mem. Orange County Ctr. for Performing Arts, Calif., 1982, dir. at large, 1991; pres. Laguna Beach Summer Music Festival, Calif., 1984. Reinhart scholar U. Calif.-San Francisco, 1972-73; R. Taussig scholar, 1974-75. Fellow ACS, Am. Acad. Ophthalmology, Internat. Coll. Surgeons; mem. Calif. Med. Assn., Keratorefractive Soc., Orange County Med. Assn., Mensa, Expts. in Art and Tech. Office: Harvard Eye Assocs 665 Camino De Los Mares Ste 102 San Clemente CA 92673-2840

KIM, GREGORY ROBERT, lawyer, entrepreneur; b. LA, May 23, 1957; BS, Yale U., New Haven, Conn., 1979; JD, MBA, U. Calif., Berkeley, 1983. Bar: Calif. 1983, Hawaii 1984. Law clk. US Ct. Appeals Ninth Cir., Honolulu, 1983—84; assoc. Pillsbury, Madison &

Sutro, San Francisco, 1984—88; ptnr. Goodsill Anderson Quinn & Stifel, Honolulu, 1988—2004; founding ptnr. Vantage Coun. LLC, Honolulu, 2004—. Dir. Entrepreneurs Found. of Hawaii, Honolulu, 2004—; founding mem. HiBEAM, Honolulu, 1999—. Editor: Hawaii Corp. Law Manual. Mem. Govs. Econ. Momentum Commn., Honolulu, 2005—06; dir. Entrepreneurs Found. Hawaii, Honolulu, 2004. Mem.: Hawaii State Bar Assn. (chair bus. law section 1995—97). Office: Vantage Counsel LLC 733 Bishop St Ste 2500 Honolulu HI 96813 Office Fax: 808-356-0487; Home Fax: 808-356-0487. Business E-Mail: gkim@vantagecounsel.com.

KIM, JAMES JOO-JIN, electronics company executive; b. Seoul, Korea, Jan. 8, 1936; came to U.S., 1955, naturalized, 1971; s. Hyang-Soo and Seung-Ye (Oh) K.; m. Agnes Chungsook Kil, Dec. 30, 1961; children— Susan, David, John. Student, Seoul Nat. U. Coll. Law, 1954-55; BS, U. Pa., 1959, MA, 1961, postgrad., 1961-63; D in Comml. Sci. (hon.), Villanova U., 1990. Asst. prof. econs. Villanova (Pa.) U., 1964-70; founder, pres. AMKOR Electronics, Inc., West Chester, Pa., 1970-98; chmn., CEO AMKOR Tech. Inc., Chandler, Ariz., 1998—. Founder, dir. Electronics Boutique Holding Corp.; bd. dirs. Visalign, LLC, Semiconductor, Inc., CFM Techs. Inc.; dir., chmn. Anam Semiconductor, Inc. (Korea), 1992—. Trustee U. Pa. Named one of Forbes' Richest Americans, 2006; recipient Presdl. Commendation award Pres. Park/Chung Hee, Republic of Korea, 1979, Korean Presdl. Order of Indsl. Svc. Merits, 1983, Korean Presdl. Tin-Tower award Pres. Roh/Tae Woo, Republic of Korea, 1990, Grand-Prix, New Industry Mgmt. Acad., 1996, Global Korea award Mich. State U., 1996, Semiconductor award as pioneer in merchant packaging industry, 1998. Mem. Union League Club (Phila.), Beta Gamma Sigma. Office: Amkor Technology 1900 S Price Rd Chandler AZ 85248

KIM, JOOCHUL, urban planner, educator; b. Seoul, Korea, June 21, 1948; came to U.S., 1969; s. Kubong and Kumsoon (Song) K.; m. Shinja Rhee Kim, Sept. 16, 1969; 1 child, Matthew. BA in Sociology, U. Calif., Berkeley, 1973; MUP, U. Mich., Ann Arbor, 1977, PhD in Urban and Regional Planning, 1979. Lectr. Boston U., 1977-80; asst. prof. Ariz. State U., Tempe, 1980-85, rsch. assoc., 1980—, assoc. prof., sch. of planning, 1985—. Participant Leadership Acad., Tempe, 1989-90; mgmt. intern Ariz. State U., 1990, dir. spl. project, 1990-2001, acad. program coord., 2001—; vis. prof., Seoul Nat. U., 1987, Hanyang U., 1986-87, vis. chief rsch. assoc., Seoul Devel. Inst., 1995. Editor: Planning Perspectives, 1983—85; author: Seoul: The Making of Metropolis, 1997; contbr. articles to profl. jours. Mem. Ariz. Solar Energy Assn., Phoenix, 1983-84; mem. task force City of Tempe, 1990—; founding bd. dirs. Friends of Internat. Films, Tempe, 1982-86; co-chair City of Phoenix Planning Com., 1982-83. Fulbright scholar Republic of Korea, 1986-87; named one of Outstanding Young Men of Am., U.S. Jaycees, 1982. Mem. Internat. Div. Planners Network, Korean Urban and Regional Planning Assn. Avocations: movies, piano, music, travel, reading. Office: Ariz State U Sch Planning PO Box 872005 Tempe AZ 85287-2005 Office Phone: 480-965-2768.

KIM, KI-YONG, physicist; s. Sam-Hyun Kim and Bok-Soon Lee; m. Yeonjung Kim, June 28, 1997; 1 child, Alex Joonwoo. BS, Korea U., Seoul, Korea (South), 1995; PhD, U. Md., College Park, 2003. Postdoc. rschr. U. Md., 2003—04; postdoc. rsch. fellow Los Alamos Nat. Lab., N.Mex., 2004—. Contbr. articles to profl. jours. Recipient Marshall N. Rosenbluth Outstanding Doc. Thesis award, Am. Phys. Soc., 2004, Gold medal, Korea U., 1995; fellow Postdoc., Los Alamos Nat. Lab., 2004. Mem.: Optical Soc. Am., Am. Phys. Soc. Achievements include research in high intensity, ultrafast laser matter interactions. Office: Los Alamos National Laboratory Mail Stop K771 Los Alamos NM 87545 Office Fax: 505-665-9030. Business E-Mail: kykim@lanl.gov.

KIM, KWANG-JIN, medical educator; s. Sang-Shin Kim and Kyung-Soo Shin; m. Soon-Ja Lee, Dec. 16, 1972; children: Min-Soo, Shirley. BSEE, Seoul Nat. U., Republic of Korea, 1971, MSEE, 1973; PhD, U. of Pa., Phila., 1980. Post-doc. training in physiology UCLA, 1980—82, asst. prof., 1982—86, Cornell U. Med. Coll., NYC, 1986—90; assoc. prof. U. of So. Calif., LA, 1991—2005, prof., 2005—. Contbr. articles to profl. jours., chapters to books. Ad hoc reviewer/editl. bd. Pharm. Rsch. Jour. Recipient New Investigator award, NIH, 1985. Mem.: Am. Physiol. Soc. (life). Office: USC - Keck School of Medicine 2011 Zonal Ave- Rm HMR914 Los Angeles CA 90033 Office Fax: 323-442-2611. Business E-Mail: kjkim@usc.edu.

KIM, LEE ANN, reporter, newscaster; b. Seoul, South Korea; arrived in US, 1971; m. Louis Song. BA in Broadcast Journalism, U. Md., Coll. Park. Gen. assignment reporter & anchor, 10News Live KGTV, San Diego, 1996—. Founder, exec. dir. San Diego Asian Film Festival, 2000—. Recipient Emmy award for investigative reporting, Calif. Teacher's Assn. award for best edu. reporting, Calif. Chicano News Media Assn. award. Mem.: Asian Am. Journalists Assn. (former pres., local chapter, Best Reporting awards). Office: KGTV 10News 4600 Air Way San Diego CA 92102

KIM, MIN JUNG, bank executive; 2 children. BSBA, U. So. Calif. Br. mgr. to v.p., lending officer Hanmi Bank, 1985—95; sr. v.p., chief credit officer Nara Bancorp, LA, 1995—2003, exec. v.p., COO, 2003—06, pres., CEO, 2006—. Active Korea Youth Cmty. Ctr. Named one of 25 Most Powerful Women in Banking, US Banker mag., 2007. Office: Nara Bank 3731 Wilshire Blvd Fl 10 Los Angeles CA 90010-2828

KIM, MOON HYUN, endocrinologist, educator; b. Seoul, Korea, Nov. 30, 1934; s. Jae Hang and Kum Chu (Choi) K.; m. Yong Cha Pak, June 20, 1964; children: Peter, Edward. MD, Yonsei U., 1960. Diplomate: Am. Bd. Ob-Gyn. (examiner 1979-98). Sr. instr. Ob-Gyn Yonsei U., Seoul, 1967-68; intern Md. Gen. Hosp., Balt., 1961-62; resident in Ob-Gyn Cleve. Met. Gen. Hosp., 1962-66; fellow in reproductive endocrinology U. Wash., Seattle, 1966-67, U. Toronto, Ont., Canada, 1968-70; asst. prof. Ob-Gyn, also chief endocrinology and infertility U. Chgo., 1970-74; asso. prof. Ob-Gyn Ohio State U., Columbus, 1974-78, prof., 1978-92, chief div. reproductive endocrinology, 1974-92, vice chmn. dept. ob-gyn, 1982-96; prof. U. Calif., Irvine, 1998—2004, prof. emeritus, 2004—. Richard L. Meiling chair in ob-gyn., Ohio State U., 1987-98. Editor: Am. Jour. Ob-Gyn., 1990-2002, editor-in-chief, 2003--; contbg. author books; contbr. articles to profl. jours. Recipient McClintock award U. Chgo., 1975; named Prof. of Yr. Ohio State U., 1976; recipient Clin. Teaching award, 1980 Fellow Am. Coll. Ob-Gyn; mem. Am. Gynecol. and Obstetric Soc., Am. Fertility Soc., Chgo. Gynecol. Soc., Endocrine Soc., Soc. Study Reprodn., Soc. Gynecol. Investigation. Home: 24 Whistler Ct Irvine CA 92612-4069 Office Phone: 714-456-7204. Business E-Mail: kimmh@uci.edu.

KIM, SABRINA S., lawyer; b. Seoul, South Korea, Oct. 9, 1969; BA magna cum laude, UCLA, 1992; JD, Univ. Calif., Hastings, 1996. Bar: Calif. 1996. Dep. atty. gen. Calif. Dept. Justice; assoc., securities litigation Milberg Weiss Bershad & Shapiro, LA. Ad. prof. Loyola Law Sch. Named a Rising Star, So. Calif. Super Lawyers, 2006. Mem.: Assn. Bus. Trial Lawyers (bd. mem.), Phi Beta Kappa. Office: Milberg Weiss Bershad & Schulman Ste 3900 300 S Grand Ave Los Angeles CA 90071 Office Phone: 213-617-1200. Office Fax: 213-617-1975. Business E-Mail: skim@milbergweiss.com.

KIM, SANG KOO, pastor, educator; b. Joongwon, Choongbuk, Korea, July 22, 1938; came to U.S., 1978; s. Seyong and Sun (Shin) K.; m. Sunok Lee, Oct. 3, 1969; children: James Han, Grace Jong. BA, Korea U., Seoul, 1964; MDiv, Presbyn. Theol. Sem., Seoul, 1966; D Ministry, San Francisco Theol. Sem., 1981. Ordained to ministry 33th Daejon Presbytery Presbyn. Ch., 1968. Sr. pastor Seattle Korean Presbyn. Ch., 1980-88, Dong Shin Presbyn. Ch., Fullerton, Calif., 1988—. Moderator Western Presbytery in U.S.A., La., 1983-84; prof. Faith Evang. Sem., Federalway, Wash., 1983-88, K.P.C.A. Presbyn. Sem., L.A., 1988—; vice moderator K.P.C.A., 1995; moderator Korean Presbyn. Ch. in Am., 1995-96. Author: The Core Theory of Salvation, 1993. Democrat. Office: Dong Shin Presbyn Ch 2121 E Wilshire Ave Fullerton CA 92831-4159 Home: 14411 Rock Canyon Ct Corona CA 92880-3704 E-mail: kimsangkoo@yahoo.com.

KIM, SHANE, computer software company executive; m. Dana Kim; 2 children. B in Economics and Internat. Rels., Stanford U.; MBA, Harvard Bus. Sch., 1990. Intern Workgroup Applications team Microsoft Corp., Redmond, Wash., 1989—90, product mgr. Workgroup Applications, mgr. internat. mktg. group, 1993—95, dir. bus. devel. Microsoft Game Studios, 1995, gen. mgr., COO Microsoft Game Studios, corp. v.p. Microsoft Game Studios, 2004—08, corp. v.p. global mktg. Interactive Entertainment Bus., 2008—. Ptnr. Social Venture Ptnrs. Office: Microsoft Corp One Microsoft Way Redmond WA 98052-6399

KIM, SUNG WAN, chemistry professor; b. Pusan, South Korea, Aug. 21, 1940; came to U.S., 1966; BS, Seoul Nat. U., 1963, MS, 1965; PhD in Physical Chemistry, U. Utah, 1969. Asst. rsch. prof. U. Utah, Salt Lake City, 1971-73, asst. prof., 1974-76, assoc. prof., 1977-79, prof., 1980—2001, dir. Ctr. Controlled Chemical Delivery, 1986—, disting. prof. pharmaceutica and pharm. chemistry, disting. prof. bioengineering, 2002—. Mem. study section SGYB, NIH, Bethesda, Md., 1985-89, 95-; founder, co-chmn., Internat. Symposium on Recent Advanced in Dryg Delivery, 1983-. Editor numerous books; editl. bd., Journal of Controlled Release (Outstanding paper award, 1989, 1991, 1998), Pharm. Rsch., Jour. Biomedical Materials Sci., Biomaterials Sci. jours.; patentee in field; contbr. articles to profl. jours. Recipient Founders award Controlled Release Soc., 1995, Clemson Basic Biomaterials award Soc. for Biomaterials, 1987, Gov.'s medal for sci., State of Utah, 1988, Inst. Soc. Blood Purification award, 1994, Japanese Biomaterials Rsch. award, 1996, Volwiler award, Am. Assn. Coll. Pharmacy, 2002, Ho-Am prize in Medicine, Ho-Am Found., 2003. Fellow Am. Assn. Pharm. Scientists (Rsch. Achievement award in Drug Delivery, 1995, Dale Wurster award, 1998), Am. Inst. Med. Bioengning, Biomaterials Soc.; mem. IOM, NAE Home: 1711 Devonshire Dr Salt Lake City UT 84108-2562 Office: U Utah Ctr Controlled Chem Delivery 30 S 2000 E BPRB Rm 201 Salt Lake City UT 84112 Office Phone: 801-581-6801.

KIM, WAN HEE, engineering educator; b. Osan, Korea, May 24, 1926; came to U.S., 1953, naturalized, 1962; s. Sang Chul and Duck Hyung (Chong) K.; m. Chung Sook Noh, Jan. 23, 1960; children: Millie, Richard K. B.E., Seoul Nat. U., 1950; MS in Elec. Engring, U. Utah, 1954, PhD, 1956. Rsch. asst. U. Ill., Urbana, 1955—56; rsch. staff IBM Rsch. Ctr., Poughkeepsie, NY, 1956—57; asst. prof. Columbia U., NYC, 1957—59, assoc. prof., 1959—63, prof. elec. engring., 1963—78; chmn., CEO Tech. Assessment Corp. Internat., Palo Alto, Calif., 1991—. Chmn. Tech. Cons., Inc., N.Y.C., 1962-69; chmn. KOMKOR Am., Inc., N.Y.C., 1970-72; spl. advisor for the pres. and govt. Republic of Korea, 1967-79; advisor Korea Advanced Inst. Sci., Seoul, 1971-73; chmn. Korea Inst. Electronics Tech., 1977-81; mem. bd. Korea Telecommunication Electric Rsch. Inst., 1977-81; pres. WHK Engring. Corp. Am., 1982-84, WHK Electronics Inc., 1982-84; chmn., chief exec. officer Industries Assn. Electronic Korea, 1978-81; chmn. WHK Industries Inc., 1984-88, AEA Corp., WHK-FJF&M Assocs., 1988-89; pres. Asian Electronics Union, 1979-83; pub. Electronic Times of Korea, 1982-83, Dr. Kim Report on Korea, 1988-2001; cons. The World Bank, Washington, other indsl. orgns.; chmn., CEO Tech. Assessment Corp. Internat. (TACI), 1991—93. Author (with R.T. Chien): Topological Analysis and Synthesis of Communication Networks, 1962; author: (with H.E. Meadows) Modern Network Analysis, 1970; author: (Auto Biography) Embracing Two Suns, 1999, numerous articles, —. U.S. rep. on U.S.-Japan Scientists Coop. Program.; trustee U.S.-Asia Inst., Washington, 1984-88. Served with Korean Army, 1950-53. Decorated Bronze Star; recipient Achievement medal U.S.-Asia Inst., Industry medal Republic of Korea, 1989; Guggenheim grantee, 1964, NSF rsch. grantee, 1958-78. Fellow IEEE, Union Radio Scientifique Internat. (mem. U.S. nat. com. Commn. Band C 1963-78), Sigma Xi, Tau Beta Pi. Achievements include being honorarily named the father of Korean electronics industry for his contbrn. to promotion of industry. Home: PO Box 778 Palo Alto CA 94302-0778 Office Phone: 650-322-1328. Personal E-mail: whkim@msn.com.

KIMBALL, BRUCE ARNOLD, soil scientist; b. Aitkin, Minn., Sept. 27, 1941; s. Robert Clinton and Rica (Barneveld) K.; m. Laurel Sue Hanway, Aug. 20, 1966; children: Britt, Rica, Megan. BS, U. Minn., 1963; MS, Iowa State U., 1965; PhD, Cornell U., 1970. Soil scientist USDA-Agrl. Rsch. Svc. U.S. Water Conservation Lab., Phoenix, 1969—2006, rsch. leader Environ. and Plant Dynamics Rsch. Group, 1990—2006. Editor: Impact of Carbon Dioxide, Trace Gases and Climate Change on Global Agriculture, 1990; co-editor: Carbon Dioxide Enrichment of Greenhouse Crops, 1986; contbr. articles to profl. jours. Named Highly Cited Rschr. in agr., Ins. for Sci. Info. Fellow: Am. Soc. Agronomy (chmn. program divsn. A3 1988, assoc. editor 1977—83, bd. dirs. 1994—97), Soil Sci. Soc. Am.; mem.: AAAS. Avocations: computers, biking. Office: Arid Land Agrl Rsch Ctr USDA-ARS 21881 N Cardon Ln Maricopa AZ 85238 Office Phone: 520-316-6369.

KIMBALL, HARRY RAYMOND, medical association administrator, educator; b. LA; MD, U. Wash., 1962. Intern King County Hosp., Seattle, 1962—63; resident in internal medicine U. Wash. Hosps., Seattle, 1963—64, 1967—68; fellow infectious diseases NIH Hosps., Bethesda, Md., 1964—67; pres. Am. Bd. Internal Medicine, Phila., 1991—2004; prof. medicine, sr. advisor to dean Sch. Medicine U. Wash., Seattle, 2004—. Office: Uw School Of Medicine 815 Mercer St # 4c Seattle WA 98109-4714 Office Phone: 206-221-4743. Office Fax: 206-221-2999. Business E-Mail: hkimball@u.washington.edu.

KIMBLE, DANIEL PORTER, psychology educator; b. Chgo., Nov. 18, 1934; s. Ralph Archibald and Ruth (Hazen) K.; m. Reeva Jacobson; children: Matthew, Evan, Sara. BA, Knox Coll., 1956; PhD, U. Mich., 1961. Asst. prof. U. Oreg., Eugene, 1963-66, assoc. prof., 1966-69, prof. psychology, 1969—, head dept., 1989-92. Author: Physiological Psychology: A Unit for Introductory Psychology, 1963, Psychology as a Biological Science, 2d rev. edit. 1977; editor: The Anatomy of Memory, 1965, The Organization of Recall, 1967, Experience and Capacity, 1968, Readiness to Remember, 1970, Contrast and Controversy in Modern Psychology, 1977, Biological Psychology, 1988, 2nd edit., 1992; contbr. articles to profl. jours. Recipient Teaching awards, 1967, 90; Woodrow Wilson fellow, 1956-57, Horace Rackham fellow, 1958-59, NIH fellow, 1961-63, NSF fellow, 1969-70. Fellow Am. Assn. Sci.; mem. Am. Psychol. Soc., Neurosci. Soc. Avocations: stamp collecting/philately, sports, water color painting. Office: U Oreg Inst Neuroscience Dept Psychology Eugene OR 97403

KIMBLE, WILLIAM EARLE, lawyer; b. Denver, May 4, 1926; s. George Wilbur and Grace (Fick) K.; m. Jean M. Cayia, Dec. 27, 1950; children: Mark, Cary, Timothy, Stephen, Philip, Peter, Michael. LL.B., U. Ariz., 1951. Bar: Ariz. 1951. Spl. agt. FBI, 1951-52; pvt. practice Bisbee, 1952-60, Tucson, 1962—; judge Superior Ct. Ariz., 1960—62; ptnr. Kimble, Nelson, Audilett & McDonough, 1962—. Commr. Ariz. Oil and Gas Commn., 1958-60; adj. prof. law U. Ariz. Coll. Law, 1962-86. Author: The Consumer Product Safety Act, 1973, Products Liability, 1977; sr. editor Consumer Products Alert newsletter, 1980-81; editor, pub. In Def. of Elec. Accidents newsletter, 1993—. Founder Naval War Coll. Found.; Rep. nominee Ariz. atty. gen., 1956; Rep. nominee Ariz. U.S. Congress, 1964. Served with USNR, 1944-46. Fellow Am. Coll. Trial Lawyers; mem. Sigma Chi, Phi Alpha Delta. Home: 3544 E Placita de Pipo Tucson AZ 85718 Office: Kimble Nelson & Audilett 335 N Wilmot Rd Ste 500 Tucson AZ 85711-2636 Office Phone: 520-748-2440. Personal E-mail: wkimble@comcast.net.

KIMNACH, MYRON WILLIAM, botanist, horticulturist; b. LA, Dec. 26, 1922; s. Elmer Edward and Ida (Johnson) K.; m. Maria Jaeger, Nov. 17, 1961. Grad. h.s. Asst. mgr. U. Calif. Botanic Garden, Berkeley, 1951-62; dir. Huntington Bot. Gardens, San Marino, 1962—86, dir. emeritus, 1986; book-dealer Monrovia, Calif. Contbr. articles profl. jours. Pres., bd. dir. Palm Soc., 1976-78. With USCG, 1943-46. Fellow Cactus and Succulent Soc. Am. (pres. 1970-71, bd. dir. 1968-74, editor jour. 1993-2003). Home and Office: 509 Bradbury Rd Monrovia CA 91016-3704 Office Phone: 626-358-3043. Personal E-mail: mkimnach@aol.com.

KIMURA, DOREEN, psychology professor, researcher; b. Winnipeg, Man., Can. 1 child, Charlotte Vanderwolf. BA, McGill U., Montreal, Que., Can., 1956, MA, 1957, PhD, 1961; LLD (hon.), Simon Fraser U., 1993, Queen's U., 1999. Lectr. Sir George Williams U. (now Concordia U.), Montreal, 1960-61; rsch. assoc. otol. rsch. lab. UCLA Med. Ctr., 1962-63; rsch. assoc. Coll. Medicine, McMaster U., Hamilton, Ont., 1964-67; assoc. prof. psychology U. Western Ont., London, 1967-74, prof., 1974-98, coord. clin. neuropsychology program, 1983-97. Supr. clin. neuropsychology Univ. Hosp., London, 1975-83; vis. prof. psychology Simon Fraser U., 1998—. Author: Neuromotor Mechanisms in Human Communication, 1993, Sex and Cognition, 1999, French, Japanese, Swedish, Spanish, Portuguese, and Polish edits.; contbr. numerous articles to profl. jours. Recipient Outstanding Sci. Achievement award Can. Assn. Women in Sci., 1986, John Dewan award Ont. Mental Health Found., 1992, Kistler prize for lifetime achievement in human rsch. Found. for the Future, 2006; fellow Montreal Neurol. Inst., 1960-61, Geigy fellow Kantonsspital, Zürich, Switzerland, 1963-64, D.O. Hebb Disting. Contbn. award, Can. Soc. Brain, Behav. & Cogn. Sciences, 2005. Fellow Royal Soc. Can., Can. Psychol. Assn. (Disting. Contbns. to Sci. award 1985); mem. Soc. Acad. Freedom and Scholarship (founding pres. 1992-93, 98-2000). Office: Simon Fraser U Dept Psychology Burnaby BC Canada V5A 1S6 Office Phone: 778-782-3356. Business E-Mail: dkimura@sfu.ca.

KINCANNON, ELIZABETH ANNE, neonatologist, hospital administrator; b. LA, Feb. 24, 1954; d. William Thomas and Inez (Stout) K.; m. Patrick Clebert Payne, Nov. 30, 1985; 1 child, MacKenzie Payne. BS with distinction, Stanford U., 1975; MD, Harvard U., 1979. Diplomate Am. Bd. Pediatrics. Resident U. Colo. Health Scis. Ctr., Denver, 1979-82; neonatologist So. Calif. Permanente Med. Group, San Deigo, 1986-93, Colo. Permanente Med. Group, Denver, 1985—86, 1994—, assoc. medical dir. network, strategy and bus. devel. Chmn. dept. pediatrics St. Joseph Hosp., Denver, 1995—; physician reviewer utilization mgmt. Colo. Permanente MEd. group, 1994—. Advisor Women Creating NewLives, San Diego, 1992-93. Neonatology fellow The Children's Hosp., Denver, 1983-84. Fellow Am. Acad. Pediatrics; mem. Phi Beta Kappa. Avocations: tennis, skiing, science fiction, entertaining. Office: Colo Permanente Med Group 2045 Franklin St Denver CO 80205-5437

KINDERWATER, JOSEPH C. (JACK KINDERWATER), publishing company executive; b. Milw., Aug. 5, 1922; s. Joseph Charles and Ida (Noll) K.; m. Jacqueline Shirley Marsh, 1948; children— Mark, Mary Jo, Nancy, Scott, Diane BA, U. Minn., 1948. Advt. copywriter C. Derosier Inc., St. Paul, 1948-50; account exec. David Advt. Agy., St. Paul, 1950-53; advt. rep. The Webb Pub. Co., St. Paul, 1953-63, advt. sales mgr., 1963-68, advt. dir., 1968-78, v.p., pub., 1979-87, exec. v.p., 1987-88, pres., chmn., 1988-89; pub. cons., 1990—; v.p. Midwest Unit Farm Publs., 1979-84, pres., 1985-88. Bd. dirs. Nat. Audit Bur. Circulation, 1985-89, Better Bus. Bur. Minn., St. Paul, 1985-89; fund vol. Am. Heart Assn., St. Paul, 1983-85, Children's Hosp., St. Paul, 1975; instr. Jr. Achievement, St. Paul, 1970-75; bus. exec. rsch. com. U. Minn., 1966. With USAAF, 1943-46; ETO Named one of Top Ten Bus. Execs., City Bus. mags., 1989. Mem. Northwest Farm Equipment Assn. (pres. 1984-87), Nat. Agr. Mktg. Assn. (v.p. 1976-77), State Farm Mag. Pubs. Assn. (dir. 1980-89), Agr. Pub. Assn. (bd. dirs. 1981-89), St. Paul Advt. Club (pres. 1974-76), Am. Advt. Fedn. (Cleo award 1965, dist. gov.

1965-69) Clubs: Minn. Press, Midland Hills Country, St. Paul Athletic, Minn. Advt. Roman Catholic. Office: 13013 N Panorama Dr Unit 101 Fountain Hills AZ 85268

KING, ALONZO, artistic director, choreographer; Student, Sch. Am. Ballet, Am. Ballet Theatre Sch., Harkness House Ballet Arts. Art dir. Lines Ballet, San Francisco, 1982—. Master tchr. working with Les Ballets de Monte-Carlo, London's Ballet Rambert, Nat. Ballet of Can., N.C. Sch. of Arts, San Francisco Ballet; inaugurator San Francisco Dance Ctr., 1989; performer Bella Lewitzsky Dance Co., DTH. Commd. to create and stage ballets for The Joffrey Ballet, Dance Theatre of Harlem, Alvin Ailey Am. Dance Theatre; ballets in repertoires of Frankfurt Ballet, Washington Ballet, Hong Kong Ballet; choreographer for Les Ballets de Monte-Carlo; choreogrpaher for prima ballerine Natalia Makarova, Patrick Swazye; original works choreographed include Who Dressed You Like a Foreigner, 1998 (2 Isadora Duncan awards for best costumes and mus. composition), Ocean (3 Isadora Duncan Dance award 1994 for outstanding achievement in choreography, original score and co. performance)), Rock, 1995, others. Mem. panels Nat. Endowment for Arts, Calif. Arts Coun., City of Columbus Arts Coun., Lila Wallace-Reader's Digest Arts Ptnrs. Program; former art commr. City and County of San Francisco. Nat. Endowment for Arts Choreographer's fellow, Prudential Fellowship, US Artists, 2006; named Master of African-Am. Choreography, Kennedy Ctr, 2005. Office: Lines Ballet Fl 5 26 7th St San Francisco CA 94103-1508

KING, ARTHUR R., JR., education educator, researcher; b. Portland, Oreg., Dec. 17, 1921; BA, U. Wash., 1943; MA, Stanford U., 1951, EdD, 1955. Tchr., counselor Punahou Sch., Honolulu, 1946-49; rsch. assoc. Stanford (Calif.) U., 1949-51; dir. curricular svcs. Sonoma County Schs., Calif., 1951-55; assoc. prof. edn. Claremont Grad. Sch., Claremont, Calif., 1955-65; prof. edn. U. Hawaii, Honolulu, 1965—, dir. Curriculum Rsch. & Devel. Group, 1966—2002, rschr. Edn. Rsch. and Devel. Ctr., 1966-74. Prin. investigator, editor courses Hawaii State Dept. Edn.; head Ocean Project, 1979-90; co-founder Pacific Cir. Consortium. Author: (with John A. Brownell) The Curriculum and the Disciplines of Knowledge: A Theory of Curriculum Practice, 1966; contbr. articles to profl. jours. Served USN, WWII; capt., USNR, ret. Office: U Hawaii at Manoa Curriculum Rsch & Devel Group 1776 University Ave Honolulu HI 96822-2463 Business E-Mail: aking@hawaii.edu.

KING, CAROLE (CAROLE KLEIN), lyricist, singer; b. Bklyn., Feb. 9, 1942; m. Gerry Goffin; m. Charles Larkey; m. Rick Evers, 1977 (dec., 1978); m. Rick Sorensen, 1982; children: Louise, Sherry, Molly, Levi. Student, Queens Coll. Co-writer (with Gerry Goffin) Will You Love Me Tomorrow?, Go Away, Little Girl, Up on the Roof, (with Jerry Wexler) Natural Woman, The Locomotion, Take Good Care of My Baby, (with Toni Stern) It's Too Late, 1971; albums include Music, 1971, Tapestry, 1971 (4 Grammy awards), Simple Things, Pearls: Songs of Goffin and King, Rhymes & Reasons, 1972, Fantasy, 1973, Wrap Around Joy, 1974, Really Rosie, 1975, Thoroughbred, 1975, Her Greatest Hits: Songs of Long Ago, 1978, One To One, 1982, Speeding Time, 1983, City Streets, 1989, Colour Of Your Dreams, 1993, In Concert, 1994, A Natural Woman, 1994, The Carnegie Hall Concert, 1996, Pearls/Time Gone By, 1998, Super Hits, 2000, Love Makes the World, 2001, The Living Room Tour, 2005, Love Makes the World-Deluxe Edition, 2007, Welcome To My Living Room (DVD), 2007; composer for films Head, 1968, Murphy's Romance, 1985, The Care Bears Movie, 1985; off-Broadway theater appearance in A Minor Incident, 1989; Broadway appearance in Blood Brothers, 1994; appeared in (films) Murphy's Romance, 1985, Russkies, 1987, (TV film) Hider in the House, 1989; (TV series) The Tracy Ullman Show, Gilmore Girls, 2002, 2005. Inducted in Rock & Roll Hall of Fame, 1990. Office: Carole King Prodns 11684 Ventura Blvd 273 Studio City CA 91604

KING, CARY JUDSON, III, chemical engineer, educator, academic administrator; b. Ft. Monmouth, NJ, Sept. 27, 1934; s. Cary Judson and Mary Margaret (Forbes) K., Jr.; m. Jeanne Antoinette Yorke, June 22, 1957; children: Mary Elizabeth, Cary Judson IV, Catherine Jeanne. B in Engring., Yale U., 1956; MS, MIT, 1958, DSc, 1960. Asst. prof. chem. engring. MIT, Cambridge, 1959-63; dir. Bayway Sta. Sch. Chem. Engring. Practice, Linden, NJ, 1959-61; asst. prof. chem. engring. U. Calif., Berkeley, 1963-66, assoc. prof., 1966-69, prof., 1969—2003, prof. emeritus, 2003—, vice chmn. dept. chem. engring., 1967-72, chmn., 1972-81, dean Coll. Chemistry, 1981-87, provost profl. schs. and colls., 1987-94, dir. Ctr. for Studies in Higher Edn., 2004—; vice provost for rsch. U. Calif. Sys., Oakland, 1994—95, interim provost, sr. v.p. acad. affairs, 1995-96, provost, sr. v.p. acad. affairs, 1996—2004; interim dir. Phoebe A. Hearst Mus. Anthropology, 2007—. Bd. assessment Nat. Bur. Stds. Programs; dir. chem. engring. program divsn. Lawrence Berkeley Lab.; chair coun. chem. rsch. Gov.'s Task Force Toxics, Waste and Tech.; chair Calif. Coun. on Sci. and Tech., 2002—04; chmn. bd. Calif. Assn. for Rsch. in Astronomy, 2003—06; chmn. bd. dirs. Am. U. of Armenia Corp., 1995—2006. Author: Separation Processes, 1971, 80, Freeze Drying of Foods, 1971; contbr. numerous articles to profl. jours.; patentee in field. Active Boy Scouts Am., 1947-86; pres. Kensington Cmty. Coun., 1972-73, dir., 1970-73. Recipient Malcolm E. Pruitt award Coun. for Chem. Rsch., 1990. Mem. AIChE (Inst. lectr. 1973, Food, Pharm. and Bioengring. Divsn. award 1975, William H. Walker award 1976, Warren K. Lewis award 1990, bd. dirs. 1987-89, Clarence G. Gerhold award 1992); mem. AAAS, NAE, Am. Soc. Engring. Edn. (George Westinghouse award 1978), Am. Chem. Soc. (Separations Sci. and Tech. award 1997). Home: 7 Kensington Ct Kensington CA 94707-1009 Office: Ctr Studies Higher Edn Univ Calif MC 4650 Berkeley CA 94720-4650 Business E-Mail: cjking@berkeley.edu.

KING, DUANE HAROLD, museum administrator; b. Bristol, Tenn., May 18, 1947; BA, U. Tenn., 1969; MA, U. Ga., 1972, PhD, 1975. Dir. Mus. Cherokee (N.C.) Nation, 1975-82; exec. dir. Cherokee Nat. Hist. Soc., Tahlequah, Okla., 1982-87, Mid. Oreg. Indian Hist. Soc., Warm Springs, 1987-90; asst. dir. George Gustav Heye Ctr. Nat. Mus. Am. Indian, NYC, 1990-95; exec. dir. Southwest Mus., LA, 1995—. Chmn. adv. com. Trail of Tears Nat. Hist. Trail Nat. Park Svc., 1991—; bd. trustees mem. Inst. Am. Indian and Alaska Native Culture and Arts Devel., Santa Fe, 1988—; exec. dir. Friends of Sequoyah Found. of Ea. Band Cherokee Indians, 1989-90; periodic cons. Cherokee Nation of Okla., 1989-94, Mus. Cherokee Indian, 1985—, Walt Disney Imagineering, Glendale, Calif., 1994; hist. advisor KUSA-TV, Denver, 1994-95; Sequoyah prof. We. Carolina U., Cullowhee, N.C., 1995, adj. asst. prof. dept. sociology and anthropology, 1976-82; adj. prof. divsn. arts and humanities Northeastern State U., Tahlequah, 1986-87; vis. asst. prof. dept. anthropology U. Tenn., Knoxville, 1974-82; asst. prof. dept. sociology and anthropology U. Tenn., Chattanooga, 1974-76. Contbr. video documentaries and articles to profl. jours. Recipient Spl. Achievement and Exceptional Svc. awards (6) Smithsonian Instn., 1992-95, Gold award Nat. Park Svc., 1995, Svc. award Confederated Tribes Warm Springs, 1990, Performance award Cherokee Nation Okla., 1985, Mayor's Merit award for exceptional achievements City of Knoxville, 1983, Disting. Svc. award Ea. Band Cherokee Indians, 1982, Vol. Svc. award Save the Children Found., 1982. Home: 311 Santa Rosa Rd Arcadia CA 91007-3040 Office: Southwest Museums 234 Museum Dr Los Angeles CA 90065-5030 Fax: 213 224-8223.

KING, EDWARD LOUIS, retired chemistry professor; b. Grand Forks, ND, Mar. 15, 1920; s. Edward Louis and Beatrice (Nicholson) K.; m. Joy Kerler, Dec. 20, 1952; children: Paul, Marcia (dec.). Student, Long Beach Jr. Coll., Calif., 1938—41; BS, U. Calif., Berkeley, 1942, PhD, 1945. Rsch. chemist Manhattan Project U. Calif., Berkeley, 1942-46; mem. chemistry faculty Harvard U., 1946-48, U. Wis., 1948-62, U. Colo., Boulder, 1963-90, chmn. dept. chemistry, 1970-72; ret., 1990. Author: How Chemical Reactions Occur, 1963, Chemistry, 1979; Editor: Inorganic Chemistry, 1964-68. Guggenheim fellow, 1957-58. Mem. Am. Chem. Soc., Phi Beta Kappa, Sigma Xi. Office: U Colo Dept Chemistry PO Box 215 Boulder CO 80309-0215

KING, GARY K., state attorney general; b. Albuquerque, Sept. 29, 1954; s. Bruce and Alice Marie (Martin) King; m. Yolanda Jones, 1986. B in Chemistry, N.Mex. State U., 1976; PhD in Organic Chemistry, U. Colo., Boulder, 1980; JD, U. N.Mex., 1983. Founding ptnr. King & Stanley LLP, Moriarity, N.Mex., 1983—90; mem. N.Mex. State Ho. Reps., 1986—98, chair consumer and pub. affairs com.; corp. gen. counsel, sr. environ. scientist Advanced Sciences, Inc.; policy adv. to asst. sec. for environ. mgmt. US Dept. Energy, Washington, 1998; dir. Office of Worker and Cmty. Transition; atty. gen. State of N.Mex., Santa Fe, 2007—. Mem.: Sierra Club, NRA. Democrat. Office: Office of Atty Gen PO Drawer 1508 Santa Fe NM 87504-1508 Office Phone: 505-827-6000. Office Fax: 505-827-5826.*

KING, GEORGE H., judge; AB, UCLA, 1971; JD, U. So. Calif., LA, 1974. Judge U.S. Dist. Ct. (cen. dist.) Calif., 1995—. Office: 255 E Temple St Los Angeles CA 90012-3332

KING, GUNDAR JULIAN, retired dean; b. Riga, Latvia, Apr. 19, 1926; came to U.S., 1950, naturalized, 1954; s. Attis K. and Austra (Dale) Kenins; m. Valda K. Andersons, Sept. 18, 1954; children: John T., Marita A. Student, J.W. Goethe U., Frankfurt, Germany, 1946-48; BBA, U. Oreg., 1956; MBA, Stanford U., 1958, PhD, 1964; DSc (hon.), Riga Tech. U., 1991; D Habil. Oecon., Latvian Sci. Coun., 1992. Asst. field supr. Internat. Refugee Orgn., Frankfurt, 1948-50; br. office mfr. Williams Form Engring. Corp., Portland, Oreg., 1952-54; project mgr. Market Rsch. Assocs., Palo Alto, Calif., 1958-60; asst. prof., assoc. prof. Pacific Luth. U., 1960-66, prof., 1966—, dean Sch. Bus. Adminstrn., 1970-90. Vis. prof. mgmt. U.S. Naval Postgrad. Sch., 1971-72, San Francisco State U., 1980, 1987-88; internat. econ. mem. Latvian Acad. Scis., 1990—; regent Estonian Bus. Sch., 1991-99; vis. prof. Riga Tech. U., 1993-97 Author: Economic Policies in Occupied Latvia, 1965, additional books on business, last six in Latvian, 1999—2007; contbr. articles to profl. publs. Gov.'s com. Wash. State Govt., 1965-88; study group on pricing U.S. Commn. Govt. Procurement, 1971-72; pres. N.W. Univs. Bus. Adminstrn. Conf., 1965-66. With AUS, 1950-52. Decorated officer Order of Three Stars, Latvian, 2006; Fulbright-Hayes scholar, Thailand, 1988, Fulbright scholar, Latvia, 1993-94, 2007; recipient Spidola prize Latvian Culture Found., 1999, Recognition award, 2005 Mem. AAUP (past chpt. pres.), Am. Mktg. Assn. (past chpt. pres.), Assn. Advancement Baltic Studies (pres.), Alpha Kappa Psi, Beta Gamma Sigma. Office Phone: 253-535-7302. E-mail: Kingga@plu.edu.

KING, HELEN EMORI, dean, nursing educator; b. Stockton, Calif., Apr. 10, 1936; d. Susumu and Sumi Emori; m. William King, Aug. 5, 1973; children: Bill, Brian, Donna, Debbie. BS, Loma Linda U., 1959, MS, 1965; PhD, Boston U., 1973. Asst. prof. Boston U., 1973-75; dept. chmn., prof. Atlantic Union Coll., South Lancaster, Mass., 1978-81; dean sch. nursing Loma Linda U., Calif., 1981—. Mem. Nat. League Nursing, Sigma Theta Tau. Office: Loma Linda U Sch Nursing Loma Linda CA 92350-0001 Office Phone: 909-558-4517. E-mail: hking@sn.llu.edu.

KING, INDLE GIFFORD, industrial designer, educator; b. Seattle, Oct. 23, 1934; s. Indle Frank and Phyllis (Kenney) K.; m. Rosalie Rosso, Sept. 10, 1960; children: Indle Gifford Jr., Paige Phyllis. BA, U. Wash., 1960, MA, 1968. Indsl. designer Hewlett-Packard, Palo Alto, Calif., 1961-63; mgr. indsl. design Sanborn Co., Boston, 1963-65; mgr. corp. design Fluke Corp., Everett, Wash., 1965-97; prof. indsl. design Western Wash. U., Bellingham, 1985—; pres., CEO Teaque Inc., 1998—. Judge nat. and. internat. competitions; cons. in field. Contbr. articles to profl. jours.; designer patents in field. Coach Mercer Island (Wash.) Boys' Soccer Assn., 1972-77; pres. Mercer Island PTA, 1973; advisor Jr. Achievement, Seattle, 1975-78. Recognized as leading one of Am.'s Top 40 Design Driven Cos., ID Jour., 1999. Mem. Idsl. Design Soc. Am. (Alcoa award 1965, v.p. Seattle chpt. 1986-88), Mercer Island Country Club. Office: 2727 Western Ave # 200 Seattle WA 98121

KING, IVAN ROBERT, astronomy educator; b. Far Rockaway, NY, June 25, 1927; s. Myram and Anne King; m. Alice Greene, Nov. 21, 1952 (div. 1982); children: David, Lucy, Adam, Jane; m. Judith Schultz, Apr. 20, 2002. AB, Hamilton Coll., 1946; AM, Harvard U., 1947, PhD, 1952; Laurea Honoris Causa (hon.), U. Padua, Italy, 2002; ScD (hon.), Hamilton Coll., 2005. Instr. astronomy Harvard U., 1951—52; mathematician Perkin-Elmer Corp., Norwalk, Conn., 1951—52; methods analyst U.S. Dept. Def., Washington, 1954—56; with U. Ill., 1956—64; assoc. prof. astronomy U. Calif., Berkeley, 1964—66, prof., 1966—93, chmn. astronomy dept., 1967—70, prof. emeritus, 1993—; rsch. prof. U. Wash., Seattle, 2002—. Mem. faint object camera team Hubble Space Telescope. Contbr. numerous articles to sci. jours. Served with USNR, 1952-54. Fellow AAAS (chmn. astronomy sect. 1974), NAS, Am. Acad. Arts & Scis., Am. Astron. Soc. (councillor 1963-66, chmn. divsn. dynamical astronomy 1972-73, pres. 1978-80), Internat. Astron. Union. Achievements include research in structure of stellar systems. Office: U Wash Dept Astronomy Seattle WA 98195-1580

KING, JAMES EDWARD, retired museum director, consultant; b. Escanaba, Mich., July 23, 1940; s. G. Willard and Grace (Magee) K. BS, Alma Coll., 1962, DSc (hon.), 2002; MS, U. N.Mex., 1964; PhD, U. Ariz., 1972. Lab asst. in biology Alma Coll., Mich., 1960-62; rsch. asst. dept. biology U. N.Mex., Albuquerque, 1962-64; teaching asst. dept. botany and plant pathology Mich. State U., East Lansing, 1964-66; plant industry inspector Mich. Dept. Agriculture, Lansing, 1966-68; rsch. asst. dept. geochronology U. Ariz., Tucson, 1968-71, rsch. assoc. dept. geoscis., 1971-72; assoc. curator paleobotany Ill. State Mus., Springfield, 1972-78, head sci. sects. and full curator, 1978-85, asst. dir. for sci., 1985-87; adj. assoc. prof. dept. geology U. Ill., Urbana, 1979-88; dir. Carnegie Mus. Natural History, Pitts., 1987-96, Cleve. Mus. Natural History, 1996—2001; mus. cons., 2001—. Adj. prof. biology Sangamon State U., Springfield, Ill., 1983-87; adj. rsch. scientist Hunt Inst. Bot. Documentation, Carnegie Mellon U., Pitts., 1988—; adj. prof. dept. geology and planetary sci., U. Pitts., 1988-96; vis. scientist in residence Alma (Mich.) Coll., 1985; mem. adv. bd. dept. geosci. U. Ariz., 2005—. Author sci. papers on topics related to geology and paleobotany; mem. editorial bd. Jour. Archaeol. Sci., 1980-87. Bd. dirs. Western Pa. Conservancy, 1996-97, Allegheny Land Trust, 1995-96; trustee Chagrin River Watershed Ptnrs., 1997-2001; mem. exec. com. Univ. Cir., Inc., 1996-2001. Fellow Ill. State Acad. Sci. (pres. 1981-82); mem. Am. Assn. Mus. (bd. dirs. 1994-97), Am. Quaternary Assn., (treas., exec. com. 1976-84), Am. Assn. Stratigraphic Palynologists, Assn. Sci. Mus. Dirs. (v.p. 1992-93, pres. 1993-96), Assn. Systematics Collections (v.p. 1989-91, pres. 1991-93), Sigma Xi (pres. Springfield chpt. 1985-86). Home and Office: Ste 326 6336 N Oracle Rd Tucson AZ 85704

KING, JAMES M., lawyer; b. Denver, July 17, 1948; BSEE with spl. honors, Univ. Colo., 1970, JD, 1976. Bar: Colo. 1976, U.S. Ct. Appeals tenth cir. 1979, U.S. Ct. Appeals ninth cir. 1984. Law clk. Colo. Ct. Appeals, 1976—77; ptnr. Baker & Hostetler, Denver, 1977—. Pres. Rocky Mountain Mineral Law Found., 2004—05. Mem.: ABA, Colo. Bar Assn., Tau Beta Pi, Order of the Coif. Office: Baker & Hostetler Suite 1100 303 E 17 Ave Denver CO 80203-1264 Office Phone: 303-861-0600. Business E-Mail: jking@bakerlaw.com.

KING, JAMES NEDWED, construction company executive, lawyer; b. Chgo., July 9, 1947; s. Ralph C. and Marie (Nedwed) K.; m. Ellen Josephine Carpenter, Jan. 29, 1977; children: Cynthia Marie, Michelle Ellen BBA, U. Notre Dame, 1969; JD, U. N.Mex., 1972. Bar: N.Mex. 1972. Pres. Bradbury & Stamm Constrn. Co., Albuquerque, 1972—. Bd. dirs. Albuquerque Econ. Devel. Corp. Mem. N.Mex. Amigos. Home: 13731 Apache Plume Pl NE Albuquerque NM 87111-8090 Office: Bradbury & Stamm Constrn Co PO Box 10850 Albuquerque NM 87184-0850 E-mail: jking@bradburystamm.com.

KING, JANET CARLSON, nutrition educator, researcher; b. Red Oak, Iowa, Oct. 3, 1941; d. Paul Emil and Norma Carolina (Anderson) Carlson; m. Charles Talmadge King, Dec. 25, 1967; children: Matthew, Samuel. BS, Iowa State U., 1963; PhD, U. Calif., Berkeley, 1972. Dietitian Fitzsimmons Gen. Hosp., Denver, 1964-67; NIH postdoctoral fellow dept. nutrition sci. U. Calif., Berkeley, 1972-73, asst. prof. nutrition dept. nutrition sci., 1973-78, assoc. prof. nutrition dept. nutrition sci., 1978-83, prof. nutrition dept. nutrition sci., 1983—, chair dept. nutrition sci., 1988-94; dir. USDA Western Human Nutrition Rsch. Ctr., Davis, Calif., 1995—2002; sr. scientist Children's Hosp. Oakland (Calif.) Rsch. Inst., 2003—; prof. emeritus U. Calif., 1995—, prof. nutrition and internal medicine, 2003—. Frances E. Fischer Meml. nutrition lectr. Am. Dietetic Assn. Found., 1985, Lotte Arnrich Nutrition lectr. Iowa State U., 1985; Massee lectr. U. ND, 1991, Lydia J. Roberts lectr. U. Chgo., 1995, Virginia A. Beal lectr. U. Mass., 1998; vis. prof. U. Calif., Davis, 1998—. Contbr. articles to Jour. Am. Diet. Assn., Am. Jour. Clin. Nutrition, Jour. Nutrition, Nutrition Rsch., Obstetrics and Gynecology, Brit. Jour. Obstetrics and Gynaecology. Recipient Lederle Labs. award in human nutrition, Am. Inst. Nutrition, 1989, Internat. award in human nutrition, 1996, Atwater award, Am. Soc. Nutritional Scis., 2004. Mem.: AAAS, Inst. Medicine of NAS, Am. Dietetic Assn., Am. Soc. for Nutritional Scis., Am. Soc. Clin. Nutrition. Office: Childrens Hosp Oakland Rsch Inst 5700 MKL Jr Way Oakland CA 94609 Office Phone: 510-450-7939. E-mail: jking@chori.org.

KING, JEFFREY J., lawyer; Dir. taxation & legal services Expeditors Internat. of Wash., 1990—92, v.p., gen. counsel, 1992—94, v.p., gen. counsel, sec., 1994—98, sr. v.p., gen. counsel, sec., 1998—. Office: Expeditors Internat of Wash 1015 Third Ave Seattle WA 98104 Office Phone: 206-674-3400.

KING, JOHN G., health service administrator; BA, Dartmouth Coll.; MHA, U. Minn. Various positions Fairview Sys., Mpls.; pres. Holy Cross Health Sys., Evang. Health Sys., 1980-91; pres., CEO Legacy Health Sys., Portland, Oreg. Bd. dirs. Blue Cross Blue Shield Oreg., Premier, HealthEast, Minn. Bd. dirs. United Way, Columbia-Willamette. Mem Am. Hosp. Assn. (trustee), Portland C. of C. Office: Legacy Health Sys 1919 NW Lovejoy St Portland OR 97209-1599

KING, KEITH C., state senator; b. Tekoa, Wash., Mar. 12, 1948; m. Sandi King; children: Jeremy, Brandon. BS, U. So. Colo.; MS, Oreg. State U. Owner Waterbed Palace, Colorado Springs, 1977—; mem. Dist. 21 Colo. House of Reps., Denver, 1998—2006; mem. Dist. 12 Colo. State Senate, Denver, 2007—. Pres. Cheyenne Mountain Charter Acad., 1995—98; mem. Cheyenne Mountain (Colo.) Sch. Bd., 1991—95. Republican. Office: Colo State Capitol 200 E Colfax Ave Denver CO 80203 Office Phone: 303-866-4880. Business E-Mail: keith.king.senate@state.co.us.*

KING, KENTON J., lawyer; b. Aberdeen, Md., 1954; BA, Stanford Univ., 1977; JD, Univ. Calif., Berkeley, 1987. Bar: Calif. 1987. Law clerk to the Hon. Kenneth W. Starr, US Ct. of Appeals (DC cir.), 1987—88; ptnr. Skadden, Arps, Slate, Meagher & Flom LLP. Editor-in-chief Calif. Law Rev., 1986—87; contbr. articles to profl. journals. Named one of The World's Leading Lawyers, Chambers Global, 2002—03, America's Leading Business Lawyers, Chambers U.S.A., 2003—05. Mem.: Calif. Law Rev. Inc. (pres. 1996—98), Boalt Hall Alumni Assn. (bd. dir.), Order of Coif. Office: Skadden Arps Slate Ste 1100 525 University Ave Palo Alto CA 94301 Office Phone: 650-470-4530. Office Fax: 888-329-2950. Business E-Mail: kking@skadden.com.

KING, MARY-CLAIRE, geneticist, educator; b. Evanston, Ill., Feb. 27, 1946; m. 1973; 1 child, Emily King Colwell. BA in Math. (cum laude), Carleton Coll., Northfield, Minn., 1966; PhD in Genetics, U. Calif., Berkeley, 1973; PhD (hon.), Carleton Coll., Bard Coll., Smith Coll., Dartmouth Coll. Postdoctoral tng. U. Calif.-San Francisco; prof. genetics and epidemiology U. Calif. Berkeley, 1976—95; Am. Cancer Soc. rsch. prof. genome scis. and medicine U. Wash., Seattle, 1995—. Mem. bd. sci. counselors Nat. Cancer Inst., Meml. Sloan-Kettering Cancer Ctr., mem. NRC com. to advise Dept. Def. on the Breast Cancer Rsch. Program., NIH Genome Study Sect.; served on Nat. Commn. on Breast Cancer of the President's Cancer Panel; mem. adv.

bd., NIH Office of Rsch. on Women's Health, Coun. of the NIH Fogarty Ctr., Nat. Action Plan for Breast Cancer, NIH Breast Cancer Program Review Group; affiliate mem. Fred Hutchinson Cancer Rsch. Ctr., Seattle; cons. Com. for Investigation of Disappearance of Persons, Govt. Argentina, Buenos Aires, 1984; carried out DNA Identifications for the UN War Crimes Tribunial; mem. UN Forensic Anthropology Team; mem. adv. bd. Robert Wood Johnson Found. Minority Med. Faculty Develop. program Contbr. articles to profl. jours. Recipient Clowes award, Basic Rsch., Am. Assn. Cancer Rsch., Jill Rose award, Am. Breast Cancer Found., Brinker award, Susan G. Komen Breast Cancer Found., 1999, Genetics prize, Peter Gruber Found., 2004, Weizmann Women & Sci. award, Am. Com. for Weizmann Inst. Sci., 2006; named Woman of Yr., Glamour Mag. Fellow AAAS, Inst. Medicine, Acad. Arts and Sciences; mem. Am. Soc. Human Genetics, Soc. Epidemiologic Research, NAS, Phi Beta Kappa, Sigma Xi. Achievements include identifying the close similarity of the human and chimpanzee genomes; discovery of a gene (BRCA1) that predisposes to breast cancer; introduced direct sequencing of PCR-amplified segments of mitochondrial DNA for identifying people or their remains by comparing their DNA to that of relatives. Office: Dept Medicine and Genome Sciences Health Sciences RM K-160 U Washington Sch Medicine Box 357720 Health Sciences Room K-160 Seattle WA 98195-7720 Office Phone: 206-616-4294. Office Fax: 206-616-4295. E-mail: mcking@u.washington.edu.

KING, NICOLE, molecular biologist, educator; BA, Ind. U., Bloomington, 1992; AM, Harvard U., 1996, PhD, 1999. Postdoctoral fellow U. Wis., 2000—03; asst. prof., genetics and develop., dept. molecular and cell biology and integrative biology U. Calif., Berkeley, 2003—, faculty affiliate, Ctr. for Integrative Genomics. Founder ChoanoBase online genetic library. Contbr. articles to profl. jour. Named a MacArthur Fellow, John D. and Catherine T. MacArthur Found., 2005. Office: Univ Calif Berkeley Dept Molecular & Cell Biology 142 Life Sciences Addition #3200 Berkeley CA 94720-3200 Office Phone: 510-643-9395, 510-643-9417 (lab). Office Fax: 510-643-6791. E-mail: nking@berkeley.edu.

KING, RAY JOHN, electrical engineering educator, engineering company executive; b. Montrose, Colo., Jan. 1, 1933; s. John Frank and Grace (Rankin) K.; m. Diane M. Henney, June 20, 1964; children: Karl V., Kristin J. BS in Electronic Engring., Ind. Inst. Tech., 1956, BS in Elec. Engring., 1957; MS, U. Colo., 1960, PhD, 1965. Instr. Ind. Inst. Tech., 1956-58, asst. prof., 1960-62, acting chmn. dept. electronics, 1960-62; research asso. U. Colo., 1962-65; research assoc. U. Ill., 1965; assoc. prof. elec. engring. U. Wis., Madison, 1965-69, prof., 1969-82, assoc. dept. chmn. for research and grad. affairs, 1977-79; staff rsch. engr. Lawrence Livermore Nat. Lab. (Calif.), 1982-90, sr. scientist high power microwaves program, 1989-90; co-founder KDC Tech. Corp., 1983, v.p., 1990—, cons. Vis. Erskine fellow U. Canterbury, N.Z., 1977; guest prof., Fulbright scholar Tech. U. Denmark, 1973-74 Author: Microwave Homodyne Systems, 1978; contbr. articles to profl. jours.; patentee in field; guest editor spl. issue Subsurface Sensing Techs. and Applications jour., 2000. NSF Faculty fellow, 1962-65. Fellow IEEE (life); mem. IEEE Soc. on Antennas and Propagation (adminstrv. com. 1989-91, chmn. wave propagation stds. com. 1986-89, gen. chmn. symposium 1989), IEEE Soc. Microwave Theory and Techniques, IEEE Soc. Instrumentation and Measurements, Forest Products Soc. (life), Electromagnetics Acad., Internat. Sci. Radio Union (commns. A, B, F), Sigma Xi, Iota Tau Kappa, Sigma Phi Delta. Home: 2595 Raven Rd Pleasanton CA 94566-4605 Office: KDC Tech Corp 2011 Research Dr Livermore CA 94550-3803 Home Phone: 925-462-8197; Office Phone: 925-449-4770. Personal E-mail: rayking@ieee.org.

KING, ROBERT WILSON, public relations specialist; b. Newport, RI, Sept. 25, 1954; BA in Lit., Boston U., 1977. With Sta. WBUR-FM, Boston, 1976-77; pub. affairs dir. Sta. KDLG-AM, Dillingham, Alaska, 1978-79, news dir., 1979-94; comm. dir. Knowles for Gov. Campaign, 1994; press sec. Office Gov. Tony Knowles, Juneau, Alaska, 1994. Bd. dirs. Juneau Symphony, Alaska Hist. Soc. Home: 419 Kennedy St Juneau AK 99801-1054 Office: Office of Gov PO Box 110001 Juneau AK 99811-0001 E-mail: Bob_King@gov.state.ak.us.

KING, SAMUEL PAILTHORPE, federal judge; b. Hankow, China, Apr. 13, 1916; s. Samuel W. and Pauline (Evans) K.; m. Anne Van Patten Grilk, July 8, 1944; children— Samuel Pailthorpe, Louise Van Patten, Charlotte Lelepoki. BS, Yale, 1937, LL.B., 1940. Bar: D.C., Hawaii bars 1940. Practiced law, Honolulu, 1941-42, 46-61, 70-72, Washington, 1942; atty. King & McGregor, 1947-53, King & Myhre, 1957-61; judge 1st Circuit Ct. Hawaii, 1961-70, Family Ct., 1966-70; sr. judge U.S. Dist. Ct. for Hawaii, 1972—, chief judge, 1974-84. Faculty Nat. Coll. State Judiciary, 1968-73, Nat. Inst. Trial Advocacy, 1976, U. Hawaii Law Sch., 1980-84 Co-translator, co-editor: (O. Korschelt) The Theory and Practice of Go, 1965. Served with USNR, 1941-46; capt. Res. ret. Fellow Am. Bar Found.; mem. ABA, Hawaii Bar Assn. (pres. 1953), Order of Coif. Republican (chmn. Hawaii central com. 1953-55, nat. com. 1971-72). Episcopalian. Home: 1717 Mott-smith Dr Apt 2814 Honolulu HI 96822-2850 Office: US Dist Ct 300 Ala Moana Blr Rm C461 Honolulu HI 96850-0461

KING, SHARON MARIE, consulting company executive; b. Clarksville, Ark., Sept. 16, 1946; d. Argie L. and Vida M. K.; m. Robert W. Warnke, Feb. 14, 1983; children: Michael R., Jenna L. AA, Coll. of Ozarks, Clarksville, 1966; BA summa cum laude, Calif. State U., Dominguez Hills, 1979. Sr. exec. asst. Computer Sci. Corp., El Segundo, Calif., 1973-79; office mgr., bookkeeper Internal Charter Brokers, Manhattan Beach, Calif., 1979-80; office mgr. Metal Box Can, Torrance, Calif., 1980-81; sec. to pres. Filtrol, LA, 1981-82; owner, mgr. Select Secretarial Svc., Manhattan Beach, 1982-89; pres., CEO Chipton-Ross, Inc., El Segundo, Calif., 1989—. Mem. Calif. C. of C. Presbyterian. Office: Chipton-Ross Inc 1756 Manhattan Beach Blvd Manhattan Beach CA 90266-6220 E-mail: sking@chiptonross.com.

KING, SHELDON SELIG, health facility administrator, educator; b. NYC, Aug. 28, 1931; s. Benjamin and Jeanne (Fritz) King; m. Ruth Arden Zeller, June 26, 1955 (div. 1987); children: Tracy Elizabeth, Meredith Ellen, Adam Bradley; m. Xenia Tonesk, 1988. AB, NYU, 1952; MS, Yale U., 1957. Adminstrv. intern Montefiore Hosp., NYC, 1952, 1955; adminstrv. asst. Mt. Sinai Hosp., NYC, 1957—60, asst. dir., 1960—66, dir. planning, 1966—68; exec. dir. Albert Einstein Coll. Medicine-Bronx Mcpl. Hosp. Ctr., Bronx, NY, 1968—72; asst. prof. Albert Einstein Coll. Medicine, NYC, 1968—72; dir. hosps. and clinics Univ. Hosp., assoc. clin. prof. U. Calif., San Diego, 1972—81; acting head div. health care scis., dept. cmty. medicine U. Calif. Sch. Medicine, 1978—81; assoc. v.p. Stanford U., Calif., 1981—85, clin. assoc. prof. cmty., family and preventive medicine; exec. v.p. Stanford U. Hosp., 1981—85, pres., 1986—89, Cedars-Sinai Med. Ctr., LA, 1989—94, CEO, 1989—94; exec. v.p. Salick Health Care, Inc., LA, 1994—99, pres. ea. region, 1996—98; interim dir. UCLA Med. Ctr., 1995; interim COO INFOHEALTH Mgmt. Corp., 1999—2000, bd. dirs., 2000—; prin. Creative Intellectual Commerce, 2001—. Mem. adminstrv. bd. Coun. of Tchg. Hosps., 1981—86, chmn. adminstrv. bd., 1985; preceptor George Washington U., Ithaca Coll., Yale U., U. Mo., CUNY; chmn. health care com. San Diego County Immigration Coun., 1974—77; adv. coun. Calif. Health Facilities Commn., 1977—82; chmn. ad hoc bd. advisors Am. Bd. Internal Medicine, 1985—91; mem. exec. com. St. Joseph Health Sys., 1990—94; acting chmn. Am. Health Properties, 1996—; nat. adv. com. Robert Wood Johnson Exec. Nurse Fellows Program, 1998—; trustee Carondelet Found., Carondelet Health Sys., Tucson, 2003—, chmn., 2009—; mem. health care adv. coun. TLContact Inc., 2003—; mem. adv. coun. Precyse Solutions, Inc., 2004—08; mem. exec. adv. coun. The Beryl Cos., 2006—. Mem. editl. adv. bd. (book) Who's Who in Health Care, 1977, mem. editl. bd. Jour. Med. Edn., 1979—84. Bd. dirs. hosp. coun. San Diego and Imperial Counties, 1974—77, treas., 1976, pres., 1977; bd. dirs. United Way San Diego, 1975—80, Vol. Hosps. Am., 1990—94; mem. Accreditation Coun. for Grad. Med. Edn., 1987—90, Prospective Payment Assessment Commn., 1987—90; bd. dirs. Hosp. Fund, 1987—2000, Tucson Zool. Soc., Reid Park Zoo, 2006—. With US Army, 1952—55. Fellow: APHA, Am. Hosp. Assn. (governing coun. Met. sect. 1983—86, coun. on fin. 1987, ho. of dels. 1987—89), Am. Coll. Health Care Execs.; mem.: Ariz. Arts, Sci. and Tech. Acad. (founder), Inst. of Medicine, Am. Podiatric Med. Assn. (project coun. 2000 1985—86), Calif. Hosp. Assn. (trustee 1978—81). Personal E-mail: xenshel@comcast.net.

KING, STEVE, state legislator; Mem. Dist. 54 Colo. House of Reps., Denver, 2007—. Republican. Office: Colo State Capitol 200 E Colfax Denver CO 80203 Office Phone: 303-866-3068. Business E-Mail: steve.king.house@state.co.us.*

KING, TALMADGE E., physician; b. Feb. 24, 1948; BA, Gustavus Adolphus Coll., 1970; MD, Harvard U., 1974. Vice chair dept. medicine U. Colo., Denver, 1992-97; exec. v.p. Nat. Jewish Med. and Rsch. Ctr., Denver, 1992-95; vice chmn. medicine U. Calif., San Francisco, 1997—2007, chair medicine, 2006—; chief med. svc. San Francisco Gen. Hosp., 1997—2007. Editor: Interstitial Lung Disease, 2003; co-editor: Medical Management of Vulnerable and Underserved Patients, 2006; sect. editor: Baum's Textbook of Pulmonary Diseases, 2004. Trustee Gustavus Adolphus Coll., St. Peter, Minn., 1993—2002. Mem.: Inst. Medicine, Am. Bd. Internal Medicine (bd. dir. 2006—), Am. Thoracic Soc. (pres. 1997—98). Office: Univ Calif 505 Parnassus Ave M-994 San Francisco CA 94143 Business E-Mail: tking@medicine.ucsf.edu.

KING-BARRUTIA, ROBBIE L., former state senator; b. Waco, Tex., Jan. 10, 1959; m. Kevin Barrutia; children: Kandace, Kenzie. Student, Coll. So. Idaho. Legis. attache; Rep. rep. dist. 20 Idaho Ho. of Reps., 1992-96; Rep. senator dist. 20 Idaho State Senate, 1996. Mem. commerce and human resources, health and welfare, judiciary and rules coms. Idaho State Senate. Mem. Owyhee County Cowbelles; mem. Mountain Home Mil. Affairs Com., Region IV Infant and Toddler Com., Idaho Rural Devel. Coun. With Idaho Air N.G. Mem. South Ctrl. Idaho Recreation and Tourism Devel. Assn., Owyhee County Cattlemens Assn., Mountain Home C. o C., Glenns Ferry C. of C. Roman Catholic. Office: PO Box 28 Glenns Ferry ID 83623 also: Idaho State Senate State Capitol PO Box 83720 Boise ID 83720-0081 E-mail: infocntr@lso.state.id.us.

KINGDON, MARK, computer software company executive; BA in Economics, UCLA; MBA, U. Pa. Ptnr. PricewaterhouseCoopers; with Idealab; CEO Organic Inc., 2001—08, Linden Lab, San Francisco, 2008—. Mem.: Young Presidents Org., Internat. Academy of Digital Arts and Sciences (Webby Judge). Office: Linden Lab 945 Battery St San Francisco CA 94111-1305

KING-NING, TU, materials science and engineering educator; b. Canton, China, Dec. 30, 1937; came to U.S., 1962; s. Ying-Chiang Tu and Sau-Yuk Chen; m. Ching Chiao, Sept. 25, 1964; children: Olivia, Stephen. BSc, Nat. Taiwan U., 1960; MSc, Brown U., 1964; PhD, Harvard U., 1968. Rsch. staff mem. IBM Watson Rsch. Ctr., Yorktown Heights, NY, 1968-93, sr. mgr. thin film sci. dept., 1978-85, sr. mgr. materials sci. dept., 1985-87; prof. dept. materials sci. & engring. UCLA, 1993—. Co-author: (textbook) Electronic Thin Film Science, 1992. Recipient Acta/Scripta Metallurgica Lecturer, 1990; grantee Alexander von Humboldt, 1996. Fellow Am. Phys. Soc., The Metall. Soc. (Applications to Practice award 1988), Churchill Coll. (U.K.), Academia Sinica Republic of China. Achievements include 8 patents on thin film technology for microelectronics. Office: UCLA Boelter Hall 6532 B Los Angeles CA 90095-0001 E-mail: kntu@ucla.edu.

KINGSMORE, STEPHEN FRANCIS, physician, research scientist; b. Motherwell, Scotland, Sept. 3, 1960; came to U.S., 1988; s. Brian and Rona K. (Ritson) K.; m. Fiona J. McQuaid, Nov. 7, 1987; children: Daniel R., Rebekah F.P., Francesca S. BSc in Med. Microbiology, Queen's U., Belfast, Ireland, 1982; MB, ChB, BAO, Queen's U., Belfast, No. Ireland, 1985. Diplomate Am. Bd. Internal Medicine. Intern Craigavon Hosp., Portadown, No. Ireland, 1985-86; resident Queen's U., Belfast, 1986-88; fellow Duke U., Durham, NC, 1988-89, intern, 1989-90, resident, 1990-91, fellow, 1991-93, assoc. in medicine, 1993-94; asst. prof. U. Fla., Gainesville, 1994-97; COO Molecular Staging Inc., New Haven; v.p. rsch. CuraGen Corp., New Haven, 1997—2004; pres., CEO Nat. Ctr. for Genome Resources, Santa Fe, 2004—. Contbr. articles to profl. jours. Recipient Sr. Scholar awrd Am. Coll. Rheumatology, 1994, Arthritis Investigator award Arthritis Found., 1995, Jr. Faculty Rsch. award Am. Cancer Soc., 1996. Mem. Am. Fedn. Clin. Rsch. (Trainee Investigator award 1994, Jr. Faculty award 1996), Internat. Mammalian Genome Soc. Office: Pres Nat Ctr for Genome Resources 2935 Rodeo Pk Dr East Santa Fe NM 87505 Home Phone: 505-820-7852; Office Phone: 505-995-4466. Business E-Mail: sfk@ncgr.org.

KINGSTON, MAXINE HONG, writer, educator; b. Stockton, Calif., Oct. 27, 1940; d. Tom and Ying Lan (Chew) Hong; m. Earll Kingston, Nov. 23, 1962; 1 child, Joseph Lawrence. BA, U. Calif., Berkeley, 1962; D (hon.), Ea. Mich. U., 1988, Colby Coll., 1990, Brandeis U., 1991, U. Mass., 1991. English tchr. Sunset HS, Hayward, Calif., 1965—66, Kahuku HS, Hawaii, 1967, Kahaluu Drop-In Sch., Hawaii, 1968, Kailua HS, Hawaii, 1969, Honolulu Bus. Coll., 1969, Mid-Pacific Inst., Honolulu, 1970—77; prof. English, vis. writer U. Hawaii, Honolulu, 1977; Thelma McCandless Disting. Prof. Ea. Mich. U., Ypsilanti, 1986; sr. lectr. emerita U. Calif., Berkeley, 1990—2003. Author: The Woman Warrior: Memoirs of a Girlhood Among Ghosts, 1976 (Nat. Book Critics Cir. award for non-fiction, cited as one of best books of yr./decade TIME mag., NY Times, Asian Mail), China Men, 1981 (Nat. Book award), Hawai'i One Summer, 1987 (Western Books Exhbn. award, Book Builders West award), Tripmaster Monkey-His Fake Book, 1989 (PEN USA West award for fiction), Through the Black Curtain, 1988, To Be The Poet, 2002, The Fifth Book of Peace, 2003 (Best Spiritual Book award, Spirituality and Health, 2003); editor: The Literature of California, 2001 (Commonwealth Club Book award, 2001), Veterans of War, Veterans of Peace, 2006 (Pacific Justice/Reconciliation Ctr.for Peace Book award, 2007); prodr., prodr.: (plays) The Woman Warrior, 1994, 1995; host (TV series) Journey to the West, 1994; contbr. articles, short stories and poems to mags. Recipient Mademoiselle mag. award, 1977, Anisfield Wolf Book award, 1978, Writers award, Nat. Endowment Arts, 1980, 1982, Calif. Arts Commn. award, 1981, Lit. award, Hawaii, 1982, Calif. Gov.'s award for art, 1989, Major Book Collection award, Brandeis U. Nat. Women's Com., 1990, Lit. award, AAAL, 1990, Lila Wallace Reader's Digest Writing award, 1992, Oakland Bus. Arts Spl. Achievement award, 1994, Cyril Magnin award for outstanding achievement in arts, 1996, Artists award, Music Ctr. LA County, 1996, Nat. Humanities medal, NEH, 1997, Fred Cody Lifetime Achievement award, 1998, John Dos Passos prize for lit., 1998, Ka Palapola Po'okela award, 1999, Profiles of Courage honor Swords to Plowshares, 1999, Gold medal, Calif. State Libr., 2002, Lifetime Achievement award, Asian Am. Writers Workshop, 2006, Medal for Disting. Contribution to Am. Letters, Nat. Book awards, 2008; named Woman of Yr., Asian Pacific Women's Network, 1981, Alumna of Yr., U. Calif., 2000; named a Guggenheim fellow, 1981, Living Treasure of Hawaii, 1980. Mem.: Am. Acad. Arts & Scis. (KPFA Peace award 2005, Red Hen Press Lifetime Achievement award 2006), Womens League Peace & Freedom, Progressive Book Club (bd. mem. 2007).

KINNEAR, GREG, actor, film producer; b. Logansport, Ind., June 17, 1963; s. Edward and Suzanne Kinnear; m. Helen Labdon, May 1, 1999; 1 child. Diploma in broadcast journalism, U. Ariz. With Armed Forces Radio, Athens, Greece. Appeared on TV series College Mad House, 1989, The Best of the Worst, 1991, Talk Soup, 1991-94, Later with Greg Kinnear, 1994-1996, TV movies What Price Victory, 1988, Murder in Mississippi, 1990, Dillinger, 1991, Based on an Untrue Story, 1993, Dinner with Friends, 2001, films, Blankman, 1994, Sabrina, 1995, Dear God, 1996, A Smile Like Yours, 1997, As Good As It Gets, 1997, You've Got Mail, 1998, Mystery Men, 1999, What Planet Are You From, 2000, Nurse Betty, 2000, Loser, 2000, The Gift, 2000, Someone Like You, 2001, We Were Soldiers, 2002, Auto Focus, 2002, Stuck On You, 2003, Godsend, 2004, The Matador, 2005, (voice) Robots, 2005, Bad News Bears, 2005, Fast Food Nation, 2006, Little Miss Sunshine, 2006 (Outstanding Performance by a Cast in a Motion Picture, SAG, 2007), Invincible, 2006, Unknown, 2006, Feast of Love, 2007, Baby Mama, 2008, Ghost Town, 2008, Flash of Genius, 2008; co-exec. prodr. TV series The Best of the Worst, 1991; exec. prodr. Talk Soup, 1991-94, Later with Greg Kinnear, 1994-1996,. Mem.: Alpha Tau Omega.

KINNEY, CAROLYN, physician; b. Philipsburg, Pa., Feb. 18, 1957; MD, Boston U., 1981. Intern Thomas Jefferson U. Hosp., Phila., 1981, resident, 1982—84; staff Good Samaritan Regional Hosp. Med. Ctr., Phoenix, 1995—; phys. Health South Meridian Point Rehab., Scottsdale, Ariz., 1996—; sec. Am. Bd. Phys. Medicine & Rehab. Office: 9630 E Shea Blvd Scottsdale AZ 85260 also: Health South Meridian Point Rehab Hospital 11250 N 92nd St Scottsdale AZ 85260

KINNEY, LISA FRANCES, lawyer; b. Laramie, Wyo., Mar. 13, 1951; d. Irvin Wayne and Phyllis (Poe) Kinney; m. Rodney Philip Lang, Feb. 5, 1971; children: Cambria Helen, Shelby Robert, Eli Wayne. BA, U. Wyo., 1973, JD, 1986; MLS, U. Oreg., 1975. Reference libr. U. Wyo. Sci. Libr., Laramie, 1975-76; outreach dir. Albany County Libr., Laramie, 1975-76, dir., 1977-83; mem. Wyo. State Senate, Laramie, 1984-94, minority leader, 1992-94; with documentation office Am. Heritage Ctr. U. Wyo., 1991-94; assoc. Corthell & King, 1994-96, shareholder, 1996-99; owner Summit Bar Rev., 1987—2004; fin. planner VALIC, 2001—. Author: (with Rodney Lang) Civil Rights of the Developmentally Disabled, 1986; (with Rodney Lang and Phyllis Kinney) Manual For Families with Emotionally Disturbed and Mentally Ill Relatives, 1988, rev. 1991, 99, Lobby For Your Library, Know What Works, 1992, Understanding Mental Illnesses: A Family Legal Guide, 2004; contbr. articles to profl. jours.; editor, compiler pub. rels. directory of ALA, 1982. Bd. dirs. Big Bros./Big Sisters, Laramie, 1980-83, Children's Mus., 1993-97; bd. dirs. Am. Heritage Ctr., 1993-97, Citizen of the Century, 1997-99, govt. chmn. 1997-99; pres. Friends Cmty. Recreation Project, 2001-06. Recipient Beginning Young Profl. award, Mt. Plains Libr. Assn., 1980, Arts and Scis. Disting. Alumni award, U. Wyo., 1997, Making Democracy Work award, Wyo. LWV, 2000, Cmty. Svc. award, Laramie and Lions Club, 2006; named Outstanding Wyo. Libr. Assn., 1977, Young Woman, State of Wyo., 1980. Mem.: ABA, Nat. Conf. State Legislatures (various coms. 1985—90), Laramie Area C. of C. (bd. dirs. 1996—2000, mem. 1999, Top Hand award 1997), Zonta, Kiwanis. Democrat. Avocations: photography, dance, reading, travel, languages. Home: 1415 E Baker St Laramie WY 82072 Office: PO Box 1710 Laramie WY 82073-1710 Office Phone: 307-742-6644. Personal E-mail: lfkl@aol.com.

KINO, GORDON STANLEY, electrical engineering educator; b. Melbourne, Australia, June 15, 1928; came to U.S., 1951, naturalized, 1967; s. William Hector and Sybil (Cohen) K.; m. Dorothy Beryl Lovelace, Oct. 30, 1955; 1 child, Carol Ann. BSc with 1st class honours in Math, London U., Eng., 1948; MSc in Math, London U., 1950; PhD in Elec. Engring, Stanford U., Calif., 1955. Jr. scientist Mullard Research Lab., Salford, Surrey, England, 1947-51; research asst., then research assoc. Stanford U., 1951-55, research assoc., 1957-61, mem. faculty, 1961—, prof. elec. engring., 1965—, assoc. dean facilities and planning Sch. Engring., 1986-92, assoc. chmn. elec. engring., 1984-88, W.M. Keck Found. chair engring., 1992-97, W.M. Keck Found. chair engring. emeritus, 1997—; dir. Ginzton Lab., 1994-96. Mem. tech. staff Bell Telephone Labs., 1955-57; cons. to industry, 1957— Author: (with Kirstein, Waters) Space Charge Flow, 1968, Acoustic Devices, 1987, (with Corle) Confocal Scanning Optical Microscopy and Related Imaging Systems, 1996; also numerous papers on microwave tubes; electron optics, plasma physics, bulk effects in semiconductors, acoustic surface waves, acoustic imaging, optical microscopy, fiber optics, non-destructive testing, optical storage. Guggenheim fellow, 1967-68; recipient Applied Research Achievement award Am. Soc. Non-destructive Testing, 1986. Fellow IEEE (Centennial medal, Sonics and Ultrasonics Group Achievement award 1984), Am. Phys. Soc., AAAS; mem. Nat. Acad. Engring. Inventor Kino electron gun, 1959; co-inventor real-time scanning optical microscope, 1987, solid immersion lens, 1989, microfabricated miniature microscope, 1995. Home: 867 Cedro Way Stanford CA 94305-1002 Business E-Mail: kino@stanford.edu.

KINSLEY, MICHAEL E., newspaper columnist; b. Detroit, Mar. 9, 1951; s. George and Lillian (Margolis) K.; m. Patty Stonesifer, 2002. AB, Harvard U., 1972, JD, 1977; postgrad., Magdalen Coll., Oxford U., Eng., 1972-74. Bar: D.C. Mng. editor The Washington Monthly, 1975, The New Republic, Washington, 1976-79, editor, 1979-81, 85-89, sr. editor, 1989-95; editor Harper's Mag., NYC, 1981-83; Am. Survey editor The Economist, London, 1988-89; contbg. writer Time mag., 1987—; Editor Slate Mag., 1996—2002, contbg. editor, 2002—04; editl. and opinion editor LA Times, 2004—05; columnist Washington Post, 2005—. Co-host CNN Crossfire, 1989-95.

KINTIGH, DENNIS J., state legislator; b. Greensburg, Pa., May 1, 1952; m. Carol Kintigh; children: Melanie, Sarah, Ashley. BS in Aerospace Engring., U. Ariz., 1975; MS in Computer Sci., West Coast U., 1981. First lt. USAF, 1975—79; engr. Hughes Aircraft Corp., 1979—82; special agent FBI, 1982—2007; pumper HEYCO, 2007; mem. Dist. 57 N. Mex. House of Reps., 2009—. Republican. Home: 1205 San Juan Dr Roswell NM 88201 Office: House of Representatives State Capitol North Rm 2031CN Santa Fe NM 87503 Home Phone: 575-623-1258; Office Phone: 505-986-4453. E-mail: askdennis@denniskintigh.com.

KINTSCH, WALTER, retired psychology professor; b. Temesvar, Romania, May 30, 1932; arrived in US, 1955; s. Christof and Irene (Hollerbach) Kintsch; m. Eileen Hoover, June 27, 1959; children: Anja, Julia. PhD, U. Kans., 1960. Prof. U. Colo., Boulder, 1968—2004; ret., 2004. Editor: Pyschol Rev, 1989—94; author: books. Office: U Colo Dept Psychology Institute Congnitive Scis Boulder CO 80309-0344 Office Phone: 303-492-8663. Business E-Mail: walter.kintsch@colorado.edu.

KINTZELE, JOHN ALFRED, lawyer; b. Denver, Aug. 16, 1936; s. Louis Richard and Adele H. Kintzele; children: John A., Marcia A., Elizabeth A.; m. Suzanne Hinsberger; stepchildren: William Karp III, Christopher Karp. BS in Bus., U. Colo., 1958, LLB, 1961. Bar: Colo. bar 1961. Assoc. James B. Radetsky, Denver, 1962-63; pvt. practice law Denver, 1963—; 2. Corp. officer, dir. Kintzele, Inc.; rep. 10th cir. U.S. Ct. of Claims Bar. Chmn. Colo. Lawyer Referral Service, 1978-83, Election commr., Denver, 1975-79, 83-86 Mem. AAJ, ABA, Colo. Bar Assn., Denver Bar Assn., Am. Judicature Soc., Roscoe Pound Found. Democrat. Roman Catholic. Home: 10604 E Powers Dr Englewood CO 80111-3957 Office: 1317 Delaware St Denver CO 80204-2704 Home Phone: 303-770-7799; Office Phone: 303-892-6494. Personal E-mail: jkintlaw@aol.com. Business E-Mail: jkintlaw@comcast.net.

KIPKE, MICHELE DIANE, education and social services administrator, former hospital director; b. Glendale, Calif., Mar. 4, 1962; d. Arthur Harold and Anne Stuart (Mills) K. BA, NYU, 1984; PhD, Yeshiva U., 1989. Rsch. asst. Montefiore Med. Ctr., Bronx, N.Y., 1984-86; psychology intern Albert Einstein Coll. Medicine, Bronx, 1986-87; dir. AIDS prevention Montefiore Med. Ctr., Bronx, 1987-89; coord. substance abuse program Childrens Hosp. L.A., Calif., 1990-92, assoc. dir. rsch. and evaluation Calif., 1992-98; dir. bd. rsch. children, youth & families Nat. Res. Council, Washington, 1998—. Cons. HHS, SAMSA, HRSA, Washington, 1990—; coun. rep. elect Homeless Caucus, APHA, 1992-93; peer reviewer NIH, Washington, 1993—; cons. WHO/Mentor Found., Geneva, 1994—; spl. advisor Primary Health Care Initiative, Office of Treatment Improvement, Alcohol, Drug Abuse and Mental Health Adminstrn.; presenter in field. Reviewer AIDS Edn. and Prevention: An Interdisciplinary Jour., Jour. Adolescent Health Care; contbr. articles to profl. jours. Grantee Ctrs. for Disease Control (AIDS Evaluation of Street Outreach Project), 1992-95, Universitywide AIDS Rsch. Program (HIV Prevention Intervention Study with Seropositive Youth, 1993-95, Nat. Inst. on Drug Abuse (Investigation of Drug Use and HIV-Risk Sexual Behaviors Among Homeless Youth, 1993—, Substance Abuse and Mental Health Svc. Adminstrn./Ctr. for Substance Abuse Treatment, 1993—, Health Resources and Svcs. Adminstrn./Bur. Health Cre and Delivery and Assistance, 1993—, others. Mem. APA, Soc. Adolescent Medicine (ad hoc com. on health needs of homeless youth).

KIPPUR, MERRIE MARGOLIN, lawyer; b. Denver, July 24, 1962; d. Morton Leonard and Bonnie (Seldin) Margolin; m. Bruce R. Kippur, Sept. 7, 1986. BA, Colo. Coll., 1983; JD, U. Colo., 1986. Bar: Colo. 1986, U.S. Dist. Ct. Colo. 1986, U.S. Ct. Appeals (10th cir.) 1987. Assoc. Sterling & Miller, Denver, 1985-88, McKenna & Cuneo, Denver, 1989-94; sr. v.p., gen. counsel, dir. First United Bank, Denver, 1994-96; prin. Merrie Margolin Kippur Assocs., PC, Denver, 1997—2002. Lectr. in field; clk. to Hon. Elizabeth E. Brown, 2001—. Author: Student Improvement in the 1980's, 1984; (with others) Ethical Considerations in Bankruptcy, 1985, Partnership Bankruptcy, 1986, Colorado Methods of Practise, 1988. Active Jr. League Denver, 1992—2005, pres.-elect, then pres., 2001—03, sustainer, 2005—; bd. dirs. BMH-BJ Women's League, 2006—09, v.p., 2007—09. Mem. Colo. Bar Assn. (ethics com.), Denver Bar Assn., Gamma Phi Beta, Phi Delta Phi, Pi Gamma Mu, Yeshiva Toras Chaim Women's Auxiliary (life). Democrat. Avocations: reading, scuba diving, wine collecting. Business E-Mail: merrie_kippur@cob.uscourts.gov.

KIPRUSOFF, MIIKKA, professional hockey player; b. Turku, Finland, Oct. 26, 1976; Goalie Ky. Thoroughblades (AHL), 1991—2001, San Jose Sharks, 2001—03, Clagary Flames, 2003—. Recipient William M. Jennings Trophy, 2006, Vezina Trophy, 2006; named to First All-Star Team, NHL, 2006, NHL All-Star Game, 2007. Office: Calgary Flames PO Box 1540 Stn M Calgary AB Canada

KIRBY, J. SCOTT, air transportation executive; BS, USAF Acad.; MS, George Washington Univ. Economist, prog. acquisition & evaluation office U.S. Dept. of Defense; ops. rsch. cons. Sabre Decision Technologies; sr. dir. Am. West Airlines, 1995—97, v.p. planning, 1997—98, v.p. revenue mgmt., 1998—2000, sr. v.p. e-bus., 2000—01, exec. v.p. sales & mktg., 2001—05, US Airways Group, Tempe, Ariz., 2005—06, pres., 2006—. Office: US Airways Group 111 W Rio Salado Pkwy Tempe AZ 85281

KIRBY, RONALD EUGENE, fish and wildlife research administrator; b. Angola, Ind., Nov. 26, 1947; s. Robert Waye and Lorraine Alice (Hoag) Kirby; m. Dona J. Kirby; children: Cyrus Robert, William Emil, Peter Waye, Joshua M. Brosten, Emily A. Brosten, Andrew J. Brosten. BS, Duke U., 1969; MA, So. Ill. U., 1973; PhD, U. Minn., 1976. Staff biologist Coop. Wildlife Rsch. Lab., So. Ill. U., Carbondale, 1969-72; collaborating biologist U.S. Forest Svc., St. Paul and Cass Lake, Minn., 1970-72; rsch. biologist Antarctic Rsch. Program NSF, McMurdo Station, Antarctica, 1974; NIH rsch. trainee dept. ecology and behavioral biology U. Minn., Mpls., 1972-76; wildlife biologist, Patuxent Wildlife Rsch. Ctr. U.S. Fish and Wildlife Svc., Laurel, Md., 1976-80, population mgmt. specialist div. refuge mgmt. Washington, 1980-82, rsch. coord. Nat. Wildlife Refuge System, 1982-83, regional assistance biologist, office info. transfer Ft. Collins, Colo., 1983-88, leader info. transfer sect., 1988-90; asst. dir. No. Prairie Wildlife Rsch. Ctr., Jamestown, ND, 1991-92, dir., 1993; dir. U.S. Nat. Biol. Svc. No. Prairie Sci. Ctr., Jamestown, ND, 1993-96; dir. U.S. Geol. Survey No. Prairie Wildlife Rsch. Ctr., Jamestown, ND, 1997-2001; dir. U.S. Geol. Survey Forest and Rangeland Ecosys. Sci. Ctr., Corvallis, Oreg., 2001—03; sr. adv. biologist We. regional office U.S. Geol. Survey, Seattle, 2003—04, sci. quality coord., 2004—06, bur. approving ofcl., 2006—. Mem. waterfowl adv. com. Minn. Dept. Natural Resources, 1970—72; mem. black duck subcom. Atlantic Flyway Coun., 1976—80; mem. tech. sect. Central Flyway, 1991—. Editorial referee to sci. jours. and profl. reports; contbr. articles to profl. jours. Active Boy Scouts Am., 1984—. Grantee AEC, 1972—76. Mem.: The Wildlife Soc., Lambda Chi Alpha. Avocations: hiking, camping, birdwatching, motorcycling, hunting. Office: Western Regional Office US Geol Survey 909 1st Ave Ste 800 Seattle WA 98104 Home Phone: 253-833-7766; Office Phone: 206-220-4640. Business E-Mail: ronald_kirby@usgs.gov.

KIRCH, PATRICK VINTON, anthropology educator, archaeologist; b. Honolulu, July 7, 1950; s. Harold William and Barbara Ver (MacGarvin) Kirch; m. Debra Connelly, Mar. 3, 1979 (div. 1990); m. Therese Babineau, Feb. 6, 1994. BA, U. Pa., 1971; MPhil, Yale U., 1974, PhD, 1975. Assoc. anthropologist Bishop Mus., Honolulu, 1975-76, anthropologist, 1976-82, head archaeology div., 1982-84, asst. chmn. anthropology, 1983-84; dir., assoc. prof. Burke Mus. U. Wash., Seattle, 1984-87, prof., 1987-89, U. Calif., Berkeley, 1989—, prof. anthropology & integrative biology, endowed chair, 1994—; curator Hearst Mus. Anthropology, 1989—, dir., 1999—2002. Adj. faculty U. Hawaii, Honolulu, 1979—84; mem. lasting legacy com. Wash. State Centennial Commn., 1986—88; pres. Soc. Hawaiian Archaeology, 1980—81; vis. prof. Ecole des Hautes Etudes en Scis. Sociale, Paris, 2002. Assoc. editor Internat. Encyclopedia of the Behavioral and Social Scis., 2002; editor: Island Societies, 1986; co-editor (with Terry L. Hunt): Historical Ecology in the Pacific Islands: Prehistoric Environmental and Landscape Change, 1997; co-editor: (with Jean-Louis Raller) Growth and Collapse of Island Societies; co-editor: (with Eric Conte) Archaeological Investigations in the Mangareva Islands, 2004; co-author (with Peter S. Chapman): Archaeological Excavations at Seven Sites, Southeast Maui, Hawaiian Islands, 1979; co-author: (with Terry L. Hunt) Archaeology of the Lapita Cultural Complex: A Critical Review, 1989; co-author: (with Marshall Sahlins) Anahulu: The Anthropology of History in the Kingdom of Hawaii, Vol. 1: Historical Ethnography, 1992, Anahulu: The Anthropology of History in the Kingdom of Hawaii, Vol. 2, 1992; co-author: (with Roger C. Green) Hawaiki, Ancestral Polynesia: An Essay in Historical Anthropology, 2001; author: Marine Exploitation in Prehistoric Hawaii: Archaeological Investigations at Kalahuipua'a Hawaii Island, 1979, Island Societies: Archaeological Approaches to Evolution and Transformation, 1986, Niuatoputapu: The Prehistory of a Polynesian Chiefdom, 1989, The Evolution of the Polynesian Chiefdoms, 1989, Wet and the Dry: Irrigation and Agricultural Intensification in Polynesia, 1994, Anahulu: The Anthropology of History in the Kingdom of Hawaii, 1994, Feathered Gods and Fishhooks: An Introduction to Hawaiian Archaeology and Prehistory, 1995, Legacy of the Landscape: An Illustrated Guide to Hawaiian Archaeological Sites, 1996, Lapita Peoples: Ancestors of the Oceanic World, 1996, On the Road of the Winds: An Archaeological History of the Pacific Islands Before European Contact, 2000; contbr. articles to profl. pubs. Trustee Berkeley Art Mus. and Pacific Film Archives, 1999—2002, Ctr. for Advanced Study in Behavioral Scis., 2003—06, Sch. Advanced Rsch., Santa Fe. Recipient J.I. Staley prize in anthropology, Sch. Am. Rsch., 1998; grantee, NSF, 1974, 1976, 1977, 1982, 1987, 1988, 1989, 1993, 1996, 1998, 2001, 2006—07, NEA, 1985, NEH, 1988, 1999, Hawaii Com. for Humanities, 1981; fellow, Ctr. for Advanced Study in Behavioral Scis., 1997—98; rsch. grantee, Nat. Geog. Soc., 1986, 1989, 1996, Wenner-Gren Found. for Anthropol. Rsch., 1998, 2005. Fellow: NAS (John J. Carty medal for the advancement of sci. 1997), AAAS, Calif. Acad. Scis. (trustee 1999—2003), Am. Philos. Soc., Am. Anthrop. Assn., Am. Acad. Arts and Scis.; mem.: Polynesian Soc., Assn. Field Archaeology, Sigma Xi. Democrat. Avocation: gardening. Office: U Calif Dept Anthropology 232 Kroeber Hall Berkeley CA 94720-3710

KIRCHER, MATT, retail executive; Mng. ptnr. Terranomics Retail Svcs., Inc., San Francisco, 1999—. Office: Terranomics Retail Svcs Inc 1350 Bayshore Hwy Ste 900 Burlingame CA 94010-1818

KIRCHHEIMER, ARTHUR E(DWARD), lawyer, business executive; b. NYC, June 26, 1931; s. Arthur and Lena K.; m. Esther A. Jordan, Sept. 11, 1965. BA, Syracuse U., 1952, LL.B., 1954. Bar: N.Y. 1954, Calif. 1973. Ptnr. Block, Kirchheimer, Lemax & Failmezger, Syracuse, NY, 1954-70; corp. counsel Norwich Pharmacal Co., NY, 1970-72; sr. v.p., gen. counsel Wickes Cos., Inc., San Diego, 1972-84; prin. Arthur E. Kirchheimer, Inc., P.C., San Diego, 1984-90; writer, cons. in bus. matters La Jolla, Calif., 1990—. Sec., dir. Corp. Fin. Council San Diego, 1975 Pres. Mental Health Assn. Onondaga County, 1970; chmn. Manlius (N.Y.) Planning Commn., 1969-72; mem. Alternatives to Litigation Spl. Panel, 1984—; mem. San Diego County Grand Jury, 1991-92. Mem. ABA, Calif. Bar Assn. Home and Office: 2876 Palomino Cir La Jolla CA 92037-7066

KIRK, CASSIUS LAMB, JR., retired lawyer, investor; b. Bozeman, Mont., June 8, 1929; s. Cassius Lamb and Gertrude Violet (McCarthy) K. AB, Stanford U., Calif., 1951; JD, U. Calif., Berkeley, 1954. Bar: Calif. 1955. Assoc. Cooley, Godward, Castro, Huddleson & Tatum, San Francisco, 1956-60; staff counsel for bus. affairs Stanford U., 1960-78; chief bus. officer, staff counsel Menlo Sch. and Coll., Atherton, Calif., 1978-81; chmn. Eberli-Kirk Properties, Inc. (dba Just Closets), Menlo Park, 1981-94; ret. Faculty Coll. Bus. Adminstrn. U. Calif., Santa Barbara, summers 1967-73; past adv. bd. Allied Arts Guild, Menlo Park; past nat. vice-chmn. Stanford U. Annual Fund; past pres. Menlo Towers Assn.; endowed 2 professorships Stanford U., 2004 Past v.p. Palo Alto C. of C. With US Army, 1954-56. Mem. VFW, Stanford Faculty Club, Order of Coif, Phi Alpha Delta. Republican. Home: 1330 University Dr Apt 52 Menlo Park CA 94025-4241 Office Phone: 650-366-0285.

KIRK, DONALD EVAN, electrical engineering educator, dean; b. Balt., Apr. 4, 1937; m. Judith Ann Sand, Sept. 4, 1962; children: Kara Diane, Valerie Susan, Dana Elizabeth. BSEE, Worcester Poly. Inst., 1959; MSEE, Naval Postgrad. Sch., Monterey, Calif., 1961; PhD in Elec. Engring., U. Ill., 1965. From asst. to full prof. Naval Postgrad. Sch., Monterey, Calif., 1965-87; assoc. dean engring. San Jose (Calif.) State U., 1987-90, prof. elec. engring., 1990-93, dean engring., 1994—2002. Vis. scientist MIT Lincoln Lab., Lexington, Mass., 1981-82; program officer NSF, Arlington, Va., 1993-94. Author: Optimal Control Theory: An Introduction, 1970; co-author: First Principles of Discrete Systems and Digital Signal Processing, 1988, Contemporary Linear Systems, 1994. Bd. dirs. Carmel (Calif.) Sanitary Dist., 1973-77. Fellow IEEE, ASEE; mem. Sigma Xi, Tau Beta Pi, Eta Kappa Nu. Personal E-mail: kirkjd@sbcglobal.net.

KIRK, GERALD ARTHUR, nuclear radiologist; b. LA, Jan. 20, 1940; s. Arthur H. and Aural (Roderick) K.; m. Cherie J. Hutson, Dec. 27, 1965; children: Shannon Richard, Joel Daryn. BA in Physics, La Sierra Coll., 1962; MD, Loma Linda U., 1967. Intern Deaconess Hosp., Spokane, Wash., 1967-68; staff physician Empress Zandith Meml. Hosp., Addis Ababa, Ethiopia, 1968-69; pvt. practice Simi Valley, Calif., 1969-70; resident in radiology Loma Linda (Calif.) Med. Ctr., 1972-75, dir. sect. nuclear radiology, 1975—. Maj. USPHS, 1970-72. Home: 1341 Pine Knolls Cres Redlands CA 92373-6545 Office: Loma Linda Univ Med Ctr 25590 Prospect Ave Apt 27c Loma Linda CA 92354-3150

KIRK, HENRY PORT, academic administrator; b. Clearfield, Pa., Dec. 20, 1935; s. Henry P. and Ann (H.) K.; m. Mattie F., Feb. 11, 1956 (dec. July 1996); children: Mary Ann, Rebecca; m. Jenny Sheldon, Dec. 13, 1997. BA, Geneva Coll., 1958; MA, U. Denver, 1963; EdD, U. Southern Calif., 1973. Counselor, ednl. Columbia Coll., Columbia, Mo., 1963-65; dean Huron (S.D.) Coll., 1965-66; assoc. dean Calif. State U., LA, 1966-70; dean El Camino Coll., Torrance, Calif., 1970-81; v.p. Pasadena (Calif.) City Coll., 1981-86; pres. Centralia (Wash.) Coll., 1986—2002; vice chancellor Univ. of Livingstonia, Malawi. Contbr. articles to profl. jours. Mem. hist. commn., City Chehalis, 1990, pres. econ. devel. coun., 1992; campaign chmn., United Way, Centralia, 1989-90. Recipient PTK Bennett Disting. Pres. award, 1990, Exemplary Contbn. to Resource Devel. award Nat. Coun. Resource Devel., 1993, Earl Norman Leadership award, 2000. Mem. Wash. Assn. Community Colls. (pres. 1998-99), C. of C. (pres. 1998) Torrance Rotary Club (pres. 1977-78), Centralia Rotary Club (pres. 1990-91), Phi Theta Kappa, Phi Delta Kappa. Presbyterian. Avocation: antique restoration. Office: Centralia Coll 600 W Locust St Centralia WA 98531-4035 E-mail: hkirk@centralia.ctc.edu.

KIRK, JUDD, real estate development executive; b. Salt Lake City, Apr. 29, 1945; s. George and Mary Kirk; m. Barbara Sharon Almvig, June 15, 1968; children: Lisa, Jon. BA in fin., U. Wash., 1967; JD, Harvard U., 1970. Bar: Wash. 1970. Ptnr. Davis, Wright & Jones, Seattle, 1970-86; pres. Skinner Devel. Co., Seattle, 1986-90, Port Blakely Communities, Seattle, 1990—. Vestryman, treas., St. Stephens Ch., Seattle, 1983-86; pres. bd. dirs., Epiphany Sch., Seattle, 1984-86. Mem. ABA, Wash. State Bar Assn. (chmn. real property, probate and trust sect. 1980-81), Urban Land Inst., Nat. Assn. Indsl. and Office Parks, Am. Coll. Real Estate Lawyers, Kirkland C. of C. (bd. dirs. 1987-90), U. Wash. Alumni Assn. (trustee 1989-97, pres., 1995-96), Issaquah C. of C. (bd. dirs. 1991—, pres. 1997-98), bd. Cascade Land Conservancy. Office: Port Blakely Communities 1325 4th Ave 10th Fl Seattle WA 98101 Office Phone: 206-624-5810. Office Fax: 206-624-9745.

KIRKHAM, JOHN SPENCER, lawyer, director; b. Salt Lake City, Aug. 29, 1944; s. Elbert C. and Emma Kirkham; m. Janet L. Eatough, Sept. 16, 1966; children: Darcy, Jeff, Kristie. BA with honors, U. Utah, 1968, JD, 1971. Bar: Utah 1971, U.S. Dist. Ct. Utah 1971, U.S. Ct. Appeals (10th cir.) 1990, U.S. Supreme Ct. 1991. Assoc. Senior & Senior, Salt Lake City, 1971-73; ptnr. VanCott, Bagley, Cornwall & McCarthy, Salt Lake City, 1973-92, Stoel Rives LLP, Salt Lake City, 1992—. Mem. exec. bd. Great Salt Lake coun. Boy Scouts Am., 1987—, exec. com. v.p. legal, 2003-06, pres., 2006—; mem. Utah Statewide Resource Adv. Coun., 1995-97; trustee Met. Water Dist. Salt Lake and Sandy, 2003; mem. bd. govs. Salt Lake Chamber, 2005-. Mem. Utah Bar Assn., Utah Mining Assn. (bd. dirs. Salt Lake City chpt. 1987—), Rocky Mountain Mineral Law Found. (trustee 1989-92). Republican. Mem. Lds Ch. Office: Stoel Rives LLP 201 S Main St Ste 1100 Salt Lake City UT 84111-4904 Office Phone: 801-328-3131. Business E-Mail: jskirkham@stoel.com.

KIRKLAND, GEORGE L., oil industry executive; b. Aug. 1950; BS in civil engring., U. Fla., 1972, MS in civil engring., 1974. Constrn. engr. Chevron, New Orleans, 1974—78; with Caltex Pacific Indonesia, Sumatra, 1978—80, project engring. mgr. Duri Steam Flood project, 1980—85; sr. project mgr. Chevron U.S.A. Prodn. Co., Denver and Midland, Tex., 1985—88, San Francisco, 1988—90; group mgr. upstream tech. Chevron Rsch. and Tech. Co., 1990—92; gen. mgr. prodn. Chevron Nigeria Ltd., 1992—96, gen. mgr. asset mgmt., chmn., mng. dir., 1996—2000; pres. Chevron U.S.A. Prodn. Co., 2000; v.p. exploration and prodn. ops. Chevron Corp., 2000—; pres. N.Am. Upstream ChevronTexaco Corp., San Ramon, Calif., 2001—02; pres. ChevronTexaco Overseas Petroleum, San Ramon, Calif., 2002—05; v.p. Chevron Corp., San Ramon, Calif., 2002—05, exec. v.p., global upstream & gas, 2005—. Trustee Africa Am. Inst.; bd. dirs. Corp. Coun. on Africa. Mem.: U.S.-Kazakhstan Bus. Assn. (bd. dirs.). Office: ChevronTexaco Corp 6001 Bollinger Canyon Rd San Ramon CA 94583-2324

KIRKORIAN, DONALD GEORGE, retired academic administrator; b. San Mateo, Calif., Nov. 30, 1938; s. George and Alice (Sergius) K. BA, San Jose State U., 1961, MA, 1966, postgrad., 1968, Stanford U., 1961, U. So. Calif., 1966; PhD, Northwestern U., 1972. Producer Sta. KNTV, San Jose, Calif., 1961; tchr. LA City Schs., 1963; instrnl. TV coord. Fremont Union HS Dist., Sunnyvale, Calif., 1963—73; assoc. dean instrn. learning resources Solano CC, Fairfield, Calif., 1973—85, dean instrnl. services, 1985-89, dean learning resources and staff devel., 1989-99; exec. dir. Learning Resources Assn. of Calif. Cmty. Colls., 1976—2007. Owner, CEO The Cruise Doctor travel agy., 1999—; owner, pres. Kirkorian and Assocs., Fairfield; field cons. Nat. Assn. Edn. Broadcasters, 1966-68; adj. faculty San Jose State U., 1968-69, U. Calif., Santa Cruz, 1970-73, U. Calif., Davis, 1973-76; chmn. Bay Area TV Consortium, 1976-77, 86-87; mem. adv. panel Speech Comm. Assn./Am. Theater Assn. tchr. preparation in speech., comm., theater and media, NYC, 1973-77. Author: Staffing Information Handbook, 1990, National Learning Resources Directory, 1991, 93; editor: Media Memo, 1973-80, Intercom: The Newsletter for Calif. CC Librs., 1974-75, Update, 1980-90, Exploring the Benicia State Recreation Area, 1977, California History Resource Materials, 1977, Time Management, 1980; contbr. articles to profl. jours. Chmn. Solano County Media Adv. Com., 1974-76; bd. dirs. Napa-Solano United Way, 1980-82; mem. adv. bd. Calif. Youth Authority, 1986-93. Mem. Nat. Assn. Ednl. Broadcasters, Assn. for Edn. Comm. and Tech., Broadcast Edn. Assn., Calif. Assn. Ednl. Media and Tech. (treas.), Western Ednl. Soc. for Telecomm. (bd. dirs. 1973-75, pres. 1976-77, State Chancellor's com. on Telecomm. 1982-86), Learning Resources Assn. Calif. Comm. Colls. (sec.-treas., pres. 1974-76), Assn. Calif. CC Adminstrs. (bd. dirs. 1985-91), Cmty. Coll. Instrnl. Network. Home: 1655 Rockville Rd Fairfield CA 94534-1373

KIRKPATRICK, ANN L., United States Representative from Arizona, lawyer; b. McNary, Ariz., Mar. 24, 1950; d. Elliot Whittington and Nancy Jeanne (Cox) K.; m. Brian Richard Sheen, Jan. 22, 1983; children: Whitney, Ashley. BA cum laude, U. Ariz., 1972, JD, 1979. Bar: Airz. 1979, U.S. Dist. Ct. Ariz. 1979. Dep. atty. Coconino County, Flagstaff, Ariz., 1980-81; pvt. practice Secona, Ariz., 1981-82; dep. atty. Pima COunty, Tucson, 1982-84; assoc. Mangum, Wall, Stoops & Warden, Flagstaff, 1985; co-founder Kirkpatrick & Harris, 1991; mem. Ariz. State House of Reps. from Dist. 2, 2004—07, US Congress from 1st Ariz. Dist., 2009—. Instr. bus. law & ethics Coconino CC, 2004. Mem. Mental Health Services Com., Phoenix, 1982-84, mayors task force Tucson City Council, 1982, Civil Practice and Procedure Com., Phoenix, 1985—; chmn. funding, bd. dirs. IMPACT Victum-Witness Program, Flagstaff, 1985—; tchr. sunday sch. Federated Community Ch., Flagstaff, 1985—; cons. Flagstaff Med. Ctr. Found., 1986—. Named one of Outstanding Young Women Am., 1985. Mem. ABA, Ariz. Bar Assn., Coconino County Bar Assn., Am. Acad. Hosp. Attys., Ariz. Hosp. Assn. Republican. Presbyterian. Avocations: piano, country fiddle, swimming, skiing, ice skating. Office: US Congress 1123 Longworth House Office Bldg Washington DC 20515-0301 also: Dist Office 240 S Montezuma St Ste 101 Prescott AZ 86303 Office Phone: 202-225-2315, 928-445-3434. Office Fax: 202-226-9739, 928-445-4160.*

KIRKPATRICK, BRUCE CHARLES, plant pathology educator; b. Davis, Calif., Aug. 20, 1949; two children. BS in Biol. Scis., U. Calif., Irvine, 1980; MS in Plant Pathology, U. Calif., Berkeley, 1983, PhD in Plant Pathology, 1986. Asst. prof. plant pathology U. Calif., Davis, 1986-92, assoc. prof., 1992-98, prof., 1999—. Mem. Am. Phytopathol. Soc. (Ruth Allen award 1996), Internat. Orgn. for Mycoplasmology, Am. Soc. Microbiology, Sigma Xi. Office: U Calif Davis Dept Plant Pathology Davis CA 95616

KIRKPATRICK, CHARLES HARVEY, immunologist, researcher; b. Topeka, Nov. 5, 1931; s. Hazen Leon and Clarice Opal (Privott) K.; m. Janice Faye Fosha, July 11, 1959; children: Heather, Michael, Brian. BA, U. Kans., 1954; MD, U. Kans., Kansas City, 1958. Diplomate Am. Bd. Internal Medicine, Am. Bd. Allergy and Immunology. Asst. prof. U. Kans., Kansas City, 1965—67, assoc. prof., 1968; sr. investigator Nat. Inst. Allergy and Infectious Diseases, NIH, Bethesda, Md., 1968-79; dir. allergy and clin. immunology Nat. Jewish Ctr., Denver, 1979-93; prof. U. Colo., Denver, 1979—; dir. rsch. Innovative Therapeutics, Inc., 1993-96; pres. Cytokine Sci., Inc., Denver, 1996-99. Active NIH study sects., Bethesda. Editor: 4 books; contbr. numerous articles to profl. jours. NIH research grantee, 1981-86. Fellow ACP, Am. Acad. Allergy and Immunology, Molecular Med. Soc.; mem. Am. Soc. Clin. Investigation, Am. Assn. Immunologists. Episcopalian. Avocations: enology, antique corkscrews, antique automobiles. Office Phone: 303-724-7197. Business E-Mail: charles.kirkpatrick@vodenver.edu.

KIRKWOOD, CAROL, literature and language educator; BA summa cum laude, Colo. State U., 1971; M in French Lang. and Lit. with honors, Middlebury Coll. Sch. French, Paris, 1972. French tchr. Laramie (Wyo.) H.S., 1973—. Named Albany County Sch. Dist. One Tchr. of Yr., 2005, Wyo. Tchr. of Yr., 2006, Most Influential Pre-Coll. Tchr. (four times), Univ. Wyo. Honors Program. Office: Laramie High Sch 1275 North 11th St Laramie WY 82073

KIRKWOOD, ROBERT KEITH, applied physicist; b. Santa Monica, Calif., Mar. 10, 1961; s. Robert Lord and Patricia Cathrine (Keith) K.; m. Kimberly DeNeve Saunders, May 2, 1991; children: Rebekah Marie, Rachel Kathryn. BS, UCLA, 1982, MS, 1984; PhD, MIT, 1989. Rsch. asst. dept. elec. engring. UCLA, 1982-84; mem. tech. staff TRW Space and Tech. Group, Redondo Beach, Calif., 1984-85; rsch. asst. MIT, Cambridge, 1985-89, vis. scientist Plasma Fusion Ctr., 1992-94; postdoctoral fellow Calif. Inst. Tech., Pasadena, 1989-91; rsch. assoc. geophysics divsn. Air Force Phillips Lab., Hanscom AFB, Mass., 1991-92, physicist, 1992-94, Lawrence Livermore (Calif.) Lab., 1994—. Contbr. articles to Nuc. Fusion, Physics of Plasmas, Rev. Sci. Instruments, Physics Letters A, Phys. Rev. Letters. Recipient Rsch. Associateship award NRC, 1991; postdoctoral fellow Dept. Energy, 1989; doctoral fellow TRW Space and Tech. Group, 1985. Mem. Am. Phys. Soc. (Simon Ramo award in plasma physics 1991), Am. Geophys. Union. Achievements include development of wave transmission diagnostics for plasmas and demonstration of the interaction between multiple laser beams in plasmas. Office: Lawrence Livermore Lab L-479 PO Box 808 Livermore CA 94551-0808 Office Phone: 925-422-1007. E-mail: kirkwood1@llnl.gov.

KIRMAN, CHARLES GARY, photojournalist; b. Chgo., Feb. 2, 1949; s. Irving A. and Sylvia Lea K.; m. Heidemarie Mocker, Nov. 15, 1976 (div.); children: Christian, Courtney. BS in Profl. Photography, Rochester Inst. Tech., NY, 1972. Staff photographer Chgo. Sun-Times, 1972-81; pres. European Beauty Culture Coll., Phoenix, 1982-86; owner Phoenician Grill, Phoenix, 1987-88; admissions dir. Al Collins Graphic Design Sch., Tempe, Ariz., 1988-92; staff photographer Ventura County (Calif.) Newspapers, 1992—. With USNR, 1966-68. Recipient Nat. Headliner award for spot news photography, 1977; named Ill. Press Photographer of Year, 1975, Chgo. Press Photographer of Year, 1974 Mem. Ill. Press Photographers Assn., Chgo. Press Photographers Assn., Nat. Headliner Club. Office: 5250 Ralston St Ventura CA 93003-7318 Home: 1300 Saratoga Ave #309 Ventura CA 93003-6403

KIRSCH, STEVEN TODD, computer company executive; b. LA, Dec. 24, 1956; s. Harold and Harriet Karol (Edelman) Kirsch. BS, MS, MIT, 1980. Mem. tech. staff Rolm Corp., Santa Clara, Calif., 1981; chmn. Mouse Sys., 1982—86, Frame Tech., San Jose, 1986—94; founder Infoseek Corp., 1994. Achievements include patents for electro-optical mouse; electronic mouse. Home: 13930 La Paloma Rd Los Altos CA 94022-2628 Office: Infoseek 1399 Moffett Park Dr Sunnyvale CA 94089-1134

KIRSCHNER, MARC ALAN, neuroscientist; b. Cin., July 3, 1956; s. Jack Robert and Lucretia (Einstein) K. BA, Middlebury Coll., 1978; MD, Case Western Res. U., 1982. Neurology resident McGill U., 1987; postdoctoral fellow Howard Hughes Med. Inst., New Haven, 1988-89; assoc. rsch. scientist Yale U., New Haven, 1989-91; instr. Oreg. Health Scis. U., Portland, 1991-92, asst. prof., 1992—; asst. clin. prof. neurology U. Wash., 1997—. Rsch. asst. prof. Vollum Inst. for Advanced Biomed. Rsch. Mem. Am. Acad. Neurology, Soc. for Neurosci. Achievements include research in isolation and characterization of mouse high-affinity excitatory amino acid transporters. Office: Univ Wash 1570 N 115th St Ste 14 Seattle WA 98133 Office Phone: 206-365-0111.

KIRSHBAUM, HOWARD M., retired judge; b. Oberlin, Ohio, Sept. 19, 1938; s. Joseph and Gertrude (Morris) K.; m. Priscilla Joy Parmakian, Aug. 15, 1964; children: Audra Lee, Andrew William. BA, Yale U., 1960; AB, Cambridge U., 1962, MA, 1966; LLB, Harvard U., 1965. Ptnr. Zarlengo and Kirshbaum, Denver, 1969-75; judge Denver Dist. Ct., 1975-80, Colo. Ct. Appeals, Denver, 1980-83; justice Colo. Supreme Ct., Denver, 1983-97; arbiter Jud. Arbiter Group, Inc., Denver, 1997—, sr. judge, 1997—2006. Adj. prof. law U. Denver, 1970-; dir. Am. Law Inst. Phila., 1982-2002, Am. Judicature Soc., Chgo., 1979-2002, Colo. Jud. Inst. Denver, 1979-89; pres. Colo. Legal Care Soc., Denver, 1974-75. Bd. dirs. Young Artists Orch., Denver, 1976-85; pres. Cmty. Arts Symphony, Englewood, Colo., 1972-74; dir. Denver Opportunity, Inc., Denver, 1972-74; vice-chmn. Denver Coun. on Arts and Humanities, 1969. Mem.: ABA (standing com. pub. edn. 1996—2001), Assn. for Conflict Resolution, Denver Bar Assn. (trustee 1981—83), Colo. Bar Assn. Avocation: music performance. Office: Jud Arbiter Group Inc 1601 Blake St Ste 400 Denver CO 80202-1328 Office Phone: 303-572-1919.

KIRST, MICHAEL WEILE, education educator, researcher; b. Westreading, Pa., Aug. 1, 1939; s. Russell and Marian (Weile) K.; m. Wdndy Burdsall, Sept. 6, 1975; children: Michael, Anne. AB summa cum laude, Dartmouth Coll., 1961; MPA, Harvard U., 1963, PhD, 1964. Budget examiner U.S. Bur. Budgets, Office of Edn., Washington, 1964-64; assoc. dir. President's comsn. on White House fellows Nat. Adv. Coun. on Edn. Disadvantaged Children, Washington, 1966; dir. program planning and evaluation Bur. Elem. and Secondary Edn., U.S. Office Edn., Washington, 1967; staff dir. U.S. Senate Subcommittee Manpower, Employment and Poverty, Washington, 1968-69; with Ca. State Bd. Edn., Sacramento, 1975-77, pres., 1977-81; prof. edn. Stanford (Calif.) U., 1969—. Prin. investigator Policy Analysis for Calif. Edn., Berkeley, 1984—, Ctr. Policy Rsch. in Edn., Rutgers U., Stanford U., Mich. State U., 1984—, Reform Up Close, 1988-92; chmn. bd. comparative studies in edn. U.S. Nat. Acad. Scis., 1994—. Author: Government Without Passing Laws, 1969; author: (with Frederick Wirt) The Political Web of American Schools, 1972, Political Dynamics of American Education, 2005; author: (with Joel Berke) Federal Aid to Education: Who Governs, Who Benefit, 1972; author: State School Finance Alternatives, 1975; author: (with others) Contemporary Issues in Education: perspectives from Australia and U.S.A., 1983, Who Controls Our Schools: American Values in Conflict, 1984; author: Betraying the College Dream, 2003, From High School to College, 2004, numerous monographs; contbr. articles numerous to profl. jours., newspapers and mags. Pres. Calif. State Bd. Edn., Sacramento, 1977-80. Mem. NAS (chmn. bd. international comparative studies in edn.), Nat. Acad. Edn., Am. Edn. Rsch. Assn. (v.p.), Internat. Acad. Edn., Phi Beta Kappa. Office: Stanford U Sch Edn MC 3096 Stanford CA 94305

KIRVEN, TIMOTHY J., lawyer; b. Buffalo, Wyo., May 26, 1949; s. William J. and Ellen F. (Farrell) K.; m. Elizabeth J. Adams, Oct. 31, 1970; 1 child, Kristen B. BA in English, U. Notre Dame, 1971; JD, U. Wyo., 1974. Bar: Wyo. 1974. Ptnr. Kirven & Kirven, PC, Buffalo, 1974—. Author Rocky Mountain Mineral Law, 1982. Mem. Johnson County Libr. Br., Buffalo. Mem. ABA (ho. of dels. 2002—), Wyo. State Bar (pres. 1998-99), Johnson County Bar Assn., Western States Bar Conf. (pres. 1998-99), Rotary (pres. Buffalo club 1988-89, youth exch. program chmn. 1993-98). Home: PO Box C Buffalo WY 82834-0060 Office: Kirven & Kirven PC 104 Fort St PO Box 640 Buffalo WY 82834-0640

KIRWAN, R. DEWITT (KYLE), lawyer; b. Albany, Calif., Aug. 30, 1942; s. Patrick William and Lucille Anne (Vartanian) K.; m. Betty-Jane Elias, June 29, 1969 (div. 1982); children: Katherine DeWitt, Andrew Elias; m. Nancy Jane Evers, Oct. 27, 1984; 1 child, Fletcher Evers. BA, U. Calif., Berkeley, 1966; JD, U. San Francisco, 1969. Bar: Calif. 1971, U.S. Dist. Ct. (ctrl. dist.) Calif. 1971, U.S. Ct. Appeals (9th cir.) 1971. Assoc. Schell & Delamer, LA, 1971-73; ptnr. Lillick & McHose, LA, 1973-90, Pillsbury Madison & Sutro, LA, 1990-98, Akin, Gump, Strauss, Hauer & Feld, LA, 1998—; commr. Calif. Commn. Judicial Nominations, 2008—. Chmn., exec. bd. U. Calif., Berkeley, 1988-97, trustee U. Calif. Berkeley Found., 1995-98; bd. dirs., trustee Pacific Crest Outward Bound Sch., 1993-99; bd. dirs. L.A. Philharm. Assn., 1985-89, pres., 1986-88, mem. bus. and profl. com.; bd. dirs. Pasadena (Calif.) Symphony Assn., 1978-82. Capt. USAR, 1966-71. Mem.: ABA, Am Bd. Trial Advs., Bohemian Club, Calif. Club. Democrat. Roman Catholic. Avocations: fly fishing, mountain climbing, hunting, skiing. Office: Akin Gump Strauss Hauer & Feld Ste 2400 2029 Century Park E Los Angeles CA 90067-3012 Office Phone: 310-229-1000. Business E-Mail: rkirwan@akingump.com.

KIRZ, JANOS, physicist; b. Budapest, Hungary, Aug. 11, 1937; came to U.S., 1957; s. Andras and Emma (Teller) K.; m. Micheline Barthez, Dec. 19, 1964 (div. Aug. 1985); 1 child, Steven; m. Regina Moreno, Jan. 5, 1988. BA, U. Calif., Berkeley, 1959; PhD, U Calif., 1963. Physicist Lawrence Berkeley Lab., Berkeley, Calif., 1964-67; lectr. U. Calif., Berkeley, 1967; assoc. prof. SUNY, Stony Brook, 1968-72, prof., 1973—2007, Disting. prof., 1995—2007, chmn. dept. physics and astronomy, 1988—2001. Acting divsn. dir. Advanced Light Source Divsn. Lawrence Berkeley Lab., 2004—06, sci. advisor, 2007—. Contbr. articles to profl. jours. Fellow Woodrow Wilson Found., 1959, A.P. Sloan Found., 1970, Guggenheim Found., 1985; recipient A.H. Compton Advanced Photon Source award, 2005 Fellow AAAS, Am. Physical Soc.; mem. Optical Soc. Am. Achievements include development of scanning X-ray microscope. Office: MS 80R0114 Lawrence Berkeley Lab Berkeley CA 94720

KISPERT, JOHN H., information technology executive; b. 1964; B in Polit. Sci., Grinnell Coll.; MBA, UCLA. Various mgmt. positions IBM; contr. instrument's wafer, reticle and SEMspec insp. divsn. KLA-Tencor, San Jose, Calif., 1995, v.p. corp. fin., 1999, CFO, 2000—06, pres., COO, 2006—08; pres., CEO Spansion Inc., Sunnyvale, Calif., 2009—. Mailing: Spansion Inc PO Box 3453 Sunnyvale CA 94088*

KISSINGER, KAREN G., energy executive; V.p., contr. UniSource Energy Corp., Tucson, 1997—. Office: UniSource Energy Corp PO Box 711 Tucson AZ 85702-0711

KISTLER, RIVES, state supreme court justice; BA, Williams Coll., 1971; MA, U. N.C., 1978; JD, Georgetown U. Law Sch., 1981. Law clerk Chief Judge Charles Clark U.S. Ct. of Appeals Fifth Circuit; law clerk Justice Lewis F. Powell, Jr. U.S. Supreme Ct.; litigation assoc. Stoel Rives, Portland, Oreg., 1983—87; asst. atty. gen. Oreg. Dept. Justice, 1987—99; judge Oreg. Ct. of Appeals, 1999—2003; justice Oreg. Supreme Ct., 2003—. Adjunct prof. constitutional law Lewis & Clark Law Sch., Portland, Oreg.; former mem., vice-chair Oreg. Bd. of Bar Examiners; former mem. Nat. Assn. of Attorneys Gen. Working Groups. Office: Oreg Supreme Ct 1163 State St Salem OR 97301 Office Phone: 503-986-5713. Business E-Mail: rives.kistler@state.or.us.

KITAEV, ALEXEI, physics and computer science professor; MS, Moscow Inst. Physics and Tech., 1986; PhD, L.D. Landau Inst. Theoretical Physics, 1989. Rsch. assoc. Landau Inst., 1989—98; rschr. Microsoft Rsch., 1999—2001; prof. theoretical physics and computer sci. Calif. Inst. Tech. Contbr. articles to profl. jours. Named a MacArthur Fellow, The John D. and Catherine T. MacArthur Found., 2008. Office: Calif Inst Tech Computer Sci 1200 E California Blvd, MC 256-80 Pasadena CA 91125 Office Phone: 626-395-8760. E-mail: kitaev@iqi.caltech.edu.

KITANIDIS, PETER K., engineering educator; Prof. civil and environ. engring. Stanford (Calif.) U. Recipient Walter L. Huber Civil Engring. Rsch. prize ASCE, 1994. Office: Stanford U Dept Civil Engring Stanford CA 94305 E-mail: peterk@stanford.edu.

KITCHEN, JOHN MARTIN, historian, educator; b. Nottingham, Eng., Dec. 21, 1936; s. John Sutherland and Margaret Helen (Pearson) K. BA with honors, U. London, 1963, PhD, 1966. Mem. Cambridge (Eng.) Group Population Studies, 1965-66; mem. faculty Simon Fraser U., Burnaby, B.C., Canada, 1966—. Author: The German Officer Corps 1890-1914, 1968, A Military History of Germany, 1975, Fascism, 1976, The Silent Dictatorship, 1976, The Political Economy of Germany 1815-1914, 1979, The Coming of Austrian Fascism, 1980, Germany in the Age of Total War, 1981, British Policy Towards the Soviet Union During the Second World War, 1986, The Origins of the Cold War in Comparative Perspective, 1988, Europe Between the Wars, 1988, 2d edit., 2006, A World in Flames, 1990, Empire and After: A Short History of the British Empire and Commonwealth, 1994, Nazi Germany at War, 1994, The Cambridge Illustrated History of Germany, 1996, Empire and Commonwealth, 1996, Kaspar Hauser, 2001, The German Offensives of 1918, 2001, Nazi Germany: A Critical Introduction, 2004, A History of Modern Germany 1800-2000, 2006, The Third Reich: Charisma and Community, 2008. Fellow Royal Hist. Soc., Royal Soc. Can. Home: 24B-6128 Patterson Ave Burnaby BC Canada V5H 4P3 Office: Simon Fraser U Dept History Burnaby BC Canada V5A 1S6 Home Phone: 604-433-0119; Office Phone: 604-291-3521. Business E-Mail: kitchen@sfu.ca.

KITE, MARILYN S., state supreme court justice, lawyer; b. Laramie, Wyo., Oct. 2, 1947; BA with honors, U. Wyo., 1970, JD with honors, 1974. Bar: Wyo. 1974. Sr. asst. atty. gen. State of Wyo., 1974—78; atty. Holland & Hart, Jackson, Wyo., 1979—2000; justice Wyo. Supreme Ct., 2000—. Contbr. articles to profl. jours. Mem. ABA (nat. resources sect., litigation sect.), Wyo. State Bar. Address: Wyo Supreme Ct 2301 Capitol Ave Cheyenne WY 82002

KITTEL, CHARLES, physicist, educator emeritus; b. NYC, July 18, 1916; s. George Paul and Helen Kittel; m. Muriel Agnes Lister, June 23, 1938; children: Ruth, Peter, Timothy. BA, Cambridge U., Eng., 1938, MA, 1993; PhD, U. Wis., 1941. Research physicist Bur. Ordnance, head USN team attached to Brit. Admiralty, Helensburgh, Scotland, 1940-42; supr. Submarine Ops. Research Grp. USN, Washington, 1943-45; research assoc. MIT, Cambridge, 1945-47; research physicist Bell Labs., Murray Hill, N.J., 1947-51; prof. physics U. Calif., Berkeley, 1951-78, prof. emeritus, 1978—. Cons. E.I. Du Pont & Co., RCA, Westinghouse Corp., Hughes Aircraft Co., Chevron Corp., numerous others. Author: Introduction to Solid State Physics, 7th edit., 1996, (with H. Kroemer) Thermal Physics, 2d edit., 1980, Quantum Theory of Solids, rev. edit., 1987. Guggenheim fellow, 1947, 57, 64, Miller fellow, U. Calif., 1959, 60; recipient Disting. Tchrs. award, U. Calif. Berkeley, 1972. Fellow Am. Acad. Arts and Scis., Am. Phys. Soc. (Oliver Buckley Solid State Physics prize 1957, coun. 1958-62); mem. NAS, Am. Assn. Physics Tchrs. (Oersted medal 1978), Am. Inst. Physics (bd. govs. 1954-58). Office: U Calif Dept Physics Berkeley CA 94720-0001 E-mail: kittel@uclink4.berkeley.edu.

KITTEL, PETER, research scientist; b. Fairfax, Va., Mar. 23, 1945; s. Charles and Muriel K.; m. Mary Ellen, Aug. 12, 1972; 1 child, Katherine. BS, U. Calif., Berkeley, 1967; MS, U. Calif., La Jolla, 1969; PhD, Oxford U., 1974. Rsch. asst. U. Calif., La Jolla, 1967-69, Oxford (Eng.) U., 1969-74; rsch. assoc., adj. assoc. prof. U. Oreg., Eugene, 1974-78; rsch. assoc. Stanford (Calif.) U., 1978; rsch. assoc. Nat. Rsch. Coun. Ames Rsch. Ctr. NASA, Moffett Field, Calif., 1978-80, rsch. scientist, 1980—2004, Ames assoc., 2005—. Dir. Internat. Cryogenic Engring. Conf., 1998—, Cryogenic Engring. Conf., 1983-89, 92—, internat. CryoCooler conf., 1996-2004; co-chmn. Internat. CryoCooler conf., 1996-98. Adv. editor: Cryogenics, 1987—; editor: Advances in Cryogenic Engineering, 1992-98; contbr. articles to profl. jours. Fellow Oxford U., 1972-74, Nat. Rsch. Coun., 1978-80; recipient medal for Exceptional Engring. Achievement NASA, 1990, Space Act award NASA, 1989, 91. Fellow: Cryogenic Soc. Am.; mem.: AAAS, Am. Phys. Soc. Home: 3132 Morris Dr Palo Alto CA 94303-4037 Office: NASA 244-10 Ames Research Ctr Moffett Field CA 94035-1000 Home Phone: 650-493-2792; Office Phone: 650-604-4297. Business E-Mail: pkittel@mail.arc.nasa.gov.

KITTO, FRANKLIN CURTIS, computer systems specialist; b. Salt Lake City, Nov. 18, 1954; s. Curtis Eugene and Margaret (Ipson) K.; m. Collette Madsen, Sept. 16, 1982; children: Melissa Erin, Heather Elise, Stephen Curtis. BA, Brigham Young U., 1978, MA, 1980. Tv sta. operator Sta. KBYU-TV, Provo, Utah, 1973-78; grad. teaching asst. Brigham Young Univ., 1978-80; cable TV system operator Instructional Media U. Utah, Salt Lake City, 1980-82, data processing mgr., 1982-83, media supr., 1983-85, bus. mgr., 1985-87; dir. computer systems tng. MegaWest Systems, Inc., Salt Lake City, 1987-90, dir. new product devel., 1990-91, mgr. tng. and installation, 1991-93, mgr. rsch. and devel., 1993; tng. and installation mgr. Total Solutions, American Fork, Utah, 1993-95, tng., support and installation mgr., 1995; EDI programmer Megawest Systems, Inc., Salt Lake City, 1996; EDI supervisor Companion Technologies (formerly Megawest Systems, Inc.), Midvale, Utah, 1996-99; software developer Nuskin Internat., Provo, Utah, 1999—2001, sr. programmer, analyst, 2001—. Recipient Kiwanis Freedom Leadership award, Salt Lake City, 1970, Golden Microphone award, Brigham Young U., 1978, Summit award, Nuskin Internat., 2002, 2003, Peak award, 2004, 2005, Summit award, 2005, Peak award, 2008. Mem. Assn. Ednl. Communications and Tech., Utah Pick Users Group (sec. 1983-87, pres. 1987-89, treas. 1989-90), Am. Soc. Tng. and Devel., Assn. for Computer Tng. and Support, Phi Eta Sigma, Kappa Tau Alpha. Mem. Lds Ch. Home: 10931 S Avila Dr Sandy UT 84094-5965 Office: NuSkin Internat IT Dept 75 W Center St Provo UT 84601-4432 Personal E-mail: fkitto@iname.com. Business E-Mail: fckitto@nuskin.net.

KITTREDGE, WILLIAM ALFRED, humanities educator; b. Portland, Oreg., Aug. 14, 1932; s. Franklin Oscar and Josephine (Miessner) K.; m. Janet O'Connor, Dec. 8, 1952 (div. 1968); children: Karen, Bradley. BS, Oreg. State U., 1953; MFA in Creative Writing, U. Iowa, 1969. Rancher Warner Valley Livestock, Adel, Oreg., 1957-67; prof. U. Mont., Missoula, 1969—, now Regents Prof. emeritus. Author: The Van Gogh Field, 1979, We Are Not In This Together, 1984, Owning It All, 1987, Hole in the Sky, 1992, Who Owns the West, 1996, The Portable Western Reader, 1997, Taking Care, 1999, Balancing Water, 2000, The Nature of Generosity, 2000, Southwestern Homelands, 2002, The Best Stores of William Kittredge, 2003, The Willow Field, 2006. With USAF, 1954-57. Named Mont. Humanist of Yr., 1989; recipient award for lit. Gov. of Mont., 1988, Charles Frankel prize in Humanities, NEH, 1994, Earl A. Chiles Lifetime Acheivement award, 2006, LA Times Kirsch Lifetime Acehivement award, 2007. Home: 42 Brookside Way Missoula MT 59802-3278 Office Phone: 406-549-6605. Personal E-mail: kittredgeb@aol.com.

KITUNDU, WALTER, sound artist, instrument designer, composer; b. Tanzania, 1973; Student, Winona State U., Minn., Gustavus Adolphus Coll. Frequently collaborates with and designs instruments for Kronos Quartet, San Francisco; multimedia artist Exploratorium Mus. Sci., Art and Human Perception, San Francisco, 2003—. Guest artist Sci. Mus. Minn., 2004; artist-in-residence Singapore Sci. Ctr., 2004, Gunnar Gunnarssonn Inst., Iceland, 2004, Montalvo Ctr. Arts, Saratoga, Calif., 2006, Headlands Ctr. Arts, 2008; Wornick vis. disting. prof. wood arts Calif. Coll. Arts, 2008—09. Named a MacArthur Fellow, The John D. and Catherine T. MacArthur Found., 2008. Office: Exploratorium Learning Studio 3601 Lyon St San Francisco CA 94123 Office Phone: 415-674-2848. E-mail: kitundu@exploratorium.edu, kitundu@gmail.com.

KITZENBERG, SAM L., state legislator; b. Williston, ND, Mar. 25, 1947; m to Ronnie; children: four. Boys State Governor, formerly & Boys Nation Senator, formerly; page, Montana House Representative, 1963; Montana State Representative, District 96, 1995-01; Montana State Senator, District 48, 2001-05, District 18, 2005-, Montana State Senate.High sch teacher, currently. Democrat. Address: 130 Bonnie St Apt 1 Glasgow MT 59230 Mailing: State Capitol Helena MT 59620 E-mail: house@state.mt.us.

KITZHABER, JOHN ALBERT, emergency physician, former governor; b. Colfax, Wash., Mar. 5, 1947; s. Albert Raymond and Annabel Reed (Wetzel) K.; m. Sharon Lacroix (div. 2003); 1 child, Logan. BA, Dartmouth Coll., 1969; MD, U. Oreg., 1973. Intern Gen. Rose Meml. Hosp., Denver, 1976-77; Emergency physician Mercy Hosp., Roseburg, Oreg., 1974-75; mem. Oreg. Ho. Reps. from 45th Dist., 1979-81, Oreg. State Senate from 23rd Dist., 1981—93, pres., 1985—93; gov. State of Oregon, 1995—2003; pres. Estes Park Inst., Englewood, Colo., 2003—; endowed chair Found. for Med. Excellence, Portland, Oreg., 2003—; pres. Kitzhaber Ctr. Lewis & Clark Coll., Portland, Oreg., 2004—. Assoc. prof. Oreg. Health Sci. U., 1989-1995; MD chmn. health policy Found. Med. Excellence, 2003-. Pres. Estes Park Inst., Colo., 2003—; founder Archimedes Movement, Oreg., 2006. Recipient Neuberger award, Oreg. Environ. Coun., 1987, Dr. Nathan Davis award, AMA, 1992. Mem. Am. Coll. Emergency Physicians, Inst. Medicine, Douglas County Med. Soc., Physicians for Social Responsibility, Am. Council Young Polit. Leaders, Oreg. Trout. Democrat. Office: Found Med Excellence Ste 800 1 SW Columbia St Portland OR 97258 E-mail: kitz@wecandobetter.org.

KIVEL, PAUL, writer; 3 children. Trainer, activist, writer, cofounder Oakland Men's Project, Calif., 1979—90. Author: You Call This Democracy, Boys Will Be Men, Uprooting Racism, I Can Make My World A Safer Place, Men's Work; co-author (with Allen Creighton): Making the Peace, Helping Teens Stop Violence, Young Men's Work; co-author: (with Allen Creighton & Ralph Cantor) Days of Respect; co-author: (with M. Nell Myhand) Young Women's Lives. Office: Paul Kivel & Assoc 658 Vernon St Oakland CA 94610 E-mail: pkivel@mindspring.com.

KIVELSON, MARGARET GALLAND, physicist; b. NYC, Oct. 21, 1928; d. Walter Isaac and Madeleine (Wiener) Galland; m. Daniel Kivelson, Aug. 15, 1949; children: Steven Allan, Valerie Ann. AB, Radcliffe Coll., 1950, AM, 1951, PhD, 1957. Cons. Rand Corp., Santa Monica, Calif., 1956-69; asst. to geophysicist UCLA, 1967-83, prof., space physics, dept. earth and space scis., Inst. Geophysics & Planetary Physics, 1983—, also chmn. dept. earth and space scis., 1984-87, acting dir. Inst. Geophys. Planet Physics, 1999—2000; prin. investigator of magnetometer, Galileo Mission Jet Propulsion Lab., Pasadena, Calif., 1977—2004. Overseer Harvard Coll., 1977-83; adv. coun. NASA, 1987-93; chair atmospheric adv. com. NSF, 1986-89, Com. Solar and Space Physics, 1977-86, com. planetary exploration, 1986-87, com. solar terrestial physics, 1989-92; adv. com. geoscis. NSF, 1993-97; space studies bd. NRC, 2002-05. Editor: The Solar System: Observations and Interpretations, 1986; co-editor: Introduction to Space Physics, 1995; contbr. articles to profl. jours. Named Woman of Yr., LA Mus. Sci. and Industry, 1979, Woman of Sci., UCLA, 1984; recipient Grad. Soc. medal Radcliffe Coll., 1983, 350th Anniversary Alumni medal Harvard U., 1986, Alfvén medal European Geophys. Union, 2005. Fellow AAAS, NAS (councilor 2007-), Internat. Inst. Astronautics, Am. Geophys. Union (Fleming medal 2005), Am. Acad. Arts and Scis., Am. Phys. Soc., Am. Philisophical Soc., Royal Astron. Soc.; mem. Am. Astron. Soc. Office: UCLA Dept Earth & Space Scis 6843 Slichter Hall Los Angeles CA 90095-1567 Home Phone: 310-454-3581; Office Phone: 310-825-3435. Business E-Mail: mkivelson@igpp.ucla.edu.

KIZER, KENNETH WAYNE, physician, executive, educator; b. Decatur, Ind., May 28, 1951; s. Homer Martin Kizer and Ellen Hope Howland; m. Suzanne A. Stoddard, Aug. 26, 1972; children: Kelli Christina, Kimberly Casey. BS with honors, Stanford U., 1972; MD with honors, MPH in Epidemiology, UCLA, 1976; DSc (hon.), NY State U., 2006, Med. U. SC, 2008. Rotating internship Naval Regional Med. Ctr., Portsmouth, Va., 1977; undersea medicine fellowship Naval Undersea Med. Inst., Groton, Conn., 1977; resident in diagnostic radiology U. Calif, San Francisco, 1980-81, resident in occupl. medicine, 1982-83; firefighter; emergency physician; dir. Emergency Med. Svcs. Authority State of Calif., 1983-84; chief dep. dir. and chief of pub. health Calif. Dept. Health Svcs., Sacramento, 1984-85, dir., 1985-91; prof., chmn. dept. cmty. and internat. health U. Calif., Davis, 1991-94; undersec. for health US Dept. Vets. Affairs, Washington, 1994-99; dir. Health Sys. Internat., Inc., 1994-97; pres., CEO Nat. Quality Forum, Washington, 1999—2005; chmn. Medsphere Sys. Corp., Aliso Viego, Calif., 2002—, pres., 2005—07, CEO, 2005—07, cons., 2007—. Contbr. numerous articles to profl. jours., chpts. to books. Chair Radiation Emergency Screening Team, 1988-91, Hazardous Waste Appeal Bd., 1990; co-chair Calif. AIDS Leadership Com.; mem. Diving Control Bd. U. Calif., 1980-91, Gov.'s Emergency Ops. Exec. Coun., 1984-91, Governing Bd. Calif YMCA Model Legislature Program, 1986-90, Chem. Emergency Planning and Response Commn., 1988-90; chair S.W. Low Level Radioactive Waste Compact Commn., 1990-91, tobacco edn. oversight com. State Calif., 1990-91, bd. dirs. Calif. Wellness Found., 1992-2003, Matthews Found., 1991-94, Ctr. for AIDS Rsch., Edn. and Svcs., 1992-94, Infection Control Coun., 1991-94; mem. adv. bd. Preventive Sports Medicine Inst., 1991-94. Lt. USN, 1976-80. Recipient Humanitarian Svc. medal Dept. of Def., 1979, Spl. Recognition award No. Calif. Emergency Med. Care Coun., 1984, Golden State Med. Assn., 1986, Calif. Div. Am. Lung Assn., 1988, Calif. Health Fedn., 1988, cert. of Recognition Calif. Asian Pacific Health Coalition, 1989, Spl. Achievement award Calif. Emergency Physician Med. Group, 1989, Jean Spencer Felton award for Excellence in Sci. Writing, 1989, spl. awards from March of Dimes, Am. Cancer Soc., Calif. State Senate, Calif. Conf. Local Health Officers, others, 1991—, Healthcare Heroes award Calif. State Assembly, 1996, Cert. of Recognition award, 1996, Dr. Nathan Davis award AMA, 1998, Literacy Achievement award Am. Coll. Physician Execs., 1998, Founders award Wilderness Med. Soc., 1998, Justin Kimball Innovator's award Am. Hosp. Assn., 1998, Lifetime Achievement award Assn. Health Systems Pharmacists, 2002, Founders award Am. Coll. Med. Quality, 2004, Gustov O. Lienhard award, Inst. Medicine/Nat. Acad. Scis., 2004, Ernest S. Codman award Joint Commn. Accreditation Healthcare Orgs., 2005, Special Recognition award Am. Legion, 2007, Award for Excellence Am. Pub. Health Assn., 2008; named Toll fellow Coun. State Govts., 1987. Fellow Am. Coll. Physician Execs. (disting.), Am. Coll. Preventive Medicine, Am. Coll. Emergency Physicians, Am. Coll. Occupl. Environ. Medicine, Am. Acad. Clin. Toxicology, Royal Soc. Health, Royal Soc. Medicine, Am. Coll. Med. Toxicology, Am. Acad. Med. Adminstrs., Explorers Club; mem. APHA, Internat. Soc. Toxicology, Inst. Medicine NAS, Wilderness Med. Soc., Undersea and Hyperbaric Med. Soc., Nat. Soc. YMCA Youth Govs., Nat. Assn. Underwater Instrs. (Outstanding Contribution to Diving award 1984), Inst. Medicine, Delta Tau Delta (Beta Rho chpt. Hall of Fame 1987), Alpha Omega Alpha, Delta Omega. Independent. Avocations: scuba diving, hiking and backpacking, photography, racquet sports, book collecting. Office: Medsphere Systems Corporation 1917 Palomar Oaks Way Ste 200 Carlsbad CA 92008-5513 Office Phone: 202-256-9706. Personal E-mail: kennethwkizer@aol.com. Business E-Mail: kenneth.kizer@medsphere.com.

KIZZIAR, JANET WRIGHT, psychologist, writer, lecturer; b. Independence, Kans. d. John L. and Thelma (Rooks) Wright; m. Mark Kizziar. BA, U. Tulsa, 1961, MA, 1964, EdD, 1969. Sch. psychologist Tulsa Pub. Schs.; pvt. practice psychology Tulsa, 1969-78, Bartlesville, Okla., 1978-88. Lectr. univs., corps., health spas, 1989—. Co-host: Psychologists' Corner program, Sta. KOTV, Tulsa.; author: (with Judy W. Hagedorn) Gemini: The Psychology and Phenomena of Twins, 1975, Search for Acceptance: The Adolescent and Self Esteem, 1979. Sponsor Youth Crisis Intervention Telephone Center, 1972-74; bd. dirs. March of Dimes, Child Protection Team, Women and Children in Crisis, United Fund, YMCA Fund, Mental Health of Washington County, Alternative H.S.; edn. dir. appt. Gov.'s Commn. on Violence Against Women, Pub. Awarness Com., 1996, Women's Found. Fresh Start Women's Found., 1995. Named Disting. Alumni U. Tulsa, Outstanding Young Woman of Okla. Mem. APA, NOW, Internat. Twins Assn. (pres. 1976-77) Home: 8029 E Greythorn Dr Apache Junction AZ 85218-1753

KLAFTER, CARY IRA, lawyer; b. Chgo., Sept. 15, 1948; s. Herman Nicholas and Bernice Rose (Maremont) K.; m. Kathleen Ann Kerr, July 21, 1974; children: Anastasia, Benjamin, Eileen. BA, Mich. State U., 1968, MS, 1971; JD, U. Chgo., 1972. Bar: Calif. 1972. Assoc. Morrison & Foerster, San Francisco, 1972-79, ptnr., 1979-96; v.p. legal and corp. affairs, dir. corp. legal, corp. sec. Intel Corp., Santa Clara, Calif., 1996—. Lectr. law Stanford Law Sch., 1990-99. Capt. USAR, 1971-78. Mem.: Soc. Corp. Secs. and Governance Profls.

KLAKEG, CLAYTON HAROLD, retired cardiologist; b. Big Woods, Minn., Mar. 31, 1920; s. Knute O. and Agnes (Folvik) K.; student Concordia Coll., Moorhead, Minn., 1938-40; BS, N.D. State U., 1942; BS in Medicine, N.D. U., 1943; M.D., Temple U., 1945; MS in Medicine and Physiology, U. Minn.-Mayo Found., 1954; children: Julie Ann, Robert Clayton, Richard Scott. Intern, Med. Ctr., Jersey City, 1945-46; mem. staff VA Hosp., Fargo, N.D., 1948-51; fellow in medicine and cardiology Mayo Found., Rochester, Minn., 1951-55; internist, cardiologist Sansum Med. Clinic Inc., Santa Barbara, Calif., 1955-2008; mem. staff Cottage Hosp., St. Francis Hosp. Bd. dirs. Sansum Med. Rsch. Found., pres., 1990. Served to capt. M.C., USAF, 1946-48. Diplomate Am. Bd. Internal Medicine. Fellow ACP, Am. Coll. Cardiology, Am. Coll. Chest Physicians, Am. Heart Assn. (mem. council on clin. cardiology); mem. Calif. Heart Assn. (pres. 1971-72, Meritorious Service award 1968, Disting. Service award 1972, Disting. Achievement award 1975), Santa Barbara County Heart Assn. (pres. 1959-60, Disting. Service award 1958, Disting. Achievement award 1971), Calif. Med. Assn., Los Angeles Acad. Medicine, Santa Barbara County Med. Assn., Mayo Clinic Alumni Assn., Santa Barbara Soc. Internal Medicine (pres. 1963), Sigma Xi, Phi Beta Pi. Republican. Lutheran. Club: Channel City. Contbr. articles to profl. jours. Home: 5956 Trudi Dr Santa Barbara CA 93117-2175

KLAUSE, KLAUS J., aircraft company executive; b. Berlin, Sept. 29, 1942; came to U.S., 1956; s. Kurt and Susan (Decker) K.; m. Betty C. DeVore, July 31, 1964; children: Gregory, Thomas, William. BS, Allegheny Coll., 1964; MBA, Golden Gate U., 1979; D in Aerospace Warfare, USAF Fighter Weapons Sch., 1982. Enlisted USAF, 1965, advanced through grades to col., cmdr. 21st Fighter Squadron Victorville, Calif., 1984-86, chief Europe/NATO divsn. Arlington, Va., 1986-88, cmdr. 37th Ops. Group Las Vegas, 1988-91, chief forces Hampton, Va., 1991-94, ret., 1994; F-117 program mgr. Boeing Aerospace Ops., Alamogordo, N.Mex., 1994—. Soccer coach Hi Desert Soccer Club, Apple Valley, Calif., 1982-86, Las Vegas Soccer Club, 1972, 76-79. Mem. Air Force Assn., River Rats Fighter Pilot Assn., Phi Gamma Delta, Order of Daedalion. Republican. Lutheran. Avocations: golf, skiing, camping, fishing. Office: Boeing 744 Delaware Ave Holloman AFB NM 88330-8014

KLAUSNER, MICHAEL DAVID, law educator; b. Phila., Dec. 12, 1954; s. Gilbert and Edith (Quitman) Klausner; m. Barbara Ann-Pei Sih, Sept. 2, 1984; children: Jill, Gregory. BA in Polit. Sci./Urban Studies, summa cum laude, U. Pa., 1976; MA in Economics, Yale U., 1981, JD, 1981. Bar: DC 1983. Law clk. to Judge David Bazelon US Ct. Appeals DC Cir., 1981-82; law clk. to Justice William Brennan US Supreme Ct., 1983-84; vis. scholar & lectr. dept. law Peking U., China, 1984-85; assoc. Paul, Weiss, Rifkind, Wharton & Garrison, Washington, 1982—83, Gibson, Dunn & Crutcher, Washington, Hong Kong, 1986-89; White House fellow, dep. assoc. dir. Office Policy Devel. White House, Washington, 1989-90; asst. prof. to prof. NYU Sch. Law, 1991—97; prof. law Stanford Law Sch., 1997—, Bernard D. Bergreen faculty scholar, 1997—2003, Nancy and Charles Munger prof. bus., 2003—, assoc. dean rsch. and academics, 2004—. Vis. prof. Stanford Law Sch., 1995—96. Avocation: scuba diving. Office: Stanford Law Sch Crown Quadrangle 559 Nathan Abbott Way Stanford CA 94305-8610 Office Phone: 650-723-6433. E-mail: klausner@stanford.edu.

KLAUSNER, RICHARD DANIEL, cell biologist, researcher; b. NYC, Dec. 22, 1951; BS, Yale U., 1973; MD, Duke U. Med. Sch., 1976. Rsch. assoc. Harvard Med. Sch., 1977-79; rscher., med. officer, mathematical biology program Nat. Insts. Health, Bethesda, Md., 1979-84; branch chief, cell biology, metabolism branch Nat. Inst. of Child Health & Human Devel., Bethesda, Md., 1984-95; dir. Nat. Cancer Inst., Bethesda, Md., 1995—2001; exec. dir. Global Health (Bill and Melinda Gates Found.), Seattle, 2002—05. Chmn., Scientific Advisory Bd., Ariad Pharmaceuticals, 1991, bd. dirs. Pathwork Diagnostics, 2006- Medicine, 1976; numerous articles in prof. journals. Recipient Meritorious Svc. Award, 1986, PHS, Damashek Prize, 1992, Am. Soc. for Hematology Mem. NAS, Am. Soc. for Clinical Investigation, Inst. Medicine.

KLAWE, MARIA MARGARET, academic administrator, engineering and computer science educator; b. Toronto, Ont., Can., July 5, 1951; d. Janusz Josef and Kathleen Wreath (McCaughan) K.; m. Nicholas John Pippenger, May 12, 1980; children: Janek, Sasha. BSc in math., U. Alberta, 1973; PhD, U. Alberta, Edmonton, Can., 1977; PhD (hon.), Ryerson U., 2001, U. Waterloo, 2003, Queens U., 2004. Asst. prof. dept. math. sci. Oakland U., Rochester, Mich., 1977-78; asst. prof. dept. computer sci. U. Toronto, Canada, 1979-80; rsch. staff mem. IBM Rsch., San Jose, Calif., 1980-89, mgr. discrete math., 1984-88, mgr. dept. math., related computer sci., 1985-87; prof., head dept. computer sci. U. BC, Vancouver, 1988-95, v.p. student and acad. svcs., 1995—98, dean sci., 1998—2002; dean Sch. Engrng & Applied Sci. Princeton U., 2003—07, prof. dept. computer sci., 2003—07; pres. Harvey Mudd Coll., Claremont, Calif., 2007—. Bd. dirs. Microsoft Corp., 2009-; spkr. in field; mem. adv. bd. univ. rels. IBM Toronto Lab., 1989; mem. sci. adv. bd. Dimacs NSF Sci. Tech. Ctr., New Brunswick, NJ, 1989-95; mem. adv. bd. Geometry Ctr., 1991-95; mem. BC Premier's Adv. Coun. on Sci. & Tech., 1993—2001, Provincial Adv. Com. on Edn. Tech., 1993; founder, dir. E-GEMS project U. BC, 1992-2002; Chair for Women in Sci. & Engrng. Nat. Sciences & Engrng. Rsch. Coun. of Can.(NSERC)-IBM, 1997-2002; co-founder, chmn. bd. Silicon Chalk, Vancouver.; bd. trustees Math. Sciences Rsch. Inst., Berkeley, chair bd. trustees Anita Borg Inst. Women and Tech. Palo Alto, Calif., 2003-08; trustee Inst. Pure & Applied Math. LA. Editor: (jours.) Combinatorica, 1985—, SIAM Jour. on Computing, 1986-93, SIAM Jour. on Discrete Math., 1987-93; contbr. articles to profl. jours. Recipient Women of Distinction Award in Sci. and Tech., Vancouver YWCA, 1997, Can. Wired Woman Pioneer Award, 2001, Disting. Alum. Award, U. Alberta, 2003, Nico Habermann award, 2004; named Can. New Media Educator of Yr., 2001, BC Sci. Coun. Champion of Yr., 2001; INCO scholar, 1968—71, NRC Can. fellow, 1973—77. Fellow Assn. Computing Machinery (mem. coun. 1998-2000, v.p. 2000-02, pres. 2002-04); mem. Am. Math. Soc. (bd. trustees 1992-97, chmn. 1995-96), Can. Math. Assn., Can. Heads Computer Sci. (pres. 1990-91), Assn. Women Math., Computing Rsch. Assn. (mem. bd. 1990-96), Soc. Indsl. and Applied Math. Math. Assn. Am. Avocations: running, painting, kayaking, windsurfing. Office: Harvey Mudd Coll Kingston Hall, Rm 201 301 Platt Blvd Claremont CA 91711 Office Phone: 909-621-8120. E-mail: klawe@hmc.edu.*

KLAWITTER, RONALD F., computer company executive; b. 1952; V.p. fin. Baker Hughes Tubular Svc., 1987-92; v.p. fin., treas. Key Tronic Corp., Spokane, Wash., 1992-95, acting sec., 1994-95, v.p. fin., sec., treas., 1995-97, exec. v.p. adminstrn., CFO, treas., sec., 1997—. Office: Key Tronic Corp N 4424 Sullivan Rd Spokane WA 99216 Fax: 509-927-5248.

KLEBANOFF, SEYMOUR JOSEPH, medical educator; b. Toronto, Ont., Can., Feb. 3, 1927; s. Eli Samuel and Ann Klebanoff; m. Evelyn Norma Silver, June 3, 1951; children: Carolyn, Mark. MD, U. Toronto, 1951; PhD in Biochemistry, U. London, 1954. Intern Toronto Gen. Hosp., 1951—52; postdoctoral fellow dept. path. chemistry U. Toronto, 1954—57; postdoctoral fellow Rockefeller U., NYC, 1957—59, asst. prof., 1959—62; assoc. prof. medicine U. Washington, Seattle, 1962—68, prof., 1968—2000, prof. emeritus, 2000—. Mem. adv. coun. Nat. Inst. Allergy and Infectious Diseases, NIH, 1987—90. Author: The Neutrophil, 1978; contbr. over 200 articles to profl. jours. Recipient Merit award, NIH, 1988, Mayo Soley award, Western Soc. for Clin. Investigation, 1991, Bristol-Myers Squibb award for Disting. Achievement in Infectious Disease Rsch., 1995, Disting. Rsch. Biomed. Sci. award, Assn. Am. Med. Coll., 2007. Fellow: AAAS; mem.: NAS, Am. Acad. Arts and Scis., Inst. of Medicine, Soc. for Leukocyte Biology (Marie T. Bonazinga rsch. award 1985), Endocrine Soc., Infectious Diseases Soc. Am. (Bristol award 1993), Assn. Am. Physicians, Am. Soc. Biol. Chemists, Am. Soc. Clin. Investigation. Home: 509 Mcgilvra Blvd E Seattle WA 98112-5047 Office: U Wash Dept Medicine Div Al & Infectious Disease PO Box 357185 Seattle WA 98195-7185 Office Phone: 206-685-1876. Business E-Mail: seym@u.washington.edu.

KLEEMAN, CHARLES RICHARD, nephrologist, educator, researcher; b. LA, Aug. 19, 1923; m. 1945; 3 children. BS, U. Calif., 1944, MD, 1947. Rotating intern San Francisco City Hosp., 1947-48; asst. resident pathology Mallory Inst.-Boston City Hosp., 1948-49; resident in medicine Newington VA Hosp., 1949-51; from instr. to asst. prof. metabolism (renal endocrine & diabetes), dept. medicine & metabolic diseases Yale U. Sch. Medicine, 1953-56; chief divsn. metabolic disease UCLA Med. Ctr., 1956—60; assoc. prof. UCLA Sch. Medicine, 1956—60, prof. medicine Cedars-Sinai Med Ctr., 1961—72, prof., dir. dept. internal medicine, 1972—94, prof. emeritus, 1994—. Nephrologist VA Med. Ctr., West L.A., 1993—; prof. medicine, dept. chief Hadassah Med. Sch.-Hebrew U., Israel, 1972-75; vis. prof. Beilinson Hosp.-Tel Aviv U., 1968, St. Francis Hosp., Honolulu, 1968, U. Queensland, 1966; chief metabolic sect. VA Hosp., L.A. 1956-60, cons., 1962—; chief metabolic sect. Wadsworth VA Med. Ctr., L.A., 1956-60. Upjohn-Endocrine Soc. scholar U. London, 1960-61. Mem. AMA, Am. Physiol. Soc., Inst. Medicine-NAS, Am. Soc. Clin. Investigation, Endocrine Soc., Am. Assn. Physicians. Office: VAMC West LA Med Divsn Nephr W111L 11301 Wilshire Blvd Los Angeles CA 90073 Office Phone: 310-794-1795. Business E-Mail: ckleeman@ucla.edu.

KLEESE, WILLIAM CARL, genealogy research consultant, financial services representative; b. Williamsport, Pa., Jan. 20, 1940; s. Donald Raymond and Helen Alice (Mulberger) K.; m. Vivian Ann Yeager, June 12, 1958; children: Scott, Jolene, Mark, Troy, Brett, Kecia, Lance. BS in Wildlife Biology, U. Ariz., Tucson, 1975, MS in Animal Physiology, 1979, PhD in Animal Physiology, 1981. Sales rep. Terminix Co., Tucson, 1971-72; pest control operator, 1973-75; fire fighter Douglas Ranger Dist. Coronado Nat. Forest US Forest Svc., 1975, biol. technician Santa Catalina ranger dist., 1975-76; lab. technician dept. animal scis. U. Ariz., 1977-78, rsch. technician dept. pharmacology, toxicology, 1978, rsch. asst. dept. biochemistry, 1979-81, rsch. specialist muscle biology group, 1981-91; genealogy rsch. cons. Tucson, 1988—; fin. svcs. rep. World Fin. Group, Tucson, 1999—2008, Ameritas Investment Corp., Tucson, 2008—. Author: Introduction to Genealogy, 1988, Introduction to Genealogical Research, 1989, Genealogical Research in the British Isles, 1991, The Genealogical Researcher, Neophyte to Graduate, 1992; contbr. numerous articles to profl. jours. Chaplain Ariz. State Prisons, Tucson, 1988—. Mem. Nat. Assn. Securities Dealers, Ariz. Geneaolgy Adv. Bd. (com. chmn. 1990-92), Herpetologists League, Lycoming County Geneal. Soc., Nat. Geneal. Soc., Nat. Wildlife Fedn., Pa. Geneal. Soc., Soc. Study Amphibians Reptiles, Soc. Vertebrate Paleontology, Ariz. State Geneal. Soc. (pres. 1990-93). Republican. Mem. Lds Ch. Avocation: photography. Home and Office: 6521 E Fayette St Tucson AZ 85730-2220 Office Phone: 520-790-5444. Business E-Mail: wmkleese@familyhistoryland.com.

KLEIMAN, EVAN, chef; BA in Film magna cum laude, UCLA. Night chef, kitchen mgr. Mangia; exec. chef Verdi Ristorante di Musica, Santa Monica, Calif.; owner, chef Angeli Caffe, LA. Host "Good Food" KCRW, Santa Monica, Calif. Author (cookbooks): Cucina Fresca, 1983; author: Cucina Rustica, 1990, Angeli: Piza, Pasta and Panini, 1997. Office: 7274 Melrose Ave Los Angeles CA 90046

KLEIN, BENJAMIN, economics professor, consultant; b. NYC, Jan. 29, 1943; s. Hyman and Beartha (Kristel) K.; m. Lynne Schneider; children: Franz, Emily, Amanda. ABA in Philosophy, Bklyn. Coll., 1964; MA in Econs., U. Chgo., 1967, PhD in Econs., 1970. Asst. prof. UCLA, 1968-72, assoc. prof., 1973-78, prof. econs., 1978—; faculty rsch. fellow Nat. Bur. Econs., NYC, 1971-72, rsch. assoc., 1976-77; pres. Econ. Analysis Corp., LA, 1980—2004; dir Law and Econs. Consulting Group, 2004—. Vis. prof. U. Wash., Seattle, 1978; cons. FTC, Washington, 1976-86, bd. govs. FRS, Washington, 1973-75. Contbr. articles to profl. jours. Ford Found. fellow, 1967-68, Scaiffe Found. fellow, 1975-76, Law and Econs. fellow U. Chgo. Law Sch., 1979; grantee Sloan Found., 1981-87; recipient ann. prize for disting. scholarship in law and econs. U. Miami Law and Econ. Ctr., 1978-79, ann. award for best articles Western Econ. Assn., 1979. Mem. Am. Econs. Assn. Office: UCLA Dept Econs 405 Hilgard Ave Los Angeles CA 90095-9000 Office Phone: 310-556-0709. Business E-Mail: bklein@lecg.com.

KLEIN, CHRISTOPHER M., federal judge; b. Seattle, 1946; BA, MA, Brown U., 1969; JD, MBA, U. Chgo., 1976. Trial atty. US Dept. Justice, 1978-80; atty. Cleary, Gottlieb, Steen & Hamilton LLP, 1980-83; dep. gen. counsel Nat. Rd. Passenger Corp., 1983-87; judge US Bankruptcy Ct. (ea. dist.) Calif., 1988—. Lt. col. USMCR, 1969-79. Office: US Courthouse 501 I St Ste 3-200 Sacramento CA 95814-7300 E-mail: christopher_klein@caeb.uscourts.gov.

KLEIN, ERIC A., lawyer; b. NYC, July 3, 1959; AB, Princeton, 1981; JD, Boston U., 1985. Bar: Calif. 1986. Ptnr. corp. group, leader west coast mergers and acquisitions and securities practices Katten Muchin Zavis Rosenman, LA. Mem.: ABA (mem. Intellectual Property Law Sect., Intellectual Tech. Transfer). Office: Katten Muchin Zavis Rosenman Ste 2600 2029 Century Park E Los Angeles CA 90067 Office Phone: 310-788-4640. Office Fax: 310-712-8482. E-mail: eric.klein@kmzr.com.

KLEIN, FREDERICK CHRISTOPHE (FREDERICK CHRISTOPHE KLEIN), actor; b. Hinsdale, Ill., Mar. 14, 1979; Attended, Texas Christian U., Ft. Worth. Actor: (films) Election, 1999, American Pie, 1999, Here on Earth, 2000, Say It Isn't So, 2001, Rollerball, 2002, We Were Soldiers, 2002, The United States of Leland, 2003, Tilt-A-Whirl, 2005, The Long Weekend, 2005, Just Friends, 2005, American Dreamz, 2006, Lenexa, 1 Mile, 2006, The Good Life, 2007, Day Zero, 2007, New York City Serenade, 2007, Hank and Mike, 2008, Street Fighter: The Legend of Chun-Li, 2009; (TV films) The Valley of Light, 2007; (TV series) Welcome to the Captain, 2008. Recipient Superstar of Tomorrow - Male award, Young Hollywood Awards, 2001. Office: c/o Brillstein-Grey Entertainment 9150 Wilshire Blvd Ste Beverly Hills CA 90212

KLEIN, HENRY, architect; b. Cham, Germany, Sept. 6, 1920; came to U.S., 1939; s. Fred and Hedwig (Weiskopf) K.; m. Phyllis Harvey, Dec. 27, 1952; children: Vincent, Paul, David. Student, Inst. Rauch, Lausanne, Switzerland, 1936-38; BArch, Cornell U., 1943. Registered architect, Oreg., Wash. Designer Office of Pietro Belluschi, Architect, Portland, Oreg., 1948-51; architect Henry Klein & Assoc., Architects, Mt. Vernon, Wash., 1952—78; pvt. practice architect Henry Klein Partnership, 1978—. Bd. dirs. Wash. Pks. Found., Seattle, 1977-92, Mus. N.W. Art, 1988-95. With U.S. Army, 1943-46. Recipient Louis Sullivan award Internat. Union Bricklayers and Allied Craftsmen, 1981; Presdl. Design award Nat. Endowment Arts, 1988; George A. and Eliza Howard Found. fellow. Fellow AIA (Seattle chpt. medal 1995). Jewish. Home: 21625 Little Mountain Rd Mount Vernon WA 98274-8003 Office: Henry Klein Partnership 314 Pine St Mount Vernon WA 98273-3852

KLEIN, HERBERT GEORGE, newspaper editor; b. LA, Apr. 1, 1918; s. George and Amy (Cordes) K.; m. Marjorie Galbraith, Nov. 1, 1941; children: Joanne L. (Mrs. Robert Mayne), Patricia A. (Mrs. John Root). AB, U. So. Calif., 1940; PhD (hon.), U. San Diego, 1989, U. So. Calif., 2006. Reporter Alhambra (Calif.) Post-Advocate, 1940-42, news editor, 1946-50; spl. corr. Copley Newspapers, 1946-50, Washington corr., 1950; with San Diego Union, 1950-68, editl. writer, 1950-52, editl. page editor, 1952-56, assoc. editor, 1956-57, exec. editor, 1957-58, editor, 1959-68; mgr. comm. Nixon for Pres. Campaign, 1968-69; dir. comm. Exec. Br., U.S. Govt., 1969-73; v.p. corp. rels. Metromedia, Inc., 1973-77; media cons., 1977-80; editor-in-chief, v.p. Copley Newspapers, Inc., San Diego, 1980—2003; nat. fellow Am. Enterprise Inst., 2004—; cons. Copley Newspapers, Inc., San Diego, 2004—. Publicity dir. Eisenhower-Nixon campaign in Calif., 1952; asst. press. sec. V.P. Nixon campaign, 1956; press sec. Nixon campaign, 1958; spl. asst., press sec. to Nixon, 1959-61; press sec. Nixon Gov. campaign, 1962; dir. comm. Nixon presdl. campaign, 1968; mem. Advt. Coun., N.Y. Author: Making It Perfectly Clear, 1980. Trustee U. So. Calif.; past chmn. Holiday Bowl; bd. dirs. Greater San Diego Internat. Sports Coun.; mem. com. Super Bowls XXII, XXIII, and XXXVII; active Olympic Tng. Site Com.; trustee U. So. Calif.; trustee U. Calif. San Diego Found; bd. dirs. San Diego Econ. Devel. Com. With USNR, 1942-46; comdr. Res. Recipient Fourth Estate award U. So. Calif., 1947, Alumnus of Yr. award U. So. Calif., 1971, Gen. Alumni Merit award, 1977, Spl. Svc. to Journalism award, 1969, Headliner of Yr. award L.A. Press Club, 1971, San Diego State U. First Fourth Estate award, 1986, Golden Man award Boys and Girls Club, 1994, Newspaper Exec. of Yr. award Calif. Press Assn., 1994; named Cmty. Champion, Hall of Champions, 1993, Mr. San Diego, 2001. Fellow Am. Enterprise Inst.; mem. Am. Soc. Newspaper Editors (past dir.), Calif. Press Assn., Pub. Rels. Seminar, Gen. Alumni U. So. Calif. (past pres.), Alhambra Jr. C. of C. (past pres.), Greater San Diego C. of C. (mem. exec. com.), Kiwanis, Rotary (hon.), Sigma Delta Chi (chmn. nat. com., chmn. gen. activities nat. conv. 1958), Scripps Inst. (dir.'s cabinet Oceanography), Delta Chi. Presbyterian. Home: 3890 Nobel Dr Apt 407 San Diego CA 92122 Office: 1855 First Ave Ste 300A San Diego CA 92101-2685 Office Phone: 619-702-1141. Office Fax: 619-702-1145. Business E-Mail: hklein@sandiegocoxmail.com.

KLEIN, JEFFREY S., lawyer, media executive; b. LA, Apr. 15, 1953; s. Norman and Shirlee Klein; m. Karyn Kitson, Sept. 29, 1984; 3 children. BA suma cum laude, Claremont Mens Coll., 1975; M in Journalism, Columbia U., 1978; JD, Stanford U., 1980. Assoc. Kaplan, Livingston, Goodwin, Berkowitz & Selvin, Beverly Hills, Calif., 1980-81, Garey, Mason & Sloane, Santa Monica, Calif., 1981-83; weekly contbr. UPI-Radio, LA, 1983-84; sr. staff counsel Times Mirror, 1983-87, asst. to pres., 1987-90; asst. to pub. L.A. Times, 1989-91; pres. L.A. Times Valley and Ventura County edits., 1991-96; v.p. L.A. Times, 1991-96, sr. v.p. consumer mktg., 1996-97, sr. v.p., gen. mgr. news, 1997-98; pres., COO 101 Comms. LLC, 1999—2001, CEO, 2002—06; chmn. bd. 1105 Media, 2006—07. Pres., CEO Calif. Cmty. News Corp., 1995-97; adj. prof. journalism U. So. Calif., 1985-87, 2002; adv. Gov. Bruce Babbitt, Phoenix, 1980. Author: (weekly column) Legal View, L.A. Times, 1985-93, various book revs.; columnist: Folio mag., 2004-05; contbr. Online Journalism Rev., 1999, Columbia Journalism Rev., 2000. Bd. dirs. Meet Each Need With Dignity, Gould Ctr. for Humanities, Claremont McKenna Coll. Recipient Angel award Vol. League of San Fernando Valley, Disting. Cmty. Svc. award Anti-Defamation League, 1994, Visionary award United Way North Angeles Region, 1995, Premiere Parents award March of Dimes, 1996. Mem. Calif. Bar Assn. Office: 101 Comm 9121 Oakdale Ave Ste 101 Chatsworth CA 91311-6517

KLEIN, MARC S., editor, publishing executive; b. Feb. 16, 1949; married; 2 children. BA in Journalism, Pa. State U., 1970. Bur. chief Courier-Post, Camden, N.J., 1970-75; asst. mng. editor Phila. Bull., 1975-81; editor Jewish Exponent, Phila., 1981-83; editor, pub. Jewish Bull. of No. Calif., San Francisco, 1984—. Pub. j. the Jewish news weekly of No. Calif.; mem. exec. com. Jewish Telegraphic Agy. Past pres. Temple Israel, Alameda; former bd. dirs. Oakland-Piedmont Jewish Community Ctr. Recipient 1st place awards Phila. Press Assn., 1973, 1st place award N.J. Press Assn., 1973; Wall St. Jour. Newspaper Fund intern, fellow, 1969. Mem. Am. Jewish Press Assn. (pres.), Soc. Profl. Journalists (past bd. dirs.). Office: 225 Bush St Ste 1480 San Francisco CA 94104-4216 E-mail: marc@jweekly.com.

KLEIN, OTTO GEORGE, III, lawyer; b. Berkeley, Calif., Dec. 7, 1950; BA, U. Wash., 1973; JD, Yale U., 1976. Bar: Wash. 1976. Atty. Perkins Coie, 1976-81; ptnr. Syrdal, Danelo, Klein, Myre & Woods, 1981—88, Heller Ehrman, 1988-97; mem. Summit Law Group, Seattle, 1997—. Office: Summit Law Group Ste 1000 315 5th Ave S Seattle WA 98104-282 Office Phone: 206-676-7000. Business E-Mail: ottok@summitlaw.com.

KLEIN, PETER, computer software company executive; B, Yale U.; MBA, U. Wash. With McCaw Cellular Comm., Orca Bay Capital, Terabeam Networks; v.p., treas. Homegrocer.com; CFO Asta Networks; joined Microsoft Corp., Redmond, Wash., 2002, CFO Server & Tools Bus. Group, corp. v.p., CFO Bus. Divsn., 2006—. Mem. Seattle bd. trustees NPower. Office: Microsoft Corp One Microsoft Way Redmond WA 98052-6399

KLEIN, ROBERT GORDON, former state supreme court justice; b. Honolulu, Nov. 11, 1947; s. Gordon Ernest Klein and Clara (Cutter) Elliot; m. Aleta Elizabeth Webb, July 27, 1986; children: Kurt William, Erik Robert. BA, Stanford U., 1969; JD, U. Oreg., 1972. Dep. atty. gen. State of Hawaii, 1973, with state campaign spening commn., 1974, with state dept regulatory agys., 1975-78; judge State Dist. Ct. Hawaii, 1978-84; judge cir. ct. State of Hawaii, 1984-92, supreme ct. justice, 1992—2000. Office: Supreme Ct 417 S King St Honolulu HI 96813-2902

KLEIN, ROBERT NICHOLAS, II, real estate developer; 3 children. BA in History with honors, Stanford U., JD. Pres. Klein Fin. Corp., Palo Alto Calif., Klein Fin. Resources. Bd. dirs. Global Security Inst.; participated in drafting of legis. to create the Calif. Housing Fin. Agy., past bd. dirs.; co-author Proposition 71, Calif., 2004; chmn. Yes on Proposition 71 campaign for the Calif. Stem Cell Rsch. & Cures initiative, 2004; interim pres. Calif. Inst. for Regenerative Medicine, 2004—05, chmn. ind. citizens oversight com., 2004—. Named one of 100 Most Influential People of 2005, Time mag. Office: Klein Fin Corp Ste 330 550 Calif Ave Palo Alto CA 94306

KLEIN, SPENCER ROBERT, physicist; b. New Brunswick, NJ, June 12, 1959; s. Sidney and Eleanor Klein; m. Ruth Ehrenkrantz; children: Solomon, Micah; 1 child, Momed. BA in Physics, U. Calif., La Jolla, 1981; PhD in Physics, Stanford U., Palo Alto, Calif., 1988. Rsch. asst. prof. Boston U., 1982—91; postgraduate rschr. U. Calif., Santa Cruz, 1991—94; staff physicist and sr. scientist Lawrence Berkeley Nat. Lab., Calif., 1994—; rsch. physicist U. Calif., Berkeley, 2007—. Spokesperson Stanford Linear Accelerator Ctr. Expt. E-146, Palo Alto, Calif., 1992—2000. Contbr. articles to profl. jours. Grantee Rsch. grant, NSF, 2007—. Mem.: Am. Phys. Soc. Office: 50R5008 Lawrence Berkeley National Lab 1 Cyclotron Rd Berkeley CA 94720

KLEINBERG, DAVID LEWIS, education administrator; b. San Francisco, Feb. 28, 1943; s. Moe and Lilyan (Abrams) K.; m. Gay Buros, Mar. 21, 1970 (div. 1983); children— Leah, Rebecca; m. Patrice Ellen Greenwood, Apr. 29, 1984; stepchildren: Aaron, Brian, Jesse. BA, San Francisco State U., 1970. Prodr. Sta. KTVU TV, Oakland, Calif., 1978-79, 89-90; writer, editor San Francisco Chronicle, 1960-80, editor Sunday Datebook, 1980-94; co-dir. Bay Area Classic Learning, San Francisco, 1994—. Served with U.S. Army, 1965-67, Vietnam Decorated Bronze Star Jewish. Avocations: basketball, post card collecting, stand-up comedy. Office: 300 Taraval St San Francisco CA 94116-1953 E-mail: bael@bael.com.

KLEINBERG, JAMES P., lawyer; b. Pitts., Mar. 28, 1943; BA, U. Pitts., 1964; JD, U. Mich., 1967. Bar: Calif. 1968. Trial atty. antitrust divsn. Dept. Justice, 1967-68; ptnr. McCutchen, Doyle, Brown & Enersen, Palo Alto, Calif. Atty. rep. 9th Cir. Jud. Conf. No. Dist. Calif., 1984-84, mem. exec. com., 1984-87; mem. adv. group No. Dist. Calif., 1990—; mem. civil trial advocacy consulting group Bd. Legal Specialization, 1979-90, mem. com. adminstrn. justice, 1984-87; panelist Ann. Fed. Practice Insts., 1992—. Mem. visitors com. U. Mich. Law Sch., 1985—. Fellow Am. Bar Found. Office: McCutchen Doyle Brown & Enersen 3150 Poster Dr Palo Alto CA 94304-1212

KLEINBERG, MARVIN H., lawyer; b. NYC, Aug. 17, 1927; s. Herman and Lillian (Grossman) K.; m. Irene Aertker, July 7, 1962; children— Sarah Elizabeth, Ethan Chaim, Joel Victor. BA in Physics, UCLA, 1949; JD, U. Calif., Berkeley, 1953. Bar: Calif. 1954, also U.S. Patent Office, U.S. Supreme Ct. 1954. Dep. pub. defender, Los Angeles County, 1954; patent atty. RCA, Camden, N.J., 1955-57, Litton Industries, Inc., Beverly Hills, Calif., 1957-61; patent counsel Modal Systems Inc., La Jolla, Calif., 1961-63; mem. firm Golove & Kleinberg, Los Angeles, 1963-70, Golove, Kleinberg & Morganstern, Los Angeles, 1970-72, Kleinberg, Morganstern & Scholnick, Los Angeles, 1973-76, Kleinberg, Morganstern, Scholnick & Mann, Beverly Hills, 1976-79; sole practice Marvin H. Kleinberg, Inc., Beverly Hills, 1979-84; ptnr. Arant, Kleinberg & Lerner, 1985-93, Arant, Kleinberg, Lerner & Ram, 1993-95, Arant, Kleinberg, Lerner & Ram, LLP, LA, 1996-97, Kleinberg & Lerner, LLP, 1998—. Adj. lectr. patent law, mem. Innovation Clinic Adv. Council Franklin Pierce Law Center, Concord, N.H., 1975—; adv. council PTC Research Found., 1981; dir., sec. Digem, Inc., Los Angeles. Active YMCA Indian Guides, 1974-79; pres. Opportunity Houses Inc., Riverside, Calif., 1973-76, UCLA Class of '49, 1979-84; co-chairperson Sholem Ednl. Inst., Los Angeles, 1974-75; chief referee Region 58, Am. Youth Soccer Orgn., 1976-84; dir. Dental Med. Diagnostic Sys., Inc. 1996-2001. Sgt. AUS, 1946-47. Mem. ABA, Los Angeles Intellectual Property Law Assn., Los Angeles County Bar Assn., Am. Intellectual Property Law Assn., Zeta Beta Tau. Home: 3901 Cody Rd Sherman Oaks CA 91403-5022 Office: Kleinberg & Lerner LLP 2049 Century Park E Ste 1080 Los Angeles CA 90067-3112 E-mail: mhk@bbs-la.com, mkleinberg@kleinberglerner.com.

KLEINER, ARNOLD JOEL, television station executive; b. NYC, Apr. 7, 1943; s. Leo and Hannah K.; m. Carol Dunn, Aug. 15, 1965; children: Kim, Kerri, Keith. BBA, Pace Coll., 1967. Acct. exec. KDKA Radio, Pitts., 1968-69, WJZ-TV, Balt., 1969-71; sales mgr. TVAR (Group W), NYC, 1974-75; acct. exec. TVAR, Chgo., 1971-72; sales mgr. WBZ-TV, Boston, 1972-74; gen. sales mgr. WJZ-TV, Balt., 1975-78; dir. sales WPVI-TV, Phila., 1978-81; v.p., gen. mgr. WMAR-TV, Balt., 1981-96; pres., gen. mgr. KABC-TV, LA, 1996—. Chmn. media rels. com. United Way Ctrl. Md., Balt., 1982-84; co-chmn. Md. reg. NCCJ, 1986-90, sr. co-chair, 1990-91; bd. dirs. Levindale, Balt., 1982-84; mem. adv. bd. Md. Fedn. Parents for Drug Free Use, Balt., 1986—, William Donald Schaefer Ctr. for Pub. Policy, Balt., 1986—; chmn. edn. com. Greater Balt. Com., 1986—, bd. dirs., 1989—, pres. chamber divsn., 1991—, Coll. of Notre Dame, Md., 1989—; mem. Mayor's Coord. Com. on Criminal Justice, Balt., 1983-88, Variety Club of Md., 1984, Johns Hopkins Children Ctr.'s Devel. Com., 1984—; bd. dirs. Balt. Reads, Inc., Greater Balt. Com.; chmn. adv. com. Mayor's Office Internat. Programs; bd. dirs. Alvin Ailey Dance Theater Found. of Md., Inc., 1990—. Recipient Victorine Q. Adams Humanitarian award, Am. Men's ORT Cmty. Achievement award, 1986. Mem. Md./D.C. Broadcasters Assn. (dir. 1984), TV Bur. Advt. (sales adv. com. 1975-78), Advt. Assn. of Balt., Advt. Club of Balt., Balt. Jewish Coun. (bd. dirs., mem. exec. com. 1985—), Nat. Assn. Broadcasters. Office: Sta KABC-TV 4151 Prospect Ave Los Angeles CA 90027-4524

KLEINER, MADELEINE A., lawyer, hotel executive; b. 1951; Grad., Cornell U.; JD, Yale Law Sch. Clk. to Hon. William P. Gray U.S. Dist. Ct. for Ctrl. Dist. of Calif.; assoc. Gibson, Dunn and Crutcher, LA, 1977—83, ptnr., 1983—95; sr. exec. v.p., chief adminstrv. officer, gen. counsel H.F. Ahmanson & Co., 1995—2001; exec. v.p., gen. counsel, corp. sec. Hilton Hotels Corp., Beverly Hills, Calif., 2001—. Bd. advisors UCLA Med. Ctr. Asst. sec. Performing Arts Coun., L.A. Music Ctr. Office: Hilton Hotels Corp 9336 Civic Ctr Dr Beverly Hills CA 90210 Office Phone: 310-205-4656.

KLEINFELD, ANDREW J., federal judge; b. 1945; BA magna cum laude, Wesleyan U., 1966; JD cum laude, Harvard U., 1969. Law clk. Alaska Supreme Ct., 1969—71; U.S. magistrate US Dist. Ct. Alaska, Fairbanks, 1971—74; pvt. practice law Fairbanks, 1971—86; judge US Dist. Ct. Alaska, Anchorage, 1986—91, US Ct. Appeals (9th cir.), San Francisco, 1991—. Contbr. articles to profl. jours. Mem.: Tanana Valley Bar Assn. (pres. 1974—75), Alaska Bar Assn. (pres. 1982—83, bd. govs. 1981—84), Phi Beta Kappa. Republican. Office: US Ct Appeals 9th Cir Courthouse Sq 250 Cushman St Ste 3-A Fairbanks AK 99701-4665

KLEINFELD, ERWIN, mathematician, educator; b. Vienna, Apr. 19, 1927; came to U.S., 1940; s. Lazar and Gina (Schönbach) K.; m. Margaret Morgan, July 2, 1968; children— Barbara, David. BS, CCNY, 1948; MA, U. Pa., 1949; PhD, U. Wis., 1951. Instr. U. Chgo., 1951-53; asst. prof. Ohio State U., 1953-56, asso. prof., 1957-60, prof., 1960-62; prof. math. Syracuse U., 1962-67, U. Hawaii, 1967-68, U. Iowa, 1968—2002, prof. emeritus, 2002—. Vis. lectr. Yale, 1956-57; cons. Nat. Bur. Standards, 1953; rsch. specialist U. Conn., 1955; research mathematician Bowdoin Coll., 1957; rsch. asso. Cornell U., summer 1958, U. Calif., LA, 1959, Stanford, 1960, Inst. Def. Analysis, 1961-62, AID-India, 1964-65; vis. prof. Emory U., 1976-77; Cons. Edn. IX Project, World Bank, U. Indonesia, 1985-86, Mucia/Ind. U.-(ITM) Shah Alam, Malaysia Project, 1988-89. Editorial bd. Jour. Algebra-Academic Press; cons. editor, Merrill Pub. Co.-Div. Bell & Howell. Contbr. articles research jours. Served with AUS, 1945-46. Wis. Alumni Rsch. Found. fellow, 1949-51, vis. rsch. fellow U. New Eng., Australia, 1992; grantee U.S. Army Rsch. Office, 1955-70, NSF, 1970-75. Mem. Am. Math. Soc., Sigma Xi. Home: 1555 N Sierra 120 Reno NV 89503 Home Phone: 775-337-0196. Business E-Mail: mkleinfd@math.uiowa.edu.

KLEINGARTNER, ARCHIE, dean, educator, academic administrator; b. Gackle, ND, Aug. 10, 1936; s. Emanuel and Ottile (Kuhn) K.; m. Dorothy Jean Hanselmann, Sept. 21, 1957; children: Elizabeth, Thomas. BA, U. Minn., 1959; MS, U. Oreg., 1961; PhD, U. Wis., 1965. Asst. and assoc. prof. UCLA, 1964-69, assoc. dean, chmn., 1969-71, prof., 1971-75, 83—, dir. entertainment mgmt. program, 1988—, founding dean Sch. Pub. Policy and Social Rsch. Berkeley, 1994—; v.p. U. Calif. Sys., Berkeley, 1975-83. Cons. in field, 1967—; arbitrator in field, 1971—; chmn. Global Window Ptnrs., Inc., 1998—. Mem. labor mgmt. disputes panel City of L.A., 1978—. With U.S. Army, 1954-56. Mem. London Sch. Econs., Alpha Kappa Psi. Republican. Methodist. Avocations: tennis, biking, gardening. Office: UCLA Sch Pub Policy Social Rsch PO Box 951656 Los Angeles CA 90095-1656 Home: 87306 Halderson Rd Eugene OR 97402-9226 Office Phone: 310-206-1589. Business E-Mail: akleinga@ucla.edu.

KLEINPETER, AMY E. CLARK, lawyer; b. Hardin County, Ky., 1970; BS, Hiram Coll., 1992; MS, Univ. Calif., Riverside, 1994; JD, Univ. So. Calif., 2002. Bar: Calif. 2002, Tex. 2004, US Dist. Ct. Ctrl. Calif., US Ct. Appeals Ninth Cir. Atty. pvt. practice, Pasadena, Calif. Bd. mem. Univ. So. Calif. Public Interest Law Found. Editor: Univ. So. Calif. Rev. Law & Women's Studies. Named a Rising Star, So. Calif. Super Lawyers, 2005—06. Mem.: ABA, LA County Bar Assn., Assn. Trial Lawyers Am., Women's Law Assn. LA, Phi Beta Kappa. Office: Law Offices Amy E Clark Klei 1489 E Colorado Blvd Ste 207 Pasadena CA 91106-2032 Office Phone: 626-507-8090. Office Fax: 626-737-6030. Business E-Mail: amykleinpeter@earthlink.net.

KLEINROCK, LEONARD, computer scientist; b. NYC, June 13, 1934; s. Bernard and Anne (Schoenfeld) K.; m. Stella Schuler, Dec. 1, 1967; 4 children BEE, CCNY, 1957; MS, MIT, 1959, PhD, 1963; DSc (hon.), CCNY, 1997, U. Mass., Amherst, 2000; degree (hon.), U. Bologna, 2005, Politecnico di Torino, 2005. Asst. elec. engr. Photobell Co. Inc., 1951-57; rsch. engr. Lincoln Labs., MIT, 1957-63; mem. faculty UCLA, 1963—, prof. computer sci., 1970—, chair, computer sci. dept., 1991—95, co-chairperson dept., 1994-95; co-founder Linkabit Corp., 1968-69, pres.; founder Computer Channel, Inc., 1988; founder, CEO, chmn. Tech. Transfer Inst., 1976—98; chmn. TTI/Vanguard, 1998—; founder, chmn. Nomadix Inc., 1995—. Cons. in field, prin. investigator govt. contracts; founding mem. computer sci. and telecommunications bd., NRC, 1986; Disting. lectr. UCLA, 1994; chair Realizing the Info. Future: The Internet and Beyond, NRC, 1994, mem. com. Computing the Future-A Broader Agenda for Computer Sci. and Engring. Towards a Nat. Rsch. Network Com.; mem. adv. bd. CCNY Powell Ctr. for Policy Studies; mem. Network Rsch. Liaison Coun.; mem. adv. bd. Gigabit Testbed; founding mem. Sci. Coun. of the Cross Industry Working Team. Author: Queueing Systems, Vol. I, 1975, Vol. II, 1976, Communication Nets: Stochastic Message Flow and Delay, 1964, Solutions Manual for Queueing Systems, Vol. I, 1982, Vol. II, 1986, Queueing Systems: Problems and Solutions, 1996; contbr. several articles to profl. jours. and chapters to books. Recipient CCNY Elec. Engring. award, 1956, Paper award ICC, 1978, Leonard G. Abraham paper award Communications Soc., 1975, Outstanding Faculty Mem. award UCLA Engring. Grad. Students Assn., 1966, Townsend Harris medal CCNY, 1982, L.M. Ericsson Prize Sweden, 1982, 12th Marconi award, 1986, Okawa prize, 2001, C&C award Found. for C&C, 2005, 2007 Nat. Medal Sci.; Named one of 50 People Who Most Influenced Bus. This Century LA Times, 1999; Guggenheim fellow, 1971-72; named to Computer Design Hall of Fame, 1982. Fellow IEEE (Disting. lectr. 1973, 76, Harry M. Goode award 1996, Internet Millennium award, 2000), Internat. Engring. Consortium, Assn. Computing Machinery (SIGCOMM award 1990, Monie A. Ferst award Sigma Xi, 1996), Inst. for Ops. Rsch. and the Mgmt. Scis. (INFORMS)(Pres. award, 1999); mem. NAE (vice chair, computer sci. and engring. peer com., 2002, Charles Stark Draper prize, 2001), Am. Acad. Arts & Scis.; Ops. Rsch. Soc. Am. (Lancaster prize 1976), Internat. Fedn. Info. Processes Sys., Amateur Athletic Union, AAAS. Jewish. Achievements include creation of the basic principles of packet switching tech. Avocations: Karate, hiking, jogging, swimming, marathon runner, puzzles. Office: UCLA Dept Computer Sci 405 Hilgard Ave 3732G Boelter Hall Los Angeles CA 90095-1596 Office Phone: 310-825-2543. Office Fax: 310-825-7578. Business E-Mail: lk@cs.ucla.edu.

KLEINSMITH, BRUCE JOHN See NUTZLE, FUTZIE

KLEPPE, JOHN ARTHUR, electrical engineer, educator, company executive; b. Oakland, Calif., Feb. 21, 1939; s. Arthur William and Musa (Anderson) K.; m. Julianna Marie Galli, Aug. 12, 1961; children: John Frederick, Johanna Beth, Judith Anne. BSEE, U. Nev., 1961, MSEE, 1967; PhD, U. Calif., Davis, 1970. Registered profl. engr., Nev., Calif. Prof. elec. engring. U. Nev., Reno, 1970—2006, prof. emeritus, 2006—, dir. Engring. Research and Devel., 1976-88; pres., research cons. Sci. Engring. Instruments, Inc., Reno, 1968-97; pres. Klepco, Inc., 1976—. Cons.; chief engr. NSF weather expdn. to Antarctica, 1977; del. White House Conf. Small Bus., 1980 Author: (textbook) Engineering Applications of Acoustics, 1989; contbr. articles, papers to publs. and confs. around the world. Served to lt. C.E. USN, 1961-65. Recipient Outstanding Engring. Achievement award for Nev., 1981, 84; Inventor of Yr. award, 1985, Olympus Lifetime award, 2006, Nev. Tech. Hall of Fame, 2006. Mem. IEEE (life), Nev. Innovation and Tech. Coun. (pres. 1981-93, pres. 1996-97), Sigma Xi, Tau Beta Pi. Home: 2776 Spinnaker Dr Reno NV 89519 Office: U Nev Dept Elec and Biomed Engring MS 260 Reno NV 89557-0260

KLEPPER, ELIZABETH LEE, retired physiologist; b. Memphis, Mar. 8, 1936; d. George Madden and Margaret Elizabeth (Lee) K. BA, Vanderbilt U., 1958; MA, Duke U., 1963, PhD, 1966. Rsch. scientist Commonwealth Sci. and Indsl. Rsch. Orgn., Griffith, Australia, 1966-68, Battelle Northwest Lab., Richland, Wash., 1972-76; asst. prof. Auburn U., Ala., 1968-72; plant physiologist USDA Agrl. Rsch. Svc., Pendleton, Oreg., 1976-85, rsch. leader, 1985-96; ret., 1996. Assoc. editor Crop Sci., 1977-80, 88-90, tech. editor, 1990-92, editor, 1992-95; mem. editl. bd. Plant Physiology, 1977-92, Irrigation Sci., 1987-92; mem. editl. adv. bd. Field Crops Rsch., 1983-91; contbr. articles to profl. jours., chpts. to books. Mem. Umatilla Basin Watershed Coun., 2005—, Umatilla County Critical Groundwater Taskforce, 2005—. Marshall scholar Brit. Govt., 1958-59; NSF fellow, 1964-66; Recipient First Citizen award, Pendleton, 2005, White Rose award, March of Dimes, Portland, 2005. Fellow: AAAS, Am. Soc. Agronomy (monograph com. 1983—90, bd. dirs. 1995—98), Soil Sci. Soc. Am. (fellows com. 1986—88), Crop Sci. Soc. Am. (fellows com. 1989—91, pres.-elect 1995—96, pres. 1996—97, Monsanto Disting. Career award 2004, Presdl. award 2006); mem.: Agronomic Sci. Found. (bd. dirs. 1993—99), Sigma Xi. Home: 1454 SW 45th Pendleton OR 97801 Home Phone: 541-276-8416. E-mail: klepperb@uci.net.

KLEWENO, GILBERT H., lawyer; b. Endicott, Wash., Mar. 21, 1933; s. Melvin Lawrence and Anna (Lust) K.; m. Virginia Symms, Dec. 28, 1958; children: Stanley, Douglas, Phillip. BA, U. Wash., 1955; LLR, U. Idaho, 1959. Bar: Wash. 1960. Assoc. Read & Church, Vancouver, Wash., 1960-68, Boettcher, LaLonde & Kleweno, Vancouver, Wash., 1968-99; sole practitioner Vancouver, 1999—. Parttime U.S. Magistrate Judge, 1979. Chmn. Bd. Adjustors, Vancouver, Civil Svc. Commn., Vancouver. Mem. Wash. State Bar Assn., Elks, Gyro Club. Office: 211 E McLoughlin Blvd #130 Vancouver WA 98663

KLINE, ADAM, state legislator; b. Red Bank, NJ, Oct. 27, 1944; m to Laura Gene (Genie) Middaugh; children: Genevieve. Washington State Senator, District 37, 97-, chairman, Judicial Committee, member, Govt Opers Committee, Washington State Senate; co-operating attorney, America Civil Liberties Union, formerly.Pvt law practice, formerly. Washington Conserv Voters (co-chair, formerly); Mothers Against Drunk Drivers (legislation director, formerly); Nat Abortion Rights Action League (chair, formerly); America Civil Liberties Union (cooperation attorney, formerly); PAC. Democrat. Jewish. Address: Seattle WA Office: State Senate 223 John A Cherberg Bldg, PO Box 40437 Olympia WA 98504 Office Phone: 360-786-7688; 800-562-6000; Dist: 206-725-1974. Fax: 360-786-1999. E-mail: kline.adam@leg.wa.gov.

KLINE, FRANK MENEFEE, psychiatrist; b. Cumberland, Md., May 14, 1928; s. Frank Huber and Margaret (Menefee) K.; m. Shirley Steinmetz, June 27, 1953; children: Frank F., Margaret L. BS, U. Md., 1950, MD, 1952; PhD, So. Calif. Psychoanalytic Inst., 1977. Diplomate Am. Bd. Psychiatry and Neurology (examiner 1970—). Intern Cin. Gen. Hosp., 1952-53; resident Brentwood VA Med. Ctr., West L.A., 1955-58; regional chief West Ctrl. Mental Svc., L.A. County Dept. Mental Health, LA, 1967—68; assoc. dir. adult psychiatry out-patient dept. L.A. County, U. So. Calif. Med. Ctr., 1968—77, acting dir. adult psychiat. dept., 1977, attending physician, 2009—; chief psychiatry VA Med. Ctr., Long Beach, Calif., 1977-91. Clin. prof., vice-chair U. Calif., Irvine, 1978—91, prof. emeritus, 1995—, U. So. Calif.; clin. prof. Drew King, 1992—2004; reviewer Hosp. Cmty. Psychiatry, 1978—, Am. Jour. Psychiatry, 1978—, Readings, 1995—2002; cons. Los Angeles County Dept. Mental Health, 1992—2008. Editor: A Handbook of Group Psychotherapy, 1983. 1st lt. M.C., U.S. Army, 1953-55. Office Phone: 310-325-3343. E-mail: frank.kline1@cox.net.

KLINE, JOHN ANTHONY, judge; b. NYC, Aug. 17, 1938; s. Harry and Bertha (Shapiro) K.; m. Fiona Fleming, Dec. 7, 1968 (div. 1977); m. Susan Sward, Nov. 25, 1982 (div.); children: Nicholas Sward Kline, Timothy Sward Kline. BA, Johns Hopkins U., 1960; MA, Cornell U., 1962; LLB, Yale U., 1965. Bar: Calif. 1966, N.Y. 1967, U.S. Supreme Ct. 1971. Assoc. atty. Davis Polk & Wardwell, NYC, 1966-69; staff atty. legal svcs. program OEO, Berkeley, Calif., 1969-70; mng. atty. Pub. Advocates Inc., San Francisco, 1970-75; legal affairs sec. to gov. Calif. Sacramento, 1975-80; judge Superior Ct., San Francisco, 1980-82; presiding justice 1st appellate dist. div. two Calif. Ct. Appeal, 1982—. Mem. Calif. Commn. on Jud. Appointments, 1995—; mem. Calif. Jud. Coun. Adv. Commn. Juvenile Law, 1997—. Bd. dirs. San Francisco Lawyers Commn. Urban Affairs, 1972-74, San Francisco Pvt. Industry Coun., 1981-89, Am. Jewish Congress of No. Calif., 1981-85, Youth Svc. Am., 1987-90; chmn. bd. dirs. Golden Gate Kindergarten Assn., 1992—, Youth Guidance Ctr. Improvement Com., 1982-90, San Francisco Conservation Corps, 1984—, Environ. Action Ctr., 1980—. Alfred P. Sloan fellow Cornell U., 1960-62; recipient Ambrose Gherini prize and Sutherland Cup Yale U., 1965. Mem. Calif. Judges Assn. Democrat. Jewish. Office: 350 McAllister St San Francisco CA 94102-4712 Office Phone: 415-865-7370. E-mail: anthony.kline@jud.ca.gov.

KLINE, RICHARD STEPHEN, communications and public affairs executive; b. Brookline, Mass., June 20, 1948; s. Paul and Helen (Chartoff) K.; m. Carroll Potter, (dec. Apr. 1984); m. Sharon Tate, June 16, 1985; stepchildren: Allison, Kevin. BA, U. Mass., 1970. Reporter, photographer Worcester (Mass.) Telegram & Gazette, 1970-71; account exec. Wenger-Michael Advt., LA, 1971; pub. rels. dir. Oakland (Calif.) Symphony Orch., 1972; asst. v.p., dir. promotions Gt. Western Savs. and Loan, Beverly Hills, Calif., 1972-75; v.p., dir. mktg. Union Fed. Savs. and Loan, LA, 1975-78; chmn. bd. dirs. Berkhemer & Kline, LA, 1978-88, Berkhemer Kline Golin/Harris, LA, 1988-93; COO Golin/Harris Comm., Chgo., 1992-95; pres. Shandwick U.S.A., NYC, N.Y., 1995-96, Kline Consulting Group, L.A., 1997; regional pres., sr. ptnr. Fleishman-Hillard, Inc., L.A., 1997—2007; v.p. comms. and pub. affairs Occidental Petroleum Corp., L.A., 2007—. Former instr. Am. Savs. and Loan Inst.; bd. dirs. Golin/Harris Communications; exec. com. Santa Barbara Old Spanish Days Fiesta Rodeo, 1992. Past pres., mem. exec. com. Big Bros. L.A.; bd. dirs. Am. Cancer Soc., L.A., Solvang (Calif.) TheatreFest; mem. Town Hall Forum, L.A.; commr. Parks and Recreation, City of Oakland, 1973-74; bd. dirs. United Way, 1988-93, TheaterFest, 1990-94, LA's Best, LA C. of C.; exec. com. Ctrl. City Assocs. Recipient Pres.'s Club award Big Bros. Greater L.A., 1987, 88, Best in West Pub. Svc. award Am. Advt. Fedn., San Francisco, 1975, Commitment to Youth award Big Bros. Greater L.A., 2001. Mem. Nat. Investor Rels. Inst., Pub. Rels. Soc. Am. (Disting. Cmty. Svc. award 1987), Internat. Assn. Bus. Communicators, Newcomen Soc., Nat. Cattlemen's Assn., Arthur W. Page Soc., Calif. Cattlemen's Assn., Am. Quarter Horse Assn., Rancheros Visitadores, Vaqueros de Los Ranchos, Jonathan Club. Avocations: horseback riding, fishing. Office: Occidental Petroleum Corp 10889 Wilshire Blvd 7th Fl Los Angeles CA 90024 Office Phone: 310-443-6249. Business E-Mail: richard_kline@oxy.com.

KLINEDINST, JOHN DAVID, lawyer; b. Washington, Jan. 20, 1950; s. David Moulson and Mary Stewart (Coxe) K.; m. Cynthia Lynn DuBain, Aug. 15, 1981. BA cum laude in History, Washington and Lee U., 1971, JD, 1978; MBA in Fin. and Investments, George Washington U., 1975. Bar: Calif. 1979, U.S. Dist. Ct. (so. dist.) Calif. 1979, U.S. Ct. Appeals (9th cir.) 1987. With comml. lending dept. 1st Nat. Bank Md., Montgomery County, 1971-74; assoc. Ludecke, McGrath & Denton, San Diego, 1979-80; ptnr. Whitney & Klinedinst, San Diego, 1980-83, Klinedinst & Meiser, San Diego, 1983-86; CEO Klinedinst PC, San Diego, 1986—. Trustee Phi Kappa Psi Endowment Fund, 2004—. Mem. law coun. Washington and Lee U., 1993-97, vice chmn. law campaign, 1991-94, trustee, 2001—; vice chmn. bd. dirs. ARC of San Diego/Imperial, 1991-97; pres. House Corp. Calif. Lambda, Phi Kappa Psi, 1999—2006. Recipient Disting. Alumnus award Washington and Lee U., 1993. Mem. ABA (standing com. on legal profl. liability), Order of the Coif (hon.), Calif. Bar Assn., San Diego Bar Assn., San Diego Def. Lawyers, San Diego/Tijuana Sister Cities Soc., Washington Soc. (bd. dirs. 1997—), Washington and Lee U. Alumni Assn. (bd. dirs. 1986-90, pres. 1989-90), Washington and Lee U. Club (pres. San Diego chpt. 1980-87, San Diego Dialogue of U. Calif. San Diego), La Jolla Beach and Tennis Club, Fairbanks Ranch Country Club, Bohemian Club, Phi Kappa Psi. Republican. Episcopalian. Home: 6226 Via Dos Valles Rancho Santa Fe CA 92067-9999 Office: Klinedinst PC 501 W Broadway Ste 600 San Diego CA 92101-3584 Office Phone: 619-239-8131. Business E-Mail: jklinedinst@klinedinstlaw.com.

KLINGER, ALLEN, engineering educator; b. NYC, Apr. 2, 1937; s. Benjamin and Evelyne Klinger; m. Judith Theresa Flesch, Aug. 31, 1958 (div. Dec. 1980); children: Deborah, Richard; m. Dorothy Joy Fisher, Feb. 14, 1988; stepchildren: Elisa, Laura Duncan, Kevin Gittleman. BEE, The Cooper Union, 1957; MS, Calif. Inst. Tech., 1958; PhD, U. Calif., Berkeley, 1966. Mem. tech. staff Hughes Aircraft Co., Culver City, Calif., 1957; teaching asst. Calif. Inst. Tech., Pasadena, 1957-58; electronics engr. ITT Labs., Nutley, NJ, 1958-59; electronics system engr. System Devel. Corp., Santa Monica, Calif., 1959-62; rsch. asst. U. Calif. Electronics Rsch. Lab., Berkeley, 1962-64; sr. rsch. engr. Jet Propulsion Lab., Pasadena, Calif., 1964-65; researcher Rand Corp., Santa Monica, Calif., 1965-67; prof. UCLA, 1967—. Mem. LA County Data Processing and Telecom. Adv. Com., 1994-95; cons. in pattern recognition, image analysis, computer systems and math. modeling; expert witness, 1990—; invited spkr. Zhejiang U., 2004. Author: Data Structures, in Ency. Phys. Sci. and Tech., 1987, 92, 2001; editor: Soviet Image Pattern Recognition Research, 1989, Human Machine Interactive Systems, 1991; co-editor: Data Structures, Pattern Recognition and Computer Graphics, 1977 Structured Computer Vision, 1980; co-guest-editor Jour. Theoretical Computer Sci., 2003; contbr. 11 chpts. to books; contbr. articles to profl. jours. Fulbright fellow India, 1990. Fellow IEEE (life, Disting vis. 1975-76, 88-90), Tau Beta Pi (nat. dist. dir. 2001—). Office: UCLA Computer Sci Dept 4532-K Boelter Hall Los Angeles CA 90095-1596 Home Phone: 310-578-5677; Office Phone: 310-825-7695. Business E-Mail: klinger@cs.ucla.edu.

KLINGER, MARILYN SYDNEY, lawyer; b. NYC, Aug. 14, 1953; d. Victor and Lillyan Judith Klinger. BS, U. Santa Clara, 1975; JD, U. Calif., Hastings, 1978. Bar: Calif. 1978. Assoc. Chickering & Gregory, San Francisco, 1978-81, Steefel, Levitt & Weiss, San Francisco, 1981-82, Sedgwick, Detert, Moran & Arnold, San Francisco and L.A., 1982-87, ptnr. San Francisco, 1988-98, LA, 1998—. Guest lectr. Stanford U. Sch. Engring., Constrn. Mgmt. Course, assoc. gen. contractors Legal Adv. Com. Calif. Mem. ABA (tort and ins. practice sect., chair surety and fidelity com. 2003-04, constrn. forum, pub. contracts sect.), Internat. Assn. Def. Counsel (assoc. builders & contractors), Nat. Bond Claims Assn. (spkr.), Surety Claims Inst. (spkr.), No. Calif. Surety Underwriters Assn., Surety Assn. L.A. (spkr.). Avocations: reading, hiking, golf. Home: 939 15th St # 10 Santa Monica CA 90403-3146 Office: Sedgwick Detert Moran & Arnold 801 S Figueroa St Fl 18 Los Angeles CA 90017-2573 Home Phone: 310-899-4494; Office Phone: 213-615-8038. Business E-Mail: marilyn.klinger@sdma.com.

KLINGER, TERRIE, science educator; BS in Biology, U. Calif., Berkeley, 1979; PhD in Biol. Oceanography, San Diego, 1989; MSc in Botany, U. BC, 1984. Cert. Internat. Bioethics Inst. Tng., Lisbon, Portugal, 2001, Premier Workshop Multivariate Stats., Ensenada, Mex., 2005. Project leader Marine Thermal Effects Lab., TERA Corp., Berkeley, 1979—80; grad. rsch. asst. and tchg. asst. U. BC, 1980—83; grad. rsch. asst. Scripps Instn. Oceanography, 1983—89; cons. Nat. Pk. Svc. Exxon Valdez Oil Spill Shoreline Assessment, 1989—92; postdoc. rsch. assoc., botany and plant scis. U. Calif., Riverside, 1989—92; vis. instr. and vis. rschr., Friday Harbor Labs. U. Wash., 1992—2001, asst. prof., marine affairs, 2001—07, assoc. prof., marine affairs, 2007—, with, Cedar Rock Res. Adv. Com., 2003—; adj. asst. prof. Sch. Aquatic and Fisheries Scis., 2005—. Vis. instr. Northeastern U., 1991—99, U. San Diego, 1992; guest lectr. U. Puget Sound, 2003—04. Editor numerous profl. jours.; author: Ecological Risks and Prospects of Transgenic Plants, 1999, Genetically Engineered Organism: Assessing Environmental and Human Effects, 2002, Marine Ecology Progress Series, 2003, J. Ocean Coastal Mgmt., 2004, Aquatic Conservation, Marine and Freshwater System, 2006, Frontiers in Ecology and the Environment, 2007; contbr. scientific papers. Recipient Outstanding Grad. Tchg. award, Coll. Ocean & Fishery Sci., 2007, Numerous Presentations and Publs. awards; nominee Outstanding Tchg. award, U. Wash., 2003, Tchg. award, 2006; Mead grant, U. Calif., 1986, Grant-in Aid, 1987, Numerous Rsch. grants. Fellow: NSF; mem.: Phycological Soc. America, Ecol. Soc. America, San Juan County Marine Resource Com. (chair, sci. subcom. 2004—, policy & mgmt. subcom. 2004—, ecosystem core planning team 2005—), Nat. Marine Sanctuary (rsch. adv. com. 2001—, chair, adv. coun. 2003—, nat. coun. chairs 2004—, chair, acoustic working group 2005—, nominee vol. of yr. 2007), Sch. Marine Affairs (academic affairs com. 2001—, student ombudsman 2004—, admissions com. 2004—). Office: Univ Wash Sch Marine Affairs Box 355685 Seattle WA 98105-6715 Business E-Mail: tklinger@u.washington.edu.

KLINMAN, JUDITH POLLOCK, biochemist, educator; b. Phila., Apr. 17, 1941; d. Edward and Sylvia Pollock; m. Norman R. Klinman, July 3, 1963 (div. 1978); children: Andrew, Douglas. BA, U. Pa., 1962, PhD (hon.), 1966, degree (hon.), 2006; PhD (hon.), U. Uppsala, Sweden, 2000, U. Penna, 2006. Postdoctoral fellow Weizmann Inst.

Sci., Rehovoth, Israel, 1966—67; postdoctoral assoc. Inst. Cancer Rsch., Phila., 1968—70, rsch. assoc., 1970—72, asst. mem., 1972—77, assoc. mem., 1977—78; asst. prof. biophysics U. Pa., Phila., 1974—78; assoc. prof. chemistry U. Calif., Berkeley, 1978—82, prof., 1982—, Miller prof., 1992, 2003—04, prof. molecular and cell biology, 1993—, chair chem. dept., 2000—03, Joel Hildebrand chair, 2002—03. Mem. ad hoc biochemistry and phys. biochemistry study sects. NIH, 1977—84, phys. biochemistry study sect., 1984—88. Mem. editl. bd.: Jour. Biol. Chemistry, 1979—84, Biofactors, 1991—98, European Jour. Biochemistry, 1991—95, Biochemistry, 1993—, Ann. Rev. Biochemistry, 1996—2000, Accts. Chem. Res., 1995—98, Current Opinion in Chemical Biology, 1997—, Chemical Record, 2000—, Advances in Physical Organic Chemistry, 2003—; contbr. articles to profl. jours. Fellow, NSF, 1964, NIH, 1964—66, Guggenheim, 1988—89. Mem.: AAAS, NAS, Royal Soc. Chemistry, Am. Philos. Soc., Am. Soc. Biochemistry and Molecular Biology (membership com. 1984—86, pub. affairs com. 1987—94, program com. 1995, pres.-elect 1997, pres. 1998, past pres. 1999, Merck award 2007), Am. Acad. Arts and Scis., Am. Chmn. Soc. (exec. coun. biol. divsn. 1982—85, chmn. nominating com. 1987—88, program chair 1991—92, Repligen award 1994, Remsen award 2005), Sigma Xi. Office: U Calif Dept Chemistry Berkeley CA 94720-0001 Office Phone: 510-642-2668.

KLIPPERT, BRAD, state legislator; b. Sunnyside, Wash., June 27, 1957; m. Kim Klippert; 1 foster child, Mason children: Alexis, Aubrey Jo. Attended, Evangel U., Springfield, Mo.; honors grad. Capt's. Career Course, USAR; grad. EMT program, Columbia Basin Coll., Pasco, Wash.; cert. Paramedic program, Ctrl. Wash. U., Ellensburg, Wash.; BA in Behavioral Sci. & Biblical Studies, NW Coll., Kirkland, Wash., 1991; M Tchg., City U., Tacoma, Wash. Lic. Min.; Nationally Cert. Paramedic Ctrl. Wash. U. Former paramedic firefighter & emergency med. technician; former correctional officer Pierce County; former patrol dep. Pierce County Sherriff's Dept.; former tchr.; min.; sch. resource officer Kiona-Benton Sch. Dist.; patrol officer Benton County Sheriff's dept.; asst. rep. whip Wash. House of Reps., mem. Dist. 8, 2008—. Adj. faculty mem. Columbia Basin Coll., Pasco, Wash. Former major Nat. Guard US Army, formerly with USAR, Haiti (Operation Uphold Democracy) & Bosnia (Operation Joint Forge), former operations officer USAR, Operation Noble Eagle, former detachment comdr. Chinook helicopter unit USAR. Recipient Medal of Valor, Pierce County Sheriff's Dept., 1987, Commanding Gen. Military Excellence award, 1988. Republican. Office: 436 John L O'Brien Bldg PO Box 40600 Olympia WA 98504-0600 Office Phone: 360-786-7882. Business E-Mail: klippert.brad@leg.wa.gov.

KLITZNER, THOMAS S., pediatric cardiologist; b. LA, Sept. 4, 1948; AB in Physics, Harvard U., Cambridge, Mass.; MS in Mech. Engring., Mass. Inst. Tech., Cambridge; MD, U. Pa. Sch. Med., 1977, PhD, 1979. Diplomate Am. Bd. Pediat., Am. Bd. Pediat. Cardiology. Intern pediat. UCLA Sch. Med., 1978—79, resident pediat., 1979—80, fellow pediat. cardiology, 1980—84, prof., chief divsn. pediat. cardiology. Vice-chair academic affairs, dept. pediat UCLA Med. Sch., dir. med. home. project; dir. Calif. children's svcs. prog. Mattel Children's Hosp., LA. Healthy Tomorrows Partnership for Children Grant, Fed. Health Resources Svcs. Adminstrn. Mem.: Joint Coun. Congenital Heart Disease, Am. Heart Assn. (past pres.), Am. Acad. Pediat. (exec. com. cardiology, cardiac surgery, Excellence in Pediat. Rsch. award). Office: David Geffen Sch Med UCLA Div Pediat Cardiology 10833 Le Conte Ave Los Angeles CA 90095 Office Phone: 310-825-7148. Office Fax: 310-825-9524. Business E-Mail: tklitzner@mednet.ucla.edu.

KLOBE, TOM, retired art gallery director; b. Mpls., Nov. 26, 1940; s. Charles S. and Lorna (Effertz) K.; m. Delmarie Pauline Motta, June 21, 1975. BFA, U. Hawaii, 1964, MFA, 1968; postgrad., UCLA, 1972-73. Vol. peace corps, Alang, Iran, 1964-66; tchr. Calif. State U., Fullerton, 1969-72, Santa Ana (Calif.) Coll., 1972-77, Orange Coast Coll., Costa Mesa, Calif., 1974-77, Golden West Coll., Huntington Beach, Calif., 1976-77; art gallery dir. U. Hawaii, Honolulu, 1977—2006; ret., 2006. Acting dir. Downey Mus. Art, Calif., 1976; exhibit design cons. Honolulu Acad. Arts, 1998-2005, Mission Houses Mus., 2003, Hawaii State Art Mus., 2002; exhibit designer John Young Mus., U. Hawaii, 1998; cons. Judiciary History Mus., Honolulu, 1982-96, Maui (Hawaii) Arts and Cultural Ctr., 1984-94, curator Keia Wai Ola: This Living Water, 1994; exhbn. coord. Schaefer Portrait Challenge, 2003; exhibit designer Inst. for Astronomy, Honolulu, 1983-86; exhibit design cons. Japanese Cultural Ctr. Hawaii, 1993—; juror Print Casebooks; project coord. Crossings '97: France/Hawaii, Crossings 2003: Korea/Hawaii. Recipient Best in Exhbn. Design award Print Casebooks, 1984, 86, 88, Vol. Svc. award City of Downey, 1977, Chevalier l'Ordre des Arts et des Letters, France, 2000, Robert W. Clopton award for Disting. Cmty. Svc., 2003; named Living Treasure of Hawaii, Honpa Hongwanji Mission of Hawaii, 2005; grantee NEA, 1979-93, State Found. Culture and the Arts, 1977—. Mem.: Am. Assn. Mus., Hawaii Mus. Assn. Roman Catholic. Business E-Mail: globetom@hawaii.edu.

KLOWDEN, MICHAEL LOUIS, think-tank executive; b. Chgo., Apr. 7, 1945; s. Roy and Esther (Siegel) K.; m. Patricia A. Doede, June 15, 1968; children: Kevin B., Deborah C. AB, U. Chgo., 1967; JD, Harvard U., 1970. Bar: Calif. 1971. From assoc. to ptnr. Mitchell, Silberberg & Knupp, LA, 1970-78; mng. ptnr. Morgan, Lewis & Bockius, LA, 1978-95; vice chmn. Jefferies & Co., Inc., LA, 1995-96; pres., COO Jefferies Group, Inc. and Jefferies Co., Inc., LA, 1996-2000, vice chmn., 2000—01; pres., CEO Milken Inst., 2001—. Trustee U. Chgo., 1986—. Office: Milken Institute 1250 Fourth St Santa Monica CA 90401 E-mail: mklowden@milkeninstitute.org.

KLUG, JOHN JOSEPH, secondary school educator, director; b. Denver, Apr. 27, 1948; s. John Joseph Sr. and Dorthea Virginia (Feely) Carlyle. BA in English, U. N.C., 1974; MA in Theatre, U. Colo., 1984. Tchr. Carmody Jr. High Sch., Lakewood, Colo., 1976-78, Golden (Colo.) High Sch., 1978—, dir. of dramatics, 1978—; producer, dir. Children's Theatre Tours, 1978—. Theatrical cons., 1983—; improvisational workshop leader, 1983—. Playwright, editor: Children's Theatre scripts, 1982—; producer, dir. Denver Theatre Sports, 1993—. Recipient Bravo/TCI Theatre award, 1995. Home: 4565 King St Denver CO 80211-1357 Office: Golden HS 701 24th St Golden CO 80401-2379

KLUM, HEIDI, model, actress; b. Bergisch-Gladbach, Germany, June 1, 1973; naturalized, US, 2008; d. Gunther and Erna Klum; m. Ric Pipino, Sept. 6, 1997 (div. Nov. 2002); 1 child, Leni; m. Seal, May 10, 2005; children: Henry Guenther, Johan Rily. Model Victoria's Secret Fashion Show, 2001, 2002, 2003; appeared on covers of major mags. including Elle, Sports Illustrated (Swimsuit Edit.), Mademoiselle, Glamour, Bride's, Cosmopolitan; appeared in campaigns including Bonne Bell, Finesse, Gerry Webber, Givenchy, Amerige, INC, Am. Express, Kathleen Madden, Katjes, Nike, Otto, Peek&Cloppenburg, Swatch, Victoria's Secret; launched line of perfume, 2002; co-creator jewelry collection The Heidi Klum Collection for Mouawad, 2007—; designer of a line of Birkenstocks. Actor: (films) 54, 1998, Blow Dry, 2001, Ella Enchanted, 2004, The Life and Death of Peter Sellers, 2004, Perfect Stranger, 2007; (TV films) Spin City, 1998—99; exec. prodr., host (TV series) Project Runaway, 2004— (Inspiration award, LA Fashion Awards, 2007), TV appearances include Sex and the City, 2001, Malcolm in the Middle, 2002, Yes, Dear, 2002, CSI: Miami, 2003; author (with Alexandra Postman): Heidi Klum's Body of Knowledge: 8 Rules of Model Behavior (To Help You Take off on the Runway of Life), 2004. Charity involvements include ARC, Elizabeth Glazer Pediatric AIDS Found. Recipient Fashion Influencer award, Accessories Coun. of Excellence, 2007; named one of World's Richest Model (#3), Forbes, 2007, The 100 Most Powerful Celebrities, Forbes.com, 2008, The 50 Most Powerful Women in NYC, NY Post, 2007. Office: William Morris Agy One William Morris Pl Beverly Hills CA 90212

KLUNDER, JACK D., publishing executive; Attended, UCLA Anderson Sch. Mgmt., Pepperdine U. With LA Times, 1976—88, dir. circulation, 1988—96; dir. sales & mktg. Fin. Mgmt. Control of Ariz., Inc., 1996—97; founding ptnr. Equant Mktg. Group, LLC, 1997—99; sr. v.p. circulation LA Newspaper Group, 2000—05, LA Times, 2005—08; pres. LA Times Newspaper, 2008—. Aztec Parent adv. bd. San Diego State U. Mem.: Major/Metro Newspaper Group, Cal Western Circulation Mgrs. Assn. Office: LA Times 202 W 1st St Los Angeles CA 90012 E-mail: jack.klunder@latimes.com.

KMIEC, DOUGLAS WILLIAM, law educator, columnist; b. Chgo., Sept. 24, 1951; s. Walter and Beatrice (Neumann) K.; m. Carolyn Keenan, June 2, 1973; children: Keenan, Katherine, Kiley, Kolleen, Kloe. BA, Northwestern U., 1973; JD, U. So. Calif., LA, 1976. Bar: Ill. 1976, Calif. 1980, U.S. Supreme Ct. 1986. Assoc. Vedder, Price, et al, Chgo., 1976-78; prof. law Valparaiso U., Ind., 1978-80, Notre Dame U., 1980-99; Caruso family chair in constitutional law Pepperdine U., 1999—2001, 2003—; dean, St. Thomas More prof. Cath. U., Washington, 2001—03. Dir. Thomas J. White Ctr. on Law and Govt., 1983-88; dep. asst. atty. gen. Ofice of Legal Counsel, Dept. Justice, Washington, 1985-87; asst. atty. gen., 1988-89; vis. scholar Stanford U., 1985; spl. asst. to sec. HUD, Washington, 1982-83; disting. chair Dorothy & Leonard Straus, Pepperdine U. Sch. Law, 1995-96, 97-98; mem. pres.'s Commn. on Manufactured Housing, Washington, 1984-85, 89-92; mem. adv. com. Civil Rights Commn., bd. trustees Housing Allowance Program, Ind., 1983-85; state chmn. Scholars for Reagan and Bush, Ind., 1984. Author: Recharting Criminal Procedure, 1984, Zoning and Planning Desk Book, 1986, The Attorney General's Lawyer, 1992, Cease-fire on the Family, 1995, (with Stephen B. Presser) The American Constitutional Order, 1998, Individual Rights and the American Constitution, 1998, The History, Philosophy and Structure of the American Constitution, 1998; host, exec. prodr. Forefront TV series WNIT-TV, 1984-85; radio commentator The American Family Perspective, 1994-96; columnist Chgo. Tribune, 1996-99. Recipient Clark Boardman prize, 1983, 87, 90, Disting. Svc. award HUD, 1983, Disting. Svc. award Dept. Justice, 1987, Edmund J. Randolph award Dept. Justice, 1989; White House fellow, Washington, 1982-83, 40th Anniversary Fulbright Disting. fellow, 1987. Mem. U.S. Supreme Ct. Bar, Ill. Bar Assn., Calif. Bar Assn., Notre Dame Club (Washington). Republican. Roman Catholic. Office: Pepperdine Univ Sch Law 24255 Pacific Coast Highway Malibu CA 90263 E-mail: Douglas.Kmiec@pepperdine.edu.

KNAPP, CHARLES LINCOLN, law educator; b. Zanesville, Ohio, Oct. 22, 1935; s. James Lincoln and Laura Alma (Richardson) K.; m. Beverley Earle Trott, Aug. 23, 1958 (dec. 1995); children: Jennifer Lynn, Liza Beth. BA, Denison U., 1956; JD, NYU, 1960. Bar: N.Y. 1961. Assoc. Paul, Weiss, Rifkind, Wharton & Garrison, NYC, 1960-64; asst. prof. law NYU Law Sch., NYC, 1964-67, assoc. prof., 1967-70, prof. law, 1970-88, Max E. Greenberg prof. contract law, 1988-98, Max E. Greenberg prof. emeritus contract law, 1998—, assoc. dean, 1977-82. Vis. prof. law U. Ariz. Law Sch., Tucson, 1973, Harvard U. Law Sch., Cambridge, Mass., 1974—75, Bklyn. Law Sch., 2003, U. Copenhagen, 2004, Hastings Coll. Law, San Francisco, 1996—97, disting. prof. law, 1998—2000, Joseph W. Cotchett Disting. prof. law, 2000—. Author: Problems in Contract Law, 1976; author: (with N. Crystal and H. Prince) 6th edit., 2007; editor-in-chief: Commercial Damages, 1986. Mem. Am. Law Inst., Order Coif, Phi Beta Kappa. Office: Hastings Coll Law 200 McAllister St San Francisco CA 94102-4707 Business E-Mail: knappch@uchastings.edu.

KNAPP, CLEON TALBOYS, publishing executive; b. LA, Apr. 28, 1937; s. Cleon T. and Sally (Brasfield) K.; m. Elizabeth Ann Wood, Mar. 17, 1979; children: Jeffrey James, Brian Patrick, Aaron Bradley, Laura Ann. Student, UCLA, 1955-58. With John C. Brasfield Pub. Corp. (purchased co. in 1965, changed name to Knapp Comm Corp. 1977, sold to Condé Nast Publs. in 1993); pres. Talwood Corp., Knapp Found., LA. Bd. visitors John E. Anderson Grad. Sch. of Mgmt., UCLA; chmn. bd. trustees Art Ctr. Coll. Design. Mem. Bel Air Country Club, Regency Club, Country Club of the Rockies, Eagle Springs Golf Club. Office: Talwood Corp 10100 Santa Monica Blvd Los Angeles CA 90067-4003

KNAPP, HOWARD RAYMOND, internist, clinical pharmacologist; b. Red Bank, NJ, Oct. 5, 1949; s. Howard Raymond and Jane Marie (Ray) K.; m. Brenda Louise Carr, 1984; 1 child, Matthew. AB in Biology, Washington U., St. Louis, 1971; MD, Vanderbilt U., 1977, PhD in Pharmacology, 1984. Diplomate Am. Bd. Internal Medicine, cert. clin. densitometrist. Asst. prof. medicine and pharmacology Vanderbilt U., Nashville, 1984-89, assoc. prof., 1990; assoc. prof. internal medicine and pharmacology U. Iowa, Iowa City, 1990-97, prof. internal medicine and pharmacology, 1997-2000, assoc. dir. NIH Clin. Rsch. Ctr., 1997-2000; exec. dir. Billings Clin. Res. Divsn., Mont., 2000—05, v.p. rsch. Mont., 2006—. Mem. NIH Nutrition Study Sect., Bethesda, Md., 1994—96; cons. pharm. firms, grant orgns. and govtl. entities; mem. applied pharmacol. task force Nat. Bd. Med. Examiners, 1997—2000; mem. expert panel on cardiovasc. and renal drugs U.S. Pharmacopeia, 2000—05. Editor-in-chief Lipids, 1995-2006; contbr. numerous articles to profl. jours., chpts. to books. Grantee NIH, Am. Heart Assn., others. Fellow ACP, Am. Heart Assn. (vascular biol. rsch. rev. com. 1993-95, arteriosclerosis coun.); mem. Ctrl. Soc. for Clin. Rsch. (chair clin. pharmacol. sect. 1992-95), Am. Soc. for Clin. Pharmacology and Therapeutics, Am. Oil chemists Soc. (gov. bd., 2002-04, v.p., 2005-06, pres., 2006-07), Am/ Diabetes Assn., NY Adad. Sci., Am. Chem. Soc. Achievements include first demonstration that calcium ionophores stimulate eicosanoid synthesis; first evidence that N-3 fatty acids reduce platelet activation and blood pressure in patients; first demonstration of the effects of 5-lipoxygenase inhibition in humans. Office: Billings Clinic Rsch Ctr 1045 N 30th St Billings MT 59101-0733 Office Phone: 406-255-8475. Business E-Mail: hknapp@billingsclinic.org.

KNAUSS, DONALD R., consumer products company executive; b. 1951; m. Ellie Knauss. BA, Ind. U. Brand mgr. Procter & Gamble; mktg. & sales mgmt. positions Frito-Lay & Tropicana div. PepsiCo Inc.; sr. v.p. mktg. The Minute Maid Co., 1994—96, sr. v.p., gen. mgr. retail ops., 1996—98, pres., CEO, 2000—04; sr. v.p., mgr. so. Africa The Coca-Cola Co., 1998—2000, pres., COO No. Am., 2004—06; chmn. CEO The Clorox Co., Oakland, Calif., 2006—. Trustee USMC Univ. Found., Morehouse Coll. Officer USMC. Office: The Clorox Co 1221 Broadway Oakland CA 94612

KNAUSS, WOLFGANG GUSTAV, engineering educator; Prof. aeronautics and applied sci. Calif. Inst. Tech., Pasadena. Editor: (with I. Emri) Mechanics of Time-Dependent Materials. Fellow ASME, Soc. Exptl. Mechanics (Murray medal 1995, Lazan award 1999), Am. Acad. Mechanics, Inst. for the Advancement of Engring.; mem. AIAA, Nat. Acad. Engring., Russian Acad. Natural Scis. (fgn., Kapitsa medal), Internat. (Russian Acad. Engring. (corr.), The Adhesion Soc., Soc. Rheology, Soc. for the Advancement Sci., Sigma Xi. Office: Calif Inst of Tech Div Engring & Applied Sci Mail Code 105 50 Pasadena CA 91125-0001

KNEBEL, JACK GILLEN, lawyer; b. Washington, Jan. 28, 1939; s. Fletcher and Amalia Eleanor (Rauppius) Knebel; m. Linda Karin Ropertz, Feb. 22, 1963; children: Hollis Anne(dec.), Lauren Beth. BA, Yale Coll., 1960; LLB, Harvard U., 1966. Bar: Calif. 1966, U.S. Dist. Ct. (no. dist.) Calif. 1966, U.S. Ct. Appeals (9th cir.) 1966. Assoc. McCutchen, Doyle, Brown & Enersen, San Francisco, 1966-74, ptnr., 1974-94, of counsel, 1994-99; owner Artema, 1999—; dir. litigation tng. Bingham, McCutchen, San Francisco, 2002—. Adv. coun. Hastings Coll. Trial Advocacy, San Francisco, 1981—91; mediator, arbitrator Am. Arbitration Assn., 1989—; chair Hastings Coll. Trial Advocacy, San Francisco, 1990—91; mem. exec. com. San Francisco Lawyers Com. Urban Affairs, 1991—93; lectr. Law Sch. Stanford U., 1998—2001, Harvard U., 2002—04. Co-chmn. Citizens to Preserve Orinda, 1983—85; bd. dirs., pres. Orinda (Calif.) Assn., 1972—74, Sea Ranch (Calif.) Assn., 1978—79. Ensign lt. (jg) USN, 1960—63, ensign lt. (jg) USNR, 1963—66. Fellow: Am. Coll. Trial Lawyers (mem. com. fed. rules civ. pro 1990—93); mem.: ABA, Maritime Law Assn. U.S. Democrat. Home: PO Box 220 Islesboro ME 04848 Office: Bingham Mccutcher Llp 3 Embarcadero Ctr Ste Pl2 San Francisco CA 94111-4074 Office Phone: 415-393-2000. Business E-Mail: jack.knebel@bingham.com.

KNECHT, JAMES HERBERT, retired lawyer; b. LA, Aug. 5, 1925; s. James Herbert and Gertrude Martha (Morris) K.; m. Margaret Paton Vreeland, Jan. 3, 1953 (dec. 1994); children— Susan, Thomas Paton, Carol. BS, UCLA, 1947; LLB, U. So. Calif., 1957. Bar: Calif. bar 1957, U.S. Supreme Ct. bar 1969. Mem. firm Forster, Gemmill & Farmer, Los Angeles, 1957-84; sole practice, 1985—2005; ret., 2005. Chmn. bd. Templeton (Calif.) Nat. Bank, 1992-95. Fellow Am. Bar Found. (life); mem. ABA, Legion Lex, Caltech Assocs., L.A. Area C. of C. (dir. 1979-83), Beta Theta Pi. E-mail: jknecht@ccaccess.net.

KNEEN, SIMON, apparel executive; b. 1962; Designer Simon Kneen collection; head designer Pret-a Porter, Paris; creative dir. Maska, 2001—03; creative design dir. Brooks Brothers Retail Brand Alliance, 2003—08; exec. v.p. design, creative dir. Banana Republic Gap Inc., 2008—. Recipient Retailer of Yr. award, Accessories Coun. Excellence Awards, 2008. Office: Gap Inc Two Folsom St San Francisco CA 94105

KNIGHT, GARY J., transportation executive; Pres. Knight Transp., Inc., Phoenix, 1990—. Office: Knight Transp Inc 5601 W Buckeye Rd Phoenix AZ 85043-4698

KNIGHT, GREG, professional sports team executive; m. Carrie Knight, 2004. Student, U. Denver Sch. Law; grad. in Bus., Kutztown U., Pa. Positions up to mgr. Denver Nuggets, 1999—2006, dir. basketball ops., 2006—. Mem.: U. Denver Sports and Entertainment Law Soc. Office: Denver Nuggets 1000 Chopper Cir Denver CO 80204

KNIGHT, KEVIN P., transportation executive; CEO Knight Transp., Inc., Phoenix, 1990—. Office: Knight Transp Inc 5601 W Buckeye Rd Phoenix AZ 85043-4698

KNIGHT, PATRICIA MARIE, biomedical engineer, consultant; BS in Engring. Sci., Ariz. State U., MSChemE; PhD in Biomed. Engring., U. Utah. Teaching and rsch. asst. Ariz. State U., Tempe; product devel. engr. Am. Med. Optics, Irvine, Calif., mgr. materials rsch.; rsch. asst. U. Utah, Salt Lake City; dir. materials rsch. Allergan Surg. Products, Irvine, dir. rsch., v.p. rsch., devel. and engring., 1991—2002; v.p. rsch., devel. Advanced Med. Optics, Santa Ana, Calif., 2002—03; cons. biomed. product rsch. and devel. Laguna Niguel, Calif., 2003—. Contbr. articles to profl. jours. Mem. Soc. Biomaterials, Am. Chem. Soc., Soc. Women Engrs., Assn. Rsch. in Vision and Opthalmology, Biomed. Engring. Soc. E-mail: pkbiomed@cox.net.

KNIGHT, PHILIP HAMPSON, apparel executive; b. Portland, Oreg., Feb. 24, 1938; s. William W. and Lota (Hatfield) Knight; m. Penelope Parks, Sept. 13, 1968; 3 children. BA/BS, U. Oreg., Eugene, 1959; MBA, Stanford U., Calif., 1962. CPA Oreg. Asst. prof. bus. adminstrn., 1964—69; co-founder Nike, Inc. (formerly Blue Ribbon Sports, Inc.), 1962, chmn. Beaverton, Oreg., 1967—, CEO, 1967—2004, pres., 1968—90, 2000—04. Bd. dirs. US-Asian Bus. Coun., Washington. 1st lt. AUS, 1959—60. Named Oreg. Businessman of Yr., 1982; named one of 1988's Best Mgrs., Bus. Week Mag., World's Richest People, Forbes Mag., 1999—, Forbes Richest Americans, 1999—, Most Influential People in the World of Sports, Bus. Week, 2007, 2008. Mem.: AICPA. Republican. Episcopalian. Avocations: tennis, running, golf. Office: Nike Inc One Bowerman Dr Beaverton OR 97005-6453 Office Phone: 503-671-6453.

KNIGHT, ROBERT EDWARD, bank executive, educator; b. Alliance, Nebr., Nov. 27, 1941; s. Edward McKean and Ruth (McDuffee) K.; m. Eva Sophia Youngstom, Aug. 12, 1966. BA, Yale U., 1963; MA, Harvard U., 1965, PhD, 1968. Asst. prof. U.S. Naval Acad., Annapolis, Md., 1966—68; lectr. U. Md., 1967—68; fin. economist Fed. Res. Bank Kansas City, Mo., 1968—70, rsch. officer, economist,

1971—76, asst. v.p., sec., 1977, v.p., sec., 1978—79; pres. Alliance Nat. Bank, 1979—94, chmn., 1983—94; pres. Robert E. Knight & Assocs., banking and econ. cons., Cheyenne, Wyo., 1979—. Chmn., CEO Eldred Found., 1985—; vis. prof., chmn. banking and fin. East Tenn. State U., Johnson City, 1988; faculty Stonier Grad. Sch. Banking, 1972-2002, Colo. Grad. Sch. Banking, 1975-82, Am. Inst. Banking, U. Mo., Kansas City, 1971-79, Prochnow Grad. Sch. Banking, U. Wis., 1980-84; extended learning faculty Park Coll., 1996-2005; mem. Coun. for Excellence for Bur. Bus. Rsch. U. Nebr., Lincoln, 1991-94, mem. Grad. Sch. Arts and Scis. Coun. Harvard, 1994—; chmn. Taxable Mcpl. Bondholders Protective Com., 1991-94. Contbr. articles to profl. jours. Bd. dirs. Stonier Grad. Sch. Banking, 1979-82, Nebr. Com. for Humanities, 1986-90, People of Faith (Royal Oaks) Found., 2000-04; trustee Knox Presbyn. Ch., Overland Park, Kans., 1965-69; bd. regents Nat. Comml. Lending Sch., 1980-83; mem. Downtown Improvement Com., Alliance, 1981-94; trustee U. Nebr. Found., 1982-94; fin. com. United Meth. Ch. Alliance, 1982-85, trustee, 1990-93; mem. Box Butte County Indsl. Devel. Bd., 1987-94; bd. mem., treas. Sun City Homeowners Found., Sun City, Ariz., 2005-07; chmn., CEO, Knight Mus. Found., 1994—. Woodrow Wilson fellow, 1963—64. Mem. Am. Econ. Assn., Am. Fin. Assn., So. Econ. Assn., Nebr. Bankers Assn. (com. state legis. 1980-81, com. comml. loans and investments 1986-87), Am. Inst. Banking (state com. for Nebr. 1980-83), Am. Bankers Assn. (econ. adv. com. 1980-83, cmty. bank leadership coun.), Western Econ. Assn., Rotary, Masons. Home and Office: 429 W 5th Ave Cheyenne WY 82001-1249

KNIGHT, STEVE, state legislator; b. Majove, Calif; m. Lily Knight; children: Christopher, Michael. High School, Palmdale High School. Assembly mem. District 36, Calif., 2008—; mem. Palmdale City Council, Calif., 2005—; officer LAPD, Calif.; former soldier United States Army, Germany. Soldier US Army. Office: PO Box 942849 Rm 2016 Sacramento CA 94249-0036 E-mail: steveknight@cityofpalmdale.org.*

KNIGHT, W. H., JR., (JOE KNIGHT), law educator, former dean; m. Susan Mask; children: Michael, Lauren. BA in Econs., Speech and Polit. Sci., U. N.C., 1976; JD, Columbia U. Adj. prof. U. Bridgeport Sch. Law, Bridgeport, Conn., 1981—83; assoc. counsel, asst. sec. Colonial Bancorp, Waterbury, Conn., 1979—83; vis. prof. Duke U. Law Sch., 1991, Wash. U. Law Sch., St. Louis, Miss., 1992, Seattle U. Law Sch.; prof. U. Iowa Coll. Law, 1988—2001; assoc. prof. U. Iowa Coll. Law, 1983—88, assoc. dean, 1991—93, vice provost, 1997—2000; prof. U. Wash. Law Sch., 2001—, dean, 2001—07. Mem.: ABA, Nat. Bar Assn., Nat. Conf. on Black Lawyers, Soc. Am. Law Tchrs., Am. Law Inst., N.Y. Bar Assn., State Farm Mut. Automobile Ins. Co. (dir.). Office: Seattle Univ Sch Law Sullivan Hall Box 353020 Seattle WA 98195-3020 Office Phone: 206-423-4315. Office Fax: 206-725-1231. Business E-Mail: whkslm@comcast.net.

KNIZE, DAVID MAURICE, plastic surgeon; b. Ennis, Tex., Apr. 2, 1938; s. Joseph Fred and Mary Elizabeth (Vavra) K. BA, Tex. U., 1959; MD, Southwestern Med. Coll., 1963. Resident in Orthopedic surgery Duke U., Durham, NC, 1964-66; resident gen. surgery U. Colo., Denver, 1966-68; resident plastic surgery N.Y.U., 1970-74; assoc., prof. surgery U. Colo., Denver, 1974--. Contbr. articles to profl. jours. Lt. comdr. USN, 1969—71. Mem.: AMA, Colo. State Soc., Am. Soc. Plastic and Reconstructive Surgeons. Republican. Avocations: bicycling, windsurfing, scuba diving. Office: 3701 S Clarkson St Englewood CO 80110-3909 Home: 112 Mayhurst Ave Colorado Springs CO 80906-3056

KNOBLOCH, FERDINAND J., psychiatrist, educator; b. Prague, Czech Republic, Aug. 15, 1916; emigrated to Can., 1970; s. Ferdin and Marie (Verunac) K.; m. Susana Hartman (dec. 1944 victim of Holocaust); m. Jirina Skorkovska, Sept. 5, 1947; children: Katerina, Gohana. Maturity degree, Realgymnasium, Prague, 1935; student, Charles U. Med. Sch., Prague, 1935—46; psychoanalytic tng., Charles U. Med. Sch., 1945-53, 1945—53. Successively lectr., asst. prof., assoc. prof. psychiatry Charles U., Prague, 1946-70; mem. faculty U. B.C., Vancouver, Canada, 1970—, prof. psychiatry, 1971-83, prof. emeritus, 1983—; clin. dir. Day House Univ. Hosp., 1972-90. Vis. prof. U. Havana, 1963, U. Ill., Chgo., 1968-69, Columbia U., 1969-70, Albert Einstein Med. Coll., 1970; pres. European seminar mental health and family WHO, 1961, 3d Internat. Congress Psychodrama, 1968; co-chmn. Internat. Symposium Non-Verbal Aspects and Techniques of Psychotherapy, 1974; hon. dir. psychodrama Moreno Inst., NYC, 1974. Author: (with Jirina Knobloch) Forensic Psychiatry, 1967 (award Czechoslovak Med. Soc. 1968), Psychotherapy, 1968, Neurosis and You, 1962, 63, 68, Integrated Psychotherapy, 1979 (transl. into German 1983, Japanese 1984, Czech 1993, 1999, Chinese, 1995), Integrated Psychotherapy in Action, 1999; contbr. articles on psychotherapy integration, psychology of music and evolutionary psychology to profl. jours. Polit. prisoner of Gestapo, 1943-45. Recipient award, Min. Foreign Affairs, 2004. Fellow Am. Psychiat. Assn. (disting. life), Czechoslovak Soc. Advancement Psychoanalysis and Integration of Psychotherapy (pres. 1968-72), Am. Acad. Psychoanalysis, Polish Psychiat. Assn. (corr.), Can. Psychiat. Assn., Am. Group Psychotherapy Assn., Can. Soc. for Integrated Psychotherapy and Psychoanalysis (pres. 1972—), World Psychiat. Assn. (co-chmn. sect. psychotherapy 1983-93, chmn. 1993-96). Personal E-mail: knobloch19@shaw.ca.

KNOELKER, MICHAEL T.F., science observatory director; b. Feb. 9, 1953; Diploma in Physics, U. Göttingen, Germany, 1978; PhD in Physics, Freiburg U., Germany, 1983. Asst. prof. U. Göttingen, 1983—90; astronomer Kiepenheuer-Instut Sonnenphysik, Freiburg, 1990—; vis. scientist High Altitude Obs. Nat. Ctr. Atmospheric Rsch., Boulder, Colo., 1987—94, affiliate scientist High Altitude Obs., 1994—95, sr. scientist, dir. High Altitude Obs., 1995—. Mem., steering com. Solar Magnetism Initiative, 1995—; mem. Assn. of Univs. for Rsch. in Astronomy (AURA) Observatory Vis. Com., 1996—. Office: High Altitude Obs Nat Ctr Atmospheric Rsch PO Box 3000 Boulder CO 80307-3000

KNOLL, JAMES LEWIS, lawyer; b. Chgo., Oct. 5, 1942; AB, Brown U., 1964; JD, U. Chgo., 1967. Bar: Ill. 1967, Oreg. 1971, Wash. 1984, Alaska 1993. Mediator, arbitrator, Portland, Oreg. Adj. prof. law Northwestern Sc. Law, Lewis and Clark Coll., 1982-91. Mem. ABA (mem. TIPS coun. 1989-92, chair property ins. com. 1984-85, mem. fidelity surety com., chair comml. tort com. 1985-86), Oreg. State Bar (editor 2 vol. text on ins. 1983, 96), Wash. State Bar, Oreg. Assn. Def. Coun. (pres. 1984). Office: 1500 SW Taylor St Portland OR 97205-1819 E-mail: jim@hamiltonmediation.com.

KNOLL, JOHN, visual effects supervisor; b. Ann Arbor, 1962; m. Jennifer Knoll; 4 children. BA in Cinema Prodn., U. Southern Calif. Tech. asst. Indsl. Light & Magic, 1986, motion control camera operator, visual effects supr.; co-creator Adobe Photoshop, 1987. Named an 50 Smartest People in Hollywood, Entertainment Weekly, 2007. Office: Industrial Light And Magic 1110 Gorgas Ave San Francisco CA 94129-1406

KNOLLER, GUY DAVID, lawyer; b. NYC, July 23, 1946; s. Charles and Odette Knoller; children: Jennifer Judy, Geoffrey David. BA cum laude, Bloomfield Coll., NJ, 1968; JD cum laude, Ariz. State U., 1971. Bar: Ariz. 1971, U.S. Dist. Ct. Ariz. 1971, U.S. Supreme Ct. 1976. Trial atty. atty. gen.'s hons. program Dept. Justice, 1971-72; atty., adv. NLRB, 1972-73, field atty. region 28 Phoenix, 1972-74; assoc. Powers, Ehrenreich, Boutell & Kurn, Phoenix, 1974-79; ptnr. Froimson & Knoller, Phoenix, 1979-81, Fannin, Terry & Hay, Phoenix, 1981—85; sole practice Phoenix, 1985—; of counsel Burns & Burns. Mem. bd. visitors Ariz. State U. Coll. Law, 1975-76; pres. Ariz. Theatre Guild, 1990, 91. Fellow Ariz. Bar Found.; mem. ABA, State Bar Ariz. (chmn. labor rels. sect. 1977-78), Ariz. State U. Coll. Law Alumni Assn. (pres. 1977). Office: 2999 N 44th St Phoenix AZ 85018 Home Phone: 602-801-9071; Office Phone: 602-230-1099. Business E-Mail: gdkpc@pcslink.com.

KNOPF, KENYON ALFRED, economist, educator; b. Cleve., Nov. 24, 1921; s. Harold C. and Emma A. (Underwood) K.; m. Madelyn Lee Siddy Trebilcock, Mar. 28, 1953 (dec. June 1999); children—Kristin Lee, Mary George. AB magna cum laude with high honors in Econs., Kenyon Coll., 1942; MA in Econs.; PhD, Harvard U., 1949; LLD (hon.), Kenyon Coll., 1993. Mem. faculty Grinnell Coll., 1949-67, prof. econs., 1960-67, Jentzen prof., 1961-67, chmn. dept., 1958-60, chmn. div. social studies, 1962-64, chmn. faculty, 1964-67; dean coll. Whitman Coll., Walla Walla, Wash., 1967-70, prof. econs., 1967-89, Hollon Parker prof. econs., 1985-89, prof. emeritus, 1989—, provost, 1970-81, dean faculty, 1970-78, acting pres., 1974-75; pub. interest dir. Fed. Home Loan Bank, Seattle, 1976-83. Mem. council undergrad. assessment program Ednl. Testing Service, 1977-80 Author: (with Robert H. Haveman) The Market System, 4th edit, 1981; A Lexicon of Economics, 1991; editor: Introduction to Economics Series (9 vols.), 1966, 2d edit., 1970-71; co-editor: (with James H. Strauss) The Teaching of Elementary Economics, 1960. Mem. youth coun. City of Grinnell, 1957—59; mem. Walla Walla County Mental Health Bd., 1968—75, Walla Walla Civil Svc. Commn., 1978—84, chmn., 1981—84; mem. Grinnell City Coun., 1964—67; pres. Walla Walla County Human Svcs. Adminstrv. Bd., 1975—77; mem. Ia. adv. coun. SBA; tax aide AARP/IRS Tax Counseling for Elderly, 1987—98, local coord., 1990—91, assoc. dist. coord. S.E. Wash., 1991—94, assoc. dist. coord. tng., 1994—98; bd. dirs. Skagit County Boys & Girls Club, 2001—07, Walla Walla United Fund, 1968—76, pres., 1973; bd. dirs. Shelter Bay Cmty., Inc., 1995—2003, v.p., 1995—97, pres., 1997—2003; bd. dirs. La Conner Cmty. Scholarship Found., 1997—, La Conner Unit Boys and Girls Club, 1999—, pres., 2001—03. With USAF, 1942—46, PTO. Social Sci. Rsch. Coun. grantee, 1951-52. Mem.: Am. Conf. Acad. Deans (exec. com. 1970—77, chmn. 1975), Am. Assn. Ret. Persons, Kiwanis (pres. LaConner club 2003—04), Delta Tau Delta, Phi Beta Kappa. Office: 223 Skagit Way La Conner WA 98257-9602

KNOPOFF, LEON, geophysics educator; b. LA, July 1, 1925; s. Max and Ray (Singer) K.; m. Joanne Van Cleef, Apr. 9, 1961; children— Katherine Alexandra, Rachel Anne, Michael Van Cleef. Student, Los Angeles City Coll., 1941-42; BS in Elec Engring, Calif. Inst. Tech., 1944, MS in Physics, 1946, PhD in Physics, 1949. Asst., then assoc. prof. physics Miami U., Oxford, Ohio, 1948-50; mem. faculty UCLA, 1950—, prof. physics, 1961—, prof. geophysics, 1959—, rsch. musicologist, 1963—; assoc. dir. Inst. Geophysics and Planetary Physics, 1972-86; prof. geophysics Calif. Inst. Tech., 1962-63, research assoc. seismology, 1963-64; vis. prof. Technische Hochschule, Karlsruhe, Germany, 1966, Harvard U., 1972, U. Chile, Santiago, 1973. Chmn. U.S. Nat. Upper Mantle Com., 1963-71; sec. Internat. Upper Mantle Com., 1963-71; chmn. com. math. geophysics Internat. Union Geodesy and Geophysics, 1971-75; mem. Internat. Union Geodesy and Geophysics (U.S. nat. com.), 1973-75; vis. prof. U. Trieste, 1984. Recipient Wiechert medal German Geophys. Soc., 1978; Gold medal Royal Astron. Soc., 1979; NSF sr. postdoctoral fellow Cambridge (Eng.) U., 1960-61; Guggenheim Found. fellow, 1976-77; Selwyn Coll. Cambridge U. fellow. Fellow AAAS, Am. Acad. Arts and Scis., Royal Astron. Soc. (Jeffreys lectr.), Am. Geophys. Union (Gutenberg lectr. 1992), Nat. Acad. Scis., Seismol. Soc. Am. (hon., medal 1990); mem. Am. Phys. Soc., Am. Philosophical Soc., Phi Beta Kappa (hon.). Office: U Calif Dept Physics Los Angeles CA 90095-0001

KNOSPE, WILLIAM HERBERT, medical educator; b. Oak Park, Ill., May 26, 1929; s. Herbert Henry and Dora Isabel (Spruce) K.; m. Adris M. Nelson, June 19, 1954. BA, U. Ill., Chgo. and Urbana, 1951; BS, U. Ill., 1952; MD, U. Ill., Chgo., 1954; MS in Radiation Biology, U. Rochester, 1962. Diplomate Am. Bd. Internal Medicine and Subspecialty Bd. on Hematology. Rotating intern Upstate Med. Ctr. Hosps-SUNY-Syracuse, 1954-55; resident in medicine Ill. Central Hosp., Chgo., 1955-56, VA Research Hosp-Northwestern U. Med. Sch., Chgo., 1956-58; investigator radiation biology Walter Reed Army Inst. Research, Washington, 1962-64, investigator hematology, asst. chief dept. hematology, 1964-66; attending physician med. service Walter Reed Gen. Hosp., Washington, 1963-64, fellow in hematology, 1964-65; asst. chief hematology service, chief hematology clinic Walter Reed Army Inst. of Rsch., Washington, 1964-66; asst. attending staff physician Presbyn. St. Luke's Hosp., Chgo., 1967-68, asst. dir. hematology radiohematology lab., 1967-74, assoc. attending staff physician, 1968-74, sr. attending staff physician, 1974—; asst. prof. medicine U. Ill.-Chgo., 1967-69, assoc. prof., 1969-72; assoc. prof. medicine Rush Med. Coll., Chgo., 1971-74, prof. medicine, 1974—; dir. sect. hematology Rush-Presbyn.-St. Luke's Med. Ctr., Chgo., 1974-93; Elodia Kehm prof. hematology Rush-Med. Coll., Chgo., 1986-94, prof. emeritus, 1994—; prof. medicine U. N.Mex., Albuquerque, 1994—2002, emeritus, 2002—. Speaker at profl. confs. U.S. and abroad; vis. prof. medicine dept. hematology U. Basel, Switzerland, 1980-81, Cancer Ctr., U. N.Mex., 1992-93. Contbr. numerous articles to profl. publs. Trustee Ill. chpt. Leukemia Soc. Am., 1977-88, v.p., 1979-80; trustee Bishop Anderson House (Rush-Presbyn.-St. Luke's Med. Ctr.), 1980-94. Served to capt. M.C., USAR, 1958-61, to lt. col., U.S. Army, 1961-66. Fellow ACP; mem. Am. Fedn. Clin. Research, AMA, Am. Soc. Hematology, Am. Soc. Clin. Oncology, Central Soc. Clin. Research, Chgo. Med. Soc., Inst. Medicine Chgo., Internat. Soc. Exptl. Hematology, Radiation Research Soc., Southeastern Cancer Study Group, Polycythemia Vera Study Group, Eastern Coop. Oncology Group, Ill. State Med. Soc., Assn. Hematology-Oncology Program Dirs., Sigma Xi, Chgo. Literary Club. Office: 310 Big Horn Ridge Dr NE Albuquerque NM 87122-1455 Home Phone: 505-858-0060.

KNOTT, DOUGLAS RONALD, dean, agricultural sciences educator, researcher; b. Fraser Mills, BC, Can., Nov. 10, 1927; s. Ronald David and Florence Emily (Keeping) K.; m. Joan Madeline Hollinshead, Sept. 2, 1950 (dec.); children: Holly Ann, Heather Lynn, Ronald Kenneth, Douglas James (dec.); m. Pat Decker, June 1, 2002 (dec.); m. Irene Sosulski, July 8, 2005. BSA, U. B.C., 1948; MS, U. Wis., 1949, PhD, 1952. Asst. prof. U. Sask., Saskatoon, 1952-56, assoc. prof., 1956-65, prof., 1965-93, head dept. crop sci., 1965-75, assoc. dean rsch. Coll. Agr., 1988-93; prof. emeritus, 1993—. Author: The Wheat Rusts—Breeding for Resistance, 1989; also numerous papers. Named to Saskatchewan Agr. Hall of Fame. Fellow Am. Soc. Agronomy, Agrl. Inst. Can.; mem. Can. Soc. Agronomy, Genetics Soc. Can., Order of Can. Mem. United Ch. of Can. Avocation: tennis. Office: U Sask Dept Plant Scis 51 Campus Dr Saskatoon SK Canada S7N 5A8 Office Phone: 306-966-5004. E-mail: dougknott@shaw.ca.

KNOTT, JACK H., dean, political science professor; b. Grand Rapids, Mich., June 14, 1947; s. Harold George and Alice (June) K.; m. Vicki Lynn Bergsma, June 6, 1969; children: Michael, Lisa, Alex. BA, Calvin Coll., 1969; MA, Johns Hopkins U., 1971; PhD, U. Calif., Berkeley, 1977. Lectr. U. Calif., Berkeley, 1977-78; prof. polit. sci. Mich. State U., East Lansing, 1978-97, dir. Inst. Pub. Policy, 1987-97; prof. polit. sci. U. Ill., Urbana-Champaign, 1997—2005, dir. Inst. Govt. and Pub. Affairs, 1997—2005; C. Erwin and Ione L. Piper dean and prof. Sch. Policy, Planning, and Devel., U. So. Calif., 2005—. Mem. adv. bd. Ill. Issues Mag., Springfield, 1997—; mem. Ill. State Govt. Accountability Coun., 2000—, Ill. Channel Planning Adv. Bd. Author: Managing the German Economy, 1980, Zero Base Budgeting, 1981, Reforming Bureaucracy, 1987; mem. editl. bd. Pub. Adminstrn. Rev., 1995-97. Sci. Ctr. fellow, Berlin, 1974-76; Russell Sage Found. fellow, 1981-82; grantee Kellogg Found., 1994—, U.S. AID/Mott Found., 1995-97. Fellow: Nat. Acad. Pub. Adminstrn. (NAPA); mem.: Assn. Pub. Policy and Mgmt., Pub. Adminstrn. Soc., Am. Polit. Sci. Assn. Avocations: skiing, tennis, handball, hiking, mountain climbing. Office: Sch Policy, Planning, and Devel U So Calif Ralph and Goldy Lewis Hall 312 A Los Angeles CA 90089-0626 Office Phone: 213-740-0350. Office Fax: 213-740-0350. E-mail: jhknott@usc.edu.*

KNOTT, WILLIAM ALAN, library director; b. Muscatine, Iowa, Oct. 4, 1942; s. Edward Marlan and Dorothy Mae K.; m. Mary Farrell, Aug. 23, 1969; children: Andrew Jerome, Sarah Louise. BA in English, U. Iowa, 1967, MA in L.S., 1968. Asst. dir. Ottumwa (Iowa) Pub. Libr., 1968-69; libr. cons. Iowa State Libr., Des Moines, 1968-69; dir. Hutchinson (Kans.) Pub. Libr., S. Cen. Kans. Libr. Sys., 1969-71, Jefferson County Pub. Libr., Lakewood, Colo., 1971—. With USAR, 1965—67. Mem.: ALA, Urban Librs Coun., Colo. Libr. Assn. Office: Jefferson County Pub Libr 10200 W 20th Ave Lakewood CO 80215-1402 Home Phone: 303-423-3160; Office Phone: 303-275-2200. Business E-Mail: wknott@jefferson.lib.co.us.

KNOWLES, ELIZABETH PRINGLE, museum director; b. Decatur, Ill., Jan. 9, 1943; d. William Bull and Elizabeth E. (Pillsbury) Pringle; m. Joseph E. Knowles; 1 child, Elizabeth Bakewell. BA in Humanities with honors, Stanford U., 1964; MA in Art History, U. Calif., Santa Barbara, 1968; grad., Mus. Mgmt. Inst., 1984; MBA, Rensselaer Poly. Inst., 1999. Cert. jr. coll. tchr. Calif. Instr. art history Murray State U., Murray, Ky., 1967-68; instr. Santa Barbara Art Inst., 1969, Santa Barbara City Coll., 1969-70, 76-78, instr. cont. edn., 1973-86; from staff coord. docents to curator edn. Santa Barbara Mus. Art, 1974-86; assoc. dir. Meml. Art Gallery, Rochester, NY, 1986-88; instr. mus. studies Calif. State U., Long Beach, 1989; exec. dir. Lyman Allyn Art Mus., New London, Conn., 1989-95; pres. Only In Conn. Spl. Interest Tours, Chester, 1995-97; supr. mus. edn. programs Mystic (Conn.) Seaport Mus., 1996-2001; exec. dir. Wildling Art Mus., Los Olivos, Calif., 2001—. Instr. continuing edn. Santa Barbara City Coll., 1973—86, 2002—. Contbr. essays to art catalogues. Bd. dirs., chmn. Met. Transit Dist., Santa Barbara, 1978—80; commr. Santa Barbara City Planning Commn., 1975—77; founding pres. Santa Barbara Contemporary Arts Forum, 1976—78. Recipient Disting. Conn. Citizen's award, U. Conn. Alumni Assn., 1994; fellow Kellogg Found., Smithsonian Inst., 1985. Mem.: New Eng. Mus. Assn. (v.p. 1993—95), Coll. Art Assn., Am. Assn. Mus. (treas. edn. com. 1986—88, regional rep. edn. com. 1982—86), Phi Beta Kappa. Office: Wildling Art Mus PO Box 907 2329 Jonata St Los Olivos CA 93441 Office Phone: 805-688-1082, 805-688-1082. E-mail: Penny@wildlingmuseum.org.

KNOWLES, JAMES KENYON, applied mathematician, educator; b. Cleve., Apr. 14, 1931; s. Newton Talbot and Allyan (Gray) K.; m. Jacqueline De Bolt, Nov. 26, 1952; children: John Kenyon, Jeffrey Gray, James Talbot. SB in Math., MIT, 1952, PhD, 1957; DSc (hon.), Nat. U. Ireland, 1985. Instr. math. MIT, Cambridge, 1957-58; asst. prof. applied mechanics Calif. Inst. Tech., Pasadena, 1958-61, assoc. prof., 1961-65, prof. applied mechanics, 1965—, William R. Kenan Jr. prof., 1991—, William R. Kenan Jr. prof. emeritus, 1996—. Vis. prof. MIT, 1993-94; cons. in field. Contbr. articles to profl. jours. Recipient Eringen medal, Soc. Engring. Sci., 1991, Goodwin medal, MIT, 1955. Fellow: AAAS, ASME (Koiter medal 2002), Am. Acad. Mechanics. Office: Calif Inst Tech Divsn Engring & Applied Sci 104-44 1201 E California Pasadena CA 91125-0001 Office Phone: 626-395-4135. Business E-Mail: knowles@caltech.edu.

KNOWLES, MARIE L., transportation executive; Sr. fin. analyst Arco Transp. Co., Long Beach, Calif., 1972-1986; asst. treas. for banking, 1986-1988; v.p. of fin., planning and control ARCO Internat. Oil and Gas Co., 1988-90; v.p. and controller ARCO, 1990-93; sr. v.p. and pres. ARCO Transp. Co., 1993-96, exec. v.p., CFO LA, 1996—. Office: Atlantic Richfield 4 Centerpointe Dr La Palma CA 90623-2502

KNOWLES, TONY (ANTHONY CARROLL KNOWLES), former governor; b. Tulsa, Jan. 1, 1943; m. Susan Morris, 1968; children: Devon, Lucas, Sara. BA in Econs., Yale U., 1968. Co-owner Downtown Deli, Anchorage, 1969—; mayor Municipality of Anchorage, 1981-87; gov. State of Alaska, 1994—2002. Mem., bd. dirs. Anchorage Conv. & Visitors Bur., 1992-93, Anchorage C. of C., 1992-94; Dem. candidate for Alaska US Senate seat, 2004. Mem. citizen's com. to develop comprehensive plan for growth and devel., Anchorage, 1972; mem. Borough Assembly, Anchorage, 1975—79. With 82d Airborne US Army, 1961—65, Vietnam. Recipient Silver Medal of Merit, VFW, 2001; named Child Advocate of the Yr., Child Welfare League Am., 1999. Democrat.

KNOWLES, WILLIAM LEROY (BILL KNOWLES), television news producer, journalism educator; b. LA, June 23, 1935; s. Leroy Edwin and Thelma Mabel (Armstrong) K.; children from previous marriage: Frank, Irene, Daniel, Joseph, Ted; m. Sharon Weaver, Dec. 28, 1990. BA in Journalism, San Jose State Coll., 1959; postgrad., U. So. Calif., 1962—63. Reporter, photographer, prodr. KSL-TV, Salt Lake City, 1963-65; prodr., editor, writer WLS-TV, Chgo., 1965-70; news writer ABC News, Washington, 1970-71, assoc. prodr., 1971-75, ops. prodr., 1975-77, So. bur. chief Atlanta, 1977-81, Washington bur. chief, 1981-82, West Coast bur. chief, 1982-85; prof. U. Mont., Missoula, 1986—2006, prof. emeritus, 2006—; jazz writer and historian; chair radio-TV dept. U. Mont., 2000—03. Advisor U. Mont. Student Documentary Unit; chair faculty senate, 2003-04; lectr. in field. Served with U.S. Army, 1959-62. Decorated Commendation medal; Gannett fellow Ind. U., 1987; Media Mgmt. fellow Poynter Inst. Media Studies, 1988; recipient Fulbright scholar, Jordon, 2007—08. Mem. Assn. for Edn. in Journalism (head radio-TV divsn. 1995-96). Office Phone: 406-544-6673. Business E-Mail: bill.knowles@umontana.edu.

KNOX, VENERRIA L., transportation executive; BS in Journalism, Northwestern U., 1978; M in Adminstrn., Willamette U., 1980. Asst. to dep. treas. Treasury Dept. State of Oreg., Salem, 1979-80; fin. analyst Pacific Power, Portland, Oreg., 1980-83; fin. officer Security Pacific Bank, Seattle, 1983-85; legis. analyst City of Seattle, 1985-87, mgr. fin. and govt. ops., 1987-91, dep. dir., program support divsn. dir. Dept. Housing and Human Svcs., 1991-93, dir. Dept. Housing and Human Svcs., 1994-99, dir. human svcs. dept., 1999—2003; dir. citywide outreach Seattle Monorail Project, 2003—. Mem. Leadership Tomorrow, 2003—04. Mem. Nat. Cmty. Devel. Assn., Nat. Forum Black Pub. Adminstrs. Office: Seattle Monorail Project 1904 3d Ave Ste 105 Seattle WA 98101 Office Phone: 206-382-1200. E-mail: ven@elevated.org.

KNUDSON, PETER C., state legislator; b. Brigham City, Utah, Oct. 26, 1937; m to Georgianna; children: four. City councilman, Bingham City, 74-78; mayor 78-90; chairman, State Job Training Coordr Coun, 92-94; Utah State Representative, District 2, 1995-98, member, Transportation Standing & Transportation & Environ Quality Appropraitions Committees, formerly, vice chairman, Busn Labor & Econ Develop Standing Committee, formerly, Utah House Representative; Utah State Senator, District 24, 1999-2002; Utah State Senator, District 17, 2003-, Majority Leader, currently, member Health & Human Serv Committee, currently, Workforce Serv and Community Committee, currently, Econ Develop Committee, currently, co-chmn, Ethics Committee, currently, Utah State Senate.Orthodontist, currently. Most Outstanding Elected Public Official, Utah League Cities & Towns. America Association Orthodontists; America Dental Association; Pierre Fauchard Acad; Utah Dental Association; Utah Association Orthodontists. Republican. Mailing: 1209 Michelle Dr Brigham City UT 84302 Home Phone: 435-723-2035; Office Phone: 435-723-6366. Office Fax: 435-723-6371. E-mail: pknudson@utahsenate.org.

KNUTH, DONALD ERVIN, computer sciences educator; b. Milw., Jan. 10, 1938; s. Ervin Henry and Louise Marie (Bohning) Knuth; m. Nancy Jill Carter, June 24, 1961; children: John Martin, Jennifer Sierra. BS summa cum laude, Case Inst. Tech., 1960, MS, 1960; PhD in Math., Calif. Inst. Tech., 1963; DSc (hon.), Case Western Res. U., 1980, Luther Coll., Decorah, Iowa, 1985, Lawrence U., 1985, Muhlenberg Coll., 1986, U. Pa., 1986, U. Rochester, 1986, U. Paris-Sud, Orsay, 1986, SUNY, Stony Brook, 1987, Oxford U., Eng., 1988, Brown U., 1988, Valparaiso U., 1988, Grinnell Coll., 1989, Dartmouth Coll., 1990, Concordia U., Montréal, 1991, Adelphi U., 1993, Masaryk U., Brno, 1996, Duke U., 1998, St. Andrews U., 1998, Williams Coll., 2000, U. Tubingen, 2001, Athens U. Econ., 2001, U. Oslo, 2002, Harvard U., 2003, U. Thessaloniki, 2003, U. Antwerp, 2003, U. Montréal, 2004, Armenian Acad. Sci., 2005, Eth Zurich, 2005, Republic of Armenia Nat. Acad. Scis., 2006; DSc, U. Bordeaux, 2007; D Tech., Royal Inst. Tech., Stockholm, 1991; Pochetnogo Doktora, St. Petersburg U., Russia, 1992; DLitt (hon.), U. Waterloo, 2000, Concordia U., Wis., 2006. Asst. prof., math. Calif. Inst. Tech., Pasadena, Calif., 1963—66, assoc. prof., math., 1966—68; prof., computer sci. Stanford U., Calif., 1968—77, prof., elec. engring. (by courtesy) Calif., 1977—, Fletcher Jones prof., computer sci. Calif., 1977—89, prof., Art of Computer Programming Calif., 1990—92, prof., Art of Computer Programming, emeritus Calif., 1993—. Cons. Burroughs Corp., Pasadena, Calif., 1960—68; staff mathematician Inst. for Def. Analysis-Comm. Rsch. Divsn., 1968—69; guest prof., math. U. Oslo, 1972—73; vis. prof., computer sci. U. Oxford, 2002—06; invited lectr. in field. Author: The Art of Computer Programming, 1968 (Steele prize, 1987), Computers and Typesetting, 1986, 3:16 Bible Texts Illuminated, and several others; mem. editl. bd. Jour. Computer and System Sciences, 1969—, Jour. Algorithms, 1979—2004, Software-Practice and Experience, 1979—, Applied Mathematics Letters, 1987—, Combinatorica, 1985—, Discrete and Computational Geometry, 1986—, Jour. Computer Sci. and Tech., 1989—, Mathematica Jour., 1990—, Random Structures & Algorithms, 1990—, Electronic Jour. Combinators, 1994—, Jour. Exptl. Algorithmics, 1996—, Jour. Graph Algorithms and Applications, 1996—, Japan Jour. Indsl. and Applied Math., 1997—, Theory of Computing, 2004—. Recipient Nat. medal of Sci., Pres. James Carter, 1979, Disting. Alumni award, Calif. Inst. Tech., 1978, Priestley award, Dickinson Coll., 1981, Golden Plate award, Am. Acad. Achievement, 1985, Franklin medal, 1988, J.D. Warnier prize, 1989, Gold Medal award, Case Alumni Assn., 1990, Adelsköld medal, Swedish Acad. Sci., 1994, Harvey prize, Israel Inst. Tech., 1995, Kyoto prize, Inamori Found., 1996, Fellow award, Computer History Mus., 1998; fellow, Guggenheim Found., 1972—73; Woodrow Wilson Fellow, 1960, NSF Fellow, 1960, Hon. Fellow, Magdalen Coll., Oxford U., 2005—. Fellow: Brit. Computer Soc. (Disting. Fellow 1980), Assn. for Computing Machinery (chmn., subcommittee on ALGOL 1963—64, nat. lectr. 1966—67, vis. scientist 1966—67, mem. gen. tech. achievement awards subcommittee 1975—79, mem. editl. bd. Tranactions on Algorithms 2004—, Grace Murray Hopper award 1971, Alan M. Turing award 1974, Computer Sci. Edn. award 1986, Software Sys. award 1986), Am. Acad. Arts and Scis., The Computer Mus.; mem.: NAS, IEEE (hon.; mem. editl. bd., Transactions on Software Engring. 1975—79, W. Wallace McDowell award 1980, Computer Pioneer award 1982, John von Neumann medal 1995), Soc. Indsl. and Applied Math., Math. Assn. Am. (Lester R. Ford award 1975, 1993), French Acad. Sciences (assoc.), Am. Math. Soc. (mem. com. on composition tech. 1978—81, Steele prize for Expository Writing 1986), Acad. Sci. (fgn. assoc. Paris, Oslo, Munich, Moscow), NAE, Royal Soc. London (fgn. mem. 2003), Am. Guild Organists. Lutheran. Achievements include patents in field. Avocations: playing pipe organ, reading, writing. Office: Stanford Univ Computer Scis Dept Gates Bldg 4B Stanford CA 94305-9045

KNUTH, ELDON LUVERNE, engineering educator; b. Luana, Iowa, May 10, 1925; s. Alvin W. and Amanda M. (Becker) K.; m. Marie O. Parrat, Sept. 10, 1954 (div. 1973); children: Stephen B., Dale L., Margot O., Lynette M.; m. Margaret I. Nicholson, Dec. 30, 1973. BS, Purdue U., 1949, MS, 1950; PhD (Guggenheim fellow), Calif. Inst. Tech., 1953. Aerothermodynamics group leader Aerophysics Devel. Corp., 1953-56; asso. research engr. dept. engring. UCLA, 1956-59, asso. prof. engring., 1960-65, prof. engring. and applied sci., 1965-91, prof. emeritus, 1991—, head chem., nuclear thermal div. dept. engring., 1963-65, chmn. energy kinetics dept., 1969-75, head molecular-beam lab., 1961-88. Gen. chmn. Heat Transfer and Fluid Mechanics Inst., 1959; vis. scientist, von Humboldt fellow Max-Planck Inst. für Strömungsforschung, Göttingen, Fed. Republic Germany, 1975-76; mem. Internat. Adv. Com. Internat. Symposium Rarefied Gas Dynamics., 2000—. Author: Introduction to Statistical Thermodynamics, 1966, Who Wrote Those Letters?, 2005, Auf den Spuren von Jürnjakob Swehn, 2005; also numerous articles; patentee radial-flow molecular pump Served with AUS, 1943-45. Recipient Fritz Reuter medal, Landsmannschaft, Mecklenburg, 2002, Johannes-Gillholf Lit. prize, Johannes-Gillhoff Soc., Mecklenburg, 2009. Mem. AIAA, Am. Soc. Engring. Edn., Am. Inst. Chem. Engrs., Combustion Inst., Soc. Engring. Sci., AAAS, Am. Phys. Soc., Am. Vacuum Soc., Sigma Xi, Tau Beta Pi, Gamma Alpha Rho, Pi Tau Sigma, Sigma Delta Chi, Pi Kappa Phi. Clubs: Gimlet (Lafayette, Ind.). Home: 18085 Boris Dr Encino CA 91316-4350

KNUTZEN, MARTHA LORRAINE, lawyer; b. Bellingham, Wash., Aug. 28, 1956; BA in Polit. Sci., Scripps Coll., 1978; MA in Polit. Sci. Practical Politics, U. San Francisco, 1981, JD, 1981. Bar: Calif. 1981. Lawyer, mgr. legal computer support svcs., San Francisco, 1981—. Mem. San Francisco Citizens' Adv. Com. on Elections, 1994-96; 3d vice chair Dem. Party, San Francisco, 1996-2000, treas., 1996-2000; mem. Resolution Com., Calif. Dem. Party, 2001—2005; chair San Francisco Human Rights Commn., 1996-2005; cmty. organizer. Recipient Civil Rights Leadership award Calif. Assn. Human Rights Commn., 1996. Office: San Francisco Dist Atty 850 Bryant # 322 San Francisco CA 94103 Home: Apt 44 601 Van Ness Ave San Francisco CA 94102-3263

KOBAYASHI, ALBERT SATOSHI, mechanical engineering educator; b. Chgo., Dec. 9, 1924; s. Toshiyuki and Taka (Torii) K.; m. Elizabeth Midori Oba, Sept. 24, 1953; children: Dori Kobayashi Ogami, Tina, Laura. BS in Engring., U. Tokyo, 1947; MSME, U. Wash., 1952; PhD, Ill. Inst. Tech., 1958. Position II engr. Konishiroku Photo Industry, Tokyo, 1947-50; design engr. Ill. Tools Works, Chgo., 1953-55; rsch. engr. Armour Rsch. Found., Ill. Inst. Tech., Chgo., 1955-58; from asst. prof. to assoc. prof. dept. mech. engring. U. Wash., Seattle, 1958-64, prof., 1964-97, Boeing Pennell prof. structural mechanics, 1988-95, prof. emeritus, 1997—. Coll. faculty assoc.The Boeing Co. Seattle, 1958—76; cons. Math. Sci. Northwest, Bellevue, Wash., 1962—82, UN Devel. Program, NY, 1984; vis. scholar U. Tokyo, 1969, 77; program dir. mech., structural and materials engring. divsn. NSF, 1987—88, expert, structural and materials program, 2005. Contbr. over 490 papers to Fracture Mechanics, Exptl. Mechanics Biomechanics and numerical analysis. Decorated Order of Rising Sun, gold rays with neck ribbons Emperor of Japan, 1997; recipient F. G. Tatnall award Soc. Exptl. Stress Analysis, 1973, B.J. Lazan award, 1981, R. E. Peterson award, 1983, William Murray Lecture medal, 1983, Burlington Resources Found. Faculty Achievement award, 1992, M. M. Frocht award, 1995, G. E. Sr. Rsch. award Am. Soc. Engring. Edn., 1995, Disting. Alumni award Univ. Student Club, U. Wash., 1997; named to Mech. Engring. Hall of Fame, U. Wash., 2006. Fellow ASME (Daniel C. Drucker medal 2007), Soc. Exptl. Mechanics (hon. life mem., pres. 1989-90), Internat. Congress on Fracture (hon.). Home: 15420 62nd Pl NE Kenmore WA 98028-4312 Office: U Wash Dept Mech Engring Box 352600 Seattle WA 98195-2600 Home Phone: 425-488-1869; Office Phone: 206-543-5488. Business E-Mail: ask@u.washington.edu.

KOBLIK, STEVEN S., academic administrator; Pres. Reed Coll., Portland, Oreg., 1992—2001, The Huntington Library, Art Collections, and Botanical Gardens, San Marino, Calif., 2002—. Office: Reed Coll Office Pres 3203 SE Woodstock Blvd Portland OR 97202-8199

KOCH, MITCHELL L., computer software company executive; married; 3 children. BA in Acct., Calif. State U. With Arthur Anderson & Co.; various positions including pres. Buena Vista Home Entertainment; corp. v.p. worldwide retail sales & mktg. for home & retail divsn. Microsoft Corp., Redmond, Wash., 2000—04, corp. v.p. global retail sales and mktg. group, entertainment and devices divsn., 2004—. Office: Microsoft Corp One Microsoft Way Redmond WA 98052-6399

KOCH, RICHARD, retired pediatrician, educator; b. ND, Nov. 24, 1921; s. Valentine and Barbara (Fischer) K.; m. Kathryn Jean Holt, Oct. 2, 1943; children: Jill, Thomas, Christine, Martin, Leslie. BA, U. Calif., Berkeley, 1958; MD, U. Rochester, 1951. Mem. staff Children's Hosp., LA, 1952—75, 1977—2003, dir. child devel. divsn., 1955-75; dep. dir. Calif. Dept. Health, 1975-76; prof. pediat. U. So. Calif., 1955—75, 1977—; dir. Phenylketonuria Collaborative Study, 1966-82; med. dir. Spastic Children's Found., LA, 1980-85. Mem. Project Hope, Trujillo, Peru, 1970; dir. Regional Ctr. for Developmentally Disabled at Children's Hosp., L.A., 1966-75; mem. rsch. adv. bd. Nat. Assn. Retarded Citizens, 1974-76; mem. Gov.'s Coun. on Devel. Disabilities, 1981-83; bd. dirs. Down's Syndrome Congress, 1974-76; prin. investigator Maternal Phenylketonuria Project Nat. Inst. Child Health and Human Devel., Washington, 1985-2003; mem. forensic assessment team South Ctrl. Regional Ctr. for Developmental Disabilities, 1999—. Author: (with James Dobson) The Mentally Retarded Child and his Family, 1971, (with Kathryn J. Koch) Understanding the Mentally Retarded Child, 1974, (with Felix de la Cruz) Downs Syndrome, 1975; contbr. articles to profl. jours. Recipient Albert L. Anderson award for outstanding health care profl., 1997, Homer Smith Rsch. award, 1998; Carrie D. Jones scholar, U. Calif., Berkeley, 1941. Mem. Am. Assn. on Mental Deficiency (pres. 1968-69), Am. Acad. Pediat., Soc. for Study Inborn Errors Metabolism, Soc. Inborn Metabolic Disorders, Sierra Club (treas. Mineral King task force 1972). Achievements include research in mental retardation, phenylketonuria and relation to pediatrics. Home: 2125 Ames St Los Angeles CA 90027-2902 Office: Children's Hosp of LA Divsn Med Genetics 4650 Sunset Blvd Los Angeles CA 90027-6062 Home Phone: 323-664-6902. Personal E-mail: rkoch8@earthlink.net.

KODA-KIMBLE, MARY ANNE, pharmacologist, educator, dean; PharmD, U. Calif., San Francisco, 1969. Lic. pharmacist Calif., 1969, cert. diabetes educator. Faculty U. Calif., San Francisco, 1970—, prof., dean Sch. Pharmacy, Thomas J. Long Endowed chair in Chain Pharmacy Practice. Mem. nonprescription drugs adv. com. FDA; mem. Calif. State Bd. of Pharmacy; lectr. and cons. in field. Co-editor (with others): Applied Therapeutics for Clinical Pharmacists, 1975, 1978, Basic Clinical Pharmacokinetics, 1980, Applied Therapeutics: Clinical Use of Drugs, 1988, Basic Clinical Pharmacokinetics, 1988, Handbook of Applied Therapeutics, 3d edit., 1996; contbr. numerous articles to profl. jours., chpts. to books.; editl. bd. Internat. Jour. Clin. Pharmacology, 1979—82, Drug Interactions Newsletter and Update, 1981, Diabetes Forecast, 1986—89, referee various jours. Numerous others. Recipient Disting. Alumna award, U. Calif.-San Francisco; named to Hall of Fame, CPhA. Mem.: Nat. Acad. of Practice in Pharmacy (founding mem., Disting. Practitioner), Am. Coun. on Pharm. Edn., Am. Coll. Clin. Pharmacy (bd. dirs., Edn. award), Calif. Soc. Health-System Pharmacists (bd. dirs., Pharmacist of the Yr.), Am. Pharm. Assn. (task force on edn.), Am. Assn. Colls. of Pharmacy (pres., commn. to implement change in pharm. edn.), Inst. of Medicine of NAS. Office: Sch Pharmacy UCSF Box 0622 San Francisco CA 94143-0622

KOECHNER, DAVID, actor; b. Tipton, Mass., Aug. 24, 1962; m. Leigh Koechner, June 27, 1998; 4 children. Degree in Polit. Sci., U. Mo. Performer Northwest Second City Touring Co., ImprovOlympic, Chgo. Actor: (films) It's Now...or Never!, 1995, Wag the Dog, 1997, Dirty Work, 1998, Dill Scallion, 1999, Austin Powers: The Spy Who Shagged Me, 1999, Man on the Moon, 1999, Dropping Out, 2000, Whatever It Takes, 2000, Out Cold, 2000, Run Ronnie Run, 2002, Life Without Dick, 2002, The Third Wheel, 2002, American Girl, 2002, Waking Up in Reno, 2002, Soul Mates, 2003, A Guy Thing, 2003, My Boss's Daughter, 2003, Anchorman: The Legend of Ron Burgundy, 2004, Wake Up, Ron Burgundy: The Lost Movie, 2004, Waiting, 2005, The Dukes of Hazzard, 2005, The 40 Year Old Virgin, 2005, Thank You for Smoking, 2005, (voice) Here Comes Peter Cottontail: The Movie, 2005, Daltry Calhoun, 2005, Yours, Mine and Ours, 2005, (voice) Farce if the Penguins, 2006, Larry the Cable Guy: Health Inspector, 2006, Talladega Nights: The Ballad of Ricky Bobby, 2006, (voice) Barnyard, 2006, Snakes on a Plane, 2006, Let's Go to Prison, 2006, Unaccompanied Minors, 2006, Reno 911!: Miami, 2007, Careless, 2007, Balls of Fury, 2007, The Brothers Solomon, 2007, The Comebacks, 2007, Semi-Pro, 2008, Drillbit Taylor, 2008, Get Smart, 2008; (TV series) Saturday Night Live, 1995—96, Late World with Zach, 2002, Still Standing, 2002—03, Reno 911!, 2003—06, The Office, 2005—07, (TV specials) Comedy Central Laughs for Life Telethon, 2003, Last Laugh '05, 2005; (TV films) Why Blitt?, 2004; actor, exec. prodr., writer (TV series) The Naked Trucker and T-Bones Show, 2007. Office: c/o William Morris Agy 1 William Morris Pl Beverly Hills CA 90212

KOEGEN, ROY JEROME, lawyer; b. Spokane, Wash., Mar. 1, 1949; s. Frank J. and Jeanne (Bardsley) K.; m. Ann Martinelli, Aug. 28, 1970; children: Jennifer, Christopher. BA, Gonzaga U., 1971; JD, U. Calif., San Francisco, 1974. Bar: Calif. 1974, Wash. 1979, U.S. Supreme Ct. 1982. Assoc. Wilson, Jones, Morton & Lynch, San Mateo, Calif., 1974-78, Blair & Koegen, Spokane, 1978-80; ptnr. Preston, Thorgrimson, Ellis & Holman, Spokane, 1980-90, Perkins Coie LLP, Seattle, Spokane, 1990—2002, Lukins & Annis, PS, Spokane, 2002—05, Koegen Edwards LLP, 2005—. Author: Washington Municipal Financing Deskbook, 1992. Chmn. exec. com. Cmty. Alcohol Ctr., Spokane, 1982—84, Century II Park Dist., Spokane, 1982—84; bd. dirs. Nature Conservancy, Wash. Nat. Pk. Found. Mem. ABA, Wash. Bar Assn., Calif. Bar Assn., Nat. Assn. Bond Lawyers, The Nature Conservancy (bd. dirs.). Roman Catholic. Office: Koegen Edwards LLP Bank of America Financial Ctr 601 W Riverside Ave Ste 1700 Spokane WA 99201 Office Phone: 509-747-4040. Business E-Mail: roy@koegenedwards.com.

KOEHL, MIMI R., integrative biology professor; BA in Biology magna cum laude, Gettysburg Coll.; PhD in Zoology, Duke U. Postdoctoral fellow Friday Harbor Lab., U. Wash., U. York, England; Virginia G. and Robert E. Gill chair, natural history U. Calif., Berkeley, prof., integrative biology. Contbr. articles to profl. jours. Recipient Borelli award, Am. Soc. Biomechanics, Presdl. Young Investigator award, Young Alumni Achievement award, Gettysburg Coll., Disting. Alumni award; Phi Beta Kappa Vis. Scholar, John Simon Guggenheim Meml. Found. Fellowship, MacArthur Found. Fellowship award. Fellow: Calif. Acad. Sci.; mem.: Am. Acad. Arts & Sciences, NAS. Office: U Calif Berkeley Dept Integrative Biology Office 4116VLSB 3060 Valley Life Sciences Bldg #3140 Berkeley CA 94720-3140 Office Phone: 510-642-8103, 510-643-9048 (lab). Office Fax: 510-643-6264. Business E-Mail: cnidaria@berkeley.edu.

KOEHLER, REGINALD STAFFORD, III, lawyer; b. Bellevue, Pa., Dec. 29, 1932; s. Reginald S. and Esther (Hawken) K.; m. Ann Ellsworth Rowland, June 15, 1956; children: Victoria Elizabeth Clark, Cynthia Rowland, Robert Steven. BA, Yale U., 1956; JD, Harvard U., 1959. Bar: N.Y. 1960, Calif., Fla., D.C. 1979, Wash. 1984, Oreg. 1985, Alaska 1985, U.S. Supreme Ct. 1973. Assoc. Davis Polk & Wardwell, NYC, 1959-68; ptnr. Donovan Leisure Newton & Irvine, NYC, 1968-84, Perkins Coie, Seattle, 1984—. Author: The Planning and Administration of a Large Estate. Fellow Am. Coll. Trust and Estate Counsel; mem. N.Y. State Bar Assn., Calif. Bar Assn., D.C. Bar Assn., Wash. Bar Assn., Oreg. Bar Assn., Alaska Bar Assn., Chi Psi. Episcopalian. Office: Perkins Coie 1201 3rd Ave Fl 48 Seattle WA 98101-3029 Office Phone: 206-359-8632. Business E-Mail: rkoehler@perkinscoie.com.

KOEPP, DAVID, screenwriter; Grad., UCLA. Screenwriter: (with Martin Donovan) Apartment Zero, 1989 (also prodr.), Bad Influence, 1990, (with Daniel Petrie Jr.) Toy Soldiers, 1991, (with Donovan) Death Becomes Her, 1992, (with Michael Crichton) Jurassic Park, 1993, Carlito's Way, 1993, (with Stephen Koepp) The Paper, 1994 (also co-prodr.), The Shadow, 1994, Mission: Impossible, 1996, The Trigger Effect, 1996 (also dir.), The Lost World: Jurassic Park, 1997, Snake Eyes, 1998, Stir of Echoes, 1999 (also dir.), Panic Room, 2002 (also prodr.), Spider-Man, 2002, Secret Window, 2004, War of the Worlds, 2005, Indiana Jones and the Kingdom of the Crystal Skull, 2008, Ghost Town, 2008, Angels & Demons, 2009, (TV films) Hack, 2002 (also exec. prodr.), (TV series) Hack, 2002-04 (also exec. prodr.). exec. prodr., dir. (TV films) Suspense, 2003. Office: c/o Creative Artists Agy 2000 Ave of the Stars Los Angeles CA 90067

KOEPPEL, JOHN A., lawyer; b. Jersey City, Aug. 9, 1947; s. A.J. and Florence (McDonald) K.; m. Susan Lynn Rothstein, Nov. 12, 1972; children: Adam, Leah. BA in Govt. cum laude, U. Notre Dame, 1969; MA in Internat. Law, Tufts U., 1970; JD, U. Calif., San Francisco, 1976. Bar: Calif. 1976, D.C. 1980, U.S. Dist. Ct. (no. dist.) Calif. 1976, U.S. Supreme Ct. 1980. Assoc. Barfield, Barfield, Dryden

& Ruane, San Francisco, 1976-80; from assoc. to shareholder Ropers, Majeski, Kohn & Bentley, San Francisco, 1980—, resident dir., 1992-95, 97-99; mediator San Francisco Superior Ct., 1993—, US Dist. Ct., 2006—. Arbitrator San Francisco Superior Ct., 1979—; legal counsel San Francisco Jaycees, 1980-81, Friends of the Americas, San Francisco, 1982-84; bd. dirs. ST. Francis Homes Assn., 1985-88; instr. Hastings Coll. Advocacy, San Francisco, 1988-91; lectr. U. Calif., San Francisco, 1990-95; sec. San Francisco Casualty Claims Assn., 1993-95; bd. dirs. and legal counsel Or Shalom, 2002—05; bd. dirs. Ropers Majeski Kohn & Bentley, 1992-99, 2003—. Active Youth Sports Coaching, 1990—2000; bd. dirs. San Francisco Sch., 1998—2000, San Francisco Food Bank, 2005—. Mem. Nat. Bd. Trial Advocacy, Calif. State Bar (certificate of recognition for pro bono legal work, 1989), D.C. Bar, San Francisco Bar Assn. (Outstanding Vol. 2004, 05). Avocations: running, skiing, hiking, rowing, travel. Office: Ropers Majeski Kohn & Bentley 201 Spear St Ste 1000 San Francisco CA 94105 Home Phone: 415-664-8453; Office Phone: 415-543-4800. Business E-Mail: jkoeppel@ropers.com.

KOERBER, ERICA, photographer; b. 1970; Owner, chief photographer Evon Photography; ops. mgr. Ventana Rsch. Corp. Involved with Susan G. Komen Race for the Cure, Women's Found. Southern Ariz., Youth On Their Own, Brewster Ctr. Domestic Violence Services, Angel Charity for Children, Tucson Indian Ctr., Arts for All & Third St. Kids, Humane Soc. Southern Ariz., Child Protective Services. Named one of 40 Under 40, Tucson Bus. Edge, 2006. Office: Ventana Research Corporation 2702 S4th Ave Tucson AZ 85713 Office Phone: 520-882-8772. Office Fax: 520-882-8762.

KOESTEL, MARK ALFRED, geologist, photographer; b. Cleve., Jan. 1, 1951; s. Alfred and Lucille (Kemeny) Koestel; life ptnr. Jennifer E. Budzak; children: Jennifer Rose, Bonnie Leigh. BS, U. Ariz., 1978. Registered profl. geologist Wyo., Alaska, Ind.; registered environ. assessor, Calif. Sr. geologist Union Oil Co. of Calif., Tucson and Denver, 1978-86; mgr. geology Harmsworth Assocs., Laguna Hills, Calif., 1986-88; sr. project mgr. Applied GeoSystems, Irvine, Calif., 1988-90; cons. geologist, photographer Adventures in Geology/Outdoor Images, Chino, Calif., 1990—. Contbr. articles and photographs to profl. jours. and mags. N.Mex. state rep. Minerals Exploration Coalition, Tucson and Denver, 1982. Sci. Found. scholarship No. Ariz. U., 1969, Acad. Achievement scholarship, 1970, Disting. Scholastic Achievement scholarship, 1971. Mem. Am. Inst. of Profl. Geologists (cert.), Soc. of Mining Engrs., Aircraft Owners and Pilots Assn., Geol. Soc. of Am., Nat. Geographic Soc. Avocations: sporting clays, backpacking, travel, tennis, flying. Home and Office: 13214 Breton Ave Chino CA 91710-5952 Office Phone: 909-629-8417. Personal E-mail: makjeb@yahoo.com.

KOFFEL, MARTIN M., engineering company executive; b. 1939; MS, MBA, Stanford U., 1971. With Homestake Mining Co., 1974-81, Cooper Labs., Inc., 1981-84, Gilette Corp., 1984-86, Cooper Vision Inc., 1986-88; chmn. bd., pres., CEO URS Corp., San Francisco, 1989—. Bd. dir. McKesson Corp., San Francisco, 2000—02, James Hardie Industries N.V., Mission Viego, Calif., 2001—02. Adv. coun. McLaren Sch. Bus., U. San Francisco; trustee Am. Enterprise Inst. Pub. Policy, Washington. Office: URS Corp 600 Montgomery St 25th Fl San Francisco CA 94111-2727 Office Phone: 415-774-2700. Office Fax: 415-398-1905.

KOGA, ROKUTARO (ROCKY KOGA), physicist; b. Nagoya, Japan, Aug. 18, 1942; came to U.S., 1961, naturalized, 1966; s. Toyoki and Emiko (Shinra) K.; m. Cordula Rosow, May 5, 1981; children: Evan A., Nicole A. BA, U. Calif., Berkeley, 1966; PhD, U. Calif., Riverside, 1974. Rsch. fellow U. Calif., Riverside, 1974-75; rsch. physicist Case Western Res. U., Cleve., 1975-79, asst. prof., 1979-81; physicist Aerospace Corp., LA, 1981-96, sr. scientist, 1996-2000, dsting. scientist, 2000—. Contbr. articles to profl. confs. Mem. IEEE, Am. Phys. Soc., Am. Geophys. Union, N.Y. Acad. Scis., Sigma Xi. Achievements include research on gamma-ray astronomy, solar neutron observation, space sciences, charged particles in space and the effect of cosmic rays on microcircuits in space. Office: Aerospace Corp Space Scis Lab Los Angeles CA 90009 Business E-Mail: rocky.koga@aero.org.

KOH, STEVE Y., lawyer; b. Seattle, Aug. 20, 1967; BBA magna cum laude, U. Wash., 1989; JD, Yale U., 1992. Bar: Wash., US Supreme Ct., US Ct. Appeals (5th Cir.), US Ct. Appeals (9th Cir.), US Dist. Ct. (We. Dist.) Wash. Intern to Hon. Jose A Cabranes US Dist. Ct., (Dist. Conn.), 1990; summer assoc. Cravath Swaine & More, NY, 1991; law clk. to Hon. Patricia Wald US Ct. Appeals (DC Cir.), 1992—93; atty. US Dept. Justice, Fraud Sect., 1993—95; ptnr., mem exec. com. Perkins Coie LLP, Seattle, chmn. hiring com. Articles editor Yale Law Jour. Bd. trustees Childhaven. Named a Super Lawyer, Wash. Law& Politics; named to best lawyers under 40, Nat. Asian-Pacific ABA. Mem.: Fed. Bar Assn. (trustee), Wash. State Bar Assn., Asian Bar Assn. Office: Perkins Coie LLP Ste 4800 1201 Third Ave Seattle WA 98101-9000 Office Phone: 206-359-8530. Office Fax: 206-359-9000. Business E-Mail: skoh@perkinscoie.com.

KOHLOSS, FREDERICK HENRY, retired engineer; b. Ft. Sam Houston, Tex., Dec. 4, 1922; s. Fabius Henry and Rowena May (Smith) K.; m. Margaret Mary Grunwell, Sept. 9, 1944; children: Margaret Ralston, Charlotte Foster, Eleanor. BS in Mech. Enging., U. Md., 1943; M in Mech. Enging., U. Del., 1951; JD, George Washington U., 1949. Enging. faculty George Washington U., Washington, 1946-50; devel. and stds. engr. Dept. Def., 1950-51; chief engr. for mech. contractors Washington, 1951-54, Cleve., 1954-55, Honolulu, 1955-56; cons. engr., 1956-61; pres. Frederick H. Kohloss & Assocs., Inc., Cons. Engrs., Honolulu, 1961-91; chmn. Lincolne, Scott & Kohloss Inc, Cons. Engrs., Honolulu, 1991-97, sr. cons., 1997-2001, cons. engr., 2001—03, ret., 2003. Contbr. articles to profl. jours. Served with AUS, 1943-46. Fellow ASME, ASHRAE, Chartered Inst. Bldg. Svcs. Engrs., Instn. Engrs. Australia, Australian Inst. Refrigeration, Air Conditioning, Heating; mem. IEEE (sr.), NSPE. Home: 2500 N Rosemont Blvd #433 Tucson AZ 85712 Office Phone: 520-325-4753. E-mail: fredpeg@cox.net.

KOHL-WELLES, JEANNE E., state legislator; b. Madison, Wis., Oct. 19, 1942; m to Alex Welles; children: Randy, Brennan, Terra, Kyle & Devon. Washington State Representative, District 36, 92-94, Majority Whip, 93-94, Washington House Representative; Washington State Senator, District 36, 94-, member, Sentencing Guidelines Comn, Joint Legislature Syst Committee, Joint Legislature Audit & Review Committees, K-20 Network, currently, chairman, Higher Education Committees, 1999-2002, ranking member, Higher Education Development & rules Committee, currently, Washington State Senate; president, Nat Conf State Legislators Women's Legislature Network Bd, Center for Women Policy Studies, fellow, Foreign Policy Inst, Center Policy Alternatives, currently; executive comt, NCSC-.Public sch teacher, formerly; lectr sociology & women's studies, Univ Washington, 85-; writer, currently. Auth, Study Guide to Accompany Marriage and the Family, Mayfield Publ Co, 1990, 4th edit, 1999, 5th edit (with Kyle Jenkins), 2002, Study Guide to Accompany Intimate Relationships, Marriages and Families, Mayfield Publ Co, 1990, 4th edit, 1999, 5th edit (with Kyle Jenkins), 2002; Auth Instructor's Manual for Windows on Society, Roxbury Publ Co, 1989; Coauth (with Jane Reisman), Explorations in Social Research: Qualitative and Quantitative Applications, Roxbury Publ Co, 1994; Coauth (with John Heeren & Marylee Mason), Windows on Society, Rosbury Publ Co, 1989; Coauth (with Pamela Macdonald), Growing Up Equal, Prentice-Hall Publ Co, 1979. Flemming Fellow, Center Policy Alternatives. Bayview Manor (board member); Queen Anne Helpline; YouthCare; Rainier Inst; Seattle Monorail Proj. Democrat. Episcopalian. Mailing: State Senate 432 John A Cherberg Bldg PO Box 40436 Olympia WA 98504-0482 Address: 157 Roy St Seattle WA 98109 Fax: 360-786-7450. E-mail: Kohl_je@leg.wa.gov.

KOHN, ALAN J., zoology educator; b. New Haven, July 15, 1931; s. Curtis and Harriet M. (Jacobs) K.; m. Marian S. Adachi, Aug. 29, 1959; children: Lizabeth, Nancy, Diane, Stephen. AB. in Biology, Princeton U., 1953; PhD in Zoology, Yale U., 1957. Asst. prof. zoology Fla. State U., Tallahassee, 1958-61, U. Wash., Seattle, 1961-63, assoc. prof. zoology, 1963-67, prof., 1976-98, prof. emeritus, 1998—. Bd. dirs. Coun. Internat. Exchange Scholars, Wash., 1986-90. Author: A Chronological Taxonomy of Conus, 1758-1840, 1992, (with F.E. Perron) Life History and Biogeography: Patterns in Conus, 1994, (with D. Röckel and W. Korn) Manual of the Living Conidae, 1995, (with others) The Natural History of Enewetak Atoll, 1987; editor: (with F.W. Harrison) Microscopic Anatomy of Invertebrates, vol. 5, Mollusca I, 1994, vol. 6 Mollusca II, 1997; mem. editl. bd. Am. Zoologist, 1973-77, Am. Naturalist, 1976-78, Malacologia, 1974—, Jour. Exptl. Marine Biology and Ecology, 1981-84, Coral Reefs, 1981-87, Am. Malacological Bull., 1983—; assoc. editor Am. Zoologist, 1999—; assoc. editor Integrative and Comparative Biology, 2002-06; contbr. articles to profl. jours. Sr. postdoctoral fellow Smithsonian Inst., 1990, John Simon Guggenheim fellow, 1974-75, Nat. Rsch. Coun. fellow, 1967; numerous rsch. grants NSF, 1960-94, 2003-07. Fellow AAAS, Linnean Soc. London; mem. Internat. Soc. Reef Studies, Soc. for Integrative and Comparative Biology (treas. 1971-74, pres. 1997-98), Am. Malacol. Union (pres. 1982-83), Marine Biol. Assn. India, Marine Biol. Assn. U.K., Malacol. Soc. London, Malacol. Soc. Japan, Inst. Matacology (v.p., 2004-05, pres.-elect 2006—), Am. Microscopical Soc., Sigma Xi (pres. U. Wash. chpt. 1971-72). Home: 18300 Ridgefield Rd NW Shoreline WA 98177-3224 Office: U Wash Dept Biology Seattle WA 98195-1800 Office Phone: 206-616-4383. E-mail: kohn@u.washington.edu.

KOHN, MATTHEW J., education educator, researcher; BS, MIT, 1986; MS, Rensselaer Poly. Inst., NYC, 1989, PhD, 1991. Asst. prof. U. of S.C., Columbia, 1998—2004, assoc. prof., 2004—. Author over 50 articles in internat. jours., NSF grad. and postdoc. fellow, 1986—89, 1991—93. Mem.: SVP, AGU, GSA, MSA. Office: Boise St Univ Dept Geoscis 1910 Univ Dr Boise ID 83725

KOHN, ROGER ALAN, surgeon; b. Chgo., May 1, 1946; s. Arthur Jerome and Sylvia Lee (Karlen) K.; m. Barbara Helene, Mar. 30, 1974; children: Bradley, Allison. BA, U. Ill., Urbana, 1967; MD, Northwestern U., Evanston, Ill., 1971. Diplomate Am. Bd. Ophthalmology. Internship UCLA, 1971-72; residency Northwestern U., Chgo., 1972-75; fellowship U. Ala., Birmingham, 1975, Harvard Med. Sch., Boston, 1975-76; chmn. dept. ophthalmology Kern Med. Ctr., Bakersfield, Calif., 1978-87; asst. prof. UCLA Med. Sch., 1978-82, assoc. prof., 1982-86, prof., 1986—. Vice chmn. dept. ophthalmology Santa Barbara Cottage Hosp., Calif., 2004—05, chmn. dept. ophthalmology, 2006—, dir. Author: Textbook of Ophthalmic Plastic and Reconstructive Surgery, 1988; contbr. numerous articles to profl. jours.; author chpts. in 16 additional textbooks; patentee in field. Bd. dirs. Santa Barbara Symphony, Calif., 1990—. Capt. USAR, 1971-77. Name applied to med. syndrome Kohn-Romano Syndrome. Mem. Am. Soc. Ophthalmic Plastic and Reconstuctive Surgery (cert.), Am. Acad. Ophthalmology (Honor award 1995), Santa Barbara Ophthalmologic Soc. (pres. 1998), Pacific Coast Ophthal. Soc. (bd. dirs. 1986—, 1st v.p. 1990). Jewish. Avocations: guitar, tennis. Office: 525 E Micheltorena St Ste 201 Santa Barbara CA 93103-4212

KOHN, STEVEN M., lawyer; b. Chgo., June 19, 1942; m. Dorine Kohn; 3 children. BA, UCLA, 1965, MBA in fin., 1967; JD, U. San Francisco, 1974. Bar: Calif. 1974. With Crosby Heafey Roach & May (combined with Reed Smith in 2003), 1977—2003, chair products liability practice group; ptnr. Reed Smith LLP, Oakland, Calif., 2003—, practice group leader products liability group, 2003—07. Mem.: Def. Rsch. Inst. (mem. drug and med. device litig. steering com., chair warnings subcom.), Internat. Assn. Def. Counsel, Alameda Bar Assn., San Francisco Bar Assn. Avocations: reading, photography, endurance sports. Office: Reed Smith LLP 1999 Harrison St, Ste 2400 Oakland CA 94612-3572 Office Phone: 510-466-6727. Office Fax: 510-273-8832. Business E-Mail: skohn@reedsmith.com.

KOHN, WALTER, physicist, retired educator; b. Vienna, Mar. 9, 1923; m. Mara Schiff; children: J. Marilyn, Ingrid E.Kohn Katz, E. Rosalind. BA, U. Toronto, Ont., Can., 1945, MA, 1946, LLD (hon.), 1967; DSc (hon.), U. Paris, 1980; PhD (hon.), Hebrew U. Jerusalem, 1981; DSc (hon.), Queens U., Kingston, Can., 1986, Fed. Inst. of Tech., Zurich, 1994, U. Wuerzburg, 1995, Tech. U. Vienna, 1996, Carnegie Mellon U., 1999, Rutgers U., 2001, Oxford U., 2001, U. Sherbrooke, Canada, 2002, Free U., Berlin, 2003; DSc, Tech. U., Dresden, 2003; PhD in Physics, Harvard U., 1948; PhD (hon.), Brandeis U., 1981, Weizmann Inst., Israel, 1997, Tel Aviv U., 1999. Indsl. physicist Sutton Horsley Co., Canada, 1941—43; geophysicist Koulomzine, Que., Canada, 1944—46; instr. physics Harvard U., Cambridge, Mass., 1948—50; asst. prof. physics Carnegie Mellon U., Pitts., 1950—60, assoc. prof. physics, 1953—57; prof. physics U. Calif., San Diego, 1960—79, chmn. dept. physics, 1961—63; dir. Inst. for Theoretical Physics, U. Calif., Santa Barbara, 1979—84; prof. dept. physics U. Calif., Santa Barbara, 1984—91, prof. of physics emeritus, rsch. prof. of physics, 1991—; rsch. physicist Ctr. for Quantized Electronic Structures, U. Calif., Santa Barbara, 1991—. Vis. scholar U. Pa., U. Mich., U. Wash., U. Paris, U. Copenhagen, U. Jerusalem, Imperial Coll., London, ETH, Zurich, Switzerland; cons. Gen. Atomic, 1960—72, Westinghouse Rsch. Lab., 1953—57, Bell Telephone Labs., 1953—66, IBM, 1978; mem. or chmn. rev. coms. Brookhaven Nat. Labs., Argonne Nat. Labs., Oak Ridge Nat. Labs., Ames Lab., Tel Aviv U. (physics dept.), Brown U., Harvard U., U. Mich., Simon Frazer U., Tulane U., Reactor Divsn. NIST, Gaithersburg, Md.; chmn. S.D. divsn. Acad. Senate, 1968—69; dir. NSF Inst. Theoretical Physics U. Calif. Santa Barbara, 1979—84; mem. senate rev. com. U. Calif. Mgmt. Nat. Labs., 1986—89; adv. bd. Statewide Inst. Global Conflict and Cooperation, 1982—92; mem. bd. govs. Weizmann Inst. Sci., 1996—. Contbr. over 200 sci. articles and revs. to profl. jours. With Can. Army Inf., 1944—45. Recipient Buckley prize, 1960, Davisson-Germer prize, 1977, Nat. medal of Sci., 1988, Feenberg medal, 1991, Niels Bohr/UNESCO Gold medal, 1998, Nobel prize in Chemistry, 1998; grantee Oersted Fellow, Copenhagen, 1951—52; fellow Lehman, Harvard U., 1946, NRC, 1950—51, sr., NSF, 1958, Guggenheim, 1963, sr. postdoctoral, NSF, 1967. Fellow: AAAS, 1993, Am. Phys. Soc. (counselor-at-large 1968—72); mem.: NAS, 1969, Bavarian Acad. Scis. (corr. mem. 2003—), Royal Soc. of London (fgn. mem.), Am. Philos. Soc., Internat. Acad. Quantum Molecular Scis. Achievements include research in electron theory of solids and solid surfaces. Office: Dept Physics U Calif Santa Barbara CA 93106

KOHNEN, KERRY, hospital administrator; B. in Finance, Cal. State U., MBA. Joined Kaiser Permanente, 1975, worked for both Kaiser Found. Health Plan and the Permanente Medical Groups in three different regions, numerous positions in health care operations and finance, v.p. bus. operations and finance Denver. Mem. common issues committee Labor Mgmt. Partnership. Office: Colo Permanente Med Group 2045 Franklin St Denver CO 80205-5437

KOIDE, FRANK TAKAYUKI, electrical engineering educator; b. Honolulu, Dec. 25, 1935; s. Sukeichi and Hideko (Dai) K.; children: Julie Anne M., Cheryl Lynne K. BSEE, U. Ill., 1958; MEE, Clarkson U., Potsdam, NY, 1961; PhD, U. Iowa, 1966. Publs. engr. to electronics engr. Collins Radio Co., Cedar Rapids, Iowa, 1958-61; tchr. Cedar Rapids Adult Edn. Sch., 1960-61; lab. instr. U. Iowa Coll. Medicine, 1963-64; asst. prof. Iowa State U., 1966-69; prin. biomed. engr. Tech., Inc., San Antonio, 1968-69; mem. faculty U. Hawaii, 1969—2002, prof. elec. engring. and physiology, 1974—95, prof. emeritus, 2002—. Cons. in field. Author papers, reports in field. NIH predoctoral fellow, 1966; NASA-Am. Soc. Enging. Edn. Space systems Design Inst. fellow, 1967; NSF Digital and Analogue Electronics Inst. fellow U. Ill., 1972. Mem. IEEE. Office: U Hawaii Dept Electrical Enging 2540 Dole St Honolulu HI 96822-2303 Office Phone: 808-956-7406. Business E-Mail: koide@spectra.eng.hawaii.edu, fkoide@hawaii.edu.

KOJIMA, SHERI S., high school business educator; married; 3 children. BA, Univ. Hawaii, Manoa; M in Occupational Studies, Univ. Calif., Long Beach. Bus. tchr., 1990—; career, tech. edn. tchr. Waiakea H.S., Hilo, Hawaii, 1994—; and lead instr. Waiakea H.S. Bus. Acad. Named Secondary Educator of Yr., Hawaii Bus. Edn. Assn., 2002, Hawaii Tchr. of Yr., 2006. Office: Waiakea High Sch 155 West Kawili St Hilo HI 96720 Office Phone: 808-974-4888 ext. 245. Business E-Mail: Sheri_Kojima/WAIAKEAH/HIDOE@notes.k12.hi.us.

KOKOTOVIC, PETAR V., electrical and computer engineering educator; b. Mar. 18, 1934; Dipl.Eng., U. Belgrade, Yugoslavia, 1958, Magistar (Elec. Engring.), 1963; Candidate of Tech. Scis., Russian Acad. Scis., Moscow, 1965. Prof. elec. engring. U. Ill., Urbana, 1966-91, Grainger prof. emeritus, 1991—; prof. elec. and computer engring. U. Calif., 1991—; dir. Ctr. for Control Engring. and Computation. Recipient Quazza medal Internat. Fedn. Automatic Control, 1990, IEEE Control Sys. Field award, 1995. Fellow: IEEE (Engring. Outstanding AC Transactions Paper award 1982—83, Axelby Outstanding Paper award 1991—92, H. Bode Prize lecture 1991, James H. Mulligan, Jr. Edn. medal 2002, Richard E. Bellman Control Heritage award 2002); mem.: NAE. Office: U Calif Electrical & Comp Eng Dept Santa Barbara CA 93106

KOLAROV, KRASIMIR DOBROMIROV, computer scientist, researcher; b. Sofia, Bulgaria, Oct. 16, 1961; came to the U.S., 1987; s. Dobromir Krastev and Margarita Georgieva (Kurukafova) K.; m. Janet Louise Barba, July 4, 1990; children: April, Kathryn, Sonia, Elena. BS in Math. with honors, U. Sofia, Bulgaria, 1981, MS in Ops. Rsch. with honors, 1982, MA in English, 1982; MS in Mech. Enging., Stanford U., 1990, PhD in Mech. Enging., 1993. Rschr. Bulgarian Acad. Scis., Sofia, 1982-83; rsch. assoc., vis. prof. Inst. Mechanics and Biomechanics, Bulgarian Acad. Scis., Sofia, 1983-87; tchg. asst. Stanford (Calif.) U., 1988-92; mem. rsch. staff Interval Rsch. Corp., Palo Alto, Calif., 1992-2000; CEO, pres., founder Droplet Tech., Menlo Park, Calif., 2000—06; v.p., bus. devel. Rapport, Inc., 2006—07; founder, v.p. Bus. Devel. Holox Tech., 2008—. Vis. prof. Inst. for Civil Enging., Sofia, 1983-86; lectr. H.S. U., Sofia, 1985; reviewer Jour. Robotic Sys., Palo Alto, 1991—, others. Contbr. articles to profl. jours. Mem. IEEE, Assn. for Computing Machinery, Soc. for Indsl. and Applied Math. Avocations: bridge, travel, skiing, bicycling, flying. Office: Rapport Inc 2603 Broadway Redwood City CA 94063 E-mail: kolarov@stanfordalumni.org.

KOLB, JAMES A., science foundation director, writer; b. Berkeley, Calif., May 31, 1947; s. James DeBruler and Evelyn (Thomas) K.; m. Mary Catherine Eames; children: Thomas, Catherine Mary. BA in Zoology, U. Calif., Berkeley, 1970, BA in Biol. Sci., Ecology, 1970, MS in Wildland Resource Sci., 1972. Rsch. asst. Sagehen Creek Rsch. Sta. U. Calif., Berkeley, 1970, tchg. asst. dept. wildlife & fisheries, 1970-71, rsch. assoc. air pollution resource ctr. Berkeley, Riverside, 1971; tchr. secondary sci. Hayward (Calif.) Unified Sch. Dist., 1972-77; dir. Marine Sci. Ctr., Poulsbo, Wash., 1981-92; exec. dir. Marine Sci. Soc. Pacific Northwest, Poulsbo, 1992-95, For Sea Inst. Marine Sci., Indianola, Wash., 1995—98; dir. academic studies West Sound Academy, Poulsbo, 1998—. Project dir. Marine Sci. Project FOR SEA, Poulsbo, 1978-81; mem. Wash. State Environ. Edn. Task Force, Olympia, 1986—, Puget Sound Water Quality Authority Edn. & Pub. Involvement, Olympia, 1987-91, Marine Plastics Debris Task Force, Olympia, 1987; dir. acad. studies, West Soun Acad., Poulsbo, 1998-; cons., tchr., trainer Hood Canal Wetlands Project, Hoodsport, Wash., 1990. Author: Marine Science Activities, 1979 (NSTA award 1986), Marine Biology and Oceanography, 1979, 80, 81 (NSTA award 1985, 86), Marine Science Career Awareness, 1984 (NSTA award 1985), The Changing Sound, 1990, Puget Soundbook, 1991, Life in the Tidal Zone, 1995, The Sea Around Us, 1995, Life in the Estuary, Begining in the Watershed, 1995, Life With Pagoo, 1995, Investigating the Ocean Planet, 1995, Ocean Studies, Ocean Issues, 1995, Marine Biology and Oceanography, 1995, Marine Explorations CD-ROM, 1997, The Tuna/Dolphin Controversy CD-ROM, 1998, Marine Science Clip Art Portfolio CD-ROM, 1998, Marine Biology and Oceanography CD-ROM, 2000, Ocean Studies, Ocean Issues CD-ROM, 2001; co-author: A Salmon in the Sound, 1991, Discovering

Puget Sound, 1991, The Puget Sound Book CD-Rom, 2003, The Electronic Whale Gray Whale Migration Simulation CD-ROM, 2004, Pacific Northwest Native Plant Habitat Garden Manual, 2007. Mem. NSTA, ASCD, Internat. Reading Assn., Nat. Marine Educators Assn. (Marine Edn. award 1997), Northwest Assn. Marine Educators (past pres.), Wildlife Soc., People for Puget Sound (v.p.).

KOLB, KEITH ROBERT, architect, educator; b. Billings, Mont., Feb. 9, 1922; s. Percy Fletcher and Josephine (Randolph) K.; m. Jacqueline Cecile Jump, June 18, 1947; children: Brooks Robin, Bliss Richards. Grad. basic engring., US Army Specialized Tng., Rutgers U., 1944; BArch cum laude, U. Wash., 1947; MArch, Harvard U., 1950. Registered arch., Wash., Mont., Idaho, Calif., Oreg., Nat. Coun. Archtl. Registration Bds. Draftsman, designer various archtl. firms, Seattle, 1946-54; draftsman, designer Walter Gropius and Archs. Collaborative, Cambridge, Mass., 1950-52; prin. Keith R. Kolb, Arch., Seattle, 1954-64, Keith R. Kolb Arch. & Assocs., Seattle, 1964-66; ptnr. Decker, Kolb & Stansfield, Seattle, 1966-71, Kolb & Stansfield AIA Archs., Seattle, 1971-89; pvt. practice Keith R. Kolb FAIA Archs., Seattle, 1989—. Instr. Mont. State Coll., Bozeman, 1947-49; asst. prof. arch. U. Wash., Seattle, 1952-60, assoc. prof., 1960-82, prof., 1982-90, prof. emeritus, 1990—. Design arch. Dist. II Hdqrs. and Comm. Ctr., Wash. State Patrol, Bellevue, 1970 (Exhbn. award Seattle chpt. AIA), Hampson residence, 1970 (nat. AIA 1st honor 1973, citation Seattle chpt. AIA 1980), Acute Gen. Stevens Meml. Hosp., 1973, Redmond Pub. Libr., 1975 (jury selection Wash. coun. AIA 1980), Tolstedt residence, Helena, Mont., 1976, Herbert L. Eastlick Biol. Scis. Lab. bldg. Wash. State U., 1977, Redmond Svc. Ctr., Puget Sound Power and Light Co., 1979, Computer and Mgmt. Svcs. Ctr., Paccar Inc., 1981 (curatorial team selection Mus. History and Industry exhbn. 100th anniversary of AIA 1994), Seattle Town House, 1960 (curatorial team selection Mus. History and Industry exhbn. 100th anniversary of AIA 1994), Comm. Tower, Pacific N.W. Bell, 1981 (nat. J.F. Lincoln bronze), Forks br. Seattle 1st Nat. Bank, 1981 (commendation award Seattle chpt. AIA 1981, nat. jury selection Am. Architecture, The State of the Art in the '80's 1985, regional citation Am. Wood Coun. 1981), Reg. ops. Control Ctr. Sacramento Dist. Corps Engrs. McChord AFB, Wash., 1982, Puget Sound Blood Ctr., 1983-88, expansion vis./dining/recreation facilities Wash. State Reformatory, Monroe, 1983, Univ. Sta. P.O., U.S. Postal Svc., Seattle, 1983, Guard Towers, McNeil Island Corrections Ctr. Wash., 1983, Magnolia Queen Anne Carrier Annex, U.S. Postal Svc., Seattle, 1986, Tolstedt residence, Seattle, 1987, Maxim residence, Camano Island, Wash., 1991, Carmean residence alterations/additions, Seattle, 1995, 96, 97, 2001, 02, Susanna Burney and Bliss Kolb residence, Seattle, 2001-04; subject of articles. Pres. Laurelhurst Cmty. Club, Seattle, 1966. Served with U.S. Army, 1943-45, ETO. Decorated Bronze Star medal ETO; recipient Alpha Rho Chi medal; selected Am. Archs., Facts on File, Inc., 1989; selected Archs. at Home, Pacific NW, The Seattle Times, 2006. Fellow AIA (dir. Seattle chpt. 1970-71, sec. Seattle chpt. 1972, Wash. state coun. 1973, pres. sr. coun. Seattle chpt. 1994-96, trustee Seattle Archtl. Found. 1994-96, Citation award Seattle chpt. for a Seattle 1960 Town House, 1990, honored Living Legends Series 2002); mem. U. Wash. Archtl. Alumni Assn. (pres. 1958-59), Phi Beta Kappa, Tau Sigma Delta. Home and Office: 3379 47th Ave NE Seattle WA 98105-5326 Office Phone: 206-527-7544.

KOLB, KEN LLOYD, writer; b. Portland, Oreg., July 14, 1926; s. Frederick Von and Ella May (Bay) K.; m. Emma LaVada Sanford, June 7, 1952; children: Kevin, Lauren, Kimrie. BA in English with honors, U. Calif., Berkeley, 1950; MA with honors, San Francisco State U., 1953. Cert. jr. coll. English tchr. Freelance fiction writer various nat. mags., NYC, 1951-56; freelance screenwriter various film and TV studios, LA, 1956-81; freelance novelist Chilton, Random House, Playboy Press, NYC, 1967—. Instr. creative writing Feather River Coll., Quincy Calif., 1969; min. Universal Life Ch. Author: (teleplay) She Walks in Beauty, 1956 (Writers Guild award 1956); (film) Seventh Voyage of Sinbad, 1957, Snow Job, 1972; (novel) Getting Straight, 1967, The Couch Trip, 1970, Night Crossing, 1974; represented in permenant collections Gotlieb Archival Rsch. Ctr.; contbr. articles to profl. jours., popular mags. Foreman Plumas County Grand Jury, Quincy, 1970; chmn. Region C Criminal Justice Planning Commn., Oroville, Calif., 1975-77; film commr. Plumas County, 1986-87. Served with USNR, 1944-46. Mem. Writers Guild Am. West, Authors Guild, Plumas Ski Club (pres. 1977-78), Mensa, Phi Beta Kappa, Theta Chi. Democrat. Avocations: skiing, tennis, travel. Home and Office: PO Box 30022 Cromberg CA 96103-3022 Office Phone: 530-836-2332.

KOLBE, JIM (JAMES THOMAS KOLBE), former United States Representative, Arizona; b. Evanston, Ill., June 28, 1942; s. Walter William and Helen (Reed) K. BA in Polit. Sci., Northwestern U., 1965; MBA in Econs., Stanford U., 1967. Asst. to coordinating architect Ill. Bldg. Authority, Chgo., 1970-72; spl. asst. to Gov. Richard Ogilvie State of Ill., Chgo., 1972-73; v.p. Wood Canyon Corp., Tucson, 1973-80; mem. Ariz. State Senate from Dist. 14, 1977-83, majority whip, 1979-80; mem. U.S. Congress from 8th dist. Ariz., 1985—2007; mem. appropriations com.; chmn. appropriations subcom. treasury, postal svc., gen. gov. Trustee Embry-Riddle Aero. U., Daytona Beach, Fla.; bd. dirs. Community Food Bank, Tucson; Republican precinct committeeman, Tucson, 1974—. Served as lt. USNR, 1968-69, Vietnam. Republican. Methodist.

KOLLER, DAPHNE, computer scientist; m. Dan Avida. BS in Math. and Computer sci., Hebrew U., Jerusalem, Israel, 1985, MSc in Computer Sci., 1986; PhD in Computer Sci., Stanford U., Calif., 1993. Postdoctoral fellow, computer sci. divsn. U. Calif., Berkeley, 1993—95; asst. prof., computer sci. Stanford U., Calif., 1995—2001, assoc. prof., computer sci. Calif., 2001—. Author: published in jour. such as Games and Economic Behavior, Artificial Intelligence, Science, and Nature Genetics. Recipient Young Investigator award, Office of Naval Rsch., 1999, Presdl. Early Career award for Scientists and Engineers, 1999, Fellow Internat. Joint Conf. on Artificial Intelligence Computers and Though award, 2001; named a MacArthur Fellow, 2004; Rothschild Grad. Fellowship, 1989—90, U. Calif. President's Postdoctoral Fellowship, 1993—95, Sloan Found. Rsch. Fellowship, 1996. Avocations: reading, music, hiking, sailing, scuba diving. Office: Computer Sci Dept Rm 142 Gates Bldg 1A Stanford U 353 Serra Mall Stanford CA 94305-9010 Office Phone: 650-723-6598. Office Fax: 650-725-1449. Business E-Mail: koller@CS.stanford.edu.

KOLLER, LOREN D., veterinary medicine educator; b. Pomeroy, Wash., June 16, 1940; s. Edwin C. and Doris K. (Shelton) K.; m. Kathleen Noel Ringness, Sept. 7, 1963; children: Susan E., Michael D., Christopher L. DVM, Wash. State U., 1965; MS, U. Wis., 1969, PhD, 1971. Head diagnostic and comparative pathology Nat. Inst. Environ. Health Scis., Research Triangle Park, NC, 1971-72; rsch. assoc. dept. vet. medicine Oreg. State U., Corvallis, 1972-76, assoc. prof., 1976-78, prof., 1995—2001, dean Coll. Vet. Medicine, 1985-95; assoc. prof. dept. vet. medicine, asst. dean U. Idaho, Moscow, 1978-81, assoc. prof., assoc. dean, 1981-82, prof., assoc. dean, 1982-85; owner Loren Koller & Assocs., LLC, 2001—. Rsch. asst. dept. vet. sci. U. Wis., Madison, 1968-71; assoc. veterinarian Blue Cross Vet. Clinic, Corvallis, 1965-66; mem. Nat. Adv. Com. to Establish Acute Exposure Guidelines for Hazardous Substances Commn.; chair expert consultation panel provisional adv. levels Nat. Homeland Security Rsch. Ctr. Office Rsch. and Devel. US EPA. Contbr. articles to profl. jours., chpts. to books. Served to capt. M.C., U.S. Army, 1966-68. Grantee NIH, USDA, Dow Chem. Co., EPA, WHO, FDA, Merck Sharp & Dohme, Warner-Lambert, Pew Found. Fellow Acad. Toxicol. Sci.; mem. AVMA, NAS (mem. com. toxicology and Inst. of Medicine). Personal E-mail: kollerl@pacifier.com.

KOLODNER, RICHARD DAVID, biochemist, educator, director; b. Morristown, NJ, Apr. 3, 1951; s. Ignace Izack and Ethel (Zelnick) Kolodner; m. Karin Ann Gregory, Aug. 6, 1983 (div. May 1991); m. Jean Y.J. Wang, Dec. 2, 2004. BS, U. Calif., Irvine, 1971, PhD, 1975; MS (hon.), Harvard U., 1988. Rsch. fellow Harvard U. Med. Sch., Boston, 1975-78; from asst. prof. to prof. biochemistry Dana Farber Cancer Inst. and Harvard U. Med. Sch., Boston, 1978—97; chmn. divsn. cellular molecular biology Dana-Farber Cancer Inst., 1991-94, head x-ray crystallography lab., 1991-97, chmn. divsn. of human cancer genetics, 1995-97; prof. medicine, mem. Cancer Ctr. U. Calif. Med. Sch., San Diego, 1997—; mem. Ludwig Inst. Cancer Rsch., San Diego, 1997—, assoc. dir. NYC, 2004—05, exec. dir. lab. sci. and tech., 2006—. Editor: PLASMID Jour., 1986—95; assoc. editor: Cancer Rsch. Jour., 1995—2000, Cell jour., 1996—; mem. editl. bd. Molecular Cellular Biology Jour., 1999—2007, Jour. Biol. Chemistry, 2000—05, DNA Repair Jour., 2003—; contbr. articles to sci. jours. Recipient Jr. Faculty Rsch. award, Am. Cancer Soc., 1981, Faculty Rsch. award, 1984, Merit award, NIH, 1993, Charles S. Mott prize, GM Cancer Rsch. Found., 1996; grantee, NIH, 1978—; rsch. grantee, Am. Cancer Soc., 1980—82. Fellow: Am. Acad. Arts Scis., Am. Acad. Microbiology; mem.: NAS, Am. Assn. Cancer Rsch. (Kirk Landon award 2007), Genetic Soc. Am., Am. Soc. Microbiology, Am. Soc. Biochemistry and Molecular Biology. Home: 13468 Kibbings Rd San Diego CA 92130-1231 Office: Ludwig Inst for Cancer Rsch 9500 Gilman Dr CMME 3058 La Jolla CA 92093-0669 Home Phone: 858-259-9027. Business E-Mail: rkolodner@ucsd.edu.

KOLVE, V. A., English literature educator; b. Taylor, Wis., Jan. 18, 1934; s. Amos and Gunda (Lien) K. BA, U. Wis., 1955; BA with honors, Oxford U., 1957, MA, DPhil, Oxford U., 1962. From asst. prof. to assoc. prof. English Stanford (Calif.) U., 1962-69; prof. English U. Va., Charlottesville, Va., 1969-78, Commonwealth prof. English, 1979-86, chmn. dept. English, 1979-81; found. prof. English UCLA, 1986—2001, prof. emeritus, 2001—. Ednl. adv. bd. Guggenheim Found., 1988—, Alexander Lectures, U. Toronto, 1993, Clark Lectures, Cambridge U., 1994 Author: The Play Called Corpus Christi, 1966, Chaucer and The Imagery of Narrative, 1984; author, editor: (with Glending Olson) Norton Critical Edition: Chaucer: The Canterbury Tales, 1989, 2d expanded edit., 2005. 1st lt. U.S. Army, 1959. Recipient Brit. Coun. Humanities prize, 1985, Harbison Teaching award Danforth Found., 1972, UCLA Disting. Teaching award, 1995, Disting. Faculty award, 1999; Jenkins Rsch. fellow Oxford U., 1958-62, Guggenheim fellow, 1968, Sr. fellow Ctr. Advanced Studies in Visual Arts, Nat. Gallery, 1984, fellow Ctr. Advanced Study in Behavioral Scis., Stanford U., 1985; Rhodes scholar, 1955-58. Fellow Medieval Acad. Am. (pres. 1992), Am. Acad. Arts and Scis.; mem. MLA (chair exec. com. Chaucer divsn. 1973-77, 86-90, James Russell Lowell prize 1985), New Chaucer Soc. (trustee 1988-92, pres. 1994-96), Early English Text Soc., AAUP, Phi Beta Kappa. Democrat. Home: 2034 Outpost Dr Los Angeles CA 90068-3726 E-mail: kolve@ucla.edu.

KOMADINA, STEVE, state legislator; New Mexico State Senator, District 9, 2001-, interim member Judicial Sys Committee, Legislature Health Subcomt, Tobacco Settlement Revenue Oversight Committee, member, Judiciary Committee, Public Affairs, New Mexico State Senate.Physician, self-employed. New Mexico Med Soc (president). Republican. Lds. Mailing: Box 2085 Corrales NM 87048 E-mail: komadina@stevekomadina.com.

KOMEN, RICHARD B., food service executive; Founder Restaurants Unlimited, Inc., Seattle. Office: Restaurants Unlimited Inc 1818 N Northlake Way Seattle WA 98103-9036

KONAN, DENISE, academic administrator, economics professor; BA, Goshen Coll.; MA, PhD, Univ. Colo., Boulder. Prof. econ. Univ. Hawaii, Manoa, 1993—, asst. vice chancellor, 2002—05, interim chancellor, 2005—07. Contbr. articles in profl. jours., chapters to books. Office: U Hawaii Manoa Dept Econ 2424 Maile Way Honolulu HI 96822

KONDRUP, STEVEN W., state agency administrator; BA in Bus. Adminstrn. Pers. adminstr. Western Mortgage Corp., Utah; ops. mgr. leasing divsn. Nev. First; v.p., banking ctr. mgr. Bank of Am.; dep. commr. Nev. Divsn. Fin. Instns., 2005—06, acting commr., 2006—. Ret. master sgt. US Army. Office: Office of Commr Nev Divsn Fin Instns 2785 E Desert Inn Rd Ste 180 Las Vegas NV 89121 Office Phone: 702-486-4120. Office Fax: 702-486-4563. E-mail: skondrup@fid.state.nv.us.

KONG, LAURA S. L., geophysicist; b. Honolulu, July 23, 1961; d. Albert T.S. and Cordelia (Seu) K.; m. Kevin T.M. Johnson, Mar. 3, 1990. ScB, Brown U., 1983; PhD, MIT/Woods Hole Oceanog. Inst., 1990. Grad. rschr. Woods Hole (Mass.) Oceanog. Instn., 1984-90; postdoctoral fellow U. Tokyo, 1990-91; geophysicist Pacific Tsunami Warning Ctr., Ewa Beach, Hawaii, 1991-93; seismologist U.S. Geol. Survey Hawaiian Volcano Obs., 1993-95; rschr. U. Hawaii, Honolulu, 1996-99; environ. specialist Dept. Transp., Honolulu, 2000—05; dir. Internat. Tsunami Info. Ctr., Honolulu, 2005—. Chair Hawaii Earthquake Adv. Bd., 1994—; tsunami advisor State of Hawaii, 1999—; mem. equal opportunity adv. bd. Nat. Earth Svc. Pacific Region, Honolulu, 1992-93, Asain-Am.-Pacific Islander spl. emphasis program mgr., 1992-93; mem. steering com. U.S. Nat. Tsunami Hazard Mitigation Program; mem. Hawaii State Hazard Mitigation Forum, Hawaii Multi-Hazard Sci. Adv. Com.; legis. rschr. Hawaii Senate, 1996-98. Contbr. articles to profl. jours.; spkr., editl. reviewer in field. Rsch. fellow Japan Govt.-Japan Soc. for Promotion of Sci., 1990; recipient Young Investigator grant Japan Soc. for Promotion of Sci., 1990. Mem. Am. Geophys. Union, Seismol. Soc. Am., Hawaii Ctr. for Volcanology, Assn. Women in Sci., Sigma Xi. Avocation: sports. Office: Nat Weather Svc Internat Tsunami Info Ctr 737 Bishop St Ste 220 Honolulu HI 96813 E-mail: laura.kong@fhwa.dot.gov.

KONISHI, MASAKAZU, neuroscientist, educator; b. Kyoto, Feb. 17, 1933; BS, Hokkaido U., Japan, 1956, MS, 1958; PhD in Zoology, U. Calif., Berkeley, 1963; degree (hon.), Hokkaido U., 1991; LLD (hon.), Hokkaido U., Japan, 1991. Postdoctoral fellow Alexander von Humboldt Found., 1963-64; fellow Internat. Brain Rsch. Orgn. and UNESCO, 1964-65; asst. prof. zoology U. Wis., 1965-66; asst. to assoc. prof. biology Princeton U., NJ, 1970-75; prof. biology Calif. Inst. Tech., Pasadena, 1975-79, Bing prof. behavioral biology, 1979—. Mem. Salk Inst., 1991—. Assoc. editor Jour. Neurosci., 1980-89, sect. editor, 1990-93; mem. editl. adv. bd. Jour. Comparative Physiology. Recipient Elliot Coues award, Am. Ornithologists Union, 1983, F.O. Schmitt prize, 1987, Internat. prize for biology Japan Soc. for Promotion Sci., 1990, David Sparks award in Integrative Neurophysiology U. Ala., 1992, Charles A. Dana award for Pioneering Achievements in Health and Edn., 1992, Sci. Writing prize Acoustical Soc. Am., 1994, Found. Ipsen prize, 1999, Kresge/Mirmelstein award for Excellence in Auditory Rsch., 2001, Lewis S. Rosenstiel award for Disting. Work in Basic Med. Sci., Brandeis U., 2004, Edward M. Scolnick prize in Neuroscience, McGovern Inst., MIT, 2004, Gerard prize, Soc. Neuroscience, 2004, Karl Spencer Lashley award, Am. Philos. Soc., 2004. Mem.: Internat. Soc. Neuroethology (pres. 1986—89, The Peter and Patricia Gruber prize in Neuroscience 2005), Am. Acad. Arts and Scis., Nat. Acad. Scis. Office: Calif Inst Tech Divsn Biology 1200 E California Blvd Pasadena CA 91125-0001

KONNEY, PAUL EDWARD, health products executive, lawyer; b. Hartford, Conn., June 24, 1948; s. William Frederick and Dorothy (Dittmer) K.; m. Elizabeth Buhl Wright Temple, July 27, 1968 (div. 1979); m. Barbara Jean Greaves, June 2, 1979; children: Gretchen Blair Konney Blanchard, Tyler Wingard. AB cum laude, Harvard U., 1966; JD, U. Pa., 1969. Bar: NY 1973. Law clk. to Hon. Chief Judge William Hastie U.S. Ct. Appeals, Phila., 1969-70; assoc. Debevoise & Plimpton, NYC, 1971-81; v.p., gen. counsel Tambrands Inc., Lake Success, NY, 1982-83, v.p., gen. counsel, sec. White Plains, NY, 1983-89, sr. v.p., gen. counsel, sec., 1989-93; v.p., gen. counsel Quaker State Corp., Oil City, Pa., 1994, v.p., gen. counsel, sec. Irving, Texas, 1995, sr. v.p., gen. counsel, sec., 1996-98, Estee Lauder Cos. Inc., NYC, 1999—2004; gen. counsel. head worldwide regulatory affairs Metagenics Inc., San Clemente, Calif., 2005—. Bd. dirs. Taylor & Dodge Inc., NYC; mem. US Del. US/USSR Legal Exchange, Russia, 1988; internat. policy com. US C of C, Washington, 1989—; forum for US-EU Legal and Econ. Affairs, 1999-. Article and book rev. editor U. Pa. Law Rev., 1968-69. Bd. dir. Visiting Nurse Assn., Dallas, 1996-99. Mem. U.S. delegation to 1st U.S.-USSR legal seminar. Mem. ABA (com. of corp. gen. counsel 1999-, exec. com. 2001-04), Am. Soc. Corp. Secs., U.S. C. of C. (internat. policy com.). Episcopalian. Office: Metagenics Inc 100 Avenida La Pata San Clemente CA 92673

KONNYU, ERNEST LESLIE, former congressman; b. Tamasi, Hungary, May 17, 1937; arrived in US, 1949; s. Leslie and Elizabeth Konnyu; m. Lillian Muenks, Nov. 25, 1959; children: Carol, Renata, Lisa, Victoria. Student, U. Md., 1960-62; BS in Acctg., Ohio State U., 1965. Mem. Calif. Assembly, Sacramento, 1980-86, 100th Congress from 12th Calif. dist., 1987-89; CEO Konnyu Financials and Taxes, Inc. Chmn. Assembly Rep. Policy Com. of State Assembly, Sacramento, 1985-86; vice chmn. Assembly Human Svcs., Sacramento, 1980-86; vice chmn. Policy Rsch. Com., Sacramento, 1985-86. Mem. Rep. State Cen. Com., Calif., 1977-88, Rep. Cen. Com., Santa Clara County, Calif., 1980-88; mem. adv. bd. El Camino Hosp., Mountain View, Calif., 1987-89. Served to maj. USAF, 1959-69. Recipient Nat. Def. Medal, 1968, Disting. Service award U.S. Jaycees, 1969, Nat. Security award Am. Security Council Found., 1987; named lifetime senator U.S. Jaycees, 1977. Mem. Am.- Hungarian C. of C. (v.p. 1995-97). Republican. Roman Catholic. Avocations: politics, golf. Office: Konnyu Financials & Taxes Inc 19437 De Havilland Ct Saratoga CA 95070-4040 Office Phone: 408-244-3299. Personal E-mail: konnyu@sbcglobal.net. E-mail: goernie@sbcglobal.net.

KONOPNICKI, BILL, state legislator, small business owner; b. Detroit; m. Cathy Konopnicki; 4 children. Student, Ariz. Western Coll.; BA in Bus. Edn., MA in Bus. Edn., Ariz. State U., EdD in Higher Edn. Adminstrn. Owner various small businesses including 9 McDonald's restaurants, 7 radio stations; mem. Dist. 5 Ariz. House of Reps., 2003—, chair natural resources & rural affairs com., mem. commerce com., judiciary com. Vol. Ronald McDonald Houses, Boys & Girls Clubs; past pres. bd. dirs. Mt. Graham Regional Med. Ctr., Safford, Ariz. Republican. Mailing: Ariz House Reps Capitol Complex 1700 W Washington Rm 219 Phoenix AZ 85007 Office Phone: 602-542-5409. Office Fax: 602-417-3105. Business E-Mail: bkonopni@azleg.gov.*

KONOWIECKI, JOSEPH SAMUEL, lawyer, health facility administrator; b. Albany, NY, May 17, 1953; BA in polit. sci. magna cum laude, UCLA, 1975; JD, U. Calif. Hastings Coll. Law, San Francisco, 1978. Bar: Calif. 1978, DC. Ptnr. K & R Law Group (formerly Konowiecki & Rank LLP), LA, 1980—2001; gen. counsel PacifiCare Health Systems, Inc., Calif., 1989—, sec. Calif., 1993—, exec. v.p. Calif., 1999—, full-time exec. v.p., gen. counsel, sec. Calif., 2002—. Adv. bd. ForestWeb Inc., 2000—. Founding editor Hastings Comm. and Entertainment Law Jour.; contbr. articles to Practicing Law Inst., law journals. Mem.: LA County Bar Assn. Office: Pacificare Health Systems Inc 3120 Lake Center Dr Santa Ana CA 92704 Office Phone: 714-825-5200.

KONTNY, VINCENT L., rancher, retired engineering executive; b. Chappell, Nebr., July 19, 1937; s. Edward James and Ruth Regina (Schumann) K.; m. Joan Dashwood FitzGibbon, Feb. 20, 1970; children: Natascha Marie, Michael Christian, Amber Brooke. BSCE, U. Colo., 1958, DSc honoris causa, 1991. Operator heavy equipment, grade foreman Peter Kiewit Son's Co., Denver, 1958-59; project mgr. Utah Constrn. and Mining Co., Western Australia, 1965-69, Fluor Australia, Queensland, Australia, 1969-72; sr. project mgr. Fluor Utah, San Mateo, Calif., 1972-73; sr. v.p. Holmes & Narver, Inc., Orange, Calif., 1973-79; mng. dir. Fluor Australia, Melbourne, 1979-82; group v.p. Fluor Engrs., Inc., Irvine, Calif., 1982-85, pres., chief exec. officer, 1985-87; group pres. Fluor Daniel, Irvine, Calif., 1987-88, pres., 1988-94, Fluor Corp., Irvine, 1990-94, COO, bd. dirs., vice chmn., 1994; ret., 1994; bd. dirs. Chgo. Bridge & Iron Co., Plainfield, Ill., 1997—; COO Washington Group Internat., Inc., Boise, Idaho, 2000—03. Purchased Last Dollar Ranch, Ridgway Co. 1989, Centennial Ranch, Colona Co., 1992, owner Double Shoe Cattle Co. Contbr. articles to profl. jours. Mem. engring. devel. coun., U. Colo.; mem.

engring. adv. coun., Stanford U. Lt. USN, 1959-65. Mem.: Nat. Acad. Constrn. (pres. 2007, v.p. 2006), Center Club (Costa Mesa, Calif.). Republican. Roman Catholic. Avocations: skiing, hunting, fishing. Home and Office: 35000 S Highway 550 Montrose CO 81401-8477 Personal E-mail: vincekontny@starband.net.

KOO, JOHN YING MING, psychiatrist, dermatologist; b. Tokyo, Jan. 9, 1955; arrived in U.S., 1967; s. Kwang Ming Koo and Amy Tsai Ma; m. Nancy Chiang, July 7, 1978; children: Kathie, Jennifer, Jocelyn, Jonathan, Karina. BA in Biochemistry, U. Calif., Berkeley, 1977; MD, Harvard U., 1981. Cert. psychiatry and dermatology. Intern UCLA Ctr. Health Scis., 1981—82; resident in psychiatry UCLA Neuropsychiatric Inst., 1982—85; resident in dermatology U. Calif.-San Francisco Med. Ctr., 1985—88; dir. Psoriasis and Skin Treatment Ctr., U. Calif., San Francisco, 1988—; prof. and vice chmn. dept. dermatology, prof. U. Calif., San Francisco, 1989—. Med. adv. bd. Nat. Psioriasis Found., Portland, Oreg., 1995; cons. in field. Mem. editl. bd.: Jour. Am. Acad. Dermatology, 1994; editor: Dermatology and Psychosomatics, 1999. Scholar Harvard Nat. scholar, Harvard Med. Sch., Boston, 1981. Mem.: Am. Psychiat. Assn., Am. Acad. Dermatology, Assn. for Psychocutaneous Medicine N.Am. (founder). Avocations: philosophy, military history. Office: U Calif San Francisco Psoriasis and Skin Treatment Ctr 515 Spruce St San Francisco CA 94118 Office Phone: 415-476-4701. Office Fax: 415-502-4126.

KOOGLE, TIMOTHY K., communications executive; MS in Engr., Stanford U. Pres. Intermec Corp.; corp. v.p. Western Atlas Inc.; with Motorola Inc.; chmn., CEO Yahoo! Corp., Santa Clara, Calif., 1999—. Chmn. bd. dirs. AIM.

KOOKESH, ALBERT M., state legislator; b. Juneau, Alaska, Nov. 24, 1948; m to Sally Woods; children: Elaine, Jaeleen, Reanna, Albert & Walter. BA, Alaska Meth. U., 1971; JD, U. Wash., 1976. Special asst for rural affairs, Off of Governor, 94-96; member, Alaska Democratic Party, formerly; precinct chairman, Cent Committee, formerly; Alaska State Representative, District 5, 1997-2004, member, Community & Regional Affairs & Transportation Committees & Select Committee on Legislature Ethics, currently, Alaska House Representative; Alaska State Senator, District C, 2005-.Bd director, Sealaska Corp, formerly; business manager, exec vice president, acting president & chief exec officer, Kootznoowoo Inc, 76-92; commercial fisherman, lodge & marketing owner & operator, currently; director, America Indian Museum Smithsonian Institution, currently. Lions (chairman, Hall of Fame Committee, currently); Alaska Sch Activities Association; Alaska Fedn Natives (co-chmn, currently); Alaska Native Brotherhood Grand Camp. Democrat. Office: State Capitol Rm 11 Juneau AK 99801 Office Phone: 907-465-3473. Office Fax: 907-465-2827. Business E-Mail: Senator_Albert_Kookesh@legis.state.ak.us.*

KOOL, ERIC T., chemist, educator; b. 1960; BS, Miami U., Ohio, 1982; PhD, Columbia U., 1988. Prof. dept. chemistry Stanford (Calif.) U. Contbr. articles to profl. jours. Recipient faculty awad Am. Cyanamid, 1994, Pfizer award Am. Chem. Soc., 2000; named Young Investigator, Office Naval Rsch., 1992, Young Investigator, Beckman Found., 1992, Young Investigator, Army Rsch. Office, 1993; Dreyfus Found. Tchr.-scholar, 1993, Arthur C. Cope scholar Am. Chem. Soc., 2000; Alfred P. Sloan Found. fellow, 1994. Achievements include research on design, synthesis and study of molecules that mimic complex biological functions such as replication. Office: Stanford U Dept Chemistry Stauffer I Rm 103 Stanford CA 94305-5080 E-mail: kool@leland.stanford.edu.

KOONTZ, DEAN RAY, writer; b. Everett, Pa., July 9, 1945; s. Raymond and Florence (Logue) Koontz; m. Gerda Ann Cerra, 1966. BS, Shippensburg U., 1966, LittD (hon.), 1989. Tchr. Appalachian Poverty Prog., Saxton, Pa., 1966-67, Mechanicsburg HS, Pa., 1967-69; freelance writer Orange, Calif., 1969—. Author: (novels) Star Quest, 1968, Fear That Man, 1969, The Fall of the Dream Machine, 1969, Hell's Gate, 1970, The Dark Symphony, 1970, Dark of the Woods, 1970, Beastchild, 1970, Anti-Man, 1970, The Crimson Witch, 1971, Warlock!, 1972, Time Thieves, 1972, Starblood, 1972, A Darkness in My Soul, 1972, The Flesh in the Furnace, 1972, A Werewolf Among Us, 1973, The Haunted Earth, 1973, Hanging On, 1973, Demon Seed, 1973, After the Last Race, 1974, Nightmare Journey, 1975, Night Chills, 1976, The Vision, 1977, Whispers, 1980, Phantoms, 1983, Darkfall, 1984, Twilight Eyes, 1985, Strangers, 1986, Watchers, 1987, Lightning, 1988, Midnight, 1989, The Bad Place, 1990, Cold Fire, 1991, Hideaway, 1992, Mr. Murder, 1993, Dragon Tears, 1993, Winter Moon, 1994, Dark Rivers of the Heart, 1994, Icebound, 1995, Intensity, 1996, Ticktock, 1996, Sole Survivor, 1997, Fear Nothing, 1998, Seize the Night, 1998, False Memory, 1999, From the Corner of His Eye, 2000, One Door Away from Heaven, 2001, By the Light of the Moon, 2002, The Face, 2003, Odd Thomas, 2003, The Taking, 2004, Life Expectancy, 2004, Velocity, 2005, Forever Odd, 2005, City of Night, 2005, Prodigal Son, 2005, The Husband, 2006, Brother Odd, 2006, The Good Guy, 2007, The Darkest Evening of the Year, 2007, Odd Hours, 2008, In Odd We Trust, 2008, Your Heart Belongs to Me, 2008, (as Leonard Chris) Hung, 1970, (as Deanna Dwyer) Legacy of Terror, 1971, Demon Child, 1972, The Dark of Summer, 1972, Children of the Storm, 1972, Dance with the Devil, 1973, (as Brian Coffey) Blood Risk, 1973, Surrounded, 1974, Wall of Masks, 1975, The Face of Fear, 1977, The Voice of the Night, 1980, (as John Hill) The Long Sleep, 1975, (as K. R. Dwyer) Chase, 1972, Shattered, 1973, Dragonfly, 1975, (as Leigh Nichols) The Key to Midnight, 1979, The Eyes of Darkness, 1981, The House of Thunder, 1982, The Servants of Twilight, 1984, Shadow Fires, 1987, (as Owen West) The Funhouse, 1980, The Mask, 1981, (as Richard Paige) The Door to December, 1985, (non-fiction) The Underground Lifestyles Handbook, 1970, The Pig Society, 1970, Writing Popular Fiction, 1972, How To Write Best-Selling Fiction, 1981, Life is Good! Lessons in Joyful Living, 2004, Christmas Is Good!: Trixie Treats And Holiday Wisdom, 2005, (short story collections) Soft Come the Dragons, 1970, Strange Highways, 1995, (children's books) Oddkins: A Fable for All Ages, 1988, Santa's Twin, 1996, The Paper Doorway: Funny Verse and Nothing Worse, 2001, Every Day's a Holiday: Amusing Rhymes for Happy Times, 2003, Robot Santa: The Further Adventures of Santa's Twin, 2004. Achievements include having ten hardcovers and thirteen paperbacks reach #1 on the NY Times Bestseller list. Mailing: PO Box 9529 Newport Beach CA 92658-9529

KOOPMANS, CHRIS, telecommunications industry executive; BS in Elec. and Computer Engring. with highest honors, U. Ill., Urbana-Champaign. Engr. Intel Corp. Microcomputer Rsch. Labs., Silicon Graphics Cray Rsch.; founding engr. Bytemobile Inc., Mountain View, Calif., 2000, arch. product integration, dir. engring., chief arch., v.p. product devel., 2008—. Fellow, NSF. Achievements include patents in field of wireless internet protocol services and optimiation technology. Office: Bytemobile Inc 2025 Stierlin Ct Ste 200 Mountain View CA 94043

KOOYMAN, GERALD LEE, physiologist, researcher; b. Salt Lake City, June 16, 1934; s. Albert John and Virginia L. (Monson) K.; m. Melba Mae Bingham, July 6, 1962; children: Carsten, Tory. AB, UCLA, 1957; PhD, U. Ariz., 1966. Postdoctoral fellow NSF, London, 1966-67; asst. rsch. physiologist U. Calif. San Diego, La Jolla, 1967-94, rsch. prof. to prof. emeritus biology, 1994—. Author: Weddell Seal, Consummate Diver, 1981; editor: Fur Seals: Maternal Behavior On Land and At Sea, 1986, Diverse Divers, Physiology and Behavior, 1989; contbr. articles to sci. jours. Recipient Antarctic medal NSF, Kenneth Norris Lifetime Achievement award, Soc. Marine Mammalogy, 2005. Fellow AAAS, London Zool. Soc., Explorers Club (Finn Ronne Meml. award, Polar Field Sci. and Exploration 2007); mem. Am. Physiol. Soc., Am. Soc. Zoologists, Sigma Xi. Office: Scripps Instn Oceanography U Calif San Diego 9500 Gilman Dr La Jolla CA 92093-0225 Office Phone: 858-534-2091. E-mail: gkooyman@ucsd.edu.

KOPEL, DAVID BENJAMIN, lawyer; b. Denver; s. Gerald Henry and Dolores B. Kopel; m. Deirdre Frances Dolan, 1987. BA in History, Brown U., 1982; JD, U. Mich., 1985. Bar: Colo. 1986, N.Y. 1986, U.S. Dist. Ct. (ea. and so. dists.) N.Y. 1986, U.S. Ct. Appeals (2d cir.) 1988, U.S. Dist. Ct. Colo. 1988, U.S. Ct. Appeals (10th cir.) 1988, U.S. Ct. Appeals (D.C. cir.) 1997, U.S. Ct. Appeals (5th cir.) 1999, U.S. Ct. Appeals (4th cir.) 2003, US Ct. Appeals (8th cir.) 2003, US Ct. Appeals (7th cir.) 2009. Assoc. Sullivan & Cromwell, NYC, 1985-86; asst. dist. atty. Manhattan Dist. Atty., NYC, 1986-88; asst. atty. gen. Colo. State Atty. Gen., Denver, 1988-92; rsch. dir. Independence Inst., Golden, Colo., 1992—. Adj. prof. NYU Sch. of Law, 1998-99. Democrat. Avocations: skiing, golf, amateur radio. Office: Independence Inst 13952 Denver West Pkwy Ste 400 Golden CO 80401

KOPITAR, ANZE, professional hockey player; b. Jesenice, Slovenia, Aug. 24, 1987; s. Matjaz and Mataja Kopitar. Center Sodertalje SK (Swedish Elite League), 2005—06, LA Kings, 2006—. Named to NHL YoungStars Game, 2007, NHL All-Star Game, 2008. Office: LA Kings Hockey Club Ste 3100 1111 S Figueroa St Los Angeles CA 90015

KOPONEN, PETTERI, Internet company executive; Grad., Helsinki U. Tech. Advisor Blyk; founder, former CEO, now bd. mem. First Hop; co-founder, CEO Jaiku (purchased by Google), 2006—07; product mgr. Google, 2007—. Chmn. bd. Alkuvoima. Home: Google 1600 Amphitheatre Parkway Mountain View CA 94043

KOPP, EUGENE HOWARD, communications and electrical engineer, consultant; b. NYC, Oct. 1, 1929; s. Jacob and Fanny (Lipschitz) K.; m. Claire Bernstein, Aug. 31, 1950; children: Carolyn, Michael, Paul. B.E.E., CCNY, 1950, M.E.E., 1953; PhD in Engring, UCLA, 1965. Registered profl. engr., Calif. Project engr. Polarad Electronics Corp., Long Island City, NY, 1950-53, Kaye Halbert Corp., Culver City, Calif., 1953-55; chief engr. Precision Radiation Instruments, Inc., Los Angeles, 1955-58; mem. faculty sch. engring. Calif. State U., Los Angeles, 1958-74, assoc. prof., 1962-66, prof., 1966-74, dean engring. Sch., 1967-73; v.p. acad. affairs West Coast U., Los Angeles, 1973-79; sr. scientist Hughes Aircraft Co., 1980-85, mgr. R & D, 1985-93, dir. advanced programs, 1994-95; v.p. mobile satellites Boeing Satellite Sys., 1996-97, chief scientist comml. satellites, 1998—2002; chief scientist homeland security The Boeing Co., 2003—05, chief engr. joint programs, 2006, consulting comm. engr., 2006—. Lectr. evening divsn. CCNY, N.Y.C., 1952-53; lectr. UCLA, 1979-91. Vis. research fellow U. Leeds, Eng., 1966-67 Fellow AIAA (assoc.); mem. IEEE, Tau Beta Pi, Eta Kappa Nu, Pi Tau Sigma. Avocation: flying. Office: PO Box 1351 South Pasadena CA 91031-1351

KOPP, MIKE, state legislator; m. Kimberly; children: Meghan, Ethan, Allie-Grace. BA, North Ctrl. U., Mpls. Clk., detention & deportation divsn. US Border Patrol; fire fighter Nat. Pk. Svc.; prin. ForwardThink Strategies; mem. Dist. 22 Colo. State Senate, 2007—, minority caucus chair. Sgt., ranger 82d Airborne Divsn. US Army. Decorated Army Commendation Medals, Combat Infantry Badge, Army Achievement Medal. Republican. Office: Colo State Capitol 200 E Colfax Denver CO 80203 Office Phone: 303-866-2638. Business E-Mail: mike.kopp.senate@state.co.us.*

KOPPEL, MICHAEL G., retail executive; B in acctg., Univ. Conn. Fin. mgmt. positions May Dept. Stores, 1984—88, v.p., controller G. Fox div., 1988—93, v.p., controller Filene's div., 1993—97; CFO Lids Corp., 1997—98; COO CML Group, 1998—99; v.p., controller, prin. acctg. officer Nordstrom Inc., Seattle, 1999—2001, exec. v.p., CFO, 2001—. Office: Nordstrom Inc 1617 6th Ave Seattle WA 98101

KORAN, DENNIS HOWARD, publisher; b. LA, May 21, 1947; s. Aaron Baer and Shirley Mildred (Kassan) K.; m. Roslynn Ruth Cohen, Apr. 6, 1979; 1 child, Michael; stepchildren: Jeff, Beth, Judy. Student, U. Leeds, Eng., 1966-67, UCLA, 1979-80; BA, U. Calif., Berkeley, 1980; postgrad., Loyola U., LA, 1982-84, 86-89. Co-founder, co-editor Cloud Marauder Press, Berkeley, 1969-72, Panjandrum/Aris Books, San Francisco, 1973-81; founder, editor Panjandrum Books, San Francisco, 1971—, Panjandrum Press, Inc., San Francisco, 1971—. Substitute tchr. L.A. Unified Sch. Dist., 1997—; co-dir. poetry reading series Panjandrum Books, 1972-76. Author: (book of poetry) Vacancies, 1975, After All, 1993; (with Mike Koran) Refrigerator Poems: Variations on 24, 48 & 120 Words, 1998, Love & Space, 2000; editor Panjandrum Poetry Jour., 1971—, Noumenal Books, 1998—; co-editor Cloud Marauder, 1969-72; author poetry pub. various jours. Liaison between U.S. Govt. and Seminole Indians VISTA, Sasakwa, Okla., 1969-70. Nat. Endowment for Arts Lit. Pub. grantee, 1974, 76, 79, 81, 82, 84, Coord. Coun. for Lit. Mags., 1971-80, grantee Lit. Pub. Calif. Arts Coun., 1985-86, L.A. Cultural Arts Found., 1986. Mem. Lovers of the Stinking Rose, Poets and Writers. Avocations: rare book collecting, travel, sports, coin collecting/numismatics.

KORBER, BETTE TINA MARIE, chemist; b. Long Beach, Calif., 1958; d. George Korber. BS in chemistry, Calif. State U., 1981; PhD in chemistry in the field of immunology, Calif. Inst. Tech., 1988. Postdoctoral fellow Los Alamos Nat. Lab., 1990, tech. staff scientist theoretical biology and biophysics (T10) group, 1993—. Elizabeth Glaser scientist Pediatric AIDS Found., 1997—2003; external faculty Santa Fe Inst., N.Mex. Recipient Los Alamos Nat. Achievement award, 1996, 2002, Elizabeth Glaser Scientist for the Pediatric AIDS Found., 1997—2003, Outstanding Alumnus award for Sch. Natural Scis., Calif. State U., Long Beach, 2001, Ernest Orlando Lawrence award, US Dept. Energy, 2004; nominee Rave award in Medicine, WIRED, 2005; grantee Los Alamos Nat. Lab. Fellow, 2002; fellow, Leukemia Soc., Harvard U., 1988—90, Dir. Funded Postdoctoral Fellow, Los Alamos Nat. Lab, 1990—92. Achievements include publishing over 100 sci. papers that have been cited over 3,700 times; conducting pioneering studies delineating the genetic characteristics of the virus population; developing the Los Alamos HIV database, a foundation for HIV research for scientific community; internationally recognized AIDS researcher. Office: Los Alamos Nat Lab MS K710 T 10 Theoretical Divsn Los Alamos NM 87545 Office Phone: 505-665-4453. Office Fax: 505-665-3493. Business E-Mail: btk@lanl.gov.

KORDESTANI, OMID, information technology executive; BSEE, San Jose State U., Calif.; MBA, Stanford U. Former positions in mktg., product mgmt., and bus. devel. 3DO Co., Go Corp., and Hewlett-Packard; dir. OEM sales Netscape, 1996—97, v.p. bus. devel. sales, 1998—99; sr. v.p. worldwide sales and field ops. Google Inc., Mountain View, Calif., 1999—. Named one of 100 Most Influential People, Time Mag., 2006, Forbes Richest Americans, 2006. Office: Google Inc 1600 Amphitheatre Pky Mountain View CA 94043

KORG, JACOB, English literature educator; b. NYC, Nov. 21, 1922; s. Reuben and Mary (Lehrman) K.; m. Cynthia Stewart, Jan. 21, 1952; 1 dau., Nora Francis. BA, CCNY, 1943; MA, Columbia U., 1947, PhD, 1952. Instr. English Bard Coll., 1947-49, CCNY, 1950-55; from asst. prof. to prof. U. Wash., Seattle, 1955-68, prof. English, 1970-91, prof. emeritus, 1991—; prof. English U. Md., 1968-70. Vis. prof. Nat. Taiwan U., 1960. Author: George Gissing, A Critical Biography, 1963, Dylan Thomas, 1965, Language in Modern Literature, 1979, rev. edit., 1992, Browning and Italy, 1983, Ritual and Experiment in Modern Poetry, 1995, Winter Love: Ezra Pound and H.D., 2003, also articles, revs.; editor: London in Dickens' Day, 1960, George Gissing's Commonplace Book, 1962, The Force of Few Words, 1966, Twentieth Century Views of Bleak House, 1968, Poetry of Robert Browning, 1971; co-editor: George Gissing on Fiction, 1978; mem. editl. bd. Victorian Poetry, 1979-2002, Nineteenth-Century Lit., 1983-95, Rivista di Studi Vittoriani. Served with AUS, 1943-46. Mem.: MLA, Assn. Literary Scholars and Critics. Office: Univ Wash Dept English Seattle WA 98195-0001 Home: 900 University St Apt 14-0 Seattle WA 98101 Business E-Mail: korg@u.washington.edu.

KORMAN, MARTIN, lawyer; b. Phila., Oct. 10, 1963; AB, Stanford U., 1985; JD, Yale U., 1989. Bar: NY 1990, Calif. 1994. Ptnr. Wilson Sonsini Goodrich & Rosati. Named one of 45 Under Forty-Five, Am. Lawyer, 2003. Office: Wilson Sonsini Goodrich & Rosati 650 Page Mill Rd Palo Alto CA 94304-1050 Office Phone: 650-493-9300.

KORMONDY, EDWARD JOHN, retired academic administrator, science educator; b. Beacon, NY, June 10, 1926; s. Anthony and Frances (Glover) Kormondy; m. Peggy Virginia Hedrick, June 5, 1950 (div. 1989); children: Lynn Ellen, Eric Paul, Mark Hedrick. BA in Biology summa cum laude, Tusculum Coll., 1950, DSc (hon.), 1997; MS in Zoology, U. Mich., 1951, PhD in Zoology, 1955. Tchg. fellow U. Mich., 1952-55; instr. zoology, curator insects Mus. Zoology, 1955-57; from asst. prof. to assoc. prof. Oberlin Coll., Ohio, 1957—67, prof., 1967—69, acting assoc. dean, 1966—67; dir. Commn. Undergrad. Edn. Biol. Scis., Washington, 1968-72; dir. Office Biol. Edn. Am. Inst. Biol. Scis., Washington, 1968-71; mem. faculty Evergreen State Coll., Olympia, Wash., 1971-79, interim acting dean, 1972-73, v.p., provost, 1973-78; sr. profl. assoc., directorate sci. edn. NSF, 1979; provost, prof. biology U. So. Maine, Portland, 1979-82; v.p. acad. affairs, prof. biology Calif. State U., LA, 1982-86; sr. v.p., chancellor, prof. biology U. Hawaii-West Oahu & U. Hawaii-Hilo, 1986—93, chancellor emeritus, 2000—; pres. U. West LA, 1995-97; pro bono spl. asst. to pres. Pacific Oaks Coll., Pasadena, Calif., 2000—05; acting pres. Tusculum Coll., Greeneville, Tenn., 2007. Author: Introduction to Genetics: A Program for Self Instruction, 1964, Readings in Ecology, 1965, General Biology, A Book of Readings, 1966, Concepts of Ecology, 1969, 4th edit., 1996, General Biology: The Integrity and Natural History of Organisms, 1977, Handbook of Contemporary World Developments in Ecology, 1981, International Handbook of Pollution Control, 1989, Biology, 1984, 1988, Fundamentals of Human Ecology, 1998, University of Hawaii-Hilo: A College in the Making, 2001, Nine University Presidents Who Saved their Institutions, 2008; contbr. articles to profl. jours. With USN, 1944—46. Postdoctoral fellow, U. Ga., 1963—64, Vis. Rsch. fellow, Georgetown U., 1978—79, Rsch. grantee, NAS, Am. Philos. Soc., NSF. Fellow: AAAS; mem.: NSF (rsch. grantee), So. Calif. Acad. Scis. (bd. dirs. 1985—86, 1993—97, v.p. 1995—96), Nat. Assn. Biology Tchrs. (pres. 1981), Ecol. Soc. Am. (sec. 1976—78), Sigma Xi. Personal E-mail: ed.kormondy@gmail.com.

KORNBERG, ROGER DAVID, biochemist, structural biologist; b. St. Louis, Apr. 24, 1947; s. Arthur and Sylvy Ruth (Levy) K.; m. Yahli Deborah Lorch, Sept. 18, 1984; children: Guy Joseph, Maya Lorch, Gil Lorch.adr BS, Harvard U., 1967; PhD, Stanford U., 1972. Mem. sci. staff MRC Lab. Molecular Biology, Cambridge, Eng., 1974-75; asst. prof. biol. chemistry Harvard Med. Sch., Cambridge, Mass., 1976-77; prof. cell/structural biology Stanford (Calif.) U., 1978—, chmn. dept., 1984-92, Winzer prof. Structural Biology. Contbr. articles to profl. jours. Recipient Eli Lilly award, 1981, Passano award, 1982, Ciba-Drew award, 1990, Harvey prize Technion, 1997, Gairdner Found. internat. award, 2000, Welch award in Chemistry, 2001, Le Grand prix Charles-Leopold Mayer, Academie des Sciences, France, Alfred P. Sloan, Jr. award, GM Cancer Rsch. Found., 2005, Nobel Prize in Chemistry, Nobel Found., 2006. Mem. NAS, Am. Acad. Arts and Sciences. Office: Stanford U Dept Structural Biology Fairchild Bldg 1st Fl 299 Campus Dr Stanford CA 94305-5126 E-mail: kornberg@stanford.edu.

KORNFIELD, JULIA ANN, chemical engineering educator; b. Oakland, Calif., July 2, 1962; BA, Calif. Inst. Tech., 1983; MS, Stanford U., 1984, PhD in Chemical Engring., 1988. Rsch. asst. Calif. Inst. Tech., 1983-84, asst. prof. chemical engring., 1990—; rsch. asst. chem. engring. Stanford U., 1984-88, tchg. asst. appl. math., 1986, 87. NSF/NATO fellow chem. engring. Max-Planck Inst., 1989. Mem. AIChE, Am. Phys. Soc. (John H. Dillon medal Rsch. in Polymer Physics 1996), Am. Chem. Soc., Soc. Rheology. Office: Calif Inst Tech Dept Chem Engring 206-41 1201 E California Blvd Pasadena CA 91125-0001

KORNSTEIN, DON ROBERT, gaming industry executive; b. NYC, Feb. 9, 1952; s. Sol and Faye (Manheim) K.; m. Leslie Gayle Harris, May 18, 1975; children: Eric Chad, Rachel Blair. BA, U. Pa., 1973;

MBA, Columbia U., 1975. Rsch. analyst Citibank, NA, NYC, 1975-77; sr. mng. dir. investment banking dept. Bear, Stearns & Co. Inc., NYC, 1977-94; pres., CEO Jackpot Enterprises, Inc., Las Vegas, Nev., 1994—. Office: 825 Lakeshore Blvd Incline Village NV 89451-9507

KORSCH, BARBARA M., pediatrician; b. Jena, Germany, Mar. 30, 1921; arrived in U.S., 1936; 1 child. BA, Smith Coll., 1941; MD, Johns Hopkins U., 1944. Cert. Am. Bd. Pediat. Asst. resident Bellevue Hosp., 1945, Mary Imogene Basset Hosp., 1946, N.Y. Hosp., 1947, fellow Inst. Child Devel., 1948—49; asst. pediats. Med. Coll. Cornell U., 1949—50, from instr. to assoc. prof., 1950—61; assoc. clin. prof. preventive medicine Sch. Medicine UCLA, 1961—64; assoc. prof. Keck Sch. Medicine, U. So. Calif., LA, 1964—69, prof. pediats. Sch. Medicine, 1969—. George Armstrong lectr. Ambulatory Pediatric Assn., 1973; Katherine D. McCormick Disting. lectr. Stanford U., 1977; Kathy Newman Meml. lectr. Tulane U., 1987; asst. outpatient pediatrician N.Y. Hosps., 1949—50, asst. attending pediatrician, 1950—55, clin. dir. pediatric outpatient dept., 1950—61, assoc. attending pediatrician, 1955—61; pediatric cons. Dept. Health, NY, 1949—51, Hosp. Spl. Surgery, 1955—61, Gen. Pediatric Childrens Hosp., LA, 1961—65, Med. Ctr., U. So. Calif., 1969—74; coord. pediatric rehab. program Nat. Found. Infantile Paralysis, 1953—61; pediatric dir. Obs. Clinic Children L.A., 1961—64; assoc. attending pediatrician Cedars of Lebanon Hosp., 1961—; vis. prof. numerous U.S. and fgn. univs., 1973—89; hon. staff mem. dept. pediat. Cedars-Sinai Med. Ctr., 1976—; attending pediatrician, dir. behavioral and devel. program, dir. dr.-patient comm. project Children's Hosp. L.A.; Philip Rothman fellow, 1999—. Author: Intelligent Patient's Guide to the Doctor-Patient Relationship, 1997; contbr. articles to profl. jours. Chmn. coun. Bayer Inst. for Health Comm., 1989—98. Recipient Disting. Career award, Ambulatory Pediatric Assn., 1991. Mem.: Soc. Pediatric Rsch., Soc. Behavioral Pediat. (pres. 1985), Am. Pediatric Soc., Am. Acad. Pediat. (C. Anderson Aldrich award 1988, Genesis award for med. ethics 1998), Inst. Medicine NAS, Sigma Xi. Office: Childrens Hosp Divsn Gen Pediats MB # 76 4650 W Sunset Blvd Los Angeles CA 90027-6062 E-mail: bkorsch@chla.usc.edu.

KOSSEFF, JEFF, reporter, news correspondent; married. BA, MA, U. Mich. Tech. reporter The Oregonian, Portland, reporter Washington, DC bur., 2004—; corr. Newhouse News Svc., Washington. Co-recipient George Polk award for Nat. Reporting, 2006. Office: The Oregonian 1320 SW Broadway Portland OR 97201 also: Newhouse News Svc 618 A St SE Apt 27 Washington DC 20003-1228 Office Phone: 503-294-7605. E-mail: jeff.kosseff@newhouse.com.

KOSTER, JOHN FREDERICK, insurance executive; b. Ancon, Canal Zone, Sept. 6, 1950; s. Frederick Eugene and Margaretta (Lillystrand) K.; m. Laura Plikerd, June 11, 1971; children: Kimberly, Erik, Krista. BS, N.Mex. Tech. U., 1972; MD, U. N.Mex., 1976. Intern Providence Hosp., Portland, Oreg., 1976; resident U. N.Mex., Albuquerque, 1977; assoc. Internal and Family Medicine Assocs., Albuquerque, 1979-88; med. dir. Blue Cross and Blue Shield N.Mex., Albuquerque, 1988-90; sr. v.p. healthcare Rocky Mountain Healthcare Corp., Denver, 1990—91; v.p. Presbyterian Healthcare Services, Albuquerque, 1992—93; v.p targeted mem. services VHA, Inc., Irving, Tex., 1993—97; dir. system ops. Providence Health System, Seattle, 1997—2002, acting pres., CEO, 2003, pres., CEO, 2003—06, Providence Health and Svc. (merger with Providence Health System), Seattle, 2006—. Cons. Govs. Health Policy Adv. Com., N.Mex., 1990-91. Mem. AMA (Physicians Recognition award 1985—). Office: Providence Health System 502 2nd Ave Ste 1200 Seattle WA 98104

KOSTOULAS, IOANNIS GEORGIOU, physicist, consultant; b. Petra, Pierias, Greece, Sept. 12, 1936; arrived in U.S., 1965, naturalized, 1984; s. Gerogios Ioannou and Panagiota (Zarogiannis) Kostoulas; m. Katina Sioras Kay, June 23, 1979; 1 child, Alexandra. Diploma in physics, U. Thessoloniki, Greece, 1963; MA, U. Rochester, 1969, PhD, 1972; MS, U. Ala., 1977. Instr. U. Thessaloniki, 1963—65; tchg. asst. U. Ala., 1966—67, U. Rochester, 1967—68; guest jr. rsch. assoc. Brookhaven Nat. Lab., Upton, NY, 1968—72; rsch. physicist, lectr. UCLA, U. Calif.-San Diego, 1972—76; sr. rsch. assoc. Mich. State U., East Lansing, 1876—1978, Fermi Nat. Accelerator Lab., Batavia, Ill., 1976—78; rsch. staff mem. MIT, Cambridge, 1978—80; sr. sys. engr., physicist Hughes Aircraft Co., El Segundo, Calif., 1980—86; sr. physisict electro-optics and space sensors Rockwell Internat. Corp., Downey, Calif., 1986—96, Boeing Corp., Downey, 1996—98; scientist Raytheon Sys. Co., El Segundo, Calif., 1998—2000; engring. specialist Northrop-Grumman Corp., Azusa, Calif., 2000—04; sr. project engr. Aerospace Corp., El Segundo, 2005—06, cons., 2006—. Contbr. articles to profl. jours. With Greek Army, 1961—63. Rsch. grantee, U. Rochester, 1968—72. Mem.: Internat. Soc. Optical Engring., N.Y. Acad. Scis., Am. Phys. Soc., Pan Macedonian Assn., Hellenic U. Club, Ahepa Lodge, Sigma Pi Sigma. Home: 2404 Marshallfield Ln B Redondo Beach CA 90278-4406 Office: 977 1/2 Hyperion Ave Los Angeles CA 90029 Office Phone: 323-669-1153. Personal E-mail: yannismacedon@aol.com.

KOTCHIAN, SARAH BRUFF, municipal official; MEd, Harvard U., 1977; MPH, U. Wash., 1985. Dir. dept. environ. health City of Albuquerque, 1982—. Office: City of Albuquerque Environ Health Dept PO Box 1293 Albuquerque NM 87103-1293

KOTLER, RICHARD LEE, lawyer; b. LA, Apr. 13, 1952; s. Allen S. Kotler and Marcella (Fromberg) Swartz; m. Cindy Jasik, Dec. 9, 1990; children: Kelsey Elizabeth, Charles Max. BA, Sonoma State Coll., 1976; JD, Southwestern U., 1979. Bar: Calif. 1980, U.S. Dist. Ct. (cen. dist.) Cal. 1980; cert. family law specialist. Sole practice, Newhall, Calif., 1980-83, 88—; sr. ptnr. Kotler & Hann, Newhall, 1983-88; pvt. practice Law Offices of Richard L. Kotler, Newhall, 1984-86. Judge pro temp Municipal Ct., 1981-84, Superior Ct., 1985—. Chmn. Santa Clarita Valley Battered Women's Assn., Newhall, 1983-87; bd. dirs. Santa Clarita Valley Hotline, Newhall, 1981-83. Recipient Commendation award L.A. County, 1983; named SCV Paintball champion. Mem. Santa Clarita Valley Bar Assn. (v.p. 1985—), L.A. Assn. Cert. Family Law Specialists, Los Angeles Astronomy Soc., Newhall Astronomy Club. Avocations: astronomy, classic cars, stamp collecting/philately, fishing. Office: Ste 204 24881 San Fernando Rd Santa Clarita CA 91321-4172

KOULES, OREN D., film producer, professional sports team executive; b. Jan. 1961; m. Rita Shapiro (div.); 1 child. Commodities trader Chgo. Mercantile Exchange; former sr. v.p. Paramount Studios; co-founder Peak Productions; co-founder, pres. Evolution Entertainment, 1998—; co-founder Twisted Pictures, 2004; mgr. OK Hockey LLC, 2008—; co-owner Tampa Bay Lightning, 2008—. Owner Helena Bighorns, Mont. Prodr.: (films) Mrs. Winterbourne, 1996, Set It Off, 1996, Lockdown, 2000, Good Advice, 2001, Diary of a Sex Addict, 2001, Run Ronnie Run, 2002, John Q, 2002, Dumb and Dumberer: When Harry Met Lloyd, 2003, Saw, 2004, Saw II, 2005, Saw III, 2006, Catacombs, 2007, Dead Silence, 2007, Saw IV, 2007; exec. prodr.: Black and White, 1999, Love Don't Cost a Thing, 2003; (TV series) Two and a Half Men, 2003—; prodr.: The Casino, 2004, Love, Inc, 2005. Office: Evolution Entertainment 901 N Highland Ave Los Angeles CA 90038

KOURLIS, REBECCA LOVE, director, former state supreme court justice; b. Colorado Springs, Colo., Nov. 11, 1952; d. John Arthur and Ann (Daniels) Love; m. Thomas Aristithis Kourlis, July 15, 1978; children: Stacy Ann, Katherine Love, Aristithis Thomas. BA with distinction in English, Stanford U., 1973, JD, 1976; LLD (hon.), U. Denver, 1997. Bar: Colo. 1976, D.C. 1979, U.S. Dist. Ct. Colo. 1976, U.S. Ct. Appeals (10th cir.) 1976, Colo. Supreme Ct., U.S. Ct. Appeals (D.C. cir.), U.S. Claims Ct., U.S. Supreme Ct. Assoc. Davis, Graham & Stubbs, Denver, 1976-78; sole practice Craig, Colo., 1978-87; judge 14th Jud. Dist. Ct., Craig, Colo., 1987-94; arbiter Jud. Arbiter Group, Inc., 1994-95; justice Colo. Supreme Ct., 1995—2006; exec. dir. Inst. Advancement Am. Legal Sys. U. Denver, 2006—. Water judge divsn. 6, 1987-94; lectr. to profl. groups. Contbr. articles to profl. jours. Chmn. Moffat County Arts and Humanities, Craig, 1979; mem. Colo. Commn. on Higher Edn., Denver, 1980-81; mem. adv. bd. Colo. Divsn. Youth Svcs., 1988-91; mem. com. civil jury instructions, 1990-95, standing com. gender and justice, 1994-97, chair jud. adv. coun., 1997-2002, chair com. on jury reform, 1996—, chair com. family issues, 2002—; co-chair com. on atty. grievance reform, 1997-2002; mem. long range planning com. Moffat County Sch., 1990; bd. visitors Stanford U., 1989-94, Law Sch. U. Denver, 1997-2002; trustee Kent Denver Sch., 1996-2002, Graland Sch., 2004—. Named N.W. Colo. Daily Press Woman of Yr., 1993; recipient Trailblazer award AAUW, 1998, Mary Lathrop award Colo. Women's Bar Assn., 2001, Jud. Excellence award Acad. Matrimonial Lawyers, 2002, Champion for Children award Rocky Mountain Children's Law Ctr., 2003, Friend of Children award Adv. for Children, 2003. Fellow: Colo. Bar Found., Am. Bar Found.; mem.: N.W. Colo. Bar Assn. (Cmty. Svc. award 1993—94), Dist. Ct. Judges' Assn. (pres. 1993—94), Colo. Bar Assn. (bd. govs. 1983—85, mineral law sect. bd. dirs. 1985, sr. v.p. 1987—88), Rocky Mountain Mineral Found. Office: 2044 E Evans Ave Ste 307 Denver CO 80208 Office Phone: 303-871-6600. Business E-Mail: legalinstitute@du.edu.

KOURLIS, THOMAS A., state commissioner; m. Rebecca Kourlis; 3 children. BS in Fin., U. Denver. Owner, operator cattle and sheep ranch, Craig, Colo., 1973—; commr. Colo. Dept. Agr., Lakewood, 1994-99. Mem. Colo. Sheep and Wool Bd.; mem. N.W. Coordinated Resource Mgmt. Steering Com.; mem. Colo. Rangeland Reform Working Group; a founder Habitat Partnership Program. Mem. Soc. Range Mgmt. (award for excellence in grazing mgmt.), Colo. Woolgrowers Assn. (pasat v.p.), Am. sheep Industry Assn. (past bd. dirs.). Office: Colo Dept Agr 5310 Nassau Cir E Englewood CO 80110-5142

KOUSSER, J(OSEPH) MORGAN, historian, educator; b. Lewisburg, Tenn., Oct. 7, 1943; s. Joseph Maximillian and Alice Holt (Morgan) K.; m. Sally Ann Ward, June 1, 1968; children: Rachel Meredith, Thaddeus Benjamin. AB, Princeton U., 1965; M.Phil., Yale U., 1968, PhD, 1971; MA, Oxford U., Eng., 1984. Instr. Calif. Inst. Tech., Pasadena, 1969-71, assoc. prof. Padadena, 1975-79, prof., 1979—. Vis. prof. U. Mich., Ann Arbor, 1980, Harvard U., Cambridge, Mass., 1981-82, Oxford U., 1984-85, Claremont Grad. Sch., 1993; expert witness Minority Voting Rights Cases; researcher. Author: Shaping of Southern Politics, 1974, Colorblind Injustice: Minority Voting Rights and the Undoing of the Second Reconstruction, 1999. Recipient Lillian Smith award So. Regional Coun., 1999, Ralph J. Bunche award Am. Polit. Sci. Assn., 2000; Guggenheim Found. fellow, 1984-85, Woodrow Wilson Ctr. fellow, 1984-85; grantee NEH, 1974, 82. Mem. Orgn. Am. Historians, Am. Hist. Assn., Social Scis. History Assn., So. Hist. Assn. Democrat. Avocation: running. Office: Calif Inst Tech 228-77 Caltech Pasadena CA 91125-7700 Office Phone: 626-395-4080. E-mail: kousser@hss.caltech.edu.

KOUYMJIAN, DICKRAN, art historian, educator; b. Tulcea, Romania, June 6, 1934; (parents Am. citizens); s. Toros S. and Zabelle I. (Calusdian) K.; m. Angèle Kapoïan, Sept. 16, 1967. BS in European Cultural History, U. Wis., 1957; MA in Arab Studies, Am. U., Beirut, 1961; PhD in Near East Lang. and Culture, Columbia U., 1969; D (hon.), Nat. Acad. Scis., Republic of Armenia, 2005. Instr. English and gen. edn. depts. Am. U. Beirut, 1959—61; instr. English Columbia U., NYC, 1961-64; dir. Am. Authors, Inc., NYC, 1965-67; asst. prof. and asst. dir. Ctr. for Arabic Studies Am. U., Cairo, 1967-71; prof., chmn. Armenian Studies dept. Haigazian U., Beirut, 1971-72; assoc. prof. history Am. U. Beirut, 1971-75; prof. art history Am. U., Paris, 1976-77; prof. history and art, dir. Armenian Studies program Calif. State U., Fresno, 1977—2008, prof. emeritus, 2008—. Dir. Ctr. for Armenian Studies, Calif. State U., Fresno, 1990—96; Fulbright disting. lectr., prof. Armenian and Am. Lit. Yerevan (Armenia, USSR), 1987; cons. archaeology UNESCO, Paris, 1976; prof., chairholder Armenian Sect., Inst. Nat. des Langs. et Civilisations Orientales, U. Paris, 1988—91; 1st incumbent Haig & Isabel Berberian endowed chair Armenian studies Calif. State U., Fresno, 1989—2008; 2nd incumbent William Saroyan endowed chair of Armenian studies U. Calif., Berkeley, 1996—97; vis. prof. Oriental Inst. U. Louvain-la-Neuve, Belgium, 2001. Author: Index of Armenian Art, part I, 1977, part II, 1979, The Armenian History of Ghazar P'arpetzi, 1986, Arts of Armenia, 1992; co-author: (with A. Kapoïan) The Splendor of Egypt, 1975, (with M. Stone, H. Lehmann) Album of Armenian Paleography, 2002, Armenian edit., 2006, (with Giusto Traina, Carlo Franco, Cecilia Veronese Arslan) History of Alexander of Macedonia: An Illustrated Armenian Manuscript of the 14th Century, 2003; author and editor: William Saroyan: An Armenian Trilogy, 1986, William Saroyan: Warsaw Visitor and Tales of the Vienna Streets, 1990; editor: (books) Near Eastern Numistatics, Iconography, Epigraphy and History, 1974, Essays in Armenian Numismatics in Honor of C. Sibilian, 1981, Armenian Studies: In Memoriam Haïg Berbérian, 1986, Movses of Khoren and Armenian HIstoriography from its Beginnings, 2000; editl. bd. Armenian Rev., 1974—, Ararat Lit. mag., 1975—, Revue des Etudes Arméniennes, 1978—, NAASR Jour. Armenian Studies, Jour. of the Soc. for Armenian Studies, 1995—; contbr. articles to profl. jours. With US Army, 1957. Recipient St. Sahag and St. Mesrob medal His Holiness Karekin I, Catholics of All Armenians, 1996, Outstanding Prof. award Am. U., Cairo, 1968-69, 69-70, Hagop Kevorkian Disting. Lectureship in Near Eastern Art and Civilization, NYU, 1979, Arthur H. Dadian Armenian Heritage award Armenian Students Assn. Am., 2003; voted Outstanding Prof. of Yr., Faculty Senate, Calif. State U., Fresno, 1986-87; Fulbright fellow, USSR, 1986-87, Michael Dukakis fellow Am. Coll. Thessaloniki, 2003; grantee NEH, Paris, 1980-81, 95, Bertha & John Garabedian Charitable Found., 1994—; chosen Scholar of U. Phi Beta Phi Calif. State U., 1999; named Man of Yr. Armenian Nat. Com. Calif., 2000-08, named one of designated Hay & Isabel prof. Am. Studies Emeritus, 2008. Mem. Am. Oriental Soc., Am. Numismatic Soc., Mid. East Studies Assn. (charter), Coll. Arts Assn., Soc. Armenian Studies (charter, pres. 1985-86, 92-94), Sociéte asiatique (Paris), Internat. Assn. of Armenian Studies, Mid. East Medievalist, Assn. Paléographique Internat., Phi Kappa Phi (nat. scholar Fresno chpt. 1998, Univ. Scholar award chpt. 962 1999), Nat. Acad. Scis. Republic Armenia (elect. fgn. mem., 2008), Achievements include selected to serve on jury for annual Francqui Fund Prize, Brussels, 2001. Avocations: music, films, bibliophile. Home: 54 rue Boussingault 75013 Paris France Office: Calif State U Armenian Studies Program 5245 N Backer Ave # PB4 Fresno CA 93740-8001 Office Phone: 559-278-2669. Business E-Mail: dickrank@csufresno.edu.

KOVACEVICH, RICHARD MARCO (DICK KOVACEVICH), bank executive; b. Tacoma, Wash., Oct. 30, 1943; m. Mary Jo Kovacevich; 3 children. BA in Industrial Engring., Stanford U., 1965, M in Industrial Engring., 1966, MBA, 1967. With strategic planning divsn. Gen. Mills, Inc., Mpls., 1967—69, gen. mgr. Kenner divsn. Cin., 1969—72; prin. Am. Photographic Corp., L.I., NY, 1972-75; v.p. consumer services Citicorp, 1975—77, mgr. internat. consumer ops., 1982—86; vice-chmn., COO banking group Norwest Corp., Mpls., 1986—89, pres., COO, 1989—93, CEO, 1993—96, chmn., 1995—96; chmn., CEO Wells Fargo & Co. (merged with Norwest Corp.), 1996—98; pres., CEO Wells Fargo & Co., San Francisco, 1998—2001, chmn., pres., CEO, 2001—05, chmn., CEO, 2005—07, chmn., 2007—. Bd. dirs. Norwest Corp., 1986—98, Dayton Hudson, 1996—2000, Wells Fargo & Co., 1998—, Target Corp., 2000—, Cisco Systems, Inc., 2005—; mem. Fed. Res. Fed. Advisory Coun., Calif. Bus. Roundtable, Calif. Commn. for Jobs and Economic Growth; chmn. San Francisco Com. on Jobs. V.p., bd. governors San Francisco Symphony; vice chmn., bd. trustees San Francisco Museum of Modern Art. Recipient Banker of the Year, Am. Banker, 2003. Republican. Office: Wells Fargo & Co 420 Montgomery St San Francisco CA 94163-1205 Office Phone: 415-396-4928.

KOVACH, ROBERT LOUIS, geophysics educator; b. LA, Feb. 15, 1934; s. Nicholas Arthur and Stefania Teresa (Rüssler) K.; m. Linda Elly Heyn, Dec. 23, 1960; children: Denise Lynn, Dianne Yvonne, John Robert, Robert John. Geophysical Engring Degree, Colo. Sch. Mines, 1955; MA, Columbia U., 1959; PhD, Calif. Inst. Tech., 1962. Registered geophysicist, Calif. Sr. scientist Jet Propulsion Lab., Pasadena, Calif., 1961-63; asst. prof. Calif. Inst. Tech., Pasadena, 1963-65, Stanford (Calif.) U., 1965-66, assoc. prof., 1966-70, prof. geophysics, 1970—. Prin. investigator Apollo Moon Seismic Expts., 1996-76; cons. DOE, 1996-97. Author: Earth's Fury, 1995, Conflict with the Earth, 1997. Lt. U.S. Army, 1956-58. Fellow John Simon Guggenheim Found., 1971; recipient Exceptional Sci. Achievement award NASA, 1973. Fellow Geol. Soc. Am.; mem. Am. Geophysical Union (pres. seismology sect. 1976-78), Can. Well Logging Soc., Seismol. Soc. Am., Soc. Exploration Geophysicists. Office: Dept Geophysics Stanford University Stanford CA 94305 Office Phone: 415-723-4827. Business E-Mail: kov@pangea.stanford.edu.

KOVACHY, EDWARD MIKLOS, JR., psychiatrist, consultant; b. Cleve., Dec. 3, 1946; s. Edward Miklos and Evelyn Amelia (Palenscar) K.; m. Susan Eileen Light, June 21, 1981; children: Timothy Light, Benjamin Light. BA, Harvard U., 1968, JD, MBA, Harvard U., 1972; MD, Case Western Reserve U., 1977. Diplomate Nat. Bd. Med. Examiners. Resident in psychiatry Stanford U. Med. Ctr., Stanford, Calif., 1977-81; pvt. practice psychiatry, mediation, exec. coaching Menlo Park, Calif., 1981—. Presenter ann. meeting Am. Psychol. Assn., 1998, Calif. Assn. Marriage and Family Therapists, 1999. Co-prodr. Jolson and Company, Century Ctr. for the Performing Arts, N.Y.C., 2002; columnist The Peninsula Times Tribune, 1983-85. Trustee Mid-Peninsula H.S., Palo Alto, Calif., 1990-2001, mem. bd. advisors, 2001—; mem. gift com. Harvard Coll. Class of 1968, 25th reunion chmn. participation, San Francisco, 1993, 30th reunion chmn. participation, West Coast, 1998, nat. co-chmn. participation and assocs. giving, 1999—, nat. co-chmn. participation, 35th reunion, 2003, nat. co-chmn. participation, 40th reunion, 2008. Recipient Albert H. Gordon award Harvard U., 2000, 05, 07, Joseph R. Hamlen award Harvard U., 2003; named to Hall of Fame, Shaker Heights Alumni Assn., 2003. Mem. Am. Psychiat. Assn. (presenter annual meetings 1984, 98), Physicians for Social Responsibility, Assn. Family and Conciliation Cts., No. Calif. Psychiat. Soc., Harvard Alumni Assn. (dir. 2006—). Presbyterian. Avocations: personal activism, musical comedy, athletics. Office: 1187 University Dr Menlo Park CA 94025-4423 Office Phone: 650-329-0600. Personal E-mail: edkovachy@aol.com.

KOVTYNOVICH, DAN, geotechnical engineer, civil engineer, scientist; b. Eugene, Oreg., May 17, 1952; s. John and Elva Lano (Robie) K. BCE, Oreg. State U., 1975, BBA, 1976. Registered profl. engr., Calif., Oreg. V.p. Kovtynovich, Inc., Contractors and Engrs., Eugene, 1976-80, pres., chief exec. officer, 1980—. Appointee State of Oreg. Bldg. Codes and Structures Bd., 1996-2005. Fellow ASCE; mem. Am. Arbitration Assn. (arbitrator/mediator 1979—, mem. dispute rev. bd. found.), N.W. China Coun., Navy League of U.S., Eugene Asian Coun. Republican. Avocations: flying, skiing, fishing, hunting. Office: Kovtynovich Inc PO Box 898 Lake Oswego OR 97034-0143

KOWALSKI, KAZIMIERZ, computer science educator, researcher; b. Turek, Poland, Nov. 7, 1946; arrived in U.S., 1986, naturalized, 1994; s. Waclaw and Helena K.; m. Eugenia Zajaczkowska, Aug. 5, 1972. MSc, Wroclaw U. Tech., Poland, 1970, PhD, 1974. Asst. prof. Wroclaw U. Tech., 1970-76, assoc. prof., 1976-86, Pan Am. U., Edinburg, Tex., 1987-88; prof. computer sci. Calif. State U.-Dominguez Hills, Carson, 1988—, chmn. computer sci. dept., 1998—2001. Lectr. U. Basrah, Iraq, 1981-85; cons. XXCal, Inc., L.A., 1987-91; conf. presenter in field; rsch. fellow Power Inst. Moscow, USSR, 1978; info. sys. tng. UNESCO, Paris, 1978; cons. Tex. Instruments, Inc., 1999-2001. Co-author: Principles of Computer Science, 1975, Organization and Programming of Computers, 1976; also articles. Recipient Bronze Merit Cross, Govt. of Poland, 1980, Knights' Cross of the Order of Merit, Republic of Poland, 1997, Disting. Tchrs. award, 1998. Mem. IEEE Computer Soc., Assn. for Advancement of Computing in Edn., Mensa, Sigma Xi. Avocations: travel, puzzles. Home: 3836 Weston Pl Long Beach CA 90807-3317 Office: Calif State U 1000 E Victoria St Carson CA 90747-0001 Office Phone: 310-243-2034. Personal E-mail: kazikk@gmail.com.

KOZBERG, JOANNE CORDAY, public affairs consultant; b. Edmonton, Alta., Can., July 4, 1944; d. Eliot and Marian (Lipkind) Corday; m. Roger A. Kozberg, May 25, 1968; children: Lindsey, Anthony. BA in history, U. Calif., Berkeley, 1966; MA in pub. policy, Occidental Coll., 1969. Assoc. prodr. KCET Cmty. Affairs Dept., LA, 1967-68; dir. So. Calif. NAACP Legal Def. and Edn. Fund, LA, 1975-77; acting exec. dir., dir. pub. affairs and the arts program CORO Found., LA, 1978-81; sr. policy cons. to US Senator Pete Wilson, LA, 1984-88; chair Calif. Arts Coun., 1988—91, exec. dir., 1991-93; sec. state and consumer affairs State of Calif., 1993-98; pres., COO Music Ctr. of LA County, 1999—2002; now ptnr. Calif. Strategies, LA. Mem. Nat. Hwy. Adv. Commn., Washington, 1980-86; dir. Western States Arts Fedn., Santa Fe, 1991-94, Nat. Assembly of State Arts Agys., Washington, 1992-94. Pres. The Blue Ribbon, LA, 1988—91; trustee Calif. Cmty. Found.; bd. dirs. Ctr. Theatre Group, LA, 1994—99; bd. regents U. Calif., 1998—; bd. trustees J. Paul Getty Trust, LA, 2005—. Recipient Rosalie M. Stern award U. Calif., Berkeley, 1984, Crystal Eagle award for pub. affairs excellence, Coro Found., 1998; CORO fellow, 1967. Mem. Calif. Club, Hillcrest Country Club. Republican. Jewish. Avocations: bicycling, tennis. Office: Calif Strategies Ste 1025 1875 Century Pk E Los Angeles CA 90067

KOZINSKI, ALEX, federal judge; b. Bucharest, Romania, July 23, 1950; came to US, 1962; s. Moses and Sabine (Zapler) K.; m. Marcy J. Tiffany, July 9, 1977; children: Yale Tiffany, Wyatt Tiffany, Clayton Tiffany. AB in Econs. cum laude, UCLA, 1972, JD, 1975. Bar: Calif. 1975, DC, 1978. Law clk. to Hon. Anthony M. Kennedy US Ct. Appeals (9th Cir.), 1975-76; law clk. to Chief Justice Warren E. Burger US Supreme Ct., 1976-77; assoc. Covington & Burling, Washington, 1979-81; dep. legal counsel Office Pres-elect, Washington, 1980; asst. counsel to Pres. The White House, Washington, 1981; spl. counsel Merit Systems Protection Bd., Washington, 1981-82; chief judge US Claims Ct., Washington, 1982-85; judge US Ct. Appeals (9th Cir.), Pasadena, Calif., 1985—, chief judge, 2007—. Lectr. law U. So. Calif., 1992. Office: US Ct Appeals Ste 200 125 S Grand Ave Pasadena CA 91105

KOZLOFF, LLOYD M., dean, microbiologist, educator; b. Chgo., Oct. 15, 1923; s. Joseph and Rose (Hollobow) K.; m. Judith Bonnie Friedman, June 16, 1947; children: James, Daniel, Joseph, Sarah BS, U. Chgo., 1943, PhD, 1948. Asst., then assoc. prof. biochemistry U. Chgo., 1949-61, prof., 1961-64; prof. microbiology U. Colo., Denver, 1964-80, chmn. dept. microbiology, 1966-76, assoc. dean, prof., 1976-80; dean, prof. U. Calif., San Francisco, 1981-91, prof., dean emeritus, 1991—. Career investigator USPHS, U. Chgo., 1962 Founding editor Jour. Virology, 1966-76; contbr. articles to profl. jours., chpts. to books. Chmn. bd. dirs. Proctor Fund., 1981-91; v.p. San Francisco Alliance for Mental Illness, 1993-96; pres. emeritus U. Calif. San Francisco Faculty Assn., 1996-2000. With USN, 1944-46. Commonwealth Fund fellow, 1953, Lederle Found. fellow, 1954; recipient Disting. Svc. award U. Chgo., 2004. Fellow AAAS, Am. Acad. Microbiol. (hon.); mem. Am. Soc. Biol. Chemistry, Am. Soc. Microbiology (head virology sect. 1974-76), Am. Chem. Soc., N.Y. Acad. Sci. Home: 43000 Lyndon Ln Fort Bragg CA 95437 Office: U Calif Grad Divsn San Francisco CA 94114-2732

KOZLOFF, THEODORE J., lawyer; b. Reading, Pa., 1941; BA, U. Pa., 1964, MA in Econ., 1964, LLB cum laude, 1967. Bar: Calif. 1967, N.Y. 1968. Mem. Comm. on Securities Regulation, Assoc. of the Bar of the City of New York, 1981—84, Skadden, Arps, Slate, Meagher & Flom, San Francisco; Board of Overseers University of Pennsylvania Law School, 1986—90; bd. trustees The Hill School, Pottstown, Pa., 1987—96. Editor U. Pa. Law Rev., 1966-67. Office: Skadden Arps Slate Meagher & Flom 4 Embarcadero Ctr San Francisco CA 94111-4106

KOZOLCHYK, BORIS, law educator, consultant; b. Havana, Cuba, Dec. 6, 1934; came to U.S., 1956; s. Abram and Chana (Brewda) D.; m. Elaine Billie Herman, Mar. 5, 1967; children: Abbie Simcha, Raphael Adam, Shaun Marcie. DCL, U. Havana, 1956; Diplome, Faculte Internat. de Droit, Luxembourg, 1958; LLB, U. Miami, 1959; LLM, U. Mich., 1960, SJD, 1966. Teaching asst. Sch. of Law U. Miami, Fla., 1957-59; asst. prof. law Sch. of Law So. Meth. U., Dallas, 1960-64; resident cons. The Rand Corp., Santa Monica, Calif., 1964-67; dir. Law Reform Project USAID, San Jose, Costa Rica, 1967-69; prof. law Coll. of Law U. Ariz., 1969—. Tchg. asst. Faculte Internat. de Droit Campare, 1958; vis. prof. law Nat. U. of Mex., 1961; vis. exch. prof. law Nat. U. of Chile, Santiago, 1962; guest lectr. Latin Am. Law seminar Stanford (Calif.) U., 1964; guest lectr. extension grad. seminar on Latin Am. law UCLA, 1965; Bailey vis. prof., Tucker lectr. La. State U., 1979; vis. prof. U. Aix en Provence, France, 1985; cons. on legal sys. U.S. Agy. Internat. Devel., 1974-77; legal cons. Overseas Pvt. Investment Corp., 1974; cons. uniformity of comml. laws Orgn. Am. States and U.S. State Dept., 1974-77; expert witness on banking and comml. law and custom issues; advisor Libr. Congress Law divsn.; Joseph Bernfeld Meml. lectr. L.A. Bankruptcy Forum, 1989; magisterial lectr. Nat. U. Mex. Sch. Law, 1989; advisor Project Lao, 1991; lectr. in field. Author of books; bd. mem. Am. Jour. of Comparative Law; mem. editl. bd. Internat. Banking Law Jour.; founder, faculty advisor Ariz. Jour. of Internat. and Comparative Law, 1982-86; reporter Ency. Comparative Law, 1989; contbr. articles to profl. jours. and publs. Selected Nat. U. Mex. rep. First Mexican congress Comml. Law, 1974; pres. Ariz. Friends of Music, 1975-76; hon. chmn. community rels. com. Jewish Fedn. So. Ariz.; mem. adv. com. Ariz.-Mex. Commn. Govs.; legal advisor Ariz.-Mex. Banking com.; del U.S. Coun. on Internat. Banking to ICC; adv. mem. U.S. del. to UNCITRAL Internal. Contract Law, 1989-95, 2009; dir., pres., bd. dirs. Nat. Law Ctr. for InterAm. Free Trade, 1992—. NSF grantee, 1973-75; recipient Extraordinary Tchg. and Rsch. Merit award Coll. Law, U. Costa Rica, 1969, Cmty. Svc. award Tucson Jewish Cmty. Coun., 1979, Man of Yr. award, 1982, Commendation award U.S. Dept. Justice, 1979, Disting. Svc. award Law Coll. Alumni Assn., 1990, Commendation award U.S. Dept. State, 1990, Ptnrs. in Democracy award Am.-Israel Friendship League, 2003, cert. of Honor Outstanding Contbn. Civil Rights and Social Justice, Tucson Human Rels. Commn., 2003, Excellence in Internat. Edn. award U. Ariz. Ctr. for ESL, 2004; named to Hall of Fame Profs. of Comml. Law, Nat. U., Mex., 1987; named One of Most Influential Hispanics, Hispanic Bus. Mag., 1991, Man of Yr., Hispanic Profl. Action Com., 1995; Guadalajara chpt. Mex. and US Student Bar Assn. was named the Boris Kozolchyk chpt., Guadalajara br. The Inst. Legal Rsch. of Tech. Monterrey named the Boris Kozolchyk Inst. Mem. ABA (task force for the revision of UCC article 5, Leonard J. Theberge award 2004), State of Ariz. Bar (Honoree at 100 Women and Minority Lawyers Dinner), Inter-ABA (co-chmn. comml. law and procedure sec. 1973-78, Best Book award 1973), Am. Soc. Internat. Law, Internat. Acad. Comml. and Consumer Law (pres. 1988-90), Am. Acad. Fgn. Law (founding), Am. Law Inst. (consultative com. to UCC articles 3, 4, 4a and 5), Nat. Mexican Notarial Bar Assn. (hon. life 1982), Internat. Acad. Comml. and Consumer Law (elected pres. 1988), Sonora Bar Assn. (1st Disting. Svc. award 1989), Nat. Law Ctr. Inter-Am. Free Trade Bldg. Home: 7401 N Skyline Dr Tucson AZ 85718-1166 Office: U Ariz Coll Of Law Tucson AZ 85721-0001 Home Phone: 520-297-1642. Personal E-mail: b.kozolchyk@natlaw.com.

KRAEMER, HELENA ANTOINETTE CHMURA, psychiatry educator; Degree, Stanford U., 1963. With Stanford U., 1964—, prof. biostats. in psychiatry, Dept. Psychiatry and Behavioral Scis., 1991—, mem. Comprehensive Cancer Ctr. Mem. editorial bd. Jour. Child & Adolescent Psychopharmacology. Co-author: How Many Subjects?: Statistical Power Analysis in Rsch., 1987, Evaluating Medical Tests: Objective & Quantitative Guidelines, 1992, To Your Health: How to Understand What Research Tells Us About Risk, 2005. Recipient Harvard award in psychiat. epidemiology and biostats., 2001. Mem.: Inst. Medicine. Office: Stanford U Dept Psychiatry and Behavioral Scis 300 Pasteur Dr Stanford CA 94305 also: Stanford Comprehensive Cancer Ctr 875 Blake Wilbur Dr Stanford CA 94305

KRAEMER, KENNETH LEO, architect, urban planner, educator; b. Plain, Wis., Oct. 29, 1936; s. Leo Adam and Lucy Rose (Bauer) K.; m. Norine Florence, June 13, 1959; children: Kurt Randall, Kim Rene. BArch, U. Notre Dame, Ind., 1959; MS in City and Regional Planning, U. So. Calif., 1964, M of Pub. Adminstrn., 1965, PhD, 1967. From instr. to asst. prof. U. So. Calif., LA, 1965-67; from asst. prof. to rsch. prof. U. Calif., Merage Sch. Bus., Irvine, 1967—, dir. Pub. Policy Rsch. Orgn., 1974-92, dir. Ctr. Rsch. Info. Tech. and Orgns., 1992—2007, dir. Ctr. Study Personal Computing Industry, 2004—, Taco Bell chair in IT for mgmt. Cons. Office of Tech. Assessment, Washington, 1980, 84-85; pres. Irvine Research Corp., 1978—. Author: Management of Information Systems, 1980, Computers and Politics, 1982, Dynamics of Computing, 1983, People and Computers, 1985, Modeling as Negotiating, 1986, Data Wars, 1987, Wired Cities, 1987, Managing Information Systems, 1989, Asia's Computer Challenge, 1998, Globalization of E-Commerce, 2006, Computerzation Monuments and Technology Diffusion, 2008. Mem. Blue Ribbon Data Processing Com., Orange County, Calif., 1973, 79-80, Telecomm. Adv. Bd., Sacramento, 1987-92. Fellow Assn. for Info. Sys.(LEO Lifetime Achievement award, 2009); mem. Am. Soc. for Pub. Adminstrn. (Disting. Research award 1985), Internat. Conf. on Info. Systems, Am. Planning Assn., Assn. for Computing Machinery, Notre Dame Club. Democrat. Roman Catholic. Office: U Calif Ctr Rsch Info Tech & Orgns Berkley Pl N Ste 3200 Irvine CA 92697-0001 E-mail: kkraemer@uci.edu.

KRAFT, ARTHUR, dean; b. Eden, NY, May 7, 1944; s. Arthur Brauer and Mary Jane (Forti) K.; m. Joan Marie Brown, Sept. 3, 1966; children: Arthur G., Stephen Michael, Leigh Judith. BS, St. Bonaventure U., 1966; MA, SUNY, Buffalo, 1969, PhD, 1970. Asst. prof. Ohio U., Athens, 1969—72, assoc. prof., 1972—75; prof. U. Nebr., Lincoln, 1975—77, assoc. dean Coll. Bus., 1977—83; dean Coll. Bus. and Econs. W.Va. U., Morgantown, 1983—87; dean sch. bus. Rutgers U., New Brunswick, NJ, 1987—93; dean Sch. Mgmt. Ga. Inst. Tech., Atlanta, 1993—97; dean Coll. Commerce, Charles H. Kellstadt Grad Sch. Bus. DePaul U., Chgo., 1997—2005; dean Robert J. and Carolyn A. Waltos, Jr. chair in bus. and econs. George L. Argyros Sch. Bus. and Econs. Chapman U., Orange, Calif., 2006—. Mem. pension adv. com. Monongalia County Hosp., Morgantown, 1985-87., 1985—87. Recipient NASA fellowship Stanford U., 1973, fellow Sears-Roebuck Fellowship Found., Washington, 1974-75; named Outstanding Young Individual Jaycees, Lincoln, 1978 Mem. Am. Econ. Assn., Am. Assembly of Collegiate Schs. of Bus. (chmn. bd. 2006-07, visitation com. 1977—, continuing accreditation com. 1987, bus. accreditation com. 1995—), North Ctrl. Assn. (evaluator 1986-87), Beta Gamma Sigma. Avocations: trivia, sports. Office: Chapman Univ George L Argyros Sch Business Economics Beckman Hall One University Dr Orange CA 92866 Office Phone: 714-628-2839. Personal E-mail: artkraft07@yahoo.com.

KRAFT, DONALD BOWMAN, advertising agency executive; b. Seattle, Mar. 20, 1927; s. Warren E. and Beulah (Bowman) K.; m. Mary Jo Erickson, Dec. 20, 1973; children: Daniel, Karen Kraft VanderHoek, Berkeley, Erika. BA, U. Wash., 1948. Pres. Kraft Advt., Seattle, 1948-54; v.p. Honig Cooper, Seattle, 1954-59; pres., chief exec. officer Kraft Smith Advt., Seattle, 1959-84, Evans, Kraft Advt., Seattle, 1984-87; chmn. emeritus EvansGroup, Publics, Seattle, 1998—. Chmn. Evans Group, Inc., Salt Lake City, 1989—. Bd. dirs. KCTS Assn., Public TV, Seattle, 1982-90. Served with USN, 1945-46. Recipient Man and Boy award Boys Club Am., 1960; named Young Man of Yr., Seattle Jaycees, 1962 Mem. Am. Assn. Advt. Agys. (chmn. we. region 1962-64, nat. sec.-treas. 1970-71, mem. nat. govt. relations com. 1983-86), Affiliated Advt. Agys. Internat. (internat. pres. 1967-68, Albert Emery Mgmt. Excellence award 1984, 92), Young Pres.'s Orgn Alumni (chmn. Pacific NW chpt. 1980-81), Greater Seattle C. of C. (bd. dirs.). Clubs: Wash. Athletic (pres. 1987-88), Rainier (pres. 1990-91), Seattle Tennis, Broadmoor Golf, Rotary Seattle (pres. 1973-74, Paul Harris fellow 1974). Republican. Methodist. Home: 6530 NE Windermere Rd Seattle WA 98105-2058 Office: 424 2nd Ave W Fl 5 Seattle WA 98119-4013

KRAFT, GEORGE HOWARD, physician, educator; b. Columbus, Ohio, Sept. 27, 1936; s. Glen Homer and Helen Winner (Howard) K.; children: Jonathan Ashbrook, Susannah Mary. AB, Harvard U., 1958; MD, Ohio State U., 1963, MS, 1967. Diplomate Am. Bd. Phys. Medicine and Rehab. (subspecialty in spinal cord injury medicine), Am. Bd. Electrodiagnostic Medicine. Intern U. Calif. Hosp., San Francisco, 1963—64, resident in phys. medicine and rehab., 1964—65, Ohio State U., Columbus, 1965—67; assoc. U. Pa. Med. Sch., Phila., 1968—69; asst. prof. U. Wash., Seattle, 1969—72, assoc. prof., 1972—76, prof., 1976—, Alvord prof. MS rsch., 2005—; chief of staff U. Wash. Med. Ctr., Seattle, 1993—95. Dir. electrodiagnostic medicine U. Wash. Hosp., 1987—, dir. Multiple Sclerosis Ctr., 1982—; co-dir. Muscular Dystrophy Clinic, 1974—; bd. dirs. Am. Bd. Electrodiagnostic Medicine, 1993-2000, chmn., 1996-2000 Co-author: Chronic Disease and Disability, 1994, Living with Multiple Sclerosis: A Wellness Approach, 2000, The M.S. Workbook, 2006; cons. editor: Phys. Medicine and Rehab. Clinics, 1990—, EEG and Clin. Neurophysiology, 1992-96; assoc. editor Jour. Neurol. Rehab. and Neurol. Repair, 1988-2000, Muscle and Nerve, 1998-2000; contbr. articles to profl. jours. Sci. peer rev. com. C Nat. Multiple Sclerosis Soc., N.Y.C., 1990-96, chmn., 1993-96, med. adv. bd., 1991—; bd. sponsors Wash. Physicians for Social Responsibility, Seattle, 1986—. Rsch. grantee Rehab. Svcs. Adminstrn., 1976-81, Nat. Inst. Handicapped Rsch., 1984-88, Nat. Multiple Sclerosis Soc., 1990-92, 94-95, 2005—Nat. Inst. Disability and REhab. Rsch., 1998—. Fellow Am. Acad. Phys. Medicine and Rehab. (pres. 1984-85, Zeiter award 1991, Krusen award 2002); mem. Am. Assn. Electrodiagnostic Medicine (pres. 1982-83. Lifetime Achievement award 2004), Assn. Acad. Physiatrists (pres. 1980-81), Am. Acad. Clin. Neurophysiology (pres. 1995-97), Am. Acad. Neurology, Internat. Rehab. Medicine Assn., Alpha Omega Alpha. Episcopalian. Office: Dept Rehab Med U Wash PO Box 956490 Seattle WA 98195 Home Phone: 206-467-0206; Office Phone: 206-543-7272.

KRAFT, JAMES ALLEN, lawyer; b. Seattle, Mar. 8, 1955; s. Warren Earl and Barbara Anne (Allen) K.; m. Dominique Patricia Posy, Aug. 4, 1984. AB in East Asian Studies cum laude, Harvard U., 1978, JD, 1982. Bars: N.Y. 1982, Wash. 1984. Assoc. Milbank, Tweed, Hadley & Mc Cloy, NYC, 1982-84; assoc. corp. counsel Burlington Northern, Inc., Seattle, 1984-88; sr. corp. counsel Burlington Resources, Inc., Seattle, 1988, asst. v.p. law, 1989; v.p. law and corp. affairs Plum Creek Timber Co., Seattle, 1989—2002, sr. v.p., gen. counsel and sec., 2002—. Contbr. articles to profl. jours. Mem. bd. trustees Pacific Northwest Ballet Co., Seattle, 1986—. Mem. ABA, Wash. State Bar Assn., N.Y. State Bar Assn., Japan Am. Soc. State Wash., (trustee 1987—). Clubs: Lincoln's Inn Soc. (Cambridge, Mass.) (co-chmn. 1981-82). Republican. Avocations: squash, gardening. Office: Plum Creek Timber Co 999 3rd Ave Ste 4300 Seattle WA 98104-4096

KRAFT, RICHARD LEE, lawyer; b. Lassa, Nigeria, Oct. 14, 1958; m. Tanya Kraft, July 14, 1984; children: Devin, Kelsey. BA in Fgn. Svc., Baylor U., 1980, JD, 1982. Bar: N.Mex. 1982, U.S. Dist. Ct. N.Mex., U.S. Ct. Appeals, U.S. Supreme Ct. Assoc. Sanders, Bruin & Baldock, Roswell, N.Mex., 1982-87, ptnr., 1987-98, Kraft & Stone, LLP, Roswell, 1998-2000; owner The Kraft Law Firm, 2000—. Vol. lawyer Ea. N.Mex. U., Roswell, 1984-98; bd. dirs. Roswell YMCA, 1983-87, Crimestoppers, 1991-94; pres. Roswell Mens Ch. Basketball League; participant Roswell Mens Ch. Softball League; asst. chair legal div. United Way Drive, 1990; pres. sch. bd. Valley Christian Acad., 2003—. Recipient Outstanding Contbn. award N.Mex. State Bar, 1987, 2000. Mem. N.Mex. Bar Assn. (bd. dirs. young lawyers div. 1983-91, pres. 1986-87, chmn. membership com., bar commr. 1986-87, 91-2003, pres. 1998-99, Outstanding Young Lawyer award 1990), Chaves County Bar Assn. (chair law day activities, chair ann. summer picnic com., rep. bench and bar com.), Roswell Legal Secs. Assn. (hon.), Roswell C. of C. (participant and pres. Leadership Roswell, exec. dir., bd. dirs. 1991-), Sertoma (bd. dirs. Roswell club 1989-91) Valley Christian Acad. (pres., bd. dirs., 2003-). Baptist. Office: Kraft & Hunter LLP 111 W Third St Roswell NM 88201-4783 Office Phone: 505-625-2000. Business E-Mail: rkraft@krafthunter.com.

KRAFT, ROBERT PAUL, astronomer, educator; b. Seattle, June 16, 1927; s. Victor Paul and Viola Eunice (Ellis) K.; m. Rosalie Ann Reichmuth, Aug. 28, 1949; children: Kenneth, Kevin. BS, U. Wash., 1947, MS, 1949; PhD, U. Calif.-Berkeley, 1955; DSc (hon.), Ind. U., 1995. Postdoctoral fellow Mt. Wilson Obs., Carnegie Inst., Pasadena, Calif., 1955-56; asst. prof. astronomy Ind. U., Bloomington, 1956-58, Yerkes Obs., U. Chgo., Williams Bay, Wis., 1958-59; staff Hale Obs., Pasadena, 1960-67; prof., astronomer Lick Obs., U. Calif., Santa Cruz, 1967-92; astronomer, prof. emeritus, 1992—. Acting dir. Lick Obs., 1968-70, 71-73, dir., 1981-91; dir. U. Calif. Observatories, 1988-91; chmn. Fachbeirat, Max-Planck-Inst., Munich, Fed. Republic Germany, 1978-88; bd. dirs. Cara corp. (Keck Obs.), Pasadena, 1985-91; bd. dirs. AURA, 1989-92. Contbr. articles to profl. jours. Jila vis. fellow U. Colo., Nat. Bur. Stds., Boulder, 1970; Fairchild scholar Calif. Inst. Tech., Pasadena, 1980, Tinsley prof. U. Tex., 1991-92; Henry Norris Russell lectr. Am. Astron. Soc., 1995; recipient Disting. Alumnus award Coll. Arts and Scis., U. Wash., 1995, Catherine Wolfe Bruce Gold medal Astron. Soc. Pacific, 2005. Mem. Nat. Acad. Sci., Am. Acad. of Arts and Scis., Am. Astron. Soc. (pres. 1974-76, Warner prize 1962, Russell prize lectr. 1995), Internat. Astron. Union (v.p. 1982-88, pres.-elect 1994-97, pres. 1997-2000), Astron. Soc. Pacific (bd. dirs. 1981-87), Royal Astron. Soc. (fgn. assoc.). Democrat. Unitarian Universalist. Avocations: contract bridge, art appreciation, classical music, opera, eonology. Office: U Calif Lick Observatory Santa Cruz CA 95064 E-mail: kraft@ucolick.org.

KRAFT, SCOTT COREY, news correspondent; b. Kansas City, Mo., Mar. 31, 1955; s. Marvin Emanuel and Patricia (Kirk) K.; m. Elizabeth Brown, May 1, 1982; children: Kate, Kevin. BS, Kans. State U., 1977. Staff writer AP, Jefferson City, Mo., 1976-77, Kansas City, 1977-79, corr. Wichita, Kans., 1979-80, nat. writer NYC, 1980-84; nat. corr. L.A. Times, Chgo., 1984-86, bur. chief Nairobi, Kenya, 1986-88, Johannesburg, South Africa, 1988-93, Paris, 1993-96, dep. fgn. editor, 1996-97, nat. editor, 1997—. Recipient Disting. Reporting in a Specialized Field award Soc. of the Silurians, 1982, Peter Lisagor award Headline Club Chgo., 1985, Feature Writing finalist Pulitzer Prize Bd., 1985, Sigma Delta Chi award, 1993. Office: LA Times Nat Editor 202 W 1st St Los Angeles CA 90012

KRAININ, JULIAN ARTHUR, film director, producer, cinematographer, writer; b. NYC, Jan. 24, 1941; s. David A. and Anne N. (Wineblatt) K.; m. Martha Wineblatt, June 17, 1967; 1 child, Todd Philip. BS, Allegheny Coll., 1962, HHD (hon.), 1993; MFA, Columbia U., 1965. Prodr. spl. projects Westinghouse Broadcasting Co., NYC, 1967-69, also prodr., dir., writer, 1967—; v.p., exec. prodr. Krainin/Sage Prodns., Inc., NYC, 1969-80, also dir., writer, 1969-80; pres. Krainin Prodns., Inc., NYC, 1976—. Nat. lectr. motion pictures at various univs. and colls., 1967—; cons. on films U. Mass., 1973; juror Mid-West Film Makers and Graphic Arts Festival, 1971-72, Nat. Emmy Awards, 1975-82, 85-90, Dirs. Guild of Am. Awards, 1987-90; mem. journalism adv. bd. Queens Coll., 1987-90; bd. dirs. Bklyn. Ctr. for Families in Crises, 1986-90; journalism adv. bd. Queens Coll. Films include: The Reluctant Revolution, 1968, Exit to Nowhere, 1967, Promises to Keep, 1967, The March, 1965, Nowhere Fast, 1968, Hide and Seek, 1966, (with Jacques Cousteau) Oceans: The Silent Crisis, 1972, Art is (Acad. award nominee, hon. screenings White House, Mus. Modern Art), 1972, The Other Americans (Emmy award), 1969, Princeton: A Search for Answers (Acad. award), 1973, The American Experiment, 1974, Going Metric, 1975, To America, 1976, The Broken Silence, 1976, The World of James Michener: Hawaii Revisited, 1977, The World of James Michener: The South Pacific, End of Eden? (hon. screening Mus. Modern Art), 1978, (with Ed Asner) The Writer, 1980, The Making of an Opera, 1980, Luciano Pavorotti At Home, 1980, La Gioconda miniseries, 1980, Heritage: Civilization and the Jews (Peabody, Emmy, Christopher awards), 1981-82, PBS series, CBS Reports: Don't Touch that Dial!: The Making of a Television Series (Emmy nominee, TV Guide citation, 1982, The Smithsonian Quadrangle: A View from the Castle, 1984,

America Undercover: The Wrong Man, 1985-86, (with Tom Peters) The Power of Excellence, 1987; (with Abba Eban) Heritage: Civilization and the Jews, Disaster at Silo 7, 1988, Memory and Imagination, New Pathways to the Library of Congress, 1990; documentary film: The Television Quiz Show Scandal, 1991, Queen's College, 1993, (feature film) Quiz Show, 1994 (4 Acad. award nominations including Best Picture), The Unabomber: Deadly Mail!, 1996, The Thousand Acre Universe, 1996, George Wallace (Golden Globe, Humanitas, Cable Ace, Peabody awards), The John Glenn Story: Return to Space and Return of the Hero, 1998-99, Something the Lord Made, 2004 (Emmy, 9 Nominations, 3 awards including Best TV Movie, Peabody, Am. Film. Inst., Dir. Guild Am., Christopher, NAACP Image, Freddie, TV Critics Assn. awards and nominations). Recipient numerous awards and citations including Acad. Award, 1973, Emmy Award, 1969, 2004, Chgo. Internat. Film Festival award, 1969, 77, 78, Florence Internat. Film Festival award, 1969, Cine Golden Eagle awards, 1969, 72, 73, 74, 76, 78, Photog. Soc. Am. award, 1968, Venice Film Festival award, 1970, Moscow Internat. Film Festival award, 1970, Cindy award Prodrs. Assn. Am., 1971, 76, San Francisco Internat. Film Festival award, 1972, Am. Film Festival award, 1974, 76, 78, Tel Aviv Internat. Film Festival award, 1970, Atlanta Internat. Film Festival award, 1969, 72, Festival of Ams. award, 1976, N.Y. Internat. Film and TV Festival award, 1969, 72, Gabriel award, 1968-70, Oberhausen Internat. Film Festival award, 1969, Columbus Film Festival award, 1973, Mannheim Internat. Film Festival award, 1969, U.S. Indsl. Film Festival award, 1973, Ohio State award, 1967, N.Y. Film Festival at Lincoln Center award, 1970. Mem. Writers Guild Am. (awards), Acad. Motion Picture Arts and scis., Photog. Soc. Am., Dirs. Guild Am. (award 1973). Office: 25211 Summerhill Ln Stevenson Ranch CA 91381-2262 Office Phone: 661-259-9700. Business E-Mail: krainin@ca.rr.com.

KRALL, DIANA, musician, singer; b. Nanaimo, BC, Can., Nov. 16, 1964; m. Elvis Costello, Dec. 2003; children: Dexter Henry Lorcan, Frank Harlan James. Student, Berklee Coll. Music, 1982—84; degree (hon.), U. Victoria. With Justin Time Records, Montreal, Que., Canada, 1993, GRP, Verve Records. Musician: (albums) Stepping Out, 1993, Only Trust Your Heart, 1995, All For You, 1996, Love Scenes, 1997, When I Look In Your Eyes, 1999 (Grammy award for Best Jazz Vocal Performance, 2000, Grammy award nomination for Album of Yr., 2000, Cert. Platinum, U.S. and Portugal, Double Platinum in Can., Gold, France, Juno award Best Vocal Jazz Album), The Look of Love, 2001 (Quadruple Platinum, Can., Platinum, Australia, New Zealand, Poland and Portugal, Gold, France, Singapore, Eng., Juno award for Best Artist, Best Album, Best Vocal Jazz Album, Record of Yr. award Nat. Jazz Awards), Live in Paris, 2002 (Grammy award for Best Jazz Vocal Album, 2002), Heartdrops: Vince Benedetti Meets Diana Krall, 2003, The Girl in the Other Room, 2004, Xmas Songs featuring the Clayton/Hamilton Jazz Orchestra, 2005, From This Moment On, 2006, Quiet Nights, 2009. Named Musician of Yr., Nat. Jazz Awards, Internat. Musician. Office: Macklam/Feldman Mgmt 1505 W 2d Ave Ste 200 Vancouver BC Canada V6H 3Y4 E-mail: management@mfmgt.com.

KRAMER, DONOVAN MERSHON, SR., newspaper publisher; b. Galesburg, Ill., Oct. 24, 1925; s. Verle V. and Sybil (Mershon) K.; m. Ruth A. Heins, Apr. 3, 1949; children: Donovan M. Jr., Diana Sue, Kara J. Kramer Cooper, Eric H. BS in Journalism, Pub. Mgmt., U. Ill., 1948. Editor, publisher, ptnr. Fairbury (Ill.) Blade, 1948-63, Forrest (Ill.) News, 1953-63; ptnr. Gibson City (Ill.) Courier, 1952-63; pres., publisher, editor Casa Grande (Ariz.) Valley Newspapers, Inc., 1963—; mng. ptnr. White Mt. Pub. Co., Show Low, Ariz., 1978—. Wrote, edited numerous articles and newspaper stories. Many award-winners including Sweepstakes award in Ill. and Ariz. Mem., chmn. Econ. Planning and Devel. Bd. State of Ariz., Phoenix, 1976-81; pres. Indsl. Devel. Authority of Casa Grande, 1977-; founding pres. Greater Casa Grande Econ. Devel. Found., exec. bd. dirs.; gov. apptd. bd. mem. Ariz. Dept. Transp., 1992-97, chmn., 1997; mem. adv. bd. dept. journalism U. Ariz. With USAAF, WWII, PTO. Recipient Econ. Devel. plaque City of Casa Grande, 1982, Lifetime Achievement award Greater Casa Grande Econ. Devel. Found., 1994. Mem. Ariz. Newspapers Assn. (pres. 1980, Master Editor-Pub. 1977, Hall of Fame, 1998), Cmty. Newspapers Ariz. (pres. 1970-71), Inland Newspapers Assn., Newspapers Assn. Am., Ctrl. Ariz. Project Assn., Nat. Newspapers Assn., Greater Casa Grande C. of C. (pres. 1981-82, Hall of Fame 1991), Soc. Profl. Journalists. Republican. Lutheran. Avocations: hiking, fishing, nature studies, travel.

KRAMER, EDWARD JOHN, materials engineering educator; b. Wilmington, Del., Aug. 5, 1939; s. Edward Noble and Irma (Nemetz) K.; m. Gail Allen Woodford, Aug. 24, 1963; children: Eric Woodford, Jeanne Noble. BChemE, Cornell U., 1962; PhD, Carnegie-Mellon U., 1967. Asst. prof. dept. materials sci. and engring. Cornell U., Ithaca, NY, 1967-72, assoc. prof., 1972-79, prof., 1979-88, Samuel B. Eckert prof. materials sci. and engring., 1988-97; prof. dept. materials & chem. engring. U. Calif., Santa Barbara, 1997—. Vis. scientist Argonne (Ill.) Nat. Lab., 1974-75; vis. prof. Akademie der Wissenschaften Inst. Metallphysik, Göttingen, Germany, 1979, Ecole Poly. Federale de Lausanne, Switzerland, 1982, Johannes Gutenberg U., Mainz, Germany, 1987-88. Contbr. over 300 articles to sci. jours. Recipient U.S. Sr. Scientist award Alexander von Humboldt Stiftung, 1987-88, Swinburne award Inst. Materials, U.K., 1996; NATO fellow, 1966-67, John Simon Guggenheim Found. fellow, N.Y.C., 1988. Fellow AAAS, Am. Phys. Soc. (High Polymer Physics prize 1985); mem. NAE, Materials Rsch. Soc., Am. Chem. Soc., Böhmische Phys. Soc. Avocation: masters swimming. Office: Univ Calif Materials Dept Engring II Santa Barbara CA 93106 Office Phone: 805-894-4999. Business E-Mail: edkramer@mrl.ucsb.edu.

KRAMER, LARRY, dean, lawyer, educator; b. Chgo., June 23, 1958; m. Sarah Delson, 1996; 1 child, Veronika. BA magna cum laude, Brown U., 1980; JD cum laude, U. Chgo., 1984. Clerk to Judge Henry J. Friendly U.S. Ct. Appeals for the Second Cir., 1984—85; to Justice William J. Brennan, Jr. U.S. Supreme Ct., 1985—86; asst. prof. U. Chgo., 1986—90, prof., 1990—91; vis. prof. U. Mich., 1990—91, prof., 1991—94; vis. prof., Golieb Fellow NYU, 1993—94, Russell D. Niles Prof. Law, 2001—04, assoc. dean Rsch. and Academics, 2002—04; dean, Richard E. Lang Prof. Law Stanford Law Sch., 2004—. Reporter Fed. Cts. Study Com., 1989—90; cons. Mayer, Brown, Rowe & Maw, New York, NY, 1991—2004; assoc. dir., instr. Inst. Judicial Adminstrn., NYU, 1994—98; dir. English-Lang. Studies The Hague Acad. Internat. Law, 1994. Co-author: Conflict of Laws: Cases-Comments-Questions, 1993, 2001; editor: Reforming the Civil Justice System, 1996; author: The People Themselves: Popular Constitutionalism and Judicial Review, 2004. Recipient L. Hart Wright Award for Excellence in Teaching, U. Mich. Law Sch., 1991, Award for Best Teacher, Assn. Am. Law Schools, 2000, Order of the Coif, U. Chicago Law Sch. Fellow: Am. Acad. Arts & Sciences; mem.: ABA, Chgo. Coun. Lawyers (bd. govs. 1989—91), Brennan Ctr. for Jusice (bd. mem. 1995—2004), Am. Assn. Law Schs. (chair Conflict Laws Sec. 1992—93, chair Fed. Cts. Sec. 1996—97), Judicature Soc., NY Bar Assn., Am. Law Inst., Phi Beta Kappa. Office: Stanford U Sch Law Crown Quadrangle 559 Nathan Abbott Way Stanford CA 94305-4985 Office Phone: 650-723-4985. E-mail: deans.office@law.stanford.edu.

KRAMER, LAWRENCE STEPHEN, journalist; b. Hackensack, NJ, Apr. 24, 1950; s. Abraham and Ann Eve (Glasser) K.; m. Myla F. Lerner, Sept. 3, 1978; children: Matthew Lerner, Erika. BS in Journalism, Syracuse U., 1972; MBA, Harvard U., 1974. Reporter San Francisco Examiner, 1974-77, exec. editor, 1986-91; reporter Wash. Post, 1977-80, asst. to exec. editor, 1982, asst. mng. editor, 1982-86; exec. editor Trenton Times, NJ, 1980-82; founder, pres., exec. editor DataSport Inc. (acquired by Data Broadcasting Corp.), San Mateo, Calif., 1991-94; v.p. news, sports, mktg. Data Broadcasting Corp., San Mateo, 1994-97; founder, pres., CEO CBS.Marketwatch.com., San Francisco, 1997—2005, CBS pres. digital media, 2005—. Guest lectr. Harvard Bus. Sch.; mem. Pulitzer Prize Jury, 1987—88; founding bd. mem. Online Pub. Assn., 2001. Recipient W.R. Hearst Found. award 1971-72, Gerald Loeb award 1977, Nat. Press Club award; named one of 100 Most Influential Bus. Journalists 20th Century, 2000 Mem. Soc. Profl. Journalists Achievements include created SporTrax; created DBC News, predecessor co. to MarketWatch.com. Home: 8 Auburn Ct Belvedere Tiburon CA 94920-1349

KRAMER, LORNE C., protective services official; BA in Pub. Mgmt., U. Redlands, 1977; MPA with honors, U. So. Calif., 1979; Advanced Exec. Cert., Calif. Law Enforcement Coll., 1987; grad., Nat. Exec. Inst., 1993. Comdr. L.A. Police Dept., 1963-91; chief police Colorado Springs (Colo.) Police Dept., 1991—. Cons., instr. drugs and gangs Nat. Inst. Justice, Office Juvenile Justice U.S. Dept. Justice. Active Colo. State DARE Adv. Bd.; bd. dirs. Ctr. Prevention Domestic Violence, Pikes Peak Mental Health. Mem. Colo. Assn. Chiefs Police (bd. dirs., major cities rep.), Internat. Assn. Chiefs Police (juvenile justice com.), Police Exec. Rsch. Forum. Office: PO Box 2169 Colorado Springs CO 80901-2169

KRAMER, REMI THOMAS, film director; b. LA, Mar. 7, 1935; s. Geprge N. and Justina Magdelene Kramer; m. Agnes Marie Gallagher, Feb. 1, 1969; children: Matthew, Christiana, Timothy, Ian, Vincent, Brigitte, Danika. BA, UCLA, 1956; MA, Calif. State U., LA, 1963. Art dir. Doyle, Dane, Bernbach Advt., LA, 1965-66, N.W. Ayer Advt., NYC, 1966-67; dir. John Urie & Assocs., Haboush Co., Hollywood, Calif., 1967-69, Columbia-Screen Gems, Hollywood, 1969-76, 79-81, 1st Asian Films, Hollywood and Manila, 1976-77, Peterson Co., Hollywood, 1977-79; freelance film dir. Hollywood, 1981-85; founder Oz Enterprises, Inc., Sandpoint, Idaho, 1985—. Author: The Legend of Lonestar Bear Series, 1988—, How Lonestar Got His Name, 1988, Soaring with Eagles, 1989, The Mystery of the Walking Cactus, 1990 (The 100 Best Products of the Yr. 1990, Best Illustration: Creativity 90, 1990); author, illustrator: Klondike Ike, 1992; writer, dir. film High Velocity, 1976; patentee children's pacifier toy; designer Lonestar Bear plush animal collection. With U.S. Army, 1958-60. Recipient Clio award, 1971, 1st Internat. Broadcast awards, 1973, Cine Golden Eagle award, 1976, The Golden Teddy award, 1990, 91. Mem. Dirs. Guild Am., Writers Guild Am. Roman Catholic. Avocations: painting, inventing. E-mail: remi@intergate.com.

KRAMER, RICHARD JAY, gastroenterologist, educator; b. Morristown, NJ, Mar. 31, 1947; s. Bernard and Estelle (Mishkin) K.; m. Leslie Fay Davis, June 28, 1970; children: Bryan Jeffrey, Erik Seth Davis. Student, UCLA, 1965-68; MD, U. Calif., Irvine, 1972. Diplomate Am. Bd. Internat. Med., Am. Bd. Gastroenterology. Intern Los Angeles County Harbor Gen. Hosp., Torrance, Calif., 1972-73; resident Santa Clara Valley Med. Ctr., San Jose, Calif., 1973-76; fellow gastroent. Stanford (Calif.) U. Hosp., 1976-78; pvt. practice San Jose, 1978—2003; tchr. gastroenterology Santa Clara Valley Med. Ctr., San Jose, 2003—. Clin. assoc. prof. of medicine Stanford (Calif.) U., 1984—; chmn. med. dept. Good Samaritan Hosp., San Jose, 1988-90. Pres. Jewish Family Service Bd., San Jose, 1974. Recipient Regents scholarship U. Calif., 1965, 68, Mosby Book award, Mosby Books, Inc., Irvine, Calif., 1972. Fellow Am. Gastroent. Assn.; mem. Am. Coll. Physicians, Calif. Med. Soc., Santa Clara County Med. Soc., No. Calif. Soc. Clin. Gastroenterologists, Internat. Brotherhood Magicians, Mystic 13 (pres. 1986-87, San Jose), Masons, Alpha Omega Alpha. Jewish. Avocations: magic, travel.

KRAMLICH, C(HARLES) RICHARD (DICK), venture capitalist; b. Green Bay, Wis., Apr. 27, 1935; m. Debra Durbrow, Apr. 26, 1961 (div.); m. Lynne Kramlich (dec. 1980); m. Pamela Kramlich; children: Mary, Richard Squire, Peter Ward, Christina. BS in History, Northwestern U., 1957; MBA, Harvard U., 1960. With Kroger Co., Cin., 1960—64; joined Gardner & Preston Moss, Boston, 1964, exec. v.p., 1968—69; gen. ptnr. Arthur Rock & Assocs., 1969—78; co-founder & gen. ptnr. New Enterprise Assocs., Menlo Park, Calif., 1978—. Bd. dirs. Fabric7Systems, Financial Engines, Force10 Networks, Foveon, Informative, Zhone Technologies, Visual Edge Tech., Silicon Valley Bancshares, 2005—, Tabula, Kor Electronics, Xoom, IPunity, Sierra Monsoon. Vice chmn. bd. dirs. San Francisco Exploratorium; bd. dirs. UCSF Found., Bay Area Video Coalition; founder New Art Trust, 1997—. Recipient Lifetime Achievement Award in Entrepreneurship & Innovation, Lester Ctr. for Entrepreneurship & Innovation, Haas Sch. Bus., U. Calif. Berkeley, 2005; named one of Top 200 Collectors, ARTnews mag., 2004. Fellow: World Tech. Network (World Tech. award (Finance) 2005); mem.: Nat. Venture Capital Assn. (pres. 1992—93, chmn. 1993—94, Lifetime Achievement Award 2001). Avocation: collector video and new media art. Office: New Enterprise Associates 2855 Sand Hill Rd Menlo Park CA 94025-7022 Office Phone: 650-854-9499. Office Fax: 650-854-9397. Business E-Mail: dkramlich@nea.com.

KRANE, SUSAN, museum director, curator; b. Gary, Ind., June 8, 1954; m. Chuck Albright. BA, Carleton Coll., 1976; MA, Columbia U., 1978; MBA, U. Colo., 2000. Rockefeller Found. intern Walker Art Ctr., Mpls., 1978-79; curator Albright-Knox Art Gallery, Buffalo, 1979—87; curator, modern and contemporary art High Mus. Art, Atlanta, 1987-95; dir. U. Colo. Art Galleries, 1996—2001, Scottsdale Mus. Contemporary Art, Ariz., 2001—08; exec. dir. San Jose Mus. Art, Calif., 2008—. Mem. fed. adv. com. Internat. Exhbns. in Washington DC, 1994—99; lectr. in field. Author catalogues: Judy Pfaff, 1982, Surfacing Images: The Paintings of Joe Zucker, 1982, Mario Merz, 1984, Jan Kotik: The Painterly Object, 1984, Hollis Frampton: Recollections Recreations, 1984, The Wayward Muse, 1987, Albright-Knox Art Gallery: The Paintings and Sculpture Collection, 19877, Creighton Michael, 1987, Sherrie Levine, 1988, Houston Conwill, 1989, Ida Applebroog, 1989, Lynda Benglis: Dual Natures, 1991, Joel Otterson, 1991, Max Weber: The Cubist Decade 1910-1920, 1991, Barbara Ess, 1992, Ray Smith, 1993, Alison Saar, 1993, Equal Rights and Justice, 1994, Tampering Artists and Abstraction Today, 1995; contbr. Striking Out: Another American Road Show, 1991, Graven Images, 1991, Conversations at the Castle: Changing Audiences and Contemporary Art, Out of Order: Mapping Social Space, 2000, Lesley Dill: A 10-Year Survey, 2002, Let's Walk West: Brad Kahlhamer, 2004 Recipient Peter Norton Found. award, 1994. Mem.: ArtTable. Office: San Jose Mus Art 110 S Market St San Jose CA 95113 Business E-Mail: skrane@sjmusart.org.

KRANS, MICHELLE M., publishing executive; b. Chgo. m. Michael Krans; 1 child, Sarah. With McCord Ins. Services, Studio City, Calif., 1985—90; mktg. & promotions mgr. Desert Sun, Palm Springs, Calif., 1990—2001, advt. & mktg. dir., 2001—05, pres., pub., 2005—. Recipient 4 Pres.'s Rings for outstanding work in advt. & mktg., Gannett Co. Inc., Chmn.'s Ring, 2006; named Advt. Exec. of Yr. for 2005. Office: The Desert Sun PO Box 2734 Palm Springs CA 92263 Office Phone: 760-322-8889.

KRANTZ, JUDITH TARCHER, novelist; b. NYC, Jan. 9, 1928; d. Jack David and Mary (Brager) Tarcher; m. Stephen Falk Krantz, Feb. 19, 1954 (dec. Jan. 4, 2007); children: Nicholas, Anthony. BA, Wellesley Coll., 1948. Fashion publicist, Paris, 1948-49; fashion editor Good Housekeeping mag., NYC, 1949-56; contbg. writer McCalls, 1956-59, Ladies Home Jour., 1959-71; contbg. west coast editor Cosmopolitan mag., 1971-79. Author: Scruples, 1978, Princess Daisy, 1980, Mistral's Daughter, 1982, I'll Take Manhattan, 1986, Till We Meet Again, 1988, Dazzle, 1990, Scruples Two, 1992, Lovers, 1994, Spring Collection, 1996, The Jewels of Tessa Kent, 1998, Sex & Shopping: Confessions of a Nice Jewish Girl, 2000. Office: St Martin Press 175 5th Ave New York NY 10010

KRANZLER, JAY D., pharmaceutical executive; b. Nyack, NY, Feb. 17, 1958; s. Moses Nathan Kranzler and Eveline Leah Shuchatowitz; m. Bryna Wincelberg, June 22, 1980; children: Michael Jared, Jesse Ryan. BA, Yeshiva U.; MD, Yale U., D of Philosophy-Pharmacology. Mgmt. cons. McKinsey & Co., 1985-89; pres., ceo Cytel Corp., San Diego, 1989—. Psychiatry prof. Yale U.; pres., ceo, chmn. bd. dirs. Sequel Therapeutics, San Diego, 1992—. Adj. mem. Rsch. Inst. of Scripps Clinic, 1989—. Office: Cypress Bioscience Inc Ste 325 4350 Executive Dr San Diego CA 92121

KRASNER, STEPHEN DAVID, political science educator, former federal agency administrator; b. NYC, Feb. 15, 1942; s. Jack and Lillian Rhoda (Weiss) K.; m. Joan Beverly Karliner, Sept. 3, 1967 (div. Sept. 1987); children: Daniel J., Rachel L.; m. Patricia L. Brandt, Feb. 13, 1999. BA, Cornell U., 1963; M in Internat. Affairs, Columbia U., 1967; PhD, Harvard U., 1972. Asst. prof. Harvard U., Cambridge, Mass., 1971-75; from asst. to assoc. prof. UCLA, 1976-81; prof. Stanford U., Calif., 1981—, chair polit. sci. dept., 1984—91, Graham H. Stuart prof. internat. rels., dep. dir. Inst. for Internat. Studies; mem. policy planning staff US Dept. State, 2001, dir. policy planning, 2005—07; dir. governance and devel. NSC, 2002. Sr. fellow Hoover Inst. Author: Defending the National Interest: Raw Materials Investment and American Foreign Policy, 1978, Structural Conflict: The Third World Against Global Liberalism, 1985, Sovereignty: Organized Hypocrisy, 1999; editor: International Regimes, 1983, Problematic Sovereignty: Contested Rules and Political Possibilities, 2001. Fellow Am. Acad. Arts and Scis.; mem. Coun. on Fgn. Rels., Am. Polit. Sci. Assn., Am. Econs. Assn. Office: Stanford U Dept Polit Sci 616 Serra St Encina Hall W Rm 405 Stanford CA 94305-2044 Business E-Mail: skrasner@stanford.edu.

KRATOCHVIL, BYRON GEORGE, chemistry educator, researcher; b. Osmond, Nebr., Sept. 15, 1932; came to Can., 1967; s. Frank James and Mabel Louise (Schneider) K.; m. Marianne Spain; children: Susan, Daniel, Jean, John. BS, Iowa State U., 1957, MS, 1959, PhD, 1961. Asst. prof. chemistry U. Wis.-Madison, 1961-67; assoc. prof. chemistry U. Alta., Edmonton, Canada, 1967-71, prof. chemistry, 1971-98, prof. emeritus, 1998—, dept. chmn., 1989-95, assoc. v.p. rsch., 1996-98, sr. advisor, v.p. rsch., 1998-2001; dir. planning and ops. Alta. Synchrotron Inst., 2002—04. Co-author: (with W.E. Harris) Chemical Analysis, 1969, Chemical Separations and Measurements, 1974, Introduction to Chemical Analysis, 1981; analytical editor Can. Jour. Chemistry, Ottawa, Ont., 1985-88, sr. editor, 1988-93; contbr. articles to profl. jours. Recipient Merit award Iowa State U. Alumni, 1990. Fellow AAAS, Chem. Inst. Can. (bd. dirs. 1977-80, Fisher Lectr. award 1990); mem. Am. Chem. Soc. Office: U Alta Dept Chemistry Chemistry Centre Edmonton AB Canada T6G 2G2 Office Phone: 780-492-4665. E-mail: ron.kratochvil@ualberta.ca.

KRAUSE, KEITH WINSTON, engineering company executive; b. Houston, Aug. 22, 1957; s. Leeland Stanford Jr. and Kay Marjorie (Keller) K.; m. Angeles Arquisola, July 3, 1991; 1 child, Kaylin Dominique; stepchildren: Michelle Economos, Steven Economos. BS in Indsl. Tech., Tex. So. U., 1980. Draftsman B-1 divsn. Rockwell Internat., LA, 1977-78, draftsman Rocketdyne divsn. Canoga Park, Calif., 1978; draftsman Schlumberger Well Svcs., Houston, 1979; pipe design quality mgr. Hughes Aircraft Co., El Segundo, Calif., 1980-97; quality mgr. Irvin Aerospace Co., Santa Ana, Calif., 1997; sr. quality project engr. Fairchild Aerospace Co., Torrance, Calif., 1997-2000; mgr. quality engring. Krause, Keith, Winston; dir. quality engring. Hydroform USA, Carson, Calif., 2001—. Author: Electronics Workmanship Criteria Manual, 1996. Indsl. Tech. scholar Tex. So. U., 1977. Mem. C. of C., Phi Beta Sigma (life, v.p. 1978-79). Avocations: Karate, sports, landscaping, interior decorating and design, electronics. Office Phone: 310-632-6353. E-mail: keithk@hydroformusa.com.

KRAUSS, GEORGE, metallurgist; b. Phila., May 14, 1933; s. George and Berta (Reichelt) K.; m. Ruth A. Oeste, Sept. 10, 1960; children: Matthew, Jonathan, Benjamin, Thomas. BS in Metall. Engring., Lehigh U., Bethlehem, Pa., 1955; MS, MIT, Cambridge, 1958, ScD, 1961. Registered profl. engr., Colo., Pa. Devel. metallurgist Superior Tube Co., Collegeville, Pa., 1955-56; prof. Lehigh U., Bethlehem, Pa., 1963-75, Colo. Sch. Mines, Golden, 1975—; dir. Advanced Steel Processing and Products Research Ctr., 1984-93; Amax Found. prof., 1975-90; prof. dept. metall. engring. Colo. Sch. Mines, Golden, 1990-92, John Henry Moore prof., 1992-97, Univ. prof. emeritus, metallurg. cons., 1997—. Author: Principles of Heat Treatment of Steel, 1980, Steels: Heat Treatment and Processing Principles, 1990, Tool Steels, 5th edit., 1998, Steels: Processing Structure and Performance, 2005; editor: Deformation Processing and Structure, 1984, Carburizing: Processing and Performance, 1989;

editor Jour. Heat Treating, 1978-82; co-editor Fundamentals of Microalloying Forging Steels, 1987; contbr. articles profl. jours. NSF fellow Max Planck Inst. fur Eisenforschung, 1962-63; recipient Adolf Martens medal, Wiesbaden, 1990, Disting. Alumni award Lehigh U., 1993, George R. Brown Gold medal, 1998; named Outstanding Educator, Colo. Sch. Mines, 1990 Fellow ASM, The Metals Soc., Internat. Fedn. Heat Treatment and Surface Engring., Japan Soc. Promotion Sci.; mem. AIME, Iron and Steel Soc.-AIME (disting. mem. 1993, Howe lectr. 2003), Iron and Steel Inst. Japan (hon.), Am. Soc. Materials Internat. (hon.; trustee 1991-94, v.p. 1995-96, pres. 1996-97, C.S. Barrett silver medal 1998, Bodeen Heat Treating Achievement award 1999, A.E. White Disting. Tchr. award 1999, Campbell lectr. 2000), Internat. Fedn. Heat Treatment (pres. 1989-91, medal, 2007), ASM Materials Edn. Found. (trustee 2004-07), Japan Inst. Metals(Hon.) Home: 3807 Ridge Rd Evergreen CO 80439-8517 Office: Colo Sch Mines Dept Metall Engring Golden CO 80401 Office Phone: 303-674-0670. Business E-Mail: gkrauss@mines.edu.

KRAUSS, MICHAEL EDWARD, linguist; b. Cleve., Aug. 15, 1934; s. Lester William and Ethel (Sklarsky) K.; m. Jane Lowell, Feb. 16, 1962; children: Marcus Feder, Stephen Feder, Ethan, Alexandra, Isaac. Bacc. Phil. Islandicae, U. Iceland; BA, U. Chgo., 1953, Western Res. U., 1954; MA, Columbia U., 1955; Cert. d'études supérieures, U. Paris, 1956; PhD, Harvard U., 1959. Postdoctoral fellow U. Iceland, Reykjavik, 1958-60; rsch. fellow Dublin Inst. Advanced Studies, Ireland, 1956-57; vis. prof. MIT, Cambridge, 1969-70; prof. linguistics Alaska Native Lang. Ctr., U. Alaska, Fairbanks, 1960—, dir., 1972-2000, head Alaska native lang. program, 1972-2000; prof. emeritus linguistics U. Alaska, Fairbanks, 2000—. Panel mem. linguistics NSF. Author: Eyak Dictionary, 1970, Eyak Texts, 1970, Alaska Native Languages: Past, Present and Future, 1980; editor: In Honor of Eyak: The Art of Anna Nelson Harry, 1982, Yupik Eskimo Prosodic Systems, 1985; mem. editorial bd.: Internat. Jour. Am. Linguistics, Arctic Anthropology; edited dictionaries and books in Alaska Eskimo and Indian langs. Halldor Kiljan Laxness fellow Scandinavian-Am. Found., Iceland, 1958-60, Fulbright fellow Leningrad, USSR, 1990; Fulbright study grantee Iceland, 1958-60; grantee NSF, 1961—, NEH, 1967; named Humanities Forum, 1981; recipient Athabaskan and Eyak rsch. award NSF, 1961—. Mem. Linguistics Soc. Am. (chair com. endangered langs. and preservation 1991-95), Am. Anthropol. Assn., Soc. Study Indigenous Langs. of the Ams. (pres. 1991). Jewish. Office: U Alaska Fairbanks Alaska Native Lang Ctr Fairbanks AK 99775

KRAVITZ, ELLEN KING, musicologist, educator; b. Fords, NJ, May 25, 1929; d. Walter J. and Frances M. (Prybylowski) Kokowicz; m. Hilard L. Kravitz, Jan. 9, 1972; children: Julie Frances, Heather Frances stepchildren: Kent, Kerry, Jay. BA, Georgian Ct. Coll., 1964; MM, U. So. Calif., 1966, PhD, 1970. Tchr. 7th and 8th grade music Mt. St. Mary Acad., North Plainfield, NJ, 1949-50; cloistered nun Carmelite Monastery, Lafayette, La., 1950-61; instr. Loyola U., LA, 1967; asst. prof. music Calif. State U., LA, 1967-71, assoc. prof., 1971-74, prof., 1974—99, emeritus prof., 1999—. Founder Friends of Music Calif. State U., LA, 1976. Mem. editl. adv. bd.: Jour. Arnold Schoenberg Inst., 1977—87; editor: Jour. Arnold Schoenberg Inst., Vol. I, No. 3, 1977, Jour. Arnold Schoenberg Inst., Vol. II, No. 3, 1978; author (with others): Catalog of Schoenberg's Paintings, Drawings and Sketches; author: (book) Music in Our Culture, 1996. Guest lectr. Schoenberg Centennial Com., 1969—, mem., 1974. Mem.: Hist. Assn. L.A. Music Ctr., Am. Musicol. Soc., L.A. County Mus. Art, Pi Kappa Lambda, Mu Phi Epsilon.

KRAVITZ, LENNY, singer, guitarist; b. May 26, 1964; 1 child, Zoe. Singer, musician: albums Let Love Rule, 1989, Mama Said, 1991, Are You Gonna Go My Way, 1993 (2 Grammy nominations), Circus, 1995, 5, 1998 (Grammy award Best Male Rock Vocal Performance for song "Fly Away", 1998, Grammy award Best Male Rock Vocal Performance for song "American Woman", 1999), Greatest Hits, 2000 (Grammy award Best Male Rock Vocal Performance for song "Again", 2000), Lenny, 2001 (Grammy award Best Male Rock Vocal Performance for song "Dig In", 2001), Baptism, 2004, It is Time for a Love Revolution, 2008; Soundtrack Cutting Edge, Waterboy, 1998, Twice Upon a Yesteryear, Austin Powers, The Spy Who Shagged Me, 1999, appeared (films) Lennon: A Tribute, 1991, Lenny Kravitz: Video Retrospective, 1992, (voice films) Rugrats: The Movie, 1999. Office: care Creative Artists Agy 9830 Wilshire Blvd Beverly Hills CA 90212-1804 also: Virgin Records 550 Madison Ave New York NY 10022-3211 also: 2100 Columbia Ave Santa Monica CA 90404

KRAW, GEORGE MARTIN, lawyer, writer; b. Oakland, Calif., June 17, 1949; s. George and Pauline Dorothy (Herceg) K.; m. Sarah Lee Kenyon, Sept. 3, 1983 (dec. Nov. 2001). BA, U. Calif., Santa Cruz, 1971; student, Lenin Inst., Moscow, 1971; MA, U. Calif., Berkeley, 1974, JD, 1976. Bar: Calif. 1976, U.S. Supreme Ct. 1980, D.C. 1992. Pvt. practice, 1976—; ptnr. Kraw & Kraw, San Jose, 1988—. Mem. adv. com. Pension Genefit Guaranty Corp., 2002—05. Mem. ABA, Internat. Soc. Cert. Employee Benefit Specialists, Nat. Assn. Health Lawyers, Inter-Am. Bar Assn. Office: Kraw & Kraw 605 Ellis St # 200 Mountain View CA 94043-2241 Business E-Mail: gkraw@kraw.com.

KREBS, EDWIN GERHARD, biochemistry educator; b. Lansing, Iowa, June 6, 1918; s. William Carl and Louise Helena (Stegeman) K.; m. Virginia Frech, Mar. 10, 1945; children: Sally, Robert, Martha. AB in Chemistry, U. Ill., 1940; MD, Washington U., St. Louis, 1943; DSc (hon.), U. Geneva, 1979; degree (hon.), Med. Coll. Ohio, 1993; DSc (hon.), U. Ind., 1993; doctorate (hon.), U. Nat. De Cuyo, 1993; DSc (hon.), U. Ill., 1995, Washington U., St. Louis, 1995. Intern, asst. resident Barnes Hosp., St. Louis, 1944-45; rsch. fellow biol. chemistry Wash. U., St. Louis, 1946-48; prof., chmn. dept. biol. chemistry Sch. Medicine U. Calif., Davis, 1968-76; from asst. prof. to prof. biochemistry U. Wash., Seattle, 1948-66, prof., chmn. dept. pharmacology, 1977-83, prof. biochemistry and pharmacology, 1984-91, emeritus prof., biochemistry and pharmacology, 1991—; investigator, sr. investigator Howard Hughes Med. Inst., Seattle, 1983-90, sr. investigator emeritus, 1991—. Mem. Phys. Chemistry Study Sect. NIH, 1963-68, Biochemistry Test Com. Nat. Bd. Med. Examiners, 1968-71, rsch. com. Am. Heart Assn., 1970-74, bd. sci. counselors Nat. Inst. Arthritis, Metabolism and Digestive Diseases, NIH, 1979-84, Internat. Bd. Rev., Alberta Heritage Found. for Med. Rsch., 1986, external adv. com. Weis Ctr. for Rsch., 1987-91; mem. subgroup interconvertible enzymes IUB Spl. Interest Group Metabolic Regulation; internat. adv. bd. Advances in Second Messenger Phosphoprotein Rsch.; external adv. com. Cell Therapeutics Inc., Seattle; adv. bd. Kinetek, Vancouver, B.C. Mem. editorial bd. Jour. Biol. Chemistry, 1965-70; mem. editorial adv. bd. Biochemistry, 1971-76; mem. editorial and adv. bd. Molecular Pharmacology, 1972-77; assoc. editor Jour. Biol. Chemistry, 1971-93; mem. internat. adv. bd. Advances in Cyclic Nucleotide Rsch., 1972—; editorial advisor Molecular and Cellular Biochemistry, 1987—. Recipient Gairdner Found. award, Toronto, 1978, J.J. Berzelius lectureship, Karolinska Institutet, 1982, George W. Thorn award for sci. excellence, 1983, Sir Frederick Hopkins Meml. lectureship, London, 1984, Rsch. Achievement award Am. Heart Assn., Anaheim, Calif., 1987, 3M Life Scis. award FASEB, New Orleans, 1989, Albert Lasker Basic Med. Rsch. award, 1989, CIBA-GEIGY-Drew award Drew U., 1991, Steven C. Beering award, Ind. U., 1991, Welch award in chemistry Welch Found., 1991, Louisa Gross Horwitz award Columbia U., 1989, Alumni Achievement award Coll. Liberal Arts and Scis. U. Ill., 1992, Nobel prize in physiology or medicine, 1992, Kaul Found. award for excellence, 1996; John Simon Guggenheim fellow, 1959, 66. Mem. NAS, Am. Soc. Biol. Chemists (pres. 1986, ednl. affairs com. 1965-68, councillor 1975-78), Am. Acad. Arts and Scis., Am. Soc. Pharmacology and Exptl. Therapeutics. Achievements include life-long study of the protein phosphorylation process. Office: Prof Emeritus U Wash HSB K540E PO Box 357750 Seattle WA 98195-7750 Home Phone: 206-325-8176; Office Phone: 206-543-8500. Business E-Mail: egkrebs@u.washington.edu.

KREGER, BRIAN FREDERICK, lawyer; b. Saginaw, Mich., Jan. 17, 1947; s. Walter L. and June R. (Schultz) K.; m. Peggy J. Martin, July 10, 1971. BA, Concordia Coll., Ft. Wayne, Ind., 1969; MA, U. Nebr., 1971, JD, 1974. Bar: Nebr. 1974, U.S. Dist. Ct. (no. dist.) Nebr. 1974, Wash. 1980, U.S. Dist. Ct. (we. dist.) Wash. 1980. Legis. com. counsel Nebr. State Legis., Lincoln, 1974-79; pvt. practice Lincoln, 1974-79; atty. Safeco Ins. Co., Seattle, 1979-85; assoc. Waitt Johnson & Martens, Seattle, 1985-87; gen. counsel, sec. Empire Ins. Co., Seattle, 1987-97; of counsel Ryan Swanson and Cleveland, Seattle, 1997—. Gen. counsel WM Ins. Co. Vol. atty. Nebr. Civil Liberties Union, Lincoln, 1974-79; dist. rep. Ravenna-Bryant Community Assn., Seattle, 1985—; elder Messiah Luth. Ch., Seattle, 1986—; bd. dirs. Compass Ctr., Seattle Internat. Children's Festival. Mem. Coll. Club (Seattle).

KREISMAN, ARTHUR, higher education consultant, retired humanities educator; b. Cambridge, Mass., June 7, 1918; s. Louis and Rose (Shechtell) K.; m. B. Evelyn Goulston, Apr. 20, 1940 (dec. July 1992); children: Peter Jon, Steven Alan, Richard Curt, James Bruce; m. Mamie Jewel Liles Tribble, July 17, 1994. AB, Brigham Young U., 1942; student, Harvard U., 1939; AM, Boston U., 1943, PhD, 1952; LittD (hon.), City U., 1988. Grad. asst. in English Boston U., 1942-43; with Signal Corps. U.S. Army, 1943-45, with Signal Corps. overseas, 1944-45; instr. U.S. Armed Forces Inst., 1945, So. Oreg. U., Ashland, 1946, asst. prof., 1947-51, assoc. prof., 1951-55, prof., 1955-81, chmn. dept. English, 1951-63, chmn. humanities div., 1955-69, dir. gen. studies, 1959-66, dean arts and scis., 1966-77, dir. curricular affairs, 1978-80, prof. emeritus, 1981—, appt. ofcl. univ. historian, 1985; co-founder with Evelyn Kreisman Edukon, Inc., 1982—. TV lectr. Network Ednl. TV, 1955-58; dir. Block Teaching Project, U.S. Office Edn., 1957-59, Nat. Def. Edn. Act Inst. for Advanced Study in English, 1966; cons. Fedn. Regional Accrediting Commns. in Higher Edn., 1974-75, Coun. on Postsecondary Accreditation, 1975-79, Chico (Calif.) State U., 1973-76, City U. Seattle, 1975-99, Lincoln Meml. U., 1976, Marylhurst Edn. Center, 1976, Oreg. Inst. Tech., 1977-79, Sheldon Jackson Coll., 1979-83, Council on Chiropractic Edn., 1982, 83, Griffin Coll., 1990-91; mem. Gov.'s Adv. Com. on Arts and Humanities, 1966-69, 71-76; mem. task force human svcs. Oreg. Ednl. Coordinating Council, 1972; mem. steering com. Oreg. Joint Com. for Humanities, 1972-74; chmn. Seminar Coll. Evaluators NW Assn. Schs. and Colls., U. Wash., 1977-84; mem. nat. adv. bd. on quality assurance in experiental learning Coun. on Advancement Experiental Learning, 1978-80; team leader Danforth Found. Workshop on Liberal Arts Edn., Colo. Coll., 1972. Author: Correspondence Courses for State System, American Literature, 1955, World Literature, 1956, Contemporary Literature, 1961, Reader's Guide to the Classics, 1961, Remembering: The History of Southern Oregon University, 2002; editor: Oregon Centennial Anthology, 1959; Contbr. poetry and articles to periodicals. Active Ashland City Coun., 1950-54; co-founder Rogue Valley Unitarian Fellowship, 1953; bd. dirs. Comty. Chest, Inst. Renaissance Studies, 1956-64, Friends of Libr., 1991-96, pres., 1994-96; steering com. Learning in Retirement Program, 1993-94; chmn. bd. trustees Ashland Cmty. Hosp., 1960-64; bd. dirs. So. Calif. U. for Profl. Studies, 1997-99; chmn. bd. dirs. North Ctrl. U., 1998-99; emeritus bd. dirs. Ashland Cmty. Hosp. Found., 2005. Recipient Bicentennial anniversary prize in humanities Columbia U., 1954, Disting. Svc. award Ashland Cmty. Hosp. Found., 1998; prize for excellence in teaching, 1966, Outstanding Svc. award Indsl. Coll. Armed Forces, 1976, Disting. Svc. award Alumni Assn., 1977; Ford Found. fellow in Oriental philosophy and religion Harvard, 1954 Mem. AAUP (past pres. Oreg. coun.), Nat. Coun. Tchrs. English (past pres. Oreg. coun.), Commn. of Pacific Assn. of Schs. and Colls. (elected 1994-95), N.W. Assn. Schs. and Colls. (examiner 1958—, trustee 1976-80, mem. comm. colls. 1972-80), Am. Legion (past post comdr.), Lambda Iota Tau, Phi Kappa Phi, Tau Kappa Alpha. Office: 1880 Green Meadows Way Ashland OR 97520-3683

KREISSMAN, STARRETT, librarian; b. NYC, Jan. 4, 1946; d. Bernard and Shirley (Relis) K.; m. David Dolan, Apr. 13, 1985; 1 child, Sonya. BA, Grinnell Coll., 1967; MLS, Columbia U., 1968. Asst. circulation libr. Columbia U., NYC, 1968-70; sci. libr. N.Y. Pub. Libr., NYC, 1970-71; outreach libr. Stanislaus County Free Libr., Modesto, Calif., 1971-73, Oakdale libr., 1974-79, acquisitions libr., 1979-85, br. supr., 1985-92, county libr., 1992—99; libr. dir. Ventura County Libr., 1999—. Writer book revs. Stanislaus County Commn. on Women. Mem. ALA, Pub. Libr. Assn., Calif. Libr. Assn. (legis. com. 1993-95, 2003—, Libr. of Yr. 1998), Rotary. Office: Ventura County Library 646 County Square Dr Ste 150 Ventura CA 93003 Office Phone: 805-477-7333.

KREITH, FRANK, research engineer, consultant; b. Vienna, Dec. 15, 1922; s. Fritz and Elsa (Klug) K.; m. Marion Finkels, Sept. 21, 1951; children: Michael, Marcia, Judith. BSME, U. Calif., Berkeley, 1945; MS in Engring., UCLA, 1946; DSc, U. Paris, 1964. Registered profl. engr., Calif., Colo. Rsch. engr. Jet Propulsion Lab. Calif. Inst. Tech., 1945-49; asst. prof. U. Calif., Berkeley, 1951-53; assoc. prof. mech. engring. Lehigh U., Bethlehem, Pa., 1953-59; prof. engring. U. Colo., 1959-77; chief solar thermal rsch. Solar Energy Rsch. Inst., Golden, Colo., 1977-87; sr. fellow Nat. Conf. State Legis., 1987—2001; pres. Environ. Cons. Svcs., 1974-77; cons. NATO, 1980-85, Nat. Renewable Energy Lab, 1990-98. Author: Principles of Heat Transfer, 1958, 2d edit., 1965, 3d edit., 1973, (with C. B. Wrenn) Nuclear Impact, 1975, (with J. F. Kreider) Principles of Solar Engineering, 1980; CRC mech. engr. series editor, 1997-, EPRI, 2005; co-editor: Solar Energy Handbook, 1981; editor-in-chief Handbook of Solid Waste Managmement, 1993, Handbook of Energy Efficiency, 1996, Handbook of Mechanical Engineering, 1997, Ground Transportation for the 21st Century, 1999, Handbook of Thermal Engineering, 2000, Handbook of Energy Efficiency and Renewable Energy, 2007. Mem. Human Rels. Commn., 1963-65, Energy Adv. Com., 1979-82. Recipient First Gen. Achievement award, 1983; Guggenheim fellow, 1950. Mem. ASME (hon. life; heat transfer meml. award 1972, medal, 1998, Washington award 1997, Edwin F. Church medal 2001, Disting. Lectr., 2002-), Internat. Solar Energy Soc.(hon.), Sigma Xi (nat. lectr. 1980-81, Charles Greeley Abbott award 1988), Phi Tau Sigma. Office Phone: 303-443-1406. E-mail: fkreith@comcast.net.

KREJCI, ROBERT HENRY, aerospace engineer; b. Shenandoah, Iowa, Nov. 15, 1943; s. Henry and Marie Josephine (Kubicek) K.; m. Carolyn R. Meyer, Aug. 21, 1967; children: Christopher S., Ryan D. BS with honors in Aerospace Engring., Iowa State U., 1967, M in Aerospace Engring., 1971. Commd. 2d lt. USAF, 1968, advanced through grades to capt., 1978; dept. mgr. advanced Navy tech. programs ATK, Brigham City, Utah, 1978-84, mgr. space programs, 1984-85, mgr. Navy advanced programs, 1986—. Lt. col. USAFR. Fellow: AIAA (assoc.). Home: 885 North 300 East Brigham City UT 84302-1310 Office: ATK PO Box 707 Brigham City UT 84302-0707 Office Phone: 435-863-3365. Business E-Mail: robert.krejci@atk.com.

KREKORIAN, PAUL, state legislator; b. San Fernando, Calif. m to Tamar; children: two. B, U. Southern Calif.; JD, U. Calif., Berkeley. California State Assemblyman, District 43, 2006-, asst. majority floor leader, currently; coun, Webster Comn, formerly; president, Burbank Bd of Education, formerly; law clerk, Organized Crime Strike Force, United States Justice Department, formerly. attorney, private practice, currently. Democrat. Office: Dist 43 620 N Brand Blvd Suite 403 Glendale CA 91203 Office Phone: 818-240-6330. Office Fax: 818-240-4632. Business E-Mail: Assemblymember.Krekorian@assembly.ca.gov.

KRENDL, CATHY STRICKLIN, lawyer; b. Paris, Tex., Mar. 14, 1945; d. Louis and Margaret Helen (Young) S.; m. James R. Krendl, July 5, 1969; children: Peggy, Susan, Anne. BA summa cum laude, North Tex. State U., 1967; JD cum laude, Harvard U., 1970. Bar: Alaska 1970, Colo. 1972. Atty. Hughes, Thorsness, Lowe Gantz & Clark, Anchorage, 1970-71; adj. prof. U. Colo. Denver Ctr., 1972-73; from asst. prof. to prof. law, dir. bus planning program U. Denver, 1973-83; ptnr. Krendl, Krendl, Sachnoff & Way, Denver, 1983—. Author: Colorado Business Corporation Act Deskbook, 2003—08; editor: Colorado Methods of Practice, 8 vols., 1983—2008, Closely Held Corporations in Colorado, vols. 1-3, 1981; contbr. articles to profl. jours. Named Disting. Alumna, North Tex. State U., 1985, Super Lawyer, Colo., 2006, 2007, 2008, Platinum Author, Thomason West, 2006, 2007, 2008; named one of Best Lawyers in Am. in Corp. Law Mergers and Aquisitions, 1996—2008. Mem. Colo. Bar Assn. (bd. govs. 1982-86, 88-91, chmn. securities subsect. 1986, bus. law sect. 1988-89, Professionalism award), Denver Bar Assn. (pres. 1989-90). Avocation: reading. Home: 1551 Larimer St Apt 1101 Denver CO 80202-1630 Office Phone: 303-629-2600. E-mail: csk@krendl.com.

KRENER, ARTHUR J., systems engineering educator; b. Bklyn., Oct. 8, 1942; BS, Holy Cross Coll., 1964, MS, 1967; PhD, U. Calif., Berkeley, 1971. Prof. math. U. Calif., 1943—. Fellow IEEE. Office: U Calif-Davis Dept Maths 660 Kerr Hall Davis CA 95616

KREPS, DAVID MARC, economist, educator; b. NYC, Oct. 18, 1950; s. Saul Ian and Sarah (Kaskin) Kreps; m. Anat Ruth Admati, Jan. 4, 1984; children: Tamar, Oren, Avner. AB, Dartmouth Coll., 1972; MA, PhD, Stanford U., 1975. Asst. prof. Stanford U., 1975-78, assoc. prof., 1978-80, prof., 1980-84, Holden prof., 1984—. Rsch. officer U. Cambridge, Eng., 1978-79, fellow commoner Churchill Coll., Cambridge, 1978-79; vis. prof. Yale U., New Haven, 1982, Harvard U., Cambridge, Mass., 1983, U. Paris, 1985; vis. prof. U. Tel Aviv, 1989-90, sr. prof. by spl. apppintment, 1991—. Author: Notes on the Theory of Choice, 1988, A Course in Microeconomic Theory, 1990, Game Theory and Economic Modelling, 1990; co-author: Strategic Human Resources, 1999; co-editor Econometrica, 1984-88. Alfred P. Sloan Found. fellow, 1983, John S. Guggenheim fellow, 1988. Fellow Econometric Soc.; mem. Am. Econ. Assn. (J.B. Clark medal 1989), Am. Acad. Arts and Scis., Nat. Acad. Scis. Office: Stanford U Grad Sch of Bus Stanford CA 94305-5015

KRESA, KENT, manufacturing executive, retired aerospace executive; b. NYC, Mar. 24, 1938; s. Helmy and Marjorie (Boutelle) K.; m. Joyce Anne McBride, Nov. 4, 1961; 1 child, Kiren BSAA, MIT, 1959, MSAA, 1961, EAA, 1966; LLD (hon.), Pepperdine U., 2003. Sr. scientist rsch. and advanced devel. divsn. AVCO, Wilmington, Mass., 1959-61; staff mem. MIT Lincoln Lab., Lexington, Mass., 1961-68; dep. dir. strategic tech. office Def. Advanced Rsch. Projects Agy., Washington, 1968-73; dir. tactical tech. office Def. Advanced Rsch. Project Agy., Washington, 1973-75; v.p., mgr. Rsch. & Tech. Ctr. Northrop Corp., Hawthorne, Calif., 1975-76, v.p., gen. mgr. Ventura divsn. Newbury Park, Calif., 1976-82, group v.p. Aircraft Group L.A., 1982-86, sr. v.p. tech. devel. and planning, 1986-87, pres., COO, 1987-90; chmn., pres., CEO Northrop Grumman Corp., L.A., 1990—2001, chmn., CEO, 2001—03, chmn. emeritus, 2003—; sr. advisor The Carlyle Group, NYC, 2003—; non-exec. chmn. Avery Dennison Corp., Pasadena, Calif., 2005—; interim chmn. Gen. Motors Corp., Detroit, 2009—. Bd. dirs. Avery Dennison Corp., 1999—, Gen. Motors Corp., 2003—, Fluor Corp., 2003—, Mannking Corp., 2004—. Bd. dirs. John Tracy Clinic for the Hearing-Impaired, W.M. Keck Found., Performing Arts Ctr. L.A. County Found.; bd. overseers Keck Sch. Medicine, U. So. Calif.; bd. governors, Broad Found; bd. visitors UCLA Anderson Sch. Mgmt.; mem. advisory bd., MIT Lincoln Laboratory; bd. trustees Haynes Found., Calif. Inst. Tech., 1994-, chmn., 2005- Recipient Henry Webb Salsbury award MIT, 1959, Arthur D. Flemming award, 1975, Calif. Industrialist of Yr. Calif. Mus. of Sci. and Industry and the Calif. Mus. Found., 1996, Bob Hope Disting. Citizen award Nat. Security Indsl. Assn., 1996; Sec. of Def. Meritorious Civilian Svc. medal, 1975, USN Meritorious Pub. Svc. citation, 1975, Exceptional Civilian Svc. award USAF, 1987, Howard Hughes Meml. award, Aero Club So. Calif., 2002, Laurel Citation, Aviation Week, 2002, Calif. Inst. Tech. Mgmt. Assn. Excellence in Mgmt. award, 2002, Ellis Island Medal of Honor, 2002; named a Manufacturer of the Century, Calif. Manufacturers & Tech. Assn., 2000; named one of The Top 25 Managers, Business Week, 2001, 2002 Fellow AIAA; mem. Aerospace Industries Assn. (past bd. govs.), Naval Aviation Mus. Found., Navy League U.S., Soc. Flight Test Engrs., Assn. U.S. Army, Nat. Space Club, Am. Def. Preparedness Assn., L.A. Country Club, NAE. Office: Avery Dennison Corp Charles D Miller Corporate Center 150 N Ornage Grove Blvd Pasadena CA 91103*

KRETSCHMER, KEITH HUGHES, investor; b. Omaha, Oct. 20, 1934; s. John G. and Mary (Hughes) K.; m. Adine Williams, Oct. 1, 1960; children: Hugh, Dara, Kurt. AA, Wentworth Acad., 1954; BS, U. Nebr., 1956; student, UCLA, 1968. With J.G. Kretschmer & Co., Omaha, 1958—60; gen. agt. Lincoln Life & Casualty, 1960—62; exec. v.p., sec.-treas. Automated Mgmt. Sys., Kansas City, Mo., 1962—68; investment exec. Shearson, Hammill & Co., LA, 1968—75; gen. ptnr. Bear Stearns & Co., LA, 1975—85; sr. mng. dir. Bear Stearns & Co. Inc., Boston, 1985—91, spl. assoc. dir., 1991—92; mng. dir. Oppenheimer & Co., Inc., Boston, 1993—94, Oppenheimer Capital, 1995—2001; bd. dirs. Visiphor Corp., 2004—. Mem. stockholders com. Tosco Corp., LA, 1982; bd. dirs. Cogent Fin. Group dba Medi Credit, 2004-06. Author: Your Option, 1978. Advanceman Rep. Pres.'s Nixon and Ford, 1970-76; trustee Lighthouse Preservation Soc., 1986-88, Wentworth Mil. Acad., Lexington, Mo., 2005—08; founding dir. Option Soc. So. Calif, 1974-85; bd. dirs. Pacific Palisades-Malibu YMCA, 1976-86, chmn. bd. dirs., 1980; bd. dirs. South Shore Art Ctr., Cohasset, Mass., 1988-97, pres., 1991-93; bd. dirs. World Affairs Coun. Boston, 1989-96; mem. pres.'s coun. Accion Internat., 1992—. Served to maj. U.S. Army, Airborne Ranger, 1956-58. Mem. The Explorers Club, Aircraft Owners and Pilots Assn., Exptl. Aircraft Assn., Seaplane Pilots Assn., CEO Club, Angel Flight, AERO Club New Eng., Vintage Sports Car Club Am., Masons, Shriners. Congregationalist. Avocation: pilot since 1952. Office: 294 Sunshine Ave Sequim WA 98382 Home: 323 North St Sequim WA 98382 Office Phone: 360-808-7788. Personal E-mail: kkretsc@aol.com.

KREUTZBERG, DAVID W., lawyer; b. Edwardsville, Ill., May 20, 1953; BA summa cum laude, Ariz. State U., 1975, JD magna cum laude, 1978. Bar: Ariz. 1978, U.S. Dist. Ct. (Ariz. dist.) 1978. Law clk. to Hon. William E. Eubank Ariz. Ct. Appeals, Phoenix, 1978-79; ptnr. Squire, Sanders & Dempsey LLP, Phoenix, 1989. Mem. ABA (mem. bus. law sect.), State Bar Ariz., Maricopa County Bar Assn., Phi Beta Kappa. Office: Squire Sanders & Dempsey LLP Two Renaissance Sq 40 N Central Ave Ste 2700 Phoenix AZ 85004-4498

KREVANS, JULIUS RICHARD, academic administrator, internist; b. NYC, May 1, 1924; s. Sol and Anita Krevans; m. Patricia N. Abrams, May 28, 1950; children: Nita, Julius R., Rachel, Sarah, Nora Kate. BS Arts and Scis, N.Y. U., 1943, MD, 1946. Diplomate: Am. Bd. Internal Med. Intern, then resident Johns Hopkins Med. Sch. Hosp., mem. faculty, until 1970, dean acad. affairs, 1969—70; physician in chief Balt. City Hosp., 1963—69; prof. medicine U. Calif., San Francisco, 1970—, dean Sch. Medicine, 1971—82, chancellor, 1982—93, chancellor emeritus, 1993—. Contbr. articles on hematology, internal med. profl. jours. With USMC, 1948—50, AUS. Mem. ACP, Assn. Am. Physicians. Address: 32 Birch Bay Dr Bar Harbor ME 04609 E-mail: krevansmaine@adelphia.net.

KREVANS, RACHEL, lawyer; b. Balt., June 15, 1957; d. Julius Richard and Patricia (Abrams) K. BA, Dartmouth Coll., 1979; JD, U. Calif., Davis, 1984. Law clk. hon. Robert Boochever U.S. Ct. Appeals for Ninth Cir., Juneau, Alaska, 1984-85; assoc. Morrison & Foerster LLP, San Francisco, 1985-90, mng. ptnr.-San Francisco office, 1991—. Office: Morrison & Foerster LLP 425 Market St San Francisco CA 94105-2482 Office Phone: 415-677-7178. Office Fax: 415-268-7522. Business E-Mail: rkrevans@mofo.com.

KRIDER, E. PHILIP, atmospheric scientist, educator; b. Chgo., Mar. 22, 1940; s. Edmund Arthur and Ruth (Abbott) K.; m. Barbara A. Reed, June 13, 1964 (div. Mar. 1983); children: Ruth Ellen, Philip Reed; m. Patricia L. MacCorquodale, Aug. 14, 1999. BA in Physics, Carleton Coll., 1962; MS in Physics, U. Ariz., 1964, PhD in Physics, 1969. Resident rsch. assoc. NASA Manned Spacecraft Ctr. NAS, Houston, 1969-71; asst. rsch. prof. Inst. Atmospheric Physics U. Ariz., Tucson, 1971-75, asst. prof. dept. atmospheric scis., 1973-75, assoc. prof. dept. atmospheric scis., Inst. Atmos. Physics, 1975-80; exec. v.p., part-time chmn. Lightning Location and Protection, Inc., Tucson, 1976-83; adj. prof. dept. elec. engring. U. Fla., Gainesville, 1988—; prof. dept. atmospheric scis. Inst. Atmospheric Physics U. Ariz., 1980—, dir. Inst. Atmospheric Physics, head dept. atmospheric scis., 1986-95. Pres. Internat. Commn. Atmospheric Electricity, 1992-99; co-chmn. panel Earth's elec. environment geophysis study com. NAS, 1982-86; mem. panel weather support for space ops. NAS, 1987-88, geostationary platform sci. steering com. NASA, 1987—; mems. rep. Univ. Corp. for Atmospheric Rsch., 1986-95; mem. U.S. nat. com. Internat. Sci. Radio Union; mem. aerospace corp. adv. team USAF Launch Vehicle Lightning/Atmospheric Elec. Constraints, Post Atlas/Centaur 67 Incident, 1987-89; sci. advisor Air Force Geophys. Lab., 1988; mem. lightning adv. com. U.S. Army Missile Command, 1986-87; lectr. in field. Author: (with others) Thunderstorms, 1983, Lightning Electromagnetics, 1990, Benjamin Franklin des Lumieres á nos Jours., 1991; contbr. numerous articles to profl. jours.; co-chief editor Jour. of Atmospheric Scis., 1990-92, editor, 1992-93; assoc. editor Jour. Geophys. Rsch., 1977-79; referee Jour. Geophys. Rsch., Geophys. Rsch. Letters, Jour. of Atmospheric Scis., Planetary and Space Sci. Fellow Am. Meteorol. Soc. (Outstanding Contbn. to Advance Applied Meteorology award 1985), Am. Geophys. Union (Smith medal selection com. 1994, com. on atmospheric and space electricity 1990-98); mem. IEEE (Transactions Prize Paper award EMC Soc. 1982), Am. Assn. Physics Tchrs., Sigma Xi, Sigma Pi Sigma. Achievements include patents for All-Sky camera apparatus for time-resolved lightning photography, photoelectric lightning detector apparatus, transient event data acquisition apparatus for use with radar systems and the like, lightning detection system utilizing triangulation and field amplitude comparison techniques, thunderstorm sensor and method of identifying and locating thunderstorms. Office: U Ariz Dept Atmospheric Scis PO Box 210081 Tucson AZ 85721-0081

KRIEGER, MARCIA SMITH, federal judge; b. Denver, Mar. 3, 1954; d. Donald P. Jr. and Marjorie Craig (Gearhart) Smith; m. Michael S. Krieger, Aug. 26, 1976 (div. July 1988); children: Miriam Anna, Matthias Edward; m. Frank H. Roberts, Jr., Mar. 9, 1991; stepchildren: Melissa Noel Roberts, Kelly Suzanne Roberts, Heidi Marie Roberts. BA, Lewis & Clark Coll., 1975; JD, U. Colo., 1979. Bar: Colo. 1979, U.S. Dist. Ct. Colo. 1979, U.S. Ct. Appeals (10th cir.) 1979. Rotary grad. fellow U. Munich, Germany, 1975—76; assoc. Mason, Reuler & Peek, P.C., Denver, 1976-83, Smart, DeFurio Brooks, Eklund & McClure, Denver, 1983-84; ptnr. Brooks & Krieger, P.C., Denver, 1984-88, Wood, Ris & Hames, P.C., Denver, 1988-90; pvt. practice U.S. Bankruptcy Court, 10th Circuit, Denver, 1990-94; judge U.S. Bankruptcy Ct., 10th Circuit, Denver, 1994-2000; chief judge U.S. Bankruptcy Ct., Denver, 2000—02, U.S. Dist. Ct., 2002—. Lectr. U. Denver Grad. Tax Program, 1987—, Colo. Soc. CPA's, Denver, 1984-87, Colo. Continuing Legal Edn., Denver, 1980—, Colo. Trial Lawyers Assn., Denver, 1987—, U. Colo. Law Sch.; adj. instr. U. Colo. Sch. Law, 1999-2001; spkr. in field. Contbr. articles to profl. publs. Vestry person Good Shepherd Episcopal Ch., Englewood, 1986—, judge and coach for H.S. mock trial. Mem. Colo. Bar Assn. (past chair Com. Court Reform; past mem. Professionalism Com.), Arapahoe Bar Assn., Arraj Inn of Ct. (v.p.), Nat. Conf. Bankruptcy Judges (past chair Internat. Law Rels. Com, Ethics Com.; past mem. Newsletter Com., Program Com.), Littleton Adv. Coun. for Gifted and Talented education, Alfred A. Arraj Inn of Court (past pres.), Colo. Jud. Coordinating Coun., Kenya Children Found. (bd. dirs.). Republican. Avocations: international relations, travel, marksmanship. Office: US Dist Ct Dist Colo Alfred J Arraj US Courthouse 901 19th St A-941 Denver CO 80294

KRIEGER, WAYNE, state legislator; Member, Oregon Bd Forestry & Govs Water Enhancement Bd, 96-, Landslide Task Force, 97, Forest Industries Coun on Taxation, Washington, DC, 97-, Oregon State Legislature; Oregon State Representative, District 1, 2001-.Owner, Skyview Ranch & Tree Farm, currently. Republican. Mailing: 900 Court St NE H-378 Salem OR 97301 Business E-Mail: rep.waynekrieger@state.or.us.

KRIENS, SCOTT GREGORY, information technology executive; b. 1957; m. Joan Kriens. BA in Economics, Calif. State U., Hayward, 1979. Co-founder StrataCom, Inc., 1986—96; v.p. sales & ops. StrataCom Inc., 1986—96; chmn., CEO Juniper Networks, Inc., Mountain View, Calif., 1996—2008, chmn., 2008—, interim CFO, 2007. Bd. dirs. Juniper Networks, Inc., 1996—, Equinox, Inc., 2000, VeriSign, Inc., 2001—. Recipient Ernst & Young Entrepreneur of the Yr. award, 2000; named one of The Top 25 Managers, Bus. Week, 2000, The Top Tech. Execs, Forbes mag., 1996, The 25 Most Powerful People in Networking, Network World, 2006. Office: Juniper Networks Inc 1194 N Mathilda Ave Sunnyvale CA 94089-1206 E-mail: scottkriens@juniper.net.

KRIKEN, JOHN LUND, architect; b. Calif., July 5, 1938; s. John Erik Nord and Ragnhild (Lund) K.; m. Anne Girard (div.); m. Katherine Koelsch, Aug. 8, 1988. BArch, U. Calif., Berkeley, 1961; MArch, Harvard U., 1968. Ptnr. Skidmore, Owings and Merrill, San Francisco, 1970—2003, cons. ptnr., 2003—. Tchr. Washington U., St. Louis, 1968, U. Calif., Berkeley, 1972, Rice U., Houston, 1979; prof. U. Calif., Berkeley, 2005—; design advisor, chief architect Ho Chi Minh City, Vietnam, 1994—; mem. design rev. bd. Port San Francisco, 1995—. Mem. Bay Conservation and Devel. Commn., Calif., 1984—; chair Design Review Bd.; mem. Arts Commn. City and County of San Francisco, 1989-95; mem. design rev. bd. Berkeley campus U. Calif., 1986-92; bd. dirs. San Francisco Planning and Rsch., 1995—; vice chair, Eng. and Des. Advisory Panel (EDAP) for the rebuilding pf San Francisco Bay Bridge, 1997—; mem. GSD's alumni coun. Harvard U, 2000—; CED's dean's adv. coun. U. Calif., Berkeley, 2000—; mem. San Francisco Arts Commn., 2006—. Fellow AIA; mem. Am. Inst. Cert. Planners, Sunday Afternoon Watercolor Soc. (founding mem.), Lambda Alpha Internat. Office: Skimore Owings & Merrill 1 Front St San Francisco CA 94111-5303 Office Phone: 415-981-1555.

KRIKORIAN, BLAKE, entrepreneur, consumer electronics company executive; B in Mech. Engring., UCLA, 1989. With General Magic; co-founder, group project mgr. Philips Mobile Computing Group, 1994—98; sr. v.p. Metis Associates (acquired by BSQUARE in 2000), 1998; pres. Mainbrace Corp. (acquired by BSQUARE in 2000), 1998—2000; founder, CEO id8 Group Holdings, Inc., San Mateo, Calif., 2000—04; co-founder, CEO Sling Media, Inc., San Mateo, Calif., 2004—. Spkr. in field. Named one of 50 Who Matter Now, CNNMoney.com Bus. 2.0, 2006. Achievements include with other members of Slingbox Media, Inc., created Slingbox Player, a device that allows a person to watch their own TV from a laptop anywhere in the world; Slingbox Player named one of PC World Innovations in 2006, Business Week Best Products of 2005, Time Best Inventions of 2005, Popular Science Best of What's New 2005 & Laptop Best of CES 2005; Slingbox Player has won awards including Mobile Trax Mobility award-Accessories in 2006 and International Consumer Electronics Show Innovations 2006 Design and Engineering Finalist; Sling Media Inc. was chosen by Fortune as one of the 25 Breakout Companies of 2005 and 2006 ACE award Finalist-Start-up Company of Year. Office: Sling Media Inc 1051 E Hillsdale Blvd Ste 500 Foster City CA 94404-1640 Office Phone: 650-293-8000. Office Fax: 650-378-4422.

KRIPPNER, STANLEY CURTIS, psychologist; b. Edgerton, Wis., Oct. 4, 1932; s. Carroll Porter and Ruth Genevieve (Volenberg) Krippner; m. Lelie Anne Harris, June 25, 1966 (div. 2002). BS, U. Wis., 1954; MA, Northwestern U., 1957, PhD, 1961; PhD (hon.), U. Humanistic Studies, San Diego, 1982. Diplomate Am. Bd. Sexology. Speech therapist Warren Pub. Schs. (Ill.), 1954-55, Richmond Pub. Schs. (Va.), 1955-56; dir. Child Study Ctr. Kent (Ohio) State U., 1961-64; dir. dream lab. Maimonides Med. Ctr., Bklyn., 1964-73; prof. of psychology Saybrook Grad. Sch., San Francisco, 1973—. Adj. prof. psychology Calif. Inst. Human Sci., 1994—; vis. prof. U. P.R., 1972, Sonoma State U., 1972-73, U. Life Scis., Bogota, Colombia, 1974, Inst. for Psychodrama and Humanistic Psychology, Caracas, Venezuela, 1975, State U. West Ga., 1976, John F. Kennedy U., 1980-82, Inst. for Rsch. in Biopsychophysics, Curitiba, Brazil, 1990; adj. prof. Calif. Inst. Integral Studies, 1991-97; lectr. Acad. Pedagogical Scis., Moscow, 1971, Acad. Scis., Beijing, 1981, Minas Gerais U., Belo Horizonte, Brazil, 1986-87. Author: (with Montague Ullman) Dream Telepathy, 1973, rev. edit., 1989, Song of the Siren: A Parapsychological Odyssey, 1975, (with Alberto Villoldo) The Realms of Healing, 1976, rev. edit., 1987, 2003, Human Possibilities, 1980, (with Jerry Solfvin) La Science et les Pouvoirs Psychiques de l'Homme, 1986, (with Alberto Villoldo) Healing States, 1987, (with Joseph Dillard) Dreamworking, 1988, (with David Feinstein) Personal Mythology, 1988, (with Patrick Welch) Spiritual Dimensions of Healing, 1992, (with Dennis Thong and Bruce Carpenter) A Psychiatrist in Paradise, 1993, (with David Feinstein) The Mythic Path, 1997, (with Andre de Carvalho) Sonhos Exoticos, 1998, (with Fariba Bogzaron and Andre de Carvalho) Extraordinary Dreams and How to Work with Them, 2002, (with Stephen Kierulff) Becoming Psychic, 2004, (with Danyl S. Paulson) Haunted by Combat, 2007; editor: Advances in Parapsychological Research, Vol. 1, 1977, Vol. 2, 1978, Vol. 3, 1982, Vol. 4, 1984, Vol. 5, 1987, Vol. 6, 1990, Vol. 7, 1994, Vol. 8, 1997, Psychoenergetic Systems, 1979, Dreamtime and Dreamwork, 1990; co-editor: Galaxies of Life, 1973, The Kirlian Aura, 1974, The Energies of Consciousness, 1975, (with Susan Powers) Future Science, 1977, Broken Images, Broken Selves, 1997, (with Mark Waldman) Dreamscaping, 1999, (with Etzel Cardeña and Steven J. Lynn) Varieties of Anomalous Experience, 2000, (with Teresa McIntyre) The Psychological Effects of War Trauma on Civilians, 2003, (with Michael Bova and Leslie Gray) Healing Stories, 2007, (with Michael Bova and Leslie Gray and Adam Kay) Healing Tales, 2007, (with Daryl Paulson) Haunted by Combat: Understanding Post Traumatic Stress Disorder in War Veterans, 2007; mem. editl. bd. Alternative Therapies in Health and Medicine, Jour. Humanistic Psychology, Jour. Transpersonal Psychology, Jour. Indian Psychology, Dream Network, Humanistic Psychologist; contbr. 1000 articles to profl. jours Mem. Joseph Plan Found.; Bd. dirs., adv. bd. Acad. Religion and Phys. Rsch., Survival Rsch. Found., Hartley Film Found. Recipient Svc. to Youth award YMCA, 1959, Citation of Merit Nat. Assn. Creative Children and Adults, 1975, Cert. Recognition Office Gifted and Talented, US Office Edn., 1976, Volker medal South Africa Soc. Psychical Rsch., 1980, Bicentennial medal U. Ga., 1985, Charlotte and Karl Bühler award, 1992, Dan Overlade Meml. award, 1994, Humanist of Yr. award Ch. of Humanism, 1996, Career Achievement award Parapsychol. Assn., 1998, J.B. Rhine Award, 2002, Ashley Montagu Peace prize, 2003; named to Wisdom Hall of Fame, 2001. Fellow: APA (pres. divsn. 32 1980, pres. divsn. 30 1997, Disting. Contbns. to Profl. Hypnosis award 2002, Disting. Contbns. to Internat. Advancement of Psychology award 2002), Western Psychol. Assn., Soc. Sci. Study Sexuality, Soc. Sci. Study Religion, Am. Psychol. Soc., Am. Soc. Clin. Hypnosis; mem.: ACA, AAAS, Soc. Clin. and Exptl. Hypnosis, Parapsychol. Assn. (pres. 1983), Nat. Soc. Study of Edn., Menninger Found., Internat. Soc. Gen. Semantics, Western Psychol. Assn., Swedish Soc. Clin. and Exptl. Hypnosis, Soc. Gen. Sys. Rsch., Soc. Accelerative Learning and Tchg., Coun. Exceptional Children, Biofeedback Soc. Am., Soc. Sci. Exploration, Sleep Rsch. Soc., Nat. Assn. for Gifted Children, Internat. Soc. for Study of Dissociation, Internat. Soc. Hypnosis, Assn. Transpersonal Psychology, Assn. Humanistic Psychology (pres. 1974—75), Inter-Am. Psychol. Assn., Soc. for the Anthropology Consciousness, Internat. Assn. for Study of Dreams (pres. 1993—94, Lifetime Achievement award 2006), Internat. Coun. Psychologists, Am. Ednl. Rsch. Assn., Am. Soc. Psychical Rsch., World Future Soc. Office: Saybrook Grad Sch 747 Front St 3rd Fl San Francisco CA 94111 Home Phone: 415-456-2153. Business E-Mail: skrippner@saybrook.edu.

KRISE, THOMAS WARREN, academic administrator, literature and language professor, retired military officer; b. Ft. Sam Houston, Tex., Oct. 27, 1961; s. Edward Fisher and Elizabeth Ann (Bradt) K.; m. Patricia Lynn Love, Sept. 5, 1987. BS, USAF Acad., 1983; MSA, Cen. Mich. U., 1986; MA, U. Minn., 1989; PhD, U. Chgo., 1995; diploma, Air Command and Staff Coll., Maxwell AFB, Ala., 1996, Air War Coll., 2001. Commd. 2d lt. USAF, 1983, advanced through grades to lt. col., ret., 2005; dep. ICBM comdr. 742d Strategic Missile Squadron, Minot AFB, ND, 1983-85, ICBM crew comdr., 1985-86, ICBM flight comdr., 1986-87; instr. English USAF Acad., Colorado Springs, 1989-91, asst. prof., 1991-92, 97-99, assoc. prof., 1999—2002, prof., 2002—05; prof., chair dept. English U. Ctrl. Fla., Orlando, 2005—07; prof., dean Coll. of Pacific, U. of Pacific, Stockton, Calif., 2008—. Sr. mil. fellow Inst. Nat. Strategic Studies, 1995—97; vice-dir. Nat. Def. U. Press, 1995—97; dir. English major program USAF Acad., 1997—2000, deputy head, dept. English and Fine Arts, 2002—03; dir. Air Force Humanities Inst., 1997—2005, pres. faculty senate, 2003—05; vis. prof. U.W.I., Mona, Jamaica, 1999. Asst. editor: War, Lit. and the Arts: An Internat. Jour. Humanities, 1991—92, assoc. editor:, 1998—2003, mng. editor:, 2003—05; editor: Caribbeana: An Anthology of English Literature of the West Indies 1657-1777, 1999; gen. editor: McNair Papers monograph series, 1995—97; contbr. articles to profl. jours. Adult literacy tutor trainer, Adult Literacy Network, Colorado Springs, 1989-92. Recipient Defense Meritorious Svc. medal, Meritorious Svc. medal, Air Force Commendation medal, Combat Readiness medal; Summer Inst. grantee Nat. Endowment for the Humanities, 1990, Seiler Rsch. grantee F.J. Seiler Rsch. Lab., A.F. Systems Command, 1991, Faculty Rsch Com. grantee, 1998-2004, Salzburg Seminar grantee, 2003, Rsch. grant USAF Inst. Nat. Security Studies, 1998, 99, CBS Bicentennial Narrators scholar, 1994; Fulbright fellow, 1999. Mem.: SAR (chpt. pres. Pikes Peak 1991—92), Fulbright Assn., Air Force Assn., Assn. Grads. USAF Acad. (bd. dirs. 1991—95, Chgo. chpt. pres. 1993—95), Mil. Officers Assn. Am., Soc. Early Americanists (exec. coord. 2003—05, v.p. 2005—07, pres. 2007—09), Soc. 18th Century Am. Studies (sec.-treas. 1995—99), Am. Soc. 18th Century Studies (conf. dir. 2002), Early Caribbean Soc. (pres. 2002—), Colorado Springs Adult Literacy Network (pres. 1991—92), Univ. Club San Francisco, Royal Air Force Club London, Army and Navy Club Washington, Toastmasters Internat. (U. Minn. chpt. pres. 1988—89), Sigma Tau Delta, Phi Kappa Phi. Democrat. Episcopalian. Avocations: travel, sailing, skiing, hiking, scuba diving. Office: U Pacific Coll Deans Office 3601 Pacific Ave Stockton CA 95211 Office Phone: 209-946-2023. Personal E-mail: krisetw@hotmail.com. Business E-Mail: tkrise@pacific.edu.

KRISTOF, KATHY M., journalist; b. Burbank, Calif., Feb. 4, 1960; d. Joseph E. and Frances S. Kristof; m. Richard R. Magnuson, Jr., Jan. 4, 1986 (div.); 2 children. BA, U. So. Calif., LA, 1983. Reporter L.A. Bus. Jour., 1984-88, Daily News, Woodland Hills, Calif., 1988-89, L.A. Times, 1989—; syndicated columnist L.A. Times Syndicate, 1991—. Author: Kathy Kristof's Complete Book of Dollars and Sense, 1997, Investing 101, 2000, Taming the Tuition Tiger, 2003; contbr. articles to mags. and profl. jours. Recipient John Hancock Fin. Svcs. award, 1992, Personal Fin. Writing award ICI/Am. U., 1994, Consumer Adv. of Yr., Calif. Alliance for Consumer Edn., 1998. Mem. Soc. Bus. Editors and Writers (pres. 2003), Calif. Newspapers Pubs. Assn. (2nd pl. Bus. and Fin. Story award 1999). Office: Los Angeles Times 202 W 1st St Los Angeles CA 90012 E-mail: kathy.kristof@latimes.com.

KRISTOF, LADIS KRIS DONABED, political scientist, writer; b. Cernauti, Romania, Nov. 26, 1918; came to U.S., 1952, naturalized, 1957; s. Witold and Maria (Zawadzki) Krzysztofowicz; m. Jane McWilliams, Dec. 29, 1956; 1 son, Nicholas. Student, U. Poznan, Poland, 1937-39; BA, Reed Coll., Portland, Oreg., 1955; MA, U. Chgo., 1956, PhD, 1969. Regional exec. dir., Sovromlemn, Romania, 1948; sales mgr. Centre du Livre Suisse, Paris, France, 1951-52; lectr. U. Chgo., 1958-59; assoc. dir. Inter-Univ. Project History Menshevism, NYC, 1959-62; mem. faculty dept. polit. sci. Temple U., 1962-64; research fellow Hoover Instn., Stanford U., 1964-67; faculty polit. sci. U. Santa Clara, 1967-68; asso. Studies Communist System, Stanford, 1968-69; mem. faculty polit. sci. U. Waterloo, Ont., Can., 1969-71; prof. polit. sci. Portland (Oreg.) State U., 1971-89, prof. emeritus, 1990—. Vis. prof. U. Wroclaw, Poland, 1990, U. Iasi, Romania, 1991, U. Punjab, India, 1992, U. Bucharest, Romania, 2004. Author: The Nature of Frontiers and Boundaries, 1959, The Origins and Evolution of Geopolitics, 1960, The Russian Image of Russia, 1967, The Geopolitical Contours of the Post-Cold War World, 1992; also articles in Romania; co-author, co-editor: Revolution and Politics in Russia, 1972. Active Internat. YMCA Center, Paris, 1950-52, NAACP, Chgo., 1957-59, Amnesty Internat., Portland, 1975—. Served with Corps Engrs. Romanian Army, 1940-45. Fulbright scholar Romania, 1971, 84 Mem. Am. Polit. Sci. Assn., Assn. Am. Geographers, Am. Assn. for Advancement of Slavic Studies, Internat. Polit. Sci. Assn., Western Slavic Assn. (pres. 1988-90), Am.-Romanian Acad. Arts and Scis. (v.p. 1995-00). Home: 23050 NW Roosevelt Dr Yamhill OR 97148-8336 Office: Portland State Univ Dept Polit Sci Portland OR 97207 Personal E-mail: kristofj@pdx.edu.

KROCHALIS, RICHARD F., federal agency administrator; BS in Environ. Sys. Engring., Cornell U.; M in City and Regional Planning, Harvard U. Dir. dept. constrn. and land use City of Seattle, Seattle, 1992-99, dir. dept. design, constrn. and land use, 1999—2001; regional adminstr. Fed. Transit Adminstrn., 2002—. Past pres. Sustainable Seattle, 2002-03; mem. coun. Cornell U., 1991-98, Cornell U. Coll. of Arch. Art, Planning Adv. Coun., 1998-. Mem. Urban Land Inst., Am. Planning Assn., Am. Inst. Cert. Planners. Office: Federal-Transit Adminstrn Ste 3142 915 Second Ave Seattle WA 98174-1002 Office Phone: 206-220-7954. E-mail: rick.krochalis@dot.gov.

KROEMER, HERBERT, electrical engineering educator; b. Weimar, Germany, Aug. 25, 1928; Diplom-Physiker, Gottingen U., Germany, 1951, Dr. rer. nat., 1952; Doctorate (hon.), Tech. U. Aachen, Germany, 1985, U. Lund, Sweden, 1998, U. Colo., 2001. Prof. elec., computer engring. U. Calif., Santa Barbara, faculty rsch. lectr., 1985—96, Donald W. Whittier chair in elec. engring., 1986—. Recipient Heinrich Welker medal Internat. Symposium on GaAs and related compounds, 1982, Alexander von Humboldt Rsch. award, 1994, NAE, 1997, Nobel Prize in physics, 2000, Grand Cross of Order of Merit, Germany, 2001. Mem. NAS, IEEE (J.J. Ebers award Electron Devices Group 1973, Nat. lectr. 1983, Jack Morton award 1986, Medal of Honor, 2002), Am. Phys. Soc., Nat. Acad. Engring. Office: Elec-Computer Engring Dept Rm 2205A Engring Sci Bldg Univ Calif Santa Barbara CA 93106-9560

KROENER, WILLIAM FREDERICK, III, lawyer; b. NYC, Aug. 27, 1945; s. William Frederick Kroener Jr. and Barbara (Mitchell) Kroener; m. Evelyn Somerville Bibb, Sept. 3, 1966; children: William F. Kroener IV(dec.), Mary Elizabeth, Evangeline Alberta, James Mitchell. AB, Yale Coll., 1967; JD, MBA, Stanford U., Calif., 1971. Bar: Calif. 1972, N.Y. 1979, D.C. 1983. Assoc. Davis Polk & Wardwell, NYC, 1971-79, London, 1974—75, ptnr. NYC, 1979-82, 1982-94, Washington, 1982—94; gen. counsel FDIC, 1995—2006; counsel Sullivan & Cromwell LLP, Washington and LA, 2006—. Lectr. Stanford U. Law Sch., 1993—94, George Washington U. Law Sch., 1995—98, Washington Coll. Law, Am. U. Law Sch., Washington, 1997—2003; mem. legal adv. group Fed. Fin. Instns. Exam. Coun., 1995—2006, chmn. legal adv. group, 2001—03. Pres. Kroener Family Found.; gov. bd. mem. St. Albans Sch., 1991—95; fin. com. mem. Protestant/Episcopal Cathedral Found.-Wash. Nat. Cathedral, 1992—95; mem. bd. visitors Stanford U. Law Sch., 1983—92, deans adv. coun., 1992—93; nat. chair Stanford Law Fund, 1990—92; dir., gen. counsel Kenwood Citizens Assn., Inc., 1993—94; governing bd. FDIC Corp. Univ., 2002—06; mem. regulatory appeals com. Dubai fin. Svcs. Authority, 2007—. Mem.: ABA, Assn. Bar City of NY, Am. Law Inst., Lido Isle Yacht Club, Kenwood Golf Club, Yale Club of NYC. Republican. Episcopalian. Office: Sullivan & Cromwell LLP 1701 Pennsylvania Ave NW Washington DC 20006-5605 also: Sullivan & Cromwell LLP 1888 Century Park E Los Angeles CA 90067-1725 Office Phone: 202-956-7095. Business E-Mail: kroenerw@sullcrom.com.

KROENERT, ROB, Internet company executive, marketing professional; BA, U. Mich.; MBA, Emory U. Mgmt. cons. IBM; co-founder, former v.p. mktg., advisor RateItAll, Inc., San Francisco, 1999—; dir. rsch. cons. TNS Prognostics; global practice mgr. customer & brand engagement The Gallup Orgn. Office: RateItAll, Inc 3338 17th St, Ste 206 San Francisco CA 94110 also: Gallup Orgn 101 California St, Ste 3000 San Francisco CA 94111 Office Phone: 415-626-6645.

KROENKE, E. STANLEY, real estate developer, professional sports team owner; b. Cole Camp, Mo. m. Ann (Walton) Kroenke; children: Whitney, Josh. Grad. in Bus., U. Mo., MBA, 1973. Chmn., owner The Kroenke Group., Columbia, Mo.; chmn. THF Realty; owner Kroenke Sports Enterprises; vice chmn., co-owner St. Louis Rams, 1995—; owner Pepsi Ctr., Denver, 2000—, Denver Nuggets, 2000—, Colo. Avalanche, 2000—, Colo. Crush, 2002—, Colo. Mammoth, 2002—, Colo. Rapids, 2003—; co-owner Dick's Sporting Goods, Colo. Bd. dirs. Cmty. Investment Partnership Funds I and II, St. Louis, Boone County Nat. Bank, Columbia, Ctrl. Bancompany, Jefferson City; co-owner Screaming Eagle Vineyard, Napa Valley, Calif., 2006-. Trustee Coll. of the Ozarks; mem. bd. Greater St. Louis Area Coun. Boy Scouts of Am., St. Louis Art Mus. Named one of 400 Richest Ams., Forbes mag., 2006, Most Influential People in the World of Sports, Bus. Week, 2008. Office: Pepsi Ctr 1000 Chopper Cir Denver CO 80204 also: St Louis Rams 1 Rams Way Earth City MO 63045-1525

KROGER, JOHN RICHARD, state attorney general, former prosecutor, law educator; b. 1966; BA magna cum laude, Yale U., 1990, MA; JD magna cum laude, Harvard U., 1996. Bar: Ct., Oreg. Legis. asst. to US Rep. Tom Foley, Senator Chuck Schumer; dep. policy dir. Bill Clinton's Presdl. Campaign, 1991—92; sr. policy analyst US Treasury Dept.; law clk. for Hon. Judge Anthony Scirica US Ct. Appeals (3rd cir.); asst. US atty. (ea. dist.) NY US Dept. Justice, prosecutor Enron Task Force.; prof. criminal law and legal philosophy Lewis & Clark Law Sch., Portland, 2002—; atty. gen. State of Oreg., 2009—. Author: Convictions: A Prosecutor's Battles Against Mafia Killers, Drug Kingpins, and Enron Thieves, 2008. Former chair Dem. Party of Oreg. Fin. Com. Served in USMC, 1983—86. Democrat. Avocations: running, bicycling, hiking. Office: Oreg Dept of Justice 1162 Court St NE Salem OR 97301-4096 E-mail: kroger@lclark.edu.

KROHN, KENNETH ALBERT, radiologist, educator; b. Stevens Point, Wis., June 19, 1945; s. Albert William and Erma Belle (Cornwell) K.; 1 child, Galen. BA in Chemistry, Andrews U., 1966; PhD in Chemistry, U. Calif., 1971. Acting assoc. prof. U. Wash., Seattle, 1981-84, assoc. prof. radiology, 1984-86, prof. radiology and radiation oncology, 1986—, adj. prof. chemistry, 1986—. Guest scientist Donner Lab. Lawrence Berkeley (Calif.) Lab., 1980-81; radiochemist, VA Med. Ctr., Seattle, 1982—; affiliate investigator Fred Hutchinson Cancer Rsch. Ctr., 1997—. Contbr. articles to profl. jours.; patentee in field. Recipient Aebersold award, 1996; fellow, NDEA. Fellow AAAS; mem. Am. Assn. for Cancer Rsch., Am. Soc. Clin. Oncology, Am. Chem. Soc., Radiation Rsch. Soc., Soc. Nuclear Medicine, Acad. Coun., Sigma Xi. Home: 550 NE Lakeridge Dr Belfair WA 98528-8720 Office: U Washington Imaging Rsch Lab Box 356004 Seattle WA 98195-6004 Office Phone: 206-598-6245. Business E-Mail: kkrohn@u.washington.edu.

KROLICKI, BRIAN KEITH, Lieutenant Governor of Nevada, former state official, state legislator; b. Providence, Dec. 31, 1960; s. Thadeus James Krolicki and Gail Carolyn (Gourdeau) Jacus; m. Kelly Lea DiGiusto, May 21, 1994; children: Katherine, Caroline, Elizabeth. BA in Polit. Sci., Stanford U., 1983. Cert. gov. fin. mgr.; lic. securities dealer. Assoc. banker Bankers Trust Co., NYC, 1984-85; sr. acct. exec. First Commodity Boston, Zephyr Cove, Nev., 1985-86; acct. exec. Smith Barney, San Francisco, 1986-87, investment banker Manama, Bahrain, 1987-89; pres. Inter Am. Mktg. Corp., Reno, London, 1989-91; chief dep. state treas. and sec. state bd. fin. State of Nev., Carson City, 1991-99, state treas., 1999—2006, lt. gov., 2007—; pres. Nev. State Senate, 2007—. Sec. Nev. Master Lease Corp., Carson City, 1992—. Mem. Rep. State Ctrl. Com., Nev., 1990; vice-chmn. planning commn. Douglas County, Minden, Nev., 1991-98; chmn. support svcs. Am. Cancer Soc., Nev., 1993-96, bd. dirs. Southwestern US divsn.; bd. dirs. found. Lake Tahoe (Calif.) C.C., 1996. Recipient Unruh award, 2004, Gritz award for Excellence in Pub. Fin. Mem. Nev. Govt. Fin. Officer Assn. (pres. 1997—). Republican. Avocations: guitar, outdoors. Office: Lieutenant Governor State Capitol Bldg 101 North Carson St Carson City NV 89701 also: Grant Sawyer Bldg 555 East Washington Ave Ste 5500 Las Vegas NV 89101 also: 401 South Carson St Rm 1220 Carson City NV 89701 Office Phone: 775-684-7111, 702-486-2400. Office Fax: 775-684-7110, 702-486-2404. Business E-Mail: ltgov@lt.nv.gov.*

KROLL, SUE (SUSAN A. KROLL), film company executive; b. 1961; m. Michael Desilets. BA in Comm., Glassboro State U., 1983. Sr. v.p. mktg. TNT, Atlanta, mng. dir. TNT Europe London, 1992—95; sr. v.p. programming & ops. Warner Bros. Internat. Channels, 1995—97; sr. v.p. internat. mktg. Warner Bros. Pictures, 1997—2000, pres. internat. mktg., 2000—08, pres. worldwide mktg., 2008—. Named an Entertainment Marketer of Yr., Advt. Age. mag., 2008; named one of The 100 Most Powerful Women in Entertainment, Hollywood Reporter, 2006, 2007. Office: Warner Bros Pictures 4000 Warner Blvd Burbank CA 91522 Office Phone: 818-954-6000. E-mail: sue.kroll@warnerbros.com.

KROM, BETH, former Mayor, Irvine, California; m. Solly Krom; children: Abby, Noah, Hershel. Councilwoman City of Irvine, 2000—04, 2008—, former mayor, 2004—08. Former mem. Mayors for Climate Protection. Rep. US Conf. Mayors, Nat. League Cities; bd. mem. Orange County Great Park Corp., Irvine Ednl. Partnership Fund, Transp. Corridor Agy., Discovery Sci. Ctr.; rep. Southern Calif. Assn. Govts., Orange County Coun. Govts. Mailing: 1 Civic Center Plaza PO Box 19575 Irvine CA 92623-9575 Office Phone: 949-724-6233, 949-724-6000. E-mail: bethkrom@ci.irvine.ca.us.*

KRUCKEBERG, ARTHUR RICE, botanist, educator; b. LA, Calif., Mar. 21, 1920; s. Arthur Woodbury and Ella Muriel K.; m. Mareen Schultz, Mar. 21, 1953; children— Arthur Leo, Enid Johanna; children by previous marriage— Janet Muriel, Patricia Elayne, Caroline. BA, Occidental Coll., Los Angeles, 1941; postgrad., Stanford U., 1941-42; PhD, U. Calif.-Berkeley, 1950. Instr. biology Occidental Coll., 1946; teaching asst. U. Calif.-Berkeley, 1946-50; mem. faculty U. Wash., Seattle, 1950—, prof. botany, 1964-88, emeritus, 1988—, chmn. dept., 1971-77. Cons. in field. Co-founder Wash. Natural Area Preserves system, 1966. Served with USNR, 1942-46. Mem. Wash. Native Plant Soc. (founder 1976), Calif. Bot. Soc. Rsch. edaphics of serpentines, flowering plants. Home: 20312 15th Ave NW Shoreline WA 98177-2166 Office: U Wash PO Box 351800 Seattle WA 98195-180o Office Phone: 206-543-1976. Business E-Mail: ark@u.washington.edu.

KRUEGER, EUGENE REX, academic program consultant; b. Grand Island, Nebr., Mar. 30, 1935; s. Rudolph F. and Alma K.; m. Karin Schubert, June 9, 1957; children: Eugene Eric, Richard Kevin, Kristina. Student, Kans. State U., 1952-53; BS in Physics, Rensselaer Poly. Inst., 1957, MS in Math, 1960, PhD in Applied Math, 1962. Research physicist IBM, 1957-58; research fellow Army Math. Research Center, U. Wis., 1962-63; prof. U. Colo., Boulder, 1965-74; vice chancellor, prof. Oreg. State System of Higher Edn., Eugene, 1974-82; exec. cons. Control Data Corp., 1982-85, v.p., 1985-89; exec. dir. tech.-based engring. edn. consortium William C. Norris Inst., 1989-96, v.p., 1996-97. Adj. prof. computer sci. U. Minn., 1989-94; adj. prof. Western Sem., 1997-01; chmn. seminar for dirs. of acad. computing facilities, 1969-82; pres. Krueger & Assocs., 1989—; cons. on computer graphics computing facility mgmt.; dir. various research grants and contracts; U.S. acad. cons. African Virtual U./World Bank, 1995-2001; interim pres. Christian Heritage Coll., 1998; interim exec. dir. WorldView/Internat. Inst. Christian Comm., 2004-05. Contbr. research papers in field to publs. Mem. Sigma Xi, Phi Kappa Phi. E-mail: rex@bendcable.com.

KRUEGER, KENNETH JOHN, nutritionist, educator; b. LA, Jan. 29, 1946; s. Charles Herbert and Adelaide Marie K.; m. Ellen Santucci, June 16, 1979 (div. 1989); children: Kenneth, Michael, Scott, David. BA in Humanities, U. So. Calif., 1968; MS in Edn. (Psychology), Mt. St. Mary's Coll., 1972. Tchr. English Corcoran H.S., Calif., 1968, Charter Oak H.S., Covina, Calif., 1969—90; instr. nutrition and exercise Mt. San Antonio Coll., Walnut, Calif., 1974—80; pres. Mega Group, Ltd., 1990, The Krueger Group, Malibu, Calif., 1991—2000; exec. Overnite Express, LA, 1993, Calif. Parcel Express, Encino, 1994—96; nutritionist Swiss Nat. Team, 1995—99; tchr. phys. edn. Hiram Johnson H.S., Sacramento, 1995—96. Adj. prof. phys. edn. Sierra Coll., Rocklin, Calif., 1996; health instr. L.A. City Coll., 1996-97, West L.A. Coll., 1998; swim coach Mt. San Antonio Coll., Walnut, Calif., 1974-77; coach, v.p. Trojan Swim Club, Newport Beach, Calif., 1976-90; bd. dirs. Nutrition and Exercise Cons., Tustin, Calif.; nutrition and exercise dir. Health Am., 1987-90; chmn., nutrition and fitness com. Internat. Eating Disorders Com., 1988; U.S. nat. team nutritionist for (FINA) World Cup 1988 Champions; recruiter Club Med, Paris, 1976-78; program coord. Pacific Am. Inst., San Francisco, 1983; asst. coach Vevey Natation, Switzerland, 1972-73; asst. swim coach Swiss Nat. Team, 1968, 85; chief marshall U.S. Olympic Swim Trials, Irvine, 1980, linguistics chmn. protocol U. So. Calif. Venue, L.A. Olympic Com., 1983-84; mem.-at-large long distance com. U.S. Swimming, Colorado Springs, 1987-91, coach So. Calif. Long Distance Swimming, 1987-89; del. chief, coach and swimmer So. Calif. Swimming for Internat. Crossing of Lake Geneva, sponsored by Internat. Olympic Com., Switzerland, 1987; meet dir. U.S. 25K Long Distance Swimming Championships/FINA World Cup Trials, Long Beach, Calif., 1988, U.S. 25K Swim Championships, Long Beach, 1989. Author: Reflections and Refractions, 1973; contbr. articles to internat. profl. nutrition and sport jours. Bd. dirs. U.S.A. Athletes Hall of Fame, 1991-92. Recipient NCAA All Am. award U. So. Calif., 1966, NCAA Nat. Champ award, 1966, U.S. Masters Swimming Champion, 1972 and annually 1974-81, Internat. Sr. Olympics Champion, 1972 and annually 1974-85; recipient commendations U.S. Congress, Calif. Senate, L.A. County Bd. Suprs; inducted into U.S.A. Athletes Hall of Fame. Mem. KC. Libertarian. Roman Catholic. Avocations: sports, reading. Mailing: 5435 Vesper Ave Sherman Oaks CA 91411 Personal E-mail: krkrueger@hotmail.com.

KRUGER, KENNETH CHARLES, architect; b. Santa Barbara, Calif., Aug. 19, 1930; s. Thomas Albin and Chleople (Gaines) K.; m. Patricia Kathryn Rasey, Aug. 21, 1955; children: David, Eric. BArch, U. So. Calif., 1953. Registered arch., Calif. Pres. Kruger Bensen Ziemer, Santa Barbara, 1960-90; part-time instr. architecture dept. Calif. Poly., San Luis Obispo, 1993-95; part-time arch., 1993—. Regent Calif. Archtl. Found., 1997-2003. Bd. dirs. United Boys and Girls Club, 2000-. Fellow AIA; mem. Archtl. Found. Santa Barbara (pres. 1987-89). Democrat. Home: 1255 Ferrelo Rd Santa Barbara CA 93103-2101

KRUGER, LON, men's college basketball coach; b. Topeka, Aug. 19, 1952; m. Barbara Miles; children: Angie, Kevin. BS in Bus., Kans. State U., 1975; MS in Phys. Edn., Pittsburg State U., Kans., 1977. Draft pick Houston Astros, 1970, St. Louis Cardinals, Atlanta Hawks, 1974, head coach, 2000—03; asst. coach Pittsburg State U., Kans., 1976-77; grad. asst. coach Kans. State U., 1977-78, asst. coach, 1978-82, head coach, 1986—90, Pan Am. U., 1982-86, athletic dir., 1982-85; head coach U. Fla., 1990—96, U. Ill., 1996—2000, UNLV, 2004—; asst. coach NY Knicks, 2003—04. Asst. coach US Pan Am. Team, 1987; head coach Big Eight Select Team, Beijing, 1987, U.S.A. Jr. World Champion Team, 1991, U.S.A. World U. Games Team, 1995; bd. dirs. Nat. Assn. Basketball Coaches, 1994—2000. Co-chairperson Alachua County's Red Ribbon Campaign, 1991-93. Named Big Eight Player of Yr., 1973, 74, Southeastern Conf. Coach of Yr., 1992, 94, Gainesville Vol. of Yr., 1995, State of Ill. Collegiate Coach of Yr., 1997; named to the Kans. Hall of Fame, 1999, Kans. State U. Hall of Fame, 2003, Topeka and Shawnee County Sports Hall of Fame, 2006. Office: Mens Basketball UNLV Athletics Dept 4505 Maryland Pky Las Vegas NV 89154 Office Phone: 702-895-3295. E-mail: lon.kruger@unlv.edu.

KRUGER, PAULA, telecommunications industry executive; b. Bklyn., July 31, 1950; d. Jean Jacques Kruger and Jo Campione; m. Lawrence C. Heller; children: Michael, Tracy, Jessica. BA in Bus. Adminstrn., C.W. Post, Brookville, NY, 1972; MBA, LI U., 1976. V.p. customer rels. Cablevision, Woodbury, NY, 1994—97; corp. v.p. customer svc. Am. Express, NYC, Citibank, NYC, v.p. devel. divsn.; v.p. consumer svcs. group Republic of Korea; v.p. teleservices Excel Comm., 1997—99, exec. v.p. customer and ind. rep. ops., 1999; gen. mgr. customer relationship mgmt. svc. line Electronic Data Systems Corp., 2002—03; exec. v.p. mass markets group Qwest Comm. Internat., Inc., Denver, 2003—. Office: Qwest Comm Internat Inc 1801 California St Denver CO 80202 Office Phone: 303-992-1400. Office Fax: 303-896-8515.

KRUGGEL, JOHN LOUIS, plastic surgeon; b. Lake Mills, Iowa, Jan. 27, 1931; s. August and Elizabeth (Gleitz) K.; m. Kathleen Ann Lawson, June 1958 (div. 1972); children: Deborah, Natalie, Victoria, Pamela, Michael; m. Donna Marie Koerner, Mar. 2, 1978; 1 child, Matthew. AS, Waldorf Coll., 1951; MD, U. Iowa, 1957. Diplomate Am. Bd. Plastic Surgery, Am. Bd. Surgery. Intern Mercy Hosp., San Diego; resident Orange Meml. Hosp., Orlando, Fla., Mercy Hosp., San Diego, U. Calif., San Francisco; pvt. practice in plastic surgery San Diego, 1966—. Capt. USAF, 1959-61. Mem. Am. Soc. Plastic and Reconstructive Surgery, Calif. Soc. Plastic and Reconstructive Surgery, Calif. Med. Soc., San Diego County Med. Soc. (del. to Calif. Med. Assn.). Avocations: skiing, water-skiing, hiking, pilot. Office: John Kruggel Md Inc 15904 Ranch Hollow Rd Poway CA 92064-2130

KRUGMAN, RICHARD DAVID, pediatrician, academic administrator, educator; b. NYC, Nov. 28, 1942; s. Saul and Sylvia (Stern) K.; m. Mary Elizabeth Kerber, July 9, 1966; children: Scott, Joshua, Todd, Jordan. AB, Princeton U., 1963; MD, NYU, 1968. Resident U. Colo. Sch. Medicine, Denver, 1968-71; staff assoc. Nat. Inst. Health, Bethesda, Md., 1971-73; asst. prof. U. Colo. Sch. Medicine, 1973-78, assoc. prof., 1978-87, prof. of pediatrics, 1988—, dean, 1992—, vice chancellor, Health Affairs, 2007—. Author: The Battered Child, 5th edit., 1997; editor: (jour.) Child Abuse/Neglect, 1986-2001. Chmn. U.S. Adv. Bd. Child Abuse and Neglect, Washington, 1989-91; dir. Kempe Nat. Ctr. for Prevention and Treatment of Child Abuse and Neglect, Denver, 1981-92; trustee Princeton U., 2001-2005. Recipient C. Henry Kempe award Nat. Conf. on Child Abuse, 1989, St. Geme award U. Colo. Sch. Medicine, 1992, 98; Paul Harris fellow Rotary Internat., Sydney, Australia, 1992. Mem. Internat. Soc. Prevention of Child Abuse and Neglect (pres. 1992-94), Am. Acad. Pediatrics (Ray Helfer award 1995, Brandt Steele award 1996), Am. Pediatric Soc., Inst. Medicine. Office: U Colo Sch Medicine 4200 E 9th Ave Denver CO 80262-0001

KRUGMAN, STANLEY LEE, international management consultant; b. NYC, Mar. 2, 1925; s. Harry and Leah (Greenberg) K.; m. Helen Schorr, June 14, 1947; children: Vicky Lee, Thomas Paul; m. Carolyn Schambra, Sept. 17, 1966; children: David Andrew, Wendy Carol; m. Gail Jennings, Mar. 17, 1974. Grad., Rensselaer Poly. Inst., Navy V-12 Program, 1945; BS in Chem. Engring., Rensselaer Poly. Inst., 1947; postgrad., Poly. Inst. NYU, Columbia U., 1947—51. Process devel. engr. Merck & Co., Rahway, NJ, 1947-51; sr. process and project engr. C.F. Braun & Co., Alhambra, Calif., 1951-55; with Jacobs Engring. Co., Pasadena, Calif., 1955-76; from chief engr. to v.p. engring. and constrn. to v.p. gen. mgr. to exec. v.p. to pres., and dir., 1974—82; exec. v.p., dir. Jacobs Engring. Group Inc., Pasadena, Calif.; pres., dir. Jacobs Constructors of P.R., San Juan, 1970-82; pres. Jacobs Internat. Inc., 1971-82, Jacobs Internat. Ltd., Inc., Dublin, 1974-82; dep. chmn. Jacobs LTA Engring., Ltd., Johannesburg, 1981-82; pres. Krugman Assocs., 1982—; internat. mgmt. cons. Patentee in field. Served to lt. (j.g.) USNR, 1944-46, PTO. Mem.: Am. Chem. Soc., Am. Inst. Chem. Engrs., U.S. Naval Inst. Presbyterian. Home and Office: 60 Condon Ln Port Ludlow WA 98365

KRUMBOLTZ, JOHN DWIGHT, psychologist, educator; b. Cedar Rapids, Iowa, Oct. 21, 1928; s. Dwight John and Margaret (Jones) K.; m. Helen Brandhorst, Aug. 22, 1954 (div. Aug. 1986); children: Ann, Jennifer; m. Betty Lee Foster, Nov. 8, 1987. BA, Coe Coll., Cedar Rapids, 1950; MA, Columbia Tchrs. Coll., 1951; PhD, U. Minn.,

1955; PhD (hon.), Pacific Grad. Sch. Psychology, 1991. Counselor, tchr. W. Waterloo (Iowa) H.S., 1951-53; from teaching asst. to instr. U. Minn., 1953-55; from asst. prof. ednl. psychology to assoc. prof. Mich. State U., 1957-61; faculty Stanford U. Sch. Edn., 1961-66, prof. edn. and psychology, 1966—. Vis. sr. research psychologist Ednl. Testing Service, 1972-73; fellow Ctr. for Advanced Study in Behavioral Scis., 1975-76, Advanced Study Ctr., Nat. Ctr. for Research in Vocat. Edn., Ohio State U., 1980-81; vis. colleague dept. psychology Inst. Psychiatry, U. London, 1983-84 Author: (with others) Learning to Study, 1960; (with Helen B. Krumboltz) Changing Children's Behavior, 1972; editor: Learning and the Educational Process, 1965, Revolution in Counseling, 1966; (with Carl E. Thoresen) Behavioral Counseling: Cases and Techniques, 1969, Counseling Methods, 1976; (with Anita M. Mitchell and G. Brian Jones) Social Learning and Career Decision Making, 1979; (with Daniel A. Hamel) Assessing Career Development, 1982; contbr. articles to profl. jours. With USAF, 1955-57. Recipient Eminent Career award Nat. Career Devel. Assn., 1994, Living Legend award Am. Counseling Assn., 2004, Outstanding Achievement award, U. Minn., 2006; Guggenheim fellow, 1967-68. Mem. APA (pres. div. counseling psychology 1974-75, award for disting. profl. contbns. to knowledge 2002), Am. Ednl. Rsch. Assn. (v.p. div. E 1966-68), Am. Pers. and Guidance Assn. (Outstanding Rsch. award 1959, 66, 68, Disting. Profl. Svcs. award 1974, Leona Tyler award 1990). Home: 933 Valdez Pl Stanford CA 94305-1008

KRUMM, CHARLES FERDINAND, electrical engineer; b. Macomb, Ill., Aug. 3, 1941; s. Harold F. and Jean Dunlap (Burns) K.; m. Patricia L. Kosanke, Dec. 9, 1967; children: Jennifer, Frederick. AS, Grand Rapids Jr. Coll., 1961; BSEE, U. Mich., 1963, MSEE, 1965, PhD, 1970. Sr. scientist Raytheon Co., Waltham, Mass., 1969-76; mem. tech. staff Hughes Rsch. Labs., Malibu, Calif., 1976-77, sect. head, 1977-79, asst. dept. mgr., 1979-81, dept. mgr., 1981-86, lab. mgr., 1986-89; program mgr. Hughes Radar and Comm. Sys., El Segundo, Calif., 1989-96; product line mgr. Hughes GaAs Operation, Torrance, Calif., 1996; divsn. mgr. Hughes Microelectronics Divsn., Newport Beach, Calif., 1996-98; v.p., dep. mgr. ctrs. excellence and strategic components, sensors, and elec. sys. segment Raytheon Sys. Co., 1998-99; gen. mgr. Raytheon RF Components, Andover, Mass., 1999-2000; progrm dir. GAAS Tech., Conexant Sys., Inc., Newbury Park, Calif., 2000—. Home: 9 Vincennes Newport Coast CA 92657-0110

KRUMMEL, JERRY, state legislator; b. Walla Walla, Wash., Jan. 31, 1953; m to Gerri; children: one. Member, Budget Committee, Wilsonville, Oregon, 89-96, city counselor, 91, mayor, 91-97; Oregon State Representative, District 27, 1999-2002; Oregon State Representative, District 26, 2003-.High sch & col teacher, athletic trainer, 75-88, private practice, 90-; medical sales/coffee store owner, 88-90. Nat & Oregon Athletic Trainers Asns; Lions; City of Wilsonville, West Linn & Sherwood Chamber of Commerce. Republican. Lutheran. Office: 900 Court St NE, Rm H-281 Salem OR 97301 Fax: Capit: 503-986-1561. E-mail: krummel.rep@state.or.us.

KRUPKA, ROBERT GEORGE, lawyer; b. Rochester, NY, Oct. 21, 1949; s. Joseph Anton and Marjorie Clara (Meteyer) Krupka; m. Pamela Banner Krupka; children: Kristin Nicole, Kerry Melissa. BS, Georgetown U., 1971; JD, U. Chgo., 1974. Bar: Ill. 1974, Colo. 1991, DC 1991, Calif. 1998, US Dist. Ct. (no. dist.) Ill. 1974, US Dist. Ct. (ea. dist.) Wis. 1974, US Ct. Appeals (7th cir.) 1976, US Supreme Ct. 1978, US Dist. Ct. (ctrl. dist.) Ill. 1980, US Dist. Ct. (so. dist.) Ill. 1988, US Dist. Ct. (no. dist.) Calif. 1980, US Dist. Ct. (ctrl. and so. dists.) Calif. 1999, US Dist. Ct. Ariz. 1998, US Dist. Ct. Colo. 1998, US Dist. Ct. Md. 2000, US Dist. Ct. (ea. dist.) Tex. 2006, US Dist. Ct. (we. dist.) Wis., 2006, US Ct. Appeals (4th and fed. cirs.) 1982, US Ct. Appeals (6th cir.) 1985, US Ct. Appeals (1st, 2nd, 3rd, 5th, 8th, 9th, 10th and 11th dists.) 1999, US Patent and Trademark Office. Assoc. Kirkland & Ellis LLP, 1974—79, ptnr. Chgo., 1979—. Author: Infringement Litigation Computer Software and Database, 1984, Computer Software, Semiconductor Design, Video Game and Database Protection and Enforcement, 1984. Mem. bd. trustees Francis W. Parker Sch., 1987-98, pres., 1994-97. Recipient Calif. Lawyer Atty. of Yr. award, Calif. Lawyer Mag., 2004; named one of Top 10 Trial Lawyers in Am., Nat. Law Jour., 1998, 2005, Leading Practitioners in the Fed. Cir., 2001, Top 100 Most Influential Lawyers, 2006, Top 30 Intellectual Property Lawyers, Daily Jour. Extra, 2005, Top 500 Lawyers in Am., Lawdragon, 2005, Top 100 Attys. in Calif., Daily Jour., 2005, World's Leading Lawyers for Bus. in Intellectual Property, Chambers Global, 2006. Mem. ABA (chmn. sec. com. 1982-88, chmn. divsn. 1988-90, 98—, coun. 1994-97, chair intellectual property law sect., mem. litig. sect.), LA Bar Assn., Internat. Bar Assn. (co-chair intellectual property and entertainment law com.), Am. Intellectual Property Law Assn. (chmn. subcommittee 1988—), LA Intellectual Property Law Assn., Chgo. Intellectual Property Law Assn., Fed. Cir. Bar Assn., Internat. Trademark Assn., ITC Trial Lawyers, Nat. Inst. Trial Advocacy (trustee 2002—), Regency Club. Office: Kirkland & Ellis LLP Ste 3700 777 S Figueroa St Los Angeles CA 90017-5800 Office Phone: 213-680-8456. Office Fax: 213-680-8500. E-mail: bkrupka@kirkland.com.

KRUPP, CLARENCE WILLIAM, lawyer, health facility administrator; b. Cleve., June 20, 1929; s. William Frederick and Mary Mae (Volchko) K.; m. Janice Margaret Heckman, June 28, 1952; children: Bruce, Carolyn. BBA cum laude, Cleve. State U., 1958, LL.B., 1959, LL.M., 1963; LL.D. (hon.), 1974. Bar: Wis. 1972. Dir. pers. Case Tech. U., Cleve., 1960—63; dir. indsl. relations and indsl. engring. Buxbaum Co., Canton, Ohio, 1963-66; mgr. indsl. relations Trane Co., La Crosse, Wis., 1966-73; dir. personnel-labor relations environ. products div. ITT, Phila., 1973; v.p. indsl. relations, gen. counsel G. Heileman Brewing Co., La Crosse, 1973-76; atty., v.p. human resources-risk control, sec. Good Samaritan Hosp., Dayton, Ohio, 1976-80; mgr. compensation and benefits State of Ariz., Phoenix, 1980-83; personnel adminstr., law/land mgmt. divsn. agt. Salt River Project, 1983-94; Indian and sch. land specialist, 1992—; chmn., pres. C.W. Krupp P.C., 1986—. Cons. on labor rels., 1969, 81-83, 88—; elec. line land impact cons., western states, 2000—. Contbr. articles to profl. jours. Mcpl. arbitrator, La Crosse, 1976; pres., mem. La Crosse Bd. Edn., 1969-72; mem. Wis. Gov.'s Task Force on Edn., 1972-73, Ohio Little White House library del.; mem. Ariz. Spinal Injury Panel, 1984-2000. Served with U.S. Army, 1951-53. Named Outstanding Ariz. State Profl. Employee, 1982, Employee of Quarter, 1990, 91; nominee Internat. Bar Assn. Mem. ABA (forum hosp. law, labor law sect.), Am. Corp. Counsel Assn., Nat. Notary Assn., Wis Bar Assn. (Continuing Edn. award 1972), Am. Assn. Hosp. Attys., Ariz. Assn. Industries (healthcare com. 1983-97, chmn. legis. subcom. 1983-97), Am. Soc. Law and Medicine, Dayton C. of C., Electric League of Ariz. (ins. advisor 1985-97), Internat. Right of Way Assn. (regional cons. Native Am. land rights 1998—), Rotary. Democrat. Roman Catholic. Home and Office: 8701 E Via De La Gente Scottsdale AZ 85258-4040 Home Phone: 480-998-7653; Office Phone: 480-998-7653. Personal E-mail: clarewk@msn.com.

KRUPP, EDWIN CHARLES, astronomer; b. Chgo., Nov. 18, 1944; s. Edwin Frederick and Florence Ann (Olander) K.; m. Robin Suzanne Rector, Dec. 31, 1968 (div., 2006); 1 son, Ethan Hembree. BA, Pomona Coll., 1966; MA, UCLA, 1968, PhD (NDEA fellow, 1970-71), 1972. Astronomer Griffith Obs., Los Angeles Dept. Recreation and Parks, 1972—, dir., 1976—. Mem. faculty El Camino Coll., U. So. Calif., extension divs. U. Calif.; cons. in ednl. TV C.C. Consortium; host teleseries Project: Universe. Author: Echoes of the Ancient Skies, 1983, The Comet and You, 1986 (Best Sci. Writing award Am. Inst. Physics 1986), The Big Dipper and You, 1989, Beyond the Blue Horizon, 1991, The Moon and You, 1993, Skywatchers, Shamans & Kings, 1996, The Rainbow and You, 2000; editor, co-author: In Search of Ancient Astronomies, 1978 (Am. Inst. Physics-U.S. Steel Found. award for best sci. writing 1978), Archaeoastronomy and the Roots of Science; editor-in-chief Griffith Obs., 1984—; contbg. editor Sky & Telescope, 1993—. Mem. Am. Astron. Soc. (past chmn. hist. astronomy divsn., solar physics divsn. writing award 2002), Astron. Soc. Pacific (past dir., Klumpke-Roberts Outstanding Contbns. to the Public Understanding and Appreciation of Astronomy award 1989, G. Bruce Blair medal for contbns. to pub. astronomy 1996, Clifford W. Holmes award for contbns. to amateur astronomy 2002), Internat. Soc. Archaeoastronomy and Astronomy in Culture (coun. mem., 2004-), Internat. Astron. Union, Explorers Club, Am. Rock Art Rsch Assn., Sigma Xi. Office: Griffith Observatory 2800 E Observatory Rd Los Angeles CA 90027-1255 Business E-Mail: eckrupp@earthlink.net.

KRUSE, JEFF, state legislator; b. Roseburg, Oreg., Sept. 7, 1951; c Shawn & Rhiannon. Oregon State Representative, District 45, formerly, chairman, House Health & Public Avocacy, currently, member House Govt Efficiency Committee, House Water & Environ Committee, House Stream Restoration & Species Recovery Committee, currently; Oregon State Representative, District 7, 2003-04; Oregon State Senator, District 1, 2004-.Farmer, Kruse Farms, currently. Republican. Office: 900 Court St NE, S-316 Salem OR 97301 also: 636 Wild Iris Ln Roseburg OR 97470 Home Phone: 541-673-7201; Office Phone: 503-986-1701. Business E-Mail: sen.jeffkruse@state.or.us.

KRUSE, SHARI, real estate agent; Sales assocs. sales mgr. Prudential Northwest Realty Assoc., Seattle. Recipient Prudential Legend award, Inspirational award. Office: Prudential Northwest Realty 4700 42nd Ave SW Ste 600 Seattle WA 98116 Office Phone: 206-932-4500. Business E-Mail: sharikruse@pnwrealty.edu.

KUBAS, GREGORY JOSEPH, research chemist; b. Cleve., Mar. 12, 1945; s. Joseph Arthur and Esther Kubas; m. Chrystal Henry, Dec. 22, 1973; children: Kelly Richmond (dec. 1997), Sherry Lopez. BS, Case Inst. Tech., 1966; PhD, Northwestern U., 1970. Postdoctoral fellow Princeton (N.J.) U., 1971-72, Los Alamos (N.Mex.) Nat. Lab., 1972-74, mem. staff, 1974—; lab. fellow, 1987—. Author: Metal Dihydrogen And Sigma Complexes, 2001; contbr. articles to profl. jours.; chpts. to books. Recipient E.O. Lawrence Meml. award US Dept. Energy, 1994. Fellow AAAS; mem. Am. Chem. Soc. (Inorganic Chemistry award 1993). Achievements include patents in field. Office: Los Alamos Nat Lab MS J582 Los Alamos NM 87545-0001 Home: 53 Avenida Las Nubes Santa Fe NM 87508

KUBIDA, WILLIAM JOSEPH, lawyer; b. Newark, Apr. 3, 1949; s. William and Catherine (Gilchrist) K.; m. Mary Jane Hamilton, Feb. 4, 1984; children: Sara Gilchrist, Kathleen Hamilton. BSEE, USAF Acad., 1971; JD, Wake Forest U., 1979. Bar: N.C. 1979, U.S. Patent Office 1979, Ind. 1980, U.S. Dist. Ct. (no. dist.) Ind. 1980, U.S. Dist. Ct. (so. dist.) Ind. 1980, U.S. Ct. Appeals (7th cir.) 1981, U.S. Dist. Ct. Ariz. 1982, U.S. Ct. Appeals (9th and fed. cirs.) 1982, Ariz. 1982, Colo. 1990, U.S. Dist. Ct. Colo. 1990, U.S. Ct. Appeals (10th cir.) 1990. Patent and trademark atty. Lundy and Assocs., Ft. Wayne, Ind., 1979-81; patent atty. Motorola, Inc., Phoenix, 1981-85; intellectual property counsel Nippon Motorola, Ltd., Tokyo, 1985-87; ptnr. Lisa & Kubida, Phoenix, 1987-89; engring. law counsel Digital Equipment Corp., Colorado Springs, Colo., 1989-92; of counsel Holland & Hart, Denver, Colorado Springs, 1992-93, ptnr., chmn. intellectual property practice group, 1993-99; ptnr., dir. intellectual property practice group Hogan & Hartson LLP, Colorado Springs, 1999—. Bd. dirs. Colorado Springs Tech Incubator, Bd. dirs. Colorado Springs Tech. Incubator. 1st lt. USAF, 1971—76. Mem. Am. Intellectual Property Law Assn. (computer software sect.), Licensing Exec. Soc. (Pacific Rim subcom.), Country Club Colo., Mensa, Intertel, Federlist Soc., Aston Martin Owners Club, Phi Delta Phi. Republican. Mem. Christ Ch. Of Col. Springs. Office: Hogan & Hartson LLP Two N Cascade Ave Ste 1300 Colorado Springs CO 80903 Office Fax: 719-448-5909. Business E-Mail: wjkubida@hhlaw.com.

KUBIK, TIMOTHY ROBERT WHITE, director, history educator; b. Sandy Point, Nova Scotia, Canada, Mar. 27, 1966; s. Robert William Kubik and Janet Ann Malins; m. Nancy J.M. Matchett, Aug. 17, 1967; children: Kenneth Ian, Sophia Lillian. PhD, Johns Hopkins U., 1997. Asst. dir. upper sch. The Ross Sch., East Hampton, NY, 1998—2002; chair history Kent Denver Sch., Englewood, Colo., 2002—07; adj. prof. homeland security U. Denver Grad. Sch. Internat. Studies, 2007—; edn. political cons. Asian Soc. Richardson for Pres. Obama Am., 2007—. Curriculum cons. UN Assn. of US, NYC, 1999—2002. Mem.: Am. Hist. Assn., UN Assn. U.S. (pres. 2005—06). Democrat. Avocations: fencing, running, historical miniatures, cross country skiing, horseback riding. Home: 4900 Meining Rd Berthoud CO 80513 E-mail: tkubik@kentdenver.org.

KUBO, EDWARD HACHIRO, JR., prosecutor; b. Honolulu, July 9, 1953; s. Edward H. and Rose M. (Coltes) K.; children: Diana K., Dawn M., Edward H. III. BA in Polit. Sci., U. Hawaii, 1976; JD, U. San Diego, 1979. Bar: Hawaii 1979. Legal asst. Legal Aid Soc. Hawaii, 1975-76; law clk. Kobayashi & Watanabe, Honolulu, 1979; dep. pros. atty. Honolulu City Prosecutor's Office, 1980-83, 85-90; assoc. Carlsmith & Dwyer, Honolulu, 1983-85; asst. US atty. Dist. Hawaii US Dept. Justice, Honolulu, 1990—2001, US atty. Dist. Hawaii, 2001—. Instr. Honolulu Police Dept. Acad., Waipahu, Hawaii, 1986-89; lectr. US Dept. Justice, Lincoln, Neb., 1997, Pearl Harbor Police Acad., 1995, Western State Vice Investigators Assn. Conf., Houston, 1997, Las Vegas, 1998; spkr. teleconf. US Dept. Justice Violence Against Women Act, 1998, Hawaii Bar Assn. H.S. Mock trial adv., 1996-99. Co-author: Concurrent Jurisdiction for Civil RICO, 1987. Recipient Nat. Art medal (France), 1992, Cert. of Appreciation, US Immigration and Naturalization Svc., 1992, Drug Enforcement Adminstrn., 1997, Plaque of Appreciation, US Border Patrol, 1995, cert. appreciation Bureau Alcohol, Tobacco & Firearms, 1999. Mem. Hawaii Bar Assn., Order of Barristers. Home: 1212 Nuuanu Ave #2905 Honolulu HI 96817

KUC, JOSEPH A., research scientist; b. NYC, Nov. 24, 1929; s. Peter and Helen (Dubec) K.; m. Karola Ingrid Maywald, July 17, 1991; children: Paul D., Rebecca R., Miriam A. BS, Purdue U., 1951, MS, 1953, PhD, 1955. Asst. prof. Purdue U., West Lafayette, Ind., 1955—59, assoc. prof., 1959—63, prof., 1963—74, U. Ky., Lexington, 1974—95, prof. emeritus, 1995—. Contbr. over 300 articles to profl. jours. Pres. Cen. Ky. ACLU, Lexington, 1977-79. Mem. Am. Chem. Soc., Am. Phytopathol. Soc., Am. Soc. Plant Physiologists, Am. Soc. for Biochemistry and Molecular Biology, N.Y. Acad. Sci., Phytochem. Soc., Ky. Acad. Sci., Sigma Xi. Avocations: hiking, gardening, conversation. Home and Office: 5502 Lorna St Torrance CA 90503

KUCHAR, THEODORE, conductor, academic administrator, musician; b. NYC; Music dir., condr. Boulder (Colo.) Philharm. Orch., 1987—. Prin. violist leading orchs. Cleve. and Helsinki, Finland; soloist, chamber musician Australia, Europe, New Zealand, U.S., Russia, festivals including Blossom, Edinburgh, Kuhmo, Tanglewood, others; dir. orchestral studies U. Colo., 1996—; artistic dir., prin. condr. Nat. Symphony Orch. Ukraine; artistic dir. Australian Festival Chamber Music, 1990—; past music dir. Queensland Philharm. Orch., Brisbane, Australia, W. Australian Ballet, Perth. Muscian Penderecki's String Trio, N.Y.C., 1994; music dir., condr. recordings with Nat. Symphony Orch. and Ukrainian Chamber Orch. including Lyatoshynsky's Symphonies Nos. 2 and 3 (Best Internat. Recording of Yr. 1994), others; music dir., condr. worldwide tours. Paul Fromm fellow, 1980; recipient bronze medal for his work in promoting that country's music Finnish Govt., 1989. Office: Boulder Philharmonic Orchestra 2995 Wilderness Pl Ste 100 Boulder CO 80301-5408

KUCHEMAN, CLARK ARTHUR, philosophy and religious studies educator; b. Akron, Ohio, Feb. 7, 1931; s. Merlin Carlyle and Lucile (Clark) K.; m. Melody Elaine Frazer, Nov. 15, 1986. BA, U. Akron, 1952; BD, Meadville Theol. Sch., 1955; MA in Econs., U. Chgo., 1959, PhD, 1965. Instr., then asst. prof. U. Chgo., 1961-67; prof. Claremont (Calif.) McKenna Coll., 1967—, Claremont Grad. Sch., 1967—. Co-author: Belief and Ethics, 1978, Creative Interchange, 1982, Economic Life, 1988; contbg. editor: The Life of Choice, 1978; contbr. articles to profl. jours. 1st lt. USAF, 1955—57. Mem. Am. Acad. Religion, Hegel Soc. Am., N.Am. Soc. for Social Philosophy. Democrat. Home: 10160 60th St Riverside CA 92509-4745 Office: Claremont McKenna Coll Dept Philosophy Religon Pitzer Hall 850 Columbia Ave Claremont CA 91711-6420 Office Phone: 909-607-7980. Business E-Mail: clark.kucheman@claremontmckenna.edu.

KUDROW, LISA (MARIE DIANE), actress; b. Encino, Calif., July 30, 1963; d. Lee and Nedra Kudrow; m. Michael Stern, May 27, 1995; 1 child, Julian Murray. BS in Biology, Vassar Coll., Poughkeepsie, NY, 1985. Actress (TV series) Mad About You, 1991-99, Friends, 1994-2004 (Emmy award outstanding supporting actress, 1998, SAG award outstanding performance female, 2000, Am. Comedy award, 2000, Golden Satellite award best actress, 2000), Hopeless Pictures, 2005; (TV guest appearances) Cheers, 1989, Newhart, 1990, Life Goes On, 1990, Coach, 1993-94, Flying Blind, 1993, Hope & Gloria, 1996, The Simpsons (voice), 1998; (films) The Crazysitter, 1995, Romy and Michele's High School Reunion, 1997, Clockwatchers, 1997, The Opposite of Sex, 1998 (NY Film Critics Circle award, 2000), Hercules (voice) 1998, Analyze This, 1998, Hanging Up, 2000, All Over the Guy, 2001, Dr. Dolittle 2 (voice), 2001, Analyze That, 2002, Marci X, 2003, Wonderland, 2003, Happy Endings, 2005, P.S. I Love You, 2007, Kabluey, 2007, Hotel for Dogs, 2009; exec. prodr.: (TV films) Picking Up and Dropping Off, 2003; actress, exec. prodr., writer (TV series) The Comeback, 2005; (music video) The Rembrandts I'll Be There For You, 1995. Named one of 50 Most Beautiful People in World, People mag., 1997. Mem.: Groundlings Improv Group.

KUECHLE, JOHN MERRILL, lawyer; b. Mpls., Dec. 18, 1951; s. Harry Bronson and Virginia (McClure) K.; m. Nancy Anderson, June 20, 1976; 1 child, David Michael. AB magna cum laude, Occidental Coll., 1974; JD cum laude, Harvard U., 1977. Bar: Calif. 1977. Assoc. Mitchell, Silberberg & Knupp, LA, 1977-83, ptnr., 1983-2000, of counsel, 2001—. Active Culver City Planning Commn. Mem. Phi Beta Kappa. Republican. Episcopalian. Avocations: track and field, orienteering, rock climbing. Home: 10733 Ranch Rd Culver City CA 90230-5458 Office: Mitchell Silberberg & Knupp 11377 W Olympic Blvd Los Angeles CA 90064-1625 Office Phone: 310-312-3139. Business E-Mail: jmk@msk.com.

KUEHL, HANS HENRY, electrical engineering educator; b. Detroit, Mar. 16, 1933; s. Henry Martin and Hilde (Schrader) K.; m. Anna Meidinger, July 25, 1965; children: Susan, Michael. BS, Princeton U., 1955; MS, Calif. Inst. Tech., 1956, PhD, 1959. Asst. prof. elec. engring. U. So. Calif., 1960-63, assoc. prof., 1963-72, prof., 1972—2004, prof. emeritus, 2004—, chmn. dept. elec. engring., electrophysics, 1987-98. Cons. Deutsch Co., L.A., 1973, Hughes Aircraft Co., Culver City, Calif., 1975. Contbr. articles to profl. jours. Recipient Tchg. Excellence award U. So. Calif., 1964, Haliburton award U. So. Calif., 1980, Lifetime Achievement award U. So. Calif., 2006; named to Royal Oak Dondero HS Hall Fame, 2006. Fellow IEEE; mem. Am. Phys. Soc., Internat. Sci. Radio Union, Eta Kappa Nu (bd. dirs. 2000-02, Outstanding Faculty award 1977). Avocations: tennis, racquetball. Office: U So Calif Elec Engring Dept PHE 622 Mc 0271 Los Angeles CA 90089-0271 Business E-Mail: kuehl@usc.edu.

KUEHL, SHEILA JAMES, state board member; b. Tulsa, Feb. 9, 1941; d. Arthur Joseph and Lillian Ruth (Krasner) K. BA, UCLA, 1962; JD, Harvard U., 1978. Actress, 1950-65; assoc. dean of students UCLA, 1969-75; pvt. practice LA, 1978-85; law prof. Loyola U. LA, 1985-89; mng. atty. Calif. Women's Law Ctr., LA, 1989-93; mem. Calif. State Assembly, Sacramento, 1995-2000, spkr. pro tem, 1997-99, chair jud. com., 1999-2000; mem. Calif. State Senate, 2001—08. Chair natural resources and water com., Calif. State Senate, 2001—06, chmn. health com., 2007-08, bd. dirs., Liberty Hill Found., bd. dirs, Calif. Women's Law Ctr. Appeared in TV series Broadside, 1964-65, as Zelda Gilroy in Dobie Gillis, 1959-63, as Jackie Erwin in Trouble with Father, 1950-56. Bd. overseers Harvard U., 1997-05. Named One of 20 Most Fascinating Women in Politics, George Mag., 1996, named One of 100 Most Influential Attys. in Calif., Calif. Law Bus., 1998; recipient Barry Goldwater Human Rights award, 1998, Legislator of Yr., Calif. Pks. and Recreation Soc., 1999, Pub. Svc. award UCLA Alumni Assn., 2000, Liberty award Lambda Legal Def.

Edn. Fund, 2002, Women in Govt. award Good Housekeeping, 2003, Courageous Leader award Women Against Gun Violence, 2005, Matthew O. Tobriner Pub. Svc. award Legal Aid Soc., 2005, Legislator of Yr., Congress Calif. Srs., 2006, Paul & Sheila Wellstone award Wellstone Democratic Club, 2007, Respect award Gay, Lesbian, Straight Edn. Network, 2007, The Soul of a Nurse award Calif. Nurses Assn./Nat. Nurses Org., 2007, Presley Honor award Calif. Partnership to End Domestic Violence, 2007, 2007, Scales of Justice award, Calif. Judges' Assoc., 2008, Pub. Ofcl. of Yr. award, Consumer Watchdog, 2008. Office: Calif Integrated Waste Mgmt Bd Sacramento CA 95814 Office Phone: 916-341-6039.

KUH, ERNEST SHIU-JEN, electrical engineering educator; b. Peking, China, Oct. 2, 1928; s. Zone Shung and Tsia (Chu) K.; m. Bettine Chow, Aug. 4, 1957; children: Anthony, Theodore. BS, U. Mich., 1949; MS, MIT, 1950; PhD, Stanford U., 1952; DEng (hon.), Hong Kong U. Sci. and Tech., 1997, Nat. Chiao Tung U., Taiwan, 1999. Mem. tech. staff Bell Tel. Labs., Murray Hill, NJ, 1952-56; assoc. prof. elec. engring. U. Calif., Berkeley, 1956-62, prof., 1962—, Miller rsch. prof., 1965-66, William S. Floyd Jr. prof. engring., 1990—, William S. Floyd Jr. prof. engring. emeritus, 1993—, chmn. dept. elec. engring. and computer sci., 1968-72, dean Coll. Engring., 1973-80. Cons. IBM Rsch. Lab., San Jose, Calif., 1957—62, NSF, 1975—84; mem. panel Nat. Bur. Stds., 1975—80; mem. vis. com. Gen. Motors Inst., 1975—79; mem. vis. com. dept. elec. engring. and computer scis. MIT, 1986—91; mem. adv. coun. elec. engring. dept. Princeton (NJ) U., 1986—98; mem. bd. councilors Sch. Engring. U. So. Calif., 1986—91; mem. sci. adv. bd. Mills Coll., 1976—80. Co-author: Principles of Circuit Synthesis, 1959, Basic Circuit Theory, 1967, Theory of Linear Active Network, 1967; Linear and Nonlinear Circuits, 1987. Recipient Alexander von Humboldt award, 1980, Lamme medal Am. Soc. Endring. Edn., 1981, U. Mich. Disting. Alumnus award, 1970, Berkeley citation, 1993, C & C prize Japanese Found. for Computers and Comm. Promotion, 1996, Phil Kaufman award EDAC, 1998; Brit. Soc. Engring. and Rsch. fellow, 1982. Fellow IEEE (Edn. medal 1981, Centennial medal 1984, Circuits and Systems Soc. award. 1988), AAAS; mem. NAE, Acad. Sinica, Chinese Acad. Scis. (fgn. mem.), Sigma Xi, Phi Kappa Phi. Office: U Calif Elec Engring & Computer Sci Berkeley CA 94720-0001 Business E-Mail: kuh@eecs.berkeley.edu.

KUHL, PATRICIA K., science educator; b. Mitchell, SD, Nov. 5, 1946; d. Joseph John and Susan Mary (Schaeffer) K.; m. Andrew N. Meltzoff, Sept. 28, 1985; 1 child, Katherine. BA, St. Cloud State U., Minn., 1967; MA, U. Minn., 1971, PhD, 1973. Postdoctoral research assoc. Cen. Inst. for Deaf, St. Louis, 1973-76; from rsch. assoc. to prof. U. Wash., Seattle, 1976—82, prof., 1982—, William P. and Ruth Gerberding prof., 1997—, dept. chair, 1994—, dir. Inst. Learning and Brain Scis., 2003—. Gov. bd. Am. Inst. Physics, 1994-96; trustee Neurosci. Rsch. Found., 1994—; bd. dirs. Wash. Tech. Ctr., U. Wash., 1994-96; invited presenter White House Conf. on Early Learning and the Brain, 1997, Early Childhood Cognitive Devel., 2001. Editor Jour. Neurosci., 1989-96. Recipient Women in Research citation Kennedy Council, 1978, Virginia Merrill Bloedel Scholar award, 1992-94. Fellow AAAS, Am. Psychol. Soc., Acoustical Soc. Am. (assoc. editor Jour. 1988-92, chair medals and awards, 1992-94, v.p. 1997, Silver medal 1997, pres. 1999—); mem. Am. Acad. Arts and Scis. Office: Inst Learning and Brain Sci Dept Speech & Hearing Sciences 357988 Seattle WA 98105-6247 Office Phone: 206-685-1921. Business E-Mail: pkkuhl@u.washington.edu.

KUHL, PAUL BEACH, lawyer; b. Elizabeth, NJ, July 15, 1935; s. Paul Edmund and Charlotte (Hetche) Kuhl; m. Janey Mae Stadheim, June 24, 1967; children: Alison Lyn, Todd Beach. BA, Cornell U., Ithaca, NY, 1957; LLB, Stanford U., Calif., 1960. Assoc. Law Offices of Walter C. Kohn, San Francisco, 1961-63, Sedgwick, Detert, Moran & Arnold, San Francisco, 1963-73, ptnr., 1973-99, of counsel, 2000—. Pro tem judge, arbitrator San Francisco Superior Ct., 1989—. Served to lt. USCG, 1961. Recipient Def. Atty. of Yr. award, San Francisco (Calif.) Trial Lawyers Assn., 2001. Mem.: Mediation Soc., Am. Platform Tennis Assn. (regional pres., bd. dirs. 2003—09), Def. Rsch. Inst., Am. Bd. Trial Advs., Am. Coll. Trial Lawyers, Tahoe Tavern Property Owners Assn. (sec. 1979—81, pres. 1981—83, bd. dirs. 2006—), Lagunitas Country Club (v.p. 1995—97, pres. 2006—08). Avocations: tennis, reading. Home: PO Box 1434 Ross CA 94957-1434 Office: Sedgwick Detert Moran & Arnold One Market St Steuart Tower 8th Fl San Francisco CA 94105 Office Phone: 415-781-7900. Business E-Mail: beach.kuhl@sdma.com.

KUHL, TONYA L., science educator; BS in Chem. Engring., U. Ariz., 1989; PhD in Chem. Engring., U. Calif., Santa Barbara, 1996. Postdoctoral fellow U. Calif., Santa Barbara, 1996—97, asst. rsch. engr., 1997—2000, asst. prof. chem. engring. Davis, Calif. Office: One Shields Ave Davis CA 95616

KUHLMAN, WALTER EGEL, artist, educator; b. St. Paul, Nov. 16, 1918; s. Peter and Marie (Jensen) K.; m. Nora McCants; 1 son, Christopher; m. Tulip Chestman, April 9, 1979. Student, St. Paul Sch. Art; BS, U. Minn., 1941; postgrad., Tulane U., Academié de la Grand Chaumierè, Paris, Calif. Sch. Fine Arts. Mem. faculty Calif. Sch. Fine Arts Stanford, U. Mich., Santa Clara (Calif.) U., U. N. Mex., prof., Sonoma State U., Calif., 1969-89, prof. emeritus, 1989-. One person shows include U. N.Mex., Walker Art Center, Mpls., The Berkshire Museum, Mass., La Jolla Museum of Contemporary Art, Calif., Santa Barbara Mus. of Art, Calif., San Francisco Mus. of Modern Art, 1958, New Arts Gallery, Houston, 1959-61, Roswell Mus. Calif. Palace of the Legion of Honor, 1956, 64, De Saisset Gallery, Santa Clara U. 20-Year Retrospective, Jonson Gallery, U. N.Mex., 1963, 64, 65, Charles Campbell Gallery, San Francisco, 1981, 83, 85, The Carlson Gallery, San Francisco, Gump's Gallery, San Francisco, 1976, 1992, University Gallery, Sonoma State U. 40 Year Retrospective, Calif. Natsoulis Gallery, Davis, Calif., Albuquerque Mus. Fine Arts, George Krevsky Fine Arts, San Francisco, 1994, 96, 99, Robert Green Gallery, Mill Valley, Calif.; group shows include N.Y. World's Fair, St. Paul Gallery, WPA Exhibition, Lawson Galleries, San Francisco, A 1948 Portfolio: 16 Lithographs (Diebenkorn, Lobdell, Hultberg), All Annual Invitational Exhibitions, San Francisco Mus. Modern Art, 1948-58, Petit Palais Mus., Paris, San Francisco Mus. Modern Art, III Biennial of Sao Paulo, Museo de Arte Moderna, Brazil, L.A. County Mus., Mus. Modern Art, Rio de Janiero, San Francisco Mus. Modern Art, 1955, 57, 66, 76, 96, Graham Found., Chgo, L.A. County Mus., Calif. Palace of the Legion of Honor, Virginia Mus. Fine Arts, Richmond, Stanford U., Gallery, Roswell Mus., 1961, 62, Univ. Art Mus., Austin, Texas Santa Fe Mus. Fine Arts, NM, Ca. Palace of Legion of Honor, Richard L. Nelson Gallery, UC Davis, Natsoulis Gallery, Northern California Figuration Expositions Art USA, 1992, 93, 94, George Krevsky Fine Art, San Francisco, Art Mus. Santa Cruz, Calif., 1993, Pasquale Ianetti Art Galleries, San Francisco, 1994, Robert Green Fine Arts, Mill Valley, Calif. 1994, 95, Am. Acad. Arts and Letters, N.Y. 1995, Dark Avenue Armory Annual Internat. Fine Print Exhbn., N.Y., Va. Mus. Modern Art Am. Paintings, Petit Palais Mus., Paris, Mus. of Modern Art, Sao Paulo British Mus., London, Nat. Mus. Am. Art, Phillip Meml. Gallery, Washington, DC, Oakland Mus. Art, Calif., Laguna Mus. of Art, Calif., 1998, The Menil Collection, Houston, Cleve. Mus. Art, Mus. Modern Art, San Francisco Mus. Modern Art, Salander O'Reilly Gallery, N.Y.; permanent collections include: The Phillips Collection, Washington, Nat. Gallery Am. Art, Washington, Walker Art Ctr., Washington, San Francisco Mus. Modern Art, Brit. Mus., Met. Mus. Art, NAD, N.Y., others. Recipient Maestro award Calif. Arts Coun.; Outstanding Calif. Working Artist and Tchr. grantee; fellow Tiffany Found., Graham Found., Chgo., Cummington Found. Mem. Nat. Acad. Design N.Y. Studio: Indsl Ctr Bldg Studio 335 480 Gate 5 Rd Sausalito CA 94965-1461

KUHN, ROBERT LAWRENCE, investment banker, corporate financier, strategist, writer; b. NYC, Nov. 6, 1944; s. Louis and Lee (Kahn) K.; m. Dora Elana Serviarian, June 23, 1967; children: Aaron, Adam, Daniella. AB in Human Biology, Johns Hopkins U., 1964; PhD in Brain Sci., UCLA, 1968; MS in Mgmt., MIT, 1980. Investment banker, fin. adv. representing various firms, N.Y.C., L.A., Beijing, Tokyo, 1980—; pres. The Geneva Cos., Irvine, Calif., 1991—2002, vice chmn., 2002—; mng. dir. Smith Barney, 2001—. Cons. corp. strategy and fin., N.YC, LA, Beijing, Tokyo, 1980—; adj. prof. Grad. Sch. Bus. Adminstrn. NYU, 1981-89; exec.-in-residence U. So. Calif., 1990; bd. advisors U. So. Calif. Sch. Bus., 1992—; internat. adviser in fin. and high tech. to govts. US, Israel, Fed. Republic Germany, China, 1984—; sr. rsch. fellow in creative amd innovative mgmt. IC2 Inst. U. Tex., Austin, 1986—; cons. and lectr. in field. Author: Mid-Sized Firms: Success Strategies and Methodology, 1982, Creativity and Strategy in Mid-Sized Firms, 1988, Man Who Changed China, 2004, (with George Geis) The Firm Bond: Linking Meaning and Mission in Business and Religion, 1984, Micromanaging: Transforming Business Leaders with Personal Computers, 1987, To Flourish Among Giants: Creative Management for Mid-Sized Firms, 1985, Japanese translation, 1986, (Macmillan Book Club main selection), (with Arie Lavie) Industrial Research and Development in Israel, 1986, Dealmaker: All the Negotiating Skills and Secrets You Need, 1988, Investment Banking: the Art and Science of High-Stakes Dealmaking, 1989, Japanese translation, 1990, Chinese translation, 1995, (with Don Gamache) The Creativity Infusion, 1989; editor: Commercializing Defense-Related Technology, 1984, (with Raymond Smilor) Corporate Creativity: Robust Companies and the Entrepreneurial Spirit, 1984, (with Margaret Maxey) Reglatory Reform: Private Enterprise and Risk Assessment, 1985, (with Eugene Konecci) Technology Venturing: American Innovation Management, 1985, (with Yuji Ijiri) New Directions in Creative and Innovative Management, 1988, Medical Strategic Defense Technologist, 1986, Commercializing SDI Technologies, (with Stewart Nozette 1987); editor-in-chief: Handbook for Creative and Innovative Managers, 1987, Libr. of Investment Banking, 7 vols., 1990; contbg. editor, columnist Jour. Bus. Strategy, 1984-90; exec. prodr. and host (TV series) Closer to Truth: Science Meaning and the Future. Sloan fellow MIT, Cambridge, 1979. Mem. Phi Beta Kappa. Avocations: weightlifting, ping pong/table tennis, chess, classical music. Office: The Geneva Coms 5 Park Plz Irvine CA 92614-5995

KUHRAU, EDWARD W., retired lawyer; b. Caney, Kans., Apr. 19, 1935; s. Edward and Dolores (Hardman) Kuhrau; m. Janiece Christal (div. 1983); children: Quentin, Clayton; m. Sandy Shreve. BA, U. Tex., 1960; JD, U. So. Calif., 1965. Bar: Calif. 1966, Wash. 1968, Alaska 1977. With Perkins Coie (and predecessor firms), Seattle, 1968—2008, ptnr., 1973—2008. Editor-in-chief Wash. Real Property Deskbook; contbr. articles to profl. jours. With USAF, 1955—58. Mem. ABA, Wash. Bar Assn., Am. Coll. Real Estate Lawyers, Pacific Real Estate Inst. (pres., founding trustee), Order of Coif, Seattle Yacht Club. E-mail: kuhre@perkinscoie.com.

KUKLIN, SUSAN BEVERLY, lawyer, librarian, educator; d. Albert and Marion (Waller) K. BA in English and History with honors, U. Ariz., 1969, JD, 1973; MLS, Ind. U., 1970; LLM in Taxation, DePaul U., 1981. Bar: Ariz. 1973, Ill. 1980, Calif. 1984, US Dist. Ct. (no. dist.) Ill. 1980. Asst. city atty. City of Phoenix, 1974-75; dep. county atty. County of Pima, Ariz., 1975-76; polit. sci., law libr., asst. prof. Northern Ill. U., 1976-78; law libr., assoc. prof. U. SD, 1978-79; dir. law libr., asst. prof. DePaul U., 1979-83; law libr., dir. Santa Clara County, San Jose, Calif., 1983—2004; faculty libr. Pima CC, Tucson, 2005—. Sec. bd. trustees Law Library Santa Clara County; sec. exec. bd. dir. Amigos de Pima Found., Pima CC, Tucson, 2007-. Mem. Am. Assn. Law Libr. (cert. law libr.), Coun. Calif. County Law Libr. (newsletter editor 1983-84), Northern Calif. Assn. Law Libr., Calif. Libr. Assn., Ariz. Librs. Assn., Phi Beta Kappa, Phi Kappa Phi, Alpha Lambda Delta, Phi Alpha Theta, Phi Delta Phi. Office: Pima CC Desert Vista Campus Libr Tucson AZ 85709 Business E-Mail: skuklin@pima.edu.

KULLAS, ALBERT JOHN, management consultant, systems engineer; b. Webster, Mass., May 5, 1917; s. Albert J. and Mary (Piechowiak) K.; m. Joyce M. Gladue, Jan. 31, 1942; children: Michael, Daniel, Mark, James. BS in Civil Engring., Worcester Poly. Inst., 1938; grad., Am. Mgmt. Assn., 1956; MS in Civil Engring., NYU, 1940; grad., Sloan Sch. Mgmt. Sr. Execs., MIT, 1973. Registered profl. engr. With Martin Marietta Corp., 1940-82, structures mgr. Balt., 1955-57, chief engr., 1957, design engring. mgr., 1957-59, tech. devel. mgr., 1959-60, Dyna Soar and Gemini Launch vehicle tech. dir., 1960-62, research and engring. dir. Denver, 1962-65, dir. tech. ops., 1965-66, dir. space sci., research, adv. tech., 1966-67, dir. Voyager program, 1967-68, dir. Planetary Systems, 1968, dir. Viking project, div. v.p., 1969-72, div. v.p. ops. rev., 1972-73, v.p. data systems, 1973-82; mgmt. and systems engring. cons. Littleton, Colo., 1982-98; pres. Albert J. Kullas, Inc. Rsch. and tech. panel space vehicles NASA, 1968-78; chmn. bd. Biax Corp., 1987-90; 1st v.p. Highlands, Inc., 1999-2004; bd. dirs. THI. Contbr. articles to profl. jours. Rsch. adv. coun. Colo. State U., 1971—; treas. Porter Hosp. Found., 1980-85, 1st v.p., 1986-88, pres., 1988-90, v.p., 1990-93, emeritus, 2003—; bd. dirs. Colo. Jud. Inst., 1980-91, chmn., 1984-86; exec. com. Rocky Mountain Sci. Coun., 1964-65; bd. dirs. MIT Alumni Colo., 1990-2002. Recipient Robert H. Goddard award Worcester Poly. Inst., 1962 Fellow AIAA (award 1967); Asso. fellow (chmn. honors and awards com. 1973-81); mem. ASCE, Sigma Xi, Tau Beta Pi. Home: 5088 W Maplewood Ave Littleton CO 80123-6729

KULONGOSKI, TED (THEODORE RALPH KULONGOSKI), Governor of Oregon, former state supreme court justice; b. Washington County, Mo., Nov. 5, 1940; married; 3 children. BA, U. Mo., 1967, JD, 1970. Bar: Oreg., Mo., U.S. Dist. Ct. Oreg., U.S. Ct. Appeals (9th cir.). Legal counsel Oreg. State Ho. of Reps., 1973-74; founding and sr. ptnr. Kulongoski, Durham, Drummonds & Colombo, Oreg., 1974-87; deputy dist. atty. Multnomah County, Oreg., 1992; atty. gen. State of Oreg., 1993-97, gov., 2003—; justice Oreg. Supreme Ct., 1997—2001. State rep. Lane County (Oreg.), 1974-77, state senator, 1977-83; chmn. Juvenile Justice Task Force, 1994, Gov.'s Commn. Organized Crime; mem. Criminal Justice Coun.; exec. dir. Met. Family Svc., 1992; dir. Oreg. Dept. Ins. and Fin., 1987-91. Mem. Oreg State Bar Assn., Mo. Bar Assn, Lane County Bar Assn. Democrat. Roman Catholic. Office: Gov's Office 254 Capitol Bldg 900 Court St NE Salem OR 97301 Office Phone: 503-378-3111. Office Fax: 503-378-8970.

KULTERMANN, UDO, architectural and art historian, educator, writer; b. Stettin, Germany, Oct. 14, 1927; came to U.S., 1967, naturalized, 1981; s. Georg and Charlotte (Schultz) K.; m. Erika Klusener, 1954 (div. 1975), children: Martin, Andrew, Eva, m. Judith Danoff, May 10, 1975. Student, U. Greifswald, Germany, 1947—50; PhD magna cum laude, U. Muenster, Germany, 1953; PhD (hon.), Art Acad. Tallinn, Estonia, 2004. Curatorial asst. Kunsthalle, Bremen, Germany, 1954-55; art editor Bertelsmann Pubs., Guetersloh, Germany, 1955-56; program dir. Am. House, Bremen, Germany, 1956-59; dir. city art mus. Schloss Morsbroich, Leverkusen, Germany, 1959-64; dir. Morsbroicher Kunsttage, Leverkusen, 1961; prof. Washington U., St. Louis, 1967-94, prof. emeritus, 1994—; participant Symposium for Islamic Architecture in Urbanism, Damman, Saudi Arabia; lectr. Art History and Nat. Identity, louvre, Paris. Ednl. leader study tours German architects to Japan, 1965, 67; arch. commn. Biennale Venice, 1979—82; ednl. leader Soviet-Am. Travelling Arch. Seminar, Russia, 1986—87, Nat. Trust for Hist. Preservation, Cruise, Copenhagen, Amsterdam, Rouen, Mont St. Michel, Bordeaux, and Lisbon, 1989; jury Nat. U., Al Ain, United Arab Emirates, 1987, Internat. Open Air Exhbn., Pistany, Czech Republic, 1969; participant 2d Biennale Arab art Govt. of Morocco; lectr. in field; cons. in field; chmn. Sec III Symposium Expanding Metropolis-Coping the Urban Growth of Cario; ednl. leader Profl. Seminar Architects to Moscow, Lelingard, Tashkent, Samarkand, Bukharin. Author: Architecture of Today, 1958, Hans und Wassili Luckhardt-Bauten und Projekte, 1958, Dynamische Architektur, 1959, New Japanese Architecture, 1960, New Architecture in Africa, 1963, Junge deutsche Bildhauer, 1963, Der Schluessel zur Architektur von heute, 1963, New Architecture in the World, 1965, History of Art History, 1966, paperback edit., 1981, English. edit., 1993, Spanish edit., 1994, Croatian edit., 2002, The New Sculpture-Assemblage and Environments, 1967, Architektur der Gegenwart, 1967, Gabriel Grupello, 1968, The New Painting, 1969, rev. edit., 1978, New Directions in African Architecture, 1969, Kenzo Tange-Architecture and Urban Design, 1970, paperback edit., 1978, 1989, Art and Life: The Function of Intermedia, 1970, New Realism, 1972, Die Architektur im 20 Jahrhundert, 1977, English edit., 1993, 6th revised edit., 2003, Ernest Trova, 1977, I Contemporanei, Storia della Scultura nel Mondo, 1979, Architecture in the Seventies, 1980, Architects of the Third World, 1980, Zeitgenoessische Architektur in Osteuropa, 1985, Spanish edit., 1989, Visible Cities-Invisible Cities-Urban Symbolism and Historical Continuity, 1988, Kleine Geschichte der Kunsttheorie, 1987, Kleine Geschichte der Kunsttheonte, 1998, Japanese edit., 1996, Korean edit., 1999, Kunst und Wirklichkeit-Von Fiedler bis Derrida-Zehn Annaeherungen, 1991, Die Maxentius-Basilika.Ein Schluesselwerk spaetantiker Architektur, 1996, Contemporary Architecture in the Arab States-Renaissance of a Region, 1999, Thirty Years After-The Future of the Past, 2002, Architecture and Revolution-The Visions of Boullée and Ledoux, 2003; co-author, (with Werner Hofmann): Modern Architecture in Color, 1970; editor: Kenzo Tange: Architecture and Urban Design, 1970, paperback edits., 1978, 1989, Architektur der Welt, Verlag und Datenbank fuer Geisteswissenschaften, Weimar, 1996—2005, St. James Modern Masterpieces: The Best of Art, Architecture, Photography and Design Since 1945, 1998, vol. VI Architecture in South and Central Africa in: World Architecture: A Critical Mosaic 1900-2000, 2000; contbr. chapters to books, scientific papers to profl. jours. Recipient Disting. Faculty award, Washington U., 1985. Mem.: Nat. Faculty Humanities, Arts, Scis., Croatian Acad. Scis. and Arts (corr.). Avocations: poetry, music, dance. Personal E-mail: ukulter@rcn.com.

KUMAR, RAJENDRA, electrical engineering educator; b. Amroha, India, Aug. 22, 1948; arrived in US, 1980; s. Satya Pal Agarwal and Kailash Vati Agarwal; m. Pushpa Agarwal, Feb. 16, 1971; children: Anshu, Shipra. BS in Math. and Sci., Meerut Coll., 1964; BEE, Indian Inst. Tech., Kanpur, 1969, MEE, 1977; PhD, U. New Castle, NSW, Australia, 1981. Mem. tech. staff Electronis and Radar Devel., Bangalore, India, 1969-72; rsch. engr. Indian Inst. Tech., Kanpur, 1972-77; asst. prof. Calif. State U., Fullerton, 1981-83, Brown U., Providence, 1980-81; prof. Calif. State U., Long Beach, 1983—, dept. chmn., 2005—. Cons. Jet Propulsion Lab., Pasadena, Calif., 1984-91, Aerospace Corp., El Segundo, Calif., 1995—. Contbr. articles. Recipient Best Paper award Internat. Telemetering Conf., Las Vegas, 1986, 10 New Technology awards NASA, Washington, 1987-91. Mem.: AAUP, AIAA, NEA, IEEE (sr.), Inst. of Navigation, Calif. Faculty Assn., Inst. Navigation, Auto Club So. Calif. (Cerritos), Tau Beta Pi (eminent mem.), Sigma Xi, Eta Kappa Nu. Achievements include patents for efficient detections and signal parameter estimation with applications to hihg dynamic GPS receivers; multiusage estimation of received carrier signal parameters under very high dynamic conditions of the receiver; fast frequency acquisition via adaptive least squares algorithms; Kalman filter ionospheric delay estimator; method and apparatus for reducing multipath signal error using deconvolution; adaptive smoothing system for fading communication channels; others. Avocations: gardening, walking, hiking, reading. Home: 13910 Rose St Cerritos CA 90703-9043 Office: Calif State U 1250 N Bellflower Blvd Long Beach CA 90840-0001 Personal E-mail: rajendrakumar@sbcglobal.net. Business E-Mail: kumar@csulb.edu.

KUMMER, WOLFGANG H., electrical engineer; b. Stuttgart, Germany, Oct. 10, 1925; BS, U. Calif., Berkeley, 1946, MS, 1947, PhD, 1954. Self-employed elec. engr. Mem. U.S. Comms. B & F, Internat. Sci. Radio Union; mem. evaluation panel NBS, Nat. Acad. Scis., 1975-81. Fellow IEEE (activities editor AP-S newsletter 1964-68, gen. chmn. AP-S internat. conv. 1971, chmn. antenna stds. subcom. 2.11 1971-77, adcom mem. AP-S 1972-79); mem. Antennas and Propagation Soc. (pres. 1975, chmn. 1985-86), Phi Beta Kappa, Tau Beta Pi, Eta Kappa Nu, Sigma Xi, Alpha Mu Gamma. Office: 1310 Sunset Ave Santa Monica CA 90405-5843

KUMMERT, TED, computer software company executive; married; 3 children. BSEE, U. Wash. With Hewlett-Packard Co., Apple Computer Co.; gen. mgr. consumer devices group Microsoft Corp., Redmond, Wash., 1989, corp. v.p. MSN Internet access and consumer devices, corp. v.p. bus. process and integration divsn., corp. v.p. security, access and solutions divsn., corp. v.p. data storage and platform divsn. Office: Microsoft Corp One Microsoft Way Redmond WA 98052-6399

KUMPFER, KAROL LINDA, research psychologist; b. Neptune, NJ, July 30, 1943; d. Beverly Donald and Mary Belle (Campbell) K.; m. Henry Overton Whiteside, Mar. 6, 1978; 1 child, Jane H. BA, Colo. Women's Coll., 1966; MA, U. Utah, 1970, PhD, 1972; postdoctoral, U. Minn., 1975. Lic. psychologist, Utah. Asst. prof. psychology Oberlin Coll., Ohio, 1971-73; research assoc. Inst. Child Devel. U. Minn., Mpls., 1975-76; asst. prof. Colo. Women's Coll., Denver, 1976-78; psychologist Salt Lake County Mental Health Dept., 1979-80; dep. dir. State Div. Alcoholism and Drugs, Salt Lake City, 1980-84; vis. assoc. prof. Grad. Sch. Social Work U. Utah, Salt Lake City, 1983—88, asst. prof. psychiatry, 1986—88, assoc. prof. dept. health promotion and edn., 1988—2005, prof. dept. health promotion and edn., 2005—; dir. Ctr. Substance Abuse and Prevention, Washington, 1998—2000; author, dir. Strengthening Families Program, Salt Lake City, 1982—; coordinating scientist Center for Disease Control, 2000—03. Editor/author: Childhood and Chemical Abuse: Prevention and Intervention, 1986. Bd. dirs. Repetory Dance Theatre, Salt Lake City, 1983-87, Western Assn. Concerned Adoptive Parents, Salt Lake City, 1985-90, Utah Alliance for Mentally Ill, Salt Lake City, 1979-80, Utah Mental Health Assn., 2000-03, House of Hope, Salt Lake City, 1994-98, Indian Walk-in Ctr., 2000—05, chair-elect, 2004-05; sec. bd. dirs. Utah Opera Guild, 1994-98; pres. U. Utah. Faculty Women's Club, 1974-75; mem. exec. com., chair Salt Lake City Mayor's Substance Abuse Prevention Coalition, 2000—. Grantee Utah Dept. Social Svcs., Salt Lake City, 1984-1986, Dept. Justice Office Juvenile Justice and Juvenile Delinquency Prevention, 1987-2003, Nat. Inst. on Drug Abuse, 1998-2004, Ctr. for Substance Abuse Prevention, 1997-2002; recipient SAMHSA/CSAP Model Prevention Program award, 2000, White House Office Nat. Drug Control Policy Dirs. award for Disting. Svc., 2000, Luther Terry Lectr. award U.S. Commd. Officers Assn., 2000. Mem.: APHA, AAAS, APA, Soc. for Prevention Rsch. (bd. dirs. 1995—2002, pres. 1997—99), Nat. Inst. Drug Abuse (spl. task force 1985—, grantee 1982—86, 1998—2004), Coun. on Social Work Edn., Nat. Inst. Alcoholism and Alcohol Abuse (spl. task force 1985—, grantee 1980, 2000—06), Am. Acad. Child Psychiatry (spl. task force 1986—88), Utah Psychol. Assn. (bd. dirs. 1985—88), Nat. Coun. Social Work Edn., Am. Pub. Health Assn. (mem. 1996—), Utah Psychologists in Pvt. Practice Assn. (pres. 1985—90), Sigma Xi. Democrat. Unitarian Universalist. Avocations: skiing, sailing, hiking, travel. Office: Health Promotion Edn U Utah 250 S 1850 East Salt Lake City UT 84112-0920 Office Phone: 801-581-7718.

KUNDIG, TOM, architect; BA magna cum laude in Environ. Design, U. Wash., 1977, MArch, 1981. Lic. Wash., 1982, Alaska, 1983, Idaho, 2000, Fla., 2002, NC, 2003, Oreg., 2004, NY, 2005, Calif., 2005, Colo., 2005. Assoc. C. Cichanski & Assocs., 1977—80; arch. Bruno Inabnit Akitectcuburo, Switzerland, 1980—81, TRA, 1981—83, The Callison Partnership, 1983, MHK Archs., 1984—85; prin. Jochman/Kundig Partnership, 1983—84; ptnr. Olsen Sundberg Kundig Allen Archs., Seattle, 1986—. Design studio instr. U. Wash., 1998—2001, instr. grad. design studio, 1999, lectr. dept. architecture, 99; vis. design critic dept. architecture Wash. State U., 1999; vis. design critic U. Oreg., Kyoto, 2001, vis. instr. dept. landscape architecture, 04; vis. design critic Tex. Tech U. Coll. Architecture, 2004; D. Kenneth Sargent vis. design critic Syracuse U. Coll. Architecture, 2006. Prin. works include Seattle Art Mus. (Blueprint award, 1981), The Meadow House (AIA Seattle Commendation award, 1993, AIA NW & Pacific Region Design Merit award, 1994), Home House (AIA Seattle Conceptual Citation award, 1996), Urban Villa (AIA Seattle Citation award, 1996, AIA NW & Pacific Region Design Honor award, 1997), Chapel of St. Ignacius (AIA Nat. Religious Architecture award, 1997, 1998, AIA Nat. Honor award, 1999), Studio House (AIA Seattle Merit award, 1997, AIA NW & Pacific Region Design Honor award, 1998, AIA Summit 2000 Western Internat. Design Merit award, 2000), The Brain: A Filmmaker's Studio (AIA Seattle Conceptual Honor award, 1999, AIA Seattle Honor award, 2000, AIA NW & Pacific Region Design Honor award, 2001, AIA Nat. Honor award, 2004), Chicken Point Cabin (AIA Seattle Honor award, 2002, AIA NW & Pacific Region Design Honor award, 2003, The Chgo. Athenaeum: Mus. Architecture and Design Am. Architecture award, 2004, AIA Nat. Honor award, 2004, Residential Arch. Grand award, 2005), Lake House (Masonry Inst. Wash. award, 2004), North Seattle Residence (Met. Home Design 100, 2005), Smithsonian's Cooper-Hewitt Nat. Design Mus., Arch.'s Office (Internat. Interior Design Assn. No. Pacific Chpt. INawards, 2005), Delta Shelter (Residential Arch. Grand award, 2006, Record House, Archtl. Record, 2006, AIA Seattle Merit award, 2006), Tyee River Cabin (AIA Seattle Merit award, 2006). Recipient Architecture award, AAAL, 2007; named one of 8 North Am. Emerging Archs., Archtl. League NY, 2004. Fellow: AIA; mem.: Tau Sigma Delta, Phi Beta Kappa. Office: Olson Sundberg Kundig Allen Archs 159 S Jackson St Ste 600 Seattle WA 98104 Office Phone: 206-624-5670. Office Fax: 206-624-3730.

KUNG, FRANK F., biotechnology and life sciences investor, venture capitalist; b. 1948; BS, Nat. Tsing Hwa U., Taiwan, 1970; MBA, U. Calif., Berkeley, 1983, PhD in Molecular Biology, 1976. Post doctoral rsch. scientist Univ. Calif., Berkeley, 1976-77; rsch. dir. Clin. Bio-Rsch., Emeryville, Calif., 1977-79; scientist, asst. to pres. Cetus Corp., Berkeley, Calif., 1979-81; dir. Cetus Immune Corp. (subs. of Cetus Corp.), Palo Alto, Calif., 1980-84; pres., CEO Genelabs Techs., Inc., Redwood City, Calif., 1984-95, chmn., 1984-96, BioAsia Investments, Palo Alto, Calif., 1996—. Office: BioAsia Investments 575 High St Ste 201 Palo Alto CA 94301-1648 E-mail: fkung@bioasia.wm.

KUNKEL, RICHARD LESTER, public radio executive; b. Syracuse, NY, Nov. 12, 1944; s. Lester DeLong Kunkel and Margaret Fanny Ralph; m. Mary Joan Goldsworthy, Aug. 10, 1968; children: Richard J., Charles J., Joseph B. BS, Syracuse U., 1967, MS, 1969. Lic. real estate broker, N.C. Program dir. Sta. WNBI, Northland Broadcasting, Park Falls, Wis., 1969-72; instr., prodn. dir. Sta. WMKY, Morehead (Ky.) State U., 1972-77; radio mgr. Maine Pub. Broadcasting Network, Orono, 1977-78; instr., sta. mgr. Sta. KNTU, U. North Tex., Denton, 1978-84; v.p., dean Southeastern Ctr. for Arts, Atlanta, 1985-88; pres., gen. mgr. Spokane (Wash.) Pub. Radio Inc., 1988—. Cons., 1978—. With Army N.g., 1968-74. Recipient Addy award 1975. Avocations: photography, computers. Office: KPBX/KIBX, KSFC & KPBZ Spokane Pub Radio 2319 N Monroe St Spokane WA 99205-4586 Home Phone: 509-467-4848. Business E-Mail: rkunkel@kpbx.org.

KUNOWSKI, HERBERT PETER, lawyer; b. LA, Dec. 7, 1958; AA with honors, El Camino Coll., 1984; BA magna cum laude, UCLA, 1987; JD, Pepperdine U., 1990. Bar: Calif. 1990; U.S. Dist. Co. (so., ea., no. and cen. dists.) Calif. 1990; U.S. Ct. Appeals (9th cir.) 1990. With Office of City Atty., LA, 1989—90, Wilson, Elser, Moskovwitz, Edelman & Dicker LLP, LA, 1990, ptnr. Judicial arbitrator and mediator LA County Superior Ct., judge pro tem. Mem. Calif. State Bar, LA County Bar Assn., The Federalist Soc., Orange County Bar Assn.

KUNZ, APRIL BRIMMER, state legislator, lawyer; b. Denver, Apr. 1, 1954; divorced. AA, Stephens Coll., 1974; BS, U. So. Calif., 1976; JD, U. Wyo., 1979. Bar: Wyo. Pres. K and R Enterprises; mem. Wyo. Ho. Reps., Cheyenne, 1985-86, 90-92, Wyo. Senate, Cheyenne, 1992—, chair jud. com., v.p., 1999—2000, majority floor leader, 2001—02, pres., 2003—04. Mem. Laramie County Rep. Women's Club. Mem. Wyo. State Bar Assn, Laramie County Bar Assn. Republican. Home: PO Box 285 Cheyenne WY 82003-0285 Office: Wyo Senate State Capitol Cheyenne WY 82002-0001

KUNZ, HEIDI, healthcare company executive; Grad., Georgetown U., 1977; MBA, Columbia U. Dir. overseas financing, asst. treas., then treas. GM Can.; fin. mgmt. positions through v.p., treas. GM, White Plains, NY, 1979—95; exec. v.p., CFO ITT, 1995-99, Gap Inc., 1999—2003, Blue Shield Calif., San Francisco, 2003—. Bd. dirs. Agilent Technologies, Inc., 2000—. Office: Blue Shield 50 Beale St San Francisco CA 94105-1808

KUNZ, PHILLIP RAY, sociologist, educator; b. Bern, Idaho, July 19, 1936; s. Parley P. and Hilda Irene (Stoor) K.; m. Joyce Sheffield, Mar. 18, 1960; children: Jay, Jenifer, Jody, Johnathan, Jana. BS, Brigham Young U., 1961, MS cum laude, 1962; PhD (fellow), U. Mich., 1967. Instr. Eastern Mich. U., Ypsilanti, 1964, U. Mich., Ann Arbor, 1965-67; asst. prof. sociology U. Wyo., Laramie, 1967-68; prof. emeritus sociology Brigham Young U., Provo, Utah, 1968—, acting dept. chmn., 1973; dir. Inst. Geneal. Studies, 1972-74; cons. various ednl. and rsch. instns., 1968—. Missionary Ch. Jesus Christ LDS, Ga. and S.C., 1956-58, mem. high coun., 1969-70, bishop; mission pres. La. Baton Rouge Mission, 1990-93. Author: 10 Critical Keys for Highly Effective Families, other books; contbr. articles on social orgn., family rels. and deviant behavior to profl. jours. Housing commr. City of Provo, 1984—. Served with AUS, 1954-56. Recipient Karl G. Maeser rsch. award, 1977 Mem. Am. Sociol. Assn., Rocky Mountain Social Sci. Assn., Am. Coun. Family Rels., Rural Sociol. Soc., Am. Soc. Criminology, Soc. Sci. Study of Religion, Religious Rsch. Assn., Sigma Xi, Phi Kappa Phi, Alpha Kappa Delta (Alcuin award 1997). Democrat. Home: 3040 Navajo Ln Provo UT 84604-4820 Office: Brigham Young Univ Dept Sociology Provo UT 84602

KUO, FRANKLIN F., computer scientist, electrical engineer; b. Apr. 22, 1934; came to U.S., 1950, naturalized, 1961; s. Steven C. and Grace C. (Huang) K.; m. Dora Lee, Aug. 30, 1958; children: Jennifer, Douglas. BS, U. Ill., 1955, MS, 1956, PhD, 1958. Asst. prof. dept. elec. engring. Poly. Inst. Bklyn., 1958-60; mem. tech. staff Bell Telephone Labs., Murray Hill, NJ, 1960-66; prof. elec. engring. U. Hawaii, Honolulu, 1966-82; exec. dir. SRI Internat., Menlo Park, Calif., 1982-94; founder, v.p. GWcom, 1994-98; sr. adv. Mtone Wireless Inc., 1998—. Dir. info. systems Office Sec. of Def., 1976-77; liason scientist U.S. Office Naval Research, London, 1971-72; cons. prof. elec. engring. Stanford U., Calif., 1982—96; vis. prof. U. Mannheim, Germany, 1995-96, Nihon U. Global Bus. Sch., 1998-2002; mem. exec. panel Chief of Naval Ops., 1980-85; mentor, Stanford U. Grad. Sch. of Bus., 1999-; advisor China Vest, 2001-03. Author: Network Analysis and Synthesis, 1962, (2d edit.), 1966, Linear Circuits and Computations, 1973; co-author: System Analysis by Digital Computer, 1966, Computer Oriented Circuit Design, 1969, Computer Communications Networks, 1973, Protocols and Techniques in Data Communication Networks, 1981, Multimedia Communications, 1997; cons. editor, Prentice-Hall Inc., 1967—; mem. editorial bd. Future Generations Computer Systems; contbr. articles to profl. jours.; developer Alohanet packet broadcast radio network Mem. Pres. coun. U. Ill.; mem. adv. bd. Beckman Inst.; mem. dean's adv. bd. U. Calif. Santa Cruz, 2002—. Recipient Alexander von Humboldt Found. Rsch. award, 1994. Fellow IEEE; mem. The Internet Soc., Tau Beta Pi, Eta Kappa Nu Home: 824 La Mesa Dr Portola Valley CA 94028 E-mail: ffkuo@mindspring.com.

KUPCHAK, MITCHELL, professional sports team executive, retired professional basketball player; b. Hicksville, NY, May 24, 1954; m. Claire Kupchak. Student, U. NC; MBA, UCLA, 1987. Player Washington Bullets, 1976—81, LA Lakers, 1981—86, asst. gen. mgr., 1986—94, gen. mgr., 1994—. Mem. US basketball team World Univ. Games, 1973, Olympics, 1976. Recipient Gold medal World Univ. Games, 1973, Olympics, 1976; named to NBA All-Rookie Team, 1977. Achievements include being a member of the NBA Championship winning: Washington Bullets, 1978, LA Lakers, 1982, 1985. Office: LA Lakers 555 N Nash St El Segundo CA 90245

KUPEL, FREDERICK JOHN, business services executive; b. Burbank, Calif., Apr. 22, 1929; s. Martin Charles and Lorene (Murray) K.; m. Nancy Kathryn Eubank, 1952 (div. 1979); children: James Frederick, Douglas Edward; m. Karen J. Jensen, 1980 (div. 1992); 1 stepchild, John Robert Jensen, Jr.; m. Beverly A. Blom, 2004. Student, Claremont McKenna Coll., 1948-50; BA in Econs., U. Calif., Berkeley, 1951; MA in Psychology, Sonoma State U., 1980. Lic. profl. counselor. Acctg., fin. and mgmt. positions, 1951-66; acctg. and ops. exec. Evans Products Co., Portland, Oreg., 1967-71; v.p. fin. Columbia Corp., Portland, 1971-77, Plantronics, Inc., Santa Cruz, Calif., 1977-78; counselor Yellow Brick Rd. Program, Portland, 1975-76; cons., 1978-84; dir. bus. devel. and acquisitions ITT Communication Services, Inc., 1985-87; v.p. fin., chief fin. officer Bohemia, Inc., Eugene, Oreg., 1987-89; pres. Bus. Devel. Corp., Lake Oswego, Oreg., 1989-93; bus. owner, 1994—2000; CEO, Kupel & Co., Portland, 2000—. With AUS, 1946-47. Office: 3735 SE Ogden St Portland OR 97202 Office Phone: 503-774-0885. E-mail: fred@kupel.com.

KUPIETZKY, MOSHE JOSEPH, lawyer; b. NYC, May 17, 1944; s. Jacob Harry and Fanny (Dresner) K.; m. Arlene Debra Usdan, June 22, 1966; children: Jay, Jeff, Jacob. BBA cum laude, CCNY, 1965; LLB magna cum laude, Harvard U., 1968. Bar: NY 1969, Calif. 1970. Law clerk to Hon. William B. Herlands U.S. Dist. Ct., NYC, 1968-69; assoc. Mitchell Silberberg & Knupp, LA, 1969-74, ptnr., 1974-80; ptnr., prin. Hayutin Rubinroit Praw & Kupietzky, LA, 1980-87; ptnr. Sidley, Austin LLP, LA, 1987—; mng. partner, LA office and head, corp. and fin. practice group Sidley, Austin, Brown & Wood, LA, mem. exec. com. Editor: Harvard Law Rev., 1967—68. Bd. dirs. Nat. Inst. Jewish Hospice, Beverly Hills, Calif., 1986-98, LA Econ. Devel. Corp.; bd. advisors Graziadio Sch. Bus. and Mgmt. Pepperdine U., LA, 1996-98. Mem. ABA, Beverly Hills Bar Assn., LA County Bar Assn., Calif. State Bar (vice-chair opinions com. 2004-05.). Office: Sidley Austin LLP 555 W 5th St Ste 4000 Los Angeles CA 90013-3000 Home Phone: 310-277-9179; Office Phone: 213-896-6000. E-mail: mkupietzky@sidley.com.

KURIAN, THOMAS, computer software company executive; B summa cum laude in Elec. Engring., Princeton U., NJ; MBA, Stanford U., Calif. Cons. McKinsey & Co., London, Brussels and San Francisco; with Oracle Corp., Redwood City, Calif., 1996, various product mgmt. and devel. positions Oracle Server Techs. Divsn., v.p. e-bus., sr. v.p. Oracle Server Techs. Devel. Office: Oracle Corp 500 Oracle Pky Redwood City CA 94065 Office Phone: 650-506-0024.

KURLAND, STANFORD L., mortgage company executive; b. 1952; BS in Bus. Adminstrn. & Acctg., Calif. State U., Northridge, 1975. With Grant Thornton; joined Countrywide Fin. Corp. (formerly Countrywide Credit Industries), Calabasas, Calif., 1979, exec. mng. dir., COO, 2000—04, pres., COO, 2004—06; chmn., CEO PennyMac (Private Nat. Mortgage Acceptance Co. LLC), Calabasas, Calif., 2008—. Bd. visitors UCLA Anderson Sch. Mgmt., 2004—. Office: PennyMac 27001 Agoura Rd Agoura Hills CA 91301*

KURN, NEAL, lawyer; b. Springfield, Mass., July 19, 1934; s. Samuel and Jane Etta (Freeman) K.; m. Barbara Agron(dec.), June 9, 1957; children: Jeffrey Howard, Sharon Ilene Marcus-Kurn, Jennifer Rose Endsley. BSBA with high honors, U. Ariz., 1956, JD with honors, 1963. Bar: Ariz. 1963; cert. specialist tax and estate and trust law, Ariz.; CPA, Ariz. Staff mem. Price Waterhouse & Co., San Francisco, L.A. and Phoenix, 1956, 58-60; assoc., ptnr. Moore, Romley, Kaplan, Robbins & Green, Phoenix, 1963-71; ptnr. Powers, Ehrenreich, Boutell & Kurn, Phoenix, 1971-82; ptnr., also bd. dirs. Fennemore Craig, Phoenix, 1982—, chmn., bd. dirs., 2007—. Adj. prof. law Ariz. State U., 1980-82. Editor-in-chief Ariz. Law Rev., 1962-63. Past chmn. tax adv. commn. Ariz. State Bd. Legal Specialization; bd. dirs. Ariz. Cmty. Found., 1986-2008, chmn. 1994-96; bd. dirs. Ariz. Bar Found., 1983-89, chmn., 1988; bd. dirs. Jewish Fedn. Greater Phoenix, pres., 1977-79; bd. dirs. U. Ariz. Found., 1998-2004; v.p. coun. Jewish Fedn., 1988-90; chmn. Jewish Cmty. Found. Greater Phoenix, 1998-2001; bd. dirs. Trust for Jewish Philanthropy, 2000-2003; chmn. adv. bd. Leave a Legacy, State of Ariz., 2001-2004. With U.S. Army, 1956-58; bd. dirs. Bannerc Alzheimers Inst. Found, 2006-, Phoenix Symphony Found., 2008-, treas. Fellow Am. Coll. Tax Counsel, Am. Bar Found., Am. Coll. Trust and Estate Counsel; mem. ABA, State Bar Ariz. (past chmn. taxation sect., bd. govs. 1991-93), Maricopa County Bar Assn., Phi Kappa Phi, Beta Gamma Sigma. Democrat. Jewish. Office: Fennemore Craig 3003 N Central Ave Ste 2600 Phoenix AZ 85012-2913 Office Phone: 602-916-5485. Business E-Mail: nkurn@fclaw.com.

KURREN, BARRY M., federal judge; BA with highest honors, U. Hawaii, 1973, JD, 1977. Law clk. to Hon. Martin Pence U.S. Dist. Ct. Hawaii, 1977-78; with Goodsill Anderson & Quinn, 1978-80, Burke, Sakai, McPheeters, Bordner & Gilardy, 1980-91; judge Dist. Ct. (1st cir.) Hawaii, 1991; apptd. magistrate judge U.S. Dist. Ct. Hawaii, 1992; acting assoc. justice Supreme Ct. of Republic of Marshall Islands, 2000—. Adj. prof. law William S. Richardson Sch. of Law, Hawaii, 1994—; arbitrator Ct. Annexed Arbitration Program, 1st Jud. Cir., Hawaii, 1986-91. Mem. ABA, Am. Judicature Soc., Am. Arbitration Assn. (panel of arbitrators 1989-91), Fed. Magistrate Judges' Assn., Fed./State Jud. Coun., Am. Inn of Ct. (bencher), Hawaii State Bar Assn., Aloha Inn, Honolulu County Med. Soc. (med. practices com. 1987-90). Office: C-229 US Courthouse 300 Ala Moana Blvd Honolulu HI 96850-0001 Fax: 808-541-3500. E-mail: Barry_Kurren@hid.uscourts.gov.

KURTH, DONALD JAMES, JR., Mayor, Rancho Cucamonga, California, medical educator; b. Newport, RI, Apr. 26, 1949; s. Donald James and Isabelle Virginia (Statchen) Kurth; m. Dee Frances Matreyck-Kurth. BA, Columbia U., NYC, 1975, MD, 1979; MBA, Loma U., 2007; MPA, Kennedy Sch. Govt., Harvard U., 2008. Cert. Emer. Medicine and Addiction Medicine. Chief addiction medicine Loma Linda U., Behavioral Med. Ctr., Redlands, Calif., 1997—; assoc. prof. Loma Linda U., Calif., 1997—; owner Urgent Care Ctr and Alta Loma Med. Group, 1983—; mayor City of Rancho Cucamonga, Calif., 2006—. Pres. California Soc. Addiction Medicine, 2004—06. Pres. Rancho Cucamonga C. of C.; bd. dir., bd. pres. Cucamonga County Water Dist.; chmn. Pub. Rels. Com.; mem. Legis. Com.; v.p. San Bernardino Spl. Dist. Assoc. Recipient Brainard award, Columbia U., 1975; named Fellow of the Am. Soc. of Addition Med.; grantee Devel. Leadership in Reducing Substance Abuse, Robert Wood Fellowship, 2003—06. Fellow: Robert Wood Johnson Found. (fellow leadership devel. 2003—06), Am. Soc. Addiction Medicine (treas. 2005—07). Achievements include development of the Children's Free Immunization Prog. Office: Cucamonga City Hall 10500 Civic Ctr Dr Rancho Cucamonga CA 91730 Office Phone: 909-477-2700. Office Fax: 909-477-2848. Business E-Mail: council@cityofrc.us.*

KURTZ, SWOOSIE, actress; b. Omaha, Sept. 6, 1944; d. Frank and Margo (Rogers) K. Student, Acad. Music and Dramatic Art, London, U. So. Calif. Appeared on TV series As the World Turns, 1956, Mary, 1978, Love, Sidney, 1981-83 (nominated Best Actress in Comedy Series 1982-83), Sisters, 1991-96 (Emmy nominee Lead Actress in Drama 1993, 94, SAG award nominee 1995), Suddenly Susan, 1996, 97, Touched by an Angel, 1997, ER, 1998, Love and Money, 1999, That's Life, 2000-01, Huff, 2004-06, Pushing Daisies, 2007-; (TV films) Ah, Wilderness!, 1976, Walking Through the Fire, 1979, Uncommon Women and Others, 1979, Marriage is Alive and Well, 1980, The Mating Season, 1980, Fifth of July, 1982, A Caribbean Mystery, 1983, Guilty Conscience, 1985, A Time to Live, 1985, The House of Blue Leaves, 1987, Baja Oklahoma, 1988 (Golden Globe nominee 1987), Terror on Track 9, 1992, The Image (Emmy nominee, Ace award nominee), 1990, The Positively True Adventures of the Alleged Texas Cheerleader-Murdering Mom, 1993, And the Band Played On, 1993 (Emmy award nominee 1994, Ace award nominee), One Christmas, 1994, Betrayed: A Story of Three Women, 1995, A Promise to Carolyn, 1996, Little Girls in Pretty Boxes, 1997, More Tales of the City, 1998, My Own Country, 1998, Harvey, 1999, The Wilde Girls, 2001, Nadine in Date Land, 2005, Category 7: The End of the World, 2005; TV guest appearances on Kojak, Carol and Co. (Emmy award); (films) Slap Shot, 1977, The World According to Garp, 1982, Against All Odds, 1984, Wild Cats, 1986, True Stories, 1986, Vice Versa, 1988, Bright Lights, Big City, 1988, Dangerous Liaisons, 1988, Stanley and Iris, 1989, A Shock to the System, 1990, Reality Bites, 1994, Citizen Ruth, 1996, Liar, Liar, 1997, Outside Ozona, 1999, Cruel Intentions, 1999, The White River Kid, 2000, Sleep Easy, Hutch Rimes, 2000, Get Over It, 2001, Bubble Boy, 2001, The Rules of Attraction, 2002, Duplex, 2003; (theater) Ah Wilderness!, 1975, Children, 1976, Tartuffe, 1977 (Tony award nominee), A History of the American Film, 1978 (Drama Desk award), Uncommon Women and Others, 1978 (Obie award, Drama Desk award), Who's Afraid of Virginia Woolf, 1980, Summer, 1980, Fifth of July, 1980-82 (Tony award, Drama Desk award, Outer Critics Circle award), Michael Bennett's Scandal, 1985, Beach House, 1986, The House of Blue Leaves, 1986-87 (Tony award, Obie award), Hunting Cockroaches, 1987 (Drama Logue award nominee), Love Letters, 1989-90, Six Degrees of Separation, 1990, Lips Together, Teeth Apart, 1991, The Mineola Twins, 1999 (Obie award, Drama Desk award nominee, Outer Critics Circle nominee), The Vagina Monologues, 2000, Imaginary Friends, 2002-03, Frozen, 2004 (Tony award nominee, Best Actress in a Play), Heartbreak House, 2006. Office: c/o William Morris Agency One William Morris Pl Beverly Hills CA 90212

KURTZMAN, JOEL ALLAN, economist; b. LA, June 25, 1947; s. Samuel Michael and Roselle (Rosencranz) K.; m. Susan Leslie Kurtzman, Dec. 28, 1969; 1 child, Eli. AB, U. Calif., Berkeley, 1969; MS, U. Houston, 1976. Cons. United Nations, various locations worldwide, 1970; economist UN, NYC, 1978; editor devel. bus. World Bank, NYC, 1984; former exec. editor Harvard Business Review; former bus. columnist NY Times; founding editor-in-chief Strategy and Business mag.; former global lead ptnr., thought leadership and innovation PricewaterhouseCoopers; chmn. Kurtzman Group LLC, Concord, Mass., 1995—; also sr. fellow, pub., Milken Inst. Rev. Milken Inst., Santa Monica, Calif. Bd. dirs. Medtec Internat., Beverly Hills, Calif., Orbit Prodns., Washington, Soc. for Trial Peoples, Bombay. Author: Crown of Flowers, 1970 (Eisner Prize 1970), Sweet Bobby, 1976, No More Dying, 1976, Futurecasting, 1980, Decline and Crash of the American Economy, 1988, The Death of Money, 1993, Thought Leaders, 1997, How the Markets Really Work, 2002, Startups That Work, 2005; Co-author: Radical E: From GE to Enron Lessons on How to Rule the Web, 2001, MBA in a Box, 2004, co-editor New International Economic Order Library, 1978-82, editor: Thought Leaders, 1997; editl. bd Sloan Mgmt. Rev, MIT; lectr. in field. Grantee Moody Found., 1976, Govt. Italy, 1980, Govt. the Netherlands, 1982. Avocation: jogging. Office: Milken Inst Rev 1250 Fourth St Santa Monica CA 90401 also: Kurtzman Group LLC 904 Lowell Rd Concord MA 01742-5513 Office Phone: 310-570-4600, 978-369-6661. Office Fax: 310-570-4601. Business E-Mail: joel.kurtzman@kurtzmangroup.com.

KURY, BERNARD EDWARD, lawyer; b. Sunbury, Pa., Sept. 11, 1938; AB, Princeton U., 1960; LLB, U. Pa., 1963. Bar: NY 1964. Assoc. Dewey, Ballantine, Bushby, Palmer & Wood, NYC, 1963-71, ptnr., 1971—2004; v.p., gen. counsel Guidant Corp., Indpls., 2004—06. Contbg. editor Ency. of Venture Capital; bd. trustees Keck Grad. Inst. (KGI), 2006—. Editor: Pa. Law Sch. Review. Mem.: NY State Bar Assn., Assn. of the Bar of the City of NY, ABA. Mailing: Keck Grad Inst 535 Watson Dr Claremont CA 91711

KURZ, MORDECAI, economics professor; b. Natanya, Israel, Nov. 29, 1934; came to U.S., 1957, naturalized, 1973; s. Moshe and Sarah (Kraus) K.; m. Lillian Rivlin, Aug. 4, 1963 (div. Mar. 1967); m 2d Linda Alice Cahn, Dec. 2, 1979. BA in Econs. and Polit. Sci., Hebrew U., Jerusalem, 1957; MA in Econs., Yale U., 1958, PhD in Econs., 1962; MS in Stats., Stanford U., 1960. Asst. prof. econs. Stanford U., 1962-63, assoc. prof., 1966-68, prof., 1969—, Joan Kenney prof. econs., 1997—, dir. econs. sect. Inst. for Math. Studies, 1971-89; sr. lectr. in econs. Hebrew U., 1963-66. Cons. econs. SRI Internat., Menlo Park, Calif., 1963-78; spl. econ. advisor Can. health and Welfare Ministry, Ottawa, Ont., 1976-78; spl. econ. advisor Pres.'s Commn. on Pension, Washington, 1979-81; rsch. assoc. Nat. Bur. Econ. Rsch., 1979-82; Lady Davis vis. prof. Hebrew U., Jerusalem, 1993; prin. investigator Smith Richardson Found., 2001-2006; mem. adv. bd. Annals of Fin., 2004—; mem. Editl. Bd. Econ. Theory, 2008-. Author: (with Kenneth J. Arrow) Public Investment, The Rate of Return and Optimal Fiscal Policy,1970, Endogenous Economic Fluctuations: Studies in the Theory of Rational Beliefs, 1997; co-editor Econ. Theory, 1997-2008, mem. adv. bd., 2008. Bd. dirs. Ben-Gurion U. of the Negev, Israel, 1998—. Ford Found. faculty fellow Stanford U., 1973; Guggenheim Found. fellow Stanford U., Harvard U., Jerusalem, 1977-78; Inst. Advanced Studies fellow Hebrew U., Mt. Scopus, Jerusalem, 1979-80; prin. investigator NSF, 1969-93, Smith-Richardson Found., 2001-2006. Fellow Econometric Soc. (assoc. editor Jour. Econ. Theory 1976-90); mem. Am. Econ. Assn. Democrat. Jewish. Office: Stanford U Econs Dept Serra St at Galvez Stanford CA 94305-6702 Office Phone: 650-723-2220.

KUSHAR, KENT, information technology executive; BS, Univ. Montana; postgrad. Advanced Bus. and Tech. Program, Harvard Bus. Sch., Kellogg Sch. at Northwestern, Chgo. Dir. IBM Consulting; gen. mgr. IBM-ROLM subs., Calif.; co-founder EDP Industries; tech. v.p. Citicorp; mng. prin. Unisys Cons.; v.p. & chief info. officer E&J Gallo Winery, Modesto, Calif. Nat. bd. advisors Univ. Ariz.; bus. advisory bd. Calif. State Univ., Stanislaus; bd. of advisors Info. Tech. Rsch. Ctr. Avocation: auto restoration. Office: VP & CIO E&J Gallo Winery PO Box 1130 Modesto CA 95353 Business E-Mail: kent.kushar@ejgallo.com.

KUSHNER, LAWRENCE, rabbi; b. Detroit; m. Karen Kushner; 3 children. BA Phi Beta Kappa, U. Cincinnati. Cert. ordained Rabbi Hebrew Union Coll, 1969. Rabbi Congregation of Beth El, Sudbury, Mass.; rabbi-in-residence Hebrew Union College-Jewish Inst. Religion, NYC; vis. prof. Jewish Spirituality Grad. Theological U., Berkeley, Calif.; Emanu-El scholar in residence Emanu-El Congregation, San Francisco. Contbr. articles to numerous profl. jours.; author: (novels) Kabbalah: A Love Story. Named one of The Top 50 Rabbis in America, Newsweek Mag., 2007. Achievements include being first Rabbinic Chairman of Reform Judaism's Commission on Religious Living. Office: The Congregation Emanu-El 2 Lake St San Francisco CA 94118 Office Phone: 415-751-2541 148.

KUSTER, ROBERT KENNETH, semi-retired scientist; b. LA, July 11, 1932; s. Arthur Rollo Kuster and Ermine Rosebud (Prittchett) Woodward. AS, Gavilan Coll., 1974, AA in Humanities, 1981; student, San Jose State U., 1955, 1974-76, UCLA, 1977. Installer Western Electric Co., Inc., Corpus Christi, Tex., 1951-52, 1955, San Jose, Calif., 1957-58, 1960-83; ptnr., scientist, cons. WE-Woodward's Enterprises, Morgan Hill, Calif., 1975—; technician Lucent Tech., Inc., San Jose, 1983-85, ret., 1985. Scientist pvt. practice, Gilroy, 1978—. Served to sgt. U.S. Army Corps Engrs., 1952-54. Mem. AAAS, Astron. Soc. Pacific, Calif. Acad. Scis., N.Y. Acad. Scis., Am. Legion, VFW. Lodges: Elks. Baptist. Avocations: photography, golf, camping, hiking, music. Home: 17506 Hoot Owl Way Morgan Hill CA 95037-6524 Office Phone: 408-427-4554. Personal E-mail: rkkuster6851@msn.com.

KUSTIN, KENNETH, chemist; b. Bronx, NY, Jan. 6, 1934; s. Alex and Mae (Marvisch) K.; m. Myrna May Jacobson, June 24, 1956; children: Brenda Jayne, Franklin Daniel, Michael Thorpe. BSc, Queens Coll., Flushing, NY, 1955; PhD, U. Minn., 1959. Postdoctoral fellow Max Planck Inst. for Phys. Chemistry, Göttingen, Germany, 1959-61; asst. prof. chemistry Brandeis U., Waltham, Mass., 1961-66, assoc. prof., 1966-72, prof., 1972-97, prof. emeritus, 1997—, chmn. dept. chemistry, 1974-77. Vis. prof. pharmacology Harvard U. Med. Sch., 1977-78; Fulbright-Hays lectr., 1978; program dir. NSF, 1985-86; adj. rsch. scientist U.S. Army, Natick RD&E Ctr., 1991—. Editor: Fast Reactions, vol. 16 of Methods in Enzymology, 1969; bd. editors Internat. Jour. Chem. Kinetics, 1983-90, Inorganic Chemistry, 1993-95; co-editor: Vanadium: The Versatile Metal, 2007; rsch. and publs. in field. Mem. AAAS, Am. Chem. Soc. (councilor 1983-85), Phi Beta Kappa.

KUSTRA, ROBERT W. (BOB KUSTRA), former state official, academic administrator; b. St. Louis, Mar. 21, 1943; s. Walter and Loretto (Shaughnessy) K.; m. Kathleen Breidert, Sept. 10, 1989; children: Jennifer, Stephen; stepchild: Matthew Breidert. BA in Polit. Sci., St. Benedict's Coll., Atchison, Kans., 1965; MA in Pub. Adminstrn., So. Ill. U., 1968; PhD in Polit. Sci., U. Ill., 1975. Prof. Northwestern U., U. Ill. at Springfield (formerly Sangamon State U.), Roosevelt U., Chgo.; exec. asst. to U.S. Senator Charles Percy Chgo., 1978-80; state rep. Ill. Ho. of Reps., 1981-83; state senator Ill. State Senate, 1983-91; lt. gov. State of Ill., Springfield, 1991; chmn. Ill. Bd. Higher Edn., 1997; pres. Eastern Ky. U., Boise State U., 2003—. Prof. Roosevelt U., Loyola U., Lincoln Land. C.C., Springfield, bd. mem. Idaho Nature Conservancy, Western Interstate Commn. Higher Edn., Inland Northwest Rsch. Alliance, Sci. Technology Adv. Coun., State of Idaho. Host (radio program) New Horizons in Edn. Trustee Village of Glenview, Ill., 1978-80. Named Best Freshman Rep., Ill. Polit. Reporter, 1981, Best Freshman Senator, 1983; Outstanding Legislator, Ill. Assn. Sch. Bds., 1987-88, Friend of Edn., Ill. State Bd. Edn., 1987-88, Heritage award Ill. Divsn. of the Polish-Am. Congress., 1992. Republican. Roman Catholic. Office: Boise State University Business Bldg Rm B-307 1910 University Dr Boise ID 83725-1000 Office Phone: 208-426-1491. Office Fax: 208-426-3779.

KUSUNOSE, TARO, lawyer; b. Tokyo, July 27, 1973; married; 2 children. BA cum laude, UCSD, 1996; JD, U. Calif. Davis Sch. Law, 1999. Bar: Wash. 2000. Assoc. atty., bus. law., corp. law, real estate Lasher Holzapfel Sperry & Ebberson, PLLC, Seattle. Bd. mem., exec. com. mem. Nikkei Concerns; mem. Seattle Japanese Bus. Owner's Group. Contbr. articles to numerous profl. jours. Bd. mem. Transportation Club Seattle, Japan Am. Soc. State Wash. Mem.: ABA, King Co. Bar Assn., Wash. State Bar Assn. Office: Lasher Holzapfel Sperry Ebberson PLLC 2600 Two Union Square 601 Union St Seattle WA 98101-4000

KUYKENDALL, GREGORY JOHN, lawyer; b. Denver, Jan. 13, 1961; s. Louis George and Mary (Spragins) Kuykendall. BA, U. Colo., 1983; MA, Tulane U., 1985; JD, Northwestern U., 1988. Bar: Ariz. 1989, U.S. Dist. Ct. Ariz. 1989, U.S. Ct. Appeals (9th cir.) 1989, U.S. Dist. Ct. Mich. (Ea. Dist.) 1990, Colo. 1991, U.S. Dist. Ct. (Ctrl. Dist. Ill.) 1996, U.S. Supreme Ct. 2003, cert. specialist criminal law: Ariz. Bd. Legal Specialization. Atty. O'Connor, Cavanagh, Tucson, 1988-92, Butler & Stein, Tucson, 1992—94; pvt. practice Tucson, 1994—. Lectr. in field. Mem.: Ariz. Attys. Criminal Justice, State Bar Ariz., Fed. Bar Assn., Colo. Bar Assn., NACDL (life), Phi Beta Kappa. Democrat. Avocations: skiing, running, bicycling. Office: Gregory Kuykendall 531 S Convent Ave Tucson AZ 85701-2612 Office Phone: 520-792-8033. Office Fax: 520-792-0113.

KVAMME, MARK D., marketing professional; BA in French, Econs. and Lit., U. Calif., Berkeley. Programmer Apple Computer; founding mem., then internat. product mgr. in U.S. Apple France; founder, pres., CEO Internat. Solutions, 1984-86; dir. internat. mktg. Wyse Tech., 1986-89; ptnr. CKS Group, Cupertino, Calif., 1989-91, chair, CEO, 1991-98; chair USWEB/CKS, Cupertino, Calif., 1998—99; ptnr. Sequoia Capital, Menlo Park, Calif., 1999—. Office: Sequoia Capital 3000 Sand Hill Rd Bldg 4 Menlo Park CA 94025-7113

KWAN, MICHELLE WING, professional figure skater; b. Torrance, Calif., July 7, 1980; d. Danny and Estella Kwan. Student, UCLA, U. Denver, 2007—. Good-will amb. US Dept. State, 2006—. Spokesperson Walt Disney Co., 2006—. Published (book series) Michelle Kwan Presents Skating Dreams, guest appearances Disney and ABC Specials; performer: (TV special) based on the music of Disney's animated film, Mulan, 1998. Nat. spokesperson, Champions Across Am. Children's Miracle Network, 1996—, co-chair, ProKid's Program; founder Chevrolet/Michelle Kwan R.E.W.A.R.D.S. scholarship program. Recipient Skating Mag. Readers' Choice award for figure skater of yr., 1993-94, U.S. Figure Skating Skater of Yr. award, 1994-96, 98, 99, 2001-03, Dial award, 1997, Sullivan award for top amateur athlete in Am., 2001, Kids' Choice award, 2002, 03, Teen Choice award, 2002, Skating Mag. Reader's Choice award, 2003; named Female Athlete of Yr. U.S. Olympic Com., 1996, 98-2001, 2003, Women's Sports Found. Sportswoman of Yr., 2003, CosmoGirl of Yr., 2002. Achievements include being the youngest World Champion in US history; most decorated figure skater in US history; third youngest World Champion; received 50 perfect 6.0 marks in major competitions; victories include: World Junior Championships, 1994, 96, Nations cup, 1995, U.S. Postal Svc. Challenge, 1995, State Farm U.S. Championships, 1996, 1999, 2001, 2003, Champions Series Final, 1996, Japan Open, 1997, 1999, Skate Am., 1995, 1997, 1999, 2000, Skate Can., 1995, 1997, 1999, US Championships, 1996, 1998-2004, World Championships, 1998, 1999, 2000, 2001, 2003, Goodwill Games, 1998, 1998 Ultimate Four, 1998, Grand Slam Figure Skating, 1998, US Pro Classic, 1998, Masters of Figure Skating, 1998, 1999, 2000, Silver Medal, Olympics, 1998, Bronze Medal, 2002; Michelle Kwan Trophy named in her honor, 2004. Office: US Figure Skating Assn 20 1st St Colorado Springs CO 80906-3624

KWAN, SIMON H., financial economist, researcher; PhD, U. NC, Chapel Hill, 1990. V.p. Fed. Res. Bank San Francisco, 2004—. Office: Fed Res Bank San Francisco 101 Market St San Francisco CA 94105 Office Fax: 415-974-2168. Business E-Mail: simon.kwan@sf.frb.org.

KWAN-RUBINEK, VERONIKA, broadcast executive; MBA, 1988. Rsch. cons. German Am. C. of C.; with internat. mktg. Lorimar Film Entertainment; sales analyst Warner Bros. Pictures Internat., sr. sales analyst, mgr. internat. sales, dir. internat. ops., v.p. internat. distbn., 1995—97, sr. v.p. internat. distbn., 1997—2001, pres. internat. distbn., 2001—. Named one of The 100 Most Powerful Women in Entertainment, Hollywood Reporter, 2005, 2006, 2007. Office: Warner Bros Pictures International Distribution 4000 Warner Blvd Burbank CA 91522 Office Phone: 818-954-1663. Office Fax: 818-954-6112. E-mail: veronika.kwan-rubinek@warnerbros.com.

KWIRAM, ALVIN L., retired chemistry professor, academic administrator; b. Riverhills, Man., Can., Apr. 28, 1937; came to U.S., 1954; s. Rudolf and Wilhelmina A. (Bilske) K.; m. Verla Rae Michel, Aug. 9, 1964; children: Andrew Brandt, Sidney Marguerite. BS in Chemistry, Walla Walla Coll., Wash., 1958, BA in Physics, 1958; PhD in Chemistry, Calif. Inst. Tech., 1963; DS (hon.), Andrews U., 1995. Alfred A. Noyes instr. Calif. Inst. Tech., Pasadena, 1962-63; research asso. physics dept. Stanford (Calif.) U., 1963-64; instr. chemistry Harvard U., Cambridge, Mass., 1964-67, lectr., 1967-70; assoc. prof. chemistry U. Wash., Seattle, 1970-75, prof., 1975—2007, chmn. dept. chemistry, 1977-87, vice provost, 1987-88, sr. vice provost, 1988-90, vice provost for rsch., 1990—2002; ret., 2007. Bd. dirs. Seattle Biomed. Rsch. Inst.; environ. and health scis. divsn. rev. com. Pacific N.W. Nat. Lab., 1998—2001, adv. com., 2000—06; exec. dir. NSF Ctr. Materials and Devices Info. Tech. Rsch., 2002—07; vis. prof. dept. chemistry U. Berkeley, Calif., 1976—77; vis. prof. dept. physics U. Stuttgart, Germany, 1985—86; vis. scholar Wolfson Coll. Oxford U., England, 2006; adv. bd. mem. Lahore U. Mgmt. Scis., Sch. Sci. & Engring., 2009—. Contbr. numerous articles to sci. jours. Bd. dirs. Seattle Econ. Devel. Commn., 1988-92, Wash. Rsch. Found., 1989-94, Seattle-King County Econ. Devel. Coun., 1989-98, Helen R. Whiteley Found., 1997-, Lumera Corp., 2001-03; mem. vis. com. divsn. chemistry and chem. engring. Calif. Inst. Tech., 1991-96; chmn. adv. bd. Sch. Engring., Walla Walla Coll., 1992-2005. Recipient Eastman-Kodak Sci. award, 1962, Univ.-Industry Rels/ award Coun. for Chem. Rsch., 1986; Woodrow Wilson fellow, 1958; Alfred P. Sloan fellow, 1968-70; Guggenheim Meml. Found. fellow, 1977-78. Fellow: AAAS (chmn.-elect, chmn., past chmn. sect. on chemistry 1991—94, program com. 1994—98), Am. Phys. Soc.; mem.: Nat. Acad. Sci. (com. on advanced rsch. instrumentation, com. sci. and pub. policy), Worldwide Univ. Network (acad. adv. bd. 2002—05, US liaison 2003—08, chmn. global acad. devel. adv. bd. 2007—08), Coun. Chem. Rsch. (bd. dirs. 1980—84, chmn. 1982—83), Am. Chem. Soc. (sec.-treas. divsn. phys. chemistry 1976—86, divsn. councilor 1986—2005, com. on sci., chmn. subcom. on fed. funding for rsch. 1990—94, adv. bd. grad. edn. 2000—08, chair 2005—08), Nat. Assn. State Univs. and Land Grant Colls. (chmn.-elect, chmn., past chmn. 2000—03, exec. com., coun. rsch. policy and grad. edn.), Sigma Xi. Office: Univ Wash Dept Chem Seattle WA 98195-1700 Office Phone: 206-543-4020. Business E-Mail: kwiram@u.washington.edu.

KWOCK, ROYAL, architect; s. Eddie Sing and Jeanie K. Kwock; m. Irene L. Leau, June 26, 1983. BArch, Calif. Poly. U., 1972. Registered architect, Calif. Draftsman Martinskis & Prodis, San Jose, 1973—74; intern architect, staff architect, assoc. Hawley, Stowers & Assoc., San Jose, 1974—83; project architect Winston & May, Santa Clara, Calif., 1983—86; prin. May & Kwock, Santa Clara, 1986—98, Ahearn & Kwock Archs., San Jose, 1998—. Mem. Nat. Trust Hist. Preservation, San Jose, 1984; bd. dirs. Youth Sci. Inst. Santa Clara Valley, 1985—95. Mem.: AIA (corr.; mem. Interiors Commn. 1982—83), Kiwanis Club of West San Jose (bd. dirs. 1993, 1998). Office: Ahearn & Kwock Archs 600 N 3rd St San Jose CA 95112-5119

KWOH, STEWART, lawyer, cultural organization administrator; BA, JD, UCLA; PhD (hon.), Williams Coll., 1996. Pres., exec. dir. Asian Pacific Am. Legal Ctr. Bd. dirs., vice chair Nat. Asian Pacific Am. Legal Consortium; adjunct instructor UCLA. Mem. steering comm. Coalition for Humane Immigration Rights of Los Angeles; bd. mem. Los Angeles Charter Reform Commn., El Pueblo Historical Monument Authority Commn.; chair, bd. dirs. Calif. Endowment, 2000—02; trustee Methodist Urban Found., Calif. Consumer Protection Found., Calif. Wellness Found., Tang Family Found., Fannie Mae Found. Recipient Professional award, L.A. County Human Relations Commn., 1992, Faith and Freedom award, UCLA U. Religious Conf., 1993, CORO Public Affairs award, 1993, Asian Pacific Heritage Month award, 1993, ACLU award, 1993, President's award, So. Christian Leadership Conf. & Martin Luther King Legacy Assn., 1994, Mayor's award, L.A. City Human Relations Commn., 1996; named MacArthur Found. fellow, 1998, Lawyer of the Yr., California Lawyer mag., 1998. Mem.: So. Calif. Chinese Lawyers Assn. (former pres.). Office: Asian Pacific Am Legal Ctr 1145 Wilshire Blvd Los Angeles CA 90017

KYL, JON LLEWELLYN, United States Senator from Arizona; b. Oakland, Nebr., Apr. 25, 1942; s. John H. and Arlene (Griffith) K.; m. Caryll Louise Collins, June 5, 1964; children: Kristine Kyl Gavin, John Jeffry. BA in Polit. Sci., with honors, U. Ariz., 1964, LLB, 1966. Bar: Ariz. 1966, US Supreme Ct. 1971. Assoc. Jennings, Strouss & Salmon, Phoenix, 1966—70, ptnr., 1971—86; mem. US Congress from 4th Ariz. Dist., 1987—95; US Senator from Ariz., 1995—; asst. minority leader (minority whip), 2007—; mem. US Senate Fin. Com., US Senate Judiciary Com. Chmn. US Senate Republican Policy Com., 2003—07, US Senate Republican Conf., 2007. Founding dir. Ariz. Crime Victim Found, 1983; mem. Phoenix C. of C. Recipient Keeper of the Flame award, Ctr. Security Policy, 1994, Champion Small Bus. Cmty. award, Small Bus. Survival Com., 2000, Legis. of Yr. award, Am. Internat. Automobile Dealers, 2005, Medal of Honor award, US Oncology and Ariz Oncology Associates, 2005; named one of America's 10 Best Senators, TIME mag., 2006. Mem.: Ariz. State Bar Assn. Republican. Presbyn. Office: District Office Ste 120 2200 E Camelback Rd Phoenix AZ 85016-3455 also: US Senate 730 Hart Senate Bldg Washington DC 20510-0001 Office Phone: 602-840-1891, 202-224-4521. Office Fax: 202-224-2207, 602-957-6838.*

KYLE, JAMES LEWIS, dean, physician; b. LA; BA in Religion, Loma Linda U., 1973; MDiv, Andrews Theological Seminary, Berrien Springs, Mich., 1977; MD, UCLA Sch. of Medicine, 1987. Internal medicine physician private practice, San Diego; pres., CEO Sharp Health Plan; chief med. officer, dir. clinical bus. develop., compliance officer and admin. dean coll. of medicine Charles R. Drew U. of

Medicine and Sci., 1996—99; former v.p. Sharp Healthcare Community Care; former pres., CEO Genesis Healthcare Strategies; former v.p., Calif. market Schaller Anderson; chair, dept. of health admin. & dean, sch. of public health Loma Linda U., 2006—. Health presentations KUSI Television in San Diego, San Diego, 1992—96. Trustee Catholic Healthcare W., Shields for Families; bd. dirs. Calif. Endowment, 2004—. Captain, primary care physician USAR, 1995—2000. Decorated Army Commendation Medal. Office: Loma Linda U Dept of Health Administration Nichol Hall Rm 1321 Loma Linda CA 92350

KYLE, ROBERT CAMPBELL, II, publishing executive; b. Cleve., Jan. 6, 1935; s. Charles Donald and Mary Alice (King) K.; children: Peter F., Kit C., Scott G. BS, U. Colo., 1956; MA, Case Western Res. U., 1958; MBA, Harvard U., 1963, DBA, 1966. Ptnr. McLagan & Co., Chgo., 1966-67; founder, pres. Devel. Sys. Corp. (subs. Longman Group USA), Chgo., 1967-82; pres. Longman Group USA, Chgo., 1982-89; chmn., CEO Dearborn Pub. Group, Inc. (formerly Longman Group USA), 1989-98. Chmn. CTS Fin. Pub., 1997-2000. Author: Property Management, 1979; co-author: Modern Real Estate Practice, 1967, How to Profit From Real Estate, 1988 (Chgo. Book Clinic Lifetime Achievement award 1998). Mem. dean's adv. coun. Coll. Bus. U. Colo., 1992-98, Ctr. for Entrepreneurship Adv. Bd., U. Colo., 1996-2002; trustee Mystic Seaport Mus., 1989—, exec. com., 1999—2004, vice chair, 2001—2004; dir. Chgo. Maritime Soc., pres. 1999-2000; trustee The Burnham Inst., 2002—, San Diego Maritime Mus., 2002—, exec. com., 2003—, chair audit com., 2003—. Mem. Real Estate Educators Assn. (pres. 1981), Internat. Assn. Fin. Planning, Chgo. Book Clinic (bd. dirs.), Harvard Club NY, Chgo. Econs. Club, San Diego Yacht Club (chair history com. 2004—, bd. dirs. 2006—), NY Yacht Club, Explorers Club, Rotary. Avocations: yacht racing, skiing. Home: 2910 Owens St San Diego CA 92106 E-mail: rckyle@aol.com.

KYLES, CEDRIC ANTONIO (CEDRIC THE ENTERTAINER), comedian, actor; b. Jefferson City, Mo., Apr. 24, 1964; s. Rosetta Kyles; m. Lorna Wells, Sept. 3, 1999; children: Croix, Lucky Rose; 1 child from previous marriage, Tiara. Bachelor's in Mass Comm., S.E. Mo. State U., 1991. Actor: (Broadway plays) American Buffalo, 2008; (films) Ride, 1998, Big Momma's House, 2000, The Smoker, 2000, Kingdom Come, 2001, (voice) Dr. Dolittle 2, 2001, Barbershop, 2002, (voice) Ice Age, 2002, Serving Sara, 2002, Intolerable Cruelty, 2003, Barbershop 2: Back in Bus., 2004, Lemony Snicket's A Series of Unfortunate Events, 2004, Man of the House, 2005, Be Cool, 2005, The Honeymooners, 2005, (voice) Madagascar, 2005, Charlotte's Web, 2006, Talk to Me, 2007, Welcome Home Roscoe Jenkins, 2008, Street Kings, 2008, (voice) Madagascar: Escape 2 Africa, 2008, Cadillac Records, 2008; (TV series) The Steve Harvey Show, 1996—2002 (Image award for outstanding supporting actor comedy series, 1999, 2000, 2001, 2002); voice actor: The Proud Family, 2001 (Image award for outstanding supporting actor comedy series, 2003); host Black Entertainment TV's Comicview, 1993—94; creator, writer, prodr., actor, host Cedric the Entertainer Presents, 2002—03; exec. prodr. and comedian: (TV spl.) Cedric the Entertainer: Starting Lineup, 2002; prodr. and actor: (films) Johnson Family Vacation, 2004; actor, exec. prodr. Code Name: The Cleaner, 2007; performer: Kings of Comedy tour, 1997—2000. Co-founder CTE Charitable Found. Inc., 1995—. Named Richard Pryor Comic of Yr., Black Entertainment TV. Office: care of Marla Winston Entertainment Enterprises 401 Le Doux Rd Ste 401 Los Angeles CA 90048

KYSAR, RAYMOND L., state legislator; b. Hays, Kans., Jan. 21, 1931; BS, N.Mex. State U. Mem. N.Mex. Legislature, Santa Fe, 1988—, mem. rules com., mem. corps. and transp. com. Republican. Office: 300 W Arrington St Ste 100 Farmington NM 87401-8432

LABA, MARVIN, management consultant; b. Newark, Mar. 17, 1928; s. Joseph Abraham and Jean Cecil (Saunders) L.; m. Sandra Seltzer, Apr. 16, 1961 (div. May 1974); children: Stuart Michael, Jonathan Todd; m. Elizabeth Luger, June 11, 1974 (div. 1979). BBA, Ind. U., 1951. Buyer Bamberger's (Macy's N.J.), Newark, 1951-67; v.p., mdse. adminstr. Macy's N.Y., 1967-73; v.p., gen. mdse. mgr. Howland/Steinback, White Plains, NY, 1973-75, Pomeroy's, Levittown, Pa., 1975-76; v.p., gen. mdse. mgr., sr. v.p., exec. v.p. May Co. Calif., North Hollywood, 1976-79; pres., chief exec. officer G. Fox & Co. (div. of the May dept. stores), Hartford, Conn., 1979-82; pres. Richard Theobald & Assocs., LA, 1983; pres., chief exec. officer Marvin Laba & Assocs., LA, 1983—. With U.S. Army, 1946-48. Avocations: coins, tennis, theater, travel. Office: Marvin Laba & Assoc 4336 Whitsett Ave Ste 5 Studio City CA 91604 Home Phone: 818-761-7555; Office Phone: 818-762-2122. Personal E-mail: marvin@marvinlaba.com.

LABELLE, PATTI (PATRICIA LOUISE HOLTE), singer, entertainer; b. Phila., May 24, 1944; d. Henry and Bertha Holte; m. Armstead Edwards, 1969 (div. 2000); 5 children. PhD (hon.), Berkeley Sch. Music, 1996, Cambridge U., Drexel U. Singer Patti LaBelle and the BlueBelles, 1961—70; lead singer musical group LaBelle, 1970-76; solo performer, 1977—; entrepreneur Patti LaBelle's Fragrances & Cosmetics, 1995. Established clothing line Patti LaBelle Clothing, 2003—. Albums (with the BlueBelles) Sweethearts of the Apollo, 1963, Over the Rainbow, 1967, (with LaBelle) LaBelle, 1971, Moon Shadows, 1972, Pressure Cookin', 1973, Nightbirds, 1974, Phoenix, 1975, Chameleon, 1976, (solo) Patti LaBelle, 1977, Live at the Apollo, 1980, Gonna Take A Miracle-The Spirit's in It, 1981, I'm in Love Again, 1983, Winner in You, 1986, The Best of Patti LaBelle, 1987, Patti, 1985, Be Yourself, 1989, Burnin', 1991 (Grammy award best r&b vocalist, 1991), Live (Apollo Theater), 1992, Gems, 1994, Live! One Night Only, 1998 (Grammy award best trad. r&b vocal perf., 1998), Greatest Hits, 1996, Flame, 1997, When a Woman Loves, 2000, Timeless Journey, 2004, Patti Labelle: Classic Moments, 2005, Miss Patti's Christmas, 2007; actress (films) A Soldier's Story, 1984, Sing, 1989, On the One, 2005, Idlewild, 2006, Cover, 2007; (TV movies) For Colored Girls Who Have Considered Suicide, 1982, Working, 1982, Unnatural Causes, 1986, Fire and Rain, 1989, Parker Kane, 1990, Santa Baby! (voice), 2001, My Life in Idlewild, 2005, Why I Wore Lipstick to My Mastectomy, 2006; (TV series) A Different World, 1990-93, Out All Night, 1992; (guest appearances) Dolly, 1987, The Nanny, 1994, Cosby, 1997, All of Us, 2004; (TV specials) Live Aid, 1985, The Patti LaBelle Show, 1985, Sisters in the Name of Love, 1986 (CableACE award best perf. music special, 1987) Motown 30: What's Goin' On!, 1990, Sinatra Duets, 1994, The Remarkable Journey, 2000, Born to Diva, 2003, Nina Simone: A Tribute, 2003, VH1 Divas Live, 2004, (plays) Your Arms Too Short to Box with God (revival), 1980; author Don't Block the Blessings: Revelations of a Lifetime, 1997, LaBelle Cuisine: Recipes to Sing About, 1999, Patti's Pearls: Lessons in Living Genuinely, Joyfully & Generously, 2001, Patti LaBelle's Lite Cuisine; host (TV show) Living It Up with Patti LaBelle, 2004—. Spokesperson Am. Diabetic Assn., Nat. Minority AIDS Council, Nat. Cancer Inst., founder The Patti LaBelle Med. Ed. Scholarship Fund. Recipient award of Merit, Phila. Art Alliance, 1987, Entertainer of Yr. Image award NAACP, 1992, Soul Train Lifetime Achievement award, 1997, Excellence in Media award, Gay & Lesbian Alliance Against Defamation, 2007, Legend award for Outstanding Contbn. to R&B, World Music Awards, 2007; Walk of Fame honoree Black Entertainment TV, 2000. Office: c/o Richard De La Font Agy Ste 505 4845 S Sheridan Rd Tulsa OK 74145 also: c/o Brian Bunnin Internat Creative Mgmt 10250 Constellation Blvd Los Angeles CA 90067

LABELLE, THOMAS JEFFREY, research executive, academic administrator; b. Owen, Wis., Sept. 21, 1941; s. Wendell Allen and Katherine (Dolan) LaB.; m. Nancy Reik, June 16, 1966 (dec. 1981); children: Katherine Anne, Jeanette Marie AA, Pierce Coll., Woodland Hills, Calif., 1962; BA, Calif. State U., Northridge, 1964; MA, U. N.Mex., Albuquerque, 1967, PhD, 1969. Prof. UCLA, 1969-86, asst. dean edn., 1971-79, assoc. dean grad. div., 1980-86; prof. comparative and internat. edn. U. Pitts., 1986-90, dean Sch. Edn., 1986-90; v.p. acad. programs, provost Ga. State U., Atlanta, 1990-93; provost, v.p. acad. affairs and rsch. W.Va. U., Morgantown, 1993-96; provost v.p. acad. affairs San Francisco State U., 1996—2002; exec. dir. internat. and area studies U. Calif., Berkeley, 2002—05. Cons. InterAm. Found., US AID, Ford Found., CBS, Acad. Ednl. Devel., Juarez and Assocs.; disting. vis. prof. Obirin U., Tokyo, 2005—; adj. prof. Grad. Sch. Edn., U. Calif., Berkeley. Author: Education and Development in Latin America, 1972, Nonformal Education in Latin America and the Caribbean, 1986, Stability, Reform or Revolution, 1986, Education and Intergroup Relations, 1985, Multiculturalism and Education, 1994, Ethnic Studies and Multiculturalism, 1996. Vol. Peace Corps, Colombia, 1964-66. Grantee Fulbright Found., 1983, 96, InterAm. Found., Latin America, 1984; recipient Andres Bello award 1st Class, Venezuela, 1987. Fellow Soc. Applied Anthropology; mem. Comparative and Internat. Edn. Soc. (pres. 1981), Coun. on Anthropology and Edn. (bd. dirs. 1977), Inter-Am. Found. (chmn. learning fellowship on social change), Golden Key, Omicron Delta Kappa, Phi Kappa Phi. Democrat. Home: 1717 Ala Wai Blvd Apt 2906 Honolulu HI 96815 Personal E-mail: 921tom@gmail.com.

LABEOUF, SHIA, actor; b. LA, June 11, 1986; s. Jeffrey LaBeouf and Shayna Saide. Attended, Hamilton Acad. Music, LA. Co-founder Element record label, Grassy Slope prodn. co. Actor: (films) The Christmas Path, 1998, Monkey Business, 1998, Holes, 2003, Dumb and Dumber: When Harry Met Lloyd, 2003, Charlie's Angels: Full Throttle, 2003, The Battle of Shaker Heights, 2003, I, Robot, 2004, Constantine, 2005, The Greatest Game Ever Played, 2005, A Guide to Recognizing Your Saints, 2006 (Spl. Jury prize, Sundance Film Festival, 2006, Best actor, Gijón Internat. Film Festival, 2006), Bobby, 2006 (Hollywood Film award, Hollywood Film Festival, 2006), Disturbia, 2007 (Choice Movie Actor: Horror/Thriller, Teen Choice Awards, 2007), Transformers, 2007, (voice) Surf's Up, 2007, Indiana Jones and the Kingdom of the Crystal Skull, 2008, Eagle Eye, 2008; (TV films) Breakfast with Einstein, 1998, Hounded, 2001, Tru Confessions, 2002, The Even Stevens Movie, 2003; (TV series) Even Stevens, 1999—2003 (Outstanding Performer in a Children's Series, Daytime Emmy awards, 2003); writer, dir. (films) Let's Love Hate, 2004 (Children's Audience award, Newport Internat. Film Festival, 2005, 2nd place, Children's Jury award, Chgo. Internat. Children's Film Festival, 2004). Recipient Choice Movie: Breakout Male, Teen Choice Awards, 2007, Orange Rising Star award, Brit. Acad. Film and TV Arts, 2008; named Male Star of Tomorrow, ShoWest Convention, 2007; named one of Top 25 Entertainers of Yr., Entertainment Weekly, 2007.

LABONGE, TOM, councilman; b. Silver Lake, Calif., Oct. 6, 1953; s. Robert and Mary Louise Learnihan LaBonge; m. Brigid Manning; children: Mary-Catherine, Charles. Grad., Cal State LA. With Councilwoman Peggy Stevenson, Dist. 13 LA City Coun., 1976—78, field dep. to coun. pres. John Ferraro, Dist. 4, 1978, councilman, Dist. 4, 2001—; chief field ops. Mayor Richard J Riordan; dir. cmty. rels. LA Department Water & Power, 1997. Recipient Humanitarian of Yr. award, LA City Employee's Assn., 1997. Office: City Hall 200 N Spring St Rm 480 Los Angeles CA 90012 Office Phone: 213-485-3337. Office Fax: 213-624-7810. Business E-Mail: councilmember.labonge@lacity.org.*

LABOVITZ, EARL A., allergist; b. Cleveland, Miss., June 12, 1949; MD, U Miss, 1975. Allergist Desert Samaritan Hosp., Mesa, Ariz. Office: Mesa Tempe Allergy Asthma Cl 2915 E Baseline Rd Ste 121 Gilbert AZ 85234-2474

LABUDA, JEANNE, state legislator; Former HS tchr.; claims rep. Social Security Adminstrn.; asst. atty. gen. Colo. State Atty. General's Office; mem. Dist. 1 Colo. House of Reps., Denver, 2007—. Mem. Girl Scouts America (leader), Peace Corps (vol.), City Denver Planning Bd., Am. Assn. Univ. Women (officer), Harvey Pk. Improvement Assn. (bd. mem., pres.), Father Ed Judy House Cmty. Adv. Bd. Democrat. Office: Colo State Capitol 200 E Colfax Denver CO 80203 Office Phone: 303-866-2966. Business E-Mail: jeanne.labuda.house@state.co.us.*

LACHENBRUCH, ARTHUR HEROLD, geophysicist, researcher; b. New Rochelle, NY, Dec. 7, 1925; s. Milton Cleveland and Leah (Herold) L.; m. Edith Bennett, Sept. 7, 1950; children: Roger, Charles, Barbara. BA, Johns Hopkins U., 1950; MA, Harvard U., 1954, PhD, 1958. Registered geophysicist and geologist, Calif. Research geophysicist U.S. Geol. Survey, 1951—. Vis. prof. Dartmouth Coll., 1963; mem. numerous adv. coms. and panels. Contbr. articles to sci. jours. Mem. Los Altos Hills (Calif.) Planning Commn., 1966-86. Served with USAAF, 1943-46. Recipient Spl. Act award U.S. Geol. Survey, 1970, Meritorious Service award, 1972, Disting. Service award U.S. Dept. Interior, 1978. Fellow AAAS, Am. Geophys. Union (Walter H. Bucher medal 1989), Royal Astron. Soc., Geol. Soc. Am. (Kirk Bryan award 1963), Arctic Inst. N.Am.; mem. Nat. Acad. Sci. Achievements include current work: solid-earth geophysics, terrestial heat flow, tectonophysics, permafrost; subspecialties: tectonics, geophysics. Office: US Geol Survey 345 Middlefield Rd Menlo Park CA 94025-3591

LACHEY, NICK (NICHOLAS SCOTT LACHEY), singer, actor; b. Harlan, Ky., Nov. 9, 1973; s. John and Cate (Fopma-Leimbach) Lachey; m. Jessica Simpson, Oct. 26, 2002 (div. July 2006). Attended, Creative and Performing Arts, Cin., Ohio; studied acting, U. So. Calif., LA, Calif.; studied sports medicine, Miami U., Oxford, Ohio. Co-owner Tacoma Rainier's AAA Baseball Affiliate, 2006—. Singer (with 98 Degrees): (albums) 98°, 1997, 98° and Rising, 1998, This Christmas, 1999, Revelation, 2000; singer: (solo albums) SoulO, 2003, What's Left of Me, 2006 (Music-Choice Love Song and Choice Red Carpet Fashion Icon (Male), Teen Choice Awards, 2006); actor: (TV series) Newlyweds: Nick and Jessica, 2003—05, (TV) Nick & Jessica's Variety Hour, 2004, Nick & Jessica's Family Christmas, 2004, Nick & Jessica's Tour of Duty, 2005, Bewitched, 2005; guest appearances City Guys, 1998, As The World Turns, 1999, Mad TV, 2000, 2004, Just Shoot Me!, 2000, The Apprentice, 2004, Charmed (6 episodes), 2004, Hope & Faith, 2004. Mem.: Sigma Alpha Epsilon Fraternity.

LACHOWICZ, RACHEL, artist, educator; b. San Francisco, 1964; BFA, Calif. Inst. Arts, 1988. Adj. faculty art Claremont (Calif.) Grad. U., 1996—. One-woman shows include Dennis Anderson Gallery, L.A., 1989, 1991, Krygier/Landau Contemporary Art, Santa Monica, Calif., 1989, 1990, Shoshana Wayne Gallery, Santa Monica, 1991, 1993, 1996, Fawbush Gallery, N.Y.C., 1992, 1995, Newport Harbor Art Mus., Newport Beach, Calif., 1992, Rhona Hoffman Gallery, Chgo., 1993, Magazin 4 Vorarlberger Kunstverein, Bregenz, Austria, 1995, Dogenhaus Galerie, Berlin, 1997, Cristinerose Gallery, N.Y.C., 1998, Peggy Phekps Gallery, Claremont (Calif.) Grad. U., 1999, Kapinos Galerie for Zeitgenossische Kunst, Berlin, 2000, Cryo-Field Snap, L.A., 2001, Represented in permanent collections Denver Art Mus., Israel Mus., Jerusalem, L.A. County Mus. Art, Mus. Fine Art, Boston, Mus. Contemporary Art, L.A., Mus. Moderner Kunst, Palais Lichtenstein, Vienna, Orange County Mus. Art, Newport Beach, Whitney Mus. Am. Art, N.Y.C. Recipient Louis Comfort Tiffany Found. award, 1997; fellow, Skowhegan Sch. Painting and Sculpture, John Simon Guggenheim Meml. Found., 2003. Office: Claremont Grad Univ Art Dept 251 E Tenth St Claremont CA 91711

LACITIS, ERIK, journalist; b. Buenos Aires, Dec. 10, 1949; came to U.S., 1960, naturalized, 1965; s. Erik and Irene Z. L.; m. Malorie Nelson, Aug. 30, 1976. Student, Coll. Forest Resources, U. Wash., 1967-71. Editor U. Wash. Daily, 1970; pub. New Times Jour., 1970-71; reporter, pop-music cons. Seattle Post Intelligencer, 1972—; reporter, columnist Seattle Times, 1974—; v.p., treas. Malorie Nelson, Inc., 1980—; cons. editor Malheur Enterprise, 2006—. Bd. mem. Wash. News Coun., 2005. Recipient numerous awards from Wash. State chpt. Sigma Delta Chi; Nat. Headliners Club award, 1978; winner gen. interest competition Nat. Soc. Newspaper Columnists, 1987, 2003, Best of the West Journalism contest, 2000. Lutheran. Office: Fairview Ave N And John St PO Box 7070 Seattle WA 98133-2070 E-mail: lacitis@prodigy.net.

LACK, WALTER J., lawyer; b. LA, Jan. 10, 1948; BA, Loyola Marymount U., 1970, JD, 1973. Bar: Calif. 1973, US Ct. Appeals, Ninth Circuit 1979, US Supreme Ct. 1981. Ptnr. Engstrom, Lipscomb & Lack, LA. Lectr. in field; Superior Ct. arbitration panel, 1976—; mem. panel arbitrators Am. Arbitration Assn., 1976—; chairperson bar fee dispute com. LA County, 1979—; mem. standing com. on discipline Cent. Dist. Calif., 1997—2000; mem. Calif. Governor's Judicial Selection Com., 1998—2003, Governor's LA Judicial Selection Adv. Com., 1999—; dep. atty. gen. State N.Mex. Recipient Top 10 Calif. Jury Verdicts, Daily Journal Calif. Law Bus. award, 1993, 1994, 1996, 1999; named one of One Hundred Most Influential Lawyers in Calif., Daily Journal, 2000—04, Top 50 Litigators LA, LA Bus. Journal, 1999, 2001, LA 25 Most Powerful Atty., LA Bus. Jour., 2002. Fellow: Internat. Acad. Trial Lawyers (bd. dir. 2000—03); mem.: Trial Lawyers Pub. Justice, Consumer Atty. Calif. (bd. gov. 2001), Assn. Trial Lawyers Am., State Bar Calif., ABA, LA County Bar Assn. Office: Engstrom Lipscomb Lack 10100 Santa Monica Blvd Los Angeles CA 90067-4003 Office Phone: 310-552-3800.

LACKLAND, JOHN, lawyer, nurseryman; b. Parma, Idaho, Aug. 29, 1939; AB, Stanford U., 1962; JD, U. Wash., 1964; Master Gardener, Colo. State U., 1996. Bar: Wash. 1965, U.S. Dist. Ct. (we. dist.) Wash. 1965, (ea. dist.) Wash. 1973, U.S. Ct. Appeals (9th cir.) 1965, Conn. 1981, U.S. Dist. Ct. Conn. 1983, U.S. Supreme Ct. 1973, U.S. Dist. Ct. (so. dist.) N.Y. 1988; cert. profl. nurseryman, Idaho, 2005. Assoc. firm Lane Powell Moss & Miller, Seattle, 1965-69; asst. atty. gen. State of Wash., Seattle, 1969-72, asst. chief U. Wash. divsn., 1969-72; v.p., sec., gen. counsel Western Farmers Assn., Seattle, 1972-76, Fotomat Corp., Stamford, Conn., 1976-80; ptnr. Leepson & Lackland, 1981-88, Lackland and Nalewaik, 1988-92; pvt. practices Westport, Conn., 1992-94; prin. Lackland Assocs., Grand Junction, Colo., 1994—2002. Profl. nurseryman, 1995—; nursery mgr. Boutique Nursery, Twin Falls, Idaho, 2005; nurseryman Kimberly Nurseries, Twin Falls, 2004—07; mgr. Snake River Garden Ctr., Buhl, Idaho, 2007—08. Bd. dirs. Mercer Island (Wash.) Congl. Ch., 1967-70, pres. bd. dirs., 1970; mem. land use plan steering com. City of Mercer Island, 1970-72; bd. dirs. Mercer Island Sch. Dist., 1970-73, v.p. bd. dirs., 1972, pres. 1973; trustee Mid-Fairfield Child Guidance Ctr., 1982-84, Norfield Congl. Ch., 1982-84; bd. dirs. Grand Junction Symphony Orch., 1995-99.

LACROIX, PIERRE, professional sports team executive; b. Montreal, Aug. 3, 1948; m. Colombe Lacroix; children: Martin, Eric. Agt. NHL; gen. mgr. Quebec Nordiques, 1994—95, Colo. Avalanche, Denver, 1995—2006, also pres., interim gen. mgr., 2009—. Recipient Stanley Cup Championship, Denver Avalanche, 1996; named NHL Exec. of Yr., The Hockey News, 1996. Achievements include being the general manager of Stanely Cup Champion Colorado Avalanche, 1996, 2001. Office: Colo Avalanche Pepsi Ctr 100 Chopper Cir Denver CO 80204-1743

LACY, JOHN ROBERT, lawyer; b. Dallas, Dec. 15, 1942; BS, San Diego State U., 1966; MS, U. So. Calif., 1971; JD, U. Calif., 1973. Bar: Calif. 1973, Hawaii 1974. Atty. Goodsill Anderson Quinn & Stifel, Honolulu. Arbitrator Ct. Annexed Arbitration Program, 1986—, Nat. Assn. Security Dealers, 2006—. Comment editor Hastings Law Jour., 1972-73. Fellow: Am. Coll. Trial Lawyers; mem.: ABA, Maritime Law Assn. US, Am. Bd. Trial Advocates, State Bar Calif., Hawaii Bar Assn., Order of Coif, Thurston Soc. Office: Goodsill Anderson Quinn & Stifel PO Box 3196 1800 Alii Pl 1099 Alakea St Honolulu HI 96813-4511 Office Phone: 808-547-5600. Business E-Mail: jlacy@goodsill.com.

LADANYI, BRANKA MARIA, chemist, educator; b. Zagreb, Croatia, Sept. 7, 1947; arrived in U.S., 1969; d. Branko and Nevenka (Zilic) Ladanyi; m. Marshall Fixman, Dec. 7, 1974. BSc, McGill U., Montreal, Can., 1969; MPhil, Yale U., 1971, PhD, 1973. Vis. prof. of chemistry U. Ill., 1974; postdoctoral research assoc. Yale U., 1974-77, research assoc., 1977-79; asst. prof. chemistry Colo. State U., Ft. Collins, 1979-84, assoc. prof. chemistry, 1985-87, prof. chemistry, 1987—. Vis. fellow Joint Inst. for Lab. Astrophysics, 1993—94.

Assoc. editor Jour. Chem. Physics, 1994—, referee articles to profl. jours., —; contbr. articles to profl. jours. Grantee, NSF, DOE, NATO, 1983—89; fellow, Sloan Found., 1982—84, Dreyfus Found., 1983—87. Fellow: AAAS, Am. Phys. Soc.; mem.: Assn. Women in Sci., Am. Chem. Soc. (PRF grant 1979—82, 1989—91, 1995—98), Sigma Xi. Office: Colo State U Dept Chemistry Fort Collins CO 80523-1872 Business E-Mail: bl@lamar.colostate.edu.

LADD, DIANE, actress, writer, film director, producer; b. Laurel, Miss., Nov. 29, 1942; m. Bruce Dern, 1960 (div. 1969); 1 child, Laura; m. William Shea, Jr., 1973 (div. 1977); m. Robert C. Hunter, Feb. 14, 1999; stepchildren: Brandon Hunter, Amy Oleson, Emily Hunter. Grad., St. Aloysius Acad. Appearances include (films) The Wild Angels, 1966, Rebel Rousers, 1967, The Reivers, 1969, Macho Callahan, 1970, WUSA, 1970, White Lightning, 1973, Alice Doesn't Live Here Anymore, 1974, Chinatown, 1974, Embryo, 1976, The November Plan, 1976, All Night Long, 1981, Something Wicked This Way Comes, 1983, Black Widow, 1987, Plain Clothes, 1988, National Lampoon's Christmas Vacation, 1989, Wild at Heart, 1990, A Kiss Before Dying, 1991, Rambling Rose, 1991, Cemetery Club, 1992, Hold Me, Thrill Me, Kiss Me, 1992, Code Name: Chaos, 1992, Carnosaur, 1993, Father Hood, 1993, Spirit Realm, 1993, Obsession, 1994, Mrs. Munck (also dir., writer, co-prodr.), 1994, The Haunted Heart, 1995, Raging Angels, 1995, Ghosts of Mississippi, 1996, Mother (also exec. prodr.), 1996, Citizen Ruth, 1996, James Dean: Race With Destiny, 1997, Primary Colors, 1998, Daddy N Them, 1999, 28 Days, 2001, Rain, 2001, Law of Enclosures, 2001, Charlies War, 2002, World's Fastest Indian, 2005, Come Early Morning, 2005-06, When I Find the Ocean, 2006, Inland Empire, 2006, Jake's Corner, 2007, American Cowslip, 2008, Woman Inside, 2009 (also dir., writer, co-prodr.); (TV series) Alice, 1980-81; (TV movies) The Devil's Daughter, 1973, Thaddeus Rose and Eddie, 1978, Black Beauty, 1978, Willa, 1979, Guyana Tragedy: The Story of Jim Jones, 1980, Desperate Lives, 1982, Grace Kelly, 1983, I Married a Centerfold, 1984, Crime of Innocence, 1985, Celebration Family, 1987, Bluegrass, 1988, The Lookalike, 1990, Rock Hudson, 1990, Shadow of a Doubt, 1991, Hush Little Baby, 1994, Ruby Ridge: An American Tragedy, 1996, Breach of Faith: Family of Cops II, 1997, The Waiting Game, 1997, The Staircase, 1998, Sharing the Secret, 2000, Christy: The Movie, 2001, Aftermath, 2001, Damaged Care, 2002, Gracie's Choice, 2004; (TV miniseries) Cold Lazarus, 1996, Kristy, James Van Praag Story, Christy, Choices of the Heart, Part I & II, 2001, Stephen King's Kingdom Hospital, ABC, 2004 (15 hour TV spl.), Montana Sky, Lifetime, 2006; author: (book) Spiraling Through the School of Life: A Mental, Physical & Spiritual Discovery, 2006. Pres. Art and Culture Taskforce; bd. advisors Nat. Found. for Alt. Medicine, Washington. Recipient award Brit. Acad., Spirit award, Golden Globe award, Tor Broadway award, 3 Acad. award nominations, 4 Golden Globe nominations, 3 Emmy nominations for Guest Actress in a Series (Grace Under Fire), 1994, Dr. Quinn, Medicine Woman, Touched by an Angel; named Woman of Yr. City of Hope, 1992; recipient Achievement award Women in Film, 1992, PATH Angel award, 1992, Disting. Artist award LA Music Ctr., 1994, Hollywood Legacy award, 1994, 1st Time Dir. award Dla. Film Festival, 1996, Tribuate award Newport Festival, 1996. Mem.: Screen Actors Guild (nat. bd. dir.).

LADD, JAMES ROGER, international business executive, consultant; b. San Diego, Mar. 5, 1943; s. Robert Dwinell and Virginia Ruth (Dole) L.; m. Sharon Patricia Smith, Aug. 22, 1964; children— Brian Andrew, Jennifer Louise, Casey James AB, Duke U., 1964. CPA, CMC. With Deloitte Haskins & Sells, Seattle, 1964-79, mng. ptnr. Tokyo, 1979-84, dir. human resources NYC, 1984-86, area mng. ptnr. Seattle, 1986-89; mng. dir. Deloitte & Touche, Seattle, 1989-92; pres. Ladd Pacific Cons., Seattle, 1992-97; pres., CEO EnCompass Globalization Inc., Kirkland, Wash., 1997—2001; CFO,sr. v.p. fin. & ops. BSquare Corp., Bellevue, Wash., 2002—03; ptnr. Tatum Ptnrs., Seattle, 2004; exec. v.p., fin. and operations City U., Bellevue, Wash., 2004—. Bd. dirs., treas. Seattle Found., 1988—97; trustee Duke U., 1991—93; chair global bus. adv. bd. U. Wash., 1995—97, 2001—03; trustee United Way of King County Endowment Fund, 1993—, Wash. CPA Found., 2001—03; treas. United Way of King County, 1990—93; dir. Softrade Internat., 2000—; mem. audit com. Children's Hosp. and Regional Ctr. Med. Ctr., Seattle, 2003—. Mem. AICPA, Japan Am. Soc. State Wash. (chmn. 1996-98), Wash. Soc. CPAs, Duke Alumni Assn. (nat. pres. 1991-92), Inst. Mgmt. Cons., Rainier Club. Office: City University 11900 NE 1st St Bellevue WA 98005

LADEHOFF, ROBERT LOUIS, bishop; b. Feb. 19, 1932; m. Jean Arthur Burcham (dec. Feb. 1992); 1 child, Robert Louis Jr. Grad., Duke U., 1954, Gen. Theol. Sem., 1957, Va. Theol. Sem., 1980. Ordained deacon, priest The Episcopal Ch., 1957. Priest in charge N.C. parishes, 1957-60; rector St. Christopher's Ch., Charlotte, N.C., 1960-74, St. John's Ch., Fayetteville, 1974-85; bishop, co-adjutor of Oreg., 1985; bishop, 1986—.

LA DUC, JOHN, manufacturing executive; b. 1943; BS, Purdue U., 1965; MBA, Stanford U., 1967. Econ. analyst Conoco Inc., NYC, 1967-69; with Kaiser Aluminum Corp., 1969—, treas., 1987-89, exec. v.p., CFO, 1989—. Office: Kaiser Aluminum 27422 Portola Pkwy Ste 350 Foothill Ranch CA 92610-2837

LAFFER, ARTHUR BETZ, economist; b. Youngstown, Ohio, Aug. 14, 1940; s. William Gillespie Laffer; m. Traci Lynn Hickman; 6 children. BA, Yale U., 1963; MBA, Stanford U., 1965, Ph.D, 1971. Faculty mem. U. Chgo., 1967—76, assoc. prof. bus. economics, 1970—76; chief economist, Office Mgmt. & Budget Exec. Office of the Pres., Washington, 1970—72; prof. fin. & bus. economics U. So. Calif., LA, 1976-84, Charles B. Thornton prof. bus. economics, 1979-84; Disting. Univ. prof. Pepperdine U., 1984—87; founder, CEO Laffer Associates, 1979—; commentator, co-host MoneyMan Report BizRadio Network, 2007—; Disting. Univ. prof. economics Mercer U., 2008—. Cons. to sec. US Dept. Treasury, 1972—77; mem. Econ. Policy Adv. Bd. Exec. Office of the Pres., Washington, 1981—89; mem. exec. com. Reagan/Bush Fin. Com., 1984; co-chmn. Policy Coun. for the Free Enterprise Fund. Author: Supply Side Economics: Financial Decision -Making for the 80's; co-author (with Stephen Moore & Peter Tanous): The End of Prosperity: How Higher Taxes Will Doom the Economy-If We Let It Happen, 2008. Bd. dirs. Com. Monetary Research and Edn.; hon. bd. dirs. Los Angeles County Mus. Natural History; mem. adv. bd. Taxpayers Found. Recipient Commerce Assocs. Dean's Facility award U. So. Calif., 1979, Teaching Excellence award U. So. Calif. Assocs., 1980, John J. Knezevich Americanism award, 1979, Daniel Webster award Internat. Platform Assn., 1982, Father of Yr. award West Coast Fathers' Day Com., 1983 Republican. Achievements include the invention of the Laffer Curve. E-mail: jax@laffer.com.

LA FORCE, JAMES CLAYBURN, JR., economist, educator; b. San Diego, Dec. 28, 1928; s. James Clayburn and Beatrice Maureen (Boyd) La F.; m. Barbara Lea Latham, Sept. 23, 1952; children: Jessica, Allison, Joseph. BA, San Diego State Coll., 1951; MA, UCLA, 1958, PhD, 1962. Asst. prof. econs. UCLA, 1962-66, assoc. prof., 1967-70, prof., 1971-93, prof. emeritus, 1993—, chmn. dept. econs., 1969-78, dean Anderson Sch. Mgmt., 1978-93; acting dean Hong Kong U. Sci. & Tech., 1991-93. Bd. dirs. Arena Pharms., Payden & Rygel Investment Trust; adv. Series Trust; chmn. adv. com. Calif. Workmen's Compensation. Author: The Development of the Spanish Textile Industry 1750-1800, 1965, (with Warren C. Scoville) The Economic Development of Western Europe, vols. 1-5, 1969-70. Bd. dirs. Nat. Bur. Econ. Rsch., 1975-88, Found. Francisco Marroquin, Lynde and Harry Bradley Found., Pacific Legal Found., 1981-86; trustee Found. for Rsch. in Econs. and Edn., 1970—, chmn., 1977—; mem. bd. overseers Hoover Inst. on War, Revolution and Peace, 1979-85, 86-93; mem. nat. coun. on humanities NEH, 1981-88; chmn. Pres.'s Task Force on Food Assistance, 1983-84. Social Sci. Research Council research tng. fellow, 1958-60; Fulbright sr. research grantee, 1965-66; Am. Philos. Soc. grantee, 1965-66 Mem.: Mont Pelerin Soc., Econ. History Assn., Phi Beta Kappa. Office: UCLA Anderson Grad Sch Mgmt 405 Hilgard Ave Los Angeles CA 90095-9000

LA FORGIA, ROBERT M., management consultant, former hotel executive; BS summa cum laude, Providence Coll.; MBA, UCLA. With Hilton Hotels Corp., Beverly Hills, Calif., 1981—, v.p., corp. contr., 1994—96, sr. v.p., contr., 1996—2004, sr. v.p., CFO, 2004—06, exec. v.p., CFO, 2006—08; prin. The Atalon Group, Henderson, Nev., 2008—. Mem.: Nat Assn. Corp. Directors, Contr. Coun. Conf. Bd., Fin. Execs. Inst. Office: Atalon Group 1605 Lake Las vegas Pkwy Henderson NV 89011 Office Phone: 702-629-7260.

LAGOMARSINO, ROBERT JOHN, former congressman; b. Ventura, Calif., Sept. 4, 1926; s. Emilio J. and Marjorie (Gates) L.; m. Norma Jean Mabrey, Nov. 10, 1960; children: Dexter, Karen, Dana. BA, U. Calif., Santa Barbara, 1950; JD, U. Santa Clara, Calif., 1954. Bar: Calif. 1954. Pvt. practice, Ventura, 1954; mem. Ojai (Calif.) City Coun., 1958-61, mayor, 1958-61; mem. Calif. Senate, 1961-74, US Congress from 19th Calif. Dist., 1974—92; chmn. Mid-State Bank & Trust, emeritus dir.; v.p. Lagomarsino's. Mem. fgn. affairs com., house interior and insular affairs com., House Rep. study com., Asian and Pacific affairs subcom. US Congress from 9th Calif. Dist., co-chmn. Congl. Task Force on Afghanistan, vice chmn. subcom. western hemisphere affairs; chmn. House POW/MIA Task Force; Congl. observer Geneva Arms Control Talks. Former sec. Rep. Conf.; chmn. Nat. Rep. Inst. for Internat. Affairs. Served with USNR, 1944-46. Recipient Pearl Chase Conservation Edn. award, 1970, Legislator Conservationist of Year award Calif. Wildlife Fedn., 1965, Honor award Calif. Conservation Coun., 1967, Peace Officers Rsch. Assn. award, 1966, Santa Barbara medal U. Calif. at Santa Barbara, 1985; named U. Calif. Santa Barbara alumnus of Yr., 1974. Mem. Calif. Bar Assn., Ventura County Bar Assn., DC Bar Assn. Clubs: Elks, Moose, Eagles, Rotary. Republican. Roman Catholic. Office: Mid-State Bank & Trust 1026 E Grand Ave Arroyo Grande CA 93420

LAGORIA, GEORGIANNA MARIE, curator, writer, editor, visual art consultant; b. Oakland, Calif., Nov. 3, 1953; d. Charles Wilson and Margaret Claire (Vella) L.; m. David Joseph de la Torre, May 15, 1982; 1 child, Mateo Joseph. BA in Philosophy, Santa Clara U., 1975; MA in Museology, U. San Francisco, 1978. Exhbn. coord. Allrich Gallery, San Francisco, 1977-78; asst. registrar Fine Arts Mus., San Francisco, 1978-79; gallery coord. de Saisset Mus., Santa Clara, Calif., 1979-80, asst. dir., 1980-83, dir., 1983-86, Palo Alto (Calif.) Cultural Ctr., 1986-91; ind. writer, editor and cons. mus. and visual arts orgns., Hawaii, 1991-95; dir. The Contemporary Mus., Honolulu, 1995—. V.p. Non-Profit Gallery Assn., San Francisco, 1980-82; bd. dirs. Fiberworks, Berkeley, Calif., 1981-85; field grant reviewer Inst. Mus. Svcs., Washington, 1984, 85, 97, 98; adv. bd. Hearst Art Gallery, Moraga, Calif., 1986-89, Womens Caucus for Art, San Francisco, 1987—; mem. adv. bd. Weigand Art Gallery, Notre Dame Coll., Belmont, Calif. Curator exhbns. The Candy Store Gallery, 1980, Fiber '81, 1981; curator, author exhbn. catalogue Contemporary Hand Colored Photographs, 1981, Northern Calif. Art of the Sixties, 1982, The Artist and the Machine: 1910-1940, 1986; author catalogue, guide Persis Collection of Contemporary Art at Honolulu Advertiser, 1993; co-author: The Little Hawaiian Cookbook, 1994; coord. exhbn. selections Laila and Thurston Twigg-Smith Collection and Toshiko Takaezu ceramics for Hui No'eau Visual Arts Ctr., Maui, 1993; editor Nuhou (newsletter Hawaii State Mus. Assn.), 1991-94; spl. exhbn. coord. Honolulu Acad. Arts, 1995; dir. The Contemporary Mus., Honolulu, 1995—. Mem. Arts Adv. Alliance, Santa Clara County, 1985-86; grant panelist Santa Clara County Arts Coun., 1987; mem. art adv. bd. Kapiolani C.C., 1994—. Exhbn. grantee Ahmanson Found., 1981, NEA, 1984, Calif. Arts Coun., 1985-89 Mem. Am. Assn. Mus., ArtTable, 1983—, Calif. Assn. Mus. (bd. dirs. 1987-89), Assn. Art Mus. Dirs., Hawaiian Craftsmen (bd. dirs. 1994-95), Honolulu Jr. League, Key Project (bd. dirs. 1993-94). Democrat. Roman Catholic. Avocations: dance, writing. Home and Office: 47-665 Mapele Rd Kaneohe HI 96744-4918

LAHTI, CHRISTINE, actress; b. Detroit, Apr. 4, 1950; d. Paul Theodore and Elizabeth Margaret (Tabar) L.; m. Thomas Schlamme, Sept. 4, 1983; children Wilson, Joseph, Emma. BA in Lang., Speech, Drama, U. Mich., 1972; MFA, Fla. State U., 1972-73; studies with William Esper, Uta Hagen, Herbert Berghof Studios. Actress: (stage prodns.) The Woods, 1978 (Theater World award 1979), Division Street, 1980, Loose Ends, 1981, Present Laughter, 1983, Landscape of the Body, 1984, The Country Girl, 1984, Cat on a Hot Tin Roof, 1985, Little Murders, 1987 (Obie award), The Heidi Chronicles, 1989, Three Hotels, 1993; regular mem. cast (TV series) Dr. Scorpion, 1978, The Harvey Korman Show, 1978, Chicago Hope, 1995-1999 (Golden Globe award, best actress in a leading role drama series, 1998, Emmy award, 1998), Jack & Bobby, 2004 (TV films) The Last Tenant, 1978, The Henderson Monster, 1980, The Executioner's Song, 1982, Single Bars, Single Women, 1984, Love Lives On, 1985, Amerika, 1987, No Place Like Home, 1989 (Golden Globe award, best actress in a leading role mini-series or TV movie, 1989), Crazy from the Heart, 1991, The Fear Inside, 1992, The Good Fight, 1985, The Four Diamonds, 1995, Subway Stories: Tales from the Underground, 1997, Hope, 1997, An American Daughter, 2000, The Pilot's Wife, 2002, Out of the Ashes, 2003, The Book of Ruth, 2004, Revenge of the Middle-Aged Woman, 2004 (feature films) ...And Justice For All, 1979, Whose Life Is It, Anyway?, 1981, Swing Shift, 1984 (N.Y. Film Critics Circle award for best supporting actress 1985, Acad. award nominee 1985, Golden Globe award nominee 1985), Ladies and Gentlemen: The Fabulous Stains, 1985, Just Between Friends, 1986, Housekeeping, 1987, Season of Dreams, 1987, Stacking, 1988, Running on Empty, 1988, Gross Anatomy, 1989, Miss Firecracker, 1989, Funny About Love, 1990, The Doctor, 1991, Leaving Normal, 1992, Hideaway, 1995, Pie in the Sky, 1995, A Weekend in the Country, 1996, Smart People, 2008, Obsessed, 2009; prodr. short action film, actress: Lieberman in Love, 1995 (Oscar award, 1995, Acad. award nominee for best live action short film, 1996). Recipient Susan B. Anthony Failure is Impossible award, High Falls Film Festival, 2005. Office: ICM c/o Toni Howard 8942 Wilshire Blvd Beverly Hills CA 90211-1934

LAIDLAW, VICTOR D., construction executive; b. 1946; Officer Moran Cons., Alhambra, Calif., 1972-88; pres. Koll Cons., 1988-2000; ptnr. Focus Real Estate L.P., Irvine, Calif. Office: Focus Real Estate LP 3184 Airway Ave Ste H Costa Mesa CA 92626-4619 E-mail: vlaidlaw@focusrelp.com.

LAING, STEVEN O., former school system administrator; MEd in Ednl. Adminstrn., Brigham Young U., EdD in Ednl. Leadership. With Cedar City high sch., 1976—87; dir. secondary edn. Iron Sch. Dist.; supt. Box Elder Sch. Dist., 1990—97; assoc. supt. Utah State Office Edn., 1997—99; state supt. pub. instrn. Utah State Bd. Edn., 1999—2004.

LAIRD, DAVID, humanities educator emeritus; b. Marshfield, Wis., Oct. 17, 1927; s. Melvin Robert and Helen Melissa (Connor) L.; m. Helen Astrid Lauritzen, Sept. 10, 1955; 1 child, Vanessa Ann. PhB, U. Chgo., 1947; BA with highest honor, U. Wis., 1950, MA, 1951, PhD, 1955; postgrad., Courtauld Inst., 1953. Instr. to asst. prof. Oberlin Coll., 1955-58; mem. faculty Calif. State U., LA, 1958—, chmn. dept. English, 1969-73, chmn. dept. Am. studies, 1977-79. Nat. Humanities Inst. fellow U. Chgo., 1978-79; sr. Fulbright lectr. U. Tunis, Tunisia, 1979-80; fellow Folger Shakespeare Libr., 1982; Fulbright lectr. Odense U. (Denmark), 1983-84; vis. prof. U. Ottawa, 1984-85; cons. to Choice. Mem. editorial bd. Jour. Forest History; contbr. articles on Shakespeare, Am. lit. and cultural history to profl. jours. Mem. Western Shakespeare Seminar, Friends of Huntington Libr. Recipient Outstanding Prof. award Calif. State U., 1987, Nat. Endowment for the Humanities Summer Seminar award Northwestern U., 1989; Uhrig Found. grantee, 1964-65; Fulbright fellow, 1953-54. Mem. MLA, Malone Soc., Am. Studies Assn., Phi Beta Kappa. Home: 208 S Cherry Ave Marshfield WI 54449-3732 Office: Calif State U Humanities Dept Los Angeles CA 90032 Business E-Mail: laird208@wctc.net.

LAIRD, JERE DON, news reporter; b. Topeka, Aug. 8, 1933; s. Gerald Howard and Vivian Gertrude (Webb) L.; m. Alexandra Berezowsky, Aug. 4, 1957; children: Lee, Jennifer, Christopher. BA in Journalism, U. Nev., 1960. Disc jockey Sta. KHBC Radio, Hilo, Hawaii, 1949-50; announcer, chief engr. Sta. KOLO Radio, Reno, Nev., 1951-58; program dir. Sta. KOLO-TV, Reno, 1958-60; news reporter Sta. KCRA Radio and TV, Sacramento, Calif., 1960-61, Sta. KRLA Radio, LA, 1962-63; news reporter, editor Sta. KNXT-TV, LA, 1964-68; news reporter, fin. editor Sta. KNX-CBS Radio, LA, 1968—; fin. reporter Sta. KCBS-TV, LA, 1990—. Lectr. U. So. Calif., L.A., 1984-85; instr. Calif. State U., Northridge, 1978-79. Cpl. U.S. Army, 1953-55. Recipient Emmy award, L.A., 1964, Peabody award, U. Ga., 1984, Best Bus. News award, L.A. Press Club, 1983, 84, 86, 87, 88, 89, Martin K. Gainsburgh award, Fiscal Policy Coun., Fla., 1978. Mem. Radio TV News Assn. (bd. dirs. 1966-68, Golden Mike award 1984), Sigma Delta Chi. Avocation: sailing.

LAIRD, JOHN, state legislator; b. Santa Rosa, Calif., 1950; California State Assemblyman, District 27, 2002-; Commr, Santa Cruz Regl Transportation Comm, 1981-90; Director, Santa Cruz Metro Transit District, 1981-90; Assistant of Monterey Bay Area Govts, 1981-93; Mayor, Santa Cruz, formerly.Analyst, Santa Cruz Co Govt. Legislator of Year, Children's Advocacy Inst, Faculty Association California Community Cols; Environ Leadership Award, California League Conserv Voters. Cabrillo Col (board director); Santa Cruz AIDS Project (exec director, 1991-94); Area Agency on Aging Advisor Coun (chairman); others. Democrat. Mailing: State Capitol PO Box 942849 Rm 6026 Sacramento CA 94249 Office Phone: 916-319-2027. Fax: 916-319-2127. E-mail: assemblymember.Laird@assembly.ca.gov.

LAITIN, DAVID DENNIS, political science professor; b. Bklyn., June 4, 1945; s. Daniel and Frances (Blumenkranz) L.; m. Delia Fortune; children: Marc Oliver, Anna Elizabeth. BA, Swarthmore Coll., 1967; PhD, U. Calif., Berkeley, 1974. Instr. Nat. Tchr. Edn. Ctr., Afgoy, Somalia, 1969; master Grenada Boys' Secondary Sch., West Indies, 1970-71; asst. prof. dept. polit. sci. U. Calif.-San Diego, La Jolla, 1975-79, prof., 1984-87, chmn., 1986-87; reader dept. polit. sci. U. Ife, Nigeria, 1979-80; prof. polit. sci., dir. Wilder House Ctr. for Study Politics, History and Culture U. Chgo., 1987-99, William R. Kenan, Jr. prof., 1992—99; prof. polit. sci. Stanford U., Calif., 1999—, James T. Watkins IV and Elise V. Watkins prof. polit. sci. Calif., 2005—. Expert witness fgn. affairs subcom. U.S. Ho. Reps., 1981; resident Rockefeller Found., Bellagio Ctr., Sept. 1996. Author: Politics, Language and Thought: The Somali Experieince, 1977, Hegemony and Culture: Politics and Religious Change Among the Yoruba, 1986, Somalia: A Nation in Search of a State, 1987, Language Repertoires and State Construction in Africa, 1992, (with James Fearon) Explaining Ethnic Couperation, 1996, Identity in Formation: The Russian-Speaking Populations of the Near Abroad, 1998, (with James Fearon) Ethnicity, Insurgency and Civil War, 2003, (with Alan B. Krueger) Misunderestimating Terrorism, 2004, Nations, States and Violence, 2007. Fellow NEH, 1979-80, Howard Found., 1984-85, German Marshall Fund, 1984-85, John Simon Guggenheim Found., 1995-96, Harry F. Guggenheim Found., 1997—, Ctr. for Advanced Study in Behavioral Scis., 1989-2000, Russell Sage Found., 2003-2004; co-prin. investigator award NSF, 1993-95, 2002—; recipient award Am. Assn. for the Advancement of Slavic Studies, Dogan award Soc. for Comparative Rsch.; co-prin. investigator award Carnegie Found., 2000-01. Mem. Am. Polit. Sci. Assn. (v.p. 2005-06, 2 awards), Am. Acad. Arts and Scis., Coun. Am. Polit. Sci. Assn., NAS. Office: Stanford U Dept Polit Sci Stanford CA 94305 Office Phone: 650-725-9556. Business E-Mail: dlaitin@stanford.edu.

LAKE, BRUCE MENO, physicist; b. LA, Nov. 22, 1941; s. Meno Truman and Jean Ivy (Hancock)_ L. BS in Engring., Princeton U., 1963; MS, Calif. Inst. Tech., 1965, PhD, 1969. Mem. tech. staff advanced instrumentation dept. TRW Corp., Redondo Beach, Calif., 1969-73, head exptl. hydrodynamics sect., 1973-81, asst. mgr. dept. fluid mechanics, 1977-81, mgr. dept. fluid mechanics, 1981-96, mgr. computational physics bus. area, 1996-2000; pvt. cons., 2000—. Contbr. articles to profl. jours. and books. Ford Found. fellow,

1964-65, TRW tech. fellow. Mem. Am. Phys. Soc., Nat. Acad. Engring. Office: 41650 Calle Pino Murrieta CA 92562 Business E-Mail: blake@alumni.princeton.edu.

LAKE, JOSEPH EDWARD, ambassador; b. Jacksonville, Tex., Oct. 18, 1941; s. Lloyd Euel and Marion Marie (Allen) L.; m. Sarah Ann Bryant (div.); children: Joseph Edward, Mary Elizabeth; m. Jo Ann Kessler, June 12, 1971; 1 child, Michael Allen. BA summa cum laude, Tex. Christian U., 1962, MA, 1967. 3rd sec. U.S. Embassy, Taipei, Taiwan, 1963-65, Bur. of European Affairs Dept. State, 1966-67; second sec. U.S. Embassy, Cotonou, Dahomey, 1967-69; with bur. intelligence and rsch. Dept. State, 1969-71; second sec. U.S. Embassy, Taipei, Taiwan, 1971-76; with office Philippine affairs Dept. State, 1976-77; second sec. U.S. Embassy, Lagos, Nigeria, 1977-78; prin. officer and consul U.S. Consulate, Kaduna, Nigeria, 1978-81; with Fgn. Svc. Inst., Washington, 1981-82; first sec. U.S. Embassy, Sofia, Bulgaria, 1982-84, charge d'affaires, 1984, counselor, dep. chief mission, 1984-85; dep. dir. regional affairs, bur. East Asian and Pacific Affairs Dept. State, 1985-86; advisor U.S. delegation 41st UN Gen. Assembly, 1986; dir. ops. ctr. Dept. State, Washington, 1987-90; amb. to Rep. of Mongolia, Ulaanbaatar, 1990-93, Rep. of Albania, Tirana, 1994-96; dep. asst. sec. of state for info. mgmt. Dept. State, Washington, 1996-97; chair com. Messaging and Interagy Collaboration, Dept. State, Washington, 2002—05; dir. internat. affairs City of Dallas, 1997—2002; sr. insp. Dept. State, Washington, 2006; rsch. assoc. Tower Ctr. So. Meth. U. Mem. adv. bd. Asian studies program So. Meth. U., 2002-07 Contbr. articles to profl. jours. Chair com. Mgmt. Return Dept. State, Washington, 2007-08 Mem.: Am. Fgn. Svc. Assn. Home: 790 SE Webbes St Apt 205 Portland OR 97202

LAKE, RICKI (PAMELA), talk show host, actress; b. NYC, Sept. 21, 1968; m. Rob Sussman (separated); children Milo Sebastian, Owen Tyler Syndicated talk show host Ricki Lake, 1993—. Movie appearances include: Hairspray, 1988, Working Girl, 1988, Cookie, 1989, Cry-Baby, 11990, Last Exit to Brooklyn, 1989, Where the Day Takes You, 1992, Inside Monkey Zetterland, 1993, Serial Mom, 1994, Cabin Boy, 1994, Skinner, 1995, Mrs. Winterbourne, 1996, Cecil B. DeMented, 2000, Park, 2006; TV appearances include (series) China Beach, 1990, Kate and Allie, Fame, King of Queens, 2001, (spls.) A Family Again, 1988, Starting Now, 1989, Gravedale High, 1990, (movies) Babycakes, 1989, The Chase, 1991, Based on an Untrue Story, (pilot) Starting Now; stage actress: A Girl's Guide to Chaos, 1990, (off-Broadway) The Early Show, Youngsters, 1983; host Game Show Marathon, 2006. Recipient Gracie Allen award, Am. Women in Radio & TV, 2001, Angel award (2), Excellence in Media. also: WMA 151 S El Camino Dr Beverly Hills CA 90212-2704 also: 8530 Wilshire Blvd Beverly Hills CA 90211

LAKEFIELD, BRUCE R., air transportation executive; b. Jan. 29, 1944; m. Bernadine J. Lakefield; 2 children. BS, US Naval Acad., 1967. With Lehman Bros. Inc., 1974—99; chmn., CEO Lehman Bros. Internat., 1995—99; mng. dir. Lehman Bros. Inc., 1996—99, COO, 1999; non.-exec. dir. Constellation Corp., PLC, 2000—04; pres., CEO US Airways, Inc., 2004—07, US Airways Group, Inc., 2004—07, vice-chmn., 2007—. Sr. adv. investment policy com. HGK Asset Mgmt., 2000—04; mem. bd. dirs. US Airways Group, 2003—; non-exec. dir. Constellation Corp. PLC. With USN, 1968—71, with USNR, 1971—90, ret. as comdr., 1990. Office: US Airways Group 111 W Rio Salado Pkwy Tempe AZ 85281

LAKOFF, GEORGE, linguistics professor; PhD in Linguistics, Ind. U., Bloomington, 1966. Lectr. Harvard U., Cambridge, Mass., 1965—69, U. Mich., Ann Arbor, 1969—71, Stanford U. Ctr. Advanced Study in the Behavioral Scis., Calif., 1971—72; prof. linguistics U. Calif., Berkeley, 1972—. Sr. fellow Rockridge Inst.; mem. adv. bd. Frameworks Inst. Co-author (with M. Johnson): Metaphors We Live By, 1980; author: Women, Fire, and Dangerous Things, 1987; co-author (with M. Turner): More Than Cool Reason, 1989; author: Moral Politics, 1996, Philosophy In The Flesh, 1999; co-author (with R. Núñez): Where Mathematics Comes From: How the Embodied Mind Brings Mathematics into Being, 2000; author: Whose Freedom?: The Battle Over America's Most Important Idea, 2006. Achievements include research in conceptual analysis within cognitive linguistics. Office: Univ Calif Berkeley Dept Linguistics 1203 Dwinelle Hall #2650 Berkeley CA 94720-2650 Office Phone: 510-642-2757. Office Fax: 510-643-5688. Business E-Mail: lakoff@berkeley.edu.*

LAKSHMI, PADMA, actress, television host, model; b. Madras, India, Sept. 1, 1970; m. Salman Rushdie, Apr. 17, 2004 (separated). BA in Theater Arts, Clark U., Mass. Founder Lakshmi Films. Actor: (films) Glitter, 2001, Boom, 2003, The Darkness and the Light, Caribbeans, Mistress of Spices; (TV miniseries) The Ten Commandments, 2006, Sharpe's Challenge, 2006; host (TV series) Dominica In, Rai TV, Padma's Passport, Food Network, Top Chef, Bravo, 2006—, (documentaries) Planet Food; author: (cookbook) Easy Exotic, 2003 (Best First Book, World Cookbook Awards, Versailles, 1999); appeared in Vogue, Elle, In Style, modeled for Ralph Lauren, Alberta Ferretti, Herve Leger, La Perla, Roberto Cavalli. Global amb. Keep a Child Alive. Named one of World's Most Successful Super Models, Max Mag., 1997, The 50 Most Powerful Women in NYC, NY Post, 2008. Office: Bravo c/o NBC Entertainment 3000 W Alameda Ave Burbank CA 91523*

LAL, DEVENDRA, nuclear geophysics educator; b. Varanasi, India, Feb. 14, 1929; s. Radhe Krishna and Sita Devi L.; m. Aruna Damany, May 17, 1955 (dec. July 1993). BS, Banaras Hindu U., Varanasi, 1947, MS, 1949, DSc (hon. causa), 1984; PhD, Bombay U., 1960. Research student Tata Inst. of Fundamental Research, Bombay, 1949-60, research fellow, fellow, assoc. prof., 1960-63, prof., 1963-70, sr. prof., 1970-72; dir. Phys. Research Lab., Ahmedabad, India, 1972-83, sr. prof., 1983-89; vis. prof. UCLA, 1965-66, 83-84; prof. Scripps Instn. Oceanography, La Jolla, Calif., 1967—. Editor: Early Solar System Processes and the Present Solar System, 1980, Biogeochemistry of the Arabian Sea, 1995. Recipient K.S. Krishnan Gold medal Indian Geophys. Union, 1965, Shanti Swarup Bhatnagar award for Phys. Sciences, Coun. Scientific and Indsl. Rsch., 1971, award for Excellence in Sci. and Tech., Gedn. of Indian Chamber Com., 1974, Pandit Jawaharlal Nehru award for Scis., 1986, Group Achievement award NASA, 1986, Raman Birth Centenary award, 1996, V.M. Goldschmidt medal, 1997. Fellow AAAS, Royal Soc. London, Indian Nat. Sci. Acad., Indian Acad. Scis., Geol. Soc. India (hon.), Phys. Rsch. Lab. Ahmedabad, Tata Inst. Fundamental Rsch., Geochem. Soc. USA, Am. Geophys. Union; mem. NAS U.S.A. (fgn. assoc.), Third World Acad. Scis. (founding mem.), Indian Geophys. Union, NAS India, Royal Astron. Soc. (assoc.), Internat. Acad. Aeronautics, Internat. Union of Geodesy and Geophysics (pres. 1984-87), Am. Acad. Arts and Scis. (fgn., hon.), Internat. Assn. Phys. Sci. of Ocean (hon., pres. 1979-83). Hindu. Avocations: chess, photography, painting, puzzles. Office: U Calif Scripps Inst Oceanography 9500 Gilman Dr GRD-0244 La Jolla CA 92093-0244 Home: No 20 Jayantilal Park Amli Bopal Rd Village Makarba Ahmedabad 380009 India Office Phone: 858-534-2134. Fax: 858-822-3310. Business E-Mail: dlal@ucsd.edu.

LALANNE, JACK (FRANÇOIS HENRI LALANNE), physical fitness specialist, entrepreneur; b. San Francisco, Calif., Sept. 26, 1914; m. Elaine LaLane, 1959; children: Jon Allen, Yvonne, Janet (dec.). Opened first gym Jack LaLanne's Physical Culture Studio, Oakland, Calif., 1936; host The Jack LaLanne Show, 1956-70, Jack LaLanne and You, 1981-83; spokesperson Jack LaLanne Juicing products. Released Jack LaLanne's Glamour Stretcher Time (album), 1959, Jack LaLalanne's Low Impact Plus Workout Featuring Kim Scott (video), 1988; books inlclude: The Jack LaLanne Way to Vibrant Good Health, 1960, Foods for Glamour, 1961, For Men Only, with a Thirty-Day Guide to Looking Better and Feeling Younger, 1973, Revitalize Your Health: Improve Your Health, Your Sex Life & Your Look after Age Fifty, 1995, Revitalize Your Life, Total Juicing; DVDs and Videoes include: The Jack LaLanne Way, The Jack LaLanne Show Commemorative Special, Hydronastics Exercises, Back to Basics Chair Exercises, Forever Young and Face-a-Tonic. Named to Calif. Hall of Fame, 2008. Office: Befit Enterprises Inc PMB 151 430 Quintana Rd Morro Bay CA 93442

LAM, CAROL CHIEN-HUA, lawyer; b. NYC, June 26, 1959; BA in Philosophy, Yale U., 1981; JD, Stanford U., 1985. Law clk. to Hon. Irving R. Kaufman US Ct. Appeals (2nd cir.), 1985—86; asst. US atty. (so. dist.) Calif. US Dept Justice, 1986—97; chief, major fraud sect. US Dept. Justice, 1997—2000, US atty. (so. dist.) Calif., 2002—07; sr. v.p., legal counsel QUALCOMM Inc., San Diego, 2007—. Recipient Spl. Achievement award, US Dept. Justice, 1990—94, 1997—99, Dir.'s award for Superior Performance as an Asst. US Atty., 1994, Health & Human Svc. Inspector Gen.'s Integrity award, 1995, Atty. Gen.'s award for Disting. Svc., 1997, Health & Human Svc. Inspector Gen.'s award for Exceptional Achievement, 1997, Outstanding Lawyer of Yr., San Diego County Bar Assn., 2007; named one of Top 100 Calif. Lawyers, LA Daily Jour., 2007, 75 Top Women Litigator, Nat. Law Jour., 2007. Office: QUALCOMM Inc 5775 Morehouse Dr San Diego CA 92121

LA MAINA, FRANCIS C., performing company executive; Formerly exec. v.p. dick clark prodns., inc., Burbank, Calif.; now pres., chief operating officer Dick Clark Prodns., inc., Burbank, Calif. Office: Dick Clark Prodns inc 3003 W Olive Ave Burbank CA 91505-7811

LAMBERSON, JOHN ROGER, insurance company executive; b. Aurora, Mo., Aug. 16, 1933; s. John Oral Lamberson and Golda May (Caldwell) Tidwell; m. Virginia Lee, Aug. 10, 1957; 1 child, John Clinton. BA, U. Calif., Berkeley, 1954. Coach, tchr. Thousand Palms (Calif.) Sch., 1954-55; underwriter trainee Fireman's Fund Ins. Co., San Francisco, 1955; surety mgr. Safeco Ins. Co. (formerly Gen. Ins. Co.), San Francisco and Sacramento, Calif., 1957-61; pres., COO Willis Corroon Corp., NYC, 1966-92, also bd. dirs., chmn. constrn. industry div., mem. exec. com., aquisition com.; pres., chmn., CEO Lamberson Consulting LLC, San Francisco, 1992—. Bd. dirs. Willis Corroon Group PLC, London, Consumers Benefit Life Ins. Co., Constrn. Inst., Griffith Co., Rosendin Electric, Sheedy Drayage Co., Valentine Corp. Mem. ASCE (bd. dirs. Construction Institute), Nat. Assn. Heavy Engring. Constructors (bd. dirs. 1985—, Golden Beavers award for outstanding svc. to industry), Constrn. Fin. Mgmt. Assn. (bd. dirs. 1987-91, exec. com.), Assoc. Gen. Contractors Am. (membership devel. com., past chmn. bd. dirs. nat. assoc. mems. coun.), Assoc. Gen. Contractors Calif. (bd. dirs. 1976), Nat. Acad. Constrn., Consulting Contractors Coun. Am., Beavers Charitable Trust(bd. trustee), Nat. Assn. Surety Bond Prodrs. (past nat. dir., regional v.p.), Am. Inst. Contractors, Soc. Am. Mil. Engrs., The Moles-Heavy Engring. Constrn. Soc., Young Pres. Orgn. (sem. leader), Bankers Club, Sharon Heights Golf and Country Club, Bermuda Dunes Country Club, Villa Taverna Club. Home: 85 Greenoaks Dr Atherton CA 94027-2160 Office: Lamberson Consulting LLC 580 California St Ste 500 San Francisco CA 94104-1000 Home Phone: 650-322-9641; Office Phone: 415-439-4822. E-mail: jrlamberson@mindspring.com.

LAMBERT, FREDERICK WILLIAM, lawyer, educator; b. Millburn, NJ, Feb. 12, 1943; m. Barbara E. Fogell, Aug. 13, 1965; children: Elisabeth, Mark. BA, U. Mich., 1965, JD, 1969. Bar: Ohio 1969, Fla. 1973, Calif. 1973, U.S. Supreme Ct. 1975. Law clk. to Stanley N. Barnes, U.S. Cir. Judge U.S. Cir. Ct., LA, 1969-70; atty. advisor Office Legal Counsel U.S. Dept. Justice, Washington, 1970-71; law clk. to Justice William H. Rehnquist U.S. Supreme Ct., Washington, 1971-72; pvt. practice LA, 1973-90; acting gen. counsel Itel Corp., San Francisco, 1981-82; ptnr. Adams, Duque & Hazeltine, LA, 1985-90, chmn. bus. law dept., 1989-90; assoc. prof. Hastings Coll. Law, U. Calif., San Francisco, 1993-99, prof. law, 1999—. Vis. prof. U. Mich. Law Sch., Ann Arbor, 1990-91, Duke Law Sch., Durham, N.C., 1992-93, U. Leiden; bd. faculty advisors William H. Rehnquist Found., 2007—. Mem. Am. Law Inst., Am. Law and Econs. Assn., Econ. Round Table of LA, Calif. State Bar Assn Home: 1100 Pilarcitos Ave Half Moon Bay CA 94019-1459

LAMBERT, JAMES L., data storage systems company executive; b. 1954; BS in Civil and Environ. Engring., MS in Civil and Environ. Engring., U. Wis. Various positions CALMA divsn. GE Co., 1979-81, v.p. R&D, 1981-84; pres., CEO, dir. Artecon, 1984; co-CEO, COO, pres., dir. Dot Hill Sys. Corp., Carlsbad, Calif., 1999, pres., CEO, 2000—. Dir. Nordic Group of Cos., Snow Valley, Inc. Office: 6305 El Camino Real Carlsbad CA 92009

LAMBERT, KENT, state legislator; m. Gretchen Ann Simpich; children: Christopher, Michael, Melissa. BA, USAF Acad., Colo.; MA, U. So. Calif., LA; MS, USAF Inst. Tech. Commd. officer through the grades to col. USAF, 1974—2004; scientific analyst, br. chief, divsn. chief USAF Studies & Analyses Agency; dep. def. intelligence officer, Europe Def. Intelligence Agency; air & def. attache, internat. security assistance officer USAF, Sweden, Jordan; dep. dir. USAF Space Command Space Analysis Divsn., 2001—04; ret., 2004; legis. aide Colo. House of Reps., Denver, mem. Dist. 14, 2007—. Chmn., exec. dir. Rep. Study Com. Colo.; mem. El Paso Rep. Exec. Com., First Presbyn. Ch.; comdr., Colo. Legis. Squadron Civil Air Patrol. Mem. NRA, VFW, Mil. Officers Assn. America, USAF Acad. Assn. Grads., Nat. Eagle Scout Assn., Disabled Am. Vets, Am. Legion, Order of Daedalians, Assn. Old Crows, Leaders Colo., The Heritage Found, Colo. Union Taxpayers, Colo. Club for Growth, The Independence Inst., Minutemen Civil Def. Corps, Pikes Peak Firearms Assn., Rocky Mountain Gun Owners. Republican. Office: Colo State Capitol 200 E Colfax Denver CO 80203 Office Phone: 303-866-2937. Business E-Mail: rep.kent.lambert@comcast.net.*

LAMBERT, SHIRLEY ANNE, marketing professional, publisher; b. Dayton, Ohio, Sept. 28, 1945; d. Norman Frank and Muriel Noreen (Atkinson) Best; m. Joseph Calvin Lambert, Apr. 27, 1968 (div. 1986); children: Joseph Calvin III, James Edward, Kristin Carole. BA in Polit. Sci., Wellesley Coll., 1967; degree in French, Universite de Paris, 1966; MLS, Simmons Coll., 1980. Mktg. asst. G.K. Hall and Co., Boston, 1969-73; cons. Info. Dynamics Corp., Reading, Mass., 1973-75, Pergamon Press, Elmsford, N.Y., 1979-82; computer lab. coordinator Cherry Creek Schs., Aurora, Colo., 1983-85; mktg. dir. Libraries Unltd., Littleton, Colo., 1985—. Author: Clip Art and Dynamic Designs for Libraries and Media Centers, vol. 1; reviewer Am. Reference Books Ann., 1987-88, Library and Info. Sci. Ann., 1986-88. Host parent Am. Field Service, N.Y., 1986-87; selection chmn. Ams. Abroad; Returnee, 1962. Mem. ALA, Rocky Mountain (Colo.) Dressage Assn. (local chpt. sec. 1984-85), Colo. Hunter/Jumper Assn., Phi Beta Kappa, Beta Phi Mu. Republican. Congregationalist. Avocations: horse breeder, bridge. Office: Librs Unltd PO Box 3988 Englewood CO 80155-3988

LAMBERT, THOMAS P., lawyer; b. Kankakee, Ill., Oct. 14, 1946; BA, Loyola U., LA, 1968; JD, UCLA, 1971. Bar: Calif. 1971. Atty. Mitchell, Silberberg & Knupp, LA, 1971—. Note and comment editor UCLA Law Rev., 1970-71. Mem. ABA (antitrust law sect., litigation sect.), State Bar Calif., Beverly Hills Bar Assn., L.A. County Bar Assn. Office: Mitchell Silberberg & Knupp 11377 W Olympic Blvd Los Angeles CA 90064-1625

LAMBIRTH, TIMOTHY A., attorney; s. Woodrow M. Lambirth and Evelyne L. Jenkins; m. Dena Hayden Lambirth, Nov. 15, 1987; children: Heather, Travis, Hayden, Jackson. BA in Polit. Sci. with honors, U. Calif., Riverside, 1974, BA in Urban Studies, 1974; JD cum laude, Whittier Law Sch., 1978. Bar: Calif. 1978, DC 1984, Md. 1985, bd. cert. civil trial adv.:. Assoc. Strumwasser & Leichter, Beverly Hills, Calif., 1978—80, Monteleone & McCrory, LA, 1980—82, Ross & Ivanjack, LA, 1982—87; mng. ptnr. Ivanjack & Lambirth, LA, 1988—2004; ptnr. Aldrich & Bonnefin, Irvine, Calif., 2005—07, Marcin Lambirth LLP, Encino, Calif., 2007—. Governing bd. mem. Mng. Ptnrs. Roundtable, LA, 2002—05. Author: (column) Big Money, 2003—; founding editor: Whittier Law Schs. Law Rev., 1978. Founder Children's Rights Clinic Whittier Law Sch., 1999; bd. trustees Whittier Coll. Named Super Lawyer in Banking and Fin., LA Mag., 2005—09. Mem.: LA County Bar Assn. PPJR (exec. com. mem. 1995—2004), Italian Am. Lawyers (treas. 1989—91), Whittier Law Sch. Alumni (pres. 1997—99, 2001—). Office: 16830 Ventura Blvd Ste 320 Encino CA 91436 Office Phone: 818-305-2800. Business E-Mail: tal@marcin.com.

LAMBORN, DOUGLAS L., United States Representative from Colorado; b. May 24, 1954; m. Jeanie Lamborn; children: Luke, Eve, Will, Nathan, Mark. B in Journalism, U. Kans., 1978, JD, 1985. Pvt. gen. practice atty., Colo. Springs, 1987—; mem. Colo. Ho. of Reps., 1995—97, Rep. whip, 1997; mem. dist. 9 Colo. State Senate, Denver, 1997—2006, pres. pro-tem, chmn. state, vets. & mil. affairs com.; mem. US Congress from 5th Colo. dist., 2006—, mem. natural resources com.,vets. affairs com., armed svcs. com. Mem. We. States Reps. Leadership Conference, 1989, 93. Mem. prin.'s adv. coun. Antelope Trails Elem. Sch., Colo. Springs; former mem. citizen's adv. com. Pikes Peak Area Coun. Govt.'s. Republican. also: 200 E Colfax Ave Ste 259 Denver CO 80203-1716 Office: 3730 Sinton Rd, Ste 150 Colorado Springs CO 80907 also: 437 Cannon House Office Bldg Washington DC 20515 Office Phone: 202-225-4422. Office Fax: 202-226-2638.

LAMBROS, VAL (VASILIOS S. LAMBROS II), plastic surgeon; b. Washington, 1948; MD, Rush Med. Coll., 1974. Diplomate Am. Bd. Plastic Surgery. Intern Rush Presbyn. St. Luke's Med. Ctr., Chgo., 1974—75, resident plastic surgery, 1980—82; associated with Calif. Emergency Physicians, 1975—76; resident surgery UCLA Ctr. for Health Scis., 1976—78; fellowship, asst. dir. microsurgical rsch. UCLA Harbor Microsurgical Lab., 1978—79; fellow burn surgery U. Calif. Irvine (UCI) Burn Unit, 1979; fellow hand surgery U. Miami, 1980; cosmetic surgical fellowship with Bruce F. Connell, MD, Santa Ana, Calif., 1982; dir. Burn Unit and Hand and Reconstructive Surgery King Faisal Hosp., Saudi Arabia, 1982—83; plastic surgeon Western Med. Ctr., Santa Ana, Calif.; pvt. practice Newport Beach, Calif., 1984—. Clin. instr. U. Calif., Irvine; spkr. in field. Contbr. articles to med. jours. Mem.: Orange County Soc. Plastic Surgeons, Orange County Med. Assn., Lipoplasty Soc. N.Am., Calif. Soc. Plastic Surgery, Am. Soc. Plastic Surgery, Am. Soc. Aesthetic Plastic Surgery. Office: 360 San Miguel, Ste 406 Newport Beach CA 92660 Office Phone: 949-759-4733. Office Fax: 949-759-5458. E-mail: LAMBROSONE@aol.com.

LAMENDOLA, WALTER FRANKLIN, technology business executive, educator; b. Donora, Pa., Jan. 29, 1943; BA in English, St. Vincent Coll., 1964; MSW in Cmty. Orgn., U. Pitts., 1966; diploma in Sociology and Social Welfare, U. Stockholm, 1970; PhD in Social Work, U. Minn., 1976. Cmty. svcs. dir. Ariz. tng. programs State Dept. Mental Retardation, Tucson, 1970-73; assoc. prof. social welfare adminstrn. Fla. State U., 1976-77; pres., CEO Minn. Rsch. and Tech., Inc., 1977-81; assoc. prof., dir. Allied Health Computer Lab. East Carolina U., 1981-84; prof., dir. info. tech. ctr. Grad. Sch. Social Work U. Denver, 1984-87, 99—, cons. info. tech., rsch. human svcs., 1987-90; v.p. rsch. Colo. Trust, Denver, 1990-93, info. tech. and rsch. cons., 1993—; dir. doctoral program U. Denever, GSSW, 2008. Cons. European Network Info. Tech. and Human Svcs.; mem. rebuilding cmtys. initiative PODER project Casey Found., 1996-97; adv. bd. ctr. Computers in Tchg. Initiative, U. Southampton, Brit. Rsch. Coun. Univs., Human Svc. Info. Tech. Applications, CREON Found., Netherlands; lectr. conf., symposia, univs. US, Europe; spkr. HUSITA conf., Hong Kong, 2004; nat. adv. bd. Native Elder Health Resource Ctr., 1994-96, Data Coord. Ctr., 1999—; co-founder Denver Free Net, 1993; adj. prof. U. Colo. Health Scis. Ctr., 1996—; dir. tech. GSSU, U. Denver, 1998—; info. tech. cons. Healthy Nations Program Robert Wood Johnson Found, 1993-96; evaluator Nat. Libr. Rsch. Program, Access Colo. grant, 1994, Nat. Info. Infrastructure grant Colo. State Libr.; cons. set up on the Internet for U.S. Cts.-Ct. for Mental Health Svcs., NIH, Frontier Mental Health Svcs. Network grant; collaborating investigator SBIR award Computerized Advance Directives, tech. plan San Mateo County and Seattle Dist. Cts.; keynote spkr. conf. Human Svc. Info. Tech. Applications, Finland, 1996; adj. prof. U. Colo., 1997-98; dir. tech., adj. prof. U. Denver, 1997-98; adj. prof.

informatics U. Colo. Health Scis. Ctr., 1998, 03-; nat. adv. coun. Ctr. Substance Abuse Prevention Dept. HHS, 1998, co-chair prevention decision support sys. steering group, 1999; pres. ActiveGuide, LLC; nat. design team Decision Support Sys., U.S. Dept. HHS, 1998—; prin. investigator bridge project Cmty. Tech. Ctr., US Dept. Edn., 2000-03; prin. investigator Bridge Cmty. Tech. Ctr. Dept. Edn., 2000-03; mem. external steering com. Date Coord. Ctr., Ctr. Substance Abuse Prevention, 2003—. Co-author: Choices for Colorado's Future, 1993, The Integrity of Intelligence: A Bill of Rights for the Information Age, 1992, Choices for Colorado's Future: Executive Summary, 1991, Choices for Colorado's Future: Regional Summaries, 1991; co-editor: A Casebook of Computer Applications in Health and Social Services, 1989; contbr. numerous articles to profl. jours. Capt. U.S. Army, 1966-69. Recipient Innovative Computer Application award Internat. Fedn. Info. Processing Socs., 1979, Lacy Stevenson award U. Denver, 2006; Nat. Lib. Rsch. Evaluator grantee, Colo., 1994—, Nat. Info. Infrastructure grantee Dept. Edn., State Libr. and Adult Literacy, 1994-95, Rural Area Edn. Tech. Assessments Sliver grantee Colo. Dept. Edn., 2005-06; Funds & Couns. Tng. scholar United Way Am., 1964-66, Donaldson Fund scholar, 1965-66, NIMH scholar, 1964-66, 73-76, St. Vincent Coll. Benedictine Soc. scholar, 1963-64; vis. fellow U. Southampton, 1992-95. Office: GSSW Univ Denver 2148 South High St Denver CO 80208 also: ActiveGuide LLC PO Box 24994 Denver CO 80224-4994 Business E-Mail: wlamendo@du.edu. E-mail: walter.lamendola@du.edu.

LAMM, RICHARD DOUGLAS, lawyer, former governor; b. Madison, Wis., Aug. 3, 1935; s. Arnold E. and Mary (Townsend) L.; m. Dorothy Vennard, May 11, 1963; children: Scott Hunter, Heather Susan. BBA, U. Wis., 1957; LLB, U. Calif., Berkeley, 1961; LHD (hon.), Regis Coll., U. Denver; LLD (hon.), Colo. Coll.; Doctorate in Pub. Adminstrn. (hon.), Drexel. U. Bar: Colo. 1962; CPA, Colo. Accountant, Salt Lake City, 1958, Ernst & Ernst, Denver, 1961-62; atty. Colo. Anti-Discrimination Commn., Denver, 1962-63, Jones, Meiklejohn, Kilroy, Kehl & Lyons, Denver, 1963-65; sole practice, 1965-74; mem. Colo. Ho. of Reps., 1966-74, asst. minority leader, 1971-74; gov. State of Colo., 1975-87; now spl. counsel Berliner, Boyle, Kaplan, Zisser & Walter (formerly O'Connor & Hannan), Denver; dir. Ctr. for Pub. Policy & Contemporary U. Denver, 1987—. Assoc. prof. law U. Denver, 1969-74; chmn. natural resource and environ. mgmt. com. Nat. Gov.'s Assn., 1978-79, mem., from 1979, also mem. exec. com. and environment com., and chmn. task force on synthetic fuels; del. Dem. Nat. Conv., 1980; adj. prof. U. Colo. Sch. Pub. Policy, Denver, 1983-87; vis. prof. U. Colo. Grad. Sch. Pub. Affairs, 1984-85; disting. prof. history U. New Orleans, Innsbruck, Austria, 1987; pub. mem. Accreditation Coun. for Grad. Med. Edn., 1994-. Co-author: Pioneers & Politicians, 1984, The Immigration Time Bomb: The Fragmenting of America, 1985; author: Megatraumas: America at the Year 2000, 1985; co-author: Nineteen Eighty-Eight, 1985. Pres. Denver Young Democrats, 1963; v.p. Colo. Young Democrats, 1964; mem. Conservation Found., Denver Center Performing Arts Center for Growth Alternatives, Central City Opera House Assn. Served as 1st lt. US Army, 1957—58. Recipient winner Peace 2010 Essay Competition, Christian Sci. Monitor, 1985, Helen Yerger/L. Vann Seawell Best Article award, Healthcare Fin. Mgmt. Assn., 1990; named Humanist of Yr., Am. Humanist Assn., 1993; named an Outstanding Your Leader in Am., Time Mag., 1974; named one of Colo. 100, Denver Post & Hist. Denver, Inc., 1992; Montgomery fellow, Dartmouth Coll., 1987, Presdl. fellow, U. Calif. Med. Sch., 1989. Mem.: Western Gov. Assn. (chmn. 1985—86), Nat. Gov. Assn. Office: Berliner Boyle Kaplan Zisser & Walter 1 United Bank Ctr 1700 Lincoln St Denver CO 80203-4500 Mailing: U Denver Ctr for Pub Policy 2199 S Univ Blvd Denver CO 80208 E-mail: rlamm@aol.com.

LAMPHERE, LOUISE, anthropology and women's studies educator; b. St. Louis, Oct. 4, 1940; d. Harold and Miriam (Bretschneider) L.; 1 child, Peter Bret. BA, Stanford U., 1962; MA, Harvard U., 1966, PhD, 1968. Vis. asst. prof. U. Rochester, 1967—68; asst. prof. anthropology Brown U., Providence, 1968—71, 1972—75, assoc. prof., 1979-85, prof. anthropology, 1985—86; assoc. prof. U. N.Mex., Albuquerque, 1976-79, adj. prof., 1979-85, prof. anthropology, 1986—99, acting dir. women studies, 1993—94, univ. regents prof., 1999—2002, disting. prof. anthropology, 2001, disting. prof. emeritus, 2009—; academic coord. women studies program. Academic vis. London Sch. Econs., 1971—72; fellow Radcliffe Inst., 1975—76; fellow Ctr. Rsch. on Women Wellesley Coll., 1981; faculty fellow Pembroke Ctr. Rsch. and Tchg. on Women, 1984—85; vis. scholar Russell Sage Found., NYC, 2001—02; vis. prof. Dept. Anthropology and Sociology U. Calif., Berkeley, 2004, Berkeley, 06. Author: From Working Daughters to Working, 1987, Weaving Together Women's Lives: Three Generations in a Navajo Family, 2007, (with others) Sunbelt Working Mothers, 1993; editor: Structuring Diversity, 1992, Newcomers in the Workplace, 1993, (with others) Woman, Culture and Society, 1974, Situated Lives: Gender and Culture in Everyday Life, 1997; editor Frontiers: A Jour. of Women Studies, Albuquerque, 1990-93. Recipient Conrad Arensberg award Soc. for Anthropology of Work, 1994; grantee NSF, 1981-83, Russell Sage Found., 1985-86, Ford Found., 1987-90. Mem. Am. Ethnological Soc. (counsellor 1981-84, pres.-elect 1987, pres. 1987-89), Am. Anthropol. Soc. (exec. com. 1987-89), Assn. for Feminist Anthropology (bd. dirs. 1989-91, pres.-elect 1993-95, pres. 1995-97), Am. Anthropology Assn. (pres.-elect 1997-99, pres. 1999-2001, Squeaky Wheel Award, 1998). Office: U New Mexico Dept Anthropology 1 University of New Mexico, MSC01-1040 Albuquerque NM 87131-0001 Business E-Mail: lamphere@unm.edu.

LAMPMAN, RICHARD H. (DICK LAMPMAN), former computer company executive; b. 1945; BSEE, MSEE, Carnegie Mellon U. With Hewlett-Packard, 1971—2007, with HP labs., 1981—86, dir. measurement sys. lab., 1986—88, dir. computer systems lab., 1988—92, dir. worldwide Computer Rsch. Ctr., 1992—99, dir. HP Labs. Palo Alto, Calif., 1999—2007, sr. v.p. rsch., 2001—07. Bd. govs. EPCglobal. Mem. adv. bd. Carnegie Inst. Tech., Ga. Inst. Tech., Internet Soc. Adv. Coun., Corp. Exec. bd.; rep. HP on the adv. bd. Bay Area Sci. Infrastructure Consortium, Computer Systems Policy Project CTO. Mem.: IEEE (sr.), Assn. Computing Machinery, Computing Rsch. Assn., Silicon Valley Computer Sci. Rsch. Dirs., Math. Scis. Rsch. Inst. (mem. adv. bd.), Internet Soc. (mem. adv. coun.).

LAMPORT, LESLIE B., computer scientist; b. NYC, Feb. 7, 1941; s. Benjamin and Hannah (Lasser) L.; m. Carol Dahl Crum, Oct. 31, 1968 (div. Feb. 1978), m. Ellen Gilkerson, 2006; 1 child, Jason Christopher. BS in Math., MIT, 1960; MA in Math., Brandeis U., 1963, PhD in Math., 1972; PhD (hon.), U. Rennes, 2003, Christian Albrechts, Kiel, 2003, U. Lugano, 2004, Ecole Polytechnique Fédérale de Lausanne, 2004, Universitá della Svizzera Italiana, Lugano, 2006, Université Henri Poincaré, Nancy, 2007. Part-time with Mitre Corp., 1962—65; mem. faculty Marlboro Coll., Vt., 1965-69; systems analyst Mass. Computer Associates, Wakefield, 1970-77; sr. computer scientist SRI Internat., Menlo Park, Calif., 1977-85; sr. cons. engr. Digital Equipment Corp., Palo Alto, Calif., 1985-98, Compaq, Palo Alto, Calif., 1998—2001; with Microsoft Rsch., Mountain View, Calif., 2001—. Contbr. several articles to profl. jours.;, author of several papers. Recipient PODC (Principles Of Distributed Computing) Influential Paper award forTime, Clocks, and the Ordering of Events in a Distributed System, 2000, Piore award, IEEE, 2004, John Von Neumann medal, 2008, Edsger W. Dijkstra Prize for Reaching Agreement in the Presence of Faults, 2005, Assn. Computing Machinery SIGOPS Hall of Fame award for Time, Clocks and the Ordering of Events in a Distributed System, 2007, Logic in Computer Science (LICS) 1988 Test of Time award for The Existence of Refinement Mappings, 2008. Mem. NAE. Achievements include being best known for LaTeX, Byzantine fault tolerance, Paxos algorithm; patents in field. Office: Microsoft Corp 1065 La Avenida Mountain View CA 94043 Office Phone: 650-693-2725. E-mail: lamport@pa.dec.com.

LANAHAN, DANIEL JOSEPH, lawyer; b. Bklyn., Jan. 13, 1940; Attended, L.I. U., Temple U.; JD, San Francisco Law Sch., 1969; LLD (hon.), Calif. State U., 2007. Bar: Calif. 1970. Dir. Ropers, Majeski, Kohn & Bentley, P.C., Santa Rosa, Calif., 1970-96; mng. ptnr. Lanahan & Reilley L.L.P., Santa Rosa, 1997—2006. Mem. State Bar Calif., Sonoma County Bar Assn., Internat. Assn. Def. Counsel, Assn. Def. Counsel. Home Phone: 707-575-5726; Office Phone: 707-524-4200. Business E-Mail: dlanahan@lanahan.com.

LAND, GEORGE AINSWORTH, philosopher, consultant, writer; b. Hot Springs, Ark., Feb. 27, 1933; s. George Thomas Lock and Mary Elizabeth Land; m. Jo A. Gunn, 1957 (dec. 1969); children— Robert E., Thomas G., Patrick A.; m. Beth Smith Jarman, 1987. Student, Millsaps Coll., 1952-54, U. Veracruz, Mexico, 1957-59; numerous hon. degrees U.S. and abroad. Program dir. Woodall TV Stas. of Ga., Columbus, 1951-52; ops. mgr. Lamar Broadcasting, Jackson, Miss., 1952-54; anthrop. research Cora, Huichole and Yaqui tribes, Latin Am. Mexico, 1955-60; dir. gen. Television del Norte (NBC), Mexico, 1960-62; v.p. Roman Corp., St. Louis, 1962-64; chmn. Transolve Inc., Cambridge, Mass., and St. Petersburg, Fla., 1964-68; chief exec., chmn. Innotek Corp., NYC; also pres. Hal Roach Studios, Los Angeles and NYC, 1969-71; chmn. emeritus Turtle Bay Inst., NYC, 1971-80, Farsight Group, NYC, 1971—80; vice chmn. Wilson Learning Corp., Mpls., 1980-86; chmn., CEO Leadership 2000 The Farsight Group, Phoenix, 1986—; chmn. Opportunity Intelligency Inc., Scottsdale, Ariz.; prof. Mankato State U., 1973-74; sr. fellow U. Minn., 1982—; chmn. Global Alliance for Creative Peace; chmn., adv. bd. Advanced Integrated Tech. Inc., 2006—. Cons.-in-residence Synplex Inc., NYC, AT&T, Forest Hosp., Des Plaines, Social Systems Inc., Chapel Hill, NC, Children's Hosp., Nat. Med. Ctr., Washington, Herman Miller Inc., Arthur Anderson & Co., strategy cons. Intermedics Orthopedics; mem. Nat. Action Com. on Drug Edn., 1974-75, sr. exec. svc. U.S. Govt. 2001-2002, Assn. Non-profit mgmt., 1999, The Congerence Bd. 1999, 2000, Ctr. for Disease Control, 2002, The Concours Group, 2002, Global Fourm Ctr., 2002, CEO, 2002; co-chmn. Syncon Conf., So. Ill. U., 1972-74; keynoter Emerging Trends in Edn. Conf., Minn., 1974, 75, Bicentennial Conf. on Limits to Growth, So. Ill. U., 1976, No. States Power Conf., 1975, U.S. Office Edn., Nat. Conf. Improvements in Edn., 1979, World Conf. on Gifted, 1977, S.W. Conf. on Arts, 1977, World Symposium on Humanity, 1979, Internat. Conf. Internal Auditors, 1977, Four Corners Conf. on Arts, 1977, Chautaugua Inst., 1977, 78, Conf. Am. Art Tchrs. Assn., 1979, Internat. Conf. on Gifted, 1982, Japan Mgmt. Assn., Nat. Conf. Art Curators, Chgo., 1985, others; keynoter, Nat. Conf. on Econ. Devel., Mex., 1988, Credit Union Roundtable, Tampa, Fla., 1988, Internat. Bihai Conf., Princeton, NJ, 1982, co-chmn. com. on society World Conf. Peace and Poverty, St. Joseph's U., Phila., 1968, Internat. Bahai Conf. Princeton U., 1987, Gov.'s Trade Corridor Conf., Phoenix, 1994, Cath. Hosp. Assn., Phila, 1994, Am. Assn. Adminstrs., 1994, Inst. Pub. Execs., 1994, Fed. Conf. Quality, Washington, 1994, MAC IS Nat. Conf., Ont., 1994, Innovative Thinking Conf., 1994, Ventana Groupware Conf., 1994, Assn. Non-Profit Orgs., 1998, The Conf. Bd., 1999-2000, Strategic Innovation Conf., 1999, Tng. Dirs. Forum, 1999, Young Pres.' Orgn., Cannes, 1993, Assn. Convn. and Visitors Bur., Phoenix, 1993, Profession Conv. Mgmt. Assn., Atlanta, Internat. Assn. Law Enforcement, 1995, Cath. Health Assn., 1995, Excellence in Govt. Fellows, 1996, U.S. Govt. Sr. Exec. Svc., 2000-01, Chautauqua Instn., 2001, PEMEX, 2002, Coca-Cola, 2002, US Fish and Wildlife Svc., 2003, Innovation Convergence, Mpls., 2003, Internat. Conference Energy, Geneva, 2003, Am. Med. Systems, France, 2003, Adv. Innovation, Zurich, Switzerland, 2003, Mex. Petroleum Inst., Mexico City, 2004, Ctr. for Competitiveness, Belfast, No. Ireland, 2004, Creative Edn. Found., Buffalo, 2004, Congress Innovation and Quality Pub. Adminstrn., Mex. DF, 2005, Internat. Petroleum Conf., Venacruz, Mex., 2005, Delphi, Xerox, Groupo, Bal (Mex.), Petroles (Mex.), others; mem. Nat. Security Sem., U.S. Dept. Def., 1975; faculty Edison Electric Grad. Mgmt. Inst., 1972-78; lectr., seminarian in transformation theory, strategic planning and interdisciplinary rsch. Menninger Found., U. Ga., Emory U., Waterloo, Can., Office of Sec. HEW, Jamestown Coll., NY, Hofstra U., U.S. Office Edn., Calif. Dept. Edn., St. Louis U., Coll. William and Mary, Webster Coll., St. Louis, Wash. State Dept. Edn., U. Ky., So. Ill. U., St. John's U., Harvard U., U. South Fla., MIT, U. Veracruz, Children's Hosp. D.C., Gov.'s Sch. NC, Scottsdale Ctr. Arts, Ariz., Humbolt U., East Berlin, AAAS, others; advanced faculty Creative Problem Solvin-gInst., SUNY, 1965—, S. Conn. Coll.; disting. lectr. Northwestern State U., La., SUNY, Coll. of the Lakes, Ill.; chmn. adv. bd. Advanced Integrated Tech., Inc., 2006—; cons. in field. Author: Innovation Systems, 1967, Innovation Technology, 1968, Four Faces of Poverty, 1968, (as George T.L. Land) Grow or Die: The Unifying Principle of Transformation, 1973, Creative Alternatives and Decision Making, 1974, The Opportunity Book, 1980, (with Vaune E. Ainsworth), Breakpoint and Beyond, 1994, (with Beth Jarman) Harper Bus. New Paradigm in Business, 1994, Community Building in Business, 1995, Forward to Basics, 1980; contbr. to profl. jours. and gen. mags. Sr. fellow U. Mich. Fellow: World Bus. Acad., NY Acad. Scis.; mem.: Authors League Am., Authors Guild, Com. for Future (colleague), World Future Soc., Am. Soc. Value Engrs. (past dir.), Creative Edn. Found. (trustee, Lifetime Achievement award 1993, named to Hall of Fame 2006), Am. Soc. Cybernetics (past v.p.), Soc. Gen. Sys. Rsch. Achievements include research on interdisciplinary unification, orginated transformation theory; invention of computer-assisted group creative thinking processes, The Innovator, CoNexus, TeamWare, Synnovas, FarSightPro, others. Home: 7470 E San Miguel Ave Scottsdale AZ 85250-6446 Office: Leadership 2000 The Farsight Group 6619 N Scottsdale Rd Scottsdale AZ 85250

LAND, KENNETH DEAN, test and balance agency executive, consultant; b. Central City, Nebr., Oct. 5, 1931; s. Adrew Kenneth Land and Marie Eveline (Weaver) Gehrke. Grad., El Camino Coll., Gardena, Calif., 1954-56; student, Long Beach City Coll., 1958, Calif. State Coll., Long Beach, 1959. Cert. quality assurance insp. for smoke removal and life safety systems; cert. test and balance engr. and commn. agent for bldg. and environ. sys. Gen. mgr. Air Heat Engrs., Inc., Santa Fe Springs, Calif., 1956-61; sales and estimating engr. Thermodyne Corp., Los Alamitos, Calif., 1962-64; pres., founder Air Check Co., Inc., Santa Ana, Calif., 1964-69; chief test balance engr. Nat. Air Balance Co., LA, 1969-73; gen. mgr. B&M Air Balance Co., South El Monte, Calif., 1973-78; CEO, founder Land Air Balance Tech. (LABTECH), Las Vegas, Nev., 1978—2007. Founder, bd. dirs. Energy Resources and Mgmt., Inc., San-I-Pac, Internat., Inc., Energy Equities Group, Inc., Utility Connection, 1980—. Active Las Vegas Founders Club-Las Vegas Invitational PGA Tournament, 1983—, player, 1992; former trustee Assoc. Air Balance Coun.-Sheet Metal Workers Internat. Apprenticeship Tng. Fund; mem. Citizens Against Govt. Waste, 1990—, YNOT Night for YMCA, 1987—; co-founder The Golf Com., operators charity golf tournament for Am. Cancer Soc., 1990, 91, Am. Diabetes Assn., 1992, Nev. Child Seekers, 1992—; nat. pres. Assn. Air Balance Coun., 1989-90. With USN, 1951-54, journalist. Mem. ASHRAE (pres. so. Nev. chpt. 1983-84, editor chpt. bull. 1979-89, Citizen of Yr. 1989), CSI (co-founder Las Vegas chpt., pres. 1989-90, editor, founder chpt. bull. 1987-90, S.W. regional mem. chmn. 1990-91), Assn. Energy Engrs., Am. Soc. Profl. Cons., Associated Air Balance Coun. (cert. test and balance engr. 1966—, internat. pres. 1988-89, bd. dirs. 1982-90, cert. commissioning agent, mem. numerous coms.), Sheet Metal Workers Internat. Tng. Fund, Internat. Conf. Bldg. Officials, Internat. Assn. Plumbing and Mech. Officials, Nat. Fedn. Ind. Businessmen, Rotary (So. El Monte Calif. Club 1977-78, Las Vegas S.W. Nev. Club 1978-94, bd. dirs. 1983-85, 88-90, photographer 1987-90, chmn. internat. svc., 4 Paul Harris fellowships, charter mem. Las Vegas West Club, Nev., 1994—), Citizens for Pvt. Enterprise, Nev. Taxpayers Assn., UNLV Golf Found., UNLV Presdl. Assocs. Group, Nev. Devel. Assn., Nev. Nuclear Waste Study Com. adv. coun., Sheet Metal and Air Conditioning Contractors Assn. (nat. and so. Nev. chpt. bd. dirs.), Associated Gen. Contractors (nat. and Las Vegas chpt.), Nat. Energy Mgmt. Inst. (cert., co-chmn. Nev. adv. coun., instr. Energy Mgmt. Tng. 1991), Las Vegas C. of C., Nat. Inst. Bldg. Scis., Nev. Assn. Ind. Businessman, Nat. Fire Protection Assn., Am. Soc. Hosp. Engrs., Nev. Profl. Facility Mgrs. Assn., Constrn. Specifivcation Inst. (founder, past pres), Soc. Fire Protection Engrs. (charter Las Vegas chpt.), Soc.Mktg. Profl. Svcs. (charter Las Vegas chpt.), Las Vegas Country Club. Avocations: golf, dance, racquetball, collecting jazz, swing and big band music. Office Phone: 702-385-7421. Office Fax: 702-385-7389. Business E-Mail: Ken@landairbalance.com.

LANDAU, ELLIS, hotel executive; b. Phila., Feb. 24, 1944; s. Manfred and Ruth (Fischer) L.; m. Kathy Suzanne Thomas, May 19, 1968 (div.); children: Rachel, David; m. Yvette Ehr Cohen, Nov. 1, 1992. BA in Econs., Brandeis U., 1965; MBA, Columbia U., 1967. Fin. analyst SEC, Washington, 1968-69; asst. treas. U-Haul Internat., Phoenix, 1969-71; v.p., treas. Ramada, Inc., Phoenix, 1971-90; CFO Boyd Gaming Corp., Las Vegas, Nev., 1990—2006; pvt. investor Pinnacle Entertainment, Inc., bd. dirs., 2007—, chmn., audit com., mem. nominating com. and Governance and Compliance com. Office: Boyd Gaming Corp 6465D S Rainbow Blvd Las Vegas NV 89118- Office Phone: 702-622-5180. Personal E-mail: ellislandau@yahoo.com.

LANDAU, YVETTE E., lawyer, resort company executive; b. Milw., Nov. 26, 1956; BS magna cum laude, Ariz. State U., 1979; JD, Northwestern U., 1984. Bar: Ariz. 1984, Nevada 1991. Assoc. Snell & Wilmer, Phoenix, 1984—89, prtnr., 1990—93; assoc. gen. counsel Mandalay Resort Group, 1993—96, v.p., gen. counsel, sec., 1996—. Mem. exec. com. Circus/Eldorado Joint Venture; mem. mngmt. com. Detroit Entertainment. Mem.: ABA, Internat. Assn. of Gaming Attys. (trustee 1997—), Nevada State Bar Assn., Ariz. State Bar Assn. Office: Mandalay Resort Group 3950 Las Vegas Blvd Las Vegas NV 89119

LANDEFELD, STEWART M., lawyer; b. Cleve., Mar. 13, 1954; BA, Yale U., 1976; JD, U. Chgo., 1980. Bar: Wash. 1980, US Ct. Appeals (9th Cir.). Ptnr. Perkins Coie LLP, Seattle, 1987—2007, 2008—, chair Nat. Bus. Practice Group, 2005—07; exec. v.p., interim chief legal officer Washington Mutual, Inc., 2007—08. Co-author: Washington Business Entities, 1991—. Chmn. bd. trustees Seattle Found.; past chmn. bd. trustees Henry Art Gallery. Named a Wash. Super Lawyer, Wash. Law & Polit. Office: Perkins Coie LLP 1201 3rd Ave Ste 4800 Seattle WA 98101-3029 Office Phone: 206-359-8430. Office Fax: 206-359-9430. Business E-Mail: slandefeld@perkinscoie.com.

LANDERS, AUDREY, actress, singer; b. Phila., July 18, 1959; d. Ruth Landers; m. Donald Berkowitz, May 1988; 2 children. BA, Barnard Coll. Records singles and albums with sister Judy Landers. Actress (films) 1941, 1979, Underground Aces, 1981, Tennessee Stallion, 1982, Deadly Twins, 1985, A Chorus Line, 1985, Getting Even, 1986, Johann Strauss: The King Without a Crown, 1987, California Casanova, 1991, Last Chance Love, 1997, Island Forever, 2005, (TV films) Our Voices Ourselves, 1982, Popeye Doyle, 1986, Ghost Writer, 1989, Dallas: J.R. Returns, 1996, (TV series) The Secret Storm, 1972—73, Somerset, 1974—76, Highcliffe Manor, 1979, Dallas, 1981—84, 1989, Lucky/Chances, 1990, One Life to Live, 1990—91, The Huggabug Club, 1995. Office: care Jo-Ann Geffen & Assocs 3151 Cahuenga Blvd W Ste 235 Los Angeles CA 90068-1749

LANDERS, TERESA PRICE, librarian; b. NYC, Dec. 28, 1954; d. Stanley and June Ethel (Novick) Price; m. Gary David Landers, Sept. 2, 1979; children: Joshua Price, Alisha Rose. BA in History cum laude, Williams Coll., 1976; MA in LS, U. Denver, 1978; postgrad., Ctrl. Wash. U., 1980; MA in Orgnl. Mgmt., U. Phoenix, 1999. Libr., asst. analyst Earl Combs, Inc., Mercer Island, Wash., 1979; reference libr. Yakima (Wash.) Valley Regional Libr., 1981-83, coord. youth svcs., 1983-84; libr. Tempe (Ariz.) Pub. Libr., 1984-85; supervisory libr. Mesa (Ariz.) Pub. Libr., 1985-90; head telephone reference Phoenix Pub. Libr., 1990-91, head bus. and scis., 1991-95, info. svcs. mgr., 1995-99; dep. dir. Corvallis-Benton County Pub. libr., 1999—. Cons. Fed. Dept. Corrections, Phoenix, 1993. Mem. ALA, Oreg. Libr. Assn., Nat. Wildlife Fedn. (life), Altrusa, Beta Phi Mu. Democrat. Unitarian Universalist. Avocations: cooking, horseback riding, gardening. Office: Corvallis-Benton County Pub Libr 645 NW Monroe Ave Corvallis OR 97330-4722 E-mail: teresa.landers@ci.corvallis.or.us.

LANDESMAN, HOWARD M., retired academic administrator; b. Bklyn., 1938; m. Lynne Landesman; 1 child, Lori. BS, UCLA, 1958; DDS, U. So. Calif., 1962, MS in Edn., 1971. Named co-dir., grad. prosthodontics program U. So. Calif. Sch. Dentistry, 1973, chair, dept. restorative dentistry, assoc. dean academic and faculty affairs, exec. assoc. dean, dean, 1991—99; dean. Sch. Dentistry U. Colo., 1999—2004; v.p. devel. U. Colo. Denver & Health Sciences Ctr. Mem.: Acad. Prosthodontics. Mailing: Colo Univ Foundation 4740 Walnut St Boulder CO 80301

LANDIS, GREGORY P., lawyer; b. 1951; BA magna cum laude, Yale U., 1973; JD cum laude, Harvard U., 1978. Bar: Calif. 1978. Ptnr. McCutchen, Doyle, Brown & Enerson, San Francisco; joined AT&T Wireless Svcs., Inc., Redmond, Wash., 1996, sr. v.p., gen. counsel, exec. v.p., gen. counsel. Chmn. bd. dirs. Equal Justice Works, 2001—03, treas., bd. dirs., 2003—; adv. bd. CoroporateProBono.Org. Recipient Corp. Pro Bono award, Am. Corp. Counsel Assn., 2000. Mem.: Cellular Telecom. Industry Assn. (bd. dirs.).

LANDON, ALLAN R., bank executive; b. 1948; m. Sue Landon, 1970; 2 children. BS in Acctg., Iowa State U., 1970. CPA. Assoc., lead audit ptnr. Ernst & Young LLP, 1970—84, ptnr., 1984—98; exec. v.p., CFO First Am. Corp., First Am. Nat. Bank, Nashville, 1998—2000; exec v.p., dir. risk mgmt. Bank of Hawaii Corp., Honolulu, 2000—01, vice chmn., CFO, 2001—03, COO, 2004, pres., 2003—, chmn., CEO, 2004—; vice chmn. Bank of Hawaii (divsn. Bank of Hawaii Corp.), 2001—03, CFO, 2001—, pres., 2003—. Bd. dirs. Bank of Hawaii (divsn. Bank of Hawaii Corp.), 2002—, Bank of Hawaii Corp., 2004—, Fed. Home Loan Bank, Seattle, The Rsch. Corp. Chmn. Hawaii Medical Svc. Assn.; bd. regents U. Hawaii Sys., 2005—; bd. dirs. Catholic Charities of Hawaii; mem. mil. affairs coun. Hawaii C. of C. Mem.: Hawaii Bus. Roundtable. Office: Bank of Hawaii Corp Hdqs 130 Merchant St Honolulu HI 96813

LANDON, JACK D., JR, state legislator; b. Sept. 1, 1949; m to Kathryn; children: two. Trustee, Sheridan Co Sch District No 1, 92-98; Wyoming State Representative, District 30, 99-.Greenhouse owner & manager, 78-98. Lions Club. Republican. Mailing: 120 Paradise Park Rd Sheridan WY 82801 Home Phone: 307-672-8431. Business E-Mail: jlandon@wyoming.com. E-mail: jlandon@cyberhighway.net.

LANDON, SUSAN MELINDA, petroleum geologist; b. Mattoon, Ill., July 2, 1950; d. Albert Leroy and Nancy (Wallace) L.; m. Richard D. Dietz, Jan. 24, 1993. BA, Knox Coll., 1972; MA, SUNY, Binghamton, 1975. Cert. profl. geologist; cert. petroleum geologist. Petroleum geologist Amoco Prodn. Co., Denver, 1974—87; mgr. exploration tng. Amoco, Houston, 1987—89; ind. petroleum geologist Denver, 1990—. Editor: Interior Rift Basins, 1993. Mem., chmn. Colo. Geol. Survey Adv. Com., Denver, 1991-98; mem. Bd. on Earth Sci. and Resources-NRC, 1992-97, chair com. on earth resources, 1998-2003; mem. Nat. Coop. Geologic Mapping Program Fed. Adv. Com., 1997—. Recipient Disting. Alumni award Knox Coll., 1986. Mem. Am. Assn. Petroleum Geologists (hon., treas., Disting. Svc. award 1995), Am. Inst. Profl. Geologists (pres. 1990, Martin Van Couvering award 1991, Ben H. Parker medal 2001), Am. Geol. Inst. (pres. 1998), Rocky Mountain Assn. Geologists (pres. 2000, Disting. Svc. award 1986, Disting. Pub. Svc. to Earth Sci. award 1995). Achievements include frontier exploration for hydrocarbons in U.S. Home: 780 Ballantine Rd Golden CO 80401-9503 Office: Susan M 780 Ballantine Rd Golden CO 80401-9503 Home Phone: 303-526-7723; Office Phone: 303-436-1930. Personal E-mail: susanlandon@att.net.

LANDRETH, KATHRYN E., lawyer; U.S. atty. Dept. Justice, Las Vegas, 1993—2001; chief of policy and planning Met. Police Dept., Las Vegas, Nev., 2001—02; metro counsel Las Vegas, 2003—.

LANDRUM-TAYLOR, LEAH N., state legislator; b. Phoenix, Aug. 23, 1966; m. Gregory Taylor; 1 child, Greyson Elijah. BA in Polit. Sci., Ariz. State U., 1989, MA in Polit. Sci., 1991; student, Harvard U. John F. Kennedy Sch. Govt. Founder, v.p. Landrum Found., Phoenix; sr. adv. Ariz. Children's Assn.; mem. Dist. 23 Ariz. House of Reps., 1999—2002, mem. Dist. 16, 2003—07, Ariz. State Senate, 2007—, mem. pub. safety & human svcs. com., edn. accountability & reform com. Adj. faculty mem. Maricopa Cmty. Coll., Tempe, Ariz.; Ariz. chair Nat. Black Caucus State Legislators; alumna Am. Coun. Young Polit. Leaders. Mem. Mountain Park Health Bd., YMCA Youth Initiatives Bd. Democrat. Roman Catholic. Office: Ariz State Senate Capitol Complex 1700 W Washington Rm 312 Phoenix AZ 85007 Office Phone: 602-926-3830. Fax: 602-542-0140; Office Fax: 602-417-3148. Business E-Mail: llandrumtaylor@azleg.gov. E-mail: llandrum@azleg.state.az.us.*

LAND-WEBER, ELLEN, photography professor; b. Rochester, NY, Mar. 16, 1943; d. David and Florence Epstein; 1 child, Julia. BA, U. Iowa, 1965, MFA, 1968. Faculty mem. UCLA Extension, 1970-74, Orange Coast Coll., Costa Mesa, Calif., 1973, U. Nebr., Lincoln, 1974; asst. prof. photography Humboldt State U., Arcata, Calif., 1974-79, assoc. prof., 1979-83, prof., 1983—. Photographer Seagram's Bicentennial Courthouse Project, 1976-77, Nat. Trust for Hist. Preservation/Soc. Photographic Edn., 1987. Author: The Passionate Collector, 1980, To Save a Life: Stories of Holocaust Rescue, 2000; contbr. sects. to books; photographs pub. in numerous books and jours. Named Humboldt State U. Scholar of Yr., 2004-2005; Nat. Endowment for Arts fellow, 1974, 79, 82; Artist's support grantee Unicolor Corp., 1982, Polaroid 20X24 Artist's support grantee, 1990, 91, 93, 94; Fulbright sr. fellow, 1993-94. Mem. Soc. for Photog. Edn. (exec. bd. 1979-82, treas. 1979-81, sec. 1981-83) Avocation: weaving. Office: Humboldt State U Art Dept Arcata CA 95521

LANE, DIANE, actress; b. NYC, Jan. 22, 1965; d. Burt Lane and Colleen Farrington; m. Christopher Lambert, Oct. 1988 (div. Mar. 1994); 1 child, Eleanor; m. Josh Brolin, Aug. 14, 2004. Actress: (stage prodns.) Medea, 1972, Agamemnon, 1977, The Cherry Orchard, 1977, Runaways, 1978, Electra, The Trojan Woman, As You Like it, The Good Woman of Setzuan, (films) A Little Romance, 1979 (Young Artist Award for best juvenile actress motion picture, 1980), Cattle Annie and Little Britches, 1981, National Lampoon Goes to the Movies, 1981, Six Pack, 1982, Ladies and Gentlemen, The Fabulous Stains, 1982, The Outsiders, 1983, Rumble Fish, 1983, The Cotton Club, 1984, Streets of Fire, 1984, Lady Beware, 1987, The Big Town, 1987, Vital Signs, 1990, Chaplin, 1992, Knight Moves, 1992, Indian Summer, 1993, Wild Bill, 1995, Judge Dredd, 1995, Jack, 1996, Mad Dog Time, 1996, The Only Thrill, 1997, Murder at 1600, 1997, Over the Moon, 1998, GunShy, 1998, A Walk on the Moon, 1999, The Setting Sun, 1999, My Dog Skip, 1999, The Perfect Storm, 2000, Hard Ball, 2001, The Glass House, 2001, Unfaithful, 2002 (Acad. Award nomination for best actress, 2003, Golden Satellite award for best actress, 2003, Nat. Soc. of Film Critics award for best actress, 2003, NY Film Critics Circle award for best actress, 2003), Under the Tuscan Sun, 2003, Fierce People, 2005, Must Love Dogs, 2005, Hollywoodland, 2006, Untraceable, 2008, Jumper, 2008, Nights in Rodanthe, 2008, Killshot, 2007; (TV movies) Child Bride of Short Creek, 1981, Miss All-America Beauty, 1982; (TV miniseries) Lonesome Dove, 1989, The World's Oldest Living Confederate Widow Tells All, 1994, A Streetcar Named Desire, 1995, Grace and Glorie, 1998. Recipient Women in Hollywood Tribute award, Elle Mag., 2007; named Actress of Yr., Hollywood Film Festival, 2003. Mem. Actors' Equity Assn., AFTRA. Office: The Endeavor Agy 9601 Wilshire Blvd Beverly Hills CA 90212

LANE, FIELDING H., retired lawyer; b. Kansas City, Mo., May 6, 1926; s. Ralph Fielding and Nancy Lee (Greene) L.; m. Patricia Cecil Parkhurst, Jan. 25, 1980 BS in Bus. Adminstrn., U. Mo.-Columbia, 1948; LL.B. cum laude, Harvard U., 1951. Bar: Mo. 1951, Calif. 1956. Assoc. Watson Ess Marshall & Enggas, Kansas City, Mo., 1951-55; assoc. Thelen Marrin Johnson & Bridges, San Francisco, 1955-66, ptnr., 1967—95. Served with USN, 1944-46; PTO; lt. comdr. Res. (ret.) Home: 163 Villa Ter San Francisco CA 94114 Office Phone: 415-369-7068.

LANE, JOHN RODGER, art association administrator, retired museum director; b. Evanston, Ill., Feb. 28, 1944; s. John Crandall Lane and Jeanne Marie (Rodger) L. Moritz; m. Inge-Lise Eckmann, 1992. BA, Williams Coll., 1966; MBA, U. Chgo., 1971; AM, Harvard U., 1973, PhD, 1976; DFA (hon.), San Francisco Art Inst., 1995. Asst. dir. Fogg Art Mus., Cambridge, Mass., 1974—75; exec. asst. to dir., adminstr. curatorial affairs, asst. dir. curatorial affairs Bklyn. Mus., NYC, 1975-80; dir. Carnegie Mus. Art, Pitts., 1980-86, San Francisco Mus. Modern Art, 1987-97; Eugene McDermott dir. Dallas Mus. Art, 1999—2008, dir. emeritus, 2008—; pres., CEO New Art Trust, San Francisco, 2008—. Author: Stuart Davis: Art and Art Theory, 1978; co-editor: Abstract Painting and Sculpture in America, 1927-1944, 1983, Carnegie International, 1985, Dallas Mus. Art 100 Years, 2003, Sigmar Polke: The History of Everything, Paintings, and Drawings, 1998-2003, Gerhard Richter Edits., 1965-2004, Lothar Baumgartern: Carbon, 2004, Fast Forward: Contemporary Collections for Dallas Mus. Art, 2007; exec. editor: The Making of a Modern Museum/SFMOMA, 1995. Mem. vis. com., Williams Coll. Mus. Art, 2007-; Trustee Fountain Valley Sch., Colorado Springs, 1999—2005, James Brooks Found. 2008-. Served to lt. USNR, 1966-69. Nat. Endowment Arts Mus. fellow, 1974-75 Mem. Assn. Art Mus. Dirs. (trustee 2000—02), Am. Assn. Museums. Office: Dallas Mus Art 1717 N Harwood St Dallas TX 75201-2398 Office Phone: 214-922-1304. Business E-Mail: jlane@DallasMuseumofArt.org.*

LANE, LARRY K., air industry service executive; b. 1948; BS in Social Scis., Oreg. Coll. Edn., 1974. With Evergreen Aviation Ground Logistics, 1967-78, 1984—, now chmn.; regional sales rep. Skyline Mobile Home Mfr., McMinnville, Oreg., 1978-84; pres. Evergreen Internat. Airlines, Inc., 1992—. Bd. dirs. Evergreen Internat. Aviation. With USAR, 1969-75. Office: Evergeen Internat Airlines Inc 3850 NE Three Mile Ln Mcminnville OR 97128-9402

LANE, LAURENCE WILLIAM, JR., retired ambassador, publisher; b. Des Moines, Nov. 7, 1919; s. Laurence William and Ruth (Bell) L.; m. Donna Jean Gimbel, Apr. 16, 1955; children: Sharon Louise, Robert Laurence, Brenda Ruth. Student, Pomona Coll., 1938-40, LLD (hon.), 1976; BJ, Stanford U., 1942; DHL (hon.), Hawaii Loa Coll., 1991. Chmn. bd. Lane Pub. Co.; pub. Sunset Mag., Sunset Books and Sunset Films; U.S. amb. to Australia and Nauru, 1985-89; ret., 1990. Bd. dirs. Calif. Water Svc. Co., Crown Zellerbach Corp., Pacific Gas and Electric Co.; bd. dirs. Time Inc.; bd. dirs. Oreg. Coast Aquarium, Internat. Bd. Advice, ANZ Bank; U.S. amb. and commr. Gen. Worlds Fair, Japan, 1975-76; hon. fellow Coll. Notre Dame, 1974. Former mem. adv. bd. Sec. Interior's Bd. Nat. Parks; mem. adv. coun. Grad. Sch. Bus., Stanford U., SRI; mem. Pres.'s Nat. Productivity Adv. Com.; mem. Pacific Basin Econ. Coun.; former bd. dirs. Pacific Forum, CSI, Nat. Parks Found.; vol. The Nat. Ctr.; mem. bd. overseers Hoover Instn. War, Revolution and Peace; mem. exec. com. Ctr. for Australian Studies, U. Tex., Austin. Lt. USNR, World War II, PTO. Decorated officer Order of Australia; recipient Conservation Svc. award Sec. Interior; Theodore and Conrad Wirth award NPF, 1994; William Penn Mott Jr. Conservationist of Yr. award NPCA, 1995; named hon. prof. journalism Stanford U. Mem. Newcomen Soc. N.Am., Pacific Asia Travel Assn. (life mem., chmn. 1980-81), Coun. of Am. Ambs., Los Rancheros Vistadores, Advt. Club San Francisco, No. Calif. Alumni Assn., Bohemian Club, Pacific Union, Men's Garden Club L.A., Alpha Delta Sigma. Republican. Presbyterian. Office: 3000 Sand Hill Rd Bldg 215 Menlo Park CA 94025-7113

LANE, NATHAN (JOSEPH LANE), actor; b. Jersey City, Feb. 3, 1956; s. Daniel and Nora Lane. Appeared in plays: (off-Broadway) A Midsummer Night's Dream, Dedication or the Stuff of Dreams, 2005; (Broadway) Present Laughter, 1982-83, Merlin, 1983, Raving, NYC, 1984, She Stoops to Conquer, NYC, 1984, The Common Pursuit, 1984-85, A Backer's Audition, NYC, 1985, The Wind in the Willows, 1985, Measure for Measure, 1985 (St. Clair Bayfield award for Shakespearean Performance, 1986), The Common Pursuit, 1986-87, Claptrap, NYC, 1987, Uncounted Blessings, 1988, The Film Society, 1988, The Lisbon Traviata, 1989 (Drama Desk award for Best Actor in a Play, 1990, Lucille Lortel award), A Pig's Valise, 1989, Some Americans Abroad, 1990, Bad Habits, 1990, Lips Together, Teeth Apart, 1991, On Borrowed Time, 1991-92, Guys and Dolls, 1992-95 (Drama Desk award for Outstanding Actor in a Musical, 1992, Obie award for Sustained Excellence of Performance, 1992, Outer Critics Cir. awards), Laughter on the 23rd Floor, 1993-94, Love!, Valour!, Compassion!, 1995 (Drama Desk award for Outstanding Featured Actor in a Play, 1995, Obie award for Ensemble Acting, 1995, Outer Critics Cir. awards), A Funny Thing Happened on the Way to the Forum, 1996-98 (Tony award for Best Actor in a Musical, 1996, Drama Desk award for Outstanding Actor in a Musical, 1996, Outer Critics Cir. awards), The Man Who Came to Dinner, 2000, The Producers, 2001-02, 2003 (Drama Desk award for Outstanding Actor in a Musical, 2001, Tony award for Best Actor in a Musical, 2001, Olivier award for Best Actor in a Musical, 2005), Trumbo Red White and Blacklisted, 2003, The Frogs, 2004, The Odd Couple, 2005-06, Butley, 2006-07, November, 2008; (TV movies) Valley of the Dolls, 1981, The Last Mile, 1992, The Wizard of Oz in Concert: Dreams Come True, 1995, The Boys Next Door, 1996, Merry Christmas, George Bailey, 1997, The Man Who Came to Dinner, 2000, Laughter on the 23rd Floor, 2001; (TV series) One of the Boys, 1982, One Saturday Morning, 1997, Encore!Encore!, 1998-99, George and Martha, 1999, Teacher's Pet, 2000-02 (Daytime Emmy award for Outstanding Performer in an Animated Program, 2001); actor, exec. prodr.: (TV series) Charlie Lawrence, 2003; actor: (films) Walls of Glass, 1985, Ironweed, 1987, The Lemon Sisters, 1990, Joe Versus the Volcano, 1990, He Said, She Said, 1991, Frankie and Johnny, 1991, Life With Mikey, 1993, Addams Family Values, 1993, (voice only) The Lion King, 1994, The Birdcage, 1996 (SAG award for Outstanding Performance by a Cast, Am. Comedy award for Best Performance by an Actor in a Motion Picture-Musical or Comedy, 1996, Golden Globe nomination), Mousehunt, 1997, (voice only) The Lion King II: Simba's Pride, 1998, The Best Man, 1999, At First Sight, 1999, (voice only) Stuart Little, 1999, Isn't She Great?, 2000, Trixie, 2000, Love's Labour's Lost, 2000, (voice only) Titan A.E., 2000, Nicholas Nickelby, 2002 (Nat. Bd. Review award for Best Ensemble Performance, 2002), (voice only) Stuart Little 2, 2002, Austin Powers in Goldmember, 2002, (voice only) Teacher's Pet, 2004, Win a Date with Tad Hamilton!, 2004, (voice only) The Lion King 1½, 2004, The Producers, 2005, (voice only) Stuart Little 3: Call of the Wild, 2006, Swing Vote, 2008; (TV guest appearances) Miami Vice, 1985, The Days and Nights of Molly Dodd, 1989, '90, '91, (voice only) The American Experience, 1991, (voice only) Timon and Pumbaa, 1995 (Daytime Emmy award for Outstanding Performer in an Animated Program, 1996), Frasier, 1995, Mad About You, 1997, Sex and the City, 2002, Absolutely Fabulous, 2004, 30 Rock, 2007 Recipient People's Choice award for Favorite Male Performer in a New TV Series, 1999, Vito Russo award, GLAAD, 2002, American Theatre Wing Honor, 2006, Trevor Project Hero award, 2007, Human Rights Campaign Equality award; named to Hollywood Walk of Fame, 2006.

LANE, NATHAN, III, lawyer; b. Phila., 1946; AB, Duke U., 1968; JD cum laude, U. Pa., 1971. Bar: Calif. 1972, registered: US Dist. Ct. (No. Dist.) Calif. 1972, US Ct. Appeals (9th cir.) 1972, US Dist. Ct. (So. Dist.) Calif. 1976, US Dist. Ct. (Ctrl. Dist.) Calif. 1980, US Ct. Appeals (10th cir.) 1985, US Dist. Ct. (Ea. Dist.) Calif. 1987, US Ct. Appeals (8th cir.) 1991, US Tax Ct. 1992, US Ct. Appeals (Fed. Cir.) 1997, US Patent & Trademark Office 1999. Ptnr. Graham & James, San Francisco, Squire, Sanders & Dempsey LLP, San Francisco, chmn., Intellectual Property Practice Group. Editl. bd. U. Pa. Law Rev., 1969—71; author: Discovery in Other Nations, 1988. Bd. dir. Legal Aid Soc., San Francisco, 1986—91. Mem.: Bar Assn. San Francisco (chmn. Antitrust Sect. 1988), ABA (Antitrust Sect., Intellectual Property Sect., Internat. Law Sect., Litig. Sect.), Order of Coif. Office: Squire Sanders & Dempsey LLP One Maritime Plaza Ste 300 San Francisco CA 94111-3492 Office Phone: 415-954-0249. Office Fax: 415-393-9887. Business E-Mail: nlane@ssd.com.

LANE, SYLVIA, economist, educator; b. NYC; m. Benjamin Lane, Sept. 2, 1939; children: Leonard, Reese, Nancy. AB, U. Calif., Berkeley, 1934, MA, 1936; postgrad., Columbia U., 1937; PhD, U. So. Calif., 1957. Lectr., asst. prof. U. So. Calif., 1947—60; assoc. prof. econs. San Diego State U., 1961-65; assoc. prof. finance, assoc. dir. Ctr. for Econ. Edn. Calif. State U., Fullerton, 1965-69, chmn. dept. fin., 1967-69; prof. agrl. econs. U. Calif., Davis, 1969-82, prof. emerita, 1982—; prof. emerita and economist Giannini Found., U. Calif.-Berkeley, 1982—; vis. scholar Stanford U., 1975-76. Cons. Calif. Adv. Commn. Tax Reform, 1963, Adv. Office Consumer Affairs, Exec. Office of Pres., 1972-77, FAO, UN, 1983, Consumer food Subsidiaries Project, 1993. Author: (with E. Bryant Phillips) Personal Finance, 1963, rev. edit., 1979, The Insurance Tax, 1965, California's Income Tax Conformity and Withholding, 1968, (with Irma Adelman) The Balance Between Industry and Agriculture in Economic Development, 1989; author video: Women in Agriculture - Africa, 1994; editl. bd. Agrl. Econs., 1986-92; also articles, reports in field. Project economist Los Angeles County Welfare Planning Coun., 1956-59; del. White House Conf. on Food and Nutrition, 1969, Pres.'s Summit Con. on Inflation, 1974; mem. adv. com. Ctr. for Bldg. Tech., Nat. Bur. Stds., 1975-79; bd. dirs. Am. Coun. Consumer Interests, 1972-74; exec. bd. Am. Agr. Econ. Assn. 1976-79. Ford Found. fellow UCLA, 1963; Ford Found. fellow U. Chgo., 1965; fellow U. Chgo., 1968; fellow Am. Agrl. Econ. Assn., 1984; fellow Sylvia Lane Fellowship Fund, 1993. Mem. Am. Econ. Assn., Am. Coun. Consumer Interests, Omicron Delta Epsilon (pres. 1973-75, trustee 1975-83, chmn. bd. trustees 1982-84). Home and Office: Pacific Regent - La Jolla 3890 Nobel Dr #1508 San Diego CA 92122 Personal E-mail: blane5@san.rr.com.

LANE, W. JAMES, Mayor, Scottsdale, Ariz., airline executive, CPA; b. Jersey City, Feb. 22, 1951; s. William James and Bernadette Ann (Berube) L.; m. Kathleen McDonald, Dec. 30, 1972 (div. June 1978); 1 child, Bill; m. Joanne Blum, June 2, 1979; children: Scott, Nancy. BS in Acctg., St. Joseph's U., Phila., 1973. CPA, Ariz. Supervising sr. Peat, Marwick, Mitchell & Co., Phoenix, 1973-78; contr. Phoenix (Ariz.) Redi-Mix Co., Inc., 1978-82; comptr. Kupanoff & Assocs., Inc., Scottsdale, Ariz., 1982-84; pres. Westrock, Inc., Phoenix, 1983-88, StatesWest Airlines, Phoenix, 1988—90; mem. Chatham Hill Group, LLC, Manacine, 1996—, Scottsdale City Coun., 2004—09; mayor City of Scottsdale, Ariz., 2009—. YMCA Bd.Mgmt., 1996-2002, chmn.Kids Campaign,1999. Scottsdale Fire & EMS Advisory Committee, 2002, Nat.League of Cities Pub.Safety, Crime Prevention Steering Com. Republican. Roman Catholic. Avocations: flying, boating. Home: 7666 E El Rancho Dr Scottsdale AZ 85260-6468 Office: Office of Mayor 3939 N Drinkwater Blvd Scottsdale AZ 85251 Office Phone: 480-312-2433. Office Fax: 480-312-2738. Business E-Mail: jlane@scottsdaleaz.gov.

LANEY, MICHAEL L., manufacturing executive; b. LA, Sept. 10, 1945; s. Roy and Wanda Laney; m. Marti Miller, Dec. 31, 1964; children: Tynna, Kristen. BS with honors, Calif. State U., Northridge, 1967; MBA, UCLA, 1969. CPA, Calif. Sr. tax acct. Haskins-Sells, Los Angeles, 1967-69; asst. prof. acctg. Calif. State U., Northridge, 1969-72; tax prin. M. Klaiman Acctg. Corp., Beverly Hills, Calif., 1972-75; pvt. practice Beverly Hills, 1975-80; v.p., controller Ducommun, Inc., Los Angeles, 1980-87; sr. v.p., fin. and adminstrn. Monarch Mirror Door Co. Inc., Chatsworth, Calif., 1987-92; v.p. ops. feature animation Walt Disney Pictures and TV (part of The Walt Disney Co.), Glendale, Calif., 1992-93; sr. v.p. ops. Warner Bros., Glendale, Calif., 1994-96; pres. Children's Wonderland, Agoura, Calif., 1996-97; CFO Dacor, Pasadena, Calif., 1997-2001; pres., CEO Cool Roof of Calif., Inc., Calabasas, 2001—; pres. M. Laney & Assocs., Portland, 2002—; CFO Energy Trust Oreg., Inc., 2004—05. Mem. Fin. Execs. Inst. (pres. Portland chpt.), Am. Inst. CPA's, Calif. Soc. CPA's; Assn. Corp. Growth., Am. Sch. Counselors Assn., Soc. Human Resources (practioner), Assn. Psychol. Type. Office Phone: 503-946-8798. Personal E-mail: mlaneyassoc@yahoo.com.

LANG, GEORGE FRANK, insurance company executive, lawyer, consultant; b. Orange, NJ, Aug. 21, 1937; s. Frank W. and Hilda I. (Pierson) L.; m. Grace B. Preisler, Jan. 30, 1960; children: Christine, Gregg, Cynthia; m. Valerie J. Hanson, Nov. 24, 1978. BS, Ill. Wesleyan U., 1960; JD, Ill. Inst. Tech., 1968. Account exec. Scarborough & Co., Chgo., 1960-67; dir. fin. inst. George F. Brown & Sons, Chgo., 1967-69; v.p., dir. Fin. Ins. Svc., Schaumburg, Ill., 1969-79; pres. City Ins. Svc., Elizabeth, N.J., 1980-84; mng. dir. Res. Fin. Mgmt., Miami, Fla., 1984-85; v.p. Beneficial Ins. Group, Newport Beach, Calif., 1985-86, Ask Ins. Svc., Irvine, Calif., 1986-89, cons. product ctr. sales, 1989; cons. Nat. Dealer Ins. Systems, 1989, New Liberty Adminstrn., 1990—, Home Crest Ins., 1991—, Great Western Ins. Agy., 1992—, Dana Harbor Ins. Svcs., Inc., 1995—. Cons. in field. Bd. dirs. Woodview Civic Assn., Mt. Prospect, Ill., 1964-70, pres., bd. dirs., 1969; bd. dirs. Chippendale Assn., Barrington, Ill., 1972-76, v.p., bd. dirs., 1976. Avocations: boating, fishing, travel. Home and Office: 1122 Morning Walk Depoe Bay OR 97341 Home Phone: 541-765-3177. E-mail: danaharbo@centurytel.net.

LANG, K. D. (KATHERINE DAWN LANG), country music singer, composer; b. Consort, Alta., Can., Feb. 11, 1961; d. Adam and Audrey L. Lang. Mem. Tex. swing fiddle band, 1982—; formed band The Reclines. Albums include A Truly Western Experience, 1984, Angel with a Lariat, 1986, Shadowland, 1988, Absolute Torch and Twang, 1990 (Can. Country Music Awards album of the yr.), Ingenue, 1992, Even Cowgirls Get the Blues (soundtrack), 1993, Drag, 1997, Australian Tour, 1997, Invincible Summer, 2000, Live By Request, 2001, Hymns of the 49th Parallel, 2004, Watershed, 2008; (with others) All You Can Eat, 1995, (with Tony Bennett) A Wonderful World, 2003 (Grammy award for Best Traditional Pop Vocal Album, 2004); actress (film) Salmonberries, 1991; Teresa's Tattoo, 1994, Eye of the Beholder, 1999, The Black Dahlia, 2006, (TV miniseries) The Last Don, 1997, TV guest appearance Ellen, 1997. Recipient Can. Country Music awards, including Entertainer of Yr., 1989, Grammy award, 1990, 1993, 2004, Best Pop Female Vocal for Constant Craving, Grammy nomination Best Pop Female Vocal for Miss Chatelaine, 1994, William Harold Moon award Soc. of Composers, Authors and Music Publishers of Can., 1994. Office: Warner Bros Records Inc 3300 Warner Blvd Burbank CA 91505-4694

LANG, LINDA A., food service executive; B in Fin., U. Calif., Berkeley; MBA, San Diego State U. Joined Jack in the Box Inc., 1985, divsn. v.p. new products and promotions, 1994—96, v.p. products, promotions and consumer rsch., 1996—99, v.p. mktg., 1999—2001, sr. v.p. mktg., 2001—02, exec. v.p. mktg. and ops., human resources, restaurant devel., quality assurance and logistics, 2002—03, pres., COO San Diego, 2003—05, chmn., CEO, 2005—. Bd. dir. WD-40 Co. Office: Jack in the Box Inc 9330 Balboa Ave San Diego CA 92123

LANG, THOMPSON HUGHES, publishing executive; b. Albuquerque, Dec. 12, 1946; s. Cornelius Thompson and Margaret Miller (Hughes) L. Student, U. N.Mex., 1965-68, U. Americas, Mexico City, 1968-69. Advt. salesman Albuquerque Pub. Co., 1969-70, pres., 1971—; pub., pres., treas., dir. Jour. Pub. Co., 1971—; pres., dir. Masthead, Internat., 1971—; pres. Magnum Systems, Inc., 1973—; pres., treas., dir. Jour. Ctr. Corp., 1979—; chmn. bd., dir. Starline Printing, Inc., 1985—. Chmn. bd. dirs. Corp. Security and Investigation, Inc., 1986—; pres., bd. dirs. Eagle Systems, Inc., 1986—. Mem. HOW Orgn., Sigma Delta Chi. Home: 8643 Rio Grande Blvd NW Albuquerque NM 87114-1301 Office: Albuquerque Pub Co PO Drawer JT 87103 7777 Jefferson St NE Albuquerque NM 87109-4343

LANGA, BRIAN D., lawyer; b. Marietta, Ga., Mar. 1, 1973; BS, Rice Univ., 1995; JD, Univ. Washington, 1998. Bar: Calif. 1998, US Dist. Ct. Ctrl. & No. Calif. Ptnr., environ. & real estate law Demetriou, Del Guerico, Springer & Francis LLP, LA. Contbr. articles to profl. jours. Named a Rising Star, So. Calif. Super Lawyers, 2006. Mem.: Fed. Bar Assn., LA County Bar Assn., Internat. Right of Way Assn., Calif. Waste Assn. (past chmn. steering com., LA county chapter), Harbor Assn. Ind. & Comm. Office: Demetriou Del Guerico Springer & Francis LLP 10th Fl 801 S Grand Ave Los Angeles CA 90017-4613 Office Phone: 213-624-8407. Office Fax: 213-624-0174. Business E-Mail: blanga@ddsffirm.com.

LANGACKER, RONALD WAYNE, linguistics educator; b. Fond du Lac, Wis., Dec. 27, 1942; s. George Rollo and Florence (Hinesley) L.; m. Margaret G. Fullick, June 5, 1966 (dec.); m. Sheila M. Pickwell, Mar. 28, 1998. AB in French, U. Ill., 1963, A.M. in Linguistics, 1964, PhD, 1966. Asst. prof. U. Calif. at San Diego, La Jolla, 1966-70, asso. prof., 1970-75, prof. linguistics, 1975—2003; ret. Author: Language and its Structure, 1968, Fundamentals of Linguistic Analysis, 1972, Non-Distinct Arguments in Uto-Aztecan, 1976, An Overview of Uto-Aztecan Grammar, 1977, Foundations of Cognitive Grammar I, 1987, Concept, Image and Symbol, 1990, Foundations of Cognitive Grammar II, 1991, Grammar and Conceptualization, 1999; Cognitive Grammar: A Basic Intro., 2008; assoc. editor: Lang, 1971-77, Cognitive Linguistics, 1989—; contbr. articles in field to profl. jours. Guggenheim fellow, 1978 Mem. Linguistic Soc. Am., Cognitive Sci. Soc., Soc. for Study Indigenous Langs. of Ams., Internat. Cognitive Linguistics Assn. (pres. 1997-99), ACLU. Home: 7381 Rue Michael La Jolla CA 92037-3915 Office: U Calif San Diego Dept Linguistics 0108 La Jolla CA 92093 E-mail: rlangacker@ucsd.edu.

LANGAN, KENNETH J., lawyer; b. Sept. 14, 1955; BSFS cum laude, Georgetown U., 1977; JD, Columbia U., 1980. Bar: N.Y. 1981, Calif. 1993, England & Wales (solicitor) 1998. Ptnr., Project Fin. Practice Group Arnold & Porter, LA. Mem.: Phi Beta Kappa. Office: Arnold & Porter 777 S Figueroa St Los Angeles CA 90017-2513 Office Phone: 213-243-4114. Office Fax: 213-243-4199. Business E-Mail: kenneth.langan@aporter.com.

LANGBERG, BARRY BENSON, lawyer; b. Balt., Nov. 24, 1942; s. Nathan and Marion (Cohen) L.; m. Vickie Williams, Mar. 27, 1978 (div. 1987); children: Mitchell, Marie, Elena. BA, U. San Francisco, 1964, JD, 1968. Bar: Calif. 1971, U.S. Dist. Ct. (cen. dist.) Calif. 1971, U.S. Supreme Ct. 1974, U.S. Tax Ct. 1976. Dep. pub. defender Los Angeles County, 1971-72; assoc. Trope & Trope, LA, 1972-74, Hayes & Hume, Beverly Hills, Calif., 1974-85; pres. David Jamison Carlyle Corp., LA, 1979-84; ptnr. Hayes, Hume, Petas & Langberg, LA, 1985-89; atty. Barry B. Langberg & Assocs., LA, 1989-97; ptnr. Bronson, Bronson & McKinnon, LA, 1997—2000; mng. ptnr., LA office, entertainment law practice area Stroock & Stroock & Lavan LLP, LA, 2000—. Prof. Mid-Valley Coll. Law, L.A., 1972-82; lectr. U. So. Calif., 1980. Mem. ABA. Democrat. Avocations: sailing, baseball. Office: Stroock & Strook & Lavan LLP 2029 Century Pk E Los Angeles CA 90067-3086 Office Phone: 310-556-5861. Office Fax: 310-556-5959. Business E-Mail: blangberg@stroock.com.

LANGDON, GLEN GEORGE, JR., electrical engineer; b. Morristown, NJ, June 30, 1936; s. Glen George and Mildred (Miller) L.; m. Marian Elizabeth Jacobsen, Aug. 10, 1963; 1 child, Karen Joan. BSEE, Wash. State U., 1957; MSEE, U. Pitts., 1963; PhD, Syracuse U., 1968. Elec. engr. Westinghouse Electric Co., East Pittsburgh, Pa., 1960-62; applications programmer Churchill Boro, Pa., 1962-63; engr. IBM Corp., Endicott, N.Y., 1963-73; rsch. staff mem. San Jose, Calif., 1974-87; prof. computer engring. U. Calif., Santa Cruz, 1987—. Vis. prof. U. São Paulo, Brazil, 1971-72; lectr. U. Santa Clara, 1975-78, Stanford U., 1984; U. Calif. affiliate lectr. Los Alamos Nat. Lab., 2001. Author: Logic Design: A Review of Theory and Practice, 1974, (with Edson Fregni) Projecto de Computadores Digitals, 1974, Computer Design, 1982; patentee in field. Lt. Signal Corps., U.S. Army, 1958-59. Recipient Armed Svcs. Comm. award Wash. State U., 1957, Outstanding Innovation award IBM, 1980, 91; Erskine fellow U. Canterbury, 1993, 99. Fellow IEEE, Computer Soc. IEEE (stds. com. 1969-70, 74-81, sec. 1982, edn. bd. 1983-86, pub. bd. 1984-85, 87-90, bd. govs. 1984-87, v.p. edn. 1986, Compcon gen. chair 1986, Hot Chips IV Symposium gen. chair 1992, cons. data compression patent disputes 1993—, mem. joint steering com. hot chips and hot interconnects 1999—); mem. Assn. Computing Machinery (vice chmn. So. Tier chpt. 1973), Soc. Photog. Instrumentation Engrs., Soc. Motion Picture and TV Engrs., Sigma Xi. Home: 220 Horizon Way Aptos CA 95003-2739 Office: U Calif Dept Computer Engring Santa Cruz CA 95064

LANGE, ANDREW E., astrophysicist; BA, Princeton U., 1980; PhD, U. Calif., Berkeley, 1987. Vis. assoc. Calif. Inst. Tech., 1993—94, prof., 1994—2001, Marvin L. Goldberger prof. physics, Observational Cosmology Group, 2001—. Named Calif. Scientist Yr., Calif. Sci. Ctr., 2003. Mem.: NAS. Achievements include expert in structure and geometry of very early universe and in measurement of irregularities in cosmic microwave background radiation. Office: Calif Inst Tech Mailcode 59-33 Pasadena CA 91125 Office Phone: 626-395-6887. Office Fax: 626-584-9929. Business E-Mail: ael@astro.caltech.edu.

LANGE, CLIFFORD ELMER, retired librarian; b. Fond du Lac, Wis., Dec. 29, 1935; s. Elmer H. and Dorothy Brick (Smithers) L.; m. Janet M. LeMieux, June 6, 1959; children: Paul, Laura, Ruth. Student, St. Norbert Coll., 1954-57; BS, Wis. State U., 1959; MSL.S. (Library Services Act scholar), U. Wis., 1960, PhD (Higher Edn. Act fellow), 1972. Head extension dept. Oshkosh Pub. Libr., Wis., 1960-62, head reference dept., 1962-63; asst. dir. Jervis Libr., Rome, 1962; dir. Eau Claire Pub. Libr., Wis., 1963-66; asst. dir. Lake County Pub. Libr., Griffith, Ind., 1966-68; asst. prof. Sch. Libr. Sci., U. Iowa, 1971-73; dir. Wauwatosa Pub. Libr., Wis., 1973-75; asst. prof. U. So. Calif., 1975-78; state libr. N.Mex. State Libr., Santa Fe, 1978-82; dir. Carlsbad City Libr., Calif., 1982—2005; ret., 2005. Served with U.S. Army, 1958. Mem. ALA, Calif. Libr. Assn. Home: 3575 Ridge Rd Oceanside CA 92056-4952 Personal E-mail: clifflange@cox.net.

LANGE, FREDERICK F., materials engineer, educator; BS in Ceramics, Rutgers U., 1961; PhD in Solid State Tech., Pa. State U., 1965. Sr. scientist, fellow sci. dept. materials Westinghouse Rsch. Labs., 1967-76; mgr., prin. scientist structural ceramics group Rockwell Internat. Sci. Ctr., 1976-86; prof. dept. materials and chem. engring. U. Calif., Santa Barbara, 1986—. Adj. prof. UCLA, 1979-86. Contbr. articles to profl. jours. Humboldt Sr. fellow German govt., 1996; recipient Centennial Fellow award Pa. State U., Max Planck Rsch. award, Max Planck Soc., Germany, 1997; named Jubilee prof. Chalmers U., Sweden, 1983, Disting. Dow lectr., Northwe. U., 1992. Fellow Am. Ceramic Soc. (Ross Coffin Purdy award 1982, Richard M. Fulrath award 1982, Sosman Meml. lecture 1987, John Jeppson award 1988, Kraner award 1989); mem. NAE, Acad. Ceramics. Achievements include research in interrelations between processing, phase relations, microstructure and properties leading to either new or improved structural ceramics and their composites; processing of ceramic microstructure that produce higher crack growth resistance, and colloidal powder. Office: U Calif Dept Materials Santa Barbara CA 93106-5050 E-mail: flange@engineering.uscb.edu.

LANGE, LESTER HENRY, mathematics professor; b. Concordia, Mo., Jan. 2, 1924; s. Harry William Christopher and Ella Martha (Alewel) L.; m. Anne Marie Pelikan, Aug. 17, 1947 (div. Oct. 1960); children: Christopher, Nicholas, Philip, Alexander; m. Beverly Jane Brown, Feb. 4, 1962; 1 son, Andrew. Student, U. Calif., Berkeley, 1943-44; BA in Math, Valparaiso U., 1948; MS in Math, Stanford, 1950; PhD in Math, U. Notre Dame, 1960. Instr., then asst. prof. math. Valparaiso U., 1950-56; instr. math. U. Notre Dame, 1956-57, 59-60. Mem. faculty San Jose State U., Calif., 1960—, prof. math., head dept., 1961-70, dean Sch. Natural Scis. and Math., 1970—, dean Sch. Sci., 1972-88, emeritus prof. math., emeritus dean, 1988—; founder Soc. Archimedes at San Jose State U., 1982; now spl. asst. to dir. Moss Landing (Calif.) Marine Labs.; founding bd. dirs. Friends of MLML, Inc. Author text on linear algebra; sr. editor Calif. Math, 1981-84; contbr. to profl. jours. Served with inf. AUS, 1943-46, ETO. Decorated Combat Infantryman's Badge and Bronze Star; Danforth fellow, 1957-58; NSF faculty fellow, 1958-59. Fellow Calif. Acad. Scis.; mem. Math. Assn. Am. (bd. govs., L.R. Ford Sr. award 1972, George Polya award 1993, Meritorious Svc. award 2003), Calif. Math. Coun., London Math. Soc., Fibonacci Assn. (bd. dirs. 1987-97). Home: 308 Escalona Dr Capitola CA 95010-3419 Office: Moss Landing Marine Labs Moss Landing CA 95039 Business E-Mail: lange@cruzio.com.

LANGELLA, FRANK, actor; b. Bayonne, NJ, Jan. 1, 1940; m. Ruth Weil, June 14, 1977 (div. 1996); 2 children. Student, Syracuse U.; studies with Seymour Falk. Apprenticed Pocono Playhouse, Mountain Home, Pa., appeared Erie (Pa.) Playhouse, 1960, mem. original, Lincoln Center repertory tng. co., 1963; actor (Broadway shows) Yerma, 1966, Seascape, 1974-75 (Tony award best featured actor, 1975, Drama Desk award, 1975), A Cry of Players, 1968 (Drama Desk award, 1968), Dracula, 1977-80 (Drama League award, 1978, Tony nom. best actor in a play, 1978), Passion, 1983, Design for Living, 1984, Hurlyburly, 1985, Sherlock's Last Case, 1987, The Father, 1996, Present Laughter, 1996-97, Fortune's Fool, 2002, Match, 2004 (Tony nom. best actor in a play, 2004), Frost/Nixon, 2007, A Man for All Seasons, 2008; other stage appearances include: The Immoralist, 1963, Benito Cereno, 1964, The Old Glory, 1964-65 (Obie award, 1965), Good Day, 1965-66 (Obie award, 1966), The White Devil, 1965-66 (Obie award, 1966), Long Day's Journey Into Night, The Skin of Our Teeth, The Cretan Woman, all 1966, The Devils, Iphigenia at Aulis, all 1967, Cyrano de Bergerac, 1971, A Midsummer Night's Dream, 1972, The Relapse, The Tooth of Crime, 1972, The Taming of the Shrew, 1973, The Seagull, 1974, Ring Round the Moon, 1975, After the Fall, 1984, Booth, 1994, The Prince of Hamburg, Cleve. Playhouse Co., 1967-68, L.I. Festival repertory, 1968, Les Liaisons Dangereuses, Frost/Nixon, 2006 (Drama Desk award outstanding actor in a play 2007, Outer Critics Cir. award outstanding actor in a play, 2007, Tony award best performance by a leading actor in a play, 2007); stage directing debut in John and Abigail, 1969; (films) Diary of a Mad Housewife, 1970 (Nat. Soc. Film Critics award, 1970), The Twelve Chairs, 1970, The Deadly Trap, 1972, The Wrath of God, 1972, Dracula, 1979, Those Lips Those Eyes, 1980, Sphinx, 1981, The Men's Club, 1986, Masters of the Universe, 1987, And God Created Woman, 1988, True Identity, 1991, 1492: Conquest of Paradise, 1992, Dave, 1993, Body of Evidence, 1993, Brainscan, 1994, Junior, 1994, Bad Company, 1995, Cutthroat Island, 1995, Eddie, 1996, Lolita, 1997, I'm Losing You, 1998, Alegría, 1998, Small Soldiers, 1998, The Ninth Gate, 1999, Stardom, 2000, Sweet November, 2001, House of D, 2004, The Novice, 2004, Breaking the Fifth, 2004, How You Look to Me, 2005, Return to Rajapur, 2005, Good Night, and Good Luck, 2005, Superman Returns, 2006, Starting Out in the Evening, 2007 (Best Actor, Boston Film Critics Awards, 2007), The Caller, 2008, Frost/Nixon, 2008 (Best Actor African Am. Film Critics Assn., 2008), (voice) The Tale of Despereaux, 2008; (TV movies) Benito Cereno, 1965, Good Day, 1967, The Mark of Zorro, 1974, The Ambassador, 1974, The Seagull, 1975, The American Woman: Portraits of Courage, 1976, Eccentricities of a Nightingale, 1976, Sherlock Holmes, 1981, I, Leonardo: A Journey of the Mind, 1983 (Emmy nom. best actor, 1983), Liberty, 1986, The Doomsday Gun, 1994, Moses, 1996, Kilroy, 1999, Jason and the Argonauts, 2000, Cry Baby Lane, 2000, 111 Gramercy Park, 2003, Now You See It..., 2005, The Water is Wide, 2006, 10.5: Apocalypse, 2006. Bd. dirs. Berkshire Festival. Named one of The Ten Most Fascinating People of 2008, Barbara Walters. Mem. Actors Equity, Screen Actors Guild. Office: Special Artists Agency 9465 Wilshire Blvd Ste 880 Beverly Hills CA 90212-2607

LANGENHEIM, JEAN HARMON, biologist, educator; b. Homer, La., Sept. 5, 1925; d. Vergil Wilson and Jeanette (Smith) Harmon; m. Ralph Louis Langenheim, Dec. 1946 (div. Mar. 1962). BS, U. Tulsa, 1946; MS, U. Minn., 1949, PhD, 1953. Rsch. assoc. botany U. Calif., Berkeley, 1954-59, U. Ill., Urbana, 1959-61; rsch. fellow biology Harvard U., Cambridge, Mass., 1962-66; asst. prof. biology U. Calif., Santa Cruz, 1966-68, assoc. prof. biology, 1968-73, prof. biology, 1973-93, prof. biology emerita, 1993—, rsch. prof. ecol. and evolution biology, 2001—. Acad. v.p. Orgn. Tropical Studies, San Jose, Costa Rica, 1975—78; chmn. com. humid tropics US Nat. Acad. Nat. Rsch. Coun., 1975—77; mem. com. floral inventory Amazon NSF, Washington, 1975—87; mem. sci. adv. bd. EPA, Washington, 1977—81. Author: (Book) Botany-Plant-Biology in Relation to Human Affairs, 1982, Plant Resins: Chemistry, Evolution, Ecology and Ethnobotany, 2003 (Klinger Best Ethnobotany Book award, Soc. Economic Botany, 2004); contbr. articles to profl. jours. Recipient Disting. Alumni award, U. Tulsa, 1979, Dedication of Madrono, Calif. Bot. Soc., 2004, Fellow's Medal, Calf. Academy Scis., 2006; grantee, NSF, 1966—88. Fellow: AAUW, AAAS, Bunting Inst., Calif. Acad. Scis.; mem.: Soc. Econ. Botany (pres. 1993—94), Assn. Tropical Biology (pres. 1985—86), Internat. Soc. Chem. Ecology (pres. 1986—87), Ecol. Soc. Am. (pres. 1986—87), Bot. Soc. Am. (Centennial award 2006). Home: 191 Palo Verde Ter Santa Cruz CA 95060-3214 Office: Univ California Dept Ecol and Evolutionary Biology Earth and Marine Scis Bldg Santa Cruz CA 95064 Home Phone: 831-426-3058; Office Phone: 831-459-2918. Business E-Mail: lang@darwin.ucsc.edu.

LANGER, JAMES STEPHEN, physicist, researcher; b. Pitts., Sept. 21, 1934; s. Bernard F. and Liviette (Roth) L.; m. Elinor Goldmark Aaron, Dec. 21, 1958; children: Ruth, Stephen, David. BS, Carnegie Inst. Tech., 1955; PhD, U. Birmingham, Eng., 1958. Prof. physics Carnegie-Mellon U., Pitts., 1958-82, assoc. dean, 1971-74; prof. physics U. Calif., Santa Barbara, 1982—, dir. Inst. for Theoretical Physics, 1989-95. Contbr. articles to profl. jours. Guggenheim fellow, 1974-75; Marshall scholar, 1955-57 Fellow AAAS, Am. Acad. Arts and Scis., Am. Phys. Soc. (chair divsn. condensed matter physics 1997-98, pres.-elect 1999, pres. 2000, Oliver E. Buckley Condensed-Matter Physics prize 1997); mem. NAS (v.p. 2001-05). Democrat. Home: 1130 Las Canoas Ln Santa Barbara CA 93105-2331 Office: U Calif Dept Physics Santa Barbara CA 93106 Business E-Mail: langer@physics.ucsb.edu.

LANGER, STEVEN, human resources specialist, consultant, psychologist; s. Israel and Anna (Glaisner) L.; m. Jacqueline White, Oct. 11, 1954 (dec. Dec. 1969); children: Bruce, Diana, Geoffrey; m. Elaine Catherine Brewer, Dec. 29, 1979 (dec. Feb. 1992). BA in Psychology, Calif. State U., Sacramento, 1950; MS in Pers. Svcs., U. Colo., 1958; PhD, Walden U., 1972. Lic. psychologist, Ill; cert. sr. human resources specialist. Asst. to pers. dir. City and County of Denver, 1956-59; pers. dir. City of Pueblo, Colo., 1959-60; pers. cons. J.L. JAcobs & Co., Chgo., 1961-64, adminstrv. mgr., 1966-67; sales selection mgr. Reuben H. Donnelly Corp., Chgo., 1964-66; pres. Abbott, Langer & Assocs., Crete, Ill., 1967—2007, Langer Human Resources Group, LLC, Boulder, Colo., 2007—. Vis. prof. mgmt. Loyola U., Chgo., 1969-71; community prof. behavioral scis. Purdue U., Calumet campus, Hammond, Ind., 1973-75. Contbr. articles to profl. jours. Mem. Ill. Psychol. Assn. (chmn. sect. indsl. psychologists 1971-72), Chgo. Psychol. Assn. (pres. 1974-75, 94-95), Chgo. Indsl./Orgnl. Psychologists, Soc. Human Resources Mgmt. (accredited, chmn. rsch. award com. 1966-69), World at Work, Chgo. Compensation Assn. (sec. 1976-77), Mensa (pres. Chgo. chpt. 1972-74). Unitarian Universalist. Office: Langer Human Resources Group LLC 247 Manhattan Dr Boulder CO 80303 Office Phone: 720-304-2171. Business E-Mail: SLanger@LangerHR.com.

LANGLEY, DONNA, film company executive; Sr. v.p. prodn. New Line Cinema, 1994—2001, Universal Pictures, 2001—03, exec. v.p. prodn., 2003—05, pres. prodn., 2005—. Exec. prodr.: (films) Austin Powers: The Spy Who Shagged Me, 1999, Drop Dead Gorgeous, 1999, The Astronaut's Wife, 1999, The Bachelor, 1999, The Cell, 2000, Lost Souls, 2000, Highway, 2002. Named one of The 100 Most Powerful Women in Entertainment, Hollywood Reporter, 2006, 2007. Office: Universal Pictures 100 Universal City Plz Universal City CA 91608

LANGONI, RICHARD ALLEN, retired civil engineer; b. Trinidad, Colo., Aug. 7, 1945; s. Domenic and Josephine (Maria) L.; m. Pamela Jill Stansberry, Aug. 19, 1972; children: Kristi, Kerri. A of Applied Sci., Trinidad State Jr. Coll., Colo., 1966; BSCE, Colo. State U., Ft. Collins, 1968; MA, U. No. Colo., Greeley, 1978. Registered profl. engr., Colo. Civil engr. Dow Chm. Co., Golden, Colo., 1968-71; city engr., dir. pub. works City of Trinidad, 1971-74; civil engr. Clement Bros. Constrn. Co., 1974-75; instr. Trinidad State Jr. Coll., 1975-78; city engr., dir. pub. works City of Durango, Colo., 1978-82; traffic engr. Colo. Dept. Transp., Durango, 1982—2005; ret., 2005. Home: 30 Moenkopi Dr Durango CO 81301-8599 Home Phone: 970-259-0750. Personal E-mail: dlangoni@hotmail.com.

LANGSLEY, PAULINE ROYAL, psychiatrist; b. Lincoln, Nebr., July 2, 1927; d. Paul Ambrose and Dorothy (Sibley) Royal; m. Donald G. Langsley, Sept. 9, 1955; children: Karen Jean, Dorothy Ruth Langsley Runman, Susan Louise. BA, Mills Coll., 1949; MD, U. Nebr., 1953. Cert. psychiatrist, Am. Bd. Psychiatry and Neurology. Intern Mt. Zion Hosp., San Francisco, 1954; resident U. Calif., San Francisco, 1954-57, student health psychiatrist Berkeley, 1957-61, U. Colo., Boulder, 1961-68; assoc. clin. prof. psychiatry U. Calif. Med. Sch., Davis, 1968-76; student health psychiatrist U. Calif., Davis, 1968-76; assoc. clin. prof. psychiatry U. Cin., 1976-82; pvt. practice psychiatry Cin., 1976-82; cons. psychiatrist Federated States of Micronesia, Pohnpei, 1984-87; fellow in geriatric psychiatry Rush-Presbyn./St. Luke Hosp., Chgo., 1989-91. Mem. accreditation rev. com. Accreditation Coun. for Continuing Med. Edn., 1996-98. Trustee Mills Coll., Oakland, 1974-78, 2001—; bd. dirs. Evanston Women's Club. Fellow Am. Psychiat. Assn. (chair continuing med. edn. 1990-96); mem. AMA, Am. Med. Womens Assn., Ohio State Med. Assn., Ill. Psychiat. Soc. (sec. 1993-95, pres.-elect 1995-96, pres. 1996-97, accreditation coun. 1996-98). Home and Office: 1111 Race St 10A Denver CO 80206 Home Phone: 303-321-4193; Office Phone: 303-321-4193.

LANGWORTHY, ROBERT H., law educator; MS, SUNY Albany, PhD, 1983. Prof. U. Cin., 1987—97, U. Alaska, Anchorage, 1997—. Mem. Cmty. Oriented Policing Project Nat Inst. Justice, 1995—96; dir. Justice Ctr. U. Alaska, Anchorage. Author: The Structure of Police Organizations, Policing in America; contbr. articles to prof. jour. Office: U Alaska Justice Ctr 3211 Providence Dr Anchorage AK 99508 Office Phone: 907-786-1810. Business E-Mail: afrhl@uaa.alaska.edu.

LANGWORTHY, WILLIAM CLAYTON, retired college official; b. Watertown, NY, Sept. 3, 1936; s. Harold Greene and Carolyn (Peach) L.; m. Margaret Joan Amos, Sept. 6, 1958; children: Kenneth, Geneva. BS magna cum laude, Tufts U., 1958; PhD, U. Calif.-Berkeley, 1962. Asst. prof. Alaska Meth. U., Anchorage, 1962-65; asst. prof. chemistry Calif. State U.-Fullerton, 1965-67, assoc. prof., 1967-72, prof., 1972-73, assoc. dean Sch. Letters Arts and Scis., 1970-73; prof. chemistry Calif. Poly. State U., San Luis Obispo, 1973-76, head dept. chemistry, 1973-76; dean Sch. Sci. and Math Calif. Poly State U., San Luis Obispo, 1976-83; v.p. acad. affairs Ft. Lewis Coll., Durango, Colo., 1983-95, prof., 1995-2000. Mem. cmty. edn. adv. comm. Skagit Valley Coll., 2008—. Author: monograph Environmental Education, 1971; contbr. articles to profl. jours. Treas. Coun. Concerned Citizens, Inc., Arroyo Grande, Calif., 1976—83; mem. Clean Air Coalition, San Luis Obispo, 1978—83; mem Skagit Valley Chorale, 2007—; mem. Jacksonville Boosters, 2001—05, treas., 2002—04, pres., 2004—05; active Mozart Festival, 1981—82; mem. Rogue Valley Harmonizers, 2001—05; mem. forestry com. City of Jacksonville, Oreg., 2002—05; mem. Stoneybrook arch. com. Corvallis, 2006; bd. dirs. Durango Choral Soc., 1984—93, San Juan Symphony League, pres, 1997—2000; bd. dirs. Durango Repertory Theatre Co., 1990—96, pres., 1992—94; bd. dirs. Skagit Symphony, 2007—. Mem. AAAS, AAHE, Am. Chem. Soc., Coun. Colls. Arts and Scis. (bd. dirs. 1982), Sierra Club, Phi Beta Kappa, Sigma Xi, Kappa Mu Epsilon, Phi Kappa Phi. Home: 3825 Carpenter St Mount Vernon WA 98274 Personal E-mail: hillsidebill@aol.com.

LANNI, TERRY (JOSEPH TERRENCE LANNI), retired hotel corporation executive; b. L.A., Mar. 14, 1943; s. Anthony Warren and Mary Lucille (Leahy) L.; m. Debbie Lanni BA in Speech, U. So. Calif., 1965. V.p. Intervest, Inc., L.A., 1967-69; treas. Republic Corp., L.A., 1969-76; treas., CFO Caesars World Inc., L.A., 1977-78, sr. v.p., 1978-79, exec. v.p., 1979-81, pres., COO, 1981—95, Caesars N.J., Inc., Atlantic City, 1981—95; pres., CEO MGM Grand, Inc., Las Vegas, 1995, chmn., CEO, 1995—99; chmn. MGM Mirage, Las Vegas, 2000—01, chmn., CEO, 2001—08. Bd. dirs. Caesars World, Inc., 1982—95, MGM Grand, Inc., 1995—2000, MGM Mirage, 2000—, KB Home, 2003—. Author: Anthology of Poetry, 1965. Trustee St. John's Hosp. and Med. Ctr., Archdiocese of L.A. Edn. Found., Loyola Marymount U.; bd. councillors U. So. Calif. Sch. Bus. Adminstrn. Mem. Calif. C. of C. (bd. dirs.), Commerce Assocs., Regency Club, Rep. Senatorial Inner Circle, Clermont Club (London), Annabel's (London. Clubs: Bachelors; Crockfords (London), Beach (London).

LANSBURY, ANGELA BRIGID, actress; b. London, Oct. 16, 1925; came to U.S., 1940; d. Edgar and Moyna (Macgill) L.; m. Richard Cromwell, Sept. 27, 1945 (div. Aug. 1946); m. Peter Shaw, Aug. 12, 1949 (dec. Jan. 29, 2003); children: Anthony, Deirdre. Student, Webber-Douglas Sch. Drama, London, 1939-40, Feagin Sch. Drama, NYC, 1940-42; LHD (hon.), Boston U., 1990. Host 41st-43d Ann. Tony Awards, 45th Ann. Emmy Awards; spokesperson ALS Assn., 2008-. Actress with Metro-Goldwyn-Mayer, 1943-50; films include: Gaslight, 1944 (Acad. award nomination), National Velvet, 1944, The Picture of Dorian Gray, 1944 (Golden Globe award, Acad. award nomination), The Harvey Girls, 1946, The Hoodlum Saint, 1946, Till the Clouds Roll By, 1946, The Private Affairs of Bel Ami, 1947, If Winter Comes, 1948, Tenth Avenue Angel, 1948, State of the Union, 1948, The Three Musketeers, 1948, The Red Danube, 1949, Samson and Delilah, 1949, Kind Lady, 1951, Mutiny, 1952, Remains to be Seen, 1953, A Life at Stake, 1955, The Purple Mask, 1956, A Lawless Street, 1956, Please Murder Me, 1956, The Court Jester, 1956, The Long Hot Summer, 1958, Reluctant Debutante, 1958, A Breath of Scandal, 1960, Dark at the Top of the Stairs, 1960, Season of Passion, 1961, Blue Hawaii, 1961, All Fall Down, 1962, Manchurian Candidate, 1962 (Golden Globe award, Acad. award nomination), In the Cool of the Day, 1963, Dear Heart, 1964, The World of Henry Orient, 1964, The Greatest Story Ever Told, 1965, Harlow, 1965, The Amorous Adventures of Moll Flanders, 1965, Mister Buddwing, 1966, Something for Everyone, 1970, Bedknobs and Broomsticks, 1971, Death on the Nile, 1978, The Lady Vanishes, 1980, The Mirror Crack'd, 1980, The Pirates of Penzance, 1982, The Company of Wolves, 1983, Beauty and the Beast, 1991, Your Studio and You, 1995, Beauty & the Beast: Enchanted Christmas (vioce), 1997, Anastasia (voice), 1997, Nanny McPhee, 2005; star TV series Murder, She Wrote, 1984-96 (Golden Globe awards 1984, 86, 91, 92, 12 Emmy nominations, Lead Actress - Drama), Murder, She Wrote: A Story to Die For, 2000, Murder, She Wrote: The Last Free Man, 2001, Murder, She Wrote: The Celtic Riddle, 2003; appeared in TV mini-series Little Gloria, Happy at Last, 1982, Lace, 1984, Rage of Angels, part II, 1986; other TV movies include: The First Olympics-Athens 1896, A Talent for Murder, Gift of Love, 1982, Shootdown, 1988, The Shell Seekers, 1989, The Love She Sought, 1990, Mrs. 'Arris Goes to Paris, 1992, (musical) Mrs. Santa Claus, 1996; appeared in plays Hotel Paradiso, 1957, A Taste of Honey, 1960, Anyone Can Whistle, 1964, Mame (on Broadway), 1966, 83 (Tony award for Best Mus. Actress 1966), Dear World, 1968 (Tony award for Best Mus. Actress 1969), All Over (London Royal Shakespeare Co.), 1971, Prettybelle, 1971, Gypsy, 1974 (Tony award for Best Mus. Actress 1975, Sarah Siddons award), The King and I, 1978, Sweeney Todd, 1979 (Tony award for Best Mus. Actress 1979, Sarah Siddons award), Hamlet, Nat. Theatre, London, 1976, A Little Family Business, 1983, Deuce, 2007; TV appearances Law & Order: SVU, 2005. Named Woman of Yr., Harvard Hasty Pudding Theatricals, 1968, Comdr. of British Empire by Queen Elizabeth II, 1994; named to Theatre Hall of Fame, 1982, TV Hall of Fame, 1996; recipient British Acad. award, 1991, Silver Mask Lifetime Ach. Award, British Acad. Film and TV Arts, 1992, Lifetime Achievement award, Screen Actors' Guild, Hollywood, 1997, Spl. citation for contbn. to Am. theater, NY Drama Critics' Cir., 2009, 16 Emmy Award Nominations, 8 Golden Globe Nominations, 6 Golden Glode Awards; received Nat. medal of the Arts from President Clinton, 1997. Office: c/o William Morris Agy 151 El Camino Dr Beverly Hills CA 90212

LANSDOWNE, WILLIAM M., police chief; b. May 10, 1944; s. Leonard M. and Grace (Dabuque) L.; m. Sharon L. Young, June 12, 1994; children: Greg, Erik. BS in Law Enforcement, San Jose State U., 1971. Asst. chief San Jose (Calif.) Police Dept., 1966-94; chief Richmond (Calif.) Police Dept., 1994—98; chief of police San Jose Police Dept., Calif., 1998—2003, San Diego Police Dept., Calif., 2003—. Mem. Internat. Assn. Chiefs of Police, Calif. Police Chiefs Assn., Police Exec. Rsch. Forum, Calif. Homeland Security Pub. Safety Adv. Com., Maj. Cities Chiefs Assn. Office: San Diego Police Dept 1401 Broadway San Diego CA 92101-5729 Office Phone: 619-531-2777.

LANSING, SHERRY LEE, foundation administrator, former film company executive; b. Chgo., July 31, 1944; d. Norton and Margo L.; m. William Friedkin, July 6, 1991. BS summa cum laude in Theatre, Northwestern U., 1966; DFA (hon.), Am. Film Inst. High sch. tchr. math., LA, 1966-69; model TV commls. Max Factor Co., 1969-70, Alberto-Culver Co., 1969-70; story editor Wagner Internat. Prodn. Co., 1972-74, dir. west coast devel., 1974-75; story editor MGM, 1975-77, v.p. creative affairs, 1977; senior v.p. prodn. Columbia Pictures, 1977-80; pres. studio 20th Century Fox Prodns., Hollywood, 1980-82; founder Jaffee-Lansing Prodns., 1983—92; pres. Paramount Comm., 1990—2005; chmn. Paramount Motion Pictures Group, LA, 1992—2005; CEO The Sherry Lansing Found., 2005—. Bd. dirs. QUALCOMM Inc., 2006—. Actress (films) Loving, 1970, Rio Lobo, 1970; (TV appearances) Ironside, 1971, Frasier, 1996; exec. prodr. (films) Racing With the Moon, 1984, Firstborn, 1984; prodr. (films) Fatal Attraction, 1987, The Accused, 1988, Black Rain, 1989, School Ties, 1992, Indecent Proposal, 1993; exec. prodr. (TV movies) When the Time Comes, 1987, Mistress, 1992. Bd. dirs. Teach for Am., Civic Ventures; bd. dirs., chair Stop Cancer; bd. dirs., mem. exec. com. Friends of Cancer Rsch.; bd. dirs., founder, chair EnCorps; adv. com. RAND Health, Donors Choose; bd. dirs. ARC, Lasker Found.; bd. regents U. Chgo., U. Calif., 1991—; bd. trustees The Carter Ctr., 2005—, Am. Assn. Cancer Rsch.; bd. dirs., Ind. Citizens' Oversight Com. Calif. Inst. Regenerative Medicine; bd. dirs., co-founder Big Sisters LA Future Fund; adv. com. Calif. Pub. Instruction Supts. P-16 Coun.; adv. com. Ednl. Excellence Gov. Schwarzenegger. Recipient Disting. Cmty. Svc. award, Brandeis U., 1982, Alfred P. Sloan, Jr. Meml. award, 1989, Producers Guild of Am. Milestone award, 2000, Woodrow Wilson award for Corp. Citizenship, 2003, Horatio Alger Humanitarian award, 2004, Exemplary Leadership in Mgmt. award, UCLA Anderson Sch. Mgmt., 2005, Legacy award, Big Brothers Big Sisters, 2005, Pub. Svc. award, Am. Assn. Cancer Rsch., 2006, Jean H. Hersholt Humanitarian award, Acad. Motion Picture Arts & Sciences, 2007, Paltrow Mentorship award, Women in Film, 2008; named Pioneer of Yr., Found. Motion Picture Pioneers, 1996; named one of 100 Most Powerful Women in Entertainment, Hollywood Reporter, 2003, 2004, Top 50 Powerful Women in Bus., Fortune Mag., 2007. Achievements include being the first woman to head a major film studio when she was named president of 20th Century Fox, 1980.

LANTZ, KENNETH EUGENE, consulting firm executive; b. Altoona, Pa., Mar. 9, 1934; s. William Martin and Alice Lucretia (Glass) L.; m. D. Arlene Yocum, Nov. 28, 1959; children: Antonia Marie, Theresa Antoinette. BS cum laude, Fordham U., 1956. Cons. Sutherland Co., 1960-62; spl. rep. IBM, LA, 1962-67; dir. info. svcs. Loyola-Marymount U., LA, 1967-70; pres. CBIS, LA, 1970-72; mgr. fin. sys. Occidental Life Ins., LA, 1973-77; pres. Kenneth Lantz Assocs., LA, 1977-82; dir. sys. Sayre & Toso, LA, 1982-83; prin. Atwater, Lantz, Hunter & Co., LA, 1983—. Lectr. computing topics Technology Transfer Inst., 1987-88. Author: The Prototyping Methodology, 1984; contbr. articles to profl. jours. 1st lt. USAF, 1957-60. Mem. Future of Automation Roundtable (dir. 1983—), Ins. Acctg. and Sys. Assn. (nat. Merit award 1984). Republican. Roman Catholic. Office: Atwater Lantz Hunter & Co PO Box 572366 Tarzana CA 91357-2366 Office Phone: 818-477-4451. Business E-Mail: kel@manageknowledge.com, info@manageknowledge.com.

LANZONE, JIM, Internet company executive; BA, UCLA; JD/MBA, Emory U., Atlanta. Product mktg. position KnowX.com (divsn. of Thomson Corp.); co-founder, pres. eTour (acquired by Ask.com), 1997—2001; v.p. product mgmt. to sr. v.p., gen. mgr. US IAC Search & Media (Ask.com), Oakland, Calif., 2001—06, CEO, 2006—08, adv., 2008—; entrepreneur-in-residence Redpoint Ventures, 2008—. Office: Redpoint Ventures 3000 Sand Hill Rd Bldg 2 Ste 290 Menlo Park CA 94025

LAO, LANG LI, nuclear scientist, physicist; b. Hai Duong, Vietnam, Jan. 28, 1954; came to US, 1972; s. Thich Cuong and Boi Phan (Loi) L.; m. Ngan Hua, Dec. 22, 1979; children: Bert J., Brian J. BS, MS, Calif. Inst. Tech., Pasadena, 1976; MS, U. Wis., Madison, 1977, PhD, 1979. Staff scientist Oak Ridge Nat. Lab., Tenn., 1979-81, TRW, Redondo Beach, Calif., 1981-82; mgr. integrated modeling br. Gen. Atomics, San Diego, 1982—. Contbr. articles to sci. jours. Recipient award for Excellence in Plasma Physics Rsch. Am. Physical Society, 1994 Fellow Am. Phys. Soc. (co-recipient excellence in plasma physics rsch. award 1994). Achievements include rsch. in equilibrium analysis of magnetic fusion plasma physics experiments; developed computer code essential for successful operation and interpretation of tokamak fusion experiments. Office: General Atomics 3550 General Atomics Ct San Diego CA 92121-1122

LAPAGLIA, ANTHONY, actor; b. Adelaide, Australia, Jan. 31, 1959; m. Gia Carides, Sept. 1998; 1 child, Bridget. Actor: (films) Cold Steel, 1987, God's Payroll (Phone Calls), 1988, Slaves of New York, 1989, Mortal Sins, 1990, Betsy's Wedding, 1990, Criminal Justice, 1990, He Said, She Said, 1991, One Good Cop, 1991, 29th Street, 1991, Keeper of the City, 1992, Whispers in the Dark, 1992, Innocent Blood, 1992, The Custodian, 1993, So I Married an Axe Murderer, 1993, Killer, 1994, Lucky Break, 1994, The Client, 1994, Mixed Nuts, 1994, Empire Records, 1995, Chameleon, 1995, Commandments, 1996, Brilliant Lies, 1996, Trees Lounge, 1996, Phoenix, 1998, The Repair Shop, 1998, Summer of Sam, 1999, Sweet and Lowdown, 1999, Company Man, 2000, Looking for Alibrandi, 2000, The House of Mirth, 2000, Autumn in New York, 2000, Jack the Dog, 2001, Lantana, 2001, The Bank, 2001, The Salton Sea, 2002, Dead Heat, 2002, I'm With Lucy, 2002, The Guys, 2002, Manhood, 2003, Happy Hour, 2003, Spinning Boris, 2003, The Architect, 2006, Played, 2006, (voice) Happy Feet, 2006,: (plays) A View From the Bridge (Tony award for Best Performance Male in a Drama, 1998); (TV miniseries) Murder One: Diary of a Serial Killer, 1997; (TV films) Police Story: Gladiator School, 1988, Frank Nitti: The Enforcer, 1988, The Brotherhood, 1991, Black Magic, 1992, Past Tense, 1994, Never Give Up: The Jimmy V. Story, 1996, Garden of Redemption, 1997, Black and Blue, 1999, Lansky, 1999, The Other Side, 2001; (TV series) Normal, Ohio, 2000, Frasier, 2000, 2002—04, Without a Trace, 2002— (Gloden Globe award for best actor in a dramatic series, 2004); exec. prodr., actor: (films) Winter Solstice, 2006; exec. prodr.: (TV films) The Away Game, 2004.

LAPEYRE, GERALD J., physics educator, researcher; b. Riverton, Wyo., Jan. 3, 1934; BS in Physics, U. Notre Dame, 1956; MS in Physics, U. Mo., 1958, PhD in Physics, 1962. Prof. physics Mont. State U., Bozeman. Dir. Ctr. Rsch. in Surface Sci.; coord. Materials Rsch. Group; interim dir. Ctr. Advanced Materials; R&D engr. Convair Astronautics, San Diego, 1957, RadioCorp. of Am., Camden, N.J., 1959; vis. prof. Stanford U., Calif., 1963, Lawrence Radiation Lab., Livermore, Calif., 1969; vis. rsch. physicist Brookhaven Nat. Lab. NSLS, 1984; mem. program com. Physics of Compound Semiconductor Interfaces, 1984, planning com. 1985—, chmn., 1988-89; local chmn. 41st Annual Conf. on Phys. Electronics, 1981; spkr. in field. Mem. internat. adv. com. Vibrations at Surfaces, 1989—, Atomically Controlled Surfaces & Interfaces, 1991—; contbr. 158 articles to scientific jours. Vis. fellow Sci. and Engring. Rsch. Coun. Cardiff Coll. U. Wales, 1991; recipient Sr. Humboldt Rsch. award Fritz-Haber, Berlin and KFA, 1992. Fellow Am. Phys. Soc. (solid state divsn.); mem. Am. Assn. Physics Tchr., Am Vacuum Soc. (sec., treas. surface sci. divsn. 1989, chmn. 1990, bd. dirs. 1991-93, mem. electronic materials and processing divsn. coun. 1994-96, Langmuir award 1996), Wis. Synchrotron Radiation Ctr. User Adv. Coun. (chmn. 1986, 93—), Materials Rsch. Soc. Achievements include contribution to the development of photoemission spectroscopy with synchrotron radiation. Office: Montana State U Dept Physics Bozeman MT 59717-0001

LAPHEN, MICHAEL W., computer services company executive; b. 1950; BS in Acctg., Pa. State U., 1972; MBA, U. Pa., Phila.; postgraduate student, Temple U., Phila. With Computer Scis. Corp., El Segundo, Calif., 1977—, pres. systems group Integrated Systems Divsn., 1992—98, pres. fed. sector Civil Group, 1998—2000, pres. European group, 2000—03, v.p. El Segundo, Calif., 2001, pres., COO, 2003—07, pres., CEO, 2007—, chmn., 2007—. With USAF. Mem.: Nat. Def. Indsl. Assn., Armed Forces Comm. and Electronics Assn., Info. Tech. Assn. Am. Office: Computer Scis Corp 2100 E Grand Ave El Segundo CA 90245 Office Phone: 310-615-0311.

LAPIN, DANIEL, rabbi; b. 1950; Studied Math., Econ., Philosophy and Theology, Jerusalem and London. Cert. ordained Rabbi. Founding Rabbi Pacific Jewish Ctr., Venice, Calif.; syndicated radio host Toward Tradition, Seattle; co-chmn. Conservative Alliance of Jews and Christians. Vis. lectr. Christian Coalition, US Army, Harvard Law Sch., Family Rsch. Coun. Contbr. articles to numerous profl. jours, mags. and newspapers incl. Wall Street Jour., National Review, Commentary, the American Enterprise, and the Washington Times; author: (nonfiction) America's Real War, Thou Shall Prosper, Buried Treasure. Named one of The Top 50 Rabbis in America, Newsweek Mag., 2007. Republican. Jewish.

LAPIROFF, JERRY, secondary school educator; b. Bklyn., Feb. 11, 1947; s. Harry and Betty (Klein) Lapiroff; m. Helen Chu, July 24, 1988 (div.); children: Harris, Mariah. Tchr. John F. Kennedy High Sch., 1971—. Fulbright exch. tchr., 1992-93; coord. Virtual H.S. Project. Named Spl. Recognition advisor Journalism, 1989, Disting. advisor Dow Jones Newspaper Fund, 1992. Office: 39999 Blacow Rd Fremont CA 94538-1913 Office Phone: 510-657-4070. Personal E-mail: jerlap@rocketmail.com.

LAPONCE, JEAN A., political scientist, educator; b. Decize, France, Nov. 1925; s. Fernand and Fernande (Ramond) L.; m. Joyce Price, July, 1950; children: Jean-Antoine, Marc, Patrice; m. Iza Fiszhaut, Apr. 10, 1972; 1 child, Danielle. Diploma, Inst. d'études politiques, Paris, 1947; PhD, UCLA, 1955; LLD (hon.), U. B.C., Can., 2003. Instr. U. Santa Clara, 1956; asst. prof. polit. sci. U. B.C., Can., Vancouver, 1956-61, assoc. prof., 1961-66, prof., 1966—; dir. Inst. Interethnic Rels. U. Ottawa, 1993-2001. Mem. grad. faculty Aichi Shukutoku U., 1994-97. Author: The Protection of Minorities, 1961, The government of France under the Fifth Republic, 1962, People vs Politics, 1970, Left and Right, 1981, Langue et territoire, 1984, Languages and Their Territories, 1987, Loi de Babel et autres régularités des rapports entre langue et politique, 2006. Fellow Royal Soc. Can. (pres. Acad. Humanities and Social Scis. 1988-91); mem. Can. Polit. Sci. Assn. (pres. 1972-73), Am. Polit. Sci. Assn., French Polit. Sci. Assn., Internat. Polit. Sci. Assn. (pres. 1973-76) Office: U BC Dept Polit Sci Vancouver BC Canada V6T 1Z1 Home Phone: 604-731-0823; Office Phone: 604-822-2832. Office Fax: 604-822-5540. Business E-Mail: jlaponce@interchange.ubc.ca.

LAPORTA, SCOTT A., recreation facility executive; V.p. corp. fin. Host Marriott Corp., treas., 1995. Office: Park Place Entertainment Corp 4th Fl 3930 Howard Huges Hwy Las Vegas NV 89109

LAPORTE, KATHLEEN DARKEN, venture capitalist; b. NYC, Sept. 23, 1961; d. John Edward and Sheila Anne (Keane) Darken; m. Brian Edward LaPorte, July 30, 1988. BS in Biology summa cum laude, Yale U., 1983; MBA, Stanford U., 1987. Fin. analyst First Boston Corp., NYC, 1983-84, fin. analyst San Francisco, 1984-85; assoc. Asset Mgmt. Co., Palo Alto, Calif., 1987-90, prin., 1990-92; gen. ptnr. The Sprout Group, Menlo Park, Calif., 1994—2005; mng. dir. New Leaf Ventures, Menlo Park, Calif., 2005—. Bd. dirs. Onyx

Pharms., Richmond, Calif., CIBUS Pharms., Sequana Therapeutics, Intrabiotics Pharms., Lynx Therapautics, Pearl Therapeutics, Inc. Founder Phil Larson Fund, Stanford U., 1988; mem. Cmty. Impact Vol. Group, Palo Alto, 1988—. Recipient Eleanor Dawson award Yale U., 1982, MacLeish Meml. trophy Yale U., 1983. Mem. Nat. Venture Capital Assn., Western Assn. Venture Capitalists (past pres.), Bay Area Bioscience Women's Group (founding), Phi Beta Kappa. Avocations: swimming, golf. Office: New Leaf Venture Partners 2500 Sand Hill Rd Ste 203 Menlo Park CA 94025 E-mail: kathy@nlvpartners.com.

LAPPEN, CHESTER I., lawyer; b. Des Moines, May 4, 1919; s. Robert C. and Anna (Sideman) L.; m. Jon Tyroler Irmas, June 29, 1941; children: Jonathan Bailey, Timothy, Andrea L., Sally Morris. AB with highest honors in Econs, U. Calif., 1940; LL.B. magna cum laude (Faye diploma), Harvard, 1943. Bar: Calif. bar 1943. Practice in, Los Angeles, 1946—; sr. partner firm Mitchell, Silberberg & Knupp, 1949—; advisory bd. Bank Am., 1962-65; chmn. bd., dir. Zenith Nat. Ins. Corp., 1975-77. Bd. dirs. Arden Group, Inc. (chmn. exec. com. 1978), 1963-91, Data Products Corp. (chmn. fin. com.), 1965-93, City Nat. Bank Corp., 1967-92; trustee, pres. Citinat, Devel. Trust; bd. dirs., chmn. bd. Pacific Rim Holding Corp., 1987-94. Editor-in-chief: Harvard Law Rev, 1942-43. Chmn. bd. trustees Immaculate Heart Coll., 1981-88; trustee UCLA Found.; v.p., dir. Ctr. for Childhood. Spl. agt., counter intelligence US Army, 1943—46. Named to Artus Econs. Honor Soc., U. Calif., 1939. Mem. ABA, Los Angeles Bar Assn. (dir. 1953), Los Angeles Jr. Bar Assn. (pres. 1953), Beverly Hills (Calif.) Bar Assn., Harvard Law Sch. Alumni Assn. So. Calif. (pres. 1973-82). Republican. Office: Mitchell Silberberg & Knupp 11377 W Olympic Blvd Los Angeles CA 90064-1625

LARA, ADAIR, columnist, writer; b. San Francisco, Jan. 3, 1952; d. Eugene Thomas and Lee Louise (Hanley) Daly; m. James Lee Heig, June 18, 1976 (div. 1989); children: Morgan, Patrick; m. William Murdock LeBlond, Nov. 2, 1991. BA in English, San Francisco State U., 1976. Reader Coll. of Marin, Kentfield, Calif., 1976-83; freelance editor, 1983-86; mng. editor San Francisco Focus mag., 1986-89; exec. editor San Francisco mag., 1988-89; columnist San Francisco Chronicle, 1989—. Author: History of Petaluma: A California River Town, 1982, Welcome to Earth, Mom, 1992, Slowing Down in a Speeded-up World, 1994, At Adair's House, More Columns by America's Funniest Formerly Single Man, 1995; contbr. articles to profl. publs. Recipient Best Calif. Columnist award AP, 1990. Democrat. Avocations: reading, photography, travel, softball, biking. Office: San Francisco Chronicle 901 Mission St San Francisco CA 94103-2905

LARET, MARK R., health facility executive; BS in Polit. sci., UCLA; M in Polit. sci., U. So. Calif. Asst. dir. UCLA Med. Ctr., 1985, assoc. dir. marketing and planning, 1990, dep. dir., 1994; CEO UCLA Med. Group, 1994, Univ. Calif. Irvine Med. Ctr., Orange, Calif., 1995—2000, exec. dir., 1995; CEO Univ. Calif. San Francisco (UCSF) Med. Ctr., 2000—, Univ. Calif. San Francisco (UCSF) Children's Hosp., 2000—. Exec. com. bd. Univ. Healthcare Consortium; bd. dir. CaloPTIMA, 1997, AAMC Coun of Teaching Hosp. and Health Systems (COTH), 2003—04. Named Orange County Manager of Year, Soc. for Advancement of Mgmt., 1999. Office: Med Ctr Adminstrn Univ Calif San Francisco Box 0296 500 Parnassus Ave MU 509E San Francisco CA 94143-0296 Office Phone: 415-353-2733. Office Fax: 415-353-2765. Business E-Mail: mark.laret@ussfmedctr.org.

LARGE, LARRY DENTON, academic administrator; b. Lewiston, Idaho, Aug. 8, 1940; s. Clifford Denton and Cleo Elva (Pixley) L.; m. Jeanne M. Large, Mar. 22, 1964 (div. 1978); children: Elizabeth, Timothy; m. Marsha Lee Lancaster, 1990. BS in Psychology, Portland State U., 1964; MA in History, U. Oreg., 1970, PhD in Edn., 1974. Dir. fin. aid U. Oreg., Eugene, 1971-72; v.p. Willamette U., Salem, Oreg., 1972-82; v.p. devel. & coll. rels. Reed Coll., Portland, Oreg., 1982-87; v.p. pub. affairs & devel. U. Oreg., 1987-89; vice chancellor pub. affairs Oreg. State System Higher Edn., Portland, 1989—; pres. Oglethorpe U., Atlanta, 1999—2005; exec. cons. Sierra Nev. Coll., Incline Village, Nev., 2005—, interim pres., 2006—. Spl. asst. to deputy commr. for postsecondary edn., U.S. Office Edn., Washington; adj. prof. U. Oreg. Coll. Edn., 1987; cons. in field; lectr. in field. Contbr. articles to profl. jours. Gov. appointed mem. Bicentennial commn., 1988-90; bd. dirs. Magna Carta Am., 1985—; vol. cons. Oreg. State Coun. Alcoholism and Drug Abuse, 1983, trustee, 1984-85; independent coll. rep. Oreg. Ednl. Coord. Comms, State Wide Planning Com., 1985-86. With U.S. Army Res., 1958-59. Mem. Coun. Advancement Support Edn. (nat. ednl. fund raising com. 1985-87. trustee), Oreg. Assn. Student Fin. Aid Officers (v.p. 1971), Assn. Independent Colls. and Univs. (trustee). Office: Sierra Nevada College Office of President 999 Tahoe Blvd Incline Village NV 89451-9500 Office Phone: 775-831-1314.

LARIVA, GLORIA, labor union administrator, advocate; b. Albuquerque; Attended, Brandeis U., Waltham, Mass. Printing profl.; pres., typographical sector Calif. Media Workers Guild, Local 39521, San Francisco. Organizer Free Nelson Mandela & Leonard Peltier tour, 1986; vol. organizer Act Now to Stop War and End Racism Coalition; coord. Nat. Com. to Free the Cuban Five; ind. US vice presdl. candidate, 1984—2000; US presdl. candidate Party for Socialism and Liberation, 2008, mem. nat. com.; gubernatorial candidate Peace & Freedom Party, Calif., 1994, 1998. Party For Socialism & Liberation. Office: Calif Media Workers Guild Local 39521 Typographical Sector 2d Fl 433 Natoma St San Francisco CA 94103 Office Phone: 415-777-0910. Business E-Mail: glariva@mediaworkers.org.*

LARKIN, THOMAS ERNEST, JR., investment management company executive; b. Wilkes-Barre, Pa., Sept. 29, 1939; s. Thomas Ernest and Margaret (Gorman) L.; m. Margaret Givan, Nov. 2, 1979; 1 child, Thomas Ernest III. BA in Econs., U. Notre Dame, 1961; postgrad., Grad. Sch. Bus., NYU, 1962-66. New bus. rep. Mfrs. Hanover Trust Co., 1963-66; mgr. pension dept. Eastman Dillon, Union Securities, 1966-69; v.p. Shearson Hayden Stone, Inc., NYC, 1969-75; sr. v.p. Bernstein Macaulay Inc., NYC, 1969-75, Crocker Investment Mgmt. Corp., San Francisco, 1975-77, Trust Co. of the West, LA, 1977, mng. dir., 1982—, pres., COO, 1989-2000; vice chmn. The TCW Group, Inc., 2000—. Trustee U. Notre Dame, Loyola Marymount U., Mt. St. Mary's Coll., Childrens Hosp. LA, Amateur Athletic Found. LA, Heart and Lung Surgery Found., Orange County Performing Arts Ctr. With US Army, 1961-63. Mem.: Investment Counsel Assn. Am., Assn. Investment Mgmt. Sales Execs., LA Country Club, Westchester Country Club, Regency Club, Wilshire Country Club, Jonathan Club, Calif. Club. Republican. Roman Catholic. Office: TCW Group 865 S Figueroa St Ste 1800 Los Angeles CA 90017-2593

LAROCCO, LARRY, former congressman; b. Van Nuys, Calif., Aug. 25, 1946; m. Christine Bideganeta, 1967; children: Anna, Matthew BA, U. Portland, 1967; MA, Boston U., 1969; student, Johns Hopkins Sch. Advanced Internat. Studies, 1968—69. N Idaho field rep. for Seantor Frank Church US Senate, 1976—81; asst. v.p., dir. mktg. Twin Falls Bank and Trust; v.p. Piper, Jaffray & Hopwood, 1989—90; mem. US Congresses from 1st Idaho Dist., 1991—95, mem. interior & insular affairs com., banking, fin. & urban affairs com.; v.p. First Idaho Corp.; fin. services cons. Shearson Lehman Hutton, Inc.; sr. lobbyist Fleishman-Hillard, Inc., 2002—04; gen. mgr. Fleishman-Hillard Govt. Rels., Washington, 2004—. Capt. US Army, 1969-72. Democrat. Roman Catholic. Office: PO Box 1068 Boise ID 83701

LAROCK, BRUCE EDWARD, civil engineering educator; b. Berkeley, Calif., Dec. 24, 1940; s. Ralph W. and Hazel M. L.; m. Susan E. Gardner, June 17, 1968; children: Lynne M., Jean E. BS in Civil Engring., Stanford U., 1962, MS in Civil Engring., 1963, PhD, 1966. Registered profl. engr., Calif. Asst. prof. U. Calif., Davis, 1966—72, assoc. prof., 1972—79, prof., 1979—2003, prof. emeritus, 2003—. Sr. vis. fellow U. Wales, Swansea, 1972-73; US sr. scientist Tech. U., Aachen, Germany, 1986-87. Author: (with D. Newnan) Engineer-in-Training Examination Review, 3d edit., 1991, (with R. Jeppson and G. Watters) Hydraulics of Pipeline Systems, 2000; contbr. over 80 tech. articles to profl. jours. Mem. ASCE, Sigma Xi, Tau Beta Pi. Lutheran. Avocation: duplicate bridge. Office: Dept Civil Environ Engring U Calif Davis CA 95616-5294 E-mail: belarock@ucdavis.edu.

LAROWE, MILES, academic administrator; m. Betsy LaRowe; children: Meighan, Margaux. BBA, MA, EdD. Instr., adminstr. Laramie County Cmty. Coll.; instr. Ea. Wyo. Coll., Chatman Coll.; dean Dodge City Coll., 1993—96; pres. Ea. Idaho Tech. Coll., 1996—2003, Northwest Coll., Powell, Wyo., 2003—. Bd. dir. Cody County C. of C. Office: Northwest Coll President's Office 231 W 6th St Powell WY 82435

LARPENTEUR, JAMES ALBERT, JR., retired lawyer; b. Seattle, Aug. 6, 1935; s. James Albert and Mary Louise (Coffey) L.; m. Hazel Marie Arntson, Apr. 23, 1965 (div. 1983); children: Eric James, Jason Clifford; 1 adopted child, Brenda Mon Fong; m. Katherine Annette Bingham, Nov. 8, 1986. BS in Bus., U. Oreg., 1957, LLB, 1961. Bar: Oreg. 1961, U.S. Dist. Ct. Oreg. 1961, U.S. Tax Ct. 1962, U.S. Ct. Appeals (9th cir.) 1962, U.S. Supreme Ct. 1965. Assoc. Schwabe Williamson & Wyatt, Portland, Oreg., 1961-69, ptnr., 1969-82, sr. ptnr., 1982—2002, mem. exec. com., 1989—93, ret., 2003. Dir. exec. com. Portland Rose Festival Assn., 1975—2004, pres., 1987; ex-officio dir. Portland Visitors Assn., 1981—2005; bd. dirs., mem. exec. com. Providence Child Ctr. Found., 1983—94, chmn. exec. com., 1986—87; bd. dirs. Willamette Light Brigade, 1987—, Cath. Charities Portland, 1989—92, Albertina Kerr Ctrs., 1996—2003, Japanese Garden Soc., 2000—07, Abbey Found. Oreg., Mt. Angel, 2002—08. Mem.: Oreg. Bar Assn. (chmn., Bus. law Sect. 1986—87, editor, writer, spkr. numerous continuing legal edn. programs, real estate, alternate dispute resolution, securities regulation sects), Thunderbird Country Club of Rancho Mirage, City Club of Portland, Waverley Country Club, Univ. Club of Portland, Multnomah Athletic Club (pres. 1984). Avocation: golf. Office: 1211 SW 5th Ave Ste 1800 Portland OR 97204-3713 Office Phone: 503-796-2920. Business E-Mail: jlarpenteur@schwabe.com.

LARRABEE, MATTHEW LLOYD, lawyer; b. Palo Alto, Calif., July 7, 1955; AB, U. Calif., Davis, 1977; JD, U. Calif., San Francisco, 1980. Bar: Calif. 1980. Atty. Heller, Ehrman, White & McAuliffe, San Francisco, 1990—2008, co-chair, San Francisco litigation dept., 1995—97, mng. ptnr., 1997—99, firm wide practice chair litigation, 1999—2005, chmn., 2005—08; ptnr. Dechert LLP, San Francisco, 2008—. Mem. ABA, Am. Law Inst., Order of Coif. Office: Dechert LLP One Maritime Plz Ste 2300 San Francisco CA 94111

LARRABEE, WAYNE FOX, JR., facial plastic surgeon; b. Ft. Benning, Ga., May 10, 1945; s. Wayne Fox and Ruth (Truex) L.; m. Tane; children: Shane, Sascha, Kai, Spencer, Gregory. BS in Math., Midland Coll., 1967; postgrad., U. Edinburgh, 1965-66; MD, MPH in Epidemiology, Tulan U., 1971. Diplomate Am. Bd. Otolaryngology; lic. MD, Wash. Intern Letterman Gen. Hosp., San Francisco, 1971-72; resident in surgery Tulane U. Svc. Charity Hosp., New Orleans, 1975-76, resident in otolaryngology and maxillofacial surgery, 1976-79; head sect. reconstructive and aesthetic plastic surgery Va. Mason Med. Ctr., Seattle, 1986-88, head sect. otolaryngology, 1985-88. Instr. dept. surgery Tulane Med. Sch., 1975-79, instr. dept. otolaryngology, 1976-79; clin. assoc. prof. U. Wash., 1979-88; clin. prof., U. Wash., 1988-2001; pres. med. bd. Virginia Mason Rsch. Ctr., 1985-88; observations fellowship Moorfields Eye Hosp., London, 1988; presenter in field; pres. Am. Bd. Facial Plastic Surgery, 2000-03. Author: Surgical Anatomy of the Face, 1993, Principles of Facial Reconstruction, 1995, Roslyn A Town's Portrait, 2d edit., 1999; mem. editl. bd. JAMA, 1999—; editor Archives of Facial Plastic Surgery, 1999—. Maj. U.S. Army Med. Corps, 1972-75, Panama Canal Zone. Fellow ACS, Am. Acad. Facial Plastic and Reconstructive Surgery (pres. 1996), Am. Soc. Head and Neck Surgery, Triological Soc., Am. Bd. Otolaryngology (bd. dirs., prs. 2002—); mem. King County Med. Soc., Am. Acad. Otolaryngology-Head and Neck Surgery. Avocations: photography, poetry. Office: Ctr for Facial Plastic Surgery 600 Broadway # 280 Seattle WA 98122 Home Phone: 206-232-8868; Office Phone: 206-386-3550. Business E-Mail: info@larrabeecenter.com.

LARRICK, JAMES WILLIAM, science administrator; b. Englewood, Colo., Jan. 4, 1950; s. William Franklin and Louise (Scatman) L. BA in Chemistry magna cum laude, Colo. Coll., 1972; MD, PhD, Duke U., 1980. Research fellow Marie Stauffer Sigall Found., Stanford U., Palo Alto, Calif., 1981-82; staff physician Kaiser Permanente Hosp., Santa Clara, Calif., 1982-88; sci. project leader Human Monoclonal Antibodies Cetus Immune Research Labs, Palo Alto, 1982-87; research scientist Cetus Immune Research Labs., Palo Alto, Calif., 1982-85, sr. research scientist, 1985, dir. research, 1985-87; dir. exploratory research Genelabs, Inc., Redwood City, 1988-91; founder, sci. dir. Palo Alto Inst. for Molecular Medicine, Mountain View, Calif., 1991—. Contbr. numerous articles to profl. jours.; chpts. to books. Staff Young Lords Free Health Clinic, Chgo., 1972-73; staff Edgemont Health Clinic, Durham, N.C., 1975-76; mem. curriculum com. Duke U. Sch. Medicine, 1974-75; active Bay Area Physicians for Social Responsibility, 1982-88; vol. physician Haight-Ashbury Free Health Clinic, San Francisco, 1983-88; bd. dirs. Emergency Relief Fund Internat., San Francisco, 1985-88. Mem. AAAS, Am. Fedn. Clin. Research, Am. Assn. Immunologists, Am. Assn. Phys. Anthropology, Calif. Acad. Scis., N.Y. Acad. Scis., Phi Beta Kappa. Avocations: cross country skiing, bicycling, scuba diving, mountain climbing, sailing. Home: Star Rte Box 48 Woodside CA 94062 Office: Palo Alto Inst Of Molecular Medicine 1230 Bordeaux Dr Sunnyvale CA 94089-1202 E-mail: jwlarrick@aol.com.

LARRUBIA, EVELYN, reporter; Reporter South Fla. Sun-Sentinel, Ft. Lauderdale, Fla.; county govt. reporter, metro desk LA Times, investigative writer. Co-recipient Livingston award for local reporting, Livingston Found., 1996, Joseph L. Brechner Freedom of Information award, 1997, Ursula & Gilbert Farfel prize for investigative reporting, Scripps Howard Found., 2006, Local Watchdog Reporting award, Am. Soc. Newspaper Editors, 2006. Office: LA Times 202 W 1st St Los Angeles CA 90012 Office Phone: 213-237-7847. Office Fax: 213-237-4712. E-mail: evelyn.larrubia@latimes.com.

LARSEN, CLIFFORD G., state legislator; m. Trish Larsen; 1 child, Tucker. Former counselor Veteran's Admin.; former educator U. Oreg., Boise State U.; former commr. Missoula Co. Airport Authority; former healthcare admin.; operator ranch/farming enterprise, LaValle Creek; mem. Dist. 50 Mont. State Senate, 2008—. Served, Vietnam War. Democrat. Office: Montana Senate PO Box 200500 Helena MT 59620-0500 Mailing: 8925 LaValle Creek Rd Missoula MT 59808-9324 Home Phone: 406-728-1601; Office Phone: 406-444-4800. Office Fax: 406-444-4875. Business E-Mail: cliff@larsenusa.com.

LARSEN, DAVID COBURN, lawyer, educator; b. Honolulu, Mar. 20, 1944; s. Harold Samuel and Eugenia Bowen (Coburn) L.; m. Pamela Ann Magee, Aug. 1, 1970; 1 child, Jennifer M. BA with honors, U. Va., 1965, MA, 1966; JD, UCLA, 1974. Bar: Calif. 1974, Hawaii 1975. Assoc. Cades Schutte, Honolulu, 1974-80, ptnr., 1980—. Tchr. U. Hawaii Law Sch., Honolulu, 1975-79, U. Hawaii Cont. Edn., 1980—. Author: Who Gets It When You Go, 1982, 2d edit. 1987, You Can't Take It With You, 1986. Lt. USN, 1967-70. Ford Found. fellow 1966. Office: Cades Schutte PO Box 939 1000 Bishop St Honolulu HI 96808

LARSEN, GARY LOY, physician, researcher; b. Wahoo, Nebr., Jan. 10, 1945; s. Allan Edward and Dorothy Mae (Hengen) L.; m. Letitia Leah Hoyt, Dec. 22, 1967; children: Kari Lyn, Amy Marie. BS, U. Nebr., 1967; MD, Columbia U., 1971. Diplomate Am. Bd. Pediat., Am. Bd. Pediatric Pulmonology (chmn. 1990-92). Pediatric pulmonologist Nat. Jewish Med. and Rsch. Ctr., Denver, 1978—, head divsn. pediatric pulmonary medicine, 1989—; mem. faculty U. Colo. Sch. Medicine, Denver, 1978—, dir. sect. pediatric pulmonary medicine, 1987—2003, prof. pediat., 1990—; head dept. respiratory medicine The Children's Hosp., Denver, 2002—03. Editl. councillor Pediat. Pulmonology; editl. adv. bd. Child Mag., 2006—07. Assoc. editor: Jour. Allergy and Clin. Immunology; contbr. articles to prof. jours. Mem. sci. adv. panel Nat. Urban Air Toxics Rsch. Ctr., 1998-2005. Maj. M.C., U.S. Army, 1974-76. Grantee Med. Rsch., NIH, 1981—2007. Mem. Am. Thoracic Soc. (chmn. pediatric assembly 1987-88), Soc. Pediatric Rsch., N.Y. Acad. Scis., Chilean Respiratory Soc. (hon.), Western Soc. Pediat. Rsch., Phi Beta Kappa, Alpha Omega Alpha. Lutheran. Office: Nat Jewish Med & Rsch Ctr 1400 Jackson St Denver CO 80206-2761

LARSEN, RICHARD LEE, city manager, consultant, retired mayor, arbitrator; b. Jackson, Miss., Apr. 16, 1934; s. Homer Thorsten and Mae Cordelia (Amidon) L.; m. Virginia Fay Alley, June 25, 1955; children: Karla, Daniel, Thomas (dec.), Krista; Lisa. BS in Econs. and Bus. Adminstrn, Westminster Coll., Fulton, Mo., 1959; postgrad., U. Kans., Lawrence, 1959-61. Fin. dir. Village of Northbrook, Ill., 1961-63; city mgr. Munising, Mich., 1963-66, Sault Ste. Marie, Mich., 1966-72, Ogden, Utah, 1972-77, Billings, Mont., 1977-79; mcpl. cons., 1979—; pub., pvt. sector labor rels. cons., arbitrator, 1979—; semi-ret., 2003. Mayor City of Billings, Mont., 1990-95; dep. gen. chmn. Greater Mich. Found., 1968. Bd. dir. Ctrl. Weber Sewer Dist., 1972-77; chmn. labor com. Utah League Cities and Towns, 1973-77, Mont. League Cities and Towns, 1977-79; bd. dir., coach Ogden Hockey Assn., 1972-77, Weber Sheltered Workshop, 1974-77, Billings YMCA, 1980-86, Rimrock Found., 1980-86; chmn. cmty. rels. coun. Weber Basin Job Corps Ctr., 1973-77; bishop LDS Ch.; missionary LDS Ch., Portland, Oreg., 2003-05. With USCG, 1953-57. Recipient Cmty. Devel. Disting. Achievement awards Munising, 1964, Cmty. Devel. Disting. Achievement awards Sault Ste. Marie, 1966-70, Citizen award Dept. of Interior, 1977, Alumni Achievement award Westminster Coll., 1990, Dist. award of merit Boy Scouts Am., 1993, Silver Beaver award Boy Scouts Am., 1994; named Utah Adminstr. of Yr., 1976. Mem. Utah City Mgrs. Assn. (pres. 1972-74), Greater Ogden C. of C. (dir.), Rotary (pres. Billings 1997-98), Phi Gamma Delta. Home and Office: 1733 Parkhill Dr Billings MT 59102-2358 Office Phone: 406-248-4252. Business E-Mail: rllarsen@bresnan.net.

LARSEN, RICHARD RAY (RICK LARSEN), United States Representative from Washington; b. Arlington, Wash., June 15, 1965; m. Tiia Larsen; children: Robert, Per. BA, Pacific Luth. U., Tacoma; M in Pub. Affairs, U. Minn. Dir. pub. affairs Wash. State Dental Assn.; econ. devel. ofcl. Port of Everett; councilman Snohomish County, Wash., County Coun. chair Wash., 1999; mem. US Congress from 2nd Wash. dist., 2001—, mem. armed svcs. com., mem. transp. and infrastructure com., mem. agr. com., co-chair Congl. Caucus to Fight and Control Methamphetamine, mem. No. Border Caucus. Named Friend of the Nat. Pks., Nat. Pks. Conservation Assn. Democrat. Office: US Ho Reps 107 Cannon Ho Office Bldg Washington DC 20515 Office Phone: 202-225-2605.

LARSON, BRIAN A., lawyer; Acct. Coopers and Lybrand, Ernst and Young; ptnr. Snell and Wilmer, Phoenix; v.p. devel. Boyd Gaming Corp., Las Vegas, 1993, assoc. gen. counsel, 1993—98, sr. v.p., gen. counsel, 1998—, sec., 2001—. Office: Boyd Gaming Corp 6465D S Rainbow Blvd Las Vegas NV 89118-

LARSON, BRYAN ALAN, lawyer; s. Byron Ancedus and Betty Marilyn Larson; m. Kathy Stevenett; children: Aaron, Adam, Conor, Kaden, Sara, Aubrey. BA, Brigham Young U., 1980, JD, 1983. Bar: Utah 1983. Assoc. Christensen, Jensen & Powell, Salt Lake City, 1983-86, McKay, Burton & Thurman, Salt Lake City, 1986-91; ptnr. Larson, Jenkins & Halliday, Salt Lake City, 1991-95, Larson, Kirkham & Turner, Salt Lake City, 1995-99, Larson Turner Fairbanks Dalby, Salt Lake City, 1999—2004, Larson, Turner, Dalby & Ethington, 2004—. Seminar lectr. in field. Editor: Backtalk Newsletter, 1995—, Utah Auto Body Watch Dawg, 2002—; contbr. articles to mags. in field. Mem. ATLA (mem. polit. action com. 1991—), Utah Bar Assn. (com. chmn. 1990-92), Utah Assn. Justice (exec. bd., pres. bd. govs.), Spkrs. Bur., Order of Barristers. Mem. Lds Ch. Avocations:

boating, skiing. Office: Larson Turner Dalby & Ethington 1218 W South Jordan Pkwy Ste B South Jordan UT 84095 Office Phone: 801-446-6464. E-mail: larson@bestattorneys.com.

LARSON, CAROL S., foundation administrator, lawyer; BA, Stanford U.; JD, Yale Law Sch. Law clerk to Judge Warren J. Ferguson U.S. Dist. Crt., Central Dist. of Calif.; former atty., civil litigation O'Donnell and Gordon; dir. rsch., grants, law and public policy, Ctr. for Future of Children David and Lucile Packard Found., 1989—94, dir. prog., 1995—2003, v.p., 2000—03, pres., CEO, 2004—. Special asst. and speechwriter for pres. Am. Bar Assn., 1998; lecturer Stanford Law Sch., 1994—96; coordinator of advocacy Exceptional Children's Found., Los Angeles, 1980—81. Former bd. mem. Grantmakers for Children, Youth and Families; bd. mem. No. Calif. Grantmakers, Am. Leadership Forum, Silicon Valley. Office: David and Lucile Packard Found 300 Second St Los Altos CA 94022 Office Phone: 650-948-7658.

LARSON, EDWARD JOHN, history and law professor; b. Mansfield, Ohio, Sept. 21, 1953; s. Rex and Jean (Uncapher) Larson; m. Lucy Marie Kaiser, July 28, 1990; children: Sarah Marie, Luke Anders. BA, Williams, 1974; MA, U. Wis., 1976, PhD, 1985; JD, Harvard U., 1979; DHL (hon.), Ohio State U., 2004. Bar: Wash. 1979, U.S. Dist. Ct. (we. dist.) Wash. 1979, U.S. Ct. Appeals (9th cir.) 1979, U.S. Tax Ct. 1981, U.S. Supreme Ct. 1984. Atty. Davis, Wright & Tremaine, Seattle, 1979—82; assoc. counsel U.S. House Com. on Edn. and Labor, Washington, 1983—86; counsel U.S. Office Edn. Rsch. and Improvement, Washington, 1986—87; Richard B. Russell prof. history and Talmadge chair law Univ. Ga., Athens, 1987—, chair history dept., 2001—04; Darling chair law and u. prof. history Pepperdine U., Malibu, Calif., 2006—. Adv. US Dept. Edn., Washington, 1987—93; vis. prof. U. Jean Moulin, Lyon, France, 1996; John Adams chair Fulbright program U. Leiden, The Netherlands, 2000—01; participant Antarctic Artists and Writers Program, NSF, 2003—04; Straus disting. vis. prof. Pepperdine Law Sch., 2005; panelist human genome project NIH, Washington, 2006—. Author: Trial & Error, 1985, Sex, Race & Science, 1995, Summer for the Gods, 1997, A Different Death, 1998, Evolution's Workshop, 2001, Evolution, 2004, Constitutional Convention, 2005, The Creation-Evolution Debate, 2007, A Magnificent Catastrophe, 2007. Counsel Wash. State House Reps., Olympia, 1981—82; analyst Wis. State Senate, Madison, 1974—76. Recipient Pulitzer prize for history, 1998, Templeton Found. Article prize, 1997, George Sarton Lectr. award, AAAS, 2000, James Livingood award, Conf. on So. Lit., 2003; scholar, Rockefeller Found., 1996. Mem.: Forum History Sci. Am. (exec. com. chair 1992—94), History Sci. Soc. (com. chair 1994—97), Wash. State Bar Assn. Avocations: travel, hiking, bicycling, birdwatching. Office: Pepperdine U Sch Law Malibu CA 90263 Home: 24323 Baxter Dr Malibu CA 90265-4751 Office Phone: 706-542-2660, 310-506-7593. Business E-Mail: edlarson@uga.edu, elarson@pepperdine.edu.

LARSON, ERIC B., medical educator, director, internist; BA in History (with great distinction), Stanford Univ., Stanford, Calif, 1969; MD, Harvard Med. Sch., 1973; MPH, U. Wash. Sch. Pub. Health, Seattle, Wash., 1977. Cert. Nat. Bd. Med. Examiners (Parts I, II, III), 1974, diplomate Am. Bd. Internal Medicine, 1977, lic. Wash., 1975. Assoc. diener, dept. pathology Children's Hosp., Boston, 1969—71; intern, medicine Beth Israel Hosp., Harvard Med. Sch., Boston, 1973—74, asst. resident, medicine, 1974—75; internist, outpatient dept. Harborview Med. Ctr., Seattle, 1975—77; rsch. assoc. Va. Mason Hosp./Rsch. Found., Seattle, 1975—77; chief resident, medicine U. Hosp., Seattle, 1977—78, attending physician, 1977—; Robert Wood Johnson Clin. scholar, sr. fellow, dept. medicine U. Wash., Seattle, 1975—77, assoc. dean clin. affairs; med dir. U. Wash. Med. Ctr., 1989—2002; sr. investigator, dir., Group Health Coop. Ctr. for Health Studies, Seattle, 2002—06, exec. dir., Group Health Coop., 2006—. Instructor, medicine Harvard Med. Sch., Boston, 1973—75; acting instructor, medicine U. Wash. Sch. Medicine, Seattle, 1977—78, assoc. dean for clin. affairs, 1989—2002; asst. prof., medicine U. Wash., Seattle, 1978—82, assoc. prof., medicine, 1982—88, prof. medicine, 1988—; adj. asst. prof., cmty. medicine Sch. Pub. Health, Seattle, 1979—82; adj. assoc. prof., health services & cmty. medicine U. Wash. Sch. Pub. Health, Seattle, 1982—88, adj. prof., health services & cmty. medicine, 1988—; sect. head, gen. internal medicine U. Hosp., Seattle, 1988—89; sr. investigator and dir. Ctr. for Health Studies, Group Health Coop., 2002; commr. Joint Commn. for Accreditation Health Care Orgns., 1999—. Contbr. articles to profl. jours.; assoc. editor: Jour. of Gen. Internal Medicine, 1989—94, editl. bd.: Annals of Internal Medicine, 1992—95, Health Services Rsch., 1994—, Am. Jour. Medicine, 1997—, Primary Care Case Reviews, 1988—, editl. adv. bd.: Rsch. and Practice, 1998—. Nat. reviewer, abstract selection Soc. of Gen. Internal Medicine (SGIM), 1984, co-chmn., NW regional mtg., 1983, chmn., NW regional mtg., 1986, regional rep., 1986—87, coun., 1986—89, pres., 1994—95; commr. Joint Commn. on Accreditation of Healthcare Orgns., 2003; nat. reviewer Am. Fedn. for Clin. Rsch.-Clin. Epidemiology-Health Care Rsch., 1983—88, western regional reviewer, 1985, chmn., abstract selection, 1990 Nat. Mtg., 1989—90; DHHS Adv. Panel on Alzheimer's Disease Office of Tech. Assessment, 1987—89, chmn., 1993—98. Henry J. Kaiser Family Found. Faculty Scholar in Gen. Internal Medicine, 1981. Fellow: ACP (regent 1998—2006, chmn. publications comm. 2000—03, chair-elect, bd. regents 2003, chair, bd. regents 2004, master 2006, George Morris Piersol Tchg. and Rsch. Scholar 1978, Laureate award, Wash. Chpt. 2006); mem.: AMA, Inst. Medicine, ACP Jour. Club (editl. adv. bd. 1990—), Wash. State Medical Soc., King County Med. Soc. (editl. adv. bd. 1987—90), Am. Fedn. for Med. Rsch. (clin. epidemiology-Health Care Rsch., Nat. reviewer 1983—88, clin. epidemiology-Health Care Rsch., Western Regional Reviewer 1985, chmn., abstract selection 1990 Nat. Mtg. 1989—90), Seattle Acad. of Medicine, Soc. Gen. Internal Medicine (co-chmn., northwest regional mtg. 1983, nat. reviewer, abstract selection 1984, chmn., Northwest Regional Mtg. 1986, regional rep. 1986—87, councilor 1986—89, pres. 1994—95, Robert J. Glaser award 2004), Am. Clin. and Climatological Assn., Am. Soc. Clin. Investigation, Am. Geriatrics Soc. (editl. bd. 1988—91, Service award 1992), Assn. Am. Physicians, Phi Beta Kappa. Office: Ctr for Health Studies Ste 1600 1730 Minor Ave Seattle WA 98101-1448 Office Phone: 206-287-2988. Business E-Mail: larson.e@ghc.org. E-mail: ebl@u.washington.edu.*

LARSON, ERIK, writer; b. Bklyn., Jan. 1, 1954; m. Christine Gleason; children: Kristin, Lauren, Erin. BA in Russian history summa cum laude, U. Pa., 1976; MA, Columbia Grad. Sch. of Journalism, 1978. Features writer The Wall St. Jour., TIME mag. Author: The Naked Consumer: How Our Private Lives Become Public Commodities, 1992, Lethal Passage: How the Travels of a Single Handgun Expose the Roots of America's Gun Crisis, 1994, Isaac's Storm: A Man, a Time and the Deadliest Hurricane in History, 1999 (Pacific Northwest booksellers award), The Devil in the White City: Murder Magic and Madness at the Fair that Changed America, 2003 (Nat. Book award nominee, Edgar award in Best Fact Crime category, 2004), Thunderstruck, 2006.

LARSON, JO ANN, government agency administrator; Student, Montgomery Coll.; AA, U. Md. From pers. clk. to equal employment specialist NASA, 1970—91, mgr. Minority Univ. Program Dryden Flight Ctr. Edwards AFB, Calif., 1991—. Avocation: travel, watercolor painting, reading.

LARSON, JOHN WILLIAM, lawyer; b. Detroit, June 24, 1935; s. William and Sara Eleanor (Yeatman) L.; m. Pamela Jane Wren, Sept. 16, 1959; 1 dau., Jennifer Wren. BA with distinction, honors in Economics, Stanford, 1957; LLB, Stanford U., 1962. Bar: Calif. 1962. Assoc. Brobeck, Phleger & Harrison, San Francisco, 1962-68, ptnr., 1968—71, 1973—2003, CEO, 1988—96; asst. sec. Dept. Interior, Washington, 1971-73; exec. dir. Natural Resources Com., Washington, 1973; counsellor to chmn. Cost of Living Coun., Washington, 1973; ptnr. Morgan, Lewis & Backius LLP, 2003—. Faculty Practising Law Inst.; bd. dirs. Sangamo Bio Scis., Inc., Wage Works, Inc., Needham Funds, Inc., MBA Polymers, Inc. Mem. 1st U.S.-USSR Joint Com. on Environment; mem. bd. visitors Stanford U. Law Sch., 1974-77, 85-87, 95-96; pres. bd. trustees The Katherine Branson Sch., 1980-83. With AUS, 1957-59. Mem. ABA, Calif. Bar Assn., San Francisco C. of C. (bd. dirs., chmn. 1996), Bay Area Coun., Calif. Acad. Sci., Order of Coif, Pacific Union Club, Burlingame Country Club, Bohemian Club, Lagunitas Country Club. Home: PO Box 349 Ross CA 94957-0349 Office: Morgan Lewis & Bockius LLP Spear St Tower 1 Market Plz San Francisco CA 94105-1420 Office Phone: 415-442-1000. Business E-Mail: jlarson@morganlewis.com.

LARSON, MARK ALLAN, financial executive; b. Milw., June 24, 1948; s. Owen Earl and Alice May (Ulmen) L.; m. Linda Rosalie Wohlschlaeger, Jan. 3, 1970; children: Craig Allan, Emily Lin. BA, Ripon Coll., 1970; postgrad., Washington U., St. Louis, 1971-74; postgrad. in bus., St. Louis U., 1974-76. Personnel supr. Barnes Hosp., St. Louis, 1970-71; various fin. and mgmt. positions Bank Bldg. Corp., St. Louis, 1971-76, G.D. Searle & Co., Skokie, Ill., Geneva, Switzerland, 1976-85; sr. v.p., chief fin. and admistrv. officer Leaf Inc., Bannockburn, Ill., 1985-89; v.p. internat. devel. and adminstrn. Carlson Cos., Inc., Mpls., 1990-91; exec. v.p. fin. and adminstrn., travel and mktg. groups, 1992-93; exec. v.p. ops. and internat., mktg. groups, 1993-95; sr. v.p. fin. Internat. Distillers & Vintners N.Am., Hartford, Conn., 1995-96; pres. IDV Wines, San Mateo, Calif., 1997-98, United Distillers & Vintners, West, San Francisco, 1998-99; pres., COO, Golden State Vinters, Napa, Calif., 2000—. E-mail: mlarson@gsvinc.com.

LARSON, MARK R., former state legislator; b. Phila., July 12, 1950; m. Margie Larson; 1 child, Kris; 1 child, Dianna. AA, N.Mex. Mil. Inst. Small bus. owner; former state rep. dist. 59 Colo. Ho. of Reps., Denver, 2000—06, vice chair transp. and energy com., mem. bus. affairs and labor com. Republican. Unitarian.

LARSON, RANDALL J., energy executive; BBA, MBA, Univ. Wis. Ptnr. KPMG, Denver & NYC, 1981—96, San Jose, Calif., 1996—2002; exec. v.p., chief acctg. officer TransMontaigne Inc., Denver, 2002—03; exec. v.p., CFO TransMointaigne Inc., Denver, 2003—06; pres., CEO, CFO TransMontaigne Partners LP, Denver, 2006—. Profl. acctg. fellow Office of Chief Acct., SEC, 1992—94. Office: TransMontaigne Inc Ste 3100 1670 Broadway Denver CO 80202 also: TransMontaigne Partners LP Ste 3100 1670 Broadway Denver CO 80202

LARSON, STEPHEN G., federal judge; b. Fontana, Calif., 1964; BS, Georgetown U., 1986; JD, U. So. Calif. Law Sch., 1989. Bar: Calif. 1989. Assoc. O'Melveny & Myers, 1989—91; asst. US atty. US Atty.'s Office (Ctrl. dist.) Calif., 1991—2000; US magistrate judge US Dist. Ct. (Ctrl. dist.) Calif., 2000—06, dist. judge, 2006—. Adj. asst. prof. Glendale Coll. Law, 1997—2001; instr. Calif. So. Law Sch., 2001—05; adj. prof. U. LaVerne Coll. Law, 2002—. Office: US Dist Ct Rm 1 3470 12th St Riverside CA 92501 Office Phone: 951-328-4464, 950-274-0844. E-mail: James_Holmes@cacd.uscourts.gov.

LARSON, WILLIAM, electronics executive; Pres., chmn. Network Assocs., Santa Clara, Calif. Office: Network Assocs 3965 Freedom Cir Santa Clara CA 95054-1203

LARSON BONCK, MAUREEN INEZ, rehabilitation consultant; b. Madison, Minn., Mar. 10, 1955; d. Alvin John and Leona B. (Bornhorst) Larson; m. Michael Bonck, Jan. 8, 2005. BFA in Psychology & Fine Arts cum laude, U. Minn., 1977; MA in Counseling & Guidance, U. N.D., 1978. Cert. rehab. counselor, disability mgmt. specialist. Employment counselor II, coordinator spl. programs Employment Security div. State of Wyo., Rawlins, 1978-80; employment interviewer Employment Security divsn. State of Wash., Tacoma, 1980; lead counselor Comprehensive Rehab. Counseling, Tacoma, 1980-81; dir. counseling Cascade Rehab. Counseling, Tacoma, 1981-87, dist. mgr., 1987-90; regional mgr. Rainier Case Mgmt., Tacoma; owner Maureen Larson and Assocs., Gig Harbor, Wash., 1992—2005, Maureen Larson Consulting, 2005—. State capt. legis. div. Provisions Project, Am. Pers. and Guidance Assn., 1980. Advocate Grand Forks (N.D.) Rape Crisis Ctr., 1977-78; mem. Pierce County YMCA; bd. dir. Boys and Girls Clubs of Tacoma, 1991-98, chair sustaining drive, 1991-98, sec.-treas., 1992-93, pres., 1994, auction com. and spl. events com.; founding bd. dir., bd. devel. chair, events chair, co-chmn. Literacy Plus!, 1999-2001; chairperson adv. bd. Gig Harbor br. Tacoma C.C., 2002—. State of Minn. scholar, 1973-77; recipient Alice Tweed Tuohy award U. Minn., 1977, Nat. Disting. Svcs. Registry award Libr. of Congress, 1987; named bd. mem. vol. of Yr. Boys and Girls Clubs of Tacoma, 1992. Mem.: Nat. Rehab. Adminstrs. Assn. (bd. dir. 1993), Nat. Rehab. Counseling Assn. (bd. dir. 1993, State of Wash. Counselor of Year 1991, Pacific Region Counselor of Year 1992), Nat. Rehab. Assn. (bd. dir. Olympic chpt. 1988—97, pres. 1990—91, chmn. state conf. planning com. 1993, 1996, 1990), Nat. Fedn. Bus. & Profl. Women (rec. sec. 1978—80, runner-up Young Careerists' Program 1980), Washington Self-Insured Assn., Rotary Gig Harbor Midday Club (charter mem., dir. vocat. svcs. 2002—08), Pi Gamma Mu. Avocations: sailing, aerobics, ballet, arts. Office: M Larson Consulting 4325 Country Club Dr NE Tacoma WA 98422-4612 Office Phone: 253-943-5272. Office Fax: 253-943-5279. Personal E-mail: mlarsonassoc@msn.com. Business E-Mail: maureen@mlarson.consulting.com.

LARSON-GREEN, JULIE, computer software company executive; married; 2 children. BBA, Western Wash. U.; M in Software Engring., Seattle U. Software engr. Adobe PageMaker desktop pub. software; program mgr. devel. tools and languages Microsoft Corp., Redmond, Wash., devel. mgr. Windows team, program mgr. Microsoft Office team, 1997, corp. v.p. Windows Experience program mgmt. Named one of Most Influential Women in Technology, Fast Company, 2009. Office: Microsoft Corp One Microsoft Way Redmond WA 98052-6399 Business E-Mail: julielar@exchange.microsoft.com.

LARSSON, WILLIAM DEAN, metal products executive; b. Newberg, Oreg., June 8, 1945; s. Richard A. and Beverly L. (Phillips) Larsson; m. Debra T. Moore, Apr. 19, 1986; children: Amy, Alexander, Anna. BS in Econs., U. Oreg., 1967, BS in Math., 1968; MBA, Calif. State U., 1970. Supr. fin. analysis Ford Motor Co., Dearborn, Mich., 1968—75; v.p., contr. Wheel Horse Products, South Bend, Ind., 1975—79; v.p. fin. Whiting Corp., Chgo., 1979—80, Precision Castparts Corp., Portland, Oreg., 1980—93, v.p. fin., CFO, 1993—2000, sr. v.p., CFO, 2000—. Bd. dir. Schnitzer Steel Industries Inc., 2006—. Home: 1210 Chandler Rd Lake Oswego OR 97034-2806 Office: Precision Castparts Corp 4600 SE Harney Dr Portland OR 97206-0825

LARWOOD, LAURIE, psychologist, artist; b. NY, Nov. 23, 1941; PhD, Tulane U., 1974. Pres. Davis Instruments Corp., San Leandro, Calif., 1966—71; cons., 1969—; asst. prof. orgnl. behavior SUNY, Binghamton, 1974—76; assoc. prof., chair dept. psychology Claremont (Calif.) McKenna Coll., 1976—83, assoc. prof. bus. adminstrn., 1976—83, Claremont Grad. Sch., 1976—85; prof., head dept. mgmt. U. Ill., Chgo., 1983—87; dean sch. bus. SUNY, Albany, 1987—90; dean Coll. Bus. Adminstrn. U. Nev., Reno, 1990—92, prof., 1990—2003, prof. emerita, 2003—; dir. Inst. Strategic Bus. Issues, 1992—2003; mng. ptnr. Quail Lane Studios, Tucson, 2003—. Western regional adv. coun. SBA, 1976-81; dir. Mgmt. Team; pres. Mystic Games, Inc.; mng. ptnr. Quail Lane Studios, 2003-. Author: (with M.M. Wood) Women in Management, 1977, Organizational Behavior and Management, 1984, Women's Career Development, 1987, Strategies-Successes-Senior Executives Speak Out, 1988, Women's Careers, 1988, Managing Technological Development, 1988, Impact Analysis, 1999; mem. editl. bd. Sex Roles, 1979-2003, Consultation, 1986-91, Jour. Orgnl. Behavior, 1987-2003, Jour. Vocat. Behavior, 1999-, Group and Orgn. Mgmt., 1982-84, editor, 1986-91; founding editor Women and Work, 1983, Jour. Mgmt. Case Studies, 1983-87; artist: artistic digital photography; contbr. articles to profl. jours. Mem.: Nat. Assn. Photoshop Profls., So. Ariz. Arts Guild. Libertarian. Office: Quail Ln Studios 10225 N Quail Ln Tucson AZ 85742 Mailing: Box 89789 Tucson AZ 85752 Personal E-mail: larwood@earthlink.net.

LASAROW, WILLIAM JULIUS, retired federal judge; b. Jacksonville, Fla., June 30, 1922; s. David Herman and Mary (Hollins) L.; m. Marilyn Doris Powell, Feb. 4, 1951; children: Richard M., Elisabeth H. BA, U. Fla., 1943; JD, Stanford U., 1950. Bar: Calif. 1951. Counsel judiciary com. Calif. Assembly, Sacramento, 1951-52; dep. dist. atty. Stanislaus County, Modesto, Calif., 1952-53; pvt. practice law LA, 1953-73; bankruptcy judge U.S. Cts., LA, 1973-94; chief judge U.S. Bankruptcy Ct., Central dist., Calif., 1978-90; judge Bankruptcy Appellate Panel 9th Fed. Cir., 1980-82; fed. judge U.S. Bankruptcy Ct., LA, 1973. Faculty Fed. Jud. Ctr. Bankruptcy Seminars, Washington, 1977-82 Contbg. author, editor legal publs.; staff: Stanford U. Law Review, 1949. Mem. ABA, Am. Coll. Bankruptcy, Am. Bankruptcy Inst., Nat. Conf. Bankruptcy Judges, Los Angeles County Bar Assn., Wilshire Bar Assn., Blue Key, Phi Beta Kappa, Phi Kappa Phi. Home: 11623 Canton Pl Studio City CA 91604-4164

LASATER, W(ILLIAM) ROBERT, JR., lawyer; b. El Dorado, Kans., Oct. 31, 1944; s. W. Robert and Marguerite Lasater; m. Janet Lynn Lasater; children: W. Robert III, Alisa Linn. BA, Kans. U., 1966, JD, 1969. Bar: Kans. 1969, U.S. Ct. Mil. Appeals 1972, N.Mex. 1974, U.S. Supreme Ct. 1976. Legal aid Wyandotte Co., Kansas City, Kans., 1969; forensic medicine cons. USAF, 1971-74; assoc. Rodey, Dickason, Sloan, Akin & Robb, Albuquerque, 1974-78, ptnr., 1978—. Bd. dirs. Bernalillo County (N.Mex.) chpt. Am. Cancer Soc., 1984. Capt. JAG, USAF, 1969-71. Named one of best lawyers in Am., 2005—06. Fellow Am. Acad. Health Care Attys.; mem. ABA, N.Mex. State Bar Assn.(chmn. Dental-Legal Panel 1981-1990, chmn. Health Law Sect. 1988-1989, Med. Legal Liaison Com. 1991-, Med. Rev. Com. 1989-), Am. Bd. Trial Advs., Am. Coll. Trial Lawyers, Kans. Bar Assn., Albuquerque Bar Assn., N. Mex Health Lawyers Assn., Am. Arbitration Assn. (panel neutrals), Phi Delta Phi. Republican. Methodist. Office: Rodey Dickason Sloan Akin & Robb PO Box 1888 Albuquerque NM 87103-1888 Office Phone: 505-768-7287. Business E-Mail: rlasater@rodey.com.

LASHOF, JOYCE COHEN, public health service officer, educator; b. Phila. d. Harry and Rose (Brodsky) Cohen; m. Richard K. Lashof, June 11, 1950; children: Judith, Carol, Dan. AB, Duke U., 1946; MD, Women's Med. Coll., 1950; DSc (hon.), Med. Coll. Pa., 1983. Dir. Ill. State Dept. Pub. Health, 1973—77; dep. asst. sec. for health programs and population affairs Dept. Health, Edn., and Welfare, Washington, 1977—78; sr. scholar in residence IOM, Washington, 1978; asst. dir. office of tech. assessment U.S. Congress, Washington, 1978—81; dean sch. pub. health U. Calif., Berkeley, 1981—91; prof. pub. health U. Calif. Sch. Pub. Health, Berkeley, 1981—94, prof. emeritus, 1994—. Co-chair Commn. on Am. after Roe vs. Wade, 1991—92; mem. Sec.'s Coun. Health Promotion and Disease Prevention, 1988—91; chair Pres.'s Adv. Com. on Gulf War Vets. Illnesses, 1995—97. Mem. editl. bd.: Wellness Letter, 1993—, Ann. Rev. of Pub. Health, 1987—90. Recipient Alumni Achievement award, Med. Coll. Pa., 1975, Sedgewick Meml. medal, APHA, 1995. Avocation: hiking. Office: U Calif Sch Pub Health 140 Earl Warren Hl Berkeley CA 94720-7360 Home: 2431 Mariner Square Dr Apt 105 Alameda CA 94501-1679 Office Phone: 510-642-2493. Business E-Mail: jlashof@berkeley.edu.

LASORDA, TOMMY (THOMAS CHARLES LASORDA), retired professional baseball team manager; b. Norristown, Pa., Sept. 22, 1927; s. Sam and Carmella (Covatto) Lasorda; m. Joan Miller Lasorda, Apr. 14, 1950; children: Laura, Tom Charles(dec.). Student pub. schs., Norristown. Pitcher Bklyn. Dodgers, 1954—55, Kans. City Athletics, 1956; with L.A. Dodgers, 1956—, mgr. minor league clubs Pocatello, Idaho, Ogden, Utah, Spokane, Albuquerque, 1965—73, coach, 1973—76, mgr., 1976—96, v.p. fin., 1996—98, interim gen. mgr., 1998, sr. v.p., 1998—2004, sr. adv. to chmn., 2004—. Co-author (with David Fisher): (autobiography) The Artful Dodger, 1985; co-author: (with Bill Plaschke) I Live for This!: Baseball's Last True Believer, 2007. With US Army, 1945—47. Recipient World Championship, 1981, 1988, Milton Richman Meml. award, Assn. Profl. Baseball Players Am.; named Pitcher of Yr., Internat. League, 1958, L.A. Dodgers winner, Nat. League pennant, 1977, 1978, 1981, 1988, 2d Nat. League mgr. to win pennant first two yrs. as mgr., Nat. League Mgr. Yr., UPI, 1977, AP, 1977, Baseball Writers' Assn. Am., 1988, Sporting News, 1988, Baseball Writers Assn. Am., 1983, 1988, coach, Nat. League All-Star team, 1977, 1983—84, 1986, 1993; named to Baseball Hall of Fame, 1997. Mem.: Profl. Baseball Players Am., Variety Club of Calif. (v.p.). Roman Catholic. Office: c/o Los Angeles Dodgers 1000 Elysian Park Ave Los Angeles CA 90012-1112

LASSETER, JOHN ALAN, film company executive, computer animator; b. Hollywood, Calif., Jan. 12, 1957; m. Nancy Lasseter; 5 children. BFA in Film, Calif. Inst. Arts, 1979; degree (hon.), Am. Film Inst. Animator The Walt Disney Co., Burbank, Calif., 1979—84; with animation divsn. Lucasfilm Industrial Light & Magic, 1984—86; founding mem. Pixar Animation Studios, Richmond, Calif., 1986, exec. v.p. creative, chief creative officer, 2006—; prin. creative advisor Walt Disney Imagineering, 2006—. Dir., writer, prodr.: (films) Luxo Jr., 1986 (Silver Berlin Bear award Berlin Internat. Film Festival, 1986, nominated Oscar for Best Short Films, Animated Films, 1986); dir., writer: Red's Dream, 1987, Tin Toy, 1988 (Acad. award for Best Achievement in Short Films, 1988), Knick Knack, 1989 (Best Short Film award Seattle Internat. Film Festival 1989), Toy Story, 1995 (Academy award for Spl. Achievement 1995), A Bug's Life, 1998, Toy Story 2, 1999, Cars, 2006 (runner-up LA Film Critics Circle awards, 2006); exec. prodr.: Geri's Game, 1997, For the Birds, 2000, Spirited Away, 2001, Monsters Inc., 2001, Finding Nemo, 2003, Boundin', 2003, Howl's Moving Castle, 2004, The Incredibles, 2004, One Man Band, 2005, Meet the Robinsons, 2007; actor: Computer Illusions, 1998. Recipient Humanitarian award ShoWest Conv., 1997, Outstanding Contribution to Cinematic Imagery award Art Directors Guild, 2004; named one of The 50 Most Powerful People in Hollywood, Premiere mag., 2002-06, The Global Elite, Newsweek mag., 2008 Fellow: Am. Acad. Arts & Scis. Office: Pixar Animation Studios 1200 Park Ave Emeryville CA 94608 Office Phone: 510-752-3000.*

LASSONDE, PIERRE, retired mining executive; BA, U. Montreal; BSEE, Polytech. Sch. Montreal; MBA, U. Utah, 1973. Registered profl. engr., Assn. Profl. Engrs. Ontario, 1976. Pres. Franco-Nev., 1982—2002; pres., CEO Euro-Nev. Mining Corp., 1985—99; pres., co-CEO Franco-Nev., 1999—2002; pres. Newmont Mining Corp., Denver, 2002—06, vice chmn., 2007. Author: Gold Book, The Complete Investment Guide to Precious Metals.

LASSWELL, MARCIA LEE, psychologist, educator; b. Oklahoma City, July 13, 1927; d. Lee and Stella (Blackard) Eck; m. Thomas Lasswell, May 29, 1950 (div. July 1990); children: Marcia Jane, Thomas Ely, Julia Lee. BA, U. Calif., Berkeley, 1949; MA, U. So. Calif., 1952; postgrad., U. Calif., Riverside, U. So. Calif., U. N.C. Individual practice psychotherapy, marriage/family therapy, Claremont, Calif.; asst. prof. Pepperdine Coll., LA, 1959—60; asst. prof. psychology behavioral sci. dept. Calif. State U., Pomona, 1960—64, assoc. prof., 1965—69, prof., 1970—, chmn. dept., 1964—69, emeritus, 2005—; assoc. clin. dir. Human Rels. Ctr. U. So. Calif., 1975—98. Vis. assoc. prof. Scripps Coll., 1968-69, U. So. Calif., 1969-70, Occidental Coll., 1971-72; lectr. various Calif. univs.; mem. staff spl. project alcoholics and narcotics offenders Calif. Prison System, 1970-73; mem. Calif. Accreditation Com. Secondary Schs. and Colls., 1965—1990; mem. commn. accreditation for marriage and family tng. US Dept. Edn., 1981-87. Author: College Teaching of General Psychology, 1967, Love, Marriage and Family, 1973, No-Fault Marriage, 1976, Styles of Loving, 1980, Marriage and Family, 1982, rev. edit., 1987, 91, Equal Time, 1983. Recipient Outstanding Tchrs. award Calif. State U., 1971, Outstanding Contbn. to Marriage and Family Therapy, 1991, Disting. Clin. Mem. award Calif. Assn. Marriage and Family Therapists, 1995, award Outstanding Marriage and Family Therapy Orgn., 1999. Fellow Am. Assn. Marital and Family Therapy (bd. dirs. 1970-72, 87-91, pres. elect 1993-95, pres. 1995-97, past pres. 1997-98); mem. AAAS, Nat. Coun. Family Rels. (exec. com. 1978-80), Am. Acad. Family Therapy, So. Calif. Assn. Marital and Family Therapy (pres. 1972-73), Groves Family Conf. Acad., Groves Family Conf. (sec. 2001-2004), Alpha Kappa Delta, Phi Delta Gamma, Pi Gamma Mu. Home: 800 W 1st St Apt 2908 Los Angeles CA 90012-2444 Office: 250 W First St # 352 Claremont CA 91711 Office Phone: 909-624-4641. Personal E-mail: mlass@aol.com.

LATHAM, JOSEPH AL, JR., lawyer; b. Kinston, NC, Sept. 16, 1951; s. Joseph Al and Margaret Lee (Tyson) L.; m. Elaine Frances Kramer, Dec. 19, 1981; children: Aaron Joshua, Adam Daniel. BA, Yale U., 1973; JD, Vanderbilt U., 1976. Bar: Calif. 1976, U.S. Dist. Ct. (cen. dist.) Calif. 1977, U.S. Ct. Appeals (9th cir.) 1977, U.S. Dist. Ct. (no. and so. dists.) Calif. 1978, Ga. 1980, U.S. Dist. Ct. (no. dist.) Ga. 1981, U.S. Ct. Appeals (5th and 11th cirs.) 1981, U.S. Dist. Ct. (mid. dist.) Ga. 1982, D.C. 1984. Assoc. Paul, Hastings, Janofsky & Walker, Orange County and L.A., 1976-80, Atlanta, 1980-83, ptnr. Orange County and L.A., Calif., 1987—; chief counsel to bd. mem. NLRB, Washington, 1983-85; staff dir. U.S. Commn. on Civil Rights, Washington, 1985-86. Instr. advanced profl. program U. So. Calif. Law Ctr., 1988, lectr. law, 1989—. Articles editor Vanderbilt Law Rev., 1975-76; editorial asst. Employment Discrimination Law, 2d edit., 1983; contbr. articles to Barron's, ABA Jour., Litigation, Employee Rels. Law Jour. Recipient Best Lawyers in Am., Fellow, Coll. Labor & Employment Lawyers. Mem. Calif. Bar Assn., Ga. Bar Assn., D.C. Bar Assn., Order of Coif., U. So. Calif. law sch.(adj. faculty), Order of Coif. Republican. Episcopalian. Home: 655 Prospect Cres Pasadena CA 91103-3245 Office: Paul Hastings et al LLP 515 S Flower St 25th Fl Los Angeles CA 90071-2201 Office Phone: 213-683-6319. Office Fax: 213-996-3319. Business E-Mail: allatham@paulhastings.com.

LATHI, BHAGAWANDAS PANNALAL, retired electrical engineering educator; b. Bhokar, Maharashtr, India, Dec. 3, 1933; came to U.S., 1956; s. Pannalal Rupchand and Tapi Pannalal (Indani) L.; m. Rajani Damodardas Mundada, July 27, 1962; children: Anjali, Shishir. BEEE, Poona U., 1955; MSEE, U. Ill., 1957; PhD in Elec. Engring., Stanford U., 1961. Rsch. asst. U. Ill., Urbana, 1956-57, Stanford (Calif.) U., 1957-60; rsch. engr. Gen. Electric Co., Syracuse, NY, 1960-61; cons. to semicondr. industry India, 1961-62; assoc. prof. elec. engring. Bradley U., Peoria, Ill., 1962-69, U.S. Naval Acad., Annapolis, Md., 1969-72; prof. elec. engring. Campinas (Brazil) State U., 1972-78, Calif. State U., Sacramento, 1979—2001, prof. emeritus, 2002—. Vis. prof. U. Iowa, Owa City, 1979. Author: Signals, Systems and Communication, 1965, Communication Systems, 1968 (transl. into Japanese 1977), Random Signals and Communication Theory, 1968, Teoria Signalow I Ukladow Telekomunikacyjnych, 1970, Sistemy Telekomunikacyjne, 1972, Signals, Systems and Controls, 1974, Sistemas de Comunicacion, 1974, 86, Sistemas de Comunicacao, 1978, Modern Digital and Analog Communication Systems, 1983, 89 (transl. into Japanese 1986, 90, Korean, 2001), Signals and Systems, 1987, Linear Systems and Signals, 1992, 2d rev. edit., 2005, Signal Processing and Linear Systems, 1998; contbr. articles to profl. jours. Fellow IEEE. Office: Calif State U 6000 J St Sacramento CA 95819-2605 Address: 3021 Scenic Height Way Carmichael CA 95608 Personal E-mail: bercamb@yahoo.com.

LATHROP, ANN, retired librarian, educator; b. LA, Nov. 30, 1935; d. Paul Ray and Margaret W.; divorced; children: Richard Harold, John Randolph, Rodney Grant. BA in History summa cum laude, Ea. N.Mex. U., 1957; MLS, Rutgers U., 1964; PhD, U. Oreg., 1988. Cert. elem. tchr., Calif.; cert. libr., Calif; adminstrv. credential, Calif. Elem. sch. tchr. Chalfont (Pa.) Boro Sch., 1960-61, Livingston Elem. Sch., New Brunswick, N.J., 1961-63, Rosedale Elem. Sch., Chico, Calif., 1964-65; libr. Chico (Calif.) H.S., 1965-72, Princeton (Calif.) H.S., 1972-73, Santa Maria (Calif.) H.S., 1973-77; libr. coord. San Mateo County Office Edn., Redwood City, Calif., 1977-89; assoc. prof. Calif. State U., Long Beach, 1989-92, prof., 1993—99; ret., 1999. Author: Online Information Retrieval as a Research Tool in Secondary School Libraries, 1988, Student Cheating and Plagiarism in the Internet Era: A Wake-Up Call, 2000, Guiding Students from Cheating and Plagiarism to Honesty and Integrity, 2005; co-author: Courseware in the Classroom, 1983. Mem. ALA, NEA, Am. Assn. Sch. Librs., Assn. State Tech. Using Tchr. Educators, Calif. Faculty Assn., Calif. Sch. Libr. Assn., Computer Using Educators, Internat. Soc. for Tech. in Edn. Avocations: travel, camping. E-mail: alathrop@csulb.edu.

LATHROP, IRVIN TUNIS, retired dean; b. Platteville, Wis., Sept. 23, 1927; s. Irvin J. and Marian (Johnson) Lathrop; m. Eleanor M. Kolar, Aug. 18, 1951; 1 child, James I. BS, Stout State Coll., 1950; MS, Iowa State U., 1954, PhD, 1958. Tchr. Ottumwa HS, Iowa, 1950-55; mem. faculty Iowa State U., 1957-58, Western Mich. U., 1958-59, Calif. State Coll., 1959-88, prof. indsl. arts, 1966-88, chmn. dept. indsl. edn., 1969-88, assoc. dean extended edn., 1978-88, prof. emeritus, 1988—. Cons. Naval Ordnance Lab., Corona, Calif., 1961—63. Author (with Marshall La Cour): Photo Technology, 1966; author: (with John LIndbeck) General Industry, 1969, with John LIndbeck: rev. edit., 1977; author: Laboratory Manual for Photo Technology, 1973, Photography, 1979, rev. edit., 1992, The Basic Book of Photography, 1979; author: (with Robert Kunst) Photo-Offset, 1979; editl. cons. Am. Tech. Soc.; contbr. articles to profl. jours. Mem. Orange County Grand Jury, 1989—90, Orange County Juvenile Justice Commn., 1991—2002; mem. adv. com. El Camino and Orange Coast Coll. Mem.: Am. Ednl. Rsch. Assn., Internat. Tech. Assn., Nat. Assn. Indsl. and Tech. Tchrs., Am. Vocat. Assn., Am. Coun. Indsl. Arts Tchr. Edn., Nat. Soc. Study Edn., Phi Kappa Phi, Phi Delta Kappa, Psi Chi, Epsilon Pi Tau. Home: PO Box 3430 Laguna Woods CA 92654-3430 Office: 1250 N Bellflower Blvd Long Beach CA 90840-0006 Personal E-mail: ilathrop@sbcglobal.net.

LATHROP, MITCHELL LEE, lawyer; b. LA, Dec. 15, 1937; s. Alfred Lee and Barbara (Mitchell) L.; m. Lynn Mara Dalton; children: Christin Lorraine Newlon, Alexander Mitchell BSc, US Naval Acad., 1959; JD, U. So. Calif., 1966. Bar: DC 1966, Calif. 1966, U.S. Supreme Ct. 1969, NY 1981; cert. arbitrator Nat. Arbitration Forum, ARIAS-US; London Ct. Internat. Arbitration; diplomate internat. arbitration law, Coll. Law, Eng., Wales, 2005. Dep. counsel LA County, Calif., 1966-68; with Brill, Hunt, DeBuys and Burby, LA, 1968-71; ptnr. Macdonald, Halsted & Laybourne, LA and San Diego, 1971-80; sr. ptnr. Rogers & Wells, NYC, San Diego, 1980-86; sr. ptnr., exec. com. Adams, Duque & Hazeltine, LA, San Francisco, NYC, San Diego, 1986-94, firm chmn., 1992-94; sr. ptnr. Luce, Forward, Hamilton & Scripps, San Diego and NYC, 1994—2003; ptnr. Duane Morris LLP, NYC, of counsel San Diego, 2003—09; mem. Mintz, Levin, Cohn, Ferris, Glovsky & Popeo, P.C, 2009—. Presiding referee Calif. Bar Ct., 1984-86, mem. exec. com., 1981-88; lectr. law Calif. Judges Assn., Practicing Law Inst. NY, Continuing Edn. of Bar, State Bar Calif., ABA, others. Author: Insurance Coverage for Environmental Claims, 1992; mem. editl. bd. Def. Counsel Jour., 1997—, Jour. Ins. Coverage. Western Regional chmn. Met. Opera Nat. Coun., 1971—81, v.p., mem. exec. com., 1971—, now chmn; trustee Honnold Libr. at Claremont Colls., 1972—80; sec. Music Ctr. Opera Assn., 1974—80; v.p. San Diego Opera Assn., 1985—89, pres.-elect, 1993, pres., 1994—96; bd. dirs. Music Ctr. Opera Assn., LA, 1973—80, San Diego Opera Assn., 1980—2003, Met. Opera Assn., NYC, 1982—; mem. adv. bd. Internat. Dominican Found., Rome. Fellow: Australian Internat. Arbitration Ctr., Ctr. Internat. Legal Studies, Chartered Inst. Arbitrators, London; mem.: ABA, Internat. Assn. Def. Counsel, Judge Advocates Assn. (dir. LA chpt. 1974—80, pres. So. Calif. chpt. 1977—78), Am. Bd. Trial Advocates, Assn. So. Calif. Def. Counsel, Assn. Bus. Trial Lawyers, San Diego County Bar Assn. (chmn. ethics com. 1980—82, bd. dirs. 1982—85, v.p. 1985), DC Bar Assn., Calif. Bar Assn., Fed. Bar Coun., Fed. Bar Assn., NY Bar Assn., S.R. (pres. 1977—79), Friends Claremont Coll. (dir. 1975—81, pres. 1978—79), Soc. Colonial Wars in Calif. (gov. 1970—72), LA Opera Assocs. (pres. 1970—72), Order St. Lazarus of Jerusalem, Brit. United Svcs. Club (dir. LA 1973—75), Mensa Internat., The Naval Club (London), Met. Club (NYC), Calif. Club (LA), Phi Delta Phi. Republican. Office: Mintz Levin Cohn Ferris Glovsky & Popeo PC 3580 Carmel Mountain Rd San Diego CA 92130 also: Chrysler Ctr 666 Third Ave New York NY 10017 Office Phone: 619-985-8262. Business E-Mail: mllathrop@mintz.com.

LATHROPE, DANIEL JOHN, law educator; BSBA, U. Denver, 1973; JD, Northwestern U., Evanston, Ill., 1977; LLM, NYU, 1979. Bar: Ariz. 1977, Calif. 1978. Assoc. Evans, Kitchel & Jenckes, Phoenix, 1977-78; instr. law NYU, 1979-80; assoc. prof. U. Calif. Hastings Coll. Law, San Francisco, 1980-86, prof., 1986—. Assoc. acad. dean U. Calif. Hastings Coll. Law, San Francisco, 1986-87, acting dean, 1987-88, acad. dean, 1988-90, dir. LLM program US legal studies, 2004-07; prof., assoc. dean, dir. grad. tax program U. Fla. Coll. Law, Gainesville, 1995-96. Co-author: (with Lind, Schwarz and Rosenberg) Fundamentals of Corporate Taxation, 6th edit., 2005, Fundamentals of Business Enterprise Taxation, 3d edit., 2005, Fundamentals of Partnership Taxation, 7th edit., 2005; (with Schwarz) Black Letter on Federal Taxation of Corporations and Partnerships, 5th edit., 2005; (with Freeland, Lind and Stephens) Fundamentals of Federal Income Taxation, 14th edit., 2006; (with McNulty) Federal Income Taxation of Individual in a Nutshell, 7th edit., 2004; author: The Alternative Minimum Tax-Compliance and Planning with Analysis, 1994 Mem. Order of Coif, Beta Gamma Sigma. Office Phone: 415-565-4636.

LATONA, VALERIE ANN, editor-in-chief; d. Salvatora and Valeria Latona; m. David Marc Contract, May 27, 2000; 2 children. Grad. magna cum laude, Canisius Coll., Buffalo; MA in Journalism, NYU. Sr. editor Allure mag. Condé Nast Publs.; various positions from beauty dir., dep. editor/editl beauty dir. active lifestyle grp. to dep. editor NY office Shape mag. Weider Publs., 2000—05, editor-in-chief, 2005—. Office: Weider Publs Llc 21100 Erwin St Woodland Hills CA 91367

LATOUR, THOMAS W., hotel executive; m. Barbara LaTour. Degree in hotel/restaurant mgmt., Mich. State U., 1966; grad. mgmt. devel., Harvard U., 1980. Gen. mgr. Sky Chef; regional mgr. Amfac, 1983, sr. v.p. adminstrn.; pres. Kimpton Hotel and Restaurant Group, Inc., San Francisco, 1983—. Office: Kimpton Hotel Restaurant Group Inc 222 Kearny St Ste 200 San Francisco CA 94108-4510

LATTA, GEORGE HAWORTH, III, neonatal/perinatal nurse practitioner; b. Chattanooga, Sept. 4, 1960; s. George Haworth Jr. and Charlotte (Major) L. BS in Physics, Ga. Inst. Tech., 1982; MD, East Tenn. State U., 1986. Cert. in pediat., neonatology. Intern, resident in pediat. Dartmouth (N.H.) U., 1986-88; resident in pediat. Stanford (Calif.) U., 1988-89; fellow in neonatology Vanderbilt U., Nashville, 1989-90, U. Tenn., Memphis, 1990-92; attending neonatologist Rose Med. Ctr., Denver, 1992-94, Forrest Gen. Hosp., Hattiesburg, Miss., 1994-95, Meth. Hosps., Memphis, 1995-99; neontalogist Intermountain Healthcare, Provo, Utah, 2000—05, Children's Hosp. Ctrl. Calif., Madera, 2006—, Kaweah Delta Hosp., 2007—. NIH pulmonary trainee grantee Vanderbilt U., 1989; March of Dimes scholar East Tenn. State U., 1984, Johnny J. Jones scholar, 1981. Fellow: Am. Acad. Pediat.; mem.: Wildnerness Med. Soc., Phi Eta Sigma. Roman Catholic. Avocations: skiing, camping, jazz, aquariums, scuba diving. Personal E-mail: ghlatta3@comcast.net. Business E-Mail: uvglatta@ihc.com.

LATTMAN, LAURENCE HAROLD, retired academic administrator; b. NYC, Nov. 30, 1923; s. Jacob and Yetta (Schwartz) L.; m. Hanna Renate Cohn, Apr. 12, 1946; children— Martin Jacob, Barbara Diane. BSChemE, Coll. City N.Y., 1948; MS in Geology, U. Cin., 1951, PhD, 1953. Instr. U. Mich., 1952-53; asst. head photogeology sect. Gulf Oil Corp., Pitts., 1953-57; asst. prof. to prof. geomorphology Pa. State U., 1957-70; prof., head dept. geology U. Cin., 1970-75; dean Coll. of Mines U. Utah, 1975-83, dean Coll. Engring., 1978-83; pres. N.Mex. Tech., Socorro, 1983-93, pres. emeritus, 1993—. Bd. dirs. Pub. Svc. Co. of N.Mex.; cons. U.S. Army Engrs., Vicksburg, Miss., 1965-69, also major oil cos. Author: (with R.G. Ray) Aerial Photographs in Field Geology, 1965, (with D. Zillman) Energy Law; Contbr. articles to profl. jours. Mem. N.Mex. Environ. Improvement Bd., 1995-2002. With AUS, 1943-46. Fenneman fellow, U. Cin., 1953. Fellow Geol. Soc. Am.; mem. Am. Assn. Petroleum Geologists, Am. Soc. Photogrammetry (Ford Bartlett award 1968), Soc. Econ. Paleontologists and Mineralogists, AIME (Disting. mem. 1981, Mineral Industries Edn., award 1986—), Assn. Western Univs. (chmn. bd. dirs. 1986-87), Sigma Xi. Home: 11509 Penfield Ln NE Albuquerque NM 87111-6526 Personal E-mail: lhlattman@comcast.net.

LATZER, RICHARD NEAL, investment company executive; b. NYC, Jan. 6, 1937; s. Paul John and Alyce A. Latzer; m. Ellen Weston, Sept. 5, 1965; children: Steven, David. BA, U. Pa., 1959, MA, 1961. Chartered fin. analyst. Security analyst Mut. Benefit Life Ins. Co., Newark, 1963-66; portfolio mgr. EquitableLife Ins., Washington, 1966-68; securities analyst Investors Diversified Svcs., Mpls., 1968-69, dir. cert. and ins. investments, 1969-77, v.p. cert. and ins. investments, 1977-84, IDS Fin. Svcs., Inc., 1984-86, IDS Fin. Corp., 1987-88; v.p. investments IDS Reins. Co., 1986-88; asst. treas. Investors Syndicate Life Ins. & Annuity Co., Mpls., 1969-72; v.p. IDS Life Ins. Co., Mpls., 1973-80, v.p. investments, 1980-88; v.p. Investors Syndicate of Am., 1973-77, v.p. investments, 1977-84; v.p. Investors Syndicate Title & Guaranty Co., 1977-83; investment officer IDS Life Ins. Co. of N.Y., 1977-88; v.p. investments IDS Life Capital Resource Fund I, Inc., 1981-88, IDS Spl. Income Fund, Inc., 1981-88, Am. Enterprise Life Ins. Co., 1986-88, Reinsurance Co., 1986-88, IDS Life Series Fund, 1986-88, IDS Life Managed Fund, Inc., 1986-88, IDS Property Casualty, 1987-88; v.p. IDS Realty Corp., 1987-88; pres., chmn. bd., bd. dirs. Real Estate Svcs. Co., 1986-88, IDS Life Moneyshare Fund, Inc., 1981-88, IDS Cert. Co., 1984-88; chmn. bd., dir. IDS Real Estate Svcs. Co., 1983-86; v.p. Fireman's Fund Am. Life Ins. Co., 1985-86; dir. Investors Syndicate Devel. Corp., Mpls., 1970-88, Nuveen Realty Corp., Mpls., 1976-80; sr. v.p., chief investment officer Transamerica Corp., San Francisco, 1988—; pres., CEO Transamerica Investments Svcs., Inc., San Francisco, 1988—; dir., chief investment officer, chmn. investment com. Transamerica Occidental Life Ins. Co., LA, 1989—; dir., chief investment officer, chmn. investment com., CEO Transamerica Life Ins. and Annuity Co., LA, 1989—. Dir., chief investment officer, mem. investment com.Transamerica Ins. Group, Woodland Hills, 1988-93; bd. dirs., mem. exec. com. Transamerica Realty Svcs., Inc., San Francisco, 1988—, pres., CEO, 1996—; dir. Transamerica Realty Investment Corp., San Francisco, 1988—; chmn. pension investment com. Transamerica Life Ins. Co. Can., Toronto, 1991—; chief investment officer, mem. operating com. ARC Reins. Corp., Honolulu, 1993—. Lt. USN, 1960-63. Mem. Security Analysts San Francisco, Chartered Fin. Analysts. Office: Transamerica Invest Mgmt LLC 1150 S Olive St Los Angeles CA 90015-2211

LAU, CHARLES KWOK-CHIU, architect, firm executive; b. Hong Kong, Oct. 19, 1954; came to U.S., 1973; s. Oi-Ting and Wai-Han L. BFA in Environ. Design, U. Hawaii Manoa, Honolulu, 1977. Registered architect, Hawaii. Designer CJS Group Architects, Honolulu, 1977-78, Fox Hawaii, Honolulu, 1978-80, Wimberly Allison Tong & Goo, Honolulu, 1980-82, Architects Hawaii, Honolulu, 1982-84; assoc., designer Stringer & Assocs., Honolulu, 1984-85; pres. AM Ptnrs., Inc., Honolulu, 1985—. Instr. U. Hawaii, Honolulu, 1987. Principal works include Crystal Fantasy, Hyatt Regency Hotel, Honolulu, 1988 (Merit award Hawaii chpt. AIA 1988), Dole Cannery Sq., Honolulu, 1989 (Merit award Hawaii Renaissance 1989), Danelle Christie's, Ala Moana Hotel, Honolulu, 1989 (Hawaii Region award Illuminating Engring. Soc. N.Am. 1989, Grand and Nat. Grand awards Hawaii Renaissance 1989, Tiger Restaurant, Lahaina, Hawaii, 1990 (Gold Key Excellence in Interior Design award Am. Hotel and Motel Assn. 1990, Nat. and Merit awards Hawaii Renaissance 1990), La Pierre du Roi, ANA Kalakaua Ctr., Honolulu, 1990 (Grand and Nat. Grand awards 1990), Crazy Shirts, Honolulu, 1991 (Grand and Overall awards Hawaii Renaissance 1991), Grand Hyatt Wailea, Maui, Hawaii, 1992 (Merit award Hawaii chpt. AIA 1992), Carrera y Carrera, Ala Moana Ctr., Honolulu, 1992 (Merit award Hawaii chpt. AIA 1992), Danelle Christie's, Outrigger Waikiki Hotel, Honolulu, 1992 (Merit award Hawaii Renaissance 1992), Exec. Ctr. Hotel,

Honolulu, 1992 (Merit award Hawaii Renaissance 1992), Centre Ct. Restaurant, Honolulu, 1993 (Merit award Hawaii Renaissance 1993), Lani Huli, Kailua, 1993 (Spl. Recognition award Parade of Homes 1993), 218 Plantation Club Dr., Kapalua, Maui, 1993 (Interior Design award Am. Soc. Interior Design 1993), Royal Garden Restaurant, Alamoana Hotel, Honolulu, 1994 (Brand and Overall award Hawaii Renaissance, 1994, Lani Huli, Kailua, Hawaii (Project of Yr., City and County of Honolulu 1994). Recipient 1994 Best in Am. Living award Profl. Builders, Kapalua Residence in Maui. Mem. AIA (mem. design award jury selection com. Honolulu chpt. 1990), C. of C. Hawaii, Chinese C. of C. Hawaii, Pacific Club. Home: 1100 Alakea St Ste 800 Honolulu HI 96813-2851

LAU, CONSTANCE H. (CONNNIE LAU), electric power industry executive; b. Honolulu; 3 children. BS, Yale Univ.; JD, Univ. Calif. Hastings Coll. Law; MBA, Stanford Univ. With Hawaiian Elec. Industries, Honolulu, 1984—99; treas. Hawaiian Elec. Industries, Hawaiian Elec. Co., 1989—99; fin. v.p., CFO HEI Power Corp.; sr. exec. vice-pres., COO Am. Savings Bank, 1999—2001, pres., CEO, 2001—, Hawaiian Elec. Industries, Honolulu, 2006—. Mem. bd. Punahou Sch., Kamehameha Sch., Charles Reed Bishop Trust, Alexander & Baldwin Inc. Named one of 25 Most Powerful Women in Banking, US Banker, 2006. Mem.: Maunalani Found., Hawaii Bus. Roundtable, Hawaiian Bankers Assn. Office: Hawaiian Elec Industries Bldg 1 900 Richards St Honolulu HI 96813 Office Phone: 800-272-2566.

LAU, H. LORRIN, obstetrician, gynecologist; b. Honolulu, Apr. 21, 1932; s. Henry S. and Helen (Lee) L.; m. Maureen Lau; children: David, Marianne, Mike, Mark, Linda. AB cum laude, Harvard U., 1950-54; MD, Johns Hopkins U., 1954-58, MPH, 1970-71. Asst. prof. Sch. Med. Johns Hopkins U. (Balt.), 1964-82; assoc. prof. U. Hawaii, 1982-84; chief ob-gyn. St. Francis West Hosp., Honolulu, 1990-92, Kuakini Hosp., Honolulu, 1994-95. Fellow AMA; mem. ACOG, Internat. Soc. Biology and Medicine. Inventor pregnancy tests, helped introduce alpha-fetoprotein tests into obstetrics in USA, 1971. Home: 1121 Wilder Ave 1700B Honolulu HI 96822 Office: 1010 S King St Honolulu HI 96814-1701 Office Phone: 808-596-0164. Personal E-mail: drhllau@yahoo.com.

LAU, JENNY KWOK WAH, theater educator, consultant, film educator; arrived in U.S.A., 1979; d. Wai-Wing and Yau-Ying L.; children: Daniel, Esther. BSc in Physics, U. Hong Kong, 1976; PhD in Cinema Studies, Northwestern U., 1989. Lectr. dept. T.V. and film Hong Kong Bapt. Coll., 1983-85, asst. prof., 1990-91; vis. prof. dept. radio, T.V., film Northwestern U., 1991-92; asst. prof. Ohio U., 1992-96, assoc. prof. sch. film, 1997; assoc. prof. cinema dept. San Francisco State U., 2005—. Radio culture critic Radio Hong Kong, 1983-86; prodr., dir. Sta. 32, Chgo., 1988-89; spkr. in field; presenter numerous confs. Contbr. articles to books and profl. jours.; creator numerous exptl. films. Recipient Best Short Film Award PBS, Chgo., Boston, 1990, Baker Award, 1995; grantee for Libr. Acquisition, 1992-93, Hong Kong Office Econ. Trade, 1995, for Devel. of Web Based Courses in Film, 1997, Coll. Fine Arts, 1997, David C. Lam Inst. for East West Studies, 1998. Mem. Hong Kong Film Scholar Assn., Soc. Cinema Studies (co-chair Asian-Asian Pacific caucus, exec. coun. mem.). Achievements include being the first Chinese national (men or women) to receive a PhD degree in Cinema Studies. Avocations: singing, piano, photography, films, debates with friends. Office: San Francisco State U Cinema Dept San Francisco CA 94132

LAUB, ALAN JOHN, engineering educator; b. Edmonton, Alta., Can., Aug. 6, 1948; came to U.S., 1970; naturalized, 1984; BSc with honors, U. B.C., 1969; MS, U. Minn., 1972, PhD, 1974. Asst. prof. Case Western Res. U., Cleve., 1974-75; vis. asst. prof. U. Toronto, Can., 1975-77; rsch. scientist MIT, Cambridge, Mass., 1977-79; assoc. prof. U. So. Calif., LA, 1979-83; prof. U. Calif., Santa Barbara, 1983-96, chmn. dept. elec. and computer engring., 1989-92; dean Coll. of Engring. U. Calif. Davis, 1996—. Contbr. articles to profl. jours. Fellow IEEE; mem. IEEE Control Systems Soc. (pres. 1991, Disting. Mem. award 1991, Control Systems Tech. award 1993), Soc. Indsl. Applied Math., Assn. Computing Machinery. Avocations: bridge, tennis. Office: U Calif Office Dean Coll Engring One Shields Ave Davis CA 95616-5294

LAUCHENGCO, JOSE YUJUICO, JR., lawyer; b. Manila, Philippines, Dec. 6, 1936; came to US, 1962; s. José Celis Sr. Lauchengco and Angeles (Yujuico) Sapota; m. Elisabeth Schindler, Feb. 22, 1968; children: Birthe, Martina, Duane, Lance. AB, U. Philippines, Quezon City, 1959; MBA, U. So. Calif., 1964; JD, Loyola U., LA, 1971. Bar: Calif. 1972, US Dist. Ct. (ctrl. dist.) Calif. 1972, US Ct. Appeals (9th cir.) 1972, US Supreme Ct. 1975. Banker First Western Bank/United Calif. Bank, LA, 1964-71; assoc. Demler, Perona, Langer & Bergkvist, Long Beach, Calif., 1972-73; ptnr. Demler, Perona, Langer, Bergkvist, Lauchengco & Manzella, Long Beach, 1973-77; sole practice Long Beach and L.A., 1977-83; ptnr. Lauchengco & Mendoza, LA, 1983-92; pvt. practice LA, 1993—. Mem. commn. on jud. procedures County of LA, 1979; tchr. Confraternity of Christian Doctrine, 1972-79; counsel Philippine Presdl. Commn. on Good Govt., LA, 1986. Chmn. Filipino-Am. Bi-Partisan Polit. Action Group, LA, 1978. Recipient Degree of Distinction, Nat. Forensic League, 1955. Mem. Philippine-Am. Bar Assn. (life), Calif. Pub. Defenders Assn., U. Philippines Vanguard Assn. (life), KC, Beta Sigma. Roman Catholic. Avocations: classical music, opera, romantic paintings and sculpture, camping, shooting. Office: PO Box 767 Los Angeles CA 90078-0767 Office Phone: 323-462-1555.

LAUDA, DONALD PAUL, retired dean; b. Leigh, Nebr., Aug. 7, 1937; s. Joe and Libbie L.; m. Sheila H. Henderson, Dec. 28, 1966; children: Daren M., Tanya R. BS, Wayne State Coll., 1963, MS, 1964; PhD, Iowa State U., 1966. Assoc. dir. Communications Center U. Hawaii, 1966-67; assoc. prof. indsl. arts St. Cloud (Minn.) State Coll., 1967-69; asst. dean Ind. State U., 1970-73; chmn. tech. edn. W.Va. U., 1973-75; dean Sch. Tech., Eastern Ill. U., Charleston, 1975-83; dean Coll. Health and Human Svcs. Calif. State U., Long Beach, 1983—2002, dean emeritus, 2002—. Cons. traditional Chinese medicine edn. Author: Advancing Technology: Its Impact on Society, 1971, Technology, Change and Society, 1978, 2d edit., 1985; contbr. articles to profl. jours. Pres. Council on Tech. Tchr. Edn.; dir. Charleston 2000 Futures Project, 1978-81. Served with USAR, 1957-59. EPDA research fellow, 1969-70; Eastern Ill. U. faculty research grantee, 1971 Mem. Future Soc. Internat. Tech. Edn. Assn., Coun. Tech. Tchr. Educators (pres., Tchr. of Yr. award 1978), World Future Soc., Internat. Tech. Edn. Assn. (pres. 1990), World Coun. Assn. Tech. Edn., Am. Vocat. Assn., Phi Kappa Phi (pres. 1993), Epsilon Pi Tau (Laureate citation 1982), Long Beach C. of C. (bd. dirs. 1995—), Japan Am. Soc. (adv. bd.). Office: Calif State U Coll Health & Human Svcs Long Beach CA 90840-0001 Office Phone: 949-916-2735. Personal E-mail: dlauda@aol.com.

LAUER, JEANETTE CAROL, dean, history educator, writer; b. St. Louis, July 14, 1935; d. Clinton Jones and Blanche Aldine (Gideon) Pentecost; m. Robert Harold Lauer, July 2, 1954; children: Jon, Julie, Jeffrey. BS, U. Mo., St. Louis, 1970; MA, Washington U., St. Louis, 1973, PhD, 1975. Assoc. prof. history St. Louis C.C., 1974-82, U.S. Internat. U., San Diego, 1982-90, prof., 1990-94, dean Coll. Arts and Scis., 1990-94, rsch. prof., 1997—. Author: Fashion Power, 1981, The Spirit and the Flesh, 1983, Til Death Do Us Part, 1986, Watersheds, 1988, The Quest for Intimacy, 5th edit., 2002, 6th edit. 2006, No Secrets, 1993, The Joy Ride, 1993, For Better of Better, 1995, True Intimacy, 1996, Intimacy on the Run, 1996, How to Build a Happy Marriage, 1996, Sociology: Contours of Society, 1997, Windows on Society, 1999, 7th edit., 2005; Becoming Family: How to Build a Stepfamily that Works, 1999, How to Survive and Thrive in an Empty Nest, 1999, Troubled Times: Readings in Social Problems, 1999, Love Never Ends, 2002, The Play Solution: How to Put the Fun Back into your Relationship, 2002, Social Problems and the Quality of Life, 10th edit., 2005, 11th edit., 2008, Marriage and the Family: The Quest for Intimacy, 6th edit., 2005, 7th edit., 2008. Woodrow Wilson fellow, 1970, Washington U. fellow, 1971-75. Mem.: Am. Hist. Assn., Orgn. Am. Historians. Democrat. Presbyterian.

LAUER, WARREN A., lawyer; b. Lusk, Wyo., Dec. 3, 1951; BS in Agr., U. Wyo., 1976, JD, 1980. Bar: Wyo. 1981. Pvt. practice Lauer Law Offices, Laramie, Wyo. Bd. dirs. U. Wyo. Coll. Law Alumni Assn., pres., 2002—03; bd. dirs., treas. Laramie Regional Airport. Contbr. articles to profl. jours. Mem. pres. coun. U. Wyo.; mem. state small bus. air quality adv. panel, 1994—97; mem. bd. adjustment Laramie Zoning Bd., 1983—89; mem. Albany County Planning and Zoning Commn., 1998—2000. Mem.: ABA, Wyo. Trial Lawyers Assn., Wyo. State Bar (commr. 1998—2001, sec.-treas. 2002—03, v.p. 2003—04, pres.-elect 2004, pres. 2005), Albany County Bar Assn. (sec., treas. 1995, v.p. 1996, pres. 1997). Office: Lauer Law Offices 208 Garfield St Ste 200 A Laramie WY 82070 Office Phone: 307-742-7288. Office Fax: 307-745-5502. E-mail: warrenlauer@lauerlegal.com.

LAUGHLIN, ROBERT B., academic administrator, physics professor; b. Visalia, Calif., Nov. 1, 1950; m. Anita Rhona Perry, Apr. 22, 1979; children: Nathaniel David, Todd William. AB in Math, U. Calif., Berkeley, 1972; PhD in Physics, MIT, 1979. Postdoctoral fellow Bell Tel. Labs., 1979—81, Lawrence Livermore Nat. Lab., 1981—82; research scientist Lawrence Livermore Nat. Lab, 1982—; assoc. prof. physics Stanford U., Calif., 1985—89, prof. physics Calif., 1989—2004, Anne T. and Robert M. Bass prof. Sch. Humanities and Scis. Calif., 1992—, prof. applied physics Calif., 1993—; pres. Korea Advanced Inst. Sci. & Tech. (KAIST), Daejeon, Republic of Korea, 2004—. Lectr. in field. Author: A Different Universe: Reinventing Physics from the Bottom Down, 2005; contbr. articles to profl. jours. With US Army, 1972—74. Recipient E.O. Lawrence award for Physics, 1985, Franklin Inst. medal, 1998, Nobel Prize in Physics, 1998; named Eastman Kodak lectr., 1989, Van Vleck lectr., 1994; fellow, IBM, 1976—78. Fellow: AAAS, Am. Acad. Arts and Scis., Am. Phys. Soc. (Oliver E. Buckley prize 1986); mem.: NAS, Aspen Ctr. Physics. Office: Stanford U Dept Physics LAM Rm 342 McCullough Bldg 476 Lomita Mall Stanford CA 94305-4045 Business E-Mail: rbl@large.stanford.edu.

LAURANCE, DALE R., oil company executive; b. Ontario, Oreg., July 6, 1945; s. Rolland D. and Frances S. (Hopkins) L.; m. Lynda E. Dolmyer, Sept. 11, 1966; children— Catherine Megan, Brandy Nichole, Holly Elizabeth. BSChemE, Oreg. State U., 1967; MSChemE, U. Kans., 1971, PhDChemE, 1973. Mem. mgmt., research staff E.I. DuPont de NeMours, Lawrence, Kans., 1967-77; mgr. process technology Olin Corp., Lake Charles, La., 1977-80, bus. mgr. urethanes Stamford, Conn., 1980-82, gen. mgr. urethane and organics, 1982-83; sr. v.p. Occidental Chem. Corp., Darien, Conn., 1983-84; exec. v.p. Occidental Petroleum Corp., LA, 1984-91, exec. v.p., sr. oper. officer, 1991, also bd. dirs., pres., 1996—; chmn., CEO Occidental Oil & Gas, LA, 1999—2004; owner Laurance Enterprises LLC, 2005—, Nightingale Properties LLC; non-exec. chmn. Ingram Micro, 2007—. Chmn. adv. bd., mem. dept. chem. and petroleum engring., U. Kans., Lawrence, 1985—; dir. Jacobs Engring. Group Inc., Ingram Micro, Inc. Contbr. articles to profl. jours. Patentee in field. Recipient Disting. Engring. Svc. award Sch. Engring., U. Kans., 1991. Mem. Am. Petroleum Inst., Chem. Mfrs. Assn., Soc. Chem. Industry, L.A. Area C. of C. (bd. dirs.). Clubs: Riveria Country (Los Angeles). Republican. Mailing: Ingram Micro Bd Directors PO Box 25125 Santa Ana CA 92799-5125

LAURIDSEN, MORTEN JOHANNES, composer, music educator; b. Colfax, Wash., Feb. 27, 1943; BA, Thornton Sch. Music, U. So. Calif., 1966, MA, 1968, DMA, 1974. Disting. prof. composition Thornton Sch. Music, U. So. Calif., 1972—, chair composition dept., 1990—2002; composer-in-residence LA Master Chorale, 1994—2001. Composer: A Winter Come, 1968, Variations for piano solo, 1972, Mid-Winter Songs, 1980, Cuatro Canciones, 1983, Madrigali: Six Firesongs on Renaissance Italian Poems, 1987, Canticle: In Memoriam, Halsey Stevens, 1990, Les Chansons des Roses, 1994, O Magnum Mysterium, 1994, Lux Aeterna, 1997, Nocturnes, 2005. Recipient Outstanding Alumnus award, Thornton Sch. Music, 1999, Phi Kappa Phi Creative Writing prize, U. So. Calif., Ramo award, Lambda Delta citation for Teaching Excellence, Dean's award, Nat. Medal Arts, 2007; named an Am. Choral Master, Nat. Endowment Arts, 2006. Office: Dept Composition MUS 308 USC Thornton Sch Music Los Angeles CA 90089-0851 Office Phone: 213-740-7416. E-mail: lauridse@usc.edu.

LAURIE, HUGH, actor; b. Oxford, Oxfordshire, Eng., June 11, 1959; s. George Ranald and Patricia Mundell; m. Jo Green, June 16, 1989; children: Charlie, Bill, Rebecca. Attended, Cambridge U. Actor, writer: (TV series) Alfresco, 1983—84; A Bit of Fry and Laurie, 1986—95; actor, dir. Fortysomething, 2003; actor: Blackadder the Third, 1987, Les Girls, 1988, Blackadder Goes Forth, 1989, (voice) Treasure Island, 1993, Tracey Takes On..., 1996, (voice) Preson Pig, 2000, Little Grey Rabbit, 2000, Stuart Little, 2003, House, M.D., 2004— (Best Performance by an Actor in a TV Series-Drama, Hollywood Fgn. Press Assn. Golden Globe award, 2006, Best Performance by an Actor in a TV Series-Drama, Golden Globe award, Hollywood Fgn. Press Assn., 2007, Outstanding Performance by a Male Actor in a Drama Series, SAG, 2007, Choice TV Actor: Drama, Teen Choice Awards, 2007, Outstanding Performance by a Male Actor in a Drama Series, SAG, 2009); (TV films) Cambridge Footlights Revue, 1982, The Crystal Cube, 1983, Mrs. Capper's Birthday, 1985, The Laughing Prisoner, 1987, Hysteria 2!, 1989, All or Nothing at All, 1993, The Adventures of Mole, 1995, The Place of Lions, 1997, The Nearly Complete Utter History of Everything, 1999, Life with Judy Garland: Me and My Shadows, 2001, The Young Visitors, 2003; (films) Plenty, 1985, Peter's Friends, 1992, A Pin for the Butterfly, 1994, Sense and Sensibility, 1995, 101 Dalmatians, 1996, The Borrowers, 1997, The Man in the Iron Mask, 1998, Cousin Bette, 1998, Stuart Little, 1999, Blackadder Back and Forth, 1999, Carnivale, 2000, The Piano Tuner, 2001, Stuart Little 2, 2002, Flight of the Phoenix, 2004, The Big Empty, 2005, Valiant, 2005, Street Kings, 2008, (voice) Monsters vs. Aliens, 2009; author: The Gun Seller. Named Favorite Male TV Star, People's Choice Awards, 2009; named an Honorary Knight Comdr. of the Most Excellent Order of the British Empire, Queen Elizabeth II, 2007. Office: The Gersh Agy 232 N Canon Dr Beverly Hills CA 90210

LAURIE, RONALD SHELDON, lawyer; b. San Francisco, June 30, 1942; s. Charles M. and Mimosa (Ezaoui) L.; m. Mina Heshmati, June 1, 1986. BS in Indsl. Engring., U. Calif., Berkeley, 1964; JD, U. San Francisco, 1968. Bar: Calif. 1969, U.S. Ct. Appeals (9th cir.) 1969, U.S. Patent Office 1969, U.S. Supreme Ct. 1971, U.S. Ct. Appeals (fed. cir.) 1972. Programmer, sys. engr. Lockheed Missiles & Space Co., Sunnyvale, Calif., 1960-64; patent atty. Kaiser Aluminum & Chem. Co., Oakland, Calif., 1968-70; ptnr. Townsend and Townsend, San Francisco, 1970-88, Irell & Manella, Menlo Park, Calif., 1988-91, Weil, Gotshal & Manges, Menlo Park, 1991-94, McCutchen, Doyle, Brown & Emersen, San Francisco, 1994-98; chmn. McCutchen Computers and Software Industry Group, 1995-98; ptnr. Skadden, Arps, Meagher & Flom, Palo Alto, Calif., 1998—; co-chair Skadden Arps' Computer and Info. Tech. Group, 1998—. Lectr. computer law Stanford U. Law Sch., 1993-94; advisor NAS, U.S. Copyright Office and U.S. Patent and Trademark Office, Washington, Office Tech. Assessment, U.S. Congress, World Intellectual Property Orgn., Geneva; lectr. patent law U. Calif., Berkeley, 1999—; permanent faculty World Law Inst., 1996—. Co-editor: International Intellectual Property, 1992; contbr. articles to profl. jours. Mem. Internat. Intellectual Property Assn. (exec. com.), State Bar Calif. (past mem. exec. com. intellectual property sect.), Computer Law Assn. (bd. dirs.). Avocation: auto racing. Office: Skadden Arps Meagher & Flom 525 University Ave Palo Alto CA 94301-1903 Home: 1037 Ramona St Palo Alto CA 94301-2444 E-mail: rlaurie@skadden.com, roulaurie@sprintmail.com.

LAURITZEN, PETER OWEN, electrical engineering educator; b. Valparaiso, Ind., Feb. 14, 1935; s. Carl W. and Edna B. (Seebach) L.; m. Helen M. Janzen, Apr. 6, 1963; children: Beth K., Margo S. BS, Calif. Inst. Tech., 1956; MS, Stanford U., 1958, PhD, 1961. Assoc. evaluation engr. Honeywell Aero. Div., Mpls., 1956-57; mem. tech. staff Fairchild Semiconductor Div., Palo Alto, Calif., 1961-65; asst. prof. elec. engring. U. Wash., Seattle, 1965-68, assoc. prof., 1968-73, prof., 1973-98, prof. emeritus, 1999—, adj. prof. social mgmt. of tech., 1977-83; engring. mgr. Avtech Corp., Seattle, 1979-80. Cons. x-ray div. Chgo. Bridge & Iron Works, 1967-71, 78, Eldec Corp., 1982-91, Energy Internat., 1986-88; conf. chair IEEE Power Electronics Specialist Conf., 1993; co-dir. NSF industry/univ. rsch. ctr., 1995-97; Fulbright lectr. IIT, Madras, India, 1997; Danfoss vis. prof. Aalborg (Denmark) U., 1999. Pres. Coalition for Safe Energy, Wash. Citizens Group, 1975-76. Danforth assoc., 1966-78; NASA-Am. Soc. Engring. Edn. summer faculty fellow, 1974 Mem. IEEE, AAAS. Home: 325 33d St Port Townsend WA 98368-5023 Office: U Wash Elec Engring Dept PO Box 352500 Seattle WA 98195-2500 E-mail: plauritz@ee.washington.edu.

LAVERNIA, ENRIQUE JOSE, materials science and engineering educator, dean; b. Havana, Cuba, July 30, 1960; arrived in US, 1965; s. Carlos Manuel and Ana Margot (Borrego) L.; m. Julie M. Schoenung, Oct. 4, 1986. BS in solid mechanics, Brown U., 1982; MS in metallurgy, MIT, 1984, PhD in materials engring., 1986. Rsch. asst. MIT, Cambridge, 1982-86, postdoctoral assoc., 1986, rsch. assoc., 1986-87; asst. prof. dept. chem. and aerospace engring. U. Calif., Irvine, 1987-91, assoc. prof. dept. chem. engring. and materials sci., 1991—95, prof., 1995—2002, dept. head, 1998—2002, dean Coll. Engring. Davis, 2002—, prof. dept. chem. engring. and materials sci., 2002—; vis. prof. Max Planck Inst., Stuttgart, Germany, 1997. Adv. bd. Advanced Composites Newsletter, 1994—, Key Engring. Materials, Trans Tech, 1996—; bd. review Jour. Applied Composite Materials, 1994—, Metallurgical and Materials Transactions, 1994—, Internat. Jour. Non-Equilibrium Processing, 1996—; co-editor Jour. Materials Synthesis and Processing, 1996—; editl. bd. Electronic Jour., Ciencia Abierta, U. of Chile, 1999—, Jour. Materials Processing Tech., 1999—; assoc. editor Jour. Metastable and Nanostructured Materials, 2000—; adv. bd. NSF-Ctr. for Advanced Materials & Smart Structures, NC State U., 1998—; mem. Nat. Materials Adv. Bd., 2002—. Recipient Faculty Career Devel. Award, U. Calif. Irvine, 1989, Chem. and Biochem. Engring. and Materials Sci. Tchr. of Yr., 1998, Young Investigator Award, Office Naval Rsch., 1990—93; co-recipient Best Paper Award, Jour. Thermal Spray Tech., 1995, Marion Howe Medal for Best Paper, Metallurgical and Materials Transaction, 1998, Marcus A. Grossmann Award for Best Paper, 1999; named Chancellor's Prof., U. Calif. Irvine, 2002, Outstanding Asst. Prof., U. Calif. Irvine Sch. Engring., 1989—90, Presdl. Young Investigator, NSF, 1989—94; Rockwell Internat. Fellowship, 1982—84, Aluminum Co. Am. Fellowship, 1990—92, Iketani Sci. and Tech. Found. Fellowship, Japan, 1993, Alexander Von Humboldt Fellowship, Germany, 1995, Ford Found. Fellowship, 1995. Fellow: AAAS; mem.: Am. Metal Powder Industries Fedn., Minerals, Metals and Materials Soc., Materials Rsch. Soc., ASM Internat. (Bradley Stoughton Award for Young Teachers 1993, Materials Sci. Divsn. Silver Medal 1995), Phi Beta Delta, Sigma Xi. Avocations: tennis, jogging, handball, scuba diving. Office: U Calif Coll Engring 1021A Kemper Hall 1 Shields Ave Davis CA 95616-5294 Home Phone: 530-758-4485; Office Phone: 530-752-0554. Business E-Mail: lavernia@ucdavis.edu.

LAVIDGE, ROBERT JAMES, marketing research executive; b. Chgo., Dec. 27, 1921; s. Arthur Wills and Mary Beatrice (James) L.; m. Margaret Mary Zwigard, June 8, 1946 (dec., Aug. 28, 2006); children: Margaret, Kathleen, William, Lynn Elizabeth. AB, DePauw U., 1943; MBA, U. Chgo., 1947. Analyst Pepsodent divsn. Lever Bros., Chgo., 1947-48, new products mktg. rsch. mgr. Pepsodent divsn., 1948-49; asst. dir. mktg. Am. Meat Inst., Chgo., 1950-51; ptnr. Elrick, Lavidge and Co., Chgo., 1951-56; pres. Elrick and Lavidge, Inc., Chgo., 1956-86; pres. emeritus Elrick and Lavidge, Scottsdale, Ariz., 1987—2002; ret. Lectr. mktg. rsch., sales adminstrn. Northwestern U., 1950-80; mem. Nat. Mktg. Adv. Com., 1967-71, exec. com.; bd. govs. Brand Names Edn. Found., 2000-02. Trustee Village

Western Springs, Ill., 1957-61, pres., 1973-77; trustee McCormick Theol. Sem., 1981-90, 92-96; mem. coun. U. Chgo. Grad. Sch. Bus.; bd. dirs. Ariz. Faith Counseling Ctr.; mem. coun. Ctr. Svcs. Leadership. Mem. Am. Mktg. Assn. (v.p. 1963-64, pres. 1966-67, trustee found. 1992—, chmn. 1992-99), Internat. Rels. Soc. (chmn. 1961-65), DePauw U. Alumni Assn. (pres. 1967-68), Klinger Lake Club (Mich.), Paradise Valley Country Club (Ariz.), Phi Beta Kappa, Beta Gamma Sigma, Sigma Delta Chi. Presbyterian. Personal E-mail: rlavidge@lavidge.com.

LAVIGNE, AVRIL, singer; b. Napanee, Ont., Can., Sept. 27, 1984; d. John and Judy Lavigne; m. Deryck Whibley, July 15, 2006. Designer Abbey Dawn clothing line, 2008. Singer: (albums) Let Go, 2002 (nominee Grammy award Best New Artist, 2002, nominee Grammy award Best Pop Vocal Album, 2002, nominee Grammy award for Best Female Rock Vocal Performance, 2002, Album of Yr. & Pop Album of Yr., Juno Awards, 2003), Under My Skin, 2004, The Best Damn Thing, 2007, (songs) Complicated, 2002 (nominee Grammy award for Song of Year, 2002, nominee Grammy award for Best Female Pop Vocal Performance, 2002, Single of Yr., Juno Awards, 2003), Sk8r Boi, 2002 (Favorite Song, Nickelodeon Kids' Choice Awards, 2003), Girlfriend, 2007 (Favorite Song, Nickelodeon Kids' Choice Awards, 2008); voice actor: (films) Over the Hedge, 2006; actor: Fast Food Nation, 2006, The Flock, 2007. Recipient Best New Artist award, MTV Video Music Awards, 2002, New Artist of Yr., Juno Awards, 2003, Best Female Pop/Rock Artist, World Music Awards, 2004, 2007, Best-selling Can. Artist, 2007, Favorite Female Singer, Nickelodeon Kids' Choice Awards, 2005. Achievements include signed with L.A. Reid of Arista Records at age 16. Avocations: hockey, basketball, skateboarding. Office: c/o Ian Volke Nettwerk Mgmt 1650 W 2nd Ave Vancouver BC V6J 4R3 Canada Office Phone: 604-654-2929. Office Fax: 604-654-1993. E-mail: nettmanagement@nettmanagement.com.

LAVIN, MATTHEW T., horticultural educator; Assoc. prof. biology dept. Mont. State U., Bozeman. Recipient N.Y. Botanical Garden award Botanical Soc. Am., 1993. Office: Montana State U Dept Biology 310 Lewis Hl Bozeman MT 59717-0001

LAVIN, STEPHEN MICHAEL, university basketball coach; b. San Francisco, Sept. 4, 1964; s. Cap and Mary Lavin. BS, Chapman U., 1987. Grad. asst. basketball coach, staff mem. Purdue U., 1988-91; staff mem. UCLA, 1991-95, asst. coach, 1995-97, recruiting coord., 1996-97, head coach, 1997—. Dir., founder Lavin Basketball Camps, 1984—; summer camp and coaches clinic spkr., 1989—; cons./advisor Korean Nat. Profl. Team, Samsung Profl. Team, 1992-96. Named Nat. Rookie Coach of Yr. Basketball Times mag., 1997; recipient Internat. Inspiration award Hugh O'Brien Youth Found., 1997. Office: UCLA 325 Westwood Plz Los Angeles CA 90095-8356

LAVINE, STEVEN DAVID, academic administrator; b. Sparta, Wis., June 7, 1947; s. Israel Harry and Harriet Hauda (Rosen) L.; m. Janet M. Sternburg, May 29, 1988. BA, Stanford U., 1969; MA, Harvard U., 1970, PhD, 1976. Asst. prof.-English Lit. U. Mich., Ann Arbor, 1974-81; asst. dir. arts and humanities Rockefeller Found., NYC, 1983-86, assoc. dir. arts and humanities, 1986-88; pres. Calif. Inst. Arts, Valencia, 1988—. Cons. Wexner Found., Columbus, Ohio, 1986-87; selection panelist Input TV Screening Conf., Montreal, Can., and Granada, Spain, 1985-86; faculty chair Salzburg Seminar on Mus., 1989; co-dir. Arts and Govt. Program, The Am. Assembly, 1991; mem. arch. selection jury L.A. Cathedral, 1996, Arch. L.A., 1998-2001; adv. com. The Asia Soc., So. Calif. Ctr., 1998-; co-chair The Arts Coalition for Acad. Progress, L.A. Unified Sch. Dist., 1997-; vis. com. J. Paul Getty Mus., 1990-1997; cons. in field. Editor: The Hopwood Anthology, 1981, Exhibiting Cultures, 1991, Museums and Communities, 1992. Bd. dirs. Sta. KCRW-FM (NPR), 1989—, Endowments, Inc., 1994—, Cotsen Family Found., 2000—, Villa Aurora, 2003—, Am. Coun. Edn., 2004—; trustee Idyllwild Arts Found., 2003—. Recipient Class of 1923 award, 1979, Faculty Recognition award, U. Mich., 1980, Highlight award, W.O.M.E.N., Inc., LA, 2005; Ford fellow, 1969—74, Charles Dexter traveling fellow, Harvard U., 1972. Jewish. Office: Calif Inst Arts Office Pres 24700 McBean Pkwy Santa Clarita CA 91355-2397 Home Phone: 818-995-7613. Business E-Mail: slavine@calarts.edu.

LAW, CLARENE ALTA, small business owner, state legislator; b. Thornton, Idaho, July 22, 1933; d. Clarence Riley and Alta (Simmons) Webb; m. Franklin Kelso Meadows, Dec. 2, 1953 (div.); children: Teresa Lin Meadows, Charisse Meadows Haws, Steven Riley; m. Creed Law, 1973. Student, Idaho State Coll., 1953. Sec., sub. tchr. Grand County Schs., Cedar City, Utah, 1954-57; UPI rep. newspaper agy. Moab, Utah Regional Papers, Salt Lake City and Denver; auditor Wort Hotel, Jackson, Wyo., 1960-62; innkeeper, CEO Elk Country Motels, Inc., Jackson, Wyo., 1962—; rep. Wyo. Ho. of Reps., Cheyenne, 1991—2004. Bd. dirs. Jackson State Bank, Snow King Resort; mem. bank bd. Wyo. State Ho. Reps., 1991-98, chmn. travel com., 1993-2000, chmn. minerals and econ. devel. com., 2001-04. Chmn. sch. bd. dirs. Teton County Schs., Jackson, 1983-86; bd. dirs. Wyo. Taxpayers Assn., Bus. Coun., 1998—2004. Named Citizen of Yr. Jackson C. of C., 1976, 99, Bus. Person of Yr. Jackson Hole Realtors, 1987, Wyo. Small Bus. Person SBA, 1977. Mem. Wyo. Lodging and Restaurant Assn. (pres., chmn. bd. dirs. 1988-89, Big Wyo. award 1987), Soroptimists (charter), Bus. Profl. Womens Orgn. (Woman of Yr. 1975, mem. Heritage steering com. 1996—), Gov.'s 15-Mem. Bus. Coun. Republican. Avocations: travel, study. Address: PO Box 575 Jackson WY 83001-0575 Office: Elk County Motels Inc Box 575 43 W Pearl Jackson WY 83001 Home Phone: 307-733-4158. E-mail: antlerjh@aol.com.

LAWER, BETSY, banker, small business owner, vintner, director; b. Anchorage, July 27, 1949; d. Daniel H. and Betti Jane Cuddy; m. David A. Lawer, June 9, 1972; 1 child. Vice chair bd., COO 1st Nat. Bank Alaska, 1974—; pres. Lawer Family Winery Inc., 2005—, Lawer Family Vineyard Properties, Inc., 2005—. Bd. dirs., mem. audit com. Fed. Res. Bank San Francisco, Seattle, 1997—2003; emeritus bd. dirs. Providence Health Care Found., 2001; bd. dirs. Commonwealth North. Named Jr. Achievement Hall of Fame Laureate, Alaska Bus., 2007; named one of Top 25 Most Powerful Alaskans, Alaska Jour. Commerce, 1999—2003, 25 Women to Watch, US Banker, 2003. Mem.: Anchorage Athena Soc. (Athena award 2001).

LAWLER, JEAN MARIE, lawyer; b. San Francisco, Aug. 7, 1954; d. Jack Wofford and Evelyn Mary (Matkovich) Suggs; m. Timothy Lawler, May 20, 1978; children: Kathleen, Megan, Colleen, Timothy. AA, Riverside City Coll., 1974; BBA, Loyola Marymount U., LA, 1976; JD, Loyola U. Law Sch., 1979. Bar: Calif. Supreme Ct. 1979, Oreg. Supreme Ct. 1981. Assoc. law firm David L. Rosner, LA, 1979—80; instr. Lane CC, Eugene, Oreg., 1981—82, chmn. legal asst. adv. com., 1981—82; sole practice law Eugene, 1981—82, Beaverton, 1982—84; with with Murchison & Cumming, LA, 1985—, sr. ptnr., chair ins. law practice. Editor: Copyright Law, 1979—80, Business Associated Review, 1974; contbr.: Coll. Poetry Rev., 1974, 1976. Named Calif. Super Lawyer, 2006, 2005, 2006; scholarship, Riverside County Bar Assn., 1977, Jesuit Cmty. scholarship, Loyola U., 1978. Mem.: ABA, Lawyers for Civil Justice (bd. dirs. 2003—06), Def. Rsch. Inst. (bd. dirs. 2003—06), Assn. Southern Calif. Def. Counsel, Fedn. Def. & Corp. Counsel (bd. dirs. 1996—2006, pres. 2004—05), Washington County Bar Assn., Oreg. State Bar Assn., State Bar Calif., Assn. So. Calif. Def. Counsel (bd. birs. 1994—2000), Jonathon Club. Democrat. Roman Catholic. Office: Murchison & Cumming 9th Fl 801 S Grand Ave Los Angeles CA 90017 Office Phone: 213-630-1019. Office Fax: 210-623-6336. Business E-Mail: jlawler@murchisonlaw.com.

LAWLESS, LUCY (LUCILLE FRANCIS RYAN), actress; b. Auckland, New Zealand, Mar. 28, 1968; m. Garth Lawless 1991 (div. 1995); 1 child, Daisy; m. Robert G. Tapert Mar. 28, 1998; children Julius Robert Bay Tapert, Judah Miro Tapert. Student, Auckland U., William Davis Ctr. Actor Study, Vancouver, Can.; trained with martial arts master, Douglas Wong. Previous jobs include TV comml. actress, gold miner, Kalgoorlie, Australia. Actress (films) A Bitter Song, 1990, Within the Law, 1990, The End of the Golden Weather, 1991, The Black Stallion, 1992, The Rainbow Warrior, 1992, Peach, 1995, Spider-Man, 2002, EuroTrip, 2004, Boogeyman, 2005, The Darkroom, 2006, Bedtime Stories, 2008, (TV) Funny Business, 1987, Typhon's People, 1993, Hercules and the Amazon Women, 1994, Women from Down Under, 1995, Xena: Princess Warrior, 1995-2005, (TV Films) Locusts, 2005, Vampire Bats, 2005; co-host Air New Zealand Holiday, 1992-93, (film, voice of Xena) Hercules and Xena-The Animated Movie: The Battle for Mount Olympus, 1998; guest appearances Shark in the Park, 1990, For the Love of Mike, 1991, High Tide, 1994, 95, Hercules: The Legendary Journeys, 1995, 97, 98, Just Shoot Me!, 2001, The X-Files, 2001, Tarzan, 2004, Less Than Perfect, 2004, Veronica Mars, 2006, Battlestar Galactica, 2005, 2006, Two and Half Men, 2005, Celebrity Duets, 2006 Office: c/o Endeavor Agy 9601 Wilshire Blvd 3rd Fl Beverly Hills CA 90212

LAWRANCE, CHARLES HOLWAY, retired civil and sanitary engineer; b. Augusta, Maine, Dec. 25, 1920; s. Charles William and Lois Lyford (Holway) L.; m. Mary Jane Hungerford, Nov. 22, 1947; children: Kenneth A., Lois R., Robert J. BS in Pub. Health Engring., MIT, 1942; MPH, Yale U., 1952. Registered profl. engr., Calif. Sr. san. engr. Conn. State Dept. Health, Hartford, 1946-53; assoc. san. engr. Calif. Dept. Pub. Health, LA, 1953-55; chief san. engr. Koebig & Koebig, Inc., Cons. Engrs., LA, 1955-75; engr., mgr. Santa Barbara County Water Agy., Santa Barbara, Calif., 1975-79; prin. engr. James M. Montgomery Cons. Engrs., Pasadena, Calif., 1979-83; v.p. Lawrance, Fisk & McFarland, Inc., Santa Barbara, 1983-96; cons. engr., retired Santa Barbara, 1996-99. Author: The Death of the Dam, 1972; co-author: Ocean Outfall Design, 1958; contbr. articles to profl. jours. Bd. dirs. Pacific Unitarian Ch., Palos Verdes Peninsula, Calif., 1956-60, chmn. bd. 1st lt. USMCR, 1942-46, PTO. Fellow ASCE (life, Norman medal 1966); mem. Am. Water Works Assn. (life), Am. Acad. Environ. Engrs. (life diplomate), Water Environment Fedn. (life). Republican. Unitarian Universalist. Home and Office: 1340 Kenwood Rd Santa Barbara CA 93109-1224 E-mail: charleslawrance@earthlink.net.

LAWRENCE, KRISTINE GUERRA, project engineer; married. MS in Aerospace Engring., U. Colo. Gravitational biology facility engr. NASA Ames Rsch. Ctr. Mem. adv. com. women NASA Ames Rsch. Ctr. Flight medic USAF Res. Business E-Mail: klawrence@mail.arc.nasa.gov.

LAWRENCE, MARTIN, actor, comedian; b. Frankfurt, Germany, Apr. 16, 1965; s. John and Chlora L.; m. Patricia Southall Jan. 7, 1995 (div. Sept. 17, 1996); 1 child. Actor (TV series) What's Happening Now, 1985, HBO One Night Stand, 1989, Kid 'N' Play, 1990 (voice), Russell Simmons' Def Comedy Jam, 1991-93 (host); (films) Do the Right Thing, 1989, House Party, 1990, House Party 2, 1991, Talkin' Dirty after Dark, 1991, Boomerang, 1992, You So Crazy, 1994 (concert film, also exec. prodr.), Bad Boys, 1995, Nothing to Lose, 1997, Life, 1997, Blue Streak, 1999, Bad Boys II, 2003, Open Season (voice), 2006, Wild Hogs, 2007, Welcome Home Roscoe Jenkins, 2008, College Road Trip, 2008; actor, exec. prodr., writer, dir. A Thin Line Between Love and Hate, 1997; actor, exec. prodr. Big Momma's House, 2000, What's the Worst That Could Happen, 2001, Black Knight, 2001, National Security, 2003, Rebound, 2005, Big Momma's House 2, 2006, (TV series) Martin, 1992-97. Office: United Talent Agy 9560 Wilshire Blvd Ste 500 Beverly Hills CA 90212

LAWRENCE, SALLY CLARK, retired academic administrator; b. San Francisco, Dec. 29, 1930; d. George Dickson and Martha Marie Alice (Smith) Clark; m. Henry Clay Judd Jr., July 1, 1950 (div. Dec. 1972); children: Rebecca, David, Nancy; m. John I. Lawrence, Aug. 12, 1976; stepchildren: Maia, Dylan. Grad., Castilleja Sch. Girls, 1948; attended, House in the Pines Jr. Coll., Norton, Mass., 1948—49, Stanford U., 1949—50. Docent Portland Art Mus., Portland, Oreg., 1958-68; gallery owner, dir. Sally Judd Gallery, Portland, Oreg., 1968-75; art ins. appraiser, cons. Portland, Oreg., 1975-81; from interim dir. Mus. Art Sch. to pres. Pacific NW Coll. Art, Portland, Oreg., 1981—2003, pres. emerita, 2003—. Bd. dirs. Contemporary Crafts Gallery, Portland, 1970—73, Art Coll. Exch., 1982—91, Portland Arts Alliance, Portland, Oreg., 1987—2003, Portland Inst. Contemporary Art, 2005—, sec., 2006, 2007—. Fellow: Nat. Assn. Sch. Art and Design (life; bd. dirs. 1984—91, 1994—2002, pres. 1996—99); mem.: Assn. Ind. Coll. of Art and Design (pres. 1995—96, sec. 1996—2001), Oreg. Ind. Coll. Assn. (bd. dirs. 1981—2003, exec. com. 1989—94, pres. 1992—93, v.p. 2001—03), Pearl Arts Found. (chair bd. dirs. 2000—03). Personal E-mail: sallyl@carrollsweb.com.

LAWSON, KARA, professional basketball player; b. Alexandria, Va., Feb. 14, 1981; d. Williams and Kathleen Lawson; m. Damien Barling, Apr. 12, 2008. Grad. in fin., U. Tenn., 2003. Guard Sacramento Monarchs, 2003—. Mem. USA Basketball Women's Sr. Nat. Team, Australia, 2006, Beijing, 08. Recipient Woody Hayes Nat. Scholar Athlete award, 2003, Francis Pomeroy Naismith award, 2003, Gold medal, FIBA Americas Championship, 2007, Gold medal, women's basketball, Beijing Olympic Games, 2008; named Kodak/WBCA All-Am., 2003. Achievements include being a member of the WNBA Championship winning Sacramento Monarchs, 2005. Office: Sacramento Monarchs ARCO Arena One Sports Pky Sacramento CA 95834

LAWTON, MATT, professional baseball player; b. Gulfport, Miss., Nov. 3, 1971; Baseball player Minn. Twins, 1995—2001, Cleveland Indians, 2002—04, Pitts. Pirates, 2004—05, Chgo. Cubs, 2004—05, New York Yankees, 2005, Seattle Mariners, 2006—. Office: Seattle Mariners PO Box 4100 Seattle WA 98194

LAY, THORNE, geosciences educator; b. Casper, Wyo., Apr. 20, 1956; s. Johnny Gordon and Virginia Florence (Lee) L. BS, U. Rochester, 1978; MS, Calif. Inst. Tech., 1980. Rsch. assoc. Calif. Inst. Tech., Pasadena, 1983; asst. prof. geosciences U. Mich., Ann Arbor, 1984-88, assoc. prof., 1988-89; prof. earth and planetary sciences U. Calif., Santa Cruz, 1989—. Cons. Woodward Clyde Cons., Pasadena, 1982—84; dir. Inst. Tectonics, 1990—94, chmn. earth sci. dept., 1994—2000; dir. Inst. Geophysics and Planetary Physics, 2002—05, assoc. dean math., 2003—05; chmn. bd. dirs. Incorp. Rsch. Instns. Seismology, 2005—07; dir. Ctr. for Study of Imaging and Dynamics of the Earth, 2007—. Author: Structure and Fate of Subducting Slabs, 1997; co-author: (with T.C. Wallace) Modern Global Seismology, 1995; contbr. numerous articles to profl. jours. NSF fellow, 1978-81, Guttenberg fellow Calif. Inst. Tech., 1978, Lilly fellow Eli Lilly Found., 1984, Sloan fellow, 1985-87, Presidential Young Investigator, 1985-90. Fellow AAAS, Royal Astron. Soc., Am. Geophys. Union (Macelwane medal 1991), Soc. Exploration Geophysicist, Seismol. Soc. Am., Am. Acad. Arts and Scis.; mem. Nat. Acad. Sci. (life assoc.). Home: 2114 Harborview Ct Santa Cruz CA 95062-1678 Office: Univ California Santa Cruz Earth Planetary Sciences Dept 1156 High St Earth Marine Sciences Bldg Santa Cruz CA 95064 Home Phone: 831-454-8246; Office Phone: 831-459-3164. Business E-Mail: thorne@pmc.ucsc.edu.

LAYBOURNE, STANLEY, computer technology company executive; CPA. With Touche, Ross & Co. (now Deloitte & Touche), 1972—85, audit ptnr., 1983—85; pres., CEO Scottscom Group, 1985—89; exec. v.p. Ovation Broadcasting Co., 1989—90; CFO, treas. Insight Enterprises, Inc., 1991—, sec., 1994—, exec. v.p. Tempe, Ariz., 2002—. Office: Insight Enterprises Inc 1305 W Auto Drive Tempe AZ 85284

LAYMAN, CHARLES DONALD, plastic surgeon; b. Portland, Oreg., Mar. 20, 1949; MD, U Oreg. Health Scis. U., 1975. Plastic surgeon St. Vincent Med. Ctr., Portland. Clin. assoc. prof. plastic surgery U. Oreg. Health Sci. Ctr. Office: 9155 SW Barnes Rd Ste 220 Portland OR 97225-6629

LAYMON, JOE W., human resources specialist; b. 1952; married; 3 children. BA, Jackson State U.; MA, U. Wis. Various sr. human resouces positions including chief labor negotiator Xerox Corp., 1979—96; dir., v.p. human resources Kodak; with agency for internat. devel. U.S. State Dept.; exec. dir., human resources ops. Ford Motor Co., 2000—01, v.p. corp. human resources, 2001—03, group v.p., corp. human resources and labor affairs, 2003—08; corp. v.p. human resources Chevron Corp., San Ramon, Calif., 2008—. Bd. dirs. Am. Soc. Employers, Nat. Action Coun. Minorities in Engring., Douglas A. Fraser Ctr. Workplace Issues, Molex Inc., Nat. Tech. Inst. Deaf Rochester Inst. Tech., U. Wis., Human Resources Policy Assn., Am. Soc. Employers, Volvo Cars. Avocations: golf, cooking. Office: Chevron Corp 6001 Bollinger Canyon Rd San Ramon CA 94583-2324 Office Phone: 313-322-3000. Office Fax: 313-845-6073.*

LAYNE, JONATHAN K., lawyer; b. July 16, 1953; BA in Econs., Coll. William and Mary, 1975; MBA, Emory U., Atlanta, 1979; JD with distinction, Emory U. Sch. Law, Atlanta, 1979. Bar: Ga. 1979, Calif. 1979. Joined Gibson Dunn & Crutcher LLP, LA, 1979—, now ptnr. and co-chair mergers and acquisitions. Mem. exec. com, Gibson Dunn & Crutcher. Mng. editor Emory Law Jour., 1978—79. Bd. dir. Calif. C. of C.; past chmn. and pres. John Thomas Dye Sch. Mem.: ABA, LA County Bar Assn., State Bar of Calif., Order of Coif, Beta Gamma Sigma. Office: Gibson Dunn & Crutcher LLP 1043 Roscomare Rd Los Angeles CA 90077-2227 Office Phone: 310-552-8641. Office Fax: 310-552-7053. Business E-Mail: jlayne@gibsondunn.com.

LAZAREFF, JORGE ANTONIO, neurosurgeon, researcher; b. Buenos Aires, Jan. 11, 1953; s. Nicolas and Vera (Budinska) L.; m. Ines Garcia Lloret, May 28, 1982; children: Nicolás, Ana Maria. MD, Nat. Univ. Buenos Aires, 1977, cert. neurosurgeon Edu. Comm. for Foreign Med. Grads., 1980, Mexican Coun. Neurosurgeons, 1991, Medical Bd. of Calif., 1993, Colegio Argentino de Neurocirujanos, 1996. Resident in neurosurgery Hosp. de Niños, Buenos Aires, 1979-83; chief resident in neurosurgery Hosp. Fernandez, Buenos Aires, 1983-84; registrar in neurosurgery Groote Schuur Hosp., Red Cross Meml. Children Hosp., Cape Town, 1984-86; rsch. fellow dept. surgery U. Alberta, Edmonton, Can., 1986-88; head dept. exptl. surgery Hosp. Infantil de Mexico, 1988-91, head dept. neurosurgery, 1991—93; assist. prof. dept. neurosurgery UCLA Med. Ctr., Los Angeles, Calif., 1993—99, dir. pediatric neurosurgery, 1997—, assoc. prof. dept. neurosurgery, 1999—, co. dir., Cerebral Palsy Clinic, co. dir., Pediatric Brain Tumor Prog. Mem. rsch. com. Hosp. Infantil de Mexico, 1991. Inventor biopsy probe for sterotactic brain surgery; separated conjoined twins, 2002; author papers on neurosurgery and neurophistology. Recipient Rsch. award for spasticity Aaron Saenz Found., 1991, Ulrich Batzdorf, M.D. Faculty Teaching award, 2001. Mem. Soc. for Neurosci., 1991, Sociedad Mexicana de Cirugia Neurologica, 1992, Research Soc. of Neurological Surgeons, 1993, Internat. Soc. for Pediatric Neurosurgery, 1993, Academic Senate, UCLA, 1994, Johnson Comprehensive Cancer Ctr. 1994. Roman Catholic. Office: UCLA Med Ctr Divsn Neurosurgery PO Box 957039 Los Angeles CA 90095-7039

LAZARUS, DAVID, journalist; Grad., U. Calif., Berkeley. Crime reporter Daily (Californian) at Berkeley; columnist Japan Times; weekend radio talk show host KGO Radio, San Francisco; with San Francisco Chronicle, 1999—2007; columnist, bus. & tech. LA Times, 2007—. Contbg. writer: Fortune, Wired, Salon.com, Nat. Geographic; author: two books. Recipient Journalist of Yr. award, Soc. Profl. Journalists, 2001, John Jacobs award, 2001, Calif. Journalism award, Ctr. Calif. Studies Calif. State U., 2002, Nat. Headliner award, 2002, C. Everett Coop award, 2003, Journalist of Yr. award, Consumer Fedn. Calif., 2004. Office: LA Times Bus Section 202 W 1st St Los Angeles CA 90012 E-mail: david.lazarus@latimes.com.

LAZARUS, JEREMY A., psychiatrist; b. Chgo. m. Debbie Lazarus; 3 children. B in chemistry, Northwestern U.; MD with honors, U. Ill. Coll. Medicine. Intern Michael Reese Hosp., Chgo.; chief resident and tchg. fellow U. Colo. Health Sci. Ctr. (UCHSC), Denver, clinical prof. psychiatry; psychiatrist pvt. practice, Denver, 1972—. Med. dir. Colo. Met. State Coll. Student Health Svc.; vol. assoc. prof. psychiatry U.

Miami Sch. Medicine. Author several articles, chpt., books and other med. publ. on issues from ethics to managed care, Entering Private Practice: A Handbook for Psychiatrists, musician, singer. Recipient Presdl. Commendation, Am. Psychiatric Assn., 2003, Assembly Warren Williams award, 2004; fellow, Am. Coll. Psychiatrists; disting. fellow, Am. Psychiatric Assn. Mem.: AMA (vice speaker Ho. Del. 2003—07, spkr. Ho. Del. 2007—, chair bd. task force on medicare/health sys. reform, mem. bd. audit and orgn. and ops. coms., liaison to the Coun. on Med. Svc., vice chair, Nat. Adv. Coun. on Violence and Abuse, (found.) Uniting for the Future of Medicine campaign steering com., rep., Ride for World Health 2007, nominee for Isaac Hays, M.D. and John Bell, M.D. award for leadership in med. ethics and professionalism 1998), Fla. Med. Assn., Am. Inst. Parliamentarians, Nat. Assn. Parliamentarians, Colo. Med. Soc. (past pres.), Colo. Psychiatric Soc. (pres., Spokesperson Yr. 1995), Arapahoe County Med. Soc. (pres.). Achievements include 13-time Ironman Triathlon finisher; 13-time marathon finisher. Office: Jeremy A Lazarus 7555 E Hampden Ave Ste 301 Denver CO 80231-4834 Office Phone: 303-771-0353.

LAZARUS, MELL, cartoonist; b. NYC, May 3, 1927; s. Sidney and Frances (Mushkin) L.; m. Eileen Hortense Israel, June 19, 1949; children: Marjorie, Suesan, Catherine; m. Sally Elizabeth Mitchell, May 13, 1995. Cartoonist-writer Miss Peach, 1957—, Momma, 1970—; author anthologies Miss Peach, Miss Peach, Are These Your Children?, Momma, We're Grownups Now!; novels The Boss is Crazy, Too, 1964, The Neighborhood Watch, 1986; plays Everybody into the Lake, Elliman's Fly, Lifetime Eggcreams, 1969-70; juvenile Francine, Your Face Would Stop a Clock, 1975; co-author Miss Peach TV spl. programs Turkey Day Pageant and Annual Heart Throb Ball. With USNR, 1945, USAFR, 1951-54. Mem. Nat. Cartoonists Soc. (pres. 1989-93, chmn. membership com. 1965, nat. rep., Humor Strip Cartoonist of Yr. 1973, 79, Reuben award 1981, Silver T-Square award 2000), Nat. Press Club, The Century Assn., Am. Mensa. Office: Creators Syndicate Inc 5777 W Century Blvd Los Angeles CA 90045-5600 Personal E-mail: kpop3@aol.com.

LAZARUS, STEVEN S., management and marketing consultant; b. Rochester, NY, June 16, 1943; s. Alfred and Ceal H. Lazarus; m. Elissa C. Lazarus, June 19, 1966; children: Michael, Stuart, Jean. BS, Cornell U., 1966; MS, Poly. U. N.Y., 1967; PhD, U. Rochester, 1974. Pres. Mgmt. Systems Analysis Corp., Denver, 1977—; dir. Sci. Application Intern Corp., Englewood, Colo., 1979-84; assoc. prof. Metro State Coll., Denver, 1983-84; sr. v.p. Pal Assocs. Inc., Denver, 1984-85; with strategic planning and mktg. McDonnell Douglas, Denver, 1985-86; mktg. cons. Clin. Reference Systems, Denver, 1986; pres. Mgmt. Sys. Analysis Corp., 1986-89, 95—; assoc. exec. dir. Ctr. Rsch. Ambulatory Health Care Adminstrn., Englewood, 1990-94. Spl. cons. State of Colo., Denver, 1976-81; mktg. cons. IMX, Louisville, 1986-87; speaker Am. Hosp. Assn., Chgo., 1983; asst. sec. Work Group for Elec. Data Interchange, 1995-96, bd. dirs., 1997—, chmn. bd. dirs., 2001-02; trustee WEDI Found., 2003—, sec., 2004-05, chmn. bd. trustees, 2006-; pres. Boundary Info. Group, 1995—; founder, bd. dirs. Train for Compliance, Inc., 2003-, vice chmn., 2003—; co-founder Health IT Cert., LLC, 2004—. Co-author: Handbook for HIPAA Security Implementation, 2003, Complete Guide to HIPAA Security Risk Analysis: A Step-by-Step Approach, 2004, Electronic Health Records: Transforming Your Medical Practice, 2005; contbr. chapters to books. NDEA fellow U. Rochester, 1968-71; recipient Book of Yr. award Healthcare Info. and Mgmt. Sys. Soc., 2006. Fellow Healthcare Info. and Mgmt. Sys. Soc.; mem. Med. Group Mgmt. Assn., Optimists (program chmn. Denver club 1976-78). Achievements include patents for med. quality assurance. Office: MSA Corp 4401 S Quebec St Ste 100 Denver CO 80237-2644 Home: 4533 Via Rio Newbury Park CA 91320-6850 Home Phone: 303-757-7562; Office Phone: 303-488-9911.

LAZEAR, EDWARD PAUL, economics professor; b. NYC, Aug. 17, 1948; s. Abe and Rose (Karp) L.; m. Victoria Ann Allen, July 2, 1977; 1 child, Julia Ann AB, A.M., UCLA, 1971; PhD, Harvard U., 1974; LLD (hon.), Albertson Coll., 1997. Asst. prof. economics U. Chgo., 1974-78, assoc. prof. indsl. relations, 1978-81, prof. indsl. relations, 1981-85, Isidore and Gladys Brown prof. urban & labor economics, 1985-92; Morris Arnold Cox sr. fellow Hoover Institution, 1985—; sr. fellow Hoover Instn. Stanford U., Calif., 1985—2002, coord. domestic studies Hoover Instn., 1987-90, prof. economics & human resource mgmt. Grad. Sch. Bus., 1992-95, Jack Steele Parker prof. economics & human resource mgmt., 1995—, mem. steering com. Stanford Inst. for Econ. Policy Rsch., 1996—; chmn., Coun. Econ. Advisers Exec. Office of the Pres., Washington, 2006—09. Econ. advisor to Romania, Czechoslovakia, Russia, Ukraine, Georgia; rsch. assoc. Nat. Bur. Econ. Rsch., Econs. Rsch. Ctr. of Nat. Opinion Rsch. Ctr.; chmn. rsch. adv. bd. World at Work; fellow Inst. Advanced Study, Hebrew U., Jerusalem, 1977-8; lectr. Inst. Advanced Study, Vienna, 1983-84, Nat. Productivity Bd., Singapore, 1982, 85, Adam Smith lectr., Seville, Spain, 2003; vis. prof. Inst. des Etudes Politiques, Paris, 1987; Wicksell lectr., Stockholm, 1993; chmn. Am. Compensation Assoc. Adv. Bd., 1999—; mem. Pres.'s Panel on Tax Reform, 2005. Author: (with R. Michael) Allocation of Income Within the Household, 1988; (with J.P. Gould) Microeconomic Theory, 1989, Personnel Economics, 1995, Personnel Economics for Managers, 1998, Education in the Twenty-First Century, 2002; editor: Economic Transition in Eastern Europe and Russia, 1995; founding editor Jour. Labor Econs., 1982-2001; assoc. editor Jour. Econ. Perspectives, 1986-89, German Econ. Rev., 2000—; co-editor: Jour. Labor Abstracts, 1996—; contbr. articles to profl. jours. Recipient Disting. Teaching award, Stanford U. Grad. Sch. Bus., 1994, Leo Melamed prize for Outstanding Scholarship, 1998, PhD Faculty Disting. Svc. award, 2000, Adam Smith prize, European Assn. Labor Economists, 2003, Prize in Labor Economics (IZA prize), Inst. for the Study of Labor, 2004, Jacob Mincer prize, Soc. Labor Economics, 2006; NSF grad. fellow, 1971-74 Fellow Am. Acad. Arts and Scis., Econometric Soc., Soc. Labor Economists (1st v.p. 1995-96, pres. 1997-98), Ctr. Corp. Performance Denmark; mem. Am. Econs. Assn., Inst. Study Labor (prize for outstanding contbns. in labor econs. 2004), Nat. Acad. Scis. (bd. testing and assessment), Bd. Tng. Assessment. Office: Stanford U Graduate School of Business 518 Meml Way Stanford CA 94305-5015 also: Hoover Institution 434 Galvez Mall Stanford CA 94305 Office Phone: 650-723-9136, 650-723-4724. Office Fax: 650-723-0498. E-mail: lazear@stanford.edu.*

LAZOR, PATRICIA ANN, interior designer; d. Charles A. and Grace E. (Siegrist) LaGattuta; m. E. Alexander Lazor; children: Pamela A., Carolyn L., Charles L., Peter A BA, Chestnut Hill Coll., 1957; MEd, Rutgers U., 1962; cert., N.Y. Sch. Interior Design, 1972. Tchr. Bridgewater Raritan Schs., NJ, 1958—60; designer Patricia A. Lazor Interior Design, Bernardsville, NJ, 1975—85; pres. Alexander Abry, Inc., Washington, 1985—87; owner, designer Patricia A. Lazor Interior Design Antiques, Inc., Bernardsville, 1985—. Designer numerous residential interior design projects throughout the U.S.; featured in 100 Designers Favorite Rooms Rep. com. woman, Somerset County, N.J., 1978; chmn. Family Counseling Svc. Somerset County, 1972-78 Mem. Garden Club Morristown, Kappa Delta Phi Office: 11304 Desert Vista Rd Scottsdale AZ 85255

LAZOWSKA, EDWARD DELANO, computer science educator; b. Washington, Aug. 3, 1950; AB, Brown U., 1972; MSc, U. Toronto, Can., 1974, PhD, 1977. Asst. prof. U. Wash., Seattle, 1977-82, assoc. prof., 1982-86, prof. dept. computer sci. & engring., 1986—, chair dept. computer sci. and engring., 1993—2001, Bill and Melinda Gates chair, 2000—. Vis. scholar computer sci. Stanford U., 1984—85; vis. scientist Digital Equipment Corp., 1984—85; vis. scholar computer sci. U. Calif., San Diego, 2001—02; tech. adv. bd. mem. Microsoft Rsch., Voyager Capital, Ignition, Madrona Venture Group, Impinj; bd. dirs. Washington Tech. Industry Assoc., Tech. Alliance of Washington; co-chair Pres.'s Info. Tech. Adv. Com., 2003—05. Chair Computing Cmty. Consortium. Fellow: AAAS, IEEE, Am. Acad. Arts and Sci., Assn. Computing Machinery (chmn. spl. interest group on measurement and evaluation 1985—89); mem.: Nat. Acad. Engring. Office: U Wash Dept Computer Sci & Engring PO Box 352350 Seattle WA 98195-2350 Home Phone: 206-789-0477. Business E-Mail: lazowska@cs.washington.edu.

LEACH, ANTHONY RAYMOND, financial executive; b. Gerrards Cross, Eng., Nov. 11, 1939; came to U.S., 1969; s. John Raymond Geoffrey and Edith Eileen (Blackburn) L.; m. Shirley Ann Kidd, Apr. 17, 1965; children: Mark Irwin, Amanda Jane, Christopher John. Supr. Ernst & Whinney, London, 1957-63, San Francisco, 1967—, mgr. Paris, 1963-69; mgr. fin. acctg. Occidental Petroleum Corp., LA, 1965-74, asst. controller, 1974-81, v.p. acctg., 1981-91, v.p., contr., exec. v.p., CFO, 1991, now v.p. fin. Fellow Inst. Chartered Accts.; mem. Fin. Execs. Inst. Clubs: Palos Verdes Breakfast. Office: Occidental Petroleum Corp 10889 Wilshire Blvd Los Angeles CA 90024-4201

LEACH, JOHN F., editor, director, journalist, educator; b. Montrose, Colo., Aug. 6, 1952; s. Darrell Willis and Marian (Hester) L.; m. Deborah C. Ross, Jan. 2, 1982; children: Allison, Jason. BS in Journalism, U. Colo., 1974, MA in Journalism, 1979; MA in Am. Studies, U. Sussex, Brighton, Eng., 1983. News reporter Boulder (Colo.) Daily Camera, 1974-79, The Ariz. Republic, Phoenix, 1979-85, asst. city editor, 1985-93; news editor The Phoenix Gazette, 1993-94; asst. mng. editor Phoenix Gazette, 1994-95, The Ariz. Republic and The Phoenix Gazette, 1995-97; sr. editor The Ariz. Republic, Phoenix, 1997-99, sr. editor for online news, 1999—2002, sr. editor digital media, 2002—06, sr. mgr. online news, 2006—07; sr. editor for online news azcentral.com, 1999—2002, sr. editor digital media, 2002—06, editor, 2006—07; mng. editor news and digital media The Arizona Republic and azcentral.com, 2007—08; mng. editor print & online operations Ariz. Republic, 2008—, Ariz. Ctrl. LLC, 2008—. Faculty assoc. Ariz. State U., Tempe, 1990—; pres., dir. Best of the West, Phoenix, 1987—; adv. bd. sch. journalism and mass comm. U. Colo., Boulder. Bd. Regents scholar U. Colo., 1970-74, Rotary Found. scholar, 1982-83. Mem. Ariz. Press Club (treas. 1984-86, pres. 1986-87), Soc. Profl. Journalists, Online News Assn., Newspaper Assn. Am. New Media Fedn. Office: The Ariz Republic 200 E Van Buren St Phoenix AZ 85004-2238 Home Phone: 602-840-7402. Personal E-mail: jfleach@hotmail.com. Business E-Mail: jleach@azcentral.com.

LEAHY, T. LIAM, business development and technology investor; s. Thomas James and Margaret May L.; m. Shannon Kelly Brooks, Apr. 21, 1990. BS, St. Louis U., 1974, MA, 1975. V.p. sales Cablecom Inc., Chgo., 1976-80, Kaye Advt., NYC, 1980-82; group pub. Jour. Graphics Pub., NYC, 1983-85; pres., gen. mgr. Generation Dynamics, NYC, 1985-86; pres., dir. Leahy & Assocs., NYC, 1982—99, LA, 1982—2001; v.p., gen. mgr., dir. RBAC, Inc., 1999—; pres. Global Area Network, 2001—. Chmn. Global Area Network; bd. dirs. RBAC, Inc. Contbr. articles to profl. jours. Mem. Turnaround Mgmt. Assn., L.A. C. of C. Avocations: jazz, woodwinds, films, music. Business E-Mail: lleahy@globalareanet.com.

LEAKE, PATRICIA ANN, medical educator, researcher; d. Donald Eugene and Ethel Irene Leake; m. Joseph Ross Trimble, 1991. BS, Baldwin-Wallace Coll., Berea, Ohio, 1970; MS in Anatomy, U. Calif., San Francisco; PhD in Anatomy, U. Calif. Postdoctoral fellow U. Calif. San Francisco, 1977—80, asst. prof., 1980—85, assoc. prof., 1985—91, Epstein lab. rsch. dir., dept. otolaryngology, 1985—, prof. in residence, dept. otolaryngology, 1991—, prof. otolaryngology, 2002—. Contbr. articles to profl. jours. Grantee Rsch. grants, NIH, Nat. Inst. Deafness and Other Comm. Disorders, 1980—. Mem.: Soc. Neurosci., Assn. Rsch. Otolaryngology (chair long range planning com. 1999—2002). Office: Univ Calif Epstein Lab U490 533 Parnassus Ave San Francisco CA 94143-0526

LEANSE, THOMAS J., lawyer; b. LA, Feb. 21, 1954; BA, U. Calif., San Diego, 1975; JD, U. San Diego, 1978. Bar: Calif. 1978, Ill. 1979, US Supreme Ct. 1982. Asst. state atty. Cook County, Ill., 1979—81; gen. counsel US Ski Assn. and US Ski Team, 1985—94; ptnr. Katten Muchin Rosenman LLP, LA. Mem.: ABA, LA County Bar Assn., Internat. Coun. of Shopping Ctrs., Calif. Bus. Properties Assn., Anti-Defamation League, Cedars-Sinai Med. Ctr. Office: Katten Muchin Rosenman LLP Ste 2600 2029 Century Park E Los Angeles CA 90067 Office Phone: 310-788-4475. Office Fax: 310-712-8426. Business E-Mail: thomas.leanse@kattenlaw.com.

LEAPHART, W. WILLIAM, state supreme court justice; b. Butte, Mont., Dec. 3, 1946; s. Charles William and Cornelia (Murphy) L.; m. Barbara Berg, Dec. 30, 1977; children: Rebecca, Retta, Ada. Student, Whitman Coll., 1965—66; BA, U. Mont., 1969, JD, 1972. Bar: Mont. 1972, U.S. Dist. Ct., U.S. Ct. Appeals (9th cir.) 1975, U.S. Supreme Ct. 1975. Law clk. to Hon. W.D. Murray U.S. Dist. Ct., Butte, 1972—74; ptnr. Leaphart Law Firm, Helena, Mont., 1974—94; justice Mont. Supreme Ct., Helena, 1995—. Former assoc. ed. Mont. Law Review. Mem.: Am. Law Inst., Am. Acad. of Appellate Lawyers. Office: Mont Supreme Ct Justice Bldg 215 N Sanders St Rm 315 Helena MT 59601-4522 also: PO Box 203001 Helena MT 59620-3001

LEAR, NORMAN MILTON, producer, writer, director; b. New Haven, July 27, 1922; s. Herman and Jeanette (Seicol) Lear; m. Lyn Davis; children: Benjamin Davis, Brianna, Madeline; children: Ellen, Kate B. Lear LaPook, Maggie B. Student, Emerson Coll., 1940-42, HHD, 1968. Engaged in pub. relations, 1945-49; founder Act III Comms., 1987—. Comedy writer for TV, 1950—54; dir.(writer): (films, and TV), 1954—59; prodr.: (films) Never Too Late, 1965, Start the Revolution Without Me, 1970; (TV series) Sanford and Son, Maude, 1972, Good Times, 1974, Hot L Baltimore, 1975, All That Glitters, A Year at the Top, 1977, The Baxters, 1979, Sunday Dinner, 1991; exec. prodr.: (films) Fried Green Tomatoes, 1991, Way Past Cool, 2000, Stand By Me, 1986, Princess Bride, 1987; (TV series) The Andy Williams Show, 1962, One Day at a Time, 1975, The Nancy Walker Show, 1976, Heartsounds, 1984, a.k.a. Pablo, 1984, 704 Hauser, 1994, Channel Umptee-3, 1997; prodr.(dir., creator): All in the Family, 1971 (4 Emmy awards 1970-73, Peabody award, 1977), The Powers That Be, 1992, (screenwriter): (films) Come Blow Your Horn, 1963, Divorce American Style, 1967, The Night They Raided Minsky's, 1968, (dir., screenwriter): Cold Turkey, 1971; screenwriter Scared Stiff, 1953, creator The Jeffersons, 1975, Fernwood 2-Night, 1977. Pres. Am. Civil Liberties Found. So., Calif., 1973—; trustee Mus. Broadcasting; founder Bus. Enterprise Trust; bd. dirs People for the American Way. With USAF, 1942—45. Decorated Air medal with 4 oak leaf clusters; recipient Humanitarian award, NCCJ, 1976, Mark Twain award, Internat. Platform Assn., 1977, William O. Douglas award Pub. Counsel, 1981, 1st Amendment Lectr. Ford Hall Forum, 1981, Gold medal Internat. Radio and TV Soc., 1981, Disting. Am. award, 1984, Mass Media award, Am. Jewish Com. Inst. of Human Relations, 1986, Internat. award of Yr., Nat. Assn. TV Program Execs., 1987, Nat. Arts Medal, 1992, Achievement award in TV, Producers Guild Am., 2006; named One of Top Ten Motion Picture Producers, Motion Picture Exhibitors, 1963, 1967, 1968, Showman of Yr., Publicists Guild, 1971—77, Assn. Bus. Mgrs., 1972, Broadcaster of Yr., Internat. Radio and TV Soc., 1973, Man of Yr. Hollywood chpt., Nat. Acad. Television Arts and Scis., 1973; named to TV Acad. Hall of Fame, 1984. Mem.: AFTRA, Writers, and Dirs., Caucus Producers, Dirs. Guild Am., Writers Guild Am. (Valentine Davies award 1977). Office: Act III Comm 100 N Crescent Dr, Ste 250 Beverly Hills CA 90210

LEAR, WILLIAM H., lawyer; b. 1939; BA magna cum laude, Yale U., 1961; JD, Duke U., 1965. Bar: Calif. 1966. Sr. v.p., gen. counsel, sec. Fleetwood Enterprises, Inc., Riverside, Calif. Office: Fleetwood Enterprises Inc 3125 Myers St PO Box 7638 Riverside CA 92513-7638

LEARY, G. EDWARD, state agency administrator; m. Betty Chamberlain; 5 children. BS in Polit. Sci., U. Utah, 1971, MBA, 1981. Cert. Internat. Rels. With collections and lending dept. Draper Bank and Trust, 1974—77; examiner Utah Dept. Fin. Instns., Salt Lake City, 1977—82, industry supr., 1982—87, chief examiner, 1987—92, commr., 1992—. Chmn. Bd. Fin. Instns.; mem. Utah Housing Fin. Agy. Bd., Utah Appraiser Registration and Cert. Bd. Served in USN, 1971—73, ret. capt. USNR, 1995. Mem. Conf. State Bank Suprs. (frmr. chmn.). Office: Utah Dept Fin Instns Box 146800 Salt Lake City UT 84114-6800 Office Phone: 801-538-8830. Office Fax: 801-538-8894. E-mail: eleary@utah.gov.

LEASE, RONALD CHARLES, financial economics educator; b. Davenport, Iowa, Feb. 3, 1940; s. Mace Duane and Mary Virginia (Marsh) L.; m. Judy Ellen Gifford, Aug. 24, 1962; 1 child, Tracy Rene. BS in Engring., Colo. Sch. Mines, 1963; MS, Purdue U., 1966, PhD, 1973. Metall. engr. Aluminum Co. Am., 1963-69; prof. U. Utah, Salt Lake City, 1973-86; prof., chmn. Tulane U., New Orleans, 1986-90, endowed prof., assoc. dean, 1988-90; endowed prof. U. Utah, Salt Lake City, 1990—. Vis. assoc. prof. U. Chgo., 1978-79; vis. prof. U. Mich., Ann Arbor, 1985-86. Mem. editorial bd. Jour. Fin. Rsch., Phoenix, 1987-93, Fin. Mgmt., Tampa, 1986-98, Jour. Corp. Fin., Pitts., 1993—; contbr. articles to profl. jours. Mem. Am. Fin. Assn., Western Fin. Assn., Fin. Mgmt. Assn. (editor Survey and Synthesis in Fin. 1984-90, pres. 1992-93, chmn. bd. dirs. 1996-99), Phi Kappa Phi, Beta Gamma Sigma. Office: U Utah Eccles Sch Bus Salt Lake City UT 84112 Home: PO Box 778 Driggs ID 83422-0778

LEAVY, EDWARD, federal judge; b. Oreg., Aug. 14, 1929; m. Eileen Leavy; children: Thomas, Patrick, Mary Kay, Paul. AB, U. Portland, 1950; LLB, U. Notre Dame, 1953. Dist. judge Lane County, Eugene, Oreg., 1957—61, cir. judge, 1961—76; magistrate US Dist. Ct. Oreg., Portland, Oreg., 1976—84, judge, 1984—87, US Ct. Appeals (9th Cir.), Portland, Oreg., 1987—97, sr. judge, 1997—; judge Fgn. Intelligence Surveillance Ct. (FISA), 2001—08. Recipient Sid Lezak award, 2003. Office: US Ct Appeals Pioneer Courthouse 700 SW Sixth Ave Ste 226 Portland OR 97204-1323

LEBDA, DOUGLAS R., Internet company executive; BBA, Bucknell U., 1992; attended, U. Va., Darden Sch. Bus., 1998. Auditor, cons. PriceWaterhouse Coopers; founder LeadingTree, LLC (acquired by IAC.InterActiveCorp in 2003), 1998; CEO, LeadingTree, LLC, GetSmart.com, RealEstate.com, INest & Domania IAC Fin. Services and Real Estate, 1998; pres., COO IAC/InterActiveCorp, 2005—07; CEO IAC Search & Media, Oakland, Calif., 2006—07; chmn., CEO fin. services & real estate bus. IAC/Interactive Corp., 2008—. Bd. dir. Eastman Kodak Co., 2007—. Bd. dir. Bucknell U. Alumni Assn.; bd. trustee Darden Sch. Found., 2002—05; mem. Charlotte C. of C. Recipient Ernst & Young Entrepreneur of Yr. award, Coun. for Entrepreneurial Development's Trailblazer award, Inman Innovator of Yr. award; vis. scholar Shermet Scholar. Achievements include patents in field. Office: IAC Search & Media 555 12th St Ste 500 Oakland CA 94607

LEBEAU, MARY DELLE, dancer, educator, writer; b. El Paso, Tex., Oct. 24, 1951; d. George Louis LeBeau, Jr. and Rachel Elaine (McGibboney) LeBeau. BA in Russian and French cum laude, U. Tex., 1974; diploma in Eurythmy, Sch. Eurythmy, Spring Valley, NY, 1982—87; MA in Russian, SUNY, Albany, 2001; PhD in Russian, U. Southern Calif., LA, 2009. Cert. tchr., secondary Edn. in French, Russian, Eng. U. Tex., 1978. Tchr. of English Kashmere Sr. High, Houston, 1980—82; tchr. of eurythmy, Russian, French Hawthorne Valley Sch., Ghent, NY, 1987—93; founding tchr. Acad. of Art of Eurythmy, Moscow, 1993—97; grad. asst. in Russian SUNY, 1999—2001; tchg. asst. U. of So. Calif., 2003—. Guest artist in eurythmy at confs., NY, 1990—97; guest spkr. on Russia at confs., NY, 1993—97; performer Acad. of the Art of Eurythmy, Moscow, 1993—97. Dir., performer, creator of program (performance: eurythmy, poetry, jazz) And Still I Rise: African Am. poetry & music (N.Y. State Grant, 1993); translator: (transl. of poems) The Russian poet, Ol'ga Sedakova. Recipient Phi Beta Kappa, U. of Tex., 1974; grantee Decentralization Grant, N.Y. State, 1993, Spl. Opportunity Grant, 1992; Admunson fellow, U. So. Calif., 2001—03. Mem.: MLA, Am. Coun. of Teachers of Russian, Assn. for Women in Slavic Studies, Am. Assn. of Slavic and East European Languages, Eurythmy Assn. Am. Avocations: gardening, observing and reading about nature, weather; reading poetry, raising exotic finches, collecting Russian folk toys & crafts, birdwatching. Office: U of So Calif SLL 2nd Fl Taper Hall Los Angeles CA 90089 Business E-Mail: mlebeau@usc.edu.

LEBER, MIKE, advertising executive; CFO Alcone Mktg. Group, Irvine, Calif. Office: Alcone Mktg Co 4 Studebaker Irvine CA 92618-2012

LE BERTHON, ADAM, lawyer; b. LA, June 12, 1962; s. Edward Lynch and Veronica Rose (Franks) Le B; m. Kelly Elizabeth McKee, Mar. 23, 1996; children: John Thomas, Ryan Michael. BA cum laude with dept. honors, U. San Diego, 1985; JD, U. So. Calif., LA, 1989. Bar: Calif. 1989, U.S. Dist. Ct. (ctrl. dist.) Calif. 1989, U.S. Ct. Appeals (9th cir.) 1989, U.S. Dist. Ct. (so. dist.) Calif. 1990, (no. dist.) Calif. 1990, (ea. dist.) Calif. 1990. Assoc. White & Case, LA, 1989-91, Straw & Gilmartin, Santa Monica, Calif., 1991-97; ptnr. Gilmartin & Le Berthon LLP, Santa Monica, 1997-99; assoc. Arnold & Porter LLP, LA, 1999—2002, ptnr., 2003—. Editor So. Calif. Law Rev., 1987-89; contbr. articles to profl. jours. Recipient Am. Jurisprudence award U. So. Calif., 1987. Mem. Calif. State Bar Assn., L.A. County Bar Assn., Order of the Coif, Phi Alpha Delta, Omicron Delta Epsilon, Kappa Gamma Pi. Home: 27621 Harwick Pl Valencia CA 91354-1925 Office: Arnold & Porter LLP 44th Fl 777 S Figueroa St Los Angeles CA 90017-5800 Office Phone: 213-243-4110. E-mail: adam_le_berthon@aporter.com.

LEBLANC, TINA, dancer; b. Erie, Pa. m. Marco Jerkunica, May 1988; children: Marinko James, Sasha Johan. Trained, Carlisle, Pa. Dancer Joffrey II Dancers, NYC, 1982-83, The Joffrey Ballet, NYC, 1984-92; prin. dancer San Francisco Ballet, 1992—. Guest tchr. Ctrl. Pa. Youth Ballet, 1992, 94—. Work includes roles in (with San Francisco Ballet) Con Brio, Bizet Pas de Deux, Swan Lake, Nanna's Lied, Handel--A Celebration, La fille mal gardée, Rubies, Tchaikovsky Pas de Deux, Wanderer Fantasy, Seeing Stars, The Nutcracker, La Pavane Rouge, Company B, Romeo and Juliet, Sleeping Beauty, The Dance House, Terra Firma, Lambarena, Fly by Night, In the Night, Ballo della Regina, The Lesson, The Tuning Game, Quartette, Etudes, Western Symphony, Maelstrom, Pacific, Criss-Cross, Giselle, Theme and Variations, Gala Performance, The Vertiginous Thrill of Exactitude, Taiko, Sandpaper Ballet, La Bayadere, Night, Serenade, Celts, Stars & Stripes, Tarantella, Symphony in C, Dances at a Gathering, Don Quixote (full length), Square Dance, Apollo, Rush, Paquita, Who Cares, Study in Motion, 7 for Eight, Symphonic Variations, Two Bits, Valses Poeticos, Sea Pictures, Elite Syncopations, Smile with Your Heart, Falling, Harlequinade, Rodeo, Other Dances, Blue Rose, Quaternary, Chaconne, Artifact Suite, The Death of a Moth, Divertimento #15, On Common Ground; (with other companies) The Green Table, Les Presages, Le sacre du printemps, Les Noces, Light Rain, Romeo and Juliet, Runaway Train, Empyrean Dances, La Vivandière, L'air D'esprit, Corsaire Pas de deux, Don Quixote pas de deux, Lacrymosa, Confetti, Kettentanz Le Beau Danube, Offenbach in the Underworld, Suite Saint Saens, Forgotten Land, Dream Dances, Postcards, Coppelia, Remembrances, Reflections, Cotillon, Forcefield Petrouchka Cabochon. Recipient Princess Grace Found. award, 1988, Princess Grace Statuette award, 1995, Isadora Duncan award, 1998-99, 2000-01. Office: San Francisco Ballet Assn 455 Franklin St San Francisco CA 94102-4471 Home Phone: 650-375-8905; Office Phone: 415-861-5600.

LEBLOND, ANTOINE, computer software company executive; m. Lucie Leblond; 2 children. BS in Math., McGill U., Montreal. With Microsoft Corp., Redmond, Wash., 1989—, software design engr., 1989—98, dir., office develop., 1998—2002, disting. engr., 2000, corp. v.p., office program mgmt., 2002—06, corp. v.p., office productivity applications, 2006—. Office: Microsoft Corp One Microsoft Way Redmond WA 98052-7329

LECHLER, SHANE (EDWARD SHANE LECHLER), professional football player; b. Sealy, Tex., Aug. 7, 1976; m. Erin Lechler. BA in History, Tex. A&M U., College Station, 2000. Punter Oakland Raiders, 2000—. Named 1st Team All-Pro, AP, 2000, 2003, 2004, 2008; named to Am. Football Conf. Pro Bowl Team, NFL, 2001, 2004, 2007, 2008. Achievements include having one punt of 50 yards or more in 33 consecutive games, the longest such streak by any player since the AFL-NFL Merger in 1970, 2003-05; leading the National Football League in: punting yards, 2003, 2008; longest punt, 2003; yards per punt, 2003-05, 2007. Office: Oakland Raiders 1220 Harbor Bay Pky Alameda CA 94502*

LECLERC, ROBERT L., mining company executive; b. 1944; Chmn., CEO Milner Fenerty, Calgary and Edmonton, Can.; dir. Echo Bay Mines, Englewood, Colo., chmn., 1996—, CEO, chmn. bd., 1997—. Office: Echo Bay Mines 670 Sierra Rose Dr Reno NV 89511-2072

LEDEBOER, NANCY, library director; b. Mont. Student, Diablo Valley Coll., Pleasant Hill, Calif., 1974—77; BA in Hist., U. Calif., 1979; MLS, U. Calif., Berkeley, 1980. Libr. Contra Costa Times, 1980—81; children's/young adult libr. Contra Costa County Libr. Sys., Calif., 1983—84, children's libr. Calif., 1989—91, El Sobrante br. mgr. Calif., 1991—92; head libr. Heritage Coll. Libr., 1985—87; info. specialist St. Mary's Coll., 1987—89; youth svcs. coord. Spokane Pub. Libr., Wash., 1992—96, dep. dir. pub. svcs. Wash., 1996—98; assoc. dir. pub. svcs. King County Libr. Sys., Wash., 1998—99; dep. dir., COO Las Vegas-Clark County Libr. Dist., Nev., 1999—2005; dir. Pima County Pub. Libr., Tucson, 2005—. Bd. dirs. Wash. Libr. Assn., 1993—95. Bd. dirs. Literacy Vols. Tucson. Recipient Spl. Citation award, Nev. Libr. Assn., 2004; named Libr. of Yr., 2004. Mem.: ALA, Ariz. Libr. Assn., Pub. Libr. Assn. (mem. Gordon M. Conable Award jury), REFORMA (pres. Nev. chpt. 2001—02). Office: Pima County Pub Libr 101 N Stone Ave Tucson AZ 85701-1501 Office Phone: 520-791-4391. Office Fax: 520-791-3213. E-mail: Nancy.Ledeboer@pima.gov.

LEDER, MIMI, television and film director, producer; b. NYC, Jan. 26, 1952; d. Paul and Etyl Leder; m. Gary Werntz, Feb. 6, 1986; 1 child, Hannah. Student, Los Angeles City College, Am. Film Inst. Dir. (TV films) A Little Piece of Heaven (also known as Honor Bright), 1991, Woman with a Past, 1992, Rio Shannon, 1992, Marked for Murder, 1992, There Was a Little Boy, 1993, House of Secrets, 1993, The Sandman, 1993, The Innocent, 1994, John Doe, 2002; dir. (TV series) L.A. Law, 1986, Midnight Caller, 1988, A Year in the Life, 1988, Buck James, 1988, Just in Time, 1988, Crime Story, 1988, ER, 1994-95 (Emmy award 1995, 96), John Doe, 2002, China Beach (also prodr.), The Beast (also exec. prodr.), 2001, Jonny Zero (also prodr.), 2005, Vanished, (also exec. prodr.), 2006, (films) The Peacemaker, 1997, Deep Impact, 1998, Sentimental Journey, 1999, Pay it Forward, 2000; supervising prodr. China Beach, 1988-91 (Emmy nominations for outstanding drama series 1989, 90, and outstanding directing in drama series 1990, 91), Nightingales, 1989. Mem. Dirs. Guild Am. Office: c/o Creative Artists Agy 9830 Wilshire Blvd Beverly Hills CA 90212-1804 also: United Talent Agy 9560 Wilshire Blvd Beverly Hills CA 90212

LEDERER, MARION IRVINE, cultural administrator; b. Brampton, Ont., Can., Feb. 10, 1920; d. Oliver Bateman and Eva Jane (MacMurdo) L.; m. Francis Lederer, July 10, 1941. Student, U. Toronto, 1938, UCLA, 1942-45. Owner Canoga Mission Gallery, Canoga Park, Calif., 1967—, cultural heritage monument, 1974—. V.p. Screen Smart Set women's aux. Motion Picture and TV Fund, 1973, pres., 2002—03; founder sister city program Canoga Park-Taxco, Mex., 1963. Mem. Mayor's Cultural Task Force San Fernando Valley, 1973—, LA Cultural Affairs Commn., 1980—85; pres. Women's Aux. of Motion Pictures, TV Fund. Recipient Pub. Svc. award, mayor, city council, C. of C. Mem.: Canoga Park C. of C. (cultural chmn. 1973—75, dir. 1973—75). Presbyterian. Home: PO Box 32 Canoga Park CA 91305-0032 Office: Canoga Mission Gallery 23130 Sherman Way Canoga Park CA 91307-1402

LEDERER, RICHARD HENRY, writer, educator, columnist; b. Phila., May 26, 1938; s. Howard Jules and Leah (Perry) L.; m. Rhoda Anne Spangenberg, Aug. 25, 1962 (div. 1986); m. Simone Johanna van Egeren, Nov. 29, 1991; children: Howard Henry, Anne Labarr, Katherine Lee. BA, Haverford Coll., 1959; student, Harvard U., 1959—60, M of Arts and Tchg., 1962; PhD, U. N.H., 1980. Tchr., coach St. Paul's Sch., Concord, NH, 1962-89. Lectr. in field. Author: Anguished English, 1987, Get Thee to a Punnery, 1988, Crazy English, 1989, The Play of Words, 1990, The Miracle of Language, 1991, More Anguished English, 1993, Building Bridge, 1994, Adventures of a Verbivore, 1994, The Cunning Linguist, 1995, The Write Way, 1995, Pun and Games, 1996, Fractured English, 1996, The Word Circus, 1998, Sleeping Dogs Don't Lay, 1999, The Bride of Anguished English, 2000, The Circus of Words, 2001, Word Play Crosswords, 2000, A Man of My Words, 2003, The Cunning Linguist, 2003, The Revenge of Anguished English, 2005, Comma Sense, 2005, The Giant Book of Animal Jokes, 2005, Word Wizard, 2006, Puns Spoken Here, 2006, Have a Punny Christmas, 2006 Literary Trivia, 2007, Classic Literary Trivia, 2007, The Ants aRe My Friends, 2007, Presidential Trivia, 2007; weekly columnist Looking at Lang.; contbr. over 3000 articles to mags. and jours.; broadcaster various radio stas.; numerous TV appearances; host A Way With Words KPBS, San Diego. Recipient Chmns. award, Am. Mensa, Ltd., 2000, Toastmasters Internat. Golden Gavel, 2002, Lifetime Achievement award Columbia Scholastic Press Assn., N.Y.C., 1989, Leadership in Comms. award San Diego Toastmasters, Odin award San Diego Writers and Editors, 2004; named Internat. Punster of Yr. Internat. Save the Pun Found., Toronto, 1990, Celebrity in Action, San Diego Found. for Ednl. Achievement, 2002; Paul Harris Rotary fellow. Mem. Am. Mensa, Phi Beta Kappa, Phi Delta Kappa. Avocations: tennis, cards, films. Office: Ste 201 9974 Scripps Ranch Blvd San Diego CA 92131-1825 Home Phone: 858-549-6788; Office Phone: 858-549-6788. E-mail: richard.lederer@pobox.com.

LEDYARD, JOHN ODELL, economics professor, consultant; b. Detroit, Apr. 4, 1940; s. William Hendrie and Florence (Odell) L.; m. Bonnie Higginbottom, May 23, 1970 (div. July 2004); children: Stephen, J. Henry, Meg; m. Elaine Fleming, Dec. 12, 2006. BA, Wabash Coll., 1963; PhD, Purdue U., 1967; PhD (hon.), Purdue U./Ind. U., 1993. Asst. prof. Carnegie-Mellon U., Pitts., 1967-70; prof. Northwestern U., Evanston, Ill., 1970-85, Calif. Inst. Tech., Pasadena, 1985—, exec. officer for social sci., 1989-92, chmn. div. humanities and social scis., 1992—2002. Contbr. articles to profl. jours. Fellow Am. Acad. Arts and Scis., Econometric Soc., Pub. Choice Soc. (pres. 1980-82); mem. Econ. Sci. Assn. (exec. com. 1986-88). Office: Calif Inst Tech Dept HHS Pasadena CA 91125-0001

LEE, ANG, film director; b. Pingtung, Taiwan, Oct. 23, 1954; m. Jane Lin, 1983; children: Haan, Mason. Grad., Nat. Taiwan Coll. Arts, 1975; BFA in Theater, U. Ill., 1980; MFA in Film, NYU, 1984. Arts & culture cons. 2008 Summer Olympics, 2006—. Dir. (films) Fine Line, 1985, Sense and Sensibility, 1996 (N.Y. Film Critics Circle award, Boston Film Critics award, Nat. Bd. Rev. award, Golden Bear award, Berlin Film Festival award, nominee Brit. Acad. Film and TV Arts award, nominee Dirs. Guild award, nominee Golden Globe award, all as best dir.), Chosen, 2001, The Hulk, 2003, Brokeback Mountain, 2005 (Best Dir., NY Film Critics Circle, 2005, Boston Soc. Film Critics award, 2005, Nat. Bd. Review, 2005, Broadcast Film Critics Assn., 2006), Outstanding Directorial Achievement in Feature Film, Director's Guild Am. 2005, Best Picture, 2005, Best Dir., Hollywood Fgn. Press Assn. (Golden Globe award), 2006, David Lean award for Achievement in Direction, British Acad. Film and TV Arts, 2006, Best Director, Spirit Independent award, 2006, Achievement in Directing, Acad. Motion Picture Arts & Sciences, 2006); dir., prodr. (films) Pushing Hands, 1991 (several Golden Horse award nominations, Taiwan, Spl. Jury prize for Direction, Best Film honors Asian Pacific Film Festival 1992), The Wedding Banquet, 1993 (Asian Am. Media award 16th Asian Am. internat. Film Festival, Golden Bear award Berlin Film Festival, nominee Acad. award for Best Fgn. Lang. Film, nominee Golden Globe award for Best Fgn. Lang. Film, several Ind. Spirit award nominations, Golden Horse awards for Best Film and Best Dir.), The Ice Storm, 1997, Crouching Tiger, Hidden Dragon, 2000, Lust, Caution, 2007; screenwriter (with Hui Ling Wang and James Schamus), Eat Drink Man Woman, 1994 (Best Fgn. Lang. Film award Nat. Bd. Rev., nominee Acad. award for Best Fgn. Lang. Film, nominee Golden Globe award for Best Fgn. Lang. Film, honored for Best Film and as Best Dir. Asian Pacific Film Festival, various Ind. Spirit award nominations), Ride With the Devil, 1999; exec. prodr. (films) One Last Ride, 2003; The Wedding Banquet and Eat Drink Man Woman included in book: Two Films by Ang Lee, 1994. Named one of 100 Most Influential People, Time Mag., 2006, 50 Most Powerful People in Hollywood, Premiere mag., 2006. Office: c/o Anonymous Content 3532 Hayden Ave Culver City CA 90232

LEE, ANN L., biotechnology company executive; BSChemE, Cornell U.; MSChemE, Yale U., New Haven, D in Engring. and Applied Scis. Sr. leadership positions up to v.p. chem. tech. and engring. in mfg. divsn. Merck & Co.; v.p. process devel. Genentech Inc., South San Francisco, 2005—. Contbr. articles to profl. publs.; assoc. editor: Biotechnology and Applied Biochemistry. Sr. adv. com. Yale U. Faculty of Engring. Fellow: Am. Inst. Med. and Biol. Engring.; mem.: NAE. Achievements include patents in field. Office: Genentech Inc 1 DNA Way South San Francisco CA 94080-4990 Office Phone: 650-225-1000. Office Fax: 650-225-6000.

LEE, BARBARA JEAN, United States Representative from California; b. El Paso, Tex., July 16, 1946; m. Michael Millben (div.); children: Tony, Craig. BA, Mills Coll., Calif., 1973; MSW, U. Calif., Berkeley, 1975. No. Calif. Presdl. campaign coord., 1972; chief of staff to Rep. Ron Dellums US Congress, 1976—86; mem. Calif. State Assembly, 1990-96, Calif. State Senate, 1996-98, US Congress from 9th Calif. Dist., Washington, 1998—, US House Appropriations Com., US House Fgn. Affairs Com. Chair Calif. Rainbow Coalition; founder Calif. Commn. Status African Am. Males; bd. mem. Calif. Coastal Conservancy/Dist. Export Coun.; co-chair Congl. Progressive Caucus; mem. Calif. Commn. Status Women, Calif. Def. Conversion Coun., Congl. Black Caucus, chair, 2009—, co-chair Haiti Task Force, Outreach Task Force, mem. Minority Bus. Task Force, chair Task Force Global HIV/AIDS. Mem. adv. bd. Alameda Boys Club; bd. dirs. Bay Area Black United Fund. Named one of Most Influential Black Americans, Ebony mag., 2006; named to Power 150, 2008. Mem.: League of Women Voters, Black Women Organized Polit. Action, Ronald V. Dellums Dem. Club (founder), John George Dem. Club. Democrat. Baptist. Office: US Congress 1724 Longworth Ho Office Bldg Washington DC 20515-0509 also: Dist Office Ste 1000 N 1301 Clay Oakland CA 94612 Office Phone: 202-225-2661, 510-763-0370. Fax: 202-225-9817; Office Fax: 510-763-6538.

LEE, BRYAN, information technology executive; m. Lisa Lee; 4 children. BA in Acctg., U. Miss. With Arthur Andersen & Co., Houston, Sony Pictures Entertainment, Inc., 1987—2000, former exec. v.p. bus. affairs; gen. mgr. bus. devel. home and entertainment group Microsoft, Redmond, Wash., 2000—02, corp. v.p., CFO worldwide mktg. and pub. home and entertainment group, 2002—07, v.p., entertainment bus. group, 2005—07.

LEE, CHAN-YUN, physicist, process engineer, educator; b. Hwa-Liang, Taiwan, July 19, 1952; came to U.S., 1988; s. Hsiao-Feng and Shu-Yun (Huang) L.; m. Chia-Li Yang, Jan. 13, 1983; children: Yifan E., Ethel Y., Elias Y. BS in Physics, Soochow U., Taipei, Taiwan, 1974; MS, U. So. Calif., 1980; PhD, U. Notre Dame, 1988. Cert. assoc. prof., lectr. Dept. Edn. Asst. prof. physics Tatung Inst. Tech., Taipei, 1982-86, assoc. prof., 1986-88, chmn. physics sect., 1986-88; cons. Tatung Semiconductor Divsn., Taipei, 1985-88; dir. Tatung Natural Sci. Mus., Taipei, 1986-88; lab. instr. U. Notre Dame, Notre Dame, Ind., 1988-94; process engr. Lam Rsch. Co., Fremont, Calif., 1994-96, sr. process engr., 1996-99, mgr. metal etch key accounts, 1998-99; assoc. prof. physics San Jose City Coll., Calif., 1998-99; regional chief process technologist Silicon Valley Group, 1999-2000; West Coast process coord., tech. staff Tokyo Electron Am., Santa Clara, Calif., 2000—. Rsch. asst. U. So. Calif., L.A., 1977-79. Contbr. numerous articles to profl. jours. 2d lt. Chinese Artillery, 1974-76. Recipient Excellent Rschrs. prize Chinese Nat. Sci. Coun., Taipei, 1986-88, Outstanding Acad. Pub. prize Hsieh-Tze Indsl. Revival Com., Taipei, 1987, 88, Sci. & Tech. Pers. Rsch. & Study award Chinese Nat. Sci. Coun., 1989. Mem. Chinese Physics Assn. Achievements include development of model of relativistic corrections to semiconducting properties of selected materials, simulated and calculated the dynamical susceptibility of square lattice antiferromagnets; successfully developed the first large size SAC process in the world on high density plasma TCP etcher with satisfactory yields; designed and developed the single chamber dry clean process with a MW downstream and RF plate chamber for metal via applications; designed and constructed a spectrophotometer to measure the absolute photoabsorption cross section of atomic potassium in VUV region. Home: 471 Via Vera Cruz Fremont CA 94539-5325 Office: Tokyo Electron Am Inc 2953 Bunker Hill Ln Santa Clara CA 95054 Personal E-mail: cylee9334@yahoo.com.

LEE, CHRIS, state legislator; b. Kailua, Hawaii; s. Gary and Connie. Grad., Ore. State Coll. Mem. Dist. 51 Hawaii House of Reps., 2008—. Dir. Breakthroughs for Youth at Risk. Mem.: Ala Wai Watershed Assn. (dir.). Democrat. Office: State Capitol 415 S Beretania St Rm 313 Honolulu HI 96813 Office Phone: 808-586-9450. Office Fax: 808-586-9456. Business E-Mail: repclee@capitol.hawaii.gov.

LEE, DALE W., lawyer; b. Spokane, Wash., Sept. 16, 1948; AB in Am. Civilization, Brown U., 1970; JD, So. Meth. U., 1974. Bar: Hawaii 1974. Investigator, dep. prosecuting atty., felony prosecutor; ptnr. Kobayashi, Sugita & Goda, Honolulu. Arbitrator Ct. Annexed Arbitration Program, Hawaii; mem. hearing com., Office Disciplinary Counsel Supreme Ct. State Hawaii; pvt. arbitrator, mediator and discovery master; adj. prof. law William S. Richardson Sch. Law. Dir. Hawaii Justice Found., Vol. Legal Services of Hawaii; bd. adv. Korean Am. Found., Hawaii. Named one of Best Lawyers in Am. Mem.: ABA (bd. gov. 2006), Am. Judicature Soc., Korean Am. Bar Assn. Hawaii, Hawaii State Bar Assn. (treas. Young Lawyers sect. 1979—80, pres. 2004), Delta Theta Phi. Office: Kobayashi, Sugita & Goda 26th Floor 999 Bishop St Honolulu HI 96813 Office Phone: 808-539-8700. Office Fax: 808-539-8799. Business E-Mail: dwl@ksglaw.com.

LEE, DAVID MALLIN, physicist; b. Bklyn., Jan. 18, 1944; s. George Francis Lee and Winifred Rita (Jones) Wyatt; m. Judith Carol Silliman, Aug. 20, 1966; children: David, Timothy, Karen, Jeffrey, Rebecca. BS, Mannhattan Coll., 1966; PhD, U. Va., 1971. Vis. mem. staff Los Alamos (N.Mex) Nat. Lab., 1971-74, mem. staff, 1974-80, 81—; U.S. tech. expert IAEA, Vienna, Austria, 1980-81. Patentee in field. Mem. Am. Phys. Soc., AAAS, Sigma Xi. Democrat. Roman Catholic. Home: 48 Wildflower Way Santa Fe NM 87506-2116 E-mail: dLee@lanl.gov.

LEE, GLENN RICHARD, medical association administrator, educator; b. Ogden, Utah, May 18, 1932; s. Glenn Edwin and Thelma (Jensen) L.; m. Pamela Marjorie Ridd, July 18, 1969; children—Jennifer, Cynthia. BS, U. Utah, 1953, MD, 1956. Intern Boston City Hosp.-Harvard U., 1956-57, resident, 1957-58; clin. asso. Nat. Cancer Inst., NIH, 1958-60; postdoctoral fellow U. Utah, 1960-63; instr. U. Utah Coll. Medicine, 1963-64, asst. prof. internal medicine, 1964-68, assoc. prof., 1968-73, prof., 1973-96, assoc. dean for acad. affairs, 1973-76, dean, 1978-83, prof. emeritus, 1996—; chief of staff Salt Lake VA Med. Ctr., 1985-95. Author: (with others) Clinical Hematology, 10th edit, 1998; Contbr. (with others) numerous articles to profl. jours.; editorial bd.: (with others) Am. Jour. Hematology, 1976-79. Served with USPHS, 1958-60. Markle Found. scholar, 1965-70; Nat. Inst. Arthritis, Metabolic and Digestive Disease grantee, 1977-82. Mem. A.C.P., Am. Soc. Hematology, Am. Soc. Clin. Investigation, Western Assn. Physicians, Am. Inst. Nutrition. Mem. Lds Ch. Home and Office: 194 Harvest Run Idaho Falls ID 83404 Personal E-mail: grichardl@cableone.net.

LEE, HI YOUNG, physician, acupuncturist; b. Seoul, Republic of Korea, Oct. 18, 1941; arrived in U.S., 1965, naturalized, 1976; s. Jung S. and Hwa J. (Kim) Lee; m. Sun M. Lee, June 4, 1965; children: Sandra, Grace, David. MD, Yon Sei U., Seoul, 1965. Diplomate Am. Bd. Family Practice. Intern Grasslands Hosp., Valhalla, NY, 1965-66; resident VA Hosp., Dayton, Ohio, 1966-70; mem. staff Eastern State Hosp., Medical Lake, Wash., 1970-74; practice family medicine, acupuncturist Empire Med. Office, Spokane, Wash., 1974—. Active staff St. Lukes Meml. Hosp., Spokane, 1974—; courtesy staff Deaconess Med. Ctr., Spokane, 1974—, Sacred Heart Med. Ctr., Spokane, 1974—; sr. disability analyst, diplomate Am. Bd. Disability Analysts, 2000. Author: Von Recklinghousen's Disease, 1970; columnist: Rainier Forum Korea Post Weekly News, 1996—. Trustee St. Georges Prep Sch., Wash., 1986—; elder First Presbyn. Ch., Spokane, 1975. Fellow: Am. Acad. Family Practice; mem.: Christian Med. Soc., Ctr. Chinese Medicine, Nat. Acupuncture Rsch. Soc., Spokane County Med. Soc. Home: 2006 W Liberty Ave Spokane WA 99205-2570 Office: Empire Med Office 17 E Empire Ave Spokane WA 99207-1707 Personal E-mail: drhileemd@yahoo.com.

LEE, JASON, actor; b. Huntington Beach, Ca., Apr. 25, 1970; m. Carmen Llywelyn, July 1995 (div. July 2001); 1 child (with Ceren Alkec), Pilot Inspektor Riesgraf Lee Profl. skateboarder, 1989—96; owner Stereo Manufacturing Corp. (skateboarding), 2003—. Actor: (films) Video Days, 1991, My Crazy Life, 1993, Mallrats, 1995, Drawing Flies, 1996, Chasing Amy, 1997, A Better Place, 1997, Kissing a Fool, 1998, American Cuisine, 1998, Enemy of the State, 1998, Dogma, 1999, Mumford, 1999, Almost Famous, 2000, Heartbreakers, 2001, Jay and Silent Bob Strike Back, 2001, Vanilla Sky, 2001, Big Trouble, 2002, Stealing Harvard, 2002, A Guy Thing, 2003, Dreamcatcher, 2003, I Love Your Work, 2003, Jersey Girl, 2004, (voice only) The Incredibles, 2004, The Ballad of Jack and Rose, 2005, Drop Dead Sexy, 2005, (voice only) Jack-Jack Attack, 2005, Clerks II, 2006, Monster House, 2006, (voice only) Underdog, 2007, Alvin and the Chipmunks, 2007; (TV films) Weapons of Mass Distraction, 1997, Sonic Youth Video Dose, 2004; actor, prodr. (TV series) My Name is Earl, 2005—. Office: c/o United Talent Agency 9560 Wilshire Blvd Beverly Hills CA 90212

LEE, JERRY CARLTON, university administrator; b. Roanoke, Va., Nov. 21, 1941; m. Joan Marie Leo; 1 child, Zan. BA, W.Va. Wesleyan Coll., 1963; postgrad., W.Va. U. Grad. Sch. Indsl. Relations, 1963-64, U. Balt. Sch. Law, 1967-69; MA, Va. Poly. Inst., 1975, EdD, 1977; LLD (hon.), Gallaudet U., 1986. Mgmt. trainee Gen. Motors Corp., 1964-65; v.p. adminstrn. Comml. Credit Indsl. Corp., Washington, 1965-71; dir. gen. services Gallaudet Coll., Washington, 1971-77, asst. v.p. bus. affairs, 1978-82, v.p. adminstrn. and bus., 1982-84; pres. Gallaudet U. (formerly Gallaudet Coll.), Washington, 1984-88, Nat. U., San Diego, 1989—. Hon. bd. dirs. D.C. Spl. Olympics; commn. in adminstrn. org. Rehab. Internat.; bd. dirs. People to People, Deafness Research Found., Am. Assn. Univ. Adminstrs., Am. Coun. on Edn. Commn. on Women in Higher Edn.; hon. advocacy bd. Nat. Capital Assn. Coop. Edn.; mem. Personnel Policies Forum Bur. Nat. Affairs. Served with USAR, 1966-72. Recipient Nat. Service award, Hon. Pres. award Council for Better Hearing and Speech, 1986, One-of-a-Kind award People-to-People, 1987, Advancement Human Rights & Fundamental Freedoms award UN, U.S.A., Disting. Alumni award Va. Poly. Inst., 1985, Pres.' award Gallaudet Coll. Alumni Assn., Gallaudet Community Relations award, U.S. Steel Found. Cost Reduction Incentive award Nat. Assn. Coll. and Univ. Bus. Officers, award Am. Athletic Assn. Deaf, 1987 Mem. Am. Assn. Univ. Adminstrs. (Eileen Tosney award 1987), Consortium of Univs. Washington Met. Area (exec. com.), Nat. Collegiate Athletic Assn. (pres.' commn.), Nat. Assn. Coll. Aux. Services (jour. adv. bd., journalism award), Alpha Sigma Pi (Man of Yr. award 1983-84). Lodges: Sertoma (life, found. nat. adv. com.). Avocations: tennis, running, weightlifting. Office: Nat Univ 11255 N Torrey Pines Rd La Jolla CA 92037-1011

LEE, JHEMON HOM, physician; b. Redwood City, Calif., July 1, 1970; s. Billy Tom and Yuen Han Lee. BA in Engring. summa cum laude, Harvard U., 1990; MD cum laude, U. Md., 1994. Diplomate Nat. Bd. Med. Examiners. Resident in diagnostic radiology U. Chgo., 1994—98, chief resident, 1997—98; fellow in abdominal imaging Brigham and Women's Hosp./Harvard Med. Sch., Boston, 1998—99; radiologist, ptnr. MemRAD Med. Group, Long Beach, Calif., 1999—2006; vice chair dept. diagnostic imaging Los Alamitos Radiology Group, 2002—08, ptnr., 2006—. Bd. dir. Radiologic Practice Mgmt., Inc., 2004—05. Editor-in-chief UMAB news, 1993; news editor East Wind, 1987-90; contbr. articles to profl. jours. Mem. steering com. United Asian Am. Orgns., Chgo., 1996-98; mem. Leadership Ctr. for Asian Ams., Chgo., 1997-98. Recipient Chgo. Chpt. Recognition award, Nat. Assn. of Asian Am. Profl., 1998, Lifetime Achievement award, 2002; named one of Am. Top Radiologists, Consumers' Rsch. Coun. of Am., 2002—03, Am. Top Physicians, 2004—05. Mem. Radiol. Soc. N.Am., Nat. Coun. Asian Pacific Islander Physicians (steering com. mem.), Assn. Asian Am. Studies, Harvard Club Southern Calif., Nat. Assn. Asian Am. Profls. (nat. pres., 1998-2000, exec. v.p. 2002-04), Chgo. Radiol. Soc., Asian Pacific Am. Med. Students Assn. (pres. adv. bd.), Asian Profl. Exch. (chair Healthcare Spl. Interest Group, dir. profl. devel. 2000-01), Orgn. Chinese Ams. (pres. Orange County chpt. 2003-06), Cold Tofu Improv, East West Players Actors Conservatory, Phi Beta Kappa, Alpha Omega Alpha. Avocations: computers, Asian American culture, writing, films. Home: 13710 Alderton Ln Cerritos CA 90703 Office Phone: 562-799-3294. Business E-Mail: jhemon@post.harvard.edu.

LEE, JIMMY S.M., electronic executive; Chmn., pres., CEO Integrated Silicon Solutions, Inc., Santa Clara, Calif. Office: Integrated Silicon Solutions Inc 2231 Lawson Ln Santa Clara CA 95054-3311

LEE, JOHN JIN, lawyer; b. Chgo., Oct. 20, 1948; s. Jim Soon and Fay Yown (Young) L.; m. Jamie Pearl Eng, Apr. 30, 1983. BA magna cum laude, Rice U., 1971; JD, MBA, Stanford U., 1975. Bar: Calif. 1976. Assoc. atty. Manatt Phelps & Rothenberg, LA, 1976-77; asst. counsel Wells Fargo Bank N.A., San Francisco, 1977-79, counsel, 1979-80, v.p., sr. counsel, 1980, v.p., mng. sr. counsel, 1981-98, v.p., asst. gen. counsel, 1998—2001; gen. counsel, sec. Westlake Realty Group, San Mateo, Calif., 2002—. Mem. governing com. Conf. on Consumer Fin. Law, 1989-93. Bd. dirs. Asian Bus. League San Francisco, 1980—, gen. counsel, 1980—81, chmn., 2004—. Fellow Am. Coll. Consumer Fin. Svcs. Lawyers, Inc. (bd. regents 1995-96); mem. ABA (chmn. subcom. housing fin., com. consumer fin. svcs., bus. law sect. 1983-90, vice chmn. subcom. securities products, consumer fin. svcs., bus. law sect. 1995-96, chmn. subcom. elec. banking, com. consumer fin. svcs., bus. law sect. 1996-2000, co-chmn. joint subcom. elec. fin. svcs., bus. law sect. 1997-2000, co-chmn. directory com. minority in-house counsel group 1995-98), Consumer Bankers Assn. (lawyers com.), Soc. Physics Students, Stanford Asian-Pacific Am. Alumni/ae Club (bd. dirs. 1989-93, v.p. 1989-91). Democrat. Baptist. Office: PO Box 1304 San Carlos CA 94070-7304 Home Phone: 650-368-1106; Office Phone: 650-579-1010 157. Business E-Mail: johnjinlee@stanfordalumni.org.

LEE, JOHN MARSHALL, mathematics professor; b. Phila., Sept. 2, 1950; s. Warren W. and Virginia (Hull) L.; m. Pm Weizenbaum, May 26, 1984; children: Nathan Lee Weizenbaum, Jeremy Lee Weizenbaum. AB, Princeton U., 1972; student, Tufts U., 1977-78; PhD, MIT, 1982. Systems programmer Tex. Instruments, Princeton, NJ, 1972-74; Geophys. Fluid Dynamics Lab., GFDL/NOAA, Princeton, 1974-75; tchr. math. and physics Wooster Sch., Danbury, Conn., 1975-77; programmer and cons. info. processing svcs. MIT, Cambridge, Mass., 1978-82; asst. prof. math. Harvard U., Cambridge, 1982-87, U. Wash., Seattle, 1987-89, assoc. prof. math., 1989-96, prof. math., 1996—. Sr. tutor Harvard U., Cambridge, 1984-87. Author: Riemannian Manifolds: An Introduction to Curvature, 1997, Introduction to Topological Manifolds, 2000, Introduction to Smooth Manifolds, 2002; contbr. articles to profl. jours. Rsch. fellow NSF, 1982. Mem. Am. Math. Soc. (Centennial fellow 1989). Avocations: hiking, wine tasting, music. Office: Univ Wash Math Dept PO Box 354350 Seattle WA 98195-4350 Home Phone: 206-524-6346; Office Phone: 206-543-1735. E-mail: lee@math.washington.edu.

LEE, KWAN MIN, communications educator, consultant; s. Youngduck and Sohyun Lee; m. Jihye Mo, Dec. 25, 1998. BA, Sogang U., Republic of Korea, 1994; MA, Mich. State U., East Lansing, 1998; PhD, Stanford U., Calif., 2002. Rschr. IBM T. J. Watson Rsch. Ctr., Hawthorn, NY, 2000; rsch. behavior analyst Quack.com (now merged to AOL), San Jose, Calif., 2001—01; cons. Samsung, Seoul, 2002—04; prof. U. So. Calif., LA, 2002—. Mem. adv. bd. World Cyber Edugames, Seoul, 2005, Beijing, 05. Contbr. articles to profl. jours. Grantee, Annenberg Found., 2003, Ministry Edn., 2004; fellow, Stanford U., 1999; Lily M. and Henry J. Budde fellow, 2001. Mem.: ACM, Korean Am. Comm. Assn. (v.p. 2005—), Nat. Comm. Assn. (assoc.), Internat. Comm. Assn. (assoc.). Achievements include research in human-computer interaction; media psychology. Office: U So Calif Annenberg Sch Comm Los Angeles CA 90089 Business E-Mail: kwanmin.lee@usc.edu.

LEE, LORRIN L., internet marketing entrepreneur, architect, writer; b. Honolulu, July 22, 1941; s. Bernard Chong and Betty (Lum) L.; m. Nina Fedoroscko, June 10, 1981. BArch, U. Mich., 1970; MBA, Columbia Pacific U., 1981, PhD in Psychology, 1981. Registered Hawaii. Arch. Skidmore, Owings & Merrill Archs., Hawaii, 1967, Clifford Young AIA, Honolulu, 1971-72, Aotani & Oka AIA, Honolulu, 1972—73, Naramore, Bain, Brady & Johansen, Hawaii, 1974, Geoffrey Fairfax FAIA, Honolulu, 1974-76; seminar leader Lorrin Lee Program, Honolulu, 1976-81; star grand master coord. Enhance Corp., 1981-83; 5-diamond supr. Herbalife Internat., LA, 1983—, mem. Global Expansion Team, 1993—; presdl. dir. Uni-Vite Internat., San Diego, 1989-92; agt. Internat. Pen Friends, 1995—; mgr. Cyber Media Sales, 1996-2000; dealer Cajun Country Candies, 2000—05; pearl distributor Tahitian Noni Internat., 2002—; agt. FriendFinder, 2001—; assoc. My World Plus, 2007—. Author: Here is Genius, 1980, How to be Rich and Happy, How to Have an Ideal Relationship, Live a Memorable Life. Editor Honolulu Chinese Jaycees, Honolulu, 1972, v.p., 1983; active Makiki Cmty. Ctr., Honolulu, 1974. 1st lt. U.S. Army, 1967-70, Okinawa, 2nd Logistical Command. Recipient Braun-Knect-Heimann award, 1959, 1st Prize in Design Kidjel Cali-Pro Internat., 1975, Kitchen Design award Sub-Zero Contest, 1994; named Honolulu Chinese Jaycee of Yr., Honolulu Chinese Jaycees, 1973. Mem. Nature Conservancy, Sierra Club. Avocations: international travel, hiking, desktop publishing, photography, reading. Office: 500 University Ave #2415 Honolulu HI 96826 Office Phone: 808-949-5000. Personal E-mail: lorrin@lorrinlee.com.

LEE, PALI JAE, retired librarian, writer; b. Nov. 26, 1925; d. Jonathan Everett Wheeler and Ona Katherine (Grunder) Stead; m. Richard H.W. Lee, Apr. 7, 1945 (div. 1978); children: Catherine Lani Honcoop, Karin Elizabeth Robinson, Ona G., Laurie Brett, Robin Louise Halbert; m. John K. Willis, 1979 (dec. 1994). Student, U. Hawaii, 1944-46, Mich. State U., East Lansing, 1961-64. Cataloguer and processor US Army Air Force, 1945-46; with US Weather Bur. Film Library, New Orleans, 1948-50, FBI, Wright-Patterson AFB, Dayton, Ohio, 1952, Ohio Wholesale Winedealers, Columbus, Ohio, 1956-58, Coll. Engring., Ohio State U., Columbus, 1959; writer tech. manual Annie Whittenmeyer Home, Davenport, Iowa, 1960; with Grand Rapids Pub. Libr., Mich., 1961-62; dir. Waterford Twp. Librs., Mich., 1962-64; acquisition librarian Pontiac Pub. Librs., Mich., 1965-71, dir. East Side br. Mich., 1971-73; rsch. asst. dept. anthropology Bishop Mus., Honolulu, 1975-83; pub. Night Rainbow Pub., Honolulu, 1984—. Author: HIstory of Wine Growing in America, 1952, House Parenting at its Best, 1960, Mary Dyer, Child of Light, 1973, Giant: Pictorial History of the Human Colossus, 1973, History of Change: Kaneohe Bay Area, 1976, English edit., 1983, Tales of the Night Rainbow, 1981, rev. edit., 1988, Mo'olelo O Na Pohukaina, 1983, Ka Ipu Kukui, 1994, Ho'opono, 1999, rev. edit., 2007, Remembrance: The History of a Family, 2003; contbr. articles to profl. jours. Chmn. Oakland County br. Multiple Sclerosis Soc., 1972-73, co-chmn. Pontiac com. of Mich. area bd., 1972-73; sec. Ohana o Kokua, 1979-83, Paia-Willis Ohana, 1982-91, Ohana Kame'ekua, 1988-91; bd. dirs. Detroit Multiple Sclerosis Soc., 1971; mem. Mich. area bd. Am. Friends Svc. com., 1961-69; mem. consumer adv. bd. Libr. for Blind and Physically Handicapped, Honolulu, 1997—, bd. dirs. 1999—; pres. Blind 55 plus Hawaii Ctr. for Ind. Living, 1990-94, pres., 1995-96; pres. Honolulu chpt. Nat. Fedn. of Blind, 1991-93, 1st v.p. #93 state affiliate, 1991-93, editor Na Na Maka Aloha newsletter, 1990-94 Recipient Mother of the Yr. award Quad City Bus. Men, 1960, Bowl of Light award Cmty. Hawaii, 1989. Mem. Soc. Friends, Talking Book Readers Club (1st vp. Hawaii chpt. 1994-95, pres., 1996, corr. sec. 2000-05), Hahamenalima Club (chmn. youth outreach com.), Peace and Social Concerns Soc. Friends (corr. dinajor, peace sub com.). Personal E-mail: palijae@juno.com, palijae@hawaii.rr.com.

LEE, PHILIP RANDOLPH, medical educator; b. San Francisco, Apr. 17, 1924; 5 children. AB, Stanford U., 1945, MD, 1948; MS, U. Minn., 1956; DSc (hon.), MacMurray Coll., 1967; PhD (hon.), Ben Gurion U., Israel, 1995, St. George U., 1998. Diplomate Am. Bd. Internal Medicine. Asst. prof. clin. phys. medicine and rehab. NYU, 1955—56; clin. instr. medicine Stanford (Calif.) U., 1956—59, asst. clin. prof., 1959—67; asst. sec. health and sci. affairs Dept. HEW, Washington, 1965—69; chancellor U. Calif., San Francisco, 1969—72, prof. social medicine, 1969—93, dir. inst. health policy studies, 1972—93; asst. sec. U.S. Dept. HHS, Washington, D.C., 1993-97; prof. emeritus, sr. advisor Inst. Health Policy, San Francisco, 1997—; cons. prof. human biology program Stanford U., 1997—. Mem. dept. internal medicine Palo Alto Med. Clinic, Calif., 1956—65; cons. bur. pub. health svc. USPHS, 1958—63, adv. com., 1978, 1978, nat. commn. smoking & pub. policy, 1977—78; dir. health svc. office tech. cooperation & rsch. AID, 1963—65; dep. asst. sec. health & sci. affairs HEW, 1965, mem. nat. coun. health planning & devel., 1978—80; co-dir. inst. health & aging, sch. nursing U. Calif., San Diego, 1980—93; pres. bd. dirs. World Inst. Disability, 1984—93; mem. population com Nat. Rsch. Coun.- Nat. Acad. Sci., 1983—86; mem. adv. bd. Scripps Clinic & Rsch. Found., 1980—86. Author (or coauthor): 15 books; contbr. more than 100 articles to profl. jours. Chmn. bd. trustees Jenifer Altman Found., 1992—93; trustee Kaiser Family Found., 1991—93, Mayo Found., 1971—75, Carnegie Fedn., 1971—79. Recipient Hugo Schaefer medal, medal Am. Pharm. Assn., 1976. Mem.: APHA, ACP, AMA, AAAS, Inst. Medicine-Nat. Acad. Sci., Assn. Am. Med. Colls., Am. Geriatric Soc., Am. Fedn. Clin. Rsch., Alpha Omega Alpha. Achievements include research in arthritis and rheumatism, especially Rubella arthritis; cardiovascular rehabilitation; academic medical administration; health policy. Home: 101 Alma St mt 805 Palo Alto CA 94301 Office: U Calif Inst Health Policy Studies 3333 California St Ste 265 San Francisco CA 94143-0001

LEE, RICHARD DIEBOLD, lawyer, educator; b. Fargo, ND, July 31, 1935; s. Sidney Jay and Charlotte Hannah (Thompson) L.; m. Patricia Ann Taylor, June 17, 1957; children: Elizabeth Carol, Deborah Susan, David Stuart. BA with distinction, Stanford U., 1957; JD, Yale U., 1960. Bar: Calif. 1961, U.S. Dist. Ct. (no. dist.) Calif. 1961, U.S. Ct. Appeals (9th cir.) 1961. Dep. atty. gen. Office of Atty. Gen., Sacramento, 1960-62; assoc. McDonough, Holland, Schwartz, Allen & Wahrhaftig, Sacramento, 1962-66, ptnr., 1966-69; asst. dean U. Calif. Sch. Law, Davis, 1969-73, assoc. dean, 1973-76; assoc. prof. law Temple U. Sch. Law, Phila., 1976-77, vis. prof., 1975-76, prof., 1977-89; dir. profl. devel. Baker & McKenzie, Chgo., NYC, 1981-83; dir. Am. Law Inst.-ABA In-House, Phila., 1985—89, mem. adv. bd., 1989—; dir. profl. devel. Morrison & Foerster, San Francisco, 1989—93; dir. Continuing Edn. of the Bar, Berkeley, Calif., 1993—97; v.p. JusLaw.com, 2000—01, LawyersTV Continue Learning Networks L.L.C., 2002; exec. v.p. Lawyer Prep, LLC, 2007—. Mem. Grad. and Profl. Fin. Aid Coun., Princeton, NJ, 1974-80; trustee Law Sch. Admissions Coun., Washington, 1976-78; mem. internat. adv. com. Internat. Juridical Orgn., Rome, 1977-88; mem. bd. advisors Lawyer Hiring and Tng. Report, Chgo., 1983-95. Author: (coursebook) Materials on International Efforts to Control the Environment, 1977, 78, 79, 80, 84, 85, 87; co-editor: Orientation in the U.S. Legal System annual coursebook, 1982-92; contbr. articles to profl. jours. Trustee Grad. Theol. Union, Berkeley, 1991—2000, vice chair, 1994—99; mem. bd. of coun. Episc. Cmty. Svcs., Phila., 1984—88; trustee Grace Cathedral, San Francisco, 1989—2004, chair bd. trustees, 1992—95; trustee Coll. of Preachers, Washington Nat. Cathedral, 1999—2004, mem. cathedral coll. bd., 2004—06; adv. bd. Ch. Div. Sch. of the Pacific, 2000—; bd. dirs. Lung Assn. of Sacramento-Emigrant Trails, 1962—69, pres., 1966—68; bd. dirs. Sacramento County Legal Aid Soc., 1968—74, pres., 1971—72; chmn. bd. overseers Phila. Theol. Inst., 1984—88, bd. overseers, 1979—80, 1984—88; mem. bd. visitors John Marshall Law Sch., Chgo., 1989—93; bd. dirs. Earplay, 2004—06; chair, bd. dirs. The Ghiberti Found., 2002—04, bd. dirs., 2004—, San Francisco Contemporary Music Players, 2007—, pres., 2009—. Mem. ABA (chmn. various coms., spl. cons. on continuing legal edn. MacCrate Task Force on Law Schs. and the Profession: Narrowing the Gap, 1991-93, standing com. on specialization 1998-2001, standing com. paralegals 2003-06), State Bar Calif. (chair standing com. on minimum continuing legal edn. 1990-92, com. mem. 1990-93), Bar Assn. San Francisco (legal ethics com., conf. of delegates 1987—), Assn. Continuing Legal Edn. (com. chair, Tech. awards 2002-07), Profl. Devel. Consortium (co-founder, chair 1990-93, mem. 1993-2006), Am. Law Inst., Yale Club (N.Y.C., San Francisco). Democrat. Episcopalian. Home and Office: 2001 Sacramento St Ste 4 San Francisco CA 94109-3342 Home Phone: 415-673-9929. Personal E-mail: RichardDLee@earthlink.net.

LEE, RICHARD KENNETH, software company executive; b. Birmingham, Eng., Dec. 10, 1942; came to U.S., 1964; s. Kenneth Jesse Lee and Eleanor Margaret (Bellsham) Dean; m. Melinda Elena Noback, Aug. 20, 1966; children: Sonja Eleanor, Alyssa Claire. BSc with upper 2d class honours, No. Poly. U. London, 1964; MS in Inorganic Chemistry, Northwestern U., 1965; PhD in Inorganic Chemistry, U. London, 1968. Various corp. rsch. positions UOP Inc., Des Plaines, Ill., 1965-74, mgr. catalyst R & D automotive products divsn., 1974-77; v.p., gen. mgr. portable battery div. Gould Inc., St. Paul, 1977-82; v.p., gen. mgr. Elgar Corp., an Onan/McGraw Edison Co., San Diego, 1982-85; v.p. R & D, Pharmaseal div. Baxter Healthcare Corp., Valencia, Calif., 1985-88; v.p. strategic bus. ops. Manville Sales Corp., Denver, 1988-92; pres., chief exec. officer Rocklite Inc., Denver, 1992-99; prin. LeeVarage Internat., Castle Rock, 1993-00; chmn., pres., CEO Value Innovations, Inc., Denver, 1999—; mng. dir. Edgeguard Internat. Ltd., Castle Rock, 2002—03. Adj. prof. masters tech. program U. Coll., U. Denver, 1993-95; bd. dirs. Q.E.D., Denver; mem. adv. bd. Kodiak, Denver, 1998-99. Author: (videotape) U.S. Competitiveness—A Crisis?, 1992; patentee for vehicle emission control system. Chmn. Summit 91, Denver, 1991, mem. organizing com. Summit 92, Pacoima, Calif., 1992; bd. dirs. Indsl. Rsch. Inst., Inc., Washington, 1991-92, chmn. emeritus, 2003-04. Recipient IR-100 award, Indsl. R & D, 1978; Fulbright travel scholar, 1964—65. Mem. Rocky Mountain World Trade Ctr. (vice chmn. 1992-94, exec. com. 1992-94, bd. dirs. 1990-95). Office Phone: 303-688-4143. Business E-Mail: dick_lee@valueinnovations.net.

LEE, RONALD DEMOS, demographer, economist, educator; b. Sept. 5, 1941; s. Otis Hamilton and Dorothy (Demetracopoulou) Lee; m. Melissa Lee Nelken, July 6, 1968; children: Sophia, Isabel, Rebecca. BA, Reed Coll., 1963; MA, U. Calif., Berkeley, 1967; PhD, Harvard U., 1971; D (hon.), Lund U., Sweden, 2004. Postdoctoral fellow Nat. Demographic Inst., Paris, 1970-71; asst. prof. to prof. U. Mich., Ann Arbor, 1971-79; prof. demography and econs. U. Calif., Berkeley, 1979—. Dir. Berkeley Ctr. Econs. and Demography Aging; chair com. population NAS, 1993—97; cons. in field. Author, editor: Population Patterns in the Past, 1977, Econometric Studies of Topics in Demographic History, 1978, Population, Food, and Rural Development, 1988, Economics of Changing Age Distributions in Developed Countries, 1988, Population Change in Asia: Transition, Development and Aging, 2000, Demographic Change and Fiscal Policy, 2000, United States Fertility: New Patterns, New Theories, 1996; contbr. articles to profl. jours. Vol. Peace Corps, Ethiopia, 1963—65. Recipient Mindel C. Sheps award, Population Assn. Am. and U. N.C. Sch. Pub. Health, 1984, MERIT award, Nat. Inst. Aging, 1994—2003, 2005—, Taeuber award, Population Assn. Am. and Princeton U.,

1999; fellow, Social Sci. Rsch. Coun., 1970—71; NIH fellow, 1965—67, NSF fellow, 1968—69, NIH grantee, 1973—, Guggenheim fellow, 1984—85. Mem.: AAAS, NAS, Am. Acad. Arts and Scis., Am. Philos. Soc., Am. Econ. Assn., Population Assn. Am. (pres. 1987), Internat. Union Sci. Study Population, Brit. Acad. (corr.). Democrat. Home: 2933 Russell St Berkeley CA 94705-2333 Office: U Calif Dept Demography 2232 Piedmont Ave Berkeley CA 94720-2120 E-mail: rlee@demog.berkeley.edu.

LEE, STAN (STANLEY MARTIN LIEBER), cartoon publisher, writer; b. NYC, Dec. 28, 1922; s. Jack and Celia (Solomon) Lieber; m. Joan Clayton Boocock, Dec. 5, 1947; children: Joan Celia, Jan(dec.). Degree (hon.), Bowling Green State U. Copy writer to asst. editor, then editor Timely Comics, NYC, 1939—42; editor, creative dir. Atlas Comics (formerly Timely Comics), 1945—61; with Marvel Comics, 1961—72, pub., editl. dir., 1972—78; creative dir. Marvel Prodns., 1978—89, chmn. Marvel comics; partnered with DC Comics, 2000—. Founder Stan Lee Media. Creator, former writer/editor Fantastic Four, Incredible Hulk, Amazing Spiderman, numerous others; author: Origins of Marvel Comics, 1974, Son of Origins, 1975, Bring On The Bad Guys, 1976, Mighty Marvel Strength & Fitness Book, 1976, Mighty Marvel Superheroes Fun Book, 1976, The Marvel Comics Illustrated Version of Star Wars, 1977, The Amazing Spiderman Vol. No. 3, 1977, The Superhero Women, 1977, The Mighty World of Marvel Pin-up Book, 1978, The Mighty Marvel Superhero Fun Book Vol. No. 3, 1978, The Silver Surfer, How to Draw Comics the Marvel Way, 1978, Marvel's Greatest Superhero Battles, 1978, Incredible Hulk, 1978, Marvelous Mazes to Drive You Mad, 1978, Fantastic Four, 1979, Doctor Strange, 1979, Complete Adventures of Spider-Man, 1979, Captain America, 1979, The Best of the Worst, 1979, Marvel Word Games, 1979, Omnibus Fun Book, 1979, Dunn's Conundrum, 1985, The Best of Spider-Man, 1986, Marvel Team-Up Thrillers, 1987, The Amazing Spiderman, No. 2, 1980, Hulk Cartoons, 1980, Marvel Masterworks Vol. 2: Fantastics Four, 1987, X-Men, 1987, Marvel Masterworks, Vol. 1: Amazing Spider-Man, 1987, Masterworks, Vol. 6: Fantastic Four, 1988, Silver Surfer: Judgement Day, 1988, Silver Surfer: Parable, 1988, Spider-Man, 1988, Avengers, 1988, The God Project, 1990, Silver Surfer: The Enslavers, 1990, Marvel Masterworks, Vol. 13: Fantastic Four, 1990, Best of Marvel Comics, 1991, Night Cat, 1991, Marvel Masterworks, Vol. 17: Daredevil, 1991, Marvel Masterworks, Vol. 18: Thor, 1991, Spider-Man Wedding, 1991, Spider-Man Masterworks, 1992, Uncanny X-Men Masterworks, 1993, Marvels Greatest Super Battles, 1994, The Ultimate Spiderman, 1994, The Very Best of Spiderman, 1994, The Incredible Hulk: A Man-Brute Berserk, 1995, others; creator (TV series), Iron Man, 1966, Hulk, 1966, The Fantastic Four, 1994, Spider-Man, 1994-98, The Incredible Hulk, 1996-97, Avengers, 1999-2000, Spider-Man: The New Animated Series, 2003, Striperella, 2003; cameos in several movie adaptations of comic book characters including X-Men, 2000, Spider-Man, 2002, Daredevil, 2003, Hulk, 2003, Spider-Man 2, 2004, Fantastic Four, 2005; guest appearences include (voice) The Incredible Hulk, 1997, (voice) Spider-Man, 1998, 2003, Turn Ben Stein On, 2001, To Tell the Truth, 2001, (voice) The Simpsons, 2002, Mad TV, 2003, 2004, several talk shows. With Signal Corps US Army, 1942—45. Recipient Alley awards, Acad. Comic Book Fans & Collectors, 1963—68, Comic Art award, Soc. Comic Art Rsch. & Preservation, 1968, Popular Culture Assn. ann. award, 1974, Nat. Medal of Arts, NEA, 2008, star on Hollywood Walk of Fame, 2008; named Pub. of Yr., Periodical & Book Assn. of America, 1978; named to Jack Kirby Hall of Fame, 1995. Mem.: AFTRA, Nat. Cartoonists Soc., Nat. Acad. TV Arts & Scis., Acad. Comic Book Arts (founder), Friars NYC. Office: Marvel Comics Group Wilshire Blvd Ste 1400 Los Angeles CA 90024 Address: Attn: Gill Champion POW! Entertainment 9440 Santa Monica Blvd Ste 620 Beverly Hills CA 90210 Office: Marvel Enterprises Inc 417 5th Ave Fl 2 New York NY 10016-2204

LEE, THOMAS L., real estate executive; Degree in Econ., Denison U.; MBA, Stanford U. Various positions The Newhall Land & Farming Co., Valencia, Calif., 1970-85, pres., COO, 1985-87, CEO, 1987—, chmn., 1989—. Bd. dirs. Blue Shield Calif., L.A. Area C. of C., chmn. bd. dirs., 1994; bd. dirs. Nat. Realty Com., bd. trustees Boys and Girls Clubs Am., Calif. Inst. Arts. With USNR, 1965-68. Mem. Calif. Bus. Roundtable, Urban Land Inst. Office: Newhall Land & Farming Co 23823 Valencia Blvd Valencia CA 91355-2103

LEE, V. PAUL, entertainment software company executive; B in Commerce, U. BC. Prin. Distinctive Software, Inc.; with Elec. Arts, Redwood City, Calif., 1991—, gen. mgr. Canada, COO, CFO sports, v.p. fin. and adminstrn., sr. v.p., COO Redwood City, Calif., 1998—2002, exec. v.p., COO, 2002—05, pres. worldwide studios, 2005—. Office: Elec Arts 209 Redwood Shores Pky Redwood City CA 94065 Office Phone: 650-628-1500.

LEE, WILLES K., political organization administrator; Chmn. rules com. Hawaii Rep. Party, vice chmn., chmn., 2007—, Hawaii State Boxing Commn. Campaign mgr. Friends of Charles Djou; dir. coalitions Linda Lingle Campaign Com.; mem. com. on resolutions Rep. Nat. Com., 2004, 08; del. Rep. Nat. Conv., 2004, 08. Mem. bd. dirs. Luth. High Sch. Ret. US Army. Republican. Office: C-105 725 Kapiolani Blvd Honolulu HI 96813 Office Phone: 808-593-8180. Business E-Mail: chairman@gophawaii.com, willes@gophawaii.com.*

LEE, YEU-TSU MARGARET, surgeon, educator; b. Xian, Shensi, China, Mar. 18, 1936; m. Thomas V. Lee, Dec. 29, 1962 (div. 1987); 1 child, Maxwell M. AB in Microbiology, U. S.D., 1957; MD, Harvard U., 1961. Diplomate Am. Bd. Surgery. Assoc. prof. surgery Med. Sch., U. So. Calif., LA, 1973-83; commd. lt. col. U.S. Army Med. Corps, 1983, advanced through grades to col., 1989; chief surg. oncology Tripler Army Med. Ctr., Honolulu, 1983-98; ret. U.S. Army, 1999; assoc. clin. prof. surgery Med. Sch., U. Hawaii, Honolulu, 1984-92, clin. prof. surgery, 1992—. Author: Malignant Lymphoma, 1974; author chpts to books; contbr. articles to profl. jours. Pres. Orgn. Chinese-Am. Women, L.A., 1981, Hawaii chpt., 1988; active U.S.-China Friendship Assn., 1991—. Decorated Nat. Def. Svc. medal, Army Commendation medal, Army Meritorious Svc. medal, Army Humanitarian Svc. medal; recipient Chinese-Am. Engrs. and Scis. Assn., 1987; named Sci. Woman Warrior, Asian-Pacific Womens Network, 1983. Mem. ACS, Soc. Surg. Oncology, Assn. Women Surgeons. Avocations: classical music, movies, hiking, ballroom dancing. Address: PO Box 29726 Honolulu HI 96820 E-mail: ytm_lee@hotmail.com.

LEEB, CHARLES SAMUEL, psychologist; b. July 18, 1945; s. Sidney Herbert and Dorothy Barbara (Fishstrom) Leeb; m. Storme Lynn Gilkey, Apr. 28, 1984; children: Morgan Evan, Spencer Douglas. BA in Psychology, U. Calif., Davis, 1967; MS in Counseling and Guidance, San Diego State U., 1970; PhD in Edn. and Psychology, Claremont Grad., 1973. Assoc. So. Regional Dir. Mental Retardation Ctr., Las Vegas, Nev., 1978—79; pvt. practice Las Vegas, 1978—79; dir. biofeedback and athletics Menninger Found., Topeka, 1979—82, dir. children's divsn. biofeedback and psychophysiology ctr., 1979—82; pvt. practice Claremont, Calif., 1982—. Dir. psychol. svcs. Horizon Hosp., 1986—88; dir. adolescent chem. dependence and children's program Charter Oak Hosp., Covina, Calif., 1989—91; founder, CEO Rsch. and Treatment Inst., Claremont, Calif., 1991—2002; co-founder, dir. Live Oak Canyon Sch., 1992—; lectr. in field. Contbr. articles to profl. jours. Mem.: APA, Calif. State Psychol. Assn. Office: 1420 N Claremont Blvd #102-A Claremont CA 91711-3358 Office Phone: 909-624-4864. Business E-Mail: ChuckL@liveoaknps.org.

LEEFE, JAMES MORRISON, architect; b. NYC, Aug. 28, 1921; s. Charles Clement and Suzanne (Bernhardt) L.; m. Miriam Danziger, Oct. 31, 1949; 1 dau., Molly Elizabeth. Cert., U.S. Mcht. Marine Acad., 1943; B.Arch., Columbia U., 1950. Practice architecture, San Francisco, 1955-60; chief architect power and indsl. div. Bechtel Inc., San Francisco, 1960-64, prin. urban designer, 1974-80; chief architect San Francisco Power div. Bechtel Power Corp., 1980-89; v.p., asst. sec. Bechtel Assos. P.C., NY, 1978-89, v.p. DC, 1978-89, Va., 1978—89; pvt. cons. architect Sausalito, Calif., 1989—; ptnr. Leefe & Ehrankrantz Architects, San Francisco, 1964-68; v.p. Bldg. Systems Devel. Inc., San Francisco and Washington, 1965-70; also dir.; dir. architecture Giffels Assos. Inc., Detroit, 1971-74. Lectr. in architecture Columbia U., 1951-52, U. Calif., Berkeley, 1954-60; mem. faculty U. for Pres's., Young Pres's. Orgn., 1967; adj. prof. U. Detroit, 1971-72; mem. adv. bd. Nat. Clearing House for Criminal Justice Planning and Architecture, 1974-76 Works include Mus. West of Am. Craftsmen's Council, San Francisco, 1964 (Archtl. Record award for interior design 1971), Wells Hydrocombine Dam and Power Generating Facility, Columbia River, Wash., 1965, Boundary Dam, Pend Orielle River, Wash., 1965 (Am. Public Power Assn. honor award 1975), Detroit Automobile Inter-Ins. Exchange Corp. Hdqrs, Dearborn, Mich., 1972 (Detroit chpt. AIA honor award 1975), PPG Industries Research Center, Allison Park, Pa., 1973 (Detroit chpt. AIA honor award 1975, Am. Inst. Steel Constrn. Archtl. award of excellence 1975, Mich. Soc. Architects honor award 1976), Gen. Electric Research Center, Twinsburg, Ohio, 1973 (Detroit chpt. AIA honor award 1977), Appliance Buyers Credit Corp. Hdqrs. Office, Benton Harbor, Mich., 1974 (Engring. Soc. Detroit Design award 1976), Standard Tng. Bldg. Commonwealth Edison, 1989-90, Strybing Arboretum, San Francisco, 1990; contbr. articles to profl. jours.; originator various techniques for analysis of human factors in the working environment. Chmn. bd. Mus. West of Am. Crafts Coun., San Francisco, 1966-68; vice chmn. Franklin (Mich.) Hist. Dist. Commn., 1973-74; trustee So. Marin Land Trust. With U.S. Mcht. Marine, 1942-46. Recipient Hirsh Meml. prize Columbia U., 1950, 1st prize (with Miriam Leefe) Dow Chem. Co. Competition for Interior Design, 1960 Fellow AIA; hon. mem. Internat. Union Architects Working Group Habitat, trustee, So. Marin Land Trust. Home and Office: James Leefe FAIA Architect 131 Spencer Ave Sausalito CA 94965-2022

LEEMANS, WIM PIETER, physicist; b. Gent, Belgium, June 7, 1963; BS in Elec. Engring., Free U. Brussels, 1985; MS in Elec. Engring., UCLA, 1987, PhD in Elec. Engring., 1991. Teaching asst. UCLA, 1986-87, rsch. asst., 1987-91; staff scientist Lawrence Berkeley Lab., Berkeley, Calif., 1991—. Group leader exptl. beam physics group, 1994—; chair ICFA panel on advanced and novel accelerators; presenter numerous seminars. Contbr. articles to profl. jours. Recipient Simon Ramo awd., Am. Physical Soc., 1992; grad. scholar IEEE Nuclear and Plasma Soc., 1987. Fellow Belgian Am. Ednl. Found., Francqui Found.; mem. IEEE (Nuclear and Plasma scis. soc. grad. scholar 1987), Soc. Photo-Optical Instrument Engrs., Am. Phys. Soc., Royal Flemish Engrs. Soc. Achievements include research in high intensity laser-plasma interaction, interaction of relativistic electrons with lasers and plasmas, novel radiation sources, advanced accelerator concepts, non-linear dynamics of free electron lasers. Office: Lawrence Berkeley Lab Divsn Accelerator Fusion Rsch 1 Cyclotron Rd Ms 71 259 Berkeley CA 94720-0001

LEES, ANDREW, computer software company executive; married; 2 children. BS in Computer Sci., Bradford U., Eng. Leader tech. consulting group, dir. mktg. offices systems Hewlett-Packard Co. U.K. subs.; product mgr. Microsoft U.K. subs., 1990, various pos., to dir. emerging mkts. group, 1990—2000; corp. v.p., US mktg., sales and ptnrs. Microsoft Corp., Redmond, Wash., 2000, corp. v.p. Microsoft server & tools mktg. and solutions group, sr. v.p. mobile comm. bus. Avocation: travel. Office: Microsoft Corp One Microsoft Way Redmond WA 98052-6399

LEESMAN, BEVERLY JEAN, artist, critic, writer, educator; b. Lincoln, Ill., Apr. 22, 1953; d. Robert Eugene and Jean (Bruner) L.; m. Paul A. Martin, Nov. 28, 1987; children: Danielle, Stewart Martin. AS in Fine Art, Springfield Coll., 1973; BS in Art History, Graphics Design, Painting, Ill. State U., 1976; postgrad., U. Grenoble, France, 1980, L'Ecole de Louvre, Paris, 1980, U. Ill., 1986. Dept. mgr. J.C. Penney, Springfield, Ill., 1979; head asst. to curator Slide Libr. Ill. State U., Normal, 1981-82; teaching asst. U. Ill., Urbana-Champaign, 1983-84, instr., 1984-85; art instr. North Syracuse Adult Edn. Program, 1992-94. Guest lectr. U. Ill., 1981-85; layout, past-up artist Dynamic Graphics, Inc., Peoria, Ill., 1976-78; tech. illustrator I-270 Project, St. Louis, 1984-85; freelance artist, 1986—. One-woman shows include Paine Br. Libr., Syracuse, N.Y., 1993, Liverpool Pub. Libr., 1994, Manlius (N.Y.) Libr., 1995, Roaster's Corner Cafe, Fayetteville, N.Y., 1995, JCC Gallery, Albuquerque, N.Mex., 2003; group shows include SUNY Inst. Tech., Utica, Rome, N.Y., 1990, 92-94, Skaneateles (N.Y.) Arts Expn., 1990, 93, Everson Mus., Syracuse, 1994-95, Canastota (N.Y.) Canal Town Mus., 1991-95, Cooperstown (N.Y.) Art Assn., 1992, 94-95, Rome Art & Cmty. Ctr., 1994, Great N.Y. State Fair, Syracuse, 1994-95, CNY Art Open, DeWitt, N.Y., 1995, North East Watercolor Soc., Goshen, N.Y., 1994, 2003, Pitts. Watercolor Soc., 1995, 2002, 16th Ann. Internat. Exhbn. Watercolor Art Soc. Houston, 2003, La. State U., Baton Rouge, 2003, 26th Internat. Exhbn., N.Mex. State Fair, Albuquerque, 2002, 2003, River Road Show, Baton Rouge, 2002-2003 (2d Pl. 2002), Hilton Head Art League's Nat. Juried Art Exhbn., Hilton Head Island, S.C., 2003, 26th Ann. Non-mem. Juried Exhbn., N.Y.C., 2003, Barnsite Gallery, Kewaunee, Wis., 2003, Masterworks, Albuquerque, 2003-2004, Salmugundi Club, N.Y.C., N.Y., 2003, Barns & Farms, Kewaunee, Wis., 2003, Wolfe Art Club, N.Y.C., N.Y., 2003, N.Mex. Watercolor Soc., 2003, Spring & Fall Shows, 2003-2004, Red River Watercolor Soc., Fargo, ND, 2004, 8th Ann. Heartland Exhbn., Merriam, Kans., 2004, Mo. Watercolor Nat., Fulton, Mo., 2004, Art For The Parks, Wyo., 2004; painter (dinosaur mural) Gold Cup Gymnastics, Albuquerque, N.Mex., 2002-2003. Recipient Cooperstown Vet. Clinic prize, 1995, Dick Blick award Pitts. Watercolor Soc. Mem. Nat. League Am. Pen Women, City N.Y. Art Guild, Inc. (founding pres. 1994-95, 2d v.p. 1995-96), Am. Artists Profl. League, Nat. Assn. Women Artists, N.Mex. Watercolor Soc. (Fall Exhibit Bd. Dirs. award 2002, 03, M. Graham and Co. Mdse. award 2003). Home: 12231 Academy Rd NE #301-221 Albuquerque NM 87111 Personal E-mail: bev@beverlyleesman.com.

LEFF, BARBARA, state legislator; b. NYC, May 14, 1947; m. Edmund Leff; 2 children. BA, Boston U., 1969; MS in Social Work, Simmons Coll., Boston, 1971. Small bus. owner, Scottsdale, Ariz., 1985—89; cert. instr. Maricopa County Cmty. Coll. Sys., Ariz., 1986—88; mem. Ariz. House of Reps., 1997—2002; mem. Dist. 11 Ariz. State Senate, 2003—, chair commerce & econ. devel. com., mem. health com., fin. com. Recipient Guardian of Small Bus. award, Nat. Fedn. Ind. Bus., 2002, Eagle for Enterprise award, Ariz. Small Bus. Assn., 2004; named a Leader of Yr. in Pub. Policy, Ariz. Capitol Times, 2008. Republican. Jewish. Office: Ariz State Senate Capitol Complex 1700 W Washington Rm 302 Phoenix AZ 85007-2890 Office Phone: 602-926-4486. Office Fax: 602-417-3270. Business E-Mail: bleff@azleg.gov.*

LEFRANC, MARGARET (MARGARET SCHOONOVER), artist, illustrator, editor, writer; b. NYC, Mar. 15, 1907; d. Abraham and Sophie (Teplitz) Frankel; m. Raymond E. Schoonover, 1942 (dec. Sept. 5, 1998). Student, Art Students League, NYC, Kunstschule des Westerns, Berlin, NYU Grad. Sch., Andre L'Hote, Paris, Acad. Grande Chaumiere, Paris. Tchr. art Adult Edn., Los Alamos, 1946, Miami Mus. Modern Art, Fla., 1975-76. One-woman shows include Mus. N.Mex., Santa Fe, 1948, 1951, 1953, Philbrook Art Ctr., Tulsa, Okla., 1949, 1951, Okla. Art Ctr., 1950, Recorder Workshop, Miami, Fla., 1958, St. John's Coll., Santa Fe, N.Mex., 1993, 1997, A Lifetime of Imaging, 1921—95, Figurative Works, 1920—30, Cline Fine Art Gallery, 1997, one-woman shows include a lifetime imaging The Art of Margaret Letrane Exhibition, exhibited in group shows at Salon de Tuileries, Paris, 1928—30, Art Inst. Chgo., 1936, El Paso Mus. Art, 1964, Mus. Modern Art, 1974, North Miami Mus. Contemporary Art, 1984, Miami Collects, 1989, Women's Caucus Invitational, 1990, Gov.'s Gallery, Santa Fe, 1992, Gene Autry Western Heritage Mus., 1995, Gilcrease Mus., Tulsa, 1996, Mus. N.Mex., Santa Fe, 1996, Brigham Young U., Provo, Utah, 1996, Art in the Embassies Program, Paris, 1998—2001, Miami Dade CC Kendall Campus, Miami, Fla., 1999—2000, Modernistic Peaks, Gerald Peters Gallery, Santa Fe, 1999, Ind. State U. and Swope Art Mus. Women Artists, Terre Haute, 1999, Gerald Peters Gallery, 2001, 2003, Purdue U., 2004, Panhandle-Plains Hist. Mus., Canyon, Tex., 2004—05, St. George Art Mus., St. George Utah, 2005, Hall of Fame, Okla. City, 2006, Archives Am. Art Smithsonian Mus., Washington, A Lifetime of Imaging: The Art of Margaret Lefranc, 2007—08, Gerald Peters Gallery, Santa Fe, Represented in permanent collections, State Capital, Belles Artes, Mexico City, Mus. Fine Arts, Santa Fe, exhibitions include Women Artists of Santa Fe 1914-1964, First Lady, Barbara Richards Painting in on Loan, pvt. collections. Bd. dir., pres. Artist Equity of Fla., 1964-68; v.p. Miami Art Assn., 1958-60; founder, dir. Guild Art Gallery, NYC, 1935-37. Recipient Illustration award Fifty Best Books of Yr., Libr. of Congress, 1948, Hon. Mention award Rodeo Santa Fe, Mus. N.Mex., 1949, others, Gov.'s award for Excellence and Achievement in the Arts, 1996. Office Phone: 505-983-1790. Personal E-mail: mckenziehi@aol.com.

LEGARIE, WARREN, sports agent; Founder, sports agent Warren LeGarie Sports Mgmt., San Francisco; founder, exec. dir. Las Vegas Summer League, Nev., 2004—. Office: Warren LeGarie Sports Mgmt 1108 Masonic Ave San Francisco CA 94117 Office Phone: 415-431-7772. Office Fax: 415-431-7774.

LEGERE, EDWARD J., health products executive; BS in Internat. Bus., Fla. Atlantic U.; MBA, U. Chgo. Pres., CEO, dir. Peregrine Pharms. Inc., Tustin, Calif., 1992—. Office: 14272 Franklin Ave Ste 100 Tustin CA 92780

LEGGE, CHARLES ALEXANDER, federal judge; b. San Francisco, Aug. 24, 1930; s. Roy Alexander and Wilda (Rampton) L.; m. Janice Meredith Sleeper, June 27, 1952; children: Jeffrey, Nancy, Laura. AB with distinction, Stanford U., 1952, JD, 1954. Bar: Calif. 1955. Assoc. Bronson, Bronson & McKinnin, San Francisco, 1956-64, ptnr., 1964-84, chmn., 1978-84; U.S. Dist. Ct. judge U.S. Dist. Ct. (no. dist.) Calif., San Francisco, 1984—. Served with U.S. Army, 1954-56. Fellow Am. Coll. Trial Lawyers; mem. Calif. Bar Assn. (past chmn. adminstrn. justice com.). Clubs: Bohemian, World Trade (San Francisco); Orinda (Calif.) Country. Republican.

LEGRAND, SHAWN PIERRE, enterprise support services manager; b. San Diego, Nov. 27, 1960; s. Roger and Violet Louise (Howe) L. BS in Computer Sci., St. Regis U., 2002. Cert. computer programmer, in neural networks U. Calif., San Diego, 1993, Founds. IT Svc. Mgmt., 2004. Computer operator Grossmont CCD, El Cajon, 1978-79; sys. engr. ICW, San Diego, 1979—2008, Enterprise support svcs. mgr., 2008—. Recipient Math. Achievement award Bank of Am., 1978. Mem.: Internat. Coun. Sys. Engring., Am. Math. Soc., Soc. Indsl. & Applied Mathematicians, Assn. Computing Machinery, IEEE computer Soc. Office: ICW 11455 El Camino Real San Diego CA 92130-2088 Office Phone: 858-350-2457. Personal E-mail: splegrand@yahoo.com.

LEGUIZAMÖ, JOHN, actor, comedian; b. Bogota, Columbia, July 22, 1964; s. Alberto and Luz Leguizamo; m. Yelba Osorio, Sept. 1994 (div. Nov. 1996); m. Justine Mauer, July 5, 2003; children: Allegra Sky, Ryder Lee. Studied, Sylvia Leigh's Showcase Theater, NY, Lee Strasberg Inst., HB Studio; studied Theater, NYU. Actor: (films) Mixed Blood, 1985, The Burning Question, 1988, Casualties of War, 1989, Street Hunter, 1990, Gentille alouette, 1990, Revenge, 1990, Die Hard 2, 1990, Poison, 1991, Hangin' with the Homeboys, 1991, Out for Justice, 1991, Regarding Henry, 1991, Time Expired, 1992, Whispers in the Dark, 1992, Night Owl, 1993, Super Mario Bros., 1993, Carlito's Way, 1993, A Pyromaniac's Love Story, 1995, To Wong Foo, Thanks for Everything, Julie Newmar, 1995, Executive Decision, 1996, The Fan, 1996, Romeo & Juliet, 1996, The Pest, 1996, A Brother's Kiss, 1997, Spawn, 1997, Frogs for Snakes, 1998, Body Count, 1998, (voice only) Doctor Doolittle, 1998, Joe the King, 1999, Summer of Sam, 1999, (voice only) Titan A.E., 2000, Moulin Rouge!, 2001, What's the Worst That Could Happen?, 2001, King of the Jungle, 2001, Empire, 2002, Zigzag, 2002, (voice only) Ice Age, 2002, Spun, 2002, Crónicas, 2004, Sueño, 2005, Assault on Precinct

13, 2005, The Honeymooners, 2005, Land of the Dead, 2005, The Alibi, 2006, (voice only) Ice Age: The Meltdown, 2006, The Groomsmen, 2006, Where God Left His Shoes, 2007, The Babysitters, 2007, The Take, 2007, Love in the Time of Cholera, 2007, Paraiso Travel, 2008, The Happening, 2008, Righteous Kill, 2008, Miracle at St. Anna, 2008, Nothing Like the Holidays, 2008; actor (TV films) Words in Your Face, 1991, N.Y.P.D. Mounted, 1991, Arabian Nights, 2000, Point of Origin, 2002, Undefeated, 2003, (also exec. prodr., dir., writer); (TV series) House of Buggin, 1995 (also writer, prodr.), The Brothers Garcia (voice), 2000, ER, 2005-06; (TV appearances) Miami Vice, 1986, 1987, 1989; actor (music video for Madonna) Borderline, 1984, Madonna: The Immaculate Collection, 1990; co-exec. prodr. Piñero, 2001; exec. prodr. Nuyorican Dream, 1999; writer, actor (Broadway plays) Freak: A Semi-Demi-Quasi-Autobiographical Comedy, 1997 (Tony award nomination), writer, prodr. John Leguizamo LIVE, Sexaholix...A Love Story, 2001; actor American Buffalo, 2008; writer (TV film) Mambo Mouth, 1991, Spic-O-Rama, 1993; author: Pimps, Hos Playa Hatas and All the Rest of My Hollywood Friends, 2006 Recipient OBIE award for Mambo Mouth, 1991, Tony award for play Freak, 1998, Entertainer of Yr. ALMA, 2002 Office: c/o William Morris Agy 151 S El Camino Dr Beverly Hills CA 90212-2775

LEHANE, CHRISTOPHER S., political consultant; b. June 2, 1967; m. Andrea Lehane; 1 child, Dominic. BA, Amherst Coll., 1990; JD, Harvard U., 1994. Mem. Clinton Presdl. Campaign, 1992; spl. asst. counsel to Pres. Bill Clinton The White House, Washington, 1995—97, press sec. to Al Gore, 1997—2000; ptnr. Fabiani & Lehane, San Francisco, 2001—; co-founder LFM Campaigns, Sacramento, 2009—. Democrat. Office: 115 Presidio Ave San Francisco CA 94115-1613*

LEHMAN, I(SRAEL) ROBERT, biochemist, educator; b. Tauroggen, Lithuania, Oct. 5, 1924; arrived in U.S., 1927; s. Herman Bernard Lehman and Anne Kahn; m. Sandra Lee, July 5, 1959; children: Ellen, Deborah, Samuel. BA, Johns Hopkins U., 1950, PhD, 1954; MD (hon.), U. Gothenberg, Sweden, 1987; DSc, U. Paris, 1992. Asst. prof. Stanford (Calif.) U., 1959-62, assoc. prof., 1962-67, prof. biochemistry, 1967—, chmn. dept. biochemistry, 1974—79. Mem. sci. adv. bd. U.S. Biochem., Cleve., 1984-98, RPI Pharms., Boulder, Colo., 1991-96, Genetrol, Oakland, Calif., 1998-2003; cons. Abbott Labs, Chgo., 1990-94. Author: Principles of Biochemistry, 7th edit., 1984. Sgt. U.S. Army, 1943-46, ETO. Recipient Merck award Am. Soc. Biochemistry and Molecular Biology, 1994, Herbert Tabor award, 2008. Fellow: Am. Acad. Arts and Scis.; mem.: Am. Soc. Biochemistry and Molecular Biology (pres. 1995), Nat. Acad. Scis. Democrat. Jewish. Office: Sch of Medicine Stanford U Stanford CA 94305

LEHMAN, MICHAEL EVANS, information technology executive; BBA in Acctg., U. Wis., Madison, 1974. Sr. mgr. Price Waterhouse, San Francisco; asst. corp. contr., external reporting mgr. Asian subs. Sun Microsystems, Inc., Hong Kong, dir. fin. and adminstrn. Asian subs., v.p., corp. contr., v.p., CFO, 1994—98, v.p. corp. resources, CFO, corp. exec. officer, 1998-2000, exec. v.p. corp. resources, CFO, 2000—02, 2006—. Bd. dirs. Sun Microsystems, Inc., 2002—06. Mem. deans adv. bd. Grad. Sch. Bus., U. Wis., Madison. Mem. Am. Electronics Assn. (exec. com.). Office: Sun Microsystems Inc 4150 Network Cir Santa Clara CA 95054 Office Phone: 650-960-1300.

LEHR, JEFFREY MARVIN, immunologist, allergist; b. NYC, Apr. 29, 1942; s. Arthur and Stella (Smellow) L.; m. Suzanne Kozak, June 10, 1946; children: Elisa, Alexandra, Vanessa, Ryan. BS, City Coll., Bklyn., 1963; MD, NYU, 1967. Intern, resident Beth Israel Hosp., NYC, 1967-69; resident in allergy/immunology, internal medicine Roosevelt Hosp., NYC, 1969-72; chief of allergy/immunology USAF, Wright Patterson AFB, Ohio, 1972-74; allergist, immunologist Monterey, Calif., 1974—. Chmn. Monterey Bay Air Pollution Hearing Bd., 1982-95; v.p. Lyceum of Monterey, 1977-83. Fellow Am. Acad. Allergy/Immunology, Am. Coll. Allergy/Immunology, Am. Assn. Cert. Allergists; mem. Am. Lung Assn. (v.p. 1989-91), Monterey County Med. Soc. (pres. 1988-89). Avocations: tennis, jogging, golf, hiking, backpacking. Office: 798 Cass St Monterey CA 93940-2918 Office Phone: 831-649-6340. Personal E-mail: lehrallergy@sbcglobal.net.

LEHRER, STEVEN, health products executive; Degree in Chem. Engring. and Econs., U. Md.; MBA, Harvard U. Former tech. brand mgr. Procter and Gamble Co., Inc.; former engagement mgr. McKinsey & Co., Inc.; former co-leader strategic bus. team, developer Integrated Protein Techs. Monsanto Group; chief bus. officer DNA Scis., Inc., Fremont, Calif., 2000—01, chmn., CEO, acting pres., COO, 2001—.

LEIBEL, STEVEN ARNOLD, oncologist; Undergrad., Mich. State U. S, 1967, Mich. State U. Coll. Medicine, 1970; MD, U. Calif., San Francisco, 1972. Cert. Am. Bd. Radiology. Intern U. Calif., San Francisco, 1972—73, resident radiation oncology, 1973—76, asst. prof., 1980—82, assoc. prof. radiation oncology, 1982—88; radiation oncologist Nat. Naval Med. Ctr., Bethesda, Md., 1976—78, chmn. radiation oncology NYC, 1977—78; asst. prof. Johns Hopkins Hosp., 1978—80; vice chmn., clin. dir. dept. radiation oncology Meml. Sloan-Kettering Cancer Ctr., NYC, 1988—98; chmn. radiation oncology Meml. Sloan Kettering Cancer Ctr., NYC, 1998—. Mem.: Am. Bd. Radiology (pres.). Office: Stanford Cancer Ctr 875 Blake Wilbur Dr Mc 5827 Stanford CA 94305-5827 Office Phone: 650-723-4250. Business E-Mail: sleibel@stanford.edu.

LEIBOW, RONALD LOUIS, lawyer; b. Santa Monica, Calif., Oct. 4, 1939; s. Norman and Jessica (Kellner) L.; m. Linda Bengelsdorf, June 11, 1961 (div. Dec. 1974); children: Jocelyn Elise, Jeffrey David, Joshua Aaron; m. Jacqueline Blatt, Apr. 6, 1986. AB, Calif. State U., Northridge, 1962; JD, UCLA, 1965. Bar: Calif. 1966, U.S. Dist. Ct. (cen. dist.) Calif. 1966, U.S. Dist. Ct. (no., so. and ea. dists.) Calif. 1971. Spl. asst. city atty. City of Burbank, Calif., 1966-67; from assoc. to ptnr. Meyers, Stevens & Walters, LA, 1967-71; ptnr. Karpf, Leibow & Warner, Beverly Hills, Calif., 1971-74, Volk, Newman Gralla & Karp, L.A., LA, 1979-81, Spector & Leibow, LA, 1982-84, Stroock & Stroock & Lavan, LA, 1984-94, Kaye Scholer LLP, LA, 1994—, mng. ptnr., 1996-97. Lectr. law UCLA, 1968-69, Practicing Law Inst., 2001-; asst. prof. Calif. State U., Northridge, 1969-71, faculty, Practising Law Inst., 2001-. Contbr. articles to profl. jours. Pres. Jewish Cmty. Ctr., Greater LA, 1983-86; vice chair Jewish Cmty. Ctr. Assn. N.Am., NYC, 1988—; vice chair Jewish Fedn. Greater LA, 1988—, chair planning and allocations com., 1998-01, chair Jewish Cmty. Rels. Com., 2006-; chair internat. bd., exec. com. Starlight Children's Found., co-chair exec. com., 2005-06; vice chair Modern and Contemporary Arts Coun., LA County Mus. Art, 2003-. Mem. ABA (bus. bankruptcy com.), Phi Alpha Delta. Avocations: writing, tennis, skiing, travel. Office: Kaye Scholer LLP 1999 Avenue Of The Stars Fl 17 Los Angeles CA 90067-6022 Office Phone: 310-788-1220. Business E-Mail: rleibow@kayescholer.com.

LEIGH, HOYLE, psychiatrist, educator, writer; b. Seoul, Korea, Mar. 25, 1942; came to U.S., 1965; m. Vincenta Masciandaro, Sept. 16, 1967; 1 child, Alexander Hoyle. MA, Yale U., 1982; MD, Yonsei U., Seoul, 1965. Diplomate Am. Bd. Psychiatry and Neurology. Asst. prof. Yale U., New Haven, 1971-75, assoc. prof., 1975-80, prof., 1980-89, lectr. in psychiatry, 1989—. Dir. Behavioral Medicine Clinic, Yale U., 1980-89; dir. psychiat. cons. svc. Yale-New Haven Hosp., 1971-89; chief psychiatry VA Med Ctr., Fresno, Calif., 1989—; prof., vice chmn. dept. psychiatry U. Calif., San Francisco, 1989—, head dept. psychiatry, 1989—; cons. Am. Jour. Psychiatry, Archives Internal Medicine, Psychosomatic Medicine. Author: The Patient, 1980, 2d edit., 1985, 3d edit., 1992; editor: Psychiatry in the Practice of Medicine, 1983, Consultation-Liaison Psychiatry: 1990's & Beyond, 1994, Biopsychosocial Approaches in Primary Care: State of the Art and Challenges for the 21st Century, 1997. Fellow ACP, Internat. Coll. Psychosomatic Medicine (v.p.), Am. Acad. Psychosomatic Medicine; mem. AMA, AAUP, World Psychiat. Assn. Avocations: reading, music, skiing. Office: U Calif Dept Psychiat 2615 E Clinton Ave Fresno CA 93703-2223

LEIGH, JENNIFER JASON (JENNIFER LEIGH MORROW), actress; b. LA, Feb. 5, 1962; d. Barbara Turner and Vic Morrow; m. Noah Baumbach, Sept. 3, 2005. Student, Lee Strasberg Inst. Appearances include (films) Eyes of a Stranger, 1980, Fast Times at Ridgemont High, 1982, Wrong is Right, 1982, Easy Money, 1983, Grandview U.S.A., 1984, Flesh & Blood, 1985, The Hitcher, 1986, The Men's Club, 1986, Sister, Sister, 1987, Under Cover, 1987, Heart of Midnight, 1988, The Big Picture, 1989, Last Exit to Brooklyn, 1989 (Critic Soc. award 1990), Miami Blues, 1990 (Critic Soc. award 1990), Fire Princess, 1990, Crooked Hearts, 1991, Backdraft, 1991, Rush, 1992, Single White Female, 1992, The Prom, 1992, Short Cuts, 1993, The Hudsucker Proxy, 1994, Mrs. Parker and the Vicious Circle, 1994, Dolores Claiborne, 1994, Georgia, 1995, Kansas City, 1996, Bastard Out of Carolina, 1996, A Thousand Acres, 1997, Washington Square, 1997, eXistenZ, 1998, The King is Alive, 2000, Skipped Parts, 2000, Beautiful View, 2000, The Quickie, 2001, The Anniversary Party, 2001, Hey Arnold! The Movie, (voice) 2002, Road to Perdition, 2002, In the Cut, 2003, The Machinist, 2004, Palindromes, 2004, Childstar, 2004 (Genie award 2005), The Jacket, 2005, Easter Sunday, 2005, Rag Tale, 2005, Margot at the Wedding, 2007, Synecdoche, New York, 2008; (TV movies) Angel City, 1980, I Think I'm Having a Baby, 1981, The Killing of Randy Webster, 1981, The Best Little Girl in the World, 1981, The First Time, 1982, Have You Ever Been Ashamed of Your Parents?, 1983, Girls of the White Orchid, 1983, Picnic, 1986, Buried Alive, 1990, The Love Letter, 1998, Crossed Over, 2002 (mini series) Thanks of a Grateful Nation, 1998; prodr., actress Georgia, 1995; writer, dir., prodr., actor The Anniversary Party, 2001; TV guest appearances include The Waltons, 1972, Tracey Takes On..., 1996, King of the Hill, 1997; (TV series) Hercules (voice), 1998; appeared in music video Last Cup of Sorrow by Faith No More; (theatre) Cabaret, Proof, Abigail's Party, 2005. Named one of America's 10 Most Beautiful Women, Harper's Bazaar mag., 1989. Office: ICM c/o Tracey Jacobs 8942 Wilshire Blvd Beverly Hills CA 90211-1934 also: care Elaine Rich 2400 Whitman Pl Los Angeles CA 90068-2464

LEIJONHUFVUD, AXEL STIG BENGT, economics professor; b. Stockholm, Sept. 6, 1933; came to U.S., 1960; s. Erik Gabriel and Helene Adelheid (Neovius) L.; m. Marta Elisabeth Ising, June 10, 1955 (div. 1977); m. Earlene Joyce Craver, June 18, 1977; children—Carl Axel, Gabriella Helene, Christina Elisabeth Fil. kand., U. Lund, Sweden, 1960; MA, U. Pitts., Pa., 1961; PhD, Northwestern U., 1967; Fil. Dr. (hon.), U. Lund, Sweden, 1983; Dr. (hon.), U. Nice, Sophia-Antipolis, France, 1995. Acting asst. prof. econs. UCLA, 1964-67, assoc. prof. econs., 1967-71, prof. econs., 1971—, chair dept. econs., 1980-83, 90-92; dir. Ctr. for Computable Econs., 1992-97; prof. monetary theory and policy U. Trento, Italy, 1995—2008. Co-dir. summer workshops Siena Internat. Sch. Econ. Rsch., 1987-91; dir. program in econ. dynamics U. Trento, 2000—; participant profl. confs.; cons., lectr., vis. prof. econs. various colls. and univs.; cons. Republic of Tatarstan, 1994. Author: On Keynesian Economics and the Economics of Keynes: A Study in Monetary Theory, 1968, Keynes and the Classics: Two Lectures, 1969, Information and Coordination: Essays in Macroeconomic Theory, 1981; co-author (with D. Heymann): High Inflation, 1995, Macroeconomic Instability and Coordination, Selected Essays, 2000; editor: Monetary Theory as a Basis for Monetary Policy, 2001, Monetary Theory and Policy Experience, 2001, Organization and Economic Instability: Selected Essays, 2006; co-editor (with Elisabella de Antoni): (in Spanish) Information, coordination and macroeconomic instability, 2004. Econ. expert com. of pres. Kazakhstan, 1991-92. Brookings Instn. fellow, 1963-64; Marshall lectr. Cambridge U., Eng., 1974; Overseas fellow Churchill Coll., Cambridge, 1974; Inst. Advanced Study fellow, 1983-84 Mem. Am. Econ. Assn., Western Econ. Assn., History of Econs. Soc. Business E-Mail: axel@ucla.edu.

LEINART, MATTHEW STEPHEN, professional football player; b. Santa Ana, Calif., May 11, 1983; s. Bob and Linda Leinart; 1 child, Cole. BA in Sociology, U. So. Calif., 2006. Quarterback Ariz. Cardinals, Phoenix, 2006—. Recipient Manning award, 2004, Heisman Meml. Trophy, Heisman Trophy Trust, 2004, Johnny Unitas Golden Arm award, 2005; named First Team All-American, AP, 2003, 2004, 2005, Pac-10 Offensive Player of the Yr., 2003, Rose Bowl MVP, 2003, Sportsman of Yr., The Sporting News, 2005; named to All-Pac-10 first team. Achievements include being a member of NCAA Division I Bowl Championship Series National Championship winning University of Southern California Trojans, 2004, 2005. Office: Ariz Cardinals PO Box 888 Phoenix AZ 85001

LEINO, DEANNA ROSE, business educator; b. Leadville, Colo., Dec. 15, 1937; d. Arvo Ensio Leino and Edith Mary (Bonan) Leino Malenck; 1 adopted child, Michael Charles Bonan. BSBA, U. Denver, 1959, MS in Bus. Adminstrn., 1967; postgrad., C.C. Denver, U. No. Colo., Colo. State U., U. Colo., Met. State Coll. Cert. tchr., vocat. tchr., Colo. Tchr. Jefferson County Adult Edn., Lakewood, Colo., 1963-67; tchr. bus., coord. coop. office edn. Jefferson HS, Edgewater, Colo., 1959-93, ret., 1993; sales assoc. Joslins Dept. Store, Denver, 1978—89; mem. ea. team. clk. office automation Denver Svc. Ctr., Nat. Pk. Svc., 1993-94; wage hour tech. US Dept. Labor, 1994—. Instr. C.C. Denver, Red Rocks, 1967—81, U. Colo., Denver, 1976—79, Parks Coll. Bus. (now Everest Coll.), 1983—2009, Front Range C.C., 1998—2000; dist. advisor Future Bus. Leaders Am. Author short story. Active City of Edgewater Sister City Project Student Exch. Com., Opera Colo. Assocs. and Guild, I Pagliacci; pres. Career Women's Symphony Guild, 1980—82, 2008—09, sec., pres., 2008—; treas. Phantoms of Opera, 1982—83; pres. Colo. Symphony Guild, 2006—07, treas., 2008—; ex-officio trustee Denver Symphony Assn., 1980—82, Colo. Symphony Assn., 2006—07. Recipient Disting. Svc. award Jefferson County Sch. Bd., 1980, Tchr. Who Makes a Difference award Sta. KCNC/Rocky Mountain News, 1990, Youth Leader award Lakewood Optimist Club, 1993; named to Jefferson HS Wall of Fame, 1981, Jefferson County Hist. Commn. Hall of Fame, 2000, countess of the Wheat Ridge Carnation Festival, 2001. Mem. NEA (life), Colo. Edn. Assn., Jefferson County Edn. Assn., Colo. Vocat. Assn., Am. Vocat. Assn., Colo. Bus. Educators, Profl. Sec. Internat., Career Women's Symphony Guild, Profl. Panhellenic Assn., Colo. Congress Fgn. Lang. Tchr., Wheat Ridge C. of C. (edn. and scholarship com.), Federally Employed Women, Tyrolean Soc. Denver, Delta Pi Epsilon, Phi Chi Theta, Beta Gamma Sigma, Alpha Lambda Delta. Republican. Roman Catholic. Avocations: decorating wedding cakes, crocheting, sewing, music, world travel. Home: 3712 Allison St Wheat Ridge CO 80033-6124 Office Phone: 720-264-3257. Personal E-mail: deannaleino@comcast.net.

LEITH, CECIL ELDON, retired physicist; b. Boston, Jan. 31, 1923; s. Cecil Eldon and Elizabeth (Benedict) L.; m. Mary Louise Henry, July 18, 1942; children: Ann, John, Paul. AB, U. Calif. at, Berkeley, 1943, PhD, 1957. Exptl. physicist Lawrence Radiation Lab., Berkeley, 1946-52, theoretical physicist Livermore, Calif., 1952-68; sr. scientist Nat. Center for Atmospheric Research, Boulder, Colo., 1968-83, div. dir., 1977-81; physicist Lawrence Livermore Nat. Lab., Calif., 1983-90. Symons Meml. lectr. Royal Meteorol. Soc., London, 1978; chmn. com. on atmospheric scis. NRC, 1978-80, sci. program evaluation com. Univ. Corp. for Atmospheric Rsch., 1991-96; mem. joint sci. com. world climate research program World Meteorol. Organ. and Internat. Council Sci. Unions, 1976-83; mem. program adv. com. Office Advanced Sci. Computing, NSF, 1984-85. Served with AUS, 1944-46. Fellow Am. Phys. Soc., Am. Meteorol. Soc. (Meisinger award 1967, Rossby research medal 1982) Home: 627 Carla St Livermore CA 94550-2316

LEITMANN, GEORGE, mechanical engineer, educator; b. Vienna, May 24, 1925; arrived in U.S., 1940, naturalized, 1944; s. Josef and Stella (Fischer) Leitmann; m. Nancy Lloyd, Jan. 28, 1955; children: Josef Lloyd, Elaine Michèle. BS, Columbia U., 1949, MA, 1950; PhD, U. Calif., Berkeley, 1956; D Engring. honoris causa, Tech. U. Vienna, 1988; D honoris causa, U. Paris, 1989, Tech. U. Darmstadt, 1990. Physicist, head aeroballistics sect. U.S. Naval Ordnance Sta., China Lake, 1950-57; mem. faculty U. Calif., Berkeley, 1957—, prof. engring. sci., 1963—, first acad. ombudsman, 1968—70, prof. grad. sch., 1995—, assoc. dean acad. affairs, 1981-90, assoc. dean rsch., 1990-94, acting dean, 1988, chair faculty, 1994-98, assoc. dean internat. rels., 2003—. Cons. to aerospace industry and govt.; lectr. in field. Author: (book) An Introduction to Optimal Control, 1966, Quantitative and Qualitative Games, 1969, The Calculus of Variations and Optimal Control, 1981; editor: (jour.) Math Analysis Applications, 1985—2002; assoc. editor Optimization Theory Applications; contbr. 300 articles to profl. jours.; assoc. editor, mem. editl. bd. (to 11 jour.); translator: The Mantle of Dreams. Chmn. bd. dirs. ARTSHIP Found.; master knight Order of Knights of Vine; mem. Acad. Italiana della Cucina. With AUS, 1944—46, ETO, combat engrs., special agent CIC. Decorated Croix de Guerre France, Fourragere Belgium, Comdr.'s Cross, Order of Merit Germany, commendatore Order of Merit Italy; recipient Pendray Aerospace Lit. award, AIAA, 1979, Mechanics and Control of Flight award, 1984, Von Humboldt U.S. Sr. Scientist award, Von Humboldt Found., 1980, Levy medal, Franklin Inst., 1981, Berkeley citation, U. Calif.-Berkeley, 1991, von Humboldt medal, von Humboldt Found., 1991, Rufus Oldenburger medal, ASME, 1995, Distng. Engring. Alumni award, 2002, Disting. Emeritus of Yr., 2004, 1st recipient Isaacs award, Internat. Soc. Dynamic Games, 2004, Werner Heisenberg medal, von Humboldt Found., 2005; named Miller Rsch. prof., 1966; Berkeley fellow, 2002. Mem.: NAE, World Innovation Found., Georgian Acad. Sci., A. V. Humboldt Assn. Am. (pres. 1994—97), Bavarian Acad. Sci., Georgian Acad. Engring., Russian Acad. Natural Sci., Argentine Nat. Acad. Engring., Internat. Acad. Astronautics, Acad. Sci. Bologna. Avocations: art, swimming, oenology, international relations. Office: U Calif Coll Engring Berkeley CA 94720-0001 Business E-Mail: gleit@berkeley.edu.

LEITZELL, TERRY LEE, lawyer; b. Williamsport, Pa., Apr. 15, 1942; s. Ernest Richard and Inez Mae (Taylor) L.; m. Lucy Acker Emmerich, June 18, 1966; children: Thomas Addison, Charles Taylor, Robert Davies. AB, Cornell U., 1964; JD, U. Pa., 1967. Bar: DC 1967. Consular officer Dept. State, Bombay, India, 1968-70, atty.-adv. for oceans affairs Washington, 1970-77, chief U.S. negotiator UN law of sea negotiations Geneva, also NYC, 1974-77; asst. adminstr. for fisheries and dir. Nat. Marine Fisheries Service, NOAA, Dept. Commerce, Washington, 1978-81; practice law Washington, 1981-92, Seattle, 1992—; gen. counsel Icicle Seafoods, Seattle. Mem.: Wash. Bar Assn. Democrat. Office: Icicle Seafoods 4019 21st Ave W Ste 300 Seattle WA 98199-1299 Home: 16 Elm St Topsham ME 04086-1402 Office Phone: 206-281-5372. Business E-Mail: terryl@icicleseafoods.com.

LEIWEKE, TIMOTHY, sports executive, marketing professional; b. St. Louis, Apr. 21, 1957; s. John Robert and Helen (Caicuey) L.; m. Bernadette Leiweke; 1 child, Francesa Leiweke. Grad. high sch., St. Louis. Salesperson New Eng. Mut. Life Ins. Co., St. Louis, 1976-79; asst. gen. mgr. St. Louis Steamers/MISL, 1979-80; gen. mgr. Balt. Blast/MISL, 1980-81; v.p., gen. mgr. Kansas City (Mo.) Comets/MISL, 1981-84; v.p. Leiweke and Co., Kansas City, 1984-85; pres. Kansas City Comets/MISL, 1986-88; v.p. sales and mktg. div. Minn. Timberwolves, Mpls., 1988-91; sr. v.p. of bus. ops. Denver Nuggets, Denver, 1991-92, pres., 1992-96, LA Kings, Los Angeles, 1996—. Bd. dirs. Kidney Found., Minn., 1989—, Spl. Olympics, Minn., 1989—, Timberwolves Community Found., Minn., 1989—; pres. Staples Ctr. Arena. Named Rookie of Yr. Mo. Life Underwriters, 1976, Kansas City Citian of Yr. Kansas City Press Club, 1983; named one of The Most Influential People in the World of Sports Bus. Week, 2007, 08; recipient William Brownfield award US Jaycees, 1978, William Brownfield award Mo. Jaycees, 1978, Excalibur award Am. Cancer Soc., 1987. Mem. Kansas City Mktg. and Sales Execs., Mpls. Club. Avocations: running, golf, cross country skiing, soccer, basketball. Office: 1111 S Figueroa St Ste 3100 Los Angeles CA 90015-1333

LEIWEKE, TOD, professional sports team executive; m. Tara Leiweke; children: Tyler, Tori. Prin. Leiweke & Co., Kansas City, 1982—87; v.p. mktg. and broadcasting Golden State Warriors, NBA, 1987—91, pres. arena devel. co., 1994; exec. v.p. Orca Bay Sports and Entertainment; exec. dir. First Tee, World Golf Found.; pres. Minn. Wild Minn. Hockey Ventures Group LP, St. Paul, 1999—2001, COO, 2001—04; CEO Seattle Seahawks, 2004—; interim gen. mgr. Portland Trailblazers, 2007—. Office: Seattle Seahawks 12 Seahawks Way Renton WA 98056-1572

LEMAN, LOREN DWIGHT, former lieutenant governor, civil engineer; b. Pomona, Calif., Dec. 2, 1950; s. Nick and Marian (Broady) L.; m. Carolyn Rae Bratvold, June 17, 1978; children: Joseph, Rachel, Nicole. BSCE, Oreg. State U., 1972; MS in Civil, Environ. Engring., Stanford U., 1973; studied Arctic engring., U. Alaska, Anchorage. Registered profl. engr., Alaska. Project mgr. CH2M Hill, San Francisco, 1973, Reston, Va., 1973-74, Ketchikan, Alaska, 1974-75, Anchorage, 1975-87; owner Loren Leman, P.E., Anchorage, 1987—; mem. Alaska Ho. of Reps., 1989-93, Alaska State Senate, Dist. G, Juneau, 1993—2003; lt. gov State of Alaska, Juneau, 2003—07. Mem. Anchorage Hazardous Materials Commn., Local Emergency Planning Com., 1989-93. Contbr. articles to profl. jours. Mem. Breakthrough Com., Anchorage, 1978; del. to conv. Rep. Party of Alaska, 1976-90; basketball coach Grace Christian Sch., Anchorage, 1985-88; commr. Pacific States Marine Fisheries Commn.; past chmn. Pacific Fisheries Legis. Task Force. Mem. ASCE, Alaska Water Mgmt. Assn., Am. Legis. Exch. Coun., Water Environment Fedn., Toastmasters (pres.). Republican. Avocations: reading, fishing, bicycling, music, basketball. Office Phone: 907-465-3520.

LEMAS, NOAH, small business owner; b. Santa Ana, Calif., 1970; married; 2 children. BA in Geography, U. Calif., Santa Barbara; MBA, Portland State U., Ore.; student in internat. fin., Euromed Marseille, France. Owner, ind. retailer Sunriver Snowboards, Side Effect Boardshop. Mem.: Beta Gamma Sigma. Democrat. Avocations: hiking, fishing, baseball, golf, snowboarding. Office: Side Effect Boardshop 137 SW Century Dr Bend OR 97702 Office Phone: 541-312-8255.

LEMIEUX, CLAUDE, professional hockey player, professional sports team executive; b. Buckingham, Que., July 16, 1965; Right wing Montreal Canadiens, 1983—90, NJ Devils, 1990—95, 1999—2000, Colo. Avalanche, 1995—99, Phoenix Coyotes, 2000—03, Worcester Sharks, 2008—09, San Jose Sharks, 2009—; pres. Phoenix Roadrunners, 2005. Mem. Stanley Cup Championship Team, 1986, 95, 96. Recipient Guy Lafleur Trophy, 1985, Conn Smythe Trophy MVP in Playoffs, 1995; named to Que. Major Jr. League All-Star 2nd Team, 1983. Achievements include being a member of Stanely Cup Champion Montreal Canadiens, 1986, New Jersey Devils, 1995, 2000, Colorado Avalanche, 1996. Office: c/o Lemieux Acad 2021 E Camelback Rd Ste A38 Phoenix AZ 85016 also: San Jose Sharks 525 W Santa Clara St San Jose CA 95113

LEMIEUX, LINDA DAILEY, museum director; b. Cleve., Sept. 6, 1953; d. Leslie Leo LeMieux Jr. and Mildred Edna (Dailey) Tutt. BA, Beloit Coll., 1975; MA, U. Mich., 1979; A cert., Mus. Mgmt. Program, Boulder, Colo., 1987. Asst. curator Old Salem, Inc., Winston-Salem, NC, 1979-82; curator Clarke House, Chgo., 1982-84, Western Mus. Mining and Industry, Colorado Springs, Colo., 1985-86, dir., 1987—. Author: Prairie Avenue Guidebook, 1985; editor: The Golden Years--Mines in the Cripple Creek District, 1987; contbr. articles to mags. and newspapers. Fellow Hist. Deerfield, Mass., 1974—. Rsch. grantee Early Am. Industries Assn., 1978. Mem. Am. Assn. Mus., Am. Assn. State and Local History, Colo.-Wyo. Mus. Assn., Colo. Mining Assn., Mountain Plains Assn. Mus., Women in Mining, Colo. Mont. Wyo. State Conf. Edn. Com. NAACP. Mem. First Congl. Ch. Home: 1337 Hermosa Way Colorado Springs CO 80906-3050 Office: Western Mus Mining & Industry 1025 N Gate Rd Colorado Springs CO 80921-3018 E-mail: director@wmmi.org, lindalemieux1@aol.com.

LEMIRE, DAVID STEPHEN, school psychologist, educator; b. Roswell, N.Mex., May 23, 1949; s. Joseph Armand and Jeanne (Longwill) Lemire. BA, Linfield Coll., McMinnville, Oreg., 1972, MEd, 1974; EdS, Idaho State U., Pocatello, 1978; postgrad., U. Wyo., Laramie, EdS in Ednl. Adminstrn. and Instrnl. Leadership, 1988, postgrad.; PhD in Curriculum and Instrn., Kans. State U., Manhattan, 2005. Cert. sch. counselor, sch. psychologist, psychotherapist. Student pers. worker, psychology instr., Calif. Sch. counselor, psychol. technician and tchr. Goshen County Sch. Dist. 1, Torrington, Wyo.; counselor Aspen (Colo.) HS; sch. counselor Unita County Sch. Dist., Evanston, Wyo., coord. R&D Lifelong Learning Ctr., 1986—87; dir. spl. svcs. and sch. psychologist Bighorn County Sch. Dist. #4, Basin, Wyo., 1989—90; sch. psychologist Sweetwater County Sch. Dist. #2, Green River, Wyo., 1990—91; dir. housing, residence supr. Pratt (Kans.) CC, 1991—92; tchr. Highland CC and Cloud County CC, Kans.; pres. David Lemire Software Enterprises, Evanston; dir. Inst. for Advanced Study of Thinkology. Author (with Richard Mueller): Instructional Psychology, Fifty or More Ethical Dilemas: Reading/Writing Activities for the Secondary and College Classroom; author: Twenty Simple and Inexpensive Learning Style/Personal Style/Self Concept Instruments for Professionals and Educators with Rsearch and Supporting Documentation; editor (former): WACD Jour.; editor: (former mng.) Jour. Humanistic Edn.; mem. editl. bd.: Jour. Humanistic Counseling, Edn. and Devel., The Profl. Sch. Counselor, Jour. Counseling and Devel., Jour. Devel. Edn.; contbr. articles to profl. jours. Mem.: APA, ASCD, Nat. Assn. Sch. Psychologists (cert.). Office: Creative Therapeutics Adminstrv Offices 2390 Riviera St Reno NV 89509-1144 Personal E-mail: lemire62@msn.com.

LEMKE, HERMAN ERNEST FREDERICK, JR., retired elementary school educator, consultant; b. Argo, Ill., July 13, 1919; s. Herman and Augusta Victoria (Statt) L.; m. Geneva Octavene Davidson, Sept. 5, 1942 (dec.); children: Patricia, Herman E.F. III, Gloria, John, Elizabeth. BA, George Peabody Coll., 1949, MA, 1952. Cert. social sci. tchr., Tenn., elem. tchr., Calif. Tchr. Cadd Parish Sch., Shreveport, La., 1950-55, Pacific Sch. Dist., Sacramento, 1956-58, Sacramento (Calif.) Sch. Dist., 1958-89; part-time tchr. Sacramento (Calif.) County Sch., 1974-84, ret., 2002. Substitute tchr., 1989—. Co-author: Natural History Guide, 1963, (field guide) Outdoor World of Sacramento Region, 1975; contbr. articles to profl. jours. Asst. dist. Commn. Boys Scouts Am., Shreveport, 1954, cubmaster, 1954; leader 4-H Club, Shreveport, 1950-54; elder Faith Luth. Ch., Fair Oaks, Calif., 1981-88. Recipient Scouter award, Boy Scouts Am., Shreveport, 1954, Honorary Svc. award Am. Winn Sch. PTA, 1982, Calif. Life Diploma Elem. Schs., 1961. Mem. Calif. Congress Parents Tchrs. Inc. (life). Democrat. Avocations: backpacking, coin collecting/numismatics, stamp collecting/philately, antiques, fishing. Home: 6795 Sylvan Rd Citrus Heights CA 95610 Personal E-mail: hermanlemke@worldnet.att.net.

LEMLEY, MARK ALAN, law educator; b. St. Louis, Nov. 20, 1966; s. Alan Norman Lemley and Linda Leigh (Allen) Huheey; m. Rose Anne Hagan, Mar. 11, 1995. AB in Econs. and Polit. Sci., Stanford U., 1988; JD, U. Calif., Berkeley, 1991. Bar: Calif. 1991, US Ct. Appeals 9th Cir. 1991, US Ct. Appeals 7th Cir. 1996, US Ct. Appeals Fed. Cir. 1997, U.S. Ct. Appeals 2nd Cir., U.S. Supreme Ct. 2002. Law clk. to Judge Dorothy W. Nelson US Ct. of Appeals 9th Cir., Pasadena, Calif., 1991-92; atty. Brown & Bain, Palo Alto, Calif., 1992-93, Fish & Richardson P.C., Menlo Park, Calif., 1993—94, of counsel Austin, Tex., 1995—2001, Keker & Van Nest, San Francisco, 2001—; asst. prof. U. Tex. Sch. Law, Austin, 1994-98, prof., 1998—99, Marrs McLean prof. law, 1999—2000; prof. law Boalt Hall Sch. Law, U. Calif., Berkeley, 2000—04, co-dir. Berkeley Ctr. for Law & Tech., 2000—04, Elizabeth Josslyn Boalt Chair in Law, 2003—04; William H. Neukom prof. law Stanford Law Sch., 2004—, dir. Program in Law, Sci. & Tech., 2004—. Vis. prof. Boalt Hall Sch. Law, U. Calif., Berkeley, 1998, Stanford Law Sch., 2003; bd. editors Am. Intellectual Property Law Assn. Quarterly Jour., 1994-2000; mem. No. Dist. Calif. Working Com. on Model Patent Jury Instruction, 2000-, Calif. Blue Ribbon Task Force on Nanotechnology, 2004-05. Co-author: Antitrust, 1996, 2004, Intellectual Property in the New Technological Age, 1997, 4th edit., 2006, Software and Internet Law, 2000, 3d edit., 2006, IP and Antitrust, 2001. Adv. bd. Electronic Frontier Found., 2004-. Recipient Thelen Marrin Prize, Boalt Hall Sch. Law, Order of the Coif; named Young Alumnus of Yr., 2002, World Econ. Forum Young Global Leader, 2007; named one of 100 Most Influential Lawyers, Nat. Law Jour., 2006, Litigation's Rising Stars, The Am. Lawyer, 2007. Mem. Am. Intellectual Property Law Assn., Am. Law and Economics Assn., U. Coop. Soc. (bd. dirs. 1995-99), Assn. of Am. Law Schools (chair law and computers sect. 1997, chair antitrust sect. 2006). Avocations: cooking, hiking. Office: Stanford Law Sch Crown Quadrangle 559 Nathan Abbott Way Stanford CA 94305 Office Phone: 650-723-4605. Office Fax: 650-725-0253. Business E-Mail: mlemley@law.stanford.edu.

LEMLY, THOMAS ADGER, lawyer; b. Dayton, Ohio, Jan. 31, 1943; s. Thomas Moore and Elizabeth (Adger) L.; m. Kathleen Brame, Nov. 24, 1984; children: Elizabeth Hayden, Joanna Marsden, Isabelle Stafford, Kate Brame. BA, Duke U., 1970; JD with honors, U. N.C., 1973. Bar: Wash. 1973, U.S. Dist. Ct. (we. dist.) Wash. 1973, U.S. Ct. Appeals (9th cir.) 1975, U.S. Supreme Ct. 1980. Assoc. Davis Wright Tremaine, Seattle, 1973-79, ptnr., 1979—. Contbg. editor Employment Discrimination Law, 1984-87, 94—; editor Wash., Oreg., Alaska and Calif. Employment Law Deskbooks, 1987—. Chmn. Pacific Coast Labor Conf., Seattle, 1983; trustee Plymouth Congregational Ch., 1980-84, Seattle Opera Assn., 1991—. Fellow Am. Coll. Trial Lawyers; mem. ABA (labor employment law sect. 1975—, subcom. chmn. 1984-90, govt. liaison com. 1982-94), Seattle-King County Bar Assn. (chmn. labor sect.), Assn. Wash. Bus. (sec.-treas. 2002-03, trustee 1992—, vice chair 2003-2004, bd. chair 2004-2005, chmn. human resources coun. 1993-2002, chmn. employment law task force 1987-93), U. N.C. Bar Found. (bd. dirs. 1973-76), Seattle Duke Alumni Assn. (pres. 1979-84), Order of Coif, Wash. Athletic Club (Seattle), Rotary. Republican. Presbytarian. Home: 1614 7th Ave W Seattle WA 98119-2919 Office: Davis Wright Tremaine 2600 Century Sq 1501 4th Ave Seattle WA 98101-1688 Office Phone: 206-628-7716. E-mail: tomlemly@dwt.com.

LEMMONS, KASI, actress, film director; b. St. Louis, Feb. 24, 1961; m. Vondie Curtis-Hall, 1995; 2 children. Actress (TV films) 11th Victim, 1979, Adam's Apple, 1986, The Court-Martial of Jackie Robinson, 1990, The Big One: The Great Los Angeles Earthquake, 1990, Before the Storm, 1991, Afterburn, 1992, Override, 1994, Zooman, 1995, (films) School Daze, 1988, Vampire's Kiss, 1989, Silence of the Lambs, 1991, The Five Heartbeats, 1991, Candyman, 1992, Hard Target, 1993, Fear of a Black Hat, 1994, Drop Squad, 1994, Gridlock'd, 1997, 'Til There Was You, 1997, Liars' Dice, 1998, Waist Deep, 2006, writer, dir. Eve's Bayou, 1997 (Outstanding Directorial Debut, Nat. Bd. Review, 1997, Spirit award for Best First Feature, Film Ind., 1998, Best Dir., Black Film award, 1998), Dr. Hugo, 1998; dir.: (films) The Caveman's Valentine, 2001, Talk to Me, 2007 (Outstanding Directing in a Motion Picture, NAACP Image award, 2008, Best Dir., African Am. Film Critics Assn., 2007). Office: c/o The Gersh Agy 232 N Canon Dr Beverly Hills CA 90210

LEMON, LESLIE GENE, retired diversified financial services company executive, lawyer; b. Davenport, Iowa, June 14, 1940; BS, U. Ill., 1962, LLB, 1964. Bar: Ill. 1964, Ariz. 1972. Asst. gen. counsel Am. Farm Bur. Fedn., Chgo., 1964-69; sr. atty. Armour and Co., Chgo., 1969-71; with Viad Corp (formerly The Dial Corp and Greyhound Corp.), Phoenix, 1971-99; gen. counsel The Dial Corp (formerly Greyhound Corp.), Phoenix, 1977-96, v.p., 1979-99; ret., 1999; chmn. State of Ariz. Citizens Clean Elections Commn., 1999—2003. Vestryman All Saints Episcopal Ch., Phoenix, 1975-81; trustee Phoenix Art Mus., 1985-98; bd. dirs. Phoenix Children's Hosp., 1985-98; bd. visitors U. Calif. Med. Sch., Davis, 1983—2008. Mem. ABA, Nat. Conf. Uniform Law Commrs., Assn. Gen. Counsel, Maricopa County Bar Assn., State Bar Ariz., Phoenix C. of C. (bd. dirs. 1989-95), Am. Arbitration Assn. (bd. dirs. 1996-2004). Home: 1136 W Butler Dr Phoenix AZ 85021-4428 E-mail: l.lemon@azbar.org.

LEMONE, MARGARET ANNE, atmospheric scientist; b. Columbia, Mo., Feb. 21, 1946; d. David Vandenberg and Margaret Ann (Meyer) LeMone; m. Peter Augustus Gilman; children: Patrick Cyrus, Sarah Margaret. BA in Math., U. Mo., 1967; PhD in Atmospheric Scis., U. Wash., 1972. Postdoctoral fellow Nat. Ctr. for Atmospheric Rsch., Boulder, Colo., 1972-73, scientist, 1973-92, sr. scientist, 1992—; chief scientist Globe, 2003—. Mem. bd. on atmospheric sci. and climate NRC, 1993-97, 2001-04; mem. sci. adv. com. U.S. Weather Rsch. Program, 1997-99. Contbr. articles to profl. jours.; contbg. author: D.C. Heath Earth Science, 1983-93; editor Jour. Atmospheric Scis., 1991-95. Woodrow Wilson fellow, NSF fellow, NDEA fellow, 1967. Fellow AAAS, Am. Meteorol. Soc. (councillor, mem. exec. com. 1992-96, Editor's award, Charles Anderson award); mem. Am. Geophys. Union, Nat. Acad. Engring. Achievements include research in dynamics of linear convection (roll vortices) in daytime atmospheric boundary layer and its relationship to clouds; demonstrating that bands of deep convection (like squall lines) can increase the vertical shear of horizontal wind (contrary to conventional wisdom at that time); developing technique to estimate small fluctuations in air pressure from aircraft flying over land, used to estimate pressure field around clouds and storms. Home: 2048 Balsam Dr Boulder CO 80304-3618 Office: Nat Ctr Atmospheric Rsch PO Box 3000 Boulder CO 80307-3000 Business E-Mail: lemone@ucar.edu.

LEMPERT, PHILIP, advertising executive, writer, news correspondent; b. East Orange, NJ, Apr. 17, 1953; s. Sol and Lillian E. L.; m. Laura Gray; 1 son BS in Mktg., Drexel U., 1974; degree in Package Design, Pratt Inst., 1978. With Lempert Co., Belleville, NJ, 1974—89; pres. Consumer Insight, Inc., 1990—; sr. v.p., sr. ptnr. AGE Wave Inc., 1991—93; pres., CEO Supermarketguru.com, 1993—. Founder, CEO Supermarket Alliance, 1993—; adj. prof. Fairleigh Dickinson U., Seton Hall U. Pub., editor newsletter The Lempert Report; editor Factus, Figures and the Future e-Newsletter; lectr. in field Author: Phil Lempert's Supermarket Shopping and Value Guide, 1996, Top Ten Trends for Baby Boomers for Business, 1997, Being the Shopper: Understanding Consumer Choices for the Second Millenium, 2002; columnist Chgo. Tribune, 1993-98, Knight-Ridder/Tribune Syndicate, L.A. Times, 2000-02, Progressive Grocer mag., 2003—; editor (newsletter) Facts, Figures and the Future, Xtreme Retail 23; food editor, corr. Today Show, KNBC-TV, BBC Radio 5; talk show host WOR Radio Network; news corr. Discovery Health Network Chmn. Tribune Food Task Force, 1996-98; bd. dirs. Powerhouse Theatre, Partnership for Food Safety; adv. bd. Partnership for Food Safety Mem. Am. Assn. Advt. Agys. (bd. govs. 1986-88, legis. liason 1988-90, legis. coord. 1987-90), Nat. Food Brokers Assn. (chmn. food svcs. com.)

LENARD, MICHAEL BARRY, merchant banker, lawyer; b. Chgo., May 20, 1955; s. Henry Madart and Jacqueline Jo Anne (Silver) L.; children: Madeline Michael, Nicholas Xavier. BBA, U. Wis., 1977; postgrad., NYU, 1981-82; JD, U. So. Calif., 1982. From assoc. to ptnr. Latham & Watkins, LA, 1984-93; mng. dir., counsellor William E. Simon & Sons, LA, 1993—; mng. dir. Indsl. Sport, LA, 2001—03; mng. dir. counsellor Paladin Group, 2003—. Bd. dir. William E. Simon & Sons, Hong Kong; spl. adv. bus. affairs U.S. Olympic Com., Washington, 2000—02. With So. Calif. Law Rev. mag., 1980-81. V.p. U.S. Olympic Com., 1989-96, mem. exec. com., bd. dirs., 1985-96, mem. athletes' adv. coun., 1981-89, vice chmn. athletes' adv. coun., 1985-89; named to Internat. Coun. for Arbitration of Sport, 1994—; bd. dirs. L.A. Sports Coun., 1988—, Atlanta Com. for Olympic Games, 1990-98. Named semi-finalist Outstanding Undergrad. Achievement award, 1977, USA Team Handball Athlete of Yr., 1985, USOC Olympian Mag. Team Handball SportsMan of Yr., 1985, Nat. Champion in Team Handball, 1975, 77, 79-80, 82, 87, 95; recipient Harry A. Bullis scholarship, 1977, Disting. Svc. award U.S. Sports Acad., 1996; mem. 1984 Olympic Team, U.S. Nat. Team, 1977-85 (capt. 1985). Mem. Order of the Coif, Phi Kappa Phi, Beta Gamma Sigma, Beta Alpha Psi, Phi Eta Sigma, Urban Land Inst. Achievements include development of A.C. Sushi Masters, 1985. Business E-Mail: mlenard@paladinrp.com.

LENDARIS, GEORGE GREGORY, systems science educator; b. Helper, Utah, Apr. 2, 1935; s. Gregory George and Argie (Xenakis) L.; m. Irene Kokinos, June 26, 1958 (dec. July 1988); children: Miriam, Dorothy. BSEE cum laude., U. Calif., Berkeley, 1957, MSEE, 1958; PhD in Electrical Engring., 1961. Registered profl. engr., Calif., Oreg. Sr. rsch. engr., program mgr. Gen. Motors Corp., Defense Rsch. Labs., Santa Barbara, Calif., 1961-69; assoc. prof. systems sci., chmn. faculty Oreg. Grad. Ctr. for Rsch., Beaverton, 1969-71; prof. systems sci., electrical engring. Portland State U. Systems Sci. PhD Program, Oregon, 1971—; with Accurate Automation Corp., Chattanooga, 1993—, also bd. dirs. Cons. various bus.; editorial bd. Internat. Jour. of Gen. Systems (Gordon & Breach), 1974—, Systems Rsch. Jour. 1985—, IEEE Transactions on Neural Networks, 1991—; chmn. gen. Internat. Joint Conf. on Neural Networks, Oreg., 1991-93; presiding officer Faculty Senate Portland State U., 1995-96. Author jour. article Diffraction Pattern Sampling, 1970, selected reprints book IEEE, 1978, chpt. in book Conceptual Graphs & Neural Networks, 1992, numerous conf. articles. Choir dir. local chs. Greek Orthodox Ch., Santa Barbara, Portland, 1962-73, pres., chmn. various coms., 1962—, mem. justice and human rights com. local ch., Portland, 1974—; mem. Gov.'s Tech. Adv. Com., Oreg., 1970-72, oreg. State Senate Task Force on Econ. Devel., 1972-73; mem. adv. panel Portland Energy Commn., 1980. NAS fellow, 1974. Fellow IEEE; mem. AAAS, Systems, Man and Cybernetics Soc., Internat. Neural Network Soc. (bd. govs. 1996—), Internat. Soc. Knowledge Engrs., Am. Helenic Edn. Progressive Assn., Sigma Xi, Tau Beta Pi, Eta Kappa Nu. Avocations: woodworking, folk dancing instructor, singing. Office: Portland State U Sys Sci PhD Program PO Box 751 Portland OR 97207-0751

LENFANT, CLAUDE JEAN-MARIE, physician, director; b. Paris, Oct. 12, 1928; arrived in U.S., 1960, naturalized, 1965; s. Robert and Jeanine (Leclerc) Lenfant; children: Philipe, Bernard, Martine Lenfant Wayman, Brigitte Lenfant Martin, Christine. BS, U. Rennes, France, 1948; MD, U. Paris, 1956; DSc (hon.), SUNY, 1988. Asst. prof. physiology U. Lille, France, 1959—60; from clin. instr. to prof. medicine physiology and biophysics U. Wash. Med. Sch., 1961—72; assoc. dir. lung programs Nat. Heart, Lung and Blood Inst. NIH, Bethesda, Md., 1970—72, dir. divsn. lung diseases, 1972—80; dir. Fogarty Internat. Ctr. NIH, 1980—82, assoc. dir. internat. rsch., 1980—82; dir. Nat. Heart, Lung and Blood Inst., 1982—2003, disting. scientist emeritus, 2003—; pres. World Hypertension League, 2000—06; exec. dir. Global Initiative Asthma, and Global Initiative Chronic Obstructive Lung Disease, 2005—. Mem. editl. bd.: Undersea Biomed. Rsch., 1973—75, Respiration Physiology, 1971—78, Am. Jour. Physiology and Jour. Applied Physiology, 1970—76, Am. Rev. Respiratory Disease, 1973—79, Jour. Applied Physiology, 1976—82, Am. Jour. Medicine, 1979—82; editor: Lung Biology in Health and Disease. Elected mem., planning group Global Alliance Against Chronic Respiratory Disease/WHO, 2007—; apptd. mem., Expert Panel Cardiovascular Disease WHO Etpest, 2007—. Recipient Nathan Davis award, AMA, 1998, Gold Heart award, Am. Heart Assn., 2002, European Lung Found. award, 2002. Fellow: Royal Soc. Medicine, Royal Coll. Physicians; mem.: French Nat. Acad. Medicine, USSR Acad. Med. Scis., Inst. Medicine of NAS, Undersea Med. Soc., NY Acad. Scis., Am. Physiol. Soc., French Physiol. Soc., Am. Soc. Clin. Investigation, Assn. Am. Physicians, Alpha Omega Alpha. Home: PO Box 65278 Vancouver WA 98665-0010 Personal E-mail: lenfantc@prodigy.net.

LENHOFF, HOWARD MAER, biological sciences educator, academic administrator; b. North Adams, Mass., Jan. 27, 1929; s. Charles and G. Sarah Lenhoff; m. Sylvia Grossman, June 20, 1954; children: Gloria, Bernard. BA, Coe Coll., 1950, D.Sc. (hon.), 1976; PhD, Johns Hopkins U., 1955. USPHS fellow Loomis Lab., Greenwich, Conn.,

1954-56; vis. lectr. Howard U., Washington, 1957-58; rsch. assoc. George Washington U., Washington, 1957-58; postdoctoral fellow Carnegie Instn., Washington, 1958; investigator Howard Hughes Med. Inst., Miami, 1958-63; prof. biology, dir. Lab. for Quantitative Biology U. Miami, Coral Gables, 1963-69; prof. biol. scis. U. Calif., Irvine, 1969—96, prof. polit. sci., 1986, assoc. dean biol. scis., 1969-71, dean grad. div., 1971-73, faculty asst. to vice chancellor of student affairs, 1986-88, 90-96, chair faculty senate, 1989-90, prof. emeritus, rsch. prof., 1993—; adj. prof. psychology U. Mass., Amherst, 2001—03. Adj. prof. biology U. Miss., Oxford, 2001—; vis. scientist, Louis Lipsky fellow Weizmann Inst. Sci., Rehovot, Israel, 1968-69; vis. prof. chem. engring., Rothschild fellow Israel Inst. Tech., 1973-74; vis. prof. Hebrew U., Jerusalem, spring 1970, fall 1971, 77-78; Hubert Humphrey Inst. fellow Ben Gurion U., Beersheva, Israel, 1981; sr. rsch. fellow Jesus Coll., U. Oxford, 1988; dir. Nelson Rsch. & Devel. Co., Irvine, 1971-73; bd. dirs. BioProbe Internat., Inc., Tustin, Calif., 1983-89, chmn. bd., 1983-86. Editor/author: Biology of Hydra, 1961, Hydra, 1969, Experimental Coelenterate Biology, 1972, Coelenterate Biology— Review and Perspectives, 1974, Hydra: Research Methods, 1983, Enzyme Immunoassay, 1985, From Trembley's Polyps to New Directions in Research on Hydra, 1985, Hydra and the Birth of Experimental Biology, 1986, Biology of Nematocysts, Conception to Birth, 1988, Williams-Beuren Syndrome, 2006, The Strangest Song, 2006, Black Jews, Jews and Other Heroes, 2007; mem. editl. bd. Jour. Solid Phase Biochemistry, 1976-80. Vice chmn. So. Calif. div. Am. Assn. Profs. for Peace in Middle East, 1972-80; bd. dirs. Am. Assn. for Ethiopian Jews, 1974-93, pres., 1978-82; bd. govs. Israel Bonds Orange County, Calif., 1974-80, Dade County Heart Assn., Miami, 1958-61, So. Calif. Technion Soc., 1976; pres. Hillel Coun. of Orange County, 1976-78; nat. chmn. faculty div. State of Israel Bonds, 1976; mem. sci. adv. bd. Am. Friends of Weizman Inst. Sci., 1980-84; bd. dirs. Hi Hopes Identity Discovery Found., Anaheim, Calif., 1982-87, pres. bd. govs., 1983-85, William Syndrome Found., trustee, 1992, 99—, pres., bd. dirs., 1993-95, exec. v.p., 1995-99; v.p. edn. Williams Syndrome Assn., 1994, bd. dirs., 1993-94, mem. adv. bd., 2001—; founder, mem. adv. bd., founder Berkshire Hills Music Acad., 2000—; founder, mem. adv. bd. Guardian Angel Initiative, 2004—. 1st lt. USAF, 1956-58. Recipient Career Development award USPHS, 1965-69; Disting. fellow Iowa Acad. Sci., 1986. Fellow AAAS; mem. Soc. Physics and Natural History of Swiss Acad. Scis. Geneva (hon.), Am. Chem. Soc., Am. Biophys. Soc., Am. Soc. Zoologists, History of Sci. Soc., Am. Soc. Cell Biologists, Am. Soc. Biol. Chemists, Biophysics Soc., Soc. Gen. Physiologists, Soc. Growth and Devel. Home: 304 Dogwood Dr Oxford MS 38655-9670 Office: U Calif Sch Biol Scis Irvine CA 92697-2300 Office Phone: 949-824-7259. Business E-Mail: hlenhoff@uci.edu.

LENK, EDWARD C. (TOBY), retail executive; BA in Econs. and Govt. summa cum laude, Bowdoin Coll., Brunswick, Maine; MBA, Harvard U. Stragegy cons. LäEäK Partnership; v.p. corp. strategic planning Walt Disney Co.; founder eToys, Inc., Santa Monica, Calif., 1997, pres., CEO, uncle of the bd., 1997—2001; co-founder, CEO GameFly, 2002—03; pres. Gap Inc. Direct Gap, Inc., San Francisco, 2003—. Office: Gap Inc 2 Folsom St San Francisco CA 94105 Office Phone: 650-952-4400.

LENO, JAY (JAMES DOUGLAS MUIR LENO), talk show host, comedian, writer; b. New Rochelle, NY, Apr. 28, 1950; s. Angelo and Cathryn Leno; m. Mavis Nicholson Nov. 30, 1980. Grad., Emerson Coll., 1972. Worked as Rolls-Royce auto mechanic and deliveryman. Stand-up comedian playing Carneigie Hall, Caesar's Palace, others; numerous appearances on Late Night with David Letterman; exclusive guest host The Tonight Show, NBC-TV, 1987-92, host, prodr., writer, 1992— (Emmy award, 1995, People's Choice award, favorite late night talk show host, 2006); host, prodr. Showtime Spl. Jay Leno and the American Dream, 1986, Saturday Night Live, 1986, Jay Leno's Family Comedy Hour (Writers Guild Am. nomination), 1987, Our Planet Tonight; film appearances include: The Silver Bears, Fun with Dick and Jane, 1977, American Hot Wax, 1978, Americathon, 1979, Collision Course, 1989, Dave, 1993, Wayne's World 2, Major League 2, The Flintstones, 1994, The Birdcage, 1996, (voice) What's up Hideous Sun Demon?, We're Back! A Dinosaur's Story, 1993, The Flinstones, 1994, (voice) Robots, 2005, Ice Age: The Meltdown, 2006, Cars, 2006, The Astronaut Farmer, 2007, (voice) Igor, 2008; (TV series) The Fairly Odd Parents (voice only), 2001; prodr. (TV films) Roadside Attractions, 2002; writer: (TV series) Good Times, 1974-79; author: Leading with my Chin, 1996, If Roast Beef Could Fly, 2004, How to be the Funniest Kid in the Whole Wide World (or Just in your Class), 2005 Named one of The 100 Most Powerful Celebrities, Forbes.com, 2007, 2008, The World's Most Influential People, TIME mag., 2009. Avocation: antique motorcycles and automobiles. Office: NBC Universal Tonight Show 100 Universal City Plz Universal City CA 91608*

LEON, BRUNO, architect, educator; b. Van Houten, N.Mex., Feb. 18, 1924; s. Giovanni and Rosina (Cunico) L.; m. Louise Dal-Bo, Sept. 4, 1948 (dec. 1974); m. Bonnie Bertram, Sept. 12, 1976; children: Mark Jon, John Anthony, Lisa Rose. Student, Wayne State U., 1942, U. Detroit, 1945-48, LHD (hon.), 1984; BArch, N.C. State U., 1953. Registered architect, Mich., N.C., Mass., N.Y., N.Mex., Fla. Head design staff Fuller Research Found., Raleigh, NC, 1954-55; archtl. designer I.M. Pei & Assos., NYC, 1955-56; instr. Mass. Inst. Tech., 1956-59; designer Catalano & Belluschi (architects), Cambridge, Mass., 1958-59; asst. prof. U. Ill., Urbana, 1959-61; dean Sch. Architecture, U. Detroit, 1961-93, dean emeritus, 1993; pvt. practice architecture, 1956—. With USAAF, 1942-45. Fellow AIA (dir. Detroit 1963-64); mem. Alpha Sigma Nu (hon.), Phi Kappa Phi. Home: 9 Redondo Ct Santa Fe NM 87508-8308 Office Phone: 505-466-1961. Personal E-mail: volterra@newmexico.com.

LEON, PAUL S., Mayor, Ontario, California; Mayor City of Ontario, 2006—. Bd. mem. Ontario Redevelopment Agy., Ontario Indsl. Devel. Authority, Ontario Redevelopment Financing Authority, Ontario Housing Authority. Office: 303 E "B" St Ontario CA 91764 Office Phone: 909-395-2000.*

LEONARD, GEOFFREY PORTER, lawyer; m. Sandy Sevier Simmons, July 9, 1988. BA, Trinity Coll., 1978; JD, Georgetown U., 1981. Bar: NY 1982, Calif. 1992. Corp. assoc. Cravath, Swaine & Moore, NYC, 1986—92; ptnr. Orrick, Herrington & Sutcliffe LLP, Menlo Park, Ropes & Gray LLP, San Francisco, 2006. Mem.: NY Bar. Assn., State Bar of Calif. Office: Ropes & Gray LLP One Embarcadero Ctr Ste 2200 San Francisco CA 94111 Office Phone: 415-315-6364. Office Fax: 415-315-4833.

LEONARD, GEORGE EDMUND, bank executive, credit manager, marketing professional; b. Phoenix, Nov. 20, 1940; s. George Edmund and Marion Elizabeth (Fink) L.; m. Gloria Jean Henry, Mar. 26, 1965 (div. Feb. 1981); children: Tracy Lynn McKinney, Amy Theresa Blanchard, Kristin Jean Steel; m. Mary C. Short, Sept. 22, 1990. Student, Ariz. State U., 1958—60; BS, U.S. Naval Acad., 1964; postgrad., Pa. State U., 1969—70; MBA, U. Chgo., 1073. Commd. ensign USN, 1964, advanced through grades to lt. comdr., 1975; v.p. 1st Nat. Bank Chgo., 1970-75; exec. v.p., chief banking, CFO, chief lending officer Mera Bank, Phoenix, 1975-90, also bd. dirs., 1982-90; pres., CEO Ctrl. Savs., San Diego, 1985-87; chmn., CEO AmBank Holding Co. of Colo., Scottsdale, Ariz., 1990-91, Consumer Guarantee Corp., Phoenix, 1996; pres., CEO Diversified Mgmt. Svcs., Inc., Phoenix, 1991-96, GEL Mgmt. Inc., Phoenix, 1991—; v.p. CFO Western Pacific Airlines, Colorado Springs, 1996-98, bd. dirs., 1996-98; exec. v.p., CFO, treas., sec., dir. fin. Radi Sys. Microware Sys. Corp., Des Moines, 1998—2002, COO, bd. dirs., 2000—01; sr. v.p., chief credit officer Harris Bank N.A., Scottsdale, Ariz., 2002—07; v.p., mktg. mgr. Business Banking, Ariz., 2007—. Active Phoenix Thunderbirds, 1979—; bd. dirs. Maricopa C.C.s Found., treas., 2nd v.p., 1991-93, 1st v.p., 1993-94, pres., 1994-95, past pres., 1995-96, Camelback Charitable Trust, 1991-92; bd. dir. Arrona Golf Found., 2008-, treas., 2009-; The Samaritan Found., 1993-96, chmn. fin. com., 1994-96, vice chmn., 1996; bd. dirs. Westminster Village, Inc., 2003—, v.p., sec., 2004—; bd. trustees Desert Bot. Gardens, 2004—09; mem. City Scottsdale Housing Bd., 2005-08, chmn. 2007-08. Mem. Phoenix Met. C. of C. (bd. dirs. 1975-82), Inst. Fin. Edn. (bd. dirs. 1980-87, nat. chmn. 1985-86), Ariz. State U. Coll. of Bus. Deans Coun. of 100, Ariz. Golf Found. (bd. dir. & treas. 2008-), Paradise Valley Country Club (bd. dirs. 1991-98, treas. 1992-95, pres. 1995-97), White Mountain Country Club (bd. dirs. 2005, pres. 2008-), Kiwanis. Republican. Roman Catholic. Office: Harris Bank NA 6720 N Scottsdale Rd Ste 111 Scottsdale AZ 85253 Home: 11113 E North Ln Scottsdale AZ 85259-4853 Office Phone: 480-951-4616. Personal E-mail: geljr@aol.com.

LEONARD, GLEN MILTON, historian; b. Salt Lake City, Nov. 12, 1938; s. Burnham J. and Allene (Green) L.; m. Karen Wright, Mar. 15, 1968; children: Cory, Kyle, Keith. BA, U. Utah, 1964, MA, 1966, PhD, 1970. Mng. editor Utah State Hist. Soc., Salt Lake City, 1970-73; sr. rsch. assoc. history divsn. Ch. of Jesus Christ of LDS, Salt Lake City, 1973-78; dir. Mus. Ch. History and Art, Salt Lake City, 1979—2004. Mem. adv. bd. editors Utah Hist. Quarterly, Salt Lake City, 1973-88; assoc. editor Jour. Mormon History, Provo, Utah, 1974-80; bd. dirs. Western Studies Ctr., Brigham Young U., Provo. Co-author: The Story of the Latter-day Saints, 1976; Author: A History of Davis County, 1999, Nauvoo: A Place of Peace, A People of Plenty, 2002. Mem. Hist. Preservation Commn., Farmington, Utah, 1986-92; mem. adv. coun. Mormon Pioneer Nat. Hist. Trail, Nat. Pk. Svc., 1980-86; mem. Utah Pioneer Sesquicentennial Celebration Coordinating Coun., 1995-97. Recipient Dale Morgan Article award Utah State Hist. Soc., 1973, Mormon History Assn. Article awards, 1990, 96. Mem. Orgn. Am. Historians, Western History Assn., Am. Assn. Mus. (mus. assessment program cons.), Western Mus. Assn., Utah Mus. Assn. (bd. dirs. 1980-83), Am. Assn. State and Local History. Avocations: photography, music, gardening.

LEONARD, HERMAN, photographer; b. Allentown, Pa., 1923; BFA, Ohio U., 1947; apprentice to master photographer Yousuf Karsh, Ottawa, 1947—48; MS in photography (hon.), Brooks Inst. Photography, Santa Barbara, Calif., 1995. Independent photographer, 1949—; personal photographer to Marlon Brando, 1956; European photographer Playboy, Paris; founder Herman Leonard Jazz Archive, 2007—. Represented in permanent collections Smithsonian Inst., Washington, Jazz at Lincoln Ctr., NYC, Ogden Mus. Southern Art, LA, George Eastman House, NY; author: The Eye of Jazz, 1985, Jazz Memories, 1995, Jazz, Giants, and Journeys: The Photography of Herman Leonard, 2006. Anesthetist 13th Mountain Med. Bn. US Army, 1943—45, Burma. Recipient Milt Hinton award for Excellence in Jazz Photography, Jazz Photographer's Assn., 1999, Excellence in Photography award, Jazz Journalists Assn., 2000, Lifetime Achievement award, Downbeat mag., 2004, Lucie award for Achievement in Portraiture, Internat. Photography Awards, 2008. Office: Herman Leonard Photography LLC 11434 Venture Blvd Ste 101 Studio City CA 91604 Office Phone: 818-509-8987. E-mail: mail@hermanleonard.com.

LEONARD, JACK, reporter; Justice writer, Orange County ed. LA Times, county govt. reporter. Co-recipient Ursula & Gilbert Farfel prize for investigative reporting, Scripps Howard Found., 2006, Local Watchdog Reporting award, Am. Soc. Newspaper Editors, 2006. Office: LA Times 202 W 1st St Los Angeles CA 90012 Office Phone: 213-237-7847. Office Fax: 213-237-4712.

LEONARD, THOMAS C., librarian, dean; BA (hon.), Univ. Mich., 1966; PhD in History, Univ. Calif., 1973. Prof., former assoc. dean, grad. sch. journalism U. Calif., Berkeley, Calif., interim univ. libr., 2000—01, libr. dir., 2001—. Spkr., cons. in field. Author: Above the Battle: War-Making in America from Appomattox to Versailles, 1978, The Power of the Press: The Birth of American Political Reporting, 1986, News for All: America's Coming of Age with the Press, 1995; contbr. numerous articles to profl. jours. Office: U Calif Berkeley Libr 245 Doe Libr MC 6000 Berkeley CA 94720-6000 Office Phone: 510-642-3773. Business E-Mail: tleonard@library.berkeley.edu.

LEONDAKIS, NIKI ANNA, food service executive; b. West Springfield, Mass., Nov. 28, 1960; B in Hotel and Restaurant Mgmt., U. Mass. Restaurant and beverage mgr. Marriott, Nashville; dir. catering Ritz Carlton Hotels, Atlanta, dir. food and beverage Marina Del Rey, Calif., San Francisco; joined Kimpton Hotel and Restaurant Group, Inc., San Francisco, 1993, regional mgr. N.W., 1993-95, v.p. restaurant ops. San Francisco, 1995—. Named Rising Star, Restaurant Hospitality Mag. Avocations: skiing, running, painting, family activities. Office: Kimpton Hotel & Restaurant Group Inc 222 Kearny St Ste 200 San Francisco CA 94108

LEONE, STEPHEN ROBERT, chemical physicist, educator; b. NYC, May 19, 1948; s. Dominic and Annie Frances (Sappa) L. BA, Northwestern U., 1970; PhD, U. Calif., Berkeley, 1974. Asst. prof. U. So. Calif., LA, 1974-76; physicist/fellow Nat. Inst. Standards and Tech., Boulder, Colo., 1976-94, acting chief Quantum Physics divsn., 1994-95; adj. prof. U. Colo., Boulder, 1994-96. Contbr. over 200 articles to profl. publs.; mem. editorial bd. Optics Letters, Jour. Chem. Physics, Chem. Revs., Jour. Phys. Chemistry, Molecular Physics, Chem. Physics Letters, Progress in Reaction Kinetics; patentee in field. Recipient silver and gold medals Dept. Commerce, 1980, 85, Coblentz award Coblentz Soc., 1984, Arthur S. Flemming award U.S. Govt., 1986, Samuel Wesley Stratton award Nat. Inst. Standards and Tech., 1992; Alfred P. Sloan fellow Sloan Found., 1977-81, Guggenheim fellow, 1988. Fellow AAAS, Optical Soc. Am., Am. Phys. Soc. (chair div. chem. physics 1987-88, Herbert P. Broida prize 1989); mem. NAS, Am. Chem. Soc. (pure chemistry award 1982, nobel laureate signature award 1983). Office: JILA PO Box 440 Boulder CO 80309-0440

LEONE, WILLIAM J., lawyer, former prosecutor; b. Trinidad, Colo., Oct. 16, 1956; BA in Polit. Sci., Colo. State U., Ft. Collins, 1978; JD, U. Colo., 1981. Bar: Colo. Assoc. Sparks Dix Enoch Suthers, Colorado Springs, Colo., 1985-86; assoc., officer, dir. Ireland, Stapleton, Pryor, Denver, 1982—94; ptnr. Cooley Godward Castro, Denver, 1994—2001; first asst. US atty. dist. Colo. US Dept. Justice, Denver, 2001—04, US atty., 2005—06; ptnr. Faegre & Benson LLP, Denver, 2006—. Author: Immunity to a Direct Action: Is It a Defense, 1978. Active Colo. and Adams County Rep. Orgn., 1978—; bd. dirs. Cath. Cmty. Svcs., Colorado Springs, 1985; pres. Brandy Chase East Homeowner's Assn., Aurora, Colo., 1981-84. Mem. ABA, Colo. Bar Assn., Denver Bar Assn., Order of Coif, Denver Athletic Club, Phi Beta Kappa. Avocations: basketball, golf. Office: Faegre & Benson LLP 3200 Wells Fargo Ctr 1700 Lincoln St Denver CO 80203 Home Phone: 303-726-6606; Office Phone: 303-607-3595. Business E-Mail: wleone@faegre.com.

LEONG, ALBIN B., pediatric pulmonologist, allergist, educator; b. Astoria, Oreg., Nov. 8, 1950; BS in Biology, Trinity Coll., Hartford, Conn., 1973; MD, U. Calif., La Jolla, Calif., 1977. Diplomate Nat. Bd. Medical Examiners, 1979, Am. Bd. Pediatrics, 1982, Am. Bd. Allergy & Immunology, 1983. Resident Children's Hosp. of L.A., 1977-79; resident in pediat. U. Calif., San Diego, 1979-80, fellow in pediat. pulmonology, immunology and allergy, 1980-82; pediat. pulmonologist and allergist Sacramento Kaiser Found. Hosp., 1993—. Contbr. articles to profl. jours. Grantee Travel grant, Am. Acad. Alelrgy, 1981, 2004—05, 2006—. Mem.: Calif. Thoracic Soc., Am. Thoracic Soc., Am. Acad. Pediatrics. Office: Sacramento Kaiser Found Hosp Pediatric Pulmonology & Allergy 2025 Morse Ave Sacramento CA 95825 Office Phone: 916-973-7324. Office Fax: 916-973-7338. Business E-Mail: albin.leong@kp.org.

LEONHARDT, THOMAS WILBURN, librarian, library director; b. Wilmington, NC, Feb. 7, 1943; s. Thomas Beauregard and Rachel Virginia (Callicutt) L.; m. Margaret Ann Pullen, Sept. 19, 1966; children: Hilary, Thomas, Rebecca, Benjamin. AA, Pasadena City Coll., Calif., 1968; AB, U. Calif., Berkeley, 1970, MLS, 1973. Head gift and exch. div. Stanford U. Librs., Calif., 1973-76; head acquisition dept. Boise State U. Libr., Idaho, 1976-79, Duke U. Librs., Durham, NC, 1980-82; asst. univ. libr. U. Oreg., Eugene, 1982-87; dean librs. U. of the Pacific, Stockton, Calif., 1987-92; dir. tech. svcs. U. Okla. Librs., Norman, 1992-97; libr. dir. Oreg. Inst. Tech., Klamath Falls, 1997—2001; founding libr. Internat. U., Bremen, Germany, 2001; cons., 2002—; dir. Scarborough-Phillips Libr./St. Edward's Univ., Austin, Tex., 2002—. Editor RTSD Newsletter, Chgo., 1986-89, Info. Tech. & Librs., Chgo., 1990-95. Editor Advances in Collection Development and Resource Management, JAI Press, 1994-97, Internat. Leads, 2004-05; publisher, editor Callicutt Family Chronicle; contbr. articles to profl. jours. Bd. dirs. No. Regional Libr. Facility, Richmond, Calif., 1988-92, Feather River Inst. for Libr. Acquisitions, Blairsden, Calif.; del. Online Computer Libr. Ctr. AMIGOS Bibliog. Coun., Inc., 1996-97; chair Orbis Coun., 1999-2001; mem. Klamath Symphony, 1997-2001; chair Am. Libr. Assn. Com. on Accreditation, 2005-08. Mem. ALA (chair com. on accreditation 2005-07), Assn. Coll. Rsch. Librs., Libr. and Info. Tech. Assn. (pres. 1997-98), Assn. for Libr. Collections and Tech. Svcs., Ctrl. Assn. Librs. (bd. dirs. Stockton chpt. 1987-92), Cath. Rsch. Resource Alliance (bd. dir. 2007-), Assn. Profl. and Specialized Accreditors (bd. dir. 2008-). Democrat. Avocations: trumpet, guitar. Office Phone: 512-448-8470. Personal E-mail: thomasleonhardt@yahoo.com. Business E-Mail: thomasl@stedwards.edu.

LEOPOLD, GEORGE ROBERT, radiologist; b. Lewistown, Pa., 1937; MD, U. Pitts., 1962. Intern York Hosp., 1962-63; resident U. Pitts., 1965-68; chmn., prof. dept. radiology U. Calif., San Diego, 1984—. Mem. Am. Coll. Radiology (Gold medal 1996), AIUM, ARRS, AUR, RSNA. Office: U Calif San Diego Med Ctr Ultrasound Divsn 8756 200 W Arbor Dr San Diego CA 92103-8756

LEPORE, DAWN GOULD, Internet pharmaceutical company executive; b. 1954; m. Kenneth Lepore. BA in Music, Smith Coll., Northampton, Mass., 1977. With Cin. Bell, Informatics, San Francisco, Charles Schwab Corp., San Francisco, 1983—2004, exec. v.p., chief info. officer, 1993—99, vice chmn., chief info. officer, 1999—2001, vice chmn. tech. & adminstrn., 2001—02, vice chmn. tech., ops., & adminstrn., 2002—03, vice chmn. tech., ops., bus. strategy, & adminstrn., 2003, vice chmn. tech., active trader, ops., bus. strategy, & adminstrn., 1999—2004; CEO drugstore.com inc., Bellevue, Wash., 2004—. Bd. dirs. eBay Inc., 1999—, Wal-Mart Stores, Inc., 2001—04, The NY Times Co., 2008—. Trustee Smith Coll. Recipient Aiming High Conf., NOW, 2003; named one of Bay Area's Most Powerful Corp. Women, San Francisco Chronicle, Top 100 Women in Computing, Open Computing mag., Ten Hottest CIOs, Future Banker mag., 1999, 50 Most Powerful Women in Am. Bus., Fortune mag., 2000, 2001, 2002. Office: drugstore.com inc 411 108th Ave NE Ste 1400 Bellevue WA 98004

LEPPER, MARK ROGER, psychologist, educator; b. Washington, Dec. 5, 1944; s. Mark H. and Joyce M. (Sullivan) L.; m. Jeanne E. Wallace, Dec. 22, 1966; 1 child, Geoffrey William. BA, Stanford U., Calif., 1966; PhD, Yale U., 1970. Asst. prof. psychology Stanford U., 1971-76, assoc. prof., 1976—82, prof., 1982—, chmn., 1990—94, 2000—04, Albert Ray Lang prof. psychology, 2004—. Fellow Ctr. Advanced Study in Behavioral Scis., 1979-80; chmn. mental health behavioral scis. rsch. rev. com. NIMH, 1982-84, mem. basic sociocultural rsch. rev. com., 1980-82. Co-editor: The Hidden Costs of Reward, 1978; cons. editor Jour. Personality and Social Psychology, 1977-85, Child Devel., 1977-86, Social Cognition, 1981-84, Jour. Ednl. Computing Rsch., 1983—, Media Psychology, 1999—; contbr. articles to profl. jours. Recipient Cattell Found. award, 1999; Woodrow Wilson fellow, 1966-67, NSF fellow, 1966-69, Sterling fellow, 1969-70, Mellon fellow, 1975; grantee NSF, 1978-82, 86-88, 2004, NIMH, 1978-86, 88, 2005—, Nat. Inst. Child Health and Human Devel., 1975-88, 90-98, U.S. Office Edn., 1972-73. Fellow APA, AAAS, Am. Psychol. Soc., Soc. Personality and Social Psychology, Soc. Psychol. Study Social Issues, Am. Acad. Arts and Scis.; mem.

Am. Ednl. Rsch. Assn., Soc. Exptl. Social Psychology, Soc. Rsch. in Child Devel. Home: 1544 Dana Ave Palo Alto CA 94303-2813 Office: Stanford U Dept Psychology Jordan Hall Bldg 420 Stanford CA 94305-2130

LEPRINO, JAMES G., food products executive; b. 1937; married; 2 children. With Leprino Foods Co., Denver, 1955—, chmn. bd., CEO. Named one of 400 Richest Americans, Forbes, 2005—. Office: Leprino Foods Co 1830 W 38th Ave Denver CO 80211-2200

LERER, SETH, literature professor, writer; b. Bklyn., 1966; BA, Wesleyan U., Middletown, Conn., 1976, U. Oxford, Eng., 1978, MA, 1986; PhD, U. Chgo., 1981. Prof. English Stanford U., Calif., 1990—2009, prof. comparative lit., 1996—2009, chair dept. comparative lit., 1997—2000, also Avalon Found. prof. humanities; disting. prof. lit., dean of arts & humanities U. Calif., San Diego, 2009—. Hurst vis. prof. Washington U., St. Louis, 1996; Helen Cam vis. scholar medieval studies Cambridge U., England, 2002; Fletcher Jones disting. fellow Huntington Libr., San Marino, Calif., 2007—08. Author: Boethius and Dialogue, 1985, Literacy and Power in Anglo-Saxon Literature, 1991, Chaucer and His Readers, 1993 (Beatrice White prize, English Assn. Great Britain), Courtly Letters in the Age of Henry VIII, 1997, Error and the Academic Self: The Scholarly Imagination, Medieval to Modern, 2002 (Harry Levin prize, Am. Comparative Lit. Assn., 2005), Inventing English: A Portable History of the Language, 2007, Children's Literature: A Reader's History, 2008 (Nat. Book Critics Circle award for Criticism, 2008); editor: (essay collections) Literary History and the Challenge of Philology, 1996, Reading from the Margins, 1996, The Yale Companion to Chaucer, 2006; contbr. articles to profl. jours. Recipient Hoagland prize for Undergrad. Tchg., Stanford U., 1993, Dean's award for Grad. Tchg., 2003; fellow NEH, Guggenheim Found., Am. Coun. Learned Societies. Office: Univ of California at San Diego 9500 Gilman Dr # 0406 La Jolla CA 92093 Office Phone: 858-534-6270. Office Fax: 858-534-0091. Business E-Mail: slerer@ucsd.edu.

LERMAN, EILEEN R., lawyer; b. NYC, May 6, 1947; d. Alex and Beatrice (Kline) L. BA, Syracuse U., 1969; JD, Rutgers U., 1972; MBA, U. Denver, 1983. Bar: NY 1973, Colo. 1976. Atty. FTC, NYC, 1972-74; corp. atty. Samsonite Corp. and consumer products divsn. Beatrice Foods, Denver, 1976-78, assoc. gen. counsel, 1978-85, asst. sec., 1979-85; ptnr. Davis, Lerman, & Weinstein, Denver, 1985-92, Eileen R. Lerman & Assocs., Denver, 1993—; corp.atty. RCA Global Communication, Inc., 1974—76. Bd. dirs. Legal Aid Soc. Met. Denver, 1979-80; mcpl. judge pro tem City Ctrl., Colo. Bd. dirs., vice chmn. Colo. Postsecondary Ednl. Facilities Authority, 1981-89; bd. dirs., pres. Am. Jewish Com., 1989-92; mem. Leadership Denver, 1983. Mem. ABA, Colo. Women's Bar Assn. (bd. dirs. 1980-81), Colo. Bar Assn. (mem. bd. govs.), Denver Bar Assn. (trustee), N.Y. State Bar Assn., Rhone Brackett Inn (pres. 1997-98), Denver Law Club, Rutgers U. Alumni Assn., Univ. Club. Home: 1018 Fillmore St Denver CO 80206-3332 Office: Lerman & Assocs PC 815 E 17th Ave Denver CO 80218 Office Phone: 303-394-3900. Personal E-mail: lerman@usa.net.

LERNER, MICHAEL, rabbi; BA, Columbia U.; studied, Jewish Theological Seminary. Ordained Rabbi 1995. Chmn. Free Students Union, 1966—68; chmn., Berkeley Chapter Students for a Democratic Soc.; lectr., Philosophy of Law San Francisco State U.; founder Seattle Liberation Front; prof., Dept. Philosophy Trinity Coll., 1972; prof., Field Study U. Calif., Berkeley, 1975—77; found. Inst. Labor and Mental Health, 1977; rabbi ALEPH: Alliance For Jewish Renewal, 1995—. Founder, current editor Tikkun Mag. Recipient Gandhi, King, Ikeda Community Builders Prize, Moorehouse Coll., 2005; named one of The Top 50 Rabbis in America, Newsweek Mag., 2007. Mem.: Atid (past pres.). Office: Tikkun Mag Ste 1200 2342 Shattuck Avenue Berkeley CA 94704 Fax: 510-644-1255.

LERNER, RICHARD ALAN, chemistry educator, scientist; b. Chgo., Aug. 26, 1938; s. Peter Alex and Lily (Orlinsky) L.; m. Diana Lynn Pritchett, June 1966 (div. 1977); children: Danica, Arik, Edward; m. Nicola Green, Sept. 1, 1979. Student, Northwestern U., 1956-59; BS, MD, Stanford U., 1964; MD (hon.), Karolinska Inst., 1990. Intern Palo Alto (Calif.) Stanford Hosp., 1964-65, rsch. fellow, 1965-68; assoc. mem. Wistar Inst., Phila., 1968-70; assoc. mem. dept. exptl. pathology Scripps Clinic and Rsch. Found., La Jolla, Calif., 1970-72, mem., 1972-74, mem. dept. immunopathology, 1974-82; chmn. and mem. dept. molecular biology Rsch. Inst. Scripps Clinic, La Jolla, 1982-87, prof. dept. chemistry, 1988—, dir., 1987—; pres. The Scripps Rsch. Inst., La Jolla. Cons. Johnson & Johnson, 1983—, PPG Industries, Inc., Pitts., 1987—; sci. advisor Igen Inc., Rockville, Md., 1986—; spl. advisor Genex Corp., Gaithersburg, Md., 1988—; bd. dirs. Cytel Corp.; chmn. Internat. Symposium on Molecular Basis Cell-Cell Interaction, 1977, 78, 79, 80; mem. organizing com. for Modern Approaches to Vaccines, Cold Spring Harbor, 1983-89. Contbr. over 250 sci. papers; mem. editorial bd. Jour. Virology, Molecular Biology and Medicine, Protein Engring., Vaccine, In Vivo, Peptide Rsch. Mem. sci. policy adv. com. Uppsala U. (Sweden), sci. adv. bd. Econ. Devel. Bd., Singapore. Decorated Oficial de La Orden de San Carlos (Colombia); recipient NIH AID Career Devel. award, 1970, Parke Davis award, 1978, John A. Muntz Meml. award, 1990, San Marino prize, 1990, Burroughs Wellcome Fund and FASEB Wellcome Vis. Prof. award, 1990-91, College de France award, 1991, 1oth Ann. Jeanette Piperno Meml. award, 1991, Arthur C. Cope scholar award in chemistry, 1991, Wolf Prize in chemistry, Wolf Found., Israel, 1994, Humboldt Rsch. award, Bonn, Germany, 1994, William B Coley award disting. rsch. in basic and tumor immunology, Cancer Rsch. Inst, NY, 199, Windaus medal, Georg-August-Universitat, Germany, 1999. Fellow ACS (screening com. Calif. div.), AAAS; mem. NAS Inst. Med. (ad hoc com. new rsch. opportunities in immunology), Am. Soc. Virology (charter), Am. Soc. Nephrology, Am. Assn. Immunologists, Am. Soc. Exptl. Pathology, Am. Soc. Microbiology, N.Y. Acad. Scis., Biophys. Soc., Royal Swedish Acad. Sci, Nat. Cancer Inst. (cancer preclin. program project rev. com. 1985-88), Royal Swedish Acad. Scis. (fgn., Lita Annenberg Hazen prof. immunochemistry 1986), 1st Thursday Club, Phi Eta Sigma, Alpha Omega Alpha. Avocations: tennis, walking, skiing, polo. Office: Scripps Rsch Inst 10550 N Torrey Pines Rd La Jolla CA 92037-1000 Office Phone: 858-784-8265.

LERNER, SANDY, cosmetics executive; b. Phoenix, 1955; BA, Calif. State U.; student, Claremont Coll., Stanford U. Co-founder Cisco Sys., 1984-90, Ampersand Capital, 1990—; CEO Urban Decay, Mountain View, Calif., 1996—. Office: Urban Decay 833 W 16th St Newport Beach CA 92663-2801

LEROY, DAVID HENRY, lawyer; b. Seattle, Aug. 16, 1947; s. Harold David and Lela Fay (Palmer) L.; 2 children. BS, U. Idaho, 1969, JD, 1971; LLM, NYU, 1972; JD (hon.), Lincoln Coll., 1993. Bar: Idaho 1971, NY 1973, US Supreme Ct. 1976. Law clk. Idaho 4th Dist. Ct., Boise, 1969; legal asst. Boise Cascade Corp., 1970; assoc. firm Rothblatt, Rothblatt, Seijas & Peskin, NYC, 1971-73; dep. prosecutor Ada County Prosecutor's Office, Boise, 1973-74, pros. atty., 1974-78; atty. gen. State of Idaho, Boise, 1978-82, lt. gov., 1983-87; ptnr. Runft, Leroy Coffin & Matthews, 1983-88, Leroy Law Offices, 1988—. Candidate for Gov. of Idaho, 1986, US Congress, 1994; US nuc. waste negotiator, 1990-93; US Presdl. elector, 1992; chmn. com. on improving practices for regulatory and mng. low-activity radioactive waste NAS, 2002-; lectr., cons. in field. Mem. State Task Force on Child Abuse, 1975; mem. Ada County Coun. on Alcoholism, 1976; del. Rep. Nat. Conv., 1976, 80, 84, 2004; chmn. Nat. Rep. Lt. Gov.'s Caucus, 1983-86; bd. dirs. United Fund, 1975-81; del. Am. Coun. Young Polit. Leaders, USSR, 1979, Am. Coun. for Free Asia, Taiwan, 1980, U.S./Taiwan Investment Forum, 1983; del. leader Friendship Force Tour USSR, 1984; legal counsel Young Reps., 1974-81; candidate for Gov. Idaho, 1986; presdl. elector, 1992; candidate U.S. Ho. Reps. 1st Dist., Idaho, 1994; Idaho Abraham Lincoln Bicentennial Commn. Com. chmn., 2006—; governor's coun. US Abraham Lincoln Bicentenniel commn. (chmn. 2007-). Mem. Nat. Dist. Attys. Assn., Idaho Prosecutors Assn., Am. Trial Lawyers Assn., Idaho Criminal Defense Lawyers Assn., Nat. Assn. Attys. Gen. (chmn. energy subcom., exec. com., del to China 1981), Western Attys. Gen. Assn. (vice chmn. 1980-83, chmn. 1981), Nat. Lt. Govs. Assn. (exec. bd. 1983), Idaho Bar Assn., Ada County Lincoln Day Assn. (pres. 2000), Am. Lung Assn. Idaho, Found. for Idaho History (pres. 2001-05), NAS (chmn. com. on improving practices for regulating and mng. low activity radioactive waste 2002-06), Idaho State Repub. Conv. (vice chmn. 2004), Sigma Alpha Epsilon. Presbyterian. Office: The Leroy Offices PO Box 193 Boise ID 83701-0193 Office Phone: 208-342-0000.

LE SAGE, BERNARD E., lawyer; b. Pasadena, Calif., Mar. 29, 1949; BA, U. Notre Dame, 1971; JD, Loyola U., LA, 1974. Bar: Calif. 1974. Extern clk. to Hon. William P. Clark Calif. Supreme Ct., 1974; with Buchalter, Nemer, Fields & Younger, LA, 1979—. Mem. ABA, State Bar Calif., Los Angeles County Bar Assn. (trustee 1982-84), Los Angeles County Bar Barristers (pres. 1983-84), Chancery Club. Office: Buchalter Nemer 1000 Wilshire Blvd Ste 1500 Los Angeles CA 90017-1730

LESAVOY, MALCOLM ALAN, plastic surgeon; b. Allentown, Pa., June 27, 1942; m. Sabine Lesavoy. BA, U. NC, 1964; MD, Chgo. Med. Sch., 1969. Diplomate Am. Bd. Plastic Surgery 1977. Resident gen. surgery U. Chgo., 1969—74; resident plastic and reconstructive surgery U. Miami, 1974—76; chief plastic surgery Harbor-UCLA Med. Ctr., Torrance, 1976—99; plastic surgeon Encino Outpatient Surgery Ctr., Calif., 1999—. Prof. plastic and reconstructive surgery UCLA Sch. Medicine, LA, 1976—99, clin. prof. plastic and reconstructive surgery and hand surgery, 1999—; nat. pres. Millard Plastic Surgery Soc., 1987—89; Frank Hawkins Kenan vis. prof. dept. surgery Duke U., Durham, NC, 2003; Kazanjian vis. prof. divsn. plastic and reconstructive surgery Harvard U., Boston, 2003; Courtemanche vis. prof. U. BC, Vancouver, 2004; vis. prof. Baylor Coll. Med., Houston, 2005. Author: Reconstruction of the Head and Neck, 1981, Hand Surgery Review, 1981, 2d edit., 1985, over 25 book chpts., over 70 articles to profl. jours. in field. Nat. pres. Reconstructive Surgeons Vol. Program, 1990—92. With USAR, 1969—76. Recipient Excellence in Clin. Tchg. award, UCLA Sch. Medicine, 1978, 1992, 1993, 2004; named a Disting. Alumnus, Chgo. Med. Sch., 1983. Mem.: ACS, World Soc. Reconstructive Microsurgery, Plastic Surgery Rsch. Coun., Plastic Surgery Ednl. Found. (bd. dirs. 1984—93, pres. 1991—92), Internat. Coll. Surgeons, Am. Soc. Plastic Surgeons (bd. dirs. 1990—94, chmn. bd. trustees 1995—96), Am. Soc. Maxillofacial Surgeons, Am. Assn. Plastic Surgery (named Clinician of Yr. 2002). Office: 16311 Ventura Blvd Ste 555 Encino CA 91436 Office Phone: 818-986-8270. Office Fax: 818-986-1342. Business E-Mail: mlesavoy@surgicalrenaissance.com.

LESCH, BARRY M., lawyer; b. NYC, Apr. 26, 1945; BA, U. Pa., 1965; MA, Ind. U., 1971; JD, U. Calif., Berkeley, 1975. Bar: Calif. 1975, U.S. Supreme Ct. 1980. With Laughlin, Falbo, Levy & Moresi, Sacramento. Mem. State Bar Calif. (cert. specialist workers compensation law). Office: Laughlin Falbo Levy & Moresi 106 K St Fl 2 Sacramento CA 95814-3218

LESHER, JOHN, film company executive; Grad., Harvard U., 1988. Film agent United Talent Agy., 1988, ptnr., co-head motion picture literature dept.; ptnr. Endeavor Talent Agy., 2002—05; founder, pres. Paramount Vantage Paramount Pictures, 2005—08, pres. Paramount Film Group, 2008—. Office: Paramount Pictures Corp 5555 Melrose Ave Ste 121 West Hollywood CA 90038

LESHY, JOHN DAVID, lawyer, solicitor, educator; b. Winchester, Ohio, Oct. 7, 1944; s. John and Dolores (King) L.; m. Helen M. Sandalls, Dec. 15, 1973 (div. 2005); 1 child, David Alexander. AB cum laude, Harvard U., 1966, JD magna cum laude, 1969. Trial atty. civil rights divsn. Dept. Justice, Washington, 1969-72; atty. Natural Resources Def. Coun., Palo Alto, Calif., 1972-77; assoc. solicitor energy and resources Dept. Interior, Washington, 1977-80, solicitor (gen. counsel), 1993-2001; prof. law Ariz. State U., Tempe, 1980—2002; spl. counsel to chair Natural Resources Com. US Ho. Reps., Washington, 1992-93. Cons. Calif. State Land Commn., N.Mex. Atty. Gen., Western Govs. Assn., Congl. Rsch. Svc., Ford Found., Hewlett Found., Pew Charitable Trusts, Wyss Found.; mem. com. Onshore Oil & Gas Leasing, NAS Nat. Rsch. Coun., 1989-90; vis. prof. Sch. Law U. San Diego, 1990; disting. vis. prof. law U. Calif. Hastings Coll. Law, 2001-02, Harry D. Sunderland disting. prof. real property, 2002-; vis. prof. Harvard Law Sch., 2004, 06, 07. Author: The Mining Law: A Study in Perpetual Motion, 1987, The Arizona State Constitution, 1993; co-author Federal Public Land and Resources Law, 6th edit., 2007, Legal Control of Water Resources, 4th edit., 2006; contbr. articles, book chpts. to profl. jours., environ. jours. Bd. dirs. Grand Canyon Trust, 1987—92, 2002—, Natural Heritage Inst., 2002—, Ariz. Raft Adventures, 1982—92, 2002—08; mem. City of Phoenix Environ. Quality Commn., 1987—90; pres. Wyss Found., 2002—07, vice-chair bd., 2007—; bd. dirs. Ariz. Ctr. Law in Pub. Interest, 1981—86, Western Progress, 2007—. Robinson Cox vis. fellow U. Western Australia Law Sch., Perth, 1985, rsch. fellow U. Southampton, Eng., 1986; Ford Found. grantee, Resources for the Future grantee. Democrat. Avocations: piano, hiking, whitewater rafting, photography. Office: Calif Hastings Coll Law 200 McAllister St San Francisco CA 94102-4978 Business E-Mail: leshyj@uchastings.edu.

LESJAK, CATHERINE A., computer company executive; b. 1959; B in Biology, Stanford U., Calif.; MBA, U. Calif., Berkeley. With Hewlett Packard Co., Palo Alto, Calif., 1986—, various fin. and risk mgmt. positions, 1986—2000, contr. HP software solutions, 2000—02, v.p. fin. HP enterprise mktg. & HP software, 2002—03, sr. v.p., treas., 2003—06, exec. v.p., CFO, 2006—. Named one of 50 Most Powerful Women in Bus., Fortune mag., 2007. Office: Hewlett Packard Co 3000 Hanover St Palo Alto CA 94304*

LESKO, DEBBIE, state legislator; married; 3 children. Mem. Dist. 9 Ariz. House of Reps., 2009—. Officer State & County Rep. Party; rep. chmn. Legis. Dist. 9; voter registration chmn. Maricopa County Rep. Party. Bd. mem. Ariz. Fedn. Taxpayers, 2005—08; adv. bd. mem. Eve's Place; mem. Glendale Fire Dept. Cmty. Emergency Response Team; hearing officer North Valley Justice Ct.; treas. PUSD Cmty. Com.; neighborhood leader Glendale Cmty. Partnership Program. Mem.: Ariz. Citizens Defense League, Parent Tchr. Assn., Arrowhead Rep. Women Club (1st v.p.), Ironwood High Sch. Booster Club. Republican. Office: Capitol Complex 1700 W Washington Rm 129 Phoenix AZ 85007-2890 Office Phone: 602-926-5413. Office Fax: 602-417-3109. Business E-Mail: dlesko@azleg.gov.*

LESLIE, LISA DESHAUN, professional basketball player; b. Gardena, Calif., July 7, 1972; d. Christine Leslie-Espinoza; m. Michael Lockwood; 1 child, Lauren Jolie Lockwood. Student, U. So. Calif., 1990—94, grad. in Comm., 1997. Ctr. Sicilgesso, Italy, 1994—95, LA Sparks, 1997—. Mem. USA Basketball Women's Sr. Nat. Team, Atlanta, 1996, Sydney, 2000, Athens, Greece, 04, Beijing, 08; color commentator U. So. Calif. Trojans Basketball; guest corr. NBA Inside Stuff. Named USA Basketball Female Athlete of Yr., 1993, WNBA All-Star Game MVP, 1999, 2001, 02, WNBA MVP, 2001, 04, 06, WNBA Finals MVP, 2001, 02, Sportswoman of Yr. for a team sport, Women's Sports Found., 2003, WNBA Defensive Player of Yr., 2004; named to All-WNBA First Team, 1997, 2000-04, 06, WNBA All-Defensive Team, 2006, WNBA All-Decade Team, 2006; recipient Gold medal, women's basketball, Goodwill Games, 1994, Atlanta Olympic Games, 1996, Sydney Olympic Games, 2000, Athens Olympic Games, 2004, Beijing Olympic Games. Achievements include being a member of the WNBA Championship winning Los Angeles Sparks, 2001, 2002. Mailing: LA Sparks 888 S Figueroa St Ste 2010 Los Angeles CA 90017

LESLIE, TIM (ROBERT LESLIE), state legislator; b. Ashland, Oreg., Feb. 4, 1942; s. Robert Tabor Leslie and Virginia (Hall) P.; m. Clydene Ann Fisher, June 15, 1962; children: Debbie, Scott. BA in Polit. Sci., Calif. State U., Long Beach, 1963; MPA, U. So. Calif., 1969. Prin. analyst Sacramento County Exec. Office, Calif., 1965-69; cons. Assn. W. & M. Commn., Sacramento, 1965-72; prin. legis. rep. County Suprs. Assn., Sacramento, 1972-80; founder bd. dirs. Cmty. Action Against Drugs, Sacramento, 1975-83; v.p. Moss & Thompson, Inc., Sacramento, 1980-84; exec. v.p. Kuhl Corp., Sacramento, 1984-86; assemblyman Calif. State Assembly, Sacramento, 1986-91; senator State of Calif., Sacramento, 1991—. Chmn. fin. Investment and Internat. Trade Com.; vice chmn. Appropriations Com.; mem. Ins. Com., Natural Resources Com. Rep. candidate for lt. gov., 1998. Recipient Hang Tough award Nat. Tax Limitation Com., Calif., 1987; named Legislator of Yr., Sacramento County Taxpayers League and Osteo. Surgeons of Calif., 1990, Women in Timber, 1994. Republican. Presbyterian. Office: 3300 Douglas Blvd Ste 430 Roseville CA 95661-3891

LESONSKY, RIEVA, editor-in-chief; b. NYC, June 20, 1952; d. Gerald and Muriel (Cash) L. BJ, U. Mo., 1974. Rschr. Doubleday & Co., NYC, 1975-78, Entrepreneur Mag., LA, 1978-80, rsch. dir., 1983-84, LFP Inc., LA, 1980-82; mng. editor Entrepreneur Mag., LA, 1985-86, exec. editor, 1986-87, editor Irvine, Calif., 1987-90; sr. v.p., editor dir. Entrepreneur Media, Inc., Irvine, 1990—2008; CEO SMB Connects; consulting editor Biznomen.Com; editorial dir. Moran Media Group; contbg. writer Microsoft; editor-at-large AllBusiness-.com, Inc., 2008—. Spkr., lectr. in field. Author: Start Your Own Business, 1998, 4th edit., 2007, Young Millionaires, 1998, Get Smart!, 1999, 303 Marketing Tips, 1999, Ultimate Guide to Franchises, 2004; editor: Complete Guide to Owning a Home-based Business, 1990, 168 More Businesses Anyone Can Start, 1991, 111 Businesses You Can Start for Under $10,000, 1991; contbr. articles to mags. Mem. adv. bd. disting. counselors Women's Leadership Exch.; nat. adv. coun. SBA, 1994—2000; bd. dirs. Students in Free Enterprise, Jr. Achievement, Orange County. Named Dist. Media Adv. of Yr., SBA, 1993, Dist. Women in Bus. Adv., SBA, 1995; Bus. Luminaries award. Mem. Women's Network for Entrepreneurial Tng. (bd. dirs., advisor, nat. steering com.). Avocations: books, magazines, baseball. Office: SMB Connects 17625 Von Karman Ave Irvine CA 92614 Office Phone: 949-769-6000. Personal E-mail: rieva7@gmail.com. Business E-Mail: rieva@smbconnects.com.

LESOWITZ, JESSICA R., lawyer; b. LA, Calif., Sept. 4, 1976; BA, Univ. Calif., Berkeley, 1998; JD, Pepperdine Univ., 2001. Bar: Calif. 2001, US Dist. Ct. No., Ea., Ctrl., So. Calif. Atty., family law practice, Beverly Hills. Named a Rising Star, So. Calif. Super Lawyers, 2006. Mem.: State Bar Calif., Beverly Hills Bar Assn., LA County Bar Assn., Santa Monica Bar Assn. Office: Jessica R Lesowitz 9663 Santa Monica Blvd Beverly Hills CA 90210 Office Phone: 310-288-1601. Office Fax: 310-858-8504. Business E-Mail: jrl@jrlesowitzlaw.com.

LESSER, HENRY, lawyer; b. London, Feb. 28, 1947; came to US, 1976; s. Bernard Martin and Valerie Joan (Leslie) L.; m. Jane Michaels, June 29, 1969. BA with honors, Cambridge U., Eng., 1968, MA with honors, 1972; LLM, Harvard U., 1973. Bar: Eng. 1969, N.Y. 1977, U.S. Dist. Ct. (so. and ea. dists.) N.Y. 1977, Calif. 1984, U.S. Dist. Ct. (cen. dist.) Calif. 1984. Pvt. practice, London, 1969-71; assoc. Spear & Hill, NYC and London, 1974-75, Webster & Sheffield, NYC and London, 1976-77, Wachtell, Lipton, Rosen & Katz, NYC, 1977-80, ptnr., 1980-83, Gibson, Dunn & Crutcher, LA, 1983-87, Fried, Frank, Harris, Shriver & Jacobson, LA, 1987-91, Irell & Manella, LLC, LA, 1991-97, Heller, Ehrman, White & McAuliffe, Palo Alto, Calif., 1997-2000, Gray, Cary, Ware & Friedenrich, Ea. Palo Alto, 2000—04; ptnr., co-chmn. Private Equity practice group DLA Piper Rudnick Gray Cary, Ea. Palo Alto, Calif., 2005—. Lectr. law Oxford (Eng.) U., 1968-69, Cambridge U., 1970-71, UCLA, 1989. Editor-in-chief emeritus (bi-monthly) Corporate Governance Adviser; contbr. articles to profl. publs. Chmn. bd. Schola Cantorum, Mountain View, Calif.; bd. mem. Redwood Symphony Orch. Harkness fellow Commonwealth Fund, N.Y., 1971; named one of No. Calif. Top 100 Super Lawyers, San Francisco mag., 2004. Mem. ABA, Internat. Bar Assn., Calif. Bar Assn. (chmn. corps. com. 1990-91, vice chmn. bus. law sect. exec. com. 1993-94), Am. Law Inst., Assn. Bar City N.Y. Avocations: running, golf. Office: DLA

Piper Rudnick Gray Cary 2000 University Ave East Palo Alto CA 94303 Home Phone: 650-036-0539; Office Phone: 650-833-2425. Office Fax: 650-833-2001. Business E-Mail: henry.lesser@dlapiper.com.

LESSER, JOAN L., lawyer; b. LA; BA, Brandeis U., 1969; JD, U. So. Calif., 1973. Bar: Calif. 1973, U.S. Dist. Ct. (cen. dist.) Calif. 1974. Assoc. Irell and Manella LLP, LA, 1973-80, ptnr., 1980—. Spkr. profl. confs. Trustee UCLA Design for Sharing, 2005—, pres.; grants com. mem. LA Women Donor's Cir. Mem.: Tech Coast Angels, Order of Coif. Office: Irell & Manella LLP 1800 Avenue Of The Stars Los Angeles CA 90067-4276 Office Phone: 310-203-7577. Business E-Mail: jlesser@irell.com.

LESSER, WENDY, editor, writer, consultant; b. Santa Monica, Calif., Mar. 20, 1952; d. Murray Leon Lesser and Millicent Dillon; m. Richard Rizzo, Jan. 18, 1985; 1 child, Nicholas 1 stepchild, Dov Antonio. BA, Harvard U., 1973; MA, Cambridge U., Eng., 1975; PhD, U. Calif., Berkeley, 1982. Founding ptnr. Lesser & Ogden Assocs., Berkeley, 1977-81; founding editor Threepenny Rev., Berkeley, 1980—. Bellagio resident Rockefeller Found., Italy, 1984. Author: The Life Below the Ground, 1987, His Other Half, 1991, Pictures at an Execution, 1994, A Director Calls, 1997, The Amateur, 1999, Nothing Remains the Same, 2002, The Pagoda in the Garden, 2005, Room for Doubt, 2007; editor: Hiding in Plain Sight, 1993, The Genius of Language, 2004. Fellow, NEH, 1983, Guggenheim Found., 1988, NEH, 1992, ACLS, 1996, Open Soc. Inst., 1998, Columbia U., 2000—01, Am. Acad. Berlin, 2003, Remarque Inst., 2004, Cullman Ctr. for Scholars and Writers, 2005—06, Dedalus Found., 2008. Democrat. Office: The Threepenny Rev PO Box 9131 Berkeley CA 94709-0131

LESSEY, SAMUEL KENRIC, JR., foundation administrator; b. Newark, Oct. 9, 1923; s. Samuel Kenric and Ruth (Turner) Lessey. BS, US Mil. Acad., 1945; student, Vanderbilt U., 1945; LLB, Harvard U., 1951; postgrad., George Washington U., 1951—52, U. Md., 1951—53; MBA, Harvard U., 1956; postgrad., Air War Coll., 1974—75. Bar: NY, US Dist. Ct. DC, S. Ct. Claims, US Tax Ct., US Ct. Mil. Appeals, US Ct. Appeals (DC cir.), US Supreme Ct. Commd. USAF, 1945, advanced through grades to brig. gen., active duty, 1942-54, 76-78; with USAFR, 1954-83; v.p., bd. dirs. Nat. Aviation Corp. Investment Trust, 1957-68; v.p. Shearson Hammill and Co., Inc., 1968-74; moblzn. asst. to dir. Fed. Emergency Mgmt. Agy., 1979-82; insp. gen. US Synthetic Fuels Corp., 1982—86; dir. Selective Svc. System, 1987-91. Civilian aide to Sec. of Army, 1992; bd. visitors US Mil. Acad., West Point, NY, 2003—, vice chmn., 2007. Bd. dirs. Nat. Stroke Assn., 1991—, chmn. bd., 1994—2000, chmn. emeritus, 2001—; bd. dirs. Dwight D. Eisenhower Soc., 2004—, vice chmn., 2006—. Decorated Legion of Merit with Oak Leaf Cluster, Army Outstanding Civil Svc. award, Selective Svc. Disting. Svc. medal, WWII Victory medal, Occupation medal, Nat. Def. Svc. medal, Am. Campaign medal, UN Svc. medal, Air Force Outstanding Unit award; Korean Svc. medal. Mem. AIAA, IEEE, Aerospace Analysts Soc. (past pres.), Am. Fighter Pilots Assn., Air Force Assn. (past v.p. Iron Gate chpt.), Am. Astronautical Soc., Am. Def. Preparedness Assn., Am. Helicopter Soc., Assn. US Army (NH pres.), Aviation Space Writers Assn., Elec. and Electronic Analysts Group, Chartered Fin. Analysts Inst., NY Soc. Security Analysts, Mil. Order of World Wars, Res. Officers Assn., Air Force Pub. Affairs Alumni Assn., Am. Assoc. Royal Acad. Arts, Def. Orientation Conf. Assn. (v.p.), Wings Club (past bd. dirs.), Ctr. for Mil. Readiness (adv. bd.), Nat. Aviation Club, NY Athletic Club, Lincoln's Inn Soc., Capitol Hill Club, Army & Navy Club. Avocations: skiing, tennis, swimming, traditional jazz, antiques. Home: Brimstone Corner PO Box 57 Hancock NH 03449-0057 Office: Nat Stroke Assn 9707 E Easter Ln Centennial CO 80112-3754

LESSIG, L. LAWRENCE, III, law educator, writer; b. Rapid City, SD, June 3, 1961; m. Bettina Neuefeind, 1999; children: Willem Dakota Neuefeind, Teo Elias Neuefeind. BA in Econs., U. Pa., 1983, BS in Mgmt., 1983; MA in Philosophy with honors, Trinity Coll., 1986; JD, Yale U., 1989. Law clk. to Hon. Richard Posner US Ct. Appeals 7th cir., 1989—90; law clk. to Hon. Antonin Scalia US Supreme Ct., 1990—91; asst. prof. law U. Chgo., 1991—95, prof. law, 1995—97, co-dir. Ctr. for the Study of Constitutionalism in Ea. Europe; prof. law Harvard U., Cambridge, 1997—2000, Jack N. and Lillian R. Berkman Prof. Entrepreneurial Legal Studies, 1998; prof. law Stanford U., 2000—, founder, exec. dir. Ctr. for Internet and Soc., 2000—, Wilson Faculty Scholar Calif., 2002, John A. Wilson Disting. Faculty Scholar Calif., 2003—; founder Creative Commons, San Francisco, 2001, CEO, bd. dirs., 2001—. Vis. prof. law Yale U., 1995, Harvard U., 1997; bd. mem. RedHat Ctr. for Pub. Domain, 2000—01; bd. dirs. Electronic Frontier Found., San Francisco, Pub. Knowledge, Washington, Free Software Found.; mem. Penn Nat. Commn. Soc., Culture and Cmty. U. Pa., Phila.; moderator Constl. Law Discussion Group Lexis Counsel Connect, 1994—95; editl. adv. bd. Lexis-Nexis Electronic Authors Press, 1995—97; monthly columnist The Industry Standard, 1998—2001, Wired Mag., 2003—; bi-monthly columnist Red Herring, 2002—03; columnist CIO Insight, 2002—03; lectr. in field. Author: Code, and Other Laws of Cyberspace, 1999, The Future of Ideas: The Fate of the Commons in a Connected World, 2001 (Editor's Choice Award for Best Non-Tech. Book, Linux Jour., 2002), Free Culture: How Big Media Uses Technology and the Law to Lock Down Creativity, 2004; contbr. articles to profl. jours. Bd. dirs. Pub. Libr. Sci., San Francisco, 2003—. Recipient Annual award, Internat. Tech. Network, 2001, World Tech. award for law, 2001, Advancement of Free Software award, Free Software Found., 2002; named one of Top 25 eBiz Leaders, BusinessWeek, 2000, 2001, 100 Most Influential Lawyers, Nat. Law Jour., 2000, 2006, Top 50 Innovators, Sci. Am., 2002, 50 Most Important People on the Web, PC World, 2007; fellow Program on Ethics and the Professions, Harvard U., 1996—97, Wissenschaftskolleg zu Berlin, Germany, 1999—2000. Fellow: Am. Acad. Arts & Sciences, World. Acad. Art and Sci. Office: Stanford Law Sch Crown Quadrangle 559 Nathan Abbott Way Stanford CA 94305-8610 also: Creative Commons 171 Second St Ste 300 San Francisco CA 94105

LESTER, W. HOWARD, retail executive; Attended, Univ. Okla. V.p. Computer Sciences Corp.; founder Centurex Corp.; CEO Williams-Sonoma Inc., San Francisco, 1978—2001, 2006—, chmn., 1986—. Bd. dir. Harold's Stores, Inc. Mem. adv. bd. Haas Sch. Bus., Univ. Calif., Berkeley, Retail Mgmt. Inst., Santa Clara Univ.; mem. exec. council Univ. Calif., San Francisco; bd. mem. Mus. Modern Art, San Francisco. Named Bus. Leader of the Yr., Haas Sch. Bus. Univ. Calif. Berkeley, 2003; named to Okla. Hall of Fame, 2001. Mem.: Internat. Assoc. Shopping Centers (assoc.). Office: Williams-Sonoma Inc 3250 Van Ness Ave San Francisco CA 94109

LESTER, WILLIAM ALEXANDER, JR., chemist, educator; b. Chgo., Apr. 24, 1937; s. William Alexander and Elizabeth Frances (Clark) L.; m. Rochelle Diane Reed, Dec. 27, 1959; children: William Alexander III, Allison Kimberleigh. BS, U. Chgo., 1958, MS, 1959; postgrad., Washington U., St. Louis, 1959-60; PhD, Cath. U. Am., 1964. Phys. chemist Nat. Bur. Stds., Washington, 1961-64; asst. dir. Theoretical Chemistry Inst./U. Wis., Madison, 1965-68; rsch. staff IBM Rsch. Lab., San Jose, Calif., 1968-75, mgr., 1976-78; tech. planning staff IBM T.J. Watson Rsch. Ctr., Yorktown Heights, NY, 1975-76; dir. Nat. Resource for Computation in Chemistry, Lawrence Berkeley (Calif.) Lab., 1978-81, also assoc. dir., staff sr. scientist, 1978-81, faculty sr. scientist, 1981—; prof. chemistry U. Calif., Berkeley, 1981—, assoc. dean Coll. Chemistry, 1991-95. Lectr. chemistry U. Wis., 1966-68; cons. NSF, 1976-77, chem. divsn. adv. panel, 1981-83, adv. com. Office Advanced Sci. Computing program, 1985-87, chmn., 1987, sr. fellow for sci. and engring., asst. to dir. for human resource devel., 1995-96; US nat. com. Internat. Union Pure and Applied Chemistry, 1976-79; com. on recommendations for U.S. Army Basic Sci. Rsch. NRC, 1984-87, steering com., 1987-88; chemistry rsch. evaluation panel AF Office Sci. Rsch., 1974-78; chmn. Gordon Conf. Atomic and Molecular Interactions, 1978; mem. NRC panel on chem. physics Nat. Bur. Stds., 1980-83; com. to survey chem. scis. NRC, 1982-84, Fed. Networking Coun. Adv. Com., 1991-95; blue ribbon panel on high performance computing NSF, 1993; com. on high performance computing and comm.: status of a major initiative NRC, 1994-95, com. on math. challenges from theoretical computational chemistry, NRC, 1994-95; tech. assessment bd. Army Rsch. Lab., NRC, 1996-99; coun. mem. Gordon Rsch. Conf., 1997-2000, selection and scheduling com., 2000-06, bd. trustees, 2006—; adv. bd. Model Instns. Excellence Spelman Coll., 1997-2004; external vis. com. Nat. Partnership Advanced Computational Infrastructure, 1999-2002; pres. com. Nat. Medal Sci., 2000-02; dept. energy adv. com. on advanced sci. computing, 2000-04; bd. on chem. scis. and tech. NRC, 2004-06. Editor: Procs. of Conf. on Potential Energy Surfaces in Chemistry, 1971, Recent Advances in Quantum Monte Carlo Methods, 1997; co-editor (with J. Govaerts and M.N. Houkonnou): Contemporary Problems in Mathematical Physics, 2000; co-editor: (with S.M. Rothstein and S. Tanaka) Recent Advances in Quantum Monte Carlo Methods, Part II, 2002; co-author (with Brian L. Hammond and Peter J. Reynolds): Monte Carlo Methods in Ab Initio Quantum Chemistry, 1994; mem. editl. bd. Jour. Phys. Chemistry, 1979—81, Jour. Computational Chemistry, 1980—87, Computer Physics Comm., 1981—86, mem. adv. bd. Sci. Yr., 1989—93, Comms. on Analysis, Geometry and Physics, 1997—, Jour. Chem. Physics, 2006—08. Recipient Alumni award in sci. Cath. U. Am., 1983; named to U. Chgo. Athletics Hall of Fame, 2004. Fellow AAAS (com. on nominations 1988-91, nat. bd. dirs. 1993-97, coun. del. chemistry sect.), Calif. Acad. Scis., Am. Phys. Soc. (chmn. divsn. chem. physics 1986); mem. Am. Chem. Soc. (sec.-treas. Wis. sect. 1967-68, chmn. divsn. phys. chemistry 1979, treas. divsn. computers in chemistry 1974-77), Nat. Orgn. Black Chemists and Chem. Engrs. (Percy L. Julian award 1979, Outstanding Tchr. award 1986, exec. bd. 1984-87), Sigma Xi (lectureships com. 1993-2002, chair 1998-2000, bd. dirs. 1998-99, com. on devel. 1999-2006, U. Calif. Berkeley chpt. v.p. 1998-2000, pres. 2000-01), Internat. Acad. Quantum Molecular Sci. Home: 4433 Briar Cliff Rd Oakland CA 94605-4624 Office: U Calif Dept Chemistry Berkeley CA 94720-1460 Office Phone: 510-643-9590. Business E-Mail: walester@lbl.gov.

LETA, DAVID EDWARD, lawyer; b. Rochester, NY, June 9, 1951; married; 2 children. BA with high honors, SUNY, Binghamton, 1973; JD, U. Utah, 1976. Bar: Utah, 1976, US Dist. Ct. Utah, US Tax Ct., US Ct. Appeals (9th and 10th cirs.), US Supreme Ct. Assoc. Roe & Fowler, 1976-80, ptnr., 1980-82, Hansen, Jones, & Leta and predecessor firms Hansen, Jones, Maycock & Leta, Hansen & Anderson, 1982-92, Snell & Wilmer, LLP, Salt Lake City, 1992—. Adj. prof. U. Utah. 1978-80; co-chair, presenter, lectr. confs., numerous seminars and CLE programs. Mem. editl. bd. law rev. Utah Coll. Law; contbr. articles to profl. jours. Trustee Ballet West. Named One of the Best Lawyers in Am., Woodward/White, Inc., 1995—; named one of The Leading Bankruptcy Lawyers in the Country, Corp. Counsel, 1995, Utah 100 Legal Elite, Utah Bus., 1995. Fellow Am. Coll. Bankruptcy; mem. ABA (bankruptcy cts., rules and legis. subcoms. bus. bankruptcy sect.), Utah State Bar (first chmn. bankruptcy sec. 1976, organizer 1976), Am. Bankruptcy Inst., Utah Bankruptcy Lawyers Forum (initial trustee) Order of the Coif, Phi Beta Kappa. Office: Snell & Wilmer LLP 15 W South Temple Ste 1200 Salt Lake City UT 84101-1547 Home Phone: 801-581-0683; Office Phone: 801-257-1928. Business E-Mail: dleta@swlaw.com.

LETTICH, SHELDON BERNARD, director, screenwriter; b. NYC, Jan. 14, 1951; s. Max and Sonja (Shapelska) L.; m. Toni Dorthera Williams, Mar. 5, 1954; children: Micheline, Jessica, Angelique. Student, Brooks Inst., Santa Barbara, Calif., 1974; AA, Santa Monica Coll., 1974-76; student, Am. Film Inst., Beverly Hills, 1977-78. Author: (with others) play Tracers, 1980 (Los Angeles Drama Critics award, 1981), film Russkies, 1987, Rambo III, 1988; author: film Bloodsport, 1988; dir., writer films Lionheart, 1990, Only the Strong, 1993, The Hard Corps, 2006; dir., writer, co-prodr. film Double Impact, 1991; dir. films Perfect Target, 1996, The Last Patrol, 2000, The Order, 2001; writer, exec. prodr. film Legionnaire, 1999. Served to cpl. U.S.M.C., 1969-72, Vietnam. Mem. Dirs. Guild Am., Writers Guild Am. Office: Hard Corps Prodns Inc Ste 1060 10100 Santa Monica Blvd Los Angeles CA 90067-4100 Office Phone: 310-201-6523.

LETTS, J. SPENCER, federal judge; b. 1934; BA, Yale U., 1956; LLB, Harvard U., 1960. Commd. U.S. Army, 1956, advanced through grades to capt., resigned, 1965; pvt. practice law Fulbright & Jaworski, Houston, 1960-66, Troy, Malin, Loveland & Letts, LA, 1973-74, Hedlund, Hunter & Lynch, LA, 1978-82, Latham & Watkins, LA, 1982-85; gen. counsel Teledyne, Inc., 1966-73, 75-78, legal cons., 1978-82; judge U.S. Dist. Ct. (cen. dist.) Calif., LA, 1986—. Contbr. articles to profl. jours. Mem. ABA, Calif. State Bar, Tex. State Bar, L.A. Bar Assn., Houston Bar Assn. Office: US Dist Ct 312 N Spring St Ste 243J Los Angeles CA 90012-4704

LETWIN, LEON, law educator; b. Milw., Dec. 29, 1929; s. Lazar and Bessie (Rosenthal) L.; m. Alita Zurav, July 11, 1952; children— Michael, Daniel, David PhB, U. Chgo., 1950; LLB, U. Wis., 1952; LLM, Harvard U., 1964. Bar: Wis. 1952, Calif. 1969. Teaching fellow Harvard Law Sch., Boston, 1963-64; faculty Law Sch. UCLA, 1964—, prof., 1968-92, prof. emeritus, 1993—. Coord. Native-Am. Grave Protection and Repatriation Act, UCLA, 1998—2002. Contbr. articles to profl. jours. Active ACLU. Mem. Lawyers Guild, State Bar Calif. Home: 2226 Manning Ave Los Angeles CA 90064-2002 Office: UCLA Law Sch 405 Hilgard Ave Los Angeles CA 90095-9000 Business E-Mail: letwin@ucla.edu.

LEUNG, DONALD Y. M., pediatric allergist; b. NYC, Oct. 1, 1949; s. Kwok Choy and Kit (Tsui) Leung; m. Susan Bertarelli, Nov. 10, 1979; children: Allison, Alexander. BA, Johns Hopkin's U., Balt., 1970; PhD, U. Chgo., 1975, MD, 1977. Diplomate Am. Bd. Pediat., Am. Bd. Allergy-Immunology, lic. Mass., Colo. Intern pediat. Children's Hosp. Medical Ctr., Boston, 1977—78, resident pediat., 1978—79, fellow, allergy and immunology, 1979-81; instr. pediat. Harvard Med. Sch., 1981—83, asst. prof. pediat., 1983—87, assoc. prof. pediat., 1987-89; head div. pediat., sr. staff physician Nat. Jewish Ctr. Immunology Respiratory Medicine, Denver, 1989—. Clin. fellow pediat. Harvard Med. Sch., 1977—79; dir. diagnostic allergy, clin. immunology lab. Children's Hosp. Med. Ctr., 1983—87; assoc. clin. dir. immunology prog., dir. allergy prog. Children's Hosp. Medical Ctr., 1987—89; assoc. prof., dept. pediat. U. Colo. Health Sci. Ctr., 1990—91, prof., 1991—, rsch. adv. com., 2006; dir. NIH Gen. Clin. Rsch. Ctr., Denver, 1994. Author: (med. text) Treatment of Atopic Dermatitis, 1991; editorial bd. mem. (to numerous med. jours.); contbr. articles to profl. jours. Recipient Sci. Achievement award, Nat. Jewish med. rsch. Ctr., 2003, Psoriasis Achievement award, Am. Skin Assn., 2004; named to Woodward & White's Best Dr.'s in America, 1992—, Cambridge Outstanding Scientists of the 21st Century, Internat. Biog. Ctr., 2002. Fellow: Am. Coll. Allergy, Asthma, Immunology, Am. Acad. Allergy, Asthma, Immunology; mem.: Am. Soc. Clin. Investigation, European Soc. Pediat. Allergy Clin. Immunology, Soc. Investigative Dermatology, Colo. Allergy Soc., Am. Assoc. Advancement of Sci., New Eng. Soc. of Allergy, Am. Fedn. Clin. Rsch., Am. Assn. Immunologists, Collegium Internat. Allergologicum, Soc. Pediat. Rsch., Eczema Assn. Sci. Edn. (adv. bd. 1988), Am. Acad. Allergy Immunology, Phi Beta Kappa. Achievements include research in treatment of atopic dermatitis and asthma with inmunomodulatory agents; pathogenesis of Kawasaki disease and inmune mechanisms in atopic dermatitis; regulation of the human IgE response; patents for treatment of atopic disorders with gamma-interferon; treatment of steroid resistant diseases. Office: Nat Jewish Med Rsch Ctr Dept Pediat 1400 Jackson St Denver CO 80206-2761 Office Phone: 303-388-4461.

LEUNG, FRANKIE FOOK-LUN, lawyer; b. Guangzhou, China, 1949; (div.); 1 child. BA in Psychology with honors, Hong Kong U., 1972; MS in Psychology, Birmingham U., Eng., 1974; BA, MA in Jurisprudence, Oxford U., Eng., 1976; JD, Coll. of Law, London, 1977. Bar: Calif. 1987. Barrister Eng. and Hong Kong, 1977—. Lectr. Chinese law for businessmen Hong Kong U., 1984-85, 85-86; vis. scholar Harvard U. Law Sch., 1983; barrister, solicitor Supreme Ct. of Victoria, Australia, 1983—, Calif. Bar, 1987—; cons. prof. Chinese Law Diploma Program, U. East Asia, 1986-87; adj. prof. Loyola Law Sch., L.A., 1988-2000, Pepperdine U. Law Sch., 1989-90; lectr. Stanford U. Law Sch., 1995-96, U. So. Calif. Law Sch., 1998-2003. Author books on Chinese and Hong Kong law, Asian politics, Asian trade and bus. mgmt.; contbr. numerous articles to profl. jours., and 6 books. Bd. advisors Hong Kong Archives Hoover Instn.-Stanford U., 1988—; adv., Ctrl. Policy Unit, Hong Kong govt., 1997-99, dir. YMCA, Pasadena, Calif., 1997-99. Mem. Am. Arbitration Assn. (bd. dirs.), Calif. State Bar (mem. exec. coun. internat. sect. 1989-92, Wiley W. Manuel award 1993), Hong Kong Bar Assn., European Assn. for Chinese Law (mem. exec. coun. 1986—, country corr. 1985—), Am. C. of C. (chmn. subcom. on Chinese intellectual property law 1985-86), Am. Soc. Internat. Law (judge moot ct. 1984-2005). Office: 444 S Flower St Ste 3010 Los Angeles CA 90071-2901 Home Phone: 213-952-8511; Office Phone: 213-228-8922. Personal E-mail: frankieleunglaw@aol.com.

LEUNG, KASON KAI CHING, computer specialist; b. Hong Kong, July 2, 1962; came to U.S., 1963; s. Patrick Kin Man and Esther Mo Chee (Shum) L. BA in Computer Sci., U. Calif., 1984. Microcomputer specialist Coopers & Lybrand, San Francisco, 1985-87; freelance computer specialist San Francisco, 1988-90; computer applications specialist T.Y. Lin Internat., San Francisco, 1990-92; tech. specialist Ziff-Davis Labs., Foster City, Calif., 1993-94; tech. analyst PC Mag., Foster City, Calif., 1995; sr. tech. analyst Ziff-Davis Benchmark Operation, Foster City, Calif., 1996; sr. tech. specialist Ziff-Davis Labs., Foster City, Calif., 1997-98; sys. adminstr. TurboLinux, Inc., Brisbane, Calif., 1999; sys. programmer II Office of the Pres., U. Calif., Oakland, Calif., 2000—08; freelance computer specialist San Fransisco, 2009. Mem. Assn. for Computing Machinery. Avocations: computers, sports, music, reading. Home: 90 Stanford Heights Ave San Francisco CA 94127-2318 Office Phone: 510-987-0345. Personal E-mail: kasonleung@netscape.net. Business E-Mail: kason.leung@yahoo.com.

LEUNG, SIMON, lawyer, electronics executive; BA, U. Calif., Davis; JD, U. Minn. Atty. Fotenos & Suttle, PC, 1995—99, Paul, Hastings, Janofsky & Walker LLP, 1999—2000; corp. counsel SYNNEX Corp., Fremont, Calif., 2000—01, gen. counsel, corp. sec., 2001—. Office: SYNNEX Corp 44201 Nobel Dr Fremont CA 94538 Office Phone: 510-656-3333.

LEVE, ALAN DONALD, electronics executive; b. LA, Dec. 15, 1927; s. Milton Lewis and Etta L.; m. Annette Einhorn, Sept. 3, 1962; children— Laura Michelle, Elise Deanne. BS, UCLA, 1951. CPA, Calif. Staff acct., mgr. Joseph S. Herbert & Co. (C.P.A.s), Los Angeles, 1951-57, ptnr., 1957-63; CFO, sec., treas. Mica Corp., Culver City, Calif., 1963-82, also bd. dirs., 1963-82, chmn. bd., chief exec. officer, 1982-83; v.p., bd. dirs. Micaply Internat. Inc., 1968-1982; v.p. Micaply AG, Switzerland, 1972-83, also bd. dirs., chief exec. officer, also bd. dirs., 1982-83; v.p., bd. dirs. Micaply Internat., Ltd., U.K., 1971-82; chmn. bd., mng. dir., chief exec. officer Micaply Internat. Ltd., U.K., 1982-83; v.p., bd. dirs. Titan Chem. Corp., Edgecraft Corp., Culver Hydro-Press, Inc., LA, 1963-75; chmn. bd., pres., chief exec. officer Ohmega Techs., Inc., Culver City, Calif., 1983—, Ohmega Electronics, Inc., Culver City, 1986—2004. Served with USAAF, 1946-47. Home: 16430 Dorado Dr Encino CA 91436-4118 Office: 4031 Elenda St Culver City CA 90232-3723

LEVEL, LEON JULES, investor, director; b. Detroit, Dec. 30, 1940; s. Leon and Madeline G. (Mayea) L.; m. Constance Kramer, June 25, 1966; children— Andrea, Aileen BBA, U. Mich., 1962, MBA, 1963. CPA, Mich. Asst. accountant Deloitte Haskins & Sells, Detroit, 1963-66, sr. accountant, 1966-69, prin., 1969-71; asst. corp. controller Bendix Corp., Southfield, Mich., 1971-81; v.p. fin. planning Burroughs Corp., Detroit, 1981-82, v.p., treas., 1982-86, Unisys Corp., Blue Bell, Pa., 1986-89; CFO, v.p. Computer Scis. Corp., 1989—2006. Mem. adv. bd. U. Mich., Ann Arbor, 1984-90, Providence Hosp., Southfield, Mich., 1984-86, Western FM Global Ins., 1995-06; bd. dirs. Allied Waste Industries, Inc., UTi Worldwide, Inc., Levi Strauss & Co. Trustee Walnut St. Theatre, Phila., 1988-89, Autry Nat. Ctr., 2000. Mem. Fin. Execs. Inst. (sec. Detroit chpt. 1983-85, v.p. 1985-86, pres. 1986-87), Am. Inst. C.P.A.s, Mich. Assn. C.P.A.s, Inst. Mgmt. Accts.

LEVEN, MICHAEL ALAN, hotel and gaming company executive; b. Boston, Nov. 13, 1937; s. David and Sara (Goldberg) L.; m. Andrea Elaine Aronson, May 29, 1961; children: Jonathan, Adam, Robert BA, Tufts U., 1959; MS, Boston U., 1961; D in Bus. Adminstrn. (hon.), Johnson & Wales U.; D in Commercial Sci. (hon.), Coll. Hospitality & Tourism Mgmt., Niagra U., 2001. Vice-pres. mktg. Sonesta Hotels, 1972-73; v.p. ops. Dunfey Hotels, Hampton, N.H., 1973-76; sr. v.p. mktg. Americana Hotels, Chgo., 1976-80, exec. v.p., 1980-84, pres., 1984-85, Days Inns of America, Atlanta, 1985—90; pres., COO Holiday Inn Worldwide, 1990—95; chmn., CEO US Franchise Systems, Inc. (USFS), 1995—2008; pres., COO Las Vegas Sands Corp, 2009—. Bd. dirs. Las Vegas Sands Corp., 2004—. Pres. New Trier Hockey Club, Winnetka, Ill., 1983-85; bd. dirs. Stamford Little League, Conn., 1976-80; bd. trustees Hersha Hospitality Trust, 2001-, The Chief Exec. Leadership Inst., Marcus Found., 2001-, vice chmn., 2006-; co-founder Asian Am. Hotel Owners Assn. (AAHOA), 1989 Recipient Hospitality Hall of Fame award Hospitality Mag., 1972, Hotel Salesman of Yr. award Wash. State U., 1973, AH&LA Coun. Inns & Suites Person of the Yr. award, 1998, Arthur Landstreet award, 1998, Ga. Hospitality & Travel Assn. Spirit of Hospitality award, 1999, Internat. Soc. Hospitality Consultants' Pioneer award, 2000, UJA Fedn. NY Hotel & Hospitality award, 2001, Above & Beyond award, The Lodging Conf., 2001, Disting. Alumni Svc. award, Tufts U., 2002, Total Quality Franchising Lifetime Achievement award, Am. Assn. Franchises & Dealers, 2005; named one of The 25 Most Extraordinary Sales & Mktg. Minds in Hospitality & Travel, 2002 Mem. Hotel Sales Mgmt. Assn. Internat. (Albert E. Koehl award 1981, Mktg. Exec. Yr. award 1982, internat. pres. 1976,) Office: Las Vegas Sands Corp 3355 Las Vegas Blvd S Las Vegas NV 89109*

LEVENSON, ALAN IRA, psychiatrist, physician, educator; b. Boston, July 25, 1935; s. Jacob Maurice and Frances Ethel (Biller) Levenson; m. Myra Beatrice Katzen, June 12, 1960 (div. 1993); children: Jonathan, Nancy; m. Linda Ann Nadell, Jan. 30, 1994. AB, Harvard U., 1957, MD, 1961, MPH, 1965. Diplomate Am. Bd. Psychiatry and Neurology. Intern U. Hosp., Ann Arbor, Mich., 1961-62; resident in psychiatry Mass. Mental Health Ctr., Boston, 1962-65; staff psychiatrist NIMH, Chevy Chase, Md., 1965-66, dir. divsn. mental health svc. programs, 1967-69; prof. psychiatry U. Ariz. Coll. Medicine, Tucson, 1969-2000, prof. emeritus, 2000—, head dept. psychiatry, 1969-89; CEO Palo Verde Mental Health Svcs., Tucson, 1971-91, chief med. officer, med. dir., 1991-93; chmn. bd. dirs., CEO Psychiatrists' Purchasing Group, 1991—; chmn. bd. dirs. Psychiatrists' Risk Retention Group, 1991-2000. Author: (book) The Community Mental Health Center: Strategies and Programs, 1972; contbr. papers and articles to profl. jours. Bd. dirs. Tucson Urban League, 1971—78, Pima Coun. Aging, 1976—83, 2006—, chmn., 2008—. With USPHS, 1965—69. Fellow: Am. Coll. Mental Health Adminstrn. (v.p. 1980—82, pres. 1982—83), Am. Coll. Psychiatrists (regent 1980—83, v.p. 1983—85, pres.-elect 1985—86, pres. 1986—87), Am. Psychiat. Assn. (treas. 1986—90); mem.: Group Advancement Psychiatry, Harvard Alumni Assn. (bd. dirs. 1988—91). Office: 75 E Calle Resplendor Tucson AZ 85716-4937

LEVENSON, MARC DAVID, optics and lasers specialist, editor; b. Phila., May 28, 1945; s. Donald William and Ethyl Jean Levenson; m. Naomi Francis Matsuda, Oct. 24, 1971. SB, MIT, 1967; MS, Stanford U., 1968, PhD, 1971. Rsch. fellow Harvard U., Cambridge, Mass., 1971-74; asst. prof. physics U. So. Calif., LA, 1974-77, assoc. prof., 1977-79; mem. rsch. staff IBM Rsch. div., San Jose, Calif., 1979-93, head mgr. OSC, 1987, mgr. quantum metrology, 1990; v.p. Focused Rsch., Inc., Sunnyvale, Calif., 1993-95; propr., cons. Marc D. Levenson Optics, Saratoga, 1993—. Vis. fellow Joint Inst. for Lab. Astrophysics, U. Colo., Boulder, 1995-96; vis. prof. Rice U., Houston, 1996. Author: Introduction to Nonlinear Laser Spectroscopy, 1988; editor: Lasers, Spectroscopy, New Ideas, 1987, Resonances, 1991; contbg. editor Solid State Tech. mag., 1993—; editor-in-chief Microlithography World Mag., 1995—; contbr. articles to profl. jours. Alfred Sloan rsch. fellow, 1975. Fellow IEEE, Optical Soc. Am. (Adolph Lomb medal 1976), Am. Phys. Soc., Bay Area Chrome Users Soc./Soc. Photog. and Instrumentation Engrs. (award 1991); mem. NAE. Avocations: gardening, reading. Home Phone: 408-867-1746; Office Phone: 650-941-3438 x26. Business E-Mail: marcl@pennwell.com.

LEVENSON, MILTON, chemical engineer, consultant; b. St. Paul, Jan. 4, 1923; s. Harry and Fanny M. Levenson; m. Mary Beth Novick, Aug. 27, 1950 (dec.); children: James L., Barbara G., Richard A., Scott D., Janet L. BChemE, U. Minn., 1943. Jr. engr. Houdaille-Hershey Corp., Decatur, Ill., 1944; research engr. Oak Ridge Nat. Lab., 1944-48; with Argonne (Ill.) Nat. Lab., 1948-73, assoc. lab. dir., 1973; dir. nuclear power div. Electric Power Research Inst., Palo Alto, Calif., 1973-80; exec. cons. Bechtel Power Corp., San Francisco, 1981-88; v.p. Bechtel Internat., 1984-89; pvt. exec. cons., 1990—. Lectr. in field. Contbr. over 150 articles to profl. jours., chpts. to 8 books; patentee in field. Served with C.E. U.S. Army, 1944-46. Bechtel fellow, 1981-89. Fellow AIChE (Robert E. Wilson award 1975), NAE, Am. Nuclear Soc. (pres. 1983-84). Office: 2319 Sharon Rd Menlo Park CA 94025-6807 E-mail: mlevenso@nas.edu.

LEVEY, GERALD SAUL, dean, internist, educator; b. Jersey City, Jan. 9, 1937; s. Jacob and Gertrude (Kantoff) Levey; m. Barbara Ann Cohen, June 4, 1961; children: John, Robin. AB, Cornell U., 1957; MD, N.J. Coll. Medicine, 1961. Diplomate Am. Bd. Internal Medicine. Med. intern Jersey City Med. Ctr., 1961—62, asst. med. resident, 1962—63; postdoctoral fellow dept. biol. chemistry Harvard U. Med. Sch., 1963—65; med. resident Mass. Gen. Hosp., Boston, 1965—66; clin. assoc. clin. endocrinology br. Nat. Inst. Arthritis and Metabolic Diseases NIH, Bethesda, Md., 1966—68, clin. assoc. Nat. Heart and Lung Inst., 1968—69, sr. investigator Nat. heart and Lung Inst., 1969—70; assoc. prof. medicine U. Miami Sch. Medicine, Fla., 1970—73, prof. medicine Fla., 1973—79; prof., chmn. dept. medicine U. Pitts. Sch. Medicine, 1979—91; physician-in-chief Presbyn.-Univ. Hosp., Pitts., 1979—91; sr. v.p. for med. and sci. affairs Merck and Co., Inc., Whitehouse Sta., NJ, 1991—94; prof., dept. medicine UCLA, dean, David Geffen Sch. of Medicine, 1994—, vice chancellor med. scis., 1994—. Harold Jeghers lectr. N.J. Coll. Medicine, 1977; Marian Blankenhorn lectr. Cin. Soc. Internal Medicine, 1982—; co-prin. investigator Nat. Study of Internal Medicine Manpower, 1984—. Mem. editl. bd.: Endocrinology, 1972—76, Am. Jour. Physiology, 1972—76, Jour. Applied Physiology, 1972—76, Annals of Internal Medicine, 1981—84, cons. editor: Hosp. Medicine, 1981—91; contbr. articles to profl. jours. Mem. United Jewish Fedn. Pitts. Leadership Devel., 1981—82; bd. dirs. Jewish Family and Children's Svcs., 1982—83, Am. Jewish Com., Miami, 1975—79. Grantee, NIH, 1971—91, Fla. Heart Assn., 1971—74. Fellow: ACP; mem.: AMA, Assn. Am. Physicians, Soc. Gen. Internal Medicine, So. Soc. Clin. Investigation, Assn. Profs. Medicine (chmn. ad hoc com. for use of animals in rsch. 1982—85, chmn. task force on internal medicine manpower 1983—90, nat. pres. 1990—91), Endocrine Soc., Am. Soc. Clin. Investigation, Am. Fedn. Clin. Rsch. (councillor so. sect. 1973—76, pres. so. sect. 1977—78), Am. Thyroid Assn. (mem. membership com. 1977—80), Alpha Omega Alpha. Office: UCLA Deans Office Sch Medicine 10833 Le Conte Ave Los Angeles CA 90095-3075*

LEVI, ALEXIS, professional sports team executive, owner, agent; Grad., Calif. State U., Hayward, 1985. Co-owner Bowden & Levi Media Grp.; co-founder LexMAR Entertainment; agent, adv. Sports Mgmt. Worldwide, 2006—; owner, gen. mgr., CEO Las Vegas Stars Internat. Basketball League, 2007—. Named to Power 150, Ebony mag., 2008. Mem.: Nat. Assn. Black Female Entertainment Media Execs. (pres.). Achievements include first African American woman to be Owner/CEO/GM of a mens professional basketball team. Office: Internat Basketball League Pvt Box 558 11124 NE Halsey Portland OR 97220

LEVIE, MARK ROBERT, lawyer; b. Chgo., Sept. 2, 1951; s. Harold M. and Muriel L.; m. Gail M., Aug. 19, 1973; children: Melissa, Allison, David. BA in Rhetoric and Composition, U. Ill., 1973; JD magna cum laude, Harvard U., 1976. Bar: Calif. 1978, U.S. Dist. Ct. (no. dist.) Calif. 1978. Clk. to Hon. James R. Browning, chief judge U.S. Ct. Appeals (9th cir.), San Francisco, 1976-77; assoc. Orrick, Herrington & Sutcliffe, San Francisco, 1977-82, ptnr., 1983—, mem. exec. com., mng. dir. transactional practices. Bd. dirs., mem. audit com. Legal Aid Soc.-Employment Law Ctr., 2006—. Mem. ABA (corp. banking and bus. law sect., com. devel. bus. fin., sub-com. on securitization of assets, fin. task force), State Bar of Calif., San Francisco Bar Assn., San Francisco Lawyers Com. for Civil Rights (treas. 1995-1998). Avocations: golf, reading. Office: Orrick Herrington & Sutcliffe LLP 405 Howard St San Francisco CA 94105 Office Phone: 415-773-5955. Office Fax: 415-773-5759. Business E-Mail: mlevie@orrick.com.

LEVIN, ANDREW, state legislator; b. NYC, May 4, 1946; m. Nicolette Levin. BA, U. Pa.; JD, Harvard U. Chief counsel Big Island, Legal Aid Soc., 1969-74, Aloha Airlines, 1971-74; asst. prof. U. Hawaii, Hilo, 1977-79; pvt. practice Hilo, 1974—; mem. Hawaii Senate, Honolulu, 1998—, co-chair ways and means com., mem. health/human svcs. com., mem. govt. ops. and housing com. Pres. Easter Seals; chair Carole Kai Bed Race; mem. Gov.'s Solid Waste Task Force; pres. Big Isle Mental Health Assn.; pres. East Hawaii Cultural Coun.; bd. dirs. BICA; mem. Vol. Action League, Humane Soc., ECOH, Puna Traffice and Crime Commn., Hist. Hawaii Found., Big Isle Rd. Runners; mem. Hawaii County Coun., 1975-76. Office: State Capitol 415 S Beretania St Honolulu HI 96813-2407

LEVIN, BARRY RAYMOND, rare book dealer, film producer; b. Phila., June 11, 1946; s. Sidney and Bertha (Zwerman) L.; m. Sally Ann Fudge, Aug. 19, 1983 (dec. June 18, 2006). Student, Santa Monica City Coll., 1964—65. Various aerospace positions McDonnell Douglas, AstroPeen, 1967-72; owner Barry R. Levin Sci. Fiction & Fantasy Lit., 1973—. Cons. sci. fiction, fantasy and horror films, 1976—; co-founder film prodn. co. Sci. Fiction Fantasy Films, Inc., 2008-. Author: (rare book catalogs) Titles from the Back Room, 1981, Great Works and Rarities of Science Fiction and Fantasy, 1982, One Small Step, 1983, Newsletters, 1980—, others; contbr. articles to profl. jours. With U.S. Army, 1965-67. Mem. Antiquarian Booksellers Assn. Am., Am. Booksellers Assn., Bibliog. Soc. Am., Bibliog. Soc. Great Britain, New Eng. Sci. Fiction Assn., So. Calif. Booksellers Assn., Internat. League Antiquarian Booksellers, Internat. Assn. of the Fantastic in the Arts, Internat. Platform Assn., Sci. Fiction Writers Am., Horror Writers Am., Manuscript Soc., Sci. Fiction Rsch. Assn., Assn. Sci. Fiction and Fantasy Artists, Lewis Carroll Soc., others. Jewish. Office: Barry R Levin Sci Fiction & Fantasy Lit 720 Santa Monica Blvd Santa Monica CA 90401-2602 also: Sci Fiction Fantasy Films Inc 406 Broadway Ste 3496 Santa Monica CA 90401 Office Phone: 310-458-6111. Business E-Mail: barry@sfffilms.com. E-mail: brl@raresf.com.

LEVIN, BARRY STEVEN, lawyer; b. St. Louis, Dec. 16, 1954; AB, Washington U., St. Louis, 1976; JD, Northwestern U., 1979. Bar: Calif. 1979. Atty. Heller Ehrman White & McAuliffe, LLP, San Francisco, 1979—, chmn. ins. coverage practice group, 1995—97, chmn. litigation dept., 1997—99, shareholder, chmn., 1999—2005. Lectr. in ins. coverage and law firm mgmt. Recipient Atty. of Yr. award, Calif., 2003; named one of Leading Ins. Coverage Attorneys in Calif., Chambers & Partners America's Leading Bus. Lawyers, 2003, 2004. Mem. ABA, Order of Coif, Bar Assn. San Francisco, Phi Beta Kappa. Office: Heller Ehrman White & McAuliffe 333 Bush St San Francisco CA 94104-2806 Office Phone: 415-772-6646. Fax: 415-772-6268. E-mail: blevin@hewm.com.

LEVIN, HARVEY ROBERT, reporter, television producer, lawyer; b. LA, Sept. 2, 1951; Grad., U. Calif., Santa Barbara, 1973; JD, U. Chgo., 1975. Tchr. Whittier Coll. Sch. Law (formerly Beverly Rubens Sch. Law), LA, 1977—96; legal reporter KCBS-TV, LA; legal analyst The People's Ct., NYC, 1996—2002; creator, exec. prodr. Celebrity Justice, 2002—05; mng. editor TMZ.com, 2005—; host TMZ on TV, 2007—. Guest The Kevin and Bean Morning Show, Larry King Live, CNN. Office: TMZ Productions, Inc 8033 W Sunset Blvd, Ste 875 Los Angeles CA 90046*

LEVIN, JACK, physician, biomedical investigator, educator; b. Newark, Oct. 11, 1932; s. Joseph and Anna (Greengold) L.; m. Francine Corthesy, Apr. 13, 1975. BA magna cum laude, Yale U., 1953, MD cum laude, 1957. Diplomate: Am. Bd. Internal Medicine. Intern in medicine Grace-New Haven Hosp., 1957-58, asst. resident in medicine, 1960-62; chief resident in medicine Yale-New Haven Med. Ctr., 1964-65; clin. assoc. Nat. Cancer Inst., Bethesda, Md., 1958-60; fellow in hematology Johns Hopkins U. Sch. Medicine and Hosp., Balt., 1962-64, mem. faculty, 1965-82, prof. medicine, 1978-82; prof. lab. medicine, prof. medicine U. Calif. Sch. Medicine, San Francisco, 1982—; dir. hematology lab. and blood bank San Francisco VA Med. Ctr., Calif., 1982-93, dir. flow cytometry facility Calif., 1987-90; dir. Anticoagulation Clinic, San Francisco VA Med. Ctr., San Francisco, 1996—. Cons. in field. Author: (with P.D. Zieve) Disorders of Hemostasis, 1976; editor: (with E. Cohen and F.B. Bang) Biomedical Applications of the Horseshoe Crab (Limulidae), 1979, (with S.W. Watson and T.J. Novitsky) Endotoxins and Their Detection with the Limulus Amebocyte Lysate Test, 1982, Detection of Bacterial Endotoxins with The Limulus Amebocyte Lysate Test, 1987, (with others) Bacterial Endotoxins. Structure, Biomedical Significance, and Detection with the Limulus Amebocyte Lysate Test, 1985, Megakaryocyte Develop. and Function, 1986, Bacterial Endotoxins. Pathophysiological Effects, Clinical Significance, and Pharmacological Control, 1988, Molecular Biology and Differentiation of Megakaryocytes, 1990, Bacterial Endotoxins: Cytokine Mediators and New Therapies for Sepsis, 1991, Bacterial Endotoxin: Recognition and Effector Mechanisms, 1993, Bacterial Endotoxins: Basic Sci. to Anti-Sepsis Strategies, 1994, Bacterial Endotoxins: Lipopolysaccharides from Genes to Therapy, 1995; mem. editorial bd. Blood, Jour. Endotoxin Rsch.; contbr. numerous articles to profl. jour; editor-in-chief, Jour. Endotoxin Rsch., 1998-2004; developer (with F.B. Bang) Limulus test for bacterial endotoxins. Mem. Yale Alumni Sch. Com. for Md., 1967-82, for San Francisco, 1986-1997; mem. sci. adv. bd. Nat. Aquarium, Balt., 1978-82; mem. corp. Marine Biol. Lab., 1965—; trustee Marine Biol. Lab., 1988-93; mem. panel ind. assessors for rsch. project grants awards Nat. Health and Med. Rsch. Coun. Australia, 1982—. Served with USPHS, 1958-60. Markle scholar, 1968-73; recipient USPHS Rsch. Career Devel. award, 1970-75; Royal Soc. Medicine fellow Oxford (Eng.) U., 1972; Josiah Macy Jr. Found. faculty scholar, 1978-79; fellow, Found. for Med. Rsch., Paris, France, 1998; Fonds Nat. de la Rechorche Scientifique (FNRS) fellowship, Liege (Belg.), 2003; Frederik B. Bang award for rsch. in bacterial endotoxins, 1986. Fellow ACP; mem. Am. Soc. Hematology, Am. Soc. Clin. Investigation, Internat. Soc. Hematology, Internat. Soc. Explt. Hematology, Am. Soc. Investigative Pathology, Am. Fedn. Clin. Rsch., Soc. Exptl. Biology and Medicine, Internat. Endotoxin Soc., So. Soc. Clin. Investigation, Western Assn. Physicians, Soc. Invertebrate Pathology, Soc. Analytical Cytology, Cell Kinetics Soc., Internat. Soc. Artificial Cells, Blood Substitutes and Immobilization Biotech., Calif. Acad. Medicine, Phi Beta Kappa, Sigma Xi. Clubs: 14 W Hamilton St, Tudor and Stuart; Yale (San Francisco). Office Phone: 415-750-6913. Business E-Mail: levinj@medicine.ucsf.edu.

LEVIN, LEWIS, computer software company executive; BA in Bus. Adminstrn., Quantitative Analysis & Fin., U. Cin.; MA, MIT. Sr. product mgr. Micropro Internat.; from mem. staff Microsoft Corp., Redmond, Wash., 1986, group product mgr. PowerPoint, dir. applications mktg., v.p., gen. mgr. Excel Group, v.p. desktop fin. divsn., pres., CEO TransPoint, corp. v.p. platforms tech. strategy, corp. v.p. office bus. applications strategy. Office: Microsoft Corp One Microsoft Way Redmond WA 98052-6399

LEVIN, ROBERT BARRY, motion picture company executive; b. Chgo., May 31, 1943; s. Albert Harold and Sally Ethel (Bloom) L.; children: Jordan, Leigh; m. Pamela Knussmann, Dec. 2, 1990; 1 stepchild, Taylor Thompson; 1 child, Spencer. BS in Journalism and Comm, U. Ill., 1965. Copywriter Sears Roebuck and Co., Chgo., 1965-66; pub. relations Natural Gas Pipeline Co. Am., Chgo., 1966-69; accounts exect. Hurvis Binzer and Churchill, Chgo., 1969-70; with McCann-Erickson, Chgo., 1975-82, acct. supr., 1975-79; mgmt. supr. Needham Harper Worldwide, Chgo., 1982-85; pres. mktg. Walt Disney Co., Burbank, Calif., 1985-94, chief corp. mktg. and comm., 1994-95; pres. worldwide mktg. Savoy Pictures, Santa Monica, Calif., 1995-96, Sony Pictures Entertainment, Culver City, Calif., 1996—2001, MGM Studios, 2001—.

LEVINE, ALISON, entrepreneur, leadership development consultant, adventurer; b. Apr. 5, 1966; BS in Social & Behavioral Sciences, U. Ariz.; MBA, Duke U., 2000. Positions in sales and mktg. in the healthcare industry in US and Asia, 1989—2000; with Goldman Sachs, 2000—03; founder, pres. Daredevil Strategies, San Francisco, 2003—. Dep. fin. dir. for Arnold Schwarzenegger, 2003; invited spkr. Guest appearences on Today Show, CNN, CNBC, Fox ABC News, CBS Evening News and other nat. programs, subject of articels in Oprah Mag., National Geographic, Lifetime Mag., Sports Illustrated Women, Outside and other publications, host of blog womenclimb-high.spaces.inc.com, featured in More Than 85 Broads, Smart Moves; performer: The Vagina Monologues, Calif. Theater, 2005. Participant North Pole Leadership Challenge, 2004; founder The Climb High Found., 2005—; founding mem. World Wildlife Fund's Young Partners in Conservation. Recipient Courage in Sports award, Anaheim Angels, 2003; named one of San Francisco's Top Bus. Leaders Under 40, Arizona's Most Interesting People. Mem.: Assn. of Women MBAS, 85 Broads (co-chair). Achievements include climbing mountains in 1998 after a second heart surgery to repair a life threatening condition called Wolff Parkinson White Syndrome; serving as team captain of the first American Women's Everest Expedition in 2002; climbed highest peaks on six continents-Kilimanjaro, Aconcagua, Elbrus, Carstensz Pyramid, McKinley and Vinson, also Rainier, Muir, Whitney and Shasta, Cotopaxi (Ecuador), Ixta and Orizaba (Mexico); skied more than 100 miles to reach the top of the world-the North Pole; created Climb High Foundation for improving the lives of jobless women in third-world countries by training them to be trekking guides or porters for the local mountains; involvment in Western Uganda was groundbreaking because it was the first time the local women had climbed mountains because it was forbidden due to cultural beliefs (subordinate status of women); raised funds to build two schools in Nepal; helped to fund the construction of a school for AIDS orphans in Uganda. Avocations: mountaineering, adventure travel, philanthropy, women's initiatives, theater, reading. Office: Daredevil Strategies 1538 Filbert St #4 San Francisco CA 94123 Office Phone: 415-595-3966. Business E-Mail: alison@daredevilstrategies.com.

LEVINE, ARTHUR M., law educator; b. NYC, Apr. 14, 1939; s. Mervin Levine and Elsie Klein. BA, Princeton U., NJ, 1960; JD, Yale U., New Haven, Conn., 1963. Assoc. atty. McGlaughlin & Stern, NYC, 1965—66; civil rights atty. Dept. of Justice, Washington, 1966—67; underwriter Ladenburg Thalmann, NYC, 1968—70; investment analyst Lehman Bros., NYC, 1971—73; prof. ethics and legal studies Calif. State U., Coll. Bus. Adminstrn., Long Beach, Calif., 1974—. Host, exec. prodr. Straight Talk TV Show, 1992—. Bd. dirs. Long Beach Transit, 1988—96, Ctr. for Water Edn., Hemet, Calif., 2004—08. Lt. USN, 1964—70. Recipient Dist. Faculty Tchg. award, Calif. State U., Long Beach, 2003. Mem.: State Bar NY, State Bar Calif. Office: Calif State Univ Coll Bus Adminstrn 1250 Bellflower Blvd Long Beach CA 90840

LEVINE, C. BRUCE, lawyer; b. Liberty, NY, Aug. 20, 1945; Student, Stanford U.; AB magna cum laude, UCLA, 1967; JD cum laude, Harvard U., 1971. Bar: Calif. 1971, US Tax Ct. Mem.

Greenberg, Glusker, Fields, Claman & Machtinger, LA, 1971—; ptnr. Greenberg Glusker, LA. Spkr. in various fields. Mem. State Bar Calif., LA County Bar Assn. (chmn. income tax com. tax sect. 1979-80), Beverly Hills Bar Assn. (chmn. taxation com. 1977-78), Phi Beta Kappa, Pi Gamma Mu. Office: Greenberg Glusker 1900 Ave of Stars 21st Fl Los Angeles CA 90067 Office Phone: 310-201-7440. Business E-Mail: blevine@ggfirm.com.

LEVINE, JEROME L., lawyer; b. LA, July 20, 1940; m. Maryanne Shields, Sept. 13, 1966; children: Aron Michael, Sara Michelle. BA, U. So. Calif. San Francisco State U., 1962; JD, U. Calif. Hastings Law Coll., 1965. Bar: Calif. 1966, U.S. Dist. Ct. (Ctrl. Dist. Calif.) 1966, U.S. Ct. Appeals (9th Cir.) 1985, U.S. Supreme Ct. 1986, U.S. Dist. Ct. (Ea. Dist. Calif.) 1988, U.S. Ct. Appeals (Fed. Cir.) 1989. Dir. operational svcs., assoc. dir. Western Ctr. on Law and Poverty, LA, 1968-72; assoc. Swerdlow, Glikbarg & Shimer, Beverly Hills, Calif., 1972-77; ptnr. Lans Feinberg & Cohen, LA, 1977-79, Albala & Levine, LA, 1980-83, Neiman, Billet, Albala & Levine, LA, 1983-90, Levine & Assocs., LA, 1991-2000, Holland & Knight LLP, LA, 2000—, exec. ptnr. L.A. office, 2006—. Lectr. U. So. Calif. Law Ctr. 1970, Loyola U. Sch. Law 1971; corp. counsel Nat. Indian Gaming Assn.(NIGA)(chmn. task force on IGRA regulations, mem. NIGA-Nat. Congress American Indians Tribal-State negotiating team (NCAI)), Calif. Nations Indian Gaming Assn. (CNIGA), Wash. Indian Gaming Assn.(WIGA); mem. bd. dir. Law and Legis. Com. 1988-92, co-chmn. 1992-95; mem. dir. com. Holland & Knight LLP, L.A., 2004—; spkr. in field. Contbr. articles to profl. jours.; regular contbr. Indian Gaming Mag., 1990—97, Internat. Gaming and Wagering Mag., oversees editing and publication Indian Gaming Handbook. Mem. ABA (sects. on corp., banking and bus. law, litig., patent, trademark and copyright law, mem. forum com. on the entertainment and sports industries 1979), Beverly Hill Bar Assn. (mem. corp. and commerical law com. 1977-, entertainment law com. 1977-), LA County Bar Assn. (mem. antitrust sect.), Fed. Bar Assn. (indian law sect.), State Bar Calif., Internat. Assn. Gaming Lawyers, Internat. Masters Gaming Law Assn. Office: Holland & Knight LLP 633 W 5th St 21st Fl Los Angeles CA 90071 Office Phone: 213-896-2565. Business E-Mail: jerry.levine@hklaw.com.

LEVINE, JESSE E., publishing executive; b. NYC, Apr. 28, 1951; one child. BA in English Lit., State U. N.Y. Sales rep. New Line Cinema, 1976-77; exec. v.p. N.Y. Syndicate Sales Corp., 1977-82; dir. L.A. Times Syndicate, 1982-88, pres., COO, 1988-93, pres., CEO, 1993—. Office: LA Times Syndicate 218 S Spring St Los Angeles CA 90012-3723

LEVINE, LAINIE See KAZAN, LAINIE

LEVINE, MARK DAVID, science administrator, director; b. Cleve., May 26, 1944; s. Hyman and Rebecca (Spector) Levine; m. Irma Herrera, June 1990. AB summa cum laude, Princeton U., 1966; PhD, U. Calif., Berkeley, 1975. Staff scientist Ford Found. Energy Policy Project, Washington, 1972-73; sr. energy policy analyst SRI Internat., Menlo Park, Calif., 1974-78; staff scientist Lawrence Berkeley Lab., Berkeley, 1978-84, dept. program leader, 1984-86, leader energy analysis program, 1986-96, dir. environ. energy techs. divsn., 1996—2006, leader China energy group, 2006—. Cons. Ford Found., TEM, Inc., Pacific Gas & Electric Co., QED Rsch., Inc., Energy Found., Peabody Energy; adv. bd. China Energy Conservation Investment Corp., 1994—98, Dow Chem. Co.; adv. bd. energy efficiency ctr. U. Calif., Davis, 2007—. Contbr. articles to profl. jours.; mem. editl. bd.: Energy Policy, Building Research and Information, Japan IEEE. Bd. dirs. Am. Coun. Energy Efficient Econ., Ctr. Clean Air Policy, Ctr. Resource Solutions, chair; bd. dirs. Calif. Clean Energy Fund, Shanghai Pacific Energy Ctr. Fulbright scholar, 1966. Fellow: Calif. Coun. Sci. and Tech.; mem.: Consortium Electricity Reliability (vice-chair). Jewish. Home: 5701 Barrett Ave El Cerrito CA 94530-1408 Office: Lawrence Berkeley Lab Bldg 90 Room 3125 Berkeley CA 94720 Business E-Mail: mdlevine@lbl.gov.

LEVINE, MELDON EDISES, lawyer, Former United States Representative, California; b. LA, June 7, 1943; s. Sid B. and Shirley B. (Blum) L.; children: Adam Paul, Jacob Caplan, Cara Emily. AB, U. Calif., Berkeley, 1964; MPA, Princeton U., 1966; JD, Harvard U., 1969. Bar: Calif. 1970, D.C. 1972. Assoc. Wyman, Bautzer, Rothman & Kuchel, 1969-71; legis. asst. U.S. Senate, Washington, 1971-73; ptnr. Levine Krom & Unger, Beverly Hills, Calif., 1973-77; mem. Calif. Assembly, Sacramento, 1977-82, 98th-102d Congresses from 27th Calif. dist., Washington, 1983-93; ptnr. Gibson, Dunn & Crutcher, LA, 1993—. Author: The Private Sector and the Common Market, 1968; contbr. articles to various publs. Mem. governing bd. U.S.-Israel Sci. and Tech. Commn., U.S. Holocaust Meml. Mus.; mem. amateur baseball team Hollywood Stars, 1971—. Mem.: LA Bar Assn., Calif. Bar Assn. Office: Gibson Dunn & Crutcher 1043 Roscomare Rd Los Angeles CA 90077-2227 Office Phone: 310-557-8098. Business E-Mail: mlevine@gibsondunn.com.

LEVINE, MICHAEL, public relations executive, author, television and radio personality; b. NYC, Apr. 17, 1954; s. Arthur and Virginia (Gaylor) L. Student, Rutgers U., 1978. Owner, operator TV News Mag., Los Angeles, 1977-83; owner Levine/Schnieder Pub. Rels., now Levine Comms. Office, Los Angeles, 1982—. Gov.'s adv. bd. State Calif., Sacramento, 1980-82; pres., owner Aurora Pub., LA, 1986—; moderator Thought Forum; lectr. in field; founder, moderator LA Media Roundtable; founder LBN ELERT Breaking News Newsletter; media expert KFWB Radio; radio host Access LA, Spiritual Seeker, Inside/Out Author: The Address Book: How to Reach Anyone Who's Anyone, 1984, The New Address Book, 1986, The Corporate Address Book, 1987, The Music Address Book, 1989, Environmental Address Book, 1991, Kid's Address Book, 1991, Guerrilla P.R., Lessons at Halfway Point, 1995, Take It From Me, Selling Goodness, 1998, The Princess & The Package, 1998, Guerrilla PR Wired, A Branded World, 2003, The 7 Life Lessons of Noah's Ark, 2004, Charming Your Way to the Top, 2004, Broken Windows, Broken Business, 2005; composer: Never, 2007; editor (newsletter): For Consideration. Mem. Ronald Reagan Pres.'s Libr.; founder The Actor's Conf., Aurora Charity, 1987; bd. dir. Felice Found., Micah Ctr.; adv. bd. Dare America; moderator U. Judaism Thought Forum. Mem. TV Acad. Arts and Scis., Entertainment Industries Coun., Musician's Assistance Program, West Hollywood C. of C. (bd. dirs. 1980-82). Jewish. Office: 1180 S Beverly Dr 301 Los Angeles CA 90035 Office Phone: 310-300-0950 ext 230. Office Fax: 310-300-0951. Business E-Mail: mlevine@lcoonline.com.

LEVINE, MICHAEL STEVEN, science educator; b. LA, Mar. 5, 1955; married; 2 children. BA, U. Calif., Berkeley, 1976; PhD, Yale U., 1981. Postdoctoral staff U. Basel, 1982—83, U. Calif., Berkeley, 1983—84; asst. prof. dept. biol. scis. Columbia U., 1984—86, assoc. prof. dept. biol. scis., 1986—88, prof. dept. biol. scis., 1988—90; prof. dept. biology U. Calif., San Diego, 1991—96, prof. divsn. genetics Berkeley, 1996—, Frances Williams prof. genetics, 2002—, dir. Ctr. for Integrative Genomics. Mem. devel. biology study sect. NSF, 1988—90, genetics study sect. NIH, 1990—94; co-dir. MBL Embryology, Woods Hole, Mass., 1991—96; vis. prof. Zoology Inst., U. Zürich, 1999—2000. Editor: (jours.) Mech. Devel., 1990—95, Devel., 1995—; mem. editl. bd. (jours.) Sci., Genes & Devel., —, Current Opinion Cell Biology, —, Procs. Nat. Acad. Sci., —; contbr. more than 120 articles to profl. jours. Recipient award in molecular biology, NAS, 1996, Singer medal, SBD, 2003; fellow Jane Coffin Childs postdoctoral, 1982—84, Alfred P. Sloan Rsch., 1985—87, Searle Scholars, 1985—88. Fellow: AAAS; mem.: NAS. Office: Univ Calif Dept MCB Divsn Genetics 401 Barker Hall Dept Mcb Berkeley CA 94720-3208 Office Phone: 510-642-5014. E-mail: mlevine@berkeley.edu.

LEVINE, PAMELA, film company executive; V.p. Marketcast, 1985—95; v.p. market rsch. Twentieth Century Fox Film Corp., LA, 1995, sr. v.p. mktg. planning, rsch., co-pres. domestic theatrical mktg., 2002—. Named an Entertainment Marketer of the Yr., Advt. Age mag., 2007; named one of The 100 Most Powerful Women in Entertainment, Hollywood Reporter, 2006, 2007. Office: Twentieth Century Fox Film Corp 10201 W Pico Blvd Los Angeles CA 90035 Office Phone: 310-277-2211. Office Fax: 310-203-1558.

LEVINE, PHILIP, classics educator; b. Lawrence, Mass., Sept. 8, 1922; s. Samuel and Jennie (Derdak) L.; m. Dinnie Moseson, June 19, 1955; children— Jared Elliott, Harlan Alcon. AB, Harvard, 1946, A.M., 1948, PhD, 1952; DHL (hon.), U. Judaism, 1986. Instr., asst. prof. classics Harvard, 1952-59; assoc. prof. classical langs. U. Tex. at Austin, 1959-61; assoc prof., prof. classics UCLA, 1961-91, prof. emeritus, 1991—, dean div. humanities, 1965-83; Biggs resident lectr. Washington U., 1993. Info. officer Coun. U. Calif. Emeriti Assn. Author: Lo Scriptorium Vercellese da S. Eusebio ad Attone, 1958, St. Augustine, City of God, Books 12-15, 1966; editor: Latin lt. sect. Twayne World Author Series, 1964—; adv. editor, U. Calif. Publs. in Classical Studies, 1963-72; assoc. editor, contbr. to U. Calif. Studies in Classical Antiquity, 1967-75, sr. co-editor, 1975-78; mem. editorial bd. Classical Antiquity, 1986-93. Mem. rev. com., sr. fellowship program Nat. Endowment for Humanities, 1966-70; bd. govs. U. Judaism, 1968-90; coun. visitors, 1990-94, acad. adv. coun., 1994—. With AUS, 1943-46. Sheldon fellow Italy; Guggenheim fellow; Fulbright Research grantee; recipient Bromberg Humanities award; decorated Cavaliere dell' Ordine al Merito della Repubblica Italiana. Mem. Am. Philol. Assn. (dir. 1968-70), Mediaeval Acad. Am. (exec. council 1969-72), Renaissance Soc., Am. Philol. Assn., Pacific Coast (chmn. gen. lit. 1964-65), Phi Beta Kappa. Office: U Calif Dept Classics Los Angeles CA 90095-0001 Home: 663 Loring Ave Los Angeles CA 90024-2552 Office Phone: 310-825-4171. Business E-Mail: levine@humnet.ucla.edu.

LEVINE, RAPHAEL DAVID, chemistry professor; b. Alexandria, Egypt, Mar. 29, 1938; brought to U.S., 1939; s. Chaim S. and Sofia (Greenberg) L.; m. Gillah T. Ephraty, June 13, 1962; 1 child, Ornah T. MSc, Hebrew U., Jerusalem, 1959; PhD, Nottingham U., Eng., 1964; DPhil, Oxford U., Eng., 1966; PhD honoris causa, U. Liege, Belgium, 1991, Tech. U., Munich, Germany, 1996. Vis. asst. prof. U. Wis., 1966-68; prof. theoretical chemistry Hebrew U., Jerusalem, 1968—2007, chmn. research ctr. molecular dynamics, 1981—89, Max Born prof. natural philosophy, 1985—2007; disting. prof. dept. chemistry and biochemistry UCLA, 1990—, disting. prof. molecular and med. pharmacology, 2007—. Battelle prof. chemistry and math. Ohio State U., Columbus, 1970-74; Brittingham vis. prof. U. Wis., 1973; adj. prof. U. Tex., Austin, 1974-80, MIT, 1980-88, UCLA, 1989—; Arthur D. Little lectr. MIT, 1978; Miller rsch. prof. U. Calif., Berkeley, 1989, A.D. White prof. at large Cornell U., 1989-95. Author: Quantum Mechanics of Molecular Rate Processes, 1969, Molecular Reaction Dynamics, 1974, Lasers and Chemical Change, 1981, Molecular Reaction Dynamics and Chemical Reactivity, 1986, Algebraic Theory of Molecules, 1995, Molecular Reaction Dynamics, 2005; mem. editorial bds. several well known scientific jours.; contbr. articles to profl. jours. With US Army, 1960—62. Recipient Ann. award, Internat. Acad. Quantum Molecular Sci., 1968, Landau prize, 1972, Israel prize in exact scis., 1974, Weizman prize, 1979, Rothschild prize, 1992, Max Planck prize for internat. cooperation, 1996, EMET prize, 2002, MOLEC award, 2004; co-recipient Wolf prize in chemistry, Wolf Found., 1988; named Ramsay Meml. fellow, 1964—66, Alfred P. Sloan fellow, 1970—72. Fellow Am. Phys. Soc.; mem. Israel Chem. Soc., Israel Acad. Scis., Max Planck Soc. (fgn. mem.), Academia Europaea (fgn.), Am. Acad. Arts and Scis. (fgn. hon. mem.), Am. Philos. Soc. (fgn.), Royal Danish Acad. Scis. and Letters (fgn.), Natl. Acad. of Sci., US, (fgn.). Office: UCLA Dept Chemistry & Biochemistry 607 Charles E Young E Dr Los Angeles CA 90095-1569 also: Hebrew U Jerusalem Fritz Haber Rsch Ctr Molecular Dynamics Jerusalem 91904 Israel Office Phone: 310-206-0476.

LEVINSOHN, PETER, film company executive; b. 1966; B in Bus. Adminstrn., Pepperdine U., 1988. Mgr., internat. theatrical divsn. 20th Century Fox, 1989, various positions, worldwide pay TV divsn., 1990—2004; pres., digital media Fox Entertainment Group, 2004—06, pres., Fox Interactive Media, 2006—09; pres. new media & digital distribution Fox Filmed Entertainment, Inc., L.A., 2009—. Named one of The 50 Most Important People on the Web, PC World, 2007. Office: Fox Filmed Entertainment Inc 10201 W Pico Blvd Los Angeles CA 90035*

LEVINSON, STEVEN HENRY, retired state supreme court justice; b. Cin., June 8, 1946; BA with distinction, Stanford U., 1968; JD, U. Mich., 1971. Bar: Hawaii 1972, US Dist. Ct. Hawaii 1972, US Ct. Appeals (9th cir.) 1972. Law clk. to Hon. Bernard H. Levinson Hawaii Supreme Ct., 1971-72; pvt. practice Honolulu, 1972-89; judge Hawaii Cir. Ct. (1st cir.), 1989-92; assoc. justice Hawaii Supreme Ct., Honolulu, 1992—2008. Staff mem. U. Mich. Jour. Law Reform, 1970-71. Active Temple Emanu-El. Recipient Allies for Justice award, Nat. Gay and Lesbian Law Assn., 2006. Mem. ABA (jud. divsn. 1989—), Hawaii State Bar Assn. (dir. young lawyers divsn. 1975-76, dir. 1982-84), Am. Judges Assn., Am. Judicature Soc. Jewish.

LEVINTHAL, ELLIOTT CHARLES, physicist, researcher; b. Bklyn., Apr. 13, 1922; s. Fred and Rose (Raiben) L.; m. Rhoda Arons, June 4, 1944; children: David, Judith, Michael, Daniel. BA, Columbia Coll., 1942; MS, Mass. Inst. Tech., 1943; PhD, Stanford U., 1949. Project engr. Sperry Gyroscope Co., NYC, 1943-46; research assoc. nuclear physics Stanford (Calif.) U., 1946-48, sr. scientist dept. genetics Sch. Medicine, 1961-74, dir. Instrumentation Research Lab., 1961-80, assoc. dean for research affairs, 1970-73, adj. prof. genetics Sch. Medicine, 1974-80, research prof. mech. engring., dir. Inst. Mfg. and Automation Sch. Engring., 1983-90, assoc. dean for research Sch. Engring., 1986-90, assoc. dean spl. programs, 1990-91, prof. emeritus, 1991—; research physicist Varian Assocs., Palo Alto, Calif., 1949-50, dir. research, 1950-52; chief engr. Century Electronics, Palo Alto, 1952-53; pres. Levinthal Electronics, Palo Alto, 1953-61; dir. def. scis. office Def. Advanced Projects Agy., Dept. Def., Arlington, Va., 1980-83. Mem. NASA Adv. Coun., 1980-84, space studies bd., NRC, 1989-91, mem. human exploration, 1991-92, army sci. bd., 1989-91; cons. HEW; chmn. bd. dirs. Eunoe, Inc. Recipient NASA Public Service medal, 1977 Mem. AAAS, IEEE, Am. Phys. Soc., Optical Soc. Am., Biomed. Engring. Soc., Sigma Xi. Democrat. Jewish. Home: 555 Byron St Apt 303 Palo Alto CA 94301-2038 Personal E-mail: levinthal@stanford.edu.

LEVIT, VICTOR BERT, lawyer, foreign representative, civic worker; b. Singapore, Apr. 21, 1930; s. Bert W. and Thelma (Clumeck) L.; divorced; children: Carson, Victoria; m. Margery K. Blum, Oct. 26, 1996. AB in Polit. Sci. with great distinction, Stanford, 1950; LL.B., Stanford U., 1952. Bar: Calif. 1953. Assoc. Long & Levit, San Francisco and Los Angeles, 1953-55, ptnr., 1955-83, mng. ptnr. San Francisco and L.A., 1971-83; ptnr. Barger & Wolen, San Francisco, L.A. and Newport Beach, 1983—; assoc. and gen. legal counsel U.S. Jaycees, 1959-61; legal counsel for consul gen. Ethiopia for San Francisco, 1964-71, hon. consul for Ethiopia, 1971-76. Guest lectr. Stanford U. Law Sch., 1958—, Haile Selassie I Univ. Law Sch., 1972-76; mem. com. group ins. programs State Bar Calif., 1980—; Mem. Los Angeles Consular Corps, 1971-77; mem. San Francisco Consular Corps, 1971-77, vice dean, 1975-76; Grader Calif. Bar Exam., 1956-61; del. San Francisco Mcpl. Conf., 1955-63, vice chmn., 1960, chmn., 1961-63 Author: Legal Malpractice in California, 1974, Legal Malpractice, 1977, 2d edit., 1983; Note editor: Stanford Law Rev, 1952-53; legal editor: Underwriters' Report, 1963—; Contbr. articles to legal jours. Campaign chmn. San Francisco Aid Retarded Children, 1960; mem. nat. com. Stanford Law Sch. Fund, 1959—; mem. Mayor's Osaka-San Francisco Affiliation Com., 1959-65, Mayor's Com. for Mcpl. Mgmt., 1961-64; mem. San Francisco Rep. Country Cen. Com., 1956-63; assoc. mem. Calif. Rep. Cen. Com., 1956-63, 70-72; campaign chmn. San Francisco Assemblyman John Busterud, 1960; bd. dirs. San Francisco Comml. Club, 1967-70, San Francisco Planning and Urban Renewal Assn., 1959-60, San Francisco Planning and Urban Renewal Assn. Nat. Found. Infantile Paralysis, 1958, Red Shield Youth Assn., Salvation Army, San Francisco, 1960-70, bd. dirs. NCCJ, San Francisco, 1959—, chmn., No. Calif., 1962-64, 68-70; mem. nat. bd. dirs., 1964-75; bd. dirs. San Francisco Tb and Health Assn., 1962-70, treas., 1964, pres., 1965-67; bd. dirs. San Francisco Assn. Mental Health, 1964-73, pres., 1968-71; mem. com. Nat. Assn. Mental Health, 1969-71; trustee United Bay Area Crusade, 1966-74, Ins. Forum San Francisco; bd. visitors Stanford Law Sch., 1969-75; mem. adv. bd. Jr. League San Francisco, 1971-75. Named Outstanding Young Man San Francisco mng. editors San Francisco newspapers, 1960, One of Five Outstanding Young Men Calif., 1961 Fellow ABA (chmn. profl. liability com. for gen. practice sect. 1979-81, council gen. practice sect. 1982-86, sec.-treas. gen. practice sect. 1986-87); mem. San Francisco Bar Assn. (chmn. ins. com. 1962, 73, chmn. charter flight com. 1962-66), State Bar Calif. (com. on group ins. programs 1980—, chmn. gen. practice sect. 1988—), Consular Law Soc., Am. Arbitration Assn. (arbitrator), World Assn. Lawyers (chmn. parliamentary law com. 1976—), Am. Law Inst. (adviser restatement of law governing lawyers 1985—), Internat. Bar Assn., San Francisco Jr. C. of C. (dir. 1959, pres. 1958), U.S. Jaycees (exec. com. 1959-61), Jaycees Internat. (life, senator), Calif. Scholarship Fedn., U.S. C. of C. (labor com. 1974-76), San Francisco C. of C. (dir.), Phi Beta Kappa, Order of Coif, Pi Sigma Alpha. Clubs: Commercial (San Francisco) (dir.); Commonwealth (quar. chmn.), California Tennis; World Trade; Bankers. Home: 2063 Broadway St San Francisco CA 94115-1537 Office: Barger & Wolen 650 California St Fl 9 San Francisco CA 94108-2702

LEVITCH, JOSEPH See LEWIS, JERRY

LEVITON, ALAN EDWARD, curator; b. NYC, Jan. 11, 1930; s. David and Charlotte (Weber) L.; m. Gladys Ann Robertson, June 30, 1952; children: David A., Charlotte A. Student, NYU, 1948; postgrad., Columbia U., 1948; AB, Stanford U., 1949, MA, 1953; student, U. Nebr., 1954; PhD, Stanford U., 1960. Asst. curator herpetology Calif. Acad. Scis., San Francisco, 1957—60, assoc. curator, 1960—61, chmn., curator, 1962—82, 1989—92, 2001—, curator, 1983—88, 1993—2000, chmn. computer svcs., 1983—92, editor sci. publs., 1994—; assoc. curator zool. collections Stanford U., 1962—63, lectr. biol. sci., 1963—70; professorial lectr. Golden Gate U., 1953—63; adj. prof. biol. sci. San Francisco State U., 1967—2000, rsch. prof., 2000—. Rsch. assoc. nat. mus. natural history Smithsonian Instn., Washington, 2005—. Author: North American Amphibians, 1970, Reptiles of the Middle East, 1992, T.H. Hittel's California Academy of Sciences, 1997; contbr. articles to profl. jours. Grantee Am. Philos. Soc., 1960, NSF, 1960-61, 77-79, 80, 83-89, 91-93, 2002—, Belvedere Sci. Fund, 1958-59, 62; recipient Disting. Svc. award, 1990, Fellows medal Calif. Acad. Scis., 1999, Gerald & Sue Friedman Disting. Svc. award Geol. Soc. Am. His. of Geol. Divsn., 2007. Fellow AAAS (coun. 1976-97, com. coun. affairs 1983-85, sec.-treas. Pacific divsn. 1975-79, exec. dir. 1980-98, 2000-2001, pres.-elect 1998, pres. 1999-2000, counselor 2001—), Calif. Acad. Scis., Geol. Soc. Am. (vice-chmn. history geology divsn. 1989-90, chmn. 1990-91); mem. Am. Soc. Ichthyologists and Herpetologists (mem. bd. govs. 1960-84), Forum Historians of Sci. Am. (coord. com. 1986-88, sec.-treas. 1988-90), History of Sci. Soc. Home: 571 Kingsley Ave Palo Alto CA 94301-3225 Office: Calif Acad Scis Golden Gate Park San Francisco CA 94118 Business E-Mail: aleviton@calacademy.org.

LEVITT, RAYMOND ELLIOT, civil engineer, educator; b. Johannesburg, Aug. 7, 1949; arrived in U.S., 1972; s. Barnard and Riva Eleanor (Lazarus) Levitt; m. Kathleen Adele Sullivan, Nov. 26, 1976; children: Benjamin John, Joanna Maurine, Zoë Ellen. BSCE, U. Witwatersrand, Johannesburg, 1971; MSCE, Stanford U., 1973, PhDCE, 1975. Project engr. Christiani & Neilsen, Cape Town, South Africa, 1971-72; asst. prof. civil engring. MIT, Cambridge, 1975-79, assoc. prof., 1979-80, Stanford (Calif.) U., 1980—, prof., 1988—, acad. dir. advanced project mgmt. program, 1999—, dir. collaboratory rsch. global projects, 2003—. Advisor U.S. Dept. Labor, Washington, 1976—77, Calif. Pub. Utilities Commn., San Francisco, 1982—84, U.S. Dept. Energy, 2002—03; chmn. bd. dirs. Vité; bd. dirs. Visual Network Design. Co-author: Union and Open-Shop Construction, 1978, Construction Safety Management, 1987, 2d edit., 1993, Knowledge-Based Systems in Engineering, 1990. Pres. Stanford Homeowners Assn., 1981—83. Recipient Marksman award, Engring.

News Record, N.Y.C., 1985, Committment to Life award, Nat. Safe Workplace Inst., 1987. Mem.: INFORMS, ASCE (Huber Prize award 1982, Computing Civil Engrng. award 2000, Peurifoy Constrn. Rsch. award 2006), Project Mgmt. Inst. Unitarian Universalist. Avocations: swimming, trout fishing, music, surfing. Office: Stanford U Dept Civil Engring # 4020 Stanford CA 94305

LEVY, BERNARD C., electrical engineer, educator; b. Princeton, NJ, July 31, 1951; Ingenieur civil des mines, Paris, 1974; PhD in Elec. Engring., Stanford U., 1979. Prof. dept. elec. and computer engr. U. Calif., Davis, 1980—, chair dept. elec. and computer engring., 1996—. Fellow IEEE (image and multidimensional signal processing tech. com. 1992—). Office: U Calif Dept Elec & Computer Engr 1 Shields Ave Davis CA 95616-5270

LEVY, CLAIRE, state legislator; m. David Driscoll; 2 children. BA in European History, cum laude, Carleton Coll., Northfield, Minn., 1978; JD, Case Western Res. U. Sch. Law, Cleve., 1982. Law clk., Judge Alan Sternberg Colo. Ct. of Appeals, 1982—83; dep. pub. defender Colo. Pub. Defender's Office Appellate Divsn., Denver, 1983—86; assoc. Buchanan, Gray, Purvis & Schuetze, Boulder, Colo., 1983—86; asst. county atty. Jefferson County Atty. Office, 1989—99; pvt. practice atty. Boulder, 1999—2008; mem. Dist. 13 Colo. House of Reps., Denver, 2007—, majority whip. Adj. prof. U. Colo. Sch. Law, 2000; bd. commr. Boulder County Housing Authority, 2000—04; mem. Boulder Planning Bd., 2004—; commr. Nat. Conf. Uniform State Laws, 2008—. Contbr. articles to profl. jours. Mem. Boulder County Parks & Open Space Adv. Com., 1994-99; bd. mem. PLAN-Boulder County, 2000-04, bd. chair 2002-04; bd. mem. Boulder Arts Acad., 2003-05, Boulder Ballet, 2005-. Mem.: Order of the Coif. Democrat. Office: Colo State Capitol 200 E Colfax Denver CO 80203 Office Phone: 303-866-2578. Business E-Mail: claire.levy.house@state.co.us.*

LEVY, EUGENE, actor, film director, screenwriter; b. Hamilton, Ont., Can., Dec. 17, 1946; m. Deborah Divine, 1977; 2 children. Appearences include (films) Cannibal Girls, 1972, Running, 1979, Nothing Personal, 1980, Heavy Metal, 1981, Strange Brew, 1983, Going Berserk, 1983, National Lampoon's Vacation, 1983, Splash, 1984, Armed and Dangerous, 1986, The Canadian Conspiracy, 1986, Club Paradise, 1986, Speed Zone, 1989, Father of the Bride, 1991, Once Upon A Crime, 1992, Stay Tuned, 1992, I Love Trouble, 1994, Father of the Bride, Part II, 1995, Waiting for Guffman, 1996, Multiplicity, 1996, Waiting for Guffman (also wrote), 1996, Dogmatic, 1996, Creature Crunch (voice only), 1996, Almost Heroes, 1998, Richie Rich's Christmas Wish, 1998, Akbar's Adventure Tours, 1998, The Secret Life of Girls, 1999, American Pie, 1999, Best in Shown (also wrote), 2000, The Ladies Man, 2000, Silver Man, 2000, Down to Earth, 2001, American Pie 2, 2001, Serendipity, 2001, Repli-Kate, 2002, Like Mike, 2002, Bringing Down the House, 2003, A Mighty Wind (also wrote), 2003, Dumb and Dumberer: When Harry Met Lloyd, 2003, American Wedding, 2003, New York Minute, 2004, The Man, 2005, Cheaper by the Dozen 2, 2005, Curious George, 2006, Over the Hedge (voice), 2006, For Your Consideration, 2006; actor: (TV) Second City TV, 1977-81, Lovebirds, 1979, From Cleveland, 1980, George Burn's Comedy Week, 1985, SCTV Network, 1981-83, The Last Polka, 1985, Dave Thomas: The Incredible Time Travels of Henry Osgood, 1986, Billy Crystal-Don't Get Me Started, 1986, Bride of Boogedy, 1987, Ray Bradbury Theatre, 1988, Autobiographies: The Enigma of Bobby Bittman, 1988, Hiller and Diller, 1997, Hercules (voice only), 1998, D.O.A., 1999, The Sports Pages, 2001, Club Land, 2001, Committed (TV series), 2001, The Kid, 2001, Greg the Bunny (TV series), 2002; dir.: (TV) Second City's 50th Anniversary Special, 1988, Once Upon a Crime..., 1992, Partners in Love, 1992, Sodbusters, 1994.

LEVY, JAY A., medical educator; b. Wilmington, Del., Nov. 21, 1938; BA, Wesleyan U., 1960; MD, Columbia U. Coll. Physicians and Surgeons, 1965; DSc (hon.), Wesleyan U., 1996. Tchg. asst. in Biology Wesleyan U., Middletown, Conn., 1959—60; researcher Coll. Physicians and Surgeons, Columbia U., 1961—65; intern in medicine Hosp. U. Pa., Phila., 1965—66, 1st yr. resident in medicine, 1966—67; staff assoc. Nat. Cancer Inst. NIH, Bethesda, Md., 1967—70; collaborator N.Y. Blood Ctr., NYC, 1970; 2d yr. resident in medicine San Francisco Sch. Medicine U. Calif., 1970—71; asst. clin. prof. dept. medicine U. Calif. Sch. Medicine, San Francisco, 1972—77, rsch. assoc. Cancer Rsch. Inst., 1972—, assoc. prof. in residence dept. medicine, 1978—82, assoc. prof. in residence, departments of medicine, microbiology and immunology, 1982—85, prof. in residence dept. medicine, 1985—96, prof. dept. medicine div. hematology/oncology, 1996—, dir. Lab. for Tumor and AIDS Virus Rsch., 1996—. Vis. scientist and NATO fellow INSERM, Paris, 1971—72; vis. scientist and Eleanor Roosevelt fellow dept. chem. immunology Weizmann Inst. Sci., Rehovot, Israel, 1978—79, vis. scientist and ICRETT fellow, 1982, mem. exec. bd. Am. com., 1987—; exec. bd. Bay Area region Am. Com. for the Weizmann Inst. Sci., 1987—, regional chair, 2001—, bd. dir., mem. exec. com., 2002—; disting. lectr. in field; mem. sci. adv. bd. Agence Nationale de Recherches sur le Sida, Govt. France, 1999—; mem. Mayor Willie Brown's AIDS Sci. Adv. Coun., 1997—; mem. sci. adv. com. Brown U./Tufts U. Ctr. AIDS Rsch., 1997—; mem. internat. sci. adv. bd. Rhone-Poulenc-Rorer, 1997; mem. sci. adv. bd. NIH HIV vaccine design and devel. team Chiron Corp., San Francisco, 2001—; mem. internat. adv. com. Internat. Conf. on AIDS, 1986—96; mem. cell and devel. biology study sect. Am. Cancer Soc., 1983—87; internat. adv. bd. Lancet, 1992—; mem. World Affairs Coun., 1999—, mem. biotechnology task force, 2002—; mem. sci. adv. com. U. Calif., Ctr. for AIDS Rsch., Davis, 2000—; mem. sci. adv. bd. Genelabs, Redwood City, Calif., 2002—; bd. dir. Alliance for Prudent Use of Antibiotics, 2002—; mem. bd. associates Whitehead Inst. for Biomedical Rsch., 2002—; mem. adv. com. Physicians for Human Rights, 2002—; vice chair, sci. adv. bd. China Integrated Programs for Rsch. on AIDS, 2002—. Editor: AIDS, 1988—2000; editor in chief:, 2000—, mem. numerous editl. bds.:; author: HIV and the Pathogenesis of AIDS, 2nd. edit.; contbr. articles in profl. jours.;, co-editor several books. Mem. adv. bd. Internat. Alliance for Haiti, 1989—; mem. adv. com. United Religious Initiative Found., 2000—; bd. trustees Wesleyan U., 1988—91; bd. dir. People to People Ethiopian/Am. AIDS Assn., 1999—. Recipient Phi Beta Kappa, Sigma Xi, Wesleyan Meml. award, 1959—60, Fulbright and French Govt. awards, 1960—61, Rsch. Career Develop. award, 1972—77, Award of Distinction, Am. Found. for AIDS Rsch., 1994, Disting. Alumnus award, Wesleyan U., 1995, Wellcome Vis. Professorship award, U. PR, 1999, Heroes in Medicine award, Internat. Assn. Physicians in AIDS Care, 2000; named Highly Cited Researcher, Microbiology, ISIHighlyCited.com, 2002; named one of Ten Most Influential People of the Bay Area, San Francisco Sunday Chronicle Examiner, 1998; named to Leon G. Smith Infectious Disease Inst. Hall of Fame, St. Michael's Med. Ctr., Newark, NJ, 2000; Fulbright and French Govt. Rsch. fellow, U. Paris, 1960—61, Fellow, Sch. Internat. and Pub. Affairs, Columbia U., 1961—63, USPHS, 1962, Lederle Med. fellow, Karolinska Inst., Stockholm, 1963, La. State U. Med. fellow in Tropical Medicine, Makerere Univ. Coll., Kampala, Uganda, 1964, Am. Cancer Soc., Eleanor-Roosevelt Internat. Cancer Fellowship, 1978—79. Fellow: Am. Acad. Microbiology, Molecular Medicine Soc., Am. Acad. Arts & Sciences, Infectious Diseases Soc. Am.; mem.: AAAS, HIV Med. Assn. Infectious Diseases Soc. Am., People to People Ethiopian/Am. AIDS Assn. (bd. dirs. 1999—), HIV Med. Assn. Infectious Diseases Soc. Am., We. Soc. Clin. Rsch., We. Assn. Physicians, Internat. AIDS Soc. (mem. adv. bd. 1993—96), Assn. IUCC Fellows, World Jewish Acad. Sciences (hon.), Assn. Am. Physicians, Am. Soc. Virology, Am. Soc. Tropical Medicine and Hygiene, Am. Soc. Microbiology (Abbott award in clinical and diagnostic immunology 2004), Am. Soc. Clin. Investigation, Am. Assn. Cancer Rsch. (mem. long-range planning com. 1987—90, bd. dirs. 1988—91, chair local com. ann. meeting 1989, mem. spl. confs. com. 1989—92, mem. long-range planning com. 1990—93, mem. minority issues com. 1990—93, chair by-laws com. 1992—93, rep. physicians for human rights 1992—, mem. legis. com. 1992—, chair fin. com. 1993—96, mem. local com. ann. meeting 1994, mem. program com. ann. meeting 1996, mem. minority issues com. 1996—2000, mem. program com. ann. meeting 1997, Spl. Recognition award for outstanding leadership as chair fin. com. 1997), Am. Assn. Immunologists, Am. Found. AIDS Rsch. (mem. sci. adv. bd. 1986—, bd. dir. 1993—, chair sci. policy com. 1994—, mem. exec. com. 1994—, mem. opportunity fund com. 1998—, mem. com. global initiatives 2001—), Internat. Union Against Cancer, The World Innovation Found. (hon.). Achievements include patents in field. Office: U Calif San Francisco Sch Medicine Dept Medicine Lab Tumor and AIDS Virus R Box 1270 S 1280 San Francisco CA 94143 Business E-Mail: jalevy@itsa.ucsf.edu.

LEVY, JOSEPH WILLIAM, department stores executive; b. Fresno, Calif., 1932; m. Sharon Sorokin; children: Felicia, Jody, Bret. BS, U. So. Calif., 1954. Asst. merchandising mgr., then mgr. Gottschalks, Inc., Fresno, 1956-72, exec. v.p., 1972-82, chmn., chief exec. officer, 1982—. Chmn. exec. com. Frederick Atkins Inc., N.Y.C., 1992—, also bd. dirs. Chmn. Fresno Econ. Devel. Corp., 1982-83; mem. Calif. Transp. Commn., 1983-91, chmn., 1986-87; sec. City of Fresno Equipment Corp.; mem. bus. adv. coun. Sch. Bus. and Adminstrv. Scis., Calif. State U., Fresno; trustee Community Hosps. Cen. Calif. With USNR, 1950-58. Mem. Calif. C. of C. (bd. dirs.), Fresno County and City C. of C. (transp. com.), U. So. Calif. Sch. Bus. Alumni Assn., San Joaquin Country Club, U. Sequoia-Sunnyside Country Club, Downtown Club (Fresno). Home: 6475 N Sequoia Dr Fresno CA 93711-1232 Office: Gottschalks Inc PO Box 28920 Fresno CA 93729-8920

LEVY, JULIA, immunology educator, researcher; b. Singapore, May 15, 1935; arrived in Can., 1940; d. Guillaume Albert and Dorothy Frances (Brown) Coppens; m. Howard Bernard Gerwing, Oct. 8, 1955 (div. 1962); children— Nicholas, Benjamin; m. Edwin Levy, June 13, 1969; 1 child, Jennifer BA with honors, U. B.C., 1955; PhD, U. London, 1958; Dr. of Univ. (hon.), U. Ottawa, 1993; DLitt (hon.), Mt. St. Vincent's U., 1994; DSc (hon.), U. Western Ont., 1997; LLD (hon.), Simon Fraser U., 1999; DSc honoris causa (hon.), U. B.C., 2001; DSc (hon.), U. Victoria, 2002; LLD (hon.), Concordia U., 2002; D of Tech. (hon.), B.C. Inst. Tech., 2002. Asst. prof. U. B.C., Vancouver, 1959-65, assoc. prof., 1965-72, prof. immunology, 1972—99, prof. emeritus, 1999—; pres., CEO QLT Inc., Vancouver, 1996—2002, exec. chmn. sci. adv. bd., 2002—. Dir. v.p. rsch. and devel. Quadra Logic Techs., Vancouver, 1980—2002; cons. Monsanto Chems., Mo., 1978—80; mem. Prime Minister's Nat. Adv. Bd. on Sci. and Tech., 1987—; exec. chmn. sci. adv. bd. QLT, Inc., 2002—. Decorated Officer of Order of Can.; recipient award, Can. Women Entrepreneur in Internat. Bus., 1998, Vision and Leadership award, BCBA, 1999, Amb.'s award for outstanding achievement of Can. women entrepreneurs, 1999, Nat. Merit award, Ottawa Life Scis. Coun., 1999, Future of Vision award, Found. Fighting Blindness, 2001, Women of Distinction award, YWCA, 2001, Friesen-Rygiel prize, 2002, Prix Galien Can. 2002 Rsch., 2002, award of leadership in Can. pharm. rsch. and devel., Can. Soc. Pharm. Scis., 2002, Helen Keller award, The Helen Keller Found. Rsch. and Edn., 2003, Leadership award, BC Export, 2003, Lifetime Achievement award, BC Biotech, 2004; named Pacific Can. Entrepreneur of Yr., 2000, Pioneer of Innovation, Bd. of Trade, 2001, Person of Yr., B.C. Tech. Industries Assn., 2001. Fellow: Royal Soc. Can.; mem.: Am. Soc. Immunology, Can. Soc. Immunology (pres. 1983—85), Can. Fedn. Biol. Sci. (pres. 1983—84). Achievements include endowed Julia G. Levy chair professorship of ophthalmology John's Hopkins Hospital, Wilmer Eye Institute. Office: QLT Inc 887 Great Northern Way Vancouver BC Canada V5T 4T5

LEVY, KENNETH, retired computer company executive; BS in Engrng., MS in Engrng. Founder KLA Instruments Corp., 1976; former CEO KLA-Tencor, San Jose, Calif., chmn., 1999—2006, chmn. emeritus, 2006—. Dir. emeritus Semiconductor Equipment Materials Inst. Recipient numerous awards. Mem.: NAE. Office: KLA-Tencor Corp One Technology Dr Milpitas CA 95035

LEVY, MARK RAY, lawyer; b. Denver, Mar. 2, 1946; s. Richard C. and Hilde (Lindauer) L.; m. Patricia Loeb, June 13, 1971; children: Betsy, Robert. BA, U. Colo., 1968, JD, 1972. Bar: Colo. 1972, U.S. Dist. Ct. Colo. 1972. Assoc. Holland & Hart LLP, Denver, 1972-78, ptnr., 1978—. Adj. prof. the lawyering process U. Denver Law Sch., 1990-93; mem. spl. adv. com. Colo. Securities Bd., 1996-97. Author: (with others) Colorado Corporations Manual, 1987, Colorado Corporation Law and Practice, 1990. Trustee Congregation Emanuel, Denver, 1984-90, mem. legal com., 2005-06; chmn. Denver Alumni Phonathon U. Colo. Law Sch., 1989-90, mem. alumni bd., 1992-96, chmn. alumni bd., 1994-95; trustee Nat. Repertory Orch., 1995-96. Mem. ABA, Colo. Bar Assn. (Blue Sky Law task force 1980-81, co-chmn. Colo. securities law rev. com. 1988-91, Article 8 of UCC com. 1995-96, chmn. ann. conv. com. 1999-00, mem. annual conv. com. 1998-02, mem. planning com. annual bus. law inst. 2000, mem. bd. dirs. Am. Jewish com. 2005-, v.p. Colo. chpt. 2005-), Denver Bar Assn. Office: Holland & Hart LLP 555 17th St Ste 3200 Denver CO 80202-3950 E-mail: mlevy@hollandhart.com.

LEVY, NAOMI, rabbi; m. Robert Eshman; children: Adin, Noa. BA summa cum laude, Cornell U. Cert. ordained Rabbi Jewish Theological Seminary. Founder, spiritual leader Nashuva. Spkr. in field of Judaism and Spirituality. Author: (Religious Books) To Begin Again, Talking to God; TV appearances: Oprah Winfrey Show; NBC's Today Show; featured Red Book, Self Mag., LA Times, The Boston Globe. Named one of The Top 50 Rabbis in America, Newsweek Mag., 2007. Office: Nashuva PO Box 64196 Los Angeles CA 90064

LEVY, RALPH, engineering executive, consultant; b. London, Apr. 12, 1932; came to U.S., 1967, naturalized, 1978; s. Alfred and Esther L.; m. Barbara Dent, Dec. 12, 1959; children: Sharon E., Mark S. BA, Cambridge U., 1953, MA, 1957; PhD, Queen Mary Coll. U. London, 1966. Mem. sci. staff GEC, Stanmore, Middlesex, Eng., 1953-59; mem. sci. staff Mullard Research Labs., Redhill, Eng., 1959-64; lectr. dept. elec. and electronic engring. U. Leeds, 1964-67; v.p. research Microwave Devel. Labs., Inc., Natick, Mass., 1967-84; v.p. engring. KW Engring., San Diego, 1984-88; v.p. research Remec Inc., San Diego, 1988-89; R. Levy Assocs., 1989—. Author: (with J.O. Scanlan) Circuit Theory, 1970, 2d vol., 1973; editor: Classic Works in RF Engineering, Vol. 2, 2007; contbr. articles to profl. jours. Fellow IEEE (editor Transactions on Microwave Theory and Techniques 1986-88, Career award IEEE Microwave Theory and Techniques Soc. 1997); mem. Instn. Elec. Tech. (London). Achievements include patents in field. Office: 1897 Caminito Velasco La Jolla CA 92037-5725 Office Fax: 858-459-6752. E-mail: r.levy@ieee.org.

LEVY, RONALD, medical educator, researcher; b. Carmel, Calif. BS, Harvard U., 1963; MD, Stanford U., 1968. Cert. Internal Medicine, 1973, Med. Oncology, 1979, lic. Commonwealth Mass., 1970, State Calif. Med. License, 1975. Intern, internal medicine Mass. Gen. Hosp., Boston, 1968-69, residency, internal medicine, 1969-70; clin. assoc., immunology branch Nat. Cancer Inst., 1970—72; Helen Hay Whitney Found. fellow in dept. chem. immunology Weizmann Inst. Sci., Rehovot, Israel, 1973-75; fellow, dept. medicine, divsn. oncology Stanford U. Sch. Medicine, 1972—73, mem. faculty Calif., 1975—, asst. prof. medicine, divsn. oncology Calif., 1975—81, assoc. prof. dept. medicine-oncology Calif., 1981—87, prof. medicine, divsn. oncology Calif., 1987—, Robert K. Summy and Helen K. Summy prof. Calif., 1987—; Frank and Else Schilling Am. Cancer Soc. Clin. Rsch. prof., 1987—; chief divsn. oncology Stanford U. Sch. Medicine, Calif., 1993—. Investigator Howard Hughes Med. Inst., 1977—82; chmn., bd. scientific counselors, divsn. cancer treatment NIH, 1989—93; mem. scientific advisory bd. Fred Hutchinson Cancer Rsch. Ctr., 1994—, Coley Pharm. Group, 2001, XTL Therapeutics, Rehovoth, Israel, Therion Inc., Cambridge, Mass., Xeyte Therapeutics, Seattle, Agensys, Santa Monica, Calif., Pointilliste, Mountain View, Calif., Cell Genesis, Foster City, Calif., Five Prime, South San Francisco, Calif.; Woodward vis. prof. Meml. Sloan Kettering Cancer Ctr., NY, 1994; Morton Mason lecture U. Tex. Southwestern, 1995; vis. prof. U. Minn. Cancer Ctr., 1996, U. Nebr. Cancer Ctr., 1999; lectr. in field. Contbr. articles to profl. jours.; Author, co-author of several books and publs. Mem. Dorothy P. Landon Am. Assn. for Cancer Rsch. Translational Cancer Rsch. com., 2001; bd. dir. Damon Runyon Cancer Rsch. Fund, 2002—; mem., Conflict of Interest Com. Stanford U. Sch. Medicine, 2001—; mem. Am. Assn. Med. Sch. Task Force on Fin. Conflicts of Interest in Clin. Rsch., 2001, GM Cancer Rsch. Found. Awards Assembly, 1992—96, 2001—. Recipient Armand Hammer award for Cancer Rsch., 1982, Ciba-Geigy/Drew award in Biomedical Rsch., 1983, Dr. Josef Steiner prize for Cancer Rsch., 1989, Karnofsky award, Am. Soc. Clin. Oncology, 1999, Charles F. Kettering award, GM Cancer Rsch. Found., 1999, Centeon award, 6th Internat. Conf. on Bispecific Antibodies, 1999, C. Chester Stock award, Meml. Sloan-Kettering Cancer Ctr., 2000, Medal of Honor, Am. Cancer Soc., 2000, Key to the Cure award, Cure for Lymphoma Found., 2000, Evelyn Hoffman Meml. award, Lymphoma Rsch. Found. Am., 2001, Jeffrey A. Gottlieb Meml. award, M.D. Anderson Cancer Ctr, 2003, Discovery Health Channel Med. Honors, 2004. Mem. ACP, Inst. Medicine, Am. Soc. Clin. Oncology, Am. Cancer Soc. (chmn. immunology study sect., 1988-92, mem., rsch. coun., 2003-), Am. Soc. Clin. Investigation, Assn. Am. Physicians, Am. Assn. for Cancer Rsch. (chmn., Joseph H. Burchinal award com., 2002, Joseph H. Burchenal Clin. Cancer Rsch. award, 1997), Am. Assn. Immunology (program com. and block chmn. for tumor immunology, 1992-96), Am. Fed. for Clin. Rsch., Am. Soc. Hematology, Western Soc. Medicine, Acad. of Cancer Immunology. Achievements include first to the development of idiotype-based therapeutic vaccines for the treatment of non-Hodgkin's B-cell lymphoma. Office: Levy Lab Divsn Oncology 269 Campus Dr CCSR 1126 Stanford CA 94305-5151 Address: Stanford Sch Medicine 300 Pasteur Dr M207 Stanford CA 94305 Office Phone: 650-725-6452. Office Fax: 650-725-1420. E-mail: levy@stanford.edu.*

LEVY, SALOMON, mechanical engineer; b. Jerusalem, Apr. 4, 1926; arrived in U.S., 1945; s. Abraham Isaac and Sultana Claire (Elyachar) Levy; m. Eileen Dolores Jaques, Oct. 14, 1951; children: Marshall Douglas, Linda C. BSME, U. Calif., Berkeley, 1949, MME, 1951, PhD in Mech. Engring., 1953. Engr. GE, Schenectady, NY, San Jose, Calif., 1953—59, mgr. heat transfer, 1959-66, mgr. sys. engring., 1966-68, mgr. design engring., 1968-71, gen. mgr. fuel, 1971-75, gen. mgr. boiling water reactor ops., 1975-77; chmn. S. Levy Inc., Campbell, Calif., 1977-98; owner Levy & Assocs., 1998—. Adj. prof. UCLA, 1986—87; Springer prof. U. Calif., Berkeley, 1979—80; bd. dirs. IES Industries, Inc. Author: Two-Phase Flow in Complex Systems, 1999. Fellow: ASME (hon.; chmn. heat transfer divsn. 1964—65, Heat Transfer Conf. award 1963, Heat Transfer Meml. award 1966, 50th Ann. Heat Transfer Divsn. award 1988), Am. Nuc. Soc. (chmn. thermal hydraulics divsn. 1985—86, Thermal Hydraulics Divsn. Achievement award 1987, Power Divsn. Walter H. Zinn award 1989); mem.: AIChE (Donald Kern award 1993), NAE, Inst. Nuc. Power Ops. (mem. adv. coun.). Democrat. Unitarian Ch. Achievements include patents in field. Avocations: racquetball, golf. Home: 1829 Dry Creek Rd San Jose CA 95124-1002 Office: Levy and Assocs Ste 225 3425 S Bascom Ave Campbell CA 95008 Office Phone: 408-369-6500. Personal E-mail: slevy112@aol.com.

LEVYN, THOMAS STANLEY, lawyer, former mayor; b. LA, Apr. 2, 1949; s. Stanley Miles and Toni (March) L.; children: Adam, Stacy. BS in Bus., U. So. Calif., LA, 1971, JD, 1974. Mng. ptnr. Agapay, Levyn & Halling, LA, 1974—2004; mem. city council City of Beverly Hills, 1992—2003, vice mayor, 1995—96, 1998—99, mayor Calif., 1996—97, 1999—2000, 2003—04; ptnr. Christensen, Miller, Fink, Jacobs, Glaser, Weil & Shapiro, LA, 2004—. Judge trial advocacy program U. So. Calif. Law Ctr., 1982—83; landlord tenant settlement officer & judge pro tempore LA mcpl. ct., 1984—86. Bd. govs. Cedars Sinai Med. Ctr., L.A., 1986—, Beverly Hills Pub. Access Corp., 1989-92; bd. trustees, Temple Isaiah, 1991-92. Jewish. Avocations: golf, reading, listening well. Office: Chritensen Miller Fink Jacobs Glaser Weil & Shapiro LLP 10250 Constellation Blvd 19th Fl Los Angeles CA 90067 Office Phone: 310-282-6214. E-mail: tlevyn@chrismill.com.

LEW, RONALD. S. W, federal judge; b. LA, 1941; m. Mamie Wong; 4 children. BA in Polit. Sci., Loyola U., LA, 1964; JD, Southwestern U., 1971. Bar: Calif. 1972. Dep. city atty. L.A. City Atty's. Office, 1972-74; ptnr. Avans & Lew, LA, 1974-82; commr. fire and police pension City of L.A., 1976-82; mcpl. ct. judge County of L.A., 1982-84, superior ct. judge, 1984-87; judge U.S. Dist. Ct. (cen. dist.) Calif., LA, 1987—. Bar: Calif. 1971. Mem. World Affairs Council of L.A., 1976—, Christian Businessmen's Com. of L.A., 1982—; active Com. of 100, Chinese Am. Heart Coun., Friends of the Mus. Chinese Am. History. 1st lt. U.S. Army, 1967-69. Recipient Vol. award United Way of L.A., 1979, cert. of merit L.A. Human Relations Commn., 1977, 82. Mem. Am. Judicature Soc., Calif. Assn. of Judges, So. Calif. Chinese Lawyer's Assn. (charter mem. 1976, pres. 1979), Chinese Am. Citizens Alliance, San Fernando Valley Chinese Cultural Assn., Delta Theta Phi. Office: US Dist Ct 312 N Spring St Los Angeles CA 90012-4701

LEWIN, DAN'L, computer software company executive; AB in Politics, Princeton U. Exec. leading sales and mktg. divsns. various cos., including Apple Computer Corp., NeXT Software, Inc., Go Corp.; cons. emerging cos. such as Kaleida and Taligent, venture capital firms, such as Kleiner Perkins Caufield & Byers, and SOFTBANK Venture Capital; CEO Aurigin Systems Inc.; corp. v.p. strategic and emerging bus. devel. Microsoft Corp., Mountain View, Calif. Office: Microsoft Corp 1065 La Avenida Mountain View CA 94043

LEWIS, ALAN JAMES, pharmaceutical executive, pharmacologist; b. Newport Gwent, UK; BSc, Southampton U., Hampshire, 1967; PhD in Pharmacology, U. Wales, Cardiff, 1970. Postdoctoral fellow biomedical sci. U. Guelph, Ont., Can., 1970-72; rsch. assoc. lung rsch. ctr. Yale U., 1972-73; sr. pharmacologist Organon Labs., Ltd., Lanarkshire, Scotland, 1973-79; rsch. mgr. immunoinflammation Am. home products Wyeth-Ayerst Rsch., Princeton, N.J., 1979-82, assoc. dir. exptl. therapeutics, 1982-85, dir., 1985-87, asst. v.p., 1987-89, v.p. rsch., 1989-93; pres. Signal Pharms. Inc., San Diego, 1994-96, pres., CEO, 1996-2000; pres. signal rsch. divsn. Celgene Corp., 2000—. Editor allergy sect. Agents & Actions & Internat. Archives Pharmacodynamics Therapy; reviewer Jour. Pharmacology Exptl. Therapy, Biochemical Pharmacology, Can. Jour. Physiol. Pharmacology, European Jour. Pharmacology, Jour. Pharm. Sci. Mem. Am. Soc. Pharmacological and Exptl. Therapeutics, Am. Rheumatism Assn., Mid-Atlantic Pharmacology Soc. (v.p. 1991-93, pres. 1993-94), Pulmonary Rsch. Assn., Inflammation Rsch. Assn. (pres. 1986-88), Pharm. Mfrs. Assn., Internat. Assn. Inflammation Socs. (pres. 1990-95), Bio Bd. Achievements include research in mechanisms and treatment of inflammatory diseases including arthritis and asthma cardiovascular diseases, metabolic disorders, central nervous system diseases, osteoporosis and viral diseases. Office: Celgene Signal Research 4550 Towne Centre Ct San Diego CA 92121-1900 E-mail: alewis@signalpharm.com.

LEWIS, CARL (FREDERICK CARLTON LEWIS), Olympic track and field athlete; b. Birmingham, Ala., May 1, 1961; s. William McKinley Lewis, Jr. and Evelyn (Lawler) Lewis. Student, U. Houston. Mem. U.S. Olympic Team, 1980, 1984, 1988, 1992, 1996. Musician: (albums) Break it Up, 1986. Founder Carl Lewis Found. Recipient James E. Sullivan award best amateur athlete, 1981, Jesse Owens award, 1982, Athlete of Yr. award Assoc. Press Sports, 1983; named World Athlete of the Decade Track & Field News, 1980-89, Olympic Athlete of the Century, 2000, U.S. Athlete of the Yr., 1981, 82, 83, 84, 87, 88, 91, World Athlete of the Yr., 1982, 83, 84, named to U.S. Olympic Hall of Fame, 1985. winner 1 Bronze medal Pan Am. Games, 1979, 2 Gold medals, 1981, 1 Gold medal World Cup, 1981, 3 Gold medals, 100m, long jump, 400m relay, World Championships, 1983, 1987, 9 Olympic Gold medals, Long Jump 1984, 1988, 1992, 1996, 100m, 1984, 1988, 200m, 1980, 4x100m relay, 1984, 1992, Silver medal, 200m, 1988; world record holder in 4x100m relay, 1981, 83, 84, 91, 92, in 4x200m relay, 1989, 100 meter dash, 1991; Am. record holder in 4x100 relay, 1981, 83, 84, 90, 91, in 200 meter dash, 1983, 100 meter dash, 1987, 88, 91, 4x200m relay, 1989; world and Am. indoor record holder in long jump, 1981, 82, 84, in 60 yd. dash, 1983, holds current world record of 37.40 seconds in the 4x100m relay, 1992-. Office: Carl Lewis Foundation 7765 W 91st St Unit F2102 Playa Del Rey CA 90293-7311

LEWIS, CHARLES EDWIN, epidemiologist, educator; b. Kansas City, Dec. 28, 1928; s. Claude Herbert and Maudie Friels (Holaday) Lewis; m. Mary Ann Gurera, Dec. 27, 1963; children: Kevin Neil, David Bradford, Matthew Clinton, Karen Carleen. Student, U. Kans., 1948—49; MD, Harvard, 1953; MS, U. Cin., 1957, ScD, 1959. Diplomate Am. Bd. Preventive Medicine (Occupl. Medicine). Intern, resident U. Kans. Hosp., 1953—54; trainee USPHS, 1956—58; fellow occupational health Eastman Kodak Co., 1958—59; asst. clin. prof. epidemiology Baylor U. Sch. Medicine, 1960—61; asso. prof. medicine U. Kans. Med. Sch., 1961—62, prof., chmn. dept. preventive medicine, 1962—69; coordinator Kan. Regional Med. Program, 1967—69; prof. social medicine Harvard Med. Sch., 1969—70; prof. pub. health, head div. health adminstrn. UCLA Med. Sch., 1970—72, prof. medicine, div. head, 1972—90; prof., 1972—89; prof. nursing Sch. Nursing UCLA Med. Sch., 1973—, prof. emeritus nursing Sch. Nursing, head div. preventive and occupational medicine, 1991—93; dir. Health Svcs. Rsch. Ctr., 1991—93, UCLA Ctr. Health Promotion and Disease Prevention, 1991—; chair acad. senate UCLA, 1995—96. Cons. Getty Trust, Walt Disney Prodns.; mem. Nat. Bd. Med. Examiners, 1964—68, 1968—83, Jt. Commn. on Accreditation Health Care Orgns., 1989—95; mem. health svcs. rsch. study sect. USPHS, 1968—76; vis. scholar Annenberg Sch. Comm., U. So. Calif., 1980—81; mem. adv. bd. Hosp. Rsch. and Edn. Trust, 1972—75. Contbr. articles to profl. jours. Capt. USAF, 1954—56. Recipient Ginsberg prize medicine, U. Kans., 1954, Glasier award, Soc. Gen. Internal Medicine, 1988. Master: ACP (regent 1988—94, Rosenthal award 1980, Laureate award So. Calif. III 1994); fellow: APHA, Acad. Occupl. Medicine; mem.: Am. Assn. Physicians, Assn. Tchrs. Preventive Medicine (pres. coun. 1977—80), Internat. Epidemiology Soc. Home: 221 S Burlingame Ave Los Angeles CA 90049-3702 Office Phone: 310-825-6709. Office Fax: 310-206-5717. Business E-Mail: lewis@ph.adm.ucla.edu. E-mail: lewis@admin.ph.ucla.edu.

LEWIS, CHARLES JEREMY (JERRY LEWIS), United States Representative from California; b. Spokane, Wash., Oct. 21, 1934; m. Arlene Lewis; 3 stepchildren; 4 children from previous marriage. BA in Govt., UCLA, 1956. Former life ins. underwriter; field rep. former US Rep. Jerry Pettis; mem. Calif. State Assembly, 1968-78; vice chmn. rules com., chmn. subcom. on air quality; mem. US Congress from 41st (formerly 35th) Calif. dist., 1978—, mem. ways & means com., chmn. appropriations com., 2005—. Mem. San Bernardino Sch. Bd., 1965—68; chmn. VA-HUD/Ind. Agencies Subcom., 1994—99, Calif. Congl. Delegation, 1996—2001. Grantee Pub. Affairs Fellowship, Coro Found., San Francisco. Republican. Presbyterian. Office: US Ho Reps 2112 Rayburn Ho Office Bldg Washington DC 20515 also: 1150 Brookside Ave, Ste J-5 Redlands CA 92373

LEWIS, CHARLES S., III, lawyer; b. Baker, Oreg., Aug. 19, 1953; Student, U. So. Calif.; BS magna cum laude, Lewis and Clark Coll., 1975; JD magna cum laude, Willamette U., 1978. Bar: Oreg. 1978, U.S. Tax Ct. 1978. Mem. Stoel Rives, LLP, Portland, Oreg., 1978—. Co-author: The Tax Reform Act of 1986: Analysis and Commentary, 1987. Mem. ABA (taxation and bus. law sects.), Delta Mu Delta. Office: Stoel Rives LLP 900 SW 5th Ave Ste 2600 Portland OR 97204-1268

LEWIS, CYNTHIA, law librarian; b. Athens, Greece; m. Jason Lewis; 2 children. BA, Wellesley Coll., 1985; MSLIS, Simmons Coll., 1991; JD, Franklin Pierce Law Ctr., 2001. Law libr., Boston; reference/computer rsch. libr. Franklin Pierce Law Ctr., Concord, NH; electronic resources libr. Hugh and Hazel Darling Law Libr., UCLA Sch. Law, 2001, assoc. law libr., acting dir., 2006—, tchr. advanced legal rsch. Contbr. articles to law jours. Office: UCLA Box 951476 Los Angeles CA 90095-1476 Office Phone: 310-267-4468. E-mail: lewis@law.ucla.edu.

LEWIS, DONALD CLYDE, lawyer; b. Evansville, Ind., Apr. 28, 1942; s. Raymond and Helen (Newman) L.; m. Brenda Cobb, Sept. 1, 1962; children: Kelly Marie, Matthew Ryan, Elaine Janel, Nicole Renee. BS, Ind. U., 1964, cert. in Urban Studies, 1964, JD, 1967. Bar: Ind., 1967, Colo., 1989. Staff atty. N. Am. Van Lines, Ft. Wayne, Ind., 1967-72, PepsiCo Inc, Ft. Wayne, 1972-74; various legal positions Ball Corp., Muncie, Broomfield, Ind. Colo., 1974-96, asst. corp. sec., asst. gen. counsel Broomfield, Colo., 1995—.

LEWIS, EDWIN REYNOLDS, biomedical engineering educator, academic administrator; b. LA, July 14, 1934; s. Edwin McMurtry and Sally Newman (Reynolds) L.; m. Elizabeth Louise McLean, June 11, 1960; children: Edwin McLean, Sarah Elizabeth. AB in Biol. Sci., Stanford U., 1956, MSEE, 1957, Engr., 1959, PhD in Elec. Engring., 1962. With research staff Librascope div. Gen. Precision Inc., Glendale, Calif., 1961-67; mem. faculty dept. elec. engring. and computer sci. U. Calif., Berkeley, 1967—, dir. bioengring. tng. program, 1969-77, prof. elec. engring. and computer sci., 1971-94, prof. grad. sch., 1994-99, prof. emeritus, 1999—, assoc. dean grad. div., 1977-82, assoc. dean interdisciplinary studies coll. engring., 1988-96. Chair joint program bioengring. U. Calif., Berkeley and San Francisco, 1988-91. Author: Network Models in Population Biology, 1977, (with others) Neural Modeling, 1977, The Vertebrate Inner Ear, 1985, Introduction to Bioengineering, 1996; contbr. articles to profl. jours. Grantee NSF, NASA, 1984, 87, Office Naval Rsch., 1990-93, NIH, 1975-2001; Neurosci. Rsch. Program fellow, 1966, 69; recipient Disting. Tchg. citation U. Calif., 1972, Berkeley citation, 1997; Jacob Javits Neurosci. investigator NIH, 1984-91. Fellow IEEE, Acoustical Soc. Am.; mem. AAAS, Assn. Rsch. in Otolaryngology, Soc. Neurosci., Toastmasters (area lt. gov. 1966-67), Sigma Xi. Office: U Calif Dept Elec Engring & Computer Scis Berkeley CA 94720-1770 Business E-Mail: lewis@eecs.berkeley.edu.

LEWIS, FRED PARKER, career officer; b. Cottonwood, Ariz., Mar. 2, 1942; BS in Physics, U. Ariz., 1972; postgrad., U. Utah, 1973, PhD in Meteorology, 1979. Commd. 2d lt. USAF, 1972, advanced through grades to brig. gen., 1996; automated program designer Air Force Global Weather Ctrl., Offutt AFB, Nebr., 1973-76, asst. chief, numerical forecast sect., 1979-81, officer-in-charge, weather forecast models unit, 1981-82; officer-in-charge, operating location B, detachment 15 30th Weather Squadron, Suwon Air Base, South Korea, 1983-84; asst. chief environtl. svcs. hd. Hdqrs. Mil. Airlift Command, Scott AFB, Ill., 1984-86; vice comdr. USAF Environtl. Tech. Applications Ctr., Scott AFB, 1986-87; comdr. 26th Weather Squadron, Barksdale AFB, La., 1987-89; dept. chief of staff, automation support Hdqrs. Mil. Airlift Command, Scott AFB, 1990; comdr. 1500th Computer Systems Group, Scott AFB, 1990-92; chief, weather divsn. U.S. Transp. Command, Scott AFB, 1992-94, dir. Joint Transp. Corp. Info. Mgmt. Ctr., 1994-96; dir. of weather, dep. chief of staff for air and space ops. Hdqrs. USAF, Washington, 1996-2000; v.p. IPS MeteoStar, Aurora, Colo., 2000—. Decorated Legion of Merit. Home: 9522 Oak Stream Ct Fairfax Station VA 22039-2650

LEWIS, GEORGE, music educator; Music prof. U. Calif., San Diego. Music curator Kitchen in N.Y.; collaborator Ctr. for Black Music Rsch., Chgo. Musician (with Anthony Braxton): (albums) Elements of Surprise, 1976; musician: The George Lewis Solo Trombone Record, 1977, George Lewis, 1977, (re-issue on CD) Shadowgraph, 1977; musician: (with Douglas Ewart) (albums) George Lewis/Douglas Ewart, 1979; musician: (with Evan Parker) From saxophone and trombone, 1980; musician: Chgo. Slow Dance, 1981;: (albums) Homage to Charles Parker, 1980, Changing With the Times, 1993; musician: (with Anthony Braxton) Donaueschingen (Duo), 1994; musician: Shadowgraph, 1994; contbr. articles in Black Music Rsch. Jour., Arcana: Musicians on Music Granary Books; improvisor-trombonist, composer: IRCAM Summer Acad. (France), De Ijsbreker, Groningen JazzMarathon, BIM-Huis (Netherlands), P3 Art and Environment (Tokyo), Centro Multimedia/Centro National de las Artes (Mex. City), Rensselaer Polytechnic Inst./iEAR Studios, Metronom (Barcelona), LA County Mus. of Art, Warsaw Autumn Internat. Festival of Contemporary Music, Bang on a Can Marathon, Alice Tully Hall (N.Y.C.), Akademie Schloss Solitude (Stuttgart), Beijing Internat. Jazz Festival, New England Conservatory Improvisation Festival, Inst. of Contemporary Arts (London), Western Front (Vancouver), Ctr. for New Music and Audio Tech. (Berkeley), Velvet Lounge (Chgo.). Mem.: Assn. for the Advancement of Creative Musicians.

LEWIS, HUEY (HUGH ANTHONY CREGG III), singer, composer, bandleader; b. NYC, July 5, 1951; s. Hugh Anthony II and Magda Cregg; m. Sidney Conroy, 1983; children: Kelly, Austin. Student, Cornell U. Mem. Clover, 1972-77; singer, composer leader Huey Lewis and the News, 1978—. Rec. artist: (with Clover) Clover, 1977, Unavailable, 1977, Love on the Wire, 1977, (with Huey Lewis and the News) Huey Lewis and the News, 1980, Picture This, 1982, Sports, 1983, Fore, 1986, Small World, 1988, Hard at Play, 1991, Best of Huey Lewis and the News, 1992, Four Chords and Several Years Ago, 1994, Time Flies...The Best of Huey Lewis, 1996, Original Gold, 2000; hit singles include Do You Believe in Love?, Workin' for a Living, I Want a New Drug, The Heart of Rock 'n' Roll (Grammy award for Best Music Video 1985), Heart and Soul, Walking on a Thin Line, Hip To Be Square, I Know What I Like, (single from Back to the Future soundtrack) The Power of Love; contbr. (single and video) We Are the World, 1984; (films) Back to the Future, 1985, Short Cuts, 1993, Sphere, 1998, Shadow of Doubt, 1998, Duets, 2000; (TV films) Dead Husbands, 1998, video: Twister: A Ritual Reality, 1994; (Broadway actor) Chicago, 2006. Office: c/o Capitol EMI Records 1750 Vine St Hollywood CA 90028-5209

LEWIS, JAMES BELIVEN, state treasurer; b. Roswell, N.Mex., Nov. 30, 1947; m. Armandie Johnson; children: Terri, James Jr., Shedra, LaRon. BS in Edn., Bishop Coll., 1970; MA in Pub. Adminstrn., U. N.Mex., 1977, BS in Bus. Adminstrn., 1981; chief staff cert., Duke U.; student minority leaders program, U. Va. Chief adminstrn. officer City of Albuquerque; dir., asst. sec. US Dept. Energy; coord., counselor pub. svcs. careers program N.Mex. State Personnel Office, Albuquerque; adminstr. consumer affairs div., investigator white collar crime sect., then dir. purchasing div. Bernalillo County Dist. Atty.'s Office, 1977—83; adminstr., educator U. Albuquerque; county treas. Bernalillo County, 1982-85; state treas. State of N.Mex., 1985-90, 2007—; chief of staff Gov. Bruce King, 1991—94; chief clerk N.Mex. State Corp. Commn., 1995—96; city adminstr. Rio Rancho, 1996; dir. oil, gas, and mineral divsn. N.Mex. Commn. Pub. Lands, 1995. Mem. State Investment Coun., Coun. Govs. (policy advisor); apptd. to U.S. Magistrate Merit Selection Panel, 1994; spkr Washington Area State Rels. Group; invitee Governance Mag. Reinventing Govt. (Va./Calif.). Mem. adv. bd. Victims of Domestic Violence; past chmn. Dem. precincts and ward, Albuquerque; mem. N.Mex. State Bd. of Fin., Edn. Found. Bd., State Investment Coun., Oil and Gas Ad-Hoc Com., NAACP. With U.S. Army, 1970-72. Recipient Toll Fellowship Coun. State Govt., Lexington, Ky. Mem. Nat. State Treas.'s Assn. (v.p.), Western State Treas.'s Assn. (pres.), Western Gov.'s Assn. Staff Coun., Pub. Employees Retirement Assn., Edn. Retirement Assn., Mortgage Fin. Authority, N.Mex. Assn. of Counties (past pres. treas.'s affiliate), Nat. Assn. County Treas. and Fin. Officers (chmn. membership com., bd. dirs.), Am. Soc. for Pub. Adminstrn. (past treas. N.Mex. chpt., pres. 1989), mem. Coun. State Govts. Internat. Com., Coun. Gov. Policy Advisors (Disting. Pub. Svc. award, pres. coun. govt. policy advs. 1994-95, apptd. U.S. magistrate merit selection panel 1994, spkr. Wash. area state rels. group), 1994, Am. GI Forum, Am. Legion, Internat. Alumni Assn. Bishop Coll., Taylor Ranch Neighborhood Assn., Western State Treas.'s Assn. (pres.), Kiwanis, Masons, Omega Psi Phi (life), Alpha Beta Psi. Office: Office of State Treas 2019 Galisteo St Bldg K PO Box 608 Santa Fe NM 87504-0608 Office Phone: 505-955-1120. Office Fax: 505-955-1195.

LEWIS, JASON ALVERT, JR., communications executive; b. Clarksville, Tex., Aug. 17, 1941; s. Jason Allen and Mary (Dinwiddie) L. Student, Stockton Coll., 1959-60, San Jose Jr. Coll., 1962-63. Field engr. telephone tech. Pacific Bell, San Francisco, 1983-84; systems technician AT&T, San Francisco, 1984—. Patentee in field. Dep. gov. 1990; With U.S. Army, 1964-66. Mem. Internat. Platform Assn., Cousteau Soc., Astron. Soc. Pacific, San Francisco Zool. Soc., Planetary Soc., U.S. Naval Inst. Democrat. Avocations: photography, astronomy. Home: 139 Pecks Ln South San Francisco CA 94080-1744

LEWIS, JEROME A., petroleum company executive, investment banker; b. 1927; married. BA in Engring., U. Okla. Geologist Shell Oil Co., 1950-51; pres. Lewmont Drilling Inc., 1951-65, Border Exploration Co., 1965-68; pres., chmn. bd., CEO Petro-Lewis Corp., 1968-87; pres. Princeps Ptnrs., Inc., 1987-97; dir. DenverAmerican Petrol., 1991-97; pres. Downing Ptnrs Inc., Denver, 1998—2009. Bd. dirs. Denver Leadership Found., Downing St. Found. Mem. Ind. Petroleum Assn. Am., Oil Investment Inst. (founding gov.), World Pres.' Orgn., Am. Assn. Petroleum Geologists. Office: Downing Ptnrs Inc 5290 E Yale Cir #209 Denver CO 80222-2808 Office Phone: 303-830-6622.

LEWIS, JERRY (JOSEPH LEVITCH), comedian; b. Newark, Mar. 16, 1926; s. Danny and Rae Levitch; m. Patti Palmer, 1944 (div., 1982); children: Gary, Ron, Scott, Chris, Anthony, Joseph; m. Sandra Pitnick, 1983; 1 child, Danielle Sara. DHL (hon.), Mercy Coll., 1987. Prof. cinema U. So. Calif.; pres. JAS Prodns., Inc., P.J. Prodns., Inc. Began as entertainer with record routine at Catskill (NY) hotel; formed comedy team with Dean Martin, 1946-56, The Martin and Lewis Show, 1949-53, performed at Copa, 1948, 1950, Las Vegas Performances, 1952; performer with Sammy Davis Jr., Playboy Afterdark, 1969; performed as a single, 1956—, The Diamond Jubilee of the Royal Variety Performance, The Palladium, London, 1966 (for Her Majesty Queen Elizabeth The Queen Mother), 1966, (Her Majesty The Queen Elizabeth II), 1969, Olympia, 1976; formed Jerry Lewis Prodns. Inc., prod., dir., writer, star, 1956; films include: How to Smuggle a Hernia Across the Border, 1949 (also dir., writer), My Friend Irma, 1949, My Friend Irma Goes West, 1950, At War with the Army, 1950, That's My Boy, 1950, Sailor Beware, 1951, The Stooge, 1952, Jumping Jacks, 1952, Road to Bali, 1952, The Stooge, 1953, Scared Stiff, 1953, The Caddy, 1953, Money From Home, 1954, Three Ring Circus, 1954, Living it Up, 1954, You're Never Too Young, 1955, Artists and Models, 1955, Pardners, 1956, Hollywood or Bust, 1956, The Delicate Delinquent, 1957(also prodr.), The Sad Sack, 1957, The Geisha Boy, 1958 (also prodr.), Rock-a-bye Baby, 1958 (also prodr.), The Jazz Singer, 1959, Don't Give Up the Ship, 1959, Li'l Abner, 1959, It's a Mad, Mad, Mad, Mad World, 1959, Visit to a Small Planet, 1960, The Bellboy, 1960 (also writer, dir., prodr., co-author), Cinderfella, 1960 (also prodr.), The Ladies Man, 1961(also dir., prodr., co-author), It's Only Money, 1962, The Errand Boy, 1962 (also dir., composer, co-author), The Nutty Professor, 1963(also dir., co-author), Who's Minding The Store, 1963, The Patsy, 1964 (also dir., co-author), The Disorderly Orderly, 1964, Ben Casey, 1964 (also dir., one episode), The Family Jewels, 1965 (also dir., prodr., co-author), Boeing-Boeing, 1965, Three On A Couch (also dir., prodr.), 1966, Way... Way... Out, 1966, The Big Mouth, 1967 (also dir., prodr., co-author), Don't Raise the Bridge, Lower the River, 1968, Hook, Line and Sinker, 1969 (also prodr.), One More Time, 1969 (also dir.), Which Way To the Front?, 1970 (also dir., prodr.), The Day the Clown Cried, 1972 (also dir., co-author), Hardly Working, 1981 (also dir., co-author), The King of Comedy, 1983, Smorgasbord, 1983 (also dir., co-author), Cracking Up, 1983 (also dir., writer), Slapstick of Another Kind, 1984, To Catch A Cop, 1984, How Did You Get In?, 1985, Fight for Life, 1987, Cookie, 1989, Boy, 1990 (also writer, dir.), Arrowtooth Waltz, 1991, Arizona Dream, 1991, Mr. Saturday Night, 1992, Funny Bones, 1994, Miss Cast Away, 2004; appeared on Broadway in Damn Yankees, 1995, on nat. tour, 1995-1997, internat. tour., 1997; (TV series) Wiseguy, 1988-89; dir. (TV Series) The Bold Ones: The New Doctors, 1969, Good Grief, 1991, Super Force, 1993; writer, exec. prodr. (films) Nutty Professor, 1996, Nutty Professor II: The Klumps, 2000; writer (TV Series) The Jerry Lewis Show, 1963; author: The Total Film-Maker, 1971, (with

Herb Gluck) Jerry Lewis in Person, 1982, (with James Kaplan) Dean & Me, 2005; guest appearances include: Toast of the Town, 1948, 1960-62, 1961, What's My Line?, 1954, 1956, 1960-62, 1966, This is Your Life, 1956, Rowan & Martin's Laugh-In, 1968, Saturday Night Live, 1983, Mad About You, 1993, (voice) The Simpsons, 2003, and several famous talk shows 1970-; principal TV appearances include master of ceremonies ann. Labor Day Muscular Dystrophy Telethon, 1966-. Comdr. Order of Arts & Letters, France, 1984; nat. chmn. Muscular Dystrophy Assn. Recipient most promising male star in TV award Motion Picture Daily's 2nd Ann. TV poll, 1950, (as team with Dean Martin), one of TV's top 10 money making stars award Motion Picture Herald - Fame poll, 1951, 53-54, 57, The Number One Top Money Actors, Independent Film Jour., 1953, best comedy team award Motion Picture Daily's 16th annual radio poll, 1951-53, Top Men in the Movies, Look Mag., 1953, Nobel Peace Prize nomination, 1978, French Legion of Honor, 1984, Lifetime Achievement award, Am. Comedy Awards, 1998, Governors award, Creative Arts Primetime Emmy Awards, 2005, Jean Hersholt Humanitarian award, Acad. Motion Picture Arts and Sciences, 2009; Honored by the Eleanor Roosevelt Inst. for Cancer Rsch.; named to NJ Hall of Fame, 2008. Mem. Screen Producers Guild, Screen Dirs. Guild, Screen Writers Guild. also: William Morris Agy Inc 151 S El Camino Dr Beverly Hills CA 90212-2704 Office: Jerry Lewis Films Inc 2820 W Charleston Blvd Ste D33 Las Vegas NV 89102

LEWIS, JOHN CHRISTOPHER, allergist; b. Boston, Oct. 15, 1950; MD, Loyola U., Maywood, 1982. Asst. prof. medicine Mayo Clinic Coll. Medicine (formerly Mayo Med. Sch.), Scottsdale, Ariz. Office: Mayo Clinic Scottsdale 13400 E Shea Blvd Scottsdale AZ 85259-5499 Home Phone: 480-451-8753; Office Phone: 480-301-8227.

LEWIS, JOHN CLARK, JR., retired manufacturing company executive; b. Livingston, Mont., Oct. 15, 1935; s. John Clark and Louise A. (Anderson) L.; m. Carolyn Jean Keesling, Sept. 4, 1960; children: Robert, Anne, James. BS, Fresno State U., Calif., 1957. With Service Bur. Corp., El Segundo, Calif., 1960-70, Computer Scis. Corp., 1970; with Xerox Corp., El Segundo, 1970-77, pres. bus. systems div., 1977; pres. Amdahl Corp., Sunnyvale, Calif., 1983-87, CEO, 1983, chmn., 1987-2000; ret., 2000. Served with USNR, 1957-60. Roman Catholic. Office: Amdahl Corp 1250 E Arques Ave Sunnyvale CA 94085-4730

LEWIS, JOHN R., state legislator; b. LA, Nov. 2, 1954; m. Suzanne Henry. BA in Polit. Sci., U. So. Calif. Mem. Calif. State Assembly, 1981-92, Calif. State Senate, 1992—, chmn. Rep. caucus elections com. Mem. Reagan for Pres. Calif. Exec. Com., 1976; del. Nat. Conv. 1976. Republican. Office: Calif State Senate State Capitol Rm 3063 Sacramento CA 95814 also: 1940 W Orangewood Ave Ste 106 Orange CA 92868-2064 Fax: 714-939-0730.

LEWIS, JOHN WILSON, political science professor; b. King County, Wash., Nov. 16, 1930; s. Albert Lloyd and Clara (Lewis) Seeman; m. Jacquelyn Clark, June 19, 1954; children: Cynthia, Stephen, Amy. Student, Deep Springs Coll., 1947-49; AB with honors, UCLA, 1953, MA, 1958, PhD, 1962; degree (hon.), Morningside Coll., 1969, Lawrence U., 1986, Russian Acad. Sci., 1996. Asst. prof. govt. Cornell U., 1961-64, assoc. prof., 1964-68, asst. prof. govt., 1961-64; prof. polit. sci. Stanford U., 1968-97, William Haas prof. Chinese politics, 1972-97, William Haas prof. emeritus, 1997—, co-dir. arms control and disarmament program, 1971-83, co-dir. NE Asia U.S. Forum on Internat. Policy, 1980-90, co-dir. Ctr. for Internat. Security and Arms Control, 1983-91, sr. fellow, 1991—; dir. Project on Peace and Cooperation in the Asian-Pacific Region, 1990—; coord. Five-Nation Project on Asian Regional Security and Econ. Cooperation, 2001—; chmn. Internat. Strategic Inst., 1983-89; chmn. joint com. on contemporary China Social Sci. Rsch. Coun.-Am. Coun. Learned Socs., 1976-79; mng. dir. Generation Ventures, 1994-99. Former vice chmn. Nat. Com. on U.S.-China Rels.; cons. Senate Select Com. on Intelligence, 1977-81, Los Alamos Nat. Lab., 1987-92, Lawrence Livermore Nat. Lab., 1982-2002, Dept. of Def., 1994-96; mem. Def. Policy Bd., 1994-96; chmn. com. advanced study in China Com. Scholarly Comm. with People's Republic of China, 1979-82; com. on internat. security and arms control Nat. Acad. Scis., 1980-83; organizer first univ. discussion arms control and internat. security matters Chinese People's Inst. Fgn. Affairs, 1978, first academic exch. agreement Dem. People's Repb. of Korea, 1988; negotiator first univ. tng. and exch. agreement People's Rep. of China, 1978; coord. Five-Nation Project on Asian Regional Security and Econ. Devel., 2002-05; co-chmn. Nat. Com. North Korea, 2004. Author: Leadership in Communist China, 1963, Major Doctrines of Communist China, 1964, Policy Networks and the Chinese Policy Process, 1986; co-author: The United States in Vietnam, 1967, Modernization by Design, 1969, China Builds the Bomb, 1988, Uncertain Partners: Stalin, Mao, and the Korean War, 1993, China's Strategic Seapower: The Politics of Force Modernization in the Nuclear Era, 1994, Imagined Enemies: China Prepares for Uncertain War, 2006, Negotiating with North Korea, 1992-2007, 2008; editor: The City in Communist China, 1971, Party Leadership and Revolutionary Power in China, 1970, Peasant Rebellion and Communist Revolution in Asia, 1974; contbr.: Congress and Arms Control, 1978, China's Quest for Independence, 1979, others; mem. editl. bd. Chinese Law and Govt., China Quarterly. Served with USN, 1954-57. Recipient Helios award, 2001. Home: 541 San Juan St Stanford CA 94305-8432 Office: Stanford U Encina Hall Stanford CA 94305-6105 Office Phone: 650-723-9627. Business E-Mail: jwlewis@stanford.edu.

LEWIS, JONATHAN, health care association administrator; BS in Applied Behavioral Scis., U. Calif., Davis. Founder, mng. ptnr., pres. JLA Advocates, Inc.; exec. dir. Calif. Commn. on Tchg. Profession; chief cons. State of Calif. State Senate Commn. on Property Tax Equity, 1990-91; exec. dir. Calif. Assn. Health Maintenance Orgns., Sacramento, 1990-93; founder, pres. Acad. for Internat. Health Studies, Inc., Davis, Calif., 1993—. Vis. faculty U. Calif., Berkeley; budget cons. State of Calif. Senate Pres. Office: Acad Internat Health Study 621 Georgetown Pl Davis CA 95616-1821

LEWIS, LOUISE MILLER, gallery director, art history educator; b. St. Louis, Dec. 4, 1940; d. Hugh Milton and Jeanne (Vical) Miller; m. Guy R. Lewis, Nov. 26, 1966; 1 child, Kevin. BA with distinction, 1963; cert. practique de la langue Francaise, U. Paris, 1963; MA in French, U. N.Mex., 1966, MA in Art History, 1972. Curator Art Mus. U. N.Mex., Albuquerque, 1966-70, asst. dir., 1970-72, acctg. dir., 1970, 71-72; assoc. dir. Art Gallery Calif. State U., Northridge, 1972-80, dir., 1980—; asst. prof. art history/recent art of internat. origins Calif. State U., 1972-79, assoc. prof., 1979-83, prof., 1983—, v.p. faculty, 1990-92, pres. faculty, 1992-94. Mem. Phi Beta Kappa. Office: Calif State U 18111 Nordhoff St Northridge CA 91330-8299 E-mail: louise.lewis@csun.edu.

LEWIS, NATHAN SAUL, chemistry professor; b. LA, Oct. 20, 1955; BS in Chemistry with highest honors, MS in Chemistry, Calif. Inst. Tech., 1977; PhD in Chemistry, MIT, 1981. Asst. prof. chemistry Stanford (Calif.) U., 1981-86, assoc. prof., 1986-88, Calif. Inst. Tech., 1988-90, prof., 1990—. Cons. Lawrence Livermore (Calif.) Nat. Lab., 1977-81, 84-88, Solar Energy Rsch. Assocs., Santa Clara, Calif., 1981-85, Am. Hosp. Supply, Irvine, Calif., 1983-85, Molecular Devices, Palo Alto, Calif., 1983-88; mem. U.S. Japan Joint Conf. Photochemistry and Photoconversion, 1983, Chem. Revs. Adv. Bd., 1989-92, long range planning com. Electrochem. Soc., 1991-94, Adv. Bd. Progress Inorganic Chemistry, 1992-94, vis. com. dept. applied sci. Brookhaven Nat. Lab., 1993—. Divisional editor Jour. Electrochemical Soc., 1984-90; mem. editorial adv. bd. Accounts Chem. Rsch., 1993—. Recipient Presdl. Young Investigator award, 1984-88, Fresenius award Phi Lambda Upsilon, 1990, Pure Chemistry award Am. Chem. Soc., 1991; Achievement Rewards Coll. Scientists Found. scholar Calif. Inst. Tech., 1975-77, Calif. State scholar, 1976-77, Carnation Co. Acad. Merit scholar, 1976-77, Camille and Henry Dreyfus Tchr. scholar, 1985-90; Fannie and John Hertz Found. fellow MIT, 1977-81, Alfred P. Sloan Rsch. fellow, 1985-87. Office: Calif Inst Tech Dept Chem 127 72 Pasadena CA 91125-0001 Office Phone: 626-395-6335. E-mail: nslewis@caltech.edu.

LEWIS, NORMAN G., academic administrator, researcher, consultant; b. Irvine, Ayrshire, Scotland, Sept. 16, 1949; came to U.S., 1985; s. William F. and Agnes H. O. L.; m. Christine I. (div. Oct. 1994); children: Fiona, Kathryn; m. Laurence Beatrice Davin, July 1997; 1 child, Sebastien. BSc in Chemistry with honors, U. Strathclyde, Scotland, 1973; PhD in Chemistry 1st class, U. B.C., 1977. NRC postdoctoral fellow U. Cambridge, Eng., 1978-80; rsch. assoc. chemistry dept. Nat. Rsch. Coun., Can., 1980; asst. scientist fundamental rsch. divsn. Pulp and Paper Rsch. Inst. Can., Montreal, 1980-82, group leader chemistry and biochemistry of woody plants, grad. rsch. chemistry divsn., 1982-85; assoc. prof. wood sci. and biochemistry Va. Poly. Inst. and State U., Blacksburg, 1985-90; dir. Inst. Biol. Chemistry, Wash. State U., Pullman, 1990—; Eisig-Tode disting. prof. Wash. State U., Pullman, regents prof., 2008—. Cons. NASA, DOE, USDA, NIH, NSF, Am. Inst. Biol. Sci., other industries, 1985—; mem. sci. adv. bd. Ctr. for Marine Sci., U. NC, 2004—, Thad Cochran Nat. Ctr. for Natural Products Rsch., U. Miss., Oxford, 2003—, Donald Danforth Plant Sci. Ctr., St. Louis, 2002—. Mem. editl. bd. Holzforschung, 1986, TAPPI, 1986, 89, Jour. Wood Chemistry and Tech., 1987, Polyphenols Actualities, 1992—; mem. editl. bd. Wood Sci. and Tech., 2001-, The Ams., Asia regional editor Phytochemistry, 1992—; exec. editor Advances in Plant Biochemistry and Molecular Biology, 2007-; monitoring editor Plant Physiology, 2005-; author or co-author more than 200 publs., books, articles to profl. jours. Hon. mem. Russian Assn. Space and Mankind. Recipient ICI Merit awards Imperial Chem. Industries, 1968-69, 69-70, 70-71, 71-72, ICI scholar, 1971-73, Chemistry awards Kilmarnock Coll., 1969-70, 70-71; NATO/SRC scholar U. B.C., 1974-77; named Local Hero, Prestwick Acad., Ayrshire, Scotland. Mem. TAPPI, Am. Chem. Soc. (at-large cellulose divsn., organizer symposia, programme subcom. cellulose, paper and textile divsn. 1987-90, editl. bd.), Am. Soc. Plant Biologists, Am. Soc. Gravitational and Space Biology (pres. 1998-99), Phytochem. Soc. N.A. (phytochem. bank com. 1989—, pres. 2006—), Chem. Inst. Can. (treas. Montreal divsn. 1982-84, Am. Inst. Chemists and Chem. Inst. Can. Montreal conf. 1982-84), Can. Pulp and Paper Assn., Societe de Groupe Polyphenole, Gordon Rsch. Conf. (vice-chmn. renewable resources com. 1993), Agricultural Biotech. Rsch. Ctr. Sci. (advisory bd.). Presbyterian. Achievements include numerous patents in field; consultant on a project on bioprospecting in Brazil (funded by FAPESP), which has goals of bioassay-guided fractionation, as well as studying biosynthetic pathways and ecological interactions. Home: 1710 NE Upper Dr Pullman WA 99163-4624 Office: Washington State U Inst Biol Chemistry Clark Hall Pullman WA 99164-6340 Office Phone: 509-335-8382. Office Fax: 509-335-8206. Business E-Mail: lewisn@wsu.edu.

LEWIS, OLI PAREPA, curator; b. Cleve., Dec. 14, 1958; d. Raymond Joseph and Yarmila Manlet; m. Fred Lewis. BA, U. Las Vegas. Gen. mgr., curator Guinness World Records Mus., Las Vegas, Nev., 1990—. Pres. Mus. and Attractions in Nev. Recipient Voluntourism award Nev. Commn. Tourism, 1994. Office: Guinness World Of Records 3901A S Maryland Pkwy Las Vegas NV 89119-7537

LEWIS, ORME, JR., real estate company executive, land use adviser; b. Phoenix, Apr. 26, 1935; s. Orme and Barbara (Smith) L.; m. Elizabeth Bruening, Oct. 17, 1964; children: Joseph Orme, Elizabeth Blaise Hazelblood. BS, U. Ariz., Tucson, 1958. Assoc. Coldwell Banker, Phoenix, 1959-64; v.p. Braggiotti Constrn., Phoenix, 1964-65; pvt. practice investment brokerage Phoenix, 1966-69; dep. asst. sec. Dept. Interior, Washington, 1969-73; dir. devel. Ariz. Biltmore Estates, 1973—76; exec. World Resources Co., Phoenix and McLean, Va., 1978-91; mng. mem. Applewhite Laflin & Lewis, Phoenix, 1979-96; gen. ptnr. Equity Interests, Phoenix, 1982—2002; mng. dir. Select Investments, Phoenix, 1996—. Co-chmn. U.S. Adv. Com. on Mining and Mineral Rsch., Washington, 1982-94; mem. U.S. Emergency Minerals Adminstrn., 1987-01, Gov.'s Regulatory Rev. Coun., 1992-95, State Plant Site Transmission Line Com., Phoenix, 1974-85; co-chmn. Biomed. Rsch. Commn., 1995-2002; adv. bd. U.S. Minerals Mgmt. Svcs., 2002—08. Mem. Ariz. Senate, 1966-70 (chmn. Phoenix Children's Hosp., 1981—; mem. bds. Boyce Thompson Arboretum, 1999—); emeritus governing bd. Polycystic Kidney Disease Found., Kansas City, Mo., 1983-2002, Ariz. Parks and Conservation Coun., 1985-96, Ariz. State U. Found., Tempe, 1981-2006, Desert Bot. Garden, 1987-89, Men's Art Coun., 1962-; emeritus Ariz. Cmty. Found., 1986-91, Ariz. Hist. Found., 1984—. Recipient Dept. Interior Conservation Svc. award, 1996; inductee Wisdom Hall of Fame, 1997. Mem. Ariz. C. of C. (dir. 1990-96), Met. Club (Washington), Ariz. Valley Field Riding and Polo Club, Paradise Valley Country Club (Scottsdale), Rotary. Republican. Home: 4325 E Palo Verde Dr Phoenix AZ 85018-1127 Office: Select Investments LLC 5070 N 40th St Ste 140 Phoenix AZ 85018-2193 Office Phone: 602-952-8800. Personal E-mail: adviser_az@msn.com.

LEWIS, RANDOLPH VANCE, molecular biologist, researcher; b. Powell, Wyo., Apr. 8, 1950; s. William (Jack) Fredrick and Evelyn Jean (Vonburg) L.; m. Lorrie Dale Emery, May 27, 1972; children: Brian, Daryl (dec.), Karren. BS in Chemistry, Calif. Inst. Tech., 1972; MS in Chemistry, U. Calif., San Diego, 1974; PhD in Chemistry, U. Calif., 1978. Postdoctoral fellow Roche Inst. Molecular Biology, Nutley, N.J., 1978-80; asst. prof. molecular biology U. Wyo., Laramie, 1980-84, assoc. prof., 1984-89, head dept., 1986-91, prof., 1989—; dir. NSF EPSCOR Program, 1990—. Cons. NIH, Bethesda, Md., 1985—91, Hoffman-LaRoche, Nutley, NJ, 1990—93, DuPont, Wilmington, Del., 1990—94, Protein Polymer Techs., San Diego, 1988—94, Nexia, 1999—; pres. Wyobigen, Laramie, Wyo., 1994—; bd. dirs. Wyo. Bus. Devel. Ctr. Author chpts. to books; contbr. articles to profl. jours. Mem. Jr. Livestock Sale Com., Laramie, 1991-98; pres. Albany County 4-H Coun., Laramie, 1994-98. Sloan Found. fellow, 1985; recipient Research Career Devel. award NIH, 1985, Jr. Faculty award Am. Cancer Soc., 1985, Burlington-North Faculty award U. Wyo., 1986. Mem. Am. Chem. Soc., Am. Soc. Biochemists and Molecular Biologists, N.Y. Acad. Scis., Protein Soc. Republican. Baptist. Achievements include discovery of opioid peptide precursor; sequencing of first spider silk protein genes; five product licenses; 4 patents. Home: 1948 Howe Rd Laramie WY 82070-6889 Office: U Wyo 1000 E University Dept 3944 Laramie WY 82071-3944 Office Phone: 307-766-2147. Business E-Mail: silk@uwyo.edu.

LEWIS, RODERIC W., electronics executive, lawyer; b. Nyssa, Oreg., May 17, 1955; BA in Econs. and Asian studies, Brigham Young U., 1980; JD, Columbia U., 1983. Bar: Utah 1983. Assoc. LeBoeuf, Lamb, Leiby & MacRae, NYC, 1983-89, Rogers, MacKay, Price & Anderson, 1989-91; asst. gen. counsel Micron Tech., Inc., Boise, 1991-95, v.p. legal affairs, gen. counsel, corp. sec., 1996—; v.p., gen. counsel, corp. sec. Micron Electronics, Inc., 1995—96. Vice-chmn. Utah Bus. Corp. Act Revision Com. Mem. ABA, Idaho State Bar, Utah State Bar (chmn. bus. law sect. 1988-89). Office: Micron Technology Inc PO Box 6 8000 S Federal Way Boise ID 83716-9632 Office Phone: 208-368-4500. E-mail: rodlewis@micron.com.

LEWIS, SHELDON NOAH, technology consultant; b. Chgo., July 1, 1934; s. Jacob Joseph and Evelyn (Mendelsohn) Iglowitz; m. Suzanne Joyce Goldberg, June 17, 1957; children: Sara Lynn, Matthew David, Rachel Ann. BA with honors, Northwestern U., 1956, MS (Univ. fellow), 1956; PhD (Eastman Kodak fellow), UCLA, 1959; postgrad. (NSF fellow), U. Basel, Switzerland, 1959-60; postgrad. cert. in research mgmt, Indsl. Research Inst., Harvard U., 1973. With Rohm & Haas Co., 1960-78, head lab., 1963-68, research supr., 1968-73, dir. splty. chem. research, 1973-74; gen. mgr. DCL Lab. AG subs., Zurich, Switzerland, 1974-75; dir. European Labs. Valbonne, France, 1975-76; corp. dir. research and devel. worldwide for polymers, resins and monomers Spring House, Pa., 1976-78; with The Clorox Co., Oakland, Calif., 1978-91, v.p. R&D, 1978, group v.p., 1978-84, exec. v.p., 1984-91, also bd. dirs.; pres. SNL Inc., Lafayette, Calif., 1991—. Mem. indsl. panel on sci. and tech. NSF. Referee: Jour. Organic Chemistry; patentee in field; contbr. articles to profl. publs. Mem. Calif. Inst. Adv. Bd., World Affairs Council, UCLA Chemistry Adv. Council, Bay Area Sci. Fair Adv. Bd., Mills Coll. Adv. Council for Sci. and Math. Recipient cert. in patent law Phila. Patent Law Assn., 1962, Roon award for coatings research Fedn. Socs. Coatings Tech., 1966, cert. of service Wayne State U. Polymer Conf. Series, 1967, cert. in mgmt. by objectives Am. Mgmt. Research, Inc., 1972 Mem. Soap and Detergent Assn. (bd. dirs.), Chem. Ind. Inst. of Toxicology (bd. dirs.), Indsl. Rsch. Inst., Am. Chem. Soc. (chmn. Phila. polymer sect. 1970-71), Soc. Chem. Industry London, Sigma Xi. Jewish. Office: SNL Inc 3711 Rose Ct Lafayette CA 94549-3030

LEWIS, SHIRLEY JEANE, retired therapist, educator; b. Phoenix, Aug. 23; d. Herman and Leavy (Hutchinson) Smith; m. Edgar Anthony Lewis (div.); children: Edgar Anthony (dec.), Roshaun, Lucy Ann, Jonathan. AA, Phoenix C.C., 1957; BA, Ariz. State U., 1960; MS, San Diego State U., 1975, MA, 1985, Azusa Pacific U., 1982; PhD, U. So. Calif., 1983. Cert. tchr. Calif. Recreation leader Phoenix Parks and Recreation Dept., 1957-62; columnist Ariz. Tribune, Phoenix, 1958-59; tchr. phys. edn. San Diego Unified Schs., 1962—; adult educator San Diego C.C., 1973—94; counselor San Diego County Schs., 1979—97; assoc. prin. Oceanside (Calif.) Unified Sch. Dist., 1997—98; head counselor Gomper Secondary Sch. San Diego (Calif.) Unified Schs., 1998—2003, ret. Gomper Secondary Sch., 2003. Instr. psychology, health, Black studies, 1977—, counselor, 1981—; cmty. counselor S.E. Counseling and Cons. Svcs. and Narcotics Prevention and Edn. Sys., Inc., San Diego, 1973-77; counselor educator, counselor edn. dept. San Diego State U., 1974-77; marriage, family, child counselor Counseling and Cons. Ctr., San Diego, 1977—; inservice educator San Diego Unified and San Diego County Sch. Dists., 1973-77; Fulbright Exch. counselor, London, 1994-96; instr. San Diego (Calif.) C.C., 1977-94, counselor, 1981-94; lectr. in field. Contbr. articles to profl. jours. Girl Scout phys. fitness cons., Phoenix, 1960-62; vol. cmty. tutor for high sch. students, San Diego, 1963; sponsor Tennis Club for Youth, San Diego, 1964-65; troop leader Girl Scouts U.S., Lemon Grove, Calif., 1972-74; vol. counselor USN Alcohol Rehab. Ctr., San Diego, 1978; mem. sch. coun.'s adv. bd. San Diego State U. Named Woman of Yr., Phoenix, 1957, One of Outstanding Women of San Diego, 1980; recipient Phys. Fitness Sch. award and Demonstration Sch. award Pres.'s Coun. on Phys. Fitness, Taft Jr. H.S., 1975, Excel award Corp. Excellence Edn., 1989; Delta Sigma Theta scholar, 1957-60; Alan Korrick scholar, 1956. Mem. NEA, Calif. Tchrs. Assn., San Diego Tchrs. Assn., Assn. Marriage and Family Counselors, Am. Personnel and Guidance Assn., Calif. Assn. Health, Phys. Edn. and Recreation (v.p. health), Am. Alliance of Health, Phys. Edn. and Recreation, Assn. Black Psychologists (corr. sec. 1993), Assn. African-Am. Educators, Delta Sigma Theta (Delta of Yr. 1987). Democrat. Baptist. Home: 1226 Armacost Rd San Diego CA 92114-3307

LEWIS, SUZANNE, parks director; b. 1956; BA magna cum laude, U. W. Fla., 1978. Various positions including seasonal park supt., park tech. park historian, supervisory park ranger, mgmt. asst. to supt. Glacier Nat. Park Gulf Islands Nat. Seashore, 1978—89; acting supt. Christiansted Nat. Historic Site, Buck Island Reef Nat. Monument U.S. Virgin Islands; supt. Timucuan Ecological and Historic Preserve, 1990—97, Chattahoochee River Nat. Recreation Area, Atlanta, 1997—2000, Yellowstone Nat. Park, 2002—. Recipient Woman of Distinction award, Girl Scout Councils of Am., 1997, Sec. of Interior Bronze Exec. Leadership award, 2004, others; named Mgr. of Year for Partnerships, Nat. Parks and Conservation Assn., 1994. Office: Yellowstone Nat Park PO Box 168 Yellowstone National Park WY 82190-0168

LEWIS, THOMASINE ELIZABETH, magazine editor-in-chief; b. Manila, Phillipines, Sept. 20; d. Thomas Donald and Elizabeth Jane (Munson) L. Student, Broward C.C., 1976, Universidad de las Americas, Mexico City, 1979, U. Fla., L.A. Valley Coll., 1981, UCLA, 1984. Copy editor, reporter Mexico City News, 1979-81; mng. editor, editor-in-chief Playgirl Mag., Santa Monica, Calif., 1984-86; exec. editor mag. devel. Petersen Pub., Hollywood, Calif.,

1986-87; exec. editor Japan Jour. Mag., Marina del Rey, Calif., 1987-88; assoc. pub., dir. Radio Guide Mag., LA, 1988-90; editor-in-chief Disney Adventures Mag., Burbank, Calif., 1991-95, Sassy Mag., LA, 1995; exec. dir. Live! Mag., LA, 1995-98; editor, chief Teen Mag., 1998—. Bd. dirs. Santa Monica Red Cross; mem. League of Women Voters, NOW, People for the Am. Way. Avocations: travel, writing, running.

LHUILLIER, (DIANE) MONIQUE, apparel designer; b. Philippines; m. Tom Bugbee. Grad., Fashion Inst. of Design and Merchandising, Los Angeles. Founder, designer Monique Lhuillier & Co., Los Angeles, 1996—; opened Monique Lhuillier Boutique, Beverly Hills, 2001—. Designs featured in numerous magazines including W, In Style, Modern Bride, Elle. Recipient Glamorous Bridal Designer award, 2001, Avant Garde Bridal Designer award, Wedding Dresses Mag., 2002, Designer of Yr. award, 2003. Mem.: Council of Fashion Designers of Am. Office: Monique Lhuillier & Co 1201 S Grand Ave 3rd Fl Los Angeles CA 90015

LIBBIN, ANNE EDNA, lawyer; b. Phila., Aug. 25, 1950; d. Edwin M. and Marianne (Herz) L.; m. Christopher J. Cannon, July 20, 1985; children: Abigail Libbin Cannon, Rebecca Libbin Cannon. AB, Radcliffe Coll., 1971; JD, Harvard U., 1975. Bar: Calif. 1975, U.S. Dist. Ct. (cen. dist.) Calif. 1977, U.S. Dist. Ct. (no. dist.) Calif. 1979, U.S. Dist. Ct. (ea. dist.) Calif. 1985, U.S. Ct. Appeals. (2d cir.) 1977, U.S. Ct. Appeals (5th cir.) 1982, U.S. Ct. Appeals (7th cir.) 1976, U.S. Ct. Appeals (9th cir.) 1976, U.S. Ct. Appeals (D.C. cir.) 1978, U.S. Supreme Ct. 2001. Appellate atty. NLRB, Washington, 1975-78; assoc. Pillsbury Madison & Sutro LLP, San Francisco, 1978-83, ptnr., 1984-99; sr. counsel SBC West Legal Dept., San Francisco, 1999—; dir. Jewish Vocat. Svcs., San Francisco, 2002—. Three Guineas fellow Harvard Law Sch., 1997; dir. Alumnae Resources, San Francisco, 1991-97. Mem. ABA (labor and employment sect.), State Bar Calif. (labor law sect.), Bar Assn. San Francisco (labor law sect.), Radcliffe Club (San Francisco).

LIBERMAN, ROBERT PAUL, psychiatry educator, researcher, writer; b. Newark, Aug. 16, 1937; s. Harry and Gertrude (Galowitz) L.; m. Janet Marilyn Brown, Feb. 16, 1973; children: Peter, Sarah, Danica, Nathaniel, Annalisa. AB summa cum laude, Dartmouth Coll., 1959, diploma in medicine with honors, 1960; MS in Pharmacology, U. Calif., San Francisco, 1961; MD, Johns Hopkins U., 1963. Diplomate Nat. Bd. Med. Examiners, Am. Bd. Psychiatry and Neurology. Intern Bronx (N.Y.) Mcpl. Hosp.-Einstein Coll. Medicine, 1963-64; resident psychiatry Mass. Mental Health Ctr., Boston, 1964-68; postdoctoral fellow in social psychiatry Harvard U., 1966-68, tchg. fellow in psychiatry, 1964-68; mem. faculty group psychotherapy tng. program Washington Sch. Psychiatry, 1968-70; asst. clin. prof. psychiatry UCLA, 1970-72, assoc. clin. prof., 1972-73, assoc. rsch. psychiatrist, 1973-76, rsch. prof. psychiatry, 1976-77, prof. psychiatry, 1977—. With nat. Ctr. Mental Health Svc., Tng. and Rsch., St. Elizabeths Hosp., also mem. NIMH Clin. and Rsch. Assocs. Tng. Program, Washington, 1968-70; dir. Camarillo-UCLA Clin. Rsch. Unit, 1970-97, dir. Clin. Rsch. Ctr. Schizophrenia and Psychiat. Rehab., 1977-2001; chief Rehab. Medicine Svc., West L.A. VA Med. Ctr., Brentwood divsn., 1980-92; cons. divsn. mental health and behavioral scis. edn. Sepulveda (Calif.) VA Hosp., 1975-80; practice medicine specializing in psychiatry, Reston, Va., 1968-70, Thousand Oaks, Calif., 1977—; staff psychiatrist Ventura County Mental Health Dept., 1970-75, Ventura County Gen. Hosp.; mem. med. staff UCLA Neuropsychiat. Inst. and Hosp., 1971—, Ventura Gen. Hosp., Camarillo State Hosp., 1970-97, West L.A. VA Med. Ctr.; dir. Rehab. Rsch. and Tng. Ctr. Mental Illness, 1980-85; prof. psychiatry, dir. psych. rehab. program UCLA Sch. Medicine. Author: (with King, DeRisi and McCann) Personal Effectiveness: Guiding People to Assert Their Feelings and Improve Their Social Skills, 1975, A Guide to Behavioral Analysis and Therapy, 1972, (with Wheeler, DeVisser, Kuehnel and Kuehnel) Handbook of Marital Therapy: An Educational Approach to Treating Troubled Relationships, 1980, Psychiatric Rehabilitation of Chronic Mental Patients, 1987, (with DeRisi and Mueser) Social Skills Training for Psychiatric Patients, 1989, (with Kuehnel, Rose and Storzbach) Resource Book for Psychiatric Rehabilitation, 1990, Handbook of Psychiatric Rehabilitation, 1992, (with Yager) Stress in Psychiatric Disorders, 1993, (with Corrigan) Behavior Therapy in Psychiatric Hospitals, 1994, International Perspectives on Skills Training with the Mentally Disabled, 1998; mem. editl. bd. Jour. Applied Behavior Analysis, 1972-78, Jour. Marriage and Family Counseling, 1974-78, Jour. Behavior Therapy and Exptl. Psychiatry, 1975-2000, Behavior Therapy, 1979-84, Assessment and Intervention in Devel. Disabilities, 1980-85; assoc. editor Jour. Applied Behavior Analysis, 1976-78, Schizophrenia Bull., 1981-87, Internat. Rev. Psychiatry, 1988—, Psychiatry, 1993—; contbr. over 300 articles to profl. jours. and chpts. to books. Bd. dirs. Lake Sherwood Cmty. Assn., 1978—, pres., 1979-81, 90-92, v.p., 1992-95, sec., 1995-97; mem. Conejo Valley Citizens Adv. Bd., 1979-81. Served as surgeon USPHS, 1964-68. Recipient Noyes award for Rsch. in Schizophrenia, 1992, Kolb award in Schizophrenia, 1994, Human Rights award Psychosocial Rehab., Lilly Reintegration prize, Human Rights award WHO, 2000, Reintegration award Eli Lilly, 2000, Disting. Investigator award Nat. Alliance for Rsch. in Schizophrenia and Depression, 2000-01; rsch. grantee NIMH, SSA, NIDA, VA, 1972—. Mem. Assn. Advancement Behavior Therapy (exec. com. 1970-72, dir. 1972-79), Am. Psychiat. Assn. (Hibbs and Van Ameringen awards, Inst. Psychiat. Svcs. Significant Achievement award), Assn. Clin. Psychosocial Rsch. (mem. coun. 1985-98, pres. 1995-97), Phi Beta Kappa. Home: 528 Lake Sherwood Dr Thousand Oaks CA 91361-5120 Office: UCLA Neuropsychiatric Inst 760 Westwood Plz Los Angeles CA 90095

LICCARDO, SAM T., councilman; BA magna cum laude, Georgetown U.; JD, Harvard U., M in Pub. Policy. Pub. prosecutor Santa Clara County Dist. Atty.'s Office; pvt. atty.; councilman, Dist. 3 San José City Coun., 2006—. Vice chair Valley Transp. Authority, chairperson congestion mgmt. com.; bd. mem. Capitol Corridor Rail Commn. Mem.: Santa Clara County Cities Assn. (mem. exec. com.), Assn. Bay Area Govts. (bd. mem.). Democrat. Office: San Jose City Coun 200 E Santa Clara St San Jose CA 95113 Office Phone: 408-535-4903. Office Fax: 408-292-6456. Business E-Mail: District3@sanjoseca.gov.*

LICHTENBERG, MAGGIE KLEE, publishing executive; b. NYC, Nov. 19, 1941; d. Lawrence and Shirley Jane (Wicksman) Klee; m. James Lester Lichtenberg, Mar. 31, 1963 (div. 1982); m. William Shaw Jones, July 2, 2000; children: Gregory Lawrence, Amanda Zoe. BA, U. Mich., 1963; postgrad., Harvard U., 1963. Cert. profl. coach Internat. Coach Fed. Book rev. editor New Woman mag., 1972-73; assoc. editor children's books Parents Mag. Press, 1974; editor, rights dir. Books for Young People, Frederick Warne & Co., NYC, 1975-78; sr. editor Simon & Schuster, NYC, 1979-80; dir. sales promotion Grosset & Dunlap, NYC, 1980-81; ednl. sales mgr. Bantam Books, NYC, 1982-84; dir. mktg. and sales Grove Press, NYC, 1984-86, dir. of sales, 1986-87; dir. sales Weidenfeld & Nicolson, NYC, 1986-87; mktg. dir. Beacon Press, Boston, 1988-95; bus. and pub. coach, 1995—. Freelance critic, 1961—; founder Open Heart Pub., Santa Fe, 2005—. Author: The Open Heart Companion: Preparation and Guidance for Open-Heart Surgery Recovery, 2006 (finalist, Book of Yr. awards, ForeWord Mag., 2006); contbr. articles, essays, stories, poetry, revs. to mags. newspapers and anthologies. Bd. dirs. Children's Book Coun., 1978. Recipient 2 Avery Hopwood awards in drama and fiction, 1962, 2 in drama and poetry, 1963; coll. fiction contest award Mademoiselle mag., 1963; Woodrow Wilson fellow, 1963. Mem. Women's Nat. Book Assn. (past pres. N.Y. chpt.), Internat. Coach Fedn. (cert.), The Coaching Collective, Independent Book Pubs. Assn. (bd. dirs. 2006—), N.Mex. Book Assn., PEN N.Mex., Adult Congenital Heart Assn. Home and Office: 4 Cosmos Ct Santa Fe NM 87508-2285 Office Phone: 505-986-8807. Business E-Mail: maggie@openheartcoach.com, maggie@maggielichtenberg.com.

LICHTER, LINDA, lawyer; b. Milw., Feb. 12, 1951; m. Nick Marck; 3 children. AB with great distinction, U. Calif., Berkeley, 1973; JD, U. Calif. Boalt Hall Sch. Law, 1976. Bar: Calif. 1976. Atty. Kaplan, Livingston, Goodwin, Berkowitz and Selvin; ptnr. Weissmann, Wolff, Bergman, Coleman & Silverman, Lichter, Grossman, Nichols & Adler, Inc., LA, 1992—. Mem. adv. bd. Ind. Feature Project West, 1985—90; lectr. Practicing Law Inst., 1996—98. Mem. exec. bd. U. Calif. Coll.Letters & Sci., Berkeley, 1993—2001; bd. mem. LA Theater Works, 1980—, Women in Film, 1998—99. Named one of 100 Power Lawyers, Hollywood Reporter, 2007. Mem.: Phi Beta Kappa. Office: Lichter Grossman Nichols & Adler Inc 9200 Sunset Blvd Ste 1200 Los Angeles CA 90069-3507 Office Phone: 310-205-6999. Office Fax: 310-205-6990.

LICHTMAN, MOSHE, computer software company executive; Degree in computer engring., Technion, Israel Inst. Tech.; M in bus., MIT. Product mgr. personal systems divsn. Microsoft Corp., Redmond, Wash., 1991, pres. Softimage, 1995—98, v.p. Digital TV platform strategy, 1998—99, head internat. internet bus., 1999, corp. v.p. TV divsn., 2002—06, corp. v.p. Israel rsch. & devel., 2006—. Co-author: Complete Guide to the C Language. Office: Microsoft Corp One Microsoft Way Redmond WA 98052-6399

LICK, WILBERT JAMES, mechanical engineering educator; b. Cleve., June 12, 1933; s. Fred and Hulda (Sunntag) L.; children—James, Sarah. BAE., Rensselaer Poly. Inst., 1955, MAE., 1957, PhD, 1958. Asst. prof. Harvard, 1959-66; sr. research fellow Calif. Inst. Tech., 1966-67; mem. faculty Case Western Res. U., 1967-79, prof. earth scis., 1970-79, chmn. dept., 1973-76; prof. mech. engring. U. Calif.-Santa Barbara, 1979—, chmn. dept., 1982-84. Home: 1236 Camino Meleno Santa Barbara CA 93111-1007 Office: U Calif Dept Mech & Environ Engring Santa Barbara CA 93106 Office Phone: 805-893-4295. Business E-Mail: willy@engineering.ucsb.edu.

LIDDELL, CHRISTOPHER P., computer software company executive; married; 2 children. BS in Engring. with honors, Auckland U., New Zealand; MA in Philosophy, Oxford U., Eng. CFO to CEO Carter Holt Harvey, 1995—2002; v.p., fin. Internat. Paper Co., Stamford, Conn., 2002—03, sr. v.p., CFO, 2003—05; CFO Microsoft Corp., 2005—. Office: Microsoft Corp 1 Microsoft Way Redmond WA 98052

LIDDLE, ALAN CURTIS, retired architect; b. Tacoma, Mar. 10, 1922; s. Abram Dix and Myrtle (Maytum) L. B.Arch., U. Wash., 1948; postgrad., Eidgenoissche Technische Hochschule, Zurich, Switzerland, 1950-51. Asst. prof. architecture U. Wash., 1954-55; prin. Liddle & Jones, Tacoma, 1957-67, Alan Liddle (architects), Tacoma, 1967-90, Liddle & Jacklin, Tacoma, 1990-98; ret., 1999. Architect oceanography bldgs, U. Wash., 1967, Tacoma Art Mus., 1971, Charles Wright Acad., Tacoma, 1962, Pacific Nat. Bank Wash., Auburn, 1965. Pres. bd. Allied Arts Tacoma, 1963-64, Civic Arts Commn. Tacoma-Pierce County, 1969; commr. Wash. Arts Commn., 1971; Bd. dirs. Tacoma Art Mus., Tacoma Zool. Soc., Tacoma Philharmonic, Inc. Served with AUS, 1943-46. Fellow A.I.A. (pres. S.W. Wash. chpt. 1967-68); mem. Wash. Hist. Soc., U. Wash. Alumni Assn. (all life) Home: 12735 Gravelly Lake Dr SW Lakewood WA 98499-1459 Office: 703 Pacific Ave Tacoma WA 98402-5207 Home Phone: 353-588-4525; Office Phone: 253-272-3155.

LIDICKER, WILLIAM ZANDER, JR., zoologist, educator; b. Evanston, Ill., Aug. 19, 1932; s. William Zander and Frida (Schroeter) L.; m. Naomi Ishino, Aug. 18, 1956 (div. Oct., 1982); children: Jeffrey Roger, Kenneth Paul; m. Louise N. DeLonzor, June 5, 1989. BS, Cornell U., 1953; MS, U. Ill., 1954, PhD, 1957. Instr. zoology, asst. curator mammals U. Calif., Berkeley, 1957-59, asst. prof., asst. curator, 1959-65, assoc. prof., assoc. curator, 1965-69; assoc. dir. Mus. Vertebrate Zoology, 1968-81, acting dir., 1974-75, prof. zoology, curator mammals, 1969-89, prof. integrative biology, curator of mammals, 1989-94, prof., curator emeritus, 1994—. Adj. rsch. scientist Inst. Ecology U. Ga., 1989—. Dancer Westwind Internat. Folk Ensemble, 1994-2000, Jubilee Am. Dance Theater, 1999—; contbr. articles to profl. jours. Bd. dir. No. Calif. Com. for Environ. Info., 1971-77; bd. trustees BIOSIS, 1987-92, chmn., 1992; N.Am. rep. steering com., sect. Mammalogy IUBS, UNESCO, 1978-89; chmn. rodent specialist group Species Survival Commn., IUCN, 1980-89; mem. sci. adv. bd. Marine World Found. at Marine World Africa USA, 1987-98; pres. Dehnel-Petrusewicz Meml. Fund, 1985-97, sec.-treas., 1999. Fellow AAAS (life, 50 Yr.), Calif. Acad. Scis., Polish Acad. Scis. (fgn. mem., 50 Yr. Anniversary medal and diploma 2004), Explorers Club; mem. Internat. Fedn. Mammalogists (bd. dir. 2006—, pres. 2007—), Am. Soc. Mammalogists (dir. 1969—, 2d v.p. 1974-76, pres. 1976-78, C.H. Merriam award 1986, hon. mem. 1995), Am. Ornithologist's Union (life), Am. Soc. Naturalists, Berkeley Folk Dancers Club (pres. 1969, tchr. 1984—, hon. mem. 2000)., Nat. Folk Orgn. (bd. trustees 2005—), Folk Dance Fedn. Calif. (bd. dir. 2005-, pres. 2007—). Office: U Calif Mus Vertebrate Zoology Berkeley CA 94720-0001 Business E-Mail: wlidicker@berkeley.edu.

LIDMAN, ROGER WAYNE, museum director; b. June 8, 1956; s. Arthur Arvid and Elna G. (Bernson) L.; m. Cynthia Louise Platt, May 26, 1988. BA in Anthropology, Ariz. State U., 1987, postgrad. studies, 1987-91. Mus. aide Pueblo Grande Mus., Phoenix, 1976-84, exhibit preparator, 1984-86, ops. coord., 1986-89, acting dir., 1989-90, dir., 1990—. Chair Ariz. Archaeol. Adv. Commn., 1998, 99-01. Bd. mem. Ariz. Tourism Alliance, 1997—; bd. mem. Ariz. Humanities Coun., 2003-05, v.p. 2004-05, chair, 2006-; mem. Ariz. State Libr. adv. coun., 2001—. Recipient Outstanding Personal Svc. award Mus. Assn. Ariz., 1998. Mem. Am. Assn. Mus. (officer small mus. adminstr. com. 1993-94, treas. 1994-96), Mus. Assn. Ariz. (v.p. 1994-95, pres. 1995-96), Ctrl. Ariz. Mus. Assn. (v.p. 1992, pres. 1993-94, 95-96), Papago Salado Assn. (treas. 1996-99), Western Mus. Assn. (at-large mem. 1998-2001, 1st v.p. 2001-02). Avocations: golf, natural history, guitar. Office: Pueblo Grande Mus 4619 E Washington St Phoenix AZ 85034-1909

LIDSTROM, MARY E., chemical engineering and microbiology professor; BS in Microbiology, Ore. State Univ., 1973; MS in Bacteriology, Univ. Wis., Madison, 1975; PhD in Bacteriology, Univ. Wis., 1977. Prof., environ. engring. sci. Calif. Tech. Inst.; Frank Jungers Chair, Engring. Univ. Wash., and prof. chem. engring, prof. microbiology, assoc. dean for new initiatives in engring. Rsch. prof. Howard Hughes Med. Inst., 2002—. Editl. bd. Jour. Bacteriology; contbr. articles to profl. journals. Recipient Prather award for Young Women in Sci., CalTech award for Excellence, NSF Faculty award for Women, Howard Hughes Med. Inst. grant, 2002. Fellow: Am. Acad. Microbiology. Office: 263 Benson Univ Wash Box 351750 Seattle WA 98195-1750 Office Phone: 206-616-5282. Office Fax: 206-616-5721. Business E-Mail: lidstrom@u.washington.edu.

LIEBECK, ROBERT H., aerospace engineer; PhD in Aero. and Astron. Engring., U. Ill., 1968. With Boeing/McDonnell Douglas; rschr., instr. U. So. Calif.; sr. fellow The Boeing Co.; prof. dept. mech. and aerospace engring. U. Calif., Irvine, 2000—. Mem. NAE. Achievements include design for high-lift airfoils, referred to as "Liebeck airfoils"; contributor to propeller design, windmill analysis, wing design for supersonic transports, and design of high-altitude unmanned aircraft; co-developer Blended-Wing Body, a revolutionary design for subsonic transports. Office: Dept Mech and Aerospace Engring 4200 Engineering Gateway U Calif Irvine Irvine CA 92697-3975 Fax: 949-824-8585.

LIEBELER, SUSAN WITTENBERG, lawyer; b. July 3, 1942; d. Sherman K. and Eleanor (Klivans) Levine; m. Wesley J. Liebeler, Oct. 21, 1971 (dec.); 1 child, Jennifer. BA, U. Mich., 1963, postgrad., 1963-64; LLB, UCLA, 1966. Bar: Calif. 1967, Vt. 1973, DC 1988. Law clk. Calif. Ct. of Appeals, 1966-67; assoc. Gang, Tyre & Brown, 1967-68, Greenberg, Bernhard, Weiss & Karma, L.A., 1968-70; assoc. gen. counsel Rep. Corp., 1970-72; gen. counsel Verit Industries, 1972-73; prof. Loyola Law Sch., LA, 1973—85; spl. counsel, chmn. John S. R. Shad, SEC, Washington, 1981-82; commr. U.S. Internat. Trade Commn., Washington, 1984-88, vice-chmn., 1984-86, chmn., 1986-88; ptnr. Irell & Manella, LA, 1988-94; pres. Lexpert Rsch. Svcs., LA, 1995—. Vis. prof. U. Tex., summer 1982; cons. Office of Policy Coordination, Office of Pres.-elect, 1981-82; cons. U.S. Ry. Assn., 1975, U.S. EPA, 1974, U.S. Price Commn., 1972; mem. Adminstrv. Conf. U.S., 1986-88. Mem. editl. adv. bd. Regulation mag. CATO Inst.; sr. editor UCLA Law Rev., 1965-66; contbr. articles to profl. jours. Mem. adv. bd. U. Calif. Orientation in USA Law; bd. govs. Century City Hosp., 1992—2002, vice chair, 1997—99, chair, 1999—2001. Stein scholar UCLA, 1966. Mem. State Bar Calif. (treas., vice chair, chair exec. com. internat. law sect.), Practicing Law Inst. (Calif. adv. com.), Washington Legal Found. (acad. adv. bd.), Order of Coif. Jewish. Office Phone: 310-589-5546. Business E-Mail: lexpert@lexpertresearch.com.

LIEBER, DAVID LEE, university president; b. Stryj, Poland, Feb. 20, 1925; came to U.S., 1927, naturalized, 1936; s. Max and Gussie L.; m. Esther, June 10, 1945; children: Michael, Daniel, Deborah, Susan. BA, CCNY, 1944; B of Hebrew Lit., Jewish Theol. Sem. Am., 1944, M of Hebrew Lit., 1948, D of Hebrew Lit., 1951; MA, Columbia U., 1947; postgrad., U. Wash., 1954—55, UCLA, 1961—63; LDH (hon.), Hebrew Union Coll., 1982. Ordained rabbi, 1948. Rabbi Sinai Temple, LA, 1950-54; dir. B'nai B'rith Hillel, Seattle, Cambridge, 1954-56; dean students U. Judaism (now The Am. Jewish U.), LA, 1956—63, Samuel A. Fryer prof. Bible, pres., 1963—92, Skovron Disting. Svc. prof. Bibl. lit., 1990—, pres. emeritus, 1992—; lectr. Hebrew UCLA, 1957-90; vice chancellor Jewish Theol. Sem., 1972-92. Mem. exec. coun. Rabbinical Assembly, 1966-69, v.p., 1994-96, pres., 1996-98; vice chmn. Am. Jewish Com., L.A., 1972-75; bd. dirs. Jewish Fedn. Coun., L.A., 1980-86. Mem. editl. bd. Conservative Judaism, 1968-70; sr. editor (bibl. commentary) ETZ Hayim. Served as chaplain USAF, 1951-53. Recipient Torch of Learning award Hebrew U., 1984, Simon Greenberg award U. Judaism, 2002, Book of Yr. award Nat. Jewish Book Coun., 2002, Tomech Torah award Nat. Jewish Edn. Assn., 2004. Mem. Assn. Profs. Jewish Studies (dir. 1970-71), Phi Beta Kappa. Office: The Am Jewish U 15600 Mulholland Dr Los Angeles CA 90077-1519 Office Phone: 310-440-1288. Personal E-mail: dllieber@aol.com.

LIEBER, MICHAEL RANDALL, biochemist, educator; b. St. Louis, June 21, 1955; s. John Warren Sr. and Matilda V. Lieber; m. Chih-Lin Hsieh, Jan. 1, 1990. BA, BS, U. Mo., 1977; PhD, U. Chgo., 1981, MD, 1983. Diplomate Am. Bd. Pathology. Resident in pathology NIH, Bethesda, Md., 1983-86, postdoctoral fellow, 1986-89; asst. prof., then assoc. prof. Stanford (Calif.) U., 1989-94; assoc. prof. pathology Washington U., St. Louis, 1994-97; prof. U. So. Calif., 1997—. Editl. bd. Molecular and Cellular Biology, JBC, DNA Repair; contbr. over 130 articles to profl. publs., including Nature, Cell, Sci., EMBO Jour., Genes & Devel. Recipient Faculty Scholar award Leukemia Soc. Am., 1994-99, Ed Heitz Meml. Rsch. Fund award Leukemia Soc. Am., 1998, award Warner-Lambert/Parke-Davis, 1998; Stohlman scholar Leukemia Soc. Am., 1999. Mem. AAAS, Am. Soc. Investigative Pathology. Achievements include patents in field. Home: 245 W Palm Dr Arcadia CA 91007 Office: USC Sch Medicine ME 9176 1441 Eastlake Ave Los Angeles CA 90089-9176

LIEBER, RICHARD LOUIS, biomedical engineering scientist, educator; b. Walnut Creek, Calif., Dec. 14, 1956; s. Richard and Janet Elizabeth (Stone) L.; children: Katelyn Suzanne, Kristin Michelle; m. Dina Lieber, Oct. 2004. BS with honors, U. Calif., Davis, 1978, PhD, 1982. Sr.rsch. career scientist VA Med. Ctr., San Diego, 1983—; prof. orthopaerics & bioengring. U. Calif., 1985—. Cons. Pref Med. Products Inc., 1987—. Contbr. sci. papers to profl. publs.; inventor surgical myometer, 1985, adaptive muscle stimulator, 1987. Faculty advisor Inter-Varsity Christian Fellowship, San Diego, 1984—. Recipient Presdl. award Am. Acad. Cerebral Palsy, 1984, Nicolas Andry award Am. Bone & Joint Inst., 1998; State of Calif. Gov.'s scholar, 1974 Mem. IEEE, Orthopaedic Rsch. Soc., Biophys. Soc. (Talbot award 1981), Rehab. Engring. Soc. N.Am., Soc. Neursci., Am. Soc. Biomechanics (Giovani Borellj award), Am. Physiol. Soc. Republican. Achievements include patent for surgical myometer; development of techniques used involving computer controlled muscle contraction and optical sensors for structure monitoring; research on skeletal muscle properties in normal and diseased muscles. Home: 10471 Mira Montana Dr Del Mar CA 92014 Office: U Calif Dept Orthopaedics V 151 San Diego CA 92161-0001 Office Phone: 858-552-8585 x 7016. Business E-Mail: rlieber@ucsd.edu.

LIEBER, STANLEY MARTIN See LEE, STAN

LIEBERFARB, WARREN N., digital media pioneer; b. Mar. 1943; BS, U. Penn; MBA, U. Mich. Financial analyst Ford Motor Co.; exec. asst. to pres. Paramount Pictures; v.p., telecommunications 20th Century Fox Film, 1973—75; sr. v.p., sales & mktg. Warner Bros., 1982—84; pres. Warner Home Video, Burbank, Calif., 1984—2002; chmn. Lieberfarb & Assoc.

LIEBERMAN, ABRAHAM NATHAN, physician, medical administrator; b. Bklyn., July 8, 1938; s. Usher and Esther (Nosenchuk) L.; m. Ina Lieberman, Feb. 14, 1965; children: Wendy, Unice, Usher, Mike. AB, Cornell U., 1959; MD, NYU, 1963. Diplomate Am. Bd. Psychiatry and Neurology. Intern Cin. Gen. Hosp., 1963-64; resident, chief resident in neurology Bellevue Hosp. Med. Ctr.-NYU, NYC, 1964-67; staff neurologist USAF Hosp., Tachikawa, Japan, 1967-69; fellow in pharmacology NYU Med. Ctr., NYC, 1969-70, from instr. to prof. neurology, 1970-89; attending physician Univ. Hosp., NYC, 1970-78, Bellevue Hosp., NYC, 1970-89, assoc. dir. EEG, 1973-79; attending physician Manhattan VA Hosp., 1972-89; chief Movement Disorders Barrow Neurol. Inst., 1989—; attending physician St. Joseph's Hosp., Phoenix, 1989-98; cons. NeuroSci. Inst. Good Samaritan Hosp., LA, 1993-98; nat. med. dir. Muhammad Ali Ctr. Excellence Nat. Parkinson Found., Miami, Fla., 1997—2005; head, Muhammad Ali Parkinson cCtr. Barrow Neurol. Inst., Phoenix. Reviewer Archives of Neurology, Annals of Internal Medicine, Annals of Neurology, JAMA, Jour. Pharmacology and Exptl. Therapeutics, Med. Letter, Movement Disorders, New Eng. Jour. Medicine, Neurology; mem. pharm. med. adv. bd., cons. Adria Labs., 1988-91, Boehringer Ingelheim, 1992-96, Elan Pharms., 1990-92, Janssen Pharms., 1990-92, Merck, Sharpe & Dohme, 1983-89, Pharmacia, 1991—, Smith Kline Beecham, 1995—, SIBIA, 1994—, Novartis (formerly Sandox), 1985—, Eli Lilly, 1996—, Hoffman LaRoche, 1993—, Dupont Pharma, 1995—; presenter papers at confs., symposiums, and seminars; lectr. in field. Editor-in-chief Neurovews Trends in Clin. Neurology, 1985-89, Neurology Forum, 1990-96; mem. editl. bd. Parkinsonism and Related Disorders, 1995—; contbr. numerous articles to profl. jours. including Neurology, JAMA, Jour. Neurol. Neurosurgery Psychiatry. Recipient numerous awards; grantee Nat. Cancer Inst., 1969-71, 72-75, 76-79, Merck, Sharp and Dohme, 1971-72, 75, Sterling Winthrop, 1971, Schering Corp., 1972-75, Nat. Inst. Neurol. and Communicative Disorders and Stroke, 1972-83, Servior Labs., 1973-75, Eli Lilly Corp., 1977-80, 79-80, 97—, Schering AG, 1979-82, Hoffman La Roche, 1982-85, 92-94, 94—, Sandoz, 1983-85, Janssen Pharms., 1984-86, Syntho Labs., 1985, Am. Home Products, 1985-87, FIDIA, 1985-87, Somerset Pharms., 1986-89, Adria Labs., 1990-92, Elan Pharms., 1990-92, Synergan, 1993-95, Smith Kline Beecham, 1993-97, MDS Harris and Scherer, 1997—, Novartis, 1997—, PSG, 1997—, Merrill-Trust, 1972, Bendheim Found., 1986-89, John and Evelyn Kossak Found., 1989-96, Frank and Donna Stanton Found., 1992-95, Wallace Found., 1994-96, among others. Fellow Am. Acad. Neurology; mem. Am. Neurol. Assn., Movement Disorder Soc., World Fed. Neurology Rsch. Coun., Internat. Tremor Found. (med. adv. bd. 1993—), Parkinson's Disease Study Group. Office Phone: 602-406-6262. Personal E-mail: abedoc@gmail.com.

LIEBERMAN, MICHAEL A., electrical engineer, educator; b. NYC, Oct. 3, 1940; married; 2 children. BS, MS, MIT, Cambridge, 1962; PhD, MIT, 1966. With dept. electrical engring. and computer sci. U. Calif., Berkeley, 1966—, prof. electronic rsch. labs., 1977-80, prof., vice-chmn. undergrad. program EECS, 1984—; asst. prof. biochem. dept. nutrition Harvard Sch. Pub. Health, Boston, 1981-83; assoc. prof. molecular genetics, biochemistry & microbiology Coll. Medicine U. Cin., 1983-84. Study sect. cellular biology & physiology NIH, 1986-89; lectr. in field. Contbr. scientific papers articles to profl. publs.; co-author (with A.J. Lichtenberg): (monograph) Regular and Stochastic Motion, 1983, Regular and Stochastic Motion, 2nd edit., 1991, Principles of Plasma Discharge and Materials Processing, 1994, Principles of Plasma Discharge and Materials Processing, 2nd edit., 2005. Recipient von Engel prize, Internat. Union Pure and Applied Physics, 2005; Guggenheim Fellow, 1972—73. Fellow IEEE (award for contbns. to rsch. in plasma-assisted materials processing, nonlinear dynamics and controlled fusion), Am. Phys. Soc.(Will Allis prize for Study of Ionized Gases, 2006), AAAS, IEEE (Plasma Sci. and Applications award, 1995), Am. Vacuum Soc., Inst. Physics (Great Britain). Office: Dept Electrical Engring and Computer Sci U Calif Berkeley Rm 467 Cory Hall Berkeley CA 94720-1770 Office Phone: 510-643-6632. Office Fax: 510-643-4976. Business E-Mail: lieber@eecs.berkeley.edu.

LIEBERMAN, SAM, political organization administrator; BA in Social Work, U. Nevada Las Vegas, 1996. Staff mem., Senator Harry Reid US Senate; staff mem., Rep. Shelley Berkley US House of Reps.; vol., staff mem., activist and donor Nev. State Dem. Party, 1986, first vice chmn., 2007—08, chmn., 2008—. Coord. vol. and cmty. rels. Las Vegas Marathon; exec. dir. Vol. Ctr. of So. Nev. Sec. UNLV Alumni Assn. Bd. Dirs. Mem.: Sigma Chi. Democrat. Office: Nev State Dem Party 1210 S Valley View Rd, Ste 114 Las Vegas NV 89102 Office Phone: 702-286-0739.*

LIEBHABER, MYRON I., allergist; b. Dec. 28, 1943; MD, U. Ariz., 1972. Allergist Coll. Hosp., Santa Barbara, Calif. Assoc. vis. clin. prof. UCLA. Office: Sansum Med Found Clinic 215 Pesetas Ln Santa Barbara CA 93110-1416 Home Phone: 805-963-8033; Office Phone: 805-681-7635. Business E-Mail: mliebhab@sansumclinic.org. E-mail: mil1258@pol.net.

LIEFF, ROBERT LAWRENCE, lawyer; b. Bridgeport, Conn., Sept. 29, 1936; BA, U. Bridgeport, 1958; JD, MBA, Columbia U., 1962. Bar: Calif. 1966, U.S. Dist. Ct., No. Dist. Calif. 1969, U.S. Ct. Appeals, Ninth Cir. 1969, U.S. Supreme Ct. 1969, U.S. Ct. Appeals, Seventh Cir. 1972, U.S. Tax Ct. 1974, U.S. Dist. Ct., Dist. of Hawaii 1986. Founding ptnr. Lieff, Cabraser, Heimann & Bernstein, LLP, 1972—2006, of counsel, 2007—; founding ptnr. Lieff Global, 2007—. Bd. visitors Columbia Law Sch., 1992—2004. Mem.: ABA (mem. Section on Corp., Banking and Bus. Law), Assn. Trial Lawyers of Am., Consumer Attys. Calif., Calif. Trial Lawyers Assn., San Francisco Trial Lawyers Assn., Lawyers Club of San Francisco, State Bar of Calif., Bar Assn. of San Francisco. Office: Lieff Cabrasser Heimann & Bernstein Embarcadero Ctr W 275 Battery St Ste 3000 San Francisco CA 94111 Office Phone: 415-965-1000. E-mail: rlieff@lchb.com, relieff@lieffglobal.com.

LIEGLER, ROSEMARY MENKE, dean; b. Fairfield, Iowa, Aug. 21, 1939; d. Vincent Thomas and Catherine Lucille Menke; m. Donald G. Liegler, June 8, 1963; children: Katherine, Jerry. BSN, St. Ambrose Coll., 1961; MS in Nursing, Marquette U., 1962; PhD, Claremont Grad. Sch., 1994. Asst. prof. Miami (Fla.)-Dade Jr. Coll., Georgetown U., Washington, U. Miami; prof., dean Sch. Nursing Azusa (Calif.) Pacific U. Bd. dirs. Huntington East Valley Hosp. Mem. ANA, Calif. Assn. Colls. Nursing, East San Gabriel Valley Vis. Nurses' Assn. (cmty. bd. 1995), Sigma Theta Tau. Home: 3226 E Whitebirch Dr West Covina CA 91791-3037 Office: Azusa Pacific U Sch Nursing 901 E Alosta Ave Azusa CA 91702-2769

LIENERT, JAMES M., oil industry executive; BS in Acctg., SUNY, Buffalo; MBA, SUNY Buffalo. CPA Tex. With Occidental Chem. Corp., Niagara Falls, NY, 1974, v.p. fin., 1998, sr. v.p. chlor-alkali bus., 2000, sr. v.p. vinyls bus., 2002, pres., 2004—06; v.p. Occidental Petroleum Corp., 2004—06, exec. v.p. fin. and planning, 2006—. Office: Occidental Petroleum 10889 Wilshire Blvd Los Angeles CA 90024-4201 Office Phone: 310-208-8800.

LIEPMANN, DORIAN, engineering educator; b. LA, Nov. 21, 1957; s. Hans Wolfgang and Dietland (Goldschmidt) L.; m. Kathleen Mary Toups, July 10, 1992; 1 child, Colin Wolfgang. BA, Occidental Coll., 1981; BS, Calif. Inst. Tech., 1981, MS, 1983; PhD, U. Calif., San Diego, 1990. Engr. Jet Propulsion Laboratory, Pasadena, Calif., 1983—84; rsch. scientist Technol. Rsch. Group Sci. Applications Internat. Corp., San Diego, 1984—92; rsch. engineer, Inst. for Non-Linear Sci. U. of Calif. San Diego, 1986—92; asst. prof. mechanical engring. U. of Calif. Berkeley, 1992—98, assoc. prof. departments of bioengineering and mechanical engring., 1998—2003; mem. faculty joint grad. group U. of Calif. Berkeley and U. of Calif. San Francisco, 1993—; Lester John and Lynne Dewar Lloyd Disting. Prof. Bioengineering U. of Calif. Berkeley, 2001—, prof. bioengineering and mechanical engring., 2003—, vice chair undergraduate affairs, dept. bioengineering, 2003—, chair dept. bioengineering, 2004—. Dir. Berkeley Sensor and Actuator Ctr. U. of Calif. Berkeley, 1998—. Mem. ASME, Am. Phys. Soc. Office: U Calif 483 Evans Hall 1762 Berkeley CA 94720-1741 Business E-Mail: liepmann@me.berkeley.edu.

LIFFICK, STEVE, computer software company executive; BA in Biochemistry, Harvard U., 1989. Developer OS/2 Microsoft Corp., Redmond, Wash., 1989, with Pen Windows, 1990, with WinPad, 1992, with Microsoft NetMeeting, 1994, with MSN Messenger, 1997, corp. v.p. MSN comm. svcs., corp. v.p. Windows Live User Experience Group, 2004—. Avocation: bicycling. Office: Microsoft Corp One Microsoft Way Redmond WA 98052-6399 Office Phone: 425-882-8080. Office Fax: 425-936-7329.

LIGHT, JANE ELLEN, library director; b. Crosby, ND, May 4, 1948; d. Ralph W. and Ethel S. (Cady) Johnson; children: Jessica, David. BA, Calif. State U., Sacramento, 1973; MLS, U. Calif., Berkeley, 1974. Project mgr. Peninsula Libr. Sys., San Mateo, Calif., 1974-78, sys. dir., 1979-83; prog. mgr. Coop. Libr. Authority, San Jose, Calif., 1978-79; asst. libr. dir. Redwood City Pub. Libr., Calif., 1983-84, libr. dir., 1984-97; city libr. San Jose Pub. Libr., Calif., 1997—. Del. On-line Computer Libr. Ctr. User's Coun., 1993—2000; chair exec. bd. Urban Librs. Coun., 2005—06. Bd. dirs. Child Care Coordinating Coun., San Mateo, 1988-97, pres. 1992-93; bd. dirs. YMCA Silicon Valley, 2001—. Mem. ALA, Calif. Libr. Assn., Pub. Libr. Assn. (Charlie Robinson award 2004), Rotary Club San Jose. Office: San Jose Pub Libr Sys 150 E San Fernando St San Jose CA 95112 Office Phone: 408-808-2150. E-mail: jane.light@sjlibrary.org.

LIGHTFOOT, WILLIAM CARL, performing arts association executive, symphony musician; b. Indpls., May 5, 1938; s. Francis H. and Margaret (Vitz) L.; m. May C. Chu, Sept. 22, 1988; children: Melissa, Tom. BME, Butler U., Indpls., 1960; cert., Vienna Acad. Music, Austria, 1965. 2d and Eb clarinetist Honolulu Symphony Orch., 1966-84, orch. mgr., 1984-88; exec. dir. Boulder (Colo.) Philharm. Orch. (now Peak Assn. of the Arts), 1988—. Pers. mgr. Honolulu Symphony Orch., 1982-84, orch. mgr., 1984-88; exec. dir. Ensemble Players Guild, Honolulu, 1969-74; gen. mgr. Honolulu Chamber Music Series, 1978, Chamber Music Hawaii, Honolulu, 1979-84. Avocations: sailing, skiing.

LIGHTNER, SHERRI, councilwoman, mechanical engineer; b. 1950; BA in Math. and Sociology, U. Calif., San Diego, MS in Applied Mechanics and Engring. Lic. Profl. Mech. Engr., Calif. Engring. aide Gen. Atomics (GA); sr. engr. structural dynamics group Rohr Industries; co-owner Lightner Engring., San Diego; councilwoman, Dist. 1 San Diego City Coun., 2008—. Pres. La Jolla Town Coun., La Jolla Shores Assn.; sec. La Jolla Cmty. Planning Assn. Office: 202 C St, MS #10A San Diego CA 92101 Office Phone: 619-236-6611. Office Fax: 619-236-6999. E-mail: SherriLightner@sandiego.gov.*

LIGHTSTONE, RONALD, lawyer; b. NYC, Oct. 4, 1938; s. Charles and Pearl (Weisberg) L.; m. Nancy Lehrer, May 17, 1973; 1 child, Dana. AB, Columbia U., 1959; JD, NYU, 1962. Atty. CBS, NYC, 1967-69; assoc. dir. bus. affairs CBS News, NYC, 1969-70; atty. NBC, NYC, 1970; assoc. gen. counsel Viacom Internat. Inc., NYC, 1970-75, v.p., gen. counsel, sec., 1976-80; v.p. bus. affairs Viacom Entertainment Group, Viacom Internat., Inc., 1980-82, v.p. corp. affairs, 1982-84, sr. v.p., 1984-87; exec. v.p. Spelling Entertainment Inc., LA, 1988-91, CEO, 1991-93; chmn. Multimedia Labs. Inc., 1994-97; CEO, pres. New Star Media Inc., 1997-99, vice chmn., 1999-2000. Lt. USN, 1962—66. Mem. ABA (chmn. TV, cable and radio com.), Assn. of Bar of City of N.Y., Fed. Comm. Bar Assn.

LIIAS, MARKO, state legislator; b. Edmonds, Wash., 1981; BS in Internat. Politics, Georgetown U., Washington, DC, 2003; studied, Belgium & Czech Rep.; student Pub. Adminstrn., Evans Sch. Pub. Affairs, U. Wash., Seattle. Former intern Congressman Eliot Engel, NY, Congressman Jay Inslee, Wash.; freelance reporter Mukilteo Beacon; former rschr. KING-5; former small business owner; former gen. contractor; mem. Dist. 21 Wash. House of Reps., 2008—. Democrat. Office: 434 John L O'Brien Bldg PO Box 40600 Olympia WA 98504-0600 Office Phone: 360-786-7972. Business E-Mail: liias.marko@leg.wa.gov.

LIKINS, PETER WILLIAM, retired academic administrator; b. Tracy, Calif, July 4, 1936; s. Ennis Blaine and Dorothy Louise (Medlin) L.; m. Patricia Ruth Kitsmiller, Dec. 18, 1955; children: Teresa, Lora, Paul, Linda, Krista. BCE, Stanford U., 1957, PhD in Engring. Mechanics, 1965; MCE, MIT, 1958; PhD (hon.), Lafayette Coll., 1983, Moravian Coll., 1984, Med. Coll. Pa., 1990, Lehigh U., 1991, Allentown St. Francis de Sales, 1993, Czech Tech U., 1993. Devel. engr. Jet Propulsion Lab., Pasadena, Calif., 1958-60; asst. prof. engring. UCLA, 1964-69, assoc. prof., 1969-72, prof., 1972-76, asst. dean, 1974-75, asso. dean, 1975-76; dean engring. and applied sci. Columbia U., NYC, 1976-80, provost, 1980-82; pres. Lehigh U., Bethlehem, Pa., 1982-97, U. Ariz., Tucson, 1997—2006. Cons. in field. Author: Elements of Engineering Mechanics, 1973, Spacecraft Dynamics, 1982; Contbr. articles to profl. jours. Mem. US Pres.'s Coun. Advisors Sci. and Tech., 1990-93. Ford Found. fellow, 1970-72; named to Nat. Wrestling Hall of Fame. Fellow AIAA; mem. Nat. Acad. Engring., Phi Beta Kappa, Sigma Xi, Tau Beta Pi. Home: 6550 Marta Hillgrove St Tucson AZ 85710 Office Phone: 520-298-0820. Personal E-mail: plikins@arizona.edu.

LIL' BOW WOW, See MOSS, SHAD

LILJENQUIST, DANIEL R., state legislator; m. Brooke Liljenquist; children: Jacob, Grace, Nathan, Joshua, Benjamin. BA in Economics, Brigham Young U.; JD, U. Chicago Law Sch. Former strategy consultant Bain & Co.; former dir. operational strategy Affiliated Computer Services; pres./ COO Focus Svcs., LLC; mem. Dist. 23 Utah State Senate, 2008—. Republican. Office: W115 State Capitol Complex Salt Lake City UT 84114 Mailing: 553 S Davis Blvd Bountiful UT 84010 Home Phone: 801-294-2378; Office Phone: 801-538-1035. Office Fax: 801-326-1475. Business E-Mail: dliljenquist@utahsenate.org.

LILLA, JAMES A., plastic surgeon; b. Comfrey, Minn., June 12, 1943; MD, Stanford U., 1969. Plastic hand surgeon Sutter Cmty. Hosp., Calif. Office: Hand Surg Assocs 1201 Alhambra Blvd Ste 410 Sacramento CA 95816-5243

LILLEGRAVEN, JASON ARTHUR, retired paleontologist, educator; b. Mankato, Minn., Oct. 11, 1938; s. Arthur Oscar and Agnes Mae (Eaton) L.; m. Bernice Ann Hines, Sept. 5, 1964 (div. Feb. 1983); children: Brita Anna, Ture Andrew; m. Linda Elizabeth Thompson, June 5, 1983. BA, Long Beach State Coll., 1962; MS, S.D. Sch. Mines and Tech., 1964; PhD, U. Kans., 1968. Professional geologist, Wyo. Postdoctoral fellow Dept. Paleontology U. Calif., Berkeley, 1968-69; from asst. prof. to prof. zoology San Diego State U., 1969-75; from assoc. prof. to prof. geology and zoology U. Wyo., Laramie, 1975—2004, Arts and Scis. Disting. prof. emeritus, 2004—. Program dir. NSF Systematic Biology, Washington, 1977-78; assoc. dean U. Wyo. Coll. Arts and Scis., 1984-85, temporary joint appointment Dept. Geography, 1986-87; U.S. sr. scientist Inst. for Paleontology Free U., Berlin, 1988-89; mem. adv. panel geology and paleontology program NSF, 1997-2000. Author, editor: Mesozoic Mammals the First Two Thirds of Mammalian History, 1979, Vertebrates, Phylogeny and Philosophy, 1986; mem. editl. bds. of Research and Exploration (Nat. Geographic Soc.), Jour. of Mammalian Evolution, Jour. of Vertebrate Paleontology, Cretaceous Rsch., Palaios; co-editor Contbns. to Geology, Rocky Mountain Geology; contbr. articles to profl. jours. Trustee Wyo. chpt. Nature Conservancy. Recipient numerous rsch. grants NSF, 1970-, George Duke Humphrey Disting. Faculty award, Humboldt prize. Mem. Am. Soc. Mammalogists, Am. Assn. Petroleum Geologists, Paleontol. Soc., Soc. Vertebrate Paleontology (hon. membership award, pres. 1985-86), Linnean Soc. London, Soc. Mammalian Evolution, Soc. Study Evolution, Nat. Ctr. Sci. Edn., Sigma Xi. Avocations: computer graphics, outdoor activities. Home Phone: 307-742-5275; Office Phone: 307-742-5275. Personal E-mail: bagpipe@uwyo.edu.

LILLY, GEORGE DAVID, broadcasting executive; b. Winchester, Mass., Nov. 4, 1934; s. George M. and Eleanor (Hamlin) L.; children: Brian, Kevin, Kristin. BS in Communication Arts, Boston U., 1956. Mgr. Sta. WGAN-TV, Portland, Maine, 1960-69, Sta. WIVB-TV, Buffalo, 1969-80; v.p. TV ops. Park TV, Ithaca, NY, 1980-83; prin., pres. BK&K, Inc., Syracuse, NY, 1986—, SJL Broadcast Mgmt. Corp., Billings, Mont. and Montecito, Calif., 1984-95, owner Kans., 1988-95; prin., dir. Fayetteville, NC, 1985—; owner Sta. KTVQ-TV, Billings, 1984—, Sta. WKFT-TV, Fayetteville, 1985—, Sta. WSTM-TV, Syracuse, 1986—; pres., CEO SJL Mgmt., Santa Barbara, Calif. Mem. CBS Affiliates Govt. Relations com., 1986; owner Sta. KSNW-TV, Wichita, Sta. KSNC-TV, Great Bend, Kans., Sta. KSNG-TV, Garden City, Kans., Sta. KSNK-TV, Overlin, Nebr., Sta. KSNT-TV, Topeka, Sta. WJRT-TV, Flint, Mich., 1989, SJL Comms., Inc., 1996—, KSBY-TV, San Luis Obispo, Calif., 1996—2002, WICU-TV, Erie, Pa., 1996—, WFXP-TV (LMA), Erie, Pa., 1996—. With U.S. Army, 1957-59. Mem. Nat. Assn. Broadcasters. Avocations: skiing, pvt. pilot. Office: KSNW 833 N Main St Wichita KS 67203-3606 also: SJL Mgmt 559 San Ysidro Rd Ste I Santa Barbara CA 93108

LILLY, LUELLA JEAN, retired academic administrator; b. Newberg, Oreg., Aug. 23, 1937; d. David Hardy and Edith (Coleman) Lilly. BS, Lewis and Clark Coll., 1959; postgrad., Portland State U., 1959—61; MS, U. Oreg., 1961; PhD, Tex. Woman's U., 1971; postgrad., various univs., 1959—72. Tchr. phys. edn. and health, dean girls Ctrl. Linn Jr.-Sr. H.S., Halsey, Oreg., 1959—60; tchr. phys. edn. and health, coach swimming, tennis, golf Lake Oswego H.S., Oreg., 1960—63; instr., intramural dir., coach Oreg. State U., Corvallis, 1963—64; instr., intercollegiate coach Am. River Coll., Sacramento, 1964—69; dir. women's phys. edn., athletics U. Nev., Reno, 1969—73, assoc. prof. phys. edn., 1971—76, dir. women's athletics, 1973-75, assoc. dir. athletics, 1975—76; dir. women's intercollegiate athletics U. Calif., Berkeley, 1976—97; ret., 1997; unr coach, volley ball, basketball. Organizer, coach Lue's Aquatic Club, 1962—64; v.p. PAC-10 Conf., 1990—91; state coach, volleyball, softball, swimming. Author: An Overview of Body Mechanics, 1966, 3d rev. edit., 1969. Vol. instr. ARC, 1951; vol. Heart Fund and Easter Seal, 1974—76, Am. Heart Assn., 1991—2007, Multiple Sclerosis Soc., 1999—2006; vol. ofcl. Spl. Olympics, 1975; mem. LA Citizens Olympic Com., 1984; bd. dirs. Las Trampas, 1993—98, sec., 1996—98. Recipient Mayor Anne Rudin award, Nat. Girls' and Women's Sports, 1993, Lifetime Sports award, Bay Area Women's Sports Found., 1994, Golden Bear award Vol. of Yr., 1995, Su Stauffer Firend of Edn. award, 2002, Pride of Nev. award, 2006, Lifetime Sport and Leadership award, 2006, Lifetime Achievment award, Lewis and Clark Coll.; named to Athletic Hall of Fame, 1988, First 125 Yrs. Women of Honor, U. Calif., Berkeley, 1995, Athletic Hall of Fame, 2005. Mem.: AAUW, AAHPERD (life), No. Calif. Athletic Conf. (pres. 1979—82, sec. 1984—85), Nev. Assn. Health Phys. Edn. and Recreation (state chmn. 1974), No. Calif. Intercollegiate Athletic Conf. (volleyball coord. 1971—72), No. Calif. Women's Intercollegiate Conf. (sec., basketball coord. 1970—71), Nev. Bd. Women Ofcls. (chmn. basketball sect. 1969, chmn. bd. dirs., chmn. volleyball sect.), Calif. Assn. Health, Phys. Edn. and Recreation (chmn.-elect jr. coll. sect. 1970), Ctrl. Calif. Bd. Women Ofcls. (basketball chmn. 1968—69), Oreg. Girls' Swimming Coaches Assn. (pres. 1960, 1963), We. Assn. Intercollegiate Athletics Women (exec. bd. dirs. 1973—75, 1979—82), We. Soc. Phys. Edn. Coll. Women (membership com. 1971—74, program adv. com. 1972, exec. bd. 1972—75), Coun. Collegiate Women Athletics Adminstrs. (membership com. 1989—92), Women's Athletic Caucus, Nat. Assn. Coll. Women Athletic Adminstrs. (divsn. 1-A women's steering com. 1991—92, Lifetime Achievement award 1999), Women's Sports Found. (awards com. 1994—2007), Nat. Soc. Profs., Soroptomists (v.p. 1989, 1992—93, sec. 1993—95, 1st v.p. 1996—97, corr. sec. 1997—98, pres. 1998—2000, sec. 2001—02, pres. 2006—08, bd. dirs., Women Helping Women award 1991, Women of Distinction award 2002), Theta Kappa, Phi Kappa Phi. Avocation: swimming. Home and Office: 60 Margrave Ct Walnut Creek CA 94597-2511 Office Phone: 925-934-3868. E-mail: luelilly@astound.net.

LILLY, MARTIN STEPHEN, retired university dean; b. New Albany, Ind., Aug. 31, 1944; s. Raymond John and Amy Elizabeth (Peake) L.; m. Marilyn Ann MacDougall, Jan. 8, 1966; children—Matthew William, Mark Christopher, Rachel Marie, Martin Stephen, Jason Wood BA, Bellarmine Coll., Louisville, 1966; MA, Peabody Coll., Nashville, 1967, Ed.D., 1969. Instr. dept. spl. edn. Peabody Coll., 1967-69; asst. prof. edn. U. Oreg., 1969-71; research coordinator N.W. Regional Spl. Edn. Instructional Materials Center, 1969-71; research coordinator div. research Bur. Edn. for Handicapped U.S. Office Edn., 1971-72; assoc. prof. dept. spl. edn. U. Minn., Duluth, 1972-75; assoc. prof., chmn. dept. spl. edn. U. Ill., Urbana-Champaign, 1975-79, prof., chmn., 1979-81, assoc. dean grad. studies Coll. Edn., 1981-84; dean Coll. Edn. Wash. State U., Pullman, 1984-90, Calif. State U., San Marcos, 1990—2004; ret. Cons. in field; U.S. Office Edn. fellow, 1966-69; pres. Tchr. Edn. Coun. State Colls. and Univs.; commr. Calif. Commn. on Tchr. Credentialing, 2002-05. Author: Children with Exceptional Needs: A Survey of Special Education, 1979, (with C.S. Blankenship) Mainstreaming Students With Learning and Behavior Problems, 1981; assoc. editor: Exceptional Children, 1969-79; cons. editor: Edn. Unltd, 1979-81; reviewer: Jour. Tchr. Edn, 1980—; mem. editorial bd. Tchr. Edn. and Spl. Edn, 1980-83, co-editor, 1983-84; contbr. chpts. to books, articles to profl. jours. Trustee Vista (Calif.) Unified Sch. Dist., 2004—. Democrat. Roman Catholic. Office: Calif State U San Marcos CA 92096-0001 Home Phone: 760-598-3304; Office Phone: 760-750-4310. Business E-Mail: slilly@csusm.edu.

LILLY, MICHAEL ALEXANDER, lawyer, writer; b. Honolulu, May 21, 1946; s. Percy Anthony Jr. and Virginia (Craig) L.; m. Cindy Lilly; children: Michael Jr., Cary J., Laura B., Claire F., Winston W. AA, Menlo Coll., Menlo Park, Calif., 1966; BA, U. Calif., Santa Cruz, 1968; JD with honors, U. of Pacific, 1974. Bar: Calif. 1974, U.S. Dist. Ct. (no., so., ctrl. and ea. dists.) Calif. 1974, U.S. Ct. Appeals (9th cir.) 1974, Hawaii 1975, U.S. Dist. Ct. Hawaii 1975, U.S. Ct. Appeals (D.C. cir.) 1975, U.S. Supreme Ct. 1978, U.S. Ct. Appeals (7th cir.) 1979. Atty. Pacific Legal Found., Sacramento, 1974-75; dep. atty. gen. State of Hawaii, Honolulu, 1975-79, 1st dep. atty. gen., 1981-84, atty. gen., 1984-85; ptnr. Feeley & Lilly, San Jose, Calif., 1979-81, Ning, Lilly & Jones, Honolulu, 1985—. Author: If You Die Tomorrow-A Layman's Guide to Estate Planning. Dir. Diamond Head Theatre, U.S.S. Mo. Meml. Assn.; Lt. USN, 1968-71, Vietnam; capt. USN, ret. Named hon. Ky. col.; decorated Legion of Merit medal, 1997. Mem. Nat. Assn. Attys. Gen., Navy Res. Assn. (pres. 14th dist. 1986-89), Navy League (dept. judge adv. to bd. Honolulu coun.), Outrigger Canoe Club. Office: Ning Lilly & Jones 707 Richards St Ste 700 Honolulu HI 96813-4623 Office Phone: 808-528-1100. Business E-Mail: michael@nljlaw.com.

LILLYMAN, WILLIAM JOHN, language educator, academic administrator; b. Sydney, Apr. 17, 1937; came to US, 1963, naturalized, 1974; s. John and Christina Mary (Munro) L.; m. Ingeborg Wolz, Sept. 14, 1962; children: Gregory, Christina. AB, U. Sydney, 1959; PhD, Stanford U., Calif., 1964. Asst. prof. Stanford U., 1964-67; assoc. prof. U. Calif., Santa Cruz, 1967-72, prof. German Irvine, 1972—, dean humanities, 1973-81, vice chancellor acad. affairs, 1981-82, exec. vice chancellor, 1982-88, 98-00. Author: Otto Ludwig's Zwischen Himmel und Erde, 1967, Otto Ludwig: Romane und Romanstudien, 1977, Reality's Dark Dream The Narrative Fiction of Ludwig Tieck, 1979, Goethe's Narrative Fiction, 1983; co-editor: Probleme der Moderne, 1983, Horizonte Festschrift für H. Lehnert, 1990, Critical Architecture and Contemporary Culture, 1994. Recipient Extraordinarius award, U. Calif.-Irvine, 1988, UCI medal, 2000. Mem. MLA, Am. Assn. Tchrs. German. Office: U Calif Exec Vice Chancellors Office 509 Administrn Bldg Irvine CA 92697-1000 Business E-Mail: wjlillym@uci.edu.

LIM, ALAN YOUNG, plastic surgeon; b. St. Louis, Apr. 11, 1953; MD, U. Calif., San Diego, 1979. Plastic surgeon Kaiser-Permanente, Sacramento, Calif. Assoc. clin. prof. U. Calif. Davis Office: Plastic Surg 1020 29th Ste 600 Sacramento CA 95816 Office Phone: 916-733-9588.

LIM, DAVID JONG-JAI, otolaryngology educator, researcher; b. Seoul, Republic of Korea, Nov. 27, 1935; came to U.S., 1964; s. Yang Sup Lim and Cha Nang Yoo; m. Young Sook Hahn, May 14, 1966; children: Michael, Robert. AB, Yonsei U., Seoul, 1955, MD, 1960. Research fellow in otolaryngology Mass. Eye & Ear Infirmary, Boston, 1965-66; research assoc. dept. otolaryngology Ohio State U. Coll. Medicine, Columbus, 1966-67, asst. prof., 1967-71, assoc. prof., 1971-76, prof. dept. otolaryngology, 1976-91, dir. otological research labs., 1967-91, prof. cell biology, neurobiology and anatomy, 1977-91, prof. emeritus otolaryngology, 1992—; rsch. prof. cell and neurobiology U. So. Calif., 1996—; dir. intramural rsch. program Nat. Inst. on Deaf and Other Communication Disorders, NIH, Bethesda, Md., 1992-94, chief lab cellular biology, 1993-95; exec. v.p., rsch. House Ear Inst., LA, 1995—. Mem. nat. adv. neurol. and communicative disorders and stroke coun. NIH, Bethesda, Md., 1979-83; mem. adv. bd. Nat. Inst. Deafness and Other Communication Disorders, 1989-91; cons., bd. dirs. Rsch. Fund Am. Otol. Soc., 1982-87; mem. adv. bd. Cen. Inst. for Deaf, 1989-91. Contbr. articles to profl. jours., chpts. to textbooks. Pres. Korean Assn. in Columbus, 1970; chmn. bd. dirs. Cen. Ohio Korean Lang. Sch., Columbus, 1986; bd. dirs. Deafness Rsch. Found., N.Y.C., 1980—. Fogarty Internat. fellow Karolinska Inst., Stockholm, 1982; recipient Disting. Scholar award Ohio State U., 1985, Javits award NIH, 1985, Claude Pepper award, 1989, Guyot prize U. Groningen, 1994, Freedom award L.A. Sertoma Club, 1996, Grand prize for med. scis. Yonsei U., 1997, Magarotto award 1998; grantee various orgns., 1969-91. Fellow Am. Acad. Otolaryngology (Gold award 1972, Paparella award 1999); mem. Internat. Symposium Recent Advances in Otitis Media (co-founder 1975, 79, 83, 87, 91, 95, 99, co-dir.), Assn. for Research in Otolaryngology (co-founder, sec./treas. 1973-75, pres. 1976-77, editor-historian 1980-93, historian, 1993—, Merit award 1993), Am. Laryngol. Rhinol. and Otol. Soc., Collegium Oto-rhino-laryngologicum Amicitiae Sacrum (Shambaugh prize 1993, v.p. 2000—), Am. Otol. Soc., Soc. Neurosci., Am. Soc. Cell Biology, Histochem. Soc., Soc. for Mucosal Immunology, Flint Canyon Tennis Club (La Canada). Methodist. Avocations: tennis, skiing. Home: 775 Panorama Pl Pasadena CA 91105-1020 Office: House Ear Inst 2100 W 3rd St Los Angeles CA 90057-1922 E-mail: dlim@hei.org.

LIM, JOHN K., state legislator; b. Yeoju, Republic of Korea, Dec. 23; son of Eun Kyu Lim & Seo Nyu Chung L; married to Grace Young Hee Park; children: Peter, Billy & Gloria. Member, Ore-Korea Econ Coop Committee, 86; national president, Korean America Fedn USA, 88-89; chairman, Asian America Voters Coalition, 89-90; cand, Oregon State Gubernatorial Race (GOP), 90; Oregon State Senator, District 11, 93 & 96, 99-2001; Republican nominee, United States Senate, Oregon, 98; Oregon State Representative, District 50, currently.President, America Royal Jelly Co, 70-92, chairman, 93-; board trustees, George Fox Univ, Newburg, Oregon, 1997—. Auth, World Korean Directory, John Lim, 89; World Korean Chamber Directory, John Lim, 90. Mok Ryan Chang Award, Republic of Korea, 2002. Fedn Korean America Chamber of Commerce (president, 89-90); Royal Rosarian; Portland Chamber of Commerce. Republican. Protestant. Mailing: 740 SE 25th St Gresham OR 97080 Address: PO Box 1616 Gresham OR 97030 Office: 900 Court St NE, H-496 Salem OR 97301 Fax: 503-238-0401; 503-665-0864. E-mail: senatorjohnlim@aol.com.

LIM, LARRY KAY, university official; b. Santa Maria, Calif., July 4, 1948; s. Koonwah and Nancy (Yao) L.; m. Louise A. Simon, Aug. 15, 1988. BA, UCLA, 1970, teaching cert., 1971. Asst. engr. Force Ltd., LA, 1969; tchg. asst. UCLA, 1970-71; tchr. L.A. Sch. Dist., 1971-82; dir. pre-coll. programs Sch. Engring., U. So. Calif., LA, 1979—. Presenter minority math.-based intervention symposium U. D.C., Washington, 1988; presenter NEMEPA/WEPAN nat. conf., 1997, ASEE conf., 2003. Newsletter editor, 1981-92. Bd. dirs. Developing Ednl. Studies for Hispanics, L.A., 1983-88. Named Dir. of Yr., Math., Engring., Sci. Achievement Ctr. Adv. Bd., 1986, 91, 92. Fellow Inst. Advancement Engring. (educator award); mem. Nat. Assn. Pre-Coll. Dirs., Nat. Assn. Minority Engring. Program Adminstr., Lotus/West Club (pres. 1981-92). Avocation: auto racing. Office: U So Calif Sch Engring Ohe 104 Los Angeles CA 90089-0001

LIM, SHIRLEY GEOK LIN, language educator; b. Malacca, Malaysia, Dec. 27, 1944; came to U.S., 1969; m. Charles Bazerman, Nov. 1972; 1 child, Gershom Kean. BA with 1st class honors, U. Malaya, 1967, postgrad., 1967-69; MA, Brandeis U., 1971, PhD in English, Am. Lit., 1973. Tchg. fellow Queens Coll. CUNY, Flushing, 1972-73; asst. prof. Hostos C.C. CUNY, Bronx, 1973-76; from assoc. prof. to prof. Westchester C.C. SUNY, Valhalla, 1976-90; prof. Asian Am. studies U. Calif., Santa Barbara, 1990-93, prof. women's studies and English, 1990—, chair women's studies, 1997-99; chair prof. English U. Hong Kong, 1999—2001. Part-time lectr. U. Malaya, Kuala Lumpur, 1967-69, U. Sains, 1974; vis. fellow Nat. U. of Singapore, 1982, writer in residence, 1985; Asia Found. fellow Ctr. for Advanced Studies, 1989; Mellon fellow Grad. Ctr. CUNY, 1983, 87; minority discourses fellow Interdisciplinary Rsch. Ctr. U. Calif., Irvine, 1993; writer in residence East-West Ctr., Honolulu, 1988; Fulbright Disting. Lectureship, Singapore, 1996; vis. prof. MIT, 2003, U. Hong Kong, 2005; presenter workshops in field. Author: Crossing the Peninsula and Other Poems, 1980 (Commonwealth Poetry prize 1980), Another Country and Other Stories, 1982, No Man's Grove, 1985, Modern Secrets: New and Selected Poems, 1989, Nationalism and Literature: English-Language Writers from the Philippines and Singapore, 1993, Monsoon History, 1994, Writing South/East Asia in English, 1994, Life's Mysteries, 1995, Among the White Moon Faces: An Asian American Memoir of Homelands, 1996 (Am. Book award 1997), Two Dreams, 1997, What the Fortune Teller Didn't Say, 1998, (novels) Joss and Gold, 2001; editor: Approaches to Teaching Kingston's "The Woman Warrior", 1991, Anthology of Asian American Literature, 1999; co-editor: Reading Asian-American Literatures, 1992, One World of Literature, 1992, Transnational Asia Pacific, 1999; co-editor, author: Introduction: The Forbidden Stitch: An Asian American Women's Anthology, 1989 (Am. Book award 1989); mem. edit. bd. Feminist studies, World Englishes, Short Story. Mem. N.Y. Gov.'s Commn. on Librs., 1990. Wein internat. fellow, 1969-72; Fulbright scholar, 1969-72; grantee NEH, 1978, 87, Westchester Found., 1987; Fulbright Disting. lectr., 1996; recipient J.T. Stewart Hedgebrook award. Mem. MLA (exec. com. divsn. Lit. in English Other Than Brit. and Am. 1986-90, founder discussion group on Asian Am. lit. 1985, chair exec. com. 1989, exec. com. divsn. ethnic lit. 1993—, chair com. langs. and lit. of the U.S. 1995), Internat. PEN, Am. Studies Assn. (programs com. 1994, chair minority scholars com. 1995—, chair women's com. 1998), Assn. Asian Am. Studies, Nat. Women's Studies Assn., Multi-Ethnic Lit. of U.S., Coord. Coun. Lit. Mags. (bd. dirs. 1983-88, chair 1986-87, exec. coun. 1987-88), Assn. Commonwealth Langs. and Lits. Office: U Calif Dept of English Santa Barbara CA 93106 Office Phone: 805-893-8711. Business E-Mail: slim@english.ucsb.edu.

LIMAN, DOUG, film director, film producer; b. NYC, July 24, 1965; s. Arthur Lawrence and Ellen (Fogelson) Liman. BA, Brown U., 1988; attended, U. So. Calif. Film Sch., 1992. Dir.: (films) Getting In, 1994, Go, 1999, Jumper, 2008; dir., cinematographer (films) Swingers, 1996 (Best New Filmmaker award, MTV, 1997, Newcomer of Yr. award, Fla. Film Critics Circle, 1997); prodr.: (films) See Jane Run, 2001; assoc. prodr. (films) Kissing Jessica Stein, 2001, prodr., dir. The Bourne Identity, 2002, Indie Is Great, 2002, supervising prodr. Otto+Anna, 2003; exec. prodr.: (films) Two Harbors, 2003, One Man's Castle, 2003, Gabriel y Gato, 2003, Terry Tate, Office Linebacker: Sensitivity Training, 2004, Mail Order Wife, 2004, The Bourne Supremacy, 2004, Cry Wolf, 2005, The Killing Floor, 2007, The Bourne Ultimatum, 2007; (TV series) The PTA, 2006; (TV films) Business Class, 2007; dir., exec. prodr. (films) Mr. & Mrs. Smith, 2005, (TV series) The O.C., 2003, Heist, 2006; actor: (TV series) The Moth, 2002. Office: c/o Creative Artists Agy 2000 Ave of the Stars Los Angeles CA 90067

LIMATO, EDWARD FRANK, talent agent; b. Mt. Vernon, NY, July 10, 1936; s. Frank and Angelina (Lacerra) L. Grad. high sch., Mt. Vernon. With IFA (formerly Ashley Famous Agency), NYC, 1966—78; sr. exec. William Morris Agy. Inc., LA, 1978—88; with Internat. Creative Mgmt., 1988—2007, talent agt. NYC, LA, co-pres., 1999—2007; talent agt. William Morris Agy. Inc., Beverly Hills, 2007—. Bd. dirs. Abercrombie & Fitch Co., 2003—, Motion Picture and TV Fund, L.A. Conservancy, Am. Cinematheque. Mem. Acad. Motion Picture Arts & Scis. (assoc.). Republican. Roman Catholic. Office: William Morris Agy Inc One William Morris Pl Beverly Hills CA 90212

LIMBAUGH, RONALD HADLEY, retired historian, cultural organization administrator; b. Emmett, Idaho, Jan. 22, 1938; s. John Hadley and Evelyn E. (Mortimore) L.; m. Marilyn Kay Rice, June 16, 1963; 1 child, Sally Ann. BA, Coll. Idaho, Caldwell, 1960; MA, U. Idaho, Moscow, 1962, PhD, 1967. Hist. libr. Idaho State Hist. Soc., Boise, 1963-66; instr. Boise Coll., 1964-66; asst. prof. history U. of the Pacific, Stockton, Calif., 1966-71, archivist, curator, 1968-87, prof. history, 1977-2000, Rockwell Hunt chair of Calif. history, 1989-2000; dir. Holt-Atherton Ctr., U. of the Pacific, Stockton, 1984-87. Exec. dir. Conf. of Calif. Hist. Socs., Stockton, 1973-76, 77-78, 82-86, 90-97, bd. trustees, 2006—; dir. John Muir Ctr. for Regional Studies, U. of Pacific, Stockton, 1989-2000; cons., evaluator NEH, 1983-86. Author: Rocky Mountain Carpetbaggers, 1982, John Muir's Stickeen and the Lessons of Nature, 1996; co-author: Calaveras Gold, 2003; co-editor: (microform) John Muir Papers, 1986, (book) Guide to Muir Papers, 1986; contbr. articles to profl. jours. With U.S. Army, 1955-56. NDEA fellow, 1960; grantee Calif. Coun. Humanities, 1976, Nat. Hist. Publs. and Records Commn., 1980-82, NEH, 1983, Inst. European Studies, 1989, Hoover Libr. Assn., 1997. Mem. Western History Assn., Mining History Assn. (pres. 2008-09). Christian Humanist. Avocation: birdwatching. Office: Univ Pacific 3601 Pacific Ave Stockton CA 95211-0197 Office Phone: 209-946-2145.

LIMERICK, PATRICIA NELSON, history professor; b. Banning, Calif., May 17, 1951; m. J. Houston Kempton. BA, U. Calif., Santa Cruz, 1972; PhD, Yale, 1980. Prof. history dept. U. Colo., Boulder. Chmn. bd. dirs. Ctr. Am. West. Author: (books) Desert Passages: Encounters With the American Deserts, 1985, The Legacy of Conquest: The Unbroken Past of the American West, 1987, Something in the Soil: Legacies and Reckonings in the New West, 1995-2000. MacArthur fellow, 1995. Office: U Colo Ctr Am West Macky 229 282 UCB Boulder CO 80309 Business E-Mail: pnl@centerwest.org.

LIMTIACO, ALICIA GARRIDO, state attorney general, former prosecutor; b. Agaba, Guam, Aug. 7, 1963; d. Francisco Perez and Julia Garrido Limtiaco; m. Vincent Untalan Muñoz; 1 child, Julia Faye Limtiaco Muñoz. BSBA, U. So. Calif., 1985; JD, UCLA Sch. Law, 1990. Law clk. Superior Ct. Guam; assoc. Arriola, Cowan & Arriola; ptnr. Torres, Limtiaco, Cruz & Sison, P.L.L.C., Limtiaco, Cruz & Sison, P.L.L.C.; lawyer rep. US Dist. Ct. Guam (9th cir.); asst. atty. gen. prosecution divsn., lead atty. criminal sexual conduct and family violence unit Guam Atty. Gen.'s Office, 1991—96, acting chief prosecutor, 1994—95; atty. gen. Territory of Guam, 2007—. Chair Gov.'s Family Violence Task Force; adj. faculty, asst. prof. pub. adminstrn. and legal studies prog. Sch. Bus. and Pub. Adminstrn. U. Guam Coll. Profl. Studies; adj. faculty basic law enforcement acad. and criminal justice prog. Guam Cmty. Coll.; mem. Family Violence Info. Network, Com. Family Violence, Sex Offender Registry Steering Com.; mem. crisis ctr. steering com. Healing Hearts. Bd. dirs. Make a Wish Found. Guam, Guam Coun. of Arts and Humanities Agy. Named Outstanding Woman of Yr., 1999. Office: Office of Atty Gen Justice Bldg 287 W O'Brien Dr Hagatna GU 96910*

LIN, FRANK C., computer company executive; Chmn. bd. dirs., pres., CEO Trident Microsys. Inc., Mountain View, Calif. Office: Trident Microsystems Inc 3408 Garrett Dr Santa Clara CA 95054-2803

LIN, LAWRENCE SHUH LIANG, lawyer; b. July 5, 1938; arrived in US, 67, naturalized, 79; s. Wan Chow and Inn Chi Lin; m. Grace Yu, July 31, 1966; children: Ray, Lester. LLB, Soochow U., 1963; MBA, Pepperdine U., 1970; JD, U. West L.A., 1998. Spl. project acctg. supr. Motown Records, Hollywood, Calif., 1975; chief acct. Elektra/Asylum/Nonesuch Records, Beverly Hills, Calif., 1976—77, United Artists Music Pub. Group, Hollywood, 1977—80; contr.-adminstr. Pasadena (Calif.) Guidance Clinics (name now Pacific Clinics), 1980—86; v.p. Stew Kettle Corp., LA, 1986—87, LKL Corp., LA, 1987—89; internat. fin. cons. Pacific Capital Mgmt., Alhambra, Calif., 1990—2001; prin. Law Offices of Lawrence Lin, Woodland Hills, Calif., 2001—05; ptnr. Lin & Chow, Monterey park, Calif., 2006—. Mem.: ABA, Los Angeles County Bar Assn., Calif. Bar Assn., Nat. Assn. Security Dealers, Inst. Mgmt. Accts. Baptist. Office: 5971 Rod Ave Woodland Hills CA 91367 Home Phone: 818-884-7942; Office Phone: 626-284-0400. Personal E-mail: larrylinlaw@yahoo.com.

LIN, ROBERT PEICHUNG, physicist, educator, researcher; b. Kwangsi, People's Republic of China, Jan. 24, 1942; s. Tung Hua and Susan Lin; m. Lily Wong, Aug. 14, 1983; 1 stepson, Linus Sun. BS, Calif. Inst. Tech., 1962; PhD, U. Calif., Berkeley, 1967. Asst. rsch. physicist Space Sci. Lab., U. Calif., Berkeley, 1967-74, assoc. rsch. physicist, 1974-79, rsch. physicist, 1979-88, sr. fellow, 1980-88; adj. prof. astronomy dept. U. Calif., Berkeley, 1988-91, prof. physics dept., 1991—, assoc. dir. space scis. lab., 1992—98, dir. space scis. lab., 1998—. Vis. prof. geophysics program U. Wash., Seattle, 1987; mem. solar physics panel Astronomy and Astrophysics Survey, Nat. Acad. Sci., 1989-91; mem. working groups for astrophysics, solar physics, space plasma, cosmic and heliospheric physics, balloons, space and applications adv. com. NASA, 1977—, mem. various rev. panels, 1977—. Contbr. articles to Jour. Geophys. Rsch., Solar Physics, Phys. Rev. Letters, Rev. Sci. Instruments, Astrophys. Jour., Geophys. Rsch. Letters. Grantee NASA, 1980—, NSF, 1981—. Mem. Am. Geophys. Union, Am. Astron. Soc., NAS; fellow Am. Acad. Arts & Sciences Achievements include research on solar and interplanetary physics, high energy astrophysics, lunar and planetary science, and physics of the earth's magnetosphere. Office: U Calif Space Scis Lab Berkeley CA 94720-0001

LINAWEAVER, WALTER ELLSWORTH, JR., physician; b. San Pedro, Calif., Oct. 16, 1928; s. Walter Ellsworth and Catherine Breathed (Bridges) L.; m. Lydia Anne Whitlock, Oct. 5, 1957 (dec. 2005); children: Catherine Ann, Nancy Alyn, Walter E. III; m. Vicki Beckham, July 30, 2005. BA cum laude, Pomona Coll., 1952; MD, Rochester U., NY, 1956. Diplomate Am. Bd. Allergy and Immunology, Am. Bd. Pediat., Am. Bd. Pediatric Allergy. Intern pediat. Med. Ctr. U. Rochester, 1956-57, resident pediat. Med. Ctr., 1958-59; asst. resident pediat. Med. Ctr. UCLA, 1957-58; fellow allergy and immunology Med. Ctr. U. Colo., Denver, 1959-61, instr. pediat. Sch. Medicine, 1961; pvt. practice Riverside (Calif.) Med. Clinic, 1962—. Asst. clin. prof. pediat. Loma Linda U. Med. Sch., 1965—. Elder Presbyn. Ch. Staff sgt. U.S. Army, 1946-48. Inducted into Athletic Hall of Fame Pomona Coll., Claremont, Calif., 1979. Fellow: L.A. Acad. Medicine, Am. Acad. Pediat., Am. Acad. Allergy, Asthma and Immunology; mem.: AMA, Calif. Med. Assn., Riverside County Heart Assn. (pres. 1965—66), Riverside County Med. Soc. (councilor 1964—66). Dfl. Avocations: American and British military history, gardening. Home: 1296 Tiger Tail Dr Riverside CA 92506-5475 Office Phone: 951-782-3681.

LINCOLN, GEORGIANNA, state legislator; b. Fairbanks, Alaska, Feb. 22, 1943; children: Gidget, Sean. Student, U. Alaska. Mem. Alaska Ho. of Reps., 1990-92, Alaska Senate, Dist. R, Juneau, 1992—; mem. resources, transp. and adminstrv. regulation rev. coms. Bd. dirs. Doyon Ltd., Doyon Drilling, Inc. Commr. Alaska Commn. on Jud. Conduct, 1984-90; U.S. del. East Asia and Pacific Parliamentarian's Conf. on Environment and Devel., 1993; mem. Local-State Tribal Rels. Task Force, 1994; vice-chair NCSL. Democrat. Avocation: working with children and people.

LINCOLN, HOWARD, manufacturing company and sports team executive; b. Oakland, Calif., Feb. 14, 1940; m. Grace; c. Brad BA in Polit. Sci., U. Calif., Berkeley, 1962; JD, U. Calif. Sch. Law, 1965. Practiced law, Seattle, 1970—83; legal work Nintendo Am. Inc., 1981—83, sr. v.p., gen. counsel, 1983—94, chmn., 1994—2000, chmn. emeritus, 2000—; chmn., CEO Seattle Mariners, 1999—. Bd. dirs. Nintendo of Am., Nintendo Co. Ltd. of Kyoto, Japan; chmn. Interactive Digital Software Assn. Instrumental in creating Nintendo's charitable contbns. program, including Starlight Found.; major initiator in Club Mario/after-sch. program with Bellevue, Wash. Boys & Girls Club; trustee Seattle Children's Hosp. Found., Western Washington U.; chmn., Washington Roundtable; hi-tech chmn. United Way of King County, Wash., 1999, campaign chair, 2003-2004; bd. dirs. Boalt Hall Alumni Assn., U. Calif., Berkeley, ArtsFund, Bellevue Boys & Girls Club, The Baseball Club of Seattle, LP, Seattle Mariners, Pacific Sci. Ctr., Corp. Coun. for the Arts, chief Seattle coun. Boys Scouts Am., others; supports Mariners Care Found. Naval officer Judge Advocate Gen. Corps USN, 1966—70. Recipient Lifetime Achievement award, Acad. of Interactive Arts & Sci., 2007. Office: c/o Seattle Mariners Safeco Field PO Box 4100 Seattle WA 98104

LIND, MARSHALL L., academic administrator; b. Sept. 27, 1942; Ed.B., U. Wisc., Milwaukee; Ed.M, U. Mont, Missoula; PhD, Education, Northwestern U. Dean Sch. Extended and Grad. Studies U. Alaska, Juneau, until 1987, chancellor, 1987-99, Fairbanks, 1999—. Office: U Alaska Office Chancellor PO Box 757500 Fairbanks AK 99775-7500

LINDE, DAVID, film company executive; b. 1960; Grad., Swarthmore Coll. With Paramount Pictures Corp., 1985—88; v.p. Fox/Lorber Associates, 1990—91; v.p. acquisitions Miramax Films, 1991—92, sr. v.p., 1992—97; exec. v.p., head of sales Miramax Internat., 1992—97; ptnr. GOOD Machine (bought by Universal Pictures and merged into new studio, Focus), NYC, 1997—2006; co-pres. Focus Features, NYC, 2002—06; pres. Rogue Pictures, 2002—06; co-chmn. Universal Pictures, Universal City, Calif., 2006—. Bd. dirs. Am. Film Mktg. Assn. Exec. prodr.: (films) The Who's Tommy, the Amazing Journey, 1993, Wonderland, 1997, Happiness, 1998, Ride with the Devil, 1999, The King is Alive, 2000, Crouching Tiger, Hidden Dragon, 2000, Storytelling, 2001, And Your Mother Too, 2001, They, 2002, How to Deal, 2003; prodr.: The Hitcher, 2007. Bd. dirs. Bklyn. Woods. Named one of 50 Most Powerful People in Hollywood, Premiere mag., 2006. Office: Universal Pictures 100 Universal City Plz Universal City CA 91608

LINDE, HANS ARTHUR, state supreme court justice; b. Berlin, Apr. 15, 1924; came to US, 1939, naturalized, 1943; s. Bruno C. and Luise (Rosenhain) L.; m. Helen Tucker, Aug. 13, 1945; children: Lisa, David Tucker. BA, Reed Coll., 1947; JD, U. Calif., Berkeley, 1950. Bar: Oreg. 1951. Law clk. U.S. Supreme Ct. Justice William O. Douglas, 1950-51; atty. Office of Legal Adviser, Dept. State, 1951-53; pvt. practice Portland, Oreg., 1953-54; legis. asst. U.S. Sen. Richard L. Neuberger, 1955-58; from assoc. prof. to prof. U. Oreg. Law Sch., 1959-76; justice Oreg. Supreme Ct., Salem, 1977-90, sr. judge, 1990—. Fulbright lectr. Freiburg U., 1967-68, Hamburg U., 1975-76; cons. U.S. ACDA, Dept. Def., 1962-76; mem. Adminstrv. Conf. U.S., 1978-82, Oreg. Law Commn., 1997—; pub. commr. Oreg. Legislature, 2005-06; disting. scholar in residence Willamette U. Coll. Law, Salem, Oreg., 1994—. Author: (with George Bunn) Legislative and Administrative Processes, 1976. Mem. Oreg. Constl. Revision Commn., 1961-62, Oreg. Law Commn., 1997—, Oreg. Commn. on Pub. Broadcasting, 1990-93, Pub. Commn. Oreg. Legislative, 2005-06; bd. dirs. Oreg. Pub. Broadcasting, 1993-99. With U.S. Army, 1943-46. Fellow Am. Acad. Arts and Scis.; mem. Am. Law Inst. (council), Order of Coif, Phi Beta Kappa. Office: Willamette U Coll Law Salem OR 97301 Business E-Mail: hlinde@willamette.edu.

LINDE, MAXINE HELEN, lawyer, corporate financial executive, investor; b. Chgo., Sept. 2, 1939; d. Jack and Lottie (Kroll) Stern; m. Ronald K. Linde, June 12, 1960. BA summa cum laude, UCLA, 1961; JD, Stanford U., 1967. Bar: Calif. 1968. Applied mathematician, rsch. engr Jet Propulsion Lab., Pasadena, Calif., 1961—64; law clk. U.S. Dist. Ct. No. Calif., 1967—68; mem. firm Long & Levit, San Francisco, 1968—69, Swerdlow, Glikbarg & Shimer, Beverly Hills, Calif., 1969—72; sec., gen. counsel Envirodyne Industries, Inc., Chgo., 1972—89; pres. The Ronald and Maxine Linde Found., 1989—; vice chmn. bd., gen. counsel Titan Fin. Group, LLC, Chgo., 1994—98. Mem. bd. visitors Stanford Law Sch., 1989—92, law and bus. adv. coun., 1991—94, dean's adv. coun., 1992—94. Mem.: Alpha Lambda Delta, Pi Mu Epsilon, Phi Beta Kappa, Order of Coif.

LINDE, RONALD KEITH, investor; b. LA, Jan. 31, 1940; s. Morris and Sonia Doreen (Hayman) L.; m. Maxine Helen Stern, June 12, 1960. BS with honors, UCLA, 1961; MS (Inst. scholar), Calif. Inst. Tech., 1962, PhD (ARCS scholar, Rutherford scholar), 1964. Cons. Litton Industries, LA, 1961-63, engr., 1961; materials scientist Poulter Labs., Stanford Rsch. Inst., Menlo Park, Calif., 1964; head solid state rsch. Stanford Rsch. Inst., Menlo Park, Calif., 1965-67; chmn. shock wave physics dept., mgr. tech. svcs. Poulter Labs., 1967, dir. shock and high pressure physics div., 1967-68, chief exec. labs., 1968-69; dir. phys. scis. Stanford Rsch. Inst., 1968-69; chmn. bd., CEO Envirodyne Industries, Inc., Chgo., 1969-89; chmn. bd. The Ronald and Maxine Linde Found., Phoenix, 1989—. Co-chmn. bd. Titan Fin. Group, LLC, Chgo., 1994-98; law and bus. adv. coun. Stanford Law Sch., 1991-94, dean's adv. coun. 1992-94. Contbr. articles to various publs.; patentee in field. Mem. adv. bd. ARCS Found., Chgo., 1993-98; mem. Northwestern U. Assocs., 1978-2005; trustee Calif. Inst. Tech., 1989—, chmn. alumni rels. com., 1997-2002, chmn. audit and compliance com., 2002—, Harvey Mudd Coll., 1989-98, vice chmn., bd. trustees, 1993-98, vice chmn. emeritus, 1998—. Mem. Sigma Xi, Tau Beta Pi, Phi Eta Sigma.

LINDEMAN, ROBERT DEAN, medical educator, researcher, consultant; b. Ft. Dodge, Iowa, July 19, 1930; s. Verlus F. and Dorothy L. (Cawelti) L.; m. Janet Ruth Lyman, Apr. 12, 1954 (div. June 1982); children: William Douglas, Ann Denise Hendrix, James Lawrence, Peter Verlus, David Matthew; m. Edith Lynn Lind, Aug. 14, 1982 (dec. Oct. 2001); stepchildren: Laurel Lind Lisinski, Lisa Lind Ringhoff, Kristine Lind Cannaday, Robert Mathew Lind; m. Judith Margaret Brown, Jan. 11, 2003; stepchildren Laura Brown Traeger, Martha Brown Swinney, Leslie Ida Brown. BS, SUNY Syracuse, 1952, MD, 1956. Diplomate Am. Bd. Internal Medicine. Intern Blodgett Meml. Hosp., Grand Rapids, Mich., 1956—57; resident in internal medicine Upstate Med. Ctr., Syracuse, 1957—60; chief renal sect. Dept. Medicine U. Okla., Oklahoma City, 1966—77; assoc. chief of staff in rsch. Oklahoma City VA Med. Ctr., 1966—76; chief of staff Louisville VA Med. Ctr., 1977—83; assoc. dean VA affairs Sch. Medicine U. Louisville, 1977—83; chief of staff VA Med. Ctr., Washington, 1983—88; assoc. dean VA affairs, prof. medicine Sch. Medicine George Washington U., Washington, 1983—88; prof. medicine, chief divsn. gerontology U. N.Mex., Albuquerque, 1988—99, prof. medicine emeritus, 1999—; dir. N.Mex. Geriatric Edn. Ctr., 1995—2001. Mem. panel nutrition U. S. Pharmacopeia, Rockville, Md., 1975-2000, chair, 1990-2000; mem. adv. bd. Am. Assn. Ret. Persons, Pharmacy Svc., Washington, 1990-2001 Contbr. articles to profl. jours. Pres. Okla. chpt. Nat. Kidney Found., Oklahoma City, 1970-71, pres.-elect and pres. Ky. chpt., Louisville, 1978-81. Recipient Ralph C. Williams Rsch. award U. N.Mex., 1992, Gerontology Assoc. award, 1992. Master Am. Coll. Nutrition (pres., pres.-elect, v.p. 1981-87); fellow ACP, Am. Geriat. Soc.; mem. Nat. Assn. VA Chiefs of Staff (pres., pres.-elect 1984-86), Gerontol. Soc. Am., Am. Soc. Nephrology, Internat. Soc. Nephrology, So. Soc. for Clin. Investigation, Ctrl. Soc. for Clin. Rsch., We. Assn. Physicians Democrat. Avocation: fly fishing. Office: Rm 215 2701 Frontier Pl NE Albuquerque NM 87131-5666 Home: 1404 Florida St NE Albuquerque NM 87110-6806 Office Phone: 505-272-3313. Business E-Mail: rlindeman@salud.unm.edu.

LINDENFELD, JOANN, physician, educator; b. Benton Harbor, Mich., Feb. 11, 1948; d. Nelson Albert and Viola C. Lindenfield. MD, U. MIch., 1973. Diplomate in internal medicine, cardiology and critical care medicine Am. Bd. Internal Medicine. Asst. prof. medicine U. Colo., Denver, 1980-85, assoc. prof. medicine, 1985-90, prof. medicine, 1990—. Mem. cardiovenal adv. panel FDA, Washington, 1995—; cons. for pharm. firms. Author: Geriatric Internal Medicine, 1995, 99; contbr. articles to profl. jours. Recipient numerous awards U. Colo., Denver. Fellow Am. Coll. Cardiology, Am. Heart Assn. (clin. coun. rep.); mem. Internat. Soc. Heart and Lung Transplant, Am. Soc. Transplant Physicians. Avocations: hiking, poetry, gardening, writing. Office: U Colo Health Scis Ctr 4200 E 9th Ave B130 Denver CO 80262-0001 Home Phone: 303-733-4352; Office Phone: 303-315-4410, 720-848-0850. Business E-Mail: joAnn.lindenfeld@uchsc.edu.

LINDER, VIRGINIA LYNN, state supreme court justice; b. Cañon City, Colo., Apr. 20, 1953; d. Irene D. Linder. BS in Polit. Sci., So. Oreg. State U., 1975; JD, Willamette U., 1980. Bar: Oreg., U.S. Dist. Ct. Oreg. 1981, U.S. Ct. Appeals (9th cir.) 1981, U.S. Supreme Ct. 1983. Asst. atty. gen. Oreg. Dept. Justice, Salem, 1980-83, atty. in charge edn. sect., gen. counsel, 1983-84, asst. solicitor gen., 1984-86, solicitor general, 1986-97; judge Oreg. Ct. Appeals, Salem, 1997—2007; assoc. justice Ore. Supreme Ct., 2007—. Presenter, spkr., panelist in fields of women's law, constnl. law, family and juvenile law, capital cases, other topics; adj. law prof. Willamette U., 1998—, U. Oreg. Law Sch., 1988; mem. Oreg. Judicial Dept. exec. com.; mem. appellate ct. tech. com., 1997—; mem. Coun. on Ct. Procedures, 1997—; mem. Appellate Cts. Settlement Conf. com., 1994; mem. Ho. Task Force on Oreg. Appellate Ct. Sys;., 1993-94; apptd. Oreg. Appellate Ct. rules com., 1990, 92-93; mem. 9th Cir. Death Penalty Task Force, 1988-91. Prin. author minority report Videotape Ct. Reporting Evaluation com., trial level, 1990, appellate level, 1991. Judge Nat. We the People (Bill of Rights) H.S. Competition, Washington, 1993; judge state-wide h.s. We the People Competition, Oreg. Law Related Edn. Program, 1992, 93; trial practice instr./judge, Willamette U., 1983—. Recipient Outstanding Alumna award, So. Oreg. State Coll., 1987; recipient Cmty. award YWCA Tribute to Outstanding Women, 1991; recipeint merit award Oreg. Gay and Lesbian Lawyers Assn., 1996. Mem. Nat. Assn. Attys. Gen. (state specialist group providing amicus support and expertise on 8th amendment issues), Oreg. State Bar (exec. com. constnl. law sect., chair appellate practice sect. 1994-95, vice chair 1993-94, chair-elect 1994-95), Oreg. Women Lawyers (bd. mem. 1997—, exec. com. mem.), Marion County Bar Assn. (Law Practices Career Day host 1991, 92), Willamette Inns of Ct. Office: Ore Supreme Ct 1163 State St Salem OR 97301-2563 Office Phone: 503-986-5555. Office Fax: 503-986-5730. E-mail: ojd.info@ojd.state.or.us.

LINDGREN, TIMOTHY JOSEPH, supply company executive; b. NYC, Dec. 7, 1937; s. Carl Herbert and Ruth Elizabeth (Pickering) L.; m. Barbara Fiorini, Feb. 7, 1957; children: Sharon, Mark, Susan. AA, Pierce Coll., Woodland Hills, Calif., 1959; BS in Prodn. Mgmt., Calif. State U., Northridge, 1961; MBA in Indsl. Relations, UCLA, 1962. Registered profl. engr., Calif. cert. tchr., Calif. Systems analyst, methods acct. Pacific Tel. & Tel., Van Nuys, Calif., 1964-65; dir. mfg. Olga Co., Van Nuys, 1965-69; dir. prodn. Calif. Almond Orchards, Bakersfield, 1970-72, gen. mgr., 1972-73; pres. United Wholesale Lumber Co., Montebello, Calif., 1973-77; pres., chief exec. officer Fruit Growers Supply Co., Sherman Oaks, Calif., 1978—. Mem. Calif. C. of C. (chair com. on agrl. & natural resources). Office: Fruit Growers Supply Co 14130 Riverside Dr Sherman Oaks CA 91423-2313

LINDHEIM, RICHARD DAVID, broadcast executive, director; b. NYC, May 28, 1939; s. Gilbert R. and Pearl (Gruskin) L.; m. Elaine Lavis, Dec. 22, 1963; children: Susan Patricia, David Howard. BS, U. Redlands, 1961; postgrad, U. So. Calif., 1963. Adminstrv. asst. story dept. CBS, LA, 1962-64; project dir. entertainment testing ASI Market Rsch., LA, 1964-69; v.p. program research NBC, LA, 1969-78, v.p. dramatic programs, 1978-79; producer Universal TV, LA, 1979-81, v.p. current programs, 1981-85, sr. v.p. series programming, 1986-87, exec. v.p. creative affairs, 1987-91; exec. v.p. program strategy MCA TV Group, 1991-92; exec. v.p. Paramount TV Group, 1992-99; exec. dir. Inst. for Creative Techs., U. So. Calif., LA, 1999—; with ICT, Marina Del Rey, Calif. Asst. prof. Calif. State U.; sr. lectr. U. So. Calif.; lectr. UCLA; reviewer NEH; bd. dirs. Am. Fgn. Svc. Intercultural Program-USA. Author: (with Richard Blum) Primetime: Network Television Programming, 1987, Inside Television Producing, 1991; contbr. articles to profl. jours. Mem. Acad. TV Arts and Scis., Producers Guild Am., Writers Guild Am. Democrat. Jewish. Avocations: model building, photography, music, travel. Office: ICT 4676 Admiralty Way Ste 1001 Marina Del Rey CA 90292 Office Phone: 310-574-5706. E-mail: lindheim@ict.usc.edu.

LINDHOLM, DWIGHT HENRY, lawyer; b. Blackduck, Minn., May 27, 1930; s. Henry Nathanial and Viola Eudora (Gummert) L.; m. Loretta Catherine Brown, Aug. 29, 1958; children: Douglas Dwight, Dionne Louise, Jeanne Marie, Philip Clayton, Kathleen Anne. Student, Macalester Coll., 1948-49; BBA, U. Minn., 1951, LLB, 1954; postgrad., Mexico City Coll. (now U. of Ams.), 1956-57. Bar: Minn. 1954, Calif. 1958. Sole practice, Los Angeles, 1958-65, 72-81, 84—; ptnr. Lindholm & Johnson, Los Angeles, 1965-69, Cotter, Lindholm & Johnson, Los Angeles, 1969-72; sole practice Los Angeles, 1972-81; of counsel Bolton, Dunn & Moore, Los Angeles, 1981-84. Mem. Calif. Rep. Ctrl. Com., 1962-63, L.A. Republican County Ctrl. Com., 1962-66; bd. dirs. Family Service L.A., 1964-70, v.p., 1968-70; bd. dirs. Wilshire YMCA, 1976-77; trustee Westlake Girls Sch., 1978-81; hon. presenter Nat. Charity League Coronet Debutante Ball, 1984; bd. dirs. Calif. State U.-Northridge Trust Fund, 1989-93; bd. dirs. Queen of Angeles/Hollywood Presbyn. Med. Ctr., 1990-98; chmn., CEO Queen of Angels, Hollywood Presbyn. Found., 1997-2000; bd. dirs., corp. sec. QueensCare, 1998-2002. Served as capt. JAG Corps USAF, 1954-56. Recipient Presdl. award LA Jr. C. of C., 1959 Mem. Calif. Bar Assn., L.A. County Bar Assn., Wilshire Bar Assn. (bd. govs. 1989-91), Internat. Genealogy Fellowship of Rotarians (founding pres. 1979-86), Calif. Club, Ocean Cruising Club Eng. (Newport Harbor port officer), Rotary (dir. 1975-78), Delta Sigma Pi, Delta Sigma Rho, Delta Theta Phi (state chancellor 1972-73). Presbyterian. Avocations: sailing, offshore cruising. Office: 3580 Wilshire Blvd Fl 17 Los Angeles CA 90010-2501

LINDL, JOHN D., physicist; Scientific dir. Inertial Confinement Fusion Program. Recipient E.O. Lawrence Meml. award U.S. Dept. Energy, 1994. Office: Lawrence Livermore Nat Lab Livermore CA 94550

LINDLEY, F(RANCIS) HAYNES, JR., foundation executive, lawyer; b. LA, Oct. 15, 1945; s. Francis Haynes and Grace Nelson (McCanne) L.; 1 child, Anne Hollinger Lindley. BA, Claremont Men's Coll., Calif., 1967; MFA, Claremont Grad. Sch., Calif., 1972; JD, Southwestern U., L.A., 1976. Bar: Calif. 1976, U.S. Supreme Ct. 1980. Deputy pub. defender Office of Pub. Defender, LA, 1977-79; staff atty., Dept. Trial Counsel The State Bar of Calif., LA, 1979-81; pvt. practice, 1981-90; pres. John Randolph Haynes and Dora Haynes Found., LA, 1987-97, pres. emeritus, 1997—. Trustee John Randolph Haynes and Dora Haynes Found., L.A., 1978—. Bd. dirs. TreePeople, L.A., 1985-87, So. Calif. Assn. Philanthropy, L.A., 1985-89; mem. bd. fellows Claremont (Calif.) U. Ctr. and Grad. Sch., 1987—2006; bd. dirs. Marin Agrl. Land Trust, 1995-2005, Family and Children Law Ctr., Marin County, 2006—. Recipient Disting. Svc. award The Claremont (Calif.) Grad. Sch., 1994. Avocations: sailing, art history, guitar. Home: PO Box 3058 Sausalito CA 94966-3058 Office: John Randolph Haynes & Dora Haynes Found 888 W 6th St Ste 1150 Los Angeles CA 90017-2737 Office Phone: 213-623-9151.

LINDSEY, CASIMIR CHARLES, zoologist, educator; b. Toronto, Ont., Can., Mar. 22, 1923; s. Charles Bethune and Wanda Casimira (Gzowski) L.; m. Shelagh Pauline Lindsey, May 29, 1948. BA, U. Toronto, 1948; MA, U. B.C., Vancouver, 1950; PhD, Cambridge U., Eng., 1952. Div. biologist B.C. Game Dept., 1952-57; with Inst. Fisheries, also dept. zoology U. B.C., 1953-66; prof. zoology U. Man., Winnipeg, 1966-79; dir. Inst. Animal Resource Ecology, U. B.C., 1980-85; mem. Fisheries and Oceans Adv. Council, 1981-86; prof. emeritus U. B.C., 1988—. Bd. govs. Vancouver Pub. Aquarium, 1956—66, 1980—95, patron, 1996—2004; external assessor univs., Singapore and Nanyang, 1979—81; cons. in field. Author papers in field. Served with Can. Army, 1943-45. Recipient Publ. award Wildlife Soc., 1972; Saunderson award for excellence in teaching U. Man., 1977; Rh Inst. award, 1979; Nuffield Found. grantee, 1973; Killam sr. fellow, 1985-86. Fellow Royal Soc. Can.; mem. Can. Soc. Zoologists (pres. 1977-78), Can. Soc. Environ. Biologists (v.p. 1974-75), Am. Soc. Ichthyologists and Herpetologists (gov.), Fedn. Can. Artists. Office: U BC Dept of Zoology 6270 University Blvd Vancouver BC Canada V6T 1Z4

LINDSTROM, KENT J., Internet company executive; BS in Economics, Northwestern U., 1988, MBA in Fin. and Mktg. CFA. Officer First Colonial Bankshares Corp.; sr. mgr., practice leader Deloitte & Touche LLP; pres. NetRead; joined Friendster, Inc., San Francisco, 2002, CFO, 2003—06, pres., 2006—08, sr. v.p. corp. devel., 2008—. Avocations: guitar, yoga, reading. Office: Friendster Inc 568 Howard St San Francisco CA 94105 Office Fax: 415-618-0074.

LINDSTROM, KRIS PETER, environmental consultant; b. Dumont, NJ, Oct. 18, 1948; s. Sven Rune and Moyra Hilda (Coughlan) L.; m. Annette Gail Chaplin, June 25, 1978; 1 child, Karl Pierce. MPH, U. Calif., Berkeley, 1973; MS in Ecology, U. Calif., Davis, 1983. Registered environ. health specialist, Calif. Sr. lab. analyst County Sanitation Dists. Orange County, Fountain Valley, Calif., 1970-72, environ. specialist, 1973-74, J.B. Gilbert and Assocs., Sacramento, 1974-78; prin. K.P. Lindstrom & Assocs., Sacramento, 1978-84; pres. K.P. Lindstrom, Inc., Pacific Grove, Calif., 1985—. Mem. rsch. adv. bd. Nat. Water Rsch. Inst., Fountain Valley, 1991—. Author: Design of Municipal Wastewater Treatment Plants, 1992; editor publs., 1989, 90. Chmn. City of Pacific Grove (Calif.) Mus. Bd., 1992-96, City of Seal Beach (Calif.) Environ. Bd., 1970; dir. Monterey Peninsula Water Mgmt. Dist., 1999—. Mem. Water Environ. Fedn. (chmn. marine water quality com. 1987-90), Calif. Water Pollution Control Assn., Pacific Grove Residents Assn. (bd. dirs., pres., v.p. 1992-98). Office: KP Lindstrom Inc PO Box 51008 Pacific Grove CA 93950-6008

LINEBERGER, WILLIAM CARL, chemistry professor; b. Hamlet, NC, Dec. 5, 1939; s. Caleb Henry and Evelyn (Cooper) L.; m. Katharine Wyman Edwards, July 31, 1979. BS, Ga. Inst. Tech., 1961, MSEE, 1963, PhD, 1965. Rsch. physicist U.S. Army Ballistic Rsch. Labs., Aberdeen, Md., 1967-68; postdoctoral assoc. Joint Inst. for

Lab. Astrophysics U. Colo., Boulder, 1968-70, from asst. prof. to prof. chemistry, 1970-83, E.U. Condon prof. chemistry, 1983—. Phi Beta Kappa nat. lectr., 1989. Capt. US Army, 1965—67. Fellow AAAS, Joint Inst. for Lab. Physics, Am. Phys. Soc. (H.P. Broida prize 1981, Bomen Michelson prize 1987, Optical Sci. Am. Meggers prize 1988, Plyler prize 1992; mem. NAS, Am. Chem. Soc. (Irving Langmuir prize 1996), Am. Acad. Arts and Scis., Sigma Xi. Office: U Colo Joint Inst Lab Astrophysics Cb 440 Boulder CO 80309-0001

LINFORD, RULON KESLER, physicist, electrical engineer; b. Cambridge, Mass., Jan. 31, 1943; s. Leon Blood and Imogene (Kesler) L.; m. Cecile Tadje, Apr. 2, 1965; children: Rulon Scott, Laura Linford Williams, Hilary Linford Henderson, Philip Leon. BSEE, U. Utah, 1966; MSEE, MIT, 1969, PhD in Elec. Engring., 1973. Staff CTR-7 Los Alamos (N.Mex) Nat. Lab., 1973-75, asst. group leader CTR-7, 1975-77, group leader CTR-11, 1977-79, program mgr., group leader compact toroid CTR-11, 1979-80, program mgr., asst. divsn. leader compact toroid CTR divsn., 1980-81, assoc. CTR divsn. leader, 1981-86, program dir. magnetic fusion energy, 1986-89, program dir., divsn. leader CTR divsn. office, 1989-91, program dir. nuc. sys., 1991-93, staff LER, 1993-94; coord. sci. and tech. U. Calif., 1994-97; assoc. vice provost lab. programs Office of the Pres., U. Calif., Oakland, 1997—2001, assoc. vice provost, 2001—03, asst. v.p. lab. programs, 2003—04; ret., 2004. Contbr. articles to profl. jours. Recipient E. O. Lawrence award Dept. of Energy, Washington, 1991. Fellow Am. Phys. Soc. (exec. com. 1982, 90-91, program com. 1982, 85, award selection com. 1983, 84, fellowship com. 1986); mem. AAAS, Sigma Xi. Home: 1055 Aquarius Way Oakland CA 94611-1939 E-mail: cecile.rulon@comcast.net.

LING, ROBERT M., JR., lawyer, consumer products company executive; b. Marquette, MI, 1957; Grad., Tufts U., 1979; JD, U. Michigan Law Sch., 1982. Bar: Wis. 1982. V.p., gen. counsel Unified Western Grocers (formerly Certified Grocers of Calif.), LA, 1996—97, sr. v.p., gen. counsel, sec., 1997—98, exec. v.p., gen. counsel, 1998—. Office: Unified Western Grocers Inc PO Box 513396 5200 Sheila St Los Angeles CA 90051-1396

LING, VICTOR, oncologist, educator; b. Mar. 16, 1943; BS in Biochemistry, U. Toronto, 1966; PhD in Biochemistry, U. BC, 1971. Staff scientist Ont. Cancer Inst., Toronto, 1971-98, head divsn. molecular and structural biology, 1989-98; asst. dean, prof., dept. biochemistry & molecular biology U. BC, Vancouver, 1998—, prof., dept. of pathology & lab. medicine, 1998—; v.p., rsch., assoc. vice chair BC Cancer Rsch Ctr., Vancouver, Canada, 1995—. Prof. med. biophysics U. Toronto, 1983-95, mem. coun. sch. grad. studies, 1984-90, mem. faculty of medicine rsch. com., 1985-95, vice-chmn., 1988—; mem. study sect. of experimental therapeutics Nat. Insts. of Health, USA, 1986—; bd. govs. Wellesly Hosp. Rsch. Inst., 1988-90; mem. MRC scholarship com. Med. Rsch. Coun. of Can., 1988—, bd. sci. advisors Hong Kong Inst. Biotech., 1989—, adv. bd. Internat. Jour. Anti-cancer Drugs, 1990—, external adv. com. U. Wis. Clin. Cancer Ctr., 1990—, bd. sci. counselors divsn. cancer treatment Nat. Insts. of Health, 1990—; bd. dirs. Hosp. for Sick Children Found., 1992—. Assoc. editor Cancer Rsch., 1986—, Jour. Cellular Physiology, 1989—, Jour. Cellular Pharmacology, 1989—, Jour. Molecular Pharmacology, 1992—, Jour. Biomed. Sci., 1992-; contbr. to 180 peer-reviewed publs. Victoria U. Alumni scholar in Life Scis., 1965, Centennial fellow MRC of Can., 1969-71; recipient C. Chester Stock award Meml. Sloan-Kettering Cancer Ctr., 1988, Cancer Rsch. award The Milken Family Med. Found., 1988, Merit award The FCCP (Ont.) Edn. Found., 1989, Internat. award Gairdner Found., 1990, Charles F. Kettering prize GM Cancer Rsch. Found., 1991, Joseph Steiner Cancer Rsch. award, 1991 Fellow Royal Soc. Can.; mem. Am. Assn. Cancer Rsch. (bd. dirs. 1992—, Bruce F. Cain Meml. award 1993), Am. Soc. Cell Biology, Can. Cancer Soc. (bd. dirs. 1992—), Can. Soc. Cell Biology, Can. Biochem. Soc., Genetics Soc. Can., Can. Breast Cancer Rsch. Initiative, Nat. Cancer Inst., Hosp. for Sick Children Found., Toronto; mem. GM Adv. Council, Cancer Rsch. Found. Achievements include revolutionizing cancer therapy and research into chemotherapy resistance with his discovery of the membrane transport protein P-glycoprotein, a protein the resists anti-cancer drugs in 1974. Office: BC Cancer Rsch Ctr 601 West 10th Ave Vancouver BC V5Z 4E6 Canada Address: Dept Biochemistry and Molecular Biology Faculty of Medicine Univ of BC 2010-2146 Health Sciences Mall Vancouver BC V6T 1Z3 Canada Office Phone: 604-877-6010, 604-822-3178, 607-877-6000 2524, 604-877-6151. Office Fax: 604-822-5227, 604-877-6150. Business E-Mail: vling@bccancer.bc.ca.

LINGENFELTER, SHERWOOD GALEN, academic administrator, retired anthropologist; b. Hollidaysburg, Pa., Nov. 18, 1941; s. Galen Miller and Kathern Margareta (Rogers) L.; m. Judith Elaine Beaumont, Aug. 10, 1962; children: Jennifer Elaine, Joel Sherwood. BA, Wheaton Coll., 1963; PhD, U. Pitts., 1971. Dir. acad. advising U. Pitts., 1964-66; instr. SUNY, Brockport, 1966-67, asst. prof, 1969-74, assoc. prof., 1974-82, prof. anthropology, 1982-83; NIH predoctoral fellow U. Pitts., 1967-69; prof. Biola U., La Mirada, Calif., 1983-88, provost, sr. v.p., 1988-99; dean Sch. of World Mission Fuller Theol. Sem., Pasadena, Calif., 1999—2002, provost, sr. v.p., 2001—. Cons. in anthropology Summer Inst. Linguistics, Dallas, 1977-2003; tng. cons. Liebenzell Mission Am., Schooleys Mountain, NJ, 1981-89; evaluating cons. Trust Ter. of the Pacific Islands, Saipan, Mariana Islands, 1969-74. Author: Yap: Political Leadership, 1975, The Deni of Western Brazil, 1980, Ministering Cross-Culturally, 1986, Transforming Culture, 1992, 2d edit., 1998, Agents of Transformation, 1996, Teaching Cross-Culturally, 2003, Breaking Tradition to Accomplish Vision, 2006, Leading Cross-Culturally, 2008; editor: Political Development in Micronesia, 1974, Social Organization of Sabah Societies, 1990. Bd. dirs. Christian Scholars Rev., 1989-95, Grace Brethren Internat. Missions, 1994—; mem. Sr. Accrediting Commn. Western Assn. Schs. and Colls., 2000-06, pres., 2002-, chair, 2007-. Recipient Disting. Tchg. award Biola U., 1987-88; grantee NSF, 1967-69, 79-81, SUNY Rsch. Found., 1970. Fellow Am. Anthrop. Assn., Soc. for Applied Anthropology, Am. Ethnol. Soc.; mem. Assn. Social Anthropology Oceania, Am. Conf. Acad. Deans. Democrat. Mem. Grace Brethern Ch. Office: Fuller Theol Sem Provost and Sr VP 135 N Oakland Ave Pasadena CA 91182-0001 Office Phone: 626-584-5205. Business E-Mail: provost@fuller.edu.

LINGLE, LINDA, Governor of Hawaii; b. St. Louis, June 4, 1953; BJ, Calif. State U., Northridge, 1975. Mayor County of Maui, Hawaii; chair. Democratic Party of Hawaii; mem. Maui County Coun., 1980—90; mayor Maui County, 1990—98; chmn. Hawaii Republican Party, 1999—2001; gov. State of Hawaii, Honolulu, 2002—. Recipient Evelyn McPhail award, 2000. Republican. Jewish. Office: Off of the Gov State Capitol Executive Chambers Honolulu HI 96813 Office Phone: 808-586-0034. Office Fax: 808-586-0006.

LINKHART, DOUG(LAS) D., state legislator; b. Norman, Okla., Dec. 17, 1955; m. Doroth Norbie. BA, MA, U. Ariz. Bus. economist; Presdl. mgmt. intern EPA, former analyst air quality divsn.; mem. Colo. Ho. of Reps., 1994-95, Colo. Senate, Dist. 31, Denver, 1995—; mem. fin. com., mem. joint legis. audit com.; mem. health, environ., welfare and instns. com. Founder Neighborhood Resource Ctr.; bd. mem. Urban League Met. Denver; active West Denver Teen Pregnancy Prevention Task Froce, Colo. Inst. for Hispanic Edn., Econ. Devel. Bd.; mem. Mayuor's Adv. Coun., 1987-88, Denver Air Pollution Regulations Adv. Com., 1990-91; capt., co-capt. Dem. Party Dist. 2A. Democrat. Office: State Capitol 200 E Colfax Ave Ste 274 Denver CO 80203-1716 Fax: 303-866-4543. E-mail: rubyg@dnvr.us.west.net.

LINKLETTER, ARTHUR GORDON, radio and television broadcaster; b. Moose Jaw, Sask., Can., July 17, 1912; s. Fulton John and Mary (Metzler) L.; m. Lois Foerster, Nov. 25, 1935; children: Jack, Dawn, Robert (dec.), Sharon, Diane (dec.). AB, San Diego State Coll., 1934. Program dir. Sta. KGB, San Diego, 1934; program dir. Calif. Internat. Expn., San Diego, 1935; radio dir. Tex. Centennial Expn., Dallas, 1936; San Francisco World's Fair, 1937-39; pres. Linkletter Prodns.; ptnr., co-owner John Guedel Radio Prodns. Chmn. bd. Linkletter Enterprises; owner Art Linkletter Oil Enterprises. Author: theme spectacle Cavalcade of Golden West, 1940; author and co-producer: theme spectacle Cavalcade of Am, 1941; writer, producer, star in West Coast radio shows, 1940-55; former star, writer: People Are Funny, NBC-TV and radio, Art Linkletter's House Party, CBS-TV and radio; Author: People Are Funny, 1953, Kids Say The Darndest Things, 1957, The Secret World of Kids, 1959, Confessions of a Happy Man, 1961, Kids Still Say The Darndest Things, 1961, A Child's Garden of Misinformation, 1965, I Wish I'd Said That, 1968, Linkletter Down Under, 1969, Oops, 1969, Drugs at My Door Step, 1973, Women Are My Favorite People, 1974, How to be a Super Salesman, 1974, Yes, You Can!, 1979, I Didn't Do It Alone, 1979, Public Speaking for Private People, 1980, Linkletter on Dynamic Selling, 1982, Old Age is not for Sissies, 1988; co-host (with Bill Cosby) series Kids Say the Darnedest Things, 1998—; lectr. convs. and univs. Nat. bd. dirs. Goodwill Industries; commr. gen. to U.S. Exhibit at Brisbane Expo 88, Australia, 1987; commr. gen. to rank of U.S. amb. to The 200th Anniversary Celebration, Australia, 1987—; bd. regents Pepperdine U.; chmn. bd. Ctr. on Aging, UCLA; chmn. bd. French Found. for Alzheimers Rsch., Solargenix; pres. USA-Next (sr.). Recipient numerous awards. Mem.: United Srs. Assn. (pres.). Address: 11601 Wilshire Blvd Ste 500 Los Angeles CA 90025

LINN, MARCIA CYROG, education educator; b. Milw., May 27, 1943; d. George W. and Frances (Vanderhoof) Cyrog; m. Stuart Michael Linn, 1967 (div. 1979); children: Matthew, Allison; m. Curtis Bruce Tarter, 1987 (div. 2003). BA in Psychology and Stats., Stanford U., 1965, MA in Ednl. Psychology, 1967, PhD in Ednl. Psychology, 1970. Prin. investigator Lawrence Hall Sci. U. Calif., 1970-87, prin. investigator Sch. Edn., 1985—, asst. dean Sch. Edn., 1983-85, prof., 1989—; prin. investigator NSF Funded Ctr.- Tech.-Enhanced Learning in Sci. (TELS), 2003—08; chancellor's prof., 2003—. Fulbright prof. Weizmann Inst., Israel, 1983; exec. dir. seminars U. Calif., 1985-86, dir. instnl. tech. program, 1988-96, chair cognition and devel., 1996—98; cons. Apple Computer, 1983—90; mem. adv. com. on sci. edn. NSF, 1978—85, Ednl. Testing Svc., 1986—90, Smithsonian Instn., 1986—, Fulbright Program, 1983-86, Grad. Record Exam. Bd., 1990-94, adv. com. edn. and human resources directorate, NSF, 2002—; chair Cognitive Studes Bd. McDonell Found., 1994-97; mem. computing svcs. adv. bd. Carnegie Mellon U., 1991-99; mem. steering com. 3d Internat. Math. and Sci. Study, U.S., 1991-2002. Author: Education and the Challenge of Technology, 1987; co-author: The Psychology of Gender-Advances Through Meta Analysis, 1986—, Designing Pascal Solutions, 1992—, Designing Pascal Solutions with Data Structures, 1996, Computers, Teachers, Peers-Science Learning Partners, 2000, Internet Environments for Science Education, 2004, Designing Coherent Science Education, 2008, Wise Science, 2009; contbr. articles to profl. jours. Sci. advisor Parents Club, Lafayette, Calif., 1984-87; mem. Internat. Women's Forum, Women's Forum West, 1992—, membership com., 1995-98; bd. dirs. Nat. Ctr. for Sci. Edn., 1997—, GIS and edn. com., 2000—; mem. bd. on behavioral, cognitive and sensory scis. Nat. Rsch. Coun., 1997-2005, mem. com. on info. tech. literacy, computer sci. and telecomms., 1997-2000; mem. nat. adv. bd. Nat. Ctr. for Improving Student Learning and Achievement in Math. and Sci., 1997—; mem. com. on info. tech. fluency and H.S. grad. outcomes NRC, 2004-05. Recipient fellow Ctr. for Adv. Study in Behavior. Scis. 1995-96, 2001-02, Excellence Ednl. Rsch. award Coun. Sci. Soc. Pres., 1998. Fellow AAAS (bd. dirs. 1996-2001, chair-elect edn. sect. 2005—), APA, AAUW (mem. commn. tech. and gender 1998-2001), Am. Psychol. Soc., Am. Ednl. Rsch. Assn. (chmn. rsch. on women and edn. 1983-85, Women Educators Rsch. award 1982, 88, edn. in sci. and tech. 1989-90, ann. mtg. program com. 1996, Willystine Goodsell award 1991); mem. Nat. Assn. Rsch. in Sci. and Teaching (bd. dirs. 1983-86, assoc. editor jour., Outstanding Paper award 1978, Outstanding Jour. Article award 1975, 83, Disting. Contbns. to Sci. Edn. Through Rsch. award 1994), Internat. Soc. Learning Svcs. (bd. dirs. 2005-, pres. 2008-09), Nat. Sci. Tchrs. Assn. (mem. rsch. agenda com. 1987-90, task force 1993-94), Soc. Rsch. in Child Devel. (editl. bd. 1984-89), Soc. Rsch. Adolescence, Nat. Acad. Edn., Sierra Club. Avocations: skiing, hiking. Office: U Calif Grad Sch Edn 4611 Tolman Hl Berkeley CA 94720-0001

LINN, STUART MICHAEL, biochemist, educator; b. Chgo., Dec. 16, 1940; s. Maurice S. and Pauline Linn; children: Matthew S., Allison D., Meagan S. BS in Chemistry with honors, Calif. Inst. Tech., 1962; PhD in Biochemistry, Stanford U., 1967. Asst. prof. biochemistry U. Calif., Berkeley, 1968-72, assoc. prof., 1972-75, prof., 1975-87, head divsn. biochemistry and molecular biology, 1987-90, 1995-2000. Mem. editl. bd. Nucleic Acids Rsch., 1974—, Jour. Biol. Chemistry, 1975—80, Molecular and Cellular Biology, 1987—91, DNA Repair, 2003—; contbr. articles to profl. jours., chapters to books. Helen Hay Whitney fellow, 1966—68, John Simon Guggenheim fellow, 1974—75, Merit grantee, USPHS, 1988—97. Mem.: AAAS, Am. Soc. Biol. Chem. Molecular Biol., Am. Acad. Arts and Scis. Office: U Calif Divsn Biochem & Molec Bio Barker Hall Berkeley CA 94720-3202 Business E-Mail: slinn@berkeley.edu.

LINNA, TIMO JUHANI, immunologist, researcher, educator; b. Tavastkyro, Finland, Mar. 16, 1937; arrived in U.S., 1968, naturalized, 1981; foster s. Gustaf Lennart and Anne-Marie (Forsstrom) Ackell; m. Rhoda Margareta Popova, May 20, 1961; children: Alexander, Fredrik, Maria. MB, U. Uppsala, Sweden, 1959, MD, 1965, PhD, 1967. Intern, resident hosps., Sweden; pvt. practice medicine hosps. and clinic; asst. prof. histology U. Uppsala, 1967-71; asst. prof. microbiology and immunology Temple U., Phila., 1970-71, dir. lab. clin. immunology hosps., 1970-72, adviser clin. immunology, 1972-80, assoc. prof. microbiology, immunology Phila., 1971-78, prof., 1978-80, research prof., 1980-90. Group leader immunology central research and devel. dept. E.I. duPont de Nemours & Co., Wilmington, Del., 1980-84, research supr., 1984-85, mgr. med. research products dept., 1986-87, assoc. med. dir., 1987-90; sr. dir. cellular immunology Applied Immune Scis., Inc., Menlo Park, Calif., 1990-91; sr. assoc. med. dir. inst. clin. immunology and infectious diseases, devel. rsch., Syntex (USA) Inc., Palo Alto, Calif., 1992-94, dir. med. rsch., 1994-95; dir. med. rsch. Roche Global Devel., Palo Alto, Calif., 1995-96; transplant med. liaison Roche Labs., Palo Alto, 1996—; immunology cons. UNDP/World Bank/WHO Spl. Program for Research and Tng. in Tropical Diseases, WHO, Geneva, 1978-79; mem. sci. adv. coun. Internat. Inst. Immunology Tng. and Research, Amsterdam, Netherlands, 1975-81. Author: books; contbr. articles to profl. jours. USPHS Internat. postdoctoral research fellow, 1968-70; spl. research fellow U. Minn., 1970; Eleanor Roosevelt Am. Cancer Soc. fellow, 1976; grantee Swedish Med. Research Council, 1969-71; grantee NIH, 1972-80 Mem. Am. Assn. Cancer Research, Am. Assn. Immunologists (chmn. edn. com. 1975-80), Am. Assn. Pathologists, Am. Soc. Microbiology, Internat. Soc. Exptl. Hematology, Internat. Soc. Lymphology, N.Y. Acad. Scis., Reticuloendothelial Soc., Royal Lymphatic Soc. Uppsala, Scandinavian Soc. Immunology, Soc. Swedish Physicians, Swedish Med. Assn. Lutheran. Home: 260 Highland Ave San Carlos CA 94070-1911 Office: PO Box 10850 3401 Hillview Ave Palo Alto CA 94304-1320 Personal E-mail: jlinna@prodigy.net.

LINSK, MICHAEL STEPHEN, real estate company executive; b. LA, Apr. 20, 1940; s. Abe P. and Helen Linsk; m. Wilma M. Stahl, Aug. 11, 1979; children from previous marriage: Cari E., Steven D. BSBA, U. So. Calif., 1965, MBA, 1969. CPA. CFO Larwin Group, Inc., Encino, Calif., 1970-75; v.p. fin., dir. Donald L. Bren Co., LA, 1976-78; v.p., CFO, treas., dir. Wilshire Mortgage/Wilshire Diversified, Burbank, Calif., 1980-81; pres., dir. subs. Wilshire Mortgage Corp., Burbank, 1981-84; pres., dir. Wilshire Realty Investments, Burbank, 1981-84, Glenfed Investments Inc., subs. Glendale Fed. Savs., 1982-84; pres. Eastern Pacific Fin. Group, LA, 1984-85; sr. v.p. Leisure Tech., Inc., LA, 1985-87; CEO Investec Realty Group, Inc., Encino, 1987-88; sr. v.p. LA Land Co., 1988-91; mng. dir. FTI Consulting (formerly Price Waterhouse Coopers), 1992—. Bd. dirs. Savs. Bank, Jewel City Ins., Verdugo Svcs., Inc. Treas., bd. dirs. Am. Theater Arts; bd. dirs. North Hollywood Cultural Ctr., Inc., Cmty. of Friends, Inc., 1996—; trustee Temple Judea, Tarzana, Calif., 1981—83, treas., 1982—83. Mem.: AICPA, Urban Land Inst., Calif. Soc. CPAs, Bldg. Industry Assn. (bd. dirs. LA chpt. 1981—88), Beta Gamma Sigma. Office: FTI Consulting Inc 633 W 5Th St Ste 1600 Los Angeles CA 90071-2030 Office Phone: 213-452-6009. Business E-Mail: michael.linsk@fticonsulting.com.

LINSTONE, HAROLD ADRIAN, management consultant, educator; b. Hamburg, Germany, June 15, 1924; came to U.S., 1936; s. Frederic and Ellen (Seligmann) L.; m. Hedy Schubach, June 16, 1946; children: Fred A., Clark R. BS, CCNY, 1944; MA, Columbia U., 1947; PhD, U. So. Calif., 1954. Sr. scientist Hughes Aircraft Co., Culver City, Calif., 1949—61, The Rand Corp., Santa Monica, Calif., 1961—63; assoc. dir. planning Lockheed Corp., Burbank, Calif., 1963—71; prof. Portland State U., Oreg., 1970—. Pres. Systems Forecasting, Inc., Santa Monica, 1971-98; cons. 1973—. Author: Multiple Perspectives for Decision Making, 1984, Decision Making for Technology Executives, 1999; co-author: The Unbounded Mind, 1993, The Challenge of the 21st Century, 1994; co-editor The Delphi Method, 1975, Technological Substitution, 1976, Futures Research, 1977; editor-in-chief Technol. Forecasting Social Change, 1969—. Recipient Disting. Svc. award World Future Soc., 2003, Leadership Tech. Mgmt. award, PICMET, 2007; NSF grantee, Washington, 1976, 79, 85. Mem. Inst. Mgmt. Scis., Ops. Rsch. Soc., Internat. Soc. Systems Scis. (pres. 1993-94). Avocation: photography. Office: Portland State U PO Box 751 Portland OR 97207-0751 Home: 76400 Sweet Pea Way Palm Desert CA 92211 Personal E-mail: linstoneh@aol.com.

LINTON, MIKE, marketing executive; b. Ohio; married; 2 children. B, Bowling Green U., Ohio; M, Duke U., Durham, NC. Brand mgmt. Proctor & Gamble; gen. mgr. Progressive Ins.; v.p., gen. mgr. James River Corp.; v.p. mktg. Remington Products Corp.; sr. v.p. strategic mktg. Best Buy Co., Inc., Mpls., 1999—2002, exec. v.p. consumer and brand mktg., chief mktg. officer, 2002—06; sr. v.p. marketplace adjacencies eBay Inc., San Jose, Calif., 2006—07, chief mktg. officer, 2007—. Bd. dirs. Peet's Coffee and Tea, chmn. nominating and governance; bd. dirs. Allen Edmonds Shoe Co. Named to Retail Advt. Hall of Fame, 2008. Office: eBay 2145 Hamilton Ave San Jose CA 95125

LINVILL, JOHN GRIMES, engineering educator; b. Kansas City, Mo., Aug. 8, 1919; s. Thomas G. and Emma (Crayne) L.; m. Marjorie Webber, Dec. 28, 1943; children: Gregory Thomas, Candace Sue. AB, William Jewell Coll., 1941; SB, Mass. Inst. Tech., 1943, SM, 1945, ScD, 1949; D of Applied Sci., U. Louvain, Belgium, 1966; DSc, William Jewell Coll., 1992. Asst. prof. elec. engring. Mass. Inst. Tech., 1949-51; tech. staff Bell Telephone Labs., 1951-55; assoc. prof. elec. engring. Stanford U., 1955-57, prof., dir. solid-state electronics lab., 1957-64, prof., chmn. dept. elec. engring., 1964-80, prof., dir. Center for Integrated Systems, 1980-90—, Canon USA prof. engring., 1988-89, prof. emeritus, 1989—; co-founder, dir. Tele Sensory Corp., 1971-2000; dir. Read-Rite Corp., 1992-2000. Author: Transistors and Active Circuits, 1961, Models of Transistors and Diodes, 1963; inventor Optacon reading aid for the blind. Recipient citation for achievement William Jewell Coll., 1963, John Scott award for devel. of Optacon, City of Phila., 1980, Medal of Achievement Am. Electronics Assn., 1983, Louis Braille Prize Deutscher Blindenverband, 1984. Fellow IEEE (Edn. medal 1976), AAAS; mem. Nat. Acad. of Engring., Am. Acad. of Arts and Scis. Office: Stanford U Dept Elec Engring Stanford CA 94305 Home: 620 Sand Hill Rd Apt 122 F Palo Alto CA 94304 Business E-Mail: linvill@ee.stanford.edu.

LINZNER, JOEL, lawyer; b. Phila., May 11, 1952; BA, Brandeis U., 1974; JD, U. Calif., Berkeley, 1977. Bar: Calif. 1977, U.S. Ct. Appeals (9th cir.) 1979, U.S. Supreme Ct. 1987. Former ptnr. Crosby, Heafey, Roach & May P.C., Oakland, Calif.; v.p. worldwide bus. affairs Electronic Arts, Calif., 1999—2002, sr. v.p. worldwide bus. affairs, 2002—04, sr. v.p. legal & bus. affairs, 2004—. Adj. prof. Sch. Law Santa Clara U., 1990, 92-93. Contbr. articles to profl. jours. Mem. ABA, State Bar Calif., Bar Assn. San Francisco. Office: Electronic Arts Inc 209 Redwood Shores Pky Redwood City CA 94065

LIONAKIS, GEORGE, architect; b. West Hiawatha, Utah, Sept. 5, 1924; s. Pete and Andriani (Protopapadakis) L.; student Carbon Jr. Coll., 1942-43, 46-47; BArch., U. Oreg., 1951; m. Iva Oree Braddock, Dec. 30, 1951; 1 dau., Deborah Jo. With Corps Engrs., Walla Walla, Wash., 1951-54; architect Liske, Lionakis, Beaumont & Engberg, Sacramento, 1954-86, Lionakis-Beaumont Design Group, 1986—. Mem. Sacramento County Bd. Appeals, 1967—, chmn., 1969, 75, 76; pres. Sacramento Builders Exchange, 1976. Served with USAAF, 1943-46. Mem. AIA (pres. Central Valley chpt., 1972—), Constrn. Specifications Inst. (pres. Sacramento chpt., 1962; nat. awards, 1962, 63, 65), Sacramento C. of C. (code com., 1970—). Club: North Ridge Country (pres. 1987). Lodge: Rotarian (pres. East Sacramento 1978-79). Prin. works include Stockton (Calif.) Telephone Bldg., 1968, Chico (Calif.) Main Telephone Bldg., 1970, Mather AFB Exchange Complex Sacramento, 1970, Base Chapel Mather AFB, Sacramento, 1970, Woodridge Elementary Sch., Sacramento, 1970, Pacific Telephone Co. Operating Center Modesto, Calif., 1968, Sacramento, 1969, Marysville, Calif., 1970, Red Bluff, Calif., 1971, Wells Fargo Banks, Sacramento, 1968, Corning, Calif., 1969, Anderson, 1970, Beale AFB Exchange Complex, Marysville, 1971, Cosumnes River Coll., Sacramento, 1971, base exchanges at Bergstrom AFB, Austin, Tex., Sheppard AFB, Wichita Falls, Tex., Chanute AFB, Rantoul, Ill., McChord AFB, Tacoma, Wash., health center Chico State U., Sacramento County Adminstrn. Center, Sacramento Bee Newspaper Plant. Home: 160 Breckenwood Way Sacramento CA 95864-6968 Office: Lionakis Beaumont Design Group 1919 19th St Sacramento CA 95814-6714

LIOTTA, RAY, actor; b. Newark, Dec. 18, 1954; s. Alfred and Mary Liotta; m. Michelle Grace Liotta, Feb. 15, 1997 (div. 2004); 1 child. Grad., U. Miami. Actor: (films) The Lonely Lady, 1983, Something Wild, 1986, Arena Brains, 1987, Dominick and Eugene, 1988, Field of Dreams, 1989, Goodfellas, 1990, Article 99, 1992, Unlawful Entry, 1992, No Escape, 1994, Corrina, Corrina, 1994, Operation Dumbo Drop, 1995, Unforgettable, 1996, Turbulence, 1997, Copland, 1997, Phoenix, 1998, Forever Mine, 1999, Muppets From Space, 1999, Pilgram, 2000, A Rumor of Angels, 2000, Hannibal, 2001, Heartbreakers, 2001, Blow, 2001, Narc, 2002 (also prodr.), John Q, 2002, Identity, 2003, The Last Shot, 2004, Control, 2004, Revolver, 2005, Slow Burn, 2005, Take the Lead, 2006 (also exec. prodr.), Even Money, 2006, Comeback Season, 2006, Smokin' Aces, 2006, Wild Hogs, 2007, Bee Movie (voice), 2007, In the Name of the King: A Dungeon Siege Tale, 2008, Crossing Over, 2009, Observe and Report, 2009; actor, prodr. (films) Narc, 2002; actor (TV movies) Hardhat & Legs, 1980, Crazy Times, 1981, Women and Men 2: In Love There Are no Rules, The Rat Pack, 1998, Point of Origin, 2002; (TV series) Another World, 1978-81, Casablanca, 1983, Our Family Honor, 1985-86, Smith, 2006; (TV appearances) St. Elsewhere, 1983, Mike Hammer, 1984, Frasier, 1995, Family Guy (voice), 2001, Just Shoot Me!, 2001, 2002, ER, 2004 (Creative Arts Primetime Emmy awards for guest actor in a drama, 2005). Mem. SAG, AFTRA. Office: Endeavor Talent Agency 9601 Wilshire Blvd Ste 300 Beverly Hills CA 90210-5200

LIPINSKI, TARA KRISTEN, retired professional figure skater; b. Phila., June 10, 1982; Prof. figure skater Stars On Ice, 1998—. Nat. spokesperson Campaign for Tobacco-Free Kids. Tara Lipinski's A Night of Skating Champions, Houston, 2003; actor(TV appearance): 7th Heaven, 2003, The Wayne Brady Show, 2003. Recipient Mary Lou Retton award, U.S. Olympic Festival, 1994, 2nd Place, Skate Can., 1996, 1st (team), Postal Svc. Challenge, 1996, 2nd Place, Nations Cup, 1996, 3rd Place, Trophy Lalique, 1996, 1st Place, Hershey's Kisses Challenge, 1997, World Championships, 1997, Champion Series Final, 1997, 1998, 1st Nat. Sr., 1997, 2nd Place, Nat. Championship, 1998, 1st Place, Rattle and Roll, 1998, Gold Medal, Winter Olympic Games, 1998. Achievements include youngest Olympic Festival gold medalist at age 12. Avocations: reading, cooking, tennis.

LIPMAN-BLUMEN, JEAN, public policy and organizational behavior educator; b. Brookline, Mass., Apr. 28, 1933; AB, Wellesley Coll., 1954, AM, 1956; PhD, Harvard U., 1970; postgrad., Carnegie-Mellon U., 1970-71, Stanford U., 1971-72; LHD (hon.), U. La Verne, 2005. Asst. dir., Nat. Inst. Edn., dir women's rsch. program, 1973-78; spl. asst., mem. domestic policy staff The White House, Office of Asst. Sec. Edn.; pres. LBS Internat., Ltd., 1979-84; prof. orgnl. behavior Claremont Grad. U., Calif., Thornton F. Bradshaw prof. pub. policy Peter F. Drucker and Masatoshi Ito Grad. Sch. Mgmt., 1983—. Vis. prof. sociology and orgnl. behavior U. Conn., 1978—80, U. Md., 1980—82; spkr. in field; cons. Exec. Office of Pres., Dept. State, Dept. Labor, Dept. HHS, Dept. Agr., Dept. Edn., Bell Labs., Singapore Airlines, MarketIndex, Finland, various fgn. govts.; tchr. exec. mgmt. and MBA programs. Author, editor (with Jessie Bernard): Sex Roles and Social Policy, 1978; author: The Paradox of Success: The Impact of Priority Setting in Agricultural Research and Extension, 1984, Metaphor for Change: The USDA Competitive Grants Program, 1978-84, 1985, Gender Roles and Power, 1984, Women in Corporate Leadership: Reviewing a Decade's Research, 1996, The Connective Edge: Leading in an Independent World, 1996 (Pulitzer prize nomination); author: (with Harold J. Leavitt) Hot Groups: Seeding, Feeding, and Using Them to Ignite Your Organization, 1999 (Best Book award Assn. Am. Pubs., 1999); author: Connective Leadership: Managing in a Changing World, 2000; author: (with Grace Gabe) Step Wars: Overcoming the Perils and Making Peace in Adult Stepfamilies, 2004, Making Adult Stepfamilies Work-Strategies for the Whole Family When a Parent Marries Later in Life, 2005; author: The Allure of Toxic Leaders: Why We Follow Destructive and Corrupt Politicians-and How We Can Survive Them, 2005, The Art of Fellowship, 2008. Fellow, Ctr. Advanced Study Behavioral Sci., 1978, 1979. Fellow: AAAS. Office: Claremont Grad U 1021 N Dartmouth Ave Claremont CA 91711 Office Phone: 909-621-8083. Personal E-mail: jeanlipman@earthlink.net.

LIPPARD, LUCY ROWLAND, writer, educator, critic, curator; b. NYC, Apr. 14, 1937; d. Vernon William and Margaret Isham (Cross) L.; m. Robert Tracy Ryman, Aug. 19, 1961 (div. 1968); 1 child, Ethan Isham Ryman. BA, Smith Coll., 1958; MA in Art History, NY Inst. Fine Arts, 1962; DFA (hon.), Moore Coll. Art, 1972, San Francisco Art Inst., 1984, Maine Coll. Art, 1994, Mass. Coll. Art, 1998, Art Inst. Chgo., 2003, Nova Scotia Coll. Art and Design, 2007; degree (hon.), Bowdoin Coll., 2008. Freelance writer, lectr., curator, 1964—; rsch. assoc. Mus. N.Mex., Santa Fe. Prof. Sch. Visual Arts, NYC, Williams Coll., Queensland U., Brisbane, Australia, U. Colo., Boulder; mem. adv. bd. Franklin Furnace, NYC, 1979—; co-founder, bd. dirs. Printed Matter, NYC; bd. dirs. Ctr. Study Polit. Graphics, LA, Time & Space Ltd., Hudson, NY, Sustainable Settings, Woody Creek, Colo., Earth Works Inst., Santa Fe, Ctr. Am. Pls., Stanton, Va.; co-founder W.E.B., Ad Hoc Women Artist's Com., Artists Meeting for Cultural Change, Heresies Collective and Jour., Artists Call Against US Intervention in Ctrl. Am., Polit. Art Documentation/Distbn.; lectr. in field. Author: Pop Art, 1966, The Graphic work of Philip Evergood, 1966, Changing: Essays in Art Criticism, 1971, Tony Smith, 1972, Six Years: The Dematerialization of the Art Object, 1973, From the Center: Feminist Essays on Women's Art, 1976, Eva Hesse, 1976, (with Charles Simonds) Cracking (Brüchig Werden), 1979, Issue: Social Strategies by Women Artists, 1980, Ad Reinhardt, 1981, Overlay: Contemporary Art and the Art of Prehistory, 1983, Get the Message? A Decade of Art for Social Change, 1984, Mixed Blessings: New Art in a Multicultural America, 1990, A Different War: Vietnam in Art, 1990, The Pink Glass Swan: Selected Feminist Essays on Art, 1995, The Lure of the Local: Senses of Place in a Multicentered Society, 1997, Florence Pierce: In Touch With Light, 1998, On the Beaten Track: Tourism, Art and Place, 1999, (with Alfred Barr and James Thrall Soby) The School of Paris, 1965, (novel) I See/You Mean, 1979; author, editor: Partial Recall: Photographs of Native North Americans, 1992; editor: Surrealists on Art, 1970, Dadas on Art, 1971; contbg. editor: Art in Am.; founding editor El Puente de Galisteo, 1997—; contbr. monthly columns Village Voice, 1981-85, In These Times, Z Mag.; contbr. articles to profl. jours., popular mags.; curator 50 exhbns.; performer in guerrilla and st. theater. Mem. Santa Fe County Open Lands and Trails Planning and Adv. Com. (COLTPAC), 1999. Recipient Frederick Douglass award North Star Fund, 1994, Frank Jewett Mather award Coll. Art Assn., 1974, Claude Fuess award Phillips Andover Acad., 1975, Curating award Penny McCall Found., 1989, citation NYC mayor David Dinkins, 1990, Smith Coll. medal, 1992, Athena award RISD, 2004, Lifetime Achievement award Coll. Art Assn., 2007, Womens Caucus for Art, 2007; Guggenheim fellow, 1968, ArtTable award, 1999; grantee Lannan Found., 2000. Avocations: hiking, rock art, local history. Home Phone: 505-466-1276; Office Phone: 505-466-1276.

LIPPE, PHILIPP MARIA, neurosurgeon, academic administrator, educator; b. Vienna, May 17, 1929; came to U.S., 1938, naturalized, 1945; s. Philipp and Maria (Goth) L.; m. Virginia M. Wiltgen, 1953 (div. 1977); children: Patricia Ann Marie, Philip Eric Andrew, Laura Lynne Elizabeth, Kenneth Anthony Ernst; m. Gail B. Busch, Nov. 26, 1977. Student, Loyola U., Chgo., 1947-50; BS in Medicine, U. Ill. Coll. Medicine, 1952, MD with high honors, 1954. Diplomate Am. Bd. Neurol. Surgery, 1965, Nat. Bd. Med. Examiners, 1955, Am. Bd. Pain Medicine, 1992. Rotating intern St. Francis Hosp., Evanston, Ill., 1954-55; asst. resident gen. surgery VA Hosp., Hines, Ill., 1955, 58-59; asst. resident neurology and neurol. surgery Neuropsychiat. Inst., U. Ill. Rsch. and Ednl. Hosps., Chgo., 1959-60, chief resident, 1962-63, resident in neuropathology, 1962, postgrad. trainee in electroencephalography, 1963; resident in neurology and neurol. surgery Presbyn.-St. Luke's Hosp., Chgo., 1960-61; practice medicine, specializing in neurol. surgery/pain medicine San Jose, Calif., 1963—93; clin. prof. neurosurgery Stanford U., Calif., 1996—; exec. v.p. Am. Bd. of Pain Medicine, 1994—; exec. med. dir. Am. Acad. of Pain Medicine, 1996—. Instr. neurology and neurol. surgery U. Ill. 1962-63; clin. instr. surgery and neurosurgery Stanford U., 1965-69, clin. asst. prof., 1969-74, clin. assoc. prof., 1974-96, clin. prof., 1996—; staff cons. in neurosurgery O'Connor Hosp., Santa Clara Valley Med. Ctr., San Jose Hosp., Los Gatos Cmty. Hosp., El Camino Hosp. (all San Jose area); chmn. divsn. neurosurgery Good Samaritan Hosp., 1989-97, chmn. dept. clin. neuroscis., 1997-99; founder, exec. dir. Bay Area Pain Rehab. Ctr., San Jose, 1979—; clin. adviser to Joint Commn. on Accreditation of Hosps.; mem. dist. med. quality rev. com. Calif. Bd. Med. Quality Assurance, 1976-87, chmn., 1976-77; cons., med. expert Med. Bd. Calif., 1996—; participant, moderator of numerous profl. seminars and sessions. Assoc. editor Clin. Jour. Pain; contbr. articles to profl. jours. Fellow ACS, Am. Coll. Pain Medicine (bd. dirs. 1991-94, v.p. 1991-92, pres. 1992-93, exec. med. dir.); mem. AMA (ho. of dels. 1981-, CPT editl. panel 1995-99, sr. adv. panel Guides to the Evaluation of Permanent Impairment 1997—, chair pain and palliative medicine splty. sect. coun. 2006-), Am. Coll. Physician Execs., Calif. Med. Assn. (ho. of dels. 1976-80, sci. bd., coun. 1979-87, sec. 1981-87, Outstanding Svc. award 1987), Santa Clara County Med. Soc. (coun. 1974-81, pres. 1978-79, Outstanding Contbn. award 1984, Benjamin J. Cory award 1987), Chgo. Med. Soc., Congress Neurol. Surgeons, Calif. Assn. Neurol. Surgeons (dir. 1974-82, v.p. 1975-76, pres. 1977-79, Pevehouse Disting. Svc. award 1997), San Jose Surg. Soc., Am. Assn. Neurol. Surgeons (chmn. sect. on pain 1987-90, dir. 1983-86, 87-90, Disting. Svc. award 1986, 90), Western Neurol. Soc., San Francisco Neurol. Soc., Santa Clara Valley Profl. Stds. Rev. Orgn. (dir., v.p., dir. quality assurance 1975-83), Fedn. Western Socs. Neurol. Sci., Internat. Assn. for Study Pain, Am. Pain Soc. (founding mem.), Am. Acad. Pain Medicine (sec. 1983-86, pres. 1987-88, Philipp M. Lippe Disting. Svc. award 1995, exec. med. dir. 1996—), Am. Bd. Pain Medicine (pres. 1992-93, exec. v.p. 1994—), Am. Soc. Law, Medicine, and Ethics, Alpha Omega Alpha, Phi Kappa Phi. Achievements include pioneer in medical application of centrifugal force using flight simulator; pioneer in the developing medical specialty of pain medicine. Avocations: photography, travel, computers, raising animals. Office: PO Box 41217 San Jose CA 95160-1217 Address: Am Acad Pain Medicine 4700 W Lake Glenview IL 60025 Personal E-mail: pmlippe@att.net.

LIPPS, JERE HENRY, biology and geology professor; b. LA, Aug. 28, 1939; s. Henry John and Margaret (Rosaltha) L.; m. Karen Elizabeth Loeblich, June 25, 1964 (div. 1971); m. Susannah McClintock, Sept. 28, 1973; children: Jeremy Christian, Jamison William. BA, UCLA, 1962, PhD, 1966. Asst. prof. U. Calif., Davis, 1967-70, assoc. prof., 1970-75, prof., 1975-88, Berkeley, 1988—, prof. paleontology, 1988-89, prof. integrative biology, 1989—; dir. Mus. Paleontology, Berkeley, 1989-97. Dir. Inst. Ecology U. Calif., Davis, 1972-73, chmn. dept. geology, 1971-72, 79-84, chmn. dept. integrative biology, Berkeley, 1991-94. Contbr. articles to sci. publs. Dir. Cushman Found., pres., 1983—84, 2002—03. Recipient U.S. Antarctic medal NSF, 1975, Darwin award NCSE, 2002, Joseph A. Cushman award, 2006; Lipps Island, Antarctica named in his honor, 1979. Fellow: Com. for the Sci. Investigation of Claims of the Paranormal, AAAS (sec. sect.), Paleontol. Soc. (pres. 1996—97), Cushman Found. (pres. 1983—84, 2001—02), Geol. Soc. Am., Calif. Acad. Scis.; mem.: Bd. Micropaleontology Project (dir. 2000—07, chair 2000—07), Coun. for Media Integrity. Avocation: scuba diving. Office: U Calif Mus Paleontology #4780 1101 Valley Life Sciences Bldg Berkeley CA 94720-4780 Home Phone: 510-531-4269. Business E-Mail: jlipps@berkeley.edu.

LIPSEY, RICHARD GEORGE, economist, educator; b. Victoria, BC, Can., Aug. 28, 1928; s. Richard Andrew and Faith Thirell (Ledingham) L.; m. Diana Louise Smart, Mar. 17, 1960; children: Mark Alexander (stepson), Mathew Richard, Joanna Louise, Claudia Amanda. BA with honours, U. BC, 1950; MA, U. Toronto, 1953; PhD, London Sch. Econs., 1955; LLD (hon.), McMaster U., 1983, Victoria U., 1985, U. Carleton, 1987, Queens U., 1990, Toronto U., 1992; DLitt (hon.), U. Guelph, 1993; LLD (hon.), U. Essex, Eng., 1996, U. BC, 1999, Simon Fraser U., 2007. Rsch. asst. B.C. Dept. Trade and Industry, 1950-53; from asst. lectr. to prof. econs. London Sch. Econs., 1955-63; prof. econs., chmn. dept., dean Sch. Social Studies, U. Essex, England, 1965-69; vis. prof. U. B.C., 1969-70, U. Colo., 1973-74; Irving Fisher vis. prof. Yale U., 1979-80; Sir Edward Peacock prof. econs. Queens U., Kingston, Ont., 1970-87; prof. Simon Fraser U., Vancouver, B.C., 1989-97, prof. emeritus, 1997—. Sr. rsch. advisor C.D. Howe Inst., 1983-89; dir. rsch. into growth in U.K. Nat. Econ. Devel. Coun. U.K., 1961-63; mem. coun. and planning com. Nat. Inst. Econ. and Social Rsch. U.K., 1962-69; mem. bd. Social Sci. Rsch. Coun. U.K., 1966-69. Author: An Introduction to Positive Economics, 11th edit, 2007, The Theory of Customs Unions: A General Equilibrium Analysis, 1971; co-author: An Introduction to a Mathematical Treatment of Economics, 3d edit, 1977, Economics, 13th edit., 2007, Mathematical Economics, 1976, An Introduction to the U.K. Economy, 1983, 4th edit., 1993, Common Ground for the Canadian Common Market, 1984, Canada's Trade Options in a Turbulent World, 1985, Global Imbalances, 1987, First Principles of Economics, 1988, 3d edit., 1996, Evaluating the Free Trade Deal, 1988, The NAFTA, What's In, What's Out, What Next, 1994, Business Economics, 1997, A Structuralist Assessment of Innovation Policies, 1998, Economic Transformations: General Purpose Technologies and Long Term Economic Growth, 2005 (Joseph Schumpeter prize, 2006); editor: Rev. Econ. Studies, 1962-64. Decorated officer Order of Can.; Can. Inst. for Advanced Rsch. fellow, 1989—2002. Fellow Econometric Soc., Royal Soc. Can., IC2 Soc. (Austin, Tex.); mem. Royal Econ. Soc. (coun. 1967-71), Econ. Study Soc. (chmn. 1965-69), Am. Econ. Assn., Can. Econ. Assn. (pres. 1980-81), Atlantic Econ. Soc. (chmn. 1986-87). Office Phone: 604-947-9714. Personal E-mail: rlipsey@sfu.ca.

LIPSIG, ETHAN, lawyer; b. NYC, Dec. 11, 1948; s. Daniel Allen and Haddassah (Adler) L. BA, Pomona Coll., 1969; postgrad., Oxford U., 1969-70; JD, UCLA, 1974. Bar: US Dist. Ct. (cen. dist.) Calif. 1974, US Ct. Appeals (9th cir.) 1974, US Tax Ct. 1978. Ptnr. Paul, Hastings, Janofsky & Walker LLP, LA, 1982—. Author: Individual Retirement Arrangements, 1980, Downsizing, 1996, Reductions in Force in Employment Law, 2007. Mem.: ABA (subcom. fed. preemption 1978—79, subcom. investments and funding 1981, employee benefits com., labor and employment law and tax sects.), European Labor Law Network (mem. adv. bd.), US C. of C., Nat. Assn. Pub. Pension Attys., State Bar Calif. (chmn. employee benefits com. 1981—84, tax. sect.), Am. Coll. Employee Benefits Counsel (charter mem.), LA Men's Garden Club, Soc. Fellows of Huntington Libr., Order Coif. Avocations: travel, horticulture, wine, music, art. Office: Paul Hastings Janofsky & Walker LLP 515 S Flower St Fl 25 Los Angeles CA 90071-2280 Office Phone: 213-683-6304. Office Fax: 213-627-0705. Business E-Mail: ethanlipsig@paulhastings.com.

LIPSON, MELVIN ALAN, technology and business management consultant; b. Providence, June 1, 1936; s. Nathan and Esta (Blumenthal) L.; m. Jacqueline Ann Barclay, July 2, 1961; children: Donna, Robert, Michelle, Judith. BS, U. R.I., 1957; PhD, Syracuse U., 1963. Chemist ICI Organics, Providence, 1963, Philip A. Hunt Chem. Co., Lincoln, R.I., 1964-67, rsch. mgr., 1967-69; tech. dir. Dynachem div. Morton Thiokol Inc., Tustin, Calif., 1969-72, v.p., 1979-82, sr. v.p., 1972-82, 1982-85, exec. v.p., 1985-86, pres., 1986-89; v.p. tech. devel. Morton Internat. Inc., Chgo., 1989-92; pres. Lipson Assocs., Newport Beach, Calif., 1993—. Chmn. bd., CEO Aurelon, Inc., Huntington Beach, Calif., 1993-96, Pivotech., Inc., Newport Beach, Calif., 1996-98; CEO Meltex, Inc., Huntington Beach, Calif., 1998—. Home and Office: 14 Belcourt Dr Newport Beach CA 92660 Office Phone: 949-644-2403. Personal E-mail: mellipson@yahoo.com.

LIPSTONE, HOWARD HAROLD, television production executive; b. Chgo., Apr. 28, 1928; s. Lewis R. and Ruth B. (Fischer) L.; m. Jane A. Nudelman, Apr. 7, 1957; children: Lewis, Gregory. BA in Cinema, U. So. Calif., 1950. Asst. to gen. mgr. Sta. KTLA, LA, 1950-54; program dir. Sta. KABC-TV, LA, 1955-61, film and program dir., 1961-63; exec. asst. to pres., exec. prodr. Selmur Prodns., Inc. subs. ABC-TV, LA, 1963-69; exec. v.p. Ivan Tors Films and Studios, Inc., 1969-70; pres. Alan Landsburg Prodns., Inc., 1970-85; pres., COO The Landsburg Co., 1985—. Mem. NATAS, Soc. Motion Picture and TV Engrs., Motion Picture Acad. Arts and Scis., Radio Club Am. Office: The Landsburg Co PO Box 49920 Los Angeles CA 90049-0920

LIPTON, JEFFREY MARC, chemicals executive; b. NYC, July 5, 1942; s. David J. and Ethel (Kuris) L.; m. Adrienne Frank, Dec. 14, 1975; children: Gregory, Dana, Erika. B in Chem. Engring., Rensselaer Poly. Inst., 1963; MBA, Harvard U., 1965. With E. I. DuPont de Nemours & Co., Wilmington, Del., 1965—, v.p. med. products, 1986-87, v.p. polymer products, 1987-90, v.p. DuPont continuous improvement, 1990-91, v.p. corp. mktg. and continuous improvement, 1991—94; sr. v.p., CFO Nova Corp., Canada, 1994—98, pres., CEO, 1998—. Chmn. dir. Methanex Corp., Trimeris, Inc., Am. Plastics Coun.; bd. dirs., mem. bd. internat. com. Am. Chemistry Coun., chmn. exec. com.; dir. Bus. Coun. on Nat. Issues., Hercules Inc.; bd. dir. Canadian Coun. Chief Executives. Chmn. bd. dirs. Med. Ctr. Del. Holding Co., Wilmington, 1987; bd. dirs. Girls Clubs of Del., 1990; trustee N.J. Acad. Aquatic Scis., Camden, 1991-92; mem. exec. com. Nat. Coun. on Econ. Edn., N.Y.C., 1991—. Mem. Soc. Chem. Industry (Am. sect. mem. exec. com., current chmn.) Office: Nova Chemicals 1000 Seventh Ave SW PO Box 2518 Calgary AB T2P 5C6 Canada also: Society Of Chemical Industry 315 Chestnut St Philadelphia PA 19106-2702

LISBAKKEN, JAMES ROBERT, lawyer; b. Washington, June 25, 1945; s. Robert Benjamin and Genevieve Louise (Roberts) L.; m. Linda Jean Alvey, Jan. 2, 1982; children: Kelly, Benjamin. BS, Oreg. State U., 1967; JD, U. Oreg., 1975. Bar: Wash. 1975, U.S. Dist. Ct. Wash. 1975. Engr. Westinghouse Electric Nuclear Power Div., Monroeville, Pa., 1967-70; assoc. Perkins Coie, Seattle, 1975-81, ptnr., 1981-83; dir., exec. v.p., sec., gen. counsel Genetic Systems Corp., Seattle, 1983-85; ptnr., Bus. Law Practice Area Perkins Coie, Seattle, 1985—. Mem. Mcpl. League, Seattle, 1976-80; organizing com. Northwest Biotech. Series. Mem. ABA, Wash. Bar Assn., Seattle King County Bar Assn., Phi Delta Phi, Tau Beta Pi, Wash. Athletic Club. Republican. Presbyterian. Avocations: tennis, skiing, mountain climbing, sailing. Office: Perkins Coie 1201 Third Ave Ste 4800 Seattle WA 98101-3099 Office Phone: 206-359-8660. Office Fax: 206-359-9000. Business E-Mail: jlisbakken@perkinscoie.com.

LISBERGER, STEPHEN G., physiologist, educator; BA in Math., Cornell U.; PhD in Physiology, U. Wash. Investigator Howard Hughes Med. Inst., 1997—; prof. physiology U. Calif., San Francisco, dir. W.M. Keck Found. Ctr. Integrative Neuroscience, co-dir. Sloan Ctr. Theoretical Neurobiology. Recipient McKnight Scholar award, Distinction in Tchg. award, U. Calif. San Francisco, McKnight Investigator award. Fellow: Am. Acad. Arts and Sciences; mem.: AAAS, Soc. Neuroscience (Young Investigator award). Office: UCSF Dept Physiology Box 0444 513 Parnassus Ave San Francisco CA 94143-0444 Office Phone: 415-476-1062. Office Fax: 415-502-4848. E-mail: sgl@keck.ucsf.edu.

LISIO, DONALD JOHN, historian, educator; b. Oak Park, Ill., May 27, 1934; s. Anthony and Dorothy (LoCelso) Lisio; m. Suzanne Marie Swanson, Apr. 22, 1958; children: Denise Anne, Stephen Anthony. BA, Knox Coll., 1956; MA, Ohio U., 1958; PhD, U. Wis., 1965. Mem. faculty overseas div. U. Md., 1958-60; from asst. prof. history to prof. emeritus Coe Coll., Cedar Rapids, Iowa, 1964—2002, prof. emeritus, 2002—. Author: (book) The President and Protest: Hoover, Conspiracy, and the Bonus Riot, 1974, Hoover, Blacks, and Lily-Whites: A Study of Southern Strategies, 1985; contbg. author: book The War Generation, 1975; contbr. articles to hist. jours. Mem. exec. com. Cedar Rapids Com. Hist. Preservation, 1975—77. With US Army, 1958—60. Grantee Am. Coun. Learned Socs., 1971—72, Rsch., U.S. Inst. Peace, 1990; fellow William F. Vilas Rsch., U. Wis., 1963—64, NEH, 1969—70, Rsch., 1984—85, Am. Coun. Learned Socs., 1977—78. Mem.: AAUP, Am. Hist. Assn., Orgn. Am. Historians, Rancho Bernardo Rotary Club. Roman Catholic. Home Phone: 858-676-1226.

LISS, WALTER C., JR., television station executive; Pres., gen. mgr. WABC-TV, NYC; chmn. Buena Vista TV, Burbank, Calif., 1999—; pres. ABC owned TV stas. ABC, Inc. Office: ABC Inc 500 S Buena Vista St Burbank CA 91521-4472

LISSAUER, JACK JONATHAN, astronomy educator; b. San Francisco, Mar. 25, 1957; s. Alexander Lissauer and Ruth Spector. SB in Math., MIT, Cambridge, 1978; PhD in Applied Math., U. Calif., Berkeley, 1982. NAS-NRC resident rsch. assoc. NASA-Ames Rsch. Ctr., Moffett Field, Calif., 1983-85; asst. rsch. astronomer U. Calif., Berkeley, Calif., 1985, vis. rschr. dept. physics Inst. for Theoretical Physics Santa Barbara, Calif., 1985-87; asst. prof. astronomy program dept. earth and space sci. SUNY, Stony Brook, 1987-93, assoc. prof., 1993-96; space scientist NASA Ames Rsch. Ctr., 1996—. Rep. Univs. Space Rsch. Assn., SUNY, Stony Brook, 1987-96; vis. scholar dept. planetary sci. and lunar and planetary lab. U. Ariz., Tucson, 1990; guest prof. dept. physics U. Paris VII et Observatoire Paris, Meudon, France, 1990; mem. Lunar and Planetary Geoscis. rev. panel, 1989, 91, 99, mem. outer planets rsch. program rev. panel, 2005-06, origins of solar sys. rev. panel 2007; vis. asst. rsch. physicist Inst. for Theoretical Physics, U. Calif., Santa Barbara, 1992, organizer Program on Plant Formation, 1992; rsch. assoc. Inst. d'Astrophysique, Paris, 1993; vis. scholar dept. astronomy U. Calif., Berkeley, 1994-95; adj. assoc. prof. SUNY, Stony Brook, 1996-2002; Yuval Ne'eman Disting. lectr. geophysics, atmosphere and space sci. Tel Aviv U., 2001, cons. prof. dept. geology and environ. sci. Stanford U., 2002—. Textbook author "Planetary Sciences" Cambridge Univ. Press; Planetary sci. editor New Astronomy Reviews; contbr. numerous articles on planet and star formation, extrasolar planets, spiral density wave theory, rotation of planets and comets to profl. jour. including Nature, Astron. Jour., Icarus, Sci., Astrophys. Jour. Letters, Astrophys. Jour., Jour. Geophys. Rsch., Astron. Astrophysics, Ann. Rev. Astron. Astrophysics, Revs. of Modern Physics. Recipient Spot Beam award Calif. Space Authority, 2006; NASA Grad. student fellow, 1981-82, Alfred P. Sloan Found. fellow, 1987-91, NASA Ames Assoc. fellow, 2007. Mem. Am. Astronomical Assn. (divsn. planetary sci., divsn. dynamical astronomy, Harold C. Urey prize divsn. planetary sci. 1992, Chambliss Astronomical Writing award 2007), Internat. Astronomical Union, Am. Geophys. Union. Achievements include research in planetary accretion, extrasolar planets, dynamics of planetary rings, cratering, binary and multiple star systems, circumstellar disks, resonances and chaos. Office: NASA Ames Rsch Ctr Space Sci Astrobiology Divsn 245-3 Moffett Field CA 94035 Business E-Mail: lissauer@jack.nasa.gov.

LIST, ERICSON JOHN, environmental engineering science educator, consultant; b. Whakatane, New Zealand, Mar. 27, 1939; came to U.S., 1962; s. Ericson Bayliss and Freda Helen (Sunkel) L.; m. Olive Amoore, Feb. 3, 1962; children: Brooke Meredith, Antonia Michael. B.E. with honors, U. Auckland, New Zealand, 1961, B.Sc., M.E., U. Auckland, New Zealand, 1962; PhD, Calif. Inst. Tech., 1965. Registered profl. engr., Calif., S.C., N.C., Ga., Fla., Nev. Sr. lectr. U. Auckland, 1966-69; asst. prof. Calif. Inst. Tech., Pasadena, 1969-72, assoc. prof., 1972-78, prof. environ. engring. sci., 1978-97, exec. officer, 1980-85, prof. emeritus, 1997; with Flow Sci. Inc., Pasadena, 1997—. Bd. dirs. Environ. Def. Scis., Pasadena; bd. chmn., prin., cons. Flow Sci. Inc., Pasadena, 1983-. Author: (with Hugo B. Fischer et al), Mixing in Inland and Coastal Waters, 1979, (with W. Rodi) Turbulent Jets and Plumes, 1982, (with Roscoe Moss Co.) Handbook of Ground Water Development, 1990. Mem. Blue Ribbon Commn. City of Pasadena, 1976-78. Recipient Spl. Creativity award NSF, 1982 Fellow ASCE (life, editor Jour. Hydraulic Engring. 1984-89, Athenaeum (Pasadena) (chmn. wine com. 1981-83). Office: Flow Sci Inc 723 E Green St Pasadena CA 91101-2111 Home: 196 Wandolea Dr Mount Pleasant SC 29464-2524 Home Phone: 843-388-8044; Office Phone: 626-233-6014. Business E-Mail: ejlist@flowscience.com.

LIST, ROBERT FRANK, former Governor of Nevada; b. Visalia, Calif., Sept. 1, 1936; s. Frank Way and Alice (Dove) L.; m. Mary Ann Minor, Feb. 23, 1991; children: Suzanne Kathryn, Franklin Mark, Michelle Alice. BS, Utah State U., 1959; JD, U. Calif., San Francisco, 1962. Bar: Nev. 1962, DC 1979. Assoc. Richard Hanna Law Firm, Carson City, Nev., 1962-66, Laxalt, Ross & Laxalt Law Firm, Carson City, 1966-67; dist. atty. Carson City County, 1967-70; atty. gen. State of Nev., Carson City, 1971-78, gov., 1979-83; ptnr. Vargas & Bartlett Law Firm, Reno, 1983-86; sr. ptnr. Beckley, Singleton, DeLanoy, Jemison & List, Chtd., Reno, 1986; CEO Robert List Co. Bd. dirs. First Interstate Bank, N.A., Reno, Clark & Sullivan Constructors, Boomtown Inc., Strotek, Inc., Am. Judicature Soc.; appointed USAF Bd./Visitors Pres. Carter; named to commn. on nat. policy toward gambling Pres. Nixon; named to planning coun. on radioactive wast mgmt. Pres. Carter. Nat. bd. dirs. Am. Cancer Soc., 1977-81. Recipient Humanitarian award Nat. Conf. Christians and Jews, 1980. Mem. ABA, Rocky Mountain Mineral Law Found., Geothermal Resources Coun., Internat. Assn. of Gaming Attys., Nat. Pub. Lands Adv. Coun., D.C. Bar Assn., Western Attys. Gen. Assn. (pres.), Nev. Dist. Attys. Assn. (pres.), Western Gov.'s Assn. (pres.), Nev. State Bar Assn., Washoe County Bar Assn., Clark County Bar Assn., Am. Jud. Soc. (bd. dirs.). Republican. Office: Robert List Co 1975 Village Ctr Cir Ste 140 Las Vegas NV 89134-6255

LISTON, LARRY G., state legislator; m. Mary Ann Liston. Fin. cons.; mem. Dist. 16 Colo. House of Reps., Denver, 2004—. Republican. Office: Colo State Capitol 200 E Colfax Denver CO 80203 Office Phone: 303-866-2965. Business E-Mail: larry.liston.house@state.co.us.*

LITEWKA, ALBERT BERNARD, entertainment executive; s. Joel and Leah L. BA summa cum laude, UCLA, 1964; postgrad., U. Calif., Berkeley, 1964-65. Mgr. purchasing McGraw-Hill Book Co., NYC, 1965-67; pres. Mktg. Innovations, Inc., NYC, 1967-69; v.p. Westinghouse Leisure Time Industries, NYC, 1972-75; exec. v.p. mktg. The Baker & Taylor Co. (W.R. Grace & Co.), NYC, 1975-77; pres. Pix of Am. (W. R. Grace & Co.), NYC, 1978; v.p. consumer services group W.R. Grace & Co., NYC, 1977-79; pres. Macmillan Gen. Books div., NYC, 1980-82; sr. v.p. Macmillan Pub. Co., Inc., 1980-82; pres. Warner Software, Inc., 1982-85; chmn., CEO Air Creative Group, L.A. and NYC, 1986-98, Creative Domain, Inc., LA, 1991—2005, Winning Entertainment, LA, 2005—. Author: Warsaw: A Novel of Resistance, 1989. Chmn. bd. trustees Oakwood Sch., 2003—06. Internat. Ladies Garment Workers Union Nat. scholar, 1959-64, U. Calif. Regents scholar, 1959-64; Woodrow Wilson Nat. Grad. fellow, 1964-65; recipient 1st prize Acad. Am. Poets, 1964. Mem. Am. Film Inst., Authors Guild, Authors League Am., Acad. TV Arts & Scis. Home: 2020 Nichols Canyon Rd Los Angeles CA 90046-1728

LITHGOW, JOHN ARTHUR, actor; b. Rochester, NY, Oct. 19, 1945; s. Arthur and Sarah Jane (Price) L.; m. Jean Taynton, Sept. 10, 1966 (div.); 1 child, Ian; m. Mary Yeager, 1981; children: Phoebe, Nathan. Grad. magna cum laude, Harvard U., 1967; postgrad., London Acad. Music and Dramatic Art, 1967-69; ArtsD (hon.), Harvard U., 2005. Printmaker, founder Lithgow Graphics. Actor: (films) Obsession, 1976, The Big Fix, 1978, Rich Kids, 1979, All That Jazz, 1979, Blow Out, 1981, I'm Dancing as Fast as I Can, 1982, The World According to Garp, 1982, Twilight Zone: The Movie, 1983, Terms of Endearment, 1983, 2010: The Year We Make Contact, 1984, Footloose, 1984, Adventures of Buckaroo Banzai Across the 8th Dimension, 1984, The Glitter Dome, 1984, Santa Claus: The Movie, 1985, Mesmerized, 1986, The Manhattan Project, 1986, Harry and the Hendersons, 1987, Distant Thunder, 1988, Out Cold, 1989, Memphis Belle, 1990, At Play in the Fields of the Lord, 1991, Richochet, 1991, Raising Cain, 1992, Cliffhanger, 1993, The Pelican Brief, 1993, Good Man in Africa, 1994, Silent Fall, 1994, Princess Caraboo, 1994, Hollow Point, 1995, (voice only)Special Effects: Anything Can Happen, 1996, Officer Buckle and Gloria, 1998, Johhny Skidmarks, 1998, Homegrown, 1998, A Civil Action, 1998, Portofino, 1999, (voice only) Rugrats in Paris: The Movie-Rugrats II, 2000, C-Scam, 2000, (voice only) Shrek, 2001, Orange County, 2002, The Life and Death of Peter Sellers, 2004, Kinsey, 2004, Dreamgirls, 2006, Confessions of a Shopaholic, 2009; (TV movies) Mom, the Wolfman and Me, 1983, Not in Front of the Children, 1982, The Day After, 1983, Resting Place, 1986, Baby Girl Scott, 1987, Traveling Man, 1989, Ivory Hunters, 1990, The Boys, 1991, The Wrong Man, 1993, Love, Cheat and Steal, 1993, Then There Were Giants, 1994, American Cinema, 1994, World War II: When Lions Roared, 1994, The Tuskegee Airmen, 1995, My Brother's Keeper, 1995, Redwood Curtain, 1995, Christmas in Washington, 1996, E=mc², 2005; (TV series) 3rd Rock from the Sun, 1996-2001 (Emmy for Outstanding Lead Actor in a Comedy Series 1996, 97, 99, Golden Globe award for Best Actor in a TV Series Musical and Comedy 1996), Twenty Good Years, 2006; (mini-series) Don Quixote, 1999; (TV appearances) Amazing Stories, 1985 (Emmy for Outstanding Guest Performer in a Drama Series 1986), Tales from the Crypt, 1989, Cosby, 1996, Paloozaville, 2008; (Broadway plays) Sweet Smell of Success, 2000-03 (Tony for Best Male Actor 2002), The Retreat from Moscow, 2004, Dirty Rotten Scoundrels, 2005, All My Sons, 2008; (one man shows) John Lithgow: Stories by Heart, 2008; singer: (albums) Singing in the Bathtub, 1999; author: (children's books) The Remarkable Farkle McBride, 2000, Marsupial Sue, 2001, I'm a Manatee, 2003, Carnival of the Animals, 2004. Named to Theater Hall of Fame, 2005.

LITMAN, ROBERT BARRY, physician, writer, television and radio commentator; b. Phila., Nov. 17, 1947; s. Benjamin Norman and Bette Etta (Saunders) L.; m. Niki Thomas, Apr. 21, 1985; children: Riva Belle, Nadya Beth, Caila Tess, Benjamin David. BS, Yale U., New Haven, Conn., 1968, MD, 1970, MS, MPhil in Anatomy, 1972. Diplomate Am. Bd. Family Practice, Am. Bd. Family Medicine, 2008. Postdoct. rsch. fellow Am. Cancer Soc. Yale U., New Haven, 1970-73, USPHS fellow, 1974-75; resident in gen. surgery Bryn Mawr Hosp., Pa., 1973-74; pvt. practice in medicine and surgery Ogdensburg, NY, 1977-93, San Ramon, Calif., 1993—; mem. staff A. Barton Hepburn Hosp., 1977-93, John Muir Med. Ctr., 1993—, San Ramon Regional Med. Ctr., 1993—, also chmn. med. edn., chmn. dept. family practice, 1998-99, chmn. med. edn., 2004—06. Commentator Family Medicine Stas. WWNY-TV and WTNY-Radio, TCI Cablevision, Contra Costa T.V.; moderator Ask the Dr.; clin. preceptor dept. family medicine State U. Health Sci. Ctr., Syracuse, 1978—. Author: Wynnefield and Limer, 1983, The Treblinka Virus, 1991, Allergy Shots, 1993; contbr. articles to numerous profl. jours. Pres. No. NY chpt. AHA. Fellow Life Ins. Med. Rsch. Fund, U. Coll. Hosp., U. London, 1969-70; recipient We. Access Video Excellence award, 1998, 2001, Bay Area Cable Excellence award, 1999, Telly award, 1999-2005, 06-08. Fellow Am. Coll. Allergy, Asthma, and Immunology, Am. Acad. Family Physicians; mem. AMA (Physicians Recognition award 1970—), Calif. State Med. Assn., Alameda-Contra Costa County Med. Assn., Joint Coun. Allergy and Immunology, Nat. Assn. Physician Broadcasters (charter), Acad. Radio and TV Health Communicators, Book and Snake Soc., Gibbs Soc. Yale U. (founder), Sigma Xi, Nu Sigma Nu, Alpha Chi Sigma. Home and Office: PO Box 1857 San Ramon CA 94583-6857

LITT, IRIS FIGARSKY, pediatrics educator; b. NYC, Dec. 25, 1940; d. Jacob and Bertha (Berson) Figarsky; m. Victor C. Vaughan, June 14, 1987; children from previous marriage: William M., Robert B. AB, Cornell U., 1961; MD, SUNY, Bklyn., 1965. Diplomate Am. Bd. Pediatrics (bd. dirs. 1989-94), sub-specialty bd. cert. in adolescent medicine. Intern, then resident in pediat. N.Y. Hosp., NYC, 1965-68; assoc. prof. pediat. Stanford U. Sch. Medicine, Palo Alto, Calif., 1982-87, prof., 1987—, dir. divsn. pediatrics and adolescent medicine, 1976—, dir. Inst. for Rsch. on Women and Gender, 1990-97. Editor Jour. Adolescent Health; contbr. articles to profl. jours including Jour. Am. Med. Assn., Pediatrics. Mem. Soc. for Adolescent Medicine (charter), Am. Acad. Pediatrics (award sect. on adolescent health), Western Soc. Pediatric Rsch., Soc. Pediatric Rsch., Am. Pediatric Soc., Inst. of Medicine/NAS. Office: 750 Welch Rd Ste 325 Palo Alto CA 94304-1510 E-mail: iris.litt@stanford.edu.

LITTLE, BRAD, Lieutenant Governor of Idaho, former state legislator; b. Emmett, Idaho, Feb. 15, 1954; m. Teresa Little; children: Adam, David. BS, U. Idaho, 1977. Mem. Idaho State Senate from Dist. 11, 2000—09, mem. Resources & Environ., State Affairs and Transp. Com., maj. caucus chmn.; lt. gov. State of Idaho, 2009—. Vice chair Emmett Pub. Sch. Found., 2004, Idaho Cmty. Found., 2004. Recipient Honorary Lifetime Membership award, Boise State U. Alumni Assn. Republican. Episcopalian. Office: State Capitol Bldg #339, PO Box 83720 Boise ID 83720-0081 also: PO Box 488 Emmett ID 83617-0488 also: Office of Lt Gov Rm 225, State Capitol Boise ID 83720-0057 Home Phone: 208-365-6566; Office Phone: 208-332-1000, 208-365-4611. Fax: 208-365-4615. E-mail: blittle@senate.state.id.us.*

LITTLE, (WILLIAM) GRADY, former professional baseball coach, team manager; b. Abilene, Tex., Mar. 30, 1950; m. Debi Little; 1 child, Eric. Minor league player-coach West Haven Yankees, Conn., 1971—73, minor league coach, 1974, Bluefield Orioles, Md., 1980; cotton farmer Tex., 1975—79; minor league mgr. Hagerstown Suns, 1981—82, 1984, Charlotte O's, 1983—84, Kinston Blue Jays, 1985, Pulaski Braves, 1986—87, Burlington Braves, 1988, Durham Bulls, 1988—91, Greenville Braves, 1992, Grand Canyon Rafters, 1992, Richmond Braves, 1993—95; bullpen coach San Diego Padres, 1996; bench coach Boston Red Sox, 1997—99, mgr., 2002—03, LA Dodgers, 2006—07; bench coach Cleve. Indians, 2000—00; spl. asst. to gen. mgr., minor league catching instr. Chgo. Cubs, 2004—05. With USMCR, 1969. Named Carolina League Mgr. of Yr., 1981, 1989, Southern League Mgr. of Yr., 1992, Minor League Mgr. of Yr., Sporting News, 1992, Baseball Am., 1992, Internat. League Mgr. of Yr., 1994; named to Ariz. Fall League Hall of Fame, 2006. Achievements include 93 wins in the 2002 season, the most by a rookie Major League manager since Jim Frey with 97 in 1980.

LITTLE, RICH (RICHARD CARUTHERS LITTLE), comedian, impressionist, actor; b. Ottawa, Ont., Can., Nov. 26, 1938; s. Lawrence Peniston and Elizabeth Maud (Wilson) L. Student, Lisgar Collegiate, Ottawa, 1953-57; student drama, Ottawa Little Theatre, 1950-60. First TV appearance in U.S. on Judy Garland Show, 1964; appearances films, TV, night clubs; host: TV series The Rich Little Show, 1975-76 (Winner Entertainer of Year award 1974), You Asked For It, 1981-83; appeared on TV series Love on a Rooftop, 1966-71, The John Davidson Show, 1969, ABC Comedy Hour, 1972, The Julie Andrews Hour, 1972-73; TV film appearance Dirty Tricks, 1981, Rich Little's Christmas Card, Rich Little's Washington Follies, Parade of Stars, The Christmas Raccoons, Rich Little and Friends in New Orleans, The Late Shift, 1996, (films) Bsetter Off Dead, 1985, One Crazy Summer, 1986, (voice) Bebe's Kids, 1992; others; rec. albums include My Fellow Canadians, The First Family Rides Again; appeared in films Dirty Tricks, 1981, Happy Hour, 1987. Recipient Maple Leaf Disting. Arts and Letters award, 1983. Office: William Morris Agy 151 S El Camino Dr Beverly Hills CA 90212-2775

LITTLE, WILLIAM ARTHUR, physicist, researcher; b. South Africa, Nov. 17, 1930; came to U.S., 1958, naturalized, 1964; s. William Henry and Margaret (Macleod) L.; m. Annie W. Smith, July 15, 1955; children— Lucy Claire, Linda Susan, Jonathan William. PhD, Rhodes U., S. Africa, 1953, Glasgow U., Scotland, 1957. Faculty Stanford, 1958—, prof. physics, 1965-94; prof. emeritus, 1994—. Cons. to industry, 1960—; co-founder, chmn. MMR Techs. Inc., 1980—, 3L&T, Inc., 1999—. Recipient Deans award disting. tchg. Stanford U., 1975-76, Walter J. Gores award for excellence in tchg., Stanford U., 1979, IR-100 award Indsl. R&D, 1981, R&D 100 award, 2006, Samuel C. Collins award, 2007; NRC Can. postdoctoral fellow Vancouver, Can., 1956-58, Sloan Found. fellow, 1959-63, John Simon Guggenheim fellow, 1964-65, NSF sr. postdoctoral fellow, 1970-71. Fellow Am. Phys. Soc.; mem. Am. Chem. Soc. Achievements include spl. research low temperature physics, superconductivity, neural network theory, cryogenics; holder 24 patents in area of cryogenics and med. instrumentation. Home: 15 Crescent Dr Palo Alto CA 94301-3106 Office: Stanford U Dept Physics Stanford CA 94305 Business E-Mail: bill@mmr.com.

LITTLE RICHARD, (RICHARD WAYNE PENNIMAN), musician, lyricist, minister; b. Macon, Ga., Dec. 5, 1932; s. Bud and Leva Mae Penniman; m. Ernestine Campbell, 1957 (div.). BA, Oakwood Coll. Sem., Huntsville, Ala., 1961. Ordained to ministry Seventh Day Adventist Ch., 1961 (performed marriage of Bruce Willis and Demi Moore, Las Vegas). Began singing and dancing on streets of Macon, Ga., 1942; won talent shows in Atlanta, 1943 and 1951; toured with Dr. Hudson's Medicine Show and other shows, 1949-51; worked with own band doing dances and clubs, 1951-52, with Tempo Toppers in New Orleans, 1953-54; recording artist Peacock Records, Houston, 1953-54, Splty. Records, 1955-58, 64; toured in Big 10 Package shows, U.S., Australia and Gt. Brit., 1957-58; recording artist Veejay Records, 1964-65. Songs include Long Tall Sally, Tutti Frutti, Slippin' and Slidin', Rip it Up, Ready Teddy, Lucille, Send Me Some Lovin', Jenny, Jenny, Miss Ann, Keep A-Knockin', Good Golly Miss Molly, Baby Face, True Fine Mama, Kansas City, Bama Lama Bama Loo, Freedom Blues, Greenwood Mississippi; albums include Here's Little Richard, 1958, Little Richard 2, 1958, The Fabulous, 1959, Well Alright, 1959, Sings Gospel, 1964, Coming Home, 1964, Sings Freedom Songs, 1964, King of Gospel Songs, 1965, Wild & Frantic, 1965, The Explosive, 1967, The Explosive & Roy Orbison, 1970, The Rill Thing, 1971, King of Rock N Roll, 1971, Second Coming, 1971, All Time Hits, 1972, Rock Hard Rock Heavy, 1972, The Very Best Of, 1975, Georgia Peach, 1980, Get Down With It, 1982, Ooh! My Soul, 1983, Lucile, 1984, Shut Up, 1988, The Specialty Sessions, 1990, Greatest Songs, 1995, Mega-Mix, 1995; film appearances include The Girl Can't Help It, 1956, Don't Knock the Rock, 1957, She's Got It, 1957, Mr. Rock and Roll, 1957, Jimi Plays Berkeley, 1970, Let the Good Times Roll, 1973, Jimi Hendrix, 1973, Down and Out in Beverly Hills, 1985 Chuck Berry Hail! Hail! Rock 'n' Roll, 1987, Purple People Eater, 1988, Scenes from the Class Struggle in Beverly Hills, 1989, Magic Years, Vols. 1-3, 1989, Sunset Heat, 1991, The Naked Truth, 1992, The Last Action Hero, 1993, The Pickle, 1993, The History of Rock 'n' Roll, Vol. 1, 1995, Why Do Fools Fall in Love, 1998, Mystery, Alaska, 1999; TV appearances include Tonight Show, Merv Griffin Show, Mike Douglas Show, Smothers Brothers Show, American Bandstand, Glen Campbell Good Time Hour, Tom Jones Show, Midnight Special, Donny & Marie Show, The Godess of Love, 1988, Mother Goose Rock 'n' Rhyme, 1990, Happy Birthday Bugs!: 50 Looney Years, 1990, Columbo: Columbo & the Murder of a Rock Star, Sinatra: 80 Years My Way, 1995, The Late Shift, 1996,

The Fifties, 1997, Motown 40: The Music is Forever, 1998, Hollywood Squares, 1998; stage appearances include Paramount Theatre, The Felt Forum, Wembley Stadium, Hollywood Paladium. Inducted Rock & Roll Hall of Fame, 1986. Achievements include being referred to as the Architect of Rock 'n Roll.

LITTMAN, IRVING, forest products company executive; b. Denver, Apr. 21, 1940; s. Maurice Littman and Cecile P. Zohn.; m. Gertrude Pepper, Aug. 16, 1964; children: Margaret R., Michael J., Elizabeth B. BS in Engring. (Applied Math.), U. Colo., 1964; MBA, U. Chgo., 1966. Mgr. corp. sys. Boise Cascade Corp., Idaho, 1966-68, corp. mgr. budgeting Idaho, 1968-71, asst. to pres. Idaho, 1971-73, asst. contr. realty group Palo Alto, Calif., 1973-76, dir. investor rels. Boise, 1976-84, treas., 1984-86, v.p., treas., 1986—. Bd. dirs. Idaho Humanities Coun., Boise, 1985-88, vice chair, 1987-88; trustee Boise H.S. Band Scholarship Endowment, 1987—; trustee Boise Art Mus., 1996—, treas., 1998—; referee US Soccer Fedn., 1982—; investment com. Idaho Cmty. Found., 1989—, chmn. investment com., 1991—, treas., 1997—. With U.S. Army, 1958-59. Mem. Bogus Basin Ski Area Assn. (bd. dirs. 1988-97, treas. 1989-94, vice-chmn. 1991-94, chmn. 1994-96), Treas. Club San Francisco, Fin. Execs. Inst., Crane Creek Country Club, Arid Club (Boise).

LITTMAN, RICHARD ANTON, psychologist, educator; b. NYC, May 8, 1919; s. Joseph and Sarah (Feinberg) L.; m. Isabelle Cohen, Mar. 17, 1941; children— David, Barbara, Daniel, Rebecca. AB, George Washington U., 1943; postgrad., Ind. U., 1943-44; PhD, Ohio State U., 1948. Faculty U. Oreg., 1948—, prof. psychology, 1959—, chmn. dept., 1963-68, vice provost acad. planning and resources, 1971-73, prof. emeritus, 1990. Vis. scientist Nat. Inst. Mental Health, 1958-59 Contbr. articles to profl. jours. Sr. postdoctoral fellow NSF, U. Paris, 1966-67; sr. fellow Nat. Endowment for Humanities, U. London, 1973-74; Ford Found. fellow, 1952-53; recipient U. Oreg. Charles H. Johnson Meml. award, 1980. Mem. APA, Western Psychol. Assn., Am. Psychol. Soc., Soc. Research and Child Devel., Psychonomics Soc., Animal Behavior Soc., Soc. Psychol. Study of Social Issues, Internat. Soc. Developmental Psychobiology, History of Sci. Soc., Am. Philos. Assn., AAUP, Sigma Xi. Home: 3625 Glen Oak Dr Eugene OR 97405-4736 Office: U Oreg Dept Psychology Eugene OR 97403 Business E-Mail: rlittman@uoregon.edu.

LITVACK, MARK D., lawyer; b. 1958; BA, Hamilton Coll., 1980; JD, Northwestern U. Sch. Law, 1995. Bar: Conn. 1983, NY 1984, Calif. 1995. Sr. atty. Texaco Inc.; v.p., dir., legal affairs, world-wide anti-piracy Motion Picture Assn. Am.; ptnr. Mitchell Silberberg & Knupp, Manatt, Phelps & Phillips, LA, 2006—. Mem.: Fed. Bar Assn., NY Bar Assn., Conn. Bar Assn., ABA (counsel mem., Sci. and Tech. com.). Office: Manatt Phelps & Phillips LLP Trident Ctr East Tower 11355 W Olympic Blvd Los Angeles CA 90064 Office Phone: 310-312-4121. Office Fax: 310-312-4224.

LITWACK, GERALD, biochemistry researcher, educator, administrator; b. Boston, Jan. 11, 1929; s. David and Edith Jean (Berkman) Lytell; m. Patricia Lynn Gorog, Feb., 1956 (div. 1973); 1 child, Claudia; m. Ellen Judith Schatz, Aug. 31, 1973; children: Geoffrey Sandor, Katherine Victoria. BA, Hobart Coll., 1949; MS, U. Wis., 1950, PhD, 1953. Postdoctoral fellow Biochem. Labs. U. Paris, 1953-54; asst. prof. Rutgers U., New Brunswick, NJ, 1954-60; trainee Oak Ridge Inst. Nuc. Studies, 1955; assoc. prof. U. Pa., Phila., 1960-64; Carnell prof., dep. dir. Fels Inst., Sch. of Medicine Temple U., Phila., 1964-91; prof., chair dept. pharmacology Thomas Jefferson U., Phila., 1991-96, also dep. dir. Kimmel Cancer Inst., 1991-97; assoc. dir. for basic sci. Kimmel Cancer Ctr., Phila., 1992-97, prof., chmn. dept. biochemistry and molecular pharmacology, 1996—2003, emeritus, 2003, dir. Ctr. Apoptosis Rsch., assoc. dean sci. affairs, 1996-2001, vice dean for rsch., 2001—03; vis. scholar Dept. Biol. Chemistry David Geffen Sch. Medicine UCLA, 2004—. Chmn. adv. com. am. Cancer Soc., NYC, 1977-80; mem. adv. panel NSF, Washington, 1980-84; mem. ad hoc panels NIH, Bethesda, 1985, 89, reviewer, 1977, 84, 91, cons. Nat. Inst. Environ. Health Sci., 1982; mem. ad hoc panels Israel Cancer Rsch. fund Sci. Rev. Panel, 1992-93, US Army Breast Cancer Study Sect., 1994; mem. US Army Neurotoxicology and Neurodegeneration Study Sect., 1997, NIH, NIDDK, subcom. B Study Sect.,1998, NIH, NIDDK Spl. Emphasis Panel, Primary Reviewer Molecular Endocrinology,2003, others; councilor Soc. for Exptl. Biology and Medicine, NYC, 1984-88; cons. Franklin Inst., 1976, Georgetown U., 1980; reviewer Haverford Coll., 1976, NIH programs, 1984, 91; mem. adv. bd. Diabetes Rsch. Ctr. U. Pa., 1996—; mem. joint steering com. for pub. policy Rockville, Md., 1997—; evaluator Roswell Park Meml. Inst., 1978; mem. sci. adv. bd. Norris Cotton Cancer Ctr. Dartmouth Med. Sch., 1984—; Jefferson rep. U. Catania, Sicily, 1994— 2001, U Naples, Italy, 2001--; mem. subcom. B study sect. NIH, NIDDK, 1998; mem. subcom. on rsch. Sharpe-Strumia Found., 1998—; external reviewer NICHD, NIH, 1999; vis. prof. U. Calif., Berkeley, 1956, U. Calif., San Francisco, 1972; hon. prof. biochemistry Rutgers U., 1957-60; vis. scientist Courthauld Inst. Biochemistry, U. London, 1971; mem. study sect. SPORE breast and prostate cancer rsch., NIH and NCI, 2000-01; vis. scholar dept. biol. chemistry David A. Geffen Sch. Medicine at UCLA, 2004—. Bd. dirs. Sharpe-Strumia Found. Bryn Mawr Hosp., 1997—2003. Recipient Rsch. Career Devel. award NIAMD, NIH, 1963-69, Pub. Svc. award Chapel of Four Chaplains, 1977, Faculty Rsch. award Temple U., 1987. Mem. Endocrine Soc. (program com. 1991-93, sci. and edn. com. 1992-93, ann. meeting steering com. 1990-93, com. on sci. and ednl. programs 1992-93), Am. Soc. Biochemistry and Molecular Biology, Am. Soc. Pharmacology and Exptl. Therapeutics, Am. Assn. Cancer Rsch. (chair task force on endocrinology 1995, endocrinology and signal transduction subcom., program com., 1995-96, Tellers Com., 2002), Am. Chem. Soc., Assn. of Am. Med. Coll. (GREAT group 1997—2003, congl. liaison 1998-2003), Assn. for Med. Sch. Pharmacology, Assn. of Med. and Grad. Dept. of Biochemistry. Achievements include discovery and identification of the glucocorticoid receptor; co-discovery of ligandin (glutathione S-Transferase family) mechanism of glucocorticoid receptor activation, studies in apoptosis, immunophilin signal transduction, basic studies in asthma, glucocorticoid induced gene expression. Office: 4610 Ledge Ave Toluca Lake CA 91602 Business E-Mail: gerry.litwack@mail.tju.edu.

LITWACK, LEON FRANK, historian, retired educator; b. Santa Barbara, Calif., Dec. 2, 1929; s. Julius and Minnie (Nitkin) L.; m. Rhoda Lee Goldberg, July 5, 1952; children: John Michael, Ann Katherine. BA, U. Calif., Berkeley, 1951, MA, 1952, PhD, 1958. Asst. prof., then assoc. prof. history U. Wis., Madison, 1958-65; dir. NDEA Inst. Am. History, summer 1965; mem. faculty U. Calif., Berkeley, 1965—2007, prof. history, 1971—2007, Alexander F. and May T. Morrison prof. history, 1987—2007, prof. emeritus, 2007, Morrison prof. history emeritus, 2007. Vis. prof. U. S.C., 1975, Colo. Coll., Sept. 1974, 79, La. State U., 1985; Fulbright prof. Am. history U. Sydney, Australia, 1991, Moscow (USSR) State U., 1980; Wentworth scholar-in-residence U. Fla., Spring 1983; mem. Nat. Afro-Am. History and Culture Commn., 1981-83; mem. screening com. Fulbright Sr. Scholar Awards, 1983-86; bd. acad. advisors The American Experience Sta. WGBH-TV, 1986—, Africans in America, WGBH-TV, 1990-98; Ford Found. prof. So. studies U. Miss., 1989; mem. exec. com. of dels. Am. Coun. of Learned Socs., 1993-96; lectr. in field. Author: North of Slavery: The Negro in the Free States, 1790-1860, 1961, Been in the Storm So Long: The Aftermath of Slavery, 1979, Trouble in Mind: Black Southerners in the Age of Jim Crow, 1998; (film) To Look for America, 1971; co-author: The United States, 1981, rev. edit., 1991, Without Sanctuary: Lynching Photography in America, 2000; editor: American Labor Movement, 1962; co-editor: Reconstruction, 1969, Black Leaders in the Nineteenth Century, 1988, Harvard Guide to African American History, 2001. Mem. Bradley Commn. on History in Schs., 1987-90, Schomburg Commn. for the Preservation of Black Culture; trustee Nat. Coun. for History Edn., 1990-96, mem. steering com. 1994 NAEP History Consensus Project; chair U. Calif. Acad. Senate Libr. Com. 1995-97. Served with AUS, 1953-55. Recipient Excellence in Teaching award U. Calif., Berkeley, 1967, 95, Disting. Tchg. award, 1971, 95 Mem. Orgn. Am. Historians (chmn. nominations bd. 1975-76, exec. bd. 1983-85, pres. 1986-87), Am. Hist. Assn. (chmn. program com. 1980-81), So. Hist. Assn. (bd. dirs. 2003-05, pres. 2007—), So. Historian Assn. (pres. 2007—), Am. Acad. Arts and Scis., Am. Antiquarian Soc., U. Calif. Alumni Assn., Assn. for the Study African Am. Life and History, PEN Am. Ctr. Office: U Calif Dept History 3229 Dwinelle Hall Berkeley CA 94720-2550 Business E-Mail: llitwack@berkeley.edu.

LIU, CHEN-CHING, electrical engineering educator; b. Tainan, Taiwan, Dec. 30, 1954; came to the U.S., 1980; m. Judy Y. Chuvan; 1 child, Wendy. BSEE, Nat. Taiwan U., 1976, MSEE, 1978; PhD, U. Calif., Berkeley, 1983. Asst. prof. U. Wash., Seattle, 1983-87, assoc. prof., 1987-91, prof., 1991—. Program dir. NSF, Arlington, Va., 1994-95; Tokyo Electric Power chair U. Tokyo, 1991; prof. invite Swiss Fed. Inst. Tech., Lausanne, 1989. Editor: Engring. Intelligent Systems, 1993—; mem. editl. bd. Procs. of IEEE; assoc. editor: IEEE Trans. Circuits and Systems. Fellow IEEE; mem. Internat. Coun. on Intelligent System Application to Power Systems (pres., steering com.), IEEE Power Engring. Soc. (chair history com. 1992—, mem. governing bd. 1992—). Achievements include pioneered artificial intelligence applications to power systems; development of theories for power system voltage dynamics, computational methods for power electronic circuits, knowledge engineering methods. Office: U Wash Dept Elec Engring Seattle WA 98195-0001

LIU, DEREK, Internet company executive; b. Kowloon, Hong Kong, Apr. 15, 1974; Tech. support Ascend Comm., network support engr., product mgr.; with Lucent Technologies; co-founder Studio XD; co-founder, chief tech. officer Gaia Interactive, 2003—. Office: Gaia Interactive, Inc Ste 125 50 Airport Parkway San Jose CA 95110

LIU, KAI, physics professor; b. Changzhou, Jiangsu, China; PhD, Johns Hopkins U., Balt., 1998. Asst. prof. U. Calif., Davis, 2001—05, assoc. prof., 2005—08, prof., 2008—. Jr. faculty rsch. fellow U. Calif. Davis, 2003, chancellor's fellow, 2007—; presenter in field. Contbr. articles to profl. jours. Grantee, Lawrence Livermore Nat. Lab., 2002—03, 2003—04, 2003—05, NSF, 2002—05, 2005—06, 2007—, U. Calif., 2003—06, 2004—06, Am. Chem. Soc., Petroleum Rsch. Fund, 2003—05, 2005—08; fellow, Alfred P. Sloan Found., 2005—07. Mem.: Neutron Scattering Soc. Am., Am. Vacuum Soc., Am. Phys. Soc. Achievements include patents in field. Office: UC Davis Physics Dept One Shields Ave Davis CA 95616 Office Fax: 530-752-4717. E-mail: kailiu@ucdavis.edu.

LIU, PETER, bank executive; Former sr. v.p. Credit Suisse First Boston; former v.p. Chase Manhattan Bank; former regional COO UBS Investment Bank; former sector head, bus. consulting svc. IBM China/Hong Kong Limited; former chief info. officer Bank of China Hong Kong; founder, vice chmn. New Resource Bank, 2006—. Adv. bd. Clean Tech. Investment Advisory Calif. Public Employees Retirement System; adv. bd. Calif. Teachers' Retirement System; co-founder, vice-chair China-U.S. Energy Efficiency Alliance. Office: New Resource Bank 405 Howard St Ste 110 San Francisco CA 94105

LIU, YOUNG KING, biomedical engineering educator; b. Nanjing, China, May 3, 1934; came to U.S., 1952; s. Yih Ling and Man Fun (Teng) L.; m. Nina Pauline Liu, Sept. 4, 1964 (div. July 1986); children— Erik, Tania; m. Anita Beeth, Aug. 14, 1994 (div. Aug. 2000). BSME, Bradley U., 1955; MSME, U. Wis.-Madison, 1959; PhD, Wayne State U., 1963. Cert. acupuncturist, Calif. Asst. prof. Milw. Sch. of Engring., 1956—59; instr. Wayne State U., Detroit, 1960—63; lectr. then asst. prof. U. Mich., Ann Arbor, 1963—69; assoc. prof. then prof. Tulane U., New Orleans, 1969—78; prof. biomed. engring., dir. dept. U. Iowa, Iowa City, 1978—93; pres. U. No. Calif., Petaluma, 1993—; interim pres., CEO Calif. Coll. Podiatric Medicine, 2000—01. COO, 3DMetrics, Inc., 2001—03. Contbr. articles to profl. jours., chpts. to books NIH spl. research fellow, 1968-69; recipient Research Career Devel. award NIH, 1971-76 Mem. Internat. Soc. Lumbar Spine (exec. com., ctrl. U.S. rep. 1983-88), Orthopedic Research Soc., Am. Soc. Engring. Edn., Sigma Xi Democrat. Office Phone: 707-765-5960, 707-636-5964. Personal E-mail: ykingliu@yahoo.com. Business E-Mail: ykingliu@uncm.edu.

LIVERMORE, ANN MARTINELLI, computer company executive; b. Greensboro, NC, Aug. 23, 1958; m. Tom Livermore. BA in Econs., U. NC, Chapel Hill, 1980; MBA, Stanford U., 1982. Various mgmt. positions Hewlett-Packard Co., Palo Alto, Calif., 1982-1995, corp. v.p., 1995—2002, pres., CEO enterprise computing divsn., 1998—2003, exec. v.p., 2002—, exec. v.p. tech. solutions group, 2004—. Bd. dirs. United Parcel Svc., 1997—; bd. advs. Stanford Bus. Sch.; bd. visitors Kenan-Flagler Bus. Sch. Named one of 100 Most Powerful Women in Bus., Forbes mag., 2005—08, 50 Women to Watch, Wall St. Jour., 2006, 50 Most Powerful Women in Bus., Fortune mag., 2006, 2007, 2008, Most Influential Women in Technology, Fast Company, 2009.*

LIVERMORE, JOHN S., geologist; Founder Pub. Resource Assocs., Reno, Nev. Recipient Daniel C. Jackling award Soc. for Mining, Metallurgy and Exploration, 1996, Disting. Nevadan award U. Nev., 1997; named to Nat. Mining Hall of Fame, 2000. Office: Pub Resource Assocs 1755 E Plumb Ln Ste 170 Reno NV 89502-3683

LIVERMORE, SAMUEL MORGAN, lawyer; s. Norman Banks Livermore, Jr. and Virginia Pennoyer Livermore; m. Cynthia Saranec Livermore, Jan. 11, 1975; children: Sealy, Morgan. AB summa cum laude, Dartmouth Coll., Hanover, NH, 1973; MSc, London U., 1974; JD, Stanford U., Palo Alto, Calif., 1978. Bar: Calif. 1978, U.S. Dist. Ct. (no. dist.) Calif. 1978. Assoc. Thelen Marrin Johnson & Bridges, San Francisco, 1978—85, ptnr., 1986—92, Sheppard Mullin Richter & Hampton LLP, San Francisco, 1992—96, Cooley Godward Kronish, LLP, San Francisco, 1996—. Mem. mgmt. com. Cooley Godward Kronish, LLP, San Francisco, 2003—, head San Francisco bus. and tech., 2003—. Bd. mem., chmn. Marin County Day Sch., Corte Madera, Calif., 1979—86; founder, bd. mem., chmn. The Yosemite Fund, San Francisco, 1988—; bd. mem. Save-the-Redwoods League, San Francisco, 1998—. Recipient Barrett Cup, Dartmouth Coll., 1973, 20th Anniversary award, Yosemite Fund, 2006. Mem.: ABA, Lagunitas Country Club, Pacific-Union Club. Avocations: outdoor recreation, camping, hunting, fishing. Office: Cooley Godward Kronish LLP 5th Fl 101 California St San Francisco CA 94111 Office Fax: 415-276-5743.

LIVINGSTON, JOHNSTON REDMOND, manufacturing executive; b. Foochow, China, Dec. 18, 1923; s. Henry Walter V and Alice (Moorehead) Livingston; m. Caroline Johnson, Aug. 17, 1946 (dec.); children: Henry, Ann, Jane, David; m. Patricia Karolchuck, Sept. 4, 1965. BS in Engring. with honors, Yale U., 1947; MBA with distinction, Harvard U., 1949. With Mpls.-Honeywell Regulator Co., 1949-55; with Whirlpool Corp., 1956-66, v.p., until 1966, Redman Industries, Dallas, 1966-67; dir. Constrn. Tech., Inc., Dallas, 1967—, pres., chmn. bd. dirs. Denver, 1974-89; chmn. bd. dirs. Enmark Corp., Denver, 1979-90. Pres. Marcor Housing Sys., Inc., Denver, 1971-74. Past mem. industry adv. com. Nat. Housing Ctr.; bd. dirs., past pres. Nat. Home Improvement Coun.; pres., chmn. bd. dirs. Denver Symphony Assn., 1977-81; bd. dirs., past chmn. bd. dirs. Rocky Mountain Regional Inst. Internat. Edn.; trustee, chmn. emeritus, bd. dirs. Bonfils-Stanton Found., Denver, 1979—; hon. trustee Inst. Internat. Edn., N.Y. Recipient Internat. Leadership award Rocky Mountain Regional Inst. Internat. Edn., 2003; Baker scholar, Harvard U., 1949. Mem. Rocky Mountain World Trade Assn. (bd. dirs., past chmn. bd. dirs.), Denver Country Club, Yale Club N.Y., Sigma Xi, Tau Beta Pi. Home: 2800 S University Blvd No 27 Denver CO 80210 Office: 5070 Oakland St Denver CO 80239-2724

LIVINGSTON, LOUIS BAYER, lawyer; b. NYC, Dec. 12, 1941; s. Norman and Helen (Bayer) L.; m. Mari Livingston, Apr. 6, 1968; children: Diana, Alex, Ann. BA, Yale U., 1963; LLB, Harvard U., 1966. Bar: N.Y. 1967, Oreg. 1971. Atty. NLRB, Memphis, 1967-68, Poletti, Freidin et al., NYC, 1968-71; ptnr. Miller Nash LLP, Portland, Oreg., 1971—. Office: Miller Nash LLP 111 SW 5th Ave Ste 3400 Portland OR 97204-3699

LIVINGSTON, STANLEY C., architect; BArch, U. So. Calif., 1961; student, U. Calif., San Diego. Lic. architect Calif., N.Mex., Nev., Ariz., Colo., Ky.; cert. Nat. Coun. Archtl. Registration. Prin. Salerno/Livingston Architects, San Diego. Lectr. numerous instns. Archtl. projects include Residence Hall Tower & Multi Purpose Bldg. San Diego State U., Pacific Southwest Airlines Adminstrv. Offices & Hangar Facility, Fujitsu Microelectronics, Inc., Belden Village Low Income Sr. Housing Project, Atkinson Marine Corp. Hdqs. & Ship Repair Facility, Campbell Industries, Islandia Hotel Tower, Marlin Club, Sportfishing Facility and 500 Boat Marina, Branch Libr., Belmont Park Master Plan, Expert Witness Projects; other comml. projects include U.S. Fin. Office Bldg., Lake Murray Office Bldg., San Diego Fed. Branch Bank (5 locations), Nat. U. Office Bldg., Harbor Boat & Yacht Shipyard Renovation, Pacific Southwest Airlines Passenger Lounges & Gates (2 locations), and others. Symposia chmn. "Frank Lloyd Wright-Living in the Wright Century...An Evaluation" San Diego Archtl. Found./San Diego Mus. Art, 1990; mem. design competition adv. panel Balboa Park Organ Pavilion Parking Garage, 1990; mem. urban design com. San Diego Centre City, 1982-86; founder Orchids and Onions Program, 1976, com. chmn. 1984, jury chmn. 1985; chmn. design adv. com. San Diego Center City Devel. Corp., 1980. Fellow AIA (San Diego chpt., past pres. 1978-79, chmn. urban design com. 1978-86, chmn. task force Balboa Pk. master plan); mem. Am. Planning Assn. (mem. bd. dirs. San Diego 1981-82), Soc. Mktg. Profl. Svcs., Am. Arbitration Assn. (mem. panel arbitrators 1988—), Urban Land Inst. (assoc.), Urban Design & Planning Com., Bldg. Industry Assn. (mem. construction quality com.), Community Assn. Inst., San Diego Archtl. Found. (bd. dirs.), SCARAB. Office: Salerno Livingston Architects 363 5th Ave Fl 3 San Diego CA 92101-6965

LIVSEY, HERBERT C., lawyer; b. Salt Lake City, Aug. 20, 1941; BS, U. Utah, 1967, JD, 1969; LLM in Taxation, NYU, 1971. Bar: Utah 1969. Shareholder, fin. dir. Ray, Quinney & Nebeker P.C., Salt Lake City, 1969—. Assoc. editor: Utah Law Review, 1968-69; graduate editor: Tax Law Review, 1970-71. Fellow Am. Coll. Trust and Estate Counsel; mem. Utah State Bar Assn. (chmn. tax sect. 1978-79), Order of the Coif, Phi Kappa Phi, Delta Theta Phi. Office: Ray Quinney & Nebeker PC PO Box 45385 Salt Lake City UT 84145-0385

LIVSEY, ROBERT CALLISTER, lawyer; s. Robert Frances and Rosezella Ann (Callister) L.; m. Renate Karla Guertler, Sept. 10, 1962; children: Scott, Rachel, Daniel, Benjamin. BS, U. Utah, 1962, JD, 1965; LLM, NYU, 1967. Bar: Utah 1965, Calif. 1967. Prof. Haile Selassie U., Addis Ababba, Ethiopia, 1965-66; spl. asst. to chief counsel IRS, Washington, 1977-79; assoc., then ptnr. Brobeck, Phleger & Harrison, San Francisco, 1967—2003; of counsel Morgan, Lewis & Bockius, San Francisco, 2003—. Adj. prof. U. San Francisco Law Sch., 1970-77; mem. adv. com. IRS Dist. Dirs., 1986-89; mem. western region liason com IRS (chmn. 1989). Research editor U. Utah Law Rev., 1964-65; editor Tax Law Rev., 1966-67; contbr. articles to profl. jours. Bd. dirs. Gilead Group, 1986-88, East Bay Habitat for Humanity, 1987-88, Morning Song, 1992-94, U. Utah Alumni Assn. Bay Area Chpt., pres. 2001-07. Mem. ABA (chmn. subcom. real estate syndications 1981-84), State Bar Calif. (chmn. taxation sect. 1984-85), San Francisco Bar Assn. (chmn. taxation sect. 1982), Am. Coll. Tax Counsel, Am. Law Inst., Tax Litigation Club (pres. 1986-87), Order of Coif, Beta Gamma Sigma. Democrat. Mem. Evangelical Covenant Ch. Club: Commonwealth (San Francisco). Home: 128 La Salle Ave Piedmont CA 94610-1233 Office: Morgan Lewis & Bockius 1 Market Plz Fl 31 San Francisco CA 94105-1100 Office Phone: 415-442-1230. Business E-Mail: rlivsey@morganlewis.com.

LJUBIMOV, ALEXANDER V., molecular biologist, cell biologist, researcher; b. Moscow, Oct. 27, 1952; s. Vladimir V. Ljubimov and Margarita S. Ljubimova; m. Julia Y. Savchenko, Apr. 1, 1989;

children: Anna A., Vladimir A. PhD, Russian Cancer Rsch. Ctr., Moscow, 1979. Staff scientist Russian Cancer Rsch. Ctr., 1979—93; rsch. scientist Cedars Sinai Med. Ctr., LA, 1993—2002, dir. Ophthalmology Rsch. Labs., 2002—; prof. UCLA Sch. Medicine, 2003—. Mem. editl. bd.: Frontiers in Biosci., Exptl. Eye Rsch., Diabetes, The Open Ophthalmology Journal, Brain Rsch. Bull.; contbr. articles to profl. jours. Grantee, NIH, 1998—. Mem.: Internat. Soc. Eye Rsch., Am. Diabetes Assn., Assn. Rsch. in Vision and Ophthalmology, Assn. UICC Fellows. Achievements include patents for cancer research and angiogenesis. Office: Cedars Sinai Med Ctr Ste D2025 8700 Beverly Blvd Los Angeles CA 90048 E-mail: ljubimov@cshs.org.

LLAURADO, JOSEP G., nuclear medicine physician, researcher; b. Barcelona, Catalonia, Spain, Feb. 6, 1927; s. José and Rosa (Llaurado) Garcia; m. Catherine D. Entwistle, June 28, 1958 (dec.); children: Thadd, Oleg, Montserrat; m. Deirdre Mooney, Nov. 9, 1966; children: Raymund, Wilfred, Mireya. BS, BA, Balmes Inst., Barcelona, 1944; MD, Barcelona U., 1950, PhD in Pharmacology, 1960; MSc in Biomed. Engring., Drexel U., 1963. Diplomate Am. Bd. Nuclear Medicine. Resident Royal Postgrad. Sch. Medicine, Hammersmith Hosp., London, 1952-54; fellow M.D. Anderson Hosp. and Tumor Inst., Houston, 1957-58, U. Utah Med. Coll., Salt Lake City, 1958-59; asst. prof. U. Otago, Dunedin, New Zealand, 1954-57; sr. endocrinologist Prizer Med. Rsch. Lab., Groton, Conn., 1959-60; assoc. prof. U. Pa., Phila., 1963-67; prof. Med. Coll. Wis., Milw., 1970-82, Marquette U., Milw., 1967-82; clin. dir. nuc. medicine svc. VA Med. Ctr., Milw., 1977—82; chief nuc. medicine svc. VA Hosp., Loma Linda, Calif., 1983—; prof. dept. radiation scis. Loma Linda U. Sch. Medicine, 1983—. U.s. rep. symposium dynamic studies with radioisotopes clin. medicine and rsch. IAEA, Rotterdam, Netherlands, 1970, Knoxville, Tenn., 74. Hon. editor: Internat. Jour. Biomed. Computing, dep. editor: Mgmt. Environ. Quality (now Mgmt. Environ. Quality: an Internat. Jour.); contbr. articles to profl. jours. Merit badge counselor Boy Scouts Am., 1972—; pres. Hales Corners (Wis.) Hist. Soc., 1981—83. Recipient Commendation cert., Boy Scouts Am., 1980, Joan d'Alos prize, Cardiovasc. Ctr. St. Jordi, Barcelona, 1999, XII Batista-Roca prize, Inst. Exterior Projection Catalan Culture, 2000. Fellow: Am. Coll. Nutrition; mem.: IEEE (life), Calif. Med. Assn. (mem. sci. adv. panel nuc. medicine 1993—), Soc. Catalana Biologia, Am. Soc. Nuc. Cardiology, Endocrine Soc., Soc. Math. Biology (founding), Am. Soc. Pharmacology and Exptl. Therapeutics, Am. Physiol. Soc., Biomed. Engring. Soc. (charter), IEEE Medicine and Biology Soc. (mem. nat. adminstrv. com. 1986—89), Soc. Nuc. Medicine (computer and acad. couns.), Royal Acad. Medicine Catalonia/Barcelona, Casal dels Catalans Calif. (pres. 1989—91). Roman Catholic. Office: VA Hosp Nuclear Med Svc Rm 115 11201 Benton St Loma Linda CA 92357-0001 Office Phone: 909-583-6102.

LLOYD, LLYN ALLAN, association executive; b. Evergreen Park, Ill., Jan. 14, 1938; s. Russell Donald and Gladys Marie (Bladholm) L.; m. Helen Elizabeth Main, Mar. 22, 1959; children: Leanne, Douglas, Bradley. BS in Pharmacy, Ohio No. U., 1960; MA in Pub. Adminstrn., Boise State U., 1980. Lic. pharmacist, Ohio, Idaho, Ariz. With various pharmacies, Ohio and Idaho, 1960-63; pharmacist, owner Arco (Idaho) Drug, 1963-76; pharmacist City of Boise, Idaho, 1976-82; exec. dir. Idaho Bd. Pharmacy, Boise, 1982-86, Ariz. State Bd. Pharmacy, Phoenix, 1986—. Chmn. Butte County unit ARC, Arco, Idaho, 1968-74; mem. forest adv. com. Challis (Idaho) Nat. Forest, 1969-72. Recipient A.H. Robbins Bowl of Hygiene award Challis Nat. Forest, 1973. Mem. Nat. Assn. Bds. Pharmacy (exec. com. 1986—), Ariz. Pharmacy Assn., Ariz. Soc. Hosp. Pharmacists (Svc. to Pharmacy award 1988), Rotary, Lions, Masons. Avocations: woodworking, gardening, travel, fishing, golf. Office: Ariz State Bd Pharmacy 4425 W Olive Ave # 140 Glendale AZ 85302 Home: 169 W Sedgewick Dr Meridian ID 83642-8367

LLOYD, MICHAEL JEFFREY, recording producer; b. NYC, Nov. 3, 1948; s. John and Suzanne (Lloyd) Sutton; m. Patricia Ann Varble, Sept. 6, 1980; children: Michael, Christopher, Jeni, Deborah. Student, U. So. Calif. V.p. artists and repertoire MGM Records, Inc., 1969-73; ind. record producer, 1973—; pres. Heaven Prodns., 1975—, Michael Lloyd Prodns., 1979—, Taines-Lloyd Film Prodns., 1984-85; music dir. TV series Happy Days; music dir. Kidsongs, Living Proof, NBC-TV movie, Kidsongs Videos; prodr. Love Lines, NBC-TV movie Swimsuit; pres., co-founder Studio M, Beverly Hills, Calif., 2000—. Guest lectr. UCLA, Pepperdine U.; judge Am. Song Festival. Composer: (music for feature films) Tough Enough, If You Could See What I Hear, Dirty Dancing, All Dogs Go to Heaven, (music and lyrics) Rudolph the Red Nose Reindeer - The Movie, 1998, Coyote Ugly, Driven, Angel Eyes, View From the Top, music for 17 Movies of the Week, 13 TV Spls., 37 TV series and 100 motion pictures. Recipient 51 Gold Album awards, 26 Platinum Album awards, 26 Gold Single awards, 2 Platinum Single awards, 3 Grammy awards, 43 Chart Album awards, 100 Chart Single awards, 10 Broadcast Music Inc. awards, Am. Music award, Dove award, 2 Nat. Assn. Record Minets, 60 Gold Album awards. Mem.: AFTRA, NARAS, SAG, ASCAP (12 awards), Am. Fedn. Musicians.

LO, BERNARD, medical educator; BA summa cum laude, Harvard Univ., 1966; MA, Univ. Sussex, England, 1968; AM, Harvard Univ., 1970; MD, Stanford Univ., 1975, postdoctoral fellow, 1978—80. Internship, residency UCLA, 1975—77; residency Stanford Univ., 1977—78; asst. prof. Univ. Calif., San Francisco, 1980—87, assoc. prof., 1987—93, co-dir. UCSF-Stanford Robert Wood Johnson Clinical Scholars prog., 1989—96, dir. prog. in Medical Ethics, 1989—, prof. medicine, 1993—. Author: Resolving Ethical Dilemmas: A Guide for Clinicians; contbr. articles to profl. jours. Mem.: Am. Soc. of Law Medicine & Ethics (bd. dir.), Inst. Medicine (mem., bd. of health sci. policy, coun. mem. 2006—), Am. Assoc. Physicians, We. Soc. for Clinical Investigation, Phi Beta Kappa. Office: U Calif Dept Medicine PO Box Cc-126 San Francisco CA 94143-0001

LOCATELLI, PAUL LEO, academic administrator; b. Santa Cruz, Calif., Sept. 16, 1938; s. Vincent Dino and Marie Josephine (Piccone) L. BS in Acctg., Santa Clara U., 1961; MDiv, Jesuit Sch. Theology, 1974; DBA, U. So. Calif., 1971. CPA, Calif.; ordained priest Roman Cath. Ch., 1974. Prof. acctg. Santa Clara (Calif.) U., 1974-86, assoc. dean Bus. Sch., 1976—78, acad. v.p., 1978—86, pres., 1988—. Mem. Silicon Valley Leadership Group, Cath. Relief Svcs.; trustee Jesuit Sch. Theology, Berkeley. Mem. acad. adv. bd. Panetta Inst.; mem. internat. com. Jesuit Higher Edn.; sec. higher edn. Soc. Jesus. Mem. Calif. Soc. CPAs (Disting. Prof. of the Yr. award 1994), Assn. Jesuit Colls. and Univs., Commonwealth Club Silicon Valley. Democrat. Office: Santa Clara U 500 El Camino Real Santa Clara CA 95053-0015

LOCHMILLER, KURTIS L., real estate entrepreneur; b. Sacramento, Cali; s. Rodney Glen and Mary Margaret (Frauen) L.; m. Mariye Susan Mizuki, Nov. 9, 1951; children: Margaux Sian, Chase Jordan. BA in Econs. and Fin., U. Denver, 1975. Dist. sales mgr. Hertz Truck Div., Denver, 1975-76; drilling foreman Shell Oil, Alaska, Mont., Colo., 1976-79; pres., owner Kurtex Mortgage & Devel. Co., Denver, 1979—, Kurtex Properties Inc., Denver, 1980-86; pres., chief exec. officer Kurtex Inc., Denver, 1981—, Bankers Pacific Mortgage, Denver, 1980—, Bankers Fin. Escrow Corp., Denver, 1984—, Northwest Title & Escrow, Denver, 1984—. Pres., chief exec. officer Steamboat Title, Steamboat Springs, Colo., 1985—, First Escrow, Denver, 1986—, Fidelity-Commonwealth-Continental Escrow, Denver, 1984—; pres. Colonnade Ltd., Denver, 1981-88; pres., bd. dirs. Breckridge (Colo.) Brewery. V.p., founder Colfax on the Hill, Denver, 1984; mediator, arbitrator Arbitrator/Mediation Assn., Denver, 1986; mem. Police Athletic League, Denver, 1988. Recipient Pres. Spl. Achievement/Founder award Colfax on the Hill, Denver, 1984, Spl. Mayor's award, City & County of Denver, 1985. Mem. Nat. Assn.of Real Estate Appraisers, Internat. Brotherhood of Teamsters, Colo. Mortgage Bankers Assn., Mortgage Banking Assn., Denver C. of C., Phi Beta Kappa, Omicron Delta Epsilon. Clubs: U.S. Karate Assn. (Phoenix) (3d degree Black Belt), Ferrari (Portland). Lodges: Internat. Supreme Council Order of Demolay. Avocations: collecting cars, Karate, fishing, art collecting. Home: 1 Carriage Ln Littleton CO 80121-2010 Office: Bankers Fin Escrow Corp 9655 E 25th Ave Ste 101 Aurora CO 80010-1056

LOCK, GERALD SEYMOUR HUNTER, retired mechanical engineering educator; b. London, June 30, 1935; arrived in Can., 1962, naturalized, 1973; s. George and Mary (Hunter) L.; m. Edna Burness, Sept. 19, 1959; children: Graeme, Gareth, Grenville. B.Sc. with honors, U. Durham, Eng., 1959, PhD, 1962. Asst. prof. mech. engring. U. Alta. (Can.), Edmonton, 1962-64, assoc. prof., 1964-70, prof., 1970-93, dean interdisciplinary studies, 1976-81; cons. mech. engr., Edmonton, 1993—. Chmn. Internat. Arctic Sci. Commn. Regional Bd., 1993-96. Vice chmn. Alta. Manpower Adv. Coun., 1979-84, chmn., 1984-89; chmn. Salvation Army Red Shield Appeal, 1980-82; bd. govs. Alta. Coll., chmn., 1982-85; founding pres. Alta. Poetry Festival Soc., 1981. Recipient Queen Elizabeth II Silver Jubilee medal, 1977 Fellow Engring. Inst. Can, Can. Soc. Mech. Engring. (pres. 1977-78), ASME; mem. Sci. Coun. Can., Can. Polar Commn. Mem. Progressive Conservative Party. Anglican. Home: 11711 83rd Ave Edmonton AB Canada T6G 0V2 Office: U Alta Edmonton AB Canada T6G 0V2

LOCKE, VIRGINIA OTIS, writer; b. Tiffin, Ohio, Sept. 4, 1930; d. Charles Otis and Frances Virginia (Sherer) L. BA, Barnard Coll., NYC, 1952; MA in Psychology, Duke U., Durham, NC, 1972, postgrad. Program officer, asst. corp. sec. Agrl. Devel. Coun., NYC, 1954-66; staff psychologist St. Luke's-Roosevelt Med. Ctr., NYC, 1973-75; freelance writer and editor NYC, 1976-85; writer-editor Cornell U. Med. Coll./N.Y. Hosp. Med. Ctr., NYC, 1986-89; sr. editor humanities and social scis. coll. divsn. Prentice Hall, Upper Saddle River, NJ, 1989-96; profl. writer behavioral scis., 1996—. Co-author: (coll. textbook) Introduction to Theories of Personality, 1985, (book) The Agricultural Development Council: A History, 1989, (coll. textbook) Child Psychology: A Contemporary Viewpoint, 6th edit., 2006; co-editor: The Life and Work of Arthur T. Mosher, 2001. Founder Help Our Neighbors Eat Yearround (H.O.N.E.Y.), Inc., N.Y.C., chmn., 1983-87, vol., 1987-99, newsletter editor, 1992-97; reader Recording for the Blind, N.Y.C., 1978-84; vol. Reach to Recovery program Am. Cancer Soc., Bergen County, N.J., 1990-96. Recipient Our Town Thanks You award, N.Y.C., 1984, Mayor's Vol. Svc. award, N.Y.C., 1986, Cert. of Appreciation for Community Svc. Manhattan Borough, 1986, Jefferson award Am. Ins. Pub. Svc., Washington, 1986. Home and Office: 9316 Bocina Ln # G Atascadero CA 93422 Personal E-mail: volwriter@att.net.

LOCKYER, BILL (WILLIAM LOCKYER), state treasurer; b. Oakland, Calif., May 8, 1941; children: Lisa, Diego. BA in Polit. Sci., U. Calif., Berkeley; cert. in sec. tchg., Calif. State U., Hayward; JD, U. of the Pacific. Past tchr., San Leandro, Calif.; Mem. Calif. State Assembly, 1973; state senator State of Calif., 1982; pres. pro tem, chmn. senate rules com., chmn. senate jud. com. Calif. State Senate, 1994—98; atty. gen. State of Calif., 1999—2007, state treas., 2007—. Active San Leandro Sch. Bd., 1968—73. Past chair Alameda County Dem. Ctrl. Com. Named Legislator of Yr., Planning and Conservation League, 1996, Calif. Jour., 1997. Democrat. Office: Calif State Treas Office PO Box 942809 915 Capitol Mall C-15 Sacramento CA 94209-0001 Office Phone: 916-653-2995. Office Fax: 916-653-3125. Business E-Mail: bill.lockyer@treasurer.ca.gov.

LODER, JOHN MARK, lawyer; b. Minot, ND, Sept. 22, 1958; s. LeRoy Albert and Ann Louise (Hennes) L.; m. Elizabeth Janet Wentz, June 1, 1985; children: Thomas A., Stephen A.C. AB, Harvard U., 1980, JD, 1983. Bar: Mass. 1985. Law clk. Judge Myron H. Bright U.S. Ct. Appeals (8th Cir.), Fargo, ND, 1983-84; assoc. Ropes & Gray LLP, Boston, 1984-92, ptnr., 1992—. Bd. dirs. New Eng. Philharm. Orch., 2003—09; bd. overseers Boston Symphony Orch., 2005—09, New Eng. Conservatory, 2008—; bd. trustees Boston Symphony Orchestra, 2009—. Avocations: mountain biking, music. Home: 36 Marsh St Dedham MA 02026-4306 Office: Ropes & Gray LLP 1 International Pl Boston MA 02110-2624 also: Ropes & Gray LLP 1 Embarcadero Ctr San Francisco CA 94111 Office Phone: 617-951-7405. Business E-Mail: john.loder@ropesgray.com.

LODGE, EDWARD JAMES, federal judge; b. 1933; BS cum laude, Coll. Idaho, 1957; JD, U. Idaho, 1961. With Smith & Miller, 1962-63; probate judge Canyon County, Idaho, 1963-65; judge Idaho State Dist. Ct., 1965-88; U.S. bankruptcy judge State of Idaho, 1988—89; dist. judge, chief judge U.S. Dist. Ct. Idaho, 1989—. Mem. Ninth Cir. Jud. Coun., 1997-98; chair Chief Dist. Judges for Ninth Cir., 1998-99. Recipient Kramer award for excellence in jud. adminstrn., award of legal merit U. Idaho Law Sch., 2000, Disting. Lawyer award, 2002; named three time All-Am., disting. alumnus Coll. Idaho, Boise State U., Professionalism award Idaho State Bar, 1997; named to Hall of Fame Boise State U., Coll. Idaho. Mem. Idaho Trial Lawyer Assn., Idaho State Bar Assn. (Professionalism award 1997), U.S. Fed. Judges Assn., Boise State Athletic Assn., Elks Club. Office: US Dist Ct MSC 040 550 W Fort St Fl 6 Boise ID 83724-0101

LOEFFLER, KAREN LOUISE, prosecutor; b. NYC, Mar. 28, 1957; d. Robert Mendelle and Marjorie (Apt) L. AB magna cum laude, Dartmouth Coll., 1979; JD cum laude, Harvard U., 1983. Bar: Minn. 1983, Alaska 1985, U.S. Dist. Ct. (9th cir.). Assoc. Faegre & Benson, Mpls., 1983-85; asst. atty. gen. State of Alaska, Anchorage, 1985-86, asst. dist. atty., 1986-89; asst. US atty. dist. Alaska US Dept. Justice, Anchorage, 1989—2009, chief criminal divsn., 1995—, acting US atty., 2009—. Avocations: various sports, sea kayaking, skiing, ice hockey, soccer. Office: US Atty's Office Fed Bldg and US Courthouse 222 W 7th Ave Rm 253 Ste 9 Anchorage AK 99513-7500 Office Phone: 907-271-5071.*

LOEHMAN, RONALD ERNEST, materials scientist; b. San Antonio, Feb. 22, 1943; s. Roland Albert and Charlotte (Herweck) L.; m. Edna Tusak, June 26, 1965 (div. Oct. 1981), 1 child, Rachel Andrea; m. Ellen Louise Griffith, July 10, 1982; 1 child, Matthew Charles. BA, Rice U., 1964; PhD, Purdue U., 1969. Asst. prof. U. Fla., Gainesville, 1970-75, assoc. prof., 1975-78; sr. materials scientist SRI Internat., Menlo Park, Calif., 1978-82; mem. tech. staff Sandia Nat. Labs., Albuquerque, 1982-86, div. supr., 1986-87, mgr. chemistry and ceramics dept., 1987-92; co-dir. Advanced Materials Lab., Albuquerque, 1992—; nat. labs. disting. prof. U. N.Mex., 1992—; sr. scientist Sandia Nat. Labs., 1998—. Contbr. articles to profl. jours.; patentee in field. Mem. AAAS, Am. Ceramic Soc. (assoc. editor jour. 1988—, Roland Snow award 1984, Fulrath award 1988), Nat. Inst. Ceramic Engrs., Sigma Xi. Office: Advanced Materials Lab 1001 University Blvd SE Albuquerque NM 87106-4325

LOEHWING, LORD RUDI CHARLES, film producer, director, publicist, radio broadcasting executive, journalist; b. Newark, July 26, 1957; s. Rudy Charles Sr. and Joan Marie (Bell) L.; m. Lady Claire Popham, Sept. 4, 1987; children: Aspasia Joyce, Tesia Victoria, Rudi Douglas, Anna Marie, Samantha Diane, Ian Ryan. Student, Biscayne U., 1975, Seton Hall U., 1977. Announcer radio stas. WNEW-FM, WHBI-FM, NYC, 1970—72; producer Am. Culture Entertainment, Belleville, NJ, 1973-74, exec. producer Hollywood, Calif., 1988-94; CEO Broadcaster's Network Internat., UK, 1988—, La Crescenta, Calif., 1989—2002. Co-founder BNI Comms., LA, 1989; bd. dirs. First Break, Hollywood, also UK, 1989-02; founder, pres. World Inst. Natural Health Scis., 2006. Author: Growing Pains, 1970; dir. exec. producer TV documentaries and comml. advertisements, 1983; narrative dir. We Become Silent, Generation Rx; patentee in field. Bd. dirs. Civic Light Opera of South Bay Cities, 1998—, LA Civic Light Opera, Tax Edn. Assn., Just Say No to Drugs, L.A., 1989, Hands Across the Atlantic, Internat. Country Top 10, The Rock of Russia, Job Search, Hollywood, U.K. and Russia, Strategic Bus. Alliances Network. Named Youngest Comml. Radio Producer and Announcer for State of NY, Broadcaster's Network Internat., 1972 Mem. Nat. Press Club, Broadcasters Network Assn. (bd. dirs. 1977—), Profl. Bus. Comms. Assn. (founder 1989), BNI News Bur. (chmn. 1991—), Civic Light Opera of South Bay Cities (bd. dirs. 1996—), Friars Club, Mensa. Avocations: music, writing, photography, martial arts (recipient awards). Home: Leicester House 11487 Mt Gleason Ave Los Angeles CA 91042-1229 Office: Broadcasters Network Internat Ltd Leicester House 11417 Mt Gleason Ave Tujunga CA 91042 Business E-Mail: rudi@loehwing.com.

LOESCHER, RICHARD ALVIN, retired gastroenterologist; b. Brockton, Mass., Feb. 6, 1940; s. Vernon Alvin and Anna Marie (Good) Loescher; m. Linda Rockwell Clifford, June 5, 1955 (div. Jan. 1982); children: Steven Clifford, Laura May. BA, DePauw U., Greencastle, Ind., 1961; MD cum laude, Harvard U., Cambridge, Mass., 1965. Diplomate Am. Bd. Internal Medicine, 1972, Am. Bd. Gastroenterology, 1973. Chief med. svc. USPHS Hosp., Lawton, Okla., 1967-69, chief med. staff, 1968-69, svc. unit dir., 1969, attending physician Seattle, 1970-71, Univ. Hosp., Seattle, 1970-71; active staff Sacred Heart Med. Ctr., Eugene, Oreg., 1973—2005, Eugene Hosp., Oreg., 1972—88; courtesy staff McKenzie-Willamette Hosp., Springfield, Oreg., 1982—2004. Recipient Rector scholarship DePauw U., 1957-61, Maimonides award Harvard Med. Sch., 1965. Mem. AMA, ACP-Am. Soc. Internal Medicine, Lane County Med. Soc., Oreg. Med. Assn., Am. Soc. for Gastrointestinal Endoscopy, Am. Acad. Med. Acupuncture, Alpha Omega Alpha, Phi Beta Kappa. Democrat. Unitarian Universalist. Avocations: physical fitness, personal growth, magic, dance. Home: 2345 Patterson St Apt 34 Eugene OR 97405-2974

LOEWENSTEIN, WALTER BERNARD, nuclear energy industry executive; b. Gensungen, Hesse, Germany, Dec. 23, 1926; arrived in U.S., 1938; m. Lenore C. Pearlman, June 21, 1959; children: Mark Victor, Marcia Beth. BS, U. Puget Sound, Tacoma, Wash., 1949; postgrad., U. Wash., Seattle, 1949-50; PhD, Ohio State U., Columbus, Ohio, 1954. Registered profl. engr., Calif. Rsch. asst., fellow Ohio State U., Columbus, 1951-54; rsch. asst. Los Alamos Nat. Lab., 1952-54; sr. physicist, divsn. dir. Argonne (Ill.) Nat. Lab., 1954-73; dept. dir., dep. divsn. dir. Electric Power Rsch. Inst., Palo Alto, Calif., 1973-89, profl. cons., 1989—, mem. large aerosol containment experiment project bd., 1983-87. Mem. Marviken project bd. Studsvik Rsch. Ctr., Stockholm, 1978-85; mem. LOFT project bd. Nuc. Energy Agy., Paris, 1982-89; mem. tech. adv. com. nuc. safety Ontario Hydro Corp., 1990-98; mem. nuc. engring. dept. adv. com. Brookhaven Nat. Lab., 1992-96; mem. advanced tech. divsn. adv. com. Los Alamos Nat. Lab., 1994-99; mem. nuc. engring. dept. adv. com. U. Calif., Berkeley, 1994-2003. With USNR, 1945-46. Recipient Alumnus Cum Laude award U. Puget Sound, 1976. Fellow Am. Phys. Soc., Am. Nuc. Soc. (v.p., pres. 1988-90); mem. Am. Assn. Engring. Socs. (sec., treas. 1990), Nat. Acad. Engring. Jewish. Avocations: history, golf. Home and Office: 515 Jefferson Dr Palo Alto CA 94303

LOFGREN, CHARLES AUGUSTIN, historian, educator; b. Missoula, Mont., Sept. 8, 1939; s. Cornelius Willard and Helen Mary (Augustin) L.; m. Jennifer Jenkins Wood, Aug. 6, 1986. AB with great distinction, Stanford U., 1961; AM, 1962, PhD, 1966. Instr. history San Jose State Coll., 1965-66; asst. prof. Claremont McKenna Coll., 1966-71; assoc. prof., 1971-76; prof., 1976—; prof. Am. history and politics, 1976—. Author: Government from Reflection and Choice, 1986, The Plessy Case, 1988, Claremont Pioneers, 1996; contbr. articles to profl. jours. Served with USAR, 1957-63. Mem. Am. Soc. Legal History, Orgn. Am. Historians, Am. Hist. Assn. Republican. Roman Catholic. Office: Claremont McKenna Coll Dept History 850 Columbia Ave Claremont CA 91711-6420 Home Phone: 909-626-6731. Business E-Mail: clofgren@cmc.edu.

LOFGREN, ZOE, United States Representative from California; b. Palo Alto, Calif., Dec. 21, 1947; d. Milton R. and Mary Violet Lofgren; m. John Marshall Collins, Oct. 22, 1978; children: Sheila Zoe, John Charles. BA in Polit. Sci., Stanford U., 1970; JD cum laude, U. Santa Clara Sch. Law, 1975. Bar: Calif., DC. Adminstrv. asst. to Representative Don Edwards US Congress, San Jose, Calif., 1970—78; ptnr. Webber & Lofgren, San Jose, 1978—80; mem. Santa Clara County Bd. Suprs., 1981-94, US Congress from 16th Calif. dist., 1994—; chair US House Standards of Official Conduct Com., 2009—; vice chair US House Adminstrn. Com.; mem. US House Judiciary

Com., US House Homeland Security Com., Joint Com. on the Library. Law tchr. U. Santa Clara Sch. Law, 1976—78, adj. prof. immigration law, 1981—94; founding exec. dir. Cmty. Housing Developers, Santa Clara County, 1978—81; mem. New Dem. Coalition, Nat. Guard & Reserve Components Caucus, Dem. Leader's High Tech. Adv. Grp.; chair Calif. Dem. Congl. Delegation. Actice People Acting in Cmty. Together; bd. trustees San Jose-Evergreen Cmty. Coll. Dist., 1979—81. Recipient Bancroft-Whitney award for Excellence in Criminal Procedure, 1973. Mem.: Santa Clara Law Sch. Alumni Assn. (v.p. 1977, pres. 1978), DC Bar Assn., Santa Clara County Bar Assn. Democrat. Lutheran. Office: US Congress 102 Cannon Ho Office Bldg Washington DC 20515-0516 also: Dist Office Ste B 635 N 1st St San Jose CA 95112-5110*

LOFTFIELD, ROBERT BERNER, biochemistry professor; b. Detroit, Dec. 15, 1919; s. Sigurd and Katherine (Roller) L.; m. Ella Bradford, Aug. 24, 1946 (dec. Dec. 1990); children: Lore Loftfield DeBower, Eric, Linda, Norman, Bjorn, Curtis, Katherine, Earl, Allison Dinsdale, Ella-Kari. BS, Harvard U., 1941, MA, 1942, PhD, 1946. Research assoc. MIT, Cambridge, 1946-48; research assoc. to sr. research assoc. Mass. Gen. Hosp., Boston, 1948-64; asst. to assoc. prof. biochemistry Harvard U. Sch. Medicine, Boston, 1948-64; prof. biochemistry Sch. Medicine U. N.Mex., Albuquerque, 1964-90, chmn. dept. biochemistry, 1964-71, 78-90, prof. emeritus, 1990—. Contbr. articles on protein biosynthesis and enzymology to profl. jours. Served as corp. U.S. Army, 1945-46. Fellow Damon Runyon Fund, 1952-53, Guggenheim Found., 1961-62; Fulbright fellow, 1977, 83; sr. fellow NIH, 1971-72. Mem. AAAS, Am. Soc. Biol. Chemists, Am. Chem. Soc., Am. Assn. Cancer Rsch., Biophys. Soc., Marine Biol. Lab. Lutheran. Avocations: sailing, hiking, camping, skiing. Home: 707 Fairway Rd NW Albuquerque NM 87107-5718 Office: U NMex Sch Medicine Dept Biochemis & Molecular Biology Albuquerque NM 87131-0001

LOFTIN, NANCY CAROL, lawyer, utilities executive; b. Phoenix, 1954; BA, Ariz. State U., 1976; JD, U. Ariz. Sch. of Law, 1979. Bar: Ariz. 1979. Special counsel & dir. enforcement Ariz. Corp. Commn.; staff atty. Ariz. Public Service, 1985—87; v.p., gen. counsel, sec. Pinnacle West Capital Corp. & Ariz. Pub. Svc. Co., 1987—. Mem. Edison Electric Inst. Bd. mem. Phoenix Children's Hospital, former bd. chair. Mem.: ABA, Am. Soc. of Corporate Secretaries, Ethics Officer Assn. Office: Pinnacle West Capital Corp PO Box 53999 Phoenix AZ 85072-3999

LOFTIS, JOHN (CLYDE), JR., language educator; b. Atlanta, May 16, 1919; s. John Clyde and Marbeth (Brown) L.; m. Anne Nevins, June 29, 1946; children: Mary, Laura, Lucy. BA, Emory U., 1940; MA, Princeton U., 1942, PhD, 1948. Instr. English Princeton, 1946-48; instr., then asst. prof. English UCLA, 1948-52; faculty Stanford U., 1952-81, prof. English, 1958-81, Bailey prof. English, 1977-81, Bailey prof. emeritus, 1981—, chmn. dept., 1973-76. Author: Steele at Drury Lane, 1952, Comedy and Society from Congreve to Fielding, 1959, La Independencia de la Literatura Norteamericana, 1961, The Politics of Drama in Augustan England, 1963, The Spanish Plays of Neoclassical England, 1973, (with others) The Revels History of Drama in English, Vol. V, 1976, Sheridan and the Drama of Georgian England, 1977, Renaissance Drama in England and Spain: Topical Allusion and History Plays, 1987; editor: (Steele) The Theatre, 1962, Restoration Drama: Modern Essays in Criticism, 1966, (with V.A. Dearing) The Works of John Dryden, Vol. IX, 1966, (Sheridan) The School for Scandal, 1966, (Nathaniel Lee) Lucius Junius Brutus, 1967, (Addison) Essays in Criticism and Literary Theory, 1975, The Memoirs of Anne, Lady Halkett and Ann, Lady Fanshawe, 1979, (with D.S. Rodes and V.A. Dearing) The Works of John Dryden, Vol. XI, 1978, (with P.H. Hardacre) Colonel Bampfield's Apology, 1993; co-editor Augustan Reprint Society, 1949-1952, English Literature, 1660-1800: A Current Bibliography, 1951-56; gen. editor: Regents Restoration Drama Series, 35 vols, 1962-81; mem. editorial bd.: Studies in English Literature, 1966-76, Huntington Library Quar., 1968-76, Wesleyan Edit. Works Henry Fielding, 1970-83, Augustan Reprint Soc., 1985-90. Served with USNR, 1942-46, PTO. Fellow Fund Advancement Edn., 1955-56; Fulbright lectr. Am. studies Peru, 1959-60; Guggenheim fellow, 1966-67; fellow Folger Shakespeare Library, 1967; NEH fellow, 1978-79 Mem. MLA, Phi Beta Kappa, Kappa Alpha. Office: Stanford Univ Dept English Stanford CA 94305 Home: 4075 El Camino Way Palo Alto CA 94306 Personal E-mail: anneloftis@gmail.com.

LOFTON, KEVIN EUGENE, medical facility administrator; b. Beaumont, Tex., Sept. 29, 1954; BS, Boston U., 1976; M Health Care Adminstrn., Ga. State U., 1979. Adminstrv. resident Meml. Med. Ctr., Corpus Christi, Tex., 1978-79; adminstr. emergency svcs. Univ. Hosp., Jacksonville, Fla., 1979-80, adminstr. material mgmt., 1980-81, asst. exec. dir. ambulatory care, 1981-82, asst. v.p. ambulatory svcs., 1982-83, v.p. profl. svcs., 1983-86; exec. v.p. Univ. Med. Ctr., Jacksonville, 1986-90; exec. dir. Howard Univ. Hosp., Washington, 1990-93, U. Ala. Hosp., Birmingham, 1993-98; group pres. Cath. Health Initiative, Louisville, 1998-99, coo Denver, 1999—2003, ceo, 2003—. Contbr. articles to profl. publs. Fellow Am. Coll. Health Care Execs. (R.S. Hudgens award 1993); mem. Am. Hosp. Assn. (bd. dirs.), Nat. Assn. Health Svcs. Execs. (past pres., bd. dirs.).

LOGAN, BEN H., III, lawyer; b. Medina, Ohio, 1951; BA magna cum laude, Duke U., 1973; JD, Stanford, 1976. Bar: Calif. 1976, US Dist. Ct. (Ctrl. Dist. Calif.) 1978, DC 1984, US Dist. Ct. (No. and So. Dists. Calif.) 1986, US Dist. Ct. (Dist. Ariz) 1990, US Dist. Ct. (Ea. Dist. Calif.) 1991, US Ct. Appeals (2nd Cir.) 1991, US Ct. Appeals (9th Cir.) 1994. Ptnr. O'Melveny & Myers LLP, Los Angeles. Mem. Stanford Law Review, 1974—76; editor: Stanford Law Review, 1975—76. Mem. ABA, State Bar Calif. (mem., debtor/creditor rels. and bankruptcy subcommittee, comml. law and bankruptcy sect.1986-91), LA County Bar Assn. (mem. bankruptcy com. 1989-92), Phi Beta Kappa; fellow Am. Coll. Bankruptcy. Office: O'Melveny & Myers 400 S Hope St Los Angeles CA 90071-2899 Office Phone: 213-430-7704. Office Fax: 213-430-6407. Business E-Mail: blogan@omm.com.

LOGAN, FRANCIS DUMMER, retired lawyer; b. Evanston, Ill., May 23, 1931; s. Simon Rae and Frances (Dummer) Logan; m. Claude Riviere, Apr. 13, 1957; children: Carolyn Gisele, Francis Dummer. BA, U. Chgo., 1950; BA Juris, Oxford U., 1954; LLB, Harvard U., 1955. Bar: N.Y. 1956, Calif. 1989. Assoc. Milbank, Tweed, Hadley & McCloy, NYC, 1955-64, ptnr. NYC and L.A., 1965-96, chmn., 1992-96. Commr. Burbank-Glendale-Pasadena Airport Authority, Calif., 2005—. Overseer Huntington Libr., Art Collections and Bot. Gardens, Calif., 2006—. Mem.: N.Y. State Bar, Pacific Coun. Internat. Policy, Am. Law Inst., Coun. Fgn. Rels., Calif. State Bar. Home: 1726 Linda Vista Ave Pasadena CA 91103-1132

LOGAN, LEE ROBERT, orthodontist, department chairman; b. LA, June 24, 1932; s. Melvin Duncan and Margaret (Seltzer) L.; m. Maxine Nadler, June 20, 1975; children: Chad, Casey. BS, UCLA, 1952; DDS, Northwestern U., Evanston, Ill., 1956, MS, 1961. Diplomate Am. Bd. Orthodontics. Gen. practice dentistry, Reseda, Calif., 1958—59; pvt. practice Northridge, Calif., 1961—, 2000—; vice chair dental dept., 2006—; chief staff dental dept. Northridge Hosp., 2008—. Med. staff Northridge Hosp., 2000—, vice chair med. staff dental dept.; owner Maxine's Prodn. Co., Maxine's Talent Agy.; guest lectr. dept. orthodontics UCLA, U. So. Calif. Contbr. articles to profl. jours. Achievements include patent and licensing agreement with 3M for a device to attach braces, 2001, Can. patent, 2004, patents U.K., Germany, France, Japan. Served to lt. USNR, 1956-58. Recipient Nat. Philanthropy award, 1987, winner, Logan's Run, 2005—08, Founder's award, Autistic Assn., 2007; named 1st Pl. winner, Autistic Jogathon, 1981—2001, (with wife) Couple of Yr., Autistic Children Assn., 1986, in his honor Logan's Run, Walk for Autism; named to Best Dentist's in Am., 2004—07. Mem. ADA, San Fernando Valley Dental Assn. (pres. 1998), Am. Assn. Orthodontists, Pacific Coast Soc. Orthodontists (dir., pres. so. sect. 1974-75, chmn. membership 1981-83), Foudn. Orthodontic Rsch. (charter mem.), Calif. Soc. Orthodontists (chmn. peer rev. 1982-93), G.V. Black Soc. (charter) Angle Soc. Orthodontists (pres. 1981-82, bd. dirs. 1982—, nat. pres. 1985-87), U. S.C. Century Club Fraternity, Northridge Hosp. Med. Ctr. (chief staff), Xi Psi Phi, Chi Phi. Achievements include patents in field. Home: 4830 Encino Ave Encino CA 91316-3813 Office: 18250 Roscoe Blvd Northridge CA 91325-4226 Home Phone: 818-788-2361. Personal E-mail: orthologan@aol.com.

LOGAN, MARK BYRON, optics corporation executive; b. Phoenixville, Pa., Dec. 1, 1938; s. Leo Joseph and Roselyn Francis (Baker) L.; m. Sharon Kathleen Logan, Sept. 3, 1960 (div. Nov. 19, 1973); 1 son, Bret; m. Anne Herndon Jones, May 9, 1975; children: Catherine, Virginia. BA, Hiram Coll., 1960; MA, NYU, 1961; postgrad., Harvard U. Grad. Sch. Bus. Adminstrn. Pres. Home Products de Mex. div., Am. Home Products, NYC, 1967-74; v.p., mktg. cons. products A.H. Robins Co., Richmond, Va., 1974-75; group pres. Becton Dickinson Co., Paramus, N.J., 1975-81; sr. v.p., pres. vision care group Bausch & Lomb Inc., Rochester, N.Y., 1981—, also dir.; chmn., Pres and CEO Insmed Pharmaceuticals, Inc.; chmn. and CEO VISX, Inc., Santa Clara, CA, 1994—. Dir. Upstate Health Systems, Rochester, Eastman Dental Ctr., Rochester, Abgenix, Inc., VIVUS, Inc. Bd. dirs. Roberts Wesleyan Coll., Rochester, 1982—. Woodrow Wilson fellow, 1960-61 Mem.: County of Rochester, Genessee Valley. Home: 109 Ambassador Dr Rochester NY 14610-3403 Office: VISX Inc 3400 Central Expy Santa Clara CA 95051-0703

LOGAN, NANCY JANE, broadcast sales and marketing executive; b. Buffalo, Oct. 29, 1957; d. Harry Lee and MaryJane (Redinger) Logan. AA, Erie Community Coll., Buffalo, 1977; BS, SUNY, Brockport, 1979. Account exec. Sta. WBUF Radio, Buffalo, 1979-80; account exec. Sta. WBEN Radio, Buffalo, 1980-82; regional mgr. Westwood One Radio Networks, LA, 1983-84; mktg. rep. TV Guide Mag., LA, 1984-88, broadcast mktg. supr., 1988-89, western mgr. tune-in advt., 1989—; sr. dir., media licensing BMI, LA; pres., foundation chair. AWRT, LA, 1999—. Mem. NATAS, Am. Women in Radio & TV (pres. so. Calif. chpt. 1988-89), Publicity Club L.A. Democrat. Presbyterian. Avocations: painting, skiing, horseback riding, bicycling, music. Home: 2627 5th St Santa Monica CA 90405-4259 Office: BMI 8730 W Sunset Blvd Fl 3 Los Angeles CA 90069-2210

LOGUE, DAN R., state legislator; m. Peggy Logue; 1 child, Cheni. Owner Logue Realty; mem. bd. supervisors Yuba County, Calif., 2002—, vice-chmn. bd. supervisors Calif.; mem. Dist. 3 Calif. State Assembly, 2006—. Yuba County co-chmn. Ronald Reagan for Pres., 1980, George Bush for Pres., 2004, Arnold Schwarzenegger for Gov., 2006. Republican. Office: PO Box 942849 Rm 2002 Sacramento CA 94249-0003 Address: 1550 Humbolt Rd Ste 4 Chico CA 95928 Office Phone: 503-895-4217, 916-319-2003. Office Fax: 530-895-4219, 916-319-2103. Business E-Mail: dstottlemeyer@co.yuba.ca.us.*

LOHMAN, LORETTA CECELIA, social scientist, consultant; b. Joliet, Ill., Sept. 25, 1944; d. John Thomas and Marjorie Mary (Brennan) L. BA in Polit. Sci., U. Denver, 1966, PhD in Am. History, 1996; MA in Social Sci., U. No. Colo., Greeley, 1975. Lectr. Ariz. State U., Tempe, 1966-67; survey researcher Merrill-Werthlin Co., Tempe, 1967-68; edn. asst. Am. Humane Assn., Denver, 1969-70; econ. cons. Lohman & Assocs., Littleton, Colo., 1971-75; rsch. assoc. Denver Rsch. Inst., 1976-86; owner, rsch. scientist Lohman & Assocs., Littleton, 1986-99; affiliate Colo. Water Resources Rsch. Inst., Ft. Collins, Colo., 1989-91; Colo. Nonpoint source outreach coord. coop. ext. Colo. State U., 1999—. Tech. adv. com. Denver Potable Wastewater Demo Plant, 1986—90; cons. Constrn. Engring. Rsch. Lab., 1984—; peer reviewer NSF, 1985—86, Univs. Coun. Water Resources, 1989; WERC consortium reviewer N.Mex. Univs.-U.S. Dept. Energy, 1989—, Co-Alliance Environ. Edn. Adv. Bd., 2000—; course cons. Regis Coll., Denver, 1992—. Contbr. articles to profl. jours. Vol. Metro Water Conservation Projects, Denver, 1986-90; co-coord. AWARE Colo., 2003--; vol. handicapped fitness So. Suburban Parks and Recreation. Recipient Huffsmith award Denver Rsch. Inst., 1983; Nat. Ctr. for Edn. in Politics grantee, 1964-65. Mem. ASCE (social and environ. objectives com.), Orgn. Am. Historians, Pub. Hist. Assn., Sigma Xi, Pi Gamma Mu, Phi Alpha Theta. Avocations: vegetable and xeriscape gardening, travel, miniature boxes. Home and Office: 3375 W Aqueduct Ave Littleton CO 80123-2903 Business E-Mail: lorettalohman@npscolorado.com.

LOHNES, WALTER F. W., German language and literature educator; b. Frankfurt, Germany, Feb. 8, 1925; came to U.S., 1948, naturalized, 1954; s. Hans and Dina (Koch) L.; m. Claire Shane, 1950; children: Kristen, Peter, Claudia. Student, U. Frankfurt, 1945-48, Ohio Wesleyan U., 1948-49, U. Mo., 1949-50; PhD, Harvard U., 1961. Asst., Inst. German Folklore, U. Frankfurt, 1947-48; instr. German U. Mo., 1949-50; head dept. German, Phillips Acad., Andover, Mass., 1951-61; asst. prof. Stanford (Calif.) U., 1961-65, assoc. prof., 1965-68, prof., 1969-95, prof. emeritus, 1995—, dir. NDEA Inst. Advanced Study, 1961-68, chmn. dept. German studies, 1973-79, dir. Inst. Basic German, 1975-95, prin. investigator NEH grant, 1978-80. Vis. prof. Woehler-Gymnasium, Frankfurt, 1956-57, Middlebury Coll., 1959, U. N.Mex., 1980, 81, 86, U. Vienna, 1990, Coll. de France, Paris, 1992; mem., chmn. various coms. of examiners Ednl. Testing Svc. and Coll. Bd.; chmn. German Grad. Record Exam. Author: (with V. Nollendorfs) German Studies in the United States, 1976, (with F. W. Strothmann) German: A Structural Approach, 1968, 4th rev. edit., 1988; (with E.A. Hopkins) Contrastive Grammar of English and German, 1982, (with Martha Woodmansee) Erkennen und Deuten, 1983, (with J.A. Pfeffer) Grunddeutsch, Texte zur gesprochenen deutschen Gegenwartssprache, 3 vols., 1984, (with D. Benseler and V. Nollendorfs) Teaching German in America: Prolegomena to a History, 1988; contbr. numerous articles to profl. jours.; editor: Unterrichtspraxis, 1971-74 Bd. dirs. Calif. Youth Symphony, 1977-78, Oakland (Calif.) Symphony Youth Orch., 1978-80, Peninsula Dem. Coalition, 1998—. Decorated Fed. Order of Merit (Germany); Medal of Honor in Gold (Austria); German Govt. grantee, 1975, 76, 78. Mem. MLA, Am. Assn. Tchrs. German (v.p. 1961-62, 70-71, Outstanding Educator award 1994; hon. 1995), Am. Assn. Applied Linguistics, Am. Coun. on Teaching Fgn. Langs., German Studies Assn., Internat. Vereinigung Germanische Sprach und Literaturwissenschaft. Home: 733 Covington Rd Los Altos CA 94024-4903 Office: Stanford U Dept German Studies Stanford CA 94305-2030

LOHRDING, RONALD K., business executive; PhD in Math. Statistics, Kans. State U. R&D mgr., scientist Los Alamos (N.Mex.) Nat. Lab., asst. dir. for indsl. and internat. initiatives, dep. assoc. dir. for environment and biosys., program dir. for energy, environment, and tech.; co-founder Cell Robotics, Albuquerque, 1988—, chmn., pres., CEO. Office: Cell Robotics International Inc 4801 Lang Ave NE Ste 110 Albuquerque NM 87109-4475

LOIACONO, JOHN P., information technology executive; married. BA in Comm., Fresno State U., 1984. Joined, various mgmt. roles in communications, advertising, sales, public relations, websites and branding Sun Microsystems, Santa Clara, Calif., 1987, chief mktg. officer, sr. v.p. operating platforms group, 2000—04, exec. v.p. software group, 2004—06; sr. v.p., creative solutions. Adobe Systems, Inc., San Jose, Calif., 2006—. Advisory bd. Design Ignites Change; bd. dirs. Adobe Found. Office: Adobe Systems Inc 345 Park Ave San Jose CA 95110-2704 Office Phone: 650-960-1300, 800-555-9786, 408-536-6000. Fax: 408-537-6000; Office Fax: 408-276-3804.*

LOMBARD, GEORGE, electronics company executive; Pres., CEO Signal Tech., Sunnyvale, Calif., chmn., CEO Danvers, Mass., 1998—. Office: Signal Tech Interpoint Corp PO Box 97005 Redmond WA 98073-9705

LOMBARD, KENNETH T., beverage and music company executive; Pres. Johnson Develop. Corp., Magic Johnson Theatres, 1992—2004; sr. v.p., pres. Starbucks Entertainment Starbucks Corp., Seattle, 2004—; chief mgr. Hear Music label, LA, 2007—.

LOMBARDI, DEAN, professional sports team executive; b. Holyoke, Mass. Grad., U. New Haven; JD with honors, Tulane U. Player agent; asst. gen. mgr. Minn. North Stars, San Jose Sharks, 1990—92, pres., dir. hockey ops., 1992—96, exec. v.p., gen. mgr., 1996—2003; pro scout Phila. Flyers, 2003—06; pres., gen. mgr. LA Kings, 2006—. Office: LA Kings Ste 3100 1111 S Figueroa St Los Angeles CA 90015

LOMBARDI, EUGENE PATSY, retired conductor, musician, educator; b. North Braddock, Pa., July 7, 1923; s. Nunzio C. and Mary (Roberto) L.; m. Jacqueline Sue Davis, Mar. 1955; children: Robert, Genanne. BA, Westminster Coll., 1948; MA, Columbia U., 1948; Edn. Specialist, George Peabody Coll., 1972; MusD, Westminster Coll., 1981. Band dir. Lincoln H.S., Midland, Pa., 1948-49; orch. dir. Du Pont Manual H.S., Louisville, 1949—50, Male H.S., Louisville, 1949-50, Phoenix Union H.S., 1950-57; orch. dir., prof. Ariz. State U., Tempe, 1957-89; ret., 1989. Condr. Phoenix Symphonette, 1954-61, 70-73, Phoenix Symphony Youth Orch., 1956-66, Phoenix Pops Orch., 1971-83, Fine Arts String Orch., Phoenix, 1995-97 With USAAF, 1943-46. Decorated Bronze Star; recipient Alumni Achievement award Westminster Coll., 1976, gold medal Nat. Soc. Arts and Letters, 1973, Disting. Tchr. award Ariz. State U. Alumni, 1974, Phoenix appreciation award, 1983 Mem. Music Educators Nat. Conf., Am. String Tchrs. Assn. (pres. Ariz. unit 1965-67), Am. Fedn. Musicians, Ariz. Music Educators Assn. (pres. higher edn. sect. 1973-75, Excellence in Teaching Music award 1989), Ind. Order Foresters, Phi Delta Kappa, Phi Mu Alpha, Alpha Sigma Phi. Republican. Methodist. Home: 2625 E Southern C-164 Tempe AZ 85282-7635 Personal E-mail: genesuelombardi@cox.net.

LOMBARDINI, CAROLANN, lawyer; b. Framingham, Mass., Dec. 29, 1954; d. Harry and Sarah (Scarano) L. m. William L. Cole, Apr. 23, 1983; children: Kevin Daniel, Kristin Elizabeth. BA, U. Chgo., 1976; JD, Stanford U., 1979. Bar: Calif. 1979. Assoc. Meserve, Mumper & Hughes, LA, 1979-80, Proskauer Rose Goetz & Mendelsohn, LA, 1980-82; from counsel to sr. v.p. legal and bus. affairs Alliance of Motion Picture and TV Prodrs., Encino, Calif., 1982—. Trustee Dirs. Guild Contract Adminstrn., Encino, 1982—, Prodr.-Writers Guild Pension & Health Plans, Burbank, Calif., 1983—, SAG-Prodr. Pension & Health Plans, Burbank, 1986—, Dirs. Guild-Prodr. Pension & Health Plans, L.A., 1987— Avocations: hiking, cooking. Office: Alliance Motion Picture & TV Prodrs 15503 Ventura Blvd Encino CA 91436-3103

LOMICKA, WILLIAM HENRY, investor; b. Irwin, Pa., Mar. 9, 1937; s. William and Carabel Lomicka; m. Carol L. Williams, Feb. 14, 1979; 1 child, Edward W. BA, Coll. Wooster, Ohio, 1959; MBA, U. Pa., 1962. Sr. securities analyst Guardian Life Ins. Co., NYC, 1962-65; treasury svcs. mgr. L. B. Foster Co., Pitts., 1966-68, Welch Foods Co., Westfield, NY, 1969-70; asst. treas. Ashland Oil, Inc., Ky., 1970-75; sr. v.p. fin. Humana Inc., Louisville, 1975-85; pres., fin. cons. Old South Life Ins. Co., Louisville, 1985-87; sec. econ. devel. Commonwealth of Ky., 1987-88; acting pres. Citizens Security Life Ins. Co., Louisville, 1988-89; pres. Mayfair Capital, Inc., Louisville, 1988-99; chmn. Coulter Ridge Capital, Tucson, 1999—. Bd. dirs. Counsel Corp. Bd. trustees Heuser Hearing Inst., Ariz.-Sonora Desert Mus., chair. With USAR, 1962—63. Home and Office: 7406 N Secret Canyon Dr Tucson AZ 85718-1435

LOMIO, J. PAUL, law librarian, researcher; B in Psychology, St. Bonaventure U., 1972; JD, Gonzaga U., 1978; LLM, U. Wash., 1979; MLS, Cath. U. Am., 1982. Bar: Wash. 1978. Law clk. for Judge T. Patrick Corbett King County Superior Ct., Seattle, 1980; reference and documents libr. Robert J. White Law Libr., Columbus Sch. Law, Cath. U. Am., Washington; reference libr. Robert Crown Law Libr., Stanford U. Law Sch., Calif., 1982, assoc. pub. svcs. libr. Calif., 1983, asst. dir. info. svcs. Calif., 1994, acting dir. Calif., 2004—05, dir. Calif., 2005—. Chair Stanford U. Pub. Svcs. Coordinating Coun., 1989; mem. Law Librarians' Adv. Com., Calif. Office of Adminstrv.

Law., Electronic Ct. Filing Task Force, US Dist. Ct. (no. dist.) Calif. Mem. editl. bd. DATABASE; contbr. articles to law jours. Recipient Marshall D. O'Neill Award. Office: Robert Crown Law Libr Stanford Law Sch 559 Nathan Abbott Way Stanford CA 94305 Office Phone: 650-725-0804. E-mail: plomio@stanford.edu.

LOND, HARLEY WELDON, editor, publishing executive; b. Chgo., Feb. 5, 1946; s. Henry and Dorothy L.; m. Marilyn Moss, Aug. 20, 1981; 1 child Elizabeth. BA in Journalism, Calif. State U., LA, 1972. Adminstrv. dir. Century City Ednl. Arts Project, LA, 1972-76, hon. dir., 1982—; founder, editor Intermedia mag., LA, 1974-80; prodn. mgr. FilmRow Publs., LA, 1981; assoc. editor Box Office mag., Hollywood, Calif., 1981-84, editor, assoc. pub., 1984-94; dir. publs. Entertainment Data, Inc., 1994-95; pres. CyberPod Prodns., 1995—; webmaster OnVideo.org, 1996—, Dreamsville.com, 2007—; asst. news editor The Hollywood Reporter, 1995-2000, news editor, 2000—07, mng. editor, 2007—. Syndicated columnist Continental Features, Washington, Tel-Aire Publs., Dallas, 1986—; hon dir. Monterey (Calif.) Film Festival, 1987; mem. media adv. bd. Cinetex Internat. Film Festival, 1988; cons. Take 3 Info. Svc.; web architect-master, OnVideo website, 1995—. Editor: Entertainment Media Electronic Info. Svc.; contbg. editor: (video) Family Style Mag.; contbr. articles to profl. publs. Calif. Arts Council grantee, 1975, Nat. Endowment for Arts grantee, 1976-77. Mem. MLA, Soc. Profl. Journalists, Assn. for Edn. in Journalism and Mass Communication, Speech Communication Assn., Soc. for Cinema Studies. Home and Office: PO Box 17377 Beverly Hills CA 90209-3377 Home Phone: 310-277-0778. Personal E-mail: harleyl@earthlink.net, harley.lond@thr.com.

LONDEN, JACK W., lawyer; b. Boulder, Colo., Feb. 11, 1953; married; 3 children. BA magna cum laude, Harvard U., 1975; JD, Yale U., 1978. Bar: Calif. 1979, Ariz. 1979. Law clerk to Hon. William W. Schwarzer U.S. Dist. Ct. (no. dist.) Calif., 1979-80; assoc. Morrison & Foerster, San Francisco, 1980—84, ptnr., 1984—. Chmn. Californians for Legal Aid; vice-chmn. Calif. Commissn. on Access to Justice. Recipient Loren Miller Legal Services Award, State Bar of Calif, 1996; named one of Top Ten Lawyers in Bay Area, San Francisco Chronicle, 2003, 100 Most Influential Lawyers, Nat. Law Jour., 2006. Mem.: Legal Aid Soc. of San Francisco (bd. dirs.). Office: Morrison & Foerster 425 Market St San Francisco CA 94105-2482 Office Phone: 415-268-7415. Business E-Mail: jlonden@mofo.com.

LONERGAN, KEVIN M., retail apparel company executive; With Gap Inc., 1971, other retail cos.; rejoined Gap Inc., 1989, co-creator, exec. v.p. Old Navy divsn., 1994, now exec. v.p., COO Old Navy divsn., 1999—. Office: Gap Inc 1 Harrison St San Francisco CA 94105-1602

LONG, ANTHONY ARTHUR, classics educator; b. Manchester, Eng., Aug. 17, 1937; came to U.S. 1983; s. Tom Arthur and Phyllis Joan (LeGrice) L.; m. Janice Calloway, Dec. 30, 1960 (div. 1969); 1 child, Stephen Arthur; m. Mary Kay Flavell, May 25, 1970 (div. 1990); 1 child, Rebecca Jane; m. Monique Marie-Jeanne Elias, Mar. 22, 1997. BA, U. Coll. London, 1960; PhD, U. London, 1964. Lectr. classics U. Otago, Dunedin, New Zealand, 1961-64, U. Nottingham, England, 1964-66; lectr. Greek and Latin U. Coll. London, 1966-71; reader in Greek and Latin U. London, 1971-73; Gladstone prof. Greek U. Liverpool, England, 1973-83, pub. orator, 1981-83; prof. classics U. Calif., Berkeley, 1982—, chmn. dept. classics, 1986-90, Irving Stone prof. lit., 1991—. Mem. Inst. Advanced Study, Princeton, NJ, 1970, 79; vis. prof. U. Munich, 1973, Ecole Normale Supérieure, Paris, 1993, 2001; Cardinal Mercier prof. philosophy U. Louvain, Belgium, 1991; Belle van Zuylen prof. philosophy, U. Utrecht, Netherlands, 2003; mem. selection com. Mellon Fellowships, 1984-90, Stanford U. Humanities Coun., 1985-86; Corbett lectr. U. Cambridge, 1998-99; faculty rsch. lectr. U. Calif., Berkeley, 1999-2000, affiliated prof. philosophy, 2005-; Brackenridge lectr., U. Tex., San Antonio, 2003. Author: Language and Thought in Sophocles, 1968 (Cromer Greek prize 1968), Problems in Stoicism, 1971, 96, Hellenistic Philosophy, 1974, 2d edit., 1986, (with Fortenbaugh and Huby) Theophrastus of Eresus, 1985, (with Sedley) The Hellenistic Philosophers, 1987, (with Dillon) The Question of Eclecticism, 1988, 96, (with Bastianini) Hierocles, 1992, (with others) Images and Ideologies, 1993, Stoic Studies, 1996, 2d edit., 2001, Cambridge Companion to Early Greek Philosophy, 1999, Epictetus, 2002-04, From Epicurus to Epictetus: Studies in Hellenistic and Roman Philosophy, 2006; editor: Classical Quar., 1975-81, Classical Antiquity, 1987-90; gen. editor: (with Barnes) Clarendon Later Ancient Philosophers, 1987—. Served to lt. Royal Arty., Eng., 1955-57 Named hon. citizen City of Rhodes, Greece; sr. fellow humanities coun. Princeton U., 1978, short-term fellow, 2002, Bye fellow Robinson Coll., Cambridge, 1982, Guggenheim fellow, 1986-87, sr. fellow Ctr. for Hellenic Studies, 1988-93, Wissenschaftskolleg fellow, Berlin, 1991-92, William Evans fellow U. Otago, New Zealand, 1995; fellow NEH, 1990-91, Ctr. Advanced Study in Behavioral Scis., Stanford, 2007-. Fellow Am. Acad. Arts and Scis., Brit. Acad. (corr.); mem. Classical Assn., Aristotelian Soc., Am. Philol. Assn., Phi Beta Kappa (hon.). Avocations: music, walking, travel, bridge. Home: 32 Sunset Dr Kensington CA 94707-1139 Office: U Calif Dept Classics Berkeley CA 94720-0001 E-mail: aalong@berkeley.edu.

LONG, GREGORY ALAN, lawyer; b. San Francisco, Aug. 28, 1948; s. William F. and Ellen L. (Webber) L.; m. Jane H. Barrett, Sept. 30, 1983; children: Matthew, Brian, Michael, Gregory. BA magna cum laude, Claremont Men's Coll., Calif., 1970; JD cum laude, Harvard U., 1973. Bar: Calif. 1973, U.S. Dist. Ct. (ctrl. dist.) Calif. 1973, U.S. Ct. Appeals (9th cir.) 1976, U.S. Supreme Ct. 1977, U.S. Ct. Appeals (fed. cir.) 1984. Assoc. Overton, Lyman & Prince, LA, 1973-78, ptnr., 1978-87, Sheppard, Mullin, Richter & Hampton, LA, 1987—. Arbitrator L.A. Superior Ct. Fellow Am. Bar Found.; mem. ABA (young lawyers divsn. exec. coun. 1974-88, chmn. 1984-85, ho. of dels. 1983-89, exec. coun. litigation sect. 1981-83), Calif. Bar Assn. (del. 1976-82, 87-88), L.A. County Bar Assn. (exec. com. 1979-82, trustee 1979-82, barristers sect. exc. coun. 1976-82, pres. 1981-82, exec. coun. trial lawyers sect. 1984-88, chair amicus briefs com. 1989-92). Office: Sheppard Mullin Richter & Hampton 333 S Hope St Los Angeles CA 90071-1406 Office Phone: 213-617-5443. Business E-Mail: glong@smrh.com.

LONG, JEANINE HUNDLEY, state legislator; b. Provo, Utah, Sept. 21, 1928; d. Ralph Conrad and Hazel Laurine (Snow) Hundley; m. McKay W. Christensen, Oct. 28, 1949 (div. 1967); children: Cathy Schuyler, Julie Schulleri, Kelly M. Christensen, C. Brett Christensen, Harold A. Christensen; m. Kenneth D. Long, Sept. 6, 1968. AA, Shoreline C.C., Seattle, 1975; BA in Psychology, U. Wash., 1977. Mem. Wash. Ho. of Reps., 1983-87, 93-94, mem. Inst. Pub. Policy; mem. Wash. Senate, Dist. 44, Olympia, 1995—2003. Ranking mem. Human Svcs. and Corr. com. Wash. Senate, 1995-96, 99-2002, chair, 1997-98; vice-chair Rep. Caucus, 1997-98; mem. Braam panel to monitor Dept. Social and Health Svcs., 2005—. Mayor protem, mem. city coun. City of Brier, Wash., 1977-80. Republican. Office: PO Box 40482 Olympia WA 98504-0482 E-mail: long_je@leg.wa.gov.

LONG, SHARON RUGEL, molecular biologist, educator; b. Mar. 2, 1951; d. Harold Eugene and Florence Jean (Rugel) Long; m. Harold James McGee, July 7, 1979 (div. 2004); 2 children BS, Calif. Inst. Tech., 1973; PhD, Yale U., 1979. Rsch. fellow Harvard U., Cambridge, Mass., 1979-81; from asst. prof. molecular biology to prof. Stanford U., Palo Alto, Calif., 1982-92, prof. biol. scis., 1992—, William C. Steere, Jr.-Pfizer Inc. prof. biological scis., dean Sch. Humanities and Scis., 2001—07. Investigator Howard Hughes Med. Inst., 1994-2001; adv. bd. Jane Coffin Childs Meml. Fund; bd. dirs. Ann. Revs. Inc., Monsanto Co. Recipient award NSF, 1979, NIH, 1980, Shell Rsch. Found. award 1985, Presdl. Young Investigator award NSF, 1984-89; grantee NIH, Dept. Energy, NSF; MacArthur fellow, 1992-97, Georges Morel fellow I.N.R.A., France, 1998; fellow Noble Found. Fellow Assn. Women in Sci., Am. Soc. Microbiology, Soc. Devel. Biology, Am. Acad. Arts Scis., Am. Soc. Plant Biologists; mem. NAS (councilor 2007—), Genetics Soc. Am., Am. Soc. Plant Physiology (Charles Albert Shull award 1989). Office: Stanford U Dept Biology 371 Serra Mall Stanford CA 94305-5020 Office Fax: 650-725-8309. Business E-Mail: srl@stanford.edu.

LONG, WILLIAM D., grocery store executive; b. Watertown, Wis., Nov. 30, 1937; s. William D. and Olive (Piper) L.; m. Doreen Loveall, Sept. 23, 1967; children: Angela, Scott, Irene, Jeffrey, William, Jennifer. Student, U. Wis., Madison. Store mgr. Safeway, Salt Lake City, 1961-68; pres., CEO WinCo Foods, Inc, Boise, Idaho, 1968—. Cpl. U.S. Army, 1957-60. Office: Winco Foods 650 N Armstrong Pl Boise ID 83704

LONGAKER, RICHARD PANCOAST, retired political science professor, academic administrator; b. Phila., July 1, 1924; s. Edwin P. and Emily (Downs) L.; m. Mollie M. Katz, Jan. 25, 1964; children—Richard Pancoast II (dec.), Stephen Edwin, Sarah Ellen, Rachel Elise. BA in Polit. Sci, Swarthmore Coll., 1949; MA in Am. History, U. Wis., 1950; PhD in Govt, Cornell U., 1953. Teaching asst. Cornell U., 1950-53, vis. asso. prof., 1960-61; asst. prof. Kenyon Coll., 1953-54, asso. prof., 1955-60; asst. prof. U. Calif., Riverside, 1954-55, faculty Los Angeles, 1961-76, chmn. dept. polit. sci., 1963-67, prof., 1975—76, dean acad. affairs grad. div., 1970-71; prof. Johns Hopkins U., Balt., 1976-87, provost and v.p. for acad. affairs, 1976-87, prof. emeritus, cons. western states office Santa Monica, Calif., 1987—; prof. in residence UCLA, 2001—. Author: The Presidency and Individual Liberties, 1961; co-author: The Supreme Court and the Commander in Chief, 1976, also articles, revs. Served with AUS, 1943-45. Mem.: Am. Polit. Sci. Assn. Office: 16550 Chalet Ter Pacific Palisades CA 90272-2344

LONGBRAKE, WILLIAM ARTHUR, bank executive; b. Hershey, Pa., Mar. 15, 1943; s. William Van Fleet and Margaret Jane (Barr) Longbrake; m. Martha Ann Curtis, Aug. 23, 1970; children: Derek Curtis, Mark William, David Robert, Dorothy Eleanor Lois. BA in Econs., Coll. of Wooster, 1965; MA in Monetary Econs., U. Wis., 1968, MBA, 1969; PhD in Fin., U. Md., 1976. Jr. asst. planner Northeastern Ill. Planning Commn., Chgo., 1966; instr. Coll. Bus. and Mgmt. U. Md., 1969-71, lectr., 1976, 79-81; fin. economist FDIC, Washington, 1971-75, sr. planning specialist Office Corp. Planning, 1975-76, spl. asst. to chmn., acting contr., 1977-78; assoc. dir. div. banking rsch. Office Compt. of Currency, Treas. Dept., Washington, 1976, dep. dir. econ. rsch. and analysis div., 1976-77, dep. compt. for rsch. and econ. programs, 1978-81, acting sr. dep. compt. for policy, 1981-82, sr. dep. compt. for resource mgmt., 1982; exec. v.p., CFO Wash. Mut. Savs. Bank, Seattle, 1982—95; CFO, dep. to chmn. FDIC, Washington, 1995—96; exec. v.p., CFO Wash. Mut. Inc., Seattle, 1996—99, mem. exec. com., 1996—2008, vice chmn., CFO, 1999—2002, vice chmn., 2002—08; bd. dirs. First Fin. Northwest, Inc., Renton, Wash., 2008—. Bd. dir. Fed. Home Loan Bank Seattle, Wash. Fin. League, America's Cmty. bankers. Assoc. editor Fin. Mgmt., 1974-78; mem. editorial adv. bd. Issues in Bank Regulation, 1977-84, Jour. Econs. and Bus., 1980-83; contbr. articles to profl. jours. Mem. College park (Md.) Citizen's Adv. Com. on Code Enforcement, 1973-74, cons., 1975; lectr. Albers Sch. Bus. Seattle U., 1985, student mentor, 1994; bd. dirs. Pget Sound Coun. Fin. Insts., Seattle, dir., 1986-90, v.p., 1988, pres., 1989-90; mem. Seattle Mcpl. League, 1986—, treas., 1988-90, pres., 1990-93; past chmn. Capitol Hill Housing Improvement Program, Seattle; mem. The King County Housing Partnership, Seattle exec. com., chmn. outreach and tech. assistance com., 1990-92; bd. visitors Sch. Nursing U. Wash., Seattle, 1983-92, chmn., 1986-90; mem. of local initiative support corp. Seattle/Tacoma Adv. Bd., 1989-91; bd. dirs. Diabetes Rsch. Coun., Seattle, 1984-89, v.p., 1987-88; bd. dirs. N.W. Symphony Orch., Seattle, 1987-89, treas., 1988-89, adv. bd.; trustee Kenney presbyn. Home, West Seattle, exec. com., chmn. fin. com.; trustee Intiman Theatre Co., Seattle, 1988-92; past chmn. tax com. Wash. Savs. league; mem. Seattle Comprehensive Plan Implement Task Force, 1993-94; past chmn. adv. bd. Wash. State Affordable Housing; dir. Nat. Assn. Housing partnerships; mem. King County Growth Mgmt., planning coun. affordable housing task force, 1992-93; co-chair Gov.'s Task force on Affordable Housing, Washington, 1992-93, chmn. bd. dirs. Threshold Housing, 1992—; mem. Impact Fees commn., 1992-92, Coun. Washington's Future, arrangement's chair, 1988-91; mem. Governor's Council Econ. Adv., Wash.; mem. adv. bd. Univ. Wsh. Bus. Sch. Recipient Kenneth E. Trefftz prize, Western Fin. Assn., 1971. Mem. Am. Econs. Assn., Am. Fin. Assn., Fin. Mgmt. Assn. (dir. 1978-80), Fin. Execs. Inst. (Puget Sound chpt., bd. dirs. 1988—, chmn. acad. rels. com. 1988-89, chmn. tec. com. 1989-90, treas. 1990-91, v.p. 1991-93, pres. 1993-94, chmn. nominating com. 1994—), Coll. of Wooster Alumni Assn. (pres. Washington Alumni Assn. 1976, pres. Seattle Alumni Assn. 1983—, trustee 1988—, mem. fin., audit, religious dimension, student rels. com. alumni bd. 1988—), Nat. Coun. Savings Instns. (mortgage fin. com. 1989), Columbia Tower Club. Avocations: jogging, painting, singing, piano. Office: First Fin Northwest Inc 201 Wells Ave S Renton WA 98057

LONGENECKER, MARTHA W., museum director; BA in Art, UCLA; MFA, Claremont Grad. Sch.; studied with Millard Sheets, Shoji Hamada, Tatsuzo Shimaoka. Owner ceramics studio, Claremont, Calif.; prof. art, now prof. emerita San Diego State U.; founder, dir. Mingei Internat. Mus., San Diego. Coord. editing, design and prodn. of exhbn. documentary publs.; condr. tours. Contbr. chpts. to books; developer videotapes; exhibited at Dalzell Hatfield Galleries. San Diego State U. Found. grantee, 1967, Calif. State U. Rsch. grantee, 1978; recipient Disting. Alumna award Claremont Grad. Sch., 1980, Essence of Life award ElderHelp of San Diego, 1993, Living Legacy award Women's Internat. Ctr., 1994, Women of Distinction award Soroptimist Internat. of La Jolla, 1994, Headliner of Yr. Art, San Diego Press Club, 1998, Disting. Svc. medal, San Diego State U., 1998, Reischauer Internat. Edn. award, Japan Soc. San Diego and Tijuana, 1999, San Diego Women Who Mean Bus. award, Foley Vardner Attys. at Law, San Diego Bus. Jour., 2000, Gold Rays with Rosette, Order of Rising Sun, Emperor of Japan, 2003, Golden Hanger Spl. award, Fashion Careers of Calif. Coll., 2004. Office: Mingei Internat Mus Balboa Park 1439 El Prado San Diego CA 92101-1617 also: Mingei International Museum 1439 El Prado San Diego CA 92101-1617

LONGO, LAWRENCE DANIEL, physiologist, obstetrician, gynecologist, educator; b. LA, Oct. 11, 1926; s. Frank Albert and Florine Azelia (Hall) L.; m. Betty Jeanne Mundall, Sept. 9, 1948; children: April Celeste, Lawrence Anthony, Elisabeth Lynn, Camilla Giselle. BA, Pacific Union Coll., 1949; MD, Coll. Med. Evangelists, Loma Linda, Calif., 1954. Diplomate Am. Bd. Ob-Gyn. Intern L.A. County Gen. Hosp., 1954-55, resident in ob-gyn., 1955-58; asst. prof. ob-gyn UCLA, 1962-64; asst. prof. physiology and ob-gyn U. Pa., 1964-68; prof. physiology and ob-gyn Loma Linda U., 1968—; dir. ctr. for perinatal biology Loma Linda U. Sch. Medicine, 1974—. Perinatal biology com. Nat. Inst. Child Health, NIH, 1973-77; co-chmn. reprodn. scientist devel. program NIH; NATO prof. Consiglio Nat. delle Rsch., Italian Govt. Editor: Respiratory Gas Exchange and Blood Flow in the Placenta, 1972, Fetal and Newborn Cardiovascular Physiology, 1978, Charles White and A Treatise on the Management of Pregnant and Lying-in Women, 1987; co-editor: Landmarks in Perinatology, 1975-76, Classics in Obstetrics Gynecology, 1993, Dearest G..., Yours W.O., William Osler's Letters from Egypt to Grace Revere Osler, 2003, William Osler's Man's Redemption of Man, 2003, Our Lords the Sick..., 2004; editor classic pages in ob-gyn. Am. Jour. Ob-Gyn.; contbr. articles to profl. jours. Served with AUS, 1945-47. Founder Frank A. and Florine A. Longo lectureship in faith, knowledge, and human values Pacific Union Coll., 1993. Fellow Royal Coll. Ob-Gyns., Am. Coll. Ob-Gyns.; mem. Am. Assn. History Medicine (coun.), Am. Osler Soc. (bd. govs., sec.-treas., pres.), Am. Physiol. Soc., Assn. Profs. Ob-Gyn., Perinatal Rsch. Soc., Soc. Gynecologic Investigation (past pres.), Neurosci. Soc., Royal Soc. Medicine. Adventist. Office: Loma Linda U Sch Medicine Ctr Perinatal Biology Loma Linda CA 92350-0001 Business E-Mail: llongo@llu.edu.

LONGVILLE, JOHN, state legislator; b. St. Paul, Sept. 21, 1949; m. Victoria Brookins, Jan. 1975 (dec. 1991); 1 child, Regan Brookins-Longville. Student, U. Minn., 1968. From polit. aide to press sec. U.S. Rep. George Brown, Calif., 1968-79; councilman City of Rialto, Calif., 1980-84, 86-88, mayor Calif., 1988—98; mem. Calif. Ho. of Reps., 1998—. Bd. dirs. Omnitrans, So. Calif. Regional Rail Authority. Vol. United Farm Workers, 1969; project dir. Viewer sponsored TV Found., L.A., 1970-71; past pres. Am. Cancer Soc., Rialto. Jr. Achievement scholar. Mem. NAACP (life), MADD, So. Calif. Assn. Govts. (pres. 1996—), Jaycees, Kiwanis.

LONNQUIST, GEORGE ERIC, lawyer; b. Lincoln, Nebr., Mar. 29, 1946; s. John Hall and Elizabeth Claire (Hanson) L.; m. Wendi Ann McDonough; children: Alethea, Courtenay, Barrett. BS, U. Tenn., 1968; JD, U. Nebr., 1971; LLM, NYU, 1974. Bar: Calif. 1983, Oreg. 1972, Nebr. 1971. Law clerk Oreg. Supreme Ct., Salem, 1971-72; dep. legis. counsel Oreg. Legislature, Salem, 1972-73; ptnr. Meysing & Lonnquist, Portland, 1974-78; v.p., assoc. gen. counsel Amfac, Inc., Portland and San Francisco, 1978-84; sr. v.p., gen. counsel Homestead Fin. Corp., Millbrae, Calif., 1984-91, Homestead Savs., Millbrae, 1984-93; pvt. practice, San Francisco, 1993—. Democrat. Roman Catholic. Avocation: woodcarving. Office: 4000 E 3rd Ave Foster City CA 94404-4805 Home: 60759 Currant Way Bend OR 97702 Office Phone: 650-235-2861. Business E-Mail: lonn@legacypartners.com.

LOO, THOMAS S., lawyer; b. 1943; BS, JD, U. So. Calif. Bar: Calif. 1969. Ptnr. Greenberg Traurig, Santa Monica, Calif., 2001—. Office: 2450 Colorado Ave Ste 400E Santa Monica CA 90404

LOOMIS, CHRISTOPHER KNAPP, metallurgical engineer; b. San Francisco, May 6, 1947; s. Richard and Evaline Elsie (Crandal) L.; m. Merril Ellen Purdy, Dec. 8, 1968; 1 child, Nicole Lee; m. Sandra Lee Marsh, Feb. 14, 1993. Profl. Engring. degree, Colo. Sch. Mines, 1969. Process engr. Alcan Aluminum Corp., Riverside, Calif., 1969-73, prodn. supt., 1973-76, process engr. Oswego, N.Y., 1976-78, maintenance engr., 1978-80; metall. engr. Hazelett Strip-Casting Corp., Colchester, Vt., 1980-81; chief engr. ARCO Metals Co., Chgo., 1981-84; maintenance supt. Cerro Metal Products, Paramount, Calif., 1984-85, mgr. engring. and maintenance, 1985-86; supt. tech. svcs. Golden Aluminum Co., Ft. Lupton, Colo., 1987-88, process devel. engr. Lakewood, Colo., 1988-91, corp. environ. and process engr., 1991; engr. IV Coors Brewing Co., Golden, Colo., 1991-93, materials engr. V, 1993-96, supr. maintenance svcs., 1999—; gen. ptnr. Loomis Engring. and Design, 1996-99. Mem. Am. Soc. for Metals, Metall. Soc., Colo. Sch. Mines Alumni Assn., Am. Soc. for Quality Control, Fedn. Fly Fishers (life), Trout Unltd. (life). Episcopalian. Avocations: fishing, camping, mechanics, home repair. Office: Coors Brewing Co PO Box 4030 Golden CO 80401-0030 Office Phone: 303-277-5097. Personal E-mail: loomisengrg@comcast.net. Business E-Mail: chris.loomis@coors.com.

LOOMIS, RICK, photographer; b. Raleigh, NC, Mar. 22, 1969; Student, Palm Beach Cmty. Coll., 1987—88; BA, Western Ky. U., Bowling Green, 1993. HS intern Palm Beach Post, 1987, lab technician, 1987—89; summer intern Ft. Wayne News Sentinel, 1990, Colo. Springs Gazette Telegraph, 1991, Seattle Times, 1992, Syracuse (NY) Newspapers, 1993; staff photographer Coll. Heights Herald, Western Ky. U., 1991—92; photographer LA Times, 1994—. Recipient Sigma Delta Chi award, Soc. Profl. Journalists, 2003, Journalist of Yr. award, LA Press Club, 2004, Sidney Hillman Found. award for Overall Excellence in Photojournalism, 2005; co-recipient Pulitzer Prize for Explanatory Reporting, 2007. Mem.: Nat. Press Photographers Assn. (Photographer of Yr. 2003), Calif. Press Photographers Assn. (Photographer of Yr. 2002, 2004). Office: LA Times 202 W 1st St Los Angeles CA 90012

LOOPER, MARSHA, state legislator; m. Lynn Looper; children: Rachelle, Travis, Justin. Attended, Mesa State Coll., Grand Junction, Colo. Former co-owner Waterworks Sales; ptnr. Big Sky Realty; owner, operator Phoenix & Associates; owner Computing Solutions Group, 1993—; mem. Dist. 19 Colo. House of Reps., Denver, 2007—. Exec. dir. Colo. Citizens Property Rights; chair Eastern Plains

Citizens Coalition; vol. Spl. Olympics; basketball coach YMCA; leader 4H; mem. Falcon Sch. Dist. Accountability Com. Mem.: NRA, El Paso County Soil & Water Conservation Soc., Pikes Peak Pivots, Pikes Peak Range Riders, Pikes Peak Firearms Coalition. Republican. Office: Colo State Capitol 200 E Colfax Denver CO 80203 Office Phone: 303-866-2946. Business E-Mail: marsha.looper.house@state.co.us.*

LOOPLOCK, PAUL, computer technician; b. Dec. 1970; s. Gerald and Maryanne Looplock; m. Janet Marie Looplock; children: William, Christine, Laura, Ian. BS in Computer Sciences, U. Wis., 1992, MSc in Computer Sciences, 1994. Asst. computer technician IBM, 1995—97, jr. computer technician, 1998—2000; head computer technician Meriks Computer Svcs., Cheyenne, Wyo., 2000—04, v.p. computer technician, 2004—. Author: How-to Rid your Computer of Viruses, 2000, Learning How To Work Your MAC, 2003. Vol. technician City Schools, 2000—. Office: Meriks Computer Services 1600 Muskogee Loop Unit A Cheyenne WY 82001

LOPACH, JAMES JOSEPH, political science professor; b. Great Falls, Mont., June 23, 1942; s. John Ernest and Alma Marie (Schapman) L.; div. Dec. 10, 1991; children: Christine, Paul. AB in Philosophy, Carroll Coll., 1964; MA in Am. Studies, U. Notre Dame, 1967, MAT in English Edn., 1968, PhD in Govt., 1973. Mgr. Pacific Telephone, Palo Alto, Calif., 1968-69; adminstr. City of South Bend, Ind., 1971-73; prof. U. Mont., Missoula, 1973—, chmn. dept. polit. sci., 1977-87, 2006—08, assoc. dean Coll. Arts and Scis., 1987-88, acting dir. Mansfield Ctr., 1984-85, spl. asst. to the univ. pres., 1988-92, assoc. provost, 1992-95, spl. asst. to provost, 1995-96. Cons. local govts., state agys., tribal govts., law firms, 1973—; expert witness. Author, editor: We the People of Montana, 1983, Tribal Government Today, 1990, 98, Planning Small Town America, 1990, Jeannette Rankin: A Political Woman, 2005; contbr. articles to profl. jours. Roman Catholic. Office: U Mont Dept Polit Sci Missoula MT 59812-0001 Office Phone: 406-243-5202. E-mail: james.lopach@umontana.edu.

LOPER, JOYCE E., plant pathologist, educator; BS in Biol. Scis., U. Calif., Davis, 1974, MS in Plant Pathology, 1978; PhD in Plant Pathology, U. Calif., Berkeley, 1983. Prof. dept. botany and plant pathology Oreg. State U., 1987—; rsch. plant pathologist USDA-Agrl. Rsch. Svc., 1985—, rsch. leader Hort. Crops Rsch. Lab., 2000—04. Mem. agr. bd. NRC, ecologically-based pest mgmt.: new solutions for a new century panel NAS, Washington, 1992-95, sci. adv. panel NSF Ctr. Microbial Ecology Mich. State U., 1992-96; councilor-at-large Am. Phytopathol. Soc., 1997-2000. Sr. editor Am. Phytopathol. Soc. Press, 1990-93; assoc. editor Molecular Plant-Microbe Interactions, 1996-99; mem. editl. com. Ann. Revs. of Phytopathology, 1996—2005; mem. editl. bd. European Jour. Plant Pathology, 1995—2005. Recipient CIBA GEIGY award Am. Phytopathological Soc., 1995. Fellow Am. Phytopathol. Soc. Office: USDA ARS Hort Crops Lab 3420 NW Orchard Ave Corvallis OR 97330-5014

LOPES, JAMES LOUIS, lawyer; b. Watsonville, Calif., Feb. 1, 1947; s. Allen M. and Norma Maxine (McElroy) L.; m. Gail R. Lopes, Mar. 24, 1979; children: Elizabeth, Jane. BS, U.Calif., Davis, 1969; JD, U. Pacific, 1974; LLM, Harvard U., 1975. Bar: Calif. 1974, U.S. Ct. Appeals (9th cir.), U.S. Dist. Ct. (no., ea., ctrl. dists.) Calif. Assoc. Gendel, Raskoff, Shapiro & Quittner, LA, 1975-78; ptnr. Gordon, Peitzman & Lopes, San Francisco, 1978-81, Howard, Rice & Nemerovski, San Francisco, 1982—. Adv. com. bankruptcy/creditors' rights Practicing Law Inst., 1992—. Fellow Am. Coll. Bankruptcy, Calif.; mem. Bankruptcy Forum (bd. dirs. 1990-93), Calif. State Bar Assn. Avocations: flying, contract bridge. Office: Howard Rice & Nemerovski 3 Embarcadero Ctr Ste 7 San Francisco CA 94111-4074 Office Phone: 415-434-1600. E-mail: jlopes@howardrice.com.

LOPES, PHIL, state legislator; b. Dos Palos, Calif., June 30, 1941; m. Pamela Lopes; children: Tobin, Mark. AA, West Hills Coll., Calif., 1961; BA in L.Am. Studies, UCLA, 1965; MA in Anthropology, U. Wis., Milw., 1967. Instr. U. Phoenix, 1981; founding faculty mem., instr. Pima Cmty. Coll., Tucson, 1969—73; exec. dir. Health Sys. Agy. Southwestern Ariz., 1981—87; asst. dir. rural health office U. Ariz., 1987—94; sr. lectr. U. Ariz. Coll. Medicine, 1989—94; asst. dir., bur. chief Ariz. Dept. Health Svcs., 1994—98; exec. dir. Ariz. Sch.-Based Health Care Coun., 1998—2003; mem. Dist. 27 Ariz. House of Reps., 2003—, former minority leader. Interim exec. dir. El Pueblo Clinic, Tucson, 2000—01, exec. dir., 2002—04; founder, bd. dirs. Ariz. Health Care Campaign. Vol. Peace Corps, Colombia, 1961—63, staff Brazil, 1963—65, country dir. Ecuador, then co-dir. Brazil, 1976—81; mem. Am. Civil Liberties Union (co. Ariz. chpt.), 1974—76, Nat. Assn. Pub. Health Policy, 1994—2000. Mem.: Am. Health Planning Assn., Ariz. Pub. Health Assn. (bd. dirs. 1982—), Am. Pub. Health Assn. Democrat. Office: Ariz House Reps Capitol Complex 1700 W Washington Rm 330 Phoenix AZ 85007 Office Phone: 602-926-3278. Office Fax: 602-417-3127. Business E-Mail: plopes@azleg.gov.*

LOPES, ROSALY MUTEL CROCCE, astronomer, planetary geologist; arrived in US, 1989, naturalized; d. Walmir Crocce and Atir (Mutel) Lopes; m. Thomas Nicholas Gautier, III, Nov. 17, 1990 (div.); 1 child, Thomas N. Gautier. BSc in Astronomy, U. London, 1978, PhD in Physics, 1986. Curator Old Royal Obs., Greenwich, Eng., 1985-88; rsch. assoc. Vesuvius Obs., Naples, Italy, 1989; NRC rsch. assoc. Jet Propulsion Lab., Pasadena, Calif., 1989-91, rsch. scientist Galileo Project, 1991—2002, rsch. scientist Cassini Project, 2002—04, prin. scientist Cassini Project, 2004—. Mem. Volcanic Eruption Surveillance Team, U.K., 1981. Author: Volcanic Worlds, 2004, The Volcano Adventure Guide, 2005, Io After Galileo, 2007, Alien Volcanoes, 2008, numerous other works in sci. field. Recipient Latinas in Sci. award Commn. Feminil Mexicana Nat., LA, 1990, NASA Exceptional Svc. medal, 2007; named Woman of the Yr. in Sci., Gems TV, 1997. Fellow AAAS, Explorers Club; mem. Internat. Astron. Union, Am. Astron. Soc. (Carl Sagan medal 2005), Am. Geophys. Union. Avocations: scuba diving, hiking, travel. Home: 278 Bonita Ave Pasadena CA 91107-4735 Office: Jet Propulsion Lab Mail Stop 183-601 4800 Oak Grove Dr Pasadena CA 91109-8001 Home Phone: 626-304-0688; Office Phone: 818-393-4584. Business E-Mail: rosaly.m.lopes@jpl.nasa.gov.

LOPEZ, BARRY HOLSTUN, writer; b. Port Chester, NY, Jan. 6, 1945; s. Adrian Bernard and Mary Frances (Holstun) L.; m. Sandra Jean Landers, June 10, 1967 (div. Jan. 16, 1999), m. Debra Arleen Gwartney, Dec. 15, 2007. Degree, NYU, 1963; BA cum laude, U. Notre Dame, 1966, MA in Teaching, 1968; postgrad., U. Oreg., 1968-69; LHD (hon.), Whittier Coll., 1988, U. Portland, 1994, Tex. Tech. U., 2000; LHD in Environ. Studies (hon.), Utah State U., 2002. Free-lance writer, 1970—. Assoc. Media Studies Ctr. at Columbia Univ., N.Y.C., 1985-96; mem. U.S. Cultural Delegation to China, 1988. Author: Desert Notes, 1976, Giving Birth to Thunder, 1978, Of Wolves and Men, 1978 (John Burroughs Soc. medal 1979, Christophers of N.Y. medal 1979, Pacific Northwest Booksellers award in nonfiction 1979), River Notes, 1979, Winter Count, 1981 (Disting. Recognition award Friends Am. Writers in Chgo. 1982), Arctic Dreams, 1986 (Nat. Book award in nonfiction Nat. Book Found. 1986, Christopher medal 1987, Pacific Northwest Booksellers award 1987, Frances Fuller Victor award in nonfiction Oreg. Inst. Literary Arts 1987), Crossing Open Ground, 1988, Crow and Weasel, 1990 (Parents Choice Found. award), The Rediscovery of North America, 1991, Field Notes, 1994 (Pacific Northwest Booksellers award in fiction 1995, Critics' Choice award 1996), Lessons From the Wolverine, 1997, About This Life, 1998, Apologia, 1998, Light Action in the Caribbean, 2000, Vintage Lopez, 2004, Resistance, 2004 (H.L. Davis Short Fiction Lit. Arts award, Oreg., 2005); also numerous articles, essays and short stories; editor: Home Ground, 2006; contbg. editor Harper's mag., 1981-82, 1984-2004, N.Am. Rev., 1977—, Ga. Rev., 2000—, Manoa, 2006—, Nat. Geog., 2007-; works translated into Japanese, Swedish, German, Dutch, Italian, French, Norwegian, Chinese, Finnish, Slovak, Spanish, Arabic. Recipient award in Lit., Am. Acad. Arts and Letters, 1986, Antarctic Svc. medal U.S. Congress, 1989, Gov.'s award for Arts, 1990, Lannan Found. award, 1990, Internat. Environ. award Prescott Coll., 1992, John Hay award, The Orion Soc., 2002, St. Francis of Assisi award DePaul U., 2002, Denise Levertov award Image mag., 2002, Robert F. Griffin award U. Notre Dame, 2007; Title V fellow HEA, 1967, fellow John Simon Guggenheim Found., 1987; residency fellow Lannan Found., 1999; Bernadine Kielty Scherman Residency fellow The Macdowell Colony in Vt., 2004; grantee NSF, 1987, 88, 91, 92, 99, vis. disting. scholar Tex. Tech U., 2003—. Fellow Explorers Club; mem. PEN Am. Ctr., PEN Ctr. USA West, Authors Guild, Poets and Writers, Amnesty Internat., Nature Conservancy (hon. life), Arctic Inst. N.Am. (life). Achievements include archive purchased for The James Sowell Family Collection in Literature, Community and the Natural World, Tex. Tech. U., 2000.

LOPEZ, DANIEL HERALDO, academic administrator; b. Puerto de Luna, N.Mex., Feb. 14, 1946; s. Julian and Tiofila (Ocaña) L.; m. Linda Vigil, July 12, 1975. BA in Polit. Sci., U. N.Mex., 1970, MA in Polit. Sci., 1972, PhD in Polit. Sci., 1982. Cabinet sec. N.Mex. Dept. Fin. and Adminstrn., Santa Fe, 1984-86; chief of staff for senate fin. and sr. staff analyst House Appropriations and Fin. Com., Santa Fe, 1987-89; assoc. and dep. dir. terminal effects rsch. and analysis N.Mex. Inst. Mining and Tech., Socorro, 1987-89, adj. prof., 1994—; v.p. institutional devel. N.Mex. Inst. Mining and Technology, Socorro, 1989-93, pres., 1993—. Exec. dir. N.Mex. Adv. Coun. on Vocat.-Tech. Edn., 1973-82; adj. prof. U. N.Mex., Albuquerque, 1975-82, N.Mex. Inst. Mining and Tech., Socorro, 1994—; cabinet sec. N.Mex. Employment Security Dept., Albuquerque, 1983-84. Mem. League of United Latin Am. Citizens, Albuquerque; mem., past pres. Albuquerque Hispano C. of C. Staff Sgt. USAF, 1968-69, Korea. Mem. N.Mex. Tech. Rsch. Found. (v.p. 1994), N.Mex. First Exec. Com. (v.p. 1994), N.Mex. Children's Found., N.Mex. Industry Network Corp. (exec. com. 1994), N.Mex. Amigos, Rio Grande Tech. Found. Avocations: running, travel. Home: One Olive Ln Socorro NM 87801 Office: NMex Inst Mining & Tech Office Pres 801 LeRoy Pl Socorro NM 87801

LÓPEZ, EUGENIO ALONSO, art gallery owner, food products executive; b. Mexico City, 1968; Dir. mktg. Grupo Jumex, Ecatepec, Mexico. Owner Chac Mool Gallery, LA, 1994—, Jumex Collection contemporary art, Ecatepec, Mexico, 2001—; trustee Mus. Contemporary Art, LA, New Mus. Contemporary Art, NYC. Named one of Top 200 Collectors, ARTNews Mag., 2006—08. Achievements include founding the largest collection of Latin American art in the world, also Latin America's largest private art collection.

LOPEZ, GEORGE, actor, comedian; b. Mission Hills, Calif., Apr. 23, 1961; m. Ann Serrano, 1993. Radio show host MEGA 92.3 (KCMG), Los Angeles, 2001; co-founder The George & Ann Lopez-Richie Alarcon Care Found. Actor: (films) Fist of Fear, Tough of Death, 1980, Ski Patrol, 1990, Fatal Instinct, 1993, Bread and Roses, 2000, Real Women Have Curves, 2002, Outta Time, 2002, Ali G In Da House, 2002, Balls of Fury, 2007, Henry Poole Is Here, 2008, Swing Vote, 2008, (voice) Beverly Hills Chihuahua, 2008; appearances (TV specials) Latino Laugh Festival, 1997, 2nd Annual Latino Laugh Festival, 1998, host Loco Comedy Jam, 4th Annual Latin Grammy Awards, 2003, 5th Annual Latin Grammy Awards, 2004, correspondent (TV series) Inside the NFL, HBO, 2003; actor: (TV miniseries) Fidel, 2002; actor, co-creator, writer, prodr. George Lopez, 2002—07, comedian (headliner) ARCO Arena, Sacramento, Shoreline Amphitheater, San Francisco, Majestic Theatre, Dallas, San Antonio, Wiltern Theatre, Los Angeles, HBO US Comedy Arts Festival, Aspen; performer: (live comedy albums) Team Leader, 2003 (Grammy nom. best comedy album, 2003), Right Now Right Now, 2004; author: Why You Crying?: My Long, Hard Look at Life, Love, and Laughter, 2004. Spokesperson Stop the Violence program, Los Angeles Police Dept. Recipient Nat. Hispanic Media Coalition Impact award, Community Spirit award, Manny Mota Found., Artist of the Yr. award, Harvard Found. for Intercultural & Race Relations, 2004; named one of 25 Most Influential Hispanics, Time Mag., 2005. Achievements include first Latino to headline a morning radio show on an English-language station in Los Angeles. Office: c/o Ron DeBlasio SDM Inc 740 N La Brea Ave Los Angeles CA 90039

LOPEZ, JENNIFER, actress, singer, dancer; b. Bronx, NY, July 24, 1970; d. David and Guadalupe Lopez; m. Ojani Noa, Feb. 22, 1997 (div. Jan. 1, 1998); m. Cris Judd, Sept. 29, 2001 (div. Jan. 26, 2003); m. Marc Anthony, June 5, 2004; children: Emme Maribel, Maximilian David. Launched clothing line J-Lo by Jennifer Lopez, 2001, lingerie line, 2004; released signature fragrance Glow, 2002, Still, 2004, Miami Glow, 2005, Live Jennifer Lopez, 2005, Love at First Glow, 2006, Deseo, 2008, other fragrances include Glow After Dark, Live Luxe; owner Madre's restaurant, Pasedena, 2002-. Won dance competition and was hired as dancer for TV series In Living Color, 1991-93; actress (TV series) Second Chances, 1993-94, South Central, 1994, Hotel Malibu, 1994; actress (films) Money Train, 1995, Jack, 1996, Blood and Wine, 1996, Anaconda, 1997 (ALMA award 1998), Selena, 1997 (ALMA award 1998), My Family, 1995, U-Turn, 1997, Antz (voice only), 1998, Out of Sight, 1998 (ALMA award 1999), Thieves, 1999, Pluto Nash, 1999, The Cell, 2000 (Blockbuster Entertainment award for Favorite Actress, MTV Movie award for Best Dressed), The Wedding Planner, 2001, Angel Eyes, 2001, Enough, 2002, Maid in Manhattan, 2002, Gigli, 2003, Jersey Girl, 2004, Shall We Dance?, 2004, Monster-in-Law, 2005, An Unfinished Life, 2005, El Cantante, 2006; (TV appearances) Will & Grace, 2004; singer (albums) On the 6, 1999, J.Lo, 2001, J to Tha L-O!: The Remixes, 2002, This Is Me...Then, 2002, Rebirth, 2005, Como Ama Una Mujer (Latin Pop Album of Yr., Billboard Latin Music Awards, 2008), 2007, Brave, 2007. Recipient ALMA Female Entertainer Yr. award 2000, Lasting Image award 1998, Lone Star Film and TV award 1998, Artists for Amnesty award, Amnesty Internat., 2007, Favorite Latin Music Artist award, Am. Music Awards, 2007; voted #1 in 100 Sexiest Women list, FHM, 2000, 2001; named one of The 50 Most Beautiful People in the World, People mag., 1997, The 25 Most Influential Hispanics, Time Mag., 2005, The 100 Most Influential Hispanics, People en Espanol, 2007, The 100 Most Powerful Celebrities, Forbes.com, 2008 Office: c/o Simon Fields Nyuorican Prodns 1100 Glendon Ave Ste 920 Los Angeles CA 90024 also: Internat Creative Mgmt c/o Jeff Berg or Ed Limato 10250 Constellation Blvd Los Angeles CA 90067

LOPEZ, JOE EDDIE, state legislator; b. Duran, N.Mex., Dec. 8, 1939; m. Rosie Lopez; children: Debbie, Eddie. Student, Ariz. State U. Mem. Ariz. Ho. of Reps., 1991-96, Ariz. Senate, Dist. 22, 1996—; mem. appropriations com., mem. edn. com. Ariz. State Senate, mem. family svcs. com., mem. joint legis. budget com. Affirmative action adminstr. Ariz. Dept. Transp.; pres. Housing Devel. Corp. Elected ofcl. Maricopa County Bd. Suprs., Phoenix, 1972-76; mem. governing bd. Phoenix Union H.S. Dist., 1990-96; bd. dirs. Tiempo Devel.; active Los Diablos, Inc., Ariz. Hispanic Cmty. Forum, Mexican-Am. Legislators Policy Inst.; past co-founder, chmn. Chicanos Por La Causa, Inc.; past co-founder, bd. mem. Valle Del Sol, Inc., Barrio Youth Project; past chmn. Phoenix Human Rels. Commn.; past bd. mem. Boy Scouts Am., Ariz. Recipient Cmty. Leadership award Chicanos Por La Causa, 1972, Cmty. Leadership award SER, 1976, Outstanding Svc. to the Cmty. award Ariz. Hispanic/Native Am. Indian Sch. Bd. Forum, 1989, El Aguila award Alma de la Gente, 1992. Mem. Nat. Coun. State Legislators (Ariz. rep. tourism and econ. devel. com.). Democrat. Roman Catholic.

LOPEZ, LINDA, state legislator; b. Logansport, Ind., Sept. 10, 1948; children: Aaron, Toni, Bobbi. Student, U. Calif., Berkley; BA in Women's Studies, U. Ariz., 1990. Clin. supr. La Frontera Ctr., Inc., Tucson, 1991—2003, prog. devel. coord., 2003—06, cmty. rels. coord., 2006—; mem. Dist. 10 Ariz. House of Reps., 2001—02, mem. Dist. 29, 2003—08, Ariz. State Senate, 2009—, minority whip. Mem. Ariz. Sch. Boards Assn., 1991—2002, 2005—06, pres., 2001; mem. gov. bd. Sunnyside Unified Sch. Dist., 1986—2002, 2005—06. Recipient Golden Apple award, Ariz. Parents for Edn., 2008; named Legislator of Yr., Ariz. Sch. Boards Assn., 2003, 2005; named to Sunnyside Sch. Dist. Hall of Fame, 2004. Mem.: NOW (Woman of Courage award 1996), NAACP, Am. Assn. Univ. Women, Bus. & Profl. Women's Assn., Nat. Assn. Latino Elected Officials, Los Descendientes Tucson. Democrat. Office: Ariz State Senate Capitol Complex 1700 W Washington Rm 315 Phoenix AZ 85007-2890 Office Phone: 602-926-4089. Office Fax: 602-417-3029. Business E-Mail: llopez@azleg.gov.*

LOPEZ, LINDA CAROL, social sciences educator; b. NYC, Dec. 26, 1949; d. Ralph B. and M. Lopez. BA, U. Wis., Madison, 1972; MA, Ohio State U., Columbus, 1974, PhD, 1976. Vis. asst. prof. U. Wis., Eau Claire, 1976-77; from instr. to asst. prof. SUNY, Oneonta, 1977-83; assoc. prof. Rockford (Ill.) Coll., 1983—89; prof. dept. social scis. Western N.Mex U., Silver City, 1989—, dir. field experience, 1989—91. Contbr. (to profl. jours. articles) including Psychol. Reports, Internat. Jour. Addiction, Hispanic Jour. Behavioral Scis., Jour. Genetic Psychology, Jour. Employment Counseling, Perceptual and Motor Skills, Reading Improvement, Counseling and Values, Social Studies. Recipient Best Paper award, New Eng. Ednl. Rsch. Orgn., 1979; Postdoctoral Faculty fellow, Northeastern U., Boston, 1980—81. Mem.: Am. Assn. Behavioral & Social Scis. Avocations: walking, reading, travel. Home: PO Box 1479 Bayard NM 88023 Office: Western NMex U Dept Social Scis 1000 W College Ave Silver City NM 88062 Business E-Mail: lopezl@wnmu.edu.

LOPEZ, MANUEL M., optometrist, former mayor; b. 1927; s. Manuel C. and Isabel (Martinez) Lopez; m. Irma J. Lopez; children: Marisa, Tiffany. Degree, Ventura C.C., U. Calif., Berkeley, degree in Optometry. Optometrist, 1962—; mem. City Coun., Oxnard, Calif., 1978—92; mayor protem Oxnard, 1980—82, 1984—86; former mayor. Founder, chmn. Vets. Meml. Com.; founder Oxnard/Ocotlan Sister City Com.; mem. Oxnard/Mexicali Sister City Com.; bd. dir. United Way, 1974—78, Boys and Girls Club, Oxnard. Recipient Patrick Henry award, 1992; named Disting. Citizen of Yr., Oxnard, Calif., 1991. Mem.: Tri-County Optometric Soc. (pres. 1973—74, named Optometrist of Yr. 1975), Calif. Optometric Soc., Am. Optometric Soc., BPOE, Oxnard (Calif.) C. of C., Hispanic C. of C., Trade Club. Address: 300 W 3rd St Oxnard CA 93030-5790

LOPEZ, STEVE, journalist; married; 2 children. With Oakland (Calif.) Tribune, San Jose (Calif.) Mercury News; reporter, columnist Phila. Inquirer, 1986—98, Time Inc., 1998—2001; reporter, Points West columnist LA Times, 2001—. Author: Land of Giants: Where No Good Deed Goes Unpunished, 1995, (novels) Third & Indiana, 1994, The Sunday Macaroni Club, 1997, In the Clear, 2002. Recipient Ernie Pyle Lifetime Achievement award, Nat. Soc. Newspaper Columnists, 2004, Media award, Nat. Alliance on Mental Illness, 2006, Nat. Journalism award for commentary, Scripps Howard Found., 2006, Ernie Pyle award for human interest writing, Nat. Headliner award for column writing, H.L. Mencken Writing award. Office: LA Times 202 W 1st St Los Angeles CA 90012 Office Phone: 213-237-7847. Office Fax: 213-237-4712. E-mail: steve.lopez@latimes.com.

LOPICCOLO, JOHN, conductor, music director; m. Mary Lopiccolo; children: Sabrina, John Michael. MusB in Music Edn., San Francisco State U.; MusM in Orchestral Conducting, Ea. Washington U. Music dir., conductor Idaho Falls (Idaho) Symphony Soc., Inc. Founder, music dir., conductor Idaho Falls Symphony Chorale; concert programmer ann. POPS concerts, Idaho; guest condr. Charlotte, Dubuque, Spokane, S.D., Bremerton, Great Falls, Lethbridge, Walla Walla, Fla. Festival Symphonies, Mont. All-State Orch.; covercondr. Boise Philharm., 1995-96. Guest condr. (play) Porgy and Bess, Vancouver, B.C. Judge Idaho State Civic Symphony, Idaho Falls Symphony Young Artist Competition, Idaho Falls Music Club Scholarship Awards. Recipient Outstanding Svc. award Greater Idaho Falls C. of C. Office: 450 A St Idaho Falls ID 83402-3617

LOQUASTO, SANTO, theatrical set designer; b. Wilkes-Barre, Pa. Grad., King's Coll., Wilkes-Barre; student, Yale U. Sch. Drama. Set designer for repertory cos. including Hartford Stage Co., Long Wharf Theater, New Haven, Conn., 1967-68, Yale Sch. Drama Repertory Theater. NYC debut Astor Place, 1970; set and costume designer

Broadway and off-Broadway prodns. Sticks and Bones, 1971, That Championship Season, Glengarry Glen Ross, 2005 (Drama Desk award, outstanding set design of a play, 2005), A Touch of the Poet, 2005, The Times They Are A-Changin', 2006, Prelude to a Kiss, 2007, Inherit the Wind, 2007, 110 in the Shade, 2007; designer other prodns. including The Secret Affairs of Mildred Wild, 1972, Siamese Connections, The Orphan, As You Like It, King Lear, A Public Prosecutor is Sick of It All, Washington, 1973, The Tempest, The Dance of Death, Pericles, The Merry Wives of Windsor, Richard III, Mert and Phil, Cherry Orchard, Hartford Stage Co., That Championship Season, London, 1974, A Midsummer Night's Dream, A Doll's House, Hamlet, The Comedy of Errors, Awake and Sing, Kennedy's Children, 1975, Murder Among Friends, Heartbreak House, Legend, Measure for Measure, The Glass Menagerie, Hartford, 1976, The Lower Depths, The Cherry Orchard, Agamemnon, Cafe Crown (Antoinette Perry award, 1989); scenery and costume design, Jakes's Women, 1992; film prodn. designer, Shadows and Fog, 1992; costumes only Golda, 1977, Curse of the Starving Class, The Play's the Thing, The Mighty Gents, Stop the World - I Want to Get Off, King of Hearts, 1978, Sarava, The Goodbye People, Bent, 1979, Grand Hotel, 1990; prin. designer costumes only, Twyla Tharp Dance Found.; other ballet design includes Don Quixote for Am. Ballet Theater, 1978, Heart of the Matter for Joffrey Ballet, 1986, costumes for La Salle des Pas Perdus for Les Grand Ballets Canadiens, 1988, set and costumes for Pastorale, Nat. Ballet Can., 1990; designer sets and costumes for opera including La Dafne, Spoleto Festival, Italy, 1973; designer sets for opera including San Diego Opera, Opera Soc. Washington, San Francisco Spring Opera; prodn. designer films Radio Days, 1987, Bright Lights, Big City, 1988, Big, 1988. Recipient Antoinette Perry award (Tony), 1990, Drama Desk award and Variety Poll of NY, Drama Critics award for Sticks and Bones and That Championship Season 1971, 72.

LORD, ROBERT JAMES, lawyer; b. Washington, Oct. 20, 1956; s. Norman W. and Maxine (Levin) Schwartzman L.; m. Janet Susan Weinstein, Jan. 14, 1987. BS cum laude, U. Md., 1977, MBA, 1979; JD, George Washington U., 1983; LLM, NYU, 1987. Bar: Calif. 1983, NY 1985, Md. 1985, US Tax Ct. 1985, Ariz. 1988. Assoc. Kronish, Lieb, Weiner & Hellman, NYC, 1984—87, O'Connor Cavanagh Anderson Westover Killingsworth Beshears, Phoenix, 1987; of counsel Buchalter Nemer, Scottsdale. Disciplinary hearing officer Ariz. Supreme Ct.; lectr. Arizona Sch. Real Estate and Bus.; former commr. Scottsdale Airport Adv. Commn. Contbr. article to law jour. Precinct chmn Dem. Party Ariz., Scottsdale, 1988. Mem. ABA, NY State Bar Assn., Scottsdale C. of C., Scottsdale Bar Assn. Democrat. Office: Buchalter Nemer 16435 N Scottsdale Rd, Ste 440 Scottsdale AZ 85254 Office Phone: 480-383-1843. Office Fax: 480-383-1608. E-mail: rlord@buchalter.com.

LORENZ, MARIANNE, curator; b. Denver, Nov. 5, 1949; d. Paul Frederick and Celesta (Johnson) Holscher. BA, U. Colo., 1971, MFA, 1981, MBA in Mktg., 1982. Tchr. French/German Adams County #50, Westminster, Colo., 1972-80; coord. pub. programs Colo. State History Mus., Denver, 1984-85, dir. edn., 1985-87; curator edn. Joslyn Art Mus., Omaha, 1987-89; asst. dir. collections and programs Dayton (Ohio) Art Inst., 1989; dir., chief exec. ofcr. Yellowstone Art Museum, Billings, Mont. Author: Theme and Improvisation Kandinsky and the American Avant-Garde, 1912-1950, 1992; contbr. Dictionary of Art, 1993. Fulbright grantee, 1975-76. Mem. Am. Assn. Museums, Coll. Art Assn. Avocations: skiing, running.

LORENZ, NANCY, artist; BFA in Painting and Printmaking, U. Mich., 1985; MFA in Painting, Tyler Sch. Art, Phila. and Rome, 1988. Instr. R.I. Sch. Design, 1996; lectr. in field. One-woman shows include Temple U., Rome, 1988, Willoughby Sharp Gallery, NY, 1990, Genovese Gallery, Boston, 1990, 1991, 1994, others, exhibited in group shows at Helander Gallery, NY, 1989—93, JG Contemporary, NYC, 2006, Helander Gallery, Palm Beach, 1989—91, NY Pub. Libr., 1994, Austin Ackles Studio, NY, 1995, PDX, Portland, 1996, 1998, 2000, Galerie Verneil des Saints-Péres, Paris, Galerie Xippas, numerous others, Represented in permanent collections Senayan Hotel, Jakarta, Yokahama Hotel, Japan, Soho Grand Hotel, NY, MIA Ins., Pan Am. Bldg., San Francisco, Muscat Hilton, Oman, David Barton Gym, NY Pub. Libr., Champion Paper, Ohio, Shinwa Med. Inc., Nagoya, Japan, Aero Studios, NY, The Boston Co., numerous others. Guggenheim fellow, 1998. Office: Pdx Gallery 925 NW Flanders St Portland OR 97209-3123 E-mail: pdxgallery@aol.com.

LORENZ, STEPHEN R., career officer; b. Houston, Oct. 17, 1951; BS in Internat. Affairs, USAF Acad., 1973; M in Pub. Adminstrn., U. Northern Colo., 1977; postgrad., Pa. State U., 1995. Commd. 2d lt. USAF, 1973, advanced through grades to brig. gen., 1996; co-pilot, aircraft comdr. 4th Airborne Command and Control Squadron, Ellsworth AFB, S.D., 1975-80; aide, T-39 pilot to comdr. Air Force Logistics Command, Wright-Patterson AFB, Ohio, 1980-82; congrl. liaison officer Office of Legis. Liaison The Pentagon, Washington, 1982-83, exec. officer to the dir. of legis. liaison, 1983; dep. chief Air Force Senate Liaison Office, Capitol Hill, Washington, 1983-86; KC-135 instr. pilot, flight comdr. 924th Air Refueling Squadron, Castle AFB, Calif., 1986-87; comdr. 93rd Air Refueling Squadron, Castle AFB, 1987-89; chief N.E. Asia br., Japan desk officer The Pentagon, Washington, 1990-91, chief European and North Atlantic Treaty Orgn. Policy br., 1991-92; comdr. 398th Ops. Group, Castle AFB, 1992-93, 22nd Air Refueling Wing, 722nd Air Refueling Wing, March AFB, 1993-94, 305th Air Mobility Wing, McGuire AFB, N.J., 1994-96; commandant of cadets, comdr. 34th Tng. Wing, USAF Acad., Colorado Springs, Colo., 1996-99. Decorated Legion of Merit with oak leaf cluster. Office: USAF Acad Commandant for Cadets 2354 Fairchild Dr Ste 5a10 U S A F Academy CO 80840-6299

LORENZINI, PAUL GILBERT, electric power industry executive; b. Portland, Oreg., Apr. 16, 1942; s. Gilbert Henry and Viola Pauline (Gates) L.; m. Janet Grace Jesperson, Aug. 19, 1967; children: Christy, Michael. BS in Marine Engring., U.S. Merchant Marine Acad., 1964; PhD in Nuclear Engring., Oreg. State U., 1969; JD, Loyola U., LA, 1975. Registered profl. engr., Calif.; bar: Calif., Oreg. Nuclear engr. Rockwell Internat., Canoga Park, Calif., 1969-76; assoc. Tooze, Kerr, Peterson, Marshall & Shenker, Portland, 1976-79; dir. health/safety/environ. Rockwell Hanford Ops., Richland, Wash., 1979-82, asst. gen. mgr., 1982-84, v.p., gen. mgr., 1984-87; dir., spl. projects Pacific Power & Light, Portland, 1987, v.p., 1987-89, exec. v.p., 1989—. Adv. bd. dept. nuclear engring. Oreg. State U., Corvallis, 1989—. Pres. Columbia Pacific Coun., Boy Scouts Am., Portland, 1991; trustee Maryhurst Coll., Lake Oswego, Oreg., 1990—; bd. dirs. Holladay Park Med. Ctr., Portland, 1990—. Recipient Tri-Cities Engr. of Yr. award NSPE, Richland, Wash., 1983-84. Mem. Arlington Club, Am. Nuclear Soc., Riverside Country Club, Oreg. Golf Club, Mountain park Tennis Club. Avocations: golf, skiing, tennis, fishing. Home: 17550 Brookhurst Dr Lake Oswego OR 97034-5095

LORIMER, MARK W., transportation company executive; Capital mkts. ptnr. Dewey Ballantine; from gen. counsel to pres., CEO Auto-By-Tel, Irvine, Calif., 1996-98, pres., CEO, 1998—. Mem. faculty Fordham U., N.Y.C., 1993-95; lectr. in field. Office: Autobytel com Inc 18872 Macarthur Blvd Ste 200 Irvine CA 92612-1400

LO SCHIAVO, JOHN JOSEPH, academic administrator; b. San Francisco, Feb. 25, 1925; s. Joseph and Anne (Re) Lo S. AB, Gonzaga U., 1948, Ph.L. and MA, 1949; S.T.L., Alma Coll., 1962. Joined S.J., Roman Catholic Ch., 1942; tchr. St. Ignatius High Sch., San Francisco, 1949-50; instr. philosophy and theology U. San Francisco, 1950-52, 56-57, 61-62, v.p. for student affairs, dean of students, 1962-68, pres., 1977-91, chancellor, 1991—. Pres. Bellarmine Coll. Prep. Sch., San Jose, 1968-75 Bd. dirs. Sch. of Sacred Heart, 1991-2000, St. Mary's Hosp., 1990-96, United Religion Initiative, 1999—. Mem. Olympic Club, Bohemian Club, Univ. Club. Office: U San Francisco 2130 Fulton St San Francisco CA 94117-1080

LOSSE, JOHN WILLIAM, JR., mining company executive; b. St. Louis, Mar. 16, 1916; s. John William and Claire (Schmedtje) L.; m. Marjorie West Penney, Mar. 7, 1942; children: John William IV, Georgia Shane, Barbara Stevens, Mary Coulter, Penney Gregersen, Jane Momberger. BS, Washington U., St. Louis, 1937; MBA, Harvard U., 1939. Sec.-treas. J.W. Losse Tailoring Co., St. Louis, 1939-41, 45-55; treas., contr., asst. sec. Uranium Reduction Co., Salt Lake City, 1955—61; v.p. fin. Atlas Minerals div. Atlas Corp., Salt Lake City, 1962-64; asst. v.p., asst. treas. Am. Zinc Co., St. Louis, 1965-66, v.p. fin., treas., 1966-70; v.p. fin. Conrad, Inc., St. Louis, 1970-71; v.p. fin., sec., dir. Fed. Resources Corp., Salt Lake City, 1971-82, pres., CEO, dir., 1982-84, 85-86, CFO, dir., 1986-88, v.p., treas., 1988—2001, also bd. dirs., 1988-89; sec.-treas. Madawaska Mines Ltd., Bancroft, Ont., Canada, 1976—82, pres., bd. dirs., 1983—2001; pres. Camp Bird Colo., Inc., Ouray, 1983-92. Pres. Utah Natural Resources Council, 1964; tax com. and fin. adv. com. Am. Mining Congress, 1965-84; bd. dirs. Episcopal Mgmt. Corp., Salt Lake City, 1988-99. Bd. dirs. St. Mark's Hosp., Salt Lake City, 1987-88, Arthritis Found., Salt Lake City, 1988-97; vice chmn., bd. dirs. St. Mark's Charities, Salt Lake City, 1987-92; mem. investment com. Corp. of the Bishop, Salt Lake City, 1989-96; mem. investment adv. com. Perpetual Trust of St. Peter and St. Paul, 1995-96. Lt. comdr. USNR, 1941-45. Mem. Utah Mining Assn. (bd. dirs., legis. and tax coms. 1971-91), Alta Club of Salt Lake City, Phi Delta Theta. Republican. Episcopalian.

LOTT, IRA TOTZ, pediatric neurologist; b. Cin., Apr. 15, 1941; s. Maxwell and Jeneda (Totz) L.; m. Ruth J. Weiss, June 21, 1964; children: Lisa, David I. BA cum laude, Brandeis U., 1963; MD cum laude, Ohio State U., 1967. Intern Mass. Gen. Hosp., Boston, 1967, resident in pediatrics, 1967-69, resident in child neurology, 1971-74; clin. assoc. NIH, Bethesda, Md., 1969-71; from clin. rsch. fellow to asst. prof. Harvard Med. Sch., Boston, 1971-82; clin. dir. Eunice Kennedy Shriver Ctr. for Mental Retardation, Waltham, Mass., 1974-82; assoc. prof. U. Calif., Irvine, 1983-91, prof., 1992—, chmn. dept. pediat., 1990-2000, dir. clin. neurosci. devel., 2000—03; assoc. dean for clin. neuroscis. U. Calif. Irvine Health Sys., 2003—. Chmn. dept. pediat. U. Calif., Irvine, 1990-2000, dir. pediat. neurology, 1983—, clin. neuroscience devel., 2000-01, assoc. dean clin. neurosciences, 2002—; pres. Prof. Child Neurology, Mpls., 1992—. Editor: Down Syndrome-Medical Advances, 1991; contbr. articles to profl. jours. Sec., treas. Child Neurology Soc., Mpls., 1987-90. Lt. comdr. USPHS, 1969-71. Recipient Career Devel. award Kennedy Found., 1976, Spotlight award Outstanding Svc. People with Devel. Disabilities as Health Care Provider, Regional Ctr. Orange County, 2005; NIH grantee, 1974—. Fellow Am. Acad. Neurology; mem. Am. Pediatric Soc., Am. Neurol. Assn., Nat. Down Syndrome Soc. (sci. acad. bd. 1985—, chmn. sci. adv. bd., 2005—, dir. sci. adv. bd. 2005, Rsch. award, 2004, Christian Puschel Meml. Rsch. award, 2005), Western Soc. for Pediatric Rsch. (councillor 1989-91). Achievements include research in relationship of Down Syndrome to Alzheimer's disease, neurometabolic disease. Office: U Calif Irvine Med Ctr Dept Pediatrics 101 The City Dr S # 2 Orange CA 92868-3201 Business E-Mail: itlott@uci.com.

LOTT, RONNIE (RONALD MANDEL LOTT), retired professional football player; b. Albuquerque, May 8, 1959; m. Karen Collmer, 1991; children: Kailey, Isaiah, Chloe. BS in Pub. Adminstrn., U. So. Calif., 1981. Defensive back San Francisco 49ers, 1981—90, L.A. Raiders, 1991—93, NY Jets, 1993—94, Kans. City Chiefs, 1994—95; analyst Fox NFL Sunday, Beverly Hills, Calif., 1996—98. Founder, chmn. All Stars Helping Kids, 1989—. Named NFL All-Pro, 1981, 1983—86, Defensive Back of Yr., NFL Alumni Assn., 1983; named to Sporting News Coll. All-Am. team, 1980, Nat. Football Conf. Pro Bowl Team, 1981—84, 1986—91, NFL All-Pro, 1986—91, The Pro Football Hall of Fame, 2000, The College Football Hall of Fame, 2002, The NFL 1980s All-Decade Team, The NFL 1990s All-Decade Team, The NFL 75th Anniversary All-Time Team, 1994. Achievements include being a member of the San Francisco 49ers Super Bowl Champion Teams, 1981, 1984, 1988, 1989. Office: All Stars Helping Kids 970 Main St Redwood City CA 94063

LOUGHEED, PETER, lawyer, former Canadian premier; b. Calgary, Alta., Can., July 26, 1928; s. Edgar Donald and Edna (Bauld) L.; m. Jeanne Estelle Rogers, June 21, 1952; children— Stephen, Andrea, Pamela, Joseph. BA, U. Alta., 1950, LL.B., 1952; MBA, Harvard U., 1954. Bar: Alta 1955. With firm Fenerty, Fenerty, McGillivray & Robertson, Calgary, 1955-56; sec. Mannix Co., Ltd., 1956-58, gen. counsel, 1958-62, v.p., 1959-62, dir., 1960-62; individual practice law, from 1962; formerly mem. Alta. Legislature for Calgary West; formerly leader Progressive Conservative Party of Alta., 1965-85; premier of Alta., 1971-85; ptnr. Bennett Jones, Calgary, 1986-99, counsel, 1999—. Named an inductee, Canadian Med. Hall of Fame, 2001. Office: Bennett Jones LLP 855 2nd St SW 4500 Bankers Hall Calgary AB Canada T2P 4K7

LOUGHLIN, MICHAEL J., bank executive; BA, Univ. Calif., Berkeley, 1978. Mgmt. positions Wells Fargo & Co., San Francisco, 1986—, regional v.p. comml. banking, head U.S. corp. banking; exec. v.p. Wells Fargo Bank, 2000—06; sr. credit officer comml. banking Wells Fargo & Co., San Francisco, 2000—03, head credit officer wholesale banking, 2003—06, dep. chief credit officer, 2006, exec. v.p. chief credit officer, 2006—. Office: Wells Fargo & Co 420 Montgomery St San Francisco CA 94163

LOUIE, STEVEN GWON SHENG, physics professor, researcher; b. Canton, China, Mar. 26, 1949; came to U.S., 1961; s. Art and Kam Shui (Lau) L.; m. Jane Yuk Wong, Aug. 3, 1975; children: Jonathan S., Jennifer Y., Sarah W. AB in Math. and Physics, U. Calif., Berkeley, 1972, PhD in Physics, 1976. IBM postdoctoral fellow IBM Watson Rsch. Ctr., Yorktown Heights, NY, 1977-79; mem. vis. tech. staff AT&T Bell Labs., Murray Hill, NJ, 1979; asst. prof. U. Pa., Phila., 1979-80; NSF postdoctoral fellow physics dept. U. Calif., Berkeley, 1976-77, assoc. prof., 1980-84, prof., 1984—, Miller rsch. prof., 1986, 95. Faculty scientist Lawrence Berkeley Lab., 1980-93, sr. faculty scientist, 1993—; cons. Exxon Rsch. & Engring. Co., Annandale, N.J., 1981-87; Closs lectr. U. Chgo., 2006. Editor Solid State Comm., 1994—; contbr. over 400 articles to sci. jours. Recipient sustained outstanding rsch. in solid state physics award Dept. Energy, 1993, Feynman prize Foresight Inst., 2003, Outstanding Overseas Chinese award Chinese Consol. Benevolent Assn., 2005; fellow A.P. Sloan Found., 1980, Guggenheim fellow, 1989. Fellow AAAS, Am. Phys. Soc. (Aneesur Rahman prize 1996, Davisson-Germer prize 1999); mem. NAS, Materials Rsch. Soc. Baptist. Achievements include patents in field. Avocations: gardening, skiing, tennis. Home Phone: 510-527-2921.

LOUIS-DREYFUS, JULIA, actress; b. NYC, Jan. 13, 1961; d. William and Judith Louis-Dreyfus; m. Brad Hall, 1987; children: Henry, Charles. Attended, Northwestern U., 1980—82, D (hon.) in Arts, 2007. Mem. Second City and the Practical Theatre Co., Chgo. Actor: (TV series) Saturday Night Live, 1982-85, Day by Day, 1986-89, The Art of Being Nick, 1986, Seinfeld, 1989-98 (Emmy award supp. actress, 1996, Emmy nom., 1992, 93, 94, 95, 97, 98, Amer. Comedy award best supp. actress, 1993, 94, 95, 97, 98, Golden Globe award supp. actress, 1994, SAG award, 1997, 98), The New Adventures of Old Christine, 2006-(Emmy award for outstanding lead actress in a comedy series, 2006); actor, prodr. Watching Ellie, 2002-2003; (TV appearances) Family Ties, 1988, Dinosaurs, 1991, The Single Guy, 1995, Hey Arnold, 1997, Curb Your Enthusiasm, 2000, 01, (voice only) The Simpsons, 2001, Arrested Development, 2002, 2004, 2005; (films) Soul Man, 1986, Troll, 1986, Hannah and Her Sisters, 1986, National Lampoon's Christmas Vacation, 1989, Jack the Bear, 1993, North, 1994, Father's Day, 1997, Deconstructing Harry, 1997, (voice only) A Bug's Life, 1998, Gilligan's Island, 1999, Speak Truth to Power, 2000; (TV movies) London Suite, 1996, (voice only) Animal Farm, 1999, Gepetto, 2000 Office: Jonas PR 240 26th St Ste 3 Santa Monica CA 90402 also: Hofflund/Polone 9465 Wilshire Blvd Beverly Hills CA 90212

LOUX, GORDON DALE, philanthropic consultant; b. Souderton, Pa., June 21, 1938; s. Curtis L. and Ruth (Derstine) L.; m. Elizabeth Ann Nordland, June 18, 1960; children: Mark, Alan, Jonathan. Diploma, Moody Bible Inst., Chgo., 1960; BA, Gordon Coll., Wenham, Mass., 1962; BD, No. Bapt. Sem., Oak Brook, Ill., 1965, MDiv, 1971; MS, Nat. Coll. Edn., Evanston,Ill., 1984; LHD (hon.), Sioux Falls Coll., 1985. Ordained to ministry, Bapt. Ch., 1965. Assoc. pastor Forest Park (Ill.) Bapt. Ch., 1962-65; alumni field dir. Moody Bible Inst., Chgo., 1965-66, dir. pub. rels., 1972-76; dir. devel. Phila. Coll. Bible, 1966-69; pres. Stewardship Svcs., Wheaton, Ill., 1969-72; exec. v.p. Prison Fellowship Ministries, Washington, 1976-84, pres., CEO, 1984-88, Prison Fellowship Internat., Washington, 1979-87; pres. Internat. Students, Inc., Colorado Springs, Colo., 1988-93, Gordon D. Loux & Co., LLC, Colorado Springs, 1994—, Trinity Cmty. Found., 1996—. Author: Uncommon Courage, 1987, You Can Be a Point of Light, 1991; contbg. author: Money for Ministries, 1989, Dictionary of Christianity in America, 1989. Bd. dirs. Evang. Coun. for Fin. Accountability, Washington, 1979-92, vice chmn., 1981-84, 86-87, chmn., 1987-89; vice chmn. Billy Graham Greater Washington Crusade, 1985-85; bd. dirs. Evang. Fellowship of Mission Agys., 1991-94, Ctr. for Christian Jewish Dialogue, Colorado Springs, 1996—, Hope and Home, Colorado Springs, 1998—, C2ure, Mechanicsburg, Pa., 1999—, Global Leaders Initiative. Named Alumnus of Yr., Gordon Coll., 1986. Mem. Broadmoor Golf Club (Colo. Springs). Republican. Home: 740 Bear Paw Ln N Colorado Springs CO 80906-3215 Office: PO Box 38898 Colorado Springs CO 80937-8898 Personal E-mail: louxco@aol.com.

LOVATO, DEMI (DEMETRIA DEVONNE LOVATO), actress; b. Dallas, Aug. 20, 1992; d. Patrick and Diana (Hart) Lovato. Actress (TV series) Barney & Friends, 2002—03, As the Bell Rings, 2007, (TV films) Camp Rock, 2008, actress (guest appearance) (TV series) Prison Break, 2006, Just Jordan, 2007. Office: c/o CESD Talent Agency Ste 130/135 10635 Santa Monica Blvd Los Angeles CA 90025

LOVE, DANIEL JOSEPH, consulting engineer; b. Fall River, Mass., Sept. 27, 1926; s. Henry Aloysius and Mary Ellen (Harrington) L.; m. Henrietta Maurisse Popper, June 10, 1950 (dec. Mar. 1986); children: Amy, Timothy (dec.), Terence, Kevin; m. Adeline Aponte Esquivel, Feb. 11, 1989; stepchildren: Eric, Brian, Jason. BSEE, Ill. Inst. Tech., 1951, MSEE, 1956; MBA, Calif. State U., Long Beach, 1973. Registered profl. engr., Calif.; cert. fire protection Calif. Test engr. Internat. Harvester Co., Chgo., 1951-52; designer Pioneer Svc. & Engring. Co., Chgo., 1952-53; project engr., ops. mgr. Panellit Co., Skokie, Ill., 1953-60; mktg. mgr. Control Data Co., Mpls., 1961-62; mktg. mgr., asst. to pres. Emerson Electric Co., Pasadena, Calif., 1963-65; pres., gen. mgr. McKee Automation Co., North Hollywood, Calif., 1965-68; engring. specialist Bechtel Co., Vernon and Norwalk, Calif., 1968-80, chief elec. engr. Madrid, 1980-83, engring. specialist Norwalk, Calif., 1983-87; cons. engr. Hacienda Heights, Calif., 1987—. Contbr. articles to jours. in field. Pres. Wilson High Sch. Band Boosters, Hacienda Heights, 1971-73. With USN, 1944-46. Named Outstanding Engr., Inst. for Advancement Engring., 1986; recipient 3d place prize paper award Industry Application Soc., 1995. Fellow IEEE (disting. lectr., chmn. Met. L.A. sect. 1973-74, chmn. L.A. coun. 1977-78, chmn. protection com. 1990-91, Richard Harold Kaufmann award 1994, Ralph H. Lee prize paper award 1995); mem. NSPE, Instrument Soc. Am. (sr.), Soc. Fire Protection Engrs. Republican. Roman Catholic. Avocations: duplicate bridge, travel, walking, writing. Home: 16300 Soriano Dr Hacienda Heights CA 91745 E-mail: dan.love@ieee.org.

LOVE, EDITH HOLMES, theater producer; b. Boston, Oct. 17, 1950; d. Theodore Rufus and Mary (Holmes) L. Student, Denison U., 1968-72; BFA, U. Colo., 1973. Freelance designer various orgns., Atlanta, 1974-75; costumer Atlanta Children's Theatre, 1975-77; prodn. acct. David Gerber Co., LA, 1980-81; bus. mgr. Alliance Theatre/Atlanta Children's Theatre, 1977-79, adminstrv. dir., 1981-83, gen. mgr., 1983-85, mng. dir., 1985-96, Dallas Theater Ctrn., 1997—2003, Portland (Oreg.) Ctr. Stage, 2003—. Adv. bd. Stage Hands, Inc., Atlanta, 1983-89; mem. exec. com. Prodn. Values, Inc.,

Atlanta, 1985-89; mem. adv. com. arts mgmt. program Carnegie Mellon U.; panelist Nat. Endowment for Arts, 1994-96; mem. Nat. Theatre Conf., 2005—; vis. prof. Yale Sch. Drama, 1997. Active Cultural Olympiad Task Force, 1996 Summer Olympic Games, 1992-96, Met. Atlanta Arts Fund Bd., 1992-97; bd. dirs. Atlanta Convention and Vistor's Bur., 1993-95, Arts Dist. Friends, Theatre Comm. Group; exec. com. Dallas Theatre League, 1999—2003. Recipient Deca award for Outstanding Bus. Women in Atlanta, 1992. Mem. League Resident Theatres (treas. 1987-97, v.p. 1997-2000), Atlanta Theatre Coalition (exec. com. 1987-91, pres. 1989), Atlanta C. of C. (bd. dirs. bus. coun. for arts 1988-97), Leadership Atlanta, Charter 100 Dallas, Bd. Arts Dist. Found. Home: 1041 Ridge Rd Unit 320 Wilmette IL 60091-1570 Office: Portland Center Stage 128 NW 11th Ave Portland OR 97209-4160

LOVE, KEITH SINCLAIR, communications executive; b. Apr. 26, 1947; s. James and Ruth L. BA, NYU, 1980. Editor N.Y. Times, NYC, 1973-79; editor, polit. writer L.A. Times, 1979-90; asst. to v.p. ops. McClatchy Newspapers, Inc., 1990-92; pub. Ellensburg (Wash.) Daily Record, 1992-98; comm. dir. Gov. State of Washington, Olympia, 1998-99; v.p. comm. St. Michelle Wine Estates, Woodinville, Wash., 1999—. Office: Stimson Lane Vineyards State Wash PO Box 1976 Woodinville WA 98072-1976

LOVE, SUSAN MARGARET, surgeon, educator, writer; b. NJ, Feb. 9, 1948; d. James Arthur and Margaret Connick (Schwab) L.; life ptnr. Helen Sperry Cooksey, Sept. 8, 1982; 1 child, Katherine Mary Love-Cooksey. BS, Fordham U., 1970; MD, SUNY, NYC, 1974. DSc (hon.), 1998; MBA, UCLA, 1998; DSc (hon.), Northeastern U., 1991, Trinity Coll., 1999; D of Humane Sci. (hon.), Simmons Coll., 1992; LHD (hon.), U. R.I., 1997. Surgery intern Beth Israel Hosp., Boston, 1974—75, surgical resident, 1975—79, chief resident, 1979, clin. fellow in pathology, 1980, asst. in surgery, 1980—87, dir. breast clinic, 1980-88, assoc. surgeon, 1987—92; clin. fellow in surgery Harvard Med. Sch., Boston, 1977-78, clin. instr. in surgery, 1980-87, asst. clin. prof. surgery, 1987-92; clin. assoc. in surg. oncology Dana Farber Cancer Inst., Boston, 1981-92; dir. Faulkner Breast Ctr. Faulkner Hosp., Boston, 1988-92; assoc. prof. clin. surgery UCLA Med. Sch., 1992-96, adj. prof. divsn. gen. surgery, 1996—2002; dir. Revlon/UCLA Breast Ctr., 1992-96; clin. prof. divsn. gen. surgery David Geffen Sch. Medicine, UCLA, 2002—; founder, chief med. officer Windy Hill Med., 2006—. Prin. investigator Nat. Surg. Adjuvant Breast and Bowel Project, 1985—96; adv. com. Women's Health Initiative Program, Washington, 1993—95; adv. coun. Breast and Cervical Cancer Program and Breast Cancer Early Detection Program, State of Calif. DHS, 1994—98; mem. Pres.'s Nat. Action Plan on Breast Cancer, DHHS, 1994—2000; co-chair Biol. Resources Working Group, 1994—98; mem. Nat. Cancer Adv. Bd., 1998—2004; nat. adv. environ. health sci. coun. NIH, 2003—04; med. dir. Dr. Susan Love Rsch. Found. (formerly Santa Barbara Breast Cancer Inst., 1983-2000, The Susan Love MD Breast Cancer Research Foundation, 2000-04), 1995—; pres. bd. dirs. Dr. Susan Love Rsch. Found.; founder, sr. ptnr., dir. LLuminari, Inc., 2000—; bd. dirs. Sanarus Med.; cons. Cytyc Health Corp., 2002. Author: Dr. Susan Love's Breast Book, 1990, 4th edit., 2005, Dr. Susan Love's Menopause and Hormone Book, 1997, 2nd edit., 2003; Atlas of Techniques in Breast Surgery, 1996; contbr. chpts. to books, articles to profl. jours. Founder, bd. dirs. Nat. Breast Cancer Coalition, 1991—; bd. dirs. Lesbian Health Found., 1992—, Soc. Menstrual Cycle Rsch., 2000—, Y-ME Nat. Breast Cancer Orgn., 2001—. Recipient Rose Kushner award, Am. Med. Writers Assn., 1991, Achievement award, Am. Assn. Physicians for Human Rights, 1992, Women Making History award, U.S. Senator Barbara Boxer, 1993, Woman of Yr. award, YWCA, 1994, Frontrunner award, Sara Lee Corp., 1994, Spirit of Achievement award, Albert Einstein Coll. of Yeshiva U., 1995, Abram L. Sachar medallion, Brandeis U., 1996, Bicentennial honoree, U. Louisville, 1997, Walker prize, Boston Mus. Sci., 1998, Radcliffe medal, 2000, Humanitarian of Yr. award, Western U. Health Sci., Pomona, Calif., 2001, Excellence in Cancer Awareness award, Cancer Rsch. Found. Am., 2002, Dir.'s award, Nat. Cancer Inst., 2004;, Dept. Def. grantee, 1994, 1996, others. Mem. Am. Med. Women's Assn. (pres. br. 39 1987, Lila Wallis Women's Health award 2004), Soc. for Study of Breast Disease, Am. Soc. Preventive Oncology, Southwestern Oncology Group (women's health and breast com. 1992-96, surg. rep. 1992-96), L.A. Med. Soc., Boston Surg. Soc., N.Am. Menopause Soc., Am. Assn. Cancer Rsch., Am. Coll. Women's Health Physicians, Assn. Women Surgeons. Office: Dr Susan Love Rsch Found PO Box 846 Pacific Palisades CA 90272-0846 Office Phone: 310-230-1712. Business E-Mail: slove@earthlink.net.

LOVE, TED W., biotechnology company executive; married; 3 children. BA in Molecular Biology, Haverford Coll.; MD, Yale U. Resident Mass. Gen. Hosp., Harvard Med. Sch.; with dept. cardiology Mass. Gen. Hosp.; rsch. physician, v.p. product devel. Genentech, 1992—98; sr. v.p. devel. Theravance, Inc., 1998—2001; COO Nuvelo, Inc., San Carlos, Calif., 2001, pres., CEO, 2001—, chmn., 2005—. Mem. Calif. Independent Oversight Commn.; bd. dirs. Predix Pharmaceuticals, Inc., Santarus, Inc. Office: Nuvelo 201 Indsl Rd Ste 310 San Carlos CA 94070-6211

LOVE, WILLIAM EDWARD, lawyer; b. Eugene, Oreg., Mar. 13, 1926; s. William Stewart and Ola A. (Kingsbury) L.; m. Sylvia Kathryn Jaureguy, Aug. 6, 1955; children: Kathryn Love Petersen, Jeffrey, Douglas, Gregory. BS, U. Notre Dame, 1946; MA in Journalism, U. Oreg., 1950, JD, 1952. Bar: Oreg. 1952. Newspaper reporter Eugene Register Guard, 1943-44, 47-52; asst. prof. law, asst. dean Sch. Law U. Wash., Seattle, 1952-56; ptnr. Cake, Jaureguy, Hardy, Buttler & McEwen, Portland, Oreg., 1956-69; pres., chmn., CEO Equitable Savs. & Loan, Portland, 1969-82; sr. ptnr. Schwabe, Williamson & Wyatt, Portland, 1983—. Chmn. Oreg. Savs. League, 1976; dir. Portland Gen. Electric, 1976-83, Fed. Home Loan Bank of Seattle, 1976-79, 85-96, adv. coun. Fed. Nat. Mortgage Assn., Washington, 1978-80; exec. dir. Oreg. Facilities Authority, 1990-2006. Author (with Jaureguy): Oregon Probate Law and Practice, 2 vols., 1958; contbr. articles to profl. jours. Commr., past chmn. Oreg. Racing Commn., 1963-79; pres. Nat. Assn. State Racing Commrs., 1977-78; commr. Port of Portland, 1979-86, pres. 1983; referee Pac-10 football, 1960-81, Rose Bowl, 1981; active United Way, Boy Scouts Am., Portland Rose Festival, polit. campaigns; mem. adv. coun. Jockey's Guild, Inc., 1990-2001. Served to lt. (j.g.) USN, 1944-47. Mem. Oreg. Bar Assn., Multnomah County Bar Assn., Multnomah Athletic Club, Golf Club (Portland). Republican. Home: 421 SW 70th Terr Portland OR 97225-4356 Office: Schwabe Williamson & Wyatt 1211 SW 5th Ave Ste 1800 Portland OR 97204-3713 Office Phone: 503-222-9981.

LOVEJOY, LYNDA M., former state agency administrator, state legislator; b. 1949; m. Randolph John Lovejoy; children: Kelly, Russell, Jacob. AA in Elem. Edn., U. N.Mex., Gallup; BSc in Pub. Adminstrn., No. Ariz. U. Exec. staff asst. office of pres. Navajo Nation; case mgr. K'e Project; personnel dir. Pueblo of Zuni Tribe; project dir. adult edn. Crownpoint Inst. Tech.; commr. Dist. 4 State Pub. Regulation Commn., Santa Fe, 1999—2006; mem. Dist. 69 N.Mex. House of Reps., 1989—98; mem. Dist. 22 N.Mex. State Senate, 1996—. U.S. del. Guatemala; spkr. in field. Exec. bd. St. Bonaventure Indian Mission, Nat. Order Women Legislatures, Nat. Women's Network. Recipient N.Mex. Woman of Yr. award, Gov.; named one of Yr. 2000 N.Mex. top 100 power brokers, N.Mex. Bus. Weekly. Republican. E-mail: lynda.lovejoy@state.nm.us, sue.beffort@nmlegis.gov.*

LOVELESS, KEITH, lawyer, air transportation executive; b. Chgo., 1956; BA, Vanderbilt U., 1979, JD, 1983. Bar: Wash. 1983, US Dist. Ct. (ea. dist) Wash. 1983, US Dist. Ct. (we. dist.) Wash. 1983. Corp. sec., asst. gen. counsel Alaska Air Group, Inc., 1996—99, v.p. legal & corp. affairs, gen. counsel, corp. sec., 1999—. Mem.: ABA. Office: Alaska Air Group Inc 19300 Internat Blvd Seattle WA 98188

LOVELY, RANDY, editor-in-chief; b. Lake City, Tenn. BA, Central Mich. U., Mt. Pleasant, 1986. Reporter & city editor Sturgis Jour., Mich., 1988—90; copy editor & designer News-Sentinel, Ft. Wayne, Ind., 1990—92; page designer Press-Telegram, Long Beach, Calif., 1992—97; asst. mng. editor News-Press, Fort Myers, Fla., 1997; mng. editor The Times, Shreveport, La., 1997—2000; exec. editor Desert Sun, Palm Springs, Calif., 2000—02; mng. editor Arizona Republic, Phoenix, 2002—05, exec. editor, 2005—08, editor, v.p. news, 2008—. Named one of 20 Under 40, Presstime Mag., 1999. Mem.: Nat. Lesbian & Gay Journalists Assn. Office: c/o Arizona Republic 200 E Van Buren Street Phoenix AZ 85004

LOVEMAN, GARY W., hotel and gaming company executive; BA in Econs., Wesleyan U., 1982; PhD in Econs., MIT, 1989. Assoc. prof. bus. adminstrn. Harvard U., 1989—98; cons. Harrah's Entertainment, Inc., exec. v.p., 1998—2001, COO, 1998—2003, pres., 2001—, CEO, 2003—, chmn., 2005—. Bd. dir. Coach, 2002—, FedEx Corp., 2007—. Co-author: The Evolving Role of Small Business and Some Implications for Employment and Training Policy, 1990; author: An Assessment of the Productivity Impact of Information Technologies, 1994; co-author: Starting Over in Eastern Europe: Entrepreneurship and Economic Renewal, 1995. Recipient Apgar award for Excellence and Innovation in Tchg., Harvard Bus. Sch.; Alfred Sloan Doctoral Dissertation fellow. Mem.: Phi Beta Kappa. Office: One Harrahs Ct Las Vegas NV 89119 Office Phone: 702-407-6316.

LOVERIDGE, RONALD OLIVER, Mayor, Riverside, California; b. Antioch, Calif., 1938; m. Marsha Jean White, 1964; 2 children. BA in Polit. Sci., U. Pacific, 1960; MA in Polit. Sci., Stanford U., 1961, PhD in Polit. Sci., 1965. Assoc. prof. polit. sci. U. Calif., Riverside, 1965—, assoc. dean coll. social scis., 1970-72, chair acad. ednl. policy com., 1990-92; mem. Riverside City Coun., 1979-94; mayor City of Riverside, Calif., 1994—. Chair land use com. Riverside City Coun., 1980-94; exec. com. Western Riverside Coun. of Govts., 1994—. Contbr. articles to profl. jours. Chair Earth Day City of Riverside, 1990; co-chair Citrus Heritage Tourism Task Force, 1991; mem. bd. dirs. League of Calif. Cities; mem. South Coast Air Quality Mgmt. Dist. Bd., 1995—; 1st v.p. Nat. League of Cities. Recipient Robert Presley Cmty. Svc. award, Friends of Calif. Sch. for Deaf, Riverside, 2001, Spirit of Citizenship award, Calif. Baptist U., 2004, Leadership award, Internat. Econ. Devel. Coun., 2004, Tom Bradley award, Nat. Assn. of Regional Couns., 2005, Disting. Citizen of Yr. award, Boy Scouts of America, Calif. Inland Empire Coun., Mt. Rubidoux Div., 2005. Mem. Greater Riverside C. of C., Northside Improvement Assn., Urban League, So. Calif. Assn. Govts. (exec. com. 1994—). Avocations: reading, hiking. Office: 3900 N Main St 7th Fl Riverside CA 92522-0001 Office Phone: 951-826-5551. Business E-Mail: rloveridge@riversideca.gov.*

LOVETT, CLARA MARIA, retired academic administrator, historian; b. Trieste, Italy, Aug. 4, 1939; came to U.S., 1962; m. Benjamin F. Brown. BA equivalent, U. Trieste, 1962; MA, U. Tex., Austin, 1967; PhD, U. Tex., 1970. Prof. history Baruch Coll. CUNY, NYC, 1971-82, asst. provost, 1980-82; chief European divsn. Libr. of Congress, Washington, 1982-84; provost, v.p. acad. affairs George Mason U., Fairfax, Va., 1988-93; on leave, dir. Forum on Faculty Roles and Rewards Am. Assn. for Higher Edn., 1993-94; pres. No. Ariz. U., Flagstaff, 1994-2001, pres. emerita, 2001—; sr. fellow, dir. Ctr. for Competency-Measured Edn. The Oquirrh Inst., 2002—03; pres., CEO Am. Assn. for Higher Ed., 2003—05; ret., 2005. Vis. lectr. Fgn. Svc. Inst., Washington, 1979-85. Author: Democratic Movement in Italy 1830-1876, 1982 (H.R. Marraro prize, Soc. Italian Hist. Studies); Giuseppe Ferrari and the Italian Revolution, 1979 (Phi Alpha Theta book award); Carlo Cattaneo and the Politics of Risorgimento, 1972 (Soc. for Italian Hist. Studies Dissertation award), (bibliography) Contemporary Italy, 1985; co-editor: Women, War, and Revolution, 1980, (essays) State of Western European Studies, 1984; contbr. sects. to publs., U.S., Italy. Organizer Dem. clubs Bklyn., 1972-76; mem. exec. com. Palisades Citizens Assn., Washington, 1985-87; vestry mem. St. David's Episc. Ch., Washington, 1986-89; bd. dirs. Blue Cross Blue Shield Ariz., 1995-2004, Nat. Coun. Tchr. Quality, 2005-, Ariz. Women's Edn. Employment Inc., 2001-; trustee Western Govs. U., 1996-2007, Thunderbird, The Thunderbind, The Sch. of Global Mgmt., 2006—, Scottsdale Cultural Coun., 2006-; mem. Ariz. State Bd. Edn., 1999-2001; vestry mem. Trinity Episcopal Cath., Phoenix, 2009-. Fellow Guggenheim Found., 1978-79, Woodrow Wilson Internat. Ctr. for Scholars, 1979 (adv. bd. West European program), Am. Coun. Learned Socs., 1976, Bunting Inst. of Radcliffe Coll., 1975-76, others; named Educator of Yr. Va. Fedn. of Bus. and Profl. Women, 1992. Mem. Am. Assn. Higher Edn. (cons. 1979—), Soc. for Italian Hist. Studies, Assn. Am. Coll. and Univs. (bd. dirs. 1990-93). Avocations: choral singing, swimming. Office Phone: 602-728-9505. Business E-Mail: clara.lovett@nau.edu.

LOVETT, RICHARD, talent agency executive; b. Wis. m. Brittany Lovett. Attended, U. Wis.-Madison. Began as mailroom employee and advanced from agent trainee to agent Creative Artists Agy., pres., 1995—. Tchr. Venice H.S., 1994—; co-founder Creative Artists Agency Found., 1996; bd. dirs. Artists Rights Found. Recipient City of Angels Helen Bernstein award, David Niven award, 2000, Champion of Children award, Fulfillment Fund, 2002, Amb. for Humanity award, Shoah Found., 2004; named one of 50 Most Powerful People in Hollywood, Premiere mag., 2004—06. Avocations: sports, yoga.

LOVETT, WAYNE J., air transportation executive, lawyer; b. 1950; m. Margaret A. Lovett, 1969; 1 child, David. BA in Mgmt., Northeastern U., 1972; JD, South Tex. Coll. Law, Houston, 1977. Bar: Tex. 1977. Trial lawyer pvt. practice; in-house counsel Centurion Petroleum Corp., 1982; corp. counsel, sec. Comm. Transmission Inc. (now Broadwing Corp.); presiding judge Lakeway Mcpl. Ct., Tex., 1993—97; gen. counsel Mercury Air Grp. Inc., LA, 1997—, corp. sec., 1999—, exec. v.p., 2001—. Avocations: history, reading. Office: Mercury Air Group Inc 5456 McConnell Ave Los Angeles CA 90066

LOVETT, WENDELL HARPER, architect, educator; b. Seattle, Apr. 2, 1922; s. Wallace Herman and Pearl (Harper) L.; m. Eileen (Whitson), Sept. 3, 1947; children: Corrie, Clare. Attended, Pasadena Jr. Coll., 1943-44; BArch, U. Wash., 1947; MArch, M.I.T., 1948. Arch., designer Naramore, Bain, Brady, and Johanson, Seattle, 1948; arch. assoc. Bassetti and Morse, Seattle, 1948-51; instr. architecture U. Wash., 1948-51; pvt. practice, arch. Seattle, 1951—; asst. prof. U. Wash., 1951-60, assoc. prof., 1960-65, prof., 1965-83, prof. emeritus, 1983—. Lectr. Technische Hochschule, Stuttgart, 1959-60. Prin. works include nuclear reactor bldg., U. Wash., 1960; Villa Simonyi Medina, Wash., 1989; patentee in field. Pres. Citizen's Planning Coun., Seattle, 1968-71; bd. dir. Seattle Baroque Orch., 1998-2002. Served in AUS, 1943-46. Recipient 2d prize Progressive Architecture U.S. Jr. C. of C., 1949; Internat. design award Decima Triennale di Milano, 1954; Arch. Record Homes awards, 1969, 72, 74; Interiors award, 1973; Sunset-AIA awards, 1959, 62, 69, 71; Fulbright grantee, 1959; AIA fellow, 1978 Mem. AIA (sec. Wash. chpt. 1953-54, bd. dirs. Found. Seattle chpt. 1991-92, Seattle chpt. medal 1993, pres. sr. coun. 1991-92, Plestcheeff Inst. bd. dir. 1992; bd.dir., Soc. of Architectural Historians, MDRC, 2002-05. Home and Office: 420 34th Ave Seattle WA 98122-6408 Home Phone: 206-329-5211.

LOVETT, WILLIAM LEE, surgeon; b. Natchez, Miss., June 12, 1941; s. Frank Lee and Lucille (Mullen) L.; m. Martha Lynn Gray, Aug. 15, 1964; children: Shelby Elizabeth Lovett Cuevas, Heather Lee Lovett Dunn, Michael Gray. BA, U. Miss., Oxford, 1963; MD, U. Miss., Jackson, 1967. Diplomate Am. Bd. Surgery, Am. Bd. Hand Surgery. Intern in surgery U. Va. Med. Ctr., Charlottesville, 1967-68, jr. asst. resident in surgery, 1968-69, sr. asst. resident in surgery, 1970-72, co-chief resident in surgery, 1972-73; fellow surg. rsch. dept. surgery U. Va., Charlottesville, 1969-70; physician S.W. Hand Surgeons Ltd., Phoenix, 1983—; vice chief of staff St. Joseph's Hosp., Phoenix, 1990-93, rep. orthopedic surgery com., 1990—, vice chair dept. orthopedics, 1991-92, chief of staff, 1996-98; physician S.W. Hand Surgeons Ltd., Phoenix; med. dir., med. staff adminstrn. St. Joseph's Hosp. and Med. Ctr., Phoenix, 2002—07. Mem. sports medicine adv. team Ariz. State U., 1991-95; presenter in field. Contbr. articles to profl. jours. Mem. Sch. Bd. Xavier High Sch., 1983-87, v.p., 1985-86, pres., 1986-87; Roosevelt coun. Boy Scouts Am., Phoenix, 1992-93, asst. scoutmaster, 1993—. Comdr. USN, 1974-76. Fellow ACS (pres. Ariz. chpt. 1983-84); mem. AMA, Am. Soc. for Surgery of the Hand, Ariz. Med. Assn. (del. 1985), Phoenix Surg. Soc. (pres. 1985-86), Muller Surg. Soc., Scottsdale Mounted Posse. Avocations: horseback riding, fly fishing, quail hunting, canoeing. Home: 6049 N 5th Pl Phoenix AZ 85012-1219 Home Phone: 602-266-0630; Office Phone: 602-406-4095, 602-266-2834. Personal E-mail: L5hand@cox.net.

LOVINS, L. HUNTER, public policy institute executive, consultant, educator; b. Middlebury, Vt., Feb. 26, 1950; d. Paul Millard and Farley (Hunter) Sheldon; m. Amory Bloch Lovins, Sept. 6, 1979 (div. 1999). BA in Sociology, Pitzer Coll., 1972, BA in Polit. Sci., 1972; JD, Loyola U., LA, 1975; LHD, U. Maine, 1982. Bar: Calif. 1975. Asst. dir. Calif. Conservation Project, LA, 1973-79; policy advisor Friends of the Earth, 1979—81; co-CEO, co-founder Rocky Mountain Inst., Snowmass, Colo., 1982—2002; co-chair Natural Capitalism Group, Snowmass, 2000—; pres. Natural Capitalism Solutions, 2004—. Vis. prof. U. Colo., Boulder, 1982; Henry R. Luce vis. prof. Dartmouth Coll., Hanover, N.H., 1982; prof. sustainable mgmt. Presidio World Coll., 2003—; pres. Nighthawk Horse Co., 1993; bd. dirs. EcoStructure Fin. Co-author: Brittle Power, 1982, Energy Unbound, 1986, Least-Cost Energy Solving the CO2 Problem, 2d edit., 1989, Factor Four, 1997, Green Development, 1998, Natural Capitalism, 1999, The Natural Advantage of Nations, 2005. Bd. dirs. Basalt and Rural Fire Protection Dist., 1987-2000, Nighthawk Horse Co., Rocky Mountain Inst., 1982-2002, Windstar Land Conservancy, 1996-2002, Internat. Ctr. Sustainable Devel., 2004-; vol. EMT and firefighter, Engrs. Without Borders, 2003, bd. dirs., 2003-; advisor Energy Ministry Afghanistan, 2004—. Recipient Mitchell prize Woodlands Inst., 1982, Right Livelihood Found. award, 1983, Best of the New Generation award Esquire Mag., 1984, Nissan prize, 1995, Lindbergh award, 1999, Bd. Govs.' award Loyola Law Sch., 2000, LOHAS award for svc. to bus., 2001, Shingo Prize for Excellence in Mfg. Rsch., 2001, Leadership in Bus. award, 2001; named Hero of Planet, Time Mag., 2000. Mem. Calif. Bar Assn., Am. Quarter Horse Assn., Am. Polocrosse Assn. Avocations: rodeo, fire rescue, polocrosse. Office: Natural Capitalism Solutions PO Box 3125 Eldorado Springs CO 80025 Office Phone: 303-554-6550.

LOW, ANDREW M., lawyer; b. NYC, Jan. 1, 1952; s. Martin Laurent and Alice Elizabeth (Bernstein) L.; m. Margaret Mary Stroock, Mar. 31, 1979; children: Roger, Ann. BA, Swarthmore Coll., 1973; JD, Cornell U., 1976. Bar: Colo. 1981, U.S. Dist. Ct. Colo. 1981, U.S. Ct. Appeals (10th cir.) 1986. Assoc. Rogers & Wells, NYC, 1977-81, Davis Graham & Stubbs LLP, Denver, 1981-83, ptnr., 1984—. Editor: Colorado Appellate Handbook, 1984, 94. Pres. Colo. Freedom of Info. Coun., Denver, 1990-92, Colo. Bar Press Com., 1989, appellate practice subcom. Colo. Bar Assn. Litig. Coun., 1994—; bd. dirs. CLE in Colo., Inc., 1993-96; trustee 9 Health Fair, Denver, 1988—; mem. Colo. Supreme Ct. Joint Com. on Appellate Rules, 1993—. Avocations: skiing, golf, fly fishing. Office: Davis Graham & Stubbs LLP Ste 500 1550 17th St Denver CO 80202 E-mail: andrew.low@dgslaw.com.

LOW, BOON CHYE, physicist; b. Singapore, Feb. 13, 1946; came to U.S., 1968; s. Kuei Huat and Ah Tow (Tee) Lau; m. Daphne Nai-Ling Yip, Mar. 31, 1971; 1 child, Yi-Kai. BSc, U. London, Eng., 1968; PhD, U. Chgo., 1972. Scientist High Altitude Observatory Nat. Ctr. for Atmospheric Rsch., Boulder, Colo., 1981-87, sect. head, 1987—90, 1997—2004, acting dir., 1989-90, sr. scientist, 1987—. Mem. mission operation working group for solar physics NASA, 1992-94; vis. sr. scientist Princeton Plasma Physics Lab., 1998-99; mem. Living With a Star steering com. for targeted rsch. and tech. NASA, 2004; mem. Theoretical Inst. for Advanced Rsch. in Astrophysics, Taiwan, 2004—; mem. rev. panel Nat. Rsch. Coun. Associateship Program, 2005-08. Mem. editl. bd. Solar Physics, 1991—2005. Named Fellow Japan Soc. for Promotion of Sci., U.

Tokyo, 1978, Sr. Rsch. Assoc., NASA Marshall Space Flight Ctr., 1980. Mem. Am. Physical Soc., Am. Astron. Soc., Am. Geophysical Union. Office: Nat Ctr for Atmosph Rsch PO Box 3000 Boulder CO 80307-3000 Home Phone: 303-554-0049; Office Phone: 303-497-1553. Business E-Mail: low@hao.ucar.edu.

LOW, HARRY WILLIAM, judge; b. Oakdale, Calif., Mar. 12, 1931; m. May Ling, Aug. 24, 1952; children: Larry, Kathy, Allan. AA, Modesto Jr. Coll., 1950; AB Polit. Sci. with honors, U. Calif., Berkeley, 1952, JD, 1955. Bar: Calif. 1955, U.S. Ct. Appeals (9th cir.) 1955. Commr. Worker's Compensation Commn., 1966; teaching assoc. Boalt Hall, 1955-56; dep. atty. gen. Calif. Dept. Justice, 1956-66; judge Mcpl. Ct., San Francisco, 1966-74, presiding judge, 1972-73; judge Superior Ct., San Francisco, 1974-82; presiding justice Calif. Ct. Appeals, 1st dist., 1982-92; commr. Calif. Ins. Dept., San Francisco, 2000—03; arbitrator/mediator JAMS, 2003—. Pres. San Francisco Police Commn., 1992-96; pres. San Francisco Human Rights Commn., 1999-2000, 2003; mem. Jud. Arbitration and Mediation Svcs., 1992-2000, 2003-, Commn. on Future of Cts., 1991-94; Calif. Ins. Commr., 2000-03, BAJI-Jury Instrn. Com. Contbr. articles to profl. jours. Chmn. bd. Chinese-Am. Internat. Sch., 1979-99; bd. visitors U.S. Mil. Acad., 1980-83; bd. dirs. Friends of Recreation and Parks, Salesian Boys Club, World Affairs Coun., 1979-85, NCCJ, San Francisco chpt. St. Vincent's Boys Home, Coro Found., 1970-76, San Francisco Zool. Trust, 1987, Union Bank Calif., 1993-2000, Calif. Health Plan Found., 2003—; pres. San Francisco City Coll. Found., 1977-87, Inst. Chinese Western History U. San Francisco, 1987-89. Mem. ABA (chmn. appellate judges conf. 1990-91, commr. on minorities, Spirit of Excellence award, 2002), San Francisco Bar Assn., Chinese Am. Citizens Alliance (pres. San Francisco chpt. 1976-77, nat. pres. 1989-93), Calif. Judges Assn. (pres. 1978-79), Calif. Jud. Coun., State Bar Calif. (rsch. editor publs. 1958-76, pub. affairs com. 1987-90, exec. bd. 1992-94), Calif. Conf. Judges (editor jour. cts. commentary 1973-76), Calif. Judges Assn. (exec. bd. 1976-79), Asian Bus. League (dir. 1986-93), Nat. Ctr. State Cts. (bd. dirs. 1986-91), San Francisco Bench Bar Media Commn. (chmn. bd. dirs. 1987-92), Boalt Hall Alumni Assn. (Distinguished Svc. award 1992, Judge Lowell Jensen award 2000), Phi Alpha Delta. Office Phone: 415-982-5267.

LOW, JOHN WAYLAND, lawyer; b. Denver, Aug. 7, 1923; s. Oscar Wayland and Rachel E. (Stander) L.; m. Merry C. Mullan, July 8, 1979; children: Lucinda A., Jan W. BA, Nebr. Wesleyan U., 1947; JD cum laude, U. Denver, 1951. Bar: Colo. 1951, U.S. Dist. Ct. (Colo. dist.) 1951, U.S. Ct. Appeals (10th cir.), U.S. Supreme Ct. 1960. Ptnr. Sherman & Howard LLC, Denver, 1951-93, counsel, 1993—. Trustee U. Denver, 1987—; chmn. bd. Denver Symphony Assn., 1989-90; vice chmn. Colo. Symphony Assn., 1990-96; pres. Colo. Symphony Found., 1995—, Mesa Verde Found., 1997-2003; chmn. Colo. Alliance of Bus., Denver, 1983-87; pres. First Plymouth Found, 1982—; dir. Public Edn. and Bus. Coalition, 1995—; dir. Inst. Internat. Edn., 2005—. 1st lt. U.S. Army, 1942-46, CBI. Recipient Learned Hand award Am. Jewish Com., 1989, Outstanding Law Alumni award U. Denver, 1994, Evans Disting. Svc. award U. Denver, 2001. Mem. ABA, Colo. Bar Assn., Denver Bar Assn., University Club of Denver, Garden of Gods Club (Colorado Springs). Republican. Mem. United Ch. of Christ. Office: Sherman & Howard 633 17th St Ste 3000 Denver CO 80202-3665 Home Phone: 303-777-2541; Office Phone: 303-299-8148. Business E-Mail: jlow@sah.com.

LOW, RANDALL, internist, cardiologist; b. San Francisco, June 24, 1949; s. Huet Hee and Betty Tai (Quan) L.; m. Dorothy Fung, May 4, 1975; children: Audrey, Madeleine, Jennifer. AA, City Coll., San Francisco, 1969; BA, U. Calif., Berkeley, 1971; MD, U. Calif., Davis, 1975. Diplomate Am. Bd. Internal Medicine, Nat. Bd. Med. Examiners, Am. Bd. Cardiovascular Diseases. Intern Hosp. of Good Samaritan, LA, 1975-76, resident, 1976-77, chief med. resident, 1977-78, fellow in cardiology, 1979-81; mem. staff St. Francis Meml. Hosp., San Francisco, 1981—, chmn. dept. cardiology, 1995—; pvt. practice internal medicine and cardiology San Francisco, 1981—; mem. staff Chinese Hosp., San Francisco, 1981—, chief of medicine, 1991-92; asst. clin. prof. U. Calif., San Francisco, 1994-2000. Courtesy staff St. Mary's Hosp., San Francisco, 1981—, Calif. Pacific Med. Ctr., San Francisco, 1990—; cardiology cons. Laguna Honda Hosp., San Francisco, 1981—. Home health quality assurance com. Self Help for Elderly, San Francisco, 1991—; bd. trustees San Francisco Health Authority, 2000—; bd. dirs. Youth Advocates, San Francisco, 1992-99. Recipient Hearst Pub. Svc. award U. Calif.-Berkeley, 1970, Homecare Recognition award Self Help for Elderly, 1993. Mem. ACP, Am. Soc. Internal Medicine, Am. Coll. Cardiology, Am. Heart Assn. (bd. govs. 1983-90), Calif. Acad. Medicine, Calif. Med. Soc., San Francisco Med. Soc. (bd. dirs. 1999-2005), Assn. Chinese Cmty. Physicians (sec.-treas. 1986-89), Chinese Cmty. Health Care Assn. (pres. 1991-96, 99-2002), Fedn. Chinese Am. and Canadia Med. Soc. (pres. 2005-06, chmn. bd.). Office: 909 Hyde St Ste 501 San Francisco CA 94109-4853

LOW, REGINALD INMAN, cardiologist; b. Stockton, Calif., June 1, 1947; MD, U. Calif. Davis, 1975. Cert. Internal Medicine 1978, Cardiovascular Disease 1981, Interventional Cardiology 1999. Intern in internal medicine U. Calif. Davis Med. Ctr., 1975—76, resident in cardiology, 1976—78, fellow in cardiology, 1978—80, chief cardiovascular medicine, 2000—, dir., Heart Ctr.; dir. coronary catherization lab. and coronary care unit U. Ky. Med. Ctr., VA Med. Ctr.; dir. Mercy Heart Inst. Mercy Gen. Hosp., Sacramento, 1989—97; prof. medicine U. Calif. Davis Sch. Medicine, 2000—. Mem., divsn. med. quality Med. Bd. Calif., Dept. Consumer Affairs, 2006—. Recipient Disting. Alumni award, U. Calif. Davis, 2007. Office: U Calif Davis Med Ctr Div Cardiology 4860 Y St Ste 2820 Sacramento CA 95817 Office Phone: 916-734-5191.

LOWBER, JOHN M., communications executive; b. 1950; Sr. mgr. KPMG Peat Marwick; CFO Gen. Comm., Inc., Anchorage, 1987—, sec., treas., 1988—, CFO, sr. v.p., 1989—. Office: Gen Comm Inc Ste 1000 2550 Denali St Anchorage AK 99503 Office Fax: 907-265-5076.

LOWBER, STEPHEN SCOTT, financial executive; b. Gainesville, Fla., Apr. 17, 1951; s. Leslie Vernon and Grace Irene (Townsend) L.; m. Susan Irene LeClair, Aug. 28, 1976; children: Jessica Renee, Allison Susanne. BA in Acctg., Western Wash. U., 1975; MBA, Seattle U., 1978. CPA, Wash. Sr. audit mgr. Ernst & Whinney, Seattle, 1978-84; v.p., chief fin. officer Xytec, Inc., Tacoma, 1984-90, Advanced Digital Info. Corp., Redmond, Wash., 1990—. Served with U.S. Army, 1969-71, Socialist Republic Vietnam. Mem. Am. Inst. CPA's, Wash. Soc. CPA's, Nat. Assn. Accts. (bd. dirs. 1983). Republican. Mem. Assembly of God. Club: Pacific West. Avocations: tennis, hiking, church activities. Home: 3006 161st St SE Mill Creek WA 98012-7838

LOWDEN, SUE, political organization administrator; m. Paul W. Lowden. MA, Farleigh Dickinson U. Reporter, anchorwoman, writer, prodr. KLAS-TV Channel 8, 1977—87; dir. Sahara Resorts, 1982—95; mem. Nev. Senate, 1992—96; dir., exec. v.p. Archon Corp., Paradise, Nev. Founding bd. mem. Comml. Bank of Nev. Chairwomen Nev. Rep. Party, 2007—. Republican. Office: Nev Rep Party 8625 W Sahara Ave Las Vegas NV 89117 Office Phone: 702-258-9182. Office Fax: 702-258-9186. E-mail: chairman@nevadagop.org.

LOWE, KATHLENE WINN, lawyer; b. San Diego, Dec. 1, 1949; d. Ralph and Grace (Rodes) Winn; m. Russell Howells Lowe, Oct. 3, 1977; 1 child, Taylor Rhodes. BA in English magna cum laude, U. Utah, 1971, MA in English, 1973, JD, 1976. Bar: Utah 1976, US Dist. Ct. Utah 1976, US Ct. Appeals (10th cir.) 1980, Calif. 1989, US Ct. Appeals (9th cir.), US Dist. Ct. Calif. Assoc. Parsons, Behle & Latimer, Salt Lake City, 1976-80, ptnr., 1980-84; v.p. law, asst. gen. counsel Am. Stores Co., Salt Lake City, 1984—89; office mng. ptnr. Brobeck, Phleger & Harrison, Newport Beach, Calif., 1999—2003; ptnr.-in-charge, So. Calif. Dorsey & Whitney LLP, Irvine, Calif. Comment editor Utah Law Rev., 1975-76. Mem. ABA, Calif. Bar Assn., Utah Bar Assn. Avocations: fly fishing, reading, skiing, golf, travel. Office: Dorsey & Whitney LLP 38 Technology Dr Irvine CA 92618-5310 Office Phone: 949-932-3600. Office Fax: 949-932-3601. Business E-Mail: lowe.kathlene@dorsey.com.

LOWE, KEVIN HUGH, professional sports team executive, former hockey player and coach; b. Lachute, Que., Can., Apr. 15, 1959; m. Karen Percy. Defenseman Edmonton Oilers, 1979-92, 98-99, capt., 1991-92; defenseman NY Rangers, 1992-98; head coach Edmonton Oilers, 1999—2000, gen. mgr., alt. gov., 2000—08, pres. hockey ops., 2008—. Player NHL All-Star Game, 1984—86, 1988—90, 1993. Recipient King Clancy Meml. Trophy, 1990; named Budweiser/NHL Man of Yr., 1990. Achievements include being a member of Stanely Cup Champion Edmonton Oilers, 1984, 1985, 1987, 1988, 1989, NY Rangers, 1994. Office: Edmonton Oilers 11230 110th St Edmonton AB Canada T5G 3H7

LOWE, KRISTIN, film company executive; b. Dec. 9, 1971; With Michael Bay Films, Metro-Goldwyn-Mayer, Inc.; creative exec. to dir. devel. Warner Bros. Pictures, 2002—04; dir. devel. Universal Pictures, 2004—06, v.p. prodn., 2006—. Prodn. asst.: Armageddon, 1998. Achievements include overseeing day-to-day production of the films Inside Man, The Break-Up and You, Me and Dupree. Office: Universal Pictures 100 Universal City Plz Ste 3200 Universal City CA 91608

LOWE, ROB, actor; b. Charlottesville, Va., Mar. 17, 1964; m. Sheryl Berkoff, July 22, 1991; 2 children. Appeared in films including The Outsiders, 1983, Class, 1983, The Hotel New Hampshire, 1984, Oxford Blues, 1984, St. Elmo's Fire, 1985, Youngblood, About Last Night..., 1986, Square Dance, 1987, Illegally Yours, Masquerade, 1988, Bad Influence, 1991, The Dark Backward, 1991, Wayne's World, 1992, Frank and Jesse (also prodr.), 1994, Billy the Third, 1995, First Degree, 1995, Eye of the Storm, 1995, Tommy Boy, 1995, Mullholland Falls, 1996, Crazy Six, 1997, Austin Powers: International Man of Mystery, 1997, Living in Peril, 1997, Contact, 1997, Hostile Intent, 1997, One Hell of a Guy, 1998, Crazy Six, 1998, Under Pressure, 1999, Statistics, 1999, Dead Silent, 1999, Austin Powers: The Spy Who Shagged Me, 1999, Proximity, 2001, Austin Powers in Goldmember, 2002, View from the Top, 2003, Thank You for Smoking, 2006; appearances include (TV series) A New Kind of Family, The West Wing, 1999-2003, The Lyon's Den, 2003-04, Dr. Vegas, 2004 (also prodr.), Brothers & Sisters, 2007-; (mini-series) Atomic Train, 1998, Beach Girls, 2005, (TV films) Thursday's Child, A Matter of Time, Schoolboy Father, Stephen King's The Stand, On Dangerous Ground, 1995, Midnight Man, 1995, Outrage, 1998; (stage) A Few Good Men, London, 2005; writer, dir. (TV films) Desert's Edge, 1997, Jane Doe, 2001, Framed, 2002, Salem's Lot, 2004, Perfect Strangers, 2004, The Christmas Blessing, 2005; TV guest appearances include The Larry Sanders Show, 1992, The Naked Truth, 1995. Recipient Hollywood Legacy award, Hollywood Entertainment Mus., 2008. Office: Brillstein Grey 9150 Wilshire Blvd Ste 350 Beverly Hills CA 90212-3453

LOWELL, FREDERICK K., lawyer; b. NYC, Aug. 9, 1948; BA, Columbia U., 1971; JD, U. Va., 1975. Bar: Va. 1975, Calif. 1975. Assoc. then ptnr. Pillsbury, Madison & Sutro, San Francisco, 1975—2001; (Pillsbury Madison & Sutro merged with Winthrop, Stimson, Putnam and Roberts, 2001); ptnr., govt. relations & polit. law Pillsbury Winthrop LLP, San Francisco, 2001—05; (Pillsbury Winthrop LLP merged with Shaw Pittman LLP, 2005); ptnr., govt. relations & polit. law, chair polit. law group Pillsbury Winthrop Shaw Pittman LLP, San Francisco, 2005—. Author: The Regulation of Politics in Calif. Immediate past chair Lincoln Club of No. Calif.; Calif. delegate Nat. Rep. Convention, 1992, 1996, 2000, 2004; volunteer counsel Bush 2000 Campaign, Bush-Cheney 2004 Campaign. Mem.: ABA, San Francisco Bar Assn., Va. State Bar Assn., Calif. State Bar Assn., Calif. Polit. Atty. Assn. (former pres.). Office: Pillsbury Winthrop Shaw Pittman LLP 50 Fremont St San Francisco CA 94105 Office Phone: 415-983-1585. Office Fax: 415-983-1200. Business E-Mail: frederick.lowell@pillsburylaw.com.

LOWELL, J(AMES) DAVID, geological consultant, cattle rancher; b. Nogales, Ariz., Feb. 28, 1928; s. Arthur Currier and Lavina (Cumming) L.; m. Edith Walmisly Sykes, Mar. 30, 1948; children: Susan, William, Douglas. BS in Mining Engring., U. Ariz., 1949, E.Geol., 1959; MS in Geology, Stanford U., 1957; D. Hon. Causa, U. N at. Mayor de San Marcos, Peru, 1998; Dsc (hon.), U. Ariz, 2000. Registered profl. engr., Ariz. Mining engr. to mine foreman Asarco, Chihuahua City, Mex., 1949-51; field geologist to dist. geologist AEC, Grand Junction, Colo., 1951-54; chief geologist to v.p. S.W. ventures Ventures Ltd. and subs., Denver, Tucson, 1955-59; dist. geologist Utah Internat., San Francisco, Tucson, 1959-61; geol. cons. Lowell Mineral Exploration, Tucson, 1961—, pres. Chile, 1985—, Acuarios Mineral, Peru, 1991-96; chmn. Areguipa Resources Ltd., Can., 1993-96; pres. Exploraciones Mineras Lowell SA de CV, Mexico, 1998—2004, Lowell Mineral Exploration LLC, Ariz., 1998—; chmn. Bear Creek Mining Co., 2002—05; pres., CEO CIC Resources, 2007—; exec. chmn. Bear Creek Mining Co., Peru Copper Inc., 2004—07. Mem. bd. dirs. Soc. Econ. Geologists Found., 1986-91; Thayer Lindsley disting. lectr. Soc. Econ. Geologists, 1978; disting. exch. lectr. Soc. Econ. Geologists, 2000-02; cons. to 120 other oil and mining cos., U.S. and fgn. countries, 1961—, to nat. govt. orgn., US; dir. Nat. Mining Hall of Fame, 2000-. Assoc. editor Econ. Geology, New Haven, 1970-75. Recipient Disting. Citizen award U. Ariz., 1974, Soc. Econ. Geol. Thayer Lindsley Dist. Lectr., 1977, Silver Medal Soc. Econ. Geologists, 1983, Medal of Merit Am. Mineral Hall of Fame, 1994; named Can. Mining Man of Yr., No. Miner, 1999; inductee Am. Mining Hall of Fame, 2002. Mem. Ariz. Geol. Soc. (pres. 1965-66), Soc. Econ. Geologists (Silver medal 1983), Am. Inst. Mining Engrs. (pres. Yavapai sect. 1957, Daniel Jackling award 1970, Robert Dreyer award 2000, Earll McConnell award 2000), Can. Inst. Mining and Metall. Engrs. (disting. lectr. 1972), Internat. Assn. on Genesis of Ore Deposits, Mining and Metallurgy Soc. Am. (gold medal award 2001, Soc. Econ. Geologists Penrose medal 2004), Mining Club S.W. (dir. 1969-70), Prescott Country Club. Republican. Episcopalian. Home: 789 Avenida Beatriz Rio Rico AZ 85648-2200 Office: Lowell Mineral Exploration 789 Avenida Beatriz Rio Rico AZ 85648-2200 Home Phone: 520-281-1911; Office Phone: 520-281-8271. Business E-Mail: davidlowell@jdlcopper.com.

LOWELL, VIRGINIA LEE, retired librarian; b. San Jose, Calif., Nov. 21, 1940; d. Earnest S. and Dorothy (Givens) Greene; children: Michael Edward, Christopher Scott. Student, Reed Coll, 1958-61; BA, U. Calif., Berkeley, 1963; MSLS, Western Res. U., 1964. Cataloger Wittenberg U., Springfield, Ohio, 1965-66, John Carroll U., Cleve., 1966-68, Cuyahoga Community Coll., Cleve., 1968-70, cons., instr., 1970; head catalog dept. Cuyahoga County Pub. Library, Cleve., 1976-78; dir. tech. svcs. Cuyahoga County Pub. Libr., Cleve., 1979-89; dir. Jackson (Mich.) Dist. Libr., 1989—98; state libr. State of Hawaii, 1998—2003. Chmn. bd. trustees Ohionet, Columbus, 1987-89. Mem. ALA, Ohio Libr. Assn. (coord. automation and tech. div. 1988—), No. Ohio Tech. Svc. Librs. (chmn. 1988-89), Ohio Women Librs. (treas. 1987-89), Am. Mgmt. Assn., Mich. Libr. Assn. Democrat. Roman Catholic. Avocation: choral singing.

LOWEN, ROBERT MARSHALL, plastic surgeon; b. Detroit; MD, U. Mich. Med. Sch., 1971. Diplomate Am. Bd. Plastic Surgery. Internship Pacific Presbyn., San Francisco, 1971-72; resident general surgery Stanford U. Med. Ctr., 1983-85; resident plastic surgery U. Okla. HSC, Okla. City, 1985-86; fellow hand surgery U. Colo. HSC, Denver, 1986-87, resident plastic surgery, 1987-88; pvt. practice Mountain View, Calif., 1988—; mem. staff El Camino Hosp., Mountain View, Calif., 1988—, Sequoia Hosp., Redwood City, Calif., 1988—. Mem. Am. Soc. Plastic Surgeons, Am. Soc. Lasers in Medicine and Surgery, Calif. Med. Soc., Santa Clara County Med. Assn., Am. Soc. for Aesthetic Plastic Surgery.

LOWENTHAL, ABRAHAM FREDERIC, international relations educator; b. Hyannis, Mass., Apr. 6, 1941; s. Eric Isaac and Suzanne (Moos) L.; m. Janet Wyzanski, June 24, 1962 (div. 1983); children: Linda Claudina, Michael Francis; m. Jane S. Jaquette, Jan. 20, 1991. AB, Harvard U., 1961, MPA, 1964, PhD, 1971; postgrad., Harvard Law Sch., 1961—62. Tng. assoc. Ford Found., Dominican Republic, 1962-64, asst. rep. Lima, Peru, 1969-72; asst. dir., then dir. of studies Coun. Fgn. Rels., NYC, 1974-76; dir. Latin Am. program Woodrow Wilson Internat. Ctr. for Scholars, Washington, 1977-83; exec. dir. Inter-Am. Dialogue, Washington, 1982-92; prof. Sch. Internat. Rels., U. So. Calif., LA, 1984—; dir., ctr. internat. studies U. So. Calif., 1992-97; pres. Pacific Coun. Internat. Policy, LA, 1995—2005; v.p. Coun. Fgn. Rels., 1995—2005. Vis. fellow, rsch. assoc. Ctr. Internat. Studies, Princeton U., 1972-74, lectr., 1974; vis. lectr. polit. sci. Cath. U. Santiago, Dominican Republic, 1966; spl. cons. Commn. U.S.-L.Am. rels., N.Y.C., 1974-76; mem. internat. adv. bd. Ctr. U.S.-Mex. Rels., U. Calif.-San Diego, 1981-94; mem. internat. adv. bd. Helen Kellogg Inst., 1984-95; cons. Ford Found., 1974-90. Author: The Dominican Intervention, 1972, 2nd edit., 1995, Partners in Conflict: The United States and Latin America in 1990s, 1991; editor, contbg. author: The Peruvian Experiment: Continuity and Change Under Military Rule, 1975, Armies and Politics in Latin America, 1976, Exporting Democracy: The United States and Latin America, 1991; co-editor, contbg. author: The Peruvian Experiment Reconsidered, 1983, The California-Mexico Connection, 1993; editor Latin Am. and Caribbean Record, vol. IV, 1985-86, vol. V, 1986-87, Latin America in a New World, 1994, Constructing Democratic Governance: Latin America, 1996; mem. editl. bd. Jour. Inter-Am. Studies and World Affairs, 1980-97, New Perspectives Quarterly, 1984—, Hemisphere, Internat. Security, 1977-85, Wilson Quar., 1977-83; contbr. articles to profl. jours. Mem. nat. adv. coun. Amnesty Internat., 1977-83, Ctr. for Nat. Policy, 1986—. Mem. Internat. Inst. Strategic Studies, Am. Polit. Sci. Assn. (coun. 1979-81), Latin Am. Studies (exec. coun. 1979-81), Coun. Fgn. Rels. Democrat. Jewish. Office: U So Calif Los Angeles CA 90089-0035 Office Phone: 213-740-0793. Business E-Mail: afl@usc.edu.

LOWENTHAL, BONNIE, state legislator; BA in Sci., Wisconsin U.; MA in Sci. Cmty. & Clinical Psychology, CSU, Long Beach. Lic. family counselor and mental health cons., 1975. First coun. dist. City of Long Beach, 2001, vice mayor, 2006—; bd. mem. Long Beach Unified Sch. Dist. Bd. Edn; mem. LA County Met. Transp. Authority, 2008—; mem. Dist. 54 Calif. State Assembly, 2008—. Democrat. Mailing: PO Box 942849 Rm 5158 Sacramento CA 94249-0054 Office: 3711 Long Beach Blvd Ste 801 Long Beach CA 90807 Office Phone: 916-319-2054, 562-997-0794. Office Fax: 916-319-2154, 562-997-0799.

LOWENTHAL, STEVEN R., lawyer; BS, U. Calif., Berkeley, 1979; JD, Stanford U., 1982. Bar: Calif. 1982, admitted to practice: US Ct. Appeals (9th Cir.), US Dist. Ct. (No. and Ctrl. Dists. Calif.), Ct. Fed. Claims, Washington, DC. Ptnr. Farella Braun & Martel LLP, San Francisco, mng. ptnr., 2005—. Faculty, trial advocacy program Stanford Law Sch. Advocacy Skills Workshop. Mem.: Assn. Bus. Trial Lawyers (v.p.). Office: Farella Braun & Martel LLP Russ Bldg 235 Montgomery St San Francisco CA 94104-3105 Office Phone: 415-954-4405. Office Fax: 415-954-4480. Business E-Mail: slowenthal@fbm.com.

LOWERY, LAWRENCE FRANK, mathematic science and computer educator; b. Oakland, Calif., June 26, 1932; AA, U. Calif., Berkeley, 1952, BA, 1954, MA, 1962, EdD, 1965. Assoc. dean Sch. Edn. U. Calif., Berkeley, 1980-84, prof., 1965—. Contbr. articles to profl. jours.; also, books, videos and films; prolific writer. Numerous leadership roles in field. With U.S. Army, 1954-56. Mem. AAAS, ASCD, Am. Edn. Rsch. Assn. (res. rev. bd.), Assn. for the Edn. Tchrs. Sci., Phi Delta Kappa. Home: 650 Diablo Rd Danville CA 94526-2802

LOWNDES, DAVID ALAN, retired programmer analyst, application developer; b. Schenectady, NY, Oct. 28, 1947; s. John Henry and Iris Anne (Hepburn) Lowndes; m. Peggy Welco, May 3, 1970; children: Diana Justine, Julie Suzanne. AB, U. Calif., Berkeley, 1969, postgrad., 1972-73. Acct., credit mgr. The Daily Californian, Berkeley, 1973-75, bus. mgr., 1975-76; acct. Pacific Union Assurance Co., San Francisco, 1976-77, acctg. mgr., 1977-78; sr. acct. U. Calif., San Francisco, 1978-88, sr. programmer analyst, 1988—2003; ret., 2003. Mem.: Nev. Hist. Soc. (docent 2007—), Calif. Genealogical Soc. (bd. dir. 2005—06). Avocations: genealogy, microcomputing. Home: 6155 S Featherstone Cir Reno NV 89511-4348

LOWRY, EDWARD FRANCIS, JR., lawyer; b. LA, Aug. 13, 1930; s. Edward Francis and Mary Anita (Woodcock) L.; m. Patricia Ann Palmer, Feb. 16, 1963; children: Edward Palmer, Rachael Louise. Student, Ohio State U., 1948—50; AB, Stanford U., 1952, JD, 1954. Bar: Ariz. 1955, D.C. 1970, U.S. Supreme Ct. 1969. Camp dir. Quarter Circle V Bar Ranch, 1954; tchr. Orme Sch., Mayer, Ariz., 1954—56; trust rep. Valley Nat. Bank Ariz., 1958—60; pvt. practice Phoenix, 1960—; assoc. atty. Cunningham, Carson & Messinger, 1960—64; ptnr. Carson, Messinger, Elliott, Laughlin & Ragan, 1964—69, 1970—80, Gray, Plant, Mooty, Mooty & Bennett, 1981—84, Eaton, Lazarus, Dodge & Lowry Ltd., 1985—86; exec. v.p., gen. counsel Bus. Realty Ariz., 1986—93; pvt. practice, Scottsdale, Ariz., 1986—88; ptnr. Lowry & Froeb, Scottsdale, 1988—89, Lowry, Froeb & Clements, P.C., Scottsdale, 1989—90, Lowry & Clements P.C., Scottsdale, 1990, Lowry, Clements & Powell, P.C., Scottsdale, 1991—. Asst. legis. counsel Dept. Interior, Washington, 1969-70; mem. Ariz. Commn. Uniform Laws, 1972—, chmn., 1976-88; judge pro tem Ariz. Ct. Appeals, 1986, 92-94. Chmn. Coun. Stanford Law Socs., 1968; bd. dirs. Scottsdale Prevention Inst., 1999-2003, Cox Comms. Charities, 2006—; vice chmn. bd. trustees Orme Sch., 1972-74, treas., 1981-83; trustee Heard Mus., 1965-91, life trustee, 1991—, pres., 1974-75; bd. dirs. Rio Salado Found., 2006—; bd. visitors Stanford Sch. Law, dir. operational bd. dirs. Rio Salado Town Lake Found., 2003-2006; magistrate Town of Paradise Valley, Ariz., 1976-83, town councilman, 1998-2004, mayor, 1998-2004; juvenile ct. referee Maricopa County, 1978-83. Capt. USAF, 1956-58. Fellow Ariz. Bar Found. (founder); mem. ABA, Maricopa County Bar Assn., Scottsdale Bar Assn., State Bar Ariz. (chmn. com. uniform laws 1979-85), Stanford Law Soc. Ariz. (past pres.), Scottsdale Bar Assn. (bd. dirs. 1991—2001, v.p. 1991, pres. 1992-95), Ariz. State U. Law Soc. (bd. dirs.), Nat. Conf. Commrs. on Uniform State Laws (life), Delta Sigma Rho, Alpha Tau Omega, Phi Delta Phi. Home: 7600 N Moonlight Ln Paradise Valley AZ 85253-2938 Office: Edward F Lowry Jr PC 4200 N 82d St Ste 2001 Scottsdale AZ 85251-2771 Office Phone: 480-423-1200.

LOWRY, MICHAEL E., former governor, former congressman; b. St. John, Wash., Mar. 8, 1939; s. Robert M. and Helen (White) L.; m. Mary Carlson, Apr. 6, 1968; 1 child, Diane. BA, Wash. State U., Pullman, 1962. Chief fiscal analyst, staff dir. ways and means com. Wash. State Senate, 1969-73; govtl. affairs dir. Group Health Coop. Puget Sound, 1974-75; mem. council King County Govt., 1975-78, chmn., 1977—78; mem. US Congress from 7th dist. Wash., 1979-1989; instr. Seattle U. Inst. Pub. Svc., 1989—92; governor State of Wash., 1993-96. Chmn. King County Housing and Community Devel. Block Grant Program, 1977; pres. Wash. Assn. Counties, 1978; co-chmn. Wash. Wildlife & Recreation Coalition. Mem.: Kappa Sigma. Democrat. Address: 3326 Park Ave N Renton WA 98056-1915

LOWY, PETER, corporate financial executive; Exec. dir. Westfield Mgmt. Ltd., 1986, Westfield Holdings Ltd., 1987, Westfield Am. Mgmt. Ltd., 1996, mng. dir. LA, 1997—, bd. dir. Bd. gov. Nat. Assn. of Real Estate Investment Trusts; bd. dir. Lowy Inst. for Internat. Policy. Office: Westfield Corp Inc 11601 Wilshire Blvd 11th Fl Los Angeles CA 90025-1748 Office Phone: 310-478-4456. Office Fax: 310-478-1267.

LOZANO, MONICA CECILIA, publishing executive; b. LA, July 21, 1956; d. Ignacio Eugenio and Marta Eloisa (Navarro) Lozano; m. Marcelo Centanino, Sept. 27, 1987 (div.); children: Santiago Alberto, Gabriela. Student, U. Oreg.; student San Francisco City Coll.; LHD (hon.), Occidental Coll., 1999. Mgr. Copy-Copia, Inc., San Francisco, 1980—85; mng. editor La Opinion, LA, 1985—89, assoc. pub., 1989—91, assoc. pub., exec. editor, 1991—2000, pres., COO, 2000—04, pub., CEO, 2004—; v.p. Lozano Comm., 2000—04; sr. v.p. ImpreMedia LLC, 2004—08, sr. v.p. newspapers, 2008—. Pub. El Eco del Valle, Calif., 1991; bd. dirs. Union Bank Calif., Nat. Coun. La Raza, Calif. Health Care Found., Tenet Healthcare Corp., 2002—05, The Walt Disney Co., 2000—, Bank of America Corp., 2006—; bd. trustees SunAmerica Asset Mgmt. Corp.; mem. President's Econ. Recovery Advisory Bd., 2009—. Trustee LA County Mus. Art, U. So. Calif., 1991—; mem. bd. regents U. Calif., 2001—; bd. dirs. Venice Family Clinic, Ctrl. Am. Resource Ctr., Weingart Found. Recipient Humanitarian award, Ctrl. Am. Refugee Ctr., LA, 1989, Outstanding achievement award, Mex. Am. Opportunities Found., LA, 1989; co-recipient José Ortega y Gasset award, Madrid, 2006; named one of 25 Best Latinos in Bus., Hispanic Mag., 2008. Mem.: Coun. Fgn. Rels., Nat. Network Hispanic Women, Calif. Chicano News Assn., Am. Soc. Newspaper Editors, Calif. Hispanic Pubs., Nat. Assn. Hispanic Journalists, Nat. Assn. Hispanic Pubs. Avocations: photography, reading, water sports. Office: La Opinion 700 S Flower St Ste 3000 Los Angeles CA 90017-4217 Office Phone: 213-748-1191.*

LU, HONG LIANG, telecommunications industry executive; b. Taiwan; BS civil engring., Univ. Calif., Berkeley. COO Unison World Inc., pres., CEO, 1983—86, Kyocera Unison, 1986—91, UTStarcom, Alameda, Calif., 1991—2003, chmn. pres., CEO, 1995—2006, CEO, 2006—08, exec. chmn., 2008—. Mem. strategic adv. bd. Pacrim Venture Partners. Office: UTStarcom 1275 Harbor Bay Pkwy Alameda CA 94502

LU, NANCY CHAO, nutrition and food science educator; b. Xian, China, May 29, 1941; came to U.S. 1963; d. Lun Yuan and Shu Mei (Tsang) Chao; m. Chyi Kang Lu, Mar. 19, 1966; 1 child, Richard H. BS, Nat. Taiwan U., 1963; MS, U. Wyo., 1965; PhD, U. Calif., Berkeley, 1973. Registered dietitian. Teaching asst. dept. nutritional sci. U. Wyo., Laramie, 1963, U. Calif., Berkeley, 1964, 70, teaching assoc. dept. nutritional sci., 1978, 79; lectr. dept. nutrition and food sci. San Jose State U., 1980-82, assoc. prof. dept. nutrition and food sci., 1982-87, prof. dept. nutrition and food sci., 1987—, acting assoc. dean, dir. divsn. health professions. Contbr. articles to profl. jours. Recipient Ellsworth Dougherty award, 1976, Calif. State U. Affirmative Action Faculty Devel. award, 1984, 85, 86, Meritorious Performance and Profl. Promise award San Jose State U., 1986, Most Outstanding Nutrition and Food Sci. Prof. award, 1989, 93; San Jose State U. Found. grantee, 1986-87, 89-90, 92-93, 93-94, 94-95, NIH grantee, 1975-76, 78-79, 73-75. Mem. Am. Dietetic Assn., Am. Inst. Nutrition, Inst. Food Technologists, Soc. Nematology, Soc. for Exptl. Biology and Medicine, Iota Sigma Pi, Sigma Xi. Office: San Jose State U Divsn Health Professions San Jose CA 95192-0001

LU, QI, computer software company executive; b. China, 1961; BS in Computer Sci., Fudan U., China, 1984, MS in Computer Sci., 1987; PhD in Computer Sci., Carnegie Mellon U. Mem. faculty Fudan U., China; rsch. assoc. Carnegie Mellon U.; rsch. staff mem. IBM Almaden Rsch. Ctr.; v.p. engring., search and marketplace bus. unit Yahoo! Inc., 1998—2006, exec. v.p. engring., search and advt. tech. group, 2006—08; pres. online services group Microsoft Corp., 2009—. Office: Microsoft Corp One Microsoft Way Redmond WA 98052-7329

LUBATTI, HENRY JOSEPH, physicist, researcher; b. Oakland, Calif., Mar. 16, 1937; s. John and Pauline (Massimino) L.; m. Catherine Jeanne Berthe Ledoux, June 29, 1968; children: Karen E., Henry J., Stephen J.C. AA, U. Calif., Berkeley, 1957, AB, 1960; PhD, U. Calif., 1966; MS, U. Ill., 1963. Research assoc. Faculty Scis. U. Paris, Orsay, France, 1966-68; asst. prof. physics MIT, 1968-69; assoc. prof., sci. dir. visual techniques lab. U. Wash., 1969-74, prof., sci. dir. visual Techniques lab., 1974-98, prof., 1998—. Vis. lectr. Internat. Sch. Physics, Erice, Sicily, 1968, Herceg-Novi, Yugoslavia Internat. Sch., 1969, XII Cracow Sch. Theoretical Physics, Zapokane, Poland, 1972; vis. scientist CERN, Geneva, 1980-81; vis. staff Los Alamos Nat. Lab., 1983-86; guest scientist SSC Lab., 1991-93; mem. physics editl. adv. com. World Sci. Pub. Co. Ltd., 1982-93; guest scientist Fermilab, 1999-2000; vis. scientist U. Rome, summers 2001-08. Editor: Physics at Fermilab in the 1990's, 1990; contbr. numerous articles on high energy physics to profl. jours. Alfred P. Sloan Rsch. fellow, 1971-75. Fellow AAAS, Am. Phys. Soc.; mem. Sigma Xi, Tau Beta Pi. Office: Elem Particle Experiment Group U Wash PO Box 351560 Seattle WA 98195-1560 Home Phone: 206-524-2496; Office Phone: 206-543-8964. E-mail: lubatti@u.washington.edu.

LUBECK, MARVIN JAY, ophthalmologist; b. Cleve., Mar. 20, 1929; s. Charles D. and Lillian (Jay) L. A.B., U. Mich., 1951, M.D., 1955, M.S., 1959. Diplomate Am. Bd. Opthamology; m. Arlene Sue Bitman, Dec. 28, 1955; children: David Mark, Daniel Jay, Robert Charles. Intern, U. Mich. Med. Ctr., 1955-56, resident ophthalmology, 1956-58, jr. clin. instr. ophthalmology, 1958-59; pvt. practice medicine, specializing in ophthalmology, Denver, 1961—; mem. staff Rose Hosp., Porter Hosp., Presbyn. Hosp., St. Luke's Hosp. With U.S. Army, 1959-61. Fellow ACS; mem. Am. Acad. Ophthalmology, Denver Med. Soc., Colo. Ophthalmol. Soc. Home: 590 S Harrison Ln Denver CO 80209-3517

LUBETKIN, ALVIN NAT, sporting goods retail company executive; b. Newark, Dec. 5, 1933; s. William and Dorothy L.; children—Wendy, Karen, Andrew. BA, Harvard U., 1956. Stockbroker L.F. Rothschild & Co., NYC, 1957-60, J.R. Williston & Beane, NYC, 1960-61; with Oshman's Sporting Goods Co., Houston, 1961—, vice chmn., 1970—, CEO, 1970—, pres., 1989—. Past bd. dirs. March of Dimes, Better Bus. Bur. Served with AUS, 1953-55. Mem. Nat. Sporting Goods Assn. (bd. dirs. 1972-78, 87-89). Office: Oshmans Sporting Goods Co 1050 W Hampden Ave Englewood CO 80110-2118

LUBIN, STANLEY, lawyer; b. May 7, 1941; children: David Christopher, Jessica Nicole; m. Barbara Ann Lubin. AB, U. Mich., 1963, JD with honors, 1966. Bar: D.C. 1967, U.S. Ct. Appeals (D.C. cir.) 1967, U.S. Ct. Appeals (4th cir.) 1967, Mich. 1968, U.S. Ct. Appeals (6th cir.) 1968, U.S. Supreme Ct. 1970, Ariz. 1972, U.S. Ct. Appeals (9th cir.) 1976, U.S. Ct. Appeals (fed. cir.) 1985, Tex. 2005, U.S. Ct. Appeals (5th cir.) 2002, U.S. Dist. Ct. (ctrl. and so. dist.) Tex. 2005. Atty. NLRB, Washington, 1966-68; asst. gen. counsel UAW, Detroit, 1968-72; assoc. Harrison, Myers & Singer, Phoenix, 1972-74, McKendree & Tountas, Phoenix, 1975; ptnr. McKendree & Lubin, Phoenix and Denver, 1975-84; shareholder Treon, Warnicke & Roush, P.A., 1984-86; pvt. practice Law Offices Stanley Lubin, Phoenix, 1986-95, The Law Offices of Stanley Lubin, P.C., 1996-98, Lubin & Enoch, P.C., Phoenix, 1999—, El Paso, Denver. Mem. Ariz. Employment Security Adv. Coun., 1975—77; vice chair Ariz. State Personnel Bd., 2008—, chair, 2009, Phoenix Employment Rels. Bd., 2009, hearing officer, 2007—. Co-author: Union Fines and Union Discipline Under the National Labor Relations Act, 1971. Active ACLU, dir. Ariz. chpt., 1974-81; vice chair Ariz. State Cen. Com. Dem. Party, 1986-91, 93-2004, sec., 1991-92, mem. state exec. com., 1986-2004, Ariz. Dem. Coun., 1987-99, chmn., 1988-93, Thomas Jefferson Forum, 1987-99, chmn., 1988-93. Fellow: Coll. Labor & Employment Lawyers; mem.: Ariz. Labor & Employment Rels. Assn. (exec. bd. 1973—, pres. 1979—80, 1984), Labor & Employment Rels. Assn. Home: 7520 N 9th Pl Phoenix AZ 85020-4138 Office: 349 N 4th Ave Phoenix AZ 85003 also: 7362 Remcon Cir El Paso TX 79912-1623 also: 999 18th St Ste 3000 Denver CO 80207 Business E-Mail: stan@lubinandenoch.com.

LUBITZ, STUART, lawyer; b. Bklyn., Dec. 17, 1934; s. Morris and Yetta (Oshinsky) L.; m. Linda Lee Garden, Dec. 24; children: Debbie Lubitz Bloch, Michael, David. BS in Elec. Engring., U. Fla., 1957, BS in Elem. Edn., 1958; JD with honors, George Washington U., 1961. Bar: U.S. Ct. Appeals (9th cir.) 1964, U.S. Dist. Ct. (no. dist.) Calif. 1964, U.S. Dist. Ct. (ctrl. dist.) Calif. 1965, U.S. Dist. Ct. (so. dist.) Calif. 1978, U.S. Ct. Customs & Patent Appeals 1981, U.S. Ct. Internat. Trade 1981, U.S. Ct. Appeals (fed. cir.) 1982, Calif. 1988. Devel. engr. IBM, 1957-60; patent examiner U.S. Patent & Trademark Office, Washington, 1960-61; staff atty. Ford Motor Co., Detroit, 1961-63; asst. patent counsel Ampex Corp., Redwood City, Calif., 1963-65; ptnr. Spensley Horn Jubas & Lubitz, LA, 1965-95, Loeb & Loeb, LA, 1995—; ptnr., intellectual property practice group Hogan & Hartson LLP. Prof. law Loyola U. Law Sch., L.A., 1972-84; bd. dirs. Kyocera Corp., Kyoto, Japan, Kyocera Internat., Inc., San Diego, AVX Corp., N.Y.C., Murata Bus. Systems, Inc., Plano, Tex., Murata Wiedemann, Charlotte, N.C. Bd. dirs. Inamori Charitable Found., Kyoto, 1985-96. Mem. ATLA, L.A. County Bar Assn., L.A. Intellectual Property Law Assn. Jewish. Avocations: tennis, golf. Office: Hogan & Hartson LLP Biltmore Tower 500 S Grand Ave Ste 1900 Los Angeles CA 90071 Office Phone: 213-337-6840. Business E-Mail: slubiz@hhlaw.com.

LUBNAU, THOMAS EDWIN, II, state legislator, lawyer; b. Laramie, Wyo., Dec. 12, 1958; s. Thomas Edwin and Cynthia L'Vere (Kirkland) Lubnau; m. Rita Lubnau; 1 child, Tommy 1 stepchild, Rachel. BS in Fin., U. Wyo., 1981, JD, 1984. Bar: Wyo. 1984, U.S. Dist. Ct. Wyo. 1984, U.S. Ct. Appeals (10th cir.) 1984, U.S. Supreme Ct. 1995. Mem. Lubnau, Bailey & Dumbrill, P.C., Gillette, Wyo., 2000—; mem. Dist. 31 Wyo. House of Reps., 2005—, spkr. pro tempore, 2007—08. Chmn. Wyo. Bd. CLE, Cheyenne, 1990-92; trustee Rocky Mountain Mineral Law, Denver, 1992-95; legal counsel Wyo. Jaycees, Gillette, 1986-94, Campbell County Rep. Party, Gillette, 1989-96 Contbr. to Land and Water Law rev., 1984. Bd. dirs. Campbell County Libr. Found.; chalice bearer, lay reader Holy Trinity Episcopal Ch., Campbell County Rep. Party (state committeeman 1988-89; mem. Campbell County Fire Dept. Mem. ABA, Assn. Trial Lawyers Am., Campbell County C. of C. (bd. dirs., chmn. 1993-94), Gillette Rotary (bd. dirs.), Wyo. State Bar (commnr. 1998-2001, v.p. 2001-02, pres.-elect 2002-03, pres. 2003-04), Campbell County Bar Assn. (pres. 2000-01), Gov.'s Probate Com. (1984-90), Bd. Continuing Ed. (chmn. 1988-91), Rocky Mtn. Mineral Law Found. (trustee 1992-95), Atty.'s Assistance Com. (co-chair, 1995-96), Jackrabbit Bar Assn. (chancellor 2004-05) Republican. Episcopal. Avocations: woodworking, photography, writing. Office: Lubnau Bailey & Dumbrill PC PO Box 1028 Gillette WY 82717-1028 Address: 213 State Capitol Building Cheyenne WY 82002 Office Phone: 307-682-1313. Fax: 307-682-9340. E-mail: tlubnau@vcn.com.*

LUCAS, GENE, academic administrator; BS, U. Calif., Santa Barbara, 1973; MS, MIT, 1975, ScD, 1978. Joined faculty U. Calif., Santa Barbara, 1978, exec. vice chancellor, 2003—. Office: Exec Vice Chancellor 5105 Cheadle Hall Univ Calif Santa Barbara CA 93106 Office Phone: 805-893-2126. Business E-Mail: gene.lucas@evc.ucsb.edu.

LUCAS, GEORGE WALTON, JR., film director, producer, scriptwriter; b. Modesto, Calif., May 14, 1944; Student, Modesto Jr. Coll.; BA, U. So. Calif., 1966. Chmn. Lucasfilm Ltd., San Rafael, Calif., 1971—. Mem. TV bd. councilors U. So. Calif.; chmn. George Lucas Ednl. Found., Artists Rights Found., Joseph Campbell Found., Film Found. Asst. to Francis Ford Coppola (films) The Rain People, 1969, creator short film, dir., co-writer THX-1138:4EB, 1970, THX-1138, 1971, dir., co-writer American Graffiti, 1973, dir., author screenplay Star Wars, 1977 (earned seven Acad. awards); exec. prodr.: (films) More American Graffiti, 1979, The Empire Strikes Back, 1980, Raiders of the Lost Ark, 1981, Indiana Jones and the Temple of Doom, 1984, Labyrinth, 1986, Howard the Duck, 1986, Willow, 1988, Tucker, 1988, Radioland Murders, 1994, (co-author screenplay) Return of the Jedi, 1983; co-exec. prodr. (films) Mishima, 1985; co-author (co-exec. prodr.): (films) Indiana Jones and the Last Crusade, 1989; dir., exec. prodr. (films) Star Wars: Episode I The Phantom Menace, 1999, Star Wars: Episode II Attack of the Clones, 2002, Star Wars: Episode III Revenge of the Sith, 2005 (Favorite Movie and Favorite Movie Drama, People's Choice award, 2006), writer, exec. prodr. Indiana Jones and the Kingdom of the Crystal Skull, 2008, Star Wars: The Clone Wars, 2008; exec. prodr.(TV series): The Young Indiana Jones Chronicles, 1992—93. Mem. adv. bd. Sci. Fiction Mus. and Hall of Fame. Recipient Irving G. Thalberg Meml. award, Academy of Motion Picture Arts and Sciences, 1991, Lifetime Achievement award, Am. Film Inst., 2005; named one of The 100 Most Powerful Celebrities, Forbes.com, 2008. Office: Lucasfilm Ltd PO Box 2009 San Rafael CA 94912-2009 Office Phone: 415-662-1800.

LUCAS, SPENCER G., paleontologist, curator, director; Grad., U. N.Mex. Paleontology curator N.Mex. Mus. Natural History & Sci., interim dir. Author: (books) Santa Rosa - Tucumcari Region: New Mexico Geological Society Thirty-si, 1985, Coryphodon From the Hannold Hill Formation Eocene of Trans-Pecos Texas, 1989, Dinosaurs: The Textbook, 1996, Chinese Fossil Vertebrates, 2001; co-author: Bisti, 1987, Color Pattern on the Selmacryptodiran Turtle Neurankylus from the Early Paleocene, 1988; editor: Late Paleocene-Early Eocene Biotic and Climatic Events in the Marine and Terrestrial Records, 1998; contbr. scientific papers to profl. jours. Avocation: chess. Office: New Mexico Mus Natural History & Sci 1801 Mountain Rd NW Albuquerque NM 87104 Office Phone: 505-841-2841.

LUCAS, WILLIAM JOHN, science educator; b. Adelaide, Australia, Feb. 23, 1945; BSc in Botany (hon.), U. Adelaide, 1971, PhD, 1975, DSc (hon.), 1990; prof. (hon.), U. Internat. des Eaux-de-Vie, 1990. Rsch. assoc. U. Toronto, Ont., Canada, 1975—77; from asst. prof. to assoc. prof. U. Calif., Davis, 1977—83, prof., 1983—. Gastprof. U. Goettingen, Germany, 1984—85; Lady Davis prof. Hebrew U. Jerusalem, 1998; hon. visitor Nat. Sci. Coun., China, 1999; vis. prof. Tokyo U. Agr. and Biotech., 1999; Internat. Franqui chair Inter-Univ., Belgium, 2001; lectr. in field. Mem. editl. bd.: Plant Physiology, 1977—92, Protoplasma, 1985—2001, Planta, 1989—2002, assoc. editor: Jour. Theoretical Biology, 1999—. Recipient rsch. grants in field. Mem.: AAAS, French Nat. Acad. Scis. (fgn. mem.), Am. Soc. Plant Physiologists (Martin Gibbs medal 1997), Am. Soc. for Virology, Internat. Soc. Photosynthesis Rsch., Soc. for Exptl. Biology U.K., N.Y. Acad. Scis., Australian Soc. Plant Physiologists (hon.), Sigma Xi. Office: U Calif-Davis 1231 Life Scis Addition 1 Shields Ave Davis CA 95616

LUCCHETTI, DAVID J., manufacturing executive; CEO, pres. Pacific Coast Bldg. Products, Sacramento. Home: Pacific Coast Bldg Products PO Box 419074 Rancho Cordova CA 95741-9074 Fax: 916-325-3697.

LUCE, R. DUNCAN (ROBERT DUNCAN LUCE), psychology professor; b. Scranton, Pa., May 16, 1925; s. Robert Rennselaer and Ruth Lillian (Downer) L.; m. Gay Gaer, June 6, 1950 (div.); m. Cynthia Newby, Oct. 5, 1968 (div.); m. Carolyn A. Scheer, Feb. 27, 1988; 1 child, Aurora Newby. BS, MIT, Cambridge, Mass. 1945, PhD, 1950; MA (hon.), Harvard U., Cambridge, Mass. 1976; D of Math. (hon.), U. Waterloo, Calif., 2007. Mem. staff research lab electronics MIT, 1950-53; asst. prof. Columbia U., 1953-57; lectr. social relations Harvard U., 1957-59; prof. psychology U. Pa., Phila., 1959-69; vis. prof. Inst. Advanced Study, Princeton, 1969-72; prof. Sch. Social Scis., U. Calif., Irvine, 1972-75; Alfred North Whitehead prof. psychology Harvard U., Cambridge, Mass., 1976-81, prof., 1981-83, Victor S. Thomas prof. psychology, 1983-88, Victor S. Thomas prof. emeritus, 1988, chmn., 1988-94; disting. prof. cognitive sci. U. Calif., Irvine, 1988-94, dir. Irvine Rsch. Unit in math. behavioral sci., 1988-92, disting. rsch. prof. cognitive sci. and rsch. prof. econs., 1994—; dir. Inst. for Math. Behavioral Sci., 1992-98. Chmn. assembly behavioral and social scis. NRC, 1976-79 Author: (with H. Raiffa) Games and Decisions, 1957, Individual Choice Behavior, 1959, (with others) Foundations of Measurement, I, 1971, II, 1989, III, 1990, Response Times, 1986, (with others) Stevens Handbook of Experimental Psychology, I and II, 1988, Sound & Hearing, 1993, Utility of Gains and Losses, 2000. Served with USNR, 1943-46. Recipient

Disting. award Rsch. U. Calif., Irvine, 1994, medal, 2001, Extraordinarius award, 2006, Gold medal Am. Psychol. Found., 2001, Daniel G. Aldrich, Jr. Disting. Svc. award U. Calif., Irvine, 2003, Ramsey medal Soc. Decision Analysis, 2003, Norman Anderson award Soc. Exptl. Psychologists, 2004, Nat. medal of Sci., 2003, with Ragnar Sbingrinham; Ctr. Advanced Study in Behavioral Scis. fellow, 1954-55, 66-67, 87-88, NSF Sr. Postdoctoral fellow, 1966-67, Guggenheim fellow, 1980-81; named Best Artic, 2005-07. Fellow: Am. Psychol. Soc. (bd. dirs. 1989—91), APA (bd. sci. affairs 1993—95, exec. com. divsn. I 2000, disting. sci. contbn. award 1970), AAAS (chair elect psychology sect. 1998—99, chair 1999); mem.: Soc. Math. Psychology (pres. 1979), Psychonomic Soc., Psychometric Soc. (pres. 1976—77), Fedn. Behavioral Psychol. and Cognitive Scis. (pres. 1988—90), Math. Assn. Am., Am. Math. Soc., Nat. Acad. Scis. (chmn. sect. psychology 1980—83, class behavioral and social scis. 1983—86, mem. dbasse bd. 2005—), Am. Philos. Soc., Am. Acad. Arts and Sci., Tau Beta Pi, Phi Beta Kappa, Sigma Xi. Home: 20 Whitman Ct Irvine CA 92617-4057 Office: U Calif Social Sci Plz Irvine CA 92697-5100 Office Phone: 949-824-6239. Business E-Mail: rdluce@uci.edu.

LUCERO, CARLOS, federal judge; b. Antonito, Colo., Nov. 23, 1940; m. Dorothy Stuart; 1 child, Carla. BA, Adams State Coll.; JD, George Washington U., 1964. Law clk. to Judge William E. Doyle US Dist. Ct., Colo., 1964—65; pvt. practice Alamosa, Colo., 1966—95; sr. ptnr. Lucero, Lester & Sigmund, Alamosa, Colo.; judge US Ct. Appeals (10th cir.), 1995—. Mem. Pres. Carter's Presdl. Panel on Western State Water Policy. Bd. dirs. Colo. Hist. Soc., Sante Fe Opera Assn. of N.Mex. Recipient Outstanding Young Man of Colo. award, Colo. Jaycees, Disting. Alumnus award, George Washington U.; fellow Paul Harris, Rotary Found. Fellow: Internat. Soc. Barristers, Internat. Acad. Trial Lawyers, Colo. Bar Found. (pres.), Am. Coll. Trial Lawyers, Am. Bar Found.; mem.: ABA (mem. action com. to reduce ct. cost and delay, mem. adv. bd. ABA jour., mem. com. on the availability of legal svcs.), Colo. Rural Legal Svcs. (bd. dirs.), Colo. Hispanic Bar Assn. (Profl. Svc. award), Nat. Hispanic Bar Assn., San Luis Valley Bar Assn. (pres.), Colo. Bar Assn. (pres. 1977—78, mem. ethics com.), Order of the Coif. Office: US Ct Appeals 1823 Stout St Denver CO 80257

LUCIA, MARILYN REED, physician; b. Boston; m. Walter M. Dickie Jr., 1951 (div. 1958); m. Salvatore P. Lucia, 1959, (dec. 1984); m. C. Robert Russell, 1985 (dec. 2000); children: Elizabeth, Walter, Salvatore, Darryl. AB with highest honors, U. Calif., Berkeley, 1951; MD, U. Calif., San Francisco, 1956. Cert. in psychiatry and child psychiatry Am. Bd. Psychiatry and Neurology. Intern Stanford U. Hosp., 1956-57; NIMH fellow, resident in psychiatry Langley Porter, U. Calif., San Francisco, 1957-60; NIMH fellow, resident in child psychiatry Mt. Zion Hosp., San Francisco, 1964-66; NIMH fellow, in cmty. psychiatry U. Calif., San Francisco, 1966—68, clin. prof. psychiatry, 1982—. Founder, cons. Marilyn Reed Lucia Child Care Study Ctr., U. Calif., San Francisco; cons. Cranio-facial Ctr., U. Calif., San Francisco; No. Calif. Diagnostic Sch. for Neurologically Handicapped Children; dir. children's psychiat. svc. Contra Costa County Hosp., Martinez. Fellow Am. Psychiat. Assn. (disting. life), Am. Acad. Child Psychiatry; mem. Am. Cleft Palate Assn., San Francisco Med. Soc., Phi Beta Kappa. Office: 350 Parnassus Ave Ste 602 San Francisco CA 94117-3608

LUCIW, PAUL A., molecular virologist, educator; BA in Microbiology, Cornell U., 1970; PhD in Microbiology, U. Pa., 1977. Scientist Chiron Corp., Emeryville, Calif., 1982—84, prin. scientist, 1984—85, sr. scientist, 1985—86; postdoctoral fellow dept. microbiology U. Calif., San Francisco, 1978—82; asst. adj. prof., dept. pathology, U. Calif., Sch. Medicine, Davis, Calif., 1986—90, assoc. adj. prof., dept. pathology, 1990—91, assoc. prof. in residence, dept. pathology, 1992—94, assoc. prof. dept. pathology, 1994—; rsch. dir. viral oncology program U. Calif., Davis, 1997—. Mem. microbiology grad. group U. Calif., Davis, 1987—, mem. biochemistry and molecular biology grad. group, 1987—, mem. genetics grad. group, 1987—, mem. comparative pathology grad. group, 1987—, co-dir., Optical Biology Program, 1997—2000, mem. exec. com., Cancer Ctr., 1997—, founding mem., Ctr. for Comparative Medicine, 1993—; rsch. affiliate Calif. Regional Primate Rsch. Ctr., Davis, 1986—99, core-staff scientist, 2000—; mem. Calif. Universitywide AIDS Rsch. program, 1992—95; mem. basic sci. coun. U. Calif. Davis Sch. Medicine, 1996—; mem. Targeted Action Group for Vaccines, AIDS Rsch. Inst. U. Calif., San Francisco, 1999—, Cancer Biology in Animals Program, 2000—. Contbr. articles to profl. jours.; mem. editl. bd. Virology, 1994—, AIDS Rsch. and Human Retroviruses, 1994—, Jour. Virology, 2001—. Achievements include patents in field. Office: U Calif Sch Medicine Dept Pathology 3444 Tupper Hall Davis CA 95616 Office Phone: 916-752-3430. Office Fax: 916-752-4548. E-mail: paluciw@ucdavis.edu.

LUCZO, STEPHEN JAMES, computer hardware company executive; b. 1957; BA in Economics & Psychology, Stanford U., MBA, 1984. Sr. mng. dir. Global Tech. Group Bear Stearns & Co. Inc., 1992—93; exec. v.p. corp. devel. Seagate Tech. LLC, Scotts Valley, Calif., 1993—97, pres., 1997—98, pres., CEO, 1998—2002, chmn., pres., CEO, 2002—04, chmn, pres., CEO, 2009—, chmn., 2004—09. Bd. dirs. Seagate Tech. LLC, 2000—. Office: Seagate Technology LLC 920 Disc Dr Scotts Valley CA 95066-4542*

LUDGUS, NANCY LUCKE, lawyer; b. Palo Alto, Calif., Oct. 28, 1953; d. Winston Slover and Betty Jean Lucke; m. Lawrence John Ludgus, Apr. 8, 1983. BA in Polit. Sci. with honors, U. Calif., Berkeley, 1975; JD, U. Calif., Davis, 1978. Bar: Calif. 1978, U.S. Dist. Ct. (no. dist.) Calif. 1978. Staff atty. Crown Zellerbach Corp., San Francisco, 1978-80, Clorox Co., Oakland, Calif., 1980-82, Nat. Semiconductor Corp., Santa Clara, Calif., 1982-85, corp. counsel, 1985-92, sr. corp. counsel, asst. sec., 1992-2000, assoc. gen. counsel, asst. sec., 2000—. Contbr. articles to profl. jours. Mem. ABA, Am. Corp. Counsel Assn., Calif. State Bar Assn., Santa Clara County Bar Assn., Phi Beta Kappa. Democrat. Avocations: travel, jogging, opera. Office: Nat Semiconductor Corp 2900 Semiconductor Dr # G3135 Santa Clara CA 95051 E-mail: nancy.lucke.ludgus@nsc.com.

LUEDTKE, ROGER A., lawyer; b. Wausau, Wis., Apr. 10, 1942; BS, U. Wis., 1964, MA, 1968, JD, 1974. Bar: Wis. 1974, Oreg. 1974. Atty. Schwabe, Williamson & Wyatt, Portland, Oreg., 1974—. Mem. Oreg. State Bar, Phi Eta Sigma. Address: Schwabe Williamson & Wyatt 1211 SW 5th Ave Ste 1600 Portland OR 97204-3716

LUENBERGER, DAVID GILBERT, electrical engineer, educator; b. LA, Sept. 16, 1937; s. Frederick Otto and Marion (Crumley) L.; m. Nancy Ann Iversen, Jan. 7, 1962; children: Susan Ann, Robert Alden, Jill Alison, Jenna Emmy. BSE.E., Calif. Inst. Tech., 1959; MSE.E., Stanford U., 1961, PhD in Elec. Engring., 1963. Asst. prof. elec. engring. Stanford (Calif.) U., 1963-67, assoc. prof. engring.-econ. systems, 1967-71, prof., 1971—, dept. chmn., 1980-91, prof. mgmt. sci. & engring., 2000—. Tech. asst. dir. U.S. Office Sci. and Tech., Exec. Office of Pres., Washington, 1971-72; vis. prof. MIT, Cambridge, 1976; guest prof. Tech. U. of Denmark, Lyngby, 1986. Author: Optimization by Vector Space Methods, 1969, Linear and Nonlinear Programming, 1973, 2d edit., 1984, Introduction to Dynamic Systems, 1979, Microeconomic Theory, 1995, Investment Science, 1998; contbr. articles to tech. jours. Recipient Hendrik W. Bode Lecture prize Control Systems Soc., 1990, Rufus Oldenburger medal, 1998. Fellow IEEE; mem. Econometric Soc., Soc. for Advancement Econ. Theory, Soc. for Promotion of Econ. Theory, Inst. Mgmt. Sci., Soc. Econ. Dynamics and Control (pres. 1987-88), Math Programming Soc., Palo Alto Camera Club, Sigma Xi, Tau Beta Pi. Lutheran.

LUI, ELWOOD, lawyer; b. LA, Feb. 4, 1941; BS, UCLA, 1962, MBA, 1964, JD, 1969. Bar: Calif. 1970, D.C. 1990; CPA, Calif. Dep. atty. gen. State of Calif., 1969-71; judge mcpl. ct. LA Judicial Dist., 1975-79, LA County Superior Ct., 1980-81; assoc. justice 2nd appellate dist. Calif. Ct. Appeals, 1981-87; mem. Jones, Day, LA; ptnr.-in-charge San Francisco office Jones Day. Mem. Judicial Coun. Calif., 1983-87; adj. prof. law U. So. Calif., 1977-87, Loyola U., LA, 1984. Recipient Bernard Witkin medal, State Bar Calif., 2006. Fellow: Am. Acad. Appellate Lawyers; mem.: Calif. Acad. Appellate Lawyers. Office: Jones Day Ste 4600 555 S Flower St Los Angeles CA 90050 also: Jones Day 26th Fl 555 California St San Francisco CA 94104 Office Phone: 213-489-3939, 415-626-3939. Office Fax: 415-875-5700. Business E-Mail: elui@jonesday.com.

LUIKART, JOHN FORD, investment banker; b. Washington, Apr. 9, 1949; s. Fordyce Whitney and Margaret Lucille (Clark) L.; m. Lorry Adele Haycock, June 2, 1973; children: Erin Kristine, James Benjamin, John Thomas. BA, Ohio Weslyan U., 1971. Ptnr. Prescott Ball and Turben, Cleve., 1977, sr. v.p., mgr. fixed income, 1982-86, exec. v.p., also bd. dirs., 1986-88; pres. Sutro & Co. Inc., San Francisco, 1989—, CEO, 1995—; bd. dirs. John Hancock Freedom Securities, San Francisco, 1996; chmn., CEO Sutro & Co., San Francisco. Pres. Selected Money Mkt. Fund, Chgo., 1986, 1331 Advisors, Cleve., 1986; mgr. Ohio Bond Fund, Cleve., 1983—; chmn. NASD Dist. Bus. Conduct Com., 1994; bd. dirs. Freedom Securities, Freedom Capital Mgmt. Chmn. Ohio Mcpl. Adv. Council, Cleve., 1978-79. Mem. Cleve. Bond Club (pres. 1980). Methodist. Avocations: sports, reading. Office: 345 California St FL 29 San Francisco CA 94104-2642

LUJAN, BEN, SR., state legislator; b. 1936; m. Carmen Lujan; children: Ben Jr., Jerome, Shirley, Jackie. Attended, Coll. Santa Fe. Former iron worker with Zia Co., Los Alamos, N.Mex.; mem. Dist. 46 N.Mex. House of Reps., 1974—, Dem. House whip under spkr. Ray Sanchez, Dem. majority leader under spkr. Ray Sanchez, spkr. of the house, 2002—. Democrat. Office: State Capitol Rm 104 Santa Fe NM 87503 also: Dist 46 05 Entrada Celedon y Nestora Santa Fe NM 87506 Home Phone: 505-455-3354; Office Phone: 505-986-4782. E-mail: ben.lujan@nmlegis.gov.*

LUJAN, BEN RAY, JR., United States Representative from New Mexico, former state official; b. Santa Fe, June 7, 1972; s. Ben and Carmen Lujan. Attended, U. N.Mex., Albuquerque, 1997—99; BBA, N.Mex. Highlands U., Las Vegas. Dep. state treas. State of N.Mex., 2003—05; dir. adminstrn. svc. & CFO N.Mex. Cultural Affairs Dept.; commr., dist. 3 State Pub. Regulation Commn., N.Mex., 2005—09; mem. Santa Fe Co. Extraterritorial Zoning Commn., US Congress from 3rd N.Mex. Dist., 2009—. Democrat. Office: US Congress 502 Cannon House Office Bldg Washington DC 20515-3103 also: Dist Office 811 St Michael's Dr Ste 104 Santa Fe NM 87505 Office Phone: 202-225-6190, 505-984-8950. Office Fax: 202-226-1331, 505-986-5047.*

LUJAN, DAVID M., state legislator; b. Phoenix, Apr. 7, 1965; BS in Mktg., Ariz. State U., 1993, JD, 1996. Asst. atty. gen. Office Ariz. Atty. Gen., 1999—2003; atty. Ariz. State Senate Judiciary Com., 2003—04, Curtis Goodwin Sullivan Udall & Schwab, 2003—05, Martinez & Curtis, 2004—; mem. Dist. 15 Ariz. House of Reps., 2005—, minority leader. Mem. Phoenix Union HS Dist. Gov. Bd., 2002—, pres. bd., 2007—09; atty. non-profit orgn. Justice for Children, 2005—07, Defenders of Children, 2008—. Vol. Valley Big Brothers Big Sisters, 1998—, Ctrl. HS Mock Trial Team, 1998—; bd. dirs. St. Joseph the Worker, 2005—; mem. adv. bd. U. Ariz. Coll. Medicine, Phoenix, 2005—; chmn. adv. bd. Ariz. Latino Leadership Inst., 2008—. Recipient Golden Apple award, Ariz. Parents for Edn., Legis. Ptnr. award, Ariz. Bus. & Edn. Coalition; named Legislator of Yr., Ariz. Students Assn., 2006. Mem.: Young Men's Christian Assn. (bd. dirs. Christown branch 2005—). Democrat. Roman Catholic. Office: Ariz House Reps Capitol Complex 1700 W Washington Rm 320 Phoenix AZ 85007 Office Phone: 602-926-5829. Office Fax: 602-417-3115. Business E-Mail: dlujan@azleg.gov.*

LULLO, THOMAS A., electronics executive; CFO Consolidated Electrical Distbrs., Inc., Westlake Village, Calif. Office: Consolidated Electronics Distbrs 31356 Via Colinas Ste 107 Westlake Village CA 91362 Office Fax: (818) 991-6858.

LUM, JEAN LOUI JIN, nursing educator; b. Honolulu, Sept. 5, 1938; d. Yee Nung and Pui Ki (Young) L. BS, U. Hawaii, Manoa, 1960; MS in Nursing, U. Calif., San Francisco, 1961; MA, U. Wash., 1969, PhD in Sociology, 1972. Registered nurse, Hawaii. From instr. to prof. Sch. Nursing U. Hawaii Manoa, Honolulu, 1961-95, acting dean, 1982, dean, 1982-89, prof. emeritus, 1995—. Project coordinator Analysis and Planning Personnel Svcs., Western Interstate Commn. Higher Edn., 1977; extramural assoc. div. Rsch. Grants NIH, 1978-79; mem. mgmt. adv. com. Honolulu County Hosp., 1982-96; mem. exec. bd. Pacific Health Rsch. Inst., 1980-88; mem. health planning com. East Honolulu, 1978-81; mem. rsch. grants adv. coun. Hawaii Med. Svcs. Assn. Found., Nat. Adv. Coun. for Nursing Rsch., 1990-93. Contbr. articles to profl. jours. Trustee Straub Pacific Health Found., Honolulu; bd. dirs. Friends of the Nat. Inst. of Nursing Rsch., 1994-97. Recipient Nurse of Yr. award Hawaii Nurses Assn., 1982, Gov.'s commendation State of Hawaii, 2006; named Disting. Practitioner in Nursing, Nat. Acads. Practice, 1986; USPHS grantee, 1967-72. Fellow Am. Acad. Nursing; mem. Am. Nurses Assn., Am. Pacific Nursing Leaders Conf. (pres. 1983-87), Council Nurse Researchers, Nat. League for Nursing (bd. rev. 1981-87), Western Council Higher Edn. for Nurses (chmn. 1984-85), Western Soc. for Research in Nursing, Am. Sociol. Assn., Pacific Sociol. Assn., Assn. for Women in Sci., Hawaii Pub. Health Assn., Hawaii Med. Services Assn. (bd. dirs. 1985-92), Western Inst. Nursing, Mortar Bd., Phi Kappa Phi, Sigma Theta Tau (Kupuna award 2003), Alpha Kappa Delta, Delta Kappa Gamma. Episcopalian. Office: U Hawaii Manoa Sch Nursing Webster Hall 2528 The Mall Honolulu HI 96822

LUMMIS, CYNTHIA MARIE, United States Representative from Wyoming, former state official, lawyer; b. Cheyenne, Wyo., Sept. 10, 1954; d. Doran Arp and Enid (Bennett) L.; m. Alvin L. Wiederspahn, May 28, 1983; children: Annaliese Alex. BS, U. Wyo., 1976, BS, 1978, JD, 1985. Bar: Wyo. 1985, U.S. Dist Ct. of Wyo. 1985, U.S. Ct. of Appeals (10th cir.) 1986. Rancher Lummis Livestock Co., Cheyenne, 1972—; law clk. Wyo. Supreme Ct., Cheyenne, 1985-86; atty., 1986—; assoc. to ptnr. Wiederspahn, Lummis & Liepas P.C., Cheyenne, 1986—95; treas. State of Wyo., 1999—2006; mem. US Dept. of Interior Royalty Mgmt., 2007, Wyo. Stock Growers Agrl. Land Trust, 2000—08, US Congress from 1st Wyoming Dist., 2009—. Mem. Wyo. Ho. Judiciary Com., 1979-86, Ho. Agriculture, Pub. Lands & Water Resources Com., 1985-86, Wyo. State Senate, 1993-94, Senate Judiciary Com., 1993-94, Senate Mines, Minerals, Econ. Devel. Com., 1993-94, U. Wyo. Inst. for Environment and Natural Resource Policy and Rsch.; chmn. County Ct. Planning Com., Wyo., 1986-88, Ho. Rev. Com., 1987-92, Joint Revenue Interim Com., 1988-89, 91-92; mem. adv. bd. U. Mont. Ctr. for the Rocky Mountain West, 1998—. Sec. Meals on Wheels, Cheyenne, 1985-87; mem. Agrl. Crisis Support Grp., Laramie County, Wyo., 1985-87; mem. adv. com. U. Wyo. Sch. Nursing, 1988-90; mem. steering com. Wyo. Heritage Soc., 1986-89. Mem.: Rep. Women's (Cheyenne) (legis. chmn. 1982). Republican. Lutheran. Office: US Congress 1004 Longworth HOB Washington DC 20515-5001 also: Dist Office 100 East B St Ste 4003 Casper WY 82602 Office Phone: 202-225-2311, 307-261-6595. Office Fax: 202-225-3057, 307-261-6597.*

LUMPKIN, LIBBY, museum director; BA in Hist., U. Houston; MA in Art Hist., U. Tex., Austin; PhD, U. N.Mex, Albuquerque. Asst. prof. art hist., cur. Donna Beam Fine Art Gallery, U. Nev.; vis. prof. U. N.Mex, Yale U., U. Calif. Santa Barbara; vis. lectr. Umea U., Sweden, Harvard U.; dir. mus. studies prog., asst. prof. art hist. Calif. State U., Long Beach; cons. exec. dir. Las Vegas Art Mus., 2005—07, dir., 2007—. Author: Deep Design: Nine Little Art Histories, Jean-Michel Basquiat, Ingrid Calame, War Paint. Office: Las Vegas Art Mus 9600 W Sahara Ave Las Vegas NV 89117

LUNA, B. MARTIN, lawyer; b. Waimea, Kauai, Hawaii, July 25, 1938; BA, Emory U., 1960, MA, 1962; LLB, George Washington U., 1967. Bar: Hawaii 1968, U.S. Dist. Ct. Hawaii, U.S. Ct. Appeals (9th cir.), U.S.Supreme Ct. Ptnr. Carlsmith Ball Wichmans Case, Wailuku, Hawaii. Office: Carlsmith Ball Wichman Case Mukai & Ichiki PO Box 1086 2200 Main St Ste 400 Wailuku HI 96793-1691

LUNA, BERNADETTE, mechanical engineer; 3 children. B in Bioengineering, U. Pa.; M in Mech. Engring., Stanford U., postgrad. Rsch. engr. NASA Ames Rsch. Ctr. Avocations: knitting, jogging. Office: NASA Ames Rsch Ctr Bldg 200 Rm 116 Moffett Field CA 94035 Business E-Mail: bernadette.luna@nasa.gov.

LUNA, THOMAS, school system administrator; m. Cindy Luna; 6 children. Grad., Thomas Edison State Coll. Former mem., chmn. Nampa Sch. Bd., Idaho; spl. asst. Office of Under Sec. of Edn., US Dept. Edn., Washington, dir. Rural Edn. Task Force; mem. Idaho Assessment and Accountability Commn.; supt. pub. instrn. Idaho Dept. Edn., Boise, 2007—. Pres. Scales Unlimited Inc., 1985. Mem.: Western Weights and Measures Assn., Nat. Conf. on Weights and Measures, Nampa Exchange Club. Republican. Office: Idaho Dept Edn 650 W State St PO Box 83720 Boise ID 83720-0027 Office Phone: 208-332-6815. E-mail: Trluna@sde.idaho.gov.

LUND, ROBERT W., newspaper editor; Editor L.A. Daily News, 1994-98, mgr. editl. ops. and fin., 1998—. Office: Los Angeles Daily News 21221 Oxnard St Woodland Hills CA 91367-5015

LUNDBERG, KEVIN, state legislator; m. Sandy Lundberg; 3 children. Farmer, near Berthoud, Colo.; owner, operator Lundberg Prodns.; co-founder Christian Home Educators, Colo.; mem. Dist. 49 Colo. House of Reps., Denver, 2002—09; mem. Dist. 15 Colo. State Senate, Denver, 2009—. Precinct committeeman, dist. capt., campaign vol. Rep. Party; participant Colo. Rep. Leadership Program, 2000; apptd. Colo. Commn on Family Medicine, 2000; bd. trustees Colo. Christian Univ., 1986-2002; bd. deacons Galilee Ch., Loveland, Colo. Republican. Office: Colo State Capitol 300 E Colfax Denver CO 80203 Office Phone: 303-866-4853. Business E-Mail: kevin@kevinlundberg.com.*

LUNDEN, JOAN, television personality; b. Fair Oaks, CA, Sept. 19, 1950; d. Erle Murray and Gladyce Lorraine (Somervill) Blunden; m. Michael Krauss, 1978 (div. 1992); children: Jamie Beryl, Lindsay Leigh, Sarah Emily; m. Jeff Konigsberg, 2000; children: Kate Elizabeth, Max Aaron, Kimberly, Jack. Student, Universidad de Las Americas, Mexico City, U. Calif., Calif. State U., Am. River Coll., Sacramento, Calif. Began broadcasting career as co-anchor and prodr. at Sta. KCRA-TV and Radio, Sacramento, 1973-75; with Sta. WABC-TV, N.Y.C., 1975—97, co-anchor, 1976-80; co-host Good Morning America, ABC-TV, 1980-97; host spl. report TV for Whittle Comm.; host Everyday with Joan Lunden, 1989, Behind Closed Doors With Joan Lunden, 1994-2000 (ABC), 2000- (A&E); pres., host Women's Supermarket Network; film appearances include: Macho Callahan, 1970, What About Bob?, 1991, Free Willy 2, 1995, Conspiracy Theory, 1997, Thank You for Smoking, 2006; spl. appearances: (TV appearances) Murphy Brown, 1992, 93, LateLine, 1998; Author: Good Morning, I'm Joan Lunden, 1986, Joan Lunden's Mother's Minutes, 1986, Your Newborn Baby: Everything You Need to Know, 1988, Joan Lunden's Healthy Cooking, 1996, Joan Lunden's Healthy Living, 1997, Joan Lunden's A Bend in the Road Is Not the End of the Road, 1998, Wake-Up Calls: Making the Most Out of Every Day, 2000; syndicated columnist: Parent's Notes. Recipient Outstanding Mother of Yr. award, Nat. Mother's Day Com., 1982; Albert Einstein Coll. of Yeshiva U. Spirit of Achievement award; Nat. Women's Polit. Caucus award; NJ Divsn. of Civil Rights award; Baylor U. Outstanding Woman of the Year award; Decoration for Disting. Civilian Svc., US Army. Office: LMNO Prodns PO Box 4361 Los Angeles CA 90028 also: Rm 4332 1271 Avenue Of The Americas New York NY 10020-1401

LUNDIN, NORMAN KENT, artist, educator; b. LA, Dec. 1, 1938; s. John R. and Louise A. (Marland) L.; m. Sylvia Johnson; children: Kelly Jean, Christopher David. BA, Sch. Art Inst. Chgo., 1961; M.F.A., U. Cin., 1963. Asst. to dir. Cin. Art Mus., 1962-63; instr. art U. Wash., Seattle, 1964-66, asst. prof., 1966-68, assoc. prof., 1968-75, prof., 1976—. Vis. artist Hornsey Coll. Art, London, 1969-70; vis. prof. Ohio State U., Columbus, 1975; prof. San Diego State U., 1978; vis. prof. U. Tex.-San Antonio, 1982, Chelsea Coll. Art, London, 1996. Exhibited one-man shows, Francine Seders Gallery, Seattle, Space, L.A., Jack Rasmussen Gallery, Washington, Allen Stone, N.Y.C., Adams Middleton Gallery, Dallas, Allport Gallery, San Francisco, Stephen Haller Fine Art, N.Y.C., 1987-94, Schmidt-Bingham Gallery, N.Y.C., 1997, Koplin Gallery, L.A., 1997, Koplin DelRio Gallery, Los Angeles, 2005; group shows include Mus. Modern Art, N.Y.C., Whitney Mus. Am. Art, N.Y.C., Denver Art Mus., Seattle Art Mus., San Joes Mus. Art, Ca, 1982-1983, Fine Art Mus., Seattle, 2000, San Francisco Mus. Modern Art Nat. Endowment Arts grantee; Fulbright-Hays grantee Norway, 1963-64; Tiffany Found. grantee, 1968; Ford. Found. grantee Soviet Union, Eastern Europe, 1978-79 Office: U Wash Sch Art Seattle WA 98105

LUNDINE, STANLEY NELSON, former congressman, former lieutenant governor, lawyer; b. Jamestown, NY, Feb. 4, 1939; m. Karol Anne Ludwig, 1962 (div.); m. Sara Sibley; children: John Ludwig, Mark Andrew. AB, Duke U., 1961; LLB, NYU, 1964; LLD (hon.), Alfred U. Bar: NY 1965. Atty., Jamestown, NY, 1965—; mayor, 1969—76; mem. from 39th and 34th Dist. NY US Ho. of Reps, 1976-87, mem. banking, fin. and urban affairs com., mem. select com. on aging, mem. sci. and tech. com.; lt. gov. State of NY, Albany, 1987—95; exec. dir. Found. for Enterprise Devel., La Jolla, CA. Mailing: PO Box 3050 Jamestown NY 14702-3050

LUNDSTROM, MARJIE, editor; Grad., U. Nebr. Columnist, editor, nat. corr. The Denver Post, 1981-89; with The Sacramento Bee, 1989-90, 91—; nat. corr. Gannett News Svc., Washington, 1990-91. Recipient Pulitzer Prize for nat. reporting, 1991. Office: The Sacramento Bee PO Box 15779 Sacramento CA 95852-0779 Business E-Mail: mlundstrom@sacbee.com.

LUNDY, ROBERT W., JR., lawyer; b. San Mateo, Calif., Aug. 12, 1950; BA cum laude, Yale U., 1972; JD, UCLA, 1975. Bar: Calif. 1975. Founding ptnr., health care law Hooper Lundy & Bookman, LA, 1987—. Contbr. articles to profl. jours.; editor: Calif. Health Law Monitor, 1995—2001. Bd. mem. Partners In Care Found., 1997—, chmn., 2002—. Named a So. Calif. Super Lawyer, LA Mag., 2004, 2005, 2006; named an Outstanding Healthcare Transaction Lawyer, Healthcare News, 2003. Mem.: Am. Health Lawyers Assn., Calif. Soc. Health Care Attys. (bd. mem. 1996—2003, pres. 2001—02), LA County Bar Assn. (chmn. health law sect. 1981—82). Office: Hooper Lundy & Bookman Ste 1600 1875 Century Park E Los Angeles CA 90067 Office Fax: 310-551-8181. Business E-Mail: rlundy@health-law.com.

LUNGREN, DANIEL EDWARD, United States Representative from California, former state attorney general; b. Long Beach, Calif., Sept. 22, 1946; s. John Charles and Lorain Kathleen (Youngberg) Lungren; m. Barbara Kolls, Aug. 2, 1969; children: Jeffrey Edward, Kelly Christine, Kathleen Marie. BA in English, with honors, Notre Dame U., 1968; student, U. So. Calif.; JD, Georgetown U., 1971. Bar: Calif. 1972. Staff asst. to senators George Murphy, William Brock US Senate, 1969—71; spl. asst. to co-chmn. Rep. Nat. Com., 1971—72; from assoc. to ptnr. Ball, Hunt, Hart, Brown & Baerwitz, Long Beach, 1973—78; mem. US Congresses from 34th Calif. Dist., 1979—83, US Congresses from 42nd Calif. Dist., 1983—89; ptnr. Diepenbrock, Wulff, Plant & Hannegan, Sacramento, 1989—90; atty. gen. State of Calif., Sacramento, 1991—99; ptnr. Venable LLP, Washington, 1999—2004; mem. US Congress from 3rd Calif. Dist., 2005—; ranking mem. US House Adminstrn. Com., 2009—; mem. US House Judiciary Com., US House Homeland Security Com. Del. Calif. State Rep. Conv., 1974—79; co-chmn. Nat. Congl. Coun., 1977—78; former chair Youth for Nixon campaign, Calif. Nat. syndicated radio talk show host, 1998. Bd. dirs. ARC Boy's Club, Long Beach, 1976—88. Recipient Good Samaritan award, L.A. Coun. Mormon Chs., 1976; fellow Harvard Univ.'s Inst. Politics. Republican. Roman Catholic. Achievements include helped write and later defended in court California's landmark Three-Strikes-and-You're Out law; sponsored legis. against sexual predators which culminated in the state's Megan's Law giving people in Calif. the right to know if their children are at risk of predators in their own neighborhoods. Office: US Ho Reps 2448 Rayburn Ho Office Bldg Washington DC 20515-0503 Office Phone: 202-225-5716.

LUNINE, JONATHAN IRVING, astronomer, educator; b. NYC, June 26, 1959; BS magna cum laude, U. Rochester, 1980; MS, Calif. Inst. Tech., 1983, PhD, 1985. Rsch. assoc. U. Ariz., Tucson, 1984-86, asst. prof. planetary scis., 1986-90; vis. asst. prof. UCLA, 1986, assoc. prof., 1990-95, prof., 1995—2003, prof. planetary sci. and physics, faculty mem. program in applied math., 1992—, chair theoretical astrophys. program, 2000—05. Interdisciplinary scientist joint U.S.-European Cassini mission to Saturn and JWST mission, James Webb Space Telescope, 2002—; mem. com. planetary and lunar exploration space sci. bd. NAS, 1986—90; disting. vis. scientist Jet Propulsion Lab., 1997—; mem. exec. com. space studies bd. NRC, 1998—2002, chmn. com. origin and evolution life in universe space studies bd., 2000—02; mem. sci. coun. NASA Astrobiology Inst., 2000—03; chair solar sys. exploration subcom. NASA, 1990—94, 2003—05, mem. internat. Mars exploration adv. panel, 1993—94, mem. space sci. adv. com., 1990—95, 2003—05, co-chair, titan saturn system mission sci. definition team; vis. prof. Inst. Physics Interplanetary Space, Rome, 2005—06; chair Exoplanet Task Force, 2007—08. Co-editor: (book) Protostars and Planets III, 1993; author: Earth: Evolution of, 1999, Astrobiology: A Multidisciplinary Approach, 2005; contbr. articles to profl. jours. Recipient Cospar Zeldovich prize, Soviet Intercosmos and Inst. for Space Rsch., 1990, Arthur Adel award sci. achievement, No. Ariz. U., 2000; named one of 50 Emerging Leaders, Time Mag., 1994; Galileo Circle fellow, U. Ariz., 2003. Fellow: AAAS, Am. Geophys. Union (Macelwane medal 1995); mem.: NAS (nat. assoc.), European Geophys. Soc., Internat. Coun. Sci. Unions, Internat. Acad. Astronautics, Am. Astron. Soc. (Harold C. Urey prize 1988), Sigma Xi. Avocation: hiking. Office: U Ariz Dept Planetary Scis PO Box 210092 Tucson AZ 85721-0092 Office Phone: 520-621-2789. Business E-Mail: jlunine@lpl.arizona.edu.

LUONG, DOMINIC, bishop; b. Ninh Cuong, Vietnam, Dec. 20, 1940; BS, St. Bernard's Coll., Rochester, NY, 1962; MS, Canisius Coll., Buffalo, 1967; LittD (hon.), Notre Dame Sem., 2006. Ordained priest Diocese of Danang, Vietnam, 1966; hospital chaplain Buffalo, 1966—75; assoc. pastor St. Louis Ch., Buffalo, 1975—76; incardinated priest Archdiocese of New Orleans, 1976, dir. Vietnamese Apostolate, 1976—83, mem. priests' coun., 1987—2003, dean New Orleans East, 2002—03; pastor Mary Queen of Vietnamese Ch., New Orleans, 1983—89; dir. Nat. Pastoral Ctr. for the Vietnamese Apostolate, New Orleans, 1989—2003; ordained bishop, 2003; aux. bishop Diocese of Orange, Calif., 2003—. Roman Catholic. Office: PO Box 14195 Orange CA 92863-1595 Office Phone: 714-282-3000. Office Fax: 714-282-3029.

LUONG, KHANH VINH QUOC, nephrologist, researcher; b. Cantho, Vietnam, Oct. 20, 1952; s. Hien Vinh Luong and Lieu Thi Huynh; m. Lan Thi Hoang Nguyen, Oct. 15, 1981. MD, U. Kans., 1981. Diplomate Am. Bd. Internal Medicine, Am. Bd. Nephrology, Nat. Bd. Med. Examiners, Am. Coll. Ethical Physicians. Intern in internal medicine St. Elizabeth Med. Ctr., Northeastern Ohio U., Youngstown, 1981; resident internal medicine Tulane U. Hosp. Program, New Orleans, 1982-83, City of Faith Med. and Rsch. Ctr., Oral Roberts U., Tulsa, Okla., 1986-87; fellow in nephrology Cedars-Sinai Med. Ctr., UCLA Program in Nephrology, LA, 1987-90; pvt. practice Westminster, Calif., 1990—; clin. assoc. prof. family medicine U. So. Calif., Keck Sch. Medicine, LA, 2002—. Vis. asst. prof. medicine UCLA, 1989—90; clin. assoc. prof. family medicine Keck Sch. Medicine, U. So. Calif., LA, 2002—; presenter at nat. and internat. meetings. Contbr. articles to profl. jours. Nat. Kidney Found. So. Calif. fellow, 1989-90. Fellow ACP, Am. Coll. Endocrinology, Am. Coll. Allergy, Asthma and Immunology, Am. Coll. Nutrition, Am. Bd. Hosp. Physicians (diplomate), Am. Soc. Nephrology, Am. Assn. Clin. Endocrinologists, Am. Coll. Chest Physicians, Endocrine Soc., Am. Soc. Bone and Mineral Rsch., Assn. Vietnamese Physicians of the Free World, Vietnamese Med. Assn. in U.S., Vietnamese Am. Med. Rsch. Found. (pres.). Office: 14971 Brookhurst St Westminster CA 92683-5556 Office Phone: 714-839-5898.

LUONGO, ROBERTO, professional hockey player; b. Montreal, Quebec, Canada, Apr. 4, 1979; Goaltender NY Islanders, 1999—2000, Florida Panthers, 2000—06, Vancouver Canucks, 2006—, capt., 2008—. Goaltender Team Can., World Championships, 2003, 04, Team Can., World Cup of Hockey, 2004. Recipient Mark Messier Leadership Award, 2007; named to NHL All-Star Game, 2004, 2007, 2008, 2009, Second All-Star Team, NHL, 2007. Achievements include being a member of gold medal winning Canadian World Championships Team, 2003, 2004; being a member of World Cup Champion Team Canada, 2004; setting NHL record for saves in a single season (2,303), 2004. Office: Vancouver Canucks 800 Griffiths Way Vancouver BC Canada*

LUPIN, LOUIS MARTIN, lawyer; b. Mar. 1955; m. Margarita I. Lupin; children: Gabe, Daniel, Leanna. BA in Psych., Swarthmore Coll., 1977; JD, Stanford U., 1985. Bar: 1985. Assoc. Cooley, Godward, Castro, Huddleson & Tatum, San Francisco, 1985—92, ptnr., 1992—95; sr. legal counsel QUALCOMM Inc., San Diego, 1995—96, v.p., proprietary rights counsel, 1996—98, sr. v.p., proprietary rights counsel, 1998—2000, sr. v.p., gen. counsel, 2000—06, exec. v.p., gen. counsel, 2006—07. Exec. com. bd. visitors Stanford Law Sch. Mem.: San Francisco Bar Assn., Santa Clara County Bar Assn., ABA.

LUSK, HARLAN GILBERT, national park superintendent, business executive; b. Jersey City, June 22, 1943; s. Harlan H. and Mary M. (Kuhl) L.; m. Mildred Dearing, Feb. 3, 1968 (div. 1986), m. Catherine Rutherford, Oct. 11, 1986. BA in History, Gettysburg Coll., 1965, PhD (hon.), 2001. Supervisory historian Cape Hatteras Nat. Seashore, Manteo, NC, 1968; historian Nat. Pk. Svc., Washington, 1968-69; programs specialist So. Utah Group, Cedar City, 1968-70; pk. supt. Wolf Trap Farm Pk., Vienna, Va., 1970-72; supervisory pk. ranger Blue Ridge Pkwy., Roanoke, Va., 1972-74; pk. supt. Appomattox (Va.) Courthouse, Nat. Hist. Pk., 1974-76, Valley Forge (Pa.), Nat. Hist. Pk., 1976-81, Big Bend (Tex.) Nat. Pk., 1981-86, Glacier Nat. Pk., West Glacier, Mont., 1986-94; pk. supt. Albright Tng. Ctr. Grand Canyon Nat. Pk., Ariz., 1994-95; chief, Divsn. Tng. and Employee Nat. Park Svc., Washington, 1995-97; retired from park svc., 1997; chmn. Gil Lusk Assocs., 1997—; group mgr. The Cholla Group, 1997—; co-adminstr. Lusk Surname DNA Project Family Tree DNA, 2004—; pres., CEO Rancho La Joya Corp., 2001—; owner Lusk Auction Svcs., 2008. First supr. Wolf Trap Farm Pk., Vienna, 1970; co-organizer 1st regional conf. Rio Grande Border, States on Pks. and Wildlife, Laredo, Tex., 1985; creator Crown of Continent Ecosystem Concept (now Y to Y Project) NW Mont., 1986; co-creator Burlington No. Environ. Stewardship Area, Glacier Nat. Pk., Montana, 1990; first nat. pk. supr. Valley Forge Nat. Hist. Pk., 1976. Author: Considered Options, 1991. Bd. dirs. Tech. Com. on Pks. and Recreation Cen. Va. Planning Dist., 1972-74, Fed. Exec. Assn. Roanoke Valley, 1972-74, Flathead Basin Commn., 1986-94, Flathead Conv. and Visitor Assn., 1986-94, Sonoran Inst., 1995-2001; prin. founder, 1st pres., Appomattox County Hist. Soc., 1974-76; trustee Sci. Mus. Assn. Roanoke Valley, 1972-74, Nature Conservancy Mont., 1994-1997; ex-officio Friends of Valley Forge, 1977-81; founder, ex-officio, bd. dirs. Valley Forge Pk. Interpretive Assn., 1977-81; founder Big Bend Area Travel Assn., chmn., 1984-86. Recipient Meritorious Svc. award. Dept. Interior, 1986, Exemplary Pub. Svc., Nature Conservancy Mont., 1993, Disting. Svc. award, 1999; first recipient Grey Towers Conservation Fellow, US Forest Svc., Yale U., 1991. Mem. Glacier Natural History Assn. (ex officio 1986-94), Glacier Nat. Pk. Assocs. (founder, ex-officio 1989-94), George Wright Soc., Lions, Rotary. Avocations: golf, antiques, computers, collecting artwork, hiking. Home and Office: 1382 N Boyce Ave Green Valley AZ 85614-6259 Personal E-mail: hglusk@msn.com.

LUSKY, JOHN ANDERSON, lawyer; b. Louisville, Oct. 30, 1951; BA, Harvard U., 1973; JD, Stanford U., 1977. Bar: Oreg. 1977. Ptnr. Miller, Nash LLP (formerly known as Miller, Nash, Wiener, Hager & Carlsen), Portland, Oreg. Mem. Oreg. State Bar. Office: Miller Nash LLP 111 SW 5th Ave Ste 3500 Portland OR 97204-3638

LUSZTIG, PETER ALFRED, dean, educator; b. Budapest, Hungary, May 12, 1930; s. Alfred Peter and Susan (Szabo) L.; m. Penny Bicknell, Aug. 26, 1961; children: Michael, Cameron, Carrie. B in Com., U. B.C., Vancouver, Can., 1954; MBA, U. Western Ont., London, Can., 1955; PhD, Stanford U., 1964. Asst. to comptroller B.C. Electric, Vancouver, 1955-57; instr. fin. U. B.C., 1957-60, asst. prof. fin., 1962-64, assoc. prof., 1965—68, Killam sr. research fellow, 1968-69, prof., 1968—95, dean faculty commerce, 1977-91, dean emeritus, 1995—. Trustee BC Health Benefit Trust; bd. dirs. Canfor Pulpco; fed. comnr. BC Treaty Commn., 1995-2003; vis. prof. IMEDE, Switzerland, 1973-74, London Grad. Sch. Bur. Studies, 1968-69, Pacific Coast Banking Sch., 1977—1982; sr. advisor B.C. Ministry of Econ. Devel., Small Bus. and Trade, 1991. Author: Report of the Royal Commission on Automobile Insurance, 2 vols., 1968, Financial Management in a Canadian Setting, 6th rev. edit., 2001, Report of the Commission on the B.C. Tree Fruit Industry, 1990. Past bd. dirs. Vancouver Gen. Hosp. Ford Found. faculty dissertation fellow, Stanford U., 1964.

LUTHY, RICHARD GODFREY, environmental engineering educator; b. June 11, 1945; s. Robert Godfrey Luthy and Marian Ruth (Ireland) Haines; m. Mary Frances Sullivan, Nov. 22, 1969; children: Matthew Robert, Mara Catherine, Jessica Bethlin. BSChemE, U. Calif., Berkeley, 1967; MS in Ocean Engring., U. Hawaii, 1969; MSCE, U. Calif., Berkeley, 1974, PhDCE, 1976; DSc (hon.), Clarkson U., 2005. Registered profl. engr. Pa.; diplomate Am. Acad. Environ. Engrs. Rsch. asst. dept. civil engring. U. Hawaii, Honolulu, 1968-69; rsch. asst. div. san. and hydraulic engring. U. Calif., Berkeley, 1973-75; asst. prof. civil engring. Carnegie Mellon U., Pitts., 1975-80, assoc. prof., 1980-83, prof., 1983—, assoc. dean Carnegie Inst. Tech., 1986-89, head dept. civil and environ. engring., 1989-96, Lord prof. environ. engring., 1996-2000; Silas H. Palmer prof. dept. civil and environ. engring. Stanford (Calif.) U., 2000—, chmn. Dept. Civil and Environ. Engring., 2003—. Shimizu Corp. vis. prof. dept. civil engring. Stanford U., 1996-97; cons. sci. adv. bd. U.S. EPA, 1983-2004, Bioremediation Action com., 1990-92; cons. U.S. Dept. Energy, 1978-93, various pvt. industries; del. water sci. and tech. bd. NAE, Washington and Beijing, 1988; mem. tech. adv. bd. Remediation Techs., Inc., Concord, Mass., 1989-94, Fostin Capital, Pitts., 1991-94, Balt. Gas & Elec., 1992-95, Pa. Dept. Environ. Protection, 1994-96; mem. sci. adv. com. Hazardous Substance Rsch. Ctr. Stanford U., 1994-99; chair Gordon Rsch. Conf. Environ. Scis., 1994; Nat. Rsch. Coun. Commn. on Innovative Remediation Tech., Com. on Intrinsic Remediation, Com. on Bioavailabilty, Water Sci. and Tech. Bd., 1997-2004, chair, 2000-04. Contbr. articles to tech. and sci. jours. Chmn. NSF/Assn. Environ. Engring. Prof. Conf. on Fundamental Rsch. Directions in Environ. Engring, Washington, 1988. Lt. C.E. Corps, USN, 1969-72. Recipient George Tallman Ladd award Carnegie Inst. Tech., 1977; AT&T Indsl. Ecology Faculty fellow, 2005. Mem. ASCE (Pitts. sect. Prof. of Yr. award 1987), Nat. Acad. Engring., Assn. Environ. Engring. Sci. Profs. (pres. 1987-88, Nalco award 1978, 82, Engring. Sci. award 1988, 2005, Svc. award 1999), Water Environ. Fedn. (rsch. com. 1982-86, awards com. 1981-84, 89-94, std. methods com. 1977—, groundwater com. 1989-90, editor jour. 1989-92, Eddy medal 1980, McKee medal 2000), Water Environ. Rsch. Found. (bd. 2003—), Internat. Assn. on Water Quality (Foudners award U.S. Nat. Com. 1986, 93, orgnl. com. 16th Biennial Conf. Washington 1992), Am. Chem. Soc. (divsn. environ. chemistry, mem. editl. adv. bd. Environ. Sci. Tech. 1992-95). Presbyterian. Business E-Mail: luthy@stanford.edu.

LUTTROPP, PETER C., city official; b. Coeur d' Alene, Idaho, Feb. 7, 1941; BS, U. Idaho, 1964; MBA, U. Calif., Berkeley, 1969. City treas. City of Tacoma, Wash., 1971-91, dir. fin., 1991—. Office: City Tacoma Tacoma Mcpl Bldg 747 Market St Ste 132 Tacoma WA 98402-3726

LUTZ, CHRIS P., research physicist; Rsch. scientist IBM Almaden Rsch. Ctr., San Jose, Calif. Recipient Newcomb Cleveland prize AAAS, 1993-94. Office: IBM Almaden Rsch Ctr 650 Harry Rd San Jose CA 95120-6099

LUTZ, FRANK WENZEL, education administration educator; b. St. Louis, Sept. 24, 1928; s. Vincent J. and Helen M. (Scrivens) L.; m. Susan Virginia Bleikamp, July 12, 1958; children: Paul E., Andrew C., Lynn S. AA, Harris Tchrs. Coll., 1948; BS, Washington U., 1950, MS, 1954, EdD, 1962. Instr. Washington U., St. Louis, 1961-62; from asst. to assoc. prof. NYU, NYC, 1964-68; dir. divsn. policy studies Pa. State U., State College, 1968-73, prof. edn. adminstrn., 1974-80; dean Sch. Edn. Eastern Ill. U., 1980-82, asst. to v.p., 1982-83; prof., dir. Ctr. Policy Studies Tex. A&M-Commerce, 1983—91, prof. edn. adminstrn., 1983—98, prof. emeritus, 1998; sr. nat. lectr. Nova S.E. U., Ft. Lauderdale, Fla., 1991-98; prof. edn. adminstrn. U. Tex.-Pan-Am., Edinburg, 1998—2002. Mem. adv. com. Opportunities Acad. Mgmt. Tng., Phila., 1975—90; mem., pres. Pattonville (Mo.) Sch. Bd., 1960—62; adv. bd. Nederland Columbine Clinic, 2001—03. Author seven books, numerous book chpts. in field; contbr. more than 200 articles to profl. jours. Chair Nederland Cmty. Ctr. Bd., 1998-2000; deacon 1st Presbyn. Ch., Commerce, Tex., 1989-91; clerk of session, Nederland Presbyn Ch., 2003-04. Doctoral fellow Washington U., 1960-61; grantee U.S. Office Edn., OEO. Mem. Am. Ednl. Rsch. Assn. (sec. Divsn. A 1970-72, dir. rsch. pre-session 1969, program com. 1970), Nederland C. of C. (bd. dirs. 2005—), Nederland Area Sr. Inc. (pres. bd. dirs. 2006—), Commerce Rotary (dist. 5810, pres. 1991-92, chair internat. svc. 1994-96, Found. award 1994, Paul Harris fellow), Peak-to-Peak Rotary (int. chair 2000—, Dist. 5450 world cmty. svc. and youth exch. com. 1999—, ambassadorial fellow com. 2006—, Rotarian of Yr. 1999-2001), Nederland C. of C. (bd. dirs. 2004—), Phi Delta Kappa (life, pres. Washington U. chpt. 1960, 1st v.p. East Tex. State U. chpt. 1985, sec. 2006, Lafferty Faculty Senate Disting. scholarship award 1996, Lifetime Achievement award 2006). Avocations: appaloosa horses, opera, classical music. Home: PO Box 51 Nederland CO 80466-0051 Personal E-mail: fslutz@msn.com.

LUTZ, RAYMOND PRICE, retired industrial engineer, educator; b. Oak Park, Ill., Feb. 27, 1935; s. Raymond Price and Sibyl Elizabeth (Haralson) Lutz; m. Nancy Marie Cole, Aug. 23, 1958. BSME, U. N.Mex., Albuquerque, 1958, MBA, 1962; PhD, Iowa State U., Ames, 1964. Registered profl. engr., N.Mex., Okla. With Sandia Corp., Albuquerque, summers 1958-63; instr. mech. engring. U. N.Mex., 1958-62; from asst. to assoc. prof. indsl. engring. N.Mex. State U., 1964-68; prof. head indsl. engring. U. Okla., 1968-73; prof., acting dean U. Tex. Sch. Mgmt., Dallas, 1973-76, dean, 1976-78, exec. dean grad. studies and rsch., 1979-92, prof. ops. mgmt., 1992-2001, ret., 2001. Cons. Bell Telephone Labs., Tex. Instruments, Kennecott Corp., Bath Iron Works, Sabre, Inc., City of Dallas, Oklahoma City; cons. US Army, USAF, US Dept. Transp., LA and Seattle public schs.; shipbldg. productivity panel NRC Editor: The Engring. Economist, 1973-77, Indsl. Mgmt., 1983-87. Pres., bd. dirs. United Cerebral Palsy, Dallas, 1978, treas., 1984-88; bd. dirs., treas. Amigos Bibliographic Network, Dallas, 1984-90; chmn., bd. dirs. S.W. Police Inst., Dallas, 1980—; v.p., bd. dirs. Santa Fe Opera, 1988—, Dallas Opera, 1989-2001; pres. bd. Santa Fe Opera Found., 1993-2000, bd. Desert Chorale, treas, 2008—. Fellow AAAS, Am. Inst. Indsl. Engrs. (v.p. industry and mgmt. divsns., trustee, dir. engring. economy divsn., systems engring. group); mem. Am. Soc. Engring. Edn. (chmn. engring. economy divsn., Eugene L. Grant award 1972), INFORMS, Dallas Classic Guitar Soc. (bd. dirs. 1993-96, v.p. 1994-96), Ops. Mgmt. Assn. (bd. dirs. 1994-98), Sigma Xi (bd. dirs. 1990-98,

99—2005, chmn. devel. 1992—, exec. com. 1992-95). Avocations: opera, hiking. Home: 1230 Turquoise Trl Cerrillos NM 87010-9716 Office Phone: 505-471-6709. Personal E-mail: rplutz@q.com.

LUTZ, WILLIAM LAN, lawyer; b. Chgo., May 18, 1944; s. Raymond Price and Sibyl (McCright) L.; m. Jeanne M. McAlister, Dec. 27, 1969; children: William Lan, David Price. BS, U. Tex., 1965, JD, 1969. Bar: Tex. 1969, N.Mex. 1970. Assoc. Martin, Lutz, Cresswell & Hubert and predecessor firms, Las Cruces, N.Mex., 1969-82; former U.S. atty. dist. N.Mex. U.S. Dept. Justice, Albuquerque, 1982-91; ptnr. Martin, Lutz, Roggow, Hosford & Eubanks, P.C., Las Cruces, 1991—. Mem. ABA, N.Mex. Bar Assn. (mem. bd. bar commrs. 1995-97); Aggie Sports Assn. (bd.dirs.) N.Mex. State U., Nat. Assn. Former U.S. Attys. (bd. dirs. 2001-). Methodist. Office: Martin Lutz Roggow Hosford & Eubanks PC 2100 N Main St Ste 2 Las Cruces NM 88001-1183

LUYENDYK, BRUCE PETER, geophysicist, educator, academic administrator; b. Freeport, NY, Feb. 23, 1943; s. Pieter Johannes and Frances Marie (Blakeney) L.; 1 child, Loren Taylor Luyendyk. BS Geophysics, San Diego State Coll., 1965; PhD Marine Geophysics, Scripps Inst. Oceanography, 1969. Geophysicist Arctic Sci. and Tech. Lab. USN Electronics Lab. Ctr., 1965; lectr. San Diego State Coll., 1967-68; postgrad rsch. geologist Scripps Inst. Oceanography, 1969; postdoctoral fellow dept. geology and geophysics Woods Hole Oceanographic Instn., 1969-70, asst. scientist dept. geology and geophysics, 1970-73; asst. prof. U. Calif., Santa Barbara, 1973-75, assoc. prof., 1975-81, prof. dept. geol. scis., 1981—, acting dir. Inst. Crustal Studies, 1987-88, dir. Inst. Crustal Studies, 1988-97, chair dept. geol. scis., 1997—2003, assoc. dean, 2005—. Participant, chief sci. oceanographic cruises, geol. expdns.; coord. bd. So. Calif. Integrated GPS Network, 1997-2000. Editorial bd. Geology, 1975-79, Marine Geophysical Rschs., 1976-92, Jour. Geophysical Rsch., 1982-84, Tectonophysics, 1988-92, Pageoph, 1988-95; contbr. articles to profl. jours., chpts. to books, encys. Co-recipient Newcomb Cleveland prize AAAS, 1980; recipient Antarctic Svc. medal U.S. NSF, Dept. Navy, 1990, Disting. Alumni award San Diego State U., 1983, numerous rsch. grants, 1971—. Fellow Geol. Soc. Am., Am. Geophys. Union. Office: U Calif Santa Barbara Dept Earth Scis Santa Barbara CA 93106

LYDON, DANIEL T., city official; s. James and Joan (O'Brien) L.; m. Pat Lydon, 1966; children: Bridget, Daniel, Kevin, Margaret, Michael. Grad. h.s., Berkeley, Calif.; grad. exec. fire officer program, Nat. Fire Acad., Emmitsburg, Md. Firefighter, lt., capt., battalion chief City of Fremont (Calif.) Fire Dept., fire chief, 1987—. Condr. profl. seminars and courses. With USMC. Office: City Fremont Fire Dept 39100 Liberty St PO Box 5006 Fremont CA 94537-5006

LYMAN, RICHARD WALL, foundation and academic administrator, historian; b. Phila., Oct. 18, 1923; s. Charles M. and Aglae (Wall) Lyman; m. Elizabeth D. Schauffler, Aug. 20, 1947; children: Jennifer P., Holly Lyman Antolini, Christopher M., Timothy R. BA, Swarthmore Coll., 1947, LLD (hon.), 1974; MA, Harvard U., 1948, PhD, 1954, LLD (hon.), 1980, Washington U., St. Louis, 1971, Mills Coll., 1972, Yale U., 1975; LHD (hon.), U. Rochester, 1975, Coll. of Idaho, 1989; DSc (hon.), Worcester Polytech. Inst., 2008. Teaching fellow, tutor, Harvard U., 1949-51; instr. Swarthmore Coll., 1952-53; instr., then asst. prof. Washington U., St. Louis, 1953-58; mem. faculty Stanford U., 1958-80, 88-91, prof. history, 1962-80, 88-91, Sterling prof., 1980-91, Sterling prof. emeritus, 1991—, assoc. dean Sch Humanities and Scis., 1964-66, v.p., provost, 1967-70, pres., 1970-80, pres. emeritus, 1980—, dir. Inst. Internat. Studies, 1988-91; pres. Rockefeller Found., 1980-88. Spl. corr. The Economist, London, 1953-66; bd. dirs. Coun. on Founds., 1982-88, Independent Sector, 1980-88, chair, 1983-86, Nat. Com. on U.S.-China Rels., 1986-92; dir. IBM, 1978-92, Chase Manhattan Corp., 1981-91. Author: The First Labour Government, 1957; editor: (with Lewis W. Spitz) Major Crises in Western Civilization, 1965, (with Virginia A. Hodgkinson) The Future of the Nonprofit Sector, 1989; editorial bd. Jour. Modern History, 1958-61. Mem. Nat. Coun. on Humanities, 1976-82, vice chmn., 1980-82; chmn. Commn. on Humanities, 1978-80; trustee Rockefeller Found., 1976-88, Carnegie Found. Advancement of Tchg., 1976-82, World Affairs Coun. of No. Calif., 1992-98; bd. dirs. Nat. Assn. Ind. Colls. and Univs., 1976-77, Assn. of Governing Bds. of Univs. and Colls., 1994-97, Am. Alliance for Rights and Responsiblities, 1993-2002; chmn. Assn. Am. Univs., 1978-79. With USAAF, 1943-46. Decorated officier Legion of Honor; recipient Clark Kerr award U. Calif., Berkeley, 1981; Fulbright fellow London Sch. Econs., 1951-52, hon. fellow, 1978—; Guggenheim fellow, 1959-60. Fellow Royal Hist. Soc.; mem. Am. Acad. Arts and Scis., Am. Hist. Assn., Council on Fgn. Relations, Am. Philos. Soc., Conf. Brit. Studies, Phi Beta Kappa. Office: Stanford U Sch Edn Stanford CA 94305-3096 Personal E-mail: rwlyman@hotmail.com.

LYNCH, BEVERLY PFEIFER, education and information studies educator; b. Moorhead, Minn. d. Joseph B. and Nellie K. (Bailey) Pfeifer; m. John A. Lynch, Aug. 24, 1968. BS, N.D. State U., 1957, L.H.D. (hon.); MS, U. Ill., 1959; PhD, U. Wis., 1972. Librarian Marquette U., 1959-60, 62-63; exchange librarian Plymouth (Eng.) Pub. Library, 1960-61; asst. head serials div. Yale U. Library, 1963-65, head, 1965-68; vis. lectr. U. Wis., Madison, 1970-71, U. Chgo., 1975; exec. sec. Assn. Coll. and Research Libraries, 1972-76; univ. librarian U. Ill.-Chgo., 1977-89; dean, prof. Grad. Sch. Libr. and Info. Sci. UCLA, 1989-94, prof. Grad. Sch. Edn. and Info. Studies, 1989—, dir. sr. fellows program, 1990—; interim pres. Ctr. for Rsch. Librs., Chgo., 2000-01; founding dir. Calif. Rare Book Sch., 2004—. Sr. fellow, vis. scholar UCLA, 1982. Author: (with Thomas J. Galvin) Priorities for Academic Libraries, 1982, Management Strategies for Libraries, 1985, Academic Library in Transition, 1989, Information Technology and the Remaking of the University Library, 1995. Recipient Cert. of Appreciation, Chinese Am. Librs. Assn., 2001, named Acad. Libr. of Yr., 1982, Disting. Alumnus award Grad. Sch. Libr. Info. Studies, U. Ill. Urbana-Champaign, 1987, one of top sixteen libr. leaders in Am., 1990; fellow Indo-U.S. Subcommn. on Edn. and Culture, 1992-93; vis. scholar U. Nebr., 1981, Disting. Alumnus, U. Wis. Sch. Libr. Info. Studies, 2009. Mem.: ALA (pres. 1985—86, coun. 1998—2004, chair 1999—2000, com. on accreditation 1999—2002, co-chair joint com. ALA, Soc. Am. Archivists and Am. Assn. Museums 2005—07, chair, Internat. Relations Com. 2008—, Joseph W. Lippincott award 2009), Bibliog. Soc. Am., Assn. for Study Higher Edn., Am. Sociol. Assn., Acad. Mgmt., Nat. Info. Stds. Org. (bd. dirs. 1996—2005, vice chair 1999—2001, chair 2001—03), Scottish Libr. Assn. (hon.), Zamorano Club, Book Club Calif., Grolier Club, Caxton Club, Phi Kappa Phi. Office: UCLA Grad Sch Edn Info Mailbox 951520 Los Angeles CA 90095-1520 Office Phone: 310-206-4294. Business E-Mail: bplynch@ucla.edu.

LYNCH, CHARLES ALLEN, investment company executive, director; b. Denver, Sept. 7, 1927; s. Laurence J. and Louanna (Robertson) L.; divorced; children: Charles A., Tara O'Hara, Casey Alexander; m. Justine Bailey, Dec. 27, 1992. BS, Yale U., 1950. With E.I. duPont de Nemours & Co., Inc., Wilmington, Del., 1950—69, dir. mktg., 1965—69; corp. v.p. SCOA Industries, Columbus, Ohio, 1969—72; corp. exec. v.p., also mem. rotating bd. W.R. Grace & Co., NYC, 1972—78; chmn. bd., CEO, Saga Corp., Menlo Park, Calif., 1978—86; chmn., CEO, DHL Airways, Inc., Redwood City, Calif., 1986—88; pres., CEO Levolor Corp., 1988—89, chmn. exec. com. of bd. dirs., 1989—90; chmn. Market Value Ptnrs. Co., Menlo Park, Calif., 1990—95, 1999—. Bd. dirs. Sigaba Corp. Bd. dirs. United Way, 1990-92, past chmn. Bay Area campaign, 1987; vice chmn., dir. Bay Area Coun.; past chmn. Calif. Bus. Roundtable; past chmn. bd. trustees Palo Alto Med. Found. Mem. Yale Club (N.Y.C.), Internat. Lawn Tennis Club, Menlo Country Club (Calif.), Pacific Union Club (San Francisco), Coral Beach and Tennis Club (Bermuda), Vintage Club (Indian Wells, Calif.), Menlo Circus Club. Republican. Home: 96 Ridge View Dr Atherton CA 94027-6464 Office: 333 Ravenswood Ave Ste Ag320 Menlo Park CA 94025-3453 Office Phone: 650-859-5884. Business E-Mail: clynch@mvp-co.com.

LYNCH, DANIEL C., multimedia executive; Degree in Math. and Philosophy, Loyola Marymount U.; M in Math., UCLA. Mgr. computing lab. Artificial Intelligence Ctr., SRI; dir. computing facilities SRI Internat.; dir. info. processing divsn. U. So. Calif., Info. Scis. Inst., Marina del Rey; founder, chmn. bd. dirs. CyberCash, Inc., Reston, Va.; owner Lynch Enterprises, Los Altos Hills, Calif. Founder Interop Co. divsn. Softbank Expos; trustee Santa Fe Inst., Bionomics Inst., CommerceNet; founder, bd. dirs. CyberCash Inc., Reston, Va. Author: Digital Money: The New Era of Internet Commerce. Mem. IEEE. Avocation: vineyards.

LYNCH, JOHN DANIEL, secondary education educator, state legislator; b. Butte, Mont., Sept. 17, 1947; s. Leo and Queenie Veronica Lynch; m. Shannon Christine Crawford, May 7, 1983; children: Kaitlin, Jennifer. BS, West Mont. Coll.; MS, No. Mont. Coll. Tchr. Butte H.S., 1970-78, Butte Vo-Tech, 1978-89, Adult Basic Edn., 1989—. Mem. Mont. State Legis., Helena, 1971-79, state senator, 1982—. Mem. KC. Democrat. Roman Catholic.

LYNCH, KEVIN, computer software company executive, application developer; Studied, Electronic Visualization Lab. Univ. Ill. Software developer FrameTechnology, 1988—92, Gen. Magic, 1992—96; chief software architect, pres. product develop. Macromedia Inc., 1996—2005; sr. v.p., chief software architect platform bus. unit Adobe Systems Inc., San Jose, Calif., 2005—08, chief tech. officer, 2008—. Named one of First Annual Web Innovators, CNET, 1998, Top 25 Innovators, CRN, 2003. Achievements include patents in field. Office: Adobe Systems Inc 345 Park Ave San Jose CA 95110

LYNCH, KEVIN J., publishing executive, media planner; BA in English and Comm., Kean U., 1978. Sales rep. McCall, 1981-83, So. Living, 1983-86, ea. regional mgr., 1986, nat. sales mgr., 1992, nat. advt. dir., 1994-95, v.p., pub., 1995—2000; sr. v.p. Sunset Pub. Corp., Menlo Pk., Calif., 2000—. Office: Sunset Publishing Corp 80 Willow Rd Menlo Park CA 94025-3691 E-mail: lynchk@sunset.com.

LYNCH, MARTIN ANDREW, retail company executive; b. Chgo., Oct. 5, 1937; s. George Irwin and Cecilia Veronica (Corley) L.; children: Kathleen Marie, Kevin Michael, Karen Ann, Daniel Patrick, Michelle Eileen. BSc, DePaul U., 1962. CPA, Ill., Calif. Audit mgr. Price Waterhouse & Co., Chgo., 1962-69; asst. to pres. Scot Lad Foods, Chgo., 1969-70; v.p. fin. N.Am. Car Corp., Chgo., 1970-76; sr. v.p. fin. Tiger Internat. Inc., LA, 1976-83; exec. v.p., chief fin. officer Duty Free Shoppers Group Ltd., San Francisco, 1983-89, Casino USA Inc., Santa Barbara, Calif., 1989—, Smart & Final Inc., Santa Barbara, 1989—. Mem. AICPA, Calif. CPA Soc., Fin. Execs. Inst., Nat. Assn. Whole Grogery, Inst. Food Distbn. Assn., Bel Air Country Club (L.A.). Roman Catholic. Avocations: jogging, swimming, skiing, golf. Office: Smart & Final Inc 600 Citadel Dr City Of Commerce CA 90040

LYNCH, PETER JOHN, retired dermatologist; b. Mpls., Oct. 22, 1936; s. Francis Watson and Viola Adeline (White) L.; m. Barbara Ann Lanzi, Jan. 18, 1964; children: Deborah, Timothy. Student, St. Thomas Coll., 1954-57; BS, U. Minn., 1958, MD, 1961. Intern U. Mich. Med. Ctr., 1961-62, resident in dermatology, 1962-65, asst. prof., then assoc. prof. dermatology, 1968-73; clin. instr. U. Minn., 1965; chief dermatology and venereal disease Martin Army Hosp., Columbus, Ga., 1966-68; asso. prof. to prof. dermatology U. Ariz., Tucson, 1973-86, chief sect. dermatology, 1973-86, asso. head dept. internal medicine, 1977-86; prof., head dermatology U. Minn. Med. Sch., Mpls., 1986-95; med. dir. ambulatory care U. Minn. Health Sys., 1993-95; prof., chmn. dept. dermatology U. Calif., Davis, 1995-2000, prof. emeritus, 2000—, tng. program dir., 2001—08, Frederick G. Novy, Jr. prof., 2005—. Co-author: (with S. Epstein) Burckhardt's Atlas and Manual of Dermatology and Venereology, 1977, Dermatology for the House Officer, 1982, 3rd edit., 1994, (with W.M. Sams) Principles and Practice of Dermatology, 1992, 2nd edit., 1996, (with I.E. Edwards) Genital Dermatology, 1994, (with M. Black, C. Rud & L. Edwards) Obstetric and Gynecologic Dermatology, 2008. With AUS, 1966-68. Decorated Army Commendation Medal; recipient Disting. Service award for faculty U. Mich., 1970, Disting. Faculty award U. Ariz., 1981 Mem.: Am. Acad. Dermatology (hon., bd. dirs. 1974-78, v.p. 1991-92, Pearson award, 2009), Assn. Profs. Dermatology (bd. dirs. 1976-80, pres. 1994-96), Internat. Soc. Study of Vulvar Disease (bd. dirs. 1976-79, pres. 1983), Soc. Investigative Dermatology, Am. Bd. Dermatology (bd. dirs. 1984-89), Gougerot Soc. (Bronze medal award), Alpha Omega Alpha. Democrat. Roman Catholic. Home: 425 Hartnell Pl Sacramento CA 95825-6615 Office: U Calif 3301 C St #1400 Sacramento CA 95816

LYNN, BOB, state legislator; b. LA, Calif., Feb. 23, 1933; m to Marlene Wagner Lynn; children: Debra, Bob, Jr, Robyn, Mary, Marla & John. BA, U. Ariz.; MA, Calif. State U., Long Beach. Inspector gen., contracts and procurement, USAF; Alaska State Representative, District 31, 2003-. Assoc-broker, realtor; Public sch tchr, ret. Mem. Alaska Outdoor Coun., MADD, Nat. Breast Cancer Coalition. Fighter pilot USAF, bandsman USAF, served in Air Def. Ops. USAF, radar site comdr. USAF, Vietnam, maj. ret. USAF. Decorated Bronze Star, Vietnamese Cross of Gallantry, others. NRA, VFW, Vietnam Veterans America, Am. Legion, AMVET, Air Force Assn. Republican. Mailing: State Capitol Rm 104 Juneau AK 99801-1182 Office: Dist 31 716 W 4th Ave Ste 650 Juneau AK 99801 Office Phone: 907-465-4931, 907-465-4931. Office Fax: 907-465-4316, 907-465-4316. Business E-Mail: representative_bob_lynn@legis.state.ak.us.*

LYNN, EVADNA SAYWELL, investment analyst; b. Oakland, Calif., June 16, 1935; d. Lawrence G. Saywell; m. Richard Keppie Lynn, Dec. 28, 1962; children: Douglas, Melisa. BA, U. Calif., Berkeley, MA in Econs. CFA. With Dean Witter, San Francisco, 1958-61, 70-71, Dodge & Cox, San Francisco, 1961-69; fin. analyst, v.p. Clark, Dodge & Co., San Francisco, 1971-73, Wainwright Securities, NYC, 1977-78; 1st v.p. Merrill Lynch Capital markets, NYC, 1978-90; sr. v.p. Dean Witter Reynolds, NYC, 1990-97; forest products cons., San Francisco, 1997—. Mem. Assn. for Investment Mgmt. and Rsch., San Francisco Security Analysts (treas. 1973-74), Fin. Women's Club San Francisco (pres. 1967). Office: Apt F 1824 Jackson St San Francisco CA 94109-2873

LYNNE, SHELBY (SHELBY LYNN MOORER), country singer; b. Quantico, Va., Oct. 22, 1968; Singer: (albums) Sunrise, 1989, Tough All Over, 1990, Soft Talk, 1991, Temptation, 1993, Restless, 1995, I Am Shelby Lynne, 2000, Love, Shelby, 2001, Identity Crisis, 2003, Suit Yourself, 2005, Just a Little Lovin', 2008, (singles) I'll Lie Myself to Sleep, 1990, Things Are Tough All Over, 1990, Feelin Kind of Lonely Tonight, 1993, (duet with George Jones) If I Could Bottle This Up, 1988; actor: (films) Walk the Line, 2005; (TV films) Another Pair of Aces: Three of a Kind, 1991; appearances (TV special) Willie Nelson and Friends, Outlaws and Angles, (TV series) Nashville Now. Recipient Horizon award, CMA, 1991, Grammy award for Best New Artist, 2001; named best new female artist, ACM, 1991. Office: Capital Records 1750 N Vine St Hollywood CA 90028

LYNTON, MICHAEL, film company executive; b. London, Jan. 1, 1960; s. Mark and Marion Lynton; m. Jamie Alter, 1993. AB in History and Lit., Harvard Coll., 1982; MBA, Harvard Bus. Sch., 1987. Assoc. mergers and acquisitions The First Boston Corp./Credit Suisse First Boston, 1982-85; pres. Disney Pub. The Walt Disney Co., 1987—92, pres. Hollywood Pictures, 1992—96; chmn., CEO, penguin group Pearson plc, NYC, 1996—2000; pres. AOL Internat., NYC, 2000—03; CEO AOL Europe, 2000—03; pres. Time Warner Internat. (formerly AOL Time Warner Internat.), NYC, 2002—03; chmn., CEO Sony Pictures Entertainment, Culver City, Calif., 2004—. Bd. dirs. JAMDAT, 2005—. Named one of 50 Most Powerful People in Hollywood, Premiere mag., 2004—06. Office: Sony Pictures Entertainment 10202 W Washington Blvd Culver City CA 90232

LYON, BRUCE ARNOLD, lawyer, educator; b. Sacramento, Sept. 24, 1951; s. Arnold E. and Arlene R. (Cox) L.; m. Patricia J. Gibson, Dec. 14, 1974; children: Barrett, Andrew. AB with honors, U. Pacific, 1974; JD, U. Calif.-Hastings Coll. Law, 1977; MTS, Harvard U., 2008. Bar: Calif. 1977, US Dist. Ct. (ea. and no. dists.) Calif. 1977; cert. in religion and conflict transformation Boston Theol. Inst., 2008. Ptnr. Ingoglia, Marskey, Kearney & Lyon, Sacramento, 1977-84; sole practice Auburn, Calif., 1984-91; ptnr. Robinson, Robinson & Lyon, Auburn, 1991-98, Robinson, Lyon & Springford LLP, Auburn, 1999—2004, Robinson & Lyon, Auburn, 2005—. Instr. in law Sierra Coll., Rocklin, Calif., 1983-98; mem. adminstrv. bd. Harvard Div. Sch., Cambridge, 2006-07. Mng. editor Comment, A Jour. of Comm. and Entertainment Law, 1974; contbr. articles to trade publs. Bd. dirs. emeritus Auburn Cmty. Found., Harvard Mediation Program; pres. Calif. Tule Elk Found. Mem.: Thurston Soc., Placer County Bar Assn., State Bar Calif., Native Sons of the Golden West, Mensa, Harvard Law Sch. Program for Negotiation, Harvard Alumni San Francisco, Harvard Faculty Club, Order of Coif. Office Phone: 916-835-8900. Personal E-mail: blyon2@mac.com. Business E-Mail: brucelyon@post.harvard.edu.

LYON, DAVID WILLIAM, research executive; b. Lansing, Mich., Mar. 26, 1941; s. Herbert Reid and Mary Kathleen (Slack) L.; m. Catherine McHugh Dillon, July 8, 1967. BS, Mich. State U., 1963; M in City and Regional Planning, U. Calif., Berkeley, 1966, PhD, 1972. Regional economist Fed. Res. Bank Phila., 1969-71; rsch. dir. human and econ. resources The NYC-Rand Inst., 1972-75, v.p., 1975; sr. economist The Rand Corp., Santa Monica, Calif., 1975-77, dep. v.p., 1977-79, v.p. domestic rsch. divsn., 1979-93, v.p. external affairs, 1993-94; pres., CEO Pub. Policy Inst. Calif., 1994—2007, founding pres. emeritus, 2007. Adj. prof. U. Pa., 1975; mem. adv. bd. Inst. for Civil Justice, 1987-93, Rand-Urban Inst. Program for Rsch. on Immigration Policy, 1988-91, Drug Policy Rsch. Ctr., 1989-93, So. Calif. Health Policy Rsch. Consortium, 1989-94, Rand Ctr. for U.S.-Japan Rels., 1989-93, Rand Ctr. for Asia-Pacific Policy, 1993-95; dir. Coll. Environ. Design Coun., U. Calif., Berkeley, 1979-90; Walker-Ames lectr., U. Wash. Mem. publs. com. Rand Jour. Econs., 1984-94; contbr. articles to profl. jours. Bd. dirs. Ctr. for Healthy Aging, Santa Monica, 1985-94, pres., 1989-91; mem. com. fgn. rels. San Francisco, Calif., 1996—, adv. coun. Coll. Environ. Design, U. Calif., Berkeley, 2000-05. Mellon fellow in city planning, 1966-68; Econ. Devel. Adminstrn. grad. fellow, 1966. Mem. Coun. on Fgn. Rels., San Francisco Com. on Fgn. Rels., World Affairs Coun. No. Calif. (trustee 1999—), Japan Am. Soc. So. Calif. (bd. dirs. 1990-94), Japan Soc. No. Calif. (bd. dirs. 2000-), Asia Soc. (So. Calif. Ctr. adv. coun. 1988-2002, No. Calif. adv. bd. 2002—), Calif. Connected (cir. of advisors 2002-05), Pacific Coun. on Internat. Policy, Delta Phi Epsilon, Lambda Alpha Internat. Office: Public Policy Institute Of Ca 500 Washington St Ste 600 San Francisco CA 94111-2932 Business E-Mail: lyon@ppic.org.

LYON, JAMES KARL, German language educator; b. Rotterdam, Holland, Feb. 17, 1934; came to U.S., 1937; s. T. Edgar and Hermana (Forsberg) L.; m. Dorothy Ann Burton, Dec. 22, 1959; children: James, John, Elizabeth, Sarah, Christina, Rebecca, Matthew, Melissa. BA, U. Utah, 1958, MA, 1959; PhD, Harvard U., 1963. Instr. German Harvard U., Cambridge, Mass., 1962-63, asst. prof., 1966-71; assoc. prof. U. Fla., Gainesville, 1971-74; prof. U. Calif. San Diego, La Jolla, 1974-94, provost Eleanor Roosevelt Coll., 1987-94; prof. dept. Germanic and Slavic langs. Brigham Young U., Provo, Utah, 1994—. Vis. prof. U. Augsburg, Germany, 1993, 2005. Author: Konkordanz zur Lyrik Gottfried Benns, 1971, Bertolt Brecht and Rudyard Kipling, 1975, Brecht's American Cicerone, 1978, Bertolt Brecht in America, 1980, Brecht in den USA, 1994, Paul Celan and Martin Heidegger: An Unresolved Conversation 1951-1970, 2006. Capt. M.I., U.S. Army, 1963-66. NEH fellow, 1970, Guggenheim Found. fellow, 1974; Ford Found. grantee, 1988, 91. Mem. MLA, Am. Assn. Tchrs. German, Internat. Brecht. Soc., Phi Beta Kappa. Democrat. Mem. Lds Ch. Avocations: backpacking, fishing. Office: Brigham Young U Dept Germanic & Slavic Lang 3106 JFSB Provo UT 84602-6120 Business E-Mail: james_lyon@byu.edu.

LYON, JOSEPH LYNN, physician, medical educator; b. Salt Lake City, May 13, 1939; s. Thomas Edgar and Hermana (Forsberg) L.; m. June Fetzer, July 3, 1964; children: Natalee, Joseph, Stephen, Maryanne, Rachael, Janet. BS, U. Utah, 1964, MD, 1967; MPH, Harvard

U., 1969. Diplomate Am. Bd. Preventive Medicine. Intern U. Calif., San Diego, 1967-68; resident Harvard U., 1968-70, Utah State Health Dept., 1971-72; asst. prof. U. Utah, Salt Lake City, 1974-80, assoc. prof., 1980-90, prof., 1990—. Contbr. articles to profl. jours. Mem.: Soc. for Epidemiologic Rsch. (sec.-treas. 1993). Mem. Lds Ch. Office: U Utah Dept Medicine Salt Lake City UT 84132-0001

LYON, RICHARD, retired mayor, military officer; b. Pasadena, Calif., July 14, 1923; s. Norman Morais and Ruth (Hollis) L.; m. Cynthia Gisslin, Aug. 8, 1975; children: Patricia, Michael, Sean; children by previous marriage: Mary, Edward, Sally, Kathryn, Patrick (dec.), Susan. B.E., Yale U., 1944; MBA, Stanford U., 1953. Commd. ensign USN, 1944; advanced through grades to Rear Adm. SEAL, 1974; served with Scout and Raider in Pacific and China, World War II; Underwater Demolition Team 5 in Korea; recalled to active duty as dep. chief Naval Res. New Orleans, 1978-81. Mem. Chief Naval Ops. Res. Affairs Adv. Bd., 1978-81; exec. v.p. Nat. Assn. Employee Benefits, Newport Beach, Calif., 1981-90; mem. Bd. Control, U.S. Naval Inst., 1978-81; pres. Civil Svc. Commn., San Diego County, 1990, Oceanside Unified Sch. Bd., 1991; mayor City of Oceanside, 1992-2000. Pres. bd. trustees Children's Hosp. Orange County, 1965, 72. Decorated Legion of Merit. Mem. Nat. Assn. Securities Dealers (registered prin.), Newport Harbor Yacht Club, Oceanside Yacht Club, Rotary (Anaheim, Calif. pres. 1966). Republican. Anglican. Home: 600 S The Strand Oceanside CA 92054-3902 Personal E-mail: lyonclan@cox.net.

LYON, WILLIAM, SR., construction executive; b. 1923; Student, U. So. Calif. With Lyon & Son, Phoenix, 1945-50, William Lyon Devel. Co., Newport Beach, Calif., 1954-72, pres.; with William Lyon Co., Newport Beach, 1972—, now chmn. bd., CEO; and owner Martin Aviation, Orange County, Calif. Served to maj. gen. USAF, Pacific, European, Middle East theaters. WWII, pilot, 75 combat missions, Korean War. Decorated DSM, DFC, Air Medal, Presdl. Unit Citation, others. Office: William Lyon Co 4490 Von Karman Ave Newport Beach CA 92660-2000

LYONS, CATHY, computer company executive; BS in Bus. Adminstrn. and Mktg., U. Colo. Gen. mgr. LaserJet Solutions Grp. European Operation Hewlett-Packard Co., Bergamo, Italy, v.p., gen. mgr. Supplies Bus. Palo Alto, Calif., 1999—2001, v.p., gen. mgr. Inkjet Supplies Divsn., 2001—03, sr. v.p. bus. and imaging printing Imaging and Personal Systems Grp., 2003—05, exec. v.p., chief mktg. officer, 2005—07, exec. v.p. imaging & printing group strategic change mgmt., 2007—. Office: Hewlett Packard Co 3000 Hanover St Palo Alto CA 94304-1185 also: Hewlett Packard Co 11311 Chinden Blvd Boise ID 83714-1021

LYONS, JAMES ELLIOTT, lawyer; b. Lexington, Mo., Mar. 10, 1951; s. james Elliott and Elouise L.; m. Mary Jane McCarthy, June 30, 1979; children: Sean Austin, Caitlan Maureen. BA with honors, U. Mo., 1973; JD, NYU, 1976. Bar: Mo. 1976, N.Y. 1977, Calif. 1984. Assoc. Stinson Mag Thompson McEvers & Fizzell, Kansas City, Mo., 1976-77; assoc. Skadden, Arps, Slate et al., NYC, L.A., 1977-84; law clk. to Hon. Robert W. Sweet U.S. Dist. Ct. (so. dist.) N.Y., 1978; ptnr. Skadden, Arps, Slate et al., L.A. and San Francisco, 1984—. Mem. ABA, Los Angeles County Bar Assn., Bar Assn. San Francisco, Mo. Bar Assn., Phi Beta Kappa Democrat. Office: Skadden Arps Slate et al 4 Embarcadero Ctr Ste 3800 San Francisco CA 94111-5974

LYONS, JAMES M., lawyer; b. Joliet, Ill., Jan. 6, 1947; AB, Coll. Holy Cross, 1968; JD, DePaul U., 1971; LLD (hon.), U. Ulster, Belfast, Ireland, 2002. Bar: Colo. 1971, Ill. 1971, U.S. Dist. Ct. Colo. 1971, U.S. Dist. Ct. (no. dist.) Ill. 1971, U.S. Ct. Appeals (7th, 10th and federal cirs.), U.S. Supreme Ct. 1971. Sr. trial ptnr., litigation & arbitration Rothgerber Johnson & Lyons LLP, Denver, 1971—. Mem. Colo. Supreme Ct. bd. law examiners, 1982-88; instr. Univ. Denver, Univ. Colo., Nat. Inst. Trial Advocacy; gen. counsel Clinton for Pres. Com., 1991-92, Office of Pres.-Elect, 1992-93; U.S. observer, Internat. Fund for Ireland, 1993-2001; spl. adv. to U.S. Pres. & Sec. State for econ. initiatives in Ireland & No. Ireland, 1997-2001; pres. Faculty of Fed. Advocates, US Dist. Ct. Colo. dist., 2003; vis. lectr. Univ. Ulster, No. Ireland, 2004; adj. prof. Univ. Denver, 2004. Assoc. editor DePaul Law Rev., 1970-71. Recipient St. Thomas More award, Catholic Lawyers Guild Colo., Learned Hand Nat. award, Am. Jewish Com., 1998. Fellow Am. Coll. Trial Lawyers, Internat. Acad. Trial Lawyers; mem. ABOTA, Ill. State Bar Assn., Colo. Bar Assn., Denver Bar Assn., Am. Bd. Trial Advocates. Office: Rothgerber Johnson & Lyons LLP Ste 3000 1 Tabor Ctr 1200 17th St Denver CO 80202 Office Phone: 303-623-9000. Office Fax: 303-623-9222. Business E-Mail: jlyons@rothgerber.com.

LYONS, LIONEL DALE, city official; b. NC; BA in Polit. Sci., N.C. Agrl. & Tech. State U.; MPA, Ohio State U. Adminstrv. intern City of Columbus (Ohio) Water Dept.; mgmt. intern City of Phoenix, 1986-87; mgmt. asst. City of Phoenix Mgr.'s Office, 1987-90; asst. to mayor City of Phoenix, 1991-94, dir. equal opportunity dept., 1995—. Bd. dirs. Valley Leadership; past mem. capital devel. program com., South Mountain YMCA; bd. dirs. Phoenix Met. YMCA, urban svcs. br. Mem. NAACP (life), Internat. City Mgmt. Assn., Nat. Forum for Black Pub. Adminstrs., Nat. Spkrs. Assn. (cert. Toastmaster 1987—), Greater Phoenix Urban League, Omega Psi Phi (pres. Phoenix chpt. 1993-95). Office: City Phoenix Equal Opportunity Dept Calvin C Goode Bldg 251 W Washington St Phoenix AZ 85003-2245

LYONS, MARY E., academic administrator; b. Calif. BA, Sonoma St. Univ., 1971; MA, San Diego St. Univ., 1976; PhD, Sonoma St. Univ., 1983. Prof. Franciscan School of Theology, Berkeley, Calif., 1984—90; pres. Calif. Maritime Acad., Vallejo, 1990-96, Coll. of St. Benedict, St. Joseph, Minn., 1996—2003, U. San Diego, 2003—. Office: Office of Pres U San Diego 5998 Alcala Pk San Diego CA 92110-2492 Office Phone: 619-260-4520. Office Fax: 619-260-6833. E-mail: president@sandiego.edu.

LYONS, PATRICK HILLER, state legislator; b. Clovis, N.Mex., Nov. 7, 1953; BS, N.Mex. State U., 1976; M in Agr., Colo. State U., 1977. Rancher, farmer, N.Mex.; mem. N. Mex. Senate, Dist. 7, Santa Fe, 1993—, mem. conservation com., mem. fin. com., mem. water and natural resource com. Mem. N.Mex. Farm and Livestock Bd. Republican. Home: Ima Rt Box 26 Cuervo NM 88417

LYONS, RICHARD KENT, dean, finance educator; b. Palo Alto, Calif., Feb. 10, 1961; s. J. Richard and Ida (Primavera) L. BS in Bus. with highest honors, U. Calif., Berkeley, 1982; PhD in Econs., MIT, 1987. Rsch. analyst SRI Internat., Menlo Park, Calif., 1983-84; summer intern Orgn. for Econ. Cooperation & Devel., Paris, 1985, Bd. Govs., Fed. Res. System, Washington, 1986; asst. prof. Columbia U., NYC, 1987-91, assoc. prof., 1991-93; asst. prof. Haas Sch. Bus., U. Calif., Berkeley, 1993-96, assoc. prof., 1996—2000, prof., 2000—04, Sylvan Coleman Chair fin., 2004—, assoc. dean for academic affairs, 2004, acting dean, 2004—05, exec. assoc. dean, 2005—06, dean; chief learning officer Goldman Sachs, NYC, 2006—08. Vis. prof. U. Toulouse, France, Stockholm U., Sweden, London Sch. Econs., Found. for Advanced Info. and Rsch., Japan, U. Aix-Marseille, France; rsch. assoc. Nat. Bur. Econ. Rsch., Cambridge, Mass., 1989—; former chmn., dir. Matthews Asian Funds; former trustee iShares; cons. IMF, World Bank, Fed. Res. Bank, European Commn.; adv. bd. Econ. Policy Review, NYC. Assoc. editor Calif. Mgmt. Rev., Jour. Fin. Markets; contbr. articles to profl. jours. NSF grad. fellow, 1984. Mem. Am. Econ. Assn., Coun. on Fgn. Rels., Phi Beta Kappa, Beta Gamma Sigma, Sigma Alpha Epsilon. Democrat. Avocations: squash, guitar, French.

LYONS, SUSANNE D., information technology executive; BA, Vassar Coll., 1979; MBA, Boston U., 1982. Mgmt. positions through sr. v.p. brokerage mktg. Fidelity Investments, 1982—92; mgmt. positions through enterprise pres. retail services Charles Schwab & Co., 1992—2001; mng. dir. Russell Reynolds Associates, San Francisco, 2003—04; exec. v.p., chief mktg. officer Visa USA, San Francisco, 2004—07; ind. cons. Hillside Home, 2007—. Bd. dirs. CNET Networks, Inc., 2007—08, GAIN Capital Holdings Inc., 2008—, WildCare, 2008—; mem. advisory bd. EPOCH, 2008—, Marketo, 2008—. Recipient Woman of the Year, American Diabetes Assn., 2005; named Woman of the Yr., San Francisco Financial Woman's Assn., 1999; named one of The 75 Most Influential Bay Area Bus. Women, San Francisco Bus. Times, 1999.*

M., K. B. See MAHDAVI, KAMAL

MA, CHUNG-PEI MICHELLE, astronomer, educator; BS, PhD, MIT, 1993. From asst. prof. to assoc. prof. physics and astronomy U. Pa., Phila., 1996—2001; assoc. prof. astronomy U. Calif., Berkeley, 2001—. Contbr. articles to profl. jours. Recipient Annie J. Cannon award, 1997, 1st prize Taiwan Nat. Violin Competition, 1983, Cottrell Scholars award Rsch. Corp., 1999, Lindback award for Disting. Tchg., U. Pa., 1999; Alfred P. Sloan fellow, 1999; Sherman Fairchild fellow, 1993. Mem. Phi Beta Kappa. Achievements include research in the formation and evolution of galaxies and large scale structure in the Universe; performed numerical simulations of the clustering of dark matter in various cosmological models of structure formation from the Early Universe until the present day; computation of the temperature variations imprinted on the cosmic microwave background radiation which provides a snapshot of the infant Universe. Office: U Calif Berkeley Dept Astronomy 601 Campbell Hall Berkeley CA 94720

MA, FAI, mechanical engineering educator; b. Canton, People's Republic of China, Aug. 6, 1954; came to U.S., 1977, naturalized, 1988; s. Rui-Qi and Shao-Fen (Luo) M. BS, U. Hong Kong, 1977; MS, PhD, Calif. Inst. Tech., 1981. Sr. rsch. engr. Weidlinger Assocs., Menlo Park, Calif., 1981-82; rsch. fellow IBM, Yorktown Heights, N.Y., 1982-83; sr. engr. Standard Oil Co., Cleve., 1983-86; prof. mech. engring. U. Calif., Berkeley, 1986—. Vis. scholar Oxford U., Eng., 1992, U. Stuttgart, Germany, 1993. Co-author: Probabilistic Analysis, 1983, Computational Mechanics, 1989; co-editor Advances in Engring., 1995--; contbr. articles to profl. jours. Young Investigator award NSF, 1987; Humboldt fellow, 1992; Fulbright awardee, 2002. Fellow: ASME. Office: U Calif Dept Mech Enging Berkeley CA 94720-1740 Business E-Mail: fma@me.berkeley.edu.

MA, FIONA, state legislator; m to Philippe Ma. BS, Rochester Inst. Tech., NY; MS in Taxation, Golden Gate U., San Francisco; MBA, Pepperdine U. CPA LA. Member, Bd Suprs, District 4, San Francisco, 2002-2006; District rep to California State Senator; member, Transportation Authority; California State Assemblywoman, District 12, 2006-, California State Assembly, majority whip, currently. Member awards comt, United States Small Bus Admin, 96; member, San Francisco Assessment Appeals Bd, California, formerly; Delegate, California State Democratic Party, formerly; co-chair, Courage & Justice Project Oversite Panel; member advisor panel, California Earthquake Authority. Bd member Democratic Women's Forum; board member San Francisco Women's Polit Commerce; founder, Westside Chinese Democratic Club; member, Sunset Neighborhood Beacon Center Community Council. Democrat. Mailing: San Francisco State Bldg Civic Ctr Complex 455 Golden Gate Ave Ste 14600 San Francisco CA 94102 Office: State Capitol PO Box 942849 Suite 2176 Sacramento CA 94249-0012 Office Phone: 415-554-2312, 916-319-2012. Office Fax: 415-554-1178, 916-319-2112. Business E-Mail: Assemblymember.Ma@assembly.ca.gov.

MABEY, RALPH R., lawyer; b. Salt Lake City, May 20, 1944; s. Rendell Noel and Rachel (Wilson) M.; m. Sylvia States, June 5, 1968; children: Kathryn, Rachel, Elizabeth, Emily, Sara. BA, U. Utah, 1968; JD, Columbia U., 1972. Bar: Utah 1972, U.S. Dist. Ct. Utah 1972, U.S. Ct. Appeals (10th cir.) 1976, N.Y. 1985, U.S. Supreme Ct. 1988, U.S. Ct. Appeals (4th cir.) 1988, U.S. Ct. Appeals (3d cir.) 1993. Law clk. Atty. Gen., Salt Lake City, 1970, US Dist. Ct., Salt Lake City, 1972-73; ptnr. Irvine, Smith & Mabey, Salt Lake City, 1973-79; US bankruptcy judge US Ct., Salt Lake City, 1979-83; ptnr. LeBoeuf, Lamb, Greene & MacRae LLP, Salt Lake City and NYC, 1983—2005, Mabey & Murray LC, Salt Lake City, 2005—06; sr. of counsel Stutman Treister & Glatt, LA, 2006—. Sr. lectr. Brigham Young U. Sch. Law, Provo, Utah, 1983—2005; prof. law U. Utah Coll. Law, Salt Lake City, 2007—. Mng. editor Norton Bankruptcy Law Adviser, 1983-85. With USAR, 1968-74. Mem. ABA (bus. bankruptcy com.), Nat. Bankruptcy Conf., Am. Law Inst., Am. Bankruptcy Inst., Am. Coll. Bankruptcy, Internat. Insolvency Inst. Republican. Mem. Lds Ch. Avocations: running, fly fishing. Home Phone: 801-295-0677. Business E-Mail: rmabey@stutman.com.

MACARTHUR, CAROL JEANNE, pediatric otolaryngology educator; b. Glendale, Calif., Aug. 23, 1957; d. Seth Gerald and Barbara Jeanne (Shaw) MacA.; m. Geoffery Buncke, Dec. 14, 1990; children: Keith Davis, Michelle Jeanne. BS, Occidental Coll., 1979; MD, UCLA, 1984. Diplomate Am. Bd. Otolaryngology. Intern U. Calif., Davis, 1984-85, resident in otolaryngology, 1985-90; fellow in pediatric otolaryngology Boston Children's Hosp., 1990-91; instr. dept. otolaryngology U. Calif.-Davis, Sacramemto, 1989-90; clin. fellow in otology and laryngology Harvard U. Med. Sch., Boston, 1990-91; asst. prof. U. Calif., Irvine, 1991—2002, asst. prof. dept. pediatrics, 1993-98, program dir. dept. otolaryngology-head and neck surgery, 1992-95; staff dept. otolaryngology Oreg. Health Scis. U., Portland, 2002—. Recipient investigator devel. award Am. Acad. Facial Plastic and Reconstructive Surgery, 1993. Fellow ACS, Am. Acad. Pediatrics; mem. Am. Soc. Pediat. Otolaryngology, Soc. for Ear, Nose and Throat Advances in Children, Am. Acad. Otorhinolaryngology-Head and Neck Surgery, Alpha Omega Alpha. Home: 4018 Canal Woods Ct Lake Oswego OR 97034 Office: Oreg Health Scis U Dept Otolaryngology 3131 SW Sam Jackson Park Rd Portland OR 97201-3011

MACAULAY, RONALD KERR STEVEN, linguistics educator, retired dean; b. West Kilbride, Ayrshire, Scotland, Nov. 3, 1927; came to U.S., 1965; s. Robert Wilson and Mary Robb (McDermid) M.; m. Janet Grey, July 25, 1956; children: Harvey, Anna. MA, U. St. Andrews, 1955; PhD, UCLA, 1971. Lectr. Brit. Inst., Lisbon, Portugal, 1955-60, Brit Council, Buenos Aires, Argentina, 1960-64; asst. prof. linguistics Pitzer Coll., Claremont, Calif., 1965-67, assoc. prof., 1967-73, prof., 1973-99, dean faculty, 1980-86, prof. emeritus, 2000—. Author: Language, Social Class and Education, 1977, Generally Speaking: How Children Learn Language, 1980, Locating Dialect in Disourse: The Language of Honest Men and Bonnie Lasses in Ayr, 1991, The Social Art: Language and Its Uses, 1994, Standards and Variation in Urban Speech: Some Examples From Lowland Scots, 1997, Talk That Counts: Age, Gender and Social Class Differences in Discourse, 2005, Extremely Common Eloquence: Constructing Scottish Identity Through Narrative, 2005; editor: (with R.P. Stockwell) Linguistic Change and Generative Theory, 1972, (with D. Brenneis) The Matrix of Language: Contemporary Linguistic Anthropology, 1996 Home: 317 W 7th St Claremont CA 91711-4312 Office: Pitzer Coll 1050 N Mills Ave Claremont CA 91711-6901

MACCOBY, ELEANOR EMMONS, psychology professor; b. Tacoma, May 15, 1917; d. Harry Eugene and Viva May (Johnson) Emmons; m. Nathan Maccoby, Sept. 16, 1938 (dec. Apr. 1992); children: Janice Carmichael, Sarah Maccoby Blunt, Mark. BS, U. Wash., 1939; MA, U. Mich., 1949, PhD, 1950. Study dir. div. program surveys USDA, Washington, 1942-46; study dir. Survey Rsch. Ctr. U. Mich., Ann Arbor, 1946-48; lectr., rsch. assoc. dept. social rels. Harvard U., Cambridge, Mass., 1950-58; from assoc. to full prof. Stanford (Calif.) U., 1958-87, Barbara Kimball Browning prof., 1979, chmn. dept. psychology, 1973-76, prof. emeritus, 1987—. Author: (with R. Sears and H. Levin) Patterns of Child-Rearing, 1957, (with Carol Jacklin) Psychology of Sex Differences, 1974, Social Development, 1980, (with R.H. Mnookin) Dividing the Child: Social and Legal Dilemmas of Custody, 1992, (with Buchanan and Dornbusch) Adolescents after Divorce, 1996, The Two Sexes: Growing Up Apart, Coming Together, 1998; editor: (with Newcomb and Hartley) Readings in Social Psychology, 1957, The Development of Sex Differences, 1966. Recipient Gores award for Excellence in Tchg., Stanford U., 1981, Disting. Contbn. to Ednl. Research award Am. Ednl. Rsch. Assn., 1984, Lectureship award Soc. for Devel. and Behavioral Pediats., 2002. Fellow APA (pres. Divsn. 7, 1971-72, G. Stanley Hall award 1982), Soc. for Rsch. in Child Devel. (pres. 1981-83, mem. governing coun. 1963-66, Disting. Sci. Contbn. award 1987), Assn. Psychol. Ssci. (Disting. Sci. Contbns. award 1988); mem. NAS, Am. Acad. Arts and Scis., Inst. Medicine, Western Psychol. Assn. (pres. 1974-75, Lifetime Achievement award 2004), Inst. for Rsch. on Women and Gender, Social Sci. Rsch. Coun. (chmn. 1984-85), Consortium of Social Sci. Assns. (pres. 1997-98), Am. Psychol. Found. (Life Achievement award 1996). Democrat. Office: Stanford U Dept Psychology Stanford CA 94305-2130 Personal E-mail: maccoby@stanford.edu.

MACCRACKEN, MICHAEL CALVIN, atmospheric scientist; b. Schenectady, May 20, 1942; s. Calvin Dodd MacCracken and Martha (McCracken) MacCracken Howard; m. Sandra Ann Svets, Mar. 12, 1967; children— Christopher, Ronald. B.S. in Engring., Princeton U., 1964; M.S. in Applied Sci., U. Calif.-Davis/Livermore, 1966, Ph.D. in Applied Sci., 1968. Atmospheric scientist Lawrence Livermore Nat. Lab., 1968—2002, prin. investigator Bay Area air quality modeling study, 1973-76, dep. div. leader atmospheric and geophys. scis. div., 1974-87, div. leader atmospheric and geophys. scis. div., 1987-93; sr. scientist, Office US Global Change Rsch. Program, 1993-2002, exec. dir. 1993-97, exec. dir. nat. assessment coord. office, 1997-2001; co-project leader study on global effects of nuclear exchange, 1983—88; prin. investigator Earth System Modeling Project, 1991-93; area mgr. CO2 research program Dept. Energy, 1979—90, project dir. multistate atmospheric power prodn. study, 1976-79, project leader bilateral on environ. working group VIII, US/USSR, 1984—90; mem. Internat. Com. Climate, 1987-2003, pres. 1995-2003; chief scientist climate change programs, Climate Inst., Washington, 2002—. mem. assesment investigation team, Arctic Climate Impact Assessment, 2003-04; Co-author: Environmental Consequences of Nuclear War, Vol. 1: Physical and Atmospheric Effects, 1986; co-author, co-editor (U.S. Dept. Energy state of the arts reports) Projecting the Climatic Effects of Increasing Carbon Dioxide, 1985; assoc. editor J. of Climate, 1987-95; co-editor, Sudden and Disruptive Climate Change: Exploring the Real Risks and How We Can Avoid Them, 2005; contbr. articles and reports to profl. pubs. Bd. dirs. Livermore Area Recreation and Park Dist., 1970-78, chmn., 1974, 78. Fannie and John Hertz Found. fellow, 1964-68. Mem. Am. Meteorol. Soc. (chmn. com. on climate variations 1983-85), Am. Geophys. Union, Am. Oceanography Soc., AAAS (fellow, chair atmosperic and hydrosperic scis., 1996-97), Internat. Assn. Meteorology and Atmospheric Scis. (pres. 2003-07), Sci. Com. Oceanic Rsch.

MACDONALD, ALAN HUGH, academic administrator; b. Ottawa, Ont., Can., Mar. 3, 1943; s. Vincent C. and Hilda C. MacDonald; children: Eric Paul Henry, Nigel Alan Christopher. BA, Dalhousie U., Halifax NS, 1963; BLS, U. Toronto, Ont., 1964. With Dalhousie U., 1964-78, law libr., 1965-67, 69-71, asst. univ. libr., 1970-72, health sci. libr., 1972-78, lectr. Sch. Libr. Svcs., 1969-78; with U. Calgary, Canada, 1979—2003, sr. advisor Info. Resources, 1999—2003, asst. to provost, 1999—2003, adj. prof. faculty comm. and culture, 2000—03, dir. Info Svcs., 1988—99, dir. librs., 1979-92, univ. orator, 1989—2003; dir. U. Calgary Press, 1984—90. Chair editl. bd. U. Calgary Press, 2001—03, libr. emeritus, 2003—; libr. N.S. Barristers Soc., 1969—74; mem. adv. bd. Nat. Libr. Can., 1972—76, Health Scis. Resource Ctr., Can. Inst. Sci. and Tech. Info., 1977—79; mem. Coun. of Prairie Univ. Librs., 1979—92, 1997—98, chair, 1984—85, 1989, 91; Bassam lectr. U. Toronto Faculty Info. Studies, 1994; Lorne MacRae lectr. Libr. Assn. Alta., 1996; mem. steering com. Alta. Libr. Knowledge Network, 1999—2002; steering com. Can. Digital Libr. Rsch. Initiative, 1999—2000. Mem. editl. bd. America: History and Life (ABC-CLIO), 1985-93. Pres. TELED Cmty. Media Access Orgn., Halifax, N.S., 1972—74; mem. Minister's Com. on Univ. Affairs, Alta., 1979—83; bd. dirs. Alta. Found. for Can. Music Ctr., 1985—92, Can. Inst. for Hist. Microreprodn., 1990—98, pres., 1996—97; bd. dirs. Calgary Learning Ctr., 1997—2004, vice-chair, 2000—04. Coun. Libr. Resources fellow, 1975; exec. fellow Univ. Microfilms Internat., 1986; recipient Disting. Acad. Librarian award

Can. Assn. of Coll. and Univ. Libraries, 1988, U. Toronto Faculty of Info. Studies Alumni Jubilee award, 1999. Mem.: Order of U. Calgary, Calgary Cmty. Network Assn. (bd. dirs. 1994—99, chair 1996—99), Can. Assn. Rsch. Librs. (bd. dirs. 1981—86, v.p. 1985—86, Disting. Svc. award to rsch. librarianship 2003), Can. Assn. Info. Sci. (pres. 1979—80), Foothills Libr. Assn., Atlantic Provinces Libr. Assn. (pres. 1977—78), Can. Libr. Assn. (treas. 1977—79, pres. 1980—81, Award for Outstanding Svc. to Librarianship 1997), Australian Libr. and Info. Assn. (assoc.), Can. Health Libr. Assn. (life; treas. 1977—79), Libr. Assn. Alta. (life; v.p. 1988—89, Pres.' award 1992), AeroSpace Mus. Assn. Calgary (bd. dirs. 2002—07, exec. dir. 2003—04, sec. 2004—07, libr. 2006—). Personal E-mail: ahmacdon@ucalgary.ca.

MACDONALD, ANDREW STEPHEN, management consulting firm executive; b. Fairbanks, Alaska, July 15, 1953; s. Bernard L. and Rosemary (Unger) MacD.; m. Josephine A. Joanne, Aug. 4, 1972; children: Peter, Stephen, Charles. BA in Acctg., Seattle U., 1974. CPA, cert. mgmt. cons. Acct. Boeing Aerospace, Seattle, 1976-79; owner, pres. Triak Corp., Seattle, 1977—; pres. Exec. Cons. Group, Inc., Seattle, 1979—. Mem. AICPA, Inst. Mgmt. Cons., Wash. Soc. CPAs, Columbia Tower Club. Home: 10030 Lake Shore Blvd NE Seattle WA 98125-8158

MACDONALD, BRIAN, computer software company executive; Attended, U. Wash., 1980—82. Head Microsoft Project devel. team Microsoft Corp., Redmond, Wash., 1989, gen. mgr. Microsoft Outlook team, sr. v.p. subscription svcs., mgr. NetDos, 1999, corp. v.p. core search program mgmt., 2007—. Office: Microsoft Corp One Microsoft Way Redmond WA 98052-6399

MACDONALD, DON, psychology educator; b. Mar. 24, 1950; BA in Psychology, U. Tex., 1972; MS in Counseling, Ind. U., 1973; PhD in Psychology, Mich. State U., 1984. Tchr. 3rd grade Northshore Sch. Dist., Kenmore, Wash., 1975-76; staff psychologist Ho. of Commons, Lansing, Mich., 1976-80; grad. asst. Mich. State U., East Lansing, 1977-80; asst. prof. coun. and family therapy Seattle Pacific U., 1980-86, assoc. prof. coun. and family and cmty. therapy, 1986-96, prof. family therapy, 1996—. Office: Seattle Pacific Univ Watson Hall Seattle WA 98119 Office Phone: 206-281-2107. Business E-Mail: eieio@spu.edu.

MACDONALD, DONALD J., marketing executive; JD, U. Lancaster, Eng., 1983. Dir. mktg. Intel Japan, 1987; dir. mktg. mobile platform grps. Intel Corp., v.p., gen. mgr. Digital Home Grp., v.p. sales, mktg. grp., dir. global mktg., 2007—. Recipient Intel Achievement award. Office: Intel Corp 2200 Mission Coll Blvd Santa Clara CA 95054

MACDONALD, ERIN E., healthcare company executive; With Sierra Health Svcs. Inc. and predecessor firms, 1978—, ops. mgr. Southwest Med. Assocs.; dir. ops. HPN Sierra Health Svcs. Inc., Reno, Nev., v.p. HMO Ops., pres. HPN, 1984, v.p. HMO and ins. ops., 1989-92, pres. SHL, 1990, sr. v.p. ops. Office: Sierra Health Svcs 2724 N Tenaya Way Las Vegas NV 89128

MACDONALD, KEN CRAIG, geophysicist; b. San Francisco, Oct. 14, 1947; m. Rachel Haymon, 1984. BS in Engring. Geoscis., U. Calif., Berkeley, 1970; PhD in Marine Geophysics, MIT/Woods Hole, 1975. Cecil H. and Ida Green postdoctoral scholar Scripps Instn. of Oceanography, 1975-76, asst. rsch. geophysicist, lectr., 1976-80; assoc. prof. U. Calif., Santa Barbara, 1980-83, prof., 1983—. Chief scientist on over 30 deep sea expeditions; prin. ALVIN diver on over 40 dives to the mid-ocean ridge. Assoc. editor Jour. of Geophys. Rsch., 1979-82, Earth and Planetary Sci. Letters, 1978-88; mem. editorial bd. Marine Sci. Revs., 1986—; editor Marine Geophys. Rschs., 1986-90; contbr. over 100 articles to profl. jours. Mem. ALVIN Rev. Com., 1979-82; mem. Ocean Sci. Bd. of NAS, 1980-83, Lithosphere Panel Advanced Ocean Drilling Project, 1983-85, Ocean Scis. Panel, NSF, 1984-86, COSOD II planning com.; mem. various RIDGE coms., RIDGE steering com., 1987-90; mem. NSF Ocean Scis. Strategic Plan for Rsch. and Edn. Com., 1993-94, U.S. Geodynamics Comm., 1997—. Regents scholar U. Calif., Berkeley, 1966-70, Mineral Tech. scholar, 1967-70, Cecil H. and Ida Green scholar Inst. Geophysics and Planetary Physics/U. Calif., San Diego, 1975-76; NSF Grad. fellow, 1970-73, World Innovation Found. fellow, 2005; recipient AAAS Newcomb-Cleveland prize, 1980, Robert L. and Bettie P. Cody prize and medal Scripps Instn. Oceanography, 1994; ISI Highly Cited Rschr., 2004. Fellow Am. Geophys. Union, Geol. Soc. Am., Am. Assoc. Advancement Sci., 2007; mem. Phi Beta Kappa, Sigma Psi. Avocations: windsurfing, fly fishing. Office: U Calif Santa Barbara Dept Earth Sci Santa Barbara CA 93106 Business E-Mail: macdonald@geol.ucsb.edu.

MACDONALD, LAURIE, film company executive; m. Walter F. Parkes, 1983; 2 children. BA in English Lit., Sonoma State U., Calif. Documentary and news prodr. K-RON, NBC affiliate, San Francisco; creative exec. Columbia Pictures, 1984—85, v.p. prodn., 1985—88; head Aerial Pictures, 1988—94; exec. prodr. Amblin Entertainment, 1994; co-head motion pictures divsn. DreamWorks Pictures, 1994—. Prodr.: (films) Hayseed, 1997, Men in Black, 1997 (nominated Golden Globe best musical or comedy), Men in Black II, 2002, The Ring, 2002, The Terminal, 2004, Lemony Snicket's A Series of Unfortunate Events, 2004, The Ring Two, 2005, Just Like Heaven, 2005, The Legend of Zorro, 2005; (TV series) SFO; exec. prodr.: (films) How to Make an American Quilt, 1995, The Trigger Effect, 1996, Twister, 1996, The Mask of Zorro, 1998, Gladiator, 2000, The Time Machine, 2002, The Tuxedo, 2002, Catch Me If You Can, 2002; exec. prodr.: (films) The Island, 2005, The Lookout, 2007. Recipient Women in Hollywood Icon award, Premiere Mag., 1999; named one of 100 Most Powerful Women in Hollywood, Hollywood Reporter, 2003, 2005, 50 Most Powerful People in Hollywood, Premiere mag., 2004—05. Office: DreamWorks SKG 100 Flower St Glendale CA 91201 Office Phone: 818-733-7000. Office Fax: 818-695-7574.

MACDONALD, NORVAL, safety engineer; b. Medford, Oreg., Dec. 8, 1913; s. Orion and Edith (Anderson) MacD.; m. Elizabeth Ann Clifford, Dec. 8, 1937; children: Linda (Mrs. Bob Comings), Peggy (Mrs. Don Lake), Kathleen (Mrs. Michael Nissenberg). Student, U. So. Calif., 1932-34. Registered profl. safety engr., Calif. Safety engr. Todd Shipyards, San Pedro, Calif., 1942-44, Pacific Indemnity Ins. Co., San Francisco, 1944-50; area safety engring. chief safety engr. Indsl. Ind., San Francisco, 1950-76; supervising safety engr. Beaver Ins. Co., 1976-82, v.p. loss control, 1982-88; cons. safety engr. MacDonald and Assocs., 1988-99. Tchr. adult evening classes U. San Francisco, 1960-63, Golden Gate U., 1969-76. Contbr. articles to profl. jours.; producer safety training films. Mem. ASME, Am. Soc. Safety Engrs. (pres. San Francisco chpt. 1958, 59), Masons, Shriners. Methodist. Home: 1199 S Dora St Apt 32 Ukiah CA 95482 Personal E-mail: nmacd@msn.com.

MACE, JOHN WELDON, pediatrician; b. Buena Vista, Va., July 9, 1938; s. John Henry and Gladys Elizabeth (Edwards) M.; m. Janice Mace, Jan. 28, 1962; children: Karin E., John E., James E. BA, Columbia Union Coll., 1960; MD, Loma Linda U., 1964. Diplomate: Am. Bd. Pediatrics, Sub-bd. Pediatric Endocrinology. Intern U.S. Naval Hosp., San Diego, 1964-65, resident in pediatrics, 1966-68; fellow in endocrinology and metabolism U. Colo., 1970-72; asst. prof. pediatrics Loma Linda (Calif.) U. Med. Ctr., 1972-75, prof., chmn. dept., 1975—2003. Med. dir. Loma Linda U. Children's Hosp., 1990-92, physician-in-chief, 1992—2003. Contbr. articles to profl. jours. Treas. Found. for Med. Care San Bernardino County, 1979-80, pres., 1980-82; mem. Congl. Adv. Bd., 1984-87; pres. So. Calif. affiliate Am. Diabetes Assn., 1985-86, dir., 1987-89; chmn. adv. bd. State Calif. Children's Svcs., 1986—; bd. dirs. So. Calif. Children's Cancer Svcs., 1993-94, Loma Linda Ronald McDonald House, 1991—2003, Aetna Health Plans of Calif., 1993-95; bd. dirs. Loma Linda U. Health Care, 1995—2003. Recipient Shirley N. Pettis award, 2002, Contrbn. to Medicine award, San Bernardino County Med. Soc., 2003; named Alumnist of Yr., Loma Linda U. Sch. Medicine, 1994; named one of Best Doctors in Am., 1998, America's Top Pediatricians, 2006. Mem. AAAS, N.Y. Acad. Sci., Calif. Med. Soc. (adv. panel genetic diseases State Calif., 1975—, chmn. acad. practice forum 1997—), Western Soc. Pediatric Rsch., Lawson Wilkens Pediatric Endocrine Soc., Assn. Med. Pediatric Dept. Chmn., Am. Acad. Pediatrics, Sigma Xi, Alpha Omega Alpha.

MACE, MICHAEL R., academic administrator, real estate development consultant, mortgage executive; b. Billings, Mont., Oct. 4, 1951; s. Robert E. and Ruth (Fox) M.; m. Karen Marie Lawrenz, June 10, 1974; children: Ann Michelle, Joseph Michael. BBA, Mont. State U., 1975. V.p. Mace Realty & Ins., Billings, 1974-84; pres. Mut. Montago Group, Billings, 1984—; pvt. practice cons. Billings and Seattle, 1986—; pres. Mut. Trade Services, Billings and Seattle, 1988—; chief ops. exec., chmn. D&M Industries; interim pres. Rocky Mountain Coll., Billings, 2005—06, pres., 2006—. Developer in field, Billings, 1983—; mortgage banker Mut. Montago Group, 1984—; cons. in field. Mem. Nat. Assn. Realtors, Rotary. Avocations: music, fishing. Office: Rockey Moauntain Coll 1511 Poly Dr Billings MT 59102 also: 735 Grand Ave Billings MT 59101-5823 Office Phone: 406-657-1026. E-mail: president@rocky.edu.

MACEY, WILLIAM BLACKMORE, oil industry executive; b. Buffalo, Aug. 1, 1920; s. Richard Charles and Doris (Bourne) M.; m. Jean Olive Mullins, Oct. 6, 1945; 1 dau., Barbara Jean. BS in Petroleum Engring, N.Mex. Sch. Mines, 1942; D.Engring. (hon.), N.Mex. Inst. Mining and Tech., 1984. Dist. engr. N.Mex. Oil Conservation Commn., 1946-48; dist. supt. Am. Republics Corp., 1948-52; chief engr. N.Mex. Oil Conservation Commn., 1952-54, state geologist, dir., 1954-56; v.p. Internat. Oil & Gas Corp. (and predecessor co., developers mineral properties), Denver, 1956-60, then pres., 1960-67; pres. Nielson Enterprises Inc., oil and gas prodn. and pipelines, livestock ranching, 1967-74; v.p., dir. Y-Tex Corp. (mfr. livestock identification tags), 1972-73; pres. GEN Oil Inc. (oil and gas prodn.), 1972-75, Col. Cody Inn (real estate and golf course devel.), 1970-73; pres., dir. Macey & Mershon Oil, Inc., 1974-93; dir. Juniper Oil and Gas Corp., Denver, 1981-83, Ruidoso (N.Mex.) State Bank Holding Co., 1987—; pres. The Macey Corp., Denver, 1985—99. Chmn. Pres.'s N.Mex. Inst. Mines and Tech., 1980-82; mem. adv. bd. U. Ariz. Heart Ctr., 1997-2002; mem. Pres.'s U. Ariz. Found. Served from 2d lt. to capt. USAAF, 1942-45. Mem.: N.Mex. Oil and Gas Assn. (exec. com. 1949—52, 1960—61), Popejoy & Pres.'s Club (U. N.Mex.), N.Mex. Jockey Club (bd. dirs. 1985—88, 1991—93, pres. 1993), Ruidoso, Tucson Country Club, Altolakes Golf and Country Club, Skyline Country Club (Tucson) (dir., treas. 1980—82, pres. 1982—83), Garden of the Gods. Episcopalian. Office: PO Box 2210 Denver CO 80201-2210 Home: 13605 Quaking Aspen Pl NE Albuquerque NM 87111-7166

MACFARLAND, CRAIG GEORGE, natural resource management professional; b. Great Falls, Mont., July 17, 1943; s. Paul Stanley and Jean Elizabeth (Graham) MacF.; m. Janice Lee Bennett, Dec. 23, 1963 (div. 1987); children: Bennett, Francisco; m. Marilyn Ann Swanson, Mar. 19, 1988 (div. 1999). BA magna cum laude, Austin Coll., 1965; MA, U. Wis., Madison, 1969, PhD in Zoology, 1993; DSc (hon.), Austin Coll., 1978. Dir. Charles Darwin Rsch. Sta., Galapagos Islands, Ecuador, 1974-78; head Wildlands and watershed mgmt. program C.Am. Centro Agronomico Tropical de Investigacion Enseñanza, Turrialba, Costa Rica, 1978-85; pres. Charles Darwin Found. for Galapagos Islands, Ecuador, 1985-96; cons. natural resources and sustainable use in L.Am. Moscow, Idaho, 1985—. Affiliate faculty dept. Resource, Recreation and Tourism, U. Idaho, Moscow, 1988—; affiliate faculty dept. natural resource recreation and tourism Colo. State U., Ft. Collins, 1992. Contbr. to numerous profl. publs. Recipient Internat. Conservation medal Zool. Soc. San Diego, 1978, Order of Golden Ark for internat. conservation, Prince Bernhard of Netherlands, 1984. Mem. World Conservation Union, World Commn. on Protected Areas, Ecol. Soc. Am., Internat. Soc. for Ecol. Econs., Internat. Soc. Tropical Foresters, Assn. Tropical Biology, Soc. Conservation Biology, Nature Conservancy, World Wildlife Fund, Greenpeace, Cultural Survival, George Wright Soc. Avocations: cross country skiing, hiking, camping, skiing. Home and Office: Box 207 Arlee MT 59821-0207 E-mail: riverbottom@blackfoot.net, craigmacfarland@hotmail.com.

MACFARLANE, SETH WOODBURY, television producer, scriptwriter; b. Kent, Conn., Oct. 26, 1973; s. Ron and Perry MacFarlane. Grad., RI Sch. Design; degree (hon.), Harvard U., 2006, RI Sch. Design, 2007. Founder, owner Fuzzy Door prodn. co. Dir., writer, voice (films) The Life of Larry, 1995, Larry & Steve, 1996, writer Zoomates, 1998, exec. prodr., writer, voice Family Guy Presents Stewie Griffin: The Untold Story, 2005, exec. prodr., writer, dir., voice American Dad: The New CIA, 2005; actor: (films) Life Is Short, 2006, A Conversation with George, 2008, Hellboy II: The Golden Army, 2008; writer (TV series) Jungle Cubs, 1996, Ace Ventura: Pet Detective, 1996, Dexter's Laboratory, 1996—2003, Cow and Chicken, 1997, Johnny Bravo, 1997—2003, The Winner, 2006, exec. prodr., writer, voice Family Guy, 1999— (Emmy award for Outstanding Music and Lyrics, 2002, Emmy award for Outstanding Voice-Over Performance, Best Voice Acting in an Animated TV Prodn., Annie Awards, 2006), American Dad, 2005—, voice Crank Yankers, 2003—05, Robot Chicken, 2005—07, writer (TV films) Dexter's Laboratory Ego Trip, 1999, voice Robot Chicken: Star Wars, 2007, (video game) Family Guy, 2006. Avocations: piano, golf. Office: c/o Greater Talent Network 437 Fifth Ave New York NY 10016 also: c/o The Family Guy Twentieth TV PO Box 900 Beverly Hills CA 90213-0900

MACGINITIE, WALTER HAROLD, psychologist, educator; b. Carmel, Calif., Aug. 14, 1928; s. George Eber and Nettie Lorene (Murray) MacG.; m. Ruth Olive Kilpatrick, Sept. 2, 1950; children: Mary Catherine, Laura Anne. BA, UCLA, 1949; A.M., Stanford U., 1950; PhD, Columbia U., 1960. Tchr. Long Beach (Calif.) Unified Sch. Dist., 1950, 1955-56; mem. faculty Columbia U. Tchrs. Coll., 1959-80, prof. psychology and edn., 1970-80; Lansdowne scholar, prof. edn. U. Victoria, B.C., Canada, 1980-84. Research assoc. Lexington Sch. Deaf, N.Y.C., 1963-69; mem. sci. adv. bd. Ctr. for Study of Reading, 1977-80, chmn. 1979-80. Co-author: Gates-MacGinitie Reading Tests, 1965, 78, 89, 2000, Psychological Foundations of Education, 1968; Editor: Assessment Problems in Reading, 1972; co-editor: Verbal Behavior of the Deaf Child, 1969. Life mem. Calif. PTA. Served with USAF, 1950-54. Fellow APA, AAAS, Assn. Psychol. Sci., Nat. Conf. Rsch. on Lang. and Literacy, N.Y. Acad. Scis.; mem. Internat. Reading Assn. (pres. 1976-77, Spl. Svc. award 1981), Reading Hall of Fame (pres. 1989-90). Home and Office: PO Box 1789 Friday Harbor WA 98250-1789

MACGOWAN, BILL, information technology executive; BA in Polit. Sci., Claremont McKenna Coll., Calif. With Northrop Grumman, Allergan; v.p. human resources Corning Inc., Quest Diagnostics; head enterprise svcs. divsn. Sun Microsystems, Inc., Santa Clara, Calif., 1998, v.p. human resources Systems, Storage and Ops. bus. groups, v.p. human resources Global Ctrs. Expertise, sr. v.p. human resources, chief human resources officer, exec. v.p. people and places. Trustee Am. Found. for Blind. Office: Sun Microsystems Inc 4150 Network Cir Santa Clara CA 95054 Office Phone: 650-960-1300.

MACGREGOR, GEORGE LESCHER, JR., freelance/self-employed writer; b. Dallas, Sept. 15, 1936; s. George Lescher and Jean (Edge) MacG.; divorced; children: George Lescher III (dec.), Michael Fordtran. BBA, U. Tex., 1958. Asst. cashier First Nat. Bank in Dallas, 1960-64, asst. v.p., 1964-68; v.p. Nat. Bank of Commerce of Dallas, 1968-70, sr. v.p., 1970-73, exec. v.p., 1973-74; pres., chief exec. officer Mountain Banks Ltd., Colorado Springs, 1974-77; chief exec. officer Highfield Fin. (U.S.A.) Ltd., 1978-83; chmn. bd., chief exec. officer, dir. Dominion Nat. Bank, Denver, 1981-84; chmn. bd., chief exec. officer Royal Dominion Ltd., Denver; chmn. bd., chief exec. officer, dir. Market Bank of Denver, 1983-84; vice chmn., dir. Bank of Aurora, Denver, 1983-84; chmn., pres., chief exec. officer Alamosa Bancorp. of Colo., Denver, 1983-84; pres., chief exec. officer Am. Interstate Bancorp., 1984-88; pres. Banco, Inc., 1984-89; sr. mng. ptnr. Scotland Co., Denver, London, 1988-91; free-lance writer, 1992—. Served with M.C. AUS, 1958-60. Mem. Am. Inst. Banking (hon.), Young Pres.'s Orgn., Coon Creek Club, Broadmoore Golf Club, Oxford Club, Phi Gamma Delta. Anglican Catholic. Home and Office: 1736 Blake St Denver CO 80202-1226 Home Fax: 303-292-9794. Personal E-mail: twotatertotts@aol.com.

MACHADO, MICHAEL, state legislator; b. Mar. 12, 1948; married. California Assemblyman, District 17, 94-2000; California State Senator, District 5, 01-. Democrat. Catholic. Mailing: State Capitol Rm 5066 Sacramento CA 95814 Office Phone: 916-445-7931. Fax: 916-327-3519. E-mail: mike.machado@assembly.ca.gov.

MACHIDA, CURTIS A., research molecular neurobiologist, molecular virologist, oral biologist, educator; b. San Francisco, Apr. 1, 1954; AB, U. Calif., Berkeley, 1976; PhD, Oreg. Health Scis. U., 1982. Postdoctoral scientist Oreg. Health Scis. U., Portland, 1982-88; asst. sci. div. neurosci. Oreg. Nat. Primate Rsch. Ctr., Beaverton, 1988-95, assoc. scie. divsn. neurosci., 1995—2002; assoc. rsch. prof. integrative biosciences Sch. Dentistry Oreg. Health Scis. U., Portland, 2002—05, rsch. prof. integrative bioscis., 2005—. Rsch. asst. prof. biochemistry and molecular biology Oreg. Health Sci. U., 1989-95, mem. faculty neurosci. and molecular and cell biology grad. programs, 1989—, adj. assoc. prof. biochemistry and molecular biology, 1995—; mem. grad. faculty biochemistry and biophysics Oreg. State U., Corvallis, 1997-01; mem. Institutional Ethics oversight com., Institutional Biosafety com., faculty bylaws com., preclin. curriculum com.; mem. Dental Sch. Rsch. Task Force; mem. biotech. program adv. com. Portland C.C. Editor Adrenergic Receptor Protocols, 1997-99, Viral Vectors for Gene Therapy: Methods and Protocols, 2000-03; mem. editl. bd. Molecular Biotechnology, Frontiers in Biosci., Internat. Jour. Biomed. Sci., World Medicine; ad-hoc reviewer Endocrinology, Molecular Pharmacology, Biochimica et Biophysica Acta, Am. Jour. Physiology, Lab. Animal Sci., NSF, Bio-Techs., Brain Rsch.; contbr. articles, revs., and abstracts to profl. jours. and internat. confs. Recipient Leukemia Assn. award, 1981, Tartar award Med. Rsch. Found. Oreg., 1980; NIH fellow, 1980-82, 85-87, grantee, 1989, 95, 98, 2002, 05; rsch. grantee Med. Rsch. Found. Oreg., Wills Found., Nat. Parkinson Found., Collins Med. Trust, Murdock Charitable Trust and Rsch. Corp., Nat. Am. Heart Assn. Mem. AAAS, Am. Soc. Biochemistry and Molecular Biology, Am. Soc. Microbiology, Soc. Neurosci., Am. Heart Assn. (basic scis. coun., established investigator 1994-99), Am. Soc. Gene Therapy, U.S.-Israel Binational Sci. Found. (reviewer). Achievements include patent on dopamine receptor and genes; cloning of several adrenergic receptor genes and simian retroviral infectious genomes; depositor, nucleotide sequence to EMBL and GenBank databases, and clones to American Type Culture Collection. Office: Oreg Health Sci U Sch Dentistry Dept Integrative Biosciences 611 SW Campus Dr Portland OR 97239-3097 E-mail: machidac@ohsu.edu.

MACHINA, MARK JOSEPH, economist; b. Detroit, Oct. 27, 1954; BA in Econs., Mich. State U., East Lansing, 1975, BA in Math., 1975; PhD in Econs., MIT, Boston, 1979. Asst. prof. econs. U. Calif., San Diego, 1979—84, assoc. prof. econs., 1984—88, prof. econs., 1988—. Vis. prof. econs. Duke U., Durham, NC, 1996; jr. rsch. officer Cambridge U., 1980—81; vis. asst. prof. econs. Princeton (N.J.) U., 1981—82; instr. People's U. China, Beijing, 1987, 90, 91, 93; Kaiser vis. prof. econs. Stanford (Calif.) U., 1999. Assoc. editor: Jour. Econ. Theory, 1983—91, Econometrica, 1984—91, Quarterly Jour. Econs., 1985—91, Jour. Econ. Perspectives, 1987—90, Jour. Econ. Surveys, 1987—91; co-editor: Theory and Decision, 1986—, Jour. Math. Econs., 1999—; founding co-editor: Jour. Risk and Uncertainty, 1988—90; contbr. articles to profl. jours. Trustee U. Calif. San Diego Found., 2001—04. Grantee, NSF, 1983—86, 1992—95, 1998—2001; fellow, Ctr. for Advanced Study in the Behavioral Scis., 1987—88; Grad. fellow, NSF, 1975—78, Vis. fellow, Australian Nat. U., Canberra, 1983, Rsch. fellow, Alfred P. Sloan Found., 1984—86, Erskine fellow, U. Canterbury, Christchurch, New Zealand, 1994. Fellow: Econometric Soc., Am. Acad. Arts and Scis.; mem.: Phi Beta Kappa. Business E-Mail: mmachina@ucsd.edu.

MACIAS, FERNANDO, state legislator, lawyer; b. Dona Ana, N.Mex., 1953; BA, N.Mex. State U.; JD, Georgetown U. Mem. N.Mex. Legislature, Santa Fe, 1984—, mem. conservation com., mem. corps. and transp. com. Democrat. Office: PO Box 1155 Mesilla NM 88046-1155

MAC INTYRE, DONALD JOHN, college president; b. Detroit, Aug. 19, 1939; s. Donald MacLellan and Ellen (McGrath) MacI.; m. Antoinette Shen, June 2, 1979; children by previous marriage: Honey, Michele, James, John. AB, U. Detroit, 1961; MA, U. Iowa, 1963, PhD, 1966. Prof. U. Pacific, Stockton, Calif., 1966-73; acad. dean/pres. St. Francis Coll., Biddeford, Maine, 1973-75; acad. v.p. U. San Francisco, 1975-79; pres. Metro. State Coll., Denver, 1979-81, Canada Coll., Redwood City, Calif., 1981-83, Skyline Coll., San Bruno, Calif., 1983-85, John F. Kennedy U., Orinda, Calif., 1985-89, Patricia Montandon & Assocs., San Francisco, 1989-91, Tie Tone, Inc., Mill Valley, Calif., 1991-92, The Fielding Inst., Santa Barbara, Calif., 1993-99; exec. v.p. e-vitro, Boulder, Colo., 1999—. Cons. Indsl. Rels. Workshops Seminars, Inc., 1978-81, State Bd. Agr. Colo., 1979; assoc. John A. Scalone & Assocs., Orinda, Calif., 1977-85; chmn. adv. com. office adult learning svcs. Coll. Entrance and Exam. Bd., 1980-81; evaluator Women's Equity in Edn. Act Program, 1981. Contbr. articles to profl. jours. Chmn. edn. div. Mile High United Way, Denver, 1980-81; bd. dirs. Nat. Hispanic Center for Advanced Studies and Policy Analysis, 1981-86, Nat. Hispanic U., 1982-86, Chinese Culture Found., 1983-89; chmn. Children As the Peacemakers Found. Recipient award for Commendable Service U. San Francisco, 1979, Henry Clay Hall award, 1976; Disting. Teaching award U. Pacific, 1971; U. Pacific grantee, 1969-71; Don Quixote award Nat. Hispanic U., 1983; hon. mem. World Trade Ctr. Club, Nanjing, Republic of China, 1985—. Mem. Assn. Public Coll. and Univ. Pres.'s (co-chmn. Colo. 1980-81), Internat. Cultural Soc. Korea. Clubs: World Trade Ctr. (hon.) (Nanjing, China). Democrat. Roman Catholic. Office: e-vitro 27 Midway Ave Mill Valley CA 94941-3438

MACK, JAMES A., parks director; b. Chgo., July 7, 1944; BS in Wildlife Mgmt., Calif. State U., Eureka, 1968; postgrad., N. Ariz. U., 1973. With Nat. Park Svcs.; chief naturalist Haleakla, Maui, Hawaii, 1975-78; chief visitor svcs. Rocky Mt. Nat. Park, 1988-97; supt. Fort Laramie, Wyo., 1997—. Office: Nat Hist Site HC 72 Box 389 PO Box 86 Fort Laramie WY 82212-0086

MACK, JAMES CURTIS, II, cultural organization administrator; b. LA, Dec. 22, 1944; s. James Curtis and Ahli Christina (Youngren) M.; m. Tamara Jo Kriner, Jan. 23, 1988; children: James Curtis III, Robert Lee, Edward Albert. BA cum laude, U. So. Calif., 1967, M in Pub. Adminstrn., 1969, MA, 1976. Asst. to regional dir. VA, Los Angeles, 1973-79; exec. dir. Citizens for the Republic, Santa Monica, Calif., 1979-85; asst. sec. oceans and atmosphere U.S. Dept. Commerce, Washington, 1985-88; pres. Los Angeles World Affairs Coun., 1988—. Adj. prof. Pepperdine U. Grad. Sch. Pub. Policy, 1999—; bd. dirs. Brentwood Bank of Calif. Mem. Pres.'s Commn. on White House Fellowships, 1984-85; mem. exec. adv. bd. European Union Ctr. Calif. Col. USAFR, 1969-99. Mem. Coun. Fgn. Rels., Nat. Space Club (bd. dirs. 1987-88). Republican. Episcopalian. Avocation: philatelist. Home: 4921 Fulton Ave Sherman Oaks CA 91423 Office: LA World Affairs Coun 345 S Figueroa St Ste 313 Los Angeles CA 90071-1002 Office Phone: 213-628-2333. Business E-Mail: jcmack@lawac.org.

MACKAY, CHARLES, opera company director; b. Albuquerque, N.Mex, 1950; s. John and Margaret MacKay. Grad., U. Minn. Box office mgr. Santa Fe Opera, asst. orchestra mgr., bus. mgr., gen. dir. designate, 2007—08, gen. dir., 2008—; dir. fin. and adminstrn. Spoleto Festival USA, 1978—84; joined Opera Theatre of St. Louis, 1984, gen. dir., 1985—. Chmn. bd. OPERA America, 2004—08. Recipient Arts Mgmt. Career Svc. Award, 1997. Office: Opera Theatre of St Louis PO Box 191910 Saint Louis MO 63119-7910 also: Santa Fe Opera PO Box 2408 Santa Fe NM 87504-2408

MACKAY, HAROLD HUGH, lawyer; b. Regina, Sask., Can., Aug. 1, 1940; s. John Royden and Grace Madeliene (Irwin) MacK.; m. Jean Elizabeth Hutchison, Dec. 27, 1963; children: Carol, Donald. BA, U. Sask., 1960; LLB, Dalhousie U., Halifax, NS, 1963; LLD (hon.), U. Regina, 2002. Bar: Sask. 1964, Queen's Counsel 1981. Assoc. MacPherson Leslie & Tyerman LLP, Regina, 1963-69, ptnr., 1969—2004, mng. ptnr., 1989-96, chmn., 1997—2003, of counsel, 2005—. Bd. dirs. Mosaic Co., Toronto-Dominion Bank; chmn. task force Future of the Can. Fin. Svcs. Sector, 1997-98; Clifford Clark vis. economist Dept. of Fin., Govt. of Can., 2002-04; non-exec. chmn. bd. Domtar Corp. Recipient Officer Order of Can., 2002. Mem. Internat. Bar Assn., Can. Bar Assn., Law Soc. Sask. Mem. United Ch. Office: 1500 1874 Scarth St Regina SK Canada S4P 4E9 Home Phone: 306-586-4089; Office Phone: 306-347-8417.

MACKENBACH, FREDERICK W., welding products manufacturing company executive; b. St. Marys, Ohio, Mar. 10, 1931; s. Frederick Jacob and Mabel (Tangeman) M.; m. Jo Ann Dietrich, Oct. 21, 1953; children: John Frederick, David Dietrich. BS in Econs., Wharton Sch. Fin. & Commerce, 1953. Various sales engr. positions The Lincoln Electric Co., Indpls., Ft. Wayne, L.A., 1956-64, asst. dist. mgr. LA, 1973-76, dist. mgr., 1976-88; pres. Lincoln Electric Mexicana, 1988-91, Lincoln Electric Latin Am., 1991-92; pres., COO The Lincoln Electric Co., Cleve., 1992-96, ret., 1996. Mem. Com. on Fgn. Rels. Mayor City of Palos Verdes Estates (Calif.) City Coun., 1999-2005. With U.S. Army 1953-55. Mem.: Am. Welding Soc., Econ. Round Table in LA. Office: Lincoln Electric Co 732 Via Somonte Palos Verdes Estates CA 90274-1629 Personal E-mail: mackenbach@aol.com.

MACKENZIE, JOHN DOUGLAS, engineering educator; b. Hong Kong, Feb. 18, 1926; came to U.S., 1954, naturalized, 1963; s. John and Hannah (Wong) MacK.; m. Jennifer Russell, Oct. 2, 1954; children: Timothy John, Andrea Louise, Peter Neil. BS, U. London, 1952, PhD, 1954. Research asst., lectr. Princeton U., 1954-56; ICI fellow Cambridge (Eng.) U., 1956-57; research scientist Gen. Electric Research Ctr., NYC, 1957-63; prof. materials sci. Rensselaer Poly. Inst., 1963-69; prof. engring. U. Calif., Los Angeles, 1969—. U.S. rep. Internat. Glass Commn., 1964-71 Author books in field (6); editor: Jour. Non-Crystalline Solids, 1968—; contbr. articles to profl. jours.; patentee in field. Fellow Am. Ceramic Soc., Royal Inst. Chemistry; mem. Nat. Acad. Engring., Am. Phys. Soc., Electrochem. Soc., ASTM, Am. Chem. Soc., Soc. Glass Tech. Office: U Calif 6532 Boelter Hall Los Angeles CA 90095-1595 Office Phone: 310-825-3539. Business E-Mail: jdmac@ucla.edu.

MACKEY, PAMELA ROBILLARD, lawyer; b. Harlingen, Tex., July 16, 1956; d. Gregory Leo and Rosanne Elizabeth (Niland) Robillard; m. Craig W. Mackey, Dec. 30, 1983. BS in Journalism with honors, U. Colo., Boulder, 1981; JD with highest honors, George Washington U., 1985. Bar: Colo. 1985, US Dist. Ct. (dist. Colo.) 1985. Assoc. Davis, Graham & Stubbs, Denver, 1985-87, Haddon, Morgan & Foreman, P.C., Denver, 1987—89; dep. state pub. defender Office of State Pub. Defender, Colo., 1989—94; shareholder Haddon, Morgan, Mueller, Jordan, Mackey & Foreman, P.C., Denver, 1994—. Exec. editor George Wash. Law Rev., 1984-85. Fellow ABA; mem. Colo. Bar Assn., Denver Bar Assn. (mem. conciliation panel), Colo. Women's Bar Assn. (bd. dirs. 1986-90, 94-95; pres. 1995-96), Colo. Criminal Def. Bar (newsletter editor 1988), NACDL. Democrat. Roman Catholic. Avocations: skiing, golf. Office: Haddon Morgan Mueller Jordan Mackey & Foreman PC 150 E Tenth Ave Denver CO 80203 Office Phone: 303-831-7364. E-mail: pmackey@hmflaw.com.

MACKIE, JERRY, state legislator, small business owner; b. Ketchikan, Alaska, Jan. 10, 1962; s. Ralph P. Mackie and Marge (Thompson) Young; divorced; 1 child, John. Grad. high sch., Ketchikan. Chmn. bd. Shaan Seet Inc., Craig, Alaska, 1981-90; comml. fisherman Craig, 1985—; rep. Alaska State Legislature, Juneau, 1990-96; owner fishing lodge Craig, 1985—; mem. State Senate AK, Juneau, AK, 1996—. Bd. dirs. Alaska Fed. Natives, Anchorage. Recipient Pub. Svc. commendation USCG, 1987. Mem. Alaska Native Brotherhood, Moose. Democrat. Avocations: fishing, basketball, racquetball, skiing. Office: Alaska State Legislature State Capitol St Juneau AK 99801-1182 Home: 5835 Prominence Pointe Dr Anchorage AK 99516-5415

MACKINNON, PEGGY LOUISE, public relations executive; b. Florence, Ariz., June 18, 1945; d. Lacy Donald Gay and Goldie Louise (Trotter) Martin; m. Ian Dixon Mackinnon, Oct. 20, 1973. BA, San Jose State U., 1967, postgrad., 1968. Cert. secondary tchr., Calif. Tchr. Las Lomas H.S., Walnut Creek, Calif., 1968-69; edn. officer Ormond Sch., Sydney, Australia, 1970-72; tchr. Belconnen H.S., Canberra, Australia, 1972-73; temp. exec. sec. various orgns., London, 1973-75; mktg. mgr. Roadtown Wholesale, Tortola, British Virgin Islands, 1975-80; sr. v.p., gen. mgr. Hill & Knowlton Inc., Denver, 1981-96; pres. Peggy Mackinnon Inc., Denver, 1996—. Bd. dirs. Rocky Mountain Poison and Drug Found., Denver, 1984-87, Denver C. of C., Boy Scouts Am., Denver coun. Avocations: tennis, skiing, fishing, travel. Home: 137 Harrison St Denver CO 80206-5538

MACKINNON, STEPHEN R., Asian studies administrator, educator; b. Columbus, Nebr., Dec. 2, 1940; s. Cyrus Leland and Helen (Wigglesworth) MacKinnon; children: Rebecca, Cyrus R.; m. Anne Feldhaus, Dec. 21, 2005. BA, Yale U., New Haven, Conn., 1963, MA, 1964; PhD, U. Calif., Davis, 1971. Acting instr. Chinese U., Hong Kong, 1968-69; dir. Asian Studies, prof. history Ariz. State U., Tempe, 1971—; vis. assoc. Chinese Acad. Social Sci., Beijing, 1979-81, 85. Mem. US State Dept. Selection Bd., Washington, 1991, Nat. Com. on US-China Rels., NYC, 1991—; cons. PBS film documentary "Dragon and Eagle." Author: Power/Politics China, 1980, Wuhan, 1938, 2008; co-author: Agnes Smedley, 1988, China Reporting, 1987; co-editor: Chinese Women Revolution, 1976 (ALA notable book 1976), Scars of War, 2001, China At War, 2007; lectr. on China to local orgns. and TV, 1981—. Commr. Phoenix Sister Cities, 1986-91; bd. dirs. Com. on Fgn. Rels., Phoenix, 1988—; bd. dirs. Marshall Fund Ariz., 1995—. Rsch. fellow Am. Coun. Learned Socs., Hong Kong, 1978, Fulbright Found., India, 1977-78; rsch. sr. Com. on Scholarly Com. People's Republic China, Washington-Beijing, 1992, Pacific Cultural Found., 1999, Am. Inst. Indian Studies, 2003, Fulbright-Hays ACLS, China, 2005-. Mem. Assn. Asian Studies (bd. dirs. 1990-91), Am. Hist. Assn. (program com. 1990-91). Avocations: tennis, hiking, jazz. Office: Ariz State U Dept History Tempe AZ 85287-4302 Office Phone: 480-965-6692. Business E-Mail: stephen.mackinnon@asu.edu.

MACLACHLAN, DOUGLAS LEE, marketing educator; b. Hollywood, Calif., Aug. 27, 1940; s. Alexander D. and Patricia E. (Culver) MacL.; m. Natalie Bowditch Knauth, July 23, 1966; children: Heather Bowditch, Trevor Douglas. AB in Physics, U. Calif., Berkeley, 1963, MBA, 1965, MA in Stats., 1970, PhD in Bus. Adminstrn., 1971; student, Hastings Sch. Law, 1965—66. Instr. bus. adminstrn. U. Calif., Berkeley, 1969-70; v.p. Hartec Corp., Newport Beach, Calif., 1965-70; from acting asst. prof. to Marion B. Ingersoll endowed prof. mktg. U. Wash., Seattle, 1970—2007, Marion B. Ingersoll endowed prof. mktg., 2007—, chair dept. mktg. and internat. bus., 2006—. Vis. prof. bus. adminstrn. U. Calif., Berkeley, 1974; vis. prof. Institut Europeen des Affaires, Fontainebleau, France, 1982—83, Cath. U. Leuven, Belgium, 1991—92, Koc U., Istanbul, 2001; dir. Univ. Book Store, 1985—2002, 2004—08. Contbr. articles to profl. jours.; mem. editl. bd.: Jour. Mktg. Rsch., 1975-81. Mem. Am. Mktg. Assn. (dir. Puget Sound chpt. 1975-77, 90-91, pres. 1978-79), Informs, Am. Statis. Assn., Assn. Consumer Rsch., Clan MacLachlan Soc. (pres. n.w. br. 1995—2009), Alpha Kappa Psi, Kappa Delta Rho, Beta Gamma Sigma. Home: 16305 Inglewood Rd NE Kenmore WA 98028-3908 Office: U Washington Box 353200 Seattle WA 98195-3200 Office Phone: 206-543-4369.

MACLAINE, SHIRLEY, actress; b. Richmond, Va., Apr. 24, 1934; d. Ira O. and Kathlyn (MacLean) Beatty; m. Steve Parker, Sept. 17, 1954 (div. 1982); 1 child, Stephanie Sachiko. Broadway appearances include Me and Juliet, 1953, Pajama Game, 1954; actress (films) The Trouble With Harry, 1954, Artists and Models, 1954, Around the World in 80 Days, 1955-56, Hot Spell, 1957, The Matchmaker, 1957, The Sheepman, 1957, Some Came Running, 1958 (Fgn. Press award 1959), Ask Any Girl, 1959 (Silver Bear award as best actress Internat. Berlin Film Festival), Career, 1959, Can-Can, 1959, The Apartment, 1959 (Best Actress prize Venice Film Festival), Children's Hour, 1960, The Apartment, 1960, Two for the Seesaw, 1962, Irma La Douce, 1963, What A Way to Go, The Yellow Rolls Royce, 1964, John Goldfarb Please Come Home, 1965, Gambit and Woman Times Seven, 1967, The Bliss of Mrs. Blossom, Sweet Charity, 1969, Two Mules for Sister Sara, 1969, Desperate Characters, 1971, The Possession of Joel Delaney, 1972, The Other Half of the Sky: A China Memoir, 1975, The Turning Point, 1977, Being There, 1979, A Change of Seasons, 1980, Loving Couples, 1980, Terms of Endearment, 1983 (Acad. award for Best Actress, 1984, Golden Globe award for Best Actress), Cannonball Run II, 1984, Madame Sousatzka, 1988 (Best Actress Venice Film Festival, Golden Globe-Best Actress), Steel Magnolias, 1989, Waiting For the Light, 1990, Postcards From the Edge, 1990, Defending Your Life, 1991, Used People, 1992, Wrestling Ernest Hemingway, 1993, Guarding Tess, 1994, Evening Star, 1995, Mrs. Winterbourne, 1996, Carolina, 2003, Bewitched, 2005, In Her Shoes, 2005, Rumor Has It..., 2005, Closing the Ring, 2007; (TV appearances) Shirley's World, 1971-72, Shirley MacLaine: If They Could See Me Now, 1974-75, Gypsy in My Soul, 1975-76, Where Do We Go From Here?, 1976-77, Shirley MacLaine at the Lido, 1979, Shirley MacLaine...Every Little Movement, 1980 (Emmy award 1980), (TV movies) Out On A Limb, 1987, The West Side Waltz, 1995, Joan of Arc, 1999, These Old Broads, 2001, Hell on Heels: The Battle of Mary Kay, 2002, (TV mini-series) Salem Witch Trials, 2002; (directorial debut) Bruno, 2000; co-dir. documentary: China The Other Half of the Sky; star U.S. tour stage musical Out There Tonight, 1990; author: Don't Fall Off the Mountain, 1970, The New Celebrity Cookbook, 1973, You Can Get There From Here, 1975, Out on a Limb, 1983, Dancing in the Light, 1985, It's All in the Playing, 1987, Going Within: A Guide for Inner Transformation, 1989, Dance While You Can, 1991, My Lucky Stars: A Hollywood Memoir, 1995, The Camino: A Journey of the Spirit, 2000, Out On A Leash: Exploring The Nature of Reality and Love, 2003, Sage-ing While Age-ing, 2007; editor: McGovern: The Man and His Beliefs, 1972 Address: C/O ICM 8942 Wilshire Blvd Beverly Hills CA 90211-1934

MACLAUGHLIN, FRANCIS JOSEPH, lawyer; b. Davenport, Iowa, Oct. 5, 1933; s. Francis Joseph and Sylvia (Boone) MacL.; m. Joan Elizabeth Pfeiffer, Oct. 17, 1959; children: Lisa Ann, Christine Ann, Francis Joseph BA, Yale U., 1955; JD, U. Mich., 1958. Bar: Ill. 1958, Calif. 1963. Assoc. Graham, Califf, Harper & Benson, Moline, Ill., 1958-59, Lillick, McHose & Charles, LA, 1963-70, ptnr., 1970-90, White and Case, 1990—97. Lt. USN, 1959—63. Mem. ABA, Calif. Bar Assn., Los Angeles County Bar Assn., Maritime Law Assn. U.S. Republican. Office: White & Case 633 W 5th St Ste 1900 Los Angeles CA 90071-2087 Home Phone: 310-459-2165; Office Phone: 213-553-7900. Personal E-mail: rusty1933@charter.net.

MACLEOD, ALEX, newspaper editor; b. Seattle; Student, Whitman Coll. Night reporter to city editor to asst. mng. editor-news Seattle Times, 1976-84, assoc. mng. editor, 1984-86, mng. editor, 1986—. Office: Seattle Times PO Box 70 Seattle WA 98111-0070

MACLEOD, HUGH ANGUS MCINTOSH, optical science educator, physicist, consultant; b. Glasgow, Scotland, June 20, 1933; came to U.S., 1979; s. John and Agnes (Maclure) M.; m. Ann Turner, May 25, 1957; children: Hugh, Ivor, Charles, Eleanor, Alexander. BSc with honors, U. Glasgow, 1954; D of Tech., Coun. for Nat. Acad. Awards, 1979; D honoris causa, U. Aix-Marseille, 1997. Chartered physicist. Grad. apprentice Sperry Gyroscope Co. Ltd., Brentford, Eng., 1954-56, engr., 1956-60; chief engr. Williamson Mfg. Co. Ltd., London, 1961-62; sr. physicist Mervyn Instruments Ltd., Woking, Eng., 1963; tech. mgr. Sir Howard Grubb Parsons & Co. Ltd., Newcastle upon Tyne, Eng., 1964-70; reader in thin-film physics Newcastle upon Tyne Poly., 1971-79; assoc. prof. U. Aix-Marseille III, France, 1979; prof. optical scis. U. Ariz., Tucson, 1979-95, prof. emeritus, 1995—; pres. Thin Film Ctr., Inc., Tucson, 1992—; dir. Precision Optics Corp., Inc., 1997—2002. Author: Thin-Film Optical Filters, 2001; editor Jour. Modern Optics, London, 1988-93; contbr. over 200 articles to profl. jours., chpts. to books. Recipient John Matteucci award, Assn. Indsl. Metallizers, Coaters and Laminators, 2000, Life for Thin Film award, European Vacuum Coaters Workshop, 2004. Fellow Inst. Physics (London), Optical Soc. Am. (dir.-at-large 1987-89, Esther Hoffman Beller award 1997), SPIE-Internat. Soc. Optical Engring. (Gold medal 1987), Am. Vacuum Soc., Soc. Vacuum Coaters (Nathaniel H. Sugerman Meml. award 2002). Anglican. Avocation: piano. Home: 2745 E Via Rotunda Tucson AZ 85716-5227 Office: Thin Film Ctr Inc 2745 E Via Rotonda Tucson AZ 85716-5227 Business E-Mail: angus@thinfilmcenter.com.

MACMILLEN, LISA BECHTLER, bank executive; b. 1959; BA in Math. & Econs., Miami U., 1981; JD, Boston U. Sch. Law. Staff atty. Fed. Home Loan Bank San Francisco, 1986—92, asst. v.p., 1992—97, v.p., assoc. gen. counsel, 1997—98, sr. v.p., corp. sec., 1998—2007, gen. counsel, 1998—2005, exec. v.p., COO, 2007—. Office: Fed Home Loan Bank San Francisco PO Box 7948 San Francisco CA 94120-7948 Office Phone: 415-616-2726. Office Fax: 415-616-2626. Business E-Mail: macmilll@fhlbsf.com.

MACMILLEN, RICHARD EDWARD, biological sciences educator, researcher; b. Upland, Calif., Apr. 19, 1932; s. Hesper Nichols and Ruth Henrietta (Golder) MacM.; m. Ann Gray, June 12, 1953 (div. 1975); children: Jennifer Kathleen, Douglas Michael; m. Barbara Jean Morgan, Oct. 23, 1980; 1 child, Ian Richard. BA, Pomona Coll., Claremont, Calif., 1954; MS, U. Mich., 1956; PhD, UCLA, 1961. From instr. to assoc. prof. Pomona Coll., Claremont, Calif., 1960-68, Wig Disting. prof., 1965; assoc. prof., then prof. U. Calif., Irvine, 1968—, chair dept. population and environ. biology, 1972-74, chair dept. ecology and evolutionary biology, 1984-90, prof. emeritus, 1993—. Award panel NSF, Washington, 1976-80; coord. U. Calif. Multi-Campus Supercourse in Environ. Biology, White Mountain Rsch. Sta., 1996-97, tchg. participant, 1998—; rev. panel, EPA Star grad. fellowship program, 2002, 04; budget com., Jackson County Fire Dist. 5, 2001—; Alumni Admissions vol., Pomona Coll., 2001—; SMART vol. Talent Elem. Sch., 2007-; vol. morphologist US Fish and Wildlife Svc. Forensics Lab., 2004—. Contbr. numerous articles to profl. jours; co-author: (with Barbara MacMillen) Meandering in the Bush: Nature History Explorations Outback Australia, 2007 Chair sci. adv. bd. Endangered Habitats League, 1991-93. Recipient Rsch. award NSF, 1961-83; Fulbright-Hays Advanced Rsch. fellow Monash U., Australia, 1966-67. Fellow AAAS; mem. Am. Soc. Mammalogists (life), Ecol. Soc. Am. (cert. sr. ecologist), Am. Ornithologists Union (life), Cooper Ornithol. Soc. (life, bd. dirs. 1982-84). Democrat. Avocations: fly fishing, camping, hiking, nature photography. Home: 705 Foss Rd Talent OR 97540-9758 Home Phone: 541-512-9884. Business E-Mail: bidmac@jeffnet.org.

MACOVSKI, ALBERT, electrical engineer, educator; b. NYC, May 2, 1929; s. Philip and Rose (Winogr) Macovski; m. Adelaide Paris, Aug. 5, 1950; children: Michael, Nancy. BEE, City Coll. N.Y., 1950; MEE, Poly. Inst. Bklyn., 1953; PhD, Stanford U., 1968. Mem. tech. staff RCA Labs., Princeton, NJ, 1950—57; asst. prof., then assoc. prof. Poly. Inst. Bklyn., 1957—60; staff scientist Stanford Rsch. Inst., Menlo Park, Calif., 1960—71; fellow U. Calif. Med. Center San Francisco, 1971—; prof. elec. engring. and radiology Stanford U., 1972—, endowed chair, Canon USA prof. engring., 1991—. Dir. Magnetic Resonance Sys. Rsch. Lab.; cons. to industry. Recipient award for color TV cirs., Inst. Radio Engrs., 1958; spl. fellow, NIH, 1971. Fellow: IEEE (Zworykin award 1973), Internat. Soc. Magnetic Resonance in Medicine (trustee 1991—94, gold medal 1997), Optical Soc. Am., Am. Inst. Med. Biol. Engring.; mem.: NAE, Am. Assn. Physicists in Medicine, Inst. Medicine, Eta Kappa Nu, Sigma Xi.

Jewish. Achievements include patents in field. Office: Stanford Univ Dept Elec Engring Stanford CA 94305 Home: 620 Sand Hill Rd Apt 407B Palo Alto CA 94304 Office Phone: 650-723-2708. Business E-Mail: macovski@stanford.edu.

MACPHERSON, SHIRLEY, clinical therapist; b. Bayonne, NJ, June 16, 1934; d. Alexander Phillip and Milldred (Gurstelle) Gottlieb; m. Duncan MacPherson, Jan. 2, 1981; children from previous marriage: Suzanne Pugsley, Brett Barber. BS, Columbia U., NYU, 1951; MS, Juilliard Sch. Music, 1955; MEd, Calif. State U., Northridge, 1967; MA in Psychology, Pepperdine U., 1992; PhD in Psychology, Pacific Western U., 1998. Concert pianist Norman Seman Prodns., NYC, 1952-61; indsl. health educator Am. Med. Internat., LA, 1968-70; cons., lectr. Hosp. Mgmt. Corp., LA, 1970-80; regional dir. Control Data Corp., LA, 1980-86; outplacement specialist Ind. Cons., LA, 1986-90; psychologist, intern Airport Marina Counseling Svcs., LA, 1990-93; staff psychologist Forensic Psychology Assocs., Sherman Oaks, Calif., 1993-94; staff clin. psychologist Pacific Psychologist Assocs., LA, 1992-94; clin. therapist employee profiling and crisis intervention MacPherson Relationship Counseling, LA, 1993—. Author: Rx for Brides, 1990, Understanding Your Man, 1998. Vol. Cmty. Alliance to Support and Empower, L.A., 1994-96, South Bay Free Clinic, L.A., 1995-97; mem. Town and Gown Scholarship program, U. So. Calif., L.A. Mem. AAUW, APA, Calif. Psychol. Assn., L.A. Psychol. Assn., L.A. World Affairs Coun., Am. Bd. Hypnotherapy, Am. Assn. Humanistic Psychology, Am. Assn. Suidiology, Juilliard Alumni Assn., Pepperdine Allumni Assn., Internat. Wound Ballistics Assn. Avocations: studying French and Italian, piano, studies. Office Phone: 310-322-9959. Personal E-mail: Shirlmac@ix.netcom.com.

MACTAVISH, CRAIG, former professional hockey coach, retired professional hockey player; b. London, Ont., Can., Aug. 15, 1958; m. Debbie MacTavish; children: Nathan, Sean, Brianna. Center Boston Bruins, 1980-85, Edmonton Oilers, 1985-94, NY Rangers, 1994, Phila. Flyers, 1994-96, St. Louis Blues, 1996-97; asst. coach NY Rangers, 1997—99, Edmonton Oilers, 1999—2000, head coach, 2000—09. Achievements include being a member of Stanely Cup Champion Edmonton Oilers, 1987, 1988, 1990, New York Rangers, 1994.

MACYS, SONJA, science association director; b. 1971; Exec. dir. Tucson Audubon Soc. Mem., Found. Bd. Rsch. Ranch Found.; mem., environ. adv. com. Raœl Grijalva; mem., exec. com. Sonoran Joint Venture, US Fish & Wildlife Svc. Named an 40 Under 40, Tucson Bus. Edge, 2006. Office: Tucson Audubon Society 300 E University Blvd 120 Tucson AZ 85705 Office Phone: 520-622-5622. Office Fax: 520-623-3476.

MADDEN, ALICE DONNELLY, lawyer; b. St. Louis, Dec. 9, 1958; d. William Joseph and Katherine (Kinsella) Donnelly; m. Peter Gerard Madden, Aug. 3, 1985; children: Thomas Joseph, Jackson Joseph. BA in Psychology, U. Colo., 1981, JD, 1989. Bar: Colo. 1989, U.S. Dist. Ct. Colo. 1989, U.S. Ct. Appeals (10th cir.) 1989. Assoc. Fairfield & Woods, P.C., Denver, 1989-94, Clayton & Stone, Boulder, Colo., 1994-96. Bd. dirs. Boulder County (Colo.) Land Trust, 1991-96, sec., 1992, pres., 1994; bd. dirs. Shannon Estates Homeowners Assn., Boulder, Colo., 1989-92; dir. alumni rels. U. Colo. Sch. of Law, 1997—. Mem. ABA, Colo. Bar Assn., Denver Bar Assn. (ct. reform com. 1991), Boulder County Bar Assn., Colo. Women's Bar Assn. Democrat. Avocations: skiing, hiking, reading. Office: U Colo Sch of Law PO Box 401 Boulder CO 80309-0401

MADDEN, JOHN PHILIP, motion picture director, actor; b. Portsmouth, Hampshire, England, Apr. 8, 1949; Dir. (theatre prodns.) Grownups, Wings, Beyond Therapy, Caritas Christ, The Bundle, Measure For Measure, The Suicide, Beyond East And West, An American Comedy, Terry By Terry, Cinders, Salonka (Am. Premiere at Pub. Theatre), (TV films) The Pigman's Protege, Poppyland, A Wreath Of Roses, Sherlock Holmes, The Return Of Sherlock Holmes, Inspector Morse, The Storyteller, also directed episodes of After The War (PBS) and TV versions of Grownups and Wings; (films) Grown Ups, 1985, Ethan Frome, 1993, Meat, 1994, Golden Gate, 1994, Prime Suspect 4: The Lost Child, 1995, Truth or Dare, 1996, Mrs. Brown, 1997, Shakespeare in Love, 1998, Captain Corelli's Mandolin, 2001, Proof, 2005, Killshot, 2009; acted in films P.K. and the Kid, 1985, Little Giants, 1994, The Replacements, 2000.

MADDEN, PALMER BROWN, lawyer; b. Milw., Sept. 19, 1945; m. Susan L. Paulus, Mar. 31, 1984. BA, Stanford U., 1968; JD, U. Calif., Berkeley, 1973. Bar: Calif. 1973, U.S. Dist. Ct. (no. dist.) Calif. 1973, U.S. Supreme Ct. 1982. Ptnr. McCutchen, Doyle Brown & Enersen, Walnut Creek, 1985-98; prin. ADR Svcs., Alamo, Calif., 1999—. Pres. State Bar Bd. Govs., 2000-01. Chair bd. govs. Continuing Edn. of the Bar, 1997; judge pro tem Contra Costa Superior Ct., 1991-98; pres. Contra Costa Coun., 1995, Kennedy-King Found., 1994; bd. dirs. Episcopal Homes Found., 2001-05, Bay Area Legal Aid, 2005-2007, Bar Fund, 2006-2007. Mem. Contra Costa County Bar Assn. (pres. 1996-97). Democrat. Episcopalian. Office: ADR Svcs 3000 Danville Blvd # 543 Alamo CA 94507 Office Phone: 925-838-8593. Business E-Mail: pbm@netvista.net.

MADDEN, RICHARD BLAINE, forest products executive; b. Short Hills, NJ, Apr. 27, 1929; s. James L. and Irma (Twining) M.; m. Joan Fairbairn, May 24, 1958; children: John Richard, Lynne Marie, Kathryn Ann, Andrew Twining. BS, Princeton U., 1951; JD, U. Mich., 1956; MBA, NYU, 1959; PhD (hon.), St. Scholastica Coll., 1994. Bar: Mich. 1956, N.Y. 1958. Gen. asst. treas.'s dept. Socony Mobil Oil Corp., NYC, 1956-57, spl. asst., 1958-59, fin. rep., 1960; asst. to pres. Mobil Chem. Co.; also dir. Mobil Chems. Ltd. of Eng., 1960-63; exec. v.p., gen. mgr. Kordite Corp.; also v.p. Mobil Plastics, 1963-66; v.p. Mobil Chem. Co., NYC, 1966-68, group v.p., 1968-70; asst. treas. Mobil Oil Corp., 1970-71; chmn. Mobil Oil Estates Ltd., 1970-71; pres., chief exec. Potlatch Corp., San Francisco, 1971-77, chmn. chief exec. officer, 1977-94; ret., 1994. From lectr. to adj. assoc. prof. fin. N.Y.U., 1960-63; bd. dir., Knight Grand Cross Magistral Grace in Obedience Order of Malta, Western Assn., pres., chief exec.; bd. govs., chmn. audit com., mem. adminstrv. compensation and labor rels. com. San Francisco Symphony. Former bd. dir. Smith-Kettlewell Eye Rsch. Inst., trustee emeritus, former chmn. Am. Enterprise Inst.; former mem. bd. Nat. Park Found.; hon. trustee Com. Econ. Devel. Lt. (j.g.) USNR, 1951-54. Mem. N.Y. Bar Assn., Mich. Bar Assn. Clubs: Bohemian (San Francisco); Lagunitas (Ross, Calif.); Metropolitan (Washington). Roman Catholic. Office Phone: 415-453-9121.

MADDOCK, JEROME TORRENCE, library and information scientist; b. Darby, Pa., Feb. 7, 1940; s. Richard Cotton and Isobel Louise (Mezger) M.; m. Karen Rhueama Weygand, Oct. 2, 1965. BS in Biology, Muhlenberg Coll., 1961; MS in Info. Sci., Drexel U., 1968. Editl. assoc. Biol. Abstracts, Phila., 1962—63; mgr. rsch. info. Merck & Co., West Point, Pa., 1963—72; sr. cons. Auerbach Assocs., Inc., Phila., 1972—79; mgr. libr. and info. svcs. Solar Energy Rsch. Inst., Golden, Colo., 1979—88; mgr. info. svcs. Transp. Rsch. Bd., Washington, 1988—99; project mgr. IHS Enterprise Solutions, Boulder, Colo., 1999—2001; ind. cons., 2002—; faculty online U. Phoenix, 1999—. Del. Gov.'s Conf. on Libr. and Info. Svc., Pa., 1978; mem. blue ribbon panel to select archivist of U.S., Washington, 1979; U.S. del. to ops. com. on transp. rsch. info. Orgn. for Econ. Cooperation and Devel., 1988-99. Bd. dirs. Paoli (Pa.) Pub. Libr., 1976-77, Boulder Friends of Jazz, 2003—; bd. trustees Louisville County Pub. Libr., 2002-07, pres. 2004. With USAFR, 1962-68. Mem. AAAS, Am. Soc. Info. Sci. (chmn. 1974-75), Elks, Beta Phi Mu, Pi Delta Epsilon. Republican. Episcopalian. Achievements include projection of information science operations 10 years into the future. Home: 545 W Laurel Ct Louisville CO 80027-1116

MADDY, PENELOPE JO, philosopher, educator; b. Tulsa, Okla., July 4, 1950; d. Richard and Suzanne (Lorimer) Parsons. BA in Math., U. Calif., Berkeley, 1972; PhD in Philosophy, Princeton U., NJ, 1979. Asst. prof. U. Notre Dame (Ind.), 1978-83; assoc. prof. U. Ill., Chgo., 1983-87, U. Calif., Irvine, 1987-89, prof., 1989—, chair philosophy dept., 1991-95, chair logic and philosophy of sci., 1998-2001. Author: Realism in Mathematics, 1990, Naturalism in Mathematics, 1997 (Lakatos award 2002), Second Philosophy, 2007; editor Notre Dame Jour. Formal Logic, 1979-84, editl. bd., 1984—; editl. bd. Jour. Philos. Logic, 1985-2004, Jour. Symbolic Logic, 1995-2000, Philosophia Mathematica, 1993—, Bull. Symbolic Logic, 2004-07. Fellow AAUW, 1982-83, U. Calif., 1988-89; NSF grantee, 1986, 88-89, 90-91, 94-95, Marshall scholar, 1982-83, Westinghouse Sci. scholar, 1968-72. Mem. Assn. Symbolic Logic (mem. exec. com. 1993-96, v.p. 2001-04, pres. 2007—), Am. Philos. Assn. (mem. exec. com. 1993-95), Philosophy of Sci. Assn. (mem. governing bd. 1993-95), Am. Acad. Arts and Scis. Office: U Calif at Irvine Dept Logic and Philosophy of Sci Irvine CA 92697-5100 Business E-Mail: pjmaddy@uci.edu.

MADERA URIBE, JOSE DE JESUS, bishop emeritus; b. San Francisco, Nov. 27, 1927; Student, Domus Studiorum of the Missionaries of the Holy Spirit, Coyoacan, D.F., Mexico. Ordained priest Missionaries of the Holy Spirit, 1957; ordained bishop, 1980; coadjutor to bishop Diocese of Fresno, 1980—91; aux. bishop Archdiocese for Mil. Svcs., Washington, 1991—2004, aux. bishop emeritus, 2004—. Roman Catholic. Office: 2330 John Still Dr Sacramento CA 95832 E-mail: maderajj@aol.com.

MADHAVAN, MURUGAPPA CHETTIAR, economics professor; b. Kandramanickam, Tamilnadu, India, Dec. 17, 1932; came to U.S., 1960; s. L. Murugappa Chettiar and Adaikkammai Achi (Meyyappan) M.; m. Nachammai Manickam, May 3, 1953; children: Nachiappa, Nataraj. BA with honors, Annamalai U., India, 1955, MA, 1958; MS, U. Wis., 1963, PhD, 1969. Lectr. in econs. Annamalai U., 1955-60; economist Europe and Mid. East World Bank, Washington, 1963-66, asst. sec. econ. com., 1966-68; dir. Ctr. for Rsch. in Econ. Devel. San Diego State U., 1969-85, prof. econs., 1974—2004, dir. Asian Studies, 1991-2000, chmn. dept. Asian Studies, 1999-2000. Prof. econs. Nat. Inst. Bank Mgmt., Bombay, 1971—72; vis. prof. econs. Indian Inst. Tech., Madras, 1979—80, Madras Sch. Econs., 1996, U. Putra, Malaysia, 2002; Father Carty Meml. lectr. U. Madras, 1980; vis. Fulbright prof. U. of the Philippines, 1987—88; cons. UN Devel. Program, NYC, 1987—88, Gen. Atomics, San Diego, 1993—99; advisor Gov. Sim Grinio, Philippines, 1988; vis. scholar IMF Inst., Washington, 2002; Fulbright sr. specialist Faculty of Law and Econs., Phnom Penh, Cambodia, summer, 2001. Co-author: The Transfer of Knowledge Through Expatriate Nationals, 1988. Chmn. World Affairs Coun. San Diego, 1991-93; pres. Tamil Nadu Found., Inc., Chgo., 1985-87, life mem.; advisor Mingei Internat. Mus., San Diego, 1985—; pres. San Diego Indian Am. Soc., 1984-99. Fulbright fellow, 1960; recipient Hon. Am. award Ams. by Choice, 1987, Leadership and Contbn. award Tamil Nadu Found., 1994; Fulbright sr. scholar Fulbright Program in Ho Chi Minh City, U. Econs., 2000, U. Putra Malaysia, 2000. Mem.: Am. Econ. Assn., Assn. Indian Econ. Studies (life), Indian Econ. Assn. (life), San Diego Indian Am. Soc. (life), Tamilnadu Found. (life), Fulbright Assn. (life). Democrat. Avocations: reading, walking, organizational activities. Home: 8727 Verlane Dr San Diego CA 92119-2033 Office: San Diego State U Coll Arts & Letters Ctr Asian Studies San Diego CA 92182 Home Phone: 619-698-5058; Office Phone: 619-594-1675. Business E-Mail: madhavan@mail.sdsu.edu.

MADISON, JAMES RAYMOND, lawyer; b. White Plains, NY, Apr. 27, 1931; s. Raymond S. and Katherine (Sherwin) M.; m. Mary Massey, Sept. 19, 1953; children: Michael, Matthew, Molly. BS, Stanford U., 1953, LLB, 1959. Bar: Calif. 1960, U.S. Dist. Ct. (no. dist.) Calif. 1960, U.S. Ct. Appeals (9th cir.) 1960, U.S. Dist. Ct. (ctrl. dist.) Calif. 1970, U.S. Supreme Ct. 1973, U.S. Dist. Ct. (ea. dist.) Calif. 1981, U.S. Dist. Ct. (so. dist.) Calif. 1988. Assoc. Orrick, Herrington & Sutcliffe, San Francisco, 1959-67, ptnr., 1968-95; pvt. practice Menlo Park, Calif., 1996—. Trustee Antioch U., Yellow Springs, Ohio, 1980-87; bd. dirs. Planned Parenthood Alameda/San Francisco, 1984-89; pres. Calif. Dispute Resolution Coun., 2001; vice-chair Calif State Bar ADR Com., 2009. Lt. (j.g.) USN, 1953-56. Mem. ABA, ASCE, State Bar Calif., Bar Assn. San Francisco, San Mateo County Bar Assn., Am. Arbitration Assn. (large complex case panel arbitrators and mediators, No. Calif. regional adv. coun.), Mediation Soc., Calif. Dispute Resolution Coun., Dispute Rev. Bd. Found., Coll. Comml. Arbitrators. Democrat. Episcopalian. Avocation: soccer. Office: 750 Menlo Ave Ste 250 Menlo Park CA 94025-4758 Office Phone: 650-614-0160. Personal E-mail: jrmcoach@aol.com.

MADISON, PAULA, broadcast executive; b. NYC, 1952; m. Roosevelt Madison; 1 child, Imani. Grad., Vassar Coll., 1974. Reporter Syracuse Herald Jour., 1974—80; investigative bur. reporter Ft. Worth Star - Telegram, 1980—82; asst. city editor Dallas Times Herald, 1982; cmty. affairs dir. WFAA-TV, Dallas, 1982—84, news mgr., 1984—86; news dir. KOTV-TV, Tulsa, 1986—87; exec. news dir. KHOU-TV, Houston, 1987—89; asst. news dir. WNBC, NYC, 1989—96, v.p., news dir., 1996—2000; v.p., sr. v.p. diversity NBC, NYC, 2000—02; pres., gen. mgr. KNBC, LA, 2000—07; regional gen. mgr. KVEA, KWHY, 2002—07; exec. v.p. diversity NBC Universal & Co., 2007—. Co. officer Gen. Electric. Bd. trustees Vassar Coll. Recipient Ida B. Wells award, Nat. Assn. Black Journalists', 1998, Ellis Island medal of honor, Nat. Ethnic Coalition of Orgns., 1999, President's award, NAACP, 2001, Frederick C. Patterson award, United Negro College Fund, 2001, Diversity award, Nat. Assoc. Minority Media Execs., 2002, Woman of the Year, Los Angeles County Commn. for Women, 2002, Excellence in Media Award, Calif. NOW Chap., 2003, TRISCCORT award, Tri-State Catholic Com. on Radio and TV, Asian-Pacific Am. Corp. Impact award, Org. Chinese Americans Greater Los Angeles Chap. Image award Corp. Achievement., Deborah award, Anti-Defamation League, 2003; named Disting. African-Am. New Yorker, N.Y.C. Comptroller Alan Hevesi, Citizen of Yr., City of LA Marathon, 2004; named to Power 150, Ebony mag., 2008. Mem.: N.Y. Assn. Black Journalists, Nat. Assn. Black Journalists. Office: NBC Universal 100 Universal City Plaza Universal City CA 91608

MADIX, ROBERT JAMES, chemical engineer, educator; b. Beach Grove, Ind., June 22, 1938; s. James L. and Marjorie A. (Strohl) M.; children: Bradley Alan, David Eric, Michaella Lynn, Evan Scott. BS, U. Ill., 1961; PhD, U. Calif., 1964. NSF postdoctoral fellow Max Planck Inst., Göttingen, Fed. Republic of Germany, 1964-65; asst. prof. chem. engr. Stanford (Calif.) U., 1965-72, assoc. prof., chem. engr., 1972-77; prof. chem. engring. Stanford U., 1977—, chmn., chem. engr., 1983-87, prof. chemistry, 1981—, Charles Lee Powell prof., 1990—2006, Charles Lee Powell prof. emeritus, 2006; sr. rsch. fellow divsn. engring. and applied sci. Harvard U., Cambridge, Mass., 2006. Cons. Monsanto Chem., St. Louis, 1975-84, Shell Oil Co., Houston, 1985-86; Peter Debye lectureship Cornell U., 1985; Eyring lectr. chemistry Ariz. State U., 1990; Barnett Dodge lectr. Yale U., 1996; disting. prof. lectr. U. Tex., Austin, 1980; Walter Robb Disting. lectr. Pa. State U., 1996; chmn. Gordon Rsch. Conf. on Reactions on Surfaces, 1995; sr. rsch. fellow divsn. engring. and applied scis. Harvard U., 2006; shah disting. leadership U. Fla., 2009. Assoc. editor Catalysis Rev., 1986—, Catalysis Letters, 1992—, Rsch. on Chem. Intermediates, 1994—; contbr. articles to profl. jours. Recipient Alpha Chi Sigma award AIChemE, 1990, Paul Emmett award Catalysis Soc. N.Am., 1984, Humboldt U.S. Sr. Scientist prize, 1978; Ford Found. fellow, 1969-72. Mem. AIChE, Internat. Precious Metal Inst. (Henry J. Alber award 1997), Am. Chem. Soc. (Irving Langmuir Disting. Leetr. award 1981, Arthur Adamson award 1997, Am. Phys. Soc., Am. Vacuum Soc., Calif. Catalysis Soc.

MADONNA, (MADONNA LOUISE VERONICA CICCONE), singer, actress, producer; b. Bay City, Mich., Aug. 16, 1958; d. Sylvio and Madonna Ciccone; m. Sean Penn, Aug. 16, 1985 (div. Sept. 14, 1989); m. Guy Ritchie, Dec. 22, 2000 (separated 2008); 1 child Rocco John; 1 child Lourdes Maria (with Carlos Leon); 1 adopted child, David. Student, U. Mich., 1976-78. Dancer Alvin Ailey Dance Co., NYC, 1979; CEO Maverick Records, LA, 1992—. Singer: (albums) Madonna, 1983, Like a Virgin, 1985, True Blue, 1986, You Can Dance, 1987, Like a Prayer, 1989, The Immaculate Collection, 1990, Erotica, 1992, Bedtime Stories, 1994, Something to Remember, 1995, Ray of Light, 1998 (Grammy award for Best Pop Album 1999), Music, 2000, GHV2: Greatest Hits Volume II, 2002, American Life, 2003, Remixed & Revisited, 2003, Confessions on a Dancefloor, 2005 (Grammy award for Best Electronic/Dance Album, 2007), I'm Going to Tell You a Secret, 2006, The Confessions Tour, 2007, Hard Candy, 2008; (soundtracks) Who's That Girl, 1987, I'm Breathless: Music From and Inspired by the Film Dick Tracy, 1990, Evita, 1996; actress: (films) A Certain Sacrifice, 1980, Vision Quest, 1985, Desperately Seeking Susan, 1985, Shanghai Surprise, 1986, Who's That Girl, 1987, Bloodhounds of Broadway, 1989, Dick Tracy, 1990, Shadows and Fog, 1992, Body of Evidence, 1992, A League of Their Own, 1992, Dangerous Game, 1993, Blue in the Face, 1995, Four Rooms, 1996, Girl 6, 1996, Evita, 1996 (Golden Globe award for Best Actress in Comedy/Musical, 1997), The Next Best Thing, 2000, Swept Away, 2002, (voice only) Arthur and the Invisibles, 2006; (TV appearances) Will & Grace, 2003; stage appearance: Speed-the-Plow, 1987, Up for Grabs, 2002; appeared in: (documentaries) Madonna: Truth or Dare, 1991, I'm Going to Tell You a Secret, 2005; writer, exec. prodr., I Am Because We Are, 2008; dir., exec. prodr.: (films) Filth and Wisdom, 2008; exec. prodr.: (films) Agent Cody Banks, 2003, Agent Cody Banks 2: Destination London, 2004; (TV films) 30 Days Until I'm Famous, 2004; author: Sex, 1992, (children's books) The English Roses, 2003, Mr. Peabody's Apples, 2003, Yakov and the Seven Thieves, 2004, Adventures of Abdi, 2004, Lotsa de Casha, 2005. Recipient Grammy award for Best Song Written for Motion Picture, 1999, World's Best Pop Artist award, World Music Awards, 2007, Best-Selling US Artist, 2007, 2008, Ivor Novello award for Internat. Hit of Yr., Brit. Acad. Composers & Songwriters, 2007, Style Icon award, Elle Mag., 2007; named one of The 100 Most Powerful Celebrities, Forbes.com, 2008; named to Rock & Roll Hall of Fame, 2008.

MADRID, PATRICIA A., former state attorney general; BA in English and Philosophy, U. N.Mex., 1969, JD, 1973; cert., Nat. Jud. Coll., U. Nev., 1978. Bar: N.Mex. Dist. judge State of N.Mex., 1978—84, atty. gen., 1999—2006. Chmn. Western Conf. of Attys. Gen.; exec. cons. Dickstein Shapiro, LLP, Washington. Recipient Trailblazer award, N.Mex. Commn. on the Status of Women, Las Primeras award, MANA, 2004, Woman of the Yr. in Govt. award, Capital Bus. and Professional Women of Santa Fe, 2004, Exec. Dir. award, Animal Protection of N.Mex., 2004; named Latina Atty. of Yr., Nat. Hispanic Bar Assn., 2001, N.Mex. Power Broker, N.Mex. Bus. Weekly. Democrat. Mailing: 2219 Vista Larga Dr Albuquerque NM 87106 Office: 20 First Plaza Ctr NW Albuquerque NM 87102 Office Phone: 505-243-0503. E-mail: patriciamadrid100@yahoo.com.

MADSEN, BARBARA A., state supreme court justice; b. Renton; BA, U. Wash., 1974; JD, Gonzaga U., 1977. Pub. defender King and Snohomish Counties, 1977—82; staff atty. Seattle City Atty.'s Office, 1982—84, spl. prosecutor, 1984—88; judge Seattle Mcpl. Ct., 1988—92; justice Wash. Supreme Ct., Olympia, 1993—. Chair Wash. State Gender and Justice Commn., Supreme Ct. Circulation Com., Ct. Personnel Com.; co-chair Internal Rules Com., Death Penalty Rules Com.; mem. Ct. Budget Com., Administrative Com., Reporter of Decisions Com. Active in Judges in the Classroom prog., Tacoma Public Sch. Recipient Wash. Women Lawyers Vanguard award, 1998, Wash. Women Lawyers Found. award, 2001, Presidents award, Nat. Assn. of Women Judges, 2002, Equal Justice Coalition Judicial award, 2004, Access to Justice award of distinction for public svc., 2006. Mem.: Judicature Soc., Nat. Assn. of Women Judges, Am. Judges Assn. Office: Wash Supreme Ct PO Box 40929 Olympia WA 98504-0929

MADSEN, REGINALD B., protective services official; b. Neopit, Wis., Sept. 15, 1940; married; 2 children. AAS, Clark Coll., Vancouver, Wash., 1967. Police officer Vancouver (Wash.) Police Dept., 1966-68; supt. Oreg. State Police Dept., Salem, 1968-93, retired,

1993; U.S. marshal U.S. Marshals Svc., Dept. Justice, Portland, 1994—. With USN, 1958-64. Office: Mark O Hatfield US Courthouse 100 SW 3d Ave Rm 401 Portland OR 97204

MADSEN, SUSAN ARRINGTON, writer; b. Logan, Utah, Aug. 25, 1954; d. Leonard J. and Grace F. Arrington; m. Dean Madsen, Aug. 20, 1974; children: Emily, Rebecca, Sarah, Rachel. BS in Journalism, Utah State U., 1975. Mem. adj. faculty Logan Latter-day Saints Inst. Religion, 1991-95. Author: Christmas: A Joyful Heritage, 1984, The Lord Needs a Prophet, 1990, I Walked to Zion: True Stories of Young Pioneers on the Mormon Trail, 1994, Growing Up in Zion: True Stories of Young Pioneers Building the Kingdom, 1996, The Second Rescue: The Story of the Spiritual Rescue of the Willie and Martin Handcart Pioneers, 1998, (with Leonard J. Arrington) Sunbonnet Sisters: True Stories of Mormon Women and Frontier Life, 1984, Mothers of the Prophets, 1987; contbr. numerous articles to Collier's Ency. Yearbooks. Chair Hyde Pk. (Utah) Bd. Adjustments, 1985-94. Honoree Utah State U. Nat. Women's History Week, 1985; recipient Cmty. Svc. award Nat. Daus. Utah Pioneers, 1990. Mem. Lds Ch. Avocations: horseback riding, skiing, genealogy, family activities.

MADSEN, VIRGINIA, actress; b. Chgo., Sept. 11, 1963; d. Cal Madsen; m. Danny Huston, Sept. 2, 1989 (div. 1992); 1 child, Jack. Represented by Creative Artists Agy., Beverly Hills, Calif. Actor: (films) Class, 1983, Dune, 1984, Electric Dreams, 1984, Creator, 1985, Fire with Fire, 1986, Modern Girls, 1986, Slam Dance, 1987, Zombie High, 1987, Mr. North, 1988, Hot to Trot, 1988, Heart of Dixie, 1989, The Hot Spot, 1990, Highlander II—The Quickening, 1991, Becoming Colette, 1992, Candyman, 1992, Blue Tiger, 1994, Caroline at Midnight, 1994, The Prophecy, 1995, Ghosts of Mississippi, 1996, The Rainmaker, 1997, Ambushed, 1998, Ballad of the Nightingale, 1998, The Florentine, 1998, The Haunting, 1999, After Sex, 2000, Lying in Wait, 2000, Almost Salinas, 2001, American Gun, 2002, Artworks, 2003, Tempted, 2003, Nobody Knows Anything!, 2003, Sideways, 2004 (Screen Actors Guild Award, outstanding performance by cast in motion picture, 2005), Firewall, 2006, A Prairie Home Companion, 2006, The Number 23, 2007, The Astronaut Farmer, 2007, Diminished Capacity, 2008, The Haunting in Connecticut, 2009; (TV films) A Matter of Principle, 1984, The Hearst and Davies Affair, 1985, Long Gone, 1987, Gotham, 1988, Third Degree Burn, 1989, Ironclads, 1991, Victim of Love, 1991, Love Kills, 1991, A Murderous Affair: The Carolyn Warmus Story, 1992, Linda, 1993, Bitter Vengeance, 1994, The Apocalypse Watch, 1997, Children of Fortune, 2000, The Inspector General, 2000, Crossfire Trail, 2001, Just Ask My Children, 2001, Tempted, 2003, Brave New Girl, 2004; (TV miniseries) Mussolini: The Untold Story, 1985; (TV series) American Dreams, 2002-03, Smith, 2006-; TV appearances include The Hitchhiker, 1987, Moonlighting, 1989, Earth 2, 1994, Star Trek: Voyager, 1998, Frasier, 1999, The Practice, 2001, (voice) Justice League, 2002, Dawson's Creek, 2003, CSI: Miami, 2003, Boomtown, 2003. Democrat.

MAEDER, GARY WILLIAM, lawyer; b. LA, Dec. 21, 1949; s. Clarence Wilbur and Norma Jean (Buckbee) M.; m. Sue Ellen; children: Stephen Gregory, Charlene Michelle. BA, UCLA, 1971, JD, 1975; student, Fuller Seminary, 1971—72. Bar: Calif. 1975. Assoc. Kindel & Anderson, LA, 1975-82, ptnr., 1982-96; shareholder Heller Ehrman LLP, LA, 1996—. Author: God's Will for Your Life, 1973, 76, 91. Elder adult edn. St. John's Presbyn. Ch., LA, 1981—86, 1994—96; bd. dirs. Christian Legal Soc. L.A., 1975—, Christian Conciliation Svc. L.A., 1983—88. Mem. Los Angeles County Bar Assn. (state and local tax com.), Christian Legal Soc. (bd. dirs. 1989-92), Order of Coif, Phi Beta Kappa. Office: 333 S Hope St Ste 3900 Los Angeles CA 90071 Office Phone: 213-689-7555. Business E-Mail: gary.maeder@hellerehrman.com.

MAEHL, WILLIAM HENRY, historian, academic administrator, consultant; b. Chicago Heights, Ill., June 13, 1930; s. William Henry and Marvel Lillian (Carlson) M.; m. Audrey Mae Ellsworth, Aug. 25, 1962; 1 child, Christine Amanda. BA, U. Minn., 1950, MA, 1951; postgrad., King's Coll., U. Durham, Eng., 1955—56; PhD, U. Chgo., 1957; LHD (hon.), Fielding Inst., 1993. Asst. prof. Montclair (N.J.) State Coll., 1957-58, Washington Coll., Chestertown, Md., 1958-59, U. Okla., Norman, 1959-64, assoc. prof., 1964-70, prof. English history, 1970-86; dean Coll. Liberal Studies, 1976-86, vice provost for continuing edn. and public service, 1979-86; pres. The Fielding Inst., Santa Barbara, Calif., 1987-93, pres. emeritus, 1993—. Prin. investigator Project for a Nation of Lifelong Learners, Regents Coll., Albany, N.Y., 1994-97; vis. prof. U. Nebr., summer 1965; vis. fellow Wolfson Coll. Oxford (Eng.) U., spring 1975; fellow Salzburg Seminar in Am. Studies, 1976. Author: The Reform Bill of 1832, 1967, Lifelong Learning at Its Best: Innovative Practices in Adult Credit Programs, 2000; contbg. author: Encyclopedia of Education, 2d edit., 2003, Encyclopedia of Distributed Learning, 2004; editor: R.G. Gammage, Chartist Reminiscences, 1981, Continuum: Jour. of the Nat. Continuing Edn. Assn., 1980-83, also articles. Mem. coun. Nat. Ctr. for Adult Learning, 1990—2001; bd. dirs. Alliance for Alternative Degree Programs, 1988—90; trustee Coun. for Adult and Exptl. Learning, 1990—94, Southwestern Coll., 2000—02. Fulbright fellow, 1955-56; Leverhulme Rsch. fellow, 1961-62; grantee Am. Philos. Soc., 1961-62, 67-68, 71, 76. Fellow: Assn. Grad. Liberal Studies Programs, Royal Hist. Soc.; mem.: Adult Higher Edn. Alliance. Home: 500 Rodeo Rd Apt 910 Santa Fe NM 87505-6364

MAES, PETRA JIMENEZ, state supreme court justice; widowed; 4 children. BA, U. N.Mex., 1970, JD, 1973. Bar: N.Mex. 1973. Pvt. pratice law, Albuquerque, 1973-75; rep., then office mgr. No. N.Mex. Legal Svcs., 1975-81; dist. judge 1st Jud. Dist. Ct., Santa Fe, Los Alamos, 1981-98; chief judge, 1984-87, 92-95; assoc. justice N.Mex. Supreme Ct., 1998—, chief justice, 2003—04. Mem. N.Mex. Commn. on Access to Justice. Mem.: Improved Task Force and Judical Info. Sys. Coun. (liason), Am. Law Instn., Am. Bar Assn., N. Mex Com. (co-chair), Nat. Hispanic Bar Assn., N. Mex. Hispanic Bar Assn., N. Mex. Women's Bar Assn., N. Mex. Bar Assn. Office: Supreme Court NMex PO Box 848 Santa Fe NM 87504-0848 Office Phone: 505-827-4883.

MAES, ROMAN M., III, state legislator, lawyer; BA, N.Mex. Highlands U.; JD, U. Denver. Mem. N.Mex. Senate, Dist. 25, Santa Fe, 1998—; mem. corps. and transp. com. N.Mex. Senate, Santa Fe, mem. ways and means com. Real estate property mgr.; investment cons. Democrat. Office: 1488 S Saint Francis Dr Ste B Santa Fe NM 87505-4096

MAFFEI, GREGORY B., media company executive, former computer software company executive; b. NYC, May 24, 1960; s. Ralph J. and Sheila (Quinn) M. AB, Dartmouth Coll., 1982; MBA, Harvard U., 1986. Analyst Dillon, Read & Co., Inc., NYC, 1982-84, assoc.; pres. Beacon Hill Cons. Co., Boston, 1984; dir. bus. devel & investments Microsoft Corp., Redmond, Wash., 1993—94, treas., 1994—96, v.p. corp. devel., 1996—97, sr. v.p., fin. & adminstrn., CFO, 1997—2000; non-exec. chmn. Expedia, Inc., Bellevue, Wash., 1999—2002; pres., CEO 360 networks, Inc., Vancouver, BC, Canada, 2000—05, chmn., 2000—05; pres., CFO Oracle Corp., Redwood City, Calif., 2005; pres., CEO Liberty Media Corp., Englewood, Colo., 2006—. Bd. dir. Starbucks Corp., Seattle, 1999—, Electronic Arts Inc., Redwood City, Calif., 2003—, Liberty Media Corp., Englewood, Colo., 2005—. Bd. trustee Seattle Pub. Libr. George F. Baker scholar Harvard U., 1986. Roman Catholic. Office: Liberty Media Corp 12300 Liberty Blvd Englewood CO 80112

MAGELITZ, LARRY L., construction company executive; CFO Dillingham Constrn. Corp., Pleasanton, Calif. Office: Dillingham Pacific Ltd PO Box 1268 Placerville CA 95667-1268

MAGER, ARTUR, retired aerospace executive; b. Nieglowice, Poland, Sept. 21, 1919; arrived in U.S., 1939, naturalized, 1944; s. Herman and Ella (Kornbluh) M.; m. Phyllis R. Weisman, Aug. 19, 1942; 1 child, Ilana Gail. BS, U. Mich., 1943; MS, Case Inst. Tech., 1951; PhD in Aeros., Calif. Inst. Tech., 1953. Aero. rsch. scientist NASA Lewis Labs., Cleve., 1946-51; rsch. scientist Marquardt Corp., Van Nuys, Calif., 1954-60; dir. Nat. Engring. Sci. Co., Pasadena, Calif., 1960-61; dir. spacecraft scis. Aerospace Corp., El Segundo, Calif., 1961-64, gen. mgr. applied mechanics divsn., 1964-68, v.p., gen. mgr. engring. sci. ops., 1968-78, v.p. engring. group, 1978-82, cons., 1982—. Mem. BSD Re-entry Panel, 1961—63; mem. NASA com. missile and space vehicle aerodynamics, 1963—65; mem. adv. com. AFML, 1971—72; mem. NASA Adv. Coun., 1982—86; chmn. NASA Space Applications Adv. Com., 1982—86; mem. Aeros. and Space Engring. Bd. NRC, 1982—87; mem. Space Sta. Task Force NRC, 1983—87, mem. Shuttle Critically and Hazard Analysts Rev. Bd., 1986—88; mem. DSB NASP Task Force, 1987—88, AFSB Hypersonic Task Force, 1987—88. Contbr. articles to profl. jours. Mem. alumni fund coun. Calif. Inst. Tech., 1972—74; trustee West Coast U., 1980—92; mem. devel. disabilities bd. Area X, 1976—80, chmn., 1976—78; 1st v.p. Calif. Assn. Retarded, 1983—85; pres. Exceptional Children's Found., 1970—72; bd. councilors U. So. Calif. Sch. Engring., 1976—86. Recipient Disting. Alumni award, U. Mich., 1969, Golden Rule award, Calif. Assn. Retarded, 1977, 1989. Fellow: AAAS, AIAA (chmn. L.A. sect. 1967—68, bd. dirs. 1975—77, pres. 1980—81), Inst. Advanced Engring.; mem.: Nat. Acad. Engring., Technion Soc., Sigma Xi. Home and Office: 1353 Woodruff Ave Los Angeles CA 90024-5129 Personal E-mail: ap.mager1@verizon.net.

MAGNESS, RHONDA ANN, retired microbiologist; b. Stockton, Calif., Jan. 30, 1946; d. John Pershing and Dorothy Waneta (Kelley) Wetter; m. Barney LeRoy Bender, Aug. 26, 1965 (div. Jan. 1977); m. Gary D. Magness, Mar. 5, 1977; children: Jay D.(dec.), Troy D. BS, Calif. State U., Sacramento, 1977. Med. asst. C. Fred Wilcox, MD, Stockton, 1965-66; clk. typist Dept. of U.S. Army, Ft. Eustis, Va., 1967, Def. Supply Agy., New Orleans, 1967-68; med. asst. James G. Cross, MD, Lodi, Calif., 1969, Arthur A. Kemalyan, MD, Lodi, 1969-71, 72-77; med. sec. Lodi Meml. Hosp., 1972; lab. aide Calif. State U., Sacramento, 1977; phlebotomist St. Joseph's Hosp., Stockton, 1978-79; microbiologist Dameron Hosp. Assn., Stockton, 1980—2004. Active Concerned Women Am., Washington, 1987—. Mem.: San Joaquin County Med. Assts. Assn., Calif. Assn. Clin. Lab. Technologists, Nat. Audubon Soc., Nat. Geog. Soc., Jobs Daus. (chaplain 1962—63). Baptist. Avocations: birdwatching, sewing, reading. Home: 14606 E Dale Ln Scottsdale AZ 85262-6895

MAGOWAN, PETER ALDEN, professional sports team and retail executive; b. NYC, Apr. 5, 1942; s. Robert Anderson and Doris (Merrill) Magowan; m. Jill Tarlau (dec. July 1982); children: Kimberley, Margot, Hilary; m. Deborah Johnston, Aug. 14, 1982. BA, Stanford U., 1964; MA, Oxford U., Eng., 1966; postgrad., Johns Hopkins U., 1967—68. Store mgr. Safeway Stores Inc., Washington, 1968—70, dist. mgr. Houston, 1970—71, retail ops. mgr. Phoenix, 1971—72, divsn. mgr. Tulsa, 1973—76, mgr. internat. divsn. Toronto, Ont., Canada, 1976—78, mgr. western region San Francisco, 1978—79, CEO Oakland, Calif., 1980—93, chmn. bd. dirs., 1980—98; pres., mng. gen. ptnr. San Francisco Giants, 1993—; ret. Safeway Stores Inc., 2005. Bd. dirs. Daimler Chrysler Corp, Caterpillar. Office: San Francisco Giants 24 Willie Mays Plz San Francisco CA 94107-2199 Office Phone: 415-972-1950. Business E-Mail: scasabat@sfgiants.com.

MAGUIRE, JOHN DAVID, academic administrator, educator, writer; b. Montgomery, Ala., Aug. 7, 1932; s. John Henry and Clyde (Merrill) M.; m. Lillian Louise Parrish, Aug. 29, 1953; children: Catherine Merrill, Mary Elizabeth, Anne King. AB magna cum laude, Washington and Lee U., 1953, Litt.D. (hon.), 1979; Fulbright scholar, Edinburgh U., Scotland, 1953-54; B.D. summa cum laude, Yale U., 1956, PhD, 1960; postdoctoral research, U. Tübingen, Germany, 1964-65, U. Calif., Berkeley, 1968-69, Silliman U., Philippines, 1976-77; HLD (hon.), Transylvania U., 1990. Dir. Internat. Student Ctr., New Haven, 1956-58; mem. faculty Wesleyan U., Middletown, Conn., 1960-70, asso. provost, 1967-68; vis. lectr. Pacific Sch. Religion and Grad. Theol. Union, Berkeley, 1968-69; pres. SUNY Coll. at Old Westbury, 1970-81, Claremont (Calif.) Grad. U., 1981-98. Sr. fellow Claremont Grad. U. Sch. Politics and Econs.; trustee (charter) Keck Grad. Inst. Applied Life Scis., 1997-98, (hon) Claremont Grad. U., 1998-, Union Theological Seminary, 2003-; dir. nat. project Renewing Democracy through Interracial/Multicultural Cmty. Bldg., 1998—; mem. adv. coun. Pacific Oaks Coll., Ga. State U., 1999-, The Advancement Project; sr. adv. Claremont Mus. Art; nat. co-dir. Inst Democratic Renewal/Project Change's joint antiracism venture, 2002-. Author: The Dance of the Pilgrim: A Christian Style of Life for Today, 1967; also numerous articles. Mem. Conn. adv. comt. US Comn. Civil Rights, 1961—70; participant White House Conf. on Civil Rights, 1966; advisor Martin Luther King Cent. Social Change, Atlanta, 1968—, permanent trustee, 1968—, 1st chmn. bd. dirs., 1968—; bd. dirs. Nassau County Health and Welfare Coun., 1971—81, pres., 1974—76; trustee United Bd. Christian Higher Ed in Asia, 1975—81, Inst. Int. Ed., 1980—86; charter trustee Tomas Rivera Policy Inst., Claremont, Calif., 1984—, vice chmn., 1987—94, treas., 1995—; with Asn. Ind. Calif. Cols. and Univs., 1985—98, chmn., 1990—92, mem. exec. comt., 1992—98; with Calif. Achievement Coun., 1985—94, chmn., 1990—94; with Transylvania Univ. Bingham Trust, 1987—, Lincoln Found. and Lincoln Inst. Land Policy, Inc., 1987—94; The JL Found., 1988—; with Educ. Found. African Ams., 1991—99; bd. dirs. Asn. Am. Cols. and Univs., 1981—86, chmn., 1984—85; bd. dirs. Legal Def. and Edu. Fund NAACP, 1991—, west coast div., 1981—91, Thacher Sch., Ojai, Calif., 1982—94, vice chmn., 1986—90; with Salzburg Seminar, 1992—96; charter mem. Pacific Coun. Int. Policy, 1995—; mem. Am. Comt. US-Soviet Rels., 1981—92, Blue Ribbon Calif. Comn. Teaching Profession, 1984—86; mem. gov. coun. Aspen Inst. Wye Faculty Seminar, 1984—94; mem. Coun. Fgn. Rels., 1983—; mem. adv. bd. RAND Cent. Research Immigration Policy, 1994—97, Peter F. Drucker Found. Non-Profit Mgt, 1990—, Andrew Young Sch. Policy Ga. State Univ., 1999—, The Eureka Communities, 1998—; mem. Pres.'s Adv. Coun. Comn. on Calif. Master Plan Higher Educ., 1986—87, Los Angeles Educ. Alliance Restructuring Now, 1992—98, Calif. Bus. Higher Educ. Forum, 1992—98; leader Idyllwild Sch. Summer Poetry Festival, 1998—. Recipient Julia A. Archibald High Scholarship award Yale Div. Sch., 1956; Day fellow Yale Grad. Sch., 1956-57; Kent fellow, 1957-60; Howard Found. postdoctoral fellow Brown U. Grad. Sch., 1964-65; Fenn lectr., 7 Asian countries, 1976-77; recipient Conn. Prince Hall Masons' award outstanding contbns. human rights in Conn., 1965; E. Harris Harbison Gt. Tchr. prize Danforth Found., 1968 Fellow Soc. Values Higher Edn. (pres. 1974-81, bd. dirs. 1972-88); mem. Phi Beta Kappa, Omicron Delta Kappa Democrat. Office: Claremont Grad U Inst for Dem Renewal 170 E 10th St Claremont CA 91711-5909 Office Phone: 909-607-9220. Business E-Mail: john.maguire@cgu.edu.

MAGUIRE, ROBERT FRANCIS, III, retired real estate company executive; b. Portland, Oreg., Apr. 18, 1935; s. Robert Francis Jr. and Jean (Shepard) M. BA, UCLA, 1960. V.p. Security Pacific Nat. Bank, L.A., 1960-64; chmn. Maguire Partners Inc., L.A., 1964—2008, chmn. emeritus, 2008—. Exec. bd. med. scis. UCLA. Bd. dirs. Los Angeles County Mus. Art; trustee UCLA Found., Bard Coll.; bd. dirs. St. John's Hosp., Music Ctr. Bd. Govs., Calif. Presidential Citation of Excellence, Am. Inst. Achitects; Real Estate Exec. Yr., NACORE. Mem.: California (Los Angeles); Valley (Montecito, Calif.), L.A. Country. Office: Maguire Partners Inc 355 S Grand Ave Ste 400 Los Angeles CA 90071 E-mail: robert.maguire@maguirepartners.com.

MAHAJAN, SUBHASH, electronic materials educator; b. Gurdaspur, India; m. Sushma Sondhi, Sept. 3, 1965; children: Sanjoy, Sunit, Ashish. BS with highest honors, Panjab U., India, 1959; BE in Metallyrgy with highest honors, Indian Inst. Sci., 1961; PhD in Materials Sci. and Engring., U. Calif., 1965. Rsch. asst. U. Calif., Berkeley, 1961-65; rsch. metallurgist U. Denver, 1965-68; Harwell fellow Atomic Energy Rsch. Establishment, Harwell, England, 1968-71; mem. tech. staff AT&T Bell Labs., Murray Hill, NJ, 1971-83, rsch. mgr., 1981-83; prof. electronic materials dept. material sci. and engring. Carnegie Mellon U., Pitts., 1983-97; prof. electronic materials Ariz. State U., Tempe, 1997—, assoc. chair, 1999, interim chair and chair dept. chem. and materials engring., 2000—06, dir. Sch. Materials, 2006—, Regents' prof., 2007. Mem. site panel Materials Rsch. Lab., 1993; vis. prof. U. Antwerp, Belgium, 1991, Ecole Ctrl. Lyon, Ecully, France, 1993; lectr., spkr., patentee, cons. in field. Editor: Handbook on Semiconductors, vol. 3, 1994, Acta Materialia, 2001; editor: (with V.G. Keramidas) Electrochemical Society Symposium Volume, 1983; editor: (with L.C. Kimerling) The Concise Encyclopedia of Semiconducting Materials and Related Technologies, 1992; editor: (with D. Bloor, R.J. Brook and M.C. Flemings) The Encyclopedia of Advanced Materials, 1994; editor: (with K.H. Jurgen Buschow, Robert W. Cahn et al) Encyclopedia of Materials: Science and Technology, 2001; coordinating editor: The Acta Materiala Jours., 2004—; contbr. more than 200 articles to profl. jours. Mem. materials rsch. adv. com. divsn. materials rsch. NSF, 1989-92. Fellow TMS, Am. Soc. Metals Internat. (trustee bd., Albert Sauveur Achievement award, Campbell Meml. Lectr.); mem. NAE, Materials Rsch. Soc. (editor symposium volume 1983, organizer symposium Am. Assn. Crystal Growers), Electrochem. Soc. (mem. electronics divsn. 1973-86, divisional editor 1976-86), Minerals, Metals and Materials Soc. (mem. phys. metallurgy com. 1976-83, vice chmn. mech. metallurgy com. 1978-79, mem. 1975-80, mem. electronic materials com. 1990-94, chmn. electronic, magnetic and photonic materials com. 1984-86, tech. dir. bd., John Bardeen award, The Educator award), Sigma Xi. Home: 8824 S Poplar St Tempe AZ 85284-4521 Office: Ariz State U Sch Materials Tempe AZ 85287 Home Phone: 480-345-9192; Office Phone: 480-727-9322. Business E-Mail: smahajan@asu.edu.

MAHAN, JAMES E., archivist, educator; s. Lowell Edward Mahan and Ora Irene Lohmeyer; m. Janet Pike, Aug. 2, 1970; children: Adam, Abby E. Hammar. BA, Wichita State U., Kans., 1969; MS, Emporia State U., Kans., 1974. Prof. Mohave CC, Lake Havasu City, Ariz., 1975—. Bd. edn. Lake Havasu Charter Sch., 2004; sec treas. Lake Havasu Charter Sch., Inc, 2004; judge Brewers Competitions, Lake Havasu City, 2005—09. Home: 2864 Glengarry Dr Lake Havasu City AZ 86404 Office: Mohave CC 1977 W Acoma Blvd Lake Havasu City AZ Business E-Mail: jimmah@mohave.edu.

MAHARAJ, DAVAN R., editor; b. 1962; BA in Polit. Sci. & Communications, U. Tenn., 1989; LLM, Yale U. Reporter LA Times, Orange County, Calif., LA, East Africa, asst. fgn. editor, dep. bus. editor, bus. editor, 2007—08, mng. editor, head fgn., nat., metro, sports and bus. depts., 2008—. Co-recipient Ernie Pyle Award for Human Interest Writing, 2005. Office: LA Times 202 W 1st St Los Angeles CA 90012 Office Phone: 213-237-5000. Office Fax: 213-237-7679.

MAHARIDGE, DALE DIMITRO, journalist, educator, writer; b. Cleve., Oct. 24, 1956; s. Steve and Joan (Kopfstein) Maharidge. Student, Cleve. State U., 1974—75. Freelance reporter various publs., Cleve., 1976, Cleve. Plain Dealer, 1978—80; reporter The Gazette, Medina, Ohio, 1977—78, Sacramento Bee, 1980—91; vis. prof. Stanford U., Palo Alto, Calif., 1992—2002; assoc. prof. Columbia U. Grad. Sch. Journalism, NYC, 2002—. Art colony resident Yaddo Residency, 2004, 07, MacDowell Colony, 2006. Author: Journey to Nowhere: The Saga of the New Underclass, 1985, Journey to Nowhere: The Saga of the New Underclass repub. with introduction by Bruce Springsteen, 1996, And Their Children After Them, 1989 (Pulitzer Prize for gen. nonfiction, 1990), The Last Great American Hobo, 1993, The Coming White Minority: California, Multiculturism and the Nation's Future, 1996, The Coming White Minority: California's Eruptions and the Nation's Future, Vintage Books edit., 1999, Homeland, 2004, Denison, Iowa: Searching for the Soul of America Through the Secrets of a Midwest Town, 2005; contbr. articles to profl. jours. Grantee, Open Soc. Inst., 2006; Freedom Forum grantee, 1995, Nieman fellow, Harvard U., 1988, Pope Found. grantee, 1994. Democrat. Office Phone: 212-854-3854. Personal E-mail: dmaharidge@yahoo.com.

MAHDAVI, KAMAL B. (K. B. M.), writer, researcher; b. Esfahan, Iran, Sept. 1, 1933; arrived in US, 1958, naturalized; s. Ebrahim B. and Ghamar (Jalilian) M. BA, U. Calif., Berkeley, 1964; MA, U Toronto, 1965; postgrad., U. Cambridge, 1965—69. Cert. coll. tchr., Calif. R&D rschr. U. Stockholm, 1969—71; freelance rschr., writer self-employed, San Francisco, San Diego, 1972—. Ind. legal rschr. San Francisco, San Diego, 1980—. Author (as K.M.B. Writer): Technological Innovation: An Efficiency Investigation, 1972; contbr. articles to profl. jours. Civil rights litigant. Avocations: swimming, chess. Office: PO Box 121164 San Diego CA 92112-1164

MAHER, BILL (WILLIAM MAHER JR.), television personality and producer, comedian; b. NYC, Jan. 20, 1956; s. Bill and Julie (Berman) Maher. BA in English and Hist., Cornell U., NYC, 1978. Host Catch a Rising Star Comedy Club, NYC, 1979; creator, host Politically Incorrect Comedy Central, NYC, 1993-96, ABC, 1996—2002; host Real Time With Bill Maher, HBO, 2003—. Stand-up performances include The Bob Monkhouse Show, Late Night with David Letterman, The Tonight Show, (HBO spls.) One Night Stand, 1989, 1992, Stuff that Struck Me Funny, 1995, The Golden Goose Special, 1997, Be More Cynical, 2000, Victory Begins at Home, 2003, I'm Swiss, 2005, The Decider, 2007, film appearances: DC Cab, 1993, Rags to Riches, 1986, Club Med, 1986, Ratboy, 1986, House II: The Second Story, 1987, Out of Time, 1988, Cannibal Women in the Avocado Jungle of Death, 1989, Pizza Man, 1991, Say What?, 1992, Don't Quit Your Day Job, 1996, Bimbo Movie Bash, 1997, EDtv, 1998, Tomcats, 2001, The Aristocrats, 2005, Swing Vote, 2008, Religulous, 2008, TV appearances: Sara, 1985, Hard Knocks, 1987, Max Headroom, 1987, Murder She Wrote, 1989—90, The Midnight Hour, 1990, Charlie Hoover, 1991, Married With Children, 1992—93, MADtv, 2005, True Blood, 2008, The Man Show; author: True Story: A Novel, 1994, Does Anybody Have a Problem With That? Politically Incorrect's Greatest Hits, 1996, Does Anybody Have a Problem with That? The Best of Politically Incorrect, 1997, When You Ride Alone You Ride With Bin Laden: What the Government Should Be Telling Us to Help Fight the War on Terrorism, 2003, Keep the Statue of Liberty Closed: The New Rules, 2004, New Rules: Polite Musings from a Timid Observer, 2005. Adv. bd. mem. The Reason Project; bd. dirs. PETA. Recipient CableACE award, Nat. Acad. Cable Programming, 1990, CableACE award for best talk show series, 1995, CableACE award for best talk show host, 1995, Pres.'s award for Championing Free Speech, LA Times Press Club, 2002, Johnny Carson Prodr. of Yr. award, Prodrs. Guild of America, 2007; named one of Comedy Central's 100 Greatest Stand-Ups of All Time. Office: Brillstein Grey Entertainment Ste 350 9150 Wilshire Blvd Beverly Hills CA 90212*

MAHLENDORF, URSULA RENATE, literature educator; b. Strehlen, Silesia, Germany, Oct. 24, 1929; arrived in US, 1953; Student, Oberschule an der Hamburgerstraße, Bremen, Fed. Republic Germany, 1950, U. Tübingen, Fed. Republic Germany, 1950-52, Brown U., Providence, 1953-57, MA in English Lit., 1956, PhD in German Lit., 1958; student, Bonn U., Fed. Republic Germany, 1953, London U.; grad., New Directions in Psychoanalysis, Washington, 2002. Teaching asst. Brown U., Providence, 1953-57; from acting instr. to prof. German U. Calif., Santa Barbara, 1957—93, prof. women's studies, 1988—93, assoc. dir., campus coord. edn. abroad program, 1967—69, chmn. dept. Germanic and Slavic langs. and lits., 1980-83, assoc. dean Coll. Letters and Sci., 1986-89, emeritus, 1993—. Chmn. symposium in honor of Harry Slochower, 1977; campus coord. edn. abroad program U. Calif., 1967-69, assoc. dir., 1969-72; co-chair Nietzsche symposium Dept. Germanic and Slavic Langs. and Lits., U. Calif., Santa Barbara, 1981. Author: The Wellsprings of Literary Creation, 1985; editor: (with John L. Carleton) Man for Man: A Multi-Disciplinary Workshop on Affecting Man's Social and Psychological Nature through Community Action (Charles C. Thomas), 1973, Dimensions of Social Psychiatry, 1979, (with Arthur Lerner) Life Guidance through Literature, 1992, The Shame of Survival: Working through a Negi Childhood, 2009; assoc. editor Am. Imago, Am. Jour. Social Psychiatry, Jour. Evolutionary Psychology; contbr. more than 90 articles to profl. jours. Recipient Alumni Tchg. award, 1981; rsch. grantee, U. Calif., 1974—, Fulbright fellow, 1951—52, Festschrift named in her honor, Calif., 2004. Mem. MLA, Am. Assn. for Aesthetics and Art Criticism (past pres. Calif. div.), Assn. for applied Psychoanalysis (profl. mem.), Am. Assn. Social Psychiatry (councillor 1977-81), Internat. Assn. Social Psychiatry (treas. 1978-83) MLA, GSA, Women in German. Avocations: sculpting, woodcarving. Office: U Calif Dept Germanic Semitic Slavic Studies Santa Barbara CA 93106 Office Phone: 805-893-2131. Business E-Mail: mahlendo@gss.ucsb.edu.

MAHLEY, ROBERT W., health facility administrator; b. July 23, 1941; m. Linda Mahley; children: Stephen, Leslyn. BS, Maryville Coll., Tenn., 1963; PhD, Vanderbilt U., 1968, MD, 1970; MD (hon.), U. Gsoteborg, Sweden. Instructor biology Maryville Coll., Tenn., 1963—64; MD and PhD program Vanderbilt U., 1964—70, pathology intern, 1970—71; staff Nat. Heart, Lung, and Blood Inst., NIH, Bethesda, Md., 1971—75, head, comparative atherosclerosis and arterial metabolism sect., lab. exptl. atherosclerosis, 1975—79; dir., sr. investigator Gladstone Inst. of Cardiovascular Disease, San Francisco, 1979—; prof. pathology and medicine U. Calif., San Francisco, 1979—; pres. J. David Gladstone Inst., U. Calif., San Francisco, 1992—; sr. investigator Gladstone Inst. of Neurological Disease, San Francisco, 1998—. Contbr. articles to profl. jours. Recipient Heinrich Wieland prize, George Lyman Duff Meml. Lectureship, Am. Heart Assn. award, CIBA-GEIGY award in Biomedical Rsch., Metropolitan Life award for Medical Rsch. in Alzheimer's Disease, Nat. Cholesterol Education Program DeWitt S. Goodman award for Basic Science Achievement, Distinguished Alumnus Award, Vanderbilt U. Sch. Medicine. Fellow: Am. Acad. Arts & Sciences; mem.: NAS, Am. Soc. for Clinical Investigation, Assn. Am. Physicians, IOM. Office: J David Gladstone Inst 1650 Owens St San Francisco CA 94158 Office Phone: 415-794-2000. Office Fax: 415-355-0826. Business E-Mail: rmahley@gladstone.ucsf.edu.

MAHLMAN, JERRY DAVID, retired meteorologist; b. Crawford, Nebr., Feb. 21, 1940; s. Earl Lewis and Ruth Margaret (Callendar) M.; m. Janet Kay Hilgenberg, June 10, 1962; children: Gary Martin, Julie Kay. AB, Chadron State Coll., Nebr., 1962, LHD (hon.), 2000; MS, Colo. State U., 1964, PhD, 1967. Instr. Colo. State U., Ft. Collins, 1964-67; from asst. prof. to assoc. prof. Naval Postgrad. Sch., Monterey, Calif., 1967-70; rsch. meteorologist NOAA Geophys. Fluid Dynamics Lab., Princeton, NJ, 1970-84, lab. dir., 1984-2000; lectr. with rank of prof. Princeton U., NJ, 1980—2002; sr. rsch. fellow Nat. Ctr. for Atmospheric Rsch., Boulder, Colo., 2001—. Chmn. panel on mid-atmosphere program NAS-NRC, 1982-84, mem. climate rsch. com., 1986-89, mem. panel on dynamic extended range forecasting, 1987-90; mem. U.S.-USSR Commn. on Global Ecology, 1989-92; mem. Bd. on Global Change, 1991-95, Bd. on Sustainable Devel., 1995-2000, Commn. to Review U.S. Climate Change Program Strategic Plan, 2002-03; U.S. rep. world climate rsch. program Joint Sci. Commn., 1991-96. Contbr. over 100 articles to profl. jours. Bd. dirs. Lawrence Non-Profit Housing Inc., 1978-88. Recipient Disting. Authorship award Dept. Commerce, 1980, 81, Gold medal, 1986, Disting. Svc. award Chadron State Coll., 1984, Presdl. Rank award disting. exec. 1994, Honor Alumnus award Colo. State U. 1995, Climate Protection award EPA, 2000. Fellow Am. Geophys. Union (Jule Charney lectr. 1993), Am. Meterol. Soc. (awards com. 1984, 95, chmn. 2000, chmn. upper atmosphere com. 1979, assoc. editor Jour. Atmospheric Sci. 1979-86, councilor 1991-94, Editor's award 1978, Carl-Gustaf Rossby Rsch. medal 1994, disting. lectr. 1999), Blue Key Nat. Honor Soc., Lambda Delta Lambda (life), Phi Kappa Phi (life), Sigma Delta Nu (life), Sigma Xi. Home: 460 Golden Ln Longmont CO 80501 Office: Nat Ctr for Atmospheric Rsch PO Box 300 Boulder CO 80307-3000 Business E-Mail: jmahlman@ucar.edu.

MAHLUM, DALE DUANE, state legislator, small business owner; b. Bowman, ND, June 12, 1930; s. Lloyd S. and Ragna (Paulson) M.; m. Sandra Sue Little, Dec. 21, 1956; children: Douglas, Connie, Thomas, Dee Ann, Michele. BS, U. Mont, 1956. Mgr. Super Foods, Kalispell, Mont., 1958—93; store owner Ace Hardware, Missoula, Mont., 1959-93; thoroughbred farm owner, breeder Missoula, Mont.; mem. Mont. Senate, Dist. 35, Helena, 1996—2003. Chmn. Mont. Bank Bd., Missoula, 1974—; bd. dirs. Mont. Hardware Implement, Helena, St. Patricks Hosp., Missoula; chmn. adv. bd. sch. bus U. Mont., Missoula, 1985-88. Mem. Western Mont. Fair Commn., Missoula, 1974-94. With USN, 1950-54. Mem. Mont. Thoroughbreds Breeders Assn. (pres.), Thoroughbred Owners/Breeders Assn. Republican. Lutheran. Home: 10955 Us Highway 93 N Missoula MT 59808-9227 Office: Mont Legislature PO Box 201706 Helena MT 59620-1706 Office Phone: 406-549-3115. Personal E-mail: mal51732@aol.com.

MAHONEY, DAVID L., former pharmaceutical wholesale and healthcare management company executive; b. Brighton, Mass., June 24, 1954; s. Thomas H.D. and K. Phyllis (Norton); m. Winn Canning Ellis, Sept. 26, 1992. AB in English, Princeton U., 1975; MBA, Harvard U., 1981. Asst. gen. mgr. Ogden Food Svc. Corp., LA, 1975-76, concessions mgr. East Boston, Mass., 1976-77, gen. mgr., 1977-78, ops. analyst, 1978-79; assoc. McKinsey & Co., San Francisco, 1981-86, prin., 1986-90; v.p. strategic planning McKesson Corp., San Francisco, 1990-94, pres. HDS, Inc., 1994-95, pres. pharm. svcs., 1995-97, group pres. pharm svcs. & internat. group, 1997-99; exec. v.p., CEO pharm. svcs. bus. McKesson HBOC, 1999, co-CEO, 1999-2001; CEO iMcKesson, 2000-01. Bd. dirs. Symantec Corp., Corcept Therapeutics, Tercica, Inc., KQED, Live Oak Sch., SF-MOMA, Mercy Corps. Mem.: Young Pres. Orgn. Avocations: outdoor activities, photography. Office: Pier 5 The Embracadero Ste 102 San Francisco CA 94111

MAHONEY, GERALD FRANCIS, manufacturing executive; b. Bklyn., July 31, 1943; s. Francis B. and Leona (Gray) M.; m. JoAnne A. Maselli, May 2, 1971; children: G. Scott, Ryan J. BA, Adelphi U., 1965; MBA, Northeastern U., 1966. CPA, N.Y. Mgr. Arthur Andersen & Co., NYC, 1966-73; asst. contr. Bairnco Corp., NYC, 1973-78, v.p. fin., 1980-81, gen. mgr. Pensauken, N.J., 1979-80, v.p., div. pres. Union, N.J., 1981-83; sr. v.p. fin. and adminstrn. Polychrome Corp., Yonkers, N.Y., 1984-87; pres. Transcrit Corp., Brewster, N.Y., 1987-90, Pavey Envelope & Tag Corp., Jersey City, 1991-94; chmn., CEO Mail-Well, Inc., Englewood, Colo., 1994—. Mem. AICPA, N.Y. State Soc. CPA's, Noyac Country Club (Sag Harbor, N.Y., bd. dirs. 1980-83), Glenmoor Country Club (Englewood, Colo.), Ridgewood Country Club (N.J.). Republican. Roman Catholic. Avocations: golf, tennis.

MAHONEY, JAMES E., information technology executive; BS in Info. Sys., Boise State Univ., 1981. Joined Micron Technology, Boise, Idaho, 1981, various mgmt. positions in info. sys., v.p. info. sys., 1997—. Achievements include being involved in devel. of software applications for Fab, Probe, Assembly, Test, Sales, Shipping, Fin. and Plant ops. depts. Office: VP Info Sys Micron Tech 8000 S Federal Way Boise ID 83716-9632

MAHONY, ROGER MICHAEL, cardinal, archbishop; b. Hollywood, Calif., Feb. 27, 1936; s. Victor James and Loretta Marie (Baron) Mahony. AA, Our Lady Queen of Angels Sem., 1956; BA, St. John's Sem. Coll., 1958, BST, 1962; MSW, Cath. U. Am., 1964. Ordained priest Diocese of Fresno, Calif., 1962; asst. pastor St. John's Cathedral, Fresno, Calif., 1962—64; diocesan dir. Cath. Charities and Social Svc., Fresno, 1964—70; exec. dir. Infant of Prague Adoption Svc., Cath. Welfare Bur., Fresno, 1964—70; adminstr. St. Genevieve's Parish, Fresno, Calif., 1964—67, pastor, 1967—68; asst. pastor St. John's Cathedral, Fresno, Calif., 1968—73, rector, 1973—80; chancellor Diocese of Fresno, 1970—77; ordained bishop, 1975; aux. bishop & vicar gen. Diocese of Fresno, Calif., 1975—80; bishop Diocese of Stockton, Calif., 1980—85; archbishop Archdiocese of LA, 1985—; elevated to cardinal, 1991; cardinal-priest Ss. Quattro Coronati, 1991—. Faculty extension divsn. Fresno State U., 1965—67; sec. U.S. Cath. bishops ad hoc com. on farm labor Nat. Conf. Bishops, 1970—75; chmn. com. on pub. welfare and income maintenance Nat. Conf. Cath. Charities, 1969—70; adminstrv. com. Nat. Conf. Cath. Bishops, 1976—79, 1982—85, 1987—90, 1992—95, 1998—2001, com. migration and refugees, 1976—95, chmn. com. farm labor, 1981—92, com. moral evaluation of deterrence, 1986—88, cons. com., chmn. for prolife activities, 1990—95; com. social devel. and world peace U.S. Cath. Conf., 1985—93, chmn. internat. policy sect., 1987—93; com. justice and peace Pontifical Couns., 1984—98, chmn. com. domestic policy, 1998—2001, pastoral care of migrants and itinerant people, 1986—91, social comms., 1989—. Active Mexican-Am. Coun. for Better Housing, 1968—72, Fed. Commn. Agrl. Workers, 1987—93, Urban Coalition of Fresno, Calif., 1968—72, Fresno County Econ. Opportunities Commn., Calif., 1964—65, Fresno County Alcoholic Rehab. Com., Calif., 1966—67, Fresno City Charter Rev. Com., 1968—70, Fresno Redevel. Agy., 1970—75, L.A. 2000 Com., 1985—88, Blue Ribbon Com. Affordable Housing City of L.A., LA, 1988; mem. commn. to draft an ethics code L.A. City Govt., 1989—90; trustee St. Agnes Hosp., Fresno, 1969—73, Cath. U. Am., 1984—88, 1998—; named chaplain to Pope Paul VI, 1967; chaplain St. Vincent de Paul Soc., 1964—70; bd. dirs. West Coast Regional Office Bishops Com. for Spanish-Speaking, 1967—70; chmn. Calif. Assn. Cath. Charities Dirs., 1965—69; trustee St. Patrick's Sem., Archdiocese of San Francisco, 1974—75; bd. dirs. Fresno Cmty. Workshop, 1965—67, Rebuild L.A., 1992—95. Named Young Man of Yr., Fresno Jr. C. of C., 1967. Mem.: Canon Law Soc. Roman Catholic. Office: Archdiocese LA 3424 Wilshire Blvd Los Angeles CA 90010-2241

MAIER, DAVID EUGENE, computer science educator; b. Eugene, Oreg., June 2, 1953; BA in Math. and Computer Sci., U. Oreg., 1974; PhD in Elec. Engring. and Computer Sci., Princeton U., 1978. Asst. prof. dept. computer sci. SUNY, Stony Brook, 1978-82; asst. prof. dept. computer sci. and engring. Oreg. Grad. Inst., Portland, 1982-83, assoc. prof. dept. computer sci. and engring., 1983-88, prof., 1988—, acting chair, 1988. Vis. scientist GIP Altair-Inst. Nat. de Rsch. en Informatique et an Automatique, Rocquencourt, France, 1989-90; vis. prof. computer scis. dept. U. Wis., Madison, 1997-98; organizer and mem. arrangements com. various confs. and workshops; cons. and presenter in field. Author: The Theory of Relational Databases, 1983, (with D.S. Warren) Computing with Logic: Introduction to Logic Programming, 1988, Query Processing for Advanced Database Systems, 1993, Persistent Object Systems, 1995; contbr. chpts. to books and articles to profl. jours. Recipient NSF Presdl. Young Investigator award, 1984-89, Innovations award Assn. Computing Machinery/Spl. Interest Group Mgmt. Data, 1997; grantee Dept. Energy Emergency Info. Mgmt. Sys., 1979, NSF, 1979-82, 81-83, 82-84, 82-84, 86-88, 88-90, 89-91, 91-94, 92-95, 93-95, 97-99, Tektronix Computer Rsch. Lab., 1983-86, Tektronix Info. Display Group, 1984-85, Microelectronics and Computer Tech. Corp., 1985-87, Apple Computer, 1988-89, Battelle Pacific N.W. Labs., 1991-92, 91, 92, 93-94, 93, 94, Sequent Computer Sys., 1991, DARPA, 1991-94, 96-99, Office Naval Rsch., 1996-99, U.S. West Advanced Techs., 1992, others; Univ. Awards Com. fellow SUNY, 1979. Fellow Assn. for Computing Machinery. Office: Data Intensive Sys Ctr Computer Sci & Engring Dept PO Box 91000 Portland OR 97291-1000

MAIER, GERALD JAMES, gas industry executive; b. Regina, Sask., Can., Sept. 22, 1928; s. John Joseph and Mary M. Student, Notre Dame Coll., Wilcox, U. Man., U. Alta., U. Western Ont.; LLD (hon.), U. Alta., 1999; LLD, U. Calgary, 2005. With petroleum and mining industries Can., U.S., Australia, U.K.; responsible for petroleum ops. Africa, United Arab Emirates, S.E. Asia; past chmn., pres., CEO TransCan. PipeLines, Calgary, Canada, 1985-99; vice-chmn. NOVA Chems. Corp., Calgary, 1998-2000. Chmn. Can. Nat. Com. for World Petroleum Congresses, 1991—94, Van Horne Inst. for Internat. Transp., 1992—2000; bd. dirs. Stream-Flo Industries, Ltd., 1998—, Master Flo Valve Inc., 1998—, Bow Valley Energy Ltd., 2006—, GEM Inc., 2006—, Willbros Group, Inc., 2007—. Chmn. bd. dirs. Notre Dame Coll. Named Hon. Col. (ret.) King's Own Calgary Rgt., Resource Man of Yr. Alta. Chamber of Resources, 1990, Officer Order of Can., 2004; named to Can. Petroleum Hall of Fame, 1999; recipient Can. Engr.'s Gold medal Can. Coun. Profl. Engrs., 1990, Disting. Alumni award U. Alta., 1992, Mgmt. award McGill U., 1993, Centennial award Alta. Assn. Engrs., Geologists and Geophysicists, 1994, Hal Godwin award U. Calgary, 1999, Can. Bus. Leader award U. Alta., 1999, Can. Engring. Leader award U. Calgary, 2003, Alta. Centennial medal, 2005. Fellow Can. Acad. Engring.; mem. Assn. Profl. Engrs., Geologists and Geophysicists Alta. (past pres.), Can. Inst. Mining and Metallurgy (Past Pres.'s Meml. medal 1971), Legion of Honour, Soc. Petroleum Engr. (mem. CDN sect. 2006). Avocations: golf, downhill skiing, shooting, fishing. Office: Granmar Investments Ltd 88 Massey Pl SW Calgary AB Canada T2V 2G8

MAIER, PAUL VICTOR, pharmaceutical executive; b. Seattle, Nov. 6, 1947; s. Norman Alvin and Rosalie (Godek) M.; m. Shirley Diehl, Aug. 11, 1979. BS, Pa. State U., 1969; MBA, Harvard U., 1975. Fin. analyst Greyhound Corp, Phoenix, 1975-76; asst. mgr. Wells Service Wells Fargo Bank, San Francisco, 1976-78; v.p. Fin. Cummins Service and Sales, Los Angeles, 1978-84; v.p., treas. ICN Pharms, Inc., Costa Mesa, Calif., 1984-90; v.p. fin. DFS West, 1990-92; sr. v.p., CFO Ligand Pharmaceuticals, Inc., San Diego, 1992—. Chmn. audit com. Entropin Inc., 2000—, also bd. dirs. Chmn. hosp. div. United Way Region V, L.A., 1983-84; bd. dirs. The Wellness Community, San Diego, 1993-2003. Served with USNR, 1969-95. Mem. Fin. Execs. Inst., The Athletic Congress, Pa. State Club of S.D., Harvard Bus. Sch. Assn. So. Calif., Ctr. for Non-Profit Mgmt., Vis. Nurse Assn. L.A. (bd. dirs. 1979-92, chmn.), Protection Mut. Inst. (West Coast adv. bd. 1985-90). Republican. Roman Catholic. Office: Ligand Pharmaceuticals 10275 Science Center Dr San Diego CA 92121-1117 E-mail: pmaier@ligand.com.

MAIER, RONALD VITT, surgeon, educator; b. Wheeling, W.Va., Oct. 23, 1947; BS, U. Notre Dame, 1969; MD, Duke U., 1973. Intern Parkland Meml. Hosp., Dallas, 1973-74; resident U. Wash. Hosps., Seattle, 1974-78; rsch. assoc. Scripps Rsch. Found., La Jolla, Calif., 1978-81; surgeon-in-chief HMC, Seattle, 1993—; vice chair U. Wash., Seattle, 1994—, Jane and Donald D. Trunkey prof., 2005—. Office: Dept Surgery 359796 Harborview Med Ctr 325 9th Ave Seattle WA 98104-2499 Office Phone: 206-744-3564. Business E-Mail: ronmaier@u.washington.edu.

MAIER, STEPHEN JOHN, college president; b. Newburgh, NY, Apr. 23, 1946; s. Gerard G. and Esther (Brandow) M.; m. Edre Jane Maier, Sept. 5, 1970. BA, St. Lawrence U., 1968; MS, SUNY, 1970; EdD, U. Colo., 1974. Dean student svcs. Miles Community Coll., Miles City, Mont., 1974-78; dean instrn. N.Mex. J.C., Hobbs, 1978-88; pres. No. Wyo. Community Coll. Dist., Sheridan, 1988—. Mem. commn. on small/rural community colls. Mem. Econ. Devel. Com., Sheridan, 1991—. Mem. C. of C. (dir. 1990—), Rotary (Sheridan chpt.). Avocations: soaring, soccer, fishing, skiing. Office: Sheridan Coll Office Pres PO Box 1500 Sheridan WY 82801

MAIN, ROBERT GAIL, communications educator, training services executive, television and film producer, retired military officer; b. Bucklin, Mo., Sept. 30, 1932; s. Raymond M. and Inez L. (Olinger) M.; m. Anita Sue Thoroughman, Jan. 31, 1955; children: Robert Bruce, David Keith, Leslie Lorraine. BS magna cum laude, U. Mo., 1954; grad. with honors, Army Commd. Gen. Staff Coll., 1967; MA magna cum laude in Comm., Stanford U., Calif., 1968; PhD, U. Md., 1978. Commd. 2d lt. US Army, 1954, advanced through grades to lt. col., 1968; mem. faculty Army Commd. Gen. Staff Coll., 1968-70; chief speechwriting and info. materials divsn. US Army Info. Office, 1971, chief broadcast and film divsn., 1972-73; dir. def. audiovisual activities Office of Info. for Armed Forces, 1973-76; ret., 1976; prof. instrnl. tech. Calif. State U., Chico, 1976—, dept. chair, 1993-98, prof. emeritus. Cons. in field. Author: Rogues, Saints and Ordinary People, 1988; prodr. (TV documentary) Walking Wounded, 1983, Army Info. Films, Army Radio Series, 1972-73; contbr. articles on computer based tng. and telecoms. to scientific and profl. jours. Decorated Legion of Merit, Meritorious Svc. medal, Commendation medal with oak leaf cluster, combat Inf. Badge; Vietnamese Cross of Gallantry; recipient Freedom Found. awards, 1972, 73, 74; Bronze medal Atlanta Film Festival, 1972; Best of Show award Balt. Film Festival, 1973; Creativity award Chgo. Indsl. Film Festival, 1973; Cine gold award Internat. Film Prodrs. Assn., 1974; named an Outstanding Prof. Calif. State U., 1987-88. Mem. Phi Eta Sigma, Alpha Zeta, Phi Delta Gamma, Omicron Delta Kappa, Alpha Gamma Rho. Personal E-mail: rmain75@aol.com.

MAINWARING, WILLIAM LEWIS, publishing company executive, author; b. Portland, Oreg., Jan. 17, 1935; s. Bernard and Jennie (Lewis) M.; m. Mary E. Bell, Aug. 18, 1962; children: Anne Marie, Julia Kathleen, Douglas Bernard. BS, U. Oreg., 1957; postgrad., Stanford U., 1957-58. With Salem (Oreg.) Capital Jour., 1958-76, editor, pub., 1962-76; pub. Oreg. Statesman, 1974-76; pres. Statesman-Jour. Co., Inc., Salem, 1974-76, Westridge Press, Ltd., 1977—, MediAmerica, Inc., Portland, 1981-96, CEO, 1988—91. Bd. dirs. MediAmerica, Inc. Author: Exploring the Oregon Coast, 1977, Exploring Oregon's Central and Southern Cascades, 1979, Exploring the Mount Hood Loop, 1992, Government, Oregon-Style, 1996, rev. edit., 1997, 99. Pres. Salem Beautification Coun., 1968, Marion-Polk County United Good Neighbors, 1970, Salem Social Svcs. Commn., 1978-79, Salem Hosp. Found., 1978-81, Marion Hist. Found., 2002-03. 2d lt. AUS, 1958; capt. Res. Ret. Mem. Salem Area C. of C. (pres. 1972-73), Oreg. Symphony Soc. Salem (pres. 1973-75), Salem City Club (pres. 1977-78), Sigma Chi. Republican. Presbyterian. Home and Office: 1090 Southridge Pl S Salem OR 97302-5947

MAISEL, DAVID, entertainment company executive; b. 1961; Mgr. entertainment and media practice The Boston Cons. Group; with Creative Artists Agy.; dir. corp. devel. and strategic planning The Walt Disney Co.; pres. Livent, Inc.; mng. dir. Chello Broadband, 1999—2001; head corp. strategy and bus. devel. Endeavor Talent Agy., 2001—03; pres., COO Marvel Studios, 2004—05, vice chmn., 2005—07, chmn., 2007—; exec. v.p. corp. devel., Office Chief Exec. Marvel Entertainment Inc., 2005—. Office: Marvel Studios 1600 Rosecrans Ave # 7A Manhattan Beach CA 90266-3708

MAISEL, SHERMAN JOSEPH, economist, educator; b. Buffalo, July 8, 1918; s. Louis and Sophia (Beck) M.; m. Lucy Cowdin, Sept. 26, 1942; children: Lawrence C., Margaret L. AB, Harvard U., Cambridge, Mass., 1939, MPA, 1947, PhD, 1949. Mem. bd. govs. FRS, 1965-72; economist, fgn. service res. officer Dept. State, 1945-46; teaching fellow Harvard U., 1947-48; asst. prof., assoc. prof., prof. bus. adminstrn. U. Calif. at Berkeley, 1948-65, 72-86; sr. economist Nat. Bur. Econ. Research-West, 1973-78; chmn., bd. dirs. Farmers Savings & Loan, 1986-88; pres. Sherman J. Maisel & Asscs. Inc., 1986—. Fellow Fund For Advancement Edn., 1952-53, Inst. Basic Math. with Application to Bus., 1959-60, Center for Advanced Study in Behavioral Scis., 1972; mem. adv. coms. to Bur. Census, FHA, State of Calif., Ford Found., Social Sci. Research Council; mem. bldg. research adv. bd. NRC. Author: Housebuilding in Transition, 1953, Fluctuations, Growth, and Forecasting, 1957, Managing the Dollar, 1973, Real Estate Investment and Finance, 1976, Risk and Capital Adequacy in Commercial Banks, 1981, Macroeconomics: Theories and Policies, 1982, Real Estate Finance, 1987, 2d edit., 1992. Bd. dirs. Berkeley Unified Sch. Dist., 1962-65. Served to capt. AUS, 1941-45. Recipient citation, U. Calif., Berkeley, 1986. Fellow Am. Fin. Assn. (pres. 1973); mem. Am. Econ. Assn. Home: 2164 Hyde St San Francisco CA 94109-1788 Office: U Calif Haas Bus Sch Berkeley CA 94720-1900

MAJOR, CLARENCE LEE, writer, painter, poet, educator; b. Atlanta, Dec. 31, 1936; s. Clarence and Inez (Huff) M.; m. Pamela Ritter, May 8, 1980. BS, SUNY, Albany; PhD, Union Inst. Prof. U. Colo., Boulder, 1977-89, U. Calif., Davis, 1989—. Author: All-Night Visitors, 1969, 2d version, 1998, Dictionary of Afro-American Slang, 1970, No, 1973, Reflex and Bone Structure, 1975, rev. edit., 1996, Emergency Exit, 1979, My Amputations, 1986, Such Was the Season, 1987, Painted Turtle: Woman with Guitar, 1988, Fun and Games, 1990, Calling the Wind, 1993, Juba to Jive: A Dictionary of African American Slang, 1994, Dirty Bird Blues, 1996; poetry: Swallow the Lake, 1970 (Nat. Coun. on the Arts award 1970), Symptoms & Madness, 1971, Private Line, 1971, The Cotton Club, 1972, Inside Diameter: The France Poems, 1985, Surfaces and Masks, 1988, Some Observations of a Stranger at Zuni in the Latter Part of the Century, 1989, Parking Lots, 1992, The Garden Thrives, 1996, Configurations: New and Selected Poems, 1958-1998, 1998 (Nat. Book Award Bronze medal 1999), Clarence Major and His Art: Portraits of an African American Postmodernist, 2001, Necessary Distance, 2001, Come By Here: My Mother's Life, 2002, Waiting for Sweet Betty, 2002, Conversations with Clarence Major, 2002, One Flesh, 2003, Myself Painting, 2008; one man shows include Kresge Mus., Mich., 2001, Hamilton Club Gallery, Paterson, NJ, 2006-07; group shows include Schacknow Mus. Fine Art, Plantation, Fla., 2003, Exploding Head Gallery, Calif., 2003-06; contbr. articles to Washington Post Book World, L.A. Times Book Rev., N.Y. Times Book Rev. Recipient Nat. Council on Arts award, Washington, 1970; Western States Book award, Western States Found., Santa Fe, 1986; Fulbright grantee, 1981-83. Office: Univ Calif Dept English 351 Voorhies Hall Davis CA 95616

MAJOR, JOHN CHARLES, judge; s. William and Elsie M.; m. Hélène Provencher, 1959; children: Suzan, Peter, Paul, Steven. BComm, Loyola Coll., Montreal, 1953; LLB, U. Toronto, 1957, LLD (hon.), 2005, Concordia U., 2003, U. Calgary, 2005. Bar: Alta. 1958, Queen's Counsel, 1972. With Bennett, Jones & Verchere, Calgary, 1957-91, sr. ptnr., 1967; sr. counsel City of Calgary Police Svc., 1975-85; counsel McDonald Commn., 1978-82; sr. counsel Province of Alta., 1987, Alta. Ct. Appeal, 1991; justice Supreme Ct. of Can., Ottawa, Ont., Canada, 1992—95. Fellow: Am. Coll. Trial Lawyers. Avocation: golf. Office: Bennett Jones LLP 4500 855-2 Str SW Calgary AB Canada T2P 4K7 Office Phone: 403-298-3166. Business E-Mail: majorj@bennettjones.ca.

MAKEPEACE, MARY LOU, foundation administrator, former mayor; 2 children. BA in Journalism, U. ND, 1962; MPA, U. Colo., Colorado Springs, 1980. Tchr. Am. Sch., Tananarive, Madagascar; asst. to Def. Attaché Am. Embassy, Prague, Czechoslavakia; adult edn. officer Ramstein AFB, Germany; case worker, adminstr. El Paso County Dept. Social Svcs., 1974-82; exec. dir. Cmty. Coun. Pikes Peak Region, 1982-84; dist. 1 rep. City Colorado Springs, 1985-97, vice mayor, 1997, mayor, 1997—2003; exec. dir. Leadership Pike's Peak, Colo. Springs, 2003—04, Gill Found. Gay and Lesbian Fund, Colo., 2004—. Exofficio mem. Econ. Devel. Coun. Bd. Dirs.; chair Econ. Devel. Com., Task Force City Svcs. to Srs., urban affairs com. Pikes Peak Area Coun. Govts.; apptd. Colo. Space Adv. Coun.; adj. prof. U. Colo.; ex-dir. leadership Pikes Peak Mem. steering com. Imagination Celebration; sr. advisor Palmer Found., Pikes Peak Partnership; mem. Nat. League Cities Leadership Tng. Coun.; past mem. Colo. Mcpl. League Exec. Bd., 1st United Meth. Ch. Gates Found. fellow, 1992; recipient Svc. Mankind award Centennial Sertoma Club, 1985, Mary Jean Larson Cmty. Svc. award Girl Scouts Wagon Wheel Coun., 2002, Spence Vanderlin Pub. Ofcl. award Am. Pub. Power Assn., 2002, Outstanding Cmty. award Econ. Devel. Corp., 2003; named Super Woman Women's Health Ctr., 1988, Best City Councilmem. Springs Mag., 1991; honored Women in Your Life dinner Women's Found. Colo., 2002. Mem. Am. Soc. Pub. Adminstrn., Pi Alpha Alpha. Personal E-mail: maryloum@gillfoundation.org.

MALA, THEODORE ANTHONY, physician, consultant; b. Santa Monica, Calif., Feb. 3, 1946; s. Ray and Galina (Liss) M.; children: Theodore S., Galina T.; 1 adopted child, Christine A. Lindholm. BA in Philosophy, DePaul U., 1972; MD, Autonomous U., Guadalajara, Mex., 1976; MPH, Harvard U., 1980. Spl. asst. for health affairs Alaska Fedn. Natives, Anchorage, 1977-78; chief health svcs. Alaska State Divsn. Corrections, Anchorage, 1978-79; assoc. prof., founder, dir. Inst. for Circumpolar Health Studies, U. Alaska, Anchorage, 1982-90; founder Siberian med. rsch. program U. Alaska, Anchorage, 1982, founder Magadan (USSR) med. rsch. program, 1988; commr. Health and Social Svcs. State of Alaska, Juneau, 1990-93; pres., CEO Ted Mala, Inc., Anchorage, 1993-97; pres., ptnr. Mexican-Siberian Trading Co., Monterrey, Mex., 1994-96; CEO, Confederated Tribes of Grand Ronde, Oreg., 1998-99; dir. tribal rels. Southcentral Found., Anchorage, 1999—, 2000—. Traditional healing dir. Southcentral Found., Anchorage, 2000—; Alaska rsch. and publs. com. Indian Health Svc., USPHS, 1987-90; advisor Nordic Coun. Meeting, WHO, Greenland, 1985; mem. Internat. Organizing Com., Circumpolar Health Congress, Iceland, 1992-93; chmn. bd. govs. Alaska Psychiat. Inst., Anchorage, 1990-93; cabinet mem. Gov. Walter J. Hickel, Juneau, 1990-93; advisor humanitarian aid to Russian Far East U.S. Dept. State, 1992-96; cons. USAID on U.S.-Russian Health Programs, 1994; apptd. adv. com. Sec. of Health and Human Svc. on Minority Health for the U.S., 2000—; mem. coun. pub. reps. NIH, 2002-05. Past columnist Tundra Times; contbr. articles to profl. jours. Trustee United Way Anchorage, 1978-79; chmn. bd. trustees Alaska Native Coll., 1993-96. Recipient Gov.'s award, 1988, Outstanding Svc. award Alaska Commr. Health, 1979, Ministry of Health citation USSR Govt., 1989, Citation award Alaska State Legislature, 1989-90, 94, Commendation award State of Alaska, 1990, Alaska State Legislature, 1994, Honor Kempton Svc. to Humanity award, 1989, citation Med. Comty. of Magadan region, USSR, 1989; named Physician of Yr. Nat. Assn. Am. Indian Physicians, 2008; Nat. Indian fellow U.S. Dept. Edn., 1979. Mem. Assn. Am. Indian Physicians (pres.), N.Y. Acad. Scis., Internat. Union for Circumpolar Health (permanent sec.-gen. 1987-90, organizing com. 8th Internat. Congress on Circumpolar Health 1987-90), Russian Acad. Polar Medicine (elected). Avocations: cross country skiing, hiking, photography, travel. Office Phone: 907-729-4955. E-mail: tmala@post.harvard.edu.

MALAMUTH, NEIL MOSHE, psychology and communication educator; BA in Psychology summa cum laude, UCLA, 1972, MA in Psychology, 1972, PhD in Social Psychology and Personality, 1975. Lectr. dept. psychology, UCLA and postdoctoral fellow Ctr. for Behavioral Therapy, Beverly Hills, Calif., 1975-77; asst. prof. psychology U. Man., Winnipeg, Can., 1977-80, assoc. prof., 1980-82; prof. comm. and psychology, chairperson dept. comm. U. Mich., Ann Arbor, 1991-94; tchg. asst. dept. psychology UCLA, 1971-73, rsch. assoc. Ctr. for Computer-Based Behavioral Studies, 1973-75, assoc. prof., 1982-86, assoc. dir. Ctr. for Study of Women, 1986-87, prof. comm. and psychology, 1982-91, 94—, chairperson comm. studies program and speech dept., 1984-91, 94—. Vis. scholar Stanford (Calif.) U., fall 1988; mem. rev. com. on violence and stress NIMH, 1989-93; Lady Davis sr. fellow Hebrew U. Jerusalem, spring 1995; participant leadership inst. Freedom Forum, Columbia U., summer 1992; participant workshop for deans and chairpersons Annenberg Programs, Washington, winter 1993; presenter various profl. and ednl. confs., most recently Oakland (Mich.) U., 1994, Nat. Assn. for Devel. of Work with Sex Offenders, Durham (Eng.) U., 1994, Soc. for Sci. Study of Sex., Miami, Fla., 1994, Ctr. for Study of Evolution and Origins of Life, UCLA, 1994, Ctr. for Evolutionary Psychology, Santa Barbara, Calif., 1995, Tel Aviv U., 1995, Bar-Ilan U., Israel, 1995, Hebrew U. Jerusalem, 1995, NRC, Washington, 1995, Soc. Exptl. Social Psychology, Washington, 1995, Nat. Assn. for Treatment of Sexual Aggression, New Orleans, 1995, Polish Nat. Acad. Sci., Warsaw U., 1995. Co-author: An Instructor's Manual and Guide for Teaching a Course in Social Psychology, 1976, Pornography, 1993; co-editor Sites and Insights in Psychology, 1976; co-editor, contbr. chpt. to: Pornography and Sexual Aggression, 1984, Sex, Power, Conflict: Evolutionary Feminist Perspectives, 1996; contbr. chpt. to: Aggression in Children and Youth, 1984, Handbook of Research on Rape and Sexual Assault, 1984, Media Violence and Pornography: An International Perspective, 1984, The psychology of Women: Ongoing Debates, 1987, Public Communication and Behavior, Vol. 2, 1989; contbr. or co-contbr. various chpts., also numerous articles; mem. editl. bd. Motivation and Emotion, 1983-89, Comm. Rsch., 1986-92, Jour. Sex Rsch., 1982-99, Sexual Abuse: A Jour. and Treatment, 1995-99; assoc. editor Comm. Concepts Series, 1989-98, Jour. Rsch. in Personality, 1990-93; co-editor issue Jour. Social Issues, 1986. Recipient John Kendall award for Outstanding Contbns. to Psychology, Gustavus Coll., Minn., 1987; rsch. grantee Social Sci. and Humanities Rsch. Coun. Can., 1979-81, NIMH, 1986-89, 89-91, 91-92; named one of 7 scholars among top 100 rschrs. in 4 categories of eminence Personality and Social Psychology Bull., 1992. Fellow APA, Am. Psychol. Soc.; mem. Internat. Comm. Assn. (presenter 1994, Top 5 Conf. Paper award mass comm. divsn. 1987), Internat. Soc. for Rsch. on Aggression, Soc. for Psychol. Study of Social Issues, Soc. for Sci. Study of Sex, Phi Beta Kappa. Office: UCLA Comm Studies Program 334 Kinsey Hall Los Angeles CA 90095-0001

MALCOLM, DAWN GRACE, family physician; b. LA, Nov. 3, 1936; d. Thomas N. and Grace S. (Salisian) M. BA, UCLA, 1959; MD, Med. Coll. Pa., 1973. Diplomate Am. Bd. Family Practice. Tchr. elem. music Fullerton (Calif.) Sch. Dist., 1960-61; tchr. Ahlman Acad., Kabul, Afghanistan, 1961-65; intern and resident in family practice Kaiser Found. Hosp., LA, 1973-76; family physician So. Calif. Permanente Med. Group, LA, 1976—. Mem. faculty family practice residency program Kaiser Found. Hosp., L.A., 1976—. Fellow Am. Acad. Family Physicians.

MALCOLM, GAROLD DEAN, architect; b. Belle Fouche, SD, Apr. 25, 1940; s. Gifford Garold Malcolm and Ellen Eve Liming; m. Breta Lois Bailey, 1966 (div. 1982); children: Heather Marie, Allison Clare; m. Lucia Eagon Stenson, 1991. BArch, U. Oreg., 1966. Ptnr. McAdoo, Malcolm & Youel, Architects, 1981—. Prin. works include Creston-Nelson Elec. Substation, Seattle (Honor award Wash. Aggregates and Concrete Assn.), Arboretum Visitor's Ctr., Seattle (Honor award Builders Community Awards Program, People's Choice award Seattle chpt. AIA), Des Moines (Wash.) Libr., Queen Anne Swimming Pool, Seattle. Mem. AIA, Matsumura Kenpo Karate Assn. (black belt). Office: McAdoo Malcolm & Youel Architects 1718 E Olive Way Seattle WA 98102-5683

MALDONADO, ABEL, state legislator; b. Santa Maria, Calif. m to Laura; children: Erika, Nicholas & Marcus. BS in Crop Sci., Calif. Polytechnic State U., San Luis Obispo. Councilman, Santa Maria, 94-96, mayor, 96-98; California State Assemblyman, District 33, 99-2004, vice chairman, Agriculture Committee, 99-2004, member, Appropriations, Budget, Govt Organization & Transportation Committees, Budget Subcomt, 99-2004, California State Assembly; California State Senator, District 15, 2004-. United Way Cent Coast; Santa Maria Kiwanis; Santa Maria Valley Chamber of Commerce; California Strawberry Comn; Santa Barbara Co Association of Govt; Santa Maria Valley Econ Develop Association. Republican. Office: State Capitol Rm 4082 Sacramento CA 95841 also: 100 Paseo de San Antonio Ste 206 San Jose CA 95113 also: Dist 15 1356 Marsh St San Luis Obispo CA 93401 Office Phone: 805-549-3784. Office Fax: 805-549-3779. Business E-Mail: Senator.Maldonado@senate.ca.gov.*

MALDONADO, GREGORY MATTHEW, music director, educator; b. Merced, Calif., June 8, 1958; s. Daniel Robert and Elaine Louise (Turrey) M. MusB, UCLA, 1990. Music dir., founder L.A. Baroque Orch., 1986—; mem. faculty U. So. Calif., 1988-97; instr. in Baroque violin UCLA, 1989-91. Founder, music dir. La Stravaganza, L.A., Eroica String Quar., L.A., L.A. Fortepiano Trio, L.A. Supporter Greenpeace Internat., San Francisco, 1989, Pesticide Watch, L.A., 1990—. Mem. So. Calif. Early Music Soc. Avocations: travel, hiking, films. Home: 2844 Avenel St Los Angeles CA 90039-2071

MALDONADO, KIRK FRANCIS, lawyer; b. Omaha, Mar. 7, 1950; s. Manuel and Orpha Mae (Kovar) Maldonado. BA, U. Nebr.-Omaha, 1975; JD, Creighton U., 1978; MLT, Georgetown U., 1981. Bar: Nebr. 1978, Calif. 1982. Atty. Employee Plans and Exempt Orgns. Divsn. Office of Chief Counsel IRS, Washington, 1978—81; assoc. Gibson, Dunn & Crutcher, Newport Beach, Calif., 1982—85; prin. Stradling, Yocca, Carlson & Rauth, Newport Beach, 1985—89, Riordan & McKinzie, Costa Mesa, Calif., 1989—2001; ptnr. Bobeck Phleger & Harrison LLP, 2001—03; mem. Sherman & Howard, LLC, Denver, 2003—. Contbr. articles to profl. jours. Mem.: ABA (employee benfits com.), State Bar Calif. Office: Sherman & Howard LLC 633 17th St Ste 3000 Denver CO 80202 E-mail: kmaldonado@sah.com.

MALECHEK, JOHN CHARLES, ecology and range science educator; b. San Angelo, Tex., Aug. 6, 1942; BS, Tex. Tech. U., 1964; MS, Colo. State U., 1966; PhD in Range Sci., Tex. A&M U., 1970. From asst. prof. to assoc. prof. Utah State U., Logan, 1970-82, prof. range sci., 1982—, head rangeland & resources. dept., 1986—. Mem. Am. Soc. Animal Sci., Soc. Range Mgmt. Office: Utah State U Dept Rangeland & Resources 5320 Old Main Hl Logan UT 84322-0001

MALENKA, ROBERT C., psychiatrist, educator; b. Boston, June 21, 1955; PhD in Neuroscis., MD, Stanford U., 1983. Resident in psychiatry Stanford Sch. Medicine; postdoctoral work U. Calif., San Francisco, asst. prof. psychiatry and physiology, prof. psychiatry and physiology; dir. Ctr. for Neurobiology of Addiction; assoc. dir. Ctr. for Neurobiology and Psychiatry; Pritzker prof. psychiatry and behavioral scis., dir. Pritzker Lab. Stanford U. Sch. Medicine, 1999—; lectr. in field. Scientific adv. bd. Renovis, Inc., 2000—, Merck, Inc., 2000—; Wendy and Stanley Marsh lectr., 2002. Mem. editl. bd. jours.:; co-author: (textbook) Molecular Neuropharmacology: A Foundation for Clinical Neuroscience, 2001; contbr. articles to profl. jours. Mem. Nat. Adv. Coun. on Drug Abuse. Recipient Alfred P. Sloan rsch. fellowship, 1990, Young Investigator award, Nat. Alliance for Rsch. in Schizophrenia and Depression, 1990, 1992, Scholars award in neurosci., McKnight Endowment Fund for Neurosci., 1990, Investigator award in neurosci., 1997, Soc. for Neurosci. Young Investigator award, 1993, Daniel H. Efron award, Am. Coll. Neuropsychopharmacology, 1998, Dargut and Milena Kemali Found. Internat. prize in neurosci., 2000, MERIT award, NIMH, 2001—11, Basic Neuroscience Rsch. award, Collegium Internationale Neuropsychopharmacologicum, 2002. Mem.: Am. Acad. Arts & Sciences, Inst. Medicine, Soc. for Neurosci. (program com.). Office: Stanford U Sch Medicine Psychiatry and Behavioral Scis MSLS P104 Mail Code 5485 Stanford CA 94305-5485 E-mail: malenka@stanford.edu.

MALICK, TERRENCE (DAVID WHITNEY II), film director; b. Waco, Tex., Nov. 30, 1943; m. Jill Jakes (div. 1978); m. Michele Malick, 1985 (div. 1998); m. Alexandra Wallace, 1998. Student, Harvard U., Oxford U.; MFA, Am. Film Inst. Dir., prodr., writer (films) Badlands, 1973 (Golden Seashell award 1974); dir., writer, Lanton Mills, 1969, Days of Heaven, 1978 (Best Dir. award Cannes Film Festival 1979, nominee Golden Globe award 1979, N.Y. Film Critics Circle award 1978), The Thin Red Line, 1998 (Acad. award nomination for Best Dir., Golden Berlin Bear award 1999, Chgo. Film Critics Assn. award 1999, Golden Satellite award, 1999), The New World, 2005; prodr. (films) Endurance, 1999, The Endurance, Shackleton's Legendary Antartic Expedition, 2000, Happy Times, 2001, The Beautiful Country, 2004, Undertow, 2004, Amazing Grace, 2006, The Unforseen, 2007; writer (films) Drive, He Said, 1971, Deadhead Miles, 1972, Pocket Money, 1972, The Gravy Train, 1974, Bear's Kiss, 2002

MALIK, OM PARKASH, electrical engineering educator, researcher; b. Sargodha, Punjab, India, Apr. 20, 1932; arrived in Can., 1966; s. Arjan Dass and Kesar Bai (Ahuja) M.; m. Margareta Fagerstrom, Dec. 22, 1968; children: Ola Parkash, Mira, Maya. Nat. Diploma in Elec. Engring., Delhi Poly., India, 1952; M in Engring., Roorkee U., India, 1962; PhD, London U., 1965; D.I.C., Imperial Coll., London, 1966. Registered profl. engr., Ont., Alta. Asst. engr. Punjab State Elec. Bd., 1953-61, asst. to chief engr., 1957-59; rsch. engr. English Elec. Co., England, 1965-66; asst. prof. U. Windsor, Ont., Canada, 1966-68; assoc. prof. U. Calgary, Alta., Canada, 1968-74, prof. Alta., 1974-97, faculty prof. Alta., 1997—2000, assoc. dean student affairs, faculty engring. Alta., 1995-98, assoc. acad. dean faculty engring. Alta., 1979-90, acting dean Alta., 1981, prof. emeritus Alta., 1997—. Cons. prof. Huazhong U. Sci. and Tech., Wuhan,

People's Republic China, 1986—; chief judge Can. Wide Sci. Fair, 2003; hon. prof. Tech. U. Cluj-Napoca, Romania, 2007—. Assoc. editor Can. Elec. and Computer Engring. Jour., 1988-97, mng. editor, 1998-2003; contbr. 700 articles to profl. jours. Indsl. tng. scholar Govt. India, 1952-53, sr. indsl. tng. scholar Confedn. Brit. Industries, 1959-60; recipient vol. svc. award APEGGA, 1990, Rsch. Excellence award Elec. and Computer Engring. Dept. U. Calgary, 1996, Can. Pacific Rwy. engring. medal Engring. Inst. Can., 1997, Disting. Lifetime Leadership award Faculty Engring. U. Calgary, 2001, Alberta Ingenuity Fund Rsch. Excellence award, 2002, L. C. Charlesworth Profl. Svc. award, APECGA, 2008; admitted Order of U. Calgary, 2006. Fellow IEEE (life, chmn. life mems. com. 2004-05, chmn. Western Can. coun. 1983-84, chmn. student activities Can. region 1979-82, chmn. life mems. com., mem. Found., Can. pres. elect 2008-, dir. Can. Found. 2005-, Centennial medal 1984, Western Can. Coun. Merit award 1986, Third Millennium medal 2000, A.G.L. McNaughton award 2001), Inst. Elec. Engrs., Can. Acad. Engring., World Innovation Found.; mem. IEEE Power Engring. Soc. (electric machinery com. 2002-, vice chmn. 2006-2007, chair 2008-, machine theory subcom. 1979-2004, excitation sys. subcom. 1988—, chmn. 2004-2007, sys. dynamic performance com. 1988-, energy devel. and power generation com. mem. 1990-, vice chmn. 2009-, sect. 2007-08), Assn. Profl. Engrs., Geologists and Geophysicists Alta. (Vol. Svc. award 1990, Alta. Ingenuity Rsch. Excellence award), Assn. Profl. Engrs. Ont., Am. Soc. Engring. Edn., Can. Elec. Assn. (assoc., controls com. 1977-92, chmn. digital control com. 1977-85, chmn. edn. com. 1983-85, mem. expert sys. com. 1989-94), Confederacion Panamericana de Ingenieria Mecanica, Electica y Ramas Afines (v.p. 1987-00, bd. dirs. region I, 1991-93), U. Calgary Emeritus Assn. (v.p. 2002-03, pres. 2003-04), Internat. Fed. Automatic Control (chmn. power plants and power sys. control commn. 2002-08). Hindu. Home: 4 6841 Coach Hill Rd SW Calgary AB Canada T3H 3T9 Office: U Calgary Dept Elec & Computer Engring 2500 University Dr NW Calgary AB Canada T2N 1N4 Home Phone: 403-217-6412; Office Phone: 403-220-6178. Personal E-mail: maliko@ucalgary.ca.

MALINS, DONALD CLIVE, biochemist, researcher; b. Lima, Peru, May 19, 1931; came to U.S., 1947; s. Richard Henry and Mabel (Madeline) M.; m. Mary Louise Leiren, 1962; children: Christopher W., Gregory S., Timothy J. BA, U. Wash., 1953; BS in Chemistry, Seattle U., 1954; PhD in Biochemistry, U. Aberdeen, 1967, DSc, 1976. Dir. environ. conservation div. Nat. Marine Fisheries Svc., Seattle, 1974-87; sr. scientific cons. U.S. Dept. Justice, Washington, 1989-91; sci. cons. NOAA, 1990-92; prin. scientist, dir. molecular epidemiology program Pacific N.W. Rsch. Inst., Seattle, 1992—2001, dir. biochem. oncology program, 2001—06, prin. scientist emeritus, 2006—; rsch. prof. dept. chemistry Seattle U., 1972-95. Affiliate prof. dept. environ. and occupl. health sci. U. Washington, 1984—. Coll. Ocean & Fishery Scis. U. Washington, 1974-91; editor-in-chief Aquatic Toxicology, 1980-95; lectr., speaker in field. Mem. editl. bd. Tech. in Cancer Rsch. and Treatment, 2001—; mem. editl. bd. Tech. in Cancer Rsch. and Treatment, 2001—; contbr. articles to profl. jours.; inventor in field. Bd. dirs. Am. Oceans Campaign, 1989-91; adv. bd. Internat. Jt. Commn., 1990-91. Recipient U.S. Dept. Commerce Gold medal, 1982. Mem. NAS, Am. Soc. Biochemistry and Molecular Biology, Am. Assn. for Cancer Rsch.

MALKIN, JOSEPH M., lawyer; b. NYC, Jan. 26, 1947; BA, Claremont Men's Coll., 1968; JD, Yale U., 1972. Bar: Calif. 1972, U.S. Dist. Ct. (ctrl. dist.) Calif. 1972, U.S. Dist. Ct. (no. dist.) Calif. 1972, U.S. Fed. Cts. 1972, U.S. Ct. Appeals (9th cir.) 1973, U.S. Supreme Ct. 1976. Mem. O'Melveny & Myers, San Francisco; ptnr. in charge-San Francisco Office Orrick, Herrington & Sutcliffe LLP, San Francisco, co-chmn. energy & project fin. group. Editor Yale Law Jour., 1970-72. Recipient Carter, Ledyard and Milburn prize Yale Law Sch., 1970. Mem. ABA, Bar Assn. San Francisco. Office: Orrick, Herrington & Sutcliffe LLP The Orrick Building 405 Howard St San Francisco CA 94105 Office Phone: 415-773-5505. Office Fax: 415-773-5759. Business E-Mail: jmalkin@orrick.com.

MALKOVICH, JOHN, actor; b. Christopher, Ill., Dec. 9, 1953; m. Glenne Headley, 1982 (div. 1988); m. Glenne Headly, Aug. 2, 1982 (div. 1988); m. Nicoletta Peyran, 1989; children: Amandine and Lorwy. Student, Eastern Ill. U., Ill. State U. Co-founder Steppenwolf Theatre, Chgo., 1976 Made N.Y.C. theatrical debut in True West, 1982 (Obie award, Clarence Derwent award); other theatrical appearances include: Death of a Salesman, 1984, Burn This, 1987, States of Shock; dir. Balm in Gilead, 1984-85, Arms and the Man, 1985, The Caretaker, 1986, Coyote Ugly, (Chgo., Kennedy Ctr. for Performing Arts, Washington) 1985, Libra, 1994, Steppenwolf, 1994; appeared in films Places in the Heart, 1984, The Killing Fields, 1984, Eleni, 1985, Making Mr. Right, 1987, Glass Menagerie, 1987, Empire of the Sun, 1987, Miles From Home, 1988, Dangerous Liaisons, 1988, The Sheltering Sky, 1990, Queen's Logic, 1991, The Object of Beauty, 1991, Shadows and Fog, 1992, Jennifer 8, 1992, Of Mice and Men, 1992, In The Line Of Fire, 1993 (Academy award nomination best supporting actor 1993), Alive, 1993, Touchstone, 1994, Para De La Nuages, 1994, Mary Reilly, 1994, Mulholland Falls, 1996, Der Unhold, 1996, The Portrait of a Lady, 1996, Primary Colors, 1997, Con Air, 1997, The Man in the Iron Mask, 1998, Rounders, 1998, Le Temps retrouvé, 1999, The Libertine, 1999, Ladies Room, 1999, Joan of Arc, 1999, Being John Malkovich, 1999 (American Comedy Award, 2000), Shadow of the Vampire, 2000, Les Ames Forte, 2001, Knockaround Guys, 2001, Je rentre a la Maison, 2001, Ripley's Game, 2002, Hotel, 2001, The Dancer Upstairs, 2002, Johnny English, 2003, The Hitchhiker's Guide to the Galaxy, 2005, Colour Me Kubrick, 2005, Klimt, 2006, The Call, 2006, Eragon, 2006, Drunkboat, 2007, Gardens of the Night, 2007, In Tranzit, 2007, Beowulf (voice), 2007, Burn After Reading, 2008, Changeling, 2008; exec. prodr. The Accidental Tourist, 1988, Somewhere Else, 2000; prodr. Ghost World, 2000, The Loner, 2001, Found in the Street, 2001, The Dancer Upstairs, 2002, Ripley's Game, 2002, Johnny English, 2003, A Talking Picture, 2003, The Libertine, 2004, Kill the Poor, 2006, Art School Confidential, 2006; co-exec. prodr. The Accidental Tourist, 1988; The Dancer Upstairs, 2002; appeared in TV films Word of Honor, 1981, American Dream, 1981, Death of a Salesman, 1985 (Emmy award 1986), Heart of Darkness, 1994, RKO 281, 1999, Les Miserables, 2000, Napoleon, 2002. Office: c/o Mr Mudd 5225 Wilshire Blvd #604 Los Angeles CA 90036

MALL, WILLIAM JOHN, JR., aerospace transportation executive, retired military officer; b. Pitts., Jan. 13, 1933; s. William John and Margaret (Henry) M.; m. Vivian Lea Fenton; children— Michele, William, Catherine BBA, U. Pitts., 1954; MBA, George Washington U., 1966; sr. mgrs. in govt. program, Harvard U., 1980. Commd. officer USAF, 1954, advanced through grades to maj. gen., 1981; insp. gen. Mil. Airlift Command., Scott AFB, Ill., 1978, comdr. 436 wing Dover AFB, Del., 1979; DCS personnel Mil. Airlift Command, Scott AFB, Ill., 1979-81; comdr. Air Rescue Service, Scott AFB, Ill., 1981-83, 23d AF/MAC, Scott AFB, Ill., 1983-85; assigned to Hdqrs USAF, Bolling AFB, DC, 1985-86; ret.; dir. integrated logistics support div. Douglas Aircraft Co., Long Beach, Calif., 1987-89, gen. mgr. human resources, 1989-91; exec. dir. LAX Two Corp., LA, 1991-99. Decorated Legion of Merit, Bronze Star, Air medal Mem. Airlift Assn., Daedalians, Jolly Green Pilots Assn. Avocations: tennis, sailing. Office: LAX Two Corp 200 World Way Los Angeles CA 90045-5859

MALLORY, FRANK LINUS, lawyer; b. Calgary, Alta., Can., May 5, 1920; s. Frank Louis and Anna Amy (Allstrum) M.; m. Jean Ellen (Lindsey), Jan. 29, 1944; children: Susan Mallory Remund, Ann M. Kenney, Bruce R. AB, Stanford U., 1941, LLB, 1947. Bar: Calif., 1948. Assoc. Gibson, Dunn, and Crutcher, LA, 1947-54; ptnr. L.A. and Orange County, 1955-88. Cert. specialist taxation law Calif. Bd. Legal Splty., 1973-89. Pres. town hall of L.A., 1970; Boys Republic, Chino. Calif., 1962-64; pres. Braille Inst. Am., L.A., 1988-92; Lt.(j.g.), USNR, 1942-46. Mem. ABA, Los Angeles County Bar Assn., Orange County Bar Assn., Newport Harbor Yacht Club, Big Canyon Country Club, Transpacific Yacht Club (staff commodore), Order of Coif, Phi Beta Kappa. Republican. Home: 25382 Sea Bluffs Dr 205 Dana Point CA 92629

MALLORY, V(IRGIL) STANDISH, geologist, educator; b. Englewood, NJ, July 14, 1919; s. Virgil Sampson and Sarah Lauris (Baum) M.; m. Miriam Elizabeth Rowan, Feb. 3, 1946; children— Charles Standish, Stefan Douglas, Peter Sommers, Ingrid Lauris. AB, Oberlin Coll., 1943; MA, U. Calif., Berkeley, 1948, PhD (Standard Oil of Calif. fellow in paleontology), 1952. Preparator U. Calif. Museum Paleontology, Berkeley, 1946-48, curator foraminifera, 1948-50, cons., 1951; lectr. paleontology U. Calif. at Berkeley, 1951; asst. prof. geology U. Wash., 1952-59, asso. prof., 1959-62; prof., chmn. div. geology and paleontology, curator of paleontology Burke Meml. Wash. State Mus., 1962-84, prof. emeritus, mus. curator, 1984—. Cons. in petroleum geology and mus. curation, in wines to restaurants; lectr. geology of wine; mem. Gov. of Wash. Commn. on Petroleum Regulations, 1956-57; mem. NSF Paris Basin Field Inst., Paris, Belgium and Luxembourg, 1964; co-dir. NSF Inst. Secondary Sch. Tchrs., Western Wash. State Coll., summers 1963, 65. Author: Lower Tertiary Biostratigraphy of California Coast Ranges, 1959, Lower Tertiary Foraminifera From Media Agua Creek Drainage Area, Kern County, California, 1970, Biostratigraphy— A Major Basis of Paleontologic Correlation, 1970; contbg. author: Lincoln Library Essential Knowledge, 1965, Ency. Brit., 15th edit, 1974; Editor paleontology: Quaternary Research Jour, 1970-77; Contbr. articles to profl. jours. Served with AUS, 1944-46, PTO. Am. Assn. Petroleum Geologists Revolving Fund grantee, 1957; U. Wash. Agnes Anderson Fund grantee, 1963 Fellow AAAS (coun. 1964—), Geologic Soc. Am.; mem. Am. Assn. Petroleum Geologists (sect. coun. 1964-84, com. on stratigrahic correlations 1979-85), Paleontologic Soc. (chmn. sect. 1956-58), Geol. Soc. Am., Soc. Econ. Paleontology and Mineralogy, Paleontol. Rsch. Soc., Paleontologische Gesellschaft, Geologische Gesellschaft, Internat. Paleontological Union, N.W. Sci. Soc., Am. Assn. Mus., Mineral Mus. (adv. coun. 1974-87), N.W. Fedn. Mineralogical Socs. (hon. award 1995, 96), N.W. Paleontol. Assn. (hon. mem.), Sigma Xi, Theta Tau. Home: 5209 Pullman Ave NE Seattle WA 98105-2139 Office: U Wash Burke Meml Wash State Mus Db10 Seattle WA 98195-0001

MALONE, JAMES RICHARD, manufacturing executive; b. Cleve., Dec. 2, 1942; s. William R. and Marian (Bentley) Malone; m. Linda Malone; children: Deanna Lynn, Lisa Suzanne, Zachary, Gabriel. BSc, Ind. U., 1965. With Gen. Motors, 1969—70, Bendix, 1969—70, Cummins Engine, 1969—70, Western Acadia, Chgo., 1970—74; pres., CEO Mgmt. Concepts Co., Pitts., 1974—79, Facet Enterprises Inc., Tulsa, 1979, Purolator Products Co., Tulsa, Anchor Glass Container Corp., Grimes Aerospace, Cenveo, 2005—. V.p. mfg. Haskell of Pitts., 1971—74; former founding, mng. ptnr. Qorval LLC, Naples, Fla.; bd. dirs. Sooner Fed. Savs. and Loan, Red Ball Freight Co., Maclenburg-Duncan Inc. Mem. exec. com. Tulsa Philharm., Indian Nations Coun. Boy Scouts America, Tulsa Global Trade Found., Gov.'s Task Force Econ. Devel.; bd. dirs. Tulsa Ballet Theatre, Jr. Achievement Tulsa, pres., 1986. Mem.: UN Bus. Coun., Young Pres. Orgn., Castle Pines Golf Club, Golf Club (Okla.), Southern Hills Country Club, Tulsa Club. Republican. Methodist.

MALONE, JOHN C., media company executive; b. Milford, Conn., Mar. 7, 1941; m. Leslie Malone; 2 children BS in Elec. Engring. and Econ., Yale U., 1963; MS in Indsl. Mgmt., John Hopkins U., 1964, PhD in Ops. Rsch., 1967; LHD (hon.), Denver U., 1992. With econ. planning rsch. and devel. Bell Telephone Labs/AT&T, 1963—68; joined McKinsey & Co., 1968; group v.p. Gen. Instrument Corp., 1970—73; formerly pres. Jerrold Electronics Corp. (subs. Gen. Instrument Corp.); pres., CEO Tele-Comms., Inc., Denver, 1973—96; chmn., CEO Tele-Comms., Inc. (merged with AT&T Corp.), Denver, 1996-99; chmn. Liberty Satellite, 1996—2000, Liberty Media Corp., Denver, 1990—, CEO, 2005—06. Bd. dirs. IAC/InterActiveCorp., 2001—04, Bank of New York, 1986—, UnitedGlobalCom, Inc., Discovery Communications, CATO Inst., Cablevision Systems Corp.; bd dirs. Liberty Media Corp.; bd. dirs. The Nature Conservancy; bd. dirs., chmn. emeritus Cable Television Laboratories, Inc. Bd. dirs. Nature Conservancy, CATO Inst. Recipient Wall Street Transcript's Gold award for cable industry's best CEO, 1982, 1985, 1986, 1987, Wall Street Transcript Silver award, 1984, 1989, NCTA Vanguard award, 1983, Women In Cable Betsy Magness Fellowship Honoree, U. Pa. Wharton Sch. Sol C. Snider Entrepreneurial Ctr. Award of Merit for Disting. Entrepreneurship, Am. Jewish Com. Sherrill C. Corwin Human Rels. award, Comm. Tech. Mag. Svc. and Tech. award, Bronze award, Fin. World CEO of Yr. Competition, 1993, Hopkins Disting. Alumnus award, 1994; named Man of Yr. award, TVC Mag., 1981; named one of Forbes' Richest Americans, 2006. Mem.: Nat. Cable. TV Assn. (dir. 1974—77, treas. 1977—78, dir. 1980—93, Vanguard award 1983). Office: Liberty Media Corp 12300 Liberty Blvd Englewood CO 80112

MALONE, KEVIN, sports team executive; b. San Diego, Aug. 6, 1957; m. Marilyn Perry; children: Shannon, Shawn. Grad., U. Louisville, 1980. Second baseman Cleve. Indians, 1980-85; scout and coach Calif. Angels, 1985-87; East Coast supr. Minn. Twins, 1989-91; coach N.Y. Penn League, 1988; dir. scouting Montreal Expos, 1991-93, gen. mgr., 1994-95, Balt. Orioles, 1995-99; exec. v.p., gen. mgr. L.A. Dodgers, 1999—.

MALONE, NANCY, actress; b. Queens Village, NY; d. James and Bridget (Sheilds) M. Freelance actress, dir., producer, writer. Performer (TV series) The First Hundred Years, Naked City, The Long, Hot Summer (Best Performance by an Actress award); Broadway debut in Time Out For Ginger, other stage performances include Major Barbara, The Makropoulis Secret, A Touch of the Poet, The Trial of the Catonsville Nine; touring performances include The Chalk Garden, The Seven Yr. Itch, A Place For Dolly; actress (films) The Violators, I Cast No Shadow, An Affair of the Skin, Intimacy, The Trial of the Cantonsville Nine, The Man Who Loved Cat Dancing, Capricorn One; producer (TV series) including Bionic Woman, 1978, Husbands, Wives and Lovers, 1978, The Great Pretender, 1984, (special) Bob Hope: The First 90 Years, 1993 (Emmy award, Outstanding Variety, Musical or Comedy Special, 1993), Womanspeak, 1983; dir. (TV series) Dynasty, 1984-87, Hotel, 1984-87, Colbys, 1985, Cagney and Lacey, 1987, Star Trek Voyager, 1997, Burning Zone, 1997, Fame l.A. 1997-98, Rosie O'Niel (Emmy nomination), Sisters (Emmy nomination), Melrose Place, 1992-99, Beverly Hills, 1990-2000, Picket Fences, Judging Amy, 1999-, Resurrection Blvd., 2000-02; producer, dir. (film) There Were Times Dear, 1986 (John Muir Trustees award, Cine Golden Eagle, Blue Ribbon); founder Nancy Malone Prodns., 1975, Lilac Prodns., 1979. Fellow Leaky Found.; mem. Am. Film Inst. (mem. founder), Women in Film (trustee, Chrystal award, Founders award 1996). Office: Guild Mgmt PHA 9911 W Pico Blvd Los Angeles CA 90035-2703 Home: 4604 Ledge Ave Toluca Lake CA 91602-1536

MALONE, ROBERT JOSEPH, retired bank executive; b. Sept. 3, 1944; With Bank of Am., 1969-81; chmn., pres., CEO First Interstate Bank Boise, Idaho, 1981-84; pres., CEO First Interstate Bank Denver, 1984-90; chmn., pres., CEO Western Capital Investment Corp. (now First Bank System, Inc.), Denver, 1990-92; chmn., CEO Bank Western/Central Banks (now First Bank System, Inc.), Denver, 1992-93; CEO Colo. Nat. Bank, Denver, 1993—; chmn. U.S. Bank (formerly Colo. Nat. Bank), Denver, 1996-2001, ret., 2001. Office: US Bank 950 17th St Denver CO 80202-2815

MALONEY, DON, professional sports team executive, retired professional hockey player; b. Lindsay, Ont., Can., Sept. 5, 1958; m. Toni Maloney; 1 child, Don. Left wing NY Rangers, 1979—89, Hartford Whalers, 1989, NY Islanders, 1989—91, asst. gen. mgr., 1991—92, gen. mgr., v.p. hockey ops., 1992—95; eastern profl. scout San Jose Sharks, 1996—97; asst. gen. mgr. NY Rangers, 1997—2007, v.p. player personnel, 2000—07; gen. mgr. Phoenix Coyotes, 2007—. Asst. gen. mgr. Team Can., World Hockey Championships, Helsinki, Finland, 2003, Czech Republic, 04. Office: Phoenix Coyotes Hockey Club 6751 N White Out Way, #200 Glendale AZ 85305

MALONEY, KRISTEN, gymnast; b. Hacketstown, NJ, Mar. 10, 1981; d. Richard and Linda. Mem. U.S. Gymnastics Team, 1994—2001, UCLA Gymnastics Team, 2000—. Mem. U.S. World Championships Team, 1997, 99, U.S. Gymnastics Team Sydney Olympics, 2000. Recipient numerous awards, 1st pl. Am. Classic, 1997, 98, 1st pl. (3) Foxsport Challenge, Sydney, 1997, 1st team, 1st balance beam, 1st floor exercise 1st AA, Internat. Team Championships, 1998, 1st team, 1st AA, Pacific Alliance Champaionships, Winnipeg, Can., 1998, 1st balance beam Goodwill Games, 1998, others. Mem. Parketts Club. Avocations: reading, music, movies, shopping. Office: UCLA Women's Gymnastics PO Box 24044 Los Angeles CA 90024

MALONEY, ROBERT E., JR., lawyer; b. San Francisco, Sept. 17, 1942; s. Robert E. and Mara A. (Murphy) M.; children: Michael, Sarah, Paul. BA magna cum laude, U. Portland, 1964; JD summa cum laude, Willamette U., Salem, Oreg., 1967. Bar: Oreg., Wash., U.S. Dist. Ct. Oreg., U.S. Dist. Ct. (we. dist.) Wash., U.S. Dist. Ct. (ea. dist.) Wash., U.S. Ct. Appeals (9th cir.). Shareholder Lane Powell PC, Portland, 1967—; chmn., profl. svcs. counsel Bounce Back Oreg., 2003. Mem. bd. visitors Willamette U. Law Sch., 1985-98, chair, 1993-95, mem. exec. com., 1992-97; past chair, mem. exec. com. Portland Trial Dept.; lawyers del. 9th Cir. Jud. Conf., 1995-98; chmn., pres. adv. coun. U. Portland, 2001—; mem. adv. com. Oreg. Ct. Appeals, 2004-. Bd. dirs. Oreg. chpt. Multiple Sclerosis Soc., 1995-02, Children's Cancer Assn., 2002—, Oreg. Ind. Coll. Found., 2004—, chmn., Oreg. Lawyers Against Hunger, 1997-99; judge pro tem Multnomah County Cir. Ct., 1994-98. Mem. ABA (co-chair products liability com., trial practice com. 1988-93), Nat. Assn. R.R. Trial Counsel, Fedn. Ins. Corp. Counsel, Oreg. Assn. Def. Counsel (bd. dirs. 1988-95 sec. 1991-92, v.p. 1993-94, pres. 1994), Fed. Bar Assn. (exec. com. Oreg. divsn. 1988-96, pres. 1994-95), Multnomah Athletic Club. Republican. Roman Catholic. Office: Lane Powell PC 601 SW Second Ave Ste 2100 Portland OR 97204-3158 Office Phone: 503-778-2105. Office Fax: 503-778-2200. Business E-Mail: maloneyr@lanepowell.com.

MALONEY, ROBERT KELLER, ophthalmologist, medical educator; b. May 1, 1958; AB in Mathematics summa cum laude, Harvard U., 1979; MA in Philosophy, Politics and Econs., Oxford U., Eng., 1981; MD, U. Calif., San Francisco, 1985. Diplomate Am. Bd. Ophthalmology. Rsch fellow dept. physiology Cambridge (Eng.) U., 1985; intern U. Calif., LA, 1985-86; resident Wilmer Ophthal. Inst. Johns Hopkins Hosp., Balt., 1986-89; Heed fellow cornea and refractive surgery Emory U., Dept. Ophthalmology, Atlanta, 1989-91; clin. prof. ophthalmology Jules Stein Eye Inst. Sch. Medicine U. Calif., 2005—, assoc. prof. ophthalmology Jules Stein Eye Inst. Sch. Medicine, 1991—2004; dir. Maloney Vision Inst., LA, Calif., 1998—. Bd. dirs. Lasik Inst., Calhoun Vision; cons. in field. Contbr. numerous articles to profl. jours.; presenter and spkr. in field; assoc. editor (N.Am.) Jour. Refractive and Corneal Surgery, 1991-95; internat. editl. bd. European Jour. Implant and Refractive Surgery, 1995; reviewer Am. Jour. Ophthalmology, Ophthalmology, Archives of Ophthalmology, Jour. Cataract and Refractive Surgery, Ophthalmic Surgery and Lasers; editl. bd. Ophthalmology Times. Rhodes scholar, 1979, Heed Found. fellow, 1989-90, Heed/Knapp fellow, 1990-91, John Harvard scholar, 1978; recipient Detur and Edward Whitaker prizes, Harvard U., Rsch. to Prevent Blindness Career Devel. award, 1992, Mericos Whittier award, 1997, VISX Star Surgeon award, 1999, 2000. Mem. Am. Acad. Ophthalmology (long-range planning com. 1989-92, quality of care com. 1987-91, retina preferred practice pattern subcom., refractive errors preferred practice pattern subcom.; chmn. ann. meeting program com. for young ophthalmologists, 1990-92; adv. group to ad hoc com. on orgnl. design 1991, young ophthalmologists' com. 1992-94; Honor award 1993, 97, Sr. Achievement award 2002, Secretariat award 2003), Assn. Rsch. in Vision and Ophthalmology, Internat. Soc. Refractive Surgery (Disting. Lans Refractive Surgery award 2001), Calif. Assn. Ophthalmology, Max

Fine Corneal Soc., Phi Beta Kappa. Office: Maloney Vision Inst Ste 900 10921 Wilshire Blvd Los Angeles CA 90024 Office Phone: 310-208-3937. Business E-Mail: info@maloneyvision.com.

MALONEY, SEAN M., electronics company executive; b. 1956; Mgr. applications engring. Intel U.K. Intel Corp., country mgr. Intel U.K., dir. mktg. Intel Europe, gen. mgr. Asia Pacific ops., tech. asst. to chmn. and chief exec., 1992—95, mgr. sales and mktg. activities Asia Pacific, 1995—98, sr. v.p., mgr. sales org., 1999—2001, exec. v.p., dir. sales org., 2001, exec. v.p., gen. mgr. Intel Comm. Group, 2001—04, exec. v.p., co-mgr. mobility group, 2004—06, exec. v.p., gen. mgr. sales & mktg. group, chief sales & mktg. officer, 2006—. Bd. dirs. Autodesk, Inc., 2007—, Cadence Design Sys., U.S./China Bus. Coun. Office: Intel Corp 2200 Mission College Blvd Santa Clara CA 95052

MALOOF, GAVIN PATRICK, professional sports team executive; b. Oct. 9, 1956; s. George and Colleen Maloof. Student, N.Mex. Mil. Inst., Roswell, N.Mex.; BA in Speech and Comm., Trinity U., San Antonio, 1979. Co-owner NBA Houston Rockets, 1979-82, Women's NBA Sacramento Monarchs, Sacramento Knights, ARCO Arena, NBA Sacramento Kings, 1999—; pres. World League of Am. Football Birmingham Fire, 1990—92; vice chmn. Maloof Cos. Co-recipient Most Involved Execs. award, World Sports Humanitarian Hall of Fame, 2001; named one of The Most Influential People in the World of Sports, Bus. Week, 2007. Avocation: golf. Office: Sacramento Kings Arco Arena One Sports Pky Sacramento CA 95834

MALOOF, GEORGE JOSEPH, JR., hotel and gaming company executive; b. Albuquerque, Sept. 2, 1964; s. George Joseph and Colleen Maloof. BBA in Hotel Mgmt., U. Nev., Las Vegas, 1987. Pres. Maloof Hotels, 1989—; co-owner Fiesta Casino, 1994—2000, The Palms Casino Resort, Las Vegas, Nev., 2001—. Exec. prodr.: (films) Feast, 2006. Mem. Patriarchal Order of Holy Cross of Jerusalem, Legatus, Las Vegas Chpt. Mem.: Kappa Sigma. Office: The Palms Casino Resort 4321 W Flamingo Rd Las Vegas NV 89103*

MALOOF, GILES WILSON, academic administrator, educator, author; b. San Bernardino, Calif., Jan. 4, 1932; s. Joseph Peters and Georgia (Wilson) M.; m. Mary Anne Ziniker, Sept. 5, 1958 (dec. Oct. 1976); children: Mary Jane, Margery Jo. BA, U. Calif., Berkeley, 1953; MA, U. Oreg., 1958; PhD, Oreg. State U., 1962. Petroleum reservoir engr. Creole Petroleum Corp., Venezuela, 1953—54; mathematician electronics divsn. rsch. dept. U.S. Naval Ordnance Rsch. Lab., Corona, Calif., 1958—59; asst. prof. math. Oreg. State U., Corvallis, 1962—68, rsch. assoc. dept. oceanography, 1963—68, vis. prof. math., 1977—78; prof. math. Boise State U., Idaho, 1968—, head dept., 1968—75, dean grad. sch., 1970—75. Author, reviewer of coll. textbooks; contbr. to profl. jours. Served with Ordnance Corps, AUS, 1950, 54-56. Recipient Carter award, 1963, Mosser prize, 1966, Oreg. State U., Alumni Found. scholar Tchg. award Boise State U., 2000. Mem. Math. Assn. Am., Am. Math. Soc., Soc. Indsl. and Applied Math., N.W. Coll. and Univ. Assn. for Sci. (dir., pres. 1990-92), N.W. Sci. Assn. (trustee 1977-80), Assn. We. Univs. (edn. and rsch. com. 1993-2001), Sigma Xi, Pi Mu Epsilon, Phi Kappa Phi. Home: 1400 Longmont Ave Boise ID 83706-3730 E-mail: giles@diamond.boisestate.edu.

MALOOF, JOSEPH, professional sports team owner; s. George and Colleen Maloof. Co-owner NBA Houston Rockets, 1979-82, NBA Sacramento Kings, 1999—, Women's NBA Sacramento Monarchs, Sacramento Knights, ARCO Arena; ptnr., pres. Maloof Cos. Bd. govs. NBA, 1999—; bd. mem. Coors Distbr. Coun. Co-recipient Most Involved Execs. award, World Sports Humanitarian Hall of Fame, 2001; named one of The Most Influential People in the World of Sports, Bus. Week, 2007. Avocation: tennis. Office: Sacramento Kings Arco Arena One Sports Pky Sacramento CA 95834

MALOOF, PHILLIP J., state legislator; BUS, U. N.Mex. Exec. v.p. Maloof Hotels; mem. N.Mex. Legislature, Santa Fe, 1993—, vice chair corps. and transp. com., vice chair Indian and cultural affairs. Democrat.

MALOTT, ADELE RENEE, editor; b. St. Paul, July 19, 1935; d. Clarence R. and Julia Anne (Christensen) Lindgren; m. Gene E. Malott, Oct. 24, 1957 BS, Northwestern U., 1957. Coordinator news KGB Radio, San Diego, 1958-60; asst. pub. relations dir. St. Paul C. of C., 1961-63; night editor Daily Local News, West Chester, Pa., 1963-65; editor, co-pub. Boutique and Villager, Burlingame, Calif., 1966-76; sr. editor mag. The Webb Co., St. Paul, 1978-84; editor GEM Pub. Group, Reno, 1985-2001. Faculty Reader's Digest Writers' Workshops. Co-author: Get Up and Go: A Guide for the Mature Traveler, 1989, The Mature Traveler's Book of Deals, 1997; columnist The Mature Traveler, 1989—. Recipient numerous awards Soc. Am. Travel Writers, Nat. Fedn. Press Women, Calif. Newspaper Pubs. Assn., San Francisco Press Club, Calif. Taxpayers Assn., White House Citations. Mem. Internat. Assn. Bus. Communicators (Merit award 1984), Press Women Minn. (numerous awards), Press Women Nev., Soc. Am. Travel Writers (v.p. 1999, chair Western chpt. 1996-98, pres. 2002-03). Avocations: golf, travel, photography, reading. E-mail: maturetrav@aol.com.

MALTIN, LEONARD, commentator, writer; b. NYC, Dec. 18, 1950; s. Aaron Isaac and Jacqueline (Gould) M.; m. Alice Tlusty, Mar. 15, 1975; 1 child, Jessica Bennett. BA, NYU, 1972. Mem. faculty New Sch. for Social Rsch., NYC, 1973-81; curator Am. Acad. Humor, NYC, 1975-76; guest curator dept. film Mus. Modern Art, NYC, 1976; film critic and corr. Entertainment Tonight, Hollywood, Calif., 1982—; columnist Modern Maturity, 1996-99; film critic Playboy Mag., 1998—2004. Adj. prof. Sch. Cinema & TV, U. So. Calif., 1998—. Author: Movie Comedy Teams, 1970, rev. edit., 1985, Behind the Camera (reprinted as The Art of the Cinematographer), 1971, The Great Movie Shorts (reprinted as Selected Short Subjects), 1971, The Disney Films, 1973, rev. edit., 2000, The Great Movie Comedians, 1978, Of Mice and Magic: A History of American Animated Cartoons, 1980, rev. edit., 1987, The Great American Broadcast, 1997; co-author: Our Gang: The Life and Times of the Little Rascals, 1977, reprinted as The Little Rascals: The Life and Times of Our Gang, 1992; editor: Leonard Maltin's Movie & Video Guide, 1969, rev. annually, Leonard Maltin's Movie Encyclopedia, 1994, Leonard Maltin's Family Film Guide, 1999; producer, writer, host (video) Cartoons for Big Kids, 1989; writer (TV spl.) Fantasia: The Making of a Disney Classic, 1990; writer, host (video) The Making of The Quiet Man, 1992, The Making of High Noon, 1992, Cartoon Madness: The Fantastic Max Fleischer Cartoons, 1993, Cliffhanger!, 1993; co-host Hot Ticket, 2001-04; co-prodr., host (film series) Walt Disney Treasures, 2001—. Recipient Distinction award, Am. Soc. Cinematographers, 2005. Mem. Authors Guild, Soc. for Cinephiles (pres. 1990-91, Man of Yr. 1973), L.A. Film Critics Assn. (pres. 1995-96). Office: c/o Entertainment Tonight Paramount TV 5555 Melrose Ave Los Angeles CA 90038-3112

MALTZAN, MICHAEL THOMAS, architect; b. Roslyn Heights, NY, Oct. 10, 1959; s. William George and Jacqueline (Cain) M.; m. Amy Louise Murphy, Sept. 25, 1988. Student, Wentworth Inst. Tech., 1977-79; BFA, RISD, 1984, BArch, 1985; MArch with letter of distinction, Harvard U., 1988. Lic. arch., Calif. Architect The Architects, Glastonbury, Conn., 1978-80, Williamd D. Warner Assocs., Exeter, RI, 1980-83, Steven Lerner Assocs., Providence, 1983-84, Schwartz/Silver Assocs., Boston, 1984-86, Machado-Silvetti Assocs., Boston, 1986-88, Frank O. Gehry Assocs., LA, 1988-95; pvt. practice architecture LA, 1995—. Prof. RISD, Providence, 1987, Harvard U., Cambridge, Mass., 1988; co-instr. UCLA, 1989, U. Waterloo, 1993, RISD, 1995, Harvard U., 1999, USC, 2002; vis. prof. GSD, 2003; invited jury critic Harvard U., RISD, Ariz. State U., Tempe, Calif. Coll. Arts and Crafts, San Francisco, U. So. Calif., L.A., UCLA, Iowa State U., Ames, Miami (Ohio) U. Prin. works include Inner-City Arts, LA, 1994 (PA award), Getty Digital Lab., 1997, Feldman-Horn Ctr. Arts, 1997 (AIA award), Hergott-Shepard Residence, 1998 (AIA awards), Kidspace Mus., Pasadena, Calif., 1998 (PA award), UCLA Hammer Mus., 1999, MOMA ONS, 2002 (AIA awards), World Trade Ctr. Team, 2002, Fresno (Calif.) Met. Mus., 2002 (AIA award), Giardini Di Porta Nuova, Milan, Italy, 2004, Vancouver (Can.) Art Gallery, 2004. Recipient Collegiate Gold medal AIA, Young Archs. award. Fellow: AIA. Office: Michael Maltzan Architecture 2801 Hyperion Ave Studio 107 Los Angeles CA 90027-2571 Office Phone: 323-913-3098. Office Fax: 323-913-5932.

MALY, MICHAEL KIP, lawyer; b. San Antonio, Tex., July 18, 1945; BA with honors, U. Tex., 1967; JD, U. Calif., 1975. Bar: Calif. 1975, U.S. Dist. Ct. Calif. (no., so., ea., ctrl. dist.). Mng. ptnr. Winston & Strawn LLP, San Francisco, 2003—. Spkr. in field; mem. arbitration panel San Francisco Superior Ct. Contbr. articles to profl. jours. Lt USN, 1967—72. Mem.: ABA. Office: Winston & Strawn LLP 101 California St San Francisco CA 94111-5802 Office Phone: 415-591-1424. Office Fax: 415-591-1400. Business E-Mail: mmaly@winston.com.

MAM, SOMALY, advocate; b. Mondulkiri province, Cambodia, 1970; m. Pierre Legros, 1993 (div.); children: Melissa, Adana, Nicolai. PhD (hon.), Regis U., Denver, 2007. Midwife Choup dist. hospital, Cambodia, 1991; social worker Maison the Retraite, France, 1993—95; with Médecin Sans Frontère, Cambodia, 1995; co-founder & pres. Acting for Women in Distressing Situations (AFESIP), Cambodia, 1996—, Somaly Mam Found., Colo., 2007—. Author: The Road of Lost Innocence: The True Story of a Cambodian Heroine, 2005 (Le Cannet Truth prize, France, 2005). Recipient Prince of Asturias award for Internat. Cooperation, 1998, Nat. Lottery award, Holland, 1999, World Children's Prize for the Rights of the Child, 2000, Festival du Scoop prize, France, 2003, Mimosa d'Oro, Italy, 2003, Internat. Cooperation prize, France, 2004, Internat. Thought and Humanities award, Spain, 2004, award of recognition, US Dept. Homeland Security, 2007, Rule of Law award, LexisNexis, 2007, Premio Alta Qualita award, Italy, 2007; named Woman of Yr., Glamour mag., 2006; named a CNN Hero, 2007; named one of Rising Leaders of the Next 10 Years, Singapore Inst. Internat. Affairs, 2008, The World's Most Influential People, TIME mag., 2009. Mem.: End Child Prostitution/Pornography and Trafficking (pres. ECPAT-Cambodia 2001), Women Confederation of Cambodian Org. (pres. 2000), Assn. Southeast Asian Nations (pres. Confederation Women Org. 1999—2002). Mailing: AFESIP Internat PO Box 2089 Phnom Penh Cambodia Office: AFESIP Internat #62CE St 598 Toul Kork Phnom Penh Cambodia also: Somaly Mam Found PO Box 1272 Wheat Ridge CO 80034 Office Phone: 855-023-884-123. Business E-Mail: somaly.mam@afesip.org.*

MAMER, JAMES MICHAEL, secondary school educator; b. LA, Oct. 8, 1948; s. James Robert and Annette (Babue) M.; m. Jessica Puma, Aug. 31, 1963. BA in Polit. Sci., Calif. Poly. U., Pomona, 1970; MA in Internat. Studies, Immaculate Heart Coll., 1990. Tchr. Irvine (Calif.) Unified Sch. Dist., 1978—. Mentor tchr. Irvine Sch. Dist., 1988-95. Mem. editl. bd. Global Pages, L.A., 1991-96. Recipient Global Teaching award Western Internat. Studies Consortium, L.A., 1991, Am. Coun. Internat. Edn. award, 1998, Human Rights Edn. award Internat. Studies Edn. Project, 2004; Fulbright-Hays grantee, India, 1977; Coe fellow, 1984. Mem. Nat. Coun. Social Studies (Nat. Social Studies Tchr. of Yr. 1992), Irvine Tchrs. Assn. Democrat. Avocation: reading. Home: 29102 Kommers Ln Silverado CA 92676-9726 Personal E-mail: jmamer@earthlink.net.

MAMER, JOHN WILLIAM, business educator; b. July 4, 1954; BA, BS, U. Calif., Davis, 1975; MS, U. Calif., Berkeley, 1978, PhD, 1982. Analyst Manalytics Inc., 1977-78; rsch. intern Xerox Corp., 1979-80; from asst. prof. to prof. U. Calif., LA, 1981-96, prof., 1996—. Lectr. in field. Referee Mgmt. Sci., 1982—, Ops. Rsch., 1984—, Jour. Econ. Dynamics and Control, 1984, 88; contbr. over 15 articles to profl. jours. Mem. Inst. Mgmt. Sci. (organizing chmn. 1994, arrangements chmn. 1995), Ops. Rsch. Soc. Am. Office: The Anderson School UCLA PO Box 951481 Los Angeles CA 90095-1481

MAN, LAWRENCE KONG, architect, art dealer, entrepreneur; b. Kowloon, Hong Kong, July 4, 1953; s. Hon-Kwong Man and Sau-Ching Luk. Student, U. Redlands, 1971-72; BArch, U. Oreg., 1977; MArch, Harvard U., 1978. Registered architect, philanthropist, Dream Help Found., Calif. Designer, project architect Shepley Bulfinch Richardson & Abbott, Boston, 1978-86; project designer, project architect E. Verner Johnson & Assoc., Boston, 1987-91; owner Lawrence Man Architect, Cambridge, Mass., 1992-95, LA, 1994—. Prin. works include Kromka House, L.A., Calif., LMAN Studio, L.A., Chu House, Downey, Calif., Fong House, San Marino, Calif., Tighe Summer House, Sagamore Beach, Mass, Frozen Fusion Juice Bar, L.A. schs., Fed. Credit Union, L.A., Pub. Mus. Grand Rapids, Mich. (AIA Grand Valley Disting. Bldg. award 1997), LCP Studio, Somerville, Mass., New Asia Restaurants, Danvers and Arlington, Mass., Tai Pan Restaurant, Cambridge, Mass. (Honor award AIA 1993, New Eng. award Excellence in Architecture 1993, Design Excellence award Nat. Orgn. Minority Architects 1993), Ti-Sales Office, Sudbury, Mass. (Design Excellence award Nat. Orgn. Minority Architects 1993), Dental Clinic, Reading, Mass. (AIA Interior Architecture award 1992, Interior Design Project award Am. Soc. Interior Designers 1991, Boston Exports citation AIA 1990, Boston Soc. of Architects/New Eng. Healthcare Assembly honor award, 1994), Mus. Ctr. Union Terminal, Cin. (Reconstrn. award 1991), Ramesses Pavilion Boston Mus. Sci. (Double Vision award/Double Silver Soc. Environ. Graphics 1990), Smithsonian South Quadrangle Mus., Washington (Boston Exports award/citation AIA 1990, Honor award AIA 1989), U. Vt. Student Ctr., Burlington, Campus Ctr. Study and Libr. addition Franklin & Marshall Coll., Andover (Mass.) Co. Corp. Hdqs., Emerson Hosp., Concord, Mass., pvt. residences, others. Avocations: dance, travel, music. Office: 949 Chung King Rd Los Angeles CA 90012 Office Phone: 213-628-3883. Business E-Mail: info@lawrencemanarchitects.com.

MANCINO, DOUGLAS MICHAEL, lawyer; b. May 8, 1949; s. Paul and Adele (Brazaitis) M.; m. Carol Keith, June 16, 1973. BA, Kent State U., 1971; JD, Ohio State U., 1974. Bar: Ohio 1974, U.S. Tax Ct. 1977, Calif. 1981, D.C. 1981. Assoc. Baker & Hostetler, Cleve., 1974-80; ptnr. Memel & Ellsworth, LA, 1980-87, McDermott, Will & Emery, LA, 1987—. Bd. dirs. Health Net of Calif. Inc. Author: Taxation of Hospitals and Health Care Organizations, 2000, (with others) Hospital Survival Guide, 1984, Navigating the Federal Physician Self-Referral Law, 1998; (with F. Hill) Taxation of Exempt Organizations, 2002; co-author quar. tax column Am. Hosp. Assn. publ. Health Law Vigil, (with L. Burns) Joint Ventures Between Hosps. and Physicians, 1987; contbr. articles to profl. jours. Chmn. bd. dirs. The Children's Burn Found.; bd. dirs. Kent State U. Found., Inc. Mem. ABA (tax, bus., real property, probate and trust sects., chair exempt orgns. com. 1995-97, coun. dir. 1999—), Calif. State Bar Assn. (tax, bus. law sects.), Ohio Bar Assn., Calif. State Bar, D.C. Bar Assn., Am. Health Lawyers Assn. (bd. dirs. 1986-95, pres. 1993-94), Calif. Soc. for Healthcare Attys., Bel Air Country Club, The Regency Club, Calif. Yacht Club. Office: McDermott Will & Emery 2049 Century Park E Fl 34 Los Angeles CA 90067-3101 E-mail: dmancino@mwe.com.

MANCUSO, FRANK G., entertainment and communications company executive; b. Buffalo, July 25, 1933; married Ed., SUNY. Film buyer, ops. supr. Basil Enterprises, 1959-63; joined Paramount Pictures Corp., 1963, booker Buffalo br., 1963-64, sales rep. Buffalo br., 1964-67, br. mgr., 1967-70; v.p., gen. sales mgr. Paramount Pictures Can. Ltd., 1970-72, pres., 1972-76; U.S. we. divsn. mgr. Paramount Pictures Corp., LA, 1976-77, gen. sales mgr. NYC, 1977, v.p. domestic distbn., 1977-79, exec. v.p. distbn. and mktg., 1979-83, pres. motion picture divsn., 1983-84, chmn., CEO NYC, 1984-91; chmn, CEO Metro-Goldwyn-Mayer, 1993-99. Bd. dirs. Metro-Goldwyn Mayer. Bd. dirs. Will Rogers Meml. Fund, N.Y.-Cornell Med. Ctr., Burke Rehab. Ctr., UCLA Med. Ctr., Mus. of Broadcasting, MGM Motion Picture TV Found. Mem. Acad. Motion Picture Arts and Scis. (bd. dirs.), Motion Picture Assn. (bd. dirs.), Am. Film Inst. (bd. dirs.), Motion Picture Pioneers (bd. dirs.), Variety Clubs Internat. (bd. dirs.). Office: Metro Goldwyn Mayer Inc 2500 Broadway Ste B-201 Santa Monica CA 90404-3065

MANCUSO, VINCE, advertising executive; CFO, sr. v.p. Rubin Postaer & Assocs., Santa Monica, Calif. Office: Rubin Postaer & Assocs 1333 2d St Santa Monica CA 90401

MANDARICH, DAVID D., real estate corporation executive; b. 1948; With Majestic Savs. and Loan, 1966-67, MDC Holdings Inc., Denver, 1977—, bd. dir., 1980—89, 1994—, chmn. Richmond Am. Homes, 1990—93, exec. v.p. real estate, 1993—94, co-COO, 1994—96, COO, 1996—, pres., 1999—. Office: MDC Holdings 4350 S Monaco St Denver CO 80237

MANDEL, BABALOO, scriptwriter; b. NYC; 6 children. Screenwriter: (with Lowell Ganz) Night Shift, 1982, (with Bruce Jay Friedman) Splash, 1984 (Academy award nomination best original screenplay 1984), (with Dan Aykroyd) Spies Like Us, 1985, Vibes, 1988, Parenthood, 1989, City Slickers, 1991, A League of Their Own, 1992, (with Billy Crystal) Mr. Saturday Night, 1992, Greedy, 1994, City Slickers II: The Legend of Curley's Gold, 1994, (with Billy Crystal) Forget Paris, 1995, Multiplicity, 1996, Father's Day, 1997, Edtv, 1999, Where the Heart Is, 2000, Robots, 2005, Fever Pitch, 2005; writer: (TV series) Happy Days, 1974-84, Laverne and Shirley, 1976-83,Herndon, 1983; writer, assoc. prodr.: Gung Ho, 1986; creator (TV series) Knight and Daye, 1989; appearances include (film) Splash, 1984, (TV) Naked Hollywood, 1991. Office: Creative Artists Agy 9830 Wilshire Blvd Beverly Hills CA 90212-1804

MANDEL, HOWIE, actor, comedian; b. Toronto, Ont., Can., Nov. 29, 1955; m. Terry Mandel, Mar. 1980; children: Jacklyn Perry, Riley, Alex. Actor: (films) Gas, 1981, The Funny Farm, 1983, (voice) Gremlins, 1984, A Fine Mess, 1986, Walk Like a Man, 1987, Little Monsters, 1989, (voice) Gremlins 2: The New Batch, 1990, Magic Kid II, 1994, Spin Cycle, 2000, Tribulation, 2000, (voice) The Tangerine Bear, 2000, Hansel & Gretel, 2002, (voice) Pinocchio 3000, 2004, (TV series) Laugh Trax, 1982, (voice) Muppet Babies, 1984-91, St. Elsewhere, 1983, 85, 88, Good Grief, 1990-91, The Amazing Live Sea-Monkeys, 1992; exec. prodr.: Howie Mandel on Ice, 1997, The Legend of Willie Brown, 1998, The Howie Mandel Show, 1998, Hidden Howie, 2005-; host: Howie Mandel's Sunny Skies, 1995, Deal or No Deal, 2005-; comedian various nighclubs and venues; opening act for Diana Ross, Las Vegas. Named one of The 100 Most Powerful Celebrities, Forbes.com, 2008. Office: c/o 3 Arts Entertainment 9460 Wilshire Blvd 7th Fl Beverly Hills CA 90212

MANDEL, JOSEPH DAVID, academic administrator, lawyer; b. NYC, Mar. 26, 1940; s. Max and Charlotte Lee (Goodman) M.; m. Jean Carol Westerman, Aug. 18, 1963; children: Jonathan Scott, Eric David. AB, Dartmouth Coll., 1960, MBA with distinction, 1961; JD, Yale U., 1964. Bar: Calif. 1965. Law clk. U.S. Ct. Appeals, 9th cir., LA, 1964-65; lectr. law U. So. Calif. Law Ctr., LA, 1965-68; assoc. atty. Tuttle & Taylor, LA, 1965-69, mem., 1970-82, 90-91, of counsel, 1984-90; vice chancellor UCLA, 1991—2007, lectr. in law, 1993, 2001—02, spl. asst. chancellor legal affairs, 2007—; v.p., gen. counsel, sec. Natomas Co., San Francisco, 1983. Bd. dirs. LRN, The Legal Knowledge Co., 1993-2005. Mem. bd. editors Yale Law Jour., 1962-64. Pres. Legal Aid Found., L.A., 1978-79; trustee Southwestern U. Sch. Law, 1982, UCLA Pub. Interest Law Found., 1981-82, L.A. County Bar Found., 1974-79, 82, Coro Found., 1989-92, UCLA Armand Hammer Mus. Art and Cultural Ctr., 1995—, Geffen Playhouse, Inc., 1995-98, Coro So. Calif. Ctr., 1985-92; bd. dirs. pub. coun., 1989-94, cmty. v.p., 1992-94; mem. L.A. Bd. Zoning Appeals, 1984-90, vice-chmn., 1985-86, 89-90, chmn., 1986-87; mem. L.A. City Charter Reform Commn., 1996-99; bd. dirs. Western Justice Ctr. Found., 1989—, v.p., 1992-95, 1st v.p., 1995-97, sr. v.p., 1997-99, pres., 1999-03; bd. dirs. Harvard Water Polo Found., 1990-96; bd. govs. Inner City Law Ctr., 1991-05; chair Blue Ribbon Screening Com. to Select Insp. Gen., L.A. Police Commn., 1999; mem. bd. overseers Inst. for Civil Justice, RAND, 1999—, bd. dirs. Children's Law Ctr. L.A., 2003-. Recipient Maynard Toll award Legal Aid

Found. of L.A., 1991, Shattuck-Price award L.A. County Bar Assn., 1993, West Coast Liberty award Lambda Legal Def. and Edn. Fund, 1994, Cmty. Achievement award Pub. Coun., 1996, Stanley Mosk Liberty Through Justice award ADL, 2003; named One of Calif.'s 100 Most Influential Attys. by Calif. Bus. Jour., 2000. Mem. State Bar Calif. (legal svcs. trust fund commn. 1985-87, chmn. 1985-86), Yale U. Law Sch. Assn. (exec. com. 1983-88, 90-96, v.p. 1986-88, chmn. planning com. 1990-92, pres. 1992-94, chmn. exec. com. 1994-96), mem. alumni Coun. Dartmouth Coll., 1992-95, Dartmouth Coll. Assn. Alumni (exec. com. 1997-2002, v.p. 2001-02), L.A. Co. Bar Assn. (trustee 1974, 1975-81, v.p. 1977-78, sr. v.p. 1978-79, pres.-elect 1979-80, pres. 1980-81, chair pro bono coun. 1986-87), Order of Coif. Democrat. Home: 15478 Longbow Dr Sherman Oaks CA 91403-4910 Office: UCLA Office of the Chancellor 2135 Murphy Hl Los Angeles CA 90095-1405 Office Phone: 310-206-1355. Business E-Mail: jmandel@conet.ucla.edu.

MANDEL, MARTIN LOUIS, lawyer; b. LA, May 17, 1944; s. Maurice S. and Florence (Byer) Mandel; m. Duree Dunn, Oct. 16, 1982; 1 child, Max Andrew. BA, U. So. Calif., 1965, JD, 1968; LLM, George Washington U., 1971. Bar: Calif. 1969, U.S. Claims Ct. 1971, U.S. Tax Ct. 1971, U.S. Dist. Ct. (ctrl. dist.) Calif. 1972, U.S. Supreme Ct. 1972. With office of gen. counsel IRS, Washington, 1968-72; ptnr. Stephens, Jones, LaFever & Smith, LA, 1972-77, Stephens, Martin & Mandel, 1977-79, Fields, Fehn, Feinstein & Mandel, 1979-83; sr. v.p., gen. counsel Investment Mortgage Internat., Inc., 1983-84; ptnr. Feinstein, Gourley & Mandel, 1984-85, Mandel & Handin, San Francisco, 1985—2000; gen. counsel LA Express Football Club, 1983-85; prin., owner Law Offices Martin L. Mande, 2000—. Instr. corps. U. West LA, 1973—83. Mem.: ABA, Los Angeles County Bar Assn., LA Athletic Club, Phi Delta Phi. Office: 2905 N Sepulveda Blvd A #319 Manhattan Beach CA 90266 Business E-Mail: martin@tmgtalent.com.

MANDEL, MORTON, molecular biologist; b. Bklyn., July 6, 1924; s. Barnet and Rose (Kliner) M.; m. Florence H. Goodman, Apr. 1, 1952; children: Robert, Leslie. BCE, CUNY, 1944; MS, Columbia U., 1949, PhD in Physics, 1957. Scientist Bell Telephone Labs., Murray Hill, NJ, 1956-57; asst. prof. physics dept. Stanford (Calif.) U., 1957-61; scientist Gen. Telephone & Telegraph, Mountain View, Calif., 1961-63; rsch. assoc. dept. genetics Stanford U., 1963-64; rsch. fellow Karolinska Inst., Stockholm, 1964-66; assoc. prof. sch. of medicine U. Hawaii, Honolulu, 1966-68, prof., 1968—; founder, dir. Hawaii Biotechnology Group, Inc., 1982-95. Cons. Fairchild Semiconductor, Hewlett Packard, Lockheed, Rheem, Palo Alto, Calif., 1957-61. Contbr. articles to profl. jours. Lt. (j.g.) USN, 1944-46. Recipient Am. Cancer Soc. Scholar award Am. Cancer Soc., 1979-80, Eleanor Roosevelt Internat. Cancer fellowship, 1979; named NIH Spl. fellow Karolinska Inst., 1964-66. Fellow Am. Phys. Soc.; mem. Sigma Xi. Achievements include citation classics; optimal conditions for mutagenesis by N-methyl-N-nitro-N-nitrosoguanidine in E. coli K12; calcium dependent bacteriophage DNA infection. Office: Dept Biochemistry 1960 E West Rd Honolulu HI 96822-2319 Home: 250 Hammond Pond Pkwy Apt 303N Chestnut Hill MA 02467-1519 E-mail: mandel321@jacaro.com.

MANDEL, OSCAR, literature and language professor, writer; b. Antwerp, Belgium, Aug. 24, 1926; arrived in U.S., 1940; m. Adrienne Schizzano. BA, NYU, 1947; MA, Columbia U., 1948; PhD, Ohio State U., 1951. Asst. prof. English U. Nebr., 1955-60; Fulbright lectr. U. Amsterdam, 1960-61; vis. assoc. prof. English Calif. Inst. Tech., 1961-62, assoc. prof. English, 1962-68, prof. lit., 1968—2005, prof. emeritus, 2005—. Author: A Definition of Tragedy, 1961, The Theater of Don Juan, 1963, Chi Po and the Sorcerer, 1964, The Gobble-Up Stories, 1967, Seven Comedies by Marivaux, 1968, Five Comedies of Medieval France, 1970, The Collected Plays, 1970—72, Amphitryon, 1976, The Land of Upside Down by Tieck, 1978, The Ariadne of Thomas Corneille, 1982, Collected Lyrics and Epigrams, 1981, Three Classic Don Juan Plays, 1981, Philoctetes and the Fall of Troy, 1981, Annotations to Vanity Fair, 1981, The Book of Elaborations, 1985, The Kukkurik Fables, 1987, Sigismund, Prince of Poland, 1989, August von Kotzebue: The Comedy, The Man, 1990, The Virgin and the Unicorn: Four Plays, 1993, The Art of Alessandro Magnasco: An Essay on the Recovery of Meaning, 1994, The Cheerfulness of Dutch Art: A Rescue Operation, 1996, Two Romantic Plays: The Spaniards in Denmark and The Rebels of Nantucket, 1996, Fundamentals of the Art of Poetry, 1998, L'Arc de Philoctète, 2002, Le Pigeon qui était fou, 2002, Prosper Mérimée: Plays on Hispanic Themes, 2003, Amphitryon, ou le Cocu béni, 2003, Le Triomphe d'Agamemnon, 2003, Chi Po et le Sorcier, 2004; contbr. articles to profl. jours. Office: Calif Inst Tech Humanities Divsn Pasadena CA 91125-0001 Home Phone: 310-476-4543; Office Phone: 626-395-4078. E-mail: om@hss.caltech.edu.

MANDELSTAM, STANLEY, physicist; b. Johannesburg, Dec. 12, 1928; came to U.S., 1963; s. Boris and Beatrice (Liknaitzky) M. BSc, U. Witwatersrand, Johannesburg, 1952; BA, Cambridge U., Eng., 1954; PhD, Birmingham U., Eng., 1956. Boese postdoctoral fellow Columbia U., NYC, 1957-58; prof. math. physics U. Birmingham, 1960-63; asst. rsch. physicist U. Calif., Berkeley, 1958-60, prof. physics, 1963-94, prof. emertitus, 1994—. Vis. prof. physics Harvard U., Cambridge, Mass., 1965-66, Univ. de Paris, Paris Sud, 1979-80, 84-85. Editorial bd. The Phys. Rev. jour., 1978-81, 85-88; contbr. articles to profl. jours. Recipient Dirac medal and prize Internat. Ctr. for Theoretical Physics, 1991. Fellow AAAS, Royal Soc. London, Am. Phys. Soc. (Dannie N. Heineman Math. Physics prize 1992). Jewish. Office: U Calif Dept Physics Berkeley CA 94720-7300

MANDLER, GEORGE, psychologist, educator; b. Vienna, June 11, 1924; came to U.S., 1940, naturalized, 1943; s. Richard and Hede (Goldschmied) M.; m. Jean Matter, Jan. 19, 1957; children: Peter Clark, Michael Allen. BA, NYU, 1949; MS, Yale U., 1950, PhD, 1953; post grad., U. Basel, Switzerland, 1947-48; PhD (hon.), U. Vienna, 2009. Asst. prof. Harvard U., 1953-57, lectr., 1957-60; prof. U Toronto, 1960—65; prof. psychology U. Calif., San Diego, 1965-94, chmn. dept. psychology, 1965-70, disting. prof. emeritus, 1994—; dir. Ctr. Human Info. Processing, U. Calif., San Diego, 1965-90. Hon. rsch. fellow Univ. Coll. London., 1977-78, 82-90, vis. prof., 1990—. Author: Mind and Emotion, 1975, (German edit.), 1980, Mind and Body, 1984, (Japanese edit.), 1987, Cognitive Psychology, 1985, Japanese edit., 1991, Human Nature Explored, 1997, Interesting Times, 2001, Consciousness Recovered, 2002, A History of Modern Experimental Psychology, 2007; co-author: (with W. Kessen) The Language of Psychology, (Italian edit.), 1959, (with J.M. Mandler) Thinking: From Association to Gestalt, 1964; contbr. articles and revs. to profl. jours.; editor: Psychol. Rev., 1970-76. Served with U.S. Army, 1943-46. Fellow Ctr. for Advanced Study in Behavioral Scis., 1959-60; vis. fellow Oxford U., Eng., 1971-72, 78; Guggenheim fellow, 1971-72. Fellow AAAS, Am. Acad. Arts and Scis.; mem. AAUP, Am. Assn. Advancement Psychology (1974-82); Psychonomic Soc. (governing bd., chmn. 1983), Am. Psychol. Soc., Am. Psychol. Assn. (pres. div. exptl. psychology 1978-79, pres. div. gen psychology 1982-83, mem. coun. reps. 1978-82, William James prize 1986), Internat. Union Psychol. Scis. (U.S. com. 1985-90), Soc. Exptl. Psychologists, Fedn. Behavioral Psychol. and Cognitive Scis. (pres. 1981). Home: 1406 La Jolla Knoll La Jolla CA 92037-5236 Office: U Calif San Diego Dept Psychology La Jolla CA 92093-0109 also: 3 Perrins Lane London NW3 1QY England Business E-Mail: gmandler@ucsd.edu.

MANDLER, JEAN MATTER, psychologist, educator; b. Oak Park, Ill., Nov. 6, 1929; d. Joseph Allen and May Roberts (Finch) Matter; m. George Mandler, Jan. 19, 1957; children: Peter Clark, Michael Allen. Student, Carleton Coll., 1947-49; BA with highest honors, Swarthmore Coll., 1951; PhD, Harvard U., 1956. Rsch. assoc. lab. social rels. Harvard U., 1957-60; rsch. assoc. dept. psychology U. Toronto, Ont., Canada, 1961-65; assoc. rsch. psychologist, lectr. U. Calif. at San Diego, La Jolla, 1965-73, assoc. prof., 1973-77, prof. psychology, 1977-88, prof. cognitive sci., 1988—96, disting. prof., 1996—2000, disting. rsch. prof., 2000—; mem. adv. com. memory and cognitive processes NSF, 1978-81. Hon. rsch. fellow U. Coll., London, 1978-89, vis. prof., 1990—; hon. mem. Med. Rsch. Coun. Cognitive Devel. Unit, 1982-98. Author: (G. Mandler) Thinking: From Association to Gestalt, 1964, Stories, Scripts and Scenes, 1984, The Foundations of Mind: Origins of Conceptual Thought, 2004 (APA Divsn. 7 Eleanor Maccoby Book award 2005, Cognitive Devel. Soc. Best Authored Book award 2006); assoc. editor Psychol. rev., 1970-76; mem. editl. bd. Child Devel., 1976-89, Discourse Processes, 1977-94, Jour. Exptl. Psychology, 1977-85, Text, 1979-97, Jour. Verbal Learning and Verbal Behavior, 1980-88, Lang. and Cognitive Processes, 1985-2008, Cognitive Devel., 1990-99, Jour. Cognition and Devel., 1999-2008; contbr. articles to profl. jours Pres. San Diego Assn. Gifted Children, 1968-71; v.p. Calif. Parents for Gifted, 1970-71; mem. alumni council Swarthmore Coll., 1975-78. Recipient Disting. Scientific Contrbn. award, Am. Psychol. Assn., 2007; NIMH research grantee, 1968—81, NSF research grantee, 1981—99. Fellow: APA (mem. exec. com. divsn. 3 1983—85), Am. Acad. Arts and Scis.; mem.: Soc. Exptl. Psychologists, Cognitive Devel. Soc., Cognitive Sci. Soc., Psychonomic Soc. (mem. governing bd. 1982—87, chmn. 1985—86), Phi Beta Kappa. Office: U Calif San Diego Dept Cognitive Sci 9500 Gilman Dr La Jolla CA 92093-0515 Business E-Mail: jmandler@ucsd.edu.

MANDLES, MARTINN HEROE, facility services company executive; b. Tacoma, Nov. 1, 1940; m. Connie Mandles; children: Melanie, Valarie Barsky. BS in Engring., Stanford U., 1964. Pilot U.S. Navy, 1964—68; dir., western corp. opers. Microdot Inc., 1969—72; v.p., mem. mgmt. com. ABM Industries Inc., LA, 1973—91, exec. v.p., mem. bd. dirs., exec. com., 1992—96, chmn. bd., 1997—. Dir. Nat. Multi-Housing Coun., Washington, 1988—90, Bldg. Owners & Mgrs. Assn. of Greater L.A., 1995—. Founding dir. Century City C. of C., 1971—, chmn. bd., 1994; trustee Jewish Big Brothers & Sisters Assn., 1977—; charter mem. Fraternity of Friends of the L.A. Music Ctr., 1978—; trustee The Hebrew U. of Jerusalem, 1996—, vice chmn., dir. western region Am. Friends, 1996—. Lt. comdr. USN. Named Century City Citizen of Yr., Century City C. of C., 1986. Mem.: The Regency Club (L.A.), Hillcrest Country Club (L.A.). Home: 2465 Century Hill at 10100 Galaxy Way Los Angeles CA 90067

MANDRA, YORK T., geology educator; b. NYC; s. Raymond and Irene (Farruggio) M.; m. Highoohi Kechijian, Jan. 26, 1946. BA, U. Calif., Berkeley, 1947, MA in Paleontology, 1949; PhD in Geology, Stanford U., 1958. From instr. to assoc. prof. geology San Francisco State U., 1950-63, prof., 1964—2004, head geology sect., chmn. dept., 1960-67, prof. emeritus, 2005—. Vis. prof. U. Aix-Marseille, France, 1959, Syracuse U., summer 1963, U. Maine, summer 1969, U. Calif., Santa Barbara, summers 1972—2002; rsch. assoc. U. Glasgow, 1959, Calif. Acad. Scis., 1966-88; vis. scientist New Zealand Geol. Survey, fall 1970; disting. fellow in geol. scis. U. Calif., Santa Barbara, 2001—. Contbr. numerous articles to profl. jours. Pres. David S. Sohigian Found., 1975—. Served with USAAF, 1942-46. Recipient Neil A. Miner Disting. Coll. Teaching award, 1984; Danforth Found. teaching fellow, 1958, NSF fellow, 1959; NSF rsch. grantee, 1967-77. Fellow Geol. Soc. Am. (Sr.), Calif. Acad. Scis., AAAS; mem. Nat. Assn. Geology Tchrs. (pres. Far Western sect. 1953-54, 73-74, Robert Wallace Webb award 1977). Avocations: walking, reading, music. Office: San Francisco State U Dept Geoscis 1600 Holloway Ave Dept Geoseis San Francisco CA 94132-1722 E-mail: ytjmandra@sfsu.edu.

MANELLA, NORA MARGARET, judge; BA in Italian with high honors, Wellesley Coll., Mass., 1972; JD, U. So. Calif., 1975. Bar: Calif. 1976, U.S. Ct. Appeals (5th cir.) 1976, D.C. Ct. Appeals 1978, U.S. Dist. Ct. (ctrl., so., no. and ea. dists.) 1980-81, U.S. Ct. Appeals (9th cir.) 1982. Law clk. to Hon. John Minor Wisdom U.S. Ct. Appeals (5th cir.), New Orleans, 1975-76; legal counsel Subcom. on Constn., Senate Com. on Judiciary, Washington, 1976-78; assoc. O'Melveny & Myers, Washington and L.A., 1978-82; asst. U.S. atty. U.S. Dept. Justice, LA, 1982—90, trial asst. major crimes, 1982-85, dep. chief, criminal complaints, 1986-87, chief criminal appeals, 1988-90; judge L.A. Mcpl. Ct., 1990—92, L.A. Superior Ct., 1992-93, U.S. Dist. Ct. (ctrl. dist.) Calif., LA, 1998—2006; justice pro tem Calif. Ct. of Appeal 2d appellate dist. LA, 1992, assoc. justice, 2006—; U.S. Atty. (ctrl. dist.) Calif. U.S. Dept. Justice, LA, 1994—98. Instr. U.S. Atty. Gen. Advocacy Inst., 1984-86, Calif. Jud. Coll., 1992-93; mem. Atty. Gen.'s Adv. Com., 1994-95. Mem. editl. bd. State Bar Criminal Law Newsletter, 1991-92. Mem. adv. bd. Monroe H.S. and Govt. Magnet, 1991-94; acad. specialist USAID Delegation, 1993; judge L.A. Times Cmty. Partnership Awards, 1993; bd. councilors Law Sch. U. So. Calif., 1996—. Mem. Am. Law Inst., Calif. Judges Assn., Nat. Assn. Women Judges, Calif. Women Lawyers, Women Lawyers L.A., Order of Coif, Phi Beta Kappa. Office: Calif Ct of Appeal 2d Appellate Dist LA 300 South Spring St Los Angeles CA 90013 Office Phone: 213-830-7443. Business E-Mail: arlene.chavez@jud.ca.gov.

MANELLI, DONALD DEAN, scriptwriter, film and television producer; s. Daniel Anthony and Mignon Marie (Dean) M.; m. Susan Linda Allen, June 16, 1964 (div. Aug. 1973); children: Daniel, Lisa. BA, U. Notre Dame, 1959. Communications specialist Jewel Cos., Melrose Park, Ill., 1959; script writer Coronet Films, Chgo., 1960-62; freelance writer Chgo., 1962-63; creative dir. Fred A. Niles Communications Ctrs., Chgo., 1963-67; sr. writer Wild Kingdom NBC-TV, Chgo., 1967-70; freelance film writer, producer Chgo., 1970-76; pres. Donald Manelli & Assocs., Inc., Chgo. and Paris, 1976—. Screenwriter, prodr. more than 225 documentary films, 1970—, numerous episodes Wild Kingdom, 1967-82 (Emmy award 1969, 70). Recipient numerous awards various orgns. including N.Y. Internat. Film Festival, Houston Internat. Film Festival, Berlin, Paris, Venice Internat. Film Festivals, CINE, 1976—. Mem. Writers Guild Am. Roman Catholic. Avocations: photography, travel, tennis. also: 1 Rue Goethe 75116 Paris France Office: Donald Manelli and Assoc 8000 McConnell Ave Los Angeles CA 90045

MANGA, MICHAEL, earth science educator, geophysicist; b. Hamilton, Ont., Can., July 22, 1968; s. Pran and Louise Manga; m. Susan Storch. BSc in Geophysics, McGill U., Montreal, Que., Can., 1990; SM in Engring. Scis., Harvard U., 1992, PhD in Earth and Planetary Scis., 1994. Miller rsch. fellow Miller Inst. Basic Rsch. in Scis., Berkeley, Calif., 1994—96; asst. prof. dept. geol. scis. U. Oreg., Eugene, 1996—2001; assoc. prof. dept. earth & planetary scis. U. Calif., Berkeley, 2001—. Contbr. articles to sci. jours.; assoc. editor: Jour. Geophys. Rsch., 2001—05, mem. editl. bd.: Geology, 2004—; editor: Revs. Geophysics, 2005—. Recipient CAREER award, NSF, 1997—2001, Ersted Award for Disting. Teaching, U. Oreg., 1999; named a MacArthur fellow, John D. and Catherine T. MacArthur Found., 2005; named one of Brilliant 10, Popular Sci. mag., 2003; fellow, Sloan Found., 2001. Fellow: Geol. Soc. Am. (Donath medal 2003), Am. Geophys. Union (James B. Macelwane medal 2002). Office: Dept Earth and Planetary Sci Univ Calif Berkeley 173 McCone Hall Berkeley CA 94720-4767 Office Phone: 510-643-8532. Office Fax: 510-643-9980. E-mail: manga@seismo.berkeley.edu.

MANGIOLA, MARK, information technology executive; Exec. v.p. KBLCOM/Time Warner; CEO @Home Solutions; pres., CEO Postive Comm.; ptnr. Canaan Ventures, Menlo Park, Calif. Mem. bd. dir. Midstream Tech., TVIA, Zolo. Office: Canaan Ventures 2765 Sand Hill Rd Menlo Park CA 94025 Office Phone: 650-854-8127. Office Fax: 650-854-8127.

MANGLONA, RAMONA V., judge, former attorney general; b. 1967; BA, U. Calif., 1990; JD, U. N.Mex., 1996. Bar: New Mex. Bar Assn. 1997, No. Mariana Islands Bar Assn. 1997. Asst. atty. gen., 1997—2002; atty. gen. No. Mariana Islands, Saipan, 2002—03; assoc. judge Commonwealth Superior Ct., 2003—. Home Phone: 670-235-5443; Office Phone: 670-236-9751.

MANHAS, RAJ, school system administrator; b. India; married; 2 children. B, Univ. Wash., M indsl. engring. With Security Pacific Bank NW, Rainier Nat. Bank; dir. facilities maintenance and devel. Seattle Dept. Parks Rec.; deputy supt. Seattle Water Dept.; dir. field ops. Seattle Pub. Utilities; COO Seattle Pub. Schools, 2001—03, interim supt., 2003, supt., 2003—. Office: Seattle Public Schools Office of the Superintendent PO BOX 34165 Seattle WA 98124-1165 Office Phone: 206-252-0000.

MANHEIM, CAMRYN, television and film actress; b. Caldwell, NJ, Mar. 8, 1961; d. Jerry and Sylvia Manheim; 1 child, Milo Jacob. BFA, UC Santa Cruz, 1984; MFA, NYU, 1987. Actor: (TV series) The Practice, 1997—2004 (Emmy award for Outstanding Supporting Actress in a Drama Series, 1998, Golden Globe award for Best Performance by an Actress in a Supporting Role, 1999); (TV films) Jackie's Back!, 1999, The Loretta Claiborne Story, 2000, Jenifer, 2001; (TV miniseries) The 10th Kingdom, 2000, A Girl Thing, 2001, Elvis, 2005; actor, prodr. (TV films) Kiss My Act, 2000; actor: (films) Bonfire of the Vanities, 1990, The Road to Wellville, 1994, Jeffrey, 1995, Eraser, 1996, Romy and Michele's High School Reunion, 1997, David Searching, 1998, Wide Awake, 1998, Mercury Rising, 1998, Happiness, 1998 (Nat. Bd. Rev. award, 1998), Fool's Gold, 1998, Joe the King, 1999, What Planet are You From?, 2000, East of A, 2000, The Laramie Project, 2002, Just Like Mona, 2003, Scary Movie 3, 2003, Twisted, 2004, Marilyn Hotchkiss' Ballroom Dancing and Charm School, 2005, Dark Water, 2005, An Unfinished Life, 2005; guest appearances Law and Order, Touched By an Angel, New York Undercover, Ally McBeal, Oh Baby, Chicago Hope, Will and Grace; writer: (off-Broadway play) Wake Up, I'm Fat, 1995; theater appearances include N.Y. Shakespeare Festival, Lincoln Ctr., Yale Repertory, N.Y. Theatre Workshop, Classic Stage Co., Home for Contemporary Theater. Office: Creative Artists Agency 2000 Avenue Of The Stars Los Angeles CA 90067-4700

MANKA, RONALD EUGENE, lawyer; b. Wichita, Kans., Dec. 12, 1944; s. James Ashford and Jane Bunn (Meeks) M.; m. Frances Ann Patterson, Aug. 7, 1965 (dec. Dec. 1985); children: Kimberly Ann, Lora Christine; m. Linda I. Bailey, Mar. 11, 1995. BBA cum laude, U. Kans., 1967; JD cum laude, U. Mich., 1970. Bar: Conn. 1970, Mo. 1974, Kans. 1985, Colo. 2001. Assoc. Day, Barry & Howard, Hartford, Conn., 1970-73, Lathrop & Gage L.C., Kansas City, Mo., 1973-78, mem., 1979-82, 85—; group counsel Butler Mfg. Co., Kansas City, 1982-83, div. gen. mgr., 1983—84. Legal com. Boulder County Cmty. Found., Colo., 2002—. Trustee, clk., elder Village Presbyn. Ch., Prairie Village, Kans.; dir., treas. Lyric Opera of Kansas City, 1995—; pres. Genesis Sch., Kansas City, 1987-89; devel. chmn. Kansas City Friends of Alvin Ailey, 1987-89; chmn. Kansas City Mus., 1988-92, gen. counsel, 1994—; gen. counsel Kansas City C. of C., 1989-2001; pres. Ctr. for Mgmt. Assistance, Kansas City, 1991-93; dir. Colo. Music Festival, 2002-. Mem. ABA, Mo. Bar Assn. (alt. dispute resolution com. 1986-2002), Lawyers Assn. Kansas City, Silicon Prairie Tech. Assn. (bd. dirs. 1990-92), Homestead Country Club (pres. 1984-85). Democrat. Avocations: bicycling, swimming. Home: 875 11th St Boulder CO 80302 Office: Colorado Venture 7542 Crestview Dr Longmont CO 80504-7301 Fax: 720-931-3001. E-mail: RManka@LathropGage.com.

MANKOFF, DAVID ABRAHAM, nuclear medicine physician; b. July 10, 1959; BS in Physics summa cum laude, Yale U., 1981; MD, PhD in Bioengring., U. Pa., 1988. Diplomate Am. Bd. Internal Medicine, Am. Bd. Nuclear Medicine. Rsch. scientist UGM Med. Sys., Phila., 1988-89, dir. engring., 1989-90; rsch. assoc. nuclear medicine sect. U. Pa., Phila., 1988-90; resident in internal medicine U. Wash., Seattle, 1990-92, resident in nuclear medicine, 1992-96, asst. prof. radiology, 1996—2001, assoc. prof. radiology, 2001, assoc. prof. medicine, 2002—06, assoc. prof. bioengring., 2005—06; prof. radiology, medicine, and bioengring. Seattle Cancer Care Alliance, 2006—.

MANN, ALFRED, pharmaceutical executive; b. Portland, Oreg., 1925; MS in Physics, UCLA; DHL (hon.), U. So. Calif., 2001, Johns Hopkins U., 2001. Chmn., CEO MannKind Corp., Sylmar, Calif.; chmn., co-CEO Advanced Bionics Corp.; chmn. emeritus MiniMed Inc.; founder, chmn. Med. Rsch. Group, Inc.; chmn., CEO Siemens-Pacesetter, Inc. and predecessor Pacesetter Sys., Inc.; pres. Spectrolab,

Heliotek. Chmn. bd. trustees Alfred Mann Found., 1985—, Alfred Mann Inst., U. So. Calif.; U. So. Calif. trustee mem. bd. overseers Keck U. So. Calif. Sch. Medicine; chmn. So. Calif. Biomed. Coun., Second Sight, LLC, Allecure Corp., Quallion, LLC, CTL Immunotherapy, Inc., Pharm. Discovery Co., Inc. Recipient Spirit of Edison award for cmty. svc., Thomas Edison State Coll., 1999, Vision of the Future award, RP Internat., 1999, Reynolds Soc. Achievement award, Harvard Med. Sch., 1999; named Man of Yr., WISE Sr. Svcs., 1999, Humanitarian of Yr., House Ear Inst., 1999; named one of 10 Most Influential People on Tch Coast, L.a. Times, 1999, Forbes' Richest Americans, 2006. Fellow: Am. Inst. Med. and Biol. Engring.; mem.: NAE. Office: MannKind Corp 28903 N Ave Paine Valencia CA 91355 also: Alfred Mann Found PO Box 905 Valencia CA 91380

MANN, BRUCE ALAN, lawyer, investment banking executive; b. Chgo., Nov. 28, 1934; s. David I. and Lillian (Segal) M.; m. Naomi Cooks, Aug. 31, 1980; children: Sally Mann Stull, Jonathan Hugh, Andrew Ross. BBA, U. Wis., 1955, SJD, 1957. Bar: Wis. 1957, N.Y. 1958, Calif. 1961. Assoc. Davis, Polk & Wardwell, NYC, 1957-60, Pillsbury, Madison & Sutro, San Francisco, 1960-66, ptnr., 1967-83; adminstrv. mng. dir. L.F. Rothschild Unterberg Towbin, 1983-87; ptnr. Morrison & Foerster, San Francisco, 1987—; sr. mng. dir. W.R. Hambrecht & Co., San Francisco, 1999—2003. Cons. SEC, 1978; vis. prof. law Georgetown U., 1978; lectr. in field. Author: (with Mattson) California Corporate Practice and Forms, 1999; contbr. articles to profl. jours. Served with USAR, 1957. Mem.: NASD (gov.-at-large 1981—83), ABA (chmn. fed. regulation of securities com. 1981—83, mem. bus. law sect. coun. 1996—99, standing com. on ethics and profl. responsibility 1997—2003, chmn. com. on venture capital 2000—03, chmn. com. investment strategies 2007—, coun. mem. sr. lawyers divsn. 2007—), Bar Assn. San Francisco (bd. dirs. 1974—75), State Bar Calif., Am. Law Inst., The Family Club. Office: Morrison & Foerster 425 Market St Ste 3100 San Francisco CA 94105-2482 E-mail: bmann@mofo.com.

MANN, MICHAEL KENNETH, film director, producer; b. Chgo., Feb. 5, 1943; m. Summer Mann, 1974; 4 children. Student, U. Wis., London Film Sch. Dir.: (documentaries) 17 Days Down the Line, 1972; screenwriter, dir. (films) The Keep, 1983, Manhunter, 1986, screenwriter, exec. prodr., dir. Thief, 1981, screenwriter, prodr., dir. The Last of the Mohicans, 1992, Heat, 1995 (Dir., Screenwriter, Prodr. Acad. award nominee), The Insider, 1999, Ali, 2001, Miami Vice, 2006, dir., prodr. Collateral, 2004, prodr. The Aviator, 2004, screenwriter (TV films) River of Promises, 1977, screenwriter, dir. The Jericho Mile, 1979 (Best Dir. award Dir. Guild Am., Emmy award, 1979), screenwriter Swan Song, 1980, screenwriter, exec. prodr., dir. L.A. Takedown, 1989, screenwriter, exec. prodr. (TV miniseries) Drug Wars: The Camarena Story, 1990 (Emmy award, 1990), screenwriter (TV series) Police Story, 1973, Starsky and Hutch, 1975, Bronk, 1975, screenwriter, dir. Vega$, 1978, screenwriter, exec. prodr. Miami Vice, 1984; exec. prodr.: (TV series) Robbery Homicide Division, 2002—03. Mem.: Dirs. Guild, Writers Guild. Office: c/o Creative Artists Agy 9830 Wilshire Blvd Beverly Hills CA 90212-1804

MANN, MICHAEL MARTIN, engineering executive; b. NYC, Nov. 28, 1939; s. Herbert and Rosalind (Kaplan) M.; m. Mariel Joy Steinberg, Apr. 25, 1965. BSEE, Calif. Inst. Tech., 1960, MSEE, 1961; PhD in Elec. Engring. and Physics, U. So. Calif., 1969; MBA, UCLA, 1984. Cert. bus. appraiser, profl. cons., mgmt. cons., lic. real estate broker, Calif. Mgr. high power laser programs office Northrop Corp., Hawthorne, Calif., 1969-76; mgr. high energy laser systems lab. Hughes Aircraft Co., El Segundo, Calif., 1976-78, mgr. E-0 control systems labs., 1978-83, asst. to v.p., space & strategic, 1983-84; exec. v.p. Helionetics Inc., Irvine, Calif., 1984-85, pres., chief exec. officer, 1985-86, also bd. dirs.; ptnr. Mann Kavanaugh Chernove, 1986-87; sr. cons. Arthur D. Little, Inc., 1987-88; chmn. bd., pres., CEO, Blue Marble Devel. Group, Inc., 1988—; exec. assoc. Ctr. Internat. Cooperation and Trade, 1989—91; sr. assoc. Corp. Fin. Assocs., 1990—91; exec. assoc. Reece and Assocs., 1991—92; mng. dir. Blue Marble Ptnrs. Ltd, 1991—; chmn. bd. dirs., CEO Blue Marble Ptnrs., 1992—; chmn., CEO, En Compass Techs., Inc., Torrance, Calif., 1994-98; chmn. En Compass Knowledge Systems, Inc., 2000—. Mem. Army Sci. Bd., Dept. Army, Washington, 1986-91; chmn. Ballistic Missile Def. Panel, Directed Energy Weapon Panel, Rsch. and New Initiatives Panel; cons. Office of Sec. of Army, Washington, 1986—, Inst. of Def. Analysis, Washington, 1978—, Dept. Energy, 1988—, Nat. Riverside Rsch. Inst., 1990—; bd. dirs. Datum, Inc.,1988—, Fail-Safe Tech., Corp., 1989-90, Safeguard Health Enterprises, Inc., 1988—, Am. Video Communications, Inc., Meck Industries, Inc., 1987-88, Decade Optical Systems, Inc., 1990—, Forum Mil. Application Directed Energy, 1992—, Am. Bus. Consultants, Inc., 1993—; chmn. bd. Mgmt. Tech., Inc. 1991—, Encompass Tech., Inc., 1994-98; bd. dirs., mem. adv. bd. Micro-Frame, Inc., 1988-91; chmn. bd. HLX Laser, Inc., 1984-86; bd. dirs. Cons's. Roundtable, 1992—, Am. Bus. Cons., Inc., 1993—, Country Home Bakers, Inc., 1999—, C.L.E.A.R., Inc., 1999—; chmn. TEC, 1999—; rsch. assoc., mem. extension teaching staff U. So. Calif., L.A., 1964-70; chmn. Ballistic Missile Def. Subgroup, 1989-90, Tactical Directed Energy Weapons Subgroup, 1988-90; chmn., chief exec. officer Mgmt. Tech., Inc., 1991—; dir. Am. Bus. Cons., Inc., 1993—; faculty mem. Asia Pacific Inst., 1998—; faculty Nat. Technol. U., 1997—. Mem. editl. bd. Calif. High-Tech Funding Jour., 1989-90; contbr. articles to profl. jours.; patentee in field. Adv. com. to Engring. Sch., Calif. State U., Long Beach, 1985—; chmn. polit. affairs Am. Electronics Assn., Orange County Coun., 1986-87, exec. com., 1986-88; adv. com. Calif. congressmen, 1985—; dean's coun. UCLA Grad. Sch. Mgmt., 1984-85; bd. dirs. Archimedes Circle U. Soc. Calif., 1983-85, Ctr. for Innovation and Entrepreneurship, 1986-90, Caltech/MIT Venture Forum, 1987-91; chmn. adv. coun., adj. prof., indsl. and sys. engring. U. So. Calif., 1996—; bd. examiners Nat. Quality Award, 1998—2000. Hicks fellow in Indsl. Rels. Calif. Inst. Tech., 1961, Hewlett Packard fellow. Mem. IEEE (sr.), So. Calif. Tech. Execs. Network, Orange County CEO's Network, Orange County CEO's Roundtable, Pres. Roundtable, Nat. Assn. Corp. Dirs., Aerospace-Def. CEO's Roundtable, Am. Def. Preparedness Assn., Security Affairs Support Assn., Acad. Profl. Cons. and Advisors, Internat. Platform Assn., Inst. Mgmt. Cons. (bd. dirs. So. Calif. chpt.), Pres. Assn., Cons. Roundtable Forum for Corp. Dirs., King Harbor Yacht Club, Fourth of July Yacht Club. Republican. Avocations: sailing, photography, writing. Home: 4248 Via Alondra Palos Verdes Peninsula CA 90274-1545 Office: Encompass Knowledge Sys Inc 100 Corporate Pointe Ste 210 Culver City CA 90230 Home Phone: 310-375-6391; Office Phone: 310-981-9201. Business E-Mail: mmann@encompassklnowledge.com.

MANN, NANCY LOUISE (NANCY LOUISE ROBBINS), entrepreneur; b. Chillicothe, Ohio, May 6, 1925; d. Everett Chaney and Pauline Elizabeth R.; m. Kenneth Douglas Mann, June 19, 1949 (div. June 1979); children: Bryan Wilkinson, Laura Elizabeth. BA in Math., UCLA, 1948, MA in Math., 1949, PhD in Biostatistics, 1965. Sr. scientist Rocketdyne Divsn. Rockwell Internat., Canoga Park, Calif., 1962-75; tech. staff Rockwell Sci. Ctr., Thousand Oaks, Calif., 1975-78; rsch. prof. UCLA Biomath., LA, 1978-87; pres., CEO, owner Quality Enhancement Seminars, Inc., LA, 1982—; pres., CEO Quality and Productivity, Inc., LA, 1987—. Curriculum adv. UCLA Ext. Dept. of Bus. and Mgmt., L.A., 1991—; mem. com. on Nat. Statistics, Nat. Acad. Scis., Washington, 1978-82; mem adv. bd. to supt. U.S. Naval Posgrad. Sch., Monterey, Calif., 1979-82. Co-author: Methods for Analysis of Reliability and Life Data, 1974; author: Keys to Excellence, 1985, The Story of the Deming Philosophy, 2d edit., 1987, 3d edit., 1989; contbr. articles to profl. jours. Recipient award IEEE Reliability Soc., 1982, ASQC Reliability Divsn., 1986. Fellow Am. Statis. Assn. (v.p. 1982-84); mem. Internat. Statis. Inst. Office: Quality Productivity Inc 185 Jaycroft Ct Lake Sherwood CA 91361-5183

MANN, WESLEY F., editor, writer, reporter; BA, Calif. State U.; MA, Northwestern U.; MBA Program Mgmt. Devel., Harvard Sch. Bus. Editor, co-author Investor's Business Daily, LA, 1988—, now editor-in-chief. Editor: (books) Investor's Business Daily Guide to the Markets, 1997. Office: Investors Business Daily 12655 Beatrice St Los Angeles CA 90066-7303

MANN, ZANE BOYD, editor, publisher; b. St. Paul, Jan. 28, 1924; s. Michael M. and Rose Lee (Reuben) M.; m. Esther Zeesman, Mar. 25, 1945; children: Michael L., Eric F. Personal Fin. Planning, U. Calif., Riverside, 1986. Registered investment advisor SEC. Mcpl. fin. cons. Ehlers Mann & Assoc., Mpls., 1956-64; v.p. mcpl. bond underwriter Ebin Robertson, Mpls., 1964-70; v.p. mcpl. dept. Piper Jaffrey & Co., Mpls., 1970-72; ret., 1972; editor, pub. monthly investment newsletter Calif. Mcpl. Bond Advisor, Palm Springs, Calif., 1984—. Author: Fair Winds and Far Places, 1978; contbr. articles to profl. jours. Mem. Twin City Met. Planning Commn., St. Paul, 1958-70; bd. dirs. CORAL, Riverside County, Calif., 1984-91. Staff sgt. U.S. Army, 1942-45. Decorated DFC with cluster, Air Medal with cluster, Soldier's medal, Purple Heart U.S. Army Air Corp. Mem. Nat. Fedn. Mcpl. Analysts, Calif. Soc. Mcpl. Analysts, Internat. Combat Camera Assn., Writers Guild Am. (ret.), Com. for the Sci. Investigation of Claims of the Paranormal (assoc.), Royal Corinthian Yacht Club (life, Cowles, Eng.), Mensa., Sports Car Club Am. Avocations: sailing, racing and cruising, scuba, scca competition driver, pilot. Home: 3155 E Ramon Rd Apt 601 Palm Springs CA 92264-7974 Office Phone: 760-320-7997. Personal E-mail: zanebm@cs.com.

MANNERS, NANCY, retired mayor; b. Catania, Sicily, Italy, Feb. 1920; d. Gioacchino Jack and Maria Providenza (Virzi) Marasa; m. George Manners, Dec. 20, 1941; children: Gene David, Nancy Ellen Manners Sieh, Joan Alice. BA in Pub. Adminstrn., U. La Verne, 1979. Asst. city mgr. City of Covina, 1963-74; mcpl. mgmt. cons., 1975-85; mem. city coun. City of West Covina, Calif., 1984-97; pres. Ind. Cities Risk Mgmt. Authority, West Covina, 1988; mayor City of West Covina, 1988-89, 92-93; pres. Ind. Cities Assn., 1989-90; ret., 1997. Pres. Covina Coord. Coun., 1970-71, Altrusa Club of Covina-West, 1971-72, Ea. San Gabriel Valley Regional Occupation Program, 1974-76, San Gabriel Valley Planning Com., 1986-87, Mid-Valley Mental Health Coun., 1988-89; regional chmn. San Gabriel Valley Lung Assn., 1971-73; trustee Covina-Valley Unified Sch. Dist., 1973-77; foreman pro tem L.A. County Grand Jury, 1980-81; chmn. L.A. County Solid Waste Mgmt. Com., 1986-89; treas., bd. dirs. San Gabriel Valley Commerce and Cities Consortium, 1991, policy and steering com. Nat. League Cities, 1991-96; chmn. employee rels. policy com. League Calif. Cities; bd. dirs. L.A. County Sanitation Dist., 1992-94, San Gabriel Valley Coun. of Govts., San Gabriel Valley Mosquito Abatement Dist., 1994-97; hon. chair, grand marshall July 4th Parade, City of West Covina, 1997. Named Covina Citizen Yr., 1977, West Covina Citizen Yr., 1983, Woman Yr., Calif. State Legislature, 1990; recipient Woman of Distinction award Today's Woman Forum, 1988, Woman of Achievement award YWCA, 1987, 88, Community Svc. award West Covina C. of C., 1989, Meritorious Pub. Svc. award Rsch. Inst. Claremont McKenna Coll., 1990, Disting. Leader award San Gabriel Valley Boy Scouts of Am., 1997, Cert. Recognition award for more than 25 Yrs. fof Svc. in League of Women Voters, 2008; others. Mem. LWV (pres. San Gabriel Valley 1978-79), Am. Heart Assn. (mem. bd. dirs.), Mcpl. Mgmt. Assts. So. Calif. (v.p. 1972-73), Queen of the Valley Hosp. 2100 (pres. 1996-97), Ind. Cities Assn. (v.p. 1988, pres. 1989), West Covina C. of C. (bd. dirs. 2001-), West Covina Hist. Soc. (v.p. 1995-99, pres. 1999-2000), Ret. Pub. Employees Assn. Calif. (chpt. 90, bd. dirs., treas. 2006-), West Covina Rotary (bd. dirs.). Home: 734 N Eileen Ave West Covina CA 91791-1042

MANNING, BRENT V., lawyer; b. Preston, Idaho, Jan. 18, 1950; s. Leon W. and Gwen Manning; m. J. Christine Coffin, Oct. 25, 1969; children: Justin, Britten, John. BA, Idaho State U., 1972; JD, Harvard U., 1975. Bar: Colo. 1975, Utah 1981, Idaho 2004, US Ct. Appeals (10th cir.) 1978. Assoc. Holme Roberts & Owen, Denver, 1975-80, ptnr., 1980-97, Salt Lake City, 1981-97; founding ptnr. Manning Curtis Bradshaw & Bednar, LLC, Salt Lake City, 1997—. Mem. panel mediators and arbitrators US Dist. Ct. Utah, 1993—; mediation and settlement judge pro tempore 3d Jud. Dist. State of Utah, 1996—; mem. jud. nominating commn. 2d Jud. Dist. Ct. Utah., judge pro tem, 2000-2003. Trustee Bountiful Davis Art Found., Utah, 1985-91, Utah Tibetan Resettlement Project; chmn. "...and Justice for All" campaign. Mem. Utah Bar Assn. (chmn. continuing legal edn. com. 1988, mem. disciplinary com. 1991-93, chmn. cts. and judges com. 1996-97, Am. Inns of Ct. (pres. 1997-98, master of bench 1988—), Am. Alpine Club (NYC) Democrat. Avocations: mountain climbing, bicycling, skiing, running. Home: 2079 Maple Grove Way Bountiful UT 84010-1005 Office: Manning Curtis 3d Fl Newhouse Bldg 10 Exchange Pl Salt Lake City UT 84111-2714 Business E-Mail: BManning@mc2b.com.

MANNING, ERIC, computer scientist, educator, dean, researcher; b. Windsor, Ont., Can., Aug. 4, 1940; g. George Gorman and Eleanor Katherine (Koehler) M.; m. Betty Goldring, Sept. 16, 1961; children: David, Paula; m. Eileen Walker, Sept. 10, 2005. BSc, U. Waterloo, Ont., 1961, MSc, 1962; PhD, U. Ill., 1965. Registered profl. engr., B.C. With MIT and Bell Tel. Labs., 1965-68; prof. computer sci. U. Waterloo, 1968-86, founding dir. computer comms. networks group, 1973-82; founding dir. Inst. for Computer Rsch., 1982-86; prof., dean engring. U. Victoria, B.C., Canada, 1986-92, prof. computer sci., elec. engring., 1993-2000, New Media Ctr./Nortel Networks Prof. Network Performance, 2000—03; prin. scientist, strategic advisor Syscor R&D Inc., 2003—05. NewMIC Chief Scientist, Networks Cluster, 2000-03; dir. Natural Sci. and Engring. Rsch. Coun. Can., exec. com., chair strategic grants com., 1982-87; dir. Comm. Rsch. Ctr., Govt. of Can., 1995-97, Consortium for Software Engring. Rsch., Ottawa, 1997-99; trustee B.C. Advanced Sys. Found., 1986-93; dir. Sci. Coun. B.C., 1988-91; bd. dirs. Can. Microelectric Corp.; adv. com. on artificial intelligence NRC, 1987-91; internat. rsch. adv. com. Alta. Informatics Cir. Rsch. Excellence, 2002-, chair, 2007—; IBM chair computer sci. Keio U., Yokohama, 1992-93; hon. prof. South East U., Nanjing, China; guest prof. Tokyo U. Tech., 2005-07. Author: Fault Diagnosis of Digital Systems, 1970; contbr. articles to profl. jours V.p. Greater Victoria Concert Band, 1995-96; trumpet sect., Sooke Philharm. & 5th Field Arty. Band, Royal Can. Arty. Fellow IEEE, Engring. Inst. Can.; mem. Assn. Computing Machinery (mem. snowbird com. 1999-2001), Assn. Profl. Engrs. B.C., Soc. for Computer Simulation, Can. Inst. for Advanced Rsch. (adv. com. on artificial intelligence and robotics 1986-90), Can. Assn. for Computer Sci. (pres. 1994-2000), Can. Soc. for Fifth Generation Rsch. (trustee 1987-88), B.C. Microelectronics Soc. (bd. dirs. 1986-87). Avocations: amateur radio, scuba diving, sailing, flying, musical performance. Home: 440 Simcoe St #1431 Victoria BC Canada V8V 1L3 Office: U Victoria Faculty Engring PO Box 3055 Victoria BC Canada V8W 3P6 Home Phone: 250-386-8039. Business E-Mail: eric.manning@engr.uvic.ca.

MANNING, J. RICHARD, lawyer; b. Seattle, Nov. 2, 1932; BA, Seattle U., 1954; LLB, Gonzaga U., 1960. Bar: Wash. 1960. Pvt. practice, Seattle. Chmn. Seattle adv. coun. Am. Arbitration Assn., 1985—96, Bd. Govs., 1997—2000; Mem. Law Adv. Bd. Gonzaga U., 1988—; pres. Wash. State Bar Assn., 2002—03. Chair US Supreme Ct. Hist. Soc., Wash., 2005—. Recipient Nat. Outstanding Svc. award, Am. Arbitration Assn., 1988, Wash. Law and Politics Super Lawyer award, Top 100 Lawyers award, 2002—04. Mem.: ABA, Wash. State Bar Assn. (pres. 2003), Assn. Trial Lawyers Am., King County Bar Found. (pres. 1991—93), Am. Judicature Soc., King County Bar Assn. (pres. 1995—96). Office: 925 Logan Bldg 500 Union St Seattle WA 98101 Office Phone: 206-623-6302. Business E-Mail: jmb@seanet.com.

MANNING, JOHN WILLARD, lawyer; b. Miles City, Mont., Mar. 8, 1950; s. Frank Willard Manning and Mary Kathryn (Williams) Murphy; m. Margaret Jean Connors, Dec. 11, 1987; children: Dan Marsh, Sean Marsh, Megan Marsh, Molly Manning. AB, Dartmouth Coll., 1972; JD, Stanford U., 1975. Bar: N.Y. 1977, Mont. 1983. Assoc. Davis Polk & Wardwell, NYC, 1975-80, Dorsey & Whitney, Great Falls, Mont., 1980-83, ptnr., corp. practice group, 1984—, ptnr.-in-charge, Great Falls and Missoula offices. Bd. dirs. Neighborhood Housing Services, Great Falls, 1986-, Native Am. Ctr., Great Falls, 1987-90, Mont. Overthrust Energy Found., Great Falls, 1983-. Mem. Mont. Securities Task Force, Mont. Venture Capital Network. Avocations: skiing, golf, sports. Office: Dorsey & Whitney Ste 600 Millenium Bldg 125 Bank St Missoula MT 59802-4407 Home: 125 Bank St Ste 600 Missoula MT 59802-4419 Office Phone: 406-727-3632, 406-721-6025. Office Fax: 406-727-3638, 406-543-0863. Business E-Mail: manning.jack@dorsey.com.

MANNING, RICHARD DALE, writer; b. Flint, Mich., Feb. 7, 1951; s. Harold J. Manning and Juanita Mayo; m. Margaret B. Saretsky, June 5, 1971 (div.); 1 child, Joshua; m. Tracy M. Stone, Sept. 8, 1990. AB in Polit. Sci., U. Mich., 1973. News dir. Sta. WATZ, Alpena, Mich., 1975-79; reporter Alpena News, 1977-79; city editor Post-Register, Idaho Falls, Idaho, 1979-81; editor, columnist Wood River Jour., Hailey, Idaho, 1981-82; city editor, columnist Times-News, Twin Falls, Idaho, 1982-85; reporter, columnist Missoulian, Missoula, Mont., 1985-89; John S. Knight fellow in journalism Stanford (Calif.) U., 1994-95; freelance writer Lolo, Mont., 1989—. Author: Last Stand: Timber, Journalism and the Case for Humility, 1991, A Good House, 1993, Grassland, 1995, One Round River, 1997, Food's Frontier, 2000, Inside Passage, 2000, Against the Grain, 2004 Recipient Blethen award for investigative reporting Allied Newspapers, 1986-87.

MANNING, ROBERT M., aerospace engineer; m. Dominique Manning; 1 child, Caline. Degree, Whitman Coll., Calif. Inst. Tech. With Jet Propulsion Lab., Pasadena, Calif., 1981—, mem. devel. team Galileo mission to Jupiter, mem. devel. team Magellan mission to Venus, chief engr. Cassini mission to Saturn, flight sys. chief engr. Mars Pathfinder. Office: Jet Propulsion Lab 4800 Oak Grove Dr Pasadena CA 91109-8001

MANNIX, KEVIN LEESE, lawyer; b. Queens, NY, Nov. 26, 1949; s. John Warren Sr. and Editta Gorrell M.; m. Susanna Bernadette Chiocca, June 1, 1974; children: Nicholas Chiocca, Gabriel Leese, Emily Kemper. BA, U. Va., 1971, JD, 1974. Bar: Oreg. 1974, U.S. Ct. Appeals (9th cir.) 1976, U.S. Supreme Ct. 1978, Guam 1979. Law clk. to judge Oreg. Ct. Appeals, Salem, 1974—75; asst. atty. gen. Oreg. Dept. Justice, Salem, 1975—77, Govt. of Guam, Agana, 1977—79; judge adminstrv. law Oreg. Workers' Compensation Bd., Salem, 1980—83; assoc. Lindsay, Hart, Neil & Weigler, Portland, Oreg., 1983—86; pres. Kevin L. Mannix Profl. Corp., Salem, 1986—. Chmn. St. Joseph Sch. Bd., Salem, 1981-86; pres. Salem Cath. Schs. Corp., 1985; v.p. Salem Cath. Schs. Found., 1985-88, pres., 1988-90, 91-94, 2000—; chmn. bd. dirs. Blanchet Sch., 1995-; vice chair Oreg. Rep. Party, 1998-2000, chmn., 2003-05; state rep., 1989-97, 99-2001; state sen., 1998-99. Mem. Marion Bar Assn., Rotary (bd. dirs. East Salem 1985-89, pres. 1987-88), KC. Republican. Avocations: photography, scuba diving, travel. Home: 375 18th St NE Salem OR 97301-4307 Office: 2009 State St Salem OR 97301-4349 Office Phone: 503-364-1913.

MANOS, CHRISTOPHER LAWRENCE, lawyer, mediator; b. Ft. Bragg, NC, July 1, 1952; m. B.J. Osmon, June 14, 1974; children: Monica, Kelly. BS, U.S. Mil. Acad., 1974; JD, U. N.D., 1982. Bar: Mont. 1983, U.S. Dist. Ct. (Mont.) 1983, U.S. Ct. Appeals (9th cir.) 1983. Assoc. to ptrn. Moore, O'Connell, Refling & Manos, Bozeman, Mont., 1982-92; ptnr. Biglen & Manos, Big Timber, Mont., 1992—97, Manos law firm, 1997—2007; part-time dep. county atty. Sweet Grass county, 1992—98; county atty., 1998—2001. Trainer for mediators Ctr. for Collaborative Solutions and Alternative Dispute Resolution Assocs., Bozeman and Palo Alto, Calif., 1990—. Contbr. articles to profl. jours. Bd. dirs. Mont. Pub. TV, Bozeman, 1985-92, Mont. Coun. for Internat. Visitors, Bozeman, 1992; mem. Mont. Stat Bar Dispute Resolution Com., Helena, Mont., 1989-2001. Capt. U.S. Army, 1974-79. Col. USAR (ret.), 1979-2004. Mem. Mont. Mediation Assn., Am. Arbitration Assn., State Bar Mont. Office Phone: 406-442-7660.

MANOSEVITZ, MARTIN, psychologist; b. Mpls., June 22, 1938; s. Julius and Ethel (Cohen) M.; m. Carolyn Heather Margulius, Sept. 17, 1959; children— Bradley, Jason. BA, U. Minn., Mpls., 1960, PhD, 1964. Diplomate in clin. psychology, psychoanalysis Am. Bd. Profl. Psychology. Asst. prof. psychology Rutgers U., 1964-67; asst. prof. psychology U. Tex., Austin, 1967-69, assoc. prof., 1969-75, prof., 1975-87; pvt. practice clin. psychology Austin, 1975-99, Aspen, Colo., 1999—. Adj. prof. psychology U. Tex., 1987-93; dir. psychol. svcs. CPC Capital Hosp., Austin, 1987-93, Shoal Creek Hosp., Austin, 1994-99; allied profl. staff Aspen Valley Hosp., 2000—; bd. dirs. Given Inst., Aspen. Trustee Austin-Travis County Mental Health-Mental Retardation Center, 1978-80. Fellow APA (bd. dirs. divsn. psychoanalysis, 1999-2000, membership chmn. 1997-2000, bd. mem. at large 1999-2000, treas. 2003-05), Acad. Psychoanalytic Psychology; mem. Colo. Psychol. Assn. (bd. dirs. 2005-06, pres.-elect 2006-07, pres 2007), Austin Soc. for Psychoanalytic Psychology (pres. 1994-95), Denver Psychoanalytic Soc. Office: 225 N Nill St Ste 203 Aspen CO 81611 Mailing: PO Box 7976 Aspen CO 81612 E-mail: mmanosev@earthlink.net.

MANSELL, L. ALMA, state legislator; b. Midvale, Utah, Jan. 23, 1944; m. Margurite Mansell. Student, U. Utah. Lic. real estate broker. Real estate broker; mem. Utah Senate, Dist. 10, Salt Lake City, 1994—; asst. majority whip Utah Senate, 1999—2000; mem. legis. mgmt. com., state and local affairs com.; co-chair econ. devel. and human resources appropriations; pres. Utah Senate, 2003—. Mem. Salt Lake Bd. Realtors (pres. 1983, Realtor of Yr. 1986), Utah Assn. Realtors (pres. 1990, Realtor of Yr. 1988, Pres.'s award 1992), Nat. Assn. Realtors (v.p. 1992), Sandy Rotary Club (past pres.). Republican. Office: 6995 Union Park Ctr Ste 100 Midvale UT 84047-4135

MANSFIELD, ELAINE SCHULTZ, molecular geneticist, automation specialist; b. Boulder, Colo., Apr. 20, 1954; d. William Varley and Juanita M. (Zingg) M.; m. Gary G. Schultz, Nov. 24, 1983; children: Matthew, Greggory Mark. BA in Molecular Biology, San Jose State U., 1975; MS in Genetics, U. Calif., Berkeley, 1978, PhD in Genetics, 1983. Diplomate Am. Bd. Med. Genetics (fellow), Am. Bd. Clin. Molecular Genetics. Customer cons. IntelliGenetics, Mountain View, Calif., 1983-86; staff scientist Applied Biosys., Foster City, Calif., 1986-93; sr. staff scientist Molecular Dynamics, Sunnyvale, Calif., 1993-98; dir. pharmacogenomics diaDexus, LLC, Santa Clara, Calif., 1998-99; prin. scientist Aclara Bio Sci., Mountain View, 1999—. Lectr. in the field. Author (with others) Mutations in the Human Genome, 1993; contb. to profl. jours.; patentee in field. U. Calif. grantee, Chancellors Patent Fund grantee U. Calif., NIH SBIR grantee, 1995-99. Mem. AAAS, Am. Soc. Human Genetics, Am. Soc. Histocompatibility and Immunogenetics, Women in Sci., Black Masque (pres. 1975). Avocations: skiing, quilting.

MANSFIELD, ROGER LEO, astronomy and space publisher; b. Boston, Feb. 18, 1944; s. Roy D. Sr. and Nellie E. Mansfield; m. Alice Lee Waring, Nov. 1, 1969 div. Mar. 1983); 1 child, Jason Benjamin; m. Karen June Sprout, June 27, 1987. BS in Chemistry with high honors., U. Cin., 1965; MA in Math., U. Nebr., 1972. Chemist Lockheed Missiles & Space Co., Palo Alto, Calif., 1967; orbital analyst USAF, Offutt AFB, Nebr., 1967-73; instr. Dept. of Math. USAF Acad., Colorado Springs, Colo., 1973-74; aerospace engr. Philco-Ford Corp., Palo Alto, 1974-75, Data Dynamics Inc., Mountain View, Calif., 1975-76, Ford Aerospace & Communications Corp., Colorado Springs, 1976-90; prin. engr. Loral Aerospace Corp., Colorado Springs, 1990-95; owner Astron. Data Svc., 1976—; asst. prof. adjoint U. Colo., Colorado Springs, 1996—99. Pub. Skywatcher's Almanac, 1976--, Local Planet Visibility Report, 1978--, Photographer's Almanac of the Sun and Moon, 1988--, Comparative Ephemeris, 1981--, Space Birds, 1988, Space Ornithology Newsletter, 1988-91, WeatherBirds Utilities, 1995, Skywatcher, 2001, Topics in Astrodynamics, 2003, Firebirds Iridium Flare Prediction, 2006; contbr. articles to profl. jours. Mem. Am. Astron. Soc., Math. Assn. Am., Rocky Mountain Planetarium Assn., Am. Astronautical Soc., Astronomical Soc. Pacific, Phi Beta Kappa, Phi Eta Sigma. Avocation: satellite tracking and orbital mechanics. Home and Office: 3922 Leisure Ln Colorado Springs CO 80917-3502

MANSON, MARILYN (BRIAN HUGH WARNER), singer, musician; b. Canton, Ohio, Jan. 5, 1969; s. Hugh and Barbara Warner; m. Dita Von Teese, Dec. 3, 2005 (div. Dec. 27, 2007). Music journalist, 1987—89; co-founded band Marilyn Manson & the Spooky Kids, 1989; band signed to Nothing Records as Marilyn Manson, 1992. Founder art movement Celebritarian Corp., 1996. Singer: (albums) Portrait of an American Family, 1994, Smells Like Children, 1995, Antichrist Superstar, 1996, Remix & Repent, 1997, Mechanical Animals, 1998, The Last Tour on Earth, 1999, Holy Wood (In the Shadow of the Valley of Death), 2000, The Golden Age of Grotesque, 2003, Lest We Forget, 2004, Eat Me, Drink Me, 2007, (songs) The Beautiful People, 1996 (one of 100 Greatest Videos Ever Made, MTV, 1999), The Dope Show, 1998 (Rolling Stone Best Video of Yr., Billboard Maximum Vision award, 1998); composer: WWF Smackdown! theme song, 2001—; co-author: (autobiography) The Long Hard Road Out of Hell, 1998; contbr.: film soundtracks From Hell, 2001, The Matrix, 1999, Book of Shadows: Blair Witch 2, 2000, Resident Evil, 2002, Queen of the Damned, 2002, Bowling for Columbine, 2002; actor: (films) Lost Highway, 1997, Jawbreaker, 1998, Party Monster, 2003, The Heart is Deceitful Above All Things, 2004, Rise, 2005, Living Neon Dreams, 2005, (video games) Area 51 (voice only), 2005; actor, dir., exec. prodr. (films) Doppelherz, 2003. Rev. Church of Satan, 1994. Recipient 4 S. Fla. Slammies; named one of 100 Greatest Artists of Hard Rock, VH1, 2000; nominee 3 Grammy Awards, 5 MTV Video Music awards. Avocations: painting, writing. Office: Interscope Geffen A&M Records 2220 Colorado Ave Santa Monica CA 90404

MANSOUR, TAG ELDIN, pharmacologist, educator; b. Belkas, Egypt, Nov. 6, 1924; came to U.S., 1951, naturalized, 1956; s. Elsayed and Rokaya (Elzayat) M.; m. Joan Adela MacKinnon, Aug. 6, 1955; children— Suzanne, Jeanne, Dean. DVM, Cairo U., 1946; PhD, U. Birmingham, Eng., 1949, DSc, 1974. Lectr. U. Cairo, 1950-51; Fulbright instr. physiology Howard U., Washington, 1951-52; sr. instr. pharmacology Case Western Res. U., 1952-54; asst. prof., assoc. prof. pharmacology La. State U. Med. Sch., New Orleans, 1954-61; assoc. prof., prof. molecular pharmacology Stanford U. Sch. Medicine, 1961—, chmn. dept. pharmacology, 1977-91, Donald E. Baxter prof., 1977-98, prof. emeritus, 1999—. Cons. USPHS, WHO, Nat. Acad. Scis.; Mem. adv. bd. Med. Sch., Kuwait U.; Heath Clarke lectr. London Sch. Hygiene and Tropical Medicine, 1981 Author: Chemotherapeutic Targets in Parasites, 2002; contrbr. sci. articles to profl. jours. Commonwealth Fund fellow, 1965; Macy Found. scholar NIMR, London, 1982. Fellow AAAS; mem. Am. Soc. Pharmacology and Exptl. Therapeutics, Am. Soc. Biochemistry and Molecular Biology, Am. Heart Assn., Sierra Club, Stanford Faculty Club. Office: Stanford Sch Medicine Dept Chem and Sys Biology CCSR 269 Campus Dr Stanford CA 94305-5174

MANUEL, VIVIAN, public relations executive; b. Queens County, NY, May 6, 1941; d. George Thomas and Vivian (Anderson) M. BA, Wells Coll., 1963; MA, U. Wyo., Laramie, 1965. Mgmt. analyst Dept. Navy, 1966-68; account supr. GE Co., NYC, 1968-72, corp. rep. bus. and fin., 1972-76; dir. corp. comm. Standard Brands Co., NYC, 1976-78; pvt. cons. NYC, 1978-80; pres. V M Comm. Inc., NYC, 1980-97; pub. info. officer Mont. Dept. Commerce, Helena, 1997—2002; adminstr. Gough, Shanahan, Johnson & Waterman, Helena, 2003—04. Mem. com. Girls Club N.Y., 1983—84; mem. adv. bd. Glenholme Sch., 1991—92; mem. allocation com. United Way Mont., 1998—; bd. dirs. Am. Lung Assn. of No. Rockies, 1999—2002; trustee Wells Coll., 1983—90. Mem. AAUW, N.Y. Women in Comms. (bd. v.p. 1983-85, chair Matrix awards 1985), Women Execs. in Pub. Rels. (bd. dirs. 1985-88), Women's Econ. Roundtable. Address: 109 Oakwood Ln Helena MT 59601-6024

MANUELITO-KERKVLIET, CASSANDRA, academic administrator; BA, U. Wyo., 1976, MS in Counselor Edn., 1987; PhD in Ednl. Policy and Mgmt., U. Oreg., 2004. Counselor, advisor, instr. ednl. opportunities program Oreg. State U., Corvallis, 1988—90, founder, dir. Indian Edn. Office, 1990—96; program specialist Am. Indian Student Svcs. U. N.Mex., Albuquerque, 1995—96; rsch. asst. Project SUSTAIN (Strategies for Understanding and Sustaining Ednl. Innovations) U. Oreg., Eugene, 1997—2000; pres. Diné Coll., Tsaile, Ariz., 2000—03, Inst. Am. Indian Arts, Santa Fe, 2006, Antioch U. Seattle, 2007—. Nat. bd. mem. Am. Indian Higher Edn. Consortium, 2000—03; nat. bd. trustees Am. Indian Coll. Fund, Denver, 2001—03; bd. dirs. Agrl. Assembly Policy Nat. Assn. State Univs. and Land Grant Colls., Washington, 2001—03; mem. Biological Scis. Adv. Bd. NSF, Arlington, Va., 2002—; spkr. in field. Office: Office of Pres Antioch U Seattle 2326 Sixth Ave Seattle WA 98121-1814

MAPES, JEFFREY ROBERT, journalist; b. San Francisco, Nov. 21, 1954; s. James Robert and Phyllis June (Bloemker) M.; m. Karen Jane Minkel, Aug. 20, 1978; children: Katharine, James. BA, San Jose State U., 1976. Reporter Napa (Calif.) Register, 1976-79; Washington corr. Scripps League Newspapers, 1979-83; reporter The Oregonian, Portland, 1984-87, chief polit. reporter, 1987—. Office: The Oregonian 1320 SW Broadway Portland OR 97201-3499

MAPLE, M. BRIAN, physics professor; b. Nov. 20, 1939; BS in Physics with distinction, San Diego State U., 1963, AB in Math with distinction, 1963; MS in Physics, U. Calif., San Diego, 1965, PhD in Physics, 1969. Asst. rsch. physicist U. Calif., San Diego, 1969—75, asst. prof. physics, 1973—75, assoc. prof. physics, 1975—81, prof. physics, 1981—90, assoc. rsch. physicist Inst. for Theoretical Physics Santa Barbara, 1980, Bernd T. Matthias endowed chair in physics San Diego, 1990—, dir. Ctr. Interface and Materials Sci., 1990—; Bernd T. Matthias scholar Ctr. for Materials Sci. Los Alamos Nat. Lab., N.Mex., 1993; dir. Inst. for Pure and Applied Phys. Scis. U. Calif., 1995—, chair dept. physics, 2004—, disting. prof. physics, 2005—. Vis. scientist U. Chile, Santiago, 1971, 1973; vis. prof. Inst. de Fisica Jose Balseiro, San Carlos de Bariloche, Argentina, 1974; lectr. in field; mem. rev. com. materials sci. and tech. divsn. Argonne Nat. Lab., 1983-90, chmn., 1987; mem. rev. com. Office of Basic Energy Scis. Rev. of the Materials Sci. Program at Lawrence Livermore Nat. Lab., 1985; mem. exec. com. High Flux Isotope Reactor User's Group, Oak Ridge Nat. Lab., 1984-91; mem. user's com. Francis Bitter Nat. Magnet Lab., 1984-87; mem. rev. com. materials scis. program rev. Ames Lab., 1990-93; mem. scientific adv. bd. CONNECT, 1990—; mem. adv. coun. Glenn T. Seaborg Inst. for Transactinium Sci. Lawrence Livermore Nat. Lab., 1991—. Co-editor: Applied Physics A, 1983-93, Superconductivity in d- and f-Band Metals, 1980, Valence Fluctuations in Solids, 1982, Superconductivity in Ternary Compounds, Vols. 32, 34, 1982, Proceedings of the Internat. Conf. on Strongly Correlated Electron Sys., 1994; guest editor Spl. Issue of Materials Rsch. Soc. Bulletin on High Tc Superconductors, 1989, 2d Spl. Issue of Materials Rsch. Soc. Bulletin on High Tc Superconductors, 1990, Handbook on the Physics and Chemistry of Rare Earths, Vols. 30, 31, High Temperature Superconductors, 2001; mem. editl. bd. Superconductivity Review. Recipient Lockheed Leadership scholarship, 1958-60, Rotary Club scholarship, 1958-60, Calif. State scholarship, 1961-62, John Simon Guggenheim Meml. Found. fellowship, 1984, Disting. Alumnus of Yr. award U. Calif., San Diego, 1987, Disting. Alumnus of Yr. award San Diego State U. Coll. Scis., 1988; inducted into Chula Vista HS Hall of Fame, 1990; Bernd T. Matthias Endowed Chair in Physics 1990; Bernd T. Matthias prize, Internat. Conf. on Materials and Mechanisms of Superconductivity and High Temperature Superconductors, 2000; hon. prof. Trzebiatowski Inst. for Low Temperature and Structure Rsch., Polish Acad. of Sci., 2006. Fellow AAAS (Alexander v. Humboldt Rsch. award, Germany 1998, Frank H. Spedding award 1999), Am. Physical Soc. (various positions selection com. for internat. prize on new materials, 1982-91, mem. exec. com. divsn. condensed matter physics 1985-89, vice-chmn. to chmn. divsn. 1986-88, mem. com. on mtgs. 1992-96, David Adler Lectureship award 1996, James C. McGroddy prize for New Materials 2000); mem. National Academy of Sciences, Am. Vacuum Soc., Materials Rsch. Soc., Calif. Catalysis Soc., Nat. Acad. Sci. (elected mem.), Sigma Xi. Achievements include research in experimental condensed matter physics including superconductivity, magnetism, valence fluctuation and heavy fermion phenomena, strongly correlated election phenomena low temperature and high pressure physics, surface science and catalysis. Office: U Calif San Diego Dept Physics IPAPS 0319 9500 Gilman Dr La Jolla CA 92093-0319

MAPLES, KAREN ELIZABETH, obstetrician, gynecologist; b. June 24, 1954; MD (hon.), UCLA, 1980. Cert. Am. Bd. Ob-gyn. Intern, ob-gyn. U. So. Calif. Womens Hosp., LA, 1980—82; resident Harbor-UCLA Med. Ctr., Torrance, Calif., 1982—84; hosp. appointment Kaiser Permanente Med. Ctr., Bellflower, Calif.; asst. clin. prof. UCLA Sch. Medicine. Mem.: Assn. Black Women Physicians Office. Achievements include being the member of a California team of doctors that delivered the second set of octuplets ever born in the US. Responsible for delivering the 8th baby, when doctors only thought there were 7 babies. Office: Kaiser Permanente Med Ctr 9400 E Rosecrans Blvd Ste 4300 Bellflower CA 90706 Address: 9449 Imperial Hwy Downey CA 90242-2814 Office Phone: 562-461-4127.*

MAR, ERIC LEE, city supervisor, college professor; b. San Francisco, Aug. 15, 1962; m. Sandra Chin; 1 child, Jade. Assoc. prof. Asian Am./Ethnic Studies San Francisco State U., 1992—; supr., Dist. 1 San Francisco Bd. Supervisors, 2009—, vice-chair govt. audits & oversight com., land use & econ. devel. com. Acting asst. dean New Coll. Calif., San Francisco, 1993—97; elected mem. San Francisco County & Ctrl. Com. Dem. Party, 1998—; commr. San Francisco Bd. Edn., 2000—; past mem. human rights com. State Bar Calif.; past mem. civil rights com. Nat. Asian Pacific Am. Bar Assn.; past dir. Northern Calif. Coalition Immigrant Rights. Recipient Cmty. Svc. award, Asian Pacific Am. Labor Alliance, 1999. Mem.: Chinese Progressive Assn., Asians & Pacific Islanders for Cmty. Empowerment (founding mem.). Democrat. Office: City Hall 1 Dr Carlton B Goodlett Pl Rm 24 San Francisco CA 94102 Office Phone: 415-554-7410. Office Fax: 415-554-7415. Business E-Mail: Eric.L.Mar@sfgov.org.*

MARADUDIN, ALEXEI A., physics professor; b. San Francisco, Dec. 14, 1931; BS, Stanford U., 1953, MS, 1954; PhD in Physics, Bristol U., 1957; D (hon.), U. Pierre et Marie Curie, Paris, 1986. Rsch. assoc. physics U. Md., College Park, 1956—57, rsch. asst. prof., 1957—58; asst. rsch. prof. Inst. Fluid Dynamics & Applied Math., 1958—60; physicist Westinghouse Rsch. Labs., Churchill Borough, Pa., 1960—65; cons. semiconductor br. U.S. Naval Rsch. Lab., Washington, 1958—60, Los Alamos Sci. Lab., N.Mex., 1965—67, 1983—89, Gen. Atomic Divsn. Gen. Dynamics Corp., 1965—71; prof. physics U. Calif., Irvine, 1965—, chmn. dept., 1968—71. Recipient Alexander von Humboldt U.S. Sr. Scientist award, 1980—81. Fellow: AAAS, Am. Phys. Soc., Optical Soc. Am., Inst. Physics (U.K.); mem.: Electromagnetics Acad., Phi Beta Kappa, Sigma Xi, Tau Beta Pi. Office: U Calif Irvine Dept Physics & Astronomy Rowland Hall 210 D Irvine CA 92697-4575 Office Phone: 949-824-5943. Business E-Mail: aamaradu@uci.edu.

MARALDO, USHANA, multimedia designer, artist, photographer, writer; b. Germany; BFA, Mich. State U.; MA in Psychology and Edn., U. Osnabruck; postgrad., U. Mexico; PhD in Metaphysical Sci., U. Sedona, 2005. Owner, dir. Sunstar Prodns., Santa Barbara, Calif., 1981—87; owner, pub. Luma Arts Pubs., Woodland Hills, Calif., 1982—92; owner, CEO Light World Pub. LLC, 2007—. Prodr. Arits in Edn. Program, San Francisco. Photographer, 2029 MAGAZIN, internat. edit., 1991—92, Art series: Humana, Cities of Light, Cosmic Calculus series: published in Printworld Directory of Contemporary Prints, 1988, Planet Earth, Kaiser Aluminum Corp., Represented in permanent collections Trump Tower, NYC, Warner Bros. Records, LA. Recipient Excellence award in Painting, Art Horizons, 1988, Excellence award, Photographer's Forum Mag., 1992. Mem.: Soc. Children's Book Writers and Illustrators.

MARAVICH, MARY LOUISE, realtor; b. Ft. Knox, Ky., Jan. 4, 1951; d. John and Bonnie (Balandzic) M. AA in Office Adminstrn., U. Nev., Las Vegas, 1970; BA in Sociology and Psychology, U. So. Calif., 1972; grad., Realtors Inst. Cert. residential specialist. Adminstrv. asst. dept. history U. So. Calif., LA, 1972-73; asst. pers. supr. Corral Coin Co., Las Vegas, 1973-80; realtor Americana Group divsn. Better Homes and Gardens, Las Vegas, 1980-85, Jack Matthews and Co., Las Vegas, 1985-93, Realty Execs., Las Vegas, 1993—. Mem. NAFE, Nev. Assn. Realtors (cert. realtors inst.), Las Vegas Bd. Realtors, Nat. Assn. Realtors, Women's Coun. of Realtors, Am. Bus. Women's Assn., Million Dollar Club, Pres.'s Club. Office: Realty Execs 1903 S Jones Blvd Ste 100 Las Vegas NV 89146-1220 Home Phone: 702-732-3977; Office Phone: 702-873-4500.

MARBLE, DUANE FRANCIS, geography educator, researcher; b. Seattle, Dec. 10, 1931; s. Francis Augustus and Beulah Belle (Simmons) M.; m. Jacquelynne Hardester, Aug. 18, 1957; children: Kimberley Eileen Wood, Douglas Craig. BA, U. Wash., 1953, MA, 1956, PhD, 1959. Asst. prof. real estate U. Oreg., Eugene, 1959; asst. prof. regional sci. U. Pa., Phila., 1960-63; from assoc. prof. geography to prof. geography Northwestern U., Evanston, Ill., 1963-73, assoc. dir. Transp. Ctr., 1966-73; prof. geography and computer sci. SUNY at Buffalo, Amherst, NY, 1973-87; prof. geography and natural resources Ohio State U., Columbus, 1987-98, prof. emeritus, 1998—; Courtesy prof. U. Oreg., 2003—07, Geosciences Oreg. State U., 2007—. Chmn. com. on geog. data sensing and processing Internat. Geog. Union, 1980-88; bd. dirs. Castlereagh Enterprises, Phoenix; founder Internat. Symposium Spatial Data Handling; founder Assn. Am. Geographers-Marble Fund Geographic Sci.; cons. on geog. info. systems to U.S. Bur. Census, UN, also pvt. orgns. Editor: Intro Readings in GIS, 1990, Taylor & Francis, 1990-95; author computer program (best software award Assn. Am. Geogs. 1990); mem. editl. bd. Annals of Assn. Am. Geography, 2000-05, Internat. Jour. of Geographic Info. Sys., 1987-97. Vice-chair Florence Urban Renewal Adv. Com., 2006—07; mem. Florence Transit Adv. Com., 2007—. Recipient Legend in Leadership award, Environ. Sys. Rsch. Inst., 1997, Making a Difference award, 2004; named GIS Educator of Yr., UCGIS, 2007. Mem.: Assn. Compitiing Machinery, Assn. Am. Geographers (sr. assoc. 2005, honors 1993, Geog. and Info. Sci. and Sys. Disting. Career award 2007). Home: 2226 Primrose Ln Florence OR 97439-7627 Personal E-mail: dmarble@oregonfast.net.

MARBLE, FRANK E(ARL), engineering educator; b. Cleve., July 21, 1918; m. 1943, 2 children. BS, Case Inst. Tech., 1940, MS, 1942; PhD in Aeronautics and Math., Calif. Inst. Tech., 1948. Head heat transfer and engine cooling sect. Lewis Flight Propulsion Lab., Nat. Adv. Com. Aeronautics, Cleve., 1942-44, chief compressor and turbine rsch. br., 1944-46; instr. aeronautics Calif. Inst. Tech., Pasadena, 1948-49, from asst. prof. to prof. jet propulsion and mech. engring., 1949-81, Richard L. and Dorothy M. Hayman prof., 1981-89, Richard L. and Dorothy M. Hayman prof. emeritus, 1990—. Instr. fluid dynamics and gas turbines Case Sch. Applied Sch., 1942-46; cons., 1948—; vis. prof. Cornell U., 1956, MIT, 1980-81, Chinese Acad. Sci., 1980; mem. various coms. NRC, NAS, 1956—. Fellow AIAA (Combustion and Propulsion award 1992); mem. NAE, NAS, Combustion Inst., Sigma Xi. Office: Calif Inst Tech Guggenheim Aeronaut Lab Ms 205 45 Pasadena CA 91125-0001 Fax: 818-449-2677. E-mail: marble@cco.caltech.edu.

MARCELLA, JOSEPH, information scientist; BA in Biochemistry, Temple U., 1970. Computer operator/sys. programmer, asst. mgr. King Kullen Grocery Co./Gen. Fire & Casualty, LI, 1971-72; asst. v.p., electronic banking Bank of Am., Las Vegas, 1972-83; sr. v.p., dir. info. svcs. Norwest/Wells of Nev., Las Vegas, 1983-96; chief info. officer, dir. info. technologies City of Las Vegas, 1997—. Chair State Nev. Entities Tech. Alliance; adv. U. Nev. Las Vegas Grad. Sch. Bd. dirs., past pres. Bank Adminstrn. Inst.; past pres., v.p. Nev. Clearing House Assn.; bd. dirs. Western Payments Alliance; mem. Rules Com. Nat. Automated Clearning House, Task Force to Build Acad. Advanced Tech., Focus Sch. Partnership program. Named one of Top 25 CIO, Ctr. Digital Dept., 2008. Office: City Las Vegas Dept Info Techs City Hall 5th Fl 400 Stewart Ave Las Vegas NV 89101-2927

MARCELYNAS, RICHARD CHADWICK, management consultant; b. New London, Conn., Aug. 21, 1937; s. Anthony F. and Elizabeth A. (Chadwick) M.; m. Betty A. Forray, July 1, 1961; children: Michael R., Thomas R. BA in Bus. Adminstrn., U. Wash., 1961; postgrad. Seattle U., 1971-72. Mgmt. trainee, installation foreman Pacific Bell, Fullerton, Calif., 1964-65; cost acct. Scott Paper Co., Everett, Wash., 1965-68; asst. v.p. pers. and adminstrn. Nat. Pub. Svc. Ins. Co., Seattle, 1968-77; pers. ops. mgr. Olympia Brewing Co., 1977-78; mgr. indsl. rels. Heath Tecna Precision Structures Inc., Kent, Wash., 1978-85; mgmt. cons., recruiter Pilon Mgmt. Co., Seattle, 1985-90; pers. adminstr. Peninsula Group Olympia, Wash., 1990-94; pres. Chadwick & Assocs., Olympia, 1994-2000; info. tech. recruiter Red Rover Solutions, Bellevue, Wash., 2000-01; career cons. Hay and Assocs., Bellevue, 2002-07. Mem. Olympia detachment Marine Corps League (comdt.); mem. Wash. State Vets. Legis. Coalition. Served to maj. USMCR, 1961-77. Decorated commendations for bravery and tech. expertise, 1962-64. Mem. Pacific N.W. Pers. Mgrs. Assn. (past pres. Tacoma chpt., Seattle chpt. Bd. Dirs. award 1975). Office: 623 Sherman St SW Olympia WA 98502-5454

MARCH, JAMES GARDNER, social sciences educator; b. Cleve., Jan. 15, 1928; s. James Herbert and Mildred (MacCorkle) M.; m. Jayne Mary Dohr, Sept. 23, 1947; children: Kathryn Sue, Gary Clifton, James Christopher, Roderic Gunn. BA, U. Wis., Madison, 1949; MA, Yale U., New Haven, Conn., 1950, PhD, 1953; PhD (hon.), Copenhagen Sch. Econs., Denmark, 1978, Swedish Sch. Econs., Helsinki, Finland, 1979, U. Wis., Milw., 1980, U. Bergen, Norway, 1980, Uppsala U., Sweden, 1987, Helsinki Sch. Econs., Finland, 1991, Dublin City U., Ireland, 1994, Göteborg U., Sweden, 1998, U. Poitiers, France, 2001, Budapest U. Econs., Hungary, 2003, York U., Toronto, 2007, Lappeenranta U., Finland, 2008. From asst. prof. to prof. Carnegie Inst. Tech., 1953-64; prof. psychology, sociology, dean Sch. Social Scis. U. Calif., Irvine, 1964-70; prof. mgmt., higher edn., polit. sci. and sociology Stanford (Calif.) U., 1970-95, prof. emeritus, 1995—. Cons. in field; mem. Nat. Council Ednl. Research, 1975-78, Nat. Sci. Bd., 1968-74; mem. sociol.-social psychology panel NSF, 1964-66; social sci. tng. com. NIMH, 1967-68; mem. math. social sci. com. Social Sci. Research Council, 1958-60; mem. Assembly Behavioral and Social Sci., NRC, 1973-79, chmn. com. on aging, 1977-82, chmn. com. on math., sci., tech. edn., 1984-86 Author: (with H.A. Simon) Organizations, 1958, 2nd edit., 1993, (with R.M. Cyert) A Behavioral Theory of the Firm, 1963, 2d edit., 1992, Handbook of Organizations, 1965; (with B.R. Gelbaum) Mathematics for the Social and Behavioral Sciences, 1969; (with M.D. Cohen) Leadership and Ambiguity, 1974, 2nd edit., 1986, Academic Notes, 1974; (with C.E. Lave) An Introduction to Models in the Social Sciences, 1975; (with J.P. Olsen) Ambiguity and Choice in Organizations, 1976, Aged Wisconsin, 1977, Autonomy as a Factor in Group Organization, 1980, Pleasures of the Process, 1980, Slow Learner, 1985; (with R. Weissinger-Baylon) Ambiguity and Command, 1986, Decisions and Organizations, 1988; (with J.P. Olsen) Rediscovering Institutions, 1989, Minor Memos, 1990, A Primer on Decision Making, 1994, Fornuft og Forandring, 1995; (with J.P. Olsen) Democratic Governance, 1995; The Pursuit of Organizational Intelligence, 1999, (with M. Schulz and X. Zhou) The Dynamics of Rules, 2000, Late Harvest, 2000; (with M. Augier) The Economics of Choice, Change and Organization, 2002, (with M. Augier), Models of a Man, 2004, Footprints, 2005, Valg, Vane ag Vision, 2005, (with T. Weil) On Leadership, 2005, Quiet Corners, 2008, Explorations in Orgn., 2008; contbr. articles to profl. jours. Fellow Ctr. Advanced Study in Behavioral Scis., 1955-56, 73-74; recipient Wilbur Lucius Cross medal Yale U., 1968, Viipuri prize, Finland, 2004, Herbert Simon award, Hungary, 2005; decorated knight 1st class Royal Norwegian Order of Merit, comdr. Order of Lion of Finland. Mem. NAS, APA, Nat. Acad. Edn., Accademia Italiana di Economia Aziendale, Royal Swedish Acad. Scis., Norwegian Acad. of Sci. and Letters, Am. Acad. Arts and Scis., Am. Econ. Assn., Am. Polit. Sci. Assn. (v.p. 1983-84, John Gaus award 1997, Wildavsky award 2004), Am. Sociol. Assn., Acad. Mgmt. (Disting. Scholar award 1999), Russell Sage Found. (trustee 1985-94, chmn. 1990-93), Finnish Soc. Scis. and Letters, Citigroup Behavioral Scis. Rsch. Coun. (chmn. 1994-2000), Am. Philos. Soc., Phi Beta Kappa, Sigma Xi. Home: 501 Portola Rd Box 8136 Portola Valley CA 94028 Office Phone: 650-424-4344. Business E-Mail: march@stanford.edu.

MARCHAK, MAUREEN PATRICIA, anthropology and sociology educator, academic administrator; b. Lethbridge, Alta., Can., June 22, 1936; d. Adrian Ebenezer and Wilhelmina Rankin (Hamilton) Russell; m. William Marchak, Dec. 31, 1956; children: Geordon Eric, Lauren Craig. BA, U. B.C., Vancouver, Can., 1958, PhD, 1970. Asst. prof. U. B.C., Vancouver, 1972-75, assoc. prof., 1975-80, prof., 1980—, head dept. anthropology and sociology, 1987-90, dean faculty arts, 1990-96, disting. scholar in residence Peter Wall Inst., 2000—, prof., dean emerita of arts, 2001—; sr. rsch. fellow Ctr. Internat. Rels. Liu Inst. for Study of Global Issues, 2002—, interim dir., 2005—06. Author: Ideological Perspectives on Canada, 1975, 2d edit., 1981, 3d edit., 1988, In Whose Interests, 1979, Green Gold, 1983 (John Porter award 1985), The Integrated Circus, The New Right and The Restructuring of Global Markets, 1991, Logging the Globe, 1995, Falldown, Forest Policy in British Columbia, 1999, Racism, Sexism and the University, the Political Science Affair at UBC, 1996, God's Assassins. State Terrorism in Argentina in the 1970's, 1999 (Wallace J. Ferguson prize, Hon. Mention), Reigns of Terror, 2003, No Easy Fix, Global Responses to Internal Wars and Crimes Against Humanity, 2008; author, co-editor: Uncommon Property, 1987; mem. editl. bd. Can. Rev. Sociology and Anthropology, Montreal, 1971-74, Studies in Polit. Economy, Ottawa, Ont., Can., 1980-87, Current Sociology, 1980-86, Can. Jour. Sociology, 1986-90, B.C. Studies, 1988-90, 2000-04. Bd. dir., chair ethics com. Univ. Hosp., 1992-93; trustee Cedar Lodge Trust Soc., 1989-92; mem. adv. coun. Ecotrust, 1991-93, bd. dir., 1993-97, Eco-trust Can., 1995-99; chmn. bd. dir. B.C. Bldgs. Corp., 1992-95; mem. B.C. Forest Appeals Commn., 1992-2002; bd. govs. U. B.C., 1999-2001; bd. dir. Pub. Svc. Employees for Environ. Ethics, 2002-04; mem. sector study steering com. Can. Coun. Profl. Fish Harvesters, 2002—05. Named Woman of Distinction, YWCA, 1999. Fellow Royal Soc. Can. (v.p. Acad. II 1994-98, pres. Acad. II 1998-2000); mem. Can. Sociology and Anthropology Assn. (pres. 1979-80, other offices), Internat. Sociol. Assn., Can. Polit. Sci. Assn., Assn. for Can. Studies, Forest History Soc. (mem. exec. com. 1991-92). Avocations: hiking, swimming, travel, listening to music. Home: 4455 W 1st Ave Vancouver BC Canada V6R 4H9 Home Phone: 604-228-1375. E-mail: patricia.marchak@gmail.com.

MARCHAND, RUSSELL DAVID, II, retired protective services official; b. Lafayette, Ind., May 14, 1950; s. Russell David and Mable May (Gean) M.; m. Sandra Green, June 12, 1951 (div. Nov. 1986); 1 child, Russell David III; m. Carol Bella Flashenburg, May 31, 1987 (div. Feb., 1996); m. Dorian L. Jones, Feb. 28, 2000. AA in Fire Sci., Clark County Community Coll., Las Vegas, Nev., 1979. Cert. fire service instr., supr. instr. Firefighter North Las Vegas Fire Dept., 1973-78, engr., 1978-82, capt., 1982-95, divsn. chief, officer-in-charge bldg. and constrn., 1990-2000, ret., 2000. Pres. Local 1607 Internat. Assn. Fire Fighters, Las Vegas, 1980— (v.p. 1976-80); instr. N. Las Vegas Fire Dept., 1986. Chmn. N. Las Vegas Firefighters Polit. Action Com., 1980—, Muscular Dystrophy Assn., 1980-83, 85. Sgt. USMC, 1968-72, South Vietnam. Named Fireman of Yr., Optimist Club, 1981, Lions Club Nev., 1989, Profl. Ins. Agts. of Am.; received citation of merit Muscular Dystrophy Assn., 1982, commendation City of N. Las Vegas, 1980, 83, 85. Mem. Fed. Firefighters Nev. (received commendation 1982), Internat. Assn. Fire Fighters (local 1607 pres. emeritus 1990). Avocations: sailing, computers. Office: 2626 E Carey Ave North Las Vegas NV 89030-6215

MARCHANT, GARY ELVIN, lawyer; b. Squamish, BC, Can., July 5, 1958; came to U.S., 1986; s. Leonard Roy and Elsie Christine (Anderson) M. BSc, U. B.C., 1980, PhD, 1986; MPP, Harvard U., 1990, JD magna cum laude, 1990. Bar: Mass. 1991, D.C. 1993. Assoc. Kirkland & Ellis, Washington, 1990-95, ptnr., 1995—99; assoc. prof. Ariz. State U. Coll. Law, Tempe, Ariz., 1999—2003, dir. Ctr. Study Law, Sci. & Tech., 2001—, prof., 2003—. Editor-in-chief, Harvard Jour. Law & Tech.; editor, Harvard Environ. Law rev.; assoc. ed., Nonlinearity in Biology, Toxicology and Medicine; contr. articles to profl. jours. Mem. ABA, Def. Rsch. Inst., Air and Waste Mgmt. Assn., Environ. Law Inst., AAAS, Soc. Risk Analysis, N.Y. Acad. Sci., Soc. Social Studies of Sci. Office: Ariz State U Sch Law PO Box 877906 Tempe AZ 85287-7906 Office Phone: 480-965-3246. Business E-Mail: gary.marchant@asu.edu.

MARCIALIS, ROBERT LOUIS, planetary astronomer; b. NYC, Sept. 14, 1956; s. Louis Angelo and Joan Regina (Dippolito) M. SB in Aero. and Astronautical Engring., MIT, 1978, SB in Earth and Planetary Scis., 1980; MS in Physics and Astronomy, Vanderbilt U., 1983; PhD in Planetary Scis., U. Ariz., 1990. Tchg. asst. dept. earth and planetary scis. MIT, Cambridge, 1976—80; lab. instr. dept. physics and astronomy Vanderbilt U., Nashville, 1981, 1982—83, rsch. asst. Arthur J. Dyer Obs., 1981—82; rsch. asst. Lunar and Planetary Lab. U. Ariz., Tucson, 1983—86, rsch. assoc., 1986—90; postdoctoral fellow Jet Propulsion Lab., Pasadena, Calif., 1990—92; adj. faculty Pima C.C., Tucson, 1992—; sr. rsch. specialist U. Ariz., 1996—. Founding mem. Pluto/Charon Mut. Eclipse Season Campaign. Contbr. articles to Nature, Bull. Am. Astron. Soc., Astron. Jour., Minor Planet Circular, Lunar and Planetary Sci., Sci., Jour. Brit. Astron. Assn., Astrophys. Jour., Icarus, also others. Instr. water safety ARC, 1981-82; ednl. counselor MIT, 1983—; fastpitch softball umpire, 1975—. Rsch. fellow NASA, 1986-89. Mem. AAAS, Am. Astron. Soc., Am. Geophys. Union, Astron. Soc. Pacific, Internat. Occultation Timing Assn., Sigma Pi Sigma. Roman Catholic. Achievements include discovery of water ice on surface of Pluto's moon Charon; construction of an albedo map for surface of Pluto; research on Pluto, Charon and Triton, icy satellites, outer solar system formation and evolution, solar system photometry, occultation astronomy, construction and calibration of Imager for Mars Pathfinder, cameras for the Mars Polar Lander and Mars Phoenix missions and Mars Odyssey gamma ray spectrometer. Office: U Ariz Lunar Planetary Lab Tucson AZ 85721-0001 E-mail: umpire@lpl.arizona.edu.

MARCIANO, MAURICE, apparel executive; b. Morocco, 1948; arrived in Calif., 1977; Co-founder MGA, 1973; co-founder, dir. Guess? Inc., LA, 1981—, exec. v.p., 1981—90, pres., 1990—92, chmn. bd., CEO, 1993—99, co-CEO, co-chmn., 1999—2007, chmn. bd., 2007—; chmn. bd., CEO Pepe Clothing USA, Inc., 1993. Office: Guess Inc 1444 S Alameda St Los Angeles CA 90021-2433

MARCIANO, PAUL L., apparel executive; b. Marseilles, France; arrived in Calif., 1981; Co-founder MGA, 1973, Guess? Inc., LA, 1981—, creative dir., 1990—, sr. exec. v.p., 1990—92, pres., COO, 1992—2000, co-chmn., co-CEO, 1999—2006, CEO, vice chmn., 2007—. Office: Guess Inc 1444 S Alameda St Los Angeles CA 90021 Office Phone: 213-765-3100.

MARCUM, WALTER PHILLIP, manufacturing executive; b. Bemidji, Minn., Mar. 1, 1944; s. John Phillip and Johnnye Evelyn (Edmiston) M.; m. Barbara Lynn Maloof, Apr. 17, 1976. BBA, Tex. Tech. U., 1967. Rschr. Collins Securities, Denver, 1968-70, Hanifin Imhoff, Denver, 1970-71; cons. Marcum-Spillane, Denver, 1971-76; with MGF Oil Corp., Midland, Tex., 1976-87, sr. v.p., 1978, exec. v.p., 1979-83, pres., CEO, 1983-87; sr. v.p. corp. fin. Boettcher & Co., Denver, 1987-90; pres., CEO Marcum Natural Gas Svcs., Inc., Denver, 1991-99, Metretek Techs., Denver, 1991—. Dir. Key Energy Group, Houston, Contour Energy, Inc., Houston. Dir. Colo. Endowment Humanities, Denver. Republican. Presbyterian. Home: 342 Monroe St Denver CO 80206-4445 Office: 303 East 17th Ave Ste 660 Denver CO 80203

MARCUS, FRANK ISADORE, cardiologist, educator; b. Haverstraw, NY, Mar. 23, 1928; s. Samuel and Edith (Sattler) M.; m. Janet Geller, June 30, 1957; children: Ann, Steve, Lynn. BA, Columbia U., 1948; MS, Tufts U., 1951; MD cum laude, Boston U., 1953. Diplomate Am. Bd. Internal Medicine (subspecialty cardiovasc. diseases). Intern Peter Bent Brigham Hosp., Boston, 1953-54, asst. resident, 1956-57, research fellow in cardiology, 1957-58; clin. fellow in cardiology Georgetown U. Hosp., 1958-59, chief med. resident, 1959-60; chief of cardiology Georgetown U. Med. Service, D.C. Gen. Hosp., Washington, 1960-68; instr. medicine Georgetown U. Sch. Medicine, 1960-63, asst. prof., 1963-68, assoc. prof., 1968; prof. medicine, chief cardiology sect. U. Ariz. Coll. Medicine, Tucson, 1969-82, disting. prof. internal medicine (cardiology), 1982-99, emeritus prof., 1999—, dir. electrophysiology, 1982—2001; prin. investigator multidisciplinary study of right ventricular dysplasia Nat. Heart, Lung and Blood Inst., 2001—08. Cons. cardiology VA Hosp., Tucson, 1969, USAF Regional Hosp., Davis-Monthan AFB, Tucson, 1969; mem. panel drug efficacy study, panel on cardiovascular drugs Nat. Acad. Scis.-NRC, 1967-68; chmn. undergrad. cardiovascular tng. grant com. HEW-NIH, 1970; dir. Arrhythmia Svcs., 1996-2001. Editor: Modern Concepts of Cardiovascular Disease, 1982—84; mem. editl. bd. Circulation, 1974—81, Current Problems in Cardiology, 1975—79, Cardiovascular Drugs and Therapy, 1986—2000, New Trends in Arrythmias, 1984—, Jour. Am. Coll. Cardiology, 1983—87, 1996—2000, Am. Jour. Cardiology, 1984—, Jour. Cardiovasc. Drugs and Therapy, 1991—2000, Pacing and Clin. Electrophysiology, 1995—, Annals of Noninvasive Electrocardiology, 1996—, Cardiology, 2000—, Jour. Electrocardiology, 2005—; contbr. articles to profl. jours. Chmn. Washington Heart Assn. High Sch. Heart Program, 1966-68. Capt. USAF, 1954-56. Recipient Career Devel. award NIH, 1965, Student AMA Golden Apple award Georgetown U. Sch. Medicine, 1968, Disting. Alumni award Boston U. Sch. Medicine, 2003, Master Clinician award Coun. Clin. Cardiology, 2005; Mass. Heart Assn. fellow, 1957-58; John and Mary Markle scholar, 1960-65; grantee Nat. Heart, Lung and Blood Inst., 2001—. Fellow Coun. on Clin. Cardiology Am. Heart Assn., ACP (Ariz. laureate award 1987), Am. Coll. Cardiology (bd. govs. Ariz. 1984-87, asst. sec. 1987-89, trustee); mem. Assn. Univ. Cardiologists, Inc. (v.p. 1989-90, pres. 1990-91), Ariz. Heart Assn. (dir. 1970, v.p. 1972-73, chmn. rsch. com. 1970-72), So. Ariz. Heart Assn. (dir. 1969), N.Am. Soc. Pacing and Electrophysiology, Alpha Omega Alpha. Home: 4949 E Glenn St Tucson AZ 85712-1212 Office: U Ariz Univ Med Ctr 1501 N Campbell Ave Tucson AZ 85724-0001 Home Phone: 520-327-1339; Office Phone: 520-626-1416. Business E-Mail: fmarcus@u.arizona.edu.

MARCUS, KAREN MELISSA, language educator; b. Vancouver, BC, Can., Feb. 28, 1956; arrived in U.S., 1962; d. Marvin Marcus and Arlen Ingrid (Sahlman) Bishop; m. Jorge Esteban Mezei, Jan. 7, 1984 (div. Mar. 1987). BA in French, BA in Polit. Sci., U. Calif., Santa Barbara, 1978, MA in Polit. Sci., 1981; MA in French, Stanford U., Calif., 1984, PhD in French, 1990. Lectr. French Stanford U., 1989—90; asst. prof. No. Ariz. U., Flagstaff, 1990—96, assoc. prof., 1996—2004, prof., 2004—07, prof. emerita, 2007—. Cons. Houghton Mifflin, 1993, Grand Canyon (Ariz.) Natural History Soc., 1994. Vol., letter writer Amnesty Internat. Urgent Action Network, 1991—95; vol. No. Ariz. AIDS Outreach Orgn., Flagstaff, 1994—95. Recipient medal for Outstanding Achievement in French, Alliance Française, Santa Barbara, 1978; named Scholarship Exch. Student, U. Geneva, 1979—80; Doctoral fellow, Stanford U., 1981—85. Mem.: MLA, Coordination Internat. des Chercheurs sur les Litteratures Maghrebines, Women in French, Am. Lit. Translators Assn., Am. Coun. Tchg. Fgn. Langs., Am. Assn. Tchrs. French, Phi Beta Kappa, Alpha Lambda Delta, Pi Delta Phi. Democrat. Jewish. Avocations: walking, yoga, reading, writing short stories. Business E-Mail: melissa.marcus@nau.edu.

MARCUS, LARRY DAVID, broadcast executive; b. NYC, Jan. 27, 1949; s. Oscar Moses and Sylvia (Ackerman) Marcus; children from previous marriage: Julia Ilene, Barbara Maureen. BBA, CUNY, 1970, MBA, 1972. Computer systems analyst Johnson & Johnson, 1972—73; acctg. mgr. Sta. WPLG-TV, Miami, Fla., 1974-75; v.p., bus. mgr. Sta. KPLR-TV-Koplar Comm., Inc., St. Louis, 1976-82; chief fin. officer Koplar Comm., Inc., St. Louis, 1982-88, River City Broadcasting Co., St. Louis, 1988-96; gen. ptnr. Marcus Investments, L.P., 1996—; CEO Peak Media Holdings LLC, San Diego, 1997—. Computer design cons. PriceWaterhouse Coopers; ptnr. San Diego Social Venture. Scholarship com. Pro Kids, San Diego; bd. dirs. St. Louis Nat. Pub. Radio, KPBS TV, FM, San Diego, Hero Broadcasting, MTV3; pres. Del Mar TV Found. Mem.: Broadcast Cable Fin. Mgmt. Assn. (bd. dirs. 1976—89, treas. 1989—90, sec. 1990—91, v.p. 1991—92, pres. 1992—93). Avocations: skiing, golf. Office: Peak Media LLC 13748 Pine Needles Dr Del Mar CA 92014 E-mail: ldmarcus@aol.com.

MARCUS, RICHARD LEON, lawyer, educator; b. San Francisco, Jan. 28, 1948; s. Irving Harry and Elizabeth (McEvoy) M.; m. Andrea June Saltzman, Apr. 26, 1981; 1 child, Ruth. BA, Pomona Coll., Claremont, Calif., 1969; JD, U. Calif., Berkeley, 1972. Bar: Calif. 1973, US Dist. Ct. (no. dist.) Calif. 1976, US Dist. Ct. (ctrl. dist.) Calif. 1978, US Ct. Appeals (9th cir.) 1981. Law clk. to judge Calif. Supreme Ct., San Francisco, 1972; assoc. Boalt Hall U. Calif., 1973-74; law clk. to judge U.S. Dist. Ct. Calif., San Francisco, 1974-75; from assoc. to ptnr. Dinkelspiel, Pelavin, Steefel & Levitt, San Francisco, 1976-81; assoc. prof. law U. Ill., Champaign, 1981-84, prof. law, 1984-89, U. Calif. Hastings Sch. Law, San Francisco, 1989-97, disting. prof. law, 1997-99, Horace O. Coil '57 prof., 1999—. Vis. prof. law U. Mich., 1986-87, U. Calif., Hastings, 1988; assoc. reporter Fed. Cts. Study Com., 1989-90; reporter com. civil motions Ill. Jud. Conf., Chgo., 1984, com. on evidence, 1985; cons. Nat. Commn. on Judicial Discipline and Removal, 1992-93; reporter Civil Justice Ref. Act Adv. Group No. Dist. of Calif., 1992-99, chair local rules adv. com. No. Dist. Calif., 1994-99; spl. reporter advisory commn. on the civil rules, jud. conf. of the US, 1996—; mem. 9th Cir. local rules and internal operating procedures com., 1996-2002, 9th Cir. task force on self-represented lit., 2002-06. Author: Complex Litigation, 1985, 4th edit., 2004, Civil Procedure: A Modern Approach, 1989, 4th edit., 2005, Federal Practice and Procedure, vols. 8, 8A, and 12, 2d edit., 1994, 1997; rsch. editor U. Calif. Law Rev., 1971-72; contbr. articles to profl. jorus. Mem.: Am. Law Inst., Am. Assn. Law Schs. (chmn. sect. civil procedure 1988, chmn. complex litigation com. 1991), Order of the Coif. Democrat. Home: 70 Domingo Ave Berkeley CA 94705-2436 Office: U Calif Coll Law 200 Mcallister St San Francisco CA 94102-4707 Office Phone: 415-565-4829. Business E-Mail: marcusr@uchastings.edu.

MARCUS, RUDOLPH ARTHUR, chemist, educator; b. Montreal, July 21, 1923; arrived in U.S., 1949, naturalized, 1958; s. Myer and Esther (Cohen) Marcus; m. Laura Hearne, Aug. 27, 1949 (dec. Jan. 2003); children: Alan Rudolph, Kenneth Hearne, Raymond Arthur. BS in Chemistry, McGill U., 1943, PhD in Chemistry, 1946, DSc (hon.), 1988, U. Chgo., 1983, Poly. U., 1986, U. Göteborg, Sweden, 1987, U. N.B., Can., 1993, Queens U., 1993, U. Oxford, Eng., 1995, Yokohama Nat. U., Japan, 1996, U. N.C., 1996, U. Ill., 1997, Technion-Israel Inst. Tech., 1998, Polytechnic U. Valencia, 1999, Northwestern U., 2000, U. Waterloo, Can., 2002. Rsch. staff RDX Project, Montreal, 1944—46; rsch. assoc. NRC of Can., Ottawa, Ont., 1946—49, U. N.C., 1949—51; asst. prof. Poly. Inst. Bklyn., 1951—54, assoc. prof., 1954—58, prof., 1958—64, acting head, div. phys. chem., 1961—62; prof. U. Ill., Urbana, 1964—78, head, div. phys. chem., 1967—68; Arthur Amos Noyes prof. chem. Calif. Inst. Tech., Pasadena, 1978—; vis. prof. theoretical chem. U. Oxford, 1975—76; Baker lectr. Cornell U., Ithaca, NY, 1991; Linnett vis. prof. chemistry Cambridge (Eng.) U., 1996; hon. prof. Fudan U., Shanghai, 1994—; hon prof. Inst. Chem. Chinese Acad. Scis., Beijing, 1995—; hon. fellow Univ. Coll., Oxford, 1995—; hon. prof. Tianjin U., China, 2002, China Ocean U., 2002, Dalian Inst. Chem. Physics, Dalian, China, 2005, Wenzhov Med. Coll., Wenzhov, China, 2005. Professorial fellow Univ. Coll., Oxford, 1975—76; mem. Courant Inst. Math. Scis., NYU, 1960—61; trustee Gordon Rsch. confs., 1966—69; assoc. mem. Ctr. Advanced Studies, U. Ill., Urbana, 1968—69; chmn. bd. dirs. Gordon Rsch. confs., 1968—69, mem. coun., 1965—68; mem. rev. panel Argonne Nat. Lab., 1966—72, chmn., 1967—68; mem. rev. panel Brookhaven

Nat. Lab., 1971—74; mem. rev. com.Radiation Lab., U. Notre Dame Radiation Lab., U. Notre Dame, 1975—80; mem. panel on atmospheric chemistry climatic impact com. NAS-NRC, 1975—78, mem. com. kinetics of chem. reactions, 1973—77, chmn., 1975—77, mem. com. chem. scis., 1977—79; lectr. in field, 1982; mem. com. to survey opportunities in chem. scis., 1982—86; mem. math. panel Internat. Benchmarking of U.S. Rsch. Fields, 1996—97; mem. panel on accountability of federally funded rsch. Com. on Sci., Engring. and Pub. Policy, 2000—01; adv. com. for chemistry NSF, 1977—80; external adv. bd. NAS Ctr. Photoinduced Charge Transfer, 1990—; mem. presdl. chairs com., Chile, 1994—96; advisor, Ctr. for Molecular Scis. Chinese Acad. Scis. and State Key Lab. for Structural Chemistry of Unstable and Stable Species, Beijing, 1995—; co-hon. pres. 29th Internat. Chemistry Olympiad, 1997; hon. visitor Nat. Sci. Coun., China, 1999. Hon. editor Internat. Jour. Quantum Chemistry, 1996—, former mem. editl. bd. Jour. Chem. Physics, Ann. Rev. Phys. Chemistry, Jour. Phys. Chemistry, Accounts Chem. Rsch., Internat. Jour. Chem. Kinetics Molecular Physics, Theoretica Chimica Acta, Chem. Physics Letters, Faraday Trans., Jour. Chem. Soc., editl. bd. Laser Chemistry, 1982—, Advances in Chem. Physics, 1984—, World Sci. Pub., 1987—, Internat. Revs. in Phys. Chemistry, 1988—, Progress in Physics, Chemistry and Mechanics (China), 1989—, Perkins Transactions 2, Jour. Chem. Soc., 1992—, Chem. Physics Rsch. (India), 1992—, Trends in Chem. Physics Rsch. (India), 1992—, Internat. Jour. Molecular Chemistry, 2007—. Recipient Anne Molson prize in chem., McGill U., 1943, Sr. U.S. Scientist award, Alexander von Humboldt-Stiftung, 1976, Electrochem. Soc. Lecture award, 1979, 1996, Robinson medal, Faraday divsn. Royal Soc. Chemistry, 1982, Centenary medal, 1988, Chandler medal, Columbia U., 1983, Wolf prize in chemistry, Wolf Found., Israel, 1985, Nat. medal of Sci., 1989, Evans award, Ohio State U., 1990, Nobel prize in Chem., 1992, Hirshfelder prize in Theoretical Chemistry, U. Wis., 1993, Golden Plate award, Am. Acad. Achievement, 1993, Lavoisier medal, French Chem. Soc., 1994, Oesper award, U. Cin., 1997, Key to City of Taipei, Taiwan, 1999, William Jost lectr. and medal, Deutsche Bunsenges and Acad. Sci., Göttingen, 1999, Susquicentennial medal, Polytech U., Bklyn.; named Hon. Citizen, City of Winnipeg, 1994, Treasure of L.A., Ctrl. City Assn., 1995; fellow Alfred P. Sloan, 1960—61, NSF sr. postdoctoral, 1960—61; scholar Sr. Fulbright-Hays, 1972. Fellow: AAAS, Royal Soc. Can. (hon.), Internat. Acad. Quantum Molecular Sci. (hon.), Chinese Acad. Scis. (hon.), Internat. Soc. for Theoretical Chem. Physics (hon.), Internat. Soc. Electrochemistry (hon.), Royal Soc. Chemistry (hon.), Royal Soc. (London) (hon.), Am. Acad. Arts and Scis. (hon.; exec. com. western sect., co-chmn. 1981—84, rsch. and planning com. 1989—91); mem.: NAS (hon.), Am. Chem. Soc. (past divsn. chmn., mem. exec. com., mem. adv. bd. petroleum rsch. fund, Irving Langmuir award in chem. physics 1978, Peter Debye award in physic. chemistry 1988, Willard Gibbs medal Chgo. sect. 1988, S.C. Lind Lecture, East Tenn. sect. 1988, Theodore William Richards medal Northwestern sect. 1990, Edgar Fahs Smith award Phila. sect. 1991, Ira Remsen Meml. award Md. sect. 1991, Pauling medal Portland, Oreg., and Puget Sound sect. 1991, Auburn-Kosolapoff award 1996, Theoretical Chemistry award 1997, Top 75 Chem. & Engring. News award 1998), Am. Phys. Soc., Lit. and Hist. Soc., Univ. Coll. Dublin (hon.), European Acad. Scis. (hon.), Korean Chem. Soc. (hon.), Am. Philos. Soc. (hon.; coun. mem. 1990), Alpha Chi Sigma. Achievements include development of the Marcus Theory of electron transfer reactions in chemical systems and RRKM theory of unimolecular reactions. Home: 331 S Hill Ave Pasadena CA 91106-3405 Office Phone: 626-395-6566. Business E-Mail: ram@caltech.edu.

MARCY, CHARLES FREDERICK, food company executive; b. Buffalo, Aug. 25, 1950; s. Charles and Mary Jane (Frederick) M.; m. Helen Jean Shank, May 6, 1972 (div. Dec. 1986); children: Michelle Catherine, Adam Charles; m. Cynthia Louise Shockey, June 17, 1989; 1 child, Brooke Allison. BA, Washington and Jefferson Coll., Washington, Pa., 1972; MBA, Harvard U., 1974. Various mktg. and strategic planning positions Gen. Foods Corp., White Plains, N.Y., 1974-84; v.p. mktg. Sara Lee Bakery, Deerfield, Ill., 1984-86; v.p., gen. mgr. Wolferman's Inc. divsn. of Sara Lee Corp., Lenexa, Kans., 1987-89; v.p. strategy and mktg. Kraft Gen. Foods Frozen Products, Glenview, Ill., 1989-90; pres. Kraft Gen. Foods Nat. Dairy Products Corp., Phila., 1991-92, Golden Grain Co., Pleasanton, Calif., 1993-95; pres., CEO Sealright Packaging Co., Inc., DeSoto, Kans., 1995-98; prin. Marcy & Ptnrs. Strategy Cons., Leawood, Kans., 1999; pres., COO Horizon Organic Dairy, Longmont, Colo., 1999, pres., CEO, 2000. Bd. dirs. Phila. Police Athletic League, 1991-92, Boys and Girls Club of Kansas City, Mo., 1987-90, Lake Forest (Ill.) Symphony, 1984-87. Office: Horizon Organic 12002 Airport Way Broomfield CO 80021-2546

MARCY, GEOFFREY W., astronomer, physicist, educator; BA in Physics & Astronomy summa cum laude, UCLA, 1976; PhD in Astronomy & Astrophysics, U. Calif., Santa Cruz, 1982. Fellow Carnegie Inst., Wash., 1982—84; full prof. physics & astronomy San Francisco State U., 1984—96, disting. prof., 1997—99, adjunct prof. physics & astronomy, 1999—; prof. astronomy U. Calif., Berkeley, 1999—. Mem. Com. on the Status of Women in Astronomy, 1994—97, NASA Working Group: Origins of Solar Systems, 1998—2000, NASA Working Group: Terrestrial Planet Finder, 1998—2001; dir. Ctr. for Integrative Planetary Sci., 2000—; Bunyan lectr., physics dept. Stanford U., 1997; G. Darwin Lecture Royal Astronomical Soc., 2000; NSF Disting. Lectr., 00; prin. investigator NASA Space Interferometry Mission, 2001; Sackler Lectr. U. Leiden, 2001; Niels Bohr Lecture N.B. Inst., 2005. Author numerous scientific articles in peer-reviewed jours., newspapers, and mag.; appearances include ABC Nightline, CBS Nightly News, NBC Today Show, BBC Horizons, CNN News, PBS, Late Show with David Letterman. Recipient Manne Siegbahn award, Swedish Acad., 1996, Internat. Assn. Universities Commn. 51 Bioastronomy Medal of Honor (First Ever Issued), 1997, Certificate of Recognition (First Ever Issued), Extrasolar Planetary Found., 1999, UCLA Alumni Profl. Achievement award, 1999, Carl Sagan award, Am. Astronautical & Planetary Soc., 2002, Exceptional Scientific Achievement medal, NASA, 2003, Shaw prize, 2005; named Person of Week, ABC News Hour, 1996, Alumnus Yr., U. Calif. Santa Cruz, 1997, Calif. Scientist of the Yr., 2000, Space Scientist Yr., Discover Mag., 2003. Fellow: Calif. Acad. of Sci.; mem.: NAS (Henry Draper medal 2001), Astronomical Soc. of Pacific (bd. dirs. 1997—99, pub. bd. 1997—2002), Am. Astronomical Soc. (bd. of councilors 1998—2000, Beatrice M. Tinsley prize 2002). Made First Zeeman Measurements of Magnetic Fields for Solor-Type Stars; found Pauncity of Brown Dwarfs Orbiting Stars; developed the method of Precise Doppler Measurements; discovered 70 of the first 100 Extrasolor Planets known; found evidence that the Solar System maybe peculiar; discoverd the first system of planets around a sun-like star; discovered first transiting planet around another star; discovered the first candidate Saturn-Mass planets; discovered the first extrasolar planet orbiting beyond 5AU; co-discovered the first Neptune-Sized Planets: Gliese 436b and 55 Cancri e. Office: U Calif 417 Campbell Hall Berkeley CA 94720 Office Phone: 510-642-1952. Office Fax: 510-642-3411.

MARDIAN, ROBERT CHARLES, JR., restaurateur; b. Orange, Calif., Feb. 1, 1947; s. Robert Charles Sr. and Dorothy Driscilla (Denniss) M.; children: Robert Charles III, Alexandra Quinn, Ashley Michele. BA, Stanford U., 1969; MBA, Pepperdine U., 1986. Gen. mgr. Loft Restaurant, San Jose, Calif., 1969-71; chief exec. officer/chmn. bd. Wind & Sea Restaurants, Inc., Dana Point, Calif., 1971—. Bd. dirs. Dana Niguel Bank, cons. U.S. Olympic Com., Colorado Springs, 1984-88. Commr. Dana Point Econ. Devel.; pres. Surfing Heritage Found. Mem. Young Pres. Orgn. Republican. Avocations: skiing, surfing, beach volleyball, running, snowboarding. Office: Wind & Sea Restaurants Inc 34699 Golden Lantern St Dana Point CA 92629-2908 Office Phone: 949-496-6500.

MARESCA, JOSEPH WILLIAM, JR., technology executive, physical oceanographer; b. Tampa, Fla., Feb. 5, 1946; s. Joseph William and Mary (Cueto) Maresca; m. Noreen Mary Angiola, June 27, 1970; children: Michele Eileen, Craig Robert. BS in Civil Engring., Lehigh U., 1968; MS in Hydraulics, Stanford U., 1969; MS in Oceanic Sci., U. Mich., 1973, PhD, 1975. Sr. oceanographer, program mgr. SRI Internat. (formerly Stanford Rsch. Inst.), Menlo Pk., Calif., 1975—84; CEO Vista Rsch., Inc., Sunnyvale, Calif., 1984—, Vista Engring. Techs., LLC, Kennewick, Wash., 2000—; pres., CEO Vista Applied Techs. Group, Inc., Sunnyvale, Calif., 2004—, Vista Leak Detection, Inc., Kennewick, Wash., 2004—. Contbr. articles to profl. jours. Served with C.E. US Army, 1969—72. NSF trainee, 1972—74, NDEA Title IV fellow, 1974—75. Mem.: Chi Epsilon, Tau Beta Pi, Sigma Xi. Roman Catholic. Home: 780 Fife Way Sunnyvale CA 94087-3526 Office: Vista Rsch Inc 755 N Mary Ave Sunnyvale CA 94085-2909 Office Phone: 408-830-3306. Business E-Mail: maresca@vistaengr.com.

MARGERUM, J(OHN) DAVID, chemist, researcher; b. St. Louis, Oct. 20, 1929; s. Donald Cameron and Ida Lee (Nunley) M.; m. Virginia Bolen, June 5, 1954; children: John Steven, Kris Alan, Julie Ellen. AB, S.E. Mo. State Coll., 1950; PhD, Northwestern U., 1956. Rsch. chemist Shell Oil Co., Wood River, Ill., 1954-55; chief spectoscopy sect. U.S. Army QMR&E Center, Natick, Mass., 1957-59; research specialist Sundstrand Corp., Pacoima, Calif., 1959-62; with Hughes Research Labs., Malibu, Calif., 1962—, sr. scientist, head chemistry sect., 1967—, head material scis. sect., 1988—, asst. dept. mgr. exploratory studies dept., 1989—, mgr. dept. materials sci., lab. chief scientist, 1991—; prin. rsch. scientist, 1993—; mgr. dept. batteries polymer sensors, prin. rsch. scientist HRL Labs., Malibu, 1997—. Contbr. articles to profl. jours.; patentee in field. Served with U.S. Army, 1955-57. Recipient Holley medal ASME, 1977 Fellow AAAS; mem. Am. Chem. Soc., Electrochem. Soc., Soc. Info. Display, Inter-Am. Photochem. Soc., Internat. Liquid Crystal Soc., Sigma Xi Democrat. Unitarian Universalist. Home: 5433 Rozie Ave Woodland Hills CA 91367-5760 Office: HRL Labs LLC 3011 Malibu Canyon Rd Malibu CA 90265-4737 E-mail: jdmargerum@HRL.com.

MARGOL, IRVING, personnel consultant; b. St. Louis, May 28, 1930; s. William and Dora (Karsh) M.; m. Myrna Levy, Dec., 1960; children— Bradley, Lisa, Cynthia. BA, Washington U., St. Louis, 1951, MA, 1952. Employment mgr. Am. Car & Foundry div. ACF, St. Louis, 1955-59; asst. personnel dir. Vickers Inc. div. Sperry-Rand, St. Louis, 1959-60; instr. personnel mgmt. Washington U. (St. Louis), 1960-62; personnel dir. Energy Controls div. Bendix Corp., South Bend, Ind., 1962-69; exec. v.p. community/employee affairs group, community rels. dept., employee assistance program Security Pacific Nat. Bank, LA, 1969-92; mng. dir. Southern Calif. Jannotta, Bray & Assocs., Inc., 1992—; pres. Security Pacific Found., LA, 1989—92; mng. dir. Jannotta Bray & Assocs., LA, 1992-94, Right and Assocs., LA, 1995-99; prin. Eddy Assocs., Inc., 2000—. Instr. UCLA Extension Div., Los Angeles; taught exec. mgmt. courses UCLA, Duke U., U. Colo., U. Wash., Grad. Sch. Banking, Rutgers U., Notre Dame U; currently teaches the Change Management course at the UCLA Ojai Program. Bd. dirs. L.A. chpt. ARC (former pres.), Am. Heart Assn., Am. Cancer Soc.(former pres.), Nat. Conf. Christians & Jews, Braille Inst.; bd. overseers Southwestern U. Law.; bd. dir. Braille Inst., UCLA Mgmt. Edn. Associates, Gateway Hosp., Holocaust Tracing Ctr., Women's Econ. Develop. Corp. Mem. Am. Bankers Assn. (exec. com. 1979—), Am. Soc. Tng. and Devel., Am. Soc. Personnel Adminstrs., Am. Inst. Banking, Washington U. Alumni Assn. Democrat. Jewish. Office: Eddy Assocs Inc 450 N Brand Blvd Ste 600 Glendale CA 91203 Office Phone: 818-291-6354.

MARGOLIN, BRUCE M., lawyer; LLB, U. So. Calif., 1963, JD, 1966. Bar: Calif. 1967, U.S. Dist. Ct. 1967, Ctrl. Dist. Calif. 1967. Pvt. practice, W. Hollywood, Calif. Dir. Nat. Orgn. Reform Marijuana Laws. Contbr. articles to profl. jours. Elected to State Calif. Dem. Com. Recipient Cert. Appreciation, ACLU. Mem.: Nat. Assn. Criminal Def. Lawyers (co-chmn. ethics com.), Criminal Cts. Bar Assn., Century City Bar Assn. (Criminal Def. Atty of Yr. 1999). Ran for governor of California in the 2003 recall election; contributed to the development of the California Prop 215 Medical Marijuana Initiative. Office: 8749 Holloway Dr West Hollywood CA 90069 Office Phone: 310-276-2231. Office Fax: 310-652-1501. E-mail: bmargolin@aol.com.

MARGOLIN, PHILLIP MICHAEL, lawyer; b. NYC, Apr. 20, 1944; s. Joseph Harold and Eleonore (Leftcourt) M.; m. Doreen Stamm, Dec. 22, 1968; children: Daniel Scott, Amy Elaine. BA, Am. U., Washington, 1965; JD, NYU, 1970. Bar: Oreg. 1972, U.S. Dist. Ct. Oreg. 1973, U.S. Ct. Appeals (9th cir.) 1974, U.S. Supreme Ct. 1977. Tchr. N.Y.C. Pub. Schs., 1968-70; law clk. to chief judge Oreg. Ct. Appeals, Salem, 1970-71; dep. dist. atty., spl. agt. Multnomah County, Portland, Oreg., 1971-72; pvt. practice Portland, 1973, 80-86; ptnr. Nash & Margolin, Portland, 1974-80, Margolin & Margolin, Portland, 1986—. Lectr. in field. Author: Heartstone, 1978, The Last Innocent Man, 1981, Gone But Not Forgotten, 1994, Heartstone, 1995, After Dark, 1995, The Burning Man, 1996, Wild Justice, 2000, The Associate, 2001, Ties That Bind, 2003, Sleeping Beauty, 2004, Lost Lake, 2005, numerous short stories; contbr. articles to profl. jours. Vol. Peace Corps., Liberia, 1965-67; coach Hayhurst Elem. Chess Team, Portland, 1981—. Mem. Oreg. Criminal Def. Lawyers Assn., Oreg. State Bar Assn. Democrat. Jewish. Avocations: chess, writing, swimming. Office: Margolin & Margolin 621 SW Morrison St Ste 1025 Portland OR 97205-3813

MARGOLIS, JULIUS, economics professor; b. NYC, Sept. 26, 1920; s. Sam and Fannie (Weiner) Margolis; m. Doris Lubetsky, Oct. 30, 1942; children: Jane S., Carl W. BSS, CCNY, 1941; PhM in Econs, U. Wis., 1943; MPA in Econs, Harvard, 1947, PhD, 1949. Instr. econs. Tufts Coll., 1947-48; asst. prof. econs. and planning U. Chgo., 1948-51; asst. prof. econs. Stanford (Calif.) U., 1951-54, prof. econs. and engring. econ. systems, 1964-69; prof. bus adminstrn. U. Calif., Berkeley, 1954-64, prof. econs. Irvine, 1976—; prof., dir. Fels Ctr. Govt. U. Pa., 1969-76. Cons. govt. and industry, 1958—; dir. Ctr. Global Peace and Conflict Studies, 1985—. Author (with others): The Public Economy of Urban Communities, 1965, The Northern California's Water Industry, 1966, Public Economics, 1969, Public Expenditure and Policy Analysis, 1984; contbr. articles to profl. jours. With US Army, 1943—46. Mem.: Royal Econ. Soc., Am. Econ. Assn. Office: U Calif Dept Econ Irvine CA 92697-0001 Home: 27356 Bellogente Apt 124 Mission Viejo CA 92691-6391 Office Phone: 949-854-3911. Business E-Mail: jmargoli@uci.edu.

MARGON, BRUCE HENRY, astrophysicist, educator; b. NYC, Jan. 7, 1948; 1 child Pamela. AB, Columbia U., 1968; MA, U. Calif.-Berkeley, 1971, PhD, 1973. Asst. rsch. astronomer U. Calif.-Berkeley, 1973—76; assoc. prof. astronomy UCLA, 1976—80; prof. astronomy U. Wash., Seattle, 1980—2001, chmn., 1981—87, 1990—95, sci. dir. Sloan Digital Sky Survey, 1998—99; assoc. dir. Space Telescope Sci. Inst., Balt., 2001—06; vice chancellor rsch., prof. astronomy and astrophysics U. Calif., Santa Cruz, 2006—. Bd. govs. Astrophys. Rsch. Consortium, Inc., Seattle; chmn. bd. dirs. AURA, Inc., Washington; co-investigator Hubble space telescope NASA, Washington, 1977—. NATO postdoctoral fellow, 1973-74; Sloan Found. rsch. fellow, 1979-83 Fellow AAAS, Am. Phys. Soc.; mem. Internat. Astron. Union, Am. Astron. Soc. (Pierce Prize 1981), Royal Astron. Soc. Office: Univ Calif Chancellors Office 1156 High St Santa Cruz CA 95064 Office Phone: 831-459-2425.

MARIANELLA, VINCENZO, bartender; b. Italy; arrived in US, 1999; Attended, Australian Bartending Acad., Dimension Bar Freestyle Team Assn. Sch., Cerviniano Del Friuli, Italy. Bartender Smollensky's on the Strand, London, 7 MOMA, NYC, Valentino, LA; bar chef Providence, LA. Named one of LA's Rising Stars, StarChefs.com, 2006. Office: Providence Restaurant 5955 Melrose Ave Los Angeles CA 90038 Office Phone: 323-460-4170.

MARIN, ROSARIO, state agency administrator, former federal agency administrator; b. Mexico City, Mex., Aug. 4, 1958; m. Alex Marin; children: Eric, Carmen, Alvaro. BS bus. adminstrn., Calif. State U., LA, 1983, LLD (hon.), 2002; grad., Harvard U., 1998. With City Nat. Bank, Beverly Hills, 1981—86; chief legis. affairs Calif. Dept. Devel. Svcs., 1992—93; chair Calif. State Coun. Developmental Disabilities, 1994—96; asst. dep. dir. Calif. State Dept. Social Svcs., 1996—97; dep. dir. Gov.'s Office Cmty. Rels., LA, 1997—98; mayor City of Huntington Park, Calif., 1999—2000; 41st U.S. treas. U. S. Dept. Treasury, Washington, 2001—03. Mem. Calif. Integrated Waste Mgmt. Bd., Sacramento, 2004—, chmn., 2004—. Recipient Rose Fitzgerald Kennedy award, U.N., 1995, Excellence in Pub. Svc. award, Latino Perspective Conf., 2000, Alumna of the Year, Calif. State U., 2002. Address: State and Consumer Svcs Agy 915 Capitol Mall #200 Sacramento CA 95814

MARINEAU, PHILIP ALBERT, apparel executive; b. Chgo., Oct. 4, 1946; s. Philip Albert and Bernice (Collins) Marineau; m. Susan Anne Graf, June 28, 1969. AB in History, Georgetown U., 1968; MBA, Northwestern U., 1970. Coordinator sales research The Quaker Oats Co., Chgo., 1972-73, mktg. asst., 1973-74, asst. brand mgr., then brand mgr., 1974-78, product group mgr., 1978-80, dir., then v.p. product mgmt., 1980-85, pres. grocery specialties div., 1985-87, exec. v.p. grocery specialties and market devel., 1987-88, exec. v.p. internat. grocery products, 1988, exec. v.p., U.S. grocery products, 1989-93, pres., COO, 1993-96; pres. & COO Dean Foods Co., 1996; pres. & CEO Pepsi-Cola N. America, 1997-99, Levi Strauss & Co., San Francisco, 1999—2006. Bd. mem. Meredith Corp. Bd. dirs. Travelers and Immigrant Aid, Chgo., 1987; bd. mem. Georgetown Univ., Kaiser Permanente, Am. Inst. Pub. Svc.; adv. bd. Kellogg Sch. Mgmt. Northwestern U., Vietnam Veterans Meml. Fund; trustee Northlight Theatre, Evanston, Ill., 1985; bd. mem. Holy Family Day Home, Golden Gate Nat. Parks Conservancy. Mem.: Am. Mktg. Assn. (Steuart Hendersen Britt award 1987), Westmoreland Country Club (Wilmette, Ill.).

MARINELLI, JANICE, broadcast executive; b. NY, 1958; m. Thomas Mazza; 3 children. BS in Comm., St. John's U., NY. Rsch. analyst TeleRep; sr. rschr. Lorimar TV, Katz TV Group; acct. exec. Disney-ABC Domestic TV (formerly Buena Vista TV), 1985, dir. sales western divsn., exec. v.p., 1996—99, pres. Burbank, Calif., 1999—. Named one of The 100 Most Powerful Women in Entertainment, Hollywood Reporter, 2006, 2007. Office: Disney-ABC Domestic TV 500 S Buena Vista St Burbank CA 91521

MARINER, WILLIAM MARTIN, chiropractor; b. Balt., Jan. 2, 1949; s. William Joseph and Ellen (Dexter) M. AA, Phoenix Coll., 1976; BS in Biology, L.A. Coll. of Chiropractic, 1980, D Chiropractic summa cum laude, 1980; DD (hon.), Universal Life Ch., Modesto, Calif., 1986. Health food restaurant mgr. Golden Temple of Conscious Cookery, Tempe, Ariz., 1974-75; health food store mgr. Guru's Grainery, Phoenix, 1975; physical therapist A.R.E. Clinic, Phoenix, 1975-76; research dir., founder G.R.D. Healing Arts Ctr., Phoenix, 1974-77; aminstrv. asst., acad. dean L.A. Coll. Chiropractic, Whittier, Calif., 1977-80; faculty Calif. Acupuncture Coll., LA, 1978-80; ednl. cons. Avanti Inst., San Francisco, 1985-91; found, dir., head clinician Pacific Healing Arts Ctr., Del Mar, Calif., 1980-93, Mt. Shasta, Calif., 1993—. Ednl. cons. John Panama Cons., San Francisco, 1991-99. Patentee in field. Co-dir. We Care We Share Charitable Orgn., San Diego, 1985-86. Named Outstanding Sr., L.A. Coll. Chiropractic, 1980. Mem. Calif. Chiropractic Assn., Am. Chiropractic Assn., Internat. Coll. Applied Kinesiology, Holistic Dental Assn., Brit. Homopathic Assn. Avocations: personal growth, natural healing methods, cooking. Office: Pacific Healing Arts Ctr PO Box 192 Mount Shasta CA 96067-0192 Home Phone: 530-926-6448; Office Phone: 530-926-6448. Personal E-mail: wmariner@jps.net.

MARIOTTA, CLAUDIO, electronics executive; Diploma in Engring., Swiss Inst. Tech., Zurich; MS, San Jose State U.; postgrad., U. Fla. With Harris Corp., SSE Telecom; from v.p. product devel. to v.p. ops. Giga-tronics Inc., San Ramon, Calif., 1999-2001, pres., gen. mgr. instrument divsn., 2001—. Office: Giga-tronics Inc 4650 Norris Canyon Rd San Ramon CA 94583-1320 Fax: 925-328-4700.

MARISTUEN, KEITH A., lawyer; b. Malta, Mont., 1953; BA with high honors, U. Mont., 1975, JD with honors, 1978. Bar: Mont. 1978, US Tax Ct. 1980, US Ct. Appeals (9th Cir.). Mem. Bosch, Kuhr, Dugdale, Martin & Kaze PLLP, Havre, Mont. Mem.: ABA (mem. gen. practice sect. and small bus. sect.), Mont. State Bar Assn. (pres. 2004—05, chmn. bd. 2002—03, trustee 1992—, chmn. ethics com. 1995—2000, chmn. bankruptcy sect. legis. com. 1990—2002). Office: Bosch Kuhr Dugdale Martin & Kaze PLLP 335 Fourth Ave PO Box 7152 Havre MT 59501 Office Phone: 406-265-6706. Office Fax: 406-265-7578. Business E-Mail: kmaristuen@bkdlaw.org.

MARITZ, PAUL, computer software company executive; b. Rhodesia, Zimbabwe, 1955; married; 3 children. Grad. in Math. and Computer Sci., U. Cape Town. Programmer Burroughs; rschr. U. St. Andrews, Scotland; with Intel Corp., 1981—86; various positions through v.p. platform strategy and developer group Microsoft, 1986—2000, exec. mgmt. team; founder, CEO Pi Corp. (acquired by EMC), 2003—08; pres., gen. mgr. cloud computing divsn. EMC, 2008; pres., CEO VMware (subs. EMC), 2008—. Chmn. bd. Grameen Found. Office: VMware 3145 Porter Dr Palo Alto CA 94304 Office Phone: 650-475-5000. Office Fax: 650-475-5005.

MARIUCCI, ANNE L., real estate development company executive; BA in Accounting/Finance, U. Ariz. In corp. fin. KPMG Peat Marwick, Am. Continental Corp.; v.p. corp. planning & devel. Del Webb Corp., 1982-86, pres, CEO Del Webb Investment Properties, 1986-87, sr. v.p. Phoenix, 1988—. Office: Del Webb Corp 15333 N Pima Rd Ste 300 Scottsdale AZ 85260-2782

MARK, JAMES B. D., surgeon, educator; b. Nashville, June 26, 1929; s. Julius and Margaret (Baer) M.; m. Jean Rambar, Feb. 5, 1957; children: Jonathan, Michael, Margaret, Elizabeth, Katherine. BA, Vanderbilt U., 1950, MD, 1953. Intern, resident in gen. and thoracic surgery Yale-New Haven Hosp., 1953-60; instr. to asst. prof. surgery Yale U., 1960-65; assoc. prof. surgery Stanford U., 1965-69, prof., 1969-97, prof. emeritus, 1997—, Johnson and Johnson prof. surgery, 1978—97, head div. thoracic surgery, 1972-97, assoc. dean clin. affairs, 1988-92; chief staff Stanford U. Hosp., 1988-92. Governing bd. Health Systems Agy., Santa Clara County, 1978-80; sr. Fulbright-Hays fellow, vis. prof. surgery U. Dar es Salaam, Tanzania, 1972-73 Mem. editl. bd.: Jour. Thoracic and Cardiovasc. Surgery, 1986-94, World Jour. Surgery, 1995-2003, The Pharos, 2002-; contbr. numerous articles to sci. jours. Bd. dirs. Stanford U. Hosp., 1992-94. With USPHS, 1955-57. Fellow ACS (pres. No. Calif. chpt. 1980-81), Am. Coll. Chest Physicians (pres. 1994-95); mem. Am. Assn. Thoracic Surgery, Am. Surg. Assn., Western Surg. Assn., Pacific Coast Surg. Assn., Halsted Soc. (pres. 1984), Western Thoracic Surg. Assn. (pres. 1992-93), Calif. Acad. Medicine (pres. 1978), Santa Clara County Med. Soc. (pres. 1976-77). Office: Stanford U Med Ctr CVRB Stanford CA 94305 Home: 81 Pearce Mitchell Pl Stanford CA 94305-8535 Office Phone: 650-723-6649. Business E-Mail: jbdm@stanford.edu.

MARK, SHELLEY MUIN, economist, educator; b. China, Sept. 9, 1922; came to U.S., 1923, naturalized, 1944; s. Hing D. and S. (Wong) M.; m. Janet Chong, Sept. 14, 1946 (dec. Mar. 1977); children—Philip, Diane, Paul, Peter, Steven; m. Tung Chow, July 8, 1978. BA, U. Wash., 1943, PhD, 1956; MS, Columbia, 1944; postgrad. (Ford Found. fellow), Harvard, 1959-60. Fgn. news reporter CBS, NY, 1945-46; instr. U. Wash., 1946-48; asst. prof. Ariz. State Coll., 1948-51; territorial economist OPS, Honolulu, 1951-53; prof. econs. U. Hawaii, 1953-62, dir. econ. rsch. ctr., 1959-62; dir. planning and econ. devel. State of Hawaii, 1962-74, state land use commr., 1962-74, state energy coord., 1973-74; dir. Office Land Use Coordination EPA, Washington, 1975-77; prof. econs. U. Hawaii, 1978—. Rsch. fellow East-West Ctr., Inst. Econ. Devel. and Policy, 1984-94; Asian advisor Internat. Ctr. Econ. Growth, 1992—; sr. advisor Dept. Bus., Econ. Devel. and Tourism, Hawaii, 1995-2002; vis. scholar Harvard U., 1986; vis. faculty Grad. Sch. People's Bank of China, 1988; also econ. cons. Philippines Inst. Devel. Studies, Devel. Rsch. Ctr. State Coun., China, Peoples Bank of China, Beijing, also other orgns.; mem. Gov.'s Adv. Com. Sci. and Tech., 1963-74, Oahu Transp. Policy Com., 1964-74, Regional Export Expansion Coun., 1964-74. Author: Economics in Action, 4th edit., 1969, Macroeconomic Performance of Asia-Pacific Region, 1985, Development Economics and Developing Economies, 1990, US Trade Policy, Asian Economic Interdependence, and the South China Growth Triangle, 1996; editor: Economic Interdependence and Cooperation in Asia-Pacific, 1993, Asian Transitional Economies, 1996; contbr. articles to profl. jours. Bd. dirs. U. Hawaii Rsch. Corp.; bd. dirs. Coun. State Planning Agys., pres., 1973-74, hon. mem., 1975—; governing bd. Coun. State Govts., 1972-74. Recipient Sackett Meml. award Columbia, 1944 Mem. Hawaii Govt. Employees Assn. (pres. univ. chpt., dir. 1958-59), Am. Econ. Assn., Royal Econ. Soc., Western Regional Sci. Assn. (pres. 1974-75, dir.), Phi Beta Kappa, Sigma Delta Chi. Mem. United Ch. of Christ. Home: 2036 Keeaumoku St Honolulu HI 96822-2526 Personal E-mail: smark5@hotmail.com.

MARKEY, BETSY (ELIZABETH HELEN MARKEY), United States Representative from Colorado; b. Cresskill, NJ, Apr. 27, 1956; d. Thomas Francis and Catherine A. (Dillon) Markey; m. James Francis Kelly, May 5, 1984; children: Katherine Angela, Erin Susan, Al. BA in Polit. Sci., U. Fla., 1978; MA in Pub. Adminstrn., Am. U., 1983; grad., Colo. Inst. Leadership Training, 2002. Staff asst. US Senator John Durkin, Washington, 1979, US Ho. of Reps., Washington, 1979-81; sr. asst. to v.p. Am. U., Washington, 1981-83; presdl. mgmt. intern US Dept. Treasury, Washington, 1983-84; chief policy and tng. divsn. office Info. Sys. Security US Dept. State, Washington, 1984-87; co-founder, CEO, CFO Syscom Svcs., Kensington, Mo., 1989—95; owner Huckleberry's, Fort Collins, Colo., 1995—2001; regional dir. 4th congl. dist. Senator Ken Salazar, 2005—07; mem. US Congress from 4th Colo. dist., 2009—. Founder No. Colo. Dem. Bus. Coalition, 2001; chair Larimer County Dem. Party, 2002—05; legis. aide Ho. Subcom. Post Office & Civil Svc. Vol. Christian Children's Fund, 1979—83, Poudre R-1 School Dist.; pres. bd. dirs. Food Bank Larimer County. Recipient Meritorious Honor award, US Dept. State, 1986; named a Presdl. Mgmt. Fellow, 1983. Mem.: NAFE, NOW, Nat. Assn. Women Bus. Owners, Internat. Network Women in Enterprise & Trade, Pi Alpha Alpha. Democrat. Avocation: outdoor sports. Office: US Congress 1229 Longworth House Office Bldg Washington DC 20515-0604 also: Dist Office 430 W Mountain Ave Fort Collins CO 80521-2605 Office Phone: 202-225-4676. Office Fax: 202-225-5870.*

MARKEY, WILLIAM ALAN, health facility administrator, consultant; b. Cleve., Dec. 29, 1927; s. Oscar Bennett and Claire (Feldman) M.; m. Irene Nelson, Oct. 31, 1954; children: Janet Ellen Markey-Hisakawa, Suzanne Katherine Markey-Johnson. Student, Case Inst. Tech., 1945—48; BA, U. Mich., 1950; MS, Yale U., 1954. Resident in hosp. adminstrn. Beth Israel Hosp., Boston, 1953-54; asst. dir. Montefiore Hosp., Pitts., 1954-56; asst. adminstr. City of Hope Med. Ctr., Duarte, Calif., 1956-57, adminstrv. dir., 1957-66; assoc. dir. cancer hosp. project, instr. pub. health U. So. Calif. Sch. Medicine, 1966-67, asst. clin. prof. pub. health and cmty. medicine, 1968-70, asst. prof., 1970-75, dep. dir. regional med. programs, 1967-71; adminstr. Health Care Agy., County of San Diego, 1971-74, health svcs. cons., 1974-75; dir. Maricopa County Dept. Health Svcs., Phoenix, 1975-79, cons., 1979-80; adminstr. Sonoma Valley Hosp., Calif., 1980—83. Lectr. pub. health Sch. Pub. Health, UCLA, 1969-74; lectr. cmty. medicine Sch. Medicine, U. Calif., San Diego, 1973-75; cons. LA County Dept. Hosps., 1966-71, cons. Hosp./Health Svcs., 1983—; CEO Chinese Hosp., San Francisco, 1985-86, 90-91; adj. instr. Golden Gate U., 1992-96. Mem. bd. edn. Duarte Unified Sch. Dist., 1967-72, pres., 1970-72; bd. dir. Hosp. Coun. So. Calif., 1963-67, sec., 1966-67, Duarte Pub. Libr. Assn., 1965-72, Duarte-Bradbury chpt. Am. Field Svc., 1965-72, Duarte-Bradbury Cmty. Chest, 1961-68, Ctrl. Ariz. Health Svcs. Agy., 1975-80, Vis. Nurse Assn. The Redwoods, Santa Rosa, Calif., 1985-86, Sonoma Greens Homeowners Assn., 1990-95, 2002-05, Sonoma City Opera, 1987, 93, United Way, Sonoma, 1996—; com. chmn. Sonoma County Bd. Realtors, 1990-92; active Sonoma County Multiple Listing Svc., 1987-97; mem. Sonoma County Human Svcs. Commn., 2003-. With AUS, 1950-52. Fellow Am. Coll. Health Care Execs. (life); mem. Am. Hosp. Assn. (life), APHA, Royal Soc. Health, Calif. Hosp. Assn. (trustee 1966-69, dir. 1966-69), Internat. Fedn. Hosps., Hosp. Coun. No. Calif. (dir. 1981-83), Kiwanis, Rotary (past pres. Duarte). Home: 866 Princeton Dr Sonoma CA 95476-4186

MARKEZICH, RON, computer software company executive; BA in Mgmt. Info. Sys., U. Notre Dame. With electronics and high tech. group Accenture (formerly Andersen Consulting); joined Microsoft, 1998; gen. mgr. fin. and adminstrn. info. tech. Microsoft Info. Tech., gen. mgr. info. tech. client svcs., gen. mgr. global tech. svcs.; CIO, v.p. managed solutions Microsoft Corp., Redmond, Wash., 2004, corp. v.p. Microsoft Online.

MARKHAM, JESSE WILLIAM, JR., lawyer; b. Nashville, Apr. 13, 1951; s. Jesse William and Penelope Markham; m. Diana Markham, Oct. 5, 2002; children: Elizabeth, Blakely. BA, Harvard U., 1974; MA in philosophy, U. Mass., 1976; JD, Vanderbilt U., 1979. Bar: Calif. Assoc. Rogers & Wells, Paris, Fine & Ambrogne, Boston; asst. atty. gen. State of Mass., 1986—88; dep. atty. gen. State of Calif., San Francisco, 1988-93; ptnr. Markham & Oshiro, San Francisco, 1993-97, Jackson Tufts Cole & Black, San Francisco, 1997-99, Orrick Herrington & Sutcliffe, San Francisco, 1999—2004, Morrison & Foerster LLP, San Francisco, 2004—. Adj. prof. antitrust law U. San Francisco Law Sch., mem. faculty Intensive Advocacy Training Inst., Stanford Law Sch. Co-author: (book) Calif. Antitrust Law, 1991, 1998, Calif. Antitrust and Unfair Competition Law, 2003; author: Calif. Atty. Gen.'s Antitrust Guidelines for the Ins. Industry. Bd. dirs. East Bay Agy. for Children, Oakland, Calif., 1998-2000. Mem.: Calif. State Bar (mem. antitrust and trade regulation law sect., treas. 1994—95, co-chair programs 1995—96, chair 1996—97). Avocations: skiing, hiking, mountain biking. Office: Morrison & Foerster 425 Market St San Francisco CA 94105-2482 Office Phone: 415-268-7448.

MARKLAND, FRANCIS SWABY, JR., biochemist, educator; b. Phila., Jan. 15, 1936; s. Francis Swaby Sr. and Willie Lawrence (Averritt) M.; m. Barbara Blake, Jun. 27, 1959 (dec. April 5, 1996; children: Cathleen Blake, Francis Swaby IV; m. Wendy Jacquemin, Dec. 20, 2007. BS, Pa. State U., 1957; PhD, Johns Hopkins U., 1964. Postdoctoral fellow UCLA, 1964-66, asst. prof. biochemistry, 1966-73; vis. asst. prof. U. So. Calif., Los Angeles, 1973-74, assoc. prof., 1974-83, prof., 1983—, acting chmn. dept. biochemistry, 1986-88, vice-chmn., 1988-92, assoc. dean for sci. affairs, 2004—08. Cons. Clin. Lab. Med. Group, LA, 1977-88, Cortech, Inc., Denver, 1983-88, Maret Corp., Wayne, Pa., 1996-2000; co-founder Pivotal BioScis., Inc., 2003-; mem. biochem., endocrinology study sect. NIH, 1986-90, mem FLAIR prog., rev. NIH NCI, 2002-2003, ad hoc. mem. NIAD Spl. Jour. Review, 2008. Contbg. editor: Toxicon, Jour. Natural Toxins; contbr. articles to profl. jours.:. Mem. Angeles Choral, L.A. Capt. USNR, 1957-59, ret. Recipient NIH rsch. career devel. award USPHS, NIH, 1968-73, 2007-; rsch. grantee Nat. Cancer Inst., 1979-86, 91-93, Nat. Heart Lung and Blood Inst., 1984-88, 95-2002, State of Calif. Breast Cancer Rsch. Program, 1995-2002, State Calif. Cancer Rsch. Program, 2000-03, U.S. Army Prostate Cancer Rsch. Program, 2004—, Komen Found., 2004-, US Army Ovarian Cancer Program, 2007-; study sect. reviewer Western region Am. Heart Assn., 2003-06. Mem. AAAS, Am. Soc. Biochem. and Molecular Biology, Am. Chem. Soc., Internat. Soc. on Toxinology, Internat. Soc. on Thrombosis and Haemostasis (subcom. exogenous hemostatic factors, chair 1994-96, co-chair 1999—), Am. Assn. Cancer Rsch., Am. Soc. Hematology, Sigma Xi, Alpha Zeta. Avocations: singing, aerobics, bicycling. Office: U So Calif Keck Sch Medicine Cancer Rsch Lab Rm 106 1303 N Mission Rd Los Angeles CA 90033-1020 Business E-Mail: markland@usc.edu.

MARKLE, DAVID A., optical engineer; Sr. v.p., chief tech. officer Ultratech Stepper, San Jose, Calif. Recipient David Richardson medal Optical Soc. Am., 1994. Mem.: NAE. Office: 3050 Zanker Rd San Jose CA 95134-2126

MARKLEY, WILLIAM C., lawyer; b. Salina, Kans., Dec. 21, 1945; m. Marcia A. Markley. BS, US Naval Acad., 1967; JD, Hastings Coll. Law, 1974. Sr. v.p., gen. counsel, sec. Jacobs Engring. Group Inc., Pasadena, Calif. Mem.: Am. Corp. Counsel Assn., State Bar Calif., ABA, LA County Bar Assn. Office: Jacobs Engring Group Inc 1111 S Arroyo Pky PO Box 7084 Pasadena CA 91109-7084 Office Phone: 626-578-6855. Office Fax: 626-578-6990. Business E-Mail: Bill.Markley@Jacobs.com.

MARKOFF, STEVEN C., finance company executive; CEO, pres., founder A. Mark Fin., Santa Monica, Calif., 1965—. Co-chmn. A. Mark Entertainment Film Prodn. Co., 2004; dir. Goldline Internat.; chmn. Careside Inc. Dir. ACLU Found. Southern Calif., 1979—; dir. Mgmt. Edn. Associates UCLA, 1986—92, dir. bd. visitors Grad. Sch. Mgmt., 1986; dir. Hollywood Cmty. Hosp., 1982—91. Office: A Mark Financial Corporation 233 Wilshire Blvd Ste 200 Santa Monica CA 90401-1227

MARKOVCHICK, VINCENT J., surgeon; b. Hazleton, Pa., 1944; MD, Temple U., 1970. Intern Presbyn. Med. Ctr., Denver, 1970-71; resident emergency medicine U. Chgo. Hosps.-Clinics, 1974-76; mem. staff Denver Gen. Hosp.; assoc. prof. U.Colo. Health Sci. Ctr.; pres. Am. Bd. Emer. Med., East Lansing; dir. emergency med. Denver Health Med. Center, Denver, 2000—. Mem. Am. Coll. Emergency Physicians, Colo. Med. Soc., STEM. Office: Denver Gen Hosp Emergency Medicine Dept 777 Bannock St Denver CO 80204-4507

MARKOWITZ, HARRY MAX, finance and economics educator; b. Chgo., Aug. 24, 1927; s. Morris and Mildred (Gruber) M.; m. Barbara Gay. PhB, U. Chgo., 1947, MA, 1950, PhD, 1954. With research staff Rand Corp., Santa Monica, Calif., 1952-60, 61-63; chmn. bd., tech. dir. Consol. Analysis Ctrs., Inc., Santa Monica, 1963-68; prof. UCLA, Westwood, 1968-69; pres. Arbitrage Mgmt. Co., NYC, 1969-72; pvt. practice cons. NYC, 1972-74; prof. Wharton Sch Bus., U. Pa., 1972—74; with research staff T.J. Watson Research Ctr. IBM, Yorktown Hills, NY, 1974-83; prof. Rutgers U., 1980—82; Marvin Speiser Disting. Prof. of Fin. and Econs. Baruch Coll. CUNY, NYC, 1982-93; dir. rsch. Daiwa Securities Trust Co, Jersey City, 1990-2000; prin., owner Harry Markowitz Co., 1993—; rsch. prof. dept. econs. U. Calif. San Diego. V.p. Inst. Mgmt. Sci., 1960-62. adv. bd. Jour. Investment Mgmt. Author: Portfolio Selection: Efficient Diversification of Investments, 1959, Mean-Variance Analysis in Portfolio Choice, 1987; co-author: SIMSCRIPT Simulation Programming Language, 1963, (with Frank J. Fabozzi) The Theory and Practice of Investment Management, 2002; co-editor: Process Analysis of Economic Capabilities, 1963. Recipient John von Neumann Theory prize Ops. Rsch. Soc. Am. and Inst. Mgmt. Sci., 1989, Nobel Prize in Econs., 1990. Fellow Econometric Soc., Am. Acad. Arts and Scis., Am. Fin. Assn. Office: Ste 245 1010 Turquoise St San Diego CA 92109

MARKOWITZ, SAMUEL SOLOMON, chemistry professor; b. Bklyn., Oct. 31, 1931; s. Max and Florence Ethel (Goldman) M.; children: Michael, Daniel, Jonah; m. 2d Lydia de Antonis, Oct. 31, 1993. BS in Chemistry, Rensselaer Poly. Inst., 1953; MA, Princeton U., 1955, PhD, 1957; postgrad., Brookhaven Nat. Lab., 1955-57. Asst. prof. chemistry U. Calif., Berkeley, 1958-64, assoc. prof., 1964-72, prof., 1972—. Faculty sr. scientist Lawrence Berkeley Lab., 1958—; vis. prof. nuclear physics Weizmann Inst. Sci., Rehovot, Israel, 1973-74. Mem. Bd. Edn. of Berkeley Unified Sch. Dist., 1969-73, pres. bd., 1971-72. Recipient Elizabeth McFeely D'Urso Meml. Pub. Ofcl. award Alameda County Edn. Assn., 1973; LeRoy McKay fellow Princeton U., 1955, Charlotte Elizabeth Proctor fellow Princeton U., 1956, NSF postdoctoral fellow U. Birmingham, Eng., 1957-58, NSF sr. postdoctoral fellow Faculte des Scis. U. Paris a Orsay, Laboratoire Joliot-Curie de Physique Nucleaire, 1964-65. Fellow AAAS; mem. Am. Chem. Soc. (bd. dirs. Calif. sect., chmn. 1991, 93-94, Nat. Councilor, 1990-, Walter Petersen award 2003), Am. Phys. Soc., Am. Inst. chemists, N.Y. Acad. Scis., Calif. Inst. Chemists, Sigma Xi. Home: 555 Pierce St # 245 Albany CA 94706 Office: U Calif Dept Chemistry Berkeley CA 94720-1460 Office Phone: 510-642-2922. Business E-Mail: markowit@cchem.berkeley.edu.

MARKOWSKI, ELIZABETH M., lawyer; JD cum laude, NYU, 1978. Law clk. to Hon. Edward Weinfeld US Dist. Ct. (so. dist.) NY, 1978—79; sr. ptnr. Baker Botts LLP, NYC, 1992—2000; sr. v.p. legal Liberty Media Corp., Englewood, Colo., 2000—04; with Liberty Media Internat., Englewood, Colo., 2004—05; sr. v.p., gen. counsel, sec. Liberty Global Inc., Englewood, Colo., 2005—. Mem.: ABA, Assn. of Bar of City of NY. Office: Liberty Global, Inc 12300 Liberty Blvd Englewood CO 80112 Office Phone: 303-220-6600. Office Fax: 303-220-6601.

MARKS, MERTON E., lawyer, international arbitrator, mediator, consultant; b. Chgo., Oct. 16, 1932; s. Alfred Tobias and Helene Fannie (Rosner) M.; m. Bernice H. Germaine, Aug. 21, 2007; children: Sheldon, Elise Marks Vazelakis, Alan, Elaine Marks Ianchiou (dec.). BS, Northwestern U., 1954, JD, 1956. Bar: Ill. 1956, U.S. Ct. Mil. Appeals 1957, Ariz. 1958, U.S. Dist. Ct. Ariz. 1960, U.S. Ct. Appeals (9th cir.) 1962, U.S. Supreme Ct. 1970; cert. arbitrator U.S. Dist. Ct. Ariz. Assoc. Moser, Compere & Emerson, Chgo., 1956-57; ptnr. Morgan, Marks & Rogers, Tucson, 1960-62; asst. atty. gen. State of Ariz., Phoenix, 1962-64, counsel indsl. commn., 1964-65; from assoc. to ptnr. Shimmel, Hill, Bishop & Gruender, Phoenix, 1965-74; ptnr. Lewis & Roca, Phoenix, 1974—2001; prin. Merton E. Marks PC Arbitration and Mediation Svcs., 2001—. Judge Pro Tempore Ariz. Ct. Appeals, 1994; CPR Inst. Dispute Resolution Inter-Insurer Arb. Panel; spl. master Ariz. Superior Ct., 2001—; US and internat. alternative dispute resolution; lectr. in field. Contbr. articles to profl. jours., columns. Past trustee Ariz. Opera Co., past chmn. endowment commn.; past mem. U.S. Olympic Com. for Ariz. Capt. JAGC, USAR, 1957-64. Fellow Chartered Inst. Arbitrators (London); mem. ABA (trial, tort and ins. practice sect., chmn. spl. com. on fed. asbestos legis. 1987-89, chmn. workers compensation and employers liability law com. 1983-84, dispute resolution sect.), Am. Bd. Trial Advs., Am. Coll. Legal Medicine, Am. Arbitration Assn., Financial Industry Regulatory Authority, Internat. Bar Assn. (arbitration com.), State Bar Ariz. (chmn. workers compensation sect. 1969-73), Fedn. Def. and Corp. Counsel (chmn. pharm. litig. sect. 1989-91, chmn. workers compensation sect. 1977-79, v.p. 1978-79, 81, bd. dirs. 1981-89, mem. products liability sect., mem. reinsurance sect., chmn. alternative dispute resolution sect. 2005-06), Internat. Assn. Def. Counsel, Ariz. Assn. Def. Counsel (pres. 1976-77), Maricopa County Bar Assn., Pima County Bar Assn., Def. Rsch. Inst. (drug and device com., chmn. workers compensation com. 1977-78), Reinsurance and Ins. Arbitration Soc., (cert. arbitrator). Office: 7868 E Via Marina Scottsdale AZ 85258-2852 also: 850 N Kolb Rd Tucson AZ 85710-1333 Home Phone: 480-544-4324; Office Phone: 480-991-3949. Business E-Mail: memarkspc@earthlink.net.

MARKS, MICHAEL E., electronics executive; BA, MA, Oberlin Coll.; MBA, Harvard U. Pres., CEO Metcal Inc., Menlo Park, Calif.; CEO Flextronics Internat. Ltd., Singapore, 1994—2005, chmn., 2006—; mem. Kohlberg Kravis Roberts & Co., Menlo Park, Calif., 2005—; interim CEO Tesla Motors. Bd. dir. SanDisk Corp.; mgr. Bigwood Capital. Office: KKR Ste 200 2800 Sand Hill Rd Menlo Park CA 94025

MARKS, ROBERT ARTHUR, lawyer, attorney general; b. Dayton, Ohio, Oct. 9, 1952; s. Arthur Kenneth and Patricia Marks; m. Victoria Scurlock, Oct. 21, 1978; 2 children. BA, U. Wis., 1974; JD, U. Cin., 1977. Bar: Ohio 1977, Hawaii 1978, U.S. Ct. Appeals (6th cir.) Ohio 1977, U.S. Ct. Appeals (9th cir.) Hawaii 1978, U.S. Supreme Ct. 1992. Pvt. practice, Honolulu, 1978—84; dep. atty. gen. State of Hawaii, Honolulu, 1984—87, supr. dep. atty. gen., 1987—92, 1st dep. atty.

gen., 1992, atty. gen., 1992—94; counsel Alston, Hunt, Floyd & Ing, Honolulu, 1995—97, Price, Okamoto Himeno & Lum, Honolulu, 1997—. Office: Price Okamoto Himeno Lum 707 Richards St Ste 728 Honolulu HI 96813-4623

MARLAR, JAMES M., federal judge; b. 1945; AB, Stanford U., 1967; JD, U. Ariz., 1970. With Teilberg, Sanders & Parks, Phoenix, Ariz.; pvt. practice Phoenix; judge pro tempore Ariz. Ct. Appeals, 1986, Ariz. Superior Ct., Phoenix, 1988; apptd. bankruptcy judge U.S. Dist. Ct. Ariz., 1993; apptd. 9th Cir. Bankruptcy Appellate Panel, 1999. Office: US Bankruptcy Court 38 S Scott Ave # 100 Tucson AZ 85701-1704 Fax: 520-620-7457.

MARLEAU, PATRICK, professional hockey player; b. Aneroid, Sask., Can., Sept. 15, 1979; m. Christina Marleau. Center San Jose Sharks, 1997—, capt., 2003—. Mem. Team Can., World Cup of Hockey, 2004. Recipient NHL All-Star Game, 2007; named San Jose Mercury News South Bay Sportsperson of Yr., 2006; named to NHL All-Star Game, 2004, 2009. Achievements include being a member of World Cup Champion Team Canada, 2004. Office: San Jose Sharks 525 W Santa Clara St San Jose CA 95113*

MARLEN, JAMES S., chemical, plastics and building materials manufacturing company executive; b. Santiago, Chile, Mar. 14, 1941; came to U.S., 1961; m. Carolyn S. Shields, Jan. 23, 1965; children: James, Andrew, John. BSChemE, U. Ala., 1965; MBA, U. Akron, 1971. With GenCorp., Akron, Ohio, 1965-93, engring., mktg. and gen. mgmt. positions domestic and internat. ops., 1977—80; group pres. fabricated plastics GTR Coated Fabrics Co., 1980-87; pres. consumer and indsl. sects. GenCorp Polymer Products, Akron, Ohio, 1988—; v.p. and officer GenCorp, Akron, 1988-93; pres., CEO Ameron Internat. Corp., Pasadena, Calif., 1993—. Bd. dirs., Ameron, Inc., chmn. bd. dirs., pres. and CEO, 1995—; dir. A. Schulman, Inc., Tamco Steel, Parsons Corp.; gen. and hon. chmn. Nat. Inventors Hall of Fame Induction, 1993. Bd. dirs. YMCA Met. L.A., The Employers Group of Calif., Town Hall of L.A., gov.; mem. the Beavers; dir. L.A. Sports Coun.; mem. bd. visitors Anderson Sch. Bus., UCLA, 1999-2001. Mem. Chem. Mfrs. Assn. (past pres.), Assocs. Caltech, Calif. C. of C., L.A. C. of C. (dir.), Portage Country Club (Akron, Ohio), Calif. Club (L.A.), Annandale Golf Club (Pasadena), L.A. Country Club, Valley Hunt Club (Pasadena), Soc. Fellows of Huntington Libr. (L.A.), Birnam Wood Golf Club (Santa Barbara, Calif.). Office: Ameron Internat Corp 245 S Los Robles Ave Pasadena CA 91101-2820

MARLETTA, MICHAEL A., biochemistry educator, researcher; b. Rochester, NY, Feb. 12, 1951; m. Margaret Gutowski, 1991. BA, SUNY, Fredonia, 1973; PhD in Pharm. Chemistry, U. Calif., San Francisco, 1978. NIH postdoctoral fellow, dept. chem. MIT, Cambridge, 1978-80, from asst. prof. to assoc. prof. toxicology, 1980-87; assoc. prof. med. chemistry U. Mich., Ann Arbor, 1987-91, assoc. prof. biol. chemistry, 1989-91, John G. Searle prof. med. chemistry, prof. biol. chemistry, 1991—2001; prof., chemistry, biochemistry and molecular biology U. Calif., Berkeley, 2001—, Aldo DeBenedictis disting. prof., chmn. dept. chemistry, 2005—, Joel Hildebrand disting. prof. chem., 2005—. Investigator Howard Hughes Med. Inst., 1997—2001; Miller vis. rsch. prof. U. Calif., Berkeley, 2000. Recipient George H. Hitchings award for innovative methods in drug discovery & design, 1991, Faculty Recognition award, U. Mich., 1992, Outstanding Achievement award, SUNY, Fredonia, 1993, Disting. Faculty Leadership award in biomed. rsch., U. Mich. Med. Sch., 2000, Disting. Faculty Achievement award, U. Mich., 2000, Emil Thomas Kaiser award, Protein Soc., 2007; named State of Mich. Scientist of Yr., 2000; named to Alumni Honor Roll, SUNY, 1996; MacArthur fellow, John D. and Catherine T. MacArthur Found., 1995. Fellow: Am. Acad. Arts and Scis., Mich. Soc. Fellows (sr.); mem.: NAS, Inst. Medicine, Am. Chem. Soc. (Repligen award in chemistry of biol. processes 2007, Esselen award for chemistry in pub. interest 2007), Am. Soc. Biochem. and Molecular Biology. Achievements include research in protein/structure function with a particular interest in enzyme reaction mechanisms and molecular mechanisms of signal transduction, study of nitric oxide synthase, guanylate cyclase and related enzymes in this signaling system. Office: Univ Calif Chemistry Dept 570 Stanley Hall Berkeley CA 94720-1460 Office Phone: 510-666-2763. Office Fax: 510-666-2765. Business E-Mail: marletta@berkeley.edu.

MARLON, ANTHONY M., healthcare company executive, cardiologist; m. Renee Marlon. Graduate, Coll. of Holy Cross, Mass., 1963; internship, residency in cardiology, Stanford Univ., 1967—72. Intern, resident, cardiology fellow Stanford (Calif.) U., 1967-72; chief cardiology U. Med. Ctr. So. Nev., 1972-85; pvt. practice cardiology, from 1972; founder, chmn. bd., CEO Sierra Health Svcs., Inc., Las Vegas, Nev., 1984—2008; exec. UnitedHealth Group, Minnetonka, Minn., 2008—. Office: Sierra Health Svcs Inc 2724 N Tenaya Way Las Vegas NV 89128

MARLOW, EDWARD A., former army officer; b. Cleve., Nov. 22, 1946; m. Gari Ann Dill, Sept. 20, 1975. AA, Long Beach City Coll., 1971; cert., Officer Candidate Sch., Ft. Benning, 1974, Basic Infantry Officer Course, 1976; student, Am. Law Inst., NYC, 1979-80; cert., Advance Armor Officer Course, Ft. Knox, 1982, U.S. Army Command and Gen. Staff Coll., 1986; BS in Bus. Mgmt. and Polit. Sci., SUNY, 1987; MPA, U. So. Calif., 1990; cert., Advance Intelligence Officer Course, Ft. Huachuca, 1991. Registered investment adv. with SEC, 1978-90. Commd. 2d lt. inf. US Army, 1974, advanced through grades to maj., 1988, ret., 1998; chief real property br. Mil. Dept., Sacramento, 1968—2004; pres. and dir. TEAM Mgmt. Corp., 1978—2006; pres. Western Res. Corp., Goldfield, Nev., 2000—, bd. dir.; CEO TEAM Internat., LLC, Sacramento, 2004—06; pres. and CEO TEAM Profl. Svcs., LLC, 2004—07; team leader Real Property Acquisition Program US Army Corps Engrs., LA, 2005—06; CEO Edward A. Marlow, LLC, 2005—. Del. Korean Svc. Vets. Revisit Program, Seoul, Republic of Korea, 1975. Mng. sr. ptnr. Caribbean Basin Latin Am. Devel. Orgn., Sacramento, 1988-98; trustee Hosp. Relief Fund Caribbean, Inc., Washington, 1989-92; mem. Caribbean Pvt. Sector Disaster Coord. subcom. White House Internat. Disaster Adv. Com., 1991-92; sr. ptnr. Caribbean Basin Latin Am. Devel. Orgn. Endowment Group, Sacramento, 1992-2003; chair bd. trustees CABALADO Relief Fund, Inc., 1993-99; provided disaster assistance and med. equipment to Glendon Hosp., Plymouth, Montserrat, West Indies, 1994-95; mem. Petersen Automotive Mus., 2005-06; supporter Santa Barbara County Sheriff's Coun., 2005-06. Mem.: Euclid City Schs. Alumni Assn., U. So. Calif. Gen. Alumni Assn., Am. Assn. Retired Persons, DAV (life). Avocations: sailing, fishing. Office Phone: 916-961-9382. Personal E-mail: emarlowe_teamwrc@yahoo.com.

MARMARELIS, VASILIS ZISSIS, engineering educator, writer, consultant; b. Mytilini, Greece, Nov. 16, 1949; arrived in US, 1972; s. Zissis P. and Elpis V. (Galinos) M.; m. Melissa Emily Orme, Mar. 12, 1989; children: Zissis Eugene and Myrl Galinos. Diploma in elec. and mech. engring., Nat. Tech. U. Athens, 1972; MS in Info. Sci., Calif. Inst. Tech., 1973, PhD in Engring. Sci., 1976. Rsch. fellow Calif. Inst. Tech., Pasadena, 1976—78; asst. prof. U. So. Calif., LA, 1978—83, assoc. prof., 1983—88, prof., 1988—, also dir. biomed. simulations resource, 1985—, chmn. dept. biomed. engring., 1990—96; pres. Multispec Corp., LA, 1986—2000. Author: Analysis of Physiological Systems, 1978, translated in Russian 1981, translated in Chinese 1990; Advanced Methods of Physiological Systems Modeling, vol. I, 1987, vol. II, 1989, vol. III, 1994, Nonlinear Dynamic Modeling of Physiological Systems, 2004; contbr. numerous articles to profl. jours. Fellow: IEEE, Am. Inst. for Med. and Biol. Engring.; mem.: N.Y. Acad. Scis., Biomed. Engring. Soc., Neural Networks Soc. Achievements include invention of Artemis mammography system. Office: Univ So Calif DRB160 Los Angeles CA 90089-1111

MARMARO, MARC, lawyer; b. Bronx, NY, Feb. 27, 1948; BA, George Washington U., 1969; JD cum laude, NYU, 1972. Law clk. to Hon. John J. Gibbons U.S. Ct. Appeals (3d cir.), 1972-73; asst. US atty. (so. dist.) N.Y. US Dept. Justice, 1975-78; with Jeffer, Mangels, Butler & Marmaro, LA. Rsch. editor NYU Law Review, 1971-72. Mem. Order of the Coif, ABA (litigation sect.), bd. trustees Assn. Bus. Trial Attys., 1986-88, N.Y. State Bar Assn., L.A. County Bar Assn. (com. fed. practice 1980-81), Assn. of Bar of City of N.Y.; bd. trustees Practicing Law Inst., 1995-, bd. dirs., Pub. Counsel, 1993-2000 Office: Jeffer Mangels Butler & Marmaro LLP 1900 Ave Stars 7th Fl Los Angeles CA 90067

MARMOR, MICHAEL FRANKLIN, ophthalmologist, educator; b. NYC, Aug. 10, 1941; s. Judd and Katherine (Stern) M.; m. C. Jane Breeden, Dec. 20, 1968; children: Andrea K., David J. AB, Harvard U., Cambridge, Mass., 1962, MD, 1966. Diplomate Am. Bd. Ophthalmology. Med. intern UCLA Med. Ctr., 1967; fellow neurophysiology NIMH, 1967-70; resident in ophthalmology Mass. Eye and Ear Infirmary, Boston, 1970-73; asst. prof. ophthalmology U. Calif. Sch. Medicine, San Francisco, 1973-74; asst. prof. surgery (ophthalmology) Stanford U. Sch. Medicine, Calif., 1974-80, assoc. prof. Calif., 1980-86, prof. Calif., 1986—, head. div. ophthalmology Calif., 1984-88, chmn. dept. Calif., 1988-92, dir. Basic Sci. Course Ophthalmology Calif., 1993—2005. Faculty mem. program in human biology Stanford U., 1982—; chief ophthalmology sect. VA Med. Ctr., Palo Alto, Calif., 1974-84; mem. sci. adv. bd. No. Calif. Soc. to Prevent Blindness, 1984-92, Calif. Med. Assn., 1984-92, Nat. Retinitis Pigmentosa Found., 1985-95; affiliate Stanford Ctr. for Biomedical Ethics, 2008-. Author: The Eye of the Artist, 1997, Degas Through his own Eyes, 2002; editor: The Retinal Pigment Epithelium, 1975, The Effects of Aging and Environment on Vision, 1991, The Retinal Pigment Epithelium: Function and Disease, 1998; editor-in-chief Doc. Ophthalmologica, 1995-99; history editor Survey of Ophthalmology, TimeOph; contbr. more than 250 articles to peer-rewiewed jours., 50 chpts. to books. Mem. affirmative action com. Stanford U. Sch. Medicine, 1984-92. Sr. asst. surgeon USPHS, 1967-70. Recipient Svc. award Nat. Retinitis Pigmentosa Found., Balt., 1981, Rsch. award Alcon Rsch. Found., Houston, 1989; rsch. grantee Nat. Eye. Inst., Bethesda, Md., 1974-94. Fellow Am. Acad. Ophthalmology (bd. councillors 1982-85, pub. health com. 1990-93, rep. to NAS com. on vision 1991-93, mus. com. 2004—, Honor award 1984, Sr. Honor award 1996), Cogan Ophthalmology Hist. Soc. (pres. 2003—); mem. Internat. Soc. Clin. Electrophysiology of Vision (v.p. 1990-98, dir. stds.), Assn. Rsch. in Vision and Ophthalmology, Internat. Soc. for Eye Rsch., Retina Soc., Macula Soc. (Green lectr. 2007). Democrat. Avocations: tennis, bicycling, chamber music (clarinet), art, history. Office: Stanford U Sch Medicine Dept Ophthalmology Stanford CA 94305-5308

MARMORSTEIN, VICTORIA E., lawyer; BA with distinction, U. Okla., 1973; JD, Am. U., 1977; LLM, U. Va., 1978. Bar: DC 1977, NY 1980, Calif. 1989. Ptnr., global chair, fin. and real estate dept. Latham & Watkins, LA. Adj. prof., UCLA Sch. of Law. Editor: Va. Jour. of Internat. Law; author: numerous articles in profl. publications. Named in Chambers & Partners Guide to America's Leading Lawyers for Bus., 2004, in Euromoney's Legal Group Guide to the World's Leading Securitization Lawyers; named one of Top Women Lawyers in LA, LA mag., 2004. Mem.: Phi Beta Kappa. Fluent in Spanish. Office: Latham Watkins 355 S Grand Ave Los Angeles CA 90071-1560

MARNELL, ANTHONY AUSTIN, II, architect; b. Riverside, Calif., Mar. 30, 1949; s. Anthony Austin and Ida Marie (Comforti) M.; m. Sandra Jean Graf, June 24, 1972 (div.); children: Anthony, Alisa. BArch, U. So. Calif., 1972. Architect, draftsman firms in Calif. and Nev., 1969-72; project coordinator Zuni Constrn. Co., Las Vegas, Nev., 1973-74; office mgr., architect Corrao Constrn. Co., Inc., Las Vegas, Nev., 1973-74, 1974-82; founder, CEO, chmn. bd. Marnell Corrao Assocs., Las Vegas, Nev., 1982—; pres. Marinelli Internat., Inc., Las Vegas, Nev., 1978—, A.A. Marnell II, Architect, Las Vegas, Nev., 1978—, Air Continental Jet Charter, Inc., Las Vegas, Nev., 1980-99; chmn., CEO Rio Hotel & Casino (acquired by Harrah's), 1986—99. Mem. ethics com. Nev. Bd. Architects, 1974; chmn. bd. Rio Hotel & Casino, Inc., 1986—, Focus 2000, Inc., 1989—. Prin. works include Mirage, Rio, Maxim Hotel, Treasure Island, Boulder Station, Sundance Hotel, Sam's Town, Excalibur; additions to Caesar's Palace, Desert Inn, Sands, Stardust, California, Frontier and Dunes Hotels (all Las Vegas), Caesar's, Atlantic City, others. Mem. Founders Bd. U. Nev., Las Vegas. Mem. Nat. Council Archtl. Registration Bds., Post Tensioning Inst. YPO (Nev. chmn. 1990). Roman Catholic. Office: Marnell Corrao Assoc Inc 222 Via Marnell Way Las Vegas NV 89119 Office Phone: 702-739-2000. Office Fax: 702-739-2005.

MAROSTICA, DON, state legislator; b. Sterling, Colo. m. Carol Marostica; 1 child, Blaine. BA, Colo. State U., Ft. Collins, 1970; MA, U. No. Colo., Greeley, 1975. Tchr., coach Rocky Mt. HS; ptnr. Loveland Commerce, LLC; mem. Dist. 51 Colo. House of Reps., Denver, 2007—. Dir. No. Colo. Legis. Alliance, Colo. Home Builder Bd.; chmn., dir. State Housing Bd., Poudre Valley Health Sys. Found., Med. Ctr. the Rockies Found.; mem. Colo. Divsn. Housing Blue Ribbon Panel. Served with US Army, capt. Colo. Army Nat. Guard. Republican. Office: 1043 Eagle Dr Loveland CO 80537-8060 also: Colo State Capital 200 E Colfax Denver CO 80203 Office Phone: 970-667-7000, 303-866-2947. Business E-Mail: don@donmarostica.com.*

MARPLE, STANLEY LAWRENCE, JR., electrical engineer, researcher; b. Tulsa, Sept. 7, 1947; s. Stanley Lawrence and Geraldine Doris M.; m. Eileen Suzanne Stevens, Aug. 31, 1974; children: Darci Leah, Rebecca Anne, Matthew Lawrence. BA, Rice U., 1969, MEE, 1970; DEng, Stanford U., 1976. Staff engr. Argo Systems, Inc., Sunnyvale, Calif., 1972-78; sr. staff engr. Advent Systems, Inc., Mountain View, Calif., 1978-79, The Analytic Scis. Corp., Mc Lean, Va., 1980-82; sr. devel. engr. Schlumberger Well Svcs., Houston, 1983-85; mgr., devel. engr. Martin Marietta Aero & Naval Systems, Balt., 1986-88; chief scientist Orincon Corp., San Diego, 1989-93, 96—, Acuson Corp., Mountain View, Calif., 1993-96; prof. Sch. Elec. Engring. and Computer Sci. Oreg. State U., Corvallis, 2003—. Author: Digital Spectral Analysis, 1987, Digital Time, Frequency, and Space Analysis, 1999. Capt. Signal Corps, U.S. Army, 1972-80. Fellow IEEE; mem. IEEE Signal Processing Soc. (editor Trans. on Signal Processing 1982-86, Sr. Paper award 1984, adminstrv. com. 1985-88, chmn. spectral estimation and array processing com. 1989-91). Avocations: stamp collecting/philately, hiking, writing. Home: 1425 SW Walking Wood Depoe Bay OR 97341 Office: Oreg State Univ Sch EECS Kelley Hall Corvallis OR 97331

MARQUARDT, DAVID F., venture capitalist; BSME, Columbia U., 1973; MBA, Stanford U., 1979. Design engr., devel. mgr. Diablo Systems; assoc. Instl. Venture Associates, 1979—80; founding ptnr. Tech. Venture Investors, 1980—95; founding gen. ptnr. August Capital, Menlo Park, Calif., 1995—. Founding mem. bd. dirs. Microsoft Corp., 1981—; bd. dirs. Alibre Inc., AutoTradeCenter Inc., NetCell Corp., Seagate Tech. Inc., Westbridge Tech. Inc., Netopia Inc., 1990—, Tumbleweed Comm. Corp. Inc., 1997—, Six Apart Ltd., 2004—. Mem.: Nat. Venture Capital Assn. (past dir.), We. Assn. Venture Capitalists (past pres.). Office: August Capital 2480 Sand Hill Rd Ste 101 Menlo Park CA 94025 Office Phone: 650-234-9900. Office Fax: 650-234-9910.

MARQUARDT, TERRY TYRONE, optometrist; b. Alamogordo, N.Mex., Nov. 20, 1949; s. Oscar Henry and June Lavonne (Weaver) Marquardt; children: Tyrone, Todd. BS, U. N.Mex., 1970; OD, Southern Coll. Optometry, 1974. Lic. optometrist. Assoc. Drs. Marquardt & Marquardt, Alamagordo, 1974—78; pvt. practice optometry Ruidoso, N.Mex., 1978—. Low vision cons. N.Mex. Svcs. Blind, N.Mex. Sch. Visually Handicapped, 1975—76; cons. HS sports vision; mem. state bd. examiners optometry; lectr. N.Mex. State U. Coach Seratoma Little League Basketball. Bausch & Lomb Contact Lens Rsch. fellow, 1973. Mem.: Coun. on Sports Vision, Optometric Extension Program Found., Am. Optometric Assn., Rotary (dir. 1980). Republican. Lutheran.

MARQUEZ, ALFREDO C., federal judge; b. 1922; m. Linda Nowobilsky. BS, U. Ariz., 1948, JD, 1950. Bar: Ariz. Practice law Mesch Marquez & Rothschild, 1957-80; asst. atty. gen. State of Ariz., 1951-52; asst. county atty. Pima County, Ariz., 1953-54; adminstrv. asst. to Congressman Stewart Udall, 1955; judge U.S. Dist. Ct. Ariz., Tucson, 1980-91, sr. judge, 1991—. Served with USN, 1942-45 Office: 23416 Everett Pl Ramona CA 92065-4211

MÁRQUEZ-MAGAÑA, LETICIA MARIA, biology professor; b. Sacramento, Aug. 15, 1963; d. Jesús José and Guadalupe María Márquez; married; children: Joaquín, Elías. BS,MS in Biol. Scis., Stanford U., 1986; PhD in Biochemistry, U. Calif., Berkeley, 1991. Postdoctoral fellow Stanford (Calif.) U., 1991—94; asst. prof. biology San Francisco State U., 1994—99, assoc. prof. biology, 1999—2004, prof. biology, 2004—, microbial geneticist, 1994—. Contbr. articles to profl. jours., including Jour. Bacteriology, Jour. Biol. Chemistry, Cell Biology Edn. Motivational spkr. to minority students, No. Calif., 1994—; mem. task force Hispanic-Serving Inst. Hispanic Assn. Colls. and Univs.; mentor to UC San Fransico Tchg. postdoctoral fellows, 2002—. Named Hispanic Powerhitter, Hispanic Engr. mag., 2003; named one of 100 Most Influential Hispanics, Hispanic Bus. mag., 1998; NSF grant. Mem.: AAAS (Mentor award 2001), Soc. Advancement of Chicanos and Native Americans in Sci. (sci. ptnr. K-12 educators 2001—, bd. dirs. 1989—91), Am. Soc. Microbiology. Office: San Francisco State U Dept Biology 1600 Holloway Ave San Francisco CA 94132 E-mail: marquez@sfsu.edu.

MÁRQUEZ-PETERSON, LEA, business broker; b. 1970; m. Daniel Harold Peterson. B in Mktg. and Entrepreneurship, U. Ariz., 1992; MBA, Pepperdine, 1996. Franchise and bus. devel. Shell Oil Co., LA; founder Am. Retail Corp., Am. Fuel, Marquez-Peterson Grp., Marquez-Peterson II, Valle Verde Partners; exec. dir. Greater Tucson Leadership; owner TucsonBizForSale.com; bus. broker Bus. Source. Founder, former chairperson Pima County Small Bus. Commn.; former chairperson City of Tucson Small Bus. Commn. Mem., Dean of Students adv. bd. U. Ariz., mem., Pres. Bus. Adv. Coun.; mem. YWCA, Regional Transportation Authority Com., Tucson Convention Ctr. Commn. Named Tucson Small Bus. of Yr., Small Bus. Devel. Coun., 2000, Tucson Minority Small Bus. Retailer of Yr., 2002, Small Bus. Leader of Yr., Tucson Metro. Chamber of Commerce, Wells Fargo Bank, 2003; named one of 40 Under 40, Tucson Bus. Edge, 2006. Mem.: Nat. Fedn. Ind. Bus., Nat. Assn. Women Bus. Owners (former pres., Woman Bus. Owner of Yr. 2001). Office: Greater Tucson Leadership 5151 E Broadway Blvd Ste 1600 Tucson AZ 85711 Office Phone: 520-512-5485. Office Fax: 520-512-5401.

MARRACK, PHILIPPA CHARLOTTE, immunologist, researcher; b. Ewell, Eng., June 28, 1945; m. John Kappler, 1974; children: Kate, Jim. BA, U. Cambridge, 1967, PhD in Biology, 1970. Post-doctoral fellow, lab. rschr. U. Calif., San Diego, 1971-73; post-doctoral rschr. fellow U. Rochester, NY, 1973-79, assoc. rschr. NY, 1974-75, asst. prof. immunology NY, 1975-79, assoc. prof. NY, 1980-85; prof. dept. microbiology and immunology U. Colo. Health Scis. Ctr., Denver, 1988—94, prof. integrated dept. of Immunology, 1994—, prof., dept. biochemistry and molecular biology, prof. medicine; head, div. of basic immunology Nat. Jewish Ctr. for Immunology and Respiratory Medicine, Denver, 1988—90; prof. dept. biophysics, biochemistry and genetics U. Colo. Health Scis. Ctr., Denver, 1985-88; head, div. of Basic Immunology Nat. Jewish Medical and Rsch. Ctr., Denver, 1998—99, sr. faculty mem., Integrated Dept. of Immunology; investigator Kappler and Marrack Rsch. Lab. Howard Hughes Med. Inst., Chevy Chase, Md., 1986—. Mem. dept. medicine Nat. Jewish Hosp. and Rsch. Ctr., Denver, 1979—. Contbr. articles to profl. jours.; mem. editl. bds. Cell, Science, and Journal of Immunology. Served on panels for Am. Cancer Soc., US NIH, Burroughs Wellcome Fund. Recipient Feodor Lynen medal, 1990, William B. Coley award Cancer Rsch. Inst., 1991, Wellcome Found. lecturer Royal Soc., 1990, Paul Ehrlich and Ludwig Darmstädter prize, 1993, Louisa Gross Horwitz prize, 1994, Women's Excellence Scis. award Fedn. Am. Socs. Exptl. Biology, 1995, Women in Sci. award, L'Oreal-UNESCO, 2004. Mem.

NAS, Royal Soc., Am. Assn. Immunologists (pres. 2000-2001, Lifetime Achievement award, 2003), Brit. Soc. Immunology, Internat. Union of Immunological Societies (past pres.). Office: Howard Hughes Med Inst Natl Jewish Med and Rsch Ctr 1400 Jackson St 5th fl Goodman Bldg Denver CO 80206

MARROW, DEBORAH, foundation administrator; d. Seymour Arthur and Adele M.; m. Michael J. McGuire; children: David Marrow McGuire, Anna Marrow McGuire. BA cum laude, U. Pa., PhD; MA, Johns Hopkins U. With Phila. Mus. of Art, 1974-75, Chrysalis Mag., LA, 1978-80, The J. Paul Getty Trust, LA, 1983—. Various positions including program officer Getty Grant Program; interim dir., The Getty Rsch. Inst.; dean for extern relations, The J. Paul Getty Trust, interim pres., CEO; dir. The Getty Found. Mem. Save Am.'s Treas. com., Nat. Trust for Historic Preservation (in partnership with White House Millenium Coun.), 1998-2001; bd. govs. U. Calif Humanities Rsch. Inst., 2000-05; mem. internat. com. for History of Art; mem. bd. trustees U. Pa., 2003-. Office: The Getty Found 1200 Getty Center Dr Ste 800 Los Angeles CA 90049 Office Phone: 310-440-7320.

MARROW, TRACY See ICE-T

MARSDEN, JERROLD ELDON, mathematician, educator, engineer; b. Ocean Falls, British Columbia, Aug. 17, 1942; married 1965; 1 child. BSc, U. Toronto, Canada, 1965; PhD in Math., Princeton U., 1968. Instr. math. Princeton U., N.J., 1968; lectr. U. Calif., Berkeley, 1968-69, asst. prof., 1969-72, assoc. prof., 1972-77, prof. math., 1977—; asst. prof. U. Toronto, Canada, 1970-71; prof. Calif. Tech., Pasadena, 1995—. Recipient Norbert Weiner Applied Math. prize Am. Math. Soc., 1990. Mem. IEEE, Am. Phys. Soc. Achievements include research in mathematical physics, global analysis, hydrodynamics, quantum mechanics, nonlinear Hamiltonian systems. Office: Control Dynamical Sys MS 107 81 Pasadena CA 91125-0001

MARSH, MALCOLM F., federal judge; b. Portland, Oreg., Sept. 24, 1928; m. Shari Marsh. BS, U. Oreg., 1952, LLB, 1954, JD, 1971. Bar: Oreg. 1954, U.S. Dist. Ct. Oreg. 1955, U.S. Ct. Appeals (9th cir.) 1968. Ptnr. Clark & Marsh, Lindauer & McClinton (and predecessors), Salem, Oreg., 1954-87; judge U.S. Dist. Ct. Oreg., Portland, 1987—98, sr. judge, 1998—. With U.S. Army, 1946-47. Fellow Am. Coll. Trial Lawyers; mem. ABA, Oreg. Bar Assn. Office: US Dist Ct 1507 US Courthouse 1000 SW 3d Ave Portland OR 97204

MARSH, MARTHA H., hospital administrator; BS, U. Rochester; MPH, MBA, Columbia U. Pres. and CEO Matthew Thornton Health Plan, Dartmouth-Hitchcock Med. Ctr., 1986—94; sr. v.p., profl. svcs. and managed care and v.p, managed care U. Pa. Health Sys., 1994—98; COO U. Calif.-Davis Health Care Sys., 1999—2002; dir., Hosp. and Clinics U. Calif.-Davis Medical Ctr., 1999—2002; pres. and CEO Stanford (Conn.) Hosp. and Clinics, 2002—. Apptd. by Pres. Bush Nat. Infrastructure Adv. Coun., 2003; bd. dirs. Calif. Healthcare Assoc., Integrated Healthcare Assoc., Blue Cross of Calif. Hosp. Relations Com. Office: Stanford Hosp 300 Pasteur Dr Ste H3200 Stanford CA 94305 Office Phone: 650-723-4000.

MARSH, MARY ELIZABETH TAYLOR, recreation administrator, nutritionist, dietician; b. Medina, NY, Dec. 10, 1933; d. Glenn Aaron and Viola Hazel (Lansill) Grimes dec; m. Wilbur Alvin Fredlund, Apr. 12, 1952 (div. Jan. 1980); 1 child, Wilbur Jr.; m. Frederick Herbert Taylor, Mar. 15, 1981 (dec. Dec. 1996); children: Martha Dayton, Jean Grout, Beth Stern, Cindy Hey, Carol Cook, Cheryl Dearborn, Robert, Marilyn Readers, Janice Emory, Gordon Marsh, Margaret Hana; m. Earl R. Marsh, Apr. 4, 1998. BS in Food and Nutrition, SUNY, Buffalo, 1973; MEd in Health Sci. Edn. and Evaluation, SUNY, 1978. Registered dietitian, 1977. Diet cook Niagara Sanitorium, Lockport, NY, 1953—56; cook Mount View Hosp., Lockport, 1958—60, asst. dietician, 1960—73, dietician, dir. food svc., 1973—79, cons. dietician, 1979—81; instr. Erie C.C., Williamsville, NY, 1979—81; coord. sch. lunch Nye County Sch. Dist., Tonopah, Nev., 1982—93, ret., 1993; food svc. mgmt. cons., fin. mgmt. advisor pvt. practice, 1994—; activity dir. Preferred Equity Corp. Recreation Vehicle Resort, Pahrump, Nev., 1993—95; tchr. maturing body and nutrition Nev. Cmty. Coll., Pahrump, 1997; nutritionist Equal Opportunity Bd. Clark County, Las Vegas, 1997—2000; ind. travel agt. Hello World Travel, 2001—02, 2002—03; activity dir. Preferred R.V. Resort, 2001—; cons. Isagenix Internat., 2003—; travel agt. mrshtrul.travelogia.com, 2003—04. Cons. dietitian Nye Gen. Hosp., Tonopah, 1983-88, Isagenix Internat., 2003-; adj. instr. Erie C.C., Williamsville, 1978-79, So. Nev. C.C., 1997; nutrition instr. for coop. extension Clark County C.C., 1990—; cons. Group Purchasing Western N.Y. Hosp. Adminstr., Buffalo, 1975-79, vice-chmn. adv. com., 1976-78; cons. BOCES, Lockport, 1979-81. Nutrition counselor Migrant Workers Clinic, Lockports, 1974-80; mem. Western N.Y. Soc. for Hosp. Food Svc. Adminstrn., 1974-81; nutritionist Niagara County Nutrition Adv. Com., 1977-81; mem. Helping Hands, Pahrump, 1997—; nutritionist Equal Opportunity Bd. Clark Conty, 1997-2000; activity dir. Perfered Equities RV Resort, 2001—; mem. adv. bd. Salvation Army, 2003— Recipient Outstanding Woman of the Yr., YWCA-UAW Lockport, 1981, Disting. Health Care Food Adminstrn. Recognition award Am. Soc. for Hosp. Food Svc. Adminstrs., 1979, USDA award Outstanding Lunch Program in Nev. and Western Region, 1986, 91. Mem. Am. Assn. Ret. Persons, Am. Sch. Food Svc. Assn. (bd. dirs. 1987, 92-93, cert. dir. II 1987, 5-yr. planning com. 1990, ann. confs. 1988-93), Am. Dietetic Assn. (nat. referral sys. for registered dietitians 1992-93), So. Nev. Dietetic Assn. (pres. 1985-86), Am. Diabetes Assn., Nev. Food Svc. Assn. (participant ann. meetings 1990-93), Nutrition Today Soc., Nev. Sch. Food Svcs. Assn. (dietary guidelines com. 1991-93), Am. Diabetes Assn, Am. Legion, Women of Moose, Red Hats with Attitude Republican. Lutheran. Avocations: travel, knitting, crocheting, sewing. Home: 481 N Murphy St Pahrump NV 89060-3851 Office Phone: 775-721-5513. Personal E-mail: mrshtrvl1@gmail.com.

MARSHAK, HARRY, plastic surgeon; b. LA, Oct. 1, 1961; s. Herbert and Pearl (Engelson) M. BS, U. Calif., Riverside, 1981; MD, UCLA, 1984. Diplomate Am. Bd. Surgery, Am. Bd. Plastic Surgery. Pvt. practice, Beverly Hills, Calif., 1991—. Fellow ACS (hon.), Internat. Coll. Surgeons; mem. Am. Soc. Plastic and Reconstructive Surgeons, Calif. Soc. Plastic Surgery, Am. Soc. for Aesthetic Plastic Surgery. Republican. Avocation: sports. Office: 120 S Spalding Dr Ste 300 Beverly Hills CA 90212-1841 Office Phone: 310-657-7600. Personal E-mail: drharrymarshak@aol.com.

MARSHALL, CONSUELO BLAND, federal judge; b. Knoxville, Tenn., Sept. 28, 1936; d. Clyde Theodore and Annie (Brown) Arnold; m. George Edward Marshall, Aug. 30, 1959; children: Michael Edward, Laurie Ann. AA, L.A. City Coll., 1956; BA, Howard U., 1958, LLB, 1961. Bar: Calif. 1962. Dep. atty., City of LA, 1962-67; assoc. Cochran & Atkins, LA, 1968-70; commr. LA Superior Ct., 1971-76; judge Inglewood Mcpl. Ct., 1976-77, LA Superior Ct., 1977-80, US Dist. Ct. (ctrl dist.) Calif., LA, 1980—, chief judge, 2001—. Lectr. U.S. Information Agy. in Yugoslavia, Greece and Italy, 1984, in Nigera and Ghana, 1991, in Ghana, 1992. Contbr. articles to profl. jours.; notes editor Law Jour. Howard U. Mem. adv. bd. Richstone Child Abuse Center. Recipient Judicial Excellence award Criminal Cts. Bar Assn., 1992, Ernestine Stalhut award; named Criminal Ct. Judge of Yr., U.S. Dist. Ct., 1997; inducted into Langston Hall of Fame, 2000, Outstanding Jurist Award, LA County Bar Assn., 2005; rsch. fellow Howard U. Law Sch., 1959-60. Mem. State Bar Calif., Century City Bar Assn., Calif. Women Lawyers Assn., Calif. Assn. Black Lawyers, Calif. Judges Assn., Black Women Lawyers Assn., Los Angeles County Bar Assn., Nat. Assn. Women Judges, NAACP, Urban League, Beta Phi Sigma. Office: US Dist Ct 312 N Spring St Los Angeles CA 90012-4701

MARSHALL, DAVID B., structural ceramics professional; BSc, Monash U., Melbourne, Australia, 1971, PhD, 1975. Rsch. fellow dept. applied physics U. NSW, Australia, 1975—79; assoc. rsch. engr. dept. materials sci. and mineral engring. U. Calif., Berkeley, 1979—83; mgr. structural ceramics dept. Teledyne Sci. and Imaging (formerly Rockwell Sci. Co.), 1983—. Adj. prof. materials dept. U. Calif., Santa Barbara, 1988-. Contbr. articles to profl. jours. Fellow Am. Ceramic Soc. (editor jour., Ross Coffin Purdy award 1989, Fulrath award 1991, J.J. Jeppson award 1996, Sosman award 1998); mem. NAE. Achievements include patents in field. Office: Materials Divsn Teledyne Sci and Imaging 1049 Camino Dos Rios Thousand Oaks CA 91360-2362 Office Phone: 805-373-4170. Office Fax: 805-373-4017. E-mail: dmarshall@rwsc.com.

MARSHALL, DONALD GLENN, English language and literature educator; b. Long Beach, Calif., Sept. 9, 1943; s. Albert Louis and Margaret Corinne (Morrison) M.; m. Kathleen Bonann, June 21, 1975; children: Stephanie Deborah, Zachary Louis AB summa cum laude, Harvard U., 1965; MPhil, Yale U., 1969, PhD, 1971. Asst. prof. English UCLA, 1969-75; from assoc. prof. to prof. English U. Iowa, Iowa City, 1975-90; honors dir. U. Iowa Coll Liberal Arts, 1981-85; prof. English dept. U. Ill., Chgo., 1990—2003, head dept., 1990—2000; prof. Great Books Pepperdine U., Malibu, Calif., 2003—. Editor: Philosophy as Literature/Literature as Philosophy, 1986, The Force of Tradition: Response and Resistance in Literature, Religion, and Cultural Studies, 2005; compiler: Contemporary Critical Theory: A Selective Bibliography, 1993; translator: (with Joel Weinsheimer) Truth and Method by Hans-Georg Gadamer, 1989; contbr. articles and revs. to profl. jours. Recipient Bell prize Harvard U., 1965, Webster prize Yale U., 1967; NEH Younger Humanist fellow, 1973-74; grantee UCLA, U. Iowa, Howard A. White award, Pepperdine U., 2008. Mem.: MLA, Ill. Humanities Coun. (bd. dirs. 1994—2000, Chgo. Humanities Festival bd. dir. 1997—2003), The Poetry Found. (trustee 1996—, pres. 1998—2000), Conf. Christianity and Lit. (bd. dirs. 2000—03). Democrat. Roman Catholic. Office: Pepperdine U Divsn Humanities and Tchr Edn 24255 Pacific Coast Hwy Malibu CA 90263 Office Phone: 310-506-7654. Business E-Mail: Donald.Marshall@pepperdine.edu.

MARSHALL, ELLEN RUTH, lawyer; b. NYC, Apr. 23, 1949; d. Louis and Faith (Gladstone) M. AB, Yale U., 1971; JD, Harvard U., 1974. Bar: Calif. 1975, D.C. 1981, N.Y. 1989. Assoc. McKenna & Fitting, LA, 1975-80; ptnr. McKenna, Conner & Cuneo, LA and Orange County, Calif., 1980-88, Morrison & Foerster, LLP, Orange County, 1988—2003, Manatt, Phelps & Phillips LLP, Orange County, 2003—. Mem. ABA (bus. law sect., mem. savs. inst. com., mem. asset securitization com., tax sect., mem. employee benefits com.), Orange County Bar Assn., Center Club (Costa Mesa, Calif.), Yale Club (N.Y.C.). Office: Manatt Phelps & Phillips LLP 695 Town Ctr Dr Costa Mesa CA 92626

MARSHALL, GRAYSON WILLIAM, JR., materials scientist, biomedical engineer, health sciences educator, dentist; b. Balt., Feb. 12, 1943; s. Grayson William and Muriel Marie Marshall; m. Sally Jean Rimkus, July 4, 1970; children: Grayson W. III, Jonathan Charles. BS in Metall. Engring., Va. Poly. Inst., 1965; PhD in Materials Sci., Northwestern U., 1972, DDS, 1986; MPH, U. Calif., Berkeley, 1992. Cert. dentist. Rsch. assoc., design and devel. ctr. Northwestern U., Evanston, Ill., 1972-73, NIH fellow, 1973, instr. Dental and Med. Schs. Chgo., 1973-74, asst. prof. Dental Sch., 1974-78, assoc. prof. Dental Sch. and Grad. Sch., 1978-87; prof. preventive and restorative dental scis. U. Calif., San Francisco, 1987—, chief biomaterials sect., 1988-92, chmn. biomaterials and bioengring. divsn., 1992—, vice chmn. rsch., 2005—. Chmn. oral and craniaofacial scis. program U. Calif., San Francisco, 2002-07, UCSF Grad. Coun., 2003-05, UCSF Inst. Regenerative Medicine; guest scientist Lawrence Livermore Nat. Lab., 1989-2000, Lawrence Berkeley Nat. Lab., 1989—; cons. oral biology and medicine study sect. NIH, 1988-92; dir. Clin. Rsch. Unit, 1992-96, Dentist-Sci. Award Program, 1996-2004, Integrated DDS-PhD Program, 1996—2009, Comprehensive Oral Health Rsch. Tng. Program, 2001-08. Contbr. articles to profl. jours. and books. Mem. City of Larkspur Heritage Preservation Bd., 1998—, chmn., 2006—08, mem. centennial com., 2007—. Recipient Spl. Dental Rsch. award Nat. Inst. Dental Rsch., 1975, Rsch. Lectr. award U. Calif., San Francisco, 1994, IADR Wilmer Souder Disting. Scientist award, 2007; vis. fellow U. Melbourne, Australia, 1981. Fellow: AAAS, Acad. Dental Materials (exec. sec. 1983—85, chmn. credentials 1984—91, bd. dirs. 1985—93, mem. editl. bd. Scanning Microscopy 1987—93, pres. 1991—93, Cells and Materials 1992—2000, sect. editor 1993—2000, Jour. Oral Rehab. 1994—, Dent Mater 1998—, Am. Jour. Dentistry 2004—), Am. Coll. Dentists, Internat. Coll. Dentists; mem.: AIME, APHA, ADA (assoc. editor Jour. ADA 2002—05), U.S. Power Squadrons, U.S. Naval Inst., Calif. Pub. Health Assn.-North, Calif. Acad. Scis., N.Y. Acad. Scis., Am. Assn. Dental Rsch. (bd. dirs. 1996—98, San Francisco coun. 1997—2007, v.p. 2007—08, pres. elect 2008—09, pres. 2009—), Microscopy Soc. Am., Am. Soc. Metals, Am. Coll. Sports Medicine, Internat. Assn. Dental Rsch. (Chgo. sect. officer 1978—80, dental materials coun. 1990—96, pres. 1998—99), Soc. Biomaterials, Am. Dental Edn. Assn. (sect. officer 1981—83), Omicron Kappa Upsilon, Sigma Gamma Epsilon, Sigma Xi, Alpha Sigma Mu. Avocations: swimming, sailing, hiking, travel. Office: U Calif Dept Preven & Restor Dental Scis San Francisco CA 94143-0758 Office Phone: 415-476-9119. Business E-Mail: gw.marshall@ucsf.edu, gwmarshall@lbl.gov.

MARSHALL, KATE, state treasurer; b. San Francisco, July 22, 1959; m. John Marshall; 2 children. Student, Univ. Calif. Boalt Hall, Berkeley, 1982; BA, Univ. Calif., Berkeley, 1982, Boalt Hall JD. Law intern Laxalt, Washington, Perito & Debuc, Washington; tchr., English, Commerce Peace Corps, Kenya; with field offices Dept. Justice, Washington, San Francisco; in-house counsel ATG, Inc., 2000; pvt. practice atty.; sr. dep. atty. gen. State of Nev., 1997—2000, state treas., 2007—. Named Woman of Achievement, Nevada Women's Fund, 2001. Democrat. Office: State Treas Capitol Bldg 101 N Carson #4 Carson City NV 89701 Office Phone: 775-684-5600. Office Fax: 775-684-5623. Business E-Mail: statetreasurer@nevadatreasurer.gov.

MARSHALL, PATRICK C., lawyer; b. San Francisco, Aug. 8, 1954; BA, Whitman Coll., 1976; JD with honors, U. Wash., 1979. Bar: Wash. 1979, Calif. 1984. Ptnr. Pillsbury Winthrop Shaw Pittman, San Francisco, 1984—, office mng. ptnr., 2004, co-leader Litigation sect., leader San Francisco Litigation sect. Mem.: San Francisco Bar Assn. Office: Pillsbury Winthrop Shaw Pittman 50 Fremont St San Francisco CA 94105 Office Phone: 415-983-7233. Office Fax: 415-983-1200. Business E-Mail: patrick.marshall@pillsburylaw.com.

MARSHALL, PENNY (C. MARSHALL, CAROLE PENNY MARSHALL), director, actress; b. NYC, Oct. 15, 1943; d. Anthony W. and Marjorie Irene (Ward) M.; m. Michael Henry (div.); 1 child, Tracy Lee; m. Robert Reiner, Apr. 10, 1971 (div. 1979). Student, U. N.Mex., 1961-64. Appeared on numerous television shows, including The Odd Couple, 1972-74, Friends and Lovers (co-star), 1974, Let's Switch, 1974, Wives (pilot), 1975, Chico and the Man, 1975, Mary Tyler Moore, 1975, Heaven Help Us, 1975, Saturday Night Live, 1975-77, Happy Days, 1975, Battle of Network Stars (ABC special), 1976, Barry Manilow special, 1976, The Tonight Show, 1976-77, Dinah, 1976-77, Mike Douglas Show, 1975-77, Merv Griffin Show, 1976-77, Blansky's Beauties, 1977, Network Battle of the Sexes, 1977, Laverne and Shirley (co-star), 1976-83, Entertainment Tonight's Presents: Laverne and Shirley Together Again, 2002; TV films More Than Friends, 1978, Love Thy Neighbor, 1984, Challenge of a Lifetime, 1985, The Odd Couple: Together Again, 1993; guest appearances include Mary Tyler Moore, 1975, Happy Days, 1975, Chico and the Man, 1975, Mork & Mindy, 1978, Bosom Buddies, 1982, Taxi, 1983, The Simpsons (voice), 1990, Frasier, 2004, I'm With Her, 2004; appeared in motion pictures How Sweet It Is, 1967, The Savage Seven, 1968, The Grasshopper, 1970, 1941, 1979, Movers and Shakers, 1985, She's Having a Baby, 1988, The Hard Way, 1991, Hocus Pocus, 1993, Get Shorty, 1995, Special Delivery, 1999, Stateside, 2004, Looking for Comedy in the Muslim World, 2005, Everybody Wants to Be Italian, 2007, Alice Upside Down, 2007, Blonde Ambition, 2007; dir. films: Jumpin' Jack Flash, 1986, Big, 1988, Awakenings, 1990 (exec. prodr.), A League of Their Own, 1992 (exec. prodr.), Renaissance Man, 1994 (exec. prodr.), The Preacher's Wife, 1996, The Time Tunnel: The Movie, 1999, Special Delivery, 1999, Riding in Cars with Boys, 2001; appeared in TV movie Jackie's Back, 1999; prodr. TV series A League of Their Own, 1993 (also dir. pilot), Dynasties, 2003, Crossover, 2004; dir. (TV Series) Working Stiffs, 1979; prodr. films Getting Away With Murder, 1996, With Friends Like These, 1998, Risk, 2003, Cinderella Man, 2005, Bewitched, 2005; exec. prodr. Calender Girl, 1993. Avocations: needlepoint, jigsaw puzzles, antique shopping. Office: c/o William Morris Agy 151 El Camino Dr Beverly Hills CA 90212

MARSHALL, PETER, actor, singer, game show host; b. Clarksburg, W.Va., Mar. 30, 1930; s. Ralph and Jeanne (Frampton) Lacock; m. Laurie L. Stewart, Aug. 19, 1989; children: Suzanne, Peter, David, Jaime. Grad. high sch., Huntington, W.Va. Big band singer; night club entertainer; part of comedy team Noonan and Marshall; appeared in motion pictures, musicals, comedies, Broadway and tv; host Hollywood Squares (5 Emmys: Best Game Show Host, 1973-74, 74-75, 79-80, 80-81, Best Day Time Entertainer, 1973-74). Master sgt. US Army, 1944—46. Avocations: golf, tennis. Personal E-mail: gloent@aol.com.

MARSHALL, RAYMOND CHARLES, lawyer; b. Aquadilia, PR, July 23, 1953; 1 child, Kyle. BA summa cum laude, Coll. Idaho, 1975; JD, Harvard U., 1978. Bar: Calif. 1978, D.C. 1989. Ptnr. Bingham McCutchen LLP, San Francisco, co-chmn. white-collar crime & bus. regulation practice group. Chmn. Calif. Supreme Ct. Adv. Multi-Jurisdictional Practice, 2004. Co-author: Environmental Crimes, 1992; contbr. chpt. to manual; contbr. articles to profl. jours. Bd. dirs. Nat. Multiple Sclerosis Soc. Northern Calif. chpt., 1992—; adv. bd. United Negro Coll. Fund Northern Bay Area Chpt., 1992—; bd. trustees Alta Bates Found., 1994—; adv. coun. mem. San Francisco Sports Coun. Recipient San Francisco Neighborhood Legal Assistance Found. award, 1989, Earl Warren Legal Svcs. award NAACP Legal Def. & Ednl. Found., 1990, Unity award Minority Bar Coalition, 1992, Cmty. Svc. award Wiley Manuel Law Found., 1994, Disting. Jesuit award Anti-Defamation League, 2001. Mem. ABA (met. bar caucus exec. com. 1992-94, vice-chmn. natural resources & energy litigation com. 1989-93, environmental crimes com. 1990-92, nominating com. conf. of minority ptnrs. in maj. corp. law firms 1991, commn. on women in the profession 1994-95, co-chmn. environmental crimes subcom. of white collar crime com. 1994-95), Nat. Bar Assn., Calif. State Bar (bd. govs. 1995—, pres. 1998-99), Charles Houston Bar Assn. Avocations: travel, sports. Office: Bingham McCutchen LLP Three Embarcadero Ctr San Francisco CA 94111 Office Phone: 415-393-2348. Business E-Mail: raymond.marshall@bingham.com.

MARSHALL, ROBERT HERMAN, retired economics professor; b. Harrisburg, Pa., Dec. 6, 1929; s. Mathias and Mary (Bubich) M.; m. Billie Marie Sullivan, May 31, 1958; children: Mellisa Frances Hansen, Howard Hylton Irion, Robert Charles. AB magna cum laude, Franklin and Marshall Coll., 1951; MA, Ohio State U., 1952, PhD, 1957. Teaching asst. Ohio State U., 1952-57; mem. faculty, then prof. econs. U. Ariz., Tucson, 1957-95, prof. emeritus, 1995; dir. Internat. Bus. Studies Project, 1969-71. Research observer Sci.-Industry Program, Hughes Aircraft Co., Tucson, summer 1959 Author: Commercial Banking in Arizona: Structure and Performance Since World War II, 1966, (with others) The Monetary Process, 2d edit, 1980. Bd. dirs. Com. for Econ. Opportunity, Tucson, 1968-69. Faculty fellow Pacific Coast Banking Sch., summer 1974 Mem. Am. Econ. Assn., Phi Beta Kappa, Beta Gamma Sigma, Pi Gamma Mu, Phi Kappa Phi, Delta Sigma Pi. Democrat. Roman Catholic. Home: 6700 N Abington Rd Tucson AZ 85743-9795 Office Phone: 520-621-6224.

MARSHALL, ROSEMARY, former state representative; b. Denver, 1942; m. Cleophus; children: three. Rep., dist. 8 Colo. House of Reps., Denver, 2000—09. Bd. mem. North City Pk. Civic Assn. Recipient Cmty. Svc. award, 1997, State Capitol Appreciation award. Mem. NAACP, CBWPA (Polit. Achievement award 1999). Democrat.*

MARSHALL, TOBY, lawyer; BA cum laude, Calif. State U., 1996; JD, U. Wash., Seattle, 2002. Bar: Wash. 2002. Assoc. atty., complex civil litig. Tousley Brain Stephens, P.L.L.C., 2001—. Contbr. articles to numerous profl. jours. Mem.: ABA, William L. Dwyer Inn of Ct., King Co. Bar Assn. Office: Tousley Brain Stephens PLLC Ste 2200 1700 Seventh Ave Seattle WA 98101-1332

MARSHALL-DANIELS, MERYL, mediator, executive coach; b. LA, Oct. 16, 1949; d. Jack and Nita Corinblit; m. Raymond Daniels, Aug. 19, 2000. BA, UCLA, 1971; JD, Loyola Marymount U., LA, 1974. Bar: Calif. 1974. Dep. pub. defender County of L.A., 1975—77; sole practice LA, 1977—78; ptnr. Markman and Marshall, LA, 1978—79; sr. atty. NBC, Burbank, Calif., 1979—80, dir. programs, talent contracts bus. affairs, 1980, asst. gen. atty. NYC, 1980—82, v.p., compliance and practices Burbank, 1982; v.p. program affairs Group W Prodns., 1987—89, sr. v.p. future images, 1989—91, TV prodr., Meryl Marshall Prodns., 1991—93; pres. Mediation Ptnrs. and Two Oceans Entertainment Group, 1991—. Chmn., Nat. Women's Polit. Caucus, Westside, Calif., 1978-80; mem. Calif. Dem. Ctrl. Com., 1978-79; mem. Hollywood Women's Polit. Com., 1988; chmn. George Foster Peabody Awards. Mem.: Women in Film, Acad. TV Arts and Scis. (treas. 1985, bd. govs. 1989—2001, treas. 1993—97, chmn. bd., CEO 1997—2001). Democrat. Jewish. Office: Two Oceans Consulting Group 2017 Lemoyne St Los Angeles CA 90026 E-mail: twooceans@mac.com.

MARSTON, MICHAEL, economist, consultant; b. Oakland, Calif., Dec. 4, 1936; s. Lester Woodbury and Josephine (Janovic) Marston; m. Alexandra Lynn Geyer, Apr. 30, 1966; children: John, Elizabeh. BA, U. Calif., Berkeley, 1959; postgrad., London Sch. Econs., 1961—63. Cert. rev. appraiser Nat. Assn. Rev. Appraisers and Mortgage Underwriters, 1984. V.p. Larry Smith & Co., San Francisco, 1969—72, exec. v.p. urban econ. divsn., 1969—72; chmn. bd. Keyser Marston Assocs., Inc., San Francisco, 1973—87; gen. ptnr. The Sequoia Partnership, 1979—91; pres. Marston Vineyard and Winery, 1982—, Marston Assocs., Inc., 1982—. Pres. The Ctr. Individual and Instnl. Renewal, 1996—. Contbr. articles to profl. jours. Mem. spkr. bus. Am. Embassy, London, 1961—63; mem. Gov.'s Issue Anlysis Com. and Spkr. Bur., 1966; v.p., bd. dirs. Dem. Forum, 1968—72; chmn. San Francisco Waterfront Com., 1969—86; v.p. People for Open Space, 1972—87, mem. exec. com., 1972—87; chmn. fin. com. San Francisco Planning and Urban Rsch. Assn., 1976—87, bd. dirs., 1976—87, mem. exec. com., 1976—87, treas., 1976—87; bd. trustees Cathedral Sch. Boys, 1981—82, Marin Country Day Sch., 1984—90; pres. Presidio Heights Assn. Neighbors, 1983—84; mem. Napa Valley Vintners, 1986—, mem. gov. affairs com.; v.p. St. Luke's Sch., 1986—91; chmn. Presidio Com., 1991—; v.p., trustee Youth for Svc. Served to lt. USNR. Mem.: Napa Valley Vintners, Calif. Vintage Wine Soc., World Congress Land Policy, Urban Land Inst., Pacific Union Club, Bohemian Club, Order of Golden Bear, Chevalier du Tastevin, Lambda Alpha. Home: 3375 Jackson St San Francisco CA 94118-2018 Personal E-mail: marstonmichael@yahoo.com.

MARSZOWSKI, BRUNO A., finance company executive; Sr. v.p., contr., CFO The Finova Group Inc., Scottsdale, Ariz. Office: The Finova Group Inc 4800 N Scottsdale Rd Scottsdale AZ 85251-7623

MARTEL, JOHN SHELDON, lawyer, writer, musician; b. Stockton, Calif., Jan. 1, 1931; s. Henry T. and Alice L. M.; m. Bonnie Martel; children: John Sheldon, Melissa Ann. BS, U. Calif.-Berkeley, 1956, JD, 1959. Bar: Calif. 1959. Dep. dist. atty., Alameda County, 1960-61; assoc. trial atty. firm Bronson, Bronson & McKinnon, San Francisco, 1961-64; ptnr. firm Farella, Braun & Martel, San Francisco, 1964—. Lectr., mem. adv. bd. Hastings Ctr. for Trial and Appellate Adv., 1983—. Author: (novels) Partners, 1988, Conflicts of Interest, 1994, The Alternate, 1999, Billy Strobe, 2001; author, editor legal publs.; composer-writer popular songs and CDs; profl. musician. Pilot USAF, 1951-54. Winner Am. Song Festival awards, 1978-80, 82, 85, 87. Fellow Am. Coll. Trial Lawyers (state chmn. 1985-87, bd. regents 1993-98); mem. ABA (litigation, antitrust, tort and ins. sects.), Calif. Bar Assn., San Francisco Bar Assn. (former chair litigation sect.), Am. Bd. Trial Lawyers (bd. dirs. 1991-93), Am. Fedn. Musicians, Phi Delta Phi, Kappa Sigma. Office: Farella Braun & Martel 235 Montgomery St Ste 3100 San Francisco CA 94104-2902 Home Phone: 831-336-3114; Office Phone: 415-954-4422. Personal E-mail: johnwriter@aol.com. E-mail: jmartel@fbm.com.

MARTEL, LISA, food service executive; Student, Regis Coll.; grad., Johnson and Wales Coll. Culinary Arts, 1986. Line cook then banquet chef The Bay Tower Room; chef Rebecca's, Boston, 150 Wooster St. and Remi, NYC, The Sherry Netherlands Hotel, NYC, 224 Boston St., Boston, 1990; chef, owner On the Park, Boston. Home: 1114 Paseo Del Robles Ct Ojai CA 93023-3051

MARTENS, DON WALTER, lawyer; b. Darlington, Wis., Mar. 25, 1934; s. Walter W. and Geraldine A. (McWilliams) M.; children: Kim Martens Cooper, Diane Martens Reed. BS in Engring. with hons., U. Wis., 1957; JD with honors, George Washington U., 1963. Bar: Supreme Ct. Calif. 1964, U.S. Ct. Appeals (9th cir.) 1964, U.S. Dist. Ct. (no. and cen. dists.) Calif. 1964, U.S. Supreme Ct. 1973, U.S. Dist. Ct. (so. dist.) Calif. 1977, U.S. Ct. Appeals (fed. cir.) 1982, U.S. Dist. Ct. (ea. dist.) Calif. 1984. Examiner U.S. Patent and Trademark Office, Washington, 1960-63; patent lawyer Standard Oil of Calif., San Francisco, 1963-65; ptnr. Knobbe, Martens, Olson & Bear, Newport Beach, Calif., 1965—. Mem. adv. comm. Fed. Cir. Ct. Appeals, 1991-96, 2000—. Lt. USN, 1957-60. Mem. Orange County Bar Assn. (pres. 1975), Orange County Legal Aid Soc. (pres. 1969), Orange County Patent Law Assn. (pres. 1984), L.A. Patent Law Assn. (pres. 1989), State Bar Calif. (bd. govs. 1984-87, v.p. 1986-87), Am. Intellectual Property Law Assn. (pres. 1995-96), State Bar Intellectual Property Assn. (chmn. 1977), 9th Cir. Jud. Conf. (del. 1985-88, 1995-98), Nat. Inventors Hall of Fame Found. (pres. 1998-99), Nat. Coun. Intellectual Property Law Assn. (chmn. 1998-99), Big Canyon Country Club, Santa Ana Country Club, Rancho La Quinta Country Club. Republican. Roman Catholic. Office: 2040 Main St 14th Fl Irvine CA 92614 E-mail: dmartens@kmob.com.

MARTER, BEN, legislative staff member; BA in history, U. Colo. Majority press sec. Colo. Senate, Denver; comm. dir. Betsy Markey for Congress, 2008; comm. dir. to Rep. Betsy Markey US House of Reps., Washington, 2009—. Office: Office of Rep Betsy Markey 1229 Longworth House Office Bldg Washington DC 20515 also: 123 N College Ave Ste 220 Fort Collins CO 80524 Office Phone: 202-225-4676, 970-221-7110. Office Fax: 202-225-5870, 970-221-7240.

MARTI, KURT, chemistry professor; b. Berne, Switzerland, Aug. 18, 1936; came to U.S., 1965; s. Werner Marti and Emma H. (Habegger) M.; children: Andres Niklaus, Stefan Kurt, Lorenz Roman. MS, U. Berne, 1963, PhD, 1965. Postgrad. research chemist U. Calif.-San Diego, La Jolla, 1965-68, asst. prof., 1969-74, assoc. prof., 1974-80, prof., 1980—; vis. prof. phys. rsch. lab. Ahmedabad, India, 1977, U. Berne, Switzerland, 1977, 95. Vis. prof. U. Bordeaux, France, 1983, 94; mem. rev. panel Lunar Sci. Inst., Houston, 1971-74, 91-93; lunar sample analysis planning team mem. Johnson Space Ctr., Houston, 1975-78; lectr. in field. Assoc. editor Geochim. Cosmochim. Acta, 1985-95. Grantee NASA, 1971—; Guggenheim fellow, 1976. Fellow Meteoritical Soc.; mem. AAAS, Am. Geophys. Union, Am. Chem Soc. Home: 13424 Calais Dr Del Mar CA 92014-3524 Office: U Calif San Diego Dept Chemistry La Jolla CA 92093-0317 E-mail: kmarti@ucsd.edu.

MARTIN, ANDREA LOUISE, actress, comedienne, writer; b. Portland, Maine, Jan. 15, 1947; m. Bob Dolman, 1980 (div.); children: Joe, Jack. Grad., Emerson Coll. Appearances include (plays) Hard Shell, 1980 (off-Broadway debut), Sorrows of Stephen, 1980, What's a Nice Country Like You Doing in a State Like This?, 1974, She Loves Me, (Broadway shows) My Favorite Year, 1992 (Tony award, Featured Actress in a Musical, 1993), Candide, 1997, Oklahoma!, 2002, Funny Girl, 2002, Fiddler on the Roof, 2005, Young Frankenstein, 2007, (films) Cannibal Girls, 1973, Black Christmas, 1974, Wholly Moses!, 1980, Soup for One, 1982, Club Paradise, 1986, Innerspace, 1987, Martha Ruth and Eddie, 1988, Worth Winning, 1989, Boris and Natasha, 1989, Rude Awakening, 1989, Too Much Sun, 1991, Stepping Out, 1991, All I Want for Christmas, 1991, (voice) The Itsy Bitsy Spider, 1992, Striking Distance, 1993, Bogus, 1996, (voice) Anastasia, 1997, Wag the Dog, 1997, The Rugrats Movie (voice), 1998, Bartok the Magnificent, 1999, Believe, 2000, Loser, 2000, Recess: Schools Out (voice), 2001, All Over the Guy, 2000, Jimmy Neutron: Boy Genius, 2001, My Big Fat Greek Wedding, 2002, New York Minute, 2004, The Producers, 2005, The TV Set, 2006, How to Eat Fried Worms, 2006, Young Triffie's Been Made Away With, 2006, Black Christmas, 2006, (TV series) Second City TV, 1977-81, Kate and Allie, 1982, The Martin Short Show, 1994, (voice) Earthworm Jim, 1995-96, Life...and Stuff, 1997, Recess, 1997, Damon, 1998, George and Martha, 1999, The New Woody Woodpecker Show, 1999, (voice) Superman, 1998-2000, Committed, 2001, (voice) The Adventures of Jimmy Neutron: Boy Genius, 2002-06, My Big Fat Greek Life, 2003, (voice) Kim Possible, 2002-07, (TV films) That Thing on ABC, 1978, Torn Between Two Lovers, 1979, The Robert Klein Show, 1981, Charles Dickens' David Copperfield, 1993, Gypsy, 1993, In Search of Dr. Seuss, 1994, Harrison Bergeron, 1995, My Funny Valentine, 2000, The Kid, 2001, Sick in the Head, 2003, Kim Possible: A Sitch in Time, 2003, (voice) Jimmy Neutron: Attack of the Twonkies, 2005; TV host Women of the Night II, 1988, Second City Fifteen Anniversary Special, 1988, Andrea Martin: Together Again, 1989; actress/writer: TV series SCTV Network 90, 1981-83 (2 Emmy awards 1982, 83), SCTV Channel, 1983-84, TV pilot From Cleveland, 1980; also The Completely Mental Misadventures of Ed Grimley, 1988-90 (voice of Mrs. Freebus).

MARTIN, CHRIS, singer; b. Devon, England, Mar. 2, 1977; m. Gwenyth Paltrow, 2003; children: Apple Blythe Alison, Moses. Student in Ancient World Studies, U. Coll. London. Sign painter; vocalist, pianist, rhythm guitarist Coldplay, 1998—. Singer: (albums) Parachutes, 2000 (Grammy award for Best Alternative Music Album, 2001), A Rush of Blood to the Head, 2002 (Grammy award for Best Alternative Music Album, 2002), Live 2003, 2003, X&Y, 2005 (Juno award for Best Internat. Album, 2006), Love, Actually, 2006; musician Viva La Vida, 2008 (Grammy award for Rock Album of Yr., 2009), (songs) In My Place, 2002 (Grammy award for Best Rock Performance By A Duo Or Group With Vocal, 2002), Clocks, 2002 (Grammy award for Record of Yr., 2003), Speed of Sound, 2005 (MTV Europe award for Best Song, 2005), Viva La Vida, 2009 (Grammy awards for Song of Yr. and Best Group Pop Vocal Performance, 2009). Recipient Favorite Alternative Artist (Coldplay), Am. Music Awards, 2005; named World's Best Rock Act, World's Best-Selling Rock Act, and Best-Selling Brit. Artist, World Music Awards, 2008. Office: Capital Records 1750 North Vine St 10th Fl Hollywood CA 90028*

MARTIN, CRAIG LEE, engineering company executive; b. Dodge City, Kans., Nov. 23, 1949; s. Ray N. and Nadia C. Martin; m. Diane E. Hensley, Mar. 19, 1977. BSCE, U. Kans., 1971; MBA, U. Denver, 1982. Project mgr. Martin K. Eby Constrn. Co., Wichita, Kans., 1972-83; exec. v.p., COO CRSS Constructors, Inc., Denver, 1983-89; exec. v.p. CRSS Comml. Group, Houston, 1989-90; sr. v.p. CRSS Capital, Houston, 1990-92, CRSS Inc., Houston, 1992-94; pres. CRSS Architects, Inc., Houston, 1992-94; sr. v.p. ops. Jacobs Engring. Group Inc., 1994-95; pres. Jacobs Constructors, Inc., 1994-95; sr. v.p. gen. sales and mktg. to pres. Jacobs Engring. Group, Inc., Pasadena, Calif., 1995—2000, exec. v.p. global sales, 2000—02, pres., 2002—06, CEO, pres., 2006—. Adv. bd. Constrn. Bus. Rev., 1993—. Bd. govs. Woodbury U. Sch. Bus. Mem. ASCE. Avocations: golf, clay shooting. Home: 930 S El Molino Ave Pasadena CA 91106-4414 Office: Jacobs Engring Group Inc 1111 S Arroyo Pkwy Pasadena CA 91105-3254 Office Phone: 626-578-6813. Business E-Mail: craig.martin@jacobs.com.

MARTIN, DARRICK DAVID, professional basketball player; b. Calif., Mar. 6, 1971; Grad., UCLA, 1992. Guard Minn., 1994-95, L.A. Clippers, 1996-99, Sacramento Kings, 1999—. Avocations: reading, video games, movies. Office: Sacramento Kings ARCO Arena 1 Sports Pkwy Sacramento CA 95834-2301

MARTIN, DAVID G., rental company executive; b. 1966; Investment banker Salmon Bros., Inc.; v.p. high yield fin. and merchant banking Nomura Securities Co., Ltd., 1991-96; mng. dir. high yield fin. NationsBanc Montgomery Securities LLC, 1996-99; exec. v.p., CFO Hollywood Entertainment Corp., 1999—. Office: Hollywood Entertainment Corp 9275 SW Peyton Ln Wilsonville OR 97070 Fax: 503-570-1680.

MARTIN, DAVID WILLIAM, JR., biomedical research company executive, educator; b. West Palm Beach, Fla., Jan. 15, 1941; s. David W. Sr. and Joanna (Law) M.; m. Kathleen McKinnon, Aug. 22, 1964; children: David McKinnon, Gillian Hope. Student, MIT, 1958-60; MD, Duke U., 1964. Intern in internal medicine Duke U. Med. Ctr., Durham, N.C., 1964-65, asst. resident dept. medicine, 1965-66; rsch. assoc. lab. molecular biology, Nat. Inst. Arthritis and Metabolic Diseases NIH, Bethesda, Md., 1966-69; instr. dept. medicine, dept. biochemistry and biophysics U. Calif., San Francisco, 1969-70, asst. prof. medicine, chief med. genetics service, lectr. dept. biochemistry and biophysics, 1970-75, assoc. prof. medicine in residence and biochemistry in residence, chief med. genetics service, 1975-79, prof. medicine in residence and biochemistry in residence, chief med. genetics service, 1979-82; sr. v.p. R&D Genentech, Inc., South San Francisco, Calif., 1983-89; exec. v.p. R & D, Du Pont Merck Pharm. Co., Wilmington, Del., 1991-93; sr. v.p. Chiron Corp., Emeryville, Calif., 1993—97; pres. Chiron Therapeutics, Emeryville, 1993—97; pres., CEO EOS Biotechnology, Inc., San Francisco, 1997—2003; chmn., CEO GangaGen Inc., 2003—04. Sci. adv. bd. Alliance for Lupus Rsch.; bd. dirs. Varian Med. Systems Inc., Palo Alto, Calif., 1994-, Cubist Pharmaceuticals Inc., BayBio; trustee, U. Pa. Med. Ctr., 1991-93; mem. bd. overseers U. Pa. Sch. Med., Phila., 1991-93; mem. adv. bd. Ctr. Health Sci. U. Calif. Irvine, 1991; investigator Howard Hughes Med. Inst., 1974-82, dir. med. scientist tng. program, 1978-82, mem. adv. com. biotech. rsch. and program, 1986-89; mem. recombinant DNA adv. com. NIH, 1981-85. Editor Harper's Rev. Biochemistry, 18th-20th edits., 1980-85, Sci. Yr., World Book Ency., 1981-86, Jour. Biol. Chemistry, 1983-87; contbr. numerous articles to profl. jours. Adv. coun. R & D Coun. Cystic Fibrosis Found., 1983-88; bd. overseers Duke U. Comprehensive Cancer Ctr., 1985-88. Sr. surgeon, USPHS. Named Disting. Alumnus of Duke U. Sch. Medicine, 1985. Mem. Am. Fedn. Clin. Research, Am. Soc. Biol. Chemists, Am. Soc. Clin. Investigation, Assn. Am. Physicians, Western Assn. Physicians, Alpha Omega Alpha. Office: BayBio 395 Oyster Point Blvd Ste 117 South San Francisco CA 94080-1929

MARTIN, DEAN, state treasurer; m. Kerry Martin. Degree in small bus. mgmt./entrepreneurship, Ariz. State U. Founder Digital Media Develop. Co.; ptnr. Mktg. Consulting Firm; senator, Dist 24 Ariz. State Senate, 2001—02, senator, Dist 6, 2002—07; state treas. State Ariz., 2007—. Mem.: Young Republicans, Phoenix Rotary 100, 100 Club. Office: 1700 W Washington St 1st Fl Phoenix AZ 85007 Office Phone: 602-604-7800. Office Fax: 602-542-7176.

MARTIN, FRED, artist, academic administrator; b. San Francisco, June 13, 1927; s. Ernest Thomas and Leona (Richey) M.; m. Genevieve Catherine Fisette, Jan. 29, 1950 (dec.); children: T. Demian, Fredericka C., Anthony J.; m. Stephanie Zuperko Dudek, 1992. BA, U. Calif., Berkeley, 1949, MA, 1954; postgrad., Calif. Sch. Fine Arts, 1949—50. Registrar Oakland (Calif.) Art Mus., 1955-58; dir. exhbn. San Francisco Art Inst., 1958-65, 1965-75, dir. coll., 1983-92, dean acad. affairs. Exhibited one man shows, Zoe Dusanne Gallery, Seattle, 1952, M.H. deYoung Meml. Mus., San Francisco, 1954, 64, Oakland Mus. Calif., 1958, 2003, San Francisco Mus. Modern Art, 1958, 73, Dilexi Gallery, San Francisco, 1961, Minami Gallery, Tokyo, 1963, Royal Marks Gallery, NYC, 1965-70, Hansen Fuller Gallery, San Francisco, 1974, 75, 76, Quay Gallery, San Francisco, 1979, 81, 84, Natsoulas Gallery, Davis, Calif., 1991, Belcher Studios Gallery, San Francisco, 1994, Frederick Spratt Gallery, San Jose, 1996, Ebert Gallery, San Francisco, 1997, 98, 99, 2001, 2003, Art and Consciousness Gallery/John F. Kennedy U., Berkeley, 1997, Shasta Coll., 1998, Han Art Contemporaine, Montreal, 1999, Sanchez Art Ctr., 2003, Collector's Gallery of Oakland Mus., 2004, Paul Sunderholm Gallery, 2004, Gallery Denovo, Sun Valley, Idaho; represented in permanent collections, Mus. Modern Art, NYC, San Francisco Mus. Modern Art, Oakland Art Mus., Whitney Mus., Fogg Mus.; author: Beulah Land, 1966, Log of the Sun Ship, 1969, Liber Studiorum, 1973, A Travel Book, 1976, From an Antique Land, 1979; Bay area corr.: Art Internat., 1967-69, 75-76; contbg. editor Art Week, 1976-93. Recipient prizes Oakland Art Mus., 1951, 58, prizes San Francisco Mus. Art, 1957, 58, prizes Richmond (Calif.) Art Ctr., 1962, prizes Nat. Found. for Arts, 1970. Home: 232 Monte Vista Ave Oakland CA 94611-4922 Office: San Francisco Art Inst 800 Chestnut St San Francisco CA 94133-2206

MARTIN, GEORGE FRANCIS, lawyer; b. Yuba City, Calif., July 7, 1944; s. John Severd and Albina Marie M.; m. Linda Louise D'Aoust, Mar. 17, 1968; children: Brandon, Bry. BA in Govt., Calif. State U., Sacramento, 1968; JD, U. Calif., Davis, 1971. Bar: Calif. Adminstr. asst. Assemblyman E. Richard Barnes, Sacramento, 1967-68; with Borton, Petrini & Conron, Bakersfield, Calif., 1971—, mng. gen. ptnr., 1977—; dean Calif. Pacific Sch. Law, Bakersfield, 1993-95. Holdings numerous ventures, partnerships; lectr. in field; founder, owner theatrical bus. Mgmt. by Martin, Inc., Shower of Stars, Frantic Records, 1962-67. Editor-in-chief Verdict Jour. of Law, 1984-85, Calif. Def. Mag.; newspaper reporter Appeal Democrat, Marysville, Calif., 1959-62. Former vice chmn. Kern County Rep. Ctrl. Com.; past pres. So. Calif. Def. Counsel; past chmn. Ctrl. Calif. Heart Inst.; bd. dirs. Calif. State U. at Bakersfield Found., chair, 1998; bd. dirs. Calif. Coun. Partnerships, Kern Econ. Devel. Corp; mem. adv. bd. Automobile Club So. Calif.; chmn. adv. bd. Witkin Legal Inst. Mem. Greater Bakersfield C. of C. (bd. dirs., past pres.). Office: Borton Petrini & Conron 1600 Truxtun Ave Bakersfield CA 93301-5111

MARTIN, GEORGE MONROE, pathologist, gerontologist, educator; m. Julaine Ruth Miller, Dec. 2, 1952 (dec. Apr. 2005); children: Peter C., Kelsey C., Thomas M., Andrew C. BS, U. Wash., 1949, MD, 1953. Diplomate Am. Bd. Pathology, Am. Bd. Med. Genetics. Intern Montreal Gen. Hosp., Que., Canada, 1953-54; resident, instr. U. Chgo., 1954-57; instr., prof. U. Wash., Seattle, 1957—2003, prof. emeritus, 2003—. Vis. scientist dept. genetics Albert Einstein Coll., NYC, 1964, Rockefeller U., 1998-99, UCLA, 2006; chmn. Gordon Confs. Molecular Pathology, Biology of Aging, 1974-79; chmn., nat. res. Plan on Aging Nat. Inst. on Aging, Bethesda, Md., 1985-89; dir. Alzheimer's Disease Rsch. Ctr. U. Wash., 1985—, assoc. dir., 1999—, dir. emeritus, 2003—; mem. bd. sci. counselors Nat. Inst. on Aging, 1994-98; mem. sci. adv. bd. Ellison Med. Found., 2998—, Benaroya Rsch. Inst., 2004—, Buck Inst. Aging Rsch., 2000-04. Editor Werner's Syndrome and Human Aging, 1985, Molecular Aspects of Aging, 1995; editor-in-chief: Science of Aging Knowledge Environment, 2000-06; contbr. articles in field to profl jours. Active Fedn. Am. Scientists, Human Rights Comm., Inst. Medicine. With USN, 1945—46. Recipient Allied Signal award in Aging, 1991, Rsch. medal Am. Aging Assn., 1992, Kleemeier award, 1994, Paul Glenn award for aging rsch., 1998, Longevity Prize, IPSEN Found., 2002, Irving Wright award of distinction Am. Fedn. Aging Rsch., 1996, Disting. Scientist award U. Urbino, 1998, others; named Disting. Alumnus, U. Wash. Sch. Medicine, 1987; USPHS rsch. fellow dept. genetics, Glasgow U., 1961-62; Eleanor Roosevelt Inst. Cancer Rsch. fellow Inst. de Biologie, Physiologie, Chimie, Paris, 1968-69; Josiah Macy faculty scholar Sir William Din Sch. Pathology, Oxford (Eng.) U., 1978-79, Humboldt Disting. scientist dept. genetics U. Wurzburg, Germany, 1991; Paul Harris fellow Rotary Internat., 1998. Fellow: AAAS, Tissue Culture Assn. (pres. 1986—88), Gerontol. Soc. Am. (chmn. Biol. Sci. 1979, pres. 2003, Brookdale award 1981, Lifetime Acheivement award for rsch. in alzheimer's disease World Alzheimer's Congress 2000); mem.: Am. Fedn. Aging Rsch. (pres. 1999—2001, sci. dir. 2003—), Am. Soc. Investigative Pathology, Am. Soc. Human Genetics, Am. Assn. Univ. Pathologists (emeritus), Inst. Medicine. Democrat. Avocations: travel, jazz, reading. Office Phone: 206-543-5088. Business E-Mail: gmmartin@u.washington.edu.

MARTIN, JAY HERBERT, psychoanalyst, literature professor, political science professor; b. Newark, Oct. 30, 1935; s. Sylvester K. and Ada M. (Smith) M.; m. Helen Bernadette Saldini, June 9, 1956; children: Helen E., Laura A., Jay Herbert. AB with honors, Columbia U., 1956; MA, Ohio State U., 1957, PhD, 1960; PhD in Psychoanalysis, So. Calif. Psychoanalytic Inst., 1983. Instr. English Pa. State U., 1957-58; instr., then asst. to assoc. prof. English and Am. Studies Yale U., New Haven, 1960-68; prof. English and comparative culture U. Calif., Irvine, 1968-79; asst. prof. psychiatry and human behavior, clin. supr. residency program Calif. Coll. Medicine Calif. Coll. Medicine U. Calif.-Irvine, 1978—96; Leo S. Bing prof. English and Am. lit. U. So. Calif., LA, 1979-96, dir. undergrad. program in Am. studies, 1968-69, dir. program in comparative culture, 1969-71, dir. edn. abroad program, 1971-75; prof. govt., Edward S. Gould prof. humanities Claremont McKenna Coll., 1996—; dir. civilization program Claremont (Calif.) McKenna Coll., 1996—2000, acting dir. Gould Ctr. for Humanistic Studies, 1998-2000, prof., English, grad. sch., 2004—. Instr. psychoanalysis So. Calif. Psychoanalytic Inst., 1984-96; Bicentennial prof. Am. lit. and culture Moscow State U., USSR, 1976, Dai Ho Chun (Wisdom) chair Prof. U. Hawaii, 2000-01; dir. NEH summer sems., 1976, 77; mem. evaluation com. dept. pvt. post-secondary edn. State of Calif., 1986; lectr. in field; cons. in field Author: (criticism and biography) Conrad Aiken: A Life of His Art, 1962, Harvests of Change: American Literature 1865-1914, 1967, Nathanael West: The Art of His Life, 1970 (U. Calif. Friends Libr. award), Robert Lowell, 1970, Always Merry and Bright. The Life of Henry Miller, 1978, (U. Calif. Friends of Libr. award, Phi Kappa Phi Best Faculty Publ. prize U. So. Calif., transl. in French, Japanese and German), (fiction) Winter Dreams: An American in Moscow, 1979, Who Am I This Time, Uncovering the Fictive Personality, 1988 (trans. Portuguese), Burlington No. Found. award 1989); Swallowing Tigers Whole, 1996, A Corresponding Leap of Love: Henry Miller, 1996, Henry Miller's Dream Song, 1996, Journey to Heavenly Mountain, 2002 (ForeWord mag. Book of Yr. prize), The Education of John Dewey, 2003; author Baseball Magic (short stories) 2008, Live All You Can: Alexander Joy Cartwright And the Invention of Modern Baseball, 2009, one hour radio drama, William Faulkner. Sound Portraits of Twentieth-Century Humanists, starring Tennessee Williams, Glenn Close, Colleen Dewhurst, Nat. Pub. Radio, 1980; author one-act docudrama Trial Days in Coyocoan, Antioch Rev., 2001; author sects. 24 books including most recently American Writing Today, vol. I, 1982, The Haunted Dusk: American Supernatural Fiction, 1820-1902, 1983, Frontiers of Infant Psychiatry, vol.II, 1986, Centenary Essays on Huckleberry Finn, 1985, Robert Lowell: Essays on the Poetry, 1987, William Faulkner: The Best from American Literature, 1989, The Homosexualities: Reality, Fantasy and the Arts, 1991, Life Guidance Through Literature, 1992, Biography and Source Studies, 1995, William Faulkner and Psychology, 1995, Psychotherapy East and West, 1996, Readings on Huckleberry Finn, 1999, John Fante: A Critical Gathering, 2000, Uncollected Works By...Paul Laurence Dunbar, 2000, American Literature of the Civil War, 2004, Blackwell Companion to Modernist Literature and Culture, 2004,Cases as Catalysts, 2005, Only God: A Biography of Ramsuratkumar, 2005, International Research on Global Affairs, 2005; editor: Winfield Townley Scott (Yale series recorded poets), 1962, Twentieth Century Interpretations of the Waste Land: A Collection of Critical Essays, 1968, Twentieth Century Views of Nathanael West, 1972, A Singer in the Dawn: Reinterpretations of Paul Laurence Dunbar (with intro.), 1975, Economic Depression and American Humor (with intro.), 1986; mem. editl. bd. Am. Lit., 1978-81, Humanities in Society, 1979-1983; editor-in-chief Psychoanalytic Edn., 1984-89; editor Humanitas/Communitas, 1998-2000; appearances on TV and radio including Connie Martinson Talks Books, Barbara Brunner Nightline, Sonya Live in LA, Oprah Winfrey Show, C-SPAN, 1988-89; contbr. numerous articles and revs. to profl. jours., bulls. Pres. Friends of Irvine Pub. Libr., 1974-75; mem. Com. for Freud Mus. Recipient Fritz Schmidl Meml. prize for rsch. applied psychoanalysis Seattle Assn. Psychoanalysis, 1982, Marie H. Briehl prize for child psychoanalysis, 1982, Franz Alexander prize in psychoanalysis, 1984, Disting. Writers award Antioch Rev., 2004; Morse rsch. fellow, 1963-64, Am. Philos. Soc. fellow, 1966, J.S. Guggenheim fellow, 1966-67, Rockefeller Found.humanities sr. fellow, 1975-76, Rsch. Clin. fellow So. Calif. Psychoanalytic Soc. 1977-81, Rockefeller fellow, Bellagio, Italy, 1983, NEH sr. fellow, 1983-84; Durfee Found. fellow to China, 2004; fellow Bogliasco Found. Liguria Ctr. for Arts and Humanities, 2004. Mem. So. Calif. Am. Studies Assn. (pres. 1969-71), Am. Studies Assn. (exec. bd. 1969-71, del. to MLA Assembly 1974, chmn. Ralph Gabriel prize com. 1975-77), MLA (chmn. prize com. Jay B. Hubbell Silver medal in Am. lit. 1978-84), Nat. Assn. Arts and Letters (prize com. 1987-88), Nat. Humanities Faculty (advisor to Valhalla High Sch., El Cajon, Calif. 1979-81), Nat. Am. Studies Faculty, Internat. Psychoanalytic Assn., Internat. Assn. Empirical Aesthetics, Internat. Assn. U. Profs. English, Internat. Karen Horney Soc., Newport Psychoanalytical Inst., Phi Beta Kappa. Home: 748 Via Santo Tomas Claremont CA 91711-1569 Home Phone: 909-624-8155; Office Phone: 909-398-0193. Personal E-mail: helenjay@ca.rr.com.

MARTIN, JERYL (JILL MARTIN), principal; BA in Secondary Edn. and English, Monmount U.; MA in Spl. Edn., U. Denver; PhD in Ednl. Leadership, U. Northern Colo. Prin. Thomas B. Doherty HS, Colorado Springs, Colo., 1999—. Recipient Colo. HS Prin. of Yr., Nat. HS Prin. of Yr., Nat. Assn. HS Principals, 2007. Office: Thomas B Doherty High School 4515 Barnes Rd Colorado Springs CO 80917 Office Phone: 719-328-6400. E-mail: martijl@d11.org.

MARTIN, JOANNE, social sciences educator; b. Salem, Mass., Sept. 25, 1946; d. Richard Drake and Nathalie (Ashton) M.; m. Beaumont A. Sheil, July 9, 1977; 1 child, Beaumont Martin Sheil. BA, Smith Coll., 1968; PhD in Social Psychology, Harvard U., 1977; PhD in Econs. and Bus. Adminstrn. (hon.), Copenhagen Bus. Sch., 2001; PhD (hon.), Vrije U., Amsterdam, 2005. Assoc. cons. McBer & Co. (formerly Behavior Sci. Ctr. of Sterling Inst.), 1968-70, dir. govt. mktg., 1970-72; asst. prof. orgnl. behavior Grad. Sch. Bus., Stanford (Calif.) U., 1977-80; assoc. prof. grad. sch. bus. Stanford U., 1980-91, prof. grad. sch. bus., 1991—, dir. doctoral programs, grad. sch. bus., 1991-95, Fred H. Merrill prof. orgn. behavior and, by courtesy, sociology, 1996—, prof. emeritus, 2008—. Sec. univ. adv. bd. Stanford U., 1995—96, vice chair adv. bd., 1996—97; vis. scholar Australian Grad. Sch. Mgmt. U. N.S.W., 1989—90, Copenhagen Bus. Sch., 1998, 2004; vis. scholar dept. psychology Sydney (Australia) U., 1989—90; Ruffin fellow bus. ethics Darden Grad. Sch. Bus. Adminstrn. U. Va., 1990; mem. bd. advisors iMahal, 1990—; bd. dirs. C.P.P., Inc., 1993—2003; mem. internat. adv. bd. Internat. Ctr. for Rsch. in Orgnl. Discourse, Strategy and Change; Bus. Sch. rep. Stanford U., 1995—; vis. scholar U. Tech. Sydney, 2004—05. Mem. editl. bd. Adminstrv. Sci. Qtrly., 1984—88, Jour. Social Issues, 1981—83, Acad. Mgmt. Jour., 1984—85, Social Justice Rsch., 1985—90, Jour. Mgmt. Inquiry, 1991—, Orgn., 1994—, Jour. Mgmt. Studies, 1996—2004, Gender, Work and Organization, 1998—, Orgn. Studies, 2003—, Scandinavian Jour. Mgmt., 2003—, consulting editor Internat. Jour. Mgmt. Reviews, 1998—; co-author: five books; contbr. over 60 articles to profl. jours. and edited books. Recipient Centennial medal for contbns. to soc. Harvard U. Grad. Sch. Arts and Scis., 2002; Lena Lake Forrest Rsch. fellowship Bus. and Profl. Women's Found., 1978, James and Doris McNamara Faculty fellowship Grad. Sch. of Bus., Stanford U., 1990-91, Grad. Sch. Bus. Trust Faculty fellow, 2005-06. Fellow: APA, Am. Psychol. Soc., Acad. Mgmt. (nat. rep.-at-large 1983—85, divsn. program chair 1985—87, divsn. chair 1987—89, nat. bd. govs. 1992—95, we. divsn. Promising Young Scholar award 1982, Nat. Disting. Educator award 2000, We. Divsn. Disting. Scholar award 2003, Nat. Orgn. and Mgmt. Divsn. Disting. Scholar career achievement award 2005, Joanne Martin Trailblazer award, Orgn. and Mgmt. Theory Divsn. 2007); mem.: Nat. Assn. Corp. Dirs. (adv. bd. 2000—04). Office: Stanford U Grad Sch Bus Littlefield Ctr 353 Stanford CA 94305 Business E-Mail: martin_joanne@gsb.stanford.edu.

MARTIN, JOHN C., pharmaceutical company executive; b. 1952; MBA in Mktg., Golden Gate U., 1974; PhD in Organic Chemistry, U. Chgo., 1977. With Syntex Corp., 1978-84; dir. antiviral chemistry Bristol-Myers Squibb Co., 1984-90; v.p. R&D Gilead Sciences, Inc., Foster City, Calif., 1990-95, COO, 1995-96, pres., CEO, 1996—2008, chmn., CEO, 2008—. Bd. dirs. Gilead Sciences, Inc., 1996—, Gen-Probe Inc., 2007—; chmn. Bay Area Bioscience Ctr., 1999—2001; mem. Nat. Inst. Allergy & Infectious Diseases Coun., 2000—03, Presdl. Advisory Coun. on HIV/AIDS, 2005—; bd. dirs. Calif. Healthcare Inst., 2003—, chmn. bd., 2005—06, 2008—. Bd. trustee U. Chgo., Golden Gate U. Recipient Isbell award, Am. Chemical Soc., Gertrude B. Elion award for Scientific Excellence, Internat. Soc. for Antiviral Rsch.; named to Nat. Acad. Engring. Nat. Academies, 2008. Mem.: Internat. Soc. for Antiviral Rsch. (pres. 1998—2000). Office: Gilead Scis Inc 333 Lakeside Dr Foster City CA 94404*

MARTIN, J(OHN) EDWARD, architectural engineer; b. LA, Oct. 23, 1916; s. Albert C. and Carolyn Elizabeth (Borchard) M.; m. Elizabeth Jane Hines, May 27, 1944; children: Nicolas Edward, Peter Hines, Sara Jane McKinley Reynolds, Christopher Carey, Elizabeth Margaret Ferguson. Student, U. So. Calif., 1934-36; BS in Archtl. Engring., U. Ill., 1939. Registered profl. engr., Calif., Ill. Structural engr. Albert C. Martin & Assocs., LA, 1939-42, ptnr., 1945-75, mng. ptnr., 1975-86. Founding mem. bd. trustees Thomas Aquinas Coll., Santa Paula, Calif., 1971-98, emeritus, 1998. Lt. CEC, USNR, 1942-45. Fellow ASCE; mem. Structural Engrs. Assn. Calif., Cons. Engrs. Assn. Calif., Jonathan Club (bd. dirs. 1978-81), Calif. Club, Ranchero Visitadores, Valley Hunt Club, Flintridge Riding Club, West Hills Hunt Club (Master of Fox Hounds 1975-88), Saddle & Sirloin Club, Heritage Found., Traditional Mass Soc. (founder), Pacific Legal Found. (charter). Republican. Roman Catholic. Avocation: horseback riding. Fax: 626-440-0889.

MARTIN, JULIE, women's healthcare company executive; BA in Liberal Arts and Scis., San Diego State U., MS in Exercise Physiology. Propr. 2 cos., 1983-90; gen. mgr. Dale Fitzmorris, 1990-92; dir. health promotion Ctr. for Women's Medicine, 1993-96; co-CEO, As We Change, LLC, 1995-98; v.p. catalog ops. Women First HealthCare, Inc., San Diego, 1998—.

MARTIN, JUNE JOHNSON CALDWELL, journalist; b. Toledo, Oct. 06; d. John Franklin and Eunice Imogene (Fish) Johnson; m. Erskine Caldwell, Dec. 21, 1942 (div. Dec. 1955); 1 child, Jay Erskine; m. Keith Martin, May 5, 1966. AA, Phoenix Jr. Coll., 1941; BA, U. Ariz., 1943-59; postgrad., Ariz. State U., 1939-40. Freelance writer, 1944—; columnist Ariz. Daily Star, Tucson, 1956-59, 70-94, book reviewer, 1970-94, co-founder Ann. Book and Author Event; editor Ariz. Alumnus mag., Tucson, 1959-70; ind. book reviewer, audio tape columnist Tucson, 1994—; coord. S.W. Books of Yr. sponsored by Pima Pub. Libr., Ariz., 2000—06; columnist So. Ariz. Authors, Ariz., 2005—. Panelist, co-producer TV news show Tucson Press Club, 1954-55, pres., 1958. Contbg. author: Rocky Mountain Cities, 1949; contbr. articles to World Book Ency., and various mags. Mem. Tucson CD Com., 1961; vol. campaigns of Samuel Goddard, U.S. Rep. Morris Udall, U.S. amb. and Ariz. gov. Raul. Castro. Recipient award Nat. Headliners Club, 1959, Ariz. Press Club award, 1957-59, 96, Am. Alumni Coun., 1966, 70, 2007, Lawrence Clark Powell Outstanding Contbn. Southwest Lit. Mem. Nat. Book Critics Circle, Ariz. Press Women, Jr. League of Tucson, Tucson Urban League, PEN U.S.A. West, Planned Parenthood So. Ariz., Tucson Press, Pi Beta Phi. Democrat. Methodist. Home: Desert Foothills Sta PO Box 65388 Tucson AZ 85728-5388

MARTIN, LOREN WINSTON, allergist; b. Albertsville, Ala., Apr. 20, 1938; s. Loren d. and Byrda G. (Crotwell) M.; m. Vivian Elizabeth Sanger Martin, Dec. 29, 1960; children: Lori Ann, Karen Lynn, James Winston. BA in Chemistry, Duke U., 1959; MD, U. Tenn., 1962. Lic. physician, Ariz. Rotating internship Fitzsimons Army Hosp., Denver, 1963; med. residency Honolulu, 1964-67; med. officer U.S. Army, 1962-70; fellowship allergy U. Colo., Denver, 1970-71; pvt. practice Tucson, 1971—. Decorated Bronze Star. Fellow Am. Acad. Allergy & Immunology, Am. Coll. Allergy & Immunology; mem. Pima County Med. Soc. Republican. Home: 4318 N Sunset Cliff Dr Tucson AZ 85750-6931 Home Phone: 520-760-0225; Office Phone: 520-795-1185.

MARTIN, LUCY Z., public relations executive; b. Alton, Ill., July 8, 1941; d. Fred and Lucille J. M. BA, Northwestern U., 1963. Adminstrv. asst., copywriter Batz-Hodgson-Neuwoehner, Inc., St. Louis, 1963-64; news reporter, Midwest fashion editor Fairchild Publs., St. Louis, 1964-66; account exec. Milici Advt. Agy., Honolulu, 1967; publs. dir. Barnes Med. Ctr., St. Louis, 1968-69; comms. cons. Fleishman-Hillard, St. Louis, 1970-74; comms. cons., CEO, pres. Lucy Z. Martin & Assocs., Portland, Oreg., 1974—. Spkr. Marylhurst Coll., 1991, 92, 93, Concordia Coll., 1992, Women Entrepreneurs of Oreg., 1992, Oreg. Assn. Hosps. and Health Sys. Trustees, 1992, Healthcare Assn. Hawaii, Honolulu, 1993, USBancorp for Not-for-Profits, 1993, Multnomah County Ret. Srs. Vol. Program, 1993, Healthcare Fin. Mgmt. Assn., N.W., 1993, Healthcare Comms. Oreg., 1994, Area Health Edn. Ctrs., OHSU/statewide, 1994, Columbia River chpt. Pub. Rels. Soc. Am., 1994, 96; spkr., workshop conducter Healthcare Assn. Hawaii, 1993, USBancorp Not-for-Profit, 1993, Healthcare Communicators Oreg., 1994, Pathways to Career Transition, 1995, among others; bd. dirs. Ctrs. Airway Sci., Oregon Coll. Arts & Crafts, 1989-95, Good Samaritan Hosp. Assn., 1991-94, Am. Mktg. Assn., Oreg. chap., 1992-93, Inst. Managerial and Profl. Women, 1992-94, YMCA Public Policy com., 1993-95, Jr. League Cmty. adv. bd., 1994—, Bus. Social Responsibility Steering com., 1996—, Ctrs. for Airway Sci. Bd., 1996—; spkr. in field. Featured in Entrepreneurial Woman mag.; contbr. articles to profl. jours. Chmn. women's adv. com. Reed Coll., Portland, 1977-79; mem. Oreg. Commn. for Women, 1984-87; bd. dirs. Ronald McDonald House Oreg., 1986, Oreg. Sch. Arts and Crafts, 1989—, Northwestern U. Alumni Coun., 1992—; bd. dirs. Good Samaritan Hosp. Assocs., 1991-94, chair 1993-94; mem. pub. policy com. YMCA, 1993-95; mem. adv. bd. Jr. League, 1994—; mem. steering com. Bus. for Social Responsiblity, 1996—; bd. dirs. Ctrs. for Airway Sci., 1996—. Recipient MacEachern Citation Acad. Hosp. Pub. Relations, 1978, Rosey awards Portland Advt. Fedn., 1979, Achievement award Soc. Tech. Comms., 1982, Disting. Tech. Comm. award, 1982, Exceptional Achievement award Coun. for Advancement and Support Edn., 1983, Monsoon award Internat. Graphics, Inc., 1984, William Marsh Achievement award PRSA, 1998; named Woman of Achievement Daily Jour. Commerce, 1980. Mem. Pub. Rels. Soc. Am. (pres. Columbia River chpt. 1984, chmn. bd. 1980-84, Oreg. del. 1984-86, jud. panel N. Pacific dist 1985-86, exec. bd. health care sect. 1986-87, mem. Counselors Acad., Spotlight awards 1985, 86, 87, 88, nat. exec. com. 1987-91; William Marsh Achievement award 1998), Portland Pub. Rels. Roundtable (chmn. 1985, bd. dirs. 1983-85), Assn. Western Hosps. (editl. adv. bd. 1984-85), Best of West awards 1978, 80, 83, 87), Oreg. Hosp. Pub. Rels. Orgn. (pres. 1981, chmn. bd. 1982, bd. dirs. 1992-93), Acad. Health Service Mktg., Am. Hosp. Assn., Am. Mktg. Assn. (Oreg. chpt. bd. dirs. 1992-93), Am. Soc. Hosp. Mktg. & Pub. Rels., Healthcare Communicators Oreg. (conf. keynote speaker 1994), Internat. Assn. Bus. Communicators (18 awards 1981-87), Oreg. Assn. Hosps. (keynote speaker for trustee, 1991, speaker, 1993, bd. dirs. 1992-93), Oreg. Press Women, Nat. and Oreg. Soc. Healthcare Planning and Mktg., Women in Comms. (Matrix award 1977), Bus. for Social Responsibility (steering com. 1996—), Inst. for Managerial and Profl. Women (bd. dirs. 1992-94). Home: 1800 Headlee Ln Lake Oswego OR 97034-5068 Fax: 503-227-1569. E-mail: lucyz@lzma.com.

MARTIN, MELISSA CAROL, radiological physicist; b. Muskogee, Okla., Feb. 7, 1951; d. Carl Leroy and Helen Shirley (Hicks) Paden; m. Donald Ray Martin, Feb. 14, 1970; 1 child, Christina Gail. BS, Okla. State U., Stillwater, 1971; MS, UCLA, 1975. Cert. radiol. physicist Am. Bd. Radiology, radiation oncology Am. Bd. Med. Physics. Asst. radiation physicist Hosp. of the Good Samaritan, LA, 1975-80; radiol. physicist Meml. Med. Ctr., Long Beach, Calif., 1980-83, St. Joseph Hosp., Orange, Calif., 1983-92, Therapy Physics, Inc., Gardena, Calif., 1993—. Cons. in field. Editor: (book) Current Regulatory Issues in Medical Physics, 1992. Fund raising campaign divsn. mgr. YMCA, Torrance, Calif., 1988-92; dir. AWANA Youth Club-Guards Group, Manhattan Beach, Calif., 1984—. Named Dir. of Symposium, Am. Coll. Med. Physics, 1992. Fellow Am. Coll. Med. Physics (chancellor western region 1992-95, treas. 2004-05, vice-chair, 2009, Williams award, 2009), Am. Assn. Physicists in Medicine (profl. coun. 1990-95, 2006—, treas. 1998-2003, bd. dirs. 1994-2003, co-dir. summer sch. 2007, vice-chair ednl. coun.), Am. Coll. Radiology (econs. com. 1992-95, councilor at large 2001-06, commn. on med. physics 2002-07, mem. mammogrtaphy accreditation com., 2006—), Govt. Relative Comm. (vice chair 1998-07); mem. Calif. Med. Physics Soc. (treas. 1991-98), Am. Soc. for Therapeutic Radiology and Oncology, Health Physics Soc. (pres. So. Calif. chpt. 1992-93), Am. Brachytherapy Soc. Baptist. Avocation: christian youth group dir. Home: 507 Susana Ave Redondo Beach CA 90277-3953 Office: Therapy Physics Inc 879 W 190th St Ste 419 Gardena CA 90248 Office Phone: 310-217-4114. Personal E-mail: melissamartin@compuserve.com. Business E-Mail: melissa@therapyphysics.com.

MARTIN, MYRON GREGORY, foundation administrator; b. Houston, Jan. 14, 1958; s. Monty Gene and Vera Mae (Saurage) M. MusB, U. North Tex., 1980; MBA, Golden Gate U., 1989. Various sales and mktg. positions Baldwin Piano Co., NYC, 1980-1990, dir. concert and artists, 1990-95; exec. dir. Liberace Found., Las Vegas, Nev., 1995-98; dir. U. Las Vegas, 1998—. Mem. adv. bd. Thelonious Monk Inst., Washington, D.C., 1994-95; bd. dirs. Cystic Fibrosis Found., Chgo., 1990, Liberace Found., 1993-95, Museums and Attractions, Las Vegas, 1996—. Recipient Special award Cystic Fibrosis Found., 1990. Mem. Nev. Mus. Assn. (bd. dirs. 1997—). Avocations: tennis, judging scholarship pageants for miss america organization. Home: 3996 Placita Del Rico Las Vegas NV 89120-2629 Office: U Las Vegas Performing Art Ctr 4505 S Maryland Pkwy Las Vegas NV 89154-9900

MARTIN, PATRICK J., technology company executive; b. 1941; BS in math., Iona Coll.; MS in Elec. Engring., Doctorate in Elec. Engring., George Washington U.; grad. exec. edn. program, Harvard U. With US Dept. Agriculture; exec. Xerox Corp., pres. N.Am. solutions group; chmn., pres., CEO StorageTek, Louisville, Colo., 2000—. Past mem. bd. dirs. US C. of C., US/China Bus. Coun.; bd. trustees George Washington U.; adv. bd. com. George Washington U. Sch. Engring.; adv. com. Ohio State U. Fisher Sch. Bus. Recipient Jonas Bronck award, Bronx Hist. Soc., 2001, Ellis Island Medal Honor, 2003. Office: Storagetek 500 Eldorado Blvd Broomfield CO 80021-3408

MARTIN, RICHARD H., national park service executive; Supt. Death Valley (Calif.) Nat. Park. Office: Death Valley Nat Park PO Box 579 Death Valley CA 92328-0579

MARTIN, RICHARD J., food wholesale executive; Exec. v.p., CFO Rykoff-Sexton, Wilkes-Barre, Pa.; sr. v.p. fin. & adminstrn., CFO Cert. Grocers Calif., 1998-2000; CFO, exec. v.p. fin. & adminstrn. Unified Western Grocers, Inc., Commerce, Calif., 2000—. Office: Unified Western Grocers Inc 5200 Sheila St City Of Commerce CA 90040

MARTIN, RICHARD JAY, medical educator; b. Detroit, May 16, 1946; s. Peter Aaron and Tillie Jean (Munch) M.; m. Helene Iris Horowitz, Dec. 23, 1967; children: Elizabeth Hope, David Evan. BS, U. Mich., 1967, MD, 1971. Diplomate Am. Bd. Internal Medicine and Pulmonary Disease. Intern, Ariz., 1971-72; resident Tulane U., New Orleans, 1974-76; pulmonary fellow, 1976-78; asst. prof. medicine U. Okla., Okla. City, 1978-80, U. Colo., Denver, 1980-85, assoc. prof.,

1985-92, prof., 1992—. Dir. Cardiorespiratory Sleep Rsch., Nat. Jewish Health Ctr., Denver, 1980-89, staff physician, 1980-, head divsn. pulmonary medicine, 1993-2005, vice-chair dept. medicine, 1997-2004, acting chair dept. medicine, 2004-2005, chair dept. medicine, 2006—. Author: Cardiorespiratory Disorders During Sleep, 1984, 2d edit., 1990, (with others) Current Therapy in Internal Medicine, 1984, Clinical Pharmacology and Therapeutics in Nursing, 1985, Interdisciplinary Rehabilitation of Multiple Sclerosis and Neuromuscular Disorders, 1984, Drugs for the Respiratory System, 1985, Current Therapy in Pulmonary Medicine, 1985, Abnormalities of Respiration During Sleep, 1986, Mitchell's Synopis of Pulmonary Medicine, 1987, Pulmonary Grand Rounds, 1990, Asthma and Rhinitis, 1994, The High Risk Patient: Management of the Critically Ill, 1995, Manual of Asthma Management, 1995, 2000, Severe Asthma: Pathogenesis and Clinical Management, 1995, Curret Pulmonology, 1995, Pulmonary and Respiratory Therapy Secrets, 1996, (book chpts.) Lung Biology in Health and Disease, 1995, 3d edit., 2000, Allergy, 1997, Asthma, 1997, Emergency Asthma, 1999, Difficult Asthma, 1999, Asthma and Rhinitis, 1999, Imaging of Diffuse Lung Disease, 2000, Manual of Asthma Management, 2000, Severe Asthma, 2001, Asthma Critical Debates, 2002, Inhaled Steroids in Asthma, 2002, The Merck Manual, 2002, Current Review of Asthma, 2003; editor: Nocturnal Asthma: Mechanisms and Interventions, 1993, Cardiothoracic Interrelationships in Clinical Practice, 1997; author, editor: Nocturnal Asthma: Mechanisms and Treatment, 1993, Combination Therapy for Asthma and Chronic Obstructive Pulmonary Disease, 2000; mem. editl. bd. Chronobiology Internat., 1997—, Am. Jour. Respiratory and Critical Care Medicine, 1994-98, Bronchial Asthma: Index and Review, 1996-97; assoc. editor: Clinical Care for Asthma, 1995-97; contbr. articles to profl. jours. Pres. Congregation Rodef Shalom, Denver, 1984-85; regional v.p. United Synagogues of Am., Denver, 1988-89. Recipient Best Paper in Internal Medicine award, Okla. Soc. Interna. Medicine, 1977—78, U. Okla. Gastroenterology sect, 1977, Amb. award, Nat. Jewish Med. and Rsch. Ctr., 2002; named Disting. Lectr., Royal Coll. Physicians and Surgeons Can., 1998, Cardio-Pulmonary Congress, Argentina, 1998, Assn. Argentina Allergy and Immunology, 2001; grantee Am. Lung Assn., Va., U. Okla. Lung Assn., NIH, Parker B. Francis Found.; Pulmonary fellow, Am. Lung Assn., 1977—79, James F. Hammarsten Outstanding fellow, U. Okla. Health Scis. Ctr., 1978. Mem. ACP, Am. Thoracic Soc., Am. Fedn. for Clin. Rsch., Am. Coll. Chest Physicians (Disting. scholar in respiratory health 2003-07, Colorado Pulmonary Hall of Fame, 2007), Colo. Trudeau Soc., Western Soc. Clin. Investigation. Avocations: biking, golf, Karate. Office: Nat Jewish Health Ctr 1400 Jackson St Denver CO 80206-2761 Office Phone: 303-398-1847, 303-398-1095. Business E-Mail: martinr@njc.org.

MARTIN, RICHARD PETER, classics educator, consultant; b. Boston, May 19, 1954; s. Nicholas Richard and Marie Eileen (Daly) M.; children: Catherine, Thomas. AB, Harvard U., 1976, AM, 1978, PhD, 1981. Teaching fellow Harvard U., Cambridge, Mass., 1978-81; from asst. to assoc. prof. Princeton (N.J.) U., 1981-94, prof., 1994—99; Antony and Isabelle Raubitschek Prof. of Classics Stanford U., 2000—. Author: Healing, Sacrifice and Battle, 1983, The Language of Heroes, 1989, Myths of the Ancient Greeks, 2003; editor: Bulfinch, Mythology, 1991. Class of 1936 preceptor Princeton U., 1984-87. Devel. grantee Apple Computer Co., 1989. Fellow Onassis Found.; mem. Am. Philol. Assn., Celtic Studies Assn. of N.Am., Irish Texts Soc. Democrat. Roman Catholic. Office: Stanford Univ Bldg 110 Main Quad Stanford CA 94305-2145 Home Phone: 650-823-4771; Office Phone: 650-723-0479. Business E-Mail: rpmartin@stanford.edu.

MARTIN, ROBERT BRUCE, chemistry professor; b. Chgo., Apr. 29, 1929; s. Robert Frank and Helen (Woellfer) M.; m. Frances May Young, June 7, 1953. BS, Northwestern U., 1950; PhD, U. Rochester, 1953. Asst. prof. chemistry Am. U., Beirut, Lebanon, 1953-56; research fellow Calif. Inst. Tech., 1956-57, Harvard U., 1957-59; asst. prof. chemistry U. Va., Charlottesville, 1959-61, assoc. prof., 1961-65, prof., 1965—, chmn. dept., 1968-71. Spl. fellow Oxford U., 1961-62; Program dir. Molecular Biology Sect., NSF, 1965-66 Author: Introduction to Biophysical Chemistry, 1964. Fellow AAAS; mem. Am. Chem. Soc. Home: 620 Sand Hill Rd #314D Palo Alto CA 94304

MARTIN, ROBERT BURTON, management and marketing consultant; b. Takoma Park, Md., Mar. 17, 1935; s. Herbert Lester and Lenora Marie (Sponseller) M.; m. Mary Lou Rushworth, Sept. 7, 1959 (div. Dec. 1982); children: Laurajean, Kenneth, Donna Beth. BEE, Cornell U., 1958; MS, Northwestern U., 1966, PhD, 1967. Dir. mgmt. systems Denver and Rio Grande Western R.R., 1967-71; v.p. Mgmt. Design Assoc., Denver, 1971-79; owner Martin & Assoc., Denver, 1979—; founder Martin Aquatics, LLC, Denver, 1993—. Treas. Rocky Mountain chpt. Inst. of Mgmt. Sci., Denver, 1968-70; opening speaker AICPAs, Las Vegas, Nev., 1988. Author, pub.: (newsletter) Martin Reports, 1981-90, Bob Martin-Chris Frederiksen Marketing and Management Report for CPAs, 1990-94. Served to lt. USN, 1958-63. Mem. Inst. Mgmt. Cons., Alpha Pi Mu, Sigma Xi. Avocations: hiking, camping, flying, water sports. Home and Office: PO Box 6886 Denver CO 80206-0886 Home Phone: 858-551-9282; Office Phone: 303-321-3655. E-mail: bob@martincmc.com.

MARTIN, ROLAND S., journalist, former editor; b. Houston, Nov. 14, 1968; m. Jacquie Hood. BS in Journalism, Tex. A&M, 1991; student, La. Bapt. U. Owner, pub. Dallas-Fort Worth Heritage; mng. editor Houston Defender, Dallas Weekly; county govt. & neighbors reporter Austin Am.-Statesman, 1991—93; city hall reporter Fort Worth Star-Telegram, 1993—95; morning drive reporter KRLD-AM, 1995; news dir., morning anchor KKDA-AM, Dallas, 1995—98; founding editor BlackAmericaWeb.com, 2001, Savoy mag., 2002—04; exec. editor, gen. mgr. Chgo. Defender, 2004—07; host The Roland S. Martin Show, WVON-AM, Chgo.; commentator TV One Cable Network, 2005—; contbr. CNN, 2007—. Author: (books) Speak, Brother! A Black Man's View of America, 2002, Listening to the Spirit Within: 50 Perspectives on Faith, 2007; appeared on MSNBC, FOX News, Court TV, BET Nightly News, NPR, and numerous others. Recipient Edward R. Murrow award, Radio TV News Dirs., Image award, NAACP, 2008; named to Power 150, Ebony mag., 2008. Mem.: Am. Soc. Newspaper Editors, Nat. Assn. Black Journalists, Alpha Phi Alpha. Office: TV One Cable Network Creators Syndicate 5777 W Century Blvd Ste 700 Los Angeles CA 90045 also: WVON-AM 1000 E 87th St Chicago IL 60619 Office Phone: 310-337-7003. Office Fax: 310-337-7625.

MARTIN, STEVE, actor, comedian; b. Waco, Tex., Aug. 14, 1945; s. Glenn and Mary Lee Martin; m. Victoria Tennant, Nov. 20, 1986 (div. 1994); m. Anne Stringfield, July 28, 2007 Student, Long Beach State Coll., UCLA. Exec. prodr. TV show Domestic Life, 1984. TV writer for Smothers Bros. (co-winner Emmy award 1969), Sonny and Cher, Pat Paulsen, Ray Stevens, Dick Van Dyke, John Denver, Glen Campbell; nightclub comedian; guest and host appearances NBC's Saturday Night Live, Tonight Show; appeared on Carol Burnett Show; starred in TV spls. Steve Martin: A Wild and Crazy Guy, 1978, Comedy is Not Pretty, 1980, Steve Martin's Best Show Ever, 1981; rec. comedy albums Let's Get Small, 1977 (Grammy award 1977), A Wild and Crazy Guy, 1978 (Grammy award 1978), Comedy is Not Pretty, 1979, The Steve Martin Brothers, 1982; actor, screenwriter: (films) The Absent Minded Waiter, 1977, The Jerk, 1979, Pennies From Heaven, 1981, Dead Men Don't Wear Plaid, 1982, The Man With Two Brains, 1983, All of Me, 1984 (Nat. Soc. Film Critics award best actor 1984, New York Film Critics' Circle award best actor 1984), Three Amigos, 1986 (also exec. prodr.), Roxanne, 1987 (also exec. prodr.), (Nat. Soc. Film Critics award best actor 1988, Los Angeles Film Critics' award best actor 1988), L.A. Story, 1991; actor (films) Sergeant Pepper's Lonely Hearts Club Band, 1978, The Muppet Movie, 1979, The Kids Are Alright, 1979, The Lonely Guy, 1984, Little Shop of Horrors, 1986, Planes, Trains and Automobiles, 1987, Dirty Rotten Scoundrels, 1988, Parenthood, 1989, My Blue Heaven, 1990, Father of the Bride, 1991, Grand Canyon, 1991, Housesitter, 1992, Leap of Faith, 1993, Mixed Nuts, 1994, A Simple Twist of Fate, 1994, Sgt. Bilko, 1995, The Spanish Prisoner, 1998, Bowfinger, 1999, Joe Gould's Secret, 2000, Novocaine, 2001, Bringing Down the House, 2003, Looney Tunes: Back in Action, 2003, Cheaper by the Dozen, 2003, Jiminy Glick in La La Wood, 2004, Shopgirl, 2005 (also writer, prodr.), Cheaper by the Dozen 2, 2005, The Pink Panther, 2006 (also writer), Baby Mama, 2008, The Pink Panther 2, 2009 (also writer); (theatre) Waiting For Godot, 1988; (TV movies) And the Band Played On, 1993, Rutles 2: Can't Buy Me Lunch, 2002; (TV appearances) 30 Rock, 2008; screenwriter (films) Easy Money, 1983, Bowfinger, 1999, Traitor, 2008; author: Cruel Shoes, 1977, Pure Drivel, 1998, Shopgirl, 2001; playwright Picasso at the Lapin Agile, 1993; author: (children's books) The Alphabet From A To Y With Bonus Letter Z!, 2007, (autobiography) Born Standing Up, 2007 Trustee L.A. Mus. Art. Recipient Georgie award, Am. Guild Variety Artists, 1977, 1978, Grammy award, 1978, Mark Twain prize for Am. Humor, 2005, Kennedy Ctr. Honors, John F. Kennedy Ctr. for Performing Arts, 2007; named one of 50 Most Powerful People in Hollywood, Premiere mag., 2006. Office: PO Box 929 Beverly Hills CA 90213

MARTIN, TERENCE D., food products executive; B in Polit. Sci., Holy Cross Coll.; M in Acctg., Northeastern U. Pub. acct. Arthur Andersen & Co., NYC, 1966—74; joined Price Waterhouse, 1974—86, ptnr., 1977—86; exec. v.p., fin. and adminstrn., also bd. dir. J. Walter Thompson, 1986—88; treas. Am. Cyanamid Co., 1988—91, CFO, mem. exec. com., 1991—95; exec. v.p., CFO Gen. Signal Corp., 1995—98; sr. v.p. fin., CFO Quaker Oats Co., Chgo., 1998—2001; dir. Del Monte Foods Co., San Francisco, 2002—. Office: Del Monte Food Co One Market @ The Landmark San Francisco CA 94105 Office Phone: 415-247-3000. Fax: 415-247-3565.

MARTIN, THOMAS REED, medical educator, medical association administrator; b. Cin., Oct. 27, 1947; BA in Chemistry, Macalester Coll., St. Paul, 1969; MD, U. Pa., 1973. Cert. Pediat. Critical Care Medicine, Pediat. Pulmonology. Intern, pulmonary medicine U. Wash., Seattle, 1973—74, resident, 1974—77, fellow, pulmonary and critical care medicine, 1978—80; asst. prof. medicine, 1982-85, assoc. prof. medicine to prof. medicine, 1985—, vice chair dept. medicine, dir., Pulmonary Rsch. Training Prog., 1990—; chief medicine svc., prof. medicine VA Pugent Sound Health Care Sys., Seattle, 2000—. Vis. scientist, dept. immunology Scripps Rsch. Inst., La Jolla, Calif., 1989—90; vis. scientist, dept. biochemsitry Geneva Biomedical Rsch. Inst. & Hosp. U. Geneva (Switzerland), 1997—98. Contbr. several articles to profl. jours. Mem.: Am. Thoracic Soc. (former pres.). Office: Pulmonary Rsch Lab VA Med Puget Sound Heath Care Sys U Wash Box 358280-151L 1660 S Columbian Way Seattle WA 98108 Office Phone: 206-764-2504, 206-764-2219. Office Fax: 206-768-5289. E-mail: trmartin@u.washington.edu.

MARTIN, THOMAS RHODES, communications executive, writer, educator; b. Memphis, July 10, 1953; s. Otis Knox and Joe Anne Coggin Martin; m. Wanda C. Benderman, Dec. 1, 1984; children: Seth Knox, Cyrus Rhodes. BA, Vanderbilt U., Tenn., 1975. Sales communication writer Schering and Plough Corp., Memphis, 1976-78; media devel. specialist, Fed. Express Corp., Memphis, 1978-81, sr. media devel. specialist, 1981-82, mgr. of mgmt. comm., 1982-84, mng. dir. employee comm., 1984-92, mng. dir. pub. rels., 1992-95, v.p. corp. comm., 1995-96; v.p. corp. rels., ITT Industries, White Plains, NY, 1996-99, sr. v.p., dir. corp. rels., 1999—2007; sr. counselor Feldman & Ptnrs., LA, 2007—; chair Adv. Coun. Dept. Comm., Coll. of Charleston, SC. Exec.-in-residence Dept. Comm. Coll. Charleston, 2007—. Contbg. editor Memphis mag., 1984—94, contbr. PR Week mag.; contbr. articles to profl. jours. Bd. dirs. Big Bros. and Big Sisters, Memphis, 1983—87, Memphis Oral Sch. for the Deaf, 1985—91, Leadership Memphis, 1986—87, 1992—96, Pub. Rels. Soc. Am. Found, 1999—2001; trustee Inst. for Pub. Rels., 1999—; bd. govs. Josephson Inst. Ethics. Recipient Journalism award, Sigma Delta Phi, 1983, Mobius Advt. award, 1998, NY ADDY Award, 2001; named to PR News Hall of Fame, 2006. Mem.: Arthur W. Page Soc. (bd. dirs. 2001—, pres. 2004—05), Pub. Rels. Soc. Am. (Silver Anvil award 1995, Bronze Anvil award 1996), Internat. Assn. Bus. Communicators, The Wisemen. Avocations: writing, backpacking, sailing, skiing, running. Office: Coll Charleston Dept Comm 66 George St Charleston SC 29424 also: Feldman & Ptnrs Ste 2000 8491 Sunset Blvd Los Angeles CA 90069 Office Phone: 843-953-6383. E-mail: tom@feldmanandpartners.com, martintr@cofc.edu.

MARTINETTO, JOSEPH R., investment company executive; BA, Claremont McKenna Coll.; MBA, Univ. Calif., Berkeley. Fin. mgmt. positions through sr. v.p. asset & liability mgmt. First Interstate Bank, 1984—96; sr. asst. treas. Transamerica Corp., 1996—97; sr. v.p. Transamerica Fin. Corp., 1996—97; sr. v.p., treas. Charles Schwab Corp., San Francisco, 1997—2001, sr. v.p. retail fin., 2001—07, exec. v.p., CFO, 2007—. Office: Charles Schwab Corp 101 Montgomery St San Francisco CA 94104

MARTINEZ, ADRIANA, photographer; Student, U. Nev., Las Vegas; BA, Brooks Inst. Photography. Photography instr. C.C. So. Nev.; wedding photographer So. Nev. News Bur.; chair Nev. State Dem. Party, Las Vegas, 2003—06. Mem.: PTA. Mailing: 1499 Sunair Cir Las Vegas NV 89110

MARTINEZ, ALEX J., state supreme court justice; b. Denver, Apr. 1, 1951; m. Kathy Carter; children: Julia, Maggie. Diploma, Phillips Exeter Acad., NH, 1969; student, Reed Coll., 1969-72; BA, U. Colo., 1973, JD, 1976. Bar: Colo. 1976. Dep. state pub. defender, Pueblo and Denver, 1976-83; county ct. judge Pueblo, 1983-88; dist. ct. judge, 1988-97; justice Colo. Supreme Ct., Denver, 1997—. Supreme Ct. liaison Colo. Criminal Rules Com., Colo. Criminal Jury Instns.; chmn. Pub. Access Com., Jud. Edn. Com.; bd. dirs. Servicios de la Raza. Chmn. Pueblo adv. bd. Packard Found., 1993-96; chmn. site-based governing coun. Pueblo Sch. Arts and Scis., 1994-95; mem. site-based governing coun. Roncalli Mid. Sch., 1993-94; bd. dirs. Colo. U. Law Alumni. Mem. Colo. Bar Assn. (regional v.p. 1995-96), Colo. Hispanic Bar Assn., Pueblo Bar Assn. (mem. exec. coun. 1994-96), Pueblo Hispanic Bar Assn. Office: Colo Supreme Ct 2 E 14th Ave Denver CO 80203-2115

MARTINEZ, ALMA R., actress, theater director, educator; b. Monclova, Coahuila, Mex. Student, U. Guadalajara-Artes Plasticas, Mex., 1972-73, Ibero-Am. U., 1976, UNAM, Mexico City, 1976-77; BA in Theatre, Whittier Coll., 1984; MFA in Acting, U. So. Calif., 1995; postgrad., Stanford U., 1994—; student, Jerzy Grotowski Para Theatre, Berkeley, Calif., 1977, Lee Strasberg Theatre Inst., Hollywood, Calif., 1982, Royal Acad. Dramatic Arts, London, Eng., 1987, Mnouchkine/Theatre du Soleil, Paris, 1993. Asst. prof. theatre arts U. Calif., Santa Cruz, 2001—. Appeared in plays including In the Summer House, Lincoln Ctr., N.Y.C., Greencard, Joyce Theatre, N.Y.C., Zoot Suit, Mark Taper Forum, L.A., Bocon, Mark Taper Forum, L.A., Macbeth, Oreg. Shakespeare Festival, The Skin of Our Teeth, Oreg. Shakespeare Festival, Hello Dolly, Long Beach Civic Light Opera, A Christmas Carol, South Coast Repertory, House of Blue Leaves, Pasadena Playhouse, Sundance Inst., Sundance, Utah, Fuente Ovejuna, Berkeley Repertory Theatre, Burning Patience, San Diego Repertory Theatre, Marriage of Figaro, Ariz. Theatre Co., Sons of Don Juan, Asolo Theatre, Fla., Wait Until Dark, Pa. Stage Co., La Carpa de los Rasquachis, Teatro Campesino; TV appearances include Gen. Hosp., Twilight Zone, Sequin, Corridos (Peabody award), Tough Love, Dress Gray, The Boys, In a Child's Name, The Gambler Returns, Quiet Killer, The New Adam 12 (series regular), 500 Nations, Nash Bridges (guest star); film appearances include Ballad of a Soldier, Jacaranda, The Novice, Trial by Terror, Dollie Dearest, Maria's Story, For A Loves One, Soldado Razo, Shattered Image, Zoot Suit, Barbarosa, Born in East L.A., Under Fire, among others; dir. (plays) Bed of Stone, 1996, La Gran Carpa de los Rasquachis, 1997, Heroes & Saints, 2001. Active Assistance with Alcohol and Sobriety Uniting Latinas, United L.Am. Youth, Med. Aid for El Salvador, Save the Children, the Christian Children's Fund; vol. and charity work in refugee camps in Ethiopia, India, Thailand, Sri Lanka, and The Philippines; bd. dirs. Mexican Mus., El Teatro Compresing. Recipient Cert. of Appreciation El Teatro Campesino, 1978, Recognition award Barrio Sta., 1980, Alumni Hall of Fame, El Rancho H.S., 1982, Outstanding Hispanic Alumni award Whittier Coll., 1984; co-recipient with Anthony Quinn and Edward James Olmos Hispanic Entertainer of Yr., The Equitable Co., 1987; Escobedo fellow Stanford U., 1996, Dorothy Danforth Compton Rsch. fellow, 1996. Mem. NATAS, AFTRA, SAG (John Dales scholar 1995-96, 98), TCG, Modern Lang. Assn., Assn. for Theatre in Higher Edn., Nat. Theatre Conf., Nat. Assn. Chicas and Chicano Studies, Actors Equity Assn. Address: JE Talent 323 Geary St #302 San Francisco CA 94102 Office: Univ Calif J-14 Theatre Arts Ctr Santa Cruz CA 95064 Home Phone: 831-423-0361. Business E-Mail: almamar@ucsc.edu.

MARTINEZ, BELINDA, health insurance company executive; MBA, U. So. Calif.; MPH, Loma Linda U. With Delta Ins.Co., 1988—, dir. acct. svcs. Delta Dental; v.p. profl. svcs. PMI Dental Health Plan Delta Ins.Co., v.p. underwriting and fin., 1999—2001, sr. v.p., COO, 2001—; COO Delta Ins.Co., 2003—. Named one of Top 10 Latinos in Healthcare, LatinoLeaders mag., 2004. Office: Delta Dental Calif 100 1st St San Francisco CA 94105

MARTINEZ, CARMEN LORENA, library director; Dir. brs. LA Pub. Libr.; dir. libr. svcs. Oakland Pub. Libr., Calif., 2000—. Mem. com. on recruitment of pub. libts. Pub. Libr. Assn., 2000, mem. bylaws and orgn. com.; mem. Spl. Presdl. Task Force on Status of Librs. Bd. mem. Calif. Cultural and Hist. Endowment. Office: Oakland Pub Libr 125 14th St Oakland CA 94612 Office Phone: 510-238-3281. E-mail: cmartinez@oaklandnet.com.

MARTINEZ, JENNY S., lawyer; b. 1974; BA cum laude, Yale U., 1993; JD magna cum laude, Harvard Law Sch., 1997. Bar: Va., DC. Law clk. to Honorable Guido Calabresi, US Ct. Appeals Second Circuit, 1997—98, Chambers of Justice Stephen Breyer, US Supreme Ct., 1998—99; assoc. legal officer to Judge Patricia Walk, UN Internat. Criminal Tribunal for Former Yugoslavia, 1999—2000; assoc. Jenner & Block LLC, 2000—03; sr. rsch. fellow, vis. lectr. Yale U., 2002—03; asst. prof. law Stanford Law Sch., 2003—. Mng. editor Harvard Law Review; cons. Internat. Ctr. Transitional Justice, 2003—. Contbr. articles to profl. jours. Vol. tutor Thurgood Marshall Acad. Charter HS, Washington, 2001; vol. atty. DC Bar Law Firm Pro Bono Project, 2001; vol. cons. atty. Human Rights First, 2003—. Recipient Sears prize, Harvard Law, Temple Bar Scholar, Am. Inns Ct., 1999; named one of Top 40 Lawyers Under 40, Nat. Law Jour., 2005, Litigation's Rising Stars, The Am. Lawyer, 2007. Mem.: Hispanic Bar Assn. DC (v.p. internal affairs 2003—). Office: Stanford Law Sch 559 Nathan Abbott Way Stanford CA 94305-8610 Office Phone: 650-725-2749. Business E-Mail: jmartinez@law.stanford.edu.

MARTINEZ, MARIA, computer software company executive; BA in elec. engring., U. PR; MA in computer engring, Ohio State U. Various mgmt. and engring. positions AT&T Bell Labs.; v.p., gen. mgr. Internet Connectivity Solutions Divsn. Motorola Inc.; CEO Embrace Network, Inc.; corp. v.p. comm. and mobile solutions unit Microsoft Corp., corp. v.p. worldwide services, 2007—. Recipient several process and quality awards; named an Elite Woman, Hispanic mag., 2004. Achievements include led Motorola's launching of first CDMA comml. sys. in world; played a leadership role in Bell Lab's devel. of UNIX sys. for symmetrics multiprocessing and high availability; patents for devel. and disk storage sys; launched first software platform and developed customer base for Embrace Networks, Inc; first female Hispanic named v.p. at Microsoft. Office: Microsoft Corp One Microsoft Way Redmond WA 98052-6399 Office Phone: 425-882-8080. Office Fax: 425-706-7329.

MARTINEZ, MATTHEW GILBERT, former congressman; b. Walsenburg, Colo., Feb. 14, 1929; children: Matthew, Diane, Susan, Michael, Carol Ann. Cert of competence, Los Angeles Trade Tech. Sch., 1959. Small businessman and bldg. contractor; mem. 97th-106th Congresses from 31st Calif. dist., 1982-2001; mem. edn. and labor com., fgn. affairs com. Mem. Monterey Park Planning Commn., 1971-74; mayor City of Monterey Park, 1974-75; mem. Monterey Park City Council, 1974-80, Calif. State Assembly, 1980-82; bd. dirs. San Gabriel Valley YMCA. Served with USMC, 1947-50. Mem. Congl. Hispanic Caucus, Hispanic Am. Democrats, Nat. Assn. Latino Elected and Apptd. Ofcls., Communications Workers Am., VFW, Am. Legion, Latin Bus. Assn., Monterey Park C. of C., Navy League (dir.) Lodges: Rotary. Democrat.

MARTINEZ, MIGUEL ACEVEDO, urologist, consultant, lecturer; b. Chihuahua, Mex., Aug. 18, 1953; came to US, 1956; s. Miguel Nuñez and Velia (Acevedo) M. AB, Stanford U., 1976; MD, Yale U., 1983. Diplomate Am. Bd. Urology. Intern U. SC Med. Ctr., 1983—84; resident in urology White Meml. Med. Ctr., LA, 1984-89, urologist, 1989—. Cons., lectr. physician asst. program U. So. Calif., LA, 1990—, clin. instr.; patient edn. cons. ICI Pharm., Del., 1991—, Zeneca's Speaker Forum; patient edn. and med. cons., lectr. Abbott Labs., 1991—; mem. edn.cons. several radio/TV stas., 1991—; mem. subcom. for diseases on kidney and transplantation NIH, Washington, 1991; mem. nat. Hispanic adv. bd. Pfizer Pharms., Inc., 1998—; mem. adv. bd. Glaxo Smith Kline, 2002—; cons. spkrs. bur. Pfizer, Bayer/ESK. Author: Intercellular Pathways, 1981. Polit. cons. Xavier Becerra, US Congress, 1992, Martin Gallegos, Gil Cedillo, Calif. State Assembly, 1993, others; bd. dirs. Latino Ctr. for Prevention and Action in Health, Orange County, calif.; bd. govs., sec., rep. Zeneca Urology Econ. Summit, Washington, 1993; mem. Pfizer Nat. Hispanic Adv. Bd. Named Nat. Male Outstanding Teenage of Am., 1971, One of Outstanding Young Men of Am., 1981; named one of America's Top Physicians, 2005, 06; recipient Philanthropic Leadership award Philanthropic Svc. Instns., 2006; Nat. Hispanic Med. Assn. Pub. Policy fellow, 2000-01. Mem. AMA, Nat. Hispanic Med. Assn. (public policy fellow), Am. Urological Assn., Calif. Med. Assn. (polit. action com. bd. dirs. 1997—, del.), LA Med. Assn. (polit. action com. 1992—), LA County Med. Assn., Yale Alumni Assn., Stanford Alumni Assn., LA Athletic Club. Office: White Meml Med Ctr Rm 500 1701 Cesar Chavez Ave Los Angeles CA 90033-2438 Office Phone: 323-224-6202. Personal E-mail: uromd@earthlink.net.

MARTINEZ, RUEBEN, entrepreneur; b. Miami, Ariz., 1940; Profl. barber; owner, founder Libreria Martinez Books and Art Gallery, 1993—. Co-founder Latino Book Festival; founding mem. Santa Ana's Reading com.; spkr. in field. Named MacArthur Fellow, John D. and Catherine T. MacArthur Found., 2004; named one of 26 Fascinating Entrepreneurs, Inc. Mag., 2005. Office: Libreria Martinez 1110 N Main St Santa Ana CA 92701 Office Phone: 714-973-7900.

MARTINEZ, VILMA SOCORRO, lawyer; b. San Antonio, Oct. 17, 1943; d. Salvador and Marina (Pina) Martinez; m. Stuart R. Singer, Nov. 1968; children: Carlos, Ricardo. BA, U. Tex., 1964; LLB, Columbia U., 1967. Bar: NY 1968, Calif. 1975. Staff atty. gen. civil rights litig. NAACP Legal Def. and Edn. Fund, 1967—70; EEO counsel NY State Divsn. Human Rights, 1970—71; litig. assoc. Cahill, Gordon & Reindel, 1971—73; pres., gen. counsel Mex.-am. Legal Def. & Ednl. Fund, Inc., 1973—82; ptnr. Munger, Tolles & Olsen LLP, LA, 1982—. Dir. Anheuser-Busch Cos., Inc; cons. US Commn. on Civil Rights, 1969—74, US Census Bur., 1975—81, US Treasury Dept., 1976, Calif. Fed. Jud. Selection Com., 1977—80, Presdl. Adv. Bd. on Ambassadorial Appointments, 1977—81, US Hispanic-Mex. Govt. Internat. Commn., 1980—82. Regent U. Calif., 1976—90, chmn., 1984—86; mem. corp. bd. Shell Oil co., 1997—2005, Sanwa Bank Calif., 1990—2005; trustee Edward W. Hazen Found. Recipient Jefferson award, Am. Idst. Pub. Svc., 1976, John D. Rockefeller III Youth award, Rockefeller Found., 1977, U. medal of Excellence, Columbia U., 1978, Valerie Kantor award, Mex. Am. Legal Def. Edn. Fund, Inc., 1982, Lex award, Mex.-Am. Bar Assn., 1983, Excellence medal, Columbia U. Law Sch., 1992, Maynard Toll award, Legal Aid Found.; named one of Boardroom Elite, Hispanic Bus. Mag., 2007; John Hay Whitney fellow, 1964, Samuel Rubin fellow, Columbia U. Sch. Law, 1983. Office: Munger Tolles & Olson LLP 355 S Grand Ave Fl 35 Los Angeles CA 90071-1560

MARTINO, SILVANA, osteopath, medical oncologist; b. Guardia Piemontese, Italy, Sept. 7, 1948; came to U.S., 1958; d. Antonio and Elena (Iannuzzi) M. BS in Psychology, Wayne State U., 1970; DO, Mich. State U., 1973. Bd. cert. internal medicine and med. oncology. Intern Detroit Osteo. Hosp., 1973-74; resident in internal medicine Botsford Hosp., Farmington, Mich., 1974-77; fellow in oncology Wayne State U. Sch. Medicine, Detroit, 1977-79, asst. prof. med., 1979-88, assoc. prof., 1988-93; med. dir. Westlake Comprehensive Breast Ctr., Westlake Village, Calif., 1993-97, Breast Ctr., Van Nuys, Calif., 1997-99; med. oncologist John Wayne Cancer Inst., Santa Monica, Calif., 1999—. Full-time staff Harper-Grace Hosps., Detroit, 1979-93, coord. oncology housestaff 1979-83; univ. affiliate, sect. of oncology, dept. medicine, Hutzel Hosp., Detroit, 1979-93; clin. advisor breast cancer prognostic study Mich. Cancer Found., Detroit, 1981-86; univ. affiliate dept. medicine Detroit Receiving Hosp., 1983-93; adj. faculty dept. medicine Wayne State U. 1989-92; mem. oncology drug adv. com. FDA, 2002—, chair, 2005—; spkr. in field. Co-author: Diet & Cancer: Markers, Prevention and Treatment, 1994; contbr. articles to profl. jours., chpt. to book. Bd. dir. Wellness Cmty., Conjeo Valley/Ventura, Calif., 1995-99; bd. dir. ACS Greater Conjeo Valley Unit, Thousand Oaks, Calif., 1994-99. Fellow Am. Coll. Osteo. Internists; mem. AAAS, Am. Osteo. Assn., Am. Soc. Clin. Oncology, Internat. Assn. Breast Cancer Rsch., Am. Soc. Preventive Oncology, Am. Assn. for Cancer Rsch., Inc., Southwest Oncology Group (chair breast com. 1992-2000, co-chair cancer control rsch. com. 87-92, oncology drug adv. com. 2002-2006, chmn. com. 2005-06). Office Phone: 310-582-7900. Business E-Mail: smartino@theangelesclinic.org.

MARTO, PAUL JAMES, retired mechanical engineering educator, consultant, researcher, dean; b. Flushing, NY, Aug. 15, 1938; s. Peter Joseph and Natalie Janet (Verrinoldi) M.; m. Mary Virginia Indence, June 10, 1961; children: Terese V. Marto Sanders, Paul J. Jr., Wayne T., Laura C., Marto Mahoney. BS, U. Notre Dame, 1960; SM, MIT, 1962, ScD, 1965. Asst. prof. Naval Postgrad. Sch., Monterey, Calif., 1965-69, assoc. prof., 1969-77, prof., 1977-85, disting. prof., 1985-96, chmn. dept. mech. engring., 1978-86, dean rsch., 1990-96, disting. prof. emeritus, 1996—. Cons. Modine Mfg. Co., Racine, Wis., 1986—. Editor: Power Condenser Heat, 1981; regional editor N.Am. Jour. of Enhanced Heat Transfer, 1993-98; editor-in-chief Internat. Jour. Transport Phenomena, 1997-2002, founding editor; contbr. articles to profl. jours. Bd. trustees Naval Postgrad. Sch. Found., Inc., 1997—. Lt. USN, 1965—67. Recipient Rear Adm. John J. Schieffelin award Naval Postgrad. Sch., 1976, Alexander von Humboldt U.S. Sr. Scientist award Humboldt Stiftung, Fed. Republic Germany, 1989-90, Disting. Civilian Svc. award Sec. of Navy, 1996. Fellow ASME (assoc. tech. editor Jour. of Heat Transfer 1984-90); mem. Am. Soc. Naval Engrs., Am. Soc. for Engring. Edn., Sigma Xi. Avocations: walking, tennis, music. Office: Naval Postgrad Sch Dept Mechanical Engring Code ME MX Monterey CA 93943 Office Phone: 831-659-0935. E-mail: pjmarto@aol.com.

MARTON, LAURENCE JAY, pathologist, researcher, educator; b. Bklyn., Jan. 14, 1944; s. Bernard Dov and Sylvia (Silberstein) M.; m. Marlene Lesser, June 27, 1967; 1 child, Eric Nolan BA, Yeshiva U., 1965, DSc (hon.), 1993; MD, Albert Einstein Coll. Medicine, 1969. Intern Los Angeles County-Harbor Gen. Hosp., 1969-70; resident in neurosurgery U. Calif.-San Francisco, 1970-71, resident in lab. medicine, 1973-75, asst. research biochemist, 1973-74, asst. clin. prof. depts. lab. medicine and neurosurgery, 1974-75, asst. prof., 1975-78, assoc. prof., 1978-79, prof., 1979-92, asst. dir. div. clin. chemistry, dept. lab. medicine, 1974-75, dir. divsn., 1975-79, acting chmn. dept., 1978-79, chmn. dept., 1979-92; dean med. sch. U. Wis., 1992-95, prof. pathology and lab. medicine and oncology, 1992-2000, prof. dept. human oncology Madison, 1993-95. Interim vice chancellor Ctr. Health Scis., U. Wis., 1993-94; adj. prof. dept. lab medicine U. Calif., San Francisco, 1992—; pres., CEO SLIL Biomed. Corp., 1998-2000, chief sci. and med. officer, 2000—; chief sci. officer Cellgate, 2004-. Co-editor: Polyamines in Biology and Medicine, 1981; Liquid Chromatography in Clinical Analysis, 1981; Clinical Liquid Chromatography, vol. 1, 1984, vol. 2, 1984 Served with USPHS, NIH, 1971-73 Recipient Rsch. Career Devel. award Nat. Cancer Inst., Disting. Alumnus award Albert Einstein Coll. Medicine, 1992. Mem. Am. Assn. Cancer Rsch., AAAS, Acad. Clin. Lab. Physicians and Scientists, Am. Soc. Investigative Pathology, Alpha Omega Alpha. Jewish. Avocations: photography, art, music, travel. Home: 581 Military Way Palo Alto CA 94306 Office: Cellgate Chief Sci Officer 3 Twin Dolphin Dr Ste 100 Redwood City CA 94065-1517 Home Phone: 650-494-1818; Office Phone: 650-610-7800 ext. 231. Business E-Mail: marton@cellgate.com.

MARTONE, FREDERICK J., judge; b. Fall River, Mass., 1943; BS, Coll. Holy Cross, 1965; JD, U. Notre Dame, 1972; LLM, Harvard U., 1975. Bar: Mass. 1972, Ariz. 1974, U.S. Dist. Ct. Mass. 1973, U.S. Dist. Ct. Ariz. 1974, U.S. Ct. Appeals (1st cir.) 1973, U.S. Ct. Appeals (9th cir.) 1974, U.S. Supreme Ct. 1977. Law clk. to Hon. Edward F. Hennessey Mass. Supreme Judicial Ct., 1972-73; pvt. practice Phoenix, 1973-85; assoc. presiding judge Superior Ct. Ariz., Maricopa County, judge Phoenix, 1985-92; justice Supreme Ct. Ariz., Phoenix, 1992—2002; U.S. dist. judge Dist. of Ariz., 2002—. Editor notes and comments Notre Dame Law Rev., 1970-72; contbr. articles to profl. jours. Capt. USAF, 1965-69. Mem. Am. Judicature Soc., State Bar Ariz., Horace Rumpole Inn of Ct. Office: US Dist Ct Sandra Day O'Conner US Courthouse 401 W Washington St Spc 62 Ste 526 Phoenix AZ 85003-2158 E-mail: Frederick_Martone@azd.uscourts.gov.

MARTORI, JOSEPH PETER, lawyer; b. NYC, Aug. 19, 1941; s. Joseph and Teresa Susan (Fezza) M. BS summa cum laude, NYU, 1964, MBA, 1968; JD cum laude, U. Notre Dame, 1967. Bar: DC 1968, U.S. Dist. Ct. DC 1968, U.S. Dist. Ct. Ariz. 1968, U.S. Ct. Appeals (9th cir.) 1969, U.S. Supreme Ct. 1977. Assoc. Sullivan & Cromwell, NYC, 1967-68, Snell & Wilmer, Phoenix, 1968-69; pres. Goldmar Inc., Phoenix, 1969-71; ptnr. Martori, Meyer, Hendricks & Victor, P.A., Phoenix, 1971-85, Brown & Bain, P.A., Phoenix, 1985-94, chmn. corp. banking & real estate dept., 1994—; chmn. bd. ILX Resorts, Inc., Phoenix. Chmn. ILX Inc., Varsity Clubs Am. Inc. Author: Street Fights, 1987; also articles. Trustee Boys' Clubs Met. Phoenix, 1974-99; consul for Govt. of Italy, State of Ariz., 1987-97. Mem. ABA, State Bar Ariz., Maricopa County Bar Assn., Lawyers Com.for Civil Rights Under Law (trustee 1976—), Phoenix Country Club, Plaza Club (founding bd. govs. 1979-90). Republican. Roman Catholic. Office: ILX Resorts Inc 2111 E Highland Ave Ste 200 Phoenix AZ 85016-4786 Business E-Mail: jmartorisr@ilxresorts.com.

MARTY, LAWRENCE A., magistrate; b. Leigh, Nebr., June 17, 1926; Student, Wayne State U., 1944-46, Creighton U. Sch. Law, 1946-48; JD, U. Wyo., 1954. Bar: Wyo. 1954. Sole practice, Green River, Wyo., 1954-67; ptnr. Mart & Clark, Green River, 1967-74, Marty & Ragsdale, Green River, 1975—; judge Green River Mcpl. Ct., 1956—58, U.S. Magistrate P.T. Dist. Wyo., 1958—2000, ret., 2000. Alt. del. Rep. Nat. Conv., 1964. Mem.: ABA, Sweetwater County Bar Assn., Wyo. Bar Assn. Office: 20 E Flaming Gorge Way Green River WY 82935-4210 Home Phone: 307-875-3332; Office Phone: 307-875-3235.

MARTZ, CLYDE OLLEN, retired lawyer; b. Lincoln, Nebr., Aug. 14, 1920; s. Clyde O. and Elizabeth Mary (Anderson) M.; m. Ann Spieker, May 29, 1947; children: Robert Graham, Nancy. AB, U. Nebr., 1941; LLB, Harvard U., 1947. Bar: Colo. 1948, U.S. Ct. Appeals (D.C. cir.) 1968, U.S. Supreme Ct. 1969. Prof. U. Colo., Boulder, 1947-58, 60-62; jud. adminstr. State of Colo., Denver, 1959-60; ptnr. Davis, Graham & Stubbs, Denver, 1962-67, 69-80, 81-87, of counsel, 1988—2008; asst. atty. gen. U.S. Dept. Justice, Washington, 1967-69; solicitor U.S Dept. Interior, Washington, 1980-81; exec. dir. dept. natural resources State of Colo., 1987. Adj. prof. U. Denver, 1961-79, U. Colo., Boulder, 1988-96; cons. Pres. Materials Policy Commn., 1951; mem. Colo. Adv. Bd. Bur. Land Mgmt., 1967-69; bd. dirs., adv. bd. Natural Resources Law Ctr., 1982-2003. Author: Cases and Materials on Natural Resources Law, 1951, Water for Mushrooming Populations, 1954; co-author: American Law of Property, 1953, Water and Water Rights, 1963; editor, co-author: American Law of Mining, 1960. Co-chmn. Jud. Reorganization Commn., 1961-63; elder Presbyn. Ch., Boulder; pres. Rocky Mountain Mineral Law Found., 1961-62, others. Comdr. USN, 1942-58, PTO, with Res. Decorated Silver Star, Bronze Star, Letter of Commendation, Disting. Svc. award; honored by creation of Clyde O. Martz Natural Resources Scholarship Fund, 2002. Mem. ABA (chmn. natural resources sect. 1985-86), Fed. Bar Assn., Am. Health Lawyers Assn., Colo. Bar Assn. (chmn. water sect. 1957, chmn. mineral sect. 1961, award of merit 1962), Nat. Mining Assn. (Disting. Svc. award 1997), Order of Coif, Phi Beta Kappa. Democrat. Avocations: horticulture, woodworking, mountain climbing, skiing. Home: 1620 Indian School Apt 255 Albuquerque NM 87107 also: 1620 Indian School Rd NE Apt 255 Albuquerque NM 87102-1755

MARTZ, JUDY HELEN, former governor; b. Big Timber, Mont., July 28, 1943; m. Harry Martz, June 23, 1965; children: Justin, Stacey. Owner, operator Martz Disposal Svc., Butte, Mont., 1971—; skater US World Speed Skating Team, Japan, 1963, US Olympic Team, Innsbruck, Austria, 1964; exec. dir. US High Altitude Speed Skating Ctr., Butte, Mont., 1985-89; field rep. Senator Conrad Burns, 1989—95; lt. gov. State of Mont., Helena, 1997-2001, gov., 2001—05. Coach Mont. Amateur Speed Skating Assn.; bd. dirs. Youth Hockey Assn.; pres. adv. bd. U.S. Internat. Speed Skating Assn.; chair, Montanans for Judge Roberts (chief justice nominee), 2006. Bd dirs. St. James Cmty. Hosp., Legion Oasis HUD Housing Project. Named Miss Rodeo Mont., 1963; inducted Butte Sports Hall of Fame, 1987. Republican. Office: Martz Disposal 119092 Juniper Acres Rd Butte MT 59750 Office Phone: 406-444-3111. Office Fax: 406-444-4648.

MARYANSKI, FRED J., academic administrator; BA in Math., Providence Coll.; MA in Computer Sci., Stevens Inst. Tech.; PhD in Computer Sci., U. Conn. Affiliate prof. Worcester Poly. Inst.; faculty Kans. State U., U. Conn., Storrs, 1983—, vice chancellor academic adminstrn., interim chancellor, provost U. affairs, 1999—2000, sr. vice provost academic affairs, provost, exec. v.p. academic affairs, 1999—2004; pres. Nev. State Coll., Henderson, 2005—. With Digital Equipment Corp., 1986—89. Office: Nev State Coll 1125 Nevada State Dr Henderson NV 89015

MARZION, KENNETH W., pension fund administrator; b. 1955; With fiscal services divsn. Calif. Pub. Employees' Retirement Sys. (CalPERS), with mem. services divsn., with benefit services divsn., asst. exec. officer, actuarial and employer services br., interim CEO, 2008—. Office: Calif Pub Employees' Retirement Sys Lincoln Plz Complex 400 Q St Sacramento CA 95821

MARZULLO, KEITH, computer science and engineering educator; PhD in Elec. Engring., Stanford U., 1984. Assoc. prof., computer sci. dept. Cornell U., Ithaca, NY; v.p. ISIS Distributed Sys., Inc., Ithaca; prof., dept. computer sci. U. Calif., San Diego, 1993—, chair, dept. computer sci. Co-PI GriPhyN Grid Phys. Network; head Distributed Sys. Lab., UCSD. Office: UCSD Dept Computer Sci Engring Mailcode 0404 9500 Gilman Dr La Jolla CA 92093-0404 Office Phone: 858-534-1126. Office Fax: 858-534-7029. Business E-Mail: marzullo@cs.ucsd.edu.

MASEK, BEVERLY, state representative; b. Anvik, Alaska, Sept. 30, 1963; m. Jan Masek; 1 child, Michael. Asst. mgr. Stuckagain Heights Lodge; bookkeeper Chena Hot Springs; operator Masek Racing Kennels; owner, operator Rustic Wilderness Lodge; spokesperson Alyeska Pipeline, Charter North, Payless Drug Stores; mem. Alaska Ho. of Reps., 1994—. Commr. Alaska Native Commn., Alaska Hist. Commn.; mem. state adv. com. U.S. Civil Rights Commn.; spkr. child abuse prevention program, goal setting and achievement program. Mem. Alaska Outdoor Coun., Hugh O'Brien Youth Found. Mem.: NRA, Alaska Boating Assn. Republican. Avocations: dog mushing, hiking, fishing. Address: 600 E Railroad Ave Ste 1 Wasilla AK 99654

MASHARIKI, ZOLA B., film company executive; b. Bklyn., Jan. 4, 1974; Grad., Dartmouth Coll., Hanover, NH, 1994; JD, Harvard Law Sch. Corp. atty. Manatt, Phelps & Phillips, L.L.P., LA, Proskauer Rose, L.L.P., NYC; prodn. intern Fox Searchlight, LA, 2000—01, creative exec., 2001—03, dir., 2003—06, v.p. prodn., 2006—. Prodr.: (films) Mboutoukou, 2002. Avocation: Tae Kwon Do. Office: Fox Searchlight 10201 W Pico Blvd Bldg 38 Los Angeles CA 90035

MASLACH, CHRISTINA, psychology professor; b. San Francisco, Jan. 21, 1946; d. George James and Doris Ann (Cuneo) M.; m. Philip George Zimbardo, Aug. 10, 1972; children: Zara, Tanya. BA, Harvard-Radcliffe Coll., 1967; PhD, Stanford U., 1971. Prof. psychology U. Calif.-Berkeley, 1971—, vice provost for tchg. & learning, 2001—08, 2008—. Author: Burnout: The Cost of Caring, 1982; co-author: Influencing Attitudes and Changing Behavior, 1977, Maslach Burnout Inventory (rsch. scale), 1981, 2d edit., 1986, 3d edit., 1996, Experiencing Social Psychology, 1979, 4th edit., 2001, Professional Burnout, 1993, The Truth About Burnout, 1997, Preventing Burnout and Building Engagement, 2000, Banishing Burnout, 2005. Recipient Disting. Teaching award, 1987, Best Paper award Jour. Orgnl. Behavior, 1994, Prof. of Yr. award Carnegie/CASE, 1997. Fellow AAAS, APA, Assn. Psychol. Sch., Soc. Clin. and Exptl. Hypnosis (Henry Guze rsch. award 1980), We. Psychol. Assn. (pres. 1989); mem. Soc. Exptl. Social Psychology. Democrat. Office: U Calif Office of Chancellor 200 California Hall # 1500 Berkeley CA 94720-1500 Business E-Mail: maslach@berkeley.edu.

MASON, CHERYL WHITE, lawyer; b. Champaign, Ill., Jan. 16, 1952; d. John Russell and Lucille (Birden) White; m. Robert L. Mason, Oct. 9, 1972; children: Robert L. II and Daniel G. BA, Purdue U., 1972; JD, U. Chgo., 1976. Bar: Calif. 1977. Assoc. O'Melveny & Myers LLP, LA, 1976-81, 84-86, ptnr., 1987—; exec. dir. Public Counsel, LA, 1981-84. Bd. dirs. Pub. Policy Inst. Calif. Chmn. State Bar, Legal Svcs. Trust Fund, 1987; trustee L.A. County Bar, 1985-88; bd. dirs. Challengers Boys and Girls Club, L.A., 1990—, Western Ctr. Law and Poverty, L.A., 1991-94; bd. dirs. James Irvine Found. Mem. ABA (co-chair environ. litigation commn. 1992-94, lawyer rep. 9th cir. jud. conf. 1993-94), Calif. Women Lawyers, L.A. County Bar Assn., Women Lawyers L.A., Black Women Lawyers L.A., Langston Bar Assn. Democrat. Office: O Melveny & Myers LLP 400 S Hope St Los Angeles CA 90071

MASON, DEAN TOWLE, cardiologist; b. Berkeley, Calif., Sept. 20, 1932; s. Ira Jenckes and Florence Mabel (Towle) M.; m. Maureen O'Brien, June 22, 1957; children: Kathleen, Alison. BA in Chemistry, Duke U., Durham, NC, 1954; MD, Duke U., 1958. Diplomate Am. Bd. Internal Medicine, Am. Bd. Cardiovasc. Diseases, Nat. Bd. Med. Examiners. Intern, then resident in medicine Johns Hopkins Hosp., 1958-61; clin. assoc. cardiology br., sr. asst. surgeon USPHS, Nat. Heart Inst., NIH, 1961-63, asst. sect. dir. cardiovascular diagnosis, attending physician, sr. investigator cardiology br., 1963-68; prof. medicine, prof. physiology, chief cardiovascular medicine U. Calif. Med. Sch., Davis-Sacramento Med. Center, 1968-82; dir. cardiac ctr. Cedars Med. Ctr., Miami, Fla., 1982-83; physician-in chief Western Heart Inst., San Francisco, 1983—2000; chmn. dept. cardiovascular medicine St. Mary's Med. Ctr., San Francisco, 1986-99, hon. med. staff, 2000—. Co-chmn. cardiovascular-renal drugs U.S. Pharmacopeia Com. Revision, 1970—75; mem. life scis. com. NASA; med. rsch. rev. bd. VA, NIH; prof. medicine (hon.) Peking Med. U., China, 1987; vis. prof. numerous univs.; cons. in field. Editor-in-chief Am. Heart Jour., 1980—96; contbr. chapters to books, articles. Recipient rsch. award, Am. Therapeutic Soc., 1965, Theodore and Susan B. Cummings Humanitarian award, Dept. State-Am. Coll. Cardiology, 1972, 1973, 1975, 1978, Skylab Achievement award, NASA, 1974, U. Calif. Faculty Rsch. award, 1978, Symbol of Excellence, Tex. Heart Inst., 1979, Disting. Alumnus award, Duke U. Sch. Medicine, 1979, award of Honor, Wisdom Soc., 1997, Medal of Honor, Winston Churchill Soc., 1998, Armand Hammer Creative Genius award, 1998, Dwight D. Eisenhower Admirable Am. of Achievement award, 1998,

Eternal Jesus Christ award, 1998, Blessed Lord's Prayer award, 1998, Dean Towle Mason Eminent Physician of Wisdom award, 1998, Dean Towle Mason, M.D. Medal of Wisdom award, 2001, Cardiologist of the Century Wisdom award, 2001, Albert Schweitzer world Humanitarian of Wisdom award, 2002, Jonas Salk award for med. rsch., 2003, Albert Einstein Sci. Rsch. award, 2003, John Wayne Pioneer of Am. award, 2003, Ernest Hemingway award for maj. contbns. to med. lit., 2003, Will Durant Philosopher-Physician award, 2004, Paul Dudley White award for disting. svc. in cardiovasc. medicine, 2004, Newton Kugelmass Children's Cardiology Crusader award, 2004, Norman Vincent Peale Healing Power of Prayer award, 2005, Lifetime Achievement award, U. Calif., Davis, 2008. Master Am. Coll. Cardiology (pres. 1977-78); fellow ACP, Am. Heart Assn., Am. Coll. Chest Physicians, Royal Soc. Medicine; mem. Am. Soc. Clin. Investigation, Am. Physiol. Soc., Am. Soc. Pharmacology and Exptl. Therapeutics (Exptl. Therapeutics award 1973), Am. Fedn. Clin. Research, NY Acad. Scis., Am. Assn. U. Cardiologists, Am. Soc. Clin. Pharmacology and Therapeutics, We. Assn. Physicians, AAUP, We. Soc. Clin. Rsch. (past pres.), El Macero Country Club, Phi Beta Kappa, Alpha Omega Alpha. Republican. Methodist. Home: 44725 Country Club Dr El Macero CA 95618-1047 Office: Western Heart Inst St Marys Med Ctr 450 Stanyan St San Francisco CA 94117-1079 Personal E-mail: deantmason@att.net.

MASON, JAMES ALBERT, retired museum director, former university dean; b. Eureka, Utah, 1929; married, 1956; 3 children. BA, Brigham Young U., 1955, MA, 1957; EdD, Ariz. State U., 1970. Cons., clinician in fine arts, 1955—; former chmn. dept. music Brigham Young U., Provo, Utah, dean Coll. Fine Arts and Comm., 1982-93, dir. Mus. of Art, 1993-96; ret., 1996. Vis. prof., lectr. Ind. U., Northwestern U., Cin. Coll.-Conservatory, U. Tex., Central Conservatory, Beijing, Internat. Soc. Music Edn., Warsaw; chmn. nat. symposium Applications of Psychology to the Teaching and Learning of Music. Editor The Instrumentalist, Orch. News, Utah Music Educator, Rsch. News column, Jour. Rsch. in Music Edn. Chmn., bd. dirs. The Barlow Endowment for Music Composition; co-founder, 1st pres. Utah Valley Symphony Orch.; past condr. Utah Valley Youth Orch.; past trustee Utah Opera Co.; commr. Utah Centennial of Statehood; bd. dirs. Presser Found.; pres. Music Educators Nat. Conf., 1978-80. Mem. Music Educators Nat. Conf. (past nat. pres., coun.), Nat. Music Coun. (past bd. dirs.), Am. Music Conf. (past bd. dirs.).

MASON, JOHN E., political association executive; b. LA, Dec. 6, 1946; m. Bianca Mason; seven children. BA with honors, UCLA, 1978; JD with highest honors, U. Calif., Berkeley, 1971. Chmn. Nev. State Rep. Party, 1995—2000; mem. Nat. Rep. Com., 1995—2000. Founder, pres. Mason, Sloane & Gilbert, 1977-90, now Law Office of John E. Mason; dir. and audit com. mem. LIVE Entertainment Inc., 1987-90; dir., mem. audit and compensations coms. Heftel Broadcasting Inc., 1992-96; v.p. music industry chpt. City of Hope, 1982-86. Assoc. editor Ecolog. Law Quar., 1969-71; mng. editor Calif. Law Rev., 1970-71. Trustee, chmn. western regional exec. bd. Nat. Found. Ileitis and Colitis, 1982-88; trustee Barton Meml. Hosp. Found., 1995-97; chmn. Nev. State Film Commn., 1996-97; mem. pres.'s com. arts and humanities, 2001-. Named Entertainment Lawyer of Yr. Billboard Mag., 1978, 80. Mem. Calif. Bar Assn., Nev. Bar Assn., Tenn. Bar Assn., Nat. Found. Ileitis and Colitis (Gold medal award for Humanitarian of Yr. 1986), Order of Coif, Order of Holy Sepulchre Jerusalem (Knight comdr.). Office: John Mason Esq Ltd 9650 Gateway Dr Ste 201 Reno NV 89521-3962 E-mail: maso007@ibm.net.

MASON, JOHN LATIMER, engineering executive; b. LA, Nov. 8, 1923; s. Zene Upham and Edna Ella (Watkins) Mason; m. Frances Howe Draeger, Sept. 1, 1950 (dec. June 1951); m. Mary Josephine Schulte, Nov. 26, 1954; children: Andrew, Peter, Mary Anne, John Edward. BS in Meteorology, U. Chgo., 1944; BS in Applied Chemistry, Calif. Inst. Tech., 1947, MS in Chem. Engring., 1948, PhD, 1950. Registered profl. engr., Calif. Engr. AiResearch Mfg. Co., Los Angeles, 1950-60; dir. engring. AiResearch Mfg. Co. div. Garrett Corp., Los Angeles, 1960-72; v.p. engring. Garrett Corp., Los Angeles, 1972-87; v.p. engring. and tech. Allied-Signal Aerospace Co., Los Angeles, 1987-88, cons., 1989-96; chmn. tech. adv. com. Indsl. Turbines Internat., Inc., Los Angeles, 1972-81, bd. dirs., 1980-88; adj. prof. engring. Calif. State U., Long Beach, 1992-96. Tech. adv. bd. Tex. Ctr. for Superconductivity, U. Houston, 1989-02, Ceryx Inc., 1998-2001; chair Calif. Coun. Sci. and Tech. Panel on Transp. R&D Ctr., 1993-94; bd. dirs. Planetary Sci. Inst., sec., 1998—; cons. Capstone Turbine Corp., 1994-98; workshop com. Transp. Rsch. Bd., 1998.; cons. Cleaire, Inc., 2001-03, Applied Rsch. and Tech., 2001-; ptnr. Applied Rsch. and Tech., 2001-06. Patentee in field. Chmn. energy and environment com. FISITA Coun., 1990-94. 1st lt. USAAF, 1943-46, PTO. With USAF, 1946—57. Fellow AIAA, assoc. Soc. Automotive Engrs., bd. dirs. 1984-87, 90-93, pres.-elect 1989-90, pres. 1990-91, Performance Rev. Inst. chmn. 1990-91, bd. dirs. 1992-93; mem. AAAS, NRC of NAS, com. on alternative energy R&D strategies 1989-90, Office Sci. and Tech. Policy, Nat. Critical Techs. panel 1992-93, Inst. Medicine of NAS, com. on health effects of indoor allergens 1992-93, Nat. Acad. Engring., US Advanced Ceramics Assn. chmn. tech. com., bd. dirs. 1985-88, Am. Chem. Soc., Am. Ceramic Soc., Caltech Assocs., Sigma Xi assoc., Am. Soc. Mech. Engrs., Eco Power, Inc. (mem. engrg. adv. bd. 2008-), Univ. of So. Calif. Office Phone: 310-375-5161. Personal E-mail: JL-Mason@cox.net.

MASON, MARILYN GELL, retired library administrator, writer, consultant; b. Chickasha, Okla., Aug. 23, 1944; d. Emmett D. and Dorothy (O'Bar) Killebrew; m. Carl L. Gell, Dec. 29, 1965 (div. Oct. 1978); 1 child, Charles E.; m. Robert M. Mason, July 17, 1981. BA, U. Dallas, 1966; MLS, N. Tex. State U., Denton, 1968; MPA, Harvard U., 1978. Libr. N.J. State Libr., Trenton, 1968-69; head dept. Arlington County Pub. Libr., Va., 1969-73; chief libr. program Metro Washington Coun. Govts., 1973-77; dir. White House Conf. on Librs. and Info. Svcs., Washington, 1979-80; exec. v.p. Metrics Rsch. Corp., Atlanta, 1981-82; dir. Atlanta-Fulton Pub. Libr., Atlanta, 1982-86, Cleve. Pub. Libr., 1986-99; founder, exec. dir. WebJunction Online Computer Library Ctr., 2002—08; ret., 2008. Evalene Parsons Jackson lectr. divsn. librarianship Emory U., 1981; trustee Online Computer Library Ctr., 1984—97; commr. Nat. Commn. Libr. Info. Scis., 1999—2002. Editor: Survey of Library Automation in the Washington Area, 1977; author: The Federal Role in Library and Information Services, 1983, Strategic Management for Today's Libraries, 1999. Bd. visitors Syracuse U. Sch. Info. Studies, 1981—85, U. Tenn. Sch. Libr. and Info. Sci., Knoxville, 1983—85; trustee Coun. Libr. Resources, Washington, 1992—2000. Recipient Disting. Alumna award, N. Tex. State U., 1979; named to Ohio Libr. Coun. Hall of Fame, 1999. Mem.: ALA (council mem. 1986—90, Herbert and Virginia White award 1999), DC Library Assn. (pres. 1976—77), Ohio Library Assn., Am. Assn. Info. Sci. Home and Office: 2929 First Ave 1122 Seattle WA 98121 Office Phone: 206-714-3009. Personal E-mail: marilyngmason@earthlink.net. Business E-Mail: m.g.mason@earthlink.net.

MASON, PAUL, small business owner, lighting designer; b. July 1946; s. Jason and Alison Mason; m. Charlotte Mason; children: Kayla, Michelle, Michael, Craig. BA in Business Administration, Mont. State U., 1968, MBA, 1971. Asst. mgr. P.C. Richards, 1972—72, regional mgr., 1972—90; owner Meriks Lighting, 1991—. Lighting show, Unique Lighting Expo, 2000 (Most Creative Ceiling Lights, 2000). Vol. coach Youngin' Soccer, 2006—; bd. dir. Better Business Bureau, 2003—. Office: Meriks Lighting 2510 Zimmerman Trl Billings MT 59102

MASON, ROBERT MCSPADDEN, information scientist, educator, dean; b. Sweetwater, Tenn., Jan. 16, 1941; s. Paul Rankin and Ruby May (McSpadden) M.; m. Betty Ann Durrence (div. 1980); children: Michael Dean, Donald Robert; m. Marilyn Killebrew Gell, July 17, 1981. SB, MIT, Cambridge, 1963, SM, 1965; PhD, Ga. Inst. Tech., Atlanta, 1973. Tech. staff mem. Sandia Labs., Livermore, Calif., 1965-68; rsch. scientist Ga. Inst. Tech., Atlanta, 1971-75, sr. rsch. scientist, 1975; prin. Metrics, Inc., Atlanta, 1975-80; pres. Metrics Rsch. Corp., Atlanta, 1980-86, Cleve., 1986-98, Tallahassee, 1998—2005, Seattle, 2005—; adj. prof. Weatherhead Sch. Mgmt. Case Western U., 1987-88, vis. prof., 1988-91, prof. for practice of tech. mgmt., 1991-98; dir. Ctr. Mgmt. Sci. and Tech., 1988-96; Sprint prof. mgmt. and prof. mgmt. info. sys. Coll. Bus. Fla. State U., Tallahassee, 1998—2005, chair mgmt. info. sys., 1998—2002; prof. info. sch. U. Wash., Seattle, 2006—, assoc. dean rsch., 2006—. Co-author: The Impact of Office Automation on Clerical Employment, 1985-00, 1985, Library Micro Consumer, 1986; co-editor: Information Services: Economics, Management, and Technology, 1981, Management of Technology V: Technology Management in a Changing World, 1996, Management of Technology, Sustainable Development, and Eco-Efficiency, 1998, Management of Technology: The Key to Prosperity in the Third Millenium, 2001; Am. editor Technovation, 1994-2005, sr. editl. bd., 2005—; contbr. articles to profl. jours. Mem. Internat. Assn. for Tech. Mgmt. (newsletter editor 1992-93, program chair internat. conf., 1996, pres. 1996-98, mem. exec. com. 1998—, Disting. Achievement award 2007). Republican. Presbyterian. Avocations: flying, skiing, sailing, scuba diving, photography. Home: 2929 1st Ave Unit 1122 Seattle WA 98121 Office: Info Sch U Wash Seattle WA 98195-2840

MASON, WILLIAM A(LVIN), psychologist, educator, researcher; b. Mountain View, Calif., Mar. 28, 1926; s. Alvin Frank and Ruth Sabina (Erwin) M.; m. Virginia Joan Carmichael, June 27, 1948; children: Todd, Paula, Nicole, Hunter. BA, Stanford U., 1950, MS, 1952, PhD, 1954. Asst. prof. U. Wis.-Madison, 1954-59; research assoc. Yerkes Labs. Primate Biology, Orange Park, Fla., 1959-63; head dept. behavioral sci. Delta Primate Research Ctr., Tulane U., Covington, La., 1963-71; prof. psychology, research psychologist U. Calif., Davis, 1971-91, leader behavioral biology unit Calif. Primate Rsch. Ctr., 1972-96, prof. emeritus, 1991. Bd. dirs. Jane Goodall Inst., 1978-92, Karisoke Rsch. Ctr., 1980-86. Mem. Editorial bd. Animal Learning and Behavior, 1973-76, Internat. Jour. Devel. Psychobiology, 1980-92, Internat. Jour. Primatology, 1980-90; contbr. numerous articles to profl. jours., chpts. to books. With USMC, 1944-46. USPHS spl. fellow, 1963-64. Fellow AAAS, APA (pres. divsn. 6 1982, disting. sci. contbn. award 1995), Am. Psychol. Soc., Animal Behavior Soc.; mem. Internat. Primatological Soc. (pres. 1976-80, 81-84), Am. Soc. Primatologists (pres. 1988-90, disting. primatologist award), Internat. Soc. Devel. Psychobiology (pres. 1971-72, Best Paper of Yr. award 1976), Sigma Xi. Home: 2809 Anza Ave Davis CA 95616-0257 Office: U Calif Regl Primate Rsch Ctr 1 Shields Ave Davis CA 95616 Home Phone: 530-756-2479. Business E-Mail: wamason@ucdavis.edu.

MASON, WILLIAM VANHORN, dermatologist; b. Pitts., Jan. 8, 1930; AB, Harvard U., 1951; MD, Baylor Coll. Medicine, Houston, 1961. Diplomate Am. Bd. Dermatology. Pvt. practice, Albuquerque, 1979—; clin. prof. dermatology Sch. Medicine U. N.Mex., Albuquerque, 2003—. Lt. (j.g.) USN, 1951-54. Mem. Phi Beta Kappa, Alpha Omega Alpha. Office: 800 Carlisle Pl SE Albuquerque NM 87108-4371

MASONIS, TODD, Internet company executive; BS, Stanford Univ. Systems developer e-steam Inc.; co-founder netElement, 1999, Natient Technologies; co-founder, v.p. products Plaxo Inc., Mountain View, Calif., 2001—. Office: Plaxo Inc 203 Ravendale Dr Mountain View CA 94043 Office Phone: 650-254-5402. Office Fax: 650-254-1435. Business E-Mail: todd@plaxo.com.

MASOTTI, LOUIS HENRY, real estate educator, consultant; b. NYC, May 16, 1934; s. Henry and Angela Catherine (Turi) Masotti; m. Iris Patricia Leonard, Aug. 28, 1958 (div. 1981); children: Laura Lynn, Andrea Anne; m. Ann Randel Humm, Mar. 5, 1988. AB, Princeton U., 1956; MA, Northwestern U., 1961, PhD, 1964. Fellow Nat. Ctr. Edn. in Politics, 1962; asst. prof. polit. sci. Case Western Res. U., Cleve., 1963-67, assoc. prof., 1967-69, dir. Civil Violence Rsch. Ctr., 1968-69; sr. Fulbright lectr. Johns Hopkins U. Ctr. Advanced Internat. Studies, Bologna, Italy, 1969-70; assoc. prof. Northwestern U., Evanston, Ill., 1970-72, prof. polit. sci. and urban affairs, 1972-83, dir. Ctr. Urban Affairs, 1971-80, dir. Program in Pub. and Not-for-Profit Mgmt., Kellogg Sch. Mgmt., 1979-80, prof. mgmt. and urban devel. Kellogg Sch. Mgmt., 1983-94, dir. Real Estate Research Ctr. Kellogg Sch. Mgmt., 1986-88. Cons. in field; vis. assoc. prof. U. Wash., 1969; exec. dir. Mayor Jane Byrne Transition Com., Chgo., 1979; vis. prof. Stanford Sch. Bus., 1989—92, UCLA Sch. Mgmt., 1989—92; prof., dir. real estate mgmt. program U. Calif. Grad. Sch. Mgmt., Irvine, 1992—98; bd. dirs. Mfd. Home Cmtys., Inc., Facilities Mgmt. Internat., S. Calif. Physicans Ins. Co. Author: (book) Educaiton and Politics in Suburbia, 1967, Shootout in Cleveland, 1969, A Time to Burn?, 1969, Suburbia in Transition, 1973, The New Urban Politics, 1976, The City in Comparative Perspective, 1976; co-editor: Metropolis in Crisis, 1968, Metropolis in Crisis, 2d edit., 1971, Riots and Rebellion, 1968, The Urbanization of the Suburbs, 1973, After Daley: Chicago Politics in Transition, 1981, Downtown Development, 1985, Downtown Development, 2d edit., 1987; editor: Edn. and Urban Soc., 1968—71, Urban Affairs Quar., 1973—80; sr. editor: Econ. Devel. Quar., 1986—92, vice chmn. bd.: Ill. Issues Jour., 1986—92, BOMA Office Mag., 1990—95. Mem. Cleveland Heights Bd. Edn., 1967—69; devel. coord. high tech. State of Ill. - City of Chgo., 1982—83; Rsch. dir. Carl Stokes for Mayor Cleve., 1967; advisor to various congl., gubernatorial and mayoral campaigns Ohio, Ill., NJ, Calif. Lt. USNR, 1956—59. Recipient Disting. Svc. award, Cleve. Jaycees, 1967; fellow, Homer Hoyt Inst. Advanced Real Estate Studies; numerous rsch. grants, 1963—2000. Mem.: Internat. Econ. Devel. Coun., Nat. Assn. Indsl. Office Properties, Internat. Devel. Rsch. Coun., Internat. Assn. Corp. Real Estate Execs., Nat. Trust Hist. Preservation, Habitat, Urban Land Inst., Lambda Alpha Internat. Address: 2010 W Twinoaks Dr Prescott AZ 86305 Office Phone: 619-750-1703. Personal E-mail: louismasotti@mac.com.

MASRI, SAMI F(AIZ), civil and mechanical engineering educator, consultant; b. Beirut, Dec. 9, 1939; came to U.S., 1956; BS in Aerospace Engring., U. Tex., 1960, MS in Aerospace Engring., 1961; MS in Mech. Engring., Calif. Inst. Tech., 1962, PhD in Mech. Engring., 1965. Research fellow Calif. Inst. Tech., Pasadena, 1965-66; asst. prof. civil and mech. engring. U. So. Calif., Los Angeles, 1966-69, assoc. prof., 1969-76, prof., 1976—. Contbr. articles to profl. jours. Research grantee NSF, NASA, NRC Mem. AIAA, ASME, ASCE, IEEE, AAAS, Sigma Xi Office: U So Calif Dept Civil Engring Mc 2531 Los Angeles CA 90089-0001 Business E-Mail: masri@usc.edu.

MASSARO, TONI MARIE, dean, law educator; BS highest distinction, Northwestern U., 1977; JD, Coll. William and Mary, 1980. Assoc. Vedder, Price, Kaufman and Kammholz, Chgo., 1980—82; asst. prof. Washington and Lee U., U. Fla., 1982—84; prof. law U. Ariz., Tucson, 1989—, regents prof., Milton O. Riepe chair constl. law James E. Rogers Coll. Law, 1997—, dean James E. Rogers Coll. Law, 1999—. Vis. asst. prof. law U. Fla., 1984—85; vis. prof. Johann Goethe U., Frankfurt, Germany, 1988, U. NC, 1989, Stanford U., 1989. Author: Constitutional Literacy: A Core Curriculum for a Multi-Cultural Nation; co-author: Civil Procedure: Cases and Problems, 3d edit., 2006; contbr. articles to law revs. Recipient Women on the Move award, YWCA, 2002, Leslie F. and Patricia Bell Faculty Award, 1998. Fellow: Am. Bar Found.; mem.: Ariz. State Bar (Access to Justice com. 2003—04, Professionalism com. 2002—), Am. Law Inst., Am. Assn. Law Schs. (Academic Freedom and Tenure com. 2000—04), Order of the Coif. Office: U Ariz Coll Law 1201 E Speedway PO Box 210176 Tucson AZ 85721-0176 Office Phone: 520-621-1498. Office Fax: 520-621-9140. Business E-Mail: massaro@law.arizona.edu.

MASSENGILL, MATTHEW H., computer company executive; BE, Purdue U., 1983. Rsch. engr., infra detectors and imaging sys. Ford Aerospace and Commn. Corp., 1982—85; product engr. Western Digital Corp., Irvine, Calif., 1985—86, v.p. mktg. personal storage divsn., 1993—97, sr. v.p., gen. mgr. enterprise storage group Rochester, Minn., 1997—98, chief operating officer Irvine, Calif., 1998—2000, CEO, 2000—05, chmn., 2001—07. Launched a startup software co., 1986; mgr. of ranch, Oreg., 1990—91; bd. dir. ViewSonic Corp., Western Digital. Bd. dir. Orange County Technology Action Network, Calif., THINK Together, (Orange County), Calif.; vice-chmn. CEO Roundtable program, Univ. Calif., Irvine; chmn. TechNet So.Calif. Recipient Outstanding Elec. Engring. Alumni award, Purdue Univ., 1998, Disting. Engring Alumni award, 2002. Office: Western Digital Corp 20511 Lake Forest Dr Lake Forest CA 92630-7741

MASSEY, HENRY P., JR., lawyer; b. Montclair, NJ, Sept. 2, 1939; AB, Cornell U., 1961, JD with distinction, 1968. Bar: Calif. 1969. Ptnr. Wilson Sonsini Goodrich & Rosati, Palo Alto, Calif., 1982—. Bd. editors Cornell Law Rev., 1967-68. Mem. ABA (sects. on corp., banking and bus. law, taxation law), State Bar Calif. (mem. corps. com. bus. law sect. 1979-82), Order of Coif, Phi Kappa Phi. Office: Wilson Sonsini Goodrich & Rosati 650 Page Mill Rd Palo Alto CA 94304-1050

MASSEY, THOMAS W., state legislator; Mem. Dist. 60 Colo. House of Reps., Denver, 2004—. Republican. Office: Colo State Capitol 200 E Colfax Denver CO 80203 Office Phone: 303-866-2747. Business E-Mail: tom.massey.house@state.co.us.*

MASSY, WILLIAM FRANCIS, education educator, consultant; b. Milw., Mar. 26, 1934; s. Willard Francis and Ardys Dorothy (Digman) M.; m. Sally Vaughn Miller, July 21, 1984; children by previous marriage: Willard Francis, Elizabeth BS, Yale U., 1956; SM, MIT, 1958, PhD in Indsl. Econs., 1960. Asst. prof. indsl. mgmt. MIT, Cambridge, 1960-62; from asst. prof. to prof. edn. and bus. adminstrn. Stanford U., Calif., 1962-96, assoc. dean Grad. Sch. Bus. Calif., 1971, vice provost for rsch. Calif., 1971-77, v.p. for bus. and fin. Calif., 1977-88, v.p. fin. Calif., 1988-91, prof. emeritus, 1996—; prof. edn., dir. Stanford Inst. Higher Edn. Rsch., Calif., 1988-96; sr. v.p. P.R. Taylor Assocs., 1995-99; sr. rschr. Nat. Ctr. for Postsecondary Imrprovement, 1996—2002; pres. The Jackson Hole Higher Edn. Group, Inc., 1996—. Bd. dirs. MAC, Inc., 1969-84, Stanford Mgmt. Co., 1991-93; mem. u. grants com. Hong Kong, 1990-2003; mem. coun. Yale U., 1980-95; mgmt. cons. Stanford Mgmt. Co., 1991-93.bd. dirs. Diebold, Inc., chmn. audit com., 2003-07. Author: Stochastic Models of Buying Behavior, 1970, Marketing Management, 1972, Market Segmentation, 1972, Planning Models for Colleges and Universities, 1981, Endowment, 1991, Resource Allocation in Higher Education, 1996, Honoring The Trust, 2003, Remaking the American University, 2005, Academic Quality Work, 2007; mem. editl. bd. Jour. Mktg. Rsch., 1964-70, Harcourt, Brace Jovanovich, 1965-71; contbr. articles to profl. jours. Bd. dirs. Palo Alto-Stanford chpt. United Way, 1978-80, Stanford U. Hosp., 1980-91, EDUCOM, 1983-86. Ford Found. faculty rsch. fellow, 1966-67; recipient Frederick W. Lanchester prize, Operations Rsch. Soc., 1981; Outstanding Contributions to Coll. and Univ. Planning award, Soc. Coll. Univ. Planning., 1995. Mem. Am. Mktg. Assn. (bd. dirs. 1971-73, v.p. edn. 1976-77), Inst. Mgmt. Scis., Tau Beta Pi, Sigma Xi. Avocations: hiking, scuba diving, travel. Office: The Jackson Hole Higher Edn Group Inc PO Box 9849 Jackson WY 83002-9849 Personal E-mail: bill@jhheg.com.

MAST, GREGORY LEWIS, lawyer; b. Waterloo, Iowa, July 29, 1954; s. Kenneth Edgar and Shirley Louise (Crandall) M.; m. Jennifer Lynn East, Dec. 30, 1978; children: Millicent Ashley, William Robert. BA, De Pauw U., 1976; JD, Harvard U., 1979. Bar: Ariz. 1979, U.S. Dist. Ct. Ariz. 1979. Ptnr. Evans, Kitchel & Jenckes, P.C., Phoenix, 1979-85, Jones, Jury, Short & Mast, P.C., Phoenix, 1986-88, Gallagher & Kennedy, P.A., Phoenix, 1988, shareholder. Mem. Ariz. Town Hall, Phoenix C. of C. (spl. events com.), Ariz. Baseball Commn., Valley Partnership, White Mountain Country Club, Thunderbirds, Phoenix Country Club, Real Estate Investment Adv. Coun. Named Am's. Leading Bus. Lawyers, by Chambers USA, Best Lawyers Valley, by Phoenix mag., Best Lawyers Am., by Woodward/White, Inc., 2007. Mem.: DePauw U. Alumni Assn., Phi

Beta Kappa, Maricopa County Bar Assn., State Bar Ariz. Office: Gallagher & Kennedy PA 2575 E Camelback Rd Ste 1100 Phoenix AZ 85016 Office Phone: 602-530-8310. Office Fax: 602-530-8500. Business E-Mail: glm@gknet.com.

MASTERS, JOSEPH, lawyer, engineering company executive; b. 1956; BSCE, Cleveland State U., 1979; JD, Case Western Reserve U., 1982. Bar: Ohio 1982. Pvt. practice; with URS Corp., San Francisco, 1992—, v.p., gen. counsel, 1997—2006, v.p., gen. counsel, corp. sec., 2006—. Mem.: ABA. Office: URS Corp 26th Fl 600 Montgomery St San Francisco CA 94111 Office Phone: 415-774-2700.

MASTERSON, WILLIAM A., retired judge; b. NYC, June 25, 1931; s. John Patrick and Helen Audrey (O'Hara) M.; m. Julie Dohrmann Cosgrove; children: Mark, Mary, Timothy, Barbara. BA, UCLA, 1953, JD, 1958. Bar: Calif. 1959, U.S. Supreme Ct. 1965. Assoc. Sheppard, Mullin, Richter & Hampton, LA, 1952-62, pntr., 1962-79; ptnr. Rogers & Wells, 1979-83, Skadden, Arps, Slate, Meagher & Flom, 1983-87; judge L.A. Superior Ct., 1987-92; justice Ct. Appeal, 1993-2000; ret., 2000. Author, editor: Civil Trial Practice: Strategies and Techniques, 1986. With inf. U.S. Army, 1953-55. Fellow Am. Coll. Trial Lawyers; mem. Order of Coif. Office: PO Box 190 Mendocino CA 95460

MASTO, CATHERINE MARIE CORTEZ, state attorney general, former county official; b. Nev., Mar. 29, 1964; d. Manny and Joanna Cortez; m. Paul E. Masto. BS in Fin., U. Nev., Reno, 1986; JD cum laude, Gonzaga U. Sch. Law, Spokane, Wash., 1990. Bar: Nev. 1990, US Dist. Ct. (dist. Nev.) 1991, US Ct. Appeals (9th cir.) 1994. Law clk. to Judge Michael J. Wendell 8th Jud. Dist. Ct., 1990—91; assoc. Raleigh, Hunt & McGarry, P.C., Las Vegas, 1991—95; staff mem. to Gov. Bob Miller State of Nev., Carson City, 1995—98, chief of staff, 1998—2000; asst. US atty. Dist. Nev. US Dept. Justice, Las Vegas, 2000—02; asst. county mgr. Clark County, Nev., 2002—05; atty. gen. State of Nev., Carson City, 2007—. Mem. So. Nev. Domestic Violence Ct. Task Force, Supreme Ct. Nev. Ct. Funding Commn. Democrat. Office: Office of Atty Gen Nev Dept Justice 100 N Carson St Carson City NV 89701-4717 Office Phone: 775-684-1100.*

MASTROLUCA, APRIL, state legislator; b. Hayward, Calif., 1968; m. Dan Mastroluca; children: Kelsey, Nicholas. Attending, Lincoln Christian Coll. and Sem., Lincoln, Ill. Pub. relations adminstr. (nev. campaign) Safe Haven Law; rep. supr. Nat. Svc.; mem. Dist. 29 Nev. State Assembly, 2008—. Democrat. Office: 401 South Carson St Room 4113 Carson City NV 89701 also: 265 Copper Glow Ct Henderson NV 89074 Office Phone: 775-684-8855. Business E-Mail: amastroluca@asm.state.nv.us.

MASUMOTO, DAVID MAS, writer, farmer; BA in Soc., U. Calif., Berkeley; MA in Cmty. Devel., U. Calif., Davis; attended, Internat. U., Tokyo, Japan. Farmer, Del Ray, Calif.; columnist USA Today, Los Angeles Times, The Fresno Bee. Writer in residence Iolani Sch., Honolulu, 2004. Author: Silent Strength, 1984, Country Voices, The Oral History of a Japanese American Family Farm Community, 1987, Home Bound, 1989, Epitaph For A Peach: Four Seasons on My Family Farm, 1995 (Julia Child Cookbook award, 1995, San Francisco Review Books Critics' Choice award, 1995), Harvest Son, Planting Roots in American Soil, 1998 (Calif. Book award, 1999), Four Seasons in Five Senses, Things Worth Savoring, 2003, Letters to the Valley, A Harvest of Memories, 2004. Bd. mem. Calif. Council for Humanities, 1994—, bd. co-chair, 1998—2001; bd. mem. James Irvine Found., 2002—. Recipient James Clavell Japanese Am. Nat. Literacy award, 1986, Breadloaf Writers Conf. fellowship, 1996. Mem.: Calif. Assn. of Family Farmers. Office: c/o Heyday Books PO Box 9145 Berkeley CA 94709

MATARAZZO, JOSEPH DOMINIC, psychologist, educator; b. Caiazzo, Italy, Nov. 12, 1925; (parents Am. citizens); s. Nicholas and Adeline (Mastroianni) M.; m. Ruth Wood Gadbois, Mar. 26, 1949; children: Harris, Elizabeth, Sara. Student, Columbia U., 1944; BA, Brown U., 1946; MS, Northwestern U., 1950, PhD, 1952. Fellow in med. psychology Washington U. Sch. Medicine, 1950-51; instr. Washington U., 1951-53, asst. prof., 1953-55; rsch. assoc. Harvard Med. Sch., assoc. psychologist Mass. Gen. Hosp., 1955-57; prof., head med. psychol. dept. Oreg. Health Scis. U., Portland, 1957-96, prof. behavioral neurosci., 1996—2007, prof. emeritus behavioral neurosci., 2007—. Mem. behavioral medicine study sect. NIH; nat. mental health adv. coun. NIMH; bd. regents Uniformed Svcs. U. Health Scis., 1974-80. Author: Wechsler's Measurement and Appraisal of Adult Intelligence, 5th edit., 1972, (with A.N. Wiens) The Interview: Research on its Anatomy and Structure, 1972, (with Harper and Wiens) Nonverbal Communication, 1978; editor: Behavioral Health: A Handbook of Health Enhancement and Disease Prevention, 1984; mem. editl. bd.: Jour. Clin. Psychology, 1962-96; cons. editor: Contemporary Psychology, 1962-70, 80-93, Intelligence: An Interdisciplinary Jour, 1976-90, Jour. Behavioral Medicine, 1977—, Profl. Psychology, 1978-94, Jour. Cons. and Clin. Psychology, 1978-85; editor: Psychology series Aldine Pub. Co, 1964-74; editor Williams & Wilkins Co, 1974-77; contbr. articles to profl. jours. With USNR, 1943-47; capt. Res. Recipient Hofheimer prize Am. Psychiat. Assn., 1962 Fellow AAAS, APA (pres. 1989-90, divsn. health psychology 1978-79, mem. coun. reps. 1982-91, bd. dirs. 1986-90, Ann. Disting. Profl. Contbn. award 1991, Ann. Gold Medal for Life Achievement in the Application of Psychology 2001); mem. Western Psychol. Assn. (pres. 1986-97), Am. Assn. State Psychology Bds. (pres. 1963-64), Nat. Assn. Mental Health (bd. dirs.), Oreg. Mental Health Assn. (bd. dirs., pres. 1962-63), Internat. Coun. Psychologists (bd. dirs. 1972-74, pres. 1976-77), Am. Psychol. Found. (pres. 1994-2000). Home: 1934 SW Vista Ave Portland OR 97201-2455 Office: Oreg Health Scis U Sch Medicine 3181 SW Sam Jackson Park Rd Portland OR 97239 Office Phone: 503-494-8644. Office Fax: 503-494-5972. Business E-Mail: matarazz@ohsu.edu.

MATEJU, JOSEPH FRANK, hospital administrator; b. Cedar Rapids, Iowa, Oct. 18, 1927; s. Joseph Frank and Adeline (Smid) M. BA, U. N.Mex., 1951; MA, N.Mex. State U., 1957. Sr. juvenile probation officer, San Diego County, 1958-64; adminstr. Villa Solano State Sch., Hagerman, N.Mex., 1965-67; state coord. on mental retardation planning N.Mex. Dept. Hosps. and Instns., Santa Fe, 1969-70; adminstr. Los Lunas (N.Mex.) Hosp. and Tng. Sch., 1968-69, 70-85. Pres. Intercare, bd. dirs. With USAF, 1946—47. Fellow Am. Assn. Mental Deficiency, Am. Coll. Nursing Home Adminstrs.; mem. Am. Assn. Retarded Children (v.p.), Albuquerque Assn. Retarded Citizens, N.Mex. Hosp. Assn., Pi Gamma Mu. Home: 405 Fontana Pl NE Albuquerque NM 87108-1168

MATERA, FRANCES LORINE, retired elementary school educator; b. Eustis, Nebr., June 28, 1926; d. Frank Daniel and Marie Mathilda (Hess) Daiss; m. Daniel Matera, Dec. 27, 1973. Luth. tchrs. diploma, Concordia U., Seward, Nebr., 1947, BS in Edn., 1956; MEd, U. Oreg., Eugene, 1963. Elem. tchr. Our Savior's Luth. Ch., Colorado Springs, Colo., 1954—57; tchr. 5th grade Monterey Pub. Schs., Calif., 1957—59; tchr. 1st grade Roseburg Schs., Oreg., 1959—60; tchr. several schs. Palm Springs Unified Sch. Dist., Calif., 1960—93; tchr. 3rd grade Vista del Monte Sch., Palm Springs, Calif., 1973—93; ret., 1993. Named Tchr. of the Yr., Palm Springs Unified Schs. Mem. Kappa Kappa Iota (chpt. and state pres.). Personal E-mail: franmatera7@aol.com.

MATHER, ANN, film company executive; b. Stockport, Cheshire, Eng., Apr. 10, 1960; came to U.S., 1993; d. Robert Joseph and Theresa (Westhead) M. Grad., Cambridge U., Eng., 1981. CPA. Sr. Peat Marwick, London, 1981-84; sr. fin. analyst Paramount Pictures, London, 1984-85, European contr. Amsterdam, 1985-87, mgr. strategic planning NYC, 1987-88; pres. art import/export Santa Fe Galleries, London/Santa Fe/San Diego, 1988-89; dir. fin. Polo Ralph Lauren Europe, Paris, 1989-91; European contr. life ins. div. AIG, Paris, 1991-92; dir. fin. and adminstrn. Europe internat. film distbn. div. The Walt Disney Co., Paris, 1992-93, v.p. fin. and adminstrn. Buena Vista Internat. Theatrical Divsn. Burbank, Calif., 1993-97, sr. v.p. fin. and adminstrn. Buena Vista Internat. Theatrical Divsn., 1998-99; exec. v.p., CFO Village Roadshow Pictures, 1999, Pixar Animation Studios, 1999—2004. Bd. dir. Google. Contbr. Descanso Gardens, La Canada, Calif., 1996. Recipient award for land values paper Royal Soc. Chartered Surveyors, 1981. Mem. Women in Film, Fin. Execs. Inst. (chmn. profl. devel. com.), Brit. Acad. Film and TV Arts. Avocations: skiing, horseback riding, travel, literature, films. Office: Pixar Animation Studios 1200 Park Ave Emeryville CA 94608

MATHERS, MARSHALL See EMINEM

MATHES, JAMES R., bishop; b. Aug. 18, 1959; m. Teresa Yvette Sutton, Aug. 15, 1981; children: Rutherford Lee, Sarah Elizabeth Nam. BA magna cum laude, U. of the South, Sewanee, Tenn., 1982; MDiv, Va. Theol. Sem., Alexandria, 1991. Assoc. campaign dir. The Webb Sch., Bell Buckle, Tenn., 1983—85; math tchr. & coach St. Andrews-Sewanee Sch., St. Andrews, Tenn., 1985—86, dir. devel., 1986—89; asst. min. All Saints Episcopal Ch., Belmont, Mass., 1991—94; rector Church of St. James the Less, Northfield, Ill., 1994—2001; canon to the ordinary Episcopal Diocese of Chgo., 2001—05; bishop Episcopal Diocese of San Diego, 2005—. Episcopalian. Avocations: woodworking, backpacking, reading. Office: Episcopal Diocese of San Diego 2728 Sixth Ave San Diego CA 92103 Business E-Mail: jmathes@edsd.org.

MATHESON, ALAN ADAMS, law educator; b. Cedar City, Utah, Feb. 2, 1932; s. Scott Milne and Adele (Adams) M.; m. Milicent Holbrook, Aug. 15, 1960; children: Alan, David Scott, John Robert. BA, U. Utah, 1953, MS, 1957, JD, 1959; postgrad., Columbia U. Bar: Utah 1960, Ariz. 1975. Asst. to pres. Utah State U., 1961-67; mem. faculty Ariz. State U., Tempe, 1967—, prof. law, 1970—, dean, 1972, 1978-84, 89, 97-98. Bd. dirs. Ariz. Found. for Legal Svcs. and Edn. Pres. Tri-City Mental Health Citizens Bd., 1973-74. With AUS, 1953-55. Mem. ABA, Utah Bar Assn., Ariz. Bar Assn., Maricopa County Bar Assn., Phi Beta Kappa, Order of Coif. Democrat. Mem. Lds Ch. Home: 720 E Geneva Dr Tempe AZ 85282-3737 Office: Ariz State U Coll Law Tempe AZ 85287 Office Phone: 480-965-6503.

MATHESON, CHARLES E., federal judge; b. 1935; BS, U. Colo., 1958, LLB, 1961. Bar: Colo. 1961. Ptnr. Fairfield and Woods, Denver, 1961-86; bankruptcy judge for Colo., U.S. Bankruptcy Ct., Denver, 1986-87, chief judge, 1987—. Office: US Bankruptcy Ct US Custom House 721 19th St Denver CO 80202-2500

MATHESON, JAMES DAVID (JIM), United States Representative from Utah; b. Salt Lake City, 1960; m. Amy Matheson; 2 children. BA in Govt., Harvard U., Cambridge, Mass., 1982; MBA, UCLA, 1987. Worked in energy industry, 12 yrs.; founder Matheson Grp., 1998; mem. US Congress from 2nd Utah dist., 2001—, mem. fin. svcs. com., mem. transp. and infrastructure com., mem. sci. com. Mem. Salt Lake Pub. Utilities bd., Scott M. Matheson Leadership Forum. Democrat. Mem. Lds Ch. Office: US Ho Reps 1222 Longworth Ho Office Bldg Washington DC 20515 Office Phone: 202-225-3011.

MATHESON, SCOTT MILNE, JR., law educator; b. Salt Lake City, July 18, 1953; s. Scott Milne and Norma (Warenski) M.; m. Robyn Kuida, Aug. 12, 1978; children: Heather Blair, Briggs James. AB, Stanford U., 1975; MA, Oxford U., Eng.; JD, Yale U., 1980. Bar: D.C., 1981, Utah 1986. Assoc. Williams & Connolly, Washington, 1981-85; assoc. prof. law U. Utah, 1985-91, assoc. dean law, 1990-93, prof. law, 1991—, dean, 1998—2006; dep. atty. Salt Lake County Attys. Office, 1988-89; U.S. atty. Dist. Utah, 1993-97; Pub. Policy scholar Woodrow Wilson Internat. Ctr. for Scholars, 2006—07. Vis. assoc. prof. JFK Sch. Govt. Harvard U., Cambridge, Mass., 1989-90; adv. com. on rules of evidence Utah Supreme Ct., 1987-93, Utah Constitutional Revision Commn., 1987-93, adv. com. on the local rules of practice, US Dist. Ct. Utah, 1993-97; gubernatorial candidate, State of Utah, 2004. Contbr. articles to profl. jours. Chmn. U.N. Day for State of Utah, 1991; mem. Univ. Com. on Tanner Lectures on Human Values U. Utah, 1993-2000, Honors Program Adv. Com. U. Utah, 1986-88, Adv. Bd. Hinckley Inst. Politics U. Utah, 1990-93; trustee Legal Aid Soc. of Salt Lake, 1986-93, pres., 1987; trustee TreeUtah, 1992-93; campaign mgr. Matheson for Gov., 1976, 1980; vol. state dir. Clinton/Gore '92. Recipient Up'n Comers award Zions Bank, 1991, Faculty Achievement award Burlington Resources Found., 1993, Disting. Svc. to Fed. Bar award Fed. Bar Assn., Utah chpt., 1998, spl. recognition award Utah Minority Bar Assn., 1999; named one of Outstanding Young Men of Am., 1987, 1988; Rhodes scholar. Mem. ABA, Assn. Am. Law Schs. (chair sect. on mass com. law 1993), Utah State Bar, Salt Lake County Bar Assn. (exec. com. 1986-92), Golden Key Nat. Honor Soc. (hon. 1990), Phi Beta Kappa. Office: Coll of Law U Utah 332 South 1400 East Salt Lake City UT 84112

MATHEWS, BARBARA EDITH, gynecologist; b. Oct. 5, 1946; d. Joseph Chesley and Pearl (Cieri) Mathews. AB, U. Calif., 1969; MD, Tufts U., 1972. Diplomate Am. Bd. Ob-Gyn. Intern Cottage Hosp., Santa Barbara, Calif., 1972-73, Santa Barbara Gen. Hosp., 1972-73; resident in ob-gyn Beth Israel Hosp., Boston, 1973-77; clin. fellow in ob-gyn Harvard U., Boston, 1973-76, instr., 1976-77; gynecologist Sansum Med. Clin., Santa Barbara, 1977-98; sr. scientist Sansum Med. Rsch. Inst., 1998—; med. dir., gynecologist Women's Health Svcs., Santa Barbara, 1998—. Faculty mem. ann. postgrad. course Harvard Med. Sch.; bd. dirs. Sansum Med. Clinic, 1989-96, vice chmn. bd. dirs., 1994-96; dir. ann. postgrad course UCLA Med. Sch. Bd. dirs. Meml. Rehab. Found., Santa Barbara, Channel City Club, Santa Barbara, Music Acad. of the West, Santa Barbara, St. Francis Med. Ctr., Santa Barbara; mem. citizen's contg. edn. adv. coun. Santa Barbara C.C.; moderator Santa Barbara Cottage Hosp. Cmty. Health Forum. Author: (with L. Burke) Colposcopy in Clinical Practice, 1977; contbg. author Manual of Ambulatory Surgery, 1982. Bd trustees Furman U., Greenville, SC, 2005—, bd. dirs., 2005—. Fellow ACOG, ACS; mem. AMA, Am. Soc. Colposcopy and Cervical Pathology (dir. 1982-84), Harvard U. Alumni Assn., Tri-counties Obstet. and Gynecol. Soc. (pres. 1981-82), Birnam Wood Golf Club (Santa Barbara), Phi Beta Kappa. Home: 2105 Anacapa St Santa Barbara CA 93105-3503 Office: 2235 De La Vina St Santa Barbara CA 93105-3815 Office Phone: 805-687-7778. Office Fax: 805-687-0012.

MATHEWS, CHRISTOPHER KING, biochemist, educator; b. NYC, 1937; s. Frank Pelletreau and Alison Barstow (Murphy) M.; m. Catherine Anne Zitcer, June 19, 1960; children: Lawrence Stuart, Anne Catherine. BA in Chemistry, Reed Coll., 1958; PhD in Biochemistry (USPHS fellow), U. Wash., 1962. USPHS postdoctoral fellow in biochemistry U. Pa., 1962-63; asst. prof. biology Yale U., 1964-67; asso. prof. biochemistry U. Ariz. Coll. Medicine, 1967-73, prof. biochemistry, 1973-77; prof., chmn. dept. biochemistry and biophysics Oreg. State U., 1978—2002, Disting. prof., 1991, emeritus, 2002—. Mem. virology study sect. NIH, 1977-79, mem. microbial chemistry study sect., 1979-81; Tage Erlander guest prof. Swedish Nat. Sci. Rsch. Coun., 1994-95. Author: Bacteriophage Biochemistry, 1971, Bacteriophage T4, 1983; co-author: (with K.E. Van Holde) Biochemistry, 1990, 96, 2000; contbr. numerous articles on nucleotide and nucleic acid metabolism, biochemistry of virus replication, and regulation of cellular metabolism to profl. jours.; editl. bd. Jour. Virology, 1970-80, Archives Biochemistry and Biophysics, 1973-80, Jour. Biol. Chemistry, 1994—, Biochem. Molecular Biology Edn., 2000-, Faseb Jour., 2006-. Grantee US Army, 2003—; Am. Cancer Soc. scholar grantee, 1973-74; USPHS research grantee, 1964-2002; Am. Heart Assn. grantee, 1968-78; NSF research grantee, 1980-82, 83-86, 90-2006; Eleanor Roosevelt Internat. Cancer fellow, 1984-85; recipient Discovery award Med. Research Found. Oreg., 1986, Disting. prof. award Oreg. State U. Alumni Assn., 1988. Mem.: AAUP, AAAS, Am. Soc. Cell Biology, Am. Chem. Soc., Am. Soc. Microbiology, Am. Soc. Biochemistry and Molecular Biology. Home: 3336 SW Willamette Ave Corvallis OR 97333-1507 Office: Dept Biochemistry and Biophysics Oreg State U Corvallis OR 97331-7305 Home Phone: 541-754-1172; Office Phone: 541-737-1865. Personal E-mail: mathewsc2@comcast.net.

MATHEWS, E. ANNE JONES, retired library educator, academic administrator; b. Phila. d. Edmond Fulton and Anne Ruth (Reichner) Jones; m. Frank Samuel Mathews, June 16, 1951; children: Lisa Anne Mathews-Bingham, David Morgan, Lynne Elizabeth Bietenhader-Mathews, Alison Fulton Sawyer. AB, Wheaton Coll., 1949; MA, U. Denver, 1965, PhD, 1977. Field staff Intervarsity Christian Fellowship, Chgo., 1949-51; interviewer supr. Colo. Market Rsch. Svcs., Denver, 1952-64; reference libr. Oreg. State U., Corvallis, 1965-67; program dir. Ctrl. Colo. Libr. Sys., Denver, 1969-70; inst. dir. U.S. Office of Edn., Inst. Grant, 1979; dir. pub. rels., prof. Grad. Sch. Librarianship and Info. Mgmt. U. Denver, 1970-76, prof., dir. continuing edn., 1977-80; dir. office libr. programs, office ednl. rsch., improvement US Dept. Edn., Washington, 1986-91; dir. Nat. Libr. Edn., Washington, 1992-94; cons. Acad. Ednl. Devel., Washington, 1994—; cons. mil. installation vol. edn. rev. Am. Coun. on Edn., 1990—; from asst. prof. to prof., 1977—85; ret., 2004. Mem. adv. com. Golden H.S., 1973—77; faculty assoc. Danforth Found., 1974—84; mem. secondary sch. curriculum com. Jefferson County Pub. Schs., Colo., 1976—78; vis. lectr. Simmons Coll. Sch. L.S., Boston, 1977; mem. book and libr. adv. com. USIA, 1981—91; spkr. in field; cons. USIA, 1984—85; del. Internat. Fedn. Libr. Assns., 1984—93; mem. adv. coun. White House Conf. on Librs. and Info. Svcs., 1991; cons. Walden U., Mpls., 2001. Author, editor 6 books; contbr. articles to profl. jours., numerous chpts. to books. Mem. rural librs. and humanities program Colo. planning and resource bd. NEH, 1982—83; bd. mgrs. Friends Found. of Denver Pub. Libr., 1976—82; pres. Faculty Women's Club, Colo. Sch. Mines, 1963—64; bd. dirs. Jefferson County Libr. Found., 1996—, v.p., 1997—2000. Mem.: ALA (visionary leaders com. 1987—89, mem. coun. 1979—83, com. on accreditation 1984—85, orientation com. 1974—77, 1983—84, pub. rels. com.), English Speaking Union, Assn. Libr. and Info. Sci. Edn. (comm. com. 1978—80, program com. 1977—78), Colo. Libr. Assn. (pres. 1974, bd. dirs. 1973—75, continuing edn. com. 1976—80), Mountain Plains Libr. Assn. (profl. devel. com. 1979—80, pub. rels. and publs. com. 1973—75, continuing edn. com. 1973—76), Am. Soc. Info. Sci. (chmn. pub. rels. 1971), Naples Philharm. League, Pelican Bay Women's League Fla., Mountain Rep. Women's Club (v.p. 1997—2000), Mt. Vernon (Colo.) Country Club, Cosmos Club (Washington). Avocations: travel, reading, museum and gallery activities, volunteer work. E-mail: afmathews2@earthlink.net.

MATHEWS, LAURIE A., state agency administrator; m. Andrew Holecek. BS in Environ. Biology, U. Colo., Boulder, 1974; M in Environ. Engring., Stanford U., 1976. Staff mem. U.S. Senate; water cons. DeLew Cather & Co.; asst. dir. Dept. Natural Resources; acting dir. Gov. Roy Romer's Policy Office; dir. State Colo., divsn. State Parks and Outdoor Recreation, Denver, 1991—. Bd. dirs. Nat. Assn. State Park Dirs. Bd. vols. Outdoor Colo. Office: State Colo Divsn State Parks & Outdoor Rec 1313 Sherman St Ste 618 Denver CO 80203-2240 Fax: 303-866-3206.

MATHEWS, MICH, computer company executive; married; 2 children. Grad., U. Brighton, England. With GM, 1987—89; pub. rels. cons., UK divsn. Microsoft Corp., 1989, gen. mgr. corp. pub. rels. grp. Redmond, Wash., 1993—99, v.p. corp. pub. rels. grp., 1999, mem. bus. leadership team, 1999—, v.p. corp. comm. to v.p. ctrl. mktg. orgn., sr. v.p. ctrl. mktg. group, 2002—. Named Marketer of Yr., BtoBonline mag., 2006, Power Player, Advt. Age mag., 2008; named one of Best Marketers, BtoB Mag., 2008. Office: Microsoft Corp One Microsoft Way Redmond WA 98052-6399

MATHEWS, SYLVIA MARY, foundation administrator; b. Hinton, W.Va., June 23, 1965; d. William Peter and Cleo P. M. AB, Harvard Coll., 1987; BA, Oxford U., 1990. Assoc. McKinsey & Co., NYC, 1990-92; dep. dir. econ. policy Clinton/Gore '92, Little Rock, 1992; staff dir. Nat. Econ. Coun., Washington, 1993-94; chief of staff to Sec. Robert Rubin U.S. Dept. Treasury, Washington, 1995-96; dep. chief of staff to Pres. The White House, Washington, 1997-98; dep. dir. Office of Mgmt. & Budget, Washington, 1998—2001; COO, exec. dir., The

Bill and Melinda Gates Found., Seattle, 2001—. Rhodes scholar, 1987. Mem. Coun. Fgn. Rels.; bd. dirs. MetLife, Inc., 2004- Democrat. Office: The Bill & Melinda Gates Found PO Box 23350 Seattle WA 98102

MATHIAS, BETTY JANE, communications and community affairs consultant, editor, educator, writer; b. Ely, Nev., Oct. 22, 1923; d. Royal F. and Dollie B. (Bowman) M.; 1 child, Dena. Student, Merritt Bus. Sch., 1941—42, San Francisco State U., 1941—42. Asst. publicity dir. Oakland (Calif.) Area War Chest and Comty. Chest, 1943-46; pub. rels. Am. Legion, Oakland, 1946-47; asst. to pub. rels. dir. Cen. Bank of Oakland, 1947-49; pub. rels. dir. East Bay chpt. Nat. Safety Coun., 1949-51; propr., mgr. Mathias Pub. Rels. Agy., Oakland, 1951-60; publicity dir. U.S. Nat. Figure Skating Championships, Berkeley, Calif., 1957; publicity dir., field trials salk polio vaccine Alameda County, 1955; gen. assignment reporter, teen news editor Daily Rev., Hayward, Calif., 1960-62; freelance pub. rels. and writing Oakland, 1962-66, 67-69; dir. corp. comms. Systech Fin. Corp., Walnut Creek, Calif., 1969-71; v.p. corp. comms. Consol. Capital cos., Oakland, 1972-79, v.p. comty. affairs Emeryville, Calif., 1981-84, v.p. spl. projects, 1984-85; v.p., dir. Consol. Capital Realty Svcs., Inc., Oakland, 1973-77, Centennial Adv. Corp., Oakland, 1976-77; comms. cons., 1979—. Cons. Mountainair Realty, Cameron Park, Calif., 1986-87; pub. rels. coord. Tuolumne County Visitors Bur., 1989-90; lectr. in field. Editor: East Bay Mag., 1966-67, TIA Traveler, 1969, Concepts, 1979-83; editor, writer souvenir program: Little House on the Prairie Cast and Crew Reunion, 1998. Bd. dirs. Oakland YWCA, 1944-45, ARC, Oakland, So. Alameda County chpt., 1967-69, Family Ctr., Children's Hosp. Med. Ctr. No. Calif., 1982-85, March of Dimes, 1983-85, Equestrian Ctr. of Walnut Creek, Calif., 1983-84, also sec.; mem. Women's Ambulance and Transport Corps of Calif., Oakland, 1942-46; active USO and Shrine Hospitality Ctrs., Oakland, USO-Travelers Aid Soc., Oakland, 1942-46; publicist Oakland Area War Bond Com., 1943-46; adult and publs. adv. Internat. Order of the Rainbow for Girls, 1953-78; comms. arts adv. com. Ohlone (Calif.) Coll., 1979-85, chmn., 1982-84; mem. adv. bd. dept. mass comms. Calif. State U.-Hayward, 1985; pres., founder San Francisco Bay Area chpt. Nat. Reyes Syndrome Found., 1981-86; vol. staff Columbia Actors' Repertory, Columbia, Calif., 1986-87, 89; mem. exec. bd., editor newsletter Tuolumne County Dem. Club, 1987; publicity chmn. 4th of July celebration Tuolumne County C. of C., 1988; vol. children's dept. Tuolumne County Pub. Libr., 1993-97; vol. Ann. Comty. Christmas Eve Dinner, Sonora, Calif., 1988-96; mem. adv. com. Ride Away Ctr. for Therapeutic Riding for the Handicapped, 1995-96, vol. Hold Your Horses Therapeutic Riding Acad., 1997; vol. Tuolumne County Visitors Bur. and Film Commn., 1996-99. Recipient Grand Cross of Color award Internat. Order of Rainbow for Girls, 1955. Mem. Order Ea. Star (life, worthy matron 1952, publicity chmn. Calif. state 1955), East Bay Women's Press Club (pres. 1960, 84). Home: 20575 Gopher Dr Sonora CA 95370-9034 Personal E-mail: honu-honu@hotmail.com.

MATHIAS, LESLIE MICHAEL, electronic manufacturing company executive; b. Bombay, Dec. 17, 1935; arrived in US, 1957; s. Paschal Lawrence and Dulcine Mathias; m. Vivian Mae Doolittle, Dec. 16, 1962. BSc, U. Bombay, 1957; BS, San Jose State U., Calif., 1961. Elec. engr. Indian Standard Metal, Bombay, 1957; sales engr. Bleisch Engring. and Tool, Mt. View, Calif., 1958-60; gen. mgr. Meadows Terminal Bds., Cupertino, Calif., 1961-63; prodn. mgr. Sharidon Corp., Menlo Park, Calif., 1963-67, Videx Corp., Sunnyvale, Calif., 1967-68, Data Tech. Corp., Mt. View, 1968-69; pres. L.G.M. Mfg., Inc., Mt. View, 1969-83; pvt. practice plating cons. Los Altos, Calif., 1983-87; materials mgr. Excel Cirs., Santa Clara, Calif., 1987—91, acct. mgr., 1991-93, materials mgr., 1993-98, internat. materials mgr., 2000—03; buyer Planned Parenthood, San Jose, Calif., 1998-2000; acct. mgr. Streamline Circuits, Santa Clara, Calif., 2003—04. Social chmn. Internat. Students, San Jose, 1958—59. Mem. Nat. Fedn. Ind. Bus., Calif. Cirs. Assn., Better Bus. Bur., Purchasing Assn., U.S. C. of C. Roman Catholic. Avocations: electronics, reading. Home: 20664 Mapletree Pl Cupertino CA 95014-0449 Personal E-mail: hopalonges@earthlink.net.

MATHIAS, ROBERT S., pediatric nephrologist; b. Bklyn., Mar. 22, 1955; MD, Rush U. Med. Coll., Chgo., 1983. Diplomate Am. Bd. Pediat., cert. Am. Bd. Pediat. Nephrology. Intern pediat. U. Calif. Med. Ctr., San Diego, 1983—84, resident pediat., 1984—85, resident pediat. nephrology, 1986—87; fellowship Children's Hosp., Boston, 1987; clin. prof. Children's Renal Ctr. U. Calif. Med. Ctr. Contbr. articles to profl. jours. Mem.: Am. Acad. Pediat. Office: UCSF Med Ctr 533 Parnassus Ave Rm U585 S San Francisco CA 94143 Office Phone: 415-476-2423. Business E-Mail: rmathias@peds.ucsf.edu.

MATHIES, ALLEN WRAY, JR., former pediatrician, hospital administrator; b. Colorado Springs, Colo., Sept. 23, 1930; s. Allen W. and Esther S. (Norton) M.; m. Lewise Austin, Aug. 23, 1956; children: William A., John N. BA, Colo. Coll., 1952; MS, Columbia U., 1956, PhD., 1958; MD, U. Vt., 1961. Rsch. assoc. U. Vt., Burlington, 1957-61; intern L.A. County Hosp., 1961-62; resident in pediatrics L.A. Gen. Hosp., 1962-64; asst. prof. pediatrics U. So. Calif., LA, 1964-68, assoc. prof., 1968-71, prof., 1971—, assoc. dean, 1969-74, interim dean, 1974-75, dean, 1975-85, head physician Communicable Disease Svc., 1964-75; pres., CEO Huntingtom Meml. Hosp., Pasadena, Calif., 1985-94, So. Calif. Healthcare Sys., Pasadena, 1992-95, pres. emeritus, 1995—. Bd. dirs. Pacific Mut. Contbr. articles to med. jours. Bd. dirs. Occidental Coll. With U.S. Army, 1953-55. Mem. Am. Acad. Pediatrics, Infectious Disease Soc. Am., Am. Pediatric Soc., Soc. Pediatric Rsch. Republican. Episcopalian. Home: 314 Arroyo Dr South Pasadena CA 91030-1623 Office: Huntington Meml Hosp PO Box 7013 Pasadena CA 91109-7013

MATHIS, DANIEL R., banking officer; Formerly with United Calif. Bank, Calif. First Bank; former regional v.p. Imperial Bank, San Diego, Calif., former exec. v.p. so. Calif. and Ariz. regions, pres., COO, bd. dirs. Inglewood, Calif. Mem. Econ. Devel. Corp. of L.A. County, L.A. Regional Technology Alliance. Bd. dirs. Jr. Achievement of So. Calif. Vet. USN, Vietnam.

MATIJEVIC, JACOB R., aerospace scientist; BS, Ill. Inst. Tech., 1969; MS, PhD in math., U. Chgo., 1973, PhD in Math. Sys. engr. NASA Jet Propulsion Lab., Pasadena, Calif., dir., mgr. Mars Pathfinder Microrover Flight Experiment, 1994—. Recipient Aerospace Laureate award Aviation Week, Sci. Tech., 1998. Office: NASA Jet Propulsion Lab 4800 Oak Grove Dr MS264 380 Pasadena CA 91109-8001

MATKOWSKI, BETTE, academic administrator; m. Joe Matkowski; 1 child, Anne. BA in English, Mount Union Coll., Alliance, Ohio; MA in English, Ohio State U., Columbus. Tchr., English Ohio pub. schools; faculty Vt. Cmty. Coll., adv., equity officer, dir. western region, dean advancement and enrollment; pres. Lamar Cmty. Coll., Colo., 2000—05, Johnson & Wales U., Denver, 2005—. Recipient Sister Elizabeth Candon award for disting. svc., Vt. Women in Higher Edn., 2000; named Communicator of Yr., Eastern Region, Nat. Coun. Mktg. and Pub. Rels., 2000; named to Salute to Women 2001, Lamar Daily News. Office: Johnson and Wales University Office of Pres 7150 Montview Blvd Denver CO 80220 Office Phone: 303-256-9398.

MATLIN, MARLEE BETH, actress; b. Morton Grove, Ill., Aug. 24, 1965; d. Don and Libby M.; m. Kevin Grandalski, Aug. 29, 1993; children Brandon Joseph, Tyler Daniel, Sara Rose, Isabelle Jane. Attended William Rainey Harper Coll. Spokeswomen Nat. Captioning Inst. Appeared in films Children of a Lesser God, 1986 (Acad. award for best actress, Golden Globe award), Walker, 1987, Linguini Incident, 1991, The Player, 1992, Hear No Evil, 1993, Snitch, 1996, It's My Party, 1996, In Her Defense, 1998, When Justice Fails, 1998, Freak City, 1999, Two Shades of Blue, 2000, Askari, 2001; TV films: Bridge to Silence, 1989, Against Her Will: The Carrie Buck Story, 1994, When Justice Fails, 1997, Dead Silence, 1997, Where the Truth Lies, 1999 (also exec. prodr.), Kiss My Act, 2001, Sweet Nothing in My Ear, 2008; TV series: Reasonable Doubts, 1991-93; guest star: Picket Fences, 1993, 94-96 (Emmy nomination, Guest Actress-Drama Series, 1994), Seinfeld, 1993 (Emmy nomination Guest Actress-Comedy Series, 1994), The Larry Sanders Show, 1992, Spin City, 1996, ER, 1999, Judging Amy, 1999, The West Wing, 2000—2006, The Practice, 2000, Gideon's Crossing, 2001, Extreme Makeover: Home Edition, 2003, The Division, 2003, Law & Order: Spl. Victims Unit, 2004-05, Desperate Housewives, 2005, My Name is Earl, 2006-07, CSI: NY, 2006, The L Word, 2007-08; performer Dancing with the Stars, 2008; author: Deaf Child Crossing, 2002; (voice) Baby Einstein: Baby Wordsworth, 2005, Baby Einstein: My First Signs, 2007 (also prodr.). Bd. dirs. Very Spl. Arts, Starlight Found. Office: c/o Spanky Taylor 3727 W Magnolia Ste 300 Burbank CA 91505 also: Fifteen Minutes Public Relations 8436 W Third St Ste 650 Los Angeles CA 90048

MATROS, RICHARD K., insurance company executive; b. Queens, NY; m. Adrienne Matros; children: Carly, Chelsea, Alex. BA in Psychology, Alfred U.; MA in Gerontology, U. S.C. Facility adminstr. Extended Care Inc., Catered Living Inc.; regional adminstr., v.p. We. Ops. Beverly Enterprises Inc.; exec. v.p. ops. Care Enterprises, 1988—91, pres., COO, 1988—91, 1991—94, pres., CEO, 1994; pres., COO Regency Health Svcs. Inc., 1994—95, pres., CEO, 1995—97, Bright Now! Dental, 1998—2000; chmn., CEO Sun Healthcare Group, 2001—. Office: Sun Healthcare Group Ste 400 18831 Von Karman Ave Irvine CA 92612

MATSCH, RICHARD P., judge; b. Burlington, Iowa, June 8, 1930; AB, U. Mich., 1951, JD, 1953. Bar: Colo. Asst. U.S. atty., Colo., 1959-61; dep. city atty. City and County of Denver, 1961-63; judge U.S. Bankruptcy Ct., Colo., 1965-74, U.S. Dist. Ct. for Colo., 1974-94, 1994—. Mem. Judicial Conf. of the U.S., 1991-94, mem. com. on criminal law, 1988-94; mem. bd. dirs. Fed. Judicial Ctr., 1995-99. Served with U.S. Army, 1953-55 Mem. ABA, Am. Judicature Soc. Office: US Court House 1929 Stout St Denver CO 80294-1929

MATSCHULLAT, ROBERT W., former consumer products company executive; b. Nov. 21, 1947; married. BA, Stanford U., 1969, MBA, 1972. CFO The Seagram Co. Ltd., 1995—99, vice chmn., 1995—2000; head worldwide investment banking Morgan Stanley & Co. Inc., 2000—04; non-exec. chmn. The Clorox Co., Oakland, Calif., 2004—05, interim chmn., CEO, 2006. Bd. dirs. The Clorox Co., 1999—, The Walt Disney Co., 2002—, McKesson Inc.

MATSEN, FREDERICK ALBERT, III, orthopedic educator; b. Austin, Tex., Feb. 5, 1944; s. Frederick Albert II and Cecilia (Kirkegaard) M.; m. Anne Lovell, Dec. 24, 1966; children: Susanna Lovell, Frederick A. IV, Laura Jane Megan. BA, U. Tex., Austin, 1964; MD, Baylor U., 1968. Intern Johns Hopkins U., Balt., 1971; resident in orthopaedics U. Wash., Seattle, 1971-74, acting instr. orthopaedics, 1974, asst. prof. orthopaedics, 1975-79, assoc. prof. orthopaedics, 1979-82, prof., 1982-85, 86—, adjunct prof. Ctr. Bioengring., 1985—, dir. residency program orthopaedics, 1978-81, vice chmn. dept. orthopaedics, 1982-85, acting chmn. dept. orthopaedics, 1983-84, prof., chmn. dept. orthopaedics, 1981—. Mem. Orthopaedic Residency Rev. Com., Chgo., 1981-86. Author: Compartmental Syndromes, 1980; editor: The Shoulder, 1990; contbr. articles to profl. jours., chpts. to textbooks; assoc. editor Clin. Orthopaedics, Jour. Orthopaedic Rsch., 1981—. Lt. comdr. USPHS, 1969-71. Recipient Traveling fellowship Am. Orthopaedic Assn., 1983, Nicholas Andry award Assn. Bone and Joint Surgery, 1979, Henry Meyerding Essay award Am. Fracture Assn., 1974. Mem. Am. Shoulder and Elbow Surgeons (founding, pres. 1991—), Am. Acad. Orthopaedic Surgeons (bd. dirs. 1984-85), Orthopaedic Rsch. Soc., Western Orthopaedic Assn., Phi Beta Kappa. Office: U Wash Dept Orthopaedics RK 10 1959 NE Pacific St Seattle WA 98195-0001 Office Phone: 206-543-3690. Business E-Mail: matsen@u.washington.edu.

MATSEN, JEFFREY ROBERT, lawyer; b. Salt Lake City, Nov. 24, 1939; s. John Martin and Bessie (Jackson) M.; m. Susan Davis, July 27, 1973; children: Gregory David, Melinda Kaye, Brian Robert, Jeffrey Lamont, Kristin Sue, Nicole, Brett Richard. BA cum laude, Brigham Young U., 1964; JD with honors, UCLA, 1967. Bar: Calif. 1968, US Dist. Ct. (ctrl. dist. Calif.) 1968, US Tax Ct. 1972, DC 1974, US Supreme Ct. 1974. Atty., LA, 1968, Newport Beach, Calif., 1971—; mng. ptnr. Jeffrey R. Matsen & Assocs., Newport Beach, Calif., 1978—. Prof. law Western State U. Coll. Law, Fullerton, Calif., 1969-85; instr. Golden Gate U. Grad. Taxation Prog., 1978-84. Author: Business Planning for California Closely-Held Enterprises; contbr. articles to legal jours. Capt., USMCR, 1968-71. Decorated Navy Commendation medal; named one of Top 100 Attys., Worth mag., 2005—06. Mem. State Bar Calif., ABA, Order of Coif. Office: Jeffrey R Matsen and Assocs 695 Town Center Dr Ste 700 Costa Mesa CA 92626 Office Phone: 714-384-6500. Office Fax: 714-384-6501. E-mail: jeff@jrmatsen.com.

MATSEN, JOHN MARTIN, academic administrator, pathologist; b. Salt Lake City, Feb. 7, 1933; s. John M. and Bessie (Jackson) M.; m. Joneen Johnson, June 6, 1959; children: Marilee, Sharon, Coleen, Sally, John H., Martin K., Maureen, Catherine, Carl, Jeri. BA, Brigham Young U., 1958; MD, UCLA, 1963; DSc (hon.), U. Utah, 2006. Diplomate Am. Bd. Pediatrics, Am. Bd. Pathology, Spl. Competence in Med. Microbiology. Intern UCLA, 1963-65; resident in pediat. LA County Harbor/UCLA Med. Ctr., Torrance, Calif., 1965—66; USPHS fellow U. Minn., Mpls., 1966-68, asst. prof., 1968-70, assoc. prof., 1971-74, prof., 1974, U. Utah, Salt Lake City, 1974—, assoc. dean, 1979-81, chmn. dept. pathology, 1981-93, univ. sr. v.p. health scis., dean Sch. Medicine, 1993-98. Pres. Associated Regional and Univ. Pathologists, Inc., Salt Lake City, 1983-93, chmn. bd. dirs., 1993-99. Author over 200 publs. in field. Recipient Becton Dickenson award Am. Soc. Microbiology, bioMèrieux Sonnenwirth award 1993, Disting. Svc. award Collegium Aesculapium Found., 2006, Am. Soc. Clin. Pathology, 2006; grantee TREK Diagnostic Sys., 2007. Fellow: Am. Acad. Microbiology; mem.: Assn. Pathology Chmn. (pres. 1990—92), Acad. Clin. Lab. Physicians and Scientists (pres. 1978—79). Mem. Lds Ch.

MATSIK, GEORGE A., packaging executive; Various mfg., operating postions Ball Corp., metal beverage divn., 1973-93, head of intenat. packaging ops., 1993—; COO Ball Corp., packaging bus., 1996—.

MATSON, PAMELA ANNE, environmental scientist, science educator; b. Eau Claire, Wis., Aug. 3, 1953; BS, U. Wis., 1975; MS, Ind. U., 1980; PhD, Oreg. State U., 1983. Prof. U. Calif., Berkeley, 1993—97; Goldman prof. environ. studies Stanford U., Calif., 1997—, Naramore dean sch. earth sci., 2002—. Contbr. articles to profl. jours.; editor: Annual Rev. of Environment & Resources. Fellow MacArthur fellow, 1995. Fellow: Am. Acad. Arts & Scis.; mem.: Nat. Acad. Sci. Achievements include research in interactions between the biosphere and the atmosphere; land-use changes on atmospheric change, analyzing the effects of greenhouse gas emissions resulting from tropical deforestization; intensive agriculture on the atmosphere, especially the effects of tropical agriculture and cattle ranching; development of agricultural productivity can be expanded without causing off-site environmental consequences. Office: Stanford U Sch Earth Scis Stanford CA 94305-2210

MATSUI, DORIS OKADA, United States Representative from California; b. Dinuba, Calif., Sept. 25, 1944; m. Robert Takeo Matsui, Sept. 17, 1966 (dec. Jan. 1, 2005); 1 child, Brian. BA in Psychology, U. Calif., Berkeley, 1966. Sr. adv. to Pres. White House, Washington, 1993—99; govt. rels. adv. Collier, Shannon & Scott PLLC, Washington, 1999—2005; mem. US Congress from 5th Calif. dist., 2005—; mem. energy and commerce com., rules com. Mem. Clinton-Gore Transition Team, 1992—93; past pres., bd. chair KVIE Pub. TV, Sacramento. Bd. trustees Woodrow Wilson Ctr., Meridian Internat. Ctr.; past bd. trustees Crocker Art Mus., Arena Stage, Sacramento Children's Home; bd. regents Smithsonian Inst. Recipient Action for Breast Cancer Awareness award, Advocates award, Nat. Assn. Mental Health, Mentor award, U. So. Calif. Sacramento Sch. Pub. Adminstrn., Newmyer award, Sidwell Friends Sch., Rosalie Stern award, U. Calif. Alumni Assn. Mem.: Junior League Sacramento, Women's Club Sacramento. Democrat. Methodist. Office: US House Reps 222 Cannon House Office Bldg Washington DC 20515-0505 also: Robert T Matsui Fed Courthouse 501 I St Ste 12 600 Sacramento CA 95814

MATSUMORI, DOUGLAS, lawyer; b. Salt Lake City, Oct. 22, 1947; BS, U. Utah, 1973; JD, Harvard U., 1976. Ptnr. Ray, Quinney & Nebeker PC, Salt Lake City. Mem. Utah State Bar, Phi Beta Kappa. Office: Ray Quinney & Nebeker PO Box 45385 Salt Lake City UT 84145-0385

MATSUNAGA, MATTHEW MASAO, state legislator, lawyer, accountant; b. Honolulu, Nov. 22, 1958; s. Spark Masayuki and Helene (Tokunaga) M.; m. Loretta Ann Sheehan, Apr. 20, 1986, children, Hannah, Sarah. BS, Bucknell U., 1980; JD, Georgetown U., 1985. Bar: Hawaii 1985, U.S. Ct. Appeals (9th cir.); CPA, Hawaii. Assoc. Carlsmith, Ball, Wichman, Murray & Case, Honolulu, 1985—; CPA Price Waterhouse, 1980-82; mem. Hawaii Senate, Dist. 9, Honolulu, 1992—. Bd. dirs. Moiliili Community Ctr., Honolulu, 1987—. Mem. ABA, Hawaii Bar Assn., Am. Judicature Soc., Hawaii Soc. CPAs. Office: Carlsmith Ball Wichman Murray & Case PO Box 656 Honolulu HI 96809-0656 Address: Hawaii State Capitol 415 S Beretania St Rm 226 Honolulu HI 96813-2407

MATSUNAKA, STANLEY T., former state legislator; b. Akron, Colo., Nov. 12, 1953; m. Kathleen Matsunaka; three children. BS, Colo. State U., 1975; JD, U. San Diego. Atty.; mem. Colo. Senate, Dist. 15, Denver, 1994—2002. Cubmaster, den leader Boy Scouts Pack 190; active Namaqua Sch. Accountability Com. Mem. ABA, Colo. Bar Assn. (former sect. young lawyers sect.), Larimer County Bar Assn. (former sec.), Loveland Sertoma Club (pres.). Democrat. Presbyterian. E-mail: stanseante@aol.com.

MATSUURA, KENNETH RAY, counseling administrator; b. Urbana, Ill., July 17, 1954; s. George Shigeo and Sally Sueko (Kawasaki) M.; m. Peggy Ai Iwata, May 27, 1995; 1 child, Claire Miya Sara. BA, U. Calif., Santa Barbara, 1976; MA, UCLA, 1978, PhD, 1996. Career counselor Calif. State U. Dominguez Hills, Carson, 1984-85; grad. recruitment coord. U. Calif., Irvine, 1985-90; counselor/articulation officer Cerritos Coll., Norwalk, Calif., 1990—. Mem. accreditation teams Western Assn. Schs. and Colls., L.A., 1994, Alameda, 1999, mem. accreditation task force Project Renewal; chair South Coast Higher Edn. Coun.; co-chair region 8 articulation officers and transfer ctre. dirs.; program reviewer Am. Coll. Pers. Assn. Ann. conf., Washington, 1988; presenter to confs. UCLA grad. advancement program fellow, 1977—78. Avocations: singing, music. Home: 101 Santa Ynez Dr Arcadia CA 91007 Office Phone: 562-860-2451 2141. Business E-Mail: matsuura@cerritos.edu.

MATTERN, DOUGLAS JAMES, think-tank executive; b. Creede, Colo., May 19, 1933; s. John A. and Ethel (Franklin) Mattern; m. Noemi E. Del Cioppo, May 4, 1963. Student, San Jose State U., 1956-58. Reliability engr. Intersil, Sunnyvale, Calif., 1973-80; sr. engr. Data Gen. Corp., Sunnyvale, 1981-87; staff engr. Apple Computer, Cupertino, Calif., 1987-97; sr. engr. Trimble Navigation, Sunnyvale, 1998-2000. Sec. Gen. World Citizens Assembly, San Francisco, 1975—86; dir. World Citizens Diplomats, Palo Alto, Calif., 1988—90; pres. Assn. World Citizens, San Francisco, 1989—; CEO World Citizens Found., San Francisco, 1979—; chmn. World Citizens Assembly, San Francisco, 1995, Taipei, Taiwan, 2001, Internat. Peace Conf., San Francisco, 2005. Author: Resolution to End the Arms Race, 1982, Looking for Square Two-Moving from War and Violence to Global Community, 2006, Looking for Square Twin a Path to the Future, 2008; contbg. author: Building a More Democratic United Nations, 1991; editor: World Citizen Newsmag., 1973—; contbr. Bd. dirs. War/Peace Found. With USN, 1951—55. Recipient Albert Einstein Peace award, Internat. World Educators for World Peace,

2001, Lifetime Achievement award for Love and Peace, Fowpal, 2005. Home: 2671 South Ct Palo Alto CA 94306-2462 Office: 55 New Montgomery St Ste 224 San Francisco CA 94105-3421 Office Phone: 415-541-9610. Business E-Mail: info@worldcitizens.org. E-mail: worldcit@best.com.

MATTES, MARTIN ANTHONY, lawyer; b. San Francisco, June 18, 1946; s. Hans Adam and Marion Jane (Burge) M.; m. Catherine Elvira Garzio, May 26, 1984; children: Nicholas Anthony, Daniel Joseph, Thomas George. BA, Stanford U., 1968; postgrad., U. Chgo., 1968-69, U. Bonn, Germany, 1971; JD, U. Calif., Berkeley, 1974. Bar: Calif. 1974, U.S. Ct. Appeals (D.C., 5th and 9th cirs.) 1978, U.S. Dist. Ct. (no. dist.) Calif. 1979, U.S. Dist. Ct. (ea. dist.) Calif. 1991. Asst. legal officer Internat. Union Conservation of Nature and Natural Resources, Bonn, 1974-76; staff counsel Calif. Pub. Utilities Commn., San Francisco, 1976-79, legal advisor to pres., 1979-82, adminstrv. law judge, 1983, asst. chief adminstrv. law judge, 1983-86; ptnr. Graham & James, San Francisco, 1986-98, Nossaman Guthner Knox and Elliott, LLP, San Francisco, 1998—. Adv. group, Calif. Senate Subcom. on Pub. Utilities Commn. Procedural Reform, 1994. Mng. editor Ecology Law Quar., 1973-74; contbr. articles to profl. jours. Mem. Conf. Calif. Pub. Utility Counsel (treas. 1988-90, v.p. 1990-91, pres. 1991-92), Internat. Coun. Environ. Law, San Francisco Bar Assn., Fed. Comms. Bar Assn., Power Assn. No. Calif. Office: Nossaman Guthner Knox Elliott LLP 50 California St Fl 34 San Francisco CA 94111-4624 Office Phone: 415-398-3600. Business E-Mail: mmattes@nossaman.com.

MATTESSICH, RICHARD VICTOR (ALVARUS), business administration researcher; b. Trieste, Venezia-Julia, Italy, Aug. 9, 1922; s. Victor and Gertrude M.; m. Hermine Auguste Mattessich, Apr. 12, 1952. Mech. engr., Engring. Coll., Vienna, Austria, 1940; Diplomkaufmann, Hochschule für Welthandel, Vienna, 1944; Dr.rer-.pol., Hochschule für Welthandel, 1945; Accademico Ordinario, Accademia Italiana di Economia Aziendale, Bologna, 1980—; D honoris causa, U. Complutense, Madrid, 1998, U. Montesquieux, Bordeaux, 2006, U. Malaga, 2006, U. Graz, 2008. Rsch. fellow Austrian Inst. Econ. Rsch., Vienna, 1945-47; instr. Rosenberg Coll., St. Gallen, 1947-52; dep. head Mt. Allison U., Sackville, Canada, 1953-59; assoc. prof. U. Calif., Berkeley, 1958-67; prof. econs. Ruhr U., Bochum, Germany, 1966-67; prof. indsl. adminstrn. U. Tech., Vienna, 1976-78; prof. bus. adminstrn. U. B.C., Vancouver, Canada, 1967-87, prof. emeritus, 1988—, Arthur Andersen & Co. Disting. chair, 1980-87. Vis. prof. Free U., Berlin, 1965, U. Social Scis., St. Gallen, Switzerland, 1965-66, U. Canterbury, 1970, Austrian Acad. Mgmt., 1971, 73, City Univ. Hong Kong, 1992, Chuo U., Tokyo, 1992; hon. prof. Centro Univ. Francesco de Vitoria, Madrid; mem. bd. nominations Acctg. Hall of Fame, Columbus, Ohio, 1978-87, 2004—; bd. govs. Sch. Chartered Accountancy, Vancouver, 1981-82; bd. dirs. Can. Cert. Gen. Accts. Rsch. Found., 1984-90, internat. adv. bd., 1993—. Author: Accounting and Analytical Methods, 1964, in German, 1970, in Japanese, 1972, in Spanish, 2002, Simulation of the Firm Through a Budget Computer Program, 1964, Instrumental Reasoning and Systems Methodology, 1978, Critique of Accounting: Foundational Research in Accounting, 1995, Professional Memoirs and Beyond, 1995, The Beginnings of Accounting and Accounting Thought, 2000, Two Hundred Years of Accounting Research, 2008; editor: Modern Accounting Research History, Survey and Guide, 1984, 89, 92, Accounting Research in the 1980s and Its Future Influence, 1991, French transl., 1993, others; mem. editl. bd. Theory and Decision Libr., Jour. Bus. Adminstrn., Economia Azlendale, Praxiology, Acctg., Bus. and Fin. History. Sec.-treas. Internat. House, U. B.C., 1969-70. Served to lt. Orgn. Todt., 1944-45. Recipient Lit. award AICPA, 1972, Haim Falk award Can. Acad. Acctg. Assn., 1991, highest rsch. award Acad. Accounting Historians, 2003, Hourglass award; Ford Found. fellow, 1961-62; Disting. Erskine fellow U. Canterbury, 1970; Killam sr. fellow U. B.C., 1971-72; nominated Nobel Meml. prize in Econs., 2002. Fellow Accademia Italiana di Economia Aziendale (accademico ordinario 1980—); mem. Am. Acctg. Assn. (lit. award 1972), Schmalenbach Gesellschaft, Verb. d. Hochschullehrer für Betriebswirtschaft (exec. adv. coun. 1976-78), Inst. Chartered Accts. of B.C. (bd. of govs. 1981-82), Austrian Acad. Scis. (corr.), Acad. Acctg. Historians (life). Achievements include pioneering analytical methods in accounting and the computerized spreadsheet. Office: U BC Sauder Sch Bus Vancouver BC Canada V6T 1Z2 Business E-Mail: richard.mattessich@sauder.ubc.ca.

MATTEUCCI, DOMINICK VINCENT, real estate developer; b. Oct. 19, 1924; s. Vincent Joseph and Anna Marie (Zoda) M.; m. Emma Irene DeGuia, Mar. 2, 1968; children: Felisa Anna, Vincent Eriberto. BS, Coll. of William and Mary, 1948, MIT, 1950. Registered profl. engr., Calif.; lic. gen. bldg. contractor, real estate broker. Owner Matteucci Constrn. Co., Newport Beach, Calif.; pres. Nat. Investment Brokerage Co., Newport Beach. Home: 2104 Felipe Newport Beach CA 92660-4040 Office: PO Box 10474 Newport Beach CA 92658-0474

MATTEUCCI, SHERRY SCHEEL, former prosecutor; b. Columbus, Mont., Aug. 17, 1947; d. Gerald F. and Shirley Scheel; m. William L. Matteucci, Dec. 26, 1969 (div. June 1976); children: Cory, Cody. Student, Kinman Bus. U., 1965-66, Mont. State U., 1967-69, Gonzaga U., 1971-72; BS, Eastern Wash. State U., 1973; JD, U. Mont., 1979. Bar: Mont., U.S. Dist. Ct. Mont., U.S. Ct. Appeals (9th cir.), U.S. Supreme Ct. Mont. Spl. asst. Commr. Higher Edn., 1974-76; assoc. Crowley, Haughey, Hanson, Toole & Dietrich, Billings, Mont., 1979-83, ptnr., 1984-93; U.S. atty. Dist. of Mont., Billings, 1993—2001. Bd. visitors U. Mont. Law Sch., 1988—. Mem. editorial bd. U. Mont. Law Rev., 1977-78, contbg. editor, 1978-79. Bd. dirs. Big Bros. & Sisters, Billings, 1982-85, City/County Library Bd., Billings, 1983-93, Billings Community Cable Corp., 1986, chmn., 1987; vice chmn., bd. dirs. Parmley Billings Library Found. Named one of Outstanding Young Women in Am., 1983. Mem. ABA, State Bar Mont. (chmn. jud. polling com. 1985-87, chmn. women's law sect. 1985-86, trustee, sec., treas. 1988—), Yellowstone County Bar Assn. (dir. 1984-87, pres.-elect 1986-87, pres. 1987-88), Billings C. of C. (leadership com. 1986, legis. affairs com. 1984). Democrat. Mem. Unitarian Ch.

MATTHEWS, BRIAN W., molecular biology educator; b. Mount Barker, Australia, May 25, 1938; came to U.S., 1967; s. Lionel A. and Ethlinda L. (Harris) M.; m. Helen F. Denley, Sept. 7, 1963; children: Susan, Kristine. BS, U. Adelaide, Australia, 1959, BS with honors, 1960, PhD, 1964, DSc, 1986. Mem. staff Med. Rsch. Coun., Cambridge, Eng., 1963-66; vis. assoc. NIH, Bethesda, Md., 1967-69; prof. molecular biology U. Oreg., Eugene, 1969—, chmn. dept. physics, 1985-86, dir. Inst. Molecular Biology, 1980-83, 90-92; Drummond lectr. U. Calgary (Can.), 1995. Advisor NSF, Washington, 1975-77; investigator Howard Hughes Med. Inst., 1989—2008; mem. U.S. Nat. Commn. for Crystallography, Washington, 1980-86, 88-90. Editor: Protein Science, 2007—. Rsch. fellow Alfred P. Sloan Found., 1971, Guggenheim fellow, 1977; recipient Career Devel. award NIH, 1973, Faculty Excellence award Oreg. Bd. Edn., 1984, Discovery award Med. Rsch. Found. Oreg., 1987, Reed Coll. Vollum award, 1994, Stein and Moore award Protein Soc., 2000. Mem. NAS, AAAS, Crystallographic Assn., Am. Chem. Soc., Protein Soc. (pres. 1995-97), Biophysical Soc. (nat. lectr. 2001). Office: U Oreg Inst Molecular Biology Eugene OR 97403 Office Phone: 541-346-2572. E-mail: brian@uoxray.uoregon.edu.

MATTHEWS, DAVID FORT, career officer; b. Lancaster, NH, Sept. 25, 1944; s. Clinton Fort and Mabel Sawin (Oaks) M.; m. Eva Mae Horton, Nov. 10, 1990. BA, Vanderbilt U., 1966; MA, Mid. Tenn. U., 1973. Cert. acquisition mgr. Rsch. and devel. officer U.S. Army Rsch. Inst., Washington, 1974-77; exec. officer 194th Maintenence Battalion-Camp Humphreys, Korea, 1978-79; career program mgr. U.S. Army Mil. Pers. Ctr., Washington, 1979-82; logistics staff officer Dep. Chief of Staff Logistics, Washington, 1982-83; team chief Chief of Staff Army Study Group, Washington, 1983-85; logistics div. chief Multiple Launch Rocket System Project Office, Huntsville, Ala., 1985-88; comdr. Ordnance Program Div., Riyadh, Saudi Arabia, 1988-90; project mgr. Army Tactical Missile System, Huntsville, 1990-94; sr. lectr. weapon systems acquisition Naval Postgrad. Sch., Monterey, Calif., 1994—. Decorated Legion of Merit, Bronze Star; recipient award as project mgr. of yr. Sec. of Army, 1991. Mem. Nat. Def. Indsl. Assn., Assn. U.S. Army. Avocations: sports, water-skiing, reading, scuba diving. Home: 83 High Meadow Ln Carmel CA 93923 Office: Naval Postgrad Sch Monterey CA 93943 Office Phone: 831-656-2360. Business E-Mail: DMatthews@nps.navy.mil.

MATTHEWS, EUGENE EDWARD, artist; b. Davenport, Iowa, Mar. 22, 1931; s. Nickolas Arthur and Velma (Schroeder) M.; m. Wanda Lee Miller, Sept. 14, 1952; children: Anthony Lee, Daniel Nickolas. Student, Bradley U., 1948-51; BFA, U. Iowa, 1953, MFA, 1957. Prof. fine arts grad. faculty U. Colo., Boulder, 1961-96, prof. fine arts emeritus, 1996—, dir. vis. artists program, 1985-96. Vis. artist Am. Acad. Rome, 1989. One-man shows include U. Wis., Milw., 1960, Brena Gallery, Denver, 1963, 65, 67, 70, 74, 76, 78, 80, 83, 88, Colorado Springs Fine Arts Ctr., 1967, Sheldon Art Gallery, U. Nebr., 1968, Denver Art Mus., 1972, James Yu Gallery, N.Y.C., 1973, 77, Dubins Gallery, L.A., 1981, Galeria Rysunku, Poznan, 1983, CU. Art Galleries, U. Colo., Boulder, 1996, Rule Art Gallery, Denver, 1998; exhibited in numerous group shows U.S., Europe, Africa, Asia; internat. watercolor exhbn. New Orleans, 1983, Louvre, Paris, Met. Mus. of Art, N.Y.C., Internat. Art Ctr., Kyoto, Japan, Mus. of Modern Art, Rijeka, Yugoslavia, Taipei Fine Arts Mus., Taiwan, Republic of China, Internat. Watercolor Biennial-East/West, Champaign, Ill., 1997; represented in permanent collections Nat. Mus. Am. Art, Washington, Denver Art Mus., Butler Inst. Am. Art, Chrysler Art Mus., others. Recipient Penello d'Argento award Acitrezza Internazionale, 1958, S.P.Q.R. Cup of Rome, Roma Olimpionica Internazionale, 1959, Gold medal of honor Nat. Arts Club, N.Y.C., 1969, Bicentennial award Rocky Mountain Nat. Watercolor Exhbn., 1976, Am. Drawings IV Purchase award, 1982, others; fellow in painting Am. Acad. Rome, 1957-60, U. Colo. Creative Rsch. fellow, 1966-67. Mem. Watercolor U.S.A. Honor Soc. (charter). Home: 2865 Jay Rd Boulder CO 80301-1605

MATTHEWS, GILBERT ELLIOTT, investment banker; b. Brookline, Mass., Apr. 24, 1930; s. Martin W. and Charlotte (Cohen) M.; m. Anne Lisbeth Barnett, Apr. 20, 1958 (div. 1975); children: Lisa Joan, Diana Kory (dec. 1995); m. Elaine Rita Siegal Pulitzer, Jan. 2, 1978 (div. 1999); 1 child, Jennifer Rachel. AB, Harvard U., 1951; MBA, Columbia U., 1953. Chartered fin. analyst. Dept. mgr. Bloomingdale's, NYC, 1953, 56-60; security analyst Merrill Lynch, NYC, 1960; investment banker Bear, Stearns & Co., NYC, 1960-95, gen. ptnr., 1979-85; mng. dir. Bear, Stearns & Co. Inc., 1985-86, sr. mng. dir., 1986-95, Sutter Securities Inc., San Francisco, 1995—, chmn. bd. dirs., 1997—. Served as lt. (j.g.) USN, 1953-56. Mem. N.Y. Soc. Security Analysts. Democrat. Jewish. Office: Sutter Securities Inc 220 Montgomery St Ste 1700 San Francisco CA 94104 Office Phone: 415-352-6336. Business E-Mail: gil@suttersf.com.

MATTHEWS, JOHN, human resources specialist, wholesale distribution executive; M in Finance. Various positions in human resources Costo Wholesale Corp., Issaquah, Wash., 1990—, sr. v.p., human resources and risk mgmt. Former comdr., logistics expert USN. Office: Costco Wholesale Corp 999 Lake Dr Issaquah WA 98027 Office Phone: 425-313-8100. Office Fax: 425-313-8103.*

MATTHEWS, LEONARD SARVER, advertising and marketing executive; b. Glendean, Ky., Jan. 6, 1922; s. Clell and Zetta Price (Sarver) M.; m. Dorothy Lucille Fessler; children: Nancy, James, Douglas. BS summa cum laude, Northwestern U., 1948. With Leo Burnett Co., Inc., Chgo., 1948-75, v.p., dir., 1958-59, exec. v.p. charge mktg. services, 1959-61, exec. v.p. client svc., 1961-69, pres., 1970-75; asst. sec. commerce for domestic and internat. bus., 1976; pres., exec. com., dir. Young and Rubicam, 1977-78; pres. Am. Assn. Advt. Agys., 1979-89; co-founder Matthews & Johnston, Stamford, Conn., 1989-92; chmn. Next Century Media, 1992—99. Mem. adv. bd. Scripps Capital, San Diego. Ensign USCGR, 1942-46. Named to Advt. Hall of Fame, 1999. Mem. Advt. Coun. (life bd. dirs.), Sky Club (N.Y.C.), Pine Valley Golf Club (N.J.), Rancho Santa Fe Golf (Calif.), Georgetown Club (Washington), Delta Sigma Pi, Beta Gamma Sigma. Republican. Lutheran. Office: PO Box 2629 Rancho Santa Fe CA 92067-2629

MATTHEWS, THOMAS J., game company executive; BS in Fin., U. So. Calif., 1986. From pres. to pres., CEO, COO Global Gaming Distributors Inc. (acquired by Anchor Gaming), Reno; pres., CEO, chmn. Anchor Gaming (acquired by Internat. Game. Tech.), 1994—2001; COO Internat. Game Tech., 2001—03, pres., CEO, COO, 2003—05, chmn., pres., CEO, COO, 2005—. Office: International Game Technology 9295 Prototype Dr Reno NV 89521-8986

MATTHEWS, WARREN WAYNE, retired state supreme court justice; b. Santa Cruz, Calif., Apr. 5, 1939; s. Warren Wayne and Ruth Ann (Maginnis) M.; m. Donna Stearns, Aug. 17, 1963; children: Holly Maginnis, Meredith Sample. BA, Stanford U., 1961; JD, Harvard U., 1964. Bar: Alaska 1965. Assoc. firm Burr, Boney & Pease, Anchorage, 1964-69, Matthews & Dunn, Matthews, Dunn and Baily, Anchorage, 1969-77; justice Alaska Supreme Ct., Anchorage, 1977—2009, chief justice, 1987—90, 1997—2000. Mem. Alaska Bar Ethics & Unauthorized Practices Com., Supreme Ct. Criminal Rules Revision Com., Alaska Sentencing Commn., 1990-93; former bd. mem., second v.p. Conference Chief Justices; chmn. Alaska Judicial Council, 1987-90, 1997-2000. Bd. dirs. Alaska Legal Services Corp., 1969-70. Mem. Alaska Bar Assn. (bd. govs. 1974-77), ABA, Anchorage Bar Assn.

MATTHEWS, WILLIAM, health products executive; PhD in Cell Biology, Southwestern Med. Sch., Dallas. Scientist in stem cell biology Genentech Inc., 1992—97; co-founder, pres. Deltagen, Inc., Menlo Park, Calif., 1997—, CEO, 1998—. Fellow postdoctoral fellow, Harvard Med. Sch., Princeton U.

MATTHIES, FREDERICK JOHN, civil and environmental engineer; b. Omaha, Oct. 4, 1925; s. Fred. J. and Charlotte Leota (Metz) M.; m. Carol Mae Dean, Sept. 14, 1947; children: John Frederick, Jane Carolyn Matthies Goding BSCE, Cornell U., 1947; postgrad., U. Nebr., 1952-53. Bd. cert. Am. Acad. Environ. Engrs.; registered profl. engr., Nebr. Civil engr. Henningson, Durham & Richardson, Omaha, 1947-50, 52-54; sr. v.p. devel. Leo A. Daly Co., Omaha, 1954-90; cons. engr., 1990—. Lectr. in field; mem. dist. export coun. U.S. Dept. Commerce, 1981-83. Contbr. articles to profl. jours. Mem. Douglas County Rep. Cen. Com., Nebr., 1968-72; bd. regents Augustana Coll., Sioux Falls., S.D., 1976-89; bd. dirs. Orange County Luth. Hosp. Assn., Anaheim, Calif., 1961-62, Nebr. Humanities Coun., 1988-94, Omaha-Shizuoka City (Japan) Sister City Orgn.; trustee Luth. Med. Ctr., Omaha, 1978-82; mem. adv. bd. Marine Mil. Acad., Harlingen, Tex. 1st lt. USMCR, 1943-46, 50-52, Korea. Fellow ASCE, Instn. Civil Engrs. (London), Euro Engr. European Econ. Commn.; mem. NSPE, Am. Water Works Assn. (life), Air Force Assn., Am. Legion, VFW. Home: 950 Southridge Greens Blvd # 15 Fort Collins CO 80525-6726

MATTIA, THOMAS GERARD, beverage company executive; b. Newark, Nov. 2, 1948; s. Anthony and Audrey Elizabeth (Murray) Mattia; m. Christine Wesche, Oct. 22, 1978 (div. 1988); m. Martha Louise Boone, July 28, 1988; children: Mary Elizabeth, Caitlin Jane, Matthew Jefferson. BA in Journalism, Rutgers U., NJ, 1970. Journalist several daily newspapers, NJ, Vt., Conn., 1970-80; various positions IBM, White Plains, NY, 1980-84, issues mgr. Armonk, NY, 1985-86, mgr. real estate/constrn. Stamford, Conn., 1986-87, mgr. sys./software White Plains, 1987-89, dir. advanced workers sta. mktg. com. Stamford, 1989-90; sr. v.p., gen. mgr. Hill and Knowlton New Eng., Waltham, Mass., 1990-91; exec. v.p., mng. dir. Hill and Knowlton Asia Ltd., Hong Kong, 1991-93; exec. v.p., gen. mgr. Hill and Knowlton LA, 1994-95; pres. GCI Jennings, San Francisco, 1994—95; various positions including v.p. Lincoln Mercury, dir. N. Am. pub. affairs and head internat. pub. affairs Ford Motor Co., 1995—2000; v.p. global comm. EDS (Hewlett-Packard Co.), 2000—06; sr. v.p., dir. worldwide pub. affairs/comm. Coca-Cola Co., 2006—. Bd. trustees Dallas Theater Ctr. Mem.: LA C. of C., Am. C. of C. Hong Kong (gov. 1993—94), Pub. Rels. Soc. America, Internat. Assn. Bus. Communicators. Avocations: golf, baseball, reading. Home: 606 Pt Gallinas Rd San Rafael CA 94903 Office: Co Hdqs 1 Coca Cola Plz Atlanta GA 30313 Office Phone: 404-676-2121.

MATTIS, LOUIS PRICE, pharmaceutical and consumer products company executive; b. Balt., Dec. 12, 1941; s. Louis Wadsworth and Sara Helene (Myers) M.; children: Louis Wadsworth, Deborah Cook Collier. AB in Internat. Affairs, Lafayette Coll., Easton, Pa., 1962; MBA, Tulane U., 1964. V.p., gen. mgr. Warner Lambert Co., Manila, 1971-74, regional dir. Hong Kong, 1974-76, region pres. Sydney, Australia, 1976-79; exec. v.p. Americas-Far East Richardson-Vicks, Inc., 1979-81, pres. Americas-Far East, 1981-84, exec. v.p., 1985-87; group v.p. Sterling Winthrop Inc., NYC, 1987-88, chmn., pres., CEO, 1988-94; dir. Salomon Bros. Fund, 1992—2005. Mem. Snowmass Club. Avocations: skiing, woodworking. Home: Sunny Mesa Ranch 5345 County Rd 100 Carbondale CO 81623

MATTOX, CLAUDE, councilman; m. Sherri Mattox. V.p. Nat. Western Vistas Real Estate; owner Desert Sun Enterprises; councilman, Dist.5 Phoenix City Coun., 2000—; vice mayor City of Phoenix, 2002. Chmn. Natural Resources, Pub. Safety & Vets. Coms.; mem. Transp. & Infrastructure, Econ., Commerce & Sustainability Coms. Chmn. Nat. League Cities EENR Steering & Policy Com.; exec. com. & bd. mem. Western Maricopa Coalition; bd. mem. Gomper's Habilitation Ctr., West Phoenix Bus. Alliance, Maryvale U.N.I.T.E., Phoenix Econ. Devel. Task Force; chmn. Maryvale Village Planning & Desert West Park Planning Coms., West Phoenix Cactus League Spring Baseball Coalition, Phoenix Surface Transp. Adv. Com., Maricopa Neighbors Airport Noise & Safety Com.; mem. Valley of the Sun West Phoenix Branch YMCA Founders Com., Desert Sky YMCA Ext. Adv. Com.; founding mem. Maryvale Citizens for Arts Programming Com. Mem.: Ariz. Mcpl. Water Users Assn. (bd. mem. & treas.). Office: 200 W Washington St 11th Fl Phoenix AZ 85003 Office Phone: 602-262-7446. Office Fax: 602-495-0628. Business E-Mail: council.district.5@phoenix.gov.*

MATTRICK, DONALD A., computer software company executive; Founder, chmn. Distinctive Software Inc. (acquired by Electronic Arts in 1991), 1982—91; sr. v.p. N.Am. Studios, exec. v.p., gen. mgr. EA Canada, v.p. Electronic Arts, Inc., 1991—96, exec. v.p. N.Am. Studios, 1996—97, pres. Worldwide Studios, 1997—2006; external adv., entertainment & devices divsn. Microsoft Corp., 2007, corp. v.p., interactive entertainment bus., entertainment & devices divsn., 2007—. Office: Microsoft Corp One Microsoft Way Redmond WA 98052-7329

MATTSON, ROBERT MARVIN, JR., lawyer; b. Phila., May 13, 1948; s. Robert Marvin and Rillie Lee (Wright) M.; m. Carlene Kay Anderson; children: Michael Tyler, Jeffery David. AB, Stanford U., 1971; M in Mgmt., Northwestern U., 1975, JD, 1975. Bar: Calif. 1975. Assoc. Morrison & Foerster, San Francisco, 1975-81, ptnr., 1981—, co-chair corp. practice, 2004—06. Mem. State Bar Calif. (exec. com. Bus. Law Sect. 1994-98, vice-chmn. 1997-98). Avocations: reading, travel, sports. Office: Morrison & Foerster LLP 19900 MacArthur Blvd Irvine CA 92612-2445 Office Phone: 949-251-7138. Office Fax: 949-251-0900. Business E-Mail: rmattson@mofo.com.

MATUSZAK, ALICE JEAN BOYER, pharmacy educator; b. Newark, Ohio, June 22, 1935; d. James Emery and Elizabeth Hawthorne (Irvine) Boyer; m. Charles Alan Matuszak, Aug. 27, 1955; children: Matthew, James. BS summa cum laude, Ohio State U., 1958, MS, 1959; postgrad., U. Wis., 1959-60; PhD, U. Kans., 1963. Registered pharmacist, Ohio, Calif. Apprentice pharmacist Arensberg Pharmacy, Newark, 1953-58; rsch. asst. Ohio State U., Columbus, 1958, lab. asst., 1958-59; rsch. asst. U. Wis., Madison, 1959-60, U. Kans., Lawrence, 1960-63; asst. prof. U. of the Pacific, Stockton, Calif., 1963-67, assoc. prof., 1971-78, prof., 1978—2000, prof. emerita, 2000—; order of Pacific, 2000. Vis. fgn. prof. Kobe-Gakuin U., Japan,

1992. Contbr. articles to profl. jours. Mem. rev. bd. U.S. Adopted Names Commn. Recipient Disting. Alumna award Ohio State U. Coll. Pharmacy, 1994, Profl. Frat. Assn. Career Achievement award, 2000, Order of Pacific award U. of Pacific, 2000; NIH grantee, 1965-66. Fellow Am. Pharm. Assn. (chmn. basic scis. 1990); mem. Am. Assn. Colls. of Pharmacy (chmn. chemistry sect. 1979-80, bd. dirs. 1993-95), Am. Inst. History of Pharmacy (exec. coun. 1984-88, 90-92, 92-95, chmn. contributed papers 1990-92, pres.-elect 1995-97, pres. 1997—99, cert. of commendation 1990), Am. Chem. Soc., Internat. Fedn. Pharmacy, Acad. Pharm. Rsch. Sci. (pres. 1993-94), Coun. Sci. Soc. Pres., U.S. Adopted Names Coun. Review Bd., U.S. Pharmacopeial Conv., Clan Irwin Assn., Donald Salvatori Calif. Pharmacy Mus., Sigma Xi, Rho Chi, Phi Lambda Sigma, Phi Kappa Phi, Kappa Epsilon (Unicorn award, award of merit 1995, Merck Vanguard leadership award 2000), Lambda Kappa Sigma, Delta Zeta. Democrat. Episcopalian. Avocation: collecting pharmacy artifacts. Home: 1130 W Mariposa Ave Stockton CA 95204-3021 Office: U Pacific Sch Pharmacy Stockton CA 95211-0001 E-mail: amatuszak@pacific.edu.

MATZ, JOSEPH S., computer software company executive; BS in Economics, Georgetown U., 1987; MBA, U. Chgo. Joined Microsoft Corp., Redmond, Wash., 1993, asst. treas., corp. v.p. Worldwide Licensing and Pricing. Recipient gold Alexander Hamilton award for Fin. Risk Mgmt., 2003. Office: Microsoft Corp One Microsoft Way Redmond WA 98052-6399

MATZDORFF, JAMES ARTHUR, investment banker, internet marketing professional; BS, U. So. Calif.; MBA, Loyola U., LA. Comml. loan officer Bank Am., LA, 1976—78; mng. dir. James A. Matzdorff and Co., Beverly Hills, Calif., 1978—. Mem. Rep. Nat. Com., 1980-. Mem. Am. Fin. Assn., Phi Delta Theta. Avocations: tennis, sailing, Karate, skiing. Home and Office: 537 Newport Ctr Dr #144 Newport Beach CA 92660 Office Phone: 800-348-4212. Business E-Mail: James@premierelender.com.

MAULDING, BARRY CLIFFORD, lawyer, director; b. McMinnville, Oreg., Sept. 3, 1945; s. Clifford L. and Mildred (Fisher) Maulding; m. Reva J. Zachow, Dec. 27, 1965; children: Phillip B., John C. BA in Psychology, U. Oreg., 1967, JD, 1970. Bar: Oreg. 1970. Sec., gen. counsel Alaska Continental Devel. Corp., Portland, Oreg., 1970—75, Seattle, 1970—75; gen. counsel Alaska Airlines, Seattle, 1975—84; dir. legal svcs., corp. sec. Univar Corp., Seattle, 1984—91; v.p., gen. counsel, corp. sec. Prime Source Corp., Seattle, 1991—. Mem. editl. bd.: law rev. Oreg. Law Rev. Trustee Good Neighbor Found., Seattle. Republican.

MAUPIN, A. WILLIAM, retired state supreme court chief justice; children: Allison, Michael. BA, U. Nev., 1968; JD, U. Ariz., 1971. Atty., ptnr. Thorndal, Backus, Maupin and Armstrong, Las Vegas, 1976—93; judge 8th Jud. Dist. Clark County, 1993—97; assoc. justice Nev. Supreme Ct., 1997—, chief justice, 2001—02, 2007—09. Bd. govs. Nev. State Bar, 1991—95. Mem.: Nev. Supreme Ct. (study com. to review jud. elections, chmn. 1995, alternate dispute resolution implementation com. chmn. 1992—96).

MAURER, ROBERT DISTLER, retired industrial physicist; b. St. Louis, July 20, 1924; s. John and Elizabeth J. (Distler) M.; m. Barbara A. Mansfield, June 9, 1951; children: Robert M., James B., Janet L. BS, U. Ark., 1948, LLD, 1980; PhD, MIT, 1951. Mem. staff MIT, 1951-52; with Corning Glass Works, NY, 1952-89, mgr. physics research, 1963-78, research fellow, 1978-89. Contbr. articles to profl. jours., chpts. to books; patentee in field. Served with U.S. Army, 1943-46. Decorated Purple Heart; recipient Indsl. Physics prize Am. Inst. Physics, 1978, L.M. Ericsson Internat. prize in telecommunications, 1979, Indsl. Rsch. Inst. Achievement award, 1988, Optical Soc. Am./IEEE Leos Tyndall award, 1987, Disting. Alumni award U. Ark, 1994, Am. Innovator award U.S. Dept. Commerce, 1995, Nat. Medal of Technology, 2000, C&C prize Japanese NEC Found, 2007. Fellow IEEE (Morris N. Liebmann award 1978), Am. Ceramic Soc. (George W. Morey award 1976), Am. Phys. Soc. (New Materials prize 1989); mem. NAE (Charles Draper prize 1999), Nat. Inventors Hall of Fame. Home: 2572 W 28th Ave Eugene OR 97405

MAURER, STEPHEN MARK, academic program director; BA summa cum laude, Yale U., New Haven, 1979; JD, Harvard Law Sch., 1982. Bar: Calif. Assoc. Brown & Bain, Phoenix, 1982—87; sr. assoc. Lasky, Haas, Cohler & Munter, San Francisco, 1988—92, Ritchey, Fisher, Whitman & Klein, Palo Alto, Calif., 1994—96, Fliesler, Dubb, Meyer & Lovejoy, San Francisco, 1998; contract atty. San Francisco and Palo Alto, Calif., 1992—94; lectr. U. Calif. Goldman Sch. Pub. Policy, Berkeley, 1999—2004, acting dir. Info. Tech. and Homeland Security Project, 2005. Cons. Diversified Risk Mgmt., Mutations Database Initiative, Virtual Physics Assocs.; mem. com. geophys. data NAS, 2003—04; adj. assoc. prof. U. Calif., Berkeley; co-founder Tropical Disease Initiative. Contbr. articles to profl. jours., to popular sci. publs. Named one of 50 Who Matter Now, CNNMoney.com Bus. 2.0, 2006. Achievements include writing a proposal to impose a code of conduct on the field of synthetic biology. Office: U Calif Berkeley 2607 Hearst Ave MC 7320 Berkeley CA 94720 Office Phone: 510-643-6990. E-mail: smaurer@berkeley.edu.

MAU-SHIMIZU, PATRICIA ANN, lawyer; b. Jan. 17, 1953; d. Herbert G. K. and Leilani (Yuen) Mau; 1 child, Melissa Rose. BS, U. San Francisco, 1975; JD, Golden Gate U., 1979. Bar: Hawaii 1979. Law clk. State Supreme Ct., Honolulu, 1979-80; atty. Bendet, Fidell & Sakai, Honolulu, 1980-81; legis. atty. Honolulu City Coun., 1981-83, House Majority Staff Office, Honolulu, 1983-84, dir., 1984-93; chief clk. Hawaii Ho. of Reps., 1993—. Mem. Hawaii Bar Assn., Hawaii Women Lawyers, Jr. League Hawaii. Democrat. Roman Catholic. Home: 7187 Hawaii Kai Dr Honolulu HI 96825-3115 Office: State House Reps 415 S Beretania St Rm 027 Honolulu HI 96813-2407 Office Phone: 808-586-6127. Business E-Mail: pat@capital.hawaii.gov.

MAVROUDI, MARIA, philologist, educator; BA, U. Thessaloniki, 1990; MA, Harvard U., 1992, PhD, 1998. Postdoctoral fellow Byzantine studies Dumbarton Oaks, 2000—01; postdoctoral tchg. fellow Hellenic studies Princeton U., 2001—02; asst. prof. U. Calif., Berkeley, 2002—05, assoc. prof., 2005. Author: A Bzyantine Book on Dream Interpretation: The Oneirocriticon of Achmet and its Arabic Sources, 2002. MacArthur fellow, 2004. Office: U Calif Berkeley 2223 Dwinelle Hall Berkeley CA 94720 Office Phone: 510-643-4413. E-mail: mavroudi@berkeley.edu.

MAXFIELD, MAX R., Secretary of State, Wyoming; b. Wis., 1945; m. Gayla Y. Maxfield; 4 children. Student, U. Wis. Dir. Wyo. Recreation Commn., 1987—89, Wyo. Dept. Commerce, 1989—94; state auditor State of Wyo., Cheyenne, 1995—2006, sec. state, 2007—. Mem. state loan and investment bd. State of Wyo., mem. bd. land commrs., mem. state bldg. commn., mem. state canvassing bd., chmn. state fin. adv. com. Dir. YMCA. Republican. Office: Office of State Auditor State Capitol Bldg Rm 114 Cheyenne WY 82002 Office Phone: 307-777-7831. Office Fax: 307-777-6983. E-mail: mmaxfi@state.wy.us.

MAXFIELD, PETER CHARLES, state legislator, lawyer, educator; b. 1941; AB, Regis Coll., 1963; JD, U. Denver, 1966; LLM, Harvard U., 1968. Bar: Colo. 1966, Wyo. 1969. Trial atty. Dept. Justice, 1966-67; assoc. Hindry, Erickson & Meyer, Denver, 1968-69; asst. prof. U. Wyo. Coll. Law, 1969-72, assoc. prof., 1972-76, prof., 1976-96, dean, 1979-87, prof. emeritus, 1996—. Vis. assoc. prof. U. N.Mex., 1972-73; Raymond F. Rice Disting. prof. U. Kans., 1984; Chapman Vis. Disting. prof., U. Tulsa, 1987; vis. prof. U. Utah, 1992. Author: (with Garr Houghton) Cases and Materials on the Taxation of Oil and Gas and Natural Resources Transactions, 1990, (with Allen and Houghton) Taxation of Mining Operation, 1981, 97, 2002; (with Trelease and Dietrich) Natural Resources Law on American Indian Lands, 1977. Coord. Wyo. State Planning 1988-89; spl. asst. Gov. Wyo. 1989-90; Dem. nominee U.S. Ho. Reps., 1990; mem. Wyo. Environ. Quality Coun., 1991-93; mem. Wyo. Senate, Laramie, 1993-97; counsel Gov. Wyo., 2006. Mem. Omicron Delta Kappa, Pi Delta Phi, Order of the Coif (faculty). Home: 1159 Escalera St Laramie WY 82072-5020 Office: PO Box 100 Laramie WY 82073 Business E-Mail: petemaxfield@earthlink.net.

MAX NIKIAS, See NIKIAS, CHRYSOSTOMOS

MAXSON, ROBERT C., academic administrator; b. May 1936; Former sr. v.p. acad. affairs U. Houston Systems, Houston; pres. U. Nev., Las Vegas, 1984-94, Calif. State U., Long Beach, 1994—2005.

MAXWELL, MARCIE, state legislator; m. Steve Maxwell; 2 children. Studied Bus. & Real Estate, Highline Coll. Worked several years as realtor & small bus. owner; several years svc. in banking branch mgmt. & lending; legis. rep. (king county sch. bd.) Wash. State Sch. Dirs. Assn.; mem. Dist. 41 Wash. House of Reps., 2008—. Founding bd. mem. Kennydale Neighborhood Assn., Renton Cmty. Found. Recipient Renton Citizen of Yr., Renton C. of C. Outstanding Business Citizen award. Democrat. Office: 324 John L O'Brien Bldg PO Box 40600 Olympia WA 98504-0600 Office Phone: 360-786-7894. Business E-Mail: maxwell.marcie@leg.wa.gov.

MAXWELL, SOPHENIA (SOPHIE), city supervisor; b. San Francisco; Supr., Dist. 10 San Francisco Bd. Supervisors, 2001—, chair land use & econ. devel. com., vice-chair pub. safety com., mem. govt. audit & oversight com., Transp. Authority. Founder, chair San Francisco Recreation Coun.; chair Bayview Project Area Com.; rep. League Calif. Cities, Peninsula Corridor Study Joint Powers Bd.; mem. San Francisco Bay Conservation & Devel. Com.; past mem. Southeast Alliance Environ. Justice, Third St. Light Rail Adv. Com., Southern Water Front Adv. Com. Vol. Neighborhood Emergency Response Team (NERT), San Francisco; bd. dirs. Bayview-Hunters Point Ctr. Arts & Tech., San Francisco. Mem.: San Francisco League Women Voters (past v.p.). Office: 1 Dr Carlton B Goodlett Pl Rm 244 San Francisco CA 94102-4689 Office Phone: 415-554-7670. Fax: 415-554-7674. E-mail: Sophie_Maxwell@ci.sf.ca.us.*

MAXWELL-BROGDON, FLORENCE MORENCY, school system administrator, educational consultant; b. Spring Park, Minn., Nov. 11, 1929; d. William Frederick and Florence Ruth (LaBrie) Maxwell; m. John Carl Brogdon, Mar. 13, 1957; children: Carole Alexandra, Cecily Ann, Daphne Diana. BA, Calif. State U., LA, 1955; MS, U. So. Calif., 1957; postgrad., Columbia Pacific U., San Rafael, Calif., 1982-86. Cert. tchr., Calif. Dir. Rodeo Sch., LA, 1961-64; lectr. Media Features, Culver City, Calif., 1964—; dir. La Playa Sch., Culver City, Calif., 1968-75; founding dir. Venture Sch., Culver City, Calif., 1974—, also chmn. bd. dirs. Bd. dirs., v.p. Parent Coop. Preschools, Baie d'Urfe Que., Can., 1964—; del. to Edni. Symposium, Moscow-St. Petersburg, 1992, U.S./China Joint Conf. on Edn., Beijing, 1992, Internat. Confedn. of Prins., Geneva, 1993, Internat. Conf., Berlin, 1994, Internat. Confedn. of Sch. Prins., Helsinki, Finland, 2000, Edinburgh, Scotland, 2003. Author: Let Me Tell You, 1973, Wet'n Squishy, 1973, Balancing Act, 1977, (as Morency Maxwell) Framed in Silver, 1985; (column) What Parents Want to Know, 1961—; editor: Calif. Preschooler, 1961-74; contbr. articles to profl. jours. Treas. Dem. Congl. Primary, Culver City, 1972. Mem. NASSP, Calif. Coun. Parent Schs. (bd. dirs. 1961-74), Parent Coop. Preschs. Internat. (advisor 1975—), Pen Ctr. USA West, Mystery Writers of Am. (affiliate), Internat. Platform Assn. Liberatarian. Home: 10814 Molony Rd Culver City CA 90230-5451 Office: Venture Sch 11477 Jefferson Blvd Culver City CA 90230-6115 Home Phone: 310-559-2678; Office Phone: 310-559-2678. Personal E-mail: morencee@aol.com. Business E-Mail: vntrschl@comcast.net.

MAXWORTHY, TONY, mechanical and aerospace engineering educator; b. London, May 21, 1933; came to U.S., 1954, naturalized, 1961; s. Ernest Charles and Gladys May (Butson) M.; m. Emily Jean Parkinson, June 20, 1956 (div. 1974); children: Kirsten, Kara; m. Anna Barbara Parks, May 21, 1979 BS in Engring. with honors, U. London, 1954; MSE, Princeton U., 1955; PhD, Harvard U., 1959. Rsch. asst. Harvard U., Cambridge, Mass., 1955-59; sr. scientist, group supr. Jet Propulsion Lab., Pasadena, Calif., 1960-67; assoc. prof. U. So. Calif., LA, 1967-70, prof., 1970—, Smith Internat. prof. mech. and aero. engring., 1988—, chmn. dept. mech. engring., 1979-89; cons. BBC Rsch. Ctr., Baden, Switzerland, 1972-82, J.P.L., Pasadena, Calif., 1968-80; lectr. Woods Hole Oceanographic Inst., Mass., summers 1965, 70, 72, 83. Forman vis. prof. aeronautics Technion Haifa, 1986; vis. prof. U. Poly., Madrid, 1988, Inst. Superiore Tech., Lisbon, 1988, Swiss Fed. Inst. Tech., Lausanne, 1989-95; assoc. prof. IMG, U. Joseph Fourier, Grenoble, 1980—, Ecole Superieure Physics and Indsl. Chemistry, Paris, 1995—; Shimizu vis. prof. Stanford U., 1996—, U. Canterbury, New Zealand, 2005—. Mem. editorial bd. Geophys. Fluid Dynamics, 1973-79, 88-96, Dynamic Atmospheric Oceans, 1976-83, Phys. Fluids, 1978-81, Zeitschrift fuer Angewandte Mathematik und Physik, 1987-96; contbr. articles to profl. jours. Recipient Humboldt Sr. Scientist award, 1981-93, G.I. Taylor medal Soc. Engring. Sci., 2003; life fellow Clare Hall, Cambridge U., 1974, 93—, Australian Nat. U., 1978, Nat. Ctr. Atmospheric Rsch., 1976, Glennon fellow U. Western Australia, 1990, F.W. Mosey fellow, 1993, Sr. Queen's fellow in marine scis. Commonwealth of Australia, 1984; sr. visitor DAMTP, Cambridge U., 1975—. Fellow: Am. Phys. Soc. (chmn. exec. com. fluid dynamics divsn. 1974—79, Otto Laporte award 1990), Am. Acad. Arts and Scis.; mem.: NAE, Oceanography Soc., European Geophys. Soc., Am. Geophys. Union. Office: U So Calif Dept Aerospace & Mech Engr Exposition Park Los Angeles CA 90089-1191 Business E-Mail: maxworth@usc.edu.

MAY, BRUCE BARNETT, lawyer; b. Portland, Oreg., Apr. 16, 1948; s. Ralph Barnett May and Barbara (Newton) Evans; m. Deborah Sue Wright, Jan. 22, 1972; children: Alexander, Christopher, Elizabeth, Andrew. BA, Princeton U., 1971; JD, U. Oreg., 1978. Bar: Ariz. 1978. Ptnr. Jennings Strouss & Salmon, Phoenix, 2004—. Lectr. various bar and trade assns. Contbr. articles to profl. jours. Dir. Phoenix Mountain Preservation Coun., 1985-89; mem. Paradise Valley Urban Village Planning Com., Phoenix, 1985-87, Men's Art Coun., 1987-91, Phoenix Valley Partnership; mem. adv. bd. Corp. Supportive Housing; bd. Phoenix Revitalogation Coun.; mem. exec. bd. Phoenix Cmty. Alliance. Lt. (j.g.) USN, 1972-75. Mem. ABA (chmn. land sales regulation com., vice chair divsn. CLE, task force future of CLE, co-chmn. brokers and brokerage com.), Am. Coll. Real Estate Lawyers, Order of Coif. Republican. Episcopalian. Avocations: book collecting, running, boxing. Office: Jennings Strouss & Salmon 201 E Washington St Ste1100 Phoenix AZ 85004-2385 Office Phone: 602-262-5923. Business E-Mail: bmay@jsslaw.com.

MAY, MIKE, state legislator; m. Traci May; children: Milissa, Stacie, Justin, Jeffrey, Alex, Lindsay. AAS in Bus. Mgmt., Salt Lake C.C.; BS in Acctg., Westminster Coll. CPA. Accountant May Co., Parker, Colo.; councilman Parker Town Coun., 1998—; mem. Dist. 44 Colo. House of Reps., Denver, 2002—, minority leader. Mem.: NRA, AICPA, Colo. Soc. CPA, Parker Econ. Devel. Coun., Parker C. of C. (past pres.), Sulfur Gulch Yacht Club. Republican. Office: Colo State Capitol 200 E Colfax Rm 323 Denver CO 80203 Office Phone: 303-866-5523. Business E-Mail: mike.may.house@state.co.us.*

MAY, RICHARD B., psychology professor; b. Seattle, Dec. 20, 1938; s. Louie B. and Ruby J. (Simmons) M.; m. Marjorie Ann Stevenson, Aug. 25, 1962; children: Robert Tobyn, Richard Forrest. BA, Whitman Coll., 1961; MA, Claremont Grad. Sch., 1963, PhD, 1966. Asst. prof. U. Victoria, B.C., Can., 1966-71, assoc. prof. B.C., 1971-81, prof. psychology, 1981-96, prof. emeritus, 1996—; rsch. assoc. Oxford U., England, 1972-73; vis. scholar U. Utah, Salt Lake City, 1995—96. Cons. Victoria Sch. Dist., 1971-72, Dept. Human Resources, Victoria, 1974-75. Author: Application of Statistics in Behavioral Research, 1990; contbr. articles to profl. jours., chpt. to book. Mem. foster care rev. bd. State of Utah, 1997-2001; gen. mgr. RMAY Investments LLC, 2001—. Fellow Social Scis. and Humanities Rsch. Coun., 1972-73, 79-80, 86-87, USPHS, 1962-66; rsch. grantee Nat. Sci. and Engrig. Coun. Rsch., 1969-71, 71-74, 74-77. Avocations: investing, reading, internet, card games. Home: 2072 S Parkwood Cir Spokane WA 99223-5037 Personal E-mail: rb.may@comcast.net.

MAY, ROBERT P., retired energy executive; b. May 1949; married; 5 children. Student, Harvard U. CEO Intelogistics divsn. Intelligence Electronics; COO Towne Air Freight; sr. exec. FedEx Corp., 1973—94; COO Cablevision Sys. Corp., 1997—99; pres., CEO PNV Inc., 1999—2000; pvt. investor, strategic cons. for telecom. and logistics cos.; interim CEO HealthSouth Corp., Birmingham, Ala., 2003—04, non-exec. chmn., 2004—05; acting pres., CEO Charter Communications, Inc., St. Louis, 2005; CEO Calpine Corp., San Jose, Calif., 2005—08. Bd. dirs. HealthSouth Corp., 2002—03, Charter Communications, Inc., 2004—. With USMC.

MAY, RONNY (RON) JOE, state legislator; b. Sherman, Tex., Sept. 16, 1934; son of Joe Danover May & Athie Fennell M; married 1956 to Onilla Essary; children: Mark D & Marisa (Mrs Rodney K Rogers), seven grandchildren. Bd member, Colorado Springs Utilities, 81-85; councilman, Colorado Springs City Coun, 81-85; board chairman, Colorado Springs Int Airport, 85-91; Colorado State Representative, District 15, 93-2001, member, Bus Affairs & Labor & Transportation & Energy Committees, formerly, Colorado House Representative; Colorado State Senator, District 10, 2001-, member, State Veterans & Military Affairs and Transportation Committees, currently, Colorado State Senate.President, The May Corp, Colorado Springs 80-; chairman, Colorado Springs Int Airport Advisor Bd, formerly. Friend of Trucking Award, Colorado Motor Carriers, 2000; Bus Legislator of the Year, Colorado Springs Chamber of Commerce, 1999; Several Awards for Work in Inf Technology Area, 1993-2005. Colorado Springs Exec Association; Sertoma Int Serv Club (charter president, 1978-79); founding member United States Internet Coun; Nat Conf State Legislature; America Legislature Exchange Coun (state chairman, currently, board member, currently). Republican. Presbyterian. Mailing: 6609 Showhorse Ct Colorado Springs CO 80922 Home Phone: 303-591-2330; Office Phone: 303-866-2737. Fax: 719-596-1216. E-mail: ronmay@ronmay.org.

MAY, STEPHEN JAMES, communications educator, writer; b. Toronto, Ont., Can., Sept. 10, 1946; s. Thomas and Claire (Thompson) M.; m. Caroline Casteel, Sept. 27, 1947; children: Trevor. BA, Calif. State U., Carson, 1975; MA, Calif. State U., LA, 1977; DLitt, Internat. U., London, 1990. Prof. and chair dept. of English and Lit. Pikes Peak C.C., Colorado Springs, Colo., 1980-91; prof. Colo. N.W. C.C., Craig, 1992-98; chair dept. of English and Lit. Pikes Peak C.C., Colorado Springs, Colo., 1998—2001; vis. prof. U. No. Colo., 2001—; prof. English Front Range CC, Ft. Collins, Colo., 2001—06. Advisor Internat. Biog. Ctr., Cambridge, Eng., 1989-95; vis. prof. U. Colo., Greeley, Colo., 2000—; spl. cons. James A. Michener Art Mus., 2006-, James A. Michener Libr. Author: Pilgrimage, 1987, Fire From the Skies, 1990, Footloose, 1993, Zane Grey, 1997, Maverick Heart, 2000, Rascals, 2002, Michener: A Writer's Journey, 2005, American Heritage; contbr. articles to profl. jours. including SouthWest Art, Ohio Review, Texas Highways, 20th Century Fox, Hawaii Mag. Mem. Western Writers Am., Colo. Authors League, Zane Grey Soc., Soc. S.W. Authors, C.C. Humanities, James A. Michener Soc. Avocations: travel, writing, drawing. Home: 731 Peregrine Run Fort Collins CO 80524 Personal E-mail: stepkm@msn.com.

MAYARAM, KARTIKEYA, electrical engineer, educator; arrived in U.S., 1981; m. Namita Gandhi. BS in Engring. with honors, Birla Inst. Tech. and Sci., 1981; MS, SUNY, 1982; PhD, U. Calif., Berkeley, 1988. Mem. tech. staff Tex. Instruments Inc., Dallas, 1988—92, Bell Labs., Allentown, Pa., 1992—96; assoc. prof. Wash. State U., Pullman, Wash., 1996—99, Oreg. State U., Corvallis, Oreg., 2000—03, prof., 2003—. Cons. Mentor Graphics Corp., Wilsonville, Oreg., 1998—2001, Lucent Bell Labs., Allentown, Pa., 1996—98, Fairchild Semiconductor, San Jose, Calif., 2000—01; tech. advisor Berkeley Design Automation, Santa Clara, Calif., 2003—. Co-author: Analog

Integrated Circuits for Communication: Principles, Simulation and Design. Grantee Career award, NSF, 1997—2001. Fellow: IEEE (fellow 2005). Business E-Mail: karti@eecs.oregonstate.edu.

MAYER, ALLAN, public relations executive, consultant; b. NYC, Mar. 15, 1950; s. Theodore H. and Phyllis (Zwick) M. BA, Cornell U., 1971. Staff reporter Wall Street Jour., NYC, 1972-73; assoc. editor, gen. editor Newsweek mag., NYC, 1973-77, fgn. corr. London, 1977-80, sr. editor NYC, 1980-82; editl. dir. Arbor House Pub., NYC, 1986-88; sr. editor Simon & Schuster, NYC, 1988-89; editor-in-chief Buzz mag., LA, 1990-95, editor-in-chief, pub., 1996; sr. ptnr. Sitrick and Co., LA, 1997—2004, mng. dir., 2004—06; ptnr. 42 West LLC, LA, 2006—. Bd. dir. Am. Apparel Inc., Film Ind. Author: Madam Prime Minister, 1980, Gaston's War: A True Story of a Hero of the Resistance in World War II, 1987; co-author: (with Michael S. Sitrick) Spin: How to Turn the Power of the Press to Your Advantage, 1998. Recipient award Overseas Press Club, 1974, Nat. Mag. award Am. Soc. Mag. Editors, 1978, William Allen White award City and Regional Mag. Assn., 1995-96. Mem. Writers Guild Am. Personal E-mail: allan.mayer@42west.net.

MAYER, GEORGE ROY, education educator; b. National City, Calif, Aug. 28, 1940; s. George Eberly and Helen Janet (Knight) M.; m. Barbara Ann Fife, Sept. 9, 1964 (div. June 1986); children: Kevin Roy, Debbie Rae Ann; m. Jocelyn Volk Finn, Aug. 3, 1986 (div. July 2003); m. Mary Rossetti, Sept. 22, 2005 BA, San Diego State U., 1962; MA, Ind. U., 1965, EdD, 1966. Cert. sch. psychologist; bd. cert. behavior analyst. Sch. counselor, psychologist Ind. U., Bloomington, 1964-66; asst. prof. guidance and ednl. psychology So. Ill. U., Carbondale, 1966-69; profl. edn. Calif. State U., LA, 1966—. Cons. in field; adv. bd. Dept. Spl. Edn., L.A., 1986-90, Jay Nolan Ctr. for Autism, Newhall, Calif., 1975-86; lectr. in field; study group on youth violence prevention Nat. Ctr. for Injury Prevention and Control, Divsn. Violence Prevention of the Ctrs. for Disease Control and Prevention, 1998. Author: Classroom Mgmt.: A Calif. Resource Guide, 2000, Teaching Alternative Behaviors Schoolwide: Preventing Schoolwide Behavior Problems, 2003; co-author: Behavior Analysis for Lasting Change, 1991, Gang Violence Prevention & Intervention Strategies for Schools, 2006; contbr. articles to profl. jour. Recipient Outstanding Prof. award Calif. State U.-L.A., 1988; U.S. Dept. Edn. grantee, 1996—. Mem. Assn. for Behavior Analysis, Nat. Assn. Sch. Psychologists, Calif. Assn. Behavior Analysis (hon. life, pres., conf. chmn., Outstanding Contbr. to Behavior Analysis award 1997), Cambridge Ctr. for Behavioral Studies (adv. bd.), Calif. Assn. Sch. Psychologists (chmn. practitioners conf. 1994—). Avocations: horseback riding, fishing, swimming. Home: 10735 Frank Daniels Way San Diego CA 92131- Personal E-mail: grmayer@aol.com.

MAYER, JAMES HOCK, lawyer, mediator; b. Neptune City, NJ, Nov. 1, 1935; s. J. Kenneth and Marie Ruth (Hock) M.; m. Carol I. Keating, Sept. 20, 1958 (div. Feb. 1981); children: Craig, Jeffrey; m. Patrisha Renk, Mar. 28, 1981 (div. July 2001); m. Judith Courtemanche, Mar. 23, 2004. AB with distinction, Dartmouth Coll., 1957; JD, Harvard U., 1964. Bar: Calif. 1965, US Dist. Ct (no. dist., so. dist.) Calif. 1965, US Ct. Appeals (9th cir.) 1965, US Supreme Ct. 1974. Assoc. Pillsbury, Madison & Sutro, San Francisco, 1964—72, ptnr., 1973—; ind. mediator, 1992—. Rear adm. USNR, 1957-93. Rufus Choate scholar Dartmouth Coll., 1956-57. Mem. Newcomen Soc., Navy League, Naval Order of US, Naval War Coll. Found. (regional v.p.), Harvard Club, La Jolla Country Club, La Jolla Beach and Tennis Club. Office: Mayer Mediation Svcs 7924 Ivanhoe Ave Ste 3 La Jolla CA 92037 Home: 2370 Avenida de La Playa La Jolla CA 92037 Office Phone: 858-551-5525. Business E-Mail: just-results@msn.com.

MAYER, MARISSA ANN, information technology executive; b. Wausau, Wis., May 30, 1975; BS in Symbolic Sys., with honors, Stanford U., MS in Computer Sci. With UBS rsch. lab, Zurich, Switzerland, SRI Internat., Menlo Park, Calif.; programmer, software engr. Google Inc., 1999, dir. consumer web products Mountain View, v.p. search products & user experience. Tchr. computer programming Stanford U. Recipient Centennial Tchg. award, Stanford U., Forsythe award; named a Maverick, Details mag., 2008; named one of 25 Masters of Innovation, BusinessWeek, 2006, America 's Top Women in Bus.-Game Changers, Pink mag. & Forté Found., 2007, 50 Most Important People on the Web, PC World, 2007, 50 Most Powerful Women in Bus., Fortune mag., 2008, Most Influential Women in Technology, Fast Company, 2009. Office: Google Inc 1600 Amphitheatre Pky Mountain View CA 94043 Office Phone: 650-253-0000. Office Fax: 650-253-0001. E-mail: marissa@google.com.

MAYER, RICHARD EDWIN, psychology professor; b. Chgo., Feb. 8, 1947; s. James S. and Bernis (Lowy) M.; m. Beverly Linn Pastor, Dec. 19, 1971; children: Kenneth Michael, David Mark, Sarah Ann. BA with honors, Miami U., Oxford, Ohio, 1969; MS in Psychology, U. Mich., 1971, PhD in Psychology, 1973. Vis. asst. prof. Ind. U., Bloomington, 1973-75; asst. prof. psychology U. Calif., Santa Barbara, 1975-80, assoc. prof., 1980-85, prof., 1985—, pres., chmn. dept., 1987-90. Vis. scholar Learning Rsch. and Devel. Ctr., U. Pitts., 1979, Ctr. for Study of Reading, U. Ill., 1984. Author: Foundations of Learning and Memory, 1979, The Promise of Cognitive Psychology, 1981, Thinking, Problem Solving, Cognition, 1983, 2d edit., 1992, BASIC: A Short Course, 1985, Educational Psychology, 1987, The Critical Thinker, 1990, 2d edit., 1995, The Promise of Educational Psychology, Vol. I, 1999, Vol. II, 2002, Multimedia Learning, 2001, Learning and Instruction, 2003, (with R. Clark) E-Learning and the Science of Instruction, 2004, Cambridge Handbook of Multimedia Learning, 2005; editor: Human Reasoning, 1980, Teaching and Learning Computer Programming, 1988; editor jours. Instructional Sci., 1983-87, Educational Psychologist, 1983-89. Sch. bd. officer Goleta (Calif.) Union Sch. Dist., 1981—. Grantee, NSF, 1975—88, 1991—. Fellow APA (divsn. 15 officer 1987—, G. Stanley Hall lectr. 1988, E.L. Thorndike award 2000), Am. Psychol. Soc.; mem. Am. Ednl. Rsch. Assn. (divsn. C officer 1986-88, 2007-), Psychonomic Soc. Democrat. Jewish. Avocations: computers, hiking, bicycling, reading, dogs. Office: U Calif Dept Of Psychology Santa Barbara CA 93016 Home Phone: 805-964-5936. Business E-Mail: mayer@psych.ucsb.edu.

MAYERI, BEVERLY, artist, ceramic sculptor, educator; b. NYC, Nov. 2, 1944; d. Bernard and Cora (Wisoff) Howard; m. Earl Melchior Mayeri, Sept. 1, 1968; 1 child, Rachel Theresa. BA, U. Calif., Berkeley, 1967; MA in Art and Sculpture, San Francisco State U., 1976. Tchr. Foothill Coll., Los Altos Hills, 1990, Natsoulas Gallery, 1992, U. Minn., Mpls., 1993, Sonoma Stae U., Rohnert Park, Calif., 1994, Mendocino (Calif.) Art Ctr., 1995, Fresno State U., 1996, CCAC, Oakland, Calif., 1996, Edinboro (Pa.) U., 1997, Scropps Coll., Claremont, Clif., 1999, Cuesta Coll., San Luis Obispo, Calif., 2001, San Diego State U., 2002. Artist: solo exhibitions include Palo Alto (Calif.) Cultural Ctr., 1979, Ivory/Kimpton Gallery, San Francisco, 1981, 83, Garth Clark Gallery, N.Y., 1985, 87, Esther Saks Gallery, Chgo., 1988, 90, Dorothy Weiss Gallery, San Francisco, 1990, 92, 94, 96, 98, 2000, San Jose Inst. Contemporary Art, 1990, Robert Kidd Gallery, Birmingham, Mich., 1993, Perimeter Gallery, Chgo., 1998, Susan Cummins Callery, Mill Valley, Calif., 2002; group exhibitions include San Francisco Mus. of Art, Northern Calif. Clay Routes: Sculpture Now, 1979, Smithsonian Instn., Renwick Gallery, 1981, Prieto Meml. Gallery, Mills Coll., Oakland, Calif. 1982, Crocker Art Mus., San Francisco, 1983, Euphrate Gallery, De Anza Coll., Cupertino, Calif., 1984, 88, Fisher Gallery, U. So. Calif., L.A., traveled to Pratt Inst., N.Y.C., 1984, Arts Commn. Gallery, San Francisco, 1984, Signet Arts Gallery, St. Louis (two person show), 1984, Garth Clark Gallery, N.Y., 1985, Robert L. Kidd Gallery, Birmingham, Mich., Animals Contemporary Vision, Major Concepts: Clay, 1986, Fresno (Calif.) Arts Ctr. and Mus., 1987, Canton (Ohio) Art Inst., 1991, Soc. for Contemporary Crafts, Pitts., 1992, Triton Mus. of Art, Santa Clara, Calif., 1992, Nat. Mus. of History Taipei, Taiwan, 1993, Lew Allen Gallery, Santa Fe, New Mex., 1993, Perimeter Gallery, 1995, Duane Reed Gallery, St. Louis, 1997, Scripps Coll., 1999, LACMA, L.A., 2000, Calif. State U., Chico, 2001, Clay Studio, Phila., 2001; works in pub. and private collections include: Nat. Mus. History, Taipei, Canton Art Inst., Long Beach (Calif.) Parks and Recreation, L.A. Arts Commn., Mr. and Mrs. Eric Lidow, L.A., Alfred Shands, Louisville, Mrs. Audrey Landy, Atlanta, Karen Johnson Boyd, Racine, Wis., Alan and Esther Saks, Chgo., Gloria and Sonny Kamm, L.A. County Mus. Art. Founder Marin Women Artists, Marin County, Calif., 1974-84. Recipient fellowship visual artist NEA, Washington, 1982, 88; grantee: Marin Arts Coun., 1987, Virgina A. Groot Found., 1991. Avocations: painting, hiking, skiing, gardening, environmentalist. Office: Dorothy Weiss Gallery 3 Indian Gulch Rd Piedmont CA 94611-3527

MAYHEW, ERIC GEORGE, medical researcher, educator, consultant; b. London, June 22, 1938; came to U.S., 1964; s. George James and Doris Ivy (Tipping) M.; m. Barbara Doe, Sept. 28, 1966 (div. 1976); 1 child, Miles; m. Karen Caruana, Apr. 1, 1978 (div. 1994); children: Ian, Andrea; m. Ludmila Khatchatrian, June 29, 1995. BS, U. London, 1960, MS, 1963, PhD, 1967, DSc, 1993. Rsch. asst. Chester Beatty Rsch. Inst., London, 1960—64; cancer rsch. scientist Roswell Pk. Meml. Inst., Buffalo, 1964—68, sr. cancer rsch. scientist, 1968—72, assoc. cancer rsch. scientist, 1979—83, dep. dir. exptl. pathology, 1988—93; prin. scientist The Liposome Co., Princeton, NJ, 1993—99, May Pharm Consulting, 2000—. Assoc. rsch. prof. SUNY, Buffalo, 1979-93; ad-hoc mem. NIH study sects., 1982-94; cons. to industry, 2000-. Editor jour. Selective Cancer Therapeutics, 1989-91; contbr. articles to Jour. Nat. Cancer Inst., Cancer Rsch. and many other profl. jours. Grantee NIH, Am. Heart Assn., and pvt. industry, 1972-93. Mem. Am. Assn. Cancer Rsch., N.Y. Acad. Sci. Achievements include development of liposomes for drug delivery and patents for new chemical entities and liposome delivery. Office: May Pharm Consulting 1782 S Seaview Ave Coupeville WA 98239 Home Phone: 360-678-2175.

MAYHEW, KARIN D., health and medical products executive; BA, Fordham U., NY; M, Wesleyan U., Middletown, Conn.; grad. Smith Coll. Mgmt. Program, U. Mich. Advanced Human Resources Exec. Program. Sr. v.p. orgn. devel. So. New Eng. Telecom. Corp.; with Health Net, Inc., Woodland Hills, Calif., 1999—, sr. v.p. orgn. effectiveness. Lectr. Babson Coll. Ctr. Exec. Edn., Wellesley, Mass. Office: Health Net Inc 21650 Oxnard St Woodland Hills CA 91367 Office Phone: 818-676-6000.

MAYNARD, KENNETH DOUGLAS, architect; b. Hackensack, NJ, Aug. 16, 1931; s. Douglas Harry and Eva (Whiting) M.; m. Myrna Myrtle James, Feb. 4, 1956; children: Colin, Vivien Noll. Cert. in Architecture, U. Natal, Durban, Republic of South Africa, 1958. Registered arch. 2008. Draftsman Morross & Graff, Johannesburg, Republic of South Africa, 1950-51, Anglo-Am. Corp., Johannesburg, Republic of South Africa, 1951-54, Moir & Llewellyn, Empangeni, Zululand, Republic of South Africa, 1955-57; architect Pearse Aneck-Hahn & Bristol, Johannesburg, 1957-60, Manley & Mayer, Anchorage, 1960-61, FAA, Anchorage, 1961-62, Crittenden Cassetta Wirum & Jacobs, Anchorage, 1962-65; prin. Schultz & Maynard, Anchorage, 1965-68, Kenneth Maynard Assocs., Anchorage, 1968-78; pres. Maynard & Partch, Anchorage, 1978-96; prin. USKH, Inc., Anchorage, 1996—. Active Western Alaska Coun. Boy Scouts. Am., Anchorage, 1965-84; bd. dirs. Salvation Army Adv. Bd., Anchorage, 1981-87, Anchorage Mus. Assn., 1969-86, Anchorage Opera Co., 1983-90; chmn. Mayor's Comprehensive Homeless Program Strategy Group, 1992-94. Fellow: AIA (pres. Alaska chpt. 1969, NW regional rep. for nat. com. on design 1976—89, nat. bd. 1999—2001); mem.: Constrn. Specification Inst. (pres. Cook Inlet chpt. 1993—94). Republican. Avocations: reading, travel. Home: 2237 Forest Park Dr Anchorage AK 99517-1324 Office: USKH 2515 A St Anchorage AK 99503-2776 Business E-Mail: kenmaynard@alaska.net.

MAYNARD, STEVEN HARRY, writer; b. San Diego, July 4, 1954; s. Harry Clark and Ruby Kristina (Odna). BA in Communications, U. Wash., 1976; MA in Theology, Fuller Theol. Seminary, 1979. Religion writer, gen. news reporter Walla Walla (Wash.) Union-Bulletin, 1979-84; religion writer Houston Chronicle, 1984-87; reporter religion South King County The News Tribune, Tacoma, 1987—. Recipient Mng. Editors award Tex. Associated Press, 1984, Wilbur award Religious Pub. Relations Council, 1981. Mem. Religion Newswriters Assn. Office: 1950 S State St Tacoma WA 98405-2817 Office Phone: 253-597-8647.

MAYNE, KAREN, state legislator; widowed; 2 children. Graduated, Henagers Bus. Coll. Para-educator Granite Sch. Dist.; mem. Dist. 5 Utah State Senate, 2008—. Democrat. Office: W115 State Capitol Complex Salt Lake City UT 84114 Mailing: 5044 W Bannock Cir West Valley City UT 84120 Home Phone: 801-968-7756; Office Phone: 801-538-1035. Office Fax: 801-326-1475. Business E-Mail: kmayne@utahsenate.org.

MAYNE, THOM, architect; b. Waterbury, Conn., Jan. 19, 1944; s. Walter and Bernice (Gornall) M.; m. Susan Burnham, Sept. 10, 1964 (div. 1970); 1 child, Richard; m. Blythe Alison Mayne, Aug. 8, 1981; children: Sam, Cooper. BArch, U. So. Calif., 1968; MArch, Harvard U., 1978. Mem. faculty UCLA Sch. Art and Architecture, Santa Monica, Calif., 1972—; bd. dirs. So. Calif. Inst. Architecture, Santa Monica, Calif., 1983—; architect Morphosis, Santa Monica, Calif. Adj. prof. UCLA, 1993; mem. vis. faculty Calif. State Coll., Pomona, 1971, Miami U., Ohio, 1982, Washington U., St. Louis, 1984, U. Tex., Austin, 1984, U. Pa., 1985, Columbia U., NYC, 1986, Harvard U., 1988, Clemson U., 1991, Yale U., 1991, UCLA, 1986, 92, U. Ill., Urbana-Champaign, 1992-93, Tech. U., Vienna, Austria, 1993, Berlage Inst., Amsterdam, 1993, Hochschule für Andgewandt Kunst, Vienna, 1991, 93; lectr. in field; adjudicator numerous awards. Archtl. one-man exhbns. include 2 AES Gallery, San Francisco, 1988, Cheney Cowles Mus., Spokane, Wash., 1989, Walker Arts Ctr., Mpls., 1989, Gallery of Architecture, LA, 1989, Contemporary Arts Ctr., Cin., 1989, San Francisco Mus. Modern Art, 1990, Graham Found., Chgo., 1990, Aedes Galerie and Architecture Forum, Berlin, 1990, Fenster Architekturgalerie, Frankfurt, Germany, 1990, Gallery MA, Toyko, 1990, Laguna (Calif.) Art Mus., 1991, G201 Gallery, Ohio, 1991, 1-Space Gallery, Chgo., 1992, Sadock & Uzzan Galerie, Paris, 1992, Diane Farris Gallery, 1993; group exhbns. include Umwelt Galerie, Stuttgart, Germany, 1978, The Archtl. Gallery, Venice, Calif., 1979, La Jolla (Calif.) Mus. of Contemporary Art, 1982, Inst. Contemporary Arts, London, 1983, Archtl. Assn., London, 1983, NAD, NYC, 1983, 88, Mus. Modern Art, San Francisco, 1983, Calif. Mus. Sci. and Industry, 1984, G.A. Gallery, Tokyo, 1985, 87, 90, Max Protech Gallery, NYC, 1985, 86, I.D.C., NYC, 1986, Axis Gallery, Tokyo, Milan, Paris, 1988, Pacific Design Ctr., LA, 1988, Australia Ctr. for Contemporary Arts, Victoria, 1988, Cooper-Hewitt Mus., NYC, 1988, Aedes Galerie für Architektur und Raum, Berlin, 1988, Kirsten Kiser Gallery, 1988, 89, Visual Arts Ontario, Toronto, 1988, Gallery Functional Art, Santa Monica, Calif., 1989, Deutsches Architektur Mus., Frankfurt, 1989, USIA, Moscow, 1989-90, Lameier Sculpture Park, St. Louis, 1989, Gwenda Jay Gallery, Chgo., 1990, Sadock & Uzzan Galerie, 1991, Bannatyne Gallery, Santa Monica, 1991, ROM Galleri for Arkitektur, Oslo, 1992, 65 Thompson Street Gallery, NYC, 1992; archtl. projects include Sequoyah Edn. and Rsch. Ctr., Santa Monica, 1977 (Progressive Architecture award 1974), Flores Residence, 1979 (Progressive Architecture award 1980), Sedlak Residence, 1980 (AIA award 1981), Western Melrose Office Bldg, 1981 (Progresstive Architecture award 1982), Hermosa Beach Ctrl. Bus. Dist. (Progressive Architecture award 1984), 72 Market Street Restaurant, 1983 (AIA award 1985, CCAIA award 1986), Bergren Residence, 1984 (AIA award 1985, CCAIA award 1986, Nat. AIA award 1986), Cedar Sinai Comprehensive Cancer Ctr., L.A., 1988 (Progressive Architecture award 1987, AIA award 1988, CCAIA award 1989), Arts Park Performing Pavilion, 1988, (Progressive Architecture award 1989), Leon Max Showroom, LA, 1988 (CCAIA award 1990, Archtl. Record Interior award 1990), Club Post Nulear, Laguna Beach, Calif., 1988, Berlin Wall Competition, 1988, Expo '90 Folly, Osaka, Japan, 1989, The Emery Ctr. Performing Arts, 1989, Temple U. CCC, Phila., 1989, Politix, 1990 (AIA award 1990), Salick Health Care Corp. Hdqs., 1990 (AIA award 1992, CCAIA award 1993), Visual Performing Arts Sch. at Thomas More Coll., Crestview, NY, 1990, MTV Studios, LA, 1990, Higashi Azabu Tower, Tokyo, 1991, Yuzen Vintage Car Mus., LA, 1991 (AIA award 1993), Disney Inst. and Town Ctr. Competition, Orlando, Fla., 1991, Cranbrook Acad. Gatehouse Competition (Pilkington Planar prize 1993), Spreebogen Master Plan, Berlin, 1993, Check Point Charlie Office Bldg., Berlin, 1993; contbr. articles to profl. jours. Rome Prize fellow Am. Acad. Rome, 1987; recipient Architecture award Am. Acad. Arts and Letters, 1992, Pritzker Architecture prize Hyatt Found., 2005. Fellow Am. Acad. Arts and Sciences; mem. AIA, Am. Acad. Design. Democrat. Avocations: skiing, travel. Office: Morphosis Architecture 2041 Colorado Ave Santa Monica CA 90404-3415 Office Phone: 310-570-0123. Business E-Mail: t.mayne@morphosis.net.

MAYO, ROBERT N., computer science researcher; b. Washington, Aug. 23, 1959; s. Robert P. and Marian A. Mayo. BS in Computer Sci., Washington U., St. Louis, 1981; MS in Computer Sci., U. Calif., Berkeley, 1983, PhD of Computer Sci., 1987. Asst. prof. U. Wis., Madison, 1988; staff Digital Equipment Corp./Compaq Computer/Hewlett Packard, Palo Alto, Calif., 1989—2006; cons., 2007—. Mem. IEEE, Assn. Computer Machinery. Home: 2800 Elliott Ave Apt 624 Seattle WA 98121

MAYO, STEPHEN L., biochemist; BS in Chemistry, Pa. State U., 1983; PhD in Chemistry, Calif. Inst. Tech., 1987; postdoctoral study, U. Calif., Berkeley, 1988—89. Co-founder Molecular Simulations, Inc., 1984, v.p. bio. scis., 1989—90; sr. rsch. fellow Calif. Inst. Tech., 1991—92, asst. prof. biology, 1992—98, assoc. prof., 1998—2001, assoc. prof. biology and chemistry, 2001—; asst. investigator Howard Hughes Med. Inst., 1994—2000, assoc. investigator, 2000—. Adj. asst. prof. U. So. Calif. Sch. Medicine, 1994—. Recipient Scholar award, Rita Allen Found., 1993—98, Searle, 1994—97, prize, Johnson Found., 1997; fellow, Packard Found., 1993—98; Miller Rsch. fellowship, 1988—89. Mem.: NAS. Office: Calif Inst Tech Divsn Biology Mail Code 114-96 Pasadena CA 91125 Business E-Mail: steve@mayo.caltech.edu.

MAYORKAS, ALEJANDRO, lawyer, former prosecutor; b. Cuba; With Patterson, Belknap, Webb & Tyler, LA, 1986-89; asst. U.S. atty., 1989-99; chief office's gen. crimes sect., 1996-98; U.S. atty. cen. dist. Calif. U.S. Dept. Justice, 1999—2001; ptnr. O'Melveny & Myers, LA, 2001—. Tchr. trial advocacy Loyola Law Sch., 1997-98. Office: O'Melveny & Myers 400 S Hope St Los Angeles CA 90071-2899 Office Phone: 213-430-6363. Business E-Mail: amayorkas@omm.com.

MAZO, ROBERT MARC, retired chemistry professor; b. Bklyn., Oct. 3, 1930; s. Nathan and Rose Marion (Mazo) M.; m. Joan Ruth Spector, Sept. 5, 1954; children: Ruth, Jeffrey, Daniel. BA, Harvard U., 1952; MS, Yale U., 1953, PhD, 1955. Rsch. assoc. U. Chgo., 1956-58; asst. prof. Calif. Inst. Tech., 1958-62; assoc. prof. U. Oreg., Eugene, 1962-65, prof. chemistry, 1965-95, prof. emeritus, 1996, head chemistry dept., 1978-81, dir. Inst. Theoretical Sci., 1964-67, 84-87, assoc. dean Grad. Sch., 1967-71; program dir. NSF, 1977-78. Alfred P. Sloan fellow, NSF Sr. Postdoctoral fellow, vis. prof. U. Libre de Bruxelles, Belgium, 1968-69; vis. prof. Technische Hochschule Aachen, Weizmann Inst., Rehovoth, Israel, 1981-82, U. New South Wales, Australia, 1989. Author: Statistical Mechanical Theories of Transport Processes, 1967, Brownian Motion, 2002, also rsch. articles. NSF Postdoctoral fellow U. Amsterdam, Netherlands, 1955-56. Fellow Am. Phys. Soc. Home: 2460 Charnelton St Eugene OR 97405-3214 Office: U Oreg Inst Theoretical Sci Eugene OR 97403 Home Phone: 541-344-0807; Office Phone: 541-346-5224. Business E-Mail: mazo@uoregon.edu.

MAZURSKY, PAUL, screenwriter, theatrical director and producer; b. Bklyn., Apr. 25, 1930; s. David and Jean (Gerson) M.; m. Betsy Purdy, Mar. 12, 1953; children— Meg, Jill. BA, Bklyn. Coll., 1951. Actor, star, TV and Films, 1951—, including film Deathwatch, Miami Rhapsody, 1995, (voice) The Majestic, 2001, Do it for Uncle Manny, 2002; (TV series) Once & Again, 1999-2001; night club comedian,

1954-60; writer Danny Kaye Show, 1963-67; co-writer film I Love You, Alice B. Toklas, 1968; writer, dir. films Bob & Carol & Ted & Alice, 1969, Alex in Wonderland, 1970, Blume in Love, 1972, Harry & Tonto, 1973, Next Stop, Greenwich Village, 1976, An Unmarried Woman, 1977-78, Willie & Phil, 1979-80, Tempest, 1982, Moscow on the Hudson, 1984; writer, prodr., dir. films Down and Out in Beverly Hills, 1986, Moon Over Parador, 1988; co-scriptwriter, prodr., dir. film Enemies, A Love Story, 1989, Scenes From a Mall, 1990, The Pickle, 1992, Faithful, 1995, Winchell, 1998, Coast to Coast, 2003.

MCALEER, WILLIAM HARRISON, technology venture capitalist; b. Pitts., Feb. 14, 1951; s. William Kearns and Helen (Harrison) McA.; m. Colleen McGinn, Aug. 9, 1975; children: William F., Lindsay J. BS, Cornell U., 1973, MBA, 1975. CPA, Wash. Sr. acct. KPMG-Peat Marwick, Seattle, 1975-78; v.p. Westin Hotels, Seattle, 1978-87; v.p. finance, CFO Ecova Corp., Seattle, 1987-88; v.p. fin., CFO, sec. Aldus Corp., Seattle, 1988-94; pres. e.liance Ptnrs.; co-founder, mng. dir. Voyager Capital, Seattle, 1996—. Bd. dirs. Avocent Corp., Valcatemy, Meloded Commerce. Pres., dir. Seattle Jr. C. of C., 1977-82; bd. dirs. Big Bros. King County, Seattle, 1994—. Mem. Fin. Execs. Ins., Software Pub. Assn., Wash. Software Assn., Evergreen Venture Capital Assn., Wash. Soc. CPAs, Cornell Alumni Club, Columbia Tower Club, Sand Point Country Club. Avocations: hiking, travel, golf, boating, gardening. Home: 3137 W Laurelhurst Dr NE Seattle WA 98105-5358 E-mail: mcaleer@voyagercap.com.

MCALISTER, MICHAEL H., architect; b. Calif. s. Doyle R. and Mary E. McAlister. AA, Bakersfield Coll.; BArch, Calif. Poly. U. Planning technician Bakersfield (Calif.) City Hall, 1963; carpenter Del Webb Corp., Kern City, Calif., 1964; archtl. draftsman Goss & Choy Archs., Bakersfield, 1965-67; arch., v.p. D.G.C. & Assocs., Bakersfield, 1971-80; dir. architecture, v.p. N.B.A. & Assocs., Archs., Bakersfield, 1980-83; arch. Michael H. McAlister, A.I.A., Bakersfield, 1983—. Nepthrology design cons. for various treatment groups and hosps., 1987—. Commr., archtl. advisor Hist. Preservation Commn., Bakersfield, 1986-87; bd. dirs. Camp Fire Coun., Kern County, Calif., 1980-84 Recipient Archtl. Pub. Bldg. Hist. award Beautiful Bakersfield Com., City of Bakersfield's City Coun. and Hist. Preservation Commn., 1985, 87, Exterior Environ. Design Excellence Bakersfield C. of C., 1988, Comml. Design Excellence award, 1984, Design Excellence and Beautification award City of Taft, Calif., 1989, Design Excellence award State of Nev., 1992, Beautiful Bakersfield Archtl. Comml. Remodel award, 2003 Mem. AIA (Calif. Coun., Golden Empire chpt.). Avocation: religious architecture and art. Office: 1302 Ironstone Dr Studio 201 Bakersfield CA 93312-4668

MCALLISTER, JAMES PATTERSON, II, research scientist, educator; b. Ann Arbor, Mich., Jan. 19, 1948; m. Elizabeth Ann Cacciatore, June 5, 1978 (div. 1983); m. Phyllis Ann Meyer, Jan. 9, 1999; 1 child, Elysha. BA, Earlham Coll., Richmond, Ind., 1970; PhD, Purdue U., West Lafayette, Ind., 1976. Sci. tchr. Eaton HS, Ohio, 1970—71; postdoc. fellow U. Vt. Coll. Medicine, Burlington, 1977—78; rsch. assoc. UCLA Mental Retardation Rsch. Ctr., 1978—81; assoc., asst. prof. Temple U. Sch. Medicine, Phila., 1981—93; assoc. prof. Cleve. Clinic Found., 1993—97; prof., dir. neurosurgical rsch. Wayne State U. Sch. Medicine, Detroit, 1997—2007; prof., dir. basic hydrocephalus rsch. Primary Children's Med. Ctr., U. Utah, Salt Lake City, 2007—. Med. adv. bd. Hydrocephalus Assn., San Francisco, 2005—; sci. reviewer NIH, Bethesda, Md., 2006—; exec. bd. BrainChild Found., Cave Creek, Ariz., 2007—. Contbr. scientific papers to profl. jours., chapters to books. Cons. STARS Hydrocephalus Support Group, Detroit, 1997—2008. Recipient Robert H. Pudenz award, Internat. Soc. Pediatric Neurosurgery, 2005. Mem.: Soc. Rsch. Hydrocephalus and Spina Bifida, Pediatric Sect., Soc. Neuroscience, Am. Assn. of Neurol. Surgeons (assoc.). Independent. Achievements include patents in field. Avocations: running, hiking, gardening, cooking. Office: Dept Neurosurgery 175 N Medical Dr E Salt Lake City UT 84132

MCALLISTER, KIRK W., lawyer; b. San Francisco, Apr. 18, 1944; BA, Stanford U., 1966; JD, U. So. Calif., 1969. Bar: Calif. 1970, US Dist. Ct., Ea. Dist. Calif. Prosecutor Stanislaus County, 1972—83; civil litigator Zuckerman, Hartmann and Walden, 1983—86; pvt. practice, atty./ptnr. criminal law, civil litigation McAllister & McAllister Law Firm, 1986—. Tchr. evidence Calif. State U., Stanislaus. Capt. US Army, 1970—72. Mem.: ATLA, Stanislaus Country Criminal Ct. Bar Assn. (pres. 1990—92), Calif. Atty. Criminal Justice, Consumer Atty. Calif., ABA, Tuolumne County Bar Assn., Stanislaus County Bar Assn. Avocations: art, acting, trap shooting. Office: 1012 11th St Ste 100 Modesto CA 95354 Office Phone: 209-575-4844. Office Fax: 209-575-0240. Business E-Mail: mcallister@mcallister.com.

MCANDREWS, BRIAN PATRICK, computer software company executive; AB in Economics, Harvard U., Cambridge, Mass.; MBA, Stanford U. Grad. Sch. Bus., Calif. Product mgr. Gen. Mills, Inc., 1984—89; exec. positions at ABC Sports, ABC Entertainment and ABC TV Network including exec. v.p. and gen. mgr. of ABC Sports ABC, 1990—99; CEO, bd. dirs. aQuantive, Inc.(acquired by Microsoft Corp.), Seattle, 1999—2007, pres., 2000—07; sr. v.p., advertiser and publisher solutions (APS) group aQuantive, Inc.(a wholly owned subs. Microsoft Corp.), Seattle, 2007—. Bd. dirs. Blue Nile, Inc., 2004—, Advt. Rsch. Found., Whitepages.com, Inc., aQuantive, Inc., 1999—, Fisher Comm., 2006—. Named Digital Exec. of Yr., Advt. Age, 2008; named one of 50 Who Matter Now, CNNMoney.com Bus. 2.0, 2006, 2007. Mem.: Nat. Assn. Corp. Dirs. (bd. dirs Seattle-N.W. chpt.). Office: aQuantive Inc 821 2nd Ave Ste 1800 Seattle WA 98104

MCANELLY, ROBERT D., physiatrist; b. Austin, Tex., Jan. 31, 1958; s. Robert C. and Betty J. McAnelly; m. Suzanne Marie Blickhan, Aug. 18, 1990. BS in Engring., Calif. Inst. Tech., 1979, BS in Physics, 1980; MD, U. Tex., 1987. Diplomate Am. Bd. Phys. Medicine and Rehab. Aerospace engr. Vought Corp., Dallas, 1980-82; resident U. Kans., Kansas City, 1987-91, chief resident, 1990-91; asst. prof. U. Tex. Health Scis. Ctr., San Antonio, 1991-98; dir. movement analysis lab. U. Tex., San Antonio, 1994-98; physiatrist Desert Rehab., Las Vegas, Nev., 1998-2000, Mountain Rehab., Las Vegas, 2000—. Contbr. chpt. Physical Medicine and Rehabilitation, 1996, 00, Cancer Rehabilitation, 1994. Mem. Assn. Acad. Physiatrists (mem. com. 1993—), Paralyzed Vets. Am. (assoc.). Avocations: gardening, music.

MCANIFF, EDWARD JOHN, lawyer; b. NYC, June 29, 1934; s. John Edward and Josephine (Toomey); m. Jane Reiss, June 11, 1960; children: John E., Maura T., Anne T. Annick, Jane A., Peter J., Kathleen A. AB magna cum laude, Holy Cross Coll., 1956; LLB cum laude, NYU, 1961. Bar: N.Y. 1962, Calif. 1963, D.C. 1976. Law clk. to Justice A.T. Goodwin Supreme Ct. Oreg., Salem, 1961-62; ptnr., of counsel O'Melveny & Myers, LA, 1962—. Adj. prof. Sch. Law Stanford U., 1974-75, 94-98, Boalt Hall Law Sch., 1992-95, UCLA Law Sch., 1996—; vis. prof. U. Oreg. Law Sch., 1999—; fgn. law counsel Freehill, Hollingdale & Page, Sydney, 1981-82; bd. dirs. Mellon Fin. Corp. Bd. dirs. L.A. Master Chorale, 1979-81, 87—, chmn., 1996—; dir., exec. com. Perf. Art Ctr. Los Angeles County, 1992—; bd. dirs. Music Ctr. Found., 1992—. Capt. USNR, 1956-87. Republican. Office: O Melveny & Myers 400 S Hope St Ste 1717 Los Angeles CA 90071-2899 E-mail: tmcaniff@omm.com.

MCANIFF, RICHARD, computer software company executive; married; 5 children. BS in Economics, U. Mass. Amherst, 1971, M in Resource Economics, 1976; M in Systems and Indsl. Engring., U. Ariz. Mem. tech. staff Sandia Nat. Laboratories, Albuquerque; joined Microsoft Corp., Redmond, Wash., 1987, sr. prog. mgr. Access 1.0 database, group prog. mgr. LAN Mgr. group, head FoxPro Database Product Unit, gen. mgr. Visual Basic devel. system, corp. v.p. Microsoft Office. Exec. alumnus U. Mass./Microsoft Partnership. Avocations: snowboarding, windsurfing, rock climbing. Office: Microsoft Corp One Microsoft Way Redmond WA 98052-6399

MCANINCH, JACK WELDON, urological surgeon, educator; b. Merkel, Tex., Mar. 17, 1936; s. Weldon Thomas and Margaret (Canon) McA.; m. Barbara B. Buchanan, Dec. 29, 1960 (div. Aug. 1972); m. Burnet B. Sumner, Dec. 29, 1987; children: David A., Todd G., Brendan J. BS, Tex. Tech U., 1958; MS, U. Idaho, 1960; MD, U. Tex., 1964. Diplomate Am. Bd. Urology (trustee 1991-97, pres. 1996-97). Commd. capt. U.S. Army, 1964-66, advanced through grades to col., 1977, ret., 1977; col. USAR; intern then resident Letterman Army Med. Ctr., San Francisco, 1964-69; chief urol. surgery San Francisco Gen. Hosp., 1977—; prof. urol. surgery U. Calif., San Francisco, 1977—. Editor: Urogenital Trauma, 1985, Urologic Clinics of North America, 1989, Smith's gen. Urology, 1995; section editor: Early Care of Injured Patient, 1990, Traumatic and Reconstructive Urology, 1996. Col. US Army, 1964-72. Recipient Disting. Alumnus award Tex. Tech U., 1994; named Disting. Alumnus U. Idaho, 1997. Fellow ACS (govt. 1992-97, regent 1998—); mem. Am. Urol. Assn. (pres. we. sect. 1992-93, bd. dirs. 1990—, pres. 1996-97), Genitourinary Reconstructive Surgeons (pres.), Am. Assn. Surgery Trauma (v.p.), Soc. U. Urologists, Am. Bd. Urology (pres. 1996-97). Office: San Francisco Gen Hosp Dept Urology 1001 Potrero Ave San Francisco CA 94110-3594 Home Phone: 415-282-1149; Office Phone: 415-476-3372. Business E-Mail: jmcaninch@urology.ucsf.edu.

MCARTHUR, ELDON DURANT, geneticist, researcher; b. Hurricane, Utah, Mar. 12, 1941; s. Eldon and Denise (Dalton) McA.; m. Virginia Johnson, Dec. 20, 1963; children: Curtis D., Monica McArthur Bennion, Denise McArthur Johnson, Ted O. AS with high honors, Dixie Coll., 1963; BS cum laude, U. Utah, 1965, MS, 1967, PhD, 1970. Postdoctoral rsch. fellow, dept. demonstrator Agrl. Rsch. Coun. Gt. Britain, Leeds, Eng., 1970-71; rsch. geneticist Intermountain Rsch. Sta. USDA Forest Svc., Ephraim, Utah, 1972-75, rsch. geneticist Shrub Scis. Lab., Intermountain Rsch. Sta. Provo, Utah, 1975-83, project leader, chief rsch. geneticist, 1983-97, Rocky Mountain Rsch. Sta., USDA Forest Svc., Provo, 1997—2006, program mgr., 2006—. Adj. prof. dept. plant and wildlife scis. Brigham Young U., Provo, 1976—. Author more than 425 rsch. papers; contbr. chpts. to books; editor symposium procs. Named USDA Forest Svc. Superior Scientist, 1990, Disting. Scientist, 1996; Sigma Xi grantee, 1970, NSF grantee, 1981, 85, 96, Coop. State Rsch., Svc. grantee, 1986, 91; recipient Eminent Sci. Publ. award Rocky Mtn. Rsch. Station, 2001, New Century of Svc. award 2002, USDI BLM Svc. 1st award USDA Forest Svc., 2007. Mem. Soc. Range Mgmt. (pres. Utah sect. 1987, Outstanding Achievement award 1992, Utah sect. Range Mgr. of Yr. 2004), Botan. Soc. Am., Soc. Study Evolution, Am. Genetic Assn., Shrub Rsch. Consortium (chmn. 1983—, Disting. Svc. award 2002), Intermountain Consortium for Aridlands Rsch. (pres. 1991—). Mem. Lds Ch. Avocations: hiking, bicycling, basketball. Home: 555 N 1200 E Orem UT 84097-4350 Office: USDA Forest Svc Shrub Scis Lab 735 N 500 E Provo UT 84606-1856 Office Phone: 801-356-5112. Personal E-mail: edmdixie@aol.com. Business E-Mail: dmcarthur@fs.fed.us.

MCARTHUR, RICHARD, state legislator; b. Lake Forest, Ill., 1943; m. Trish McArthur; 1 child, Michele; 1 child, Kimberly. BA in. Econ., U. Calif., Davis. Ret. special agent Fed. Bur. Investigation; candidate Nev. State Assembly, Dist. 4, 2004; mem. Dist. 4 Nev. State Assembly, 2008—. Capt. USAF, 1966—72, Vietnam. Republican. Office: 401 South Carson St Room 4123 Carson City NV 89701 Home: 4640 Panoramic Ct Las Vegas NV 89129 Home Phone: 702-396-1065; Office Phone: 775-684-8829. Business E-Mail: rmcarthur@asm.state.nv.us.

MCARTHUR, STEVEN B., Internet company executive; B, Queen's U., Belfast; MBA, Harvard Bus. Sch. Strategy cons. Bain & Co., founder Toronto office; pres., CEO AOL Can. AOL, exec. v.p.; pres. North Am. Travel Group Expedia Inc.; pres. Classmates Online. Office: Classmates Online 21301 Burbank Blvd Woodland Hills CA 91367-6677

MCAULIFFE, ROSEMARY, state legislator; b. Camaro, Wash., Aug. 1, 1940; m to Jim; children: six, ten grandchildren. Member, Northshore Sch Bd, 77-91, president, 81-82; chairwoman, Bothell Downtown Management Association, 87-90; member, Food & Safety Handling Committee, Department Health, currently; member, Student Conduct Task Force, OSPI, currently; co-chairwoman, Joint Select Committee Education Restructuring, currently; member, Education Comn of States, currently; member, Students with Behav Disabilities Subcomt, Special Education Advisor Coun, currently; member, Food Safety Advisor Coun, currently; Washington State Senator, District 1, 93-, member, Envrion Qual & Water Resources & Higher Education Committees, currently, chairwoman, Education Committee, currently, Washington State Senate.Member, Association Children with Learning Disabilties, 76-82, Together for Drug-Free Youth Committee, 89 & Lake Health Committee, 97-98; appointed member, Northshore Juv Court Conf Committee, Diversion Committee, 78-80; repr, Washington Sch Director's Association Legislature Network, 90-91; member, Northshore Econ Develop Committee, currently; delegate, Pacific NW Econ Region, currently; owner & manager, Hollywood Sch House, currently. Outstanding Citizen Award for Excellence in Education, Washington PTA, 87; Outstanding Community Leader Award, Northshore Chamber of Commerce, 89; C P Johnson Humanitarian Award, 89, 90 & 91; Outstanding Serv Award, Champion for Children, PTA, 91; Appreciation Award, Northshore Sch District, 91; Legislator of Year, Washington Voc Association, 94; Golden Gavel Award, Washington Association Sch Administrator, 95 & 96. Northshore & Woodinville Chamber of Commerce. Democrat. Roman Catholic. Address: Bothell WA Mailing: 402A John A Cherberg Bldg PO Box 40482 Olympia WA 98504-0482 also: 403 Legislative Bldg PO Box 40401 Olympia WA 98504 Fax: Olympia Off: 360-786-1999. E-mail: mcauliff_ro@leg.wa.gov.

MCAVOY, JOHN MARTIN, plastic surgeon; b. White Plains, NY, Jan. 8, 1947; s. Joseph Patrick and Claire Margaret (Boucher) McAvoy; m. Laurel Ann Streeter, June 21, 1969; children: Holly, Ian. BS in Biology, Tufts U., Medford, Mass., 1968; MD, Tufts U., Boston, 1972. Cert. Am. Bd. Surgery, Am. Bd. Plastic Surgery, Nat. Bd. Med. Examiners, ACLS. Resident dept. surgery UCLA Med. Ctr., 1972—77, chief resident dept. surgery, 1976—77; resident plastic surgery U. Colo. Med. Ctr., Denver, 1977—79, chief resident plastic surgery, 1978—79; chief plastic surgery Santa Rosa Meml. Hosp., Calif., 1986—91; pvt. practice Santa Rosa, Calif., 1979—. Presenter in field. Contbg. editor: Hosp. Physician mag., 1976—81; contbr. articles to profl. jours. Youth baseball coach Santa Rosa Babe Ruth Rincon Valley Little League, 1992—96. Reinach-Turnesia Caddie scholar, Westchester County, 1964. Fellow: ACS; mem.: Am. Soc. Plastic Surgeons (membership com.), Calif. Soc. Plastic Surgeons (ins. mediation com.), Am. Soc. for Aesthetic Plastic Surgery. Avocations: woodworking, gardening, poetry. Office: 4773 Hoen Ave Santa Rosa CA 95405 Personal E-mail: dr.jmcavoy@yahoo.com.

MCBRAYER, SANDRA L., educational director, homeless outreach educator; AA, San Diego Mesa Coll., 1981; BA in Applied Arts and Scis., San Diego State U., 1986, MA in Edn., 1990. Cert. presch.-kindergarten, grs. 1-12, adult edn., Calif. Tchr. asst. group homes Oz, The Bridge, Gatehouse, 1984-87; tchr. Hillcrest Receiving Home, 1987-88, Juvenile Hall, 1987-88, Comprehensive Adolescent Treatment Ctr., 1987-88; head tchr. the Monarch HS, 1988-96; CEO The Children's Initiative, San Diego. Lectr., cons. Ctrs. Careers Edn., Sch. Tchr. Edn. San Diego State U., 1990—; collaborator sch. dists. State Dept. Edn., Equity/Homeless Office, 1992—; staff devel. tng.; adj. prof. Coll. Edn., San Diego (Calif.) State U. Recipient award Exceptional Vols. Svc. Family Care Ctr., 1988, San Diego's 10 Leadership award Sta. KGTV, 1991, Celebrate Literacy award Internat. Reading Assn., 1992, Women of Vision in Edn. award LWV San Diego, 1992, Disting. Alumna of Yr.-Edn. award San Diego State U., 1992, Golden Bell award Calif. Sch. Bds. Found., 1992, Coun. of State Sch. Officers Nat. Tchr. of Yr. award 1994; named San Diego County Tchr. of Yr. by San Diego County Office of Edn., 1993, Calif. Tchr. of Yr. by State Dept. Edn., 1993, Nat. Tchr. of Yr., Pres. Clinton, 1994, Tech. Tchr. of Yr., Coun. on Tech. Tchr. Edn., 1994, Exceptional Svc. award Calif. State PTA, Humanitarian award Youth Advocacy Assn., Living Legacy award Internat. Women's Ctr.; recognized by local and nat. news media. Mem. NEA, Calif. Tchrs. Assn., Assn. Educators, Nat. Dropout Prevention Network, Calif. Homeless Coalition, Phi Kappa Phi. Office: The Childrens Initiative 4438 Ingraham St San Diego CA 92109

MCBRIDE, JAMES M., school system administrator; m. Sandi McBride; children: Jim, Monique. MBA, La. Tech. U., 1981; EdD, U. NC, 1983. Tchr. Caesar Rodney Jr. HS, Dover, Del., Air Force Acad.; pres. CC of Air Force (CCAF), 1996—2001; supt. schs. Bennett, Colo., 2001—03; tech. adminstr. Wyo. Dept. Edn., 2003—05, supt. pub. instrn., 2005—. Mem. Coun. Chief State Sch. Officers, Midcontinent Rsch. for Edn. and Learning. Mem. Montgomery Trust Fund for Visually Impaired, Wyo. Higher Edn. Assistance Authority, Wyo. Early Childhood Coun., Wyo. Workforce Develop. Coun., Wyo. Edn. Planning and Coord. Coun. With USAF, 1975—2001. Office: Wyo Dept Edn Hathaway Bldg, 2nd Fl 2300 Capitol Ave Cheyenne WY 82002-0050 Office Phone: 303-777-7675. Business E-Mail: jmcbri@educ.state.wy.us. E-mail: supt@educ.state.wy.us.

MCCABE, EDWARD R. B., hospital administrator, educator, physician; b. Balt., Mar. 26, 1946; BA in Biology, Johns Hopkins U., 1967; PhD in Pharmacology, U. So. Calif., 1972, MD, 1974. Diplomate Am. Bd. Pediatrics. Resident in pediatrics U. Minn. Hosps., Mpls., 1974—76; pediatric metabolism fellow Sch. Medicine U. Colo., Denver, 1976—78, instr., asst. prof., assoc. prof. pediatrics Sch. Medicine, 1978—86; from assoc. prof. to prof. genetics, pediatrics Baylor Coll. Medicine, Houston, 1986—94; exec. prof., chmn. dept. pediatrics David Geffen Sch. Medicine UCLA, 1994—. Physician-in-chief Mattel Children's Hosp. UCLA, 1995—; mem. med. genetics residency rev. com. Accreditation Coun. Grad. MEd. Edn., 1993—97; chmn. conf. gaucher disease NIH, Bethesda, Md., 1994—96; mem. NICHD Coun., 1995—99. Editor: Biochem. and Molecular Medicine, 1990—97, Molecular Genetics and Metabolism, 1998—. Chair sci. adv. bd. HEreditary Disease Found., LA, 1998—99; chmn. Basil O'Connor award March Dimes, White Plains, NY, 1997—99. Mem.: Inst. Medicine, Soc. Pediatric Rsch. (E. Mead Johnson award 1993), Am. Coll. Med. Genetics (chair sec.'s adv. com. genetics, health and society 2002—, maternal and child health bur. 1999—2000, pres. 2001—02, co-chair newborn screening screening task force), Am. Soc. Biochem. and Molecular Biology, Am. Pediatric Soc., Am. Fedn. Clin. Rsch., Am. Soc. Human Genetics, Am. Bd. Med. Genetics (bd. dirs. 1992—97, pres. Bethesda 1995—96, diplomate), Am. Acad. Pediatrics (chmn. com. genetics Elk Grove Village, Ill. 1987—91, co-founder, chmn. sect. genetics Elk Grove Village 1990, 1993—95), Alpha Omega Alpha, Sigma Xi, Phi Kappa Phi. Achievements include First to describe the Continguous Gene Syndrome Complex Glyverol Kinase Deficiency; first to extract DNA from blood in newborn screening blotters; first to set up molecular genetic diagonosis for sickle cell disease as part of newborn screening; development of concept of molecular genetic triage of bacterial infection. Office: UCLA Pediatrics Box 951752 22-412 MDCC Los Angeles CA 90095 Office Phone: 310-825-5095. E-mail: emccabe@mednet.ucla.edu.

MCCABE, JOHN L., lawyer; b. Chgo., Oct. 17, 1941; BA, U. Notre Dame, 1963; LLB, Harvard U., 1966. Bar: Ill. 1967, Colo. 1967. Ptnr. Davis Graham & Stubbs LLP, Denver. Office: Davis Graham & Stubbs LLP 1550 Seventeenth St Ste 500 Denver CO 80202 Office Phone: 303-892-9400. Business E-Mail: john.mccabe@dgslaw.com.

MCCAFFREY, CINDY, information technology executive; BA in journalism, U. Nebr. Former reporter, editor publ. including Omaha World-Herald, Springfield (Mo.) Leader & Press, Kansas City Bus. Jour., Contra Costa Times, Macintosh Today; former comm. dir./mgr. co. including Apple Computer, E*TRADE, 3DO Co., and Smart Force; current v.p. corp. mktg. Google Inc., Mountain View, Calif.

MCCAIN, CINDY (CINDY LOU HENSLEY MCCAIN), philanthropist, wholesale distribution executive; b. Phoenix, May 20, 1954; d. James and Marguerite Hensley; m. John Sidney McCain III, May 17, 1980; 1 adopted child, Bridget children: Meghan, Jack, Jimmy.

BA in Edn., U. So. Calif., LA, 1976, MA in Spl. Edn., 1978. Tchr. Agua Fria HS, Phoenix, 1979—83; founder Am. Vol. Med. Team, 1988—95, Hensley Family Found., 1995—; v.p., dir., vice chair Hensley & Co., Phoenix, chmn., 2000—. Chairwoman, Ariz. delegation Republican Nat. Convention, 2000; bd. trustees HALO Trust; bd. dirs. Operation Smile, CARE USA. Mem.: Kappa Alpha Theta. Office: Hensley & Co 4201 N 45th Ave Phoenix AZ 85031 also: John McCain 2008 PO Box 16118 Arlington VA 22215 Office Phone: 703-418-2008, 602-264-1635. Office Fax: 623-247-7094.

MCCAIN, JOHN (JOHN SIDNEY MCCAIN III), United States Senator from Arizona; b. Canal Zone, Panama, Aug. 29, 1936; s. John Sidney and Roberta (Wright) McCain; m. Carol Shepp, July 3, 1965 (div. Apr. 2, 1980); 1 child, Sidney Ann stepchildren: Douglas, Andrew; m. Cindy Lou Hensley, May 17, 1980; 1 adopted child, Bridget children: Meghan, Jack, Jimmy. Grad. US Naval Acad., 1958; grad., Nat. War Coll., 1973-74; degree (hon.), Johns Hopkins U., 1999, Colgate U., 2000, U. Penn., 2001, Wake Forest U., 2002, U. So. Calif., 2004. Dir. Navy Senate Liaison Office, Washington, 1977-81; mem. US Congress from 1st Ariz. Dist., 1983—86; US Senator from Ariz., 1987—; ranking mem. US Senate Armed Services Com., 2009—; mem. US Senate Energy & Nat. Resources Com., 2009—, US Senate Health, Edn., Labor & Pensions Com., 2009—, US Senate Homeland Security & Governmental Affairs Com., 2009—, US Senate Indian Affairs Com., chmn., 1995—97, 2005—07, US Senate Commerce Sci. & Transp. Com., 1997—2001, 2003—05. Bd. dirs. Nixon Ctr. for Peace & Freedom, Cmty. Assistance League, Phoenix, 1981—; chmn. Internat. Republican Inst., 1993—; candidate for Republican presdl. nomination, 2000, 08; Republican presdl. nominee, 08; mem. Commn. on Intelligence Capabilities of US Regarding Weapons of Mass Destruction, 2004; speaker Republican Nat. Convention, NYC, 2004. Co-author (with Mark Salter): Faith of My Fathers, 1999, Worth the Fighting For: What I Learned from Mavericks, Heroes, and Politics, 2002, Why Courage Matters: The Way to a Braver Life, 2004, Character Is Destiny: Inspiring Stories Every Young Person Should Know and Every Adult Should Remember, 2005, Hard Call: Great Decisions and the Extraordinary People Who Made Them, 2007. Served in USN, 1958—81, prisoner of war, 1967—73, Vietnam, became captain USN, 1977. Decorated Legion of Merit, Silver Star, Bronze Star, Purple Heart, Disting. Flying Cross, Vietnamese Legion of Honor; recipient Excellence in Pub. Svc. award, Am. Acad. Pediat., 1999, Friendship award, League Latin Am. Citizens, 1999, Freedom award, Intrepid Mus. Found., 1999, John F. Kennedy Profile in Courage award, John F. Kennedy Library Found., 1999, Paul H. Douglas Ethics in Govt. award, U. Ill. Inst. Govt. & Pub. Affairs, 2000, William Penn Mott Jr. Park Leadership award, Nat. Parks Conservation Assn., 2001, Citizen Patriot award, Citizen Patriot Orgn., 2003, Arthur T. Marix Congl. Leadership award, Mil. Officers Assn. America, 2004, Econ. Patriot award, Concord Coalition, 2004, Evelyn F. Burkey award, Writers Guild America East, 2004, Disting. Leadership award, Am. Ireland Fund, 2005; named Cancer Survivor of Yr., Cancer Rsch./Treatment Fund, 2004; named one of The 25 Most Influential People in America, TIME mag., 1997, The 100 Most Influential People in the World, 2006, 2008, 10 People Who Mattered, Newsweek, 2008. Mem.: VFW, Soc. of the Cin., Am. Legion. Republican. Baptist. Office: US Senate 241 Russell Office Bldg Washington DC 20510 also: District Office Ste 105 5353 North 16th St Phoenix AZ 85016-3282 Office Phone: 202-224-2235, 602-952-2410. Office Fax: 202-228-2862, 602-952-8702.*

MCCALL, JENNIFER JORDAN, lawyer; b. NYC, Feb. 15, 1956; m. James W. McCall; children: Caroline, Hillary. BA cum laude in English Lit., Princeton U., 1978; JD, U. Va. Sch. Law, 1982; LLM in Taxation, NYU, 1988. Bar: N.Y. 1983, Calif. 2002. Assoc. Lord Day & Lord, NYC, 1982-92; ptnr. Lord Day & Lord, Barrett Smith, NYC, 1992-94; ptnr. Pvt. Client Group Cadwalader, Wickersham & Taft, NYC, 1994—2003; ptnr. Pillsbury Winthrop, LLP, NYC & Palo Alto, Calif., 2003—05; ptnr., co-chmn. Wealth Mgmt. & Individual Client practice Pillsbury Winthrop Shaw Pittman, NYC & Palo Alto, Calif., 2005—. Trustee Charitable Founds. and Trusts and advisor to numerous high net worth individuals; spkr. in field on estate and tax planning and adminstrn. Co-author: Estate Planning for Authors and Artists, 1998; contbr. chpt. to Estate Tax Techniques. Steering com., Planned Giving Adv. Com., The Mus. of Modern Art; mem. Profl. Advisor's Coun., Lincoln Ctr., Inc.; trustee League for the Hard of Hearing, N.Y.C., 1992-2003, East Side House Settlement, Bronx, N.Y., 1995-2002, Chapin Sch., N.Y.C., 1998-2001; chairperson Ethel Gray Stringfellow Art Case Com., N.Y.C.; bd. trustees San Francisco Ballet. Fellow Am. Coll. Trust and Estate Counsel; mem. ABA (real property, probate and trust law sects.), N.Y. State Bar Assn. (com. on trusts and estates adminstrn.; chairperson subcom. on proposed legislation on executor's commns.), Calif. State Bar Assn. Office: Pillsbury Winthrop Shaw Pittman 2470 Hanover St Palo Alto CA 94304-1114 also: Pillsbury Winthrop Shaw Pittman 1540 Broadway New York NY 10036 Office Phone: 650-233-4020. Office Fax: 650-233-4545. Business E-Mail: jenniferjordan.mccall@pillsburylaw.com.

MCCAMMON, JAMES ANDREW, chemistry professor; b. Lafayette, Ind., Feb. 8, 1947; s. Lewis Brown and Jean Ann (McClintock) McC.; m. Anne Elizabeth Woltmann, June 6, 1969. BA magna cum laude, Pomona Coll., 1969; MA, Harvard U., 1970, PhD, 1976. NSF/NIH postdoctoral research fellow Harvard U., Cambridge, Mass., 1976-78; asst. prof. chemistry U. Houston, 1978-81, full prof., 1981, M.D. Anderson prof. chemistry, 1981-94, dir. Inst. for Molecular Design, 1987-94, prof. biochemistry, 1989-94; Joseph E. Mayer chair theoretical chemistry U. Calif. San Diego, 1995—; prof. pharmacology U. Calif. San Diego Sch. Medicine, 1995—; investigator Howard Hughes Med. Inst., 2000—. Adj. prof. molecular physiology and biophysics Baylor Coll. Medicine, Houston, 1986-94, adj. prof. biochemistry, 1992-94; cons. to Sterling-Winthrop Pharma., Stardent Computers, Rhone-Poulenc, Accelrys, Kimberly-Clark, DuPont-Merck Pharm., Merck — Co., and Bristol-Myers Squibb; mem. adv. bd. NAS, NSF, NIH and other agencies. Author: Dynamics of Proteins and Nucleic Acids, 1987; contbr. articles to profl. jours. Recipient Tchr.-scholar award Camille and Henry Dreyfus Found., 1982-87, NIH Rsch. Career Develop. award, 1980-85, George H. Hitchings award for Innovative Methods in Drug Design, Burroughs-Wellcome Fund, 1987, Smithsonian award for Breakthrough Computational Sci., 1995, Chancellor's Associates award for Rsch., 2002; named Alfred P. Sloan Rsch. fellow, 1980-84, Centennial lectr., U. Chgo., 1991 Fellow AAAS, Am. Phys. Soc., Biophys. Soc., Am. Acad. Arts & Sciences; mem. Am. Chem. Soc.(Computers in Chemical and Pharm. Rsch., 2008), Protein Soc., Phi Beta Kappa. Achievements include development of the molecular dynamics simulation method for proteins and nucleic acids, of the thermodynamic cycle perturbation method for studying molecular recognition, and of the Brownian dynamics method for simulating diffusion-controlled reactions. Office: U Calif San Diego Dept Chemistry La Jolla CA 92093-0365 E-mail: jmccammon@ucsd.edu.

MCCANDLESS, BRUCE, II, aerospace engineer, retired astronaut; b. Boston, June 8, 1937; s. Bruce and Sue McCandless; m. Alfreda Bernice Doyle, Aug. 6, 1960; children: Bruce III, Tracy. BS, U.S. Naval Acad., 1958; MSEE, Stanford U., 1965; MBA, U. Houston, Clear Lake, 1987. Commd. ensign USN, 1958, advanced through grades to capt., 1979, naval aviator, 1960, with Fighter Squadron 102, 1960-64; astronaut Johnson Space Ctr., NASA, Houston, 1966-90; mem. Skylab 1 backup crew Johnson Space Center, NASA, Houston, mem. STS-11 shuttle crew, mem. STS-31 Hubble Space Telescope deployment crew; ret. USN, 1990; prin. staff engr. Lockheed Martin Astronautics, Denver, 1990-97, chief scientist Advanced Space Transp. Sys. Co., 1997—2005, prin. staff scientist civil space, 2005—. Mem. Hubble salvage strategy panel NASA. Decorated Legion of Merit; recipient Def. Superior Service medal, NASA Exceptional Service medal, NASA Spaceflight medal, NASA Exceptional Engring. Achievement medal, Collier Trophy, 1985, Haley Space Flight award AIAA, 1991; named to Astronaut Hall Fame, 2005. Fellow Am. Astron. Soc.; mem. U.S. Naval Inst., Nat. Audubon Soc., Houston Audubon Soc. (past pres.) Episcopalian. Achievements include executing 1st untethered free flight in space using Manned Maneuvering Unit. Home: 21852 Pleasant Park Rd Conifer CO 80433-6802 Office: Lockheed Martin Space Sys Co Sensing & Exploration Sys Product Area PO Box 179 Denver CO 80201-0179 Office Phone: 303-971-6308. Personal E-mail: bruce2mc@logcabin.com.

MCCANN, BIFF (RAYMOND BIFF MCCANN), plastic surgeon; b. Fayetteville, Ark., Dec. 24, 1966; BS (cum laude) in Natural Scis., U. Ark., Fayetteville, 1989; MD, U. Ark. for Med. Scis., Little Rock, 1993. Intern, gen. surgery U. Ark. for Med. Scis., Little Rock, 1993—94, resident, gen. surgery, 1994—96; fellow, plastic surgery Scott & White Clinic, Temple, Tex., 1996—98; staff plastic surgeon U. Med. Ctr., Las Vegas, Nev., Mountain View Hosp., Las Vegas, Nev., Sunrise Hosp., Las Vegas, Nev.; chief, plastic surgery Valley Hospital, Las Vegas, Nev.; private practice Ctrl. Tex. to practice in Las Vegas, Nev., 1998—. Guest appearances on Plastic Surgery Before and After. Recipient Best Scientific Presentation by Resident Candidate, Am. Soc. for Aesthetic Plastic Surgery Ann. Mtg., NYC, 1997, Am. Soc. for Aesthetic Plastic Surgery Ann. Mtg., Dallas, Tex., 1999; named one of Las Vegas Top 10 Plastic Surgeons. Mem.: Golden Key, Gamma Beta Phi, Alpha Epsilon Delta. Office: 241 N Buffalo Dr Las Vegas NV 89145 Office Phone: 702-360-9500.

MC CANN, CECILE NELKEN, writer, artist; b. New Orleans; d. Abraham and Leona Nelken; children: Dorothy Collins, Cecile Isaacs, Annette Arnold, Denise Bachman, Albert Hews III. Student, Vassar Coll., Tulane U.; BA, San Jose State Coll., 1963, MA, 1964; postgrad., U. Calif.-Berkeley, 1966-67; doctorate (hon.), San Francisco Art Inst., 1989. Tool designer Convair Corp., New Orleans, 1942-45; archtl. draftsman, various companies New Orleans and Clinton, Iowa, 1945-47, 51-53; owner, operator ceramics studio Clinton, 1953-58; instr. San Jose State Coll., 1964-65, Calif. State U., Hayward, 1964-65, Chabot Coll., Hayward, 1966-69, Laney Coll., 1967-70, San Francisco State U., 1977-78; founder, editor, pub. Artweek mag., Oakland, Calif., 1970-89; freelance writer, art advisor Kensington, Calif., 1989—. Cons. Nat. Endowment Arts, 1974—78, fellow in art criticism, 1976; panelist numerous confs. and workshops. One-woman shows include Davenport Mus. Art, Robert North Galleries, Chgo., Crocker Art Mus., Sacramento, Calif. Coll. Arts and Crafts, Oakland, exhibited in group shows at DeYoung Mus., San Francisco, Everson Mus. Art, Syracuse, N.Y., Oakland Mus., Pasadena Mus., Los Angeles County Mus. Art, Represented in permanent collections San Jose State Coll., Mills Coll., Coll. Holy Names, City of San Francisco, State of Calif. Trustee emerita Rene and Veronica di Rosa Found.; mem. Pub. Art Adv. Com., Oakland. Recipient Vesta award, Woman's Bldg., 1988, Media award, Bay Area Visual Arts Coalition, 1989. Mem.: Internat. Assn. Art Critics, Art Table (Honor award 1988, Achievement award 1992).

MCCANN, ELIZABETH HARRISON, state legislator, lawyer; b. Radford, Va., Feb. 10, 1949; d. James Henry and Elizabeth (Roberts) McC.; m. Christopher Scott Linsmayer, Feb. 27, 1988; children: Christopher Harrison Linsmayer, Kathryn E. Linsmayer. Student, London Sch. Econs., 1968, Am. U., 1970; BA, Wittenberg U., 1971; JD, Georgetown U., 1974. Bar: Colo. 1974, US Dist. Ct. Colo. 1974, US Ct. Appeals (10th cir.) 1985. Law clk. to judge Sherman G. Finesilver US Dist. Ct. Colo., Denver, 1974-75; dep. dist. atty. Denver Dist. Atty.'s Office, 1976-81, chief dep. dist. atty., 1981-83, dep. atty. gen., civil litig. and employment law sect., 1999—; assoc. Cooper & Kelley PC, Denver, 1984-85, ptnr., 1985-91; mgr. safety Denver Dept. Excise & Lic., 1991-94, safe city coord., 1994-95, dir., 1995—99; mem. Dist. 8 Colo. House of Reps., Denver, 2009—. Faculty NITA, 1984-86, 88, 90; spkr. at numerous seminars. Bd. dirs. Leadership Denver, 1988-91, Colo. Domestic Violence Coalition, Denver, 1980-81; mem. exec. com. WIN-Colo. Dem. Women's Polit. Action Com., Denver, 1988—; mem. events com. Women's Found., Denver, 1990; participant Leadership Denver, 1988; mem. Montview Blvd. Presbyn. Ch. Recipient East HS Angel award, 2007. Mem. Denver Bar Assn. (1st v.p., 2nd v.p. 1982-83, exec. coun. young lawyers sect. 1981-84, Outstanding Young Lawyer of Yr. 1985), Colo. Bar Assn. (bd. govs. 1979-81, 82-83, 90), pres. 1985-86, chmn. jud. com. 1978-80), Colo. Womens Bd. Assn., Denver Law Club. Democrat. Avocations: skiing, photography, travel, theater, hiking, jogging. Office: Colo State Capitol 200 E Colfax Denver CO 80203 Office Phone: 303-866-2959. Business E-Mail: beth.mccann.house@state.co.us.*

MCCANN, RICHARD EUGENE, lawyer; b. Billings, Mont., Aug. 14, 1939; s. Oakey O. and Edith May (Miller) McC.; children: Tami, Todd (dec.), Jennifer. BA magna cum laude, Rocky Mountain Coll., 1965; JD with highest honors, U. Mont., 1972. Bar: Mont. 1972, Washington 1977, Alaska 1982. Law clk. to Judge W. Jameson U.S. Dist. Ct., Billings, 1972-73; assoc. Crowley, Haughey, Hansen, Toole & Dietrich, Billings, 1973-77, Perkins Coie, Seattle, 1977-80, ptnr., 1981—2002, sr. counsel, 2003—. Contbr. articles to profl. jours. Trustee Rocky Mountain Coll., Billings., 1973-77. Served with USMC, 1957-61. Mem. ABA, Mont. Bar Assn., Wash. Bar Assn., Alaska Bar Assn. Office: Perkins Coie 1201 3rd Ave Fl 40 Seattle WA 98101-3029 Office Phone: 206-359-8616. Business E-Mail: rmccann@perkinscoie.com.

MCCARTHY, ANN PRICE, lawyer; b. LA, Jan. 30, 1947; d. Frank Judson and Marianna (Chase) Price; 1 child, Sundae Jan Cloe; m. Joseph Stephen McCarthy, Dec. 15, 1974; 1 child, Caitlin Price. BA, Old Coll., Reno, 1983; JD, Nev. Sch. Law, 1987. Bar: Nev. 1987, Calif. 1988, U.S. Dist. Ct. (no. dist.) Calif. 1988, U.S. Ct. Appeals (9th cir.) 1989. Legal asst. Aebi, FitzSimmons & Lambrose, Carson City, Nev., 1981-84; ind. legal researcher Reno, 1985; law clk. Martin H. Wiener, Esquire, Reno, 1985-87, Hon. Robin C. Wright, Reno, 1987-88, Hon. John C. Mowbray, Carson City, 1988; ptnr. Eck & McCarthy, Carson City, 1988-90; pvt. practice Ann Price McCarthy, Ltd., Carson City, 1990-91; ptnr. Aebi & McCarthy, Carson City, 1991—. Lectr. Nat. Bus. Inst., Reno, 1992, 93; instr. Juvenile Drug and Alcohol Edn. Program, Carson City, 1992. Bd. dirs., sec. Brewery Arts Ctr., Carson City, 1992, bd. dirs., pres., 1993-95. Mem. Am. Trial Lawyers Assn., Nev. Trial Lawyers Assn., Washoe County Bar Assn., First Jud. Dist. Bar Assn. (pres. 1991-92, 92-93), State Bar of Nev. (pres. 2004). Address: Ann Price McCarthy & Assoc 777 E William St Ste 201 Carson City NV 89701 Office: Aebi and McCarthy Ste 201 777 E William St Carson City NV 89701-4058

MCCARTHY, BERNARD FRANCIS, lawyer; b. Butte, Mont., Aug. 20, 1955; s. John Joseph and Helen Patricia (Ryan) McC.; m. Helen Jean Waldbillig, Sept. 1, 1990; children: Sean Michael, Patrick Nicholas. BA, Carroll Coll., 1977; JD, U. Mont., 1983. Bar: Mont. 1983, U.S. Dist. Ct. Mont. 1983. Mgmt. analyst Mont. Supreme Ct., Helena, 1978-79; ptnr. O'Leary & McCarthy, Helena, 1983-85; justice of peace Lewis and Clark County, Helena, 1984-89; clk. US Bankruptcy Ct. (Dist. Mont.), Butte, Mont., 1990—. Chair edn. com. Fed. Jud. Ctr., Washington, 1994—; mem. State Bar Mont., Helena, (law practice com. 1994, sec.-treas. 2000, pres-elect 2004); Nat. Conf. Bankruptcy Clks., Dayton, Ohio, (v.p., pres.-elect, 1996-98, pres., 1998-2000; mem. Nat. Integrated Bankruptcy System user group Adminstr. Office U.S. Cts., Washington, 1996—; sec., treas. State Bar Mont., 2001-04, pres.-elect, 2004-05, pres., 2005-06. Pres. bd. Big Bros. and Sisters, Helena, 1985-86. Mem. KC, Lions (pres./sec. 1992-94). Democrat. Roman Catholic. Avocations: horse riding, fishing, reading, travel, ranching. Home: PO Box 523 176 Paul Gulch Rd Whitehall MT 59759 Office: Us Bankruptcy Court 400 N Main St Rm 303 Butte MT 59701-8866 Office Phone: 406-497-1243. Business E-Mail: bernard-mccarthy@meb.uscacts.gov.

MCCARTHY, DENIS M., medical educator; b. Galway, Ireland, July 16, 1938; s. Michael Denis and Mary Beatrice McCarthy; m. Sallie Susan Schirmer; children: Michael, Kevin, Anne, Brian, Jessica, Ben. MB BCh, BAO, U. Coll. Dublin, Ireland, 1962, MD, 1970; BSc in Physiology and Biochemistry with 1st Class honors, U. Coll. Cork, Ireland, 1963, MSc in Physiology, 1965. Cert. E.C.F.M.G. Exam., 1970, bd. eligible ABIM, 1973, in FLEX exam. State Bd., Md., 1974; gastroenterologist Md., 1975, registered Eng., 1963, Ireland, 1963, Calif., 1976, Washington, 1977, Va., 1977, lic. N.Mex., 1980. Attended U. Coll. Dublin, Med. Sch., 1956—62; med. internship Mater Misericordial Hosp., Dublin, 1962—63, sr. med. registrar, gastroenterology, 1969—70; asst. lectr. physiology U. Coll. Cork, 1963—65; med. residency London U., Royal Postgrad. Med. Sch. Fedn., Hammersmith, Dept. Gastroenterology, 1966—69, Brompton Hosp. Diseases Chest, Cardio-Pulmonary and Pediat. Cardiology Dept., London, 1966—69, Royal Free Hosp., Gastroenterology Dept., London, 1967—69; postdoc. rsch. fellow, biochemistry and gastroenterology U. Calif. Med. Ctr., San Francisco, 1970—74, asst. prof. medicine, gastroenterology, Vet. Adminstrn. Hosp., 1973—74; vis. scientist NIH, Bethesda, Md., 1974—77, attending physician, clin. ctr., 1974—80, supr., clin. rsch. digestive diseases, 1974—80, sr. investigator, Digestive Disease Br., 1977—80, capt., USPHS, 1977—80, dir., 2006; prof. medicine, GI U. N.Mex., Sch. Med., Albuquerque, 1980—, adj. prof. biochemistry, adv. com., NIH clin. rsch., exec. com., chief gastroenterology, 1988—2000, dir., GI fellowship tng. program, 1988—2001; chief gastroenterology Vets. Adminstrn. Health Care Svc., N.Mex. Regional Fed. Med. Ctr., 1980—2002, hepatologist, 2007, adj. prof., sect. gastroenterology and hepatology. Mem. US Food and Drug Adminstrn., cons., gastrointestinal and arthritis adv. com., 1985—92. Contbr. scientific papers to profl. med. jours., chapters to books. Recipient Leonard prize, Mater Hosp., Dublin, 1962, Gold medal, 1962, Irish Nat. Maternity Hosp., 1962; named one of Am. Top Physicians, Consumer Rsch. Coun. America, 2007. Master: RCP (fellow specialty bds., Ireland 1975, fellow specialty bds., London 1998); fellow: ACP; mem.: Am. Digestive Disease Soc. (exec. com. 1975—80, v.p. 1978—80, bd. mem. 1980—84), NY Acad. Scis., Western Assn. Physicians, NY Acad. Scis., Western Soc. Clin. Investigation, Brit. Soc. Gastroenterology, Gastroent. Rsch. Group, Am. Gastroent. Assn. (fellow 2006—, Disting. Mentorship award, Am. Digestive Health Found. 2005). Democrat. Roman Catholic. Avocations: music, history, travel, mountain climbing, skiing. Office: NM Vets Adminstrn Health Care Svc Med Ctr 111F Dept Vet Affairs 1501 San Pedro Blvd SE Albuquerque NM 87108 also: Univ NM HSC Divsn Gastroenterology MSC10 5550 Albuquerque NM 87131 Home: 3012 Don Quixote Dr NW Albuquerque NM 87104-3036 Office Fax: 505-256-2803; Home Fax: 505-256-5751. Business E-Mail: denis.mccarthy2@med.va.gov, bmccarthy@salud.unm.edu.

MC CARTHY, FRANK MARTIN, oral surgeon, educator; b. Olean, NY, Aug. 27, 1924; s. Frank Michael and Joan (Quinn) McC.; m. Julia Richmond, Nov. 24, 1949; children: Robert Lee, Joan Lee. BS, U. Pitts., 1943, DDS, 1945, MD, 1949; MS in Oral Surgery, Georgetown U., 1954; ScD (hon.), St. Bonaventure U., 1956. Med. intern Mercy Hosp., Pitts., 1949-50; practice oral surgery LA, 1954-75; tchg. fellow Georgetown U., 1952-53; rsch. fellow NIH, 1953-54; prof. oral surgery U. So. Calif. Sch. Dentistry, 1966-75, prof., chmn. sect. anesthesia and medicine, 1975-90, prof. emeritus, 1990—, chmn. dept. surg. scis., 1979-84, assoc. dean adminstrv. affairs, 1977-79, asst. dean hosp. affairs, 1979-84. Dir. anesthesiology U.So. Calif. oral surgery sect. L.A. County Hosp., 1958-89; clin. supr., lectr. dental hygiene program Pasadena City Coll., 1992—; v.p. Am. Dental Bd. Anesthesiology, 1984-89; lectr. in field; mem. adv. panel on dentistry sect. anesthesizing agts. Nat. Fire Protection Assn., 1971-79; mem. Am. Nat. Stds. Com., 1974-86, 95—; cons. in field. Author: Emergencies in Dental Practice, 1967, rev., 1972, 79, Medical Emergencies in Dentistry, 1982, Safe Treatment of the Medically Compromised Patient, 1987, Essentials of Safe Dentistry for the Medically Compromised Patient, 1989; mem. editorial bd.: Calif. Dental Assn. Jour; contbr. articles to profl. publs. Bd. councilors Sch. Dentistry, U. So. Calif., 1972-75. Served as lt., M.C. USNR, 1950-52. Recipient Lifetime Achievement award, So. Calif. Orofacial Acad., Palm Springs, Calif., 2006. Fellow Internat. Assn. Oral Surgeons (founder), Am. Coll. Dentists, Internat. Coll. Dentists; mem. ADA (editl. bd. jour.), Am. Dental Soc. Anesthesiology (Heidbrink award 1977), Am. Assn. Oral-Max Surgeons (chmn. anesthesia com. 1971), So. Calif. Soc. Oral Surgeons (pres. 1974), Calif., L.A. County Dental Assns., Delta Tau Delta, Psi Omega, Phi Rho Sigma, Omicron Kappa Upsilon. Home and Office: 480 S Orange Grove Blvd Apt 11 Pasadena CA 91105-1720 Home Phone: 626-577-0369.

MCCARTHY, J. THOMAS, lawyer, educator; b. Detroit, July 2, 1937; s. John E. and Virginia M. (Hanlon) McC.; m. Nancy Irene Orrell, July 10, 1976 BS, U. Detroit, 1960; JD, U. Mich., 1963. Bar: Calif. 1964. Assoc. Julian Caplan, San Francisco, 1963—66; prof. law U. San Francisco, 1966—; counsel Morrison and Foerster, 2001—. Founding dir. McCarthy Inst. Intellectual Property and Tech. Law; mem. Trademark Rev. Commn., 1986—88; cons. in field. Author: McCarthy on Trademarks and Unfair Competition, 7 vols., 4th edit., 1996, McCarthy on Rights of Publicity and Privacy, 1987, 2d edit., 2000, McCarthy's Desk Encyclopedia of Intellectual Property, 3d edit., 2004. Recipient Jefferson medal N.J. Intellectual Property Assn., 1994, Ladas award Brand Names Ednl. Found., 1997, Pattishall medal Brand Names Found., 2000, Pres.'s award Internat. Trademark Assn., 2003. Mem. IEEE, Am. Intellectual Property Law Assn. (Watson award 1965, Centennial award in Trademark law 1997), Am. Law Inst. (adv. com. on restatement of law of unfair competition).

MCCARTHY, KEVIN, United States Representative from California, former state legislator; b. Bakersfield, Calif., Jan. 26, 1965; m. Judy McCarthy; children: Connor, Meghan. Student, Bakersfield Coll.; BS in Bus. Adminstrn., Calif. State U., Bakersfield, 1989, MBA, 1994. Owner Bakersfield Batting Range, Kevin O's Deli; dist. dir. to Rep. Bill Thomas US Congress; mem. Calif. State Assembly, 2002—07, minority leader, 2004—06; mem. US Congress from 22nd Calif. dist., 2006—, asst. whip, 2006—, mem. agrl com., house adminstrn. com., joint com. on printing. Chmn. Young Republican Nat. Fedn., 1999—2001; bd. dirs. Kern Econ. Opportunity Corp. Trustee dist. bd. Kern C.C., 2000—02; exec. dir. McCarthy Found., 2000—; coach YMCA, 1999—; mem. Kern County Rep. Ctrl. Com., 1992—; bd. dirs. First Book, 2001—, Head Start, Kern County Food Bank. Mem.: Rotary. Republican. Baptist. Office: 1523 Longworth House Office Bldg Washington DC 20515 also: 4100 Empire Dr Ste 150 Bakersfield CA 93309

MCCARTHY, LAURENCE JAMES, physician, pathologist; b. Boston, Aug. 11, 1934; s. Theodore Clifford and Mary Barrett (Moran) McC.; m. Cynthia Marion DeRoch, Aug. 28, 1978; children: Laurence J. Jr., Jeffrey A., Karen E., Patrick K., Ryan N. BA, Yale U., 1956; student, Georgetown U. Sch. Med., 1956-58; MD, Harvard U., 1960; MS, U. Minn., 1965. Cert. Am. Bd. Pathology, 1965. Intern Boston City Hosp., 1960-61; resident in pathology Mayo Clinic, Rochester, Minn., 1961-65; pathologist Honolulu Heart Program, 1965-67; chief pathology Kelsey-Seybold Clinic, Houston, 1967-68; clin. asst. pathologist M.D. Anderson Hosp., Houston, 1967-68; chief pathology Straub Clinic, Honolulu, 1968-72; assoc. pathologist Wilcox Hosp., Lihue, Hawaii, 1972-74; chief pathology A.R. Gould Hosp., Presque Isle, Maine, 1975-78; assoc. pathologist Kuakini Med. Ctr., Honolulu, 1978—. Med. dir. USPHS, 1965-67. Fellow Coll. Am. Pathologists, Am. Soc. Clin. Pathologists; mem. AMA, Hawaii Soc. Pathologists (pres. 1970), Am. Acad. Forensic Sci., Hawaii Med. Assn., Honolulu County Med. Soc. (del. 1982-83). Roman Catholic. Office: Kuakini Med Ctr 347 N Kuakini St Honolulu HI 96817-2306 Home: 6575 Sundance Ln Bainbridge Island WA 98110

MCCARTHY, NIALL P., lawyer; b. San Francisco, May 6, 1967; BA, U. Calif., 1989; JD, Santa Clara U., 1992. Bar: Calif. 1992, U.S. Supreme Ct. 2001. Assoc. Cotchett, Pitre, Simon & McCarthy, San Francisco, 1992—98, ptnr., 1998—2002, principal, 2002—. Spkr. in field. Contbr. articles to profl. jours. Chmn. bd. dirs. Cmty. Gatepath. Recipient Super Lawyer, San Francisco Mag., 2003—05, rated AV, Martindale-Hubbell; named one of Top 20 Lawyers Under 40 in Calif., L.A. Daily Jour., 2002, San Francisco Daily Jour., 2002, Most Successful Litigators in Am. Under 40, Nat. Law Jour., 2002. Mem.: ABA, U. San Francisco Am. Inn. of Ct. (barrister), Consumer Attys. Calif., We. Trial Lawyers Assn., Assn. Bus. Trial Lawyers, Assn. Trial Lawyers Am., San Mateo County Trial Lawyers Assn. (pres. 2005, dir. 1998—, officer 2001—), San Mateo County Barristers, San Mateo County Bar Assn. (dir. 1993—98, pres. 1997, chmn. San Mateo bus. litigation sect. 2001—02). Office: Cotchett Pitre Simon & McCarthy San Francisco Airport Office Ctr Ste 200 840 Malcolm Rd Burlingame CA 94010 Office Phone: 650-697-6000. Office Fax: 650-697-0577, 650-692-1112, 650-692-3606.

MCCARTHY, ROGER LEE, mechanical engineer; AB in Philosophy with high distinction, U. Mich., 1972, BS in Mech. Engring. summa cum laude, 1972; MS in Mech. Engring., MIT, 1973, D in Mech. Engring., 1975, PhD in Mech. Engring., 1977. Registered profl. engr., Calif., Ga., Ariz. Project engr. machine design and devel. engring. divsn. Proctor & Gamble, Inc., Cin., 1973-74; program mgr. Spl. Machinery Group Foster-Miller Assocs., Inc., Waltham, Mass., 1976-78; prin. design engr. Failure Analysis Assocs., Inc. (became Exponent Failure Analysis Assocs., Inc. in 1998), Menlo Park, Calif., 1978—, chmn. bd. dirs., 1988—; chmn. emeritus Failure Analysis Assocs., Inc., Menlo Park, 2005—; CEO The Failure Group, Inc., Menlo Park, 1988-96, chief tech. officer, 1996-98; chmn. Exponent Failure Analysis Assocs., Inc., Menlo Park, 1998—. Co-contbr. numerous articles to profl. jours. Mem. Pres.' Commn. on Nat. Medal of Sci., 1992-94. Recipient Outstanding Civilian Svc. Gold medal U.S. Army, 1998; NSF fellow, 1972-75. Mem. ASME, ASHRAE, ASTM, NAE, Am. Soc. Metals, Soc. Automotive Engrs., Am. Welding Soc., Human Factors Soc., Nat. Fire Protection Assn., Phi Beta Kappa, Sigma Xi (James B. Angell scholar). Office: Exponent Failure Analysis Assn Inc 149 Commonwealth Dr Menlo Park CA 94025 Home Phone: 650-330-1828; Office Phone: 650-688-7100. Office Fax: 650-688-7366. E-mail: sfrlm@exponent.com.

MC CARTHY, WALTER JOHN, JR., retired utilities executive; b. NYC, Apr. 20, 1925; s. Walter John and Irene McC.; m. Linda Lyon, May 6, 1988; children by previous marriage: Walter, David, Sharon, James, William. B.M.E., Cornell U., 1949; grad., Oak Ridge Sch. Reactor Tech., 1952; D.Eng. (hon.), Lawrence Inst. Tech., 1981; D.Sc. (hon.), Eastern Mich. U., 1983; LHD, Wayne State U., 1984; LLD, Alma Coll., Mich., 1985. Engr. Public Service Electric & Gas Co., Newark, 1949-56; sect. head Atomic Power Devel. Assos., Detroit, 1956-61; gen. mgr. Power Reactor Devel. Co., Detroit, 1961-68; with Detroit Edison Co., 1968-90, exec. v.p. ops., 1975-77, exec. v.p. divs., 1977-79, pres., chief operating officer, 1979-81, chmn., chief exec. officer, 1981-90. Author papers in field. Past chmn., bd. dirs. Inst. Nuclear Power Ops., Fed. Mogul Corp., Comerica Bank; past pres. Monterey County Symphony Orch., Detroit Symphony Orch.; past chmn. Detroit Econ. Growth Corp., Detroit Area Coun. Boy Scouts of Am. Fellow Am. Nuc. Soc., Engring. Soc. Detroit; mem. ASME, NAE. Methodist.

MCCARTY, DAVID J., lawyer; BA summa cum laude, Claremont Men's Coll.; JD cum laude, Harvard U., 1977. Bar: Calif. 1977, US Supreme Court 1981. Ptnr. Bankruptcy and Fin. Restructuring Group Sheppard, Mullin, Richter & Hampton LLP, LA. Mem.: ABA (mem. Bus. Bankruptcy Com.), LA Bankruptcy Forum, Fin. Lawyers Conf., LA County Bar Assn. (mem. Exec. Com. 1984—), Am. Bankruptcy Inst. (bd. co-chair Bankruptcy Battleground West 2000—02). Office: Sheppard Mullin Richter & Hampton LLP 48th Fl 333 S Hope St Los Angeles CA 90071 Office Phone: 213-617-4171. Office Fax: 213-620-1398. Business E-Mail: dmccarty@sheppardmulin.com.

MCCARTY, FREDERICK BRIGGS, electrical engineer, consultant; b. Dilley, Tex., Aug. 11, 1926; s. John Frederick Briggs and Olive Ruth (Snell) Briggs McCarty; m. Doris Mary Cox, May 3, 1950 (div. 1970); children: Mark Frederick, David Lambuth, Jackson Clare; m. Nina Lucile Butman, Aug. 17, 1973. BSEE, U. Tex., 1949. Design engr. GE, Schenectady, NY, 1949-51; sr. design engr. Convair, Ft. Worth, 1951-55; sr. engr. Aerojet Gen., Azusa, Calif., 1955-61; sr. engring. specialist Garrett Corp., Torrance, Calif., 1961-91; v.p., founder Patio Pacific, Inc., Torrance, 1973-84; owner, operator Textiger Co., Torrance, 1980-91; cons., 1991—. With USNR, 1944—46, PTO. Mem.: IEEE (sr.), Eta Kappa Nu, Tau Beta Pi. Democrat. Achievements include patents in field; design of superconducting acyclic motor for USN and high speed elec. machines for aerospace and transp. Home and Office: 1366 Stonewood Ct San Pedro CA 90732-1550

MCCARTY, PERRY LEE, civil and environmental engineering educator; b. Grosse Pointe, Mich., Oct. 29, 1931; m. Martha Davis Collins, Sept. 5, 1953; children: Perry Lee, Cara L., Susan A., Kathleen R. BSCE, Wayne State U., Detroit, 1953; MS in San. Engring., MIT, Cambridge, 1957, ScD, 1959; DEng (hon.), Colo. Sch. Mines, Golden, 1992. Field engr. Edwin Orr Co., Dearborn, Mich., 1951-52; engr. Pate & Hirn, Detroit, 1952-53; field engr. Hubbell, Roth & Clark, Detroit, 1953; instr. civil engring. Wayne State U., 1953-54; field engr. George Jerome & Co., Detroit, 1954; engr. Civil Engrs., Inc., Detroit, 1956; assoc. Rolf Eliassen Assocs., Winchester, Mass., 1958-61; asst. prof. san. engring. MIT, 1958-62; faculty Stanford U., Calif., 1962—, prof. civil engring., 1967-75, Silas H. Palmer prof., 1975-99, Silas H. Palmer prof. emeritus, 1999—, chmn. dept. civil engring., 1980-85; chair prof. environ. sci. and engring. Tsinghua U., 2004—07. Chmn. Gordon Rsch. Conf. Environ. Scis., 1972; vice chmn. environ. studies bd. NRC-NAS, 1976-80, mem. com. on phys. scis., math. and resources, 1985-88, bd. on radioactive waste mgmt., 1989-96, mem. com. geoscis., environment, resources, 1994-97. Co-author: Chemistry for Environmental Engineering and Science, 5th edit., 2003, Environmental Biotechnology Principles and Applications, 2001. Served with AUS, 1954-56. Recipient Tyler Prize for Environ. Achievement, 1992, Clarke Prize Outstanding Achievement Water Sci. and Tech., 1997, Stockholm Water prize, 2007; NSF faculty fellow, 1968-69. Fellow AAAS, Am. Acad. Microbiology, Am. Acad. Arts and Scis.(Named to Hall of Fame Water Industry, 2009.); mem. ASCE (Walter L. Huber Rsch. prize 1964, Simon W. Freese Environ. Engring. award 1979, James R. Croes medal 1995), NAE, Am. Water Works Assn. (hon., life, chmn. water quality divsn. 1972-73, trustee rsch. divsn. 1980-85, Best Paper award 1985, A.P. Black Rsch. award 1989), Am. Soc. for Microbiology, Water Environment Fedn. (hon. 1989, Harrison P. Eddy award 1962, 77, Thomas Camp award 1975), Assn. Environ. Engring. Sci. Profs. (Disting. Faculty award 1966, Oustanding Publ. award 1985, 88, 98, 2003, Founders award 1992), Am. Soc. Engring. Edn.(vice-chmn. environ. engring. divsn. 1968-69), Sigma Xi, Tau Beta Pi (fellow 1957-58), Am. Acad. Environ. Engrs., 2009 Home: 823 Sonoma Ter Stanford CA 94305-1024 Office: Stanford U Civil Environ Engring Dept Stanford CA 94305-4020 Office Phone: 650-723-4131. Business E-Mail: pmccarty@stanford.edu.

MCCARTY, SHIRLEY CAROLYN, retired aerospace executive; b. Minot, ND, May 2, 1934; d. Harry and Cecelia Marie (Engene) Wolhowe; m. John Myron McCarty, Apr. 3, 1958. BSBA, U. ND, Grand Forks, 1956. Mem. tech. staff Douglas Aircraft, El Segundo, Calif., 1960-62, The Aerospace Corp., El Segundo, 1962-72, mgr., 1972-73, dir., 1973-79, prin. dir., 1979-89, gen. mgr., 1989—96; ret., 1996; pres. Shamrock Consulting, 1996—. Mem. adv. coun. Calif. State U., Northridge, 1979-01, chmn., 1984-86; mem. indsl. adv. bd. Purdue U. Soc. Women Engrs., West Lafayette, Ind., 1979-82, 85-; mem. adv. bd. Calif. Acad. Math. and Sci., 1991-96; apptd. mem. aerospace safety adv. panel NASA, 1998, chair, 2002-03; spkr. in field. Named Woman of Yr. The Aerospace Corp., 1976, Pres.'s award, 1987; named to Hall of Fame Women in Tech. Internat., 2003; recipient Spl. Judges Award for Leadership, Los Angeles YWCA, 1977, Sioux Alumni Award, U. N.D, 1982, Achievement award Los Angeles County Commn. for Women, 1987. Fellow Soc. Women Engrs.; mem. IEEE, Assn. for Computing Machinery, Soc. Women Engrs., Bus. and Profl. Women (Woman of Achievement 1984, Golden Nike award 1985), Women in Bus.(corp. achievement award, 1987), Women in Computing (founding mem., bd. dirs.). Avocations: raising and training siberian huskies, travel, writing, architecture.

MCCARTY-PUHL, J-PETRINA, chemistry educator; BS in Botany, Univ. Nev., Reno; MA in Curriculum and Instruction, Nova Southeastern Univ.; Crime Investigator Technician Degree, Kaplan Coll., 2005. Cert. Nat. Bd. Tchg. Standards, 2001. Tchr. Washoe County Sch. Dist., 1987—; chemistry, forensics tchr. Robert McQueen H.S., Reno. Recipient Outstanding H.S. tchr. award, Ariz.-Nev. Acad. Sci., 2003, Presdl. Excellence award for Secondary Sci. Tchr., Best of Edn. award, Subaru Sci. award for Excellence in Tchg., We. Region, The I CAN Learn-NEA Found. awards for Tchg. Excellence, 2007; named Nev. Tchr. of Yr., 2006; grantee Brandywine Fellowship. Office: Robert McQueen High Sch 6055 Lancer St Reno NV 89523 Business E-Mail: pmccarty@washoe.k12.nv.us.

MCCASLIN, BOB, state legislator; b. Warren, Ohio, Apr. 20, 1926; m to Linda Callahan; children: Janie & Bob. Washington State Senator, District 4, 80-, member, State & Local Govt, Growth Management Impact Fee, Growth Management Policy Advisor Joint Admin Rules Rev Committees, ranking member, Judiciary Committee, currently, Washington State Senate.Owner & manager, real estate firm, formerly; production management, Kaiser Aluminum & Chemical Corp, formerly. Republican. Mailing: 112 Irving R Newhouse Bldg PO Box 40482 Olympia WA 98504-0482 Address: PO Box 1384 Veradale WA 99037 E-mail: mccaslin_bo@leg.wa.gov.

MCCAW, CRAIG OLIVER, communications executive; b. Centralia, Wash., Aug. 11, 1949; s. John Elroy and Marion (Oliver) McCaw; m. Wendy McCaw, 1974; m. Susan Rasinski, 1998; 3 children. BA in History, Stanford U., 1973. Pilot; chmn., CEO McCaw Comm., 1968-88, McCaw Cellular Comm., Inc. (acquired MCI's cellular and paging ops. in 1986 sold to AT&T in 1994), Kirkland, Wash., 1982-94; founder, chmn., CEO Eagle River Investments, LLC, Kirkland, Wash., 1993; chmn., CEO XO Communications, Inc. (formerly NEXTLINK Communications, Inc.), 1994—97; chmn. Clearwire Corp., 2003—, CEO, 2003—06, co-CEO, 2006—07. Bd. dirs. Nextel Communications, Inc., 1995—2003, XO Communications, Inc. (formerly NEXTLINK Communications, Inc.), 1997—2002, ICO Global Communications Holdings Ltd., 2000—, Clearwire Corp., 2003—, ICO North America, Inc., 2004—, RadioFrame Networks, Inc., China Unicom Ltd., 2000—, non-exec. dir., 2002—; mem. Nat. Security Telecom. Adv. Com. Named one of 400 Richest Ams., Forbes mag., 2006; named to Gallery of Achievers Hall of Bus., 1989, Horatio Alger Assn. of Disting. Ams., 1999. Republican. Avocation: boating. Office: Clearwire Corp 3525 E Post Rd Ste 210 Las Vegas NV 89120 also: 5808 Lake Washington Blvd NE Ste 300 Kirkland WA 98033

MCCAW, JOHN ELROY, JR., investment company executive, professional sports team executive; s. John Elroy McCaw; married; 4 children. Grad., U. Wash. Co-founder McCaw Cable Vision, McCaw Cellular Comm., Orca Bay Ptnrs., Vancouver, BC; former chmn. Orca Bay Sports and Entertainment; chmn. Orca Bay Capital Corp.; former chmn., gov. Vancouver Canucks; owner, bd. dirs. Seattle Mariners, 1992; co-founder Tahoma Fund. Bd. dirs. Kistler Aerospace Corp. Bd. mem. Conservation Internat. Office: Orca Bay Ptnrs 1301 First Ave Seattle WA 98101

MCCLAIN, DAVID STANLEY, academic administrator, business and management professor; b. St. Joseph, Mo., Nov. 11, 1946; s. Stanley Russell and Veletta Mabel (Willis) McC.; m. Gayla Sue Webb, Dec. 30, 1967 (div. 1978); 1 child, Molly; m. Wendie Susan Kastler, Jan. 13, 1979; children: Emily, Jenna. BA, U. Kans., 1968; PhD, MIT, 1974. Dir. internat. econs. Data Resources, Inc., Lexington, Mass., 1974-78; sr. staff economist Coun. Econ. Advisers to Pres. Jimmy Carter, Washington, 1979—80; asst. prof. Sch. Mgmt. Boston U., 1978—83, assoc. prof., 1983—91, chmn. fin. and econs. dept., 1985—88; Henry A. Walker Jr. Disting. Prof. Univ. Hawaii, Manoa, 1991—99, dean Coll. Bus. & 1st Hawaiian Bank Disting. Prof. Mgmt., 2000—03; v.p. academic affairs Univ. Hawaii Sys., Honolulu, 2003—04, interim pres., 2004—06, pres., 2006—. Econ. advisor Babson-United, Boston, 1984—2002; lectr. Sloan Sch. Mgmt. MIT, Boston, U. Gabriela Mistral, Santiago, Chile; founding dir. Mgmt. Devel. Program-Japan Boston U.; vis. scholar Keio U., Japan, Meiji U., Japan; bd. dirs. ML Resources, Inc., First Ins. Co. Author Apocalypse on Wall Street; contbr. On the Money tv series, 1984-85, articles to profl. jours. Bd. dirs. non-profits. 1st lt. US Army, 1968—71, Vietnam. Fellow, Woodrow Wilson Ctr., NSF. Mem. Am. Econ. Assn., Phi Beta Kappa, Sigma Chi, Beta Gamma Sigma. Democrat. Avocations: golf, hiking. Office: University of Hawaii Bachman 204 2444 Dole St Honolulu HI 96822 Office Phone: 808-956-9704. Office Fax: 808-956-9943.

MCCLAUGHERTY, JOE L., lawyer, educator; b. June 1, 1951; s. Frank Lee and Elease (Terrell) McClaugherty. BBA with honors, U. Tex., 1973, JD with honors, 1976. Bar: Tex. 1976, N.Mex 1976, U.S. Dist. Ct. N.Mex 1976, U.S. Ct. Appeals (10th cir.) 1976, U.S. Supreme Ct. 1979, Colo. 1988. Assoc. Rodey, Dickason, Sloan, Akin & Robb, P.A., Albuquerque, 1976-81, ptnr., dir., 1981-87, resident ptnr. Santa Fe, 1983-87, mng. ptnr., 1985-87; ptnr. Kemp, Smith, Duncan & Hammond, P.C., 1987-92, mng. ptnr., 1987-92; ptnr. McClaugherty & Silver, P.C., Santa Fe, 1992—. Adj. prof. law U. N.Mex, Albuquerque, 1983—; faculty Nat. Inst. Trial Advocacy, So. Meth. U. Law Sch., 1983—, Hastings Ctr. Trial and Appellate Advocacy, 1985—, U. Denver Law Sch., 1986—, U. Colo. Law Sch., 1987; bd. dirs. MCM Corp., Brit.-Am. Ins. Co., Ltd., Nassau, 1985—91. Mem.: N.Mex Assn. Def. Lawyers (pres. 1982—83, bd. dirs. 1982—85), N.Mex Bar Assn. (bd. dirs. trial practice sect. 1976—85, chairperson 1983—84, dir. young lawyers divsn. 1978—80). Office: McClaugherty & Silver PC PO Box 8680 Santa Fe NM 87504-8680 Office Phone: 505-988-8804.

MCCLAVE, DONALD SILSBEE, academic administrator; b. Cleve., May 7, 1941; s. Charles Green and Anne Elizabeth (Oakley) McC.; m. Christine Phyllis Mary Tomkins, Feb. 19, 1966; children: Andrew Green, Susan Elizabeth (dec.). BA, Denison U., 1963. Mktg. rsch. officer Bank of Calif., San Francisco, 1968-70; v.p. Cen. Nat. Bank, Chgo., 1970-75, First Interstate Bank, Portland, Oreg., 1975-77, sr. v.p., 1977-79, exec. v.p., 1979-86; pres., CEO Portland Met. C. of C., 1987—2002; asst. to pres. Portland State U., 2002—. Instr. Pacific Coast Sch. Banking, Seattle, 1976-78, Grad. Sch. Mktg. and Strategic Planning, Athens, Ga., 1982-84; dir., mem. exec. com. Bank Mktg. Assn., 1976-82; bd. mem. Oreg. Nanosci. and Microtechs. Inst., 2003, dir. and chair fin. com. Pres. Oreg. Episc. Sch. Bd., Portland, 1983-84; pres. Assn. Oreg. Industries Found., Salem, 1984-85; pres., co-chmn. Japan-Am. Conf. Mayors and C. of C., Portland, 1985, trustee, 1991-98, exec. com., 1992-97; trustee YMCA of Columbia-Willamette, 1990-92, Portland Student Svcs. Corp., 1991-93; mem. METRO Urban Growth Mgmt. Adv. Com., 1989-92; mem. adv. com. Downtown Housing Preservation Partnership Adv. Com., 1989-94; mem. City of Portland Mayoral Transition Team, 1992, Mayor's Bus. Roundtable, 1993—; bd. dirs. Oreg. Trail chpt. ARC, 1994-95, Tri-Met, 1994—, chair fin. com., 1995—, United Way Columbia Willamette, 1978-83, 2000-01, Urban League Portland, 2000-01, Oreg. Nanoscience and Microtechnologies Inst., 2003-. Capt. USAF, 1963-68. Mem. Oreg. Chamber Execs. Assn. (pres. 1998). Avocations: reading, travel, golf, model building. Office: Portland State U PO Box 751 Portland OR 97207-0751

MCCLEARY, LLOYD E(VERALD), education educator; b. Bradley, Ill., May 10, 1924; s. Hal and Pearl McC.; m. Iva Dene Carter, June 13, 1971; children: Joan Kay, Victoria Lea, Karen Ann. Student, Kans. U., 1941—42; BS, U. Ill., 1948, MS, 1950, EdD, 1956; postgrad., Sorbonne U., Paris, 1946. Tchr., asst. prin. Portland (Oreg.) Pub. Schs., 1949-51; asst. prin. Univ. H.S., Urbana, Ill., 1951-52, prin., 1953-56; asst. supt. Evanston Twp. (Ill.) H.S., 1956-60; assoc. Roosevelt U., 1957-69; mem. faculty U. Mich., summers, 1958-59; prof. ednl. adminstrn. U. Utah, 1969—, chmn. dept., 1969-74. Assoc. CFK Ltd. Found., 1971-76; dir. projects in L.Am. for AID, World Bank, Ford Found., Bolivian Govt.; dir. Nat. Sch. Prin. Study, 1976-79, 86-89, res. project Families in Edn., 1992-94; edn. rep. to Utah People to People Program; keynoter Asian Conf. Edn., 1985; edn. adviser Office of the Queen, Jordan, 1985-86; advisor Nat. Commn. on Stds. in the Principalship; U.S. del. Conf. on Status Children, Senegal, 1992, Yr. of the Family, Malta, 1993; J. Lloyd Trump lectr., New Orleans, 1994. Author: Organizational Analysis X-Change, 1975, Politics and Power in Education, 1976, The Senior High School Principalship, 1980, Educational Administration, Today, 1984, High School Leaders and Their Schools, vols. 1 and 2, 1990, Leadership, 1996; editor Western Hemisphere Edn. Sch. Orgn., 1989—. Served with inf. AUS, 1941-46. Decorated Bronze Star with oak leaf cluster, Army Commendation medal; S.D. Shankland fellow, 1956; grantee Ford Found., 1968, 72, AID, 1966, 67, 70, 72, 74, 76, CFK Ltd., 1970-74, Rockefeller Family Found., 1979-80, U.S. Dept. State, 1981, 86-87, U.S. Dept. Def., 1986—; recipient Hatch Prize, 1988-89. Mem. Nat. Assn. Secondary Sch. Prins. (cert. of merit 1978, scholar-in-residence fall 1989, grantee 1969, 77, 86—), Assn. Supervision and Curriculum Devel., Nat. Assn. Elem. Sch. Prins., Phi Delta Kappa, Kappa Delta Pi. Methodist. Home: 1470 Wilton Way Salt Lake City UT 84108-2549 Office: U Utah 339 MBH Salt Lake City UT 84112 E-mail: www.birdsphoto@aol.com.

MCCLELLAN, CRAIG RENE, lawyer; b. Portland, Oreg., June 28, 1947; s. Charles Russell and Annette Irene (Benedict) McC.; m. Susan Armistead Nash, June 7, 1975; children: Ryan Alexander, Shannon Lea. BS in Econs., U. Oreg., 1969; JD magna cum laude, Calif. We. U., 1976. Bar: Calif. 1976, U.S. Dist. Ct. (so. dist.) Calif. 1976, U.S. Dist. Ct. (ea., ctrl., no. dists.) Calif. 1991, U.S. Supreme Ct. 1991. Compliance specialist Cost of Living Coun. and Price Commn., Washington, 1972—73, dir. Oil Policy subcom., 1973; ptnr. Luce, Forward, Hamilton & Scripps, San Diego, 1976—87; owner McClellan Law Firm, San Diego, 1987—. Chmn. annual fundraising auction KPBS, 1984. Capt. USMC, 1969-72. Fellow Am. Coll. Trial Lawyers; mem. Inner Circle of Advs., Assn. Trial Lawyers Am., Am. Bd. Trial Advocates, Am. Inns of Ct. (master), Calif. State Bar Assn., San Diego County Bar Assn., Calif. Trial Lawyers Assn. (bd. govs. 1985-87), San Diego Trial Lawyers Assn. (bd. dirs. 1983-90), Nat. Forensics League, Phi Gamma Delta, Phi Alpha Delta. Presbyterian. Avocations: reading, running, tennis, chess, civic activities. Office: McClellan Law Firm 1144 State St San Diego CA 92101-3529 Office Phone: 619-231-0505. E-mail: craig@mcclellanlaw.com.

MCCLELLAN, ROGER ORVILLE, toxicologist; b. Tracy, Minn., Jan. 5, 1937; s. Orville and Gladys (Paulson) McC.; m. Kathleen Mary Dunagan, June 23, 1962; children: Eric John, Elizabeth Christine, Katherine Ruth. DVM with highest honors, Wash. State U., 1960; M of Mgmt., U. N.Mex., 1980; DSc (hon.), Ohio State U., 2005. Diplomate Am. Bd. Vet. Toxicology, Am. Bd. Toxicology. From biol. scientist to sr. scientist Gen. Electric Co., Richland, Wash., 1957-64; sr. scientist biology dept. Pacific N.W. Labs., Richland, Wash., 1965; scientist med. rsch. br. divsn. biology and medicine AEC, Washington, 1965-66; asst. dir. rsch., dir. fission product inhalation program Lovelace Found. Med. Edn. and Rsch., Albuquerque, 1966-73; v.p., dir. rsch. adminstrn., dir. Lovelace Inhalation Toxicology Rsch. Inst., Albuquerque, 1973-76, pres., dir., 1976-88; chmn. bd. dirs. Lovelace Biomed. and Environ. Rsch. Inst., Albuquerque, 1988-96; pres., CEO Lovelace Respiratory Rsch. Inst., Triangle Park, NC, 1988-99; pres. emeritus Hamner Inst. Health Sci., Triangle Park, NC, 1999—; pvt. advisor Toxicology and Human Health Risk Analysis, 1999—. Mem. rsch. com. Health Effects Inst., 1981-92, mem. future techs. com., 2000—; bd. dir. Toxicology Lab. Accreditation Bd., 1982-90, treas., 1984-90; adj. prof. Wash. State U., 1980-95, U. Ark., 1970-88; clin. assoc. U. N.Mex., 1971-85, adj. prof. toxicology, 1985—; adj. prof. toxicology and occupl. and environ. medicine Duke U., 1988—; adj. prof. toxicology U. N.C., Chapel Hill, 1989-2000; adj. prof. toxicology N.C. State U., 1991-2008; cons. faculty Colo. State U., 2002—; regents lectr. UCLA, 1999-2000; mem. dose assessment adv. group U.S. Dept. Energy, 1980-87, mem. health and environ. rsch. adv. com., 1984-85, 1999-2004; mem. exec. com. sci. adv. bd. EPA, 1974-95, mem. environ. health com., 1980-83, chmn., 1982-83, chmn. radionuclide emissions rev. com., 1984-85, chmn. Clean Air Sci. Adv. Com., 1987-92, Diesel Exhaust Panel, 1996-2001, chmn. rsch. strategies adv. com., 1992-94, mem. Particulate Matter Panel, 1993-97, 99-2006; mem. com. toxicology NAS-NRC, 1979-87, chmn., 1980-87; mem. com. risk assessment methodology for hazardous air pollution NAS-NRC, 1991-94, com. biol. effects of Radon NAS NRC, 1994-98, com. rsch. priorities airborne particulate matter, 1998-2004; mem. Environ. Roundtable, Inst. Medicine, 1998-2002; mem. com. on environ. justice Inst. of Medicine, 1996-99, trustee toxicology excellence in risk assessment, 2000-07, chmn. bd. trustees, 2002-04, mem. coord. com. strengthening sci.-based decision making, 2002—; pres. Am. Bd. Vet. Toxicology, 1970-73; mem. adv. coun. Ctr. for Risk Mgmt., Resources for the Future, 1987-2001; mem. Nat. Coun. for Radiation Protection, 1970-2001, hon. mem., 2002—; bd. dirs. N.C. Assn. Biomed. Rsch., 1989-91, N.C. Vet. Med. Found., 1990-95, pres., 1993-94; bd. govs. Rsch. Triangle Inst., 1994-2001; mem. adv. com. alternative toxicol. methods Interagy. Ctr. Evaluation Alternative Methods, Health and Human Svcs., 1998-2001, mem. sci. adv. com. on Alternative Toxic and Logical Methods Nat. Inst. Environ. Health Scis., 2006-; mem. sci. adv. bd. strategic environ. rsch. strategies program Dept. Def./Dept. Energy/EPA, 1997-99; mem. adv. com. Ctr. for Environ. Health, Agy. for Toxic Substances and Disease Registry, CDC, 2002-04, lunar dust toxicity panel NASA, 2005—; mem. bd. sci. counselors Ctr. for Environ. Health/Agy. Toxic Substances Disease Registry, 2004-06; mem. sci. adv. com. alternative toxicol. methods Nat. Inst. Environ. Health Scis., 2006-08. Jour. Toxicology, 1984—89, assoc. dir., 1987—89; editor: Critical Revs. in Toxicology, 1987—; mem. editl bd.: Regulatory Toxicology and Pharmacology, 1993—, Risk Analysis, 1998—, Ullman's Ency. of Indsl. Chemistry, 1999—, Non-Linearity in Biology-Toxicology-Medicine, 2003—08; contbr. articles to profl. jours. Trustee Wash. State U. Found., 2001—; mem. bd. of vis. Wash. State Univ., Coll. Sci., 2002—; mem. dean's adv. coun. Coll. Vet. Medicine Wash. State U., 2003—, chair dean's adv. coun., 2003—05. Recipient Herbert E. Stokinger award Am. Conf. Govtl. Indsl. Hygienists, 1985, Alumni Achievement award Wash. State U., 1987, Disting. Assoc. award Dept. Energy, 1987, 88, Arnold Lehman award Soc. Toxicology, 1992, Disting. Vet. Medicine Alumnus award Wash. State U., 1999, Regents Disting. Alumnus award, 2008, N.Mex. Disting. Pub. Svc. award, 2006; co-recipient Frank R. Blood award Soc. Toxicology, 1989, Merit award Soc. Toxicology, 2005, Founders award, 2009, Disting. Pub. Svc. award N.Mex., 2006,; named Robert Leader Meml. lectr. Mich. State U., 1999, H.M. Parker Meml. lectr. H.M. Parker Found., 1999; named to Hall of Fame Robert O. Anderson Schs. of Mgmt., U. N.Mex., 2002; fellow Internat. Aerosol Rsch. Assembly, 1998. Fellow: AAAS, Acad. Toxicol. Sci., Gesellschaft fur Zerosol Forschung, Health Physics Soc. (chmn. program com. 1972, fellow 1997, Elda E. Anderson award 1974), Soc. Risk Analysis (fellow 1992), Am. Vet. Med. Assn., Am. Acad. Vet. and Comparative Toxicology; mem.: Internat. Soc. Aerosols in Medicine (Thomas Mercer Joint prize for Aerosol Rsch. 1997), Am. Assn. Aerosol Rsch. (bd. dir. 1982—94, treas. 1986—90, v.p. to pres. 1990—93, fellow 2008), Toxicology Edn. Found. (founding pres. 1990—91), Internat. Congress Toxicology VII (treas. 1995), Soc.Toxicology (chmn. 1983—85, inhalation splty. sect. v.p. to pres. 1983—86, bd. publs. 1983—86, v.p.-elect to pres. 1987—90, Amb.mid-Atlantic chpt. 1995, founding chair endowment fund bd. 2006—09), Am. Conf. Govtl. Indsl. Hygienists, Internat. Regulatory Pharmacology and Toxicology (Internat. Achievement award 1999), Am. Assn. Cancer Rsch., Am. Thoracic Soc., Radiation Rsch. Soc. (chmn. fin. com. 1979—82, sec.-treas. 1982—84), Inst. Medicine (elected mem. 1990, chair other health professions sect. 1999—2001), Am. Chem. Soc., Phi Zeta, Phi Kappa Phi, Sigma Xi. Republican. Lutheran. E-mail: roger.o.mcclellan@att.net.

MCCLELLAND, JAMES LLOYD, psychologist, educator, cognitive neuroscientist; b. Cambridge, Mass., Dec. 1, 1948; s. Walter Moore and Frances (Shaffer) McClelland; m. Heidi Marsha Feldman, May 6, 1978; children: Mollie S., Heather Ann. BA in Psychology, Columbia U., 1970; PhD in Cognitive Psychology, U. Pa., 1975. Asst. prof. dept. psychology U. California, San Diego, 1974-80, assoc. prof., 1980-84, Carnegie-Mellon U., Pitts., 1984-85, prof. psychology, 1985—2006, co-dir. Ctr. for Neural Basis of Cognition, 1994—2006, univ. prof., 2001—06, Walter Van Dyke Bingham chair in psychology and cognitive neurosci., 2002—06; prof. psychology, dir. Ctr. Mind, Brain and Computation Stanford U., Calif., 2006—. Rev. panel for cognition, emotion and personality NIMH, 1983-87, Cognitive Functional Neurosci., 1995-99, chair 1997-99; mem. Nat. Adv. Mental Health Coun., 2000-2003. Author: (with others) Parallel Distributed Processing: Explorations in the Microstructure of Cognition, Vols. I, II, 1986; co-author: A Handbook of Models, Programs, and Exercises, 1988, Semantic Cognition: A Parallel-Distributed Processing Approach, 2004; contbr. numerous articles, reports, book chpts. to profl. publs.; sr. editor Cognitive Sci., 1988-91; sect. editor (Cognitive Neuroscience), Internat. Ency. of The Social and Behavioral Sciences; mem. numerous jour. edit. bds. Recipient William W. Cumming prize, Columbia U., 1970, Rsch. Scientist Career Devel. award, NIMH, 1981—86, 1987—97; co-recipient Grawemeyer prize in psychology, 2002; grantee, NSF, 1976—79, 1980—84, 1986—87, 1988—. Office Naval Rsch., 1982—87; fellow, NSF, 1970—73. Fellow: APA (Disting. Sci. Contbn. award 1996), AAAS, Am. Psychol. Soc. (William James Fellow award 2003—04); mem.: NAS, Fedn. Behavioral Psychol. and Cognitive Scis. (pres. elect 2008—), Soc. Exptl. Psychologists (Warren medal 1993), Internat. Assn. for Study Attention and Performance (lectr. 1986, governing bd. 1986—94), Psychonomics Soc., Cognitive Sci. Soc. (governing bd. 1988—93, chmn. 1991), Phi Beta Kappa. Office: Stanford Univ Dept Psychology Jordan Hall Bldg 420 450 Serra Mall Stanford CA 94305-2130 Business E-Mail: mcclelland@stanford.edu.

MCCLENNEN, CRANE, judge; b. July 31, 1946; s. Louis McClennen and Dorothy (Petrovich) Johnson; m. Deborah Ann Hass, Feb. 19, 1995. BS, Ariz. State U., 1968, JD cum laude, 1972. Bar: Ariz. 1972, U.S. Dist. Ct. (Ariz.) 1972, U.S. Ct. Appeals (9th cir.) 1977, U.S. Supreme Ct. 1977. Atty. Snell & Wilmer, Phoenix, 1972-75; asst. atty. gen. Ariz. Atty. Gen.'s Office, 1975-97; judge Ariz. Superior Ct., Maricopa County, 1997—. Lectr. State Bar of Ariz., 1987—, continuing legal edn. commn., 1987—, chair, 1996-97, appellate handbook com., 1985—, criminal jury inst. com., 1996—, bd. legal specialization, 1991-96, chair, 1993-95, peer review com., 1992-95, criminal rules com., 1990-94, alternative dispute resolution com., 1984-86, criminal justice sec., 1980-87, chair, 1984-86; editl. bd. Ariz. Atty., 1987-98; spkr. in field. Author: Arizona Courtroom Evidence Manual, 3rd edit., 1998, Arizona Legal Forms, Criminal Procedure, 1990. Named Disting. Public Lawyer, State Bar Ariz., 1991, Mem. of Yr. State Bar of Arizona, 1995. Fellow Ariz. Bar Found.; mem. Phi Delta Theta, Ariz. Supreme Ct. (appellate case processing implementation task force, criminal jury com.). Office: 201 W Jefferson St SPC 47 Phoenix AZ 85003-2244 also: 1501 W Washington Phoenix AZ 85007-3231 Office Phone: 602-542-9300.

MCCLINTOCK, JESSICA, fashion designer; b. Frenchville, Maine, June 19, 1930; d. Rene Gagnon and Verna Hedrich; m. Frank Staples (dec. 1964); 1 child Scott. BA, San Jose State U., 1963. Elem. sch. tchr., Marblehead, Mass., 1966-68, Long Island, N.Y., 1968, Sunnyvale, Calif., 1964-65, 68-69; fashion designer Jessica McClintock, Inc., San Francisco, 1969—. Active donor, AIDS and Homeless programs; scholarship sponsor Fashion Inst. Design and Merchandising. Recipient Merit award Design, 1989, Dallas Fashion award, 1988, Tommy award, 1986, Pres. Appreciation award, 1986, Best Interior Store Design, 1986, Calif. Designer award, 1985, Earnie award, 1981, numerous others. Mem. Coun. Fashion Designers of Am., Fashion Inst. Design & Merchandising (adv. bd. 1979—), San Francisco Fashion Industry (pres. 1976-78, bd. dirs. 1989). Office: Jessica McClintock Inc 1400 16th St San Francisco CA 94103-5181

MCCLINTOCK, RICHARD POLSON, dermatologist; b. Lancaster, NH, Dec. 16, 1933; s. Richard P. and Dorothy Grace McClintock; m. Barbara Wyatt, June 1959 (div. Mar. 1970); children: Peter, Pamela; m. Mary Joy Fitzgerald, Mar. 21, 1970; children: Wayne, Patrick. BA, Dartmouth Coll., 1956; MD, Harvard U., 1960. Diplomate Am. Bd. Dermatology, Am. Bd. Dermatopathology. Intern in medicine U. N.C., Chapel Hill, 1960-61; resident in dermatology Stanford U., Palo Alto, Calif., 1964-67; pvt. practice Ukiah, Calif., 1967—; clin. instr. dermatology Stanford U., Palo Alto, 1967-78, clin. asst. prof., 1978-86, assoc. clin. prof., 1986-92, lectr., 1992-98, assoc. clin. prof., 1998—. Mem. hosp. staff Ukiah Valley Med. Ctr., chief of staff, 1974. Contbr. articles to profl. jours. Trustee Found. for Med. Care for Mendocino and Lake Counties, 1990-2008, pres., 1992-94. Lt. Med. Corps, USN, 1961-64. Mem. San Francisco Dermatol. Soc. (Practitioner of Yr. 2004), Pacific Dermatol. Assn., Am. Acad. Dermatology, Calif. Med. Soc., Mendocino Lake County Med. Soc., Internat. Soc. Dermatopathology. Office: 723 S Dora St Ukiah CA 95482-5335 E-mail: fitzmac@pacific.net.

MCCLINTOCK, TOM (THOMAS MILLER MCCLINTOCK II), United States Representative from California, former state senator; b. Bronxville, NY, July 10, 1956; s. Thomas Miller and Marianne (Christy) McClintock; m. Lori McClintock; children: Justin, Shannah. BA, UCLA, 1978. Chief of staff to Senator Ed Davis Calif. State Senate, 1980—82; mem. Calif. House of Reps. from Dist. 28, 1982—92, Calif. House of Reps. from Dist. 38, 1996—2000, Republican whip, 1984—89; mem. Calif. State Senate from Dist. 19, 2000—09, vice chmn. transp. & housing com., mem. revenue & taxation com., pub. employment & retirement com., com. on legis. ethics, joint com. on rules, joint legis. audit com.; mem. US Congress from 4th Calif. Dist., 2009—. Mem. housing and cmty. devel. Calif. Ho. of Reps. Recipient Benjamin Franklin award, Calif. Printing Industry, Medal of Merit, Ventura County Peace Officers Assn. Republican. Office: US Congress 508 Cannon House Office Bldg Washington DC 20515-0504 also: Dist Office 4230 Douglas Blvd Ste 200 Granite Bay CA 95746 Office Phone: 202-225-2511, 916-786-5560. Office Fax: 202-225-5444, 916-786-6364.*

MCCLOSKEY, PETE (PAUL NORTON MCCLOSKEY JR.), lawyer, former congressman; b. San Bernardino, Calif., Sept. 29, 1927; s. Paul Norton & Vera McNabb McCloskey; m. Caroline Wadsworth, 1949 (div.); children: Nancy, Peter, John, Kathleen; m. Helen Virginia Hooper, 1982 AB, Stanford, 1950, LL.B., 1953; JD, Santa Clara Law Sch., 1974. Bar: Calif., 1953. Dep. dist. atty. Alameda County, Calif., 1953-54; mem. firm McCloskey, Wilson, Mosher & Martin, Palo Alto, 1956-67; mem. US Congress from 11th Calif. Dist., 1967-83; ptnr. Brobeck Phleger & Harrison, 1983-89; counsel McClung & Davis, Laguna Hills, Calif.; founder, ptnr. Law Office of Paul McCloskey; ptnr. McCloskey, Hubbard, Ebert & Moore, LLP; prin. Cotchett, Pitre & McCarthy, San Francisco, 2008—. Del. UN Law of Sea Conf.; lectr. in law Stanford Law Sch., 1964-67, Santa Clara Law Sch., 1964-67; co-chair, Earth Day, 1970; mem., US Commn. on Nat. & Cmty. Svc., 1990-92 Author: Guide of Professional Conduct for New Practitioners, 1961, Text on the US Constitution, 1961, Truth and Untruth: Political Deceit in America, 1972, The Taking of Hill 610, 1992 Served with USN, 1945-47, to col. USMC, 1950-52. Decorated Navy Cross, Silver Star, Purple Heart; named Young Man of Yr. Palo Alto Jr. C. of C., 1961; recipient Edgar Wayburn award, Sierra Club, 2006 Mem. ABA, Palo Alto Bar Assn. (pres. 1960-61), Santa Clara County Bar Assn. (trustee 1965-67), State Bar Calif. (pres. conf. barristers 1961-62), Family Svc. Assn., Phi Delta Phi. Democrat. Presbyterian. Achievements include co-authoring the 1973 Endangered Species Act. Office: Cotchett Pitre & McCarthy San Francisco Airport Ctr 840 Malcolm Rd Burlingame CA 94010

MCCLOSKEY, THOMAS HENRY, mechanical engineer, consultant; b. Phila., Dec. 11, 1946; s. Thomas H. McCloskey; m. Rosemary Loscalzo, July 11, 1970. BSME, Drexel U., 1969. Rsch. engr. Westinghouse Elec. Corp., Phila., 1969-80; mgr. turbo-machinery Elec. Power Rsch. Inst., Palo Alto, Calif., 1980-92, cons. turbomachinery, 1992—. Mem. adv. bd. Internat. Pump Symposium, Houston, 1987—. Author: ASME Specification Guidelines for Large Steam Turbines, 1987; contbr. articles to profl. jours. Recipient George Westinghouse Gold medal Am. Soc. of Mechanical Engineers, 1995. Fellow ASME (dir. turbine design course 1988—, mem. rsch. bd. 1989—, Edison Elec. Prime Mover award 1984, 97, George Westinghouse Gold medal 1995). Achievements include 6 patents in turbomachinery design; development and field application of finite element/fracture mechanic techniques and erosion/corrosion resistant materials for life assessment/optimization of large turbine generators and pumps.

MCCLOUGHAN, SCOT G., professional sports team executive; b. San Leandro, Calif., 1971; s. Kent McCloughan; m. Kelli A. McCloughan; children: Caden, Adison, Avery. Attended, Wichita State U. Minor league baseball player St. Catharines Blue Jays; scout Green Bay Packers, 1994—97; dir., coll. scouting Seattle Seahawks, 2000—04; v.p. pro personnel San Francisco 49ers, 2004—07, gen. mgr., 2008—. Office: c/o San Francisco 49ers Marie P DeBartolo Sports Ctr 4949 Centennial Blvd Santa Clara CA 95054*

MCCLUGGAGE, KERRY, film and television executive; Studied broadcasting and film, U. So. Calif., 1976; MBA, Harvard U., 1978. With MCA/Universal, 1979—90; chmn. Paramount TV Group, Viacom, 1991—2002; founder, independent prodr., CEO Craftsman Films, 2002—; acquired with Jeff Sagansky, also co-chmn. Ardustry Home Entertainment, Woodland Hills, Calif., 2005—. Co-founder UPN Network, 1995. Supervised and developed programs such as: The A-Team, Coach, Deadwood, The Equalizer, Frasier, JAG, Northern Exposure, Law & Order, Miami Vice, Murder She Wrote, Quantum Leap and a few Star Trek Series. Address: Ardustry Home Entertainment 21250 Califa St Ste 102 Woodland Hills CA 91367

MCCLURE, R. DALE, physician; b. Jan. 4, 1943; MD, U. Western Ontario, Can., 1968. Prof. urology U. Wash. Sch. Medicine, 1991—. Fellow: RCS; mem.: Pacific Coast Reproductive Soc., Am. Soc. Reproductive Medicine (mem. exec. bd. 2004—, pres. elect, pres. 2008—09). Office: Virginia Mason Med Ctr 1100 9th Ave Seattle WA 98101-2756

MCCLUSKEY, BOB R., state representative; b. Denver, Aug. 17, 1950; BA in Econs., Stanford U., 1972, MBA, 1975. Pres. Poudre Valley Creamery, Colo.; state rep. dist. 52 Colo. Ho. of Reps., Denver, 2002—, mem. agr. livestock and natural resources, and bus. affairs and labor coms. Chmn. Colo. 4-H Youth Fund, 1991—93, Ft. Collins Cmty. Found., 2001—02; city councilman Ft. Collins City Coun., 1993—97; chmn. Poudre Fire Authority, 1995—96; pres. Ft. Collins Parks and Recreation Bd., 1991—93; chmn. Juvenile Svcs. Planning Com., 1994—95. Mem.: Ft. Collins Cmty. Found. (bd. dirs.), Ft. Collins Rotary. Republican. Methodist. Office: State Capitol # 318 200 E Colfax Ave Denver CO 80203

MCCOLLAM, CRAIG A., manufacturing executive; b. 1960; Dir. fin., corp. controller Dionex Corp, Sunnyvale, Calif., 1993-99, v.p. fin. & adminstrn., CFO, 1999—. Office: PO Box 3603 1228 Titan Way Sunnyvale CA 94085-4015 Office Phone: 408-481-4107. Business E-Mail: craig.mccollam@dionex.com.

MCCOLLAM, SHARON L., retail executive; b. 1962; BS in Acctg., U. Ctrl. Okla. CPA. Acctg. Ernst & Young; v.p., CFO fresh vegetables divsn. Dole Food Co., Inc., 1996—2000; v.p. fin. Williams-Sonoma, Inc., San Francisco, 2000, sr. v.p., CFO, 2000—03, exec. v.p., CFO, 2003—06, exec. v.p., CFO, COO, 2006—. Bd. dirs. Del Monte Foods Co., 2007—. Office: Williams-Sonoma Inc 3250 Van Ness Ave San Francisco CA 94109

MC COMIC, ROBERT BARRY, real estate company executive, lawyer; b. Selmer, Tenn., Nov. 6, 1939; s. Richard Donald and Ila Marie (Prather) McC.; children: Thomas Christopher, Robert Geoffrey. BS, Union U., 1961; LLB, Tulane U., 1964; postgrad. in law, U. Freiburg, W. Ger., 1964-65, Hague Internat. Acad. Law, Netherlands, 1965. Bar: Tenn. 1964, N.Y. 1966, Calif. 1971. Assoc. Donovan Leisure Newton & Irvine, NYC, 1965-68; assoc. gen. counsel Avco Corp., Greenwich, Conn., 1968-70; exec. v.p., pres., CEO Avco Cmty Developers, Inc., 1973-82; chmn., CEO R.B. McComic, Inc., 1982-92, McComic Consolidated, Inc., 1992—; CEO Trans West Housing, Inc., 1994—, Globelink, LLC, 1995—. Pres. emeritus U. Calif. San Diego Found.; bd. dirs. World Affairs Coun. Honoree Human Relations Inst. Am. Jewish Com., 1981, Kellog's Celebrity Tribute, 1988. Mem. ABA, Calif. Bar Assn., San Diego County Bar Assn., Assn. of Bar of City of N.Y., San Diego Bldg. Industry Assn., San Diego Yacht Club, Order of Coif, Sigma Alpha Epsilon, Omicron Delta Kappa, Lambda Alpha. Home: 7180 Fairway Rd La Jolla CA 92037-5623 Office: Mccomic Consolidated Inc 10721 Treena St Ste 200 San Diego CA 92131-1039 E-mail: bMcComic@Yahoo.com.

MCCOMISH, JOHN, state legislator; b. Youngstown, Ohio, Feb. 11, 1943; m. Karen McComish; children: John, Margaret. BA, Colgate U., Hamilton, NY, 1965. Nat. sales mgr. Johnson & Johnson, 1974—82; v.p. Becton, Dickinson & Co., 1982—89; owner Little Prof. Book Store, Ariz., 1989—95; pres. Ahwatukee Foothills C. of C., Phoenix, 1996—2006, ret., 2006; mem. Dist. 20 Ariz. House of Reps., 2007—, majority leader, mem. rules com. Mem. Ahwatukee Village Planning Com., 1997—99, chair, 2001—04; mem. City of Phoenix Planning Commn., 2000—02. Mem.: Ahwatukee Kiwanis Club. Republican. Presbyterian. Office: Ariz House Reps Capitol Complex 1700 W Washington Rm 206 Phoenix AZ 85007 Office Phone: 602-926-5898. Office Fax: 602-417-3020 602-417-3020. E-mail: jmccmos@azleg.gov.*

MCCONNEL, RICHARD APPLETON, aerospace company official; b. Rochester, Pa., May 29, 1933; s. Richard Appleton Sr. and Dorothy (Merriman) McC.; m. Mary Francis McInnis, 1964 (div. 1984); children: Amy Ellen, Sarah Catherine; m. Penny Kendzie, 1993. BS in Naval Engring., U.S. Naval Acad., 1957; MS in Aerospace Engring., USN Postgrad. Sch., 1966. Commd. ensign USN, 1957; naval aviator Operation ASW, 1959-63, 68-71, 75-79; asst. prof. math. U.S. Naval Acad., 1966-68; program mgr. P3C update Naval Air Devel. Ctr., 1971-75; range program mgr. Pacific Missile Test Ctr., 1979-82; ret. USN, 1982; program mgr. Electromagnetic Systems div. Raytheon Co., Goleta, Calif., 1982-87; sr. engr. SRS Techs., Inc., Camarillo, Calif., 1987-92, High Tech. Solutions, Inc., Camarillo, Calif., 1992—. Mem. Internat. Test and Evaluation Assn., Assn. Old Crows. Republican. Office Phone: 805-485-5217 ext 103. Personal E-mail: r.mcconnel@earthlink.net. Business E-Mail: dmcconnel@htshq.com.

MCCONNELL, MICHAEL W., federal judge, law educator; b. Louisville, Ky., May 18, 1955; m. Mary Cargill Norton McConnell; 3 children. BA, Mich. State U., 1976; JD, U. Chgo., 1979. Bar: DC 1981. Law clk. to Hon. J. Skelly Wright US Ct. Appeals (DC cir.), 1979-80; law clk. to Hon. William J. Brennan Jr. US Supreme Ct., Washington, 1980-81; asst. gen. counsel US Office of Mgmt. and Budget, Washington, 1981-83; asst. to the solicitor gen. US Dept. Justice, Washington, 1983-85; asst. prof. U. Chgo., 1984-89, prof., 1989—92, William Graham prof. law, 1992—96; Presdl. prof. U. Utah Coll. Law, 1997—2002; vis. prof. Harvard Law School, 1999; special consultant Mayer, Brown & Platt, 1989—2002; judge US Ct. Appeals (10th cir.), 2002—. Mem. Am. Acad. Arts and Scis., Order of Coif, Phi Beta Kappa, Phi Kappa Phi. Office: 10th Circuit Ct Appeals 125 S State St # 6404 Salt Lake City UT 84138

MCCORD, JOE MILTON, biochemist, educator; b. Memphis, Mar. 3, 1945; s. James Charles and Clara Elizabeth (Brown) McC. BS in Chemistry, Rhodes Coll., 1966; PhD in Biochemistry, Duke U., 1970. Research assoc. Duke U. Med. Ctr., Durham, N.C., 1971, assoc. in exptl. medicine, 1972-76, asst. med. research prof., 1976; assoc. prof. U. South Ala., Mobile, 1976-80, prof., dept. co-chmn., 1980-81, chmn. dept. biochemistry, 1981-90; prof. medicine and biochemistry Webb-Waring Inst. Biomed. Rsch. U. Colo., Denver, 1990—. Sci. cons. BioTech. Gen., N.Y., 1985—, CIBA-GEIGY Corp., Summit, N.J., 1984-85. Co-recipient Elliott Cresson medal Franklin Inst., 1997. Mem. Am. Soc. Biol. Chemists, Ala. Acad. Sci., Reticuloendothelial Soc., Am. Heart Assn. (council on basic sci.). Home: 390 S Hudson St Apt 6 Denver CO 80246-1448 Office: U Colo Webb Waring Lung Inst PO Box C-321 Denver CO 80262-0001

MC CORMACK, FRANCIS XAVIER, lawyer, former oil company executive; b. Bklyn., July 9, 1929; s. Joseph and Blanche V. (Dengel) Mc C.; m. Margaret V. Hynes, Apr. 24, 1954; children: Marguerite, Francis Xavier, Sean Michael, Keith John, Cecelia Blanche, Christopher Thomas. AB cum laude, St. Francis Coll., Bklyn., 1951; LLB, Columbia U., 1954. Bar: N.Y. 1955, Mich. 1963, Calif. 1974, Pa. 1975. Assoc. Cravath, Swaine & Moore, NYC, 1956-62; sr. atty. Ford Motor Co., 1962-64, asst. gen. counsel, 1970-72; v.p., gen. counsel, sec. Philco-Ford Corp., 1964-72; v.p., gen. counsel Atlantic Richfield Co., 1972-73, sr. v.p., gen. counsel, 1973-94. Editor Columbia U. Law Rev., 1954. Decorated commendatore Ordine al Merito (Italy); Stone scholar Columbia U., 1954. Mem. Calif. Club, Chancery Club, Annandale Golf Club.

MCCORMACK, MIKE, former congressman; b. Basil, Ohio, Dec. 14, 1921; s. Henry Arthur and Nancy (Jenkins) McCormack; m. Margaret Louise Higgins, June 21, 1947; children: Mark Alan, Steven Arthur, Timothy Arnold. BS, Wash. State U., 1948, MS in Chemistry, 1949; postgrad. studies in law, Gonzaga U., 1965—66; DEng (hon.), Stevens Inst. Tech., 1976; LLD (hon.), Salisbury State Coll., 1981. Instr. U. Puget Sound, 1949—50; chemist, engr. supr. Hanford plant GE, 1950—64; rsch. scientist Battelle-Northwest Lab., Richland, Wash., 1965—70; nuclear energy cons. Wash. Assn. Pub. Utility Dists., 1970; mem. Wash. Ho. of Reps., 1955—60, Wash. State Senate from Dist. 16, 1960—70, chmn. natural resources com., 1961, 1963, mem. edn. com., 1965, mem. revenue and taxation com., 1967—70; mem. US Congress from 4th Wash. Dist., 1971—81, mem. pub. works, transp., sci. and tech. com., chmn. energy rsch., prodn. subcom., chmn. Dem Freshman caucus; pres. McCormack Assocs., Inc., 1982—90, Chelan Assocs., Washington, 1985—89; dir. Inst. Sci. & Soc., Elleneburg, Wash., 1990—2000. Dir. engring. and sci. policy seminars Sch. Engring. and Applied Sci., George Washington U., 1984; dir. Universal Voltronics Corp., Mt. Kisco, NY; dir., sci. policy advisor Council of Sci. Soc. Pres., Washington. Advisor youth groups Wash. YMCA, Boy Scouts Am., Little League, Campfire Girls; mem. Wash. State Higher Edn. Bd, 1994—97. Served as First Lt. US Army, 1943—46, World War II. Recipient Charles Lathrop Parsons award, Am. Chemical Soc., 1999, Disting. Pub. Svc. award, IEEE, 1980; named Solar Energy Man of Yr., Solar Energy Industry Assn., 1975; named one of The Top 100 Innovators in the World, Tech. mag., 1981. Mem.: AAAS (former dir.), Am. Chem. Soc. (Charles Lathrop Parsons award 1999), Am. Nuclear Soc. (nat. com. pub. info.), Masons, Am. Legion, VFW. Democrat.

MCCORMICK, FRANK, research scientist; BSc in Biochemistry, U. Birmingham, 1972; PhD in Biochemistry, U. Cambridge, 1975; postdoctoral fellow, SUNY, Stony Brook, 1975—78, Imperial Cancer Rsch. Fund, 1978—81. Dir. molecular biology Cetus Corp., 1981—90, v.p. rsch., 1990—91, Chiron Corp., 1991—92; founder and chief sci. officer Onyx Pharm., 1992—96; dir. Comprehensive Cancer Ctr. and Cancer Rsch. Inst. U. Calif., San Francisco, 1997—, mem. Biomedical Sci. Program, 1997—, mem. Herbert Boyer Program in Bio. Sci., 1997, David A. Wood endowed chair in tumor biology and cancer rsch., 1997—. Mem. sci. adv. bd. Iconix Pharm. Recipient AACR-GHA Clowes Meml. award, 2002; fellow, Royal Soc., 1996. Mem.: Inst. Medicine. Office: Comprehensive Cancer Ctr Univ Calif San Francisco 2340 Sutter St Box 0128 San Francisco CA 94143 also: Comprehensive Rsch Ctr Univ Calif San Francisco Box 0128 San Francisco CA 94143-0128

MCCORMICK, HOMER L., JR., lawyer; b. Frederick, Md., Nov. 11, 1928; s. Homer Lee McCormick and Rosebelle Irene Biser; m. Jacquelyn R.; children: Deidre Ann and Thomas Lee. Student, George Washington U., 1946-48; AB, San Jose State U., 1951; JD, U. Calif., San Francisco, 1961. Bar: Calif. 1961, U.S. Dist. Ct. Ctrl. Dist. Calif. 1972, U.S. Dist. No. Calif. 1961, U.S. Dist. Ct., So. Dist. Calif. 1976, U.S. Dist. Ct. of Appeals (9th cir. 1961), U.S. Tax Ct. 1977, U.S. Ct. Claims 1977, U.S. Supreme Ct. 1977. Atty. Holiway Jones State of Calif., 1961-63; atty. assoc. Rutan & Tucker, Santa Ana, Calif., 1963-66, atty. ptnr., 1966-70, atty., sr. ptnr. Costa Mesa, Calif., 1970-88, dept. head pub. law, 1974-88, mng. ptnr., 1984-88; founding ptnr., sr. ptnr. McCormick, Kidman & Behrens, Costa Mesa, 1988—. Arbitrator Am. Arbitration Assn., 1966-88; judge pro tem Orange County Superior Ct., 1975, 81, 84; profl. designation Internat. Right of Way Assn.; elected mem. Calif. Condemnation Lawyers, 1994—; spkr., lectr. in field. Contbg. author: Real Property Remedies, 1982; contbr. articles to profl. jours. Bd. govs. Bus. Com. Arts, Orange County Philharm. Soc. Lt. USMCR, 1951—56, pilot, Korea. Named Alumnus of Year Hastings Law Sch., 1992. Mem. ABA (com. chair 1991), Am. Bd. Trial Adv. (pres. O.C. chpt. 1973), Orange City Atty. Assn. (pres. 1972), Fed. Bar Assoc., Consumer Attys. Calif., Am. Judicature Soc., Orange County Bar Assn. (com. chair 1991-92), Orange County Bus. Trial Lawyers, Order Coif, Thurston Soc., Hastings Alumni Assn. (pres. 1973), US Supreme Ct. Hist. Soc., 9th Cir. Hist. Soc., Hastings 1066 Found. (pres. 1974), Springs Country Club, Delta Theta Pi Republican. Episcopalian. Avocations: boating, fishing, flying, golf, foreign travel. Office Phone: 714-755-3100. Business E-Mail: mmccormick@mkblawyers.com.

MCCOY, HARRY E., II, lawyer; b. Parkersburg, W.Va., June 27, 1938; BA, U. Utah, 1967, JD, 1970. Bar: Utah 1970, Tex. 1974. Ptnr. Ballard Spahr Andrews & Ingersoll, LLP, Salt Lake City. Founding dir. ARDA Internat. Found., 1983—; bd. dirs., chair legis. coun., Am. Resort Devel. Assn. Mem. Utah State Bar. Office: Ballard Spahr Andrews & Ingersoll LLP 201 S Main St Ste 600 Salt Lake City UT 84111-2221 E-mail: mccoy2@ballardspahr.com.

MCCOY, THOMAS M., information technology executive; BA in History, Stanford U.; JD, U. So. Calif. Law clk. US Ct. Appeals (9th cir.); assoc. to ptnr. O'Melveny and Meyers, 1977—95; gen. counsel Advanced Micro Devices, Sunnyvale, Calif., 1993—95, sec., 1995—2003, sr. v.p., gen. counsel, 1998—2003, exec. v.p. legal affairs, chief adminstrv. officer, 2003—. Office: Advanced Micro Devices One AMD Pl PO Box 3453 Sunnyvale CA 94088-3453

MCCRACKEN, HARRY, journalist; b. Boston; s. Samuel and Natalie (Jacobson) McC. BA in History, Boston U., 1986. Editor Animato Mag., Cambridge, Mass., 1987-91; sr. editor CorpTech, Woburn, Mass., 1987-91; reviews editor Computer Buying World Mag., Wakefield, Mass., 1991-92; features editor Infoworld Direct mag., Boston, 1992-94; sr. assoc. editor PC World mag. and pcworld-.com, 1994—2000, exec. features editor, 2000—02, editor, 2002—04, editor-in-chief, 2004—, v.p, 2004—. Chmn. Jesse H. Neal award competition Am. Bus. Media, 2007—. Contbg. editor: Multimedia World Mag., San Francisco, 1994-96; mem. editl. bd. Am. Bus. Media; contbr. articles to profl. jours. Office: PC World Communications 501 Second Street San Francisco CA 94107

MCCRACKEN, STEVEN CARL, lawyer; b. Artesia, Calif., Oct. 29, 1950; s. Glenn A. and Helen V. (Fears) McCracken; m. Susan Lee Waggener, July 29, 1979; children: Casey James, Scott Kevin. BA magna cum laude, U. Calif., Irvine, 1972; JD, U. Va., 1975. Bar: Calif. 1975, U.S. Dist. Ct. (cen. dist.) Calif. 1975, U.S. Ct. Appeals (9th cir.) 1976, U.S. Dist. Ct. (no. dist.) Calif. 1977, D.C. 1979, U.S. Supreme Ct. 1985, U.S. Dist. Ct. (so. dist.) Calif. 1990. Assoc. Gibson, Dunn & Crutcher, LA, 1975-82, ptnr. Irvine, Calif., 1983-94; v.p., sec. and gen. counsel Callaway Golf Co., Carlsbad, Calif., 1994-96, exec. v.p., gen. counsel and sec., 1996-97, exec. v.p. licensing, chief legal officer, sec., 1997-2000, sr. exec. v.p., chief legal officer, sec., 2000—. Lawyer rep. Ninth Cir. Jud. Conf., 1989-91. Editor Va. Law Rev., 1973-75, mng. bd. 1974-75, bd. editors The Computer Lawyer, 1984-96. Mem. ABA (antitrust sect.), Orange County Bar Assn. (bd. dirs. 1988-90, chmn. fed. ct. com. 1988-89, chmn. bus. litigation sect. 1990, sec. 1991, treas. 1992, pres.-elect 1993, pres. 1994). Democrat. Office: Callaway Golf Co 2180 Rutherford Rd Carlsbad CA 92008-8815

MCCRADY, BARBARA SACHS, psychologist, educator; b. Evanston, Ill., May 7, 1949; d. James Frederick and Margaret Maxine (Miller) Sachs; m. Dennis D. McCrady, June 13, 1969; 1 child, Eric Paul. BS, Purdue U., 1969; PhD, U. R.I., 1975. Lic. clin. psychologist. Clin. project evaluator Butler Hosp., Providence, 1974-75, chief psychol. assessment program, 1975-76, chief problem drinkers' project, 1976-83; assoc. prof. psychology Rutgers U., Piscataway, NJ, 1983-89, prof. psychology, 1989-2000, prof. II, 2000—07. From instr. to assoc. prof. psychiatry Brown U., Providence, 1975—83; reviewer Nat. Inst. on Alcohol Abuse and Alcoholism, Washington, 1979—82, extramural sci. adv. bd., 1989—93; cons. Inst. Medicine, Washington, 1988—89; acting dir. Rutgers Ctr. Alcohol Studies, Piscataway, 1990—92, dir. clin. tng. dept. psychology, 1993—2005, chair dept. psychology, 2005—07; dir. Ctr. on Alcoholism, Substance Abuse, and Addictions U. N. Mex., Albuquerque, 2007—, prof. dept. psychol., 2007—. Author: The Alcoholic Marriage, 1977; editor: Marriage and Marital Therapy, 1978, Directions in Alcohol Abuse Treatment Research, 1985, Research on Alcoholics Anonymous: Opportunities and Alternatives, 1993, Addictions: A Comprehensive Guidebook, 1999. Grantee Nat. Inst. on Alcohol Abuse and Alcoholism, 1979-83, 1988—. Fellow Am. Psychol. Assn. (past pres. divsn. addictions); mem. Assn. for Advancement Behavior Therapy, Rsch. Soc. on Alcoholism (bd. dirs., 1999-2003). Avocations: horseback riding, skiing, piano. Office: Univ N Mex CASAA 2560 Yale Blvd SE MSCII 6280 Albuquerque NM 87106 Home Phone: 505-856-1161; Office Phone: 505-925-2388. Business E-Mail: bmccrady@unm.edu.

MCCRAY, RICHARD ALAN, astrophysicist, educator; b. LA, Nov. 24, 1937; s. Alan Archer and Ruth Elizabeth (Woodworth) McC.; m. Sandra Broomfield; children: Julia, Carla BS, Stanford U., 1959; PhD, UCLA, 1967. Rsch. fellow Calif. Inst. Tech, Pasadena, 1967-68; asst. prof. astronomy Harvard U., Cambridge, Mass., 1968-71; assoc. prof. astrophysics U. Colo., Boulder, 1971-75, prof., 1975—, chmn. Joint Inst. Lab. Astrophysics, 1981-82, chmn. Ctr. for Astrophysics and Space Astronomy, 1985-86, George Gamow prof. astrophysics, 1998—; corr. prof. astronomy Nanjing (China) U., 1996—. Contbr. articles to profl. jours. Guggenheim fellow, 1975-76; NSF Disting. Tchg. scholar, 2002. Mem. NAS, Am. Astron. Soc. (councilor 1980-83, chmn. high energy astrophysics div. 1986-87, Heineman Prize for Astrophysics, 1990), Internat. Astron. Union Office: U Colo Joint Inst Lab Astrophysics Boulder CO 80309-0440 E-mail: dick@jila.colorado.edu.

MC CRAY, RONALD DAVID, lawyer, apparel executive; b. Bronx, NY, July 2, 1957; s. Sylvester David and Vivian Marie (Bethea) McCray; m. Monica Ann Simon, Sept. 28, 1985; children: Morgan Marie, Adriane Michelle, Jordan Ellyse. BA, Cornell U., Ithaca, NY, 1979; JD, Harvard U., 1983. Bar: NY 1984, Tex. 1994. Assoc. Weil, Gotshal & Manges, NYC, 1983-85, Jones, Day, Reavis & Pogue, Dallas, 1985-87; sr. atty. Kimberly-Clark Corp., Dallas, 1987—93, sr. counsel, 1993—96, v.p., chief counsel, 1996—99, v.p., sec., 1999—2001, v.p., assoc. gen. counsel, sec., 2001—03, sr. v.p. law and govt. affairs, 2003—08, chief compliance officer, 2004—08; v.p., chief adminstrv. officer Nike Inc., Beaverton, Oreg., 2008—. Bd. dirs. Knight-Ridder Inc., 2003—. Editor: Pattern Discovery: Anti-Trust, 1982, Harvard CR/CL Law Rev., 1981-82. Trustee The Hockaday Sch., Dallas. Mem. ABA (wire payment systems subcommittee 1988—), NY Bar Assn., Tex. Bar Assn. (comml. code com. 1989-93), Dallas Bar Assn., Tex. Bus. Law Found. (bd. dirs. 1990-93), Nat. Assn. Securities Profls., Am. Corp. Counsel Assn., Coun. Fgn. Rels. Roman Catholic. Avocations: reading, sports, music. Office: Nike Inc 1 Bowerman Dr Beaverton OR 97005-6453

MCCREA, SHAUN S., lawyer; b. 1956; d. Robert McCrea. BA, U. Oreg.; JD, 1983. Bar: Oreg. Atty. McCrea P.C., Eugene, Oreg. Vice chmn. Oreg. Pub. Def. Svcs. Commn. Mem.: Nat. Assn. Criminal Def. Lawyers, Oreg. Criminal Def. Lawyers Assn. (past pres.). Avocation: mythology. Office: McCrea PC 1147 High St Eugene OR 97401 Office Phone: 541-485-1182. Office Fax: 541-485-6847. E-mail: smccrea@callatg.com.

MCCREARY, LORI L., film company executive; b. Antioch, Calif., Feb. 14, 1961; d. Ronald Royce and Sharon A. (Rich) McC. BS in Computer Sci., UCLA, 1984. V.p. tech. svcs. CompuLaw Inc., Culver City, Calif., 1982-85; owner McCreary and Assocs., Santa Monica, Calif., 1985-95; CEO, pres. Revelations Entertainment, Santa Monica, 1996—. Named one of The 100 Most Powerful Women in Entertainment, Hollywood Reporter, 2006, 2007. Office: Revelations Entertainment 1221 2nd St Fl 4 Santa Monica CA 90401-1150

MCCRONE, ALISTAIR WILLIAM, retired academic administrator; b. Regina, Can., Oct. 7, 1931; BA, U. Sask., 1953; MSc, U. Nebr., 1955; PhD, U. Kans., 1961. Instr. geology NYU, 1959-61, asst. prof., 1961-64, assoc. prof., 1964-69, prof., 1969-70, supr. Rsch. Ship Sea Owl on L.I. Sound, 1959-64, asst. dir. univ. program at Sterling Forest, 1965-66, resident master Rubin Internat. Residence Hall, 1966-69, chmn. dept. geology, 1966-69, assoc. dean Grad. Sch. Arts and Scis., 1969-70; prof. geology, acad. v.p. U. Pacific, 1970-74, acting pres., 1971; prof. geology, pres. Calif. State U. Sys. Humboldt State U., Arcata, 1974—2002. Exec. coun. Calif. State U. Sys., 1974-2002, acad. senate Humboldt State U., 1974-2002, chancellor's com. on innovative programs, 1974-76, trustees' task force on off-campus instrn., 1975-76, exec. com. Chancellor's Coun. of Pres., 1976-79, Calif. state del. Am. Assn. State Coll. and Univ., 1977-80; mem. Commn. on Ednl. Telecomm., 1983-86; chair Calif. State U. Statewide Task Force on Earthquake and Emergency preparedness, 1985-88, 95-97; chmn., accreditation teams Western Assn. Sch. and Coll.; chair com. on energy and environ. Am. Assn. State Coll. and Univ., 1980-84; chair program com. Western Coll. Assn., 1983-84, panelist, 1983. Contbr. articles to profl. jour.; lectr. on geology Sunrise Semester program CBS Nat. Network, 1969-70; various appearances on local TV stas. Bd. trustees Presbyn. Hosp.-Pacific Med. Ctr., San Francisco, 1971-74; mem. Calif. Coun. for Humanities, 1977-82; mem. local campaign bd. United Way, 1977-83; mem. Am. Friends Wilton Park, 1980—; bd. dirs. Humboldt Convention and Visitors Bur., 1980-87, Redwood Empire Assn., 1983-87; bd. dirs. Calif. State Automobile Assn., 1988-2007, Am. Automobile Assn., 1990-93; bd. trustees Calif. State Parks Found., 1994-2000. Recipient Erasmus Haworth Disting. Alumnus award U. Kans., 2000; Shell fellow in geology U. Nebr., 1954-55; Danforth assoc. NYU, 1964. Fellow Calif. Acad. Sci.; mem. AAAS, Geol. Soc. Am., Am. Assn. U. Adminstrs. (nat. bd. 1986-89, 96-99, 2001-2002), Assn. Am. Coll. (bd. dir. 1989-92, chair 1991), St. Andrews Soc. NY (life), Rotary, Sigma Xi (pres. NYU chpt. 1967-69), Phi Kappa Phi. Avocation: golf. Office: Humboldt State U Univ Campus Arcata CA 95521 Office Phone: 707-826-5074. Business E-Mail: mccrone@humboldt.edu.

MCCROSKEY, WILLIAM JAMES, retired aeronautical engineer; b. San Angelo, Tex., Mar. 9, 1937; s. J. M. and W. Elizabeth McC.; m. Elizabeth W. Wear, Jan. 31, 1960; children: Nancy E., Susan C. BS, U. Tex., 1960; MS, Princeton U., 1962, PhD, 1966. Rsch. assoc. Princeton U., 1966; rsch. engr. U.S. Army Aeromechanics Lab., Moffett Field, Calif., 1966-80; sr. rsch. scientist U.S. Army and NASA Aeronautics Directorate, 1980—2000; ret., 2000. Exch. scientist Office Nat. Etudes et Recherches Aérospatiale, Châtillon, France, 1972-73; mem. fluid dynamics panel NATO Adv. Group for Aerospace R & D, 1976-94, chmn., 1989-91. With U.S. Army, 1966-68. Recipient French Medaille l'Aeronautique, 1994, AGARD von Kármán medal, 1995, Nat. Acad. Engring., 1996. Fellow AIAA (Outstanding Engr. San Francisco sect. 1975, fluid dynamics tech com. 1984-88, internat. activities com. 1990—); mem. ASME (Freeman scholar award 1976), Am. Helicopter Soc. (Howard Hughes award 1991). Office: Ames Rsch Ctr N258-1 Moffett Field CA 94035

MCCULLOCH, LINDA HARMAN, state official, former school system administrator; b. Mont., Dec. 21, 1954; m. Bill McCulloch, 1978. BA in Elem. Edn., U. Mont., 1982, MA in Elem. Edn., 1990. Pub. sch. tchr., Ashland, Missoula, Bonner, Mont., 1978—95; mem. Dist. 70 Mont. House of Reps., 1995—2001; supt. pub. instrn. State of Mont., 2002—09, sec. state, 2009—. Faculty affiliate U. Mont., 1995—2000; mem. judiciary, highways & transportation, local govt. edn. and house rules committees Mont. House Reps., 1997, interim com. assignments included juvenile justice & mental health, Indian Affairs, and edn. & local govt.; minority caucus leader House Reps., Helena, Mont., 1999; vice chair edn. com. Mont. House Reps., 1999. Mem., officer PTA Assn., Helena, 1985; bd. dirs. Missoula Developmental Services. Corp.; mem. adv. com. Missoula Youth Homes Foster Care; bd. mem. Pub Edn., Bd. Reagents, Mont. Libr. Commn. and Land Board, N.W. Regional Ednl. Lab., Mont. Heritage Project, Profl. Tchg. Found. Recipient Mike and Maureen Mansfield Libr. scholaship, 1981, J.C. Penny Vol. Program award, 1998. Mem.: AAUW, LWV, Five Valleys Reading Assn., Mont. State Reading Coun., Mont. Fedn. Tchrs., Mont. Ednl. Assn., Mont. Libr. Assn.

(Legislator of Yr. award 1997), Mont. Family Union, Mont. Dem. Womens Club. Democrat. Methodist. Office: Office Sec State State Capital Rm 260 PO Box 202801 Helena MT 59620 Office Phone: 406-444-2034. Office Fax: 406-444-3976. Business E-Mail: sos@mt.gov.*

MC CULLOCH, SAMUEL CLYDE, history professor; b. Ararat, Australia, Sept. 3, 1916; came to U.S., 1936, naturalized, 1944; s. Samuel and Agnes Almond (Clyde) McC.; m. Sara Ellen Rand, Feb. 19, 1944; children: Ellen (Mrs. William Henry Meyer III), David Rand, Malcolm Clyde. AB with highest honors in History, UCLA, 1940, MA (grad. fellow history), 1942; PhD, U. Calif. at Los Angeles, 1944. Asst. U. Calif. at Los Angeles, 1943-44; instr. Oberlin Coll., 1944-45; asst. prof. Amherst Coll., 1945-46; vis. asst. prof. U. Mich., 1946-47; mem. faculty Rutgers U., 1947-60, prof. history, assoc. dean arts and scis., 1958-60; dean coll., prof. history San Francisco State Coll., 1960-63; dean humanities, prof. history U. Calif. at Irvine, 1963-70, prof., 1970-87, prof. emeritus, 1987—, coordinator Edn. Abroad Program, 1975-85, dir. Australian Study Ctr., 1986, 87. Vis. summer prof. Oberlin Coll., 1945, 46, U. Calif. at Los Angeles, 1947, U. Del., 1949; Fulbright Research prof. Monash U., Melbourne (Australia) U., 1970; Am. Philos. Soc. grantee, 1970 Author: British Humanitarianism, 1950, George Gipps, 1966, River King: The Mc Culloch Carrying Company and Echura, 1865-1898, 1986, Instant University: A History of U.C.I., 1957-1993, 1995, William McCulloch, 1932-1909, 1997, A Collection of Book Reviews, 1948-93, 2000; contbr. numerous articles, revs. to profl. jours.; assoc. editor Jour. Brit. Studies, 1960-68, bd. advisors, 1968-70; bd. corrs. Hist. Studies: Australia and New Zealand, 1949-83. Mem. Calif. Curriculum Commn., 1961-67, Highland Park (N.J.) Bd. Edn., 1959-60. Grantee Am. Philos. Soc., Social Sci. Rsch. Coun. and Rutgers U. Rsch. Coun. to Australia, 1951; Fulbright rsch. fellow U. Sydney, Australia, 1954-55; grantee Social Sci. Rsch. Coun. to Eng., summer 1955 Fellow Royal Hist. Soc.; mem. Am. Hist. Assn., Church, Royal Australian Hist. Socs., A.A.U.P., N.Am. Conf. Brit. Studies (exec. sec. 1968-73, pres. 1975-77, Liftime Disting. Contbns. Brit. Studies award 1995), English Speaking Union (pres. New Brunswick 1957-59), Phi Beta Kappa, Pi Gamma Mu; Clubs: Univ. Club Irvine (forum moderator 1981-2008). Episcopalian (vestry). Home: 2121 Windward Ln Newport Beach CA 92660-3820

MCCUNE, BRENDA L., lawyer; BS, Western State Univ., 1994, JD, 1995. Bar: Calif. 1996. Atty. McCune Family Law, Yorba Linda, Calif. Contbr. articles to profl. jours. Named a Rising Star, So. Calif. Super Lawyers, 2004—06. Mem.: ABA, State Bar Calif., Orange County Bar Assn. (dir. family law sect. 2001—04), Peter M. Elliott Inns of Ct. Office: McCune Family Law Ste 206 4676 Lakeview Ave Yorba Linda CA 92886 Office Phone: 714-695-0502. Office Fax: 714-695-0568. Business E-Mail: brenda@bmccunefamilylaw.com.

MCCUNE, SARA MILLER, foundation executive, publisher; b. NYC, Feb. 4, 1941; d. Nathan M. and Rose (Glass) M.; m. George D. McCune, Oct. 16, 1966 (dec. May 1990). BA, Queens Coll., 1961. Asst. to v.p. sales Macmillan Pub. Co., NYC, 1961-63; sales mgr. Pergamon Press Ltd., Oxford, England, 1963-64; pres., pub., founder Sage Publs. Inc., NYC, 1965-66, pres., pub. Beverly Hills, Calif., 1966-83, pub., chmn. Newbury Park, Calif., 1984—; bd. dirs. Sage Publs. Ltd., London, chmn., 1990-95; bd. dirs. Sage Publs. India, New Delhi; pres. McCune Found., Newbury Park, Calif., 1990—. Mem. bd. dirs. UCSB Comm. Dept. Adv. Bd., Santa Barbara, Calif., 1994—, USCB Bd. Trustees, 1994—, The Fielding Inst., 1994—, Am. Acad. Pol. Scis., Phila., 1994—. Bd. dirs. USCB Found. Bd. Trustees, 1994—, sec., 1996-97, treas., 1997-98, vice-chair, 1998—. Mem. Am. Evaluation Assn. (spl. award for disting. contbns. 1988). Office: Sage Publications Inc 2455 Teller Rd Newbury Park CA 91320-2234

MCCUNE-DAVIS, DEBBIE, state legislator; b. Braddock, Pa., Aug. 12, 1951; d. Harry Valentine and Ernestine (Skrabak) Ponte; m. Glenn Davis; children: Cara Lynn, Michael Eric, Courtney Elizabeth, Josh, Lauren. AA, Glendale Cmty. Coll., 1971; BS in Sociology, Ariz. State U., 1975. Mem. Dist. 20 Ariz. House of Reps., 1979—94, minority whip, 1982—94; cmty. rels. specialist ComCare, 1982—94; prog. dir. Ariz. Partnership Immunization, 1996—, Ariz. Assn. Cmty. Health Centers, 1997—; mem. Dist. 14 Ariz House of Reps., 2003—06, Ariz State Senate, 2007—, mem. fin. com., rules com. Founding bd. mem. Nat. Bd. Am. Immunization Registry Assn. Democrat. Roman Catholic. Office: Ariz State Senate Capitol Complex 1700 W Washington,Rm 311 Phoenix AZ 85007 Office Phone: 602-926-4485. Office Fax: 602-926-3429. Business E-Mail: dmccunedavis@azleg.gov.*

MCDADE, SANDY D., lawyer, paper company executive; BA, Whitman Coll., 1974; JD cum laude, Seattle U., 1979. Mem. law dept. Weyerhaeuser Co., Federal Way, Wash., 1980—2000, corp. sec., 1993—2000, v.p. strategic planning, 2000—03, sr. v.p. Can., 2003—05, sr. v.p., indsl. wood products and internat. bus., 2005—06, sup. gen. counsel, 2006—. Mem.: World Trade Ctr. (bd. of governors, Seattle), Bd. of Arts Fund, Wash. State Bar Assn. (past chmn. corp. law dept. sect.). Office: Weyerhaeuser Co PO Box 9777 Federal Way WA 98063-9777

MCDANIEL, RODERICK ROGERS, petroleum engineer, consultant; b. High River, Alta., Can., 1926; s. Dorsey Patton and Daisy (Rogers) McD.; m. Trudy Ethier, Apr. 15, 2000; children: Nancy, Leslie. BS, U. Okla., 1947. Petroleum reservoir engr. Creole Petroleum Corp., 1947, Imperial Oil Ltd., 1948-52, chief reservoir engr., 1952-55; founder McDaniel Cons., Calgary, Canada, 1955—; chmn. Can. Airlines Ltd., Calgary, 1974-91, Can. Regional Airlines, Calgary, 1991-92. Hon. dir. Calgary Exhbn. and Stampede, 1979-88, hon. bd. dirs., 1988—; dir. Calgary Stampeder Football Team, 1988. Mem. Assn. Profl. Engrs. Alta (hon. life), Can. C. of C. (bd. dirs. 1973), Calgary C. of C. (past pres.), Calgary Petroleum Club (past pres.), Calgary Highlanders (hon. col. ret.), Calgary Golf and Country Club, Outrigger Club (Honolulu), Mission Hills Country Club. Home: # 2200 255 5 Ave SW Calgary AB Canada T2P 3G6 Office: McDaniel & Assoc 2200 255 5th Ave SW Calgary AB Canada T2P 3G6

MCDANIEL, THOMAS R., retired utilities executive; BS in Civil Engring., UCLA; postgrad., Calif. State U., LA, U. So. Calif. Joined So. Calif. Edison, 1971; CEO, dir. Edison Capital, 1987—2005; CEO, pres. Edison Mission Energy, Irvine, Calif., 2002—05, chmn., 2003—05; exec. v.p., CFO, treas. Edison Internat., Rosemead, Calif., 2005—08. Active Huntington Youth Shelter; dir. Sr. Care Action Network.

MCDANIELS, JOSH, professional football coach; b. Barberon, Ohio, Apr. 22, 1976; s. Thom McDaniels; m. Laura McDaniels; children: Jack Thomas, Maddie. Grad., John Carroll U., University Heights, Ohio. Grad. asst. Mich. State U. Spartans, 1999—2000; pers. asst. New Eng. Patriots, 2001, defensive coaching asst., 2002—03, quarterbacks coach, 2004—06, offensive coord., quarterbacks coach, 2006—09; head coach Denver Broncos, 2009—. Achievements include member of Super Bowl championship winning New England Patriots, 2004, 2005. Office: Denver Broncos 13655 Broncos Pky Englewood CO 80112*

MCDAVID, DOUGLAS WARREN, executive research consultant; b. San Francisco, Feb. 25, 1947; s. James Etheridge and Elizabeth Rae (Warren) McD.; m. Nancy Kathleen Somers, June 1968 (div. 1982); 1 child, Amy Kemp; m. Carleen Ann Richmond, Feb. 14, 1987; 1 child, Amanda Claire. BA in Sociology, U. Calif., Santa Cruz, 1969; MA in Libr. Sci., San Jose State U., 1972. Libr. Palo Alto (Calif.) City Libr., 1969-81; systems analyst Tymnet (Tymshare), Cupertino, Calif., 1981-84; mgr. systems architecture Tymnet McDonnell Douglas, San Jose, Calif., 1984-86; data modeling cons. Fireman's Fund Ins., Terra Linda, Calif., 1986-87, Bank of Calif., San Francisco, 1988; systems cons. Pacific Bell, San Ramon, Calif., 1989-93; prin. Integrated Info., 1993—; exec. cons. IBM Global Svcs., 1995—, IBM Almaden Rsch Ctr., 2002—. Mem. IBM Acad. Tech., 2000—; spkr. Entity/Relationship Conf. Internat., Burlingame, Calif., 1991, DAMA Internat. Conf., 1994—; sr. cons. in bus. semantic modeling for object oriented applications IBM Corp., 1994—; 1996 spkr. Bus. Rules Conf. OOPSLA, IBM Object Technology Conf., Ind. Labor & Mgmt. Coun.; cons. IBM, 1994-98, mgr. knowledge devel., 1999—; consulting rschr. IBM Almadea Rsch. Ctr., 2002—; spkr. in field. Assoc. editor: Handbook of Object Technology. Mem. IEEE, Assn. for Computing Machinery, Data Adminstrn. Mgmt. Assn. (San Francisco bd. dirs. 1987-91, Sacramento bd. dirs. 1992, spkr. 1991, 92), Data Processing Mgmt. Assn. (spkr. 1992), Am. Assn. Artificial Intelligence (spkr. 1993), Internat. Soc. Sys. Sci. (spkr. 1999), New Media Consortium (visionary bd. mem. 2007—). Avocations: golf, gardening, creative writing, investing, swimming. Home and Office: 8611 Kingslynn Ct Elk Grove CA 95624-3135 Office Phone: 916-549-4600. Business E-Mail: mcdavid@us.ibm.com.

MCDERMOTT, JAMES A., United States Representative from Washington, psychiatrist; b. Chgo., Dec. 28, 1936; m. Therese Hansen; 2 children. BS, Wheaton Coll., Ill., 1958; MD, U. Ill. Med. Sch., Chgo., 1963. Intern Buffalo Gen. Hosp., 1963-64; resident adult psychiatry U. Ill. Hosps., Chgo., 1964-66; resident child psychiatry U. Wash. Hosps., Seattle, 1966-68; asst. clin. prof. dept. psychiatry U. Wash., Seattle, 1970-83; mem. Wash. State House Reps. from 43rd Dist., 1971-72, Wash. State Senate, 1975-87; regional med. officer US Fgn. Svc., 1987-88; mem. US Congress from 7th Wash. dist., 1989—, mem. ways and means com., ranking minority mem. human resources subcommittee. Mem. exec. and edn. com. Nat. Conf. State Legislatures, chair ethics com.; co-chmn. Congl. task force internat. HIV/AIDS, Congl. Caucus on India and Indian Ams., Africa Trade and Investment Caucus, Congl. Kidney Caucus. Mem. Wash. State Arts Commn., Wash. Coun. for Prevention Child Abuse and Neglect; Dem. nominee for gov., 1980. Lt. comdr. M.C. USN, 1968—70. Mem. Am. Psychiat. Assn., Wash. State Med. Assn., King County Med. Soc. Democrat. Episcopalian. Office: US House Reps 1035 Longworth House Office Bldg Washington DC 20515 Office Phone: 202-225-3106.

MCDERMOTT, JOHN E., lawyer; b. Ravenna, Ohio, Oct. 25, 1946; BA, Ohio Wesleyan U., 1968; JD, Harvard U., 1971. Bar: Calif. 1972, US Supreme Ct., US Dist. Cts. (no., ea., ctrl. & so. dists.) Calif., DC, (ea. dist.) Ohio, (ea. dist.) Va., US Cts. of Appeals (9th & DC cirs.). Lectr. U. So. Calif. law Sch., 1974—81; ptnr. Howrey LLP, LA. Dir. Western Ctr. on Law and Poverty, Inc, 1977—81. Editor (Book): Indeterminacy in Education, McCutchan, 1976. Recipient So. California's Super Lawyers, Law & Politics mag., LA mag. Mem. ABA, State Bar Calif. 1972-, LA County, Phi Beta Kappa, mem. Assn. Bus. Trial Lawyers. Office: Howrey LLP 550 S Hope St Ste 1100 Los Angeles CA 90071 Office Phone: 213-892-1815. Office Fax: 213-892-2300. Business E-Mail: mcdermottj@howrey.com.

MCDERMOTT, KATHLEEN E., lawyer, corporate executive; b. July 1949; BS in fgn. svc., Georgetown U., JD. Bar: 1975. Assoc. Collier, Shannon, Rill & Scott, Washington DC, 1975—80, ptnr., 1981—93, 2000—01; exec. v.p., chief legal officer Am. Stores Inc. (now Albertson's Inc.), Salt Lake City, 1993—99; sr. v.p., gen. counsel Nash Finch Inc., Mpls., 2002—06. Mem.: FTC Com. (chair), ABA (former vice chair corp. counseling com. antitrust sect.). Home: 29 E Churchhill Dr Salt Lake City UT 84103-2267 Office Phone: 801-703-1143. Personal E-mail: mcdermott.kathleen@gmail.com.

MCDERMOTT, THOMAS JOHN, JR., lawyer; b. Santa Monica, Calif., Mar. 23, 1931; s. Thomas J. Sr. and Etha Irene (Cook) McD.; m. Yolanda Amante Jatap; children: Jodi Friedman, Kimberly E., Kish S. BA, UCLA, 1953, JD, 1958. Bar: Calif. 1959. Ptnr. Gray, Binkley and Pfaelzer, LA, 1964-67, Kadison, Pfaelzer, Woodward, Quinn and Rossi, LA, 1967-87, Rogers & Wells, LA, 1987-93, Bryan Cave, LA, 1993-95, Manatt, Phelps & Phillips, LLP, LA, 1995-99, Shanks and Herbert, San Diego, 1999—2003. Served with U.S. Army, 1953-56, Korea, 1999-2003. Fellow Am. Coll. Trial Lawyers; mem. ABA, Assn. Bus. Trial Lawyers (pres. 1980-81, mem. exec. com. 9th cir. jud. conf. 1993—, chair 1997), State Bar Calif. (chair litigation sect. 1993-94), UCLA Law Alumni Assn. (pres. 1961-62), Order of Coif. Office: Law Offices Thomas J McDermott 74-770 Hwy 111 Ste 201 Indian Wells CA 92210 Office Phone: 760-779-5800. Business E-Mail: tmcdermott@mcdelaw.com.

MCDEVITT, CHARLES FRANCIS, retired judge, lawyer; b. Pocatello, Idaho, Jan. 5, 1932; s. Bernard A. and Margaret (Hermann) McDevitt; m. Virginia L. Heller, Aug. 14, 1954; children: Eileen A., Kathryn A., Brian A., Sheila A., Terrence A., Neil A., Kendal A. LLB, U. Idaho, 1956. Bar: Idaho 1956. Ptnr. Richards, Haga & Eberle, Boise, 1956-62; gen. counsel, asst. sec. Boise Cascade Corp., 1962—68; mem. Idaho State Legislature, 1963-66; sec., gen. counsel Boise Cascade Corp., 1965-67, v.p. sec., 1967-68; pres. Beck Industries, 1968-70; group v.p. Singer Co., NYC, 1970-72, exec. v.p., 1973-76; pub. defender Ada County, Boise, 1976-78; co-founder Givens, McDevitt, Pursley & Webb, Boise, 1978-89; justice Idaho Supreme Ct., Boise, 1989-97, chief justice, 1993-97; ptnr., founder McDevitt & Miller, LLP, Boise, 1997—. Served on Gov.'s Select Com. on Taxation, Boise, 1988-89; mem. State Select Com. on Campaign Ethics and Campaign Finances, State Select Com. on Legis. Compensation. Chair Idaho Jud. Coun., 1993-97, Cts. Advisors Coun., 1994-98; mem. Multi-State Tax Com. Recipient Legal Merit award, Univ. of Idaho, 2002, Professionalism award, Idaho State Bar, 2005. Home: 4940 Boise River Ln Boise ID 83716-8816 Office: McDevitt Miller 420 W Bannock Boise ID 83702-6034 Office Phone: 208-343-7500. Business E-Mail: chas@McDevitt-Miller.com.

MCDEVITT, HUGH O'NEILL, immunologist, educator; b. Cin., Aug. 26, 1930; MD, Harvard U., 1955. Diplomate: Am. Bd. Internal Medicine. Intern Peter Bent Brigham Hosp., Boston, 1955-56, sr. asst. resident in medicine, 1961-62; asst. resident Bell Hosp., 1956-57; research fellow dept. bacteriology and immunology Harvard U., 1959-61; USPHS spl. fellow Nat. Inst. Med. Research, Mill Hill, London, 1962-64; physician Stanford U. Hosp., Calif., 1966—; assoc. prof. Stanford U. Sch. Medicine, Calif., 1969-72, prof. med. immunology Calif., 1972—, prof. med. microbiology Calif., 1980—2001, Burt and Marian Avery Prof. Immunology Calif., 1988—2001. Cons. physician VA Hosp., Palo Alto, Calif., 1968— Served as capt. M.C., AUS, 1957-59. Recipient Abbott Lab. award in Clin. and Diagnostic Immunology, Am. Soc. Microbiology, 2003. Mem. NAS, AAAS, Am. Fedn. Clin. Rsch., Am. Soc. Clin. Investigation, Am. Assn. Immunologists, Transplantation Soc., Inst. Medicine, Royal Soc. (fgn.). Office: Sherman Fairchild Bldg Stanford U Sch of Medicine 299 Campus Dr MC5124 Stanford CA 94305-5124 Business E-Mail: hughmcd@stanford.edu.

MCDEVITT, JAMES A., prosecutor, lawyer; b. July 1943; B, U. Wash.; MBA, JD, Gonzaga U. Asst. atty. gen. State of Wash., Office of Atty. Gen., 1975—77; from sr. ptnr. to mng. ptnr. Reed & Geisa, Spokane, Wash., 1977—94; ptnr. Preston, Gates & Ellis, Spokane, Wash., 1994—2002; US atty. (ea. dist.) Wash. US Dept. Justice, 2002—. With USAF, 1965—71, brig. gen. Wash. Air Nat. Guard, ret. Office: US Attys Office PO Box 1494 Spokane WA 99210 Office Phone: 509-353-2767.

MCDEVITT, RAY EDWARD, lawyer; b. San Francisco, Nov. 15, 1943; s. Edward Anthony and Margaret Ann (Peterson) McD.; m. Mary Rolfs, July 1, 1967; children— Jessica, Devon. B.A., Stanford U., 1966, J.D., 1969; Diploma in Law, Oxford U., 1973. Bar: Calif., 1970, U.S. Supreme Ct., 1975. Law clk. Calif. Supreme Ct., 1970; atty. EPA, 1973-75, assoc. gen. counsel, 1975-76; ptnr. Hanson, Bridgett, Marcus, Vlahos & Rudy, San Francisco, 1976—; adj. prof. Sch. Law U. San Francisco, 1994—. Editor: Courthouses of California: An Illustrated History, 2001. Mem. ABA, Calif. Supreme Ct. Hist. Soc. (pres. 2005—), Order of Coif. Office: 425 Market St Ste 2600 San Francisco CA 94105

MCDONALD, DANIEL ROBERT, state legislator; b. Seattle, Feb. 4, 1944; s. Robert William and Josephine Dorothy (Quigley) McD.; m. Norah Jane Cornwall, Dec. 28, 1966; children: Tod Robert, Evan Daniel. BSME, U. Wash., 1965, MA in Econs., 1975. Registered profl. engr., Calif., Wash. Mem. Wash. Ho. of Reps., Olympia, 1979-83, floor leader, 1983; mem. Wash. Senate, Dist. 48, Olympia, 1983—; floor leader Wash. Senate, Olympia, 1985-86, chmn. Ways and Means Com., 1988-92. Mem. revenue forecast coun. Olympia, 1984—, chmn. 1984-85; mem. legis. evaluation and accountability program, Olympia, 1983-90; commr. exec. bd. Western Interstate Com. on Higher Edn., 1983-87; mem. State Investment Bd.; Senate minority leader, 1995-96, 1999, Senate majority leader, 1997-98. Mem. Seattle/King County Drug Commn., 1978-79, Mcpl. League, Seattle, 1979—. Served to lt. (j.g.) USN, 1966-69, Vietnam. Mem. Bellevue (Wash.) C. of C., Rotary, Spec. Olympics Bd., Municipal League. Lodges: Rotary. Republican. Presbyterian. Home: 4650 92nd Ave NE Bellevue WA 98004-1335 Office: Wash State Senate 204 Irving Newhouse Ofc Bldg Olympia WA 98504-0001

MCDONALD, DENNIS, rancher, political organization administrator; b. Salina, Kans, 1944; m. Sharon McDonald; children: Kelly, Courtney, Casey, Clay. JD, San Francisco Law Sch. Owner, operator Open Spear Ranch; chmn. Mont. State Dem. Party, 2005—. Former mem. Agrl. Trade Adv. Com. for Livestock. Co-founder R-CALF. Mem.: US Cattlemen's Assn. (interim dir. Region VI), Mont. Cattlemen's Assn. (former pres.). Democrat. Office: Mont Dem Party PO Box 802 Helena MT 59624 also: Open Spear Ranch 856 Tony Creek Rd Melville MT 59055 Office Phone: 406-537-2333. Office Fax: 406-537-2334. E-mail: mcdonald@mcn.net.

MCDONALD, JOHN GREGORY, financial investment educator; b. Stockton, Calif., 1937; m. Melody McDonald. BS, Stanford U., 1960, MBA, 1962, PhD, 1967. Mem. faculty Grad. Sch. Bus. Stanford U., Calif., 1968—, now The Stanford Investors prof. fin. Grad. Sch. Bus. Vis. prof. U. Paris, 1972, Columbia Bus. Sch., 1975, Harvard Bus. Sch., 1986; gov., vice-chmn., bd. govs. NASD/NASDAQ Stock Market, 1987—90; mem. adv. bd. InterWest Venture Capital; bd. dirs. Growth Fund of Am., New Perspective Fund, Inc., Plum Creek Timber Co., Scholastic Corp., EuroPacific Growth Fund. Contbr. articles to profl. jours. Bd. overseers vis. com. Harvard U. Bus. Sch., Cambridge, Mass., 1994-2000. Fulbright scholar, Paris, 1967—68. Office: Stanford U Grad Sch Bus 518 Memorial Way Stanford CA 94305

MC DONALD, JOHN RICHARD, lawyer; b. Connersville, Ind., Aug. 8, 1933; s. Vernon Louis and Thelma (Venham) McD.; m. Mary Alice Boyd, Aug. 17, 1957; children: Anne Elizabeth, John Richard, Colleen Lynn. BA, U. Ariz., 1957, LL.B., 1960. Bar: Ariz. 1960. Since practiced in, Tucson; assoc. Richard N. Roylston, 1961-62; pvt. practice, 1963-65; ptnr. McDonald & Rykken, 1965-68, DeConcini & McDonald (now DeConcini, McDonald, Yetwin, Lacy, and Richardson P.C.), 1968—. Mem. adv. bd. Dependable Nurses, Inc., 1994—. Mem. Ariz. Law Rev. Pres., bd. dirs. emeritus Comstock Children's Hosp. Found.; v.p. Ariz. Sch. Bds. Assn., 1979, pres., 1981; v.p. All Ariz. Sch. Bd., 1981; v.p., bd. dirs. Tucson Assn. for Blind, 1966-86; trustee Catalina Foothills Sch. Dist., 1976-82; bd. dirs. Tucson Unified Sch. Dist. Ednl. Enrichment Found., 1994-2003, Ariz. Acad., 1981-89, Tucson Symphony Soc., 1997-2003, Catalina Foothills Sch. Dist. Found., 1998-2004, Grand Canyon Music Festival, 2003—. Recipient Outstanding Svc. in Sch. Law award, Ariz. Sch. Bds. Assn., 2006. Mem. Ariz. Bar Assn., Ariz. Law Rev. Assn. (pres. 1994), Pima County Bar Assn. (dir. 1978-86, pres. 1984-85), Nat. Coun. Sch. Attys. (dir. 1992-96), Delta Chi. Independent. Presbyterian. Home: 6151 N Camino Almonte Tucson AZ 85718-3729 Office: 2525 E Broadway Blvd Tucson AZ 85716-5398 Home Phone: 520-299-9077; Office Phone: 520-322-5000. Personal E-mail: mjm85718@aol.com. Business E-Mail: jmcdonald@dmyl.com. E-mail: mjm@aol.com.

MCDONALD, JOHN W., oil industry executive; b. Ont., Can., 1951; BS in Geophysics, U. Western Ont., 1975. Geophysicist to various positions of increasing responsibility Texaco, Calgary, Alta., Canada, 1975—91, strategic adviser, asst. to chmn., 1992—94; asst. divsn. mgr. Texaco Exploration and Prodn., New Orleans, 1994—96, v.p.

exploration and prodn. offshore divsn., 1996—98; v.p. prodn. Texaco Internat., London, 1998—99; mng. dir. Texaco Ltd., 1998—2001, ChevronTexaco Upstream Europe, Aberdeen, Scotland, 2001—02; v.p. strategic planning ChevronTexaco Corp., San Ramon, Calif., 2002—08, v.p., chief tech. officer, 2008—. Mem.: U.K. Industry/Govt. Forum, U.K. Offshore Operators Assn. (past pres. exec. officer), Soc. Exploration Geophysicists, Am. Assn. Petroleum Geologists. Office: ChevronTexaco Corp 6001 Bollinger Canyon Rd San Ramon CA 94583-2324

MCDONALD, MARIANNE, classicist; b. Chgo., Jan. 2, 1937; d. Eugene Francis and Inez (Riddle) McD.; children: Eugene, James, Bryan, Bridget, Kirstie (dec.), Hiroshi. BA magna cum laude, Bryn Mawr Coll., 1958; MA, U. Chgo., 1960; PhD, U. Calif., Irvine, 1975; doctorate (hon.), Am. Coll. Greece, 1988; diploma (hon.), Am. Archaeol. Assn.; DLitt (hon.), U. Athens, 1994, U. Dublin, 1994, Aristotle U., 1997, U. Thessalonika, 1997, Nat. U. Ireland, 2001. Instr. Greek, Latin, English, mythology, cinema U. Calif., Irvine, 1975-79; founder, rsch. fellow Thesaurus Linguae Graecae Project, 1975-97. Tchg. asst. U. Calif., Irvine, 1972-74; vis. prof. U. Ulster, Ireland, 1997, U. Dublin, 1990—, Univ. Coll. Dublin, 1999, 2002, U. Cork, 1999-; adj. prof. theatre U. Calif., San Diego, 1992-94, prof. theatre and classics, 1994—; bd. dirs. Centrum. Author: (novels) Semilemmatized Concordances to Euripides' Alcestis, 1977, Semilemmatized Concordance to Euripides Cyclops, 1978, Terms for Happiness in Euripides, 1978, Cyclops, Andromache, Medea, 1978, Heraclidae, Hippolytus, 1979, Hecuba, 1984, (play) And Then He Met A Woodcutter, 2005 (San Diego Critics Cir. award for best play, 2005), (critical works) Hercules Furens, 1984, Electra, 1984, Ion, 1985, Trojan Women, 1988, Iphigenia in Taurus, 1988, Euripides in Cinema: The Heart Made Visible, 1983, The Living Art of Greek Tragedy, 2003; translator: The Cost of Kindness and Other Fabulous Tales (Shinichi Hoshi), 1986, Views of Clytemnestra, Ancient and Modern, 1990, Classics and Cinema, 1990, Modern Critical Theory and Classical Literature, 1994, A Challenge to Democracy, 1994, Ancient Sun/Modern Light: Greek Drama on the Modern Stage, 1990, Star Myths: Tales of the Constellations, 1996, Sole Antico Luce Moderna, 1999, Mythology of the Zodiac: Tales of the Constellations, 2000, Antigone by Sophocles, 2000, Mythology of the Zodiac, 2000, Sing Sorrow: Classics, History, Heroines in Opera, 2001; translator: (with Michael Walton) Euripides Andromache, 2001; translator: Euripides' Electra, 2004, Euripides' Hecuba, 2005; editor (with M. McDonald and Michael Walton): Six Greek Tragedies, 2002; editor: (with Michael Walton) Amid Our Troubles: Irish Versions of Greek Tragedy, 2002, Canta la tua Pena, 2002; contbr. chapters to books, articles in field to profl. jours., reviews. Bd. dirs. Am. Coll. of Greece, 1981-90, Scripps Hosp., 1981, Am. Sch. Classical Studies, 1986-; mem. bd. overseers U. Calif., San Diego, 1985-; nat. bd. advisors Am. Biog. Inst., 1982—; pres. Soc. for the Preservation of the Greek Heritage, 1990-, Asian Am. Repertory Theatre, 2003; founder Hajime Mori Chair for Japanese Studies, U. Calif., San Diego, 1985, McDonald Ctr. for Alcohol and Substance Abuse, 1984, Thesaurus Linguarum Hiberniae, 1991-, Hiroshi McDonald Mori Performing Arts Ctr. Recipient Ellen Browning Scripps Humanitarian award, 1975, Disting. Svc. award U. Calif., Irvine, 1982, 2001, Irvine medal, 1987; named one of the Cmty. Leaders Am., 1979-80, Philanthropist of Yr., 1985, Headliner San Diego Press Club, 1985, Philanthropist of Yr. Honorary Nat. Conf. Christians and Jews, 1986, Woman of Yr. AHEPA, 1988, San Diego Woman of Distinction, 1990, Woman of Yr. AXIOS, 1991; recipient Bravissimo gold medal San Diego Opera, 1990, Gold Medal Soc. Internationalization of Greek Lang., 1990, Athens medal, 1991, Piraeus medal, 1991, award Desmoi, 1992, award Hellenic Assn. of Univ. Women, 1992, Acad. of Achievement award AHEPA, 1992, Woman of Delphi award European Cultural Ctr. Delphi, 1992, Civis Universitatis award U. Calif., San Diego, 1993, Hypatia award Hellenic U. Women, 1993, Am.-Ireland Fund Heritage award, 1994, Contbn. to Greek Letters award Aristotle U. Thessaloniki, 1994, Mirabella Mag. Readers Choice One of 1000 Women for the Nineties, 1994, citations from U.S. Congress and Calif. Senate, Alexander the Gt. award Hellenic Cultural Soc., 1995, made hon. citizen of Delphi and gold medal of the Amphiktuonon, Del. Bus. award for Fine Arts San Diego Bus. Jour., 1995, Vol. of Decade Women's Internat. Ctr., 1994, 96, Gold Star award San Diego Arts League, 1997, Golden Aeschylus award Inst. Nat. Drama Antkg. Siracusa, 1998, Women Who Mean Bus., Fine Arts award San Diego Bus. Jour., 1998, Fulbright award, 1999, Ellis Island award, 1999, Spirit of Scripps award 1999; Theatre Excellence award KPBS Patte, 2001, Laud and Laurels, U. Calif. Disting. Alumni award Hellenic Cultural Soc. San Diego, 2003, Sledgehammer Theatre award, 2003, New Path award, 2003, Egeria award Women's Internat. Ctr., 2004, Billie award, 2004, Patté award, 2004. Mem. MLA, AAUP, Am. Philol. Assn. (disting. svc. award 1999), Soc. for the Preservation of the Greek Heritage (pres.), Libr. of Am., Am. Classical League, Philol. Assn. Pacific Coast, Am. Comparative Lit. Assn., Modern and Classical Lang. Assn. So. Calif., Hellenic Soc. (coun. award 2000), Calif. Fgn. Lang. Tchrs. Assn., Internat. Platform Assn., Royal Irish Acad., Greece's Order of the Phoenix (comdr. 1994), KPBS Prodrs. Club, Hellenic Univ. Club (bd. dirs.). Avocations: Karate, harp (medieval), skiing, diving. Home: PO Box 929 Rancho Santa Fe CA 92067-0929 Office: U Calif at San Diego Dept Theatre La Jolla CA 92093 Office Phone: 858-481-0107. E-mail: mmcdonald@ucsd.edu.

MC DONALD, MEG, public relations executive; b. Santa Monica, Calif., Oct. 11, 1948; Dir. radio & TV svcs. Fran Hynds Pub. Rels., 1969-75; owner, CEO Mc Donald Media Svcs., 1975—. Recipient Buccaneer award PIRATES, 1980, 82, Prisms award Pub. Rels. Soc. Am., 1981, Pro awards Publicity Clubs. of L.A. Mem. Pub. Rels. Soc. Am. (sec. 1985), Radio ane TV News Assn. of So. Calif. (mem. bd. dirs. 1973-88), Publicity Club of L.A. (pres. 1979-80), L.A. Advt. Women (v.p. 1984-85), Print Interactive Radio and TV Edni. Soc. (pres. 1998-00), Radio and TV News Assn. Office: Mc Donald Media Svcs 11076 Fruitland Dr Studio City CA 91604-3541 Business E-Mail: mcdmedia@earthlink.net.

MCDONALD, MICHAEL BRIAN, economist, consultant; b. Tulsa, Okla., Jan. 1, 1948; s. William Gerald and Agnes Gertrude (Sellman) McD.; m. Jane Anne Fahey, Aug. 25, 1969; children: Kelly, Anne. BA in Econs. cum laude, Georgetown U., 1969; PhD in Econs., U. Pa., 1978. Teaching fellow U. Pa., Phila., 1976-77; rsch. fellow Logistics Mgmt. Inst., Washington, 1977-78; assoc. dir. Bur. Bus. and Econ. Rsch. U. N.Mex., Albuquerque, 1978-82, dir. Bur. Bus. and Econ. Rsch., 1982—. Dir. Kirtland Fed. Credit Union, Albuquerque, 1982—. Contbr. articles to profl. jours. Lt-Col. USAFR, 1978—. Capt. USAF, 1972-76. NDEA Title IV fellow U. Pa., 1969-72. Mem. Phi Beta Kappa. Avocations: tennis, golf, fishing.

MCDONALD, MICHAEL LEE, health facility administrator, retired military officer; b. Salt Lake City, Oct. 23, 1949; s. Jack Alex and Dorothy Elsie (Mantle) McD.; m. Celia McKean Smoot, June 23, 1975; children: Sarah Lynn, Michelle Elise, AnnMarie, Jeffrey Michael, Matthew David, Emily Jane. BA, U. Utah, 1973; MA, U. Iowa, 1977. Commd. ensign USN, 1975; advanced through grades to comdr., 1991; patient adminstr. Naval Hosp., Great Lakes, Ill., 1977-80, Oakland, Calif., 1980-82; med. recruiter Navy Recruiting Dist., San Francisco, 1982-84; adminstr. Navy Environ. and Preventative Medicine Unit # 7, Naples, Italy, 1984-87; staff officer Navy Med. Commd. Europe, London, 1987-89; healthcare advisor U.S. Naval Forces Europe, London, 1989-91; exec. officer Naval Med. Clinic, Seattle, 1991-93, commdg. officer, 1993-94; officer in charge Branch Med. Clinic, Everett, Wash., 1994-96; ret., 1996; clinic adminstr. Medalia Healthcare, 1996—, Providence Med. Group, 1999—, Swedish Physicians Group, 1999—. Coach Northshore Little League, Bothell, Wash., 1992-93; scoutmaster Boy Scouts Am., Dublin, Calif., 1981-85, instl. sponsor, Naples, Italy, 1985-87; bd. dirs. North Bothell Little League, 1998—2000; bishop LDS Ch., 1996-2001. Fellow Am. Coll. Healthcare Execs. Avocations: golf, basketball, literature, bicycling. Home and Office: 1600 E Jefferson Ste 510 Seattle WA 98122 Office Phone: 206-320-4898. E-mail: michael.mcdonald@swedish.org.

MCDONOUGH, RUSSELL CHARLES, retired state supreme court justice; b. Glendive, Mont., Dec. 7, 1924; s. Roy James and Elsie Marie (Johnson) McD.; m. Dora Jean Bidwell, Mar. 17, 1946; children: Ann Remmich, Michael, Kay Jensen, Kevin, Daniel, Mary Garfield. JD, George Washington U., 1949. Bar: Mont. 1950. Pvt. practice, Glendive, Mont., 1950-83; judge Gen. Jurisdiction State of Montana, Glendive, 1983-87; justice Mont. Supreme Ct., Helena, 1987-93, ret., 1993. City atty. City of Glendive, 1953-57; county atty. Dawson County, Mon., 1957-63; del. Mont. Constl. Conv., Helena, 1972. 1st lt. USAAF, 1943-45, ETO. Decorated DFC. Mem. Mont. Bar Assn. Roman Catholic. Home: 210 Gresham St Glendive MT 59330 Personal E-mail: swedemc@yahoo.com.

MCDOUGALL, IAIN ROSS, nuclear medicine educator; b. Glasgow, Scotland, Dec. 18, 1943; came to U.S., 1976; s. Archibald McDougall and Jean Cairns; m. Elizabeth Wilson, Sept. 6, 1968; children: Shona, Stewart. MB, ChB, U. Glasgow, 1967, PhD, 1973. Diplomate Am. Bd. Nuclear Medicine (chmn. 1985-87), Am. Bd. Internal Medicine (gov. 1984-86). Lectr. in medicine U. Glasgow, 1969-76; fellow Harkness-Stanford Med. Ctr., 1972-74; assoc. prof. radiology and medicine Stanford U., Calif., 1976-84, prof. radiology and medicine, 1985—. Contbr. numerous articles to sci. jours. Fellow Royal Coll. Physicians (Glasgow), Am. Coll. Physicians; mem. Am. Thyroid Assn., Soc. Nuclear Medicine, Western Assn. for Clin. Research. Office: Stanford U Med Ctr Divsn Nuclear Medicine Stanford CA 94305 Office Phone: 650-725-4711. Business E-Mail: rossmcdougall@stanford.edu.

MCDOUGALL, JOHN ROLAND, civil engineer; b. Edmonton, Alta., Can., Apr. 4, 1945; s. John Frederick and Phyllis Eirene (Sladden) McD.; m. Susan Carley, July 2, 1971 (div. 1995); children: John Christopher, Jordan Page, Michael Tait; m. Irene Makar, May 15, 1996. BSCE, U. Alta., Edmonton, 1967. Registered profl. engr., Alta. Engr. Imperial Oil Ltd., Calgary, Alta., 1967-69, sr. engr. Edmonton, Alta., 1969-75; treas. McDougall & Secord, Edmonton, 1969-85; v.p. McDougall & Secord, Ltd., 1975-90, pres., 1990—; pres., chief exec. officer Dalcor Cos., Edmonton, 1975-91; chmn. Trade Innoventures, Inc., 1992—2002; chair engring. mgmt. U. Alta., Edmonton, 1991-98. Chmn. D.B. Robinson & Assocs., Edmonton, 1994-2002; CEO Alberta Rsch. Coun., 1997—; chmn. World Trade Centre, Edmonton, 1994-98; mem. adv. bd. Royal Trust Corp., 1984-94, Royal Glenora Club, Faculty Club; dir. PFB Corp., 1998-. Chmn. Edmonton Civic Govt. Assn., 1975-77; mem. Premiers Coun. on Sci. and Tech., 1990. Fellow Can. Acad. Engrs. (bd. dirs. 1992—); mem. Can. Coun. Profl. Engrs. (pres. 1990-91), Assn. Profl. Engrs. Alta. (hon. life, pres. 1980-81), Can. Engring. Manpower Bd. (chmn. 1985-88), Edmonton C. of C. (pres. 1989), Loyal Edmonton Regiment (hon.), Edmonton Club (pres. 1983-84), 8 Field Engring. Regiment (hon. col.). Anglican. Avocations: skiing, travel, bicycling, stamp collecting/philately, railroad modeling. Office: Alberta Rsch Coun 250 Karl Clark Rd Edmonton AB Canada T6N 1E4

MCDOUGALL, RODERICK GREGORY, lawyer; BBA in Econs., U. Ariz., JD. Bar: Ariz. 1965, U.S. Ct. Claims 1965, U.S. Supreme Ct. 1970, U.S. Dist. Ct. Ariz. 1972, U.S. Ct. Appeals (9th cir.) 1972. Law clk. Ariz. Supreme Ct., 1964, Ariz. Ct. Appeals, 1965; dep. county atty. Maricopa County, 1965-67; staff atty. Ariz. State Senate, 1967; asst. atty. gen., 1967-74; chief asst. Atty. Gen., Ariz., 1974-84; city atty. City of Phoenix, 1984-2000; pvt. practice, 2000—. Advisor Ariz. Supreme Ct. Mem. ABA, Internat. Mcpl. Lawyers Assn. (bd. dirs. 1994-2000), Ariz. Bar Assn., Maricopa County Bar Assn. E-mail: rodmcdougall@cox.net.

MCDOWELL, JENNIFER, sociologist, composer, playwright; b. Albuquerque; d. Willard A. and Margaret Frances (Garrison) McD.; m. Milton Loventhal, July 2, 1973. BA, U. Calif., 1957; MA, San Diego State U., 1958; postgrad., Sorbonne, Paris, 1959; MLS, U. Calif., 1963; PhD, U. Oreg., 1973. Tchr. English Abraham Lincoln H.S., San Jose, Calif., 1960-61; free-lance editor Soviet field, Berkeley, Calif., 1961-63; editor, pub. Merlin Papers, San Jose, 1969-80, Merlin Press, San Jose, 1973—; rsch. cons. sociology San Jose, 1973—; music pub. Lipstick and Toy Balloons Pub. Co., San Jose, 1978—, Abbie & Dolley Records, 2003—; composer Paramount Pictures, 1982-88. Tchr. writing workshops; poetry readings, 1969-73; co-producer radio show lit. and culture Sta. KALX, Berkeley, 1971-72. Author: (with Milton Loventhal) Black Politics: A Study and Annotated Bibliography of the Mississippi Freedom Democratic Party, 1971 (Smithsonian Inst. 1992), Contemporary Women Poets, Anthology of California Poets, 1977; co-author: (plays off broadway) Betsy and Phyllis, 1986, Mack the Knife Your Friendly Dentist, 1986, The Estrogen Party To End War, 1986, The Oatmeal Party Comes to Order, 1986, (plays) Betsy Meets the Wacky Iraqi, 1991, Bella and Phyllis, 1994; author numerous poems; contbr. articles and short stories to profl. jours, local newspapers; writer: (songs) Money Makes a Woman Free!, 1976, 2004; 3 songs featured in Parade of Am. Music, 1976-77; co-creator mus. comedy Russia's Secret Plot To Take Back Alaska, 1988; (Cassingle) Intern Girl, 1998, Smithsonian, 2002; (CDs) Our Women Are Strong, 2000, 02, The Wearing of the Green Burkas, 2003; (musical revs., CD) She, A Tapestry of Women's Lives, 2004. Recipient 8 awards Am. Song Festival, 1976-79, Service to Poetry award, 1977, Bill Casey Award in Letters (Soviet Studies), 1980, SHE award, Calif. State U.-ERFA Found., 2004, collected by Nobel Inst. for 2003 Nobel Peace Prize laureate Shirin Ebadi, award USA Songwriting Competition, 2006; doctoral fellow AAUW, 1971-73; grantee Calif. Arts Coun., 1976-77. Mem. AAUW, Am. Assn. for Advancement of Slavic Studies, Soc. Sci. Study of Religion, Am. Sociol. Assn., Dramatists Guild, Phi Beta Kappa, Sigma Alpha Iota, Beta Phi Mu, Kappa Kappa Gamma. Democrat. Office: care Abbie and Dolley Records PO Box 5602 San Jose CA 95150-5602 Office Phone: 800-889-8305. Business E-Mail: jeditorphd@earthlink.net.

MC DUFFIE, MALCOLM, oil industry executive; b. San Francisco, Nov. 14, 1915; s. William Chester and Mary (Skaife) McD.; m. Mary Sutherland de Surville, Dec. 8, 1951; children: Cynthia de Surville, Duncan de Surville. AB in Econs, Stanford U., Calif., 1940. With O.C. Field Gasoline Corp., 1940-41, Wilmington Gasoline Corp., 1941-42; with Mohawk Petroleum Corp., 1945-80, pres., dir., 1969-80; dir. Res. Oil & Gas Co., 1973-80, sr. v.p., 1977-80; sp. asst. to pres. Getty Oil Co., Los Angeles, 1980-82. Bd. overseers Huntington Library, Art Gallery and Bot. Gardens, 1972-98; bd. dirs. Calif. Inst. Tech. Assos., 1976-82. Mem. Nat. Petroleum Refiners Assn. (Dir. 1970-80), Ind. Refiners Assn. Calif. (pres. 1967-69, 77-78, dir. 1950-80), Rancheros Visitadores. Clubs: California (Los Angeles); Bohemian (San Francisco); Valley Hunt (Pasadena, Calif.), Annandale Golf (Pasadena, Calif.); Birnam Wood (Santa Barbara, Calif.), Valley (Montecito, Calif.). Republican. Episcopalian. Home: 300 Hot Springs Rd # 7 Santa Barbara CA 93108-2037

MCEACHERN, ALEXANDER, electronics executive; b. Boston, Feb. 18, 1955; s. Alexander William and Elisabeth Helena McEachern; m. Barbara Ruth Pereira, Dec. 18, 1975; children: Alexander Wallis, Ian Wallis. V.p. Mac Systems, 1975-79; dir. R&D Lomac Corp., Santa Clara, Calif., 1979-80; chmn., founder Basic Measuring Instruments, Santa Clara, 1981-99; pres. Electrotek Concepts, Inc., 1996-97, Power Stds. Lab., 2000—. Dir. WPT, 1997—, Dranetz/BMI/Electrotek, 1997—; founder Infrastructure Instruments Inc., 1996—; bd. dirs. Basic Measuring Instruments. Author: Handbook of Power Signatures; contbr. articles to profl. jours. Mem. IEEE (sr.).

MCELHANY, ANDREW (ANDY), state legislator; b. San Francisco, Apr. 28, 1940; son of Keet McElhany & Virginia M; children: Andrew, Mary Katherine & Virginia. Member, Colorado Springs Parks & Recreation Advisor Bd, currently, chairman, 92-94; Colorado State Representative, District 17, 94-01, member, State, Vet & Mil Affairs & Transportation & Energy Committees, formerly, Colorado House Representative; Colorado State Senator, District 12, 2001-, member, Bus, Labor & Technology, Finance and Capital Develop, currently, Colorado State Senate.Real estate broker, Shields Corp, currently. Distinguished Serv Award, Colorado Association Realtors, 89 & 90; Realtor of Year, 93. Pikes Peak Association Realtors. Republican. Mailing: 95 W Boulder St Denver CO 80903-3371

MCELHINNY, HAROLD JOHN, lawyer; b. San Francisco, Jan. 5, 1947; s. Harold James and Margaret I. (Mahoney) McE.; m. Mary Ellen McElhinny, June 22, 1968; children: Hannah, Jennifer, William. BA in Polit. Sci., U. Santa Clara, 1970; JD, U. Calif., Berkeley, 1975. Bar: Calif. 1976, U.S. Supreme Ct. 1983. Vol. Peace Corps., Tripoli, Libya, 1968-69; juvenile counselor Santa Clara County (Calif.) Juvenile Hall, 1969-72; law clk. U.S. Dist. Ct., Hartford, Conn., 1975-76; ptnr. Morrison & Foerster, San Francisco, 1976—. Mem. ABA, Calif. Bar Assn., State Bar Calif. (rev. dept. 1986-89, chmn. 1988), San Francisco Bar Assn., Am. Intellectual Property Law Assn., Assn. Bus. Trial Lawyers (bd. govs. 1992-97, pres. 1997). Democrat. Roman Catholic. Office: Morrison & Foerster 425 Market St Fl 34 San Francisco CA 94105-2482 Office Phone: 415-268-7265. E-mail: hmcelhinny@mofo.com.

MCELHINNY, WILSON DUNBAR, banker; b. Detroit, July 27, 1929; s. William Dunbar and Elizabeth (Wilson) McE.; m. Barbara Cheney Watkins, June 6, 1952 (dec.); children: David Ashton, Ward Cheney, Edward Wilson, William Dunbar; m. Lisa Lesher, Mar. 27, 1993. BA, Yale U., 1953. With Union and New Haven Trust Co., 1952-63, Reading Trust Co., Pa., 1963-68, pres., 1968-70, Nat. Ctrl. Bank (formerly Reading Trust Co.), Pa., 1970-79, CEO, 1975-79; chmn. bd. dirs., pres., CEO Hamilton Bank (formerly Nat. Ctrl. Bank), Lancaster, Pa., 1979-81, chmn. bd. dirs., CEO, 1981-83, chmn. bd. dirs., 1981-90; pres. CoreStates Fin. Corp., Phila., 1983-86, vice chmn., 1986-90; pres., chmn. Hamilton Bank, Lancaster, 1988-90. Bd. dirs. chmn. Silicon Valley Bank and 1st Bank Idaho, SIGCO, Portland, Maine. Mem. Sun Valley Summer Symphony Bd. Mem. Pa. C. of C. (chmn. 1990-92), Yale Club N.Y., The Valley Club, Franklin & Marshall Coll. (bd. visitors). Home and Office: PO Box 3070 Ketchum ID 83340-3070

MCELROY, LEO FRANCIS, communications consultant, journalist; b. LA, Oct. 12, 1932; s. Leo Francis and Helen Evelyn (Silliman) McE.; m. Dorothy Frances Montgomery, Nov. 3, 1956 (div. 1981); children: James, Maureen, Michael, Kathleen; m. Judith Marie Lewis, May 30, 1992. BS in English, Loyola U., LA, 1953. News dir. KFI, KRLA, KABC Radio, LA, 1964-72; pub. affairs host TV Sta. KCET, LA, 1967-74; v.p. Sta. KROQ AM/FM, LA, 1972-74; polit. editor Sta. KABC-TV, LA, 1974-81; pres. McElroy Comm., Sacramento, 1981—2003. Pres. sec. Lt. Gov.'s Office, Sacramento, 1982-84; chmn. Calif. AP Broadcasters, 1972-74; cons. State Office Migrant Edn., Sacramento, 1974, Californians for Water, L.A., 1982, Calif. Water Protection Coun., Sacramento, 1982, Planning and Conservation League, Sacramento, 1984—, Common Cause, Sacramento, 1988—. Author: Uneasy Partners, 1984; author plays: Mermaid Tavern, 1956, To Bury Caesar, 1952 (Christopher award), Rocket to Olympus, 1960, The Code of Whiskey King, 1995. State del. Western Am. Assembly on Prison Reform, Berkeley, Calif., 1973; chmn. State Disaster Info. Task Force, Calif., 1973-74; campaign media cons. statewide issues, various candidates, Sacramento, L.A., 1981—; bd. dirs. Vols. in Victim Assistance, Sacramento, 1984, Rescue Alliance, Sacramento, 1987-92, Mental Health Assn., Sacramento, 1985-89, Leukemia Soc., 1992-97, Calif Fire Safe Coun., 2002—. Recipient Gabriel award Cath. Archdiocese, L.A., 1972, Golden Mike award Radio-TV News Assn., L.A., 1973; Hon. Resolution, Calif. State Assembly, Sacramento, 1981. Mem. ASCAP, AFTRA, Screen Actors Guild, Am. Assn. Polit. Cons. Roman Catholic. Home: 2262 Swarthmore Dr Sacramento CA 95825-6608 E-mail: mcelcom@comcast.net.

MCEVOY, NAN TUCKER, publishing company executive, olive rancher; b. San Mateo, Calif., July 15, 1919; d. Nion R. and Phyllis (de Young) Tucker; m. Dennis McEvoy, 1948 (div.); 1 child, Nion Tucker McEvoy. Student, Georgetown U., 1975. Newspaper reporter San Francisco Chronicle, 1944-46, N.Y. Herald Tribune, NYC, 1946-47, Washington Post, 1947-48; rep. in pub. rels. John Homes, Inc., Washington, 1959-60; spl. asst. to dir. U.S. Peace Corps,

Washington, 1961-64; mem. U.S. delegation UNESCO, Washington, 1964-65; dir. Population Coun., Washington, 1965-70; co-founder, dep. dir. Preterm, Inc., Washington, 1970-74; former chmn. bd. Chronicle Pub. Co., San Francisco, 1975-95, dir. emeritus, 1995—. Mem. nat. bd. dirs. Smithsonian Instn., Washington, 1994—; bd. dirs. Am. Farmland Trust; mem. coun. Brookings Instn., Washington, 1994—; mem. U. Calif. San Francisco Found., 1993—; dir. emeritus Nat. Mus. Am. Art; mem. Nat. Coun. Fine Arts Museums; formerly arbitrator Am. Arbitration Assn., Washington. Named Woman of Yr., Washingtonian Mag., 1973. Mem. Am. Art Forum, Burlingame Country Club, The River Club, Commonwealth Club of Calif., World Affairs Coun., Villa Taverna. Office: 655 Montgomery St Ste 1430 San Francisco CA 94111-2635

MCEVOY, NION TUCKER, editor; b. San Mateo, Calif., May 23, 1952; s. Dennis Griffin and Nan (Tucker) McE.; m. Karen Ira Polcyn, July 19, 1986. BA, U. Calif., Santa Cruz, 1974; JD, Hastings Coll. Law, San Francisco, 1979. Bar: Calif. 1980, Oreg. 1984. Bus. affairs exec. William Morris Agy., Beverly Hill, Calif., 1980-83; atty. Legal Svcs. Orgn., Portland, Oreg., 1983-84; dir. of bus. affairs Wescom Prodns., LA, 1984-86; editor Chronicle Books, San Francisco, 1986-87, editor-in-chief, 1990—. Office: Chronicle Books 85 2nd St Fl 6 San Francisco CA 94105-3464

MCEWEN, ALFRED SHERMAN, planetary geologist; b. Lawrence, Kans., July 22, 1954; s. William Edwin and Miriam Sherman McEwen; m. Eileen Haney; 1 child, Ian. BS, SUNY-Syracuse, 1975, No. Ariz. U., 1981, MS, 1983; PhD, Ariz. State U., 1988. Vol. Peace Corps, Guatemala, Ctrl. Am., 1975—77; soil conservationist Soil Conservation Svc., USDA, 1978—80; geologist US Geol. Survey, Flagstaff, Ariz., 1981—96, U. Ariz., 1996—, dir. Planetary Image Rsch. Lab. Mem. Galileo, Cassini, Mars Global Surveyor, and Clementine Spacecraft Sci. Teams. Contbr. articles to profl. jours. Mem.: Am. Astron. Soc., Am. Geophys. Union. Home: 4135 E Cooper St Tucson AZ 85711-3464 Office: U Ariz Dept Planetary Sci Lunar Planetary Lab 1629 E University Blvd CPS-204 Tucson AZ 85721-0001 Office Phone: 520-621-4573. Business E-Mail: mcewen@lpl.arizona.edu.

MCFADDEN, DANIEL LITTLE, economist, educator; b. Raleigh, NC, July 29, 1937; s. Robert S. and Alice (Little) McFadden; m. Beverlee Tito Simboli, Dec. 15, 1962; children: Nina, Robert, Raymond. BS in physics, U. Minn., 1957, PhD in econs., 1962; LLD, U. Chgo., 1992; degree (hon.), U. Coll. London, 2003; PhD in Sci. (hon.), No. Carolina St. Univ., 2006. Asst. prof. econs. U. Pitts., 1962-63, U. Calif., Berkeley, 1963—66, assoc. prof. econs, 1966—68, prof., 1968—79, E. Morris Cox Chair, prof. econs. Coll. Letters & Sci., 1991—, dir. Econometrics Lab., 1991—95, 1996—, chmn. dept. of econ., 1995—96; vis. assoc. prof. U. Chgo., 1966—67; Irving Fisher research prof. Yale U., New Haven, 1977—78; prof. econs. MIT, Cambridge, Mass., 1978—91, James R. Killian Chair, 1984—91, dir. Stats. Rsch. Ctr. Cambridge, Mass., 1986—88; Sherman Fairchild Disting. Scholar Calif. Inst. Tech., 1990. Mem. econs. adv. panel NSF, 1969—71, Univs. Nat. Bur., 1974—77; chmn. NSF-NBER Conf. Econs. of Uncertainty, 1970—; bd. dirs. Nat. Bur. Econ. Rsch., 1976—77, 1980—83; mem. book com. Sloan Found., 1977—79; mem. rev. com. Calif. Energy Com. Forecasts, 1979; chmn. awards com. AEA, 1981—84. Editor: Jour. Statis. Physics, 1968—70, Econometric Soc. monographs, 1980—83; mem. bd. editors Am. Econ. Rev., 1971—74, Jour. Math. Econs., 1973—77, Transp. Rsch., 1978—80; assoc. editor: Jour. Econometrics, 1977—78; adv. com. Jour. Applied Econs., 1996—; co-editor: Essays on Economic Behavior Under Uncertainty, 1974, Production Economics, Vols. I and II, 1978, Structural Analysis of Discrete Data with Econometric Applications, 1981, Preferences, Uncertainty, and Optimality, 1990, Handbook of Econometrics Vol. IV, 1994; co-author: Urban Travel Demand: A Behavioral Analysis, 1975, Microeconomic Modeling and Policy Analysis, 1984. Mem. adv. com. Transp. Models Project, Met. Transp. Commn., 1975, City of Berkeley Coordinated Transit Project, 1975—76. Recipient Outstanding Tchr. Award, MIT, 1981, Nobel Prize in Econs., 2000, Nemmers prize in Econs., Northwestern U., 2000, Richard Stone prize in Applied Econs., Jour. Applied Economtrics, 2000—01; Ford Found. Behavioral Sci. Fellow, 1958—62, Earhart Fellow, 1960—61, Mellon Post-Doctoral Fellow, 1962—63, Ford Faculty Rsch. Fellow, 1966—67. Mem.: NAS (mem. com. basic rsch. social scis. 1982—87, mem. com. energy demand modelling 1983—84, mem. commn. behavioral and social scis. and edn. 1989—94, mem. commn. sci. engring., pub. policy 1995—, chair sect. 54 econ. scis. 2003—, chair com. forecasting demand/supply of doctoral scientists and engrs. 1997—2000), Am. Phil. Soc., Transp. Rsch. Bd. (mem. exec. com. 1975—78), Math. Assn. Am., Am. Statis. Assn., Econometrics Soc. (Fisher-Schultz lectr. 1979, mem. exec. com. 1983—86, v.p. 1984, pres. 1985, fellow 1969, Frisch Medal 1986), Am. Econ. Assn. (mem. exec. com. 1985—87, v.p. 1994, pres.-elect 2004, John Bates Clark Medal 1975), Am. Acad. Arts and Scis. Democrat. Avocations: bicycling, tennis, squash, sailing, skiing. Office: U Calif Berkeley Dept Econs 549 Evans Hall # 3880 Berkeley CA 94720-3880 Office Phone: 510-643-8428. Office Fax: 510-642-0638. Business E-Mail: mcfadden@econ.berkeley.edu.

MCFADDEN, DARREN, professional football player; b. North Little Rock, Ark., Aug. 27, 1987; s. Graylon McFadden and Mini Muhammad. Student, U. Ark., 2005—08. Running back Oakland Raiders, 2008—. Featured on the covers of Sports Illus. and ESPN Mag. Recipient Doak Walker award, 2006, 2007, Walter Camp Player of Yr. award, 2007; named SEC Offensive Player of Yr., 2006, 2007, Nat. Player of the Yr., The Sporting News, 2007, First Team All-American, AP, 2007. Achievements include being the first sophomore to win the Doak Walker award; becoming only the second two-time winner of the Doak Walker award, joining Ricky Williams; becoming only the second running back in the Razorbacks' history to rush for 1,000 yards or more in three consecutive years; becoming the all-time rusher in the University of Arkansas' history with 4,485 yards. Office: Oakland Raiders 1220 Harbor Bar Pkwy Alameda CA 94502*

MCFADDEN, NANCY ELIZABETH, utilities executive; b. Wilmington, Del., Oct. 20, 1958; d. William P. and Mary Elizabeth (Adams) McF. BA, San Jose State U., Calif., 1984; JD, U. Va., Charlottesville, 1987. Jud. clk. to Hon. John P. Wiese US Claims Ct., Washington, 1987-88; atty. O'Melveny & Myers, Washington, 1988-91; deputy comm. dir. Office of Pres.-Elect, Washington, 1992-93; asst. atty. gen. US Dept. Justice, Washington, 1993, prin. dep. assoc. atty. gen., 1993-95; gen. counsel Dept. Transp., Washington, 1996—2000; dep. chief of staff V.P. Al Gore, Washington; sr. advisor, dep. chief of staff Gov. Gray Davis Adminstrn., Calif.; with Gov. Arnold Schwarzenegger Adminstrn., Calif.; sr. v.p. pub. affairs PG&E Corp., San Francisco. Nat. dep. polit. dir. Clinton for Pres. Campaign, 1992, nat. surrogate dir. Clinton-Gore for Pres. Campaign, 1992; bd. trustees Calif. Mus. for History, Women and the Arts. Named one of 40 Best Lawyers Under 40, Washingtonian mag. Office: PG&E Corp One Market Spear Tower Ste 2400 San Francisco CA 94105-1126 Office Phone: 415-267-7070. Office Fax: 415-267-7268.

MCFADDEN, P. MICHAEL, physician, surgeon; b. Hobbs, N.Mex., June 16, 1946; s. Paul Marion and Venita Lenora (Bowen) McF.; m. Jennifer Marie James, Apr. 8, 1990; children: Heather Anne, Jennifer Suzanne, Bryn Ellen, Callan Michael. BS, La. State U., 1968; MD, Tulane U., 1974. Diplomate Am. Bd. Surgery, Am. Bd. Thoracic Surgery. Surg. intern, resident Tulane U. Sch. Medicine, New Orleans, 1974-79, instr. surgery, 1974-79, clin. prof. surgery, 1991—; resident in thoracic surgery Ochsner Clinic, New Orleans, 1979-81, cardiovascular and thoracic surgeon, 1991—2006, surg. dir. lung transplantaion, 1991—2006, dir. thoracic surgery program, 1998—2006; cardiovascular and thoracic surgeon Stanford U. Hosp., Calif., 1981-91; chief cardiovascular surgery Palo Alto Med. Clinic, Calif., 1983-91; prof. cardiothoracic surgery, surg. dir. lung transplantation Keck Sch. Medicine, U. So. Calif., 2006—. Contbr. articles to profl. jours. Bd. dirs. YMCA, Palo Alto area, 1988-91; bd. dirs. U. Tulane Health Svcs., 2006—. Capt USNR, 1984-94. Fellow ACS, Am. Coll. Cardiology, Am. Coll. Chest Physicians; mem. AMA, Alton Ochsner Surg. Soc., Am. Assn. for Thoracic Surgery, Am. Soc. Vascular Surgery, Am. Soc. Transplant Surgeons, Am. Heart Assn. (coun. on cardiovascular surgery), Assn. Mil. Surgeons U.S., Internat. Soc. for Cardiovascular Surgery, Internat. Soc. for Heart and Lung Transplantation, Norman E. Shumway Surg. Soc., Pacific Coast Surg. Assn., So. Surg. Assn., So. Thoracic Surg. Assn., Thoracic Surgery Found., Tulane Surg. Soc., Tulane U. Med. Alumni Assn., Western Thoracic Surg. Assn., Alpha Omega Alpha, Alpha Epsilon Delta, Nu Sigma Nu, Kappa Alpha. Republican. Presbyterian. Office: Dept Cardiothoracic Surgery U So Calif Keck Sch Medicine 1520 San Pablo St Ste 4300 Los Angeles CA 90033 Office Phone: 323-442-5849. Business E-Mail: mmcfadden@surgery.usc.edu.

MCFADDEN, THOMAS, former academic administrator; b. NYC, Nov. 12, 1935; m. Monica A. Dowdall; children: Monica, David. BA, Cathedral Coll., 1957; STL, Gregorian U., 1961; STD, Cath. U., 1963. Asst. prof. St. Joseph's Coll., Bklyn., 1963-66; chmn. theology dept. Cathedral Coll., Douglaston, NY, 1966-68; asst. prof. Loyola Coll., Balt., 1968-69; prof. St. Joseph's U., Phila., 1970-82, dean Coll. Arts & Scis., 1982-87; acad. v.p. St. John Fisher Coll., Rochester, NY, 1987-92; pres. Marymount Coll., Calif., 1992—2006. Vis. prof. Cath. U., Washington, 1967-68, LaSalle U., Phila., summer 1974-79. Author, editor: New Cath. Ency., 1974, 791 editor: Dictionary of Religion, 3 vols., 1979, Liberation, Revolution and Freedom, 1975, America in Theological PErspective, 1976. Recipient Disting. Teaching award Lindback, 1978, N.Y. State Excelsior award Bd. Examiners, 1991; HEW grantee, 1972, CAPHE grantee, 1985. Mem. AAUP, Coll. Theology Soc. (chmn. pubs. com. 1973-77). Democrat. Roman Catholic. Office: Marymount Coll 30800 Palos Verdes Dr E Rancho Palos Verdes CA 90275-6273 Business E-Mail: tmcfadden@marymountpv.edu.

MCFADYEN, LIANE (BUFFIE MCFADYEN), state legislator; m. Paul Ray; 1 child. B, Adams State Coll., Alamosa, Colo., 1991, M, 1993. Caseworker Alamosa County Dept. Social Svc., Colo.; operator Rocky Mt. Specialized Cleaning; owner, operator Alliance Bus. Strategies, Pueblo, Colo.; mem. Dist. 47 Colo. House of Reps., Denver, 2002—. Co-founder Young Dems. So. Colo. Democrat. Office: Colo State Capitol 200 E Colfax Rm 271 Denver CO 80203 Office Phone: 303-866-2905. Business E-Mail: mcfadyen2002@hotmail.com.*

MCFANN, MAURICE L., JR., career officer; b. June 10, 1950; BA, Calif. State U., Chico, 1972; MS, Vanderbilt U., 1981. Commd. 2d lt. USAF, 1972, advanced through grades to brig. gen., 1997; flight examiner 100th Air Refueling Wing, Beale AFB, Calif., 1973-77; pilot tng. 82nd Flying Tng. Wing, Williams AFB, Ariz., 1977-78; flight examiner 1st Tactical Reconnaissance Squadron, Royal Air Force, Alconbury, Eng., 1979-82; flight comdr. 12th Tactical Reconnaissance Squadron, Bergstrom AFB, Tex., 1982-83; air-to-surface br. chief, inspector's gen.'s office Hdqrs. Tactical Command, Langley AFB, Va., 1983-85; asst. chief tactical forces divsn., dep. chief of staff Hdqrs. USAF, The Pentagon, Washington, 1986-88, dep. dir. modeling and simulation, dep. chief of staff, 1994-95, exec. officer, dep. chief of staff to dep. dir. of ops., 1995-96; comdr. 363rd Tactical Fighter Wing, Shaw AFB, S.C., 1988-90, 12th Ops. Group, 12th Flying Tng. Wing, Randolph AFB, Tex., 1991-92; chief Joint Simulation and Interoperability Divsn. The Joint Staff, The Pentagon, Washington, 1992-94; comdr. E-3A component NATO Airborne Early Warning Force, Geilenkirchen AB, Germany, 1996-98; comdr. 552nd Air Control Wing, Tinker AFB, Okla., 1998—. Dir. plans, NORAD, Colorado Springs. Deocrated Legion of Merit. Office: Hdqs NORAD 250 S Peterson Blvd Ste 116 Colorado Springs CO 80914-3180

MCFARLAND, NORMAN FRANCIS, bishop; b. Martinez, Calif., Feb. 21, 1922; Attended, St. Patrick's Sem. Ordained to ministry Cath. Ch., 1946, consecrated bishop Cath. Ch., 1970. Ordained priest Archdiocese of San Francisco, 1946, aux. bishop, 1970—74; ordained bishop, 1970; apostolic adminstr. Diocese of Reno, 1974—76; bishop Diocese of Reno-Las Vegas, 1976—87, Diocese of Orange, Calif., 1987—98, bishop emeritus, 1998—. Roman Catholic. Office: 200 W La Veta Ave Orange CA 92866-1936

MCFARLANE, SETH WOODBURY, television producer, animator; b. Kent, Conn., Oct. 26, 1973; s. Ron and Perry McFarlane. Grad., RI Sch. Design. Animator Hanna-Barbera Prodns. (now Cartoon Network Studios); writer Walt Disney Animation, Fox Broadcasting Co. Writer, dir. (TV series) Shnookums and Meat Funny Cartoon Show, 1993, writer, dir., actor The Life of Larry, 1995, Larry & Steve, 1996, writer Dexter's Laboratory, 1996—, Jungle Cubs, 1996—98, Ace Ventura: Pet Detective, 1996, Cow and Chicken, 1997—2001, Johnny Bravo, 1997—, writer, dir. Zoomates, 1998, exec. prodr., writer, creator, actor Family Guy, 1999—, cons. prodr. The Pitts, 2003, exec. prodr., writer, dir., actor American Dad!, 2005—.

MCFARLANE, STEPHEN C., dean, researcher; BS, MS, Portland State U.; PhD, U. Wash. Prof. Portland State U., U. Washington; asst. prof. U. Nev. Sch. Medicine, Reno, 1975, chmn. dept. speech pathology and audiology, 1977—, vice dean, 1995—96, 2001, assoc. dean acad. affairs, 1990—94, dean, 2002—04; interim pres. U. Nev., 2000—01. Rschr. in field. Author: The Voice and Voice Therapy, 2000; contbr. articles to profl. jours. Recipient Honors award, Am. Speech Language Hearing Assn., 1999. Office: Manville Bldg Mailstop 357 Reno NV 89557

MCFARLING, USHA LEE, journalist; b. Landstuhl, West Germany, June 28, 1967; m. Michael Dickinson; children: Phoebe, Peter. BA in Biology, Brown U., 1988; MA in Biol. Psych., U. Calif., Berkeley, 1998. Sci. reporter Brown Daily Herald, RI, 1988—89; asst. city editor & med. writer San Antonio Light, 1990—92; hlth. & sci. writer Boston Globe, 1994—95; freelance writer, 1995—98; former reporter with Washington bur. Knight Ridder, 1998—2000; sci. writer planetary and earth scis. LA Times, 2001—07. Mem. sci. and soc. journalism awards com. Nat. Assn. Sci. Writers, Inc.; mem. judging com. Wistar Inst., 2004—; spkr. in field; freelance journalist. Recipient award, Wistar Inst., 2004; co-recipient John B. Oakes award for Outstanding Environmental Journalism, Columbia U. Grad. Sch. Journalism, 2006, George Polk award for Environmental Reporting, 2006, Walter Sullivan award for Excellence in Sci. Journalism, Am. Geophys. Union, 2007, Pub. Comm. award, Am. Soc. Microbiol., 2007, Print Media award, Am. Inst. Biol. Scis., 2007, Pulitzer Prize for Explanatory Reporting, 2007; fellow Knight Sci. Journalism, MIT, 1992—93.

MC FERON, DEAN EARL, mechanical engineer, educator; b. Portland, Oreg., Dec. 24, 1923; s. Wallace Suitor and Ruth Carolyn (Fessler) McF.; m. Phyllis Grace Ehlers, Nov. 10, 1945; children: David Alan, Phyllis Ann, Douglas Dean, Donald Brooks. Student, Oreg. State Coll., 1942-43; BSME with spl. honors, U. Colo., 1945, MSME, 1948; PhD, U. Ill., 1956. Instr. U. Colo., Boulder, 1946-48; assoc. prof. U. Ill., 1948-58; rsch. assoc. Argonne (Ill.) Nat. Lab., 1957-58; prof. mech. engring., assoc. dean U. Wash., Seattle, 1958-82, prof. emeritus, 1983—. Cons. to industry, 1959-80. Served with USNR, 1942-46, to comdr. Res., 1946-72. Co-recipient Outstanding Tech. Applications Paper award ASHRAE, 1974; Ednl. Achievement award Soc. Mfg. Engrs., 1970; NSF faculty fellow, 1967-68 Mem. ASME, Am. Soc. Engring. Edn., U.S. Naval Inst. (life), Sigma Xi (nat. dir. 1972-80, nat. pres. 1978), Tau Beta Pi, Sigma Tau, Pi Tau Sigma. Office: U Wash Dept Mech Engring Seattle WA 98195-0001 Home: Heartstone Apt 1027 6720 E Green Lake Way N Seattle WA 98103-5458

MCGAGH, WILLIAM GILBERT, financial consultant; b. Boston, May 29, 1929; s. Thomas A. and Mary M. (McDonough) McG.; m. Sarah Ann McQuigg, Sept. 23, 1961; children: Margaret Ellen, Sarah Elizabeth. BSBA, Boston Coll., 1950; MBA, Harvard U., 1952; MS, MIT, 1965. Fin. analyst Ford Motor Co., Dearborn, Mich., 1953-55; mem. staff treas. office Chrysler Corp., Detroit, 1955-64, compt., treas. Canadian divsn. Windsor, 1965-67, staff exec.-fin. Latin Am. ops. Detroit, 1967-68, asst. treas., 1968-75, treas., 1975-76, v.p., treas., 1976-80; sr. v.p. fin., dir. Northrop Grumman Corp., LA, 1980-88. Mem. adv. bd. Santa Monica-UCLA and Orthopaedic Hosp. Mem. bd. regents Mt. St. Mary's Coll.; bd. dirs. L.A. Orthop. Hosp.; bd. dirs. John Tracy Clinic. Sloan fellow MIT, 1965. Mem. Fin. Execs. Inst. (pres. Detroit chpt. 1979-80), L.A. Country Club, Calif. Club (L.A.), Eastward Ho Country Club (Chatham, Mass.). Home: 2189 Century Hill Los Angeles CA 90067 Home Phone: 310-557-0992; Office Phone: 310-248-4395. Personal E-mail: wgm9601@aol.com.

MCGANN, JOHN MILTON, real estate executive; b. Omaha, Mar. 18, 1948; s. John Byron and Donna M. (Rehnquist) McG.; m. Barbara June Scott, June 2, 1978. BSBA, cert. real estate, U. Nebr., Omaha, 1971. Property mgr. Boetel & Co., Omaha, 1971-73; asst. office bldg. mgr. The Irvine Co., Newport Beach, Calif., 1973-74; property mgr. Harbor Investment Co., Corona Del Mar, Calif., 1974-76, Robert A. McNeil Corp., Santa Ana, Calif., 1976-78; gen. mgr. Daon Mgmt., Newport Beach, 1978-80; v.p. August Mgmt. Inc., Long Beach, Calif., 1980-82, Calif. Fed. Asst. Mgmt., LA, 1982-83; pres. Wespac Mgmt. Realty Corp., Newport Beach, 1983-87; v.p., dir. asset mgmt., pres. CalFed Asset Mgmt. Co., LA, 1987-90; v.p. com. ops. Pinnacle Realty (formerly Sovereign/Ring), Santa Monica, 1990-95; pres., ptnr. Churchill McGann, LLC, 1995-97; pres. McGann Enterprises Inc. dba Churchill McGann & Round Table Pizza, Lakewood, Long Beach, Calif., 1997—; pres. McGann Asset Mgmt., Inc., 2002—. Mem. Inst. Real Estate Mgmt. (L.A. chpt., cert. property mgr.), Internat. Coun. Shopping Ctrs. (cert. shopping ctr. mgr.), Lambda Chi Alpha, Delta Sigma Pi, Rho Epsilon (pres.), Lambda Alpha Internat. Republican. Mem. Christian Sci. Ch. Home: 626 Avery Pl Long Beach CA 90807-3234 also: McGann Enterprises Inc DBA Round Table Pizza 5250 Faculty Ave Lakewood CA 90712-2508 Office: Mcgann Asset Management 4401 Atlantic Ave Ste 420 Long Beach CA 90807-2244 Office Phone: 562-951-1199. Personal E-mail: jbmcgann@charter.net.

MC GAUGH, JAMES LAFAYETTE, psychobiologist; b. Long Beach, Calif., Dec. 17, 1931; s. William Rufus and Daphne (Hermes) McG.; m. Carol J. Becker, Mar. 15, 1952; children: Douglas, Janice, Linda. BA, San Jose State U., 1953; PhD (Abraham Rosenberg fellow), U. Calif. - Berkeley, 1959; sr. postdoctoral fellow, NAS-NRC, Istituto Superiore di Sanitá, Rome, 1961-62; DSc (hon.), So. Ill. U., 1991. Asst. prof., assoc. prof. psychology San Jose State U., 1957-61; assoc. prof. psychology U. Oreg., 1961-64; assoc. prof. U. Calif., Irvine, 1964-66, founding chmn. dept. psychobiology, 1964-67, 71-74, 86-89, prof., 1966-94; rsch. prof., 1994—; dean Sch. Biol. Sci. U. Calif., Irvine, 1967-70, vice chancellor acad. affairs, 1975-77, exec. vice chancellor, 1978-82, founding dir. Ctr. Neurobiology of Learning and Memory, 1983—. Mem. adv. coms. NIMH, 1965-78, Mental Health Coun. NIMH, 1992-95. Author: (with J.B. Cooper) Integrating Principles of Social Psychology, 1963, (with H.F. Harlow, R.F. Thompson) Psychology, 1971, (with M.J. Herz) Memory Consolidation, 1972, Learning and Memory: An Introduction, 1973, (with R.F. Thompson and T. Nelson) Psychology I, 1977, (with C. Cotman) Behavioral Neuroscience, 1980; editor: (with N.M. Weinberger, R.E. Whalen) Psychobiology, 1966, Psychobiology-Behavior from a Biological Perspective, 1971, The Chemistry of Mood, Motivation and Memory, 1972, (with M. Fink, S.S. Kety, T.A. Williams) Psychobiology of Convulsive Therapy, 1974, (with L.F. Petrinovich) Knowing, Thinking, and Believing, 1976, (with R.R. Drucker-Colín) Neurobiology of Sleep and Memory, 1977, (with S.B. Kiesler) Aging, Biology and Behavior, 1981, (with G. Lynch and N. M. Weinberger) Neurobiology of Learning and Memory, 1984, (with N.M. Weinberger and G. Lynch) Memory Systems of the Brain, 1985, Contemporary Psychology, 1985, (with C.D. Woody and D.L. Alkon) Cellular Mechanisms of Conditioning and Behavioral Plasticity, 1988, (with N.M. Weinberger and G. Lynch) Brain Organization and Memory: Cells, Systems and Circuits, 1990, (with R.C.A. Frederickson and D.L. Felten) Peripheral Signaling of the Brain, 1991, (with L. Squire, G. Lynch and N.M. Weinberger) Memory: Organization and Locus of

Change, 1991; (with N.M. Weinberger and G. Lynch) Brain and Memory: Modulation and Mediation of Neuroplasticity, 1995; author over 400 sci. papers; founding editor Behavioral Biology, 1972-78, Behavioral and Neural Biology, 1979-94, Neurobiology of Learning and Memory, 1995-98, Plasticity in the Central Nervous System; Learning and Memory, 1995, Brain Processes and Memory, 1996. Recipient medal U. Calif., Irvine, 1992; recipient John P. McGovern award, 1996. Fellow AAAS, Am. Acad. Arts and Scis., Soc. Exptl. Psychologists, Am. Psychol. Soc. (William James fellow 1989, pres. 1989-91), Western Psychol. Assn. (pres. 1992-93); mem. NAS (chmn. psychol. secat. 1992-95), APA (chief sci. advisor 1986-88, Sci. Contbn. award 1981), Internat. Brain Rsch. Orgn., Soc. Neurosci., Am. Coll. Neuropsychopharmacology, Brazilian Acad. Sci. (fgn. mem.), Collegium Internat. Neuropsychopharmacologicum, Psychonomic Soc., European Behavioral Pharmacology Soc., Phi Beta Kappa, Sigma Xi. Office: U Calif Dept Neurobiology Behavior Ctr Neurobiology Learning Irvine CA 92697-0001

MCGEE, DANIEL W., state legislator; b. Shreveport, La., Sept. 30, 1947; m to LaRae; children: three. Montana State Representative, District 21, 1995-2002; Montana State Senator, District 11, 2003-05, District 29, 2005-, Montana State Senate.Land surveyor & geologist, currently. Republican. Address: 1925 Pinyon Dr Laurel MT 59044-9381 Mailing: State Capitol PO Box 201706 Helena MT 59620 E-mail: house@state.mt.us.

MCGEE, HAROLD JAMES, writer; b. Cambridge, Mass., Oct. 3, 1951; s. Charles Gilbert and Louise (Hanney) McGee; m. Sharon Rugel Long, July 7, 1979; children: John, Florence. BS, Calif. Inst. Tech., 1973; PhD, Yale U., 1978. Co-founder Senomyx, Inc., La Jolla, Calif., 1999. Author: On Food and Cooking, 1984 (André Simon Meml. Fund award, 1985), 2nd edit., 2004, The Curious Cook, 1990 (James T. Grady-James H. Stack award, Am. Chem. Soc., 2008); contbr. articles to profl. jours. Recipient Pioneer award, Chefs Assn.; named one of the 100 Most Influential People in the World, TIME mag., 2008.

MCGEE, JAMES SEARS, historian, educator; b. Houston, July 12, 1942; s. William Sears and Mary Elizabeth (Peterson) McG.; m. Mary Arnall Broach, Aug. 20, 1966; children: Elizabeth, Claude. BA, Rice U., 1964; MA, Yale U., 1966, M in Philosophy, 1968, PhD, 1971. Asst. prof. Ga. So. Coll., Statesboro, 1969-71; asst. prof. history U. Calif., Santa Barbara, 1971-78, assoc. prof., 1978-84, prof., 1984—, chmn. dept., 1990-95, 2006—07. Pres. Pacific Coast Conf. on Brit. Studies, 1998-2000. Author: The Godly Man in Stuart England, 1976; co-author: The West Transformed, 2000; editor: The Miscellaneous Works of John Bunyan, Vol. 3, 1987. Named Disting. Tchr. in Soc. Scis., U. Calif., Santa Barbara, 1989; fellow Abraham Found., 1962-63; Woodrow Wilson fellow, 1964-65; recipient summer stipend NEH, 1975. Fellow Royal Hist. Soc.; mem. Am. Soc. Ch. History, Am. Hist. Assn., N.Am. Conf. on Brit. Studies. Democrat. Episcopalian. Avocation: gardening. Office: U Calif Dept History Santa Barbara CA 93106

MCGEER, EDITH GRAEF, retired neurological science educator; b. NYC, Nov. 18, 1923; d. Charles and Charlotte Annie (Ruhl) Graef; m. Patrick L. McGeer, Apr. 15, 1954; children: Patrick Charles, Brian Theodore, Victoria Lynn. BA, Swarthmore Coll., 1944; PhD, U. Va., 1946; DSc (hon.), U. Victoria, 1987, U. B.C., 2000; DSc, Shiga U., 2006. Rsch. chemist E.I. DuPont de Nemours & Co., Wilmington, Va., 1946—54; rsch. assoc. divsn. neurol. sci. U. B.C., Vancouver, Canada, 1954-74, assoc. prof., 1974—76, prof., acting head, 1976—83, prof., head, 1983—89, prof. emerita, 1989—. Author: (with others) Molecular Neurobiology of the Mammalian Brain, 1978, 2d edit., 1987; editor: (with others) Kainic Acid as a Tool in Neurobiology, 1978, Glutamine, Glutamate, and GABA, 1983; contbr. articles to profl. jours. Decorated officer Order of B.C., Order of Can.; recipient citation, Am. Chem. Soc., 1958, Rsch. award, Clarke Inst., 1992, Lifetime Achievement award, Sci. Coun. B.C., 1995, Hon. Alumnus award, 1996, cert., Internat. Sci. Inst., 2001, medal of svc., Dr. Cam Coady Found., 2003, Lifetime Achievement award, U. B.C. Med. Faculty, 2006. Fellow Can. Coll. Neuropsychopharmacology, Royal Soc. Can.; mem. Can. Biochem. Soc., Internat. Brain Rsch. Orgn., Internat. Soc. Neurochemistry, Soc. Neurosci., Am. Neurochem. Soc. (councilor 1979-83), North Pacific Soc. Neurology and Psychiatry (hon. fellow), Lychnos Soc., Sigma Xi, Phi Beta Kappa. Office: U BC Divsn Neurol Sci 2255 Wesbrook Mall Vancouver BC Canada V6T 1Z3 Home Phone: 604-224-6403; Office Phone: 604-822-7380. Business E-Mail: mcgeer@interchange.ubc.ca.

MCGEGAN, NICHOLAS, music director; b. Eng. Student, Cambridge U., Oxford U. Music dir. Philharmonia Baroque Orch., San Francisco, 1985—, Irish Chamber Orch; artistic dir. Göttingen Handel Festival, Germany, 1990, Killaloe Festival; prin. guest condr. Scottish Opera, 1992-98; prin. condr. Drottningholm Ct. Theatre, 1993-95; founder, dir., harpsichordist The Arcadian Acad. Guest condr. San Francisco, St. Louis, Houston, Detroit, Indpls., Minn., Nat. Symphony orchs., City of Birmingham Symphony Orch., Halle Orch., Acad. of St. Martin-in-the-Fields in Breat Britain, Montreal Symphony, Nat. Arts Ctr. Orch., Ottawa, Orchestra de la Suisse Romande, Jerusalem Symphony, NY Philharm., Phila. Orch.; condr. Hanover Band, Freiburg Baroque Orch., Orch. of the Age of Enlightment; artist-in-residence, Milw. Symphony Orch.; condr. over 40 operas in Europe and US; artistic ptnr. St. Paul Chamber Orch. Condr. (Operas) Mostly Mozart Festival, NYC, 2003. Office: The St Paul Chamber Orchestra Third Fl of the Hamm Bldg 408 St Peter St Saint Paul MN 55102-1497 also: Philharmonia Baroque Orch 180 Redwood St, Ste 200 San Francisco CA 94102

MCGETTIGAN, CHARLES CARROLL, JR., investment banker; b. San Francisco, Mar. 28, 1945; s. Charles Carroll McGettigan and Molly (Fay) McGettigan Pedley; m. Katharine Havard King, Nov. 1, 1975 (div. 1981); m. Meriwether Lewis Stovall, Aug. 6, 1983; 1 child, Meriwether Lewis Fay. AB in Govt., Georgetown U., Washington, DC, 1966; MBA in Fin., U. Pa., Phila., 1969. Assoc., asst. v.p., v.p. Blyth Eastman Dillon, NYC, 1970-75, 1st v.p., 1975-78, sr. v.p. San Francisco, 1978-80, Dillon, Read & Co., San Francisco, 1980-83; gen. ptnr. Woodman Kirkpatrick & Gilbreath, San Francisco, 1983-84; prin. corp. fin. Hambrecht & Quist, Inc., San Francisco, 1984-88; mng. dir., founder McGettigan, Wick & Co., Inc., San Francisco, 1988—; gen. ptnr., founder Proactive Ptnrs., L.P., San Francisco, 1990—, Proactive Investment Mgrs., L.P., San Francisco, 1991—. Gen. ptnr. Fremont Proactive Ptnrs., 1991—2001; bd. dirs. Cuisine Solutions, Inc., Alexandria, Va., Trader Vic's Mgmt. Corp., Emeryville, Calif.; chmn. Modtech, Inc., Perris, Calif., Onsite Energy Corp., Carlsbad, Calif., Popco Entertainment Ltd, Hong Kong, Tanknology, Inc., Austin, Tex.; adv. dir. Chesapeake Ventures, Balt., 1984—94. Trustee St. Francis Meml. Hosp., San Francisco, 1980-86, 2009-, dir. Wm. H. Adams Found. ALS Rsch.; mem. United San Francisco Rep. fin. com., 1983—, steering com., 1986—; adv. bd. dirs. Leavey Sch. Bus. Adminstrn., Santa Clara U., Calif., 1984-90. With USN, 1966. Mem. The Brook, Racquet and Tennis Club (NY), The Pacific Union Club, Bohemian Club (San Francisco), San Francisco Golf Club, Burlingame Country Club (Hillsborough, Calif.), Boston (New Orleans), White's (London). Republican. Roman Catholic. Home: 3375 Clay St San Francisco CA 94118-2006 Office: McGettigan Wick & Co Inc 50 Osgood Pl San Francisco CA 94133-4622 Office Phone: 415-986-4433. Business E-Mail: Chas@McGettigan-Wick.com.

MCGIHON, ANNE LEE, state legislator, lawyer; b. Newport, RI, June 1, 1957; d. Robert Sidney and Clara Lee (Denman) McG. BA, McGill U., 1978; MSW, Fla. State U., 1980, JD with honors, 1984. Bar: Fla. 1984, US Dist. Ct. (mid. dist.) Fla. 1984, US Ct. Appeals (11th cir.) 1984, US Ct. Claims 1986, US Supreme Ct. 1988, US Dist. Ct. (DC) 1987, Colo. 1990. Social worker Tallahassee Meml. Regional Med. Ctr., Fla., 1980-81; assoc. Akerman, Senterfitt & Eidson, Orlando, Fla., 1984-86, Kirkpatrick & Lockhart, Washington, 1987-89, Holland & Hart, Denver, 1989-93, McGihon's Assoc., LLC, Denver, 1993—; mem. Dist. 3 Colo. House of Reps., Denver, 2003—. Contbr. articles to profl. jours. Vol. Fla. Dem. Com., Orlando, 1986, Dem. Nat. Com., Nat. Lawyers Coun., 1987-88. Mem. ABA (litig. and bus. law sect. 1989-91, apptd. to banking com. 1991-96), Fla. Bar Assn. (vice chmn. out of state practitioners com. 1989-91, bus. law sect., vice chmn. fin. instns. com. 1989-90, comml. litig. com.), DC Bar Assn. (litig. and corp. sect.). Democrat. Episcopalian. Office: Dist Office 837 Sherman St Denver CO 80203-2943 also: Colo State Capitol 200 E Colfax Denver CO 80203 Office Phone: 303-866-2921. Business E-Mail: anne.mcgihon.house@state.co.us.*

MC GILL, ARCHIE JOSEPH, venture capitalist; b. Winona, Minn., May 29, 1931; s. Archibald Joseph and Anne (Lettner) McG.; m. Jeanne Sullivan, Mar. 17, 1974; children: Archibald Joseph, III, Mark E., Gregory P., Debora, Susan, Brian. BA in Econs., St. Mary's Coll., Winona, 1956. With IBM Corp., 1956-69, v.p. market ops. White Plains, N.Y., 1956-69; founder, pres. McGill Assocs., White Plains, 1970-73; dir. market mgmt. AT&T Co., 1973-78, v.p. bus. mktg., 1978-83; pres. Advanced Info. Systems Am. Bell, Inc., 1983; pres., chief exec. officer Rothschild Ventures, Inc., 1983; now pres. Chardonnay, Inc. Dir. various cos. Bd. dirs. Steadman/Hawkins Found. With USAF, 1951-54. Named Mktg. Statesman of Year Sales Execs. Club, 1978 Home and Office: 10216 E Venado Trl Scottsdale AZ 85262-2961 E-mail: archmgill@cox.net.

MCGILL, LEONARD JOHN, lawyer; b. Edinburgh, Oct. 26, 1957; s. Alexander and Mary (Thomson) McG.; m. Nancy Ann Fasulo, Sept. 29, 1981. LLB with honors, U. Edinburgh, 1979; JD magna cum laude, Georgetown U., 1985. Bar: D.C. 1986, Calif. 1988. Assoc. Skadden, Arps, Slate, Meagher & Flom, Washington, 1986-87, Gibson, Dunn & Crutcher, LA, 1987—2002; v.p., dep. gen. counsel Fleetwood Enterprises, Inc., 2002—03, sr. v.p., corp. fin. & chief governance officer, 2003—, gen. counsel, sec., 2005—. Mem. ABA (internat. law and practice sect. 1986—, bus. law sect. 1986—), Masons. Democrat. Presbyterian. Avocations: golf, football. Office: Fleetwood Enterprises Inc 3125 Myers St Riverside CA 92503

MCGILL, THOMAS CONLEY, physics educator; b. Port Arthur, Tex., Mar. 20, 1942; s. Thomas Conley and Susie Elizabeth (Collins) McG.; m. Toby Elizabeth Cone, Dec. 27, 1966; children: Angela Elizabeth, Sara Elizabeth. BS in Math., Lamar State Coll., 1963, BEE, 1964; MEE, Calif. Inst. Tech., 1965, PhD, 1969. NATO postdoctoral fellow U. Bristol, Eng., 1969-70; NRC postdoctoral fellow Princeton (N.J.) U., 1970-71; from asst. to assoc. prof. applied physics Calif. Inst. Tech., Pasadena, 1971-77, prof., 1977—. Cons. United Techs. Corp., 1988-95, Advance Projects Agy./Def. Sci. Rsch. Coun., Arlington, Va., 1979—; chief Naval Ops. Exec. Panel, 1995-2000; mem. Semiconductor Tech. Coun., 1995-98; mem. adv. bd. Sematech U., 1992-95. Alfred P. Sloan Found. fellow, 1974. Fellow Am. Physical Soc.; mem. AAAS, IEEE, Am. Vacuum Soc., Sigma Xi. Office: Calif Inst Tech Mail Code 128 # 95 Pasadena CA 91125-0001

MCGINLEY, JOHN C., actor; b. NYC, Aug. 3, 1959; m. Lauren Lambert, 1997 (div. 2001); 1 child, Max; m. Nichole Kessler, Apr. 7, 2007; 1 child, Billie Grace. Attended, Syracuse U.; MFA, NYU. Ptnr. McGinley Entertainment Inc. Actor: (TV series) Another World, 1985—86, Scrubs, 2001—; (films) Sweet Liberty, 1986, Platoon, 1986, Wall Street, 1987, Shakedown, 1988, Talk Radio, 1988, Prisoners of Inertia, 1989, Suffering Bastards, 1989, Lost Angels, 1989, Fat Man and Little Boy, 1989, Born on the Forth of July, 1989, Highlander II: The Quickening, 1991, Point Break, 1991, Article 99, 1992, A Midnight Clear, 1992, Little Noises, 1992, Hear No Evil, 1993, Car 54, Where Are You?, 1994, On Deadly Ground, 1994, Mother's Boys, 1994, Surviving the Game, 1994, Wagons East, 1994, Born to Be Wild, 1995, Se7en, 1995, Nixon, 1995, Psalms from the Underground, 1996, Hollywood Boulevard, 1996, The Rock, 1996, Mother, 1996, Set It Off, 1996, Johns, 1996, Flypaper, 1997, Truth or Consequences, 1997, Nothing to Lose, 1997, Office Space, 1999, Three to Tango, 1999, Any Given Sunday, 1999, Get Carter, 2000, The Animal, 2001, Crazy as Hell, 2002, Highway, 2002, Stealing Harvard, 2002, Identity, 2003, (voice) Lil' Pimp, 2005, A.W.O.L., 2006, Two Tickets to Paradise, 2006, Puff, Puff, Pass, 2006, American Crude, 2007, Wild Hogs, 2007, Are We Done Yet?, 2007; (TV films) Clinton and Nadine, 1988, Cruel Doubt, 1992, Long Island Fever, 1995, The Return of Hunter, 1995, Intensity, 1997, Target Earth, 1998, The Pentagon Wars, 1998, Sole Survivor, 2000; actor, prodr. (films) Watch It, 1993, Colin Fitz, 1997, actor, exec. prodr. (TV films) The Jack Bull, 1999; actor: (TV appearances) Spenser: For Hire, 1988, The Practice, 1997, Spider-Man, 2003, (voice only) Kim Possible, 2003, Justice League, 2003—05, American Dragon: Jack Long, 2005; prodr.: (films) Sex & the Other Man, 1995. Nat. spokesperson Nat. Down Syndrome Soc.'s Buddy Walks. Office: c/o Innovative Artists 1505 10th St Santa Monica CA 90401

MCGINNESS, MIKE (JOSEPH M. MCGINNESS), state legislator; b. Fallon, Nev., Apr. 12, 1947; m. Dee Pearce; children: Ryan, Brett, Shannon. BA, U. Nev. Radio sta. mgr. Sta. KVLV AM-FM; mem. Nev. State Assembly, Carson City, 1989-91; mem., Ctrl. Nev. Dist. Nev. State Senate, Carson City, 1993—, mem. judiciary com., mem. natural resources com., chair taxation com. Past chair Churchill County Rep. Ctrl. Com., Churchill County Sch. Bd., Churchill County Pks. and Recreation Commn., 1986-87; past pres. Citizens for Pvt. Enterprise-Fallon Chpt., 1987-88, Nev. State Fair Bd. Dirs., 1985. With Nev. Air Nat. Guard, 1969-75. Mem. Nat. Conf. State Legislatures, Churchill County Ducks Unltd. (steering com.), Churchill County C. of C. (past pres. 1975-76), Kiwanis Club Fallon (past pres., sec., treas.). Republican. Methodist. Office: Nev Senate 401 S Carson St Rm 2100 Carson City NV 89701 Office Phone: 775-684-1442. Business E-Mail: mmcginness@sen.state.nv.us.*

MCGINNIS, ROBERT E., lawyer; b. Caldwell, Ohio, May 1, 1931; s. Earl Peregoy and Mary Ethel (Richner) McG.; m. Jane Ann Lindenmeyer, Sept. 12, 1953; children: Sharon Ann, David E. BA, Ohio Weslayan U., 1952; JD summa cum laude, Ohio State U., 1954. Bar: Ohio 1954, Calif. 1956. Asst. judge advocate USAF, 1954-56; sr. ptnr. Luce, Forward, Hamilton, & Scripps, San Diego, 1956—. Counsel to pub. utilities, pub. agys., savs. and loan instns., ins. cos. and contractors. Trustee Wesley Meth. Ch., San Diego, Fine Arts Soc., First Meth. Ch., La Mesa, Calif.; counsel Kensington Community Ch.; dir. San Diego Opera Assn., corp. sec., v.p. Mem. Order of Coif. Republican. Mem. United Ch. Christ. Office: Luce Forward Hamilton & Scripps 600 W Broadway Ste 2600 San Diego CA 92101-3372 Office Phone: 619-699-2441. Business E-Mail: rmcginnis@luce.com.

MCGLYNN, J. CASEY, lawyer; BS, Santa Clara U., 1975, JD with highest honors, 1978. With Wilson Sonsini Goodrich & Rosati, Palo Alto, Calif., 1978—, ptnr., chmn. life sci. practice group, mem. policy com., exec. nominating com., compensation com. Office: Wilson Sonsini Goodrich & Rosati 650 Page Mill Rd Palo Alto CA 94304-1050 Office Phone: 650-493-9300. Office Fax: 650-493-6811. Business E-Mail: cmcglynn@wsgr.com.

MC GOVERN, WALTER T., federal judge; b. Seattle, May 24, 1922; s. C. Arthur and Anne Marie (Thies) McG.; m. Rita Marie Olsen, June 29, 1946; children: Katrina M., Shawn E., A. Renee. BA, U. Wash., 1949, LL.B., 1950. Bar: Wash. 1950. Practiced law in, Seattle, 1950-59; mem. firm Kerr, McCord, Greenleaf & Moen; judge Municipal Ct., Seattle, 1959-65, Superior Ct., Wash., 1965-68, Wash. Supreme Ct., 1968-71, U.S. Dist. Ct. (we. dist.) Wash., 1971-87, chief judge, 1975-87, sr. judge, 1987—. Mem. subcom. on supporting personnel Jud. Conf. U.S., 1981-87, chmn. subcom., 1983, mem. adminstrn. com., 1983-87, chmn. jud. resources com., 1987-91. Mem. Am. Judicature Soc., Wash. State Superior Ct. Judges Assn., Seattle King County Bar Assn. (treas.), Phi Delta Phi. Clubs: Seattle Tennis (pres. 1968). Office: US Dist Ct US Courthouse 700 Stewart St Seattle WA 98101

MCGOWN, JOHN, JR., lawyer; b. Bowling Green, Ky., June 15, 1949; s. John Stanley and Margaret (Deatherage) McG.; m. Mary Grunewald, Apr. 20, 1978; children: Erin Margaret, Brenna Kathryn. BS, U. Ky., Lexington, 1971; JD, U. Colo., Boulder, 1974; LLM in Taxation, U. Denver, 1981. Bar: Colo. 1975, US Tax Ct. 1981, Idaho 1982. Dep. dist. atty. Weld County, Colo., 1974-78; assoc. Montgomery, Little, Young, Campbell, & McGrew, Denver, 1979-80; rschr. appellate divsn. IRS, Denver, 1980-81; mem. staff tax dept. Price Waterhouse, Denver, 1981-82; ptnr. Hawley Troxell Ennis & Hawley, LLP, Boise, Idaho, 1982-99, of counsel, 2000—. Adj. prof. Boise State U., 1983, assoc. prof., 2000-02; guest lecturer U. Idaho Coll. Law, Moscow, 1990, 2003, 04, 05, adj. prof., 06; guest speaker various tax seminars, 1983—. Contbr. over 90 articles to profl. jours. Bd. dirs. Assn. for Retarded Citizens Ada County, Inc., 1987-93, pres. 1991-92, Assoc. Taxpayers Idaho, Inc., 1993-2002, exec. com., 1995-2002; audit review panel United Way Ada County, 1986-91; IRS vol. tax asst. program 1982, 87. Fellow Am. Coll. of Trust and Estate Counsel; mem. ABA (taxation sect.), Idaho State Bar Assn. (founding mem., taxation probate and trust law sect.), Idaho Soc. CPAs (fed. and state taxation com. 1984-89, bus. legis. com. 1989-91, pers. fin. com. 2000—), Boise Bar Assn., Pioneer Club, Toastmasters (pres. 1991), Beta Gamma Sigma, Sigma Chi. Home: 282 S Mobley Ln Boise ID 83712-8329 Office: Hawley Troxell Ennis & Hawley LLP 877 Main St Ste 1000 Boise ID 83702-5883

MCGRATH, DAVID M., lawyer; BA, Brigham Young U., 1986, JD, 1989. Bar: Colo. 1989, Utah 1994. Assoc. Holland & Hart, 1989—92, Nelson, Hoskin & Farina, 1992—93; ptnr. Parry Anderson & Mansfield, 1993—2000; gen. counsel Zions Bancorp., Salt Lake City, 2000—04.

MCGRATH, DON JOHN, bank executive; b. Springfield, Ill., June 15, 1948; s. Donald John and Wilma P. (Beck) McG.; m. Patriaia Ratti, May 7, 1983. BS in Mktg., U. Ill., 1970; MBA, Boston U., 1973. Investment officer Banque Nationale de Paris, San Francisco, 1975-76, treas. San Francisco and L.A., 1976-78, v.p., treas., 1978-80, Bank of the West, San Francisco, 1980, v.p., CFO, 1980-81, sr. v.p., CFO, 1981-84, sr. exec. v.p., CFO, 1984-87, sr. exec. v.p., CEO, 1987-91, pres., COO, 1991-95, pres., CEO, 1996—, chmn., CEO, 2005; pres., COO, dir. BancWest Corp., 1998—2004, pres., CEO, dir., 2005—. Bd. dirs. Commonwealth Club Calif., Nature Conservancy Calif., Dominican Univ. San Rafael, Calif. Mem. Calif. Bankers Assn., Univ. Club, St. Francis Yacht Club (San Francisco), Diablo (Calif.) Country Club. Office: BancWest Corp 180 Montgomery St 25th Fl San Francisco CA 94104 Office Phone: 415-765-4823.

MCGRATH, MARY HELENA, plastic surgeon, educator; b. NYC, Apr. 12, 1945; d. Vincent J. and Mary M. (Manning) McG.; children: Margaret E. Simon, Richard M. Simon. BA, Coll. New Rochelle, 1966; MD, St. Louis U., 1970; MPH, George Washington U., 1994. Diplomate Am. Bd. Surgery, Am. Bd. Plastic Surgery, lic. physician Calif. Resident in surg. pathology U. Colo. Med. Ctr., Denver, 1970-71, intern in gen. surgery, 1971-72, resident in gen. surgery, 1971-75; resident in plastic and reconstructive surgery Yale U. Sch. Medicine, New Haven, 1976—78, chief resident plastic and reconstructive surgery, 1977-78; fellow in hand surgery U. Conn.-Yale U., New Haven, 1978; instr. in surgery divsn. plastic and reconstructive surgery Yale U. Sch. Medicine, New Haven, 1977-78, asst. prof. plastic surgery, 1978-80; attending in plastic and reconstructive surgery Yale-New Haven Hosp., 1978-80, Columbia-Presbyn. Hosp., NYC, 1980-84, George Washington U. Med. Ctr., Washington, 1984-2000, Children's Nat. Med. Ctr., Washington, 1985-2000, Loyola U. Med. Ctr., 2000—02, Hines VA Hosp., 2001—02, U. Calif., San Francisco, 2003—, San Francisco VA Ctr., 2003—, San Francisco Gen. Hosp., 2003—; asst. prof. plastic surgery Columbia U., NYC, 1980-84; assoc. prof. plastic surgery Sch. Medicine, George Washington U., Washington, 1984-87, prof. plastic surgery, 1987-2000, Loyola U. Med. Ctr., 2000—02, U. Calif., San Francisco, 2003—. Bd. dirs. Am. Bd. Plastic Surgery, 1989-95, historian, 1991-95; examiner certifying exam., 1986—; mem. Residency Rev. Com. Plastic Surgery, 2006—; senator med. faculty senate George Washington U., bd. govs. Med. Faculty Assocs.; presenter, cons. in field. Co-editor: (with M.L. Turner) Dermatology for Plastic Surgeons, 1993; assoc. editor: The Jour. of Hand Surgery, 1984-89, Annals of Plastic Surgery, 1984-87, Plastic and Reconstructive Surgery, 1989-95, Contemporary Surgery,

1999-2006, Archives of Surgery, 2004—; advt. editor Plastic and Reconstructive Surgery, 2003-06; guest reviewer numerous jours.; contbr. chpts. to books and articles to profl. jours Recipient numerous rsch. grants, 1978—. Fellow ACS (DC chpt. program ann. meeting chmn., 1992, pres. 1994-95, bd. govs. 1995-98, exec. com. 1996-97, chmn. adv. coun. plastic surgery 1995-98, regent 1997—2006, vice-chair bd. regents 2005-06, 1st v.p. 2007-08); mem. AAAS, Am. Surg. Assn., Am. Assn. Hand Surgery, Am. Assn. Plastic Surgeons (trustee 1997-00), Am. Burn Assn., Am. Soc. for Aesthetic Plastic Surgery, Am. Soc. Maxillofacial Surgeons, Am. Soc. Plastic and Reconstructive Surgery (chmn. ethics com. 1985-87, chmn. device/tech. evaluation com. 1993-94, chmn. workforce task force 1997-00, bd. dirs. 1994-96, chmn. endowment bd. dirs. 2000-04, trustee 2004—07, chmn. bd. trustees 2006-07, ednl. found. bd. dirs. 1985-96, treas. 1989-92, v.p. 1992-93, pres.-elect 1993-94, pres. 1994-95), Am. Soc. Reconstructive Microsurgery (edn. com. 1992-94), Am. Soc. Surgery of Hand (chmn. 1987 ann. residents' and fellows conf. 1986-87, rsch. com. 1988-90), Assn. Acad. Chmn. Plastic Surgery (bd. dirs. 1999—), Assn. Acad. Surgery, Chgo. Soc. Plastic Surgeons (treas. 2001-02), Calif. Soc. Plastic Surgeons, San Francisco Surg. Soc., Chgo. Surg. Soc., Internat. Soc. Reconstructive Surgery, Met. D.C. Soc. Surgery Hand (pres. 1995-97), N.Y. Surg. Soc., Northeastern Soc. Plastic Surgeons (treas. 1993-96, pres. 1997-98), Pacific Coast Surg. Assn., Plastic Surgery Rsch. Coun. (chmn. 1990), Surg. Biology Club III, The Wound Healing Soc Office Phone: 415-353-4389. Business E-Mail: mary.mcgrath@ucsfmedctr.org.

MCGRATH, MIKE, state supreme court chief justice, former state attorney general; b. Aug. 22, 1947; BS, U. Mont., 1970; JD, Gonzaga U., 1975. Bar: Wash. 75, Mont. 77, U.S. Ct. Appeals (9th cir.) 80, U.S. Supreme Ct. 80. Reginald Heber Smith cmty. lawyer fellow; atty. Washoe County Legal Svcs., Reno, 1975—76; asst. atty. gen. State of Mont., Helena, 1977—82, atty. gen., 2001—09; county atty. Lewis and Clark County, Helena, 1983—2001; chief justice Mont. Supreme Ct., 2009—. Bd. dirs. Mont. Legal Svcs. Assn., 1980—2003, pres., 1984—85, 1995—96; bd. dirs. Mountain chpt. Nat. Com. for Prevention of Child Abuse, 1985—90, Big Bros. Sisters, Helena, 1977—83, Friendship Ctr. Helena, 1989—2003, pres., 1995—97; chmn. Conf. Western Atty. Gens., 2003—04. With USAF, 1970—72. Mem.: Mont. County Attys. Assn. (pres. 1996—97), Nat. Dist. Attys. Assn., Mont. Bar Assn., Rock Mountain Elk Found. Home: 514 Hayes Ave Helena MT 59601-6106 Office: Mont Supreme Ct Justice Bldg - 215 N Sanders PO Box 203001 Helena MT 59620-3001 Office Phone: 406-444-5490.*

MCGRATH, PATRICK JOSEPH, bishop; b. Dublin, July 11, 1945; came to US, 1970; Grad., St. John's Coll. Sem., Waterford, Ireland; D in Canon Law, Lateran U., Rome, 1977. Ordained priest Archdiocese of San Francisco, 1970, aux. bishop, 1989-98; rector, pastor St. Mary Cathedral, 1986; ordained bishop, 1989; co-adjutor bishop Diocese of San Jose, 1998-99, bishop, 1999—. Roman Catholic. Office: Diocese San Jose 900 Lafayette St Ste 301 Santa Clara CA 95050-4934

MCGRAW, DONALD JESSE, biologist, science historian, writer; b. Altadena, Calif., Oct. 27, 1943; s. Jesse E. and Mary L. (Hajostek) McG.; m. Laura Lee Hansen, July 13, 1968; children: Adrienne, Holly, Rachel. BS in Biol. Scis., Calif. State Poly. Coll., 1965; MS, Utah State U., 1967; PhD, Oreg. State U., 1976. Registered microbiologist Am. Acad. Microbiology; CCR fed. registration. Research asst. microbiology Utah State U., 1965-66, teaching asst. food and aquatic microbiology, 1966-67; grad. teaching asst. gen. biology Oreg. State U., 1970-72, instr., 1972-73; tchr. phys. and biol. scis. U.S. Bur. Indian Affairs Boarding Sch., Shonto, Ariz., 1974-75; asst. prof. biology Franklin Coll., Ind., 1975-78; adj. asst. prof. biology Ind. Central U., Indpls., 1977-78; adj. asst. prof. Ind. U.-Purdue U., Columbus, 1978; mem. faculty Yavapai C.C., Prescott, Ariz., 1978-79; assoc. dir. Ute Research Lab., Ft. Duchesne, Utah, 1980-81, dir., 1981-82; asst. prof. biology Coll. St. Thomas, Minn., 1985-87; assoc. provost U. San Diego, 1988—2004, prof., 2001—04; independent fed. contractor, 2005—. Summer ranger/naturalist U.S. Nat. Park Svc., 1970—79, 1983—86; vis. prof. Bard Coll., NYC, 1984. Author: Andrew Ellicott Douglass and the Role of the Giant Sequoia in the Development of Dendrochonology, 2001, Edmund Schulman and the Living Ruins: Bristlecome Pines, Tree Rings and Radiocarbon Dating, 2007; contbr. articles to profl. jours. Commr. San Diego County Columbian Quincentenary Commn., 1990-93, chmn. edn. com., 1990-93; mem. pres.'s adv. com. San Diego Zool. Soc., 1995-97; trustee Quail Bot. Gardens Found., 1995-98. Capt. (0-6) USPHS Res. Recipient Disting. Alumnus award, Calif. State Poly. U., 1991, Monrovia H.S., 1991, Meritorious Pub. Svc. award USN, 2003; Eli Lilly doctoral grantee Oreg. State U., 1973-74; NSF grantee, 1998. Mem. AAAS, Cabrillo Hist. Assn. (bd. dirs. 1989-94, vice chair 1992, chair 1993, 94), History of Sci. Soc., Tree Ring Soc., Alpha Scholastic Honor Soc. of Franklin Coll. (pres. 1976-78), Sigma Xi (sec. San Diego chpt. 1996-97, v.p. 1997-98, pres. 1999-2000, assoc. dir. S.W. region 2000-02, bd. dirs. 2004—, Silver medal of achievement San Diego (Calif.) chpt. 2002), Beta Beta Beta. Office Phone: 619-216-4650. Personal E-mail: granttree@yahoo.com.

MCGRAW, JACK WILSON, federal agency administrator; b. Balt., May 19, 1943; s. P.W. and Nina (Gwinn) McG.; m. Nancy F. Foster, Aug. 31, 1974; children— David, Mark BA, Morris Harvey Coll., 1964; B.Div., Tex. Christian U., 1967. Ordained minister Christian Ch. (Disciples of Christ). Dir. temporary housing HUD, Washington, 1979-82; asst. assoc. dir. Fed. Emergency Mgmt. Agy., Washington, 1982, dep. asst. dir., 1982-83; dep. asst. adminstr. EPA Office Solid Waste and Emergency Response, Washington, 1983-88, acting asst. adminstr.; dep. regional adminstr. EPA Regional Office, Denver, 1988—2005, ret., 2005; prin., owner Jack McGraw and Assocs. LLC, Englewood, Colo., 2005—. Nominee William H. Jump award HUD, 1972; recipient Presdl. Meritorious award, Presdl. Disting. Exec. award. Presbyterian. Home: 8074 S Oneida Ct Englewood CO 80112-3128 Office: EPA Regional Office 8074 S Oneida Ct Englewood CO 80112

MCGRAW, PHILLIP CALVIN See DR. PHIL

MCGRAW, TIM, country music singer; b. Delhi, La., May 1, 1967; s. Tug McGraw; m. Faith Hill, Oct. 6, 1996; children: Gracie Katherine, Maggie Elizabeth, Audrey Caroline. Musician: (albums) Tim McGraw, 1993, Not a Moment Too Soon, 1994 (triple-platinum, Album of Yr., Acad. County Music, 1994), All I Want, 1995, Everywhere, 1997 (Album of Yr., Country Music Assn., 1998), A Place in the Sun, 1999 (Album of Yr., Country Music Assn., 1999), Tim McGraw Greatest Hits, 2000, Set the Circus Down, 2001 (Best Country Album, Am. Music Awards, 2002), Tim McGraw and the Dancehall Doctors, 2002, Live Like You Were Dying, 2004 (Most Inspiring Video of Yr., Country Music Television Music award, 2005, Single Record of Yr., Acad. Country Music Awards, 2005, Am. Music Awards Favorite Country Album, 2005), Tim McGraw Reflected Greatest Hits Vol. 2, 2006 (Favorite Country Album Am. Music Awards, 2006), Let it Go, 2007, (single) Welcome to the Club, 1992, It's Your Love, 1997 (Single & Song of Yr., Acad. Country Music, 1998), Grown Men, 2001 (Single of Yr., Radio Music Assn., 2001), Live Like You Were Dying, 2004 (Single & Song of Yr., Country Music Assn., 2004, Song of Yr., Acad. Country Music Awards, 2005), (with Nelly) Over and Over, 2004, (songs) (with Tracy Lawrence & Kenny Chesney) Find Out Who Your Friends Are, 2007 (Musical Event of Yr., Country Music Assn., 2007, Vocal Event of Yr., Acad. Country Music, 2008); vocal collaboration (with Faith Hill) Let's Make Love, 2001 (Grammy award, 2001); actor: (films) Black Cloud, 2004, Friday Night Lights, 2004, Flicka, 2006, Four Christmases, 2008, (TV appearances) The Jeff Foxworthy Show, 1997. Recipient Favorite New Artist, Am. Music Awards, 1995, Favorite Male Country Artist, 2002, 2001, 2003, 2005, 2007, Top Male Vocalist, Acad. Country Music, 1994, 1999, 1998, Vocal Event of Yr., 1997, 1998, Country Music Assn., 1997, Male Vocalist of Yr., 1999, 2000, Entertainer of Yr., 2001, Male Artist of Yr., TNN/Music City News, 1999, Favorite Male Artist, Blockbuster Award, 2001, Country Male Artist, Radio Music Awards, 2003, Favorite Male Musical Performer, People's Choice Awards, 2004, Favorite Male Performer, 2006, Best Country Collaboration With Vocals (with Faith Hill), 2006. Office: care Curb Records 3907 W Alameda Ave Burbank CA 91505-4332

MCGREGOR, JOHN JOSEPH, lawyer; b. Fort Knox, Ky., Nov. 18, 1946; s. Arden Durham and Ruth Marguerite (Funkner) McG.; m. Rebecca Lounsbury, 1989. AB, U. San Francisco, 1968; JD, U. Calif. Hastings Coll. Law, 1971; LLM, NYU, 1974. Bar: Calif. 1972, U.S. Dist. Ct. (no. dist.) Calif. 1972, U.S. Ct. Appeals (9th cir.) 1979, U.S. Dist. Ct. (ea. dist.) Calif. 1988; cert. specialist in taxation law. Sports info. dir. U. San Francisco, 1966-68; staff atty. Community Legal Svcs., San Jose, Calif., 1972-73; cons. IRS Project, Washington, 1974-75; assoc. Thomas, Snell, Jamison, Russell, Williamson & Asperger, Fresno, Calif., 1975-78; shareholder Thomas, Snell, Jamison, Russell & Asperger, Fresno, 1978-91, McGregor, Dahl, Sullivan & Klug, Fresno, 1991—. Asst. sec., gen. counsel The Vendo Co., Fresno, 1985-88; mem. Fresno County Assessment Appeals Bd., 1993-98. Author: Taxation of Real Property Transfers, 1981. Bd. dirs. Fresno (Calif.) Storyland, 1976-81; mem. Fresno Ski Patrol, 1976-93, Sierra Summit Ski Patrol, Lakeshore, Calif., 1985-93, The Acad., Fresno, 1981—. Named Vol. Atty. of the Year Fresno County Bar Assn., 1983. Mem. Am. Law Inst., Calif. State Bar Assn. (dir. taxation sect., exec. com. 1983-86, chair standards of tax practice com. 1995, 98), Fresno County Bar Assn. (dir. 1982-86). Roman Catholic. Avocations: skiing, golf, reading. Home: 4774 N Wishon Ave Fresno CA 93704-3144 Office: McGregor Dahl Sullivan & Klug PO Box 28485 Fresno CA 93729-8485 Office Phone: 559-322-9292. Business E-Mail: jmcgregor@mdsklaw.com.

MCGREGOR, RUTH VAN ROEKEL, state supreme court chief justice; b. Le Mars, Iowa, Apr. 4, 1943; d. Bernard and Marie Frances (Janssen) Van Roekel; m. Robert James McGregor, Aug. 15, 1965. BA summa cum laude, U. Iowa, 1964, MA, 1965; JD summa cum laude, Ariz. State U., 1974; LLM, U. Va., 1998. Bar: Ariz. 1974, U.S. Dist. Ct. Ariz. 1974, U.S. Ct. Appeals (9th cir.), U.S. Supreme Ct. 1982. Assoc. Fennemore, Craig, von Ammon, Udall & Powers, Phoenix, 1974-79, ptnr., 1980-81, 82-89; law clk. to justice Sandra Day O'Connor U.S. Supreme Ct., Washington, 1981-82; judge Ariz. Ct. Appeals, 1989-98, vice chief judge, 1993-95, chief judge, 1995-98; justice Ariz. Supreme Ct., 1998—, vice chief justice, 2002—05, chief justice, 2005—. Mem. disciplinary commn. Ariz. Supreme Ct., 1984-89, City of Mesa jud. adv. bd., 1997. Mem., newsletter editor Charter 100, Phoenix, 1981—; bd. dirs., mem. Ctr. for Law in Pub. Interest, Phoenix, 1977-80. Named Dwight D. Operman award for Top Judge in the Nation, Am. Judicature Soc., 2005. Mem. ABA (chmn. state memberships 1985-89; named fellow), Ariz. Bar Assn. (disciplinary com. 1984-89), Ariz. Judges Assn. (exec. com. 1990-98, sec. 1991-92, v.p. 1992-93, pres. 1993-94), Nat. Assn. Women Judges (chair first time attendees com. 1990-91, 1994 conv. com.; exec. com. 1995—), Ariz. Woman Lawyers Assn., 1975-. Democrat. Lutheran. Office: Ariz Supreme Ct 1501 W Washington St Phoenix AZ 85007-3231

MCGREGOR, SCOTT A., electronics company executive; BS, MS, Stanford Univ. Dir., interactive intelligence group Microsoft; sr. mgmt. Digital Equip. Corp., 1985—90; sr. v.p. & gen. mgr. Santa Cruz Ops., 1990—98; pres. & CEO, semiconductor div. Royal Philips Electronics, 2001—04; pres., CEO, dir. Broadcom Co., Irvine, Calif., 2005—. Office: Broadcom Corporation 5300 California Ave Irvine CA 92617-3038

MCGUCKIN, JOHN HUGH, JR., lawyer; b. Bryn Mawr, Pa., Nov. 8, 1946; AB magna cum laude, Harvard Coll., 1968, JD, 1971. Bar: Mass. 1971, Calif. 1973. Assoc. Orrick, Herrington, Rowley & Sutcliffe, 1972-79; sr. counsel legal divsn. Bank Am., 1979-81; exec. v.p., gen. counsel, corp. sec. UnionBanCal Corp./Union Bank Calif., N.A., San Francisco, 1981—. Adj. instr. Hastings Coll. Law U. Calif., 1980-82; judge pro tem San Francisco Superior Ct. Contbr. articles to profl. jours. Mem. ABA, State Bar Calif. (v.p., treas., bd. govs., chmn. subcom. duties and liabilities trustees probate and trust law sect. 1985-86, legal svcs. trust fund commn. 1989-90, minimum CLE com.), Assn. Corp. Coun. (chmn. 2003-04), Phi Beta Kappa. Office: Union Bank Calif NA 16th Fl 400 California St San Francisco CA 94104-1320

MCGUIRE, BARBARA G., state legislator; b. Ray-Sonora, Ariz., July 20, 1954; married; 2 children. Svc. extension unit dir. Salvation Army, 1991—; mem. Dist. 23 Ariz. House of Reps., 2007—, mem. mil. affairs & pub. safety com., environ. com. Vol. Angel Tree Christmas Prog., Summer Youth Camp Prog. Mem.: NRA, Casa Grande C. of C., Copper Basin C. of C. (v.p., Citizen of Yr. 2004). Democrat. Office: Ariz House Reps Capitol Complex 1700 W Washington Rm 322 Phoenix AZ 85007 Office Phone: 602-926-3012, 602-926-3012. Office Fax: 602-417-3123. Business E-Mail: bmcguire@azleg.gov. E-mail: barbmcguire@hotmail.com.*

MCGUIRE, LESIL, state legislator; b. Portland, Oreg., Jan. 22, 1971; BA, Willamette U., 1989—93, JD, 1995—98. Legal intern, United States Attorneys Office, 1996; law clerk, Oregon Department Justice, 1996-98; Alaska State Representative, District 17, 2000-02, coun member, Judiciary Committee, 2000, Alaska House Representative; Alaska State Representative, District 28, 2003-2006; Alaska State Senator, District N, 2007-. America Diabetes Association; Habitat for Humanity; Salem's Women's Crisis Center; CASA for Children; Commonwealth North; Covenant House; Anchorage Republican Women's Club; Young Reps. Republican. Avocations: fishing, hiking, skiing, flying, scuba diving, reading. Office: Dist N 716 W Fourth Ave Ste 430 Anchorage AK 99501 also: State Capitol Rm 125 Juneau AK 99801 Office Phone: 907-465-2995. Office Fax: 907-465-6592, 907-269-0249. Business E-Mail: Representative_Lesil_McGuire@legis.state.ak.us.*

MCGUIRE, MICHAEL FRANCIS, plastic surgeon; b. St. Louis, Oct. 4, 1946; s. Arthur Patrick and Virginia Claribel (Gannon) McG. BA, Columbia U., 1968, MD, 1972. Diplomate Am. Bd. Surgery, Am. Bd. Plastic Surgery. Intern UCLA, 1972-73, resident in gen. surgery, 1973-77, resident in plastic surgery, 1978-80; fellow in plastic surgery rsch. Stanford (Calif.) U., 1977-78; traveling fellow in plastic surgery Gt. Britain, 1980; chief plastic surgery L.A. County-Olive View Med. Ctr., Sylmar, Calif., 1980-85; pvt. practice Santa Monica, Calif., 1980—; chief plastic surgery St. John's Health Ctr., 1990—; asst. clin. prof. surgery UCLA, 1980-97, assoc. clin. prof., 1998—. Bd. dirs. Calif. Med. Rev., Inc., sec.-treas., 1997, v.p., 1997-99, chmn. bd. dirs. 1999-2003; chmn. surg. rev. St. Johns Health Ctr., 1996-98, chief plastic surgery, 1992-; pres. Pacific Coast Plastic Surgery Ctr., 1988—. Charter patron LA Music Ctr. Opera, 1983—; sponsoring patron LA County Art Mus., 1986—2005; patron Colleague Helpers in Philanthropic Svc., Bel Air, Calif., 1987, 93, 95; pres. Found. for Surg. Reconstrn., 1996-2007. Fellow ACS, Royal Soc. Medicine; mem. Am. Soc. Plastic Surgeons (membership chmn. 1997-2000, bd. dirs. 2002-05, sec. 2005-2007, v.p. 2007-08, pres.-elect, 2008-, chmn. leadership devel. com. 2004-07), Am. Soc. Aesthetic Plastic Surgery (ethics chmn. 1998-99, bd. dirs. 2004—07, pub. edn. chmn. 2004-05, commr. comm., 2005-2007, publications chair, 2007-), Am. Health Quality Assn. (bd. dirs. 1999—2005), LA County Med. Assn. (v.p. 1995-97, sec.-treas. 1997-99), Calif. Med. Assn. (del., exec. com., splty. delegation 1994-99), Calif. Soc. Plastic Surgery (exec. com., auditor 1988-89, program chmn. 1990, exec. coun. 1991-94, treas. 1994-97, v.p. 1997-98, acting pres. 1997, pres.-elect 1998-99, pres. 1999-2000, nominating com. chmn. 2000-01, strategic planning com. chmn. 2005—), Am. Assn. Accreditation of Ambulatory Surgery Facilities (ops. com. 1995-96, bd. dirs. 1996-, treas. 1996-98, sec. 1998-2000, v.p. 2000-02, pres. 2002-04), Surgery Facilities Resources (founding pres. 2005-07), Alpha Omega Alpha. Avocations: golf, travel, collecting antique glass, opera, art. Office: 1301 20th St Ste 460 Santa Monica CA 90404-2054 Office Phone: 310-315-0121. Business E-Mail: mmcguire@ucla.edu.

MCGUIRE, MICHAEL JOHN, environmental engineer; b. San Antonio, June 29, 1947; s. James Brendan and Opal Mary (Brady) McG.; m. Deborah Marrow, June 19, 1971; children: David, Anna. BS in Civil Engring., U. Pa., 1969; MS in Environ. Engring., Drexel U., 1972, PhD in Environ. Engring., 1977. Diplomate Am. Acad. Environ. Engring.; registered profl. engr., Pa., N.J., Calif., Ariz., Tex. San. engr. Phila. Water Dept., 1969-73; rsch. assoc. Drexel U., Phila., 1976-77; prin. engr. Brown & Caldwell Cons. Engrs., Pasadena, Calif., 1977-79; water quality engr. Met. Water Dist. of So. Calif., LA, 1979-84, water quality mgr., 1984-86, dir. water quality, 1986-90, asst. gen. mgr., 1990-92; pres. McGuire Environ. Cons., Inc., Santa Monica, Calif., 1992—2005, Michael J. McGuire Inc., LA, 2008—; v.p. Malcolm Pirnie Inc., Santa Monica, 2005—08. Cons. to subcom. on adsorbents, safe drinking water com. Nat. Acad. Scis., 1978-79, NRC, Drinking Water Contaminants (comm. mem.), 1998-99; cons. mem. Techs. Workgroup U.S. EPA, DBP Reg. Neg., 1992-93, 97, 98-2000. Editor: (with I.H. Suffet) Activated Carbon Adsorption of Organics from the Aqueous Phase, 2 vols., 1980, Treatment of Water by Granular Activated Carbon, 1983, (with J.L. McLain and A. Obolensky) Information Collection Rule Data Analysis, 2003; contbr. articles to profl. jours. Recipient Best Paper award, Water Quality Tech. Divsn., 2007. Mem. ASCE, Internat. Water Assn. (specialist group on taste and odor control 1982—, chmn. organizing com. 1991, off-flavor symposium 1987-91), Internat. Ozone Assn. (internat. bd. dirs. 1992-95), Am. Water Works Assn. (Calif.-Nev. sect. chmn. water quality and resources divsn. 1982-83, governing bd. 1984-87, 89-96, exec. com. 1989-96, chmn. 1991-92, nat. edn. divsn. chmn. 1982-83, dir. 1994-96, chair taste and odor com. 1993-98, exec. com. 1994-96, water quality and tech. divsn. trustee 2004—, Acad. Achievement award 1978, Fuller award 1994, Publs. award 2001, George A. Elliot award 2005, Hon. Membership award 2006, WQTD Best Paper award 2007, A.P. Black Rsch. award, 2009), Am. Chem. Soc., Sigma Xi, Sigma Nu, Sigma Tau, Nat. Acad. Engring.

MCGUIRE, ROBIN K., engineering company executive; SB in Civil Engring., MIT, Cambridge; MS in Structural Engring., U. Calif., Berkeley, 1969; PhD in Structural Engring., MIT, Cambridge. Pres., prin. Risk Engring., Inc., Boulder, Colo., 1984—. Author: Seismic Hazard and Risk Analysis, 2004. Mem.: NAE. Office: Risk Engring Inc 4155 Darley Ave Ste A Boulder CO 80305 Office Phone: 303-499-3000. Office Fax: 303-499-4850.

MCGUIRE, SUSAN GRAYSON, legislative staff member; BA in Polit. Sci., U. Mich., 1962. Legis. asst. select com. on equal ednl. opportunity U.S. Senate, Washington, 1970-73; staff dir. subcom. on employment opportunities U.S. Ho. of Reps., Washington, 1973-84, staff dir. com. on edn. and labor, 1984-91; pub. policy cons. McGuire & Assocs., Cedar Crest, N.Mex., 1991-93; exec. dir. Indian Arts and Crafts Assn., Albuquerque, 1995-98; state dir. U.S. Senator Jeff Bingaman, Albuquerque, 1998—. Pres. N.Mex. Arts and Crafts Fair, Albuquerque; sec. bd. dirs. Albuquerque Literacy Program; active N.Mex. Clinton for Pres. Com., 1992. Office: 625 Silver Ave SW Ste 130 Albuquerque NM 87102-3185 Fax: 505-346-6780. E-mail: Susan_McGuire@Bingaman.senate.gov.

MCGUIRE, THOMAS ROGER, distribution company executive; b. Marshfield, Wis., Aug. 29, 1943; s. James Gilbert and Gene Elizabeth (Connor) McG.; m. Patricia Mae Ainsworth, Aug. 25, 1962; children: Elizabeth Anne, Amy Lynn. Chief exec. officer, chmn. bd. dirs. Coast Fabrication, Inc., San Jose, Calif., 1964-83, Coast R.V., Inc., San Jose, 1977—. Republican. Methodist. Avocation: basketball. Home: 1480 Calaveras Ave San Jose CA 95126-2502 Office: Coast Distbn System PO Box 1449 Morgan Hill CA 95038-1449

MCGULPIN, ELIZABETH JANE, nurse; b. Toledo, Oct. 18, 1932; d. James Orville and Leah Fayne (Helton) Welden; m. David Nelson Buster, Apr. 9, 1956 (div. Nov. 1960); children: David Hugh, James Ray, Mark Stephen; m. Fredrick Gordon McGulpin, Oct. 7, 1973. AA in Nursing, Pasadena City Coll., 1968. RN Wash. Lic. nurse Las Encinas Hosp., Pasadena, Calif.; nurse Hopi Indian Reservation HEW, Keams Canyon, Ariz., 1969—70; nurse, enterostomal therapist Pasadena Vis. Nurse Assn., 1972—74; nurse Seattle King County Pub. Health, 1977—81; home care nurse Victorville, Calif., 1983—85;

nurse Adult Family Home, Woodinville, Wash., 1986—; sch. nurse Apple Valley United Sch. Dist., Calif., 2006—; RN Mojave Mesa Elem. Sch., Apple Valley United Sch. Dist., 2006—; nurse Cycle Valley United Sch. Dist., Calif., 2006—. Vol. nurse, counselor Child Protective Svcs., Victorville, 1984; realtor Century 21, Lynden, Wash., 1993—. Vol. nurse Am. Cancer Soc., Pasadena, 1973-75, United Ostomy Assn., Los Angeles, Victorville, 1973-84; RN, ARC, 1996—. Am. Cancer Soc. grantee. Mem. Nat. Assn. Realtors, Wash. Assn. Realtors, Whatcom County Assn. Realtors, Vis. Nurse Assn. (Enterostomal Therpay grantee 1973). Avocations: reading, gardening, travel. Home: 18238 Deauville Dr Victorville CA 92392 Personal E-mail: spunky@intlaccess.com.

MCGURK, CHRISTOPHER JAMIE, film company executive; b. 1957; BS, Syracuse U., 1978; MBA, U. Chgo. Various positions including CFO Pepsico, 1982—88; sr. v.p. fin. Walt Disney Studios, 1988-90, exec. v.p., CFO, 1990—94, pres. motion pictures group, 1994—96; various positions including pres., CEO Universal Pictures, 1996—99; vice chmn., COO Metro-Goldwyn-Mayer Inc., 1999—2005; sr. adv. new ventures IDT Entertainment, 2006—; CEO Overture Films, 2006—. Bd. dirs. DivX, Inc., 2006—. Exec. prodr.: (films) The Brothers Grimm, 2005.

MCHENRY, HENRY MALCOLM, anthropologist, educator; b. LA, May 19, 1944; s. Dean Eugene and Emma Jane (Snyder) McH.; m. Linda Jean Conway, June 25, 1966; children: Lindsay Jean, Annalisa Jane. BA, U. Calif., Davis, 1966, MA, 1967; PhD, Harvard U., 1972. Asst. prof. anthropology U. Calif., Davis, 1971-76, assoc. prof. anthropology, 1976-81, prof. anthropology, 1981—, chmn. dept. anthropology, 1984-88. Fellow AAAS, Am. Anthrop. Assn., Calif. Acad. Sci.; mem. Am. Assn. Phys. Anthropologists (exec. com. 1981-85), Soc. Study Evolution, Soc. Vertebrate Paleontology, Phi Beta Kappa, Phi Kappa Phi. Democrat. Buddhist. Avocation: winemaker. Home: 330 11th St Davis CA 95616-2010 Office: U of Calif Davis Dept Of Anthropology Davis CA 95616 Office Phone: 530-752-1588. Business E-Mail: hmmchenry@ucdavis.edu.

MCHUGH, PETER, mayor; b. Boston; m. Gail Marie Parnagian; children: Sean Michael, Tatia Marie. Student, Boston U. Sch. Bus. Adminstrn., 1963; BS in Bus. Adminstrn., UCLA, 1969. With IBM, 1964; mem. city coun. Milpitas, Calif., 1976-78, 82-90; mayor, 1978-82, 90-96; bd. suprs. dist. 3 County of Santa Clara, 1996—. Recipient numerous honors and acknowledgments for cmty. svc. including Calif. State Assembly, Calif. State Senate, U.S. Congress. Office: 70 W Hedding St Fl 10 San Jose CA 95110-1705

MCHUGHEN, ALAN, geneticist, educator; b. Ottawa, Ontario, Can., Apr. 13, 1954; m. Donna Greschner; children: Stephanie, Nicola. PhD, Oxford U., Eng., 1979. Lectr. Yale U., New Haven, 1979—82; prof. U. Saskatchewan, Canada, 1982—2001; prof., botany and plant scis. U. Calif., Riverside, 2002—. Author: Pandora's Picnic Basket (Book of Yr., Can. Sci.Writers Assn., 2000); contbr. articles to profl. jours. Pres. Internat. Soc. for Biosafety Rsch., Riverside, 1988—2004. Fellow, Am. Coll. Nutrition, 2002, Am. Assn. Advancement Sci., 2009. Fellow: AAAS. Achievements include patents in field, including one of the first for a higher lifeform; development of public sector commercial transgenic and conventional crop cultivars. Office: Univ Calif University Ave Riverside CA 92521-0124 Office Fax: 951-827-5717. Business E-Mail: alanmc@ucr.edu.

MCILWAIN, CARL EDWIN, physicist; b. Houston, Mar. 26, 1931; s. Glenn William and Alma Ora (Miller) McI.; m. Mary Louise Hocker, Dec. 30, 1952; children— Janet Louise, Craig Ian. BA, N. Tex. State Coll., Denton, 1953; MS, State U. Iowa, 1956, PhD, 1960. Asst. prof. State U. Iowa, 1960-62; assoc. prof. physics U. Calif.-, San Diego, 1962-66; prof. U. Calif., 1966—. Mem. space scis. steering com., fields and particles subcom. NASA, 1962-66; mem. antisubmarine warfare panel President's Sci. Adv. Com., 1964-67; mem. com. potential contamination and interference from space expts. Space Sci. Bd., Nat. Acad. Scis.-NRC, 1964-71; mem. advisory com. for radiation hazards in supersonic transports FAA, 1967-71; mem. Fachbeirat Inst. Extraterrestrial Physics, Max Planck Inst., Garching, Fed. Republic Germany, 1977-83, Space Sci. Bd., NRC, 1983-86. Author; patentee in field. Guggenheim fellow, 1968, 72; recipient Space Sci. award Am. Inst. Aeros. and Astronautics, 1970, Computer Art award U.S. Users Automatic Info. Display Equipment, 1971, Sr. U.S. Scientist award Alexander von Humboldt Found., Ger., 1976, Hannes Alfven medal European Geogphys. Soc., 2000. Fellow Am. Geophys. Union (John A. Fleming award 1975); mem. Am. Phys. Soc., Am. Astron. Soc. Home: 6662 Avenida Manana La Jolla CA 92037-6228 Office: U Calif San Diego Cass 0424 La Jolla CA 92093-0424 E-mail: cmcilwain@ucsd.edu.

MC INTOSH, J(OHN) RICHARD, retired biologist, educator; b. NYC, Sept. 25, 1939; s. Rustin and Millicent Margaret (Carey) McI.; m. Marjorie Rogers Keniston, Aug. 30, 1961; children— Robert K. (dec.), Elspeth R., Craig T. BA in Physics, Harvard U., 1961, PhD in Biophysics, 1968. Instr. in math. and physics Cambridge Sch., Weston, Mass., 1961-63; asst. prof. biology Harvard U., 1968-70; asst. prof. U. Colo., Boulder, 1970-72, assoc. prof., 1972-76, prof., 1977—2006, chmn. dept. molecular, cellular and devel. biology, 1977-78, dir. Lab for High Voltage Electron Microscopy, 1986—2005, disting. prof., 1999—2006; disting. emeritus prof., 2006—. Mem. editl. bd. Jour. Cell Biology, 1978-82, 1986-90, Cell Motility, 1986-87, Jour. Structural Biology, 1990-97, Molecular Biology Cell, 1995-2006; contbr. articles to profl. jours. Recipient Teaching Recognition award U. Colo., 1974, Scholar award Am. Cancer Soc., 1976, 90; Am. Cancer Soc. grantee, 1971-90, NSF grantee, 1970-82, NIH grantee, 1973-78, 80—; Eleanor Roosevelt Internat. Cancer fellow, 1984; Guggenheim fellow, 1990-91, Fulbright fellow Uganda, 2003-03. Mem. Am. Soc. Cell Biology (coun. 1977-80, 86-89, pres. 1994), Am. Cancer Soc. (cell biology panel 1983-87, rsch. prof. 1994-2005, adv. coun. 1997-2001), NIH (molecular cytology study sect. 1988-92), Nat. Acad. Sci., Am. Acad. Arts and Sci. Home: 870 Willowbrook Rd Boulder CO 80302-7439 Office: U Colo Dept Molec Devel & Devel Bio Boulder CO 80309-0001

MCINTOSH, TERRIE TUCKETT, lawyer; b. Ft. Lewis, Wash., July 20, 1944; d. Robert LeRoy and Elda Tuckett; m. Clifton Dennis McIntosh, Oct. 13, 1969; children: Alison, John. BA, U. Utah, 1967; MA, U. Ill., 1970; JD, Harvard U., 1978. Bar: NY 1979, Utah 1980. Assoc. Hughes, Hubbard & Reed, NYC, 1978-79, Fabian & Clendenin, Salt Lake City, 1979-84, shareholder, 1984-86; staff atty. Questar Corp., Salt Lake City, 1986-88, sr. atty., 1988-92, sr. corp. counsel, 1992—. Instr. philosophy Douglass Coll. Rutgers U., New Brunswick, N.J., 1971-72; mem. adv. com. civil procedure Utah Supreme Ct., Salt Lake City, 1987—; mem. jud. nominating com. 5th Cir. Ct., Salt Lake City, 1986-88. Mem. Utah State Bar (ethics and discipline screening panel 1989-96, vice chair ethics and discipline com. 1996-99, 2006—, co-chair law related edn. com. 1985-86, bar examiner rev. com. 2005—), Women Lawyers of Utah (chair exec. com. 1986-87, Woman Lawyer of Yr. award 2005), Salt Lake Legal Aid Soc. (trustee 1999-2008), Harvard Alumni Assn. Utah (bd. dirs. 1987—), Phi Beta Kappa, Phi Kappa Phi Office Phone: 801-324-5532.

MC INTYRE, JAMES A., diversified financial services executive; b. 1932; BS, U. So. Calif., 1954. With Ernst & Ernst, LA, 1958-63; pres. Fremont Indemnity Co., 1963-80; pres., CEO, chmn. Fremont Gen. Corp., Santa Monica, Calif., 1980—. Office: Fremont Reinsurance Co 2727 E Imperial Hwy Brea CA 92821-6713

MCINTYRE, JERILYN SUE, academic administrator; b. June 24, 1942; d. Frank Otto and Maxine (Ward) McIntyre; m. W. David Smith. Student, Stanford U., Italy, 1962; AB in History with distinction, Stanford U., 1964, MA in Journalism, 1965, cert. Summer Radio-TV Inst., 1965, tchrs. cert., 1968; PhD in Comms., U. Washington, 1973; postgrad. Inst. Ednl. Mgmt., Harvard U., 1993. Corr. World News Bureau McGraw-Hill Pub. Co., LA, 1965-67; asst. prof. dept. mass comm. Chico (Calif.) State Coll., 1968-70; asst. prof. Sch. Journalism U. Iowa, Iowa City, 1973-77; assoc. prof., prof. dept. comm. U. Utah, Salt Lake City, 1977-2000, assoc. dean Coll. Humanities, 1984-88, assoc. v.p. acad. affairs, 1988-90, interim pres., 1997, v.p. acad. affairs, 1990-98; pres. Ctrl. Wash. U., Ellensburg, 2000—. Dir. Wall St. Jour. Publs. Workshop, Chico State Coll., 1968; mem. edn. adv. bd. NFL, 1996; mem. exec. com. coun. acad. affairs Nat. Assn. State Univs. and Land Grant Coll., 1995—98, chair, 1997; mem. steering com. Utah Edn. Network, 1995—98. Editl. asst. Chemical Week Mag., 1965-66, World News Bureau, 1966-67; mem. editl. bd. Journalism History; co-author: Symbols & Society; contbr. articles to profl. jours., chpts. to books. Mem. Utah Women's Forum. Recipient Yesterday's Girl Scout Today's Successful Woman, Utah Girl Scout Coun., 1996, Salt Lake City chpt. Disting. Woman, AAUW, 1994; named a David P. Gardner fellow, 1984. Mem.: Assn. Edn. in Journalism and Mass Comm. Office: 400 E University Way Ellensburg WA 98926-7501 E-mail: mcintyrej@cwu.edu.

MC INTYRE, VONDA NEEL, writer; b. Aug. 28, 1948; d. H. Neel and Vonda Barth (Keith) McI. BS, U. Wash., Seattle, 1970. Author: The Exile Waiting, 1976, 85, Dreamsnake, 1978 (Hugo award, Nebula award), Fireflood and Other Stories, 1979, The Entropy Effect, 1981, The Wrath of Khan, 1982, Superluminal, 1983, The Search for Spock, 1984, Barbary, 1986, Enterprise: The First Adventure, 1986, The Voyage Home, 1986, Starfarers, 1989, Transition, 1991, Metaphase, 1992, Nautilus, 1993, Star Wars: The Crystal Star, 1994, The Moon and the Sun, 1997 (Nebula award); editor: (with Susan Janice Anderson) Aurora: Beyond Equality, 1976. Mem. ACLU. Recipient Nebula award, 1973, 78 Mem. Sci. Fiction Writers Am., Planetary Soc., Cousteau Soc., NOW, Space Studies Inst., Authors Guild, Greenpeace, Nature Conservancy.

MCKAGUE, SHIRLEY, state legislator; b. Nampa, Idaho, Dec. 4, 1935; m. Paul McKague; children: Rhonda, Van, Dan, Randy, Rick, Robert. Legal sec. Carey Nixon, 1964—78; bus. ptnr., book keeper Family Svc. Station, 1969—96; co-owner Paul's Meridian Stinker, 1970; columnist Valley Times, 1980—82; mem. Dist. 14B Idaho House of Reps., Boise, 1997—2003, mem. Dist. 20B, 2003—07; mem. Dist. 20 Idaho State Senate, Boise, 2007—. Mem. Alec Info. Tech. Com., 2007. Mem. Miss Meridian Pageant com., Rep. Precinct Com., 1980—. Mem.: Meridian C. of C., Idaho Farm Bur. Republican. Address: Dist 20 933 East Pine Meridian ID 83642 Office Phone: 208-888-2842. Office Fax: 208-888-3379. Business E-Mail: smckague@senate.idaho.gov.*

MCKAY, DIANNE BRENDA, nephrologist; b. Nov. 11, 1954; MD, Chgo. Med. Sch., 1983. Bd. cert. Nephrology, Internal Medicine, United Network for Organ Sharing (UNOS) cert. Transplant Nephrologist. Nephrologist Scripps Clin., La Jolla, Calif.; and Scripps Ctr. Organ and Cell Transplantation, La Jolla, Calif. Mem.: Am. Assn. Immunologists, Am. Soc. Nephrology (Women in Nephrology), Am. Soc. Transplantation (founder, Com.on Women and Transplantation, Wyeth Clin. Sci. Career Devel. award (Asst. Prof. Level) 2007). Office: Scripps Clin Torrey Pines 10666 N Torrey Pines Rd IMM-1 La Jolla CA 92037 Office Phone: 858-784-9716. Office Fax: 858-784-8069.

MCKAY, JOHN, law educator, former prosecutor; b. Seattle, June 19, 1956; s. John Larkin and Kathleen (Tierney) M. BA, U. Wash., 1978; JD, Creighton U., 1982. Bar: Wash. 1982, US Dist. Ct. (we. dist.) Wash. 1982, US Supreme Ct. 1990, US Ct. Appeals (9th cir.) 1990, DC 1999. Ptnr. Lane Powell Spears Lubersky, Seattle, 1982-92, Cairncross & Hempelmann, Seattle, 1992-97; pres. Legal Svcs. Corp., Washington, 1997—2001; US atty. (we. dist.) Wash. US Dept. Justice, 2001—07; sr. v.p., gen. counsel Getty Images, Inc., Seattle, 2007. Law prof. Seattle U. Law Sch., 2007—. White House fellow, Washington, 1989-90; named Pro Bono Lawyer of Yr. Wash. State Bar Assn., 1995, Assn. Award of Merit, 2001, Courageous Award, 2007 Mem. ABA (bd. govs. 1991-94), Wash. State Bar Assn. (pres. young lawyers divsn. 1988-89). Republican. Roman Catholic. Avocations: soccer, golf. Office: Seattle U Sch Law Sullivan Hall PO Box 222000 901 12th Ave Seattle WA 98122-1090 Business E-Mail: jmckay@seattleu.edu.

MCKAY, LAURA L., bank executive, consultant; b. Watonga, Okla., Mar. 3, 1947; d. Frank Bradford and Elizabeth Jane (Smith) Drew; m. Cecil O. McKay, Sept. 20, 1969; 1 child, Leslie. BSBA, Oreg. State U., 1969. Cert. cash mgr., Treasury Mgmt. Assn. New br. rsch. U.S. Bank, Portland, Oreg., 1969-80, cash mgmt. officer, 1980-82, asst. v.p., 1982-87, v.p., 1987-94; founder, cons. LLM Cons., Milw., 1994-97; co-founder, mng. ptnr. DMC & Assocs. LLC, Portland, 1997—2001; v.p. treasury mgmt., sales mgr. West Coast Bank, 2000—06, sr. v.p. mgr., treasury mgmt., 2006—. Cert. trainer Achieve Global and Edge Learning. Chmn. Budget Com., North Clackamas Sch. Dist., 1982-84. Mem. Assn. for Fin. Profls., Nat. Assn. Bank Women (chmn. Oreg. group 1979-80), Portland Treasury Mgrs. Assn., Portland C. of C. Republican. Office: Ste 100 5000 Meadows Rd Lake Oswego OR 97034 Home Phone: 503-632-3564; Office Phone: 503-603-8052. E-mail: mckayl@wcb.com.

MCKAY, MICHAEL DENNIS, lawyer; b. Omaha, May 12, 1951; s. John Larkin and Kathleen (Tierney) McK.; m. Nancie Miller McKay.; children: Kevin Tierney, Kathleen Lindsay, John Larkin. BA in Polit. Sci. with distinction, U. Wash., 1973; JD, Creighton U., 1976. Bar: Wash. 1976, U.S. Dist. Ct. (we. dist.) Wash. 1978, U.S. Dist. Ct. (ea. dist.) Wash. 1982, U.S. Ct. Appeals (9th cir.) 1982, U.S. Supreme Ct. 1993. Sr. dep. pros. atty. King County, Seattle, 1976-81; ptnr. McKay & Gaitan, Seattle, 1981-89; U.S. atty. we. dist. Wash. Seattle, 1989-93; ptnr. Lane Powell Spears Lubersky, Seattle, 1993-95, McKay Chadwell PLLC, Seattle, 1995—. Bd. dirs. Mental Health North, Seattle, 1982-85, St. Joseph Sch. Bd., 1984-87, Our Lady of Fatima Sch. Commn., 1994-97, stadium adv. bd., Seattle Kingdome, 1987-89; mem. U.S. Atty. Gen. Adv. Com., 1991-93, vice chmn., 1992; mem. Washington Citizens' Commn. on Salaries for Elected Officials, 1997-2001; vice chmn., 1999-2001; vice chmn. Seattle Expert Rev. Panel, 1999; vice chair Washington State George W. Bush Campaign, 2000, 2004; co-chair McLain 2008 Wash. State Steering Com. Mem. Creighton U. Alumni Assn. (pres. 1988-90, nat. alumni bd. 1988-92, bd. dirs.), Wash. Athletic Club. Republican. Roman Catholic. Avocations: golf, reading. Office: McKay Chadwell PLLC 600 University St Ste 1601 Seattle WA 98101 Business E-Mail: mdm@mckay-chadwell.com.

MCKAY, MONROE GUNN, federal judge; b. Huntsville, Utah, May 30, 1928; s. James Gunn and Elizabeth (Peterson) McK.; m. Lucile A. Kinnison, Aug. 6, 1954; children: Michele, Valanne, Margaret, James, Melanie, Nathan, Bruce, Lisa, Monroe. BS, Brigham Young U., 1957; JD, U. Chgo., 1960. Bar: Ariz. 1961. Law clk. Ariz. Supreme Ct., 1960-61; assoc. firm Lewis & Roca, Phoenix, 1961-66, ptnr., 1968-74; assoc. prof. Brigham Young U., 1974-76, prof., 1976-77; judge US Ct. Appeals (10th cir.), Denver, 1977-91, chief judge, 1991-94, sr. judge, 1994—. Mem. Phoenix Community Council Juvenile Problems, 1968-74; pres. Ariz. Assn. for Health and Welfare, 1970-72; dir. Peace Corps, Malawi, Africa, 1966-68; bd. dirs., pres. Maricopa county Legal Aid Soc., 1972-74. Served with USMCR, 1946-48. Mem. Ariz. Bar Assn. Mem. Lds Ch. Office: US Ct Appeals 10th Cir Fed Bldg 125 S State St Ste 6012 Salt Lake City UT 84138-1181

MCKEACHNIE, GAYLE F., former lieutenant governor; b. Vernal, Utah, Jan. 26, 1943; s. Colton Orville and Helen (Fletcher) McK.; m. Kathlene Argyle, Dec. 16, 1967; children: Brett, Michelle, Jared, Ashley, Dana Marie, Jonathan, Jacob. BA, Coll. So. Utah, 1967; JD, U. Utah, 1970. Bar: Utah 1970, U.S. Dist. Ct. Utah 1970, U.S. Ct. Appeals (10th cir.) 1970, U.S. Tax Ct. 1985, U.S. Supreme Ct. 1985. Assoc. Senior & Senior, Salt Lake City, 1970-72; adj. prof. UT State U., 1972—2000; prin. Gayle F. McKeachnie & Assocs., Vernal, 1972-78; ptnr. McKeachnie & Allred, Vernal, 1978-81, Nielson & Senior, Vernal, 1981-89, pres., 1988-89, also bd. dirs.; adj. prof. BYU J. Reuben Clark Law School, 1996—2000; lt. gov. State of UT, Salt Lake City, 2003—05. Atty. Daggett County, Manila, Utah, 1974-79; dep. atty. Uintah County, Vernal, 1976-79; appointed to Utah Commn. on Adminstrn. Justice in the Dist. Cts. 1986; chmn. Utah Constl. Review Commn., 1989-01; mem. task force Mgmt. and Regulation of the Practice of Law, Utah Supreme Ct., 1990-92; bd. dirs. Utah Bar Commrs., 1990-94; adv., rural affairs advisor Utah Gov. Mem. Utah Ho. of Reps., Vernal, 1979-88; Utah Bd. State Lands and Forestry, 1992-94. Recipient Disting. Lawyer of Yr. award, Utah Bar Assn., 1997, Disting. Alumnus award, So. Utah U., 1995. Mem. Kiwanis (pres. 1977-78), Utah State U. (chmn., bd. trustees 1994-04), BYU J. Reuben Clark Law Sch. (adj. prof. 1998-2002). Office Phone: 435-789-4908. Business E-Mail: gmckeachnie@mckeachnie.com.

MCKEAN, MICHAEL, actor; b. NYC, Oct. 17, 1947; s. Gilbert and Ruth McKean; m. Susan McKean; children: Colin Russell, Fletcher. Student, Carnegie Inst. Tech., NYU. Toured with satirical comedy group The Credibility Gap; TV appearances include The Goodtime Girls, More Than Friends, American Bandstand, The TV Show; regular on ABC-TV series Laverne and Shirley, 1976-83, Grand, 1989, Dream On, 1990, Sessions, 1991, Spinal Tap Anniversary Spl., 1992, Saturday Night Live, 1994, Road Rovers, 1996, Clerks: The Animated Series, 2000, Life's Too Short, 2000, The Lone Gunmen, 2001, Primetime Glick, 2002; actor: (films) 1941, 1979, Used Cars, 1980, Young Doctors in Love, 1982, This is Spinal Tap, 1984, Clue, 1985, D.A.R.Y.L., 1985, Jumpin Jack Flash, 1986, Light of Day, 1987, Planes, Trains, & Automobiles, 1987, Short Circuit II, 1988, Earth Girls Are Easy, 1989, Flashback, 1989, The Big Picture, 1989, Book of Love, 1991, True Identity, 1991, Memoirs of an Invisible Man, 1992, Man Trouble, 1992, Mojo Flats, 1993, Coneheads, 1993, Airheads, 1994, Radioland Murders, 1994, The Brady Bunch Movie, 1995, The Pompatus of Love, 1996, Jack, 1996, Still Breathing, 1997, That Darn Cat, 1997, Nothing to Lose, 1997, Small Soldiers (voice), 1998, Mystery, Alaska, 1999, Teaching Mrs. Tingle, 1999, True Crime, 1999, Best in Show, 2000, Beautiful, 2000, Little Nicky, 2000, My First Mister, 2001, Never Again, 2001, Dr. Doolittle 2, 2001, Teddy Bear's Picnic, 2001, The Guru, 2002, Auto Focus, 2002, 100 Mile Rule, 2002, A Mighty Wind, 2003, Haunted Lighthouse, 2003, Candor City Hospital, 2003; (Broadway) Accomplice, 1989, Hairspray, 2004; (off-broadway) A Second Hand Memory, 2004; (TV movies) More Than Friends, 1978, Classified Love, 1986, Murder in High Places, 1991; (video) Casper: A Spirited Begining, 1997, The Pajama Game, 2006, Love Song, 2006; rec. artist: (with David Lander) Lenny and the Squiggtones, This is Spinal Tap; songwriter (with co-writers Christopher Guest and Eugene Levy), A Mighty Wind (Grammy award for Best Song Written For A Motion Picture, Television Or Other Visual Media 2004). Office: care William Morris Agy 151 S El Camino Dr Beverly Hills CA 90212-2704

MCKEE, CATHERINE LYNCH, lawyer, educator; b. Boston, June 7, 1962; d. Robert Emmett and Anne Gayle (Tanner) Lynch; m. Bert K. McKee Jr., Dec. 25, 1990; children: Timothy Kingston, Shannon Lancaster. BA in Biol. Sci., U. Calif. Berkeley, 1984; JD, U. San Diego, 1988. Bar: Calif. 1988, U.S. Dist. Ct. (cen., so. and ea. dists.) Calif. 1989, U.S. Ct. Appeals (9th cir.) 1989. Assoc. Parkinson, Wolf, Lazar & Leo, LA, 1988—89, McCormick & Mitchell, San Diego, 1989—91; prof. Mt. San Antonio Coll., Walnut, 1994—, mock trial coach, 1994—2000, dir. paralegal program, 1999—2003, 2004—05, 2007. Cert. rev. hearing officer, Orange County, 1994-2004; legal counsel Imperial Valley Lumber Co., Valley Lumber and Truss Co., 1998—; coach nat. champion C.C. mock trial team, 2000; mem. acad. senate exec. coun. Mt. San Antonio Coll., 1996-2000, chmn. campus equivalency com., 1999, chair paralegal program adv. com., 1999-2003, 04-05, 07, verifier for cert. of online tchg., 2005—, adv. student club Paralegal Soc., 2006; mem. East San Gabriel Valley regional occupl. program adv. com., 2003—, Faculty Assn. Rep. Five Coun., 2009-. Contbr. weekly newspaper column, 1993-99; prodr., star videos An Attorney's Guide to Legal Research on the Internet, 1998, 99; co-author: Jeff and Catherine's World's Best List of Legal (and Law-related) Internet Sites. Chair scholarship com. U. Calif. Alumni Assn., Berkeley, 1995—; capt. auction team SCATS Gymnastics, 2000—02; sec. bd. dir. AC Alliance Youth Soccer Club, Calif. Polytech. U., Pomona, 2007—08. Named Cmty. Person of Yr.,

Diamond Bar C. of C., 1995. Mem. NEA, State Bar Calif. (probation monitor 1993—), Ea. Bar Assn. L.A. (trustee 2000—, sec., 2007), Calif. Tchrs. Assn., Am. Inns of Ct., Calif. Assn. Lanterman-Petris-Short Hearing Officers. Avocations: weightlifting, photography, reading. Office: Mount San Antonio Coll 1100 N Grand Ave Walnut CA 91789-1341 Office Phone: 909-594-5611 ext. 4907. Business E-Mail: cmckee@mtsac.edu.

MCKEE, CHRISTOPHER FULTON, physicist, astronomer, educator; b. Washington, Sept. 6, 1942; m. Suzanne P. McKee; 3 children. AB in Physics summa cum laude, Harvard U., 1963; PhD in Physics, U. Calif., Berkeley, 1970. Physicist Lawrence Livermore (Calif.) Labs., 1969-70, cons., 1970—; rsch. fellow in astrophysics Calif. Inst. Tech., Pasadena, 1970-71; asst. prof. astronomy Harvard U., Cambridge, Mass., 1971-74; asst. prof. physics and astronomy U. Calif., Berkeley, 1974-77, assoc. prof., 1977-78, prof., 1978—, Miller Rsch. prof., 1984-85, 99, 2001, chair dept. physics, 2000—04; assoc. dir. Space Scis. Lab., Berkeley, 1978-83, acting dir., 1983-84, dir., 1985-98, Theoretical Astrophysics Ctr., Berkeley, 1985. Co-chair Astronomy and Astrophysics Survey com. NRC, 1998-2001. Fannie and John Hertz Found. fellow, 1963-69, Guggenheim fellow, 1998; Sherman Fairchild Disting. scholar, 1981, NAS, 1992. Fellow AAAS, Am. Phys. Soc. (exec. com. astrophysics divsn. 1986-88); mem. Am. Astron. Soc. (councillor 1981-84), Am. Acad. Arts and Scis., Internat. Astron. Union, Phi Beta Kappa. Office: U Calif Dept Physics Berkeley CA 94720-0001

MCKEE, KATHRYN DIAN GRANT, human resources consultant; b. LA, Sept. 12, 1937; d. Clifford William and Amelia Rosalie (Shacher) G.; m. Paul Eugene McKee, June 17, 1961; children: Scott Alexander, Grant Christopher. BA, U. Calif., Santa Barbara, 1959; grad. Anderson Sch. Mgmt. Exec. Program, UCLA, 1979. Cert. compensation and benefits. Mgr. Mattel, Inc., Hawthorne, Calif., 1963-74; dir. Twentieth Century Fox Film Corp., LA, 1975-80; sr. v.p. 1st Interstate Bank, Ltd., LA, 1980-93; sr. v.p. and human resources dir. Am.'s Std. Chartered Bank, 1993-95; pres. Human Resources Consortia, Santa Barbara, Calif., 1995—. V.p. cons. Right Mgmt. Cons., 1997-98; dir. Accordia benefits of Southern Calif., 1991-96, mem. exec. com. H.R. div. of Am. Bankers Assn., 1991-93; bd. dirs. Bank Certification Inst. Am. Bankers Assn., 1992-94; treas. Pers. Accreditation Inst., 1983-86, pres., 1986. Co-author: Leading People Through Disaster, 2006; contbr. articles to profl. jours. Pres. GEM Theatre Guild, Garden Grove, Calif., 1984-86; bd. dirs. Vis. Nurses Assn., L.A., 1984-88, SHRM, 1986-92, treas., 1989, vice-chmn., 1990, chmn., 1991, pres. SHRM Found., 1994, 95; bd. dirs. Laguna Playhouse, 1996-2000, pres., 1998-99; dir. Old Spanish Days, 2001-, Ensemble Theatre Co., 2002-; mem. U. Calif. Santa Barbara Found., 2001-, vice chmn. stewardship, 2001-. Recipient Sr. Honor Key award U. Calif., Santa Barbara, 1959, William Winter award Am. Compensation Assn., 1986, Excellence award L.A. Pers. Indsl. Rels. Assn., 1990, Profl. Excellence award SHRM, 1994; named Outstanding Sr. Woman, 1959. Mem. Internat. Assn. Pers. Women (various offices, past nat. pres., Mem. of Yr. 1986), U. Calif. Santa Barbara Alumni Assn. (bd. dirs. 1995-2001, pres.-elect 1999, pres. 1999-2000). Office: Human Resources Consortia 3730 Cedar Vis Santa Barbara CA 93110-1578 E-mail: kmckee3730@cox.net.

MCKEE, ROGER CURTIS, retired federal judge; b. Waterloo, Iowa, Feb. 11, 1931; s. James A. and Leonace (Burrell) McK.; m. Roberta Jeanne Orvis, Sept. 3, 1954; children: Andrea Jane, Brian Curtis, Paul Robert. BA, State Coll. of Iowa, 1955; MA, U. Ill., 1960; JD, U. San Diego, 1968. Bar: US Dist. Ct. (so. dist.) Calif. 1969, Calif. 1970, US Ct. Appeals (9th cir.) 1971. Telegrapher, agt. Ill. Cen. R.R., 1950-55; tng. asst. No. Ill. Gas Co., Aurora, 1959-60; with indsl. rels. dept. Convair div. Gen. Dynamics Corp., San Diego, 1960-68; contract adminstr. and supr. Datagraphix div. Gen. Dynamics Corp., San Diego, 1968-69, asst. counsel, 1969-70; ptnr. Powell & McKee, San Diego, 1970-75, Millsberg, Dickstein & McKee, San Diego, 1975-83; magistrate judge U.S. Dist. Ct. for So. Dist. Calif., San Diego, 1983-97; presiding magistrate judge, 1993-97. Bd. trustees So. Calif. Presbyn. Homes, LA, 1979-81; moderator Presbytery of San Diego, 1980. Capt. USNR, 1949-85. Mem. Calif. Bar Assn., Fed. Magistrate Judges Assn., Navy League US, Naval Res. Officers Assn., Res. Officers Assn., Dixieland Jazz Soc. (bd. dirs. San Diego chpt. 1984—). Republican. Home Fax: 858-277-0444. Personal E-mail: rcmckee10@aol.com.

MCKELL, CYRUS M., retired dean, range plant physiologist, consultant; b. Payson, Utah, Mar. 19, 1926; s. Robert D. and Mary C. (Ellsworth) McK.; m. Betty Johnson; children: Meredith Sue, Brian Marcus, John Cyrus. BS, U. Utah, 1949, MS, 1950; PhD, Oreg. State U., 1956; postgrad., U. Calif., Davis, 1957. Instr. botany Oreg. State U., Corvallis, 1955-56; range rsch. plant physiologist U. Calif. USDA-Agrl. Research Service, Davis, 1956—61; prof., dept. chmn. U. Calif., Riverside, 1961—69; prof. dept. head., dir. Utah State U., Logan, 1969-80; v.p. research NPI, Salt Lake City, 1980-88; dean Coll. of Sci. Weber State U., Ogden, Utah, 1988-94; pres., prin. Applied Ecol. Svcs. Inc., Logan, Utah, 1995—2008. Cons. Ford Found. 1968-72, Rockefeller Found., 1964-70, 89, UN, 1978, 90, NAS, 1980, 89, 91-93, USAID, 1972, UN Devel. Program, 1989; mem. faculty of sci. adv. bd. UAE Nat. U., 2000-02. Editor: Grass Biology and Utilization, 1971, Useful Wildland Shrubs, 1972, Rehabilitation of Western Wildlife Habitat, 1978, Paradoxes of Western Energy Development, 1984, Resource Inventory and Baseline Study Methods for Developing Countries, 1983, Shrub Biology and Utilization, 1989, Wilderness Issues, Arid Lands of the Western United States, 1992; contbr. over 230 articles to profl. jours. Chmn. Cache County Planning Commn., Logan, 1974-79; mem. Utah Energy Conservation and Devel. Coun., 1976-79, Gov.'s Sci. Adv. Coun., 1988-97, chmn., 1990-91, 96-97; mem. Commn. of the Californias, Riverside, 1965-68; mem. Holladay City Planning Commn., 2003-2009. Recipient Utah Gov.'s Sci. and Tech. medal, 1990, Gardner Prize in Sci., awarded by Utah Acad. Scis., Arts and Letters, 1999; Fulbright scholar Spain, 1967-68; World Travel grantee Rockefeller Found., 1964. Fellow: AAAS (com. chmn. 1979—89, sci. exchange to China grantee 1984—85, 1989, sci. panel U.S.-Chile 1987); mem.: Am. Soc. Agronomy, Soc. Range Mgmt. (pres. Calif. sect. 1965, pres. Utah sect. 1982). Mem. Lds Ch. Avocations: travel, photography, history. Home: 2248 E 4000 S Holladay UT 84124-1864 Home Phone: 801-278-6469.

MCKENNA, ROB, state attorney general, former councilman; b. Ft. Sam Houston, Tex., Oct. 1, 1962; m. Marilyn McKenna; children: Madeleine, Katie, Robert, Connor. BA in Econs. and Internat. Studies, 1985; JD, U. Chgo., 1988. Bar: Wash., 9th Cir. US Ct. Appeals, US Supreme Ct. Atty. Perkins Cole, Bellevue, Wash., 1988—95; councilman King County, Wash., 1996—2004; atty. gen. State of Wash., 2005—. Co-founder, bd. mem. Eastside Human Svcs. Forum; bd. mem. Econ. Devel. Coun. of Seattle & King County; mem. Sound Transit Bd., 1996—2001; chair Eastside Transp. Partnership, 1999—2001, Wash. State Transp. Improvement Bd., 2001—03. Mem. King County Open Space Citizens Oversight Com., 1990—94; founder, bd. dirs. Advance Bellevue, 1991—2001; past pres., bd. mem. Bellevue Schs. Found., 1993—2002; mem. Bellevue Rotary, 1993—; bd. mem. King County Open Space Citizens Oversight Com., 1995—98; co-chair City of Hope Walk for Hope to Cure Breast Cancer, 1998, 1999; co-founder, bd. mem. Evergreen Forest Trust, 2000—; bd. mem. Bellevue CC Found., 2000—; mem. steering com. Citizens for Renton Schs., 2002—03; mem. exec. bd. Chief Seattle Coun. Boy Scouts Am., 2003—; mem. St. Louise Cath. Parish, 1977—; Eagle Scout. Recipient Doug Mason Meml. award, Mcpl. League King County, 1991, 40 under 40 award, Puget Sound Bus. Jour., 2000, Advance Bellevue 10th Anniversary Legacy award, 2003; named Elected Ofcl. of Yr., Nat. Assn. Indsl. and Office Properties, 1999; named one of The 25 Smartest People in Wash., Wash. Law & Politics, 2003. Mem.: King County Bar Assn., Wash. State Bar Assn. Republican. Office: Office Atty Gen 1125 Washington St SE PO Box 40100 Olympia WA 98504-0100 Office Phone: 360-753-6200. Business E-Mail: rob.mckenna@atg.wa.gov.*

MCKENNON, KEITH ROBERT, chemical company executive; b. Condon, Oreg., Dec. 25, 1933; s. Russel M. and Lois E. (Edgerton) McK.; m. Patricia Dragon, Sept. 30, 1961; children: Brian, Marc, Kevin. BS, Oreg. State U., 1955. Rsch. chemist Dow Chem. Co., Pittsburg, Calif., 1955—67, sales mgr. Houston, 1967, from research mgr. to exec. v.p. Midland, Mich., 1968—87, bd. dirs., 1983—92, 2003—06, exec. v.p., 1987-92; pres. Dow USA, 1987-90; chmn., chief exec. officer Dow Corning Corp., 1992-94, also bd. dirs.; chmn. PacifiCorp, Portland, Oreg., 1994-99, CEO, 1998-99. Patentee. Recipient Chemical Industry medal Soc. of Chemical Industry, 1994 Republican. Presbyterian. E-mail: kmck96@aol.com.

MCKENZIE, BRIAN BRUCE, finance educator; b. Kelowna, BC, Canada, Nov. 23, 1948; arrived in U.S., 2003; s. Rex Bruce and Dorothy McKenzie; m. Molly Kathleen Farrend, Mar. 21, 1970. BA, U. BC, Vancouver, Can., 1974; MBA, U. Victoria, Can., 1997, PhD, 2003. Cert. qualification - boatbuilding Province of BC, 1990. Pres. Brian McKenzie Boatbuilding, Inc, Victoria, Canada, 1982—97; lectr. U. Victoria, 1997—2002; asst. prof. U. Calif., East Bay, 2003—. Vis. instr. Worcester (Mass.) Poly. Inst., 1999—2000. Contbr. scientific papers, rsch. to profl. jours. Recipient Entrepreneurship Theory and Practice Best Conceptual Paper award, 2004. Fellow: Students Free Enterprise (Sam Walton fellow 2005—06); mem.: Can. Anthrop. Assn., Small Bus. Inst., N.Am. Case Rsch. Assn., Acad. Mgmt. (chair nontraditional academics com.entrepreneurship divsn., Innovations in Pedagogy award 1999), U.S. Assn. Small Bus. and Entrepreneurship (Model Undergraduate Program award 2000), Oral History Assn. Office: Calif State U 25800 Carlos Bee Blvd Hayward CA 94542 Personal E-mail: brian@brian-mckenzie.com. Business E-Mail: brian.mckenzie@csueastbay.edu.

MCKENZIE, CURTIS DAVID, lawyer; b. Corvallis, Oreg., Feb. 9, 1969; s. Ray and Symone McK.; m. Renee S., Aug. 7, 1993; 1 child, Jackson. BA, Northwest Nazarene Coll., 1992; JD, Georgetown U., 1995. Bar: Md. 1995, D.C. 1996, U.S. Dist. Ct. Md. 1996, Idaho 1997. Assoc. Arter & Hadden, Washington, 1995-97; deputy prosecutor Ada County Prosecutor, Boise, 1997-98; assoc. Stoel Rives, Boise, 1998—. Mem. Order of Coif. Republican.

MCKEON, HOWARD PHILLIP (BUCK MCKEON), United States Representative from California; b. Tujunga, Calif., Sept. 9, 1938; m. Patricia Kunz; 6 children. BS, Brigham Young U., 1985. Mem. Santa Clarita City Council, Calif., 1987—92; mayor City of Santa Clarita, 1987—88; mem. US Congress from 25th Calif. Dist., 1992—, mem. armed services com. Co-owner Howard & Phil's Western Wear, Inc., 1963—; founding dir., chmn. Valencia Nat. Bank, 1987—92; mem. Calif. Rep. State Ctrl. Com., 1988—92. Hon. chmn. Leukemia Soc., 1990, Red Cross Cmty. Support Campaign, 1992; sch. bd. mem., bd. trustees William S. Hart Union HS Dist., 1978—87; active dist. com. Boy Scouts of America, Little League; bd. dirs. Henry Mayo Newhall Meml. Hosp., 1983—88, Santa Clarita Valley Sml. Bus. Devel. Ctr., 1990—92. Recipient Silver Spur award for Outstanding Cmty. Svc., Coll. of Canyons Found., 2000, Robert J. Collier award, Nat. Aeronautic Assn., 2001, Advocacy of Ind. Higher Edn. award, Nat. Assn. Ind. Colls. & Univs., 2002; named Newsmaker of Yr., Santa Clarita Press Club, 1996. Mem.: Nat. Guard & Reserve Components Orgn., Canyon Country C. of C. (bd. dirs. 1988—92). Republican. Mem. Lds Ch. Office: US House Reps 2184 Rayburn House Office Bldg Washington DC 20515-0525 E-mail: tellbuck@mail.house.gov.*

MCKEON, JAMI WINTZ, lawyer; b. Mar. 13, 1957; BA, Pa. State U., 1978; JD, Villanova U., 1981. Bar: Pa. 1981, U.S. Supreme Ct. 1984. Ptnr. Morgan, Lewis & Bockius LLP, San Francisco, chmn. firm bus. & corp. litig. practice, firm adv. com. Frequent instr. Nat. Inst. Trial Advocacy. Office: Morgan Lewis & Bockius LLP One Market Spear St Tower San Francisco CA 94105 Office Phone: 415-442-1001. Office Fax: 415-442-1405. Business E-Mail: jmckeon@morganlewis.com.

MCKEOWN, ASHLEY, biological anthropologist, educator; PhD, U. Tenn., Knoxville, 2000. Biol. anthropologist, faculty mem. U. Mont., Missoula, Mont. Office: Dept Anthropology U Mont 32 Campus Dr Missoula MT 59812 Office Phone: 406-243-2145. Business E-Mail: ashley.mckeown@umontana.edu.

MCKEOWN, MARY MARGARET, federal judge; b. Casper, Wyo., May 11, 1951; d. Robert Mark and Evelyn Margaret (Lipsack) McKeown; m. Peter Francis Cowhey, June 29, 1985; 1 child, Megan Margaret. BA in Internat. Affairs and Spanish, U. Wyo., 1972; JD, Georgetown U., 1975. Bar: Wash. 1975, DC 1982. Assoc. Perkins Coie, Seattle, 1975—79, Washington, 1979—80; spl. asst. US Dept. Interior, Washington, 1980—81, The White House, Washington, 1980—81; ptnr., mem. exec. com. Perkins Coie, Seattle, 1981—98, mng. dir. strategic planning and client rels., 1990—95; judge US Ct. Appeals (9th cir.), San Diego, 1998—. Trustee The Pub. Defender, Seattle, 1982—85; rep. 9th Cir. Judicial Conf., San Francisco, 1985—89; mem. gender bias task force, 1992—93; jud. conf. Com. on Codes of Conduct, 2001—; exec. com. 9th Cir., 2001—; lect. U. Wash. Law Sch., 2000—01; adj. prof. U. San Diego, 2003—; bd. dirs. RAND Inst. for Civil Justice, 2003—. Author: Girl Scout's Guide to New York, 1990; contbr. chpt. to book and articles to profl. jours. Nat. bd. dirs. Girl Scouts US, NYC, 1976—87; mem. exec. com. Corp. Coun. for the Arts, Seattle, 1988—98; bd. gen. counsel Downtown Seattle Assn., 1986—89; mem. exec. com. Wash. Coun. Internat. Trade, 1994—; bd. dirs. YMCA Greater Seattle, 1998—, Family Svcs., Seattle, 1982—84. Recipient Rising Stars of the 80's award, Legal Times Washington, 1983; named one of 100 Young Women of Promise, Good Housekeeping, 1985, Washington's Winningest Trial Lawyers, Washington Jour., 1992, Top 50 Women Lawyers, Nat. Law Jour., 1998; fellow Japan leadership, 1992—93. Fellow: ABA (ho. of dels. 1990—, Jud. Adv. Com. to Standing Com. on Ethics 2000—, chair 2002—, Joint Commn. to Evaluate Code of Jud. Conduct 2003—); mem.: Louis M. Welsh Chpt. Am. Inns of Ct., Am. Judicature Soc. (bd. dirs. 2001—), Assn. Bus. Trial Lawyers (bd. dirs. 2003—), Am. Intellectual Property Law Assoc., Am. Law Institute, Nat. Assn. Iolta Programs (bd. dirs. 1989—91), Wash. Women Lawyers (bd. dirs., pres. 1978—79), Legal Found. Wash. (trustee, pres. 1989—90), Seattle-King County Bar Assn. (trustee, sec. 1984—85, Outstanding Lawyer award 1992), Wash. Bar Assn. (chmn. jud. recommendations 1989—90), Fed. Bar Assn. (trustee western dist. Wash. 1980—90), White House Fellows Found. (bd. dirs. 1998—, pres. 2000—01). Avocations: travel, classical piano, hiking, gourmet cooking, tennis. Office: US Ct Appeals 401 West A St Ste 2000 San Diego CA 92101-7908 E-mail: Judge_McKeown@ca9.uscourts.gov.

MCKIBBEN, HOWARD D., federal judge; b. Apr. 1, 1940; s. James D. and Bernice McKibben; m. Mary Ann McKibben, July 2, 1966; children: Mark, Susan. BS, Bradley U., 1962; MPA, U. Pitts., 1964; JD, U. Mich., 1967. Assoc. George W. Abbott Law Office, 1967-71; dep. dist. atty. Douglas County, Nev., 1969-71, dist. atty. Nev., 1971-77; dist. ct. judge State of Nev., 1977-84; judge U.S. Dist. Ct. Nev., Reno, 1984—. Mem. Nev. Bar Assn., Am. Inns of Ct. (pres. Nev. chpt. 1986-88). Methodist. Avocations: tennis, golf, racquetball. Home: PO Box 588 Verdi NV 89439-0588 Office: US Dist Ct 400 S Virginia St Ste 804 Reno NV 89501-2197

MCKIBBEN, RYAN TIMOTHY, newspaper executive; b. Watertown, SD, June 25, 1958; s. Bernard Dean and Patricia Martha (Loehr) McK.; m. Mary Elizabeth O'Donnell, Oct. 3, 1981; children: Sean Robert, Michael Patrick. Grad. high sch., Janesville, Wis. Classified advt. exec. Green Bay (Wis.) Press Gazette, 1977-79; display advt. exec. Racine (Wis.) Jour. Times, 1979-80; advt. dir. Oshkosh (Wis.) Northwestern, 1980-82, dir. sales/mktg., 1982-84; advt. dir. Reno Gazette-Jour., 1984-85, Madison (Wis.) Newspapers Inc., 1985-88; v.p., advt. dir., sr. v.p. advt. and mktg. Denver Post, 1988-90, exec. v.p., gen. mgr., 1990-93, pub., 1993-98; pres. Western Color Print, Denver, 1998—. Bd. dirs. Newspapers First, N.Y.C. Mem. mktg. com. Metro Area Boys Clubs, Denver, 1988—; bd. dirs. Nat. Jewish Ctr. for Immunology and Respiratory Medicine, Denver, Denver Metro Conv. Bur., Denver Ctr. for Performing Arts, Colo. Symphony, Colo. Forum, Colo. Concer, Castle Pines Golf Club. Mem. Am. Press Inst., Newspaper Advt. Coop. Network (bd. dirs. 1989—), Internat. Newspaper Advt./Mktg. Execs., (com. mem. 1989—), Denver Advt. Fedn., Boys and Girls Club, Columbine Country Club. Republican. Roman Catholic. Home: 8 Augusta Dr Littleton CO 80123-6688 Office: Western Color Print 16580 Wedge Pkwy Ste 300 Reno NV 89511-3258

MCKIM, ROBERT, state legislator; b. Laramie, Wyo., Jan. 18, 1946; m. Lyniece McKim; 4 children. BS, BYU, 1971. Mem. Dist. 21 Wyo. House of Reps., 2009—. Republican. Mem. Lds Ch. Office: 213 State Capitol Bldg Cheyenne WY 82002 also: 10964 Hwy 238 Afton WY 83110-9746 Home Phone: 307-248-2564; Office Phone: 307-777-7881. Office Fax: 307-777-5466. Business E-Mail: rmckim@wyoming.com.

MCKINLEY, WES, state legislator; m. Jan McKinley; 4 children. HS math and science tchr.; rancher; mem. Dist. 64 Colo. House of Reps., Denver, 2004—. Democrat. Office: Colo State Capitol 200 E Colfax Denver CO 80203 Office Phone: 303-866-2398. Business E-Mail: wes.mckinley.house@state.co.us.*

MCKINNEY, JUDSON THAD, broadcast executive; b. Sacramento, Aug. 21, 1941; s. Judson Bartlet and Mildred Eoline (Taylor) McK. Student, Sacramento State U., 1959-61, Western Bapt. Bible Coll., 1961-62, Am. River Coll., 1962-63. Prodn. dir. Sta. KEBR, Sacramento, 1962-65; prodn. dir. Sta. KEAR, Merced, Calif., 1965-68; sta. mgr. Sta. KAMB, 1968-75, Sta. KEAR, San Francisco, 1975-78, 79-88, WFME, Newark, 1978; western regional mgr. Family Stas. Inc., 1988—. Pres. Abounding Love Ministries, 2000-04; instr-.for study of electronic Christian media Grad. Theol. Union. V.p. New Millennium Strings, 2003—04, pres., 2005—; sec., treas. Trinity Lyric Opera, 2005—08; chmn. 1st. Bapt. Ch. San Francisco, 1985—91; recording engr. 1st Bapt. Ch. Los Altos, Calif., 2000—08. Mem. Gideons. Republican. Baptist. Office: Family Stations Inc 290 Hegenberger Rd Oakland CA 94621-1436 Business E-Mail: thad@familyradio.org.

MCKINNEY, SALLY VITKUS, state official; b. Muncie, Ind., Aug. 6, 1944; d. Robert Brookins and Mary (Mann) Gooden; m. Alan George Vitkus (div. Jan. 1979); m. James Larry McKinney, Feb. 1, 1986. AA, William Woods U., 1964; BS, U. Ariz., 1966; postgrad., U. Nev., Las Vegas, 1966-68. Tchr. Las Vegas Day Sch., 1972—76; salesperson Globe Realty, Las Vegas, 1976—79; owner, pres. Realty West, Las Vegas, 1979—96; chief investigator State of Nev. Real Estate Divsn., 1996—2000; prin., owner McKinney Realty, Las Vegas, 2000—; corp. broker, v.p., dir. bus. and devel. Real Estate Temps, Las Vegas. Rec. sec. Clark County Rep. Cen. Com., Las Vegas, 1982, 1st vice chmn., 1985; vice-chmn. Nev. Rep. com., 1986, chmn., 1987-88; active Assistance League Las Vegas; state chmn. Nev. Rep. Party. Mem. Nat. Assn. Realtors, Nat. Assn. Home Builders, Las Vegas Bd. Realtors, Greater Las Vegas C. of C., Gen. Fedn. Womens Clubs (nominee Outstanding Young Woman Am. 1979, exec. bd. 1980-82), Jr. League Las Vegas (sustaining), Mesquite Club (chmn. pub. affairs com. 1986-87, past pres., secret witness exec. bd. 1994-96, vice chmn.). Presbyterian. Avocations: bridge, fly fishing. Home: 511 Mountain Dell Ave Henderson NV 89012-2509

MCKINNEY, VIRGINIA ELAINE ZUCCARO, educational administrator; b. San Francisco, Nov. 18, 1924; d. Salvadore John and Elaine Agnes (Shepard) Zuccaro; BA, Calif. State U., LA, 1968; MA, Calif. State U., Northridge, 1969; PhD, Claremont Grad. Sch., 1983; children: Joe, Walter Clifton. Official ct. reporter LA County Superior Cts., 1948-59; tchr. speech-reading, adult edn. LA Bd. Edn., 1966-71; lang., reading specialist Marlton Sch. for the Deaf, LA, 1971-79; founder, pres., dir. communication skills program Ctr. for Communicative Devel., Inc., LA, 1969-; part-time lectr. spl. edn. Calif. State U., LA, 1971-1978; cons. for various univs. and programs for the hearing-impaired; mem. State Ind. Living Coun., 1993-2000, adv.

com. for deaf Calif. Dept. Rehab., 1979—1984, Atty.'s Gen. Commn. on Disability, 1987-1990. Recipient Leadership award Nat. Leadership Tng. Program in Area of Deaf, Calif. State U., Northridge, 1974; NEA Project Life grantee, 1970, Gallaudet Coll. Ctr. for Continuing Edn. grantee, 1974. Mem. Calif. Educators for Deaf and Hard of Hearing, Calif. Assn. For Postsecondary Edn. and Disability, Beverly-Hollywood (Calif.) Hearing Soc. (pres. 1967-68). Republican. Presbyterian. Author: The Picture Plus Dictionary, 1997, (CD) Picture Plus Vocabulary, 2000, developer, producer audio-visual media, including 22 films and 4 books, to aid in speechreading and auditory tng., 1963-68; participant research project with Project Life on devel. of communication skills for multiply-handicapped deaf adults, 1970; developer, pub. Toe-Hold Literacy Packet, 1973, Linguistics 36, interactive computer lang. devel. program, 1986. Office: 3460 Wilshire Blvd Ste 200 Los Angeles CA 90010 Office Phone: 213-738-8176. Personal E-mail: ccdcom40@yahoo.com.

MC KINNON, CLINTON DAN, aerospace transportation executive; b. San Bernardino, Calif., Jan. 27, 1934; s. Clinton Dotson and Lucille V. McK.; m. Janice Bernard; children: Holly Jean, Sherri Lynn, Clinton Scott, Lisa Caroline BA, U. Mo., 1956; doctorate (hon.), Nat. U., 1987. Page U.S. Ho. of Reps., 1950-52; reporter, photographer, advt. salesman Sentinel Newspaper, San Diego, 1960-62; owner, pres. KSON Radio, San Diego, 1962-85, KSON-FM, San Diego, 1964-85; pub. La Jolla (Calif.) Light Jour., 1969-73; owner House of Hits (book and music pub.), San Diego, 1972—; co-owner KIII-TV, Corpus Christi, Tex., 1964—, KBMT-TV, Beaumont, Tex., 1976—, KUSI-TV, San Diego, 1992—; chmn. CAB, Washington, 1981-84; with spl. projects CIA, 1985-86; founder, chmn., pres. North Am. Airlines, Jamaica, NY, 1989—2005. Author: Bullseye--One Reactor (aka Bullseye Iraq), 1986, The Ten Second Message, 1994, Words of Honor, 1995, Rescue Pilot, 2002, Safe Air Travel Companion, 2002. Chmn. exec. com. Greater San Diego Billy Graham Crusade, 1976, commr., Nat. Guard and Reserves Commn., 2005-08. Served as aviator USNR, 1956—60. Recipient Advt. Man of Year award San Diego Advt. and Sales Club, 1971; Radio Sta. Mgr. of Year award Billboard Mag., 1973; Internat. Pres.'s award Youth for Christ, 1975; Man of Distinction award Mexican-Am. Found., 1976; George Washington Honor medal Freedoms Found., 1976; Headliner of Yr. (govt.), San Diego Press Club, 1985; named to Country Radio Hall of Fame, 2003. Mem. Country Music Assn. (pres. 1977, Pres. award 1980), C. of C. (dir.), Nat. Assn. Broadcasters (bd. dirs. 1970-74), Calif. Broadcasters Assn. (dir.), Navy League (Media Man of Yr. 1980), Wings Club (bd. govs. 1995-2003, pres. 2002-2003), San Diego Rotary, Nat. Guard and Reserves (commr., 2005-08). Achievements include setting Navy helicopter peacetime rescue record of 62 air/sea rescues, 1958; 1st person to close down fed. govt. regulatory agy., CAB, 1984. Office: 1125-101 Pacific Beach Dr San Diego CA 92109

MCKINNON, F(RANCIS) A(RTHUR) RICHARD, utilities executive; b. Delburne, Alta., Can., Mar. 5, 1933; s. John Donald and Ruth Rebecca (Sundberg) McK.; m. Elma Lorraine Lebsack, June 1, 1957; children: Kenneth Richard, Stephen David, Karen Diane. B. Commerce, U. Alta., 1954; postgrad., Stanford Exec. Program, Stanford U., 1982. With Alta. Gas Trunk Line Co. Ltd., Calgary, 1960-75, treas., 1971-75; dir. fin. TransAlta Utilities Corp. (formerly Calgary Power Ltd.), 1975—, treas., 1976-81, v.p. fin., 1981—, Trans Alta Energy Corp., Trans Alta Corp.; pres. ELM FARMS CONS., INC., Calgary, 1996—. Bd. dirs. AEC Power Ltd. Past bd. dirs. Foothills Gen. Hosp., Calgary. Fellow Inst. Chartered Accts. of Alta.; mem. Can. Inst. Chartered Accts., Fin. Execs. Inst. Can. (past chmn., past pres., bd. dirs. Calgary chpt., v.p.), Fin. Execs. Inst. (bd. dirs.). Clubs: Calgary Petroleum, Canyon Meadows Golf and Country. Office: ELM FARM CONS INC 1412 Windsor St NW Calgary AB Canada T2N 3X3

MCKIRAHAN, RICHARD DUNCAN, classics and philosophy educator; b. Berkeley, Calif., July 27, 1945; s. Richard Duncan and Helen Marion (Hixson) McK.; m. Voula Tsouna, June 3, 1961; 1 child, Helen Hamilton. AB, U. Calif., Berkeley, 1966; BA, U. Oxford, Eng., 1969; MA, Oxford U., Eng., 1979; PhD, Harvard U., 1973. Teaching fellow, tutor Harvard U., Cambridge, Mass., 1971-73; asst. prof. classics and philosophy Pomona Coll., Claremont, Calif., 1973-79, assoc. prof., 1979-87, E.C. Norton prof. classics and philosophy, 1987—, chair dept. classics, 1992—. Author: Socrates and Plato, A Comprehensive Bibliography, 1958-1973, 1978, Plato's Meno, 1986, Principles and Proofs: Aristotle's Theory of Demonstrative Science, 1992, Philosophy Before Socrates, 1994, A Presocratics Reader, 1996, Cicero, De Natura Deorum I, 1997, Simplicius, On Aristotle's Physics, book 8, chpts. 6-10, 2001, Philoponus on Aristotle's Posterior Analytics, Book 1, chpts. 1-8, 2008; contbr. articles on Greek philosophy, math. and scis. Marshall Aid Commemoration Commn. scholar, U. Oxford, 1966-69, Fulbright Sr. scholar, 1999, Overseas Vis. scholar St. John's Coll., Cambridge, 1999; Woodrow Wilson Found. fellow, 1966-67; NEH grantee, 1975, 85, 90, 98, 2004. Mem. Am. Philol. Assn., Soc. Ancient Greek Philosophy, Phi Beta Kappa. Office: Pomona Coll Dept Classics 140 W 6th St Claremont CA 91711-4301 Business E-Mail: rmckirahan@pomona.edu.

MCKNIGHT, FREDERICK L., lawyer; b. Kansas City, Mo., Nov. 28, 1947; s. Harry A. and Donna Ruth (Breining) McK.; m. Linda Jean McKnight, June 20, 1970; children: Justin Teague, Cristin Ruth. AB honors, Princeton U., 1969; JD, U. Calif., Berkeley, 1972. Bar: Calif. 1973, N.Y. 1973. Regional mng. ptnr. Jones Day Reavis & Pogue, LA, 1997; now ptnr.-in-charge LA office Jones Day. Adv. com. Jones, Day, Reavis & Pogue, Cleve. Bd. dirs. Econ. Devel. Corp., L.A., 1992—, St. Vincent Med. Ctr. Found., L.A., 1994—. Fellow Am. Coll. of Trial Lawyers; mem. Assn. Bus. Trial Lawyers. Office: Jones Day 555 S Flower St # 50 Los Angeles CA 90071-2300 Office Phone: 213-243-2777. Office Fax: 213-243-2539. Business E-Mail: fmcknight@jonesday.com.

MCKNIGHT, ROBERT B., JR., sporting goods manufacturing executive; BS, Univ. So. Calif. Co-founder, bd. dir. Quiksilver Inc., Huntington Beach, Calif., 1976—, pres., 1979—91, chmn., CEO, 1991—2008, chmn., pres., CEO, 2008—. Office: Quiksilver Inc 15202 Graham St Huntington Beach CA 92649

MC KOY, BASIL VINCENT CHARLES, theoretical chemist, educator; b. Trinidad, W.I., Mar. 25, 1938; came to U.S., 1960, naturalized, 1973; s. Allan Cecil and Doris Augusta McK.; m. Anne Ellen Shannon, Mar. 18, 1967; 1 son, Christopher Allan. B.Chem. Eng., N.S. Tech. U., 1960; PhD in Chemistry (Univ. fellow), Yale U., 1964. Instr. chemistry Calif. Inst. Tech., 1964-66, asst. prof. chemistry, 1966-69, asso. prof., 1969-75, prof. theoretical chemistry, 1975—, chmn. of faculty, 1985-87. Cons. Lawrence Livermore Lab., U. Calif., Livermore, 1974—, Inst. Def. Analysis, 1984—; vis. prof. Max Planck Inst., Munich, Ger., 1976—, U. Paris, 1968—, U. Campinas, Brazil, 1976—; lectr. Nobel Symposium, Goteborg, Sweden, 1979. Contbr. articles to Jour. Physics, London, chem. Physics Lettters, Phys. Rev., Jour. Chem. Physics; bd. editors; Chem. Physics Jour., 1977-79, mem. adv. editoral bd., 1992—; co-editor: Electron-Molecule and Photon-Molecule Collisions, 1979, 83, Swarm Studies and Inelastic Electron-Molecule Collisions, 1986; co-author: Electron-Molecule Collisions and Photoionization Processes, 1982. Recipient medal Gov.-Gen. Can., 1960; Alfred P. Sloan Found. fellow, 1969-73; Guggenheim fellow, 1973-74 Fellow Am. Phys. Soc. Home: 3855 Keswick Rd La Canada Flintridge CA 91011-3945 Office: Calif Inst Tech Divsn Chemistry Pasadena CA 91125-0001 Office Phone: 626-395-6545. Business E-Mail: mckoy@caltech.edu.

MCKUSICK, MARSHALL KIRK, computer scientist; b. Wilmington, Del., Jan. 19, 1954; s. Blaine Chase and Marjorie Jane (Kirk) McK.; domestic ptnr. Eric P. Allman. BSEE with distinction, Cornell U., 1976; MS in Bus. Adminstrn., U. Calif., Berkeley, 1979, MS in Computer Sci., 1980, PhD in Computer Sci., 1984. System designer Hughes Aircraft Co., 1977-79; software cons., 1982—; rsch. computer scientist U. Calif., Berkeley, 1984-93. Author: The Design and Implementation of the FreeBSD Operating System, 2004; contbr. articles to profl. publs. Mem. IEEE, Usenix Assn. (pres. 1990-92, 2000-04, bd. dirs. 1986-92, 2000-06, Lifetime Achievement award 1992), Assn. Computing Machinery. Democrat. Avocations: swimming, scuba diving, wine collecting. Office: 1614 Oxford St Berkeley CA 94709-1608 Office Phone: 510-843-9542. E-mail: mkm@mckusick.com.

MCLACHLAN, SARAH, musician, composer; b. Halifax, Nova Scotia, Jan. 28, 1968; m. Ashwin Sood, Feb. 7, 1997 (separated 2008); children: India Ann Sushil, Taja Summer. Founder, performer Lilith Fair. Singer: (albums) Touch, 1989, Solace, 1991, Live EP, 1992, Fumbling Towards Ecstasy, 1994, Freedom Sessions, 1995, Rarities, B-Sides, and Other Stuff, 1996, Surfacing, 1997, Mirrorball, 1999, Sarah McLachlan Remixed, 2001, Afterglow, 2003, Wintersong, 2006, Mirrorball: The Complete Concert, 2006, Live from Etown: 2006 Christmas Special, 2007, Closer: The Best of Sarah McLachlan, 2008 Recipient Order of Canada, Best Female Pop Vocal Performance award Grammy, 1997, 1999, Best Pop Instrumental Performance award, 1997; nominated for Grammy for Best Female Pop Vocal Performance for "Fallen," 2003. Achievements include founding Lilith Fair, all-female peformance concert tour, 1997-1999. Office: Nettwerk Mgmt 1650 W 2nd Ave Vancouver BC V6J 4R3 Canada

MCLAIN, CHRISTOPHER M., lawyer; b. San Luis Obispo, Calif., July 21, 1943; s. James Latane and Marjorie Patricia (McNalley) McL.; m. Barbara McFarland, Nov. 23, 1968; children: Beth, Brian, Amy. BS in Bus. Adminstrn., U. Calif.-Berkeley, 1965, JD, 1968. Assoc. Knox, Goforth & Ricksen, Oakland, Calif., 1968-69, Donahue, Gallagher, Thomas & Woods, Oakland, 1969-73, ptnr., 1973-83; sec., counsel Lucky Stores, Inc., Dublin, Calif., 1984-89, v.p., 1985-89; ptnr. Sonnenschein, Nath & Rosenthal, San Francisco, 1989-90; sr. v.p., gen. counsel, sec. Transam. Corp., San Francisco, 1990-94; of counsel Sonnenschein Nath & Rosenthal, San Francisco, 1994-95; sr. v.p., gen. counsel, sec. Crown Vantage Inc., Oakland, Calif., 1995-99; ptnr., sr. v.p., gen. counsel Sequoia Assocs., LLC, Menlo Park, Calif., 1999—2003; pres., CEO, Creativity Inc., Van Nuys, Calif., 2003—. Mem. ABA, State Bar Calif., San Francisco Bar Assn., Am. Soc. Corps. Secs. Avocation: skiing. Office: Creativity Inc 7855 Hayvenhurst Ave Van Nuys CA 91406

MCLANE, FREDERICK BERG, lawyer; b. Long Beach, Calif., July 24, 1941; s. Adrian B. and Arlie K. (Burrell) McL.; m. Lois C. Roberts, Jan. 28, 1967; children: Willard, Anita. BA, Stanford U., 1963; LLB, Yale U., 1966. Bar: Calif. 1967, U.S. Dist. Ct. (cen. dist.) Calif. 1967. Assoc. prof. law U. Miss., Oxford, 1966-68; assoc. O'Melveny & Myers LLP, LA, 1968-74, ptnr., 1975—2005, of counsel, 2005—. Lectr. in field. Pres., bd. dirs. Legal Aid Found., L.A., 1974-83; deacon Congl. Ch., Sherman Oaks, Calif., 1979-83; vice-chair L.A. Music Ctr., Unified Fund, 1992-94; bd. dirs. Calif. Sci. Ctr. Found., 1991-2000. Mem.: ABA (banking com., fed. regulation of securities com.), Calif. Bar Assn. (fin. insts. com., uniform comml. codes), L.A. Country Club, The Quarry at La Quinta, Order of Coif. Avocations: golf, walking, reading. Office: O'Melveny & Myers LLP 1999 Ave of the Stars Los Angeles CA 90067-6035 Office Phone: 310-246-8554. Business E-Mail: fmclane@omm.com.

MCLAUGHLIN, CALVIN STURGIS, biochemistry professor; b. St. Joseph, Mo., May 29, 1936; s. Calvin Sturgis and Agnes Jane McLaughlin; m. Chin Helen Moy, Sept. 7, 1960; children: Heather Chin Chu, Christine Leng Oy, Andrew Calvin Moy. BS, King Coll., 1958; postgrad., Yale U., 1958-59; PhD, MIT, 1964. Postdoctoral fellow Institut de Biologie Physico-Chimique, Paris, 1964-66; prof. biochemistry U. Calif., Irvine, 1966—, dir. Cancer Rsch. Inst., 1981-83; vis. prof. Sch. Botany Oxford U., Eng., 1976, 80. Mem. peer rev. panels Am. Cancer Soc., NSF, NIH, VA Contbr. numerous articles to profl. jours.; mem. editl. bds. Jour. Bacteriology, 1975-80, Exptl. Mycology, 1980-86; reviewer profl. jours. Bd. dirs. Am. Cancer Soc., Orange County, 1980-89; mem. Traffic Affairs Com., Newport Beach, Calif., 1972-78. Named Outstanding Tchr. U. Calif.-Irvine, 1978, Gabriel Lester Meml. Lectr. Reed Coll., 1979; fellow Rockefeller Found., 1958-59, Upjohn Found., 1959-60, Nutrition Found., 1960-61, NIH, 1961-64, Am. Cancer Soc., 1964-66 Mem.: Am. Soc. Biochemistry and Molecular Biology. Episc. Office: U Calif Irvine Dept Biol Chemistry Irvine CA 92697-1700 Office Phone: 949-824-5325. Business E-Mail: cal@uci.edu.

MCLAUGHLIN, GLEN, financial services company executive; b. Shawnee, Okla., Dec. 21, 1934; s. Champe and Mattie Bet (Jenkins) McL.; m. Ellen Marr Schnake, Aug. 29, 1964; children: Helen Elizabeth, Glen Wallace. BBA, U. Okla., 1956; MBA, Harvard U., 1964. Asst. treas. Foremost-McKesson, Inc., San Francisco, 1964-69; exec. v.p., dir. MacFarlane's Candies, Oakland, Calif., 1969-70; dir. fin. and adminstrn. Memorex Corp., London, 1970-71; sr. v.p. fin. Four-Phase Systems, Inc., Cupertino, Calif., 1971-82; pres., chmn. Four-Phase Fin., Inc., Cupertino, 1977-82; chmn. bd. Four-Phase Systems, Ltd., Toronto, Ont., Can., 1977-82, Four-Phase Systems Internat., Inc., 1977-82, DeAnza Ins. Co. Ltd., Cayman Islands, 1979-82; gen. ptnr. Matrix Ptnrs., L.P., San Jose and Boston, 1982-86; chmn. bd. Venture Leasing Assocs., 1986—2003; chmn. bd. dirs. Cupertino Nat. Bank, Calif., 1990-96; dir. Greater Bay Bancorp, E. Palo Alto, Calif., 1996—2009. Author: The Mapping of California as an Island, 1995. Served USAF 1956-62, USAFR 1964-65 (capt. and pilot), pres. Jr. Achievement Santa Clara County, 1978-79, chmn. bd., 1980-81; chmn. bd. Jr. Achievement Found. Santa Clara County, 1980-87; mem. bus. sch. adv. bd. U. Santa Clara, 1981-84; pres. Boy Scouts Am., Santa Clara County, 1986-87, mem. exec. coun., 1982—, pres. No. Calif. Area, 1988-91; pres. Boy Scouts Am. Meml. Found., 1991-95, mem. nat. adv. coun., 2000-06, chmn. 2003-06, nat. exec. bd., 2003-; mem. pvt. sector investment adv. panel City of San Jose, 1984-92; bd. visitors Sch. Acctg., Coll. Bus. Adminstrn., U. Okla., 1991-94, endowed chair in bus. ethics, 1997, bd. advs., 1998—, Regents award, 2001; trustee Gould Acad., Bethel, Maine, 1993-99, O'Connor Hosp. Found., San Jose, 1994-97; bd. dirs. Am. Cancer Soc., Santa Clara County, 1994-98, Libr. Congress Map Divn., Phillips Soc., 1995—, co-chair, 1998-2000; founding angel Band of Angels, Silicon Valley, Calif., 1995-2003. Recipient Silver Leadership award Jr. Achievement, 1981, Silver Beaver award Boy Scouts Am., 1985, Silver Antelope award Boy Scouts Am., 1990, Disting. Eagle Scout award Boy Scouts Am., 1994, Silver Buffalo award, 2003, pub. svc. citations Calif. State Senate, Calif. State Assembly, Santa Clara County Suprs.; Baden-Powell World fellow, 1986; decorated Order of St. John, 1989; inducted to Jr. Achievement Bus. Hall of Fame, 2003, Disting. Alumni award, Coll. Bus., 2008. Fellow Royal Geog. Soc.; mem. Fin. Execs. Inst., English Speaking Union, Commonwealth Club, Harvard U. Bus. Sch. Club, Roxburghe Club, Book Club Calif., Beta Gamma Sigma, Sigma Alpha Epsilon. Home: 155 El Pinar Los Gatos CA 95032-1147 Home Phone: 408-871-0251; Office Phone: 408-741-1607. Personal E-mail: vla@ix.netcom.com.

MC LAUGHLIN, JEROME MICHAEL, lawyer, shipping company executive; b. St. Louis, Jan. 11, 1929; s. John Thomas and Mary Adelaide (White) McL.; m. Delphine M. McClellan, June 15, 1957; children— Margaret D., Mary Martha, Elizabeth O., Jerome Michael, John T. AB, St. Louis U., 1950, JD, 1954. Bar: Mo. 1954, U.S. Supreme Ct. 1972. V.p. Internat. Indemnity, St. Louis, 1955-56; asst. circuit atty. City of St. Louis, 1957-58; partner firm Willson, Cunningham & McClellan, St. Louis, 1958-78; v.p., gen. counsel Alexander & Baldwin, Inc., Honolulu, 1978-79; sr. v.p. Philippines, Micronesia & Orient Navigation Co., San Francisco, 1979-87, chmn. bd. dirs., 1996—. Instr. philosophy St. Louis U., 1955-60 Served to capt. USMC, 1951-53, Korea. Mem. Mo. Bar Assn. Republican. Roman Catholic. Home: 820 Smoketree Ct San Marcos CA 92078-4980 Office: 353 Sacramento St San Francisco CA 94111-3620

MCLAUGHLIN, JOSEPH MAILEY, lawyer; b. LA, July 10, 1928; s. James Aloysius and Cecilia Ann (Mailey) McL.; m. Beverly Jane Walker, July 24, 1949; children: Stephen Joseph, Lawrence James, Suzanne Carol, Eileen Louise. JD, Loyola U., LA, 1955. Bar: Calif. 1955, U.S. Supreme Ct. 1959. Mem. firm McLaughlin and Irvin, LA, 1955—. Lectr. labor relations Loyola U., L.A., 1958-60, mem. bd. visitors law sch., 1987—; pres. Food Employers Coun., Inc., 1984-89; pres. L.A. Stock Exch., 1972. Contbg. author: Labor Law for General Practitioners, 1960. Served to 1st lt. USAF, 1951-53. Mem. San Francisco, Long Beach, Los Angeles County, Fed., Am., Internat., Inter-Am. Bar Assns., State Bar Calif., Am. Judicature Soc., Assn. Bus. Trial Lawyers, Am. Soc. Internat. Law, Calif. Club. Office: 11957 Wood Ranch Rd Granada Hills CA 91344

MCLAUGHLIN, LEIGHTON BATES, II, retired journalist, reporter, educator; b. Evanston, Ill., Apr. 10, 1930; s. Leighton Bates and Gwendolyn I. (Markle) McL.; m. Beverly Jean Jeske, May 5, 1962; children: Leighton Bates III, Jeffrey, Steven, Patrick. Student, Kenyon Coll., Gambier, Ohio, 1948-50, Northwestern U., 1951; BA in English Lit., UCLA, 1983; MA in Comms., Calif. State U., Fullerton, 1990. Copyboy, reporter, rewriteman City News Bur., Chgo., 1957-58; reporter, rewriteman Chgo. Sun-Times, 1958-62; rewriteman, asst. city editor Ariz. Jour., Phoenix, 1962; reporter Miami (Fla.) Herald, 1962-64; successively rewriteman, night city editor, 1st asst. city editor, telegraph editor Chgo. Sun-Times, 1964-74; dir. Chgo. Daily News/Sun-Times News Service, 1974-79; editorial coord. electronics newspaper div. Field Enterprises, 1975-79; adminstr. reference libr. and communications ctr. Field Newspapers, 1976-79; editor News Am. Syndicate, Irvine, Calif., 1979-85; mng. editor San Gabriel Valley Daily Tribune, 1986; assoc. prof. journalism Riverside (Calif.) C.C., 1987-96, chmn. performing arts and media dept., 1993-96, coll. publs. editor, ret., 1996-99; lectr. in journalism Calif. State U.-Fullerton, 1984-96. Copy editor The Press-Enterprise, Riverside, Calif., 1988-95; lectr., condr. seminars in field. Author articles in field. Served to 1st lt. USMC, 1951-54. Recipient Stick-o-Type award for best feature story Chgo. Newspaper Guild, 1961, Best News story award Ill. AP and UPI, 1967 Mem. Chgo. Journalists Assn., Verban Soc., Psi Upsilon.

MCLAUGHLIN, MARGUERITE P., state legislator, logging company executive; b. Matchwood, Mich., Oct. 15, 1928; d. Harvey Martin and Luella Margaret (Livingston) Miller; m. George Bruce McLaughlin, 1947; children: Pamela, Bruce Jr., Cynthia. Owner, operator contract logging firm, Orofino, Idaho; mem. Idaho Ho. of Reps., 1978-80, Idaho Senate, 1980—, asst. Dem. Leader, 1990-93, Dem. leader, 1997-98. Chair Democrat Caucus, 1995-96; mem. Senate Fin. Com., 1987—, Gov.'s Adv. Coun. Workers Compensation, 1990-96, State of Idaho Endowment Fund Investment Bd., 1991-95, legis. coun., 1989-94, 95—. Mem. State of Idaho Job Tng. Coun., 1989-98, State Ins. Fund Commn., 1998—; trustee Joint Sch. Dist. 171, 1976-80; pres. Oro Celebration, Inc. Office: Idaho State Senate State Capital Boise ID 83720-0001

MCLEAN, HUGH ANGUS, management consultant; b. Salt Lake City, Feb. 19, 1925; s. George Mark and Rose (Powell) McLean; m. Martha Lane Green, Nov. 23, 1949; children: Michael Hugh, Merrie Smithson. Student, U. Kans., 1943—44; BSME, Iowa State U., 1946; postgrad., U. Utah, 1946, postgrad., 1961—66. Registered profl. engr., Utah. With Utah Oil Refining Co., Boise, Idaho, Twin Falls, Idaho and Salt Lake City, 1953—61, Am. Oil Co., Salt Lake City and 11 wc. states, 1961—66; cons. Std. Oil Ind., Chgo., 1966—69; v.p. Mahler Assocs., Midland Park, NJ, 1969—76; pres. McLean Mgmt. Sys., Wyckoff, NJ, 1976—84, Heber City, Utah, 1984—. Author: (book) Developmental Dialogues, 1972, Career Planning Program, 1975, There is a Better Way to Manage, 1982; creater, host TV live shows and commls., 1956—57, creator stewardship mgmt. sys., 1987; author: Stewardship Management: How to Manage Your Entire Job, Plus: Continuous Innovation, Productivity Improvement, Costs and Customer Satisfaction, Leadership at all Levels, Achievement Motivation, 2003. Introduced SAFE HOMES, county and state, 1987; chmn. bd. dirs. Town Hall Playhouse, 1990—96; emergency preparedness coord. Daniels Canyon area Wasatch County, Utah, 2000—05; Rep. election judge Salt Lake City, 1964, Operation Eagle Eye, Chgo., 1968; mem. Daniel Twp. Planning Commn., 1996—2000; pub. comm. dir. Ch. Jesus Christ LDS, NYC, 1981—84. Served to lt. (j.g.) USNR, 1943—46. Recipient Silver award, Am. Petroleum Inst.,

1957. Mem.: ASTD (chmn. N.Y. metro chpt. field trips 1972—74). Office: McLean Mgmt Sys PO Box 251 Heber City UT 84032-0251 Home Phone: 801-550-5274; Office Phone: 435-654-3384.

MCLEOD, BRUCE ROYAL, electrical engineering educator, consultant; b. Greeley, Colo, Jan. 17, 1939; s. Royal and Alma McLeod; m. Peggy Sue Hubbard, Sept. 30, 1961; children: Robert Royal, Cathryn Alaine McLeod. BSEE, Colo. State U., 1961; MSEE, U. Colo., 1965, PhD in Elec. Engring., 1968. Elec. engr. light mil. electronics dept. GE Co., Utica, NY, 1961-64; rsch. engr. Boeing Aerospace Group, Seattle, 1968-70; asst. prof. elec. engring. Mont. State U., Bozeman, 1970-74, assoc. prof., 1974-79; owner, operator Spear Lazy U Ranch, Wilsall, Mont., 1974—; prof. Mont. State U., Bozeman, 1979, 1979-89, 90-96, head dept. elec. engring., 1996—99, dean coll. grad. studies, 1999—2005, prof. elec. and computer engring., 2005—. Pres. Life Resonances Inc., Bozeman, 1987—, cons., 1990—; vis. rsch. scientist Columbia Presbyn. Hosp., N.Y.C., VA Hosp., U. Ky. Med. Ctr., 1981-82; cons. Devel. Tech. Corp., Bozeman, 1972, Infosystems, Bozeman, 1972, La Jolla (Calif.) Tech. Inc., 1983-85, Finnegan, Henderson, Farabow, Garret & Dunner, Washington, 1983, 85-86, IatroMed Inc., Phoenix, 1989-90. Contbr. over 38 articles to profl. jour. and books; presenter over 40 abstracts at nat. & internat. meetings; invited spkr. in field; holder of 27 US patents, 8 Australian patent, 2 Can. patent, 1 Japanese patent. Pres. Park County Legis. Assn., Livingston, Mont., 1988-90. Mem. IEEE (sr., chmn. Mont. sect. 1983-84), AAAS, Bioelectromagnetics Soc. (program com., bd. dirs. 2000-04, pres. 2004-05, tech. program chair 2005-06), Bioelec. Repair and Growth Soc. (program com. 1985-86, chmn. program com. 1988-90, coun. 1986-88, pres. 1991), Nat. Cattleman's Assn., Park County Stockgrowers Assn., Masons, Shriners, Sigma Xi (v.p. Mont. State U. chpt. 1979-80, pres. 1980-81), Sigma Tau, Eta Kappa Nu, Kappa Mu Epsilon, Sigma Xi. Avocations: hunting, fly fishing, woodcarving, trap and skeet clay pigeon shooting. Office: Mont State Univ Dept Elec and Computer Engring Rm 619 Cobleigh Hall Bozeman MT 59717-3780 Office Phone: 406-994-5960. Business E-Mail: mcleod@montana.edu.

MCLOUGHLIN, HILARY ESTEY, broadcast executive; B in Broadcasting and Film, Boston U. Rsch. analyst Seltel, Inc, 1984—86, Lorimar-Telepictures, 1986—89; dir. devel. Telepictures Prodns., 1989—92, v.p. devel., 1992, v.p. programming, sr. v.p. programming and devel., 1999—2002, exec. v.p., gen. mgr., 2002—06, pres., 2006—. Exec. prodr.: (TV series) The Rosie O'Donnell Show (Daytime Emmy award for Outstanding Talk Show, 1998, 1999). Named one of The 100 Most Powerful Women in Entertainment, Hollywood Reporter, 2007. Office: Telepictures Prodns 4000 Warner Blvd Burbank CA 91522

MC LURE, CHARLES E., JR., economist, consultant; b. Sierra Blanca, Tex., Apr. 14, 1940; s. Charles E. and Dessie (Evans) McL.; m. Patsy Nell Carroll, Sept. 17, 1962. BA, U. Kans., 1962; MA, Princeton U., 1964, PhD, 1966. Asst. prof. econs. Rice U., Houston, 1965-69, assoc. prof., 1969-72, prof., 1972-79, Allyn R. and Gladys M. Cline prof. econs., 1973-79; exec. dir. for research Nat. Bur. Econ. Research, Cambridge, Mass., 1977-78, v.p., 1978-81; sr. fellow Hoover Instn., Stanford U., 1981—; dep. asst. sec. Dept. Treasury, 1983-85. Sr. staff economist Coun. Econ. Advisers, Washington, 1969-70; vis. lectr. U. Wyo., 1972; vis. prof. Stanford U., 1973; cons. U.S. Treasury Dept., Labor Dept., World Bank, UN, OAS, Interam. Devel. Bank, Tax Found., Com. Econ. Devel., IMF, Internat. Tax and Investment Ctr., govts. Can., Colombia, Malaysia, Panama, Jamaica, Bolivia, Indonesia, New Zealand, Brazil, Trinidad and Tobago, Venezuela, Guatemala, Peoples Republic China, Egypt, Malawi, Mex., Bulgaria, Brazil, Russia, Ukraine, Romania, Kazakhstan, South Africa, Vietnam, Chile, Argentina. Author: Fiscal Failure: Lessons of the Sixties, 1972, (with N. Ture) Value Added Tax: Two Views, 1972, (with M. Gillis) La Reforma Tributaria Colombiana de 1974, 1977, Must Corporate Income Be Taxed Twice?, 1979, Economic Perperspectives on State Taxation of Multijurisdictional Corporations, 1986, The Value Added Tax: Key to Deficit Reduction, 1987; co-author: Taxation of Income from Business and Capital in Colombia, 1989; also numerous articles on econs., tax law and public finance. Ford Found. faculty research fellow, 1967-68, Disting. Svc. medal, US Treas. Dept., 1985, Daniel M. Holland medal, Nat. Tax Assn., 2004. Mem. Am. Econ. Assn., Nat. Tax Assn., Beta Theta Pi. Home: 250 Yerba Santa Ave Los Altos CA 94022-1609 Office: Stanford U Hoover Instn Stanford CA 94305-6010 Office Phone: 650-723-2657. Business E-Mail: mclure@hoover.stanford.edu.

MCLUSKIE, ED, communications educator; s. Clarence Edward and Francis McLuskie, Irma McLuskie (Stepmother); m. Ariel Thomas Haney, Oct. 4, 2004; m. Mary Elizabeth Trapp, Aug. 11, 1974 (div. Jan. 11, 1986); 1 child, Melissa Davis. BA, Mont. State U., Billings, 1970; PhD, U. Iowa, Iowa City, 1975. Prof. U. Wis., Whitewater, 1974—78, Fla. Atlantic U., Boca Raton, 1978—80, Boise State U., 1981—; Fulbright prof. U. Vienna, 1996—97, guest prof., 2002; Fulbright prof. Tbilisi State U., Georgian Inst. Pub. Affairs, Georgia, 2004—05. Contbr. articles to profl. jours., chapters to books. Bd. dirs. Snake River Alliance, Boise, 1987—88; keynote spkr. Leadership Boise, 2005. Grantee, Can. Embassy, 1983; fellow, NEH, 1979, Fulbright Commn., 1996—97, 2004—08. Mem.: Javnost - The Pub. (edtl. bd. mem., Ljubljana 2004), Media & Zeif (edtl. bd. mem., Vienna 1997), Internat. Comm. Assn. (life). Office: Boise State Univ Dept Communication 1910 Univ Dr Boise ID 83725-1920 Personal E-mail: emclusk@gmail.com. Business E-Mail: emclusk@boisestate.edu.

MCMAHON, FRANK V., insurance company executive; m. Vikki McMahon; 3 children. B in Econs., Villanova U., Pa.; MBA, Duke U., Durham, NC. With Merrill Lynch, 1994—99; positions up to mng. dir. Lehman Bros. Holdings, Inc., 1999—2006; vice chmn., CFO First Am. Corp., Santa Ana, Calif., 2006—. Bd. dirs. First Advantage Corp., 2006—. Office: First Am Corp 1 First American Way Santa Ana CA 92707 Office Phone: 714-250-3000.

MCMAHON, GERALD LAWRENCE, lawyer; b. Youngstown, Ohio, July 16, 1935; s. Lawrence J. and Lee Z. McM.; m. Donna Ghio, June 17, 1956; children: Maria, Michael, Mark, Matthew, Angela. BS cum laude, U. So. Calif., 1956; JD summa cum laude, U. San Diego, 1964. Bar: Calif. 1965, U.S. Dist. Ct. (so. dist. Calif.), U.S. Ct. Claims 1966, U.S. Ct. Appeals (9th cir.) 1966, U.S. Supreme Ct 1966. Chief of contracts Centaur space vehicle program Gen. Dynamics Astronautics, San Diego, 1960-64; from assoc. to chmn. & head litigation dept. Seltzer Caplan McMahon Vitek, San Diego, 1964—. Adj. prof. Univ. San Diego Sch. Law, 1969—72; lectr. Calif. Western Law Sch. Editor: San Diego Law Rev., 1963-64; frequent speaker & legal edn. panelist. Trustee, Sidney Kimmel Cancer Ctr.; chmn. bd. vis., U. San Diego Law Sch., 1979-80, 1996-98. Aviator with USN, 1956-59. Fellow Am. Coll. Trial Lawyers; mem. ABA, San Diego Bar Assn. (vp., dir. 1974-77), State Bar of Calif. (disciplinary referee pro tem 1977-79), Am. Judicature Soc., Am. Bd. Trial Advocates (pres. San Diego chpt. 1981), Calif. Trial Lawyers Assn., Am. Arbitation Assn., Am. Acad. Matrimonial Lawyers, San Diego Inn of Ct. (panelist 1975, dir. 1979), Phi Alpha Delta, Order of the Coif. Republican. Roman Catholic. Avocations: tennis, skiing, lic. pvt. pilot. Office: Seltzer Caplan McMahon Vitek Symphony Towers 750 B St San Diego CA 92101 Office Fax: 619-702-6803. Business E-Mail: mcmahon@scmv.com.

MCMAHON, JAMES W., federal magistrate judge; b. 1941; BA, Santa Clara U., 1962; LLB, Harvard U., 1968. Pvt. practice, LA, 1986-94; apptd. magistrate judge cen. dist. U.S. Dist. Ct. Calif., 1994. Dep. pub. defender L.A. County, 1969-79. With Peace Corps, 1963-65. Office: Courtroom 580 255 E Temple Los Angeles CA 90012-4712 Fax: 213-984-4402.

MCMANUS, MICHAEL S., federal judge; b. 1953; BA, U. Calif., Berkeley, 1975; JD, UCLA, 1978. With Morris & Polich, 1978-79, Diepenbrock, Wulff, Plant & Hannegan, 1979-94; apptd. bankruptcy judge ea. dist. U.S. Courthouse, 1994. Office: 501 I St Ste 3-200 Sacramento CA 95814 Fax: 916-930-4552. Business E-Mail: michael_mcmanus@caeb.uscourts.gov.

MCMANUS, PATRICK FRANCIS, editor, educator, writer; b. Sandpoint, Idaho, Aug. 25, 1933; s. Francis Edward McManus and Mabel Delana (Klaus) DeMers; m. Darlene Madge Keough, Feb. 3, 1954; children: Kelly C., Shannon M., Peggy F., Erin B. BA in English, Wash. State U., 1956, MA in English, 1962, postgrad., 1965-67. News reporter Daily Olympian, Olympia, Wash., 1956; editor Wash. State U., Pullman, 1956-59; with Ea. Wash. U., Cheney, 1959—; ret., 1983; news reporter Sta. KREM-TV, 1960-62; assoc. prof. Ea. Wash. U., Cheney, 1971-74, prof., 1974-83, prof. emeritus, 1983—. Author: A Fine and Pleasant Misery, 1978, Kid Camping from Aaaaiii! to Zip, 1979, They Shoot Canoes, Don't They?, 1981, Never Sniff a Gift Fish, 1983, The Grasshopper Trap, 1985, Rubber Legs & White Tail-Hairs, 1987, The Night The Bear Ate Goombaw, 1989, Whatchagot Stew, 1989, Real Ponies Don't Go Oink!, 1991, The Good Samaritan Strikes Again, 1992, How I Got This Way, 1994, Never Cry "Arp!" and Other Great Adventures, 1996, Into the Twilight, Endlessly Grousing, 1997, The Deer on a Bicycle, Excursions Into the Writing of Humor, 2000, The Bear in the Attic, 2002, The Blight Way, 2006, Avalanche, 2007, Kerplunk!, 2007, The Double Jack Murders, 2009; (stage play) A Fine and Pleasant Misery: The Humor of Patrick F. McManus, 1994, Misery II: McManus In Love, 1995, Pat McManus, Endlessly Grousing, 1997, Pott's Luck, 1999; assoc. editor Field & Stream mag., 1977-81; editor-at-large Outdoor Life, 1981—2009. Recipient Booksellers award P.N.W. Booksellers, 1983, Trustees medal EWU, 1984, Gov.'s award Wash. State Libr., 1985, Excellence in Craft award OWAA, 1986, Disting. Achievement award WSU, 1994, Founder's Day award EWU, 1994, Circle of Honor award The Outdoor Channel, 2004; named to Idaho's Hall of Fame, 1995, Legendary Communicator, Nat. Fresh Water Fishing Hall Fame, 2004, OWAA Legends, 2007. Mem.: Mystery Writers America, Outdoor Writers Am. (bd. dirs. 1981—84, Excellence award 1986), Authors Guild. Roman Catholic. Avocations: outdoor sports, woodworking, travel.

MCMANUS, RICHARD PHILIP, lawyer, agricultural products executive; b. Keokuk, Iowa, Oct. 20, 1929; s. Edward William and Kathleen (O'Connor) M.; m. Marjorie Theresa Mullaney, Nov. 5, 1955; children: Michael L., Mark J., Matthew A. BA, St. Ambrose U., Davenport, Iowa, 1949; JD, U. Mich., 1952; MBA, Roosevelt U., Chgo., 1965. Bar: Calif. 1982, Ill. 1958, Iowa 1952. Ptnr. McManus & McManus, Keokuk, 1953-63; div. counsel USN Facility Engring. Command, Great Lakes, Ill., 1963-66; v.p., dir. law Household Fin. Corp., Chgo., 1966-81; exec. v.p., sec. Security Pacific Fin. Svcs., Inc., San Diego, 1981-91, gen. counsel, 1981—91; exec. v.p./sec. Bank Am. Fin. Svcs., San Diego, 1991-92, gen. counsel, 1991—92; pres., chmn. bd. dirs. Mosamac Co., Inc., 1992—. Mem. gen. com. Conf. Consumer Fin. Law, Chgo., 1975-92; mem. adv. bd. Hostler Inst. Internat. Affairs, San Diego State U., 2005-08. Contbr. articles to profl. jours. Bd. dir., treas., atty. Tijuana/San Diego Habitat for Humanity, Inc., 1992-95; trustee Village of Lake Bluff, Ill., 1974-78; bd. dir. Charles Hostler Inst. World Affairs, San Diego State U., 2004-07. Recipient San Diego Vol. Lawyer Disting. Svc. award, 1995-, Pres. Calif. Bar Pro Bono Svs. award, 1998; named San Diego Pro Bono Atty. of Yr., 2005. Mem. Calif. Bar Assn., San Diego Bar Assn., Calif. Fin. Svcs. Assn. (chmn. law com. 1981-92), Am. Fin. Svcs. Assn. (chmn. law forum 1980-81, Disting. Svc. award 1990), Lions, Elks, KC, Beta Gamma Sigma. Democrat. Roman Catholic. Avocations: golf, flying, sailing, woodworking. Personal E-mail: mcman1000@gmail.com.

MCMASTER, JULIET SYLVIA, English language educator; b. Kisumu, Kenya, Aug. 2, 1937; emigrated to Can., 1961, naturalized, 1976; d. Sydney Herbert and Sylvia (Hook) Fazan; m. Rowland McMaster, May 10, 1968; children: Rawdon, Lindsey. BA with honors, Oxford U., Eng., 1959; MA, U. Alta., Can., 1963, PhD, 1965. Asst. prof. English U. Alta., Edmonton, Canada, 1965—70, assoc. prof., 1970—76, prof. English, 1976—86, univ. prof., 1986—2000, prof. emeritus, 2000—. Author: Thackeray: The Major Novels, 1971, Jane Austen on Love, 1978, Trollope's Palliser Novels, 1978; author: (with R.D. McMaster) The Novel from Sterne to James, 1981; author: Dickens the Designer, 1987, Jane Austen the Novelist, 1995, Reading the Body in the Eighteenth Century Novel, 2004, Woman Behind the Painter: The Diaries of Rosalie, Mrs. James Clarke Hook, 2006; co-editor: Jane Austen's Business, 1996, Cambridge Companion to Jane Austen, 1997, The Child Writer From Austen to Woolf, 2005; gen. editor: Juvenilia Press, 1993—2002, illustrator/editor: children's picture book (by Jane Austen) The Beautifull Cassandra, 1993, 2007; contbr. articles to profl. jours. Fellow Can. Coun., 1969-70, Guggenheim Found., 1976-77, Killam Found., 1987-89; recipient Molson prize in Humanities for Outstanding Contbn. to Canadian Culture, 1994, Alberta Centennial medal, 2005. Fellow Royal Soc. Can.; mem. Victorian Studies Assn. Western Can. (founding pres. 1972), Assn. Can. Univ. Tchrs. English (pres. 1976-78), MLA, Jane Austen Soc. N.Am. (dir. 1980-91). Business E-Mail: juliet.mcmaster@ualberta.ca.

MCMICHAEL, J(ACK) RICHARD, real estate developer; b. Berkeley, Calif., Mar. 9, 1943; s. Jack R. and Dorothy (Dwyer) McM.; m. Karen Lois Moore, Nov. 15, 1964; children: J. Richard IV, Erik C. BA, U. Calif., Berkeley, 1964, JD, 1969. Bar: Calif.; lic. real estate broker, Calif. Assoc. Pettit and Martin, San Francisco, 1969-71; pres. Sutter Hill Ltd., Palo Alto, Calif., 1971-78; exec. v.p. Genstar Pacific Corp., San Francisco, 1978-79; gen. mgr. investment property div. Citation Builders, San Leandro, Calif., 1979-84; prin. JRM Properties, Palo Alto, 1984-88; pres. The Fairway Land Co., Laguna Niguel, Calif., 1988-90; v.p., gen. mgr. Quadrant Corp., San Ramon, Calif., 1990-92; v.p. Weyerhauser Real Estate Co., Federal Way, Wash., 1992—. Bd. dirs., Western Real Estate Fund, Inc., Menlo Park, Calif. Chmn., Scholar Opera, Palo Alto, 1982-85; bd. mgrs., Palo Alto YMCA, 1987-91; chmn. troop com., Palo Alto area Boy Scouts Am., 1987-88. Comdr. USN, 1964-66, Vietnam. Mem. Internat. Coun. Shopping Ctrs. Republican. Presbyterian. Avocations: running, golf. Office: Weyerhaeuser Real Estate Co EC3-3B9 PO Box 9777 Federal Way WA 98063 E-mail: rick.mcmichael@wreco1.com.

MCMILLAN, LEE RICHARDS, II, lawyer, mining executive; b. New Orleans, Aug. 26, 1947; s. John H. and Phoebe (Skillman) McM.; m. Lynne Clark Pottharst, June 27, 1970; children: Leslie Clark, Hillary Anne, Lee Richards III. BS in Commerce, Washington and Lee U., 1969; JD, Tulane U., 1972; LLM in Taxation, NYU, 1976. Bar: La. 1972. Assoc. Jones, Walker, Waechter, Poitevent, Carrere & Denegre, New Orleans, 1976-79, ptnr., 1979—2007, sect. head, corp. and securities sect., 1987—90, 1994—2002, exec. com., 1990—94, 1996—99, 2001—02, chmn. exec. com., 1991—94, 1996—98, 2001—02; sr. v.p., gen. counsel Freeport-McMoRan Copper & Gold Inc., Phoenix, 2007—. Vice chmn. Mech. Equipment Co., Inc., New Orleans, 1980—86, chmn. bd., 1986—, pres., 1989—99; mem. The Bus. Coun. Greater New Orleans, 1998—, exec. com., 1999—; bd. dirs. The Chamber/New Orleans and the River Region, 1996—98; trustee Alton Ochsner Med. Found., 1995—2003. Trustee New Orleans Mus. Art., 1989-95; bd. dirs. Bur. Govt. Rsch. New Orleans, 1987-93, Louise S. McGehee Sch., New Orleans, 1982-88, co-chmn. capital fund dr., 1984-86, pres. bd. dirs., 1986-88; bd. govs. Isidore Newman Sch., New Orleans, 1991-95. Lt. JACG USNR, 1972-75. Mem. ABA (com. on negotiated acquisitions 1986-94), La. State Bar Assn. (chmn. corp. and bus. law sect. 1985-86, mem. com. on bar admissions 1986-87), Young Pres. Orgn., Washington and Lee U. Alumni Assn. (bd. dirs. 1995-99). Republican. Episcopalian. Avocation: sailing. Office: Freeport McMoRan 1 N Ctrl Ave Phoenix AZ 85004

MCMILLAN, M. SEAN, lawyer; Diploma, U. Munich, 1963; cert., Internat. Sch., Copenhagen, Denmark, 1962; SB, U. So. Calif., 1967; JD, Harvard U., 1970. Bar: Calif. 1971. Spl. projects dir. Mass. Gen. Hosp., Boston, 1967-70; ptnr. Keatinge, Libbott, Bates & Loo, Los Angeles, 1970-74, Loo, Merideth & McMillan, Los Angeles, 1974-85, Bryan Cave LLP, Los Angeles/Santa Monica, 1986—2001, Greenberg Traurig LLP, LA, 2001—. Editor: Harvard Internat. Law Jour., 1968-70. Mem. ABA, Am. Soc. Internat. Law. Office: Greenberg Traurig LLP 2450 Colorado Ave Ste 400E Santa Monica CA 90404 Office Phone: 310-586-7700. Business E-Mail: mcmillan@gtlaw.com.

MCMILLAN, NATHANIEL (NATE MCMILLAN), professional basketball coach; b. Raleigh, NC, Aug. 3, 1964; m. Michelle McMillan; children: Jamelle, Brittany Michelle. Student, Chowan Coll., Murfreesboro, NC, 1982—84, NC State U., 1984—86. Player Seattle SuperSonics, 1986—98, asst. coach, 1998—2000, interim head coach, 2000—01, head coach, 2001—05, Portland Trail Blazers, 2005—. Asst. coach US Men's Sr. Nat. Basketball Team, Beijing, 2008. Named to All-NBA Defensive Second Team, 1994, 1995, Nat. Jr. Coll. Men's Basketball Coaches Assn. Hall of Fame, 2001. Achievements include holding the NBA single-game record for rookie assists. Avocation: football. Office: Portland Trail Blazers Rose Garden One Center Ct Portland OR 97227

MCMILLAN, PAUL FRANCIS, chemistry educator; b. Edinburgh, June 3, 1955; BSc with honors, U. Edinburgh, 1977; PhD, Ariz. State U., 1981. Asst. prof. Ariz. State U., Tempe, 1983-88, assoc. prof., 1988-92, prof. chemistry, 1992—, presdl. prof. scis., dir., 1998—. Dir. Materials Rsch. Ctr. Ariz. State U., 1996—, dir. Ctr. for Solid State Sci., 1997—. Editor: Structure and Dynamics of Silicate Melts, 1995, Spl. Issue European Jour. Solid State Inorganic Chemistry, 1997; contbr. articles to profl. jours. Materials Rsch. Ctr. grant NSF, 1996. Fellow Mineralogical Soc. Am.; mem. Fgn. Assn., Materials Rsch. Soc., Am. Chem. Soc. Achievements include 2 patents on nitride glasses; research on density driven phase transition in liquids, synthesis of icosahedral borides.

MCMORRIS, JERRY, transportation company, sports team executive; Past CEO NW Transport Svc, Denver; chair, pres., CEO Colorado Rockies, Denver, 1993—. Office: 4765 Oakland St Denver CO 80239-2717

MCMORRIS-RODGERS, CATHY, United States Representative from Washington; b. Salem, Oreg., May 22, 1969; m. Brian Rodgers, Aug. 5, 2006; 1 child, Cole McMorris. BA in Pre-Law, Pensacola Christian Coll., Fla., 1990; MBA, U. Wash., 2002. Mem. Wash. State House Reps. from 7th Dist., 1994—2004, minority leader, 2002—03; mem. US Congress from 5th Wash. Dist., 2005—; vice chair US House Republican Conf., 2009—; mem. US House Armed Services Com., US House Edn. & Labor Com., US House Nat. Resources Com. Recipient Cornerstone award, Assn. Wash. Bus., 1995—96, Sentinal award, Wash. State Law Enforcement Assn., 1996, Guardian of Small Bus. award, Nat. Fedn. Ind. Bus., 1996, Gold Medal, Ind. Bus. Assn., 1996. Mem.: Wash. Women for Survival of Agr., Wash. Rural Health Assn., Wash. State Farm Bur. (Legislator of Yr. 1997), Wash. State Cattlemen's Assn., N.E. Wash. Women in Timber. Republican. Office: US Congress 1323 Longworth House Office Bldg Washington DC 20515-4705 also: 10 N Post 6th Fl Spokane WA 99201 Office Phone: 202-225-2006.

MCMURDO, C(HARLES) GREGORY, state official, lawyer; b. Klamath Falls, Oreg., Apr. 30, 1946; s. Charles Andrew and Juanita Berniece (Bell) McM. BA Oreg. State U., 1968, JD Lewis and Clark Coll., 1972. Bar: Oreg. 1972, U.S. Dist. Ct. Oreg. 1975, U.S. Ct. Appeals (9th cir.) 1980, U.S. Supreme Ct. 1984. Legal counsel Oreg. Ho. of Reps., Salem, 1972—76; asst. sec. state State of Oreg., Salem, 1976—81, dep. sec. state, 1981—85; mem. Workers Compensation Bd., 1985—88; dir. of govt. rels. Metro, Portland, 1988—90; dep. supt. of pub. instrn. State of Oreg., 1990—2000, exec. legal officer, 2000—01. Mem.: Oreg. State Bar. Republican. Episcopalian. E-mail: gmcmcmurdo@attbi.com.

MCNALL, SCOTT GRANT, sociologist, educator, academic administrator; b. New Ulm, Minn., Jan. 16, 1941; s. Everett Herman and Dorothy Grant (Brown) McNall; m. Sally Anne Allen, Oct. 31, 1960; children: Miles Allen, Amy Ellen. BA, Portland State U., 1962; PhD, U. Oreg., 1965. Instr. sociology U. Oreg., Eugene, 1964-65; asst. prof. U. Minn., Mpls., 1965-70; from assoc. prof. to prof. Ariz. State U.,

Tempe, 1970-76; prof., chmn. dept. sociology U. Kans., Lawrence, 1976-89, prof, chmn. dept. Am. studies, 1989-90; dean Coll. Arts and Scis. U. Toledo, 1990-94; provost Calif. State U., Chico, 1994—2007, interim pres., 2003—05; dir. Inst. Sustained Devel., 2007—. Fulbright lectr., Greece, 1968—69; vis. lectr. Mid-Am. State U. Assn., 1982—83. Author: (book) The Sociological Experience, 1969, 3d edit., 1974, The Greek Peasant, 1974, Social Problems Today, 1975, Career of a Radical Rightist, 1975; author: (with Sally A. McNall) Plains Families: Exploring Sociology Through Social History, 1983, The Road to Rebellion, 1988; editor: The Sociological Perspective, 1968, 4th edit., 1977, Theoretical Perspectives in Sociology, 1979, Current Perspectives in Social Theory, 1980, 6th edit., 1985, Political Economy: A Critique of American Society, 1981; editor: (with others) Studies in Historical Social Change, 1986—, The Road to Rebellion: Class Formation and Kansas Populism, 1865-1900, 1988; editor: (with Rhonda Levine) Bringing Class Back in, 1991; editor: (with Sally A. McNall) Sociology, 1992; editor: Current Perspectives in Social Theory, 1980—87; adv. editor: Sociol. Quar., 1969—72, assoc. editor: Am. Sociologist, 1975—78, Jour. Polit. and Mil. Sociology, 1982—; contbr. articles to profl. jours. East-West Ctr. Vis. fellow, 1978, Fulbright grantee, 1983. Mem.: Pacific Sociol. Soc., Am. Sociol. Assn. (chair Marxist sect. 1989—90), Midwest Sociol. Soc. (pres. 1982—83). Democrat. Congregationalist. Home: 520 Crestwood Dr Paradise CA 95969-3825 Office: Calif State U VPAA Office Chico CA 95929 Office Phone: 530-898-6101. Business E-Mail: smcnall@csuchico.edu.

MCNALLY, THOMAS CHARLES, III, lawyer; b. San Francisco, Dec. 5, 1938; s. Thomas Charles and Claire Marie (Egan) McN.; m. Paula Ann Berger, Sept. 3, 1960; children: Megan, Martin, J. Tevis. BS, U. San Francisco, 1960; JD, U. Calif., San Francisco, 1963. Bar: Calif. 1964. Dep. atty. gen., Calif., 1964; assoc. firm Bohnert, Flowers & McCarthy, San Francisco, 1965-68; asst. sec., counsel DiGiorgio Corp., San Francisco, 1968-73, sec., counsel, 1974-75; sec., gen. counsel Consol. Fibres, Inc., San Francisco, 1975-88, v.p., 1981-88, also bd. dirs.; of counsel McInerney & Dillon, P.C., Oakland, Calif., 1989-91; pvt. practice San Francisco, 1991—. Lectr. McGeorge Bar Rev., 1964-65, Continuing Edn. of Bar, U. Calif., 1975-76; judge moot ct. U. San Francisco, 1974-84; arbitrator Am. Arbitration Assn., NASD, 1988—. Co-chmn. Mill Valley Citizens Adv. Com., 1974-76; mem. pub. affairs com. San Francisco Assn. Mental Health, 1965-69; commr. Mill Valley Park and Recreation Commn., 1988-93, chmn., 1990; commr. Larkspun Park & Recreation Commn., 2005-; lector Roman Cath. ch. Mem. ABA, State Bar Calif., San Francisco Bar Assn., Olympic Club (bd. dirs. 1999—, v.p. 2001), Scott Valley Tennis Club (founder, bd. dirs. 1971-76, 80-82, pres. 1980-82), World Trade Club. Republican. Home: 108 Hawthorne Ave Larkspur CA 94939 Office: 455 Market St Ste 1900 San Francisco CA 94105-2448 E-mail: tmcnally@lmi.net.

MCNAMARA, JOHN STEPHEN, artist, educator; b. Cambridge, Mass., Feb. 16, 1950; s. John Stephen and Mary (Adams) McN. BFA in Painting, Mass. Coll. Art, Boston, 1971, MFA in Painting, 1977. Tchr. Mus. Fine Arts Sch., Boston, 1983, 90-92; undergrad. and grad. painting tchr. Mass. Coll. Art, Boston, 1988; undergrad. painting tchr. Boston Archtl. Ctr., Boston, 1977; color fundamentals tchr. Mass. Coll. Art, Boston, 1987, undergrad. drawing and painting, 1975-88. Vis. lectr. San Francisco Art Inst., 1992, 93, U. Calif., Berkeley, 1993—. One-man shows include The Exhbn. Space at 112 Greene St., N.Y.C., 1982, Stavaridis Gallery, Boston, 1983-85, 86-89, Bess Cutler Gallery, N.Y.C., 1984, 85, 86, 88, Mass. Coll. Art, 1986, Honolulu Acad. Fine Art, 1987, Nielsen Gallery, 1990, 92, Miller Block Gallery, Boston, 1995, Ebert Gallery, San Francisco, Clark Gallery, Lincoln, Mass., 2002, Humanities, Townsgurd Ctr., U. Calif., Berkeley, 2008,others; exhibited in group shows at Boston Collects, Mus. Fine Arts, Stavaridis Gallery, 1986, Bess Cutler Gallery, N.Y.C., 1987, Am. Painters and Sculptors, Met. Mus. Art, N.Y.C., 1988, Resonant Abstraciton, Fuller Mus. Art, Brockton, Mass., 1989-90, Tucson Mus. Fine Art, 1996, DeCordova Mus., Lincoln, Mass., 2002, Painting in Boston, 1950-2000, Honolulu Acad. Fine Arts "Decades Abstration", 2008-09. Recipient Outstanding Alumnus award, Mass. Coll. Art, 1986, Faculty Outstanding Mentorship award, Grad. Student Instr., U. Calif., Berkley, 2005; grantee, Mass. Arts and Humanities Grant, 1980, 1983, 1986, 1989, Equitable Life and the Rockefeller Found. Awards in the visual arts, 1982, Equitable Life and the Rockefeller Found., 1983, 1986, 1989, Nat. Endowment Arts, 1981; McDowell Colony fellow, Peterborough, NH, 1985. Home: 1501 Park Ct Novato CA 94945-1472 Office Phone: 510-642-2582. Business E-Mail: namara@berkeley.edu.

MC NAMARA, JOSEPH DONALD, researcher, retired protective services official; b. NYC, Dec. 16, 1934; s. Michael and Eleanor (Shepherd) McN.; divorced; children: Donald, Laura, Karen. BS, John Jay Coll., 1968; fellow, Harvard Law Sch., 1970; DPA (Littauer fellow), Harvard U., 1973. Served to dep. insp. Police Dept., NYC, 1956-73; police chief Kansas City, Mo., 1973-76, San Jose, Calif., 1976-91; rsch. fellow Hoover Instn., Stanford U., 1991—. Adj. instr. Northeastern U., 1972, John Jay Coll., 1973, Rockhurst Coll., 1975-76, San Jose State U., 1980; cons. U.S. Civil Rights Commn., 1978; lectr., appearances on nat. TV; apptd. nat. adv. bd. U.S. Bur. Justice Stats., 1980, U.S. Drug Control Policy Office, 1993; commentator Pub. Broadcasting Radio. Author: (non-fiction) Safe and Sane, 1984, (novel) The First Directive Crown, 1985, Fatal Command, 1987, The Blue Mirage, 1990, Code 211 Blue, 1996; contbr. articles to profl. publs. Bd. dirs. Drug Policy Found., Washington; active NCCJ. Served with U.S. Army, 1958-60. Named one of 200 Young Am. Leaders Time mag., 1975; recipient disting. alumni award John Jay Coll., 1979, Pres.'s award Western Soc. Criminology1979, Morrison Gitchoff award Western Soc. Criminology, 1992, H.B. Spear award Drug Policy Found., 1992; Kansas City police named Best in Country by Nat. Newspaper Enterprises, 1974, San Jose Police Dept. named Nat. Model U.S. Civil Rights Commn., 1980; named Law Enforcement Officer of Yr., Calif. Trial Lawyers Assn., 1991. Mem. Internat. Assn. Chiefs of Police, Calif. Police Chiefs Assn., Calif. Peace Officers Assn., Major Cities Police Chiefs Assn., Police Exec. Research Forum (dir.) Office: Hoover Instn Stanford CA 94305 Office Phone: 650-723-1475. Business E-Mail: mcnamara@hoover.stanford.edu.

MCNAMARA, MARGARET M., pediatrician; MD, U. Conn., 1990. Diplomate Am. Bd. Pediatrics. Resident in pediatrics U. Calif., San Francisco; chief of pediatrics U. Calif. San Francisco/Mount Zion Pediatric Practice, San Francisco. Office: UCSF Mount Zion Pediat Practice 2330 Post St Ste 320 San Francisco CA 94115-3466

MCNAMEE, BRIAN, medical products executive; B in Journalism, St. Bonaventure U., NY; M in Indsl. and Labor Rels., Cornell U., Ithaca, 1987. Various human resources positions GE, 1988—99; sr. v.p. human resources NBC, 1998—99; v.p. human resources Dell Computer Corp., 1999—2001; sr. v.p. human resources Amgen, Inc., Thousand Oaks, Calif., 2001—. Office: Amgen Inc One Amgen Center Dr Thousand Oaks CA 91320-1799 Office Phone: 805-447-1000. Office Fax: 805-447-1010.

MCNAMEE, STEPHEN M., federal judge; b. 1942; BA, U. Cinn., 1964; MA, U. Ariz., 1967, JD, 1969. Atty. legal & fin. dept. Florsheim Shoe Co., 1969—71; asst. US atty. Dist. Ariz., US Dept. Justice, 1971—79, 1st asst. US atty., 1980, chief asst. US atty., 1981—85, US atty. Phoenix, 1985-90; judge US Dist. Ct. Ariz., Phoenix, 1990—2006, chief judge, 1999—2006, sr. judge, 2007—. Lectr. U. Ariz. Coll. Bus., 1975—79. Office: US Dist Judge Sandra Day O'Connor US Ct 401 W Washington St SPC 60 Phoenix AZ 85003-2158 Office Phone: 602-322-7555.

MCNEAL, DALE WILLIAM, JR., biological sciences educator; b. Kansas City, Kans., Nov. 23, 1939; s. Dale William and Geraldine Estelle (Reed) McNeal; m. Arlene Joyce Purvis, Feb. 26, 1966. BA, Colo. Coll., 1962; MS, SUNY Coll. Environ. Sci. and Forestry, Syracuse, 1964; PhD, Wash. State U., 1969. Asst. prof. dept. biol. scis. U. Pacific, Stockton, Calif., 1969-74, assoc. prof., 1974-79, prof., 1979—2002, chmn. dept., 1978-84, prof. emeritus, 2002—. Contbr. articles to profl. jours. With US Army, 1964—66. Mem.: Calif. Acad. Scis., Internat. Soc. Plant Taxonomy, Am. Soc. Plant Taxonomists, Calif. Bot. Soc. (pres. 1987—88), Am. Bot. Soc., Sigma Xi. Republican. Episcopalian. Office: U Pacific Dept Biol Scis Stockton CA 95211-0001 Office Phone: 209-946-3019. Business E-Mail: dmcneal@pacific.edu.

MCNEALY, SCOTT GLENN, information technology executive; b. Columbus, Ind., Nov. 13, 1954; s. Raymond William and Marmaline McNealy; m. Susan Ingemanson, 1994; 4 children. BA, Harvard U., Cambridge, Mass., 1976; MBA, Stanford U., Calif., 1980. With Rockwell Internat. Corp., Troy, Mich., 1976-78, sales engr.; staff engr. FMC Corp., Chgo., 1980-81; dir. ops. Onyx Systems, San Jose, Calif., 1981-82; co-founder Sun Microsystems, Inc., Santa Clara, Calif., 1982, v.p. ops., 1982—84, COO, 1984, pres., 1984—99, 2002—04, CEO, 1984—2006, chmn., 1984—. Bd. dirs. Sun Microsystems, Inc., 1982—. Named one of World's Richest People, Forbes Mag., 400 Richest Ams., Am.'s Most Powerful People. Avocation: hockey. Office: Sun Microsystems Inc 4150 Network Cir Santa Clara CA 95054 Office Phone: 650-960-1300.

MCNEILL, DANIEL RICHARD, writer; b. San Francisco, June 1, 1947; s. Daniel Harry and Maureen Evangeline (Sherriff) McN.; m. Rosalind Deborah Gold, Dec. 20, 1984. AB, U. Calif., Berkeley, 1975; JD, Harvard U., 1982. Author: Fuzzy Logic, 1993 (L.A. Times Book prize in sci. and tech. 1993), The Face, 1998. Mem. Authors Guild. Avocations: photography, bodybuilding. Home and Office: 8110 Redlands St #306 Playa Del Rey CA 90293

MCNEILL, JOHN HUGH, pharmaceutical sciences educator; b. Chgo., Dec. 5, 1938; s. John and Agnes Margaret (McLean) McN.; m. Sharon Keneflly, July 27, 1963; children: Sandra, Laurie. BS, U. Alta., Can., 1960, MS, 1962; PhD, U. Mich., 1967. Lectr. pharmacy Dalhousie U., 1962-63, U. Alta., 1963; research assoc. U. Mich., Ann Arbor, 1963-65, teaching fellow, 1965-66; asst. instr. Mich. State U., East Lansing, 1966-67, asst. prof., 1967-71; assoc. prof. U. B.C., 1971-72, assoc. prof., chmn. div. pharmacology and toxicology, 1972-75, dir. rsch. and grad. studies Faculty Pharm. Scis., 1977-78, prof. Faculty Pharm. Scis., 1975—2004, dean Faculty Pharm. Scis., 1985-96, asst. dean, 1978-81, Med. Rsch. Coun. rsch. prof., 1981-82, prof., assoc. dean rsch. and grad. studies, 1982-84, prof. and dean emeritus, 2004—. Contbr. more than 800 tech. articles to profl. jours. Fellow Royal Soc. Can., Internat. Acad. Cardiovasc. Scis., Can. Acad. Health Scis., Am. Coll. Nutrition; mem. Pharm. Soc. Can. (various coms. 1974-88, coun. 1977-83, v.p. 1979, pres. 1980-81), Am. Soc. for Pharm. and Therapeutics (J.J. Abel award com. 1981, Upjohn award com., 1978-80, chmn. mem. com. 1983-86), Western Pharm. Soc. (coun. 1977-81, pres. 1979-80, past pres. 1980-81), N.Y. Acad. Scis., Internat. Soc. for Heart Rsch. (coun. 1986-95), AAAS, B.C. Coll. Pharms. (coun. 1985-96), Internat. Union Pharmacologists (Can. rep. 1982-88), Am. Pharm. Assn. Office: Univ BC Fac Pharm Scis 2146 East Mall Vancouver BC Canada V6T IZ3 Home Phone: 604-224-5456; Office Phone: 604-822-9373. E-mail: jmcneill@interchange.ubc.ca.

MCNERNEY, JERRY (GERALD M. MCNERNEY), United States Representative from California, engineer; b. Alburquerque, June 18, 1951; m. Mary McNerney; children: Michael, Windy, Gregory. Attended, US Mil. Acad., West Point, NY; BS, U. N.Mex., 1973, MS, 1975, PhD in Engring. and Math., 1981. Contractor Sandia Nat. Labs., Kirkland Air Force Base; sr. engr. US Wind Power/Kenetech Inc., 1985—94; energy cons. various cos. PG&E, FloWind, Electric Power Rsch Inst., 1994—98; sr. engr., field mgr. Wind Turbine Co., 1999—2003; CEO Hawt Power Inc., 2003—04; founder, CEO pvt. manufacture of wind turbines, 2004—; mem. US Congress from 11th Calif. dist., 2007—, mem. vets affairs com., transp. & infrastructure com., sci. & tech. com., select com. on energy independence & global warming. Mem.: Am. Math. Soc., Am. Soc. Mech. Engineers. Democrat. Roman Catholic. Avocations: reading, hunting, running, hiking. Office: 312 Cannon House Office Bldg Washington DC 20515 also: 5776 Stoneridge Mall Rd Ste 175 Pleasanton CA 94588

MCNEVIN, CHRISTOPHER J., lawyer; b. Davenport, Iowa, Sept. 6, 1958; BS summa cum laude, U. Miami, 1979; JD, Stanford U., 1983. Bar: Calif. 1983, Calif. Supreme Ct., US Dist. Ct. (all Calif. dist., we. dist. Pa.), US Ct. Appeals (3d, 9th cir.). Ptnr. Pillsbury Winthrop Shaw Pittman, LA. Spl. counsel Orange County Water Dist.; co-leader environ. litig. team Pillsbury Winthrop Shaw Pittman, LA. Contbr. articles to profl. jours. Named a So. Calif. Super Lawyer, LA Mag., 2004, 2005, 2006. Office: Pillsbury Winthrop Shaw Pittman LLP 725 S Figueroa St Ste 2800 Los Angeles CA 90017-5406 Office Phone: 213-488-7507. Office Fax: 213-629-1033. Business E-Mail: chrismcnevin@pillsburylaw.com.

MCNIFF, PETER J., federal judge; b. 1940; Bankruptcy judge U.S. Bankruptcy Ct. Wyo., Cheyenne, 1994—. Office: 2120 Capitol Ave Rm 8024 Cheyenne WY 82001-3633

MC NIVEN, HUGH DONALD, engineering science educator, earthquake engineering researcher; b. Toronto, Ont., Can., Aug. 6, 1922; came to U.S., 1953; s. James and Pearl Mary (Jackson) Mc N.; m. Marion Fitzhugh, Sept. 12, 1959; 1 dau., Carolyn Fitzhugh. BASc., U. Toronto, 1944; M.C.E., Cornell U., 1948; PhD, Columbia U., 1957. Prof. engring. sci. U. Calif.-Berkeley, 1957—91, dir. Earthquake Engring. Research Ctr., 1980-85, prof. emeritus, 1991—. Contbr. articles to profl. jours. Pres. Univ. Art Mus. U. Calif.-Berkeley, 1970-72. Served to capt. Can. Army, 1944-46. Fellow Acoust. Soc. Am.; mem. ASCE, ASME, Earthquake Engring. Research Inst., Seismology Soc. Am. Clubs: Bohemian (San Francisco); Mira Vista Golf (El Cerrito, Calif.); Fox House, American (London). Home: 1440 Hawthorne Ter Berkeley CA 94708-1804

MCNULTY, FRANK, state legislator; m. Kim Hall. Grad., U. Colo., Boulder; JD, U. Denver Coll. Law. With Office of Congressman & Senator Wayne AllarD, Office of Gov. Bill Owens; asst. dir., water Colo. Dept. Natural Resources; mem. Dist. 43 Colo. House of Reps., Denver, 2007—. Mem. St. Mark Cath. Ch. Mem. Douglas/Elbert Bar Assn., Colo. Bar Assn., Firearms Coalition Colo., Colo. State Shooting Assn., Douglas County Rep. Party. Republican. Roman Catholic. Office: 200 E Colfax Boulder CO 80302 Office Phone: 303-866-2936.*

MCNULTY, JAMES F., construction company executive; m. Judy McNulty; children: Darby, Anne, Brigid. BS in Engring., US Mil. Acad., 1964; MS in Nuc. Physics, Ohio State U., 1970; MS in Mgmt., MIT, 1985. Rsch. assoc. Lawrence Livermore Nat. Lab., 1972—74; asst. dir. Office Mil. Applications US Dept. Energy, 1978—80; officer nuc. weapon requirements Ops. and Plans Office Dept US Army, 1980—82, sys. mgr. Pershing II Missle Sys., 1982—84, program mgr. ground based laser sys., 1985—88; dir. bus. devel. Parsons Corp., 1988—89, v.p. Washington, 1991—92, sr. v.p., mgr. sys. divsn. Pasadena, 1992—95, pres. infrastructure and tech. group, 1996, pres., CEO, 1996—, chmn., 1998—. Fellow Alfred P. Sloan, MIT. Avocations: hiking, walking, golf, reading. Office: Parsons Corp 100 W Walnut St Pasadena CA 91124-0001 Office Phone: 626-440-2000. Office Fax: 626-440-2630.

MCNULTY, JOHN KENT, lawyer, educator; b. Buffalo, Oct. 13, 1934; s. Robert William and Margaret Ellen (Duthie) McN.; m. Linda Conner, Aug. 20, 1955 (div. Feb. 1977); children: Martha Jane, Jennifer, John K. Jr.; m. Babette B. Barton, Mar. 23, 1978 (div. May 1988). AB with high honors, Swarthmore Coll., 1956; LLB, Yale U., 1959. Bar: Ohio 1961, U.S. Supreme Ct. 1964. Law clk. Justice Hugo L. Black US Supreme Ct., Washington, 1959—60; vis. prof. Sch. Law U. Tex., 1960; assoc. Jones, Day, Cockley & Reavis, Cleve., 1960—64; prof. law U. Calif., Berkeley, 1964—91, Roger J. Traynor prof. law, 1991—2002, Roger J. Traynor prof. emeritus, 2002—. Of counsel Baker and McKenzie, San Francisco, 1974-75; acad. visitor London Sch. Econs., 1985, Cambridge U., 1994, U. Edinburgh, 1994; vis. fellow Wolfson Coll., Cambridge, 1994, U. Innsbruck, 1996, Trinity Coll., Dublin, 1997; vis. prof. Yale U., U. Tex., U. Leiden, U. Tilburg, U. Tokyo, U. San Diego, Hastings, Vienna Econ. U., Cologne, others; lectr. in field; mem. adv. bd. Tax Mgmt. Author: Federal Income Taxation of Individuals, (with Lathrope) 7th edit., 2004, Federal Estate and Gift Taxation, (with McCouch) 6th edit., 2003, Federal Income Taxation of S Corporations, 1992; (with Westin & Beck) Federal Income Taxation of Business Enterprises, 1995, 2d edit., 1999; mem. bd. overseers Berkeley Jour. Internat. Law. Guggenheim fellow, 1977 Mem. ABA, Am. Law Inst. (life), Internat. Fiscal Assn. (coun. U.S. br.), Order of Coif, Phi Beta Kappa. Home: 1176 Grizzly Peak Blvd Berkeley CA 94708-1741 Office: U Calif Sch Law 463 Boalt Hl Berkeley CA 94720-7200 Home Phone: 510-549-1750; Office Phone: 510-642-1928. Business E-Mail: jmcnulty@law.berkeley.edu.

MCNUTT, WALTER L., state legislator; b. Worland, Wyo., Nov. 8, 1940; m to Karen; children: two. Member, Solid Waste District Bd, Richland, currently, Montana Essential Air Serv Task Force, currently; Montana State Senator, District 50, 1997, chairman, Conf Committee & Select Committee on Const Amendments, formerly, vice chairman, Agriculture, Livestock & Irrigation Committees, formerly, member, Committee on Committees & Judiciary & Labor & Employ Relations Committees, formerly, Montana State Senate; Montana State Representative, District 37, 2005-, Montana House Representative.Agriculture implement dealer, Richland Develop Corp, currently; director, United Bank of Sidney, currently; member, Richland Airport Authority Bd, currently. Chamber of Commerce. Republican. Address: 110 12th Ave SW Sidney MT 59270-3614 Mailing: Mont Senate State Capitol PO Box 200400 Helena MT 59620 Office Phone: 406-444-4800. Office Fax: 406-444-4825. E-mail: walt@midrivers.com.*

MCPHERSON, BRUCE A., former state official, former state legislator; b. Santa Cruz, Jan. 7, 1944; m. Mary McPherson; children: Tori, Hunter (dec. 2001). Mem. Calif. State Assembly from 27th dist., 1993-96, Calif. State Senate from 15th dist, 1996—2004; vice-chair edn. com. Calif. State Senate from 15th dist., mem. appropriations com., environ. quality com., pub. safety com., revenue and taxation com.; sec. state State of Calif., Sacramento, 2005—07. Mem. joint coms. on arts, headwaters forest and fisheries/aquaculture. Active Santa Cruz City Sch. Dist.; active literacy program Santa Cruz County. Recipient Friend of Higher Edn. award Calif. State U. Alumni Coun., 1995, Simon Wiesenthal Mus. of Tolerance award, 1998; named Legislator of Yr., U. Calif. Alumni Assn., 1997, Pub. Ofcl. of Yr., Monterey Bay Nat. Marine Sanctuary Coun., 1997, 1998 Friend of C.C., Assn. Calif. C.C. Adminstrs., 1998. Mem. Calif. Coastal Conservancy, Santa Cruz Rotary Club (pres.). Republican.

MC PHERSON, ROLF KENNEDY, clergyman, religious organization administrator; b. Providence, Mar. 23, 1913; s. Harold S. and Aimee (Semple) McP.; m. Lorna De Smith, July 21, 1931 (dec.); children— Marlene (dec.), Kay; m. Evangeline Carmichael, Jan. 31, 1997. Grad., So. Cal. Radio Inst., 1933; D.D. (hon.), L.I.F.E. Bible Coll., 1944; LLD (hon.), L.I.F.E. Bible Coll., Los Angeles, 1988. Ordained to ministry Internat. Ch. Foursquare Gospel, 1940. Pres. Internat. Ch. Foursquare Gospel, LA, 1944-88, dir., 1944-92; pres. emeritus, 1988—; pres., dir. L.I.F.E. Bible Coll., Inc., LA, 1944-88. Mem. Echo Park Evangelistic Assn. (pres. 1944—). Mem. Internat. Ch. Foursquare Gospel. Office: Internat Ch Foursquare Gospel 1910 W Sunset Blvd Ste 200 Los Angeles CA 90026-3295 E-mail: drrolfe@pacbell.net.

MCPHERSON, SANDRA JEAN, poet, educator; b. San Jose, Calif., Aug. 2, 1943; d. John Emmet and Joyce (Turney) Todd, adopted d. Walter James and Frances K. (Gibson) McPherson; m. Henry D. Carlile, 1966 (div. 1985); 1 child, Phoebe; m. Walter D. Pavlich, 1995 (dec. 2002). BA in English, San Jose State U., Calif., 1965; postgrad., U. Wash., 1965-66. Vis. lectr. U. Iowa Writers Workshop, 1974-76,

78-80; Holloway lectr. U. Calif., Berkeley, 1981; tchr. poetry workshop Oreg. Writers Workshop, Portland, 1981-85; prof. English U. Calif., Davis, 1985—. Editor and pub. Swan Scythe Press. Author: (poetry) Elegies for the Hot Season, 1970, Radiation, 1973, The Year of Our Birth, 1978, Patron Happiness, 1983, Streamers, 1988, The God of Indeterminacy, 1993, The Spaces Between Birds: Mother/Daughter Poems, 1996, Edge Effect: Trails and portrayals, 1996, A Visit to Civilization, 2002. Recipient Nat. Endowment for the Arts awards; award in lit. Am. Acad. and Inst. Arts and Letters, 1987; Ingram Merrill Found. fellow; grantee Guggenheim Found., 1976, Oreg. Arts Commn., 1984-85. Democrat. Avocation: collector and exhibitor of African-Am. quilts. Office: Univ Calif Dept English 1 Shields Ave Dept English Davis CA 95616-5271

MCPHERSON, STEPHEN, broadcast executive; b. Pitts., Oct. 28, 1967; BA in Polit. Sci., Cornell U., 1986. Fgn. exchange trader Commodities Corp., NYC, 1986—91; dir. devel. Witt-Thomas Prodns., LA, 1991—93; dir. current programming Fox Broadcasting Co., LA, 1993—94; sr. v.p. creative affairs ABC Prodns., Burbank, Calif., 1994—95; v.p. Primetime Series NBC, Burbank, 1995—98; exec. v.p. Buena Vista Prodns. Walt Disney Co., 1998—2000, pres. Touchstone TV, 2000—04, pres. ABC Primetime Entertainment, 2004—. Recipient Diversity award, Director's Guild America, 2005; named a Maverick, Details mag., 2007. Office: ABC Entertainment 500 S Buena Vista St Burbank CA 91521

MCQUAID, ROBERT A., JR., federal judge; Apptd. magistrate judge U.S. Dist. Ct. Nev., 1996. Office: US Courthouse 400 S Virginia St Rm 405 Reno NV 89501-2193 Fax: 775-686-5865.

MCQUEEN, JUSTICE ELLIS (L. Q. JONES), actor, television director; b. Beaumont, Tex., Aug. 19, 1927; s. Justice Ellis and Pat (Stephens) McQ.; m. Sue Helen Lewis, Oct. 10, 1950 (dec.); children: Marlin Randolph, Marilyn Helen, Steven Lewis. Student, Lamar Jr. Coll., 1944, Lon Morris Coll., 1949, U. Tex., 1950-51. Actor, writer, dir.: motion picture films including A Boy and His Dog, 1975 (Hugo award, Sci. Fiction Achievement award for dramatic presentation, Golden Boot award, Internat. Star award, Reel Cowboys Silver Spur award, Western Walk of Fame); actor White Line Fever, 1975, Mother, Jugs & Speed, 1976, Winterhawk, 1976, Fast Charlie, The Moonbeam Rider, 1979, Timerider: The Adventures of Lyle Swann, 1982, The Beast Within, 1982, Sacred Ground, 1983, Lone Wolf McQuade, 1983, Bulletproof, 1988, River of Death, 1989, The Legend of Grizzly Adams, 1990, Lightning Jack, 1994, The Friends of Harry, 1995, Casino, 1995, Ben Johnson: Third Cowboy on the Right, 1996, The Edge, 1997, The Patriot, 1998, The Mask of Zorro, 1998, Route 666, 2001, Prairie Home Companion, 2006, numerous others; tv movies include The Sacketts, 1979, Tornado!, 1996, In Cold Blood, 1996, The Jack Bull, 1999, numerous others; appeared in tv series including Gunsmoke, 1955, Alias Smith and Jones, 1971, Cannon, 1971, Cade's County, 1971, Kung Fu, 1972, Matt Helm, 1975, Charlie's Angels, 1976, Columbo: The Conspirators, 1978, The Dukes of Hazzard, 1979, The Fall Guy, 1981, The Yellow Rose, 1983, The A-Team, 1983, Walker, Texas Ranger, 1993, numerous others; producer The Big Thickett, Come In, Children, The Witchmaker; author, prodr.: The Brotherhood of Satan, 1971; dir., prodr. The Devil's Bedroom, 1964, (tv series) The Incredible Hulk, 1978. Served with USNR, 1945-46. Nominee 4 Emmy awards. Mem. Screen Actors Guild, Dirs. Guild Am. Republican. Methodist. Home and Office: 2144 1/2 N Cahuenga Blvd Los Angeles CA 90068-2708 Office Phone: 323-465-4201, 325-465-4426.

MCQUILLEN, MICHAEL PAUL, neurologist, educator; b. NYC, Sept. 9, 1932; s. Paul and Dorothy Marian (Moore) McQ.; m. Louise Devlin; children: Daniel, Thomas, Patrick, Kathleen. BA cum laude, Georgetown U., 1953, MD, 1957; MA, U. Va., 1994. Diplomate Am. Bd. Psychiatry and Neurology (bd. dirs. 1991-95, exec. com. 1995), added qualification in clin. neurophysiology. Rotating intern Royal Victoria Hosp., Montreal, Que., Canada, 1957—58; resident in neurology Georgetown U. Med. Center, 1958—60; fellow in physiology Johns Hopkins U. Med. Sch. and Hosp., 1960—62, instr. medicine, 1962—65; mem. faculty U. Ky. Med. Center, 1965—74, prof. neurology, 1972—74, prof., chmn. neurology, 1987—93; prof. neurology, chmn. dept. Med. Coll. Wis., Milw., 1974—87; clin. faculty mem. dept. neurology U. Va. Health Sci. Ctr., Charlottesville, 1993—94; prof. neurology U. Rochester, NY, 1995—2005; clin. prof. neurology and neurol. scis. Stanford (Calif.) U., 2006—. Vis. sci. Inst. Neurophysiology U. Copenhagen, 1971-72; vis. prof. U. Ky. Med. Ctr., 1978, Royal Coll. Surgeons, Ireland, 1983. Contbr. articles to profl. jours. Mem. Cath. Commn. on Intellectual Affairs. Recipient Neurology medal Georgetown U. Med. Sch., 1957; Clin. Teaching award Med. Coll. Wis., 1976; Disting. Service award N.Y. Med. Coll., 1983; named to Johns Hopkins Soc. Scholars, 1981 Fellow Am. Acad. Neurology; mem. AMA, Royal Acad. Medicine Ireland, Nat. Myasthenia Gravis Found. (chmn. 1981-83), Am. Neurol. Assn., Wis. Neurol. Assn. (pres. 81-82), Alpha Omega Alpha. Office: Stanford Univ 300 Pasteur Dr Rm H3152 Stanford CA 94305 Home: 3611 Louis Rd Palo Alto CA 94303 Office Phone: 650-723-5297. Personal E-mail: michael_mcquillen@comcast.net. Business E-Mail: mmcquillen@stanfordmed.org.

MCREE, LISA, television host, producer; b. Ft. Worth; m. Don Granger. BA in Comm., U. Calif., San Diego. Co-anchor news broadcasts WFAA-TV, 1989-91; anchor Lifetime Mag. ABC News; reporter ABC News mag.; anchor World News Now ABC News, NYC, 1992-94; co-anchor news broadcasts KABC-TV Eyewitness News, LA, 1994-97; co-anchor Good Morning America ABC News, NYC, 1997-99; host & corr. California Connected, LA, 2002—. Recipient Alfred I DuPont-Columbia U. award, 2007, Nat. Headliner award for Documentary/Series, 2007.

MCREYNOLDS, NEIL LAWRENCE, management consultant; b. Seattle, July 27, 1934; s. Dorr E. and Margaret (Gillies) McR.; m. Nancy Joyce Drew, June 21, 1957; children: Christopher, Bonnie. BA in Journalism, U. Wash., 1956, postgrad. bus. and fin., 1973-76. Assoc. editor Bellevue (Wash.) Am., 1956-60, editor, 1960-67; press sec. to Gov. Dan Evans State of Wash., Olympia, 1967-73; N.W. regional mgr. for pub. rels. and pub. affairs ITT Corp., Seattle, 1973-80; v.p. corp. rels. Puget Sound Power & Light, Bellevue, 1980-87, sr. v.p., 1987-95; prin. McReynolds Assocs., Seattle, 1995-97; v.p. external affairs Kaiser/Group Health, Seattle, 1997-99; pres. McReynolds Assocs., Inc. (Donworth/McReynolds), Seattle, 1999—; strategic dir. Buerk Dale Victor, Seattle, 2002—. Bd. dirs. HomeStreet Bank, Seattle, 1986—, Eastern Wash. U., Cheney, 2000—; chmn. exec. adv. com. Edison Electric Inst., 1984—88; rsch. adv. coun. Electric Power Rsch. Inst., 1989—90; adj. prof. Grad. Sch. Bus. U. Wash., 2002—. Nat. pres. Electric Info. Coun., 1988; chmn. bd. trustees Bellevue CC, 1976—77; chmn. bd. dirs. Leadership Tomorrow, Seattle, 1987, Fred Hutchinson Cancer Rsch. Ctr., 1993—95, Seattle-King County Econ. Devel. Coun., 1994, Eastside Bus. Roundtable, Bellevue, 2003—04; pres. Seattle Ctr. Found., 1979—80, Horizon House, Seattle, 2007—; bd. dirs. Seattle Symphony, 1980—89, Ind. Colls. of Wash., 1984—95, Corp. Coun. for Arts, 1985—94, Mus. History and Industry, 1995—2006, Wash. Nat. Pks. Fund, 1995—2000, Seattle Repertory Theatre, 1996—2002, Wash. Dental Svc. Found., 2002—, United Way of King County, 2002—08; state chmn. Nature Conservancy, 1988—90; chmn. King County 2000, 1988—90; mem. Wash. State Commn. on Trial Cts., 1990; chair U. Wash. Bus. and Econ. Devel. Ctr., 1996—98. Named Citizen of Yr., Bellevue, One of Wash. State's Three Outstanding Young Men; recipient Pres. medal Pacific Luth. U. Mem. Pub. Rels. Soc. Am. (accredited; lifetime achievement award, 2003), N.W. Elec. Light and Power Assn. (pres. 1982-83), Greater Seattle C. of C. (officer 1979-81), Soc. Profl. Journalists, Rainier Club (trustee 1995-01, v.p. 1997-98, pres. 1999-2000), Heritage Soc. (pres. 2004-05, 2007-08), Overlake Golf and Country Club (trustee 1993-96), Rotary (pres. Downtown Seattle Club 1991-92). Episcopalian. Avocations: golf, hiking, skiing, photography, mountain climbing. Home: 14315 SE 45th St Bellevue WA 98006 Office Phone: 206-621-7272. Personal E-mail: nmcreyolds@seanet.com.

MC SHEFFREY, GERALD RAINEY, architect, educator, city planner, author; b. Belfast, Ireland, Aug. 13, 1931; s. Hugh and Jane (Piggot) McS.; m. Norma Isabella Lowry, June 4, 1956; children: Laurence, Niall, Aidan. Student, Belfast Coll. Tech., 1950-56; Diploma in Architecture, Univ. Coll., U. London, 1959; Diploma in Civic Design, U. Edinburgh, Scotland, 1963. Archtl. asst. various archtl. firms, Belfast, 1950-57; design architect Munce and Kennedy, Belfast, 1957-62; architect/planner Liverpool (Eng.) City Planning Dept. and Livingston New Town, 1963-65; asso. partner James Munce Partnership, Belfast, 1965-68; prin. planning officer (design) Belfast City Planning Dept., 1968-71; prof. architecture U. Kans., 1971-73, dir. archtl. studies, 1976-79; Belfast regional architect, dir. devel. No. Ireland Housing Exec., 1973-76; prof. architecture, dean Coll. Architecture, Planning and Design, Ill. Inst. Tech., 1979-82; dean Coll. Architecture and Environ. Design Ariz. State U., Tempe, 1982-86, prof. architecture, 1988-98; v.p. Ariz. State U., West Campus, Phoenix, 1985-88; prof. and dean emeritus, 1998—. Vis. fellow Princeton (N.J.) U., 1989; external examiner in urban design and landscape studies U. Edinburgh, 1973-76 Author: (with James Munce Partnership) Londonderry Area Plan, 1968, Planning Derry: Planning and Politics in Northern Ireland, 2000. Fulbright award, 1965 Fellow Royal Inst. Brit. Architects, Royal Town Planning Inst.; mem. AIA. Episcopalian.

MCSWEENEY, FRANCES KAYE, psychology professor; b. Rochester, NY, Feb. 6, 1948; d. Edward William and Elsie Winifred (Kingston) McSweeney. BA, Smith Coll., 1969; MA, Harvard U., 1972, PhD, 1974. Lectr. McMaster U., Hamilton, Ont., Canada, 1973—74; asst. prof. Wash. State U., Pullman, 1974—79, assoc. prof., 1979—83, prof. psychology, 1983—2004, Regents prof. psychology, 2004—, chmn. dept. psychology, 1986—94, vice provost for faculty affairs, 2003—. Cons. in field. Contbr. articles to profl. jours. Woodrow Wilson fellow, Sloan fellow, 1968—69, NIMH fellow, 1973. Fellow: APA, Assn. Behavior Analysis (pres. 2005—06), Assn. for Psychol. Sci.; mem.: Psychonomic Soc., Phi Kappa Phi, Sigma Xi, Phi Beta Kappa. Home: 860 SW Alcora Dr Pullman WA 99163-2053 Office: Wash State U Dept Psychology Pullman WA 99164-4820 Home Phone: 509-332-2320; Office Phone: 509-335-2738. Business E-Mail: fkmcs@wsu.edu.

MCTAGUE, JOHN PAUL, materials scientist, educator, chemist, researcher; b. Jersey City, Nov. 28, 1938; s. James Aloysius and Teresa Eugenia (Hanley) McT.; m. Carole Frances Reilly, Dec. 30, 1961 (dec. Jan. 1997); children: Kevin W., Catherine E., Margaret A., Maureen E.; m.Margaret Ann Danna, Oct. 15, 2004. BS in Chemistry with honors, Georgetown U., 1960; PhD in Phys. Chemistry, Brown U., 1965, DSc (hon.), 1997. Mem. tech. staff N.Am. Rockwell Sci. Ctr., Thousand Oaks, Calif., 1964—70; prof. chemistry, mem. Inst. Geophysics and Planetary Physics UCLA, 1970—82; chmn. Nat. Synchrotron Light Source Dept. Brookhaven Nat. Lab., 1983; dep. dir. Office Sci. and Tech. Policy, Exec. Office of Pres., Washington, 1983—86, acting sci. advisor to Pres. Reagan, 1986; v.p. rsch. Ford Motor Co., Dearborn, Mich., 1986—90, v.p. tech. affairs, 1990—99; v.p. lab. mgmt., Office of Pres. U. Calif., Oakland, 2001—03, prof. materials Santa Barbara, 2001—. Adj. prof. chemistry Columbia, U., 1982-83. Mem. Pres.'s Coun. Advisors on Sci. and Tech., 1990-93; mem. adv. bd. Sec. Energy, 1990—; chmn. bd. overseers Fermilab, 1994-99. Alfred P. Sloan Research fellow, 1971-73; NATO sr. fellow, 1973; John Simon Guggenheim Meml. fellow, 1975-76. Fellow AAAS, Am. Phys. Soc. (George E. Pake prize 1998), Calif. Coun. Sci. and Tech.; mem. Am. Chem. Soc. (Calif. sect. award 1975), Nat. Acad. Engring., Sigma Xi. Personal E-mail: jmctague1@aol.com.

MCVANEY, C. EDWARD, computer software executive; b. 1940; Ptnr. Alexander, Grant & Co.; co-founder, chmn. bd. dirs., CEO J.D. Edwards & Co., 1977—. Office: JD Edwards & Co One Technology Way Denver CO 80257

MCWILLIAMS, ROBERT HUGH, federal judge; b. Salina, Kans., Apr. 27, 1916; s. Robert Hugh and Laura (Nicholson) McW.; m. Catherine Ann Cooper, Nov. 4, 1942 (dec.); 1 son, Edward Cooper; m. Joan Harcourt, Mar. 8, 1986. AB, U. Denver, 1938, LL.B., 1941. Bar: Colo. bar 1941. Dep. dist. atty. Denver, Co, 1941—42; special agent US Office of Naval Intelligence, 1942—45; sgt. US Army, Office of Strategic Services, 1945—46; dist. atty. Denver, Co., 1946—49; private practice Denver, Co, 1949—52; judge municipal ct., Denver, 1949—52, dist., city, and county, Denver, 1952—61, supreme ct. of Co., 1967—70; instructor U. of Denver, 1954—60; judge US Ct. Appeals (10th cir.), Denver, 1970—84, sr. judge, 1984—. Served with AUS, World War II. Mem. Phi Beta Kappa, Omicron Delta Kappa, Phi Delta Phi, Kappa Sigma. Republican. Episcopalian. Home: 137 Jersey St Denver CO 80220-5918 Office: Byron White US Courthouse 1823 Stout St Rm 216 Denver CO 80257-1823

MCWRIGHT, MICHAEL J., historic site administrator; b. Mandan, ND, July 5, 1950; Mem. pk. svc. staff Colo. region, 1974-75; facility mgr. Grant-Kohrs Ranch Nat. Hist. Site, Deerlodge, Mont., 1975—. Office: 266 Warren LN Deer Lodge MT 59722-1002

MEAD, CARVER ANDRESS, computer science educator emeritus; b. Bakersfield, Calif., May 1, 1934; BS, Calif. Inst. Tech., 1956, MS, 1957, PhD, 1960; doctorate (hon.), U. Lund, 1987, U. So. Calif., 1991. Instructor inelec. engring. Calif. Inst. Tech., Pasadena, 1958—59, prof. engring. and applied sci., 1959—, Gordon and Betty Moore prof. engring. and applied sci., 1980-99, Gordon and Betty Moore prof. engring./applied sci. emeritus, 1999—. Founder Actel Corp., Silicone Compilers, Synaptics, Sonic Innovations; founder, chmn. Foveon. Author: Introduction to VLSI Systems, 1979 (Electronic Achievements award 1981, Harold Pender award 1984, John Price Wetherhill award 1985), Analog VLSI and Neural Systems, 1989, Collective Electrodynamics, 2000. Recipient T.D. Callinan award Electrochem. Soc., 1971, Centennial medal IEEE, 1984, Harry Goode Meml. award Am. Fedn. Info. Processing Socs., Inc., 1985, award for Outstanding Rsch., INNS, 1992, Robert Dexter Conrad award USN, 1994, Phil Kaufman award EDAC, 1995, Allen Newell award ACM, 1997, Lemelson-MIT award, 1999, Nat. Medal Tech., US Dept. Commerce, 2002, Fellow award, Computer History Mus., 2002. Fellow IEEE (John von Neumann medal 1996), Am. Phys. Soc., Franklin Inst. (life), Am. Acad. Arts and Scis.; mem. NAE (Founders Award, 2003), NAS, Royal Swedish Acad. Engring. Sci. (fgn.), Sigma Xi. Achievements include spearheading the development of tools and techniques for modern integrated-circuit design; laying the foundation for fabless semiconductor companies; catalyzing the electronic-design automation field; built the first GaAs MESFET; first to use a physics-based analysis to predict a lower limit to transistor size; developed the first techniques for designing big, complex microchips; created the first software compilation of a silicon chip; created the first neurally inspired chips, including silicon retina and chips that learn from experience; patents in field. Office: Calif Inst Tech Computer Sci MC 256-80 204 Jorgensen 1200 E California Blvd Pasadena CA 91125 Office Phone: 626-395-2814.

MEAD, MATTHEW HANSEN, rancher, former prosecutor; b. Jackson, Wyo., 1962; s. Peter and Mary (Hansen) Mead; m. Carol Mead; 2 children. BA, Trinity U., San Antonio, Tex., 1984; JD, U. Wyo. Sch. Law, 1987. Dep. county atty. Cambell Co. Atty Office, Wyo., 1987—90; asst. US atty. US Dept. Justice, 1991—95; pvt. law practice Cheyenne, 1995—97; ptnr. Mead & Phillips, 1997—2001; US atty. dist. Wyo. US Dept. Justice, 2001—07; owner Mead Land & Livestock, LLC. Bd. dirs. Wyo. Bank & Trust. Office: Mead Land & Livestock LLC 6583 Red Cloud Trail Cheyenne WY 82009

MEAD, TRAY C., museum director; b. Mesa, Ariz., Apr. 1, 1950; s. Norman Wesley and Peggy Lee (Barrows) M.; Barbara Celaya, Feb. 9, 1981; children: Michael Adam, Kristiana Nicole. BA in Edn., Ariz. State U., 1973. Cert. tchr., Ariz. Publisher Ariz. Northland Mag., Flagstaff, 1973-77; mus. dir. Mesa Southwest Mus., 1977—. Founding dir. Ariz. Fed. Credit Union, Phoenix, 1980-85. Author: Mesa, Beneath the Superstitions, 1988, Sirrine House Story, 1992; editor: Mesa Grande, 1979, Capturing the Canyon, 1987; field editor Ariz. White Mountain Mag., 1965—; contbg. editor Tonto Trails Mag., 1970—. Founding dir. Mesa Conv. and Tourism Bureau, 1989—; founding chmn. S.W. Svc. Corp., Phoenix, 1981-85; bd. dirs., founding pres. Arts in Mesa, 1980—. Recipient Excellence award Centennial Com., 1978, Golden Quill award Caligraphic Soc. Ariz., 1987, Native Am. Heritage award U.S.M.C. Netherlands, 1991; named Hon. Medicine Man, Ft. Apache Tribe, 1973, Hon. Chmn. Mesa Parade, Mayor City of Mesa, 1980. Mem. Nat. Trust Hist. Preservation, Am. Assn. State and Local Histories, Am. Assn. Mus., Mus. Assn. Ariz. (founding mem., v.p. 1982—), Ctrl. Ariz. Mus. Assn. (founding pres. 1978—), Mesa C. of C. (com. chmn. 1979-89). Avocations: sculpting, painting, hiking, reading. Home: 370 E Pinon Way Gilbert AZ 85234-4573 Office: Mesa Southwest Mus 53 North MacDonald Dr Mesa AZ 85201-7325

MEAD, WILLIAM CHARLES, physicist; b. Hazleton, Pa., Dec. 6, 1946; s. Norman Joseph and Ruth Crawford Mead; m. Carol Edna Jerome, May 24, 1969; 1 child, Bennett R. BS, Syracuse U., Syracuse, NY, 1968; MA, Princeton U., Princeton, NJ, 1970, PhD, 1974. Physicist Lawrence Livermore Nat. Lab., 1973—83; physicist, mgr. Los Alamos Nat. Lab., 1983—94; pres., chief scientist Adaptive Network Solutions Rsch. Inc., 1995—. Cons. Lawrence Livermore Nat. Lab., Livermore, Calif., 1995—99, Whistlesoft, Inc., Los Alamos, N.Mex., 1996—98, Ctr. for Adaptive Sys. Applications, Inc., Los Alamos, N.Mex., 1999, Complexica, Inc., Santa Fe, 1999—2004, Impulse Devices Inc., Grass Valley, Calif., 1999—2003, Los Alamos (N.Mex.) Nat. Lab., 2000—03, Gen. Fusion, Inc., 2003, Environ. Safety Svcs., 2004—06. Contbr. articles to profl. jours. Second lt. USAF, 1973—73. Fellow: Am. Phys. Soc. (fellowship 1987); mem.: Internat. Neural Network Soc. Achievements include being head designer for Cairn 50X Intermediate density target, the first laser-driven target to achieve compression of DT to 10 g/cc and a major milestone of the Inertial Confinement Fusion Program; designed and developed C++ engine for Agent-Based Crisis Simulator; development of the Connectionist Hyperprism Classification network to perform task of automated ion mobility spectrum analysis; Adaptive Teaching and Learning Lab. and an Adaptive Tutor for teaching basic arithmetic facts; research in theoretical and computational effort to explore feasibility of Sonic-Cavitation-Driven Fusion; numerical simulations extending knowledge in areas such as the behavior of fluid instabilities in high-gain ICF pellets and the scaling of laser-driven ablation; testing and extending the understanding of ICF physics, providing ideas, simulations and guidance for laser-plasma coupling experiments. Avocations: classical music, photography. Office: Adaptive Network Solutions Research 10 Bonito Pl Los Alamos NM 87544

MEADOR, ROSS DESHONG, lawyer; b. Mexico City, Aug. 23, 1954; s. Bruce Staffel and Betty Lee M.; m. Michelle Hyunae Chang, Mar. 14, 1997; children: Amy Chang, Leah Chang, Daniel Ross. BA in Comm. and Visual Arts, U. Calif., San Diego, 1980; JD, U. Calif., Berkeley, 1986. Bar: Calif. Co-dir. Overseas Operations Friends of Children of Vietnam, 1974—75; atty. Morrison & Foerster, San Francisco, 1986—89; fgn. legal advisor Kim & Chang, Seoul, 1989—95, Soewito, Suhardiman, Eddymurthy & Kardono, Jakarta, Indonesia, 1996—97; of counsel Morrison & Foerster, 1997—99, Howard, Rice et al, 2000; ptnr. Preston Gates & Ellis, 2001—02, Rogers & Meador, 2003—; internat. legal adv. Vietnam Internat. Law Firm, 2005—. Photographer Escape From Saigon, Gerald Ford Presdl. Mus. Permanent Collection; one man shows include U. Calif. San Diego, 1980; exec. editor Internat. Tax & Bus. Lawyer, 1985-86. Nominee Presdl. Medal of Freedom, 2005. Mem.: Am. C. of C. Vietnam, Calif. Bar Assn. (mem. exec. com. internat. law sect. 2001—04, sec. 2004—05, advisory emeritus 2006—). Avocations: travel, photography. Home: 1270 Campus Dr Berkeley CA 94708-2045

MEADOWS, JUDITH ADAMS, law librarian, educator; b. Spartanburg, SC, June 5, 1945; d. Thomas Taylor and Virginia (Dayton) Adams; m. Bruce R. Meadows; children: Beth Ann Blackwood, Ted

Adams Meadows. BA, Am. U., 1967; MLS, U. Md., College Park, 1979. Law libr. Aspen Sys. Corp., Gaithersburg, Md., 1979-81; dir. Fairfax (Va.) Law Libr., 1981-84, State Law Libr., Helena, Mont., 1984—. Vis. prof. U. Wash., Seattle, 1994; adj. prof. U. Great Falls, Mont., 1989-96; presiding ofcl. Gov.'s Conf. on Libr. Info. Svc., Helena, Mont., 1991; cons. Nat. Ctr. for State Cts., 2000—. Author: (book chpts.) From Yellow Pads to Computers, 1991, Law Librarianship, 1994, Encyclopedia of Library and Information Science, 2009; contbr. articles to profl. jours. Bd. dirs. Helena Presents, 1986-92, Holter Mus. Art, 1995-2002, Mont. Supreme Ct. Commn. on Tech., Mont. Equal Justice Task Force, 2001-; bd. dirs. Helena Edn. Found., v.p., 2003, pres. 2005-06; chair Mont. Supreme Ct. Commn. on Self-Represented Litigants, 2004—; mem. Mont. Commn. Continuing Legal Edn., 2006—. Recipient Disting. Svc. award State Bar of Mont., 1991, Pro Bono Pub. award, 2002. Mem. Am. Assn. Law Librs. (treas. 1992-95, v.p. 1996—, pres. 1997-98, past pres. 1998—), N.W. Consortium of Law Librs. (pres.), Mont. Libr. Assn. (sec. 1986-88). Office: State Law Libr Mont PO Box 203004 Helena MT 59620-3004

MEALS, PAMELA F., publishing executive; b. Ill. 1 child, Laura. Student, We. Oreg. State Coll. With advtsg. The Oreg. Statesman and Capital Jour., Salem; advtsg. mgr. The Idaho Statesman, Boise, 1979, pres., publ., 1994-99; publ. Coffeyville (Kans.) Jour., 1979-82, The Palladium-Item, Richmond, Ind., 1982-85, The Olympian, Olympia, Wash., 1985-94, Bellingham Herald, Bellingham, Wash., 1999—. Bd. dirs. Boise Pub. Schs. Edn. Found., Idaho Shakespeare Festival, Albertson Coll. Annual Fund, FUNDSY, William Allen White Found. Mem. Boise Area C. of C. (bd. dirs.), Rotary Club, Idaho Bus. Coun., Pacific N.W. Newspaper Assn. (bd. dirs.), Newspaper Assn. Am. Office: The Bellingham Herald 1155 N State St Ste 1 Bellingham WA 98225-5086

MEANS, JAMES ANDREW, retired engineer; b. Heavener, Okla., Oct. 11, 1937; s. Edward Andrew and Lorena (Nobles) M.; Therese Louise Zimmermann, Feb. 21, 1959; children: James A. Jr., William R., Charles E., Vicky M. BSEE, U. Ariz., 1962, MSEE, 1966; PhD, U. Calif., Santa Barbara, 1972; MS in Computer Sci., Chapman U., Orange, Calif., 1988. Engr. Pacific Missile Test Ctr., Pt Mugu, Calif., 1962-72, engr. mgr., 1972-79; tech. dir. Space and Missile Test Orgn., Vandenberg AFB, Calif., 1979-89; sr. tech. advisor SRI Internat., Menlo Park, Calif., 1990—2006. Cons. Agri-Craft, Camarillo, Calif., 1968-70, Astro-Geo-Marine, Ventura, Calif., 1972-74; pres. Internat. Found. for Telemetering, 1989-95. Patentee in field. Recipient Allen R. Matthews award, Internat. Test and Evaluation Assn., 1991, Pioneer award, Internat. Found. Telemetering, 2006. Democrat. Baptist. Avocations: water-skiing, fishing, hunting, old cars. Home: 284 St Andrews Way Lompoc CA 93436-1355 Personal E-mail: jim_means@verizon.net.

MEAUX, ALAN DOUGLAS, facilities technician, artist; b. Joliet, Ill., Sept. 10, 1951; s. Berry Lee and Luella Ann (Ferguson) M.; m. Letta Sue Nygaard, Sept. 15, 1984; children: Ashley Nicole, Lacey Marie. Student, Joliet Jr. Coll., 1969-71, Bradley U., 1971-72, U.S. Dept. Agr. Grad. Sch., 1972, Skagit Valley Coll., 1983-85. Cert. specialist water distbn. Wash. state, 2002, Wash. state, 2003. Photographer J.J.C. Blazer, Joliet Herald News, Joliet, 1969-71; auto mechanic Pohanka Olds and Fiat, Hillcrest Heights, Md., 1972-74, Hoffman Olds and Rolls Royce, Hartford, Conn., 1974-75; carpenter Klappenbach Constrn. Co., Moscow, Idaho, 1975-79; property mgr. Olympic Builders, Oak Harbor, Wash., 1979-86; maintenance technician Troubleshooters Inc., Oak Harbor, 1986-87; facilities technician Island County Govt., Coupeville, Wash., 1987—. Chmn. safety com. Island County Govt., 1997, 98, 99, 2000, 03; bronze sculptor Ronin Art Prodns., Oak Harbor, 1979—; appraiser class A Mid-Am. Appraisers Assn., Springfield, Mo., 1986—; bd. dirs. North West Token Kai, U. Wash., Seattle, 1989—, lectr., 1985; contbr. Nanka Token Kai, L.A., 1985-. Author: Japanese Samurai Weapons, 1989; prin. works exhibited at Mini Guild Children's Orthopedic Show, Ballard, Wash., 1986, Worldfest/Ethnic Heritage Coun., Seattle, 1988, 89, 90, Stanwood (Wash.) Invitational Art Show, 1988. Asst. coach Whidbey Islanders Soccer League, 1997-99; safety com. chmn. Island County Govt., 1998-2003. Mem. NRA (life), Law Enforcement Alliance Am. (life), Japanese Sword Soc. U.S. (life), N.W. Token Kai (charter, bd. dirs. 1989-91), Western Mus. Conf., Wash. Mus. Assn., Ethnic Heritage Coun., Nanka Token Kai, Japan Soc., Wash. Arms Collectors Assn., North Whidbey Sportmen's Assn. (chmn. range com., trustee), Leisure Acres Water Assn. (pres. 1998-2000), Internat. Defensive Pistol Assn., Ctrl. Whidbey Sportmen's Club, Whidbey Islanders Futbol Club (asst. coach for girls under 12, 1997-99). Avocations: hunting, fishing, woodworking, reading, collecting Japanese antiques. Office: Ronin Art Prodns 1287 E Hideaway Ln Oak Harbor WA 98277

MEBANE, JULIE S., lawyer; b. San Antonio, Mar. 13, 1957; d. John Cummins and Mildred (Hill) Mebane; m. Kenneth Jerome Stipanov, Jan. 21, 1984; children: Thomas Kenneth Stipanov, Kristen Hill Stipanov. BA in Polit. Sci., UCLA, 1978, JD, 1981. Bar: Calif. 1981, U.S. Dist. Ct. (so. dist.) Calif. 1981. Assoc. Gray, Cary, Ames & Frye, San Diego, 1981-85, Sheppard, Mullin, Richter & Hampton, San Diego, 1986-90; ptnr. Scalone, Stipanov, Yaffa & Mebane, San Diego, 1990-94, Stipanov & Mebane, San Diego, 1994—2004, Duane Morris LLP, San Diego, 2005—. Panelist Calif. Continuing Edn. Bar, 2000—01, Lorman Edn. Svcs., 2006—07. Bd. dirs. Episcopal Diocese San Diego, 1992—95, Francis Parker Sch., 2003—. Mem.: San Diego Lawyers Club, San Diego County Bar Assn., ABA, Nat. Assn. Women Bus. Owners (bd. dirs. San Diego chpt. 1996—97), UCLA Alumni Assn. (gen. counsel, bd. dirs. 1992—96), Phi Beta Kappa, Kappa Alpha Theta. Avocations: sports, travel. Office: Duane Morris LLP 101 W Broadway Ste 900 San Diego CA 92101-3544 Office Phone: 619-744-2211. Business E-Mail: jmebane@duanemorris.com.

MECHANIC, WILLIAM M., former television and motion picture industry executive; b. Detroit; BA in English, Mich. State U.; PhD in Film, U. So. Calif. Dir. programming SelecTV, 1978—80, v.p. programming, 1980—82; v.p. pay TV Paramount Pictures Corp., 1982—84; v.p. pay TV sales Walt Disney Pictures and TV, 1984—85, sr. v.p. video, 1985—87, pres. internat. theatrical distbn. and worldwide video, 1987—93; pres., COO 20th Century Fox Film Entertainment, 1993—96, chmn., CEO, 1996—2000.

MECKEL, PETER TIMOTHY, arts administrator, educator; b. Yankton, SD, Nov. 28, 1941; s. Myron Eugene and Cynthia Ann (Turnblom) Meckel; m. Louise Gloria Mudge, Sept. 8, 1962; children: Christina Louise, Christopher Mark; m. Adrienne Dawn Maravich, Dec. 30, 1972; children: Moya Ann, Jon-Peter. Student, Rockford Coll., Occidental Coll. Founder, gen. dir. Hidden Valley Music Seminars, Carmel Valley, Calif., 1963—; dir. Hidden Valley Opera Ensemble, Masters Festival of Chamber Music, Master Class Series. Cons. in field. Mem. Music Educators Nat. Conf. Congregationalist. Office: Hidden Valley Opera Ensemble PO Box 116 Carmel Valley CA 93924-0116 Office Phone: 831-659-3115. E-mail: hvms@aol.com.

MEDAK, PETER, film director; b. Budapest, Hungary; arrived in Eng., 1956; came to U.S., 1979; s. Gyula and Elisabeth (Diamonstein) M.; m. Julia Migenes, July 31, 1989 (div. 2004); children: Christopher, Karen, Joshua, Cornelia, Martina, Jessica. Dir. (films) Negatives, 1968, A Day in the Death of Joe Egg, 1970, The Ruling Class, 1971, Ghost in a Nonnday's Sun, 1973, The Odd Job, 1977, The Changling, 1979, Zorro the Gay Blade, 1980, The Men's Club, 1986, The Krays, 1989, La Voix Humane, 1990, Let Him Have It, 1991, Romeo is Bleeding, 1992, Pontiac Moon, 1994, Hunchback of Notre Dame, 1996, Species 2, 1997, David Copperfield, 1998-99, Feast of All Saints, 2000, (stage) Miss Julie, 1977 (opera) Salome, 1988, La Voix Humane, and others. Mem. Dir.'s Guild of Am., Dir.'s Guild of U.K., Assn. of Cinematographers, Allied Technicians, Dir.'s Guild of Can. Jewish. Office: George Harvey's Office 10100 Santa Monila Blvd Los Angeles CA 90067

MEDAK, SUSAN LEE, performing company executive; b. Chgo., Dec. 30, 1953; d. Herman and Vivian Hannah (Fried); m. Gregory Scott Murphy, Aug. 1, 1982. BA cum laude, Lawrence U., 1976. Tour asst. The Guthrie Theater, Mpls., 1974; regional svcs. dir. Milw. Repertory Theatre, 1976-80, dir. audience devel., 1980-83; mng. dir. The People's Light and Theatre Co., Malvern, Pa., 1983-84, Northlight Theatre, Evanston, Ill., 1984—, Berkeley Repertory Theatre, 1990—. Sec. League of Resident Theatres, 1988; treas. League of Chgo. Theatres, Chgo., 1987-89. Adv. bd. Evanston Jr. League, 1988—, Cameron Kravit Found. of Evanston Hosp., 1989—. Office: Berkeley Repertory Theatre 2025 Addison St Berkeley CA 94704

MEDOFF, MARK HOWARD, playwright, scriptwriter; b. Mt. Carmel, Ill., Mar. 18, 1940; s. Lawrence Ray and Thelma Irene (Butt) M.; m. Stephanie Thorne, June 24, 1972; children: Debra, Rachel, Jessica. BA, U. Miami, 1962; MA, Stanford U., 1966; DHL, Gallaudet Coll., 1981. Instr. English and drama N.Mex. State U., 1966-79, dramatist-in-residence, 1974—, head dept. drama, 1978-87, prof. drama, 1979-93, artistic dir., 1982-87, Am. S.W. Theatre Co., 1984-87. Artistic dir. Creative Media Inst. N.Mex. State U., 2006. Author: (plays) When You Comin' Back, Red Ryder?, 1974, The Wager, 1975, The Kramer, 1975, The Halloween Bandit, 1978, The Conversion of Aaron Weiss, 1978, Firekeeper, 1978, The Last Chance Saloon, 1979, Children of a Lesser God, 1980 (Soc. West Theatres best play award 1982), The Majestic Kid, 1981, The Hands of Its Enemy, 1984, Kringle's Window, 1985, The Heart Outright, 1986, Road to a Revolution, 2001, Prymate, 2004, The Same Live Over, 2004, (novel) Dreams of Long Lasting; (films) When You Comin' Back, Red Ryder?, 1979, Off Beat, 1986, Apology, 1986, Children of a Lesser God, 1986, Good Guys Wear Black, 1978, Clara's Heart, 1988, The Majestic Kid, 1988, City of Joy, 1992, Homage, 1995, Santa Fe, 1997, Who Fly On Angel's Wings, 2000, Children On Their Birthdays, 2002, 100 MPG, 2006; works appear in Best Plays, 1973-74, 75-75, 79-80, Best Short Plays, 1975, The Homage that Follows, 1987; plays Stumps, 1989, Stefanie Hero, 1990, Showdown On Rio Road, 1995, Gila, 1995, A Christmas Carousel, 1996, Crunch Time, 1996, Gunfighters, A Gulf War Chronicle, 1997, A Christmas Carousel, 1998, Tommy J and Sally, 2000, Prymate, 2004; dir. (film) Children on Their Birthdays. Guggenheim fellow, 1974-75; recipient Obie award, Drama Desk award, Outer Critics Circle award, Media award Pres.'s Com. Employment Handicapped, Tony award, Kennedy Ctr. medal Excellence in Edn. and Artistic Achievement, 2006; Oscar award nominee for Best Screenplay for Children of A Lesser God, 1987; Reynolds Eminent scholar Fla. State U., 2003-06, Artistic Dir. Creative Media Inst N.Mex. State U., 2006-. Mem. SAG, Coll. Fellows Am. Theater, Dramatists Guild, Writers Guild Am., Actors Equity Assn., PEN, Coll. Fellows of the Am. Theatre.

MEDVED, MICHAEL, film critic, author, talk show host; b. Phila., Oct. 3, 1948; s. David Bernard and Renate Rosa (Hirsch) M.; m. Nancy Harris Herman, Aug. 5, 1972 (div. 1983); m. Diane Elvenstar, Jan. 27, 1985; children: Sarah Julia, Shayna Elana, Daniel Joshua. BA, Yale U., 1969; MFA, Calif. State U., San Francisco, 1974. Speech writer, polit. cons. various campaigns and politicians, Conn., Calif., D.C., 1970-73; advt. creative dir. Anrick Inc., Oakland, Calif., 1973-74; freelance writer LA, 1974—; on-air film critic People Now, Cable News Network, LA, 1980-83; on-air film critic, co-host Sneak Previews PBS, 1985-96; chief film critic N.Y. Post, 1993-98; Hollywood corr. The Sunday Times of London; nationally syndicated radio talk show host Salem Radio Network, Seattle, 1998—. Radio talk show host KVI AM, Seattle, 1996—98; critic The Worst of Hollywood Channel 4, England, 1982. Author: What Really Happened to the Class of '65?, 1976, The Shadow Presidents, 1979, Hospital, 1983, Hollywood vs. America, 1992; co-author: (with Harry Medved) The 50 Worst Films of All Time, 1978, The Golden Turkey Awards, 1980, The Hollywood Hall of Shame, 1984, Son of Golden Turkey Awards, 1986, (with Diane Medved) Saving Childhood, 1998. Co-founder, pres. Pacific Jewish Ctr., Venice, Calif., 1977-94; pres. Emanuel Streisand Sch., Venice, 1980-85. Mem. Writers Guild Am., AFTRA. Avocation: classical music. Office: 509 Olive Way Ste 852 Seattle WA 98101

MEDVED, ROBERT ALLEN, lawyer; b. Cleve., July 22, 1945; s. Joseph Jack and Mary (Blasko) Medved. BBA, Kent State U., 1968; JD cum laude, Seattle U., 1975. Bar: Wash. 1976, US Ct. Appeals (9th cir.) 1976, US Dist. Ct. (we. dist.) Wash. 1976, US Dist. Ct. (ea. dist.) Wash. 1979, US Supreme Ct. 1981, US Ct. Appeals (DC cir.) 1989. Fin. analyst Ford Motor Co., Sandusky, Ohio, 1972; rsch. asst. Seattle U., 1973—75; law clk Judge U.S. Ct. Appeals (9th cir.), 1974; asst. to labor arbitrator Tacoma, 1975; law clk. to Judge U. S. Dist. Ct. (ctrl. dist.) Calif., 1976; assoc. Graham & Dunn, Seattle, 1976—81, ptnr., 1981—82, Drake and Whiteley, Bellevue, Wash., 1982—86, Foster, Pepper & Shefelman, Seattle, 1986—97; pvt. practice Mercer Island, 1997—. Spl. dist. counsel 8th Congl. Dist., Wash., 1983—86. Editor-in-chief: Seattle U. Law Rev. Bd. dirs. Bellevue CC found., 1986—98. Lt. USN, 1968—71. Seattle U. scholar, 1974. Mem.: Wash. State Bar Assn., Fed. Bar Assn. (chair intellectual property com.). Roman Catholic. Office: 7238 SE 32nd St Mercer Island WA 98040-2641 Office Phone: 206-232-5800. Business E-Mail: bob@ramedved.com.

MEEHAN, MICHAEL JOSEPH, lawyer; b. St. Louis, Aug. 28, 1942; s. Joseph Michael and Frances (Taylor) M.; m. Sharon Kay McHenry (div. 1988); m. Patricia Ann Shive, July 8, 1989 (dec. 1999); m. Shelley Fujiko Lee, 2002. BS in Engring., U.S. Coast Guard Acad., 1964; JD with high distinction, U. Ariz., 1971. Bar: Ariz. 1971, US Ct. Appeals (6th, 8th, 9th and 10th cirs.), US Supreme Ct. 1975. Law clk. Assoc. Justice William H. Rehnquist, US Supreme Ct., 1972; assoc. Molloy, Jones & Donahue, P.C., Tucson, 1971-75, shareholder, 1975-93; chmn. exec. com., head trial dept., 1986-93; founder Meehan & Assocs., Tucson, 1993-2001; ptnr. Quarles & Brady/Striech Long, Tucson, 2001—03; pvt. practice Tucson, 2003—; of counsel Munger Chadwick P.L.C., Tucson, 2006—. Mem. fed. appellate rules adv. com. Jud. Conf. US, 1994-99; mem. adv. bd. William H. Reinquist Ctr. Constl. Structures Govt., 2006—. Author chpt. on appellate advocacy: State Bar of Arizona Appellate Practice Handbook. Fellow Am. Acad. Appellate Lawyers (past pres.); mem. Am. Law Inst., Ariz. Bar Assn. (past chair appellate practice sect. 1999-00), Nat. Conf. Appellate Justice (mem. steering com. 2005). Lutheran. Avocation: golf. Office: Munger Chadwick PLC 333 North Wilmot Rd Ste 300 Tucson AZ 85711 Office Phone: 520-721-1900. Business E-Mail: mmeehan@mungerchadwick.com.

MEEKER, ROBERT ELDON, retired manufacturing company executive; b. Moline, Ill., Sept. 6, 1930; s. Paul Edwin and Esther (Carlson) M.; m. Dorothy Elaine Nelson, Dec. 23, 1951; children: Julie Lynn Meeker Gratton, Laurie Allison Meeker Gamel, Bradford Nelson (dec.). BS in Chemistry, Ill. Wesleyan U., 1952; PhD in Phys. Chemistry, Northwestern U., 1955. Chemist, supr. Shell Devel. Co., Emeryville, Calif., 1955-64; mgr.-dir. synthetic rubber tech. ctr. Shell Chem. Co., Torrance, Calif., 1964-66, mgr. new projects NYC, 1966-69; dir. exploratory sci., exploration and prodn. rsch. ctr. Shell Devel. Co., Houston, 1969-71; gen. mgr., head new enterprises divsn. Royal Dutch-Shell Co., London, 1971-72; v.p. comml., gen. mgr. Billiton Aluminum B.V. Billiton Internat. Metals subs. Shell Co., The Hague, Netherlands, 1972-74; pres. Roxana Shale Oil Co. subs. Shell Co., Houston, 1974-76; v.p., gen. mgr. energy systems mgmt. divsn. TRW, Inc., Redondo Beach, Calif., 1976-80, v.p., gen. mgr. maj. programs, 1980-86; pvt. practice cons., real estate investor Tucson, 1986-94. Trustee Ill. Wesleyan U., Bloomington, 1982-94, trustee emeritus, 1994—; v.p., bd. dirs. Cobblestone Homeowners Assn., 1991-92, pres. bd. dirs., 1992-94, security chmn., 1994-97. Recipient Disting. Alumnus award, Ill. Wesleyan U., 1981. Mem. Am. Parkinson Disease Assn. Inc. (pres. Ariz. chpt. 1996-2000, nat. bd. dirs. 1996—), Mercedes Benz Club Am. (pres. Chaparral sect. 1992-94). Republican. Lutheran. Achievements include patents in field. Avocations: photography, swimming, travel. Home: 7900 N La Canada Dr Apt 2218 Tucson AZ 85704-2081 Office Phone: 520-577-2760. E-mail: remeeker@theriver.com.

MEEKINS, DEBORAH, bank executive; b. 1953; 2 children. Pres., CEO Sonoma Nat. Bank, Santa Rosa, Calif., 1991—. Bd. mem. Western Ind. Bankers, Cmty. Bankers. Bd. mem. Santa Rose Jr. Coll. Found., Santa Rosa Meml. Hosp. Found., United Way, Santa Rosa Chamber of Commerce. Named one of 25 Women to Watch, US Banker, 2006. Achievements include first woman Sonoma County Bank Pres. Office: Sonoma National Bank 801 Fourth St Santa Rosa CA 95404

MEENAN, ALAN JOHN, clergyman, theology studies educator; b. Belfast, No. Ireland, Feb. 7, 1946; arrived in US, 1970, naturalized, 2001; s. John and Elizabeth (Holland) M.; m. Vicky Lee Woodall, May 6, 1974; children: Kelly Elizabeth, Katie Michelle, Kimberly Brooke. BA, Queen's U., Belfast, 1970; MDiv, Asbury Theol. Sem., Wilmore, Ky., 1972, ThM, 1975; PhD, Edinburgh U., 1981. Ordained to ministry Presbyn. Ch., U.S.A., 1973. Pastor Wilmore Presbyn. Ch., 1972-74; asst. pastor St. Giles' Cathedral, Edinburgh, 1974-77; sr. pastor 3d Presbyn. Ch., Richmond, Va., 1977—84, Canoga Park Presbyn. Ch., Calif., 1984-89, First Presbyn. Ch., Amarillo, Tex., 1989-97, Hollywood Presbyn. Ch., Calif., 1997—2005; founder, pres. The Word Is Out Internat., LA, 2005. Vis. lectr. Nairobi Grad. Sch. Theology, Kenya, 1983, 89; adj. prof. W. Africa Theol. Sem., Lagos, Nigeria, 2004-. Contbr. revs. to religious publs., including Asbury Bible Commentary. Tchr. Chogoria High Sch., Meru, Keyna, 1965-66. Yale U. rsch. fellow, 1976—77. Mem. Tyndale Fellowship for Bibl. Rsch., Theta Phi. Avocations: travel, photography, reading, swimming, squash racquets. Office: 11271 Ventura Blvd Ste 509 Studio City CA 91604 Office Phone: 323-969-9090.

MEER, JON DOUGLAS, lawyer; b. Amherst, NY, Dec. 8, 1963; s. Ronald Lewis and Sharon (Fisher) M. BS with honors, Cornell U., 1986; JD, Boston U., 1989. Bar: Calif. 1989, US Dist Ct. (no. & ctrl. dist Calif., Nev., ea. dist Mich.), US Ct. Appeals (6th, 9th cir.). Assoc. Paul, Hastings, Janofsky & Walker, LA; atty. Akin, Gump, Strauss, Hauer & Feld LLP, LA; ptnr., chmn. LA sect. Labor & Employment practice DLA Piper Rudnick Gray Cary, LA, 2002—. Lectr. Lawyer in Classroom prog., Constitutional Rights Found. Named a So. Calif. Super Lawyer, LA Mag., 2004. Mem. ABA, LA County Bar Assn., Beverly Hills Bar Assn., Phi Kappa Phi, Phi Eta Sigma. Office: DLA Piper Rudnick Gray Cary 4th Fl 1999 Ave of the Stars Los Angeles CA 90067-6022 Office Phone: 310-595-3004. Office Fax: 310-595-3304. Business E-Mail: jon.meer@dlapiper.com.

MEESTER, LEIGHTON (LEIGHTON MARISSA CLAIRE MEESTER), actress; b. Marco Island, Fla., Apr. 9, 1986; Actor(guest appearance): (TV series) Law & Order, 1999, Boston Public, 2001, Family Affair, 2002, Crossing Jordan, 2004, 7th Heaven, 2004, North Shore, 2004, Entourage, 2004, 24, 2005, 8 Simple Rules... for Dating My Teenage Daughter, 2005, Veronica Mars, 2005, Numb3rs, 2006, House M.D., 2006, CSI: Miami, 2007, Shark, 2007,; (films) The Jackalope, 2003, Hangman's Curse, 2003, Flourish, 2006, Inside, 2006, Drive Thru, 2007, The Beautiful Ordinary, 2007, Killer Movie, 2008; (TV series) Tarzan, 2003, Surface, 2005—06, Gossip Girl, 2007—; (TV films) Hollywood Division, 2004, The Haunting of Sorority Row, 2007. Office: c/o Leverage Mgmt 3030 Pennsylvania Ave Santa Monica CA 90404

MEHDI, YUSUF, computer software company executive; m. Stephanie Mehdi; 3 children. BA in Econs., Princeton U.; MBA, U. Wash. Product mgr. Reuters Group PLC; dir. mktg. Microsoft Windows op. sys. Microsoft Corp., Redmond, Wash., dir. mktg. Microsoft Internet Explorer, 1995—99, corp. v.p. MSN Personal Svcs. and Bus., 2002—05, sr. v.p., chief advt. strategist, sr. v.p. Strategic Partnerships. Office: One Microsoft Way Redmond WA 98052-6399

MEHRABADI, MORTEZA M., engineer, researcher, educator; m. Fatemeh Mirahmadi, June 6, 1975; 1 child, Roxana. BS, Tehran U., 1969; MS, Tulane U., 1973, PhD, 1979. Post doctoral fellow Northwestern U., Evanston, Ill., 1979—82; asst. prof. mech. engring. Tulane U., 1982—85, assoc. prof., 1985—92, prof., 1992—2007, chair, 1998—2007; prof., mech. engring. San Diego State U., 2007—, chair, mech. engring., 2007—. Recipient Tchg. Excellence award, Tulane U., 1983, 1999, 2006, Ralph R. Teetor Ednl. award, Soc. Automotive Engrs., 1984, Harold A. Levey award, Tulane U., 1985,

Tchg. Excellence award, Soc. Tulane Engrs., 1992; Newton and Mary Ebaugh Faculty fellow, Tulane U., 1982—83. Fellow: ASME; mem.: AAUP (v.p. Tulane U. chpt. 2006—07), Am. Soc. Engring. Edn., Am. Acad. Mechanics, Soc. Engring. Sci. Achievements include has contributed to the understanding of mechanics of anisotropic materials. Office: San Diego State Univ Dept Mech Engring 5500 Campanile Dr San Diego CA 92182-1323 Business E-Mail: mehrabadi@mail.sdsu.edu.

MEHRINGER, CHARLES MARK, medical educator; b. Dickinson, ND, Nov. 21, 1945; m. Ruth Herrman; 1 child, Sydney. BS in Biology, Lamar U., 1966; MD, U. Tex., 1970. Diplomate Am. Bd. Radiology, Am. Bd. Neuroradiology. Intern UCLA Hosp., 1970-71; resident in diagnostic radiology Harbor-UCLA Med. Ctr., Torrance, Calif., 1971-74, fellow in neuroradiology, 1976-77; asst. prof. dept. radiology UCLA Sch. Medicine, 1977-80, dir. spl. procedures, 1980-94, assoc. prof. dept. radiology, 1986-96, prof. dept. radiology, 1996—, acting chmn. radiology, 1996—. Vice-chmn. dept. radiological scis. UCLA Sch. Medicine, Torrance, 1992—, acting chmn. dept. radiology, 1992—, chief diagnostic radiology, 1983-92; chief radiological svcs., cons. U.S. Air Force for Japan and Korea, 1974-76; cons. U. Calif./Irvine (Calif.) Med. Ctr., 1988—, St. Marys Med. Ctr., Long Beach, Calif., 1986—, Long Beach VA Hosp., 1979—, L.A. County Dept. Chief Med. Examiner-Coroner, 1977—; bd. dirs. Rsch. and Ednl. Inst.; presenter in field. Co-author: (with others) Neurological Surgery of the Ear and Skull Base, 1982, Vascular Surgery, 1984, 2d edit., 1994, Youman's Neurological Surgery, 1990, Common Problems in Infertility and Impotence, 1990, Intraluminal Imaging of Vascular and Tubular Organs: Diagnostic and Therapeutic Applications, 1993, Neuroradiology, A Study Guide, 1995; contbr. articles to profl. jours. Bd. dirs., exec. com. Med. Found. Harbor-UCLA Med. Ctr., 1992—. Recipient numerous grants for rsch., 1977—. Mem. Am. Coll. Radiology, Am. Soc. Neuroradiology (sr. mem.), Western Neuroradiologic Soc., L.A. Radiologic Soc. Office: Harbor UCLA Med Ctr Box 27 1000 W Carson St Torrance CA 90502-2004

MEHTA, SIDDARTH N., credit services company executive; b. 1958; BS, London Sch. Econs.; MS, U. Chgo. V.p. Info. Bus. Divsn. Citicorp; sr. v.p. Boston Cons. Group, LA; joined Household Internat. Inc., 1996—, group exec. domestic MC/Visa bus., 1998—. Office: Household Internat Inc 1441 Schilling Pl Salinas CA 93901-4543

MEI, TOM Y. K., lawyer; b. Kuantan, Malaysia, July 24, 1940; came to U.S., 1958. s. Hung Po and Hannah (Chung) M.; m. Margene Suzuki Mei, Sept. 1964; children: Rodney, Todd. BA in econ., Calif. State U. at L.A., 1963; JD, Western State U. Coll. Law, 1975. Bar: Calif. 1976. Claim rep. CNA Ins., LA, 1964-66, claim supr. San Diego, 1966-76; assoc. attorney Murchison & Cumming, Santa Ana, 1976-88, ptnr., 1988—. Pres. San Diego Claims Mgr. Council, 1973. Mem. Am. Bd. Trial Advocates (bd. dirs.), Defense Rsch. Inst., Orange County Bar Assoc. Avocations: skiing, travel. Office: Murchison & Cumming 200 W Santa Ana Blvd Ste 801 Santa Ana CA 92701-4134 Office Phone: 518-605-6476.

MEIER, CURT, state legislator; b. Greeley, Colo., Jan. 1, 1953; m. Charlene Meier. BS, U. Wyo. Mem. Dist. 3 Wyo. State Senate, 1995-; mem. Chmn's Advisor Coun., Republican Nat. Com., Goshen Co. Econ. Devel. Bd. & Wyo. State Bd. Ed.; farm/ranch/produce. Stockgrowers; Farm Bur.; Wyo. Agr. Leadership Coun.; Goshen Co. C of C; AG Unity; fellow LEAD. Republican. Mailing: 4799 CR 18 Lagrange WY 82221 Office Phone: 307-834-2344. Business E-Mail: cmeier@wyoming.com.

MEIER, GEORGE KARL, III, minister, lawyer; b. Glen Ridge, NJ, Jan. 13, 1944; s. George Karl and Mary Claire (Myers) M.; children: G.K., Leslie; m. Therese DesCamp, Oct. 10, 1992. BS, Washington and Lee U., 1966; JD, Dickinson Sch. Law, 1969; MDiv, Pacific Sch. of Religion, 1992. Bar: N.J. 1969, Oreg. 1970, U.S. Dist. Ct. N.J. 1969, U.S. Dist. Ct. Oreg. 1970, U.S. Ct. Appeals (9th cir.) 1971, U.S. Ct. Appeals (fed. cir.) 1987, U.S. Supreme Ct. 1973. Law clk. N.J Superior Court Appellate Div., 1969-70; assoc. Stoel, Rives, Boley, Jones & Grey, Portland, Oreg., 1970-75, ptnr., 1976-89; spl. dep. atty. gen. State of Idaho, 1988-89; spl. asst. to pres. Pacific Sch. Religion, Berkeley, Calif., 1992; pastor Pioneer Congl. Ch., Sacramento, Calif., 1992-1998, Cmty. Ch. Monterey Peninsula, Carmel, Calif., 1998—. Co-founder Ctrl. City Concern, 1978, SW Youth Svc. Ctr., Portland; chmn. ctrl. adv. bd. Dept. Human Resources; pres. consistory Hillside Cmty. Ch., Portland, 1984-85; acad. com. Pacific Sch. Religion, 1989-91; interim dir. youth programs Epwirth Meth. Ch., 1992; bd. dirs. No. Calif. Nev. Conf. the United Ch. Christ, 1993-97; v.p., 1995-96, pres., 1996-97, Francis House, 1992-98; chmn. 1995-96, Cathedral Pioneer Ch. Homes, Inc., 1992-98; Samaritan Counseling Ctr., 1997-98;co-founder, bd. dirs. InterFaith Pastoral Counseling Ctr. Monterey County, 1999-2005; panel vol. United Way Fund Distbn., 1999-2000; Leadership Monterey Peninsula Class of 2000; bd. dirs. Legal Svcs. for Srs., 2004—. Recipient Outstanding Svc. award Cen. City Concern 1976-89. Mem. Oreg. State Bar Assn; mem. Carmel Valley Rotary Club, 1999—. Mem. United Ch. of Christ. Office Phone: 831-624-8595.

MEIER, GERALD MARVIN, economics professor; b. Tacoma, Wash., Feb. 9, 1923; s. Max and Bessie (Nagel) M.; m. Gilda Slote, Oct. 23, 1954; children: David, Daniel, Jeremy, Andrew. BA in Econs., Reed Coll., 1947; BLitt in Econs., Oxford U., Eng., 1952; PhD, Harvard U., 1953; MA (hon.), Wesleyan U., Middletown, Conn., 1959. Instr. Williams Coll., Williamstown, Mass., 1952-54; asst. prof. Wesleyan U., 1954-59, prof. econs., 1959-63; prof. economics Stanford U., Calif., 1963—, Konosuke Matsushita prof., Grad. Sch. Bus., prof. emeritus, mem. academic coun. Research assoc. Oxford U., 1957-58; vis. lectr. Yale U., New Haven, 1955-56, vis. assoc. prof., 1956-59, vis. prof., 1959-61; vis. prof. Stanford U., 1962; cons. Asia Soc., Bank Am., East-West Ctr., Food and Agrl. Orgn., Goodyear Internat., NSF, others; internat. lectr. in field. Author: International Trade and Development, 1963, Leading Issues in Development Economics, 1964, The International Economics of Development, 1968, 2d edit., 1978, Leading Issues in Economic Development: Studies in International Poverty, 7th edit., 2000; (with R.E. Baldwin) Economic Development, 1957; gen. editor: Econ. Devel. Series, Econ. Theory and the Underdevel. Countries, Human Resources as the Wealth of Nations, 1973, Fin. Deepening in Econ. Devel., 1975, Agrl. and Structural Transformation, 1975, Gen. X-Efficiency Theory of Econ. Devel., 1978; editor: International Economic Reform: Collected Papers of Emile Despres, 1973, Problems of Trade Policy, 1973, Problems of a World Monetary Order, 1982, Problems of Cooperation for Development, 1977, Toward a New International Development, 1982, La Nueva Era de Desarollo, 1978, Internat. Econs. of Development, International Economics: Theory of Policy, 1982, New International Development Policy, 1982, Pricing Policy for Development Management, 1983, Pioneers in Development, 1985, Emerging from Poverty: The Economics that Really Matters, 1984, Financing Asian Development, 1986, Pioneers in Development, 1987, Asian Development: Economic Success and Policy Lessons, The International Environment of Business, 1998, (with Joseph Stiglitz) Frontiers of Development Economics, 2001; author numerous chpts. to books and articles to profl. jours. Rhodes scholar, 1948-52, Rockefeller Found. Study Ctr. resident scholar, 1981; Guggenheim fellow, 1957-58, Brookings Nat. Research fellow, 1961-62, Russel Sage Found. resident fellow, 1976-77; Social Sci. Research Council Faculty research grantee, 1968, Internat. Legal Ctr. research grantee, 1970, Rockefeller Found. research grantee, 1974-75 Mem. Am. Assn. Rhodes Scholars, Am. Econ. Assn., Royal Econ. Soc., Am. Soc. Internat. Law, Phi Beta Kappa. Office: Stanford U Grad Sch Bus Stanford CA 94305-5015 Office Phone: 650-723-2851. E-mail: meier_gerald@gsb.stanford.edu.

MEIER, MARK FREDERICK, research scientist, educator, artist, small business owner; b. Iowa City, Dec. 19, 1925; s. Norman C. and Clea (Grimes) M.; m. Barbara McKinley, Sept. 16, 1955; children: Lauren G., Mark S., Gretchen A. BSEE, U. Iowa, 1949, MS in Geology, 1951; PhD in Geology and Applied Mechanics, Calif. Inst. Tech., 1957. Instr. Occidental Coll., LA, 1952-55; chief glaciology project office U.S. Geol. Survey, Tacoma, 1956-85; dir. Inst. Arctic and Alpine Rsch. U. Colo., Boulder, 1985-94; owner MeierArt, 2005—. Vis. prof. Dartmouth Coll., Hanover, N.H., 1964; rsch. prof. U. Wash., Seattle, 1964-86; prof. geol. scis. U. Colo., 1985-96, prof. emeritus, 1997—; pres. Internat. Comn. on Snow and Ice, 1967-71; pres. Internat. Assn. Hydrol. Scis., 1979-83; Mendenhall lectr. U.S. Geol. Survey, 1982, Walter Orr Roberts Disting. lectr. Aspen Global Change Inst., 1992. Contbr. articles to profl. jours. With USN, 1945—46. Recipient 3 medals, Acad. Scis., Moscow, 1970—85, Disting. Svc. award (Gold medal), U.S. Dept. Interior, 1968, Internat. Hydrology prize, Internat. Assn. Hydrol. Scis./World Meteor. Orgn./UNESCO, 1999, Goldthwait Polar medal, Ohio State U., 2002; named Meier Valley (Antarctica) in his honor. Fellow: AAAS (John Wesley Powell Meml. lectr. 1994), Am. Geophys. Union (com. chmn., Robert E. Horton medal 1996); mem.: Arctic Inst. N.Am. (gov. 1987—93), Internat. Glaciol. Soc. (v.p., coun., Seligman Crystal 1985), Geol. Soc. Am. (com. mem.). Office: U Colo Inst Arctic Alpine Rsch 1560 30th St Boulder CO 80309-0450 Business E-Mail: mark.meier@colorado.edu.

MEIERAN, EUGENE STUART, materials scientist; b. Cleve., Dec. 23, 1937; s. Elias and Rae (Linetsky) M.; m. Rosalind Berson, Mar. 25, 1962; children: Sharon Elizabeth, Andrew Marc. BS in Metallurgy, MIT, 1961, ScD in Material Sci., 1963; Doctorate (hon.), Purdue U., 2004. Mem. tech. staff Fairchild R&D, Palo Alto, Calif., 1963-73; engring. mgr. Intel Corp., Santa Clara, Calif., 1973-77, sr. mgr. quality assurance, 1977-84, Intel fellow, 1984—, mgr. applications lab., 1989—, Intel sr. fellow, 2003. Dir. rsch. LFM program MIT, 1993—; vis. lectr. Technion, Haifa, Israel, 1970-71, H.H. Wills Physics Lab., Bristol, Eng., 1970-71; mem. adv. bd. Lawrence Berkeley Lab., 1984— Contbr. articles to profl. jours. AEC fellow, 1960; recipient Internat. Reliability awards, 1970, 79, 85, Carnegie medal, 2004; named Disting. Engring. Alumnus Purdue U., 1988, Purdue Band Alumni, 2000, GIA Wall of Fame, 2004. Mem. AIME (chmn. electronic material symposium 1973—), NAE, Electron Microscope Soc. U.S.A., Tau Beta Pi, Phi Lambda Upsilon. Democrat. Jewish. Home: 5421 E Camello Rd Phoenix AZ 85018-1910 Office: Intel Corp 5000 W Chandler Blvd Chandler AZ 85226-3699 Personal E-mail: gene.s.meieran@att.net. Business E-Mail: gene.s.meieran@intel.com.

MEIKLEJOHN, ALVIN J., JR., state legislator, lawyer, accountant; b. Omaha, June 18, 1923; m. Lorraine J. Meiklejohn; children: Pamela Ann, Shelley Lou, Bruce Ian, Scott Alvin. BS, U. Denver, JD, 1951; LLD (hon.), U. No. Colo., 2000. Mem. Colo. state Senate from 19th Dist., 1976-96, chmn. com. edn.; mem. Edn. Commn. of States, 1981-96; chmn. Colo. Commn. on Ach. in Edn., 1995, mem., 1993-96, Jefferson Sch. Dist. No. R-1 Bd. Edn., 1971-77, pres., 1973-77; commr. Commn. on Uniform State Laws, 1988-96. Dir. Red Rocks C.C. Found.; emeritus dir. Wings Over the Rockies Air and Space Mus. Capt. US Army, 1940—46, maj. USAF, 1947—51. Mem. Arvada C. of C., Masons, Shriners, Transp. Lawyers Assn. (pres. 1972-73). Republican. Home: 7540 Kline Dr Arvada CO 80005-3732 Office: Jones & Keller PC 1625 Broadway Ste 1600 Denver CO 80202-4727 Office Phone: 303-573-1600. E-mail: ajmeiklejohn@joneskeller.com.

MEINDL, ROBERT JAMES, language educator, poet; b. Wausau, Wis., Sept. 17, 1936; s. George Martin and Adeline Emilie (Goetsch) M.; m. Victoria Lynn Chavez; children: Karin Rose, George Andrew, Damian Kurt, Erika Wittmer, Christopher Smith, Gabrielle Remelia. BS, U. Wis., 1958; MA, U. Conn., 1960; PhD, Tulane U., 1965; postgrad., U. Calif., Berkeley, 1967—68, Goethe Inst., Liblar, Germany, 1970, U. Cologne, Germany, 1970. Teaching asst. U. Conn., Storrs, 1958—60; teaching fellow Tulane U., 1960—62; lectr. U. Wis., Green Bay, 1963—65; asst. prof. to full prof. English Calif. State U., Sacramento, 1965—2002, prof. emeritus English, 2002—. Translator: Studies in John Gower, 1981; book rev. editor Studia Mystica Jour., 1984-89; contbr. numerous articles to profl. jours. With USNR, 1953-61, 79-96. Fellow, NEH, 1982. Mem. MLA (life), Medieval Acad. Am. (life), John Gower Soc. Office: Calif State U 6000 J St Sacramento CA 95819-2605 Office Phone: 916-278-7704. Business E-Mail: rmeindl@csus.edu.

MEISINGER, LOUIS M., lawyer; b. NYC, Dec. 12, 1942; BA, UCLA, 1964, JD, 1967. Bar: Calif. 1968. Atty. Hill Wynne Troop & Meisinger, LA; exec. v.p., gen. coun. Walt Disney Co., Burbank, Calif., 1997—2003; sr. advisor Sheppard, Mullin, Richter & Hampton, LLP, Los Angeles, Calif., 2003—. Editor: UCLA Law Rev., 1965-67. Recipient Entertainment Lawyer of the Yr., Beverly Hills Bar Assoc./ Calif., 1999. Mem. State Bar Calif., L.A. County Bar Assn., Century City Bar Assn., Order of Coif, Phi Beta Kappa, Sigma Delta Pi, Phi Delta Phi. Office: Sheppard Mullin Richter & Hampton 333 S Hope St Los Angeles CA 90071

MEISLIN, HARVEY WARREN, emergency healthcare physician, professional society administrator; b. Rochester, NY, June 19, 1946; s. Milton M. and Celia (Weiner) M.; m. Loretta Marie Bielski, Apr. 30, 1977; children: Justin, Jonathan, Megan. BS in Chemistry, Purdue U., 1968; MD, Ind. U., 1972. Diplomate Am. Bd. Emergency Medicine (chmn.), Am. Bd. Med. Spltys. (del. 1990, fin. com. 1992, exec. com. 1994); cert. cardiac life support, ACLS instr., advanced trauma life support instr. Intern U. Chgo. Hosps. and Clinics, 1973-75, resident, 1975-77, dir. div. emergency medicine, 1975-77; asst. prof. internal and emergency medicine UCLA Emergency Med. Ctr., 1977-80, resident dir. emergency medicine, 1977-80, assoc. dir., 1977-80; assoc. prof. dept. surgery emergency medicine Coll. Medicine, U. Ariz., Tucson, 1980-83, assoc. prof., 1983-85; assoc. head, dept. surgery U. Ariz., Tucson, 1995—; prof. Coll. Medicine, U. Ariz., Tucson, 1985—; chief emergency medicine U. Ariz., Tucson, 1980—; chief sect. emergency medicine dept. surgery Ariz. Health Scis. Ctr., Tuscon, 1980—, dir. emergency svcs. Univ. Med. Ctr., 1980—, dir. Ariz. Emergency Med. Rsch. Ctr., 1990—; med. dir. MEDTRAN-Aeromed. Ambulance Corp., 1985-88. Mem. emergency med. svc. com. Mid-South Health Planning Orgn., Chgo., 1974; coord. Mid-South Disaster Plan, Chgo., 1974; mem. com. revision of Disaster Plan Billings Hosp., 1974-76; mem. faculty Am. Hosp. Assn. Inst. Disaster Preparedness, 1975; vis. prof. dept. emergency medicine Denver Gen. Hosp., 1977; bd. trustees Emergency Med. Found., 1978-81; mem. med. adv. com. L.A. City Fire Dept., 1979-80; chmn.-elect Tuscon Met. EMS Coun., 1983-84, chmn., 1984-85; chmn. Tuscon Pre-Hosp. Care Coun., 1981; mem. trauma steering com. So. Ariz. Regional Trauma Ctr., 1986-88; mem. ETHICON emergency physicians adv. panel Johnson & Johnson Co., 1987-92; presenter and lectr. in field. Editor: Purdue Rivet, 1971-72, abstract sect. Annals Emergency Medicine, 1982-90, EMS sect., 1989-90; guest editor: Topics in Emergency Medicine, 1979; sci. editor: Drug Therapy, 1984—; mem. editorial bd.: Annals Emergency Medicine, 1977-90, Emergency Dept. News, 1979-87, Emergency Dept. and Ambulatory Care News, 1987-90, Digest of Emergency Medicine Care, 1981-87; contbr. articles and revs. to profl. jours. Mem. select med. adv. com. City of Tucson, 1981, med. dir. emergency med. svcs., 1982-83, 84-85; bd. dirs. so. Ariz. divsn. Am. Heart Assn., 1985-90; mem. emergency cardiac care com. so. divsn. Ariz. Heart Assn., 1986-88; mem. med. dirs. commn., dept. health svcs. State of Ariz., 1992—, also mem. Mex. border commn., 1991—; mem. med. direction commn. State of Ariz. (appointed by gov.), 1993—. Recipient Pres. gavel and plaque Am. Bd. Emergency Medicine. Fellow Am. Coll. Emergency Physicians (State of Ill. chpt.): mem. sci. adv. com. 1975, mem. sci. edn. com. 1975-76, mem. grad./undergrad. edn. com. 1976-79, mem. ethics com. 1976-77, mem. surgery/trauma task force bd. cert. exam. 1976-77, bd. dirs. 1976-77, chmn. edn. com. 1976-77; State of Calif. chpt.: mem. hosp. and contract com. 1978-79, mem. EMS and legis. com. 1978-79, mem. spl. task force on emergency dept. distbn. 1979-80, mem. membership com. 1979-80, mem. legis. com. 1979-80, mem. sci. assembly planning com. 1980-81, bd. dirs. 1979-81, mem. rsch. com. 1981; State of Ariz. chpt.: bd. dirs. 1982-92, 92—, chmn. pub. rels. com. 1982-83, v.p. and sec. 1983-84, counselor 1984-87, mem. credentials com. 1986-91, chmn. 1987-90, mem. test com. 1986-87, mem. ad hoc com. for combined tng. 1987-88, chmn. task force on emergency medicine 1987-89, mem. exec. com. 1988—, mem. fin. com. 1988—, sec./treas. 1989-90, mem. EMS com. 1990—, pres.-elect 1990-91, pres. 1991-92, chair stds. com., mem. faculty Nat. Sci. Assembly 1974-76, Cert. Appreciation award 1990); mem. APHA, Am. Coll. Physician Execs., Am. Trauma Soc., Am. Bd. Med. Specialties (mem. fin. com. 1992, mem. exec. com. 1995—, pres., 2004), Ariz. Med. Assn., Pima County Med. Soc. (bd. dirs. 1991—), Phi Rho Sigma. Avocations: racquetball, golf, skiing, automobiles. Office: U Ariz Med Ctr Sect Emergency Med 1501 N Campbell Ave Tucson AZ 85724-0001

MEISSNER, KATHERINE GONG, municipal official; b. Stockton, Calif., 1955; BA, U. Phoenix, Stockton, Calif., 1999. Mem. comty. planning dept. staff City of Stockton, Calif., 1982-85, exec. asst. city clk., 1985-96, city clk., 1996—. Office: City Stockton Office City Clk 425 N El Dorado St Stockton CA 95202-1997 Office Phone: 209-937-8458. Business E-Mail: city.clerk@ci.stockton.ca.us.

MEJIA, BARBARA OVIEDO, retired chemistry professor; b. San Francisco, Apr. 14, 1946; d. Louis Jerome and Alice May (Beall) O. AA, Sierra Coll., 1967; BS, U. Calif., Davis, 1969, PhD, 1973. Cert. community coll. tchr., Calif. Lectr. U. Calif., Davis, summer 1977, Calif. State U., Chico, 1973-76, asst. prof., 1976-80, assoc. prof., 1980-85, prof., 1985—2001, emeritus, 2001—. Contbr. articles to profl. jours. Judge Calif. Cen. Valley Sci.-Engring. Fair, Chico, 1977, 89, 81, 81, 88, bd. dirs., 1978-79; judge Butte County Sci. Fair, Chico, 1985-90. Mem. AAAS, Am. Chem. Soc., Congress of Faculty Assns., Cal Aggie Alumni Assn., Assn. Calif. State Univ. Profs., Sigma Xi. Home: 6 Laguna Ct Chico CA 95928-7431 Office: Calif State U Dept Chemistry Chico CA 95929-0001 Business E-Mail: Bmejia@csuchico.edu.

MELBY, DONNA D., lawyer; b. 1950; BA, U. Calif., Santa Barbara, 1972; attended, Loyola U. Sch. Law, 1977—78, Calif. Western Sch. Law, 1975—77, JD, 1978. Bar: Calif. 1979. Ptnr. Sonnenschein Nath & Rosenthal LLP, LA, 2002—05; ptnr. employment dept. Paul, Hastings, Janofsky & Walker, LA. Mem. Calif. Judicial Selection Adv. Coun., 2004. Recipient Rothchild Pro Bono Award, Sonnenschein Nath & Rosenthall LLP, 2004; named one of The Most Influential & Talented Women Trial Lawyers in Calif., LA Daily Jour. & San Francisco Recorder, 2002—06, 16 leading litigators in the US, Minority Corp. Counsel Assn., 2004, The 100 Most Influential Attorneys in State of Calif., LA Daily Jour. & San Francisco Recorder, 2004, The 50 Most Influential Women Lawyers in Am., Nat. Law Jour., 2007; named to Top 5% So. Calif. Super Lawyers, LA Mag., 2003—06. Fellow: Internat. Soc. Barristers, Am. Coll. Trial Lawyers; mem.: Fed. Bar Assn., Women Lawyers of LA, Calif. Women Lawyers, Assn. Bus. Trial Lawyers, Assn. So. Calif. Def. Counsel, Def. Rsch. Inst. (labor & employment com.), Fedn. Def. and Corp. Counsel, Internat. Assn. Def. Counsel (faculty mem. trial sch.), Am. Bd. Trial Advocates (faculty mem. trial sch. 1993—, mem. bd. dirs. 1994—, mem. found. bd. trustees 2001—, v.p. 2003, pres.-elect 2004, pres. 2005, pres. LA chpt. 2004, Guardian of Constitution award), Chancery Club. Office: Paul Hastings Janofsky & Walker 515 S Flower St 25th Fl Los Angeles CA 90071 Office Phone: 213-683-6098. Office Fax: 213-996-3098. E-mail: donnamelby@paulhastings.com.

MELCHER, TRINI URTUZUASTEGUI, retired finance educator; b. Somerton, Ariz., Dec. 1, 1931; d. Francisco Juan and Dolores (Barraza) Urtuzuastegui; m. Arlyn Melcher, Aug. 3, 1957 (div. Feb. 1972); children: Teresa Dolores, Michael Francis, Jocelyn Marie. BS, Ariz. State U., 1954, PhD, 1977; MBA, Kent State U., 1964. Acct. CPA firm, LA, 1954—56; instr. LA Sch. Dist., 1956—58, Dolton (Ill.) Sch. Dist., 1958—61; asst. prof. Kent (Ohio) State U., 1962—72; prof. Calif. State U., Fullerton, 1976—89, founding faculty mem. San Marcos, 1990—, prof. emeritus, 2003—. Author: Intermediate Accounting Study Guide, 1984; co-author: International Accounting: A Global Perspective, 1997. Treas. Cmty. Devel. Coun., Santa Ana, Calif., 1985-88, chmn. bd., 1989; mem. com. U.S. Dept. Labor,

1989—. Named Outstanding Educator, League of United Latin Am. Citizens, Stanton, Calif., 1987, Mex. Am. Women's Nat. Assn., Irvine, Calif., 1987, One of Ten Women of Merit, N. County Times, 1999, One of 80 Elite Hispanic Women, Hispanic Bus., 2002; recipient Outstanding Faculty award Calif. State U. Sch. Bus., 1983, Pub. Svc. award Am. Soc. Women CPAs, San Antonio, 1996; Affirmative Action grantee, 1990. Mem. AICPA (editl. bd. The Woman CPA), Am. Acctg. Assn., Calif. Soc. CPAs (Merit award 1991), Hispanic CPAs. Avocations: music, travel. Home: 2024 Sequoia St San Marcos CA 92078-5454 Office: Calif State U San Marcos CA 92096-0001 Home Phone: 760-598-1840; Office Phone: 760-750-4213. Business E-Mail: tmelcher@csusm.edu.

MELDRUM, PETER DURKEE, venture capitalist, biotechnology company executive; b. Salt Lake City, June 26, 1947; s. Benjamin Nibley and Grace Natalie (Durkee) M.; m. Catherine Roper, June 16, 1970; children: Christopher Shawn. BSChemE, U. Utah, 1970, MBA, 1974. Asst. to pres. Terra Tek, Inc., Salt Lake City, 1974-78; pres., CEO Resource Enterprises, Inc., Salt Lake City, 1978-81, AgriDyne Techs., Salt Lake City, 1981-91, Founder's Fund Inc., 1991—93, Myriad Genetics Inc., Salt Lake City, 1991—. Bd. dirs. Dairy Equipment Co. Utah, Salt Lake City, Amedica, Golden Pine Ventures LLC (sec., chmn.), 2004-. Bd. dirs., vice chmn. ARC Golden Spike, Salt Lake City, 1980-90; mem. State of Utah Coun. Sci. and Tech., 1984-89; mem. adv. bd. Coll. of Sci. U. Utah, Engr. Adv. Bd. U. Utah, adv. bd. High Tech Mktg. Rev., Austin, Tex., 1986-88; mem. Gov.'s Task Force on Entrepreneurship; Gov.'s Com. on Biomed. Industry, 1988-91; bd. arbitrators NASD, 1991-98; bd. dirs. Ballet West. 1st lt. USAR, 1970-72, bd. trustees, Pioneer Theatre Co. Recipient Utah Gov. Medal for Sci. and Tech., 1998; named Entrepreneur of Yr., 2001; named one of Top 50 Scientific Visionaries in World, Scientific Am. Mag., 2002. Mem. Utah Life Scis. Assn. (bd. dirs. 1995—), Tau Beta Pi, Phi Kappa Phi, Beta Gamma Sigma. Republican. Presbyterian. Avocations: skiing, backpacking, basketball, photography. Office: Myriad Genetics 320 Wakara Way Salt Lake City UT 84108-1214

MELICHER, RONALD WILLIAM, finance educator; b. St. Louis, July 4, 1941; s. William and Lorraine Norma (Mohart) M.; m. Sharon Ann Schlarmann, Aug. 19, 1967; children: Michelle Joy, Thor William, Sean Richard. BSBA, Washington U., St. Louis, 1963, MBA, 1965, DBA, 1968. Asst. prof. fin. U. Colo., Boulder, 1969-71, assoc. prof., 1971-76, prof. fin., 1976—, chmn. fin. divsn., 1978-86, 90, chmn. fin. and econ. divsn., 1993-2000, MBA/MS programs dir., 1990-93, chmn. fin. divsn., 2003—. Assoc. dir. space law bus. and policy ctr. U. Colo., 1986-87; rsch. cons. FPC, Washington, 1975-76, GAO, Washington, 1981, RCG/Hagler, Bailly, Inc., 1985—, Ariz. Corp. Commn., 1986-87, Conn. Dept. Pub. Utility Control, 1989, US SEC, 1992-95; cons. tech. edn. IBM Corp., 1985-91; dir. ann. Exch. Program for Gas Industry, 1975-94; instr. ann. program Nat. Assn. Regulatory Utility Commrs., Mich. State U., 1981-94. Co-author: Real Estate Finance, 1978, 3d edit., 1989, Financial Management, 5th edit., 1982, Finance: Introduction to Markets, Institutions and Management, 1980, 1984, 1988, 1992, Finance: Introduction to Institutions, Investments and Management, 9th edit., 1997, 12th edit., 2006, 13th edit., 2008, Entrepreneurial Finance, 2003, 2d edit., 2006, 3rd edit., 2009; assoc. editor Fin. Mgmt. Jour., 1975—80, The Fin. Rev., 1988—91. Recipient News Ctr. 4 TV Tchg. award, 1987, MBA/MS Assn. Tchg. award, 1988, Boulder Faculty Assembly Tchg. award, 1988, Grad. Bus. Students Tchg. award, 1995, 98; grantee NSF, 1974, NASA, 1986, 87; scholar W.H. Baughn Disting., 1989-2000, U. Colo. Pres.'s Tchg., 1989—. Mem. Fin. Mgmt. Assn. (mem. com. 1974-76, regional dir. 1975-77, v.p. ann. mtg. 1985, v.p. program 1987, pres. 1991-92, exec. com. 1991-93, bd. trustees 1992-99, chmn. 25th Anniversary com. 1994-95, mem. search com. for editor of Fin. Mgmt. Jour., 1995-96, chmn. search com. editor of Fin. Practice and Edn. Jour. 1996, mem. search com. for sec./treas. 1999, 2001), Am. Fin. Assn. Western Fin. Assn. (bd. dirs. 1974-76), Fin. Execs. Inst. (acad. mem. 1975—), Ea. Fin. Assn., Southwestern Fin. Assn., Midwest Fin. Assn. (bd. dirs. 1978-80), Alpha Kappa Psi, Beta Gamma Sigma. Office: U Colo Coll Bus PO Box 419 Boulder CO 80303 Office Phone: 303-492-3182. Business E-Mail: ronald.melicher@colorado.edu.

MELLINKOFF, SHERMAN MUSSOFF, medical educator; b. McKeesport, Pa., Mar. 23, 1920; s. Albert and Helen Mussoff Mellinkoff; m. June Bernice O'Connell, Nov. 18, 1944; children: Sherrill, Albert. BA, Stanford U., 1941, MD, 1944; LHD (hon.), Wake Forest U., 1984, Hebrew Union Coll., LA, 1988. Diplomate Am. Bd. Internal Medicine, Am. Bd. Gastroenterology, Am. Bd. Nutrition. Intern asst. resident Stanford U. Hosp., San Francisco, 1944—45; asst. resident Johns Hopkins Hosp., Balt., 1947—49, chief resident, 1950—51, instr. in medicine, 1951—53; fellow in gastroenterology Hosp. of U. Pa., Phila., 1949—50; from asst. prof. to prof. medicine UCLA Sch. of Medicine, LA, 1962—86; dean UCLA Sch. Medicine, LA, 1962—86, emeritus prof. of medicine, 1990—; disting. physician of VA Wadsworth VA Medical Ctr., LA, 1990-93. Mem. sci. adv. panel Rsch. to Prevent Blindness, Inc., NYC, 1975—93; mem. program devel. com. Nat. Med. Fellowships, Inc., NYC, 1984—. Editl. bd.: The Pharos, 1986; contbr. articles to profl. jours. Apptd. by Gov. of Calif. to McCone Com., 1965. Capt. US Army, 1945—57. Recipient Abraham Flexner award, Assn. Am. Med. Colls., 1981, J.E. Wallace Sterling Disting. Alumnus award, Stanford U. Sch. of Medicine, 1987. Master: ACP; fellow: Royal Coll. of Physicians; mem.: The Johns Hopkins Soc. of Scholars, Am. Acad. of Arts and Scis., Inst. of Medicine of NAS, Assn. Am. Physicians, Am. Gastroenterol. Assn. Assn. Avocations: reading, hiking.

MELLOR, ROBERT E., building materials company executive, lawyer; b. 1943; BA, Westminster Coll., 1965; JD, So. Meth. U., 1968. Atty. legal dept. Union Oil Co. of Calif., 1968-73; atty. U.S. Leasing Internat. Inc., 1973-75; v.p. dir. Alexander & Bolton Inc., 1975-76; with Di Giorgio Corp., San Francisco, 1976-79, v.p., 1979-80, v.p., gen. counsel, 1980-81, v.p., sec., gen. counsel, 1981-87, sr. v.p., gen. counsel, sec., 1987, chief adminstrv. officer, exec. v.p., gen. counsel, sec.; counsel Gibson, Dunn & Crutcher, San Francisco, 1990—97; pres., CEO Building Materials Holding Co., San Francisco, 1997—2002, chmn., pres., CEO, 2002—. Bd. dir. Coeur d'Alene Mines Corp., The Ryland Group, Inc., Monroe Muffler Brake, Inc. Office: c/o BMHC 4 Embarcadero Center San Francisco CA 94111

MELLOR, RONALD JOHN, history professor; b. Bklyn., Sept. 30, 1940; s. Ronald Green and Eleanor Teresa (Walsh) M.; m. Anne Tidaback Kostelanetz, June 7, 1969; 1 child, Ronald Blake. AB, Fordham Coll., 1962; cert., U. Louvain, Belgium, 1961; AM, Princeton U., 1964, PhD in Classics, 1968. Asst. prof. Classics Stanford (Calif.) U., 1965-75; assoc. prof. history UCLA, 1976-82, prof. history, 1982—. Vice-chmn. history UCLA, 1985-86, 1991-92, 1998-99, chmn. history, 1992-97; visitor Princeton Inst. Advanced Studies, 1997-98. Author: Thea Rhome, 1975, Tacitus, 1993, Tacitus and the Classical Tradition, 1995, The Roman Historians, 1999, The Ancient Roman World, 2004, The World in Ancient Times: Primary Sources and Reference Volume, 2005; editor: From Augustus to Nero: The First Dynasty of Imperial Rome, 1990, The Historians of Ancient Rome, 2d edit., 2004, Text and Tradition: Studies in Greek History and Historiography in Honor of Mortimer Chambers, 1999, Augustus and the Creation of the Roman Empire, 2005. Fellow NEH, 1969, Am. Coun. Learned Socs., 1972, Humanities Rsch. Ctr. Australian Nat. U., Canberra, Australia, 1990; hon. fellow U. Coll. London, Eng., 1969, 72, 83-85. Mem. Am. Hist. Assn., Am. Philol. Assn., Assn. Ancient Historians, Soc. for the Promotion of Roman Studies. Democrat. Avocations: opera, travel, theater, tennis. Home: 2620 Mandeville Canyon Rd Los Angeles CA 90049-1004 Office: UCLA Dept History 405 Hilgard Ave Los Angeles CA 90095-1473 E-mail: mellor@history.ucla.edu.

MELNICK, ALICE JEAN (AJ MELNICK), counselor; b. St. Louis, Dec. 25, 1931; d. Nathan and Henrietta (Hausfater) Fisher; m. Harold Melnick, May 24, 1953; children: Susan, Vikki, Patrice. BJ, U. Tex., Austin, 1952; MEd, U. North Tex., Denton, 1974. Reporter San Antonio Light, 1952-53; instr. journalism project Upward Bound So. Meth. U., Dallas, 1967-71. Instr. writing El Centro Dallas County CC, Dallas, part time 1972-74; instr. human devel. Richland CC, Dallas, part-time 1974-79; tchr. English, journalism and psychology Dallas Ind. Sch. Dist., 1969-81; counselor Ursuline Acad., 1981-94; part-time instr. human devel. Santa Fe CC, 1994-2007; freelance documentary photographer. Author: They Changed the World: People of the Manhattan Project, 2006; exhibitions include People of Manhattan Project, Los Alamos Hist. Mus., 2005—08, Bradbury Sci. Mus., Las Alamos, 2007—08, Women Making a Difference, Los Alamos Hist. Mus., 2009. Mem. Dallas Sports Car Club, N.Mex. Jewish Hist. Soc., Temple Beth Shalom. Jewish. Home: 101 Monte Alto Rd Santa Fe NM 87508-8865 Personal E-mail: aj@melnick.net.

MELNICK, MICHAEL, geneticist, educator; b. NYC, Sept. 24, 1944; s. Lester and Evelyn (Rosenberg) M.; m. Anita Goldberger, June 19, 1966; children: Cliff, Lynn. BA in Biology, NYU, 1966, DDS, 1970; PhD in Genetics, Ind. U., 1978. Instr. oral medicine Ind. U., Indpls., 1973-74, fellow in med. genetics, 1974-77, asst. prof. med. genetics, 1977-78; rsch. assoc. prof. U. So. Calif., LA, 1978-85, assoc. prof., 1985-89, prof. genetics, 1989—. Cons. in human genetics NIH, Bethesda, Md., 1977-88, grant reviewer, 1978—; manuscript referee Am. Jour. Human Genetics, Chgo., 1980—, Am. Jour. Med. Genetics, Helena, Mont., 1980—; MRC vis. prof. McGill U., Montreal, que., 1990. Author, editor 5 books on human genetics; editor-in-chief Jour. Craniofacial Genetics, 1980-2000; contbr. more than 100 articles to profl. jours. Mem. nat. bd. Com. of Concerned Scientists, N.Y.C., 1983—; vice chmn. Youth Towns of Israel, L.A., 1986—. Capt. M.C. U.S. Army, 1970-73. Recipient Ind. U. Disting. Alumnus award, 1984; Warwick James fellow U. London/Guy's Hosp., 1992. Fellow AAAS; mem. Soc. Craniofacial Genetics (pres. 1978-79), Soc. for Developmental Biology, Am. Soc. Human Genetics, Sigma Xi. Achievements include research in delineated major gene causation of cleft lip and palate; delineated insulin-like growth factor, type 2, receptor control of fetal lung, salvary gland and palate development; delineated molecular pathogenesis of viral-induced birth defects; application of probability neural networks to multi-gene analysis; molecular pathology of embryonic CMV infection. Avocations: art, philosophy, chess. Office: Univ So Calif Den 4266 Mc 0641 Los Angeles CA 90089-0641 Business E-Mail: mmelnick@usc.edu.

MELNICK, ROB, research administrator; b. Mt. Vernon, NY, May 6, 1950; BA in Govt., Dartmouth Coll., 1972; postgrad., NYU, 1972; MA in Media, Ariz. State U., 1973, PhD in Ednl. Tech., 1980. Dir. media ctr., tchr. social studies Glendale (Ariz.) Union H.S., 1973-75; instr. dept. ednl. tech., assoc. dir. univ. media sys. Ariz. State U., Tempe, 1975-80; v.p. Desert Mountain Assocs. Inc., Phoenix, 1980-82; sr. rsch. fellow, v.p. Hudson Inst., Indpls., 1982-87; dir. Morrison Inst. for Pub. Policy Ariz. State U., Tempe, 1987—. Cons. in areas of policy analysis, prodn. of pub. info. and program evaluation for numerous govt., corp., and ednl. orgns.; mass media presentations. Contbr. numerous articles to profl. jours. Bd. dirs. Noble Ctrs., Inc., Indpls., 1986, Phoenix Ctr. for Law-Related Studies, 1987—, Inst. for Ednl. Leadership of Ariz., 1990—, Succes by Six, 1990—, Work Force Solutions for Am.'s Future Inc., 1992—; mem. Phoenix Commn. on Edn., 1987-92; bd. dirs., sec. Ariz. Sch.-to-Work Partnership, Inc., 1990—; mem., moderator Gov.'s Task Force on Edn., 1991; mem., facilitator State Supt.'s Task Force on Sch. Violence, 1993, Gov.'s Task Force on Employment and Tng., 1993; other activities. Project dir., author or co-author numerous funded policy studies. Office: Morrison Inst Pub Policy PO Box 874405 Tempe AZ 85287-4405

MELNICK, ROBERT, dean; Dean architecture and applied arts U. Oreg., Eugene; interim exec. dir. Jordan Schnitzer Mus. Art, U. Oreg., Eugene. Office: Architecture Dept Univ Oregon Eugene OR 97403

MELODY, MICHAEL EDWARD, publishing company executive; b. Streator, Ill., Dec. 22, 1943; s. Giles Lambert and Rose Mary (Moreschi) M.; m. Carol Ann Weir, June 8, 1968 (div.); 1 dau., Alison Anne; m. Bonnie Kaye Binkert, Mar. 26, 1983. BA, Ala. Coll., 1966. Exec. editor, asst. v.p. Prentice-Hall, Inc., Englewood Cliff, NJ, 1974-79; v.p., editor-in-chief coll. divsn. Macmillan Pub. Co., NYC, 1979-80, sr. v.p., pres. coll. divsn., 1980-87, pres. sch. divsn., 1987—88; v.p. higher edn. group Simon & Schuster, NYC, 1988-90; sr. v.p. Houghton Mifflin Co., Boston, 1990-91, exec. v.p., 1991-95; prin. Michael E. Melody Cons., Boston, 1995-96; v.p., gen. mgr. info. prodn. Inso Corp., Boston, 1996-99; pres, CEO, bd. dirs. Sage Pubs., Inc., Thousand Oaks, Calif., 1999—2005. Chmn. bd. dirs. Appleton & Lange, N.Y.C., 1989-90; bd. dirs. Sage Publs., Ltd., London. Bd. overseers Huntington Theatre Co., Boston, 1993-96; bd. advisors Boston U. Sch. for the Arts, 1997-2000; bd. dirs. Judge Baker Ctr. for Children, Harvard U. Med. Sch., 1997-99, mem. exec. com.; pres. adv. coun. Calif. Luth. U., 2001-05; trustee New West Symphony, 2003-05, So. N.H. U., 2003—06; treas. Santa Fe Symphony Orch., 2006-08, pres., bd. dirs. 2008-. Mem. Assn. Am. Pubs. (vice chmn. coll. divsn. 1981-83, chmn. coll. divsn. 1983-86, exec. com. sch. divsn. 1987-88, exec. com. higher edn. divsn. 1990—), Nat. Assn. Coll. Stores (trustee 1986-87, 94-95). E-mail: michael.melody@gmail.com.

MELTON, ARTHUR RICHARD, public health administrator; b. Ysleta, Tex., Apr. 28, 1943; s. Francis Charles and Jean (Graham) M.; m. Frances Bay, Aug. 19, 1965; children: David Bay, Amy Elizabeth. BS, U. Utah, 1969; MPH, U. N.C., 1974, D in Pub. Health, 1976. Dir. labs. S.D. Dept. Health, Pierre, 1976-87; microbiologist Utah Dept. Health, Salt Lake City, 1970-73, dir. divsn. lab. svcs., 1987-92, dep. dir., 1992—. Mem.: Assn. State and Territorial Health Ofcls. (pres. elect 1999—2000, pres. 2000—01), SD Pub. Health Assn. (pres. 1980—81, past. pres. 2001—06), Am. Pub. Health Assn. (governing coun. 1980—83). Mem. Lds Ch. Home: 6835 Heather Way West Jordan UT 84084-2304 Office: PO Box 141000 Salt Lake City UT 84114-1000 Office Phone: 801-538-6111. Personal E-mail: dickmelton@yahoo.com. Business E-Mail: dmelton@utah.gov.

MELTZER, CLIFF, information technology executive; MS in Computer Sci., Univ. Rochester. With IBM, 1975—91, rschr., T.J. Watson Rsch. Ctr. Rochester Ctr. Yorktown Heights, NY, 1981—91; sr. v.p. IOS Tech. divsn. Cisco Sys., 1992—98, sr. v.p., network mgmt. tech. group San Jose, Calif., 2003—; CEO, pres. Digital Fountain, 1999—2003. Entrepreneur in residence Redpoint Ventures, Menlo Park, Calif., 1999; spkr. in field. Office: Cisco Sys 170 W Tasman Dr San Jose CA 95134 Fax: 408-526-4100.

MELVILL, MICHAEL W., aircraft company executive, experimental test pilot; b. 1941; arrived in US, 1970; m. Sally Melvill; 1 child. FAA coml. cert., cert. ASEL, AMEL, instrument airplane, Rotorcraft-helicopter and Glider. V.p., gen. mgr., test pilot Scaled Co., Inc., Mojave, Calif., 1985—. Recipient Ivan C. Kincheloe trophy for work on devel. high altitude flight testing of model 281 Proteus, 1999. Mem.: Experimental Aircraft Assn., Aircraft Owners' and Pilots' Assn., Soc. Experimental Test Pilots (assoc. fellow). Achievements include participated in flight testing for Beech Starship prototype (NGBA), Fairchild's Next Generation Trainer for US Air Force (NGT), Ares, Pond Racer; built and flight tested Model 27 Varividgen; built, tested and flew around world in 1997 with Dick Rutan Model 61 Long-EZ; first flight of Model 72 Grizzly prototype, Model 77 Solitaire prototype, Model 81 Catbird prototype, Model 120 Predator prototype, Model 144 UAV prototype, Model 202 Boomerang, Model 226 Raptor; first flight of Model 281 Proteus, Model 316 Spaceshipone; first flight firing of GAU-12/U25mm cannon in Model 151 Ares jet fighter; only person to have flown Voyager Aircraft besides Dick Rutan and Jeana Yeager; holds 4 World and Nat. speed and altitude records in Catbird and Proteus Aircraft; first private manned mission to space, first civilian to fly a spaceship out of the atmosphere, first private pilot to earn astronaut wings, June 21, 2004; Guinness Book of World Records dubbed rocket launch "first ever privately funded manned spaceflight"; manned SpaceShipOne flight on Sept. 29, 2004, which will mark the first of two successful flight that are needed to win the Ansari X Prize. Office: Scaled Composites Inc 1624 Flight Line Mojave CA 93501 Office Phone: 661-824-4541. Office Fax: 661-824-4174.

MELVIN, ALBERT A., state legislator; b. Helena, Mont., Nov. 3, 1944; m. Kou Marie Melvin. BS, US Merchant Marine Acad., Kings Point, NY, 1969; MBA, Thunderbird Grad. Sch. Internat. Mgmt., Glendale, Ariz., 1972; grad., US Naval War Coll., Newport, RI, 1994. Numerous tours of duty US Navy Reserve, 1969—99, ret. as capt., 1999; ship's officer Am. Maritime Officers, 1999—2002; owner, cons. Am. Quality Internat. Consulting, 2002—; mem. Dist. 26 Ariz. State Senate, 2008—, vice chair appropriations com., mem. vets. & mil. affairs com., pub. health & human svcs. com. Mem. Nat. Rep. Com., 1996—2006; adj. lectr. U. Ariz., 2002—; instr. Western Internat. U., U. Phoenix. Mem.: Rotary Internat., Pima County Rep. Club, Saddlebrooke Rep. Club. Republican. Roman Catholic. Office: Ariz State Senate Capitol Complex 1700 W Washington Rm 303 Phoenix AZ 85007 Office Phone: 602-926-4326. Office Fax: 602-417-3259. Business E-Mail: amelvin@azleg.gov.*

MELZER, RICHARD ANTHONY, historian, educator; b. NYC, Mar. 15, 1949; s. Ben and Gladys Melzer; m. Rena Chavez, Mar. 9, 1984; children: Kam Coveyou, Patrick Richard. PhD, U. N.Mex, 1979. Prof. history U. N. Mex., Valencia, 1979—. Pres. Hist. Soc. N.Mex, 2005—. Author: (books) Buried Treasures: Famous and Unusual Gravesites in New Mexico History, When We Were Young in the West (Gaspar Perez de Villagra award, 2004), Coming of Age in the Great Depression. Named Tchr. of Yr., U. N.Mex., 1995. Office: U N Mex Valencia 280 La Entrada Los Lunas NM 87031

MENAHAN, MIKE, state legislator; m. Stacy Tureck; 2 children. Dep. co. atty., 1994—; mem. Dist. 82 Mont. House of Reps., 2008—. Democrat. Office: Montana House of Representatives PO Box 200400 Helena MT 59601-0400 Mailing: 40 Olive St Helena MT 59601-6285 Home Phone: 406-443-3759; Office Phone: 406-444-4800. Office Fax: 406-444-4825. Business E-Mail: mike@mikemenahan.com.

MENASHE, ALBERT ALAN, lawyer; b. Portland, Oreg., Apr. 24, 1950; s. Solomon A. and Faye F. (Hasson) Menashe; m. Laura L. Richenstein, July 23, 1972 (div. Oct. 1979); 1 child, Shawn Nathan; m. Sandra J. Laniado, June 28, 1980 (div. Jan. 1994); m. Julie D. Howe, Oct. 25, 2003. BS in Polit. Sci., U. Oreg., 1971; JD, Willamette U., 1976. Bar: Oreg. 1977, U.S. Dist. Ct. Oreg. 1977, U.S. Ct. Appeals (9th cir.) 1977, U.S. Supreme Ct. 1980. Assoc. Bullivant, Wright et al, Portland, 1976—79; ptnr. Samuels, Samuels et al, Portland, 1979—80; mng. shareholder Gevurtz, Menashe, Larson & Howe, P.C., Portland, 1982—. Frequent spkr. on family law, 1979—; former pro tem judge County of Clackamas, Oreg. Editor-in-chief: Willamette Law Jour. 1st lt. US Army, 1971—73. Mem.: ABA, Multnomah County Bar Assn. (pres. 1997—98), Oreg. State Bar Assn. (chair family law sect. 1981—82, bd. govs. 2004—07, pres. 2007), Am. Acad. Matrimonial Lawyers (pres. Oreg. chpt. 1996—97), Phi Beta Kappa, Phi Kappa Phi. Office: Gevurtz Menashe Larson & Howe PC 111 SW 5th Ave Ste 900 Portland OR 97204

MENCER, SUE (CONSTANCE SUZANNE MENCER), former federal agency administrator; b. Nov. 15, 1947; m. John Mencer; children: Jessie, Alex. BA in Spanish, Ohio St. U., 1968; Grad., JFK Sch. Govt., Harvard U., 2003. Tchr. Spanish, 1968—78; spl. agt. FBI, 1978—85, supervisory spl. agt., 1985—90, supr., 1990—98; pvt. cons. Anti-Terrorism Tng., Denver; exec. dir. dept. pub. safety State of Colo., Denver, 2000—03; exec. dir. Office of State & Local Govt. Coordination & Preparedness US Dept. Homeland Security, Washington, 2003—05; sr. policy advisor govt. rels. group Brownstein Hyatt & Farber, PC, Denver, 2005—. Mem.: Commn. on Jud. Discipline, Soc. Former Spl. Agents. Office: Brownstein Hyatt & Farber PC 410 17th St 22nd Fl Denver CO 80202 E-mail: smencer@bhf-law.com.

MENDE, HOWARD SHIGEHARU, mechanical engineer; b. Hilo, Hawaii, Nov. 19, 1947; s. Tsutomu and Harue (Kubomitsu) M. BS in Mech. Engring., U. Hawaii, 1969; MS in Mech. Engring., U. So. Calif., 1975. Registered profl. engr., Calif. Mem. tech. staff I Rockwell

Internat., Anaheim, Calif., 1970-71, LA, 1971-73, mem. tech. staff II, 1973-77, mem. tech. staff IV, 1984-86; devel. engr. AiRsch. Mfg. Co., Torrance, Calif., 1977-83; mech. engr. Def. Contracts Mgmt. East, Santa Ana, Calif., 1987-94, electronics engr., 1994—. Lectr. Pacific States U., LA, 1974-75. Mem. ASME. Democrat. Buddhist. Home: 1946 W 180th Pl Torrance CA 90504-4417 Office: Def Contract Mgmt Agy 2000 E Imperial Hwy El Segundo CA 90245-2463 Personal E-mail: hmende@socal.rr.com. Business E-Mail: howard.mende@dcma.mil.

MENDEL, JERRY MARC, electrical engineering educator; b. NYC, May 14, 1938; s. Alfred and Eleanor (Deutch) M.; m. Letty Susan Grossman, June 26, 1960; children: Jonathan, Aileen. BMechE cum laude, Poly. U., 1959, MEE, 1960, PhD in Elec. Engring., 1963. Registered profl. engr., Calif. Instr. elec. engring. Poly. Inst. Bklyn., 1960—63; engring. scientist and sect. chief McDonnell-Douglas Astronautics Co., Huntington Beach, Calif., 1963-74; prof. dept. elec. engring. systems U. So. Calif., LA, 1974—, chmn. dept., 1984-91, dir. Signal and Image Processing Inst., 1991-94, assoc. dir. edn. Integrated Media Sys. Ctr., 1996—2004. Pres., founder MENTECH, Culver City, Calif., 1983—; pres. United Signals and Systems, Inc., 1989-2001. Author: Discrete Techniques of Parameter Estimation: The Equation Error Formulation, 1973, Optimal Seismic Deconvolution: An Estimation Based Approach, 1983 (Phi Kappa Phi award 1984), Lessons in Digital Estimation Theory, 1987, Maximum-Likelihood Deconvolution, 1990, Lessons in Estimation Theory for Signal Processing, Communications and Control, 1995; editor: Prelude to Neural Networks: Adaptive and Learning Systems, 1994, Uncertain Rule-Based Fuzzy Logic Systems: Introduction and New Directions, 2001; co-editor: Adaptive Learning and Pattern Recognition Systems, 1970. Fellow IEEE (Centennial medal 1984, Third Millennium medal 2000), IFSA; mem. IEEE Control Systems Soc. (Disting.; pres. 1986), IEEE Computational Intelligence Soc.(AdCom 2004-; Fuzzy Sys. Pioneer award, 2008). Office: U So Calif Dept Elec Engring Sys Eeb 400 Los Angeles CA 90089-2564 Home Phone: 310-837-1993; Office Phone: 213-740-4445. Business E-Mail: mendel@sipi.usc.edu.

MENDEL, JOHN W., automotive executive; With US ops. divsn. Ford Motor Co., 1976, various sales mktg. positions Lincoln Mercury, major markets/dealer advt. mgr., 1990—92, regional ops. mgr. Chgo., 1992, San Francisco, LA, 1993—98, dir. mktg. Ford of Britain, 1999—2002, exec. v.p., COO Mazda N.Am., 2002—04; sr. v.p. automobile ops. Honda/Acura Am. Honda Motor Co., Inc., 2004—. Bd. dirs. Sirius XM Radio, Inc., 2008—. Named a Power Player, Advt. Age mag., 2008. Office: Am Honda Motor Co 1919 Torrance Blvd Torrance CA 90501 Office Fax: 310-783-3023.

MENDELSOHN, DANIEL, writer, humanities professor; b. Long Island, NY, 1960; BA summa cum laude in Jour., U. Va., 1982; PhD Mellon Fell. in Humanities, Princeton U., 1994. Weekly book critic NY Mag., 2000—02; freelance jour., 2002—; lectr., dept. Classics Princeton U., 1994—2002; Charles Ranlett Flint Professor of Humanities Bard Coll., 2002—. Contbr. articles NY Times, New Yorker, NY Review of Books, Esquire Mag., The Nation, The Paris Review (Nat. Book Critics Circle award for Reviewing, 2001); author: (memoirs) The Elusive Embrace: Desire and the Riddle of Identity, 1999 (NY Times Notable Book Yr., 1999), The Lost: A Search for Six of Six Million, 2006 (Nat. Books Critics Circle award for Autobiography, 2006); contbr. chapters to books incl. Best Am. Travel Writing, Republicans Can Be Cured!, Best Am. Humor Writing. Recipient George Jean Nathan Prize for Drama Criticism; grantee Guggenheim Fell., 2005. Office: c/o Paradigm Agency 360 N Crescent Dr Beverly Hills CA 90210 Office Fax: 310-288-2000.

MENDELSOHN, HAROLD, sociologist, educator; b. Jersey City, Oct. 30, 1923; s. Louis and Bessie (Yulinsky) M.; m. Irene Sylvia Gordon, Apr. 10, 1949; 1 dau., Susan Lynn. BS, CCNY, 1945; MA, Columbia U., 1946; PhD, New Sch. Social Research, 1956. Sr. survey analyst U.S. Dept. State, Washington, 1951-52; research assoc. Bur. Social Sci. Research, Am. U., Washington, 1952-56; assoc. mgr. mktg. communications McCann-Erickson Advt., NYC, 1956-58; assoc. dir. Psychol. Corp., NYC, 1958-62; prof. dept. mass communications U. Denver, 1962-89, prof. emeritus, 1989—, chmn., 1970-78, dean faculty social scis., 1984-86, spl. asst. to chancellor, 1986-88. Morton vis. disting. prof. Ohio U., spring 1981; cons. FTC, Denver Rsch. Inst., U.S. Consumer Product Safety Commn., The Gallup Orgn., Ford Found., Fedn. Rocky Mountain States, CBS, ABC, Children's TV Workshop; vis. prof. London Sch. Econs., 1973, Hebrew U., 1973. (Emmy award Nat. Acad. TV Arts Scis. 1968, Gold Camera award U.S. Indsl. Film Festival 1972); Author: Mass Entertainment, 1966, (with David H. Bayley) Minorities and the Police: Confrontation in America, 1969, (with Irving Crespi) Polls, Television and the New Politics, 1970, (with others) Television and Growing Up: The Impact of Televised Violence, 1972, (with Garrett O'Keefe) The People Choose a President, 1976; editor: Mass Communications series, 1967-69; contbr. articles to profl. jours. Mem. Denver Coun. Pub. TV, 1970-78; mem. U.S. Surgeon Gen.'s Sci. Adv. Com. on TV and Social Behavior, 1969-71; bd. dirs. Nat. Safety Coun., 1963-69; mem. pub. affairs adv. bd. Air Force Acad. Found., 1972-76; mem. cancer control and rehab. adv. com. Nat. Cancer Inst., 1976-81; mem. adv. coun., prevention div. Nat. Inst. Alcoholism and Alcohol Abuse, 1977-82; trustee Colo. Med. Svc., Inc., 1973-78. Recipient award TV Bur. Advt., 1962, Met. Life award Nat. Safety Council, 1967; Gold Eagle award, 1973; Silver award Internat. Festival Film and TV, 1974 Fellow Am. Psychol. Assn., Am. Sociol. Assn.; mem. Am. Assn. Pub. Opinion Research (pres. 1973-74), AAAS, N.Y. Acad. Scis., Sigma Delta Chi, Omicron Delta Kappa. Clubs: Chicago Press.

MENDELSON, ALAN CHARLES, lawyer; b. San Francisco, Mar. 27, 1948; s. Samuel Mendelson and Rita Rosalie (Spindel) Brown; children: Jonathan Daniel, David Gary; m. Agnès Marie Barbariol. BA with great distinction, U. Calif., Berkeley, 1969; JD cum laude, Harvard U., 1973. Bar: Calif. 1973. Assoc. Cooley Godward LLP, San Francisco, 1973-80, ptnr. Palo Alto, 1980-2000, mng. ptnr. Palo Alto office, 1990-95, 96-97; sec. acting gen. counsel Amgen Inc., Thousand Oaks, Calif., 1990-91; acting gen. counsel Cadence Design Sys., Inc., San Jose, Calif., 1995-96; sr. ptnr. Latham & Watkins LLP, Menlo Park, Calif., 2000—. Co-chair venture & tech. group Latham & Watkins; mem. bd. advisors Santa Clara Computer and High Tech. Law Jour., 2004—08; bd. adv. vc Berklay Chemistry Dept., 2007—; mem. emerging cos. sect. governing body Biotech. Industry Orgn., 2004—; mem. US Bd. Dir., Rambam Hosp. Bd. dirs. Bay Bio, Calif. Alumni Assn., 2005—; chmn. Piedmont (Calif.) Civil Svc. Commn., 1978-80; fundraiser Harvard Law Sch. Fund, U. Calif. Berkeley Health Scis. Initiative, Lucille Packard Children's Hosp.; pres., mem. exec. com., bd. dirs. No. Calif. chpt. Nat. Kidney Found., 1986-98; mem. Overseers' Com. to visit Harvard Law Sch., 2005—.bd. trustee U. Calif. Berkley Found., 2008-, With USAR, 1969-75. Recipient Disting. Svc. award Nat. Kidney Found., 1992; named U. Calif. Berkeley Alumni scholar, 1966, Scaife Found. scholar, 1966, One of 100 Most Influential Attys. in U.S. Nat. Law Jour., 1994, 97, 2000, 06. Mem. Bohemian Club, Phi Beta Kappa. Jewish. Home: 76 De Bell Dr Atherton CA 94027-2253 Office: Latham & Watkins LLP 140 Scott Dr Menlo Park CA 94025 Home Phone: 650-853-1343; Office Phone: 650-463-4693. Business E-Mail: alan.mendelson@lw.com.

MENDELSON, LEE M., film company executive, producer, director, writer; b. San Francisco, Mar. 24, 1933; s. Palmer C. and Jeanette D. (Wise) M.; children: Glenn, Linda, Jason, Sean. BA, Stanford U., 1954. With Sta. KPIX-TV, 1961-63; chmn. bd., pres. Lee Mendelson Film Prodns. Inc., Los Angeles and Burlingame, Calif., 1963—. Guest instr. in communications Stanford U. Exec. producer, co-writer (miniseries) This Is America, Charlie Brown; producer: Charlie Brown, Cathy, Betty Boop, (TV spls.) John Steinbeck's Travels with Charley, American and Americans, The Fantastic Funnies, You Asked for It, Here Comes Garfield, (animated films) A Boy Named Charlie Brown, Snoopy Come Home, Race for Your Life Charlie Brown, Peanuts, Bon Voyage Charlie Brown (And Don't Come Back), Garfield and Friends, Mother Goose and Grim. Served to 1st lt. USAF, 1954-57. Recipient 7 Emmy awards, 3 Peabody awards. Mem. Writers Guild Am., Dirs. Guild Am. Office: Lee Mendelson Film Prodn Inc 330 Primrose Rd Ste 215 Burlingame CA 94010-4028

MENDENHALL, BRONCO, college football coach; b. Alpine, Utah; s. Paul Mendenhall; m. Holly Johnston; children: Cutter, Breaker, Raeder. Attended, Snow Coll., Ephraim, Utah, 1984—85; BS in Phys. Edn., Oreg. State U., Corvallis, 1988, MEd in Exercise Physiology, 1990. Grad. asst., defensive line coach Oreg. State U. Beavers, 1989—90, defensive line coach, 1995, defensive coord., secondary coach, 1996, Snow Coll. Badgers, 1991—92; secondary coach No. Ariz. U. Lumberjacks, 1993—94, co-defensive coord., 1994; secondary coach La. Tech. U. Bulldogs, 1997; defensive coord., secondary coach U. N.Mex. Lobos, 1998—2002, asst. head coach, 2002; defensive coord. Brigham Young U. Cougars, 2003—04, head football coach, 2005—. Recipient Leo Gribkoff Meml. award, Oreg. State U., 1987; named Asst. Coach of Yr., BYU Cougar Club, 2003, Region IV Coach of Yr., Am. Football Coaches Assn., 2006; finalist Eddie Robinson Nat. Coach of Yr. award, 2006. Office: Brigam Young Univ Athletics Dept Student Athlete Bldg 220 SAB Provo UT 84602*

MENDENHALL, HARRY BARTON, lawyer; b. Oct. 31, 1946; BA, Colo. Coll., 1968; JD, U. Colo., 1971. Bar: Colo. 1971. Ptnr. Mendenhall & Malouff, R.L.L.P., Rocky Ford, Colo., 1971—. Mem. nominating com. Colo. Supreme Ct., Denver, 1986-91; pres. Colo. Lawyer Trust Account Found., Denver, 1995-97. Mem. Colo. Bar Assn. (pres. 1999-2000). Office: Mendenhall & Malouff 805 Chestnut Ave Rocky Ford CO 81067-1224 Office Phone: 719-254-7606. E-mail: bmendenhall@centurytel.net.

MENDENHALL, MICHAEL, computer company executive; B, Emerson Coll., Boston. Various sr. mktg. positions to exec. v.p. mktg., comm. Walt Disney Co.; sr. v.p., chief mktg. officer Hewlett-Packard Co., 2007—. Bd. mem. USA Swimming Found.; bd. mem. San Gabriel Valley coun. Boy Scouts America. Named a Power Player, Advt. Age mag., 2008; named one of Best Marketers, BtoB Mag., 2008. Mem.: Exec. Mktg. Coun. (sr. adv. bd.), Acad. TV Arts & Sciences, Mktg. 50. Office: Hewlett Packard Co 3000 Hanover St Palo Alto CA 94304-1185 Office Phone: 650-857-1501. Office Fax: 650-857-5518.

MENDENHALL, ROBERT W., education technology executive; b. Pasadena, Calif., Nov. 18, 1954; s. Winton L. and Margaret E. (Kerr) Mendenhall; m. Kathleen A. White, 1978; children: Jamie, Robert, Christina, Virginia, Kathleen, Lori, Emily. BS in Univ. Studies, Brigham Young U., Provo, Utah, 1977, PhD in Instrnl. Psychology and Tech., 2003. Gen. mgr. Wicat Inst., Orem, Utah, 1977-80; pres., dir. Wicat Systems Inc., Orem, Utah, 1980—92; exec. v.p., dir. Jostens Learning Corp., San Diego, 1992—94; gen. mgr. IBM K-12 Edn., Atlanta, 1994—96, exec. cons., 1997—98; pres. Western Govs. U., Salt Lake City, 1999—. Mem. bd. bus. and econ. devel. State of Utah, 1997—2001; mem. Commn. Tech. and Adult Learning, 1999—2000; adv. bd. Partnership for 21st Century Skills, 2003—04; mem. Sec. of Edn.'s Commn. on Future of Edn., 2005—06. Missionary and bishop LDS Ch.; bd. dir. Oquirrh Inst., 2002—07; bd. dir. and chair Gina Bachauer Internat. Piano Found., 1980—2000. Office: Western Gov U Ste 700 4001 South 700 East Salt Lake City UT 84107 Home Phone: 801-209-4400; Office Phone: 801-274-3280. Business E-Mail: rwm@wgu.edu.

MENDEZ, JOHN ANTHONY, federal judge; b. Oakland, Calif., 1955; married; 3 children. BA, Stanford U., 1977; JD, Harvard Law Sch., 1980. Bar: Calif. 1980. Assoc. Chickering & Gregory, 1980—81, Orriock, Herrington and Sutcliffe, 1981—84; asst. US atty. (no. dist.) Calif. US Dept. Justice, 1984—86, 1992—93; assoc., ptnr. Downey, Brand, Seymour and Rohwer, 1986—92; of counsel Brobeck, Phleger and Harrison, 1993—95; shareholder Somach, Simmons and Dunn, 1995—2001; judge Sacramento County Superior Ct., Calif., 2001—07, US Dist. Ct. (ea. dist.) Calif., 2008—. Bd. dirs. Children's Receiving Home. Instr., lector, Eucharistic min. Cath. Ch., Calif. Mem.: Rotary. Office: US Dist Ct 501 I St Ste 4-200 Sacramento CA 95814 Office Phone: 916-930-4000.

MENDOZA, MARTHA, reporter; b. LA, 1969; BA, U. Calif. Santa Cruz, 1988. Reporter Madera Tribune, Bay City News Svc., Santa Cruz County Sentinel; nat. investigative reporter Associated Press, San Jose, Calif., 1995—. Co-author: The Bridge at No Gun RI: A Hidden Nightmare from the Korean War, 2001. Recipient Pulitzer prize, 2000, Alumni Achievment award, U. Calif. Santa Cruz, 2002; John S. Knight fellow, Stanford U., 2001. Office: Associated Press 675 N 1st St San Jose CA 95112

MENDOZA, STANLEY ATRAN, pediatric nephrologist, educator; b. Pitts., May 7, 1940; s. Joseph William and Marian Ruth (Atran) M.; m. Carole Ann Klein, June 23, 1963; children: Daniel, Joseph. Student, Harvard U., 1957—59; BA, Johns Hopkins U., 1961, MD, 1964. Diplomate Am. Bd. Pediat. Intern Johns Hopkins Hosp., Balt., 1964-65; jr. asst. resident dept. medicine Children's Hosp. Med. Ctr., Boston, 1965-66; asst. attending physician, dir. renal rsch. labs. Children's Meml. Hosp., Chgo., 1969-71; asst. prof. pediat. U. Calif. Sch. Medicine, San Diego, 1971—73, assoc. prof., 1973—79, prof. pediat. dept. pediat. divsn. pediatric nephrology, 1979—, vice chmn. dept. pediat., 1986—87, chmn. dept. pediat., 1992—2000. Contbr. article in field to profl. publ. Served With USPHS, 1966-69. Fogarty Sr. Internat. fellow, 1978-79; Alan J. Wurtzburger rsch. scholar, 1964; recipient Johns Hopkins Med. Soc. award, 1964, hon. mention Borden Undergrad. rsch. award in medicine, 1964; Eleanor Roosevelt internat. fellow Internat. Union Against Cancer, 1984-85. Mem. Am. Fedn. Clin. Rsch., Am. Pediatric Soc., Am. Physiol. Soc., Am. Soc. Nephrology, Am. Soc. Pediatric Nephrology, Internat. Soc. Nephrology. Office: U Calif San Diego Dept Pediat 9500 Gilman Dr # 0696 La Jolla CA 92093-5004 Home Phone: 858-459-0979. E-mail: samendoza@ucsd.edu.

MENDOZA, TONY, state legislator; m. to Leticia; children: three. B in Polit. Sci./Pub. Adminstrn., Calif. State U., Long Beach. California State Assemblyman, District 56, 2006-; 4th grade tchr., Bklyn. Ave. Elem. Sch.; mem. Artesia City Coun., 1997-. Democrat. Office: Dist 56 12501 E Imperial Hwy Ste 210 Norwalk CA 90650 Office Phone: 562-846-5600. Office Fax: 562-863-7466. Business E-Mail: Assemblymember.Mendoza@assembly.ca.gov.

MENELL, PETER SETH, law educator; b. Jersey City, Dec. 2, 1958; s. Allan and Carole M.; m. Claire Marie Sylvia. SB in Econs., MIT, 1980; MA in Econs., Stanford U., Calif., 1982; PhD in Econs, 1986; JD, Harvard U., 1986. Law clk. to presiding judge US Ct. Appeals (2d cir.), Hartford, Conn., 1986-87; assoc. prof. law Georgetown U. Law Ctr., Washington, 1987-90; prof. sch. law U. Calif., Berkeley, 1990—, dir. Ctr. Law and Tech., 1995—. Vis. prof. Harvard Law Sch., 1990, Stanford Law Sch., 1992-93. Co-author (with Richard Stewart): Environmental Law and Policy, 1994; co-author: (with J. Dwyer) Property Law and Policy, 1998; co-author: (with R. Merges & M. Lemley) Intellectual Property in the New Technological Age, 2006; co-author: (with M. Lemley, R. Merges and P. Samuelson) Software and Internet Law, 2006; author: Environmental Law, 2002; contbr. articles to profl. jour. Stanford U. fellow, 1980, Olin fellow Harvard U., 1985, Olin Found. fellow, 1989. Mem. Am. Econs. Assn., Calif. Bar Assn. Jewish. Office: University of California School of Law Boalt Hall, Rm 355 Berkeley CA 94720-7200 Office Phone: 510-642-5489. Business E-Mail: pmenell@law.berkeley.edu.

MENENDEZ, BELINDA, broadcast executive; Student, St. Andrews U., Scotland. With internat. TV sales Televisa, 1986—95; mgr. TV sales Cisneros; internat. tv distbn. ops. mgr. Michael Solomon's S.I.E.; exec. v.p. sales Studio Canal (formerly Canal Plus DA); co-pres. NBC Universal Internat. TV Distbn., Universal City, Calif., 2001—04, pres., 2004—. Named one of The 100 Most Influential Hispanics, Hispanic Bus. Mag., The Most Powerful and Influential Latinos, Imagen Found., The 100 Most Powerful Women in Entertainment, Hollywood Reporter; named to Hispanic Women in Entertainment Power 25, Latino Power 50. Office: Universal TV Distbn USA Bldg 1440/3030 100 Universal City Plaza Universal City CA 91608-1002

MENG, TERESA H., electrical engineer, educator; b. Taiwan; BSEE, Nat. Taiwan U., 1983; MS in Elec. Engring. and Computer Sci., U. Calif., Berkeley, 1984, PhD in Elec. Engring. and Computer Sci., 1988. Mem. faculty elec. engring. dept. Stanford U., Calif., 1988—, Reid Weaver Dennis prof. elec. engring. Calif., 2003—; founder, bd. dirs. Atheros Comm., Inc., Calif., 1998—, pres., CEO, 1998—99. Contbr. articles to sci. jours., chapters to books; author: Synchronization Design of Digital Systems, 1990; co-editor: VLSI Signal Processing IX, 1996. Bd. trustees Computer Hist. Mus. Recipient Eli Jury award, U. Calif. Berkeley, 1988, Best Paper award, IEEE Signal Processing Soc., 1989, Presdl. Young Investigator award, NSF, 1989, Young Investigator award, Office of Naval Rsch., 1989, IBM Faculty Devel. award, 1989, Disting. Lectr. award, IEEE Signal Processing Soc., 20/20 Vision award, Chief Info. Officer Mag., 2002, Demo@15 World-Class Innovator award, 2005; named Innovator of Yr., MIT Sloan Sch. eBusiness Awards, 2002; named one of Top 10 Entrepreneurs, Red Herring, 2001. Fellow: IEEE; mem.: NAE. Achievements include patents in field. Office: Dept Elec Engring 209 CIS Bldg 420 Via Palou Mall Stanford CA 94305-4070 Office Phone: 650-725-3636. Office Fax: 650-725-3383. E-mail: meng@ee.stanford.edu.

MENHALL, DALTON WINN, lawyer, insurance executive, professional association administrator; b. Edgerton, Wis., Aug. 1, 1939; s. Joseph Laurence and Mary Winn (Dalton) M.; m. Lilian Marilyn Christie, Oct. 19, 1968; children: Dalton Winn II, Rebecca Lynn, Katherine Elizabeth BA, Ill. Coll., 1962; JD, Vanderbilt U., 1965. Bar: Wis. 1965; cert. assn. exec. Staff asst. State Bar of Wis., Madison, 1965-72, dir., 1972-76, legis. counsel, dir. continuing legal edn., 1972-76; exec. dir. N.J. State Bar Assn., Trenton, 1976-86; nat. programs dir. Herbert L. Jamison & Co., 1987-91; v.p. Edward Poll & Assocs., 1995; exec. dir. San Diego County Bar Assn., 1995—. Trustee St. Patricks' Day Sch., 1994-96. Exec. v.p. Phi Alpha Delta Pub. Svc. Ctr., Washington, 1991-94; exec. dir. Phi Alpha Delta Law Frat. Internat., Granada Hills, Calif., 1992-94; bd. dirs. San Diego unit Am. Cancer Soc., 1996-98, sec.-treas., 1998, pres.-elect, 1998-99, pres., 1999-2000, bd. dirs. Calif. divsn., 1999—; mem. vestry St. John's Episcopal Ch., 1997, sr. warden, 1998-99. Fellow Am. Bar Found.; mem. ABA (cons., youth edn. and citizenship com 1993-97), Nat. Assn. Bar Execs. (pres. 1985-86), N.J. State Bar Assn., State Bar Wis., Am. Soc. Assn. Execs., Am. Judicature Soc., Nat. Assn. Bar Execs. (hon.), So. Calif. Soc. Assn. Execs., San Diego Soc. Assn. Execs. (bd. dirs. 1997-98, sec. 1998-99).

MENKEN, JANE AVA, demographer, educator; b. Phila., Nov. 29, 1939; d. Isaac Nathan and Rose Ida (Sarvetnick) Golubitsky; m. Matthew Menken, 1960 (div. 1985); children: Kenneth Lloyd, Kathryn Lee; m. Richard Jessor, Nov. 13, 1992. AB, U. Pa., 1960; MS, Harvard U., 1962; PhD, Princeton U., NJ, 1975. Asst. in biostats. Harvard U. Sch. Pub. Health, Boston, 1962-64; math. statistician NIMH, Bethesda, Md., 1964-66; rsch. assoc. dept. biostats. Columbia U., NYC, 1966-69; mem. rsch. staff Office of Population Rsch. Princeton U., 1969-71, 75-87, asst. dir., 1978-86, assoc. dir., 1986-87, prof. sociology, 1980-82, prof. sociology and pub. affairs, 1982-87; prof. sociology and demography U. Pa., Phila., 1987-97, UPS Found. prof. social scis., 1987-97, dir. Population Studies Ctr., 1989-95; prof. sociology U. Colo., Boulder, 1997—, faculty assoc. Population Program, Inst. Behavioral Sci., 1997—; dir. Population Aging Ctr., 2000—, Inst. Behavioral Sci., 2001—, disting. prof., 2002—. Mem. social scis. and population study sect., NIH, Bethesda, 1978-82, chmn., 1980-82, dirs. adv. com., 1995-2000, Nat. Adv. Child Health and Human Devel. Coun., 1988-91, adv. com. Fogarty Internat. Ctr., 2000-02, population adv. com. Rockefeller Found., NYC, 1981-93, com. on population and demography, NAS, Washington, 1978-83, com. on population, 1983-85, 1996-2002, chair 1998-2002, com. nat. stats., 1983-89, com. on AIDS rsch., 1987-93, chair 1990-93; co-chair panel data and rsch. priorities for arresting AIDS in sub-Saharan Africa, 1994-96, Com. on Behavioral and Social Scis. and Edn., 1991-97, chair, steering com., workshop on aging in Africa, 2003-06, chair, sci. adv. com., INDEPTH newtwork, 2002-; cons. Internat. Centre for Diarrhoeal Disease Rsch., Bangladesh, Dhaka, 1984—. Author: (with Mindel C. Sheps) Mathematical Models of Conception and Birth, 1973, (with Ann Blanc and Cynthia Lloyd) Training and Support of Developing Country Population Scientists, 2002; editor: (with Henri Leridon) Natural Fertility, 1979, (with Frank Furstenberg, Jr. and Richard Lincoln) Teenage Sexuality, Pregnancy and Childbearing, 1981, World Population and U.S. Policy: The Choices Ahead, 1986, (with Barney Cohen) Aging in Sub-Saharan Africa: Recommendations for Furthering Research, 2006; contbr. articles to profl. jours. Bd. dirs. Alan Guttmacher Inst., NYC, 1981-90, 93-2000, African Population and Health Rsch. Ctr., Nairobi, Kenya, 2000—. Nat. Merit scholar, 1957; John Simon Guggenheim Found. fellow, 1992-93, Ctr. for Advanced Study in Behavioral Scis. fellow, 1995-96. Fellow AAAS, Am. Statis. Assn.; mem. NAS, Inst. of Medicine, Am. Acad. Arts and Scis., Population Assn. Am. (pres. 1985, Mindel Sheps award 1982), Am. Pub. Health Assn. (Mortimer Spiegelman award 1975), Am. Sociol. Assn., Soc. for Study of Social Biology, Internat. Union for Sci. Study of Population (coun. 1989-97), Sociol. Rsch. Assn. (exec. com. 1991-96, pres. 1996). Office: U Colo IBS#1 483 UCB Boulder CO 80309-0483 Office Phone: 303-492-8148. Business E-Mail: menken@colorado.edu.

MENO, LIONEL R., academic administrator; Commr. edn. Tex. Edn Agy., Austin; dist. supt. Board of Coop. Education Services, Angola, NY, 1995—99; dean Coll. Edn. San Diego State U., 1999—. Office: 5500 Cempanile Dr San Diego CA 92182

MENSE, ALLAN TATE, research and development engineering executive; b. Kansas City, Mo., Nov. 29, 1945; s. Martin Conrad Mense and Nancy (Tate) Johnson; children from previous marriage: Melanie Georgia Thomas, Eileen Mense Hartzell. BS, U. Ariz., 1968, MS, 1970; PhD, U. Wis., 1977; MS in Indsl. Engring., Ariz. State U., 1999. Registered profl. indsl. engr., ASQ cert. reliability engring. Scientist Oak Ridge (Tenn.) Nat. Lab, 1976-79; sr. staff sci. and tech. comm. U.S. Ho. Reps., Washington, 1979-81; sr. scientist McDonnell Douglas Astro. Co., St. Louis, 1981-85; from dep. chief scientist to chief scientist Dept. Def. Strategic Def. Initiative Orgn., Washington, 1985-88; v.p. rsch. Fla. Inst. Tech., Melbourne, 1988-92; pres. Advanced Tech. Mgmt., Inc., Tempe, Ariz., 1992-97; lead sys. engr. Motorola Space Sys. Tech. Group, Chandler, Ariz., 1998—2001; chief engr., prin. engring. fellow Raytheon Missile Sys., 2002—. Vis. scholar Sloan Sch., MIT, 1995-96; mem. U.S. Army Sci. Bd., 2005—. Contbr. over 60 articles to profl. jours. Ariz. State U. scholar, 1996-97. Mem. AIAA (sr. mem.), IEEE (chmn. energy com. 1985—, sr. mem.), Nat. Def. Industries Assn., Am. Phys. Soc., Am. Nuclear Soc., Inst. Indsl. Engrs., Fla. Com. Nat. Space Club (charter), Sigma Xi, Theta Tau, Pi Mu Alpha. Episcopalian. Office: 1151 E Hermans Rd B840/MS8 Tucson AZ 85706 Home: 116 E Camino Limon Verde Sahuarita AZ 85629 Office Phone: 520-794-4720. Business E-Mail: allan_t_mense@raytheon.com.

MERCER, D. SCOTT, telecommunications industry executive; BS, Calif. Poly. State U., Pomona, 1976. With Price Waterhouse, San Jose, Calif.; CFO, controller LSI Logic Corp., Milpitas, Calif.; CFO Western Digital Corp., Lake Forest, Calif., 1991—96, sr. v.p., interim CFO, 2001—04, sr. v.p., adv. to CEO, 2004, exec. v.p., CFO, chief adminstrv. officer, 2004; v.p., fin., European ops. Dell Computer Corp., 1998—2000; v.p., CFO TeraLogic, Inc., Mountain View, Calif., 2000—01; interim CEO Adaptec, Inc., Milpitas, 2005—08; CEO Conexant Systems, Inc., Newport Beach, Calif., 2008—. Bd. dirs. Polycom, Inc., SMART Modular Techs., Inc., Palm, Inc., Conexant Systems, Inc., 2008; chmn. Adaptec, Inc. Office: Conexant Systems Inc 4000 MacArthur Blvd Newport Beach CA 92660-3095 Office Phone: 949-483-4600. Office Fax: 949-483-4078.

MERCER, JAMES LEE, management consultant; b. Sayre, Okla., Nov. 7, 1936; s. Fred Elmo and Ora Lee (Davidson) M.; m. Karolyn Lois Prince, Nov. 16, 1962; children: Tara Lee, James Lee. BS, U. Nev., Reno, 1964, MBA, 1966; postgrad. exec. devel. program, Cornell U., Ithaca, NY, 1979. Cert. in mcpl. adminstrn. U. NC, 1971, lifetime Jr. coll. tchng. credential Calif., cert. mgmt. cons. Methods and results supr. Pacific Tel. & Tel., Sacramento, 1965-66; prodn. control supr. Gen. Dynamics, Pomona, Calif., 1966-67; nuclear submarine project mgr. Litton Industries, Pascagoula, Miss., 1967-70; asst. city mgr. City of Raleigh, NC, 1970-73; nat. program dir. Pub. Tech., Inc., Washington, 1973-76; gen. mgr. Battelle So. Ops., Atlanta, 1976-79; v.p. Korn/Ferry Internat., Atlanta, 1979-81; pres. James Mercer & Assocs. Inc.; mgmt. cons. Atlanta, 1981-86; chief Indsl. Ext. Divsn. Ga. Inst. of Tech., Atlanta, 1981-83, dir. Ga. Productivity Ctr.; dir. govtl. cons. svc. Coopers & Lybrand, 1983-84; regional v.p. Wolfe & Assocs., Inc., 1984-86; pres., CEO, chmn. Mercer, Slavin & Nevins, Inc., 1986-90. The Mercer Group, Inc., 1990—. Ad hoc prof. NC State U., 1972-73; bd. dirs. Taratec Corp., lectr., spkr. in field. Author: Public Management Systems, 1978, Public Technology, 1981, Managing Urban Government Services, 1981, Strategic Planning for Public Managers, 1990, Public Management in Lean Years, 1992; contbr. numerous articles to profl. jours. Chmn. Raleigh Mayor's Civic Ctr. Authority Study Commn., 1971; founding bd. dirs. Mordecai Sq. Hist. Soc., Nat. Civic League; founding mem. Calif. Poly. State U., adv. coun. Coll. Bus. Adminstrn., San Luis Obispo, 1980-95, bd. mem. emeritus, 1995—; founding mem., bd. trustees U. Nev. Found., Reno, 1985-91, trustee emeritus, 1991—; founding mem. U. SC and Coll. Charleston, M Pub. Adminstrn. adv. bd., 1987-97. Mem.: NC League of Municipalities (George C. Franklin award 1971), Instit. Mgmt. Cons. (Atlanta Chpt. (v.p. membership 1991—97, bd. dirs. 1991—97), Contract Svcs. Assn. Am. (bd. dirs. Wash. DC 1990—2006), Ga. Indsl. Devel. Assn., Tech. Transfer Soc. (dir. 1978—87, treas. 1985—86), Internat. Pers. Mgmt. Assn., Govtl. Fin. Officers Assn., Inst. Indsl. Engrs. (chpt. pres. 1969—70, past pres.'s award 1970), Am. Soc. Pub. Adminstrn., Internat. City-County Mgmt. Assn., Raleigh Forward Leadership Orgn., U. Nev. Alumni Assn. (exec. com. 1969—79, Oustanding Alumnus), Shriners, Rotary, Atlanta C. of C., Masons, Beta Gamma Sigma. Home: 28 Sierra del Sol Santa Fe NM 87508-2136 Office: 551 W Cordova Rd Ste 726 Santa Fe NM 87505-1825 Office Phone: 505-466-9500. Personal E-mail: mercer@mindspring.com.

MERCER, JOHN A., former state legislator; b. Missoula, Mont., Jan. 21, 1957; m. Tine Mercer; children: Thomas, Michael. BA in Bus., U. Mont., 1979; JD, Northwestern U., 1982. Pvt. practice, Polson, Mont., 1982; mem. Mont. Ho. of Reps., 1984—, minority whip, 1989-90, minority leader, 1991-92, house spkr., 1993—2000, mem. rules com., mem. legis. administrv. com.; gov. bd. mem. Mont. St. U. Office: Montana St U MT Higher Education Complex 2500 Broadway Helena MT 59620 E-mail: john@polsonlaw.com.

MERCER, WILLIAM W., prosecutor; b. Jan. 7, 1964; BA in Polit. Sci., U. Mont., 1986; MPA, Harvard U., 1988; JD, George Mason U., 1993. Counselor to asst. atty. gen., sr. policy analyst Office of Policy Devel. US Dept. Justice, 1989—94, prin. assoc. dep. atty. gen. Washington, 2005—06, acting assoc. atty. gen., 2006—07, asst. US atty. Dist. Mont. Billings, Mont., 1994—2001, US atty., 2001—. Mem. president's adv. coun. U. Mont.; mem. bd. visitors U. Mont. Sch. Law; mem. atty. gen.'s adv. com. Office: US Attys Office PO Box 1478 Billings MT 59103 E-mail: askdoj@usdoj.gov.

MERCHANT, P. GLENN, JR., military officer, physician; b. Quonset Point, RI, Jan. 6, 1953; s. Paul Glenn and Mary Jean Merchant; m. Debra Colleene Brown, Nov. 25, 1951; children: Nicholas Ryan, Kaitlin Elizabeth, Joshua Daniel. BS in Biology, The Citadel, 1980—83; MD, Med. U. of SC., 1983—87; BA in Polit. Sci., The Citadel, 1971—75; Masters in Pub. Health and Tropical Medicine, Tulane U. Sch. of Pub. Health & Tropical Medicine, 1991—92. Diplomate Am. Bd. of Preventive Medicine, 1994. Marine aviator VMA-542, Cherry Point, NC, 1975—80; commd. 2d lt. USMC, 1975, advanced through grades to capt., 1980; intern in family medicine Naval Hosp., Charleston, SC, 1987—88; flight surgeon 2d MAW, 1988—91; resident in aerospace medicine Naval Aerospace Med. Inst., Charleston, SC, 1992—94; sr. med. officer USS John C. Stennis (CVN 74), Norfolk, 1994—97; prof. Uniformed Svcs. U., Bethesda, 1997—2005; mem. Med. Exam. Review Bd. Dept. of Def., USAF Acad., Colo., 2005—07, dir. Med. Exam Review Bd., 2007—. Chair Am. Bd. Preventive Medicine, Chgo., 2003—07. Recipient Delta Omega Scholastic Honor Soc., Tulane U. Sch. of Pub. Health, 1992, Phi Kappa Phi Honor Soc., The Citadel, 1983. Fellow: Am. Coll. of Preventive Medicine, Aerospace Med. Assn. (v.p. 2001—03); mem.: Am. Bd. Preventive Medicine (chair). Methodist. Office: Dept of Def Med Exam Review Bd 8034 Edgerton Dr Ste 132 U S A F Academy CO 80840-2200 Business E-Mail: glenn.merchant@dodmerb.tma.osd.mil.

MERGES, ROBERT PATRICK, law educator, writer; BS, Carnegie-Mellon U., 1981; JD, Yale Law Sch., 1985; LLM, JSD, Columbia Law Sch., 1988. Assoc. prof. Boston U. Sch. Law, 1988—92, prof., 1992—95; prof. law Boalt Hall Sch. Law, U. Calif., Berkeley, 1995—97, co-dir. Berkeley Ctr. Law and Tech., 1997—, Wilson Sonsini Goodrich & Rosati Prof. Intellectual Property Law, 1997—. Vis. prof. U. Calif., Davis Sch. Law, 2002—03; spl. cons. U.S. Dept. Justice; mem. U.S. Dept. Justice Task Force on Intellectual Property. Co-author: Patent Law and Policy: Cases and Materials, Legal Protection for Computer Technology, Intellectual Property in the New Technological Age, 2003, Foundations of Intellectual Property, 2004; contbr. articles to law jours. Grantee Alfred P. Sloan Foundation Grant, 1989—90, Office of Tech. Assessment Contract Rsch. Award, 1993, Sloan Foundation, 1994—, Dept. of Energy grant, 1998. Office: U Calif Sch Law Boalt Hall Berkeley CA 94720 E-mail: rmerges@law.berkeley.edu.

MERKER, STEVEN JOSEPH, lawyer; b. Cleve., Feb. 21, 1947; s. Steven Joseph and Laverne (Zamenik) Merker; m. Janet L. Whyatt; children: Steven, Rena, Ashley, Matthew. BS, Case Inst. Tech., 1968; MS, U. Fla., 1973; JD, George Washington U., 1976. Bar: Ohio 1976, US Dist. Ct. (no. dist.) Ohio 1976, US Dist. Ct. Colo. 1979, US Ct. Appeals (10th cir.) 1979, US Supreme Ct. 1989, US Patent & Trademark Office. Assoc. Jones, Day, Reavis & Pogue, Cleve., 1976-78, Davis, Graham & Stubbs, Denver, 1978-82, ptnr., 1983-96, chmn. labor and employment group, 1989-96; chmn. litig., labor and employment groups Merrick, Calvin & Merker, LLP, 1996-97; ptnr. Dorsey & Whitney LLP, Denver, 1997—, mng. ptnr. Denver office, 2000—. Mem. Tenth Cir. Adv. Com., 1997—2000. Bd. dirs. Very Spl. Arts, Colo., 1994—, Am. Liver Found., 2002—; legal counsel Coloradans for Lamm-Dick campaign, Denver, 1982, Nancy Dick for US Senate Com., Denver, 1984, Cantrell for Dist. Atty., Jefferson County, Colo., 1984. Capt. USAF, 1969—72. Mem.: ABA, Am. Intellectual Property Law Assn., Intellectual Property Owners Assn., Denver Bar Assn., Colo. Bar Assn. Office: Dorsey & Whitney LLP 370 17th St Ste 4700 Denver CO 80202-5644 Office Phone: 303-628-1514. Business E-Mail: merker.steve@dorsey.com.

MERKIN, ALBERT CHARLES, pediatrician, allergist; b. Chgo., Sept. 4, 1924; s. Harry A. and Goldie (Lamasky) M.; m. Eunice Aprill, Aug. 22, 1948; children: Audrey, Ellen, Joseph. Student, U. Ill., 1942-44; MD, U. Ill., Chgo., 1949. Diplomate Am. Bd. Allergy and Immunology, Am. Bd. Pediat. Intern, resident Cook County Hosp., Chgo.; resident Children's Meml. Hosp., Chgo.; with Valley Pediatric and Allergy Clinic, Las Vegas, Nev. Capt. USAF, 1950-53. Fellow Am. Acad. Pediatrics (state chmn. Nev. 1961-64, sect. allergy and immunology), Am. Coll. Allergy; mem. Am. Acad. Allergy, Allergy Subsplty. Group of Acad. Pediatrics (cert. pediatric allergist). Avocations: reading, travel. Office Phone: 702-341-8695.

MERKLEY, JEFFERY A., United States Senator from Oregon; b. Eugene, Oreg., Oct. 24, 1956; m. Mary Sorteberg; 2 children. BA, Stanford U., 1979; MA, Princeton U., 1982. Presdl. intern, 1982—85; analyst Congrl. Budget Office, 1985—89; mng. ptnr. Computer Medics, 1989—91; exec. dir. Portland Habitat for Humanity, 1991—94; dir. Housing Devel., Human Solutions, 1995—96; exec. dir. World Affairs Coun. Oreg., 1996—2003; mem. Oreg. Ho. of Reps., 1998—2009, spkr., 2007—09; US Senator from Oreg., 2009—. Democrat. Protestant. Office: PO Box 33167 Portland OR 97292-3167 also: B40B Dirksen Senate Office Bldg Washington DC 20510 Office Phone: 202-224-3753.*

MERRIFIELD, DONALD PAUL, ministries coordinator; b. Los Angeles, Nov. 14, 1928; s. Arthur S. and Elizabeth (Baker) M. BS in Physics, Calif. Inst. Tech., 1950; MS, U. Notre Dame, 1951; A.M., Ph.L. in Philosophy, St. Louis U., 1957; PhD, MIT, 1962; S.T.M., U. Santa Clara, Calif., 1966; S.T.D. (hon.), U. So. Calif., 1969; D.H.L. (hon.), U. Judaism, 1984, Hebrew Union Coll.-Jewish Inst. Religion, 1986. Joined Soc. of Jesus, 1951; ordained priest Roman Cath. Ch., 1965; instr. physics Loyola U., Los Angeles, 1961-62; lectr. Engring. Sch., Santa Clara, 1965; cons. theoretical chemistry Jet Propulsion Lab., Calif. Inst. Tech., 1962-69; asst. prof. physics U. San Francisco, 1967-69; pres. Loyola Marymount U., Los Angeles, 1969-84, chancellor, 1984—2002; regent, sr. rsch. fellow Chaminade U., Honolulu, 2002—; mem. religious ministry Catholic Diocese of Hawaii, 2002—. Contbr. chapters to books. Mem. Sigma Xi. Office: 2727 Pamoa Rd Honolulu HI 96822-1838 Home Phone: 808-988-3464. Personal E-mail: dmerrifield@calprov.org. Business E-Mail: dmerrifi@chaminade.edu.

MERRIFIELD, LANE, Internet company executive; b. Lethridge, Alta., Canada, 1978; With Disneyland, Burbank, Calif., 1995; sales rep. New Horizon Prodns., Kelowna, BC, 2003—05; co-founder, CEO Club Penguin, 2005—07, gen. mgr., 2007—; exec. v.p. Walt Disney Internet Grp., Burbank, Calif., 2007—. Office: Club Penguin 410-1620 Dickson Ave Kelowna BC V1Y-9Y2 Canada

MERRIFIELD, MICHAEL, state legislator; b. Ottowa, Colo., Jan. 3, 1947; m. Ginger Spencer; 2 children. Tchr. Colo. Pub. Schs.; tchr., choir dir. Coronado HS, Colorado Springs; operator, theater prodn. co. Ariz.; operator The Annex Cafe, Manitou Springs; councilman Manitou Springs City Coun., 1996—2000; mem. Dist. 18 Colo. House of Reps., 2002, chmn. edn. com. Author: (mountain bike guidebook) Colorado Gonzo Rides. Recipient Crystal Apple award, Colorado Springs Sch. Dist. 11. Mem.: Trails & Open Space Coalition. Democrat. Office: Colo State Capitol 200 E Colfax Rm 271 Denver CO 80203 Office Phone: 303-866-2932. Business E-Mail: michael.merrifield.house@state.co.us.*

MERRILL, HARVIE MARTIN, retired manufacturing executive; b. Detroit, Apr. 26, 1921; s. Harvie and Helen (Nelson) M.; m. Mardelle Merrill; children— Susan, Linda. BS in Chem. Engring, Purdue U., 1942, Bd Che magma cum laude. Devel. engr. Sinclair Refining Co., 1946-47; research and gen. mgr. 3M Co., St. Paul, 1947-65; v.p. fabricated products Plastics div. Stauffer Chem. Co., NYC, 1965-69; with Hexcel Corp., San Francisco, 1969-86, pres., chief exec. officer, 1969-86, chmn. bd., 1976-88. With USAF, 1942-46. Mem.: Interlachen Country Club. Home: 664 Osceola Ave Winter Park FL 32789 Home Fax: 407-628-3130.

MERRILL, RICHARD JAMES, retired educational director; b. Milw., Apr. 15, 1931; s. Henry Baldwin and Doris (Lucas) M.; m. Kathleen Emden Keely, June 14, 1953 (dec. Jan. 1974); children: Wendy Ann, Vicki Louise, Robin Kay, Christina Suzanne; m. Terry Bradley Alt, Aug. 10, 1974 (div. 1976); m. Shannon Ann Lynch, June 19, 1977. BS, U. Mich., 1953; MA, Columbia U., 1957, EdD, 1960. Tchr. sci. Ramona H.S., Riverside, Calif., 1958-62; secondary sci. coord. Riverside City Schs., 1960-62; exec. dir. chem. edn. material study Harvey Mudd Coll. and U. Calif. at Berkeley, 1962-65; curriculum specialist Mt. Diablo Unified Sch. Dist., Concord, Calif., 1965-91, dir. curriculum, 1980-81; assoc. dir. Inst. for Chem. Edn. and Project Phys. Sci., U. Calif., Berkeley, 1990—94; ret. Bd. dirs. San Francisco Bay Area Sci. Fair; mem. sci. adv. com. Calif. Assessment Program, 1983-89, also mem. assessment adv. com. to state supt., pub. instrn., 1984-86; dir. N. Calif. W. Nev. Jr. Sci. and Humanities Symposium, 1993-2004; lectr. Calif. State U., Hayward, 1996-99. Author: (with David W. Ridgway) The CHEM Study Story, 1969; co-author: National Science Teachers Association Guidelines for Self-Assessment of Secondary Science Programs, 1975, Science Framework for California Public Schools, 1978, 84; co-author, editor: The Physical Science of Living in California, 1993. Bd. dirs. Ctr. for New Ams., Concord, 1984-91. Served from ensign to lt. (j.g.) USN, 1953-56. Named to Hall Of Fame, Washington Pk. HS, 2008. Mem. NSTA (past pres., past mem. exec. com.), Nat. Sci. Suprs. Assn., Elem. Sch. Sci. Assn. (coun. 1975-82, pres. 1983), Calif. Sci. Tchrs. Assn. (Disting. Svc. award 1990), Assn. Calif. Sch. Adminstrs., Acacia, Phi Delta Kappa. Home: 1862 2d Ave Walnut Creek CA 94597-2553 E-mail: randsmerrill@sbcglobal.net.

MERRIMAN, SHAWNE DEANDRE, professional football player; b. Washington, May 25, 1984; Student in Criminology and Criminal Justice, U. Md., College Park, 2002—04. Linebacker San Diego Chargers, 2005—. Named NFL Defensive Rookie of Yr., AP, 2005, First Team All-Pro, NFL, 2006; named to Am. Football Conf. Pro Bowl Team, 2005—07. Achievements include leading the NFL in: sacks (17), 2006. Office: San Diego Chargers PO Box 609609 San Diego CA 92160-9609

MERRIN, SEYMOUR, computer company executive; b. Bklyn., Aug. 13, 1931; s. Joseph and Esther Bella (Manelis) M.; m. Elaine Cohen, Sept. 4, 1960 (dec. May 1962); m. Elizabeth Jenifer Slack, Oct. 12, 1963 (dec. Mar. 1995); children: Charles Seymour, Mariamne Jenifer Weights; m. Helene Claire Singer, Sept. 1, 2001 BS, Tufts Coll., 1952; MS, U. Ariz., 1954; PhD, Pa. State U., 1962. Geologist Magma Copper Co., Superior, Ariz., 1954, U.S. Geol. Survey, 1956-58; chemist IBM, Poughkeepsie, NY, 1962-64; mgr. package devel., mgr. reliability and failure analysis Sperry Semiconductor divsn. Sperry Rand, Norwalk, Conn., 1965-68; cons. materials tech. Fairfield, Conn., 1967-69; v.p., dir. Innotech Corp., Norwalk, 1969-74; divsn. mgr. Emdex divsn. Exxon Enterprises, Milford, Conn., 1974-78; chmn., dir. Computerworks, Westport, Conn., 1978-85; v.p., dir. personal computing svc. Gartner Group, Inc., Stamford, Conn., 1984-87; pres. Merrin Resources, Southport, Conn., 1987-89, Merrin Info. Svcs., Inc., Santa Fe, 1987—. Bd. dirs. Micrografx Corp., Allen, Tex.; adv. panel Apple Computer Co., Cupertino, Calif., 1982-83; adv. bd. Compaq Computer Corp., Houston, 1984-85, Computer and Software News, NYC, 1984-89; program adv. bd. Comdex, Boston, 1985—; lectr. in field. Contbr. numerous articles to profl. publs.; patentee in field. Bd. dirs. Futures for Children, Albuquerque, 2004—, Santa Fe Internat. Folk Market, Couse Found., Taos, N.Mex. With US Army, 1954—56. Fellow Geol. Soc. Am., Am. Inst. Chemists; Computing Tech. Industry Assn. (founder, pres. 1981-83, bd. dirs. 1981-84). Home and Office: 840 Camino de las Trampas Santa Fe NM 87501 Personal E-mail: smerrin@aol.com.

MERRITT, LAVERE BARRUS, engineering educator, civil engineer; b. Afton, Wyo., Mar. 11, 1936; s. Joseph M. and Lera (Barrus) M.; m. Jackie Call, Jan. 5, 1956 (dec. Sept. 1999); m. Diane Mainord, July 14, 2001; children: Teri, Lynn, Rachel, Shaun; stepchildren: Julia, Aaron, Benjamin, Annie. BSCE, U. Utah, 1963, MSCE, 1966; PhD, U. Wash., 1970. Registered profl. engr., Utah, Ariz. Prof. civil and environ. engring. Brigham Young U., Provo, Utah, 1970—, chmn. dept. civil engring., 1986-92; co-chmn. faculty senate, 1996-97. Cons. engring. firms, 1970—. Chmn. Provo Met. Water Bd., Utah, 1978-87. Named Utah Engring. Educator of Yr., Utah Joint Engring. Coun., 1987, Educator of Yr., Am. Water Resources Assn., Utah, 2004. Mem. ASCE (nat. dir. 1982-85), Am. Acad. Environ. Engrs., Water Environment Fedn. (nat. dir. 1981-84, Bedell award), Am. Water Works Assn., Am. Soc. Engring. Edn., Sigma Xi. Republican. Mem. Lds Ch. Home: 562 E 3050 N Provo UT 84604-4264 Home Phone: 801-373-2445; Office Phone: 801-422-6333.

MERRITT, NANCY-JO, lawyer; b. Phoenix, Sept. 24, 1942; d. Robert Nelson Meeker and Violet Adele Gibson; children: Sidney Kathryn, Kurt, Douglas. BA, Ariz. State U., 1964, MA, 1974, JD, 1978. Bar: Ariz. 1978, U.S. Dist. Ct. Ariz. 1978, U.S. Ct. Appeals (9th cir.) 1984. Shareholder Fennemore Craig, P.C., Phoenix. Author:

Understanding Immigration Law, 1993; sr. editor: Immigration and National Law Handbook, 1993—; contbr. articles to profl. jours. Chair bd. dirs. TERROS, 1995-97. Fellow Ariz. Bar Found.; mem., bd. dirs. Orizona Lost Boys Ctr., ABA, Am. Immigration Lawyers Assn. (chairperson Ariz. chpt. 1985-87, several coms., Pro Bono award), Ariz. Bar Assn. (immigration sect.), Nucleus Club. Democrat. Avocations: modern literature, south american literature, hiking, gardening. Office Phone: 602-916-5411, 702-692-8003. Business E-Mail: njmerritt@fclaw.com.

MERTENS, LYNNE G., retail executive; CEO, pres. Waller, The Graphics Resource, San Francisco, Calif. Office: Waller 339 Harbor Way South San Francisco CA 94080-6919 Fax: 650-589-0578.

MERTZ, EDWIN THEODORE, retired biochemist, emeritus educator; b. Missoula, Mont., Dec. 6, 1909; s. Gustav Henry and Louise (Sain) M.; m. Mary Ellen Ruskamp, Oct. 5, 1936; children: Martha Ellen, Edwin T.; m. Virginia T. Henry, Aug. 1, 1987. BA, U. Mont., 1931, D.Sc. (hon.), 1979; MS in Biochemistry, U. Ill., 1933, PhD in Biochemistry, 1935; D.Agr. (hon.), Purdue U., 1977. Rsch. biochemist Armour & Co., Chgo., 1935-37; instr. biochemistry U. Ill., 1937-38; rsch. assoc. in pathology U. Iowa, 1938-40; instr. agrl. chemistry U. Mo., 1940-43; rsch. chemist Hercules Powder Co., 1943-46; prof. biochemistry Purdue U., West Lafayette, Ind., 1946-76, emeritus prof., 1976—. Vis. prof. U. Notre Dame, South Bend, Ind., 1976-77; cons. in agronomy Purdue U., 1977-94; affiliate prof. crops and soils Mont. State U., Bozeman, 1995—. Author: Elementary Biochemistry, 1969; author, editor: Quality Protein Maize, 1964-94. Recipient McCoy award Purdue U., 1967; John Scott award City of Phila., 1967; Hoblitzelle Nat. award Tex. Research Found., 1968; Congressional medal Fed. Land Banks, 1968; Disting. Service award U. Mont., 1973; Browning award Am. Soc. Agronomy, 1974; Pioneer Chemist award Am. Inst. Chemists, 1976 Mem. AAAS, AAUP, Nat. Acad. Scis., Am. Soc. Biol. Chemists, Am. Inst. Nutrition (Osborne-Mendel award 1972), Am. Chem. Soc. (Spencer award 1970), Am. Assn. Cereal Chemists. Lutheran. Achievements include co-discovering high lysine corn, 1963. Office: Montana State Univ Dept Plant And Soils Bozeman MT 59717-0001

MESAROS, KENNETH LEE, state legislator, rancher; b. Great Falls, Mont., June 17, 1950; s. Albert and Hilda (Heiman) M.; m. Rebecca Lynn Mesaros; children: Mathew, Michael, Scot, Kimberly. BS in Agr. Edn., Mont. State U., 1973. Owner, operator Mesaros Ranch, Cascade, Mont., 1969—; senator State of Mont., Helena, 1992—. Dir. Am. Inst. Cooperatives, Mpls., 1978; chmn., dir. Foothill Livestock Assn., Cascade County, Mont., 1982-88, Equity Co-op Assn., Ulm, Mont., 1977-84. Sch. bd. chmn. Sch. Dist. # 95, Deep Creek, Mont., 1986-90. Staff sgt. Mont. Air N.G., 1969-75. Mem. Mont. Stockgrowers Assn. (dir. 1990-94), Cascade Lions Club, Great Falls Elks Club, NRA, Mont. Farm Bureau, Mont. Cattleman's Assoc., Mont. Graingrowers Assoc. Republican. Roman Catholic. Avocations: hunting, fishing, skiing, golf. Home: 2191 Milligan Rd Cascade MT 59421-8001

MESCHKOW, JORDAN M., lawyer; b. Bklyn., Mar. 25, 1957; s. Gerald Meschkow and Florence Y. (Katz) Silverman; m. Susan G. Scher, Aug. 10, 1980; children: Sasha Hayley, Alisha Sadie. BS in Biology, SUNY, Stony Brook, 1979; JD, Chgo. Kent Coll. Law, 1982. Bar: Ariz. 1982, Fla. 1983; registered U.S. Patent Trademark Office 1983. Assoc. James F. Duffy, Patent Atty., Phoenix, Ariz., 1982; ptnr. Duffy & Meschkow, Phoenix, 1983-84; sole practice Phoenix, 1984-92; sr. ptnr. Meschkow & Gresham, P.L.C., Phoenix, 1992—. Frequent talk radio guest spkr. seminars patent, trademark, copyright law. Contbr. article series to profl. jours.; patentee in field. Exec. bd. City Phoenix Fire Pub. Awareness League, 1996—. Mem. Am. Intellectual Property Law Assn., State Bar Ariz. (intellectual property sect. 1982—), State Bar Fla. Avocations: gardening, motorcycling, bicycling, skating, swimming. Office: 5727 N 7th St Ste 409 Phoenix AZ 85014-5818 Home Phone: 480-951-4191; Office Phone: 602-274-6996. Business E-Mail: MG@patentmg.com.

MESEREAU, THOMAS ARTHUR, JR., lawyer; b. West Point, NY, 1951; m. Heidi Gold (div.). BA cum laude, Harvard U., 1973; MSc, London Sch. Econ., 1975; JD, U. Calif., 1979. Bar: Calif. 1979. Assoc. Hunton & Williams, Washington, 1979—81; dep. dist. atty. Orange County, Calif., 1981—82; exec. Getty Synthetic Fuels Inc., 1982—85; ptnr. Collins, Mesereau, Reddock & Yu, LLP, LA, 1985—. Vol. legal clinic First African Meth. Episcopal Ch. Recipient Pro Bono award, State Bar Calif., Commendation, LA Bd. Supr., Sarah Allen Trailblazer award, Cert. Appreciation, LA County Supr., Compton award, Calif. Sch. Bd., Humanitarian award, Nat. Assn. Blacks in Criminal Justice; named Criminal Def. Lawyer Yr., Century City Bar Assn.; named one of The 10 Most Fascinating People of 2005, Barbara Walters Special. Mem.: Italian Am. Lawyers Assn. (former mem. bd. gov.), Calif. Atty. Criminal Justice. Achievements include leading def. atty. in Michael Jackson child molestation trial, 2005. Office: Mesereau Nuyu LLP 10390 Santa Monica Blvd Ste 220 Los Angeles CA 90025 Office Phone: 213-384-0982. Office Fax: 213-380-4820. Business E-Mail: mesereau@mesereauyu.com.

MESHII, MASAHIRO, materials science educator; b. Amagasaki, Japan, Oct. 6, 1931; arrived in US, 1956; s. Masataro and Kazuyo M.; m. Eiko Kumagai, May 21, 1959; children: Alisa, Erica. BS, Osaka U., Japan, 1954, MS, 1956; PhD, Northwestern U., 1959. Lectr., rsch. assoc. dept. materials sci. and engring. Northwestern U., Evanston, Ill., 1959-60, asst. prof., assoc. prof., then prof., 1960-88, chmn. dept. materials sci. and engring., 1978-82, John Evans prof., 1988—2003, John Evans prof. emeritus, 2003—. Vis. scientist Nat. Rsch. Inst. Metals, Tokyo, 1970-71; NSF faculty rsch. participant Argonne (Ill.) Nat. Lab., 1975; guest prof. Osaka U., 1985; Acta/Scripta Metallurgica lectr., 1993-95. Co-editor: Lattice Defects in Quenched Metals, 1965, Martensitic Transformation, 1978, Science of Advanced Materials, 1990; editor: Fatigue and Microstructures, 1979, Mechanical Properties of BCC Metals, 1982; contbr. over 245 articles to tech. publs. and internat. jours. Recipient Founders award Midwest Soc. Electron Microscopists, 1987, Albert Easton White Disting. Tchr. award, 2008; named Best Tchr. of Yr., Engring. Students of Northwestern U., 1978; Fulbright grantee, 1956; Japan fellow, 1957. Fellow ASM (Henry Marion Howe medal 1968, Best Acad. Paper award 1994), Japan Soc. Promotion of Sci.; mem. AIME (Meritorious award for Best Paper Iron and Steel Soc. 1993), Metall. Soc., Japan Inst. Metals (hon., Achievement award 1972), Toastmasters Internat. (Disting. Toast Master, 1987, 2007). Office: 22879 NE 127th Way Redmond WA 98053-5657 Office Phone: 425-836-2334. Personal E-mail: mmeshii@hotmail.com.

MESKE, SANDY, government agency administrator; BSBA. From clk. to tech. asst. Dryden Flight Rsch. Ctr. NASA, Edwards AFB, Calif., 1985—2000, adminstrv. ops. specialist Dryden Flight Rsch. Ctr., 2000—. Office: NASA Dryden Flight Rsch Ctr PO Box 273 MS 2004 Edwards AFB CA 93523-0273

MESSENGER, GEORGE CLEMENT, engineering executive, consultant; b. Bellows Falls, Vt., July 20, 1930; s. Clement George and Ethel Mildred (Farrar) M.; m. Priscilla Betty Norris, June 19, 1954; children: Michael Todd, Steven Barry, Bonnie Lynn. BS in Physics, Worcester Poly U., 1951, PhD (hon.) in Engring., 2008; MSEE, U. Pa., 1957; PhD in Engring., Calif. Coast U., 1986. Rsch. scientist Philco Corp., Phila., 1951-59; engring. mgr. Hughes Semicondr., Newport Beach, Calif., 1959-61; divsn. mgr. Transitron Corp., Wakefield, Mass., 1961-63; staff scientist Northrop Corp., Hawthorne, Calif., 1963-68; cons. engr. Las Vegas, Nev., 1968—. Lectr. UCLA, 1969-75; v.p., dir. Am. Inst. Fin., Grafton, Mass., 1970-78; gen. ptnr. Dargon Fund, Anaheim, Calif., 1983—; v.p., tech. dir. Messenger and Assoc., 1987—, registered investment adviser, 1989—. Co-author: The Effects of Radiation on Electronic Systems, 1986, Single Event Phenomena, 1997; contbg. author: Fundamentals of Nuclear Hardening, 1972, Nonvolatile Semiconductor Memory Technology, 1998; contbr. articles to profl. jours.; patentee microwave diode, hardened semicondrs. Recipient Naval Rsch. Lab. Alan Berman award, 1982, Best Paper award HEART Conf., 1983, Spl. Merit award, 1983, Pete Haas award, 1992, Goddard award for outstanding profl. achievement Worcester Poly. Inst., 1996, Archimedes award for contbns. to semicondr., solid state and nuc. physics rsch., 2006. Fellow IEEE (Merit award 1986); mem. Rsch. Soc. Am., Am. Phys. Soc. Congregationalist. Home and Office: 3111 Bel Air Dr Apt 7F Las Vegas NV 89109-1510

MESSER, DONALD EDWARD, theology educator, administrator; b. Kimball, SD, Mar. 5, 1941; s. George Marcus and Grace E. (Foltz) M.; m. Bonnie Jeanne Nagel, Aug. 30, 1964; children: Christine Marie, Kent Donald. BA cum laude, Dakota Wesleyan U., 1963, LHD (hon.), 1977; MDiv magna cum laude, Boston U., 1966, PhD, 1969. Asst. to commr. Mass. Commn. Against Discrimination, Boston, 1968-69; asst. prof. Augustana Coll., Sioux Falls, SD, 1969-71; assoc. pastor 1st United Meth. Ch., Sioux Falls, 1969-71; pres. Dakota Wesleyan U., Mitchell, SD, 1971-81, Iliff Sch. Theology, Denver, 1981-2000, pres. emeritus and prof. practical theology, 2000—; exec. dir. Ctr. for the Ch. and Global AIDS, 2007—. Author: Christian Ethics and Political Action, 1984, Contemporary Images of Christian Ministry, 1989, Send Me? The Intineracy in Crisis, 1991, The Conspiracy of Goodness, 1992, Caught in the Crossfire: Helping Christians Debate Homosexuality, 1994, Calling Church and Seminary Into the 21st Century, 1995, Unity, Liberty, and Charity: Building Bridges Under Icy Waters, 1996, How Shall We Die? Helping Christians Debate Assisted Suicide, 1997, The Befuddled Stork: Helping Persons of Faith Debate Beginning of life Issues, 2000, Breaking the Conspiracy of Silence: Christian Churches and the Global AIDS Crisis, 2004; co-author: (with George McGovern, Bob Dole) Ending Hunger Now, 2005; co-editor: Connected Spirits: Friends and Spiritual Journeys, 2007; contbr. articles to Face to Face, The Christian Century, The Christian Ministry. Active Edn. Commn. of U.S., 1973-79; co-chmn. Citizens Commn. Corrections, 1975-76; vice chmn. SD Commn. on Humanities, 1979-81. Dempster fellow, 1967-68; Rockefeller fellow, 1968-69; named to SD Hall of Fame, 2008 Mem. Soc. Christian Ethics, Am. Acad. Religion, Assn. United Meth. Theol. Schs. (v.p. 1986-91, pres. 1991-92). Democrat.

MESSERLE, KENNETH C., state senator; b. Coos Bay, Oreg., May 8, 1940; m. Lola Messerle; children: Anthony, Blaine, Molly. BS, Oreg. State U., 1962. Owner, mgr. Messerle and Sons, Cattle and Timber, 1962-96; dir. Security Bank Holding Co., 1992—, Lincoln Security Bank, 1997—; Rep. rep. dist. 48 Oreg. Ho. of Reps., 1996-2000; Rep. senator dist. 24 Oreg. State Senate, 2000—. Mem. full ways and means com. Oreg. Ho. of Reps., mem. Pacific fisheries legis. task force, 1997—, natural resources ways and means subcom., 1999, interim task force on children and families, gen. govt. ways and means subcom., 1999, environ. and land use transp. task force, 1999—, co-chair salmon recovery and stream restoration. Chmn. Port of Bandon Relending Corp.; commr. Port of Bandon; dir. Coquille Sch. Bd.; mem. Coos County Water Resources Com.; dir. Coos Soil and Water Dist. Mem. Oreg. Coastal Zone Mgmt. Assn. Roman Catholic. Office: 94271 Coos Sumner Ln Coos Bay OR 97420 also: Oreg State Senate H-381 State Capitol Salem OR 97310 Fax: 541 269-2510; 503 986-1336. E-mail: repMessLola@harborside.com, messerle.rep@state.or.us.

MESSERSCHMITT, DAVID GAVIN, engineering educator; b. Denver, May 21, 1945; s. Darwin Erwin and Helen Marilla (Dentan) M.; m. Dorothy Margaret Seegers, May 2, 1970; 1 child, Laura Joanne. BS, U. Colo., 1967; MS, U. Mich., 1968, PhD, 1971. Mem. tech. staff Bell Labs., Holmdel, N.J., 1968-77, supr., 1974-77; prof. dept. elec. engring. and computer sci. U. Calif., Berkeley, 1977—, chair dept., 1993-96. Bd. dirs. Teknekron Communication Systems, Berkeley. Contbr. articles to profl. jours. Patentee in field. Recipient Pres.'s award U. Colo., 1967, named Outstanding Grad. Engr., 1967; NSF fellow, 1967. Fellow IEEE (bd. govs. communications soc. 1981-84); mem. NAE. Office: U Calif 231 Cory Hall Berkeley CA 94720-1770 Home: 1315 Alma Ave #121 Walnut Creek CA 94596

MESSING, DEBRA, actress; b. Bklyn., Aug. 15, 1968; m. Daniel Zelman, Sept. 3, 2000; 1 child, Roman Walker. Grad., Brandeis U.; M in Drama, NYU. Actor: (films) Walk in the Clouds, 1995, McHale's Navy, 1997, Prey, 1997, Celebrity, 1998, Mothman Prophecies, 2002, Hollywood Ending, 2002, Along Came Polly, 2004, (voice) Garfield, 2004, The Wedding Date, 2005, (voice) Open Season, 2006, Purple Violets, 2007, Lucky You, 2007, The Women, 2008, Nothing Like the Holidays, 2008; (TV series) Ned and Stacey, 1995, Prey, 1998, Will & Grace, 1998—2006 (Emmy award best actress in a comedy, 2003); (TV miniseries) The Starter Wife, 2007—; TV appearances include: NYPD Blue, 1994, 1995; Partners, 1995; Seinfeld, 1996, 1997; (voice) King of the Hill, 2002. Office: c/o Gersh Agy 232 N Canon Dr Beverly Hills CA 90210

MESSMER, HAROLD MAXIMILIAN, JR., (MAX MESSMER), consulting company executive; b. Jackson, Miss., Feb. 20, 1946; s. Harold Maximilian and Margaret (Dee) M.; m. Marcia Elizabeth Nesmith, Apr. 5, 1973; children: Michael Christopher, Matthew Gordon. AB summa cum laude, Loyola U., 1967; JD cum laude, NYU, 1970. Ptnr. corp. law and securities O'Melveny & Myers, Los Angeles, 1970-81; sr. v.p., gen. counsel Pacific Holding Corp., Los Angeles, 1981-82, pres., chief operating officer, 1982-85; pres., dir., chief operating officer Cannon Mills Co. (subs.), Kannapolis, N.C., 1982-85; chmn., dir. Castle & Cook Inc., San Francisco, 1985; chmn., pres., chief exec. officer Robert Half Internat. Inc., Menlo Park, 1985—2004, chmn., CEO, 2004—. Adj. prof. Claremont Grad. Sch. Bus.(exec. mgmt. program), 1979-82; bd. dirs. Health Care Property Investors, Los Angeles, BF Enterprises Inc., N.C. Nat. Bank, Charlotte. Trustee Davidson (N.C.) Coll., 1984—; appointee Pres. Reagan's Adv. Com. on Trade Negotiations, 1985-87. Served with USAR, 1971-75. Mem. ABA, Los Angeles County Bar Assn., Calif. Bar Assn. Served with USAR, 1971-75. Office: Robert Half Internat Inc 2884 Sand Hill Rd Ste 200 Menlo Park CA 94025-7059

MESTRES, RICARDO A., III, film company executive; b. NYC, Jan. 23, 1958; s. Ricardo Angelo Jr. and Ann M.; m. Tracy Stewart (div.); children: Alexander Carson, Carrie Ann (dec.). AB, Harvard U., 1980; postgrad., U. So. Calif., 2007—. Creative exec. Paramount Pictures, LA, 1981-82, exec. dir. prodn., 1982-84, v.p. prodn., 1984-85, Walt Disney Pictures, Burbank, Calif., 1985-86, sr. v.p. prodn., 1986-88; pres. prodn. Touchstone Pictures, Burbank, Calif., 1988-89; pres. Hollywood Pictures, Burbank, Calif., 1989-94; co-founder Great Oaks Entertainment, Burbank, Calif., 1995-97; prin. Ricardo Mestres Prodns., Disney Studios, Burbank, Calif., 1997. Prodr: Jack, 101 Dalmations, Flubber, Home Alone 3, The Visitors, The Hunted. Mem. Acad. Motion Picture Arts and Scis. Personal E-mail: mestres@usc.edu. Business E-Mail: ricardo@rmp.com.

METCALF, WAYNE C., III, retired insurance company executive; m. Shirley Imada Metcalf. BA in Polit. Sci., U. Hawaii, 1975; JD, 1978; student, Tufts U., 1992-93. Atty. pvt. practice, 1979—; spl. cons. UN, 1994; ins. commr. Dept. Commerce and Consumer Affairs State Hawaii, 1994—97, 2002—. Staff Senate Jud. Com., 1973-75; staff dir. Senate Pres.'s Office, 1975-78; vice-chmn. House Com. on Jud., 1984-86; chmn. House Com. on Jud., 1986-92; mem. house coms. Comsuner Protection and Commerce, 1984-92, Land Use and Hawaiian Affairs Plannong, 1984-86, Labor and Pub. Employment Transp., 1985-88, Housing, Health Humand Svcs, 1988-90, Housing, Health, 1990-92. Recipient Disting. Alumni award U. hawaii, 1988, Disting. Legislator award, Nat. Dem. State LEgis. Leaders Assn., 1988; named one of Hawaii's five best legislators by polit. columnist Dan Boylan, 1990, 92.

METROS, MARY TERESA, librarian; b. Denver, Nov. 10, 1951; d. James and Wilma Frances (Hanson) Metros. BA in English, Colo. Women's Coll., 1973; MA in Librarianship, U. Denver, 1974. Adult svcs. libr. Englewood Pub. Libr., Colo., 1975—81, mgr. adult svcs., 1983—84; sys. cons. Dataphase Sys., Kansas City, Mo., 1981—82; circulation libr. Westminster Pub. Libr., Colo., 1983; supr. pub. svcs. Tempe Pub. Libr., Ariz., 1984—90, libr. dir., 1990—. Mem.: ALA, Ariz. Libr. Assn., Pub. Libr. Assn. Democrat. Office: Tempe Pub Libr 3500 S Rural Rd Tempe AZ 85282-5405 Home Phone: 480-777-8530; Office Phone: 480-350-5551. Business E-Mail: teri_metros@tempe.gov.

METSGER, RICK T., state legislator; b. Sandy, Oreg., Aug. 16, 1951; m to Kay. Oregon State Senator, District 14, 1999-2002; Oregon State Senator, District 26, 2003-.Teacher, Sam Barlow High Sch, 73-76; news reporter/anchor, KOIN TV, 77-92; owner, NewsMedia Dynamics, Inc, 92-; vice chairman, Portland Teachers Credit Union, currently; board director, Oregon Film & Video Found, currently. N Clakamas Chamber of Commerce. Democrat. Protestant. Office: 900 Court St NE S-315 Salem OR 97301 Office Phone: 503-986-1726. Business E-Mail: sen.rickmetsger@state.or.us.

METZ, ERIC D., professional sports agent; b. Monroeville, Pa., Mar. 1961; married; 3 children. Grad., Pa. State U., 1983. Sports agent Lock, Metz & Malinovic, LLC, Tempe, Ariz. Office: Lock Metz Malinovic Llc PO Box 28245 Tempe AZ 85285-8245 Office Phone: 480-921-9770.

METZ, MARY SEAWELL, retired foundation and academic administrator; b. Rockhill, SC, May 7, 1937; d. Columbus Jackson and Mary (Dunlap) Seawell; m. F. Eugene Metz, Dec. 21, 1957; 1 dau., Mary Eugena. BA summa cum laude in French and English, Furman U., 1958; postgrad., Institut Phonetique, Paris, 1962-63, Sorbonne, 1962-63; PhD magna cum laude in French, La. State U., 1966; HHD (hon.), Furman U., 1984; LLD (hon.), Chapman Coll., 1985; DLT (hon.), Converse Coll., 1988. Instr. French La. State U., 1965-66, asst. prof., 1966-67, 1968-72, assoc. prof., 1972-76, dir. elem. and intermediate French programs, 1966-74, spl. asst. to chancellor, 1974-75, asst. to chancellor, 1975-76; prof. French Hood Coll., Frederick, Md., 1976-81, provost, dean acad. affairs, 1976-81; pres. Mills Coll., Oakland, Calif., 1981-90; dean of extension U. Calif., Berkeley, 1991-98; pres. S.H. Cowell Found., San Fransisco, 1999—. Vis. asst. prof. U. Calif.-Berkeley, 1967-68; mem. commn. on leadership devel. Am. Coun. on Edn., 1981-90, adv. coun. Stanford Rsch. Inst., 1985-90, adv. coun. Grad. Sch. Bus., Stanford U.; bd. dirs. PG&E, AT&T, Inc., Union Bank, Longs Drug Stores. Author: Reflets du monde francais, 1971, 78, Cahier d'exercices: Reflets du monde francais, 1972, 78, (with Helstrom) Le Francais a decouvrir, 1972, 78, Le Francais a vivre, 1972, 78, Cahier d'exercices: Le Francais a vivre, 1972, 78; standardized tests; mem. editorial bd. Liberal Edn., 1982—. Trustee Am. Conservatory Theater. NDEA fellow, 1960-62, 1963-64; Fulbright fellow, 1962-63; Am. Council Edn. fellow, 1974-75 Mem. Western Coll. Assn. (v.p. 1982-84, pres. 1984-86), Assn. Ind. Calif. Colls. and Univs. (exec. com. 1982-90), Nat. Assn. Ind. Colls. and Univs. (govt. rels. adv. coun. 1982-85), So. Conf. Lang. Teaching (chmn. 1976-77), World Affairs Coun. No. Calif. (bd. dirs. 1984-93), Bus.-Higher Edn. Forum, Women's Forum West, Women's Coll. Coalition (exec. com. 1984-88), Phi Kappa Phi, Phi Beta Kappa. Address: PO Box 686 Stinson Beach CA 94970-0686

METZENBERG, ROBERT L., education educator; Prof. rsch. and biol. scis. Stanford U.

METZGER, ROBERT STREICHER, lawyer; b. St. Louis, Sept. 27, 1950; s. Robert Stanley and Jean Harriet (Streicher) M.; children: Michael, Kristen, Marisa. BA, Middlebury Coll., 1974; JD, Georgetown U., 1977. Bar: Calif. 1978, D.C. 1978. Legis. aide US Rep. Robert F. Drinan, Washington, 1972-73; legis. asst. US Rep. Michael J. Harrington, Washington, 1973-75; rsch. fellow Ctr. for Internat. Affairs Harvard U. Grad. Sch. Arts and Sci., Cambridge, Mass., 1977, Harvard U., Cambridge, Mass., 1978; assoc. Latham & Watkins, LA, 1978-84, ptnr., 1984-90, Kirkland & Ellis, LA, 1990-93, Troop, Meisinger, Steuber & Pasich and predecessor, LA, 1993-97, Gibson, Dunn & Crutcher LLP, LA, 1997—2007; ptnr. corp. and securities Pillsbury Winthrop Shaw Pittman LLP, LA, 2007—. Chmn. Aerospace and Govt. Practice Group, 1997—2006, Telecom. Practice Group, 2000-06; cons. Congl. Rsch. Svc., Washington, 1977-78.

Contbr. articles to profl. jours. Trustee Sierra Canyon HS Found.; mem. dean's alumni leadership coun. Kennedy Sch. Govt. Harvard U., 2005—. Mem. ABA (litig. pub. contracts sect.), Fed. Comm. Bar Assn., Internat. Inst. for Strategic Studies, Pacific Coun. on Internat. Policy, Jonathan Club. Office: Pillsbury Winthrop Shaw Pittman LLP 725 S Figueroa St Ste 2806 Los Angeles CA 90017-5406 also: Pillsbury Winthrop Shaw Pittman LLP 2300 North St NW Washington DC 20037-1122 Office Phone: 213-488-7437, 310-729-9392. Business E-Mail: robert.metzger@pillsburylaw.com.

METZLER, ROGER JAMES, JR., lawyer; b. East Orange, NJ, Feb. 4, 1945; s. Roger James and Dorothy Marie (Clark) M.; m. Marilyn Carol Schick, Apr. 19, 1969; children: Andrea C., Maria N. BS, Brown U., 1967; JD, Santa Clara U., 1975. Bar: Calif. 1975. Ptnr. Farrand, Cooper, Metzler & Bruiniers, San Francisco, 1975-88, McQuaid, Bedford, Clausen & Metzler, San Francisco, 1988-89, Keck, Mahin & Cate, Chgo. and San Francisco, 1990-96, McQuaid, Metzler, Bedford & Van Zandt, San Francisco, 1996—. Avocation: soccer. Office: McQuaid Metzler Bedford Van Zandt PO Box 2187 Sonoma CA 95476-2187

METZNER, RICHARD JOEL, psychiatrist, psychopharmacologist, educator; b. LA, Feb. 15, 1942; s. Robert Gerson and Esther Rebecca (Groper) M.; children: Jeffrey Anthony, David Jonathan; m. Leila Kirkley, June 26, 1993. BA, Stanford U., 1963; MD, Johns Hopkins U., 1967. Diplomate Am. Bd. Psychiatry and Neurology. Intern Roosevelt Hosp., NYC, 1967-68; resident in psychiatry Stanford U. Med. Ctr., 1968-71; staff psychiatrist divsn. manpower and tng. NIMH-St. Elizabeths Hosp., Washington, 1971-73; chief audiovisual edn. sys. VA Med. Ctr. Brentwood, LA, 1973-79; from asst. prof. psychiatry to assoc. clin. prof. UCLA Neuropsychiat. Inst., 1980-96, clin. prof., 1996—. Lectr. Sch. Social Welfare, 1975-84; pvt. practice medicine specializing in psychiatry, Bethesda, Md., 1972-73, L.A., 1973—, Sedona, Ariz., 1997—; dir. Western Inst. Psychiatry, L.A., 1977—; pres. Psychiat. Resource Network, Inc., 1984-90, chair, Clin. Neuropharmacology, UCLA, 2007. Contbr. articles to profl. jours.; prodr., writer numerous films and videotapes. With USPHS, 1968-71. Recipient 6 awards for film and videotape prodns., 1976-80, Career Achievement award, Psychiat. Clin. Faculty Assn., UCLA 2006 Fellow: Am. Psychiat. Assn. (life Disting.); mem.: UCLA Psychiat. Clin. Faculty Assn. (pres. 2001—02), Mental Health Careerists Assn. (chmn. 1972—73), So. Calif. Psychiat. Soc., Phi Beta Kappa. Democrat. Jewish. Office: 25 Cindercone Cir Sedona AZ 86336 Office Phone: 928-204-5850. E-mail: rmetzner@ucla.edu, rmetzner@earthlink.net.

MEULI, LARRY, state representative; b. Abilene, Kans., June 30, 1936; m. Vicki Meuli; children: Matthew, Melinda, Margaret. BA, U. Kans., 1958; MD, Kans. U., 1962; MPH, San Diego State U., 1986. Resident pediat. Children's Hosp., 1967; pediatrician Loveland, Colo., 1971—80, Tulsa, Okla., 1971—71, Missoula, Mont., 1967—69; adminstr. Wyo. Dept. Health and Social Svcs., 1981—87, adminstr., state health officer, 1987—91; dir., health officer City County Health Dept., Cheyenne, 1991—2002; state rep. dist. 8 Wyo. State Legis., Cheyenne, 1997—. Mem. Labor, Health and Social Svcs. com. Wyo. State Legis., Cheyenne, mem. Travel, Recreation, Wildlife and Cultural Resources, Appropriations; adminstr. Improved Pregnancy Outcome Program Wyo. Dept. Health and Social Svcs., 1979—84. Capt. med. corp US Army, 1963—65. Recipient Dr. Nathan Davis award for outstanding govt. svc., AMA, 2004. Mem.: Nat. Assn. County City Health Ofcls., Wyo. Med. Soc. (Physician of Yr. 2002), Nat. Soc. County Health Ofcls., Am. Acad. Pediat. (past pres. Wyo. chpt.), Greater Cheyenne C. of C., Cheyenne Rotary. Republican. Presbyterian. Home: PO Box 1302 Cheyenne WY 82003 Office: Capitol Bldg Wyo State Legis Cheyenne WY 82002

MEURLIN, KEITH W., airport manager; BA, Univ. of Vermont, 1972; MS, Univ. of Southern California, 1977. Served in U.S. Air Force and Nat. Guard, 1972—; now gen. mgr. Washington Dulles Internat. Airport; mobilization asst. Langley AFB, Va. Recipient Meritorious Service Medal, Air Force Outstanding Unit Award, National Defense Srvc. Medal. Office: Hdq Air Reserve Personnel Cntr Office of Public Affairs Denver CO 80280

MEYER, ANN JANE, human development educator; b. NYC, Mar. 11, 1942; d. Louis John and Theresa Meyer. BA, U. Mich., 1964; MA, U. Calif., Berkeley, 1967, PhD, 1971. Asst. prof. dept. human devel. Calif. State U., Hayward, 1972-77, assoc. prof., 1977-84, prof., 1984—. Mem. APA. Office: Calif State U Dept Human Devel Hayward CA 94542 Office Phone: 500-885-3076. Business E-Mail: ameyer@csuhayward.edu.

MEYER, BARRY MICHAEL, motion picture executive; b. NYC, Nov. 28, 1943; s. Perry and Lillian Helen (Katz) M.; m. Barbara Patricia, June 12, 1966; children: Matthew, Elizabeth. BA, U. Rochester, 1964; JD, Case Western Res. U., 1967. Bar: NY, Ohio. Legal counsel ABC, NYC, 1968-70, dir. bus. affairs LA, 1970-71, Warner Bros. TV, LA, 1971—72, v.p. bus. affairs, 1972—78, exec. v.p., 1978—84, Warner Bros. Entertainment, Inc., LA, 1984—94, exec. v.p., COO, 1994—99, chmn., CEO, 1999—. Mem. bd. councilors USC Sch. Cinema-TV; bd. dirs. Motion Picture Assn. Am., Mus. Radio and TV, Am. Film Inst. Contbr. articles to profl. jours. Bd. dirs. Human Rights Watch, San Fernando Valley Child Guidance Clinic, Calif.; bd. trustees U. Rochester. Named one of 50 Most Powerful People in Hollywood, Premiere mag., 2004—06. Mem. Hollywood Radio and TV Soc., Nat. Acad. TV Arts and Scis. (former gov.), Am. Mgmt. Assn., Acad. Motion Pictures Arts & Scis. Office: Warner Bros Entertainment Inc 4000 Warner Blvd Burbank CA 91522-0002 Office Phone: 818-954-1464.

MEYER, BRUCE D., lawyer; b. Aug. 31, 1945; BA, U. Ill., 1967, JD with high honors, 1970. Bar: Calif. 1971. Assoc. Gibson Dunn & Crutcher, LA, 1970—73, ptnr., 1979—81, Riyadh, Saudi Arabia, 1981—83, ptnr. corp. transactions and securities LA, 1983—; v.p., asst. gen. counsel Whittaker Corp., LA, 1973—79. Mem. exec. com. Gibson Dunn & Crutcher. Mem.: ABA (chmn. Middle East law com., internat. law section 1984—85), LA County Bar Assn., Order of Coif. Office: Gibson Dunn & Crutcher LLP 333 Grand Ave Los Angeles CA 90071-3197 Office Phone: 213-229-7979. Office Fax: 213-229-6979. Business E-Mail: bmeyer@gibsondunn.com.

MEYER, C. RICHARD, architect; BArch, U. Calif., Berkeley, 1968. Registered architect, Wash. With The Callison Partnership, Seattle, 1977—, dir. quality assurance. Mem. adv. bd. cert. program project mgmt. U. Wash.; contracts rev. panelist Soc. Archtl. Adminstrs.; mem. faculty Pacific real estate symposium N.W. Real Estate Inst.; guest lectr. Archtl. Registration Exam. Seminar; guest lectr. coll. architecture and urban planning U. Wash.; guest panelist Internat. Conf. of Bldg. Ofcls. Nat. Conf., 1991. Mem. AIA (treas. Seattle chpt., mem. steering com. Pacific NW regional conf., vice-chair nat. risk mgmt. com., mem. steering com. nat. practice com., liaison to Am. Arbitration Assn.), Nat. Inst. Bldg. Scis. Office: The Callison Partnership Ltd 1420 5th Ave Ste 2400 Seattle WA 98101-2343

MEYER, CATHERINE DIEFFENBACH, lawyer; b. Seattle, Mar. 27, 1951; d. Patrick Andrew and Hope Dieffenbach; m. Michael E. Meyer, Nov. 21, 1982; children. AB, Bryn Mawr Coll., 1973; JD, Northwestern U., 1979. Bar: Calif. 1979, U.S. Dist. Ct. (cen. dist.) Calif., 1979, U.S. Ct. Appeals (9th cir.) 1982, U.S. Dist. Ct. (ea., no. and so. dists.) Calif. 1987. Assoc. Lillick, McHose & Charles, LA, 1979-85, ptnr., 1985-88, Lillick & McHose, LA, 1988-90, Pillsbury Madison & Sutro, LA, 1990—2001, Pillsbury Winthrop LLP, LA, 2001—05; past co-chmn. Privacy & Data Protection practice, co-chmn. LA Bus. dept. Pillsbury Winthrop Shaw Pittman LLP, LA, 2005—, counsel, 2005—. Bd. dirs. House Ear Inst. Mem.: ABA (past co-chmn. Extraterritorial Application of Law subcommittee), LA County Bar Assn. Office: Pillsbury Winthrop Shaw Pittman Suite 2800 725 S Figueroa St Los Angeles CA 90017 Office Phone: 213-488-7362. Office Fax: 213-629-1033. Business E-Mail: catherine.meyer@pillsburylaw.com.

MEYER, CHARLES G., museum director; Exec. dir. Bakersfield (Calif.) Mus. Art, 1995—. Office: Bakersfield Museum Of Art 1930 R St Bakersfield CA 93301-4815

MEYER, DAVID J., energy executive, lawyer; m. Anni Ryan; 4 children. BA in Polit. Sci., BA in Econs., Valparaiso U.; JD, Cornell U., 1978. Ptnr. Paine Hamblen et. al., 1978-98; sr. v.p., gen. counsel Avista Corp., Spokane, Wash., 1998—. Pres. bd. dirs. Lilac Blind Found. Mem. Fed. Energy Bar Assn., Wash. State Bar Assn., Spokane County Bar Assn. Office: Avista Corp 1411 E Mission Ave Spokane WA 99202-2600

MEYER, DIRK (DERRICK R. MEYER), information technology executive; b. La Grange, Ill., 1961; BS in Computer Engring., U. Ill.; MBA, Boston U. With microprocessor design group Intel Corp.; with Digital Equipment Corp., 1985—95; joined Advanced Micro Devices, Inc., Sunnyvale, Calif., 1995—, dir. engring. Austin, Tex., 1996—99, v.p. engring., computation products group Sunnyvale, Calif., 1999—2001, group v.p., computation products group, 2001—02, sr. v.p., computation products group, exec. officer, 2002—04, exec. v.p., computation products group, 2004—05, pres., COO, microprocessor solutions sector, 2005—06, pres., COO, 2006—08, pres., CEO, 2008—. Bd. dirs. Advanced Micro Devices, Inc., 2007—. Recipient Maurice Wilkes award, Assn. Computing Machinery, 2003. Office: Advanced Micro Devices Inc 1 AMD Pl Sunnyvale CA 94088

MEYER, EDMOND GERALD, retired chemistry professor, energy scientist, academic administrator; b. Albuquerque, Nov. 2, 1919; s. Leopold and Beatrice (Ilfeld) M.; m. Betty F. Knobloch, July 4, 1941 (dec.); children: Lee Gordon, Terry Gene, David Gary. BS in Chemistry, Carnegie Mellon U., 1940, MS, 1942; PhD, U. N.Mex., 1950. Chemist Harbison Walker Refractories Co., 1940-41; instr. Carnegie Mellon U., 1941-42; asst. phys. chemist Bur. Mines, 1942-44; chemist research div. N.Mex. Inst. Mining and Tech., 1946-48; head dept. sci. U. Albuquerque, 1950-52; head dept. chemistry N.Mex. Highlands U., 1952-59; dir. Inst. Sci. Rsch., dean Grad. Sch. U. Wyo., 1957—63, dean Coll. Arts and Sci., 1963-75, v.p. rsch., 1974-80, prof. energy and natural resources, 1981-89, prof. and dean emeritus, 1989—; pres., CEO Advanced Clean Coal Techs. LLC, 1999—. Exec. cons. Diamond Shamrock Corp., 1980; sci. adviser Gov. of Wyo., 1964-90; pres. Coal Tech. Corp., 1981—; cons. Los Alamos Nat. Lab., NFS, HHS, GAO, TVA, Wyo. Bancorp; contractor investigator Rsch. Corp., Dept. Interior, AEC, NIH, NSF, Dept. Energy, Dept. Edn.; Fulbright exch. prof. U. Concepcion, Chile, 1959. Co-author: Chemistry-Survey of Principles, 1963, Legal Rights of Chemists and Engineers, 1977, Industrial Research & Development Management, 1982; contbr. articles to profl. jours.; patentee in field. Mem. Laramie Regional Airport Bd., 1989-93, treas., 1994-97, chair; active Laramie City Coun., 1997-2001, vice mayor, 1998-2001. Lt. comdr. USNR, 1944-46, ret. Recipient Disting. Svc. award Jaycees; rsch. fellow U. N.Mex., 1948-50. Fellow: AAAS, Am. Inst. Chemists (hon.; pres. 1992—93, chmn. 1994—95); mem.: AIChE (sr.), Coun. Coll. Arts and Scis. (pres. 1971, sec.-treas. 1972—75, dir. Washington office 1973), Biophys. Soc., Am. Chem. Soc. (councilor 1962—90, chmn. Wyo. sect. 1997, 2002, nat. vol. svc. award 2006), Assn. Western Univs. (chmn. 1972—74), Laramie C. of C. (pres. 1984), Sigma Xi. Home: 1058 Colina Dr Laramie WY 82072-5015 Office: U Wyo Coll Arts Scis Laramie WY 82073-0965 Office Phone: 307-766-5445. Business E-Mail: egmeyer@uwyo.edu.

MEYER, ERIC, state legislator; b. 1961; m. Sarah Snell; children: Sophie, Clay. BS in Econ., U. Southern Calif., 1983; MD, U. Ariz. Coll. Medicine, 1988. Practicing physician, 1988—96; dir. Providence Med. Ctr. Dept. Emergency Medicine, Portland, Oreg., 1994—96; bd. mem. Scottsdale Unified Sch. Dist., 2004—08; mem. Dist. 11 Ariz. House of Reps., 2008—. Rep. Arcadia Neighborhood Learning Ctr. Parent Coun., 2001—04; mem. SUSD Parent Budget Com., 2002—04; v.p. Scottsdale Parent Coun. PTO, 2002—03; liaison Scottsdale Parent Coun. C. of C., 2002—04; legis. liaison Scottsdale Parent Coun., 2003—04; pres. Arcadia Neighborhood Learning Ctr. PTO, 2003—04; mem. SUSD All-City Athlete Banquet Bd.; gov. mem. Children's Mus. Phoenix. Democrat. Office: Capitol Complex 1700 W Washington Rm 121 Phoenix AZ 85007-2890 Office Phone: 602-926-3037. Office Fax: 602-417-3111. Business E-Mail: emeyer@azleg.gov.*

MEYER, FREDERICK G., lawyer; b. Temple, Tex., 1945; BA, Dartmouth Coll., 1967; JD, Columbia U., 1970; LLM, NYU, 1979. Bar: Conn. 1970, N.Y. 1971, Colo. 1979. Atty. Holland & Hart, Denver, Reinhart, Boerner, Van Deuren, Norris & Rieselbach, P.C., Denver, 1998—. Vis. lectr. grad. tax program law sch. U. Denver, 1982-83. Co-author: Colorado Probate: Beyond the Basics, 1984, Colorado Probate & Estate Planning, 1986, An Attorney's Look at Tax Planing for the Small Business Owner, Rancher and Farmer: Asset Protection Planning, 1996; co-editor: Colorado Estate Planning Handbook, rev. edit., 1989; editor trust and estate forum Colo. Lawyer, 1981-82; contbr. articles to profl. jours. Fellow Am. Coll. Trust and Estate Counsel, Colo. Bar Found.; mem. ABA (vice chair agrl. tax com. 1996-97), Greater Denver Tax Counsels Assn., Rocky Mountain Estate Planning Counsel (pres. 1987). Office: Ste 1950 1200 17th St Denver CO 80202-5855

MEYER, JAROLD ALAN, oil company research executive; b. Phoenix, July 28, 1938; s. Lester M. and Anita (Walker) M.; m. Diane Louise Wheeler; children: Ronald Alan, Sharon Lynne. BSChemE, Calif. Inst. Tech., 1960, MS, 1961. Mgr. process devel. Chevron Rsch., Richmond, Calif., 1978-82; tech. mgr. Chevron U.S.A., El Segundo, Calif., 1982-84; v.p. process rsch. Chevron Rsch., Richmond, 1984-86, pres., 1986—; sr. v.p. Chevron Rsch. and Tech., Richmond, 1990-93; ret., 1993; prin. J.A. Meyer Assocs., Martinez, Calif., 1993—. Bd. dirs. Solvent Refined Coal Internat., Inc., San Francisco; mem. adv. bd. Surface Sci. and Catalysis Program Ctr. for Advanced Materials, Lawrence Berkeley Lab., 1988-91; mem. adv. coun. Lawrence Hall Sci., 1989-94; indsl. advisor Accreditation bd. for Engring. and Tech. Inventor petroleum catalysts; contbr. articles to profl. jours. Bd. visitors U. Calif., Davis, 1986-93, trustee found., 1989—. Mem. Nat. Acad. Engring., Am. Chem. Soc., Nat. Petroleum Refining Assn., Indsl. Rsch. Inst., Conf. Bd. Internat. Rsch. Mgmt. Coun., Accreditation Bd. for Engring. and Tech. Indsl. Advisor, Sigma Xi, Tau Beta Pi. Avocations: electronics design and construction, photography. Home and Office: 849 Corte Briones Martinez CA 94553-5950

MEYER, JEROME J., diversified technology company executive; b. Caledonia, Minn., Feb. 18, 1938; s. Herbert J. and Edna (Staggemeyer) M.; m. Sandra Ann Beaudoin, June 18, 1960; children— Randall Lee, Lisa Ann, Michelle Lynn Student, Hamline U., 1956-58; BA, U. Minn., 1960. Devel. engr. Firestone Tire & Rubber Co., Akron, Ohio, 1960-61; v.p., gen. mgr. Sperry Univac, St. Paul, 1961-79; group v.p. Honeywell, Inc., Mpls., 1979-84; pres., COO Varian Assocs., Palo Alto, Calif., 1984-86, also bd. dirs.; pres., CEO Honeywell Inc., 1986-90; from pres. to chmn., CEO Tektronix Inc., Beaverton, Oreg., 1990-99, chmn., 1999—. Bd. dirs. Oreg. Pub. Broadcasting, Esterline Tech., Oregon Bus. Coun., AMP, Std. Ins. Co. Trustee Oreg. Grad. Inst., Willamette U., Oreg. Children's Found. Mem. Oregon Golf Club. Avocation: golf.

MEYER, JOSEPH B., state treasurer; b. Casper, Wyo., 1941; m. Mary Orr; children: Vincent, Warren. Student, Colo. Sch. Mines; BA, U. Wyo., 1964, JD, 1967; postgrad., Northwestern U., 1968. Dep. county atty. Fremont County, Wyo., 1967-69; assoc. Smith and Meyer, 1968-71; asst. dir. legis. svc. office State of Wyo., Cheyenne, 1971-87, atty. gen., 1987-95, sec. state, 1999—2006, state treas., 2007—; spl. asst. to pres. govt. rels. U. Wyo., Laramie, 1995-98. Condr. numerous govt. studies on state codes including Wyo. probate, criminal, state adminstrn., banking, domestic rels.; negotiator with Office of Surface Mining for Wyo. state preemption; instr. Wyo. Coll. Law, fall, 1986; lectr. Rocky Mountain Mineral Law Found., 1977; chmn. Conf. Western Atty. Gen., 1992—93; mem. exec. com. Nat. Assn. Attys. Gen.; mem. Bush-Cheney Transition Team, 2000—01. Chmn. Cheyenne Bd. of Health, 1999—; bd. dirs. Longs Peak coun. Boy Scouts Am., Wyoming Cmty. Devel. Authority. Named BSA Citizen Yr., Longs Peak Coun., 2007, UPRR Honoree, RNC Nat. Convention, 2008. Mem. Rotary. Republican. Congregationalist. Avocations: golf, tennis, gardening, wood carving, rock hunting. Home Phone: 307-634-8117; Office Phone: 307-777-7409. Office Fax: 307-777-5411. Business E-Mail: jmeyer3@state.wy.us.

MEYER, KEVIN, state legislator; b. Beatrice, Nebr., May 9, 1956; m. Marty Meyer; children: Karly, Valentina. BS in Bus. Adminstrn., U. Nebr., Lincoln, 1978; MPA, U. N.Mex., Albuquerque, 1982; MBA, Alaska Pacific U., Anchorage, 1992. Anchorage Assemblyman, 1993-2000; Alaska State Representative, District 19, 2000-02; Alaska State Representative, District 30, 2001-2008; mem. Alaska State Senate from Dist. O, 2009-. Chairman, United Way Drive; jr. achievement advisor, purchasing repr, Conoco Phillips Alaska. Republican. Presbyterian. Office: Dist O 716 W Fourth Ave Ste 310 Anchorage AK 99501-2133 also: State Capitol Rm 515 Juneau AK 99801 Office Phone: 907-654-4945, 207-269-0199. Office Fax: 907-465-3476, 207-269-0197. Business E-Mail: Senator_Kevin_Meyer@legis.state.ak.us.*

MEYER, LYNN NIX, lawyer; b. Vinita, Okla., Aug. 10, 1948; d. William Armour and Joan Ross Nix; children: Veronica, Victoria, David. BA, Baldwin Wallace Coll., 1978; JD, Case Western Res. U., 1981. Bar: Ky. 1982, Colo. 1984. Paralegal Texaco Devel., Austin, Tex., 1976-77; legal asst. Alcan Aluminum, Cleve., 1977-79; assoc. Wyatt, Tarrant & Combs, Lexington, Ky., 1982-83; ptnr. Meyer, Meyer & Assocs., P.C., Denver, 1984-85; gen. counsel Carbon Fuels Corp., 1985-95; in pvt. practice Denver, 1996-97; asst. gen. counsel products Gambro, Inc. (now Gambro BCT), Lakewood, Colo., 1997—. Mem. ABA, Colo. Bar Assn., Ky. Bar Assn., Arapahoe County Bar Assn. Home: 10487 E Ida Ave Englewood CO 80111-3746 Office: Gambro BCT 10810 W Collins Ave Lakewood CO 80215-4439 E-mail: lynn.meyer@gambrobct.com.

MEYER, MARGARET ELEANOR, retired microbiologist; b. Westwood, Calif., Feb. 8, 1923; d. Herman Henry and Eleanor (Dobson) M. BS, U. Calif., Berkeley, 1945; PhD, U. Calif., Davis, 1961. Pub. health analyst USPHS, Bethesda, Md., 1945-46; swine Brucellosis control agt. Dept. Agr., Davis, 1946-47; bacteriologist U. Calif., Davis, 1947-61; research microbiologist U. Calif. (Sch. Vet. Medicine), 1961-77, prof. vet. pub. health and microbiologist exptl. sta., 1977—; rsch. microbiologist U. Calif. Med. Sch., LA, 1961-77; supr. Brucella identifications lab. WHO, U. Calif., Davis, 1964—87, prof. vet. pub. health, 1973—87, dir. program in preventive vet. medicine, 1987; ret., 1987. Cons. subcom. on Brucella Internat. Com. Bacterial Taxonomy, 1962—, mem., 1966—; mem. 5th Pan Am. Congress Veterinary Medicine, Venezuela, 1966; mem. Internat. Congress Microbiology, Moscow, 1966, Mexico City, 1970, Munich, Ger., 1978, mem., officer, Eng., 1986; mem. Internat. Conf. Culture Collections, Tokyo, 1968; mem. adv. com. to Bergey's Manual Determative Bacteriology, 1967; cons. in resident Pan Am. Health Orgn., Zoonoses Lab., Buenos Aires, 1968; mem. brucellosis tech. adv. com. U.S. Animal Health Assn., 1977; FAO cons. on brucellosis control in dairy animals, Tripoli, Libya, 1981, mem. 3d internat. brucellosis symposium, Algiers, 1983; cons. Alaska Dept. Fish and Game, 1976, FAO, Libya, 1981, Bering Straits Reindeer Herders Assn., Nome, Alaska, 1981; invited speaker Internat. Symposium on Advances in Brucellosis Rsch., Tex. A&M U., 1989, Internat. Bison Conf.; resident cons. on brucellosis control in sheep and goats Am. Near East Refugee Aid, East Jerusalem, 1989; cons. on brucellosis in Yellowstone Nat. Pk., Nat. Pk. Svc., 1991—; invited mem. nat. symposium on brucellosis in the Greater Yellowstone Area, Jackson Hole, Wyo., 1994; cons. on brucellosis control in livestock for Armenia, 1994—. Contbr. articles to profl. jours. Bd. dirs. Carmichael Park and Recreation Dist., Calif., 1975; mem. Sacramento County Grand Jury, 1999-2000. Recipient Research Career Devel. award USPHS-NIH, 1963 Fellow Am. Pub. Health Assn., Am. Acad.

Microbiology; mem. Soc. Am. Microbiologists, N.Am. Conf. Animal Disease Research Workers, Am. Coll. Vet. Microbiologists (hon. affiliate), US Animal Health Assn. (chmn. brucellosis tech. advisory com. 1978-79), Internat. Assn. Microbiol. Socs. (mem. 1st intersect. congress 1974), AAUW, No. Calif. Women's Golf Assn., U. Calif. Alumni Assn., Sigma Xi. Clubs: U. Calif. Faculty (Davis); El Dorado Royal Country (Shingle Springs, Calif.); Reno Women's Golf. Home: 5611 Fair Oaks Blvd Carmichael CA 95608-5503 Office: U Calif Sch Vet Medicine Dept Epidemiology & Preventive Medicine Davis CA 95616

MEYER, MICHAEL EDWIN, lawyer; b. Chgo., Oct. 23, 1942; s. Leon S. and Janet (Gorden) M.; m. Catherine Dieffenbach, Nov. 21, 1982; children: Linda, Mollie, Patrick, Kellie. BS, U. Wis., 1964; JD, U. Chgo., 1967. Bar: Calif. 1968, U.S. Supreme Ct. 1973. Assoc. Lillick & McHose, LA, 1967-73, ptnr., 1974-90, mng. ptnr., 1986-87; ptnr. Pillsbury Madison Sutro, 1990—, mem. mgmt. com., 1990-92; mng. ptnr. Pillsbury Winthrop, LA, 1999—2003, Piper Rudnick LLP (now DLA Piper Rudnick Gray Cary), 2004—. Judge pro tem Beverly Hills Mcpl. Ct., Calif., 1976-79, Los Angeles Mcpl. Ct., 1980-86; lectr. in field. Bd. dirs. Bldg. Owners and Mgrs. Assn. Greater L.A., L.A. coun. Boy Scouts Am., L.A. Sports and Entertainment Commn., L.A. Econ. Devel. Corp.; pub. counsel United Way Greater L.A., Los Angeles County Bar Found., trustee, 1997—, Reviving Baseball in Inner Cities; mem. L.A. County Sheriff Youth Found., Jackie Robinson Found. Recipient Good Scout award L.A. Coun. Boy Scouts Am., 1992, Man of Yr. award United Way, 1996, Real Estate Profl. of Yr. award NACORE, 2002, Reviving Baseball in Inner-Cities CB award Major League Baseball, 2005, Spirit L.A. award L.A. Hdqs. Assn., 2005, Outstanding Cmty. Svc. award Weingart Ctr., 2006; named to Top Ten So. Calif. Super Lawyers LA Mag., 2006, Top Five Calif. Real Estate Lawyers Chambers USA, 2005. Mem. ABA, Am. Arbitration Assn. (arbitrator), Calif. Bar Assn., Los Angeles County Bar Assn. (trustee 1997—), L.A. Bar Assn., Am. Coll. of Real Estate Lawyers, U. Chgo. Alumni Assn. So. Calif. (pres. 1980-82), Calif. Club, U. L.A. Club (dir. 1979-85, pres. 1984-85), L.A. Country Club. Jewish. Office: DLA Piper Rudnick Gray Cary Ste 2300 550 S Hope St Los Angeles CA 90071 Home Phone: 310-546-5500, 213-505-2113; Office Phone: 213-330-7777. Office Fax: 213-330-7577. Business E-Mail: michael.meyer@dlapiper.com.

MEYER, ROBERT LEE, secondary school educator; b. St. Joseph, Mo., July 9, 1952; s. Robert James and Jerry Lee (Patterson) M.; m. Barbara Anita Stickles, Aug. 2, 1986. BS in Edn., Mo. Western State U., 1974; MA in Edn., Alliant Internat. U., 1988. Cert. tchr., Calif., Mo.; cert. specialist learning handicapped, resource specialist cert., adminstr., Calif. Spl. edn. tchr., learning handicapped Mann Jr. HS, San Diego, 1978-80, Serra HS, San Diego, 1980-84, Morse HS, San Diego, 1984-85; magnet seminar tchr. Bell Jr. HS, San Diego, 1985-91; project resource tchr., dir. student activities Serra High Sch., San Diego, 1991-94, resource specialist, 1994-95; magnet coord. Ctr. for Sci., Math. and Computer Tech. Samuel Gompers Secondary Sch., San Diego, 1995-97; dean of students, attendance coord. Scripps Ranch HS, non-athletic event coord., 1997-98; asst. prin. Mountain Empire Jr./Sr. HS, 1998—2001; dean of students Gompers Secondary Sch., 2001—03; resource specialist Gompers Mid. Sch., 2003—04; coord. Calif. High Sch. Exam, 2004—05; dean students San Diego Sch. Creative and Performing Arts, 2004—05, site based diagnostic resource tchr., 2005—06, tchr. world history, 2008—; site based diagnostic resource tchr. Creative and Performing Media Arts Mid. Sch., San Diego, 2005—06, O'Farrell Cmty. Charter Sch., San Diego, 2006—08. Chmn. resource com. Western Assn. Schs. & Colls. accreditation Serra High Sch., San Diego, 1995, chmn. process com. Western Assn. Schs. and Colls. accreditation Gompers Secondary Sch., San Diego, 1996-97, sch. site coun., 1992-97, gov. team mem., 1992-95, chair spl. edn. dept., 1983, mem. sch. leadership team, 1992-95, sr. class advisor, 1994-95, liaison Partnerships in Edn., 1996-97; monitor City Schs. Race Human Rels. Monitoring Team, 1991-92, African Am. students pupil advocate program adv. coun., 1995-97; restructuring coord. Senate Bill 1274 Grant, 1993-95, resource specialist, 1994-95; chmn. process com. Western Assn. Schs. and Colls. accreditation Gompers Sec. Sch., adv. com. mem. African Am. students program; co-chmn. race/human rels. com. Scripps Ranch H.S., 1997-98. Contbr. chapters to books. Alternate del. Dem. Party 6th Dist. and State Conventions, Holt County, Mo., 1976; mem. Nat. Conf. Minitown Race/Human Rels. Camp Coord., Scripps Ranch H.S. Recipient star adminstr. award Calif. FFA, 2000. Mem. Assn. Calif. Sch. Adminstrs., Optimist Club, Delta Chi. Democrat. Roman Catholic. Avocations: collecting political buttons, antiques, travel.

MEYER, RON, film company executive; b. 1944; m. Kelly Chapman; children, Jennifer, Sarah, Carson, Eli. With Paul Kohner Agency, 1964-1970; agent William Morris Agency, Beverly Hills, CA, 1970-1975; co-founder, pres. Creative Artists Agency, Inc., Beverly Hills, CA, 1975-95; pres., COO Universal Studios Inc., Universal City, 1995—. Served with USMC. Recipient Milestone award, Producers Guild Am., 2007; named one of 50 Most Powerful People in Hollywood, Premiere mag., 2004—06. Office: Universal Studios Inc 100 Universal City Plz Universal City CA 91608 Office Phone: 818-777-1000.*

MEYER, THOMAS JAMES, editorial cartoonist; b. Fort Benning, Ga., May 8, 1955; s. Edward Charles and Carol (McCunniff) M. BA, U. Mich., 1977. Congl. aide U.S. Ho. of Reps., Washington, 1977-79; free lance cartoonist, illustrator Washington Post, Fed. Times, Bus. Rev. of, Washington, 1979-81; editorial cartoonist San Francisco Chronicle, 1981—. Roman Catholic. Office: San Francisco Chronicle 901 Mission St San Francisco CA 94103-2905

MEYERINK, VICTORIA PAIGE, film producer, actress; b. Santa Barbara, Calif., Dec. 27, 1960; d. William Joseph Meyerink and Jeanne Baird; m. Lawrence David Foldes, Apr. 24, 1983. Student, U. So. Calif., 1978-80. Actress, 1962—; v.p. Star Cinema Prodn. Group, Inc., 1981-85; pres. Star Entertainment Group, Inc., LA, 1985—. Mem. faculty Internat. Film & TV Workshops, 1991—; lectr. colls. & film festivals, co-editor Indeependence Filom Festival, Colo., 2007-. Prodr. (motion pictures) The Great Skycopter Rescue, 1982, Young Warriors, 1984, Night Force, 1987, Prima Donnas, 1996, Finding Home, 2004; actress (TV series) The Danny Kaye Show, Green Acres, My Three Sons, Family Affair, The FBI, Adam 12, (motion pictures) Speedway, Night of The Grizzly, Seconds, Brainstorm, The Littlest Hobo, (TV spl.) It Isn't Easy Being a Teenage Millionairess, numerous commls. Recipient Mayoral Proclamation for Outstanding Achievement award City of LA, 1984, Recognition Cert. for 25 Yrs. Outstanding Contbns. to the Entertainment Industry City of LA, 1985, Outstanding Achievement award Acad. Family Films & TV, Former Child Star Lifetime Achievement award, 2006. Mem. Acad. Motion Picture Arts & Scis. (exec. com. Student Acad. Awards 1996—), L.A. Film Tchrs. Assn. Avocations: languages, travel, music, scuba diving, gourmet cooking.

MEYEROWITZ, ELLIOT MARTIN, biology professor; b. Washington, May 22, 1951; s. Irving and Freda (Goldberg) Meyerowitz; m. Joan Agnes Kobori, June 17, 1984; 2 children. AB, Columbia U., 1973; MPhil, Yale U., 1975, PhD, 1977; D (hon.), École Normale Supérieure, Lyon, France, 2007. Rsch. fellow Stanford U., Calif., 1977-79; asst. prof. biology Calif. Inst. Tech., Pasadena, 1980-85, assoc. prof., 1985-89, prof., 1989—, George W. Beadle prof. biology, 2002—, chair, divsn. biology, 2000—. Mem. editl. bd. Trends in Genetics, Current Biology, Cell, Devel, Genome Biology, Philos. Transactions Royal Soc. B, 2006; mem. editl. bd.: Current Opinion in Plant Biology, Jour. of Biology; contbr. articles to profl. jours. Recipient LVMH Sci. pour l'Art Sci. prize, 1996, Internat. prize for biology, Japan, 1997, Mendel medal, UK, 1997, Wilbur Cross medal, Yale U., 2001, Ross Harrison prize, Internat. Soc. Devel. Biologist, 2005, Balzan prize, 2006; Jane Coffin Childs Meml. Fund fellow, 1977—79, Sloan Found. fellow, 1980—82. Fellow: AAAS; mem.: NAS (councilor 2006—, Lounsbery award 1999), Royal Soc., Soc. Devel. Biology (pres. 2005—06), Academie des Scis. (fgn. mem. France), Internat. Soc. for Plant Molecular Biology (pres. 1995—97), Genetics Soc. Am. (pres. 1999, medal 1996), Bot. Soc. Am. (Pelton award 1994, Centennial award 2006), Am. Soc. Plant Biologists (Gibbs medal 1995), Am. Acad. Arts and Scis., Am. Philos. Soc. Office: Calif Inst Tech Divsn Biology 156 29 Pasadena CA 91125-0001 Home Phone: 626-844-4555; Office Phone: 626-395-6889. Business E-Mail: meyerow@caltech.edu.

MEYERS, CHRISTOPHER, humanities educator, consultant; s. Diana Meyers and Ehrhard Bahr (Stepfather); m. Donna Elsdon, Apr. 6, 1997; 1 child, Natasha Leigh Meyers-Cherry stepchildren: Renee Elsdon, Jonathon Elsdon. BA, U. Calif., Santa Cruz, 1980; cert. in clin. ethics, U. Tenn., 1984, D, 1986. Prof. philosophy Calif. State U., Bakersfield, 1986—, exec. dir. Kegley Inst. Ethics, 1987—; clin. ethicist Kern Med. Ctr., Bakersfield, 1997—. Ethics cons., instr. Mercy Healthcare, Bakersfield, 1991—, San Joaquin Cmty. Hosp., Bakersfield, 1995—. Author: (book) A Practical Guide to Clinical Ethics Consulting: Ethics, Power & Expertise, 2007; contbr. articles to profl. jours. Ethics cons., instr. Multiple Bus. and Philanthropic Groups, Bakersfield, 1987—2006. Mem.: Am. Soc. Bioethics and Humanities, Assn. Practical and Profl. Ethics, Am. Philos. Assn. Avocations: fly fishing, hiking, bicycling. Office: Calif State U Bakersfield 9001 Stockdale Hwy Bakersfield CA 93311 Business E-Mail: cmeyers@csub.edu.

MEYERS, DAVID L., food products executive; With Standard Brands, 1973—83, RJR Nabisco, 1983—89, Del Monte Foods, San Francisco, 1989—, CFO, 1992—, dir., 1994—97, exec. v.p., adminstrn., CFO. Office: Del Monte Foods PO Box 193575 San Francisco CA 94119-3575

MEYERS, GERALD A., metal products executive; With Logan Aluminum Inc., Bowling Green, Ky., Alcan & Logan, U.S. and Canada; pres., coo Ravenswood Aluminum Corp., W.Va., pres & CEO, Century Aluminum Corp., Monteray, Calif., 1992—. Office: Century Aluminum Corp 2511 Garden Rd Monterey CA 93940

MEYERS, KEVIN O., oil industry executive; BS in Chemistry and Math., Capital U., Columbus, Ohio, 1975; PhD in Chem. Engring., MIT. Joined exploration and prodn. tech. ARCO, Plano, Tex., 1980, various positions in exploration and prodn. ops. Tex., Alaska, 1980—96, sr. v.p., Prudhoe Bay bus. unit, 1996—98, pres., ARCO Alaska, Inc., 1998, CEO, ARCO Alaska, Inc., 1998—2000; sr. v.p. Atlantic Richfield Co., 1998—2000; sr. v.p. Alaska prodn. and ops. and pres., CEO Phillips Alaska, Inc., 2000—01; exec. v.p. Alaska prodn. ops. Phillips Petroleum Co., 2001—02; pres., Alaska Conoco-Phillips, 2002—04, pres., Russia & Caspian region Moscow, 2004—06, pres., Can., 2006—. Bd. dirs. LUKOIL, CAPP. Bd. regents U. Alaska; bd. dirs. Alaska Oil and Gas Assn., Anchorage Symphony Orch., Nature Conservancy Alaska, Anchorage Mus. Found., Kenai River Sportfishing Assn., USAF Civilian Adv. Bd., Alaska Command. Office: ConocoPhillips Can 401 9 Ave SW Calgary AB T2P 3C5 Canada

MEYERS, MARLENE O., retired hospital administrator; m. Eugene Meyers; children: Lori, Lisa, Dean. BSN, U. Sask., 1962; postgrad., U. Oslo, Norway, 1973; MSc, U. Calgary, Alta., Can., 1976; continuing edn., Harvard U., 1980, Banff Sch. Mgmt., 1985, U. Western Ont., Can., 1993; EMT-B, Scottsdale C.C., 2000. RN, Ariz. Various nursing positions, Alta. and B.C., Can., 1962-69; instr., chair Mount Royal Coll. Allied Health, Calgary, 1969-82; asst. exec. dir. Rockyview Hosp., Calgary, 1982-85; v.p. patient svcs. Calgary Gen. Hosp., 1985-91, pres., CEO, 1991-95, Meyers and Assocs. Health Care Mgmt. Cons., Calgary, 1995—98; clin. nurse Scottsdale Behavioral Health Ctr., 1999—2006. Surveyor Can. Coun. on Health Facilities Accreditation, 1986-97; mem. adv. com. for South Caucasus Health info. project, Can. Adv. Com. Named Calgary Woman of Yr. in field of Health, 1982; recipient Heritage of Svc. award, 1996. Mem. Alta. Assn. RNs (hon.), Can. Coll. Health Svcs. Orgn., Can. Exec. Svcs. Orgn., Can. Soc. for Internat. Health (bd. dirs. 1997-2001, South Caucasus adv. com. 2001—), Rotary Internat. PEO also: 10464 E Cannon Dr Scottsdale AZ 85258-4929

MEYERS, NANCY JANE, screenwriter, producer, director; b. Phila., Dec. 8, 1949; d. Irving H. and Patricia (Lemisch) M; m. Charles Shyer. BA, Am. U., Washington, 1971. Writer, prodr.: (films) Private Benjamin (Acad. award nominee, Writers Guild award 1980), Baby Boom, 1987, Father of the Bride, 1991, A Place to be Loved (assoc. prodr.), 1991, I Love Trouble, 1994, Father of the Bride Part II, 1995, Ted Hawkins: Amazing Grace (co-prodr.), 1996, The Affair of the Necklace, 2001, writer: (films) Irreconcilable Differences, 1984, Protocol, 1985, Once Upon A Crime..., 1992; writer, prodr., dir.: (films) Something's Gotta Give, 2003, The Holiday, 2006; prodr., dir.: (films) What Women Want, 2000; writer, dir.: (films) The Parent Trap, 1998. Mem. ASCAP, Acad. Motion Picture Arts and Scis., Writers Guild Am. West. Office: Creative Artists Agency 2000 Avenue Of The Stars Los Angeles CA 90067-4700

MEYERS, REBECKA LOUISE, pediatric general surgeon; b. Salt Lake City, May 11, 1958; MD, Oreg. Health Scis. U. Sch. Medicine, 1985. Cert. Gen. Surgery, Pediatric Gen. Surgery. Intern, gen. surgery U. Calif. Med. Ctr., San Francisco, 1985—88, fellow, cardiovascular diseases, 1988—90, resident, gen. surgery, 1990—92; fellow St. Christopher's Hosp. for Children in Pediatric Surgery, Phila., 1992—94; pediatric surgeon Primary Children's Med. Ctr., Salt Lake City, 1994—; chief, divsn. pediatric surgery Univ. Utah Hosp. (now called U. Utah Health Scis. Ctr.), Salt Lake City, 2001—; asst. prof. U. Utah, Salt Lake City, 1994—99, assoc. prof., 1999—2007, prof., 2007—. Mem.: Utah Med. Assn., Pacific Assn. of Pediatric Surgeons, Internat. Pediatric Endosurgery Grp., Assn. Women Surgeons, Am. Pediatric Surgical Assn., Am. Coll. Surgeons, Am. Acad. Pediat. Office: U Utah Health Services Ctr 50 N Medical Dr Salt Lake City UT 84132 also: Primary Childrens Med Ctr 100 N Mario Capecchi Dr Ste 2600 Salt Lake City UT 84113 Office Phone: 801-662-2950.

MEYERSON, IVAN D., lawyer, former corporate financial executive; AB, U. Calif., Berkeley, 1966; JD, Stanford U., 1969. Bar: Calif. 1970. Assoc. Herzstein & Maier, San Francisco, 1970-75, ptnr., 1976-78; atty. SEC, 1975-76; assoc. gen. counsel McKesson Corp., San Francisco, 1984-87, v.p., gen. counsel, 1987-98; exec. v.p., gen. counsel McKesson - HBOC Inc., San Francisco, 1998—2006.

MEYERSON, RONALD L., city official; b. Mar. 23, 1947; BA, U. Ariz. Adminstrv. asst. II City of Tucson, 1974-76, adminstrv. asst. III, 1976-80, asst. dir. ops., 1980-89, dir. ops., 1989—. Office: City Tucson PO Box 27210 Tucson AZ 85726-7210

MEZA, ROBERT, state legislator; Mem. Dist. 14 Ariz. House of Reps., 2003—, mem. commerce com., banking & ins. com. Mem. Ariz. Housing Commn., 2007—. Democrat. Office: Ariz House Reps Capitol Complex 1700 W Washington Rm 339 Phoenix AZ 85007 Office Phone: 602-926-3425. Office Fax: 602-417-3114. Business E-Mail: rmeza@azleg.gov.*

MEZEY, ROBERT, poet; b. Phila., Feb. 28, 1935; s. Ralph and Clara M.; m. Olivia Simpson (div.); children: Naomi, Judah, Eve. Student, Kenyon Coll., 1951-53; BA, U. Iowa, 1959; postgrad., Stanford U., 1960-61. Lectr. Western Res. U., Cleve., 1963-64, Franklin & Marshall Coll., Lancaster, Pa., 1965-66; asst. prof. Fresno (Calif.) State U., 1967-68, U. Utah, Salt Lake City, 1973-76; prof., poet-in-residence Pomona Coll., Claremont, Calif., 1976-99; ret., 1999. Author: (poems) The Lovemaker, 1960 (Lamont award), White Blossoms, 1965, The Door Standing Open, 1970, Selected Translations, 1981, Evening Wind, 1987 (Bassine citation, PEN prize 1989), Collected Poems 1952-1999, 2000 (Poets prize 2002); editor Naked Poetry, 1968, Poems from the Hebrew, 1973, Collected Poems of Henri Coulette, 1990, Selected Poems of Thomas Hardy, 1998, The Poetry of E.A. Robinson, 1999, Poems of the American West, 2002, A Word Like Fire: Selected Poems of Dick Barnes, 2005; translator: Tungsten (César Vallejo), 1988. With US Army, 1953—55. Fellow Ingram Merrill, 1973, 89, Guggenheim Found., 1977, Stanford U., 1960, NEA, 1987; recipient Poetry prize Am. Acad. Arts and Letters, 1982. Avocations: tennis, chess. Home: 960 E Bonita Ave # 28 Pomona CA 91767 Personal E-mail: mezteadancer@gmail.com.

MEZGER, JEFFREY T., construction executive; b. Chgo., 1955; BA in Econs., DePauw U., Greencastle, Ind., 1977. Pres. ctrl. Calif. divsn. US Home, Calif., 1983—93; pres. Antelope Valley divsn. KB Home Corp., LA, 1993—95, pres. KB Home Ariz., sr. v.p., regional mgr. SW divsn., 1995—99, exec. v.p., COO, 1999—2006, pres., CEO, 2006—. Mem. exec. bd. USC Lusk Ctr. for Real Estate; mem. policy adv. bd. Harvard Joint Ctr. for Housing Studies. Mem.: Nat. Assn. Home Builders (mem. high prodn. builders coun.). Office: KB Home Corp 10990 Wilshire Blvd 7th Fl Los Angeles CA 90024

MEZZULLO, LOUIS ALBERT, lawyer; b. Balt., Sept. 20, 1944; m. Judith Scales, Jan. 2, 1970. BA, U. Md., 1967, MA, 1976; JD, T.C. Williams Law Sch., 1976. Bar: Va. 1976, Calif. 2006. Sales rep. Humble Oil (name now Exxon), Richmond, Va., 1970-72; acctg. Marcoin, Inc., Richmond, 1972-73; pvt. practice bookkeeping, tax preparation, Richmond, 1973-76; assoc. McGuire, Woods, Battle and Boothe, Richmond, 1976-79; dir. Mezzullo & McCandlish, Richmond, 1979-2000; mem. Mezzullo & Guare, PLC, Richmond, 2000—03, McGuire Woods, 2004—06, Luce, Forward, Hamilton & Scripps, Carlsbad, Calif., 2006—. Contbr. articles to profl. jours. Former pres. Southampton Citizens Assn., Richmond, 1986; former bd. dirs. Richmond Symphony; bd. dirs. Va. Mus. Fine Arts Found., San Diego Opera. Served with USAR, 1969—75. Mem.: ABA (tax sect., vice chair publs.), Am. Coll. Employee Benefits Counsel, Trust Adminstrs. Coun., Estate Planning Coun. Richmond, Va. Law Found., Am. Bar Found., Va. Bar Assn., Am. Coll. Employee Benefit Counsel, Va. State Bar (tax sect.), Am. Coll. Tax. Counsel (chair), Am. Coll. Trust and Estate Counsel (sec.), Internat. Acad. Estate and Trust Law, Willow Oaks Country Club. Home: 7326 Grebe Dr Carlsbad CA 92011 Office Phone: 858-381-8014. Business E-Mail: lmezzullo@luce.com.

MICHAEL, ERNEST ARTHUR, mathematics professor; b. Zurich, Switzerland, Aug. 26, 1925; came to U.S., 1939; s. Jakob and Erna (Sondheimer) M.; m. Colette Verger Davis, 1956 (div. 1966); children: Alan, David, Gerard; m. Erika Goodman Joseph, Dec. 4, 1966; children: Hillary, Joshua. BA, Cornell U., 1947; MA, Harvard U., 1948; PhD, U. Chgo., 1951. Mem. faculty dept. math. U. Wash., Seattle, 1953—, asst. prof., 1953-56, assoc. prof., 1956-60, prof., 1960-93, prof. emeritus, 1993—. Mem. Inst. for Advanced Study, Princeton, 1951-52, 56-57, 60-61, 68, Math. Research Inst., E.T.H., Zürich, 1973-74; vis. prof. U. Stuttgart, Ger., 1978-79, U. Munich, Fed. Republic Germany, 1987, 88, 92-93. Editor: Procs. Am. Math. Soc., 1968-71, Topology and Its Applications, 1972-94, Set-Valued Analysis, 1993—; contbr. articles to profl. jours. With USNR, 1944—46. Grantee, AEC, Office Nav. Rsch., NSF, Guggenheim Found., Humboldt Found. Mem. Am. Math. Soc., Math. Assn. Am., ACLU, Amnesty Internat. Jewish. Home: 22200 Chinook Rd Woodway WA 98020-7200 Office: U Washington Dept Math Box 354350 Seattle WA 98195-4350 Home Phone: 425-640-3200. Personal E-mail: ernie@eemichael.net.

MICHAEL, MARK DIXWELL, lawyer; b. Palo Alto, Calif., Feb. 27, 1951; s. J.L. and Elizabeth (Ketcham) M.; m. Eileen Susan Landauer; children: Sarah Kristen Michael, Emily Christine Landauer. BA, Stanford U., 1972; JD, UCLA, 1977. Bar: Hawaii 1977, Calif. 1979. Assoc. Carlsmith, Carlsmith, Wichman & Case, Honolulu, 1977-78, Char, Hamilton, Taylor & Thom, Honolulu, 1979-81, Law Offices of Jerry E. Berg, San Francisco, 1981-84; sr. v.p., gen. counsel, sec. 3Com Corp., Santa Clara, Calif., 1984—2003. Dir. Nollenberger Capital Ptnrs., Inc., Natus Med., Inc. Mem. ABA, Am. Soc. Corp. Secs., Silicon Valley Assn. Gen. Counsel, Calif. State Bar Assn., Hawaii State Bar Assn. E-mail: mark_michael@myway.com.

MICHAELS, MIA, choreographer, dancer; b. Fla. Choreographer for Celine Dion, Ricky Martin, Gloria Estefan, Cirque du Soleil, Anna

Vissi, Angelica, Prince, Jimmy Ray, and many others; founder Miami Movement Dance Co., 1989; founder, artistic dir. & choreographer R.A.W. (Reality At Work), NYC; judge, choreographer So You Think You Can Dance?, 2005—. Choreographer (theater) Celine Dion: A New Day, 2003, Fort Chaffee, Arkansas Repertory Theater, WestSide Story, If These Shoes Could Talk, Angelinos Eyes, Coconut Grove Playhouse, Miami, Hello, Dolly, Papermill Playhouse, NJ, 2006, Cirque Du Soleil: Delirium, (TV series) So You Think You Can Dance?, 2005—; contbr. Movment mag., 2006—. Recipient Primetime Creative Arts Emmy Award for Outstanding Choreography on a TV Series, 2006—07. Mem.: AFTRA. Office: c/o Julie McDonald McDonald/Selznick Assocs Inc 1611A N El Centro Ave Hollywood CA 90028 also: c/o Mark D Sendroff Sendroff & Baruch LLP 1500 Broadway Ste 2001 New York NY 10036 Office Phone: 323-957-6680. Office Fax: 323-957-5694, 323-957-6688.

MICHAELSON, JON, lawyer; b. Jersey City, Apr. 2, 1948; BA, Pomona Coll., 1969; MA, Univ. Tex., Austin, 1973; JD, Boalt Sch. Law, Univ. Calif., Berkeley, 1978. Bar: Calif. 1978, US Dist. Ct. (Calif. districts), US Ct. Appeals (9th & Fed. cir.), US Supreme Ct. Ptnr., Global Intellectual Property practice Coudert Bros. LLP, San Francisco. Editor (mng.): Indsl. Rels. Law Jour., 1976—77; editor: (articles), 1977—78. Mem.: ABA, Internat. Trademark Assn., State Bar Calif., Santa Clara County Bar Assn.

MICHAILIDES, THEMIS J., plant pathology educator; Prof. plant pathology U. Calif., Parlier. Recipient Lee M. Hutchins award Am. Phytopathological Soc., 1995. Office: U Calif Kearny Agrl Ctr 9240 S Riverbend Ave Parlier CA 93648-9757

MICHALKO, JAMES PAUL, library association administrator; b. Cleve., May 13, 1950; s. Paul James and Lillian (Fanta) M.; 1 child, Alexandra. BA, Georgetown U., 1971; MLS, MBA, U. Chgo., 1974. Asst. to v.p., adminstrn. Technicare Inc. (formerly BCC Industries), Cleve., 1971-72; asst dir., adminstrn. U. Pa. Librs., Phila., 1974-80; dir. bus. and fin. Rsch. Librs. Group, Stanford, Calif., 1980-85, v.p. fin. and adminstrn., 1985-87, acting pres., 1988-89, pres. Mountain View, Calif., 1989—. Contbr. to Libr. Quar., Coll. & Rsch. Librs.; reviewer for Libr. Quar., Coll. & Rsch. Librs., Acad. of Mgmt. Rev., Jour. Acad. Librarianship, Jour. Libr. Adminstrn.

MICHEL, MARY ANN KEDZUF, retired nursing educator; b. Evergreen Park, Ill., June 1, 1939; d. John Roman and Mary Kedzuf; m. Jean Paul Michel, 1974. Diploma in nursing, Little Company of Mary Hosp., Evergreen Park, 1960; BSN, Loyola U., Chgo., 1964; MS, No. Ill. U., 1968, EdD, 1971. Staff nurse Little Co. of Mary Hosp., 1960-64; instr. Little Co. of Mary Hosp. Sch. Nursing, 1964-67, No. Ill. U., DeKalb, 1968-69, asst. prof., 1969-71; chmn. dept. nursing U. Nev., Las Vegas, 1971-73, prof. nursing, 1975—2008, dean Coll. Health Scis., 1973-90, prof. emeritus coll. health scis., 2006—08; pres. PERC, Inc.; mgmt. cons., 1993—95. Mgmt. cons. Nev. Donor Network, 1993; mem. So. Nev. Health Manpower Task Force, 1975; mem. manpower com. Plan Devel. Commn., Clark County Health Sys. Agy., 1977-79, mem. governing body, 1981-86; mem. Nev. Health Coordinating Coun., Western Inst. Nursing, 1971-85; mem. coordinating com. assembly instnl. adminstrs. dept. allied health edn. and accreditation AMA, 1985-88; mem. bd. advisors So. Nev. Vocat. Tech. Ctr., 1976-80; sec.-treas. Nev. Donor Network, 1988-89, chmn. bd., 1988-90. Contbr. articles to profl. jours. Trustee Desert Spring Hosp., Las Vegas, 1976-85; bd. dirs. Nathan Adelson Hospice, 1982-88, Bridge Counseling Assocs., 1982, Everywoman's Ctr., 1984-86; chair Nev. Commn. on Nursing Edn., 1972-73, Nursing Articulation Com., 1972-73, Yr. of Nurse Com., 1978; moderator Invitational Conf. Continuing Edn., Am. Soc. Allied Health Professions, 1978; mgmt. cons. Nev. Donor Network, 1994-95, Donor Organ Recovery Svc., Transplant Recipient Internat. Orgn., SW Eye Bank, SW Tissue Bank. Named Outstanding Alumnus, Loyola U., 1983; NIMH fellow, 1967-68. Fellow Am. Soc. Allied Health Professions, 1991, (chair nat. resolutions com. 1981-84, treas. 1988-90, sec's. award com. 1982-83, 92-93, nat. by-laws com. 1985, conv. chair 1987); mem. AAUP, Am. Nurses Assn., Nev. Nurses Assn. (dir. 1975-77, treas. 1977-79, conv. chair 1978), So. Nev. Area Health Edn. Coun., Western Health Deans (co-organizer 1985, chair, 1988-90), Nat. League Nursing, Nev. Heart Assn., So. Nev. Mem. Hosps. (nursing recruitment com. 1981-83, mem. nursing practice com. 1983-85), Las Vegas C. of C. (named Woman of Yr. Edn.) 1988, Slovak Catholic Sokols, Phi Kappa Phi (chpt. sec. 1981-83, pres.-elect 1983, pres. 1984, v.p. Western region 1989-95, editl. bd. jour. Nat. Forum 1989-93), Alpha Beta Gamma (hon.), Sigma Theta Tau, Zeta Kappa. Personal E-mail: m.a.michel@worldnet.att.net.

MICHELS, DIRK, lawyer; b. Wupperful, Germany, Mar. 10, 1962; s. Wolfgang and Ingrid Michels; m. Claudia I. Olson, Aug. 2, 1995. BWL Vordiplom, U. Hamburg, Germany, 1986, JD Erstes Staatsexamen, 1988; LLM, U. San Diego, 1996. Bar: Hamburg 1992, Calif. 1996. Law clk. Hamburg Ct. Appeals, 1989-92; assoc. Huth Dietrich Hahn, Hamburg, 1992-95, Hillyer & Irwin, San Diego, 1996-2000; assoc. to ptnr. Kirkpatrick & Lockhart Preston Gates Ellis LLP, San Francisco, 2000—. Contbr. articles tp profl. jours. Mem. ABA (internat. sect.), Council of Bars & Law Soc. of European Cmty., German-Am. Bus. Assn. (bd. dir.), Internat. Angel Investor Inst. (bd. adv.), German-Am. Lawyers Assn., German-Am. Cultural Soc., Am. Coun. on Germany. Office: K&L Gates 630 Hansen Way Palo Alto CA 94304 Office Phone: 650-798-6709. Business E-Mail: dirk.michels@klgates.com.

MICHELSON, LILLIAN, librarian, researcher; b. NYC, June 21, 1928; d. Louis and Dora (Keller) Farber; m. Harold Michelson, Dec. 14, 1947; children: Alan Bruce, Eric Neil, Dennis Paul. Vol. Goldwyn Libr., Hollywood, Calif., 1961-69; owner Former Goldwyn Rsch. Libr., Hollywood, 1969—; ind. location scout, 1973—. Mem. Motion Picture Libr. Found., 2002—, Friends L.A. Pub. Libr. Mem.: Acad. Motion Picture Arts and Scis. Office: c/o Dreamworks SKG Rsch Libr 1000 Flower St Glendale CA 91201-3007 Home Phone: 323-654-7177. E-mail: lmichelson@dreamworks.com.

MICHIE, SARA H., pathologist, educator; b. Tulsa, Okla., Jan. 3, 1955; BS in Biology, Stephen F. Austin U., 1977; MD, U. Tex., Houston, 1981. Diplomate Am. Bd. Pathology. Resident anatomic pathology Stanford (Calif.) U. Med. Ctr., 1981—83, postdoctoral fellow immunology dept. pathology, 1983—84, 1986—87, postdoctoral fellow diagnostic immunopathology, 1984—85; resident dept. pathology U. Iowa, Iowa City, 1985—86, postdoctoral fellow, 1986; assoc. investigator lab. svc. VA Hosp., Palo Alto, Calif., 1988—89, staff physician, 1989—, assoc. investigator, 1990—91; clin. instr. pathology dept. Stanford U., 1989—92, asst. prof. pathology, 1992—. Contbr. articles to profl. jours. Recipient Rsch. award, Am. Diabetes Assn., 1996. Mem.: Bay Area Flow Cytometry Group, Soc. Investigative Pathology, Am. Soc. Investigative Pathology, Alpha Omega Alpha, Sigma Xi. Office: VA Hosp Palo Alto 3801 Miranda Ave Stop 154F Palo Alto CA 94304-1207

MICKUS, DONALD V., real estate development corporation executive; BS in Acctg., Wayne State U. CPA. Mgr. Ernst & Young, Greyhound Corp., Del Webb Corp., Phoenix, 1983-85, v.p., treas., sec., 1985—. Office: Del Webb Corp 15333 N Pima Rd Ste 300 Scottsdale AZ 85260-2782

MIDDLEBROOK, ROBERT DAVID, electronics educator; b. England, May 16, 1929; BA, Cambridge U., England, 1952, MA, 1956; MS, Stanford U., 1953, PhD in Elec. Engring., 1955. Sr. tech. instr., mem. trade testing bd. Radio Sch. No. 3, Royal Air Force, Eng., 1947-49; asst. prof. electrical engring. Calif. Inst. Tech., Pasadena, 1955-58, assoc. prof., 1958-65, prof. electronics, 1965-98, prof. emeritus, 1998—. Mem. hon. editorial adv. bd. Solid State Electronics, 1960-74; mem. WESCON tech. program com., 1964; lectr. 23 univs. and cos. in Eng., The Netherlands, Germany, 1965-66; mem. rsch. and tech. adv. coun. com. on space propulsion and power, NASA, 1976-77; gen. chmn. Calif. Inst. Tech. Indsl. Assocs. Conf. Power Electronics, 1982; cons. in field. Author: An Introduction to Transistor Theory, 1957, Differential Amplifiers, 1963, (with S. Cuk) Advances in Switched-Mode Power Conversion, Vols. I and II, 1981, 2d edit., 1983, Vol. III, 1983; mem. editorial bd. Internat. Jour. Electronics, 1976-82; presented 77 profl. papers; patentee in field. Recipient Nat. Profl. Group Indsl. Engrs. award, 1958, Indsl Rsch. 100 award Indsl. Rsch. Mag., 1980, award for the Best Use of Graphics Powercon 7, 1980, Powercon 8, 1981, William E. Newell Power Electronics award Inst. Elec. & Electronics Engrs., 1982, PCIM award for Leadership in Power Electronics Edn., 1990, Edward Longstreth Medal Franklin Inst., 1991, Richard P. Feynman prize for excellence in tchg. Calif. Inst. Tech., 1997. Fellow IEEE (exec. com. San Gabriel Valley sect. 1964-65, treas. 1977-78, gen. chmn. power electronics specialists conf. 1973, AES-S elec. power/energy systems panel 1977-87, program chmn. applied power electronics conf. 1986, 87), Instn. Elec. Engrs. (Eng.); mem. Sigma Xi. Achievements include research in new solid state devices, their development, representation and application; electronics education (design-oriented analysis techniques); power conversion and control. Office: Calif Inst Tech 136 93 Engring Applied Sci Pasadena CA 91125-0001

MIDDLEKAUFF, ROBERT LAWRENCE, historian, educator, academic administrator; b. Yakima, Wash., July 5, 1929; s. Harold and Katherine Ruth (Horne) M.; m. Beverly Jo Martin, July 11, 1952; children: Samuel John, Holly Ruth. BA, U. Wash., 1952; PhD, Yale U., 1961. Instr. history Yale U., New Haven, 1959-62; asst. prof. history U. Calif., Berkeley, 1962-66, assoc. prof., 1966-70, prof., 1970-80, Margaret Byrne prof. history, 1980-83, prof. history, 1988-92, emeritus prof., 2000—, Preston Hotchkis prof., 1992—; dir. Huntington Libr., Art Gallery and Bot. Gardens, San Marino, Calif., 1983-88; Harmsworth prof. history Oxford (Eng.) U., 1996-97. Mem. coun. Inst. Early Am. History and Culture, Williamsburg, Va., 1974-76, 85-88, chair exec. bd., 1992-96. Author: Ancients and Axioms, 1963, The Mathers, 1971, The Glorious Cause: The American Revolution, 1763-1789, 1982, 2nd edit., rev., 2005, Benjamin Franklin and His Enemies, 1996. Served to 1st lt. USMC, 1952-54, Korea. Recipient Bancroft prize, 1972, Commonwealth Club Gold medal, 1983; fellow Am. Coun. Learned Socs., 1965, NEH, 1973, Huntington Libr., 1977. Fellow Am. Acad. Arts and Scis.; mem. Am. Hist. Assn., Orgn. Am. Historians, Am. Philos. Soc., Soc. Am. Historians, Am. Antiquarian Soc., Assocs. Early Am. History and Culture (chmn. exec. com.), Colonial Soc. Mass. (corr.), Mass. Hist. Soc. Home: 5868 Ocean View Dr Oakland CA 94618-1535 Office: Univ Calif Dept History Berkeley CA 94720-2550 Office Phone: 510-642-1971.

MIDDLETON, JAMES ARTHUR, oil and gas company executive; b. Tulsa, Mar. 15, 1936; s. James Arthur and Inez (Matthews) M.; m. Victoria Middleton; children: Robert Arthur, James Daniel, Angela Lynn; stepson: Andrew Davis Fitzhugh. BA, Rice U., 1958, BS in Mech. Engring., 1959. With Atlantic Richfield Co., 1959-96; design engr. Dallas, 1962-67; tech. planner, 1967-69; mgr. shale devel. Grand Junction, Colo., 1969-72; mgr. engring. dept. Los Angeles, 1972-74; mgr. Prudhoe Bay project Pasadena, Calif., 1974-80; v.p., mgr. corp. planning Los Angeles, 1980-81; pres. ARCO Coal Co., Denver, 1981-82; sr. v.p. ARCO Oil and Gas Co., Dallas, 1982-85, pres., 1985-90, sr. v.p. parent co., 1981-87, exec. v.p. parent co., 1987-94, also bd. dirs.; chmn., CEO Crown Energy Corp., Salt Lake City, 1996-2000; pres. Jam Energy Co., 2000—. Bd. dirs. Tex. Utilities Co., Dallas., ARCO Chem. Co., Berry Petroleum Co. Corp. rep. Circle Ten coun. Boy Scouts Am.; bd. dirs. L.A. coun. Boy Scouts Am., United Way Met. Dallas, Dallas Coun. on World Affairs, Jr. Achievement So. Calif. 2d lt. C.E., AUS, 1959-60 Reicpient ASME Petroleum div. Oil Drop award. Mem. Soc. Petroleum Engrs. of AIME, Tex. Mid-Continent Oil and Gas Assn., Am. Petroleum Inst., Rocky Mountain Oil and Gas Assn., We. States Petroleum Assn. (chmn. bd. dirs.), Nat. Gas Suppliers Assn. (chmn.), L.A. C. of C. (bd. dirs.), L.A. Music Ctr. Founders, Ctr. for Strategic and Internat. Studies (CSIS)-Dallas Round Table, Am. Enterprise Forum Chief Execs. Round Table, Dallas Petroleum Club, Tower, Northwood, Calif. Club, Bel-Air Country Club, L.A. Country Club, Preston Trail Golf Club.

MIDDLETON, KAREN, state legislator; b. Salisbury, Md., Feb. 24, 1966; m. Larry Beer; stepchildren: Katie, Molly. BA in Polit. & Women's Studies, Mt. Holyoke Coll., 1988; MA in Polit. Sci., U. Colo., Denver, 1996; MA in Higher Edn. Policy, U. Denver, 2006. Mem. 7th Congl. dist. Colo. State Bd. Edn., 2004—08; mem. Dist. 42 Colo. House of Reps., 2008—, majority caucus chair. Democrat. Office: State House 200 E Colfax Denver CO 80203 Office Phone: 303-866-3911. Business E-Mail: karen@karenmiddleton.com.*

MIDDLEWOOD, MARTIN EUGENE, writer, consultant; b. Galesburg, Ill., Mar. 21, 1947; s. Martin and Bernetta Maxine (Henderson) M.; m. Mona Marie Jarmer, Sept. 10, 1971; children: Erin, Martha, Emily, Margaret. BA, Ea. Wash. U., 1973, MA, 1980. Writer tech. manuals Tektronix, Inc., Beaverton, Oreg., 1976-77, tech. writer, 1977-79, sr. tech. writer, 1979-82, supr. pub. rels., 1982-84, mgr. pub. rels., 1984-85, mgr. mktg. communications Vancouver, Wash., 1985-86; dir. info. strategy and svcs. Waggener Edstrom, Portland, Oreg., 1986-98; pub. Cognizer Report, Portland, Oreg., 1990-94. Chmn. adv. bd. sci. and tech. writing, Clark Coll., Vancouver, 1984-2004; owner communications cons. firm, Vancouver, 1978-98; pres., owner Frontline Strategies, Inc., 1998—. Author: (ednl. brochure series) Oscilloscope Measurements, 1979 (award of excellence Willamette Valley chpt., Network Svcing., won Awd. of Distinction, 1980, Soc. Tech. Communication, 1980); assoc. pub. Builder News, 2004-2005; contbr. articles to profl. jours. Served with USMC, 1967-70. Recipient cert. recognition Clark Coll., Vancouver, 1984, 86, 89, 92-99, award of excellence Pacific N.W. chpt. Internat. Assn. Bus. Communicators, 1985. Mem. Soc. Tech. Communication (pres. Willamette Valley chpt. 1983-85, award of recognition 1986, chpt. pub. achievement award 1985, awards of distinction, 1980, 81). Avocations: photography, martial arts. Home and Office: 10816 NW Oxbow Ridge Dr Vancouver WA 98685 Office Phone: 360-882-1164. Personal E-mail: martinm@pacifier.com.

MIDGETT, LEON A., manufacturing executive; b. Flat Rock, Ill., Oct. 31, 1942; BA, U. Ill., 1965. Plant contr., metal beverage container plant Ball Corp., Findlay, Ohio, 1972-74, adminstr. mgr., Findlay and Fairfield plants, 1974-78, mgr. mfg. svcs., 1978, dir. mfg. svcs. Westminister, Colo., 1979-90, v.p., mfg., 1990—, pres., 1995-00, COO, 2000—.

MIDKIFF, ROBERT RICHARDS, trust company, finance company executive, consultant; b. Honolulu, Sept. 24, 1920; s. Frank Elbert and Ruth (Richards) M.; m. Evanita Sumner, July 24, 1948; children: Mary Lloyd, Robin Starr, Shelley Sumner, Robert Richards Jr., David Wilson. BA, Yale U., 1942; grad. Advanced Mgmt. Program, Harvard U., 1962; LHD, U. Hawaii, 2002. Asst. sec. Hawaiian Trust Co., 1951—56, asst. v.p., 1956—57, v.p., 1957—65; dir. Am. Factors, Ltd., 1954—65; v.p. Amfac, Inc., 1965—68; exec. v.p., dir. Am. Security Bank, Honolulu, 1968—69, pres., dir., 1969—71; pres., CEO, dir. Am. Trust Co. Hawaii, Honolulu, 1971—93; chmn. bd. dirs. Bishop Trust Co. Ltd., Honolulu, 1984—93; pres., CEO Am. Fin. Svcs. of Hawaii, 1984—93. Co-chmn. Gov.'s Archtl. Adv. Com. on State Capitol, 1960-65; co-chmn. Gov.'s Adv. Com. on Fine Arts for State Capitol, 1965-69; past chmn., bd. dirs. Hawaii Visitors Bur.; past pres., bd. dirs. Downtown Improvement Assn., Lahaina Restoration Found., Hawaii Cmty. Found.; bd. dirs., pres. Atherton Family Found.; past chmn. Profit Sharing Rsch. Found.; chmn., bd. dirs. Hawaii Theatre Ctr.; past chmn. bd. dirs. Good Beginnings Alliance; chmn. bd. dirs. Honolulu Cultural and Arts Dist. Mem. Coun. on Founds. (past bd dirs.), Profit Sharing Coun. Am. (past bd. dirs.), Small Bus. Coun. Am. (past bd. dirs.), ESOP Assn. Am. (past bd. dirs.), Pacific Club, Waialae Golf Club, Phi Beta Kappa. Episcopalian. Home: 4389 Malia St Apt 416 Honolulu HI 96821-1171 Office Phone: 808-734-8132. Office Fax: 808-737-9007. Personal E-mail: rrmhi@aol.com.

MIDLER, LAURENCE H. (LARRY), lawyer, real estate company executive; BA with hon., U. Va., 1987; JD, NYU, 1990. Bar: NY State 1990. Former assoc. atty. Latham & Watkins Law Offices, NYC; former v.p., gen. counsel Serviscope Corp.; former head facilities corp. svcs. dept., gen. counsel Micro Warehouse, Inc.; exec. v.p., gen. counsel CB Richard Ellis Group, 2006—. Office: CB Richard Ellis Ste 2700 355 S Grand Ave Los Angeles CA 90071

MIEL, VICKY ANN, city official; b. South Bend, Ind., June 20, 1951; d. Lawrence Paul Miel and Virginia Ann (Yeagley) Hernandez. BS, Ariz. State U., 1985. Master mcpl. clk. Internat. Inst. Mcpl. Clks. Word processing coordinator City of Phoenix, 1977-78, word processing adminstr., 1978-83, chief dep. city clk., 1983-88, city clk. dir., 1988—. Assoc. prof. Phoenix Community Coll., 1982-83, Mesa (Ariz.) Community Coll., 1983; speaker in field, Boston, Santa Fe, Los Angeles, N.Y.C. and St. Paul, 1980—. Author: Phoenix Document Request Form, 1985, Developing Successful Systems Users, 1986. Judge Future Bus. Leaders Am. at Ariz. State U., Tempe, 1984; bd. dirs. Fire and Life Safety League, Phoenix, 1984. Recipient Gold Plaque, Word Processing Systems Mag., Mpls., 1980, Green Light Productivity award City of Phoenix, 1981, Honor Soc. Achievement award Internat. Word Processing Assn., 1981, 1st Ann. Grand Prize Records Mgmt. Internat. Inst. Mcpl. Clks., 1990, Olsten Award for Excellence in Records Mgmt., 1991, Tech. Award of Excellence, 1995. Mem. ASPA, Assn. Info. Systems Profls. (internat. dir. 1982-84), Internat. Inst. Mcpl. Clks. (cert., 2d v.p. 1996-97, 1st v.p. 1997-98, pres. 1998-99, tech. award of excellence 1995, immediate past pres. 1999-2000), Am. Records Mgrs. Assn., Assn. Image Mgmt., Am. Mgmt. Assn. Office: City Phoenix 200 W Washington St Ste 1500 Phoenix AZ 85003-1611

MIELKE, CLARENCE HAROLD, JR., hematologist; b. Spokane, Wash., June 18, 1936; s. Clarence Harold and Marie Katherine (Gillespie) M.; m. Marcia Rae, July 5, 1964; children: Elisa, John, Kristina. BS, Wash. State U., 1959; MD, U. Louisville, 1963. Intern San Francisco Gen. Hosp., 1963-64; resident in medicine Portland VA Hosp., 1964-65, San Francisco Gen. Hosp., 1965-67; fellow in hematology U. So. Calif., 1967-68; tchg. fellow, asst. physician, instr. Tufts-New Eng. Med. Ctr. Hosps., Boston, 1968-71; sr. scientist Med. Rsch. Inst., San Francisco, 1971-90; chief hematology Presbyn. Hosp., San Francisco, 1971-82; asst. prof. clin. medicine U. Calif. Sch. Medicine, San Francisco, 1971-80, assoc. clin. prof., 1979-90, bd. dirs. Inst. Cancer Rsch., 1992—. Trustee, bd. dirs. Med. Rsch. Inst. San Francisco, Sacred Heart Hosp. Found., 1997-2000, Rockwood Clinic Found., 1994—; dir. emeritus Inst. Cancer Rsch.; trustee emeritus, bd. dirs. Med. Rsch. Inst., 1988—; dir. Health Rsch. and Edn. Ctr., Wash. State U., 1989-2005, prof. pharmacology, 1989—, prof. vet. medicine, 1989—, assoc. dean rsch., 1992-2004; dir. Spokane (Wash.) Heart Study, 1994-2006. Editor emeritus Jour. Clin. Aphesis, 1981; contbr. chpts. to books, articles to med. jours. Named Nat. Disting. Eagle Scout, 1998; NIH grantee, 1973-88. Fellow ACP, Am. Heart Assn.; mem. AAAS, AMA, Am. Heart Assn., Internat. Acad. Clin. and Applied Thrombosis and Hemostasis, Internat. Soc. Hematology, Am. Coll. Angiology; mem. Am. Soc. Internal. Medicine, Internat. Soc. Thrombosis and Hemostasis, N.Y. Acad. Scis., Spokane Med. Soc., Internat. Soc. Angiology. Office: 25415 E Misson Ave Liberty Lake WA 99019 Office Phone: 509-358-7630. Business E-Mail: mielkeh@wsu.edu, harry@arborcrest.com.

MIELKE, PAUL WILLIAM, JR., statistician, consultant; b. St. Paul, Feb. 18, 1931; s. Paul William and Elsa (Yungbauer) M.; m. Roberta Roehl Robison, June 25, 1960; children: William, Emily Spear, Lynn Basila. BA, U. Minn., 1953, PhD, 1963; MA, U. Ariz., 1958. Tchg. asst. U. Ariz., Tucson, 1957—58, U. Minn., Mpls., 1958—60, statis. cons., 1960—62, lectr., 1962—63; from asst. to assoc. prof. dept. statis. Colo. State U., Fort Collins, 1963—72, prof. dept. stats., 1972—. Co-author: Permutation Methods: a Distance Function Approach; contbr. articles Am. Jour. Pub. Health, Jour. of Statis. Planning and Inference, Ednl. and Psychol. Measurement, Biometrika, Earth-Sci. Revs., Weather and Forecasting, Jour. Behavioral and Ednl. Stats. Capt. USAF, 1953-57. Fellow Am. Statis. Assn.; mem. Am. Meteorol. Soc. (Banner I. Miller award 1973, 94), Biometric Soc. Achievements include rsch. in common statistical methods (t test and analysis of variance) based on counter intuitive geometric foundations and provided alternative statistical methods which are based on appropriate foundations. Home: 736 Cherokee Dr Fort Collins CO 80525-1517 Office: Colo State U Dept Stats Fort Collins CO 80523-1877 Office Phone: 970-491-6465. Business E-Mail: paul.mielke@colostate.edu.

MIGHT, THOMAS OWEN, newspaper company executive; b. Fort Walton Beach, Fla., Apr. 22, 1951; s. Gerald William and Rosina (Bugner) M.; m. Sept. 22, 1973; children— Matthew, Daniel BS in Indsl. Engring., Ga. Tech. U., 1972; MBA, Harvard Bus. Sch., 1978. Asst. to pub. Washington Post, 1978-80, mgr. plant, 1980-81, v.p. prodn., v.p. marketing; now pres., CEO, divsn. Cable One The Washington Post Co., Phoenix, 1981—. Served to capt. U.S. Army, 1972-76 Roman Catholic.

MIGIELICZ, GERALYN, photojournalist; b. St. Louis, Feb. 15, 1958; d. Edward J. and Mary Ann (McCarthy) M. BJ, U. Mo., 1979. Photographer Emporia (Kans.) Gazette, 1979-80; chief photographer St. Joseph (Mo.) News-Press & Gazette, 1980-83; photo editor, photographer Seattle Times, 1984; picture editor Rocky Mountain News, Denver, 1985-86; graphics editor San Jose (Calif.) Mercury News, 1986-92, dir. photography, 1992—. Mem. faculty Poynter Inst., U. Mo. Workshop, Latin Am. Photojournalism Conf., Stan Kalish Picture Editing Workshop. Knight fellow Stanford U., 2005; recipient Individual Editing awards Soc. Newspaper Designers, 1988-04, Editing awards, 91-01; named for Overall Excellence in Editing, Picture of Yr. Contest, U. Mo., 1993. Office: San Jose Mercury News 750 Ridder Park Dr San Jose CA 95131-2432

MIGUEL, LUIS, musician; b. San Juan, Apr. 19, 1970; m. Aracely Arámbula, 2006; 1 child, Miguel. Albums include Directo Al Corazon, 1982, Un Sol, 1982, Decidete, 1983, Fiebre de Amor, 1985, Soy Como Quiero Ser, 1987, Busca Una Mujer, 1988, 20 Anos, 1990, Romance, 1991, Del Corazon del Hombre, 1992, El Idolo De Mexico 1992, Los Idolos De Mexico, 1993, Aries, 1993 (Grammy award, Best Latin Pop Perfomance), Segundo Romance, 1994 (Grammy award, Best Latin Pop Performance), Musipistas, 1995, El Concierto, 1995, Nada Es Igual, 1996, Romances, 1997 (Grammy award, Best Latin Pop Performance), Amarte Es Un Placer, 1999 (Album of the Yr. award Latin Grammy Awards, Best Pop Album award Latin Grammy Awards), Vivo, 2000, 21 Black Jack, 2000, Vallenato, 2001, Mis Romances, 2001, Amandote a la Italiana, 2002, 33, 2003, Palabra de Honor, 2004, Mexico en la Piel, 2005 (Grammy award, Best Mexican-Am. Album), Perfil, 2006, Navidades, 2006; songs include Me Gustas Tal Como Eres, 1984 (Grammy award, Best Mexican-Am. Music Performance). Recipient 5 Grammy awards, star, Hollywood Walk of Fame, 1996.

MIHALAS, DIMITRI MANUEL, astrophysicist, educator; b. LA, Mar. 20, 1939; s. Emmanuel Demetrious and Jean (Christo) M.; children: Michael Demetrious, Alexandra Genevieve. BA with highest honors, UCLA, 1959; MS, Calif. Inst. Tech., 1960, PhD, 1963. Asst. prof. astrophys. scis. Princeton U., 1964-67; asst. prof. physics U. Colo., 1967-68; asso. prof. astronomy and astrophysics U. Chgo., 1968-70, prof., 1970-71; adj. prof. astrogeophysics, also physics and astrophysics U. Colo., 1972-80; sr. scientist High Altitude Obs., Nat. Center Atmospheric Research, Boulder, Colo., 1971-79, 82-85; astronomer Sacramento Peak Obs., Sunspot, N.Mex., 1979-82; mem. staff Los Alamos (N.Mex.) Nat. Lab., 1998—2004, fellow, 2004—; G.C. McVittie prof. astronomy U. Ill., 1985-98, g. c. prof. astronomy emeritus, 1998—. Cons. Los Alamos Nat. Lab, 1981-98; vis. prof. dept. astrophysics Oxford (Eng.) U., 1977-78; sr. vis. fellow dept. physics and astronomy Univ. Coll., London, 1978; mem. astronomy adv. panel NSF, 1972-75 Author: Galactic Astronomy, 1969, 2d edit, 1981, Stellar Atmospheres, 1970, 2d edit., 1978, Theorie des Atmospheres Stellaires, 1971, Foundations of Radiation Hydrodynamics, 1984; assoc. editor Astrophys. Jour, 1970-79, Jour. Computational Physics, 1981-87, Jour. Quantitative Spectroscopy, 1984-94; mem. editorial bd. Solar Physics, 1981-89. NSF fellow, 1959-62; Van Maanen fellow, 1962-63; Eugene Higgins vis. fellow, 1963-64; Alfred P. Sloan Found. Research fellow, 1969-71; Alexander von Humboldt Stiftung sr. U.S. scientist awardee, 1984. Mem. U.S. Nat. Acad. Sci., Internat. Astron. Union (pres. commn. 36 1976-79), Am. Astron. Soc. (pub. bd. 1995-99, mem. coun. 2000—03, Helen B. Warner prize 1974), Astron. Soc. Pacific (dir. 1975-77) Office: Los Alamos Nat Lab X-3 MS-F644 Los Alamos NM 87545-0001 Home: 15 Withers Peak Santa Fe NM 87508 Office Phone: 505-665-4529. Business E-Mail: dmihalas@lanl.gov.

MIKEL, THOMAS KELLY, JR., laboratory administrator; b. Aug. 27, 1946; s. Thomas Kelly and Vrazo Anne (Katherine) M. BA, San Jose State U., 1973; MA, U. Calif., Santa Barbara, 1975. Asst. dir. Santa Barbara Underseas Found., 1975—76; marine biologist PJB Labs., Ventura, Calif., 1981—88; lab. dir. ABC Labs., Ventura, 1988—. Instr. oceanography Ventura Coll., 1980—81; chair joint task group, sect. author 20th edit. Stds. Methods Exam. Water & Wastewater APHA, 1996; biol. coord. Anacapa Underwater Natural trail U.S. Nat. Park Svc., 1976; designer ecol. restoration program of upper Newport Bay, Orange County, Calif., 78; rsch. contbr. 3d Internat. Artificial Reef Conf., Newport Beach, Calif., 1983, Ann. Conf. Am. Petroleum Inst., Houston. With US Army, 1968—70. Mem.: ASTME (rsch. contbr. 10th ann. symposium 1986), Soc. Environ. Toxicology and Chemistry (bd. dirs. 2000—), Soc. Population Ecologists, Assn. Environ. Profls. Democrat. Office Phone: 805-643-5621. E-mail: aquario@pacbell.net.

MIKLOSI, JOE, state legislator; m. Jennifer Miklosi. BA in Polit. Sci. & Religion, Hope Coll., Holland, Mich., 1992; MA in Pub. Adminstrn., U. Colo. Grad. Sch. Pub. Affairs, 2004. Intern White House Office Pub. Policy; health care legis. aide former US Senator Howard Metzenbaum; dir. dem. state house caucus Speaker Andrew Romanoff; dir. ops. Rep. Dan Grossman, 2002; chief of staff & dir. ops. former House Minority Leader Jennifer Veiga, 2003; mem. Dist. 9 Colo. House of Reps., Denver, 2008—; currently with Project C.U.R.E. Cons. Aristotle Industries; bus. devel. mgr. Cyveillance-.com; software cons. Computer Assocs., Veritas Software. State dir. Colo. Progressive Majority. Mem.: Rotary Club. Democrat. Office: State House 200 E Colfax Denver CO 80203 Office Phone: 303-866-2910. Business E-Mail: joe@joemiklosi.com.*

MIKULAS, MARTIN M., JR., aerospace engineer, educator; BS, MS, PhD, Va. Polytechnic Inst. Vis. prof. aerospace structures U. Colo., Boulder. Mem. NAE. Office: Aerospace Structures U Colo Campus Box 429 Boulder CO 80309 E-mail: Martin.Mikulas@Colorado.edu.

MILANO, ADAM, film company executive; b. July 17, 1978; Student, U. So. Calif. Intern Columbia Pictures, Culver City, Calif., dir. devel. Achievements include invention of acting as studio executive on such films as Gridiron Gang, The Grudge 2 and Monster House, as well as the upcoming releases Vantage Point and 30 Days of Night. Office: Columbia Pictures 10202 W Washington Blvd Culver City CA 90232

MILANOVICH, NORMA JOANNE, training services executive; b. Littlefork, Minn., June 4, 1945; d. Lyle Albert and Loretta (Leona) Drake; m. Rudolph William Milanovich, Mar. 18, 1943 (dec.); 1 child, Rudolph William Jr. BS in Home Econs., U. Wis., Stout, 1968; MA in Curriculum and Instrn., U. Houston, 1973, EdD in Curriculum and Program Devel., 1982. Instr. human svcs. dept. U. Houston, 1971-75; dir. videos project U. N.Mex., Albuquerque, 1976-78, dir. vocat. edn. equity ctr., 1978-88, asst. prof. occupational edn., 1982-88, coord. occupational vocat. edn. programs, 1983-88, dir. consortium rsch. and devel. in occupational edn., 1984-88; pres. Alpha Connection Tng. Corp., Albuquerque, 1988—; exec. dir. Trinity Found., 1991—; pres. Athena Leadership Ctr., 1994—. Adj. instr. Cen. Tng. Acad., Dept. Energy, Wackenhut; faculty U. Phoenix; adj. faculty So. Ill. U., Lesley Coll., Boston; lectr. in field Author: Model Equitable Behavior in the Classroom, 1983, Handbook for Vocational-Technical Certification in New Mexico, 1985, A Vision for Kansas: Systems of Measures and Standards of Performance, 1992, Workplace Skills: The Employability Factor, 1993; editor: Choosing What's Best for You, 1982, A Handbook for Handling Conflict in the Classroom, 1983, Starting Out...A Job Finding Handbook for Teen Parents, Going to Work...Job Rights for Teens; author: JTPA Strategic Marketing Plan, 1990, We, The Arcturians, 1990, Sacred Journey to Atlantis, 1991, The Light Shall Set You Free, 1996; editor: Majestic Raise newsletter, 1996—, Celestial Voices newsletter, 1991—; conf. presenter in field; dir. (film and book) Building Feng Shui Dream Homes, 2009. Del. Youth for Understanding Internat. Program, 1985—90; adv. bd. Southwestern Indian Poly. Inst., 1984—88; com. mem. Region VI Consumer Exch. Com., 1982—84; coord. various countries Worldwide Conf. for Peace on Earth, 1999—2009; coord. Customized Leadership Programs, 2003—09; bd. dirs. Albuquerque Single Parent Occupational Scholarship Program, 1984—86. Grantee N.Mex. Dept. Edn., 1976-86, HEW, 1979-81, 83-87. Mem. ASTD, Am. Vocat. Assn., Vocat. Edn. Equity Coun., Nat. Coalition for Sex Equity Edn., Am. Home Econs. Assn., Inst. Noetic Scis., N.Mex. Home Econs. Assn., N.Mex. Vocat. Edn. Assn., N.Mex. Adv. Coun. on Vocat. Edn., Greater Albuquerque C. of C., NAFE, Feng Shui Conf. and Modules for Success, Phi Delta Kappa, Phi Upsilon Omicron, Phi Theta Kappa. Democrat. Roman Catholic. Avocation: fung shui. Office: Athena Leadership Ctr Scottsdale AZ 85259 Office Phone: 480-767-5346. Business E-Mail: info@athenalctr.com.

MILEDI, RICARDO, neurobiologist; b. Mexico City, Mex., Sept. 15, 1927; m. Ana Mela Garces, Dec. 17, 1955; 1 child, Rico. BSc, Instituto Cientifico y Literario, Chihuahua, Mex., 1945; MD, U. Nacional Autonoma de Mex., 1955. Researcher Instituto Nacional de Cardiologia, Mexico, 1954-56; fellow John Curtin Sch. Med. Res., Canberra, Australia, 1956-58; mem. faculty U. Coll., London, 1959-85, Foulerton research prof. of Royal Soc., 1975-85, head dept. biophysics, 1978-85; disting. prof. dept. neurobiology and behavior U. Calif., Irvine, 1984—. Recipient Principe de Asturias prize, Spain, 1999. Fellow Royal Soc. London (Royal medal 1999), Am. Acad. Arts and Scis.; mem. AAAS, NAS, 3d World Acad. Scis., (titular) European Acad. Arts, Scis., Humanities, N.Y. Acad. Scis., Hungarian Acad. Scis. (hon.), Mex. Acad. Scis., Mex. Acad. Medicine. Home: 9 Gibbs Ct Irvine CA 92612-4032 Office: U Calif Dept Neurobiology Behavior 2205 Bio Sci Ii Irvine CA 92697-4550 Office Phone: 949-824-4730. Business E-Mail: rmiledi@uci.edu.

MILES, DON CLIFFORD, architect; b. Ft. Knox, Ky., Sept. 17, 1942; s. Don and Kathrine Eva (Gray) M.; m. Pamela Wait, Aug. 6, 1972; children: Katherine Wait, Lesley Gray, Nicole Conel. BArch with honors, U. Wash., 1966; MArch, M of City Planning in Urban Design, Harvard U., 1971. Registered architect, Wash. Assoc. ptnr. Zimmer, Gunsul, Frasca Partnership, Seattle. Cons., lectr. numerous orgns., cities, corps. Prin. projects include Pedestrian Corridor, Major Pub. Open Spaces, CBD Transit Ctr., Bellevue, Wash., Banfield Light Rail Project, Portland, Boise (Idaho) Downtown Major Pub. Open Space, Street Improvements and Transit Malls, Honolulu Rapid Transit Project, Revitalization of State St., Chgo., Midway Corridor Project, Mpls., High Capacity Transit Project, Seattle, Ctrl. Orange County Aerial Fixed Guideway, Mission Valley West Extension Light Rail Project, San Diego, Master Plan for Capitol of State of Wash., Seattle Union Sta. Redevel. Plan, Weyerhauser Corp. Campus, Quadrant Corp. site, Lake Union, Seattle, Whitman Coll. Bd. dirs., founder Project for Pub. Spaces, 1975—; bd. dirs. Seattle Children's Mus., 1978-82; trustee Queen Ann Community Coun., 1978-80. Fellow AIA, Inst. Urban Design. Avocations: skiing, jogging. Home: 611 W Comstock St Seattle WA 98119-3422 Office: Zimmer Gunsul Frasca 925 4th Ave 2400 Seattle WA 98104-1146

MILES, JACK (JOHN RUSSIANO), journalist, educator; b. Chgo., July 30, 1942; s. John Alvin and Mary Jean (Murphy) Miles; m. Jacqueline Russiano, Aug. 23, 1980; 1 child, Kathleen. LittB, Xavier U., Cin., 1964; PhB, Pontifical Gregorian U., Rome, 1966; student, Hebrew U., Jerusalem, 1966—67; PhD, Harvard U., 1971. Asst. prof. Loyola U., Chgo., 1970—74; asst. dir. Scholars Press, Missoula, Mont., 1974—75; postdoctoral fellow U. Chgo., 1975—76; editor Doubleday & Co., NYC, 1976—78; exec. editor U. Calif. Press, Berkeley, 1978—85; book editor L.A. Times, 1985—91, mem. editl. bd., 1991—95; dir. Humanities Ctr. Claremont (Calif.) Grad. U., 1995—97; Mellon vis. prof. Calif. Inst. Tech., 1997—98; sr. advisor to pres. J. Paul Getty Trust, LA, 1999—. Contbg. editor: Atlantic Monthly, 1995—; author: Retroversion and Text Criticism, 1984, God: A Biography, 1995, Christ: A Crisis in the Life of God, 2001; contbr. learned and popular articles to various periodicals; book reviewer. Recipient Pulitzer Prize for biography, 1996; Guggenheim fellow, 1990—91, 2002—, MacArthur fellow, 2003—. Mem.: PEN, Amnesty Internat., Am. Acad. Religion, Nat. Book Critics Cir. (pres. 1990—92). Episcopalian. Office: J Paul Getty Trust 1200 Getty Center Dr Ste 1100 Los Angeles CA 90049-1688

MILES, JOANNA, actress, playwright, director; b. Nice, France, Mar. 6, 1940; came to U.S., 1941, naturalized, 1941; d. Johannes Schiefer and Jeanne Miles; m. William Burns, May 23, 1970 (div. 1977); m. Michael Brandman, Apr. 29, 1978; 1 child, Miles. Grad. H.S., Putney, Vt., 1958. Mem. Actors Studio, Playwrites and Dirs. Workshop, NYC, 1966; co-founder, mem. LA Classic Theatre, 1986. Founder, artistic dir. Playwrights Group/LAWW, 1991-98. Starred in: (motion pictures) The Way We Live Now, 1969, Bug, 1975, The Ultimate Warrior, 1975, Golden Girl, 1978, Cross Creek, 1983, As Is, 1986, Blackout, 1988, Rosencrants and Guildenstern are Dead, 1991, The Rhinghart Theory, 1994, Judge Dredd, 1994, Alone, 1996, Sex & Breakfast, 2006; numerous television films including In What America, 1965, My Mothers House, 1963, Glass Managerie, 1974, Born Innocent, 1974, Aloha Means Goodbye, 1974, The Trial of Chaplain Jensen, 1975, Harvest Home, 1977, Fire in the Sky, 1978, Sophisticated Gents, 1979, Promise of Love, 1982, Sound of Murder, 1983, All My Sons, 1987, The Right to Die, 1987, The Habitation of Dragons, 1991, Heart of Justice, 1991, Water Engine, 1991, Cooperstown, 1992, Legionnaires, 1992, Life Lessons, 1992, Willing to Kill, 1992, The American Clock, 1993, Dark Reflections, 1993, Outcry, 1994, Everything to Gain, 1995, Small Vices, 1998, Crossfire Trail, 1999, Thin Aire, 1999, Monty Walsh, 2002, Jane Doe: Shaken & Stirred, 2006; episodes in numerous TV series including: Barney Miller, Dallas, St. Elsewhere, The Hulk, Trapper John, Kaz, Cagney and Lacey, Studio 5B, 1989, Star Trek: The Next Generation, 1990, 91, Life Stories, 1991, HBO Life Stories, 1993, Total Security, 1997, Nothing Sacred, 1998, Chicago Hope, 1998-99, ER, 2000, 01, Family Law, 2000, Judging Amy, 2003; stage plays include Once in a Life Time, 1963, Cave Dwellers, 1964, Drums in the Night, 1968, Dracula, 1968, Home Free, 1964, One Night Stands of a Noisy Passenger, 1972, Dylan, 1973, Dancing for the Kaiser, 1976, Debutante Ball, 1985, Kramer, 1977, One Flew Over the Cuckoo's Nest, 1989, Growing Gracefully, 1990, Cut Flowers, 1994; performed in radio shows Sta. KCRW Once in a Lifetime, 1987, Babbit, 1987, Sta. KPFK, Grapes of Wrath, 1989, The White Plague, Sta. KCRW, 1991, Chekhov Short Stories, Sta. KCRW, 1992; playwright, v.p. Brandman Productions; author: (plays) Ethanasia, A Woman in Reconstruction, Hostages, Feathers, On the Shelf, (films) An Offereing of Oranges, Breaking the Rules. Pres. Children Giving to Children. Recipient 2 Emmy awards, 1974, Women in Radio and TV award, 1974, Actors Studio Achievement award, 1980, Dramalogue award, 1996, Vision award 2003; nominated Golden Globe, 1974. Mem. Acad. Motion Picture Arts and Scis. Office: Brandman Prodns 2062 Vine St Apt 5 Hollywood CA 90068-3928 Office Phone: 323-463-3224. Personal E-mail: jmilesb@aol.com.

MILES, RAYMOND EDWARD, retired dean, organizational behavior and industrial relations educator; b. Cleburne, Tex., Nov. 2, 1932; s. Willard Francis and Wilma Nell (Owen) M.; m. Lucile Dustin, Dec. 27, 1952; children: Laura, Grant, Kenneth. BA with highest honors, U. North Tex., 1954, MBA, 1958; PhD, Stanford U., 1963. Clk. Santa Fe R.R., Gainesville, Tex., 1950-55; instr. mgmt. Sch. Bus. U. North Tex., Denton, 1958-60; asst. prof. organizational behavior and indsl. relations Sch. Bus. Adminstrn. U. Calif.-Berkeley, 1963-68, assoc. prof., 1968-71, prof., 1971—, assoc. dean Haas Sch. of Bus., 1978-81, dean, 1983-90; dir. Inst. Indsl. Relations, 1982-83; cons. various pvt., pub. orgns. Author: Theories of Management, 1975; (with Charles C. Snow) Organization Strategy, Structure and Process, 1978, Fit, Failure, and the Hall of Fame, 1994; co-author: Organizational Behavior: Research and Issues, 1976, (with Grant Miller and Charles C. Snow) Collaborative Entrepeneurship, 2005; co-editor, contbg. author: Organization by Design: Theory and Practice, 1981. Served to 1st. lt. USAF, 1955-58. Mem.: Acad. Mgmt. Democrat. Unitarian Universalist. Home: 8640 Don Carol Dr El Cerrito CA 94530-2733 Office: U Calif Walter A Haas Sch Bus Berkeley CA 94720-0001 Business E-Mail: miles@haas.berkeley.edu.

MILGROM, PAUL ROBERT, economics educator; b. Detroit, Apr. 20, 1948; s. Abraham Isaac and Anne M. (Finkelstein); m. Eva Meyersson Milgrom, Sept. 17, 2000; m. Jan Thurston, Dec. 10, 1977; children: Joshua, Elana. AB in Math. with high honors, U. Mich., 1970; MS in Stats., Stanford U., 1978, PhD in Bus., 1979; MA (hon.), Yale U., 1983. Actuarial trainee Met. Life Ins. Co., 1970-71; conulting actuary Nelson and Warren, Inc., 1972-75; asst. prof. dept. managerial econs. and decision scis. Kellogg Grad. Sch. Mgmt. Northwestern U., 1979-81, assoc. prof., 1981-82, prof., 1982-83; prof. econs. and mgmt. Yale U., 1983-85, Williams Bros. prof. mgmt. studies, prof. econs., 1985-87; prof. econs. Stanford U., 1987—, Shirley R. and Leonard W. Ely, Jr. prof. humanities and scis., 1993—. Vis. rsch. assoc. econs. Stanford U., 1981; vis. prof. Yale U., 1982-83; Ford vis. prof. econs. U. Calif. Berkeley, 1986-87; IBM rsch. chair Northwestern U., 1981; Williams Bros. chair mgmt. studies Yale U., 1985; Olin disting. lectr. Princeton U., 1988; dir. Stanford Inst. for Theoretical Econs., 1989-1991; past cons. So. New Eng. Telephone Co., Rand Corp., Arctic Slope Regional Corp., Ga. Pacific, Exxon, Pacific Telesis, Bell Atlantic, Google, Yahoo, Microsoft Network, Govt. of Mex., others; lectr. in field. Author: (with John Roberts) Economics, Organization and Management, 1992, (with John Roberts), Instructor's Manual for Economics, Organization and Management, 1992; assoc. editor Jour. Econ. Theory, 1983-87, Rand Jour. Econs., 1985-89, Econometrica, 1987-90, Jour. Fin. Intermediation, 1989-92, Games and Econ. Behavior, 1990-92; co-editor Am. Econ. Review, 1990-93; contbr. over 50 articles to profl. jours. Recipient Leonard J. Savage Meml. Thesis award, 1980, Rsch. grant NSF, 1980, 82, 85, 88-91, 89, 91, 07, Rsch. award Actuarial Edn. and Rsch. Fund, 1983, John Simon Guggenheim fellowship, 1986, Best Paper of Yr. award, 1987, Rsch. grant Ctr. Econ. Policy, 1988, 90, Erwin Plein Nemmers Prize in Econs., Am. Math. Soc., 2008. Fellow Am. Acad. Arts and Scis., Econometric Soc. (plenary lectr. 5th World Congress 1985, mem. exec. com. 2005), Morse Coll., Inst. Advanced Studies Hebrew U. Jerusalem, Ctr. Advanced Study in Behavioral Scis., Soc. Actuaries (Triennial Paper prize 1976); mem. NAS, Am. Econ. Assn., Western Econ. Assn. Internat. (pres. 2007). Office: Stanford Univ Dept Econs Stanford CA 94305 E-mail: milgrom@stanford.edu.

MILKEN, MICHAEL R., think-tank executive, philanthropist; b. Calif., July 4, 1946; m. Lori Milken, Aug. 11, 1968; 3 children. Grad. summa cum laude, U. Calif., Berkeley; MBA, U. Pa. Securities trader Drexel Burnham Lambert, until 1990; chmn. The Milken Inst., 1991—; founder Prostate Cancer Found. (formerly CaPCure), 1993—; chair Knowledge Universe, 1996—; chmn. FasterCures/Ctr. for Accelerating Med. Solutions, 2003—. Author: Taste for Living Series cookbooks. Chair Assn. Cure of Cancer of the Prostate; co-founder Milken Family Found., 1982. Named one of 400 Richest Ams., Forbes mag., 2006. Office: Milken Inst 1250 Fourth St Ste 200 Santa Monica CA 90401

MILLAN, CESAR, television personality; b. Culiacán, Mex., May 12, 1969; s. Felipe Millan Guillen and Maria Teresa Favela de Millan; m. Ilusion Wilson Millan; children: Andre, Calvin. Owner, founder, dog trainer Dog Psychology Ctr., LA; CEO Cesar Millan, Inc.; co-founder Cesar and Ilusion Millan Found., Burbank, Calif., 2007—. Host (TV series) Dog Whisperer with Cesar Millan, 2004—; co-author: (books) Be the Pack Leader: Use Cesar's Way to Transform Your Dog...and Your Life, 2007, Cesar's Way: The Natural, Everyday

Guide to Understanding and Correcting Common Dog Problems, 2007; creator: (instructional DVDs) People Training for Dogs; Become a Pack Leader; Your New Dog: First Day and Beyond; cinematographer:. Active K-9 Connection, Pups on Parole, Pets911; founder Cesar and Ilusion Millan Found. Recipient Genesis award, Nat. Humane Soc., 2005, Michael Landon award, 2007. Mem.: Internat. Assn. Canine Profls. (hon.). Office: Cesar Ilusion Millan Foundation PO Box 2039 Burbank CA 91507-2039

MILLAR, JOCELYN G., entomologist, educator; PhD in Organic Chemistry, Simon Fraser U., Burnaby, B.C. Canada, 1983. From asst. to prof. dept. entomology U. Calif., Riverside, 1988—. Assoc. editor: Jour. Chem. Ecology, 2003—; contbr. articles to profl. jours., chapters to books. Fellow: AAAS; mem.: Internat. Soc. Chem. Ecology (pres. 2005—06), Entomol. Soc. Am. (Syngenta Recognition award Crop Protection 2001, Recognition award 2001, IPM award 2005, C.W. Woodworth award 2006, IPM award 2006), Am. Chem. Soc. Office: U Calif Dept Entomology Riverside CA 92521 Office Fax: 1 951 827 3086.

MILLAR, RICHARD WILLIAM, JR., lawyer; b. LA, May 11, 1938; LLB, U. San Francisco, 1966; JD (hon.), Western State U., Coll. Law, 2008. Bar: Calif. 1967, US Dist. Ct. (cen. dist.) Calif. 1967, US Dist. Ct. (no. dist.) Calif. 1969, US Dist. Ct. (so. dist.) Calif. 1973, US Supreme Ct. Assoc. Iverson & Hogoboom, Los Angeles, 1967-72; ptnr. Eilers, Stewart, Pangman & Millar, Newport Beach, Calif., 1973-75, Millar & Heckman, Newport Beach, 1975-77, Millar, Hodges & Bemis, Newport Beach, 1979—. Trustee Western State U. Coll. Law, 2004—. Fellow: Am. Bar Found. (life); mem.: ABA (litigation sect. trial practice com., ho. of dels. 1990—), Orange County Bar Assn. (chmn. bus. litig. sect. 1981, chmn. judiciary com. 1988—90, sec. 1999, treas., dir. charitable fund 2000, pres.-elect 2001, pres. 2002, treas., dir. charitable fund 2003), Calif. Bar Assn. (lectr. CLE), Pacific Club, Bohemian Club (San Francisco). Home: 71 Hillsdale Newport Beach CA 92660 Office: Millar Hodges & Bemis One Newport Pl Ste # 900 Newport Beach CA 92660 Office Phone: 949-752-7722. Personal E-mail: millar@mhblaw.net.

MILLAR, ROBERT, artist; b. LA, Mar. 6, 1958; s. Thomas A. and Josephine E. (Alford) M. BA, Calif. State U., Northridge, 1980. Exhibited work at L.A. Metro Rail Sta., 1990 (progressive Arch. citation 1992), Newport Harbor Art Mus., 1991, Rose Theatre Site, London, 1992, S.D. Alvarado Filtration Plant, 1993. Arts commr. City of Manhattan Beach, Calif., 1985-94; mem. pub. art adv. com. Calif. Arts Coun., 1992. Grantee Pollock-Krasner Found., 1989. Studio: 1420 Old Topanga Canyon Rd Topanga CA 90290-3923

MILLARD, NEAL STEVEN, lawyer, educator; b. Dallas, June 6, 1947; s. Bernard and Adele (Marks) Millard; m. Janet Keast, Mar. 12, 1994; 1 child, Kendall Layne. BA cum laude, UCLA, 1969; JD, U. Chgo., 1972. Bar: Calif. 1972, US Dist. Ct. (ctrl. dist.) Calif. 1973, US Tax Ct. 1973, US Ct. Appeals (9th cir.) 1987, NY 1990. Assoc. Willis, Butler & Schiefly, LA, 1972-75; ptnr. Morrison & Foerster, LA, 1975-84, Jones, Day, Reavis & Pogue, LA, 1984-93, White & Case, LA, 1993—. Instr. Calif. State Coll., San Bernardino, 1975—76; lectr. Practising Law Inst., NYC, 1983—90, Calif. Edn. Bar, 1987—90; adj. prof. U. So. Calif. Law Ctr., LA, 1994—. Mem. citizens adv. com. LA Olympics, 1982—84; trustee Altadena Libr. Dist., Calif., 1985—86; bd. dirs. Woodcraft Rangers, LA, 1982—90, pres., 1986—88; bd. dirs. LA County Bar Found., 1990—2000; pres. Los Angeles County Bar Found., 1997—98; mem. Energy Commn. county/cities of LA, 1995—99; mem. jud. procedures commn. LA County, 1999—, chair, 2000—02; mem. Pub. Safety Commn. LaCanada-Flintridge, 2006—, chair, 2008—; bd. dirs. Inner City Law Ctr., 1996—99; bd. dirs., sec. LaCanada-Flintridge Ednl. Found., 2002—06; bd. dirs. Alliance Coll.-Ready Pub. Schs., 2004—. Mem.: Am. Law Inst., Pub. Counsel (bd. dirs. 1984—87, 1990—93), LA County Bar Assn. (trustee 1985—87), NY State Bar Assn., Calif. Bar Assn., U. So. Calif. Inst. Corp. Counsel (mem. adv. bd. 1998—2006), U. Chgo. Law Alumni Assn. (pres. 1998—2001), Flintridge Riding Club, Calif. Club, Chancery Club, Beach Club, Phi Beta Kappa, Phi Delta Phi, Pi Gamma Mu. Office: White & Case 633 W 5th St Ste 1900 Los Angeles CA 90071-2087 Home Phone: 818-952-3700; Office Phone: 213-620-7773. Business E-Mail: nmillard@whitecase.com.

MILLARD, RICHARD STEVEN, lawyer; b. Pasadena, Calif., Feb. 6, 1952; s. Kenneth A. and Kathryn Mary (Paden) M.; m. Jessica Ann Edwards, May 15, 1977; children: Victoria, Elizabeth, Andrew. AB, Stanford U., 1974; JD magna cum laude, U. Mich., 1977. Bar: Calif. 1977, Ill. 1985. Assoc. Heller, Ehrman, White & McAuliff, San Francisco, 1977-81, Mayer, Brown & Platt, Chgo., 1982-83, ptnr., 1984-99, Weil, Gotshal & Manges, Redwood Shores, Calif., 1999—. Mem. ABA, Order of Coif. Office: Weil Gotshal & Manges 201 Redwood Shores Pkwy Redwood City CA 94065 Office Phone: 650-802-3015. Business E-Mail: richard.millard@weil.com.

MILLER, ANN G., lawyer; b. San Francisco, Nov. 1, 1944; BA, U. San Diego, 1966; JD, U. San Francisco, 1970. Bar: Calif. 1971. Law clk. U.S. Dist. Ct. (no. dist.) Calif., 1970-71; ptnr. Lillick & Charles, San Francisco, Nixon Peabody LLP, San Francisco, 2001—. Mem. Ninth Cir. Judicial Nominating Com. Mem.: ABA, Computer Law Assn., Bar Assn. San Francisco, Maritime Law Assn. (chair Passenger Vessel and Cruise Com.). Office: Nixon Peabody Llp 1 Embarcadero Ctr Ste 1800 San Francisco CA 94111-3716 Office Phone: 415-984-8236. Office Fax: 415-984-8300. E-mail: amiller@nixonpeabody.com.

MILLER, ARNOLD, electronics executive; b. NYC, May 8, 1928; s. Sam and Mina (Krutalow) M.; m. Beverly Shayne, Feb. 5, 1950; children: Debra Lynn, Marla Jo, Linda Sue BS in Chemistry, UCLA, 1948, PhD in Phys. Chemistry, 1951; DHL (hon.), So. Calif. Coll. Optometry, 2007. Registered profl. engr., Calif. Rsch. phys. chemist Wrigley Rsch. Co., Chgo., 1951; supr. phys. chemistry Armour Rsch. Found., Chgo., 1951-54, mgr. chemistry and metals, 1954-56; chief materials sci. dept. Borg-Warner Rsch. Ctr., Des Plaines, Ill., 1956-59; dir. rsch. Rockwell Corp., Anaheim, Calif., 1959-66, dir. microelec. ops., 1967-68; group exec. materials ops. Whittaker Corp., LA, 1968-70; pres. Theta Sensors, Orange, Calif., 1970-72; mgr. xeroradiography Xerox Corp., Pasadena, Calif., 1972-75, corp. dir. rsch. and adv. devel. Stamford, Conn., 1975-78, El Segundo, Calif., 1978-81, v.p. electronics div., 1981-84, pres. electronics div., 1984-87, corp. officer Stamford, 1984-87; pres. Tech. Strategy Group, Fullerton, Calif., 1987—; prodr. Remembrance Films, 2004—. Bd. dirs. Spectro Diode Labs, San Jose, Calif., Semicondr. Rsch. Corp., Colorep Inc., Carlsbad, Calif.; bd. dirs., chair audit com. Merisel Computer Products, El Segundo, Calif., lead dir., 1989—; mem. vis. com. on materials sci. U. So. Calif., L.A., 1966-68; mem. State of Calif. Micro Bd., 1984-2000. Editorial adv. bd. Advances in Solid State Chemistry; co-editor Electronics Industry Development, Trends in IT, Trends In IT; contbr. numerous articles to profl. jours. and monographs; patentee in field. Mem. civilian adv. group Dept. Commerce, 1959-60; mem. 5th decade com., also adv. com. on engring. and mgmt. program UCLA, 1984-; mem. com. on scholarly commn. with People's Republic of China, Tech. Transfer Task Force, Nat. Acad. Sci., Washington, 1985; bd. dirs. Orange County Pacific Symphony, Fullerton, Calif., 1982-; mem. univ.'s adv. bd. Calif. State U.-Fullerton, 1986-2006, chair, 1991-2006; v.p., bd. dirs. Heritage Pointe Home for the Aging, 1987-97; chmn. indsl. Assocs. sch. engring. and computer sci. Calif. State U., 1987-97, trustee continuing learning ctr., 1993-; mem. Overseas Devel. Coun., 1988-; mem. Nat. Com. U.S.-China Rels., 1990-; trustee So. Calif. Coll. of Optometry, 1996-, sec.-treas. 1997-2003; bd. mem. Cmty. Found., 1995-, v.p., 1997-. Recipient Sci. Merit award Navy Bur. Ordnance/Armour Rsch. Found., 1952, IR-100 award, 1964, 69, U. medal Inst. Gerontology Calif. State U., Fullerton, 2002; named Hon. Alumnus Calif. State U., Fullerton, 1996, Hon. Dr. Humane Letters So. Calif. Coll. Optometry, 2007. Fellow AAAS; mem. IEEE, Am. Chem. Soc., So. Calif. Coalition Edn. Mfg. Engring. (bd. dirs. 1994-98, ind. living partnership, 2009-), Independent Living Partnership (bd. dirs. 2009-), Elec. Industry Assn. (past chmn. microelectronics), Phi Beta Kappa, Sigma Xi, Phi Lamda Upsilon Home: 505 Westchester Pl Fullerton CA 92835-2706 Office: Tech Strategy Group PO Box 5769 Fullerton CA 92838-0769 Home Phone: 714-738-0368; Office Phone: 714-447-8887. Business E-Mail: amiller@fullerton.edu.

MILLER, BARRY, researcher, psychologist; b. NYC, Dec. 25, 1942; s. Jack and Ida (Kaplan) M.; m. Susan Hallermeier; children: Eric, Arianne, Kristina, Barrie. BS in Psychology, Bklyn. Coll., 1965; MS in Psychology, Villanova U., 1967; PhD in Psychiatry, Med. Coll. Pa., 1971. Instr. psychology Villanova (Pa.) U., 1971-73; asst. dir. dept. behavioral sci., med. rsch. scientist Ea. Pa. Psychiatric Inst., Phila., 1971-73, sr. med. rsch. scientist, 1973-80; dir. Pa. Bur. Rsch. and Tng., Harrisburg, 1973-81; asst. prof. psychology U. Pa. Med. Sch., Phila., 1975-78, asst. clin. prof. psychology, 1978—; assoc. prof. psychiatry Med. Coll. Pa., Phila., 1981-90, rsch. assoc. prof. medicine, 1983-90, assoc. dean for rsch., 1981-90; dir. for rsch. devel. Albert Einstein Healthcare Network, Phila., 1990-95; dir. The Permanente Med. Group Rsch. Inst., Oakland, Calif., 1995-99; adj. assoc. prof. psychiatry Med. Coll. Pa., Phila., 1990—; rsch. assoc. prof. psychiatry Temple U. Sch. Med., Phila., 1990—; adminstrv. dir. rsch. ops. Divsn. Rsch., Oakland, Calif., 1999—. Mem. sci. and tech. task force Pa. Econ. Devel. Partnership, Harrisburg, 1987-88, adv. com. Clin. Rsch. Ctr. Psychopathology of Elderly, Phila., 1985-88; mem. cancer control prgram Pa. Dept. Health, 1994; vis. rsch. assoc. prof. Med. Coll. Pa., Phila., 1991—. Contbr. articles to profl. jours.; mem. editorial bd. Jour. Mental Health Adminstrn., 1988—, assoc. editor, 1989—. Bd. dirs. Community Mental Health Ctr. 6A, Phila., 1969-73, Northwest Jewish Youth Ctrs., Phila., 1974-75; mem. Lafayette Hill Civic Assn., 1973-86, Citizens Coun. Whitemarsh (Pa.) Twp., 1975-86; pres., bd. dirs. Golden Eagle Luxury Homeowners Assn., Pleasanton, Calif., 1995-97. Grantee HHS, NIH. Mem. AAAS, Am. Psychol. Assn., Assn. Mental Health Adminstrs., Assn. Univ. Tech. Mgrs., Soc. Rsch. Adminstrs., Calif. Psychol. Assn. Avocation: hiking. Office: Divsn Rsch 2000 Broadway Oakland CA 94612-3429 Office Phone: 510-891-3408. Business E-Mail: barry.x.miller@kp.org.

MILLER, CAROLE ANN LYONS, writer, editor, publisher, marketing executive; b. Newton, Mass. d. Markham Harold and Ursula Patricia (Foley) Lyons; m. David Thomas Miller, July 4, 1978. BA, Boston U., 1964. Cert. in Bus. Hickox Sch. Boston, 1964, advt./mktg. profl. UCLA, 1973, retail mgmt. profl. Ind. U., 1976. Editor Triangle Topics, Pacific Telephone, LA; programmer LA Ctrl. Area Spkrs. Bur., 1964-66; mng. editor, mktg. dir. Teen mag., LA, NYC, 1966-76; advt. dir. L.S. Ayres & Co., Indpls., 1976-78; v.p. mktg. The Denver, 1978-79; founder, editor, pub. Clockwise mag., Ventura, Calif., 1979-85; mktg. mgr., mgr. pub. rels. and sp. events Robinson's Dept. Store, LA, 1985-87; exec. v.p., dir. mktg. Harrison Svcs., LA, San Francisco, 1987-93; pres. divsn. Miller & Miller MillerMania, Video Image and Mktg., Camino, Calif., 1993—. Instr. retail advt. Ind. U., 1977-78. Author: AICI Publicity Handbook, 2005; editor: Style Source: The Power of the Seven Universal Styles for Women and Men, 2008. Recipient Pres.'s award Adv. Women of NY, 1974, Seklemian award, 1977, Pub. Svc. Addy award, 1978, Disting. Svc. award Bay Area chpt. Assn. Image Cons., Internat., 2003. Mem. Image Cons., Internat. (1st Ever Oustanding Svc. award Bay Area chpt. 2004), Advt. Women NY, Retail Advt. and Mktg. Assn., Fashion Group Internat., Bay Area Integrated Mktg., San Francisco Fashion Group, UCLA Alumni Assn. (life), Media Coms. (life), Assn. Image Cons. Internat. Home Phone: 530-644-3104; Office Phone: 530-644-4919. E-mail: caroleann@millermania.com.

MILLER, CHRISTOPHER JAMES, professional football coach, retired professional football player; b. Pomona, Calif., Aug. 9, 1965; Student, Oreg. State U. Quarterback Atlanta Falcons, 1987—93, St. Louis Rams, 1994—95, Denver Broncos, 1999; head football coach South Eugene HS, Oreg., 2001—06; quarterbacks coach Ariz. Cardinals, 2006—. Named to Nat. Football Conf. Pro Bowl Team, NFL, 1991, Oreg. Sports Hall of Fame, 2005. Office: Ariz Cardinals PO Box 888 Phoenix AZ 85001-0888*

MILLER, CLIFFORD ALBERT, merchant banker; b. Salt Lake City, Aug. 6, 1928; s. Clifford Elmer and LaVeryl (Jensen) M.; m. Judith Auten, Sept. 20, 1976; 1 child, Courtney; children by previous marriage, Clifford, Christin, Stephanie. Student, U. Utah, 1945-50, UCLA, 1956. Pres. Braun & Co., LA, 1955-82, chmn., 1982-87; exec. v.p. Gt. Western Fin. Corp., Beverly Hills, Calif., 1987-91; chmn. Clifford Group, Inc., bus. cons., 1992—; mng. dir. Shamrock Holdings, Inc., 1992—, Shamrock Capital Advisors, L.P., 1992—. Bd. dirs. Frontier Bank, Park City, Utah, Triad Broadcasting Co., Inc., Monterey, Calif., 2005—, Western Cmty. Bancshares, Park City, Utah; cons. to White House, 1969—74. Trustee Harvey Mudd Coll., Claremont, Calif., 1974—, chmn. bd. trustees, 1991-98; chmn. bd. dirs. L.A. Master Chorale, 1989-93, chmn. emeritus, 1993; mem. chmn.'s coun. Music Ctr. Unified Fund Campaign; bd. trustees Keck Grad. Inst. Applied Life Scis., Claremont, 1997—. Mem. Calif. Club, Wilshire Country Club, Park Meadows Country Club, Pi Kappa Alpha. Office: Shamrock Holdings Inc 4444 W Lakeside Dr PO Box 7774 Burbank CA 91510-7774 Office Phone: 818-973-4297.

MILLER, CLIFFORD JOEL, lawyer; b. LA, Oct. 31, 1947; s. Eugene and Marian (Millman) M. BA, U. Calif., Irvine, 1969; JD, Pepperdine U., 1973. Bar: Calif. 1974, Hawaii 1974, U.S. Dist. Ct. Hawaii 1974. Ptnr. Rice, Lee & Wong, Honolulu, 1974-80, Goodsill Anderson Quinn & Stifel, Honolulu, 1980-89, McCorriston Miller Mukai MacKinnon, Honolulu, 1989—. Mem. ABA, Calif. Bar Assn., Hawaii Bar Assn., Am. Coll. Real Estate Lawyers. Avocations: sailing, volleyball, swimming, history. Office: McCorriston Miller Mukai MacKinnon 5 Waterfront Plz 500 Ala Moana Blvd Ste 400 Honolulu HI 96813-4920 Office Phone: 808-529-7300. Business E-Mail: cmiller@m4law.com.

MILLER, D. CRAIG, cardiovascular surgeon; b. Dec. 3, 1946; Student in Chemistry and Math., Dartmouth Coll., 1965-68; BS in Basic Med. Scis., Stanford U. Sch. Medicine, 1969, MD, 1972. Lic. Calif., cert. Am. Bd. Surgery, Am. Bd. Thoracic Surgery, Am. Bd. Surgery (spl. qualifications gen. vascular surgery). Resident, gen. surgery Stanford U. Med. Ctr. and Affiliated Hosps., Calif., 1972—75; chief resident, peripheral vascular surgery Stanford U. Med. Ctr., Calif., 1975—76, chief resident, cardiovasc. surgery Calif., 1976—77, chief resident, thoracic surgery Calif., 1977, program dir., vascular surgery residency Calif., 1985—93; chief, cardiac surgery sect. VA Med. Ctr., Palo Alto, Calif., 1978—86, staff surgeon, cardiac surgery sect., 1978—96; clin. asst. prof., cardiovasc. surgery Stanford U. Sch. Medicine, Calif., 1978, assoc. prof., cardiovasc. surgery Calif., 1983—89, prof., cardiovasc. surgery Calif., 1989—; Thelma and Henry Doelger Prof., Cardiovasc. Surgery Stanford U., 1998—. Invited lectr. in field. Guest editor, circulation supplement Cardiovasc. Surgery, 1990—92, mem. editl. bd. Jour. Thoracic and Cardiovasc. Surgery, 1984—91, assoc. editor (acquired heart disease), 1998—2007, mem. editl. bd. Jour. Cardiac Surgery, 1985—95, Cardiac Chronicle, 1985—93, Jour. Surgical Rsch., 1990—94, Circulation, 1991—93, Jour. Heart Valve Disease, 1992—, Heart and Vessels, 1998—, ad hoc referee for several peer-reviewed publications; contbr. several articles to peer-reviewed jours. Lt. med. corps. USNR, 1970—82. Recipient Stanford U. Med. Sch. Disting. Alumni award, 1997, Wilfred Bigelow award, Canadian Cardiovasc. Soc., 2000, Antoine Marfan award, Nat. Marfan Found., 2001. Mem.: Santa Clara County Med. Soc. (mem. ethics com. 1980—82, Outstanding Achievement in Medicine award 2004), AMA, Calif. Med. Assn., San Francisco Surgical Soc., Am. Fedn. for Clin. Rsch., Pan-Pacific Surgical Assn., Sociedad de Cardiocirujanos (Spain) (pres. 1987—88), Soc. Thoracic Surgical Edn., Soc. for Clin. Vascular Surgery, Bay Area Soc. Thoracic Surgeons, Northern Calif. Vascular Soc., Am. Coll. Chest Physicians, Am. Coll. Cardiology (scientific abstract review com. 1986, 1990, peripheral vascular disease com. 1994—98), ACS (cardiovasc. surgery com. 1986—88, exec. com. 1987—88), Soc. Heart Valve Disease, Am. Heart Assn. (bd. dirs., Santa Clara County Chpt. 1980—82, mem. rsch. com., Santa Clara County Chpt. 1981—83, optimal resources for vascular surgery com. 1985—89, program com., cardiovasc. surgery coun. 1988—92, chmn. 1989—92, vice-chmn., cardiothoracic-vascular surgery coun. 1993—95, chmn., cardiothoracic and vascular surgery coun. 1995—97, chmn., cardiothoracic-vascular surgery coun. 1995—97, Disting. Scientist 2003), Western Vascular Soc. (co-chmn., com. scientific sessions 1992—93), Soc. for Thoracic Surgeons, Western Thoracic Surgical Assn. (prog. com. 1983—88, sec. 1989—93, v.p. 1993—94, pres. 1994—95), Soc. for Vascular Surgery (chmn. 1986—88), Soc. Univ. Surgeons, Am. Assn. for Thoracic Surgery (coun. 2003—07, pres. 2007—08), Am. Surgical Assn., Soc. Clin. Surgery, Cardiac Soc. Australia and New Zealand (corr.) (hon.), Sociedad Chilena de Cardiologia y Cirugia Cardiovasc. (Chile) (hon.), Sociedad Colombiana de Cirugia (Columbia) (hon.), Sociedad Espanola de Cirugia Cardiovasc. (Spain) (hon.), European Assn. for Cardio-Thoracic Surgery (hon.), Cardiac Surgery Biology Club. Office: Dept Cardiothoracic Surgery Falk Cardiovasc Rsch Ctr Stanford U Sch Medicine 300 Pasteur Dr Stanford CA 94305-5407 Office Phone: 650-723-5771, 650-725-3826. Office Fax: 650-725-3846. Business E-Mail: dcm@stanford.edu.

MILLER, DAN, information technology executive; m. Sheryl Miller; 2 children. BSBA, U. Colo., Boulder. Various product mktg., sales and mgmt. positions NBI, Inc., Colo.; dir. Reseller Channel Orgn. Sun Microsystems, Inc., dir. Telco Sales for US Western Market, various leadership positions in Global Sales Orgn. including v.p. US Telecom. Market Area, v.p. Global Svc. Provide Strategy Group, pres. Global Electric Motors Japan, sr. v.p. global systems practice. Office: Sun Microsystems Inc 4150 Network Cir Santa Clara CA 95054 Office Phone: 650-960-1300.

MILLER, DIANE WILMARTH, retired human resources director; b. Clarinda, Iowa, Mar. 12, 1940; d. Donald and Floy Pauline (Madden) W.; m. Robert Nolen Miller, Aug. 21, 1965; children: Robert Wilmarth, Anne Elizabeth. AA, Colo. Women's Coll., 1960; BBA, U. Iowa, Iowa City, 1962; MA, U. No. Colo., Greeley, 1994. Cert. tchr., Colo.; vocat. credential, Colo.; cert. sr. profl. in human resources; lic. Colo. Ins. Prodr. Sec.-counselor U. SC Rep., Myrtle Beach AFB, 1968-69; instr. Coastal Carolina Campus U. SC, Conway, 1967-69; tchr. bus. Poudre Sch. Dist. R-1, Ft. Collins, Colo., 1970-71; travel cons. United Bank Travel Svc., Greeley, Colo., 1972-74; dir. human resources Aims C.C., Greeley, 1984—2001, ret., 2001. Instr. Aims CC, 1972—89; bd. dirs. U. No. Colo. Found., Greeley, 2003—, chair, 2007—08. Bd. trustees 1st Congl. Ch., Greeley, 2005—. Mem.: Philanthropic Ednl. Orgn. (pres. 1988—89), Women's Investment Network (pres. 2007—08), Women's Panhellenic Assn. (pres. 1983—84), Questers (pres. 2002—04), WTK Club (pres. 2006—07), Scroll and Fan Club (pres. 1985—86). Home: 3542 Wagon Trail Rd Greeley CO 80634-3405

MILLER, ELIZABETH RODRIGUEZ, city official; b. Tucson, Feb. 22, 1954; d. Tony S. Martinez and Maria (Corral) Rodriguez; m. Marc Alan Miller, Nov. 5, 1972; children: Andrea Eve, Matthew Luke, Meredith C. BA in Spanish, U. Ariz., 1976, MLS, 1978. Unit mgr. S. Tucson Libr., 1978-80; activities coord. community cable com. City of Tucson, 1980; info./reference mgr. Tucson Pub. Libr., 1981-84, agy. mgr., 1984-85, regional mgr., 1985-87, asst. dir. pub. svcs., 1987-89; dep. exec. dir. divsn. ALA Libr. Adminstrn. & Mgmt. Assn., Chgo., 1990; dep. dir. Tucson Pima Libr., 1990-91, libr. dir., 1991-96; asst. city mgr. City of Tucson, 1996—. Co-editor: Great Library Promotion Ideas V, 1990; contbr. articles to profl. jours. Mem. adv. bd. libr. power grant Tucson Unified Sch. Dist., 1992-95; bd. dirs. Tucson area Literacy Coalition, 1992-95, YWCA, 1998—2001; active Hispanic Profl. Action Com., 1992—. Mem. ALA (mem. pres. program com. 1987, mem. nominating com. 1991-93), REFORMA (chair elections com. 1983-84, 85, chair conf. program 1987, pres. 1987-88), Libr. Adminstrn. and Mgmt. Assn. (mem. cultural diversity com. 1991-92, chair 1992-93, mem. nominating com. 1992-93), Pub. Libr. Assn. (mem. Pub. Libr. Assn.-Libr. Adminstrn. and Mgmt. Assn. cert. com. 1991-92, chair 1992-93, chair Allie Beth Martin Award com. 1987-88, mem. 1989), Ariz. Libr. Assn. (Libr. of Yr. 1995), Ariz. State Libr. Assn. (chair svcs. to Spanish-speaking Roundtable 1980-82, pres. pub. libr. divsn. 1984-85, chair ann. conf. 1986), Internat. City/County

Mgmt. Assn. (assoc., participant Comparative Performance Measurement Consortium 1994-96, U. Ariz. Hispanic Alumni Assn., Women at the Top (mem. Carondelet health network fin. com). Office: City Hall 255 W Alameda St Tucson AZ 85701 Office Phone: 520-791-4204. Office Fax: 520-791-5198.

MILLER, EUGENE H., lawyer; b. Chgo., Dec. 21, 1947; s. Clifford and Birdie M.; m. Judith Miriam Bolef, June 15, 1969; children: Adam, Rachel. BS, U. Ill., 1969, JD, 1973. Bar: Ill. 1973, Calif. 1973, U.S. Dist. Ct. (no. dist.) Calif. 1973, U.S. Supreme Ct. 1977, U.S. Tax Ct. 1983. Acct. Lester Witte, Chgo., 1969-70, Price Waterhouse, Oakland, Calif., 1973-74; atty. Heizel, Leighton, Brunn & Deal, Oakland, 1974-77, Brunn, Leighton & Miller, Oakland, 1977-79, Miller, Starr & Regalia, Oakland, 1980—, mng. ptnr. Author: (with others) Closely Held Corporations, 1988. Office: Miller Starr & Regalia 1331 N California Blvd Fl 5 Walnut Creek CA 94596-4537

MILLER, GALE TIMOTHY, lawyer; b. Kalamazoo, Sept. 15, 1946; s. Arthur H. and Eleanor (Johnson) M.; m. Janice Lindvall, June 1, 1968; children: Jeremy L., Amanda E., Timothy W. AB, Augustana Coll., 1968; JD, U. Mich., 1971. Bar: Mich. 1971, Colo. 1973, U.S. Dist. Ct. Colo. 1973, U.S. Ct. Appeals (10th cir.) 1979, U.S. Supreme Ct. 1997. Trial atty. FTC, Washington, 1971-73; assoc. Davis Graham & Stubbs LLP, Denver, 1973-77, ptnr., 1978—2008, chmn. exec. com., 1998—2001; judge Colo. Ct. Appeals, 2009—. Bd. dirs. Colo. Jud. Inst., 1999—, v.p., 2005—06, chair, 2006—08, Colo. Lawyers Com., 1989—91, bd. dirs., 1987—2006, mem. exec. com., 2004—06. Recipient Cmty. Svc. award Colo. Hispanic Bar Assn., 1996: named Individual Lawyer of Yr. Colo. Lawyers Com., 1994, Outstanding Sustainal Contbn., 2005. Mem. ABA (antitrust sect. task force on model civil antitrust jury instrns. 1985-87), Colo. Bar Assn. (mem. bd. govs., 2007—, chair antitrust sect. 1996-98), Denver Bar Assn. Democrat. Lutheran. Office: Colo Ct Appeals 2 E 14th Ave Denver CO 80203 Home Phone: 303-399-2845.

MILLER, GARY G., United States Representative from California; b. Huntsville, Ark., Oct. 16, 1948; m. Cathy Miller, 1972; children: Matt, Brian, Elizabeth, Loren. Student, Mt. San Antonio CC. Founder G. Miller Devel. Co., 1970—; mem. Diamond Bar City Council, 1989—95, mayor, 1993—94; mem. Calif. State Assembly, 1995—98, US Congress from 42nd Calif. dist., Washington, 1998—, asst. whip, mem. budget com., fin. svcs. com., sci. com., trans. & infrastructure com. Mem. Nat. Guard & Reserve Components Caucus, Rep. Study Com.; chair Highway, Infrastructure & Transp. Caucus, Building a Better America Caucus, 2001—. Bd. dirs. Sunrise Christian Sch., 1982—90. Served with US Army, 1967—68. Mem.: Diamond Bar C. of C., Building Industry Assn. Republican. Achievements include proposing 24 bills signed into law; negotiating funding of 1st class size reduction program, producing a balanced budget that reduced bus. tax. to 1973 levels while maintaing a $310 million reserve. Office: US Ho Reps 1037 Longworth Ho Office Bldg Washington DC 20515-0542

MILLER, GEORGE, former mayor; b. Detroit, 1922; m. Roslyn Girard; 4 children. BA, U. Ariz., 1947, MEd, 1952. Tchr. high schs.; owner, prin. painting contracting co., until 1989; mayor City of Tucson, 1991-99. Active mem. Dem. Party So. Ariz., 1960—, treas. Pima County div., state chmn. Presdl. Del. Selection Reform Commn.; bd. dirs. Tucson Jewish Community Ctr., Anti-Defamation League of B'nai B'rith; councilman Tucson City Coun., 1977-91, also vice mayor. With USMC, WWII. Decorated Purple Heart; recipient Recognition award United Way, Cmty. Svcs. Support award Chicano Por La Causa (2), Met. Edn. Commn. Crystal Apple award, cert. appreciation San Ignacio Yaqui Coun., Old Pasqua, Dr. Martin Luther King Jr. Keep the Dream Alive award, 1995; named Father of Yr. 1995, Man of Yr. So. Ariz. Home Builders Assn., Outstanding Pub. Ofcl. Ariz. Parks and Recreation Assn., 1995.

MILLER, GEORGE, III, United States Representative from California; b. Richmond, Calif., May 15, 1945; s. George and Dorothy (Rumsey) Miller; m. Cynthia Caccavo, 1964; children: George, Stephen. BA in Am. Problems, San Francisco State U., 1968; JD, U. Calif., Davis, 1972. Legis. counsel to Senator George Moscone Calif. State Senate, 1969—74; mem. US Congress from 7th Calif. dist., 1975—, US House Nat. Resources Com., chmn., 1991—94, US House Edn. & Labor Com., 2007—, US House Democratic Steering & Policy Com., 2003—. Founding mem. Progressive Caucus. Author: Giving Children A Chance: The Case for More Effective National Politics, 1989. Recipient Excellence in Pub. Svc., Am. Acad. Pediatrics, 1984, Cleve. Armory Capitol Courage award, Fund for Animals, 2002, William Steiger Meml. award, Am. Conf. Govt. Industrial Hygienists, 2002, Farmworker Justice award, Farmworker Justice Fund, Inc., 2003, N.Am. Govt. Leadership award, Global Semiconductor Industry Assn., 2007. Mem.: Davis Law Sch. Alumni Assn., Calif. Bar Assn., Martinez Dem. Club. Democrat. Roman Catholic. Office: US Congress 2205 Rayburn House Office Bldg Washington DC 20515-0507 also: 375 G St Ste 1 Vallejo CA 94592

MILLER, HAROLD WILLIAM, nuclear geochemist; b. Walton, NY, Apr. 21, 1920; s. Harold Frank and Vera Leona (Simons) M. BS in Chemistry, U. Mich., 1943; MS in Chemistry, U. Colo., 1948, postgrad. Control chemist Linde Air Products Co., Buffalo, 1943-46; analytical research chemist Gen. Electric Co., Richland, Wash., 1948-51; research chemist Phillips Petroleum Co., Idaho Falls, Idaho, 1953-56; with Anaconda (Mont.) Copper Co., 1956; tech. dir., v.p. U.S. Yttrium Co., Laramie, Wyo., 1956-57; tech. dir. Colo. div. The Wah Chang Co., Boulder, Colo., 1957-58; analytical chemist The Climax (Colo.) Molybdenum Co., 1959; with research and devel. The Colo. Sch. of Mines Research Found., Golden, 1960-62; cons. Boulder, 1960—; sr. research physicist Dow Chem. Co., Golden, 1963-73. Bd. dirs. Sweeney Mining and Milling Corp., Boulder; cons. Hendricks Mining and Milling Co., Boulder; instr. nuclear physics and nuclear chemistry Rocky Flats Plant, U. Colo. Contbr. numerous articles to profl. jours. Recipient Lifetime Achievement award Boulder County Metal Mining Assn., 1990. Mem. Sigma Xi. Avocations: mineralogy, history. Home and Office: PO Box 1092 Boulder CO 80306-1092 Office Phone: 303-443-5699.

MILLER, HARRIET SANDERS, former art center director; b. Apr. 18, 1926; m. Milton H. Miller, June 27, 1948; children: Bruce, Jeffrey, Marcie. BA, Ind. U., 1947; MA, Columbia U., 1949; MS, U. Wis., 1962, MFA, 1967. Dir. art sch. Madison (Wis.) Art Ctr., 1963-72; acting dir. Ctr. for Continuing Edn., Vancouver, B.C., Canada, 1975-76; mem. fine arts faculty Douglas Coll., Vancouver, 1972-78; exec. dir. Palos Verdes (Calif.) Arts Ctr., 1978-84; dir. Jr. Arts Ctr., LA, 1984-98. One woman exhibits at Gallery 7, Vancouver, 1978, Gallery 1, Toronto, Ont., Can., 1977, Linda Farris Gallery, Seattle, 1975, Galerie Allen, Vancouver, 1973.

MILLER, JACK DAVID R., radiologist, physician, educator; b. Johannesburg, Apr. 15, 1930; s. Harold Lewis and Inez (Behrman) M.; m. Miriam Sheckter, Dec., 1988. B.Sc., M.B., Ch.B., U. Witwatersrand, Johannesburg, 1956. Diplomate: Am. Bd. Radiology. Intern Coronation Hosp., Johannesburg, 1957-58; resident in radiology Passavant Meml. Hosp., Chgo., 1959-62, Wesley Meml. Hosp., Chgo., 1959-62; fellow in radiology Northwestern U. Med. Sch., 1962-63; chmn. dept. radiology U. Hosp., Edmonton, Alta., Canada, 1971-83; radiologist, dept. radiology U. Alta Hosp., 1963—2004, head, dir. neuroradiology, 1984—92; prof. emeritus radiology U. Alta., 1997—. Clin. prof. radiology U. Alta., 1971— Fellow Royal Coll. Physicians Can., Am. Coll. Radiology. Personal E-mail: miribud@shaw.ca.

MILLER, JAMES MCCALMONT, pediatrician; b. Springfield, Mass., Sept. 25, 1938; s. John Haynes and Josephine (Darrah) M.; m. Jane Rose, July 7, 1975; children: John, Charlotte, Willard. AB, Hamilton Coll., 1960; MD, Cornell U., 1964. Resident U. Colo. Med. Ctr., Denver, 1964-67; staff pediatrician Kaiser Permanente Med. Ctr., Walnut Creek, Calif., 1969-87, chief pediatrician, 1971-82, Pleasanton, Calif., 1982-87; staff pediatrician Appalachian Regional Health, Hazard, Ky., 1987-92, N.W. Pediat. Ctr., Centralia, Wash., 1992—. Clin. assoc. U. N.Mex., Albuquerque, 1967-69; instr. U. Calif., San Francisco, 1969-87, U. Ky., Lexington, 1988-92. With U.S. Army, 1967-69. Fellow Am. Acad. Pediat.; mem. Wash. State Med. Assn. Office: Northwest Pediatric Ctr 1911 Cooks Hill Rd Centralia WA 98531-9027 Office Phone: 360-736-6778. E-mail: jmiller@localaccess.com.

MILLER, JAMES RUMRILL, III, finance educator; b. Phila., Dec. 21, 1937; s. James Rumrill and Elizabeth Pleasants (King) M.; m. Bettie M. Studer, May 1, 1989 (div. Jan. 2007); children from previous marriage: Elizabeth, Katharine, Kerry. AB, Princeton U., 1959; MBA (Woodrow Wilson fellow), Harvard U., 1962; PhD, MIT, 1966. Sys. analyst MITRE Corp., Bedford, Mass., 1962—67; asst. prof. bus. adminstrn. Stanford U., Calif., 1967—69, assoc. prof., 1970—73, prof., 1973—97, Walter and Elise Haas prof. bus. adminstrn., 1977—97, assoc. dean Bus. Sch., 1974—76, Walter and Elise Haas prof. bus. adminstrn. emeritus, 1997—. Cons. in field. Author: Professional Decision Making, 1970; contbr. numerous articles to profl. jours. Mem. Phi Beta Kappa. Republican. Episcopalian. Office: 16641 W Loma Verde Trail Surprise AZ 85387 E-mail: mdmsinc@aol.com.

MILLER, JAN DEAN, metallurgy educator; b. Dubois, Pa., Apr. 7, 1942; s. Harry Moyer and Mary Virginia (McQuown) M.; m. Patricia Ann Rossman, Sept. 14, 1963; children: Pamela Ann, Jeanette Marie, Virginia Christine. BS, Pa. State U., University Park, 1964; MS, Colo. Sch. of Mines, Golden, 1966, PhD, 1969; D (hon.), U. Pretoria, South Africa, 2007; prof. appointment (hon.), Ctrl. South U., Changsha, P.R. China, 2007. Rsch. engr. Lawrence Livermore Lab., Calif., 1972, Anaconda Co., Mont., 1966; asst. prof. metallurgy U. Utah, Salt Lake City, 1968-72, assoc. prof., 1972-78, prof., 1978-2000, Ivor D. Thomas prof., 2000—, dept. chmn., 2002—, disting. prof., metallurgical engring., 2008. Cons. on processing of mineral resources to various cos. and govt. agys. Editor: Hydrometallurgy, Research, Development, and Plant Practice, 1983, others; contbr. over 500 articles to profl. jours.; 25 patents in field. Recipient Marcus A. Grossman award Am. Soc. Metals, 1974, Van Diest gold medal Colo. Sch. of Mines, 1977, Student award excellence in tchg. metall. engring. U. Utah, 1978, 82, 94, Extractive and Processing Lectr. award The Minerals, Metals and Materials Soc., 1992, Disting. Achievement medal Colo. Sch. of Mines, 1994, Best Paper award for fundamental rsch. 2000 TAPPI Recycling Symposium, 2000, Oustanding Tchg. award Coll. Mines and Earth Scis. U. Utah, 2000, J.D. Miller Symposium honor for innovations in resource processing, SME Annual meeting, Salt Lake City, 2005, Spl. Meritorious Recognition medal Gdansk U. Tech., Poland, 2005, Utah Govs. medal award for sci. and tech., 2006; Centennial fellow Coll. of Earth and Mineral Scis., Pa. State U., 1996. Mem. NAE, AIME (Henry Krumb lectr. 1987, Richards award 1991, Mineral Industry Edn. award 1997, Aplan award 2003), Soc. Mining, Metallurgy and Exploration (chmn. mineral processing divsn. 1980-81, Disting. Mem. award 1992, Antoine M. Gaudin award 1992), Am. Chem. Soc., Soc. Mining Engrs. (bd. dirs. 1980-83, program chmn. 1982-83, Taggart award 1986, 05, Stefanko award 1988, 02, symposium honoring J.D. Miller, 2005), Metall. Soc. (Extractive Metallurgy Tech. award 1988), Salt Lake Swim and Tennis Club, U. Utah Faculty Club. Baptist. Office: U Utah Metall Engring 135 S 1460 E Rm 412 Salt Lake City UT 84112-0114 Office Phone: 801-581-5160. Business E-Mail: jan.miller@utah.edu.

MILLER, JEAN RUTH, retired librarian; b. St. Helena, Calif., Aug. 4, 1927; d. William Leonard and Jean (Stanton) M. BA, Occidental Coll., 1950; MLS, U. So. Calif., Los Angeles, 1952. Base librarian USAF, Wethersfield, Eng., 1952-55; post librarian USMC Air Sta., El Toro, Calif., 1955-63; data systems librarian Autonetics (Rockwell), Anaheim, Calif., 1963-65; mgr. library services Beckman Instruments, Inc., Fullerton, Calif., 1966-92. Mem. adv. com. Library Technician Program, Fullerton Coll., 1969-1995. Author: (bibliography) Field Air Traffic Control, 1965, Electrical Shock Hazards, 1974. Chair Fullerton Are U. So. Calif. Scholarship Alumni Interview Program, Fullerton, 1974-1993; vol. Beckman Heritage Ctr. Mem. Orange County Libr. Assn., Spl. Libraries Assn. (pres. So. Calif. chpt. 1975-76, chair Sci./Tech. Div. 1985-86), Santa Ana Elks Lodge (scholarship chair 2003—). Republican. Avocations: travel, reading, swimming. Home: 4701 E Fairfield St Anaheim CA 92807-3651

MILLER, JEFF, state legislator; m. Debora Miller; 2 children. Grad., Cal State, Fullerton, 1985. Parks commr. in Corona, Corona, 1995; mem. Corona City Coun., Corona, 2000; del. Rep. Nat. Conv., 2004; chmn./spl. elections chair Riverside County Rep. Party, 2001—07; mayor City of Corona, Corona; mem. Dist. 71 Calif. State Assembly, Calif., 2008—. Republican. Office: State Capital Room 3147 Sacramento CA 95814 also: 1940 N Tustin St Ste 102 Orange CA 92865 Office Phone: 714-998-0980, 916-319-2171. Office Fax: 714-998-7102, 916-319-2171.*

MILLER, JOEL STEVEN, inorganic and organic materials chemist, educator; b. Detroit, Oct. 14, 1944; s. John and Rose M.; m. Elaine J., Sept. 20, 1970; children: Stephen D., Mark A., Alan D. BS in Chemistry, Wayne State U., 1967; PhD, UCLA, 1971. Postdoctoral assoc. Stanford U., Calif., 1972; mgr. rsch. Occidental Rsch. Corp., Irvine, Calif., 1979-83; supr. rsch. Ctrl. R & D Lab. E. I. Du Pont Nemours & Co., Wilmington, Del., 1983-93; prof. chemistry U. Utah, 1993—, adj. prof. materials sci., 1994—2000. Disting. prof., assoc. Inorganic Synthesis Corp., Chgo.; vis. prof. U. Calif., Irvine, 1980, Weizmann Inst., Rehovot, Israel, 1985, U. Pa., Phila., 1988, U. Paris-Sud, 1991; Schmidt lectr. Weizmann Inst. Sci. Editor 16 books; mem. adv. bd. Jour. Materials Chemistry, 1991—2003, Advanced Materials, 1994—; mem. editl. bd. CrystEngComm, 1999-; mem. editl. adv. bd. Inorganic Chemistry, 2001-03, Chemistry-A European Jour.; contbr. over 450 articles to sci. jours. Indsl. fellow in material sci. Northwestern U., 1991-93; Wilhelm Manchot rsch. fellow 1996; fellow Japan Soc. Promotion Sci., 2000; recipient Disting. Rsch./Creative award, U. Utah, 2001, Gov. of Vt.'s medal for sci. and tech., 2004, James C. McGroddy prize for New Materials, Am. Phys. Soc., 2007. Mem. Am. Chem. Soc. (chmn. solid state subdiv. 1989, Utah award, 2003, Award Chemistry of Materials, 2000). Achievements include discovery and development of organic magnets and conductors. Office: Dept Chemistry U Utah Salt Lake City UT 84112 Home Phone: 801-273-9647; Office Phone: 801-585-5455. Office Fax: 801-581-8433. E-mail: jsmiller@chem.utah.edu.

MILLER, JON HAMILTON, forest products company executive; b. Des Moines, Jan. 22, 1938; s. Victor George and Virginia Adelaide (Hamilton) M.; m. Sydney Gail Fernald, June 4, 1966; children: Emily, Sara. AB in Econs., Stanford U., 1959, MBA in Mktg. and Fin., 1961. Asst. to pres. Boise (Idaho) Cascade Corp., 1961-62, prodn. service mgr., 1962-65, sr. v.p. bus. products and services and packaging Portland, Oreg., 1971-74; exec. v.p. paper and paper products Boise Cascade Corp., Boise, Idaho, 1974-76, exec. v.p. timber/wood products/bldg. materials, 1976-78, pres. and chief operating officer, 1978—, also dir. Bd. dirs. Northwestern Mut. Life Ins. Co., St. Luke's Regional Med. Ctr., Idaho Power Co. Mem. bd. trustees Inst. Paper Science and Technology. With U.S. Army, 1959-60. Recipient Top Mgmt. award Sales & Mktg. Execs. of Boise, 1984; named Idaho Bus Leader of Yr. Alpha Kappa Psi, Idaho State U., 1986. Mem. Greater Boise C. of C. (pres. 1977), Bronco Athletic Assn. (bd. dirs. 1987—). Clubs: Arid (Boise) (bd. dirs. 1987); Multnomah Athletic (Portland). Republican. Methodist. Home: 3330 Mountain View Dr Boise ID 83704-4637

MILLER, JON PHILIP, marketing professional, pharmaceutical executive; b. Moline, Ill., Mar. 30, 1944; s. Clyde Sheldon and Alice Lenora (Taes) M.; m. Shirley Ann Hymes, Aug. 21, 1965; children: Melissa, Elizabeth. AB, Augustana Coll., 1966; PhD, St. Louis U., 1970; MBA, Pepperdine U., 1983. Rsch. assoc. to sr. biochemist ICN Pharm., Inc., Irvine, Calif., 1970—72, leader molecular pharmacology group, 1972—73, head molecular pharmacology/drug metabolism dept., 1973—76, dir. biology divsn., 1975—76; dir. SRI-NCI liaison group SRI Internat. (formally Stanford Rsch. Inst.), Menlo Park, Calif., 1976—78; sr. bioorganic chemist SRI Internat., Menlo Park, 1978—80, head medicinal biochemistry program, 1980—84, dir. biotech. rsch. dept., 1982—85, dir. biotech. and biomed. rsch. lab., 1985—92, assoc. dir. life scis. divsn., 1989—92; dir. bus. devel., strategic mktg. MDS Panlabs, Inc., Bothell, Wash., 1992—98; dir. pharm. mktg. Applied Biosys., Foster City, Calif., 1998—2001; dir. bus. devel. ACLARA Bioscis., Mountain View, Calif., 2001—03; pres. Miller & Co., Foster City, 2003—. Office: Miller & Co 1147 Blythe St Foster City CA 94404 Personal E-mail: jm330@sbcgobal.net.

MILLER, JOSEPH S., astronomy researcher; b. LA, Sept. 7, 1941; s. William George and Bertha Florence (Standard) M.; m. Nina Armstrong Parker, Dec. 22, 1971; children: Miriam Q., Samuel A. BA, UCLA, 1963; MA, U. Wis., 1966, PhD, 1967. Dir. U. Calif. Lick Observatory, Santa Cruz, Calif., 1967-68; prof. astronomy Lick Obs., Santa Cruz, 1968—, dir., 1991—. Fellow Am. Acad. Arts and Scis. Office: Lick Obs Univ Calif Santa Cruz CA 95064

MILLER, JOYCE ELLEN, oceanographer, hydrographer; b. Indpls., June 14, 1947; d. Robert Arthur Miller and Lucille Emily Miller nee Scoville; m. James Scott Ferguson, Apr. 16, 1982. MS in Edn., Ind. U., Bloomington, 1969; postgrad. in Marine Geology, U.Hawaii, Honolulu, 1979. Cert. offshore hydrographer Am. Congress on Surveying and Mapping, 1996. Tchr. math, English and bus. US Peace Corps., Cape Palmas, Liberia, 1969—71; german translator Gesellschaft for Klaranlagen und Wasserversorgungen, Mannheim, Germany, 1971—72; rsch. assoc. U. Hawaii, Honolulu, 1979—81; survey technician NOAA, Seattle, 1981—82, seafloor mapping coord., oceanographer Coral Reef Ecosys. Divsn. Honolulu, 2001—; geophysicist Naval Oceanog. Office, Bay St. Louis, Miss., 1982—83; ops. and data mgr. U. RI Sea Beam Group, Narragansett, 1985—92; sr. scientist Sci. Applications Internat. Corp., Newport, RI, 1992—98; hydrog tng. coord. Philippine Navy, Manila, Philippines, 1997—98. Recipient Best Paper award, Internat. Hydrog Orgn., 1998; nominee Best Employee of Yr., Rsch. Corp. U. Hawaii, 2006. Mem.: Am. Geophys. Union. Achievements include research in multibeam mapping of US Pacific Islands including American Samoa, the Mariana Archipelago and Pacific Remote Island Areas; conducted first shallow water multibeam mapping for nautical charting in US. Avocations: sailing, travel, swimming. Home: 350 Ward Ave #106-259 Honolulu HI 96814 Office: NOAA Coral Reef Ecosys Divsn 1125B Ala Moana Blvd Honolulu HI 96813 E-mail: joyce.miller@noaa.gov.

MILLER, JUDSON FREDERICK, lawyer, retired military officer; b. Tulsa, Dec. 5, 1924; s. Herbert Frederick and Martha (Davidson) M.; m. June Hirakis, Aug. 4, 1967; children by previous marriage: Kathleen, Shelley, Douglas, Judson Frederick. BS, U. Md., 1961; postgrad., Army War Coll., 1961-62; MA, George Washington U., 1962; JD, U. Puget Sound, 1980. Bar: Wash. 1981. Commd. 2d lt. U.S. Army, 1943, advanced through grades to maj. gen., 1975; platoon leader, co. comdr. 4th Cav. Group, Europe, 1944-46, 82d Airborne Div., 1947-50; with 187th Airborne RCT and Hdqrs. 8th Army, 1950-52; instr. Armored Sch., 1953-56; bn. comdr. 14th Armored Cav., 1958-60; with Hdqrs. U.S. Strike Command, 1963-65; brigade comdr., chief of staff 4th Inf. Div., Vietnam, 1966-67; mem. gen. staff Dept. Army, 1967-68; dep. comdg. gen. Ft. Ord, Cal., 1968-69; asst. chief of staff Hdqrs. Allied Forces Central Europe, 1969-71; asst. comdr. 3d Inf. Div., Germany, 1971-73; chief of staff I Corps Group, Korea, 1973-75; dep. comdg. gen. VII Corps, Germany, 1975-77; ret., 1977; assoc. F.G. Enslow and Assocs., Tacoma, 1981—. Decorated Silver Star, Legion of Merit, Bronze Star with V device and oak leaf cluster, Joint Service Commendation medal, Air medal with 8 oak leaf clusters, Purple Heart, Vietnamese Gallantry Cross with palm; named to Okla. Mil. Acad. Hall of Fame, 1988. Mem. ABA, Assn. U.S. Army.

Clubs: Tacoma Country, Lakewood Racquet. Home: 8009 75th St SW Tacoma WA 98498-4817 Office: Tacoma Mall Office Bldg 4301 S Pine St Ste 205 Tacoma WA 98409-7205 Personal E-mail: jud7@comcast.net.

MILLER, LARRY G., professional sports team executive; b. Phila. BBA in Acctg., Temple U., Phila., 1982; MBA, La Salle U., Phila., 1987. Exec. v.p., contr. Jantzen, Inc., Portland, Oreg., pres., 1992—97; v.p. USA apparel Nike, Inc., Oreg., 1997—99, pres. Brand Jordan, 1999—2006, v.p., gen. mgr. basketball, 2006—07; pres. Portland Trail Blazers, 2007—. Bd. mem. Urban League Portland, Portland Sports Authority. Office: Portland Trail Blazers One Center Ct Ste 200 Portland OR 97227

MILLER, LEE TODD, pediatrician, educator; b. NYC, Aug. 1, 1957; BA, Bowdoin Coll.; MD, U. Va., 1982. Cert. Pediat., 1987. Intern pediat. U. Va. Med. Ctr., Charlottesville, 1982—83, resident, 1983—86, chief resident pediat.; vice chair edn. program, dir. pediat. residency training program Cedars-Sinai Med. Ctr., LA; co-dir. med. student tchg. program pediat. David Geffen Sch. Med., UCLA. Recipient Golden Apple Tchg. Award. Mem.: Assn. Pediat. Program Dirs., Ambulatory Pediat. Assn., Am. Acad. Pediat. Office: Cedars-Sinai Med Ctr 8700 Beverly Blvd Los Angeles CA 90048 Office Phone: 310-423-4467. Office Fax: 310-423-0145. E-mail: lee.miller@cshs.org.

MILLER, MARK A., information technology training executive; B in Bus. Adminstrn., U. Mich. V.p. Nutri/System, Inc., sr. v.p., pres.; founder, pres. Foxboro Group; chmn., CEO Signature Plastic Surgery, Inc., 1997—2000; group exec. v.p. Ea. U.S. Right Mgmt. Cons., Inc.; CEO New Horizons Worldwide, Inc., 2006—. Office: New Horizons Computer Learning Center 1900 S State College Blvd Ste 120 Anaheim CA 92806-6136 Office Phone: 714-940-8000. Office Fax: 714-938-6002.

MILLER, MAURICE LIM, cultural organization administrator; BS in Mech. Engring., U. Calif., Berkeley, 1968, M in Design, 1977; Cert. in Housing and Bus. Develop., Develop. Training Inst., 1985. Exec. dir. Asian Neighborhood Design, San Francisco, 1981—2003; founder Family Independence Initiative, 2001—. Bd. dirs. Corp. for Enterprise Develop., Public Private Ventures, Calif. Endowment, 2005—. Recipient Asian Pacific Heritage Month's Local Hero of Yr. award; named Gerbode Found. Fellow, 1993, Eureka Leadership Fellow, 1997. Office: Family Independence Initiati 3746 39th Ave Oakland CA 94619-2010

MILLER, MAYNARD MALCOLM, geologist, educator, geoscience institute director, former state legislator; b. Seattle, Jan. 23, 1921; s. Joseph Anthony and Juanita Queena (Davison) M.; m. Joan Walsh, Sept. 15, 1951; children: Ross McCord, Lance Davison. BS magna cum laude, Harvard U., 1943; MA, Columbia U., 1948; PhD, St. John's Coll., Cambridge U., 1957; student, Naval War Coll., Air War Coll., Nat. Def. U., Oak Ridge Inst. Nuc. Sci.; DSc (hon.), U. Alaska, 1990. Registered profl. geologist, Idaho. Asst. prof. naval sci. Princeton U., NJ, 1946; organizer, dir. Office Naval Rsch., Juneau Icefield Rsch. project Am. Geog. Soc., NYC, 1946—55, rsch. assoc., 1948—55; geologist Gulf Oil Co., Cuba, 1947; staff scientist Swiss Fed. Inst. for Snow and Avalanche Rsch., Davos, 1952—53; instr. dept. geography Cambridge U., 1953—56; assoc. prodr., field project dir. film Seven Wonders of the World Cinerama Corp., Europe, Asia, Africa, Mid. East, 1954—55; rsch. assoc. Lamont Geol. Obs., NYC, 1955—59; sr. scientist dept. geology Columbia U., NYC, 1957—59; asst. prof. geology Mich. State U., East Lansing, 1959—61, assoc. prof., 1961—63, prof., 1963—75; dean Coll. Mines and Earth Resources U. Idaho, Moscow, 1975—88, dean emeritus, prof. geology, dir. Glaciological and Arctic Scis. Inst., 1975—2008; dir., state geologist Idaho Geol. Survey, 1975—88, dir. emeritus; rep. Legislature of State of Idaho, Boise, 1992—2000. Geophys. cons. Nat. Park Svc., NASA, USAF, NAS; mapping expdn. Brady Icefield and Glacier Bay, Alaska, 1940-41; leader Mt. St. Elias Expdn. USAF-Harvard Mountaineering Club, Alaska, 1946; geologist Am. Mt. Everest Expdn., Nepal, 1963; dir. Nat. Geog. Soc. Alaskan Glacier Commemorative Project, 1964—; organizer leader Nat. Geog. Soc. Joint U.S.-Can. Mt. Kennedy Yukon Meml. Mapping Expdn., 1965; leader Muséo Argentino de Ciencias Naturales, Patagonian expdn. and glacier survey for Inst. Geologico del Peru and Am. Geog. Soc., 1949-50; adv. missions People's Republic of China, 1981, 86, 88, 98; geol. expdns. Himalaya, Nepal, 1963, 84, 87; USAF ice survey mission to Ellesmere Land, North Pole and Polar Sea, 1951; organizer, ops. officer USN-LTA blimp geophysics flight to Ice Island T-3 and North Pole area Office Naval Rsch., 1958; ONR-LTA coord. SS Nautilus First Transit North Pole; prin. investigator U.S. Naval Oceanog. Office sea and pack ice rsch. Ice Island T-3 Polar Sea, 1967-68, 70-73; dir. lunar field sta. project Mt. Rainier summit simulation USAF-Boeing Co., 1959-60; prin. investigator Nat. Geog. Soc. 30 Yr. Remap of Lemon, Taku and Cathedral Massif Glaciers, Juneau Icefield, 1989-2005; dir. Found. for Glacier and Environ. Rsch., Pacific Sci. Ctr., Seattle, 1955-95, 97—, chmn., 1992—, pres., 1955-85, trustee, 1960—, cons. Dept. Hwys. State of Alaska, 1965; chmn., dir. World Ctr. for Exploration Found., NYC, 1968-71; dir., adv. bd. Idaho Geol. Survey, 1975-88; chmn. nat. coun. JSHS program U.S. Army Rsch. Office and Acad. Applied Sci., 1982-90; sci. dir. U.S. Army Rsch. Office and DOD Nat. Sci. and Humanities Symposia programs, 1991—; disting. guest prof. China U. Geoscis., Wuhan, 1981—, Changchun U. Earth Scis., People's Republic of China, 1988—; adj. prof. U. Alaska, 1986-. Author: Field Manual of Glaciological and Arctic Sciences; co-author books on Alaskan glaciers and Nepal geology; contbr. articles to profl. jours., chpts. to books. Past mem. nat. exploring com., nat. sea exploring com. Boy Scouts Am.; past mem. nat. adv. bd. Embry Riddle Aero. U.; bd. dirs. Idaho Rsch. Found.; pres. state divsn. Mich. UN Assn., 1970-73; mem. Centennial and Health Environ. Commns., Moscow, Idaho, 1987—. With USN, 1943-46, PTO. Decorated 11 campaign and battle stars; Fulbright scholar Cambridge U., 1951-53; named Leader of Tomorrow Seattle C. of C. and Time mag., 1953, one of Ten Outstanding Young Men U.S. Jaycees, 1954; recipient commendation for lunar environ. study USAF, 1960, Hubbard medal Nat. Geog. Soc., 1963, Elisha Kent Kane Gold medal Geog. Soc. Phila., 1964, Karo award Soc. Mil. Engrs., 1966, Franklin L. Burr award Nat. Geog. Soc., 1967, Nat. Commendation Boy Scouts Am., 1970, Disting. Svc. plaque UN Assn. U.S., Disting. Svc. commendation State of Mich. Legis., 1975, Outstanding Civilian Svc. medal U.S. Army Rsch. Office, 1977, Outstanding Leadership in Minerals Edn. commendations Idaho Mining Assn., 1985, 87, Nat. Disting. Tchg. award Assn. Am. Geographers, 1996; grantee NSF, Nat. Geog. Soc., NASA, ARO, M.J. Murdock Trust, Dept. of Interior, others, 1948—. Fellow Geol. Soc. Am., Arctic Inst. N.Am., Explorers Club; mem. AAAS (councilor, Pacific divsn. 1978-88), AIME, ASME (hon. nat. lectr.), Am. Geophys. Union, Internat. Glaciological Soc. (past councilor), Assn. Am. State Geologists (hon.), Am. Legis. Exch. Coun., Am. Assn. Amateur Oarsmen (life), Am. Alpine Club (hon., life), Fulbright Assn., Alpine Club (London), Appalachian Club (hon. corr.), Brit. Mountaineering Assn. (hon., past v.p.), The Mountaineers (hon.), Cambridge U. Mountaineering Club (hon.), Himalayan Club (Calcutta), English Speaking Union (nat. lectr.), Naval Res. Assn. (life), Dutch Treat Club, Circumnavigators Club (life), Adventurers Club N.Y. (medalist), Am. Legion, VFW, Harvard Club (N.Y.C. and Seattle), Sigma Xi, Phi Beta Kappa (past pres. Epsilon chpt.), Phi Kappa Phi. Republican. Methodist. Avocations: skiing, mountaineering, photography. Home: 514 E 1st St Moscow ID 83843-2814 Address: Found Glacier & Environ Rsch 4470 N Douglas Hwy Juneau AK 99801-9403 Office Phone: 208-882-1237. Office Fax: 208-882-6207. Business E-Mail: jirp@foundglres.edu, jirp@fqcr.edu.

MILLER, MILTON ALLEN, lawyer; b. LA, Jan. 15, 1954; s. Samuel C. and Sylvia Mary Jane (Silver) Miller; m. Mary Ann Toman, Sept. 10, 1988; 1 child, Mary Ann. AB in Econs. with distinction and honors, Stanford U., 1976; JD with honors, Harvard U., 1979. Bar: Calif. 1979, US Ct. Appeals 9th cir.) 1979, US Supreme Ct. 1989, Calif. (US Dist. Ct. (cen., no. and so. dists.)) 1981. Law clk. US Ct. Appeals (9th cir.), Sacramento, 1979—80; assoc. Latham & Watkins, LA, 1979—87, ptnr., 1987—. Chmn. global ethics com. Latham & Watkins, LA, 1986—. Author: (non fiction) Attorney Ethics, 1993; editor: (articles) Harvard Law Rev., 1978—79; contbr. articles to profl. jours. Mem.: ATLA, ABA, Royal Shakespeare Com., LA County Bar Assn. (chmn. profl. responsibility and ethics com.), Calif. State Bar Assn. (mem. com. on profl. responsibility), Harvard Club (Boston and NY), Phi Beta Kappa. Office: Latham Watkins 355 S Grand Ave Los Angeles CA 90071-1560 Office Phone: 213-485-1234. Business E-Mail: milt.miller@lw.com.

MILLER, PAULA J., library director; m. Jay Miller; children: Jason, Jon, James. BA in Psychology, Kent State U.; MLIS, U. Md. Positions including head circulation, reference libr., children's asst. and adminstrv. coord. Kent Free Libr., Ohio; dir. Dover Pub. Libr., Del., Westlake Porter Pub. Libr., Ohio, 1992—2006; adminstr. Eastern Shore Regional Libr., Md.; exec. dir. Pikes Peak Libr. Dist., Colorado Springs, 2006—. Office: Pikes Peak Libr Dist PO Box 1579 Colorado Springs CO 80901 Office Phone: 719-531-6333 ext. 2010.

MILLER, RANDY, state legislator, lawyer; b. Portland, Oreg., Dec. 10, 1946; m. Gini Miller; 4 children. BS, U. Oreg., 1968, MEd, 1970; JD, Lewis & Clark U., 1974. Mem. Oreg. Legislature, Salem, 1992—, mem. bus. and consumer affairs com., chair rev. com., vice chair rules and elections com., mem. subcom. on edn. Mem. Nat. Policy Forum on the Environment; chair State Rep. Orgn. Mem. Oreg. State Bar Assn. Republican. Presbyterian. Office: PO Box 1795 Lake Oswego OR 97035-0524 E-mail: rm13@teleport.com.

MILLER, RANNE B., lawyer; b. Claremore, Okla., Aug. 22, 1940; BBA, U. Wash., 1963; JD, U. N.Mex., 1967. Bar: N.Mex. 1967. Sr. ptnr. Miller Stratvert, P.A., Albuquerque. Bd. editors Nat. Resources Jour., 1966-67. Mem. Am. Bd. Trial Advocates (pres. N.Mex. chpt. 1976-77), Am. Coll. Trial Lawyers, State Bar N.Mex., Albuquerque Bar Assn., Phi Kappa Phi. Office: Miller Stratvert PA PO Box 25687 Albuquerque NM 87125-0687

MILLER, RICHARD SHERWIN, law educator; b. Boston, Dec. 11, 1930; s. Max and Mollie Miller; m. Doris Sheila Lunchick, May 24, 1956 (dec. April 23, 2005); children: Andrea Jayne Armitage, Matthew Harlan. BSBA, Boston U., 1951, JD magna cum laude, 1956; LLM, Yale U., New Haven, Conn., 1959. Bar: Mass. 1956, Mich. 1961, Hawaii 1977. Pvt. practice law, Boston, 1956—58; assoc. prof. law Wayne State U., Detroit, 1959—62, prof., 1962—65; prof. law Ohio State U., Columbus, 1965—73, dir. clin. and interdisciplinary programs, 1972—73; prof. U. Hawaii, Honolulu, 1973-95, prof. emeritus, 1995—, dean, 1981-84, dir. summer externship program, 2006—. Vis. prof. law USHA/U. Hawaii, Hiroshima U. Affiliation Program, Japan, 1986, Victoria U., Wellington, New Zealand, 1987; del. Hawaii State Jud. Conf., 1989-92 Author: Courts and the Law: An Introduction to our Legal System, 1980; editor: (with Roland Stanger) Essays on Expropriations, 1967; editor-in-chief: Boston U. Law Rev., 1955-56; contbr. articles to profl. jours. Mem. Hawaii Substance Abuse Task Force, 1994-95; mem. Hawaii Patients Rights Task Force, 2005-06; arbitrator Hawaii Ct. Annexed Arbitration Program, 1995-99; bd. dirs. Drug Policy Forum Hawaii, 1996—, Kokua Coun., 2007—; mem. Save our Star-Bulletin Com., 1999-2001, Citizens for Competitive Air Travel, 2002, Citizens Against Gasoline Price Gouging, 2003-; cons. Hawaii Coalition for Health, 1997-. 1st Lt. USAF, 1951—53. Sterling-Ford fellow Yale U., 1958-59; named Lawyer of Yr. Japan-Hawaii Lawyers Assn., 1990; recipient Cmty. Svc. award Hawaii Med. Assn. Alliance, 1999. Mem. ABA, Hawaii State Bar Assn., Hawaii ACLU, Am. Inn of Ct. IV (emeritus founding mem., master of the bench), Am. Law Inst., Honolulu Cmty.-Media Coun. (chair 1994-89, treas. 2000-02, vice chair 1998-2000), Yale Club of Hawaii., Am Humanist Assoc. 2007- Democrat. Office: U Hawaii Richardson Sch Law 2515 Dole St Honolulu HI 96822-2328 Business E-Mail: rmiller@aya.yale.edu.

MILLER, ROBERT A., JR., lawyer; b. LA, July 30, 1954; BSBA, U. ND, 1976; JD, Loyola Law Sch., 1983. Bar: Calif. 1984. Fin. & acctg. positions airline industry, 1976—83; ptnr. Paul, Hastings, Janofsky & Walker LLP, LA, vice chmn. corp. dept. Office: Paul Hastings Janofsky & Walker LLP 515 S Flower St 25th Floor Los Angeles CA 90071-2228 Office Phone: 213-683-6254. Office Fax: 213-627-0705. Business E-Mail: robertmiller@paulhastings.com.

MILLER, ROBERT CARMI, JR., microbiology educator, university administrator; b. Elgin, Ill., Aug. 10, 1942; s. Robert C. and Melba I. (Steinke) M.; m. Patricia A. Black, Aug. 29, 1964; children: Geoffrey T., Christopher J. BS in Physics, Trinity Coll., Hartford, Conn., 1964; MS in Biophysics, Pa. State U., 1965; PhD in Molecular Biology, U. Pa., 1969. USPHS trainee U. Pa., Phila., 1966-69; postdoctoral fellow U. Wis., Madison, 1969-70; rsch. assoc., Am. Cancer Soc. postdoctoral fellow MIT, Cambridge, 1970-71; asst. assoc. prof. U. B.C., Vancouver, 1971-79, prof. microbiology, 1980-96, head dept. microbiology, 1982-85, dean sci., 1985-88, v.p. rsch., 1988-95, univ. senate, 1985-88; assoc. vice provost for rsch., dir. technology transfer U. Wash., Seattle, 1995-2000, vice provost, 2000—01; vice chancellor rsch. U. Calif., Santa Cruz, 2001—. Vis. prof. Inst. Molecular Biology, U. Geneva, Switzerland, 1976; mem. grants com. on genetics Med. Rsch. Coun., 1980-82; mem. Grants Panel A Nat. Cancer Inst., 1981-85; biotech. com. B.C. Sci. Coun., 1981-87, univ./industry program grant com., 1987-92; biotech. com. Med. Rsch. Coun., 1983; assoc. com. for biotech. NRC, 1983-86; strategic grant com. biotech. NSERC, 1985-87; bd. dirs. Paprican, Discovery Found., Sci. Coun. B.C., TRIUMF. Assoc. editor: Virology, 1974—85, Jour. Virology, 1975—84, contbr. over 125 articles to profl. jours.:, author rsch. papers:. Recipient gold medal Nat. Sci. Coun. B.C., 1993; grantee Natural Sci. and Engring. Rsch. Coun., 1971-96, Med. Rsch. Coun., 1981, 86-89, Nat. Cancer Inst., 1982-86. Fellow: Royal Soc. Can. Office: U Calif Santa Cruz Social Scis II Rm 261 Santa Cruz CA 95060 Business E-Mail: rcmiller@cats.ucsc.edu.

MILLER, ROBERT JOSEPH, lawyer, former governor; b. Evanston, Ill., Mar. 30, 1945; s. Ross Wendell and Coletta Jane (Doyle) Miller; m. Sandra Ann Searles, Oct. 17, 1949; children: Ross, Corrine, Megan. BA in Polit. Sci., U. Santa Clara, 1967; JD, Loyola U., 1971. First legal advisor Las Vegas (Nev.) Met. Police Dept., 1973—75; justice of the peace Las Vegas Twp., 1975—78; dep. dist. atty. Clark County, Las Vegas, 1971—73, dist. atty., 1979—86; lt. gov. State of Nev., 1987—89, gov., 1989—98; sr. ptnr. Jones Vargas, Las Vegas, 1999—2005; prin. Dutko Worldwide, Las Vegas, Nev., 2005—. Bd. dir. Newmont Mining Corp., Zenith Nat. Ins. Corp., Wynn Resorts Ltd. Chmn. Nev. Commn. on Econ. Devel., Carson City, 1987—91, Nev. Commn. on Tourism, Carson City, 1987—91; mem. Pres. Reagan's Task Force on Victims of Crime, 1982; chmn. Nev. divsn. Am. Cancer Soc., 1988—90. Res. E-6 USAF, 1967—73. Recipient Nat. Advisor on Victim's Rights award, Nat. Org. for Victim Assistance, 1982, Life Achievement award, 1999, Women's Dem. Club award, 1983, Appreciation award, Am. Cancer Soc., 1983—84, Excalibur award, 1997, Silver Lily award, Easter Seals, 1985, Common Cause Ethics in Govt. award, 1990, Inaugural award for State Art Leadership, Americans for Arts, 1997, Breaking the Glass Ceiling award, Women Exec. in State Govt., 1997, Pres.'s medal, Claremont Grad. U. Ctr. for Edn. Studies, 1998, Monarch award, Nathan Adelson Hospice, 1998, Cmty. Hero Medallion, Nat. Conf. Cmty. and Justice, 1998, Life Achievement award, Nev. Mining Assn., 1998; named Law Enforcement Man of Yr., Downtown Optimist Club, Nev., 1980, Man of Yr., B'nai B'rith, 1985. Mem.: Nev. Dist. Attys. Assn. (pres. 1979, 1983), Nat. Govs. Assn. (vice chmn. exec. com. 1995—96, chmn. 1996—97, past chmn. com. on justice and pub. safety, chmn. legal affairs com. 1992—94, lead gov. on transp. 1992—, Bldg. Block award for Progress in Edn. 1998), Western Govs. Assn. (chmn. 1993—94), Nat. Dist. Attys. Assn. (pres. 1984—85, Pres.'s award 1983). Democrat. Roman Catholic. Office: Dutko Worldwide 900 S Pavilion Ctr Dr Las Vegas NV 89144 Office Phone: 702-240-0831.

MILLER, ROBERT NOLEN, lawyer; b. Monmouth, Ill., May 30, 1940; s. Robert Clinton and Doris Margaret (Nolen) M.; m. Diane Wilmarth, Aug. 21, 1965; children: Robert Wilmarth, Anne Elizabeth. BA, Cornell Coll., Mt. Vernon, Iowa, 1962; JD, U. Colo., 1965. Bar: Colo. 1965. Assoc. firm M. Quiat, Denver, 1965-66, Fischer & Beaty, Ft. Collins, Colo., 1969-70; dist. atty. Weld County Dist. Atty's. Office, Greeley, Colo., 1971-81; U.S. atty. U.S. Dept. Justice, Denver, 1981-88; chief counsel litigation and security US West Inc., Englewood, Colo., 1988-93; of counsel Patton, Boggs & Blow, Denver, 1993-94; ptnr., head litig. LeBoeuf, Lamb, Greene & Mac Crae, Denver, 1994—2003; mng. ptnr. Perkins Coie, Denver, 2003—. Instr. bus. law Am. U., U. SC, Myrtle Beach, 1966-69; mem. Gov.'s Commn. for Columbine and Civil Justice Reform, 1999-2000; mem. Supreme Ct. Nominating Commn., 1999-2005; bd. dir., pres. Colorado Judicial Inst. 2004-. Co-author: Deathroads, 1978; White Color Law, 2007. Bd. dirs. Boys Club, Greeley, 1974-78, 1st Congl. Ch., Greeley, 1975-78; Rep. candidate for atty. gen. Colo., 1977-78. Capt. USAF, 1966-69. Recipient Citizen of Yr. award Elks Club, Greeley, Colorado Super Lawyer, Best Lawyers Am. Mem. Denver Bus. Jour., Fed. Bar Assn. (pres. Colo. chpt. 1983-84), Colo. Dist. Atty's Coun. (pres. 1976-77), Colo. Bar Assn., Weld County Bar Assn., Rotary (pres. local chpt. 1980-81). Republican. Avocations: fishing, hunting, reading. Office: Perkins Coie 1899 Wynkoop Ste 700 Denver CO 80202-1043 Office Phone: 303-291-2313. Business E-Mail: rmiller@perkinscioe.com.

MILLER, RONALD, journalist, critic; b. Santa Cruz, Calif., Feb. 28, 1939; s. Fred Robert and Evelyn Lenora Miller; m. Darla-Jean Irene Rode, Nov. 2, 1963. AA, Monterey Peninsula Coll., 1958; BA, San Jose State U., 1961. Reporter Santa Cruz (Calif.) Sentinel, 1959-62; reporter, chief news bur. San Jose (Calif.) Mercury News, 1962-77, editor T.V., 1977-99; syndicated TV columnist Knight Ridder Syndicate, 1978-99. Commentator, critic Sta. KLOK, San Jose, 1981-83; nat. judge Cableace awards, 1987; adj. instr. Whatcom C.C., Bellingham, Wash., 2001-04, Western Wash. U., 2003—. Author: (foreword) Les Brown's Encyclopedia of Television, 1992; co-author: Masterpiece Theatre, 1995, Author: Mystery! A Celebration, 1996 (Agatha, Anthony, and Macavity award nominee 1996-97); columnist, mng. editor The Columnists.com website, 1999—; mystery columnist Alibris.com. website, 2000, PBS mystery.com website, 2001-2002; program host Am. Mus. Radio and Electricity, 2003; TV columnist Mystery Scene Mag., 2004-. Recipient Nat. Spot News Photo award Sigma Delta Chi, 1961, Outstanding Alumnus award San Jose State U. Dept. Journalism and Mass Comm., 1985, Nat. Headline award Press Club Atlantic City, 1994. Democrat. Home and Office: 5437 Canvasback Rd Blaine WA 98230

MILLER, RONALD ALFRED, family physician; b. Orange, Calif., Sept. 27, 1943; s. Alfred Casper and Inez Geraldine (Gunderson) M.; m. Jean Ilene Andrews, June 18, 1966; children: Jon, Lauri, Bryan. BA, Pacific Luth. U., 1965; MD, U. Wash., 1969. Diplomate Am. Bd. Family Practice (bd. dirs. 1985-90, pres. bd. 1989-90). Intern in medicine Parkland Meml. Hosp., Dallas, 1969-70; gen. practice residency USPHS Gallup Indian Med. Ctr., Gallup, N.Mex., 1970-72; prin. Medical Doctor Glacier Med Assocs., Whitefish, Mont., 1972—. Clin. prof. U. Wash., Seattle, 1975—; coord. community clin. unit in family medicine, U. Wash., Whitefish, 1975—; bd. dirs. Utah Med. Ins. Assn., Salt Lake City, 1987—. Bd. dirs. Whitefish Housing Authority, 1977-82; mem. alumni bd. Pacific Luth. U., Tacoma, 1976-81, pres., 1979-80; mem. Glacier Community Chorale, Whitefish, 1984—, bd. dirs., 1990-92. Lt. comdr. USPHS, 1970-72. Mem. Am. Acad. Family Physicians (com. on continuing med. edn. 1977-81, com. on edn. 1984-89, Mead Johnson award Grad. Edn. in Family Practice 1972), Mont. Acad. Family Physicians (bd. dirs., sec./treas, v.p., pres. 1982-83, del. nat. congress 1978-84), Rotary, Alpha Omega Alpha. Republican. Lutheran. Avocations: hunting, fishing, skiing, backpacking, singing. Home: 1046 7th St W Whitefish MT 59937-3227 Office: 1111 Baker Ave Whitefish MT 59937-2905

MILLER, RONALD D., medical educator, researcher; Prof. cellular & molecular pharmacology Univ. Calif., San Francisco, chmn. Dept Anesthesia and Perioperative Care. Office: Univ Calif Dept Anesthesia C-450 Box 0648 521 Parnassus St San Francisco CA 94143-0648 E-mail: millerr@anesthesia.ucsf.edu.

MILLER, ROSS JAMES, secretary of state; b. Las Vegas, Mar. 26, 1976; s. Bob and Sandy Miller; m. Lesley Miller; 1 child, Cameron Elise. BA in English, Stanford U., Calif., 1999; student, Monterrey Technol. Inst., Mex.; JD/MBA, Loyola Marymount U., LA, 2002. Dep. dist. atty. Clark County, Nev.; sec. state State of Nev., Carson City, 2007—. Past pres. Citizen Alert, Nev.; bd. mem. HELP of So. Nev.; bd. mem. Legacy Soc. Boys and Girls Clubs. Democrat. Office: Office Sec State 101 N Carson #3 Carson City NV 89701 Office Phone: 775-684-5708. Business E-Mail: sosexec@sos.nv.gov.

MILLER, SCOTT D., lawyer; b. Redondo Beach, Calif., 1961; BSE, Ariz. State U., 1982; JD, Columbia U., 1985. Bar: Calif. 1987. Law clk. William A. Norris, US Ct. of Appeals (9th cir.), 1985—86; assoc. Sullivan & Cromwell, Palo Alto, ptnr., and co-head, tech. practice specialty group. Named one of 12 "Dealmakers of the Yr.", The American Lawyer, 2003—04. Office: Sullivan & Cromwell 1870 Embarcadero Rd Palo Alto CA 94303-3308 Office Phone: 650-461-5620. Office Fax: 650-461-5700. Business E-Mail: millersc@sullcrom.com.

MILLER, SEAN, men's college basketball coach; b. Pa., Nov. 17, 1968; B, U. Pitts., 1992. Asst. coach U. Wis. Badgers, 1992—93, Miami U. Red Hawks, Ohio, 1993—95, U. Pitts. Panthers, 1995—96, NC State U. Wolfpack, 1996—2001; assoc. head coach Xavier U. Musketeers, 2001—04, head coach, 2004—09, U. Ariz. Wildcats, 2009—. Named Dist. 10 Coach of Yr., Nat. Assn. Basketball Coaches. Office: Univ Ariz Athletics McKale Ctr 1 National Championship Dr PO Box 210096 Tucson AZ 85721-0096*

MILLER, SUSAN CALABRESE, lawyer, consumer products company executive; b. Groton, Conn., June 5, 1959; AB summa cum laude, Duke Univ., 1980; JD, Harvard Univ., 1984. Bar: Pa. 1984, Calif. 1985. Assoc. Latham & Watkins, LA; sr. counsel Avery Dennison, Pasadena, Calif., 1991—95, sr. counsel Asia Pacific Hong Kong, 1995—98, asst. gen. counsel Pasadena, Calif., 1998—2007, v.p., gen. counsel, 2007—08, sr. v.p., gen. counsel, 2008—. Mem.: ABA, LA County Bar Assn., Phi Beta Kappa. Office: Avery Dennison Corp 150 N Orange Grove Blvd Pasadena CA 91103

MILLER, TERRY W., dean, educator, legal association administrator; b. Clinton, Okla., July 7, 1948; s. Gerald and Bess Miller; m. Julie Randolph, May 5, 1979; children: Celeste, Cody, Haley, Harrison BS, U. Okla., 1971, BSN, 1974; MSN, U. Tex., 1977, PhD, 1991. Mem. faculty East Ctrl. Okla. State U., 1975-79; prof. San Jose (Calif.) State U., 1980-98; dir. adult health NCLEX-RN, CTB/MGraw-Hill, Monterey, Calif., 1987-88; prof., dean Sch. Nursing, Pacific Luth. U., Tacoma, Wash., 1998—. Owner, cons. Miller-Randolph & Assocs., Okla., Tex., Calif., Wash.; mem. exec. adv. bd. Calif. Nursing/NURSEweek; cons. HCOP grant; project dir. advanced edn. nursing tng. program, 1998. Author: Clinical Nursing Skillls, 1985, Community Health Nursing, 1995; (with others) Community Health Nursing: Concepts and Practice, 3d edit., 1990; contbg. author: Nurses Taking the Lead, 1999. Mem. statewide acad. senate Calif. State Univ. System. Post-baccalaureate fellow, 1989-91; Shirley C. Titus scholar, 1988. Mem. ANA (del. biennial conv. 1980, chair med.-surg. div. on practice for Okla. 1978-80). E-mail: millertw@plu.edu.

MILLER, THOMAS ROBBINS, lawyer, publisher; b. Chgo., Mar. 8, 1938; s. William Whipple and Helen (Robbins) M.; m. Tran Tuong Nhu, July 3, 1974; children: Toby, Teddy, Nathalie, Gabriella. BA, Yale U., 1960; LLB, Stanford U., 1965; cert., Parker Sch. Fgn. and Comparative Law, Columbia U., 1966. Bar: N.Y. 1966, Calif. 1974. Assoc. Webster & Sheffield, NYC, 1965-68; sole practice NYC, 1968-74, Berkeley, 1974-89; pub. Lancaster Miller Pubs., Berkeley, 1974-89; sr. ptnr. Miller & Ngo, PLC, Oakland, Calif., 1989—. Founder, pres. Internat. Children's Fund, Berkeley, 1974—; cons. Peace Corps, Washington, 1961, Ctr. for Constl. Rights, UNICEF, N.Y.C., 1973-76; dep. dir. Calif. Rural Legal Assistance, San Francisco, 1977-79; gen. counsel Global Exch.; co-founder Parwaz Afghan Women's Microlending Fund. Named 1 of 10 Outstanding Young Men in U.S., U.S. Jaycees, 1974 Democrat. Office: Miller & Ngo 725 Washington St Oakland CA 94607-3924 Office Phone: 510-891-0616. Personal E-mail: viasco@aol.com.

MILLER, TIMOTHY ALDEN, plastic and reconstructive surgeon; b. Inglewood, Calif., Dec. 11, 1938; s. Henry Bernard and Florence Algena (Maddock) M.; 1 child, Matthew Christopher. Student, U. Calif., Berkeley; MD, UCLA, 1963. Diplomate Am. Bd. Surgery, Am. Bd. Plastic Surgery (dir. 1991-97). Intern Vanderbilt U. Hosp., Nashville, 1963-64; resident in surgery, dept. surg. pathology UCLA, 1966-67, resident, then chief resident gen. and thoracic surgery, 1967-69, acting asst. prof., 1969-70, prof. surgery, 1981—; asst. surg. resident John Hopkins Hosp., 1967; fellow plastic and reconstructive surgery U. Pitts., 1970-72; chief plastic surgery West Wadsworth VA Med. Ctr., 1973—; prof., chief plastic and reconstructive surgery UCLA Sch. Medicine, 2002—. Author: (novel) Practice to Deceive, 1991; assoc. editor Jour. Plastic & Reconstructive Surgery, 1987-93, co-editor, 1994-99. Trustee Children's Inst. Internat., 1995-2000. Capt. U.S. Army, 1964-66, Vietnam (Bronze Star, 1966, Vietnam Spl. Forces Parachute award, 1966). Recipient Thomas Symington award Pitts. Acad. Medicine, 1971, Ralph Goldman Rsch. award, 1996, 1999. Mem. Am. Soc. for Plastic Surgery (co-editor Jour. Plastic and Reconstructive Surgery), Am. Soc. for Aesthetic Plastic Surgery (bd. dirs. 1990-95), Am. Soc. Surgery of Hand, Am. Soc. Maxillofacial Surgeons, Plastic Surgery Ednl. Found. (bd. dirs. 1991-95), Plastic Surgery Rsch. Coun.; Phi Beta Kappa. Office: UCLA Med Ctr 200 UCLA Med Plz Ste 465 Los Angeles CA 90095-8344 Office Phone: 310-825-5644. Business E-Mail: tmiller@mednet.ucla.edu.

MILLER, WALKER DAVID, federal judge; b. Denver, Colo., 1939; m. Susanne Hauk; 3 children. LLB, U. Colo., 1963; M in Comparative Law, U. Chgo., 1965. Bar: Colo. 1963, U.S. Dist. Ct. 1965, U.S. Ct. Appeals 1971, U.S. Supreme Ct. 1970. Asst. prof. law U. Kans. Sch. Law, Lawrence, 1966-69; ptnr. Miller & Ruyle, Greeley, Colo., 1969, Miller, Ruyle, Steinmark & Shade, Greeley, 1970-74; pvt. law practice Greeley, Colo., 1974-92; ptnr. Karowsky, Witwer, Miller and Oldenburg, Greeley, 1992-96; judge US Dist. Ct. Colo., Denver, 1996—2008, sr. judge, 2008—. Office: US Dist Ct Colo 901 19th St Rm A938 Denver CO 80294-1929 Office Phone: 303-844-2468. E-mail: walker_d_miller@cod.uscourts.gov.*

MILLER, WALTER LUTHER, scientist, pediatrician, educator; b. Alexandria, Va., Feb. 21, 1944; s. Luther Samuel and Beryl (Rinderle) M. SB, MIT, 1965; MD, Duke U., 1970. Diplomate Am. Bd. Pediatrics. Intern, then resident Mass. Gen. Hosp., Boston, 1970-72; staff assoc. NIH, Bethesda, Md., 1972-74; sr. resident U. Calif., San Francisco, 1974-75, rsch. fellow, 1975-78, asst. prof. pediatrics, 1978-83, assoc. prof., 1983-87, prof., 1987—, dir. Child Health Rsch. Ctr., 1992—2003, faculty biomed. scis. grad. program, 1982—, faculty genetics grad. program, 1998—, dir. pediat. endocrinology tng. program, 1994—, chief divsn. endocrinology, 2000—, assoc. prof. metabolic rsch. unit, 1983-87, prof., 1987—. Bd. scientific counselors Nat. Inst. of Child Health & Human Devel., 2004—. Editor DNA and Cell Biology Jour., 1983—; mem. editl. bds. numerous sci. jours.; contbr. articles to profl. jours., chpts. to books. Del. Dem. Nat. Conv., NYC, 1976. Served with USPHS, 1972-74. Recipient Nat. Rsch. Svc. award NIH, 1975, Clin. Investigator award, 1978, Albion O Bernstein award NY Med. Soc., 1993, Clin. Endocrinology Trust medal Brit. Endocrine Soc., 1993, Henning Andersen prize European Soc. Pediatric Endocrinology, 1993, Samuel Rosenthal Found. prize for excellence in acad. pediatrics, 1999. Fellow: AAAS, Molecular Medicine Soc.; mem.: Androgen Excess Soc. (founding mem., bd. dirs. 2002—05), Am. Soc. Biochem. Molecular Biology, Lawson Wilkins Pediat. Endocrine Soc. (edn. com. 1992—96, coun. 1995—96, corp. adv. bd. 1998—2002, program dirs. com. 2004—), Am. Soc. Clin. Investigation, Am. Soc. Human Genetics, Endocrine Soc. (fin. com. 1999—2002, annual meeting steering com. 2005—07, Edwin B. Astwood lecture award 1988, Clin. Investigator Lectr. award 2006), European Soc. for Paediatric Endocrinology (hon.), Japanese Soc. for Pediat. Endocrinology (hon.), We. Soc. Pediat. Rsch. (Ross Rsch. award 1982), Soc. Pediat. Rsch., Am. Pediat. Soc., Am. Acad. Pediats., Assn. Am. Physicians, Am. Soc. for Microbiology, Theta Delta Chi. Achievements include patents in field; published in over 330 publs. Office: U Calif Med Ctr Dept Pediat Rm 672 S San Francisco CA 94143-0978

MILLER, WILLIAM, broadcast executive; b. Chgo., June 17, 1943; Gen. mgr. KTVK-TV, Phoenix, 1994—. Office: KTVK TV 5555 N 7th Ave Phoenix AZ 85013-1701

MILLER, WILLIAM CHARLES, architect, educator; b. San Francisco, May 11, 1945; s. Francis Leland and Ethel Lorene (Britt) M.; m. Beverly Jean McConnell, Dec. 22, 1968; children: Britt A., David A. BArch, U. Oreg., 1968; MArch, U. Ill., 1970. Cert. arch. Nat. Coun. Archtl. Registration Bds., Ariz., Kans., Utah. Asst. prof. Coll. Architecture U. Ariz., Tucson, 1970—77; assoc. prof. dept. architecture Kans. State U., Manhattan, 1977-86, prof., 1986-92, head dept., 1990-92; prof. Coll. of Architecture and Planning U. Utah, Salt Lake City, 1992—, dean, 1992—2002; architect various firms. Guest lectr. in field; presenter numerous profl. socs. and orgns.; dir. west ctrl. region Assn. Collegiate Schs. Architecture, 1988-91, chair theme paper sessions ann. meeting, San Francisco, 1990, chair regional paper sessions ann. meeting, Washington, 1991, co-chair adminstrv. conf., Milw., 1995; bd. dirs. Nat. Archtl. Accrediting Bd., 1996-99; mem. Utah Architects Lic. Bd., 2000-08; chair edn. com. NCARB, 2005-08; vis. disting. prof. U. Ill., Urbana Champain, 2003; chair nomenclature commn., NAAB, 2003. Author: Alvar Aalto: An Annotated Bibliography, 1984; co-editor: The Architecture of the In-Between, 1990, Architecture: Back to Life, 1991; contbr. over 60 articles to profl. jours., chpts. to books. Bd. dirs. Assist, Inc., 1992-2002, Artspace, Inc., 1997-2002, Contemporary Arts Group, 1992-96, Salt Lake City Art Design Bd., 1995-2003. Recipient Disting. Prof. award Assn. Collegiate Schs. Architecture, 2004, Svc. awards Nat. Coun. Archtl. Registration Bds., Nat. Archtl. Accrediting Bd. Fellow AIA (ALA Utah Bronze medal award, 2007, pres-elect Flint Hills, treas. Utah, exec. com., treas., exec. com. Western Mountain region, elected coll. of fellows 1997, adv. com. 2007—); mem. Am.-Scandinavian Found., Soc. for Advancement Scandinavian Studies, Tau Sigma Delta, NCARB(chair com. edu.) Office: U Utah Coll Architecture & Planning Salt Lake City UT 84112 Office Phone: 801-581-8254. Business E-Mail: miller@arch.utah.edu.

MILLER, WILLIAM FREDERICK, research and development company executive, educator, financial consultant; b. Vincennes, Ind., Nov. 19, 1925; s. William and Elsie M. (Everts) M.; m. Patty J. Smith, June 19, 1949; 1 son, Rodney Wayne. Student, Vincennes U., 1946-47; BS, Purdue U., 1949, MS, 1951, PhD, 1956; DSc (hon.), 1972. Mem. staff Argonne Nat. Lab., 1955-64, assoc. physicist, 1956-59, dir. applied math. div., 1959-64; prof. computer sci. Stanford U., Palo Alto, Calif., 1965-97, Herbert Hoover prof. pub. and pvt. mgmt. emeritus, 1997—, assoc. provost for computing, 1968-70, v.p. for rsch., 1970-71, v.p., provost, 1971-78; mem. Stanford Assocs., 1972—; pres emeritus., CEO SRI Internat., Menlo Park, Calif., 1979-90; chmn. bd., CEO SRI Devel. Co., Menlo Park, David Sarnoff Rsch. Ctr., Inc., Princeton, NJ, 1987—90. Chmn. emeritus bd. dirs. Borland Software, Sentius Corp.; founder, chmn. Nanostellar, Inc.; professorial lectr. applied math. U. Chgo., 1962-64; vis. prof. math. Purdue U., 1962-63; vis. scholar Ctr. for Advanced Study in Behavioral Scis., 1976; mem. adv. coun. BHP Internat., 1990-97; computer sci. and engring bd. NAS, 1968-71; mem. Nat. Sci. Bd., 1982-88; corp. com. computers in edn. Brown UU., 1971-79; mem. policy bd. EDUCOM Planning Coun. on Computing in Edn., 1974-79, chmn., 1974-76; mem. ednl. adv. bd. Guggenheim Meml. Found., 1976-80; com. postdoctoral and doctoral rsch. staff NRC, 1977-80, computer sci. and telecom.; dir. Fund Am., 1977-91, Fireman's Fund Ins., 1977-91, Wells Fargo Bank and Co., 1996-97, Varian Assocs. Inc., 1973-96. Mem. editl. bd. Pattern Recognition Jour, 1968-72, Jour. Computational Physics, 1970-74. Served to 2d lt. F.A. AUS, 1943-46. Recipient Frederic B. Whitman award United Way Bay Area, 1982, Sarnoff Founders medal, 1997, David Packard Civic Entrepreneurship Team award, 1998, Robert K. Jaedicke Silver Apple award Stanford U. Bus. Sch. Alumni, 1998, The Dongbaeg medal Order of Civil Merit, The Rep. of Korea, 2000, The Okawa prize, The Okawa Found. for Info. and Telecoms., 2000, Most Mentor award Internat. Angel Investors, 2002; named to Silicon Valley Engring. Hall of Fame, 2001, Jr. Achievement Bus. Hall of Fame, 2002. Fellow IEEE (life), Am. Acad. Arts and Scis., AAAS; mem. Soc. Indsl. and Applied Math., Assn. Computing Machinery, Nat. Acad. Engring., Sigma Xi, Tau Beta Pi (Eminent Engr. 1989). Office: Stanford U Grad Sch Bus Stanford CA 94305

MILLER, WILLIAM HUGHES, theoretical chemist, educator; b. Kosciusko, Miss., Mar. 16, 1941; s. Weldon Howard and Jewel Irene (Hughes) M.; m. Margaret Ann Westbrook, June 4, 1966; children: Alison Leslie, Emily Sinclaire. BS in Chemistry, Ga. Inst. Tech., 1963; AM, Harvard U., 1964, PhD in Chemical Physics, 1967. Jr. fellow Harvard U. Soc. Fellows, 1967-69; NATO postdoctoral fellow Freiburg U., Germany, 1967-68; asst. prof. chemistry U. Calif., Berkeley, 1969-72, assoc. prof., 1972-74, prof., 1974—, dept. chmn., 1989-93, chancellor's prof., 1998—2001, Kenneth S. Pitzer disting. prof., 1999—. Fellow Churchill Coll., Cambridge (Eng.) U., 1975-76; hon. prof. Shandong U., People's Republic of China, 1994. Alfred P. Sloan fellow, 1970-72; Camille and Henry Dreyfus fellow, 1973-78; Guggenheim fellow, 1975-76, Christensen fellow St. Catherine's Coll., Oxford, 1993; recipient Alexander von Humboldt-Stiftung U.S. Sr. Scientist award, 1981-82, Ernest Orlando Lawrence Meml. award, 1985, Hirschfelder prize in theoretical chemistry, U. Wis., 1996, Alumni Achievement award Ga. Inst. Tech., 1997, Spiers medal Faraday divsn. Royal Soc. Chemistry, London, 1998. Fellow AAAS, Am. Acad. Arts and Scis., Am. Phys. Soc. (Irving Langmuir in Chem. Physics award 1990); mem. NAS, Am. Chem. Soc. (Theoretical Chemistry award 1994, Ira Remsen award 1997, Peter Debye award 2003), Internat. Acad. Quantum Molecular Sci. (Ann. prize 1974), Herschbach award in chem. dynamics 2007, Welsh award in chemistry 2007). Office: U Calif Dept Chemistry Berkeley CA 94720-0001

MILLER, WILLIAM NAPIER CRIPPS, lawyer; b. Long Branch, NJ, June 7, 1930; adopted s. Julia (Erwin) M.; m. Carolyn Anderson, Jan. 19, 1951 (div. 1963); children: Bruce Douglass, Jennifer Erwin; m. Hannelore Steinbeck, Dec. 4, 1970 AA, Coll. Marin, 1949; student, U. Calif.-Berkeley, 1949-51, JD, 1955. Bar: N.Y., Calif. 1956, U.S. Supreme Ct. 1983. Assoc. Mudge, Stern, Baldwin & Todd, NYC, 1955-58, Pillsbury, Madison & Sutro, San Francisco, 1959-65; ptnr. Pillsbury, Winthrop Shaw Pittman LLP, San Francisco, 1966—; staff NYU Law Sch., 1957-58; ct. adv. com. Calif. State Assembly Judiciary Com., 1979-80. Author: Long Pig, 2002. Bd. dirs. Laguna Honda Hosp., San Francisco, 1966—; bd. visitors U. Calif.-Hastings Law Sch. Served with USAF, 1951-52. Served USAF, 1950—52. Recipient Bur. Nat. Affairs award U. Calif.-Hastings, 1955; recipient Thurston Soc. award, 1953. Fellow Am. Coll. Trial Lawyers; mem. ABA, San Francisco Bar Assn., Order of Coif, St. Francis Yacht Club. Home: 16 George Ln Sausalito CA 94965-1890 Office: Pillsbury Winthrop Shaw Pittman LLP PO Box 7880 San Francisco CA 94120-7880 Home Phone: 415-332-6665; Office Phone: 415-983-1464. Business E-Mail: william.miller@pillsburylaw.com.

MILLER, WILLIAM RICHEY, JR., lawyer; b. Oklahoma City, Apr. 4, 1947; s. William Richey and Edna Rosalind (Nielsen) M.; m. Susan Hammond, Aug. 2, 1970; children: Brooke, Karen. BA, Pomona Coll., Claremont, Calif., 1969; MA, Claremont Grad. Sch., 1972; JD, Lewis and Clark Coll., 1975. Bar: Oreg. 1975, U.S. Dist. Ct. Oreg. 1976, U.S. Ct. Appeals (9th cir.) 1976. Staff atty. Oreg. Ct. Appeals, Salem, 1975-76; with firm Griffith, Bittner, Abbott & Roberts, Portland, Oreg., 1976-83; ptnr. Davis Wright Termaine, Portland, 1983—. Adj. prof. Lewis and Clark Law Sch., 1975-78. Bd. dirs. Portland Civic Theatre, 1988-91, Am. Lung Assn. Oreg., Portland, 1985-88, Oreg. Bus. Com. for the Arts, Portland, 1991-93. Mem. Oreg. State Bar (sect. chair 1990-91), Comml. Fin. Assn., Oreg. Bankers Assn., Lewis and Clark Alumni Assn. (bd. dirs. 1989-92). Presbyterian. Home: 843 Lakeshore Rd Lake Oswego OR 97034-3704 Office: Davis Wright Tremaine 1300 SW 5th Ave Ste 2300 Portland OR 97201-5682 Office Phone: 503-778-5304.

MILLETT, CHARISSE E., state legislator; b. Feb. 11, 1964; m. Curtis Millett; children: Zachery, Ashley, Zane. Attended, U. Alaska, Anchorage, 1981—83. Airline employee & mgmt., 1981—2005; commercial fisher, 1992—; legis. aid, spl. asst., legis. liaison, spl. asst. comm. Dept. Adminstrn., 2005—07; mem. Alaska House of Reps from Dist. 30, 2008—. Former v.p. Abbott Loop Cmty. Coun.; former mem. Alaska Sch. Dist. Minority Edn. Concerns Adv. Com., Valdez, Kenai, Soldotna, & Homer C. of C.; former chmn. Dist. 30 Republicans; former bd. mem. Arctic Winter Games; mem. The Alliance, Resource Devel. Coun. Mem.: Am. Red Cross Alaska (bd. mem.), NRA (former bd. mem.). Republican. Office: State Capitol Terry Miller Bldg Ste 111 Rm 412 Juneau AK 99801-1182 Office Phone: 907-465-4648, 907-465-3879. Office Fax: 907-465-2864. Business E-Mail: Representative_Charisse_Millett@legis.state.ak.us.

MILLIGAN, JOHN F., information technology executive; PhD in Biochemistry, U. Ill. Rsch. scientist Gilead Sciences, Inc., 1990—96, dir. project mgmt., project team leader, Gilead Hoffmann-La Roche Tamiflu collaboration, 1996—98, corp. devel., 1998—2000, v.p. corp. devel., 2000—02, sr. v.p., 2002—03, prin. acctg. officer, CFO, 2002—08, exec. v.p., 2003—08, COO, 2007—, pres., 2008—. Named Bay Area CFO of Yr., 2006, Top Biotech. Industry CFO in the US, Instl. Investor mag., 2006—08; Am. Cancer Soc. postdoctoral fellow, U. Calif. San Francisco. Office: Gilead Sciences Inc 333 Lakeside Dr Foster City CA 94404 Office Phone: 650-574-3000. Office Fax: 650-578-9264.

MILLIGAN, SISTER MARY, theology studies educator, consultant; b. LA, Jan. 23, 1935; d. Bernard Joseph and Carolyn (Krebs) M. BA, Marymount Coll., 1956; Dr. de l'Univ., U. Paris, 1959; MA in Theology, St. Mary's Coll., Notre Dame, Ind., 1966; STD, Gregorian U., 1975; D. honoris causa, Marymount U., 1988. Tchr. Cours Marymount, Neuilly, France, 1956-59; asst. prof. Marymount Coll., Los Angeles, 1959-67; gen. councillor Religious of Sacred Heart of Mary, Rome, 1969-75, gen. superior, 1980-85; asst. prof. Loyola Marymount U., Los Angeles, 1977-78, provost, 1986-90, prof., 1990—96, dean liberal arts, 1992-97, provincial superior, 1997—2003; prof. St. John's Sem., 2003—. Pres. bd. dirs. St. John's Sem., Camarillo, Calif., 1986-89; mem. exec. com. Internat. Union Superiors Gen., Rome, 1983-85; mem. planning bd. spiritual renewal program Loyola Marymount U., Los Angeles, 1976-78. Author: That They May Have Life, 1975; compiler analytical index Ways of Peace, 1986; contbr. articles to profl. jours. Vis. scholar Grad. Theol. Union, Berkeley, 1986. Mem. Coll. Theology Soc., Cath. Biblical Assn. Democrat. Roman Catholic. Business E-Mail: mmilligan@stjohnsem.edu.

MILLIKAN, CLARK HAROLD, physician; b. Freeport, Ill., Mar. 2, 1915; s. William Clarance and Louise (Chamberlain) M.; m. Gayle Margaret Gross, May 2, 1942 (div. Apr. 1966); children: Terri, Clark William, Jeffry Brent; m. Janet T. Holmes, July 21, 1966 (div. Dec. 1987); m. Nancy Futrell, Dec. 28, 1987. Student, Parsons Jr. Coll., Kans., 1935; MD, U. Kans., 1939. Diplomate Am. Bd. Psychiatry and Neurology. Intern St. Luke's Hosp., Clev., 1939-40, asst. resident medicine, 1940-41; from resident neurology to asst. prof. neurology State U. Iowa, Iowa City, 1941-49; staff Mayo Clinic, Rochester, Minn., 1949—, cons. neurology, 1958—; dir. Mayo Center for Clin. Rsch. in Cerebrovascular Disease; prof. neurology Mayo Sch. Medicine; physician-in-chief pro tem Cleve. Clinic, 1970; prof. neurology U. Utah Sch. Medicine, Salt Lake City, 1976-87, U. Miami (Fla.) Sch. Medicine, 1987-88; scholar in residence, dept. neurology Henry Ford Hosp., Detroit, 1988-92; prof. neurology Sch. of Medicine Creighton

U., Omaha, 1992-94; clin. prof. neurology Med. Coll. Ohio, Toledo, 1994-97; dir. acad. affairs Intermountain Stroke Rsch. Found., Salt Lake City, 1997—. Asst. chmn., editor trans. 2d Princeton Conf. Cerebrovascular Disease, 1957, chmn. confs., 1961, 64; chmn. com. classification and nomenclature cerebrovascular disease USPHS, 1955-69; mem. council Nat. Inst. Neurologic Diseases and Blindness, NIH, USPHS, 1961-65, div. regional med. program, 1965-68; A.O.A. lectr. Baylor U., Waco, Tex., 1952; James Mawer Pearson Meml. lectr., Vancouver, B.C., Can., 1958; Conner Meml. lectr. Am. Heart Assn., 1961; Peter T. Bohan lectr. U. Kans., 1965, 73 Editor: Jour. Stroke, 1970-76, assoc. editor, 1976—. Recipient Outstanding Alumnus award, U. Kans., 1973. Fellow ACP, Am. Acad. Neurology (founding chmn. sect. on stroke and vascular neurology 1994), Royal Soc. Medicine; mem. AMA, AAUP, AAAS, Assn. Rsch. Nervous and Mental Disease (pres. 1961), Am. Neurol. Assn. (1st v.p. 1969-70, pres. 1973-74), Minn. Med. Assn., Four County Med. Soc. South Minn., Cen. Neuropsychiat. Assn., N.Y. Acad. Sci., Am. Heart Assn. (chmn. coun. cerebrovascular disease 1967-68, Gold Heart award 1976, Spl. Merit award 1981), Nat. Stroke Assn. (pres. 1986, editor Jour. Stroke and Cerebrovascular Disease 1990—), Sigma Xi. Office Phone: 801-263-0611. Office Fax: 801-263-9141.

MILLIKEN, MARY SUE, chef, television personality, writer; Former mem. staff Le Perroquet, Chgo., Restaurant d'Olympe, Paris; formerly chef, co-owner City Cafe, LA; chef, co-owner CITY, LA, 1985—94, Border Grill, LA, 1985—91, Santa Monica, 1990—, Las Vegas, 1999—, Ciudad, LA, 1998—. Co-host (TV series) Too Hot Tamales, 1995—, Tamales' World Tour, (radio show) Good Food; co-author: City Cuisine, 1989, Mesa Mexicana, 1994, Cantina, 1996, Cooking with Too Hot Tamales, 1997, Mexican Cooking for Dummies; guest appearances (TV series) Oprah Winfrey Show, Maury Povich, Today Show, Sabrina the Teenage Witch, featured in USA Today, People Mag., Entertainment Weekly. Active Scleroderma Rsch. Found. Named Chef of Yr., Calif. Restaurant Writers, 1993. Mem.: Chef's Collaborative 2000, Women Chefs and Restaurateurs. Office: Border Grill Santa Monica 445 S Figueroa St Ste 2950 Los Angeles CA 90071-1634

MILLIN, LAURA JEANNE, museum director; b. Elgin, Ill., June 11, 1954; d. Douglas Joseph and Patricia Ruth (Feragen) M. BA in Interdisciplinary Studies, The Evergreen State Coll., 1978. Dir. On The Boards, Seattle, 1979; art dir. City Fair Metrocenter YMCA, Seattle, 1980; dir. Ctr. on Contemporary Art, Seattle, 1981; co-owner Art in Form Bookstore, Seattle, 1981-89; co-dir. 3d internat festical of films by women dirs. Seattle Art Mus. & 911 Contemporary Arts, 1988; auction coord. Allied Arts of Seattle, 1989; exec. dir. Missoula Mus. of Arts, Mont., 1990—. Dir. Visual AIDS Missoula Mus. of the Arts, 1989; curator Radio COCA, Ctr. on Contemproary Art, Seattle, 1986, co-curator, 1981, 83; lectr. in field. Co-editor: Another (ind. feminist newspaper), Seattle, 1989, editor: (exhibition catalog) James Turrell: Four Light Installations, 1981. Bd. dirs. Internat. Festival of Films by Women Dirs., Seattle, 1987, 89, Nine One One Contemporary Arts Ctr., Seattle, 1981-87, bd. chmn. 1981-85; bd. advisors REFLEX (art mag.), Seattle, 1988-89, Ctr. on Contemporary Art, Seattle, 1983-86; state vis. Mont. Arts. Coun., Missoula, 1991, NEA, Mpls., 1988, Chgo., 1987; panelist Mont. Arts Coun., Helena, 1990; cons. Seattle Arts Commn., 1989, juror, 1985. Home: 1721 S 9th St W Missoula MT 59801-3432 Office: Missoula Art Mus 335 N Pattee St Missoula MT 59802-4520 Office Phone: 406-728-0447.

MILLIS, ROBERT LOWELL, astronomer, science observatory director; b. Martinsville, Ill., Sept. 12, 1941; m. Julia Drean, 1965; children: David, Daniel. BA, Ea. Ill. U., 1963; PhD in Astronomy, U. Wis., 1968. Staff astronomer Lowell Obs., Flagstaff, Ariz., 1967—86, assoc. dir., 1986—90, acting dir., 1989—90, dir., 1990—. Bd. dir. Mus. of No. Ariz., United Way of No. Ariz. Mem. Am. Astron. Soc., Internat. Astronomy Union, Divsn. Planetary Sci. (sec.-treas. 1985-88, chmn. 1994-95). Achievements include discovery of the Rings of Uranus (with J.L. Elliot); research in planetary satellites and ring systems; the occultation studies of solar system objects; comet and Kuiper belt objects. Office: Lowell Observatory 1400 W Mars Hill Rd Flagstaff AZ 86001-4499 Office Phone: 928-774-3358. Business E-Mail: rim@lowell.edu.

MILLNER, F. ANN, academic administrator; BS, Univ. Tenn.; MS, Southwest Tex. State Univ.; EdD, Brigham Young Univ. Assoc. dean, asst. v.p., dir. outreach edn. Weber State Univ., Ogden, Utah, 1982—93, v.p. univ. rels., 1993—2002, pres., 2002—. Trustee Intermountain Health Care; past pres. Ogden/Weber C. of C. Recipient Athena award, Ogden/Weber C. of C. Mem.: Am. Assn. State Colleges and Universities (mem. Coun. State Representatives), Phi Kappa Phi. Office: Weber State Univ President's Office 3850 University Circle Ogden UT 84408

MILLS, A(LVIN) J(ACKSON), JR., (JACK), lawyer; b. 1937; m. Cirrelda Mills; 3 children. BBA in acctg., U. Okla., 1960, LLB, 1963. Bar: 1963. Asst. athletic dir. U. Colo.; pvt. practice A.J. Mills Jr., P.C., 1966—. Adj. prof. U. Colo. Sch. Law; mem. agents adv. com. NFL Players Assn. Bd. dirs. Fellowship Christian Athletes, Colo. Served US Army. Recipient Joseph E. O'Neill award, Nat. Sports Law Inst., 1993. Mem.: Sports Lawyers Assn. (dir., past pres.), Colo. Bar Assn., Calif. Bar Assn. Office: AJ Mills Jr PC 1919 14th St #300 PO Box 187 Boulder CO 80306 Office Phone: 303-443-7770.

MILNER, HAROLD WILLIAM, hotel executive; b. Salt Lake City, Nov. 11, 1934; s. Kenneth W. and Olive (Schoettlin) Milner; m. Susan Emmett, June 19, 1959 (div. 1976); children: John Kenneth, Mary Sue; m. Lois Friemuth, Aug. 14, 1977; 1 child, Jennifer Rebecca. BS, U. Utah, 1960; MBA, Harvard, 1962. Instr. Brigham Young U., Provo, Utah, 1962-64; v.p. Gen. Paper Corp., Mpls., 1964-65; dir. finance Amalgamated Sugar Co., Ogden, Utah, 1965-67; corp. treas. Marriott Corp., Washington, 1967-70; pres., chief exec. officer, trustee Hotel Investors, Kensington, Md., 1970-75; pres., CEO Americana Hotels Corp., Chgo., 1975-85, Kahler Corp., Rochester, Minn., 1985-97, Kensington Co., Salt Lake City, 1997—. Trustee Baron Asset Funds, 1987—. Author: A Special Report on Contract Maintenance, 1963. Lt. US Army, 1960. Mem.: Minn. Bus. Partnership (bd. dirs. 1991—). Mem. Lds Ch. Office: The Kensington Co 2293 Morning Star Dr Park City UT 84060-6725 Office Phone: 435-640-1129. Personal E-mail: hmilner@aol.com.

MILONE, ANTHONY MICHAEL, bishop emeritus; b. Omaha, Nebr., Sept. 24, 1932; BA, Conception Sem., 1954; STB, Gregorian U., Rome, 1956, STL, 1958. Ordained priest Archdiocese of Omaha, Nebr., 1957; ordained bishop, 1982; aux. bishop Archdiocese of Omaha, Nebr., 1981—87; bishop Diocese of Great Falls-Billings, Mont., 1987—2006, bishop emeritus Mont., 2006—. Roman Catholic. Office: St Bernadette Ch So 42nd St Bellevue NE 68147-1702 also: Chancery Office 121 23rd St S PO Box 1399 Great Falls MT 59403-1399 Office Phone: 406-727-6683. Office Fax: 406-454-3480. E-mail: bishop@dioceseofgfb.org.

MILONE, EUGENE FRANK, astronomer, educator; b. NYC, June 26, 1939; arrived in Can., 1971; s. Frank Louis and Vera Christine (Joeckle) M.; m. Helen Catherine Louise (Ligor), Mar. 1, 1959; children: Bartholomew Vincenzo Llambro, Marie Christina Milone. AB, Columbia U., 1961; MS, Yale U., 1963, PhD, 1967. Astronomer, space sci. divsn., rocket spectroscopy br. Naval Rsch. Lab., Washington, 1967—79; asst. prof. Gettysburg (Pa.) Coll., 1968-71; asst. prof. dept. physics and astronomy U. Calgary, Alta., Canada, 1971—75, assoc. prof., 1976-81, prof., 1981—2005, Faculty prof., 2005—, prof. emeritus, 2005—; co-dir. Rothney Astrophys. Obs., 1975—2002, dir., 2002—04, dir. emeritus, 2005—. Organizer Internat. Symposium on the Origins, AAS Topical Sessions: Light Curve Modeling Improvements, 1997; Short-Period Binary Staus, 2006; Evolution and Destinies of Binary Stars in Clusters, U. Calgary, June 1995; chair rsch. grants com. U. Calgary, 1995-96. Author: Light Curve Modeling of Eclipsing Binary Stars, 1993, Solar System Astrophysics: Background Science and the Inner Solar System, vol. 1, 2008, Solar System Astrophysics: Planetary Atmospheres and the Outer Solar System, Vol. 2, 2008; editor: Infrared Extinction and Standardization, 1989, The Origins, Evolution, and Destinies of Binary Stars in Clusters, 1996; co-editor: Short-Period Binary Stars, 2007; co-author: Challenges of Astronomy, 1991, 2008, Eclipsing Binary Stars: Modeling and Analysis, 1999, Exploring Ancient Skies: An Encyclopedic Survey of Archaeoastronomy, 2005; contbr. articles to profl. jours. Elected mem. com. for coll. and univ. svcs. Evang. Luth. Ch. in Can., Synod of Alba. and the Territories, Edmonton, Alta., 1989-93. Grantee, Sci. Awareness and Promotion Program, 2002—06; Operating and Equipment grantee, Natural Scis. and Engring. Rsch. Coun. Can., 1972—, Innovation and Sci. program grantee, 2001—04, Killam resident, Killam Found. U. Calgary, 1982, 88. Mem. Internat. Astron. Union (mem. organizing com., commn. 25 1985-91, 94-2004, 2006-12, v.p. 2006-09, chair infrared astronomy working group 1988—), Am. Astron. Soc. (chmn. local organizing com. Calgary meeting 1981, co-chair 2006), Can. Astron. Soc., Sigma Xi (pres. U. Calgary chpt. 1979-80). Liberal Democrat. Lutheran. Achievements include development of Rothney Astrophysical Observatory, the Rapid Alternate Detection System, of light curve modeling techniques; research on the O'Connell Effect, on a new passband system for infrared photometry, research on binary stars in clusters, work on behalf of the proposed GAIA European space agency satellite. Home: 1031 Edgemont Rd NW Calgary AB T2N 1N4 Canada T3A 2J5 Office: U Calgary Dept Physics Astronomy 2500 University Dr NW Calgary AB Canada T2N 1N4 Home Phone: 403-239-2940; Office Phone: 403-220-5412. Business E-Mail: milone@ucalgary.ca.

MILSOME, DOUGLAS, cinematographer; Cinematographer: (TV movies) Dirty Dozen, Family of Spies, 1986, Hollywood Detective, Spies, Diana: Her True Story, Seasons of the Heart, Following Her Heart, 1995, Glory and Honor, (TV mini-series) Great Expectations, 1988, Lonesome Dove (Emmy nomination), Lonesome Dove II-The Return (Emmy nomination, ASC award), Old Curiosity Shop, Elizabeth Taylor, (films) Race for the Yankee Zephyr, Wild Horses, Full Metal Jacket (British Critics Cir. award 1987, Oscar nomination 1987), 1985, Hawks, The Beast, 1987, Desperate Hours, If Looks Could Kill-Teenagent, 1989, Robin Hood-Prince of Thieves, Last of the Mohicans (1st 7 weeks of the 1st Unit principal photography), 1990, Sunset Grill, Body of Evidence, Rumpelstulskin, Sunchaser, Breakdown, 1996, Legionnaire, Dungeons and Dragons; 2d unit dir./2d unit dir. of photography: (TV miniseries) Buffalo Girls, (movies) The Bounty, The Shining. Home: 4344 Promenade Way Unit 209 Marina Del Rey CA 90292-6291

MILSTEIN, LAURENCE BENNETT, electrical engineering educator, researcher; b. Bklyn., Oct. 28, 1942; s. Harry and Sadie (Kaplan) M.; m. Suzanne Barbara Hirschman, Oct. 3, 1969; children: Coreen Roxanne, Renair Marissa. BEE, CUNY, 1964; MSEE, Poly. Inst. Bklyn., 1966, PhD in Elec. Engring., 1968. Mem. tech. staff Hughes Aircraft Co., El Segundo, Calif., 1968-69, staff engr., 1969-72, sr. staff engr., 1972-74; asst. prof. Rensselaer Poly. Inst., Troy, NY, 1974-76, U. Calif.-San Diego, La Jolla, 1976-79, assoc. prof., 1979-82, prof. elec. engring., 1982—, chmn. dept., 1984-88, Ericsson endowed chair, 2005. Cons. Hughes Aircraft Co., Culver City, Calif., 1976—78, Lockheed Missiles and Space Co., Sunnyvale, Calif., 1978—93, Motorola Satellite Comm., 1992—96, InterDigital Comm. Corp., 1992—96, Golden Bridge Tech., 1995—99; cons. various govt. agys., pvt. cos., 1975—. Contbr. articles to profl. jours.; co-editor: Tutorials in Modern Communications, 1983, Spread Spectrum Communications, 1983. Recipient Outstanding Tchr. award Warren Coll., U. Calif.-San Diego, La Jolla, 1982, Disting. Tchg. award, 1999; grantee Army Rsch. Office, 1977-84, 86-89, 91-2001, Office of Naval Rsch., Arlington, Va., 1982-05, 07—, TRW, San Diego, 1983-89, 92-97, NSF, 1993-04, 2006—, Air Force Office Sci. Rsch. 2008—. Fellow IEEE (Millennium medal 2000, Edwin Armstrong Achievement award 2000, MILCOM long term tech. achievement award 1998, F.W. Ellersick MILCOM prize paper award 2002), IEEE Coms. Soc. (bd. govs. 1983, 85-87, 93-95, v.p. for tech. activities 1990-91), IEEE Info. Theory Soc. (bd. govs. 1989-94). Jewish. Office: U Calif San Diego Dept Elec Computer Engring La Jolla CA 92093 Office Phone: 858-534-3096. Business E-Mail: milstein@ece.ucsd.edu.

MILTON, CATHERINE HIGGS, entrepreneur; b. NYC, Jan. 6, 1943; d. Edgar Homer and Josephine (Doughty) Higgs; m. A. Fenner Milton (div.); m. Thomas F. McBride, Aug. 25, 1974 (dec. Oct. 31, 2003); children: Raphael McBride, Luke McBride. BA, Mt. Holyoke Coll., 1964, PhD (hon.), 1992. Reporter, travel writer Boston Globe, 1964-68; with Internat. Assn. Chiefs Police, Washington, 1968-70; asst. dir. Police Found., Washington, 1970-75; spl. asst. US Treasury Dept., Washington, 1977-80; project staff Spl. Com. Aging/Senate, Washington, 1980-81; spl. asst. to pres., founder/exec. dir. Stanford U. Haas Ctr. for Public, Calif., 1981-91; exec. dir. Commn. for Nat. and Cmty. Svc., Washington, 1991-93; v.p. Corp. for Nat. Svc., Washington, 1993-95; exec. dir. Presidio Leadership Ctr., 1995-96; exec. dir. US Programs Save the Children, Westport, Conn., 1996—2002; pres. Friends of the Children, Portland, Oreg., 2002—05; vis. fellow John Gardner Ctr., Stanford U., 2008. Mem. US Atty. General's Task Force on Family Violence, 1981-82; chair nat. forum Kellogg Found., 1990; bd. dirs. Inst. Higher Edn. Policy, Generation United. Author: Women in Policing, 1972, Police Use of Deadly Force, 1976; co-author: History of Black Americans, 1965, Team Policing, Little Sisters and the Law, 1970. Bd. dirs. Youth Svc. Calif., L.A., 1986-91, Trauma Found., San Francisco, 1982-90, Generation United, 1985-, Inst. Higher Edn. Policy, 1985-; spl. advisor Campus Compact, 1986-91. Nat. Kellogg Found. fellow, Battle Creek, Mich., 1985-88; recipient Dedication and Outstanding Efforts award Bd. Suprs., Santa Clara, Calif., 1989, Outstanding Vol. Contbn. award Strive for Five, San Francisco, 1991, Dinkelspiel award Stanford U., 1991; named Outstanding Campus Adminstr. COOL, 1987. Avocations: backpacking, skiing, hiking, travel. Home: 3652 SE Oak St Portland OR 97214

MILTON-JONES, DELISHA, professional basketball player; b. Riceboro, Ga., Sept. 11, 1974; d. Beverly Milton; m. Roland Jones, June 30, 2003. Attended, Stetson U., Fla.; BA in Sports Mgmt., U. Fla., Gainesville, 1997. Forward Am. Basketball League Portland Power, 1997—99, LA Sparks, 1999—2004, 2008—, Washington Mystics, 2005—07. Forward EuroLeague Ekaterinburg team, Russia, 2002; mem. USA Basketball Women's Sr. Nat. Team, Sydney, 2000, Athens, Greece, 04, Beijing, 08. Recipient Gold Medal, US Olympic Festival, 1994, World Univ. Games, 1997, World Championships, 1998, 2002, US Olympic Cup, 1999, Gold medal, women's basketball, Sydney Olympic Games, 2000, Athens Olympic Games, 2004, Beijing Olympic Games, 2008, President's Recognition award, U. Fla., 1997; named to Western Conf. All-Star Team, WNBA, 2000, Ea. Conf. All-Star Team, 2007. Achievements include being a member of WNBA Championship winning Los Angeles Sparks, 2001, 2002. Office: Los Angeles Sparks 555 N Nash St El Segundo CA 90245

MIN, SOO BONG, bank executive; b. Hwanghae Province, Korea, 1938; BA in Economics, Seoul U. Various positions including COO, pres. Comml. Bank Korea, Seoul, Republic of Korea, 1959—94; pres., CEO Hanmi Bank, 1995—99; pres., CEO, dir. Wilshire Bancorp, LA, 1999—. Office: Wilshire Bancorp Inc 3200 Wilshire Blvd Los Angeles CA 90010 Office Phone: 213-387-3200. Office Fax: 213-427-6584.

MINAHAN, JOHN P., academic administrator; BA in Philos., Canisius Coll.; PhD in Philos., Georgetown U. With Xavier U., U. North Fla., SUNY Buffalo; dean, coll. liberal arts and sciences Western Oreg. U., Monmouth, Oreg., 1986—98, prof. philos., 1986—98, provost, 1998—2004, interim pres., 2005—06, pres., 2006—. Office: Office of President Western Oreg University 345 N Monmouth Ave Monmouth OR 97361 Office Phone: 503-838-8888. Business E-Mail: president@wou.edu.

MINC, HENRYK, mathematics professor; b. Lodz, Poland, Nov. 12, 1919; s. Izrael and Haja (Zyngler) M.; m. Catherine Taylor Duncan, Apr. 16, 1943; children: Robert Henry, Ralph Edward, Raymond. MA with honors, Edinburgh U., Scotland, 1955, PhD, 1959. Tchr. Morgan Acad., Dundee, Scotland, 1956-58; lectr. Dundee Tech. Coll., 1957-58, U. BC, Vancouver, Canada, 1958-59, asst. prof., 1959-60; assoc. prof. U. Fla., Gainesville, 1960-63; prof. U. Calif., Santa Barbara, 1963-90, prof. emeritus, 1990—. Vis. prof. Technion Israel Inst. Tech., Haifa, 1969-80. Author: A Survey of Matrix Theory and Matrix Inequalities, 1964, Russian translation, 1972, Chinese translation, 1990, Introduction to Linear Algebra, 1968, Spanish translation, 1968, Modern University Algebra, 1966, Elementary Linear Algebra, Spanish translation, 1971, New College Algebra, 1968, Elementary Functions and Coordinate Geometry, 1969, Algebra and Trigonometry, 1970, College Algebra, 1970, College Trigonometry, 1971, Integrated Analytic Geometry and Algebra with Circular Functions, 1973, Permanents, 1978, Russian translation, 1980, Chinese translation, 1991, Nonnegative Matrices, 1988, Chinese translation, 1991; contbr. over 80 rsch. articles to math. jours., 9 rsch. papers to archaeol. and ancient numismatic jours., 12 articles to Burns Chronicle; referee and reviewer math. jours. 2nd lt. Polish Army, 1940-48, France, UK. Recipient Lester Ford award Math. Assn. Am., 1966, rsch. contract Office Naval Rsch., 1985-88, Air Force Office Sci. Rsch. grantee, 1960-83, Lady Davis fellow, 1975-78. Mem.: Scottish Soc. Santa Barbara (past chieftain), Robert Burns World Fedn. (hon. pres.), Am. Math. Soc. Democrat. Home: 4076 Naranjo Dr Santa Barbara CA 93110-1213 Office: U Calif Dept Math Santa Barbara CA 93106 Home Phone: 805-687-1824. Personal E-mail: hmincburns@cox.net.

MINDEL, LAURENCE BRISKER, restauranteur; b. Toledo, Oct. 27, 1937; s. Seymour Stewart and Eleanor (Brisker) M.; m. Deborah Dudley, Oct. 20, 1978; children: Katherine Dudley, Nicolas Laurence; children by previous marriage, Michael Laurence, Laura Beth, Anthony Jay. BA, U. Mich., 1959. Gen. mgr. Western Coffee Instants, Inc., Burlingame, Cal., 1962-64, dir., ptnr., 1964, chmn., dir. Caswell Coffee Co., San Francisco, 1964-70; pres. Coffee Instants, Inc., Long Island City, N.Y., 1966-70; v.p. Superior Tea and Coffee Co., 1970-72; chmn., chief exec. officer Spectrum Foods, Inc., 1970-85; pres. Restaurant Group Saga Corp., Menlo Park, Calif., 1985-86; founder Il Fornaio (Am.) Corp. Mem. adv. bd. Stanislaus Ptnrs.; chmn. trustees The Branson Sch. Mem. World Pres'. Orgn., Inst. Am. Entrepreneurs. Home: 86 San Carlos Ave Sausalito CA 94965-2048 Office: Il Fornaio Am Corp 770 Tamalpais Dr Ste 400 Corte Madera CA 94925

MINER, JOHN BURNHAM, industrial relations educator, writer; b. NYC, July 20, 1926; s. John Lynn and Bess (Burnham) M.; children by previous marriage: Barbara, John, Cynthia, Frances; m. Barbara Allen Williams, June 1, 1979; children: Jennifer, Heather. AB, Princeton U., 1950, PhD, 1955; MA, Clark U., 1952. Lic. psychologist, N.Y. Rsch. assoc. Columbia U., 1956-57; mgr. psychol. svcs. Atlantic Refining Co., Phila., 1957-60; mem. faculty U. Oreg., Eugene, 1960-68; prof., chmn. dept. orgnl. sci. U. Md., College Park, 1968-73; rsch. prof. Ga. State U., Atlanta, 1973-87, Disting. prof., 1974; pres. Orgnl. Measurement Systems Press, Eugene, Oreg., 1976—; prof. human resources SUNY, Buffalo, 1987-94, chmn. dept. orgn. and human resources, 1989-92; profl. practice Eugene, Oreg., 1995—. Cons. McKinsey & Co., N.Y.C., 1966-69; vis. lectr. U. Pa., Phila., 1959-60; vis. prof. U. Calif., Berkeley, 1966-67, U. South Fla., Tampa, 1972; researcher on orgnl. motivation, theories of orgn., human resource utilization, bus. policy and strategy, entrepreneurship. Author: Personnel Psychology, 1969, Personnel and Industrial Relations, 1969, 1973, 1977, 1985, The Challenge of Managing, 1975; author: (with Mary Green Miner) Policy Issues Personnel and Industrial Relations, 1977; author: (with George A. Steiner) Management Policy and Strategy, 1977; author: (with M.G. Miner) Employee Selection Within the Law, 1978; author: Theories of Organizational Behavior, 1980, Theories of Organizational Structure and Process, 1982, People Problems: The Executive Answer Book, 1985, The Practice of Management, 1985, Organizational Behavior: Performance and Productivity, 1988, Industrial-Organizational Psychology, 1992, Role Motivation Theories, 1993; with Donald P. Crane Human Resource Management: The Strategic Perspective, 1995; author: The 4 Routes to Entrepreneurial Success, 1996; author: (with Michael H. Capps) How Honesty Testing Works, 1997; author: A Psychological Typology of Successful Entrepreneurs, 1997, Organizational Behavior: Foundations, Theories and Analyses, 2002, Organizational Behavior: Essential Theories of Motivation and Leadership, 2005, Organizational Behavior: Essential Theories of Process and Structure, 2006, Organizational Behavior: Historical Origins, Theoretical Foundations, and the Future, 2006, Organizational Behavior: From Theory To Practice, 2007, Organizational Behavior: From Unconscious Motivation to Role Motivated Leadership, many other books and monographs; contbr. numerous articles, papers to profl. jours. With US Army, 1944—46, ETO. Decorated Bronze Star, Combat Infantryman's badge. Fellow APA, Acad. of Mgmt. (editor Jour. 1973-75, pres. 1977-78), Soc. for Personality Assessment, Am. Psychol. Soc.; mem. Soc. for Human Resource Mgmt., Inst. Operations Rsch. Mgmt. Sci., Am. Sociolog. Assn., Indsl. Rels. Rsch. Assn., Internat. Coun. for Small Bus., Strategic Mgmt. Soc., Internat. Pers. Mgmt. Assn., Human Resource Planning Soc. Republican. Home and Office: 34199 Country View Dr Eugene OR 97408-9440 Office Phone: 541-484-2715.

MINERVINO, JIM, computer software company executive; married; 2 children. B in Economics, Boston U. Mgmt. position Toshiba, Internat. Data Corp.; joined Microsoft Corp., Redmond, Wash., 1988, corp. v.p. corp. mktg. strategy & insights; lead mktg. cons. Visio Corp.; founder Genesis Cap. Mgmt., Inc., Seattle, 1994. Office: Microsoft Corp One Microsoft Way Redmond WA 98052-6399

MING, JENNY J., former retail executive; b. Canton, China, 1955; arrived in US, 1964; married; 3 children. BA in Clothing Merchandising, San Jose State U. Mdse. mgr. brand activewear Gap Inc., 1986—89, v.p., divsn. mdse. mgr., 1989—94, sr. v.p. merchandising, Old Navy, 1994—96, exec. v.p. merchandising, Old Navy, 1996—99, pres., Old Navy, 1999—2006, mem., sr. oper. com., 1999—2006. Bd. dirs. Epiphany, Inc., 2001—. Bd. dirs. Big Brothers Big Sisters, San Francisco; mem. Com. of 100. Recipient Award for Leadership in Bus. & Community Svc., Merage Found. for the American Dream, 2006; named one of 50 Most Powerful Women in Am. Bus., Fortune mag., 2003.

MINNICH, DIANE KAY, legal association administrator; b. Iowa City, Feb. 17, 1956; d. Ralph Maynard Minnich and Kathryn Jane (Obye) Tompkins. BA in Behavioral Sci., San Jose State U., 1978. Tutorial program coord./instr. Operation SHARE/La Valley Coll., Van Nuys, Calif., 1979-81; field exec. Silver Sage Girl Scout Coun., Boise, Idaho, 1981-85; continuing legal edn. dir. Idaho State Bar/Idaho Law Found. Inc., Boise, 1985-88, dep. dir., 1988-90, exec. dir., 1990—. Sec.-treas. Western States Bar Conf., 2001-2005; bd. dirs. Atty. Liability Protection Soc.--A Fmily of Profl. Svc. Cos.; mem. adv. bd. legal asst. program Boise State U. Mem. Assn. CLE Adminstrs., Chgo., 1985-90; bd. dirs. Silver Sage coun. Girl Scouts, Boise, 1990-93, 99-2001, mem. nominating com., 1990-94, 97-2001, chair nominating com., 1991-92; mem. legal asst. program adv. bd. Boise State U.; bd. dirs. Boise Schs. Found., 2004—. Named one of Outstanding Young Women in Am., 1991. Mem. ABA (standing com. on pub. edn. adv. commn. 2004—07), Nat. Orgn. Bar Execs. (membership com. 1992-97, chair 1996-97), Zonta Club Boise (pres. 1991-92, bd. dirs. 1989-93), Rotary Club Boise (chair mem. com. 1994-97, bd. dirs. 1996-97, 99—2005, pres. 2003-04). Avocations: jogging, golf. Office: Idaho State Bar Idaho Law Found PO Box 895 525 W Jefferson St Boise ID 83702-5931 Home: 1118 Harrison Blvd Boise ID 83702-3448 Office Phone: 208-334-4500. E-mail: dminnich@isb.idaho.gov.

MINNICK, MALCOLM DAVID, lawyer; b. Indpls., July 5, 1946; s. Malcolm Dick and Frances Louise (Porter) M.; m. Heidi Rosemarie Klein, May 24, 1972. BA, U. Mich., 1968, JD, 1972. Bar: Calif. 1972, U.S. Dist. Ct. (ctrl. dist.) Calif. 1972, U.S. Ct. Appeals (9th cir.) 1984, U.S. Dist. Ct. (no. dist.) Calif. 1986, U.S. Supreme Ct. 1986. Assoc. Lillick McHose & Charles, LA, 1972-78; ptnr. Lillick & McHose, LA, 1978-91, Pillsbury Winthrop Shaw Pittman LLP, San Francisco, 1991—. Group mgr. Creditors Rights and Bankruptcy Group, 1993-98; panelist Calif. Continuing Edn. of Bar, LA, 1982-86, 88, San Francisco, 2005, Practicing Law Inst., 1992, 93, 94, Banking Law Inst., 1999, 2000; bd. govs. Fin. Lawyers Conf., LA, 1981-84; mem. exec. com. Lillick & McHose, 1982-85. Co-author: Checklist for Secured Commercial Loans, 1983. Pres. Ross Sch. Found., 1997-98. Mem. ABA (corp., banking and bus. law sect.), Am. Bankruptcy Inst., Calif. Bar Assn. (Uniform Comml. Code com. 1983-86), LA County Bar Assn. (exec. com. comml. law and bankruptcy sect. 1987-90), Bar Assn. San Francisco (comml. law and bankruptcy sect., panelist 2004), LA Country Club, Univ. Club (bd. dirs. 1983-86, pres. 1985-86). Avocation: golf. Office: Pillsbury Winthrop Shaw Pittman LLP 50 Fremont St San Francisco CA 94105-2230 Office Phone: 415-983-1351. Business E-Mail: dminnick@pillsburylaw.com.

MINNICK, WALTER CLIFFORD, United States Representative from Idaho, former building materials company executive; b. Walla Walla, Wash., Sept. 20, 1942; s. Walter Lawrence and Dorothy (Waldron) M.; children from previous marriage: Amy Louise, Adam Wade; m. A.K. Lienhart. BA summa cum laude in Econs., Whitman Coll., 1964; MBA with high distinction, Harvard U., 1966, JD magna cum laude, 1969. Bar: Oreg. and Wash. bars. Assoc. firm Davies, Biggs, Strayer, Stoel & Boley, Portland, Oreg., 1969-70; staff asst. to pres. Domestic Council, Washington, 1971-72; dep. asst. dir. Office Mgmt. and Budget, Washington, 1972-73; with T.J. Internat., Boise, Idaho, 1974-95, v.p. div. ops., 1976-79, pres., COO, 1979-95, pres., CEO, 1986-95, also past chmn. bd. dirs., trustee; mem. US Congress from 1st Idaho Dist., 2009—. Bd. dir. Eljer Corp., MacMillan Bloedel, Ltd.; chmn. Bogus Basin Ski Area Chmn. Albertson Coll. of Idaho, 1989-1993; Served to 1st Lt. U.S. Army, 1970-72. Named Idaho Bus. Leader of Yr., 1992. Mem. Wash. State Bar Assn., Oreg. State Bar Assn., Idaho Conservation League, Nature Conservancy, Boise Fgn. Affairs Soc. (mem. exec. com.), Bogus Basin Recreation Assn. (past chmn.). Democrat. Unitarian Universalist. Office: US Congress 1517 Longworth House Office Bldg Washington DC 20515-1201 also: Dist Office 802 W Bannock Ste 101 Boise ID 83702 Office Phone: 202-225-6611, 208-336-9831. Office Fax: 202-225-3029, 208-336-9891.*

MINNILLO, VANESSA JOY, news correspondent; b. Pampanga, Philippines, Nov. 9, 1980; d. Vince Minnillo and Helen Berecero, Donna (Stepmother). News correspondent Entertainment Tonight, 2005—08. Appearances on (TV series) That's Life, 2001, City Guys, 2001, Bold and the Beautiful, 2001, Maybe it's Me, 2002, How I Met Your Mother, 2008, host Top of the Pops, 2002, MTV's Prom Date, 2004, The Road to Stardom with Missy Elliott, 2005, co-host Total Request Live, 2003—07, correspondent Entertainment Tonight, 2005—08, host (TV films) The Break, 2003, (TV spl.) 2 Punk Rock 4 This: The Real World San Diego Reunion, High School Stories, Spring Break Celebrity Fantasies, Miss Teen USA, 2004, correspondent 50th Ann. Miss USA Pageant, 2001, judge Miss Teen USA, 2003, 2007, co-host Miss Universe Pageant, 2007, actress (films) Fantastic Four: Rise of The Silver Surfer, 2006, Disaster Movie, 2008. Named Miss Teen USA, 1998, Miss Congeniality, 1998. Avocations: Flag Football, tennis, volleyball. Office: c/o Adam Sher William Morris Agy LLC 151 El Camino Dr Beverly Hills CA 90212

MINNIS, JOHN MARTIN, state legislator, protective services official; b. Garden City, Kans., Dec. 14, 1953; s. Elbert William and Helen R. Logerwell) M.; m. Karen Marie Bartrug, Oct. 14, 1972; children: Steven, Michael, Jennifer. Student, Portland State U. Machinist-apprentice Bingham-Willamette Co., Portland, Oreg., 1973-74; rsch. dep. sheriff Multnomah County, Oreg., 1976; police officer Portland Police Dept., 1976-92, detective, 1992—; mem. Oreg. Ho. of Reps., Salem, 1985-98, minority whip, 1989, asst. majority leader, 1991, also co-chmn. joint ways and means com.; mem. Oreg. Senate from 11th dist., Salem, 2001—. Sgt. USAF and Oreg. Air Guard, 1972-78. Mem. Am. Legis. Exch. Coun., Nat. Conf. State Legislatures (vice chmn. com. on fed. budget and taxation), Am. Profl. Soc. on Abuse of Children. Home: 23765 NE Holladay St Troutdale OR 97060-2903

MINNIS, KAREN, state legislator; b. Portland, Oreg., May 20, 1954; m to John Minnis; children: three. Member, Precinct Committee, 86-; legislation aide, 87-; Oregon State Representative, District 20, 1999-2002; Oregon State Representative, District 49, 2003-, House Speaker, currently, Oregon House Representative.Small business owner, 95-97. Republican. Protestant. Office: 900 Court St NE, Rm 269 Salem OR 97301 Fax: Capit: 503-669-2765. E-mail: minnis.rep@state.or.us.

MINOGUE, ROBERT BROPHY, retired nuclear engineer; b. Covington, Ky., Jan. 31, 1928; s. Joseph and Catherine Ann (Brophy) M.; m. Marie Joan Clarke, June 12, 1954; children: Patrick, Margaret, Marie, Francis. BS, Thomas More Coll., 1949; MS, U. Cin., 1951; grad., Oak Ridge Sch. Reactor Tech., 1952. Nuclear engr., then head nuclear tech. sect. naval reactors br. AEC, Washington, 1952-56; head research reactor design and enngring., then head nuclear power plant engring. sect. Gen. Atomic div. Gen. Dynamics Corp., 1957-67; chief spl. projects br. div. reactor standards AEC, Washington, 1967-72, asst. dir., then dep. dir. regulatory standards, 1972-74; dir. office standards devel. Nuclear Regulatory Commn., Washington, 1975-80, dir. office research, 1980-86; pvt. practice Temecula, Calif., 1986—. U.S. mem. sr. adv. group Safety Standards IAEA, 1974-86; mem. Com. on Interagy. Radiation Research and Policy Coordination, 1982-86. Author: Reactor Shielding Design Manual, 1956; patentee: Triga Research Reactor. Served with AUS, 1946-48. Recipient Bernard F. Langer award, ASME, 1982. Roman Catholic. Home and Office: 16 Pico Vista Novato CA 94947

MINOR, HALSEY, multimedia company executive; married; 3 children. BA in Anthropology, U. Va., 1987. Investment banker Merrill Lynch Capital Markets, San Francisco, 1987—89; founder, CEO Global Publishing Corp., 1989—90; cons. Russell Reynolds Associates, 1991—92; founder, chmn., CEO CNET: The Computer Network, San Francisco, 1992—2000; chmn. emeritus CNET Networks, Inc., 2000—; founder, chmn., CEO Grand Central Communications, 2000—. Founding investor Listen.com (acquired by Real Media and Salesforce.com); bd. dirs. salesforce.com, Inc. Office Phone: 415-344-3200. Office Fax: 415-344-3250.

MINSON, DIXIE L., legislative staff member; Student, Weber State U. Dir. dept. bus. regulation Utah's Divsn. Consumer Protection; dep. chief of staff Office of Gov. Norman H. Bangerter, Utah; commr. safety, health and indsl. accidents divsn. Indsl. Commn. Utah; state dir. Office of Senator Robert F. Bennett, Salt Lake City, 1993—. Active Utah Hearing Panel for Safety Auto and Inspection Stas., League Utah Consumers; Utah liaison U.S. Product Safety Commn.; v.p. Wester Assn. Worker's Compensation Bd. and Commn.; rep. Funeral Svc. Consumer Action Panel for Western States and Hawaii. Mem. Nat. Assn. Govtl. Labor Ofcls., Nat. Assn. Consumer Agy. Adminstrs., Nat. Assn. Unemployment Ins. Appellate Bds. Office: 1779 W 550 N Clearfield UT 84015

MINTON, DWIGHT CHURCH, manufacturing executive; b. North Hills, NY, Dec. 17, 1934; s. Henry Miller and Helen Dwight (Church) M.; m. Marian Haven Haines, Aug. 4, 1956; children: Valerie Haven, Daphne Forsyth, Henry Brewster. BA, Yale U., 1959; MBA, Stanford U., 1961. With Church & Dwight Co., Inc., Princeton, N.J., 1961—, asst. v.p., 1964-66, v.p., 1966-67, bd. dir., 1966—2006, chem., 1981—2001, chem. emeritus, 2001—, pres., 1967-81, chief exec. officer, 1969-95, chmn., 1981—, chmn. bd., 1966—2001, chmn. emeritus Princeton, NJ, 2001—. Bd. dirs. Crane Corp. Trustee Atlanta U., 1971-88, Morehouse Coll., 1971—2008, Spelman Coll., 1971-80; Greater Yellowstone Coalition, 1991-99, Nat. Parks Conservation, With U.S. Army, 1956-57. Mem. Chem. Mfrs. Assn. (bd. dirs. 1980-83), Grocery Mfrs. Am. (dir. 1983-87). Clubs: Racquet and Tennis, Yale, Lotos. Office: 120 W Cleveland St PO Box 4727 Bozeman MT 59715 Office Phone: 406-551-2018.

MINTS, GRIGORI EFROIM, mathematics specialist; b. Leningrad, USSR, June 7, 1939; s. Efroim B. and Lea M. (Novick) M.; m. Marianna Rozenfeld, July 21, 1987; 1 child, Anna. Diploma, Leningrad U., 1961, PhD, 1965, ScD, 1989. Rsch. assoc. Steklov Inst. Math., Leningrad, 1961-79; with Nauka Pubs., Leningrad, 1979-85; sr. rsch. assoc. Inst. Cybernetics, Tallinn, Estonia, 1985-91; prof. dept. philosophy Stanford U., Calif., 1991—, prof. dept. math., 2003—. Mem. ed. bd. Jour. Symbolic Logic, 1987-90; program orgn. com. Logic in Computer Sci., 1991-94, ASL mtg., CSLI Workshop on Logic, Language and Computation. Author: (book) A Short Introduction to Modal Logic, 1992, Selected Papers in Proof Theory, 1992, A Short Introduction to Intuitionistic Logic, 2000; editor: Mathematical Investigation of Logical Deduction, 1967, COLOG-88, 1989, Logic Colloquium, 1996, Games, Logic and Constructive Sets, 2003; mem. editl. bd.: jour. Jour. Philos. Logic, Jour. of Logic and Computation, IGPL; contbr. articles to profl. jours. Mem. Assn. Symbolic Logic (mem. coun. 1990-93), Internat. Union History and Philosophy and Sci. (assessor 1991-95). Business E-Mail: mints@csli.stany.com.

MINTZ, MARSHALL GARY, lawyer; b. Detroit, May 28, 1947; BA, UCLA, 1968, JD, 1971. Bar: Calif. 1972. Law clk. appellate dept L.A. County Superior Ct., 1971-72; ptnr. Kelly Lytton Mintz & Vann, LLP, LA, Calif., 1995-2001; of counsel Sidley & Bell LLP, LA, 2001—03; mem. Mintz & Werner, LA, 2003—. Moderator, panelist Calif. Continuing Edn. of Bar, 1980—; mem. arbitration adminstrv. com. L.A. County Superior Ct., 1979, mem. 1984 Olympics spl. settlement panel; mem. arbitration panel L.A. Superior Ct., 1999—; lectr. Lorman Ednl. Seminars, 2002-. Mem. ABA, State Bar Calif., L.A. County Bar Assn. (arbitrator arbitration and client rels. com. 1978-99), Assn. Bus. Trial Lawyers (bd. govs. 1976-77, program chmn. 1976). Office: 1801 Century Park E Ste 2400 Los Angeles CA 90067-2326 Home Phone: 310-446-9440; Office Phone: 310-556-9692. E-mail: mgmintz@earthlink.net.

MINUDRI, REGINA URSULA, librarian, consultant; b. San Francisco, May 9, 1937; d. John C. and Molly (Halter) M. BA, San Francisco Coll. for Women, 1958; MLS, U. Calif., Berkeley, 1959. Reference libr. Menlo Park (Calif.) Pub. Libr., 1959-62; regional libr. Santa Clara County (Calif.) Libr., 1962-68; project coord. Fed. Young Adult Libr. Svcs. Project, Mountain View, Calif., 1968-71; dir. profl. svcs. Alameda County (Calif.) Libr., 1971, asst. county libr., 1972-77; libr. dir. Berkeley Pub. Libr., 1977-94; city libr. San Francisco Pub. Libr., 1997-2000. Lectr. U. San Francisco, 1970-72, U. Calif., Berkeley, 1977-81, 91-93, San Jose State U., 1994-97; cons., 1975-90; mem. adv. bd. Miles Cutter Ednl., 1992-98. Author: Getting It Together, A Young Adult Bibliography, 1970; contbr. articles to publs. including Sch. Libr. Jour., Wilson Libr. Bull. Bd. dirs. No. Calif. ACLU, 1994-96, Cmty. Memory, 1989-91, Berkeley Pub. Libr. Found., 1996-99; bd. dirs. Berkeley Cmty. Fund, 1995-99, chair youth com., 1994-96; mem. bd. mgrs. ctrl. br. Berkeley YMCA, 1988-93. Recipient proclamation Mayor of Berkeley, 1985, 86, 94, Citation of Merit, Calif. State Assembly, 1994; named Woman of Yr., Alameda County North chpt. Nat. Women's Polit. Caucus, 1985, Outstanding Alumna, U. Calif. Sch. Libr. and Info. Scis., Berkeley, 1987, Lifetime Achievement award Berkeley Cmty. Fund, 2001. Mem. ALA (pres. 1986-87, exec. bd. 1980-89, coun. 1979-88, 90-94, Grolier award 1974), Calif. Libr. Assn. (pres. 1981, coun. 1965-69, 79-82), LWV (dir. Berkeley chpt. 1980-81, v.p. comm. svcs. 1995-97). Home and Office: Reality Mgmt 836 The Alameda Berkeley CA 94707-1916

MIRANDA, BEN, state legislator; m. Catherine Miranda; children: Elisa, Maritza. Student, Phoenix Coll.; B, Ariz. State U.; JD, Ariz. State U. Law Sch. Pvt. practice atty.; mem. Dist. 16 Ariz. House of Reps., 2003—, mem. judiciary com., rules com. Active Am. Red Cross. Served with US Army, Vietnam. Decorated Bronze Star; recipient John S. Martinez Leadership award, Nat. Hispanic Caucus State Legislators, 2007. Mem.: Ariz. Trial Lawyers Assn. Democrat. Office: Ariz House Reps Capitol Complex 1700 W Washington Rm 323 Phoenix AZ 85007 Office Phone: 602-926-4893. Fax: 602-417-3116. Business E-Mail: bmiranda@azleg.gov.*

MIRANDA, RICHARD, state legislator; b. Phoenix, Mar. 6, 1956; Dir. migrant health programs Ariz. Assn. Cmty. Health Centers; mem. Dist. 22 Ariz. House of Reps., 1999—2002; mem. Dist. 13 Ariz. State Senate, 2002—, minority whip, 2005—. Chmn. Ariz. Legis. Latino Caucus. Vol. Boys & Girls Clubs of America, Mountain Park Cmty. Healthcare Ctr.; bd. dirs. Cesar E. Chavez Mus. Recipient Disting. Achievment award, Ariz. State U. Mary Lou Foulton Coll. Edn., 2006; named Legislator of Yr., Ariz. Chiropractors Assn., 2003, Ariz. Assn. Cmty. Health Centers, 2004. Democrat. Roman Catholic. Office: Ariz State Senate Capitol Complex 1700 W Washington Rm 308 Phoenix AZ 85007 Office Phone: 602-926-5911. Office Fax: 602-417-3271. Business E-Mail: rmiranda@azleg.gov.*

MIRISCH, LAWRENCE ALAN, motion picture agent; b. LA, Oct. 10, 1957; s. Walter and Patricia (Kahan) M. BA Radio & TV, Film, Calif. State U., Northridge, 1980. Apprentice film editor, 1975-77; 2nd asst. dir., 1978-81; agent The Gersh Agency, Los Angeles, CA, 1982-84, Adams, Ray & Rosenberg, Los Angeles, CA, 1984, Triad Artists, Los Angeles, CA, 1984-92; pres. The Mirisch Agency, Los Angeles, CA, 1992—. Mem. Mot. Picture Editors Guild, 1975; Directors Guild of Amer., 1978; Academy of Motion Pictures Arts & Sciences, 1987; Amer. Cinema Editors, 1988; adv. bd., Amer. Film Inst., 1990; special products comm., Dir. Guild of Amer., 1991. Bd. of governors, Cedars Sinai Hosp., 1991.

MIRKARIMI, ROSS, city supervisor; b. Chgo., Aug. 4, 1961; s. Hamid Mirkarimi and Nancy Kolman. B in Polit. Sci., St. Louis U.; M in Internat. Econs. and Affairs, Golden Gate U., San Francisco; MS in Environ. Sci., U. San Francisco; grad., San Francisco Police Acad. Cert. Commn. on Peace Officer Standards & Training (POST). Formerly with San Francisco Dist. Atty.'s Office; supr., Dist. 5 San Francisco Bd. Supervisors, 2004—, chair govt. audits & oversight com., Transp. Authority, vice-chair budget & fin. com., pub. safety com. Dir. San Francisco Nuclear Freeze Zone Coalition; mem. exec. bd. Assn. Bay Area Govt.'s; mem. Children & Families First Commn., Local Agy. Formation Commn.; co-founder Calif. Green Party, 1990; coord. Ralph Nader Presdl. Campaign, Calif., 2000; campaign mgr. Harry Britt for State Assembly, San Francisco, 2002, Matt Gonzalez for Mayor, San Francisco, 2003. Mem.: NOW, Iranian-Am. C. of C., Harvey Milk Lesbian/Gay/Bisexual/Transgender Dem. Club. Green Party. Office: City Hall 1 Dr Carlton B Goodlet Pl Rm 244 San Francisco CA 94102-4689 Office Phone: 415-554-7630. Fax: 415-554-7634. E-mail: ross.mirkarimi@sfgov.org.*

MIRSKY, PHYLLIS SIMON, librarian; b. Petach Tikva, Israel, Dec. 18, 1940; d. Allan and Lea (Prizant) Simon; m. Edward Mirsky, Oct. 21, 1967; 1 child, Seth (dec.). BS in Social Welfare, Ohio State U., 1962; postgrad., Columbia U., 1962-63; AMLS, U. Mich., 1965. Caseworker field placement Children's Aid Soc., NYC, 1962-63; hosp. libr. hosp. and instns. divsn. Cleve. Pub. Libr., 1963-64; reference libr. UCLA Biomed. Libr., 1965-68, reference/acquisitions libr., 1968-69, head cons./continuing edn. Pacific S.W. Regl. Med. Libr. Sv., 1969-71, asst. dir. Pacific S.W. Regl. Med. Libr. Sv., 1971-73, faculty coord. Biomed. Libr. program Cen. San Joaquin Valley Area Health Edn. Ctr., 1973-77, assoc. dir. Pacific S.W. Regl. Med. Libr. Sv., 1973-79; head reference sect., coord. libr. assoc. program Nat. Libr. of Medicine, Bethesda, Md., 1979-81; asst. univ. libr., scis. U. Calif.-San Diego, La Jolla, 1981-86, acting univ. libr., 1985, 92-93, 98-99, asst. univ. libr. adminstrv. and pub. svcs., 1986-87, assoc. univ. libr. adminstrv. and pub. svcs., 1987-92, assoc. univ. libr., 1993-95; dep. univ. libr., 1995—. Guest lectr. Libr. Schs. UCLA and U. So. Calif., 1967-78, Grad. Sch. Libr. Sci. Cath. U., Washington, 1980, Grad. Sch. Libr. and Info. Sci. UCLA, 1984; mem. task force on role of spl. libr. nationwide network and coop. programs Nat. Commn. on Libr. and Info. Svcs./Spl. Libr. Assn., 1981-83; facilitator AASLD/MLA Guidelines Scenario Writing Session, L.A., 1984; mem. users coun. OCLC Online Computer Libr. Ctr., Inc., 1991-94; U. Calif.-San Diego rep. Coalition for Networked Info., 1992—; instr. Assn. Rsch. Librs., Office Mgmt. Studies, Mgmt. Inst., 1987; peer reviewer Coll. Libr. Tech. and Cooperation Grant Program U.S. Dept. Edn., 1988-94; cons. Nat. Libr. Medicine, Bethesda, Md., 1988, San Diego Mus. Contemporary Art Libr., La Jolla, Calif., 1993, Salk Inst., 1995; mem. Libr. of Congress Network Adv. Com.,

1994-96, chair steering com., 1995-96. Contbr. articles to profl. jours. and bulls. Mem. fin. com. City of Del Mar, 1995-98, chair, 1997-98, facility adv. com., 2000—. NIH fellow Columbia U., 1962-63; sr. fellow UCLA/Coun. on Libr. Resources, 1987. Fellow Med. Libr. Assn. (bd. dirs. 1977-80); mem. ALA (site visitors panel com. on accreditation 1990-92, libr. adminstrn. and mgmt. assn. 1990-92), Med. Libr. Group Soc. Calif. and Ariz. (sec. 1970-71, v.p. 1971-72, pres. 1972-73), Documentation Abstracts, Inc. (bd. dirs. 1985-90, vice chair bd. dirs. 1988-90), Med. Libr. Assn. (pres. 1984-85), U. Mich. Sch. Libr. Sci. Alumni Assn. Office: U Calif San Diego U Libr 0175G 9500 Gilman Dr La Jolla CA 92093-0175

MISHELEVICH, DAVID JACOB, medical products executive; b. Pitts., Jan. 26, 1942; s. Benjamin and Sarah (Bachrach) M.; m. Bonnie Gray McKim, Dec. 6, 1981; 1 child, Cory Jane. BS in Physics, U. Pitts., 1962; MD, Johns Hopkins U., 1966, PhD in Biomed. Engring., 1970. Lic., Md., Tex. Intern in medicine Balt. City Hosps. (now The John Hopkins Bayview Med. Ctr.), 1966-67; active duty USPHS, 1967—69, inactive reserve, 1969—; staff assoc. Nat. Inst. Neurol. Diseases and Stroke, NIH, Bethesda, Md., 1967-69; exec. v.p. Nat. Ednl. Consultants, Balt., 1971-72; prof., dept. chairperson, dir. med. computing resources ctr. U. Tex. Health Sci. Ctr., Dallas, 1972-82; attending physician/sr. attending physician internal med. Dallas County Hosp., Dist. Parkland Meml. Hosp., 1973-82; v.p. computer and software tech. EAN-TECH, Mountain View, Calif., 1983-84; CEO Garden Gate Software, Cupertino, Calif., 1984-86; dir., then v.p. and gen. mgr. applications and rsch. divsn. IntelliCorp, Inc., Mountain View, 1986-89; v.p. mktg. and sales Viewpoint Engring., Mountain View, 1989-90; v.p. engring. AirWays Med. Techs., Inc., Palo Alto, Calif., 1991-93; dir., then v.p. R&D, chief tech. officer Circadian, Inc., San Jose, Calif., 1993-95, v.p., gen. mgr. AirWays Asthma Ctrs. divsn., 1995-96; CEO Sterling Healthcare Outcomes, Inc., Cupertino, 1996—2002, Playa del Rey, Calif., 2002—; founder, exec. v.p., chief tech. officer QENM.com, 1999-2001; chief tech. officer HealthShore, Inc., 2001—04; lead technologist Outbreak! Music Sys., 2002—; chief tech. officer TeleCath, 2003—05. Pres. Mishelevich Assocs., Dallas, 1982-83, Cupertino, 1990-91, cons. prof. of neurosurgery Stanford U. Sch. Medicine, 2003-; dir. biomed. engring. and med. affairs Aubrey Group, Inc., Irvine, Calif., 2005—; mem. biomed. libr. rev. com. NIH-Nat. Libr. Medicine, 1978-82; cons. in field. Former tech. reviewer IBM Sys. Jour., Jour. of AMA; rev. IEEE computer Soc. Internet, 2001-03; contbr. numerous articles to profl. jours.; patentee in field. V.p. Dallas chpt. Am. Jewish Congress, 1980-84, Am. Jewish Fund, 1980-81; pres. Westport Bch. Club Villas, Homeowners Assn., 2003-06. Fellow Am. Coll. Med. Informatics; mem. AAAS, IEEE, IEEE Computer Soc. (exec. bd. tech. com. on computational medicine 1981-83), Am. Assn. for Artificial Intelligence, Assn. for Computing Machinery (chair Dallas chpt. 1974-75), Am. Med. Informatics Assn., Internat. Tandem Users Group (past pres.), Model T Ford Club of Am., Am. Radio Relay League (life), Phi Beta Kappa, Omicron Kappa. Democrat. Jewish. Home and Office: 7301 Vista del Mar #B111 Playa Del Rey CA 90293 Office Phone: 310-305-2791. Personal E-mail: david@mishelevich.com.

MISHELL, DANIEL R., JR., obstetrician, gynecologist, educator; b. Newark, May 7, 1931; s. Daniel R. and Helen Mishell; m. Carol Goodrich; children: Sandra, Daniel III, Tanya. BA, Stanford U., 1952, MD, 1955. Diplomate Am. Bd. Ob-Gyn. (examiner 1975-95, bd. dirs., dir. subspecialty divsn. reproductive endocrinology 1985-89, pres. 1986-90, chmn. 1990-94). Intern L.A. County Harbor Gen. Hosp., Torrance, 1955-56; resident in internal medicine Bellevue Hosp., NYC, 1956-57; resident in ob-gyn. UCLA-Harbor Gen. Hosp., Torrance, 1959-63; rsch. fellow Univ. Hosp., Uppsala, Sweden, 1961-62; from asst. prof. to assoc. prof. dept. ob-gyn. UCLA Sch. Medicine, 1963-69; prof. U. So. Calif., LA, 1969—, assoc. chmn. dept., 1972-78, chmn. dept. ob/gyn., 1978—. Editor-in-chief Contraception, 1969—; editor Jour. Reproductive Medicine, 1982—, Year Book of Obstetrics and Gynecology, 1987—, Year Book of Infertility, 1989-96; adv. com. Core Jours. in Ob-gyn., 1982—; mem. editl. bd. New Trends in Gynecology and Obstetrics, 1998—. Capt. USAF, 1957-59. Recipient Lester T. Hibbard award U. So. Calif., L.A., 1983, Joseph Bolivar DeLee Humanitarian award Chgo. Lying-In Hosp., 1985, Arthur and Edith Wippman Sci. Rsch. award Planned Parenthood Fedn. Am., 1992, Disting. Scientist award Soc. Gynecologic Investigation, 1994. Mem. Am. Gyn-Ob Soc., Am. Soc. Reproductive Medicine, Am. Coll. Obstetricians and Gynecologists, Am. Fedn. Clin. Rsch., Endocrine Soc., Soc. for Gynecologic Investigation (pres. 1985-86), L.A. Ob-Gyn. Soc. (v.p. 1984-85, pres. 1985-86), Assn. Profs. Gynecology and Obstetrics (exec. coun. 1982-85), Pacific Coast Fertility Soc. (pres. 1973-74), Salerni Collegium, L.A. Athletic Club, Phi Beta Kappa, Alpha Omega Alpha. Avocations: tennis, fishing. Office: U So Calif 1240 N Mission Rd Los Angeles CA 90033-1019 E-mail: mishell@hsc.usc.edu.

MISHKIN, PAUL J., lawyer, educator; b. Trenton, NJ, Jan. 1, 1927; s. Mark Mordecai and Bella (Dworetsky) M.; m. Mildred Brofman Westover; 1 child, Jonathan Mills Westover. AB, Columbia U., 1947, JD, 1950; MA (hon.), U. Pa., 1971. Bar: N.Y. State bar 1950, U.S. Supreme Ct. bar 1958. Mem. faculty Law Sch. U. Pa., Phila., 1950-72; prof. law U. Calif., Berkeley, 1972-75, Emanuel S. Heller prof., 1975—2000, Emanuel S. Heller prof. emeritus, 2000—. Cons. City of Phila., 1953; reporter study div. jurisdiction between state and fed. cts. Am. Law Inst., 1960-65; mem. faculty Salzburg Seminar in Am. Studies, 1974; Charles Inglis Thompson guest prof. U. Colo., 1975; John Randolph Tucker lectr., 1978, Owen J. Roberts Meml. lectr., 1982; vis. fellow Wolfson Coll., Cambridge U., 1984; vis. prof. Duke U. Law Sch., 1989. Author: (with Morris) On Law in Courts, 1965, (with others) Federal Courts and the Federal System, 2d edit. 1973, 3d edit, 1988; contbr. articles to profl. jours. Trustee Jewish Publ. Soc. Am., 1966-75, Ctr. for Law in the Pub. Interest, 2001-04; mem. permanent com. Oliver Wendell Holmes Devise, 1979-87. With USNR 1945-46. Rockefeller Found. rsch. grantee, 1956; Center for Advanced Study in Behavioral Scis. fellow, 1964-65; recipient Russell Prize for Excellence in Teaching, 1996. Fellow Am. Acad. Arts Scis., Am. Bar Found.; mem. Am. Law Inst., Order of Coif, Phi Beta Kappa. Home: 91 Stonewall Rd Berkeley CA 94705-1414 Office: U Calif Sch Law Boalt Hall Berkeley CA 94720 Business E-Mail: pjm@law.berkeley.edu.

MISRACH, RICHARD LAURENCE, photographer; b. LA, July 11, 1949; s. Robert Laskin and Lucille (Gardner) M.; m. Debra Bloomfield, Jan. 18, 1981 (div. 1987); 1 son, Jacob Luke; m. Myriam Weisang, Apr. 17, 1989. AB in Psychology, U. Calif., Berkeley, 1971. Instr. Assoc. Students Studio, U. Calif., Berkeley, 1971-77; vis. lectr. U. Calif.-Berkeley, 1982; lectr. U. Calif.-Santa Barbara, 1984. Juror Nat. Endowment Arts, 1986; lectr. Calif. Inst. for Arts, 1990. Exhbns. include Whitney Biennial, 1981, 91, Musée d'Art Moderne, Paris, 1979, Mus. Modern Art, NYC, 1978, Grapestake Gallery, San Francisco, 1979, 81, Young-Hoffman Gallery, Chgo., 1980, Oakland Mus., 1982, 87, San Franciso Mus. Modern Art, 1983, Centre Georges Pompidou, Paris, 1983, LA County Mus. Art, 1984, Fraenkel Gallery, San Francsico, 1985, 89, 91, 95, 97, 99, Min Gallery, Tokyo, 1975-87, Univ. Art Mus., Berkeley, Curt Marcus Gallery, 1995, 96, 97, 2000, James Danziger Gallery, 1995, Robert Mann Gallery, NY, 1999, Melbourne Internat. Festival, Australia, 1995, G. Gibson Gallery, 2000, High Mus. Art, Atlanta, 2000, Froehel Gallery, 2002, 04, 06, Grant/Selwyn Fine art, 2003, Pace MacGill Chelsea, 2004, 06, Marc Selwyn Fine Art, 2005, others; one person exhbns. at Art Inst. Chgo., 1988, Milw. Art Mus., 1988, Carpenter Ctr., Harvard U., 1988, Fotomann, Inc., NY, 1989, 91, Photographers Gallery, 1990, Parco Gallery, Tokyo, 1990, Arles Festival, France, 1990, Jan Kesner Gallery, 1990, 91, 94, 2000, Houston Mus. Fine Arts, 1996, Ctr. Creative Photography, Tucson, 1996, Mus. Contemporary Art, Chgo., 1997, Contemporary Mus. of Art Art, Hawaii, 1997, San Jose Mus. of Art, 1998, Diputacion de Granada, Spain, 1999; art commn. cover Time mag., July 4, 1988; books include Telegraph 3 A.M., 1974, Grapestake Gallery, 1979, (A Photographic Book), 1979, Hawaii portfolio, 1980, Graecism dye-transfer portfolio, 1982, Desert Cantos, 1987, (Internat. Ctr. of Photography award 1988), Bravo 20: The Bombing of the American West, 1990 (Pen Ctr. USA West award for nonfiction 1991), Richard Misrach, Minn. Gallery, 1988, Violent Legacies, Aperture, 1992, Crimes and Splendors, 1996, Cantos del Desierto, Di putacion de Granada, 1999, The Sky Book, 2000, Richard Misrach: Golden Gate, 2001, Pictures of Paintings, 2002, Chronologies, 2006, On the Beach: A Picture, 2007. Recipient Koret Israel prize, 1992, Kulturpreis for Lifetime Achivement in Photography, 2002, Lucie award for Achievement in Fine Art, Internat. Photography Awards, 2008; Guggenheim fellow, 1978, Eureka fellow, 1991; Ferguson grantee, 1976, NEA grantee, 1973, 77, 84, 92; AT&T commn.grantee, 1979.

MISSETT, JUDI SHEPPARD, dancer, jazzercise company executive; b. Iowa; BA in Theater, Radio/TV, Northwestern U., Chgo., 1966. Profl. dancer, Chgo., 1966-77; jazzercise instr., choreographer, tchr. Calif., 1977—; pres. worldwide dance-fitness franchise orgn. Jazzercise, Inc., Carlsbad, Calif.; prin. JM TV Prodns.; prin. mail-order catalog bus. Jazzertogs. Instr. convs., children's fitness progs. Author: (comprehensive nutrition prog.) The Jazzercise Know More Diet; author weekly fitness column for Los Angeles Times Syndicate; performer, prodr. home exercise videos. Mem. Calif. Gov.'s Coun. on Phys. Fitness & Sports; bd. dirs. San Diego Inner-City Games; contbr. millions of dollars for charities by leading spl., large-scale workout classes. Recognized for contbns. to growth and advancement of fitness industry by Pres. Reagan in his White House Conf. on Women in Bus., 1986, Aerobics and Fitness Assn. Am., Am. Coun. on Exercise, Pres.' Coun. on Phys. Fitness & Sports; named Entrepreneur of Year, Working Woman Mag., 1988; recipient Lifetime Achievement award Internat. Assn. Fitness Profls., 1991, Women Who Mean Bus. award San Diego Bus. Jour., 1995, A Woman of Accomplishment award Soroptimist Internat. of San Diego, 1996; inducted into Internat. Assn. Fitness Profls. Hall of Fame, 1992. Mem. Nat. Fitness Leaders Assn. (exec. dir., Charles Bucher Meml. award 1996). Office: Jazzercise Inc 2460 Impala Dr Carlsbad CA 92008-7226

MITCHELL, BEVERLY SHRIVER, hematologist, oncologist, educator; b. Balt., May 14, 1944; m. John Robert Pringle; children: Robert Mitchell, Elizabeth Greene. AB summa cum laude in Biochemistry, Smith Coll., 1965; MD, Harvard U., 1969. Hematology fellow U. Mich., Ann Arbor, 1975-77, from instr. to asst. prof. internal medicine, 1977-81, assoc. prof., 1981-87, prof. internal medicine and pharmacology, 1987-91, U. N.C., Chapel Hill, 1991—, divsn. chief hematology/oncology, 1994—2003; assoc. dir. Lineberger Cancer Ctr., Chapel Hill, 1994—2005; deputy dir. Stanford Cancer Ctr., Stanford U., 2005—. Mem. bd. sci. counselors Cancer Treatment divsn. Nat. Cancer Inst. Vice chair med. and sci. affairs Leukemia and Lymphoma Soc., 2003—05. Recipient Stohlman award Leukemia Soc., 1988. Mem. Am. Soc. Hematology (treas. 1991-96, v.p. 1998, pres. 2000), Phi Beta, Inst. Medicine. Achievements include research in nucleotide metabolism and the development of novel therapies for hematologic malignancies. Office: Stanford Blood Center 3373 Hillview Ave Palo Alto CA 94304-1204 Office Phone: 650-736-7716. Business E-Mail: bmitchell@stanford.edu.

MITCHELL, BRIANE NELSON, lawyer; b. Seattle, July 4, 1953; s. Robert Max and Frances Marie (Nelson) M.; m. Suzanne Harmatz; children: Brianne Nelson, Brittany Suzanne. AB, Columbia U., 1975; JD, U. Idaho, 1978. Law clk. U.S. Ct. Appeals (9th cir.), 1978-80; assoc. Debevoise & Plimpton, NYC, 1980-84, Paul, Hastings, Janofsky & Walker, LA, 1984-86, ptnr., 1986-93, McCambridge, Deixler & Marmaro, LA, 1994-95, Shapiro, Mitchell & Dupont LLP, Santa Monica, 1996-2000, Manatt, Phelps & Phillips LLP, LA, 2000—03. Assoc. dir. Pacific regional office SEC, 2004—. Mem.: ABA, Calif. Bar Assn., N.Y. State Bar Assn., Idaho Bar Assn.

MITCHELL, BRUCE TYSON, lawyer; b. San Francisco, Nov. 6, 1928; s. John Robert and Lorraine C. (Tyson) M.; m. Adrienne Means Hiscox, Oct. 14, 1951; 1 son, Mark Means. AB with great distinction, Stanford U., Calif., 1949, JD, 1951. Bar: Calif. 1952, US Dist. Ct. (no. dist.) Calif 1952, US Ct. Appeals (9th cir.) 1952, US Supreme Ct. 1971. Estate adminstr. Crocker Nat. Bank, San Francisco, 1955-57; atty. Utah Internat. Inc., San Francisco, 1957-87, sec., 1974-87, sr. counsel, 1961—87, ret., 1987; pvt. practice securities arbitrator. Mem. non-securities panel arbitrators NY Stock Exch., NASD Bd. Arbitrators; mem. adv. bd. archaeology, Stanford U. Chmn. San Mateo County Rep. Ctrl. Com., 1964-70; mem. Calif. Rep. Ctrl. Com., 1964-74, 77-83; alt. del. Rep. Nat. Conv., 1968; co-chmn. San Mateo (Calif.) County Pres. Ford Com., 1976; mem. bd. visitors sch. law Stanford U., 1980-83; exec. v.p., bd. dirs. San Francisco Jr. C. of C., 1961; bd. dirs. No. Calif. chpt. Arthritis Found., 1972-85, 1987-92, St. Francis Hosp. Found., San Francisco, 1992-98, 99—, hon. dir., 1998-99—. Lt. (j.g.) USNR, 1952-55, Japan. Mem. ABA, Calif. Bar Assn., San Francisco Bar Assn., Am. Judicature Soc., Am. Soc. Corp. Secs. (v.p. 1976-77, dir. 1976-79), Assn. Former Intelligence Officers, Commonwealth Club of Calif. (pres. San Francisco 1973), Stanford Assocs., Pacific Union Club, Olympic Club, Capitol Hill Club, Travelers Century Club, Masons. Congregationalist. Home: 165 Redwood Dr Hillsborough CA 94010-6971 Office: 165 Redwood Dr Hillsborough CA 94010 Office Phone: 415-439-8801.

MITCHELL, DAVID WALKER, lawyer; b. Oakland, Calif., Nov. 11, 1935; s. Theodore Boyd and Helen Louise (Walker) M.; m. Carolyn Hilliard Graves, July 29, 1961; children: Sarah, Betsy. AB in History, Stanford U., 1957; JD, Harvard U., 1960. Bar: Calif. 1961. Assoc. Kindel & Anderson, LA, 1961-65, Weir, Hopkins, Donovan, San Jose, Calif., 1965-68; ptnr. Hopkins, Mitchell & Carley, San Jose, 1968-87, McCutchen, Doyle, Brown & Enersen, San Jose, 1987-93, Hoge, Fenton, Jones & Appel, San Jose, 1993-2000, of counsel, 2001—. Bd. dirs. Peninsula Open Space Trust, Menlo Park, Calif., 1982—2005, pres., 1984-92; bd. dirs. Cmty. Found. Silicon Valley., San Jose, 1977-94, 99-2003; chair bd. trustees United Way Santa Clara County, 1983-85. Fellow Am. Bar Found., Am. Leadership Forum (sr.); mem. Santa Clara County Bar Assn. (trustee 1972-75), San Jose C. of C. (bd. dirs. 1975-80). Mem. United Ch. of Christ. Avocations: music, hiking. Office: Hoge Fenton Jones Appel 60 S Market St Ste 1400 San Jose CA 95113-2396 Office Phone: 408-287-9501. Business E-Mail: dwm@hogefenton.com.

MITCHELL, HARRY E., United States Representative from Arizona, former state legislator; b. Tempe, July 18, 1940; s. Harry Casey and Irene Gladys (Childres) M.; m. Marianne Prevratil, May 5, 1962; children: Amy, Mark. BA, Ariz. State U., 1962, MPA, 1981. Tchr. Tempe (Ariz.) H.S., 1964—; city councilman City of Tempe, 1970—76, vice mayor, 1976—78, mayor, 1978—94; mem. Ariz. State Senate, 1999—2006, US Congress from 5th Ariz. dist., 2007—, mem. sci. & tech. com., transp. & infrastructure com., vets affairs com. Chmn., Ariz. Dem. Party, 2005-06; Bd. dirs. Tempe Sister City; trustee Tempe St. Lukes Hosp., Rio Salado Devel. Dist.; state rep. Sister Cities Internat., Washington; mem. Ariz. State U. Liberal Arts Alumni Adv. Bd., Adv. Council Ctr. Pub. Affairs, Ariz. Commn. Post Secondary Edn.; mem. Nat. League Cities Resolutions Com.; exec. com. League Ariz. Cities; bd. dirs. Ariz. Mcpl. Water Users. Recipient Disting. Svc. award Tempe Jaycees, Pub. Programs Disting. Achievement award, Ariz. State U. Mem. Ariz. State U. Alumni Bd. (chmn.), Ariz. State U. Advanced Pub. Exec. Program. Democrat. Roman Catholic. Office: 2434 Rayburn House Office Bldg Washington DC 20515 also: 7201 E Camelback Rd Ste 335 Scottsdale AZ 85253

MITCHELL, JAMES ANDREW, education educator; b. Fort Campbell, Ky., Feb. 16, 1953; s. James Andrew and Joyce Anne (Smith) M.; 1 child, Magdalena Amelie. AB, Vassar Coll., 1975; MA, Princeton U., 1979, PhD, 1985. Instr. Princeton U., Princeton, NJ, 1981—82; asst. prof. Haverford Coll., Pa., 1981—82, U. Redlands, Calif., 1982—85; escort/interpreter U.S. Dept. State, Washington, 1983—86; project mgr. Delphi Internat. Group, Washington, 1986—89; asst. prof. Mt. Vernon Coll., Washington, 1990—94; assoc. prof. Calif. State U., Northridge, 1994—2003, prof., 2003—. Vis. faculty fellow Am. U. in Kygyzstan, 2001, U. Bucharest, 2001; bd. dirs. South East European Inst. of Internat. Affairs; Am. fgn. policy adv. bd. Dushkin Publ., 2006—. Contbr. articles to profl. jours. Mem. African policy issues group George Bush for Pres. Campaign, Washington, 1988. J. William Fulbright fellow CIES and USIA, U. Bucharest, 1977, NEH fellow, Washington, 1989, John Parker Compton pre-doctoral fellow Ctr. for Internat. Studies, Princeton U., 1981; Rsch. grantee Woodrow Wilson Sch., Princeton U., 1989 Mem.: Princeton Club of N.Y. Avocations: exercise, aerobics. Office: Dept Polit Sci/Calif State 18111 Nordhoff St Northridge CA 91330-0001 Office Phone: 818-677-3488. Business E-Mail: james.mitchell@csun.edu.

MITCHELL, JOAN LAVERNE, research scientist; b. Palo Alto, Calif., May 24, 1947; d. William Richardson and Doris LaVerne (Roddan) M. BS in Physics, Stanford U., 1969; MS in Physics, U. Ill., 1971, PhD in Physics, 1974. Rsch. staff mem. T.J. Watson Rsch. Ctr. IBM, Yorktown Heights, NY, 1974-88, 96-98, mgr. T.J. Watson Rsch. Ctr., 1979-88, image tech. cons. mktg. White Plains, NY, 1989-91, rsch. staff mem. T.J. Watson Rsch. Ctr. Hawthorne, NY, 1991-94, mgr. T.J. Watson Rsch. Ctr., 1992-94, supplemental employee Burlington, NY, 1994-96; vis. prof. U. Ill., Urbana, 1996; with IBM Printing Systems Divsn., Boulder, Colo., 1999—2007, IBM fellow, 2001—07; InfoPrint Solutions Co. fellow InfoPrint Solutions Co., 2007—. Del. CCITT Study Group XIV, 1978-79, ISO JPEG Com., 1987-94, ITU-T Study Group 16 Working Party 3, 2005-07. Co-author: JPEG Still Image Data Compression Standard, 1993, MPEG Video Compression Standard, 1997, (mentoring book) Straight Talk About Talking Change Of Your Career, 2007; contbr. articles to profl. jours. Recipient U. Ill. Coll. Engring. Disting. Alumni Svc. award, 2006, Leadership award Internat. Multimedia Telecoms. Consortium, 2006; Xerox Indsl. fellow, 1970-71. Fellow IEEE; mem. NAE, Am. Phys. Soc., Soc. for Imaging Sci. and Tech., Sigma Xi (chpt. sec. 1976, v.p. 1977, pres. 1978), Phi Beta Kappa, Phi Kappa Phi. Democrat. Achievements include co-inventor on numerous patents. Home: 1172 Fall River Cir Longmont CO 80501 Office: InfoPrint Solutions Co 6300 Diagonal Hwy MS004N Boulder CO 80301-9270 Office Phone: 720-663-3525. Business E-Mail: joan.mitchell@infoprint.co.

MITCHELL, JOHN HENDERSON, management consultant, retired career officer; b. Atlanta, Sept. 9, 1933; s. William Lloyd and Jessie (Henderson) M.; m. Joan Ann Cameron, Apr. 8, 1961; children: John Cameron, Christopher Lloyd, Colin MacKenzie. BABA, St. Bonaventure U., 1956, PhD in Sci., 1991; MA in Pub. Adminstrn., Shippensburg State U., 1973. Commd. 2nd lt. U.S. Army, 1956, advanced through grades to maj. gen., 1982, comdr. 8th Bn., 6th Arty., 1st Inf. divsn. Vietnam, 1968; chief officer assignments Field Arty. br. Officer Pers. Directorate, U.S. Army, Washington; chief of staff 8th divsn. U.S. Army, 1973-75, asst. dept. chief of staff for personnel, Hdqrs. U.S. Army Europe and 7th Army Heidelberg, Germany, 1975-77, comdr. Arty. divsn., chief of staff 1st Inf. divsn. Ft. Riley, Kans., 1977-79, comdr., Field Command, Def. Nuclear Agy. Kirtland AFB, N.Mex., 1979-81, dir. Human Resources Devel. Office, dept. chief staff for pers. Washington; U.S. comdr. Berlin, 1984-88; ret., 1989; pres. Intersys., Inc., Englewood, Colo., 1989-94, Pease, Orr, Mitchell Enterprises, Colorado Springs, Colo., 1994-97; chmn. Berlin Sculpture Fund, Denver, 1997—. Bd. dirs. Nat. Safety Coun., 1982-84. Decorated D.S.M. with oak leaf cluster, Legion of Merit with oak leaf cluster, D.F.C. with oak leaf cluster, Bronze Star with oak leaf cluster and V., Air medals. Mem. Assn. U.S. Army, VFW, Army Navy Club, Army War Coll. Alumni, Soc. of First Inf. Div. Republican. Roman Catholic. Avocations: tennis, history, reading. Home: 375 Hidden Creek Dr Colorado Springs CO 80906-4386

MITCHELL, LAURA REMSON, public policy analyst, writer; b. Mpls., May 12, 1945; d. Sidney and Dora (Blustein) Remson; m. Neil Jay Mitchell, June 25, 1967; 1 child, Brian Jason. BA in Journalism magna cum laude, San Fernando Valley State Coll., 1967. Reporter, copy editor Valley News, Van Nuys, Calif., 1967-71; freelance writer, 1971—. Instr. journalism Calif. State Univ., Northridge, 1970-71 Columnist San Fernando Valley Mag., Calif., 1980. Legis. cons. gov. fin. LWV Calif., 1976-84, cons. emeritus, 1984; adv. econ. Joy Picus for City Coun. campaign, L.A., 1977; mem. Assessment Practices Adv. Coun., L.A. County, 1978-85; govt. issues coord. So. Calif. chpt. Nat. Multiple Sclerosis Soc., Glendale, 1988-89, Multiple Sclerosis

Calif. Action Network, 1990-2000; co-chmn. health and welfare com. Californians for Disability Rights, 1991-95; chair health com., legis. com. Calif. Disability Leadership Forum, 1991-95; mem. steering com. Health Access, Calif., 1991-2000, steering com. Calif. Access Specialty Care, 1999-, Calif. Citizens for Right to Know, 1994—; coord. So. Calif. Disability Campaign for Health-Care Reform, 1994; bd. dirs. Western Law Ctr. for Disability Rights, L.A., 1995-2004; co-founder Calif. Disability Alliance, 1999, legis. coord., mem. exec. com., 1999—. Recipient Shevy Healey Outstanding Achievement award So. Calif. chpt. Nat. Multiple Sclerosis Soc., 1990, MS Pub. Edn. award Nat. Multiple Sclerosis Soc., 1990, Access award Los Angeles County Commn. on Disabilities, 1996. Mem. Soc. Profl. Journalists (bd. dirs. L.A. chpt. 1970-2005). Avocations: playing, composing and listening to music.

MITCHELL, REGINALD EUGENE, mechanical engineering educator; b. Houston, May 16, 1947; s. Clifford Eugene and Juanita Beatrice (Thomas) M.; 1 child, Erika Gene; m. Shirley Ann Myers, Nov. 9, 1990. BS in Chem. Engring., U. Denver, 1968; MS in Chem. Engring., N.J. Inst. Tech., Newark, 1970; ScD in Chem. Engring., MIT, 1975. Mem. tech. staff Sandia Nat. Labs., Livermore, Calif., 1975-89, disting. mem. tech. staff, 1989-91; assoc. prof. mech. engring. dept. Stanford (Calif.) U., 1991—. Recipient Outstanding Tchr. award Tau Beta Pi, 1994. Mem.: Nat. Orgn. Black Chemists and Chem. Engrs. (Percy Julian award 1987), Combustion Inst., Sigma Xi. Avocations: board games, card games, tennis. Home: 6143 Viewcrest Dr Oakland CA 94619-3728 Office: Stanford U Mech Engring Dept Bldg 520 Rm 520C Stanford CA 94305-3032 Business E-Mail: remitche@stanford.edu.

MITCHELL, RIE ROGERS, psychologist, counselor, educator; b. Tucson, Feb. 1, 1940; d. Martin Smith and Lavaun (Peterson) Rogers; m. Rex C. Mitchell, Mar. 16, 1961; 1 child, Scott Rogers. Student, Mills Coll., 1958-59; BS, U. Utah, 1962, MS, 1963; postgrad., San Diego State U., 1965-66; MA, PhD, UCLA, 1969. Diplomate Am. Bd. Psychology; registered play therapist, supr.; cert. sandplay therapist. Tchr. Coronado (Calif.) Unified Sch. Dist., 1964-65; sch. psychologist Glendale (Calif.) Unified Sch. Dist., 1968-70; psychologist Glendale Guidance Clinic, 1970-77; asst. prof. ednl. psychology Calif. State U., Northridge, 1970-74, assoc. prof., 1974-78, prof., 1978—. Chmn. dept. ednl. psychology, 1976-80, 2000—06, acting exec. asst. to pres. Calif. State U., Dominguez Hills, 1978-79; cons. to various Calif. sch. dists.; pvt. practice psychology, Calabasas, Calif. Author: Sandplay: Past Present & Future, 1994, Supervision of Sandplay Therapy, 2008; contbr. numerous articles to profl. jours. Recipient Outstanding Educator award Maharishi Soc., 1978, Woman of Yr. award U. Utah, 1962, Profl. Leadership award Western Assn. Counselor Edn., 1990, Disting. Tchg. award Calif. U. Northridge, 1994. Mem. APA, Calif. Assn. Counselor Edn., Supervision and Adminstrn. (dir. 1976-77), Western Assn. Counselor Edn. and Supervision (officer 1978-82, pres. 1980-81), Assn. Counselor Edn. and Supervision (dir. 1980-81, program chmn. 1981-82, treas. 1983-86, Presdl. award 1986, Leadership award 1987), UCLA Doctoral Alumni Assn. (pres. 1974-76), Am. Ednl. Rsch. Assn., Calif. Women in Higher Edn. (pres. chpt. 1977-78), Calif. Concerns (treas. 1984-86), Sandplay Therpists of Am. (pres., 2008, fin. officer 1996-2000, bd. mem. 1993—, exceptions com. chair, 1995-96, pres. 2008-), Internat. Soc. Sandplay Therapy (bd. mem., 2004-, v.p., 2006-), Pi Lambda Theta (pres. chpt. 1970-71, chairwoman nat. resolutions 1971-73). Home: 4503 Alta Tupelo Dr Calabasas CA 91302-2516 Office: Calif State U Counselor Edn Dept Northridge CA 91330-0001 Office Phone: 818-677-4976. Business E-Mail: rie.mitchell@csun.edu.

MITCHELL, SHAWN, state legislator; m. Yvette Mitchell. BA, Brigham Young U., Provo, Utah; JD, U. Calif., Berkeley. Spl. counsel Office of Colo. Atty. Gen.; mem. Dist. 33 Colo. House of Reps., Denver, 1998—2004; mem. Dist. 23 Colo. State Senate, Denver, 2004—. Republican. Mem. Lds Church. Office: Colo State Capitol 200 E Colfax Denver CO 80203 Office Phone: 303-866-4667. Business E-Mail: shawnmitch@aol.com.*

MITCHELL, TERENCE EDWARD, materials scientist; b. Haywards Heath, Sussex, Eng., May 18, 1937; came to U.S., 1963, naturalized, 1978; s. Thomas Frank and Dorothy Elizabeth (Perrin) M.; m. Marion Wyatt, Dec. 5, 1959; children: Robin Norman, Jeremy Neil. BA, St. Catharine's Coll., Cambridge U., Eng., 1958, MA, 1962, PhD in Physics, 1962; ScD, U. Cambridge, 1994. Research fellow Cavendish Lab., Cambridge, 1962-63; asst. prof. metallurgy Case Inst. Tech., 1963-66; assoc. prof. Case Western Res. U., 1966-75, prof., 1975-87, adj. prof., 1987—, chmn. dept., 1983-86, dir. high voltage electron microscopy facility, 1970-82, co-dir. materials research lab., 1982-83; vis. scientist NASA at Ames Lab., Stanford U. and Electric Power Research Inst., Palo Alto, Calif., 1975-76; scientist Ctr. Materials Sci. Los Alamos (N.Mex.) Nat. Lab., 1987—, lab fellow, 1991—; lab fellows chair Los Alamos (N.Mex.) Nat. Lab., 1993-95. Chmn. steering com. Electron Microscopy Ctr. Argonne (Ill.) Nat. Lab., 1979-83; cons. in field; mem. vis. com. metals and ceramics div. Oak Ridge Lab., 1987-91; vis. com. solid state scis. div. Ames Lab., 1987-89; sci. adv. com. Sci. and Tech. Ctr. for Superconductivity, 1989-93. Materials sci. editor Microscopy Rsch. and Technique, 1986—; sr. editor North Am., 1994—; contbr. 400 articles to profl. jours. Pres. Cleve. Ethical Soc., 1970-72; bd. dirs Am. Ethical Union, 1972-74; steward Los Alamos Unitarian Ch., 1992-94; mem. policy com. Univ. Materials Coun., 1986-89; mem. policy com. Argonne Electron Microscopy Steering Com., chmn. 1978-82. Electric Power Research Inst. fellow, 1975-76; NSF grantee, 1966-88; Dept. Energy grantee, 1970-86, 87—; NIH grantee, 1969-72; NASA grantee, 1974-77, 81-87; USAF Office Sci. Research grantee, 1974-85; U.S. Army Research Office grantee, 1970-75, 79-83, EPRI grantee, 1986-89; spl. issue in his honor Philos. Mag. A, Sept. 1998; spl. symposium in his honor TMS Ann. Meeting, San Diego, 2003; named Van Horn Disting. Lectr., Case Western Res. U., 2004. Fellow Am. Soc. Metals, Am. Phys. Soc., Am. Ceramics Soc. (assoc. editor jour. 1989-, v.p 1999-2000), Minerals, Metals & Materials Soc., Los Alamos Nat. Lab., Japan Inst. Metals; mem. Japan Soc. Promotion of Sci., Electron Microscopy Soc. Am. (program chmn. 1981-82, dir. 1984-86, pres.-elect 1994, pres. 1995, past pres. 1996), Materials Rsch. Soc., Soc. Francaise de Microscopie Electronique (sci. com. 1982-90). Office: Los Alamos Nat Lab Ctr Materials Sci Ms # G755 Los Alamos NM 87545-0001 Home Phone: 505-662-3323; Office Phone: 505-667-0938. E-mail: temitchell@lanl.gov.

MITCHELL, THEODORE REED, educational association administrator, former academic administrator; b. San Rafael, Calif., Jan. 29, 1956; s. Theodore Robert and Genevieve Dolores (Doose) Mitchell; m. Christine M. Beckman, July 8, 1995; children: Caroline Mitchell Beckman, Theo Beckman. BA, Stanford U., 1978, MA, 1980, PhD, 1983. Asst. prof. Dartmouth Coll., Hanover, NH, 1981—86, assoc. prof., 1986—87, chair dept. edn., 1987—91; dep. to pres. and provost Stanford U., Calif., 1991—92; dean Sch. Edn. and Info. Studies UCLA, 1992—96, vice chancellor, 1996—98; v.p. for edn. and strategic initiatives The J. Paul Getty Trust, 1998—99; pres. Occidental Coll., 1999—2005; CEO NewSchools Venture Fund, San Francisco, 2005—. Trustee Stanford U., 1985—90, Thetford Acad., Vt., 1989—91; bd. dirs. L.A. Edn. Partnership, L.E.A.R.N. Author: Political Education, 1985, Sociology of Education, 1998. Bd. dirs. Children Now, Oakland, Calif., 1994—, Gateway Learning Corp., 1996—. Office: NewSchools Venture Fund 49 Stevenson St, Ste 575 San Francisco CA 94105 Office Phone: 415-615-6860. Fax: 415-615-6861.

MITCHELL, WILLIAM H., computer software company executive; BS in Computer Sci., U. Minn.; M in Computer Sci., PhD in Computer Sci., Ariz. State U. CAD engr. Intel Corp.; co-founder software startup, Tempe, Ariz.; application arch. Microsoft Corp., Redmond, Wash., 1992, co-founder Windows CE, Handheld PC projects, 1993, dir. Handheld PC group, 1996, gen. mgr. Mobile Electronics group., 1998—2000, founder Smart Personal Objects Team, 2000—03, corp. v.p. PC 3 effort, 2003—. Office: Microsoft Corp One Microsoft Way Redmond WA 98052-6399

MITRA, SANJIT KUMAR, electrical and computer engineering educator; b. Calcutta, West Bengal, India, Nov. 26, 1935; came to U.S., 1958; MS in Tech., U. Calcutta, 1956; MS, U. Calif., Berkeley, 1960, PhD, 1962; D of Tech. (hon.), Tampere U. Tech, Finland, 1987; Academician, Acad. Finland, 2000; D in Tech. (hon.), Tech. U. Bucharest, Romania, 2004; D in Tech., U. Iasi, Romania, 2007. Asst. engr. Indian Statis. Inst., Calcutta, 1956-58; from teaching asst. to assoc. Univ. Calif., Berkeley, 1958-62; asst. prof. Cornell U., Ithaca, NY, 1962-65; mem. tech. staff Bell Telephone Labs., Holmdel, NJ, 1965-67; prof. U. Calif., Davis, 1967-77, prof. elec. and computer engring. Santa Barbara, 1977—, chmn. dept. elec. and computer engring., 1979-82; dir. Ctr. for Info. Processing Rsch., 1993-96. Cons. Lawrence Livermore (Calif.) Nat. Lab., 1974-95; cons. editor Van Nostrand Reinhold Co., N.Y.C., 1977-88; mem. adv. bd. Coll. Engring. Rice U., Houston, 1986-89; mem. adv. coun. Rsch. Inst. for Math. and Computing Sci., U. Groningen, The Netherlands, 1995—; mem. adv. bd. Internat. Signal Processing Ctr., Tampere U. of Tech., Finland, 1997—; external assessor Faculty of Engring., U. Putra Malaysia, Serdang, 1997—2000; hon. prof. No. Jiatong U., Beijing, China, 1985, Tech. U. Cluj-Napoka, 2005. Author: Analysis and Synthesis of Linear Active Networks, 1969, Digital and Analog Integrated Circuits, 1980; co-editor: Modern Filter Theory and Design, 1973, Two-Dimensional Digital Signal Processing, 1978, Miniaturized and Integrated Filters, 1989, Multidimensional Processing of Video Signals, 1992, Handbook for Digital Signal Processing, 1993, Digital Signal Processing: A Computer-Based Approach, 1997, 3d edit., 2005, Nonuniform Discrete Fourier Transform and Its Signal Processing Applications, 1998, Digital Signal Processing Laboratory Using MATLAB, 1999, Nonlinear Image Processing, 2000. Recipient F.E. Terman award, 1973, award, AT&T Found., 1985, Edn. award, Am. Soc. Eng. Edn., 1988, U. medal, Tech. U. Slovakia, 2005; named Disting. Fulbright Prof., Coun. for Internat. Exch. of Scholars, 1984, 1986, 1988, Disting. Sr. Scientist, Humboldt Found., 1989, Hon. Citizen, Cluj-Napoca, Romania, 2007. Fellow: IEEE (Tech. Achievement award 1996, Mac Van Valkenburg award 1999, Millennium medal 2000, McGraw-Hill/Jacob Millman award 2001, Best Paper award 2002, James H. Mulligan Jr. Edn. medal 2006, Soc. award 2006, Edn. award 2006), AAAS, Internat. Soc. Optical Engring. (Tech. Achievement award 2005); mem.: India NAS, Indian Nat. Acad. Engring., IEE UK (Blumlein-Browne-Wilans premium 2000), Acad. Engring. Mex., US Nat. Acad. Engring., Norwegian Acad. Technol. Scis., Croatian Acad. Arts and Scis., Acad. of Finland, European Assn. for Signal Processing (Tech. Achievement award 2001). Achievements include patents for two-port networks for realizing transfer functions; non-reciprocal wave translating device; discrete cosine transform-based image coding and decoding method; method and apparatus for multipath channel shaping; method for embedding and extracting digital data in images and videos. Office: Univ Calif Dept Elec and Computer Engring Santa Barbara CA 93106-9560

MITTELSTAEDT, ROBERT E., JR., dean; married; 3 children. BS in Mech. Engring., Tulane U., 1965; MBA, U. Pa., 1971. Founder, pres. Intellego, Inc., 1985—89; mem. faculty Wharton Sch. of U. Pa., Phila., 1973—2004, vice dean exec. edn., 1990—2004, vice dean Wharton West, 2000—01; dean Ariz. State U. W.P. Carey Sch. Bus., Tempe, Ariz., 2004—. Bd. dirs. Lab. Corp. of Am., 1996—, HIP Found., Inc., 1997—, IS&S Inc., 1988—, chmn., 1988—97. Served USN, 1965—70. Office: Ariz State U WP Carey Sch Bus Main Campus PO Box 873506 Tempe AZ 85287-3506 Office Phone: 480-965-2468. Office Fax: 480-965-5539. E-mail: Robert.Mittelstaedt@asu.edu.

MITTERMILLER, JAMES JOSEPH, lawyer; b. Washington, Apr. 13, 1953; s. Jack and Alice Marie (Froeba) M.; m. Elizabeth Gaillard Simons, June 23, 1979; children: Samuel Stoney, Paul Andrew, Laurie Alice, Claire Mary. Student, U. Heidelberg, 1973-74; BA, Claremont McKenna Coll., 1975; JD, U. Calif. Berkeley, 1978. Bar: Calif., U.S. Dist. Ct. (so., ctrl. and ea. dists.) Calif., U.S. Ct. Appeals (9th cir.), U.S. Supreme Ct. Assoc. Sheppard, Mullin, Richter & Hampton, LA, 1978-86, ptnr., 1986—. Panelist Calif. Continuing Edn. of Bar, L.A. and San Diego, 1984—. Dir. Legal Aid Soc. of San Diego, 1990—, pres., 1998-2000; bd.dirs., LaJolla YMCA, 2001-04. Recipient Wiley Manuel Pro Bono award Calif. State Bar, 1992, 2001. Mem. Assn. Bus. Trial Lawyers (bd. dirs. 1998-2001), Am. Inns of Ct., Claremont McKenna Coll. Alumni Assn. San Diego (bd. dirs.). Avocations: swimming, surfing. Office: Sheppard Mullin Richter & Hampton 501 W Broadway Fl 19 San Diego CA 92101-3536

MITZNER, KENNETH MARTIN, electrical engineer, consultant; b. Bklyn., May 7, 1938; s. Louis Bernard and Dora (Sandler) Mitzner; m. Ruth Maria Osorio, Dec. 26, 1968; children: Camille Lorena Mitzner Zeiter, Esther Jeannette Mitzner Lin, Sharon Michelle Mitzner Mentkowski. BS, MIT, 1958; MS, Calif. Inst. Tech., 1959, PhD, 1964. Mem. tech. staff Hughes Aircraft, Malibu, Calif., 1959-64; prin. engr. B-2 divsn. Northrop Corp., Pico Rivera, Calif., 1964-94; owner Mitzner Sci. and Tech., Oceanside, Calif., 1995—. Instr. U. Calif., Santa Barbara, 1964—65; lectr. in field. Author: (handbook) Demonstrations Against Abortion & Death Selection, 1970; contbr. chapters to books, articles to profl. jours. Bd. dirs. Nat. Right to Life Com., 1980—81; pres. Mobilization for Unnamed, Oceanside, 1970—; bd. dirs. Ams. United for Life, 1971—94; sec. Calif. Pro Life Coun., Sacramento, 1972; mem. Los Angeles County Select Citizens Com. Life Support Policies, LA, 1983—85; bd. dirs. Jewish Life Issues Com., Solana Beach, 1983—. Recipient Pres.'s award, 1979; named Patron of Life, Calif. Pro Life Coun., 1976; Howard Hughes fellow, 1959—64, Fulbright Found. grantee, Govt. of Italy, 1961—62. Fellow: IEEE (life); mem.: Electromagnetics Acad., U.S. Nat. Commn. Internat. Union Radio Sci. (del. 20th gen. assembly). Jewish. Avocations: history, stamp collecting/philately, birdwatching. Personal E-mail: kmitzner@aol.com.

MIYASAKI, GEORGE JOJI, artist; b. Kalopa, Hawaii, Mar. 24, 1935; BFA, Calif. Coll. Arts and Crafts, 1957, MFA, 1958. Asst. prof. art Calif. Coll. Arts and Crafts, Oakland, 1958-64; mem. faculty dept. art U. Calif., Berkeley, 1964-94, prof. emeritus, 1994—. Grantee John Hay Whitney fellow, 1957—58; Tamarind printing fellow, 1961, Guggenheim fellow, 1963—64, Nat. Endowment for Arts fellow, 1980—81, 1985—86. Mem.: NAD. Home: 2844 Forest Ave Berkeley CA 94705-1309

MIYATA, KEIJIRO, culinary arts educator; b. Tokyo, Mar. 8, 1951; came to U.S., 1967; s. Yataro Miyata and Hekkiken (Liu) Choy; m. Connie Joyce Nelson, Mar. 8, 1976; children: Michelle, Kelly, Adam. Assoc. in Occupational Study, Culinary Inst. Am., Hyde Park, NY, 1972, cert. of nutrition, 1991; cert., Seattle Wine Sch., 1991. Cert. exec. chef; cert. culinary educator. Garde mgr. Mid-Pacific Country Club, Kailua, Hawaii, 1972; working chef Waikiki Yacht Club, Honolulu, 1972-74, Sagano Japanese Restaurant, New Rochelle, N.Y., 1974-76; asst. pastry chef Rye Town (N.Y.) Hilton Hotel, 1976-77; working chef The Explorer, Everett, Wash., 1977-79; exec. chef Holiday Inn, Everett, 1979-81, Mill Creek (Wash.) Country Club, 1981; culinary art instr. Everett Community Coll., 1981-85, North Seattle (Wash.) Community Coll., 1985-90, Seattle Cen. Community Coll., 1990—. Cons. Chalon Corp., Redmond, Wash., Chiang-Mai Restaurant, Mukilteo, Wash., 1988, Holiday Inn Crown Plaza, Seattle, Satsuma Japanese Restaurant, 1996; USA rep. Winterlude Crystal Garden Ice Masters Invitational, Ottawa, Can. Participant Nagano Winter Olympic Ice Sculpture Festival, Karuizawa, Japan, 1998. Recipient Gold awards Am. Culinary Fedn., Oreg. State Chef's Assn., Portland, 1983, Gold and Bronze medals World Culinary Olympic, Frankfurt, Germany, 1984, 1988, Grand Champion award U.S. Nat. Ice Carving Contest, N.Y.C., 1986, 2d place award, All Japan Ice Carving Assn., Asahikawa, 1988, Ednl. Excellence award Oreg. and Wash. Community coll. Couns. Wash. Fedn. of Tchrs./Am. Fedn. of Tchrs./AFL-CIO, 1988, 1989, ACF Seafood Challenge State finalist, Charlotte, N.C., 1989, New Orleans, 1990, 1st place, Pacific Rim Invitational World Ice Sculpting Classic, 1989, Seymour Ice Sculpting Competition, 1991, 3d Ann. Internat. Ice Sculpting Competition, Lake Louise, Alta., Can., 1993, award of Excellence, Wash. Fedn. Tchrs./Am. Fedn. Tchrs./AFL-CIO, 1993, 1st place, Wash. State Seafood Festival Recipe Contest, Shelton, Wash., 1993, Grand Champion, 1994, 1st place, ICE ART'94 Ice Sculpting Competition, Fairbanks, Alaska, 1994, Most Artistic award Asahikawa Internat. Ice Sculpting Competition, 1996, 1st place Ice Carver's Choice, People's Choice Awards--8th Internat. Ice Carving Championship, Anchorage, Alaska, 1997, selected as Snow Sculpting Team Mem. of Sister City of Portland, Internat. Snow Sculpting Competition, Sapporo, Japan, 1997, participant, Nagano Winter Olympic Ice Sculpture Festival, Karuizawa, Japan, 1998, NICA, Gold Medal Ice Carver's Choice Awd., People's awd., Crystal Gall. of Ice, Internatl. Carving Comp., Alaska, 1999, 1st place, People's Choice Awards--7th Annual Internat. Sculpting Competition, Lake Louise, Alberta, Canada, 2000, 2d Place Hokkaido Newspaper award, Asahikawa Internat. Ice Sculpting competition, 2000, 3rd place team, Ice Alaska, Ice Art, Fairbank, Alaska, 2001, 1st place, People's Choice Award, 9th Ann. Internat. Ice Sculpting Competition, Lake Louise, Alta., 2002, Trustees Lifelong Learning award, Seattle CC, 2003—04. Mem. Wash. State Chefs Assn. (bd. dirs. 1982, 83, 86, 87, 88, cert. chmn. 1986-92, Chef of Yr. 1986), Am. Acad. Chefs, Nat. Ice Carving Assn. Office: Seattle Ctr Cmty Coll 1701 Broadway Seattle WA 98122-2413 Business E-Mail: kmiyat@sccd.ctc.edu.

MIZEL, LARRY A., housing construction company executive; b. 1942; married. BA, U. Okla., 1964; JD, U. Denver, 1967. Founder, dir. MDC Holdings Inc., Denver, 1972—, pres., 1996—99, chmn. bd., CEO, 1999—. Past trustee Marsico Investment Fund; dir. Richmond Am. Homes. Chmn. bd. Simon Weisenthal Ctr., 2003—. Office: MDC Holdings Inc 4350 S Monaco St Denver CO 80237-1867

MIZGALA, HENRY F., physician, consultant, retired medical educator; b. Montreal, Can., Nov. 28, 1932; s. Louis and Mary (Ropeleski) M.; m. Pauline Barbara Delaney, Oct. 26, 1957; children: Paul Stephen, Cynthia Louise, Liane Mary Mizgala Sizemore, Melanie Frances Mizgala Dressler, Nancy Elizabeth Mizgala Lewis. BA magna cum laude, Loyola Coll., Montreal, 1953; MD, CM, McGill U., 1957. Rotating intern, then resident in medicine St. Mary's Hosp., Montreal, 1957—59, asst. physician, 1963—66; resident in medicine Royal Victoria Hosp., Montreal, 1959—60; Dazian fellow cardiology Mt. Sinai Hosp., NYC, 1960—61, USPHS fellow cardiology, 1961—62; resident in cardiology Montreal Gen. Hosp., 1962—63, assoc. physician, 1966—74; asst. physician, cons. cardiology Lachine Gen. Hosp., Que., 1964—80; mem. faculty McGill U. Med. Sch., Montreal, 1968—74, assoc. prof. medicine, 1973—74; assoc. prof., then prof. Montreal U. Med. Sch., 1974—81; cardiologist Montreal Heart Inst., also dir. CCU, 1974—80; prof. medicine U. B.C., 1980—87, prof. medicine, head divsn. cardiology, 1980—87, prof. medicine emeritus, 1998—; hon. attending med. staff, cardiologist Vancouver Hosp. and Health Scis. Ctr. Cons. Centre Hosp. Baie des Chaleurs, Gaspe, Que., 1975—80, B.C. Cancer Agy., Vancouver, 1981—; cons. staff Univ. Hosp., U. B.C. site, 1981—94; hon. cons. Montreal Heart Inst., 1980—. Mem. editl. bd. Can. Jour. Cardiology, 1988-99, Jour. Am. Coll. Cardiology, 1992-95; contbr. articles to profl. jours. Fellow Royal Coll. Physicians and Surgeons Can., Am. Coll. Cardiology, Am. Heart Assn. (coun. clin. cardiology); mem. Can. Med. Assn., Can. Cardiovasc. Soc. (treas. 1974-90), Que. Med. Assn., B.C. Med. Assn., B.C. and Yukon Heart and Stroke Found. (bd. dirs., sr. bd. dirs.), Alpha Omega Alpha. Office: UBC Hosp Dept Cardiology 511 211 Wesbrook Mall Vancouver BL V6T 2B3 Canada Office Phone: 604-822-1747.

MLADENICH, RONALD E., publishing executive; BA in Bus. Adminstrn., U. Puget Sound, 1965. Buyer Boeing Co., Renton, Wash., 1965-68; sales/contracts Stellar Hydraulics, Sun Valley, Calif., 1968-74; circulation mgr. News Tribune, Tacoma, 1974—, transp. mgr., 1999—. Carl Burkheimer Meml. scholar N.W. Internat. Circulation Execs., 1993. Mem. Internat. Circulation Mgr. Assn. (promotions award chairperson 1986), N.W. Internat. Circulation Execs. (pres. 1984-92), Western Conf. Circulation Execs. (pres. 1985, 86). Office: News Tribune 1950 S State St Tacoma WA 98405-2817

MOBERG, JENS WINTHER, computer software company executive; married; 2 children. Grad., Copenhagen Bus. Sch. IT consulting and application devel. IBM; joined Microsoft Corp., 1995, mktg. dir. Nordic countries, 1997—98, gen. mgr. Microsoft Denmark, 1998, regional dir. Nordic and Baltic countries, regional dir. Ctrl. and So. Europe, EMEA v.p., regional dir. Western Europe, corp. v.p. US Enterprise & Ptnr. Group, 2005—. Mem.: Danish IT Industry Assn. (chmn.). Avocations: skiing, hiking, jogging, tennis. Office: Microsoft Corp One Microsoft Way Redmond WA 98052-6399

MOBLEY, KAREN RUTH, art director; b. Cheyenne, Wyo., Aug. 26, 1961; d. David G. and Marlene G. (Franz) M. BFA, U. Wyo., 1983; MFA, U. Oka., 1987. Sales assoc. Morgan Gallery, Kansas City, Mo., 1984-85; grad. asst. U. Okla. Mus. Art, Norman, 1985-87; dir. Univ. Art Gallery N.Mex. State U., Las Cruces, 1988-93; exec. dir. Nicolaysen Art Mus., Casper, Wyo., 1993-96; dir. Spokane Arts Com., 1997—. Guest artist Oklahoma City C.C., 1986. Exhbns. include Phoenix Triennial, 1990, New Am. Talent, Laguna Gloria Art Mus., Austin, Tex., 1992, Adair Margo Gallery, El Paso, 1992-94, Wyo. Arts Coun. Gallery and Casper Coll., 1995, Mont. State U., 1996, Whitworth Coll., 2004, Good Works Gallery, 2005 Trustee Westminster Congl. Ch.; bd. dirs. Spokane Pub. Radio. Wyo. Arts Coun. Individual Artist grantee 1994, Lit. fellow, 1995-96; named Outstanding Young Women Am. Mem. Am. Assn. Mus., Coll. Art Assn., Wash. State Arts Alliance, Rotary 21, Phi Beta Kappa, Phi Kappa Phi. Office: Spokane Arts Com 808 W Spokane Falls Blvd Spokane WA 99203 Office Phone: 509-625-6050. Business E-Mail: kmobley@spokanecity.org.

MOCHIDA, PAULA T., library director; Reference libr. to head Sinclair Libr. U. Hawaii, Manoa, 1974—98; spl. asst. distance learning U. Hawaii Sys., 1998—2005; interim assoc. univ. libr. adminstrn. and pub. svcs. U. Hawaii, Manoa, 2006, acting univ. libr., 2006—. Mem. adv. bd. U. Hawaii Libr. and Info. Sci. prog. Editor: Ke Kukini Library Newsletter. Office: U Hawaii Manoa Libr 2550 McCarthy Mall Honolulu HI 96822 Office Phone: 808-956-2472. E-mail: paula@hawaii.edu.

MOCK, HENRY BYRON, lawyer, writer, consultant; b. Greenville, Tex., Feb. 1, 1911; s. Henry Byron and Ellena (Edmonds) M.; m. Mary Morris, Nov. 11, 1949. AB, U. Ariz., 1933; JD, Georgetown U., 1939, George Washington U., 1940. Asst. sec. to Congresswoman Isabella Greenway of Ariz., 1934-35; office mgr., legal research asst., recreation div. WPA, Washington, 1935-38, asst. atty., 1938; legal adv. President's Adv. Com. on Edn., 1938-39; asst. solicitor Dept. Interior, 1939-41; chief counsel U.S. Grazing Service, Salt Lake City, 1941-42; adminstr. region IV U.S. Bur. Land Mgmt., Colo., Utah, 1947-54, area adminstr. Idaho, Ariz., Utah, Nev., 1954-55; exec. resource cos., 1955—. Adj. prof. law U. Utah, 1979— Contbr. profl. publs. Chmn. Dept. Interior storm relief com. Western U.S., 1949; mem. U.S. Pub. Land Law Rev. Commn., 1964-70, vice chmn., 1965-70; mem. Interior Oil Shale Com., 1964. Served pvt. to capt. with AUS, 1942-46, MTO. Mem. D.C., Va., Utah bar assns. Bar Supreme Ct. of U.S., Am., Fed. bar assn., U.S. C. of C., Bar of Ct. Mil. Appeals, Am. Inst. Mining and Metall. Engrs., Am. Soc. Range Mgmt., Am. Soc. Pub. Adminstrn. (past Utah pres.), Western Polit. Sci. Assn., Am. Forestry Assn., Pi Kappa Alpha. Clubs: Rotary (Salt Lake City), Alta (Salt Lake City). Home and Office: 900 Donner Way Apt 101 Salt Lake City UT 84108-4113

MOCK, THEODORE JAYE, finance educator; b. Traverse City, Mich., May 28, 1941; s. Raymond Doris and Georgeann (Lardie) M.; m. Mary Jo Icenhower, Mar. 25, 1962; children: Christopher, Cameron BS in Math., Ohio State U., 1963, MBA in Fin., 1964; PhD in Bus. Adminstrn., U. Calif.-Berkeley, 1969. Dir. AIS Research Ctr. UCLA, 1969-73; dir. Ctr. Acctg. Research, Arthur Andersen Alumni prof. acctg. U. So. Calif., 1982—. Vis. prof. Norwegian Sch. Econs. and Bus., Bergen, 1988, Bond U., Gold Coast, Australia, 1990, 92, So. Cross U., Lismore, Australia, 1994, Australia Nat. U., 2002-; adj. prof. U. Maastricht, The Netherlands, 1991—; hon. prof. Hong Kong City U., 1995-98; bd. dirs. Maastricht (The Netherlands) Acctg. Rsch. Ctr., U. Limburg, 1991—; Shaw prof. Nanyang Tech. U., Singapore, 1997, Tang Peng Yeu; vis. prof. Nat. U. Singapore, 2000. Author: (monographs) Risk Assessment, 1985, Internal Accounting Control (Am. Acctg. Assn. Wildman medal), 1983, Measurement and Accounting Information Criteria, 1976, Impact of Future Technology on Auditing, 1988, Auditing and Analytic Review, 1989, Belief Functions in Business Decisions, 2002; mem. editorial bd. Auditing: A Jour. of Practice & Theory, 1983-86, 88-93, 99—, editor, 1993-96; mem. editorial bd. The Acctg. Rev., 1972-78, Internat. Jour. Auditing, 1998—. Recipient CPA Faculty Excellence award Calif. CPA Found. for Edn. and Rsch., 1983; Fulbright scholar U. Otago, Dunedin, New Zealand, 1988, U. Limburg, Maastricht, The Netherlands, 1993. Mem. Acctg., Orgns. and Soc. (editorial bd. 1978-93), Am. Acctg. Assn. (dir. rsch. 1982-84, acad. vice chmn. auditing sect. 1990-91, chair auditing sect. 1991-92, Collaboration award with AICPA, 1998, Outstanding Auditing Educator award 2003). Office: U So Calif Sch Acctg Los Angeles CA 90089-0001

MODABBER, ZIA F., lawyer; b. Jan. 9, 1962; BA, U. Calif., Berkeley, 1984; JD, Loyola Law Sch., 1988. Bar: Calif. 1988, US Dist. Ct. (ctrl. dist.) Calif., US Dist. Ct. (no. dist.), US Ct. Appeals (9th cir.). Assoc. Wyman Bautzer Kuchel & Silbert, LA; ptnr. Katten Muchin Rosenman, LA. Mem.: ABA, LA County Bar Assn., St. Thomas More Law Honor Soc. Office: Katten Muchin Rosenman Ste 2600 2029 Century Park E Los Angeles CA 90067 Office Phone: 310-788-4627. Office Fax: 310-712-8462. Business E-Mail: zia.modabber@kattenlaw.com.

MODISETT, JEFFREY A., lawyer, former state attorney general; b. Windfall, Ind., Aug. 10, 1954; s. James Richard and Diana T. Modisett; m. Jennifer Ashworth, June 9, 1990; children: Matthew Hunter Ashworth, Haden Nicholas. BA, UCLA, 1976; MA, Oxford U., Eng., 1978; JD, Yale U., 1981. Bar: Ind., Calif., D.C. Clk. to Hon. R. Peckham U.S. Dist. Ct. (no. dist.) Calif., San Francisco, 1981—82; asst. U.S. atty. Office U.S. Atty. (ctrl. dist.) Calif., LA, 1982—88; issues dir. Evan Bayh for Gov., Indpls., 1988; exec. asst. to gov. State of Ind., Indpls., 1988—90; prosecutor Marion County, Indpls., 1991—94; sr. counsel Ice Miller Donadio & Ryan, Indpls., 1995—96; atty. gen. State of Ind., 1997—2000; dep. CEO, gen. counsel Dem. Nat. Conv., 2000; co-CEO TechNet, Palo Alto, Calif., 2000—01; ptnr. Manatt Phelps & Phillips LLP, 2001—02; mng. ptnr. Bryan Cave LLP, LA, 2002—. Chmn. Gov. Commn. for Drug Free Ind., Indpls., 1989—, Gov. Coun. on Impaired and Dangerous Driving, Indpls., 1989—; pres. Family Advocacy Ctr., Indpls., 1991—94, Hoosier Alliance Against Drugs, Indpls., 1993—96; dir. Cmty. Couns. of Indpls., 1991—93; chmn. Ind. Criminal Justice Inst., Indpls., 1989—90, dir., 1989—; vice chmn. Juvenile Justice and Youth Gang Study Com., Indpls., 1992—94; legal analyst Sta. WTHR-TV, Indpls., 1995—96. Author: Prosecutor's Perspective, 1991—94; editor-in-chief: Yale Jour. Internat. Law, 1980—81. Co-chair Ind. State Dem. Coordinated Campaign, Indpls., 1996. Recipient Spl. Enforcement award, U.S. Customs, 1988, Child Safety Adv. award, Automotive Safety for Children, 1997, STAR Alliance Impact award, 1998, Spirit of Ind. award, Am. Lung Assn., 1999; named Top Lawyer, Indpls. Monthly mag., 1993; named to Sagamore of Wabash, State of Ind., 1995. Mem.: Indpls. Bar Assn., Ind. Bar Assn. Democrat. Avocation: bicycling. Office: Bryan Cave LLP 120 Broadway, Ste 300 Santa Monica CA 90401 Office Phone: 310-576-2370. Office Fax: 310-576-2200. E-mail: jamodisett@bryancave.com.

MODJTABAI, AVID, bank executive; b. 1961; 1 child. BS in Indsl. Engring., Stanford U.; MBA in Fin., Columbia U. With McKinsey & Co.; exec. v.p., dir. Internet svcs. Wells Fargo, San Francisco, head online personal fin. svcs., exec. v.p., dir. HR, 2005—07, exec. v.p., CIO, dir. tech. and info. group, 2007—. Active The B.A.Y. Fund. Named one of 100 Most Influential Women in Bay Area Bus., San Francisco Bus. Times, 2004—05, 25 Most Powerful Women in Banking, US Banker, 2004, 25 Women to Watch, 2006, 2007. Office: Wells Fargo 420 Montgomery St San Francisco CA 94104

MODNY, CYNTHIA JEAN, dermatologist; b. Jan. 23, 1945; d. Michael Theodore and Mary (Tabaka) M. BA, Mt. Holyoke Coll., 1967; MD, U. Va., Charlottesville, 1971. Diplomate Am. Bd. Dermatology. Intern Lenox Hill Hosp., NYC, 1971-72; resident N.Y. Hosp./Cornell Med. Ctr., NYC, 1972-75, instr. dermatology, 1976—81; practice medicine specializing in dermatology Montclair, N.J., 1976-92, Phoenix, 1994—2006. Pvt. practice cons. undersea medicine, Montclair, 1982-92; clin. instr. dermatology Skin and Cancer Unit, NYU Med. Ctr., N.Y.C., 1981-92; participant Physicians' Undersea Medicine Tng., NOAA, Miami, Fla., 1982; dir. Skin Cancer Inst., Montclair, 1984. Med. editor Dive Travel Report (monthly), 1983-92; contbr. article to Skin Diver mag. Bd. dirs. Montclair Sr. Citizens, 1984. Fellow Am. Acad. Dermatology; mem. Undersea Med. Soc., Am. Soc. Dermatologic Surgery, Princeton Club, Mt. Holyoke Club (N.Y.C.).

MOECKEL, STEVEN, concertmaster; b. Germany, 1978; Studied, Ind. U. Co-concertmaster Ulm Philharmonic; concertmaster Tucson Symphony Orch., 2002—. Mem., master class and recital Greater Oro Valley Arts Coun. Fundraiser uninsured cancer patients; mem. Tucson Arthritis Support League. Named one of 40 Under 40, Tucson Bus. Edge, 2006. Office: Tucson Symphony Center 2175 N Sixth Ave Tucson AZ 85705-5606 Office Phone: 520-792-9155.

MOEHLE, JACK P., civil engineer, engineering executive; BSCE, MSCE, U. Ill., 1977, PhD, 1980. Registered civil engr., Calif. From asst. to assoc. prof. U. Calif., Berkeley, 1980-90, prof., 1990—, Roy W. Carlson Disting. prof. civil engring., vice-chair tech. svcs. civil engring., 1990-91, dir. earthquake engring. rsch. ctr., 1991—. Tech. advisor Double Deck Peer Rev. Panel, Caltrans, 1990—; mem. sci. adv. com. Nat. Ctr. Earthquake Engring. Rsch.; proposal reviewer NSF; cons. in field; bd. dirs. Calif. Univs. Rsch. Earthquake Engring., Cooperating Orgns. No. Calif. Earthquake Rsch. and Tech. Contbr. articles to profl. jours.; reviewer tech. papers. Recipient Chi Epsilon Excellence Teaching award, 1986; Regents Jr. Faculty fellow, 1981. Fellow Am. Concrete Inst. (chmn. detail and proportion earthquake resisting structural elements and systems com. 1988—, mem. various coms.); mem. ASCE (publs. sec. com. seismic effects, Huber Rsch. prize 1990), Structural Engrs. Assn. Calif. (mem. seismology com., reinforced concrete com., bd. dirs.), Earthquake Engring. Rsch. Inst. Office: U Calif Berkeley Earthquake Engring Rsch Ctr 1301 S 46th St Richmond CA 94804-4600

MOELLEKEN, BRENT RODERICK WILFRED, plastic surgeon; b. Vancouver, BC, Can., Apr. 19, 1960; m. Dayna Devon; 2 children. BA, Purdue U., 1979; MD, Yale U., 1985; postgrad., Harvard U., 1980-81. Diplomate Am. Bd. Surgery, Am. Bd. Plastic Surgery. Intern U. Calif., San Francisco, 1985-86, resident in gen. surgery, 1986-92, rsch. fellow in plastic surgery, 1988-90, resident in plastic surgery, 1992-94; fellow in aesthetic surgery UCLA, 1994-95; pvt. practice Beverly Hills, Calif., 1995—, Santa Barbara, Calif., 1995—. Attending surgeon UCLA Hosp., Cedars-Sinai Hosp., LA, Century City Hosp.; instr. U. Calif. Sch. Medicine, San Francisco, 1992-94, clin. instr. UCLA, 1994-99, assoc. clin. prof., 1999-2007; surgeon ABC-TV Extreme Makeover, Oprah, Discovery Channel, E!, CNN, NBC. Plastic surgery before and after lead surgeon: (TV series) Discovery Health Channel; contbr. several articles to profl. jours.; appeared in: over 60 TV shows. Founder About Face surg. found. Fellow ACS; mem. AMA, AAAS, Am. Soc. Plastic Surgeons, Am. Soc. Aesthetic Plastic Surgery, Calif. Med. Assn., Calif. Soc. Plastic Surgeons, Santa Barbara County Med. Soc., LA County Med. Assn., LA Soc. Plastic Surgeons, LA Surg. Soc., Wound Healing Soc. (founding mem.), Lipoplasty Soc. N.Am. Achievements include invention of Livefill graft; superficial cheek lift operation; hybrid abdominoplasty 360 facelift. Office: 120 S Spalding Dr Ste 340 Beverly Hills CA 90212 Office Phone: 310-273-1001. Office Fax: 310-205-4881. Personal E-mail: drbrent@drbrent.com. Business E-Mail: info@drbrent.com.

MOERBEEK, STANLEY LEONARD, lawyer; b. Toronto, Ont., Can., 1951; arrived in U.S., 1953; s. John Jacob and Mary Emily Moerbeek; m. Carol Annette Mordaunt, Apr. 17, 1982; children: Sarah, Noah. BA magna cum laude, Calif. State U., Fullerton, 1974; student, U. San Diego-Sorbonne, Paris, 1977; JD, Loyola U., 1979. Bar: Calif. 1980; cert. in internat. bus. transactions, bankruptcy and bus. rehab., and civil trial practice. From law clk. to assoc. McAlpin Doonan & Seese, Covina, Calif., 1977-81; assoc. Robert L. Baker, Pasadena, Calif., 1981-82, Miller Bush & Minnott, Fullerton, 1982-83; prin. Law Office of Stanley L. Moerbeek, Fullerton, 1984—. Notary pub. lt. gov. 9th cir. law student divsn. ABA, 1979; judge pro tem Orange County Superior Ct., 1984—96. Mem. Heritage Found., Washington, 1989—. Recipient plaque of Appreciation, Fullterton Kiwanis, 1983; Calif. Gov.'s Office scholar, 1970. Mem.: Orange County Bar Assn. (Coll. Trial Advocacy 1985), Calif. Assn. Realtors (referral panel atty. 1985—), Phi Kappa Phi. Roman Catholic. Avocations: history, politics, sports. Office: 1370 N Brea Blvd Ste 210 Fullerton CA 92835-4128 Office Phone: 714-773-5396. Personal E-mail: slmlaw@sbcglobal.net.

MOERNER, WILLIAM ESCO, physical chemist, educator; b. Pleasanton, Calif., June 24, 1953; s. William Alfred and Bertha Frances M.; m. Sharon Judith Stein, June 19, 1983; 1 child, Daniel Everett. BS in Physics and Elec. Engring., Washington U., St. Louis, 1975. AB in Math., 1975; MS in Physics, Cornell U., 1978, PhD in Physics, 1982. Langsdorf engring. fellow Washington U., St. Louis, 1971-75; NSF grad. fellow Cornell U., Ithaca, N.Y., 1975-78, rsch. asst., 1978-81; mem. rsch. staff IBM Almaden Rsch. Ctr., San Jose, Calif., 1981-88, mgr. Laser-Materials Interactions, 1988-89, rsch. staff mem. and photorefractive polymer project leader, 1989-95; prof. and disting. chair phys. chemistry and biochemistry U. Calif., San Diego, 1995-98; prof. chemistry Stanford U., Calif., 1998—, Harry S. Mosher prof. chemistry Calif., 2002, prof. applied physics Calif., 2005. Gen. chair Topical Meeting on Persistent Spectral Hole-Burning, 1991; Samuel L. McElvain lectr., dept. chemistry, U. Wis., 1993; Ehrenfest Colloquium lectr., U. Leiden, The Netherlands, 1994; vis. guest prof., lab. for phys. chemistry, Swiss Inst. Tech., Switzerland, 1993-94; A.D. Little Lectr., Dept. Chemsitry, MIT, 1995; Robert Burns Woodward vis. prof. Harvard U., 1997-98. Author, editor: Persistent Spectral Hole-Burning: Science and Applications, 1988, Single Molecule Optical Detection, Imaging, and Spectroscopy, 1997; guest editor, spl. issue, Accounts of Chem. Rsch. on Single Molecules and Atoms, 1996; adv. editor Chemical Physics Letters, Chem. Phys. Chem.; contbr. articles to tech. publs. Tenor San Jose Symphonic Choir, 1983-91, Stanford Symphonic Chorus, 2000—; ofcl. observer Am. Radio Relay League, Santa Clara Valley, Calif., 1987-88, asst. tech. coord., 1990-95, asst. emergency coord., 2000—08. Named Wilkinson Outstanding Young Elec. Engr. award, Nat. Winner Eta Kappa Nu, 1984; recipient IBM Outstanding Technical Achievement awards for Photon-Gated Persistent Spectral Hole-Burning, 1988, Single-Molecule Detection and Spectroscopy, 1992, Earle K. Plyler prize for molecular spectroscopy, 2001; co-recipient Wolf Found. prize in Chemistry, Israel, 2008, Irving Langmuir prize, 2009. Fellow Am. Phys. Soc.(symposium organizer, laser sci. topical group, 1992, March mtg., 1993), Optical Soc. Am.(chair fundamental and applied spectroscopy technical group, 1992-94, gen. chair and founder, adv. chair topical conf. on persistent spectral hole-burning sci. and applications, 1991, 1993, 1994, co-editor), Am. Acad. Arts and Scis., AAAS, Geoffrey Frew Fellow Australian Acad. Scis.,; mem. IEEE (sr. mem., asst. treas. Lasers and Electro-Optics Soc. ann. meeting 1988, 1989, symposium organizer, ann. mtg. 1989), Am. Chem. Soc. (organizer, symposium on chemistry of single molecules, 1997), Biophys. Soc., IBM Amateur Radio Club (pres. 1987-88), Materials Rsch. Soc. (symposium organizer, 1991), Soc. Photo-Optical Instrumentation Engrs. (mem. program com., 1996-98), NAS. Achievements include single molecule detection and spectroscopy being a patentee in strain-sensitive spectral features detection method, device, photorefractive polymers. Office: Dept Chemistry, M/C 5080 Stanford Univ 375 N-S Mall Stanford CA 94305-5080 Office Phone: 650-723-1727. Office Fax: 650-725-0259. Business E-Mail: wmoerner@stanford.edu.

MOFFETT, KENNETH LEE, superintendent; b. Mt. Vernon, Wash., May 6, 1935; s. Charles R. and Edith May Moffett; m. Diane Muriel Buckley, July 30, 1966; children: Kendis Charlene, Patrick Charles. BA, Western Wash. State U., 1957; MA, Calif. State U., LA, 1958—60; EdD, U. So. Calif., 1972. Tchr. pub. schs., Inglewood, Calif., 1957—61, 1963—65; asst. prin., 1965—69; prin., 1969—73; tchr. U.S. Dependent Sch., Pirmasens, Fed. Republic Germany, 1961—62; asst. prin. Erlangen, Fed. Republic Germany, 1962—63; asst. supt. Inglewood Sch. Dist., Calif., 1973—76; supt. Lennox Sch. Dist., Calif., 1976—86, ABC Unified Sch. Dist., Cerritos, Calif., 1986—96; interim supt. Oak Pk. Unified Sch. Dist., Calif., 2003, Pleasant Valley Sch. Dist., Calif., 2006—. Mem. adv. bd. Ad Hoc Com. on Mental Health for Tchrs., LA, 1980—81; chmn. scholarship com. Bank of Am., 1979—84; educator in residence Pepperdine U., 1994—2001. Mem. adv. com. LA Area coun. Boy Scouts Am., 1981—83; mem. support group for U. So. Calif., 1978—84; bd. dirs. Centinela Valley Guidance Clinic, Inglewood, 1978—82. Recipient Svc. awards, PTA, Inglewood, 1973, Lennox, 1982; named Nat. Supt. of the Yr., Am. Assn. School Adminstrators, 1994. Mem.: Centinela Valley Trustees and Adminstrs. Assn. (sec.-treas. 1977—78), Centinela Valley Supts. Group (chmn. 1980—84), Assn. Calif. Sch. Adminstrs. (region chmn. 1980—82, Svc. award 1982), Centinela Valley Adminstrs. Assn. (charter pres. 1979—80). Republican. Methodist. Office: Pleasant Valley School Dist 600 Temple Ave Camarillo CA 93010

MOGEL, LEONARD HENRY, writer; b. Bklyn., Oct. 23, 1922; s. Isaac and Shirley (Goldman) M.; m. Ann Vera Levy, Oct. 23, 1949; children: Wendy Lynn, Jane Ellen. BBA, CCNY, 1947. Salesman N.Y. Printing Co., NYC, 1946-48; sales mgr. Pollak Printing Co., NYC, 1948-52; advt. dir. Diners Club, Inc., NYC, 1952-56; pub. Diners Club for Signature and Bravo mags., 1956-67; pres. Leonard Mogel Assos., Inc. (nat. advt. reps.), NYC, 1952-67; prin. owner San Francisco Warriors Profl. Basketball Team, 1963-64; pres. Twenty First Century Comm. Inc., NYC, 1967-72; pub. Cheetah and Weight Watchers mags., 1967-75; dir. Regents Pub. Co. divsn. Simon & Schuster, 1960-67; advt. cons. Harvard Lampoon, 1968; pub. Nat. Lampoon, 1970-86, Liberty mag., 1971-73, Ingenue mag., 1973-75, Heavy Metal mag., 1977-86. Adj. prof. NYU Sch. Continuing Edn., 1973—78; panelist Folio Mag. Pub. Conf., 1975—76. Exec. prodr.: (feature films) Heavy Metal, 1981; author: Everything You Need to Know to Make It in the Magazine Business, 1979, Making It in the Media Professions, 1988, Making It in Advertising, 1993, Making It in Public Relations, 1993, Making It in Broadcasting, 1994, Making It in Book Publishing, 1996, Creating Your Career in Communications, the Media and Entertainment, 1998, The Newspaper: Everything You Need to Know to Make It in the Newspaper Business, 2000, This Business of Broadcasting, 2004. Sponsor Albert Einstein Med. Coll., Birch Wathen Sch., N.Y.C. Served with AUS, 1942-46, CBI. Personal E-mail: mogelpub@aol.com.

MOGG, JIMMY W., gas industry executive; b. Hydro, Okla., 1949; m. Freda Mogg; 2 children. B in Math., Southwestern Okla. State U., 1971; grad. advanced mgmt. program, Harvard U. With gas supply dept. Panhandle Ea. Pipe Line Co., Liberal, Kans., 1973—80; mgr. forcasting and ops. Panhandle Ea., Kansas City, 1980—86; gen. mgr. gas supply Trunkline Gas Co., Houston, 1986—88; gen. mgr. contracts and ops., gas supply Panhandle Ea., Trunkline, 1988; v.p. gas supply Panhandle Ea., Trunkline, Tex. Ea. Transmission Corp., 1989—91; sr. v.p. Panhandle Ea., 1991; pres. Centana Energy Corp., 1992—94; pres., CEO Duke Energy Field Svcs. LP, Denver, NC, 1994—99, chmn., pres., CEO, 1999—2004; group v.p. Duke Energy, Charlotte, NC, 2004—06, chief devel. officer, 2004—06, advisor to chmn., 2006; chmn. DCP Midstream Partners, 2005—. Chmn. bd. dirs. TEPPCO Ptnrs. LP, 1997—2005. Bd. dirs. Rocky Mountain chpt. Jr. Achievement. Mem.: Gas Processors Assn. (past pres.), Soc. Petroleum Engrs. Office: DCP Midstream Partners 370 17th St Ste 2775 Denver CO 80202

MOGUL, LESLIE ANNE, business development and marketing consultant; b. Balt., Mar. 9, 1948; d. Harry and Elaine Mogul; m. William Kasper. AS, Miami Dade Jr. Coll., 1969; BA, Temple U., 1976; MBA, U. Phoenix, 1996. Accredited pub. rels. Account exec. Gray & Rogers, Inc., Phila., 1976-80; pres. Leslie Mogul, Inc., Phila., 1980-84; v.p. McKinney, Inc., Phila., 1984-87; assoc. dir. comm. Scripps Meml. Hosps., San Diego, 1987-93; dir. pub. rels. Scripps Health, San Diego, 1993, dir. customer rels. and mktg., 1994-95; dir. bus. devel. Harborview Med. Ctr. Hosp., San Diego, 1995-96; cons. Projectworks, San Diego, 1996—, pres., 1996—. Recipient over 25 awards local and nat. pub. rels. and comm. orgns. Mem. Pub. Rels. Soc. Am. (dir.-at-large 1993-94), Alumni Leadership Calif. Office: Project Works PO Box 301395 Escondido CA 92030-1395 E-mail: leslie@projectworksmarketing.com.

MOHAJER, DINEH, cosmetics company executive; b. Bloomfield Hills, Mich., Sept. 2, 1972; d. Reza and Shahnaz Mohajer. B in Pre-medicine, U. So. Calif. Founder, CEO Hard Candy, Inc., Beverly Hills, Calif., 1996—. Office: Hardcandy 833 W 16th St Newport Beach CA 92663-2801

MOHAMED, JOSEPH, SR., real estate broker, developer, farmer; b. Omar, W.Va., Mar. 19, 1928; s. Mose and Minnie Elizabeth (Martin) M.; m. Shirley Ida Medeiros; children: Joseph Jr., John W., James R., Leslie Louise. BBA Personnel, Sacramento State U., 1952; postgrad., U. Pacific, U. Calif., Davis, Am. River Coll. Farmer, 1949—; founder comml. trucking operation Calif., 1949-52; founder Mexican Co. of Agr. and Livestock Ltd., Ensenada, Baja, Calif., Mexico, 1953-57; owner Quintair, Inc., Calif., 1954—; contractor, real estate developer, 1949—; owner Joseph's Landscape Svc., Sacramento, 1952—, Joseph Mohamed Enterprises, 1971—. Pest control adviser, Calif., 1970—. Mem. Rep. Nat. Com., Rep. Presdl. Task Force, 1965—, Govs.' Emergency Drought Task Force, 1977, Civil Affairs Assn., Calif. Rental Assn., 1975—, Sacramento Apartment Assn., Calif. Apt. Assn., Nat. Apt. Assn.; dir. McClellan Aviation Museum Found., Sacramento County Sheriff's Mounted Posse, 1961—; pres. First Spiritual Enlightenment Ctr., 1994-. With US Army, 1946—48, col. USAR, 1978, ret. Decorated Legion of Merit; recipient Master Aviator Badge. Mem. Sacramento U. Alumni Assn., Sacramento State U. Horseman's Assn., Calif. State Horseman's Assn., Sacramento Metro. C. of C., Navy League of U.S., Res. Officer's Assn., Assn. of U.S. Army, Mil. Civil Affairs Assn., Sacramento Bd. Realtors, Calif. Assn. Realtors, Nat. Assn. Realtors, Masons, Shriners.

MOHAN, CHANDRA, research biochemistry educator; b. Lucknow, India, Aug. 3, 1950; came to U.S., 1977; s. Prithivi Nath and Tara Rani (Sharma) Shastri; m. Nirmala Devi Sharma, July 23, 1978; children: Deepak, Naveen. BS, Bangalore U., India, 1970, MS, 1972, PhD, 1976. Research assoc. U. So. Calif. Med. Sch., L.A., 1977-83, asst. prof., 1983-93; sr. dir. tech. svc., sr. tech. writer EMD Bioscis., San Diego, 1993—. Assoc. editor Biochem. Medicine, 1986-93; contbr. articles to profl. jours. Recipient BRSG award U. So. Calif., 1983. Mem. AAAS, Am. Diabetes Assn., Am. Soc. for Biochemistry and Molecular Biology, N.Y. Acad. Scis., Am. Inst. Nutrition. Hindu. Avocations: photography, coin collecting/numismatics. Home: 13638 Dicky St Whittier CA 90605-2949 Office: EMD Bioscis Inc 10394 Pacific Center Ct San Diego CA 92121-4340 Office Phone: 858-450-5554. Personal E-mail: csharma4@aol.com. Business E-Mail: chandra.mohan@emdbiosciences.com.

MOHR, GARY ALAN, physician; b. Erie, Pa., Aug. 17, 1952; s. Arthur John and Sue (Richardson) m. Christina Wiser; children: Benjamin, Nathan, Elizabeth, Katelyn, Eric. BS, Pa. State U., 1975; MD, Jefferson Med. Coll., 1979. Cert. Am. Bd. Family Practice. Intern, resident in family medicine St. Vincent Health Ctr., Erie, Pa., 1979-82; pvt. practice Canon City, Colo., 1982—. Asst. clin. prof. family medicine U. Colo. Health Scis. Ctr. Founder, treas. Jefferson Soc., Fremont County, Colo., 1991. Fellow Am. Acad. Family Physicians; mem. Fremont County Med. Soc. (past pres.), Mensa. Lutheran. Achievements include climbing Mt. Kilimanjaro, Oct. 2000. Office: 730 Macon Ave Canon City CO 81212-3314 Office Phone: 719-275-1618.

MOHRAZ, JUDY JOLLEY, foundation administrator; b. Houston, Oct. 1, 1943; d. John Chesler and Mae (Jackson) Jolley; m. Bijan Mohraz; children: Andrew, Jonathan. BA, Baylor U., 1966, MA, 1968; PhD, U. Ill., 1974. Lectr. history Ill. Wesleyan U., 1972-74; asst. prof. history So. Meth. U., Dallas, 1974-80, coord. women's studies, 1977-81, assoc. prof. history, 1980-94, asst. provost, 1983-88, assoc. provost for student academics, 1988-94; pres. Goucher Coll., Towson, Md., 1994-2000, Virginia G. Piper Charitable Trust, Scottsdale, Ariz., 2000—. Cons. Ednl. Testing Svc., Princeton, NJ, 1984-93, Nat. Park Svcs., Seneca Falls, NY, 1992-93; bd. dirs. Balt. Equitable Soc., 1996-00, The Assocs. First Capital, 1999-00, Coun. Foundations, 2005-; bd. visitors US Naval Acad., 1996-01. Trustee St. Mark's Sch. Tex., 1993-94; adv. bd. U. Tex. Southwestern Med. Sch., 1992-94; active Leadership Dallas, 1994; bd. dirs. Nat. Assn. Ind., The Balt. Cmty. Found., Coun. of Founds., 2005—; pres. Ariz. Grantmakers Forum, 2003-05; mem. Ariz. State Sch. Readiness Bd., 2003-07; bd. dirs. Greater Phoenix Leadership, 2005—. Recipient Disting. Alumni award Baylor U., 1993; named Woman of Merit, Omicron Delta Kappa, 1993. Office: Virginia G Piper Charitable Trust 1202 E Missouri Ave Phoenix AZ 85014-2921 Home Phone: 602-957-9433; Office Phone: 480-948-5853. Business E-Mail: jmohraz@pipertrust.org.

MOHRMAN, KATHRYN J., academic administrator; BA, Grinnell Coll., 1967; MA, U. Wis., 1969; PhD, George Washington U., 1982. Dean undergrad. studies U. Md., College Park, 1988—93; pres. The Colo. Coll., Colorado Springs, 1993—2002; exec. dir. Hopkins-Nanjing Ctr. for Chinese and Am. Studies, Johns Hopkins U., 2003—08; dir. Inst. Univ. Design, prof. sch. pub. affairs Ariz. State U., 2008—. Office: 1619 Massachusetts Ave NW Washington DC 20036 Office Phone: 202-496-0463. Business E-Mail: kmohrman@asu.edu.

MOLDAW, STUART G., venture capitalist, retail clothing stores executive; b. 1927; Student, Syracuse U. With Allied Stores, NYC, 1949-51, G. Fox Co., Hartford, Conn., 1951-55; founder Foxmoor Casuals, 1959; co-founder U.S. Venture Ptnrs., 1981; chief exec. officer Ross Store Inc., Newark, Calif., from 1987, chmn. bd., 1988—. Office: Gymboree Corp 700 Airport Blvd Ste 200 Burlingame CA 94010

MOLDENHAUER, SUSAN, museum director, curator; BFA, No. Ill. U., 1974; MFA, Pa. State U., 1982. Gallery mgr. Sch. Visual Arts, Pa. State U.; exec. dir. Second Street Gallery, Charlottesville, Va.; curator mus. progs. U. Wyo. Art Mus., Laramie, 1991—96, asst. dir., 1996—2000, interim dir., 2000—02, dir., chief curator, 2002—. Office: U Wyo Art Mus 2111 Willett Dr Laramie WY 82071-3807 Office Phone: 307-766-6620. E-mail: uwartmus@uwyo.edu.

MOLINA, ALFRED, actor; b. London, May 24, 1953; m. Jill Gascione, 1985; 2 children. Grad., Guildhall Sch. Music and Drama. Film appearances include Raiders of the Lost Ark, 1981, Meantime, 1983, Number One, 1984, Eleni, 1985, Ladyhawke, 1985, Water, 1985, Letter to Brezhnev, 1986, Prick Up Your Ears, 1987, Manifesto, 1988, Not Without My Daughter, 1991, Enchanted April, 1992, American Friends, 1993, The Trial, 1993, Meverick, 1994, White Fang 2: Myth of the White Wolf, 1994, The Steal, 1994, Species, 1995, Scorpoin Spring, 1995, Hideaway, 1995, Dead Man, 1995, Drowning in the Shallow End, 1989, When Pigs Fly, 1993, White Fang II: Myth of the White Wolf, 1994, Maverick, 1994, The Steal, 1994, Hideaway, 1995, The Perez Family, 1995, Dead Man, 1995, Species, 1995, Nervous Energy, 1995, Before and After, 1996, Mojave Moon, 1996, Anna Karenina, 1997, Scorpion Spring, 1997, Further Gesture, 1997, Boogie Nights, 1997, The Man Who Knew Too Little, 1997, Impostors, 1998, The Treat, 1998, Pete's Meteor, 1998, Dudley Do-Right, 1999, Magnolia, 1999, Chocolat, 2000, Texas Rangers, 2001, Frida, 2002, Plots with a View, 2002, Ape, 2002, My Life Without Me, 2003, Identity, 2003, Coffee and Cigarettes, 2003, Luther, 2003, Chronicles, 2004, Spider-Man 2, 2004, (voice) Steamboy, 2004, Sian Ka'an, 2005, The Da Vinci Code, 2006, As You Like It, 2006, The Hoax, 2006, Orchids, 2006, The Moon and the Stars, 2007, Silk, 2007, The Little Traitor, 2007, (voice) The Ten Commandments, 2007, Nothing Like the Holidays, 2008, The Pink Panther 2, 2009; (TV films) The Accountant, 1990, Virtuoso, 1991, Angels, 1992, Ashenden, 1992, A Year in Provence, 1993, The Marshal, 1993, Requiem Apache, 1994, The Place of Lions, 1997, Rescuers: Stories of Courage: Two Couples, 1998, Miracle Maker (voice), 2000, Murder on the Orient Express, 2001; (Broadway shows) Art, 1998, Fiddler on the Roof, 2004 (Tony nom. best actor in a musical, 2004); other stage appearances include Destiny, 1977, Troilus and Cressida, 1977, Bandits, 1977, The Bundle, 1977, Frozen Assets, 1977, That Good Between Us, 1977, King Lear, 1977, Dingo, 1978, Irish Eyes and English Tears, 1978, Willie, 1978, Accidental Death of an Anarchist, 1979 (Plays and Players award for most promising new actor), Destry Rides Again, 1982, Dreyfus, 1982, Viva, 1985, The Night of the Iguana, 1992, Molly Sweeney, 1995 (Theatre World award, 1996, Drama Desk award, 1996), True West, 2001, The Cherry Orchard, 2002, Howard Katz, 2007. Office: William Morris Agy 151 S El Camino Dr Beverly Hills CA 90212-2775

MOLINA, GLORIA, municipal official; b. Montebello, Calif., May 31, 1948; d. Leonardo and Concepcion Molina; m. Ron Martinez, 1 child, Valentina Student, East L.A. Coll., 1968, Calif. State U., LA, 1968-70. Staffing specialist Office Presdl. Pers., Washington, 1977-79; dir. intergovtl and congl. affairs region IX US Dept. Health & Human Services, San Francisco, 1979-81; So. Calif chief dep. Calif. State Rep. Willie L. Brown Jr., 1981; mem. Calif. State Assembly, 1982—86, L.A. City Coun., 1987—91, L.A. County Bd. Supervisors, 1991—, chair, 2005—. Mem. Revenue & Taxation, Labor & Employment, Utilities & Comm. Coms., Select Com. on Small Bus., 1982—, Consumer Protection, 1984—; chairwoman Subcom. Mental Health & Devel. Disabilities, 1984—. Named Hispanic of the Yr. Caminos mag., 1982, Dem. of the Yr. L.A. County Dem. Ctrl. Com., 1983, Woman of the Year Mexican-Am. Opportunity Found., 1983, MS mag, 1984, Woman of the Yr. Hispanic Bus. mag., 2006 Mem. Comision Femenil Mexicana Nacional. Office: LA County 500 W Temple St Ste 856 Los Angeles CA 90012-2723

MOLINA, JOSEPH MARIO (MARIO MOLINA), medical administrator; b. Long Beach, Calif., May 16, 1958; s. C. David and Mary R. (Salandini) M.; m. Therese Ann Flynn; children: Carley, Colleen, David, Mary Clare. BA, Calif. State U., Long Beach, 1980; MD, U. So. Calif., 1984. Diplomate Am. Bd. Internal Medicine. Intern and residency Johns Hopkins U., 1984—87; assoc. investigator VA, San Diego, 1988-90; asst. clin. prof. U. So. Calif., LA, 1990-91; med. dir. Molina Healthcare, Inc., Long Beach, 1991-94, v.p. HMO, 1994—96, chmn., pres., CEO, 1996—. Bd. dirs. New Am. Alliance. Nat. trustee Boys and Girls Club Am. Recipient Ernst & Young Gr. L.A. Entrepreneur of Yr. award, 2002; named one of Top 10 Latinos in Healthcare, LatinoLeaders mag., 2004, 25 Most Influential Hispanics, Time Mag., 2005; named to Hall of Fame, Long Beach Cmty. Coll., 2002. Mem. ACP, Am. Diabetes Assn., Calif. Med. Assn. Avocation: collecting antique medical books. Office: Molina Health Care 200 Oceangate Ste 100 Long Beach CA 90802-4317 Office Phone: 562-435-3666. Business E-Mail: mario.molina@molinahealthcare.com.

MOLINA, MARIO JOSE, physical chemist, educator; b. Mexico City, Mar. 19, 1943; arrived in U.S., 1968; s. Roberto Molina-Pasquel and Leonor Henríquez; m. Alvarez Guadalupe, Feb. 11, 2006; 1 child, Felipe. Bachillerato, Acad. Hispano Mexicana, Mexico City, 1959; Ingeniero Químico, U. Nacional Autónoma de México, 1965; postgrad., U. Freiburg, Fed. Republic Germany, 1966—67; PhD, U. Calif., Berkeley, 1972. Asst. prof. U. Nacional Autónoma de México, 1967—68; research assoc. U. Calif.-Berkeley, 1972—73, U. Calif.-Irvine, 1973—75, asst. prof. phys. chemistry, 1975—79, assoc. prof., 1979—82; sr. rsch. scientist Jet Propulsion Lab., 1983—89; prof. dept. earth, atmospheric and planet sci., dept. chemistry MIT, Cambridge, 1989—96, Martin prof. atmospheric chemistry, 1997—2004, Inst. prof., 1997—2004; prof., chemistry and biochemistry Univ. Calif., San Diego, 2004—; faculty, Ctr. for Atmospheric Sci. Scripps Inst. of Oceanography, 2004—. Bd. dirs. MacArthur Found. Recipient Tyler Ecology award, 1983, Esselen award for chemistry in pub. interest, 1987, Max-Planck-Forschungs-Preis, Alexander von Humboldt-Stiftung, 1994, Nobel Prize in Chemistry, 1995, Sasakawa prize, UNEP, 1999; named a Trailblazer in Sci., Sci. Spectrum Mag., 2005; named one of 50 Most Important Hispanics in Govt., Edn., Hispanic Engineer and Info. Tech. mag., 2005. Mem.: NAS, Pontifical Acad. Sci., Inst. of Medicine, Am. Geophys. Union (Pres.'s Com. on Advisors on Sci. and Tech. 1994—2000), Am. Phys. Soc., Am. Chem. Soc. Achievements include discovery of the theory that fluorocarbons deplete ozone layer of stratosphere. Office: Dept Chem & Biochem UCSD 3050-E 9500 Gilman Dr La Jolla CA 92093-0356 Office Phone: 858-534-1696.

MOLINDER, JOHN IRVING, engineering educator, consultant; b. Erie, Pa., June 14, 1941; s. Karl Oskar and Carin (Ecklund) M.; m. Janet Marie Ahlquist, June 16, 1962; children: Tim, Karen. BSEE, U. Nebr., 1963; MSEE, Air Force Inst. Tech., 1964; PhD EE, Calif. Inst. Tech., 1969. Registered profl. engr., Calif. Project officer Ballistic Systems Div., Norton AFB, Calif., 1964-67; sr. engr. Jet Propulsion Lab., Pasadena, Calif., 1969-70; prof. engring. Harvey Mudd Coll., Claremont, Calif., 1970—; prin. engr. Qualcomm Inc., 1996-97; contractor Boeing Satellite Systems, 2000—02. Part-time lectr. Calif. State U., L.A., 1970-74; mem. tech. adv. panel Kinemetrics, Pasadena, 1985-86; part-time mem. tech. staff Jet Propulsion Lab., Pasadena, 1974-97, rep. NASA Hdqrs., Washington, 1979-80; vis. prof. elec. engring. Calif. Inst. Tech., 1982-83. Contbr. articles to profl. jours. Served to capt. USAF, 1963-67. Mem.: IEEE (sr.). Avocations: bicycling, reading, computers. Office: Harvey Mudd Coll Dept Engring 301 Platt Blvd Claremont CA 91711-5901 Home Phone: 909-593-0982. Business E-Mail: John_Molinder@hmc.edu.

MOLL, RUSSELL ADDISON, aquatic ecologist, science administrator; b. Bound Brook, NJ, Aug. 12, 1946; s. Addison and Celeste (Carrier) M. PhD, SUNY, Stony Brook, 1974; MS, U. Mich., 1983. Rsch. assoc. Brookhaven Nat. Lab., Upton, N.Y., 1972-74; rsch. investigator U. Mich., Ann Arbor, 1974-76, asst. rsch. scientist, 1976-81, assoc. rsch. scientist, 1981—; asst. dir. Mich. Sea Grant, Ann Arbor, 1988—; dir. Coop. Inst. Limnology and Ecosystems Rsch., U. Mich., 1989—. Univ. rep. Mich. Aquatic Scis. Consortium, 1989—; cons. Applied Scis. Assocs., Narragansett, R.I., 1988. Contbr. articles to profl. jours. Recipient numerous rsch. grants including NOAA, EPA, NSF, NASA, Agy. Internat. Devel. Mem. AAAS, Am. Soc. Limnology and Oceanography, Ecol. Soc. Am., Oceanographic Soc. Achievements include research in study of phytoplankton and bacteria dynamics in Great Lakes, effects of toxic materials on phytoplankton and bacteria, and ecological analysis of a large river and estuary in West Africa.

MOLLAND, MARIA U., Internet company executive; b. 1974; BA, Northwestern U.; MBA, Harvard U. With Disney Internet Group, Volpe Brown Whelan; bus. devel. mgr. Yahoo Finance, 2002—05; gen. mgr. MarketWatch, Inc. Dow Jones & Co., San Francisco, 2005—.

MOLLARD, JOHN DOUGLAS, engineering and geology executive; b. Regina, Sask., Can., Jan. 3, 1924; s. Robert Ashton and Nellie Louisa (McIntosh) M.; m. Mary Jean Lynn, Sept. 18, 1952; children: Catherine Lynn, Jacqueline Lee, Robert Clyde Patrick. BCE, U. Sask., 1945; MSCE, Purdue U., 1947; PhD, Cornell U., 1952; LLD (hon.), U. Regina, 1995. Registered profl. engr., profl. geologist Sask., Alta. and B.C., Can. Resident constrn. engr. Sask. Dept. Hwys. and Transp., 1945; grad. asst. Purdue U., West Lafayette, Ind., 1946-47; rsch. engr. sch. civil engring. Cornell U., Ithaca, NY, 1950-52; air surveys engr., soil and water conservation and devel. Prairie Farm Rehab. Adminstrn., Govt. of Can., 1947-50, chief, airphoto analysis and engring. geology divsn. Regina, 1953-56; pres. J.D. Mollard and Assocs. Ltd., Regina, 1956—. Aerial resource mapping surveys tech. adv. Colombo plan, Govts. Ceylon and Pakistan, 1954-56; adv. Shaw Royal Commn. on Nfld. Agr.; lectr. in field. Author: Landforms and Surface Materials of Canada, 8 edits.; co-author: Airphoto Interpretation and the Canadian Landscape, 1986; contbr. over 100 articles to profl. publs. Organizer, canvasser United Appeal campaigns; bd. dirs. Regina Symphony Orch., 2002; gov. gen. Can. Adrian Clarkson Rideau Hall. Decorated officer Order of Can.; recipient First Meritorious Achievement award, Lt. Gov. Sask., 2002, Engring. Achievement award, Assn. Profl. Engrs. Sask., 1984, Massey medal, Royal Can. Geog. Soc., 1989, Allied Arts medal, Royal Archtl. Inst. Can., 1998, Sask. Geotech. Achievement award, Sask. Geotech. Group, 2002, Sask. Centennial medal, Govt. of Sask., 2005, Roger Brown award, Can. Geotechnical Soc., 2006, numerous awards, Alumni of Influence, 2007; named one of 100 Persons of Influence, U. Sask., 2007; named to Engring. Alumni Wall of Distinction, 2000. Fellow: ASCE, Engring. Inst. Can. (Keefer medal 1948, Julian C. Smith medal 1999), Internat. Explorers Club, Can. Acad. Engring., Geol. Soc. Can., Geol. Soc. Am., Am. Soc. Photogrammetry and Remote Sensing (award for contbns. airphoto interpretation and remote sensing 1979); mem.: Can. Soc. Petroleum Engrs., Geol. Soc. Sask., Regina Geotech. Soc., Can. Geotech. Soc. (1st R.M. Hardy Meml. Keynote lectr. 1987, Thomas Roy award with engring. geology divsn. 1989, R.F. Legget award 1992, Rogert J.E. Brown award 2006), Assn. Cons. Engrs. Can., Regina YMCA (former dir.), Rotary (former dir. Regina club). Mem. United Ch. of Can. Avocations: jogging, reading, golf, tennis, nature study. Office: 810 Avord Tower 2002 Victoria Ave Regina SK Canada S4P 0R7 Office Phone: 306-352-8811 8855. Office Fax: 306-352-8820. Business E-Mail: mollard@jdmollard.com.

MOLLEUR, RICHARD RAYMOND, lawyer; b. Adams, Mass., May 14, 1932; s. Raymond Emory and Germaine (Ouellette) M.; m. Rita M. Desaulniers, Sept. 5, 1955; children: Denis Richard, Michelle Annette, Suzanne Nicole, Celeste Marie. AB, Assumption Coll., Worcester, Mass., 1954; JD, Georgetown U., 1957. Bar: D.C. 1958. Counsel Office of Architect of the Capital, Washington, 1957-60; trial atty. U.S. Dept. Justice, Washington, 1960-65; dir. D.C. bail project Georgetown Law Center, Washington, 1965-66, D.C. bail agy., 1966, asst. dean, asso. prof. law, 1967-69; v.p., gen. counsel Fairchild Industries, Inc., Germantown, Md., 1979-85; ptnr. Herron & Burchett, 1986-90, Winston & Strawn, 1990; corp. v.p., gen. counsel Northrop Corp., LA, 1991. Author: Bail Reform in Nation's Capital, 1966. Recipient Alumni Achievement award Georgetown Law Center, 1966 Office: Northrop Corp 1840 Century Park E Los Angeles CA 90067-2199

MOLLICA, JOSEPH A., pharmaceutical executive; b. 1940; Various positions, sr. v.p. drug devel. Ciba-Geigy, Ardsley, NY, 1966—86; v.p. med. products E.I. Du Pont De Nemours & Co., Inc., Wilmington, Del., 1987—90; CEO Du Pont Merck Pharm. Co., Wilmington, Del., 1991—93; CEO, chmn. Pharmacopeia, Princeton, NJ, 1994—2004, chmn., 2004—, Neurocrine Biosciences, Inc., San Diego. Office: Neurocrine Biosciences Inc 12790 El Camino Real San Diego CA 92130 also: Pharmacopeia Inc 3000 Eastpark Blvd Cranbury NJ 08512-3516 Business E-Mail: mollica@pcop.com.

MOLLMAN, JOHN PETER, publishing executive; b. Belleville, Ill., Feb. 8, 1931; s. Kenneth John and Maurine (Farrow) M.; m. Carol J. Piper, Apr. 4, 1998; children: Sarah Chase Underhill, Eric Cleburne. BA, Washington U., St. Louis, 1952; cert. in advanced mgmt. program, Harvard Bus. Sch., 1986. Advt. specialist Gen. Electric Co., Schenectady and Boston, 1952-54; mgr. Enterprise Printing Co., Millstadt, Ill., 1956-66; dir. prodn. Harper & Row Pubs., NYC, 1967-74; pub. Harper's Mag. Press, NYC, 1971-74; v.p. prodn. Random House Inc., NYC, 1974-81; sr. v.p. World Book-Childcraft Inc., Chgo., 1981-88; pres. World Book Pub., 1988-91; pub. cons., 1991-92; dir. intellectual property devel. Multimedia Publishing Microsoft, 1992-96; cons. in electronic pub. Carmel, Calif., 1996—. Mem. vis. com. Washington U.; mem. pub. com. Art Inst. Chgo.; bd. dirs. Yerba Buena Ctr. for the Arts, San Francisco; pres. Internat. ebook Award Found., NY; dir. Carmel Pub.Libr. Found.,Calif. Mem.

Golf Club at Quail Lodge, Phi Delta Theta, Sigma Delta Chi, Omicron Delta Kappa. Unitarian Universalist. Home: 25340 Vista Del Pinos Carmel CA 93923-8804 Office Phone: 831-622-7532. Personal E-mail: pmollman@msn.com.

MOLLOY, DONALD WILLIAM, federal judge, lawyer; b. Butte, ID, July 18, 1946; BA, U. Mont., 1968, JD with honors, 1976. Bar: Mont. 1976, U.S. Dist. Ct. Mont. 1976, U.S. Ct. Appeals (9th cir.) 1977, U.S. Supreme Ct. 1984. Law clk. to Hon. James F. Battin U.S. Dist. Ct., Billings, Mont., 1976-78; ptnr. Berger, Anderson, Sinclair & Murphy, Billings, Mont., 1978-81, Anderson, Edwards & Molloy, Billings, Mont., 1981-90, Anderson & Molloy, Billings, Mont., 1990-91; ptnr., sr., owner The Molloy Law Offices, Billings, Mont., 1991-96; judge US Dist. Ct. Mont., Missoula divsn., 1996—, chief judge, 2001—. Lawyer rep. 9th Cir. Jud. Conf., San Francisco, 1989-92. Aviation lt. USNR, 1968—72. Mem. ABA, Yellowstone County Bar Assn. (pres. 1984-95), Mont. Trial Lawyers Assn. (Trial Lawyer of Yr. 1993), Am. Trial Lawyers, Am. Bd. Trial Advocates, Am. Judicature Soc., Mont. Bar Assn., Pa. Trial Lawyer's Assn., Tex. Trial Lawyers Assn., Am. Law Inst. Roman Catholic. Avocations: aviation, pilot. Office: US Dist Ct Dist Mont PO Box 7309 Missoula MT 59807-7309

MOLONEY, STEPHEN MICHAEL, lawyer; b. LA, July 1, 1949; s. Donald Joseph and Madeline Marie (Sartoris) M.; m. Nancy Paula Barile, Jan. 15, 1972; children: Michael, John, Kathleen. Student, St. John's Sem., Camarillo, Calif., 1967-69; BS, U. Santa Clara, 1971, JD, 1975. Bar: Calif. 1975, U.S. Dist. Ct. (cen. dist.) Calif. 1976, U.S. Supreme Ct. 1990. Assoc. Gilbert, Kelly, Crowley & Jennett, LA, 1975-80, from ptnr. to sr. ptnr., 1980—. Arbitrator, settlement officer Los Angeles Superior Ct., 1985—. Contbr. articles to profl. jours. Dir. Calif. Def. Polit. Action Com., Sacramento, 1991—. With USAR. Recipient Svc. award to Pres. of So. Calif. Def. Counsel, Def. Rsch. Inst., Chgo., 1992. Mem. Assn. So. Calif. Def. Counsel (pres. 1992-93), Calif. Def. Counsel (dir. 1991—), L.A. County Bar Assn. (vols. in parole, 1976-77, exec. com. alternative dispute resolution com. 1992-96), Oakmont Country Club, La Quinta Resort and Club. Democrat. Roman Catholic. Avocations: politics, golf, reading, travel. E-mail: smm@gilbertkelly.com.

MOLONEY, WILLIAM J., school system administrator; BA in History and Polit. sci., MA in History and Polit. sci., Harvard U.; PhD in Ednl. Mgmt., Harvard U., Cambridge, Mass.; postgrad. studies in Slavic History, Oxford and U. of London. Served as a tchr., asst. prin., prin. Prin., headmaster, asst. supt., & supt. Mass., RI, NY, Pa. and Md.; dir. Am. Sch., London; supt. Calvert county pub. schools, Prince Frederick, Md., 1993—97; commr. edn. Colo. Dept. Edn., Denver, 1997—; sec. Colo. Bd. Edn., 1997—. Chmn. Edn. Leaders Coun., Washington; adj prof. Various Univs.; bd. dirs. Bds. of the Ctr. for Workforce Preparation, Ednl. Excellence Network; spkr. in field; cons. in field. Co-author: (Books) The Content of America's Character, Education Innovation: An Agenda to Frame the Future; newspaper columnist:. Office: Colo Dept Education 201 E Colfax Ave Rm 500 Denver CO 80203 Office Phone: 303-866-6646. Office Fax: 306-866-6938. E-mail: moloney_w@cde.state.co.us.

MOMADAY, NAVARRE SCOTT, writer, poet; b. Lawton, Okla., Feb. 27, 1934; s. Alfred Morris and Natachee (Scott) M.; m. Gaye Mangold, Sept. 5, 1959; children: Cael, Jill, Brit; m. Regina Heitzer, July 21, 1978; 1 dau., Lore. AB, U. N.Mex., 1958; AM, Stanford U., 1960, PhD, 1963. Asst. prof. U. Calif., Santa Barbara, 1963-65, assoc. prof. English, 1968-69, assoc. prof. English and comparative lit. Berkeley, 1969-73; prof. English and comparative lit. Stanford U., 1973—82, U. Ariz., Tucson, 1982—85, Regents prof. English; staff scholar Sch. Am. Rsch., Santa Fe. Cons. Nat. Endowment for Humanities, Nat. Endowment for Arts, 1970—. Author: Owl in the Cedar Tree, 1965, The Journey of Tai-me, 1967 (pub. as The Way to Rainy Mountain, 1969), House Made of Dawn, 1968 (Pulitzer Prize for fiction 1969), Colorado: Summer/Fall/Winter/Spring, 1973 (Western Heritage award 1974), Angle of Geese and Other Poems, 1974, The Gourd Dancer, 1976, The Names: A Memoir, 1976, The Ancient Child, 1989, In the Presence of the Sun, 1991, Circle of Wonder: A Native American Christmas Story, 1993, The Native Americans: Indian Country, 1993, The Man Made of Words: Essays, Stories, Passages, 1997, In the Bear's House, 1999, Three Plays, 2007; co-author: American Indian Photographic Images, 1868-1931, 1982; editor: The Complete Poems of Frederick Goddard Tuckerman, 1965, American Indian Authors, 1972. Founding trustee Mus. of Am. Indian, 1978-; founder and dir. Buffalo Trust. Named Poet Laureate of Okla., 2007-08; named to Acad. Achievement, 1993; named an Artist for Peace, UNESCO, 2004; recipient Acad. Am. Poets prize for "The Bear", 1962, Pulitzer Prize for Fiction, 1969, Premio Letterario Internazionale Mondello Italy, 1979, Nat. Medal Arts, 2007; Guggenheim fellow, 1966-67, Nat. Inst. Arts and Letters grantee, 1970. Mem. MLA, Am. Studies Assn., PEN; fellow AAAS. Office: Sch Am Rsch PO Box 2188 Santa Fe NM 87504-2188

MONAGHAN, KATHLEEN M., art museum director; b. Waterville, Maine, Sept. 6, 1936; d. Russell Vernon and Gloria Beatrice (LeClair) M. BA in Art History, U. Calif.-Santa Barbara, 1979, MA in Art History, 1981. Curatorial fellow Whitney Mus., NYC, 1979, dir. Equitable Br., 1985-93; asst. curator Santa Barbara Mus., Calif., 1980-81, curator of art Calif., 1983-84; curator, dir. Akron Art Mus., Ohio, 1984-85; dir. The Hyde Collection, Glens Falls, NY, 1994—99; exec. dir. Fresno Metropolitan Museum, Fresno, Calif., 1999—. Mem. Internat. Com. on Mus., Coll. Art Assn. Office: Fresno Metropolitan Museum 1540 Fulton St Fresno CA 93721-1612

MONARCHI, DAVID EDWARD, retired information science educator; b. Miami Beach, Fla., July 31, 1944; s. Joseph Louis and Elizabeth Rose (Muller) M.; 1 child by previous marriage, David Edward. BS in Engring. Physics, Colo. Sch. Mines, 1966; PhD (NDEA fellow), U. Ariz., 1972. Asst. dir. bus. rsch. divsn. U. Colo., Boulder, 1972—75, assoc. prof. mgmt. sci. and info. sys., 1975—97, prof. info. sys., 1997—2006; ret., 2006; asst. prof. mgmt. sci./info. sys. U. Colo., 1972—75, assoc. dir. divsn. info. sci. rsch., 1982—84, chair info. sys. divsn., 1999—2006. Asst. prof. mgmt. sci./info. sys. U. Colo., 1972—75, assoc. dir. divsn. info. sci. rsch., 1982—84, chair info. sys. divsn., 1999—2006; prin. investigator socio-econ. environ. sys. for govtl. agys. and local govt. orgns., State of Colo., info. sys. for pvt. firms, 1972-77, virtual reality distance learning Colo. Commn. Higher Edn., 1996—; chair, information sys. Divsn., 1999—. Contbr. numerous articles on socio-econ. modeling, object-oriented sys., info. sys. and artificial intelligence to profl. jours. Mem. Gov.'s Energy Task Force Com., 1974. Mem. IEEE, Inst. for Mgmt. Sci., Assn. Computing Machinery, Am. Assn. Artificial Intelligence. Home: 32 Benthaven Pl Boulder CO 80305-6210 E-mail: david.e.monarchi@colorado.edu.

MONDINO, BARTLY J., ophthalmologist; b. Sacramento, May 24, 1945; married; children: Kara, Kristen. BA in Med. Scis., Stanford U., 1967, MD, 1971. Diplomate Am. Bd. Ophthalmology. Intern Stanford (Calif.) U. Hosp., 1971-72; ophthalmology resident N.Y. Hosp., Cornell U., NYC, 1972-75; fellow in cornea, external disease U. Pitts. Sch. Medicine - Eye and Ear Hosp., Pitts., 1975-76, asst. prof. ophthalmology, 1976-79, assoc. prof. ophthalmology, 1979-82; dir. Charles T. Campbell Microbiology Lab. Eye and Ear Hosp., Pitts., 1978-82; assoc. prof. ophthalmology UCLA - Jules Stein Eye Inst., LA, 1982-83, prof. ophthalmology, 1983—, Wasserman Endowed chair dept. ophthalmology, 1988—; chief cornea-external disease divsn. UCLA, 1991-99, chmn. dept. ophthalmology, 1994—; dir. UCLA - Jules Stein Eye Inst., 1994—; with exec. program for acad. healthcare mgmt. The John E. Anderson Grad. Sch. Mgmt./UCLA, 1992. Bd. dirs. Charles R. Drew U. of Medicine and Sci., L.A., Braille Inst., L.A.; mem. adv. com. Rsch. Study Club, Murrieta, Calif., 1994—, scientific adv. panel on ophthalmology Calif. Med. Assn., San Francisco, 1994—. Editl. bd.: Am. Jour. Ophthalmology, Chgo., 1992—, ophthalmic Surgery and Lasers, 1995—, Ophthalmology Times, 1996—, Ophthalmic Practice (Can.), 1996—; editor-in-chief: EYE Newsletter, 1994—; co-chair corneal diseases program planning panel of Nat. Eye Inst.'s Vision Rsch. Program Planning Subcom., Bethesda, md., 1997—, others. Recipient scholarship Stanford U. Sch. Medicine, Rsch. to Prevent Blindness Manpower award 1983-84, Rsch. to Prevent Blindness Sr. Scientific Investigator's award 1994, various lectureships, others. Mem. AMA, Assn. for Rsch. in Vision and Ophthalmology, Assn. Univ. Profs. of Ophthalmology, Am. Acad. Ophthalmology, Calif. Assn. Ophthalmology, Calif. Cornea Club, Calif. Med. Assn., Contact Lens Assn. of Ophthalmologists, Eye Bank Assn. of Am., L.A. County Med. Assn., L.A. Soc. Ophthalmology, Ophthalmology Rsch. Found., Ophthalmic Surgery and Laser Therapy, Rsch. Study Club. Office: 100 Stein Plz # 2-142 Los Angeles CA 90095-7000 Business E-Mail: mondino@jsei.ucla.edu.

MONDRY, LAWRENCE N., automotive executive; V.p., nat. mdse. mgr. Highland Superstores, Inc., 1983-88, 88-90; sr. v.p., gen. mdse. mgr. CompUSA, Inc., Dallas, 1990-93, exec. v.p. merchandising, 1993—2000, pres., COO, 2000—03, CEO, 2003—06; pres., CEO CSK Auto Inc., Phoenix, 2007—. Bd. dir. Micron Technology, Golfsmith Inc. Office: CSK Auto Inc 645 E Missouri Ave Phoenix AZ 85012

MONEY, DAVID R., lawyer, information technology executive; BS, MBA, U. Utah, Salt Lake City; student, U. Oreg. Sch. Law; JD, U. Utah, Salt Lake City. Ptnr. Jones, Waldo, Holbrook and McDonough, Salt Lake City; dep. gen. counsel First Data Corp., Greenwood Village, Colo., 2004—07, exec. v.p., gen. counsel, sec., 2007—. Mem.: Utah Bar Assn., Colo. Bar Assn. Office: First Data Corp 6200 S Quebec St Greenwood Village CO 80111 Office Phone: 303-488-8000.

MONGER, DOUG J., state agency administrator; Park ranger State Mont. Fish, Wildlife and Parks Dept., Mont., park mgr. Helena, Mont., regional mgr. Mont., adminstr. Helena, Mont., 1998—. Office: State Mont Fish Wildlife & Park Dept PO Box 200701 Helena MT 59620-0701 Fax: 406-444-4952.

MONIÉ, ALAIN, information technology executive; Degree in automation engring. studies with high honors, Ecole Nationale Supérieure d'Arts et Metiers, France; MBA, Institut Supérieur des Affaires, Jouy en Josas, France. Civil constrn. engr., Mexico City; contr. Renault, France; gen. mgmt. positions Sogitec Inc.; regional sales mgr. to head of Asia-Pacific ops. Allied Signal; pres. Latin Am. divsn. Honeywell Internat.; exec. v.p. Ingram Micro, Inc., Santa Ana, Calif., 2003—04, pres. Asia-Pacific region, 2004—07, pres., COO, 2007—. Office: Ingram Micro 1600 E St Andrew Pl PO Box 25125 Santa Ana CA 92799 Office Phone: 714-566-1000.

MONISMITH, CARL LEROY, civil engineering educator; b. Harrisburg, Pa., Oct. 23, 1926; s. Carl Samuel and Camilla Frances (Geidt) M. BSCE, U. Calif., Berkeley, 1950, MSCE, 1954; D of Engring. (hon.), Carleton U., Ottawa, 2004. Registered civil engr., Calif., 1961. From instr. to prof. civil engring. U. Calif., Berkeley, 1951—, chmn. dept. civil engring., 1974-79, Robert Horonjeff prof. civil engring., 1986—, prof. emeritus, 1996. Cons. Chevron Rsch. Co., Richmond, Calif., 1957-93, U.S. Army CE Waterways Expt. Sta., Vicksburg, Miss., 1968-00, B.A. Vallerga, Inc., Oakland, Calif., 1980-98, ARE, Austin, Tex. and Scotts Valley, Calif., 1978-92; cons. Bechtel Corp., San Francisco, 1982-86; keynote speaker Hoover Mentoring Workshop, Iowa State U., 2007. Contbr. numerous articles to profl. jours. Served to 2d lt. C.E., U.S. Army, 1945-47. Recipient Rupert Myers medal U. NSW, 1976; named Henry M. Shaw Lectr. in Civil Engring., N.C. State U., 1993, First Paul Kraser Kent lectr. dept. civil and environ. engring. U. Ill., Urbana-Champaign, 2007; sr. scholar Fulbright Found., U. NSW, 1971, Nat. Asphalt Pavelent Assn. R.D. Kenyon Rsch. and Edn. award for Outstanding Contbns. for Hot Mix Asphalt Tech., 2002, Hall of Fame, 2005; named Disting. Engring. Alumnus, Coll. Engring., U. Calif., Berkeley, 1996 Fellow: AAAS; mem.: ASTM, NAE, NRC (assoc.), NAS (assoc.), ASCE (hon.; pres. San Francisco sect. 1979—80, ednl. activities com. 1989—91, State of Art award 1977, James Laurie prize 1988), Nat. Assn. of the Nat. Acads., Asphalt Inst. (Roll of Honor 1990), Calif. Asphalt Pavement Alliance (award 2002), Am. Soc. Engring. Edn., Internat. Soc. Asphalt Pavements (hon.; chmn. bd. dirs. 1988—90, Disting. Lectr. 2004), Assn. Asphalt Paving Technologists (hon.; pres. 1968, W.J. Emmons award 1961, 1965, 1985), Transp. Rsch. Bd. (assoc.; chmn. pavement design sect. 1973—79, K.B. Woods award 1972, 1st disting. lectureship 1992, Roy W. Crum award 1995). Avocation: stamp collecting/philately. Office: U Calif Dept Civil Engring 215 Mclaughlin Hall Berkeley CA 94720-1712 Office Phone: 510-665-3560. Business E-Mail: clm@maxwell.berkeley.edu.

MONIZ, GLENN, state legislator; b. Laramie, Wyo., Sept. 8, 1944; m. Sharry Moniz; 2 children. Owner Feed Store; mem. Dist. 46 Wyo. House of Reps., 2009—. Republican. Office: 213 State Capitol Bldg Cheyenne WY 82002 also: PO Box 784 Laramie WY 82073 Office Phone: 307-777-7881. Office Fax: 307-777-5466. Business E-Mail: gmoniz@bresnan.net.

MONK, ALLAN JAMES, baritone; b. Mission City, BC, Can., Aug. 19, 1942; m. Marlene Folk; 3 children. Student, Elgar Higgin and Boris Goldovsky. Operatic debut in Old Maid and the Thief, San Francisco, 1967; joined touring co., later main co. San Francisco Opera; appeared with Tulsa Opera, Pitts. Opera, Edmonton Opera, Vancouver Opera, So. Alta. Opera, Chgo. Opera, Balt. Opera, Miami Opera, Colo. Opera, Mont real Opera, Hawaii Opera Theatre, Portland Opera.;, 1976. Met. Opera debut as Schaunard in La Boheme, 1976, sang title role in Wozzeck, Wolfram in Tannheuser, Dr. Malatesta in Don Pasquale, Rodrigo in Don Carlo, Sharpless in Madame Butterfly, Herald in Lohengrin; sang with Can. Opera Co. as Abelard in Heloise and Abelard, Macbeth, Rigoletto, Belcore in L'Elisir D'Amoure, Jago in Otello, as Ford in Falstaff, four villains in Les Contes d'Hoffman; with Nat. Arts Ctr. Opera Festival, Ottawa, Ont., Can., title role in Don Giovanni, Almaviva in Le Nozze Di Figaro, gulielmo in Cossi Fan Tutti, Tomsky in Pique Dame, Marcello in La Boheme; Carnegie Hall debut as Vladislav in Dalibor, 1977; European debut as Wozzeck, 1980; solo recitalist; toured with Nat. Arts Ctr. Orch. in USSR, Poland, Italy, 1973; movie debut as Baron Douphol in La Traviata, 1983. Named Artist of Yr. Can. Music Council, 1983, laureat Order of Can., 1985. Office: 14415 Parkland Blvd SE Calgary AB Canada T2J 4L5 Home Phone: 403-281-9640; Office Phone: 403-281-9640.

MONNING, WILLIAM W., state legislator; m. Dana T. Kent; children: Laura, Alexandra. BA, U. Calif., Berkeley; grad., U. San Fran. Sch. Law. Former pres., co-founder Global Majority, Inc.; prof. Internat. Negotiation & Conflict Resolution Monterey Inst. Internat. Studies; prof. Monterey Coll. Law; mem. Dist. 27 Calif. State Assembly, Calif., 2008—. Democrat. Office: 701 Ocean St Rm 318 B Santa Cruz CA 95060 also: PO Box 942849 Rm 5150 Sacramento CA 94249 Office Phone: 831-425-1503, 916-319-2027. Office Fax: 831-425-2570.*

MONROY, GLADYS H., lawyer; d. Henry B. and Leonora E. (Low) Chu; m. Jaime L. G. Monroy (div.); m. C. Lawrence Marks, Nov. 29, 1980. BA, Hunter Coll., NYC, 1957; MS, NYU, 1968, PhD, 1973; JD, U. San Francisco, 1986. Bar: Calif.; registered U.S. Patent and Trademark office. Lab. technician Sloan-Kettering Inst., NYC, 1957-60, Pub. Health Rsch. Inst., NYC, 1960-63, rsch. asst., 1963-68; post doctoral fellow Albert Einstein Coll. Medicine, Bronx, NY, 1973-77; asst. prof. N.Y. Med. Coll., Valhalla, 1977-79; acquisitions editor Acad. Press, Inc., 1979-81; reseach assoc. U. Calif., San Francisco, 1981-83; atty. Irell & Manella, Menlo Park, Calif., 1986-90, ptnr., 1990-91, Morrison & Foerster, Palo Alto, Calif., 1991—. Co-chair I.P. Group, 1997—2005, Life Scis. Group, 1997-2002; treas. Silicon Valley Intellectual Property Assn., 1993, sec., 1994, v.p., 1995, pres., 1996; bd. dir. Calif. State Bar Intellectual Property Sect., 1997-99; co-chair IP HIV Vaccine Enterprise, 2002-. Contbr. articles to profl. jours. Mem. bd. dirs. Project Hogar De Los Ninos, Menlo Park, Calif., 1987, 89, mem. Profl. Women's Network, San Francisco, 1988—90; mem. bd. dirs. Child Advocates of Santa Clara and San Mateo Counties, 1995—99. Named one of Best Lawyers in Am., 2004-07; named Leading Lawyer in Silcon Valley, 2002-2007; elected to Patent Hall of Fame, Global Practice Law Co. Mem. ABA, Am. Intellectual Property Law Assn., Am. Soc. Human Genetics, Am. Chem. Soc., Calif. Bar Assn., San Francisco Intellectual Property Law Assn. (chair patent com. 1992-94), Peninsula Patent Law Assn. (program chair 1993-94, treas. 1994-95, sec. 1995-96, v.p. 1996-97, pres. 1997—98), Am. Soc. Microbiology, Phi Alpha Delta. Avocations: swimming, bicycling, skiing, reading, opera. Office: Morrison & Foerster LLP 755 Page Mill Rd Palo Alto CA 94304-1018 Office Phone: 650-813-5600. Office Fax: 650-494-0792. Business E-Mail: gmonroy@mofo.com.

MONSEES, JAMES EUGENE, engineering executive, consultant; b. Sedalia, Mo., Mar. 27, 1937; s. Olen Owen and Ruth Caroline (Weiffenbach) M.; m. Leda L. Hoehns, Oct. 8, 1961; children: Brenda G., Mark E. BSCE, U. Mo., 1960, MSCE, 1961; PhDCE, U. Ill., 1970. Registered profl. engr., Ill., Md., Washington, Ohio, Calif., Wash., Colo. Grad. asst. U. Mo., Columbia, 1958-61; project mgr. USAF Spl. Weapons Ctr., Albuquerque, 1961-64; engr. Exxon, Baton Rouge, 1964-66; rsch. assoc. U. Ill., Champaign, 1967-69; sr. v.p. A.A. Mathews, CRS Engrs., Arcadia, Calif. and Rockville, Md., 1969-80; dept. mgr. Battelle Meml. Inst., Columbus, Ohio, 1980-82; v.p.-engr. Lachel L. Hanson & Assocs., Golden, Colo., 1982-83; chief tunnel engr. Metro Rail Transit Couns., LA, 1983-1990; project mgr. Collider/SSC The PB/MK Team, Dallas, 1990-94; sr. v.p., tech. dir., prin. profl. assoc. Parsons Brinckerhoff, NYC. Mem. Seismic Lifeline Com., San Francisco, 1987—; mem. exec. com. Rapid Excavation/Tunnel Conf., Denver, 1989—. Author: (with others) Guidelines for Tunnel Lining Design, 1984, Mining Handbook, 1992, Tunnel Engineering, 1994, Tunnel Engineering Handbook, 1996. Mem. U.S. Nat. Com. for Rock Mechanics, Wash., D.C., 1983-86, 88-94, Internat. Soc. for Rock Mechanics, 1983—. 1st Lt. USAF, 1961-64. Recipient Mo. Honor award U. Mo., 1992. Fellow ASCE; mem. NAE, Am. Underground Space Assn. (bd. dirs. 1995—), The Moles, Underground Tech. Rsch. Coun. Republican. Avocations: shooting, bicycling, tennis, reading. Home: 10141 Hummingbird Cir Orange CA 92861-4155 Office: Parsons Brinckerhoff 505 S Main St Ste 900 Orange CA 92868-4529

MONSEN, ELAINE RANKER, nutritionist, educator, editor; b. Oakland, Calif., June 6, 1935; d. Emery R. and Irene Stewart (Thorley) Ranker; m. Raymond Joseph Monsen, Jr., Jan. 21, 1959; 1 dau., Maren Ranker Grainger-Monsen. BA, U. Utah, 1956; MS (Mead Johnson grad. scholar), U. Calif., Berkeley, 1959, PhD (NSF fellow), 1961; postgrad. NSF sci. faculty fellow, Harvard U., 1968-69. Dietetic intern Mass. Gen. Hosp., Boston, 1956-57; asst. prof. nutrition, lectr. biochemistry Brigham Young U., Provo, Utah, 1960-63; mem. faculty U. Wash., 1963—, prof. nutrition, adj. prof. medicine, 1976-84, prof. nutrition and medicine, 1984—2004, prof. emeritus, 2004—, chmn. div. human nutrition, dietetics and foods, 1977-82, dir. grad. nutritional scis. program, 1994-99, mem. Council of Coll. Arts and Scis., 1974-78; chmn. Nutrition Studies Commn., 1969-83; bd. dirs. U. Wash. Found., 2007—. Vis. scholar Stanford U., 1971-72; mem. sci. adv. com. food fortification Pan-Am. Health Orgn., São Paulo, Brazil, 1972; tng. grant coordinator NIH, 1976-97. Editor-in-chief Jour. Am. Dietetic Assn., 1983-2003; Editor Emeritus, Jour. Am. Dietetic Assn., 2003—; mem. editorial bd. Coun. Biology Editors, 1992-96; author rsch. papers on lipid metabolism, iron absorption. Bd. dirs. A Contemporary Theatre, Seattle, 1969-72; trustee, bd. dirs. Seattle Found., 1978-95, vice chmn., 1987-91, chmn., 1991-93; pres. Seattle bd. Santa Fe Chamber Music Festival, 1984-85; mem. Puget Sound Blood Ctr. Bd., 1996-99. Grantee Nutrition Found., 1965-68, Agrl. Rsch. Svc., 1969-84; recipient Disting. Alumnus award U. Utah, F. Fischer Meml. Nutrition Lectr. award, 1988, L.F. Cooper Meml. Lectr. award, 1991, L. Hatch Meml. Lectr. award, 1992, Goble Lectr. award Purdue U., 1997. Fellow: Am. Soc. Clin. Nutrition (sec. 1987—90),

Am. Inst. Nutrition; mem.: Wash. Heart Assn. (nutrition coun. 1973—76), Am. Soc. Parenteral and Enteral Nutrition, Soc. Nutriton Edn., Am. Dietetic Assn. Office: U Wash PO Box 353410 Seattle WA 98195-3410

MONSON, DAN, men's college basketball coach; b. Spokane, Wash., Oct. 6, 1961; BS in Math., U. Idaho, 1985; MS in Athletic Adminstrn., U. Ala., 1988. Asst. coach Oregon City HS, 1985—86; grad. asst. U. Ala., Birmingham, 1986—88; asst. coach Gonzaga U., Spokane, 1988—94, assoc. head coach, 1994—97, head coach, 1997—99, U. Minn., 1999—2006, Long Beach State U., Calif., 2007—. Dir. Gopherball Basketball Camp, Mpls.; asst. coach World Univ. Games, 1999, USA Basketball's 20-and-under team, 2004. Named Coach of Yr., 1998, Nat. Rookie Coach of Yr., Basketball Times, 1998. Achievements include coaching the West Coast Conf. Champions, 1998; reached NCAA Sweet 16, 1998-99. Office: Long Beach State U Mens Basketball Athletic Dept 1250 Bellflower Blvd Long Beach CA 90840

MONSON, JAMES EDWARD, electrical engineer, educator; b. Oakland, Calif., June 20, 1932; s. George Edward and Frances Eleanor M.; m. Julie Elizabeth Conzelman, June 25, 1954; children: John, Jamie, Jennifer BSEE, Stanford U., 1954, MSEE, 1955, PhD in Elec. Engring., 1961. Mem. tech. staff Bell Telephone Labs., Murray Hill, NJ, 1955-56; devel. engr. Hewlett-Packard Co., Palo Alto, Calif., 1956-61; Robert C. Sabini prof. engring. emeritus Harvey Mudd Coll., 1961—. Governing bd. Claremont Unified Sch. Dist., 1966—71, pres., 1969—70, Claremont Civic Assn., 1974—75; bd. dirs. Claremont YMCA, 1978—82, Coastal Health Alliance, 1999—2006, West Main Sr. Svcs., 2007—. Fellow NSF, 1954-55, Japan Soc. Promotion Sci., 1984; Fulbright Rsch. grantee, 1975-76; Fulbright sr. lectr., 1980. Fellow IEEE (life); mem. Phi Beta Kappa, Sigma Xi. Home: PO Box 1029 Point Reyes Station CA 94956-1029 Office: Harvey Mudd Coll 301 E 12th St Claremont CA 91711-5901 Personal E-mail: j.monson@ieee.org.

MONSON, THOMAS SPENCER, religious organization administrator, retired publishing executive; b. Salt Lake City, Aug. 21, 1927; s. George Spencer and Gladys (Condie) M.; m. Frances Beverly Johnson, Oct. 7, 1948; children Thomas L., Ann Frances, Clark Spencer. BS with honors in mktg, U. Utah, 1948; MBA, Brigham Young U., 1974, LLD (hon.), 1981; D in Bus. (hon.), U. Utah, 2007. With Deseret News Press, Salt Lake City, 1948-64, mgr., 1962-64; mem., Coun. Twelve Apostles Ch. of Jesus Christ of Latter-day Saints, 1963-85, bishop, Coun. Twelve Apostles, 1950-55, second counselor in the first presidency, 1985—95, first counselor to ch. pres. Gordon B. Hinckley, simultaneously becoming Pres. of the Quorum of the Twelve Apostles, 1995—2008, pres., 2008—, Canadian Mission, 1959-62; chmn. bd. Deseret News Pub. Co., 1977-96. Vice chmn. Deseret Mgmt. Corp.; pres. Printing Industry Utah, 1958; bd. dirs. Printing Industry Am., 1958-64; mem. Utah exec. bd. U.S. West Comm.; bd. dir. KSL-TV, Beneficial Life Ins. Co. Author Be Your Best Self, 1979, Inspiring Experiences That Build Faith: From the Life and Ministry of Thomas S. Monson, Favorite Quotations from the Collection of Thomas S. Monson, Live the Good Life, Faith Rewarded: A Personal Account of Prophetic Promises to the East German Saints, Christmas Gifts, Christmas Blessings, The Search for Jesus, Meeting your Goliath, A Christmas Dress for Ellen, Invitation to Exaltation, Pathways to Perfection. Mem. Utah Bd. Regents; mem. nat. exec. bd. Boy Scouts Am.; trustee Brigham Young U. With USNR, 1945-46. Recipient Recognition award, 1964, Disting. Alumnus award U. Utah, 1966; Silver Beaver award Boy Scouts Am., 1971; Silver Buffalo award, 1978; Bronze Wolf award World Orgn. of the Scout Movement, 1993. Mem. Utah Assn. Sales Execs., U. Utah Alumni Assn. (dir.), Salt Lake Advt. Club, Alpha Kappa Psi. Clubs: Exchange (Salt Lake City). Mem. Lds Ch. Office: LDS Ch 47 E South Temple Salt Lake City UT 84150-9701

MONTAGUE, L. DAVID, aerospace engineer; b. Washington, Apr. 17, 1933; Bachelor's, Cornell U., 1956. Assoc. engr. Lockheed Missiles & Space Co., 1956-65; chief Poseidon Missile Devel.; project engr., mgr. Poseidon Sys. Engring.; mgr. Advance Def. Sys.; v.p. Tactical & Def. Sys.; program mgr., asst. chief engr. Missile Sys. Div.; v.p. Missile Sys Div., pres., 1988-96, L. David Montague Assocs., Menlo Park, Calif. Advisor Dept. Def.; mem. Def. Sci. Bd. Task Force. Contbr. articles to profl. jours.; patentee in field. Fellow AIAA (Missile Sys. award 1991); mem. NAE. Office: L David Montague Assocs 1205 Hillview Dr Menlo Park CA 94025

MONTANDON, MICHAEL, Mayor, North Las Vegas, Nevada; m. Antoinette Montandon; 5 children. BS in Fin., Ariz. State U., Tempe; completed Harvard Univ. Sr. Exec. Program, John F. Kennedy Sch. Govt., Cambridge. Treas. Appraisal Inst., Las Vegas Chpt., 1995—96; pres. Hidden Canyon Homeowners Assn., 1995—97; current bus. devel. consultant Nev. Constrn. Svcs., Core Constrn.; mayor City of North Las Vegas, Nev., 1997—. Served on North Las Vegas Mayor's Task Force for Wages, Benefits and Fin. Vol. leader Boy Scouts; exec. bd. mem. Civilian Military Coun. Southern Nev.; mem. Clean Water Coalition, Las Vegas Conv. and Visitors Authority, North Las Vegas Redevelopment Agy., North Las Vegas Housing Authority; rep. Clark County Debt Mgmt. Commn.; chmn. Southern Nev. Regional Planning Coalition Fed. Lands Subcommittee; ex-officio mem. Deferred Compensation Adv. Com. Republican. Avocations: dirt bike riding, racquetball. Office: 2200 Civic Center Dr North Las Vegas NV 89030 Office Phone: 702-633-1007.*

MONTEITH, MATTHEW, photographer; b. Howell, Mich., 1974; Student, Internat. Ctr. Photography, NYC, 1995; MFA, Yale U., 2004. One-man shows include Galerie de la Butte, Cherbourg-Octeville, France, 2002, 779 Galerie + Editions, Paris, 2003, Prinz Galerie, Kyoto, Japan, 2004, Hotel Nord Pinus, Arles, 2005, exhibited in group shows at Small Works, P.S. 122, NYC, 1999, Ville/Visages, Regional Ctr. Cherbourg-Octeville, France, 2000, Advance Notice, Internat. Ctr. Photography, NYC, 2002, Pictures for People Like Us, Wallspace Gallery, NYC, 2003, Emerging Photographers Festival, NYC, 2004, Stilled Life, Placemaker Gallery, Miami, 2004, Let's Talk About, Larissa Goldston Gallery, NYC, 2006, Clinic, Les Nuits Blanches and Paris Photo, Paris, 2006. Recipient Abigail Cohen Rome prize, Am. Acad. Rome, 2008. Mailing: 140 16th St Brooklyn NY 11215 Office: Rosier Gallery 98 San Pablo Ave San Francisco CA 94127

MONTENEGRO, STEVE B., state legislator; BS in Polit. Sci. magna cum laude, Ariz. State U. Immigration office US Congressman Trent Franks, Glendale; mem. Dist. 12 Ariz. House of Reps., 2008—. Tchr. Ariz. Charter Acad., Superior Sch. Asst. & youth pastor Surpise Apostolic Assembly. Mem.: Ariz. Messengers Peace (pres.). Republican. Office: Capitol Complex 1700 W Washington Rm 309 Phoenix AZ 85007-2890 Office Phone: 602-926-5955. Office Fax: 602-417-3168. Business E-Mail: smontenegro@azleg.gov.*

MONTGOMERY, DAVID BRUCE, marketing educator; b. Fargo, ND, Apr. 30, 1938; s. David William and Iva Bernice (Trask) Montgomery; m. Toby Marie Franks, June 11, 1960; children: David Richard, Scott Bradford, Pamela Marie. BSEE, Stanford U., 1960, MBA, 1962, MS in Stats., 1964, PhD in Mgmt. Sci., 1966; D honoris causa, Limburgs U. Centrum, Belgium, 1998. Asst. prof. mgmt. MIT, 1966-69, assoc. prof., 1969-70; assoc. prof. mktg. and mgmt. sci. Stanford U., 1970-73, prof., 1973-78, Robert A. Magowan prof. mktg., 1978-92, Sebastian S. Kregge prof. mktg. strategy, 1992-99, prof. emeritus, 1999—; dean Sch. Bus. Singapore Mgmt. U., 2003—05, cons. and vis. prof., mktg. and mgmt., 2006—. Prin. MAC Group, Inc., 1969-91; adv. bd. LEK Partnership, London; sci. adv. bd. Univ. Connection, Bonn, Germany; acad. trustee Mktg. Sci. Inst., 1994-2000, exec. dir., 1995-97; exec. dir. coun., 2000-; cons. Mktg. & Mgmt. Singapore Mgmt. U., 2006-, vis. prof., 2006-; chair mktg. dist. scholar Hong Kong Poly.U., 2008. Author: (with Glen L. Urban) Management Science in Marketing, 1969, (with Massy and Morrison) Stochastic Models of Buying Behavior, 1970, (with Day et al) Planning: Cases in Computer and Model Assisted Marketing, 1973, (with others) Consumer Behavior: Theoretical Sources, 1973, (with G. J. Eskin) Data Analysis, 1975; editor 5 books; editor: Management Science, Marketing Department; cons. editor Jour. Internat. Mktg., 2000-03; mem. editl. bd. Mgmt. Sci., Jour. Mktg., Jour. Mktg. Rsch., Mktg. Sci., Jour. acad. of Mktg. Sci., Jour. Internat. Mktg.; contbr. more than 100 articles and tech. reports to sci. and profl. jours. Trustee Family Service Assn. of Mid Peninsula, 1972-73. Recipient citation for outstanding contbns. to use of computers in mgmt. edn. Hewlett Packard, 1977, Best Paper award Strategic Mgmt. Soc., 1996. Fellow: INFORMS Soc. Mktg. Sci. (inagural fellow 2008); mem.: Am. Mktg. Assn. (Contribution to Mktg. Strategy award 2002), Inst. Mgmt. Scis., Tau Beta Pi. Presbyterian. Office: Stanford U Grad Sch Bus Stanford CA 94305 Home: 2462 Mountain Dr Lenoir City TN 37772 Business E-Mail: montgomery_david@gsb.stanford.edu.

MONTGOMERY, JAMES FISCHER, savings and loan association executive; b. Topeka, Nov. 30, 1934; s. James Maurice and Frieda Ellen (Fischer) M.; m. Diane Dealey; children: Michael James, Jeffrey Allen, Andrew Steven, John Gregory. BA in Acctg., UCLA, 1957. With Price, Waterhouse & Co., C.P.A.'s, LA, 1957-60; controller Conejo Valley Devel. Co., Thousand Oaks, Calif., 1960; asst. to pres. Gt. Western Fin. Corp., Beverly Hills, Calif., 1960-64; fin. v.p., treas United Fin. Corp., LA, 1964—69, exec. v.p., 1967—74, pres., 1974—75; chmn., CEO Great Western Financial Corp., Chatsworth, Calif., 1975-96, chmn. bd. dirs., 1996—97; founder, CEO Frontier Bank, Park City, Utah, 1998—2002, chmn., 1998—. Pres. Citizens Savs. & Loan Assn., Los Angeles, 1970-75. Served with AUS, 1958-60. Office: Frontier Bank 1245 Deer Valley Dr PO Box 981180 Park City UT 84098-1180

MONTGOMERY, MICHAEL DAVIS, research and development company executive, real estate investor; b. San Luis Obispo, Calif., June 4, 1936; s. Harold Ray and Elva Dee (Davis) M.; m. Rita Martin, Dec. 28, 1957 (div. Sept. 1975); children: Jeanne, Gwen, Michele. MSEE, Stanford U., 1959; PhD, U. N.Mex., 1967. Group leader Max Planck Inst. for Astrophysics, Munich, 1974-76; group leader advanced concepts Los Alamos (N.Mex.) Nat. Labs., 1976-83; program mgr. for simulation Maxwell Labs. Inc., San Diego, 1983-84, dep. for DNA programs, 1984-85, v.p. rsch. and devel., 1986-91, sr. v.p. applied tech., 1991-92, sr. cons., 1992—97; owner Casa Del Mar Inn, Santa Barbara, Calif., 1991-97; real estate investor Montgomery Investments, LLC, 1997—. Owner and cons. All Santa Fe Reservations Assoc., 1999—2005. Assoc. editor Jour. Geophys. Research; contbr. articles to sci. jours. Served to lt. comdr. USN, 1959-62. Recipient (charter) Sr. Scientist award Alexander Von Humboldt Found., 1972. Mem. AAAS, Am. Phys. Soc., Phi Beta Kappa, Sigma Xi, Tau Beta Pi. Avocation: amateur radio. Home and Office: 872 Muirfield Dr Oceanside CA 92058 Home Phone: 760-231-9225. Personal E-mail: mikedmont@cox.net.

MONTGOMERY, MIKE, men's college basketball coach; b. Long Beach, Calif., Feb. 27, 1947; m. Sarah Montgomery; children: John, Anne. BA in Phys. Edn., Long Beach State U., Calif., 1968; MS in Phys. Edn., Colo. State U., 1976. Asst. coach U. Fla. Gators, The Citadel Bulldogs, Colo. State U. Rams, USCG Acad., Boise State U. Broncos, U. Mont. Grizzlies, 1975—77, head coach, 1977—86, Stanford U. Cardinal, Calif., 1986—2004, asst. to athletic dir., 2007—08; head coach Golden State Warriors, 2004—06, U. Calif. Golden Bears, 2008—. Head coach USA Basketball 22-and-Under Select Team, 1996; asst. coach USA Basketball, 2002. Named Devel. Coach of Yr., USA Basketball, 1996, US Olympic Com. 1996, Pac-10 Coach of Yr. 1999, 2000, 03, 04, Nat. Coach of Yr. Basketball Times 2000, 04; named to Long Beach State Hall of Fame; recipient John R. Wooden Legends of Coaching Lifetime Achievement award, 2004. Office: U Calif c/o Dept Athletics University Ave Berkeley CA 94720

MONTGOMERY, ROBERT F., state legislator, retired surgeon, rancher; b. Ogden, Utah, May 13, 1933; s. William Floyd and Adrianna (Van Zweden) M.; m. Jelean Skeen, June 24, 1953; children: Lance, Dana, Kristen, Keri, Tanya. AS, Weber State U., 1953; BS, Brigham Young U., 1957; MD, U. Utah, 1961. Pvt. practice, Anaheim, Calif., 1966-88; senator Utah State Senate, 1992—. Chief surgery Anaheim Gen. Hosp., 1970, Anaheim Meml. Hosp., 1972-74. Rep. chmn. Weber County, Utah, 1991-93; pres. Am. Cancer Soc., Salt Lake City, 1992-93. Sgt. U.S. Army, 1953-55, Korea. Mem. Rotary, Utah Elephant Club, Traveler's Century Club. Mem. Lds Ch. Avocations: travel, reading, hunting, fishing, golf. Home: 1825 Mountain Rd Ogden UT 84414-2903

MONTOYA, MICHAEL A., state official, accountant; b. Albuquerque, May 4, 1952; s. Orlando (Reno) and Nancy (Maestas) M. BS, U. Colo., 1982. CPA, N.Mex. Tax mgr. Ernst and Young, Albuquerque, 1985-90; dep. state auditor State of N.Mex., Santa Fe, 1993-94, treas., 1995—. V.p., bd. dirs. Albuquerque Hispano C. of C., 1986-90; bd. dirs. Belen (N.Mex.) C. of C., 1986-90; bd. dirs. Healthnet of N.Mex., Albuquerque, 1987-90, Recreational Health Occupl. Ctr., Inc., Albuquerque, 1986-90. Mem. AICPAs, Assn. Hispanic CPAs. Democrat. Avocations: racquetball, hunting, fishing. Home: PO Box 414 Los Lunas NM 87031-0414 Office: NMex State Treasurer PO Box 608 Santa Fe NM 87504-0608

MONTOYA, PATRICIA T., federal agency administrator; b. Albuquerque; BSN, U. N.Mex., 1975, MA in Pub. Health Adminstrn., 1983. Asst. dir. ANA, Washington, 1987-89; exec. dir. N.Mex. Health Resources, 1989-93; practice mgr. Presbyn. Family Healthcare, Albuquerque, 1993-94; regional dir. HHS, Dallas, 1994-98, commr. adminstrn. children, youth and families Washington, 1998—2001; mem., board of dir. New Mexico Voices for Children, Albuquerque. Office: New Mexico Voices For Children 2340 Alamo Ave SE Ste 120 Albuquerque NM 87106-3523

MOOD, DOUG, Commissioner, Montana Public Serv Comn; b. Grand Rapids, Minn., Nov. 3, 1943; m. Marion Mood; 4 children. V.p. sawmill, 1970—2001; mem. Mont. Ho. Reps., 1997—2005, vice chmn. rules com., mem. state adminstrn. com., mem. natural resources com., mem. joint select com. jobs and income; commr. Mont. Public Service Commn., 2005—. Mem. White House Conf. Small Bus., 1995, Site Select Com. for Womens Prison. Mem.: Western Conf. of Public Utility Commisioners (pres. 2007—), Nat. Fedn. Ind. Bus., Mont. C. of C. Republican. Lutheran. Office: Mont Public Service Commn PO Box 202601 Helena MT 59620-2601

MOOERS, CHRISTOPHER NORTHRUP KENNARD, physical oceanographer, educator; b. Hagerstown, Md., Nov. 11, 1935; s. Frank Burt and Helen (Miner) M.; m. Elizabeth Eva Fauntleroy, June 11, 1960; children: Blaine Hanson MacFee, Randall Walden Lincoln. BS, U.S. Naval Acad., 1957; MS, U. Conn., 1964; PhD, Oreg. State U., 1969. Postdoctoral fellow U. Liverpool, Eng., 1969-70; asst. prof. U. Miami, Fla., 1970-72, assoc. prof., 1972-76, U. Del., Newark, 1976-78, prof., 1978-79; prof., chmn. dept. oceanography Naval Postgrad. Sch., Monterey, Calif., 1979-86; dir. Inst. for Naval Oceanography, Stennis Space Ctr., Miss., 1986-89; sci. advisor to dir. Inst. for Naval Oceanography, 1989; rsch. prof. U. N.H., Durham, 1989-91; prof., chmn. divsn. applied marine physics U. Miami, 1991—2008, dir. Ocean Pollution Rsch. Ctr., 1992—2002, dir. Ocean Prediction Exptl. Lab., 1993—. Coord. Coastal Ocean Sci. Program, 1991—2008; chmn. modeling and analysis steering team Integrated Ocean Observing Sys., 2006—08; rsch. prof. Portland State U., Dept. Civil Environ. Engring., Oreg., 2008—. Editor Jour. Phys. Oceanography, 1991-96; mng. editor Coastal and Estuarine Studies, 1978-99. With USN, 1957-64. NSF fellow, 1964-67; NATO fellow, 1969-70; Sr. Queen Elizabeth fellow, 1980 Mem.: AAAS, Coastal Estuarine Res. Fedn., Marine Tech. Soc., Am. Meteorol. Soc. (chmn. sci.and tech. com. meterology and oceanography of Coastal Zone 1996—2002), U. Nat. Oceanog. Lab. Sys./Fleet Improvement Com. (chair 1994—97), U.S. Nat. Com. Internat. Union Geodesy and Geophysics (chmn. 1995—99), Ea. Pacific Oceanic Conf. (chmn. 1979—86), Am. Geophys. Union (pres. ocean sci. sect. 1982—84), The Oceanography Soc. (interim councilor 1987—88), Sigma Xi (U. Miami chpt. pres. 2006—08). Achievements include pioneering direct observation of transient coastal ocean currents and fronts plus mesoscale and coastal ocean prediction rsch. Home: 2520 NE Siskiyou St Portland OR 97212-2565 Office: Dept Civil & Environ Engring Portland State Univ PO Box 751 Portland OR 97207-0751 Office Phone: 503-954-2772. Business E-Mail: cmooers@rsmas.miami.edu, cmooers@cecs.pdk.edu.

MOON, RONALD T.Y., state supreme court chief justice; b. Sept. 4, 1940; m. Stella H. Moon. B in Psychology and Sociology, Coe Coll., 1962, LLD (hon.), 2001; LLB, U. Iowa, 1965; LLD (hon.), Inha U., Incheon, Korea, 2003. Bailiff, law clk. to Chief Judge Martin Pence U.S. Dist. Ct., 1965-66; dep. prosecutor City and County of Honolulu, 1966-68; assoc. Libkuman, Ventura, Ayabe, Chong & Nishimoto (predecessor firm Libkuman, Ventura, Moon & Ayabe), Honolulu, 1968-72, ptnr., 1972-82; judge 9th div. 1st cir., Cir. Ct., State of Hawaii, Honolulu, 1982-90; assoc. justice Hawaii Supreme Ct., Honolulu, 1990-93, chief justice, 1993—. Bd. dirs. Nat. Consortium on Racial and Ethnic Fairness in Ctr., 2004—; adj. prof. law U. Hawaii, 1986—88; lectr., guest spkr. numerous events. Recipient Disting. Svc. award, Nat. Ctr. for State Cts., 2003, Grand Prize award, Kyungmin Mission Schs., Korea, 2003. Mem. ATLA, ABA (Pursuit of Justice award tort, trial and ins. practice sect. 2006), Hawaii Bar Assn. (Golden Gavel award 2001), Am. Bd. Trial Advocates (pres. 1986-93, nat. sec. 89-91), Am. Inns of Cts. IV (bencher 1983—, bd. trustees 2004—), Am. Judicature Soc., Hawaii Trial Judges' Assn., Conf. Chief Justices (bd. dirs.). Office: Supreme Ct Hawaii 417 S King St Honolulu HI 96813-2902 Office Phone: 808-539-4700. Business E-Mail: ronald.t.moon@courts.state.hi.us.

MOONEN, RICK, chef, restaurant owner; b. Sept. 12, 1956; Grad., Culinary Inst. Am., 1976—78. Saucier La Cote Basque, 1980; chef Le Cirque, NYC; exec. chef Le Relais, Century Café, Chelsea Central, The Water Club, NYC, 1988, Oceana, NYC; owner, exec. chef rm, NYC, 2002—05, Branzini, NYC, 2002—05, RM Seafood, Las Vegas, 2005—. Mem. Corp. Culinary Inst. Am., Am. Inst. Wine Food Day's of Taste children's prog.; mem. restaurant com. Share Our Strength; mem. bd. adv. French Culinary Inst.; founding mem. Seafood Choices Alliance, Chef's Coalition; Am. rep. Oliviers & Co.; chef's adv. bd. mem. Ecofish. Contbg. editor: Food & Wine Mag.; guest appearances include (TV series) Today, Good Morning Am., The Early Show, Cooking Live with Sara Moulton, Lou Dobbs Tonight; author: (cookbooks) Fish Without a Doubt, 2008. Recipient Chef of Yr. award for Northeast Region, Chefs in Am., 1993, Epicurean award for Best Seafood in Las Vegas, Las Vegas Life Mag., 2007. Mem.: Wildlife Conservation Soc. Office: RM Seafood Mandalay Bay Resort & Casino 3950 Las Vegas Blvd S Las Vegas NV 89119 Office Phone: 702-795-7155.

MOONEY, JEROME HENRI, lawyer; b. Salt Lake City, Aug. 7, 1944; s. Jerome Henri and Bonnie (Shepherd) M.; m. Carolyn Lasrich, Aug. 10, 1965 (div. Dec. 1978); 1 child, Dierdre Nicole; m. Kaitlyn Cardon, Sept. 23, 1995. BS, U. Utah, 1966, JD, 1972. Bar: Utah 1972, Calif. 1998, U.S. Ct. Appeals (10th cir.) 1974, U.S. Supreme 1984, U.S. Ct. Appeals (7th cir.) 1999, U.S. Ct. Appeals (9th cir.) 2001, U.S. Ct. Appeals (4th cir.) 2002. Sole practice, Salt Lake City, 1972-75, 79-83; sr. ptnr. Mooney, Jorgenson & Nakamura, Salt Lake City, 1975-78, Mooney & Smith, Salt Lake City, 1983-87, Mooney & Assoc., Salt Lake City, 1987-94, Mooney Law Firm, Salt Lake City, 1995—98, 2001—06, Larsen & Mooney Law, Salt Lake City, 1999—2001, Weston, Garrou, Walters & Mooney, 2007—. Bd. dirs. Mooney Real Estate, Salt Lake City; mem. Active Music, Calif. Copyright Conf. Active Gov.'s Coun. on Vet. Affiars, Salt Lake City, 1982-89; trustee Project Realty, Salt Lake City, 1976—; SAMHSA sponsor Project Reality, 1994—; vice-chair State Mil. Acad. Assoc. With U.S. Army N.G., 1992-93. Mem. ABA (criminal justice sect. U.S. Sentencing Commn. com.), Utah Bar Assn. (chmn. criminal bar sect. 1987-88), Beverly Hills Bar Assn., Nat. Assn. Rec. Industry Profls., Utah NG Assn. (trustee 1976), 1st Amendment Lawyers Assn. (v.p. 1986-88, pres. 1988-89), Nat. Assn. Criminal Def. Lawyers, Families Against Mandatory Minimums (adv. coun.), VFW. Democrat. Jewish. Avocations: sailing, computers. Office: 50 W Broadway Ste 1000 Salt Lake City UT 84101-2066 Office Phone: 801-364-5635, 310-442-0072. Business E-Mail: jerrym@mooneylaw.com.

MOOR, CARL H., lawyer; b. Evanston, Ill., Mar. 22, 1961; BA with high honors in Polit. Sci., Swarthmore Coll., 1983; JD, Yale U., 1988. Bar: Calif. 1988. Clk. to Judge Mariana R. Pfaelzer US Dist. Ct. (ctrl. dist. Calif.), 1988—89; civil litigator Hall & Phillips, LA, 1989—94; asst. US atty. criminal divsn., major frauds sect. Ctrl. Dist. Calif., 1994—2001; atty. Munger, Tolles & Olson, 2001—. Henry Luce Found. scholar, Tokyo, 1986—87. Mem.: Phi Beta Kappa. Office: Munger Tolles & Olson LLP 35th Fl 355 S Grand Ave Los Angeles CA 90071-1560 Office Phone: 213-683-9247. Office Fax: 213-683-4047. E-mail: Carl.Moor@mto.com.

MOORAD, JEFF, professional sports team executive; b. Modesto, Calif., 1956; m. Jan Moorad; 3 children. AA, Modesto Jr. Coll., 1976; BA in Polit. Sci., UCLA, 1978; JD, Villanova U. Sch. Law, Pa., 1981. Founder, pres., CEO Moorad Sports Mgmt., 1983—2004; gen. ptnr., CEO Ariz. Diamondbacks, 2004—09; co-owner Hall of Fame Racing, 2007—; vice chmn., CEO San Diego Padres, 2009—. Tech. cons., cameo appearance: (films) Jerry Maguire, 1996; For Love of the Game, 1999. Named one of The 100 Most Powerful People in Sports, The Sporting News. Office: San Diego Padres 9449 Friars Rd San Diego CA 92108*

MOORADIAN, GEORGE T., lawyer; BA with high distinction, U. Mich., 1976; JD, U. Mich. Law Sch., 1978; LLM, NYU, 1980. Bar: DC 1979, Mich. 1979, Calif. 1983. Ptnr.-in-charge Baker & Hostetler, Costa Mesa, Calif., coord., tax, personal planning and employee benefits. Office: Baker & Hostetler 600 Anton Blvd Ste 900 Costa Mesa CA 92626-7221

MOORCROFT, WILLIAM HERBERT, retired bio-psychologist, educator, researcher; b. Detroit, Feb. 1, 1944; s. Leonard and Elsie Moorcroft; m. Christina Louise Perrin, Nov. 27, 1971; children: Marcile Louise Cappel, Partick Richard, Andrew William. PhD, Princeton U., 1970. Prof. psychobiology Luther Coll., Decorah, Iowa, 1971—2002; adj. prof. psychology Colo. State U., Ft. Collins, Colo., 2001—04. Cons. No. Colo. Sleep Consultants, Fort Collins, 2005—. Author: (textbook) Understanding Sleep and Dreaming. Mem.: APA, Am. Acad. Sleep Medicine, Phi Beta Kappa. Democrat. Episcopalian. Avocations: sailing, internationaltravel. Home: 4443 Vista Dr Fort Collins CO 80526 Office: 4500 E 9th Ave Ste 550 Denver CO E-mail: bill@sleeplessincolorado.com.

MOORE, ANNETTE B., aide; b. Salt Lake City, Nov. 8, 1946; Sec., chief adminstrv. officer Utah State Senate, Salt Lake City, 1994—. Mem.: Am. Soc. Legislative Clks. and Secs. (chair mem. and comm. com. 2000—01, chair profl. com. 2001—02, editor Jour. of Profl. Com. 2002—03, mem. exec. com. 2003, chair site selection 2003—04, vice chair Internat. Com. & Devel. 2004—05). Office: Utah State Senate State Capitol Complex Ste W-115 Salt Lake City UT 84114 Home Phone: 801-467-0715; Office Phone: 801-538-1458. E-mail: amoore@utahsenate.org.

MOORE, BROOKE NOEL, philosophy educator; b. Palo Alto, Calif., Dec. 2, 1943; s. Ralph Joseph and Dorothy Louise (Noll) M.; children: Sherry, Bill. BA, Antioch Coll., 1966; PhD, U. Cin., 1973. Asst. prof. Calif. State U., Chico, 1970-74, assoc. prof., 1974-79, prof., 1980—. Author: Philosophical Possibilities Beyond Death, 1981; co-author: Critical Thinking, 1987, 5th edit., 1997, 6th edit., 2000, The Power of Ideas, 1990, 4th edit., 1998, The Cosmos, God and Philosophy, 1992, Moral Philosophy, 1993, The Power of Ideas: A Brief Edition, 1995, Making Your Case, 1995; mem. editl. bd. Tchg. Philosophy, 1972. Mem. Am. Philos. Assn. Office: Calif State U Chico Dept Of Philosophy Chico CA 95929-0001

MOORE, C. BRADLEY, chemistry professor; b. Boston, Dec. 7, 1939; s. Charles Walden and Dorothy (Lutz) Moore; m. Penelope Williamson Percival, Aug. 27, 1960; children: Megan Bradley, Scott Woodward. BA magna cum laude, Harvard U., 1960; PhD, U. Calif., Berkeley, 1963. Predoctoral fellow NSF, 1960-63; asst. prof. chemistry U. Calif., Berkeley, 1963-68, assoc. prof., 1968-72, prof., 1972-2000, prof. emeritus, 2000—, vice chmn. dept., 1971-75, chmn. dept. chemistry, 1982-86, dean Coll. Chemistry, 1988-94; v.p. rsch. Ohio State U., Columbus, Disting. prof. math. and phys. sci., prof. chemistry, 2000—03, prof. emeritus, 2003—; prof. chemistry Northwestern U., 2003—08, v.p. rsch., 2003—07, prof. emeritus, 2008—. Assoc. prof. Faculty Scis., Paris, 1970, 75; Miller Rsch. Prof. U. Calif., Berkeley, 1972-73, 87-88, mgr. strategy & planning energy biosci. inst.; vis. prof. Inst. for Molecular Sci., Okazaki, Japan, 1979, Fudan U., Shanghai, 1979, adv. prof., 1988—; vis. fellow Joint Inst. for Lab. Astrophysics, U. Colo., Boulder, 1981-82; vis. prof., U. Göttingen, 1994, University Heidelberg, 1994, Max Planck Inst., Für-Umlant Quantum Optic, 1997; faculty sr. scientist (Chemical Sci. Div.) Lawrence Berkeley Nat. Lab., 1974-2000, divsn. dir., 1998-2000; mem. editl. bd. Jour. Chem. Physics, 1973-75, Chem. Physics Letters, 1980-85, Jour. Phys. Chemistry, 1981-87, Laser Chemistry, 1982—; mem. Basic Energy Scis. adv. com. Office Sci. U.S. Dept. Energy, 2000-03; mem. gov. bd. Fermi Nat. Accelator Lab., 2006-07; mem. bd. Chgo. Coun. Sci. & Tech., 2006-08 Editor: Chemical and Biochemical Applications of Lasers; assoc. editor Annual Review of Physical Chemistry, 1985-90; contbr. articles to profl. jours. Trustee Sci. Svc., 1995-2007, Sci. and Tech. Campus, 2000-03; mem. bd. govs. Ohio Supercomputer Ctr., 2000-03; rsch. officer Coun. of Ohio Bd. of Regents, 2000-03; pres., chmn. bd. Ohio State U. Rsch. Found., 2000-03; mem. governing bd. Argonne Nat. Lab., 2005-07, mem. sci. policy coun., 2005-07. Recipient Coblentz award, 1973, E.O. Lawrence Meml. award U.S. Dept. Energy, 1986, Lippincott award, 1987, 1st award Inter-Am. Photochem. Soc., 1988; nat. scholar Harvard U., 1958-60; fellow Alfred P. Sloan Found., 1968, Guggenheim Found., 1969, Humboldt Rsch. award for Sr. U.S. Scientists, 1994. Fellow AAAS (coun. 2007-, com. coun. affairs, 2008-), Am. Acad. Arts and Scis., Am. Phys. Soc. (Plyler award 1994); mem. NSF adv. com. for education and human resources directorate, chair subcom. policy and planning 1997-99, NAS (chmn. com. undergrad. sci. edn. 1993-97, class I membership com., 1998-2000, 2002, 2000 nominating com.), Am. Chem. Soc. (past chmn. divsn. phys. chemistry, Calif. sect. award 1977). Avocation: bicycling. Office: Univ Calif Dept Chemistry Consulting Univ Rsch Program Devel Infrastructure Berkeley CA 94720-1460 Office Phone: 510-206-1409. E-mail: moorecb@berkeley.edu.

MOORE, CARLETON BRYANT, geochemistry educator; b. NYC, Sept. 1, 1932; s. Eldridge Carleton and Mabel Florence (Drake) M.; m. Jane Elizabeth Strouse, July 25, 1959; children: Barbara Jeanne, Robert Carleton; m. Diane Beets, Apr. 23, 2000. BS, Alfred U., 1954, DSc (hon.), 1977; PhD, Cal. Inst. Tech., 1960. Asst. prof. geology Wesleyan U., Middletown, Conn., 1959-61; mem. faculty Ariz. State U., Tempe, 1961—; nat. rsch. coun. rsch. assoc. NASA Ames Rsch. Ctr., 1974; prof., dir. Ctr. for Meteorite Studies Ariz. State U., Regents' prof., 1988—. Vis. prof. Stanford U., 1974; Prin. investigator Apollo 11-17; preliminary exam. team Lunar Receiving Lab., Apollo, 12-17. Author: Cosmic Debris, 1969, Meteorites, 1971, Principles of Geochemistry, 1982, Grundzügeder Geochemie, 1985; editor: Researches on Meteorites, 1961, Jour. Meteoritical Soc.; contbr. articles to profl. jours. Asteroid 5046 named Carletonmoore in his honor, 2000. Fellow Am. Geophys. Union, Ariz.-Nev. Acad. Sci. (pres. 1979-80), Meteoritical Soc. (life hon., pres. 1966-68), Geol. Soc. Am., Mineral. Soc. Am., AAAS (council 1967-70); mem. Geochem. Soc., Am. Chem. Soc., Am. Ceramic Soc., Sigma Xi. Office: Ariz State U Ctr Meteorite Studies Tempe AZ 85287-2504 Address: PO Box 26137 Tempe AZ 85285 Home Phone: 480-838-3353; Office Phone: 480-965-3576. Business E-Mail: cmoore@asu.edu.

MOORE, DAN STERLING, insurance executive, sales trainer; b. Lincoln, Nebr., June 27, 1956; s. Jack Leroy and Carolyn Marie (Bachman) M.; m. Marla Janine Collister, June 2, 1979; children: Tyler David, Anna Rose. Student, Red Rocks Coll., 1977. Lic. ins. exec. Asst. mgr. European Health Spa, Englewood, Colo., 1975-78; sales mgr. Colo. Nat. Homes, Westminster, 1979-80; sales assoc. Dale Carnegie, Denver, 1981; sales mgr. Paramount Fabrics, Denver, 1981-84; sales assoc. Mighty Distbg., Arvada, Colo., 1984-87; divsn. mgr. Nat. Assn. for Self Employed/United Group Assn., Englewood, Colo., 1987—2007; ret., 2007. Divsn. mgr. Communicating for Agr. Assn., 1993-98, Am. Bus. Coalition, 1997-2000, Am. for Financial Security, 1999—; owner Capital City Landscaping LLC, Capital City Equipment, LLC, Paradise Properties, LLC; master gardener U. Wyo. Ext.; agt. Megal Life and Health Ins. Co. Leader, trainer Alpine Rescue Team, Evergreen, Colo., 1971-74; minister Jehovah's Witnesses, 1972—. Avocations: golf, skiing, backpacking, scuba diving, tennis. Home: 1412 Sherman Mountain Loop Cheyenne WY 82009 Office: Nat Assn Self Employed/United Group Assn 1002 W 17th St Cheyenne WY 82001 Office Phone: 307-637-5296. Personal E-mail: sterlingmoore@gmail.com.

MOORE, DANIEL ALTON, JR., retired state supreme court justice; b. 1933; BBA, U. Notre Dame, 1955; JD, U. Denver, 1961. Dist. ct. magistrate judge, Alaska, 1961-62; pvt. practice law, 1962-80; judge 3d Jud. Dist. Superior Ct., 1980-83; justice Alaska Supreme Ct., Anchorage, 1983-92, chief justice, 1992-95; ret., 1995. Mediator for J.A.M.S./Endispute, 1996—.

MOORE, DANIEL CHARLES, retired anesthesiologist; b. Cin., Sept. 9, 1918; s. Daniel Clark and May (Strebel) M.; m. Betty Maxine Tobias, Aug. 5, 1945 (div. 1988); children: Barbara, Nancy, Daniel, Susan. Grad., Amherst Coll., Mass., 1940; MD, Northwestern U., 1944. Diplomate Am. Bd. Anesthesiologists. Intern Wesley Meml. Hosp., Chgo., 1944, resident, 1945; dir. anesthesia Va. Mason Hosp., Seattle, 1947-72; anesthesiologist (Mason Clinic), 1947-72, sr. cons. in anesthesia, 1972-83. Clin. prof. U. Wash. Sch. Medicine, 1963—89. Author: Regional Block, 1953, Stellate Ganglion Block, 1954, Complications of Regional Anesthesia, 1955, Anesthetic Techniques for Obstetrical Anesthesia and Analgesia, 1964, also papers. Served as capt. M.C. AUS, 1945-47. Recipient Ralph M. Waters award Ill. Soc. Anesthesiologists, Carl Koller Gold medal European Soc. Regional Anaesthesia, 1995, Eagle Scout, 1930. Mem. Am. Soc. Anesthesiologists (1st v.p. 1953-54, 2d v.p. 1954-55, pres. 1958-59, distinguished service award 1976), AMA (sec. anesthesiology sect. 1956-58), Am. Acad. Anesthesiology, Am. Soc. Regional Anesthesia (adv. bd., Gaston Labat award 1977), Wash. Soc. Anesthesiologists (pres. 1949-50), Wash. Med. Soc., King County Med. Soc., Faculty Anaesthetists Royal Coll. Surgeons (hon.), Northwest Forum, Beta Theta Pi, Nu Sigma Nu. Home: Madison Park Pl # 103 2000 43rd Ave E Seattle WA 98112-2704 Office: PO Box 900 Seattle WA 98111-0900 Home Phone: 206-726-9832; Office Phone: 206-223-6980. Fax: 206-223-6982. E-mail: daniel.moore@vmmc.org.

MOORE, DAVID GENE, academic administrator; b. Tonasket, Wash., Oct. 2, 1938; s. Leonard W. and Peggy (Furst) M.; m. Diane Russell, June 15, 1965 (div. 1984); children: John, Kathy, Alan, m. Kathryn Welsch, Nov. 24, 1999. BA in Polit. Sci., Seattle U., 1960; MBA, U. Puget Sound, 1973; MS in Computer Sci., Kans. State U., 1978; postgrad., U. Mich., 1978—. Commd. 2d lt. U.S. Army, 1960, advanced through grades to col., 1979, ret., 1980; dean mgmt. info. systems Mott Community Coll., Flint, Mich., 1980-82, dean mgmt., 1982-84, pres., 1985-92; pres DeVry Inst. Tech., Los Angeles, Calif., 1992-94; pres. Nat. Edn. Centers, Inc., 1994-95; founder, chmn., pres and CEO Corinthian Colleges, Inc., Santa Ana, 1995—. Bd. dirs. Greater Flint Edn. Consortium. Contbr. articles to profl. jours. Mem. exec. com. Orange County Performing Arts Ctr., Opera Pacific. Decorated Silver Stars (2), Legion of Merit (2); recipient numerous civic and profl. awards. Mem. Soc. Automotive Engrs. (chmn. robotics sect. 1986—), Data Processing Mgmt. Assn. Avocations: skiing, woodworking. Office: Corinthian Colleges Inc 6 Hutton Centre Dr Ste 400 Santa Ana CA 92707-5764 E-mail: dmoore@cci.edu.

MOORE, DEMI (DEMI GUYNES, DEMETRIA GENE GUYNES), actress; b. Roswell, N.Mex., Nov. 11, 1962; d. Danny and Virginia Guynes; m. Freddy Moore, 1980 (div. 1984), m. Bruce Willis, Nov. 21, 1987 (div. 2000); 3 daughters: Rumer Glenn, Scout LaRue, Tallulah Belle; m. Ashton Kutcher, Sept. 24, 2005. Studies with Zina Provendie. Owner Moving Pictures. Actress: (feature films) Choices, 1981, Parasite, 1981, Young Doctors in Love, 1982, Blame it on Rio, 1984, No Small Affair, 1984, Master Ninja 1, 1984, St. Elmo's Fire, 1985, About Last Night..., 1986, Wisdom, 1986, One Crazy Summer, 1987, The Seventh Sign, 1988, We're No Angels, 1989, Ghost, 1990, Mortal Thoughts, 1991 (also co-producer), The Butcher's Wife, 1991, Nothing But Trouble, 1991, A Few Good Men, 1992, Indecent Proposal, 1993, Disclosure, 1994, The Scarlet Letter, 1995, Now and Then, 1995 (also prodr.), Undisclosed, 1996, Striptease, 1996, The Juror, 1996, G.I. Jane, 1997 (also prodr.), Deconstructing Harry, 1997, Passion of Mind, 2000, Charlie's Angels: Full Throttle, 2003, Half Light, 2006, Bobby, 2006, Mr. Brooks, 2007, Flawless, 2007; (TV series) General Hospital, 1982-83; (TV movies) If These Walls Could Talk, 1996 (also exec. prodr.), (voice) The Magic 7, 2006; (voice) Beavis and Butt-Head Do America, 1996, The Hunchback of Notre Dame, 1996, The Hunchback of Notre Dame II, 2002; Producer: Austin Powers: International Man of Mystery, 1997, Austin Powers: The Spy Who Shagged Me, 1999, Austin Powers in Goldmember, 2002; guest appearances on Saturday Night Live (host), 1988, Moonlighting, 1989, Tales of the Crypt, 1990, Will & Grace, 2003. Named one of 50 Most Beautiful People in the World, People, 1996.

MOORE, EMMETT BURRIS, JR., physical chemist, educator; b. Bozeman, Mont., June 14, 1929; s. Emmett Burris and Iris Marie (Brown) M.; m. Diane Elizabeth Girling, Oct. 1, 1960; children: Karen Elizabeth, Robin Diane. BS in Chemistry with honors, Wash. State U., 1951; PhD in Phys. Chemistry (Shell fellow), U. Minn., 1956. Teaching asst. U. Minn., Mpls., 1951-55, asst. prof. physics Duluth, 1957-59; staff scientist Boeing Sci. Research Labs., Seattle, 1959-73. Lectr. chemistry Seattle U., 1973; dir. power plant siting Minn. Environ. Quality Bd., St. Paul, 1973-76; gen. mgr. Richland (Wash.) Divsn. Olympic Engring. Corp., 1976-78; staff scientist Pacific N.W. Nat. Lab., 1978-96; mem. environ. engring. rev. panel EPA, 1989-95; alt. mem. Hanford Adv. Bd., 1995-2000, 2007-; adj. prof. environ. sci. Wash. State U., 1990—. Author: (book) The Environmental Impact Statement Process and Environmental Law, 1997, 2d edit., 2000, An Introduction to the Management and Regulation of Hazardous Waste, 2000, 2nd edit., 2007; contbr. articles to profl. jours. Trustee Mid-Columbia Symphony Soc., 1978-85, v.p., 1980-81, pres., 1981-83; trustee Richland Light Opera Co., 1984-88, bus. mgr., 1984-88. Recipient Land Grant Faculty Excellence award Wash. State U., 1999. Fellow AAAS; mem. Am. Phys. Soc., Am. Chem. Soc. (chmn. Pauling award com. 1971, sec. Puget Sound sect. 1971-73, mem. energy panel of com. on chemistry and pub. affairs 1983-86), Am. Assn. Physics Tchrs. (v.p. Wash. sect. 1965-66, pres. 1966-67), Phi Beta Kappa, Phi Kappa Phi, Phi Eta Sigma, Alpha Chi Sigma, Phi Lambda Upsilon, Sigma Alpha Epsilon (v.p. province 1972-73) Episcopalian (vestryman 1967-69, 76-79, 91, sr. warden 1969, del. diocesan conv. 1969-72). Home: 2323 Greenbrook Blvd Richland WA 99352-8427 Office: Wash State U 2710 University Dr Richland WA 99354-1671 Office Phone: 509-372-7276. Business E-Mail: ebmoore@wsu.edu.

MOORE, ERNEST EUGENE, JR., surgeon, educator; b. Pitts., June 18, 1946; s. Ernest Eugene Sr. and Mary Ann (Burroughs) M.; m. Sarah Van Duzer, Sept. 2, 1978; children: Hunter Burroughs, Peter Kitrick. BS in Chemistry, Allegheny Coll., 1968; MD, U. Pitts., 1972. Surg. resident U. Vt., Burlington, 1972-76; chief of trauma Denver Health Med. Ctr., 1976—, chief dept. surgery, 1984—. Prof. surgery, vice chmn. dept. U. Colo., 1984—; dir. facilities Colo. Trauma Inst., 1984-95. Editor: Critical Decisions in Trauma, 1987, Trauma, 1988, rev. edits., 1991, 96, 00, 05, 07, Early Care of the Injured, 1989, Surgical Secrets, 1996, rev. edit., 2002, 05, Trauma Manual, 2003, World Jour. Emergency Surgery; assoc. editor Jour. Trauma, Am. Jour. Surgery, World Jour. Surgery, Surgery-Problem Solving Approach, 2d edit., 1994, others; patentee retrohepatic vena cava shunt. Fellow ACS (com. on trauma, vice chair 1990), Soc. Univ. Surgeons (pres. 1989), Am. Assn. Surgery of Trauma (pres. 1993), Internat. Assn. Surgery of Trauma and Surg. Intensive Care (pres. 1998-99), Pan Am. Trauma Assn. (pres. 1991), Southwestern Surg. Congress (pres. 1998), Western Trauma Assn. (pres. 1989). Republican. Avocations: skiing, mountaineering, hunting, ultramarathons, fishing. Home: 2909 E 7th Avenue Pky Denver CO 80206-3839 Office: Denver Health Med Ctr Dept Surgery Denver CO 80204 Office Phone: 303-436-6558. Business E-Mail: ernest.moore@dhha.org.

MOORE, GORDON E., electronics executive, researcher; b. San Francisco, Jan. 3, 1929; s. Walter Harold and Florence Almira (Williamson) Moore; m. Betty I. Whittaker, Sept. 9, 1950; children: Kenneth, Steven. BS in Chemistry, U. Calif., Berkeley, 1950; PhD in Chemistry and Physics, Calif. Inst. Tech., 1954. Tech. staff Shockley Semicondr. Lab., 1956—57; mgr. engring. Fairchild Camera & Instrument Corp., 1957—59, dir. R & D, 1959—68; co-founder Intel Corp., Santa Clara, Calif., 1968, exec. v.p., 1968—75, pres., CEO, 1975—79, CEO, 1979—87, chmn., 1979—97, chmn. emeritus, 1997—. Bd. dirs. Varian Assocs. Inc., Transamerica Corp., Gilead Sciences, Inc. Founder, chmn. Gordon & Betty Moore Found.; bd. trustee Calif. Inst. Tech., 1995—2001, sr. trustee, 2001—. Recipient Nat. Medal Tech., President George Bush, 1990, Fellow award, Computer History Mus., 1998, Bower award for Bus. Leadership, Franklin Inst., 2002, Perkin medal, Soc. Chem. Industry, 2004; named one of Forbes' Richest Americans, 1999—, World's Richest People, Forbes mag., 2001. Fellow: IEEE (Founders medal 1977, Medal of Honor 2008); mem.: Am. Phys. Soc., NAE. Achievements include having a pygmy owl named after him for his donations to environ. rsch. Avocations: fishing, golf. Office: Intel Corp 2200 Mission College Blvd Santa Clara CA 95054-1549 also: Betty & Gordon Moore Library Wilberforce Rd Cambridge CB3 0WD England

MOORE, GREGORY L., editor; b. Cleve., Sept. 16, 1954; m. Nina Henderson Moore; children: Michael Langston, Jasmine Henderson. B. Journalism & Polit. Sci., Ohio Wesleyan U., 1976. Reporter Dayton Journal Herald, 1976—80, Cleveland Plain Dealer, 1980—83, political editor, 1983—86; asst. metro editor Boston Globe, 1986—94, mng. editor, 1994—2002; editor Denver Post, 2002—. Mem. Pulitzer Prize Bd., 2004—; mem. bd. trustees Ohio Wesleyan U. Named Journalist of Yr., New Eng. ch., Nat. Assn. Black Journalists, 1996. Mem.: Am. Soc. Newspaper Editors, Nat. Assn. Black Journalists. Office: Denver Post 101 W Colfax Ave Denver CO 80202 Office Phone: 303-820-1400. E-mail: gmoore@denverpost.com.

MOORE, HAL G., retired mathematician, educator; b. Vernal, Utah, Aug. 14, 1929; s. Lewis Henry and Nora (Gillman) M.; m. D'On Empey, July 20, 1956; children: David, Nora (Mrs. Bret C. Hess), Alison (Mrs. Samuel M. Smith). BS, U. Utah, 1952, MS, 1957; PhD, U. Calif., Santa Barbara, 1967. Tchr. Salt Lake City Pub. Schs., 1952-53; instr. math. Carbon Jr. Coll., also Carbon H.S., Price, Utah, 1953-55, Purdue U., Lafayette, Ind., 1957-61, adminstrv. asst. dept. math, 1960-61; from asst. prof. math. to assoc. prof. math. Brigham Young U., Provo, Utah, 1961-71, prof., 1971-95, prof. emeritus, 1995—, assoc. chmn. dept. math., 1986-89. Author: Precalculus Mathematics, 2d edit, 1977, (with Adil Yaqub) Elementary Linear Algebra With Applications, 1980, College Algebra and Trigonometry, 1983, A First Course in Linear Algebra, 1992, 3d edit., 1998; contbr. articles to profl. jours. Mem. High Coun., LDS Ch., 1985-91, MTC br. pres., 1991-94, Bishop, 1958-61, 78-82. NSF faculty fellow, U. Calif., Santa Barbara, 1964—66. Mem. Am. Math. Soc., Math. Assn. Am. (bd. govs. 1989-92), Utah State Math. Coalition (planning dir. 1990, bd. dir. 1991-92), Sigma Xi (dir. 1974-80, 82-85, com. chmn. 1982-90), Phi Kappa Phi. Home and Office: 631 W 650 S Orem UT 84058-6027 Home Phone: 801-225-7125. Personal E-mail: mooreh@math.byu.edu.

MOORE, JAMES C., museum director; Assoc. dir. Albuquerque Mus., now dir. Office: Albuquerque Mus 2000 Mountain Rd NW Albuquerque NM 87104-1459

MOORE, JAMES R., lawyer; b. Longview, Wash., Sept. 14, 1944; s. James Carlton and Virginia (Rice) M.; m. Patricia Riley, Aug. 25, 1967 (div. 1978); 1 child, Katherine M.; m. Christine M. Monkman, July 14, 1979 (div. 1996); stepchildren: Amy McKenna, John McKenna; 1 foster child, Zia Sunseri; m. Kathryn Lindquist, Aug. 26, 1996; stepchildren: Matthew Elggren, Adam Elggren, Erin Elggren, David Heilner. BA, Whitman Coll., 1966; JD, Duke U., 1969. Bar: Wash. 1970, U.S. Ct. Appeals (4th cir.) 1972, U.S. Supreme Ct. 1973, U.S. Ct. Appeals (9th cir.) 1974, D.C., 1995. Law clk. to Hon. J. Barnes U.S. Ct. Appeals (9th cir.), LA, 1969-70; trial atty. pollution control, land/natural resources div. U.S. Dept. Justice, Washington, 1970-74; asst. U.S. atty. U.S. Atty.'s Office, Seattle, 1974-82; regional counsel U.S. EPA Region 10, 1982-87; counsel Perkins Coie, 1987-88, ptnr., 1989-98; sr. environ. counsel, v.p. Huntsman Corp., Salt Lake City, 1999—; dep. gen. counsel Huntsman Internat., 2002—04, Huntsman LLC, Salt Lake City, 2004—, Huntsman Corp., Salt Lake City, 2005—. Spkr. in field. Contbr. articles to profl. jours. Bd. dirs. Environ. Law Inst., 1995-2000; chmn. audit com. Whitman Coll., 1994-2007, ethics com. Bd. Environ. Auditors Cert., 1998—, bd. overseers 2003—; mem. Athlete's Hall of Fame Com., 2003—; pres. W Club, 2008-. Mem. ABA (sect. environ., energy and resources 1987—, vice chmn. in-house counsel com., 2003-04, chmn. 2004-06), Wash. State Bar Assn. (environ. and land use sects. 1974—, spl. dist. coun. 1988-95), DC Bar, Utah Bar. Democrat. Office: Huntsman Corp 500 Huntsman Way Salt Lake City UT 84108-1235 Home Phone: 801-583-0830; Office Phone: 801-584-5828. Business E-Mail: jim_moore@huntsman.com.

MOORE, JAY WINSTON, director cytogenetics laboratory; b. Madison, Wis., Apr. 20, 1942; s. Millard Harold and Leona J. (Miller) M.; m. Nancy E. Shimits; children: Meredith, Steven. BS, Cedarville Coll., 1964; MS, U. Nebr., 1966; PhD, U. Mass., 1970. Diplomate Am. Bd. Med. Genetics. From asst. prof. to prof. Eastern Coll., St. David's, Pa., 1970-84; fellow pediatric genetics Johns Hopkins Sch. of Medicine, Balt., 1984-86; asst. dirs. cytogenetics U. Iowa, Iowa City, 1986-90; dir. cytogenetics lab. Children's Hosp., Columbus, Ohio, 1990-98; asst. clin. prof. Ohio State U., Columbus, 1991-98; dir. cytogenetics lab. Genzyme Genetics, Santa Fe, N.Mex., 1998—. Fellow Am. Coll. Med. Genetics; mem. Am. Soc. Human Genetics. Office: Genzyme Genetics 2000 Vivigen Way Santa Fe NM 87505-5600 E-mail: jay.moore@genzyme.com.

MOORE, JULIANNE (JULIE ANNE SMITH), actress; b. Fayetteville, NC, Dec. 3, 1960; m. Sundar Chakravarthy, Nov. 21, 1983 (div. Oct. 12, 1985); m. John Gould Rubin, May 3, 1986 (div. Aug. 25, 1995); m. Bart Freundlich, Aug. 23, 2003; 2 children. BFA, Boston Univ. With The Guthrie Theater, 1988-89. Actress: (theatre) Serious Money, 1987, Bone-the-Fish, 1988, Ice Cream with Hot Fudge, 1990, Uncle Vanya; (Broadway) The Vertical Hour, 2006; (TV soap operas) As the World Turns (Emmy award outstanding ingenue in daytime drama series 1988), The Edge of Night; (TV films) Money, Power, Murder, 1989, Lovecraft, 1991; (feature films) The Hand That Rocks the Cradle, 1992, The Gun in Betty Lou's Handbag, 1992, Body of Evidence, 1993, Benny & Joon, 1993, The Fugitive, 1993, Short Cuts, 1993, Vanya on 42nd Street, 1994, Roommates, 1995, Nine Months, 1995, Safe, 1995, Assassins, 1995, Surviving Picasso, 1996, The Myth of Fingerprints, 1997, The Lost World: Jurassic Park, 1997, Hellcab, 1997, Boogie Nights, 1997, Chicago Cab, 1998, The Big Lebowski, 1998, Psycho, 1998, Map of the World, 1999, Magnolia, 1999, Cookie's Fortune, 1999, An Ideal Husband, 1999, The End of the Affair, 1999, Hannibal, 2001, Evolution, 2001, The Shipping News, 2001, Far From Heaven, 2002, The Hours, 2002, Marie and Bruce, 2004, Laws of Attraction, 2004, The Forgotten, 2004, The Prize Winner of Defiance, Ohio, 2005, Freedomland, 2006, Children of Men, 2006, Next, 2007, I'm Not There, 2007, Savage Grace, 2007, Blindness, 2008. Office: c/o Kevin Huvane Creative Artists Agy 9830 Wilshire Blvd Beverly Hills CA 90212-1825

MOORE, KENNETH G., foundation administrator, former manufacturing executive; b. Los Altos Hills, Calif. BA in Bus. Admin. Trustee Gordon & Betty Moore Found., 1986—; various positions in ops. planning and control, computer systems develop., supply chain and logistics mgmt. Signetics Corp., Sunnyvale, Calif., 1978—94, Philips Semiconductors, 1995—2002; dir. evaluation & IT Gordon & Betty Moore Found., 2003—. Bd. dirs. Exploratorium, San Francisco; sch. bd. Bullis Charter Sch. Office: Gordon & Betty Moore Found Presidio of San Francisco 1661 Page Mill Rd Palo Alto CA 94304-1209

MOORE, MARY TYLER, actress; b. Bklyn., Dec. 29, 1936; d. George and Marjorie Moore; m. Richard Meeker, 1955 (div. 1961); 1 child, Richard (dec.); m. Grant Tinker, 1963 (div. 1981); m. Robert Levine, 1983. Chmn. bd. MTM Enterprises, Inc., Studio City, Calif. Stage appearances include (Broadway debut) Breakfast at Tiffany's, 1966, Whose Life Is It, Anyway?, 1980, Sweet Sue, 1988, The Players Club Centennial Salute, 1989, Rose's Dilemma, 2003; actress: (TV series) Richard Diamond, Private Eye, 1957-59, Dick Van Dyke Show, 1961-66, Mary Tyler Moore Show, 1970-77, Mary, 1978, Mary Tyler Moore Hour, 1979, Mary, 1985, Annie McGuire, 1988, New York News, 1995, Mary and Rhoda, 1998; (TV miniseries) Gore Vidal's Lincoln, 1988, New York News, 1995; (TV movies) Love American Style, 1969, Run a Crooked Mile, 1969, First You Cry, 1978, Heartsounds, 1984, Finnegan Begin Again, 1984, The Last Best Year, 1990, Thanksgiving Day, 1990, Stolen Babies, 1993 (Emmy award, Outstanding Supporting Actress in a Miniseries or Special, 1993), Payback, 1997, Mary and Rhoda, 2000, Like Mother, Like Son: The Strange Story of Sante and Kenny Kimes, 2001, Miss Lettie & Me, 2002, The Gin Game, 2003, Blessings, 2003; (films) X-15, 1961, Thoroughly Modern Millie, 1967, Don't Just Stand There, 1968, What's So Bad About Feeling Good?, 1968, Change of Habit, 1969, Ordinary People, 1980 (Acad. Award nominee for Best Actress, 1981), Six Weeks, 1982, Just Between Friends, 1986, Keys to Tulsa, 1996, Flirting with Disaster, 1996, Reno Finds Her Mom, 1997, Labor Pains, 1999; (plays) Whose Life Is It Anyway?, 1980, Sweet Sue, 1987, Labor Pains, 2000, Cheats, 2002; (TV specials) How to Survive the Seventies, 1978, How To Raise a Drug Free Child; author: After All, 1995, Growing Up Again: Life, Loves, and Oh Yeah, Diabetes, 2009 Chair Juvenile Diabetes Found., 1985—. Recipient Emmy award Nat. Acad. TV Arts and Scis. 1964-65, 73-74, 76, Golden Globe award 1965, 81, Star on the Hollywood Walk of Fame, 1992; named to TV Hall of Fame, 1985. Office: William Morris Agy care Betsy Berg 151 S El Camino Dr Beverly Hills CA 90212-2775

MOORE, NICHOLAS G., retired finance company executive; m. Jo Ann Moore; children: Kelly, Garrett, Patrick, Katy. BS in Acctg., St. Mary's Coll.; JD, U. Calif., Berkeley. With Coopers & Lybrand (now PriceWaterhouseCoopers), 1968—98, ptnr. tax practice San Jose, Calif., 1974-81, coun. NYC, 1984, exec. com., 1988, vice chmn. west region, 1991-92, client svc. vice chmn., 1992-94, chmn., CEO, 1994-98; chmn., CEO U.S. global divsn. PriceWaterhouseCoopers, NYC, 1998—2001; mem. bd. dirs. Nextance, 2002—. Compensation com., chmn. audit com., bd. dir. Gilead Sciences, 2004—; bd. dir. Bechtel Group, Inc., Network Appliance, Inc., Brocade Comm. Systems, Inc., Hudson Highland Group, Inc. Mem. US C. of C., Ctr. for Workforce Preparation; vice chmn. bus. com. Met. Mus. of Art; adv. coun., Weissman Ctr. for Internat. Bus. Baruch Coll.; bd. trustees St. Mary's Coll., Calif.; trustee Fin. Acctg. Found.; bd. dir., bus. coun. NY State, bd. trustees com. for econ. devel.; bd. dir. Co-Operations Ireland; mem. Bus.-Higher Edn. Forum, NYC Partnership. Mem.: Fin. Acctg. Found. (trustee), NY State Soc. CPAs, Calif. Soc. CPAs, Calif. Bar Assn., AICPA.

MOORE, RICHARD ALAN, landscape architect; b. St. Louis, Jan. 17, 1930; s. Ira Mack and Helen Adoline (Fakes) M.; m. Patricia Ruth Burke, Mar. 15, 1952 (div. 1967); children: Sheryl Louise, Richard Dennis, Sara Lynn, Sandra Lee. BS, U. Mo., 1951; MLA, U. Oreg., 1957. Registered landscape architect, Calif., Hawaii. Asst. prof. landscape architecture Calif. State Poly. Coll., Pomona, 1957-61; assoc. prof., head dept. landscape architecture N.C. State U., Raleigh, 1962-67; pvt. practice landscape architecture Pomona, Calif., 1957-61; dir. land devel. and planning Oceanic Properties Inc., Honolulu, 1967-69; pvt. practice Honolulu, 1969-70, 79—; dir. ops. Eckbo, Dean, Austin & Williams, Honolulu, 1970-71, v.p. ops., 1971-73; pres. EDAW, Inc., San Francisco, 1973-76, chmn. bd., 1976-78; prof. landscape architecture Tex. A&M U., Bryan, 1977-79. Prin. works include Whispering Pines Motor Lodge, N.C., 1964 (award of merit N.C. chpt. AIA 1964), North Shore Devel. Plan, Kauai, Hawaii, 1973, Comprehensive Zoning Ordinance, County of Kauai, 1973 (Am. Soc. Landscape Architects honor award 1973, HUD honor award 1974), Lihue Devel. Plan, Kauai, 1975, Koloa, Poipu, Kalaheo Devel. Plan, Kauai, 1978, Gen. Plan Update, Kauai, 1982, Mililani Town Devel. Plan, 1967-69 (Am. Soc. Landscape Architects merit award 1970), Lanai Land Mgmt. and Devel. Study, 1969 (Am. Soc. Landscape Architects merit award 1970), Wailea Master Devel. Plan, 1971, Kukuiula Devel. Plan, 1983, Lanai Project Dist. Master Plan, 1983-89, Maliu Ridge Devel. Plan, North Kohala, 1985, Mililani Mauka Devel. Plan, 1988, Devel. Plan, Lanai City Comml. Dist., 1990, Dandan Golf Course, Guam, 1991. Fst lt. U.S. Army, 1951-53, Korea. Fellow Am. Soc. Landscape Architects; mem. Masons. Avocations: sports, drawing, painting.

MOORE, STANLEY WAYNE, retired political science professor; b. Camden, NJ, Feb. 11, 1937; s. Frank Stafford and Alma Beatrice (Law) M.; m. Nancy Joan Crawford, Sept. 1, 1961; children: David Crawford, Andrea Katrina, Stanley Edward Stafford Moore, Sonia Elizabeth. AB magna cum laude, Wheaton Coll., 1959; MA and PhD in Govt., Claremont Grad. U., 1971. Asst. prof. polit. sci. Calif. State U.-Stanislaus, Turlock, 1967—69, Monterey Inst. for Internat. Studies, Calif., 1969—72; vis. assoc. U. Redlands, Calif., 1972—73; assoc. prof. Pepperdine U., Malibu, Calif., 1973—79, prof. polit. sci., 1979—, emeritus prof. polit. sci. Pres. Calif. Ctr. for Edn. in Pub. Affairs, Inc., 1981-2002. Author: A Child's Political World: A Longitudinal Perspective, 1985; contbr. articles to profl. jours. Scoutmaster troop 761 Boy Scouts Am., 1981-92, adv. bd. LA Area Coun., 1993-1999, chair advancement com., 1994-98; vice chmn. Ventura County Air Pollution Control Bd., 1981-92; mem. Ventura County Beyond the Yr. 2000 Commn., 1988-90, Nat. Dem. Com., Calif. Dem. Com., Christians in Polit. Sci.; bd. dirs. Calif. Bicentennial Found. for US Constn., 1987-91; moderator Camps and Conf. Ministry Bd., 1998-2004; bd. dir. Friends Southwest Mus. Coalition; bd. Staff of Hope, 2003—; elder Presbyn. Ch., USA, del. Gen. Assembly, 2000; San Gabriel Presbytery, Com. on Preparation for Ministry, 2005-; elected to Hist. Highland Pk. Neighborhood Coun., 2002—, treas. 2006-, v.p. 2008-; mem. Congress LA Neighborhood Couns., 2006—, Dept. Water and Power Oversight Com., 2006-, steering com. Peace Northeast March, 2008-. Recipient Medal of Honor, Boy Scouts Am., 1989; grantee Spencer Found. Chgo., 1979, 81. Fellow Am. Sci. Affiliation; mem. Am. Polit. Sci. Assn., We. Polit. Sci. Assn., So. Calif. Polit. Sci. Assn. (pres. 1988-2002), So. Calif. Soc. for Internat. Devel. (pres. 1988-98), Coun. Soc. for Internat. Devel., Sierra, Aubudon Soc., Nat. Wildlife Fedn., Highland Pk. C. of C. (bd. dirs., sec. 2003-), Kiwanis (bd. dirs. 2003—, pres.elect 2007-). Presbyterian (elder). Avocations: backpacking, fishing, photography, community activity.

MOORE, STEVEN E., foundation administrator; b. Palo Alto, Calif. s. Gordon and Betty Moore. BS in Bus. Mgmt., Santa Clara U., 1983. Exec. dir., trustee Gordon & Betty Moore Found., 1986—. Mem. environment council Tech Museum. Avocations: camping, hiking, scuba diving, fishing, skiing, travel. Office: Gordon & Betty Moore Found Presidio of San Francisco 1661 Page Mill Rd Palo Alto CA 94304-1209

MOORE, THOMAS DAVID, academic administrator; b. Rochester, NY, July 26, 1937; s. Robert Franklin and Hilda (Kennedy) M.; m. Virginia Muller, June 13, 1959; children: Kathleen Mary, Michael David, Thomas David. BSS, St. John Fisher Coll., 1959; MS, SUNY, Brockport, 1962; EdD, Rutgers U., 1966. Tchr. Rochester City Schs., 1959-62; grad. asst. Rutgers U., New Brunswick, NJ, 1963-65; from asst. to full prof. Kent (Ohio) State U., 1965-93, asst. v.p. acad. affairs, 1976-83, v.p. faculty affairs and personnel, 1984-86, provost, v.p. acad. and student affairs, 1987-91, prof. emeritus ednl. philosophy, 1991—; provost, v.p. acad. affairs Ctrl. Washington U., 1993-97, prof. edn. and philosophy, 1997—. Roman Catholic. Avocations: sports, films, public affairs, music. Office Phone: 330-524-0688. Personal E-mail: vmoore4860@sbcglobal.net.

MOORE, THOMAS GALE, economist, educator; b. Washington DC, Nov. 6, 1930; s. Charles Godwin and Beatrice (McLean) M.; m. Cassandra Chrones, Dec. 28, 1958; children: Charles G., Antonia L. BA, Geroge Washington U., 1957; MA, U. Chgo., 1959, PhD, 1961. Fgn. research analyst Chase Manhattan Bank, NYC, 1960-61; asst. prof. econs. Carnegie Inst. Tech., 1961-65; assoc. prof., then prof. econs. Mich. State U., East Lansing, 1965-74; sr. staff economist Council Econ. Advisers, 1968-70; hon. research fellow Univ. Coll., London, 1973-74; adj. scholar Am. Enterprise Inst., 1971—, CATO Inst., 1982—; sr. fellow Hoover Inst. on War, Revolution and Peace-Stanford U., 1974—, dir. domestic studies program, 1974-85; mem. Council Econ. Advisers, Washington, 1985-89. Mem. Nat. Critical Materials Council, 1985-89; mem. econ. adv. bd. Dept. Commerce, 1971-73; mem. adv. com. RANN, 1975-77, NSF, 1975-77; cons. Dept. Transp., 1973-74, 81-83; mem. adv. panel Synthetic Fuels Corp., 1982; mem. adv. bd. Reason Found., 1982—; dir. Stanford Savs. & Loan, 1979-82, chmn., 1982. Author: The Economics of American Theater, 1968, Freight Transportation Regulation, 1972, Trucking Regulation: Lessons from Europe, 1976, Uranium Enrichment and Public Policy, 1978, Climate of Fear: Why We Shouldn't Worry About Global Warming, 1998; co-author: Public Claims on U.S. Output, 1973; contbr. articles to profl. jours. Served with USN, 1951-55, Korea. Fellow Earhart Found., 1958-59; fellow Walgreen Found., 1959-60, Hoover Instn., 1973-74 Mem. Am. Econ. Assn., Mont. Pelerin Soc., Chevy Chase Club. Home: 3766 La Donna Ave Palo Alto CA 94306-3150 Office: Stanford U Hoover Instn Stanford CA 94305 Office Phone: 650-723-1411. Business E-Mail: moore@hoover.stanford.edu.

MOORE, TIRIN, neuroscientist, educator; b. Oakland, Calif., June 12, 1969; s. Walter Peter Moore and Mary Lucille Salmon; m. Giovanna Ceserani, June 21, 2003; 1 child, Emilia T. PhD, Princeton U., NJ, 1995. Asst. prof. neurobiology Stanford U., Calif., 2003—. Mem. Bio-X. Contbr. several articles to profl. jours. Recipient Nat. Rsch. Svc. award, NIH, 1999—2002, Early Career award, NSF, 2006—; co-recipient Troland Rsch. award, NAS, 2009; fellow, Alfred P. Sloan Found. fellow, 2004—06; scholar, Pew Charitable Trust, 2004—08, McKnight Endowment Fund Neurosci., 2006—;, NSF fellow, 1990—93, MIT fellow, 1995—99, Princeton U. fellow, 1999—2003. Mem.: Soc. Neurosci. Achievements include research in neurophysiology of vision, movement and cognition. Avocations: travel, movies. Office: Stanford U Sch Medicine 300 Pasteur Dr Stanford CA 94305 Business E-Mail: tirin@stanford.edu.*

MOORE, WALTER DENGEL, rapid transit system professional; b. Chgo., Sept. 16, 1936; s. Walter D. and Velma Louise (Rhode) M.; m. Sandra M. Stetzel, Jan. 23, 1965 (div. 1980); children: Thomas, Timothy; m. Janice Masilun, Nov. 30, 1996. BA in Liberal Arts and Scis., U. Ill., 1958; BSE in Major Applied Math., Ill. Inst. Tech., Chgo., 1972. Cert. keel boat sailor. Supt. maintenance of way Chgo. Transit Authority, 1963-89; supr. track and rail tech. support Met. Transp. Assn. Los Angeles County, LA, 1989-99, ret., 1999; cons. in rapid transit maintenance and tech. support, 1999—. With US Army, 1958—60, Germany. Mem. Am. Pub. Transp. Assn. (vice chmn. power com. 1974-75), Am. Ry. Engring. Assn. (vice chmn. subcom. on power signals and comm. 1990-99), Underwater Soc. Am. (N.Am. record in spear-fishing 1988), Calif. Pub. Utilities Commn. (gen. order 1995), Nat. Rsch. Coun., NAS (transp. rsch. bd.), Nat. Acad. Engrs. (project C3 and D6 light rail track manual), Alumni Assn. U. Ill., Morro Bay Art Assn. (life, pres.), Morro Bay Yacht Club (chmn. summer sailing, port fin. officer, vice commodore), Baywood Navy Retirees. Avocations: diving, theater, sailing, photography. Home: 1180 9th St Los Osos CA 93402-1325 Personal E-mail: ascrubj@charter.net.

MOORHEAD, CARLOS J., former congressman; b. Long Beach, Calif., May 6, 1922; s. Carlos Arthur and Florence (Gravers) M.; m. Valery Joan Tyler, July 19, 1969; children: Theresa, Catharine, Steven, Teri, Paul. BA, UCLA, 1943; JD, U. So. Calif., 1949. Bar: Calif. 1949, U.S. Supreme Ct. 1973. Pvt. practice law, Glendale, Calif., 1949-72; dir. Lawyers Reference Service, Glendale, 1950-66; mem. 93d-104th Congresses from 22d (now 27th) Dist. Calif., 1973-96; mem. judiciary com.; chmn. subcom. on cts. and intellectual property; vice chmn. commerce com.; mem. subcom. on energy & power, subcom. on telecomm. & fin.; dean Calif. Congl. Rep. Delegation. Apptd. to Fed. Cts. Study Com.; sr. fellow Sch. Pub. Policy, UCLA. Pres. Glendale Hi-Twelve Club; mem. Verdugo Hills council Boy Scouts Am.; mem. Calif. Assembly, 1967-72; mem. Calif. Law Revision Commn., 1971-72; pres. 43d Dist. Republican Assembly, Glendale Young Republicans; mem. Los Angeles County Rep. Central Com., Calif. Rep. Central Com.; bd. dirs. Glendale La Crescenta Camp Fire Girls, Inc.; mem. Found. Bd., Glendale Hosp., Glendale C.C.; mem. adv. bd. Salvation Army of Glendale. Served to lt. col. AUS, 1942-46. Recipient Man of Yr. award USO, 1979 Mem. Calif. Bar Assn. L.A. County Bar Assn., Glendale Bar Assn. (past pres.), Glendale C. of C., Masons, Shriners, Lions, Moose, VFW. Presbyterian. Office: 1354 J Lee Cir Glendale CA 91208-1730

MOOS, RUDOLF H., psychologist, researcher; b. Berlin, Sept. 10, 1934; s. Henry R. and Herta M. (Ehrlich) M.; m. Bernice Schradski, June 9, 1963; children: Karen, Kevin. BA in Psychology, U. Calif., Berkeley, 1956, PhD, 1960. Mem. faculty psychiatry Stanford (Calif.) U., 1962—, dir. psychiatry research tng. program, 1967-92, prof. psychiatry, 1972—, dir. social ecology lab., 1967-92; sr. rsch. career scientist VA Med. Center, Palo Alto, Calif., 1981—, dir. Ctr. for Health Care Evaluation, 1984—2002, dir. Program Evaluation and Resource Ctr., 1990-99. Vis. prof. Inst. Psychiatry, also Maudsley and Royal Bethlem Hosp., London, 1969-70 Author: Issues in Social Ecology, 1974, Evaluating Treatment Environments, 1974, Health and the Social Environment, 1974, Evaluating Correctional and Community Settings, 1975, Human Adaptation Coping with Life Crises, 1976, The Human Context, 1976, Environment and Utopia, 1977, Coping with Physical Illness, 1977, Evaluating Educational Environments, 1979, Coping with Physical Illness: New Perspectives, 1984, Coping with Life Crises: An Integrated Approach, 1986, Alcoholism Treatment: Content, Process and Outcome, 1990, Group Residential Facilities for Older Adults, 1994, Evaluating Residential Facilities, 1996; mem. editl. bd. Jour. Behavioral Medicine, 1984-04, Internat. Jour. Therapeutic Cmtys., Prevention in Human Svcs., Psychosomatic Medicine, Evaluation and Program Planning, 1977-99, Jour. Personality and Social Psychology, 1985-91, Health Psychology: An Internat. Jour., 1985-97, Violence, Agression, and Terrorism, 1985-94, Jour. Substance Abuse, 1986-2001, Jour. Applied Gerontology, 1988-2005, Jour. Cmty. and Applied Social Psychology, Psychology and Aging, 1986-91, Environ. and Behavior, 1987-91, Indian Jour. Clin. Psychology, 1996-2002, Jour. Studies Alcohol, 1997, Am. Jour. Cmty. Psychology, 1998—, Pakistan Jour. Psychol. Rsch., 2005, Internat. Jour. Clin. and Health Psychology, 2006; assoc. editor: Ency. of Psychological Assessment. Fellow APA, Acad. Clin. Psychology, Acad. Behavioral Medicine, Soc. Behavioral Medicine, Am. Orthopsychiat. Assn., Nat. Inst. on Alcohol Abuse and Alcoholism (mem. coun.); mem. Am. Sociol. Assn., Am. Psychosomatic Assn. (mem. coun.). Home: 25661 W Fremont Rd Los Altos CA 94022-1600 Office: Stanford U Dept Psychiatry MC 5550 Palo Alto CA 94305

MOOS, WALTER HAMILTON, pharmaceutical company executive; AB in Chemistry cum laude, Harvard U., 1976; PhD in Chemistry, U. Calif., Berkeley, 1982. Scientist Parke-Davis Rsch. Divsn. Warner Lambert Co., Ann Arbor, Mich., 1982-83, sr. scientist, 1984, rsch. assoc., 1984-86, sr. rsch. assoc., 1986-87, sect. dir. chemistry, 1987-89, dir. chemistry, 1989, sr. dir. chemistry, 1990, v.p. neuroscis. and biol. chemistry, 1990-91; v.p. rsch. devel. Chiron Corp., Emeryville, Calif., 1991-97; chmn., CEO MitoKor, San Diego, 1997—2004; v.p. bioscience div. SRI Internat., Menlo Park, Calif.,

2005—. Adj. asst. prof. dept. medicinal chemistry Coll. Pharmacy, U. Mich., 1990, adj. assoc. prof., 1990-91; adj. prof. dept. pharm. chemistry U. Calif., San Francisco, 1992—; bd. dirs. Migenix, Rigel Pharm., Biotech. Industry Orgn., Alnis, Anterion, Axiom, Keystone Symposia, Mimotopes, Oncologic, Onyx; presenter to numerous sci. confs. Co-editor: Drug Discovery Technologies, 1990, Cognitive Disorders: Pathophysiology and Treatment, 1991; editor-at-large Medicinal Chemistry, 1988-2004; cons. editor Bio-Organic and Medicinal Chemistry Letters. Mem. Am. Peptide Soc. (charter mem.), U. Mich. Enzyme Discussion Group (co-founder), ACS Divsn. Medicinal Chemistry (chmn. membership com. 1989, councilor 1990), Am. Chem. Soc. Office: SRI Internat 333 Ravenswood Ave Menlo Park CA 94025

MOOSSA, A. R., surgeon, educator; b. Port Louis, Mauritius, Oct. 10, 1939; s. Yacoob and Maude (Rochecoute) M.; m. Denise Willoughby, Dec. 28, 1973; children: Pierre, Noel, Claude, Valentine. BS, U. Liverpool, Eng., 1962, MD (hon.), 1965; postgrad., Johns Hopkins U., 1972—73, U. Chgo., 1973—74. Intern Liverpool Royal Infirmary, 1965—66; resident United Liverpool Hosps. and Alder Hey Children's Hosp., 1966—72; from asst. prof. surgery to assoc. prof. U. Chgo., 1975-77, prof., dir. surg. rsch., chief gen. surgery svc., vice chmn. dept., 1977-83; chmn. dept. surgery U. Calif.-San Diego Med. Ctr., 1983—2004, disting. prof., surgery, emeritus chmn., assoc. dean, spl. counsel clin. affairs, 2004—. Litchfield lectr. U., Oxford, Eng., 1978; praelector in surgery U. Dundee, Scotland, 1979; Hampson Trust vis. prof. U. Liverpool, 1992, G.B. Ong. vis. prof. U. Hong Kong, 1993, Philip Sandblon vis. prof. U. Lund, Sweden. Editor: Tumors of the Pancreas, 1982, Essential Surgical Practice, 1983, 4th edit., 2000, Comprehensive Textbook of Oncology, 1985, 2d edit., 1991, Gastrointestinal Emergencies, 1985, Problems in General Surgery, 1989, Operative Colorectal Surgery, 1993. Fellow Royal Coll. Surgeons (Hunterian prof. 1977); mem. ACS, Am. Surg. Assn., Soc. Univ. Surgeons, Am. Soc. Clin. Oncology, European Surg. Assn. Office: U Calif San Diego Thornton Hosp 9300 Campus Point Dr 7212 La Jolla CA 92037 Office Phone: 858-657-6112. Business E-Mail: amoossa@ucsd.edu.

MORA, JIM (JAMES LAWRENCE MORA), professional football coach; b. LA, Nov. 19, 1961; s. James Earnest and Connie Beatrice Mora; m. Shannon Mora; children: Cole, Lillia, Ryder, Trey. Grad., U. Wash., Seattle, 1983. Asst. coach U. Wash. Huskies, 1984; secondary asst. San Diego Chargers, 1985—88, secondary coach, 1989—91, New Orleans Saints, 1992—96, San Francisco 49ers, 1997—98, defensive coord., 1999—2003; head coach Atlanta Falcons, Flowery Br., Ga., 2004—07; asst. head coach/secondary Seattle Seahawks, 2007—08, head coach, 2009—. Office: Seattle Seahawks 12 Seahawks Way Renton WA 98056-1572

MORALES, HUGO, broadcast executive; BA with honors, Harvard Coll.; JD, Harvard Law Sch.; D (hon.), Calif. State U., Fresno. Founder, exec. dir. Radio Bilingüe, Inc., Fresno, 1976—. Bd. dirs. Calif. Endowment, 2004—, Central Calif. Legal Services, Nat. Alliance for Hispanic Health; bd. mem. Calif. Postsecondary Ed. Commn., Accrediting Commn. for Sr. Coll. and U., We. Assn. of Sch. and Coll., Rosenberg Found., San Francisco Found., Calif. Tomorrow, Calif. Wellness Teen Pregnancy Prevention Initiative Adv. Comm., Fresno Arts Council Folk Arts Program Adv. Comm., Alliance for Calif. Traditional Arts. Recipient Edward R. Murrow award, Corp. for Public Broadcasting, 1999, Susan Hadden award, Alliance for Public Tech., Cesar Chavez award, Assn. of Mexican-Am. Educators; fellow MacArthur Found., 1994. Office: Radio Bilingue Inc 5005 E Belmont Ave Fresno CA 93727

MORAN, NANCY A., ecologist, educator; b. Dallas, Dec. 21, 1954; BA in biology, U. Tex., 1976; MS in zoology, U. Mich., 1978, PhD in zoology, 1982. Asst. prof. entomology U. Ariz., 1986—91, assoc. prof. ecology and evolutionary biology, 1991—96, prof. ecology and evolutionary biology, 1996—2001, regent's prof. ecology and evolutionary biology, 2001—. NSF postdoctoral fellow, No. Ariz. U., 1984-1986, NAS postdoctoral fellow, Inst. Entomology, Czech, 1984, MacArthur Fellow, John D. and Catherine T. MacArthur Found., 1997. Mem. NAS, Soc. Study Evolution (pres. 2002), Am. Naturalists Soc. (v.p. 2001, Pres. award, 1988); fellow Am. Acad. Arts & Sciences Office: U Ariz Dept Ecology and Evolutionary Biology PO Box 210088 Biosciences W 310 1041 E Lowell St Tucson AZ 85721 Office Phone: 520-621-3581. Office Fax: 520-621-9190. E-mail: nmoran@email.arizona.edu.

MORAN, RACHEL, law educator; b. Kansas City, Mo., June 27, 1956; d. Thomas Albert and Josephine (Portillo) Moran. AB, Stanford U., 1978; JD, Yale U., 1981. Bar: Calif. 1984. Assoc Heller, Ehrman, White & McAuliffe, San Francisco, 1982-83; prof. law U. Calif., Berkeley, 1984—, Robert D. and Leslie-Kay Raven prof. law, 1998—. Vis. prof. UCLA Sch. Law, 1988, 2002, Stanford (Calif.) U. Law Sch., 1989, NYU Sch. Law, 1996, U. Miami Sch. Law, 1997, U. Tex. Law Sch., 2000, Fordham Law Sch., 2005, UC Irvine, 2008—; chair Chicano/Latino Policy Project, 1993—96; dir. Inst. for Study Social Change, 2003—08. Contbr. articles to profl. jours. Recipient Disting. Tchg. award, U. Calif. Mem.: Assn. Am. Law Schs. (pres.), Calif. Bar Assn., Am. Law Inst., Phi Beta Kappa. Democrat. Unitarian Universalist. Avocations: jogging, aerobics, reading, listening to music. Office: U Calif Sch Law Boalt Hall Berkeley CA 94720 Home Phone: 510-420-0992; Office Phone: 510-643-6351. Business E-Mail: moran@law.berkeley.edu.

MORAVCSIK, JULIUS MATTHEW, philosophy educator; b. Budapest, Hungary, Apr. 26, 1931; came to U.S., 1949; s. Julius and Edith (Fleissig) M.; m. Marguerite Germain Truninger, Sept. 14, 1954; children: Adrian Clay, Peter Matthew. BA, Harvard U., 1953, PhD, 1959. Asst. prof. U. Mich., Ann Arbor, 1960-66, assoc. prof., 1966-68; prof. Stanford (Calif.) U., 1968—. Lectr. in 25 countries. Author: Understanding Language, 1975, Thought and Language, 1990, Plato and Platonism, 1992, Meaning, Creativity, and the Partial Inscrutability of the Human Mind, 1998, Was Menschen Verbindet, 2003 The Ties That Bind, 2005. Recipient Sr. Humanist prize Humboldt Found., 1983; fellow Ctr. Advanced Studies Behavioral Scis., 1986-87, Inst. Advanced Studies, 2001-02. Fellow Inst. Advanced Studies Budapest; mem. Am. Philos. Assn. (pres. Pacific divsn. 1987-88), Am. Soc. Aesthetics (trustee 1988-92), Soc. Ancient Greek Philosophy (pres. 1989-91, bd. dirs. Jour. History Philosophy, James Wilbur Award Value Theory 2000), Hungarian Acad. Arts and Scis. (external mem.). Avocations: golf, tennis. Office: Stanford U Dept Of Philosophy Stanford CA 94305 Business E-Mail: julius@csli.stanford.edu.

MORE, MICHAEL, state legislator; b. Saint Paul, Minn., June 14, 1963; BS in Polit. Sci., U. Santa Clara, 1985. Sales/mktg. Big Sky & Snowbird Resorts, 1986—93; property mgmt. Elk Ridge Ranch, Big Sky, 1993—95; sales Rocky Mountain Timberlands, 1995—98, Terrell's Office Machines, 2000—02; freelance carpentry More Rustic Finishes, 2002—07; Precinct Capt. Gallatin Co. Rep. Party, 2008; mem. Dist. 70 Mont. House of Reps., 2008—. Republican. Roman Catholic. Office: Montana House of Representatives PO Box 200400 Helena MT 59620-0400 Mailing: 450 N Low Bench Rd Gallatin Gateway MT 59730-8546 Home Phone: 406-763-5513; Office Phone: 460-444-4800. Office Fax: 460-444-4825. Business E-Mail: mp_more@yahoo.com.

MOREAU, ETHAN, professional hockey player; b. Huntsville, Ont., Can., Sept. 22, 1975; m. Ornella Moreau; children: Trey, Mia. Left wing Chgo. Blackhawks, 1996—99, Edmonton Oilers, 1999—, capt., 2007—. Office: Edmonton Oilers Hockey Club 11230 - 110 St Edmonton AB T5G 3H7 Canada

MOREL-SEYTOUX, HUBERT JEAN, civil engineer, educator; b. Calais, Artois, France, Oct. 6, 1932; came to U.S., 1956; s. Aimé and Suzanne Claire (Rousseau) M.-S.; m. Margery K. Keyes, Apr. 16, 1960; children: Aimée, Claire, Sylvie, Marie-Jeanne. BS, Ecole St. Genevieve, Versailles, France, 1953; MS, Ecole Nationale des Ponts et Chaussées, Paris, 1956; PhD, Stanford U., 1962. Research engr. Chevron Oil Field Research Co., La Habra, Calif., 1962-66; prof. Colo. State U., Ft. Collins, 1966-91, prof. emeritus, 1991—; chargé de recherches U. Grenoble, France, 1972-73; maitre de recherches Ecole des Mines de Paris, Fontainebleau, France, 1982; directeur de recherches ORSTOM, Montpellier, France, 1991—; cons. hydrology Atherton, Calif., 1992—. Cons. AID, Dakar, Senegal, 1985-86, 88, Ministry of Agriculture and Water, Riyadh, Saudi Arabia, 1978-83, City of Thornton, Colo., 1986-88, King Abdulaziz U., Jeddah, Saudi Arabia, 1987, 89, Ford Found., India, 1976, 79, South Fla. Water Mgmt. Dist., West Palm Beach, 1991-93, Battelle Pacific Northwest Labs., Richland, Wash., 1991-94, City of Paris, France, 1992—, Agence de l'Eau Seine-Normandie, 1992-2000, Utah State U., Logan, 1994-95, Reservoir Engring. Rsch. Inst., Palo Alto, 1994-95, Bay Delta Modeling forum, 1997—, U.S. Bur. Reclamation, 1998-2006, Stockholm Environment Inst., 2006-07; vis. prof. Ecole Polytechnique Federale de Lausanne, 1987; vis. scholar Stanford U., 1992-96, 2006-; adj. prof. U. Colo., Boulder, 1992—; lectr. U. Calif., Berkley, 1993. Editor: Hydrology Days, 1981—2000, 3d Internat. Hydrology Symposium, 1977, Unsaturated Flow in Hydrologic Modeling, 1989. Pres. Internat. Ctr., Ft. Collins, 1984-86. Served to lt. French Army Marine Corps Engrs., 1959-62. Sr. Fulbright scholar, France, 1972-73; recipient Abell Faculty Rsch. award Colo. State U. Coll. Engring., 1985. Mem. Am. Geophys. Union, ASCE (best paper award, Water Resources Planning and Mgmt., 1999), Soc. Petroleum Engrs., Am. Meteorol. Soc., Am. Soc. Agrl. Engrs. Home: 57 Selby Ln Atherton CA 94027-3926 Office: Hydroprose Internat Cons Hydrology Days Publs 57 Selby Ln Atherton CA 94027-3926 Office Phone: 650-365-4080. Personal E-mail: hydroprose@batnet.com. Business E-Mail: hydroprose@sbcglobal.net.

MORENO, ARTURO (ARTE MORENO), professional sports team executive, former advertising executive; b. Tucson, 1946; s. Arturo and Mary Moreno; m. Carol Moreno, 1986; 3 children. BS in Mktg., U. Ariz., 1973. With Eller Outdoor, 1973—84; pres., COO Outdoor Systems Inc., 1984—99; former owner Salt Lake Trappers minor league baseball club; former minority owner Arizona Diamondbacks, Phoenix Suns; owner, pres. L.A. Angels of Anaheim, 2003—. Bd. dir. Nelnet. Cofounder (with Carol Moreno) Moreno Family Found. Served US Army, 1966—68, Vietnam. Named one of Forbes' Richest Americans, Forbes mag., 2006, The Most Influential People in the World of Sports, Bus. Week mag., 2007. Office: Los Angeles Angels of Anaheim 2000 Gene Autry Way Anaheim CA 92806

MORENO, CARLOS R., state supreme court justice; b. L.A., Nov. 4, 1948; m. Christine Moreno; children: Keiko, Nicholas. BA in Polit. Sci., Yale U., 1970; JD, Stanford U., 1975. Dep. city atty. L.A. City Atty.'s Office; atty. Mori & Ota (now known as Kelley, Drye & Warren), 1979; justice Mcpl. Ct., 1986—93, L.A. County Superior Ct., 1993—97, US Dist. Ct. (ctrl. dist.) Calif., 1998—2001; assoc. justice Supreme Ct. Calif., 2001—. Bd. visitors Stanford Law Sch.; bd. govs. Assn. Yale Alumni; dir. Arroyo Vista Family Health Ctr. Recipient Criminal Justice Superior Ct. Judge of Yr. award, L.A. County Bar Assn., 1997, For God, For Country and For Yale award, Yale U., 2001. Mem.: Municipal Ct. Judges Assn., Presiding Judges Assn., Calif. Judges Assn., Mexican Am. Bar Assn. (past pres.). Avocations: theater, opera, crossword puzzles. Office: Calif Supreme Ct 350 McAllister St San Francisco CA 94102-4783

MORENO, ERNEST H., college president; BA in Polit. Sci., Calif. State U., LA; MPA in Ednl. Adminstrn., Calif. State U., Long Beach. Employee rels. specialist, pers. analyst L.A. Cmty. Coll. Dist., 1969-78, asst. dir. of labor rels., 1978-85; v.p. acad. affairs East L.A. Coll., 1991-93, pres., 1993—. Instr. L.A. Trade Tech. Coll., 1976-84, West L.A. Coll., 1984-94. Bd. dirs. Santa Marta Hosp.; pres., bd. trustees Santa Clarita C.C. Dist.; bd. trustees L.A. County Med. Ctr. Sch. of Nursing; chmn. ARC; mem. pers. com. United Way, East L.A. Occpl. Ctr., Bienvenidos Family Ctr., LAPD Hispanic Cmty. Forum. With U.S. Army, 1970-72. Mem. Assn. of Negotiations and Contract Adminstrs., Assn. of Calif. Coll. Adminstrs., Am. Coun. on Edn. (commr.), Hispanic Assn. of Colls. and Univs., East L.A. Rotary, East L.A. C. of C., Am. Diabetes Assn. Office: East Los Angeles Coll 1301 Avenida Cesar Chavez Monterey Park CA 91754-6001

MORENO, WILLIAM A., museum director; Degree in bus. mgmt., St. Mary's Coll., 1989. Dir. sales & mktg., mgr. staff devel. Citibank; founder William Moreno Fine Art, 1998—2001; dir. Aguirre Gallery, San Mateo, Calif., 2001—03; exec. dir. Mex. Mus., San Francisco, 2003—06, Claremont Mus. Art, Claremont, Calif., 2007—. Mem.: Calif. Assn. Museums (bd. dirs.). Office: Claremont Mus Art 536 W 1st St Claremont CA 91711 Office Phone: 909-621-3200 ext. 101. Office Fax: 909-625-1629. E-mail: wm@claremontmuseum.org.

MORETTI, AUGUST JOSEPH, pharmaceutical executive, lawyer; b. Elmira, NY, Aug. 18, 1950; s. John Anthony and Dorothy M. (De Blasio) M.; m. Audrey B. Kavka, Nov. 8, 1981; children: David Anthony, Matthew Alexander. BA magna cum laude, Princeton U., 1972; JD cum laude, Harvard U., 1975. Assoc. Heller, Ehrman, White and McAuliffe, San Francisco, 1976-82, ptnr., 1982-2000; CFO, gen. counsel Surro Med, Inc., 2001—05; CFO Alexza Pharms., 2005—. Lectr. bus. adminstrn. U. Calif. Berkeley, 1977-79; bd. dirs. AviGenics. Bd. dirs. Ann Martin Children's Ctr.; mem. adv. panel U. Calif. Berkeley Entrepreneur Program. Mem. ABA.

MOREY, CHARLES LEONARD, III, theatrical director, playwright; b. Oakland, Calif., June 23, 1947; s. Charles Leonard Jr. and Mozelle Kathleen (Milliken) M.; m. Mary Carolyn Donnet, June 10, 1973 (div. 1975); m. Joyce Miriam Schilke, May 29, 1982; 1 child, William. AB, Dartmouth Coll., 1969; MFA, Columbia U., 1971. Artistic dir. Peterborough (N.H.) Players, 1977-88, Pioneer Theatre Co., Salt Lake City, 1984—. Actor: N.Y. Shakespeare Festival, Playwrights Horizons, New Dramatists, ARK Theatre Co., Ensemble Studio Theatre, Cubiculo, Folger Theatre, Syracuse Repertory Theatre, Theatre by Sea, others; over 200 plays acted in or directed; guest dir. Ensemble Studio Theatre, ArK Theatre, Am. Stage Festivel, McCarter Theatre, Pioneer Theatre Co., PCPA Theatrefest, The Repertory Theater of St. Louis, Meadow Brook Theatre, Utah Shakespearean Festival, Asolo Theatre Co.; author Laughing Stock (Best Original Play, N.H. Theatre Assn. 2004) and Alexandre Dumas and the Lady of the Camelias (Slammy award 2004), new adaptations Alexandre Dumas' The Three Musketeers, Bram Stoker's Dracula, Charles Dickens' A Tale of Two Cities, Victor Hugo's The Hunchback of Notre Dame, Alexandre Dumas' The Count of Monte Cristo. Trustee Utah Arts Endowment, Inc., Nat. Theatre Conf.; panelist Nat. Endowment for Arts. Mem. AEA, SAG, AFTRA, Soc. Stage Dirs. and Choreographers, Dramatists Guild, Salt Lake City C. of C. (Honors in the Arts award 1991), Utah Assn. Gifted Children (Community Svc. award 1991), Peterborough Players (Edith Bond Stearns award 1990). Democrat. Episcopalian. Office: Pioneer Theatre Co 300 S 1400 E Salt Lake City UT 84112-0660 E-mail: charles.morey@ptc.utah.edu.

MORGAN, ALFRED VANCE, management consulting company executive; b. Liberal, Kans., Apr. 13, 1936; s. Forest Francis and Gertrude Irene (Henning) M.; m. Peggy Ann Riley, June 29, 1960; children: Trudie Marie, Vance Riley, Allen Forest, Bradley Augustus, Kelly James. BBA, U. Kans., 1958; MBA, U. So. Calif., 1966; postgrad., Am. Inst. Banking, 1965. Asst. mgr. Fruehauf Trailer Co., LA, Calif., 1960-61; asst. mktg. dir. Security Pacific Nat. Bank, 1961-65; mktg. exec. Doyle, Dane, Bernbach Advt., 1965-66; cons. Harbridge House, Inc., Boston, 1966-71; pres. Morgan Bus. Assocs., Inc., Santa Barbara and Boston, 1971—; instr. bus. L.A. City Coll., 1971-72; instr. mgmt. Santa Barbara City Coll., 1973. Pres. Exptl. in Internat. Living, 1980-81. Contbr. articles to profl. publs. Mem. Lobero Theatre Bd., 1984-88; mem. vestry All Saints Espiscopal Ch., 2003-06, jr. warden, fin. com. 2006-; v.p. El Escorial Condo Assn., 2003-08. With AUS, 1958-60. Mem. ASTD, Am. Mktg. Assn. L.A., Am. Soc. Profl. Cons., U. So. Calif. Grad. Sch. Bus. Alumni Assn. Office: Morgan Bus Assocs 8096 Puesta del Sol Carpinteria CA 93013 Office Phone: 805-684-6191. Personal E-mail: almorgan@morganba.com.

MORGAN, BARBARA R., science educator, former astronaut; b. Fresno, Calif., Nov. 28, 1951; m. Clay Morgan; 2 children. BA in Human Biology with distinction, Stanford U., 1973; tchg. credential, Coll. Notre Dame, Belmont, Calif., 1974; PhD (hon.), Boise State U., 2008. Tchr. remedial reading and math Flathead Indian Reservation Arlee Elem. Sch., Mont., 1974; tchr. remedial reading/math McCall-Donnelly Elem. Sch., Idaho, 1975—78, tchr., 1975—78, 1979—85, 1986—98; tchr. elem. English and sci. Colegio Americano de Quito, Ecuador, 1978—79; astronaut, educator mission specialist candidate NASA, Johnson Space Ctr., Houston, 1998—2008; disting. educator-in-residence Boise State U., 2008—. Backup candidate for Tchr. in Space Program NASA, 1985, mem. edn. divsn., office human resources and edn.; mem. fed. task force for women and minorities in sci. and engring. NSF; worked with NASA, speaking to ednl. organizations throughout the country, 1986; crew mem. STS-118 mission (Endeavour), 2007. Recipient Citizen of Yr. award, USA Today, 1986, Edn. award, Women in Aerospace, 1991, Wright Bros. "Kitty Hawk" Sands of Time Edn. award, L.A. C. of C., 1991, Space Pioneer award for edn., Nat. Space Soc., 1992, Pres.'s Medallion award, U. Idaho, 1998, Idaho Fellowship award, 1998, Women in Aerospace award, 2003. Mem.: NEA, Challenger Ctr. for Space Sci. Edn. (Challenger 7 award 1995), Internat. Tech. Edn. Assn. (Lawrence Prakken Profl. Cooperation award 1996), Internat. Reading Assn., Nat. Sci. Tchrs. Assn., Nat. Coun. Tchrs. Math., Idaho Edn. Assn., Nat. PTA (hon.; hon. life mem.), Phi Beta Kappa. Avocations: playing the flute, reading, hiking, swimming, skiing. Office: Boise State U 1910 University Dr Boise ID 83725

MORGAN, BEVERLY CARVER, pediatrician, educator; b. NYC, May 29, 1927; d. Jay and Florence (Newkamp) Carver; children: Nancy, Thomas E. III, John E. MD cum laude, Duke U., 1955. Diplomate Am. Bd. Pediat. (oral examiner 1984-90, mem. written examination com. 1990—), Nat. Bd. Med. Examiners. Intern, asst. resident Stanford U. Hosp., San Francisco, 1955-56; clin. fellow pediat., trainee pediatric cardiology Babies Hosp.-Columbia Presbyn. Med. Ctr., NYC, 1956-59; rsch. fellow cardiovasc. diagnostic lab. Columbia-Presbyn. Med. Ctr., NYC, 1959-60; instr. pediat. Coll. Physicians and Surgeons, Columbia U., NYC, 1960; dir. heart sta. Robert B. Green Meml. Hosp., San Antonio, 1960-62; lectr. pediat. U. Tex., 1960-62; spl. rsch. fellow in pediatric cardiology Sch. Medicine, U. Wash., Seattle, 1962-64, from instr. to prof. pediat., 1962-73, chmn. dept. pediat., 1973-80; mem. staff U. Wash. Hosp., chief of staff, 1975-77; mem. staff Harborview Med. Ctr., Children's Orthop. Hosp. and Med. Ctr., dir. dept. medicine, 1974-80; prof., chmn. dept. pediat. U. Calif., Irvine, 1980-88, prof. pediat. and pediatric cardiology, 1980—; pediatrician in chief Children's Hosp. Orange County, 1988. Mem. pulmonary acad. awards panel Nat. Heart and Lung Inst., 1972-75; mem. grad. med. edn. nat. adv. com. to sec. HEW, 1977-80; mem. Coun. on Pediatric Practice; chmn. Task Force on Opportunities for Women in Pediat., 1982; mem. nursing rev. com. NIH, 1987-88. Contbr. articles to profl. jours.; mem. editl. bd. Clin. Pediat., Am. Jour. Diseases of Children, Jour. of Orange County Pediatric Soc., Jour. Am. Acad. Pediat., LA Pediatric Soc. Recipient Women of Achievement award Matrix Table, Seattle, 1974; Disting. Alumnus award Duke U. Med. Sch., 1974; Ann. award Nat. Bd. Med. Coll. Pa., 1977; Career Devel. award USPHS, 1966-71; Moseby scholar, 1955. Mem. Am. Acad. Pediat. (chmn. com. on pediat. manpower 1984-86), Am. Coll. Cardiology, Soc. for Pediat. Rsch., Am. Fedn. Clin. Rsch., Am. Pediat. Soc., Assn. Med. Sch. Pediat. Dept. Chmn. (sec.-treas. 1981-87), Western Soc. for Pediat. Rsch., Alpha Omega Alpha. Office: U Calif Irvine Med Ctr Dept Pediatrics 101 The City Dr S Orange CA 92868-3201 Office Phone: 714-456-6483. Business E-Mail: bcmorgan@uci.edu.

MORGAN, CARL, JR., state representative; b. Upper Kalskag, Alaska, Jan. 21, 1950; m. Angela Morgan; children: Mona, Mary, Carl, Sophia, Philip. Grad., Northrup Inst Tech., 1972. Apprentice, 1972—74; mayor Aniak, Alaska, 1991—96; mem. Alaska Ho. of

Reps., 1998—; co-chair cmty. regional affairs com.; co-chmn. fisheries com. Mem. Aniak Traditional Coun., 1990—2001. Mem.: NRS. Republican. Avocations: hunting, fishing, boating.

MORGAN, DAVE, editor; Sports writer, San Francisco, LA Times, sr. asst. sports editor, dep. sports editor; exec. editor Yahoo! Sports, Santa Monica, Calif., 2006—. Named one of Most Influential People in the World of Sports, Bus. Week, 2008. Office: Yahoo! Sports 2700 Pennsylvania Ave Ste 1000 Santa Monica CA 90404 Office Phone: 310-255-0244.

MORGAN, ELIZABETH, plastic surgeon; b. Washington, July 9, 1947; d. William James and Antonia (Bell) Morgan; 1 child, Elena. BA magna cum laude, Harvard U., 1967; postgrad. (fellow), Oxford U., 1967-70; MD, Yale U., 1971; PhD in Psychology, U. Canterbury, Christchurch, New Zealand, 1995. Cert. Am. Bd. Plastic Surgery, Am. Bd. Surgery, 1988. Intern Yale-New Haven Hosp., 1971-72, resident, 1972-73, 76-77, Tufts-New Eng. Med. Center, Boston, 1973-76, Harvard-Cambridge Hosp., Mass., 1977-78; columnist Cosmopolitan mag., 1973-80; pvt. practice specializing in cosmetic plastic surgery Washington, 1978-87, McLean, Va., 1998—2006, Chevy Chase, Md., 1998—2006; chief plastic surgery Beverly Hills Physicians, Calif., 2006—07; asst. clin. prof. dept. plastic surgery UCLA, 2006—. Faculty dept. psychology U. Md., 1995; assoc. faculty dept. law, justice and soc. Am. U., 1998. Author: The Making of A Woman Surgeon, 1980, Solo Practice, 1982, Custody, A True Story, 1986, The Complete Book of Cosmetic Surgery for Men, Women and Teens, 1988. Fellow: ACS, Am. Soc. Plastic Surgeons; mem.: APA. Episcopalian. Avocations: ballet, opera, exercise, writing, travel. Office: 333 S Doheny Dr 202 Los Angeles CA 90048-3527 Home Phone: 310-858-1561; Office Phone: 310-858-1561. Business E-Mail: morgan52650@gmail.com.

MORGAN, JAMES C., retired manufacturing executive; b. 1938; BSME, MBA, Cornell U.; DEng (hon.), De Anza Coll., 1994. Corp. staff Textron Inc., 1963—72; sr. ptnr. West Ven Mgmt., San Francisco, 1972—76; pres. Applied Materials, Inc., Santa Clara, Calif., 1976—87, CEO, 1977—2003, chmn., 1987—2009, chmn. emeritus, 2009—. Apptd. by Pres. Clinton to Commn. U.S.-Pacific Trade and Investment Policy, 1996; mem. Nat. Adv. Com. Semiconductors, 1988—92; bd. dirs. Cisco Sys.; apptd. to U.S.-Japan Sector Govt. Commn., 2002; adv. bd. mem. Ctr. Sci. Tech. &: Soc. Santa Clara U., Calif.; vice-chmn. Presdl. Export Council, 2003—. Co-author: Cracking the Japanese Market: Strategies for Success in the New Global Economy. Bd. gov. Nature Conservancy; trustee Nature Conservancy Calif. Recipient Cmty. Svc. award, NCCJ, 1995, Nat. Medal of Tech., Pres. Clinton, 1996, Global Humanitarian Award, Tech. Mus. Innovation, Cmty. Svc. Award, Nat. Conf. Cmty. & Justice; named Internat. Citizen of Yr., World Forum of Silicon Valley, 1995; named to Jr. Achievement Hall of Fame, 1991. Mem.: Semiconductor Equipment and Materials Internat. (dir. emeritus, past pres.), Pacific Basin Econ. Coun. (chmn.'s circle), Coun. Competitiveness, Nat. Ctr. Asia-Pacific Econ. Cooperation (bd. dirs.), Congrl. Econ. Leadership Inst. (bd. dirs.), World Presidents Orgn., Semiconductor Equipment and Materials Internat./SEMATECH (past bd. dirs., Global Pioneer Award), Am. Electronics Assn. (past bd. dirs.). Office: Applied Materials Inc 3050 Bowers Ave Santa Clara CA 95054-3298*

MORGAN, JAMES EARL, librarian, administrator; b. Wheeling, W.Va., June 30, 1941; s. James H. L. and Ethel Irene (Goodwin) M.; m. Carman H. Head, Dec. 23, 1966; 1 child, Scott Andrew BS in Edn., Ariz. State Coll., 1965; MSLS, Fla. State U., 1966. Reference asst. social scis. Fla. State U., Tallahassee, 1965-66; head pub. services Ga. Coll., Milledgeville, 1967-69; dir. pub. services U. Tex. Med. Br., Galveston, 1969-73; dir. libraries U. Conn. Health Ctr., Farmington, 1973-76, Oreg. Health Sci. U., Portland, 1976—. Contbr. articles to profl. jours. Grantee Nat. Library Medicine, 1974-76, 78-81 Mem. ALA (life), Med. Libr. Assn. (chmn. Pacific N.W. chpt. 1981), Oreg. Health Scis. Librs. Assn., Pacific N.W. Libr. Assn., Spl. Libr. Assn., Oreg. Libr. Assn., Portland Area Spl. Librarians Assn., Assn. Coll. and Rsch. Librs., Am. Med. Informatics Assn., Nat. Rural Health Assn. Democrat. Office: Oreg Health & Sci U 3181 SW Sam Jackson Park Rd Portland OR 97239-3098 E-mail: morgan@ohsu.edu.

MORGAN, JAMES JOHN, environmental engineering educator; b. NYC, June 23, 1932; s. James and Anna (Treanor) M.; m. Jean Laurie McIntosh, June 15, 1957; children— Jenny, Johanna, Eve, Michael, Martha, Sarah BCE, Manhattan Coll., 1954; MSCE, U. Mich., 1956; postgrad., U. Ill., 1956-60; PhD, Harvard U., 1964; ScD (hon.), Manhattan Coll., 1989. Instr. civil engring. U. Ill., Urbana, 1956-60; assoc. prof. U. Fla., Gainesville, 1963-65, Calif. Inst. Tech., Pasadena, 1965-69, prof. environ. engring., 1969-87, Marvin L. Goldberger prof. environ. engring. sci., 1987—, dean of students, 1972-75, dean grad. studies, 1981-84, v.p. student affairs, 1980-89; exec. officer environ. engring. sci., 1993-96. Mem. environ. studies bd., NRC, 1974-80, Abel Wolman lectr., 2004; chmn. Acid Deposition Sci. Adv. Com., Calif., 1983-98; chmn. Gordon Rsch. Conf. on Environ. Sci.; Water, 1970. Author: (with Werner Stumm) Aquatic Chemistry, 1970, 2d edit., 1981, 3rd edit. 1996; editor Environ. Sci. and Tech., 1966-74; contbr. articles to profl. jours. Recipient Stockholm Water prize, 1999, Clarke Water prize, 1999. Mem. ASCE (award 1997), Am. Chem. Soc. (award 1980), AAAS, Am. Soc. Limnology and Oceanography (editorial bd. 1977-80), Nat. Acad. Engring., Assn. Environ. Engring. Profs. (award 1981, 83, 94), Am. Water Works Assn. (award 1963), Sigma Xi, Chi Epsilon. Democrat. Roman Catholic. Avocations: tennis, music. E-mail: morgan_j@caltech.edu.

MORGAN, JEFF SCOTT, research engineer; b. Salt Lake City, Sept. 3, 1954; s. David Nyle and Dene Huber (Olsen) M.; m. Linda Mae Marquez, May 28, 1982 (div.); m. Stephanie Sugamura, Oct. 25, 1998. BS, U. Calif., San Diego, 1976; MS, U. Hawaii, 1978, PhD, 1982. Rsch. assoc. U. Hawaii, Honolulu, 1982-85; sr. rsch. assoc. Stanford U., Palo Alto, Calif., 1985—90; rsch. engr. U. Wash., Seattle, 1990—. Mem. Am. Astron. Soc.

MORGAN, LANNY, musician; b. Des Moines, Mar. 30, 1934; s. Harold Ira and Ruth (Maddick) M.; m. Marty Shelton Morgan; children: Breck, Wynter. Student, LA City Coll., 1952. Instr. Stanford U. Summer Jazz Workshops, L.A. Jazz Workshop, Grove Sch. Music, Many others; guest artist, instr. at coll., high schs. throughout U.S.; played on recordings, films, TV; guest solo U.K. clubs, festivals. Played lead alto saxophone with Maynard Ferguson, Rey De Michele Orch., Oliver Nelson, Bill Holman Band, Bob Florence Band, Supersax; appeared, recorded Steely Dan, Natalie Cole, Diane Schurr, Shirley Horn, Andy Williams, Mel Torme, Frank Sinatra, Julie Andrews, and many others; lead quartet/quintet in L.A.; recordings include Lanny Morgan Quartet, 1993, Pacific Standard, 1997, A Suite for Yardbird, Fresh Sounds Records, Carl Saunders/Lanny Morgan Quintet, Woofy Productions. With U.S. Army, 1957-59. Home: 6470 Gaviota Ave Van Nuys CA 91406-6401

MORGAN, MARK QUENTEN, astrophysics educator; s. Walter Quenten and Barbara Gene M. BA in Astronomy, San Diego State U., 1972; PhD in Astronomy, U. Addison, Ont., Can., 1976. Jet engine and power plant engr. N.Am. Aviation, Palmdale, Calif., 1966-68; astron. observer San Diego State U., 1970-74; engr., solar observer U. Md.-Clark Lake Radio Obs., Borrego Springs, Calif., 1978-82; engr., lectr. Sci. Atlanta, San Diego, 1979-97; adv. rsch. engr. Intel Corp., 1998—. Inventor continuous wave laser, high intensity sound acoustic screening system. Mem. Inst. Environ. Scis., Acoustic Soc. Am., Astrophys. Soc. Am., Union Concerned Scientists, Planetary Soc. Office: Sci Atlanta PO Box 4254 San Diego CA 92164-4254

MORGAN, MICHAEL BREWSTER, publishing executive; b. LA, Dec. 30, 1953; s. Brewster Bowen and Eleanor (Boysen) M.; m. Debra Hunter, July 20, 1986. BA, Conn. Coll., 1975. Coll. sales rep. Addison Wesley Pub. Co., Chapel Hill, NC, 1977—81, sponsoring editor Reading, Mass., 1981—84; CEO Morgan Kaufmann Pubs., San Francisco, 1984—2002, Morgan and Claypool Pubs., San Rafael, Calif., 2002—. Mem. Am. Assn. Artificial Intelligence, Assn. Computing Machinery. Office: Morgan and Claypool Pubs 40 Oak View Dr San Rafael CA 94903 Home Phone: 415-492-9415. Business E-Mail: morgan@morganclaypool.com.

MORGAN, NEIL, editor, journalist, writer; b. Smithfield, NC, Feb. 27, 1924; s. Samuel Lewis and Isabelle (Robeson) M.; m. Caryl Lawrence, 1945 (div. 1954); m. Katharine Starkey, 1955 (div. 1962); m. Judith Blakely, 1964; 1 child, Jill. AB, Wake Forest Coll., 1943. Columnist San Diego Daily Jour., 1946-50; columnist San Diego Evening Tribune, 1950-92, assoc. editor, 1977-81, editor, 1981-92; assoc. editor, sr. columnist San Diego Union-Tribune, 1992—2004. Syndicated columnist Morgan Jour., Copley News Service, 1958—; sr. editor, dir., commentator KPBS, 2004—; cons. on Calif. affairs Bank of Am., Sunset mag.; lectr. in field. Author: My San Diego, 1951, It Began With a Roar, 1953, Know Your Doctor, 1954, Crosstown, 1955, My San Diego, 1959, 1960, Westward Tilt, 1963, Neil Morgan's San Diego, 1964, The Pacific States, 1967, The California Syndrome, 1969; author: (with Robert Witty) Marines of Margarita, 1970; author: The Unconventional City, 1972; author: (with Tom Blair) Yesterday's San Diego, 1976; author: This Great Land, 1983, Above San Diego, 1990; author: (with Judith Morgan) Dr. Seuss & Mr. Geisel, 1995, Roger: The Biography of Roger Revelle, 1997; author: (forewords) Under Cover for Wells Fargo, 1999, San Diego's Navy, 2001; contbr. non-fiction articles to Nat. Geog., Esquire, Redbook, Reader's Digest, Holiday, Harper's, San Diego Mag., Travel and Leisure, Ency. Brit., commentator KPBS, 2004—, sr. editor Voice of San Diego website, 2005—. Lt. USNR, 1943-46. Recipient Ernie Pyle Meml. award, 1957, Bill Corum Meml. award, 1961, Disting. Svc. citation, Wake Forest U., 1966, Grand award for travel writing, Pacific Area Travel Assn., 1972, 1978, Fourth Estate award, San Diego State U., 1988, The Morgan award, Leadership Edn. Awareness Devel. San Diego, 1993, Chancellors medal, U. Calif., San Diego, 2000, News Editors award for best column, AP Mng. Editors, 2004; co-recipient Ellen and Roger Revelle award, 1986; named Outstanding Young Man of Yr., San Diego, 1959, 1st place news commentary, Calif. News Pub. Assn., 1993, Harold Keen award, 1996, Mr. San Diego, Rotary, 1999. Mem. Authors Guild, Soc. Profl. Journalists (award for best column 1999), Soc. of Am. Travel Writers, Bohemian Club, Phi Beta Kappa. Home: 7930 Prospect Pl La Jolla CA 92037-3721 Personal E-mail: nmorgan@san.rr.com. Business E-Mail: neil.morgan@uniontrib.com.

MORGAN, STEPHEN CHARLES, academic administrator; b. Upland, Calif., June 2, 1946; s. Thomas Andrew and Ruth Elizabeth (Miller) M.; m. Ann Marie McMurray, Sept. 6, 1969; 1 child, Kesley Suzanne. BA, U. La Verne, 1968; MS, U. So. Calif., 1971; EdD, U. No. Colo., 1979. Devel. officer U. La Verne, Calif., 1968-71, asst. to pres. Calif., 1971-73, dir. devel. Calif., 1973-75, v.p. devel. Calif., 1975-76, pres. Calif., 1985—; dir. devel. U. So. Calif., LA, 1976-79; exec. dir. Ind. Colls. No. Calif., San Francisco, 1979-85. Dir. Ind. Colls. So. Calif., L.A., 1985—. Bd. dirs. Mt. Baldy United Way, Ontario, Calif., 1988-98, McKinley Children's Ctr., San Dimas, Calif., 1989-99, LeRoy Haynes Ctr. for Family and Children's Svcs., 2000—; chair nat. com. on higher edn. Ch. of Brethren, Elgin, Ill., 1988-90; dir. Pomona Valley Hosp. Med. Ctr., 1992-98, 99—, Inter Valley Health Plan, 1992-97, PFF Bank and Trust, 2001—. Mem. Assn. Ind. Calif. Colls. and Univs. (exec. com. 1989—, vice-chmn. 1996-2000, chmn. 2000-2002), L.A. County Fair Assn. (bd. dirs., chmn. 2002—), Western Coll. Assn. (exec. com. 1992-98, pres. 1996-98), Western Assn. Schs. and Colls. (sr. accrediting commn. 1996-2001), Pi Gamma Mu. Avocations: orchid culture, gardening, travel. Home: 2518 N Mountain Ave Claremont CA 91711-1579 Office: U LaVerne Office Pres 1950 3rd St La Verne CA 91750-4401 E-mail: morgans@ulv.edu.

MORGAN, SUSAN H., state legislator; b. Nanaimo, BC, Sept. 1, 1949; m to Kip; children: three. Member, S Umpqua Co Planning Advisor Committee, 80-98; advisor board, Myrtle Creek Public Library, 88-96; Oregon State Representative, District 46, 1999-2002; Oregon State Representative, District 2, 2003-.Off manager, Morgan Loggin, M&M Hardwoods, 78-90; information system manager, Weyerhauser Pole Facil, 90-93; lumber sales, C&D Lumber Co, 93-98; parent volunteer, Girl Scout Troop 291, currently. WOOD; founding member Oregon Lands Coalition; Douglas Co Grass Roots Association; Lions; Nat Rifle Association; Roseburg Rod & Gun Club. Republican. Christian. Office: 900 Court St NE, H-381 Salem OR 97301 Fax: 541-863-5491. E-mail: morgan.rep@state.or.us.

MORGAN, WAYNE JOSEPH, medical educator, medical association administrator; arrived in USA, 1980; DCS, McGill U., Montreal, 1971, MD, CM, McGill U., Montreal, 1976. Asst. prof., pediat., pediatric pulmonary sect. U. Ariz., Tucson, 1982—87, 1989—90, rsch. asst. prof., physiology dept., 1987—89, rsch. asst. prof., pediat., pediatric pulmonary sect., 1987—89, asst. prof., physiology dept., 1989—90, assoc. prof., physiology dept., 1990—97, assoc. prof., pediat., pediatric pulmonary sect., 1990—97, dir., Tucson Cystic Fibrosis Ctr., 1990—, chief, pediat., pediatric pulmonary sect., 1991—, prof., pediat., pediatric pulmonary sect., 1997—, prof., physiology dept., 1997—, assoc. head, academic affairs, dept. pediat., 1997—. Recipient Wood Gold medal, 1976, Alexander D. Stewart prize, 1976, Robert Forsyth prize, 1976, Clin. Investigator award, NIH-NHLBI, 1984, award, Am. Thoracic Soc., 1987, Coll. Medicine, U. Ariz., 1987—88, Vernon and Virginia Furrow award, 1989, Outstanding Lectr. award, U. Ariz., 2001, Vernon and Virginia Furrow award, 2005—06; named Best Dr. America, Woodward, White, 1994; Clin. fellow, Can. Cystic Fibrosis Found., 1980, Rsch. fellow, Med. Rsch. Coun. Can., 1981. Mem.: Royal Coll. Physicians & Surgeons Can., Am. Thoracic Soc. Office: Univ Ariz 1501 N Campbell Ave Tucson AZ 85724 Office Phone: 520-626-6754. Office Fax: 520-626-9465.

MORGENROTH, EARL EUGENE, entrepreneur; b. Sidney, Mont., May 7, 1936; s. Frank and Leona (Ellison) M.; m. Adrienne Smith; children: Dolores Roxanna, David Jonathan, Denise Christine BS, U. Mont., Missoula, 1961. From salesman to gen. mgr. Sta. KGVO-AM Radio, Missoula, Mont., 1958-65; sales mgr. Stas. KGVO-TV, KTVM-TV and KCFW-TV, Missoula, Butte, Kalispell, Mont., 1965-66, gen. mgr., 1966-68, Sta. KCOY-TV, Santa Maria, Calif., 1968-69; v.p., gen. mgr. Western Broadcasting Co., Missoula, 1966-69, gen. mgr., pres., 1969-81, numerous cos. in Mont., Calif., Idaho, PR, Ga., 1966-84; pres., chmn. Western Broadcasting Co., Missoula, 1981-84, Western Comm., Inc., Reno, 1984-90; prin. Western Investments, Reno, 1984—. Chmn. Western Fin., Inc., Morgenroth Music Ctrs. Inc., Mont. Band Instruments, Inc., E&B Music Inc., Times Square, Inc., Rio Plumas Ranches, LLC; mem. pres. adv. coun. U. Mont., 1991—, mem. biol. scis. adv. coun., 1999—. Mem. Mont. Bank Bd., Helena; commencement spkr. U. Mont., 1988, mem. pres.' adv. coun., 1992—, mem. biol. scis. adv. coun., 2001—; bd. dirs. U. Mont. Found., 1985-95. With. US Army, 1954-57. Named Boss of Yr. Santa Maria Valley J.C.s, 1968, Alumnus of the Yr., U. Mont. Bus. Sch., 1998. Mem. U. Mont. Century Club (pres.), Missoula C. of C. (pres.), Rocky Mountain Broadcasters Assn. (pres.), Craighead Wildlife-Wildlands Inst. (bd. dirs. 1991-97), Boone and Crockett Club (pres. 2001-02), Grizzly Riders Internat. (bd. dirs., v.p. 1991—, pres. 2005-), Bldg. A Scholastic Heritage (bd. dirs. 1987-97), Mont. Mus. Arts & Culture (bd. mem. 2001-), Wildlife Biology U. Mont. (bd. mem. 2000-). Republican. Methodist.

MORGENSEN, JERRY LYNN, construction company executive; b. Lubbock, Tex., July 9, 1942; s. J. J. and Zelline (Butler) Morgensen; m. Linda Dee Austin, Apr. 17, 1965; children: Angela, Nicole. BS in Civil Engring., Tex. Tech U., 1965. Area engr. E.I. Dupont Co., Orange, Tex., 1965-67, div. engr. La Place, La., 1967-73; project mgr. Hensel Phelps Constrn. Co., Greeley, Colo., 1973-78, area mgr., 1978-80, v.p., 1980-85, pres., CEO, 1985—, chmn. bd. Mem. bd. trustees UNC; Member Constn. Indus. Devel. Coun. CSU; mem. Tex. Tech. Civil Engring. Acad. Office: 420 6th Ave Greeley CO 80631-2332

MORGENSTERN, JOE, film critic; b. NYC, Oct. 3, 1932; s. Mark E. and Mollie (Fisch) M.; m. Rosetta Jacobs, Jan. 21, 1962 (div. Apr. 1981); 1 child, Anna. BA in English magna cum laude, Lehigh U., 1953. Film critic Newsweek mag., NYC, 1965-72; columnist LA Herald Examiner, 1982-87; film critic Wall Street Jour., NYC, 1995—. Co-founder Nat. Soc. Film Critics. Author: World Champion, 1968 (TV scripts) Boy in the Plastic Bubble, Law & Order, 10,000 Black Men Named George. Recipient Pulitizer Prize for criticism, 2005. Mem. Phi Beta Kappa, NY Film Critics Cir., LA Soc. Film Critics. Office: Wall Street Jour PO Box 1946 Santa Monica CA 90406-1946 E-mail: joe.morgenstern@wsj.com.

MORGESE, JAMES N., broadcast executive; b. Bronx, NY, Jan. 5, 1951; s. George N. and Tina C. (Papa) M.; m. Zoe A. Larsen, July 11, 1976; children: Mila, Lane. BA in Mass Comm., U. Denver, 1973, MA in Pub. Comm., 1979. Prodn. asst. NBC, NYC, 1971-74; mem. creative staff Prodns. Unltd., Denver, 1974-75; prodn. asst. Sta. KOA-TV, Denver, 1975-79; prodn. mgr. WKYU-TV, Bowling Green, Ky., 1980-82; mgr. prodn. ops. Sta. KUID-TV, Moscow, Idaho, 1982-85; local program mgr. Sta. WUFT-TV, Gainsville, Fla., 1985-86, sta. mgr., 1986-90, KRMA-TV, Denver, 1990-93, pres., gen. mgr., 1993-97, Rocky Mountain Pub. Broadcasting Network, Denver, 1997—. Exec. prodr. Borah Symposium, Moscow, 1980; adv. bd. Alachua County Cable T.V., Fla., 1989-90; exec. in charge prodn. And Learning For All, Denver, 1992-93, A Place to Call Home, Denver, 1992-93; bd. dirs. 5 Points Media Ctr.; mem. state bd. Am.'s Pub. Telephone. Mem. adv. commn. U. Denver Alumni, 1991-92. Mem. NATAS, Colo. Hispanic Media Assn., Denver Advertising Fedn., Urban League Met. Denver, Rotary. Office: 1089 Bannock St Denver CO 80204-4067

MORGRIDGE, JOHN P., computer systems network executive; b. Elmhurst, Ill., July 23, 1933; m. Tashia F. Morgridge; three children. BBA in Mktg. & Fin., U. Wis., 1955; MBA, Stanford U., 1957; DSc (hon.), U. Wis., 1994; LLD (hon.), Carleton U., 2002; LHD, Lesley Coll., No. Ill. U. Mktg. profl. Honeywell Info. Systems, 1960-80; v.p. mkgt., sales and svc. Stratus Co., Inc., 1980-86; pres., chief ops. officer GRiD Systems (now part of Tandy Corp.), 1986-88; pres., CEO Cisco Systems, Inc., San Jose, Calif., 1988-95, chmn., 1995—2006, chmn. emeritus, 2006. Lectr. Stanford U. Bus. Sch., 1997—. Bd. dirs. Coun. on Competiveness, CARE, The Cisco Found., The Cisco Learning Inst., Interplast, The Nature Consevancy, Wis. Alumni Rsch. Found.; trustee Stanford U., 2002—. Capt. USAF, 1957—60. Recipient Leadership in Tech. award Tech. Corps, 1988, Ernest C. Arbuckle award, Stanford U., 1998, Philanthropist of the Yr., Ctr. for Excellence in Nonprofits, 1999, Deveneck Hamanitarian award, Hidden Villa, 1999; named one of 400 Richest Americans, Forbes, 2006. Office: Cisco Systems Inc 170 W Tasman Dr San Jose CA 95134-1700

MORHAIME, MIKE, video game company executive; B, UCLA, 1990. Co-founder, pres. Blizzard Entertainment (originally Silicon & Synapse), Irvine, Calif., 1991—. Prodr.: (video games) The Lost Vikings, 1992, Orcs & Humans, 1994, The Death and Return of Superman, 1994, BlackThorne, 1994, Warcraft II: Tides of Darkness, 1995, Justice League Task Force, 1995, Diablo, 1997, Warcraft II: The Dark Saga, 1997, Norse by Norse West: The Return of the Lost Vikings, 1997, StarCraft: Brood War, 1998, StarCraft, 1998, Warcraft II: Battle.net Edition, 1999, StarCraft 64, 2000, Diablo II, 2000, Diablo II: Collector's Edition, 2000, Diablo II: Lord of Destruction, 2001, Warcraft III: Reign of Chaos, 2002, Warcraft III: Reign of Chaos Collector's Edition, 2002, Warcraft III: The Frozen Throne, 2003, Rock 'n Roll Racing, 2003, World of Warcraft, 2004, World of Warcraft: The Burning Crusade, 2007. Named one of 50 Who Matter Now, CNNMoney.com Bus. 2.0, 2006, 50 Most Important People on the Web, PC World, 2007. Office: Blizzard Entertainment PO Box 18979 Irvine CA 92623

MORI, ALLEN ANTHONY, retired academic administrator; b. Hazleton, Pa., Nov. 1, 1947; s. Primo Philip and Carmella (DeNoia) M.; m. Barbara Epoca, June 26, 1971; 1 child, Kirsten Lynn. BA, Franklin and Marshall Coll., Lancaster, Pa., 1969; MEd, Bloomsburg U. Pa., 1971; PhD, U. Pitts., 1975. Spl. edn. tchr. White Haven (Pa.)

State Sch. and Hosp., 1969-70, Hazleton Area Sch. Dist., 1970-71, Pitts. Pub. Schs., 1971-74; supr. student tchrs. U. Pitts., 1974-75; prof. spl. edn. U. Nev., Las Vegas, 1975-84; dean coll edn. Marshall U., Huntington, W.Va., 1984-87; dean coll. edn. Calif. State U., LA, 1987—2003, provost, v.p. acad. affairs Dominquez Hills, 2003—07. Hearing officer pub. law 94-142 Nev. Dept. Edn., Carson City, 1978—; mem. Nev. Gov.'s Com. on Mental Health and Mental Retardation, 1983-84; cons. Ministry Edn., Manitoba, Can., 1980-82; pres. Tchr. Edn. Coun. State Colls. and Univs., 1993-94. Author: Families of Children with Special Needs, 1983; co-author: Teaching the Severely Retarded, 1980, Handbook of Preschool, Special Education, 1980, Adapted Physical Education, 1983, A Vocational Training Continuum for the Mentally and Physically Disabled, 1985, Teaching Secondary Students with Mild Learning and Behavior Problems, 1986, 93, 99; author numerous articles, book revs. and monographs. Bd. dirs. Assn. Retarded Citizens San Gabriel Valley, ElMonte, 1989—94. Recipient grants U.S. Dept. Edn., 1976-91, Nev. Dept. Edn., W.Va. Dept. Edn., Calif. State U. Chancellor's Office. Mem. Assn. Tchr. Educators, Coun. for Exceptional Children (div. on Career Devel. exec. com. 1981-83), Nat. Soc. for Study of Edn., Phi Beta Delta, Phi Delta Kappa, Pi Lambda Theta, Phi Kappa Phi. Avocations: wine collecting, travel. Home: 1761 Avenida Entrada San Dimas CA 91773 Business E-Mail: stelerfn1@roadrunner.com.

MORIE, G. GLEN, lawyer, manufacturing executive; BA, Bowdoin Coll., 1964; LLB, U. Pa., 1967. Bar: Wash. 1968. Pvt. practice law, Wash., 1970-73; asst. counsel PACCAR, Inc., Bellevue, Wash., 1973-79, asst. gen. counsel, 1979-82, gen. counsel, 1983-85, v.p., gen. counsel, 1985—2004. Sec. bd. dirs. Seattle Virtuosi Found.

MORIGUCHI, TOMIO, gift and grocery store executive; b. Tacoma, Apr. 16, 1936; s. Fujimatsu and Sadako (Tsutakawa) M.; m. Lovett Keiko Tanaka, Nov. 15, 1969; children: Tyler Minoru, Denise Ritsuko. BSME, U. Wash., 1961. With missile div. Boeing Co., Seattle, 1961-62; with Uwajimaya Inc., Seattle, 1962—, pres., 1965—. Bd. dirs. Seafirst Corp., Seattle 1st Nat. Bank, Wash. Energy Co. Bd. dirs. Wash. Inst. Applied Tech., Seattle, Seattle Found., Leadership Tomorrow, Pacific Celebration; mem. Wash. Econ. Devel. Bd., Wash. Adv. Council on Internat. Trade and Devel.; v.p., bd. dirs., past chmn. Nikkei Concerns, Inc.; treas. Nat. Japanese Am. Citizens League, 1974-76; trustee Seattle Community Coll. Dist., 1985—, also past chmn.; past chmn. Chinatown-Internat. Dist. Preservation and Devel. Authority; bd. dirs., past pres. Internat. Dist. Improvement Assn., many others. Recipient Outstanding Vol. Civic Leadership award Four Seasons Hotel, Seattle, 1987; named Alumni Legend, U. Wash., 1987. Mem. Seattle C. of C. (past v.p.), Internat. Dist. Econ. Assn. (v.p., past pres.), Japan Am. Soc. State Wash. (pres. 1985), Rotary. Office: Uwajimaya Inc 519 6th Ave S Seattle WA 98104-2812

MORING, JOHN FREDERICK, lawyer; b. Farmville, Va., Oct. 30, 1935; s. Scott O'Ferrall and Margaret Macon (Mitchell) M.; m. Margaret Ann Clarke, Mar. 30, 1959; children: Martha, Elizabeth, Scott, Lee. BS, Va. Poly. Inst., 1957; JD, George Washington U., 1961. Bar: Va. 1961, DC 1962, US Supreme Ct. 1964; cert. mediator civil disputes Supreme Ct. Va. 2004, US Dist. Ct. Va., 2004, US Cir. Ct., 2004. Assoc. Morgan, Lewis & Bockius, Washington, 1961-68, ptnr., 1969-78, Jones, Day, Reavis & Pogue, Washington, 1978-79; founding ptnr. Crowell & Moring, Washington, Irvine, NY, London, Brussels, 1979—2000. Sec. Associated Gas Distbrs., Inc., 1977-2000. Local gas utility columnist: Nat. Gas Jour., 1989—2000; mem. editl. bd. Natural Gas Contracts, 1994—2001. Mem. nat. panel neutrals Am. Arbitration Assn., 2003—; chmn. bd. dirs. Washington Legal Counsel for Elderly, 2000—01; Rep. candidate 23d Dist./Va. Gen. Assembly, Alexandria, 1973; mem. bd. govs. St. Stephen's and St. Agnes Sch., Alexandria, 1989—95; pres. St. Stephen's Found., Inc., 1990—93; sr. warden Immanuel Ch. on the Hill, Alexandria, 1988, 1989; trustee Ch. Schs. of Diocese of Va., 1996—2008; mem. found. bd. Shrine Mont Conf. Ctr. Episc. Diocese Va., Orkney Springs, Va., 2001—; mem. bd. govs. St. Margaret's Sch., Tappahannock, Va., 2002—08. 2d lt. US Army, 1958. Mem.: ABA (natural resources law sect. 1982—86, coun.), Am. Arbitration Assn., Fed. Energy Bar Assn. (sec. 1963—66, pres. 1982—83), Indian Creek Yacht and Country Club (Kilmarnock, Va.). Episcopalian. Avocations: golf, fishing, canoeing. Home: PO Box 224 White Stone VA 22578 Office: Crowell & Moring 1001 Pennsylvania Ave NW Fl 10 Washington DC 20004-2595 also: 3 Park Plaza 20th Fl Irvine CA 92614-8505 also: 11 Pilgrim St London EC4V 6RN England also: 71 Rue Royale B 1000 Brussels Belgium also: 153 E 53rd St 31st Fl New York NY 10022-4611 Business E-Mail: fmoring@kaballero.com.

MORIS, LAMBERTO GIULIANO, architect; b. Siena, Tuscany, Italy, Mar. 29, 1944; arrived in US, 1972; s. Gualtiero Luigi and Giovanna (Avanzati) M.; m. Tracy P. Schilling, 1970 (div. 1985); children: Giacomo, Stefano; m. Beverly Chiang, Mar. 28, 1986; 1 child, Christopher. MA in Arch., U. Florence, Italy, 1970. Assoc. Marquis Assocs., San Francisco, 1972-78, prin., 1978-85, Simon Martin-Vegue Winkelstein Moris, San Francisco, 1985—2005, Moris/Marino and Assoc., San Francisco, 2005—. Tchr. San Francisco City Coll., 1982—84; juror DuPont Antron Design Awards, 1989, AIA Hon. Awards, 1995, AIA Interior Architecture Awards, Chgo. chpt., 1997; mem. interior design adv. coun. Acad. Art Coll., San Francisco, 1992—2001; lectr. AIA Nat. Conf., 1996, Aircraft Interiors Expo, Canne, France, 2000, Aircraft Interiors Conf. and Exhbn., Long Beach, Calif., 2001, AIA- Italy Summit, San Francisco, 2003. Mem. design com. Clairmont Pines Task Force, 1991; charter mem. Forecast 21 Principals Roundtable, 1993; mem. Bldg. Industry Conf. Bd. (BICB), 2001—; mem. bd. dirs. ItaLingua Inst., 1984—. Mem.: FAIA (mem. selection com. 2003), AIA (mem. internat. com. 2003), Interior Architecture, No. Calif. chpt., Am. Inst. Architects, Coll. Fellows, Am. Inst. Architects (corp. mem. 1979—), Am. C. of C. in Italy, Oakland Met. C. of C., Accademia Italiane della Cucina, Cath. Prof. Bus. Club, San Francisco Opera Assn., Il Cenacolo (bd. dirs. 1991), San Francisco Heritage Assn., Engr. Club. Roman Catholic. Avocations: coin collecting/numismatics, skiing, travel. Office: Page and Moris 48 2d St San Francisco CA 94105 Home Phone: 510-654-7581; Office Phone: 510-381-5083. Personal E-mail: lgmoris@mindspring.com.

MORISHITA, AKIHIKO, trading company executive; b. Osaka, Japan, Oct. 14, 1941; came to U.S., 1981; s. Sueyoshi and Toshiko Morishita; m. Fumiko Okamura; children: Shizuko, Kumiko, Okamura. BA in Econs., Wakayama U., Wakayama, Japan, 1965. Mgr. Hanwa & Co. Ltd., Osaka, 1965-80; cons. oil dept. Pacific Southwest Trading Co., San Diego, 1981-82; exec. Pacific Marine Bunkering, Inc., LA, 1982—. Mem.: Club Leconte. Home: 4610 Don Pio Dr Woodland Hills CA 91364-4205 Fax: 908-673-1179.

MORITA, RICHARD YUKIO, microbiology and oceanography educator; b. Pasadena, Calif., Mar. 27, 1923; s. Jiro and Reiko (Yamamoto) M.; m. Toshiko Nishihara, May 29, 1926; children—Sally Jean, Ellen Jane, Peter Wayne BS, U. Nebr., 1947; MS, U. So. Calif., 1949; PhD, U. Calif., 1954. Microbiologist Mid-Pacific Expdn., 1950, Danish Galathea Deep-Sea Expdn., 1952, Trans-Pacific Expdn.; Postdoctoral fellow U. Calif., Scripps Inst. Oceanography, 1954-55; asst. prof. U. Houston, 1955-58; asst. prof., assoc. prof. U. Neb., 1958-62; prof. microbiology and oceanography Oreg. State U., Corvallis, 1962-89, prof. emeritus microbiology and oceanography, 1989—. Prog. dir. biochemistry NSF, 1968-69; Disting. vis. prof. Kyoto Univ.; cons. NIH, 1968-70; rschr. in field. Contbr. articles to sci. lit. Patentee in field. Served with US Army, 1944—46. Grantee NSF, 1962—, NIH, 1960-68, NASA, 1967-72, Office Naval Research, 1966-70, Dept. Interior, 1968-72, NOAA, 1975-82, Bur. Land Mgmt., 1982, EPA, 1986—; recipient awards including King Fredericus IX Medal and Ribbon, 1954, Sr. Queen Elizabeth II Fellowship, 1973-74, Hotpack lectr. and award Can. Soc. Fellow Japan Soc. for Promotion Sci.; mem. Am. Soc. Microbiology (Fisher award). Home: 1515 NW 14th St Corvallis OR 97330 Home Phone: 541-753-0337. Personal E-mail: dickmorita@aol.com.

MORITZ, TIMOTHY BOVIE, psychiatrist; b. Portsmouth, Ohio, July 26, 1936; s. Charles Raymond and Elisabeth Bovie (Morgan) M.; m. Joyce Elizabeth Rasmussen, Oct. 13, 1962 (div. Sept. 1969); children: Elizabeth Wynne, Laura Morgan; m. Antoinette Tanasichuk, Oct. 31, 1981; children: David Michael, Stephanie Lysbeth. BA, Ohio State U., 1959; MD, Cornell U., 1963. Diplomate Am. Bd. Psychiatry and Neurology. Intern in medicine N.Y. Hosp., NYC, 1963-64, resident in psychiatry, 1964-67; spl. asst. to dir. NIMH, Bethesda, Md., 1967-69; dir. Community Mental Health Ctr., Rockland County, NY, 1970-74, Ohio Dept. Mental Health, Columbus, Ohio, 1975-81; med. dir. psychiatry Miami Valley Hosp., Dayton, Ohio, 1981-82; med. dir. N.E. Ga. Community Mental Health Ctr., Athens, Ga., 1982-83, Charter Vista Hosp., Fayetteville, Ark., 1983-87; clin. dir. adult psychiatry Charter Hosp., Las Vegas, Nev., 1987-94; pvt. practice psychiatry Las Vegas, 1987—; med. dir. Problem Gambling Cons., Las Vegas, 2000—. Prof. Wright State U., Dayton, Ohio, 1981-82; asst. prof. Cornell U., N.Y.C., 1970-73; mem. human subjects biomed. scis. rev. com. U. Nev., Las Vegas, 2000-2001; cons. NIMH, Rockville, Md., 1973-83. Author: (chpt.) Rehabilitation Medicine and Psychiatry, 1976; mem. editorial bd. Directions in Psychiatry, 1981-1993. Dir. dept. mental health and mental retardation Gov.'s Cabinet, State of Ohio, Columbus, 1975-81. Recipient Svc. award Ohio Senate, 1981, Svc. Achievement award Ohio Gov., 1981. Fellow Am. Psychiat. Assn. (disting. life, Disting. Svc. award 1981); mem. AMA, Nev. Assn. Psychiat. Physicians, Nev. State Med. Assn., Am. Assn. Chronic Fatigue Syndrome, Clark County Med. Soc., Cornell U. Med. Coll. Alumni Assn., Ohio State U. Alumni Assn. (life). Office: 2330 Paseo del Prado Ste C-109 Las Vegas NV 89102-4336 Office Phone: 702-363-3633.

MORIUCHI, K. DEREK, secondary school educator; b. LA, 1958; BA, UCLA, 1981; MA, Calif. State U., 1982; MA in Ednl. Adminstrn., Calif. State U., LA, 2005. Cert. single subject tchg. credential in math., cross cultural lang. acquisition devel., nat. bd. cert. tchr., lic. in adminstrv. svcs. Tchr. math. Marshall Mid. Sch., 1986—90, Ganesha H.S., 1991—93; tchr. history Stevenson Middle Sch., LA, 1993—2003, chairdept. math.; secondary math. expert L.A. Unified Sch. Dist., LA, 2003—. Spkr. in field. Mem.: Calif. Math. Coun. (spkr. 2000—03), Nat. Bd. for Profl. Tchg. Stds. (bd. mem. 2001—), Pi Lambda Theta. Office: Local Dist 5 LA Unified Sch Dist 2151 N Soto St Los Angeles CA 90032 Office Phone: 323-224-3132. Personal E-mail: k12536@aol.com. E-mail: derek.moriuchi@lausd.net.

MORK, STUART R., land and farming company executive; BS in Fin., Acctg., MBA in Fin., Acctg., U. So. Ca. Treas. The Newhall Land & Farming Co., 1987-92, v.p., fin., 1992-95, CFO, 1995-98, sr. v.p., CFO, 1998—. Mem. Urban Land Inst., exec. com. mem. Lusk Ctr. Real Estate Devel. USC, bd. dirs. Henry May Newhall Meml. Hosp., bd. dirs. Boy Scouts Am. L.A. Coun., trustee San Marino Schs. Found. Office: The Newhall Land & Farming Co 23823 Valencia Blvd Valencia CA 91355-2103

MORRILL, RICHARD LELAND, geographer, educator; b. LA, Feb. 15, 1934; s. Robert W. and Lillian M. (Riffo) M.; m. Joanne L. Cooper, 1965; children: Lee, Andrew, Jean. BA, Dartmouth Coll., 1955; MA, U. Wash., 1957, PhD, 1959. Asst. prof. geography Northwestern U., 1959-60; NSF research fellow U. Lund, Sweden, 1960-61; asst. prof. U. Wash., Seattle, 1961-65, asso. prof., 1965-69, prof., 1969—, chmn. dept. geography, 1974-83, asso. dir. environ. studies, 1974-98; chmn. urban planning PhD program, 1992-98. Vis. asso. prof. U. Chgo., dir. Chgo. Regional Hosp. Study, 1966-67; cons. population, regional and urban planning. Author: Geography of Poverty, 1970, Spatial Organization of Society, 1973, Political Redistricting and Geographic Theory, 1981, Spatial Diffusion, 1987. Mem. King County Boundary Rev. Bd. Guggenheim fellow, 1983-84 Mem. Assn. Am. Geographers (Meritorious Contbn. award 1970, mem. coun. 1970-73, sec. 1979-81, pres. 1981-82), Regional Sci. Assn., Wash. Regional Sch. Assn. (pres. 1993-94), Population Assn. Am., Lambda Alpha. Office: U Wash Dept Geography Seattle WA 98195-0001 Business E-Mail: morrill@uwashington.edu.

MORRIS, ARLENE MYERS, marketing professional; b. Washington, Pa., Dec. 29, 1951; d. Frank Hayes Myers and Lula Irene (Slusser) Kolcun; m. John L. Sullivan, Feb. 17, 1971 (div. July 1982); m. David Wellons Morris, July 27, 1984. BA, Carlow Coll., 1974; postgrad., Western New England Coll., 1981-82. Sales rep. Syntex Labs., Inc., Palo Alto, Calif., 1974-77; profl. sales rep. McNeil Pharm., Spring House, Pa., 1977-78, mental health rep., 1978-80, asst. product dir., 1981-82, dist. mgr., 1982-85, new product dir., 1985-87, exec. dir. new bus. devel., 1987-89, v.p. bus. devel., 1989-93, Scios Inc., Mountain View, Calif., 1993-96, Coulter Pharma., 1996—. Mem. Found. of Ind. Colls., Phila., 1989. Mem. Pharm. Advt. Coun., Am. Diabetes Assn., Am. Acad. Sci., Healthcare Bus. Womens Assn., Lic. Execs. Soc.

MORRIS, BRIAN, state supreme court justice; b. Butte, Mont., Sept. 5, 1963; m. Cherche Prezeau; 3 children. BA in Economics, Stanford U., 1986, MA in Economics, 1987; JD, Stanford Law Sch., 1992. Law clerk for Judge John T. Noonan, Jr. U.S. Ct. of Appeals for Ninth Circuit, 1992—93; law clerk for Justice William H. Rehnquist U.S. Supreme Ct., 1993—94; legal asst. Iran-U.S. Claims Tribunal, The Hague, 1994—95; prtnr. Goetz, Gallik, Baldwin & Dolan, 1995—99; sr. legal officer UN Compensation Commn., 2000—01; state solicitor Mont. Dept. of Justice, 2001—04; justice Mont. Supreme Ct., 2005—. Author several law review and professional jour. articles. Office: Mont Supreme Ct PO Box 203003 Helena MT 59620-3003

MORRIS, DAVID JOHN, mining engineer, consultant, mining executive; b. Seattle, May 6, 1945; s. Jack Abraham and Alice Jean (Hanson) M.; m. Melania F. Kearney, July 28, 1978; children: Whitney Elizabeth, Benton James, Sienna Elise. BA in Math. and Physics, Whitman Coll., 1968; BS in Mining Engring., Columbia U., 1968. Registered profl. engr., Colo., Utah, Wash., Tex. Mining engr. Union Oil of Calif., Los Angeles, 1968-69, John T. Boyd Co., Denver, 1974-76, sr. mining engr., 1976-78, v.p., mgr., 1978-87; exec. cons., 1998; mng. ptnr. Palmer Coking Coal Co., Black Diamond, Wash., 1976-82, 90—; pres. Pacific Coast Coal Co., Black Diamond, Wash., 1982—, Pacific Hydropower Devel., Inc., Seattle, 1995—. Mem. Bd. Overseers Whitman Coll., Walla Walla, Wash., 1986-2001, vice chair, 1993-95, chmn. Rep. campaign for Whitman, Denver, 1985; coach youth athletics. Served as lt. USN, 1969-74, Vietnam. Henry Krumb scholar Columbia U., N.Y.C., 1967-68. Mem. NSPE, Soc. Mining Engrs. (admissions com. 1985-88, Howard Eavenson award com. 1984-87, Woomer award com. 1990-93, chair 1993—, Ramsay award com. 1992-95, 1999-2002, chair 1995, 2002), Nat. Coal Assn. (bd. dirs. 1990-98, exec. com. 1993-94, 96-98), Nat. Coal Coun. (appointed by Sec. of Energy 1992, 94, 96, 98, 2000), Nat. Mining Assn. (bd. dirs. 1995-98), Seattle C. of C. (chmn. energy com. 1991-94), Western Rugby Football Union (sec. 1980), Broadmoor Golf Club, Rotary. Republican. Avocations: golf, hunting, fishing, gardening, handball. Office: Pacific Coast Coal Co Inc PO Box 450 Black Diamond WA 98010-0450 Office Phone: 206-720-1899. E-mail: djmcoal@aol.com.

MORRIS, DONALD CHARLES, real estate company executive; b. Iowa City, Nov. 15, 1951; s. Lucien Ellis and Jean (Pinder) M.; m. Barbara Louise Small, Apr. 28, 1973 (div. Apr. 1980); m. Jana Susan Moyer, Aug. 28, 1982; children: Alexander Charles, Elisa Jean. Student, Cantab Coll., Toronto, Can., 1970-71; BSc, U. Guelph, Can., 1974; MSC, U. Guelph, 1975; PhD, U. B.C., Vancouver, 1978. Instr. U. B.C., Vancouver, 1975-77; pres. Morley Internat., Inc., Seattle, 1976-81; self-employed Comml. Investment Real Estate, Seattle, 1981-83; v.p., regional mgr. DKB Corp., Seattle, 1983-86; pres. Morris Devel. Svcs., Inc., Seattle, 1986—, Washington Group, Inc., Seattle, 1986—; sec.-treas., exec. v.p. Interactive Imagination Corp., Seattle, 2000—. Bd.dirs., sec., treas., exec. v.p. Interactive Imagination Corp., Seattle, 2000—. Bd. dirs. Perservation Action, Washington, 1985-90; mem. Nat. Trust for Historic Preservation. Mem. Nat. Assn. Realtors, Wash. Assn. Realtors. Avocations: skiing, sailing, boating. Office: Wash Group Morris Devel PO Box 4584 Rollingbay WA 98061-0584

MORRIS, DONNA JONES, library director; Dir. Ark. Valley Regional Libr. Svc. Sys., Pueblo, Colo., 1985—2004; state libr., dir. Utah State Libr., Salt Lake City, 2004—. Former pres. Colo. Assn. Librs. Recipient Francis Keppel award, 2005; named Colo. Libr. of Yr., 1992. Mem.: ALA (Nat. Advocacy Honor Roll 2000), Utah Libr. Assn., Chief Officers of State Libr. Agencies, Western Coun. State Librs., Utah Academic Libr. Consortium, Mountain Plains Libr. Assn. (Disting. award 2005). Office: Utah State Libr 250 N 1950 W Ste A Salt Lake City UT 84116-7901 Office Phone: 801-715-6770. Office Fax: 801-715-6767. E-mail: dmorris@utah.gov.

MORRIS, ERDIE L., dean, medical educator; b. Moline, IL, Apr. 10, 1936; s. Erdie L. Morris, Sr. and Eunice V. Johnson; m. Claudia Mae Troncin, Apr. 13, 1941; children: Michael Eric, Terry Lee. BS in Biology, Ariz. State U., 1960, MA in Biology, 1964; PhD, Purdue U., 1966; MPH, U. Calif., Berkeley, 1970. Asst. prof. biology Erskine Coll., Due West, SC, 1966-69; assoc. prof. biology Grand Canyon Coll., Phoenix, 1970-99; founding dean, prof. health sci. Grand Canyon U. Coll. Sci. and Allied Health, Phoenix, 1994—. Instr. Elder Hostel Internat., Boston, 1980-97; pres. Ariz. Biological Conf., Phoenix, 1976-78. Vol. Terros Drug Abuse Crisis Ctr., Phoenix (mem. 1984-93, pres. 1987-89), 1970-93; mem. Govnr.'s Com. on Environ. Health exec. branch, 1982-84. Recipient Tri Beta award, Am. Biological Assn., 1968, Rho Chi award, Am. Pharmaceutical Assn., 1966. Mem. N. Am. Assn. Environmental Edn., Ariz.-Nev. Acad. Sci., Sigma Xi. Democrat. Southern Baptist. Avocations: hiking, playing piano, archaeology. Home: 12346 S Shoshoni Dr Phoenix AZ 85044-2028 E-mail: csah@grand-canyon.edu.

MORRIS, GRANT HAROLD, law educator; b. Syracuse, NY, Dec. 10, 1940; s. Benjamin and Caroline Grace (Judelson) Morris; m. Phyllis Silberstein, July 4, 1967; children: Joshua, Sara. AB, Syracuse U., 1962, JD, 1964; LLM, Harvard U., 1971. Bar: N.Y. 1964. Atty. NY Mental Hygiene Law Recodification Project, Inst. Public Adminstrn., NYC, 1964-66; from asst. prof. to assoc. prof. Wayne State U. Law Sch., 1967—70, prof., 1970-73, dean acad. affairs, 1971-73; prof. U. San Diego Law Sch., 1973—, univ. prof., 1996-97, 2007—, acting dean, 1977-78, 88-89, assoc. dean grad. legal edn., 1978-81, interim dean, 1997-98; prof. law in psychiatry Wayne State U. Med. Sch., 1970-73; adj. prof. U. Calif. -San Diego Med. Sch., 1974-84; clin. prof. dept. psychiatry U. Calif. Med. Sch., San Diego, 1984—. Legal counsel Mich. Legis. Com. to Revise Mental Health Statutes, 1970-73; organizer law and psychiatry sect. Assn. Am. Law Schs., 1973, chmn., 1973-74; patients advocate, San Diego County, 1977-78; cons. Criminal Code Commn., Ariz. Legis., 1974; reporter task force on guidelines governing roles of mental health profls. in criminal process Am. Bar Assn. standing com. on assn. standards for criminal justice, 1981-84; cert. rev. hearing officer San Diego Superior Ct., 1984-90, ct. commr./judge pro tem, 1990-92, mental health hearing officer, 1992-97; hearing officer San Diego Housing Commn., 1988-92; mem. exec. com. sect. law and mental disability Assn. Am. Law Schs., 1990-97. Author: The Insanity Defense: A Blueprint for Legislative Reform, 1975, Refusing the Right to Refuse: Coerced Treatment of Mentally Disordered Persons, 2006; co-author: Mental Disorder in the Criminal Process: Stan Stress and the Vietnam/Sports Conspiracy, 1993; editor, contbr.: The Mentally Ill and the Right to Treatment, 1970. Mem. Atascadero State Hosp. adv. bd., 2000-07, chair, 2003-07. Mem. Phi Alpha Delta (faculty adv. 1970-73, 75-92). Office: U San Diego Law Sch 5998 Alcala Park San Diego CA 92110-2492 Office Phone: 619-260-2321. Business E-Mail: gmorris@sandiego.edu.

MORRIS, JAMES T., insurance company executive; BA, UCLA, 1982. Asst. actuary, spl. mktg. Pacific Life Ins. Co., Newport Beach, Calif., 1982—86, asst. v.p. product rsch. & develop., 1986—87, 2d v.p. product design & develop., 1987—90, v.p. product design, 1990—93, v.p. m-ops., 1993—96, sr. v.p. m-ops., 1996—2002, exec. v.p. life ins. div., 2002—05, exec. v.p. chief ins. officer, 2005—06,

COO, 2006—07, pres., CEO, 2007—08, chmn., pres., CEO, 2008—. Fellow: Soc. Actuaries; mem.: Am. Acad. Actuaries, LA Actuarial Club. Office: Pacific Life Ins Co 700 Newport Ctr Dr Newport Beach CA 92658-9030

MORRIS, JOHN WILLIAM, JR., metallurgy educator; b. Birmingham, Ala., June 7, 1943; s. John William and Lillian Lucille (Burnette) M.; m. Pamela Mary Dryer, Dec. 30, 1966 (div. 1978); 1 child, McKinley Lee. BS in Metall. Engring., MIT, 1964, ScD in Materials Sci., 1969. Rsch. scientist Bell Aerospace Co., Buffalo, 1968-70, mgr. materials sci., 1970-71; sr. sci. faculty mem. Lawrence Berkeley Nat. Lab., 1971—; asst. prof. dept. materials sci. and mineral engring. U. Calif., Berkeley, 1971-74, assoc. prof., 1974-77, Miller rsch. prof., 1976-77, prof. metallurgy, materials sci. and mineral engring., 1977—. Prog. leader structural materials Ctr. Advanced Materials Lawrence Berkeley Lab., 1985—; lectr., chmn. various tech. confs. Author: The Structure and Propeties of Dual Phase Steels, 1979; patentee various steels and alloys; contbr. articles to profl. jours. Disting. exch. scholar Peoples Republic of China, 1985; recipient Materials Rsch. award US Dept. Energy, 1981, Tech. 100 Citation for advancement of tech. in US Tech. Mag., 1981, Disting. Tchg. award U. Calif. Berkeley, 1988. Fellow Am. Soc. Metals (chmn. Golden Gate chpt. 1979-80, edn. com., Bradley Stoughton Tchg. award 1975); mem. NAE, Metall. Soc.- AIME (chmn. chemistry and physics of metals com. 1978-80, chmn. publs. com. 1978-79, heat treatment com., Robert Lansing Hardy gold medal 1972), Am. Phys. Soc., Am. Soc. Engring. Edn. (AT&T Found. award 1989), Internat. Cryogenic Materials Conf. (bd. dirs.), Phi Delta Theta. Republican. Avocation: golf. Office: Dept Materials Sci and Engring U Calif Berkeley 210 Hearst Meml Mining Bldg Rm 228 Berkeley CA 94720 Office Phone: 510-486-6482. Office Fax: 510-643-5792. E-mail: jwmorris@berkeley.edu.

MORRIS, MICHAEL H., computer company executive; b. 1948; BA, Northwestern U., 1970; JD, U. Mich., 1974. Ptnr. DeFrancesco & Morris, St. Joseph, Mich., 1977-79; gen. coun., sec. ROLM Corp., 1979-86, US Teleceters Corp., 1986-87, Sun Microsystems, Inc., Mountain View, Calif., 1987-2000, sr. v.p., gen. coun., sec., 2000—. Office: Sun Microsystems 4150 Network Cir Santa Clara CA 95054-1778

MORRIS, PATRICK J., Mayor, San Bernardino, California; m. Sally Morris. Grad. cum laude, U. Redlands; JD, Stanford U. Dep. Office Dist. Atty., San Bernardino, Calif.; atty. pvt. practice San Bernardino, Calif.; supervising judge family law divsn. Superior Ct. Calif., 1978—81, presiding judge, 1981—84, presiding judge juvenile ct., 1984—89, supervising criminal law judge, 1990—96, presiding judge juvenile ct.; mayor City of San Bernadino, Calif., 2006—. Trustee U. Redlands; pres. bd. edn., San Bernardino; chmn. Jud. Coun. Task Force on Drug Cts.; chmn. bd. dirs. Nat. Assn. of Drug Ct. profl., 1998; chief justice Jud. Coun., 1991—93. Bd. mem. San Bernadino Assoc. Govts.; chmn. Planning and Productivity Com.; bd. dirs. Southern Calif. Regional Rail Authority; pres. San Bernadino Internat. Airport Authority; founder Children's Network, 1985; co-chmn. Inland Valley Devel. Agy. Recipient Meritorious Svc. award, Nat. Coun. Juvenile and Family Ct. Judges, 1991, Disting. Svc. award, 1994, Trial Jurist of Yr. award, Jud. Coun. of Calif., 1994; named a Inland Southern California's Trial Judge of Yr., 1981. Office: Office of Mayor 300 N D St 6th Fl San Bernardino CA 92418 Office Phone: 909-384-5133. Office Fax: 909-384-5067. E-mail: meier_sh@sbcity.org.*

MORRIS, SANDRA JOAN, lawyer; b. Chgo., Oct. 13, 1944; d. Bernard and Helene (Davies) Aronson; m. Richard William Morris, May 30, 1965 (div. Jan. 1974); children: Tracy Michelle, Bretton Todd; m. William Mark Bandt, July 12, 1981 (div. Oct. 2004); 1 child, Victoria Elizabeth. BA, U. Ariz., 1965; JD, Calif. Western U., 1969. Bar: Calif. 1970, U.S. Dist. Ct. (so. dist.) Calif. 1970, diplomate: Am. Coll. Family Trial Lawyers. Ptnr. Morris & Morris, APC, San Diego, 1970-74; sole practice San Diego, 1974—. Mem. Adv. Commn. on Family Law, Calif. Senate, 1978—79. Contbr. articles to profl. jours. Pres. San Diego Cmty. Child Abuse Coordinating Coun., 1977; mem. human rsch. rev. bd. Children's Hosp., San Diego, 1977-92. Fellow: Internat. Acad. Matrimonial Lawyers, Am. Acad. Matrimonial Lawyers (chpt. pres. 1987—88, nat. bd. govs. 1987—89, parliamentarian 1989—91, nat. bd. govs. 1993—94, treas. 1994—97, v.p. 1997—2000, 1st v.p. 2000—01, pres. 2002—03); mem.: San Diego Cert. Family Law Specialists (chair 1995—96), State Bar Calif. (cert. family law specialist 1980—), ABA (family law sect. exec. com. marital property 1982—83, 1987—94, faculty mem. Trial Advocacy Inst. 2001—), Lawyers Club San Diego (bd. dirs. 1973). Republican. Jewish. Avocations: art, travel, skiing. Office: 3200 4th Ave Ste 101 San Diego CA 92103-5716 Office Phone: 619-296-6060.

MORRIS, SANDRA K., computer company executive; b. Paxtang, Pa., 1954; BS with honors and distinction, U. Del., 1976, MS, 1981; postgrad., U. Pa. Faculty mem. U. Del.; with RCA Corp. David Sarnoff Rsch. Ctr.; product mgr. Intel Corp., 1985, v.p. e-bus. group, 1999—2002; CIO, and V.P. Intel Corp, 2002—. Co-author: Multimedia Application Development Using Indeo video and DVI Technology, 1982. Office: Intel Corp PO Box 58119 2200 Mission College Blvd Santa Clara CA 95052-8119

MORRIS, SHARON HUTSON, city manager; BA in Home Econs., Calif. State U., 1976; MA in Urban Planning, UCLA, 1979. Legislative analyst So. Calif. Gas Co., LA, 1983-86, dist. mgr., 1986-90, cmty. outreach coord., 1990; dir. intergovt. affairs South Coast Air Quality Mgmt. Dist., Diamond Bar, Calif., 1990-94; commr. Bd. Pub. Works City of L.A., 1994-96, dep. mayor Office of Mayor Richard J. Riordan, 1996-97, gen. mgr. Dept. Animal Regulation, 1997-98, exec. dir. Dept. on Disability LA, 1998—; alt. pub. mem. South Coast Air Quality Hearing Bd., 1998—. Mem. KCET cmty. adv. bd. Hollywood Cmty. Housing Corp. Recipient Outstanding Alumna award Calif. State U., L.A., 1997. Mem. Am. Assn. Blacks in Energy, Nat. Forum for Black Pub. Adminstrn., The Ethnic Coalition (bd. dirs.), Women of Color, Inc. (past co-presiding officer), Calif. League Conservative Voters (bd. dirs.), Alpha Kappa Alpha, Phi Kappa Phi.

MORRISETTE, WILLIAM E., state legislator; b. Anaconda, Mont., Oct. 18, 1931; m to Janice; children: eight. City councilman, Springfield, Oregon, 87-89, mayor, 89-; Oregon State Representative, District 42, 1999-2002; Oregon State Senator, District 6, 2003-. Democrat. Catholic. Office: 900 Court St NE S-207 Salem OR 97301 Office Phone: 503-986-1706. Fax: 541-726-4343. Business E-Mail: sen.billmorrisette@state.or.us.

MORRISON, CHARLES EDWARD, think-tank executive; b. Billings, Mont., 1944; m. Chieko Hayashi; children: Karen, Erica, Kenneth, Douglas. BA in Internat. Studies, Johns Hopkins U., MA, PhD, Johns Hopkins U. Legis. asst. U.S. Senate, 1972-80; part-time sr. rsch. assoc. Japan Ctr. for Internat. Exch., 1980-92; asst. to pres. East-West Ctr., 1986-92, dir. program on internat. econs. and politics, 1992-95, pres., 1998—; chair U.S. Consortium of APEC Study Ctrs., 1996-98; internat. chair Pacific Econ. Cooperation Coun., 2006—. Author: wide range of books, papers and analyses; widely quoted by major news media on issues of regional cooperation, internat. rels., U.S. Asia policy and trade policies. Mem.: U.S. Asia Pacific Coun. (founding mem. 2003). Office: East West Ctr 1601 E West Rd Honolulu HI 96848-1601 Office Phone: 808-944-7111.

MORRISON, DAVID FRED, communications executive; b. Columbus, Ohio, Aug. 15, 1953; s. Fred Liew and Sophie Ann (Snider) M.; 1 child, Ian. BA, Stanford U., 1975; MBA, U. So. Calif., 1978. Sr. corp. planning analyst Tiger Internat., LA, 1978-80, mgr. new bus. devel., 1980-81; dir. planning and controls Hall's Motor Transit Co., Mechanicsburg, Pa., 1981-82; mng. dir., gen. mgr. Consol. Freightways Export-Import Svc., San Francisco, 1984-86; asst. treas. McKesson Corp., San Francisco, 1987-90, treas., 1990-91; dir. strategic planning Consol. Freightways, Inc., Palo Alto, Calif., 1982-84, 86-87, v.p., treas., 1991-96; exec. v.p., CFO Consol. Freightways Corp., 1996-99; CEO The Ladder Group, 1999—. Bd. dirs. Am. Sports Inst., Mill Valley, Calif., 1992-99; trustee Ctrl. States Pension Fund, 1997-99. Fellow State of Calif., 1977, Commerce Assocs., 1977. Mem. Fin. Execs. Inst. (silver medal 1978), Turnaround Mgmt. Assn, San Francisco Treas. Club (pres.). Avocations: bicycling, scuba diving, skiing.

MORRISON, DAVID LEE, librarian, educator; b. New London, Conn., Aug. 28, 1948; s. Samuel and Beatrice (Kinslinger) M. BA in Classics with highest honors, U. Calif., Santa Barbara, 1979; MLS, U. Ariz., 1986. Documents libr. Marriott Libr., U. Utah, Salt Lake City, 1987—, instr. libr. literacy course, 1990—. Patent fellowship libr. U.S. Patent and Trademark Office, 1996-97; workshop presenter in field; guest lectr. U. Ariz. Grad. Libr. Sch., fall 1988-94; participant confs. in field. Fay and Lawrence Clark Powell scholar U. Ariz., 1983. Mem. ALA (govt. docs. round table info. tech. com. 1987-89), Utah Libr. Assn. (GODORT bylaws com. 1987-88, 91-92, chmn. nominating com. 1987-88, continuing edn. com. 1987-89, vice chmn., chmn.-elect 1992-93, chmn. GODORT 1993-94), Patent and Trademark Depository Libr. Assn. (fin. com. 1988-97, sec.-treas. 1989-90, 92—), Patent Documentation Soc. Home: 859 S Blair St Salt Lake City UT 84111 Office: U Utah Documents Div Marriott Libr Salt Lake City UT 84112

MORRISON, GLENN LESLIE, minister; b. Cortez, Colo., Feb. 26, 1929; s. Ward Carl Morrison and Alma Irene (Butler) Anderson; m. Beverely Joanne Buck, Aug. 26, 1949; children: David Mark, Betty Jo Morrison Mullen, Gary Alan, Judith Lynn Morrison Oltmann, Stephen Scott. Student, San Diego State U., 1948-49, Chabot Coll., 1968-69. Ordained ministry Evang. Ch. Alliance, 1961. Dir. counseling follow-up Oakland (Calif.) Youth Christ, 1954-56; pres. Follow Up Ministries, Inc., Castro Valley, Calif., 1956—. Assoc. pastor 1st Covenant Ch., Oakland, 1956-58; exec. dir. East Bay Youth Christ, Oakland, 1960-66; supervising chaplain Alameda County (Calif.) Probation Dept., 1971-90; vol. chaplain Alameda County Sheriff's Dept., 1971—; founder, dir. God Squad Vol. Program Prison Workers, 1972—; seminar leader Calif. Dept. Corrections, Sacramento, 1978—, mem. chaplains coordinating com., 1988—. Author: Scripture Investigation Course, 1956, Tired of the Same Ol' Same Ol'? There is a Better Way, 1978. Mem. Am. Correctional Assn., Am. Protestant Correctional Chaplains Assn. (regional pres., sec. 1980-86, nat. sec. 1986-88, nat. 2nd v.p. 1996-98). Office: Follow Up Ministries Inc PO Box 2514 Castro Valley CA 94546-2514 Personal E-mail: fumi2000@cox.net.

MORRISON, GREGG SCOTT, executive; b. Rome, Ga., Mar. 9, 1964; s. Glen Warren and Joyce (Lannom) M.; m. Laura Edge, Jan. 21, 1995. BS in Acctg., U. Ala., 1986; MDiv, Samford U., 1996; postgrad., Emory U., 1998-2000; PhD, Catholic U. Tax assoc. Coopers & Lybrand, Atlanta, 1986, tax specialist, 1987-88, tax supr. Birmingham, Ala., 1988-89, sr. tax assoc., 1990-91, tax mgr., 1991-93; min. outreach Shades Mountain Bapt. Ch., 1993-96; dir. external rels. Beeson Div. Sch., Samford U., Birmingham, Ala., 1996—2001; interim pastor New Prospect Bapt. Ch., Jasper, Ala., 1998, Bluff Park Bapt. Ch., Birmingham, 1999, Woodward Ave Bapt. Ch., 2005, Flint River Baptist Ch., 2005, Cottondale Christian Ch., 2006; asst. prof. Simpson U., Redding, Calif., 2006—07; trust protector McDonald Group, Inc., 2007—. Adj. faculty Beeson Divinity Sch., Bethel Sem. of the East, John Leland Ctr. for Theol. Studies. Active Cystic Fibrosis Golf Fundraising Com., United Way Ctrl. Ala., Inc., Birmingham, 1989; pres. student govt. assn. Beeson Div. Sch. of Samford U., 1995-96; bd. dirs. Ctr. for Urban Missions, Inc., Birmingham, chmn. fin. com., 1991-94, 96-2001; bd. dirs. U. Cmty. Coop., Inc., Tuscaloosa, sec.-treas., pres. ACCESS; treas. Martin Luther King Unity Breakfast Planning Com.; southside campaign capt. Boy Scouts Am.; mem. planned giving adv. group Bapt. Hosp. Found., Inc.; deacon Shades Mt. Bapt. Ch., 1992-94, 96-99, mem. strategic planning com. chmn. Innercity Ministry Partnership Task Force, 1996-2001; adv. bd. Baptist Ctr. Leadership Devel; mem. long range planning com. City of Vestavia Hills, Ala; bd. dirs. Oakseed Ministries Internat.; steering com. golf tournament Cystic Fibrosis Fedn., 2005; head coach Vestavia Hills Youth Baseball, 2005; bd. dirs. Renasant Bank Ala., 2008-. Named one of Outstanding Young Men Am., 1996. Mem. Soc. Bibl. Lit., Evang. Theol. Soc., Inst. Bibl. Rsch., Tyndale Fellowship Biblical Theol. Rsch., Birmingham Hist. Soc. (planning com. 1990-91), PGA (fin. com.), Cath. Bibl. Assn., Vestavia Country Club, Theta Chi (treas. Alpha Phi house corp. 1992-94). Republican. Baptist. Avocations: golf, tennis, reading, politics. Office: 2211 College View Dr Redding CA 96003 Office Phone: 205-879-0456. Personal E-mail: gsm@wwminvest.com.

MORRISON, PATRICIA B., former electronics executive; BA in Math. & Stats. summa cum laude, Miami Univ., BS in Secondary Edn. Sys. mgmt., IT positions Procter & Gamble; CIO GE Indsl. Sys. Gen. Electric, 1997—2000; CIO Quaker Oats Co., Chgo., 2000—02; exec. v.p., CIO Office Depot, Inc., Delray Beach, Fla., 2002—05; sr. v.p., chief info. officer Motorola Inc., Schaumburg, Ill., 2005—07, exec. v.p., CIO, 2007—08. Bd. dir. Jo-Ann Stores, Inc., SPSS Inc., 2007—; mem. adv. bd. UST Global, 2009—. Bd. mem. Chgo. Symphony Orch., Lyric Opera Chgo. Named to CIO Hall of Fame, CIO Mag., 2008. Mailing: UST Global Ste 500 120 Vantis Aliso Viejo CA 92656

MORRISSEY, J. RICHARD, lawyer; b. LA, Jan. 8, 1941; BA, Santa Clara Univ., 1963; JD, Univ. Calif., Berkeley, 1966. Bar: Calif. 1966, US Ct. Mil. Appeals 1967, US Supreme Ct. 1980. Ptnr., co-leader Product Liability practice, head LA Litigation sect. Pillsbury Winthrop Shaw Pittman, LA. Mem.: ABA, LA County Bar Assn. Office: Pillsbury Winthrop Shaw Pittman Suite 2800 725 S Figueroa St Los Angeles CA 90017 Office Phone: 213-488-7525. Office Fax: 213-629-1033. Business E-Mail: richard.morrissey@pillsburylaw.com.

MORRISSEY, JOHN CARROLL, SR., lawyer; b. NYC, Sept. 2, 1914; s. Edward Joseph and Estelle (Caine) M.; m. Eileen Colligan, Oct. 14, 1950; children: Jonathan Edward, Ellen (Mrs. James A. Jenkins), Katherine, John, Patricia, Richard, Brian, Peter. BA magna cum laude, Yale U., 1937, LLB, 1940; JSD, N.Y. U., 1951; grad., Command and Gen. Staff Sch., 1944. Bar: N.Y. State 1940, D.C. 1953, Calif. 1954, U.S. Supreme Ct. 1944. Asso. firm Dorsey and Adams, 1940-41, Dorsey, Adams and Walker, 1946-50; counsel Office of Sec. of Def., Dept. Def., Washington, 1950-52; acting gen. counsel def. Electric Power Adminstrn., 1952-53; atty. Pacific Gas and Electric Co., San Francisco, 1953-70, assoc. gen. counsel, 1970-74, v.p., gen. counsel, 1975-80; individual practice law San Francisco, 1980-2000. Dir. Gas Lines, Inc. Bd. dirs. Legal Aid Soc., San Francisco; chmn. Golden Gate dist. Boy Scouts Am., 1973-75; commr. Human Rights Commn. of San Francisco, 1976-89, chmn., 1980-82; chmn. Cath. Social Svc. of San Francisco, 1966-68; adv. com. Archdiocesean Legal Affairs, 1981—; regent Archdiocesan Sch. of Theology, St. Patrick's Sem., 1994-99; dir. Presidio Preservation Assn., 1995-99. Served to col. F.A. U.S. Army, ETO, 1941-46. Decorated Bronze star, Army Commendation medal. Mem. NAS, AAAS, ABA, Calif. State Bar Assn., Fed. Power Bar Assn., N.Y. Acad. Scis., Calif. Conf. Pub. Utility Counsel, Pacific Coast Electric Assn., Pacific Coast Gas Assn., Econ. Round Table of San Francisco, World Affairs Council, San Francisco C. of C., Calif. State C. of C., Harold Brunn Soc. Med. Rsch., Electric Club, Serra Club, Commonwealth Club, Yale Club of San Francisco (pres. 1989-90), Pacific-Union Club, Sometimes Tuesday Club, Sovereign Mil. Order Malta, Phi Beta Kappa. Roman Catholic. Office: 1661 Pine St # 1135 San Francisco CA 94109-0426 Personal E-mail: dadjcm@aol.com.

MORROW, BARRY NELSON, screenwriter, producer; b. Austin, Minn., June 12, 1948; s. Robert Clayton and Rose Nell (Nelson) M.; m. Beverly Lee McKenzie, Mar. 3, 1969; children: Clayton McKenzie, ZoeAnna Rachel. BA, St. Olaf Coll., 1970; DHL (hon.), U. La Verne, Calif., 1990. Media specialist U. Iowa, Iowa City, 1974-81; freelance screenwriter Los Angeles, 1981-90; pres. Morrow-Heus Prodns., 1990-00. Storywriter (TV film) Bill, 1981 (Emmy award 1982); screenwriter: (TV films) Bill: On His Own, 1983, Conspiracy of Love, 1987, Silent Victory, 1988, The Karen Carpenter Story, 1989, (feature film) Rain Man, 1988 (co-recipient Acad. award Best Original Screenplay 1989); screenwriter, exec. prodr.: Christmas on Division Street, 1991; exec. prodr.: Switched at Birth, 1991 (Emmy nomination), Gospa, 1995, The Fifties, 1997, Behind the Mask, 1999; screenwriter, prodr. Race the Sun, 1996; monologist: Bill for Short, 1992. Recipient Pres.'s award Am. Acad. for Devel. Medicine, 1978, Outstanding Contbn. award Mid-Am. Congress on Aging, 1983, SI award NASW, 1991, Pope John XXIII award Viterbo Coll., 1992. Mem. Writers Guild Am. West, Acad. TV Arts and Scis., Acad. Motion Picture Arts and Scis., Motion Picture Screen Cartoonists Guild.

MORROW, BILL, state legislator; b. Monterey Park, Calif., Apr. 19, 1954; married; 1 child. BA, U. Calif., LA, 1976; JD, Pepperdine U., 1979. Commd. officer, mil. judge adv. USMC, 1979-87; civil litig. atty., 1987—; mem. Calif. State Assembly, 1993-98, Calif. State Senate, 1998—, vice chmn. judiciary com., mem. coms. on bus., edn., chmn. vet. Active Spl. Olympics, Boys and Girls Club, Salvation Army. Named Legislator of Yr. Orange County League of Cities., Legislator of Yr. Pro-Life PAC Orange County, 1995, Civil Justice Reform Legislator of Yr. Orange County Citizens Against Lawsuit Abuse, 1996, Legislator of Yr., Calif. Rep. Assembly, 1996, Legislator of Yr. Golden State Mobilehome Owners League Calif., 1997, Small Bus. Legislator of Yr. Calif. Rep. Assembly, 2002, Legislator of Yr. Calif. Rifle and Pistol Assn., 2002. Mem. NRA, Am. Legion, Marine Corps League, Gun Owners Calif., Ducks Unlimited, Calif. Waterfowl Assn., Oceanside C. of C., San Juan C. of C., North County Armed Forces, Amvets, Kiwanis, YMCA. Republican. Office: State Capitol Rm 4048 Sacramento CA 95814 also: 27126A Paseo Espada # 1621 San Juan Capistrano CA 92675-2725 Office: Senator Bill Morrow 1800 Thibodo Rd Ste 300 Vista CA 92081-7515 E-mail: bill.morrow@assembly.ca.gov.

MORROW, DONALD L., lawyer; b. Inglewood, Calif., Apr. 14, 1951; BA cum laude, U. So. Calif., 1972, JD, 1975. Bar: Calif. 1975. Ptnr. Paul, Hastings, Janofsky & Walker, Costa Mesa, Calif., mem. policy com., chmn. profl. devel. com. Lawyer rep. 9th Cir. Jud. Conf., 1989, 91-92. Dir. Pacific Symphony Orch., 1990-91. Fellow Am. Coll. Trial Lawyers; mem. Orange County Bar Assn. (dir. 1992—), Orange County Bar Found. (pres. 1993, dir. 1990—), Robert A. Banyard Am. Inn of Ct. (master bencher 1987-92). Office: Paul Hastings Janofsky & Walker 17th flr 695 Town Center Dr Costa Mesa CA 92626-1924 Office Phone: 714-668-6291. Office Fax: 714-668-6391. Business E-Mail: donaldmorrow@paulhastings.com.

MORROW, GEORGE J., medical products executive; m. Katherine Morrow; 3 children. BA, Southampton Coll.; MA in Biochemistry, Bryn Mawr Coll., Pa.; MBA, Duke U., Durham, NC. V.p., gen. mgr. sales and mktg. divsn. Glaxo, Inc., 1992, group v.p. comml. ops., 1993—96; mng. dir. Glaxo Wellcome UK, 1997—98; pres., CEO Glaxo Wellcome Inc., Research Park Triangle, NC, 1999—2001; exec. v.p., worldwide sales and mktg. Amgen, Inc., Thousand Oaks, Calif., 2001—03, exec. v.p. global comml. ops., 2003—. Mem. adv. bd. Duke U. Fuqua Sch. Bus.; bd. visitors Duke U. Med. Ctr. Office: Amgen Inc 1 Amgen Ctr Dr Thousand Oaks CA 91320-1799 Office Phone: 805-447-1000. Office Fax: 805-447-1010.

MORROW, JAMES FRANKLIN, lawyer; b. Shenandoah, Iowa, Oct. 23, 1944; s. Warren Ralph and Margaret Glee (Palm) M. BS, Kans. State U., 1967; JD, U. Ariz., 1973. Bar: Ariz. 1973, U.S. Dist. Ct. Ariz. 1973. Ptnr. Bilby, Shoenhair, Warnock & Dolph, Tucson, 1973-83, Quarles & Brady Streich Lang LLP, Tucson, 1984—. Mng. editor U. Ariz. Law Rev., 1972-73. Past chmn. bd. trustees Palo Verde Mental Health Svcs.; past pres. U. Ariz. Alumni Assn.; past chmn. bd. Palo Verde Hosp., Ariz. Tech. Devel. Corp.; past pres. bd. Cath. Cmty. Svcs.; past chmn. bd. dirs. U. Ariz. Found. Capt. U.S. Army, 1967-70. Mem. Am. Coll. Real Estate Lawyers, Am. Coll. Mortgage Attys., State Bar Ariz. (cert. real estate specialist, adv. com. real estate specialists, past chmn. real estate property sect.). Pima County Bar Assn., Calif. Bar Assn. Democrat. Roman Catholic. Avocation: golf. Office: Quarles & Brady Streich Lang LLP Ste 1700 One South Church Ave Tucson AZ 85701

MORROW, JAMES THOMAS, energy executive; b. Seattle, Apr. 24, 1941; s. James Elroy and Helen Margaret (Helzer) M.; 1 child, Shannon F. BSEE, BS Gen. Sci., Oreg. State U., 1964; MBA, U. Santa Clara, 1966, PhD, 1973. Registered investment advisor, SEC; profl. engr., Calif., Oreg. Engr. GE Co., San Jose, Calif., 1964—66; mgr. engring. Beckman Instruments, Inc., Palo Alto, Calif., 1966—69; pres. MSA Cons., Inc., Portland, Oreg., 1969—75; mgr. A.T. Kearney, Inc., San Francisco, 1975—78; v.p. mktg. Pierce Pacific Mfg., Portland, 1978—79; chmn., CEO Lanco Internat., Inc., Clackamas, Oreg., 1979—81; regional mgr., v.p. Case & Co., Portland, 1981—82; chmn. bd., exec. v.p. Morley Fin. Svcs. Inc., 1982—94; exec. v.p., dir. Bioject Med. Tech. Inc., 1983—92; chmn., pres., CEO Capital Devel. Group, Inc., Portland, 1994—96; chmn., CEO Apollo Fin. Group, NYC, 1996—98, Olympic Healthcare Tech., Inc., Portland, NYC, 1998—2002; sr. v.p. El Rincon Resort, Cabo San Lucas, Mexico, 2002—03; pres., CEO, dir. Naanovo Energy, Inc., Calgary, Alta., Canada, 2003—07; CEO Naanovo Energy USA, Inc., Lincoln City, Oreg., 2003—07; pres., CEO Naanovo Internat. Free Zone N.V., Oranjestad, Aruba, 2005—07, Naanovo Internat. FZC, Dubai, United Arab Emirates, 2005—07, Caanov SA, Guatemala City, 2006—; mgr. T Squared LLC, Newport, Oreg., 2005—; pres., dir., CEO Green Energy 1, Inc., New Port, Oreg., 2008—. Chmn. bd. dirs. Ship Harbor Resort and Marina, Inc., 1998-2004, Turtle Cove Resort, Inc., 1998, Olympic Capital, Inc., 1998-2003; bd. dirs. Naanove Energy, Accucom Data Network, Inc., Pierce Pacific Mfg., Lanco Internat., Energy Guard, Inc., G&R Devel. Co., Inc., MSA Cons., Inc.; sec.-treas. Everybody's Record Co., Inc. Contbr. articles to profl. jours., chpts. to textbooks Bd. dirs. Found. for Oreg. Rsch. and Edn., Jr. Achievement, First August Fin., Inc., Met. Youth Symphony; chmn. steering com. R.S. Dow Neurol. Scis. Inst.; mem. Russian ANT-25 Aviation Com. Mem.: Oreg. Pilots Assn. (pres. Beaverton chpt. 2001—02). Republican. Congregationalist. Achievements include patents for waste to energy technology; solar energy to electricity; biojector needleless syringe. Office: 1070 NE 7th Dr Newport OR 97365 Home: 515 NW Saltzman Rd Portland OR 97229 Office Phone: 971-223-0628. Business E-Mail: tmorrow@greenenergy1.com.

MORROW, JENNIFER LEIGH See **LEIGH, JENNIFER**

MORRY, G. RICHARD, retired lawyer; b. Seattle, Mar. 2, 1943; BA cum laude, U. Wash., 1965, JD with honors, 1970. Bar: Wash. 1971, Hawaii 1973, U.S. Ct. Appeals (9th cir.) 1973, U.S. Supreme Ct. 1974. Ptnr. Rush Moore Craven Sutton Morry & Beh, Honolulu, of counsel, 1998—. Pres. Hawaii Inst. for CLE, 1996. Exec. editor Wash. Law Rev., 1969-70; bd. editors Hawaii Bar Jour., 1975-97. Mem. ABA, Wash. State Bar Assn., Hawaii State Bar Assn., Am. Judicature Soc., Maritime Law Assn. of U.S. Address: Rush Moore Craven Sutton Morry Beh 737 Bishop St #2400 Honolulu HI 96813-3214

MORSE, DANIEL E., biochemistry educator, science administrator; b. NYC, May 20, 1941; BA, Harvard U., 1963; PhD in Molecular Biology, Albert Einstein Coll. Medicine, 1967. Fellow in molecular genetics Stanford U., 1967-69; from Silas Arnold Houston asst. prof. to Silas Arnold Houston assoc. prof. med. sch. Harvard U., 1969-73; prof. molecular genetics and biochemistry U. Calif., Santa Barbara, 1973—, chmn. sect. molecular biology and biochemistry dept. biol. sci., 1981-85, chmn. Marine Biotechnology Ctr., 1986—. Mem. NRC, U.S. Nat. Com. Internat. Union Biol. Sci., 1986—; chmn. task force biotechnology in ocean sci. NSF, 1987—. Fellow AAAS; mem. Am. Soc. Molecular Biology and Biochemistry, Am. Soc. Limnology and Oceanography, Am. Soc. Microbiology, Am. Soc. Zoology, N.Y. Acad. Sci., Internat. Soc. Chem. Ecology. Achievements include research on molecular mechanisms controlling reproduction, larval metamorphosis, development and gene expression; signal molecules, receptors, and transducers; molecular marine biology; molecular neurobiology; molecular chemosensory mechanisms. Office: U Calif Marine Biotech Ctr Dept Biology Santa Barbara CA 93106

MORSE, FRANK, state legislator; b. Lebanon, Oreg., Sept. 9, 1943; m. Linda Morse; children: Scot, Kerry. BTh, Northwest Christian Coll., 1966; MA, Oreg. State U., 1970. Former pres. MDU Resources Group; former bd. chmn. Environ-Metal Inc; vice pres. Morse Brothers Inc., 1975—80, pres., 1980—96, chmn./ CEO, 1996—98; mem. Dist. 8 Oreg. State Senate, 2002—, former asst. Republican Leader. Republican. Protestant. Office: Capitol 900 Court St NE S-311 Salem OR 97301 also: 3616 NW Eagle View DR Albany OR 97321 Office Phone: 503-986-1708. E-mail: sen.frankmorse@state.or.us.

MORSE, JOHN P., state legislator; BBA, U. Colo., Colo. Springs, 1980, MPA, 1996, PhD, 2001; MBA, Regis Coll., Weston, Mass., 1984. Cert. pub. accountant; EMT; sgt. Colo. Springs Police Dept.; police chief Fountain Police Dept.; pres., CEO Silver Key Sr. Svc., 2004—; mem. Dist. 11 Colo. State Senate, Denver, 2007—. Bd. dirs. Cmty. Corrections Colo. Springs Inc.; mem. steering com. El Paso County Justice Adv. Coun.; bd. mem. Fourth Jud. Dist. Spl. Investigations Fund; adv. bd. Nat. Alliance the Mentally Ill.; mem. Am. Assn. Pub. Adminstrn., PPACG Cmty. Adv. Com., Colo. Assn. Chiefs Police & Legislature Affairs Com., Colo. Coalition Against Domestic Violence Legislature Affairs Com., Colo. Orgn. Victim Advocates Pub. Policy Com. Mem. Internat. Assn. Chiefs Police, Fountain Downtown Events Assn., Colo. Soc CPA's. Democrat. Office: Colo State Senate 200 E Colfax Denver CO 80203 Office Phone: 303-866-6364. Business E-Mail: john.morse.senate@state.co.us.*

MORSE, JOSEPH GRANT, chemistry educator; b. Colorado Springs, Colo., Oct. 16, 1939; s. Grant Addison and Faris Ellen (Winninger) M.; m. Karen Dale Williams, Apr. 6, 1963; children: Robert Grant, Geoffrey Easton. BS, S.D. State Coll., 1961; MS in Chemistry, U. Mich., 1963, PhD, 1966. Instr. U. Mich., Ann Arbor, 1965-66; asst. prof. Utah State U., Logan, 1968-74, assoc. prof., 1974-93; prof. Western Wash. U., Bellingham, 1993-2000, dir. sci. edn., 1996-2000. Councilman Cache County, Utah. Capt. U.S. Army, 1966-68. Fellow AAAS; mem. Am. Chem. Soc.

MORSE, KAREN WILLIAMS, academic administrator; b. Monroe, Mich., May 8, 1940; m. Joseph G. Morse; children: Robert G., Geoffrey E. BS, Denison U., 1962; MS, U. Mich., 1964, PhD, 1967; DSc (hon.), Denison U., 1990. Rsch. chemist Ballistic Rsch. Lab., Aberdeen Proving Ground, Md., 1966-68; lectr. chemistry dept. Utah State U., Logan, 1968-69, from asst. to assoc. prof. chemistry, 1969-83, prof. chemistry dept., 1983-93, dept. head Coll. Sci., 1981-88, dean Coll. Sci., 1988-89, univ. provost, 1989-93; pres. Western Wash. U., Bellingham, 1993—. Mem., chair Grad. Record Exam in chemistry com., Princeton, N.J., 1980-89, Gov.'s Sci. Coun., Salt Lake City, 1986-93, Gov.'s Coun. on Fusion, 1989-91, ACS Com. on Profl. Tng., 1984-92; cons. 1993; nat. ChemLinks adv. com. NSF, 1995; bd. advisor's orgn. com. 2008 summer Olympic Games, Seattle, 1995; faculty Am. Assn. State Colls. and Univs. Pres.'s Acad., 1995, 96; chair Wash. Coun. of Pres., 1995-96; bd. dirs. Whatcom State Bank; NCAA Divsn. II Pres.'s Coun., 1999—, CHEA bd., 2000—; Nat. Rsch. Coun. Chem. Svcs. Roundtable, 1999—. Contbr. articles to profl. jours. Mem. Cache County Sch. Dist. Found., Cache Valley, Logan, 1988-93; swim coach, soccer coach; trustee First United Presbyn. Ch., Logan, 1979-81, 82-85; adv. bd. Sci. Discovery Ctr., Logan, 1993, KCTS-TV, Bellingham, 1996—, Seattle Opera Bd., 1999—; mem. bd. dirs. United Way, Whatcom County, 1993—; exec. com. Bellingham-Whatcom Econ. Devel. Com., 1993—. Recipient Disting. Alumni in Residence award U. Mich., 1989, Francis P. Garvan and John M. Olin medal, 1997. Fellow AAAS; mem. Am. Chem. Soc. (Utah award Salt Lake City and Cen. dists. 1988, Garvan-Olin medal 1997), Am. Assn. State Colls. and Univs. (mem. policy and purposes com. 1995, chair 1996), Bus. and Profl. Women Club (pres. 1984-85), Philanthropic Edn. Orgn., Phi Beta Kappa, Sigma Xi, Phi Beta Kappa Assocs., Phi Kappa Phi, Beta Gamma Sigma. Avocations: skiing, bicycling, photography. Office: Office of the Pres Western Washington U 516 High St Old Main 450 MS 9000 Bellingham WA 98225-5946

MORSE, RICHARD JAY, human resources and organizational development specialist, consultant; b. Detroit, Mich., Aug. 2, 1933; s. Maurice and Belle Rosalyn (Jacobson) M. BA, U. Va., 1955; MA in Clin. Psychology, Calif. State U., LA, 1967. Area pers. adminstr. Gen. Tel. Co. of Calif., Santa Monica, 1957-67; sr. v.p. human resources The Bekins Co., Glendale, Calif., 1967-83; pvt. cons. human resources and orgn. devel. Cambria, 1983—. Contbr. articles to profl. jours. Fund raiser various orgns., So. Calif., 1970—. Mem. Internat. Soc. Performance Improvement (founding mem. 1958—). Democrat. Jewish. Avocations: travel, tennis, walking, swimming. Home and Office: 6410 Cambria Pines Rd Cambria CA 93428-2009 Office Phone: 805-927-3457. Personal E-mail: dickmorse@earthlink.net.

MORTENSEN, VIGGO, actor, writer; b. NYC, Oct. 20, 1958; s. Viggo P. and Grace Mortensen; m. Christine Cervenka, July 8, 1987 (div. Mar. 13, 1998); 1 child, Henry. BA in Govt. and Spanish, St. Lawrence U., Canton, NY, 1980; ArtsD (hon.), St. Lawrence U., 2006. Owner Perceval Press, 2002—. Actor: (films) Witness, 1985, Salvation!, 1987, Fresh Horses, 1988, Prison, 1988, Leatherface: Texas Chainsaw Massacre III, 1990, Young Guns II, 1990, Reflecting Skin, The, 1990, Tripwire, 1990, The Indian Runner, 1991, Boiling Point, 1993, Ruby Cairo, 1993, Carlito's Way, 1993, The Young Americans, 1993, Ewangelia wedlug Harry'ego, 1993, Desert Lunch, 1994, Floundering, 1994, The Crew, 1994, American Yakuza, 1994, Crimson Tide, 1995, Black Velvet Pantsuit, 1995, The Prophecy, 1995, Gimlet, 1995, Albino Alligator, 1996, The Portrait of a Lady, 1996, Daylight, 1996, G.I. Jane, 1997, La Pistola de mi hermano, 1997, A Perfect Murder, 1998, Psycho, 1998, A Walk on the Moon, 1999, 28 Days, 2000, Lord of the Rings: The Fellowship of the Ring, 2001, Lord of the Rings: The Two Towers, 2002, Lord of the Rings: The Return of the King, 2003, Hidalgo, 2004, A History of Violence, 2005, Alatriste, 2006, Eastern Promises, 2007, Appaloosa, 2008; (TV films) Once In a Blue Moon, 1990; (TV miniseries) George Washington, 1984; author: (poetry) Ten Last Night, 1993, (essays) I Forget You Forever, 2006; musician: (albums) One Man's Meat, 1999, One Less Thing to Worry About, 1999, The Other Parade, 1999, 3 Fools 4 April, 2008, Time Waits for Everyone, 2008.

MORTIMER, EMILY, actress; b. London, Eng., Dec. 1, 1971; d. John Mortimer and Penelope Glossop; m. Alessandro Nivola, Jan. 3, 2003; 1 child, Sam. Actress (TV miniseries) The Glass Virgin, 1995, No Bananas, 1996, A Dance to the Music of Time, 1997, (TV series) Silent Witness, 1996, Jack and Jeremy's Real Lives, 1996, Midsomer Murders, 1997, 30 Rock, 2007, (TV films) Sharpe's Sword, 1995, Heartstones, 1996, Lord of Misrule, 1996, Coming Home, 1998, Cider with Rosie, 1998, Noah's Ark, 1999, Jeffrey Archer: The Truth, 2002, (films) The Ghost and the Darkness, 1996, The Last of the High Kings, 1996, The Saint, 1997, Elizabeth, 1998, Notting Hill, 1999, Killing Joe, 1999, Scream 3, 2000, Love's Labour's Lost, 2000, The Kid, 2000, Lovely & Amazing, 2001 (Ind. Spirit award for Best Supporting Female, 2003, Best Supporting Actress, Chlotrudis Awards, 2003, Best Supporting Actress, Ctrl. Ohio Film Critics Assn., 2003), The 51st State, 2001, A Foreign Affair, 2003, Nobody Needs to Know, 2003, The Sleeping Dictionary, 2003, Bright Young Things, 2003, Young Adam, 2003, Dear Frankie, 2004, Match Point, 2005, The Pink Panther, 2006, Paris, I Love You, 2006, Chaos Theory, 2007, Lars and the Real Girl, 2007, Transsiberian, 2008, Redbelt, 2008, The Pink Panther 2, 2009, (plays) Parlour Song, 2008. Office: c/o Aleen Keshishian Brillstein-Grey Entertainment 9150 Wilshire Blvd #350 Beverly Hills CA 90212

MORTIMER, KENNETH P., retired academic administrator; Pres. Western Wash. U., Bellingham, 1988-93, U. Hawaii Sys., Honolulu, 1993—2001. Office: U Hawaii Sys Bachmann Hall 202 2444 Dole St Honolulu HI 96822-2302

MORTIMER, WENDELL REED, JR., retired judge; b. Alhambra, Calif., Apr. 7, 1937; s. Wendell Reed and Blanche (Wilson) M.; m. Cecilia Vick, Aug. 11, 1962; children: Michelle Dawn, Kimberly Grace. AB, Occidental Coll., 1958; JD, U. So. Calif., LA, 1965. Bar: Calif. 1966. Trial atty. Legal div. State of Calif., LA, 1965-73; assoc. Thelen, Marrin, Johnson & Bridges, LA, 1973-76, ptnr., 1976-93; pvt. practice San Marino, Calif., 1994-95; judge L.A. Superior Ct., 1995—2008, mem. complex litigation panel, 2000—08; arbitrator & mediator ADR Svcs. Inc., 2008. With U.S. Army, 1960-62. Mem. ABA, Internat. Acad. Trial Judges, Los Angeles County Bar Assn., Calif. Judges Assn., Am. Judicature Soc., Am. Judges Assn., Legion Lex., Irish-Am. Bar Assn., Am. Bd. Trial Advocacy (nat. bd. dirs., exec. com. L.A. chpt.), San Marino City Club (past pres.), Pasadena Bar Assn., Balboa Yacht Club, San Gabriel Country Club Home: 1420 San Marino Ave San Marino CA 91108-2042

MORTON, DONALD CHARLES, astronomer; b. Kapuskasing, Ont., Can., June 12, 1933; s. Charles Orr and Irene Mary (Wightman) M.; m. Winifred May Austin, Dec. 12, 1970; children: Keith James, Christine Elizabeth. BA, U. Toronto, 1956; PhD, Princeton U., 1959. Astronomer U.S. Naval Rsch. Lab., Washington, 1959-61; from rsch. assoc. to sr. rsch. astronomer with rank of prof. Princeton (N.J.) U., 1961-76; dir. Anglo-Australian Obs., Epping and Coonabarabran, Australia, 1976-86; dir. gen. Herzberg Inst. Astrophysics, NRC of Can., Ottawa and Victoria, 1986—2000; rschr. emeritus NRC of Can., 2001—. Contbr. numerous articles to profl. jours. Fellow Australian Acad. Sci.; mem. Internat. Astron. Union, Royal Astron. Soc. (assoc. 1980), Astron. Soc. Australia (pres. 1981-83, hon. mem. 1986), Royal Astron. Soc. Can., Am. Astron. Soc. (councilor 1970-73), Can. Astron. Soc., Can. Assn. Physicists, U.K. Alpine Club, Am. Alpine Club, Alpine Club Can. Avocations: mountain climbing, rock climbing, ice climbing, marathon running. Office: Herzberg Inst Astrophysics NRC Can 5071 W Saanich Rd Victoria BC Canada V9E 2E7 Home Phone: 250-721-4942.

MORTON, FREDERIC, author; b. Vienna, Oct. 5, 1924; s. Frank and Rose (Ungvary) M.; m. Marcia Colman, Mar. 28, 1957; 1 dau., Rebecca. BS, Coll. City N.Y., 1947; MA, New Sch. Social Research, 1949. Author: The Hound, 1947, The Darkness Below, 1949, Asphalt and Desire, 1952, The Witching Ship, 1960, The Schatten Affair, 1965, Snow Gods, 1969, An Unknown Woman, 1976, The Forever Street, 1984, Crosstown Sabbath, 1987, (biography) The Rothschilds, 1962, A Nervous Splendor-Vienna 1888-89, 1979, Budapest 2007, Tokyo 2008, Thunder at Twilight-Vienna 1913/14, 1989, Runaway Waltz--A Memoir From Vienna To New York, 2005; books translated into 14 langs.; actor (documentary) Crosstown Sabbath, 1995; contbg. editor: Vanity Fair; contbr. to publs. including Best Am. Short Stories, 1965, Best Am. Essays of 2003, and other anthologies, N.Y. Times, Harper's mag., Atlantic mag., Nation, Playboy, Esquire, N.Y. Mag., Hudson Rev., Wall Street Jour., Vanity Fair, L.A. Times, others; columnist Village Voice, Conde-Nast Traveler, Wall Street Jour.3.2 Recipient Author of Year award Nat. Anti-Defamation League, B'nai B'rith; Hon. Professorship award Republic of Austria, 1980, Tom Osborne Disting. lectureship U. Nebr., 1989; Dodd, Mead Intercollegiate Lit. fellow, 1947; Yaddo residence fellow, 1948, 50; Breadloaf Writers' Conf. fellow, 1947; Columbia U. fellow, 1953; recipient Golden Merit award City of Vienna, 1986, City of Vienna medal of honor in gold, 2001, Cross of Honor for Achievements in Arts, Republic of Austria, 2003. Mem. Author's Guild (exec. coun.), P.E.N. Home: 110 Riverside Dr New York NY 10024-3715 Office: Sandra Diskstra Agy PMB 515 1155 Camino Del Mar Del Mar CA 92014 Office Phone: 212-721-6938.

MORTON, HARRY B (BOB), state legislator; b. 1934; m to Linda; children: Bettina, Laura, Shawn, Scott & Roxanne, eleven grandchildren. Washington State Representative, District 7, 90-94; Washington State Senator, District 7, 94-, Agriculture & Rural Econ Develop, Natural Resources Ocean & Recreation, & Water Energy & Telecommunications comts.Cattleman, currently. 100 Percent Voting Record, Washington State Farm Bureau; Guardian of Small Bus, Nat Fedn Independent Bus; Legislature of Year, Association Washington Bus, 2006. Kettle River Grange; Stevens Counties & Washington Cattlemen's Association; Citizens for Great Northwest; Washington State Pilot's Association; Kettle Falls Chamber of Commerce. Republican. Protestant. Mailing: Irving R Newhouse Bldg Room 115D, PO Box 40407 Olympia WA 98504-0407 Fax: 360-786-1999. E-mail: morton.bob@leg.wa.gov.

MORTON, JOHN DOUGLAS, retail executive; b. 1951; With Wolfe's Sporting Goods, 1972-80; dist. mgr. sporting goods divsn. Malone and Hyde, 1980-86; divsn. mgr. Utah region Gart Sports Co., Denver, 1986-88, divsn. v.p. Utah region, 1988-90, v.p. ops., 1990-94, exec. v.p., 1994-95, pres., CEO, chmn. bd., 1995—2003; vice chmn., CEO The Sports Authority, Englewood, Colo., 2003—04, chmn., pres., CEO, 2004—. Office: The Sports Authority 1050 W Hampden Ave Englewood CO 80110 Fax: 303-829-1511.

MORTVEDT, JOHN JACOB, soil scientist, researcher; b. Dell Rapids, SD, Jan. 25, 1932; s. Ernest R. and Clara M.; m. Marlene L. Fodness, Jan. 23, 1955; children: Sheryl Mortvedt Jarratt, Lori Mortvedt Klopf, Julie Mortvedt Stride. BS, SD State U., 1953, MS, 1959; PhD, U. Wis., 1962. Soil chemist TVA, Muscle Shoals, Ala., 1962-87, sr. scientist, 1987-92, regional mgr. field programs dept., 1992-93; ext. soils specialist Colo. State U., Ft. Collins, 1994-95, ext. environ. and pesticide edn. specialist, 1996. Agr. cons. U.S. Borax, 1997-2007. Co-author: Fertilizer Technology and Application, 1999; editor: Micronutrients in Agriculture, 1972, 2d edit., 1991; contbr. articles to profl. jours. 1st lt. U.S. Army, 1953-57. Fellow AAAS, Soil Sci. Soc. Am. (pres. 1988-89, editor-in-chief 1982-87, Profl. Svc. award 1991, Disting. Svc. award 1996), Am. Soc. Agronomy (exec. com. 1987-90, Agronomic Svc. award 2003); mem. Internat. Union Soil Sci., Colombian Soil Sci. Soc. (hon.), Exch. Club (pres. Florence, Ala. chpt. 1987-88), Toastmasters (pres. Florence chpt. 1964-65), Phi Kappa Phi. Avocations: photography, golf. Office: Colo State U Dept Soil And Crop Scis Fort Collins CO 80523-1170

MOSBY, DOROTHEA SUSAN, retired municipal official; b. Sacramento, Calif., May 13, 1948; d. William Laurence and Esther Ida (Lux) M. AA in Sociology, Bakersfield Coll., Calif., 1966-69; BS in Recreation, San Jose State U., 1969-72; MPA, Calif. State U. Dominguez Hills, Carson, 1980-82. Asst. dept. pers. officer San Jose Pks. and Recreation Dept., 1972-73, neighborhood ctr. dir., 1973-74; sr. recreation leader Santa Monica Recreation and Pks. Dept., 1974-76, recreation supr., 1976-83; head bus. divsn. Santa Monica Recreation and Parks Dept., 1983-88; bus. adminstr. Santa Monica Cultural & Recreation Svcs., 1988-91; dir. pks. and recreation City of South Gate, Calif., 1991—2003; ret., 2003; cons. in field. Bd. dirs., officer Santa Monica City Employees Fed. Credit Union, 1980-89, pres. 1986-87; mem. citizens adv. com. L.A. Olympic Organizing Com., 1982-84, fine arts commn. Calif. State U. Bakersfield, 2008-. Mem. choir, flute soloist Pilgrim Luth. Ch., Santa Monica, 1974-98, treas. ch. coun., 1984-86, Christ Luth. Ch., Downey, Calif., 1999-2002, First Presbyn. Ch., Bakersfield, Calif., 2003—; vol. driver XXIII Olympiad, LA, 1984; contbr. local housing assistance U.S. Olympic Com., LA, 1984; adv. com. Windsor Sq. Hancock Park Hist. Soc., LA, 1983, dir. Christmas carolling, 1980-2000, chmn. Olympic com., 1984, trustee, 1984-90, chmn. pub. programs, 1985, co-chmn. pub. programs, 1986, co-vice chair, 1987, chmn., 1988, 89; Downey Symphony Guild; bd. dirs. Downey Symphony; mem. Samuel C. May Grad. Student Rsch. Paper Judging Com., Western Govt. Rsch. Assn., 1994; trustee Calif. Found. for Parks and Recreation; v.p. Bakersfield Symphony Assocs., 2004—07, pres., 2007-, ball chair, 2004, 05; mem. Assistance League Bakersfield, 2004—, Chez Noel home tour chair, 2005, pub. rels. chair, 2006; bd. mem. Kern County Acad. Decathlon, 2006-, bd. dirs., 2006—, Fox Theater Found., 2006—, 1st v.p., 2007, pres., 2008-, sec. Kern Vets. Meml. Found., 2007-. Recipient Outstanding Profl. of Yr. award Los Angeles Basin Pk. and Recreation Commrs. and Bd. Mems., 1993. Mem. Calif. Pk. and Recreation Soc. (bd. dirs. 1979-82, 86, chair. Calif bd. pk. and recreation cert. 2003, 04, Scholarship Found. Bd. 1992-2002, chair 1996-2002, dist. 10 v.p. 1994-96, Dist. 10 Spl. Recognition award 1998, State CPRS Citation award 1999), Nat. Recreation and Pk.

Assn., Calif. Found. Pks. Recreation (trustee), Mgmt. Team Assocs. (sec., treas. 1979-83), Western Govtl. Rsch. Assn., Nat. Assn. Univ. Women, South Gate C. of C., Kiwanis, Bakersfield Coll. Alumni Assn. (bd. dirs. 2005—), Chi Kappa Rho (pres. 1986), Pi Alpha Alpha. Avocations: flute, piano, reading, bicycling. Home: 104 Durham Ct Bakersfield CA 93309

MOSELEY, CHRIS ROSSER, marketing executive; b. Balt., Apr. 13, 1950; d. Thomas Earl and Fern Elaine (Coleman) Rosser; m. Thomas Kenneth Moseley. BA with honors, The Coll. of Wooster, 1972. Asst. dir. advt. and promotion Sta. WBAL-TV, Balt., 1972-74; dir. pub. rels. Mintz & Hoke Advt. Inc., Hartford, Conn., 1974-75; promotion mgr. Sta. WFSB-TV, Hartford, 1975-77; audience promotion mgr. Sta. WTVJ-TV, Miami, Fla., 1977-78; pres. CMA Mktg. Cons., Hyde Park, NY, 1979-82; promotion mgr. Ind. Network News-Sta. WPIX-TV, NYC, 1982-84; sr. v.p., mgmt. supr. Christopher Thomas Muller Jordan Weiss, NYC, 1984-89, Earle Palmer Brown/N.Y., NYC, 1989-90; sr. v.p. advt., promotion Discovery Networks, U.S., Bethesda, Md., 1990-99; exec. v.p. mktg. ABC, Inc., NYC, 1999—2000; exec. v.p., chief mktg. officer Hallmark Channel, Studio City, Calif., 2000—. Bd. dirs. Promax/BDA, Cable Positive, WICT, CTAM. Recipient Best Bus.-to-Bus. award Art Direction mag., 1984, achievement award in media rels. and edn. Nat. Resources Coun. Am., 1991, Best Editorial Excellence award Mag. Age, 1992, Best Overall Mktg. Campaign award MIP/MIPCOM, 1994, 1st Place Print award: Media Promotion, London Internat. Advt. awards, 1993, Gold award Broadcast Designers, 1993, Mktg. 100 award Ad Age, 1995, Cable Marketer of Yr. award Ad Age, 1995. Mem.: Advt. Women N.Y., Nat. Cable TV Assn. (conv. com. 1995, 1996, named one of Multichannel News' Wonderwomen of Yr. 2002, Vanguard award 1996), Cable and Telecom. Assn. Mktg. (chair Mark award 1995, bd. dir. 1996, co-chair 1997, bd. dir. 1997). Avocations: horticulture, travel. Office: Hallmark Channel 12700 Ventura Blvd Ste 100 Studio City CA 91604-6201 Home: PO Box 590 Riderwood MD 21139-0590 Office Phone: 818-755-2587. E-mail: chrismoseley@hallmarkchannel.com.

MOSELEY, JOHN TRAVIS, academic administrator, physicist, researcher; b. New Orleans, Feb. 26, 1942; s. Fred Baker and Lily Gay (Lord) M.; m. Belva McCall Hudson, Aug. 11 1964 (div. June 1979); m. Susan Diane Callow, Aug. 6, 1979; children: Melanie Lord, John Mark, Stephanie Marie, Shannon Eleanor. BS in Physics, Ga. Inst. Tech., 1964, MS in Physics, 1966, PhD in Physics, 1969. Asst. prof. physics U. West Fla., Pensacola, 1968-69; sr. physicist SRI Internat., Menlo Park, Calif., 1969-75, program mgr., 1976-79; vis. prof. U. Paris, 1975-76; assoc. prof. U. Oreg., Eugene, 1979-81, dir. chem. physics inst., 1980-84, prof. physics, 1984—, head physics dept., 1984-85, v.p. rsch., 1985-94, v.p. acad. affairs, provost, 1994-2001, sr. v.p., provost, 2001—06, spl. asst. to pres. and provost, 2006—. Mem. exec. com., coun. on acad. affairs NASULGC, 1994-2000, chair, 1996-97; bd. dirs. Oreg. Resource and Tech., Portland; mem. com. on Atomic and Molecular Sci., 1983-85. Contbr. numerous articles to profl. jours. Mem. So. Willamette Rsch. Corridor, Eugene, 1985-00, Lane Econ. Devel. Com., Eugene, 1988-94; bd. dirs. Eugene/Springfield Metro Partnership, 1985-01, Oreg. Bach Festival, Eugene, 1987-94, Eugene Arts Found., 1995-97. Recipient Doctoral Thesis award Sigma Xi, 1969; Fulbright fellow, 1975; numerous rsch. grants, 1969—. Fellow AAAS, Am. Physical Soc.; mem. AAUP, Am. Chem. Soc. Avocations: skiing, backpacking. Home: 2140 Essex Ln Eugene OR 97403-1851 Office: U Oreg Office of Sr VP and Provost Eugene OR 97403-1258 Business E-Mail: jtm@uoregon.edu.

MOSER, ROBERT HARLAN, internist, educator, writer; b. Trenton, NJ, June 16, 1923; s. Simon and Helena (Silvers) Moser; m. Linda Mae Salsinger, Mar. 18, 1989; children from previous marriage: Steven Michael, Jonathan Evan. BS, Loyola U., Balt., 1944; MD, Georgetown U., Washington, DC, 1948. Diplomate Am. Bd. Internal Medicine. Commd. 1st lt. U.S. Army, 1948, advanced through grades to col., 1966, intern D.C. Gen. Hosp., 1948—49, fellow pulmonary disease D.C. Gen. Hosp., 1949—50, bn. surgeon Republic of Korea, 1950—51; asst. resident Georgetown U. Hosp., 1951—52; chief resident Georgetown U. Hosp. U.S. Army, 1952—53, chief med. service U.S. Army Hosp. Salzburg, Austria, 1953—55, Wurzburg, Germany, 1955—56, resident in cardiology Brooke Gen. Hosp., 1956—57, asst. chief dept. medicine Brooke Gen. Hosp., 1957—59, chief Brooke Gen. Hosp., 1967—68, fellow hematology U. Utah Coll. Medicine, 1959—60, asst. chief U.S. Army Tripler Gen. Hosp., 1960—64, chief William Beaumont Gen. Hosp., 1965—67, chief Walter Reed Gen. Hosp., 1968—69, ret., 1969; chief of staff Maui (Hawaii) Meml. Hosp., 1969—73, chief dept. medicine, 1975—77; exec. v.p. Am. Coll. Physicians, Phila., 1976—86; v.p. med. affairs The NutraSweet Co., Deerfield, Ill., 1986—91. Assoc. prof. medicine Baylor U., 1958—59; clin. prof. medicine Hawaii U., 1969—77, Washington U., 1970—77, Abraham Lincoln Sch. Medicine, 1974—75; adj. prof. medicine U. Pa., 1977—86, Northwestern U., 1987—91; adj. prof. Uniformed Svcs. U. Health Scis., 1979—97; clin. prof. medicine U. N.Mex. Coll. Medicine, 1992—96, emeritus, 1996—; flight contr. Project Mercury, 1959—62; cons. mem. med. evaluation team Project Gemini, 1962—66; cons. Project Apollo, 1967—73, Tripler Gen. Hosp., 1970—77, Walter Reed Army Med. Ctr., 1974—86; sr. med. cons. Canyon Cons. Corp., 1991—2004; mem. cardiovascular and renal adv. com. FDA, 1978—82; chmn. life scis. adv. com. NASA, 1984—87, mem. adv. coun., 1983—88; chmn. gen. med. panel Hosp. Satellite Network, 1984—86; mem. adv. com. NASA Space Sta., 1988—93; mem. Dept. Def. Com. on Grad. Med. Edn., 1986—87, Life Scis. Strategic Planning Study Group, 1986—88; mem. space studies bd. NRC, 1988—93, space exploration initiation study, 1990; mem. NASA Space Sta. Commn., 1992—93, mem. com. adv. tech. human supp. space, 1996—97; mem. med. adv. bd. the patient channel GE Healthcare, 2001—. Editor, chief divsn. sci. publs. Jour. AMA, Chgo., 1973—75, contbg. editor Med. Opinion and Rev., 1966—75, chmn. editorial bd. Diagnosis mag., 1986—89, mem. editorial bd. Hawaii Med. Jour., Family Physicians, Archives of Internal Medicine, 1967—73, Western Jour. Medicine, 1975—87, Chest, 1975—80, Med. Times, 1977—84, Quality Rev. Bull., 1979—91, The Pharos, 1991—, book rev. editor, 2000—05, mem. editorial bd. Travel Medicine, 1994—96; contbr. over 200 articles to med. sci. jours. and med. books; author: Diseases of Medical Progress, 1955, 1969, House Officer Training, 1970, Decade of Decision, 1992, Past Imperfect A Personal History of Life In and Around Medicine, 2003; co-author Adventures in Medical Writing, 1970, editor chief divsn. sci. publs. Jour. AMA, Chgo., 1973—75, contbg. editor Med. Opinion and Rev., 1966—75, chmn. editl. bd. Diagnosis mag., 1986—89; contbr. articles to med. sci. jours. and med. books. Master: ACP (exec. v.p. 1977—86); fellow: Am. Clin. and Climatol. Assn., Am. Coll. Cardiology, Royal Coll. Physicians and Surgeons Can. (hon.); mem.: AMA (adv. panel registry of adverse drug reactions 1960—67, coun. on drugs 1967—73), Soc. Med. Cons. to Armed Forces, Coll. Physicians Phila., Chgo. Soc. Internal Medicine, Nat. Assn. Physician Broadcasters, Inst. Medicine-NAS, Am. Osler Soc., Am. Therapeutic Soc., Am. Med. Writers Assn., Alpha Omega Alpha, Alpha Sigma Nu. Democrat. Jewish. Avocations: hiking, travel, writing. Home and Office: 943 E Sawmill Canyon Pl Green Valley AZ 85614 Office Phone: 520-399-2526. Personal E-mail: rhmoser@earthlink.net.

MOSER, ROYCE, JR., preventive medicine physician, educator; b. Versailles, Mo., Aug. 21, 1935; s. Royce and Russie Frances (Stringer) M.; m. Lois Anne Hunter, June 14, 1958; children: Beth Anne Moser McLean, Donald Royce. BA, Harvard U., Cambridge, Mass., 1957, MD, 1961; MPH, Harvard Sch. Pub. Health, Boston, 1965. Diplomate Am. Bd. Preventive Medicine (trustee 1989-98). Commd. officer USAF, 1962, advanced through grades to col., 1974; resident in aerospace medicine USAF Sch. Aerospace Medicine, Brooks AFB, Tex., 1965-67; chief aerospace medicine Aerospace Def. Command, Colorado Springs, Colo., 1967-70; comdr. 35th USAF Dispensary Phan Rang, Vietnam, 1970-71; chief aerospace medicine br. USAF Sch. Aerospace Medicine, Brooks AFB, 1971-77; comdr. USAF Hosp., Tyndall AFB, Fla., 1977-79; chief clin. scis. divsn. USAF Sch. Aerospace Medicine, Brooks AFB, 1979-81, chief edn. divsn., 1981-83, sch. comdr., 1983-85, ret., 1985; prof. dept. family and preventive medicine U. Utah Sch. Medicine, Salt Lake City, 1985—, vice chmn. dept., 1985-95; dir. Rocky Mountain Ctr. for Occupl. and Environ. Health, Salt Lake City, 1987—2003. Cons. in occupl., environ. and aerospace medicine, Salt Lake City, 1985—; presenter in field. Author: Effective Management of Health and Safety Programs, 1992, 3d. edit. 2008; contbr. chpts. to books, articles to profl. jours. Past pres. 1st Bapt. Ch. Found., Salt Lake City, 1987-89, moderator, 2006; chmn. numerous univ. coms., Salt Lake City, 1985—; bd. dirs. Hanford Environ. Health Found., 1990-92; preventive medicine residency rev. com. Accreditation Coun. Grad. Med. Edn., 1991-97; ednl. adv. bd. USAF Human Sys. Ctr., 1991-96; chmn. long-range planning com. Am. Bd. Preventive Medicine, 1992-95; mem. alumni coun. Harvard Sch. Pub. Health, 2003-06, chair alumni award of merit com., 2005—, chair elect, 2007—; pres. elect Harvard Sch. Pub. Health Alumni Assn., 2007—. Decorated Legion of Merit (2); recipient Harriet Hardy award New Eng. Coll. Occupl. and Environ. Medicine, 1998, Rutherford T. Johnstone award Western Occupl. and Environ. Med. Assn., 2002. Fellow Aerospace Med. Assn. (pres. 1989-90, chair fellows group 1994-97, Harry G. Mosely award 1981, Theodore C. Lyster award 1988, Eric Liljencrantz award 2001, Pres.'s citation, 2006), Am. Coll. Preventive Medicine (regent 1981-82), Am. Coll. Occupl. and Environ. Medicine (v.p. med. affairs 1995-97, Robert A. Kehoe award 1996); mem. Internat. Acad. Aviation and Space Medicine (selector 1989-94, chancellor 1994-98), Soc. of USAF Flight Surgeons (pres. 1978-79, George E. Schafer award 1982), Phi Beta Kappa. Avocations: photography, fishing. Home: 664 Aloha Rd Salt Lake City UT 84103-3329 Office: Rocky Mountain Ctr Occupl & Environ Health 391 Chipeta Way Ste C Salt Lake City UT 84108 Office Phone: 801-581-4800. Business E-Mail: Royce.Moser@hsc.utah.edu.

MOSES, RAPHAEL JACOB, lawyer; b. Girard, Ala., Nov. 6, 1913; s. William Moultrie and Anna (Green) M.; m. Marian Eva Beck, Aug. 22, 1938 (dec. Feb. 1976); 1 child, Marcia (Mrs. William S. Johnson); m. Fletcher Lee Westgaard, Jan. 20, 1979. AB, U. Colo., 1935, JD, 1937. Bar: Colo. 1938. Practiced in, Alamosa, 1938-62, Boulder, 1962—; pres. Moses, Wittemyer, Harrison & Woodruff (P.C.), from 1970, now of counsel. Spl. asst. atty. gen. Rio Grande Compact, 1957-58; mem. Colo. Water Conservation Bd., 1952-58, chmn., counsel, 1958-76, cons., 1976-77; research asso., faculty law U. Colo., 1962-66, vis. lectr., 1966-76, resident counsel, 1964-66, regent, 1973-74; grad. faculty Colo. State U., 1963-67; mem. Western States Water Council, 1965-77, chmn., 1966-70. Trustee Rocky Mountain Mineral Law Inst., 1964-66; bd. dirs. U. Colo. Found., 1977-97, chmn., 1977-79, mem. chancellor's adv. coun., 1981-97; bd. dirs. Colo. Open Lands, 1983-91, U. Colo. Improvement Corp., 1980-90, Colo. Endowment for Humanities, 1986-89; mem. adv. bd. Natural Resources Ctr., U. Colo. Sch. Law, 1983-92, chmn., 1986-88; mem. Sr. Citizens Adv. Bd., Boulder, Colo., 2003—. Served to lt. (s.g.) USNR, 1942-45. Decorated Purple Heart; recipient William E. Knous award U. Colo. Sch. Law, 1971, Norlin award U. Colo., 1972; Raphael J. Moses Disting. Natural Resources professorship established U. Colo., 1994. Fellow Am. Bar Found. (life), Colo. Bar Found. (trustee 1977-90), Am. Coll. Trial Lawyers; mem. ABA (chmn. water rights com. sect. natural resources 1959-60), Colo. Bar Assn. (pres. 1959-60, Award of Merit 1972), San Luis Valley Bar Assn. (pres. 1942), Am. Counsel Assn., Order of Coif (hon.), Boulder Country Club Presbyterian (elder) Home: 4913 Clubhouse Cir Boulder CO 80301-3715 E-mail: raymoise@aol.com.

MOSICH, ANELIS NICK, accountant, writer, educator, consultant; b. Croatia, Aug. 30, 1928; came to U.S., 1939, naturalized, 1951; s. Dinko and Josephine (Ursich) M.; m. Dorothy V. Rasich, June 15, 1958; children: Lori, Lisa, Jeffrey. BS, UCLA, 1951, MBA, 1953, PhD, 1963. CPA, Calif. Mem. faculty UCLA, 1955-63, Calif. State U., Northridge, 1963-64; examiner for Calif. State Bd. Accountancy, 1964-70; prof. acctg. U. So. Calif., LA, 1964-74, William C. Hallett prof. acctg., 1974-81, Ernst & Young prof., 1981-90, chmn. acctg. dept., 1970-74, 77-78, prof. emeritus, 1993. Cons. various bus. orgns., 1953—; expert witness; guest spkr. various profl. and bus. groups in Calif., Oreg., NY, Tex., Fla., Hawaii, Mex., 1963—95; bd. dirs. Metro-Goldwyn-Mayer, Inc., 2003—05. Author: Intermediate Accounting, rev. 6th edit., 1989, Financial Accounting, 1970, 75, Accounting: A Basis for Business Decision, 1972, Modern Advanced Accounting, 4th edit., 1988, The CPA Examination: Text, Problems and Solutions, 1978; editor: Education column Calif. CPA Quar., 1965-66; contbg. editor: Education and Professional Training column Jour. Accountancy, 1971-77; contbr. numerous articles to jours. and acctg. Mem. productivity commn. City of L.A., 1993—94; bd. dirs. Bill Hannon Found. With US Army, 1953—55. Fellow UCLA, 1963; recipient Dean's award Sch. Bus. Adminstrn., U. So. Calif., 1973, 78, Fred B. Olds Support Group award U. So. Calif., 1994, Disting. Svc. award for Leventhal Sch. Acctg., 1999, Mosich Endowment Chair award, U. So. Calif., 2006 Office: U So Calif Leventhal Sch Acctg University Park Los Angeles CA 90089-1425

MOSIER, HARRY DAVID, JR., physician, educator; b. Topeka, May 22, 1925; s. Harry David and Josephine Morrow (Johnson) M.; m. Nadine Oclea Merilatt, Aug. 24, 1949; children: Carolyn Josephine Mosier Pohlmeyer, William David, Daniel Thomas, Christine Elizabeth Mosier Mahoney; m. Marjorie Knight Armstrong, Sept. 26, 1963. BS magna cum laude, U. Notre Dame, 1948; MD, Johns Hopkins U., 1952. Diplomate Am. Bd. Pediatrics, Am. Bd. Pediatric Endocrinology. Intern Johns Hopkins Hosp., Balt., 1952-53; resident in pediat. Los Angeles Children's Hosp., 1953-54, resident pediatric pathology, 1954-55; fellow pediatric endocrinology Johns Hopkins U., 1955-57; asst. prof. pediat. UCLA, 1957-61, assoc. prof., 1961-63; dir. rsch. Ill. State Pediatric Inst., Chgo., 1963-67; assoc. prof. U. Ill., 1963-67; prof. pediat. U. Calif.-Irvine, 1967—2002, emeritus, 2002—, head divsn. pediat. endocrinology, 1967-2000; staff Children's Hosp. Med. Ctr., Long Beach, Calif., 1970—2005, U. Calif. Irvine Med. Ctr., Orange, 1979—; dist. cons. Med. Bd. Calif., 1995—. Contbr. articles to med. jours. With AUS, 1943-46, col. U.S. Army Med. Corps, 1990-91, Persian Gulf War. USAR Med. Corps. 1952-62, 83-93 (ret.). Office: U Calif Dept Pediat 101 City Dr S Orange CA 92868-3201

MOSK, RICHARD MITCHELL, judge; b. LA, May 18, 1939; s. Stanley and Edna M.; m. Sandra Lee Budnitz, Mar. 21, 1964; children: Julie, Matthew. AB with great distinction, Stanford U., 1960; JD cum laude, Harvard U., 1963. Bar: Calif. 1964, US Supreme Ct. 1970, US Ct. Mil. Appeals 1970, US Dist. Ct. (no., so., ea., and cen. dists.) Calif 1964, US Ct. Appeals (9th dist.) 1964. Staff Pres.'s Commn. on Assassination Pres. Kennedy, 1964; rsch. clk. Calif. Supreme Ct., 1964-65; ptnr. Mitchell, Silberberg & Knupp, LA, 1965-87; prin. Sanders, Barnet, Goldman, Simons & Mosk, PC, LA, 1987-2000; justice Calif. Ct. Appeal, 2nd Dist., 2001—. Spl. dep. Fed. Pub. Defender, LA, 1975—76; instr. U. So. Calif. Law Sch., 1978; judge Iran-U.S. Claims Tribunal, 1981—84, 1997—2001, substitute arbitrator, 1984—97; mem. L.A. County Jud. Procedures Commn., 1973—82, chmn., 1978; chmn., co-chmn. Motion Picture Assn. Classification and Rating Adminstrn., 1994—2000; mem. panel Ct. Arbitration for Sport-Geneva, 1998—2001; lectr. internat. law Hague Acad., 2003. Contbr. articles to profl. jours. Mem. L.A. City-County Inquiry on Brush Fires, 1970; bd. dirs. Calif. Mus. Sci. and Industry, 1979-82, Vista Del Mar Child Ctr., 1979-82; trustee L.A. County Law Libr., 1985-86; bd. govs. Town Hall Calif., 1986-91; mem. Christopher Commn. on L.A. Police Dept., 1991; mem. Stanford U. Athletic Bd., 1991-95. With USNR, 1964-75. Hon. Woodrow Wilson fellow, 1960; recipient Roscoe Pound prize, 1961. Mem.: ABA (coun. internat. law sect. 1986—90), Am. Law Inst., L.A. County Bar Assn., Beverly Hills Bar Assn., Am. Bar Found., Phi Beta Kappa. Office: Ct Appeal 300 S Spring St Los Angeles CA 90013

MOSKOS, HARRY, columnist, editor; b. Chgo., Oct. 8, 1936; m. Victoria Marie Poulos; 3 children. BA, U. N.Mex., Albuquerque, 1958. With Albuquerque Tribune, 1953-59; editor Grants (N.Mex.) Daily Beacon, 1959-60; newsman AP, Albuquerque, 1960, state editor, 1961-63, chief of bur. Honolulu, 1963-69; city editor Albuquerque Tribune, 1969-73, mng. editor, 1973—80; editor El Paso Herald-Post, 1980—84, Knoxville News-Sentinel, 1984—2001; columnist, letters editor Albuquerque Jour., 2001—. Office: 7777 Jefferson St NE Albuquerque NM 87109 Office Phone: 505-823-3837. Business E-Mail: hmoskos@abqjournal.com.

MOSKOVITZ, DUSTIN AARON, Internet company executive, entrepreneur, application developer; b. May 22, 1984; s. Richard A. Moskovitz and Nancy Siegel. Econ. major, Harvard U., 2002—04. Co-founder & v.p. engring. Facebook, Inc., Palo Alto, Calif., 2004—08. Achievements include development of one of the most widely used networking websites among college and high school students with over 11 million users throughout the US, Canada and Europe; the ninth most highly trafficked website in US. Office: Facebook Inc 151 University Ave Ste 200 Palo Alto CA 94301-1675

MOSKOWITZ, BARRY T., judge; BA, Rutgers U., 1972, JD, 1975. Judge U.S. Dist. Ct. (so. dist.) Calif., 1996—. Office: US Courthouse 940 Front St San Diego CA 92101-8994

MOSKOWITZ, DAVID K., lawyer; b. Glen Burnie, Md., Apr. 24, 1958; m. Hallie A. Moskowitz. BA summa cum laude, Western Md. College, 1980; JD with honors, George Washington U., 1983. Corp. counsel MDC Holdings Inc., 1986—90; with Echostar Communications, Englewood, Colo., 1990, exec. v.p., gen. counsel, sec., dir. Mem.: Am. Corp. Counsel Assn., Denver Bar Assn., Colo. Bar Assn., ABA. Office: Echostar Communications 9601 S Meridan Blvd Englewood CO 80112 Home: 7 Waterside Ter Englewood CO 80113-4141 Office Phone: 303-723-1040. Office Fax: 303-723-1699. Business E-Mail: david.moskowitz@echostar.com.

MOSKOWITZ, JOEL STEVEN, lawyer; b. NYC, Jan. 14, 1947; s. Jack I. and Myra (Shor) M.; m. Anna Boucher; children: David, Michael, Ellen. BA, UCLA, 1967, JD, 1970. Bar: Calif. 1971, U.S. Ct. Appeals (9th cir.) 1971, U.S. Ct. Appeals (D.C. cir.) 1975, U.S. Supreme Ct. 1975, U.S. Ct. Appeals (2d cir.) 1979. Dep. atty. gen. Calif. Dept. Justice, Sacramento, 1970-83; dep. dir. Calif. Dept. Health Svcs., Sacramento, 1983-85; of counsel Gibson, Dunn & Crutcher, LA, 1985-88, ptnr., 1988-96, Moskowitz, Brestoff, Winston & Blinderman LLP, 1996—. Author: Environmental Liability in Real Property Transactions, 1995; contbr. articles to legal publs. Mem. Phi Beta Kappa. Office: 1880 Century Park E Ste 300 Los Angeles CA 90067-1631 Home Phone: 310-373-9790; Office Phone: 310-373-9790. Personal E-mail: joel_s_moskowitz@yahoo.com. Business E-Mail: joel@moskowitzhq.com.

MOSLEY, SHANE, boxer; b. Lynwood, Calif., Sept. 7, 1971; m. Jin Mosley (separated 2009); children: Shane Jr., Norman, Najee, Tai, Mee-Yon Jinae. Profl. boxer, 1993—. Winner internat. title vs. Philip Holiday by unanimous decision, lightweight divsn. Internat. Boxing Fedn., 1997, winner internat. title def. vs. Manuel Gomez by knockout, lightweight divsn., 97, winner internat. title def. vs. Demetrio Ceballos by tech. knockout, lightweight divsn., 98, winner internat. title def. vs. John John Molina by tech. knockout, lightweight divsn., 98, winner internat. title def. vs. Wilfredo Ruiz by knockout, lightweight divsn., 98, winner internat. title def. vs. Eduardo Bartolome Morales by tech. knockout, lightweight divsn., 98, winner internat. title def. vs. Jesse James Leija by tech. knockout, lightweight divsn., 98, winner internat. title def. vs. Golden Johnson by knockout, lightweight divsn., 99, winner internat. title def. vs. John Brown by tech. knockout, lightweight divsn., 99; winner internat. title vs. Oscar de la Hoya by split decision, welterweight divsn. Internat. Boxing Assn., 2000; winner world title vs. Oscar de la Hoya by split decision, welterweight divsn. World Boxing Coun., 2000, winner world title def. vs. Antonio Diaz by tech. knockout, welterweight divsn., 00, winner world title def. vs. Shannan Taylor by tech. knockout, welterweight divsn., 01, winner world title def. vs. Adrian Stone by knockout, welterweight divsn., 01, winner world title vs. Oscar de la Hoya by unanimous decision, light middleweight divsn., 03, World Boxing Assn., 2003; winner internat. title vs. Oscar de la Hoya by unanimous decision, light middleweight divsn. Internat. Boxing Assn., 2003; winner world title vs. Luis Collazo by unanimous decision, welterweight divsn. World Boxing Coun., 2007; winner inter-continental title vs. Ricardo Mayorga by knock out, light middleweight divsn. World Boxing Assn., 2008, winner world title vs. Antonio Margarito by tech. knock out, welterweight divsn., 09. Achievements include being the only boxer to beat Oscar de la Hoya twice. Mailing: c/o Sugar Shane Inc PO Box 8318 La Verne CA 91750*

MOSS, ERIC OWEN, architect; b. LA, July 25, 1943; BA, UCLA, 1965; MArch with honors, U. Calif., Berkeley, 1968, Harvard U., 1972. Prof. design So. Calif. Inst. Architecture, 1974—, dir., 2002—; prin. Eric Owen Moss Archs., Culver City, Calif., 1973—; Eliot Noyes chair Harvard U., Cambridge, Mass., 1990; Eero Saarinen chair Yale U., New Haven, 1991. Lectr. Hirshhorn Mus. Symposium, Washington, 1990, Nat. AIA Conv., 1990, Mus. Contemporary Art, LA, 1991, NY Archtl. League, 1991, Archtl. Assn. Ireland, Dublin, Archtl. Assn., London, 1991, Royal Coll. Art, London, 1991, Smithsonian Instn., Washington, 1992, U. Calif., Berkeley, 1992, Osterreichisches Mus. fur Angewandte Kunst, Vienna, 1992, UCLA, 1992, Royal Danish Acad. Fine Arts, Copenhagen, 1993, U. Lund, Sweden, 1993, Mus. Finnish Architecture, Helsinki, 1993, Royal Acad. Arts, London, 1993, U. Pa., Phila., 1994, others; tchr. U. Tex., Austin, 1983, Wash. U., St. Louis, 1984, U. Ill., Chgo., 1985, Tulane U., New Orleans, 1985, U. Minn., Mpls., 1985, Columbia U., NYC, 1986, Rice U., Houston, 1988; participant various confs. Exhbns. of work include World Biennial of Architecture, Sofia, Bulgaria, 1989, Salle des Tirages du Credit Foncier de France, Paris, 1990, Bartlett Sch. Architecture and Urban Design, London, 1991, Gallery of Functional Art, Santa Monica, Calif., 1992, GA Gallery, Tokyo, 1992, Mus. fur Gestaltung Zurich, Switzerland, 1993, Santa Monica Mus. Art, 1993, Fonds Regional D'Art Contemporain du Centre, 1993, Aspen Art Mus., Colo., 1993, Centro de Arte y Comunicacion, Buenos Aires, 1993, Contemporary Arts Ctr., Cin., 1993, Philippe Uzzan Galerie, Paris, 1993, Contemporary Arts Ctr., Tours, France, 1993, Internat. Exhbn. Contemporary Architecture, Havana, Cuba, 1994, others. Recipient Progressive Architecture Design award, 1978, 92, Winning Interior Archtl. Record award, 1984, Interiors Design award, 1991, Award in Architecture, AAAL, 1999, Andrew W. Brunner Meml. prize, Architecture, 2007. Fellow AIA (LA awards 1977, 79, 83, 88, 90, Calif. Coun. awards 1981, 86, 88, LA Honor awards 1991, Nat. Honor awards 88, 89, Calif. Coun. Urban Design/Adaptive Re-Use awards 1991, Nat. Interior Design awards 1992, 94, LA Design awards 1992, 93, LA Gold Medal award 2001, Educator of Yr., 2006). Achievements include being subject of monographs and numerous articles in mags. and jours. Office: Eric Owen Moss Archs 8557 Higuera St Culver City CA 90232-2535 Office Phone: 310-839-1199. Office Fax: 310-839-7922. E-mail: mail@ericowenmoss.com.

MOSS, GARY CURTIS, lawyer; b. Taylorville, Ill., Feb. 17, 1944; s. William Clary and Sophronia Irene (McClellan) Moss; m. Judith K. Jones; children: Gary Curtis, Kristin Suzanne. BA, U. Ill., Champaign, 1966; JD, U. Iowa, 1969. Bar: Iowa 1969, Calif. 1970, US Dist. Ct. (ctrl. dist.) Calif. 1972, Nev. 1991, US Ct. Appeals (9th cir.) 1974, US Dist. Ct. (so. and no. dists.) Calif. 1981, US Dist. Ct. Nev. 1991. Assoc. O'Melveny & Myers, LA, 1969—75, Seyfarth, Shaw, Fairweather & Geraldson, 1975—78, ptnr., 1978—87; judge pro tem West LA Mcpl. Ct., 1981—83, Pasadena Mcpl. Ct., 1983—. Ptnr.-in-charge Las Vegas Office DLA Piper Rudnick Gary Cary. Mem.: ABA, LA County Bar Assn., State Bar Iowa, State Bar Calif. (hearing referee, arbitrator mandatory fee arbitrations), Athletic Club LA. Republican. Office: DLA Piper Rudnick Gray Cary Ste 400 3960 Howard Hughes Pkwy Las Vegas NV 89109-0993 Office Phone: 702-737-3433, 702-737-1612. Business E-Mail: gary.moss@piperrudnick.com.

MOSS, JOEL M., physicist; BS, Fort Hayes State U., 1964; PhD in Nuclear Chem., U. Calif., Berkeley, 1969. Postdoc. fellow Ctr. Nuclear Studies, Saclay, France, 1969-71, Physics Dept U. Minn., Mpls., 1971-73; faculty Physics Dept. Texas A&M U., 1973-79; Los Alamos (N. Mex.) Nat. Lab., 1979—. Mem. Nuclear Scis. Adv. Com. Recipient Tom W. Bonner prize 1998. Fellow Am. Physical Soc.

MOSS, MYRA ELLEN (MYRA MOSS ROLLE), philosophy educator; b. LA, Mar. 22, 1937; m. Andrew Rolle, Nov. 5, 1983. BA, U. Rome, Italy, 1958; PhD, Johns Hopkins U., Balt., 1965. Asst. prof. Santa Clara (Calif.) U., 1968-74; prof. Claremont McKenna Coll., 1975—2007, emeritus prof., 2007—, chmn. dept. philosophy, 1992—95. Assoc. dir. Gould Ctr. for Humanities, Claremont, Calif., 1993-94; adv. coun. Milton S. Eisenhower Libr./Johns Hopkins U., 1994-96, 2001— Author: Benedetto Croce Reconsidered, 1987, Mussolini's Fascist Philosopher: Giovanni Gentile Reconsidered, 2004, Italian edit., Armando, 2007, rev. Mussolini's Brain Trust, 2006; translator: Benedetto Croce's Essays on Literature & Literary Criticism, 1990; co-author: Values and Education, 1998; assoc. editor Special Issues; Journal of Value Inquiry, 1990-95 (Honorable Mention, Phoenix award); cons. editor Jour. Social Philosophy, 1988—; assoc. editor: Value Enquiry Book Series, 1990-95; editor: The Philosophy of José Gaos, by Pio Colonnello, Value Inquiry Book Series, 1997. Bogliasco fellow, Liguria, Italy, 2000; vis. scholar Am. Acad. Rome, 2005. Mem. Am. Philos. Assn., Am. and Internat. Soc. for Value Inquiry, Soc. for Aesthetics, Internat. Ctr. for the Arts, Humanities and Value Inquiry (assoc.), Collingwood Soc. (life), Phi Beta Kappa. Avocations: gardening, horseback riding. Office: Claremont McKenna Coll 850 Columbia Ave Claremont CA 91711-3901

MOSS, PATRICIA L., bank executive; m. Greg Moss; children: Jennifer, Jeffrey. BS in Bus. Adminstrn., Linfield Coll., Oreg.; grad. studies, Portland State U. Cert. U. Okla., ABA Comml. Banking Sch. Various banking positions Cascade Bancorp, Bend, Oreg., 1977—98, pres., CEO, 1998—; CEO Bank of the Cascades, Bend, 1998—. Bd. dirs. Cascade Bancorp, Bank of the Cascades, Aquilla Tax-Free Trust of Oreg., Ctrl. Oreg. Ind. Health Svcs., MDU Resources Group Inc., 2003—. Adv. bd. Oreg. State U. Cascade Campus. Named Disting. Citizen of Yr., Bend C. of C., Ctrl. Oreg. Bus. Woman of Yr.; named one of 25 Most Powerful Women in Banking, US Banker, 2006, 2007. Mem.: Ind. Cmty. Bankers Assn. Am., Oreg. Bankers Assn. (bd. dir.), Oreg. Women's Forum. Office: Cascade Bancorp 1100 NW Wall St Bend OR 97701

MOSS, SHAD GREGORY (BOW WOW, LIL' BOW WOW), rap artist; b. Columbus, Ohio, Mar. 9, 1987; s. Teresa and Alfonso Moss, Rodney Caldwell (Stepfather). Singer: (albums) Beware of Dog, 2000, Doggy Bag, 2001, Unleashed, 2003, Wanted, 2005, Signal Fire, 2006, The Price of Fame, 2006, New Jack City, Part II, 2009, (with Omarion) Face Off, 2007, (songs) Bounce With Me, 2000, Let Me Hold You, 2005, Fresh Azimiz, 2005, Like You, 2006, (featured on film soundtracks) Hardball, 2001, Like Mike, 2002; actor: (TV films) Carmen: A Hip Hopera, 2001; (films) All About the Benjamins, 2002, Like Mike, 2002, Johnson Family Vacation, 2004, Roll Bounce, 2005, The Fast & the Furious: Tokyo Drift, 2006. Achievements include youngest solo rapper to ever hit number one. Office: Bow Wow Found Ste 307 6555 Sugarloaf Pkwy PMB 223 Duluth GA 30097 also: c/o Jeff Frasco or Ken Stovitz Creative Artists Agy LCC 2000 Ave of the Stars Los Angeles CA 90067 Office Fax: 678-376-5911.

MOSS, THOMAS E., prosecutor; b. 1937; BA, U. Idaho; JD, U. Idaho Coll. Law, 1965. Prosecuting atty. Bingham County Dist. Ct., 1967—71, 1979—99; ptnr. Moss, Cannon and Romrell, Blackfoot, Idaho; mem. Idaho Ho. Reps., 2001; US atty. dist. Idaho US Dept. Justice, Boise, 2001—. Faculty mem. Nat. Advocacy Ctr., Columbia, SC; adv. coun. U. Idaho Coll. of Law; mem. Atty. Gen. Adv. Com., 2005—, Atty. Gen. Exec. Working Grp. Pres. Blackfoot Chamber of Commerce, Blackfoot Rotary Club; mem. Governor's Coordinating Coun. for Families and Children. Fellow: Am. Coll. Trial Lawyers; mem.: Idaho Prosecuting Attorneys' Assn. (pres.), Seventh Jud. Dist. Bar Assn. (pres.), Idaho State Bar Assn. (pres.), Idaho Ho. of Reps. Office: US Attys Office MK Plaza IV Ste 600 800 Park Blvd Boise ID 83712-9903

MOTT, FREDERICK B., JR., publishing executive; b. Miami, 1947; m. Shirlene Mott; children: Jaimie, Alissa. B. in Acctg., Fla. State U., 1972. CPA Deloitte & Touche LLP; with Knight Ridder, 1979—2005; gen. mgr. Tallahassee Democrat, Fla., 1984—91; pub. Post-Tribune, Gary, Ind., 1991—95; pres., publ. The State, Columbia, SC, 1995—2002; pres., gen. mgr. Philadelphia Newspapers Inc., 2002—05; pub., CEO ANG Newspapers, Oakland, Calif., 2006—. Avocations: golf, saltwater fishing. Office: Ang Newspaper 2640 Shadelands Dr Walnut Creek CA 94598-2513

MOTT, RANDY (RANDALL D. MOTT), computer company executive; b. 1956; BS in Math., U. Ark., Fayetteville, 1978. Various positions Wal-Mart Stores, Inc., 1978—94, sr. v.p., chief info. officer, 1994—97, mem. exec. com., 1997; sr. v.p., chief info. officer Dell, Inc., Round Rock, Tex., 2000—05; exec. v.p., chief info. officer Hewlett-Packard Co., Palo Alto, Calif., 2005—. Mem. Pres. Info. Tech. Adv. Com., 2003—. Named Chief Info. Officer of Yr., Info. Week mag., 1997. Disting. Alumni, Fulbright Coll. Alumni Acad., 2005. Office: Hewlett-Packard Co 3000 Hanover St Palo Alto CA 94304-1185 Office Phone: 650-857-1501. Office Fax: 650-857-5518.

MOTTO, JEROME ARTHUR, psychiatrist, educator; b. Kansas City, Mo., Oct. 16, 1921; MD, U. Calif., San Francisco, 1951. Diplomate Am. Bd. Neurology and Psychiatry. Intern San Francisco Gen. Hosp., 1951-52; resident Johns Hopkins Hosp., Balt., 1952-55; sr. resident U. Calif., San Francisco, 1955-56; from instr. to prof. U. Calif. Sch. Medicine, San Francisco, 1956—91, prof. emeritus, 1991—. Pres. Am. Assn. Suicidology, 1972—73; sec. gen. Internat. Assn. Suicide Prevention, 1973—77. Contbr. articles to profl. jours. With AUS, 1942-46, ETO. Recipient Outstanding Achievement award, Northern Calif. Psychiatric Soc., 2009. Fellow: Am. Psychiatric Assn. (life; disting. fellow).

MOTULSKY, ARNO GUNTHER, internist, geneticist, educator; b. Fischhausen, Germany, July 5, 1923; arrived in U.S., 1941; s. Herman and Rena (Sass) Molton; m. Gretel C. Stern, Mar. 22, 1945; children: Judy, Harvey, Arlene. Student, Cen. YMCA Coll., Chgo., 1941—43, Yale U., 1943—44; BS, U. Ill., 1945, MD, 1947, DSc (hon.), 1982, MD (hon.), 1991. Diplomate Am. Bd. Internal Medicine, Am. Bd. Med. Genetics. Intern, fellow, resident Michael Reese Hosp., Chgo., 1947—51; staff mem. charge clin. investigation dept. hematology Army Med. Service Grad. Sch., Walter Reed Army Med. Ctr., Washington, 1952—53; research assoc. internal medicine George Washington U. Sch. Medicine, 1952—53; from instr. to assoc. prof. dept. medicine U. Wash. Sch. Medicine, Seattle, 1953—61, prof. medicine, prof. genetics, 1961—; head div. med. genetics, dir. genetics clinic Univ. Hosp., Seattle, 1959—89; dir. Ctr. for Inherited Diseases, Seattle, 1972—90. Attending physician Univ. Hosp., Seattle; cons. Pres.'s Commn. for Study of Ethical Problems in Medicine and Biomed. and Behavioral Rsch., 1979—83; cons. various coms. NRC, NIH, WHO, and others. Editor: Am. Jour. Human Genetics, 1969—75, Human Genetics, 1969—97. Fellow Commonwealth Fund in human genetics, Univ. Coll., London, 1957—58, Ctr. Advanced Study in Behavorial Scis., Stanford U., 1976—77, Inst. Advanced Study, Berlin, 1984; scholar John and Mary Markle in med. sci., 1957—62. Fellow: AAAS, ACP; mem.: NAS, Am. Philos. Soc., Am. Acad. Arts and Scis., Inst. of Medicine, Am. Assn. Physicians, Am. Soc. Clin. Investigation, Am. Soc. Human Genetics, Western Soc. Clin. Rsch., Genetics Soc. Am., Am. Fedn. Clin. Rsch., Internat. Soc. Hematology. Home: 4347 53rd Ave NE Seattle WA 98105-4938 Office: Univ Wash Medicine and Genome Scis PO Box 355065 Seattle WA 98195-5065 Business E-Mail: agmot@u.washington.edu.

MOUDON, ANNE VERNEZ, urban design educator; b. Yverdon, Vaud, Switzerland, Dec. 24, 1945; came to U.S., 1966; d. Ernest Edouard and Mauricette Lina (Duc) Moudon; children: Louisa Moudon Seferis, Constantine Thomas Seferis. BArch with honors, U. Calif., Berkeley, 1969; DSc, Ecole Poly. Fed., Lausanne, Switzerland, 1987. Fed. Register of Swiss Archs. Rsch. assoc. Bldg. Sys. Devel., Inc., San Francisco, 1969-70; sr. project planner J.C. Warnecke and Assocs., NYC, 1973-74; archtl. cons. McCue, Boone & Tomsick, San Francisco, 1974-76; asst. to assoc. prof. architecture MIT, Cambridge, Mass., 1975-81, Ford internat. career chair, 1977-79; sec. Assn. Collegiate Schs. Arch., 1978-80; assoc. prof. urban design U. Wash., Seattle, 1981-87, prof. architecture, landscape architecture, urban design and planning, 1987—, dir. urban design program, 1987-93, assoc. dean acad. affairs Coll. Arch. and Urban Planning, 1992-95; dir. Cascadia Cmty. and Environ. Inst., Seattle, 1993-98. Lectr. architecture U. Calif., Berkeley, 1973-75; sr. rschr. Kungl Tekniska Hogskolan, Sch. Architecture, Stockholm, 1989; faculty assoc. Lincoln Inst. Land Policy, 1997—2005; mem. adv. com. Robert Wood Johnson Found., 2002—. Author: Built for Change, 1986; editor: Public Streets for Public Use, 1987, 91, (monograph) Master-Planned Communities, 1990, Urban Design: Reshaping Our Cities, 1995, Land Supply Monitoring with Geographic Information Systems, 2000; contbr. articles to profl. jours. Recipient Applied Rsch. award, Progressive Architecture, 1983; grantee Nat. Endowment for the Arts, 1976—89, Wash. State Dept. Transp., 1991—, CDC, 2001—04; fellow Nat. Endowment for the Arts, 1986—87, Urban Land Inst., 1999—2006; grant, NIH, 1995—2000, 2007—, Robert Wood Johnson Found., 2007—. Fellow: Inst. for Urban Design. Avocations: walking, gardening, skiing. Office: U Wash Box 355740 PO Box Jo-40 Goul Seattle WA 98195-5740 Home: 2125 First Ave #1006 Seattle WA 98121 Business E-Mail: moudon@uwashington.edu.

MOULD, JEREMY RICHARD, astronomer; b. Bristol, Eng., July 31, 1949; s. Michael Thomas and Sheila Patricia (Pickering Clarke) Mould; m. Joan Mary Milesi, Dec. 11, 1971; children: Helen, Kate. BSc with honors, U. Melbourne, Australia, 1971; PhD, Australian Nat. U., 1975. Rsch. fellow Royal Greenwich Obs., England, 1976; postdoctoral fellow Kitt Peak Nat. Obs., Tucson, 1976—78, asst. astronomer, 1980—82; Carnegie fellow Hale Obs., 1978—79; prof. Calif. Inst. Tech., Pasadena, 1982—93, exec. officer for astronomy, 1987—90; prof. Australian Nat. U., Canberra, 1993—2001; dir. Mt. Stromlo & Siding Obs., Weston, Australia, 1993—2001, Nat. Optical Astronomy Obs., Tucson, 2001—. Mem. Anglo Australian Telescope Bd., 1993—2001, chair, 1999; mem. Australia Telescope Steering Com., 1995—2000; mem. space sci. adv. com. NASA. Mem.: Australian Acad. Sci., Assn. Univ. Rsch. Astronomy (bd. dirs. 1997—2001), Astron. Soc. Pacific, Astron. Soc. Australia, Am. Astron. Soc. Office: NOAO Mail Stop DODP 950 N Cherry Ave Tucson AZ 85726-6732 Business E-Mail: jmould@noao.edu.

MOULDS, JOHN F., judge; m. Elizabeth Fry, Aug. 29, 1964; children: Donald B., Gerald B. Student, Stanford U., 1955-58; BA with honors, Calif. State U., Sacramento, 1960; JD, U. Calif, Berkeley, 1963. Bar: U.S. Supreme Ct., U.S. Dist. Ct. (no. dist.) Calif., U.S. Dist. Ct. (ea. dist.) Calif. 1968, U.S. Ct. Claims 1982, U.S. Ct. Appeals (9th cir.) 1967, Calif. Rsch. analyst Calif. State Senate Fact-Finding Com. on Edn., 1960-61; adminstrv. asst. Senator Albert S. Rodda, Calif., 1961-63; staff atty. Calif. Rural Legal Assistance, Marysville, 1966-68, dir. atty. Marysville field office and Sacramento legis. adv. office, 1968-69; staff atty. Sacramento Legal Aid, 1968-69; ptnr. Blackmon, Isenberg & Moulds, 1969-85, Isenberg, Moulds & Hemmer, 1985; magistrate judge U.S. Dist. Ct. (ea. dist.) Calif., 1985—, chief magistrate jdge, 1988-97. Moot ct. and trial practice judge U. Calif. Davis Law Sch., 1975—, U. of Pacific McGeorge Coll. Law, 1985—; part-time U.S. magistrate judge U.S. Dist. Ct. (ea. dist.) Calif., 1983-85; mem. 9th Cir. Capital Case Com., 1992—, U.S. Jud. Conf. Com. on the Magistrate Judge Sys., 1992—, Adv. Com. to the Magistrate Judges' Divsn. Adminstv. Office of U.S. Jud. Conf., 1989—. Author: (with others) Review of California Code Legislation, 1965, Welfare Recipients' Handbook, 1967; editor: Ninth Circuit Capital Punishment Handbook, 1991. Atty. Sacramento Singlemen's Self-Help Ctr., 1969-74; active Sacramento Human Relations Commn., 1969-75, chair, 1974-75; active community support orgn. U. Calif. at Davis Law Sch., 1971—; mem., atty. Sacramento Community Coalition for Media Change, 1972-75; bd. dirs. Sacramento Country Day Sch., 1982-90, Sacramento Pub. Libr. Found., 1985-87; active various polit. orgns. and campaigns, 1960-82. Mem. ABA, Fed. Bar Assn., Nat. Coun. Magistrates (cir. dir. 1986-88, treas. 1988-89, 2d v.p. 1989-90, 1st v.p. 1990-91), Fed. Magistrate Judges Assn. (pres.-elect 1991, pres. 1992-93), Calif. State-Fed. Jud. Coun. Conf. (panelist capital habeas corpus litigation 1992), Fed. Jud. Ctr. Training Conf. for U.S. Magistrate Judges (panel leader 1993), Milton L. Schwartz Inns of Ct. Office: 16-400 US Courthouse 501 I St 16th Fl Ste 1640 Sacramento CA 95814-7300

MOUNT, MINDY (MELINDA J. MOUNT), computer software company executive; BBA, U. Wis.-Madison; MBA, Harvard U. V.p. mergers and acquisitions Morgan Stanley & Co.; v.p. corp. strategy and devel. Time Warner; exec. v.p., co-mng. dir. AOL UK, London; joined Microsoft Corp, 2006, corp. v.p. Ops. and Fin. Group, CFO Entertainment and Devices Divsn. Redmond, Wash., 2006. Bd. dirs. U. Wis. Found.; advisor to students Applied Corp. Fin. Program, U. Wis.-Madison Sch. Bus. Avocations: golf, hiking, bicycling. Office: Microsoft Corp One Microsoft Way Redmond WA 98052-6399

MOUNTJOY, RICHARD, state legislator; b. LA; m. Earline Winnett; children: Michael, Dennis, Judy. Mayor, city councilman City of Monrovia, Calif., 1968-76; mem. Calif. Assembly, 1978-95, mem. assembly rules com., Rep. caucus chmn., 1982-84; mem. Calif. State Senate, Sacramento, 1995—, mem. appropriations com., vice chair energy, utilities and comm. com., vice chair indsl. rels. com., health and human svcs. com. With USN, Korea. Named Legislator of Yr., Calif. Wildlife Fedn., Calif. Rep. Assembly, San Gabriel Valley Units, Calif. Bus. Properties Assn., Calif. Rifle and Pistol Assn., Roofing Contractors Assn., Rep. Statesman of Yr., United Reps. Calif., Outstanding State Assemblyman, Young Ams. for Freedom. Mem. Commn. of the Californias, Associated Builders and Contractors Calif., Aircraft Owners and Pilots Assn. (Presdl. citation), Elks (hon. life, past exalted ruler), Monrovia Kiwanis Club, VFW (life). Republican. Avocations: fishing, hunting, flying. Office: State Capitol Rm 4052 Sacramento CA 95814 also: 500 N 1st Ave Ste 3 Arcadia CA 91006-7100

MOWE, GREGORY ROBERT, lawyer; b. Aberdeen, Wash., Feb. 23, 1946; s. Robert Eden and Jeannette Effie (Deyoung) M.; m. Rebecca Louise Nobles, June 14, 1969; children: Emily, Tom. BA, U. Oreg., 1968, MA, 1969; JD magna cum laude, Harvard Law Sch., 1974. Bar: Oreg. 1974, U.S. Dist. Ct. Oreg. 1974, U.S. Ct. Appeals (9th cir.) 1974. Assoc. atty. Stoel Rives Boley Jones & Grey, Portland, Oreg., 1974-79, ptnr., 1979—. Pres. bd. dirs. Planned Parenthood of Columbia/Willamette, Portland, 1989-90. 1st lt. U.S. Army, 1969-71, Vietnam. Mem. ABA, Phi Beta Kappa. Office: Stoel Rives Boley Jones & Grey 900 SW 5th Ave Ste 2300 Portland OR 97204-1229 Home Phone: 503-294-9458; Office Phone: 503-294-9458. Business E-Mail: grmowe@stoel.com.

MOXLEY, JOHN HOWARD, III, internist; b. Elizabeth, NJ, Jan. 10, 1935; s. John Howard Jr. and Cleopatra (Mundy) Moxley; m. Doris Banchik; children: John Howard IV, Brook, Mark. BA, Williams Coll., 1957; MD, U. Colo., 1961; DSc (hon.), Sch. Medicine Hannemann U. Diplomate Am. Bd. Internal Medicine. Intern Peter Bent Brigham Hosp., Boston, 1961—62, resident in internal medicine, 1962—66; with Nat. Cancer Inst., USPHS, 1963—65; asst. to dean, instr. medicine Harvard Med. Sch., Boston, 1966—69; dean Sch. Medicine, U. Md., 1969—73; vice chancellor health scis., dean Med. Sch., U. Calif.-San Diego, 1973—79; asst. sec. for health affairs Dept. Def., Washington, 1979—81; sr. v.p. Am. Med. Internat., Beverly Hills, Calif., 1981—87; pres. MetaMed. Inc., Playa Del Rey, Calif., 1987—89; mgr. dir. Korn/Ferry Internat., LA, 1989—. Cons. FDA, NIH; dir. Nat. Fund for Med. Edn., 1986—94, chmn., 1993—94; dir. Henry M. Jackson Found. for Adv. Mil. Medicine. Contbr. articles to profl. jours. Dir. Polyclinic Health Svcs. Games of XXIII Olympiad. Recipient Gold and Silver award, U. Colo. Med. Sch., 1974, commr.'s citation for outstanding svc. to over-the-counter drug study, FDA, 1977, spl. achievement citation, Am. Hosp. Assn., 1983, Sec. of Def. medal for disting. pub. svc., 1981. Fellow: ACP, Am. Coll. Physician Execs. (disting.); mem.: AMA (chmn. coun. sci. affairs 1985), Am. Hosp. Assn. (trustee 1979—81), Soc. Med. Adminstrs., Calif. Med. Assn. (chmn. sci. bd. 1978—83, councilor), Inst. Medicine NAS, San

Diego C. of C., Rotary, Alpha Omega Alpha. Office: Korn Ferry Internat 1900 Ave of the Stars Ste 2600 Los Angeles CA 90067-1512 Office Phone: 310-200-1296. E-mail: moxleyj@kornferry.com.

MOYA, PATRICK ROBERT, lawyer; b. Belen, N.Mex., Nov. 7, 1944; s. Adelicio E. and Eva (Sanchez) Moya; m. Sara Dreier, May 30, 1966; children: Jeremy Brill, Joshua Dreier. AB, Princeton U., 1966; JD, Stanford U., 1969. Bar: Calif. 1970, Ariz. 1970, DC 1970, U.S. Dist. Ct. (no. dist.) Calif. 1970, U.S. Ct. Claims 1970, U.S. Tax Ct. 1970, U.S. Ct. Appeals (DC cir.) 1970, U.S. Supreme Ct. 1973. Assoc. Lewis and Roca, Phoenix, 1969—73, ptnr., 1973—83; sr. ptnr. Moya, Bailey, Bowers & Jones, P.C., Phoenix, 1983—84; ptnr., mem. nat. exec. com. Gaston & Snow, Phoenix, 1985—91; ptnr. Quarles & Brady LLP, Phoenix, 1991—2003, mem. nat. exec. com., 2000—02, of counsel, 2005—; exec. v.p. Insight Enterprises, Inc., Tempe, Ariz., 2002—05, chief adminstrv. officer, 2003—05, sec., 2002—05, gen. counsel, 2002—05; sr. v.p., gen. counsel and sec. Apollo Group, Inc., Phoenix, 2007—. Instr. Sch. of Law, Ariz. State U., 1972; bd. dirs. Plusnet, plc, InPlay Techs., Inc. Mem. Paradise Valley Bd. Adjustment, 1976-80, chmn., 1978-80; mem. Paradise Valley Town Coun., 1980-82; bd. dirs. Phoenix Men's Arts Coun., 1973-81, pres., 1979-80; bd. dirs. The Silent Witness, Inc., 1979-84, pres., 1981-83; bd. dirs. Enterprise Network, Inc., 1989-94, pres., 1991-92; bd. dirs. Phoenix Little Theatre, 1973-75, Interfaith Counseling Svc., 1973-75; precinct committeeman Phoenix Rep. Com., 1975-77; dep. voter registrar Maricopa County, 1975-76; mem. exec. bd. dirs. Gov.'s Strategic Partnership for Econ. Devel.; pres. GSPED, Inc.; mem. of Steering Com. for Sonora-Ariz. Joint Econ. Plan; mem. Gov.'s Adv. Com., Ariz. and Mex., Ariz. Corp. Commn. Stock Exch. Adv. Coun., Ariz. Town Hall. Mem. ABA, Nat. Hispanic Bar Assn., Los Abogados Hispanic Lawyers Assn., Nat. Assn. Bond Lawyers, Ariz. Bar Assn., Maricopa County Bar Assn., Paradise Valley Country Club, Univ. Club. Office Phone: 602-230-5580.

MOYE, JOHN EDWARD, lawyer; b. Deadwood, SD, Aug. 15, 1944; s. Francis Joseph and Margaret C. (Roberts) M.; children: Kelly M., Mary S., Megan J. BBA, U. Notre Dame, 1965; JD with distinction, Cornell U., 1968; LLD, U. Denver, 1999. Bar: N.Y. 1968, Colo. 1971. Prof. law U. Denver, 1972-78, assoc. dean Coll. Law, 1974-78; prof. law So. Meth. U., Dallas, 1973; ptnr. Moye White, LLP and predecessor firms, Denver, 1976—. Lectr. Harcourt Brace Jovanovich, Chgo., 1972-95, Profl. Edn. Group, Minnetonka, Minn., 1982-95, West Profl. Tng. Program, 1995-98; chmn. Bd. Law Examiners, Denver, 1988-92. Chmn. Denver Urban Renewal Authority, 1988-93, Colo. Hist. Found., Denver, 1987—; pres. Downtown Denver, Inc., 1986-88; mem. Consumer Credit Commn., 1985-99; chmn. Stapleton Devel. Corp., 1995—; bd. dirs. Denver Bot. Gardens, 1996-2003, Colo. Pub. Radio, 1998-99. Named Prof. of Yr., U. Denver, 1972-74, 76-78, Outstanding Faculty Mem., 1997. Fellow Am. Bar Found.; mem. ABA, Colo. Bar Assn. (chmn. corp., banking and bus. sect. 1982-84, pres. 2002-03, Young Lawyer of Yr. award 1980, Merit award 2005), N.Y. State Bar Assn., Denver Bar Assn. (Young Lawyer of Yr. award 1980), Law Club (pres. 1982-84). Republican. Roman Catholic. Office: 1400 16th St Ste 600 Denver CO 80202-1486

MOYER, ALAN DEAN, retired newspaper editor; b. Galva, Iowa, Sept. 4, 1928; s. Clifford Lee and Harriet (Jacques) M.; m. Patricia Helen Krecker, July 15, 1950; children: Virginia, Stanley, Glenn. BS in Journalism, U. Iowa, 1950. Reporter, copy editor Wis. State Jour., Madison, 1950-53; reporter, photographer Bartlesville (Okla.) Examiner-Enterprise, 1953; telegraph editor Abilene (Tex.) Reporter-News, 1954-55; makeup editor Cleve. Plain Dealer, 1955-63; mng. editor Wichita (Kans.) Eagle, 1963-70; exec. editor Wichita Eagle and Beacon, 1970-73; mng. editor Phoenix Gazette, 1973-82, Ariz. Republic, 1982-89; ret., 1989. Pres., dir. Wichita Profl. Baseball, Inc., 1969-75; mem. jury Pulitzer Prizes, 1973-74, 85, 86, 88. Mem. AP Mng. Editors Assn. (dir. 1973-78), Am. Soc. Newspaper Editors, Wichita Area C. of C. (dir. 1970-72), Sigma Delta Chi. Office: Phoenix Newspapers Inc 200 E Van Buren St Phoenix AZ 85004-2238 Personal E-mail: moyeralan@cox.net.

MOYES, JERRY C., transportation executive, professional sports team executive; b. Plain City, Utah; m. Vickie Moyes; 10 children. Grad., Weber State Coll. Co-founder Swift Transp. Co., Inc., 1966—, v.p., 1966—84, chmn., pres., CEO Phoenix, 1984—2005, 2007—; owner SME Steel. Limited ptnr. Ariz. Diamondbacks, Phoenix Suns; co-owner Phoenix Coyotes, 2001—. Mem.: Am. Trucking Assn. (v.p.), Ariz. Motor Transportation Assn. (pres. 1987—88). Office: Swift Transp Co 2200 S 75th Ave Phoenix AZ 85043-7410 also: PO Box 29243 Phoenix AZ 85038-9243 Fax: 623-907-7380.

MOYLE, PETER BRIGGS, marine biologist, educator; b. May 29, 1942; s. John Briggs and Evelyn (Wood) M.; m. Marilyn Arneson, June 11, 1966; children: Petrea Ruth, John Noah. BA, U. Minn., 1964, PhD, 1969; MS, Cornell U., 1966. Asst. prof. Calif. State U., Fresno, 1969-72; from asst. prof. to prof. U. Calif., Davis, 1972—, chmn. dept. wildlife and fisheries, 1982-87, Pres.'s chair in undergrad. edn., 2003—06. Head, Delta Native Fishes Recovery Team, 1993-95. Author: Inland Fishes of California, 1976, 2d edit., 2002, Fishes: An Introduction to Ichthyology, 5th edit., 2003, Fish: An Enthusiast's Guide, 1993. Fellow Calif. Acad. Sci.; mem. Am. Fisheries Soc. (life, award of excellence West divsn. 1991, Outstanding Educator award 1995, award of excellence, 2007), Ecol. Soc. Am., Am. Soc. Ichthyologists and Herpetologists, Soc. Conservation Biology, Natural Heritage Inst. (v.p. 1994-2007). Home: 612 Eisenhower St Davis CA 95616-3031 Office: U Calif Dept Wildlife Fish & Conservation Biolog 1 Shields Ave Davis CA 95616 E-mail: pbmoyle@ucdavis.edu.

MOZENA, JOHN DANIEL, podiatrist; b. Salem, Oreg., June 9, 1956; s. Joseph Iner and Mary Teresa (Delaney) M.; m. Elizabeth Ann Hintz, June 2, 1979; children: Christine Hintz, Michelle Delaney. Student, U. Oreg., 1974-79; B in Basic Med. Scis., Calif. Coll. Podiatric Medicine, D in Podiatric Medicine, 1983. Diplomate Am. Bd. Podiatric Surgery. Resident in surg. podiatry Hillside Hosp., San Diego, 1983-84; pvt. practice podiatry Portland, Oreg., 1984—; dir. residency Med. Ctr. Hosp., Portland, 1985-91. Lectr. Nat. Podiatric Assn. Seminar, 1990, Am. Coll. Gen. Practitioners, 1991, Am. Coll. Family Physician, 1995; adj. faculty health profl. sect. Portland CC, 1999; legis. chmn. OPMA, 2002-. Cons. editor Podiatry Today Mag., 1999—, Podiatry Today, 1999—; contbr. articles to profl. jours.; patentee sports shoe cleat design, 1985. Podiatric adv. coun. Oreg. Bd. Med. Examiners, 1994-97. Named Clinician of the Yr., Eastmoreland Hosp., 2000-01. Fellow Am Coll. Ambulatory Foot Surgeons, Am. Coll. Foot Surgeons, Oregon Podiatric Med. Assn. (legis. chmn.) Republican. Roman Catholic. Avocations: softball, basketball, piano, electric bass guitar, running, ironman traithlon. Office: Town Ctr Foot Clinic 8305 SE Monterey Ave Ste 101 Portland OR 97086-7728 Office Phone: 503-652-1121.

MOZILO, ANGELO R., retired mortgage company executive; b. NYC, 1938; m. Phyllis Mozilo; 5 children. BS, Fordham U., 1960; LLD (hon.), Pepperdine U. Co-founder, vice chmn. Countrywide Fin. Corp., Calabasas, Calif., 1969—99, pres., 2000—03, CEO, 1998—99, chmn., CEO, 1999—2008. Bd. dirs. The Home Depot, Inc., 2006—07. Bd. mem. Nat. Housing Endowment, Joint Ctr. for Housing Studies, Harvard U., Homes for Working Families; trustee Gonzaga U. Recipient Boy Scouts of Am. James E. West Fellowship award, Ellis Island Medal of Honor, Albert Schweitzer award, Special Achiev. award, Nat. Italian Am. Found., Horatio Alger Assn. of Disting. Am. award, Lifetime Achievement award, Am. Banker mag, 2006; named one of The 30 Most Respected CEOs, Barron's mag., 2005; named to Nat. Assn. of Home Builders' Hall of Fame. Mem.: Mortgage Bankers Assn. of Am. (pres. 1991—92).

MUCHNIC, SUZANNE, art writer, educator, lecturer; b. Kearney, Nebr., May 16, 1940; d. Walter Marian Ely and Erva Nell Liston; m. Paul D. Muchnic, 1963. BA, Scripps Coll., 1962; MA, Claremont Grad. Sch., 1963. Art instr. Weber State Coll., Ogden, Utah, 1972—73; art history instr. LA City Coll., 1974—82; editor for So. Calif., Artweek, 1976—78; art writer LA Times, 1978—. Art criticism instr. Claremont Grad. Sch., 1984; LA corr. Arthews mag., 1990—2003. Author: (catalogues) Tim Nordin retrospective catalogue, 1982, Martha Alf retrospective catalogue, 1984, Mark Lere catalogue, 1986, (catalogue essay) Taiwan Mus. of Art, 1988, (art essay) The World Book Yr. Book, 1993—95, Odd Man In: Norton Simon and the Pursuit of Culture, 1998. Recipient Disting. Alumna award, Claremont Grad. Sch., 1982, Scripps Coll., 1987, 1st prize for Arts and Entertainment Reporting, Greater LA Press Club, 1993, Donald H. Pflueger History award, Hist. Soc. Southern Calif., 2002. Mem.: Internat. Assn. Art Critics, Coll. Art Assn. Office: LA Times 202 W 1st St Los Angeles CA 90012

MUDD, JOHN O., lawyer; b. 1943; BA, Cath. U., 1965, MA, 1966; JD, U. Mont., 1973; LLM, Columbia U., 1986; JSD of Law, 1994. Bar: Mont. 1973. Pntr. Mulroney, Delaney, Dalby & Mudd, Missoula, Mont., 1973-79; lectr. U. Mont., Missoula, 1973-74, 75-76, prof. law, dean, 1979-88; ptnr. Garlington, Lohn & Robinson, Missoula, 1988—99; sr. v.p. Providence Svcs., 2000—05, also bd. dir.; sr. v.p. Providence Health & Svcs., 2006—. Pres. Mid-Continent Assn. Law Schs., 1982—83; chmn. bd. dir. Ascension Health, 2004—. Editor: Mont. Law Rev., 1972—73. Chmn. Mont. Commn. Future of Higher Edn.; Dem. candidate U.S. Senate, 1994; bd. dir. St. Patrick Hosp., 1985—90. With US Army, 1967—73. Mem.: State Bar Mont., Am. Judicature Soc. (bd. dirs. 1985—89).

MUDGE, LEWIS SEYMOUR, theologian, educator, university dean; b. Phila., Oct. 22, 1929; s. Lewis Seymour and Anne Evelyn (Bolton) M.; m. Jean Bruce McClure, June 15, 1957; children: Robert Seymour, William McClure, Anne Evelyn. BA, Princeton U., 1951, M Div, 1955, PhD (Kent fellow), 1961; BA with honors in Theology, Oxford U., Eng., 1954, MA (Rhodes scholar), 1958. Ordained to ministry Presbyn. Ch., 1955. Presbyn. univ. pastor Princeton, 1955-56; sec. dept. theology World Alliance Ref. Chs., Geneva, 1957-62; minister to coll. Amherst Coll., 1962-68, asst. prof. philosophy and religion, 1962-64, assoc. prof., 1964-70, prof. philosophy and religion, 1970-76, chmn. dept. philosophy and religion, 1968-69, 75-76; dean faculty, prof. theology McCormick Theol. Sem., Chgo., 1976-87, San Francisco Theol. Sem., 1987—; prof. Grad. Theol. Union, Berkeley, Calif., 1987-95; dir. Ctr. for Hermeneutical Studies, Grad. Theol. Union/U. Calif., Berkeley, 1990-97; Stuart prof. theology Grad. Theol. Union, Berkeley, Calif., 1995—. Mem. commn. on faith and order Nat. Council Chs., 1965-70; sec. spl. com. on confession faith United Presbyn Ch., 1965-67, chmn. spl. com. on theology of the call, 1968-71; chmn. theol. commn. U.S. Consultation on Ch. Union, 1977-89; co-chmn. Internat. Ref.-Roman Cath. Dialogue Commn., 1983-90; observer Extraordinary Synod Bishops, 1985. Author: One Church: Catholic and Reformed, 1963, Is God Alive?, 1963, Why is the Church in the World?, 1967, The Crumbling Walls, 1970, The Sense of a People: Toward a Church for the Human Future, 1992, The Church as Moral Community, 1998, Rethinking the Beloved Community, 2001; also numerous articles and revs.; editor: Essays on Biblical Interpretation (Paul Ricoeur), 1980, (with James Poling) Formation and Reflection: the Promise of Practical Theology, 1987, (with Thomas Wieser) Democratic Contracts for Sustainable and Caring Societies, 2000 Pres. Westminster Found. in New Eng., 1963-67; chmn. bd. Nat. Vocation Agy., 1972-75; mem. com. selection Rhodes Scholars, Vt., 1966, Wis., 1983-85, Iowa, 1986; mem. adv. com. social witness policy Presbyn. Ch., U.S.A., 2005— Mem. Phi Beta Kappa. Democrat. Home: 2444 Hillside Ave Berkeley CA 94704-2529 Office: Grad Theol Union 2905 Dwight Way Berkeley CA 94704-2514 Office Phone: 510-845-5958. E-mail: lewismudge@aol.com.

MUELLER, EDWARD A., telecommunications industry executive; b. St. Louis, Mo. BCE, U. Mo.; MBA, Wash. U. Pres., CEO Southwestern Bell Telephone, Pacific Bell, 1997—99; pres. SBC Internat. Ops., 1999—2000; pres., CEO SBC Ameritech, San Antonio, 2000—02; CEO Williams-Sonoma, Inc., 2003—06; chmn. VeriSign, Inc., 2007—; chmn., CEO Qwest Communications Internat. Inc., Denver, 2007—. Chmn. Nat. Security Telecommunications Advisory Com., 2008—; bd. dirs. VeriSign, Inc., 2005—, Clorox Co., McKesson Corp., 2008—. Office: Qwest Communications International Inc 1801 California St Denver CO 80202

MUETH, JOSEPH EDWARD, lawyer; b. St. Louis, Aug. 8, 1935; s. Joseph and Marie Clare (Reher) M.; m. Ellen Agnes O'Heron, Dec. 24, 1973; children: Erin R., Patricia A. B.Chem. Engring., U. Dayton, 1957; LL.B., Georgetown U., 1960, LL.M., 1961. Bar: Calif. 1964. Practice law, LA; ptnr. Wills, Green & Mueth, LA, 1974-83; pvt. practice law Calif., 1983-94; of counsel Sheldon & Mak, Pasadena, Calif., 1994—. Adj. prof. law U. Calif. Hastings Coll. Law, San Francisco, 1972-75; lectr. Claremont Grad. Sch., 1982—. Author: Copyrights Patents and Trademarks, 1974. Chmn. bd. Rio Hondo council Camp Fire Girls Inc., 1967-72. Mem. AAAS, Am., Los Angeles County bar assns., State Bar Calif., N.Y. Acad. Scis., L.A. Athletic Club. Home: PO Box 3369 1217 Seal Way Seal Beach CA 90740-6419 Office: 100 E Corson St Pasadena CA 91103

MUGGERIDGE, DEREK BRIAN, engineering executive, consultant; b. Godalming, Surrey, U.K., Oct. 10, 1943; arrived in Can., 1956; s. Donald William and Vera Elvina (Jackson) M.; m. Hanny Meta Buurman, Dec. 4, 1965; children: Karen Julie, Michael Brent. BS in Aero. Engring., Calif. State Polytech. U., 1965; MASc in Aerospace Engring., U. Toronto, 1966, PhD in Aerospace Engring., 1970. Grad. fellow U. Toronto, 1965—66, NRC, Canada, 1967—70, indsl. post-doctoral fellow, 1971—72, Fleet Mfg. Co., Fort Erie, Ont., 1970-72; spl. lectr. U. Toronto, Ont., Canada, 1971; from asst. prof. to prof. Meml. U. of Nfld., St. John's, 1972-93, univ. rsch. prof., 1990-93; dir. Ocean Engring. Rsch. Ctr., 1982-93; dean Okanagan U. Coll., Kelowna, B.C., Canada, 1993—2003, assoc. v.p. rsch., 1998—2003; pvt. practice Lake County, B.C., Canada, 2003—. Pres. Offshore Design Assocs. Ltd., St. John's, Nfld., 1980—; sec., ptnr. Nfld. Ocean Cons., St. John's, 1981-93; ptnr. LNF Joint Venture Ltd., St. John's, 1984-90; vis. prof. Norwegian Inst. Tech., Trondheim, Norway, 1976, NRC, Ottawa, Can., 1976, U. Victoria, B.C., 1988-89. Co-author: Ice Interaction with Offshore Structures, 1988; contbr. articles to profl. jours.; contbr. conf. articles, reports. Mem. Assn. Profl. Engrs. and Geoscientists of Province of B.C. Marine and Naval. Avocations: windsurfing, sailing, rock collecting. Home and Office: 16438 Carr's Landing Rd Lake Country BC Canada V4V 1C3 Office Phone: 250-766-1023. Business E-Mail: dmuggeridge@shaw.ca.

MUGLIA, BOB (ROBERT L. MUGLIA), computer software company executive; BS in Computer Sci., U. Mich., 1981. Devel. mgr. ROLM Co.; with Microsoft Corp., Redmond, Wash., 1988—, v.p. enterprise storage svcs. group, 2001—03, sr. v.p. server and tools bus. Platforms & Svcs. Divsn., 2003—. Mem. Sr. Leadership Team, Bus. Leadship Team, Microsoft. Office: Microsoft One Microsoft Way Redmond WA 98052-6399

MUHLBACH, ROBERT ARTHUR, lawyer; b. LA, Apr. 13, 1946; s. Richard and Jeanette (Marcus) M.; m. Kerry Eldene Mahoney, July 26, 1986. BSME, U. Calif., Berkeley, 1967; JD, U. Calif., San Francisco, 1976; MME, Calif. State U., 1969; M in Pub. Adminstrn., U. So. Calif., 1978. Bar: Calif. 1976. Pub. defender County of Los Angeles, 1977-79; assoc. Kirtland & Packard LLP, Los Angeles, 1979—85, ptnr., 1986—2001, sr. ptnr., 2001—. Chmn. Santa Monica Airport Commn., Calif., 1984-87, chmn., bd. dirs. Hawthorne Airport Cmty. Assn. Inc. Served to capt. USAF, 1969-73. Mem. AIAA, Internat. Assn. Def. Counsel, Am. Bd. Trial Advs. Office: Kirtland & Packard LLP 2361 Rosecrans Ave 4th Fl El Segundo CA 90245 Office Phone: 310-536-1000. Business E-Mail: ram@kirtland-packard.com.

MUHLESTEIN, ROBERT M., state senator; b. Price, Utah, Oct. 10, 1965; m. Amy L. Muhlestein; 3 children. BA in Am. Studies with honors, Brigham Young U., 1990, MA in Internat. and Area Studies, 1991. With State of Utah Dept. Human Svcs., 1991-96; mem. Utah State Senate, 1996—, chair human svcs. com., mem. health and environment com., co-chair health and human svcs. appropriations. Republican. Home: 5626 W 11450 S Payson UT 84651-3627

MUIR, WILLIAM KER, JR., political science professor; b. Detroit, Oct. 30, 1931; s. William Ker and Florence Taylor (Bodman) M.; m. Paulette Irene Wauters, Jan. 16, 1960; children: Kerry Macaire, Harriet Bodman. BA, Yale U., 1954, PhD, 1965; JD, U. Mich., 1958. Bar: N.Y. 1960, Conn. 1965. Instr. U. Mich. Law Sch., 1958-59; assoc. firm Davis Polk & Wardwell, NYC, 1959-60; lectr. in polit. sci. Yale U., 1960-64, 65-67; from assoc. to ptnr. Tyler Cooper Grant Bowerman & Keefe, New Haven, 1964-68; prof. emeritus polit. sci. U. Calif., Berkeley, 1968-98, dept. chmn., 1980-83; speechwriter v.p. U.S., 1983-85; columnist Oakland (Calif.) Tribune, 1992-93; writer Gov. of Calif., Sacramento, 1994. Sr. cons. Calif. State Assembly, Sacramento, 1975-76; cons. Oakland Police Dept., 1969-74; vis. prof. polit. sci. Harvard U., summers 1976, 79; vis. prof. Hawaii Pacific U., 2000, U. Ariz., 2002. Author: Prayer in the Public School, 1967, later republished as Law and Attitude Change, 1974, Police: Streetcorner Politicians, 1977, Legislature: California's School for Politics, 1982, The Bully Pulpit: The Presidential Leadership of Ronald Reagan, 1993, Memoirs, 2003. Mem. Berkeley Police Rev. Commn., 1981-83; chmn. New Haven Civil Liberties Coun., 1965-68; Rep. candidate Calif. State Assembly, 1996. Recipient Hadley B. Cantril Meml. award, 1979, Disting. Tchg. award U. Calif., Berkeley, 1974, Phi Beta Kappa No. Calif. Assoc. Excellence in Tchg. award, 1994. Mem. Am. Polit. Sci. Assn. (Edward S. Corwin award 1966). Republican. Presbyterian. Office: U Calif Dept Polit Sci Berkeley CA 94720-1950 Personal E-mail: sandymuir@aol.com.

MUIRHEAD, BRIAN K., aerospace engineer; BSME, U. N.Mex.; MSAE, Calif. Inst. Tech. Scientist Jet Propulsion Lab., Pasadena, Calif., 1978—, builder flight hardware Galileo spacecraft, mgr. Advanced Spacecraft Devel. Group, leader SIr-C Antenna Mech. sys., leader MSTI I mech. subsys., leader Mars Pathfinder flight sys., 1992-97, project mgr. Mars Pathfinder, mgr. Deep Space 4/Champollion project. Office: Jet Propulsion Lab 4800 Oak Grove Dr Pasadena CA 91109-8001

MUKHERJEE, AMIYA K., metallurgy and materials science educator; PhD, Oxford U., Eng., 1962. Prof. U. Calif., Davis. Recipient Alexander von Humboldt award Fed. Republic Germany, 1988, Albert Easton White Disting. Tchr. award Am. Soc. Materials, 1992, Pfeil medal and prize Inst. Materials, 1993, U. Calif. prize and citation, 1993, Anatoly Bochvar medal U. Moscow, 1996, Inst. medal Max Planck Inst. for Metallforschung, 1997. Office: U Calif Davis Dept Chem Engring & Material Sci Davis CA 95616 E-mail: akmukherjee@ucdavis.edu.

MULCAHY, BENJAMIN R., lawyer; BA magna cum laude, St. John's U., 1991; JD cum laude, U. Minn., 1994. Law clk. to Justice Paul Anderson Minn. Supreme Ct., 1994—95; spl. asst. city atty. LA; ptnr. Shappard, Mullin, Richter, & Hampton. Spkr. in field. Contbr. articles to profl. jours. Named one of Top 40 Lawyers Under 40, Nat. Law Jour., 2005. Mem.: ABA, State Bar Calif., Minn. State Bar Assn., Beverly Hills Bar Assn. Office: Sheppard Mullin Richter & Hampton Century City 1901 Avenue of the Americas Los Angeles CA 90067 also: 30 Rockefellar Plz 24th Fl New York NY 10112 Office Phone: 310-228-3738, 212-332-3800. Office Fax: 310-228-3940, 212-332-3888. E-mail: bmulcahy@sheppardmullin.com.

MULFORD, RAND PERRY, health products executive, consultant; b. Denver, Sept. 30, 1943; s. Roger Wayne and Ann Louise (Perry) M.; 1 child, Conrad Perry; m. Paula Marie Skelley, 1987. BS in Basic Engring., Princeton U., 1965; MBA, Harvard U., 1972. Mgmt. cons. McKinsey & Co. Inc., Chgo., 1972-80; v.p. planning and control splty. chem. group Occidental Chem. Co., Houston, 1980-82; pres. Technivest Inc., Houston, 1982-85; exec. dir. corp. planning Merck & Co., Inc., Rahway, N.J., 1985-88; v.p. fin. Advanced Tissue Scis., Inc., La Jolla, Calif., 1989-90; CEO Chiron Mimotopes Peptide Systems, San Diego, Calif., 1991-94; COO Xytronyx, Inc., San Diego, 1994-95;

chmn. of bd. Medication Delivery Devices, San Diego, 1991-95; CEO World Blood, Inc., 1997-99; mng. dir. bus strategy Spencer Trask, Inc. Bd. dirs. ZymeTx, Inc., Oklahoma City, Diamonex Inc., Allentown, Pa. Lt. USN, 1965-70. Home: 13252 Caminito Pointe Del Mar Del Mar CA 92014-3857

MULLARKEY, MARY J., state supreme court chief justice; b. New London, Wis., Sept. 28, 1943; d. John Clifford and Isabelle A. (Steffes) M.; m. Thomas E. Korson, July 24, 1971; 1 child, Andrew Steffes Korson. BA, St. Norbert Coll., 1965, LLD (hon.), 1989; LLB, Harvard U., 1968. Bar: Wis. 1968, Colo. 1974. Atty.-advisor U.S. Dept. Interior, Washington, 1968-73; asst. regional atty. EEOC, Denver, 1973-75; 1st atty. gen. Colo. Dept. Law, Denver, 1975-79, solicitor gen., 1979-82; legal advisor to Gov. Lamm State of Colo., Denver, 1982-85; ptnr. Mullarkey & Seymour, Denver, 1985-87; justice Colo. Supreme Ct., Denver, 1987—, chief justice, 1998—. Fellow: Colo. Bar Found., ABA Found.; mem.: ABA, Denver Bar Assn. (Jud. Excellence award 2003), Colo. Women's Bar Assn. (Mary Lathrop award 2002), Colo. Bar Assn., Thompson G. Marsh Inn of Ct. (pres. 1993—94). Office: Supreme Ct Colo Jud Bldg 2 E 14th Ave Denver CO 80203-2115

MULLARKEY, MAUREEN T., former game company executive; b. 1959; m. Steve Miller. BS in Geology, U. Tex., 1980; MBA, U. Nev., 1988. With Internat. Game Tech., Reno, 1989—99, v.p. fin., CFO, treas., 1999—2000, sr. v.p., CFO, treas., 2001—03, exec. v.p., CFO, treas., 2003—07; CFO Zoho Corp., 2000—01. Bd. dirs. Sierra Pacific Resources, 2008—. Chair Nev. Mus. Art; bd. mem. Desert Rsch. Inst.; mem. advisory bd. Community Found. We. Nev. Recipient Alumni Assn. Profl. Achievement award, U. Nev. Reno, 2007; named a Great Woman of Gaming, 2005.

MULLEN, JOHN H., lawyer; b. Middletown, NY, Apr. 16, 1942; BA cum laude, St. Johns U.; LLB, Columbia U.; LLM in Tax., N.Y. U. Bar: N.Y., 1968, Calif., 1997. Lawyer; with Northrop Grumman, 1975—, dep. gen. counsel, 1994-95, sr. corp. counsel, 1995-98, acting sect., 1998-99, corp. v.p., sect., 1999—. Office: Northrop Grumman Corp 1840 Century Park E Los Angeles CA 90067-2101

MULLEN, WILLIAM JOSEPH, III, retired career army officer; b. Plattsburg, NY, Dec. 26, 1937; s. William Joseph Jr. and Georgia (Cook) M.; m. Norma Sturgeon, Aug. 6, 1962; 1 child, William Joseph IV. BS, U.S. Mil. Acad., West Point, NY, 1959; MS in Internat. Affairs, George Washington U., Washington, 1971. Commd. 2d lt. U.S. Army, 1959, advanced through grades to brig. gen., 1987; various assignments in U.S., Vietnam, Korea, Panama, Germany, Saudi Arabia, 1959-92; mem. staff, faculty U.S. Mil. Acad., West Point, 1967-70; comdr. 1st Brigade, 1st Inf. Div., Ft. Riley, Kans., 1983-86; asst. div. comdr. 5th Inf. Div., Ft. Polk, La., 1986-87; comdg. gen. U.S. Army Combined Arms Tng. Activity, Ft. Leavenworth, Kans., 1987-89, 1st Inf. Div. (Forward), Germany, 1989-91; dep. dir. ops. J3 Forces Command, Ft. McPherson, Ga., 1991-92; sr. mgr. mil. tng. and analysis sys. BDM Fed., Inc., Monterey, Calif., 1992-98; sr. program mgr. tng. mgmt. sys. Northrop Grumman Mission Sys., Monterey, 1998—2004; ret., 2004; cons. Army Operations and Tng., 2004—08. Co-author: Changing an Army, An Oral History of Gen. W.E. DePuy, 1979; contbr. articles, book revs. to Mil. Rev. Decorated D.S.C., D.S.M. Mem. Assn. U.S. Army, Assn. Grads. U.S. Mil. Acad. (bd. dir. West Point Soc. of Monterey Peninsula 2005-08), Soc. 1st Div. (chpt. officer 1968, assoc. 1989-93, trustee found. 1989-93, bd. dir.), Legion of Valor (bd. dir. 2005-08), Nat. Infantry Assn. (Order of St. Maurice). Avocations: sports, reading.

MÜLLER, HANS-GEORG, statistician; b. Stuttgart, Germany; s. Siegfried Otto Paul and Frida (Mantel) M. MD, U. Heidelberg, 1982; PhD, U. Ulm, 1983. Asst. prof. U. Marburg, Germany, 1984-87; assoc. prof. U. Erlangen, Germany, 1987-88; from assoc. prof. to prof. U. Calif., Davis, 1988—. Author: Nonparametric Regression Analysis, 1988; co-editor: Change-Point Problems, 1993. Fellow AAAS, Inst. Math. Statistics, Am. Statis. Assn.; mem. Internat. Statis. Inst., World Innovation Found. Office: U Calif Dept Statistics Davis CA 95616

MULLER, RICHARD STEPHEN, electrical engineer, educator; b. Weehawken, NJ, May 5, 1933; s. Irving Ernest and Marie Victoria Muller; m. Joyce E. Regal, June 29, 1957; children: Paul Stephen, Thomas Richard. ME, Stevens Inst. Tech., Hoboken, NJ, 1955; MSEE, Calif. Inst. Tech., Pasadena, 1957, PhD in Elec. Engring. and Physics, 1962. Test engr. Wright Aero/Curtiss Wright, Woodridge, NJ, 1953-54; mem. tech. staff Hughes Aircraft Co., Culver City, Calif., 1955-61; instr. U. So. Calif., LA, 1960-61; asst. prof., then assoc. prof. U. Calif., Berkeley, 1962-72, prof., 1973—. Guest prof. Swiss Fed. Inst. Tech., 1993; founder, dir. Berkeley Sensor & Actuator Ctr., 1985—; chmn. sensors electron devices NRC Army Rsch. Lab., 2003-04, chmn. microtech. adv. com. Helmholtz Assn., Germany, 2003—; chmn. steering com. Internat. Sensor and Actuator Meeting. Co-author: Device Electronics for Integrated Circuits, 1977, 3d, rev. edit., 2002, Microsensors, 1990; editor-in-chief IEEE/ASME Jour. Microelectromech. Sys., 1998—; contbr. over 200 articles to profl. jours. Pres. Kensington Mcpl. Adv. Coun., Calif., 1992-98; trustee Stevens Inst. Tech., 1996-2005. Fellow NSF Grad. Res., 1959-62, NATO postdoctoral fellow, 1968-69, Fulbright fellow, 1982-83, Alexander von Humboldt Rsch. Prof., 1993, Tech. U. Berlin, 1994; Berkeley citation, 1994, Stevens Renaissance award, 1995, Career Achievement award Internat. Conf. on Sensors and Actuators, 1997. Fellow IEEE (life, Cledo Brunetti award 1998, Millennium prize 2000); mem. IEEE Press Bd., NAE, NRC (chmn. sensors adv. bd. U.S. Army Rsch. Lab. 2003-04, liaison between NAE and NRC 2003—), Nat. Acad. Engring., Nat. Materials (adv. bd. 1994-98), Electron Devices Soc. (adv. com. 1984-98, Disting. Svc. award 2007). Achievements include 22 patents in field; development of world's first operating micromotor and introduction of silicon surface micromachining. Office: U Calif Dept EECS # 1770 401 Cory Hall Berkeley CA 94720-1770 Office Phone: 510-642-0614. Business E-Mail: r.muller@ieee.org.

MULLIGAN, DAVID COBOURN, medical educator; b. Louisville, Mar. 30, 1959; s. Robert Cobourn and Marguerite Stevens Mulligan; m. Pamela Christine Argue, Apr. 2, 1999; children: Madeline Rose, Benjamin Cobourn, Grace Anne. BA in Chemistry and Biology, Bellarmine Coll., 1981; MD, U. Louisville, 1986. Diplomate Nat. Bd. Med. Examiners, 1987, lic. in multi-organ transplant surgery Am. Soc. Transplant Surgeons, 1995, diplomate Am. Bd. Surgery, 2003. Internship in gen. surgery U. Louisville, 1986—87, residency in gen. surgery, 1987—88, residency in urol. surgery, 1988—91; residency in gen. surgery Case We. Reserve U., 1991—93, asst. prof. surgery Cleve., 1995—2008; fellowship in multi-organ transplantation Baylor U. Med. Ctr., 1993—95; prof. surgery Mayo Clinic Med. Sch., Phoenix, 2006—. Chair transplant, hepatobiliary and pancreatic surgery Mayo Clinic Ariz., Phoenix, 1998—; surg. dir., divsn. transplant surgery, dept. surgeryA Mayo Clinic, Scottsdale. Region 5 councilor United Network Organ Sharing, Richmond, Va., 2005—08; bd. dirs. Donor Network Ariz., Phoenix, 1999—2008. Named Outstanding Clinician for Mayo Clinic, Mayo Clinic Ariz., 2006. Fellow: ACS (licentiate). Avocations: running, swimming, rock climbing, travel. Office: Mayo Clinic Hosp 5777 E Mayo Blvd Phoenix AZ 85054 Office Fax: 480-342-2324. Business E-Mail: mulligan.david@mayo.edu.

MULLIGAN, MICHAEL K., headmaster; m. Joy Mulligan; 1 child. BA, Middlebury Coll.; EdM, Harvard U.; MA in English, Middlebury Coll. History and English teacher & soccer, lacrosse, and wrestling coach Gov. Dummer Acad., 1977—82, dir., coll. placement, 1982—86; dean of administration, teacher, and coach The Thacher Sch., Ojai, Calif., 1986—93, head of sch., 1993—. Mem.: Assn. of Boarding Schools. Office: Thacher Sch 5025 Thacher Rd Ojai CA 93023 E-mail: mmulligan@thacher.org.

MULLIN, CHRISTOPHER PAUL, professional sports team executive, retired professional basketball player; b. NYC, July 30, 1963; m. Liz Mullin; children: Sean, Christopher, Liam. Student, St. John's U., 1981—85. Player Golden State Warriors, 1985—97, 2000—01, Ind. Pacers, 1997—2000; exec. v.p. basketball ops. Golden State Warriors, 2004—, gen. mgr., 2007—. Mem. US Men's Olympic Basketball Team, LA, 1984, Barcelona, 92. Recipient Olympic Gold medal, 1984, 1992, Wooden award, 1985; named to Sporting News All-Am. First Team, 1985, NBA All-Star Team, 1989-93, All-NBA First Team, 1992. Office: Golden State Warriors 1011 Broadway Oakland CA 94607

MULLIN, HADLEY (MARY HADLEY MULLIN), private equity firm executive; b. 1974; BA in Govt., Dartmouth Coll., Hanover, NH, 1996; MBA, Stanford U. Grad. Sch. Bus., Calif., 2002. Various positions in consumer products, retail and healthcare Bain & Co.; joined TSG Consumer Ptnrs. (formerly Shansby Group), San Francisco, 2004, ptnr., mng. dir., 2006—. Bd. dirs. Radio Sys. Corp., 2006—. Named an Arjay Miller Scholar, Stanford U. Grad. Sch. Bus., 2002. Office: TSG Consumer Ptnrs 600 Montgomery St Ste 2900 San Francisco CA 94111 Office Phone: 415-217-2336. Business E-Mail: hmullin@tsgconsumer.com.*

MULLIN, STAN, real estate company executive; BS, U. Southern Calif., 1980. Cert. Comml. Investment Member, 1988. Joined Grubb & Ellis, 1982—, sr. v.p. Named Broker of Yr., 1984, 1991, 1997, 1999, 2000, 2001. Mem.: Counselors of Real Estate, Soc. Industrial and Office Realtors (chpt. pres. 1997, chmn. rsch. and publications com. 2001, com. restructure task force 2001, chmn. comm. com. 2002, mem. bd. dirs. 2002, chmn. edn. com. 2003, leadership develop. com. 2003, v.p. 2004, pres.-elect 2005, Roy Seeley award 2002), Am. Industrial Real Estate Assn. (pres. 2006). Office Phone: 949-422-0864. Office Fax: 949-417-5750. E-mail: stan@stanmullin.com.

MULLINEAUX, DONAL RAY, geologist; b. Weed, Calif., Feb. 16, 1925; s. Lester Ray and Mary Lorene (Drew) M.; m. Diana Suzanne Charais, Nov. 21, 1951; children: Peter, Lauren, Keith. Student, U. Wash., 1942, BS in Math., 1947, BS in Geology, 1949, MS in Geology, 1950, PhD in Geology, 1961. Drilling insp. U.S. Army C.E., 1948; geologist U.S. Geol. Survey, 1950-86; contracting geologist, 1987-90; scientist emeritus U.S. Geol. Survey, 1990—2005. Author articles on volcanic activity and hazards, Mt. St. Helens, other Cascade Range volcanoes, stratigraphy and engring. geology of Puget Sound Lowland, Wash. With USNR, 1943-54, active duty, 1943-46, 51-53. Rsch. fellow Engring. Expt. Sta. U. Wash., 1949-50. Fellow Geol. Soc. Am. (E.B. Burwell Jr. award 1983); mem. Colo. Sci. Soc. Home: 14155 W 54th Ave Arvada CO 80002-1513 Home Phone: 303-278-7245. Personal E-mail: don@mullineaux.us.

MULLIS, KARY BANKS, biochemist; b. Lenoir, NC, Dec. 28, 1944; s. Cecil Banks Mullis and Bernice Alberta (Barker) Fredericks; m. Richards Mullis (div.); 1 child, Louise; m. Cynthia Mullis (div.); children: Christopher, Jeremy; m. Nancy Lier Cosgrove, 1998. BS in Chemistry, Ga. Inst. Tech, 1966; PhD in Biochemistry, U. Calif., Berkeley, 1973; DSc (hon.), U. S.C., 1994. Lectr. biochemistry U. Calif., Berkeley, 1972, postdoctoral fellow San Francisco, 1977—79, U. Kans. Med. Sch., Kansas City, 1973—76; scientist Cetus Corp., Emeryville, Calif., 1979—86; dir. molecular biology Xytronyx, Inc., San Diego, 1986—88; cons. Specialty Labs, Inc., Amersham, Inc., Chiron Inc. and various others, Calif., 1988—96; chmn. StarGene, Inc., San Rafael, Calif.; v.p. Histotec, Inc., Cedar Rapids, Iowa; v.p. molecular biology chemistry Vyrex Inc., La Jolla, Calif.; disting. rschr. Children's Hosp., Rsch. Inst., Oakland, Calif. Disting. vis. prof. U. S.C. Coll. of Sci. and Math. Author: (autobiography) Dancing Naked in the Mind Field, 1998; contbr. articles to profl. jours.; patentee in field. Bd. dir. Nat. Orgn. Reform of Marijuana Laws, 2000—. Recipient Preis Biochemische Analytik award, German Soc. Clin. Chem., 1990, Allan award, 1990, award, Gairdner Found. Internat., 1991, Nat. Biotech. award, 1991, Robert Koch award, 1992, Chiron Corp. Biotechnology Rsch. award, Am. Soc. Microbiology, 1992, Japan prize, Sci. and Tech. Found. Japan, 1993, Nobel Prize in Chemistry, Nobel Foundation, 1993; named Scientist of Yr., R&D Mag., 1991, Calif. Scientist of Yr., 1992; named to National Inventors Hall of Fame, 1998. Mem.: Inst. Further Study (dir. 1983—), Am. Acad. Achievement, Am. Chem. Soc. Achievements include invention of Polymerase Chain Reaction (PCR). Avocations: astrology, surfing.

MULRYAN, HENRY TRIST, mining executive, consultant; b. Palo Alto, Calif., Jan. 6, 1927; s. Henry and Marian Abigail (Trist) M.; m. Lenore Hoag, Aug. 25, 1948; children: James W., Carol. Student, Yale U., 1945-46; AB in Econs., Stanford U., 1948; postgrad., Am. Grad. Sch. Internat. Bus., 1949, Columbia U., 1983. V.p. mktg. Sierra Talc Co., South Pasadena, Calif., 1955-65, United Sierra, Trenton, NJ, 1965-67, v.p., gen. mgr., 1967-70, pres., 1970-77; v.p. Cyprus Mines Corp., Los Angeles, 1978-80; sr. v.p. ops. Cyprus indsl. minerals div. Amoco Minerals Co., Englewood, Colo., 1980-85; pres. Cyprus Indls. Minerals Co., Englewood, 1985-87; v.p. Cyprus Minerals Co., Englewood, 1985-87, sr. v.p. mktg., corp. adminstr., 1987-89; pres. Mineral Econs. Internat., 1989—. Vol. exec. Internat. Exec. Svc. Corps., Zimbabwe, 1998, Romania, 98, Jordan, 2000, Jordan, 01, Jordan, 02, Jordan, 04, Armenia, 03; dir. Jonathan Art Found., 1997—2005, pres., 2004—05. Served with U.S. Army, 1944-46. Mem.: Rotary (pres. South Pasadena club 1964—65, bd. dir. Princeton, N.J. club 1969—75), Jonathan Club. Office: 539 Muskingum Ave Pacific Palisades CA 90272-4252 E-mail: htmulryan@verizon.net.

MUMFORD, CHRISTOPHER GREENE, corporate financial executive; b. Washington, Oct. 21, 1945; s. Milton C. and Dorothea L. (Greene) Mumford. BA, Stanford U., 1968, MBA, 1975. Cons. Internat. Tech. Resources Inc., 1974; asst. v.p. Wells Fargo Bank, San Francisco, 1975-78; asst. treas. Arcata Corp., San Francisco, 1978-82, v.p. fin., 1982-87, exec. v.p. fin., 1987-94. Gen. ptnr. Scarff, Sears & Assocs., San Francisco, 1986—95; mng. dir. Questor Ptnrs. Fund, L.P., San Francisco, 1995—98; v.p. bd. dirs. Triangle Pacific Corp., Dallas, 1986—88, Norton Enterprises Inc., Salt Lake City, 1988—90, Crown Pacific Ptnrs., Portland, Oreg., 1991—2004, Ryder TRS, Inc., Miami, Fla., 1996—98, Ockham PLC, London, 1996—98, Impco Technologies, Inc., Cerritos, Calif., 1998—2000. Office: PO Box 1340 Mill Valley CA 94942-1340 Office Phone: 415-601-6800. Personal E-mail: cgmumford@aol.com.

MUMMERY, DANIEL R., lawyer; b. Miami, Fla., Mar. 4, 1959; s. Charles R. Mummery and Kathleen M. Osborne; m. Frances D. Nuelle, Oct. 11, 1997; children: Amanda F., William G., Alexander G. AB, Bowdoin Coll., 1977—81; JD, Fordham U. Sch. Law, 1985—88. Bar: Mass. 1989, NY 1989, Calif. 2002. Assoc. Milbank, Tweed, Hadley & McCloy, New York, NY, 1988—96, ptnr., 1996—2001, Cooley Godward LLP, Palo Alto, Calif., 2001—04, Latham & Watkins LLP, Menlo Park, Calif., 2004—. Editor-in-chief Fordham Urban Law Jour., 1987. Recipient Chambers and Ptnrs., 2000—05. Mem.: ABA (assoc.), NYC Bar. Assn. (assoc.). Avocations: tennis, wine, films. Office: Latham & Watkins LLP 140 Scott Dr Menlo Park CA 94025-1008 Office Fax: 650-463-2600. Business E-Mail: daniel.mummery@lw.com.

MUND, GERALDINE, judge; b. LA, July 7, 1943; d. Charles J. and Pearl M. BA, Brandeis U., 1965; MS, Smith Coll., 1967; JD, Loyola U., 1977; MA, Calif. State U., Northridge, 2007. Bar: Calif. 1977. Bankruptcy judge U.S. Ctrl. Dist. Calif., 1984—, bankruptcy chief judge, 1997—2002. Past pres. Temple Israel, Hollywood, Calif.; past mem. Bd. Jewish Fedn. Coun. of Greater L.A. Mem.: Nat. Confs. Bankruptcy Judges, Am. Coll. Bankruptcy. Office: 21041 Burbank Blvd Woodland Hills CA 91367-6606 Office Phone: 818-587-2840.

MUNDIE, CRAIG JAMES, computer software company executive; b. 1949; BEE, Ga. Inst. Tech., M in Info. Theory and Computer Sci. Software developer Data Gen. Corp., 1972; co-founder, CEO Alliant Computer Systems Corp., 1982—92; with Microsoft Corp., Redmond, Wash., 1992—, gen, mgr., advanced consumer tech., 1992—93, v.p., advanced consumer tech. group, 1993—96, sr. v.p., consumer platforms divsn., 1996—2001, sr. v.p. advanced strategies and policy, 2001—02, chief tech. officer, advanced strategies & policy, 2001—06, sr. v.p., advanced strategies & policy, 2001—06, chief rsch. & strategy officer, 2006—. Presdl. appointee Nat. Security Telecom. Adv. Com., 2000; mem. Coun. on Fgn. Rels., 2002—, Task Force on Nat. Security in the Info. Age, 2002—; trustee Fred Hutchinson Cancer Rsch. Ctr., Seattle; adv. bd. mem. Coll. of Computing Ga. Inst. Tech., Atlanta; mem. adv. bd., Live Labs (Rsch. partnership between MSN and Microsoft Rsch.) Microsoft Corp., 2006—. Office: Microsoft Corp One Microsoft Way Redmond WA 98052-6399

MUNECHIKA, KEN KENJI, research center administrator; b. Waimea, Kauai, Hawaii, June 18, 1935; s. Masako (Yasutake) Kitamura; m. Grace Shizue Wakayama, June 10, 1958; children: Curtis K., Stacy M., Kenny K. BS, U. Hawaii, 1958; MS, U. So. Calif., 1976, PhD, 1979. Commd. 2d lt. USAF, 1958, advanced through grades to col., 1980, ret., 1989; exec. dir. State of Hawaii, Honolulu, 1992-93; dir. Ames Rsch. Ctr. NASA, Mountain View, Calif., 1994-96, dir. Moffett Fed. Airfield Calif., 1996—. Mem. AIAA, Air Force Assn. Baptist. Avocations: golf, jogging, fishing. Office: 98 809 Kahaea Pl Aiea HI 96701-2771

MUNGER, CHARLES T., diversified company executive; b. Omaha, Nebr., 1924; m. Nancy Munger; 8 children. Student, U. of Mich., 1941—42, Calif. Inst. Technol., 1943; JD, Harvard Law Sch., 1948. Joined Musick Peeler & Garrett, Los Angeles, Calif.; co-founder Munger, Tolles & Olson, 1962—, ptnr., 1962—65, Wheeler Munger & Co., LA, 1962—75; chmn., CEO, Blue Chip Stamps, 1976—; vice chmn. Berkshire Hathaway, Inc., Omaha, 1978—, also chmn., CEO Wesco Fin. subs., 1983—. Chmn. Daily Jour. Corp.; bd. dirs. Costco, 1997—. Meteorological officer USAF, World War II. Named one of Forbes' Richest Americans, 2006. Office: Berkshire Hathaway Inc 1440 Kiewit Plz Omaha NE 68131-3302 also: Munger Tolles and Olson 355 S Grand Ave Los Angeles CA 90071-1560

MUNGER, EDWIN STANTON, political geography educator; b. LaGrange, Ill., Nov. 19, 1921; s. Royal Freeman and Mia (Stanton) M.; m. Ann Boyer, May 2, 1970; 1 child, Elizabeth Stanton Gibson. B.Sc., U. Chgo., 1948, M.Sc., 1949, PhD, 1951. Fulbright fellow Makerere U., 1949-50; research fellow U. Chgo.; field assoc. Am. Univs. Field Staff, 1950-60; faculty Calif. Inst. Tech., Pasadena, 1961—, prof. polit. geography, 1960—. Research fellow Stellenbosch U., 1955-56; vis. prof. U. Warsaw, 1973 Author books including Afrikaner and African Nationalsim, 1968, The Afrikaners, 1979, Touched by Africa: An Autobiography, 1983, Cultures, Chess and Art: A Collector's Odyssey Across Seven Continents, Vol. 1 Sub Saharan Africa, 1996, Vol. 2, Americas, 1997, Pacific Islands and the Asian Rim, Vol. 3, 1999, 10 short stories for kids--L.A. Times on Africa, 2001-02; editor books including Munger Africana Library Notes, 1969-82; contbr. chpts. to books and numerous articles to profl. jours. Evaluator Peace Corps, Uganda, 1966, Botswana, 1967; chmn. State Dept. Evalustion Team South Africa, 1971; trustee African-Am. Inst., 1956-62; acting pres. Pasadena Playhouse, 1966; chmn. bd. trustees Crane Rogers Found., 1979-82, fellow, 1950-54; mem. exec. com. NAACP, Pasadena, 1979—, nat. del., 1984, 85; trustee Leakey Found., 1968—, pres., 1971-84; pres. Cape of Good Hope Found., 1985—; pres. Internat. Vis. Coun., L.A., 1991-93, bd. dirs., 1979-93. Recipient Alumni Citation award for pub. svc. U. Chgo., 1993, Gandhi Martin Luther King-Ikeda award Morehouse U., 2002. Fellow South African Royal Soc., Royal Soc. Arts, African Studies Assn. (founding bd. dirs. 1963-66, Martin L. King Ikeda-Mahatma Gandhi award 2002); mem. PEN USA West (v.p.), Coun. Fgn. Rels., Cosmos Club, Athenaeum Club, Twilight Club, Chess Collectors Internat. (bd. dirs. 1998—). Office: Calif Inst Tech Divsn Humanities & Social Scis 1201 E California Blvd Pasadena CA 91125-0001 E-mail: munger@hss.caltech.edu.

MUNICH, MARIO ENRIQUE, research scientist, electronics executive; Elec. Technician, Instituto Politécnico Gen. San Martín, Rosario, Argentina, 1985; Elec. Engr., U. Nacional de Rosario, Argentina, 1991; Electronic Systems Design Specialist, U. Politécnica de Madrid, 1993; MS in Elec. Engring., Calif. Inst. Tech., 1994, PhD in Elec. Engring., 2000. Rsch. scientist VocalPoint Technologies, San Francisco, 2000—01; v.p. engring., prin. scientist Evolution Robotics, Pasadena, 2001—. Contbr. articles to profl. jours. Recipient J. Walker von Brimer award, 2000, Leadership and Acad. Accomplishments award, Jr. Chamber of Rosario, 1991;, Iberoam. Cooperation Inst. fellow, 1993. Mem.: ACM, IEEE. Achievements include patents for Apparatus and Method for Tracking Handwriting from Visual Input; Camera-Based Handwriting Tracking. Office: Evolution Robotics 130 W Union St Pasadena CA 91103 E-mail: mariomu@ieee.org.

MUNITZ, BARRY A., former foundation administrator; b. Bklyn., July 26, 1941; m. Anne Tomfohrde. BA, Bklyn. Coll., 1963; MA, Princeton U., 1965, PhD, 1968; cert., U. Leiden, Netherlands, 1962; doctorate (hon.), Claremont U., Calif. State Univ. Sys., Whittier Coll., U. Notre Dame. Asst. prof. lit. and drama U. Calif., Berkeley, 1966-68; staff assoc. Carnegie Commn. Higher Edn., 1968-70; acad. v.p. U. Ill. System, 1971—76; v.p., dean faculties Central Campus U. Houston, 1976-77, chancellor, 1977-82; pres., COO Federated Devel. Co., 1982-91; vice chmn. Maxxam Inc., LA, 1982-91; chancellor Calif. State U. System, Long Beach, Calif., 1991-98; prof. English lit. Calif. State U., LA, 1991—98; pres., CEO, trustee J.Paul Getty Trust, LA, 1998—2006; chmn. P-16 Edn. Council Calif. Dept. Edn., Sacramento, 2004—; trustee prof. Calif. State U., LA, 2006—. Bd. dirs. KCET-TV, SLM Holdings, KB Home; trustee Princeton U. Author: The Assessment of Institutional Leadership, also articles, monographs. Mem. art mus. vis. com. Princeton and Harvard; former chair bd. dirs. ACE; former co-chair trustees planning com. Gardner Mus.; former chair Calif. Gov. Transition Team. Recipient Disting. Alumnus award Bklyn. Coll., 1979, U. Houston Alumni Pres.'s medal, 1981; Woodrow Wilson fellow. Fellow Am. Acad. Arts and Scis.; mem. Phi Beta Kappa.

MUNK, WALTER HEINRICH, geophysics educator; b. Vienna, Oct. 19, 1917; arrived in U.S., 1933; m. Edith Kendall Horton, June 20, 1953; children: Edith, Kendall. BS, Calif. Inst. Tech., 1939, MS, 1940; PhD in Oceanography, U. Calif., 1947; PhD (hon.), U. Bergen, Norway, 1975; PhD (hon.), Cambridge U., Eng., 1986; PhD (hon.), U. Crete, 1996. Asst. prof. geophysics Scripps Inst. Oceanography, U. Calif., San Diego, 1947—54, prof., 1954—; dir. Inst. Geophysics and Planetary Physics, U. Calif., La Jolla, 1960—82; prof. geophysics, dir. heard island expt. Scripps Inst., U. Calif. Author (with MacDonald): The Rotation of the Earth: A Geophysical Discussion, 1960; author: (with Worcester and Wunsch) Ocean Acoustic Tomography, 1995; contbr. over 200 articles to profl. jours. Recipient Albatross award, Am. Misc. Soc., 1959, Gold medal, Royal Astron. Soc., 1968, Nat. Medal of Sci., 1985, Marine Tech. Soc. award, 1969, Capt. Robert Dexter Conrad award, Dept. Navy, 1978, G. Unger Vetlesen prize, Columbia U., 1993, Presdl. award, N.Y. Acad. Scis., 1993, Rolex Lifetime Achievement award, 1997, Kyoto prize, 1999, Prince Albert I medal, 2001, Albert A. Michelson award, Navy League of the U.S., 2001; named Calif. Scientist of Yr., Calif. Mus. Sci. and Industry, 1969; fellow Guggenheim Found., 1948, 1955, 1962, Overseas Found., 1962, 1981—82, Fulbright Found., 1981—82, sr. Queen's, 1978. Fellow: AAAS, Marine Tech. Soc. (Compass award 1991), Acoustical Soc. Am., Am. Meteorol. Soc. (Sverdrup Gold medal 1966), Am. Geophys. Union (Maurice Ewing medal 1976, William Bowie medal 1989); mem.: N.Y. Acad. Scis. (Presdl. award 1994), Am. Geol. Soc., Am. Acad. Arts and Scis. (Arthur L. Day medal 1965), Deutsche Akademie der Naturforscher Leopoldina, Russian Acad. Sci., Royal Soc. London (fgn. mem.), Am. Philos. Soc., NAS (chmn. ocean studies bd. 1985—88, Agassiz medal 1976). Office: U Calif San Diego Scripps Inst Oceanography 0225 La Jolla CA 92093 E-mail: wmunk@ucsd.edu.

MUNOFF, GERALD J., university librarian; BA in Art and Photography, Antioch Coll., Ohio; MLS, U. Ky. Past libr. Berea Coll., Ky., U. Ky.; dir. adminstrv. svc. Ky. Dept. Libr. and Archives, dep. state libr. and dep. commr.; asst. dir. adminstrv. svc. U. Chgo. Libr., 1985—89, dept. dir., 1989—98; univ. libr. U. Calif. Irvine, 1998—. Office: U Calif Irvine 566 Main Libr PO Box 19557 Irvine CA 92623-9557 Office Phone: 949-824-5213. Office Fax: 949-824-2472. E-mail: gmunoff@uci.edu.

MUNOZ, JOHN JOSEPH, retired transportation company executive; b. Salinas, Calif., Jan. 18, 1932; s. John Fernando and Naomal (Smith) M.; m. Phyllis Taylor, Feb. 6, 1961 (div. 1978); children: Sam, Kathy, Toni; m. Rachel Canales, Nov. 24, 1979; children: Michelle, Monique. AA, Allan Hancock Coll., 1956; student, San Jose State U., 1981, Western Sierra Law Sch. Ops. mgr. So. Pacific Milling Co., Santa Maria, Calif., 1971-77; cons. Govt., Venezuela, 1977-78; fleet supt. Granite Rock Co., San Jose, Calif., 1978-80; plant mgr. Granite Constrn. Co., Greenfield, Calif., 1980-85; mgr. transpn. Ball, Ball. & Brosmer Inc., Danville, Calif., 1985-86; ops. mgr., bd. dirs. Sorrento Ready Mix Co., Del Mar, Calif., 1986-89; trans. cons. Greenfield, Calif., 1991-96; ret., 1996. Cons. Dept. Agrl. Devel., Maricaibo, Venezuela, 1976—. Commr. Planning Commn., Greenfield, Calif., 1982-85; mem. fund raising com. Broccoli Festival, Greenfield, 1983-85; dir. Soledad Prison Vocat. Tng., 1982-85. Lt. 11th Ranger Airborne, U.S. Army, 1950-52, Korea. Mem. Am. Concrete Inst., Calif. Trucking Assn., Los Californianos, Rotary, Lions, Elks. Republican. Avocations: hunting, fishing, auto racing, photography. Home and Office: PO Box 3654 Greenfield CA 93927-3654 Business E-Mail: jmunoz@redshift.com.

MUNSON, JOHN BACKUS, computer scientist, retired data processing executive; b. Chgo., May 1, 1933; s. Mark Frame and Catherine Louise (Cherry) M.; m. Anne Lorraine Cooper, July 6, 1957; children: David B., Sharon A. BA, Knox Coll., Galesburg, Ill., 1955. With Unisys Corp., McLean, Va., 1957-93, v.p. corp. software engring., 1977-81, v.p. tech. ops., 1981-84, v.p. gen. mgr. space transp. systems, 1984-89, 89-93, v.p., gen. mgr. Space Systems divsn., 1989-94, ret., 1994. Mem. sci. adv. bd. USAF, 1981-86, mem. USN panel on F14D issues, 1987-88. Mem. bd. advisors U. Houston, Clear Lake, 1988-93, chmn. 1990-92; bd. dirs. Bay Area YMCA, 1988-93, chmn. 1992, Clear Lake Am. Heart Assn., 1989-93; co-chmn. Bay Area United Way, 1988—, chmn., 1992; Disting. visitor IEEE Computing Soc., 1981-94. Capt. US Army, 1955-57. Recipient Exceptional Civilian Svc. award USAF, 1986, Superior Pub. Svc. award USN, 1988, cert. of appreciation NATO, 1984; named to Mgmt. Assn. Hall of Fame, 1994. Fellow IEEE (editor Trans. of Software Engring. 1982-84, bd. dirs. tech. com. software engring. 1982—); mem. AIA, Am. Astronautical Soc. (bd. dirs. S.W. sect. 1989-94), Aerospace Industries Assn. (space com. 1989-94), US Army Assn., Nat. Security Indsl. Assn., Armed Forces Comm. Electronics Assn. (pres. Houston chpt. 1987-90), S.W. Regional Coun. Corp. CEOs. Home and Office: 1018 Westcreek Ln Westlake Village CA 91362-5462 Personal E-mail: JaxG3@aol.com.

MUNTZ, ERIC PHILLIP, aerospace and mechanical engineering educator, consultant; b. Hamilton, Ont., Can., May 18, 1934; came to U.S., 1961, naturalized, 1985; s. Eric Percival and Marjorie Louise (Weller) M.; m. Janice Margaret Furey, Oct. 21, 1964; children: Sabrina Weller, Eric Phillip. BASc., U. Toronto, 1956, MASc., 1957, PhD, 1961. Halfback Toronto Argonauts, 1957-60; group leader Gen. Electric, Valley Forge, Pa., 1961-69; assoc. prof. aerospace engring. and radiology U. So. Calif., Los Angeles, 1969-71, prof., 1971-87, chmn. aerospace engring., 1987-97, A.B. Freeman prof. engring., 1992—, chmn. aerospace and mech. engring., 2000—03. Cons. to aerospace and med. device cos., 1967—; mem. rev. of physics (plasma and fluids) panel NRC, Washington, 1983-85 Contbr. numerous articles in gas dynamics, micromech. sys., and med. diagnostics to profl. publs., 1961—; patentee med. imaging, isotope separation, nondestructive testing, net shape mfg., transient energy release micromachines, microscale vacuum sys., micropropulsion sys. Mem. Citizens Environ. Avc. Coun., Pasadena, Calif., 1972-76. Pilot RCAF, 1955-60. U.S. Air Force grantee, 1961-74, 82—; NSF grantee, 1970-76, 87-92; NASA grantee, 1990-94, 2001—; FDA grantee, 1980-86. Fellow AIAA (aerospace Contbn. to Soc. award 1987), Am. Phys. Soc.; mem. NAE. Epsicopalian. Home: 1560 E California Blvd Pasadena CA 91106-4104 Office: U So Calif Univ Pk Los Angeles CA 90089-1191 Office Phone: 213-740-5366. Business E-Mail: muntz@usc.edu.

MURAI, KEVIN M., electronics executive; b. 1964; BSEE, U. Waterloo, Ontario. Former mgr. mgmt. info. svcs. Verifact, Inc., Ontario, Canada; joined Ingram Micro Inc., 1988; v.p., operations Ingram Micro Can., Canada, 1993—97, pres., 1997—2000; sr. v.p. Ingram Micro Inc., 1997—2002, exec. v.p. Santa Ana, Calif., 2000—05; pres. Ingram Micro US, 2000—01, COO, 2000—02; pres., COO Ingram Micro N. Am., 2002—05, Ingram Micro Inc., 2005—07; co-CEO Synnex Corp., Fremont, Calif., 2008, pres., CEO, 2008—. Office: Synnex Corp 44201 Nobel Dr Fremont CA 94538 Office Phone: 714-566-1000. Office Fax: 714-566-7900.

MURANAKA, JAMI, biology educator; m. Garett Muranaka; children: Emi, Misa. BS in Biology, UCLA; MEd, U. Hawai'i-Manoa. Cert. Nat. Bd. Profl. Tchg. Standards. Sci. tchr. Kaimuki H.S., Honolulu, 1999—. Named Honolulu Dist. Tchr. of Yr., Hawaii Tchr. of Yr., 2007. Office: Kaimuki High Sch 2705 Kaimuki Ave Honolulu HI 96816 Business E-Mail: jami_muranaka@notes.k12.hi.us.

MURANE, WILLIAM EDWARD, lawyer; b. Denver, Mar. 4, 1933; s. Edward E. and Theodora (Wilson) M.; m. Rosemarie Palmerone, Mar. 26, 1960; children: Edward Wheelock, Peter Davenport, Alexander Phelps. AB, Dartmouth Coll., 1954; LLB, Stanford U., 1957. Bar: Wyo. 1957, Colo. 1958, D.C. 1978, U.S. Supreme Ct. 1977. Assoc. then ptnr. Holland & Hart, Denver, 1961-69; dep. gen. counsel U.S. Dept. Commerce, Washington, 1969-71; gen. counsel FDIC, Washington, 1971-72; ptnr. Holland & Hart, Denver, 1972—2000. Pub. mem. Adminstrv. Conf. of the U.S., Washington, 1978-81. Bd. dirs. Ctr. for Law and Rsch., Denver, 1973-76, Colo. Bus. Com. for Arts, 2002—; trustee Colo. Symphony Orch., 1994-2000; mem. bd. visitors Stanford U. Law Sch.; mem. vestry St. John's Cathedral, Denver, 2007-. Capt. USAF, 1958-61. Fellow Am. Coll. Trial Lawyers; mem. ABA (ho of dels. 1991-96), U. Club, Cactus Club. Avocations: fishing, classical music. Office: Holland & Hart 555 17th St Ste 2700 Denver CO 80202-3950 Business E-Mail: wmurane@hollandhart.com.

MURAYAMA, HITOSHI, physicist, educator; b. Tokyo, Mar. 21, 1964; permanent resident; married; 3 children. BSc in Physics, U. Tokyo, 1986, PhD in Theoretical Physics, 1991. Rsch. assoc. Tohoku U., 1991—95; postdoctoral fellow Lawrence Berkeley Lab., Calif.; asst. prof. physics, dept. physics U. Calif., Berkeley, 1995—98, assoc. prof. physics, dept. physics, 1998—2000, prof. physics, dept. physics, 2000—. Faculty sr. staff Lawrence Berkeley Nat. Lab., Calif.; mem. high energy physics adv. panel, subpanel on long range planning for U.S. High Energy Physics Dept. Energy/NSF, 2001—02, High Energy Physics Adv. Panel Quantum Universe Com., Discovery the Quantum Universe Subpanel; mem. organizational com. Snowmass 2001 Meeting; mem. physics adv. com. Fermilab, 2002—06; mem. neutrino facilities assessment com. NRC, 2002; mem. sch. natural scis. Inst. for Advanced Study, Princeton, NJ, 2003—04; mem. physics adv. com. KEK Lepton Collider, 2003—06; mem. exec. com. Am. Linear Collider Physics Working Group; chair Edn. and Outreach com. Snowmass ILC Physics and Detector Workshop, 2005; coun. mem. Physics Working Group in Internat. Scoping Study of a Future Neutrino Factory and Super-Beam Faculty, 2005—06; mem. policy com. Stanford Linear Accelerator Ctr., 2007—. Recipient Nishinomiya Yukawa Commemoration prize in theoretical physics, 2002; fellow, Japan Soc. for Promotion Sci., 1990—91; Alfred P. Sloan fellow, 1996—99, rsch. grantee, NSF, 1996—2001, 2001—. Fellow: Am. Phys. Soc. (exec. com., educ. & outreach com., divsn. particles & fields 2002—06). Office: Dept Physics Univ Calif Berkeley CA 94720 Office Phone: 510-486-5589. Office Fax: 510-486-6808. E-mail: murayama@lbl.gov, murayama@physics.berkeley.edu.

MURDOCH, COLIN, academic administrator; BA summa cum laude, Case Western Reserve U.; MusM, U. Ill. Faculty mem. music Lawrence U., Appleton, Wis.; dean Lawrence U. Conservatory of Music, Appleton, Wis., 1978, San Francisco Conservatory Music, Calif., 1988—92, pres. Calif., 1992—. Mem. New Orleans Symphony. Recipient Excellence Award, Pacific Musical Soc. Mem.: Nat. Assn. Schs. Music (mem. Futures Com., Commn. on Accreditation). Office: Office of the President San Fancisco Conservatory of Music 50 Oak St San Francisco CA 94102-6011 Office Phone: 415-503-6230.

MURDOCH, JOHN, museum director; Asst. dir. collections Victoria and Albert Mus., London; dir. Gallery Courtauld, U. London, 1993—2002, Huntington Art Collections, San Marino, Calif., 2002—. Office: Huntington Art Collections 1151 Oxford Rd San Marino CA 91108

MURDOCH, WILLIAM WILSON, ecologist, educator; b. Glassford, Scotland, Jan. 28, 1939; came to US, 1963; m. Joan Murdoch; children: Helen, Stephen. BSc with honors in Zoology, U. Glasgow, Scotland, 1960; PhD in Population Ecology, Oxford U., Eng., 1963. Postdoctoral rschr. U. Mich., Ann Arbor, 1963—65; asst. prof. U. Calif., Santa Barbara, 1965—69, assoc. prof., 1969—74, prof. biology, 1974—, chair biol. scis. dept., 1991—95, Charles A. Storke II prof. biology, 2000—, dir. Natural Res. Sys., 2001—. Chmn. Marine Rev. Com., Santa Barbara, 1980; vis. prof. Imperial Coll., London, Adelaide U., Canberra U., Australia, U. Mich., U. Strathclyde, Glasgow, U. Calif., Berkeley, Internat. Ctr. Insect Physiology and Ecology, Nairobi, Kenya; bd. dirs. Nature Conservancy, 2000—; founding dir. Nat. Ctr. Ecol. Analysis and Synthesis, Santa Barbara. Author: Poverty of Nations, 1980; contbr. articles to sci. jours., chpts. to books; editor various sci. books; editor-in-chief Issues in Ecology, 2002-. Recipient Huffaker medal in Population Biology, U. Calif., Berkeley, Disting. Scientist award, Internat. Orgn. Biol. Control, Outstanding Svc. award, Am. Inst. Biol. Scis., 2007; grantee, NSF, 1970—; Guggenheim fellow, 1977—78. Mem. Ecol. Soc. Am. (Robert H. MacArthur award 1990-91), Brit. Ecol. Soc., Am. Soc. Naturalists (Pres.'s award 1985), Am. Acad. Arts & Scis. Office: Dept Ecology Evolution & Marine Biology U Calif Santa Barbara CA 93106-9610 Office Phone: 805-893-4887. Office Fax: 805-893-3777. E-mail: murdoch@lifesci.ucsb.edu.

MURDOCK, DAVID H., food products executive; b. Kansas City, Mo., Apr. 10, 1923; m. Gabriele Bryant Murdock (dec. 1985); children: Gene, David H. Jr., Justin M.; m. Tracy Vakzad. LLD (hon.), Pepperdine U., 1978; LHD (hon.), U. Nebr., 1984, Hawaii Loa Coll., 1989. Sole proprietor, chmn., CEO Murdock Holding Co. (formerly Pacific Holding Co.), LA, 1995—; chmn., CEO Dole Food Co., LA, 1985—2007, chmn., 2007—; owner, chmn. Castle & Cooke, Inc., 1985—. CEO Huntington Tile, Yankie Hill Brick, Murdock Devel. Corp., Wiscassett Mills, Flexi-Van Leasing, Goettel, Stair Co., Ventura Farms. Trustee Asia Soc., NYC, LA; founder, bd. dirs. Found. for Advanced Brain Studies, LA; bd. visitors UCLA Grad. Sch. Mgmt.;bd. govs. Performing Arts Coun. of Music Ctr., LA; bd. govs. East-West Ctr., LA; patron Met. Opera, NYC. With USAAC, 1943-45. Served US Army. Named one of Forbes' Richest Americans, 1999—, Forbes' Exec. Pay, 1999—, World's Richest People, Forbes mag., 2001—, 25 Most Influential Republicans, Newsmax Mag., 2008. Mem. Regency Club (founder, pres.) Bel-Air Bay Country Club, Sherwood Country Club (founder, pres.), Met. Club (N.Y.C.). Office: Murdock Holding Co 10900 Wilshire Blvd Ste 1600 Los Angeles CA 90024-6530*

MURDOCK, IAN, information technology executive; m. Debra Murdock; children: Regan, Keely, Nolan. BS in Computer Sci., Purdue Univ., 1996; attended grad. sch. in computer sci., Univ. Ariz., 1997—2000. Staff programmer Univ. Ariz., 1997—2000; co-founder, chmn., chief stategist Progeny, 2000; chief tech. officer Free Standards Group, Linux Found. (formed through merger of OSDL and the Free Standards Group); chair Linux Standard Base; chief operating platforms officer Sun Microsystems, Inc., 2007—. Founding dir. Linux Internat., 1993—95, Open Source Initiative, 1998—2001. Host (web blog) ianmurdock.com. Achievements include being founder of the Debian project in 1993. Avocations: reading, history, politics, music, gardening, investing. Office: Sun Microsystems Inc 4150 Network Circle Santa Clara CA 95054 E-mail: imurdock@imurdock.com.

MURDY, WAYNE WILLIAM, retired mining executive; b. LA, July 4, 1944; s. Lee Robert and Louise Marie (Kleinemas) M.; m. Diana Yvonne DeCruse, Nov. 23, 1968; children: Dawn Marie, Christopher John, Joseph William, Elizabeth Anne. AA, El Camino Coll., 1966; BS, Calif. State U., Long Beach, 1968. C.P.A., Calif. With Atlantic Richfield Co., Los Angeles, 1969-78; gen. auditor Getty Oil Co., Los Angeles, 1978-81; group v.p. Texaco Trading & Transp. Inc., Denver, 1981-87; sr. v.p., chief fin. officer Apache Corp., Denver, 1987-92, Newmont Mining Corp., Denver, 1992—99, pres., 1999—2002, CEO, 2001—07, chmn., 2002—07. Mem. Am. Inst. C.P.A.s Clubs: University (Denver); Village (Cherry Hills Village, Colo.). Roman Catholic.

MUREN, DENNIS E., special effects expert; b. Glendale, Calif., Nov. 1, 1946; s. Elmer Ernest and Charline Louise (Clayton) M.; m. Zara Pinfold, Aug. 29, 1981; children: Gregory, Gwendolen. AA, Pasadena City Coll., Calif., 1966; student, Calif. State U., LA. Freelance spl. effects expert, 1968-75; camera operator Cascade of Calif., Hollywood, 1975-76; visual effects dir. photography Indsl. Light & Magic, San Rafael, Calif., 1976-80, visual effects dir., 1980—. Guest speaker Berlin Film Festival, UCLA, Film Dept., U. Calif. Berkeley Film Series, Liverpool (Eng.) U. Film Program, Mill Valley Film Festival Program, Siggraph '86, Siggraph '87, Am. Film Inst., Portland Creative Conf. '89. Cameraman, photographer various films including Star Wars, 1977, Close Encounters of the Third Kind, 1977, Battlestar Galactica, 1978, The Empire Strikes Back, 1980 (Oscar award); visual effects supr. films include Dragonslayer, 1981 (Oscar nomination), ET: The Extraterrestrial, 1982 (Oscar award), Return of the Jedi, 1983 (Oscar award, Brit. Acad. of Film and TV award), Indiana Jones and the Temple of Doom, 1984 (Oscar award, Brit. Acad. of Film and TV award), Young Sherlock Holmes, 1985 (Oscar nomination), Captain Eo, 1986, Star Tours, 1986, Innerspace, 1987 (Oscar award), Empire of the Sun, 1987, Willow, 1988 (Oscar nomination), Ghostbusters II, 1989, The Abyss, 1989 (Oscar award), Terminator 2, 1991 (Oscar award, Brit. Film and TV award), Jurassic Park, 1993 (Oscar award, Brit. Film and TV award), Casper, 1995; visual effects supr. (TV program) Caravan of Courage (Emmy award); creative advisor Twister, 1995, Mission Impossible, 1995, Jurassic Park: The Lost World, 1997 (Academy award nomination), Star Wars: The Phantom Menace, 1999, (Acad. award nomination, Saturn award for best visual effects, Best Action Sequence award MTV), A.I., 2001 (acad. award nomination), Star Wars: The Attack of the Clones, 2002, The Hulk, 2003, The Day After Toorrow, 2004, War of the Worlds 2005 (Acad. award nomination, Hollywood Film Festival award for Best Visual Effects, Visual Cons. Wall E, 2008); prodr., dir. The Equinox, 1967. Recipient Acad. Sci./Tech. Award for the devel. of a Motion Picture Figure Mover for animation photography, 1981, Edit/VES Honors award, 2003; star on Hollywood Walk of Fame, 1999, Nikola Tesla award, 2007. Mem.: Visual Effects Soc. (Lifetime Achievement award 2007), Acad. Motion Picture Arts and Scis., Am. Soc. Cinematographers. Office: Indsl Light & Magic Box 29909 San Francisco CA 94129-0909

MURKOWSKI, FRANK HUGHES, former Governor of Alaska; b. Seattle, Mar. 28, 1933; s. Frank Michael and Helen (Hughes) M.; m. Nancy Rena Gore, Aug. 28, 1954; children: Carol Victoria Murkowski Sturgulewski, Lisa Ann Murkowski Martell, Frank Michael, Eileen Marie Murkowski Van Wyhe, Mary Catherine Murkowski Judson, Brian Patrick. Student, Santa Clara U., Calif., 1952—53; BA in Econs., Seattle U., 1955. With Pacific Nat. Bank of Seattle, 1957-58, Nat. Bank of Alaska, Anchorage, 1959-67; asst. v.p., mgr. Nat. Bank of Alaska (Wrangell br.), 1963-66; v.p. charge bus. devel. Nat. Bank of Alaska, Anchorage, 1966-67; commr. dept. econ. devel. State of Alaska, Juneau, 1967-70; pres. Alaska Nat. Bank, Fairbanks, 1971-80; US Senator from Alaska, 1981—2002; ranking mem. Com. on Energy and Natural Resources; mem. Com. on Fin., Vets Affairs Com., Indian Affairs Com., Japan-US Friendship Com.; mem. intelligence com. fgn. affairs; gov. State of Alaska, Juneau, 2002—06. Rep. nominee for U.S. Congress from Alaska, 1970; chmn. Can.-U.S. Interparliamentary Group. Former v.p. B.C. and Alaska Bd. Trade; mem. U.S. Holocaust Mus. Coun. Served with U.S. Coast Guard, 1955-57. Mem. AAA, AMVETS, NRA, Am. Legion, Ducks Unlimited, Res. Officer's Assn., Alaska World Affairs Coun., Coalition Am. Vets., Alaska Native Brotherhood, Am. Bankers Assn., Alaska Bankers Assn. (pres. 1973), Young Pres.'s Orgn., Alaska C. of C. (pres. 1977), Anchorage C. of C. (bd. dirs. 1966), Fairbanks C. of C. (bd. dirs. 1973-78), Pioneers of Alaska, Internat. Alaska Nippon Kai, Capital Hill Club, Washington Athletic Club, Elks, Lions. Republican. Catholic. Mailing: PO Box 70049 Fairbanks AK 99707 Office Phone: 907-360-0601. Personal E-mail: nrgdc@earthlink.net.

MURKOWSKI, LISA ANN, United States Senator from Alaska; b. Ketchikan, Alaska, May 22, 1957; d. Frank Hughes Murkowski & Nancy 9Gore); m. Verne Martell, Aug. 22, 1987; children: Nicholas, Matthew. BA in Economics, Georgetown U., 1980; JD, Willamette Coll., 1985. Dist. coun. atty., Anchorage, 1987-89; comml. atty. Hoge and Lekisch, 1989-96; pvt. law practice, 1989—96; mem. Alaska House of Reps., Anchorage, 1999—2002, majority leader, 2002; US Senator from Alaska, 2002—; mem. US Senate Appropriations Com., 2009—. Dir. First Bank; mem. Mayor's Task Force Homeless, 1990-91; state ctrl. com. Dist. 14 Rep. chair, 1993-98; commr. Anchorage Equal Rights Commn., 1997-2002; citizens adv. bd. Joint Com. Mil. Bases in Alaska, 1998—. Trustee Cath. Svcs.; pres. Govt. Hill Elem. PTA; dir. Alaskan Drug Free Youth; mem. YWCA, Arctic Power. Recipient Comunity Leadership award, FBI Dir., 1993, Outstanding Volunteer award, Alaska Sch. Dist., 1998, 2000, Food Safety award, Nat. Food Processors Assn., 2003. Mem. Alaska Bar Assn., Anchorage Bar Assn., Alaska Fedn. Rep. Women (bd. dirs.), Anchorage Rep. Womens Club, Midnight Sun Rep. Women. Republican. Roman Catholic. Office: US Senate 709 Hart Senate Office Bldg Washington DC 20510 also: 510 L St # 550 Anchorage AK 99501 Office Phone: 202-224-6665.*

MURPHREE, A. LINN, ophthalmologist; b. Houston, Miss., June 6, 1945; d. John Alan and Maxine (Linn) M. BS, U. Miss., 1967; MD, Baylor Coll., 1972. Cert. Am. Bd. Ophthalmology. Resident affiliated hosps., 1973-76, chief resident ophthalmology, 1975-76; fellow ophthalmic genetics and pediatrics The Wilmer Inst., Johns Hopkins U. Hosp., 1976-77; asst. prof. ophthalmology and pediatrics U. So. Calif., Los Angeles, 1978-83, assoc. prof., 1983—91, prof., 1991—, dir. pediatric and devel. ophthalmology Los Angeles, 1978—; head, div. ophthalmology Children's Hosp. Los Angeles, 1978—, dir. Clayton Found. Ctr. Ocular Oncology, 1978—; chief med. ops. Childrens Hosp. of Los Angeles, 1986-87. Profl. adv. com. Blind Children's Ctr., Los Angeles, 1980—; med. adv. bd. Nat. Assn. Visually Handicapped, 1980—. Contbr. numerous articles to profl. jours. Served to capt. med. corps., USAR, 1972-80. Dolly Green scholar Research to Prevent Blindness, 1984, Fulbright scholar U. Copenhagen, 1967-68; Medical Genetics fellow Baylor Coll. of Med. Affiliated Hosps., 1972-73. Mem. Calif. Assn. Ophthalmology, Calif. Med. Assn., Los Angeles County Med. Assn., Los Angeles Ophthalmol. Soc., Los Angeles Pediatric Soc., Ophthalmology Research Study Club Los Angeles, Pacific Coast Oto-Ophthalmol. Soc., Salerni Collegium, Am. Acad. Ophthalmology (honor award 1983), Am. Assn. Pediatric Ophthalmology and Strabismus, Am. Orthoptic Council, Assn. Research in Vision and Ophthalmology, Ophthalmic Genetics Study Club, Am. Bd. Ophthalmology (assoc. examiner), Internat. Soc. Genetic Eye Disease (sec. 1986—). Office: Childrens Hosp Los Angeles 4650 Sunset Blvd Mailstop 88 Los Angeles CA 90027-6016

MURPHY, EDDIE, actor, comedian; b. Bklyn., Apr. 3, 1961; s. Vernon and Lillian Murphy Lynch; m. Nicole Mitchell, March 18, 1993 (div. Apr. 17, 2006); children: Bria, Myles Mitchell, Shayne Audra, Zola Ivy, Bella Zehra; 1 child with Melanie Brown, Angel Iris; m. Tracey Edmonds, Jan. 1, 2008 (separated 2008). Student pub. schs., Bklyn. Began performing Richard M. Dixon's White House, LI, N.Y.; performed at various N.Y.C. clubs, including The Comic Strip; with Saturday Night Live, NYC, 1980-84; host 35th Ann. Emmy Awards, 1983. Actor: (films) 48 Hrs., 1982, Trading Places, 1983, Best Defense, 1984, Beverly Hills Cop, 1984, The Distinguished Gentleman, 1992, Beverly Hills Cop III, 1994, The Nutty Professor, 1996, Metro, 1997, Mulan (voice only), 1998, Dr. Dolittle, 1998, Holy Man, 1998, Bowfinger, 1999, Shrek (voice only), 2001, Dr. Dolittle 2, 2001, Showtime, 2002, The Adventures of Pluto Nash, 2002, I Spy, 2002, Daddy Day Care, 2003, The Haunted Mansion, 2003, Shrek 2 (voice only), 2004, Dreamgirls, 2006 (Best Supporting Actor, African-American Film Critics Assn., 2006, 2006 Best Supporting Actor, Critics Choice award, Broadcast Film Critics Assn., 2007, Best Performance by an Actor in a Supporting Role in a Motion Picture, Golden Globe award, Hollywood Fgn. Press Assn., 2007, Outstanding Performance by a Male Actor in a Supporting Role, SAG, 2007), Shrek the Third (voice only), 2007, Meet Dave, 2008; actor, exec. prodr.: The Golden Child, 1986; The Nutty Professor II: The Klumps, 2000; Harlem Nights, 1989; actor(actor, prodr.): Vampire in Brooklyn, 1995; actor, prodr.: Life, 1999; actor, writer, prodr. Norbit, 2007; actor, writer Beverly Hills Cop II, 1987; Coming to America, 1988; Another 48 Hrs., 1990; actor, writer: films Boomerang, 1992; actor: (TV films) Eddie Murphy Delirious, 1983, Eddie Murphy Raw, 1987; actor (voice only), exec. prodr. (TV series) The PJ's, 1999—2001. Office: c/o Rogers & Cowan Pacific Design Ctr 8687 Melrose Avenue 7th fl Los Angeles CA 90069

MURPHY, EDWARD FRANCIS, sales executive; b. Chgo., July 30, 1947; s. Edward F. and Marjorie (Mooney) M.; m. Kay A. Worcester, Apr. 17, 1970; 1 child, Dean D. BA in Mktg., No. Ill. U., 1976. Dist. mgr. Midas Internat. Corp., Chgo., 1977-85; sales mgr. Raybestos, McHenry, Ill., 1985-89, Wagner Brakes, St. Louis, 1989-99; owner Displays of Distinction, Mesa, Ariz., 1998—. V.p. Associated Roof Structures, Mesa, 1999-2007; sales mgr. Stellar Structure, 2008-. Author: Vietnam Medal of Honor Heroes, 1987, Heroes of World War II, 1990, Korea's Heroes, 1990, Dak To, 1993, Semper Fi-Vietnam, 1996, Khe Sahn-The Hill Fights, 2000; hist. cons. (book) Above and Beyond, 1985. Sgt. U.S. Army, 1965-68. Recipient Dist. Svc. award Congl. Medal of Honor Soc., 1989. Mem. Medal of Honor Hist. Soc. (founder, pres. 1975—). Republican. Avocations: writing, flying. Home: 2659 E Kael St Mesa AZ 85213-2363 Office: 1237 S Val Vista Dr Mesa AZ 85204 Office Phone: 480-279-6296.

MURPHY, (FRANCES) ELAINE, musician, harpist, flutist; b. Chattanooga, July 15; MusB, Boston U., 1982; postgrad., Aspen Sch. Music, 1988; MM, Rice U., 1990; DMA, U. So. Calif., 1997, MMEd, 2002. Flutist Brookline (Mass.) Symphony Orch., 1982-84; piccolo player North Shore Symphony Orch., Marblehead, Mass., 1982-83, Cape Ann Symphony Orch., Gloucester, Mass., 1983-84; prin. flutist Orch. Sinfonica Del Valle, Cali, Colombia, 1984-87; flutist Pro Musica Chamber Orch., El Paso, Tex., 1987-88; prin. flutist Internat. Orchestra and Internat. Chamber Players, San Diego, 1990-91; harpist Lake Ave. Orch., 2005—. Solo harpist Beverly Hills Hotel, Harp Palace Hotel, Tokyo; music instr. LAUSD, 2001-. Musician Scotia Festival of Music, 1988; participant in Festival de Hispanidad, Houston, 1990, Schladming Wind Festival, Austria, 2007; albums Thou Shalt Play Upon the Harp, 2001; CD An Angel's Harp for the Holidays. Scholar Boston U., 1978-82, Crescendo Club Boston, 1982, Aspen Music Sch., 1988-89, Rice U., 1988-90; recipient Shepherd Soc. Award. U. SC, D.M.A.,1991-97 Office: Murphy's Music PMB 449 3175 South Hoover St Los Angeles CA 90007 E-mail: murphynews@aol.com.

MURPHY, GLENN T., retail executive; BA, Univ. We. Ontario. Mgmt. positions A.C. Nielsen, Loblaw Companies Ltd., Canada; pres., CEO Chapters, Canada; chmn., CEO Shoppers Drug Mart, Canada, 2001—07. The Gap Inc., San Francisco, 2007—. Office: The Gap Inc 2 Folsom St San Francisco CA 94105

MURPHY, IRENE HELEN, publishing executive; b. Boston; d. Charles Leo and Irene Muriel (Finney) M. BA, Regis Coll., 1958; MA, Boston Coll., 1963, Northeastern U., Boston, 1968, Manhattanville Coll., 1969. Tchr. elem. sch., Boston; high sch. dir. guidance; ednl. adminstr.; prof. master tchr. program, 1969—; prof. NYC; dir. sch. svcs. Glencoe/McGraw Hill Pub. Co., Woodland Hills, Calif., 1969—; v.p. Glencoe Pub. Co., Mission Hills, Calif. Vis. lectr. univs., including Boston Coll., Sacred Heart U., St. John, Nfld., Regis Coll., Teachers Coll., Sidney, Australia, Teachers Coll., Melbourne, Australia, McGill U., Mont., Providence (R.I.) Coll. Author series ednl. games for children. Recipient Gold Seal Recognition award Today's Cath. Tchr., 1987, Leadership award in religious edn., 1992. Mem. AAUW, Nat. Cath. Edn. Assn., Nat. Assn. Female Execs., Jordan Hosp. Club, St. Peter Cath. Women's Club, Adminstrs. Club, Passport Club, Admirals Club. Roman Catholic. Avocations: sports, music, art, poetry, literature. Home: 59 Summer St Plymouth MA 02360-3462 also: 2677 SW Thunderbird Trl Stuart FL 34997-8944 Office: Benziger Pub Co 21600 Oxnard St Ste 500 Woodland Hills CA 91367-4947

MURPHY, JEREMIAH T., professional sports team, construction executive; b. NYC, July 21, 1944; m. Sandra Murphy; children: Lisa, Tara, Gregory. BA, Bernard Baruch Coll. CPA Calif. Sr. ptnr. Bowman and Co., Stockton, Calif., 1971-82; CFO A.G. Spanos Companies, Stockton, Calif., 1982—; v.p. San Diego Chargers. Mem.: Calif. Soc. of CPAs, Am. Inst. of CPAs. Office: AG Spanos Companies 10100 Trinity Pky Stockton CA 95219 also: San Diego Chargers 4020 Murphy Canyon Rd San Diego CA 92123

MURPHY, KATHLEEN ANNE FOLEY, marketing communications executive; b. Fresh Meadows, NY, Oct. 15, 1952; d. Thomas J. and Audrey L. Finn; m. Timothy Sean Murphy, Sept. 26, 1992; 1 child, G. David. BA, Marymount Coll., 1974; postgrad., Smith Coll., 1985. V.p. acct. supr., sr. v.p. mgmt. supr., sr. v.p. group dir. Ogilvy & Mather Inc., NYC, 1974-90; sr. v.p., worldwide account dir. Young & Rubicam, San Francisco, 1990-92, sr. v.p., dir. account svcs., 1992-95, exec. v.p., dir. acct. svcs., 1995-97, exec. v.p., gen. mgr., 1997—2002, COO, 2002—03; dir. network devel. WPP, San Francisco, 2003—, dir. Western region integration, 2003—. Mem. Family Caregivers Alliance. Roman Catholic. Home: One Brookside Ave Berkeley CA 94705 Office: WPP 303 Second St S Tower 9th Fl San Francisco CA 94107

MURPHY, KIM, newspaper bureau chief; b. Indpls., Aug. 26, 1955; married; 2 children. BA in English Lit. magna cum laude, Minot State Univ., ND, 1977. Asst. editor North Biloxian, Miss., 1973—74; reporter Minot Daily News, ND, 1978—80, Orange Co. Register, Calif., 1980—83, asst. metro editor Calif., 1982—83; gen. assignment staff writer, Orange Co. edition LA Times, 1983—89, nat. and fgn. corr., including Moscow Bur. chief, 1990—. Recipient ND Press Women award best news story, 1979, ND Sigma Delta Chi award, 1979, Orange Co. Press Club award, 1980, 1981, 1982, 1983, 1984, Orange Co. Press Club Watchdog award, 1985, LA Sigma Delta Chi award for fgn. corr., 1993, Pulitizer Prize for internat. reporting, 2005; named a finalist, deadline reporting, ASNE awards, 2005.

MURPHY, SISTER LILLIAN, sister, not-for-profit organization executive; BS in Social Sci., U. San Francisco; MS in Pub. Health, U. Calif., Berkeley; LHD (hon.), U. San Francisco, 1998. Mem. Religious Order Sisters of Mercy, Burlingame, Calif., 1959—; pres., CEO Mercy Housing, Inc., Denver, 1987—. Bd. dirs. Nat. Housing Trust, Fannie Mae Nat. Housing Adv. Coun., Washington Mutual Nat. Cmty. Coun.; mem. editl. adv. bd. Affordable Housing Fin. mag.; past adv. com. mem. Fed. Home Loan Bank, Bank of America Cmty. Devel. Bank. Bd. dirs. Alegent Health Sys., Omaha; past bd. dirs. Cath. Health Corp., Cath. Healthcare West, Low Income Investment Fund, Colo. Trust; former pub. interest dir. Fed. Home Loan Bank, Topeka. Recipient Affordable Housing Leadership award for Lifetime Achievement, Non-Profit Housing Assn. No. Calif., 1999, Woman of Distinction award, Girl Scouts of America, 2002, 25th Ann. Housing Leadership award, Nat. Low Income Housing Coalition, 2006. Roman Catholic. Office: Mercy House 1999 Broadway Ste 1000 Denver CO 80202 Office Phone: 303-830-3300. Office Fax: 303-830-3301.

MURPHY, MATT, information technology executive; Bus. devel. mgr., network sys. group Sun Microsystems, product line mgr.; product mgmt. NetBoost; ptnr. Kleiner Perkins Caulfield and Byer. Mem. bd. dir. IPUnity, Kodiak Networks, RGB Networks, Stoke, XSIGO, eASIC, Oakley Networks, Scintera, Quorum Sys., Endforce, Devicescape. Office: 2750 Sand Hill Rd Menlo Park CA 94025 Office Phone: 650-233-2750. Office Fax: 650-233-0300.

MURPHY, MICHAEL JOSEPH, former state treasurer; b. Seattle, May 24, 1947; s. John Anthony and Helen Elizabeth (Domick) M.; m. Theresa Ann Smith. BA in History, Seattle U., 1969; MBA, Pacific Luth. U., 1978. Chief adjudicator vet.'s program Office of the State Treas., Olympia, Wash., 1972-75, adminstr. pub. deposit protection commn., 1975-81, internal auditor to state treas., 1981-87; treas. Thurston County, Olympia, 1987-96, State of Wash., Olympia, 1997—2007. Mem. adv. bd. asset/liability com. Twin County Credit Union, Olympia, 1987-96; instr. profl. orgns., govt. Treas. Thurston County Dems., 1973-77. Mem. Wash. Assn. County Treasurers (bd. dirs., officer 1987-96, legis. coord. 1989-96, Pres. award 1994), Wash. Assn. County Ofcls. (bd. dirs. 1989-90), Wash. Mcpl. Treasurers Assn. (bd. dirs. 1990—, Cert. Excellence for investment policy 1992), Wash. Fin. Officers Assn. (profl. fin. officer 1988—, bd. dirs. 1997—), Nat. Assn. State Treasurers, Olympia Yacht Club, Olympia Country and Golf Club, Valley Athletic Club. Roman Catholic. Avocations: sailing, golf, travel.

MURPHY, MICHAEL R., federal judge; b. Denver, Aug. 1947; s. Roland and Mary Cecilia (Maloney) M.; m. Maureen Elizabeth Donnelly, Aug. 22, 1970; children: Amy Christina, Michael Donnelly. BA in History, Creighton U., 1969; JD, U. Wyo., 1972. Bar: Wyo. 1972, US Ct. Appeals (10th cir.) 1972, UT 1973, US Dist. Ct. UT 1974, US Dist. Ct. Wyo. 1976, US Ct. Appeals (5th cir.) 1976, US Tax Ct. 1980, US Ct. Appeals (9th cir.) 1981, US Ct. Appeals (fed. cir.) 1984. Law clk. to chief judge US Ct. Appeals (10th cir.), Salt Lake City, 1972-73; with Jones, Waldo, Holbrook & McDonough, Salt Lake City, 1973-86; judge 3rd Dist. Ct., Salt Lake City, 1986-95, presiding judge, 1990-95; judge US Ct. Appeals (10th cir.), Salt Lake City, 1995—. Mem. adv. com. on rules of civil procedure UT Supreme Ct., 1985—95, mem. bd. dist. ct. judges, 1989—90; mem. UT State Sentencing Commn., 1993—95, UT Adv. Com. on Child Support Guidelines, 1989—95, UT Child Sexual Abuse Task Force, 1989—93; mem. com. on fed.-state jurisdiction Jud. Conf. of US, 2001—07. Recipient Freedom of Info. award, Soc. Profl. Journalists, 1989, UT Minority Bar Assn. award, 1995, Alumni Achievement citation, Creighton U., 1997; named Judge of Yr., UT State Bar, 1992. Fellow Am. Bar Found.; mem. ABA (editl. bd. Judges' Jour. 1997-99), UT Bar Assn. (chmn. alternative dispute resolution com. 1985-88), Sutherland Inn of Ct. II (past pres.). Office: 5438 Federal Bldg 125 S State St Salt Lake City UT 84138-1102 Office Phone: 801-524-5955.

MURPHY, MICHAEL THOMAS, lawyer; b. Winton, Australia, Feb. 15, 1963; came to U.S., 1992; B of Commerce, U. Melbourne, Australia, 1986; LLB, U. Melbourne, 1986. Bar: Victoria, Australia 1987, NY 1996, Calif. 2002. Solicitor Arthur Robinson & Hedderwicks, Melbourne, 1986-91, sr. assoc., 1991-92; assoc. Shaw Pittman LLP, Washington, 1992, ptnr. Global Sourcing Group San Francisco. Mem. ABA, DC Bar Assn., Australia-Am. Assn., Calif. Bankers Assn., Fgn. Lawyer's Forum, Southwestern Legal Found. (Acad. Comparative & Internat. Law), The Phillip Collection. Office: Shaw Pittman LLP 50 Fremont St San Francisco CA 94105 Office Phone: 415-983-1303. E-mail: michael.murphy@pillsburylaw.com.

MURPHY, PATRICE ANN (PAT MURPHY), writer; b. Spokane, Wash., Mar. 9, 1955; m. Dave Wright, Feb. 14, 1999. BA in Biology, U. Calif., Santa Cruz, 1976. Sr. rsch. writer ednl. graphics dept. Sea World, 1978—82. Former instr. Clarion Speculative Fiction Workshop, Mich. State U.; former tchr. sci. fiction U. Calif., Santa Cruz; tchr. sci. fiction writing Creative Writing Program, Stanford U., 1995, 96, 97, 98. Author: The Shadow Hunter, 1982, The Falling Woman, 1987 (Nebula award 1987), Adventures in Time and Space with Max Merriwell, 2002, (novelette) Rachel in Love (Nebula award 1987, Isaac Asimov Reader's award 1987, Theodore Sturgeon Meml. award 1987), (short story collection) Points of Departure, 1990 (Philip K. Dick award 1990), (novella) Bones, 1991 (World Fantasy award 1991), (novelette) An American Childhood, Nadya-The Wolf Chronicles, There and Back Again, The City, Not Long After, 1984, By Nature's Design, The Color of Nature, 1996, The Science Explorer, 1996, Explorabook Bat Science, The Science Explorer, Out and About. Avocation: Karate. Office: c/o Tor Books 14th Fl 175 5th Ave Fl 14 New York NY 10010-7703 also: c/o Exploratorium 3601 Lyon St San Francisco CA 94123

MURPHY, PETER E., corporate financial executive; BA, Dartmouth Coll.; MBA, Wharton Sch. Bus. With The Walt Disney Co., Burbank, Calif., 1988—; sr. v.p., CFO ABC, Inc., Burbank, Calif., 1997-98; exec. v.p., chief strategic officer The Walt Disney Co., Burbank, Calif., 1998-99, sr. exec. v.p., chief strategic officer, 1999—. Office: The Walt Disney Co 500 S Buena Vista St Burbank CA 91521

MURPHY, PHILIP EDWARD, broadcast executive; b. Chgo., May 11, 1945; s. Edward Curtis and Mary Francis (D'Incecco) M.; m. Carol Jean Sefton, Mar. 11, 1967 (div. 1985); children: Mandy Jean, Patrick Jeffrey; life ptnr. Robert G. McCracken, 1985—. BS, Ind. U., 1967. Prodn. mgr. Sta. WFIU-FM, Bloomington, Ind., 1968; news reporter, photographer, editor Sta. WTHR-TV, Indpls., 1969, sr. account exec., 1970—80; acct. exec. Blair TV, LA, 1980—81; pres. Am. Spot Cable Corp., Hollywood, Calif., 1981—82; sr. v.p. TV group ops., overseer asset protection program Paramount Pictures, Hollywood, 1982—2005, CBS TV Distribution, Hollywood, 2005—. Responsible for tech. preparation and distbn. material provided to worldwide electronic ancillary markets; spkr. film preservation, in field; advisor Libr. of Congress, Washington, Nat. Archives, Washington. Lighting designer Civic Theatre, Indpls., 1979; tech. dir. Footlite Mus., Indpls., 1970-78; bd. dirs. Cathedral Arts, Indpls., 1978-80. Mem. Assn. Moving Image Archivists, Human Rights Campaign (Washington), Gay and Lesbian Alliance Against Defamation L.A., Hollywood Supports Assn., Soc. Motion Picture and TV Engrs. Avocations: photography, videography, audio, theater. Office: CBS TV Distribution Stage 3 212 5555 Melrose Ave Los Angeles CA 90038-3197

MURPHY, RICHARD (RICK) A., state legislator; b. Phoenix; m. Penny Murphy; 2 children. Realtor, small bus. owner, 1992—; mem. Dist. 9 Ariz. House of Reps., 2005—, chair ways & means com., mem. health & human svcs. com., appropriations com. Mem.-at-large, Congl. Dist. 2 Ariz. Rep. Party, 1st vice-chair, Dist. 9; chair Ariz. Fedn. Taxpayers Assn. Active Christ's Ch. of the Valley; founding mem., bd. dirs. Hemophilia Assn. Republican. Office: Ariz House Reps Capitol Complex 1700 W Wachington Rm 111 Phoenix AZ 85007 Office Phone: 602-926-3255. Office Fax: 602-417-3009. Business E-Mail: rmurphy@azleg.gov.*

MURPHY, ROBERT F., lawyer; Pvt. practice law; with FHP Internat., Fountain Valley, Calif., 1986-95; gen. counsel and sec. Sun Healthcare Group, Albuquerque, 1996—. Office: Sun Healthcare Group 101 Sun Ave NE Albuquerque NM 87109

MURPHY, TERENCE MARTIN, biology professor; b. Seattle, July 1, 1942; s. Norman Walter and Dorothy Louise (Smith) M.; m Judith Baron, July 12, 1969; 1 child, Shannon Elaine Knotts. BS, Calif. Inst. Tech., 1964; PhD, U. Calif. San Diego, La Jolla, 1968. Sr. fellow dept. biochemistry U. Wash., Seattle, 1969-70; asst. prof. botany U. Calif., Davis, 1971-76, assoc. prof., 1976-82, prof. plant biology, 1982—, chmn. dept. botany, 1986-90. Author: Plant Molecular Development, 1988; co-author: Plant Biology, 1998, 2nd edit. 2006; N.Am. exec. editor, N.Am. office, Physiologia Plantarum, 1988-98; contbr. articles to profl. jours. Mem. AAAS, Am. Soc. Plant Biologists, Am. Soc. Photobiology, Scandinavian Soc. Plant Physiology. Home: 725 N Campus Way Davis CA 95616-3518 Office: U Calif Plant Biology Davis CA 95616 Home Phone: 530-753-3783; Office Phone: 530-752-2413. E-mail: tmmurphy@ucdavis.edu.

MURRAY, ANNE, singer; b. Springhill, NS, Can., June 20, 1945; d. Carson and Marion (Burke) M.; m. William M. Langstroth, June 20, 1975; children: William Stewart, Dawn Joanne. B.Phys. Edn., U. N.B., 1966, D.Litt. (hon.), 1978, St. Mary's U., 1982. Rec. artist for Arc Records, Canada, 1968, Capital/EMI Records, 1969—. Appeared on series of TV spls. CBC, 1970—81, 1988—93; star CBS spls., 1981—85; toured N. Am., Japan, Englan, Germany, Holland, Ireland, Sweden, Australia and New Zealand, 1977—82. Singer: (31 albums including) A Little Good News, 1984, (albums) As I Am, 1988, Greatest Hits, vol. I, 1981, vol. II, 1989, Harmony, 1987, You Will, 1990, Yes I Do, 1991, Croonin', 1993, The Best So Far, 1994, Now and Forever, Anne Murray, 1996, An Intimate Evening with Anne Murray-Live, 1997, What A Wonderful World, 1999, What A Wonderful Christmas, 2001, Country Croonin', 2002. Hon. chmn. Can. Save the Children Fund, 1978-80. Recipient Juno awards as Can.'s top female vocalist, 1970-81; Can.'s Top Country Female Vocalist, 1970-86; Grammy award as top female vocalist-country, 1974; Grammy award as top female vocalist-pop, 1978; Grammy award as top female vocalist-country, 1980, 83; Country Music Assn. awards, 1983-84; named Female Rec. Artist of Decade, Can. Rec. Industry Assn., 1980, Top Female Vocalist 1970-86; star inserted in Hollywood Walkway of Stars, 1980; Country Music Hall of Fame Nashville; decorated companion Order of Can.; inducted Juno Hall of Fame, 1993. Mem. AFTRA, Assn. Canadian TV and Radio Artists, Am. Fedn. Musicians. Office: Bruce Allen Talent No 500 425 Carrall St Vancouver BC Canada V6B6E3 also: Emi Music 1750 Vine St Los Angeles CA 90028-5209

MURRAY, ANTHONY, lawyer; b. LA, Apr. 25, 1937; s. Bernard Anthony and Frances Louise (Simpson) M.; children— Matthew Anthony, Thomas Andrew. JD, Loyola U., LA, 1964. Bar: Calif. 1965. Ptnr. Loeb & Loeb LLP, LA, 1995—. Fellow Am. Coll. Trial Lawyers (bd. regents 1995-99, mem. ABA, Chancery Club, LA County Bar Assn., Long Beach Bar Assn., State Bar Calif. (bd. govs. 1980-83, pres. 1982-83, numerous other positions). Democrat. Office: Loeb & Loeb LLP 10100 Santa Monica Blvd Ste 2200 Los Angeles CA 90067-4120 Office Phone: 310-282-2000.

MURRAY, BOB (ROBERT FREDERICK MURRAY), professional sports team executive, former professional hockey player; b. Kingston, Ont., Can., Nov. 26, 1954; m. Betsy Murray; children: Kevin, Andrew, Amanda, Katie. Defenseman Chgo Blackhawks, 1975—90; dir. player personnel Chgo. Blackhawks, 1991—97, gen. mgr., 1997—99; scouting cons. Anaheim Ducks (formerly Mighty Ducks of Anaheim), 1999, sr. v.p. hockey ops., 2005—08, gen. mgr., 2008—; profl. scout Vancouver Canucks, 1999—2005; gen. mgr. Iowa Chops (Am. Hockey League), 2008—. Named to NHL All-Star Game, 1981, 1983. Office: Anaheim Ducks Honda Ctr 2695 E Katella Ave Anaheim CA 92806

MURRAY, CAROLE R., state legislator; b. Ill. m. Lisle Gates; 5 children. Former county clerk & recorder Douglas County; mem. Dist. 45 Colo. House of Reps., Denver, 2008—. Pres. Castle Rock C. of C. Republican. Office: State House 200 E Colfax Denver CO 80203 Office Phone: 303-866-2948. Business E-Mail: murrayhouse45@gmail.com.*

MURRAY, CHAD MICHAEL, actor; b. Buffalo, Aug. 24, 1981; m. Sophia Bush, Apr. 16, 2005 (div. Dec. 29, 2006). Actor(guest appearances): (TV series) Diagnosis Murder, 2000, CSI: Crime Scene Investigation, 2002,: (TV films) Murphy's Dozen, 2001, Aftermath, 2001, The Lone Ranger, 2003; (films) Megiddo: The Omega Code 2, 2001, Freaky Friday, 2003, A Cinderella Story, 2004 (Choice Movie Breakout Male, Teen Choice Awards, 2004), House of Wax, 2005 (Choice Movie Actor: Action/Adventure/Thriller, Teen Choice Awards, 2005), Home of the Brave, 2006; (TV series) Gilmore Girls, 2000—01, Dawson's Creek, 2001—02, One Tree Hill, 2003— (Choice TV Breakout Star Male, Teen Choice Awards, 2004, Choice TV Actor: Drama, Teen Choice Awards, 2008). Office: Simmons And Scott Entertainment 7942 Mulholland Dr Los Angeles CA 90046-1225

MURRAY, CHERRY ANN, physicist, researcher; b. Ft. Riley, Kans., Feb. 6, 1952; d. John Lewis and Cherry Mary (Roberts) M.; m. Dirk Joachim Muehlner, Feb. 18, 1977; children: James Joachim, Sara Hester. BS in Physics, MIT, 1973, PhD in Physics, 1978. Rsch. asst. physics dept. MIT, Cambridge, Mass., 1969-78; rsch. assoc. Bell Labs., Murray Hill, NJ, 1976-77; mem. tech. staff AT&T Bell Labs., Murray Hill, NJ, 1978-85, disting. mem. tech. staff, 1985-87, dept. head low-temperature and solid-state physics rsch., 1987-90, dept. head condensed matter physics rsch., 1990-93, dept. head semicond. physics rsch., 1993-97, dir. phys. rsch. lab., 1997—2000, sr. v.p. physical sciences, 2000—01, sr. v.p. for rsch. strategy, physical sci. & wireless rsch., 2001—04; prin. assoc. dir. for sci. & tech. Lawrence Livermore Nat. Laboratory, Livermore, Calif., 2004—. Co-chair Gordon Rsch., Wolfeboro, N.H., 1982, chair, 1984; mem. vis. com. Harvard U. Dept. Physics, 1993-2004 Contbr. numerous articles to profl. jours. and chpts. to books. NSF fellow, 1969; IBM fellow MIT, 1974-76; recipient Maria Goeppert-Mayer award, American Physical Soc. (APS), 1989, George E. Pake Prize, 2005; named one of The 50 Most Important Women in Sci., Discover mag., 2002 Fellow AAAS, Nat. Acad. Engring., Am. Phys. Soc. (Maria Goeppart-Mayer award 1989), Nat. Acad. Sciences, American Physical Soc. (v.p., 2007-) Sigma Xi. Office: Lawrence Livermore National Laboratory PO Box 808 Livermore CA 94551*

MURRAY, JEAN, communications executive, writer, speaker; b. Portland, Oreg., Aug. 29, 1943; d. Edward Howard and Dorothy Eugenia (Ross) Brown. BA in English, Portland State U., 1965. Cert. tchr., Oreg. Tchr., dept. head Beaverton (Oreg.) Sch. Dist., 1967-88; pres., founder Write Communications, Portland, 1988—. Adj. faculty Portland C.C., Concordia U., Portland State U.; nat. trainer, cons.State of Oreg., City of Portland, Nike, Inc., Oreg. Health Scis. U., Oreg. Mil. Acad., Oreg. Fin. Instns. Assn., Freightliner, Automated Data Processing, Calif. State U. Systems, others, 1988—; spkr. Tektronix, Fred Meyer, Pacific Power, Am. Inst. of Banking, Utah Power, Pacific Telecom, Inc., other; writing dir. U.S. Army C.E., USDA Forest Svcs., PacifiCare, LawTalk MCLE, Wash. State Bar Assn., others, 1989-90; owner Wiggles & Wags Self and Full-Svc. Dog Wash. Author: Grammar Gremlins: An Instant Guide to Perfect Grammar for Everybody in Business, 1994; TV appearances include Stas. KATU-TV and KGW-TV. Vol. Dove Lewis Emergency Vet. Clinic, Portland, 1989—, Doerbecher Children's Hosp., Oreg. Humane Soc., B.O.N.E. Rescue Mem. Oreg. Speakers Assn. (pres. bd. dirs. 1997—), Nat. Speakers Assn. Republican. Avocations: target-shooting, travel, speaking, exercise, animals. Office: Write Comm PMB 201 14845 SW Murray Schools Dr #110 Beaverton OR 97007 Office Phone: 800-293-6150, 503-579-6065. Personal E-mail: jean@paws4thoughts.com.

MURRAY, JOHN FREDERIC, cardiologist, educator; b. Mineola, NY, June 8, 1927; s. Frederic S. and Dorothy Murray; m. Diane Lain, Nov. 30, 1968; children— James R., Douglas S., Elizabeth. AB, Stanford, 1949, MD, 1953; D.Sc. (hon.), U. Paris, 1983, U. Athens, 2000. From instr. to asso. prof. medicine U. Calif. at Los Angeles, 1957-66; mem. sr. staff Cardiovascular Research Inst., U. Calif., San Francisco, 1966-94; asso. prof. medicine Cardiovascular Research Inst., U. Calif. (Sch. Medicine), 1966-69, prof., 1969-94; chief chest service San Francisco Gen. Hosp., 1966-89. Vis. prof. Brompton Inst. for Diseases of the Chest, London, 1972-73; Macy faculty scholar Inst. Nat. de la Santé et de la Recherche Medicale, Paris, 1979-80; mem. adv. council and pulmonary disease adv. com. Nat. Heart, Lung and Blood Inst.; mem. clin. studies panel NRC.; bd. govs. Am. Bd. Internal Medicine, Am. Bd. Emergency Medicine. Author: The Normal Lung, 1976, 2d edit., 1986; co-author: Diseases of the Chest, 5th edit., 1980; co-editor: Textbook of Respiratory Medicine, 1988, 2d edit., 1994, 3rd edit., 2000; editor: Am. Rev. Respiratory Disease, 1973-79; contbr. articles to profl. jours. Chmn. Internat. Union Against Tb and Lung Disease. Served with USNR, 1945-46. Sr. Internat. fellow Fogarty Inst.; recipient Pres.'s award European Respiratory Soc., 1996. Fellow Royal Coll. Physicians; mem. Assn. Am. Physicians, Am. Soc. Clin. Investigation, Am. Physiol. Soc., Western Soc. Clin. Research, Western Assn. Physicians, Am. Thoracic Soc. (pres. 1981-82, Trudeau medal 1994), Académie Nationale de Médecine Francaise. Office: U Calif PO Box 0841 San Francisco CA 94143-0841 Home: PO Box 542 Bolinas CA 94924-0542 Personal E-mail: johnfmurr@aol.com.

MURRAY, KATHLEEN ANNE, lawyer; b. LA, Feb. 14, 1946; d. Francis Albert and Dorothy (Thompson) M.; 1 child, Anne Murray Ladd; m. Arthur T. Perkins Jr., June 29, 1991. BA, U. Mich., 1967; JD, Hastings Coll. Law, 1973. Bar: Calif. 1973, U.S. Dist. Ct. (no. dist.) Calif. 1973, U.S. Ct. Appeals (9th cir.) 1973. Sr. staff atty Child Care Law Ctr., San Francisco, 1979—84, cons. child day care law and regulation, 1984—86; atty Epstein & Harris, San Francisco, 1985—86; gen. counsel Fisher Friedman Assocs., San Francisco, 1986—89; assoc. gen. counsel Calif. State Automobile Assn., San Francisco, 1989—98; sr. counsel Firemen's Fund Ins. Co., San Francisco, 1998—2002; prin. Mercer, 2003—. Exec. dir., editl. adv. bd. Parenting Mag., 1985-87; chair Labor and Employment Law Com. Assn. Corp. Coun. Am., 2001-03 Editor: Child Care Center Legal Handbook; Tax Guide for California Child Care Providers; contbr. articles to profl. jours. Mem. adv. coun. Humanities West, Inc., 1986-96; vestry Episcopal Ch. of St. Mary the Virgin, 1990-92; pres. Parents' Assn., Lick-Wilmerding H.S., 1993-94; Pers. Practices Com. Episcopal Diocese of Calif., 1998-2003. Mem.: Assn. Corp. Counsel (chair labor and employment law com. 2001—03). Democrat. Episcopalian. Office: Mercer Four Embarcadeo Ctr Ste 400 San Francisco CA 94111-4156 Business E-Mail: kathleen.murray@mercer.com.

MURRAY, PATRICIA, electronics company executive; b. Detroit; BA, Michigan St. U.; BS, St. Louis U.; JD, U. Mich., 1986. Nurse, intensive care unit, nursing adminstr. U. Mich. Hospitals; employment litigator Morrison & Foerster, Palo Alto, Calif., 1986—90; atty. human resources legal staff Intel Corp., 1990—91, mgr. human resoures legal staff, 1992—95, dir., v.p. human resources Santa Clara, 1996—97, sr. v.p., dir human resources, 1997—. Chmn. Intel Found. Office: Intel Corp PO Box 58119 2200 Mission College Blvd Santa Clara CA 95052-8119 E-mail: patricia.murray@intel.com.*

MURRAY, PATTY (PATRICIA LYNN MURRAY), United States Senator from Washington; b. Seattle, Wash., Oct. 11, 1950; d. David L. and Beverly A. (McLaughlin) Johns; m. Robert R. Murray, June 2, 1972; children: Randy P., Sara A. BA, Wash. State U., 1972. Sec. various companies, Seattle, 1972-76; citizen lobbyist various ednl. groups, Seattle, 1983-88; legis. lobbyist Orgn. for Parent Edn., Seattle, 1977-84; instr. Shoreline Community Coll., Seattle, 1984-88; mem. Wash. State Senate, Seattle, 1989-92; US Senator from Wash., 1993—; mem. US Senate Appropriations Com., US Senate Veterans Affairs Com., US Senate Health, Edn., Labor, & Pensions Com., US Senate Budget Com., US Senate Rules & Adminstrn. Com., Joint Congressional Com. on Printing. Chairwoman Democratic Senatorial Campaign Com. (DSCC), 2001—03; sec. US Senate Democratic Conf., 2007—. Co-author (with Catherine Whitney): Nine and Counting: The Women of the Senate, 2000. Mem. bd. Shoreline Sch., Seattle, 1985-89; mem. steering com. Demonstration for Edn., Seattle, 1987; founder, chmn. Orgn. for Parent Edn., Wash., 1981-85; 1st Congl. rep. Wash. Women United, 1983-85. Recipient Outstanding award Washing. Women United, 1986, Recognition of Svc. to Children award Shoreline PTA Coun., 1986, Golden Acorn Svc. award, 1989; Outstanding Svc. award Wash. Women United, 1986, Outstanding Svc. to Pub. Edn. award Citizens Ednl. Ctr. NW, Seattle, 1987, Wash. State Legis. of Yr., 1990, George Falcon Spike award Nat. Assn. Railroad Passengers, 2003, Person of Yr. award Wash. State VFW, 2004. Democrat. Roman Catholic. Office: US Senate 173 Russell Senate Office Bldg Washington DC 20510-0001 also: Henry M Jackson Federal Bldg Ste 2988 915 Second Ave Seattle WA 98174-4067 Office Phone: 202-224-2621, 206-553-5545. Office Fax: 202-224-0238, 206-553-0891. E-mail: senator_murray@murray.senate.gov.*

MURRAY, RICHARD M., engineering educator; BS with honors in elec. engring., Calif. Inst. Tech., 1985; MS in elec. engring. and computer sciences, U. Calif., Berkeley, 1989, PhD, 1991. Asst. prof. mech. engring. Calif. Inst. Tech., 1991—97, assoc. prof. mech. engring., 1997—2000, prof. mech. engring., 2000—05, chair Divsn. Engring. and Applied Sci., 2000, prof. Control and Dynamical Sys., 2005—; dir. mechatronic systems United Technologies Rsch. Ctr., 1998—2000. Mem. info. sci. and tech. study group Def. Advanced Rsch. Projects Agy., Dept. Def., 2000—; mem. R&D strategy adv. com. Rockwell Sci. Co., 2001—; mem. Jet Propulsion Lab. adv. coun. NASA, 2001—; mem. vis. com. Dept. Mech. Engring., MIT, 2001—; chair exec. bd. Collaborative Ctr. on Control Sci., 2002—; mem. sci. adv. bd. USAF, 2002—; cons. Alphatech, Raytheon, United Technologies Rsch. Ctr., Northrop Corp. Recipient Eliahu Jury Award, U. Calif. Berkeley, 1991, Early Faculty Career Devel. Award, NSF, 1995, Young Investigator Award, Office Naval Rsch., 1995, Donald P. Eckman Award, Am. Automatic Control Coun., 1997; Richard P. Feynman-Hughes Faculty Fellowship, Calif. Inst. Tech., 1993. Achievements include patents for Actuator Bandwidth and Rate Limit Reduction for Control of Compressor Rotating Stall (with Simon Yeung), US Patent 5,984,625, Nov. 1999. Office: Control and Dynamical Systems 107-81 Calif Inst Tech MC 107-81 Pasadena CA 91125

MURRAY, TY, professional rodeo cowboy; b. Phoenix, Oct. 11, 1969; s. Harold "Butch" and Joy M. Student, Odessa Coll., Tex. Seven-time world champion all-around world cowboy Profl. Rodeo Cowboys Assn., 1989-94, 98, two-time world champion bullrider, 1993, 98. Named Nat. H.S. Rodeo All-Around Champion, 1987, PRCA Rookie of the Year Profl. Rodeo Cowboy Assn., 1988, Nat. Intercollegiate Rodeo All-Around Champion, 1988, World Champion All Around Cowboy, World Champion Bull Rider, 1998. Achievements include holding the record for single season earnings, 1991. Office: Profl Rodeo Cowboy Assn 101 Pro Rodeo Dr Colorado Springs CO 80919-4300 also: R&R Advt Tony Garritano 8076 W Sahara Ave Las Vegas NV 89117-1957

MURREN, JAMES JOSEPH, hotel corporation executive; b. 1961; s. John and Jean-Marie Murren; m. Heather Hay. BA in Art History & Urban Studies, Trinity Coll., 1983. Chartered Fin. Analyst. Various positions Deutsche Morgan Grenfell, 1984—94; mng. dir., dir. rsch. Deutsche Bank, 1994—98; exec. v.p., CFO MGM Mirage, Las Vegas, 1998—99, pres., CFO, 1999—2007, treas., 2001—07, pres., COO, 2007—08, chmn., CEO, 2008—. Bd. dirs. MGM Mirage, 2000—, Delta Petroleum Corp., 2008—. Co-founder, bd. dirs. Nevada Cancer Inst., 2005—; trustee U. Nev. Las Vegas Found., U. Nevada Reno Found. Office: MGM Mirage 3600 Las Vegas Blvd South Las Vegas NV 89109

MUSFELT, DUANE CLARK, lawyer; b. Stockton, Calif., Sept. 14, 1951; s. Robert H. and Doris E. (Roth) M.; m. Linh T. To, Sept. 6, 1980. Student, U. Calif., Davis, 1969-71; BA in Econs., U. Calif., Berkeley, 1973; JD, UCLA, 1976. Bar: Calif. 1976, U.S. Dist. Ct. (cen. dist.) Calif. 1977, U.S. Ct. Appeals (9th cir.) 1980, U.S. Dist. Ct. (no. dist.) Calif. 1982, U.S. Dist. Ct. (ea. and so. dists.) Calif. 1983, U.S. Supreme Ct. 1987. Assoc. Haight, Dickson, Brown & Bonesteel, LA, 1976-77, Mori & Ota, LA, 1977-79, Lewis, D'Amato, Brisbois & Bisgaard, LA, 1979-82; ptnr. Lewis, Brisbois, Bisgaard & Smith, San Francisco, 1982—. Mem. State Bar Calif., Bar Assn. San Francisco. Democrat. Presbyterian. Avocations: tennis, skiing, bridge. Office: Lewis Brisbois Bisgaard & Smith One Sansome St Ste 1400 San Francisco CA 94104-4431 Office Phone: 415-362-2580. Business E-Mail: musfelt@lbbslaw.com.

MUSIHIN, KONSTANTIN K., electrical engineer; b. Harbin, China, June 17, 1927; came to US, 1967, naturalized, 1973; s. Konstantin N. and Alexandra A. (Lapitsky) M.; m. Natalia Krilova, Oct. 18, 1964; 1 child, Nicholas. Student, YMCA Inst., 1942, North Manchurian U., 1945, Harbin Poly. Inst., 1948. Registered profl. engr., Calif., NY, Pa., Wash. Asst. prof. Harbin Poly. Inst., 1950-53; elec. engr. Moinho Santista, Sao Paulo, Brazil, 1955-60; constrn. project mgr. Caterpillar-Brazil, Santo Amaro, 1960-61; mech. engr. Matarazzo Industries, Sao Paulo, 1961-62; chief of works Vidrobras, St. Gobain, Brazil, 1962-64; project engr. Brown Boveri, Sao Paulo, 1965-67; sr. engr. Kaiser Engrs., Oakland, Calif., 1967-73, Bechtel Power Corp., San Francisco, 1973-75; supr. power and control San Francisco Bay Area Rapid Transit, Oakland, 1976-78; chief elec. engr. L.K. Comstock Engring. Co., San Francisco, 1978-79; prin. engr. Morrison Knudsen Co., San Francisco, 1979-84, Brown & Caldwell, Cons. Engrs., Pleasant Hill, Calif., 1984-85; cons. engr. Pacific Gas and Electric Co., San Francisco, 1986-89; sr. engr. Bechtel Corp., San Francisco, 1989. Mem. IEEE (life, sr.), NSPE, Calif. Soc. Profl. Engrs. Mem. Christian Orthodox Ch.

MUSK, ELON, aerospace transportation executive; b. South Africa, June 28, 1971; m. Justine Musk; 5 children. Student, Queen's U., Kingston, Ont.; BS in Economics, U. Pa., 1994, BS in Physics, 1994; postgraduates studies, Stanford U. With Pinnacle Rsch.; software devel. Rocket Sci., Microsoft; co-founder, chmn., CEO, chief tech. officer Zip2 Corp. (acquired by Compaq), 1995—99; co-founder, chmn., CEO X.com (changed legal name to PayPal in 2001, acquired by eBay in 2002), 1999—2002; founder, CEO, chief tech. officer Space Exploration Tech. Corp. (SpaceX), 2002—; product architect, chmn. Tesla Motors, Inc., San Carlos, 2003—. Prin. owner, chmn. bd. Tesla Motors; primary investor, chmn. bd. Solar City; bd. dirs. The Planetary Society, 2003—. Chmn. Musk Found.; bd. trustee X-Prize Found. Named one of 50 Who Matter Now, Business 2.0, 2007. Fellow: World Tech. Network; mem.: US NAS (bd. dir, Aeronautics and Space Engring.). Office: Space Exploration Tech Corp 1310 E Grand Ave El Segundo CA 90245 also: Tesla Motors Inc 1050 Bing St San Carlos CA 94070

MUSOLF, LLOYD DARYL, political science professor, educational association administrator; b. Yale, SD, Oct. 14, 1919; s. William Ferdinand and Emma Marie (Pautz) M.; m. Berdyne Peet, June 30, 1944; children: Stephanie, Michael, Laura. BA, Huron Coll., 1941; MA, U. SD, 1946; PhD, Johns Hopkins U., 1950. Mem. faculty Vassar Coll., Poughkeepsie, NY, 1949-59, assoc. prof. polit. sci., 1955-59; chief of party adv. group Mich. State U., East Lansing, 1959-61, prof. polit. sci., 1961-63, U. Calif.-Davis, 1963-87, prof. emeritus, 1988—, dir. Inst. Govtl. Affairs, 1963-84. Vis. prof. Johns Hopkins U., Balt., 1953, U. Del., 1954, U. Mich., 1955-56; US Nat. rapporteur for Internat. Congress Adminstrv. Scis., Berlin, 1983; cons., lectr. in field. Author: Federal Examiners and the Conflict of Law and Administration, 1953, Public Ownership and Accountability: The Canadian Experience, 1959, Promoting the General Welfare, Government and the Economy, 1965, (with others) American National Government-Policies and Politics, 1971, Mixed Enterprise-A Developmental Perspective, 1972, (with Springer) Malaysia's Parliamentary System-Representative Politics and Policymaking in a Divided Society, 1979, Uncle Sam's Private Profitseeking Corporations-Comsat, Fannie Mae, Amtrak and Conrail, 1983; editor: (with Krislov) The Politics of Regulation, 1964, Communications Satellites in Political Orbit, 1968, (with Kornberg) Legislatures in Developmental Perspective, 1970, (with Joel Smith) Legislatures in Development-Dynamics of Change in New and Old States, 1979; contbr. monographs, chpts. to books, articles to profl. jours. Served to lt. USNR, 1942-45. Johnston scholar Johns Hopkins U., 1946-48; Faculty fellow Vassar Coll., 1954-55; sr. assoc. East-West Ctr., Honolulu, 1968-69; vis. scholar Brookings Instn., Washington, 1980. Mem. ASPA (exec. coun. 1967-70), Nat. Assn. Schs. Pub. Affairs and Adminstrn. (exec. coun. 1972-75), Western Govtl. Rsch. Assn. (exec. bd. 1966-68), Am. Polit. Sci. Assn., Nat. Assn. State Univs. and Land Grant Colls. (rsch. com. divsn. urban affairs 1980-81). Office: U Calif Dept Polit Sci Davis CA 95616 Home Phone: 530-747-6536; Office Phone: 530-752-0946.

MUSSEHL, ROBERT CLARENCE, lawyer; b. Washington, May 1, 1936; s. Chester Carl and Clara Cecelia (Greenwalt) Mussehl; m. Misook Chung, Mar. 22, 1987; 1 child, Omar;children from previous marriage: Debra Lee(dec.), David Lee. BA, Am. U., 1964, JD, 1966. Bar: Wash. 1967, U.S. Dist. Ct. (we. dist.) Wash. 1967, U.S. Ct. Appeals (9th cir.) 1968, U.S. Supreme Ct. 1971. Sr. ptnr. Thom, Mussehl, Navoni, Hoff, Pierson & Ryder, Seattle, 1967-78, Neubauer & Mussehl, Seattle, 1978-80, Mussehl & Rosenberg, Seattle, 1980—2001, Mussehl & Khan, 2004—06. Spkr. law convs. and other profl. orgns.; chmn. bd. dirs., CEO Seattle Smashers, 1976—80; moot ct. judge Nat. Appellate Adv. Competition, San Francisco, 1987; panel mem. ABA Symposium Compulsory Jurisdiction World Ct., San Francisco, 1987. Contbr. articles to profl. jours. Mem. Wash. Vol. Lawyers Arts, 1976—80; bd. dirs. Wash. State Pub. Interest Law Ctr., 1976—81; founder, past chair Lawyers Helping Hungry Children, bd. dirs., 1991—2008; founder, past chair Wash. State Lawyers Campaign Hunger Relief, 1991—; statewide chair Lawyers for Duming for Gov., 1976; mem. task force single adult and ch. Ch. Coun. Greater Seattle, 1976—78. Recipient Jefferson award for Cmty. and Pub. Svc., State of Wash., Am. Inst. Pub. Svc., 1997. Fellow: Am. Acad. Matrimonial Lawyers, Am. Bar Found. (life); mem.: ABA (ho. dels. 1979—91, mem. assembly resolutions com. 1979—91, chair marriage and family counseling and concilliation com. 1981—83, mem. world order under law standing com. 1983—89, chair 1986—89, chair ad hoc com. assembly 1986—89, mem. blue ribbon com. world ct. 1987—88, mem. spl. adv. com. internat. activities 1989—91, mem. standing com. dispute resolution 1992—93, mem. exec. coun. sect. dispute resolution 1993—95, asst. budget officer 1995—97, budget officer 1997—99, chair 2001—02, sect. liaison commn. racial and ethnic diversity 2002—04, ho. dels. 2003—, commn. racial and ethnic diversity 2004—06, editor Goal IX newsletter 2004—), World Assn. Lawyers World Peace through Law Ctr. (founding mem.), Am. Arbitration Assn. (panel arbitrators), Seattle-King County Bar Assn. (mem. other coms. 1970—, chmn. young lawyers sect. 1971—72, mem. family law sect. 1971—90, sec. 1972—73, trustee), Wash. State Trial Lawyers Assn., Wash. State Bar Assn. (mem. exec. com. family law sect. 1973—75, chmn. internat. law com. 1974—76, sec.-treas., mem. exec. com. world peace through law sect. 1980—, chair 1981—82, mem. editl. bd. Family Law Deskbook 1987—89), UN Assn. USA (bd. dirs. Seattle chpt. 1989—91), Heritage Club YMCA Greater Seattle (charter 1977—). Avocations: squash, bicycling, tennis, weightlifting, painting. Office: 520 Pike St Ste 2210 Seattle WA 98101 Home: 2415 34th Ave W Seattle WA 98199 Office Phone: 206-386-7200. Personal E-mail: bobmussehl@earthlink.net.

MUSSELMAN, ERIC, former professional basketball coach; b. Ashland, Ohio, Nov. 19, 1964; s. Bill Musselman; m. Wendy Musselman; children: Michael, Matthew. BS, U. San Diego, 1987. Draft pick Continental Basketball Assn. Albany Patroons, 1987; asst. dir. scouting LA Clippers, 1987—90; asst. coach Minn. Timberwolves, 1990—91, Orlando Magic, 1998—2000, Atlanta Hawks, 2000—02, Memphis Grizzlies, 2004—06; gen. mgr. Continental Basketball Assn. Fla. Beach Dogs, 1990—98, head coach, 1991—98, US Basketball League Fla. Sharks, 1995—96, Golden State Warriors, Oakland, Calif., 2002—04, Sacramento Kings, 2006—07. Head coach Continental Basketball Assn. All-Star Game, 1990, 92, 93, 94, 97.

MUSSEY, JOSEPH ARTHUR, health and medical product executive; b. Cleve., July 17, 1948; s. Arthur Glenn and Mary Jane (Silvaroli) M.; m. Mary Elizabeth Stone, July 11, 1975; 1 child, Joanna Lee. BS in Indsl. Engring. with distinction, Cornell U., 1970; MBA, Harvard U., 1976. Engring. mgmt. officer U.S. Navy Pub. Works Ctr., Pearl Harbor, Hawaii, 1971-75; mktg. exec. B.F. Goodrich, Akron, Ohio, 1976-80, fin. exec., 1980-84; v.p. fin. Combustion Engring., Stamford, Conn., 1984-85, v.p. ops., 1985-86; exec. v.p. Process Automation Bus. Combustion Engring., Columbus, Ohio, 1987-90; pres., CEO Danninger Med. Tech., Inc., Columbus, 1990—98; pres., CEO, dir. Interpore Cross Internat., Irvine, Calif., 1998—. Served as lt. U.S. Navy, 1971-75. Decorated Disting. Naval Grad. (USN), 1971, Disting. Grad. U.S. Navy Civil Engring. Corps., 1971. Mem. Alpha Pi Mu, Tau Beta Pi, Phi Eta Sigma. Clubs: Skull & Daggar. Republican. Roman Catholic. Office: Interpore Cross International 181 Technology Dr Irvine CA 92618 Home: 812 NE Bay Isle Dr Boca Raton FL 33487-1731

MUSTACCHI, PIERO, preventive medicine physician, educator; b. Cairo, May 29, 1920; came to U.S., 1947; naturalized, 1962; s. Gino and Gilda (Rieti) M.; m. Dora Lisa Ancona, Sept. 26, 1948; children: Roberto, Michael. BS in Humanities, U. Florence, Italy, 1938; postgrad. in anatomy, U. Lausanne, Switzerland, 1938-39; MB, ChB, Fouad I U., Cairo, Egypt, 1944, grad. in Arabic lang. and lit., 1946; D Medicine and Surgery, U. Pisa, 1986; Degree (hon.), U. Aix-Marseille, France, 1988, U. Alexandria, Egypt, 1985. Qualified med. examiner, Calif. Indsl. Accident Commn., 1994. House officer English Hosp., Ch. Missionary Soc., Cairo, 1945-47; clin. affiliate U. Calif., San Francisco, 1947-48; intern Franklin Hosp., San Francisco, 1948-49; resident in pathology U. Calif., San Francisco, 1949-51; resident in medicine Meml. Ctr. Cancer and Allied Diseases, NYC, 1951-53; rsch. epidemiologist Dept. HEW, Nat. Cancer Inst., Bethesda, Md., 1955-57; cons. allergy clinic U. Calif., San Francisco, 1957-70, clin. prof. medicine and preventive medicine, 1970-90, clin. prof. medicine and epidemiology, 1990-96, head occupl. epidemiology, 1975-90, head divsn. internat. health edn. dept. epidemiology and internat. health, 1985-90; médecin agréé, official physician Consulate Gen. of France, San Francisco, 1995—2006; sr. cons. internat. health care U. Calif., San Francisco. Med. cons., vis. prof. numerous ednl. & profl. instns., U. Marseilles, 1981—82, U. Pisa, Italy, 1983, U. Gabon, 1984, U. Siena, Italy, 1985; cons. U. Calif., 1975—, U. El Azhar, 1986; sr. cons. internat. med. care U. Calif., San Francisco, 2000—. Contbr. chpts. to books, articles to profl. jours. Editorial bd. Medecine d'Afrique Noire, Ospedali d'Italia. With USPHS USN, 1955—57. Decorated comdr. Order of Merit (Italy), officer Ordre de la Legion d'Honneur (France), Medal of St. John of Jerusalem, Sovereign Order of Malta, Order of the Republic (Egypt); Scroll, Leonardo da Vinci Soc., San Francisco, 1965; award Internat. Inst. Oakland, 1964; Hon. Vice Consul. Italy, 1971-90. Fellow ACP, Am. Soc. Environ. and Occupational Health; mem. AAAS, Am. Assn. Cancer Rsch., Calif. Soc. Allergy and Immunology, Calif. Med. Assn., San Francisco Med. Soc., West Coast Allergy Soc. (founding), Mex. Congress on Hypertension (corr.), Internat. Assn. Med. Rsch. and Continuing Edn. (U.S. rep.), Acad. Italiana della Cucina, Acta Medico Historica Adriatica, 2007. Democrat. Avocations: music, math, languages. also: 3838 California St San Francisco CA 94118-1522 Office Phone: 415-668-2626.

MUTU, WANGECHI, collage artist, painter; b. Nairobi, Kenya, 1972; Grad., United World Coll. of the Atlantic, Wales, 1991; BFA, Cooper Union for the Advancement Sci. and Art, 1996; MFA, Yale U., 2000. One-woman shows include Jamaica Ctr. Arts and Learning, Queens, NY, 2003, Susanne Vielmetter LA Projects, 2003, 2005, 2008, Miami Art Mus., 2005, San Francisco Mus. Modern Art, 2006, Sikkema Jenkins & Co., NYC, 2006, SITE Santa Fe, 2006—07, exhibited in group shows at Out of the Box, Queens Mus., NY, 2001, Africaine, Studio Mus. Harlem, NYC, 2002, Figuratively, 2004, African Queen, Black President, traveling, 2003, Open House, Bklyn. Mus. Art, 2003, 2004, Only Skin Deep, Internat. Ctr. Photography, NYC, 2003, New, Susanne Vielmetter LA Projects, 2004, Cut, 2005, Pin-Up: Contemporary Collage and Drawing, Tate Modern, London, 2004, Greater NY, P.S.1 Contemporary Art Ctr., 2005, Drawing from the Modern, Mus. Modern Art, NYC, 2005, Matisse and Beyond, San Francisco Mus. Modern Art, 2005, After Cezanne, Mus. Contemporary Art LA, 2005, Triumph of Painting, Saatchi Gallery, London, 2006, USA Today, Royal Acad. Arts, London, 2006, Collage: The Unmonumental Picture, New Mus., NYC, 2008. Recipient Richard Leakey merit award, 1994; grantee Joan Mitchell Found., 2007, Louis Comfort Tiffany Found., 2008; fellow Fannie B. Pardee Found., 2000, Jamaica Ctr. Arts, 2001. Studio: 849 Lafayette Ave Brooklyn NY 11221-1901 Office: c/o Sikkema Jenkins & Co 530 W 22nd St New York NY 10011 also: c/o Susanne Vielmetter LA Projects 5795 W Washington Blvd Culver City CA 90232

MUZYKA-MCGUIRE, AMY, marketing professional, nutritionist, consultant; b. Chgo., Sept. 24, 1953; d. Basil Bohdan and Amelia (Rand) Muzyka; m. Patrick J. McGuire, June 3, 1977; children: Jonathan, Elizabeth. BS, Iowa State U., 1975, postgrad., 1978—; registered dietitian, St. Louis U., 1980. Cert. dietitian. Home economist Nat. Livestock and Meat Bd., Chgo., 1975-77; dietary cons. various hosps. and nursing homes, Iowa, 1978-79; supr. foodsvc. Am. Egg Bd., Park Ridge, Ill., 1980-83; assoc. dir., mgr. foodsvc. Cole & Weber Advt., Seattle, 1984-85; prin., owner Food and Nutrition Comms., Federal Way, Wash., 1986—. Co-author: Turkey Foodservice Manual, 1987; editor: (newsletter) Home Economists in Business, 1975-77, Dietitians in Business and Industry, 1982-85; Food Net on Internet, 1995, Food and Culinary Profls. Newsletter, 1999-2001; contbr. articles to profl. jours. Named Outstanding Dietitian of Yr. North Suburban Dietetic Assn., 1983, Tastemaker of the Month, 2001, 02, 03. Mem. Am. Dietetic Assn., Internat. Foodsvc. Editl. Coun., Cons. Nutritionists, Internat. Assn. Culinary Profls. (CCP; chair nutritional food scis. group 2003-05). Avocations: gardening, travel, music, food and beverage tastings. Home: 5340 SW 315th St Federal Way WA 98023-2034

MYCIELSKI, JAN, retired mathematics professor; b. Wisniowa, Poland, Feb. 7, 1932; s. Jan and Helena (Bal) M.; m. Emilia Przezdziecka, Apr. 25, 1959. MS, U. Wroclaw, Poland, 1955, PhD, 1957. With Inst. Math., Polish Acad. Scis., Wroclaw, 1956-68; prof. math. U. Colo., Boulder, 1969—2002, prof. emeritus, 2002—. Vis. prof. Case Western Res. U., Cleve., 1967, U. Colo., 1967, Inst. des Hautes Etudes Scientifiques, Bures-sur-Yvette, 1978-79, dept. math. U. Hawaii, 1987; attache de recherche Centre National de la Recherche Scientifique, Paris, 1957-58; asst. prof. U. Calif., Berkeley, 1961-62, 70; long-term vis. staff mem. Los Alamos Nat. Lab., 1989-90. Author over 150 rsch. papers. Recipient Stefan Banach prize, 1965, Alfred Jurzykowski award, 1977, Waclaw Sierpinski medal, 1990. Mem. Am. Math. Soc., Math. Assn. Am., Polish Math. Soc., Assn. for Symbolic Logic. Office: U Colo Dept Math Boulder CO 80309-0395

MYERS, ALBERT F., aerospace executive; b. New Orleans, Jan. 11, 1946; BS in Mech. Engring., U. Idaho, 1969, MS in Mech. Engring., 1971; MS in Indl. Mgmt., MIT, 1992. Active duty U.S. Army, 1972-75; various positions Dryden Flight Rsch. Ctr., 1975-81; mgr. flight controls engring. Northrop Grumman, 1981, corp. v.p., Bus. Stategy, 1992-94, corp. v.p., treas., 1994—2003, corp. v.p., Strategy and Technology, 2003—. Mem.: NAE. Office: Northrop Grumman Corp 1840 Century Park E Los Angeles CA 90067-2101

MYERS, CHRISTOPHER D., bank executive; b. Calif. BA, Harvard U.; MBA, U. Calif. Various positions including v.p., mgr. First Interstate Bank; comml. bank ctr. mgr. Bank of the West (Sanwa Bank of Calif.); chmn., CEO Mellon First Bus. Bank, LA, 1996—2006; pres., CEO, chmn. CVB Fin. Corp., Citizens Bus. Bank, 2006—. Office: CVB Fin Corp 701 North Haven Ave Ste 350 Ontario CA 91764 Office Phone: 909-980-4030. Office Fax: 909-481-2130.

MYERS, DOUGLAS GEORGE, zoological society administrator; b. LA, Aug. 30, 1949; s. George Walter and Daydeen (Schroeder) Myers; m. Barbara Firestone Myers, Nov. 30, 1980; children: Amy, Andrew. BA, Christopher Newport Coll., 1981. Tour and show supr. Annheuser-Busch (Bird Sanctuary), Van Nuys, Calif., 1970-74, mgr. zool. ops., 1974-75, asst. mgr. ops., 1975-77, mgr. ops., 1977-78; gen. services mgr. Annheuser-Busch (Old Country), Williamsburg, Va., 1978-80, park ops. dir., 1980-81; gen. mgr. San Diego Wild Animal Park, 1981-83, dep. dir. ops., 1983-85; CEO, Exec. Dir. Zool. Soc. San Diego, 1985—. Mem. Balboa Park Cultural Partnership, Steering Com. Conservation Breeding Specialists Group, Ctrl. Balboa Park Assn. Bd. dirs. Nat. Mus. Libr. Svcs., 2007—. Mem.: Calif. Assn. Zoos and Aquariums, World Assn. Zoos and Aquariums, Am. Zoo and Aquarium Assn., Am. Assn. Museums (bd. dir.), Rotary Club San Diego. Office: Zool Soc San Diego PO Box 120551 San Diego CA 92112-0551

MYERS, ELMER, psychiatric social worker; b. Blackwell, Ark., Nov. 12, 1926; s. Chester Elmer Myers and Irene Lewis; widowed; children: Elmer Jr., Keith, Kevin. BA, U. Kans., 1951, MA, 1962; student, U. Calif., Santa Barbara, 1977-78. Lic. clin. social worker; C.C. counselor credentials. Psychiat. social worker Hastings (Nebr.) State Hosp., 1960-62, State of Calif. Bur. Social Tng. Com., Sacramento, 1962-75; supr. psychiat. social worker State of Calif., Sacramento, 1975-80, Alta Calif. Regional Ctr., Sacramento, 1980-85. Exec. dir. Tri-County Family Svcs., Yuba City, Calif., 1966-69; cons. to four convalescent Hosps., Marysville and Willows, Calif., 1969-71; lectr. Yuba Coll., Marysville, 1971-76; assoc. prof. Calif. State U., Chico, 1972-73; cons. in field, Marysville, 1985—; group and individual therapist Depot Homeless Shelter, 1996-2008, facilitator HIV support group, 1993-2002, counselor, 1995—; cons., therapist New Millennium Group Home, 2000. Bd. dirs. Habitat for Humanity, 1993; juror Yuba County Grand Jury, Marysville, 1965, 1987—88; sec. Y's Men's Club, Yuba City, 1964—65; chmn. Tri-County Home Health Agy., Yuba City, 1974—76; vice-chmn. Gateway Projects, Inc., Yuba City, 1974—75; bd. dirs. Yuba County Truancy Bd., Marysville, 1964—67; asst. dir. Marysville Adult Activity Ctr., 1990—; active Yuba-Sutter United Way, 1971—73, 1991—92; active, sec. Tri-County Ethnic Forum, 1991—93; steering com. Yuba County Sr. Ctr. Assn., 1992, 1995—; chmn. Yuba County Cmty. Svcs. Commn., 1997—99; bd. dirs. Yuba-Sutter Gleaners, 1997—2004, 2006—, fin. sec., 2006; chmn. Yuba-Sutter Commn. on Aging, 1996, bd. dirs., 1998, 2001; chmn. H.E.L.P. Working Group, HIV Prevention, 2000; bd. dirs. Christian Assistance Network, 1993, Golden Empire Health Sys. Agy., Sacramento, 1972—76, Youth Svcs. Bur., Yuba City, 1967, Bi-County Mental Retardation Planning Bd., Yuba City, 1972, Yuba County Juvenile Justice Commn., Marysville, 1982—90, Am. Cancer Soc., Marysville, 1985—92, Yuba County Rep. Ctrl. Com., 1983—90, Salvation Army, 1990—96, facilitator care proj., 1992—2002. Recipient Cert. Spl. Recognition, Calif. Rehab. Planning Project, 1969, Cert. Spl. Recognition, State of Calif., 1967, Cert. Spl. Recognition, Alta Calif. Regional Ctrs., 1985; named Vol. of Week, Appeal Dem. newspaper, 1999. Mem. Nat. Assn. Social Workers (cert.), Kern County Mental Health Assn. (chmn. 1978-79). Lodges: Rotary (bd. dirs. Marysville club 1975-76). Avocations: gardening, reading, computers. Home and Office: 3920 State Hwy 20 Marysville CA 95901-9003 E-mail: elm@syix.com.

MYERS, HARDY, former state attorney general; b. Electric Mills, Miss., Oct. 25, 1939; m. Mary Ann Thalhofer, 1962; children: Hardy III, Christopher, Jonathan. AB with distinction, U. Miss., 1961; LLB, U. Oreg., 1964. Bar: Oreg., U.S. Ct. of Appeals (9th cir.), U.S. Dist. Ct. (Dist. of Oreg.). Law clk. to US Dist. Judge William G. East, 1964—65; pvt. practice Stoel Rives LLP and predecessor firms, 1965—96; atty. gen. State of Oreg., 1997—2009. Mem. Oreg Ho. Reps., 1975—85, spkr. of the ho., 1979—83; chair Com. on Judiciary, 1977—78, 1983—84; councilor Met. Svc. Dist. (now Metro), 1985—86. Bd. editors Oregon Law Rev. Pres. Portland City Planning Commn., 1973—74; chair Oreg. Jail Project, 1984—86, Citizens' Task Force on Mass Transit Policy, 1985—86, Oreg. Criminal Justice Coun., 1987—91, Portland Future Focus, 1990—91, Metro Charter com., 1991—92, task force on state employee benefits, 1994; co-chair gov. task force on state employee compensation, 1995; mem. Commn. on Jud. Br., 1983—85. Mem.: Multnomah County Bar Assn., Oreg. State Bar, Omicron Delta Kappa, Phi Kappa Phi, Phi Eta Sigma. Democrat. Office: PO Box 9236 Portland OR 97207 Office Phone: 503-378-6002, 503-378-4732.*

MYERS, JAMES M., pet products executive; BS in Acctg., John Carroll Univ. CPA. Various positions to sr. audit mgr. KPMG LLP, 1980—90; v.p., fin. to v.p., controller PETCO, San Diego, 1990—96, sr. v.p., fin., 1996—98, exec. v.p., CFO, 1998—2004, CEO, 2004—. Office: PETCO 9125 Rehco Rd San Diego CA 92121 Office Phone: 858-453-7845.

MYERS, LOU, actor; b. Charleston, W.Va., Sept. 26, 1945; s. Dorothy (Brown) Jeffries; divorced; 1 child, Melvin L. BS in Sociology, W.Va. State Inst., 1964; M in Sociology, NYU, 1975. Chmn. Lou Myers Scenario Motion Picture Inst./Theatre & Global Bus. Incubation. Broadway appearances include Ma Rainey's Black Bottom, The First Breeze of Summer, 1975, The Piano Lesson, 1990, The Color Purple, 2005, Cat on a Hot Tin Roof, 2008; appeared off-Off-Broadway in Fat Tuesday (Audience Devel. Com. Audelco award), King Hedley II (NAACP Image award, Audelco award for Best Actor); actor (TV films) The First Breeze of Summer, 1976, The Piano Lesson, 1995, Mama Flora's Family, 1998, A Private Affair, 2000, Lackawanna Blues, 2005, (films) Missing Pieces, 1991, Cobb, 1994, The Passion of Darkly Noon, 1995, Tin Cup, 1996, Volcano, 1997, Bulworth, 1998, Goodbye Lover, 1998, How Stella Got Her Groove Back, 1998, The Stand-In, 1999, The Big Confession, 1999, Everything's Jake, 2000, The Wedding Planner, 2001, All About You, 2001, The Fighting Temptations, 2003, Sweet Oranges, 2003, Team Player, 2004, Kings of the Evening, 2008, (TV series) A Different World, 1988-93, All About the Andersons, 2003; toured Far East and Africa, US with one-man show Me and the Blues; organizer, dir. Tshaka Ensemble. Served with USAF. Recipient Living Legend award, Nat. Black Theatre Festival. Office: Scenario Movie Inst/Theatre & GBI Ste 330 6410 Green Valley Cir Culver City CA 90230 Office Phone: 310-649-6623.

MYERS, MARILYN GLADYS, pediatric hematologist, oncologist; b. Lyons, Nebr., July 17, 1930; d. Leonard Clarence and Marian N. (Manning) M.; m. Paul Frederick Motzkus, July 24, 1957 (dec. Aug. 1982). BA cum laude, U. Omaha, 1954; MD, U. Nebr., 1959. Diplomate Am. Bd. Pediat. Intern Orange County Gen. Hosp., Orange, Calif., 1959-60, resident, 1960-62; fellow in hematology/oncology Orange County Gen. Hosp./Children's Hosp. L.A., 1962-64; assoc. in rsch., chief dept. hematology/oncology Children's Hosp., Orange, 1964-80, dir. outpatient dept., 1964-73, assoc. dir. leukapheresis unit, 1971-80; clin. practice hematology, oncology, rheumatology Orange, 1964-80; instr. Coll. Medicine U. Calif., Irvine, 1968-71, asst. clin. prof. pediatrics, 1971—; pvt. practice hematology, oncology, rheumatology Santa Ana, Calif., 1980—. Clin. rschr. exptl. drugs. Contbr. articles to med. jours. Med. adv. com. Orange County Blood Bank Hemophiliac Found. Grantee Am. Leukemia Soc., 1963, Am. Heart Assn., 1964. Fellow Am. Acad. Pediat.; mem. AMA, Calif. Med. Assn., LA County Med. Assn., Orange County Med. Assn., Orange County Pediat. Soc., Southwestern Pediat. Soc., LA Pediat. Soc., Internat. Coll. Pediat., Orange County Oncologic Soc., Am. Heart Assn. (Cardiopulmonary Coun.). Republican. Methodist. Avocation: reading. Office: 2220 E Fruit St Ste 217 Santa Ana CA 92701-4459

MYERS, MIKE, actor, scriptwriter, film producer; b. Toronto, Ont., Can., May 25, 1963; s. Eric and Bunny (Hind) M.; m. Robin Ruzan, 1993 (separated). Stage appearances: The Second City, Toronto, 1986-88, Chgo., 1988-89; actor, writer: Mullarkey & Myers, Can., 1984-86, (TV show) Saturday Night Live, 1989-94 (Emmy award for outstanding writing in a comedy or variety series 1989), (film) Wayne's World, 1992, So I Married an Axe Murderer, 1993, Wayne's World II (also screenwriter, prodr.), 1993, Austin Powers: International Man Of Mystery (also screenwriter, prodr.), 1997, Pete's Meteor, 1998, It's a Dog's Life, 1998, 54, 1998, Austin Powers: The Spy Who Shagged Me (also screenwriter, prodr.), 1999, Austin Powers: The Animated Series, 1999, Shrek (voice), 2001, Austin Powers Goldmember (also writer, prodr.), 2002, View from the Top, 2003, Shrek 4-D (voice), 2003, The Cat in the Hat, 2003, Shrek 2 (voice), 2004, Shrek the Third (voice), 2007, The Love Guru (also writer, prodr.), 2008; actor: (TV movie) John and Yoko, 1985, Elvis Stories, 1989, Saturday Night Live: The Best of Phil Hartman, 1998, Saturday Night Live: the Best of Mike Myers, 1998, Saturday Night Live: 25th Anniversary, 1999, Madonna: The Video Collection 93.99, 1999; screenwriter: (tv movie) Murderers Among Us: The Simon Wiesenthal Story, 1989, Saturday Night Live: The Best of Mike

Myers, 1998; (video) Far Far Away Idol (voice), 2004; (video game voice) Shrek: Smash n' Crash Racing, 2006; TV appearances The Littlest Hobo, 1979, Russell Gilbert Show, 1998, Night of Too Many Stars: An Overbooked Event for Autism Edn., 2006; dir. (film) The Bacchae, 1999. Recipient Can. comedy award, 2000, MTV Generation award, 2007. Office: c/o David O'Connor Creative Artists Agy 9830 Wilshire Blvd Beverly Hills CA 90212-1804

MYERS, MILES ALVIN, educational association administrator, researcher; b. Newton, Kans., Feb. 4, 1931; s. Alvin F. and Katheryn P. (Miles) M.; m. Celeste Myers; children: Royce, Brant, Roslyn. BA in Rhetoric, U. Calif., Berkeley, 1953, MAT in English, 1979, MA in English, 1982, PhD in Lang. and Literacy, 1982. Cert. secondary tchr. English. Tchr. English Washington Union High Sch., Fremont, Calif., 1957-59, Oakland (Calif.) High Sch., 1959-67, 69-74, Concord High Sch., Mt. Diablo, Calif., 1967-69; chmn. bd. dirs. Alpha Plus Corp. Preschs., Piedmont, Calif., 1968—2002; dir. All City High, 1973-74; tchr. English Castlemont High Sch., Oakland, 1974-75; mem. faculty U. Calif., Berkeley, 1975-85, adminstrv. dir. Bay Area writing project Sch. Edn., 1976-85, adminstrv. dir. nat. writing project Sch. Edn., 1979-85; pres., CEO Calif. Fedn. Tchrs., 1985-90; exec. dir. Edschool-.com of Edvantage/Riverdeep, 1999—2001; dir. Inst. Rsch. on Learning and Tchg., Berkeley, Calif., 1998—; sr. rschr. Inst. for Stds. Curricula and Assessment, United Tchrs. LA, 2000—. Co-dir. Nat. Standards Project for English Language Arts, 1992-96; adj. prof. English U. Ill., Champaign-Urbana, 1991-94; vis. lectr. at numerous colleges and Univs.; rschr. in field. Author: The Meaning of Literature, 1973; co-author: Writing: Unit Lessons in Composition, Book III, 1965, The English Book-Composition Skills, 1980; author: A Procedure for Holistic Scoring, 1980, Changing our Minds, 1996; co-author: Exemplars of Standards for English Language Arts, 3 vols., 1997, Asilomar Testing Report, 2001, CSC Professional Code for English/ELA Teachers, 2005; editor Calif. Tchr., 1966-81; contbr. articles to profl. jours. Sgt. US Army, 1953—55. Recipient cert. of Merit, Ctrl. Calif. Coun. Tchrs. of English, 1969, Commendation award Oakland Fedn. Tchrs., 1970, First Place award Internat. Labor Assn., 1971, Disting. Svc. award Calif. Coun. Classified Employees, 1991, Svc. award Nat. Writing Project, 1996. Fellow Nat. Conf. Rsch. in English; mem. Nat. Coun. Tchrs. English (exec. dir. 1990-97), Nat. Conf. on Rsch. in English, Am. Fedn. Tchrs. (legis. dir. Calif. Fedn. Tchrs. 1971-72, Union Tchr. Press awards 1969-75, 86-89, 91, Ben Rust award Calif. Fedn. Tchrs. 1994), Am. Edn. Rsch. Assn., Calif. Assn. Tchrs. English (Disting. Svc. award 86), U. Calif. Berkeley Alumni Assn. Home: 5823 Scarborough Dr Oakland CA 94611-2721 Office: Dir Inst Rsch on Learning & Tchg Berkeley CA 94704 Home Fax: 510-531-0409. Business E-Mail: milesmye@pacbell.net.

MYERS, PETER SCOTT, lawyer; 2 children. BA in Lit., Am. U., Washington, DC, 1981; JD, U. Calif., San Francisco, 1984. Bar: Calif. 1984, US Dist. Ct. (no. dist. Calif.) 1984, US Dist. Ct. (so. dist. Calif.) 1986, US Ct. Appeals (9th cir.) 1986, US Dist. Ct. (ea. dist. Calif.) 1987, US Dist. Ct. (ctrl. dist. Calif.) 1988, US Tax Ct. 1997. Assoc. Bartko, Tarrant & Miller, San Francisco, 1985-87, Pillsbury, Madison & Sutro, San Francisco, 1987-92; prin. Fritz & Myers, San Francisco, 1992; ptnr. Myers Law Firm, San Francisco, 1992—. Adj. prof. Hastings Coll. Law, 1988-90; del. State Bar Conf. Dels., 1992-95. Dir. Barristers' Club, San Francisco, 1993-94, Holy Family Day Home, San Francisco, 1993-94; dir., pres. Redwood Heights Improvement Assn., Oakland, Calif., 1992-94. Named a Super Lawyer, No. Calif. Super Lawyers, 2004, 05, 06; Named one of Top 100 Attys., Worth mag., 2005-06; recipient Wiley Manuel Pro Bono award State Bar Calif., 1991-92, 92-93, Outstanding Pro-Bono Atty. award BASF, 1991. Mem.: Bar Assn. San Francisco. Office: Myers Law Firm PC 100 Spear St Ste 1430 San Francisco CA 94105 Office Phone: 415-896-1500. Office Fax: 415-896-5068.

MYERS, R(ALPH) CHANDLER, lawyer; b. LA, Jan. 9, 1933; s. Ralph Cather and Winifred (Chandler) M.; m. Rebecca Blythe Borkgren, Jan. 11, 1963. BA, Stanford U., 1954, JD, 1958; LLD (hon.), Whittier Coll., 1988. Bar: Calif. 1959, U.S. Dist. Ct. (ctrl. dist.) Calif. 1959, U.S. Supreme Ct. 1971. Law clk., then assoc. Parker, Stanbury, Reese & McGee, LA, 1958-63; assoc. Nicholas, Kolliner & Van Tassel, LA, 1963-65; ptnr. Myers & D'Angelo and predecessors, L.A. and Pasadena, Calif., 1965—. Nat. panelist Am. Arbitration Assn., LA, 1964-2000; bd. visitors Stanford U. Law Sch., Calif., 1970-73; judge pro tem panel LA Mcpl. Ct., 1971-81; mem. LA County Dist. Atty.'s Adv. Coun., 1976-83. Nat. vice chmn. Keystone Gifts, Stanford Centennial Campaign, 1987—92; trustee Whittier Coll., Calif., 1973—2001, chmn. bd. trustees Calif., 1981—87, trustee emeritus Calif., 2001—; trustee Flintridge Prep. Sch., LaCanada-Flintridge, Calif., 1981—88, chmn. bd. trustees, 1985—88; co-founder Whittier Law Sch., 1975, trustee, 1975—2001, chmn. bd. trustees, 1981—87, trustee emeritus, 2001—; bd. dirs. Opera Guild So. Calif., LA, 1971—83, pres., 1980—82; bd. dirs. Guild Opera Co. L.A., 1974—83, pres., 1975—77; bd. dirs. Western Justice Ctr. Found., 1993—2008, pres., 2003—05, adv. coun., 2008—; bd. dirs. L.A. Child Guidance Clinic, 1972—83, pres., 1977—79; bd. dirs. Opera Assocs. of the Music Ctr., LA, 1976—78. Recipient Stanford Assocs. award, 1984, Centennial Medallion award, 1991, Gold Spike award Stanford U., 1989, Disting. Svc. award Whittier Law Sch., 1993, Outstanding Achievement award Stanford Assocs., 1998; named R. Chandler Myers Dean's Suite in his honor Whittier Law Sch., 1997; Master's Cir. honoree Flintridge Prep. Sch., 1989. Mem. Wilshire Bar Assn. (bd. govs. 1972-81, pres. 1979-80), LA County Bar Assn. (trustee 1979-81), Stanford Law Soc. So. Calif. (bd. dirs. 1967-72, pres. 1970-71), Stanford Assocs. (bd. govs. 1992-97, treas. 1995-97), Jonathan Club, Univ. Club (Pasadena), Stanford Club LA (bd. dirs. 1963-70, pres. 1968-69). Home: La Canada 5623 Burning Tree Dr La Canada Flintridge CA 91011-2861 Office: Myers & D'Angelo 301 N Lake Ave Ste 800 Pasadena CA 91101-4108 Home Phone: 818-790-0888; Office Phone: 626-792-0007.

MYERS, REX CHARLES, historian, educator, retired dean; b. Cleve., July 1, 1945; s. Charles F. and Merial W. (Jones) M.; m. Susan L. Richards, Jan. 10, 1987; children: Gary W., Laura M. BA, Western State Coll., 1967; MA, U. Mont., 1970, PhD, 1972; postgrad., U. Wash., 1983, Harvard U., 1990. Instr. Palo Verde Coll., Blythe, Calif., 1972-75; reference librarian Mont. Hist. Soc., Helena, 1975-78; prof., divsn. chmn., dean Western Mont. Coll., Dillon, 1979-86; dean S.D. State U., Brookings, 1986-91; acad. dean Lyndon State Coll., Lyndonville, Vt., 1991-95; lectr. Western State Coll., Gunnison, Colo., 1995-98, Mesa State Coll., 1998-99, Lawrence U., 1999—2005, Northwest Coll., Powell, Wyo., 2005—. Author: Montana Symbols, 1976, Montana Trolleys, 1970, Lizzie, 1989; co-author: Marble Colorado, 1970, Montana: Our Land and People, 1978, Montana and the West, 1984; contbr. articles to profl. jours. Bd. dirs. Ctr. for Western Studies, Sioux Falls, SD, 1990—, Gunnison Arts Ctr., Gunnison County Libr., Fox Valley Arts Alliance, Meml. Park Arboretum and Gardens, Park County Arts Coun. Summer stipend NEH, 1973; fellow James J. Hill Library, 1985. Mem.: AAUW, Mont. Oral History Assn. (chmn. 1980—83), Am. Conf. Acad. Deans, Western History Assn. (chmn. membership com. 1980—83), N.E. Kingdom C. of C. (bd. dirs.), Westerners (sheriff, Cody 2007), Kiwanis (pres. Dillon 1983, lt. gov. 1984, 1997, pres. Gunnison 1997, lt. gov. 2003, pres. Powell 2007), Masons (master 1984), Phi Alpha Theta, Phi Kappa Phi. Unitarian Universalist. Office: Nortwest Coll 231 W Sixth St Powell WY 82435 Home: PO Box 503 Powell WY 82435 Office Phone: 307-754-6172.

MYERS, ROBERT DAVID, judge; b. Springfield, Mass., Nov. 20, 1937; s. William and Pearl (Weiss) M.; m. Judith G. Dickenman, July 1, 1962; children: Mandy Susan, Jay Brandt, Seth William. AB, U. Mass., 1959; JD, Boston U., 1962. Bar: Ariz. 1963. Pvt. practice, Phoenix, 1963—89; judge Ariz. Superior Ct., 1989—2002; presiding judge civil dept. Superior Ct. Ariz. Maricopa County, Phoenix, 1991—92, presiding judge probate and mental health dept., 1992—95, presiding judge, 1995—2000; pro tem judge Ariz. Ct. Appeals, Phoenix; chief dep. Ariz. Atty. Gen., 2003—04; gen. counsel Ariz. Dept. Corrections, Phoenix, 2004—06. Adj. prof. Ariz. State U. Sch. Law, 1997—, Phoenix Sch. Law, 2007-; chmn. com. on exams and admissions Ariz. Supreme Ct., 1974-75, chmn. com. on character and fitness, 1975-76, mem. multi-state bar exam. com., 1976-85; bd. dirs. Nat. Conf. Met. Judges, 1997—, pres., 1998-99. Pres. Valley of Sun chpt. City of Hope, 1965-66, Cmty. Orgn. for Drug Abuse Control, 1972-73, Valley Big Bros., 1975; chmn. Mayors Ad Hoc Com. on Drug Abuse, 1974-75; bd. dirs. Maricopa County Legal Aid Soc., 1978. Recipient award for outstanding svc. and dedication to improving the legal profession and professionalism of the bar and bench Maricopa County Bar Assn., 1999, Superior Svc. award Ariz. chpt. ASPA, 2000, Justice Tom C. Clark award Nat. Conf. Metro. Cts., 2000. Mem. ATLA (nat. chmn. gov.), Ariz. Bar Assn. (gov., com. chmn., sect. pres., Top 50 Pro Bono Atty's of Yr., 2008), Maricopa County Bar Assn. (dir., pres. 1979-80, Judge of yr., 1999, Henry S. Steven award 2000, Pro Bono Advocate of Yr., 2008), Ariz. Trial Lawyers Assn. (pres., dir., co-editor newsletter), Phoenix Trial Lawyers Assn. (pres., dir.), Western Trial Lawyers Assn. (pres. 1977), Am. Judicature Soc. (spl. merit citation outstanding svc. improvement of adminstrn. justice 1986), Am. Bd. Trial Advocates (Phoenix chpt. Judicial Officer of Yr. award 2001), Sandra Day O'Connor Inn of Ct. (pres. 1991-92), Thurgood Marshall Inn Ct. Office Phone: 602-980-0848. Personal E-mail: bojudy62@cox.net.

MYERS, WALTER E., protective services official; Chief of police, Salem, Oreg. Office: 555 Liberty St SE Rm 130 Salem OR 97301-3513

MYERS, WILLIAM GERRY, III, lawyer; b. Roanoke, Va., July 13, 1955; AB, Coll. of William and Mary, 1977; JD, U. Denver, 1981. Bar: Colo. 1981, Wyo. 1982, DC 1987, US Supreme Ct. 1990, Idaho 1997. Assoc. Davis & Cannon, Sheridan, Wyo., 1981-85; legis. counsel US Sen. Alan K. Simpson, Wyo., 1985-89; asst. to atty. gen. US Dept. Justice, Washington, 1989-92; dep. gen. counsel for progs. US Dept. Energy, Washington, 1992-93; dir. fed. lands Nat. Cattlemen's Assn., 1993-97; exec. dir. Pub. Lands Coun., Washington, 1993-97; atty. Holland and Hart, Boise, Idaho, 1997—2001, of counsel, 2003—; solicitor US Dept. of Interior, 2001—03. Office: Holland and Hart US Bank Plz 101 S Capitol Blvd Ste 1400 Boise ID 83702-7714 Office Phone: 208-342-5000. E-mail: wmyers@hollandhart.com.

MYERSON, ALAN, television director, film director; b. Cleve., Aug. 8, 1936; s. Seymour A. and Vivien I. (Caplin) M.; m. Irene Ryan, June 2, 1962; 1 son, Lincoln; m. Leigh French, May 15, 1977; children: Sierra French-Myerson, Darcy French-Myerson. Student, Pepperdine Coll., 1956-57, UCLA, 1957. Mem. theater/cinema faculty U. Calif., Berkeley, 1966, San Francisco State U., 1967, Internat. Film and TV Workshops, 2002, U. So. Calif, 2005—. Dir. (Broadway, Off Broadway) including This Music Crept By Me Upon the Waters, The Committee; dir.: Second City, N.Y.C. and Chgo., 1961, 62; founder, prodr., dir. The Committee, San Francisco, L.A. and N.Y., 1963-74; dir.: (films) Steelyard Blues, 1972, Private Lessons, 1981, Police Academy 5, 1988, It's Showtime, 1976; numerous TV shows, 1975—, including Ally McBeal, Judging Amy, Joan of Arcadia, Larry Sanders Show, Friends, Frazier, Picket Fences, Miami Vice, Dynasty, Laverne and Shirley, Ed, Boston Public, Gilmore Girls, Lizzie McGuire; TV films The Love Boat, 1976, Hi, Honey, I'm Dead, 1991, Bad Attitudes, 1991, Holiday Affair, 1996. Active in civil rights, peace, anti-nuclear movements, 1957-. Recipient Emmy nomination 1997, Cable ACE award nominations, 1995, 96, 97, TV Comedy award nomination Dirs. Guild, 1997. Mem. ASCAP, Acad. Motion Picture Arts and Scis., Acad. TV Arts and Scis., Dirs. Guild Am. Home Phone: 310-463-2805; Office Phone: 310-559-7756.

MYHRE, BYRON ARNOLD, pathologist, educator; b. Fargo, ND, Oct. 22, 1928; s. Ben Arnold and Amy Lillian (Gilbertson) M.; m. Eileen Marguerite Scherling, June 16, 1953; children: Patricia Ann, Bruce Allen. BS, U. Ill., Champaign/Urbana, 1950; MS, Northwestern U., Evanston, Ill., 1952, MD, 1953; PhD, U. Wis., Madison, 1962. Intern Evanston Hosp., Ill., 1953-54; resident Children's Meml. Hosp., Chgo., 1956-57, U. Wis. Hosp., Madison, 1957-60; assoc. med. dir. Milw. Blood Ctr., 1962-66; sci. dir. L.A. Red Cross Blood Ctr., 1966-72; dir. Blood Bank Harbor-UCLA Med. Ctr., Torrance, Calif., 1972-85, chief clin. pathology, 1985-2000; prof. pathology UCLA, 1972-2000, prof. emeritus, 2000—. Author: Quality Control on Blood Banking, 1974; (with others) Textbook of Clinical Pathology, 1972, Paternity Testing, 1975; editor seminar procs.; contbr. articles to profl. jours., chpts. to books. With USAF, 1954—56. Mem.: AMA, Harbor-UCLA Faculty Soc. (past pres.), Wis. Blood Bank Assn. (past pres.), LA Acad. Medicine (past pres.), Calif. Blood Bank Sys. (past pres.), Calif. Med. Assn., Assn. Clin. Scientists (past pres.), Coll. Am. Pathologists (chmn. blood bank survey com.), Am. Assn. Blood Banks (pres. 1978—79), Am. Soc. Clin. Pathology (dep. commr. commn. on continuing edn.), Palos Verdes Breakfast Club (past pres.). Home: 4004 Via Larga Vista Palos Verdes Estates CA 90274-1122 Personal E-mail: bamyhre@cox.net.

MYHRE, JANET, statistician, educator, consultant; b. Tacoma, Wash., Sept. 24, 1932; d. Leif Christian Klippen, Thelma Gladys Klippen; m. Philip Cushman Myhre, June 12, 1954 (div. Dec. 1984); 1 child, Karin Elizabeth; m. Leon Hollerman, May 29, 1988; 1 child, Jeremy Hollerman. BA summa cum laude, Pacific Luth. U., 1954; MA, U. Wash., 1956; PhD in Math. Stats, U. Stockholm, 1968. Prof. math. Claremont McKenna Coll., Claremont, Calif., 1962—2008. Vis. prof. U. Stockholm, 1971—72, Swiss Fed. Inst. Tech., Zurich, 1971—72, Wash. State U., Pullman, 1978; prof. math. Claremont Grad. U., 1968—; founder, pres. Math. Analysis Rsch. Corp., Claremont, 1973—; dir. Reed Inst. for Decision Sci. Claremont McKenna Coll., Claremont, 1975—2008; cons. Strategic Sys. Programs USN, Washington, 1968—; cons. EPA, Washington, 1976—77. Contbr. chpts. in books, articles to profl. jours. Bd. trustees mem. The Webb Schs., Claremont, 1984—88; officer Padua Hills Homeowners Assn., Claremont, 1988—94; mem. numerous blue ribbon com. USN involving reliability, nuclear safety and risk assessment, 1972—. Recipient Austin Bonis award, Am. Soc. Quality Control, 1984, hon. alumna, Claremont McKenna Coll., 1996; Rsch. grant, Office Naval Rsch., 1973—83. Fellow: Am. Statis. Assn. (assoc. editor Technometrics 1969—75, coun. rep. 2001—03, pres. So. Calif. chpt. 2003—05); mem.: Claremont Mus. Art (bd. trustees 2007—), Padua Hills Mus. Com., Phi Beta Kappa (pres. CMC chpt. 2004—07). Achievements include development of models/statistical theory used since 1972 by USN Ballistic Missile Program for reliability assessments; software/theory used by Fleet Ballistic Missile Program since 1990 for safety and risk assessment. Avocations: gardening, cooking, hiking, weaving. Office: Math Analysis Rsch Corp 4239 Via Padova Claremont CA 91711 Office Phone: 909-624-5298. Personal E-mail: MARCmath@aol.com.

MYHREN, TRYGVE EDWARD, communications company executive; b. Palmerton, Pa., Jan. 3, 1937; s. Arne Johannes and Anita (Blatz) M.; m. Carol Jane Enman, Aug. 8, 1964; children: Erik, Kirsten, Tor; m. 2d Victoria Hamilton, Nov. 14, 1981; 1 stepchild, Paige. BA in Philosophy and Polit. Sci., Dartmouth Coll., 1958, MBA, 1959. Sales mgr., unit mgr. Procter and Gamble, Cin., 1963-65; sr. cons. Glendinning Cos., Westport, Conn., 1965-69; pres. Auberge Vintners, 1970-73; exec. v.p. Mktg. Continental, Westport, 1969-73; v.p., gen. mgr. CRM, Inc., Del Mar, Calif., 1973-75; from v.p. mktg. to pres. Am. TV and Comm. Corp., Englewood, Colo., 1975-80, chmn. bd., CEO, 1981-88; pres. Myhren Media Inc., Denver, 1989—. V.p., then exec. v.p. Time Inc., N.Y.C., 1981-88; mem. exec. com., treas., vice chmn., then chmn. bd. dirs. Nat. Cable TV Assn., Washington, 1982-91; mem. adv. com. on HDTV, FCC, 1987-89, pres. Providence Jour. Co.; bd. dirs. Advanced Mktg. Svcs., Inc., La Jolla, Calif.; Dreyfus Founders Funds, Inc., J. D. Edwards, Inc., Verio, Inc., Nat. Cable TV Ctr., Denver, Cable Labs, Inc., Boulder, Colo., Peapod, Inc., Skokie, Ill.; pres. Myhren Media, 1989—; pres., CEO King Broadcast Co., 1991-96. Mem. Colo. Forum, 1984—, chmn. higher edn. com., 1986; bd. dirs., co-founder Colo. Bus. Com. for the Arts, 1985-91; mem. exec. coun. Found. for Commemoration U.S. Constn., 1987-90; mem. Nat. GED Task Force, 1987-90, Colo. Baseball Commn., 1989-91, Colo. Film Commn., 1989-91; trustee Nat. Jewish Hosp., 1989— (Humanitarian award 1996), R.I. Hosp., 1991-95, Lifespan Health Sys., 1994-97, U.S. Ski and Snowboard Team Found., 1998—; chmn. Local Organizing Commn. 1995 NCAA Hockey Championship; trustee, exec. com., chmn. fin. com. U. Denver, 1997—. Lt. (j.g.) USNR, 1959-63. Recipient Disting. Leader award Nat. Cable TV Assn., 1988. Mem. Cable TV Adminstrn. and Mktg. Soc. (pres. 1978-79, Grand Tam award 1985, One of A Kind award 1994), Cable Adv. Bur. (co-founder 1978), Cable TV Pioneers. Episcopalian. Address: Myhren Media Inc 280 Detroit St # 200 Denver CO 80206-4807 E-mail: trygm@earthlink.net.

MYHRVOLD, NATHAN P., technology executive; b. Seattle, Aug. 3, 1959; BS in Math., UCLA, 1979, MS in Geophysics and Space Physics, 1979; M in Math. Econs., Princeton U., 1981; D in Theoretical and Math. Physics, 1983. Fellow dept. applied math. and theoretical physics Cambridge U., 1981-83; founder, pres., CEO Dynamical Sys., 1984-86; dir. spl. projects Microsoft Corp., Redmond, Wash., 1986, v.p. applications and content; chief tech. officer Advanced Tech. and Rsch., Redmond, Wash., Microsoft Corp., Redmond, Wash., 1996—99; founder, mgr. Microsoft Rsch.; CEO Intellectual Ventures, Bellevue, Wash., 2000—. Bd. trustees Inst. Advanced Study, Princeton, N.J.; mem. Nat. Info. Infrastructure Adv. Coun.; adv. bd. Princeton U. dept. physics. Photographer America 24/7, Washington 24/7; contbr. scientific papers articles to Science, Nature, Paleobiology, Physical Review, Fortune, Time, National Geographic Traveler and online mag. Slate; provided forward Juice: The Creative Fuel that Drives World Class Inventors. Mem. United Way Million Dollar Roundtable; co-contbr. with Paul Allen SETI Found. for Allen Telescope Array, 2000. Recipient 1st and 2nd Place title, World Championship of Barbecue, Memphis, James Madison medal, Princeton U., 2005. Achievements include patents in field; patents pending in field. Avocations: mountain climbing, photography, French Cooking, Formula Car Racing. Office: Intellectual Ventures 1756 114th Ave SE Ste 110 Bellevue WA 98004

NABOKOV, EVGENI, professional hockey player; b. Ust-Kamenogorsk, Kazakhstan, July 25, 1975; m. Tabitha Nabokov; 1 child, Emily. Goaltender San Jose Sharks, 2000—. Mem. Team Russia, Olympic Games, Torino, Italy, 2006. Recipient Calder Meml. Trophy, 2001; named to All-Rookie Team, NHL, 2001, NHL All-Star Game, 2008, First All-Star Team, NHL, 2008. Avocations: golf, tennis. Office: San Jose Sharks 525 W Santa Clara St San Jose CA 95113

NABORS, JAMES THURSTON, actor, singer; b. Sylacauga, Ala., June 12, 1930; s. Fred Nabors. Grad. in bus. adminstrn., U. Ala. Formerly film editor, then jr. cutter for TV; singer at cabaret-theatre, The Horn, Santa Monica, Calif.; first TV appearance on Steve Allen Show; appeared in: own series Gomer Pyle-USMC, 1964-72, Andy Griffith Show, 1963-64, Jim Nabors Hour, 1969-71, Lost Saucer, 1975-76, Sylvan in Paradise, 1986, The Jim Nabors Show, 1987; TV guest appearances on Redd Foxx Show; dramatic appearances in The Rookies; night club headliner in Las Vegas and Lake Tahoe, Nev.; recs. include albums Very Special, The Special Warmth of Jim Nabors, 1986; also 16 single recs.; star: Jim Nabors Polynesian Extravaganza, Honolulu, 1979-81; movie appearances include The Best Little Whorehouse in Tex., 1982, Stroker Ace, 1983, Cannon Ball II, 1984; other TV work includes (movie) Return to Mayberry. Recipient 5 gold albums, 1 platinum album Office: c/o William Morris Agy 151 S El Camino Dr Beverly Hills CA 90212-2704

NACHT, SERGIO, biochemist; came to U.S., 1965; s. Oscar and Carmen (Scheiner) N.; m. Beatriz Kahan, Dec. 21, 1958; children: Marcelo H., Gabriel A., Mariana S., Sandra M. BA in Chemistry, U. Buenos Aires, 1958, MS in Biochemistry, 1960, PhD in Biochemistry, 1964. Asst. prof. biochemistry U. Buenos Aires, 1960-64; asst. prof. medicine U. Utah, Salt Lake City, 1965-70; rsch. scientist Alza Corp., Palo Alto, Calif., 1970-73; sr. investigator Richardson-Vicks Inc., Mt. Vernon, NY, 1973-76, asst. dir. rsch., 1976-83; dir. biomed. rsch. P&G, Shelton, Conn., 1983-87; sr. v.p. rsch. and devel. Advanced Polymer Sys., Redwood City, Calif., 1987-93, sr. v.p. sci. and tech.,

1993-98, sr. v.p. dermatology and skin care, 1998-2000, Cardinal Health, Redwood City, 2000—02; sr. v.p., chief sci. officer Riley-Nacht, LLC, Las Vegas, 2002—. Lectr. dermatology dept. SUNY Downstate Med. Ctr., Bklyn., 1977-87. Contbr. articles to profl. jours.; patentee in field. Mem. Soc. Cosmetic Chemists (award 1981), Dermatology Found., Am. Acad. Dermatology. Democrat. Jewish. Office Phone: 702-547-1611. Personal E-mail: sergnacht@aol.com.

NACKEL, JOHN GEORGE, health venture capital executive; b. Medford, Mass., Nov. 4, 1951; s. Michael and Josephine (Maria) N.; m. Gail Helen Becker, Oct. 30, 1976; children: Melissa Anne, Allison Elizabeth. BS, Tufts U., 1973; MS in Pub. Health and Indsl. Engring., U. Mo., 1975, PhD, 1977. Sr. mgr. Ernst & Young, Chgo., 1977—83; nat. dir. health care cons. Cleve., 1983—87; regional dir. health industry svcs., 1987—91; mng. dir. health care Ernst & Young, Cleve., 1991—93; mng. dir. Health Consulting, LA, 1993—99, New Ventures, 1999—2000; CEO, Sogeti USA, LLC, 2000—01; chmn., CEO, Sértan Corp., Santa Fe Springs, Calif., 2002—03; exec. v.p. US Tech., Beverly Hills, Calif., 2003—05; pres., COO Salick Cardiovascular Ctrs., 2006—07; CEO Three Sixty Group, 2007—. Author: Cost Management for Hospitals, 1987 (Am. Hosp. Assn. book award 1988); mem. editl bd. Jour. Med. Systems, 1983-; contbr. articles to profl. jours Grantee Dept. Health Edn. Welfare, Washington, 1973-76. Fellow Am. Coll. Healthcare Execs., Healthcare Info. and Mgmt. Systems Soc. (articles award); mem. Inst. Indsl. Engrs. (sr.), U. Mo. Health Svcs. Mgmt. Alumni Assn. (pres.), L.A. Country Club, Annandale Golf Club. Republican. Avocations: golf, tennis, squash, paddle, photography. Home: 666 Linda Vista Ave Pasadena CA 91105-1145 Office Phone: 310-674-9360.

NADEAU, MARK ALLEN, lawyer; b. Portland, Maine, Sept. 13, 1953; s. Albert Henry and Eugenia B. (McCallum) Nadeau; m. Marilyn Louise Nadeau, Aug. 29, 1982; children: Kate Louise, Barry Christopher. BA, U. Colo., 1976; JD, U. Pitts., 1981. Bar: Colo. 1981, registered: US Dist. Ct. (Dist. Colo.) 1981, US Ct. Appeals (10th cir.) 1981, bar: Ariz. 1987, registered: US Dist. Ct. (Dist. Ariz.) 1987, US Ct. Appeals (9th cir.) 1987, US Dist. Ct. (Ea. Dist.) Mich. 1991, US Dist. Ct. (Ctrl. Dist.) Ill. 1994, US Ct. Appeals (1th cir.) 2001, US Ct. Appeals (3rd cir.) 2004. Dep. Boulder County (Colo.) Sheriff's Dept., 1975-79; jud. clk. U.S. Dist. Ct., Denver, 1981-82; assoc. Calkins, Kramer, Denver, 1982-87, Streich Lang P.A., Phoenix, 1987-90; ptnr. Morrison & Hecker, Phoenix, 1990-93; ptnr., dir. litigation svcs. for the western U.S. Squire, Sanders & Dempsey, Phoenix, 1993—, co-chmn., Internat. Dispute Resolution Practice Group. Author: The Banking Law Journal, 1992, 90, Arizona Discovery Pre-Trial and Trial Procedures, 1988. Co-chmn. ARC, Phoenix, 1989—91, bd. dir., 1989—90. Mem.: Colo. Bar Assn., ABA, Maricopa County Bar Assn., Internat. C. of C. (Panel of Arbitrators), State Bar Ariz., Ariz. Club, Order of Barristers. Avocations: soviet and american history, horses, skiing, golf. Office: Squire Sanders & Dempsey Two Renaissance Sq 40 N Central Ave Ste 2700 Phoenix AZ 85004-4498 Office Phone: 602-528-4001. Office Fax: 602-253-8129. Business E-Mail: mnadeau@ssd.com.

NADELLA, SATYA, computer software company executive; b. 1967; MS in Computer Sci., U. Wis.; MBA, U. Chgo. Software devel. engr. Sun Microsystems Inc.; with Microsoft Corp., 1992—, from group product mgr. to leader bCentral mktg. & bus. devel., leader bCentral mktg. & bus. devel., 1999—2002, corp. v.p. Microsoft Bus. Solutions (MBS), 2002—08, sr. v.p. Search, Portal & Advertising Platform Group, 2008—. Office: Microsoft Corp One Microsoft Way Redmond WA 98052-6399

NADER, LAURA, anthropologist, educator; b. Winsted, Conn., Sept. 30, 1930; m. Norman Milleron, Sept. 1, 1962; 3 children BA, Wells Coll., Aurora, NY, 1952; PhD, Radcliffe Coll., Cambridge, Mass., 1961. Faculty mem. U. Calif., Berkeley, 1960—, prof. anthropology; vis. prof. Yale Law Sch., New Haven, fall 1971; Henry R. Luce prof. Sch. Law Harvard Wellesley Coll., Mass., 1983-84; vis. prof. Stanford U. Law Sch., 1987-89. Field work in Mex., Lebanon, Morocco and US; mem. adv. com. NSF, 1971-75; mem. cultural anthropology com. NIMH, 1968—, chmn. to 1971, chmn. social scis. rsch. tng. rev. com., 1976-78; mem. NAS-NRC assembly behavioral and social scis., 1969-71, 73-75, 75—; mem. com. Nuclear and Alternative Energy Forms, NAS, 1976-80. Editor: Law in Culture and Society, 1969, The Disputing Process, 1978, No Access to Law-Alternatives to the American Judicial System, 1980, Harmony Ideology, 1990, Naked Science, 1996, The Life of the Law, 2000; co-author (with U. Mattei): Plunder: When the Rule of Law is Illegal, 2008; contbr. articles to profl. jours.; author ednl. films, mem. editl. com. Law and Soc. Rev., 1967—. Mem. Calif. Coun. for the Humanities, 1975—79, Carnegie Coun. on Children, 1972—77; active Coun. Librs. at Libr. of Congress, Washington, 1988—. Radcliffe Coll. grantee, 1954-59; Thaw fellow Harvard U., 1955-56, 58-59; Peabody Mus. grantee, 1954-59; Am. Philos. Assn. grantee, 1955; Mexican Govt. grantee, 1957-58; Milton Fund grantee, 1959-60, Wellness Found. grantee, 1993-96; fellow Ctr. Advanced Study in Behavioral Scis., Stanford, Calif., 1963-64; NSF grantee, 1966-68; Wenner Gren Found. grantee, 1964, 66, 73; Carnegie Corp. grantee, 1975; Woodrow Wilson fellow, 1979-80; Wells Coll. Alumnae award, 1980; Radcliffe Coll. Alumnae award, 1984. Mem.: AAAS, Soc. Women Geographers (Outstanding Achievement award 1990), Am. Acad. Arts and Scis., Ctr. for Study of Responsive Law (trustee 1968—), Law and Soc. Assn. (trustee 1967—72, Harry Kalven prize 1995), Social Sci. Rsch. Coun., Am. Anthrop. Assn. (planning and devel. com. 1968—71, 1975—76), Am. Acad. Arts and Scis. Office: U Calif Dept Anthropology 313 Kroeber Hl Berkeley CA 94720-0001 Office Phone: 510-642-1218. Office Fax: 510-643-8557.

NADLER, GEORGE L., orthodontist; b. Bklyn., Jan. 13, 1939; s. Rudolph M. and Hannah (Helfman) N.; m. Essie Rubinstein, June 4, 1961; children: Rudolph M., Eric Marc. Student, Bkly. Coll., 1956-59; DDS, NYU Coll. of Dentistry, 1963, postgrad., 1966-70. Diplomate Am. Bd. Orthodontia, 1979. Intern L.I. Coll. Hosp., Bklyn., 1963-64; pvt. practice Bklyn., 1966-70, Tucson, Ariz., 1970—. Cons. El Rio Health Ctr., Tucson, 1973—. Contbr. articles to profl. jours. Cons. Ariz. Crippled Children Svc., Tucson, 1973—; exec. bd. Congregation Anshei Israel, 1988—. With USPHS, 1964-66. Fellow NIH, 1961, 62. Mem. ADA, Ariz. Dental Assn., So. Ariz. Dental Assn., Am. Assn. Orthodontists, Pacific Coast Orthodontic Assn., Ariz. Orthodontic Study Club, Tucson Orthodontic Study Club, Tucson Orthodontic Soc. (pres. 1980-81), Ariz. State Orthodontic Soc. (pres. 1988-90), Angle Orthodontic Soc., Golden Key, Skyline Country Club, Omicron Kappa Upsilon. Avocations: tennis, golf, gardening. Office: 5610 E Grant Rd Tucson AZ 85712-2239 Home: 5052 E Calle Brillante Tucson AZ 85718-1819

NADLER, GERALD, management consultant, educator; b. Cin., Mar. 12, 1924; s. Samuel and Minnie (Krumbein) N.; m. Elaine Muriel Dubin, June 22, 1947; children: Burton Alan, Janice Susan, Robert Daniel. Student, U. Cin., 1942-43; BSME, Purdue U., 1945, MS in Indsl. Engring, 1946, PhD, 1949. Instr. Purdue U., 1948-49; asst. prof. indsl. engring. Washington U., St. Louis, 1949-52, assoc. prof., 1952-55, prof., head dept. indsl. engring., 1955-64; prof. U. Wis., Madison, 1964-83, chmn. dept. indsl. engring., 1964-67, 71-75; prof., chmn. dept. indsl. and sys. engring. U. So. Calif., LA, 1983-93, IBM chair engring. mgmt., 1986-93, IBM chair emeritus, prof. emeritus, 1993—; v.p. Artcraft Mfg. Co., St. Louis, 1956-57; dir. Intertherm Inc., St. Louis, 1969-85. Pres. Ctr. for Breakthrough Thinking Inc., L.A., 1989—; vis. prof. U. Birmingham, Eng., 1959, Waseda U., Tokyo, 1963-64, Ind. U., 1964, U. Louvain, Belgium, 1975, Technion-Israel Inst. Tech., Haifa, 1975-76; spkr. in field. Author: The Planning and Design Approach, 1981; (with S. Hibino) Breakthrough Thinking, 1990, 2d edit., 1994, Creative Solution Finding, 1995; (with G. Hoffherr, J. Moran) Breakthrough Thinking in Total Quality Management, 1994, (with W. Chandon) Ask the Right Questions, 2003, Smart Questions, 2004; contbr. articles to profl. jours.; reviewer books, papers, proposals. Mem. Ladue Bd. Edn., St. Louis County, 1960-63, L.A. County Quality and Productivity Commn., 1997—; chmn. planning com. Wis. Regional Med. Program, 1966-69; bd. dirs. USC Credit Union, 1994—. Served with USN, 1943-45. Gilbreth medal Soc. Advancement Mgmt., 1961, Editl. award Hosp. Mgmt. Mag., 1966, Disting. Engring. Alumnus award Purdue U., 1975, Outstanding Indsl. Engr. award, 1997; Book of Yr. award Inst. Indsl. Engrs., 1983, Frank and Lillian Gilbreth award, 1992; Phi Kappa Phi Faculty Recognition award U. So. Calif., 1990, Engring. Disting. Svc. award U. Wis. Madison, 2000. Fellow AAAS, Inst. Indsl. Engrs. (pres. 1989-90), Inst. Operations Rsch. and Mgmt. Scis., Inst. for Advancement Engrs., Am. Soc. Engring. Edn.; mem. NAE, Japan Work Design Soc. (hon. adv. 1968—), World Future Soc., Acad. Mgmt., Engring. Mgmt. Soc., Sigma Xi, Alpha Pi Mu (nat. officer), Pi Tau Sigma, Omega Rho, Tau Beta Pi. Office: Univ Park GER 240 Dept Of I&se Los Angeles CA 90089-0193 Office Phone: 213-740-6415. Personal E-mail: gnadler@breakthroughthinking.com. Business E-Mail: nadler@usc.edu.

NADLER, HENRY LOUIS, pediatrician, educator, geneticist; b. NYC, Apr. 15, 1936; s. Herbert and Mary (Kartiganer) N.; m. Benita Weinhard, June 16, 1957; children: Karen, Gary, Debra, Amy. AB, Colgate U., 1957; MD, Northwestern U., 1961; MS, U. Wis., 1965. Diplomate Am. Bd. Pediatrics, Am. Bd. Med. Genetics. Intern NYU Med. Ctr., 1961-62, sr. resident pediatrics, 1962-63, chief resident, 1963-64; teaching asst. NYU Sch. Medicine, 1962-63, clin. instr., 1963-64, U. Wis. Sch. Medicine, 1964-65; practice medicine specializing in pediatrics Chgo., 1965—; fellow Children's Meml. Hosp. dept. pediatrics Northwestern U., 1964-65; assoc. in pediatrics Northwestern U. Med. Sch., 1965-66, asst. prof., 1967-68, assoc. prof., 1968-70, prof., 1970-81, chmn. dept. pediatrics, 1970-81; prof. Northwestern U. Med. Sch. (Grad. Sch.), 1971-80; mem. staff Children's Meml. Hosp., 1965-81, head div. genetics, 1969-81, chief of staff, 1970-81; dean, prof. pediatrics, ob-gyn Wayne State U. Med. Sch., Detroit, 1981-88; prof. U. Chgo., 1988-89, U. Ill., 1989—; pres. Michael Reese Hosp. and Med. Ctr., Chgo., 1988-91; market med. dir. Aetna Health Plans, Phoenix, 1993-94, mktg. v.p., CEO, 1994-95; v.p. managed care/physician integration, med. dir. Am. Healthcare Sys., San Diego, 1995. Mem. vis. staff, div. medicine Northwestern Meml. Hosp., 1972-81; staff Children's Hosp. of Mich., 1981-88. Mem. editl. bd. Comprehensive Therapy, 1973-84, Am. Jour. Human Genetics, 1979-83, Pediatrics in Rev., 1980-83, Am. Jour. Diseases of Children, 1983-91; contbr. articles to profl. jours. Recipient E. Mead Johnson award for pediatric rsch., 1973, Meyer O. Cantor award for Disting. Svc. Internat. Coll. Surgeons, 1987; Irene Heinz Given and John La Porte Given rsch. prof. pediatrics, 1970-81. Fellow Am. Acad. Pediatrics; mem. Am. Soc. for Clin. Investigation, Am. Soc. Human Genetics, Am. Pediatric Soc., Soc. for Pediatric Rsch., Midwest Soc. for Pediatric Rsch., Pan Am. Med. Assn., Alpha Omega Alpha. Home and Office: 17720 Camino de La Mitra PO Box 3665 Rancho Santa Fe CA 92067-3665 Personal E-mail: hlnadler@aol.com.

NAEF, WESTON JOHN, retired museum curator; b. Gallup, N.Mex., Jan. 8, 1942; s. Weston John and Kathleen Winifred (Skerry) N.; m. Mary Dawes Meghan, Apr. 4, 1964; children: Edward Weston, Ella Dawes BA, Claremont Men's Coll., 1964; MA, Ohio State U., 1966; postgrad., Brown U., 1966-69. Vis. scholar Boston Pub. Library, 1968; dir. art gallery Wheaton Coll., Mass., 1969; staff dept. prints and photographs Met. Mus. Art, NYC, 1970-84, asst. curator, 1971-81, curator, 1981-84; curator photographs J. Paul Getty Mus., Malibu, Calif., 1984—2009. Cons. in field Author, exhbn. dir. Behind the Great Wall of China, 1971, The Painterly Photograph, 1973, The Truthful Lens: A Survey of Victorian Books Illustrated with Photographs, 1974, Era of Exploration, The Rise of Landscape Photography in the American West 1860-1885, 1975, Pioneer Photographers of Brazil 1939-1914, 1976, The Collection of Alfred Stieglitz, 1978, Georgia O'Keeffe by Alfred Stieglitz, 1978, Eliot Porter, The Intimate Landscapes, 1979, After Daguerre: Masterworks of 19th Century French Photography from the Bibliotheque Nationale, Paris, 1980, Counterparts: Form and Emotion in Photographs, 1982, Whisper of the Muse: Photographs by Julia Margaret Cameron, 1986, Edward Weston in Los Angeles: The Home Spirit and Beyond, 1986, Rare States and Unusual Subjects: Photographs by Paul Strand, Andre Kertesz and Man Ray, 1987, Capturing Shadows: Notable Acquisitions, 1985-1990, 1990; August Sander: Faces of the German People, 1991; Atget's Magical Analysis: Photographs, 1915-27, 91, Two Lives: O'Keeffe by Stieglitz, 1917-23, 1992, Being and Becoming: Photographs by Edmund Teske, 1993, André Kertesz: A Centennial Tribute, 1994, Palette of Light: Handcrafted Photographs, 1898-1914, 1994, Frederick Sommer: Poetry and Logic, 1994, Hidden Witness: African Americans in Early Photography, 1995, Carrie Mae Weems Reacts to Hidden Witness, 1995, Alfred Stieglitz: Seen and Unseen, 1995, The J. Paul Getty Museum Handbook of the Photographs Collection, 1995, In Focus: Andre Kertesz, 1994, In Focus: Alfred Stieglitz, 1995, The Eye of Sam Wagstaff, 1997, Capturing Time, 1997, The Art of the Daguerreotype, 1998. Kress fellow, 1968 Mem.: Grolier (N.Y.C.). Office: J Paul Getty Mus Dept Photographs 1200 Getty Center Dr Ste 1000 Los Angeles CA 90049-1687

NAFTALI, TIMOTHY J., library director, historian, educator, writer; BA magna cum laude, Yale U., 1983; MA in Internat. Econs., Johns Hopkins U., 1987; MA in History, PhD in History, Harvard U., 1993. Asst. prof. dept. history U. Hawaii, 1993—97; assoc. prof. U. Va., 1998—2006, dir. Presdl. recordings program, Kremlin decision-making project, 1999—2006; dir. Richard Nixon Presdl. Libr. & Mus., Yorba Linda, Calif., 2006—. Vis. prof. Dept. History Yale U., 1996—98; hist. cons. Nazi War Crimes and Imperial Japanese Govt. Records Interagency Working Group, Nat. Archives, US Dept. Justice, Nat. Commn. Terrorist Attacks upon US (9/11 Commn.), 2003—04; instr. Centre Counterintelligence and Security Studies, 2003—. Co-author: US-Canadian Softwood Lumber: Trade Dispute Negotiations, 1987, One Hell of a Gamble: Khrushchev, Castro and Kennedy, 1958-1964, 1997, The Presidential Recordings: John F. Kennedy, 2001, US Intelligence and the Nazis, 2004, 2005, Blindspot: The Secret History of American Counterterrorism, 2005; gen. editor Presdl. Recordings Series, 2003—; contbr. articles to profl. jours. Co-recipient Akira Iriye Prize for Internat. Hist., 1997—98; named prin. investigator, Nat. Hist. Publs. and Records Commn., 2002—; grantee MacArthur Fellowship in Internat. Security, 1990—91, Rsch. Fellowship, Kennan Inst. for Advance Russian Studies, Woodrow Wilson Internat. Ctr. for Scholars, 1996, Olin Fellowship in Nat. Security, 1996—98. Office: Richard Nixon Presdl Libr 18001 Yorba Linda Blvd Yorba Linda CA 92886 Office Phone: 714-983-9120. Office Fax: 714-983-9111. Business E-Mail: timothy.naftali@nara.gov.

NAGATA, ROLSTON H., state agency administrator; Dir. State of Hawaii, Dept. Land and Natural Resources, Honolulu, 1998—. Office: State Hawaii Divsn State Parks Dept Land & Nat Resources 1151 Punchbowl St Rm 310 Honolulu HI 96813

NAGATANI, PATRICK ALLAN RYOICHI, artist, art educator; b. Chgo., Aug. 19, 1945; s. John Lee and Diane Yoshiye (Yoshimura) N.; m. Rae Jeanean Bodwell, June 17, 1979; children: Methuen, Hart Gen, Louis-Thomas. BA, Calif. State U., LA, 1967; MFA, UCLA, 1980. Cert. tchr. K-12, Calif. Instr. Alexander Hamilton High Sch., LA, 1968-80, West. L.A. C.C., 1980-83; artist in residency Calif. Arts Coun., Juvenile Ct. and Cmty. Schs., LA, 1986-87; instr. Otis Art Inst. Parson Sch. of Design, LA, 1987; asst. prof. dept. art/art history Loyola Marymount U., LA, 1980-87; prof. dept. art & art history U. N.Mex., Albuquerque, 1987—. Instr. Fairfax Cmty. Adult Sch., L.A., 1976-79; vis. artist/instr. The Sch. of the Art Inst., Chgo., 1983; conductor numerous seminars and workshops; lectr. in field. One man shows include Pal Gallery, Evergreen State U., Olympia, Wash., 1976, BC Space, Laguna Beach, Calif., 1978, Cityscape Gallery, Pasadena, Calif., 1978, Exploratorium Gallery, Calif. State U., L.A., 1979, Orange Coast Coll., Costa Mesa, Calif., 1980, Susan Spiritus Gallery, Newport Beach, Calif., 1981, 83, 85, Canon Photo Gallery, Amsterdam, The Netherlands, 1982, John Michael Kohler Arts Ctr., Sheboygan, Wis., 1983, 86, Arco Ctr. Visual Arts, L.A., 1983, Clarence Kennedy Gallery, Boston, 1984, Colo. Mountain Coll., Breckenridge, 1984, Jayne H. Baum Gallery, N.Y.C., 1985, 87, 89, 91, 94, Torch Gallery, Amsterdam, 1985, 87, Fotografie Forum Frankfurt, Fed. Rep. Germany, 1986, Frederick S. Wight Art Gallery, U. Calif., L.A., 1987, San Francisco Cameraworks, 1988, Koplin Gallery, L.A., 1988, 90, 92, 95, Shadai Gallery, Tokyo Inst. Polytech., 1989, Lubbock (Tex.) Fine Arts Ctr., 1990, Haggerty Mus. Art, Marquette U., Milw., 1991, Richard Levy Gallery, Albuquerque, 1992, Stanford (Calif.) Mus. Art, 1993, numerous others; exhibited in group shows at Friends of Photography, Carmel, Calif., 1976, 81, 85, Ctrl. Wash. State Coll., Ellensburg, 1977, Humboldt State U., Arcata, Calif., 1977, Soho/Cameraworks Gallery, L.A., 1978, Libra Gallery, Claremont (Calif.) Grad. Sch., 1978, Cirrus Gallery, L.A., 1979, Skidmore Coll. Art Gallery, Saratoga, N.Y., 1980, Tortue Gallery, Santa Monica, Calif., 1981, Palos Verdes (Calif.) Cmty. Art Ctr., 1982, Fine Arts Gallery, Cypress (Calif.) Coll., 1982, Fay Gold Gallery, Atlanta, 1982, Mus. Photographic Arts, San Diego, 1983, 84, Jayne H. Baum Gallery, N.Y.C., 1983, 87, Arco Ctr. Visual Art, L.A., 1984, Alt. Mus., N.Y.C., 1984, 88, Black Gallery, L.A., 1985, Mus. N.Mex., Santa Fe, 1986, Whitney Mus. Am. Art, Stamford, Conn., 1986, Balt. Mus. Art, 1987, Ctr. Photography, Woodstock, N.Y., 1988, Oakland Mus., Calif., 1989, Alinder Gallery, Gualala, Calif., 1990, 92, Coll. Santa Fe, 1990, Art Ctr., Waco, Tex., 1991, Lintas Worldwide, N.Y.C., 1991, Dirs. Guild of Am., L.A., 1992, Burden Gallery, N.Y.C., 1992, Nat. Arts Club, N.Y.C., 1992, Knoxville (Tenn.) Art Mus., 1993, G. Ray Hawkins Gallery, L.A., 1994, Houston FotoFest, 1994, Riverside (Calif.) Art Mus., 1994, Mass. Coll. Art, Boston, 1994, numerous others; represented in permanent collections Albuquerque Mus., Balt. Art Mus., Continental Ins., N.Y.C., Chrysler Mus. Art, Norfolk, Va., Denver Art Mus., Ga. Power Co., Atlanta, Honolulu Advertiser, L.A. County Mus. Art, Loyola Marymount U., L.A., Mass. Coll. Art, Boston, Met. Mus. Art, N.Y.C., Mus. Fine Arts, Houston, Mus. N.Mex., Santa Fe, Nev. Mus. Art, Reno, Oakland (Calif.) Mus., Prudential Ins. Co. Am., Newark, Roswell (N.Mex.) Mus., St. Louis Art Mus., Shearson/Am. Express, N.Y.C., Tampa (Fla.) Mus. Art, Tokyo Inst. Polytech., numerous others. Travel grantee Ford Found., 1979; Faculty Rsch. grantee Loyola Marymount U., L.A., 1981, 83, U. N.Mex., 1988, 90; Artist-In-Residence grantee Calif. Arts Coun., 1982-83; Visual Artist fellow Nat. Endowment for the Arts, 1984-85, 92-93; Brody Arts Fund fellow, 1986; Polaroid fellow, 1983-90; named Art Waves competition and exhbn. finalist Cmty. Redevel. Agy. L.A., 1987; recipient Calif. Disting. Artist award Nat. Art Edn. Assn. Conv., Mus. Contemporary Art, L.A., 1988, Kraszna-Krausz award and Photographic Book Innovation award Kraszna-Krausz Found., 1992. Avocations: gardening, gambling.

NAGLER, MICHAEL NICHOLAS, peace and conflict studies educator; b. NYC, Jan. 20, 1937; s. Harold and Dorothy Judith (Nocks) N.; m. Roberta Ann Robbins (div. May 1983); children: Jessica, Joshua. BA, NYU, 1960; MA, U. Calif., Berkeley, 1962, PhD, 1966. Instr. San Francisco State U., 1963-65; prof. classics, peace studies and comparative lit. U. Calif., Berkeley, 1966-91, prof. emeritus, 1991—. Author: Spontaneity and Tradition, 1974, America Without Violence, 1982, Is There No Other Way: The Search for a Nonviolent Future, 2001, Am. Book award, 2002; co-author: The Upanishads, 1987; contbr. articles to profl. publs. Pres. bd. dirs. METTA Ctrs. for Nonviolence Edn. Fellow Am. Coun. Learned Socs., NIH; MacArthur Found. grantee, 1988. Mem. Am. Philolog. Soc. Office: U Calif Peace and Conflict Studies Berkeley CA 94720-0001 E-mail: mnagler@igc.org.

NAGY, STEPHEN MEARS, JR., physician, allergist; b. Yonkers, NY, Apr. 1, 1939; s. Stephen Mears and Olga (Zahoruiko) N.; m. Brenda Yu Nagy, 1966; children: Catherine, Stephen III. BA, Princeton U., 1960; MD, Tufts U., 1964. Diplomate Am. Bd. Internal Medicine, Am. Bd. Allergy and Immunology. Pvt. practice, Sacramento, Calif., 1971-2000; prof. Sch. Medicine U. Calif., Davis, 1974—. Author, editor Evaluation & Management of Allergic and Asthmatic Diseases, 1981; mem. editl. bd. Clinical Reviews in Allergy; creator Famous Teachings in Modern Medicine-Allergy Series slide collection. Capt. U.S. Army, 1966-68, Vietnam. Fellow Am. Acad. Allergy, Am. Coll. Allergy; mem. CMA, Sacramento-El Dorado Med. Soc. (bd. dirs. 1971-95, 1989-95). Avocations: bicycling, book collecting, opera, fencing. Office: 4801 J St Ste A Sacramento CA 95819-3746 Office Phone: 916-456-4782.

NAHAT, DENNIS F., performing company executive, choreographer; b. Detroit, Feb. 20, 1946; s. Fred H. and Linda M. (Haddad) N. Hon. degree, Juilliard Sch. Music, 1965. Prin. dancer Joffrey Ballet, NYC, 1965-66; prin. dancer Am. Ballet Theatre, NYC, 1968-79; co-founder Cleve. Ballet, 1976, Sch. of Cleve. Ballet, 1972; founder, artistic dir. Sch. Cleve. San Jose Ballet, 1996; founder New Sch. of Cleve. San Jose Ballet, 1996—; founder, artistic dir. San Jose Cleve. Ballet (now Ballet San Jose), San Jose, 1985—. Co-chair Artists Round Table Dance USA, 1991; trustee Cecchetti Coun. Am., 1991; mem. adv. bd. Ohio Dance Regional Dance Am.; dir. dance USDAN Ctr. for the Creative Performing Arts, NY, 1999—. Prin. performer Broadway show Sweet Charity, 1966-67; choreographer Two Gentlemen of Verona (Tony award 1972), 1969-70; (ballet) Celebrations and Ode (resolution award 1985), 1985, Green Table, Three Virgins and a Devil (Isadora Duncan award 1985); conceived, directed, choreographed Blue Suede Shoes, PBS, 1997-98. Grantee Nat. Endowment Arts, 1978, Andrew Mellow Found., 1985; recipient Outstanding Achievement award Am. Dance Guild, 1995, 96, 2000—. Avocation: cooking. also: Ballet San Jose PO Box 1666 40 N 1st St San Jose CA 95109-1666 Office Phone: 408-288-2820 Ext.225. Business E-Mail: dnahat@balletsanjose.org.

NAHMAN, NORRIS STANLEY, electrical engineer; b. San Francisco, Nov. 9, 1925; s. Hyman Cohen and Rae (Levin) Nahman; m. Shirley D. Maxwell, July 20, 1968; children: Norris Stanley, Vicki L., Vance W., Scott T. BS in Electronics Engring, Calif. Poly. State U., 1951; MSE.E., Stanford U., 1952; PhD in Elec. Engring, U. Kans., 1961. Registered profl. engr., Colo. Electronic scientist Nat. Security Agy., Washington, 1952-55; prof. elec. engring., dir. electronics rsch. lab. U. Kans., Lawrence, 1955-66; sci. cons., chief pulse and time domain sect. Nat. Bur. Stds., Boulder, Colo., 1966-73, chief time domain metrology, sr. scientist, 1975-83, group leader field characterization group, 1984-85; v.p. Picosecond Pulse Labs, Inc., Boulder, 1986-90, scientific advisor, co-chair tech. adv. bd., 1990—; cons. elec. engr., 1990—; prof., chmn. dept. elec. engring. U. Toledo, 1973—75; prof. elec. engring. U. Colo., Boulder, 1966—; affiliate staff Los Alamos Nat. Lab., N.Mex., 1990—2006. Disting. lectr., prin. prof. Ctr. Nat. d'Etudes des Telcom. Summer Sch., Lanion, France, 1978; disting. lectr. Harbin Inst. Tech., China, 1982; mem. faculty NATO Advanced Study Inst., Castelvecchio, Italy, 1983, Internat. Radio Sci. Union/NRC; chmn. Internat. Intercomm. Group Waveform Measurements, 1981—90, Commn. A, 1985—86. Contbr. articles to profl. jours. Asst. scoutmaster Longs Peak coun. Boy Scouts Am., 1970—73, 1975—89. With US Mcht. Marine, 1943—46, with US Army, 1952—55. Recipient Disting. Alumnus award, Calif. Poly. State U., 1972, Order of Arrow, Boy Scouts Am., 1976; Ford Found. Faculty fellow, MIT, 1962, Nat. Bur. Stds. Sr. Staff fellow, 1978—79. Fellow: IEEE (life), Internat. Sci. Radio Union; mem.: Electromagnetic Acad., Am. Assn. Engring. Edn. (life), Instrumentation and Measurement Soc. of IEEE (mem. admnstrv. com. 1982—84, editl. bd. Trans. 1982—86, Andrew H. Chi Best Tech. Paper award 1984, Tech. Leadership and Achievement award 1987), Am. Mcht. Marine Vets., Stanford U. (life), U. Kans. (life), Calif. Poly. State U. Alumni Assn. (life), US Mcht. Marine Vets. World War II (life), Am. Radio Relay League Club (life), Am. Legion, Sigma Xi, Sigma Tau, Eta Kappa Nu, Tau Beta Pi, Sigma Pi Sigma. Achievements include patents in field.

NAHRA, LYNDA J., bank executive; b. 1951; Gard., Calf. Western U., Pacific Coast Banking School. Various positions Bank of America; management Community West Bancshares, Goleta, Calif., 1997—, pres., CEO, 2000—. Dir. Women's Economic Ventures; mem., Loan Com. Community West Bancshares, mem., Asset/Liability Com., mem., Compliance Com., mem., Mgmt. Succession Com. Mem. United Way, Santa Barbara; mem., Fin. Com. Goleta Montessori Ctr. Sch. Named one of 25 Women to Watch, US Banker, 2006. Mem.: Montecito Rotary Club. Office: c/o Community West Bank 5827 Hollister Avenue Goleta CA 93117

NAIDORF, LOUIS MURRAY, architect; b. LA, Aug. 15, 1928; s. Jack and Meriam (Abbott) N.; m. Dorise D. Roberts, June 1948 (div.); children: Victoria Beth Naidorf; m. Patricia Ann Shea, June 1, 1968 (div.); m. Patricia Ruth Allen, Dec. 6, 1992 (dec.); m. Sandra Chronis, Apr. 20, 2004. BA, U. Calif., Berkeley, 1949, MA, 1950; Doctorate (hon.), Woodbury U., 2000. Registered architect, Calif. Designer Welton Becket Assocs., LA, 1950-51, Pereira and Luckman, LA, 1951-52; project designer Welton Becket Assocs., LA, 1952-55, sr. project designer, 1955-59, v.p. asst., dir. design, 1959-70, sr. v.p., dir. rsch., 1970-73; sr. v.p., design prin. Ellerbe Becket Assocs., LA, 1973-95; dean Sch. Architecture and Design Woodbury U., LA, 1990-2000; prin. Allen/Naidorf Design Cons., 1995—. Mem. peer rev. panel Nat. Endowment Arts, 1995—; vis. lectr. Calif. Poly. Sch. Architecture, San Luis Obispo, 1975-82; instr. UCLA Sch. Architecture, 1985, UCLA Landscape Archtl. Program, 1980-85, Otis-Parsons, L.A., 1986-92. Prin. works include Capitol Records Bldg., Century City, Los Angeles, Hyatt Regency, Dallas, Restoration Calif. State Capitol Bldg. Bd. dir. Inst. for Garden Studies, L.A., 1986—, ARC, 2000; trustee Woodbury U., 2000. Recipient Honor award Nat. Trust for Hist. Preservation, 1985. Fellow AIA (bd. dir. L.A. chpt. 1977-79, Silver Medal 1950, Nat. Honor award 1985, Educator of Yr. 1997, Legacy award 2005, Lifetime Achievement award 2009). Personal E-mail: naidorf@msn.com.

NAIMARK, NORMAN M., academic administrator; b. NYC; BA, Stanford U., 1966, PhD, 1972. Prof. History Boston U.; fellow Russian Rsch. Ctr. Harvard U., 1994-97; former vis. Catherine Wasserman Davis chair of Slavic Studies Wellesley Coll.; Robert and Florence McDonnell chair in East European Studies Stanford U. Chmn. dept. History, sr. fellow Hoover Instn.; dir. Stanford's Ctr. Russian and East European Studies; joint com. Am. Coun. Learned Soc.; program com. Internat. Rsch. and Exchange Corp.; exec. com. Am. Assn. Advancement Slavic Studies. Author: The Russians in Germany, 1995, Terrorists and Social Democrats, 1983; lectr., author, co-editor in field. Grantee IREX, ACLS, Alexander von Humbolt Found, Fulbright-Hays, Nat. Coun. Soviet and East European Studies, Hist. Commn. in Berlin; recipient Officer's Cross of Order of merit, Fed. Republic of Germany, 1996, Richard W. Lyman award, 1995. Office: Stanford U Dept History Stanford CA 94305

NAKAMURA, ROBERT MOTOHARU, pathologist; b. Montebello, Calif., June 10, 1927; s. Mosaburo and Haru (Suematsu) N.; m. Shigeyo Jane Hayashi, July 29, 1957; children: Mary, Nancy. AB, Whittier Coll., 1949; MD, Temple U., 1954. Cert. of spl. qualification in pathologic anatomy, clin pathology, immunopathology, Am. Bd. Pathology. Prof. pathology U. Calif., Irvine, 1971-74, adj. prof. pathology, 1974-75; chmn. dept. pathology Scripps Clinic and Rsch. Found., La Jolla, Calif., 1974-92; sr. cons., 1992—; pres. Scripps Clinic Med. Group, La Jolla, 1981-91; prof. dept. immunology and exptl. and molecular medicine Scripps Rsch. Inst., 1997—; chmn. pathology Scripps Clinic, 1998-99, chmn. emeritus pathology, 1999—. Adj. prof. pathology U. Calif., San Diego, 1975-93. Coeditor: Jr. Clin. Lab. Analysis, 1989—; contbr. articles to profl. jours. Fellow: Coll. Am. Pathologists, Am. Soc. Clin. Pathologists, Assn. Clin. Scientists, Am. Coll. Nutrition; mem. Internat. Acad. Pathology. Avocation: reading. Home: 8841 Nottingham Pl La Jolla CA 92037-2131 Office Phone: 858-410-2804. Personal E-mail: rnakamura@pol.net.

NAKAMURA, SHUJI, engineering educator; b. Seto, Japan, May 22, 1954; BEE, U. Tokushima, Japan, 1977; MEE, U. Tokushima, 1979, DEng, 1994. R&D staff Nichia Chem. Industry, Ltd., 1979—84, group head R&D 1st sect., 1985—88, group head R&D 2nd sect., 1989—93, sr. rschr. dept. R&D, 1993—99; prof. materials dept. U. Calif., Santa Barbara, 1999—, dir., Solid State Lighting & Display Ctr. Vis. rsch. assoc. electronic engring. U. Fla., 1988—89. Mem. editl. bd.: Applied Physics Soc., 1998—2000; published several papers. Recipient Nikkei Bus. Publications Engring. award, 1994, 1996, Best Paper award, Japanese Applied Physics Soc., 1994, 1997, Sakurai award, 1995, Nishina Meml. award, 1996, IEEE Lasers and Electro-Optics Soc. Engring. Achievement award, 1996, Spl. Recognition award, Soc. for Info. Display, 1996, Okochi Meml. award, 1997, medal award, Materials Rsch. Soc., 1997, Innovation in Real Materials award, 1998, C&C award, Jack A. Morton award, IEEE, 1998, Brit. Rank prize, 1998, Julius-Springer prize for applied physics, 1999, Takayanagi award, 2000, Carl Zeiss Rsch. award, 2000, Honda award, 2000, Crystal Growth and Crystal Tech. award, 2000, Asahi award, 2001, OSA Nick Holonyak award, 2001, LEOS Disting. Lectr. award, 2001, Benjamin Franklin medal in engring., Franklin Inst., 2002, Millennium Tech. prize for his inventions in light and laser tech., Millennium Prize Found., 2006; named Cree Prof. in Solid State Light and Display Endowed chair, 2001. Mem.: NAE. Achievements include development of first group-III nitride-based blue/green LEDs; design of first group-III nitride-based violet laser diodes; patents in field. Office: Materials Dept Univ Calif Santa Barbara CA 93106-5050 Office Phone: 805-893-5552. E-mail: shuji@engineering.ucsb.edu.

NAKANISHI, ALAN, state legislator; m Sue Nakanishi; children: Pamela, Jennifer & Jon. Mayor, Livermore, California, currently; California State Assemblyman, District 10, 2003-.President, Delta Eye Med Group, 71-, Dameron IPA, currently. Fellow America Col Surgeons; America Med Association; California Med Association; San Joaquin Med Soc; Lodi Rotary service Club. Mailing: State Capitol PO Box 942849 Rm 5175 Sacramento CA 94249 Fax: 209-333-6807.

NAKANISHI, DON TOSHIAKI, Asian American studies educator, writer; b. LA, Aug. 14, 1949; m. Marsha Hirano; 1 child, Thomas. BA in Polit Sci. cum laude, Yale U., 1971; PhD in Polit. Sci., Harvard U., 1978. Instr. dept. urban studies Yale U., 1971; lectr. Coun. on Ednl. Devel. UCLA, 1973, instr. Asian Am. Studies Ctr., 1974, acting asst. prof. dept. polit. sci., 1975-78; vis. scholar Sophia U., Inst. Internat. Relations, Tokyo, 1978-89; adj. asst. prof. dept. polit. sci. UCLA, 1979-82, asst. rschr. Asian Am. Studies Ctr., 1979-82, from asst. prof. to full prof. Grad. Sch. Edn., 1982—, assoc. dir. Asian Am. Studies Ctr., 1985-87, chair interdepartmental program Asian Am. studies, 1989—90, dir. Asian Am. Studies Ctr., 1990—. Co-founder and publr. Amerasia Jour., 1970-75, edtl. bd., 1975—; researcher Social Sci. Rsch. Coun. of N.Y. and the Japan Soc. for the Promotion of Sci. of Tokyo Joint-Project on Am.-Japanese Mut. Images, 1971-73; mem. Asian Am. task force for social studies guideline evaluation, Calif. State Dept. Edn., 1973; guest spkr. Ctr. for the Study of Ednl. Policy, Grad. Sch. Edn., Harvard U., 1974, Metropathways, Ethni-City Sch. Desegregation Program, Boston, 1974; researcher, co-project chair Hispanic Urban Ctr., Project Sch. Desegregation, L.A., 1974; numerous coms. UCLA; numerous conf. chmns.; cons., rschr., speaker, presenter in field. Co-editor: (with Marsha J. Hirano-Nakanishi) The Education of Asian and Pacific Americans: Historical Perspectives and Prescriptions for the Future, 1983, (with Halford H. Fairchild, Luis Ortiz-Franco, Lenore A. Stiffarm) Discrimination and Prejudice: An Annotated Bibliography, 1991, (with Tina Yamano Nishida) The Asian Pacific American Educational Experience: A Sourcebook for Teachers and Students, 1995, (with James Lai) National Asian Pacific American Political Almanac, 1996, 98, 2000; contbr. numerous articles to profl. jours., monographs, book reviews and reports. Chair Yale U. Alumni Schs. Com. of So. Calif., 1978—; bd. dirs. Altamed and La Clinica Familiar Del Barrio of East L.A., 1982—; commr. Bd. Transp. Commrs., City of L.A., 1984-90; v.p. Friends of the Little Tokyo Pub. Libr., 1986-88; co-chair nat. scholars adv. com. Japanese Am. Nat. Mus., 1987—; mem., bd. govs. Assn. of Yale Alumni, 1988-91; mem. exec. coun. Mayor's LA's Best Aftersch. Program, City of Los Angeles, 1988-90. Rsch. fellow Japan Soc. for the Promotion of Sci., 1978; recipient Nat. Scholars award for Outstanding Rsch. Article on Asian Pacific Am. Edn., Nat. Assn. for Asian and Pacific Am. Edn., 1985, Civil Rights Impace award Asian Am. Legal Ctr. of So. Calif., 1989; grantee Chancellors' Challenge in the Arts and Humanities, 1991, Calif. Policy Seminar, 1992, U. Calif. Pacific Rim Studies, 1992; recepient numerous other research and conference grants. Mem. Nat. Assn. for Interdisciplinary Ethnic Studies (bd. dirs. 1976-79), Assn. Asian Am. Studies (nat. pres. 1983-85), Nat. Assn. for Asian and Pacific Am. Edn. (exec. bd. dirs., v.p. 1983—). Home: 4501 N Berkshire Ave Los Angeles CA 90032 Office: UCLA Asian Am Studies Ctr 3230 Campbell Ave Los Angeles CA 90024-1546 E-mail: dtn@ucla.edu.

NAKANO, GEORGE SAKAYE, principal; b. LA, Nov. 24, 1935; s. Shigeto and Sumie (Asada) Nakano; m. Helen Michiyo Unno; children: Laurie Tamiyo, Kevin Michio. BS in Math., Calif. State U., 1970, MEd, 1977. Cert. tchr. Calif. Rsch. asst. Hughes Aircraft Co., Culver City, Calif., 1962—68, sr. rsch. asst., 1968—71; tchr. math. Jordan HS, LA, 1971—74; asst. project dir. Inglewood Unified Sch. Dist., 1974—76, project dir., 1976—78; asst. prin. Centinela Sch., Inglewood, Calif., 1978—82, Worthington Sch., Inglewood, 1982—. Master ceremonies, mem. exec. planning com. 1st US Nat. Kendo Championship, 1978. Co-founder Gardena Pioneer Project; councilman City of Torrance, 1984—98; mem. Calif. House Reps., 1998—. Torrance Rose Float Assn., Torrance Sister City Assn. With Calif. Air NG, 1954—60, mem. Res., 1960—62. Mem.: Nat. Coun. Tchrs. Math., Nat. Assn. Educators Computing, Internat. Coun. Computer in Edn., Calif. Math. Coun., Assn. Supervision and Curriculum Devel., Torrance Hist. Soc., Calif. State U. Alumni Assn., Southern Calif. Kendo Fedn. (exec. sec. 1975—79, v.p. 1981—), Kendo Fedn. USA (bd. dirs. 1970—), Charter Club (Torrance). Democrat. Buddhist. Office: PO Box 942849 Sacramento CA 94249

NAKAYAMA, PAULA AIKO, state supreme court justice; b. Honolulu, Oct. 19, 1953; m. Charles W. Totto; children: Elizabeth Murakami, Alexander Totto. BS, U. Calif., Davis, 1975; JD, U. Calif., 1979. Bar: Hawaii 1979. Dep. pros. atty. City and County of Honolulu, 1979-82; ptnr. Shim, Tam & Kirimitsu, Honolulu, 1982-92; judge 1st Cir. Ct. State of Hawaii, Oahu, 1992-93; assoc. justice Hawaii Supreme Ct., Honolulu, 1993—. Mem. Am. Judicature Soc., Hawaii Bar Assn., Sons and Daughters of 442. Office: Hawaii Supreme Ct Ali'iolani Hale 417 S King St Honolulu HI 96813-2902

NALCIOGLU, ORHAN, radiologist, educator; b. Istanbul, Turkey, Feb. 2, 1944; came to U.S., 1966, naturalized, 1974; s. Mustafa and Meliha Nalcioglu. BS, Robert Coll., Istanbul, 1966; MS, Case Western Res. U., 1968; PhD, U. Oreg., 1970. Postdoctoral fellow dept. physics U. Calif., Davis, 1970-71; rsch. assoc. dept. physics U. Rochester, NY, 1971-74, U. Wis., Madison, 1974-76; sr. physicist EMI Med. Inc., Northbrook, Ill., 1976-77; prof. depts. radiol. scis., elec. engring., medicine and physics U. Calif., Irvine, 1977—, head divsn. physics and engring., 1985—, dir. biomed. magnetic resonance rsch., 1987—2002, dir. Rsch. Imaging Ctr., 1992—, vice chair dept. radiology, 2000—. Cons. UN, 1980-86; gen. chmn. IEEE Nuc. Sci. Symposium and Med. Imaging Conf., 1996, 99. Editor several books; guest editor IEEE Nuclear Sci. Symposium and Med. Imaging Conf., 1997; contbr. articles to profl. jours. Mobil scholar, 1961-66; recipient Athalie Clarke award for rsch. excellence, 2001, Outstanding Achievement in the Arts and Scis. award ATAA, 2002, Outstanding Scientist award Assembly of Turkish-Am. Assns., Washington, 2002. Fellow IEEE (pres. Nuclear and Plasma Scis. Soc. 1993-94, Millennium medal 2000, NPSS Richard Shea award 2000), Am. Assn. Physicists in Medicine, Internat. Soc. Magnetic Resonance in Medicine; mem. Nuclear and Plasma Scis. Soc., Internat. Soc. Magnetic Resonance in Medicine, Am. Assn. for Cancer Rsch., Soc. Nuc. Medicine. Office: Univ Calif Rsch Imaging Ctr Irvine CA 92697-5020 Business E-Mail: nalci@uci.edu.

NAM, SAE WOO, physicist; Grad. in Physics and Elec. Engring., MIT, Cambridge, 1991; MS in Physics, PhD in Physics, Stanford U., Calif., 1998. NRC postdoctoral fellowship Nat. Inst. Standards and Technology, staff scientist electronics and elec. engring. Boulder, Colo., 2001—. Contbr. articles to sci. jours. Recipient Presdl. Early Career award for Scientists and Engrs., 2002; named one of Brilliant 10, Popular Sci. mag., 2003. Office: Electronics and Elec Engring Nat Inst Standards and Tech 325 Broadway MC 815 04 Boulder CO 80305-3328 Office Phone: 303-497-3148. E-mail: saewoo.nam@nist.gov.

NANDA, VED PRAKASH, law educator, director, academic administrator; b. Gujranwala, India, Nov. 20, 1934; arrived in U.S., 1960; s. Jagan Nath and Attar (Kaur) N.; m. Katharine Kunz, Dec. 19, 1982; 1 child, Anjali Devi. MA, Punjab U., 1952; LLB, U. Delhi, 1955, LLM, 1958, Northwestern U., 1962; postgrad., Yale U., 1962-65; LLD, Soka U., Tokyo, 1997, Bundelkhand U., Jhansi, India, 2000, doctorate (hon.), 2000, Soka U., Tokyo, 1997. Asst. prof. law U. Denver, 1965—68, assoc. prof. law, 1968—70, prof. law, dir. Internat. Legal Studies Program, 1970—, Thompson G. Marsh prof. law, 1987—, Evans U. prof., 1992—, asst. provost, 1993—94, vice provost, 1994—. Vis. prof. Coll. Law U. Iowa, Iowa City, 1974—75; vis. prof. Fla. State U., 1973, U. San Diego, 1979, U. Colo., 1992; disting. vis. prof. internat. law Kent Coll. Law, 1981, Calif. We. Sch. Law, San Diego, 1983—84; disting. vis. scholar Sch. Law U. Hawaii, Honolulu, 1986—87; cons. Solar Energy Rsch. Inst., 1978—81, Dept. Energy, 1980—81; vis. prof. numerous summer programs. Co-author (with David Pansius): Litigation of International Disputes in U.S. Courts, 1987; editor: Law in the War Against International Terrorism, 2005; co-editor (with M. Cherif Bassiouni): A Treatise on International Criminal Law, 1973, Water Needs for the Future, 1977; co-editor: (with George Shepherd) Human Rights and Third World Development, 1985; co-editor: (with others) Global Human Rights, 1981, The Law of Transnational Business Transactions, 1981, World Climate Change, 1983, Breach and Adaption of International Contracts, 1992, World Debt and Human Conditions, 1993, Europe Community Law After 1992, 1993, International Environmental Law and Policy, 1995, European Union Law After Maastricht, 1996; co-editor: (with William M. Evan) Nuclear Proliferation and the Legality of Nuclear Weapons, 1995; co-editor: (with S.P. Sinha) Hindu Law and Legal Theory, 1996; co-editor: (with D. Krieger) Nuclear Weapons and the World Court, 1998; co-editor: (with George Pring) International Environmental Law and Policy for the 21st Century, 2003; co-editor: Law in the War Against International Terrorism, 2004; editor, contbr. Refugee Law and Policy, 1989, mem. editl. bd. Jour. Am. Comparative Law, Indian Jour. Internat. Law, Transnational Pubs.; columnist: Denver Post. O-chmn. Colo. Pub. Broadcasting Fedn., 1977—78; mem. Gov.'s Commn. on Pub. Telecomm., 1980—82; UN day chair State of Colo., 2000—; vice chair exec. coun. World Fedn. UN Assn., Geneva; bd. dir. various nat. and state civic orgns. Recipient Univ. Gold Medal, Delhi U. Faculty of Law, Internat. Excellence award, Colo. Coun. Internat. Orgns., 1985, Burlington Northern Found. Scholar award, U. Denver, 1990, World Legal Scholar award, World Peace Through Law Ctr., Beijing, 1990, Highest honor award, Soka U., Tokyo, 1994, Alumni Faculty award, U. Denver Coll. Law, 1994, India Devel. Assn. award, 1996, Civil Right's award, Anti-Defamation League, 1996, Pioneer award, U. Denver, 1997, Medal of Honor, World Congress of Ukranian Lawyers, 1999, Rotary fellowship established in his honor, Denver Rotary, 2000, Gold Medal established in his honor, Bundelkhand U., 2000, Spl. Achievement award, Indo-Am. Assn., 2002, Cmty. Peace Bldg. award, Gandhi King Ikeda, 2004, Highest Order of Justice award, World Jurist Assn., 2005, Human Rights award, India-Can. Assn., 2006; co-recipient Hyde Prize in Internat. Law, Northwestern U. Law Sch.; named Thompson G. Marsh Prof. of Law, 1987—, John Evans U. Prof., 1994—, Amb. for Peace, Interreligious and Internat. Fedn. for World Peace, 2001; graduate fellow, U. Delhi Faculty of Law, Yale Law Sch., Northwestern U. Law Sch. Mem. World Jurist Assn. (v.p. 1991—, pres. 1998-2000, hon. pres. 2000—), World Assn. Law Profs. (pres. 1987-93), UN Assn. (v.p. Colo. divsn. 1973-76, pres. 1986-88, 93-96, nat. coun. UNA-USA 1990—, mem. governing bd. UNA-USA 1995-2005, Arthur Goodman Leadership award 1995, Human Rights award 1997), World Fedn. UN Assns. (vice-chmn. 1995-2001), Am. Assn. Comparative Study Law (bd. dirs.), Am. Soc. Internat. Law (v.p. 1987-88, exec. coun. 1969-72, 81-84, bd. rev. and devel. 1988-91, hon. v.p. 1995-96, counselor 2000—), Assn. Am. Law Schs., U.S. Inst. Human Rights, Internat. Law Assn. (exec. com. 1986—, hon. pres. 2001—), Colo. Coun. Internat. Orgns. (pres. 1988-90), Assn. U.S. Mems. Internat. Inst. Space Law (bd. dirs., exec. com. 1980-88), Internat. Acad. Comparative Law (assoc.), Acad. Internat. Commercial and Consumer Law, Order St. Ives (pres.), Rotary, Cactus Club, Univ. Club, Colo. Athletic Club. Office Phone: 303-871-6276. Business E-Mail: vnanda@law.du.edu.

NANIS, LEONARD, engineering educator, consultant; s. Albert and Ida Nanis; children: Michael Steven, Leonard Alexander. BS, MIT, Cambridg, 1952; MS, MIT, 1954; PhD in Engring. Sci., Columbia U., NYC, 1960. Prof. chem. engring. U. Pa., Phila., 1965—75; mgr. electrochemistry group Sri Internat., Menlo Park, Calif., 1975—82; v.p., founder Seagate Magnetics-genrex, Sunnyvale, Calif., 1982—84; v.p., tech. DASTEC-IMC-XEBEC, San Jose, Calif., 1984—89; pres. Ln3-Electrochem. Engring., San Jose, 1989—; consulting prof. materials sci. Stanford U., Calif., 2000—. Dir., founder Trufocus X-ray Tubes, Watsonville, Calif., 1988—. Chmn., indsl. electrolytics Electrochem. Soc., 1980—82. Recipient Templin award, ASTM, 1970. Independent. Achievements include patents for manufacture Pvd sputter targets; sputtered thin film nucleation of electroless nickel plating; low temperature flux for soldering nickel-titanium alloy; contact burnish head for memory disks; wear resistant contacts for wafer probes; extractive metallurgy for low cost silicon for solar cells. Avocations: painting, sculpting. Home: 2114 Rosswood Dr San Jose CA 94124 Office: Ln3 Electrochemical Engring 1004 Hanson Ct Milpitas CA 95035 Office Fax: 408-945-5966. Personal E-mail: nanislen@juno.com.

NANOS, GEORGE PETER, JR., former science administrator, military officer, physicist; b. Torrington, Conn., Apr. 11, 1945; s. George N.; m. Joanne Louise Knowles, July 5, 1969; 1 child, George. Grad., U.S. Naval Acad., 1967; PhD in Physics, Princeton U., 1974; attended, U.S. Naval Destroyer Sch., Newport, RI, 1974, Def. Sys. Mgmt. Coll., Ft. Belvoir, Va., 1991. Joined US Navy, 1967; commd. ensign USN; advanced through grades to vice admiral; antisub warfare gunnery officer USS Glennon (DD-840), 1967-69; engr. officer USS Forrest Sherman (DD-931), 1974-76; material officer mem. staff destroyer squadron 10, 1976-78; mgr. tech. devel. high energy laser program offie (NAVSEA PMS-405), 1978-82; engring. duty officer, 1980; combat sys. officer Norfolk Naval Shipyard, 1982-84; engr. officer USS America (CV-66); dep. dir. warfare sys. engring. space and naval warfare sys. cmd., 1984-86; head navigation br., 1988-90; head missile br. devel., prodn., operational support missile subsys., 1990-92; dir. tech. divsn. strategic syss. program, 1992-94; dir. strategic sys. program, 1994-98; commr. naval sea sys. command, 1998—2002, retired, 2002; prin. dep. assoc. dir. Threat Reduction Directorate Los Alamos Nat. Lab., N.Mex., 2002—03, interim dir. N.Mex., 2003, dir. N.Mex., 2003—05. Decorated Legion of Merit, Disting. Svc. medal, Meritorious Svc. medal, Navy Achievement medal.

NANULA, RICHARD D., former heath products company executive; b. Los Angeles, 1960; married; 3 children. BA in economics, U. Calif., Santa Barbara; MBA, Harvard Bus. Sch. Joined Walt Disney Co., 1986, exec. v.p., CFO, 1991—94, pres. Disney Stores, 1994—96, CFO, 1996—98; pres., CEO Starwood Hotels and Resorts, NYC, 1998—99; chmn., CEO Broadband Sports, 1999—2001; exec. v.p., CFO Amgen Inc., 2001—07. Bd. dirs. The Boeing Co., 2005—; bd. trustees Healthcare Leadership Coun. Avocations: basketball, tennis.

NAPOLES, VERONICA, graphic designer, consultant; b. NYC, July 9, 1951; d. Florencio Andres and Elena (Colomar) N.; 1 child, Samuel Andres. BA, U. Miami, 1972; BArch, U. Calif., Berkeley, 1979. Account supr. Marsh & McLennan, Miami, Fla., 1974-76; designer Mus. of Anthropology, San Francisco, 1977-79; project dir. Landor & Assocs., San Francisco, 1979-81; prin. Communications Planning, Kentfield, Calif., 1981—. Bd. dirs. Mind Fitness, Mill Valley, Calif., Main Arts Coun., Mykytyn Cons. Group; instr. U. Calif.-Berkeley, San Francisco, 1983—, Sonoma State U., Santa Rosa, Calif., 1983-84; tchr. Dynamic Graphics Ednl. Found., San Francisco. Author: Corporate Identity Design, 1987; exhibited at San Francisco Airport, 1992. Bd. dirs. Marin Arts Coun. Recipient Bay Area Hispanic Bus. Achiever award, 1988, Design award PRINT, 1988, Excellence award Am. Corp. Identity, 1989, 90, 91, 92, 93, 94, 95, 96, Excellence award N.Y. Art Dirs. Show, 1989; finalist Sundance Inst., 1991. Mem. Am. Inst. Graphic Arts, Women in Communications. Avocations: painting, writing. Office: Napoles Design 189 Madrone Ave Larkspur CA 94939-2113

NAPOLITANO, GRACE FLORES, United States Representative from California; b. Brownsville, Tex., Dec. 4, 1936; d. Miguel and Maria Alicia (Ledezma) Flores; m. Frank Napolitano, 1982; children: Yolando, Fred, Edward, Michael, Cynthia. Student, Cerritos Coll., LA Trade-Tech. Coll., Tec Southwest Coll. Councilwoman City of Norwalk, Calif., 1986—92, mayor, 1989—90; mem. Calif. Assembly, 1993-98, US Congress from 38th Calif. dist., Washington, 1999—, mem. resources com., transp. & infrastructure com., chair water & power subcom. Dir. LA County Sanitation Dist.; mem. Am. Legion Auxiliary, Norwalk Internat. Friendship Commn., Health Task Force, Mfg. Task Force, Women's Caucus, New Dem. Coalition; founder Southeast Coalition Safe Drinking Water; founder, co-chair Congl. Mental Health Caucus; chair Southeast LA County Pvt. Industry Coun.; former chair Congl. Hispanic Caucus. Active Cerritos Coll. Found. Mem.: US/Mex. Sister Cities Assn., Vets. of Foreign Wars, Lions Club. Democrat. Roman Catholic. Office: US House Reps 1610 Longworth House Office Bldg Washington DC 20515-0538 Office Phone: 202-225-5256.

NAPOLITANO, LEONARD MICHAEL, anatomist, university administrator; b. Oakland, Calif., Jan. 8, 1930; s. Filippo Michael and Angela (De Fiore) N.; m. Jane M. Winer, July 9, 1955; children—Leonard M., Janet Ann, Nancy Angela. BS, Santa Clara U., 1951; MS, St. Louis U., 1954, PhD, 1956. Instr. anatomy Cornell Med. Coll., NYC, 1956-58; instr. U. Pitts. Sch. Med., 1958-59, asst. prof., 1959-64; asso. prof. U. N.Mex., 1964-68; prof. dept. anatomy U. N.Mex. (Sch. Medicine), 1968—, acting chmn. dept., 1971-72, dean pro tem, 1972-73, dean, 1973—, interim v.p. for health scis., 1976—; dir. U. N.Mex. (Med. Center); dean U. N.Mex. (Sch. Medicine), 1977-86, dean emeritus, 1996—. Mem. NIH Rsch. Resource Coun., 1988-91, ret. cons., 1994. Contbr. articles on lipid research and ultra structure of cholesterol to profl. jours.; Asso. editor: Anatomical Record, 1968-74. Mem. Am. Assn. Anatomists, Am. Soc. Cell Biology, Electron Microscope Soc. Am., Albuquerque, Bernalillo county Med. Assn. (hon.), Assn. Am. Med. Colls. Council of Deans. Home: 2308 Calle De Panza NW Albuquerque NM 87104-3070 Office: U N Mex Dean Sch Medicine Health Sci Center Albuquerque NM 87131

NARASIMHAN, PADMA MANDYAM, physician; b. Bangalore, India; came to U.S., 1976; d. Alasingracher Mandyam and Alamela Mandyam Narasimhan; 1 child, Ravi. MD, Maulana Azad Med. Coll., New Delhi, 1970. Diplomate Am. Bd. Internal Medicine. Intern in internal medicine Flushing Hosp., NYC, 1976-77; resident in internal medicine Luth. Med. Ctr., NYC, 1977-79; fellow hematology, oncology Beth-Israel Med. Ctr., NYC, 1979-81; asst. prof. King Drew Med. Ctr., LA, 1983-87, Harbor UCLA, Torrance, 1987—2000, USC, 2003—. Mem. editorial bd. Jour. Internal Medicine, 1986—. Mem. ACP, AAPI, Am. Soc. Clin. Oncology, So. Calif. Acad. Clin. Oncology. Hindu. Avocations: travel, reading, music, walking. Home: 6604 Madeline Cove Dr Palos Verdes Peninsula CA 90275-4608 Office Phone: 310-377-9555. Personal E-mail: padmanarasim@yahoo.com.

NARAYAN, ASH, lawyer; b. 1965; BS in Acctg., Valparaiso U., Ind.; JD, Loyola Law Sch. Mng. ptnr. RGT Capital Mgmt., Irvine, Calif. Editor: Loyola Law Sch. Law Review. Mem.: Sports Lawyers Assn. (bd. dirs.), Inst. Cert. Fin. Planners, several State Bar Assn. and CPA Soc. Office: RGI Capital Mgmt 1 Park Plz #970 Irvine CA 92614 Office Phone: 949-955-5525. Business E-Mail: anaryan@rgtnet.com.

NARAYEN, SHANTANU, computer software company executive; BS in Elec. Engring., Osmania U., India; MS in Computer Sci., Bowling Green U.; MBA, U. Calif. Berkeley, Haas Sch. Bus., 1993. Sr. mgr. Apple Computer, Inc.; dir. desktop & collaboration products Silicon Graphics, Inc.; co-founder Pictra, Inc.; v.p., gen. mgr. engring. tech. group Adobe Systems, Inc., San Jose, Calif., 1998—99, sr. v.p. worldwide products, 1999—2001, exec. v.p. worldwide product mktg. & devel., 2001—05, pres., COO, 2005—07, pres., CEO, 2007—. Bd. dirs. Adobe Systems, Inc., 2007—; spkr. in field. Adv. bd. Haas Sch. Bus., U. Calif., Berkeley. Achievements include patents in field. Office: Adobe Sys Inc 345 Park Ave San Jose CA 95110-2704 Office Phone: 408-536-6000.

NASH, CYNTHIA JEANNE, journalist; b. Detroit, Dec. 24, 1947; d. Frederick Copp and Carolyn (Coffin) N.; 1 child, Lydia Anne Maza; m. Richard Zahler, July 22, 1994. BA, U. Mich., 1969. Reporter Detroit News, 1970-75, sports columnist, 1975-77, Life Style columnist 1977-79, Life Style editor, 1979-82; news features editor Seattle Times, 1983; asst. mng. editor Sunday Seattle Times, 1983-86, assoc. mng. editor, 1986-97, dir. content devel., 1986-2000, dir., brand and content devel., 2000—. Mem. Harbor Sq. Club. Office: Seattle Times PO Box 70 Fairview Ave N & John St Seattle WA 98111-0070 E-mail: cnash@seattletimes.com.

NASH, HORACE LYONS, lawyer; b. San Jose, Calif., Dec. 19, 1955; BA with honors, U. Chgo., 1975; PhD, Stanford U., 1982; JD cum laude, Harvard U., 1985. Bar: Calif. 1985. Ptnr. Fenwick & West LLP, Mountain View, Calif., chair securities group. Named a Dealmaker of the Yr., Am. Lawyer mag., 2006. Mem.: State Bar Calif. Office: Fenwick & West LLP Silcon Valley Ctr 801 California St Mountain View CA 94041 Office Phone: 650-988-8500, 650-335-7934. Office Fax: 650-938-5200. E-mail: hnash@fenwick.com.

NASH, JILL, communications executive; BA in Journalism, San Diego State U. Head corp. comm. Transamerica Life Companies; with KPMG; v.p. corp. comm. Charles Schwab Corp.; v.p. employee comm. Gap, Inc., 2003—05, v.p. corp. comm., 2005—07; sr. v.p., chief comm. officer Yahoo! Inc., 2007—09; chief comm. officer, v.p. corp. affairs Levi Strauss & Co., San Francisco, 2009—. Past pres. Orgn. of Women Executives. Recipient multiple Gold Quill awards. Office: Levi Strauss & Co 155 Battery St San Francisco CA 94111*

NASH, MIKE, computer software company executive; married; 3 children. B in Computer Sci. with honors, Cornell U. Coll. Engring.; MBA with Distinction, Wharton Sch. Bus., U. Pa. Project leader, software developer Gen. Data Corp.; joined Microsoft Corp., Redmond, Wash., 1991, various positions in Windows mktg., 1991, gen. mgr. bus. Windows product mgmt., corp. v.p. content devel. and delivery group, corp. v.p. security tech. unit, 2002—06, corp. v.p. Windows product mgmt., 2007—. Palmer Scholar, Wharton Sch., U. Pa. Office: Microsoft Corp One Microsoft Way Redmond WA 98052-6399 Office Phone: 425-882-8080.

NASH, STEVE, professional basketball player; b. Feb. 7, 1974; Degree, Santa Clara Coll., 1996. Player Phoenix Suns, 1996, Dallas Mavericks, 1998—2004, Phoenix Suns, 2004—. Named Best NBA Player, ESPY awards, 2005, MVP, NBA, 2005—06, Man of Yr., GQ mag., 2005; named one of 100 Most Influential People, Time Mag., 2006; named to Western Conf. All-Star Team, NBA, 2002, 2003, 2005, 2007, 2008, All-NBA Third Team, 2002, 2003, All-NBA First Team, 2005—07. Office: c/o Phoenix Suns 201 E Jefferson St Phoenix AZ 85004

NASH, STEVEN ALAN, museum director, curator, art historian; b. Wadsworth, Ohio, Apr. 8, 1944; s. Frank W. N. and LaDema (Siffert) N.; m. Carol Ostrowski, June 14, 1969; children: Colin H., Jessica K. BA, Dartmouth Coll., 1966; PhD, Stanford U., 1973. Curator Albright-Knox Art Gallery, Buffalo, 1973-80; dep. dir., chief curator Dallas Mus. Art, 1980-88; assoc. dir., chief curator, European Arts Fine Arts Mus. of San Francisco, 1988; dir. Nasher Sculpture Ctr., Dallas, 2001—07; exec. dir. Palm Springs Desert Mus., Calif., 2007—. Panelist Nat. Endowment for the Arts, Washington, 1986—, Inst. Mus. Svcs., Washington, 1979—; bd. dirs. Oberlin (Ohio) Intermus. Conservation Labs., 1976-80. Author: Catalogue: Albright-Knox Art Gallery, 1976, Ben Nicholson, 1977, Naum Gabo: Constructivism, 1986, Century of Modern Sculpture, 1987. Bd. dirs. Lakehill Prep. Sch., Dallas, 1987-88, Buffalo Archtl. Guidebook, 1979-80. Mus. Profl. fellow Nat. Endowment for Arts, 1980; fellow Mabelle McLeod Lewis Found., 1970-71. Mem. Coll. Art Assn., Am. Assn. Mus., Dartmouth Alumni Club. Office: Palm Springs Desert Mus 101 N Museum Dr Palm Springs CA 92262 Business E-Mail: kcarr@psmuseum.org.

NASON, ROCHELLE, conservation organization administrator; b. Oakland, Calif., May 21, 1959; d. Milton and Ann Frances (Reed) Nason. BA, U. Calif., Berkeley, 1984; JD, U. Calif., San Francisco, 1987. Bar: Calif. 1987. Law clk. to Chief Justice Malcolm Lucas Supreme Ct. of Calif., San Francisco, 1987-88; litigation assoc. Morrison & Foerster, San Francisco, 1988-92; staff lawyer League to Save Lake Tahoe, South Lake Tahoe, Calif., 1992-93, exec. dir., 1993—. Adj. instr. Sierra Nev. Coll., Incline Village, 1992—94, Lake Tahoe C.C., 1992—96. Editor: The Traynor Reader, 1987; sr. rev. editor: Hastings Law Jour., 1986—87; editor: (jour.) Keep Tahoe Blue, 1992—; columnist: newspaper Tahoe Daily Tribune; contbr. articles to profl. jours. Mem. leadership coun. Tahoe-Truckee Regional Econ. Coalition, Stateline, Nev., 1992—94; v.p., bd. dirs. Jewish Cmty. South Lake Tahoe/Temple Bat Yam, 1992—99; bd. dirs. Tahoe Ctr. Sustainable Future, Glenbrook, Nev., 1995—98, Earthshare Calif., 2002—. Mem.: Thurston Soc., Order of Coif. Jewish. Avocations: backpacking, skiing. Office: League to Save Lake Tahoe 955 Emerald Bay Rd South Lake Tahoe CA 96150-6410

NASSETTA, CHRISTOPHER J., hotel executive; b. 1962; m. Paige Nassetta; 6 children. BS in Fin., McIntire Sch. Commerce, U. Va., 1984. Various positions Oliver Carr Co., 1984-91, chief devel. officer; pres. Bailey Realty Corp., 1991-95; exec. v.p. Host Hotels and Resorts Inc., 1995—97, COO, 1997—2000, pres., CEO Bethesda, Md., 2000—07, Hilton Hotels Corp., Beverly Hills, Calif., 2007—. Bd. dirs. CoStar Group Inc.; trustee Prime Group Realty Trust. Adv. bd. McIntire Sch. Commerce, U. Va. Office: Hilton Hotels 9336 Civic Ctr Dr Beverly Hills CA 90210

NATCHER, STEPHEN DARLINGTON, retired lawyer, electronics executive; b. San Francisco, Nov. 19, 1940; m. Carolyn Anne Bowman, Aug. 23, 1969; children: Tanya Michelle, Stephanie Elizabeth. AB in Polit. Sci., Stanford U., 1962; JD, U. Calif., San Francisco, 1965. Bar: Calif. 1966. Assoc. firm Pillsbury, Madison & Sutro, San Francisco, 1966-68; counsel Douglas Aircraft div. McDonnell Douglas Corp., Long Beach, Calif., 1968-70; v.p., sec. Security Pacific Nat. Bank, 1971-79; asst. gen. counsel Security Pacific Corp., 1979-80; v.p., sec., gen. counsel Lear Siegler, Inc., Santa Monica, Calif., 1980-87; v.p., gen. counsel Computer Sci. Corp., El Segundo, Calif., 1987-88; exec. v.p., gen. counsel, sec. CalFed Inc., 1989-90; sr. v.p. adminstrn., gen. counsel, sec. Wyle Electronics, Irvine, Calif., 1991-98; gen. counsel VEBA Electronics LLC, Santa Clara, Calif., 1998—2002, ret., 2002. With USCG, 1965-71. Mem.: St. Francis Yacht Club (San Francisco). Republican. E-mail: snatcher@starstream.net.

NATHANSON, DAVID, communications executive; b. 1977; Grad., U. Pa. Corp. analyst Comcast Cable Comm.; mgr., Strategic Planning Cablevision Systems Corp.; dir., Mktg. News Corp.; dir., Broadband Strategy Fox Cable Networks Grp., 2000, v.p., Broadband Strategy and Channel Devel., 2001; gen. mgr. Fox Sports Digital Nets, 2001; sr. v.p., gen. mgr. TVG Network, 2005—. Mem. Cable & Telecom. Assn for Mktg. Cable Network ITV Coun.; chmn. CablePositive, LA. Named one of 100 Most Influential Executives in Cable TV, Cable Fax Mag., 2000—01, 40 Executives Under 40, Multichannel News, 2006. Office: TVG Network 19545 NW Von Neumann Dr Ste 210 Beaverton OR 97006

NATHANSON, PAUL S., lawyer, educator; b. 1943; BA, Tulane U., 1964; JD, Duke U., 1967; MCL, U. Chgo., 1969. Bar: Calif., N. Mex. Assoc. O'Melveny & Myers, LA; founding dir. Nat. Sr. Citizens Law Ctr., LA, 1972—80; rsch. prof. U. N.Mex Sch. Law, 1980—2005, rsch. prof. emeritus, 2005—, dir. Inst. Public Law, 1983—2005; assoc. provost academic affairs U. N.Mex. Mem. bd. dir. Nat. Sr. Citizens Law Ctr., Internat. Ctr. for Not-For-Profit Law, Nat. Com. Preserve Social Security & Medicare, 1998—, vice chmn., 2001—03, chmn., 2003—; chmn. bd. KNME PBS TV, N.Mex.; mem. bd. dir. N.Mex Legal Aid Found. Mem.: ABA (founding mem., Commn. on Elderly), Am. Soc. Aging (past pres.), Gray Panthers (past nat. sec.).

NATION, JOSEPH EDWARD, public policy analyst, researcher; b. Dallas, July 18, 1956; s. Joseph B. and Doris C. (Koeninger) N.; m. Linda Nicolay, May 7, 1983; children: Kristen, Alexandra. BA, U. Colo., 1979; MS in Fgn. Svc., Georgetown U., 1985; PhD in Policy Analysis, Rand Grad. Sch., 1989. Asst. to sr. fgn. policy advisor to Vice-Presdl. Candidate Geraldine Ferraro, 1984; assoc. economist, devel. officer The RAND Corp., 1985—; dir. devel. & studies Calif. Seminar on Internat. Security & Fgn. Policy, 1987-88; postdoctoral fellow Ctr. for Internat. Security & Arms Control, Stanford U., Palo Alto, Calif., 1989-90; mem. Calif. Ho. of Reps., 2000—. Editor: Back From The Brink: De-escalation of Nuclear Crises, 1991; author numerous RAND Corp. reports; contbr. articles to profl. jours. Candidate for U.S. Congress, 1992. Democrat. Avocation: hiking. Office: PO Box 942849 Sacramento CA 94249

NATSUYAMA, HARRIET HATSUNE KAGIWADA, mathematician, educator; b. Honolulu, Sept. 2, 1937; d. Kenjiro and Yakue Natsuyama; children: Julia, Conan. BA, U. Hawaii, 1959, MS, 1960; PhD, Kyoto U., 1965. Math. Rand Corp., Santa Monica, Calif., 1961—68, cons., 1968-77; adj. assoc. prof. U. So. Calif., LA, 1974-79; sr. scientist Hughes Aircraft Co., El Segundo, 1979-87; chief engr. Infotec Devel. Inc., Camarillo, 1987-89; prof. systems engring. Calif. State U., Fullerton, 1990-96; co-founder Planet Aura, Inc., 2002—. Fgn. spl. vis. prof. Oita U., 1995, Kyoto Sch. of Computer Sci., 1997—2000; vis. prof. Sci. U., Tokyo, 1998; co-founder Planet Aura, Inc., 2002—; sec. Yeru Bon Ctr., LA, 2005; founder U. Hawaii, Kenjiro and Yakue Natsuyama Scholarship, 2006. Author: Invariant Imbedding and Time-Dependent Transport Processes, 1963, System Identification: Methods and Applications, 1974, Integral Equations via Imbedding Methods, 1974, Multiple Scattering Processes: Inverse and Direct, 1975, Numerical Derivatives and Nonlinear Analysis, 1986, Terrestrial Radiative Transfer: Modeling, Computation, Data Analysis, 1998. Recipient Disting. Alumna, U. Hawaii, 1991. Mem. Inst. Noetic Scis., Grad. Women in Sci. (pres. 1990-91), Phi Beta Kappa, Phi Kappa Phi.

NAUGHTON, JAMES LEE, internist; b. 1946; AB, Dartmouth Coll., 1968; MD, Harvard U., 1972. Intern U. Calif. Moffitt Hosp., San Francisco, 1972-73; resident in medicine U. Calif. Affiliated Hosps., San Francisco, 1973-75, San Francisco Gen. Hosp., 1975-76; fellow in nephrology U. Calif., San Francisco, 1976-77, assoc. clin. prof. medicine, 1982—; pvt. practice internal medicine, ptnr. Alliance Med. Group, Pinole, Calif., 1982—. Mem. Am. Bd. Internal Medicine (bd. dirs. 1995-2002, exec. com. 1997-2002, trustee found. 2000—). Office: Alliance Med Group 2160 Appian Way Ste 200 Pinole CA 94564-2524

NAUGLE, DAVID N., federal judge; b. 1943; BA, Stanford U., 1965, JD, 1967. With U.S. Army, 1968-73. Mem. ABA, San Bernardino County Bar Assn., Riverside County Bar Assn. Office: 3420 12th St Riverside CA 92501-3801

NAULTY, SUSAN LOUISE, archivist; b. Abington, Pa., May 28, 1944; d. Charles J. and Ruth E. (Schick) N. BA, Whittier Coll., 1967; MA, Loyola U., LA, 1972. Tchr. history and English, Whittier (Calif.) H.S., 1968-70; from libr. asst. to asst. curator Huntington Libr., San Marino, Calif., 1972-91; archivist Richard Nixon Libr. and Birthplace, Yorba Linda, Calif., 1991—.

NAVA, CYNTHIA L., state legislator; b. Dona Ana, N. Mex., 1953; children: Ali, Mima, Xochitl. BS, Western Ill. U.; MA, Ea. Ill. U. Dep. supt. Gadsden Schools; mem. Dist. 31 N.Mex. State Senate, Santa Fe, 1993—. Democrat. Lutheran. Home: 3002 Broadmoor Dr Las Cruces NM 88001-7501 Office: N Mex Senate State Capitol Rm 301 Santa Fe NM 87503-0001 Home Phone: 575-526-4111; Office Phone: 575-882-6200.*

NAYLOR-JACKSON, JERRY, public relations consultant, retired, entertainer, broadcaster; b. Chalk Mountain, Tex., Mar. 6, 1939; s. William Guy and Mary Bernice (Lummus) Jackson; m. Pamela Ann Robinson, Jan. 30, 1966; children: Geoffrey K. Naylor, Kelli A. Naylor-Dobrzynski, Gregory K. Naylor. Grad., Elkins Electronics Inst., Dallas, 1957. Life first class radio/TV engring. lic. FCC. Broadcaster various local TV and AM radio stas., San Angelo, Texas, 1955-57; lead singer Buddy Holly and the Crickets, 1960-65; solo entertainer, performer, recording artist and producer, 1965-87; sr. v.p. corp. devel. Newslink Internat. Satellite Broadcast Comms. Co., Inc., Washington, 1986-88; pres. Internat. Syndications, Inc. subs. Newslink, Inc., Washington, 1986-88; pres., CEO, owner The Jerry Naylor Co./Nayco Entertainment, Inc., McMinnville, Oreg., 1984—; v.p. capital programs, sr. cons. Calif. Luth. Univ., Thousand Oaks, 1990-92. Sr. cons., dir. ann. fund Calif. Luth. U., 1989-90; polit./media cons. various Rep. candidates and orgns., 1968-93; spl. cons. to Violeta Barrios de Chamarro, Pres. of Republic of Nicaragua, 1990-92; disc jockey Sta. KHEY-AM, Sta. KINT-AM, El Paso, Tex., 1959; on-air personality Sta. KRLA-AM, Sta. KDAY-AM, L.A., 1960; on-air disc jockey, air personality, celebrity host KLAC-AM, L.A., 1974-83; on-camera and voice-over spokesman for Safeway Stores, Inc., Avis Rent-a-Car, Mut. of Omaha, Wrigley Co., 1968-83; U.S. presdl. appointee, chmn. Job Tng. Partnership Act work group/youth at risk subcom. Nat. Commn. for Employment Policy, 1985-91; nat. dir. spl. events Reagan for Pres., 1979-81; apptd. mem. commn. for employment policy Pres. Ronald Reagan, 1985-91. Rec. artist maj. labels including Capitol/Tower Records, Mercury/Smash Records, CBS/Columbia Records, Mike Club Prodns., Warner/Curb Records, Motown Records, Warner Bros. Records, EMI Records, 1965-84; solo rec. artist, prodr. Phonograph Records and TV Documentaries; host weekly nat. and internat. syndicated radio program Continental Country (Number 1 syndicated country music radio show in Am., Billboard Mag., Country Music Assn., 1974), weekly syndicated TV variety show Music City, USA, 1966-67. Nat. dir. spl. events Reagan for Pres., 1975-76, 79-80; sr. cons. to White House, 1981-88, 89-92. With U.S. Army, 1957-58, Germany. Named to Top 40 Male Vocalists of Yr., Cashbox Mag., 1970, named #1 Rock Group (Crickets), New Musical Express Mag., U.K., 1962, named to Rockabilly Hall of Fame, 2000. Mem. NARAS, Country Music Assn., Acad. Country Music (Telly award for TV documentary 1991, 92), Pi Kappa Phi (alumni), founding mem. West Tex. Music Hall of Fame/Mus. Found. Avocation: writing prose and poetry. Mailing: Jerry Naylor Co LLC No 307 1301 N Highway 99W Mcminnville OR 97128 Office Fax: 503-435-0526. Business E-Mail: naycoent@comcast.net.

NAZARIAN, SAM, hotel executive, film producer; b. Tehran, Iran, 1975; s. Younes Nazarian. Founder, CEO SBE Entertainment Group, LLC, 2002—. Owner Area, Hyde and Privilige. Exec. prodr.: (films) Home of Phobia, 2004, The Beautiful Country, 2004, Trespassing, 2004, Waiting..., 2005, Down in the Valley, 2005, Five Fingers, 2006, The Last Time, 2006, Pride, 2007, Mr. Brooks, 2007, College, 2008. Named one of The Top 100 Most Powerful People in So. Calif., West mag., 2006. Office: SBE Entertainment Group LLC 8000 Beverly Blvd Los Angeles CA 90048

NAZEM, FARZAD, information technology executive; BS in Computer sci., Calif. Polytechnic State. Various tech. positions Sydis, Inc., Rolm Corp.; v.p., media and web server divsn. Oracle Corp., Redwood Shores, Calif.; exec. v.p. engring. and surfing Yahoo! Inc., Sunnyvale, Calif., 1996, chief tech. officer, 1997—2007.

NEAL, JOSEPH M., JR., state legislator; b. Mounds, La., July 28, 1935; m. Estelle Ann DeConge; children: Charisse, Tania, Withania, Dina Amelia, Joseph. BA, So. U.; postgrad., Inst. Applied Sci. Mem. Nev. Senate, Dist. 4, 1972—; asst. majority fl. leader Nev. Senate, 1985, 87; minority fl. leader Nev. State Senate, 1989, pres. pro tempore, 1991, mem. fin. com., mem. govt. affairs com., mem. taxation com. Active State Dem. Ctrl. Com., Clark County Dem. Ctrl. Com., Nev. Cath. Welfare; past chair Clark County Econ. Opportunity Bd., Greater Las Vegas Plan; candidate Nev. Gov., 1998. Mem. Elks Lodge, Phi Beta Sigma. Democrat. Home: 304 Lance Ave North Las Vegas NV 89030-3844 Office: Nev State Legis Bldg 401 S Carson St Rm 204 Carson City NV 89701-4747 Fax: 702-687-8206. E-mail: jneal@sen.state.nv.us.

NEAL, STEPHEN CASSIDY, lawyer; b. San Francisco, Mar. 26, 1949; AB, Harvard U., 1970; JD, Stanford U., 1973. Bar: Ill 1973, Calif. 1993. Ptnr. Kirkland & Ellis, Chgo.; ptnr., bus. litigation Cooley Godward Kronish LLP (formerly Cooley Godward LLP), Palo Alto, Calif., 1995—, CEO, 2001—08, chmn., 2001—. Named one of 100 Most Influential Lawyers, Nat. Law Jour., 2006. Fellow: Am. Coll. Trial Lawyers. Office: Cooley Godward Kronish LLP 5 Palo Alto Square #400 3000 El Camino Real Palo Alto CA 94306-2155 Office Phone: 650-843-5182. Office Fax: 650-857-0663. Business E-Mail: nealsc@cooley.com.

NEALE, ERNEST RICHARD WARD, retired university official, consultant; b. Montreal, Que., Can., July 3, 1923; s. Ernest John and Mabel Elizabeth (McNamee) N.; m. Roxie Eveline Anderson, June 3, 1950; children: Richard Ward, Owen Curtis. B.Sc., McGill U., Montreal, 1949; MS, Yale U., 1950, PhD, 1952; LL.D. (hon.), Calgary U., Alta., Can., 1977; DSc (hon.), Meml. U., Nfld., Can., 1989. Asst. prof. geology U. Rochester, N.Y., 1952-54; sect. chief Geol. Survey Can., Ottawa, Ont., 1954-63, div. chief, 1965-68, Calgary, 1976-81; commonwealth geol. liaison officer London, 1963-65; prof., head geology Meml. U., St. John's, Nfld., Can., 1968-76, v.p. acad., 1982-87; cons., Calgary, Alta., Can., 1987—. Chmn. nat. adv. bd. on sci. publs. NRC-Natural Scis. and Engring. Rsch. Coun., Ottawa, 1982-88. Author: Geology and Geophysics in Canadian Universities, 1980. Editor: Some Guides to Mineral Exploration, 1967, Geology of the Atlantic Region, 1968, The Geosciences in Canada, 1980; editor: Can. Jour. Earth Sci., 1974-79. Bd. dirs. Unitarian Ch. Calgary, 1993-1997, pres., 1995-96. Petty officer Royal Can. Navy, 1943-45. Decorated officer Order of Can.; recipient Queen's Jubilee medal, Govt. Can., 1977, 125 medal Can., 1992, Golden Jubilee medal Can., 2002, Integrity award, Calgary Rotary, 2003, William Irvine award, Unitarian Ch. Calgary, 2004, Alta. Centennial medal, 2005. Fellow Royal Soc. Can. (coun. 1972-75, chmn. com. pub. awareness of sci. 1987-91, Bancroft medal 1975), Geol. Assn. Can. (pres. 1973-74, Ambrose medal 1986, 1st E.R. Ward Neale medal 1995), Can. Geosci. Coun. (pres. 1975-76), R.T. Bell medal (Can. Mining Jour. 1977), Geol. Soc. Am.; mem. Assn. Earth Sci. Editors, Nat. Def. (chmn. biol. and chem. def. rev. com. 1990-93), Univ. Club Calgary, Chancellor's Club, Crows Nest Club, Calgary Sci. Network (pres. 1989), Sigma Xi (nat. lectr. New Haven 1976, chmn. Avalon chpt. 1986). Avocations: golf, cross country skiing, hiking, canoeing. Home and Office: 5108 Carney Rd NW Calgary AB Canada T2L 1G2

NEALE-MAY, DONOVAN, marketing executive; Degree in journalism, Rhodes U., South Africa. Leader pub. rels. ops. Ogilvy & Mather, Calif.; founder, mng. ptnr. GlobalFluency, Inc.; founder, exec. dir. Chief Mktg. Officer (CMO) Coun. Mem. adv. bd. pub. rels. degree program San Jose State U., Calif.; cons. with various clients; several acct. mgmt., sr. exec. positions comm. agys., England. Mem. bd. Travelzoo.com; mem. bd. Rhodes U. Charitable Trust. Scholar Cape Times. Office: GlobalFluency 4151 Middlefield Rd Palo Alto CA 94303 Office Phone: 650-433-4200. Office Fax: 650-328-5016. E-mail: donovan@globalfluency.com, donovan@cmocouncil.org.

NEAR, TIMOTHY, theater director; Grad., San Francisco State U., Acad. Music and Dramatic Art, London. Artistic dir. San Jose Repertory Theatre, 1987—. Past actress, dir. with numerous prestigious theaters including The Guthrie Theatre, Berkeley (Calif.) Repertory Theater, La Jolla (Calif.) Playhouse, The Alliance Theatre, Atlanta, The Mark Taper Forum, L.A., Ford's Theatre, Washington, Repertory Theatre of St. Louis, N.Y. Shakespeare Festival, Stage West, Mass., A.C.T., Seattle. Dir. Ghosts on Fire, La Jolla Playhouse (Drama League award), Singer in the Storm, Mark Taper Forum (Drama League award), Thunder Knocking on the Door (Drama League award). Recipient 1997 Woman of Achievement in the Arts, San Jose Mercury News and The Woman's Fund. Office: San Jose Repertory Theatre 101 Paseo De San Antonio San Jose CA 95113-2603

NEARY, PATRICIA ELINOR, ballet director; b. Miami, Fla. d. James Elliott and Elinor (Mitsitz) N. Corps de ballet Nat. Ballet of Can., Toronto, Ont., 1957-60; prin. dancer N.Y.C. Ballet, 1960-68; ballerina Geneva Ballet, Switzerland, 1968-70, ballet dir., 1973-78; guest artist Stuttgart Ballet, Germany, 1968-70; asst. ballet dir., ballerina West Berlin Ballet, 1970-73; ballet dir. Zurich Ballet, Switzerland, 1978-86, La Scala di Milano ballet co., Italy, 1986-88; tchr. Balanchine ballets, Balanchine Trust, 1987—.

NEBELKOPF, ETHAN, psychologist; b. NYC, June 13, 1946; s. Jacob and Fannie (Carver) N.; m. Karen Horrocks, July 27, 1976; children: Demian David, Sarah Dawn. BA, CCNY, 1966; MA, U. Mich., 1969; PhD, Summit U., 1989. Social worker Project Headstart, NYC, 1965; coord. Project Outreach, Ann Arbor, 1968-69; program dir. White Bird Clinic, Eugene, Oreg., 1971-75; counseling supr. Teledyne Econ. Devel. Corp., San Diego, 1976-79; dir. planning and edn. Walden House, San Francisco, 1979-89, dir. tng., 1990-93; program evaluator United Indian Nations, Oakland, Calif., 1994-96; clin. dir., Family and Child Guidance Clinic Indian Health Ctr., Oakland, Calif., 1997—; clin. dir. Family and Child Guidance Clinic Native Am. Health Ctr., Oakland, Calif., 1997—. Adj. prof. dept. social work San Francisco State U., 1982-87; cons. Berkeley (Calif.) Holistic Health Ctr., 1979-84, Medicine Wheel Healing Co-op, San Diego, 1976-79; alternate del. Nat. Free Clinic Coun., Eugene, 1972-74; clin. dir. Urban Indian Health Bd., Oakland, Calif., 1997. Author: White Bird Flies to Phoenix, 1973, The New Herbalism, 1980, The Herbal Connection, 1981, Speaking in Red, 2004 Mem. Mayor's Task Force on Drugs, San Francisco, 1988; mem. treatment com. Gov.'s Policy Coun. on Drugs, Sacramento, 1989; task force Human Svcs. Tng., Salem, Oreg., 1972; organizer West Eugene Bozo Assn., 1973; founder Green Psychology, 1993. Named Outstanding Young Man of Am., U.S. Jaycees, 1980; recipient Silver Key, House Plan Assn., 1966. Mem. Calif. Assn. Family Therapists, World Fedn. of Therapeutic Communities, Nat. Writer's Club, N.Y. Acad. Scis., Internat. Assn. for Human Rels. Lab. Tng., Calif. Assn. of Drug Programs and Profls. (pres. 1988-90), Phi Beta Kappa. Avocations: herbs, rocks, cactus, yoga, baseball cards. Office: 6641 Simson St Oakland CA 94605-2220

NEBLETT, CAROL, soprano; b. Modesto, Calif., Feb. 1, 1946; m. Philip R. Akre; 3 children. Studies with, William Vennard, Roger Wagner, Esther Andreas, Ernest St. John Metz, Lotte Lehmann, Pierre Bernac, Rosa Ponselle, George London, Jascha Heifetz, Norman Treigle, Sol Hurek, Dorothy Kirsten, Maestros Julius Rudel, Claudio Abbado, Daniel Barenboin, Erich Leinsdorf, James Levine, others. Soloist with Roger Wagner Chorale; performed in U.S. and abroad with various symphonies; debut with Carnegie Hall, 1966, N.Y.C. Opera, 1969, Met. Opera, 1979; sung with maj. opera cos. including Met. Opera, N.Y.C., Lyric Opera Chgo., Balt. Opera, Pitts. Opera, Houston Grand Opera, San Francisco Opera, Boston Opera Co., Milw. Florentine Opera, Washington Opera Soc., Covent Garden, Cologne Opera, Vienna (Austria) Staatsoper, Paris Opera, Teatro Regio, Turin, Italy, Teatro San Carlo, Naples, Italy, Teatro Massimo, Palermo, Italy, Gran Teatro del Liceo, Barcelona, Spain, Kirov Opera Theatre, Leningrad, USSR, Dubrovnik (Yugoslavia) Summer Festival, Salzberg Festival, others; rec. artist RCA, DGG, EMI; appearances with symphony orchs., also solo recitals, (film) La Clemenza di Tito; filmed and recorded live performance with Placido Domingo, La Fancuilla del West; numerous TV appearances, artist, Residence Chapman U, assoc. dir., Opera Program; tchr, master Voice & Opera Acting.

NEE, D.Y. BOB, think tank executive, engineering consultant; b. Shanghai, Dec. 13, 1935; came to U.S., 1953; m. Flora Hsu, Sept. 19, 1959; children: Winifred, Vivian, William BS, Purdue U., 1957; PhD, 1963; MS, U. Mo., Rolla, 1959. Sr. engr. Westinghouse Electric, Pitts., 1967-83; project mgr. U.S. Govt., San Francisco Bay, 1984-91; founder, pres. Inst. for Sys. Monitor, Tiburon, Calif., 1992—; pres. World Humanity Inst., Honolulu, 1995—. Pres. Acad. for Critical Edn.; sci. and tech. cons. ASTM, 1994. Author: Radicalizing the World Through Social Engineering, 1993, Destiny of Humanity, 1998, The New Globalism, 2002. Mem. adv. bd. Reagan for Pres., Washington, 1980 Office: Inst for Sys Monitor PO Box 26723 San Francisco CA 94126-6723 E-mail: whi187114@aol.com.

NEEDLEMAN, JACK, education educator, researcher; b. NYC, May 12, 1948; s. Charles and Bella Needleman; m. Barbara Berney, May 30, 1981; children: Rachel Berney Needleman, David Berney Needleman. BS, CCNY, 1969; MA, Syracuse U., NY, 1973; PhD, Harvard U., Cambridge, Mass., 1995. V.p. Lewin/ICF, Washington, 1973—90; asst. prof. Harvard U. Sch. Pub. Health, Boston, 1995—2003; assoc. prof. UCLA Sch. Pub. Health, 2003—. Mem. nursing adv. coun. Joint Commn., Oakbrook Terrace, Ill., 2003—. Recipient Health Svcs. Rsch. Impact award, Acad. Health, 2006; numerous grants, NIH, US Agy. Healthcare Rsch. and Quality and Robert Wood Johnson Found. Fellow: Acad. Nursing; mem.: Phi Beta Kappa. Jewish. Achievements include conducted widely-cited landmark studies on the association of hospital nurse staffing and quality of care. Office: UCLA Sch Pub Health PO Box 951772 Los Angeles CA 90095-1772 Business E-Mail: needlema@ucla.edu.

NEEDLEMAN, JACOB, philosophy educator, writer; b. Phila., Oct. 6, 1934; s. Benjamin and Ida (Seltzer) Needleman; m. Carla Satzman, Aug. 30, 1959 (div. 1989); children: Raphael, Eve; m. Gail Anderson, Dec. 1989. BA, Harvard U., 1956; grad., U. Freiburg, 1957-58; PhD, Yale U., 1961. Clin. psychology trainee West Haven (Conn.) Veterans Hosp. Adminstrn., 1960-61; rsch. assoc. Rockefeller Inst., NY, 1961-62; from asst. prof. to assoc. prof. philosophy San Francisco State U., 1962-66, prof philosophy, 1967—, chair dept. philosophy, 1968-69. Vis. scholar Union Theol. Seminary, 1967-68; dir. Ctr. Study New Religions, 1977-83; lectr. psychiatry, cons. med. ethics U. Calif., 1981-84. Author: Being-in-the-World, 1963, The New Religions, 1970, Religion for a New Generation, 1973, A Sense of the Cosmos, 1975, On the Way to Self-Knowledge: Sacred Tradition and Psychotherapy, 1976, Lost Christianity, 1980, Consciousness and Tradition, 1982, The Heart of Philosophy, 1982, Sorcerers, 1986, Sin and Scientism, 1986, Lost Christianity: A Journey of Rediscovery to the Centre of Christian Experience, 1990, Money and the Meaning of Life, 1991, Modern Esoteric Spirituality, 1992, The Way of the Physician, 1993, The Indestructible Question, 1994, A Little Book on Love, 1996, Time and the Soul, 1998; The American Soul, 2002, The Wisdom of Love, 2005, Why Can't We Be Good?, 2007; (trans.) The Essential Marcus Aurelius, 2008, The Primary World of Senses, 1963, Essays on Ego Psychology, 1964; editor Care of Patients with Fatal Illness, 1969, The Sword of Gnosis, 1973, Sacred Tradition and Present Need, 1974, Understanding the New Religions, 1978, Speaking of My Life: The Art of Living in the Cultural Revolution, 1979, Real Philosophy: An Anthology of the Universal Search for Meaning, 1991, The American Soul, 2002; contbr. Death and Bereavement, 1969, To Live Within, 1971, My Life with a Brahmin Family, 1972, The New Man, 1972, The Universal Meaning of the Kabbalah, 1973, The Phenomenon of Death. Grantee Religion in Higher Edn., Marsden Found., 1967—68, Ella Lymna Cabot Trust, 1969, Far West Inst., 1975. Office: San Francisco State U Dept Philosophy 1600 Holloway Ave San Francisco CA 94132-1722 Office Phone: 415-338-2216. Business E-Mail: jneedle@sfsu.edu.

NEEDLEMAN, PHILIP, cardiologist, pharmacologist; b. Bklyn., Feb. 10, 1939; m. Sima Needleman. BS in Pharmacology, Phila. Coll. Pharm. & Sci., 1960, MS in Pharmacology, 1962; PhD in Pharmacology, U. Md. Med. Sch., 1964. Fellow Sch. Medicine Washington U., St. Louis, 1965—67, from asst. prof. to prof. Sch. Medicine, 1967—75, prof. Sch. Medicine, 1975—89, adj. prof., 1976—89, chmn., dept. pharmacology, 1989, chief scientist, 1991, assoc. dean, spl. projects, 2004; sr. v.p., chief scientist Monsanto, 1989—93; pres. Searle Pharma. Co., 1993—2000; sr. exec. v.p., chief scientist, chmn. R&D Pharmacia (fomerly Monsanto/Searle), 2000—03; ptnr. Prospect Ventures Ptnrs., 2003—. Served on com. NIH study sects.; adv. com. FDA, NIH, Nat. Coun. Washington Univ. Med. Sch. Contbr. numerous articles to profl. jours. Bd. trustee Washington U.; bd. dir. Barnes-Jewish Hosp., St. Louis Plant and Biotechnology consortium, St. Louis Sci. Ctr.; sci. advisor to pres. for R&D Ben Gurion U., 2002—, bd. trustee; mem. adv. com. for the creation of Nat. Inst. for Biotechnology in the Negev; bd. trustee Donald Danforth Plant Sci. Ctr. Recipient John Jacob Abel award, Am. Pharmacology Soc., 1974, Rsch. Career Devel. award, NIH, 1974, 1976, Wellcome Creesy award in clin. pharmacology, 1977, 1978, 1980, 1987, Cochems Thrombosis Rsch. prize, 1980, Rsch. Achievement award, Am. Heart Assn., 1988, Second Century award, 1994, C. Chester Stock award Lectureship, Meml. Sloan Kettering Cancer Ctr., 2001, Indsl. Rsch. Inst. medal, 2001, Am. Soc. Exptl. Therapeutics award, Dart/NYU Biotechnology Achievement awards, Biotechnology Study Ctr. NYU Sch. Medicine, 2005. Mem.: IOM, NAS (chair phamacology-physiology sect. 2001—04, bd. trustee NAS Coun. 2004, award for Indsl. Application of Sci. 2005). Achievements include pioneering studies on the role of Cox 1 and Cox 2 enzymes in inflammation, cardiovascular and renal disease, and in tumor progression; developing the first angiotensin receptor antagonist, the first thromboxane synthetase inhibitor; discovering atriopeptin, the atrial natriuretic factor, a novel endocrine peptide that allows the heart to communicate with the kidneys and blood vessels. Office: Prospect Venture Ptnrs 435 Tasso St Ste 200 Palo Alto CA 94301 Office Phone: 650-327-8800. Office Fax: 650-324-8838.

NEELIN, J. DAVID, meteorologist, educator; arrived in U.S., 1983; BS with honors, U. Toronto, 1981, MS, 1983; PhD, Princeton U., NJ, 1987. Postdoctoral assoc. dept. Earth, atmospheric and planetary scis. MIT, Cambridge, Mass., 1987—88, vis. assoc. prof., 1994—95; asst. prof. dept. atmospheric scis. UCLA, 1988—92, assoc. prof., 1992—95, prof., 1995—. Mem. Inst. Geophysics and Planetary Physics, LA, 1995—; vice chair dept. atmospheric and oceanic scis. UCLA, 2004—. Contbr. articles to profl. jours.; assoc. editor: Jour. Climate, 1996—. Recipient Presdl. Young Investigator award, 1991—96, Spl. Creativity award, NSF, 1999—2000; grantee Guggenheim fellowship, 2007. Fellow: Am. Meteorol. Soc. (C. L. Meisinger award 1996), Royal Meteorol. Soc.; mem.: AAAS, Can. Meteorol. and Oceanog. Soc., Am. Geophys. Union. Office: Dept Atmospheric and Oceanic Scis UCLA 405 Hilgard Ave Los Angeles CA 90095-1565 E-mail: neelin@atmos.ucla.edu.

NEELY, ALEXIS, lawyer; 2 children. Grad., Georgetown U. Law Ctr. Founding ptnr. Martin Neely & Assocs., Redondo Beach, Calif., 2003—. Founder Family Wealth Planning Inst. Named a Rising Star, LA Mag.; named one of Top 100 Attys., Worth mag., 2005—06. Office: Martin Neely & Assocs 417 Beryl St Redondo Beach CA 90277 Office Phone: 310-697-0411. Office Fax: 310-531-7395. E-mail: alexis@martinneely.com.

NEELY, PEGGY, councilwoman; m. Brian Neely; children: Gloria, Mackenzie. Lic. real estate broker. Former owner Ariz. Home Team; councilwoman, Dist. 2 Phoenix City Coun., 2001—. Chmn. Transp. & Infrastructure Com.; mem. Downtown & Aviation, Seniors, Families & Youth, Census coms. Chmn. Paradise Village Planning Com., Phoenix Water & Sewer Rate Adv. Com.; vice chmn. Maricopa Assn. Govts. Regional Coun. Exec. Com.; bd. mem. Phoenix Women's Sports Assn., Greater Phoenix Conv. Ctr. & Visitors Bur.; former pres. Paradise Valley Sch. Dist. United Parent Coun.; mem. Paradise Valley Cmty. Coll. Pres. Roundtable. Mem.: Women's Coun. Realtors Phoenix Chpt. (former pres.), Phoenix Assn. Realtors (bd. dirs.), Ariz. Assn. Realtors (bd. dirs.). Office: 200 W Washington 11th Fl Phoenix AZ 85003 Office Phone: 602-262-7445. Office Fax: 602-495-0527. Business E-Mail: council.district.2@phoenix.gov.*

NEELY, SALLY SCHULTZ, lawyer; b. LA, Mar. 2, 1948; BA, Stanford U., 1970, JD, 1971. Bar: Ariz. 1972, Calif. 1977. Law clk. to judge U.S. Ct. Appeals (9th cir.), Phoenix, 1971-72; assoc. Lewis and Roca, Phoenix, 1972-75; asst. prof. Law Sch. Harvard U., Cambridge, Mass., 1975-77; assoc. Shutan & Trost, P.C., LA, 1977-79; ptnr., sr. counsel Sidley Austin LLP (and predecessor firms), LA, 1980—. Co-chair Am. Law Inst.-ABA Chpt. 11 Bus. Reorgns., 1989-95, 97—, Banking and Comml. Lending Law, 1997-99, Nat. Conf. Bankruptcy Judges, 1988, 90, 95, 96, 97, 99, 02, 06 Fed. Jud. Ctr., 1989, 90, 94-95, Southeast Bankruptcy Law Inst., 2002, 2006 Workshop Bankruptcy and Bus. Reorgn. NYU, 1992—; rep. 9th cir. jud. conf., 1989-91; mem. Nat. Bankruptcy Conf., 1993—, co-chair com. on legis., 2001—, mem. exec. com. Chair Stanford U. Law Sch. Reunion Giving, 1996; bd. vis. Stanford U. Law Sch., 1990-92; mem. bd. dir. LA Children's Chorus, 2006-. Mem.: ABA, Calif. Bar Assn., Am. Coll. Bankruptcy (mem. bd. regents 1998—2003, bd. dirs. 2003—05, co-chair ednl. programs com. 2003—, v.p. 2005—). Office: Sidley Austin LLP 555 W 5th St Ste 4000 Los Angeles CA 90013-3000 Office Phone: 213-896-6024. Business E-Mail: sneely@sidley.com.

NEERKEN, JULIE P., lawyer; b. Denver, Nov. 26, 1949; BS cum laude, U. Mich., 1971; MA, U. Wis., 1974; JD cum laude, U. Mich., 1979. Bar: Ill. 1979, N.Mex. 1981, Tex. 2000. Ptnr. Rodey, Dickason, Sloan, Akin & Robb PA, Albuquerque. Author: Med. Plans Involve Many Choices, 1993, Reviewing Actuarial Report, 1984. Named one of best lawyers in Am., 2003—04. Mem.: State Bar N. Mex., ABA. Office: Rodey Dickason Sloan Akin & Robb PA 201 Third St NW Ste 2200 PO Box 1888 Albuquerque NM 87103 Office Phone: 505-766-7557. Office Fax: 505-768-7395. Business E-Mail: jneerken@rodey.com.

NEESON, LIAM, actor; b. Ballymena, No. Ireland, June 7, 1952; s. Barney and Kitty N.; m. Natasha Richardson, July 3, 1994 (dec. March 18, 2009); children: Michael Richard Antonio, Daniel Jack. PhD (hon.), Queen's U., Belfast, 2009. Theatrical appearances include (Broadway) The Judas Kiss, 1998, Anna Christie, 1993 (Theatre World award, 1993); films include Excalibur, 1981, Krull, 1983, The Bounty, 1984, The Innocent, 1984, Lamb, 1986, Duet for One, 1986, The Mission, 1986, A Prayer for the Dying, 1987, Suspect, 1987, Satisfaction, 1988, The Good Mother, 1988, Next of Kin, 1989, Darkman, 1990, Crossing the Line, 1990, Ruby Cairo, 1991, Shining Through, 1992, Under Suspicion, 1992, Husbands and Wives, 1992, Leap of Faith, 1992, Ethan Fromme, 1992, Schindler's List, 1993 (Best Actor Acad. award nominee 1994), Nell, 1994, Rob Roy, 1995, Before and After, 1996, Michael Collins, 1996, Les Miserables, 1998, Star Wars: Episode I-The Phantom Menace, 1999, The Haunting, 1999, Gun Shy, 2000, K-19: The Widowmaker, 2002, Gangs of New York, 2002, Love Actually, 2003, Kinsey, 2004 (Best Actor, Los Angeles Film Critics Assn. award, 2004), Kingdom of Heaven, 2005, Batman Begins, 2005, Breakfast on Pluto, 2005, (voice) The Chronicles of Narnia: The Lion, the Witch, and the Wardrobe, 2005, (voice) The Chronicles of Narnia: Prince Caspian, (voice) Ponyo on the Cliff, 2008, The Other Man, 2008, Taken, 2008, Five Minutes of Heaven, 2009. Officer of the Order of the British Empire, 1999.

NEHRING, RON, political organization administrator; b. Islip, NY, May 22, 1970; BS in Polit. Sci., SUNY Stony Brook, 1988—92. Sr. cons. American's for Tax Reform; founder Nehring Strategies; chmn. Rep. Party San Diego County, 2001—07; vice chmn. Calif. Rep. Party, 2005—07, chmn., 2007—. Mem. Internat. Rep. Inst., Leadership Inst., Project for California's Future. Mem. Calif. Bd. Forestry and Fire Protection, 2005—06; trustee Grossmont Union High Sch. Dist., 2004—06. Mem.: Calif. Rep. County Chairmen's Assn. (pres. 2003). Republican. Office: Calif Rep Party 1201 K St #740 Sacramento CA 95814*

NEHRING, RONALD E., state supreme court justice; b. Wis., 1947; BA in History, Cornell U., 1976; JD, U. Utah, 1978. Bar: Utah 1978. Atty. Utah Legal Svcs.; shareholder Prince, Yeates and Geldzahler, Salt Lake City, 1982—94; judge U.S. Dist. Ct. (3d dist.) Utah, 1995—2003, Utah Supreme Ct., Salt Lake City, 2003—. Chmn. Bd. Dist. Ct. Judges; mem. adv. com. rules profl. conduct Utah Supreme Ct. Fellow: ABA. Office: Utah Supreme Ct PO Box 140210 Salt Lake City UT 84114-0210

NEIDHART, JAMES ALLEN, oncologist, educator; b. Steubenville, Ohio, Aug. 30, 1940; s. James Leonard and Mary Jane (Daniels) N.; m. Patricia Irene Harpkamp, Aug. 16, 1966 (div. Apr. 1985); children— James, Jeffrey, Jennifer; m. Mary Gagen, Feb. 1986; children: Andrew, Rae Ann. BS, Union Coll., Alliance, Ohio, 1962; MD, Ohio State U., 1966. Diplomate Am. Bd. Internal Medicine, Am. Bd. Hematology and Oncology. Intern Bronson Hosp., Kalamazoo, Mich., 1966-67; resident Ohio State U., Columbus, Ohio, 1969-71; postdoctoral fellow Coll. Medicine, Ohio State U., Columbus, 1972-74, asst. prof. medicine, 1974-78, assoc. prof., 1978-84, dir. interdisciplinary oncology unit Comprehensive Cancer Ctr., 1975-80, dep. dir. Comprehensive Cancer Ctr., 1980-84; prof. medicine U. Tex.-Houston-M.D. Anderson Hosp. and Tumor Inst., 1984-86, Hubert L. and Olive Stringer prof. oncology, 1984-86, dep. head div. medicine, 1984-86, chmn. dept. med. oncology, 1984-86; dir. Cancer Rsch. and Treatment Ctr., U. N.Mex., Albuquerque, 1986-96, chief hematology and oncology, 1986-91; dir. Cancer Rsch. and Treatment Ctr. San Juan Regional Cancer Ctr., 1996—. Contbr. chpts. to Recent Advances in Clinical Therapeutics, Clinical Immunotherapy Former mem. bd. dirs. Am. Cancer Soc., Columbus; former v.p. Ohio Cancer Research Assocs. Served to lt. USN, 1967-69, Vietnam Mem. Am. Soc. Hematology, Am. Soc. Clin. Oncology, Am. Assn. Cancer Research, ACP, S.W. Oncology Group, Wilderness Soc., Sierra Club Home: 66 Road 2577 Aztec NM 87410-1020 Office: San Juan Regional Cancer Ctr Farmington NM 87401

NEILSEN, CRAIG H., hotel executive; b. 1942; MBA, JD, U. Utah. Pres. Cactus Pete, Inc., Jackpot, Nev., 1984—, Ameristar Casino Vicksburg, Miss., 1993—. Pres. & chmn. bd. dir. Cactus Pete's Inc. Named best performing CEO, Am. Gaming Assn., 2002. Office: Ameristar Casinos Inc 3773 Howard Hughes Pkwy Las Vegas NV 89109

NEINAS, CHARLES MERRILL, sports association executive, consultant; b. Marshfield, Wis., Jan. 18, 1932; s. Arthur Oscar and Blanche Amelia (Reeder) N.; children: Andrew, Toby. BS, U. Wis., 1957. Asst. exec. dir. Nat. Collegiate Athletic Assn., Kansas City, Mo., 1961-71; commr. Big Eight Conf., Kansas City, 1971-81; exec. dir. Coll. Football Assn., 1981—97; Dr. Patricia L. Pacey prof. econs. U. Colo., Boulder, 1981—85; with Pacey Ecometrics Group, Inc., 1985—. Adviser Am. Football Coaches Assn., 1997—; cons. NCAA Football, 1997—. Served with USNR, 1952-54. Office: Neinas Sports Svcs 6630 Gunpark Dr Boulder CO 80301-3372 Home: 5344 Westridge DR Boulder CO 80301-6501

NEISER, BRENT ALLEN, foundation executive, public affairs and personal finance speaker, consultant; b. Cin., 1954; s. Rodger and Hazel Neiser; m. Marion, Apr. 1, 1978; children: Christy Jean, Steven José, April Reneé. BA in Pub. Affairs, George Washington U., 1976; MA in Urban Studies, Occidental Coll., 1978; MBA, U. Louisville, 1979; M in Global Studies Internat. Security, U. Denver, 2005. Cert. fin. planner, 1985; cert. assn. exec., 1994; cert. in Homeland Security U. Denver, 2005; chartered mut. fund counselor, 1996; accredited asset mgmt. specialist, 1998. Project mgr., analyst Legis. Research Com., Frankfort, Ky., 1978-84; pres. Moneyminder, Denver and Frankfort, 1983-91; dir. edn., govt. affairs Inst. Cert. Fin. Planners, Denver, 1985-91, exec. dir., 1991-94; pub. affairs, govt. rels. bus. strategies cons. The Brent Neiser Co., Englewood, Colo., 1994—97; dir. collaborative program Nat. Endowment for Fin. Edn., 1995—97, 1997—2007, dir. pub. edn. ctr., 1995—97, dir. strategic programs and alliances, 2007—. Mng. dir. Fin. Products Stds. Bd., Denver, 1985-91; co-creator Personal Econ. Summit '93, Washington; spkr. in field. Author: EPCOT/World Showcase External Directions, Walt Disney Imagineering, 1977, Personal Management, 1996, 2000, 03, Ignoring the Obvious: Public Diplomacy U.S. Foreign and Defense Policy, 2005; mem. editl. adv. bd. Jour. Fin. Planning, 2007. Vol., v.p. Big Bros./Big Sisters, Frankfort, 1982; del. Colo. Model Constn. Conv., 1987; mem. citizens budget rev. com. Greenwood Village; mem. long range planning com. Adoption Exch., Denver, 1992-93, bd. dirs., 1993-99; polit. action dir. Frankfort NAACP, 1983, legis. chmn. state conf., 1984; troop com. mem., asst. scoutmaster Boy Scouts Am., Englewood, 1993-99; bd. dirs. Young Ams. Bank Edn. Found., 1993-99, chair edn. coun.; mem. Leadership Denver, 1994; vol. host com. Denver Summit of the Eight, 1997; nat. spokesperson Protect our Children Campaign, 1996; active Annie E. Casey Found.: Nat. Foster Care Awareness Project, 1999-02; citizen's panelist News Hour with Jim Lehrer (PBS), 1998—; founding ptnr. Social Venture Ptnrs., Denver, 2000-04, Colo. Coun. of Advisors on Consumer Credit, 2000-07, chmn., 2005-07; mem. CFP bd. Consumer Adv. Coun. on Fin. Planning, 2001-03, 05-; bd. advisors Coll. Visual and Performing Arts, Winthrop U., 2002-05; mem. cmty. rels. bd. Daniels Coll. Bus., 2006-, U. Denver; mem. Leadership Program of Rockies, 2007. Lt. (j.g.) USNR, 1985-92. Recipient award of Excellence, Assn. Advance Am., 1996, 98, Summit award, Am. Soc. Assn. Exec., 2004; Pub. Affairs fellow Coro Found., 1976-77; fellow Ctr. for Social Innovation Stanford U., 2003, exec. seminar Aspen Inst., 2006, exec. edn. performance measurement Harvard Bus. Sch., 2006, Brookings Instn., 2007, Columbia U. Leadership Devel., 2008. Mem. Denver World Affairs Coun., Denver Coun. on Fgn. Rels., Investors Edn. Assn. Colo. (bd. dirs. 1995-01), Nat. Assns. in Colo., Denver C. of C. (pub. affairs coun.), N.Am. Securities Adminstrs. Assn. (investment adviser and fin. planner adv. com.), Nat. Soc. Compliance Profls. (bd. dirs. 1987-89), Am. Film Inst. (writers workshop), Am. Polit. Items Collectors, Fin. Planning Assn. (Foresight Group, chair awards task force, judge Fin. Frontier Awards), Alliance for Investor Edn., Nat. Eagle Scout Assn., Snowboard Outreach Soc. Achievements include co-inventor Trivia Express Game, Denver, 1986; developer over 100 projects for disaster victims, low income families and children. Avocations: snowboarding, drums (jazz) and latin percussion music, golf, swimming, modern design. Office: 5860 Big Canyon Dr Englewood CO 80111-3516 Office Phone: 303-224-3501. E-mail: ban@nefe.org.

NEITER, GERALD IRVING, lawyer; b. LA, Nov. 11, 1933; s. Harry and Ida Florence (Alperin) N.; m. Margaret P. Rowe, Mar. 5, 1961; children: David, Karen, Michael. BSL, JD, U. So. Calif., 1957. Bar: Calif. 1958. Judge pro tem Mcpl. Cts., L.A. and Beverly Hills, 1970-94, Calif. Superior Ct., L.A. County, 1974-94, family law mediator, 1976—; prin. Gerald I. Neiter, P.C., LA, 1981—. Lectr. State Bar of Calif., 1968, 76, 79, 81; former referee State Bar Ct.; arbitrator Am. Arbitration Assn.; mediator L.A. Superior Ct. Mem. ABA, Los Angeles County Bar Assn. (arbitrator), Beverly Hills Bar Assn., State Bar Calif. Office: 1925 Century Park E Ste 2000 Los Angeles CA 90067-2701 Office Phone: 310-277-2236. E-mail: Neitlaw@aol.com.

NEKRITZ, EDWARD STEVEN, lawyer; b. Chgo., Nov. 11, 1965; s. Barry Benjamin and Susan Ellen (Moss) N.; m. Wendy Nekritz, children: Jessica, Matthew AB, Harvard U., 1987; JD, U. Chgo. Law Sch., 1990. Bar: Ill. 1990. Assoc. Mayer, Brown & Platt (formerly Mayer, Brown, Rowe & Maw), Chgo., 1990-95; v.p. asset mgmt. Security Capital Indsl. Trust, Aurora, Colo., 1995-98; sr. v.p., gen. counsel, sec. ProLogis, Aurora, Colo., 1998—. Mem. Harvard Club of Chgo. (dir. 1989—).

NELIGAN, PETER C., plastic surgeon, educator; b. July 20, 1952; married; 2 children. BA, U. Dublin, Trinity Coll., 1973, MBBCh, 1975. Cert. Ont., 1985. Clin. fellow, plastic surgery The Hosp. for Sick Children, Toronto, Canada, 1983—84, rsch. fellow, plastic surgery, 1984—85, assoc. staff surgeon, 1995, rsch. project dir., rsch. inst., 1995; clin. fellow, microvascular surgery Toronto Gen. Hosp., Canada, 1985; clin. burn fellow The Ross Tilley Burn Ctr., Wellesley Hosp., Toronto, Canada, 1986; dir. The Ross Tilley Burn Ctr., The Wellesley Hosp., Toronto, Canada, 1992—93; attending plastic surgeon Laurentian Hosp., Sudbury, Canada, 1987—91, Sudbury Gen. Hosp., Canada, 1987—91, Sudbury Meml. Hosp., Canada, 1987—91, The Wellesley Hosp., Toronto, Canada, 1991—93, assoc. staff, 1993—2000; asst. prof., dept. surgery U. Toronto, Canada, 1991—97, chair, divsn. plastic surgery, 1996, assoc. prof., dept. surgery, 1997—2002, prof., dept. surgery, 2002—07; attending plastic surgeon The Toronto Hosp., Canada, 1993—2007, dep. head, divsn. plastic surgery, 1994—96; assoc. staff surgeon Mt. Sinai Hosp., Toronto, Canada, 1993; cons., dept. surg. oncology Princess Margaret Hosp., Toronto, Canada, 1995, Wharton chair in reconstructive plastic surgery, 1999; prof. surgery U. Wash., 2007—. Mem. editl. bd. Can. Jour. of Plastic Surgery, 1996—, Annals of Plastic Surgery, 2002—, Jour. of Reconstructive Microsurgery, 2002—, Brit. Jour. of Plastic Surgery, 2003—, editor-in-chief Jour. of Reconstructive Microsurgery, —. Fellow: Royal Coll. Physicians and Surgeons of Can., Am. Coll. Surgeons (mem., adv. com. on plastic and maxillofacial surgery 2000—03), Royal Coll. Surgeons Ireland; mem.: Plastic Surgery Ednl. Found. (nominating com. mem. 2002—, joint outcomes com. mem. 2002—, pres.), Ontario Soc. Plastic Surgery, Am. Burn Assn., Can. Med. Protective Assn., Irish Assn. Plastic Surgeons, Internat. Soc. for Burn Injuries, Can. Med. Assn., World Soc. Reconstructive Microsurgery (adv. coun. mem. 2001—), Plastic Surgery Rsch. Coun. (Snyder Award 1998, Hardesty Award 2000), Internat. Confederation for Plastic Reconstructive and Aesthetic Surgery, Internat. Microsurg. Soc., Ontario Med. Assn., N.Am. Skull Base Soc. (program com. mem. 2003—, v.p. 2007—08, pres.-elect), Can. Soc. Plastic Surgeons, Am. Soc. Plastic and Reconstructive Surgeons (mktg. com. mem. 1999—2002, scientific program com. mem. 1999—, bd. dirs. 2001—, ethics com. mem. 2003—, Certificate of Merit, Investigator award 1984), Am. Soc. for Reconstructive Microsurgery (nominating com. mem. 1999—2001, membership com. mem. 1999—, program com. mem. 2001—, pres.-elect), Am. Assn. Plastic Surgeons (comm. com. mem. 1999—), Inst. Med. Sci. Office: U Wash Med Ctr / Dept Surgery 1959 NE Pacific St Box 356410 Seattle WA 98195-6410 Office Phone: 206-543-5516. Office Fax: 206-543-8136. E-mail: pneligan@u.washington.edu.

NELLERMOE, LESLIE CAROL, lawyer; b. Oakland, Calif., Jan. 26, 1954; d. Carrol Wandell and Nora Ann (Conway) N.; m. Darrell Ray McKissic, Aug. 9, 1986; 1 child, Devin Anne. BS cum laude, Wash. State U., 1975; JD cum laude, Willamette U., 1978. Bar: Wash. 1978, U.S. Dist. Ct. (ea. dist.) Wash. 1979, U.S. Dist. Ct. (we. dist.) Wash. 1983. Staff atty. Wash. Ct. Appeals, Spokane, 1978-79; asst. atty. gen. Wash. Atty. Gen. Office, Spokane, 1979-83, Olympia, 1983-85; assoc. Syrdal, Danelo, Klein, Myre & Woods, Seattle, 1985-88; ptnr. Heller Ehrman White & McAuliffe, Seattle, 1990—. Bd. dirs. N.W. Environ. Bus. Coun., 1996—, Campfire Boys & Girls, Seattle, 1991-97. Mem. ABA, Wash. State Bar Assn., King County Bar Assn., Wash. Environ. Industry Assn. (bd. dirs.). Office: Heller Ehrman White & McAuliffe 701 5th Ave 6100 Columbia Ctr Seattle WA 98104-7043

NELLIS, NOEL W., lawyer; b. Concord, Calif., 1941; AB, U. Calif. Berkeley, 1963; JD, U. Calif. Berkeley, Boalt Hall, 1966. Bar: Calif. 1966. Ptnr. Orrick, Herrington & Sutcliffe LLP, San Francisco, chmn. real estate group. Asst. editor Calif. Real Property Law Reporter, 1978—; adj. prof. U. Calif. Berkeley, Haas Sch. Bus. Mem.: ABA-Real Property, Probate & Trust Law Sect. (chmn. real property financing com. 1981—83, mem. coun. 1983—88), Nat. Assn. Real Estate Investment Trusts, Pension Real Estate Assn., Assn. Attys. & Execs. Corp. Real Estate, Am. Coll. Mortgage Attys., Anglo-Am. Real Property Inst., Am. Coll. Real Estate Lawyers (charter mem., bd. gov. 1983—89), Urban Land Inst., Calif. State Bar (chmn. real property law sect. 1982—83), ABA-Young Lawyers Sect. (exec. coun. 1974—76, dir. 1976—77), Calif. Young Lawyers Assn. (bd. dir. 1972—76, pres. 1974—75), San Francisco Lawyers Com. Urban Affairs (exec. com. 1972—77), San Francisco Bar Assn. (bd. dirs. 1972—73), U. Art Museum, Berkeley (bd. trustees 1987—, pres.), U. Calif., Berkeley Found. (bd. trustees 1985—), Lambda Alpha Nat. Land Econ. Soc. Office: Orrick Herrington Sutcliffe LLP The Orrick Building 405 Howard St San Francisco CA 94105 Office Phone: 415-773-5806. Office Fax: 415-773-5759. Business E-Mail: nnellis@orrick.com.

NELSON, BERNARD WILLIAM, foundation executive, educator, physician; b. San Diego, Sept. 15, 1935; s. Arnold B. and Helene Christina (Falck) N.; m. Frances Davison, Aug. 9, 1958; children—Harry, Kate, Anne, Daniel AB, Stanford U., 1957, MD, 1961. Asst. prof., asst. dean medicine Stanford U., Palo Alto, Calif., 1965-67, assoc. dean medicine, 1968-71, cons. assoc. prof., 1980-86; assoc. dean U. Wis., Madison, 1974-77, acting vice chancellor, 1978-79; exec. v.p. Kaiser Family Found., Menlo Park, Calif., 1979-81, 1981-86; prof., chancellor U. Colo. Health Sci. Ctr., Denver, 1986-95, prof. dept. preventive med. and biometrics, 1995—. Mem., v.p., pres. Nat. Med. Fellowships, 1969-77 Trustee Morehouse Med. Sch., 1981-83 Fellow Inst. Medicine; mem. Calif. Acad. Sci., Alpha Omega Alpha (bd. dirs. 1978—) Avocations: fishing, photography, gardening, carpentry. Office: U Colo Health Sci Ctr Box C245 4200 E 9th Ave Denver CO 80262-3706

NELSON, CAROL KOBUKE, bank executive; m. Ken Nelson; 2 children. BA in fin. magna cum laude, Seattle U., Wash., 1978, MBA, 1984; attended grad. sch. Credit & Fin. Mgmt., Santa Clara U., Calif. With SeaFirst Bank (now Bank of Am.); sr. v.p., northern regional consumer exec. Bank of America; pres., CEO Cascade Bank, Everett, Wash., 2001—; pres., COO Cascade Fin. Corp., Everett, Wash., 2001—02, pres., CEO, 2002—. Exec. adv. bd. Albers Sch. Bus. and Economics Seattle U. Chair bd. dirs. United Way, Snohomish County; bd. dirs. Boys and Girls Club, Snohomish County, Econ. Devel. Coun., Snohomish County; adv. bd. Leadership Snohomish County; bd. pub. facilities dist. Washington States Baseball Stadium. Named one of 25 Women to Watch, US Banker Mag., 2003, 25 Most Powerful Women in Banking, 2004, 2005, 2007. Mem.: Wash. Bankers Assn. (bd. dirs.), Wash. Fin. League (bd. dirs.). Office: Cascade Financial Corp 2828 Colby Ave Everett WA 98201

NELSON, CHRISTINA GERRISH, lawyer; b. Kalispell, Montana, June 5, 1975; BA in English Lit., Pepperdine Univ., Malibu, Calif., 1994; JD, Gonzaga Univ., 1999. Bar: Wash. 1999. Former fed. pub. defender Spokane; assoc. atty., construction, real estate litig. Short Cressman & Burgess PLLC, Seattle. Contbr. articles to numerous profl. jours. Named Wash. Rising Star, SuperLawyer Mag., 2006. Mem.: ABA, Spokane Co. Bar Assn., King Co. Bar Assn., Wash. State Bar Assn. Office: Short Cressman & Burgess PLLC Ste 3000 Wells Fargo Ctr 999 Third Ave Seattle WA 98104-4088

NELSON, CRAIG ALAN, management consultant; b. San Rafael, Calif., July 11, 1961; s. Kenneth Alfred and Anne Catherine (Laurie) N. BS in Fin., San Diego State U., 1984. Loan assoc. Union Bank, San Diego, 1984-85, comml. loan officer, 1985-86, corp. banking officer, 1986-87, asst. v.p., 1987-89, v.p. corp. banking, 1989-93; v.p. Alexander & Alexander, San Diego, 1993-95; sr. assoc. Goreham-Moore & Assocs., San Diego, 1995-98; v.p. Sedgwick Tech. Group Sedgwick of Calif., Inc., San Diego, 1998; v.p., dir. tech. Marsh Inc., La Jolla, Calif., 1998—; regional v.p. Comerica Tech. Banking Group, San Diego; regional v.p., sr. mgr. Bank of the West, San Diego, 2002—05; exec. v.p. First Nat. Bank. V.p. Sedgwick Tech. Group, 1997; pres. MIT Enterprise Forum, San Diego. Community group chair San Diego chpt. Am. Cancer Soc., 1989; mem. com. Juvenile Diabetes Assn.; bd. dirs. San Diego State Found., 1989—; pres. Am. Lung Assn., San Diego and Imperial counties, San Diego State U. Athletic Found., 2004-. Mem. San Diego State U. Young Alumni Assn. (pres. 1988-89, bd. dirs. emeritus 1989). Home: 429 Santa Dominga Solana Beach CA 92075 Office: First Nat Bank 401 W A St Ste 200 San Diego CA 92101 Office Phone: 619-235-1205. Personal E-mail: cnelson_madison@hotmail.com. Business E-Mail: cnelson@banksandiego.com.

NELSON, DAVID, state legislator; b. Pendleton, Oreg., Aug. 6, 1941; m to Alice; children: four, two grandchildren. District attorney, Pondera Co, Montana, 71-75; Oregon State Senator, District 29, 96-, chairman, Bus & Consumer Affairs Committee, 99-, member, Info Management & Technology, Judiciary Committees & Joint Committees on Restoration & Species Recovery & Ways & Means Subcomt Education, currently, Oregon State Senate.Farmer, wheat & canola, 63-; atty-at-law, 67-81. Republican. Address: 1407 NW Horn Pendleton OR 97801 Mailing: 900 Court St NE S-211 Salem OR 97301 Office Phone: 503-986-1729, 541-278-2332. Business E-Mail: sen.davidnelson@state.or.us.

NELSON, DENNIS R., energy executive; Sr. v.p. gen. coun., corp. sec. UniSource Energy Corp., Tucson, 1997—. Office: UniSource Energy Corp PO Box 711 Tucson AZ 85702-0711

NELSON, DONALD ARVID (NELLIE NELSON), professional basketball coach; b. Muskegon, Mich., May 15, 1940; m. Joy Wolfgram, June 19, 1991; children: Julie, Donn, Christie, Katie, Lee. Student, U. Iowa. Player Chgo. Zephyrs, 1962-63, LA Lakers, 1963-65, Boston Celtics, 1965-76; asst. to head coach Milw. Bucks, 1976-87, dir. player pers.; exec. v.p., part owner, gen. mgr. Golden State Warriors, Oakland, Calif., 1987-95, head coach, 1988-95, 2006—, NY Knicks, 1995-96; head coach, gen. mgr. Dallas Mavericks, 1997—2005. Head coach NBA Western Conf. All-Star Team, 1992; head coach US Nat. Team World Championships (gold medal), Toronto, 1994. Named NBA Coach of Yr. 1983, 85, 92; named one of Top 10 Coaches in NBA Hist., 1997. Achievements include winning NBA Championships as a member of the Boston Celtics, 1966, 68, 69, 74, 76. Mailing: Golden State Warriors 1011 Broadway Oakland CA 94607

NELSON, DONNA GAYLE, state legislator; b. Paducah, Tex., June 13, 1943; d. Jack Harold Williams and Hazel Louise (Cooper Moss) Stephens; m. Douglas Caldwell Nelson, June 24, 1966 (div. 1976); children: Kellye Lou Fetters, Robert Kreg Nelson, J. Graigory. AB, South Plains Coll., Levelland, Tex., 1963; BBA, West Tex. A&M U., Canyon, 1965, MBA, 1967. Founder Evergreen Mut., McMinnville, Oreg., 1975; co-founder Evergreen Life Line, McMinnville, 1978—; founder, corp. dir. AAA Profl. Promotions, McMinnville, 1977—; pres. Evergreen Bus. Mgmt. Co., McMinnville, 1978—; sr. v.p. Evergreen Helicopters, Inc., McMinnville, 1978—, Evergreen Internat. Aviation, Inc., McMinnville, 1978—; mem. Oreg. State Ho. of Reps., 2000—, chair veterans commn., vice chair edn. bus. com., vice chair govt. com., vice chair agr. com. Bd. dirs. Evergreen Air Ctr., Inc., Marana, Ariz., Evergreen Aircraft Sales & Leasing Co., Evergreen Aviation Ground Logistics Enterprises, Inc.; sr. v.p., bd. dirs. Evergreen Internat. Aviation, Inc., McMinnville; speaker Nat. Speakers' Assn., Phoenix, 1986—; mem. adv. bd. Chemeketa Community Coll., McMinnville, 1984-85; owner 3N & Assocs. Inc., Donna G. Nelson Auctions, LLC; founder Yamhill Co. Market; teacher Tex., Calif., and Oregon; author, journalist. Poet World's Most Beloved Poetry, 1985 (Silver poet); writer Aviation/Space Writers' Assn., 1989-90; columnist It Takes Grit. Mem. Team 100 Rep. party, Washington, 1989; co-founder Poyama Land Treatment Ctr., Independence, Oreg., 1973; den mother, sustained membership chmn. Boy Scouts Am., McMinnville, 1977-79; dr. mem. March of Dimes, Heart Fund, McMinnville, 1973-75; sr. mem. transportation, budget and parks com., Yamhill Co. Budget Parks, Elks Lions, Red Cross, NRA, N7IB Farm Bur.; founder Newcomers Club, Fund for Hope, Free Enterprise Fund for Kids; bd. dirs. Humane Soc., Linfield Chamber Orch., WOU Found., Salvation Army. Named Woman of Excellence, Portland, Oreg., 1985. Mem. DAR, C. of C., McMinnville Duplicate Bridge Assn. (founder), Soroptimists Club, Elks, Lions, Beta Sigma Phi (pres. 1974-75, Woman of Yr. 1990). Republican. Baptist. Avocations: music, sports, bridge, writing, fishing, speaking, travel, fishing, charity auctioneer. Home and Office: 2150 St Andrews Dr Mcminnville OR 97128-2436 Home Phone: 503-472-7446; Office Phone: 503-472-8015. Business E-Mail: donnanelson@state.or.us.

NELSON, DOROTHY WRIGHT, federal judge; b. San Pedro, Calif., Sept. 30, 1928; d. Harry Earl and Lorna Amy Wright; m. James Frank Nelson, Dec. 27, 1950; children: Franklin Wright, Lorna Jean. BA, UCLA, 1950, JD, 1953; LLM, U. So. Calif., 1956; LLD (hon.), Western State U. Coll. Law, 1980, U. So. Calif., 1983, Georgetown U., 1988, Whittier U., 1989, U. Santa Clara, 1990, U. San Diego, 1997, Pepperdine U. Sch. of Law, 2003. Bar: Calif. 1954. Rsch. assoc. fellow U. So. Calif., 1953—56, instr., 1957, asst. prof., 1958—61, assoc. prof., 1961—67, prof., 1967—, assoc. dean., 1965—67, dean., 1967—80; judge US Ct. Appeals (9th cir.), 1979—95, sr. judge, 1995—. Com. to consider stds. for admission to practice in fed. cts. Jud. Conf. US, 1976—79; cons. project STAR Law Enforcement Assistance Adminstrn.; select com. on internal procedures Calif. Supreme Ct., 1987—; co-chair Sino-Am. Seminar on Mediation and Arbitration, Beijing, 1992. Contbr. articles to profl. jours.; author: Judicial Adminstration and The Administration of Justice, 1973; author: (with Christopher Goelz and Meredith Watts) Federal Ninth Circuit Civil Appellate Practice, 1995. Co-chair Confronting Myths in Edn. for Pres. Nixon's White House Conf. on Children, Pres. Carter's Commn. for Pension Policy, 1974—80; pres. Reagon's Madison Trust; mem. Nat. Spiritual Assembly of Bahais of US, 1967—; bd. dirs. Dialogue on Transition to a Global Soc., Weinacht, Switzerland, 1992; bd. vis. US Air Force Acad., 1978; bd. dirs. Coun. on Legal Edn. for Profl. Responsibility, 1971—80, Constl. Right Found., Am. Nat. Inst. for Social Advancement; adv. bd. Nat. Ctr. for State Cts., 1971—76; adv. com. to promote equality for woman and men in cts. Nat. Jud. Edn. Program; bd. dirs. Pacific Oaks Coll., Childrens Sch. & Rsch. Ctr., 1996—98; adv. bd. World Law Inst., 1997—, Tahirih Justice Inst., Washington, 1998—; chmn. bd. Western Justice Ctr., 1986—; chair 9th Cir. Standing Com. on Alternative Dispute Resolution, 1998—. Recipient Profl. Achievement award, 1969, AWARE Internat. award, 1970, Ernestine Stalhut Outstanding Woman Lawyer award, 1972, Humanitarian award, U. Judaism, 1973, Pax Orbis ex Jure medal, World Peace thru Law Ctr., 1975, Pub. Svc. award, Coro Found., 1978, Hollzer Human Rights award, Jewish Fedn. Coun., 1988, Medal of Honor, UCLA, 1993, Emil Gumpert Jud. ADR Recognition award, LA County Bar Assn., 1996, Julia Morgan award, YWCA, 1997, Samuel E. Gates Litigation award, Am. Coll. Trial Lawyers, 1999, Bernard E. Witkin award, State Bar Assn. Calif., 2000, Judge of Yr. award, Pasadena Bar Assn., 2002, Thurgood Marshall Career Achievement award, 2005, Harry Sheldon award, Pasadena Human Relations Comm., 2006, Meritorious Svc. award, U. Oreg. Sch. Law, 2007; named Law Alumnus of Yr., UCLA, 1967, Woman of Yr., Times, 1968, Disting. Jurist, Ind. U. Law, 1994; fellow, Davenport Coll.; Lustman fellow, Yale U., 1977. Fellow: Davenport Coll., Am. Bar Found.; mem.: ABA (sect. on jud. adminstrn., chmn. com. on edn. in jud. adminstrn. 1973—89, D'Alemberte/Raven award 2000), Assn. Am. Law Schs. (chmn. com. edn. in jud. adminstrn.), Am. Judicature Soc. (bd. dirs., Justice award 1985), Bar Calif. (bd. dirs. continuing edn. bar commn. 1967—74), Order of Coif (nat. v.p. 1974—76), Phi Beta Kappa. Office: US Ct Appeals Cir 125 S Grand Ave Ste 303 Pasadena CA 91105-1621 Office Phone: 626-229-7400. Business E-Mail: dorothy-nelson@ca9.uscourt.gov.

NELSON, GRANT STEEL, law educator; b. Mitchell, SD, Apr. 18, 1939; s. Howard Steel and Clara Marie (Winandy) N.; m. Judith Ann Haugen, Sept. 22, 1962; children: Mary Elizabeth, Rebekah Anne, John Adam. BA magna cum laude, U. Minn., 1960; JD cum laude, 1963. Bar: Minn. 1963, Mo. 1971. Assoc. Faegre & Benson, Mpls., 1963-67; mem. law faculty U. Mo., Columbia, 1967-91, assoc. prof., 1970-72, prof., 1972-91, Enoch H. Crowder prof. law, 1974-91; prof. UCLA, 1991—2007; William H. Rehnquist prof. law Pepperdine U., Malibu, Calif., 2007—. Bd. legal advisors Gt. Plains Legal Found., 1978-85; vis. asst. prof. U. Mich., Ann Arbor, 1969-70, Brigham Young U., Provo, Utah, 1976; vis. prof. U. Minn., Mpls., 1981-82, UCLA, 1989-90; disting. vis. prof. Pepperdine U., 1987-88, 2006; vis. endowed Campbell prof. U. Mo., Columbia, 1996-98; commr. Nat. Conf. Commrs. Uniform State Laws, 1983-91; adv. bd. West Pub. Law Sch Author: (with Van Hecke and Leavell) Cases and Materials on Equitable Remedies and Restitution, 1973; (with Whitman) Cases and Materials on Real Estate Finance and Development, 1976, Cases and Materials on Real Estate Transfer, Finance and Development, 1981, (with Osborne and Whitman) Real Estate Finance Law, 1979, (with Leavell and Love) Cases and Materials on Equitable Remedies and Restitution, 1980; (with Whitman) Land Transactions and Finance, 1983, 4th edit., 2004, Real Estate Finance Law, 1985, 5th edit., 2007, Cases and Materials on Real Estate Transfer, Finance and Development, 1987, 8th edit., 2009; (with Leavell, Love and Kovacic-Fleischer) Cases and Materials on Equitable Remedies, Restitution and Damages, 1986, 7th edit., 2005; (with Browder, Cunningham, Stoebuck and Whitman) Basic Property Law, 1989; (with Stoebuck and Whitman) Contemporary Property, 1996, 3rd edit., 2008; co-reporter ALI Restatement of Property-Mortgages; contbr. articles to profl. jours. 1st lt. AUS, 1964-65. Recipient award for meritorious service and achievement U. Mo. Law Sch. Found., 1974, Disting. Faculty Svc. award U. Mo.-Columbia Alumni Assn., 1978, Disting. Faculty award, 1986, Disting. Non-Alumnus award, 1991, Rutter award UCLA Law Sch., 2000, Disting. Tchg. award UCLA Alumni Assn., 2002. Mem. Am. Law Inst., Assn. Am. Law Schs. (sect. chmn. 1976-77), Am. Coll. Real Estate Lawyers, Am. Coll. Mortgage Attys., Mo. Bar Assn. (vice chmn. property law com. 1974-75, chmn. 1975-77), Order of Coif, Phi Beta Kappa, Phi Delta Phi. Office: Pepperdine Sch Law 24255 Pacific Coast Hwy Malibu CA 90263 Office Phone: 310-506-4605. Business E-Mail: grant.nelson@pepperdine.edu.

NELSON, HAROLD BERNHARD, museum director; b. Providence, May 14, 1947; s. Harold B. and Eleanor (Lavina) N. BA, Bowdoin Coll., 1969; MA, U. Del., 1972. Rsch. fellow NMAA Smithsonian Inst., Washington, 1976-77; curator Am. art Mus. Art & Archeol., U. Mo., Columbia, 1977-79; registrar Solomon R. Guggenheim Mus., NYC, 1979-83; exhibition program dir. Am. Fedn. Arts, NYC, 1983-89; dir. Long Beach (Calif.) Mus. of Art, 1989—. Juror Mus. Art, Sci. & Industry, Bridgeport, Conn., 1988, Clark County Dist. Libr., Las Vegas, Nev., 1984; speaker Am. Assn. Mus. Annual Conf., Detroit, 1985, Western Mus. Conf., Portland, Oreg., 1987, Grantmakers in Art Symposium, N.Y.C., 1986, Western Mus. Conf., Salt Lake City, 1985; adv. com. APA, Assn. Sci. and Tech. Ctrs.; panelist Aid to Spl. Exhibitions, NEA, Washington, 1986; participant Am. Legal Assn., ABA Conf., San Francisco, 1986; observer, respondent Mus. Symposium, NEA, Dallas, 1985. Author: Sounding the Depths: 150 Years of American Seascape, 1989, New Visions: Selina Trieff, 1997, Bountiful Harvest: American Decorative Arts from the Gail-Oxford Collection, 1997, For a New Nation: American Decorative Arts from the Gail-Oxford Collection, 1998, In Ye Grandest Manner and After Ye Newest Fashion, 2000, Conjunction: The Melba and Al Langman Collection, 2000, Tulips, Pomegranates and Kings: Delftware from the Collection of Benjamin F. Edwards III, 2000, Imps on a Bridge: Wedgwood Fairyland and Other Lustres, 2001, The Enamels of Annemarie Davidson, 2004, For the People: American Folk Art From the Collection of Thomas H. Oxford and Victor Gail, 2004, Engaging Nature: Contemporary Baskets From the Collection of Lloyd and Margit Cotsen, 2005, Crossing Boundries: The Ceramic Sculpture of Mineo Mizuno, 2005, Greene & Greene in Long Beach, 2005, Painting with Fire: Masters of Enameling in America 1930-1980, 2005. Office: Long Beach Mus Art 2300 E Ocean Blvd Long Beach CA 90803-2442 Office Phone: 562-439-2119.

NELSON, HARRY, journalist, medical writer; b. Interlachen, Fla., Apr. 18, 1923; s. Knut Alfred and Edith Farr (Wilkes) N.; m. Diane Gabriella Meerschaert, Aug. 29, 1948 (div. 1977); children— Tanya Ann, Lawrence Stephen, Ronald Gerard, James Anthony, John Christopher; m. Gita Doris Wheelis, Jan. 29, 1984 BA, U. So. Calif., 1949. Reporter, photographer Bakersfield Press, Calif., 1949; reporter, photographer Bakersfield Community Chest, Calif., 1949; promotion writer Los Angeles Times, 1949-57, reporter, 1957-58, med. writer, 1958-88, sr. writer, 1977-80; freelance med. writer, 1988—; staff writer Milbank Meml. Fund, 1993—. Charter mem. bd. dirs. Los Angeles County Comprehensive Health Planning Assn., Los Angeles, 1968-69. Served with USAAF, 1941-45 Recipient spl. commendation AMA, 1974, John Hancock award John Hancock Ins. Co., 1978, Journalism award Am. Acad. Pediatrics, 1979, Disting. Svc. by non-physician award Calif. Med. Assn., 1988, Lifetime Achievement in med. writing award AMA, 1988, Peter Lisagor award for exemplary journalism Chgo. Headliners Club, 1988. Mem. Nat. Assn. Sci. Writers (pres. 1966). Avocations: sailing; hiking; ceramics. Address: Med Writers Internat PO Box N 14016 Yellowstone Dr Frazier Park CA 93222

NELSON, HOWARD JOSEPH, geographer, educator; b. Gowrie, Iowa, Jan. 12, 1919; s. Joseph A. and Hannah (Swanson) N.; m. Betty Marie Garlick, June 18, 1944; children: Linda Ann, James Allan. BA with high honors, Iowa State Tchrs. Coll., 1942; MA, U. Chgo., 1947, PhD, 1949. Mem. faculty UCLA, 1949—, prof. geography, 1963-86, prof. emeritus, 1986—, chmn. dept., 1966-71. Author: (with W.A.V. Clark) Los Angeles, The Metropolitan Experience, 1976, The Los Angeles Metropolis, 1983. Served with AUS, 1943-46. Mem. Assn. Am. Geographers (regional councillor 1968-71), Sigma Xi. Home: 3939 Walnut Ave #162 Carmichael CA 95608 Office: Univ Calif Dept Geography Los Angeles CA 90024

NELSON, JAMES ALONZO, radiologist, educator; b. Cherokee, Iowa, Oct. 20, 1938; s. Joe George and Ruth Geraldine (Jones) N.; m. Katherine Metcalf, July 16, 1966; children: John Metcalf, Julie Heaps. AB, Harvard U., 1961, MD, 1965. Asst. prof. radiology U. Calif., San Francisco, 1972-74; assoc. prof. U. Utah, Salt Lake City, 1974-79, prof., 1979-86, U. Wash., Seattle, 1986-2000, prof. emeritus, 2000—04; ptnr. Integra Ventures, Seattle, 2004. Dir. radiol. rsch. U. Calif./Ft. Miley VA Hosp., 1973—74, U. Utah, 1974—85, U. Wash., 1986—98; mem. bd. sci. advisors NeoVision, 1995—96, Oreg. Life Scis., 1995—; co-founder Circulation, Inc., 1996; mem. adv. panel on non-radioactive diagnostic agts. USP, 1984—96; mem. NIH RSN study sect., 1998—; RSN study sect., 1998—2004. Contbr. chpts. to books, articles to Am. Jour. Roentgenology, Radiology, Investigative Radiology, others. Capt. USAF, 1967-69. John Harvard scholar, 1957-61, James Picker Found. scholar, 1973-77; recipient Mallinkrodt prize Soc. Body Computerized Tomography, 1990, Roscoe Miller award Soc. Gastrointestinal Radiology, 1991. Fellow Am. Coll. Radiology (diplomate); mem. Radiol. Soc. N.Am., Assn. Univ. Radiology. Achievements include patents (with others) for Non-Surgical Peritoneal Lavage, Recursive Band-Pass Filter for Digital Angiography, for Unsharp Masking for Chest Films, Oral Hepatobiliary MRI Contrast Agent, non-surgical myocardial revascularization, magnetic gut motility monitor, k-edge brachy therapy enhancement, self-debriding catheter. Office: Integra Ventures 300 E Pine Seattle WA 98122 Home Phone: 206-523-4546; Office Phone: 206-832-1995. Business E-Mail: jalonzonel@comcast.net, nelson@integraventures.net.

NELSON, JAMES AUGUSTUS, II, real estate company executive, architect; b. Damrascotta, Maine, July 26, 1947; s. Robert Maynard and Margret Rebbeca (Harmision) Nelson; 1 child, Jennifer Alexandria. BArch, Columbia U., 1973, MBA, 1974. Resident v.p. Citibank, NYC, 1974-77; group v.p. Bank of Am., San Francisco, 1977-82; assoc. John Portman and Assocs., Atlanta, 1983-85; pres. J.A. Nelson and Assocs., LA, 1986-88; dir. real estate planning and devel. Universal Studios, LA, 1988-94; founder Mother Co., Hollywood, Calif., 1995. Master planner, Internat. Gateway of the Ams., San Yisedro, Calif. Author: Banker's Guide to Construction, 1978, Doing Business in Saudi Arabia, 1979. Chmn. Eco. Dev. Com., L.A. Conservancy-Broadway Iniative, Laurel Canyon Coalition, L.A.; bd. dirs. Laurel Canyon Assn., Hollywood Heritage, Hillside Fedn., L.A., Lookout Mountain Assocs., L.A.; developer Universal CityWalk Project. Recipient Innovative Design award for Universal CityWalk, Internat. Coun. Shopping Ctrs., 1994, best new home of yr. award Metro. Home, 1989, commendation and pres.'s award Hillside Fedn., 1989, 1992. Avocations: gardening, architecture. Office: Mother Co 8306 Grand View Dr Los Angeles CA 90046-1918 E-mail: motherco@aol.com.

NELSON, JAMES C, state supreme court justice; b. Moscow, Idaho, Feb. 20, 1944; m. Chari Werner; 2 children. BS, U. Idaho, 1966; JD cum laude, George Washington U., 1974. Fin. analyst SEC, Washington, 1970—73; pvt. practice Werner, Nelson and Epstein, Cut Bank, Mont., 1974—93; county atty. Glacier County, 1980—93; assoc. justice Mont. Supreme Ct., 1993—. Former mem. State Bd. Oil and Gas Conservation, also chmn.; former mem. State Gaming Adv. Counsel, Gov. Adv. Coun. on Corrections and Criminal Justice Policy; liaison to Commn. of Cts. of Ltd. Jurisdiction, mem. adv. com. Ct. Assessment Program. Former pres. Cut Bank Chamber of Commerce. First lieutenant US Army, 1966—69. Office: Supreme Ct PO Box 203004 Helena MT 59620

NELSON, JERRY EARL, astrophysics educator; b. Glendale, Calif., Jan. 15, 1944; BS, Calif. Inst. Tech., 1965; PhD in Physics, U. Calif., Berkeley, 1972. Fellow in particle physics Lawrence Berkeley Lab. U. Calif., Berkeley, 1972-75, prof. astrophysics, 1975-96, prof. Santa Cruz, 1996—. Recipient Joseph Fraunhofer/Robert M. Burley prize Optical Soc. Am., 1997. Mem. Am. Phys. Soc., Am. Astron. Soc. (Dannie Heineman prize for Astrophysics 1995). Office: U Calif Santa Cruz Santa Cruz CA 94710-1625

NELSON, JOHN B., state legislator; b. Antigo, Wis., Jan. 12, 1936; s. Walter I. and Elnora (Bremer) Nelson; m. Monica G. Nourie, 1959; children: John B. II, Reine Jo, Amy. BSCE, Ind. Inst. Tech., 1962; MPA, Ariz. State U., 1975. Rodman, chainman, instrument man, draftsman Tyson Engring. Svc., Kankakee, Ill., 1957-59; resident engr. Benoit-Tyson Contractors & Engrs./Tyson Engring. Svc., 1962-65; project engr. City of Phoenix, 1965-72, Coe & Van Loo Cons. Engring., Inc., Phoenix, 1972-77, v.p., sr. engr., 1977-79, sr. v.p. engring., prin. engr., pres., 1979—2000; mem. from Dist. 4 Ariz. City Coun., 1984-91, mem. from Dist. 5, 1991—2000, vice mayor, 1999; mem. Ariz. House of Reps., 2001—07; mem. Dist. 12 Ariz. State Senate, 2008—. Apptd. mem. Cartwright Sch. Bd., 1997. Past pres. Maryvale Citizens' Assn.; vice-chmn. bd. trustees Maryvale Hosp. Med. Ctr., Phoenix. Cpl. US Army, 1955—57. Recipient Excellence award for Cmty. Involvement, Ariz. Civil Engrs. Assn., 1996; named Maryvale Man of Yr., 1978, Engr. of Yr., 1990. Fellow: Am. Consulting Engineers Coun. (Cmty. Svc. award 1996); mem.: Am. Water Works Assn., Ariz. Consulting Engineers Assn., Ariz. Profl. Land Surveyors Assn., Alpha Gamma-Upsilon. Republican. Lutheran. Office: Ariz State Senate Capitol Complex 1700 W Washington Rm 305 Phoenix AZ 85007 Office Phone: 602-926-5872. Office Fax: 602-417-3112. Business E-Mail: jnelson@azleg.gov.*

NELSON, KADIR, illustrator, artist; b. Washington; BFA with honors, Pratt Inst., Bklyn. Prin. works include Life of Marvin Gaye, Swizz Beatz: Ghetto Stories, Angel, Represented in permanent collections Debbie Allen, Denzel Washington, Will and Jada Pinckett Smith, Spike Lee, others, exhibitions include Simon Weisenthal Ctr., Acad. Motion Pictures and Sciences, LA, Mus. African Am. History, Detroit, Smithsonian Anacostia Mus., Washington, Soc. of Illustrators and Studio Mus., Harlem, Bristol Mus., Eng., Citizens Gallery, Yokohama, Japan, Ctr. for Culture, Tijuana, Mex., commissions, Dreamworks Studio, Sports Illustrated, Coca-Cola, NY Times, Major League Baseball, illustrator: (children's picture books), Brothers of the Knight, 1999, Big Jabe, 2000, Dancing in the Wings, 2000, Salt in His Shoes, 2000, Just the Two of Us, 2001 (NAACP Image Award), The Village that Vanished, 2002, Under the Christmas Tree, 2002, Please, Baby, Please, 2002, Thunder Rose, 2003, Ellington Was Not a Street, 2004 (Coretta Scott King Illustrator award, 2005), Tales from Shakespeare, 2004, Please, Puppy, Please, 2005, Hewitt Anderson's Great Big Life, 2005, The Real Slam Dunk, 2005, Moses: When Harriet Tubman Led her People to Freedom, 2006, Michael's Golden Rules, 2007, Henry's Freedom Box, 2007; author, illustrator: He's Got the Whole World in his Hands, 2005, We Are the Ship:The Story of Negro League Baseball, 2008 (Coretta Scott King Book award, 2009, Robert F. Sibert Informational Book medal, 2009). Recipient Silver Medal, Soc. of Illustrators. Achievements include being conceptual artist for feature film "Amistad" and animated feature "Spirit: Stallion of the Cimarron.". Office: Ste 124 6977 Navaho Rd San Diego CA 92119 Office Phone: 888-310-3222.*

NELSON, KIMBERLY TERESE, computer software company executive, former federal agency administrator; b. Phila., 1956; m. Kevin Cadden; children: Kelsey, Mackenzie. B, Shippensburg U., 1978; MPA, U. Pa., 1987. Spl. asst. to sec., spl. asst. to deputy sec. adminstrn., spl. asst. deputy sec. field ops. Pa. Dept. Environ. Resources, 1987—95; dir. program integration and effectiveness then chief info. officer Pa. Dept. Environ. Protection, 1999—2001; asst. adminstr. for environ. info. EPA, Washington, 2001—05; exec. dir. e-govt. Microsoft Corp., Redmond, Wash., 2006—. Office: Microsoft Corp 1 Microsoft Way Redmond WA 98052 also: Microsoft 5335 Wisconsin Ave NW Ste 600 Washington DC 20015

NELSON, LINDA J., state legislator; b. Plentywood, Mont., June 12, 1942; m. Roger Nelson. Grad., Medicine Lake H.S. Farmer, rancher; mem. Mont. Ho. of Reps., 1989-94, Mont. Senate, Dist. 49, Helena, 1994—2004; mem. ethics com., mem. rules com., mem. fin. and claims com.; mem. agr., livestock and irrigation com.; mem. jt. appropriations subcom. natural resources/commerce; minority whip Mont. Senate, 1999—2002, dean of senate, 2003—04. Mem. Medicine Lake (Mont.) Sch. Bd., 1981-88, chair, 1984-88; active Mont. Dem. Party; dir. Nemont Tel. Coop.; bd. mem., chair Mont. Oil and Gas Conservation; mem. Mont. ELCA Synod Coun. Mem. N.E. Mont. Land and Mineral Owners Assn., Sheridan County Dem. Women. Democrat. Lutheran. Home: 469 Griffin Medicine Lake MT 59247-9708

NELSON, PAUL WILLIAM, real estate broker; b. Mpls., Mar. 7, 1952; s. William H. and Jean (Darrington) N.; m. Jill Brownson, Oct. 18, 1986 (dec. Nov. 1990); children: Emily J., Joshua C.; m. Robin K. Carpenter, Aug. 14, 1993. BS, U. Colo., 1974. Lic. real estate broker, Colo. Advt. dir. Denver Beechcraft, 1976-77; real estate broker Coldwell Banker, Grand Junction, Colo., 1977—. Bd. dirs. Colo. Assn. Realtors, Denver, 1981-83. Mem. Grand Junction City Coun., 1985-93, also mayor pro tem; mem. Downtown Devel. Authority, Grand Junction, 1985-91; bd. dirs. Mesa County Planning Commn., Grand Junction, 1980-85, Colo. Nat. Monument Assn., 1989-91, Grand Junction Visitors and Conv. Bur., 1993-96; Lobbying Group; mem. Mesa County Uranium Mill Tailings Removal Citizens Com.; mem. co-chmn. Mesa County Riverfront Commn., 1993-99; mem. dist. resource adv. coun. Bur. Land Mgmt., 1990-92, Grand Junction Visitors and Conv. Bur. bd. dirs., 1992-96; mem. Colo. Juvenile Parole Bd., 2000—; trustee Colo. Riverfront Found., 1999—. Recipient Citizen Svc. award Mesa County, 1985, winner Parade Mag. Millennium Photo Contest. Mem. Mesa County Assn. Realtors (bd. dirs. 1981-83, treas. 1999—), Rotary, Club 20 (bd. dirs. 1994-96). Republican. Avocations: flying, skiing. Office: Coldwell Banker PO Box 3117 Grand Junction CO 81502-3117 E-mail: pablonelsoni@yahoo.com.

NELSON, ROGER HUGH, corporate financial executive, educator, consultant; b. Spring City, Utah, Mar. 7, 1931; s. Hugh Devere and Maudella Sarah (Larsen) N.; m. DeEtte Munk, Aug. 26, 1955 (dec. Sept. 1998); children: Steven R., Deanne, Mark L. BS, MS, U. Utah, 1953; Ed.D., Columbia U., 1958. Mem. faculty U. Utah Coll. Bus., 1953-97; mem. faculty Utah Mgmt. Inst., 1968-75; asst. dean U. Utah Coll. Bus., 1969-74, prof. mgmt., 1970-97, chmn. mgmt. dept., 1976-82, dir. programs in emerging bus., 1989-97, dir. MBA integrative field studies, 1993-96, prof. emeritus, 1997—; v.p. Computer Logic Corp., 1970-73; pres. Oil Resources, Inc., 1980-88, Puma Energy Corp., 1981-88, The Ultimate Choice Catalog Co., 1986—, David Eccles Sch. of Bus. Faculty, 1995-96; chmn. bd. Am. Recreation & Sports, 1996—. Fin. and mgmt. cons., 1965—; founder Utah Small Bus. Devel. Ctr., U. Utah, 1979; trustee Utah Tech. Fin. Corp., 1998-2003. Author: Personal Money Management, 1973, The Utah Entrepreneur's Guide, 1995, also articles, reports, manuals. Active local Am. Heart Assn., Am. Cancer Soc. campaigns; mem. exec. bd. Utah Opera Co., 1981-85, gen. bd., 1985-89. Danforth Teaching fellow, 1957 Mem. Acad. Mgmt., Adminstrv. Mgmt. Soc., NEA, AAUP, Phi Kappa Phi, Beta Gamma Sigma, Phi Delta Kappa, Delta Phi Epsilon. Inventor comml. color separation camera and related dye-transfer processes. Home: 2662 Skyline Dr Salt Lake City UT 84108-2855

NELSON, RUSSELL MARION, surgeon, educator; b. Salt Lake City, Sept. 9, 1924; s. Marion C. and Edna (Anderson) N.; m. Dantzel White, Aug. 31, 1945 (dec.); children: Marsha Nelson McKellar, Wendy Nelson Maxfield, Gloria Nelson Irion, Brenda Nelson Miles, Sylvia Nelson Webster, Emily Nelson Wittwer (dec.), Laurie Nelson Marsh, Rosalie Nelson Ringwood, Marjorie Nelson Helsten, Russell Marion Jr.; m. Wendy Lee Watson, April 6, 2006. BA, U. Utah, 1945, MD, 1947; PhD in Surgery, U. Minn., 1954; ScD (hon.), Brigham Young U., 1970; DMS (hon.), Utah State U., 1989; LHD (hon.), Snow Coll., 1994. Diplomate: Am. Bd. Surgery, Am. Bd. Thoracic Surgery (dir. 1972-78). Intern U. Minn. Hosps., Mpls., 1947, asst. resident surgery, 1948-51; first asst. resident surgery Mass. Gen. Hosp., Boston, 1953-54; sr. resident surgery U. Minn. Hosps., Mpls., 1954-55; practice medicine (specializing in cardiovascular and thoracic surgery), Salt Lake City, 1959-84; staff surgeon LDS Hosp., Salt Lake City, 1959-84, dir. surg. research lab., 1959-72, chief cardiovascular-thoracic surg. div., 1967-72, also bd. govs., 1970-90, vice chmn., 1979-89; staff surgeon Primary Children's Hosp., Salt Lake City, 1960; attending in surgery VA Hosp., Salt Lake City, 1955-84, Univ. Hosp., Salt Lake City, 1955-84; asst. prof. surgery Med. Sch. U. Utah, Salt Lake City, 1955-59, asst. clin. prof. surgery, 1959-66, asso. clin. prof. surgery, clin. prof., 1966-69, research prof. surgery, 1970-84, clin. prof. emeritus, 1984—; staff services Utah Biomed. Test Lab., 1970-84. Dir. tng. program cardiovascular and thoracic surgery at Univ. Utah affiliated hosps., 1967-84; mem. policyholders adv. com. New Eng. Mut. Life Ins. Co., Boston, 1976-80 Contbr. articles to profl. jours. Mem. White House Conf. on Youth and Children, 1960; bd. dirs. Internat. Cardiol. Found.; bd. govs. LDS Hosp., 1970-90, Deseret Gymnasium, 1971-75, Promised Valley Playhouse, 1970-79; mem. adv. com. U.S. Sec. of State on Religious Freedom Abroad, 1996-99. 1st lt. to capt. M.C., AUS, 1951-53. Markle scholar in med. scis., 1957-59; Fellowship of Medici Publici U. Utah Coll., 1967; Gold Medal of Merit, Argentina, 1974; named Hon. Prof. Shandong Med. U., Jinan, People's Republic of China, 1985; Old People's U., Jinan, 1986; Xi-an (People's Republic of China) Med. Coll., 1986, Legacy of Life award, 1993. Fellow A.C.S. (chmn. adv. council on thoracic surgery 1973-75), Am. Coll. Cardiology, Am. Coll. Chest Physicians; mem. Am. Assn. Thoracic Surgery, Am. Soc. Artificial Internal Organs, AMA, Dirs. Thoracic Residencies (pres. 1971-72), Utah Med. Assn. (pres. 1970-71), Salt Lake County Med. Soc., Am. Heart Assn. (exec. com. cardiovascular surgery 1972, dir. 1976-78, chmn. council cardiovascular surgery 1976-78), Utah Heart Assn. (pres. 1964-65), Soc. Thoracic Surgeons, Soc. Vascular Surgery (sec. 1968-72, pres. 1974), Utah Thoracic Soc., Salt Lake Surg. Soc., Samson Thoracic Surg. Soc., Western Soc. for Clin. Research, Soc. U. Surgeons, Am., Western, Pan-Pacific surg. assns., Inter. Am. Soc. Cardiology (bd. mgrs.), Phi Beta Kappa, Sigma Xi, Alpha Omega Alpha, Phi Kappa Phi, Sigma Chi. Mem. Ch. of Jesus Christ of Latter-day Saints (pres. Bonneville Stake 1964-71, gen. pres. Sunday sch. 1971-79, regional rep. 1979-84, Quorum of the Twelve Apostles 1984—). Office: 47 E South Temple Salt Lake City UT 84150-1200

NELSON, SARAH MILLEDGE, archaeology educator; b. Miami, Fla., Nov. 29, 1931; d. Stanley and Sarah Woodman (Franklin) M.; m. Harold Stanley Nelson, July 25, 1953; children: Erik Harold, Mark Milledge, Stanley Franklin. BA, Wellesley Coll., 1953; MA, U. Mich., 1969, PhD, 1973. Instr. archaeology U. Md. extension, Seoul, Republic Korea, 1970-71; asst. prof. U. Denver, 1974-79, assoc. prof., 1979-85, prof. archaeology, 1985—2004, rsch. prof., 2004—, chair dept. anthropology, 1985-95, dir. women's studies program, 1985-87, John Evans prof., dir. Asian studies, 1996, vice provost for rsch., 1998—2002, interim vice provost grad. studies and rsch., 2001—02. Vis. asst. prof. U. Colo., Boulder, 1974; resident Rockefeller Ctr. in Bellagio, Italy, 1996. Author: Archaeology of Korea, 1993, Gender in Archaeology: Analyzing Power and Prestige, 1997, 2d rev. edit., 2004, Shamanism in East Asian Archaeology, 2007; (novel) Spirit Bird Journey, 1999, Ancient Queens: Archaelogical Perspectives, 2003, Jade Dragon, 2004; co-author: Denver: An Archaeological History, 2001, new edit., 2008; editor: The Archaeology of Northeast China, 1995, Ancestors for the Pigs: Pigs in Prehistory, 1998, Handbook of Gender in Archeology, 2006, Women in Antiquity: Theoretical Approaches to Gender and Archaeology, 2007, Worlds of Gender, The Archaeology of Women's Lives Around the Globe, 2007; co-editor: Powers of Observation, 1990, Equity Issues for Women in Archaeology, 1994, Archaeology of the Russian Far East, 2005, In Pursuit of Gender: Worldwide Archaeological Perspectives, 2001, Korean Social Archaeology, 2005, Archeology of the Russian Far East, 2006, Integrating the Diversity of the 21st Century Anthropology, 2006. Active Earthwatch, 1989. Recipient Outstanding Scholar award U. Denver, 1989; grantee S.W. Inst. Rsch. on Women, 1981, Acad. Korean Studies, Seoul, 1983, Internat. Cultural Soc. Korea, 1986, Colo. Hist. Fund, 1995-97, Rockefeller Found. Residency, Bellagio, Italy, Wenner-Gren Found., 2000-02, Nat. Geographic Soc., 2000—. Fellow Am. Anthrop. Assn.; mem. Soc. Am. Archaeology, Assn. Asian Studies, Royal Asiatic Soc., Sigma Xi (sec.-treas. 1978-79), Phi Beta Kappa. Democrat. Avocations: travel, gardening. Home: 5878 S Dry Creek Ct Littleton CO 80121-1709 Office: U Denver Dept Anthropology Denver CO 80208-0001 Business E-Mail: snelson@du.edu.

NELSON, SHARON, state legislator; m. John Nelson; 2 children. BA in Psychol. summa cum laude, Whitman Coll., Walla Walla, Wash., 1973. Chief of staff Councilmember Dow Constantine, Metropolitan King County; several years of svc. in fin. industry (night data entry clk. to v.p.); mem. Dist. 34 Wash. House of Reps., 2007—. Found. pres. Preserve Our Islands. Democrat. Office: 338 John L O'Brien Bldg PO Box 40600 Olympia WA 98504-0600 Office Phone: 360-786-7952. Business E-Mail: nelson.sharon@leg.wa.gov.

NELSON, THOMAS G., federal judge; b. Idaho Falls, Idaho, 1936; Student, U. Idaho, 1955—59, LLB, 1962. Ptnr. Parry, Robertson, and Daly, Twin Falls, Idaho, 1965—79, Nelson, Rosholt, Robertson, Tolman and Tucker, Twin Falls, 1979; judge US Ct. Appeals (9th cir.), Boise, Idaho, 1990—2003, sr. judge, 2003—. With Idaho Air N.G., 1962—65, with USAR, 1965—68. Mem.: ABA, Idaho Law Found., Am. Bd. Trial Advocates (pres. Idaho chpt.), Idaho Assn. Def. Counsel, Idaho State Bar (pres., bd. commrs.), Am. Coll. Trial Lawyers, Am. Bar Found., Phi Alpha Delta. Office: US Ct Appeals 9th Circuit 304 N Eighth St Boise ID 83702

NELSON, WILLIAM RANKIN, retired surgeon, educator; b. Charlottesville, Va., Dec. 12, 1921; s. Hugh Thomas and Edith (Rankin) N.; children: Robin Page Nelson Russel, Susan Kimberly Nelson Wright, Anne Rankin Nelson Cron; m. Pamela Morgan Phelps, July 5, 1984. BA, U. Va., Charlottesville, 1943, MD, 1945. Diplomate Am. Bd. Surgery. Intern Vanderbilt U. Hosp., Nashille, 1945-46; resident in surgery U. Va. Hosp., Charlottesville, 1949-51; fellow surg. oncology Meml. Sloan Kettering Cancer Ctr., NYC, 1951-55; instr. U. Colo. Sch. Medicine, Denver, 1955-57, asst. clin. prof., 1962-87, clin. prof. surgery, 1987—. Asst. prof. Med. Coll. Va., Richmond, 1957-62; mem. exec. com. U. Colo. Cancer Ctr.; mem. nat. bd., nat. exec. com. Am. Cancer Soc. Contbr. articles to profl. jours. and chpts. to textbooks. Capt. USAAF, 1946-48. Recipient Nat. Div. award Am. Cancer Soc., 1979. Fellow Am. Coll. Surgeons (bd. govs. 1984-89); mem. AMA, Internat. Soc. Surgery, Brit. Assn. Surg. Oncology, Royal Soc. Medicine (UK), Soc. Surg. Oncology (pres. 1975-76), Soc. Head and Neck Surgeons (pres. 1986-87), Am. Cancer Soc. (pres. Colo. div. 1975-77, exec. com., nat. bd. dirs., del. dir. from Colo. div. 1985-94), Am. Soc. Clin. Oncology, Western Surg. Assn. Colo. Med. Soc., Denver Med. Soc., Denver Acad. Surgery, Rocky Mt. Oncology Soc., Univ. Club, Rotary. Republican. Episcopalian. Avocations: skiing, backpacking, travel, bicycling, fly fishing. Personal E-mail: wrn3@msn.com.

NEMIRO, BEVERLY MIRIUM ANDERSON, author, educator; b. St. Paul, May 29, 1925; d. Martin and Anna Mae Anderson; m. Jerome Morton Nemiro, Feb. 10, 1951-75; children: Guy Samuel, Lee Anna, Dee Martin. Student, Reed Coll., 1943-44; BA, U. Colo., 1947; postgrad., U. Denver. Tchr. Seattle Pub. Sch., 1945-46; fashion coord., dir. Denver Dry Goods Co., 1948-51; fashion dir. Denver Market Week Assn., 1952-53; free-lance writer Denver, 1958—. Moderator TV program Your Presch. Child, Denver, 1955-56; instr. writing and comm. U. Colo. Denver Ctr., 1970—, U. Calif., San Diego, 1976-78, Met. State Coll., 1985; dir. pub. rels. Fairmont Hotel, Denver, 1979-80; freelance fashion and TV model. Author, co-author: The Complete Book of High Altitude Baking, 1961, Colorado a la Carte, 1963, Colorado a la Carte, Series II, 1966, (with Donna Hamilton) The High Altitude Cookbook, 1969, The Busy People's Cookbook, 1971 (Better Homes and Gardens Book Club selection 1971), Where to Eat in Colorado, 1967, Lunch Box Cookbook, 1965, Complete Book of High Altitude Baking, 1961, (under name Beverly Anderson) Single After 50, 1978, The New High Altitude Cookbook, 1980. Co-founder, pres. Jr. Symphony Guild, Denver, 1959-60; active Friends of Denver Libr., Opera Colo.; mem. Friends of Painting and Sculpture, Denver Art Mus. Recipient Top Hand award Colo. Authors' League, 1969, 72, 79-82, 100 Best Books of Yr. award NY Times, 1969, 71; named one of Colo. Women of Yr., Denver Post, 1964. Mem. Am. Soc. Journalists and Authors, Colo. Authors League (dir. 1969-79), Authors Guild, Friends Denver Libr., Denver Women's Press Club, Kappa Alpha Theta. Address: Park Towers 1299 Gilpin St Apt 15W Denver CO 80218-2556

NEN, ROBERT ALLEN (ROBB NEN), retired professional baseball player; b. San Pedro, Calif., Nov. 28, 1969; s. Dick Nen. Grad. high sch., Los Alamitos, Calif. Pitcher Tex. Rangers, 1993, Fla. Marlins, 1993-97, San Francisco Giants, 1998—2002; ret., 2005. Office: San Francisco Giants 3 Com Park 24 Willie Mays Plz San Francisco CA 94107-2199

NERI, MANUEL, sculptor, educator; b. Sanger, Calif., Apr. 12, 1930; s. Manuel and Guadalupe (Penilla) N.; children: Raoul Garth, LaTicia Elizabeth, Noel Elmer, Maximilian Anthony, Ruby Rose Victoria, Julia Marjorie, Gustavo Manuel Student, San Francisco City Coll., 1949-50, U. Calif., Berkeley, 1951-52, Calif. Sch. Arts and Crafts, 1952-57, Calif. Sch. Fine Arts, 1957-59; D (hon.), San Francisco Art Inst., 1990, Calif. Coll. Arts and Crafts, 1992, Corcoran Sch. Art., Washinton, 1995. Mem. faculty art Calif. Sch. Fine Arts, San Francisco, 1959—65; prof. art U. Calif., Berkeley, 1963—64, Davis, 1965—90. One-man shows of sculpture, from 1957, recent exhbns. include, Oakland Mus. Art, Oakland, Calif., 1976, Western Assn. Art Mus. Travelling Exhbn., 1980-83, Seattle Art Mus., 1981, Charles Cowles Gallery, N.Y.C., 1981, 82, 86, 89, 93, 95, 97, 2002, 2003, Middendorf Gallery, Washington, 1983, 84, Gimpel-Hanover & Andre Emmerich Galerien, Zurich, Switzerland, 1984, San Francisco Mus. Modern Art, 1989, Dia Ctr. for the Arts, Bridgehampton, N.Y., 1993, 1997, Corcoran Gallery Art, Washington, D.C., 1997, Palm Springs (Calif.) Desert Mus., 1998, Riva Yares Gallery, Scottsdale, Ariz., 2002, 05, Hackett Freedman Gallery, San Francisco, 2001, 2003, 05, Fresno (Calif.) Art Mus., 2005; numerous group shows, from 1955, including San Francisco Mus. Modern Art, 1980, 83, 84, 85, 86, Am. Acad. Arts and Letters, N.Y.C., 1981, 82, 84, Oakland Mus. (Calif.), 1982, 84, 85, Seattle Art Mus., 1983, 84, Inst. Contemporary Art, Richmond, Va., 1983, Hirshhorn Mus., 1984, Contemporary Arts Ctr., Cin., 1985, Mus. Fine Arts, Houston, 1987, Bronx Mus. Arts, 1988, Whitney Mus., N.Y., 1992, 95, The White Ho., Washington, D.C., 1994, 99, Mus. Moderner Kunst, Vienna, 1997, Isetan Mus., Japan, 1999; represented in permanent collections: Oakland Mus., Seattle Art Mus., San Francisco Mus. Modern Art, Honolulu Acad. Arts, Des Moines Arts Ctr., also numerous pvt. collections including Verlaine Found., New Orleans, Bank Am. Corp., San Francisco, Lannan Found., L.A., Portland (Oreg.) Art Mus., Fine Arts Mus. San Francisco, Calif., San Jose (Calif.) Mus. Art, others Recipient 1st Award in Sculpture Oakland Art Mus., 1953, Nat. Art Found. award, 1965, award San Francisco Art Inst., 1963, award in art Am. Acad. and Inst. Arts and Letters, 1982, award of merit in sculpture San Francisco Arts Commn., 1985; Guggenheim fellow, 1979; Nat. Endowment for the Arts grantee, 1980 Roman Catholic.

NESMITH, MICHAEL, film producer, video specialist; b. Houston, Dec. 30, 1942; s. Warren and Bette Nesmith; m. Phyliss Nesmith; children: Christian, Jonathan, Jessica; m. 2d, Kathryn Nesmith. Chmn., chief exec. officer Pacific Arts Corp. (div. Nesmith Enterprises), LA, 1987—. Author, producer, performer various records, 1968-77; mem. (rock group) The Monkees; co-author, exec. producer: (films) including Timerider; actor: (films) Head, 1968, Burglar, 1987, (TV series) The Monkees, Hey Hey It's the Monkees, 1997; exec. producer: (films) Repo Man, 1984, Square Dance, 1986, Tapeheads, 1988; exec. producer, actor: (video) Dr. Duck's Super Secret All-Purpose Sauce, Michael Nesmith Live, 1992; producer: (series) Television Parts, 1985; co-author, producer: (pilot) for TV Pop Clips, original concept for MTV.; creator PBS Home Video. Trustee Gihon Found., 1970—, McMurray Found., 1970—. Recipient 1st Video Grammy for Elephant Paris Christian Scientist. Office: William Morris Agy 151 S El Camino Dr Beverly Hills CA 90212-2775

NESTANDE, BRIAN, state legislator; m. Gina Nestande; 7 children. BA in Polit. Sci., Calif. State U. Dep. campaign mgr. for Michael Huffington US House of Reps., 1992, field rep. for Michael Huffington, 1992—94, campaign mgr. for Sonny Bono, 1998, Chief of Staff for Representative Sonny Bono, 1994—98, campaign mgr. for Mary Bono, 1998, chief of staff for Representative Mary Bono, 1998—2000; founder, owner Nestande & Assocs.; mem. Dist. 64 Calif. State Assembly, 2008—. Republican. Mailing: PO Box 942849 Rm 4153 Sacramento CA 94249-0064 Office: 1223 University Ave Ste 230 Riverside CA 92507 Office Phone: 916-319-2064, 760-674-0164. Office Fax: 916-319-2164, 760-674-0184.*

NESTER, EUGENE WILLIAM, microbiology educator; b. Johnson City, NY, Sept. 15, 1930; married, 1959; 2 children. BS, Cornell U., 1952; PhD, Western Reserve U., 1959. Am. Cancer Soc. rsch. fellow genetics Stanford U., 1959-62, instr. microbiology, 1962-63, from asst. to assoc. prof. microbiology and genetics, 1963-72; prof. microbiology U. Wash., Seattle, 1972—, chmn. microbiology, 1982-96. Recipient Chiron Corp. Biotechnology Rsch. award, Australia prize, 1990. Fellow NAS, AAAS, Am. Acad. Microbiology; mem. Am. Soc. Microbiology. Achievements include bacterial-plant relationships. Office: U Wash Microbiology Dept Box 357242 Seattle WA 98195-7242

NETHERCOTT, MARK A., physics educator; Secondary tchg. cert. Named Wy. Tchr. of Yr., 2007. Mem.: Am. Assn. Physics Tchrs., Geology Soc. Am., Nat. Sci. Tchr.'s Assn. Office: Star Valley High Sch 455 West Swift Creek Ln PO Box 8000 Afton WY 83110 Business E-Mail: mnethercott@lcsd2.org.

NETZEL, PAUL ARTHUR, fundraising management executive, consultant; b. Tacoma, Sept. 11, 1941; s. Marden Arthur and Audrey Rose (Jones) Netzel; m. Diane Viscount, Mar. 21, 1963; children: Paul M., Shari Ann. BS in Group Work Edn., George Williams Coll., 1963. Program dir. S. Pasadena-San Marino YMCA, 1963—66; exec. dir. camp and youth programs Wenatchee YMCA, 1966—67; exec. dir. Culver-Palms Family YMCA, Culver City, Calif., 1967—73; v.p. met. fin. devel. YMCA Met. LA, 1978—78, exec. v.p. devel., 1979—85; pres. bd. dirs. YMCA Employees Credit Union, 1977—80; founding chmn. N. Am. Fellowship of YMCA Devel. Orricers, 1980—83; chmn., CEO Netzel Assocs., Inc., 1985—; pvt. practice cons., fund raiser. Adj. faculty U. So. Calif. Coll. Continuing Edn., 1983—86, Loyola Marymount U., 1986—90, Calif. State U., 1991—92, UCLA Extension, 1991—2002. Bd. mgrs. Culver-Palms YMCA, Culver City, 1985—2002, chmn., 1989—91, 1991—93; mem. Culver City Bd. Edn., 1975—79, pres., 1977—78; mem. Culver City Edn. Found., 1982—91, Culver City Redevel. Agy., 1980—88, chmn., 1983—84, 1987—88, vice chmn., 1985—86; chmn. bd. dirs. Calif. Youth Model Legislature, 1987—92; mem. World Affairs Coun., 1989—92; mem. adv. bd. Automobile Club So. Calif., 1996—2002; mem. Culver City City Coun., 1980—88, vice mayor, 1980—82, 1984—85, mayor, 1983—84, 1986—87; bd. dirs. L.A. Psychiat. Svc., 1971—74, Goodwill Industries of So. Calif., 1993—97, L.A. County Sanitation Dists., 1982—83, 1985—87, Western Region United Way, 1986—93, vice chmn., 1991—92. Recipient Man of Yr. award, Culver City C. of C., 1972. Mem.: Cmte RI Biuro (chairman exec. 2008—), Assn. Fundraising Profls. (v.p. bd. dirs. Greater L.A. chpt. 1986—88, pres. bd. dirs. 1989—90, nat. bd. dirs. 1989—91, vice chmn. 1994, Profl. of Yr. 1983), Mountain Gate Country Club, Rotary Internat. (L.A. # 5 pres. 1992—93, treas. L.A. found. 1995—96, gov. dist. 5280 1997—98, worldwide bd. dirs. 2007—, chmn. L.A. conv., founding chmn. internat. convention 2008 host orgn. com., chmn. exec. com., RI bd. dirs. 2008—09, named to Dist. 5280 Hall Fame 2005), Calif. Club. Office: Netzel Grigsby Assocs Inc 9696 Culver Blvd Ste 105 Culver City CA 90232-2753 Home: 12336 Ridge Cir Los Angeles CA 90049-1151

NEUFELD, ELIZABETH FONDAL, biochemist, educator; b. Paris, Sept. 27, 1928; married, 1951. PhD, U. Calif., Berkeley, 1956; DHc (hon.), U. Rene Descartes, Paris, 1978; DSc (hon.), Russell Sage Coll., Troy, NY, 1981; DSc (hon.), Hahnemann U. Sch. Medicine, 1984; DSc (hon.), Queens Coll., 1996. Asst. rsch. biochemist U. Calif., Berkeley, 1957—63; with Nat. Inst. Arthritis, Metabolism and Digestive Diseases, Bethesda, Md., 1963—84, rsch. biochemist, 1963—73, chief sect. human biochem. genetics, 1973—79, chief genetics and biochem. br., 1979—84; prof. Dept. Biol. Chemistry Sch. Medicine U. Calif., 1984—, chmn. Dept. Biol. Chemistry Sch. Medicine, 1984—2004. Recipient Dickson prize, U. Pitts., 1974, Hillenbrand award, 1975, Gairdner Found. award, 1981, Albert Lasker Clin. Med. Rsch. award, 1982, William Allan award, 1982, Elliott Cresson medal, 1984, Wolf Found. prize, 1988, Christopher Columbus Discovery award for biomed. rsch., 1992, Nat. Medal of Sci., 1994; named Passano Found. sr. laureate, 1982, Calif. Scientist of Yr., 1990. Fellow: Fellow AAAS; mem.: NAS, Am. Soc. Gene Therapy, Am. Soc. Clin. Investigation, Am. Soc. Cell Biology, Am. Soc. Biochemistry and Molecular Biology (pres. 1992—93), Am. Chem. Soc., Am. Soc. Human Genetics, Am. Philos. Soc., Am. Acad. Arts and Scis, Inst. Medicine of NAS. Office: UCLA David Geffen Sch Medicine Dept Biol Chemistry 350B BSRB Box 951737 Los Angeles CA 90095-1737 Business E-Mail: eneufeld@mednet.ucla.edu.

NEUFELD, MACE, film company executive; b. NYC, July 13, 1928; s. Philip M. and Margaret Ruth (Braun) N.; Feb. 28, 1954; children: Bradley David, Glenn Jeremy, Nancy Ann. BA, Yale U., 1948; postgrad., NYU, 1958-60. Photographer various N.Y. pubs., 1943-45; prodn. asst. Raymond E. Nelson, 1949-50; founder, owner Ray Bloch Assos., Inc., NYC, 1951-59; ptnr. BNB Prodns., NYC, 1959-70, Neufeld-Davis Prodns., Inc., Beverly Hills, Calif., 1981—. Trustee Am. Film Inst., 1978—; chmn. life achievement award nominating com. and scholarship fund. Producer in assn. with Harvey Bernhard The Omen, 1976, Damien - Omen II, 1977, Omen III - The Final Conflict, 1980; producer: The Frisco Kid, 1979, Angel on My Shoulder, 1980, The American Dream, 1980; ABC-TV mini-series East of Eden, 1981; CBS-TV series Cagney and Lacey, 1984; MGM film The Aviator, 1984, ABC-TV A Death in California, 1985; producer films Transylvania 6-5000, 1985, No Way Out, 1987, The Hunt for Red October, 1989, Flight of the Intruder, 1990, Necessary Roughness, 1991, Patriot Games, 1992, Clear and Present Danger, 1994, Gettysburg, 1994, Beverly Hills Cop 3, 1994, The Saint, 1996, The General's Daughter, 1998. Photograph entitled Sammy's Home voted Picture of Yr. N.Y. World Telegram-Sun, 1955; recipient Grand prize Eastman Kodak's First Nat. Salon of Photography, 1945; named N.A.T.O./Showest Producer of the Yr., 1993. Mem. Acad. TV Arts and Scis., Acad. Motion Picture Arts and Scis., ASCAP, Am. Film Inst. Clubs: Friars, Yale of N.Y. Democrat. Office Phone: 310-401-6868.

NEUFELD, NAOMI DAS, endocrinologist; b. Butte, Mont., June 13, 1947; d. Dilip Kumar and Maya (Chaliha) Das; m. Timothy Lee Neufeld, Nov. 27, 1971; children: Pamela Anne, Katherine Louise. AB, Pembroke Coll., 1969; M. in Med. Sci., Brown U., 1971; MD, Tufts U., 1973. Diplomate Am. Bd. Pediatrics, Am. Bd. Endocrinology. Intern R.I. Hosp., Providence, 1973-74, resident in pediatrics, 1974-75; fellow in pediatric endocrinology UCLA, 1975-78; staff endocrinologist Cedars-Sinai Med. Ctr., Los Angeles, 1978-79, chief pediatric endocrinology sect., 1979-85, dir. pediatric endocrinology, 1985—. Asst. research pediatrician UCLA, 1978-79, asst. prof.-in-residence pediatrics, 1979-85, assoc. prof.-in-residence, 1985—; med. dir. Kidshape Program Children's Weight Control, 1986—; pres. Neufeld Med. Group, Inc., 1996—; consulting physician Ventura County Med. Ctr., 1989—; attending physician Cedars Sinai Med. Ctr., 1995—; clin. prof. pediatrics Sch. Med. UCLA, 1995—; med. dir., owner, founder Kidshape, 1986—; cons. physician Pasadena Diabetes & Endoscopy Med. Group, 1998-2002 Contbr. articles to profl. jours. Mem. bd. deacons Pacific Palisades Presbyn. ch. 1988—. Named Clin. Investigator, NIH, 1978; grantee United Cerebral Palsy Soc., 1979, March of Dimes, 1981, NIH, 1983-88. Fellow Am. Coll. Endocrinology; mem. Am. Diabetes Assn., Soc. Pediatric Research, Endocrine Soc., Juvenile Diabetes Found. (research grantee 1980). Presbyterian. Avocations: sailing, reading, sewing, cooking. Home: 16821 Charmel Ln Pacific Palisades CA 90272-2218 Office: 8635 W 3rd St Ste 295 Los Angeles CA 90048-6113

NEUGEBAUER, MARCIA, physicist, researcher; b. NYC, Sept. 27, 1932; d. Howard Graeme MacDonald and Frances (Townsend) Marshall; m. Gerry Neugebauer, Aug. 25, 1956; children: Carol, Lee. BS, Cornell U., 1954; MS, U. Ill., 1956; D of Physics (hon.), U. New Hampshire, 1998. Grad. asst. U. Ill., Urbana, 1954-56; vis. fellow Clare Hall Coll., Cambridge, Eng., 1975; sr. research scientist Jet Propulsion Lab. Calif. Inst. Tech., Pasadena, 1956-96, disting. vis. scientist, 1996—2003; vis. prof. planetary sci. Calif. Inst. Tech., Pasadena, 1986-87. Mem. com. NASA, Washington, 1960-96, NAS, Washington, 1981-94; Regents lectr. UCLA, 1990-91; adj. sr. rsch. sci. Lunar & Planetary Lab., U. Ariz., 2002-; bd. dirs. Ariz. Sr. Acad., pres., 2004—. Contbr. numerous articles on physics to profl. jours. Named Calif. Woman Scientist of Yr. Calif., Mus. Sci. and Industry, 1967, to Women in Tech. Internat. Hall of Fame, 1997; recipient Exceptional Sci. Achievement medal NASA, 1970, Outstanding Leadership medal NASA, 1993, Disting. Svc. medal NASA, 1997, COSPAR award for space sci., 1998. Fellow Am. Geophys. Union (sec., pres. solar planetary relationships sect. 1979-84, editor-in-chief Rev. Geophysics 1988-92, pres.-elect 1992-94, pres. 1994-96) mem. governing bd. Amer. Inst. Physics, 1995-97. Democrat. Home: 7519 S Eliot Ln Tucson AZ 85747-9627 Office: U Ariz Lunar & Planetary Lab 1629 E Univ Blvd Tucson AZ 85721 Business E-Mail: nmeugeb@lpl.arizona.edu.

NEUKOM, WILLIAM H., lawyer; b. Chgo., Nov. 7, 1941; s. John Goudey and Ruth (Horlick) N.; m. Diane McMakin, Dec. 28, 1963 (div. Jun. 1977); children: Josselyn, Samantha, Gillian, John. BA, Dartmouth Coll., 1964; LLB, Stanford U., 1967. Bar: Calif., Wash., U.S. Dist. Ct. (we. dist.) Wash., U.S. Dist. Ct. (no. dist.) Calif., U.S. Ct. Appeals (9th cir.) 1968, U.S. Supreme Court 1974. Atty. MacDonald, Hoague & Bayless, Seattle, 1968—77; ptnr. Preston, Gates & Lucas (formerly Shidler, McBroom, Gates & Lucas), Seattle, 1978—85; v.p., law, corp. affairs Microsoft Corp., Redmond, Wash., 1985—93, exec. v.p. law & corp. affairs, sec., 1994—2002; ptnr. Bus. Practice Group Preston Gates & Ellis LLP, Seattle, 2002—, mem. exec. com.; chair Preston Gates & Ellis LLP (now Kilpatrick & Lockhart Preston Gates Ellis), Seattle, 2004—. Wash. State Delegate House of Delegates, 1999—2005; chair Decennial Governance Commn. Trustee Seattle Art Mus., 1993-99; mem. Assn. Gen. Counsel, 1994—; bd. dirs. Greater Seattle C. of C., 1987—, exec. com. 1988—, YMCA Greater Seattle, 1988—, Corporate Coun. Arts, 1988—, exec. com. 1993—, Nature Conservance (Wash. chpt.), 1991-99, Oreg. Shakespeare Festival, 1993-99. Fellow: ABA (chmn. young lawyers divsn. 1977—78, ho. of dels. 1978—80, sec. 1983—87, ho. of dels. 1983—98, pres.-elect 2006—07, pres. 2007—); mem.: Wash. State Trial Lawyers Assn., Wash. State Bar Assn., Seattle-King County Bar Assn. (chmn. young lawyers divsn. 1972—73). Avocations: fly fishing, skiing, running, golf, jazz. Office: Kilpatrick & Lochart Preston Gates & Ellis LLP 925 Fourth Ave Seattle WA 98104 Office Phone: 206-370-8120. Office Fax: 206-370-6165. E-mail: bill.neukom@klgates.com.

NEUMAN, SHLOMO P., hydrologist, educator; b. Zilina, Czechoslovakia, Oct. 26, 1938; came to U.S., 1963, naturalized, 1970; s. Alexander Neumann and Klara (Pikler) Lesny; m. Yael B. Neuman, Jan. 30, 1965; children: Gil, Michal, Ariel. BSc in Geology, Hebrew U., Jerusalem, 1963; MS in Engring. Sci., U. Calif., Berkeley, 1966, PhD in Engring. Sci., 1968. Cert. profl. hydrogeologist. Acting asst. prof., asst. rsch. engr. dept. civil engring. U. Calif., Berkeley, 1968-70, vis. assoc. prof. dept. civil engring., 1974-75; sr. scientist, assoc. rsch. prof. Inst. Soil and Water Agrl. Rsch. Orgn., Bet-Dagan, Israel, 1970-74; prof. hydrology dept. hydrology and water resources U. Ariz., Tucson, 1975-88, Regents' prof. dept. hydrology and water resources, 1988—. Cons. to U.S., Can. and Swedish govts. on hydrologic issues concerning nuc. waste disposal; vis. scientist dept. isotope Weizmann Inst. Sci., Rehovot, Israel, 1976; maitre de rsch. Ctr. d'Informatique Geologique, Ecole Mines Paris, Fountainebleau, France, 1978, dir. rsch., 1981; vis. prof. dept. fluid mechanics and heat transfer Tel-Aviv U., 1981; hon. appointment concurrent prof. Nanjing U., China; disting. lectr. in field; hon. prof. Nanjing Hydraulic Rsch. Inst., China, 1998—. Mem. editl. bd. Jour. Hydrology, 1977—84, Water Sci. and Tech. Libr. (The Netherlands), 1983—86, Stochastic Environmental Research and Risk Assessment, 1992—, Water Resources Rsch. Jour., 2006—, Hydrogeology Jour., 1999—2004, guest editor spl. issue in memory of Eugene S. Simpson, 1997—98; contbr. more than 300 profl. publs. including papers, books and reports. Hebrew U. scholar, 1962-63, Edwin Letts Oliver scholar, 1965-66; Jane Lewis fellow, 1966-68; recipient Cert. of Appreciation award USDA, 1975, C.V. Theis award Am. Inst. Hydrology, 1990. Fellow Geol. Soc. Am. (O.E. Meinzer award 1976, Birdsal Disting. Lectr. 1987), Am. Geophys. Union (4th Walter B. Langbein lectr. hydrology 1996, Robert E. Horton award 1969, Robert E. Horton medal, 2003), mem. ISI highly cited rschrs. database, Soc. Petroleum Engrs. of AIME, NAE, Assn. Groundwater Scientists and Engrs. of Nat. Well Water Assn. (Sci. award 1989), Ariz. Hydrol. Soc., Internat. Assn. Hydrogeologists. Jewish. Office: U Ariz Dept Hydrology & Water Resou Tucson AZ 85721-0001 Business E-Mail: neuman@hwr.arizona.edu.

NEUMANN, EDWARD SCHREIBER, transportation engineering educator; b. Harvey, Ill., Mar. 6, 1942; s. Arthur Edward Schreiber and Adeline Ruth (Spenks) N.; m. Carole Ann Dunkelberger, Apr. 19, 1969; children: Edward Schreiber, Jonathan David. BSCE, Mich. Technol. U., 1964; MS, Northwestern U., 1967, PhD, 1969, Cert. in Prosthetics, 2000. Registered profl. engr., W.Va., Nev.; cert. prosthetist Am. Bd. Certification. Mem. faculty W.Va. U., Morgantown, 1970-90, prof. transp. engring., 1980-90, interim dir. Harley O. Staggers Nat. Transp. Ctr., 1982-95, dir., 1985-90, 2009—; prof. U. Nev., Las Vegas, 1991—, chmn. dept., 1991-99, 2009—, dir. Transp. Rsch. Ctr., 1991-98, dir. Ctr. Disability and Applied Biomechanics, 2003—. Founder Human Kinetics Engring., LLC; chair rsch. coun. Am. Acad. Orthotists and Prosthetists. Editor numerous conf. procs.; contbr. articles and rsch. reports to profl. lit. Bd. dirs. Mason Dixon Hist. Park Assn., 1978-90; chmn. new transp. systems and tech. com. transp. rsch. bd. mem, 1998-2004, emeritus, 2004. Capt., C.E., AUS, 1969-70. Resources for Future fellow, 1969. Fellow Inst. Transp. Engrs.; mem. ASCE (chmn. com. on automated people movers, chmn. exec. com. urban planning and devel. divsn., chmn. exec. com. urban transp. divsn., James Laurie prize 1996), Nat. Soc. Profl. Engrs., Am. Soc. Engring. Edn., OITAF-NACS, Advanced Transit Assn. (bd. dirs., pres. 1988-90), Sigma Xi, Tau Beta Pi, Phi Kappa Phi, Phi Eta Sigma, Chi Epsilon. Presbyterian. Home: 935 E Eldorado Ln Las Vegas NV 89123-0515 Office: UNLV Dept Civil Environ Engring Las Vegas NV 89154-4015 Office Phone: 702-895-1072. Business E-Mail: edward.neumann@unlv.edu.

NEUMANN, HERSCHEL, retired physics professor; b. San Bernardino, Calif., Feb. 3, 1930; s. Arthur and Dorothy (Greenhood) N.; m. Julia Black, June 15, 1951; 1 child, Keith. BA, U. Calif., Berkeley, 1951; MS, U. Oreg., 1959; PhD, U. Nebr., 1965. Theoretical physicist GE, Richland, Wash., 1951—57; instr. physics U. Nebr., Lincoln, 1964—65; asst. prof. physics U. Denver, 1965—71, assoc. prof. physics, 1971—85, prof. physics, 1985—2006; ret., 2006; chmn. physics and astronomy U. Denver, 1985—97, assoc. chmn. physics and astronomy, 2001—04, interim chmn. physics and astronomy, 2004—06, chmn. physics and astronomy, 2006. Contbr. over 20 articles to profl. jours. Dir. numerous pub. outreach programs in physics. Home: 964 Salem Aurora CO 80011-6344 Office: U Denver Dept Physics Astronomy Denver CO 80208-2238 Home Phone: 303-366-0315. Business E-Mail: hneumann@du.edu.

NEUMANN, PETER GABRIEL, computer scientist; b. NYC, Sept. 21, 1932; s. J.B. and Elsa (Schmid) N.; m. Elizabeth Susan Neumann; 1 child, Helen K. AB, Harvard U., 1954, SM, 1955; Dr rerum naturarum, Technische Hochschule, Darmstadt, Fed. Republic Germany, 1960; PhD, Harvard U., 1961. Mem. tech. staff Bell Labs, Murray Hill, NJ, 1960-70; Mackay lectr. Stanford U., 1964, U. Calif., Berkeley, 1970-71; prin. scientist SRI Internat., Menlo Park, Calif., 1971—. Adj. prof. U. Md., 1999. Author: Computer-Related Risks, 1995. Recipient Nat. Computer Sys. Security award, 2002; Fulbright grantee, 1958—60. Fellow AAAS, IEEE, Assn. for Computing Machinery (editor jour. 1976-93, chmn. com. on computers and pub. policy 1985—). Avocations: music, tai chi. Office: SRI Internat EL-243 333 Ravenswood Ave Menlo Park CA 94025-3493 Business E-Mail: pneumann@acm.org.

NEUMEYER, ZACHARY T., hotel executive; Pres., CEO Sage Hospitality Resources LP, Denver. Office: Sage Hospitality Resources LLC 1512 Larimer St Ste 800 Denver CO 80202-1623

NEUPERT, PETER, computer software company executive; BA, Colo. Coll.; MBA, Dartmouth Coll. With Microsoft Corp., Redmond, Wash., 1987—98, dir. oper. sys., v.p. news and pub., Interactive Media Group, corp. v.p. Health Solutions Group, 2005—; pres., CEO Drugstore.com Inc., 1998—2001, chmn. bd. dirs., 1999—2004. Mem. Inf. Tech. Adv. Com. (PITAC), 2003—05, co-chaired Health Info. Tech. subcommittee; mem. Inst. Medicine's Roundtable on Evidence-Based Medicine, Pacific Health Summit Adv. Bd.; bd. mem. infiLearn.com, Cranium, Inc.; spkr. in field. Recipient Ernst & Young Entrepreneur of Yr. award, 2004. Office: Microsoft Corp One Microsoft Way Redmond WA 98052-6399

NEUREUTHER, ANDREW R., engineering educator; b. Decatur, Ill., July 30, 1941; BSEE, U. Ill., 1963, MSEE, 1964, PhD in Elec. Engring., 1966. With U. Calif., Berkeley, 1966—, prof. Cons. lithography modeling IBM Almaden Rsch. Ctr., 1977-90, optical lithography inspection Siemens, Perlach, 1984. Contbr. articles to IEEE Trans., SPIE, Jour. Vac. Sci. Tech. Fellow IEEE; mem. NAE. Achievements include research in microelectronics process technology and simulation, lithographic materials and tool characterization, simulation of lithography and inspection, wafer topography simulation. Office: U Calif Electronics Rsch Lab 5th Fl Berkeley CA 94720-1774

NEUWIRTH, BEBE (BEATRICE NEUWIRTH), dancer, actress; b. Newark, Dec. 31, 1958; d. Lee Paul and Sydney Anne Neuwirth; m. Paul Dorman, 1984 (div.); m. Michael Danek. Student, Juilliard Sch., 1976-77. Performer: (on Broadway) A Chorus Line (as Sheila), 1975-90, Dancin', 1978-82, Little Me, 1982, Sweet Charity, 1986-87 (Tony award for best featured actress in a musical, 1986), Damn Yankees, 1994-95, Chicago, 1996 (Tony award for best actress in a musical, 1997, Outer Critics Circle award for best actress in a musical, 1997, Drama League Award for disting. performance, 1997, Drama Desk Award for outstanding actress in a musical, 1997, Astaire Award for best female dancer, 1997), Fosse, 1999-2001, Funny Girl, 2002, Here Lies Jenny, 2004, Chicago, 2007; (off Broadway) West Side Story, 1981, Upstairs at O'Neal's, 1982-83, The Road to Hollywood, 1984, Just So, 1985, Waiting in the Wings: The Night the Understudies Take the Stage, 1986, Showing Off, 1989, Kiss of the Spider Woman (London), 1993, Pal Joey, 1995, Here Lies Jenny, 2004, Prin. dancer on Broadway Dancin', 1982; leading dance role Kicks, 1984. Actor: (TV series) The Edge of Night, 1981, Cheers, 1986-93 (Emmy award for Best Supporting Actress in a Comedy Series 1990, 91), (voice) Aladdin, 1994, (voice) All Dogs Go to Heaven: The Series, 1996, Deadline, 2000-01, Law & Order: Trial by Jury, 2005-06; (TV series guest appearances) Frasier, 1994-2003; (TV miniseries) Wild Palms, 1993; (TV films) Without Her Consent, 1990, Unspeakable Acts, 1990, Dash and Lilly, 1999, Cupid & Cate, 2000, Sounds From a Town I Love, 2001; (films) Say Anything, 1989, Green Card, 1990, Bugsy, 1991, The Paint Job, 1992, Malice, 1993, Jumanji, 1995, (voice) All Dogs Go to Heaven 2, 1996, The Adventures of Pinocchio, 1996, The Associate, 1996, Dear Diary, 1996, Celebrity, 1998, The Faculty, 1998, (voice) An All Dogs Christmas Carol, 1998, Summer of Sam, 1999, Liberty Heights, 1999, Getting to Know You, 1999, Tadpole, 2002, How to Lose a Guy in 10 Days, 2003, Le Divorce, 2003, The Big Bounce, 2004, Game 6, 2005, Adopt a Sailor, 2007. Vol. performances for March of Dimes Telethon, 1986, Cystic Fibrosis Benefit Children's Ball, 1986, Ensemble Studio Theater Benefit, 1986, Circle Repertory Co. Benefit, 1986, all in N.Y.C. Recipient Dance Mag. award, 2007. Democrat. Office: c/o Brian Mann Internat Creative Mgmt 10250 Constellation Blvd Los Angeles CA 90067

NEVILLE, MARGARET COBB, physiologist, educator; b. Greenville, SC, Nov. 4, 1934; d. Henry Van Zandt and Florence Ruth (Crozier) Cobb; m. Hans E. Neville, Dec. 27, 1957; children: Michel Paul, Brian Douglas. BA, Pomona Coll., 1956; PhD, U. Pa., 1962. Asst. prof. physiology U. Colo. Med. Sch., Denver, 1968-75, assoc. prof., 1975-82, prof., 1982—, dir. med. scientist tng. program, 1985-94, prof. ob-gyn., 2002—, chief sect. basic reprodn. sci., 2002—. Editor: Lactation: Physiology, Nutrition, Breast Feeding, 1983 (Am. Pubs. award 1984), Human Lactation I, 1985, The Mammary Gland, 1987, Jour. Mammary Gland Biology and Neoplasia, 1995-2001; contbr. numerous articles to profl. jours. Recipient Rsch. Career Devel. award NIH, 1975, NIH merit award, 1993. Mem. AAAS, Am. Physiol. Soc., Am. Soc. Cell Biology, Internat. Soc. Rsch. in Human Milk and Lactation, Soc. Gynecol. Investigation, Phi Beta Kappa. Office: U Colo Divsn Basic Reprodn Sci PO Box 6511 Mail Stop 6511 Aurora CO 80045 Home Phone: 303-333-3461; Office Phone: 303-724-3506. E-mail: peggy.neville@uchsc.edu.

NEVIN, JAMES PATRICK, lawyer; b. San Francisco, July 25, 1975; m. Brigit Nevin. BA cum laude, Boston Coll., 1997; MA in Asian Studies, Stanford U., 1998; JD, UCLA, 2002. Bar: Calif. 2002, US Dist. Ct. (no., so., ea. and ctrl. dists.) Calif., US Ct. of Appeals (9th cir.). Law clk. Wash. State Ct. Appeals; assoc. Brayton Purcell, Novato, Calif., 2002—. Tchr. English, US history and polit. sci., China. Contbr. articles to law jours. Mem.: ABA, Assn. of Trial Lawyers of Am., Consumer Attys. Assn. of LA, Trial Lawyers for Pub. Justice, Consumer Attys. Calif., State Bar of Calif. Avocations: golf, hiking. Office: Brayton Purcell 222 Rush Landing Rd PO Box 6169 Novato CA 94948-6169 Office Phone: 415-898-1555. E-mail: jnevin@braytonlaw.com.

NEWBERRY, ELIZABETH CARTER, greenhouse and floral company owner; b. Blackwell, Tex., Nov. 25, 1921; m. Weldon Omar Newberry, Sept. 24, 1950 (dec. Nov. 1984); 1 child. Student Hardin Simmons U., 1938-39. Office mgr. F. W. Woolworth, Abilene, Tex., 1939-50; acct. Western Devel. & Investment Corp., Englewood, Colo., 1968-72; owner, operator Newberry Bros. Greenhouse and Florist, Denver, 1972—; bd. dirs. Western Devel. and Investment Corp. Englewood, Colo., 1979-87. Pres. Ellsworth Elem. Sch. PTA, Denver, 1961-62; v.p. Hill Jr. High Sch. PTA, Denver. Home: 201 Monroe St Denver CO 80206-5505 Office Phone: 303-322-0443.

NEWBERRY, STEPHEN G., semiconductor equipment company executive; BS, USNA, Annapolis, 1975; MBA, Harvard Univ. Mgmt. positions through group v.p. global ops. & planning Applied Materials Inc., 1980—97; exec. v.p., COO Lam Rsch. Corp., Fremont, Calif., 1997—98, pres., COO, 1998—2005, pres., CEO, 2005—. Bd. dir. Nextest Systems Corp., Semiconductor Equip. & Materials Internat. Office: Lam Rsch Corp 4650 Cushing Pkwy Fremont CA 94538

NEWBRUN, ERNEST, oral biology and periodontology educator; b. Vienna, Dec. 1, 1932; came to U.S., 1955; s. Victor and Elizabeth (Reichl) N; m. Eva Miriam, June 17, 1956; children: Deborah Anne, Daniel Eric, Karen Ruth. BDS, Sydney U., Australia, 1954; MS, U. Rochester, 1957; DMD, U. Ala., 1959; PhD, U. Calif., San Francisco, 1965; Odont. Dr. (hon.), U. Lund, Sweden, 1988; DDSc (hon.), U. Sydney, 1997. Cert. periodontology, 1983. Rsch. assoc. Eastman Dental Ctr., Rochester, NY, 1955-57, U. Ala. Med. Ctr., Birmingham, 1957-59; rsch. fellow Inst. Dental Rsch., Sydney, 1960-61; rsch. tchr. trainee U. Calif., San Francisco, 1961-63, postdoctoral fellow, 1963-65, assoc. prof., 1965-70, prof. oral biology, 1970-83, prof. oral biology and periodontology, 1983-94, prof. emeritus, 1994—; prof. Fromm Inst. Lifelong Learning U. San Francisco, 2000—. Cons. FDA, 1983—. Author: Cariology, 1989, Pharmacology and Therapeutics for Dentistry, 2004, (with others) Pediatrics, 1991; editor: Fluorides and Dental Caries, 1986; mem. editl. bd. Jour. Periodontal Rsch., 1985-90, Jour. Periodontology, 1990-2005. Bd. dirs. Raoul Wallenberg Dem. Club, San Francisco, 1987-92. Fellow AAAS (chmn. dental section, 1988-89), Internat. Assn. Dental Rsch. (pres. 1989-90) Jewish. Avocations: gardening, hiking, skiing, opera, theater. Office Phone: 415-476-1004. Business E-Mail: ernest.newbrun@ucsf.edu.

NEWCOM, JENNINGS JAY, lawyer, director; b. St. Joseph, Mo., Oct. 18, 1941; s. Arden Henderson and Loyal Beatrice (Winans) N.; m. Cherry Ann Phelps, Apr. 4, 1964; children: Shandra Karine, J. Derek Arden. BA, Graceland U., Lamoni, Iowa, 1964; JD, Harvard U., 1968; LLD (hon.), Graceland U., 1999. Bar: Ill. 1968, Calif. 1973, Mo. 1979, Kans. 1981, Colo. 1999. Atty. McDermott, Will & Emery, Chgo., 1968-73; ptnr. Rifkind, Sterling & Lockwood, Beverly Hills, Calif., 1973-79, Shook, Hardy & Bacon L.L.P., Kansas City, Mo., 1979-99, Davis, Graham & Stubbs, LLP, Denver, 1999—; gen. counsel Lovell Minnick Ptnrs. LLC, LA, 1999—; dir. Skillpath Seminars, Overland Park, Kans.; bd. dirs. Atlantic Asset Mgmt. LLC, Berkeley Capital Mgmt., LLC, ClariVest Asset Mgmt. LLC, Mercer Advisors Inc. Trustee Hubbard Found., Linde Found., Graceland U. Mem. Denver Bar Assn., State Bar Assn. Calif. Office: Davis Graham & Stubbs LLP 1550 17th St Ste 500 Denver CO 80202-1500 Office Phone: 303-892-7318. Business E-Mail: j.newcom@dgslaw.com.

NEWCOMBE, GEORGE MICHAEL, lawyer; b. Newark, Nov. 11, 1947; s. George Anthony and Mary Hellen Newcombe; m. Joan Sharon Hanlon, May 30, 1969; children: Sean Michael, Scott Ryan, Jennifer Leigh. BSChemE, N.J. Inst. Tech., 1969; JD, Columbia U., 1975. Bar: N.J. 1975, N.Y. 1976, U.S. Dist. Ct. N.J. 1975, U.S. Ct. Appeals (2d cir.) 1975, U.S. Dist. Ct. (so. dist.) N.Y. 1976, U.S. Dist. Ct. (we. dist.) Tex. 1985, U.S. Ct. Appeals (5th cir.) 1986, U.S. Supreme Ct. 1987, U.S. Ct. Appeals (3d cir.) 1992, U.S. Ct. Appeals (fed. cir.) 1995, Calif. 1999, U.S. Dist. Ct. (no., ea., and so. dists.) Calif. 1999, U.S. Ct. Appeals (9th cir.) 1999. Ptnr. Simpson, Thacher & Bartlett, NYC, 1975—. Dir. Columbia Law Sch. Assn., Inc., Columbia Jour. Environ. Law; dir., legal sec. Am. Ditchley Found., 1994; bd. visitors Columbia Law Sch., 1997—; bd. overseers N.J. Inst. Tech., 1998—. Mem. coun. com. law offices vol. divsn. Legal Aid Soc., N.Y.C., 1980-86. Lt. USPHS, 1970-72. James Kent scholar Columbia Law Sch., 1974, Harlan Fiske Stone scholar Columbia Law Sch., 1975. Mem. Am. Law Inst., ABA, AICE, Assn. of Bar of City of N.Y., Tau Beta Epsilon, Omicron Delta Kappa. Office: Simpson Thacher & Bartlett 3373 Hillview Ave Palo Alto CA 94304-1204

NEWCOMBE, RICHARD SUMNER, newspaper syndicate executive; b. Chgo., Aug. 8, 1950; s. Leo Raymond and Ann (Lombard) N.; m. Caroline Eleanor Bermeo; children: Sara Caroline Ann, John Richard D'Arcy. BA, Georgetown U., 1972; postgrad. in bus., U. Chgo., 1973-74. Reporter/editor UPI, Balt., 1974-78; v.p., gen. mgr. Los Angeles Times Syndicate, 1978-84; pres., chief exec. officer News Am. Syndicate, Irvine, Calif., 1984-87, Creators Syndicate, Los Angeles, 1987—. Bd. dirs., 1st v.p. Newspaper Features Coun., Greenwich, Conn.; chmn. The Jester's Com. Author: Businessman's Guide to Shaping Up, 1983. Mem. Phi Beta Kappa. Avocations: weightlifting, jogging. Office: Creators Syndicate 5777 W Century Blvd Ste 700 Los Angeles CA 90045-5675

NEWELL, LINDA, state legislator; b. Calif. 2 children. BA, U. Calif., Irvine. Registered org. devel. profl. Bus. cons. Human Resources, Corp. Edn. & Workforce Devel.; mem. Dist. 26 Colo. State Senate, 2008—. Outplacement trainer & coach Drake Beam Morin; sr. dir. learning & devel. StarTek. Vol. AXIS Intervention & Training Inst., Conflict Ctr.; vol Season for Non-Violence; vol. Spl. Olympics; on-air fundraiser KBDI Channel 12, Colo.; performing arts chmn. Lakewood Arts Coun.; former bd. adv. Stalking Rescue; vol. Piton Found.-Denver Workforce Initiative. Mem.: Women's Profl. Network, Soc. for Human Resource Mgmt., Nat. Forensics League (judge), Nat. Bus. Exec., Am. Soc. for Training & Devel., Am. Assn. U. Women (bd. mem., vol., former Edn. Found. chmn.), Am. Red Cross (Youth Leadership conf., Orange County Disaster Squad), Organizational Devel. Inst., March of Dimes (music dir.). Democrat. Office: State House 200 E Colfax Denver CO 80203 Office Phone: 303-866-4846 303-866-4846. Business E-Mail: linda.newell.senate@gmail.com.*

NEWELL, MARTIN EDWARD, computer scientist; b. Eng. m. Sandra Newell. PhD, U. Utah, 1975. Mem. computer sci. faculty U. Utah, 1977—79; with Xerox Palo Alto Rsch. Ctr., Calif.; founder Ashlar, Inc., 1988; Adobe fellow Adobe Systems Inc., San Jose, Calif. Contbr. articles to sci. jours. Mem.: NAE. Achievements include creating the Utah Teapot, a 3D model that has become a standard reference object in the computer graphics community; patents in field. Office: Adobe Systems Inc 345 Park Ave San Jose CA 95110-2704

NEWHART, BOB (GEORGE ROBERT NEWHART), entertainer; b. Oak Park, Ill., Sept. 5, 1929; m. Virginia Quinn, Jan. 12, 1963; 4 children. BS, Loyola U., Chgo., 1952. Acct. U.S. Gypsum Co.; copywriter Fred Niles Film Co.; star TV variety show Bob Newhart Show, 1961; star TV series The Bob Newhart Show, 1972—78, Newhart, 1982-90, Bob, 1992, George & Leo, 1997. Rec. artist (album) The Button Down Mind of Bob Newhart, 1960, The Button Down Mind Strikes Back, 1961, Behind the Button Down Mind, 1961, The Button Down Mind on TV, 1962, Bob Newhart Faces Bob Newhart, 1964, Windmille Are Weakening, 1965, This Is it, 1967, The Best of Bob Newhart, 1971, Very Funny Bob Newhart, 1973; royal command performance, London, 1964; appeared in films Hell is for Heroes, 1962, Hot Millions, 1968, Catch 22, 1970, On a Clear Day You Can See Forever, 1970, Cold Turkey, 1971, First Family, 1980, Little Miss Marker, 1980, In and Out, 1997, Rudolph the Red-Nosed Reindeer: The Movie (voice), 1998, Legally Blonde 2: Red, White & Blonde, 2003, Elf, 2003; TV films include Thursday's Game, 1974, Marathon, 1980, The Librarian: Quest for the Spear, 2004; TV appearances (1960-) include The Ed Sullivan Show (a.k.a. Toast of the Town, (8 Times), Jack Parr Show, 1960, The Andy Williams Show, 1962, 1964, & 1966, The Dean Martin Show (24 Times), Rowan & Martin's Laugh-In, 1968 & 1969, The Tonight Show Starring Johnny Carson (also guest host), It's Garry Shandling's Show, 1990, Late Night with David Letterman, 1993, Murphy Brown, 1994, The Simpsons (voice), 1996, Mad TV, 2001, ER, 2003, Saturday Night Live (host 1980, 1995), Desperate Housewives, 2005, (PBS) Bob Newhart: Unbuttoned (Honored Am. Master 2005), 2005, and numerous others. Grand marshall Tournament Roses Parade, 1991. With U.S. Army, 1952-54. Recipient Emmy award, 1961, Peabody award, 1961, Sword of Loyola award, 1976, Legend to Legend award, 1993, three Grammy awards 1960, Kennedy Ctr. Mark Twain award, 2002, Icon award, TVLand, 2005; named to TV Acad. of Arts & Sci. Hall of Fame, 1993, Broadcasting Hall of Fame, Nat. Assn. Broadcasters, 2009; honored as an American Master (Bob Newhart: Unbuttoned), PBS, 2005. Best Known Trademarks: Stammering delivery while talking; Telephone monologues as part of act; One-sided conversations. Office: c/o Capell Rudolph 11601 Wilshire Blvd Ste 1840 Los Angeles CA 90025-1759*

NEWIRTH, RICHARD SCOTT, cultural organization administrator; b. NYC; BA in Maths. magna cum laude, Brown U., 1980; MBA, U. Calif., Berkeley, 1990. Dividend analyst, actuarial asst. Met. Life Ins. Co., San Francisco, 1980-83, sr. underwriter, 1983-85, mgr. renewal svcs., 1985-87, dir. fin. analysis, 1988; benefits and ins. adminstr. San Francisco Symphony, 1990-92; asst. dir. San Francisco Art Commn., 1993-95, dir. cultural affairs, 1995—. Cons. Berkeley (Calif.) Repertory Theatre, 1990; spkr. Nat. Conf. State Legislators, 1997, Far W. Region Cultural Tourism Leadership Forum, 1997; dist. chair Calif. Assembly of Local Arts Agys.; v.p. Urban Arts Fedn., 1998-99, pres., 2000. Mem. mktg. com., vol. Under One Roof. Recipient Pub. Managerial Excellence award, 2001, Ca. Arts Coun. Exemplary Leadership award, 2001. Office: City San Francisco San Francisco Art Commn 25 Van Ness Ave Ste 240 San Francisco CA 94102-6053 Fax: 415-252-2595. E-mail: richard.newirth@sfgov.org.

NEWLAND, CHESTER ALBERT, public administration educator; b. Kansas City, Kans., June 18, 1930; s. Guy Wesley and Mary Virginia (Yoakum) N. BA, U. N. Tex., Denton, 1954; MA, U. Kans., 1955, PhD, 1958. Social Sci. Rsch. Coun. fellow U. Wis. and U.S. Supreme Ct., 1958-59; instr. polit. sci. Idaho State U., Pocatello, 1959-60; mem. faculty U. North Tex., Denton, 1960-66, prof. govt., 1963-66, dir. dept. govt., 1963-66; prof. polit. sci. U. Houston, 1967-68; dir. Lyndon Baines Johnson Libr., Austin, Tex., 1968-70; prof. pub. adminstrn. U. So. Calif., 1966-67, 68-71, 76-82, 84-92, Duggan disting. prof. pub. adminstrn., 1992—; prof. George Mason U., Fairfax, Va., 1982-84. Faculty Fed. Exec. Inst., 1971-76, dir. 1973-76, 80-81; mgr. task force on fed. labor-mgmt. rels. US Pers. Mgmt. Project, Pres.'s Reorgn., Washington, 1977-78. Editor in chief Pub. Adminstrn. Rev., 1984-90; contbr. articles to profl. jours. Chmn. Mcpl. Rsch. Coun., Denton, 1963-64; city councilman, Denton, 1964-66; mem. Pub. Sector Commn. on Productivity and Work Quality, 1974-78; trustee Sacramento (Calif.) Mus. History, Sci. and Tech., 1993-95; mem. UN Devel. Program Kazakhstan, 1997-2000, strategy review program, 2002, Moldova, 1994, Kuwait, 1991, 95-96; cons. Poland, 1990-91, Hungary, 1991, Czech and Slovak Republics, 1992, Bank of Greece, 1999-2002, 04, Taiwan, 2001. Fellow Nat. Acad. Pub. Adminstrn., (trustee 1979-82, nominating com. 2006—07); mem. Southwestern Social Sci. Assn. (chmn. govt. sect. 1964-65), Am. Soc. Pub. Adminstrn. (pres. Dallas-Ft. Worth chpt. 1964-65, nat. coun. 1976, 78-81, editl. bd. jour. 1972-76, chmn. publ. com. 1975-79, program chmn. 1977, nat. pres. 1981-82, Dimock award 1984, Van Riper award 2002, Waldo Lifetime Scholarly Pubs. award 2007), Am. Polit. Sci. Assn., Internat. Pers. Mgmt. Assn. (program chmn. 1978, Stockberger award 1979), Am. Acad. Polit. and Social Sci., Internat. City Mgmt. Assn. (hon., Calif. bd. 2003—, credentialing adv. bd. 2006—), Nat. Assn. Schs Pub. Affairs and Adminstrn. (Staats Pub. Svc. award 1989), Sacramento Charter Review Com. Office: Univ Southern California 1800 I St Sacramento CA 95811-3004

NEWLAND, RUTH LAURA, small business owner; b. Ellensburg, Wash., June 4, 1949; d. George J. and Ruth Marjorie (Porter) N. BA, Cen. Wash. State Coll., 1970, MEd, 1972; EdS, Vanderbilt U., 1973; PhD, Columbia Pacific U., 1981. Tchr. Union Gap (Wash.) Sch., 1970-71; owner Newland Ranch Gravel Co., Yakima, Wash., 1998; ptnr. Arnold Artificial Limb, Yakima, 1981-86, owner, pres. Yakima and Richland, Wash., 1986—. Owner Newland Ranch, Yakima, 1969—. Contbg. mem. Nat. Dem. Com., Irish Nat. Caucus Found.; mem. Pub. Citizen, We The People, Nat. Humane Edn. Soc.; charter mem. Nat. Mus. Am. Indian. George Washington scholar Masons, Yakima, 1967. Mem. NAFE, NOW, Am. Orthotic and Prosthetic Assn., Internat. Platform Assn., Nat. Antivisection Soc. (life), Vanderbilt U. Alumni Assn., Peabody Coll. Alumni Assn., Columbia Pacific U. Alumni Assn., World Wildlife Fund, Nat. Audubon Soc., Greenpeace, Mus. Fine Arts, Humane Soc. U.S., Wilderness Soc., Nature Conservancy, People for Ethical Treatment of Animals, Amnesty Internat., The Windstar Found., Rodale Inst., Sierra Club (life), Emily's List. Democrat. Avocations: reading, gardening, sewing, handcrafts. Home: 2004 Riverside Rd Yakima WA 98901-8540 Office: Arnold Artificial Limb 9 S 12th Ave Yakima WA 98902-3106

NEWLIN, L. MAX, parks and recreation director; b. June 4, 1942; BS, Wilmington Coll., 1968. Mgr. Massacre Rocks State Pk., American Falls, Idaho, 1996—. Exec. dir. Friends Massacre Rocks Inc.; v.p. S.E. Idaho Travel Coun. Idaho Parks and Recreation Assn. fellow, 1990. Mem. Power County/Am. Falls Hist. Soc. (chmn.). Office: Massacre Rocks State Pk 3592 Park Ln American Falls ID 83211-5556

NEWMAN, ANITA NADINE, surgeon; b. Honolulu, June 13, 1949; d. William Reece Elton and Margie Ruth (Pollard) Newman; children: Justin Ellis, Chelsea Newman, Andrew Frank, Tyler William. BA, Stanford U., 1971; MD, Dartmouth Coll., 1975. Diplomate Am. Bd. Otolaryngology. From intern to resident in gen. surgery Northwestern Meml. Hosp., Chgo., 1975-77, resident in otolaryngology, 1977-78; resident UCLA Hosp. and Clinics, 1979-82; assoc. prof. UCLA, 1982-96; staff surgeon Wadsworth VA Hosp., LA, 1982-84; rsch. fellow in neurotology, 1984-88; surgeon USC Head and Neck Group, 1997-2000; pvt. practice LA, 2000—. Contbr. articles to profl. jours. Mem. alumni admissions support com. Dartmouth Med. Sch. Alumni Coun., 1983-87. Fellow ACS; mem. Am. Acad. Otolaryngology, Am. Med. Women's Assn., L.A. County Med. Women's Assn., L.A. Soc. Otolaryngology (pres. 2005—), Stanford Women's Honor Soc. Democrat. Office: 8631 W 3rd St Ste 440E Los Angeles CA 90048 Office Phone: 310-657-7704, 310-285-0929. Personal E-mail: entdoc49@hotmail.com.

NEWMAN, CAROL L., lawyer; b. Yonkers, NY, Aug. 7, 1949; d. Richard J. and Pauline Frances (Stoll) N. AB/MA summa cum laude, Brown U., 1971; postgrad., Harvard U. Law Sch., 1972-73; JD cum laude, George Washington U., 1977. Bar: D.C. 1977, Calif. 1979. With antitrust divsn. U.S. Dept. Justice, Washington and L.A., 1977-80; assoc. Alschuler, Grossman & Pines, LA, 1980-82, Costello & Walcher, LA, 1982-85, Rosen, Wachtell & Gilbert, LA, 1985-88, ptnr., 1988-90, Keck, Mahin & Cate, LA, 1990-94; pvt. practice LA, 1994—. Adj. prof. Sch. Bus., Golden Gate U., spring 1982. Commr. L.A. Bd. Transp. Commrs., 1993—98, v.p., 1995—96; pres. Bd. Taxicab Commrs., 1999—2001; candidate for State Atty. Gen., 1986; bd. dirs. Women's Progress Alliance, 1996—98. Mem. State Bar Calif., L.A. County Bar Assn., LGLA (co. pres. 1991-92, bd. mem. 2008-), Log Cabin (bd. dirs. 1992-97, 2003-06, pres. 1996-97), Calif. Women Lawyers (bd. govs. 1991-94), Order of Coif, Phi Beta Kappa. Office Phone: 818-225-0056. E-mail: cnewman540@aol.com.

NEWMAN, DAVID WHEELER, lawyer; b. Salt Lake City, Apr. 5, 1952; s. Donnell and Vera Mae (Siratt) N.; m. Mahnaz Navai, Mar. 14, 1981; 1 child, Anthony Dara. BA magna cum laude, Claremont Men's Coll., 1973; JD, UCLA, 1977; LLM in Taxation, NYU, 1979. Bar: Calif. 1978, US Dist. Ct. (ctrl. dist. Calif.) 1978, US Tax Ct. 1979. Tax ptnr. Mitchell, Silberberg & Knupp, LLP, LA, 1982—. Mem. exec. com. tax sect. L.A. County Bar, 1991-2000. Trustee New Visions Found., 1995—; trustee, pres. New Rds. Sch., 2000—. Named one of Top 100 Attys., Worth mag., 2005. Mem. Calif. Club, Men's Garden Club L.A. (dir. 2000—). Avocations: tennis, skiing, gardening. Office: Mitchell Silberberg & Knupp 11377 W Olympic Blvd Los Angeles CA 90064-1625 Office Phone: 310-312-3171. Office Fax: 310-231-8371. E-mail: dwn@msk.com.

NEWMAN, DEAN GORDON, business consultant; b. North Branch, Iowa, Mar. 17, 1929; s. Floyd William and Hazel Jane (Covault) N.; m. Maggie Newman; children: Gary Dean, Craig William. BA, Simpson Coll., 1950; MBA, Stanford U., 1952. From trainee to mgr. GE, Syracuse, NY, Chgo., Milw., 1952—62, mgr. employee and cmty. rels. DeKalb, 1963—69; v.p. employee and pub. rels. United Nuclear Corp., Elmsford, NY, 1969—71; v.p. employee rels. Apache Corp., Mpls., 1971-83, v.p. human resources and comm., 1983-87; v.p. mktg. Nelson Cons. Group, Mpls., 1989-92; chmn., CFO Linear Fitness Systems, Inc., Allenspark, Colo., 1998—2004. Pres. Apache Found., 1973—87; v.p., bd. dirs. Boys Clubs, Mpls., 1978—85; chmn. Boys and Girls Club Mpls., 1985—88, exec. com., 1988—89; v.p. fin., bd. Boys and Girls Club Larimer County, 1993—96; vice chmn. Bus. Econs. Edn. Found., 1986—88, chmn. fin. com., 1988—89; com. mem., treas. Allenspark Sr. Adv. Com., 1999—2003; treas. Allenspark Fire Protection Dist., 2000—05, bd. dirs., 2000—05, Aging Svcs. Found., 2006—, pres., 2007—. With USNR, 1952—55, Korea. Nat. Meth. scholar, 1946—50, Hicks fellow, 1952. Mem.: Nat. Assn. Mfrs. (dir. 1981—87), Allenspark Area Club (bd. dirs., treas. 2000—03, Founder's award 2002, Boulder County Honoring Our Elders award 2003), Pi Gamma Mu, Sigma Tau Delta, Epsilon Sigma, Alpha Tau Omega. Republican. Methodist. Home and Office: 2930 Bryn Mawr Pl Longmont CO 80503 Personal E-mail: mdnewman85@msn.com.

NEWMAN, FRANCIS A., medical device company executive; b. 1947; Sr. v.p. merchandising F.W. Woolworth, 1980-84, exec. v.p. household merchandising, 1984-85; pres., CEO, dir. F&M Distributors, Inc., 1986-93; pres., COO Eckerd Fleet, Inc., Largo, Fla., 1993-98, pres., COO, chmn., 1998-2000; pres., CEO More.com, San Francisco, 2000—. Address: PO Box 4689 Clearwater FL 33758-4689

NEWMAN, JEANNE, lawyer; BA, Conn. Coll., New London, 1977; JD, U. So. Calif. Law Ctr., LA, 1980. Ptnr. Hansen, Jacobson, Teller, Hoberman, Newman, Warren & Richman, LLP, Beverly Hills. Named one of 100 Power Lawyers, Hollywood Reporter, 2007, The 100 Most Powerful Women in Entertainment, 2007; named to Southern Calif. Super Lawyers, 2007, 2008. Office: Hansen Jacobson Teller Hoberman Newman Warren & Richman LLP 450 N Roxbury Dr 8th Fl Beverly Hills CA 90210-4222 Office Phone: 310-271-8777. Office Fax: 310-276-8310. Business E-Mail: jn@hjth.com.

NEWMAN, JOHN SCOTT, chemical engineer, educator; b. Richmond, Va., Nov. 17, 1938; s. Clarence William and Marjorie Lenore (Saucerman) Newman; m. Nguyen Thanh Lan, June 30, 1973; children: Natalie Diane, Michael Alexander. BS, Northwestern U., 1960; MS, U. Calif., Berkeley, 1962, PhD, 1963. Asst. prof. chem. engring. U. Calif., Berkeley, 1963-67, assoc. prof., 1967-70, prof., 1970—; prin. investigator environ. energy tech. divsn. Lawrence Berkeley Nat. Lab., 1963—. Vis. prof. U. Wis., Madison, 1973; Onsager prof. Norwegian U. Sci. and Tech., 2002; summer participant Oak Ridge Nat. Lab., 1965, 66. Author: Electrochemical Systems, 1973, 3d edit., 2004; assoc. editor Jour. Electrochem. Soc., 1990—2000; contbr. articles to profl. jours. Fellow: Electrochem. Soc. (Young Author's prize 1966, 1969, David C. Grahame award 1985, Henry B. Linford award 1990, Olin Palladium medal 1991, Rsch. award Battery Divsn. 2004); mem.: AIChE (Excellence in Indsl. Rsch. award No. Calif. sect. 2000), NAE. Home: 114 York Ave Kensington CA 94708-1045 Office: U Calif Dept Chem Engring Berkeley CA 94720-1462 Home Phone: 510-524-8945. Business E-Mail: newman@newman.cchem.berkeley.edu.

NEWMAN, MICHAEL RODNEY, lawyer; b. NYC, Oct. 2, 1945; s. Morris and Helen Gloria (Hendler) Newman; m. Cheryl Jeanne Anker, June 11, 1967; children: Hillary Abra, Nicole Brooke. Student NASA Inst. Space Physics, Columbia U., 1964; BA, U. Denver, 1967; JD, U. Chgo., 1970. Bar: Calif. 1971, U.S. Dist. Ct. (cen. dist.) Calif. 1972, U.S. Ct. Appeals (9th cir.) 1974, U.S. Dist. Ct. (no. dist.) Calif. 1975, U.S. Supreme Ct. 1978, U.S. Dist. Ct. (so. dist.) Calif. 1979, U.S. Tax Ct. 1979, U.S. Dist. Ct. (ea. dist.) Calif. 1983. Assoc. David Daar, 1971-76; ptnr. Daar & Newman, 1976-78, Miller & Daar, 1978-88, Miller, Daar & Newman, 1988-89, Daar & Newman, 1989—; judge pro-tem L.A. Mcpl. Ct., 1982—, L.A. Superior Ct., 1988—. Vice chmn., bd. dirs. German-Am. C. of C., 2001—02; bd. govs., fin. and phys. devel. com. U. Haifa, Israel; bd. dirs., mem. adv. bd., chmn. bus. generation com. Consulegis EEIG, 1995—; founder, facilitator 1st, 2d and 3d Ann. German-Am. Strategic Partnership Confs., 1992—2000; guest lectr., internat. law Calif. State U., Fullerton, 2006, 07, 09. Mem. L.A. Citizens Organizing Com. for Olympic Summer Games, 1984, mem. govtl. liaison adv. commn., 1984; mem. So. Calif. Com. for Olympic Summer Games, 1984; cert. ofcl. Athletics Congress of U.S., co-chmn. legal com. S.P.A.-T.A.C., chief finish judge; trustee Massada lodge B'nai Brith; bd. dirs. Ctr. for the Study of Emerging Markets, Calif. State U. Fullerton Grad. Sch. Bus. and Econs., 1997—. Recipient NYU medal, 1962, Maths. award, USN Sci., 1963. Mem.: TAC (bd. dirs., Disting. Svc. award 1988), ABA (multi-dist. litigation subcom., com. on class actions), German Am. Lawyers Assn. So. Calif. (mem. bd.), Lawyers Profl. Liability Bar Assn., Conf. Ins. Counsel, Los Angeles County Bar Assn. (chmn. attys. errors and omissions prevention com. 1995—2005, mem. cts. com., state cts. coord. com. litigation sect., exec. com., mem. internat. law sect. exec. com.), Rotary Club (internat. com.), City Club on Bunker Hill, Breakfast Club, Porter Valley Country Club. Office: Daar & Newman 865 S Figueroa St Ste 2300 Los Angeles CA 90017-2567 Office Phone: 213-892-0999. Business E-Mail: mnewman@daarnewman.com.

NEWMAN, MURRAY ARTHUR, aquarium administrator; b. Chgo., Mar. 6, 1924; emigrated to Can., 1953, naturalized, 1970; s. Paul Jones and Virginia (Murray) N.; m. Katherine Greene Rose, Aug. 8, 1952; 1 child, Susan. BSc, U. Chgo., 1949; postgrad., U. Hawaii, 1950; MA, U. Calif., Berkeley, 1951; PhD, U. B.C., Vancouver, Can., 1960. Curator fisheries UCLA, 1951-53; curator fisheries Ichthyology Mus. U. B.C., 1953-56; curator Vancouver Pub. Aquarium, 1956-66, dir., 1966-93; pres. Mana Aquarium Cons. Fgn. adv. Nat. Mus./Aquarium Project, Taiwan; past chmn. adv. com. Western Can. Univs. Marine Biol. Soc.; co-chmn. Enoshima (Japan) Internat. Aquarium Symposium, 1997; spl. advisor Enoshima Aquarium, 1998, Port of Nagoya Pub. Aquarium, 1999, 2000; hon. com. Fifth Internat. Congress, Monaco, 2000, Sixth Internat. Congress, Monterey, 2004, grand opening new Enoshima Aquarium, 2004. Author: Life in a Fishbowl: Confessions of an Aquarium Director, 1994, People Fish and Whales The Vancouver Aquarium Story, 2006. Served with USN, 1943-46. Decorated Order of Can., Order of British Columbia, 2006; recipient Man of Yr. award City of Vancouver, 1964; Centennial award Govt. Can., 1967, cert. of merit, 1988; Harold J. Merilees award Vancouver Visitors Bur., 1976, 75 Achievers award, 1987, Silver Bravery medal Royal Soc. Can., 1992, Can. 125 medal, 1992, Golden Jubilee medal, 2002. Mem. Am. Assn. Zool. Parks and Aquariums, Internat. Union Dirs. Zool. Gardens, Can. Assn. Zool. Parks and Aquariums (pres. 1978-79), Vancouver Club, Round Table Club. Office: Vancouver Pub Aquarium PO Box 3232 Vancouver BC Canada V6B 3X8

NEWMAN, RICHARD G., engineering company executive; BSCE, Bucknell U.; MSCE, Columbia U.; grad. Exec. Mgmt. Program, UCLA. Former CEO AECOM Tech. Corp., LA, 2002—, chmn. Bd. dirs. Southwest Water Co., 13 mutual funds under Capital Rsch. and Mgmt. Co., Sempra Energy, San Diego, 2002—, mem. audit and corp. governance coms. Fellow: Inst. for Advancement of Engring.; mem.: NSPE, Am. Soc. Civil Engrs., Chief Executives Orgn. Office: AECOM Tech Corp 555 S Flower St Ste 3700 Los Angeles CA 90071-2300 Office Phone: 215-593-8000. Office Fax: 213-593-8729.

NEWMAN, STEVEN HARVEY, insurance company executive, director; b. Bklyn., Apr. 26, 1943; s. Charlotte Newman Bart; m. Lenore Blaustein, June 14, 1964; children: Richard, Michael, Stephanie. BS, Bklyn. Coll., 1963. Actuarial asst. Royal Globe Ins. Co., NYC, 1963-65; asst. sec. Ins. Rating Bd., NYC, 1965-69; v.p., sr. casualty actuary Am. Internat. Group, NYC, 1969-82; exec. v.p. Home Ins. Co., NYC, 1982-85, pres., 1985-86, also bd. dirs.; chmn., CEO Underwriters Reinsurance Co., Woodland Hills, Calif., 1987—2001; now chmn. Platinum Underwriters Holdings, Ltd., Bermuda, 2002—. Chmn. GCR Holdings, 1993-97, Reins. Assn. Am., 1995-96. Fellow Casualty Actuarial Soc. (pres. 1981-82); mem. Am. Acad. Actuaries, Internat. Actuarial Assn.

NEWMAN, THOMAS, composer; s. Alfred Newman; m. Anne Marie Zirbes; children: Evan, Julia, Jack. Scores include: (films) Grandview, U.S.A., 1984, Reckless, 1984, Revenge of the Nerds, 1984, Girls Just Want to Have Fun, 1985, Desperately Seeking Susan, 1985, The Man with One Red Shoe, 1985, Real Genius, 1985, Gung Ho, 1986, Jumpin' Jack flash, 1986, Quicksilver, 1986, Light of Day, 1987, The Lost Boys, 1987, Less Than Zero, 1987, The Great Outdoors, 1988, The Prince of Pennsylvania, 1988, Cookie, 1989, Men Don't Leave, 1990, Naked Tango, 1990, Welcome Home, Roxy Carmichael, 1990, Career Opportunities, 1991, Deceived, 1991, The Rapture, 1991, Fried Green Tomatoes, 1991, The Linguini Incident, 1992, The Player, 1992, Whispers in the Dark, 1992, Scent of a Woman, 1992, Flesh and Bone, 1993, Josh and S.A.M., 1993, The Favor, 1994, Threesome, 1994, The Shawshank Redemption, 1994 (Acad. award nominee for best original score, 1994), Little Women, 1994 (Acad. award nominee for best original score, 1994), Unstrung Heroes, 1995 (Acad. award nominee for best original score, 1996), How to Make an American Quilt, 1995, Up Close & Personal, 1996, Phenomenon, 1996, American Buffalo, 1996, The People vs. Larry Flynt, 1996, Mad City, 1997, Red Corner, 1997, Oscar and Lucinda, 1997, The Horse Whisperer, 1998, Meet Joe Black 1998, American Beauty, 1999 (Golden Globe award nominee for best original score, 2000, Acad. award nominee for best original score, 2000, Grammy award for best soundtrack album, 2001), The Green Mile, 1999, Erin Brockovich, 2000, My Khmer Heart, 2000, Pay It Forward, 2000, In the Bedroom, 2001, The Execution of Wanda Jean, 2002, The Salton Sea, 2002, Road to Perdition, 2002 (Acad. award nominee for best original score, 2003), White Oleander, 2002, Finding Nemo, 2003 (Acad. award nominee for best original score, 2004), Lemony Snicket's A Series of Unfortunate Events, 2004 (Acad. award nominee for best original score, 2005), Cinderella Man, 2005, La Femme dans la chambre, 2005, Jarhead, 2005, Little Children, 2005, The Good German, 2006 (Acad. award nominee for best original score, 2007), Nothing is Private, 2007, WALL[00b7]E, 2008 (Best Instrumental Arrangement, Best Song Written for Motion Picture, Grammy Awards, 2009), Revolutionary Road, 2008; (TV movies) The Seduction of Gina, 1984, Heat Wave, 1991, Those Secrets, 1992, Citizen Cohn, 1992; (TV miniseries) Angels in America, 2003; composed themes for (TV series) Against the Law, 1990, Six Feet Under, 2001 (Emmy award for Outstanding Main Title Theme Music, 2002). Recipient Composer of Yr. award, Hollywood Film Festival, 2004. Office: The Gorfaine Schwartz Agency Inc 4111 W Alameda Ave Ste 509 Burbank CA 91505-4171

NEWMAN-GORDON, PAULINE, French language and literature educator; b. NYC, Aug. 5, 1925; d. Bernard and Eva Newman; m. Sydney A. Gordon, Sept. 13, 1959 (dec.); m. Richard Yellin, Feb. 9, 1997. BA, Hunter Coll., 1947; MA, Columbia U., 1948; PhD, Sorbonne U., Paris, 1951. Instr. French Wellesley (Mass.) Coll., 1952-53; mem. faculty Stanford (Calif.) U., 1953—, prof. French lit., 1969-93, prof. emerita, 1994—. Author: Marcel Proust, 1953, Eugene Le Roy, 1957, Corbiere, Laforgue and Apollinaire, 1964, Helen of Troy Myth, 1968, (poetry) Mooring to France, (prose poem) Sydney: editor: Dictionary of Ideas in Marcel Proust, 1968, also articles in field; contbr. articles to profl. jours. Scholar Internat. Inst. Edn., 1948-51, MLA, 1956-57, AAUW, 1962-63, Am. Philos. Soc., 1970-71, NEH, 1989; elected to Hall of Fame, Alumni Assn. Hunter Coll. of CUNY, 1990 Mem. MLA, Am. Assn. Tchrs. French, Soc. Friends Marcel Proust. Office: Stanford U Dept French Italian Stanford CA 94305

NEWMARK, CRAIG ALEXANDER, Internet company executive; b. Morristown, NJ, Dec. 6, 1952; s. Leon and Joyce Newmark. BS, Case Western Reserve U., 1975, MS in Computer Sci., 1977. Computer programmer IBM, NJ, 1979—93; systems security architect, gen. cons. Charles Schwab, Calif., 1993—95; ind. contractor, software sys. architect Bank of America, Calif., 1995—97, Intel, Calif., 1995—97, Sun Microsystems, Calif., 1995—97; founder, chmn., customer service rep. Craigslist, San Francisco, 1995—. Featured in AP, Wall Street Journal, NY Times, LA Times, USA Today, Business Week, Time Mag., and Esquire Mag. Adv. bd. Climate Theatre, Haight-Ashbury Food Program; supporter of local writers through Grotto Nights. Named #1 Most Efficient US Job Site, Forrester Rsch. Report, Wall St. Jour., 2000, Best Cmty. Website - People's Voice, Webby Awards, 2001, The Elite of the Online Employment Industry, WEDDLE's User's Choice Awards, 2004, 50 online destinations for the quarterlifer, Hatch Mag., 2004, 50 Coolest Websites, Time mag., 2004, Person of the Year, Webby Awards, The Internat. Acad. Digital Arts and Sciences, 2005, Webby Person of Yr., 2005; named one of World's 100 Most Influential People, Time Mag., 2005, 26 Most Fascinating Entrepreneurs, Inc.com, 2005, 50 Most Important People on the Web, PC World, 2007. Fellow: World Tech. Network (World Tech. award-Comm. Tech. 2006). Achievements include millions of people use Craigslist to research subjects such as: jobs, housing, goods & services, events, friendships, and advice; first commercial transmission of a website into space by Deep Space Communications Network, March 11, 2005. Office: Craigslist 1319 9th Ave San Francisco CA 94122-2308 Office Phone: 415-566-6394. Office Fax: 415-504-6394. Business E-Mail: craig@craigslist.org.

NEWMARK, LEONARD DANIEL, linguistics educator; b. Attica, Ind., Apr. 8, 1929; s. Max Jacob and Sophie (Glusker) N.; m. Ruth Broessler, Sept. 16, 1951; children: Katya, Mark. AB, U. Chgo., 1947; MA, Ind. U., 1951, PhD, 1955. Instr. English U. Ill., Urbana, 1951; vis. asst. prof. linguistics U. Mich., Ann Arbor, 1961; assoc. prof. English Ohio State U., 1954-62; assoc. prof. linguistics Ind. U., Bloomington, 1962-63; prof. linguistics U. Calif., San Diego, 1963-91, prof. emeritus, 1992—, chmn. dept., 1963-71, 79-85, head program in Am. lang. and culture, 1979-84, rsch. linguist Ctr. for Rsch. in Lang., 1992—. Author: Linguistic History of English, 1963, Spoken Albanian, 1997, Standard Albanian, 1982, Albanian-English Dictionary, 1998, Albanian Handbook, 1999; founding editor UCSD Emeriti Newsletter: Chronicles, 2001-2004. Mem. Linguistics Soc. Am., Dictionary Soc. N.Am., Phi Beta Kappa. Achievements include invention of memory aid device. Business E-Mail: ldnewmark@ucsd.edu.

NEWMEYER, FREDERICK JARET, linguist, educator; b. Phila., Jan. 30, 1944; s. Alvin S. and Fritzie B. (Nisenson) N.; m. Carolyn V. Platt, Apr. 28, 1968 (div. 1974); m. Marilyn M. Goebel, Dec. 25, 1993. BA, U. Rochester, 1965, MA, 1967; PhD, U. Ill., 1969. Asst. prof. linguistics U. Wash., Seattle, 1969-75, assoc. prof., 1975-81, prof., 1981—, chair, 1990-2000. Vis. prof. U. London, 1979, Cornell U., 1981, U. Md., 1982, UCLA, 1982-83, La Trobe U., Australia, 1987, adj. prof., U. Brit. Columbia & Simon Fraser U., 2007-. Author: English Aspectual Verbs, 1975, Linguistic Theory in America, 1980, Grammatical Theory, 1983, Politics of Linguistics, 1986, Generative Linguistics, 1995, Language Form and Language Function, 1998, Possible and Probable Languages, 2005; editor: Linguistics: The Cambridge Survey, 1988, Natural Language and Linguistic Theory, 1987-2003; assoc. editor: Language, 1980-85. NEH fellow, 1973-74. Fellow AAAS; mem. Linguistic Soc. Am. (sec.-treas. 1989-94, v.p. 2001, pres. 2002). Office: 1068 Seymour St Vancouver BC V6B 3M6 Canada Home: 428 Beach Crescent # 702 Vancouver BC V6Z 3G1 Canada E-mail: fjn@u.washington.edu.

NEWSOM, GAVIN CHRISTOPHER, mayor, San Francisco; b. San Francisco, Oct. 10, 1967; s. William and Tessa Newsom; m. Kimberly Guilfoyle Newsom, Dec. 8, 2001 (div. 2006); m. Jennifer Siebel, July 26, 2008. BA in Polit. Sci., Santa Clara U., 1989. Founder PlumpJack Wines Mgmt. Group, San Francisco, 1992—; pres. Pkg. and Traffic Commn., San Francisco, 1996—97; mem. Office of Bd. Suprs., San Francisco, 1996—2004; mayor City of San Francisco, 2004—. Named one of 17 People Who Matter, TIME mag., 2004. Office: City Hall Room 200 1 Dr Carlton B Goodlett Place San Francisco CA 94102 Office Phone: 415-554-6141. Office Fax: 415-554-6160. Business E-Mail: gavin.newsom@sfgov.org.*

NEWSOME, RANDALL JACKSON, judge; b. Dayton, Ohio, July 13, 1950; s. Harold I. and Sultana S. (Stone) N. BA summa cum laude, Boston U., 1972; JD, U. Cin., 1975. Bar: Ohio 1975, U.S. Dist. Ct. (so. dist.) Ohio 1977, U.S. Ct. Appeals (6th cir.) 1979, U.S. Supreme Ct. 1981. Law clk. to chief judge U.S. Dist. Ct. (so. dist.) Ohio, 1975-77; assoc. Dinsmore & Shohl, Cin., 1978-82; judge U.S. Bankruptcy Ct. (so. dist.) Ohio, 1982-88, U.S. Bankruptcy Ct. (no. dist.) Calif., Oakland, 1988—2004, chief judge, 2004—. Faculty mem. Fed. Jud. Ctr., ALI-ABA, 1987—; mem. Nat. Conf. of Bankruptcy Judges, 1983—, mem. bd. govs., 1987-88, pres., 1998-99; advisor USAID, Kosovo, 2007-. Contbg. author: Chapter 11 Theory and Practice, 1994—, Collier on Bankruptcy, 1997—. Recipient Disting. Alumus award, U. Cin. Law Alumni Assn., 2008. Fellow Am. Coll. Bankruptcy; mem. Am. Law Inst., Phi Beta Kappa. Democrat. Office: US Bankruptcy Ct PO Box 2070 Oakland CA 94604-2070 Office Phone: 510-879-3530.

NEWTON, JIM, editor; b. Palo Alto, Calif. m. Karlene Goller; 1 child, Jack. BA with high honors, Dartmouth Coll., 1985. Clk. for James Reston at NY Times, with fgn. desk; reporter Atlanta Journal-Constitution, LA Times, 1989—92, LA Police Dept. reporter, 1992—97, Calif. govt. & politics editor, 2001, city-county bur. chief, editl. page editor, 2007—. Author: Justice for All: Earl Warren & the Nation He Made, 2006. Co-recipient Pulitzer Prize, 1992, 1994; named Times Mirror Journalist of Yr., 1995; John Jacobs fellow, Inst. Govtl. Studies, 2003—04. Office: LA Times 202 W 1st St Los Angeles CA 90012 E-mail: jim.newton@latimes.com.

NEWTON-JOHN, OLIVIA, singer, actress; b. Cambridge, Eng., Sept. 26, 1948; arrived in Australia, 1954, arrived in England, 1964, arrived in Am., 1975; d. Brin and Irene (Born) Newton-John; m. Matt Lattanzi, Dec. 1984 (div. 1995); 1 child, Chloe Rose Lattanzi; m. John Easterling, June 21, 2008. Student pub. schs. Co-owner Koala Blue, 1982—. Singer, actress in Australia, Eng. and US, 1965—; actress: (films) Funny Things Happen Down Under, 1965, Tomorrow, 1970, Grease, 1978, Xanadu, 1980, Two of a Kind, 1983, It's My Party, 1996, Sordid Lives, 2000; (TV) Timeless Tales from Hallmark, 1990, A Mom for Christmas, 1990, A Christmas Romance, 1994, Snowden on Ice (voice), 1997, The Christmas Angel: A Story on Ice, 1998, The Wilde Girls, 2001; singer: (albums) If Not for You, 1971, Let me Be There, 1973, If You Love Me Let Me Know, 1974, Long Live Love, 1974, First Impressions, 1974, Have You Ever Been Mellow, 1975, Clearly Love, 1975, Come on Over, 1976, Don't Stop Believin', 1976, Making a Good Thing Better, 1977, Greatest Hits, 1977, Totally Hot, 1978, Grease, 1978, Xanadu, 1980, Physical, 1981, Greatest Hits, 1982, (with John Travolta) Two of a Kind, 1984, Soul Kiss, 1985, The Rumour, 1988, Warm And Tender, 1989, Back To Basics-The Essential Collection, 1992, Gaia, 1994, Heathcliff, 1995, Back With A Heart, 1998, The Main Event, 1998, Two, 2002, Indigo-Women of Song, 2004, Stronger Than Before, 2005; TV prodn. In Australia, 1988. Decorated as Officer, Order Brit. Empire, 1979, Order of Australia, 2006; named one of 50 Most Beautiful People in the World, People mag., 1998, one of 100 Greatest Women of Rock N Roll, VH1.; recipient Acad. Country Music, 1973, Country Music Assn. U.K., 1974-75, Country Music Assn. award, 1974, Grammy award, 1973-74, AGVA award, 1974, Billboard Mag. award, 1974-75, People's Choice award 1974, 1976, 1979, Record World award, 1974-76, 1978, Nat. Assn. Retail Merchandisers/Cashbox, 1974-75, Am. Music award 1974-76, Nat. Juke Box award, 1980, Lifetime Achievement award, Australian Record Industry Assn., 2002. Office: c/o Mark Hartley Fitzgerald-Hartley 34 N Palms St Ste 100 Ventura CA 93001 Office Phone: 805-641-6441. Office Fax: 805-641-6444.

NEZAMI, ELAHE, medical educator; arrived in US, 1980; d. Mahmoud and Jaleh Nezami; BA cum laude in Psychology, Assumption Coll, Worcester, Mass., 1981; MA in Clin. Counseling Psychology, U. Houston, Clear Lake City, 1983; MA in Clin. Psychology, PhD in Clin. Psychology, U. Southern Calif., LA, 1991; predoc. intern, U. Calif., Irvine Med. Ctr., 1993. Rsch. assoc. U. Tex., Med. Br., 1985—88, clin. cons., behavioral medicine lab., dept. psychology, 1985—88; grad. rschr., dept psychology U. Southern Calif., 1988—93, counselor, dept psychology, 1988—93, therapist, dept psychology, 1988—93, tchg. asst., 1989—93, instr., 1997—, chair, Adv. Com. Work Family Life, 2007—; instr. Health Promotion Disease Prevention Studies, U. Southern Calif., 1996—97, dir., undergrad. program, 1997—; asst. prof. Clin. Preventive Medicine, 2000, assoc. prof., 2008. Chair Asia Pacific Academic Consortium Pub. Health, 2004—; bd. mem. Assn. Prof. Scholars Iranian Heritage, Internat. Soc. Health Psychology Rschrs.; exec. bd. mem. Assn. Suicide Prevention; advisor Health Promotion Student Assn., Cmty. Health Involvement Project, Africa Dream Project; chair U. Southern Calif. Women Mgmt. Recipient Tchg. Has No Boundaries award, U. Southern Calif., 2004, Gamma Sigma Alpha Prof. Year award, 2004, Outstanding Faculty award, Mortar Bd., 2004; fellowship, U. Southern Calif., Inst. Health Promotion Disease Prevention Rsch., Nat. Cancer Inst. Postdoc. Rsch., 1994—97, grant, Tran Disciplinary Prevention Rsch. Ctr. Mem.: AAUW, APHA, Assn. Prevention Tchg Rsch. (grant 2006), Western Assn. Coll. Admission Counseling, Nat. Assn. Advisors Health Professions, Nat. Assn. Grad. Admission Profls., Nat. Assn. Coll. Admission Counseling, Nat. Academic Advising Assn. Achievements include research in psychological factors, social norms, cultural values, and levels of acculturation in relation to smoking among youth, translation of mmpi-t2o standardization and implementation. Home: 3771 McClintock Ave #4108 Los Angeles CA 90007 Office Phone: 213-821-1600. Office Fax: 213-821-1733. Business E-Mail: nezami@usc.edu.

NG, DOMINIC, bank executive; b. Hong Kong, Jan. 24, 1959; BBA in Acctg., U. Houston, 1980. CPA Calif., Texas. Dir. Chinese bus. svcs., sr. mgr. Deloitte & Touche, LLP, L.A., Houston, 1980—90; pres., CEO Seyen Investment, Inc., LA, 1990—92, East-West Fed. Bank f.s.b., San Marino, Calif., 1992—. Bd. dirs. Fed. Res. Bank, San Francisco, LA, Mattel Inc. Office: East West Bank 135 N Los Robles Ave 7th Fl Pasadena CA 91101 Office Phone: 626-768-6800. Business E-Mail: carmen.pan@eastwest.com.

NG, KIM (KIMBERLY J. NG), professional sports team executive; b. Wu Peiqin, China, Nov. 17, 1968; m. Tony Markward. BA in Pub. Policy, U. Chgo., 1990. Front office arbitration intern Chgo. White Sox, 1990, spl. projects analyst, 1991, asst. dir., baseball ops., 1991—95; dir. waivers, player records MLB Am. League, 1995—97; v.p., asst. gen. mgr. NY Yankees, 1998—2001; v.p. baseball ops., asst. gen. mgr. LA Dodgers, 2001—, interim dir. player devel., 2004. Named one of 10 to Watch, Baseball America, 2008; named to Young Leaders Forum, Nat. Com. on US-China Rels., 2007—. Office: Los Angeles Dodgers 1000 Elysian Park Ave Los Angeles CA 90012-1199

NGUYEN, HUONG TRAN, former elementary and secondary language educator, former district office administrator; b. Haiphong, Vietnam, Nov. 16, 1953; came to the U.S., 1971; d. Joe (Quang) Trong Tran and Therese (Nguyet-Anh) (Do) Dotran; m. Tony (Phu) The Nguyen; children: Long Tran Nguyen, Ty Tran Nguyen. B in Liberal Studies, San Diego State U., 1976, tchg. credential grades K-12, 1977; M in Curriculum Devel., Point Loma Coll., 1984; lang. devel. specialist cert., Calif. Commn. Credentialing, 1991; PhD in Edn., Curriculum & Instrn., U. Calif. Riverside, 2004. ESL tchr. San Diego (Calif.) Job Corps, 1978-80; resource tchr. grades K-12 San Diego (Calif.) Unified Sch. Dist., 1980-82; resource tchr. SEAL project grades K-12 Long Beach (Calif.) Unified Sch. Dist., 1982-83, ESL specialist, 1983-85, 85-92, English lang. devel. tchr., chair, 1992-95; adminstr., 1996-98; sr. fellow officer U.S. Dept. Edn., Office Bilingual & Minority Lang. Affairs, Washington, 1995-96; from disting. tchr.-in-residence to asst. prof. Calif. State U., Long Beach, 1998—2004, asst. prof., 2003—. Instr. curriculum PhD Program Calif. State U., 2004. Named Outstanding Tchr. of 1994, Disney Co. Am. Tchr. Awards, Washington, 1994, Outstanding Tchr. in Fgn. Lang./ESL, Disney Co. Am. Tchr. Awards, Washington, 1994. Mem.: Pacific Am. Edn., Calif. Assn. Asian Pacific Bilingual Edn., Calif. Coun. Tchr. Edn., Am. Ednl. Rsch. Assn., Nat. Coun. Tchrs. English. Avocations: reading, travel, gardening, meditation, yoga. Office: Calif State U Coll Edn Dept Tchr Edn 1250 N Bellflower Blvd Long Beach CA 90840-0001 Office Phone: 562-985-4536. Business E-Mail: hnguye10@csulb.edu.

NGUYEN, KHANH GIA, medical educator; b. Hanoi, Vietnam, Dec. 17, 1940; arrived in Can., 1972; s. Lien Bich and Lan Chi Nguyen; m. Nga Thi Ho, Dec. 30, 1940; children: Van Thanh Nguyen-Ho, Phong Nguyen-Ho. Cert. of physics, chemistry and biology, Saigon U., 1961, MD, 1969. Diplomate Am. Bd. Pathology, Am. Bd. Pathology in Cytopathology, cert. pathologist Royal Coll. Physicians and Surgeons, Can. Asst. prof. pathology U. Sask., Saskatoon, Canada, 1978—82; pathologist Plains Health Ctr., Regina, Canada, 1978—80; pathologist, head provincial cytology lab. Pasqua Hosp., Regina, Canada, 1980—82; asst. prof. pathology U. Alta., Edmonton, Alberta, Canada, 1982—84, assoc. prof. pathology, 1984—92, prof. lab. medicine and pathology, 1992—2006, prof. emeritus lab. medicine and pathology, 2006—; pathologist U. Alta. Hosp., Edmonton, Alberta, Canada, 1982—2006, pathologist and head of electron microscopy, 1987—2000, pathologist and head of cytology, 1997—2004; pathologist BC Cancer Agy., Vancouver, Canada, 2006—. Cons. pathologist Can. Tumor Reference Ctr., Ottawa, Ontario, Canada, 1982—87. Author: Essentials of Aspiration Biopsy Cytology, 1991, Essentials of Exfoliative Cytology, 1992, Essentials of Cytology: An Atlas, 1993, Critical Issues in Cytopathology, 1996, Essentials of Lung Tumor Cytology, 2007, Essentials of Abdominal Fine-Needle Aspiration Cytology, 2007, Essentials of Head and Neck Cytology, 2009; mem. editl. bd.: Acta Cytologica Jour., 1985—2006, Vietnamese Med. Jour., 2001—06; contbr. articles to profl. jours. Accreditation com. for Can. sch. cytotechnology Can. Med. Assn., Ottawa, Ont., Canada, 1992—2000. Recipient Med. Excellency award, Vietnamese Am. Rsch. Found., Westminster, CA, USA, 2004. Fellow: Internat. Acad. Cytology (assoc.; membership com. 1989—92, editl. com. 1992—95, exam. bd. 1995—2002); mem.: European Acad. Scis., Royal Coll. Physicians and Surgeons of Can., Can. Soc. Cytology (hon.; chmn. 1984—85, sec.-treas. 1985—89), Papanicolaou Soc. Cytopathology (assoc.; member-at-large 1991—99). Achievements include research in cytopathology, pathology, patient care. Personal E-mail: khanhnguyen1730@hotmail.com. Business E-Mail: gknguyen@bccancer.bc.ca.

NGUYEN, MADISON, councilwoman; b. Vietnam; BA in History, U. Calif., Santa Cruz; M in Social Sci., U. Chgo. Assoc. ombudsperson County of Santa Clara's Office of Human Rels.; pres. Franklin-McKinley Bd. Edn.; teacher sociology and Vietnamese Am. culture De Anza Cmty. Coll., Evergreen Valley Cmty. Coll.; councilwoman, Dist. 7 San José City Coun., 2005—. Mem. cmty. adv. bd. United Way Silicon Valley; mem. Asian Am. Cmty. Adv. Coun., San Jose State U. Office: San Jose City Coun 200 E Santa Clara St 18th Fl San Jose CA 95113 Office Phone: 408-535-4907. Office Fax: 408-292-6468. Business E-Mail: District7@sanjoseca.gov.*

NGUYEN, TAI ANH, minister; Supt. Vietnamese Ministry Dist. of the Christian and Missionary Alliance, 1989. Office: 2275 W Lincoln Ave Anaheim CA 92801-6551

NGUYEN, THINH VAN, internist; b. Vietnam, Apr. 16, 1948; came to U.S., 1971; s. Thao Van and Phuong Thi (Tran) N.; m. Phi Thi Ho, Jan. 2, 1973; children: Anh-Quan, Andrew. BS, U. Saigon, 1970; MS, U. Mo., 1973; MD, U. Tex., 1982. Diplomate Am. Bd. Internal Medicine, Am. Acad. Pain Mgmt., Fed. Lic. Examination. Rsch. asst. U. Tex. Med. Sch., Dallas, 1974-78; intern U. Tex. Med. Br., Galveston, 1982-83, resident, 1983-85; internist Family Health Plan, Inc., Long Beach, Calif., 1985-88, internist, area chief, 1988-89; pvt. practice San Jose, Calif., 1990—; chmn. quality assurance/UM com. Premier Care of No. Calif. Med. Group, Inc., 1996-99, also bd. dirs.; chief medical officer Healthglobe, Inc., 2000—. Chmn. interdisciplinary com. Charter Cmty. Hosp., Hawaiian Gardens, Calif., 1988-89, San Jose Med. Ctr., 1993-2004 Fellow ACP-Am. Soc. Internal Medicine, Am. Acad. Otolaryngic Allergy (affiliate), Am. Soc. Laser Med. Surgery, 1998—; mem. AMA, Am. Acad. Pain Mgmt., Calif. Assn. Med. Dirs. (bd. dirs. 1988-92), Calif. Med. Assn., Santa Clara County Med. Assn. Office: 2470 Alvin Ave Ste 70 San Jose CA 95121-1664

NICE, CARTER, conductor; b. Jacksonville, Fla., Apr. 5, 1940; s. Clarence Carter and Elizabeth Jane (Hintermister) N.; m. Jennifer Charlotte Smith, Apr. 4, 1983; children: Danielle, Christian, Olivia. MusB, Eastman Sch. Music, 1962; MusM, Manhattan Sch. Music, 1964. Asst. condr., concert master New Orleans Philharm., 1967-79; condr., music dir. Sacramento Symphony, 1979-92; music dir., condr. Bear Valley Music Fest., 1985—. Office: 579 Kevington Ct Sacramento CA 95864 Office Phone: 916-973-1138. Personal E-mail: ccniii@aol.com.

NICHOL, ALICE J., state legislator; b. Denver, Feb. 6, 1939; m. Ron Nichol; 4 children. Grad. H.S. Ret. sch. sec.; beauty cons. Mary Kay; mem. Colo. Ho. of Reps., 1992-98, Colo. Senate, Dist. 24, Denver, 1998—. Active Tri-City Bd. Health, Grassroots Adams City Dem. Party. Democrat. Roman Catholic. Office: State Capitol 200 E Colfax Ave Ste 274 Denver CO 80203-1716 also: 891 E 71st Ave Denver CO 80229-6806 Fax: 303-287-7742.

NICHOLAS, BLAIR, lawyer; b. Mesa, Ariz., July 9, 1970; BA in Economics, U. Calif., Santa Barbara, 1992; JD, U. San Diego, 1995. Bar: Calif. 1995, US Dist. Ct., Southern Dist. Calif. 1996, US Dist. Ct., Northern Dist. Calif. 1996, US Dist. Ct., Ctrl. Dist. Calif. 1996, US Dist. Ct., Ariz., US Ct. of Appeals, Ninth Cir. 1996. Ptnr. Bernstein Litowitz Berger & Grossmann LLP, San Diego. Named one of Litigation's Rising Stars, The Am. Lawyer, 2007. Mem.: Consumer Attorneys of San Diego, Assn. Bus. Trial Lawyers, San Diego Fed. Bar Assn. (v.p.), San Diego County Bar Assn. Office: Bernstein Litowitz Berger & Grossmann LLP 12481 High Bluff Dr Ste 300 San Diego CA 92130 Office Phone: 858-793-0070. Office Fax: 858-793-0323.

NICHOLAS, HENRY THOMPSON, III, former electronics company executive; b. 1959; BSEE, MSEE, UCLA, PhD in EE. With TRW; dir. microelectronics PairGain Techs.; co-founder, pres., CEO Broadcom Corp., Irvine, Calif., 1991—2003. Recipient Engrepreneur of the Yr. award, Ernst & Young, 1996, Forbes Richest Americans, 2006; named one of Top 20 Entrepreneurs, 1997 Red Herring, 1997, World's Top Cyber Elite, 1997 Time Digital Mag., 1997.

NICHOLAS, THOMAS PETER, municipal official; b. Laramie, Wyo., Dec. 6, 1948; s. Thomas Lloyd Nicholas and Frances (Collins) Chambers; m. Tanya Michelle Villont; 1 child, Ja'el Michelle. AA in Fine Arts, Cabrillo Coll., 1970; BA in English, U. Colo., 1972; MS in Librarianship and Info. Sci., U. Denver, 1982. V.p. Nicholas Properties, Denver, 1971—77; real estate salesperson Sun Country, Lakewood, Colo., 1972—74; libr. City of Aurora, Colo., 1975—80, sys. support mgr. Colo., 1981—83, dir. libr. and TV svcs. Colo., 1984—95, dir. libr., recreation & TV svcs., 1995—2000, dir. libr., recreation and cultural svcs., 2000—. Pres. bd. Irving Libr. Network Inc., Denver, 1985; adv. CL Sys. Inc., Boston, 1985; acting pers. dir. City of Aurora. Exec. prodr. TV progs.: Election Night 85 (Franny award 1986), Miss Plumjoy's Fl., 1988 (Starwards 1988), Aurora's Can't Afford Not To, 1988 (Starwards 1988). Mem. exec. bd., chmn. Arapahoe Pub. Access to Librs., 1984-85; site coord. Am. Cancer Soc., Aurora, 1988; adv. Youth at Risk, Aurora, 1989; bd. dirs. Ctrl. Colo. Libr. Sys., Lakewood, 1985-87; mem. exec. bd. Colo. Libr. Legis. Com., Denver, 1988; pres. Greater Metro Cable Consortium, 1992; acting dep. city mgr. City of Aurora, 1993. Recipient Denver Regional Coun. Govt. award for Cmty. Svc. and Govt. Coop., 1995. Mem. ALA, Colo. Libr. Assn. (adv. 1982-83, dir. libr., recreation and TV 1995, Programming award 1982, 1st Colo. Childrens Prog. award 1983, 88), Nat. Assn. Telecom. Officers and Advs. (regional pres. 1983-84, TV Prog. award 1986), Rotary (prog. chmn. 1987-88, v.p. 1997-98), Eastgate Lions Club (pres. 1989-90), pres. elect Gatway Rotary, 1998. Democrat. Greek Orthodox. Avocations: art, poetry, auto restoration, martial arts. Office: Aurora Pub Libr 14949 E Alameda Pky Aurora CO 80012-1500 Office Phone: 303-739-6600. E-mail: library@auroragov.org.

NICHOLAS, WILLIAM RICHARD, lawyer; b. Pontiac, Mich., June 19, 1934; s. Reginald and Edna Irene (Bartlett) N.; m. Diana Lee Johnson, Aug. 20, 1960; children: Susan Lee, William Richard Jr. BS in Bus., U. Idaho, 1956; JD, U. Mich., 1962. Bar: 1963. Of counsel Latham & Watkins, Los Angeles, 1962-96. Contbr. numerous articles on taxation. Lt. (j.g.) USN, 1956-59. Mem. Calif. Bar Assn., Los Angeles County Bar Assn., Am. Coll. Tax Counsel. Home: 1808 Old Ranch Rd Los Angeles CA 90049-2207 Office: Latham Watkins 355 S Grand Ave Los Angeles CA 90071-1560 Office Phone: 310-485-1234.

NICHOLS, IRIS JEAN, retired illustrator; b. Yakima, Wash., Aug. 2, 1938; d. Charles Frederick and Velma Irene (Hacker) Beisner; (div. June 1963); children: Reid William, Amy Jo; m. David Gary Nichols, Sept. 21, 1966. BFA in Art, U. Wash., 1978. Freelance illustrator, graphic designer, Seattle, 1966—2004; med. illustrator, head dept. illustration Swedish Hosp. Med. Ctr., Seattle, 1981-86; owner, med. and sci. illustrator Art for Medicine, Seattle, 1986—2003; ret., 2003. Med. illustrator U. Wash., Seattle, 1966-67; part-time med. illustrator, graphic coord. dept. art The Mason Clinic, 1968-78; instr. advanced illustration Cornish Coll. Arts, Seattle, 1988-90; organized, coordinated and gifted the artwork of Prof. Glen E. Alps of U. Wash. after his death in 1996 Illustrator various books including Bryophytes of Pacific Northwest, 1966, Microbiology, 1973, 78, 82, 94, 98, Introduction to Human Physiology, 1980, Understanding Human Anatomy and Physiology, 1983, Human Anatomy, 1984 Regional Anesthesia, 1990, many other med. and sci. books, and children's books on various subjects; exhibited in group shows at Seattle Pacific Sci. Ctr., summer 1979, 82, Am. Coll. Surgeons (1st prize 1974), N.W. Urology Conf. (1st prize 1974, 76, 2d prize 1975); pub. illustrations Constellation Pk. and Marine Res., City Seattle Pk., 1999, Whale Tail Park, Seattle. Pres. ArtsWest (formerly West Seattle Arts Coun.), 1983; chmn. West Seattle (Wash.) H.S. Art Acquisition Com., 2003—. Named to West Seattle H.S. Alumni Hall of Fame, 1986, Matrix Table, 1986-96. Mem. Assn. Med. Illustrators (Murial McLatchie Fine Arts award 1981), Nat. Mus. Women in the Arts (Wash. state com., bd. dirs. 1987-95, pres. 1993-94), Women Painters of Wash. (pres. 1987-89), U. Wash. Alumni Assn., Lambda Rho Art Assn. (pres. alumni assn. 1995-98, treas. 2002-04) Avocations: artwork, printmaking, small books.

NICHOLS, MARY D., state official, former federal agency administrator; b. Mpls., Apr. 10, 1945; m. John F. Daum; 2 children. BA, Cornell U., 1966; JD, Yale U., 1971. Atty. Ctr. for Law in Pub. Interest, L.A., 1971—74; sec. environ. affairs State of Calif., 1974—78; chief asst. city atty. City of L.A., 1978—79; pvt. cons., 1983—88; sr. staff atty. Nat. Resources Def. Coun., L.A., 1989—93; asst. adminstr. for air & radiation EPA, Washington, 1993—97; sec. resources State of Calif., Sacramento, 1999—2003; prof.-in-residence UCLA. Chair Calif. Air Resources Bd., 1974-78, 1979-1983, 2007-; campaign mgr. TYom Bradlery for Gov. of Calif., 1985-86; bd. commissioners L.A. Dept. Water and Power; instr. U. So. Calif., UCLA; founding trustee Calif. Environ. Trust; bd. dirs. L.A. 2000 Partnership; cons. in field. Office: Calif Air Resources Bd 1001 I St PO Box 2815 Sacramento CA 95812 also: UCLA Box 951476 Los Angeles CA 90095 E-mail: nichols@law.ucla.edu.

NICHOLS, MIKE, stage and film director; b. Berlin, Nov. 6, 1931; s. Nicholaievitch and Brigitte (Landauer) Peschowsky; m. Patricia Scott, 1957 (div.); m. Margot Callas, 1974 (div.); 1 child; m. Annabel Davis-Goff (div.); 2 children; m. Diane Sawyer, Apr. 29, 1988. Student, U. Chgo., 1950-53; student acting, Lee Strasberg. Ptnr. with Elaine May in comedy act; first appeared at Playwrights Theatre Club, Compass Theatre, Chgo.; NY debut An Evening with Mike Nichols and Elaine May, 1960; acted in A Matter of Position, Phila., 1962; dir.: (plays) Barefoot in the Park, 1963 (Tony award best dir.), The Knack, 1964, Luv, 1964 (Tony award best dir.), The Odd Couple, 1965 (Tony award best dir.), The Apple Tree, 1966, The Little Foxes, 1967, Plaza Suite, 1968 (Tony award best dir.), The Prisoner of 2d Avenue, 1971 (Tony award best dir.), Uncle Vanya (co-adapted), 1973, Streamers, 1976, Comedians, 1976, The Gin Game, 1977, (LA Drama Critics award), Drink Before Dinner, 1978, Lunch Hour, 1980, Fools, 1981, The Real Thing, 1984 (Tony award 1984), Hurlyburly, 1984, Social Security, 1984, Elliot Loves, 1990, Death and the Maiden, 1992, The Play What I Wrote, 2003, Whoopi, 2004, Spamalot, 2005 (Outer Critic Cir., outstanding direction of a musical, 2005, Julia Hansen award for excellence in directing, Drama League, 2005, Tony award for best direction of a musical, 2005, Julia Hansen Award excellence in directing, The Drama League, 2005), The Country Girl, 2008; (films) Who's Afraid of Virginia Woolf?, 1966, (Academy award nomination best director 1966), The Graduate, 1967 (Academy award best director 1967), Catch-22, 1970, Carnal Knowledge, 1971, The Day of the Dolphin, 1973, The Fortune, 1975, Heartburn, 1986, Biloxi Blues, 1987, Working Girl, 1988 (Academy award nomination best director 1988), Wolf, 1994; dir., prodr.: Silkwood, 1983 (Academy award nomination best director 1983), Postcards From the Edge, 1990, Regarding Henry, 1991, The Birdcage, 1996, Primary Colors, 1998, What Planet Are You From?, 2000, Closer, 2004, Charlie Wilson's War, 2007; prodr. All the Pretty Horses, 2000; prodr.: (musical) Annie, 1977; dir., exec. prodr. (TV movies) Wit, 2001; (mini-series) Angels in America, 2003 (Emmy award Outstanding Directing for a Miniseries, Movie or Dramatic Special, 2004); performed at NY musical Pres. Johnson's Inaugural Gala, 1965.

NICHOLS, WARDE V., state legislator; b. Gilbert, Ariz., Mar. 29, 1969; m. Paula Nichols; children: Sage, Alexandria, Grant. Student, Mesa Cmty. Coll., Brigham Young U. Small bus. owner; mem. Dist. 21 Ariz. House of Reps., 2003—, chair rules com., mem. govt. com. Vol. Boy Scouts of America; campaign vol. Eddie Farnsworth for Ariz. State Rep., J.D. Hayworth for US Rep., Karen Johnson for Ariz. State Senate; bd. dirs. Never Again Found. Republican. Office: Ariz House Reps Capitol Complex 1700 W Washington Rm 306 Phoenix AZ 85007 Office Phone: 602-926-5168. Office Fax: 602-417-3021. Business E-Mail: wnichols@azleg.gov.*

NICHOLS, WILLIAM FORD, JR., foundation, health science association administrator, educator; b. Palo Alto, Calif., July 4, 1934; s. William Ford and Elizabeth (Woodyatt) N.; m. Rosemary Peterson, 1988; children: Deborah, John, Andrew. AB, Stanford U., 1956, MBA, 1958. CPA, Calif. With Price Waterhouse, San Francisco, 1958-69, Price Waterhouse & Co., Sydney, Australia, 1966; asst. contr. Saga Corp., Menlo Park, Calif., 1969-72, contr., 1972—, asst. treas., 1981-83; assoc. prof. San Jose State U., 1983-88; treas. William and Flora Hewlett Found., Menlo Park, 1985-2000. Trustee Investment Fund for Founds., 1991-2001. Bd. dirs. Lucile Packard Found. for Children's Health, Palo Alto, Calif., 1999—2006; trustee Oreg. Shakespeare Festival Endowment Fund, 2005-, chair 2009-. Mem. AICPA, Calif. Soc. CPA's, Inst. Mgmt. Accts. (nat. v.p. 1974-75, bd. dirs.), Fin. Execs. Inst. (pres. Santa Clara Valley chpt. 1979-80), Palo Alto Club, Alpha Omega Alpha (asst. treas. 1985—). Home: 620 Sand Hill Rd Apt 220-D Palo Alto CA 94304-2098

NICHOLSON, JACK, actor; b. Neptune, NJ, Apr. 22, 1937; raised by John and Ethel May N.; m. Sandra Knight, June 17, 1962 (div. Aug. 8, 1968); children: Jennifer, Lorraine Broussard. Acting debut: (Hollywood stage prodn.) Tea an Sympathy; actor: (films) Cry-Baby Killer, 1958, Studs Lonigen, 1960, Little Shop of Horrors, 1960, Ensign Pulver, 1964, The Trip, 1967, Easy Rider, 1969 (Acad. award nomination best supporting actor), Five Easy Pieces, 1970, Carnal Knowledge, 1971, A Safe Place, 1971, The Last Detail, 1974 (Cannes Film Festival prize, BAFTA award best actor), Chinatown, 1974 (BAFTA award best actor, Acad. award nomination, NY Film Critics Circle award, Golden Globe award best actor), Tommy, The Passenger, 1975, The Fortune, 1975, One Flew Over the Cuckoo's Nest, 1975 (Golden Globe award best actor, Acad. award best actor, NY Film Critics Circle award, BAFTA award best actor), The Missouri Breaks, 1976, The Last Tycoon, 1976, The Shining, 1980, The Postman Always Rings Twice, 1981, Reds, 1981 (BAFTA award best supporting actor, Acad. award nomination best supporting actor), The Border, 1982, Terms of Endearment, 1983 (Acad. award best supporting actor, Golden Globe award best actor), Prizzi's Honor, 1985, Heartburn, 1986, The Witches of Eastwick, 1987, Broadcast News, 1987, Ironweed, 1987 (Acad. award nomination best actor), Batman, 1989, Man Trouble, 1991, A Few Good Men, 1992, Hoffa, 1992, Wolf, 1994, The Crossing Guard, 1995, Mars Attacks!, 1996, The Evening Star, 1996, Blood and Wine, 1996, As Good As It Gets, 1997 (Acad. award best actor, Golden Globe award best actor, SAG award best actor), The Pledge, 2001, About Schmidt, 2002 (Acad. award nomination best actor, Golden Globe award best actor), Anger Management, 2003, Something's Gotta Give, 2003, The Departed, 2006 (MTV Movie award best villain, 2007), The Bucket List, 2007; prodr.: Head, 1968, Ride the Whirlwind, The Shooting; dir.: Drive, He Said, 1971; dir., actor: (films) Goin' South, 1978, The Two Jakes, 1990. Recipient Life Achievement award, Am. Film Inst., 1994, Cecil B. DeMille award, 1999; co-recipient (with Bobby McFerrin) Grammy award for best recording for children, 1987; named to Calif. Hall of Fame, 2008. Office: Bresler Kelly & Assocs 11500 W Olympic Blvd Ste 510 Los Angeles CA 90064-1578

NICHOLSON, JOSEPH BRUCE, real estate developer; b. San Jose, Calif., Jan. 21, 1940; s. Wilmot Joseph and Ruth (Russell) N.; m. Susan Knight, Nov. 1963 (div. 1972); children: Kelsey Erin, Craig Wilmot; m. Linda Mirassou, Aug. 1992. BArch, U. Oreg., 1963. Exec. v.p. Nicholson-Brown Inc., Santa Clara, Calif., 1967-80; prin. Nicholson Assocs., Aptos, Calif., 1977—; v.p., gen. mgr. Nicholson-Wilson Co., Santa Clara, 1980-83; prin. The Nicholson Co., Campbell, Calif., 1984—; v.p. Pacific Property Ventures Inc., Campbell, 1988—; pres. Nicholson Constrn. Inc., Campbell, 1989—; v.p. Nicholson Property Mgmt. Inc., Campbell, 1989—; pres. The Nicholson Family Found., 1996—. Bd. dirs. Transmetrics Inc., San Jose, DITZ Bros. Colo. Springs, 2008-. Bd. dirs. Triton Mus., Santa Clara, 1979, Hope Rehab. Svc., San Jose, 1979, United Way Ctrl. Area, San Jose, 1991. Devel. Engring. Rsch. Inst., Carmel, Calif., 1999—, Tannery Art Ctr., Santa Cruz, 2003—; pres. adv. bd. de Saisset Mus., Santa Clara U., 1991; trustee Mus. of Art and History, Santa Cruz, 1993; pres. Cabrillo Festival of Contemporary Music, Santa Cruz, Calif., 2000—. Lt. USN, 1963—67. Mem. Rotary, Commonwealth Club (San Francisco), Tennis Club Rio Del Mar. Republican. Avocations: travel, reading, art, painting, tennis. Home: 218 Shoreview Dr Aptos CA 95003-4621 Business E-Mail: brucenicholson@thenicholsonco.com.

NICHOLSON, MARILYN LEE, arts administrator; b. San Jose, Calif., Feb. 7, 1949; d. John Hart Nicholson and Betty Ann (Price) Shepardson; m. Neal Luit Evenhuis. BA in English and History, U. Ariz., 1972; BFA in Studio, U. Hawaii-Manoa, Honolulu, 1977, MA in English, 1977, AS, 1984. Edn. coord., dir. Bishop Mus. Arts and Crafts Sch., Honolulu, 1977-79; owner Fiber Arts Store, Kailua, Hawaii, 1978-82; field coord. Hawaii State Found. on Culture and Arts, Honolulu, 1981-85; exec. dir. Sedona (Ariz.) Arts Ctr., 1986-92, Volcano (Hawaii) Art Ctr., 1992—. Mem. bd. artist selection com. Ariz. Indian Living Treasures, 1988-92; bd. dirs., treas. Sedona Cultural Arts Ctr., 1987-92; conf. speaker Nat. Assembly Arts Agys., 1988. Founding Chmn. Sedona Gallery Assn., 1990-92; mem. com. Sedona Acad., 1986-92; mem. steering com. community plan City of Sedona, 1989-91; commr. Arts & Cultural Ctr., Sedona, 1989-91; mem. exec. com. planning Volcano Community Assn., 1993-96. Recipient Mayor's award for Disting. Svc., Sedona City Coun., 1992. Mem. Hawaii Mus. Assn. (bd. dirs. 1995-00), Cooper Ctr. Coun. (bd. dirs. 1992—), Aloha Festivals-Hawaii Island (bd. dirs. 1992-99). Office: Volcano Art Ctr PO Box 129 Volcano HI 96785

NICHOLSON, WILL FAUST, JR., bank executive; b. Colorado Springs, Colo., Feb. 8, 1929; s. Will Faust and Gladys Olivia (Burns) N.; m. Shirley Ann Baker, Nov. 26, 1955; children: Ann Louise Nicholson Naughton, Will Faust III. S.B., M.I.T., 1950; MBA, U. Denver, 1956. V.p. Van Schaack & Co., Denver, 1954-66; pntr. N. G. Petry Constrn. Co., Denver, 1966-70; sr. v.p. Colo. Nat. Bankshares, Inc., Denver, 1970-75, pres., 1975-95, chmn. bd., chief exec. officer, 1985-95; chmn. Rocky Mountain Bankcard Sys., Denver, 1995—2001. Bd. dirs. Boys and Girls Clubs of Metro Denver; active Downtown Denver, Inc., Colo. Assn. of Commerce and Industry, chmn. 1990-91, Denver Urban Renewal Authority, 1958-59, Denver Bd. Water Commrs., 1959-65, pres. 1964, 65; Nat. Western Stock Show. With USAF, 1950-53. Mem. Assn. Bank Holding Cos. (bd. dirs. 1979-87, 89-91, exec. com. 1980-85, vice chmn. 1981-82, chmn. 1983-84), US C. of C. (bd. dirs. 1990-2005, chmn. 1999-2000), US Golf Assn. (exec. com. 1974-82, v.p. 1978, 79, pres. 1980, 81), Denver Country Club, Univ. Club Colo., Univ. Club NY, Castle Pines Golf Club, Royal and Ancient Golf Club (St. Andrews, Scotland), Augusta (Ga.) Nat. Golf Club. Republican. Episcopalian. Home: 37 Polo Club Cir Denver CO 80209-3307 Office: Rocky Mountain BankCard Sys Inc PO Box 5168 Denver CO 80217-5168

NICKELL, ROBERT E., electric power industry executive; b. Reedley, Calif. s. Ernest and Selma Helen (Mullen) N.; m. Margaret Mary Harrold, July 18, 1964; children: Steven Dana, Kristen Elena. BS, U. Calif., Berkeley, 1963, MS, 1964, PhD, 1967. Mem. tech. staff Rohm & Haas Co., Huntsville, Ala., 1967-68, Bell Tel. Labs., Whippany, NJ, 1968-71, Sandia Nat. Labs., Albuquerque, 1973-77; vis. assoc. prof. Brown U., Providence, 1971-73; v.p. Pacific Tech., Del Mar, Calif., 1977-79; cons. to pres. Applied Sci. and Tech., Poway, Calif., 1978—; prog mgr. Electric Power Rsch. Inst., Palo Alto, Calif., 1980-84. Tech. dir. SGI Internat., La Jolla, Calif., 1992-95. Assoc. editor Computer Methods in Applied Mechanics and Engring; contbr. numerous articles to profl. publs. Bella Zellerbach Cross scholarship, 1962-63; recipient Structural Mechanics award ONR/AIAA, 1972; NDEA Title IX fellowship, 1964-66. Fellow ASME, AAAS; mem. ASCE, NAE, Am. Nuc. Soc., Pressure Vessel Rsch. Coun., Nat. Coal Coun., Internat. Assn. Structural Mechanics in Reactor Tech., Phi Kappa Phi, Tau Beta Pi (treas. 1962), Chi Epsilon, Sigma Xi, Upper Divsn. Honor Students Soc. Home: 2500 6th Ave Apt 204 San Diego CA 92103-6629

NICKELS, GREG, Mayor, Seattle; b. Chgo., Aug. 7, 1955; s. Bob and Kathie Nickels; m. Sharon Nickels; children: Jacob, Carey. Legis. asst. to Council member Norm Rice City of Seattle, 1979—87; mem. King County Coun., 1987—2002; mayor City of Seattle, 2002—. Chair Seattle/King County Bd. Health, 1996—2001; mem. exec. com. & bd. dirs. Dirs. of Sound Transit. Recipient First Ann. Greg Nickels award for Econ. Develop., U. Dist. Bus. Improvement Assn., 2003, First Place City Livability award, US Conf. Mayors, 2005, Charles R. Imbrecht Blue Sky Innovation award, Calstart, 2005, Nat. Conservation Achievement award, Nat. Wildlife Fedn., 2006, Edgar Wayburn award, Nat. Sierra Club award for Environ. Leadership, 2006, Climate Protection award, US EPA, 2006, Global Warming Globie awards, Environ. Def. Fund, 2007, Inaugural Visionary award, Urban League Contractor Develop. & Competitiveness Ctr., 2007, Innovations in Am. Govt. award, Harvard U. John F. Kennedy Sch. Govt., 2007, Ancil Payne Civic Leader of Yr. award, Washington CeaseFire, 2008, Energy Leadership award, Energy Efficiency Forum, 2008, Economic Develop. Pub. Sector Champion award, EnterpriseSeattle, 2009; named Local Official Yr., Nat. Assn. Home Builders, 2003, Pub. Official of Yr., Nat. Assn. Indsl. and Office Properties, 2005, Low Carbon Leader, Climate Group, 2005; named one of 25 Leaders who are fighting to stave off the planetwide catastrophe: The Pied Piper, Rolling Stone Mag., 2006. Mem.: Am. Soc. Landscape Architects (hon.). Office: Office of the Mayor Seattle City Hall 600 4th Ave 7th Fl Seattle WA 98124 also: City Hall PO Box 94749 Seattle WA 98124-4749 E-mail: gjnickels@seattle.gov.*

NICKERSON, GUY ROBERT, lumber company executive; b. Salt Lake City, May 20, 1956; s. Charles Augustus and Florence May (Fogel) N.; m. Maggie Rose McDonnell, May 30, 1992; children: Melissa Marie, Rebecca Rose. B Acctg., U. Utah, 1977, M Profl. Accountancy, 1978. CPA, Utah. Sr. mgr. Deloitte Haskins & Sells, Salt Lake City and NYC, 1978-87; v.p. fin. Anderson Lumber Co., Ogden, Utah, 1987-96, v.p. ops., 1996—2001; pvt. investor Salt Lake City, 2001—.

NICOL, ROBERT DUNCAN, architect; b. La Jolla, Calif., Sept. 16, 1936; s. Duncan and Catherine (Muffly) N.; m. Susann Kay Larson; 1 child, Jennifer E. AA, Principia Coll., 1956; BArch, U. Calif., Berkeley, 1961. Registered arch., Ariz., Calif., Mont., Wash. Designer Kawneer Mfg. Co., Richmond, Calif., 1961-62, Claude Oakland, San Francisco, 1962-64; project arch. David T. Johnson, Oakland, Calif., 1964-68; pvt. practice Oakland, Calif., 1968—. Mem. bd. appeals City of Alameda, 1971-73, vice chair planning commn., 1973-77, founder, chair, vice chair design rev. bd., 1974-80, founder, chair, vice chair hist. adv. bd., 1976—, co-founder, chair, vice chair mayor's com. for handicapped, 1980-86; mem. Calif. State Access Bd., 1995—. Recipient Design award Am. Registered Archs., 1969, Harper Plz. Design award Calif. Bldg. Ofcls. Assn., 1985. Fellow AIA; mem. Soc. Am. Registered Archs., Nat. Coun. Archtl. Registration Bds. (sr.), Alexander Graham Bell Assn. for Deaf (lectr.), Oral Hearing Impaired Sec., San Leandro Hist. Railway Soc. (founder, charter mem., chair, vice-chair), Alameda Jr. C. of C. (project dir. 1969), Alameda Victorian Preservation Soc. Republican. Home: 7440 Wild Horse Vly Rd Napa CA 94558-4071

NICOLAI, THOMAS R., lawyer; b. Frazer, Mich., Dec. 1, 1943; BA cum laude, Kalamazoo Coll., 1965; JD, U. Mich., 1970. Bar: Ill. 1972, Oreg. 1973. Fellow in Econs. U. Bonn., Germany, 1965-67; fellow Alexander von Humbolt Found. at Max Planck Inst. for Fgn. and Internat. Patent, Copyright and Unfair Competition Law, Munich, West Germany, 1970-72; ptr. Stoel Rives LLP, Portland, Oreg., 1973—. Mem. Phi Beta Kappa. Office: Stoel Rives LLP 900 SW 5th Ave Ste 2600 Portland OR 97204-1229 Office Phone: 503-224-3380. Business E-Mail: trnicolai@stoel.com.

NICOLAOU, KYRIACOS COSTA (K. C. NICOLAOU), chemistry professor; b. Karavas, Kyrenia, Cyprus, July 5, 1946; came to U.S., 1972; s. Costa and Helen (Yettimi) N.; m. Georgette Karayianni, July 15, 1973; children: Colette, Alexis, Christopher, Paul. BSc, Bedford Coll., London, 1969; PhD, U. Coll., London, 1972; DSc, U. London, 1994; D (hon.), U. Thessaloniki, 1996, U. Cyprus, 1997, U. Alcala, Madrid, 1998, U. Crete, 1998, Agrl. U. Athens, 2000, U. Patras, Greece, 2002, U. Rome, 2003. Rsch. assoc. Columbia U., NYC, 1972-73, Harvard U., Cambridge, Mass., 1973-76; from asst. prof. to Rhodes-Thompson prof. chemistry U. Pa., Phila., 1976-89; prof. chemistry U. Calif. at San Diego, La Jolla, 1989—; Darlene Shiley prof. chemistry, chmn. dept. The Scripps Rsch. Inst., La Jolla, Calif., 1989—, Aline W. & L.S. Skaggs prof., Skaggs Inst. Chem. Biology, 1996—. Vis. prof. U. Paris, 1986; mem. exec. com. Diann. Cyprus Conf. on Drug Design; mem. med. study sect. D, NIH, 1988-90; mem. internat. adv. bd. Angewandte Chemie, 1994—. Author: (with N. A. Petasis) Selenium in Natural Products Synthesis, 1984, (with E. J. Sorensen) Classics in Total Synthesis, 1996; co-editor: Synthesis, Germany, 1984-90, Chemistry and Biology, 1994; editl. bd. Prostaglandins, Leukotrienes and Medicine, 1978-88, Synthesis, 1990—, Accounts of Chem. Rsch., 1992—, Carbohydrate Letters, 1993—, Chemistry-A European Jour., 1994—, Perspectives in Drug, Discovery and Design, 1994—, Indian Jour. of Chemistry, Sect. B, 1995—; mem. bd. consulting editors Tetrahedron Publs., 1992—; mem. adv. bd. Contemporary Organic Synthesis, 1993—; mem. regional adv. bd. J. C. S. Chem. Comm., 189—, J. C. S. Perkin I, 1991—; contbr. articles to profl. jours.; patentee in field. Decorated Hon. medal Order of the Comdr., Greece, 1998; recipient Japan Soc. for Promotion Sci. award 1987-88, US Sr. Scientist award Alexander von Humboldt Found., 1987-88, Alan R. Day award Phila. Organic Chemists Club, 1993, Pfizer Rsch. award, 1993-94, Paul Janssen prize, 1994, Alexander the Great award Hellenic Cultural Soc. San Diego, 1994, Rhone-Poulenc medal Royal Soc. Chemistry, 1995, Chem. Pioneer Am. Inst. of Chemists, 1996, Inhoffen Medal of Gesellscaft fur Biotechnologische Forschung mbH (GBF) Tech. U. Braunschweig, 1996, Aspirin prize, 1999, Yamada prize, 1999, Max Tischler prize, 2000, Paul Karrer Gold medal, 2000, Schering prize, 2001, Nagoya medal, 2001, Centenary medal Royal Soc. Chemistry, 2001-02, Petrahedron prize, prize Bodossaki Found., 2004, Burkardt-Helferich prize, 2006; fellow A.P. Sloan Found., 1979-83, J. S. Guggenhiem Found., 1984; Camille and Henry Dreyfus scholar, 1980-84, Arthur C. Cope scholar, 1987. Fellow NY Acad. Scis., Am. Acad. Arts and Scis., Indian Acad. Scis. (hon.), Chem. Rsch. Soc. India (hon.); mem. Nat. Acad. Scis., Am. Chem. Soc. (Creative Work in Synthetic Organic Chemistry award 1993, William H. Nichols medal 1996, Ernest Guenther award in chemistry of natural products 1996, Linus Pauling award 1996, Esselen award for chemistry in pub. interest 1998, Nobel Laureate Signature award 2003, Auburn G.M. Kosolapoff award 2006), Chem. Soc. London, German Chem. Soc., Japanese Chem. Soc., Acad. Athens (fgn. mem.). Office: Scripps Rsch Inst Dept Chemistry 10550 N Torrey Pines Rd La Jolla CA 92037-1000 also: U Calif San Diego 9500 Gilman Dr La Jolla CA 92093

NIEDERAUER, GEORGE H., archbishop; b. LA, June 14, 1936; s. George and Elaine N. BA Philosophy, St. John's Seminary, Camarillo, CA, 1959; BA Sacred Theology, Catholic U., Washington, DC, 1962; MA English Lit., Loyola U., LA, 1962; PhD English Lit., USC, 1966. Ordained priest Archdiocese of LA, Calif., 1962; asst. pastor Our Lady of the Assumption Parish, Claremont, Calif., 1962—63; priest in residence Holy Name of Jesus Parish, Los Angeles, 1963—65; instr. English Lit. St. John's Seminary Coll., Camarillo, Calif., 1965—79; instr. of English Lit. Mt. St. Mary's Coll., Los Angeles, 1967—74; English Dept. chmn. St. John's Seminary Coll., Camarillo, 1968—77, spiritual dir., 1972—79; part-time instr. of Spiritual Theology St. John's Seminary Theologate, 1976—79, full-time instr. of Spiritual Theology, 1979—87; part-time instr. of English Lit. St. John's Seminary Coll., 1979—92; rector St. John's Seminary, 1987—92, spiritual dir., 1979—95; co-dir. Cardinal Manning House of Prayer for Priests, Los Angeles, 1992—95; ordained bishop, 1995; bishop Diocese of Salt Lake City, 1995—2005; archbishop Archdiocese of San Francisco, Calif., 2005—. Mem. Nat. Fedn. of Spiritual Dirs., pres., 1975—77; mem. bd. of the Comm. of Priests' Retreat Archdiocese L.A.; mem. select comm. for revision of U.S. Cath. Conf. "Program for Priestly Formation" 3rd edit.; mem. Vatican Visitation Team for Theologates; spkr. World Vision Internat., Fuller Theol. Sem., Calif. Lutheran Coll. Mem.: Camarillo Ministerial Assn., Western Assn. of Spiritual Dirs. (pres. 1973—75), Alpha Sigma Nu (Jesuit Honor Soc. - LMU chpt.). Roman Catholic. Avocations: classical music, stamp collecting/philately, reading, film appreciation. Office: The Roman Catholic Archdiocese of San Francisco One Peter Yorke Way San Francisco CA 94109

NIEDERMAYER, SCOTT, professional hockey player; b. Edmonton, Alta., Can., Aug. 31, 1973; m. Lisa Niedermayer; children: Logan John, Jackson Robert, Joshua Leo, Luke Scott. Defenseman NJ Devils, 1991—2005, Anaheim Ducks (formerly Mighty Ducks of Anaheim), 2005—, capt., 2005—07, 2008—. Mem. Team Can., Olympic Games, Nagano, Japan, 1998, Salt Lake City, 2002, Team Can., World Cup of Hockey, 1996, 2004. Recipient James Norris Meml. Trophy, 2004, Mark Messier Leadership Award, 2006, Conn Smythe Trophy, 2007; named to All-Rookie Team, NHL, 1993, Second All-Star Team, 1998, First All-Star Team, 2004, 2006, 2007, NHL All-Star Game, 1998, 2001, 2004, 2007, 2008, 2009. Achievements include being a member of Stanley Cup Champion New Jersey Devils, 1995, 2000, 2003, Anaheim Ducks, 2007; being a member of gold medal winning Canadian Hockey Team, Salt Lake City Olympic games, 2002; being a member of World Cup Champion Team Canada, 2004. Office: c/o Anaheim Ducks 5695 E Katella Ave Anaheim CA 92806*

NIELDS, MORGAN WESSON, medical supply company executive; b. Springfield, Mass., Jan. 25, 1946; s. Robert Littleton and Florence (Wesson) N.; m. Belinda Gammon, Aug. 14, 1968; children: William, Michael, Stefan, Morgan, Lindsey, Hunter. Cert. d'Etudes Francaises, Université de Lausanne, Switzerland, 1966; BA, Williams Coll., 1968; MBA, Dartmouth Coll., 1970. Mgr. mgmt. svcs. Graco Inc., Paris, 1970-73; chmn., chief exec. officer Fischer Imaging Corp., Denver, 1973—, also bd. dirs.; pres., chief operating officer Diasonics Inc., Milpitas, Calif., 1983-84. Bd. dirs. Scinticor, Inc., Milw., Columbia Hosp. Corp., Ft. Worth. Trustee Humana, Mountain View Hosp., Thornton, Colo., 1988-89. Mem. Nat. Elec. Mfrs. Assn. (bd. govs. 1986-87, 91—, bd. dirs. diagnostic imaging and therapy systems div. 1976-89), U.S. Ski Assn. (masters div., pres. Rocky Mountain region 1987-88). Avocations: ski racing, tennis, golf. Office: Fischer Imaging Corp 12300 N Grant St Denver CO 80241-3128

NIELSEN, GREG ROSS, lawyer; b. Provo, Utah, Sept. 24, 1947; s. Ross T. and Carma (Peterson) N.; m. Jo Rita Beer, Sept. 3, 1971; children: Jennifer, Jerilyn, Eric Michael, Brittany Anne. BA in Polit. Sci. magna cum laude, Brigham Young U., 1971; JD cum laude, Harvard U., 1975. Bar: Ariz. 1975, U.S. Dist. Ct. Ariz. 1975, U.S. Ct. Appeals (9th cir.) 1977, Utah 1990, Nev. 2003. Assoc. Snell & Wilmer, Phoenix, 1975-80, ptnr., 1981—2004, mng. ptnr. Salt Lake City, 1991—2002, adminstrv. coord. real estate practice group Phoenix, 1988-90; gen. counsel franchise fin. GE Comml. Fin., Scottsdale, Ariz., 2004—. Mem. dist. com. Theodore Roosevelt coun. Boy Scouts Am., 1988-90; trustee Utah Heritage Found., 1998-2000, Swaner Nature Preserve, 2002-04. Hinckley scholar Brigham Young U., 1970; fellow Ford Found., 1970. Mem. ABA. Republican. Mem. Lds Ch. Office: GE Comml Fin Franchise Fin 8377 E Hartford Dr Ste 200 Scottsdale AZ 85255 Home Phone: 480-290-0917; Office Phone: 480-585-2234. Business E-Mail: greg.nielsen@ge.com.

NIELSEN, JAKOB, computer interface engineer; b. Copenhagen, Oct. 5, 1957; arrived in U.S., 1990, naturalized, 2001; s. Gerhard and Helle (Hofner); m. Hannah Kain, Feb. 18, 1984. MS in Computer Sci., Aarhus U., Denmark, 1983; PhD in Computer Sci., T.U. of Denmark, 1988. Rsch. fellow Aarhus U., 1983-84; vis. scientist IBM User Interface Inst., Yorktown Heights, NY, 1985; adj. asst. prof. T.U. Denmark, Lyngby, 1986-90; mem. rsch. staff Bell Comm. Rsch., Morristown, NJ, 1990-94; disting. engr. Sun Microsystems, Mountain View, Calif., 1994-98; principal Nielsen Norman Group, Fremont, Calif., 1998—. Author: Hypertext and Hypermedia, 1990, Usability Engineering, 1993, Multimedia and Hypertext: The Internet and Beyond, 1995, Designing Web Usability: The Practice of Simplicity, 2000, Homepage Usability: 50 Websites Deconstructed, 2001, Prioritizing Web Usability, 2006, Eyetracking Web Usability, 2008; editor: Coordinating User Interfaces for Consistency, 1989, Designing User Interfaces for International Use, 1990, Usability Inspection Methods, 1994, International User Interfaces, 1996, Eyetracking Web Usability, 2007; mem. editl. bd.: Behavior and Info. Tech., 1989—, Hypermedia Jour., 1989—95, Interacting with Computers, 1989—, Internat. Jour. Human-Computer Interaction, 1989—, Internat. Jour. Man-Machine Studies, 1991—94, ACM Networker, 1997—2000, Personal Technologies, 1997—2004; contbr. articles to profl. jours. Mem.: Assn. for Computing Machinery (papers co-chair internat. conf. 1993, editl. bd. Networker 1997—2000, spl. interest group on computer human interaction). Achievements include holder 79 patents in field; founding of discount usability engineering approach; invention (with R. Molich) of heuristic evaluation method for cost-effective improvement of user interfaces; demonstration (with T.K. Landauer) that user testing and heuristic evaluation both follow same mathematical model; definition of the parallel design method for rapidly exploring user interface alternatives; patents for.

NIELSEN, JAMES WILEY, state legislator; b. Fresno, Calif., July 31, 1944; s. Woodrow E. and Geraldine P. Nielsen; m. Marilyn Nielsen; children: Prima, Brandi, Kelly, Chris. BS in Agribus., Fresno State Coll. Farm mgr., farmer; mem. Calif. State Senate, 1978; minority leader Calif. Senate, 1983—87; involved in libr. funding, edn. and welfare reform, econ. devel., rural aid, coll. support throughout Calif., 1983—; mem. Dist. 2 Calif. State Assembly, 2008—. Chmn. Sacramento Valley Water Task Force. Named Agrl. Spokesman of Yr., 1976, Legislator of Yr., Calif. Rifle and Pistol Assn., 1982, Calif. Bus. Edn. Assn., 1982, Calif. Ind. Producers Assn., 1983; Agrl. Leadership Program fellow, 1975—76. Mem.: Calif. Welfare Fraud Investigators Assn., Farm Bur., Coun. State Legislators (life), Native Sons Golden West. Republican. Baptist. Home: 4990 Country Club Dr Rohnert Park CA 94928-1404 Office: State Capitol Rm 6031 Sacramento CA 95814 Office Phone: 916-319-2002. Office Fax: 916-319-2102.

NIELSEN, KENNETH RAY, academic administrator; b. Oct. 15, 1941; s. Frank and Elinor (Hansen) N.; children: Elizabeth, Mary. BEd, U. Wis., Whitewater, 1965; MS, U. Wis., Stout, 1966; EdD, U. Wyo., 1968. Dir. student activities Cornell U., Ithaca, N.Y., 1968-72; adminstr., prof. Tchr. Tng. Coll., San Juan, P.R., 1974-77; v.p. student affairs Northland Coll., Ashland, Wis., 1972-77; v.p. student life Seattle U., 1977-84; pres. Coll. St. Mary, Omaha, 1984-96, Woodbury U., Burbank, Calif., 1996—. Bd. dirs. Boy Scouts Am., Girl Scouts U.S.A., Nat. Coun. Christians and Jews, Providence Hosp. Found.; chmn. edn. sect. United Way Bd.; mem. Gov.'s Community Svcs. and Continuing Edn. Mem. Am. Coun. Edn., Am. Assn. Higher Edn., Am. Assn. Univ. Adminstrs., Coun. Ind. Colls. Roman Catholic. Avocations: reading, exercise. Office: Woodbury U 7500 N Glenoaks Blvd Burbank CA 91504-1099

NIELSEN, LESLIE, actor; b. Regina, Sask., Can., Feb. 11, 1926; s. Ingvard and Maybelle Nielsen; m. Monica Bayar, 1950 (div. 1955); m. Sandy Ullman, 1958 (div.); children: Thea, Maura; m. Brooks Nielsen, 1981 (div. 1983). Student, Neighborhood Playhouse, NYC. Former announcer, disk jockey, Can. radio; feature films include The Vagabond King, 1956, Forbidden Planet, 1956, Ransom!, 1956, The Opposite Sex, 1956, Hot Summer Night, 1957, Tammy and the Bachelor, 1957, Night Train to Paris, 1964, Harlow, 1965, Dark Intruder, 1965, Beau Geste, 1965, Gunfight in Abilene, 1967, The Reluctant Astronaut, 1967, Rosie, 1967, Counterpoint, 1967, Dayton's Devils, 1969, How to Commit Marriage, 1969, Change of Mind, 1969, The Resurrection of Zachary Wheeler, 1971, The Poseidon Adventure, 1972, Viva, Knievel, 1977, City of Fire, 1979, Airplane!, 1980, Wrong is Right, 1982, Creepshow, 1983, Spaceship, 1983, Soul Man, 1986, The Patriot, 1986, Nuts, 1987, Nightstick, 1987, Home Is Where the Hart Is, 1987, The Naked Gun, 1988, Dangerous Curves, The Repossessed, The Naked Gun 2 1/2: The Smell of Fear, 1991, All I Want for Christmas, 1991, Surf Ninjas, 1993, The Naked Gun 33 1/3: The Final Insult, 1994, Rent-a-Kid, 1995, Dracula: Dead and Loving It, 1995, Spy Hard, 1996; Family Plan, 1997, Mr. Magoo, 1997, Wrongfully Accused, 1998, 2001: A Space Travesty, 1999, Camouflage, 2001, Kevin of the North, 2001, Men with Brooms, 2002, Scary Movie 3, 2003, Scary Movie 4, 2006, Music Within, 2007, Superhero Movie, 2008; TV films include Crime Syndicated, 1952, Man Behind The Badge, 1954, See How They Run, 1964, Shadow Over Elveron, 1968, Hawaii Five-O, 1968, Companions in Nightmare, 1968, Trial Run, 1969, Deadlock, 1969, Night Slaves, 1970, The Aquarians, 1970, Hauser's Memory, 1970, Monty Nash, 1971, They Call It Murder, 1971, Incident in San Francisco, 1972, Snatched, 1973, The Letters, 1973, Can Ellen Be Saved?, 1974, Brinks! The Great Robbery, 1976, Little Mo, 1978, miniseries Back Stairs At the White House, 1979, Institute For Revenge, 1979, Ohms, 1980, The Night The Bridge Fell Down, 1980, Murder Among Friends, 1982, Cave-In, 1983, Blade in Hong Kong, 1985, The Loner, Fatal Confession: A Father Dowling Mystery, Chance of a Lifetime, 1991, Harvey, 1996, Mr. Willowby's Christmas Tree, 1995, Safety Patrol, 1998, Santa Who?, 2000, Noël Noël, 2003; numerous other TV appearances including dramatic series Studio One, Armstrong Circle Theater, Goodyear Playhouse; TV series include The New Breed, 1961, The Bold Ones, 1963-67, Peyton Place, 1965, Bracken's World, 1969-70, Shaping Up, 1984, Police Squad, 1982, The Golden Girls, 1992, (voice) Pumper Pups, 2000, Liography, 2001, Zeroman, 2004; toured country in one man show Darrow, 1979; co-author: The Naked Truth, 1993. With Can. Air Force, WWII. Office: c/o Sandy Bresler Bresler Kelly & Assocs 11500 W Olympic Blvd #352 Los Angeles CA 90064

NIELSEN, PETE, state legislator; b. Burley, Idaho, Mar. 15, 1938; m. Connie Nielsen; 8 children. Farmer self-employed, 1970—; life & health insurance agent Beneficial Life-Blue Cross & Blue Shield, 1989—; mem. Dist. 22 Idaho House of Reps., 2008—. Dist. chmn. & county chmn. Rep. Party. Mem.: Elywhee Sugar Beet Growers Assn. (chmn. & dir.), Elywhee Growers Assn. (pres. 1970), Elmore County Nat. Farmers Org. (pres. 1970), Sugar Beet Growers Assn. (pres. 1970—80), Elywhee County Republicans (pres. & chmn. 1990). Republican. Mem. Lds Ch. Office: Capitol Annex PO Box 83720

Boise ID 83720-0054 also: 4303 SW Easy St Mountain Home ID 83647 Office Phone: 208-334-2475, 208-832-4382. Office Fax: 208-832-4013; Home Fax: 208-334-2125. Business E-Mail: pnielsen@house.idaho.gov.*

NIELSEN, TOD, information technology executive; BS, Cent. Wash. U. Various mgmt. positions Microsoft Corp., 1988—2000; CEO CrossGain (acquired by BEA Systems, Inc.), 2000—01; sr. v.p. developer programs BEA Systems, Inc., San Jose, Calif., 2001, exec. v.p. engring., chief mktg. officer, 2001—05; sr. v.p., global sales support Oracle Corp., Redwood Shores, Calif., 2005; pres., CEO Borland Software Corp., Cupertino, Calif., 2005—. Office: Borland Software Corp 20450 Stevens Creek Blvd Ste 800 Cupertino CA 95014 Office Phone: 800-817-4BEA, 408-570-8000, 408-863-2800. Office Fax: 408-570-8901.

NIELSEN, WILLIAM FREMMING, federal judge; b. 1934; BA, U. Wash., 1956, LLB, 1963. Law clk. to Hon. Charles L. Powell U.S. Dist. Ct. (ea. dist.) Wash., 1963-64; mem. firm Paine, Hamblen, Coffin, Brooke & Miller, 1964-91; judge to chief judge U.S. Dist. Ct. (ea. dist.) Wash., Spokane, 1991—. Lt. col. USAFR. Fellow Am. Coll. Trial Lawyers; mem. ABA, Wash. State Bar Assn., Spokane County Bar Assn. (pres. 1981-82), Fed. Bar Assn. (pres. 1988), Spokane County Legal Svcs. Corp. (past pres.), Lawyer Pilot Bar Assn., Assn. Trial Lawyers Am., Wash. State Trial Lawyers Assn., Assn. Def. Trial Attys., Am. Inns of Ct., Charles L. Powell Inn (pres. 1987), The Spokane Club, Rotary, Alpha Delta Phi, Phi Delta Phi. Office: US Dist Ct PO Box 2208 920 W Riverside Ave 9th Fl Spokane WA 99210-2208

NIELSON, THEO GILBERT, protective services official, university official; b. Roosevelt, Utah, June 29, 1938; s. John Gilbert and Mazie (Alexander) N.; m. Martha Perez, May 22, 1961; children: Lucille Marie, Sherry Lou, Mark Andrew, Rex Alexander, Theo Gilbert Jr., Cristal Ina, Gregory Angus, Mazie Leah, Rosanna Alma. Grad., FBI Nat. Acad., 1970; BA, Ariz. State U., 1975, MS, 1977. Officer Univ. Police, Ariz. State U., Tempe, 1963-67, sgt., 1967-70, lt., 1970-79; chief police Douglas (Ariz.) Police Dept., 1979-82; div. adminstr. Ariz. Criminal Intelligence Systems Agy., Tucson, 1982-84; dir. campus safety and security No. Ariz. U., Flagstaff, 1984-92; chief of capitol police Ariz. Dept. Adminstrn., Phoenix, 1992—2001, ret., 2001. Ordinance worker LDS Temple, Mesa, Ariz. Mem. Am. Soc. for Indsl. Security (chmn. No. Ariz. chpt. 1987), Internat. Assn. Chiefs Police, Internat. Assn. Campus Law Enforcement Adminstrs., Ariz. Assn. Campus Law Enforcement (pres. 1989-90). Republican. Mem. Lds Ch. Avocations: genealogy, hiking. Home: 3335 E Hampton Ave Mesa AZ 85204-6410 E-mail: budnielson@mstar2.net.

NIEMI, JANICE, retired lawyer, state legislator, judge; b. Flint, Mich., Sept. 18, 1928; d. Richard Jesse and Norma (Bell) Bailey; m. Preston Niemi, Feb. 4, 1953 (div. 1987); children: Ries, Patricia. BA, U. Wash., 1950, LLB, 1967; postgrad., U. Mich., 1950-52; cert., Hague Acad. Internat. Law, The Netherlands, 1954. Bar: Wash. 1968. Assoc. firm Powell, Livengood, Dunlap & Silverdale, Kirkland, Wash., 1968; staff atty. Legal Svc. Ctr., Seattle, 1968-70; judge Seattle Dist. Ct., 1971-72, King County Superior Ct., Seattle, 1973-78; acting gen. counsel, dep. gen. counsel SBA, Washington, 1979-81; mem. Wash. State Ho. of Reps., Olympia, 1983-87, chmn. com. on state govt., 1984; mem. Wash. State Senate, 1987-95; sole practice Seattle, 1981-94; superior ct. judge King County, 1995-2000; chief criminal judge, 1997-2000; ret., 2000; mem. Wash. State Gambling Commn., 2002—08. Mem. White Ho. Fellows Regional Selection Panel, Seattle, 1974—77, chmn., 1976, 77; incorporator Soudn Savs. & Loan, Seattle, 1975. Bd. visitors dept. psychology U. Wash., Seattle, 1983—87, bd. visitors dept. sociology, 1988—98; mem. adv. bd. Tacoma Art Mus., 2008—; mem. Wash. State Gender and Justice Commn., 1987—89; Bd. dirs. Allied Arts, Seattle, 1971—78, Ctr. Contemporary Art, Seattle, 1981—83, Women's Network, Seattle, 1981—84, Pub. Defender Assn., Seattle, 1982—84, Artist's Trust, 2002—05. Named Woman of Yr. in Law, Past Pres.'s Assn., Seattle, 1971, Woman of Yr., Matrix Table, Seattle, 1973, Capitol Hill Bus. and Profl. Women, 1975. Mem. Wash. State Bar Assn., Wash. Women Lawyers, Am. Arbitration Assn. (panel 2003—). Democrat. Home: PO Box 20516 Seattle WA 98102-1516 Personal E-mail: janicen@aol.com.

NIJHUIS, MICHELLE, freelance journalist; BA, Reed Coll., Portland, Oreg., 1996. Biol. tech. US Geo. Survey, 1994—97; staff reporter High Country News, 1998—99, sr. editor/assoc. editor, 1999—2001, contributing editor, 2003—; corr. Orion mag.; freelance writer, 2001—. Recipient John M. Collier award for Journalism in Forest and Conservation History, 2005, Best Profile award, American Soc. Journalists and Authors, 2006, Walter Sullivan award for Excellence in Sci. Journalism, Am. Geophys. Union, 2006, AAAS Sci. Journalism award (small newspaper), 2006. Mem.: Phi Beta Kappa.

NIJINSKY, TAMARA, actress, puppeteer, author, librarian, educator; b. Vienna; arrived in U.S., 1961; d. Waslaw and Romola (de Pulszky) Nijinsky; widowed; 1 child, Kinga Maria Szakats-Gaspers. Student, Europe; postgrad. studies in U.S. Mem., actress Nat. Theater of Budapest; owner, tchr. Tamara Nijinsky Performing Art Studio, Montreal; tchr. speech/drama, French and German, libr. Cath. H.S., Phoenix; founder, exec. dir. Waslaw and Romola Nijinsky Found., Inc., 1991—. Lectr. in field. Author: Nijinsky and Romola, 1991. Decorated chevalier de l'Ordre des Arts et des Lettres, officier de l'Ordre des Arts et des Lettres (France); recipient Nijinsky medal, Pagart, Poland, Polish Order of Arts and Letters, 1997, La Medaille Vermeil de Paris, 2000. Roman Catholic. Avocations: reading, computer, swimming. Office: Nijinsky Foundation Inc PO Box # 15981 Phoenix AZ 85060-5981 Office Phone: 602-840-9605.

NIKAIDO, HIROSHI, microbiologist; b. Tokyo, Mar. 26, 1932; arrived in U.S., 1962; s. Tatsuya and Ryo Nikaido; m. Kishiko Jokura, Mar. 11, 1963; children: Michio, George. MD, Keio U., Tokyo, 1955, D in Med. Sci., 1961. Assoc. bacteriology Harvard Med. Sch., Boston, 1963-64, asst. prof., 1965-69; assoc. prof. U. Calif., Berkeley, 1969-71, prof., 1971—. Sci. adv. Essential Therapeutics, Mountain View, Calif., 1992—2002. Co-author: Microbial Biotechnology, 1995, 2nd edit., 2007; contbr. articles to profl. jours. Recipient Paul Ehrlich award, Paul Ehrlich Found., 1969, Freedom to Discover Achievement award, Bristol-Myers Squibb, 2004. Fellow: Am. Acad. Microbiology; mem.: Am. Acad. Arts and Scis., Am. Soc. Biochemistry and Molecular Biology, Am. Soc. Microbiology (editor Jour. Bacteriology 1998—2002, Hoechst-Roussel award 1984).

NIKIAS, CHRYSOSTOMOS L. (MAX NIKIAS), engineering educator; b. Cyprus, Greece; arrived in US, 1979; m. Niki Nikias. Diploma in elec. and mech. engring., Nat. Tech. U., Athens, Greece, 1977; MS in elec. engring., SUNY, Buffalo, 1980, PhD in elec. engring., 1982; PhD (hon.), U. Cyprus, 2000. Prof. elec. and computer engring. U. Conn., Northeastern U.; prof. elec. engring.-systems U. So. Calif., 1991—, assoc. dean engring., 1992—2001, founding dir. Integrated Media Systems Ctr., 1996—2001, dean Andrew and Erna Viterbi Sch. Engring., 2001—05, Zohrab A. Kaprielian Chair in Engring., provost, sch. engring., sr. v.p. academic affairs, 2005—. Bd. dirs. Lord Found., Calif., Alfred Mann Inst. Biomedical Engring. Bd. trustees Chadwick Sch., Palos Verde Peninsula, Calif. Recipient Outstanding Tchr. Award, Nat. Technol. U., 1993. Fellow: Calif. Coun. on Sci. and Tech., IEEE (Signal Processing Best Paper Award 1988, Fred W. Ellersick Award of Outstanding Unclassified Paper at Mil. Comm. 1992, AH Reeves Premium Award 2002, Simon Ramo medal 2008); mem.: Russian Acad. Nat. Sci. (fgn. mem.), Phi Kappa Phi. Office: U So Calif Sch Engring Office of the Dean Los Angeles CA 90089-1450

NIKKEL, B.J., state legislator; m. Phil Nikkel; children: Jonathan, Christopher. Dist. dir., Rep. Marilyn Musgrave US House of Reps., Colo.; pub. rels. cons.; sr. devel. dir. Nat. Guard Assn. Colo.; mem. Dist. 49 Colo. House of Reps., Denver, 2009—. Mem. State Commn. on Jud. Performance, Colo. Editl. columnist: Fort Collins Coloradoan. Del. Rep. National Convention, NYC, 2004; mem. Larimer County Youth Services Adv. Bd. Republican. Office: Colo State Capitol 200 E Colfax Rm 271 Denver CO 80203 Office Phone: 303-866-2907. Business E-Mail: rep.nikkel@gmail.com.*

NILES, JOHN GILBERT, lawyer; b. Dallas, Oct. 5, 1943; s. Paul Dickerman and Nedra Mary (Arendts) N.; m. Marian Higginbotham, Nov. 21, 1970; children: Paul Breckenridge, Matthew Higginbotham. BA in History, Stanford U., 1965; LLB, U. Tex., 1968. Bar: Tex. 1968, Calif. 1969, U.S. Dist. Ct. (cen. dist.) Calif. 1973, U.S. Ct. Appeals (9th cir.) 1973, U.S. Dist. Ct. (so. dist.) Calif. 1977, U.S. Supreme Ct. 1979, U.S. Dist. Ct. (no. dist.) Calif. 1983. Assoc. O'Melveny & Myers, Los Angeles, 1973-77, ptnr., 1978-99; of counsel, 1999—. Judge pro tem mcpl. ct. L.A.; spkr., panel mem. Practicing Law Inst., Calif. C.E.B. Served to lt. comdr. USNR, 1968-72, Vietnam. Mem. ABA, Los Angeles County Bar Assn., Am. Judicature Soc. Clubs: Bel-Air Bay (Pacific Palisades, Calif.); Calif. (Los Angeles). Avocation: sailing. Home: 1257 Villa Woods Dr Pacific Palisades CA 90272-3953 Office: O'Melveny & Myers 400 S Hope St Los Angeles CA 90071-2899 Office Phone: 213-430-6050.

NILSSON, A. KENNETH, investor; b. LA, Mar. 16, 1933; s. Arthur V. and Esther (Dean) N.; m. Lesley Swanson, Sept., 1965; children: Kerstin, Keith. BA, U. So. Calif., 1955; MA, U. Calif., 1960; grad., U.S. Defense Language Inst., 1956. Founder Koken, Ltd., Tokyo, 1960-63; mng. dir. Pfizer Internat., Tokyo, 1963-66; pres. Pfizer Inc., Manila, The Philippines, 1966-68, Max Factor & Co. Japan Ltd., Tokyo, 1968-72, Cooper Labs Internat., Inc., Geneva and Brussels, 1972-80, Cooper Labs, Inc., NYC and Palo Alto, Calif., 1980-85, Cooper Lasersonics, Inc., Palo Alto, 1982-85; dir. Monterey County Bank, Monterey, Calif., 1982-86; vice chmn. The Cooper Cos., 1986-89; chmn. Eureka Group, Monterey, 1989—. Chmn. Monterey Inst. Internat. Studies, 1983-99; dir. U.S. China Indsl. Exch., 1996—, Calif. State Automobile Assn., 2000—. Contbr. articles to profl. jours. Mem. Coun. on Foreign Rels., World Affairs Coun., Pacific Coun. on Internat. Policy. 1st lt. U.S. Army, 1955-58. Fellow Am. Soc. Laser Medicine, Internat. Inst. Stragetic Studies. Avocations: languages, literature.

NIMNI, MARCEL EPHRAIM, biochemistry educator; b. Buenos Aires, Feb. 1, 1931; came to U.S., 1955; s. Sam and Sarah Dora (Freedman) N.; children: Elizabeth, Brian Sam; m. Fabiola Cordoba, Dec. 21, 1996. BS in Pharmacy, U. Buenos Aires, 1954, PhD, 1960; MS, U. So. Calif., 1957; MD honoris causae (hon.), Maimonides U., 2002. Cert. nutrition specialist. Rsch. fellow U. So. Calif., LA, 1960-61, asst. prof. biochemistry, 1963-66, assoc. prof., 1966-72, prof., 1972—, prof. surgery, 1990—, prof. orthop., 1980—; dir. biology Don Baxter Labs., Glendale, Calif., 1962. Cons. Hancock Labs., Glendale, Calif., 1962; cons. Hancock Labs., Anaheim, Calif., 1970-78, pathobiochemistry study sect. NIH, 1980-85, orthopaedics and biomechanics study sect., 1987-90; mem. NASA Tissue Engring. Rev. Bd., 2002—; dir. biochemistry rsch. Orthopaedic Hosp., L.A., 1980-91; cons. Tillots Pharma Labs., Basle, Switzerland, 1986-94; dir. surg. rsch. Chidlren's Hosp. of L.A., 1991-98, dir. Tissue Engring. Lab., 1998—; mem. adv. bd. Maimonides U., Buenos Aires. Editor: Collagen: Biochemistry, Biotechnology and Molecular Biology, Vols. I-V,1987-91; editor Matrix, 1980-93, Connective Tissue Rsch., 1973-91, Jour. Orthopaedic Rsch., 1989-94; patentee collagen tech., transderman drug delivery. Recipient Merit award NIH, 1987; rsch. grantee NIH Arthritis Inst., 1966-94, NIH Aging Inst., 1982-2000. Fellow AAAS, Am. Coll. Nutrition, Soc. Biomaterials (Founders award 1986); mem. Am. Inst. Nutrition, Am. Assn. Biochem. and Molecular Biology. Office: Univ So Calif EDM-191 Keck Sch Medicine Los Angeles CA 90033 Office Phone: 323-224-5067. Personal E-mail: nimni007@aol.com.

NINOW, KEVIN J., chemicals executive; With Huntsman Corp., Salt Lake City, 1989—, project engr., process control group leader, mgr. tech., ops. mgr. C4's; plant mgr. C4's; plant mgr. oxides and olefins Huntsman Corp., v.p. internat. mfg., v.p. European Petrochemicals, sr. v.p. European Petrochemicals, 1999—2003, divsn. pres. base chems. and polymers, 2003—. Office: Huntsman Corp 500 Huntsman Way Salt Lake City UT 84108 Office Phone: 801-584-5700.

NISBET, TOMA A., nursing administrator; Diploma with honors, St. Mark's Hosp. Sch. Nursing, 1967; BSN with honors, No. Ill. U., 1969, MSN with honors, 1973. Internship Winnebago County Dept. Pub. Health-Health Adminstrn. & Family Planning; night staff nurse Sycamore Municipal Hosp., Ill., 1967-68; evening relief supr., charge nurse DeKalb County Nursing Home, Ill., 1969; pub. health nurse DeKalb County Health Dept., Ill., 1969-71; divsn. dir. nursing svcs. Winnebago County Dept. Pub. Health, Rockford, Ill., 1974-84; pub. dir. nursing svcs. divsn. of health & med. svcs. State of Wyo., Cheyenne, 1985-87, policy devel. & spl. projects state program mgr. divsn. of health & med. svcs., 1987-88, state bd. nursing exec., 1988—. Spokesperson for NLX D-A-Y Pub. Rels. for Burroughs Welcome, N.Y.C., 1987; project coord. for health svcs. No. Ill. U. Sch. Nursing, DeKalb, 1973-74, instr. 1979-84. Author of numerous articles. Awarded numerous rsch. grants. Mem. ANA, Nat. Coun. State Bds. of Nursing (del. 1988-95, AEC com. mem. 1990-94, mem. nomination com. 1991-92, ednl. program task force 1994-95, alternate examination com. 1994-95), Wyo. Commn. on Nursing & Nursing Edn., Wyo. Orgn. Nurse Execs., Wyo. State Bd. of Nursing Home Adminstrs. (sec. 1988-89, vice-chmn. 1990-95), Wyo. Advanced Practitioner of Nursing Orgn.

NISE, NORMAN S., engineering educator; m. Ellen L. Becker, June 4, 1961; children: Benjamin E., Alan H., Sharon L. Miller. BSEE, Drexel U., Phila., 1960; MSEE, Lehigh U., Bethlehem, Pa., 1962. Mem. tech. staff Hughes Aircraft Co., Fullerton, Calif., 1961—70, Rockwell Internat., Downey, Calif., 1980—93; prof. emeritus Calif. State Poly. U., Pomona, 1963—. Author: (book) Control Systems Engineering. Mem.: IEEE, ASEE, Eta Kappa Nu, Tau Beta Pi, Tau Epsilon Phi. Office: Calif State Polytechnic Univ 3801 W Temple Ave Pomona CA 91768 Office Fax: 909-869-4687. Business E-Mail: nsnise@csupomona.edu.

NISHIMURA, PETE HIDEO, oral surgeon; b. Hilo, Hawaii, Aug. 7, 1922; s. Hideichi and Satsuki N.; m. Tomoe Nishimura, June, 1949; children— Dennis Dean, Grant Neil, Dawn Naomi. Student, U. Hawaii, 1940-44; D.D.S., U. Mo., 1947; MSD., Northwestern U., 1949. Practice dentistry specializing in oral surgery, Honolulu, 1952—; pres. Oral Surgery Group, 1978—. Mem. coun. Nat. Bd. Dental Examination; dir. Hawaii Dental Svc., 1962-85, pres., 1970-72, 76-78; pres. State Bd. Dental Examiners, Delta Sigma Delta, Fedn. Dentaire Internat. Served with U.S. Army, 1952-54. Recipient Citation for outstanding pub. svc. toward the devel. of state plan for emergency mgmt. resources, Dir. Emergency Planning, Exec. Office of Pres. of U.S., 1968, Lifetime Achievement award, Hawaii Dental Assn.; named Disting. Alumni, U. Mo. Hawaii, 2004. Fellow Am. Coll. Dentists, Internat. Coll. Dentists; mem. ADA, Hawaii Dental Assn. (past pres., Lifetime Achievement award 2006), Delta Dental Plans Assn. (dir.), Honolulu County Dental Soc., Hawaii Soc. Oral Surgeons, Am. Assn. Oral and Maxillofacial Surgeons, Western Soc. Oral and Maxillofacial Surgeons, Am. Assn. Dental Examiners, Pierre Fauchard Acad. (citation for oustanding contbn. to arts and sci. of dentistry 1987). Democrat. Home: Apt 606 4389 Malia St Honolulu HI 96821 Office: 848 S Beretania St Honolulu HI 96813-2551 Personal E-mail: hilopete@aol.com.

NISSENSON, ALLEN RICHARD, physician, educator; b. Chgo., Dec. 10, 1946; s. Harry and Sylvia Lillian (Chapnitsky) N.; m. Charna H. Karp, May 28, 1978; 1 child, Ariel Rose. BS in Medicine, Northwestern U., 1967, MD, 1971. Diplomate Am. Bd. Internal Medicine, bd. cert. internal medicine and nephrology. Intern in medicine Michael Reese Hosp. and Med. Ctr., Chgo., 1971-72, resident in internal medicine, 1972-74; fellowship in nephrology Northwestern U., Chgo., 1974-76; assoc. medicine Northwestern U. Med. Sch., Chgo., 1976-77; asst. prof. medicine UCLA Sch. Medicine, 1977-82, assoc. prof. medicine, 1982-88, prof. medicine, 1988—; dir. dialysis program UCLA Ctr. for the Health Scis., 1977—, med. dir. renal mgmt. strategies, assoc. dean David Geffen Sch. Medicine, 2006—. Adj. attending physician Northwestern Meml. Hosp., Chgo., 1976-77; asst. attending physician UCLA Ctr. for Health Scis., 1977-82, assoc. attending physician, 1988—; attending physician nephrology Wadsworth VA Hosp., 1978—; cons. on peritoneal dialysis Baxter-Travenol Labs., 1981—; mem. nephrology adv. com. Nephrology Nursing Edn. Grant, Calif. State U., 1983-90; vice chmn. Forum of End Stage Renal Disease Networks, 1988-91; mem. sci. adv. bd. Nat. Kidney Found., 1989-91, chmn. coun. on clin. nephrology, dialysis and transplantation, 1989-91; cons. on End Stage Renal Disease reimbursement Rand Corp., 1990—, others. Editor-in-chief Advances in Renal Replacement Therapy, 1993—, Hemodialysis Internat., 2004—, Medscape Nephrology, 2006; mem. editl. bd. Dialysis and Transplantation, 1978—, UCLA Health Insights, 1981-89, Perspectives in Peritoneal Dialysis, 1983—, Internat. Jour. Artificial Organs, 1984—, Seminars in Dialysis, 1987—, Am. Jour. Nephrology, 1989—, Am. Jour. Kidney Diseases, 1989—, Geriat. Nephrology and Urology Jour., 1989—; mem. editl. adv. bd. Contemporary Dialysis, 1983—, Nephrology Practice Today, 1989—, Hematopoietic Therapy Index and Revs., 1993—, Primary Care Reports, 1994—; editl. cons. Am. Jour. Nephrology, 1981-88; contbr. chpts. to books, abstracts and articles to profl. publs. Recipient Nat. Kidney Found. So. Calif. Cmty. Svc. award, 1981, Pres.'s award Nat. Kidney Found., 1998, Lifetime Achievement award in hemodialysis U. Mo., 2007; Robert Wood Johnson policy fellow Office of Sen. Paul Wellstone, 1994-95. Fellow ACP; mem. Am. Soc. for Artifical Internal Organs, Am. Fedn. for Clin. Rsch., Am. Soc. Nephrology, Internat. Soc. Nephrology, Internat. Soc. Artificial Organs, Western Soc. for Clin. Investigation, European Dialysis and Transplant Assn., N.Am. Soc. for Dialysis and Transplantation, Renal Physicians' Assn. (bd. dirs. 1993—, sec. bd. dirs. 1994—, pres. 1999-2001), Calif. Renal Physicians (bd. dirs. 1987—). Office: UCLA Med Ctr Dialysis Ctr Ste 565-59 200 Medical Plaza Los Angeles CA 90024-6945 Office Phone: 310-536-2549. E-mail: anissenson@mednet.ucla.edu.

NISSLY, KENNETH L., lawyer; b. Mesa, Ariz., Oct. 25, 1952; m. Marjorie J. Nissly, Aug. 17, 1974; children: Jennifer, Peter. BA, San Diego State U., 1974; JD, U. Calif., San Francisco, 1977. Bar: Calif. 1977, US Dist. Ct. (No. Dist.) Calif., US Dist. Ct. (Ea. Dist.) Calif., US Ct. Appeals (9th Cir.), US Dist. Ct. (Ea. Dist.) Tex., US Dist. Ct. (Ea. Dist.) Va., US Dist. Ct. (Dist. Del.), US Ct. Appeals (Fed. Cir.). Assoc. Thelen, Marrin, Johnson & Bridges, San Jose, Calif., 1977-85, ptnr., 1985—98; ptnr., litig. dept. Thelen Reid & Priest LLP, 1998—, mng. ptnr. Silicon Valley office. Mem.: Calif. State Bar Assn., Santa Clara County Bar Assn. (judge pro tem neighborhood small claims ct. program 1985—), ABA, Order of Coif, Phi Beta Kappa. Avocation: flying. Office: Thelen Reid & Priest LLP 225 W Santa Clara St Ste 1200 San Jose CA 95113-1723 Office Phone: 408-292-5800. Office Fax: 408-287-8040. Business E-Mail: kennissly@thelenreid.com.

NISWENDER, GORDON DEAN, physiologist, educator; b. Gillette, Wyo., Apr. 21, 1940; s. Rex Lel and Inez Irene (Dillinger) N.; m. Joy Dean Thayer, June 14, 1964; children: Kevin Dean, Kory Dean. BS, U. Wyo., 1962; MS, U. Nebr., 1964; PhD, U. Ill., 1967. NIH postdoctoral fellow U. Mich., 1967-68, asst. prof. physiology, 1968-72; mem. faculty Colo. State U., Ft. Collins, 1972—, prof. physiology, 1975—; assoc. dean research Coll. Veterinary Medicine and Biomed. Scis., 1982-95, dir. animal reproduction and biotech. lab., 1986—, disting. prof., 1987—. Mem. rev. panels NIH; cons. FDA. Recipient Merit award NIH, 1988-99, grantee, 1968—. Mem.: Soc. Study Reprodn. (treas. 1972-75, pres. 1981-82, editor-in-chief Biology of Reprodn. 1995—99, Rsch. award 1988, Disting. Svc. award, 2001), Am. Assn. Animal Scientists (Outstanding Young Scientist award western sect., 1974, animal Physiology and Endocrinology award 1983). Office: Colo State U Animal Reprod & Biotech Lab College Of Veterinary Med Fort Collins CO 80523-1683

NITTA, JEFFREY W., real estate executive; V.p. Weyerhaeuser Real Estate Co., Tacoma, 1997—. Office: Weyerhaeuser PO Box 9777 Federal Way WA 98063-9777

NIX, NANCY JEAN, librarian, designer; b. Denver; d. James Frederik and Josephine (Britt) N. AB in History, U. So. Calif., LA, 1959, MLS, 1960; prof. 1st level, Ikenobo Ikebana, LA. Group shows including Ikenobo Ikebana Hist. Flower Arrangement Exhibit, Japanese Am. Cultural Ctr., 1992, 97, Invitational Iemoto Floral Design Exhibit, Lakewood, Calif., 2002. Cons. libr. Inner City Cultural Ctr., L.A., 1971; mem. guiding com. Art Assn. Egg and the Eye Gallery, 1973-76; participant Arts Humanities Symposium, Palm Desert, Calif., 1974; patron Cultural Symposium LA Garden Club, 1975. Recipient Kakan Monpyo award Ikenobo Ikebana Soc. Floral Art, 1988; com. org. 5th Teen Comic Arts Festival, LA, 2002. Mem. Ikebana Internat. (bd. dirs. LA chpt. 1972-1982, mem. chmn. 1980-82), Japanese Am. Citizens League (exec. bd. LA Downtown chpt. 1990—, chpt. historian), Japanese Am. Nat. Mus. (charter, del. participant Japanese Am. Nat. Mus. Conf. 1993), Japanese Am. Cultural and Cmty. Ctr, LA Nisei (Woman of Yr. selection com. 1990—) Republican. Jewish.

NIXON, CAROL HOLLADAY, retired park and recreation director; b. Salt Lake City, Dec. 25, 1937; m. William L. Nixon; children: William H., Joan, Michael, Jennifer, Jacqueline, John. From dep. chief of staff to chief of staff to gov. State of Utah, Salt Lake City, 1991-93, dir. Cmty. Devel. Divsn., 1993-96; pres., CEO This Is the Place Heritage Park, Salt Lake City, 1996—2001, ret., 2001. Fax: 801-584-8325.

NIXON, CYNTHIA, actress; b. NYC, Apr. 9, 1966; d. Walter and Anne Nixon; children: Samantha Mozes, Charles Ezekiel Mozes. BA in English, Barnard Coll., 1988. Founding member The Drama Dept., 1996. Actor: (plays) The Philadelphia Story, 1980 (Theatre World Award, 1981), The Real Thing, 1984, Hurly Burly, 1984, Indiscretions, 1996 (Tony Award nom., 1996, Tony award, best performance by leading actress in a play, 2006), Rabbit Hole, 2006, The Prime of Miss Jean Brodie, 2006; (films) Little Darlings, 1980, Prince of the City, 1981, Tattoo, 1981, I Am the Cheese, 1983, Amadeus, 1984, The Manhattan Project, 1986, O.C. and Stiggs, 1987, Let It Ride, 1989, Through an Open Window, 1992, The Pelican Brief, 1993, Addams Family Values, 1993, Baby's Day Out, 1994, The Cottonwood, 1996, 'M' Word, 1996, Marvin's Room, 1996, Advice From a Caterpillar, 1999, The Out-of-Towners, 1999, Igby Goes Down, 2002, The Paper Mache Chase, 2003, Sex and the City: The Movie, 2008; (TV series) Sex and the City, 1998—2004 (Emmy nom. for Outstanding Supporting Actress in a comedy series, 2002, Emmy award Outstanding Supporting Actress in a Comedy Series, 2004); (TV miniseries) Tanner '88, 1988; (TV films) The Seven Wishes of a Rich Kid, 1979, The Private History of a Campaign That Failed, 1981, Rascals and Robbers: The Secret Adventures of Tom Sawyer and Huck Finn, 1982, My Body, My Child, 1982, Fifth of July, 1982, The Murder of Mary Phagan, 1988, Women & Wallace, 1990, Love She Sought, The, 1990, Face of a Stranger, 1991, Love, Lies and Murder, 1991, Kiss-Kiss, Dahlings!, 1992, Sex and the Matrix, 2000, Papa's Angels, 2000, Stage on Screen: The Women, 2002, Tanner on Tanner, 2004, Warm Springs, 2005. Office: c/o William Morris Agy One William Morris Place Beverly Hills CA 90212

NOBE, KEN, chemical engineering professor; b. Berkeley, Calif., Aug. 26, 1925; s. Sidney and Kiyo (Uyeyama) N.; m. Mary Tagami, Aug. 31, 1957; children: Steven Andrew, Keven Gibbs, Brian Kelvin. BS, U. Calif., Berkeley, 1951; PhD, UCLA, 1956. Jr. chem. engr. Air Reduction Co., Murray Hill, NJ, 1951-52; instr. engring. UCLA, 1955—57, asst. prof. chem. engring., 1957-62, assoc. prof., 1962-68, prof., 1968—2004, prof. emeritus, 2004—, chmn. dept. chem., nuclear and thermal engring., 1978-83, founding chmn. chem. engring., 1983-84. Mem. tech. staff Ramo-Wooldridge Corp., El Segundo, Calif., 1958-59 Div. editor: Jour. Electrochem. Soc, 1967-91, Electrochimica Acta, 1977-85 With US Army, 1944—46. Recipient Disting. Tchg. award, UCLA, 1962. Mem. Electrochem. Soc. (Henry B. Linford award 1992), Am. Chem. Soc., Internat. Soc. Electrochemistry, Am. Electroplaters Surfacing Fin. Soc. (Abner Brenner Gold medal 2000), Sigma Xi. Office: UCLA Dept Chemical Engring Los Angeles CA 90095-1592 Business E-Mail: nobe@seas.ucla.edu.

NOBERT, FRANCES, music educator; b. Winston-Salem, NC, Dec. 12, 1936; d. Henry Carrington and Frances Mozelle (Harrison) Cuningham; m. Jon Marshall Nobert (div. Jan. 1980). BM in Music Edn., Salem Coll., 1959; Fulbright Cert. in Organ, Conservatory of Music, Frankfurt am Main, Germany, 1961; MM in Organ, Syracuse U., 1963; DMA in Choral Music, U. So. Calif., 1980. Organist, choir dir. United Ch., Fayetteville, N.Y., 1961-67; choral, gen. music tchr. Fayetteville Manlius Sch. Dist., 1963-67; vocal music tchr. U.S. Grant HS, Van Nuys, Calif., 1967-80; organist United Ch. Christ Congregational, Claremont, Calif., 1981-83; organist, choir dir. St. Matthias Episc. Ch., Whittier, Calif., 1983-94; organist First United Meth. Ch., Pasadena, Calif., 2000—03, Santa Monica, 2006—07; prof. music, coll. organist Whittier Coll., 1982-98, coord. women's studies, 1995-98, disting. svc. prof. music, 1998—99, prof. emerita, 1999—. Singer L.A. Master Chorale, 1972-86; vis. instr. of key bd. theory, L.A. Valley Coll., Van Nuys, 1980-81, spring 1982; bd. dirs., program chair, sub-dean, dean Pasadena chpt. Am. Guild of Organists, Calif., 1991-95, dean, 1998-99, south coast dist. convenor, 1999-2004, Region IX councillor, 2004—; v.p. Mader Corp., 2005-; resident dir. for Denmark's Internat. Study Program, Whittier Coll., 1994. Faculty Rsch. grantee Whittier Coll., 1984, devel. grantee, 1986, 88, 90, 91, 93. 96, 97, Irvine grantee, 1995. Mem. NOW, Internat. Alliance for Women in Music (treas. 1997-2000, v.p. 2000-03), Am. Guild Organists, Organ Hist. Soc., Rio Hondo Symphony Guild, Whittier Cultural Arts Found., Mader Corp. (v.p. 2005—), Feminist Majority, Pi Kappa Lambda, Mu Phi Epsilon. Episcopalian. Avocations: travel, languages. Personal E-mail: fnobert99organ@aol.com.

NOBLE, DOUGLAS, architecture educator; BS in Architecture, Calif. State Poly. U., 1981, BArch, 1982; MArch, U. Calif., Berkeley, 1983, PhD in Architecture, 1991. Registered Calif., 1985. With Cashion-Horie-Cocke-Gonzalez Architects, 1978—84; tchg. asst. U. Calif., Berkeley, 1983—88, lectr., 1988—91, rsch. asst., 1988—89; prof. U. So. Calif., 1991—; with Kenneth S. Wing and Assocs., 1985—86. Co-editor: Software for Architects; A Guide to Software for the Architectural Profession, (conf. procs.) Mission, Method, Madness; Computer Supported Design in Architecture, 1992. Fellow: AIA; mem.: Assn. for Computer Aided Design in Architecture (pres. 1998), Phi Kappa Phi. Office: 204 Watt Hall U So Calif Sch Architecture Los Angeles CA 90089-0291 Business E-Mail: dnoble@usc.edu.

NOBLE, ERNEST PASCAL, pharmacologist, biochemist, educator, psychiatrist; b. Baghdad, Iraq, Apr. 2, 1929; came to U.S., 1946; s. Noble Babik and Barkev Grace (Kasparian) Babikian; m. Inga Birgitta Kilstromer, May 19, 1956; children: Lorna, Katharine, Erik BS in Chemistry, U. Calif.-Berkeley, 1951; PhD in Biochemistry, Oreg. State U., 1955; MD, Case Western Res. U., 1962. Diplomate Nat. Bd. Med. Examiners. Sr. instr. biochemistry Western Res. U., Cleve., 1957-62; intern Stanford Med. Ctr., Calif., 1962-63, resident in psychiatry Calif., 1963-66, research assoc., asst. prof. Calif., 1965-69; assoc. prof. psychiatry, psychobiology and pharmacology U. Calif.-Irvine, 1969-71, prof., chief neurochemistry, 1971-76, 79-81; dir. Nat. Inst. Alcohol Abuse and Alcoholism HEW, 1976-78, assoc. adminstr. sci., alcohol, drug abuse and mental health, 1978-79; Pike prof. alcohol studies, dir. Alcohol Research Ctr. UCLA Sch. of Medicine, 1981—. Mem. various med./sci. jour. editorial bds.; contbr. numerous articles to profl. jours., chpts. to books V.p. Nat. Coun. on Alcoholism 1981-84; pres. Internat. Commn. for the Prevention of Alcoholism and Drug Dependency, 1988. Fulbright scholar, 1955-56; Guggenheim fellow, 1974-75; Sr. Fulbright scholar, 1984-85; recipient Career Devel. award NIMH, HEW, 1966-69 Fellow Am. Coll. Neuropsychopharmacology; mem. Internat. Soc. Neurochemistry, Am. Soc. Pharmacology and Exptl. Therapeutics, Research Soc. on Alcoholism. Office: UCLA 760 Westwood Plz Los Angeles CA 90095-8353 Business E-Mail: epnoble@ucla.edu.

NOBLE, PHILLIP D., lawyer; b. Oakland, Calif., Aug. 1, 1946; BA, AD in Bus., U. Wash., 1968, JD, 1971. Bar: Wash. 1971. Law clk. to Hon. Morell Sharp Wash. State Supreme Ct., 1971, U.S. Dist. Ct. (we. dist.) Wash., 1972; ptnr. Helsell, Fetterman LLP, Seattle, 1978—. Editor: Justice on Trial, 1971. Mem. ABA, Wash. State Bar Assn., Seattle-King County Bar Assn. Office: Helsell Fetterman LLP 1500 Puget Sound Plz PO Box 21846 Seattle WA 98111-3846

NOCAS, ANDREW JAMES, lawyer; b. LA, Feb. 2, 1941; s. John Richard and Muriel Phyliss (Harvey) Nocas; m. Cassandra Nocas; 1 child, Scott Andrew. BS, Stanford U., 1962, JD, 1964. Bar: Calif. 1965. Assoc. Thelen, Marrin, Johnson & Bridges, LA, 1964-71, ptnr., 1972-91; pvt. practice LA, 1992-2000; atty. real property divsn. Office L.A. City Atty., 2000—. Del. Calif. Bar Conv., 1972—92. Served to capt. JAGC USAR. Fellow: Am. Bar Found.; mem.: ABA (chmn. arbitration com. 1981), Los Angeles County Bar Found. (trustee 1992—99), Am. Bd. Trial Advs., Los Angeles County Bar Assn. (chmn. sect. law office mgmt. 1980—82, chair errors and ommissions com. 1987—88, chair litig. sect. 1988—89). Office: Office LA City Atty 200 N Main St 7th Fl Los Angeles CA 90012 Home Phone: 626-683-9644; Office Phone: 213-978-8197. Business E-Mail: anocas@atty.lacity.org.

NOCE, WALTER WILLIAM, JR., hospital administrator; b. Neptune, NJ, Sept. 27, 1945; s. Walter William and Louise Marie (Jenkins) N.; m. Susan Harris, Nov. 6, 2005; children: Krista Suzanne, David Michael. BA, LaSalle Coll., Phila., 1967; M.P.H., UCLA, 1969. Regional coordinator USPHS, Rockville, Md., 1969-71; v.p. Hollywood Presbyn. Hosp., LA, 1971-75; sr. v.p. Hollywood Presbyn. Med. ctr., 1975-77; v.p. adminstrn. Huntington Meml. Hosp, Pasadena, Calif., 1977-83; pres., CEO St. Joseph Hosp., Orange, Calif., 1983-90, Children's Hosp., LA, 1995—2006, vice chmn., 2006—; pres. so. Calif. region St. Joseph Health Sys., 1987-90, exec. v.p., 1990-94. Preceptor UCLA Health Svcs. Mgmt. Program, 1977—; chmn. bd. Health Plan of Am., 1985-91; chmn. Hosp. Coun. So. Calif., 1989. Exec. v.p. Mental Health Assn. in LA County, 1979-82; regional v.p. Calif. Mental Health Assn., 1982-83; vice chmn., bd. trustees Childresn's Hosp. LA, 2006-07. W. Glenn Ebersole finalist Assn. Western Hosp., 1969; recipient USPHS letter commendation, 1971, leadership in health affairs award Healthcare Assn. So. Calif., 1997. Mem. Am. Coll. Hosp. Adminstrs., Am. Hosp. Assn. (ho. of dels. 1994—), Nat. Assn. Children's Hosps. (bd. dirs. 1995—), Calif. Assn. Cath. Hosps. (chmn. 1990-91), Calif. Assn. Hosps. and Health Sys. (chmn. 1992), UCLA Hosp. Adminstrn. Alumni Assn. (pres. 1979-80), Pasadena C. of C. (v.p. 1980-82). Home: 1012 Glen Oaks Blvd Pasadena CA 91105-1108 Office: Childrens Hosp LA 4650 Sunset Blvd Los Angeles CA 90027 Home Phone: 626-796-3809; Office Phone: 323-671-1779. Business E-Mail: wnoce@chla.usc.edu.

NOCHIMSON, DAVID, lawyer; b. Paterson, NJ, June 19, 1943; s. Samuel S. and Mildred (Singer) N.; m. Roberta Maizel, June 5, 1966 (div. 1972); m. Gail Burgess, May 26, 1978. BA, Yale U., 1965; LLB, Columbia U., 1968; LLM, Australian Nat. U., Canberra, 1969. Bar: N.Y. 1970, Calif. 1977. Assoc. Paul, Weiss, Rifkind, Wharton and Garrison, NYC, 1970-72; sr. v.p. Comprop Equities Corp., NYC, 1972-76; assoc. Mitchell, Silberberg and Knupp, LA, 1977-80, ptnr., 1980-83, Ziffren, Brittenham, Branca, Fischer, Gilbert-Lurie & Stiffelman, LA, 1983—. Adv. com. UCLA Entertainment Symposium, 1979-99, co-chmn., 1981-82. Contbr. articles to Encyclopedia of Investments, 1982, profl. jours. Pres. Friends of the L.A. Free Clinic, 1994-96; trustee Santa Monica (Calif.) Mus. of Art, 1995—. Fulbright scholar, Australia, 1968-69. Mem. ABA (forum com. on entertainment and sports industries 1982—, editor The Entertainment and Sports Lawyer 1982-89, chmn. 1989-92), Internat. Bar Assn. (Vice chmn. entertainment com. 1986-90), Am. Bar Found., Beverly Hills Bar Assn. Democrat. Jewish. Avocations: tennis, racquetball, yoga, playing piano, hiking. Office: Ziffren Brittenham Branca Fischer Gilbert-Lurie and Stiffelman 1801 Century Park W Los Angeles CA 90067-6406 Office Phone: 310-552-3388.

NOCIONI, ANDRES MARCELO, professional basketball player; b. Santa Fe, Argentina, Nov. 30, 1979; m. Paula Nocioni; 1 child, Laureano. Profl. basketball player Tau Ceramica, Spain, 2003—04; forward Chgo. Bulls, 2004—09, Sacramento Kings, 2009—. Mem. Argentinean Nat. Team, 1999—. Recipient Gold medal, Tournament of the Americas, Neuquen, Argentina, 2001, Gold medal, men's basketball, Athens Olympic Games, Greece, 2004. Office: Sacramento Kings Arco Arena One Sports Pky Sacramento CA 95834*

NODAL, ADOLFO V., city manager; b. Cienfuegos, Cuba, Mar. 6, 1950; AA, Miami Dade C.C., 1970; BA in Graphics/Art History, Fla. Sttae U., 1972; MA in Contemporary Art, San Francisco State U., 1976; postgrad. cert., U. Calif., Berkeley, 1982. Exec. dir. Washington Project for the Arts, 1978-83; dir. MacArthur Park Pub. Art Program, LA; dir. exhbns. Exhbn. Ctr. Otis Parsons Sch. of Design, LA, 1983-87; exec. dir. Contemporary Arts Ctr., New Orleans, 1988; gen. mgr. Cultural Affairs Dept. City of L.A., 1988—. Mem. selection panel NEA, 1979-81, D.C. Commn. for the Arts, 1981, Md. State Arts Coun., 1981, Awards for the Visual Arts, 1983, Calif. State Arts Coun., 1985-87, City of L.A. Cultural Affairs Dept., 1985, Capp Street Project, San Francisco, 1986-91, City of Palo Alto Bixbee Park Renovation, 1986, Long Beach Corp. for the Arts Press Art Project, 1987, City of Concord, 1987, Fleishaker Found. Artists Fellowship, 1987. Founding bd. dirs. L.A. Works, 1991; v.p. MacArthur Park Found., 1988-90; sec. MacArthur Park Cmty. Coun., 1984-87; mem. Diverse Works Art Ctr., Houston, 1984-87, New Music Am. '85, 1984-85, Cultural Alliance of Greater Washington, 1982; mem. adv. com. Market Sq. Park, Houston, 1985-88, L.A. Children's Mus., 1986, L.A. Edn. Alliance for Restructuring Now, 1992; mem. overview panel NEA, 1988; mem. art adv. com. Cmty. Redevel. Agy. L.A., 1986-88; mem. Mayor Tom Bradley's Arts Task Force, 1987; mem. founding com. Latino Mus., 1990; mem. cultural masterplan com. Arts Coun. New Orleans, 1988; mem. design adv. group Pershing Sq. Mgmt. Assn., 198; mem. Metro-Dade County Pub. Art program Crandon Park Zoo, Miami, Fla., 1987; mem. pub. art in Am. conf. Fairmount Park Art Assn., Phila., 1986. Recipient Washingtonian of Yr. Washingtonian Mag. and Washington Jaycees, 1981, Mayor's Art award Washington Project for the Arts, Mayor Marion Barry, 1981, numerous pub. svc. citations, Padrino award Bilingual Found. for the Arts, 1991, Humanitarian award Ctrl. Am. Refugee Ctr. 1991, Japan Found., 1990. Mem. Am. Coun. for the Arts, So. Calif. Inst. Arch., Wilshire Blvd. C. of C., Nat. Assn. Artists Orgn., Nat. Assembly Local Arts Agys., Ams. for the Arts (adv. com. 1996—), Office: City Los Angeles Cultural Affairs Dept 433 S Spring St Fl 10 Los Angeles CA 90013-2009

NOEL, CRAIG, performing arts company executive, producer; LHD (hon.), U. San Diego. Actor Old Globe Theatre, San Diego, 1937—, dir., 1939—, exec. prodr. Instituted Globe Ednl. Tours, 1974, Old Globe's multicultural theater component Teatro Meta, 1983; established Play Discovery Program, 1974—, Shakespeare Festival, 1949—; founder Calif. Theatre Coun.; former v.p. Calif. Confedn. Arts.; introduced various playwrights, including Beckett and Ionesco, to San Diego at La Jolla Mus. Contemporary Art, then Falstaff Tavern (renamed Cassius Carter Centre Stage, 1969). Dir. more than 200 works; prodr. 290 works; recent prodns. include Morning's at Seven, Shirley Valentine, The Norman Conquests, 1979, Taking Steps, 1984, Intimate Exchanges, 1987, The Night of the Iguana, 1987, The Boiler Room, 1987, The White Rose, 1991, Mr. A's Amazing Maze Plays, 1994. Named Outstanding Citizen, U. Ariz. Alumni Assn., One of 25 Persons Who Shaped City's History, San Diego Union; Recipient Gov.'s award for Arts, San Diego's Living Treasure award, Conservator Am. Arts award, Am. Conservatory Theatre, Headliner award, San Diego Press Club, San Diego Gentlemen of Distinction award, combined tribute, Pub. Arts Adv. Coun. and San Diego County Bd. Suprs., Nat. Medal Arts, 2007; Year proclaimed in his honor, Mayor Maureen O'Connor, San Diego, 1987. Office: Old Globe Theatre PO Box 2171 San Diego CA 92112-2171

NOGALES, LUIS GUERRERO, investment company executive; b. Madera, Calif., Oct. 17, 1943; s. Alejandro Cano and Florence (Guerrero) N.; children: Alicia Fipp, Maria Cristina. BA in Polit. Sci., San Diego State U., 1966; JD, Stanford U., 1969. Asst. to pres. Stanford U., Calif., 1969-72; White House fellow, asst. to sec. U.S. Dept. Interior, Washington, 1972-73; exec. v.p., dir. Golden West Broadcasters, LA, 1973-80; pres. Nogales, Bermudex, Chase and Tamayo, LA, 1981-82; chmn., chief exec. officer UPI, Washington, 1983-86; pres. ECO Internat. News Svc., 1987, Univision, 1987-88; gen. ptnr. Nogales Castro Ptnrs., 1989-90; mng. ptnr. Nogales Investors Mgmt. LLC, LA, 1990—. Bd. mem. Edison Internat., KB Home, Arbitron Inc. Bd. dirs. State of Calif. Bd. Higher Edn., Sacramento, 1973-79, LA Redevelopment Agy., 1973-76, United Way Am., Alexandria, Va., 1984-88; trustee Claremont U. Ctr. and Grad. Sch., 1987; chmn. MALDEF, 1980-82; bd. trustees J. Paul Getty Trust, LA, 2000-, Mayo Clinic, Rochester, Minn., 2003-. Office: Nogales Investors Mgmt LLC Ste 900 9229 W Sunset Blvd Los Angeles CA 90069 Office Phone: 310-276-7439. Office Fax: 310-276-7405.

NOGUCHI, THOMAS TSUNETOMI, writer, pathologist; b. Fukuoka, Japan, Jan. 4, 1927; arrived in U.S., 1952; s. Wataru and Tomika Narahashi Noguchi. Doctorate of Medicine, Nippon Med. Sch., Tokyo, 1951; DSc (hon.), Worcester State Coll., 1985. Dep. med. examiner LA County Dept. Chief Med. Examiner, 1961-67, coroner, 1967-82; prof. forensic pathology U. So. Calif. Med. Sch., LA, 1982-99; prof. emeritus forensic pathology, 1999—. Author: Coroner, 1983 (N.Y. Times Bestseller, 1984), Coroner at Large, 1985, Unnatural Causes, 1988, Physical Evidence, 1990. Recipient Imperial medal Order Sacred Treasure, His Majesty the Emperor of Japan, 1999, Helpern Laureate medal, Nat. Assn. Med. Examiners, 2006. Fellow: Am. Acad. Forensic Sci. (chmn. sect. 1966, Disting. Fellow award 2007); mem.: AMA, AAAS, Calif. Soc. Pathologists, LA Soc. Pathologists, World Assn. Med. Law (treas.), Calif. Assn. Criminalists, Calif. State Coroners Assn. (pres. 1974—75), Nat. Assn. Med. Examiners (pres. 1983), Internat. Acad. Legal and Social Medicine, Am. Soc. Law, Medicine and Ethics, Am. Coll. Legal Medicine. Republican. Avocations: fine arts, gourmet oriental cooking, painting stills and abstracts. Office: U So Calif Med Ctr 1200 N State St Rm 2520 Los Angeles CA 90033-1029 Business E-Mail: noguchi@hse.usc.edu.

NOLAN, MARY, state legislator; b. Chicago, Ill., 1954; Attended, Dartmouth Coll. Former chmn. Portland Pvt. Industry Coun.; former dir. Portland Environ Svcs.; former bd. dir. Oreg. Constrn. Contractors; pres. Electronics Co.; bus. owner; mem. Dist. 36 Oreg. House of Reps., 2001—, House Majority Leader. Democrat. Office: 900 Court St NE H-295 Salem OR 97301 also: PO Box 1686 Portland OR 97207 Office Phone: 503-986-1436, 503-221-4999. Business E-Mail: rep.marynolan@state.or.us.*

NOLAN, MIKE, professional football coach; b. Balt., Mar. 7, 1959; s. Dick Nolan; m. Kathy Nolan; children: Michael, Christopher, Laura, Jennifer. Attended, U. Oreg. Asst. coach U. Oreg., 1981—82, Stanford U., 1982—83, Rice U., 1984—85; head coach LSU, 1986; linebackers coach, spl. teams asst. Denver Broncos, 1987—92, defensive coord., 2009—, NY Giants, 1993—96, Wash. Redskins, 1997—99, NY Jets, 2000; wide receivers coach Balt. Ravens, 2001, defensive coord., 2002—04; head coach San Francisco 49ers, 2005—08. Office: Denver Broncos 13655 Broncos Pky Englewood CO 80112*

NOLAN, STEVE, Mayor, Corona, California; Owner Backwoods BBQ; former chmn. Parks & Recreation Commn.; councilman City of Corona, 2004—08, mayor, 2008—. Rep. Infrastructure & Econ. Devel. Ad Hoc Com., Homeless Shelter Funding Ad Hoc Com. Pres. Corona Youth Sports Found.; dir. Partners for Parks & Recreation Found.; bd. mem. Corona C. of C. Named Citizen of Yr., Corona C. of C., 2003. Mem.: Circle City Rotary. Office: 400 S Vicentia Ave Corona CA 92882 Office Phone: 951-736-2400. E-mail: SNolan@ci.corona.ca.us.*

NOLL, ROGER GORDON, economist, educator; b. Monterey Park, Calif., Mar. 13, 1940; s. Cecil Ray and Hjordis Alberta (Westover) Noll; m. Robyn Schreiber, Aug. 25, 1962 (dec. Jan. 2000); 1 child, Kimberlee Elizabeth; m. Ann Seminara, Dec. 2, 2001. BS, Calif. Inst. Tech., 1962; AM, Harvard U., 1965, PhD in Econs, 1967. Mem. social sci. faculty Calif. Inst. Tech., 1965-84, prof., 1973-82, inst. prof., 1982-84, chmn. div. humanities and social scis., 1978-82; prof. econs. Stanford U., 1984—2006, Morris M. Doyle centennial prof. of pub. policy, 1990—2002, dir. pub. policy program, 1986—2002, dir. Am. Studies Program, 2001—02, dir. Ctr. for Internat. Devel., 2002—06, prof. emeritus, 2006—; Jean Monnet prof. European U. Inst., 1991; vis. fellow Brookings Instn., 1995-96, non-resident sr. fellow, 1996—2000, vis. scholar, 2003. Sr. staff economist Coun. Econ. Advisors, Washington, 1967—69; sr. fellow Brookings Instn., Washington, 1970—73; mem. tech. adv. bd. Com. Econ. Devel., 1978—82; mem. adv. coun. NSF, 1978—89, NASA, 1978—81, SERI, 1982—90; mem. Pres.'s Commn. Nat. Agenda for Eighties, 1980; chmn. L.A. Sch. Monitoring Com., 1978—79; mem. Commn. Behavioral Social Scis. and Edn. NAS, 1984—90, mem. bd. sci., tech. and econ. policy, 2000—06; mem. energy rsch. adv. bd. Dept. Energy, 1986—89; mem. Sec. Energy Adv. Bd., 1990—94, Calif. Coun. Sci. and Tech., 1995—2000; mem. bd. on sci., tech. and econ. policy NRC, 2001—. Author: (book) Reforming Regulation, 1971, The Economics and Politics of Deregulation, 1991, The Economics and Politics of the Slowdown in Regulatory Reform, 1999; co-author: Economic Aspects of Television Regulation, 1973, The Political Economy of Deregulation, 1983, The Technology Pork Barrel, 1991; editor: Government and the Sports Business, 1974, Regulatory Policy and the Social Sciences, 1985, Challenges to Research Universities, 1998; co-editor: Constitutional Reform in California, 1995, Sports, Jobs and Taxes, 1997, A Communications Cornucopia, 1998; supervisory editor: Info. Econs. and Policy Jour., 1984—92. Recipient 1st ann. book award, Nat. Assn. Ednl. Broadcasters, 1974; grantee NSF, 1973—82; fellow Guggenheim, 1983—84. Mem.: Am. Econ. Assn. Democrat. Home: 4153 Hubbartt Dr Palo Alto CA 94306-3834 Office: Stanford U Dept Econs Stanford CA 94305 Office Phone: 650-723-2297. Business E-Mail: rnoll@stanford.edu.

NOMURA, MASAYASU, biological chemistry professor; b. Hyogo-Ken, Japan, Apr. 27, 1927; s. Hiromichi and Yaeko N.; m. Junko Hamashima, Feb. 10, 1957; children— Keiko, Toshiyasu. PhD, U. Tokyo, 1957. Asst. prof. Inst. Protein Research, Osaka (Japan) U., 1960-63; assoc. prof. genetics U. Wis., Madison, 1963-66, prof., 1966-70, Conrad Elvehjem prof. in Life Sci. genetics and biochemistry, 1970-84, co-dir. Inst. for Enzyme Research, 1970-84; prof. biol. chemistry, Grace Bell chair U. Calif., Irvine, 1984—. Contbr. articles to profl. jours. Recipient U.S. Steel award in molecular biology Nat. Acad. Scis., 1971, Acad. award Japanese Acad. Arts and Sci., 1972, Abbot-ASM Lifetime Acheivement award Am. Soc. Microbiology, 2002. Mem. Am. Acad. Arts and Scis., NAS, Royal Danish Acad. Scis. and Letters, Royal Netherlands Acad. Arts and Scis., Japanese Biochem. Soc. Home: 74 Whitman Ct Irvine CA 92612-4066 Office: U Calif Dept Biol Chemistry Mail Code 1700 240D Med Sci I Dept 109 Plumwood House Irvine CA 92697-1700 Office Phone: 949-824-4673. E-mail: mnomura@uci.edu.

NONINI, ROBERT P., state legislator; b. Wallace, Idaho, Aug. 7, 1954; m. Cathyanne Nonini. Agent, rep. Northwestern Mutual Life Instn., Union Ctrl. Life Instn., 2003—; cons. Settlement Associates, Brant Hickey & Associates, 2004—; mem. Dist. 5 Idaho House of Reps., Boise. Mktg. com. Post FMLS Sr. Ctr.; mem. Idaho Dept. Ins. Continuing Edn., Coeur d'Alene Libr. Found.; chmn. Kootenai County Rep. Ctrl. Com., 1998-2004, Idaho Rep. Party, 2002-04; bd. mem. Idaho Pachyderm Club. Mem. Post Falls C. of C., Coeur d'Alene Rotary Club (past pres.), Spokane River Property Owners Assn. (past pres.), Idaho Assn. Ins. & Fin. Advisors (past pres.). Republican. Roman Catholic. Office: Dist Office 5875 W Harbor Dr Coeur D' Alene ID 83814 also: Legis Services Office PO Box 83720 Boise ID 83720-0054 Office Phone: 208-667-5762. Office Fax: 208-667-5959.*

NOOLAN, JULIE ANNE CARROLL, management consultant; b. Adelaide, South Australia, Australia, June 14, 1944; came to U.S., 1966; d. Archibald Henry and Norma Mae (Gillett) Noolan; m. Daniel Thuering Carroll, Aug. 20, 1977. MA, U. Chgo., 1968, PhD, 1974, Exec. MBA, 1983. With State Library of South Australia, 1962-63, Repatriation Dept. South Australia, 1962-66; asst. librarian U. Chgo. Libraries, 1966-68; dir. edn. Med. Library Assn., Chgo., 1972-77; exec. dir. Assn. Coll. and Research Libraries, Chgo., 1977-84; COO Carroll Group, Inc., Chgo., 1984-95; pres. COO Carroll Group, Inc., Chgo., 1995—. Mem. faculty U. Chgo., 1968-89, Am. U., 1995—. Author: Libraries and Accreditation in Higher Education; contbr. articles to jours. U. Chgo. fellow, 1967-68, Higher Edn. Act fellow, 1969-72; Nat. Library of Medicine grantee, 1967-69; named Outstanding Young U.S. Leader 1985 Coun. on the U.S., Mem. ALA, Am. Soc. Assn. Execs., Am. Mgmt. Assn., Spol. Librs. Assn., Am. Soc. for Info. Scis. (past pres., doctoral award, Watson Davis award), ASTD, Nat. Tng. Labs. (bd. dirs. 1990-94), Orgn. Devel. Network, Internat. Assn. Neuro-Linguistic Programming (bd.dirs. 1990-93), Internat. Plant Genetic Resources Inst. (Rome, bd. dirs. 1991-98), Internat. Ctr. Agrl. Rsch. in Dry Areas (Syris, bd. dirs. 1992-98), Beta Phi Mu.

NOONAN, JOHN T., JR., federal judge, educator; b. Boston, Oct. 24, 1926; s. John T. and Marie (Shea) Noonan; m. Mary Lee Bennett, Dec. 27, 1967; children: John Kenneth, Rebecca Lee, Susanna Bain. BA, Harvard U., 1946, LLB, 1954; student, Cambridge U., 1946—47; MA, Cath. U. Am., 1949, PhD, 1951, LHD, 1980, Holy Cross Coll., 1980, Loyola U., Chgo., 1999; LLD, U. Santa Clara, 1974, U. Notre Dame, 1976, Loyola U. South, 1978, St. Louis U., 1981, Duquesne U., 1995, Valparaiso U., 1996, U. San Diego, 1999, Gonzaga U., 1986, U. San Francisco, 1986. Bar: Mass. 1954, US Supreme Ct. 1971. Mem. spl. staff Nat. Security Council, 1954-55; pvt. practice Herrick & Smith, Boston, 1955-60; prof. law U. Notre Dame, 1961-66, U. Calif., Berkeley, 1967-86, chmn. religious studies, 1970-73, chmn. medieval studies, 1978-79; judge US Ct. Appeals (9th cir.), San Francisco, 1985-96, sr. judge, 1996—. Oliver Wendell Holmes, Jr. lectr. Harvard U. Law Sch., 1972; Pope John XXIII lectr. Cath. U. Law Sch., 1973; Cardinal Bellarmine lectr. St. Louis U. Div. Sch., 1973; Ernest Messenger lectr. Cornell U., 1982; John Dewey Meml. lectr. U. Minn., 1986; Baum lectr. U. Ill., 1988; Strassberger lectr. U. Tex., 1989; chmn. bd. Games Rsch., Inc., 1961—76; overseer Harvard U., 1991—97; Maguire chair in ethics Libr. of Congress, 2002; vis. prof. U. Catania, Sicily, Italy, 2002; vis. Disting. prof. kaw Emory U., 2000; Erasmus lectr. U. Notre Dame, 2003. Author: The Scholastic Analysis of Usury, 1957, Contraception: A History of Its Treatment by the Catholic Theologians and Canonists, 1965, Power to Dissolve, 1972, Persons and Masks of the Law, 1976, The Antelope, 1977, A Private Choice, 1979, Bribes, 1984, The Responsible Judge, 1993, Professional and Personal Responsibilities of the Lawyer, 1997, Canons and Canonists in Context, 1997, The Lustre of Our Country, 1998, Narrowing the Nation's Power, 2002, A Church That Can and Cannot Change, 2005; editor: Natural Law Forum, 1961—70, Am. Jour. Jurisprudence, 1970, The Morality of Abortion, 1970. Chmn. Brookline Redevel. Authority, Mass., 1958—62; cons. Papal Commn. on Family, 1965—66, Ford Found., Indonesian Legal Program, 1968, NIH, 1973, 1974; expert Presdl. Commn. on Population and Am. Future, 1971; pres. Thomas More-Jacques Maritain Inst., 1977—; trustee Population Coun., 1969—76, Phi Kappa Found., 1970—76, U. San Francisco, 1971—75; mem. com. theol. edn. Yale U., 1972—77; cons. U.S. Cath. Conf., 1979—86; sec., treas. Inst. for Rsch. in Medieval Canon Law, 1970—88; trustee Grad. Theol. Union, 1970—73; exec. com. Cath. Commn. Intellectual and Cultural Affairs, 1972—75; bd. dirs. Ctr. for Human Values in the Health Scis., 1969—71, S.W. Intergroup Rels. Coun., 1970—72, Inst. for Study Ethical Issues, 1971—73. Recipient St. Thomas More award, U. San Francisco, 1974, Christian Culture medal, 1975, Laetare medal, U. Notre Dame, 1984, Campion medal, Cath. Book Club, 1987, Alemany medal, Western Dominican Province, 1988; fellow Guggenheim fellow, 1965—66, 1979—80, Ctr. for Advanced Studies in Behavioral Scis. fellow, 1973—74, Wilson Ctr. fellow, 1979—80, Kluge chair in Am. law and govt., Libr. Congress Ctr. for Scholars, 2002. Fellow: Am. Acad. Arts and Scis., Am. Soc. Legal Historians (hon.); mem.: Am. Law Inst., Canon Law Soc. Am. (gov. 1970—72), Am. Soc. Polit. and Legal Philosophy (v.p. 1964), Phi Beta Kappa (senator United chpts. 1970—72, pres. Alpha of Calif. chpt. 1972—73). Office: US Ct Appeals 9th Cir 95 7th St San Francisco CA 94103-1526

NOONAN, PAT, state legislator; Mem. Dist. 73 Mont. House of Reps., 2008—. Democrat. Office: Montana House of Representatives PO Box 200400 Helena MT 59620-0400 Mailing: PO Box 29 Ramsay MT 59748-0029 Home Phone: 406-560-3429; Office Phone: 406-444-4800. Office Fax: 406-444-4825. Personal E-mail: pnoonan73@yahoo.com.

NOONE, LAURA PALMER, academic administrator, lawyer; BBA, U. Dubuque; MBA, JD, U. Iowa; PhD in higher edn. adminstrn., Union Inst. Atty gen. civil practice, Iowa, Ariz.; judge City of Chandler, Ariz.; faculty mem. U. Phoenix, 1987—91, dir. acad affairs, 1991—94, provost, sr. v.p. acad. affairs, 1994—2000, pres., 2002—06, pres. emerita, 2006—. Adj. faculty Grand Canyon Univ., Chandler-Gilbert Cmty. Coll.; mem. Ariz. State Bd. for pvt. postsecondary edn.; trustee Phoenix Internat. Sch. Law. Mem.: ABA, Ariz. State Bar Assn., Maricopa County Bar Assn. Office: University of Phoenix 4615 E Elwood St Phoenix AZ 85040

NORA, AUDREY HART, physician; b. Picayune, Miss., Dec. 5, 1936; d. Allen Joshua and Vera Lee (Ballard) H.; m. James Jackson Nora, Apr. 9, 1966; children: James Jackson Jr., Elizabeth Hart. BS, U. Miss., 1958, MD, 1961; MPH, U. Calif., 1978. Diplomate Am. Bd. Pediat., Am. Bd. Hematology and Oncology. Resident in pediat. U. Wis. Hosp., Madison, 1961-64; fellow in hematology/oncology Baylor U., Tex. Childrens Hosp., Houston, 1964-66, asst. prof. pediat., 1966-70; assoc. clin. prof. pediat. U. Colo. Sch. Medicine, Denver, 1970—; dir. genetics Denver Childrens Hosp., 1970-78; commd. med. officer USPHS, 1978, advanced through grades to asst. surgeon gen., 1983, cons. maternal and child health Denver, 1978-83, asst. surgeon gen. regional health adminstr., 1983-92, dir. maternal & child health bur., health resources and svc. adminstrn., 1992-99. Mem. adv. com. NIH, Bethesda, 1975-77; mem. adv. bd. Metronet Health, Inc., Denver, 1986-92; mem. adv. bd. Colo. Assn. Commerce and Industry, Denver, 1985-92, WIC Adu Bd. USDA, 1989-99; mem. adv. coun. NICHD, 1992-99; bd. mem. RMC for Health Promotion and Edn., pres., 2004-05. Author: (with J.J. Nora) Genetics and Counseling in Cardiovascular Diseases, 1978, (with others) Blakiston's Medical Dictionary, 1980, Birth Defects Encyclopedia, 1990, (with J.J. Nora and K. Berg) Cardiovascular Diseases: Genetics, Epidemiology and Prevention, 1991; contbr. articles to profl. jours. Recipient Virginia Apgar award Nat. Found., 1976. Fellow Am. Acad. Pediat.; mem. Am. Pub. Health Assn. (governing coun. 1990-92, coun. mem. maternal and child health 1990-93), Commd. Officers Assn., Am. Soc. Human Genetics, Teratology Soc., Western Soc. Pediatric Rsch. Presbyterian. Avocations: cooking, hiking, quilting. Office: 1973 S Kenton Ct Aurora CO 80014-4709

NORBECK, JANE S., retired nursing educator; b. Redfield, SD, Feb. 20, 1942; d. Sterling M. and Helen L. (Williamson) N.; m. Paul J. Gorman, June 28, 1970. BA in Psychology, U. Minn., 1965, BSN, 1965; MS, U. Calif., San Francisco, 1971, DSN, 1975. Psychiat. nurse Colo. Psychiat. Hosp., Denver, 1965-66, Langley Porter Hosp., San Francisco, 1966-67; pub. health nurse San Francisco Health Dept., 1968-69; prof. U. Calif. Sch. of Nursing, San Francisco, 1975—2003, dean, 1989-99, dept. chair, 1984-89, prof. and dean emeritus, 2003. Chair study sect. Nat. Inst. of Nursing Rsch., 1990-93, mem. editl. bd. Archives of Psychiat. Nursing, 1985-95, Rsch. in Nursing and Health, 1987-2003. Co-editor: Annual Review of Nursing Research, 1996-97; contbr. articles to profl. jours. Mem. ANA, Am. Acad. Nursing, Inst. of Medicine, Sigma Theta Tau.

NORBERG, DEBORAH DORSEY, museum administrator; b. New Haven, Conn., Jan. 31, 1950; d. Gray Lankford and Jeanne (DeVall) Dorsey; m. Henry F. Norberg, Sept. 11, 1971; children: Sarah E., Daniel G. BA, Stanford U., 1968; M in Mus. Practice, U. Mich., 1974; JD, Stanford U., 1980. Rsch. asst. San Jose (Calif.) Mus. Art, 1975, asst. to curator, 1975-76, exhibition coord., 1987-88, asst. curator, 1988-89, assoc. registrar, assoc. permanent collection curator, 1989-90, registrar, assoc. permanent collection curator, 1990—91, registrar, permanent collection curator, 1991—92, dep. dir., 1992—; assoc. Hopkins and Carley, San Jose, 1980-82. Ford Found. fellow, 1972. Mem. Phi Beta Kappa. Office: San Jose Mus Art 110 S Market St San Jose CA 95113-2383

NORBY, MARK ALAN, lawyer; b. Cadillac, Mich., July 5, 1955; s. Walter Carl and Nadine Kaye (Hunt) N.; m. Connie Lynn Perrine, Feb. 26, 1983. BS in Polit. Sci., Agr., Oreg. State U., 1977; JD, U. Mich., 1980. Bar: Oreg. 1980, U.S. Dist. Ct. Oreg. 1980. Assoc. Stoel, Rives, Boley, Fraser & Wyse, Portland, 1980-86; ptnr. Stoel, RivesLLP, Portland, 1986—. Office: Stoel Rives LLP 900 SW 5th Ave Ste 2600 Portland OR 97204-1268

NORCROSS, DAVID WARREN, physicist, researcher; b. Cin., July 18, 1941; s. Gerald Warren and Alice Elizabeth (Downey) Norcross; children: Joshua David, Sarah Elizabeth. AB, Harvard Coll., 1963; MSc, U. Ill., 1965; PhD, U. Coll., London, 1970. Rsch. assoc. U. Colo., Boulder, 1970—74; physicist Nat. Bur. Standards, Boulder, 1974—; chief quantum physics divsn. Nat. Inst. Stds. and Tech., 1989—93; dir. Boulder Labs., 1994—; fellow Joint Inst. Lab. Astrophysics, Boulder, 1976—. Contbr. articles to profl. jours. Recipient Bronze medal, Nat. Bur. Standards, 1982, Silver medal, U.S. Dept. Commerce, 1994. Fellow: Am. Phys. Soc.

NORD, LARRY B., federal judge; BA, San Jose State U., 1961; JD, U. Calif., San Francisco, 1963. Pvt. practice, Eureka, Calif.; dep. dist. atty. Humboldt County, Calif., 1968-70; apptd. part-time magistrate judge no. dist. U.S. Dist. Ct. Calif., 1971. Office: 518 W Clark St Eureka CA 95501-0103 Fax: 707-443-6535.

NORD, PAUL ELLIOTT, lawyer, accountant; b. Mar. 22, 1936; s. Abe and Rose (Guss) N.; m. Marcia B. Gross, June 13, 1965; children: Howard, Aimee, Samuel. Student, U. Utah, 1952-56; JD, John F. Kennedy U., 2000. CPA, Calif.; bar: Calif., 2000, U.S. Tax Ct., U.S. Ct. Appeals (9th cir.). Staff acct. Robinson, Nowell & Co. (merged with Muncy McPherson & Co.), 1966-73, ptnr., 1973-81, mng. ptnr., 1981-87; ptnr. BDO Seidman, 1988-95, sr. ptnr., 1995—2000; pvt. practice Walnut Creek, Calif., 2000—. Bd. dirs. Congregation Beth Sholom, San Francisco, 1969-87, pres. 1979-81; mem. budget and allocations com. Jewish Fedn., East Bay, 1981-84. With US Army, 1957—58, 1961—62. Ford Found. scholar. Mem. Am. Inst. CPAs (acctg. standards exec. com. 1979-81), Calif. Soc. CPAs (chmn. sub-com. acctg. principles 1981-83), Contra Costa County Bar Assn., Trust and Estates Section, Calif. State Bar. Jewish. Home: 931 Walnut Ave Walnut Creek CA 94598-3738 Office: Paul E 3075 Citrus Cir Ste 105 Walnut Creek CA 94598-2629 Office Phone: 925-906-9300. Business E-Mail: paulnordlaw@gmail.com.

NORDGREN, RONALD PAUL, retired engineering educator, researcher; b. Munising, Mich., Apr. 3, 1936; s. Paul A. and Martha M. N.; m. Joan E. McAfee, Sept 12, 1959; children: Sonia, Paul. BS in Engring., U. Mich., 1957, MS in Engring., 1958; PhD, U. Calif., Berkeley, 1962. Rsch. asst. U. Calif., Berkeley, 1959-62; mathematician Shell Devel. Co., Houston, 1963-68, staff rsch. engr., 1968-74, sr. staff rsch. engr., 1974-80, rsch. assoc., 1980-90; Brown prof. civil and mech. engring. Rice U., Houston, 1989-2000, prof. emeritus, 2001—. U.S. nat. com. on theoretical and applied mechanics NRC, 1984-86, U.S. nat. com. for rock mechanics, 1991-95. Contbr. articles to profl. jours.; assoc. editor Jour. Applied Mechanics, 1972-76, 81-85; patentee in field. Fellow: ASME; mem.: NAE, Sigma Xi. Office: 3989 Pebble Beach Dr Longmont CO 80503-8358 Home Phone: 303-440-1047. Business E-Mail: nordgren@rice.edu.

NORDLUND, DONALD CRAIG, lawyer, electronics executive; b. Chgo., May 23, 1949; s. Donald E. and Jane (Houston) N.; m. Sally Baum, Sept. 7, 1975; children: Courtney Elizabeth, Michael Andrew, Laurie Katherine. AB in Polit. Sci. and Journalism, Stanford U., 1971; JD, Vanderbilt U., 1974. Assoc. Ware & Freidenrich, Palo Alto, Calif., 1974-77; atty. Hewlett-Packard Co., Palo Alto, 1977-87, assoc. gen. counsel, sec., dir., 1987-99; sr. v.p., gen. counsel, sec. Agilent Technologies, Inc., 1999—. Panelist ann. disclosure doc. seminar Practicing Law Inst., 1982—2005, co-chmn., 2002—04; bd. dirs. Addison Ave. Fed. Credit Union, 1985—; sec., dir. Agilent Tech. Found. and various Agilent Tech. subsidiaries, 1999—; mem. corp. law com. ABA, 2005—. Chmn. bd. dirs. Santa Clara County chpt. Jr. Achievement, 1995-97. Mem.: Assn. Gen. Counsel (pres. 2006—07), Assn. Corp. Counsel (bd. dirs. San Francisco chpt. 1984—2000, pres. 1989—90, nat. bd. dirs. 1995—2001, Founding dir. Bay Area Chapter), Soc. Corp. Sec. and Governance Profl. (pres. San Francisco region 1986—88, bd. dirs. 1987—90, mem. exec. com. 1988—89, chmn. securities law com. 1995—98, nat. chmn. 1999—2000). Avocations: tennis, skiing, sailing, golf. Office: Agilent Technologies Inc 5301 Stevens Creek Blvd Santa Clara CA 95051

NORDSTROM, BLAKE W., retail executive; b. 1960; With Nordstrom, Inc., Seattle, 1974—, v.p. & gen. mgr. Wash./Alaska region, 1991—95, co-pres. Seattle, 1995—2000, pres., 2000—, bd. dir., 2005—. Office: Nordstrom Inc 1617 Sixth Ave Seattle WA 98101-1742

NORDSTROM, BRUCE A., department store executive; b. 1933; married. BA, U. Wash., 1956. With Nordstrom, Inc., Seattle, 1956—, v.p., 1964-70, pres., 1970-75, chmn., 1975-77, co-chmn., 1977—2006, dir. Office: Nordstrom Inc 1617 6th Ave Seattle WA 98101-1742

NORDSTROM, JOHN N., department store executive; b. 1937; married. BA, U. Wash., 1958. With Nordstrom, Inc., Seattle, 1958—, v.p., 1965-70, exec. v.p., 1970-75, pres., 1975-77, co-chmn., 1977—2002, dir., 1966—. Bd. dirs. Fed. Res. Bank San Francisco. Office: Nordstrom Inc 1617 6th Ave Seattle WA 98101-1742

NORGAARD, RICHARD BRUCE, economist, educator, consultant; b. Washington, Aug. 18, 1943; s. John Trout and Marva Dawn (Andersen) N.; m. Marida Jane Fowle, June 19, 1965 (div.); children: Kari Marie, Marc Anders; m. Nancy A. Rader, June 5, 1993; children: Addie Nelle, Mathiesen Rader. BA in Econs., U. Calif., Berkeley, 1965; MS in Agrl. Econs., Oreg. State U., 1967; PhD in Econs., U. Chgo., 1971. Instr. Oreg. Coll. Edn., 1967-68; asst. prof. agrl. and resource econs. U. Calif., Berkeley, 1970-76, assoc. prof., 1976-77, 80-87, assoc. prof. energy and resources, 1987-92, prof. energy and resources, 1992—. Project specialist Ford Found., Brazil, 1978-79; environ. cons. to internat. devel. agencies; sci. com. on problems of the environment U.S. Nat. Rsch. Coun.; founding chmn. bd. Redefining Progress, 1993-97; sci. adv. bd. US EPA, 2000-04; mem. ind. sci. bd. Calif. Bay-Delta Authority. Author: Development Betrayed: The End of Progress and a Coevolutionary Revisioning of the Future, 1994; chpt. rev. editor Millenium Ecosys. Assessment, 2004-05; mem. editl. bd. numerous academic jours.; contbr. articles to profl. jours. Active civil rights, environ., and peace orgns. Recipient Kenneth E. Boalding award, Inst. Soc. Ecological Economics, 2006, Faculty Mentoring award, Berkeley Grad. Student Assoc., 2007. Mem. AAAS, Am. Econs. Assn., Internat. Soc. Ecol. Econs. (pres. 1998-2001, past pres. 2002-2003), Fedn. Am. Scientists, Assn. Environ. and Resource Econs., Am. Inst. Biol. Scis. (bd. dirs. 2000-, treas. 2004—). Home: 1198 Keith Ave Berkeley CA 94708-1607 Office: U Calif Energy & Resources Program 310 Barrows Hall Berkeley CA 94720-3050 Business E-Mail: norgaard@berkeley.edu.

NORLING, RICHARD ARTHUR, healthcare executive; b. Waterbury, Conn., Dec. 9, 1945; s. Arthur and Alice Norling; m. Jeanne Marie Bone, Oct. 1, 1946; children: Jennifer, Stephanie. BS in Math., Tufts U., 1967; MS in Systems Engring., U. Ariz., 1969; MHA, U. Minn., 1975. Systems analyst Univ. Hosp., Tucson, 1969-70, mgr. systems engring., 1970-72, asst. to adminstr., 1972-73; adminstrv.

resident Presbyn. Hosp. Ctr., Albuquerque, 1974-75; asst. dir. Calif. Med. Ctr., Los Angeles, 1975-77, assoc. dir., 1977-79, pres., exec. dir., 1979-86; exec. v.p. LHS Corp., Los Angeles, from 1986; former pres., CEO Fairview Hosp. and Healthcare Svcs., Mpls.; now chmn., CEO Premier Inc., San Diego. Mem. Joint Commn. on Accreditation of Healthcare Orgn.'s Adv. Group, 1993; chmn., Foun. for the Malcolm Balridge Nat. Quality Award, 2001-. Bd. mem. Am. Healthcare Systems, 1989, Augsburg Coll., 1992, Benefit Panel Svcs., 1991, Express Scripts, Inc., 1992, Hosp. Edn. and Rsch. Found., 1989, Minn. Bus. Partnerships, Inc., 1991; bd. trustees Healthcare Leadership Coun. Kings Fund fellow, 1984-90; named Emerging Health Care Leader Assn. of Western Hosps. Mem. Am. Hosp. Assn. (chmn. various coms., coun. on fin. 1980-83), Am. Coll. Healthcare Execs., Edina Country Club, Mpls. Club. Congregationalist. Avocations: golf, gardening, raquetball. Office: Premier Inc 12255 El Camino Real Ste 100 San Diego CA 92130-4088

NORMAN, JEAN REID, journalist; b. Phoenix, Feb. 13, 1957; d. James August and V. Janice (Radford) R.; m. James E. Norman, Jr., Dec. 30, 1982; children: James R., Janiece C. BS in Journalism, Northwestern U., 1979. Reporter Fallon (Nev.) Eagle-Standard, 1979-80; reporter, spl. sections editor North Las Vegas Valley Times, 1980-81; mng. editor Good Times, Santa Cruz, Calif., 1981-83; copy editor Daily Review, Hayward, Calif., 1983-85, Journal-Bulletin, Providence, R.I., 1986-89, Contra Costa Times, Walnut Creek, Calif., 1989, The Washington Post, 1990, USA Today Money Sect., Rosslyn, Va., 1990-93; mng. editor Navy Times, Springfield, Va., 1993-98; asst. metro editor Las Vegas Sun, 1998—. Vestry mem. St. Mark's Episcopal Ch., 1996-98. Democrat. Office: Las Vegas Sun 2275 Corporate Cir Ste 300 Las Vegas NV 89074 E-mail: jeannorman@earthlink.net.

NORMAN, JOHN BARSTOW, JR., graphics designer, educator; b. Paola, Kans., Feb. 5, 1940; s. John B. and Ruby Maxine (Johnson) N.; m. Roberta Jeanne Martin, June 6, 1967; children: John Barstow III, Elizabeth Jeanne. BFA, U. Kans., 1962, MFA, 1966. Designer and illustrator Advt. Design, Kansas City, Mo., 1962-64; asst. instr. U. Kans., Lawrence, 1964-66; art dir. Hallmark Cards, Inc., Kansas City, 1966-69; instr. dept. art U. Denver, 1969-73, asst. prof., 1973-78, assoc. prof., 1978-93, disting. prof., 1980-93, prof. emeritus, 1993—; sr. designer Mo. Coun. Arts & Humanities, 1966-67; cons. designer Rocky Mt. Bank Note Corp., Denver, 1971—. Cons. designer Signage identity System, U. Denver; bd. dirs. comm. U. Denver; tech. cons. Denver Art Mus., 1974—, designed exhbns, 1974-75; adv. cons. Jefferson County (Colo.) Sch. System, 1976—; chmn. Design and Sculpture Exhbn., Colo. Celebration of the Arts, 1975-76. One-man shows include GalleryCortina, Aspen, Colo., 1983; commd. works include Jedda, Saudi Arabia, Synegistics Corp., Denver; represented in permanent collections Pasadena Ctr. for Arts, N.Y. Arts Dirs. Club, Calif. State U./Fiber Collection, Pasadena Ctr. Arts, N.Y. Art Dirs. Club, Midland Art Coun./Fiber Collection, Geologic Soc. Am.; represented in traveling exhbns. L.A. Art Dirs. Show and N.Y. Art Dirs. Show, U.S., Europe, Japan, 1985; featured in Denver Post, 1984, Post Electric City Mag., 1984, Rocky Mt. News, 1984, Douglas County Press, 1984, Mile High Cable Vision, 1985, Sta. KWGN-TV, 1985, Les Krantz's Am. Artists, 1988; illustrated Survey of Leading Contemporaries, 1988, U.S. Surface Design Jour., 1988; co-work represented in film collectin Mus. Modern Art, N.Y.C.; selected fashion show designs displayed Sister City dels., Denver, 1987. Recipient Silver medal award N.Y. Internat. Film and Video Competition, 1976, Design awards Coun. ADvancement and Support Edn., 1969, 71, 73, 76, Honor Mention award L.A. Art Dirs. Club, 1984, Honor Mention award N.Y. ARt Dirs. Club, 1984, Native Am. Wearable Art Competition, 1985, 5th pl. Nat. Wind Sail Am. Banners Competition, Midland, Mich., 1985, also awards for surface designs in Colo. Ctr. for Arts Wearable ARt Competition, 1984-85, Foothills Art Gallery Nat. Wearable Competition, 1984-85, Fashion Group Denver Competition, 1984-85. Mem. Art Dirs. Club Denver (Gold medals 1974-82, Best of Show Gold medal 1983, Honor Mentin award 1984, 3 gold medals 1989), Univ. Dirs. Assn. Home: PO Box 507 Lake George CO 80827-0507 Home Phone: 719-339-1751; Office Phone: 719-216-4990. Personal E-mail: normanranch@earthlink.net.

NORMAN, JOHN EDWARD, petroleum landman; b. Denver, May 22, 1922; s. John Edward and Ella (Warren) Norman; m. Hope Sabin, Sept. 5, 1946; children: J. Thomas, Gerould W., Nancy E., Susan G., Douglas E. BSBA, U. Denver, 1949, MBA, 1972. Clk., bookkeeper Capitol Life Ins. Co., Denver, 1940—42, 1945—46; salesman Security Life and Accident Co., Denver, 1947; bookkeeper Ctrl. Bank and Trust Co., Denver, 1947—50; automobile salesman H.A. Hennies, Denver, 1950; petroleum landman Continental Oil Co. (name changed to Conoco Inc. 1979), Denver, 1950—85; ind. petroleum landman, 1985; ind. investor, 1985—. Lectr. pub. lands Colo. Sch. Mines, 1968—85; lectr. mineral titles and landmen's role in oil industry Casper Coll., 1969—71. Mem. Casper Mcpl. Band Commn., 1965—71, mem. band, 1961—71, mgr., 1968—71; former musician, bd. dirs. Casper Civic Symphony; former bd. dirs. Jefferson Symphony, performing mem., 1972—75; mem. choir, vestryman, past dir. acolytes Episc. Ch. Served US Army, World War II. Mem.: Rocky Mountain Petroleum Pioneers, Rocky Mountain Oil and Gas Assn. (pub. lands com. 1981—85), Denver Assn. Petroleum Landmen, Wyo. Assn. Petroleum Landmen (pres.), Assn. Petroleum Landmen (dir. at large, chmn. publs. for regional dir.), Elks. Episcopalian. Home and Office: 2710 S Jay St Denver CO 80227-3856

NORMILE, ROBERT J., lawyer, consumer products company executive; b. July 1959; BA in econ. & philosophy, Fordham U.; JD, NYU. Atty. Latham & Watkins, Sullivan & Cromwell; asst. gen. counsel Mattel Inc., El Segundo, Calif., 1992—94, v.p., asst. gen. counsel, 1994—98, v.p., assoc. gen. counsel, sec., 1998—99, sr. v.p., gen. counsel, sec., 1999—. Office: Mattel Inc 333 Continental Blvd El Segundo CA 90245-5012 Office Phone: 310-252-2000. Office Fax: 310-252-2180.

NORRINGTON, LORRIE M., Internet company executive; b. 1960; BBA, U. Md., 1982; MBA, Harvard U., Cambridge, Mass., 1989. With GE, 1982—2001; pres., CEO GE FANUC Automation; exec. v.p. small bus. and personal fin. Intuit Inc., Mountain View, Calif., 2001—05, mem. Office of CEO, 2003—05; pres., CEO Shopping.com Ltd., 2005—06; pres. eBay Internat., San Jose, 2006—08, eBay Marketplaces, San Jose, 2008—. Mem. adv. bd. Catalyst Group. Named one of 50 Most Powerful Women in Bus., Fortune mag., 2008. Office: eBay Inc 2145 Hamilton Ave San Jose CA 95125

NORRIS, WILLIAM ALBERT, lawyer, mediator, retired judge; b. Turtle Creek, Pa., Aug. 30, 1927; s. George and Florence (Clive) Norris; m. Jane Jelenko, Feb. 17, 1991; children: Barbara, Donald, Kim, Alison, David Jelenko. Student, U. Wis., 1945; BA, Princeton U., 1951; JD, Stanford U., 1954. Bar: Calif. 1955, D.C. 1955. Assoc. Northcutt Ely, Washington, 1954—55; law clk. to Justice William O. Douglas US Supreme Ct., Washington, 1955—56; sr. mem. Tuttle & Taylor, Inc., LA, 1956—80; judge U.S. Ct. Appeals (9th cir.), LA, 1980—97; atty. Folger, Levin & Kahn, LA, 1997—2000, mediator, 1997—; sr. counsel Akin Gump Strauss Hauer & Feld, LLP, 2000—. Spl. counsel Pres.' Kennedy's Com. on Airlines Controversy, 1961; mem. Calif. State Bd. Edn., 1961—67; mem. bd. dir. L.A. Eye Inst., 2001—. Trustee Calif. State Colls., 1967—72, Craft and Folk Art Mus., 1979—87; pres. L.A. Bd. Police Commrs., 1973—74; founding pres., trustee Mus. Contemporary Art, LA, Calif., 1980—92; Dem. nominee for atty. gen. State of Calif., 1974. With USN, 1945—47. Office: Akin Gump Strauss Hauer & Feld LLP Ste 2400 2029 Century Park E Los Angeles CA 90067 Home Phone: 310-472-2238; Office Phone: 310-229-1047. Business E-Mail: wnorris@akingump.com.

NORTH, DOUGLAS MCKAY, academic administrator; b. Albany, NY, Oct. 14, 1940; s. Henry Saxe and Elsie (Sewell) N.; m. Ellen Cole, Dec. 10, 1975; children: Jeffrey, Lisa, Anton, Gabriel. BA, Yale U., 1962; MA, Syracuse U., 1964; PhD, U. Va., 1970. Asst. prof. SUNY, New Paltz, 1964-67, Wesleyan U., Middletown, Conn., 1970-71; prof. Goddard Coll., Plainfield, Vt., 1973-81, dir. devel., 1982-89; pres. Prescott (Ariz.) Coll., 1989—94; prof., pres. Alaska Pacific U., 1995—. Contbr. articles to profl. jours. Dept. Edn. grantee, Washington, 1988-91. Mem. Nat. Consortium Single Parent Educators (bd. dirs. 1988—). Office: Office of Pres 4101 University Dr Anchorage AK 99508 E-mail: dnorth@alaskpacific.edu.

NORTH, ROBERT L., computer software executive; b. Topeka, Sept. 19, 1935; BEE, Stanford U., 1953, MEE, 1958; postgrad., UCLA Grad. Bus. Sch., 1977; post grad., Stanford Grad. Bus. Sch., 1981. Tech. staff mem. Aerospace Corp., 1962-65; various positions TRW, 1965-81, v.p., gen. mgr., 1981-86; CEO HNC Software, Inc., San Diego, 1987-2000, chmn., 2000—. Mem. San Diego C. of C., 1983-84; bd. dir. San Diego Econ. Devel. Coun., 1983-84, United Way Pres. Coun., 1984 Office: Fair Isaac Corp 3661 Valley Centre Dr San Diego CA 92130-3317

NORTH, WARREN JAMES, government official; b. Winchester, Ill., Apr. 28, 1922; s. Clyde James and Lucille Adele (Bishop) N.; m. Mary Strother; children— James Warren, Mary Kay, Susan Lee, Diane. BS in Engring, Purdue U., 1947; MS, Case Inst. Tech., 1954, Princeton, 1956. Engr. and test pilot NACA, Cleve., 1947-55, asst. chief aerodynamics br., 1955-59; chief manned satellites NASA, Washington, 1959-62; chief flight crew support div. NASA (Manned Spacecraft Center), Houston, 1962-71; asst. dir. space shuttle NASA (Flight Ops. Directorate), 1972-85; pres. Spalding Edn. Found., Glendale, Ariz., 1986—. Contbr. articles to profl. jours. Served with USAAF, 1943-45. Recipient DeFlorez tng. award, 1966; NASA award for exceptional service, 1968, 69 Mem. Am. Inst. Aero. and Astronautics (asso. fellow 1955), Tau Beta Pi, Pi Tau Sigma. Clubs: Mason. Home: 6933 W Kimberly Way Glendale AZ 85308-5757 Office: Spalding Edn Found 2814 W Bell Rd Ste 1405 Phoenix AZ 85053-7531

NORTON, JANE ELLEN BERGMAN (JANE BERGMAN), former lieutenant governor; b. Grand Junction, Colo. d. Walter F. and Elinor (Pitman) Bergman; m. Mike Norton; children: Lacee, Tyler. BS in Health Sci., with distinction, Colo. State U., 1976; MS in Mgmt., Regis U. With Med. Group Mgmt. Assn., Englewood, Colo.; mem. Colo. Ho. Reps., 1986—87; regional dir. US Dept. Health and Human Svcs.; exec. dir. Colo. Dept. Pub. Health Environment, 1999—2002; lt. gov. State of Colo., Denver, 2003—07. Chair Colo. Commn. on Indian Affairs; del. Aerospace State Assn., Edn. Commn. of States; co-chair Colo. Space Coalition; Colo. spokesperson Go Red for Women Campaign Am. Heart Assn.; hon. chair Prematurity Campaign Colo. March of Dimes; hon. chair Colo. Freedom Meml. Bd. dirs. Internat. Found. Electronic Systems, Am. Coun. Young Polit. Leaders; nat. bd. adv. Inst. Sci. and Space Studies; adv. bd. women's health U. Colo.; bd. adv. Colo. History Day; co-chair Colo. Health Disparities Commn. Recipient Disting. Veterans Advocate award, United Veterans Com. Colo., Legislator of Yr. award, Persons Living with HIV Action Network of Colo., David M. Clark, S.J. Innovative Leadership award, Regis U., Family Values award, State of Colo., Honor Alumna award, Colo. State U. Coll. Applied Human Sci., US Public Health Svc. award outstanding accomplishment increasing childhood immunization rates, Outstanding Svc. to Seniors award, US Adminstn. on Aging; named Woman of Distinction, Girls Scouts, 2005, Public Servant of Yr., Rocky Mt. Family Coun. Mem.: Nat. Lt. Governors Assn. (chair-elect 2006), Omicron Kappa Upsilon (hon.). Republican. Avocations: hiking, skiing.

NORTON, KAREN ANN, accountant; b. Nov. 1, 1950; d. Dale Francis and Ruby Grace (Gehlhar) N. BA, U. Minn., 1972; postgrad., U. Md., 1978; MBA, Calif. State Poly. U., Pomona, 1989. CPA Md. Securities transactions analyst Bur. of Pub. Debt, Washington, 1972-79, internal auditor, 1979-81, IRS, Washington, 1981; sr. acct. World Vision Internat., Monrovia, Calif., 1981-83, acctg. supr., 1983-87; sr. sys. liaison coord. Home Savs. Am. (name changed to Washington Mut.), 1987-97, sys. auditor, 1997-2000, sect. mgr., 2000—02, group mgr., v.p., 2003—04, v.p., 2005—; project mgr. II Indy Mac Bank, 2004—05, v.p., 2005—08; Sr. fin. controls mgr. Kaiser Permanente, 2008—. Author: (poetry) Ode to Joyce, 1985 (Golden Poet award 1985). 2d v.p. chpt. Nat. Treasury Employees Union, Washington, 1978, editor chpt. newsletter; mem. M-2 Prisoners Sponsorship Program, Chino, Calif., 1984-86. Recipient Spl. Achievement award Dept. Treasury, 1976, Superior Performance award Dept. Treasury, 1977-78; Charles and Ellora Alliss scholar, 1968. Mem. Angel Flight, Flying Samaritans, Habitat for Humanity. Avocations: flying, chess, tennis. Office: Kaiser Permanente 393 E Walnut St Pasadena CA 91188 Office Phone: 626-405-3006. Personal E-mail: skypilot@pacbell.net.

NOSANOW, BARBARA SHISSLER, museum director, curator; b. Roanoke, Va. d. Willis Morton and Kathryn Sabin (Bradford) Johnson; m. John Lewis Shissler Jr., July 28, 1957 (dec. May 1972); children: John Lewis Shissler III, Ada Holland Shissler; m. Lewis Harold Nosanow, Oct. 15, 1973. AB, Smith Coll., 1957; MA, Case Western Res. U., 1958; ABD, U. Minn., 1972. Asst. mng. editor Jour. Aesthetics and Art Criticism, Cleve. Mus. Art, 1958-63; dir. publs. and rsch. Mpls. Inst. Arts, 1963-72; dir. U. Minn. Art Mus., Mpls., 1972-76; dir. exhbns. and edn. Nat. Archives, Washington, 1976-79; curator Smithsonian Instn., Washington, 1979-82; asst. dir. Nat. Mus. Am. Art, Smithsonian Instn., 1982-88; dir. Portland (Maine) Mus. Art, 1988-93, Art Spaces, 1993—; study leader, lecturer Smithsonian Study Tours of France and Russia, 1997—. Lectr. in field. Past mem. various rev. panels NEH, Washington. Bd. dirs. Md. Com. for Humanities, Balt., 1980-83. Mem. Internat. Women's Forum. Avocation: travel. Office: Art Spaces 7005 Crystalline Dr Carlsbad CA 92011 Office Phone: 760-804-9714. Business E-Mail: lhnosanow@yahoo.com.

NOSKI, CHARLES H., former telecommunications executive; b. Aug. 1952; Degree, Calif. State U., Northridge, 1973, degree, 1995. Corp. v.p., controller Hughes Elec. Corp., 1990—92, senior v.p., CFO, 1992—99, vice chmn., 1996—97; with Haskins & Sells (now Deloitte & Touche), 1973-83, ptnr., 1983-90; pres., COO At&T Corp., NYC, 1997—99, sr. exec. v.p., CFO, 1999—2002; vice chmn. bd. dirs. AT&T Corp., 2002; corp. v.p., CFO Northrop Grumman Corp., 2003—05. Past mem. standing adv. group Pub. Co. Accounting Oversight Bd.; past mem. Fin. Accounting Standards Adv. Coun.; bd. dirs. Northrop Grumman Corp., 2002—05, Microsoft Corp., 2003—, Air Products and Chemicals Inc., 2000—04, 2005—, Morgan Stanley, 2005—, Automatic Data Processing Inc., 2008—; sr. advisor Blackstone Group, 2003. Bd. dir. Performing Arts Ctr. of LA County. Mem.: Fin. Execs. Internat., Am. Inst. CPAs.

NOSLER, PETER COLE, construction company executive; b. Portland, Oreg., May 7, 1940; s. Lyle and Elizabeth (Lewis) Nosler; m. Kay Hanson, Apr. 25, 1971; 1 child, Alexander. BS in Physics and Math., Walla Walla Coll., 1962; postgrad., U. Wash., 1962-63, U. Calif., Berkeley, 1965-70. Physicist GE, Richland, Wash., 1963-65; pvt. practice Portland, 1970-72; project mgr. Stolte Constrn., San Leandro, Calif., 1972-75; v.p. ops. Rudolph & Sletten, Foster City, Calif., 1975-90; founder, pres. DPR Constrn. Inc., Redwood City, Calif., 1990, CEO. Lectr. Stanford U., Palo Alto, Calif., 1988—. Recipient Young Constrn. Profl. of Yr. award, Jour. Bldg. Design and Constrn., 1978. Mem.: Soc. Model Exptl. Engring. Avocations: model engineering and construction, history. Office: DPR Constrn Inc 1450 Veterans Blvd Redwood City CA 94063-2612

NOTARI, PAUL CELESTIN, communications executive; b. Chgo., Sept. 8, 1926; s. Peter and Mae Rose (Luvisi) N.; m. Marlene Fineman, Feb. 21, 1969; children: Cathy Notari Davidson, Kenneth, Sharon Notari Christian, Mindy Nielsen, Debbie McGrath. BS in Physics, DePaul U., 1952; MS in Comml. Sci., Rollins Coll., 1968. Mgr. publs. and tng. Motorola Inc., Chgo., 1952-65; supr., publs. engr. Martin Co., Orlando, Fla., 1966-67; dir. comm. Bus. Equipment Mfrs. Assn., NYC, 1967-70; dir. publs., pub. jour. Am. Water Works Assn., Denver, 1971-79; mgr. tech. info. Solar Energy Rsch. Inst., Denver, 1979-91; pres. SciTech Comm., Inc., Denver, 1992—. Lectr. bus. comm. Northwestern U. Served with USNR, 1944-46. Mem. Assn. Computer Programmers and Analysts (founding pres. 1970-73), Soc. Tech. Writers and Pubs. (chmn. chpt. 1965-66), Am. Solar Energy Soc. (nat. chmn. 1990-91, 2004), Colo. Renewable Energy Soc. (founder, bd. dirs. 1996-2001).

NOTEBAERT, RICHARD C., retired telecommunications industry executive; b. 1947; m. Peggy Notebaert; 2 children. BA, U. Wis., 1969, MBA, 1983; four hon. degrees. With Wis. Bell, 1969-83; v.p. mktg. and ops. Ameritech, Chgo., 1983-86; pres. Ameritech Mobile Comm., 1986-89, Ind. Bell Tel. Co., 1989-92, Ameritech Svcs., 1992-93, pres., COO, 1993-94; chmn., pres., CEO Ameritech Corp., Chicago, 1994—99; pres., CEO Tellabs, 2000—02; chmn., CEO Qwest Comm. Internat., Inc., Denver, 2002—07. Bd. dirs. AON Corp., Cardinal Health, Inc., Qwest Comm. Internat., Inc.; trustee, corp. leadership bd. dirs. U. Notre Dame, mem., bus. coun.; chmn. Reliability and Interoperability Coun. FCC, 2002—; apptd. mem. Nat. Security Telecom. Adv. Com., 2003—. Co-chmn. Alexis de Toqueville Soc. United Way; bd. dirs. Denver Ct. Performing Arts; vice chmn. civic com. The Comml. Club Chgo.; bd. dirs. The Execs. Club, Chgo. Recipient Dist. Alumni award, U. Wis., 1999. Office: Qwest Commn Internat Inc 1801 California St Denver CO 80202 Office Phone: 303-992-1414. Office Fax: 303-896-8515.

NOTH, CHRIS, actor; b. Madison, Wis., Nov. 13, 1954; 1 child, Orion Christopher. Grad., Yale Sch. Drama. Co-owner The Cutting Room, NYC, 1999—. Actor: (films) Smithereens, 1982, Waitress!, 1982, Off Beat, 1986, Baby Boom, 1987, Jakarta, 1988, Naked in New York, 1993, Burnzy's Last Call, 1995, The Deli, 1997, Cold Around the Heart, 1997, The Broken Giant, 1998, The Confession, 1999, Getting to Know You, 1999, A Texas Funeral, 1999, Pigeonholed, 1999, The Acting Class, 2000, Cast Away, 2000, Double Whammy, 2001, The Glass House, 2001, Searching for Paradise, 2002, Mr. 3000, 2004, Tooth Fairy, 2004, The Perfect Man, 2005, Sex and the City: The Movie, 2008; (TV films) Killer in the Mirror, 1986, Apology, 1986, At Mother's Request, 1987, In the Shadows, Someone's Watching, 1993, Where Are My Children, 1994, Nothing Lasts Forever, 1995, Abducted: A Father's Love, 1996, Born Free: A New Adventure, 1996, Rough Riders, 1997, Medusa's Child, 1997, Julius Caesar, 2002, This Is Your Country, 2003; actor, writer (TV films) Exiled, 1998, actor, prodr. The Judge, 2001, actor, exec. prodr. Bad Apple, 2004; actor: (TV series) Hill Street Blues, 1986, Law & Order, 1990—95, Sex and the City, 1998—2004, Law & Order: Criminal Intent, 2005—07; (TV miniseries) I'll Take Manhattan, 1987; (Broadway plays) The Best Man, What Didn't Happen; (plays) American Buffalo. Office: The Cutting Room 19 W 24th St New York NY 10010 also: c/o United Talent Agy 9560 Wilshire Blvd Ste 500 Beverly Hills CA 90212-2401

NOTTINGHAM, EDWARD WILLIS, JR., former federal judge; b. Denver, Jan. 9, 1948; s. Edward Willis and Willie Newton (Gullett) N.; m. Cheryl Ann Card, June 6, 1970 (div. Feb. 1981); children: Amelia Charlene, Edward Willis III; m. Janis Ellen Chapman, Aug. 18, 1984 (div. Dec. 1998); 1 child, Spencer Chapman. AB, Cornell U., 1969; JD, U. Colo., 1972. Bar: Colo. 1972, U.S. Dist. Ct. Colo. 1972, U.S. Ct. Appeals (10th cir.) 1973. Law clk. to presiding judge US Dist. Ct. Colo., Denver, 1972-73; assoc. Sherman & Howard, Denver, 1973-76, 78-80, ptnr., 1980-87, Beckner & Nottingham, Grand Junction, Colo., 1987-89; asst. US atty. (dist. Colo.) US Dept. Justice, Denver, 1976-78; judge US Dist. Ct. Colo., Denver, 1989—2008, chief judge, 2007—08. Mem. Jud. Conf. of the U.S. Com. on Automation and Tech., 1994-2000, chmn., 1997-2000. Bd. dirs. Beaver Creek Met. Dist., Avon, Colo., 1980-88, Justice Info. Ctr., Denver, 1985-87, 21st Jud. Dist. Victim Compensation Fund, Grand Junction, Colo., 1987-89. Mem. ABA, Colo. Bar Assn. (chmn. criminal law sect. 1983-85, chmn. ethics com. 1988-89), Order of Coif, Denver Athletic Club, Delta Sigma Rho, Tau Kappa Alpha. Episcopalian.

NOVAK, JAMES F., physician; b. Portland, May 5, 1944; s. John Martin and Mary Ruth Novak; m. Marilynn L. Grosso, July 10, 1971; children: Vincent, Mark. BS, U. San Francisco, 1966; MD, Oreg. Health Science U., Portland, 1970. Diplomate Am. Bd. Family Practice; cert. Md. Intern Hennepin County Gen. Hosp., Mpls., 1970-71; physician emergency room Merle West Med. Ctr., Klamath Falls, Oreg., 1971-72; physician and ptnr. Klamath (Oreg.) Med. Clinic, 1972—; clin. instr. Cascade East Family Practice Residency, Klamath Falls, 1994—. Chief of staff Merle West Meml. Ctr., Klamath Falls, 1978-79; pres. Oreg. Acad. Family Practice, 1997-98; past pres., bd. dirs. Klamath Youth Devel. Ctr., Klamath Falls, 1980—, Klamath Lake CARES, PHP Health Plan; Oreg. del. to Am. Acad. Family Physicians Congress of Dels., 2001—. Pres. Klamath County Rotary Club, 1995-96. Fellow Am. Acad. Family Practice; mem. AMA, Oreg. Med. Assn., Klamath County Med. Soc. (pres.). Avocations: sailing, fishing, skiing, wine making. Office: Klamath Med Clinic 1905 Main St Klamath Falls OR 97601-2649 Home Phone: 541-882-6920. Personal E-mail: novja@aol.com. E-mail: jfnovak@klamathmedicalclinic.com.

NOVAK, TERRY LEE, dean, educator; b. Chamberlain, SD, Sept. 1, 1940; s. Warren F. and Elaine M. N.; m. Barbara Hosea, Aug. 29, 1981; 1 child, David. B.Sc., S.D. State U., 1962; postgrad. (Rotary fellow), U. Paris, 1962-63; M.P.A., Colo. U., 1965, PhD, 1970. Asst. city mgr. City of Anchorage, 1966-68; city mgr. City of Hopkins, Minn., 1968-74, City of Columbia, Mo., 1974-78, City of Spokane, Wash., 1978-91; v.p. bus. and fin. Ea. Wash. U., Cheney, 1991—94, prof. public adminstrn., 1992—, dir. grad. program pub. administrn., 1994-95; dir. Spokane Joint Ctr. for Higher Edn., 1995-98; bus. mgr. Riverpoint campus Wash. State U., 1998-99; prof pub. adminstrn. Eastern Wash. U., 1999—. Asst. adj. prof. U. Mo., Columbia, 1975, 77; adj. instr. Gonzaga U., Spokane, 1986-88; mem. nat. adv. coun. on environ. policy and tech. EPA. Author: Special Assessment Financing in American Cities, 1970; contbr. articles to profl. jours. Mem. ASPA, Internat. City Mgrs. Assn. (Acad. Profl. Devel.). Episcopalian. Office: 668 N Riverpoint Blvd Spokane WA 99202-1677 E-mail: tnovak@terrynovak.net.

NOVINS, DOUGLAS K., psychiatrist, educator; Prof. psychiatry divsn. child and adolescent psychiatry U. Colo., Denver. Recipient Presdl. Scholar award Am. Acad. Child and Adolescent Psychiatry, 1993. Office: U CO Divsn Child & Adolescent Psychiatry Health Scis Ctr PO Box C-259 42 Denver CO 80262-0001

NOWAKOWSKI, MICHAEL, Councilman; m. Delia Nowakowski; children: Victor, Michael Ray, Irene, Carlos Raul, Raymond Casmir. BA in Religious Studies, Ariz. State U. Gen. mgr. non-profit radio station; former asst. dir. Cath. Diocese Phoenix Office of Youth and Young Adult Ministry; councilman, Dist. 7 Phoenix City Coun. Chmn. Census Com.; mem. Downtown & Aviation, Housing & Neighborhoods Coms. Founding mem. Mayor's Anti-Graffiti Task Force; mem. City of Phoenix Census, 2000, Police Chief Adv. Bd.; co-chmn. City of Phoenix Hist. Bond Com., 2006; chmn. Santa Rosa Neighborhood Coun.; supt. adv. bd. Phoenix Union High Sch. Office: 200 W. Washington St 11th Fl Phoenix AZ 85003 Office Phone: 602-262-7492. Office Fax: 602-534-4816. Business E-Mail: council.district.7@phoenix.gov.*

NOWICK, ARTHUR STANLEY, metallurgy and materials science educator; b. NYC, Aug. 29, 1923; s. Hyman and Clara (Sperling) N.; m. Joan Franzblau, Oct. 30, 1949; children: Jonathan, Steven, Alan, James. AB, Bklyn. Coll., 1943; A.M., Columbia U., 1948, PhD, 1950. Physicist NACA, Cleve., 1944-46; instr. U. Chgo., 1949-51; asst. prof., then assoc. prof. metallurgy Yale U., 1951-57; mgr. metallurgy research IBM Corp Research Center, Yorktown Heights, NY, 1957-66; prof. metallurgy Columbia U., 1966-90, Henry Marion Howe prof. metallurgy and materials sci., 1990-95, prof. emeritus, 1996—. Adj. prof. chem. engring. and materials sci. dept. U. Calif., Irvine, 2001; Frank Golick lectr. U. Mo., 1970; vis. prof. Technion, Haifa, Israel, 1973; co-chmn. Internat. Conf. Internal Friction, 1961, 69; cons. in field. Author: Crystal Properties Via Group Theory, 1995; co-author: Anelastic Relaxation in Crystalline Solids, 1972; co-editor: Diffusion in Solids, 1975, Diffusion in Crystalline Solids, 1984; contbr. articles to profl. jours. Named David Turnbull lecturer Materials Rsch. Soc., 1994; gold medalist Internat. Conf. Internal Friction, 1989. Fellow AIME, Am. Phys. Soc.; mem. Materials Rsch. Soc. (Turnbull lectr. 1994), Sigma Xi (pres. Kappa chpt. 1983-85). Home: 24 Hillsdale Dr Newport Beach CA 92660-4234 Office: U Calif Irvine 916 Engineering Tower Irvine CA 92697-2575 Business E-Mail: anowick@uci.edu.

NOWICK, JAMES S., chemistry educator; AB, Columbia U., 1985; PhD, MIT, 1990. Postdoc. fellow Mass. Inst. Tech., Cambridge, 1990-91; prof. U. Calif., Irvine, 1991. Contbr. articles to profl. jours. includingJ. Am. Chem. Soc., J. Organic Chem. Recipient Nat. Sci. Found. fellowship, Am. Chem. Soc. Division of Organic Chemistry grad. fellowship, Camille and Henry Dreyfus Found. Disting. New Faculty award 1991, Am. Cancer Soc. Jr. Faculty Rsch. award 1992, Nat. Sci. Found. Young Investigator award 1992, Arnold and Mabel Beckman Found. Young Investigator award 1994, Camille Dreyfus Tchr.-Scholar award 1996, Alfred P. Sloan rsch. fellowship 1997, Arthur C. Cope Scholar award 1998. Office: U Calif Irvine Dept Chemistry 535B Psi Irvine CA 92697-0001

NOWINSKI, PETER A., federal judge; b. 1943; BA, San Jose State U., 1966; JD, U. Calif., San Francisco, 1969. Ptnr. Wilke, Fleury, Hoffelt, Gould & Birney; chief assoc. dep. atty. gen.; 1st asst., U.S. atty. ea. dist. U.S. Dist. Ct. Calif.; dir. torts br. civil divsn. Dept. Justice, Washington; apptd. magistrate judge ea. dist. U.S. Dist. Ct. Calif., 1991. Office: 5074 US Courthouse 650 Capitol Mall Sacramento CA 95814-4708

NOYES, HENRY PIERRE, physicist; b. Paris, Dec. 10, 1923; s. William Albert and Katharine Haworth (Macy) N.; m. Mary Wilson, Dec. 20, 1947; children— David Brian, Alan Guinn, Katharine Hope. AB magna cum laude, Harvard U., 1943; PhD, U. Calif., Berkeley, 1950. Physicist MIT, 1943-44, U. Calif., Berkeley, 1949-50; Fulbright fellow U. Birmingham, England, 1950-51; asst. prof. U. Rochester, NY, 1951-55; group leader Lawrence Livermore Lab., 1955-62; Leverhulme lectr. U. Liverpool, England, 1957-58; adminstrv. head theory sect. Stanford Linear Accelerator Center, 1962-69; asso. prof. Stanford U., 1962-67, prof., 1967-2000, prof. emeritus, 2000—; prin. investigator Mereon, 2005—. Vis. scholar Center Advanced Study Behavioral Scis., Stanford, 1968—69; prin. investigator Mereon, 2005—; cons. in field. Author papers in field. Chmn. Com. for Direct Attack on Legality of Vietnam War, 1969-72; mem. steering com. Faculty Political Action Group, Stanford U., 1970-72; mem. policy com. U.S. People's Com. on Iran, 1977-79. Served with USNR, 1944-46. Fellow NSF, 1962; Fellow Nat. Humanities Faculty, 1970; recipient Alexander von Humboldt U.S. Sr. Scientist award, 1979. Mem. Alternative Natural Philosophy Assn. (pres. 1979-87, 1st alternative natural philosopher award 1989), Am. Phys. Soc., AAAS, Sigma Xi. Achievements include research in bit-string physics. E-mail: noyes@slac.stanford.edu.

NOYES, RICHARD HALL, bookseller; b. Evanston, Ill., Feb. 12, 1930; s. George Frederick and Dorothy (Hall) N.; m. Judith Claire Mitchell, Oct. 10, 1953; children— Catherine, Stephanie, Matthew. BA, Wesleyan U., Middletown, Conn., 1952. Tng. program, elementary-high sch. salesman Rand McNally & Co., Colo., Utah, Idaho, Wyo., 1955-59; founder, owner, mgr. The Chinook Bookshop, Colorado Springs, Colo., 1959—. Contbr. to A Manual on Bookselling, 1974, The Business of Book Publishing, 1984; contbr. articles to newspapers and trade jours. Co-chmn. Colo. Media Coalition, 1974—; bd. dirs. Colorado Springs Fine Arts Ctr., 1977-81, Citizens Goals for Colorado Springs, 1976-88; trustee Fountain Valley Sch., 1979-81; vice chmn. Colorado Springs Charter Rev. Commn., 1991-92; mem. adv. com. U. Colo., Colorado Springs, 1997—, Downtown Partnership, 1998—. Served with AUS, 1952-54. Recipient Intellectual Freedom award Mountain Plains Librs. Assn., 1977, Disting. Svc. award U. Colo., 1980, Recognition award Pikes Peak Arts Coun., 1989, Charles S. Haslam award, 1990), Entrepreneur of Yr. award U. Colo., 1992, Gordon Saull award for outstanding bookseller Mountains and Plains Booksellers Assn., 1996. Mem. Am. Booksellers Assn. (pres., dir.) Home: 1601 Constellation Dr Colorado Springs CO 80906-1609

NUAIMI, MARK N., Mayor, Fontana, California; m. Susanne Nuaimi; children: Jessica, Marcus, Davis. BS in Elec. Engring., Calif. State Poly. U., Pomona; MA in Bus. Adminstrn., U. LaVerne. Chmn. Fontana Industrial Devel. Authority; current asst. mgr. City of Colton, Calif.; chmn. City of Fontana Area Coun., 1998—; mayor City of Fontana, Calif., 2002—. Rep. I-10 Corridor Com., Fontana Unified Sch. Dist. Sub-Com., Route 30 Corridor Com., City of Fontana Annexation and Pub. Rels., City of Fontana Recreation, City of Fontana C. of C., San Bernardino Associated Govt., Southern Calif. Assn. Govts. Mem.: Fontana Boys & Girls Club (pres. 1995—97, treas. 1997—99). Avocation: youth sports coach. Office: City Hall 8353 Sierra Ave Fontana CA 92335 Office Phone: 909-350-7600. Business E-Mail: mnuaimi@fontana.org.*

NUCHI, LIOR O., lawyer; b. Tiberius, Israel, Aug. 8, 1960; BA, Columbia Univ., 1982; JD, NYU, 1987. Bar: Calif. Sr. bus. ptnr. Bingham McCutchen, East Palo Alto, Calif.; ptnr., chmn. Cross-Border Transactions group & Israel practice Pillsbury Winthrop Shaw Pittman, Palo Alto, Calif., 2004—. Mem.: Nat. Assn. of Corp. Directors, Silicon Ventures, Calif.-Israel C. of C. Office: Pillsbury Winthrop Shaw Pittman 2475 Hanover St Palo Alto CA 94304-1114 Office Phone: 650-233-4803. Office Fax: 650-233-4545. Business E-Mail: lior.nuchi@pillsburylaw.com.

NUCKOLLS, JOHN HOPKINS, physicist, researcher; b. Chgo., Nov. 17, 1930; s. Asa Hopkins and Helen (Gates) N.; m. Ruth Munsterman, Apr. 21, 1952 (div. 1983); children: Helen Marie, Robert David; m. Amelia Aphrodite Liaskas, July 29, 1983. BS, Wheaton Coll., 1953; MA, Columbia U., 1955; DSc (hon.), Fla. Inst. Tech., 1977. Physicist U. Calif., Lawrence Livermore Nat. Lab., 1955—2007, assoc. leader thermonuclear design divsn., 1965-80, assoc. leader laser fusion program, 1975-83, divsn. leader, 1980-83, assoc. dir. physics, 1983-88, dir., 1988-94, assoc. dir. at large, 1994-97, dir. emeritus, 1997—, Lawrence Livermore Nat. Security, 2007—. Mem. emeritus U.S. Strategic Command Strategic adv. group; tech. adv. bd. Network Physics, Inc.; cons. def. sci. bd. Dept. Def., Intellectual Ventures; mem. adv. coms. to dir. CIA, 1989-99. Recipient E.O. Lawrence award Pres. and AEC, 1969, Fusion Leadership award, 1983, Edward Teller medal Am. Nuc. Soc., 1991, Resolution of Appreciation, U. Calif. Regents, 1994, Sec. of Def. Outstanding Pub. Svc. medal, 1996, Disting. Assoc. award U.S. Dept. Energy, 1996, Career Achievement award Fusion Power Assocs., 1996. Fellow: AAAS (J.C. Maxwell prize 1981), Am. Phys. Soc.; mem.: NAE. Office: Lawrence Livermore Nat Lab PO Box 808 Livermore CA 94551-0808 Home Phone: 925-736-8018; Office Phone: 925-422-5435. Personal E-mail: jhnuckel@comcast.net.

NUFFER, DAVID O., judge; BA in Humanities, Brigham Young U., 1975, JD, 1978. Bar: Utah 1978, Ariz. 1989. Ptnr. Snow Nuffer, St. George, 1979—2003. City atty. City of Kanab, Utah, 1981-92; mem. spl. task force for mgmt. and regulation of practice of law Utah Supreme Ct., 1990-91; Utah State Bar commr., 1994-2001; U.S. magistrate judge, 1995—. Mem. Utah State Bar (pres. 2000-2001). Office: 350 S Main 483 Salt Lake City UT 84101 Office Phone: 801-524-6150.

NUGENT, ROBERT J., JR., fast food company executive; b. 1942; BBA, U. Cin., 1964. Loan officer Citizens Savs., 1964-67; asst. v.p. Gem City Savs., 1967-69; v.p. Ponderosa System Inc., 1969-78, Ky. Fried Chicken, 1978-79, Foodmaker Inc., San Diego, from 1979, exec. v.p. ops., mktg., 1985-95, CEO, pres., 1995-99, Jack in the Box, Inc., San Diego, 1999—. Office: Jack in the Box Inc 9330 Balboa Ave San Diego CA 92123-1598

NULL, PAUL BRYAN, minister; b. Oakland, Calif., May 7, 1944; s. Carleton Elliot and Dorothy Irene (Bryan) N.; m. Renee Yvonne Howell, Aug. 23, 1969; children: Bryan Joseph, Kara Renee. BS, Western Bapt. Coll., 1973; MDiv, Western Conservative Bapt. Sem., 1979; DMin, Trinity Theol. Sem., 1994. Ordained to ministry Bapt. Ch., 1982. Asst. pastor Bethel Bapt. Ch., Aumsville, Oreg., 1972-74, sr. pastor, 1974-87, The Calvary Congregation, Stockton, Calif., 1987-94; pastor Sierra Cmty. Ch., South Lake Tahoe, Calif., 1994—99; exec. pastor Dayspring Fellowship, Salem, Oreg., 1999—2004; gen. dir. Conservative Bapt. Assn. No. Calif. and Nev., 2004—. Trustee Conservative Bapt. Assn. of Oreg., 1982-85, mem. Ch. extension com., 1975-85. Radio show commentator Food for Thought, 1987. Panel mem. Presdl. Anti-Drug Campaign, 1984; bd. dirs. Western Bapt. Coll., Salem, 1998—. Served with U.S. Army, 1965-67. Named Outstanding Young Man Am., 1979. Mem. Conservative Bapt. Assn. of Am., No. Calif. Conservative Bapt. Assn. (pres. 1992-93), Delta Epsilon Chi. Avocations: weight training, aerobics, writing, hiking, cross country skiing. Home: 2922 Lonnie Beck Way Stockton CA 95209 Office: 1545 St Marks Plz Ste 1 Stockton CA 95207 Home Phone: 209-477-2851; Office Phone: 209-954-0499. Personal E-mail: nextgenpbn@sbcglobal.net. Business E-Mail: paul@nextgenchurches.com.

NUNES, DEVIN, United States Representative from California; b. Tulare, Calif., Oct. 1, 1973; m. Elizabeth Tamariz. BS in Agrl. Bus., Calif. Poly. State U., 1995, MS in Agrl., 1996. Cert. Calif. Agr. Leadership Fellowship Prog., 2000. Farmer, mgr. Nunes Dairy, 1998—2000; Calif. state dir. USDA, 2001; mem. US Congress from 21st Calif. dist., 2002—, mem. ways and means com., former asst. majority whip. Mem. Western Caucus, Rep. Main Street Partnership, Prescription Drug Action Team, Portuguese Caucus, Ho. Impact Aid Coalition, Congl. Youth Civic Caucus, Congl. Working Grp. Combat Govt. Waste, Congl. Wine Caucus, Congl. Mining Caucus, Congl. Farmer Cooperative Caucus, Congl. Caucus to Fight/Control Methamphetamine, Congl. Caucus Am. Issues; mem., former co-chair Congl. Hispanic Caucus; chair Dairy Caucus. Mem. bd. trustees Coll. Sequoias, 1996—2002. Republican. Roman Catholic. Office: US Ho Reps 1013 Longworth Ho Office Bldg Washington DC 20515-0521

NUNEZ, ANDY K., state legislator; b. Roswell, N.Mex., Nov. 30, 1935; m. Carolyn Nunez; children: Dolores, Kelly, Kimberly, Kyla, Shannon. BS, N.Mex. State U., 1962, MS, 1974. Dir. Agr. Stabilization and Conservation Svc. USDA, 1963—70; dir. Internat. Programs N.Mex. State U., 1970—78; exec. dir. Puerto Rico Farm Bur., 1978—80; farmer/rancer N.Mex., 1980—99; legis. liaison N.Mex. State U., 1991—2001; mem. dist. 36 N.Mex. House of Reps., Santa Fe, 2000—. Mem. Water and Resources com. N.Mex. State Legis., Santa Fe, mem. Taxation and Revenue com.; mem. South Ctrl. Coun. Govt., 2001—; bd. trustees City of Hatch, N.Mex., 2001—; mem. Gov.'s Rural Econ. Response Coun., 1992—96. Pres. Ben Archer Health Ctr. Bd., 1988—89; bd. mem. Las Cruces Affordable Housing Inc.; pres. Immaculate Heart of Mary Sch. Bd., 1973—74. Sgt. USMC, 1953—56. Mem.: N.Mex. Farm and Livestock Bur., Lions (sec. 1964), Jaycees (sec. 1963), Am. Legion Post 42 (dir.). Democrat. Roman Catholic. Home: PO Box 746 Hatch NM 87937 Office: New Mexico State Capitol Rm 204A Santa Fe NM 87503 Home Phone: 575-267-3451. E-mail: annunez@zianet.com.*

NUNEZ, OSCAR, actor; b. Cuba, Nov. 18, 1958; m. Carla Nunez. Attended, F.I.T., Parsons Sch. Design, NYC; grad., Magna Inst. Dental Tech. Cert. Dental Tech. Former mem. Shock of the Funny Comedy Troupe, Groundlings Sunday Co. Actor: (films) The Italian Job, 2003, When Do We Eat?, 2005, The Chipotle Diamonds, 2005, Glory Road, 2006, Reno 911!: Miami, 2007; (TV series) Resurrection Blvd., 24, Arrested Development, The Steve Harvey Show, That's Life, Ally McBeal, Curb Your Enthusiasm, 2000, The Bad Girl's Guide, 2003, Reno 911!, 2004—06, The Office, 2006— (Outstanding Performance by an Ensemble in a Comedy Series, SAG, 2007, 2008); actor, exec. prodr. (TV series) Halfway Home, 2007—. Office: OmniPop Talent Group Ste 201 4605 Lankershim Blvd Toluca Lake CA 91602

NUNN, ROBERT WARNE, lawyer; b. Salem, Oreg., Sept. 20, 1950; s. Warne Harry and Delores Nunn; m. Kandis Brewer; 1 child, Hayley Elisabeth. Student, U. Vienna, Austria, 1971; BS, Willamette U., 1972; MS in Acctg., Northeastern U., Boston, 1973, MBA, 2000; JD, U. Oreg., 1976. Bar: Oreg 1976, U.S. Dist. Ct. Oreg. 1977, U.S. Ct. Appeals (9th cir.) 1977, U.S. Supreme Ct. 1982, Wash. 1986. Ptnr. Schwabe, Williamson &, Wyatt, Portland, Oreg., 1976-92; ptnr., chmn. corp. dept. Preston, Gates & Ellis, Portland, 1992-96; founder, mng. ptnr. Nunn Motschenbacher & Blattner LLP, Portland, 1996—. Dir. Oreg. State Bar Profl. Liability Fund, 1996—2004; ptnr. Sussman Shankman LLP, 2001—. Mem. exec. com. Am. Leadership Forum, 1988-94, sr. fellow, 1988—; bd. mgrs. Multnomah Metro Br. YMCA, Portland, 1983-86, chmn., 1984-85; pres. Oreg. divsn. Am. Cancer Soc., Portland, 1986-87, bd. dirs., 1982-88; trustee Marylhurst Coll., Oreg., 1985-91, Willamette U., 1991—; trustee World Affairs Coun. Oreg., 1991-97, pres., 1995-96; bd. dirs. United Way of Columbia-Willamette, Portland, 1984-87. Named Order of Red Sword, Am. Cancer Soc., 1985; fellow Am. Leadership, 1987. Mem. ABA, Oreg. Bar Assn. (past chmn. CPA joint com., past chmn. legal assts. and legal investigators com., cert. subcom., fee arbitration panel), Univ. Club, Multhnomah Athletic Club (Portland). Republican. Lutheran. Avocations: rowing, skiing, sailing. Office: Sussman Shank LLP 1000 SW Broadway Ste 1400 Portland OR 97205 Office Phone: 503-227-1111.

NUNN, TODD L., lawyer; b. Seattle, Apr. 7, 1968; BA, Univ. Wash., 1990, JD, 1993. Bar: Wash. 1993, U.S. Dist. Ct., Western Dist. Wash. 1994, U.S. Dist. Ct., Eastern Dist. Wash. 1997, U.S. Ct. Appeals, Ninth Circuit 1997. Assoc. atty., class action, complex litig. Preston Gates & Ellis, LLP, Seattle. Contbr. articles to numerous profl. jours. Named Wash. Rising Star, SuperLawyer Mag., 2006. Mem.: ABA, Wash. Defense Trial Lawyers Assn., Wash. Bar Assn. Office: Preston Gates & Ellis LLP Ste 2900 925 Fourth Ave Seattle WA 98104-1158

NUSSBAUM, LEONARD MARTIN, lawyer; b. Amarillo, Tex., Nov. 8, 1951; s. Leonard J. and Elizabeth Marie (Gulde) N.; m. Melissa Musick, Jan. 5, 1974; children: Abraham, Elisabeth, Mary Margaret, Anna Catherine, Andrew. BA in Theology (summa cum laude), U. Notre Dame, 1974; JD, U. Tex. at Austin Law Sch., 1985. Bar: Colo. 1985, U.S. Dist. Ct. Colo. 1985. V.p. A to Z Tire and Battery, Amarillo, 1974-82; atty. Sparks, Dix, Enoch, Suthers & Winslow, P.C., Colorado Springs, Colo., 1985-89; shareholder Sparks Dix, P.C., Colorado Springs, 1989-97; ptnr. Rothgerber Johnson & Lyons LLP, Denver, 1997—. Dean's adv. com. U. Colo. at Colorado Springs, Coll. of Letters, Arts & Sci., 1987-92; co-chair, religious institutions group, Rothgerber Johnson & Lyons, LLP; mem. employment law group, Rothgerber Johnson & Lyons, LLP. Nat. Editor, Harvard Jour. Law and Public Policy, 1983-85; editor, First Freedom. Dir. Western Ctr. Law and Religious Liberty. Weaver fellow Intercollegiate Studies Inst., 1982l; named to Colo. Super Lawyers, 2006. Mem. Nat. Diocesan Attys. Assn. (mem. litig. com., 2001-), Fed. Soc. Law and Pub. Policy (ex officio dir. 1985-86), Tex. Federalist Soc. of Law and Pub. Policy (founder, pres. 1983-85), El Paso County Bar Assn. (employment law com. 1988—, program chmn. 1989-91, trustee 1991-92), Christian Legal Soc., Ctr. Law and Religious Freedom (mem. case selection com., 2001-), Phi Beta Kappa. Office: Rothgerber Johnson & Lyons LLP 90 S Cascade Ave 1100 Colorado Springs CO 80903 Office Phone: 719-386-3004.

NUSSBAUM, LUTHER JAMES, computer company executive; b. Decatur, Ind., Jan. 13, 1947; s. Leo Lester and Janet Nell (Gladfelter) N.; m. Ginger Mae McCown, Aug. 24, 1968; children: Kari, Kris. BA, Rhodes Coll., 1968; MBA, Stanford U., 1972. Dir. compensation Cummins Engine Co., Columbus, Ind., 1974-75, v.p. distbn. cos., 1977-79, v.p. parts bus., 1979-82, v.p. strategic planning, 1982-83, gen. mgr. Mex. region Mexico City, 1975-77; v.p. field ops. Businessland, San Jose, Calif., 1983-84, v.p. ops., 1984-85, sr. v.p. mktg., ops., 1985-86; pres., chief operating officer Ashton-Tate, Torrance, Calif.,

1986—. Bd. dirs. Interbase, Bedford. Mem. Dem. Nat. Fin. Council, 1986—, Dem. Nat. Bus. Council, 1987—. Mem. Young Pres's. Orgn., Phi Beta Kappa. Avocations: tennis, running. Home: 5818 E Bay Shore Walk Long Beach CA 90803-4463 Office: 1st Consulting Group Inc 111 W Ocean Blvd Ste 1000 Long Beach CA 90802

NUTTALL, RICHARD NORRIS, management consultant, physician; b. Hamilton, Ont., Can., Feb. 7, 1940; s. James William and Margaret Gay (Walsh) N.; m. Ethel Jane Pickering, July 9, 1977; children: Andrew Richard, John Patrick. BSA, U. Toronto, 1961; MPA, Harvard U., 1964; MB, BS, U. London, 1974; TM, MPH, James Cook U., 2003; MSc, U. Western Ont., 2005. Cert. mgmt. cons. Zone dir. Health and Welfare Can., Prince Rupert, B.C., 1977-79, regional dir. Edmonton, Alta., 1980-82; pres. Rutland Consulting Group, Ltd., Vancouver, B.C., Canada, 1982-87, Richmond Assocs. Internat., Vancouver, 1988-90; med. health officer Govt. N.W. Ters., Yellowknife, B.C., Canada, 1990-93, Regina (Can.) Health Dist., 1993-97; pres. Anjohn Med. Svcs., Inc., Victoria, Canada, 1997—. Staff physician Royal Jubilee Hosp. Fellow Am. Coll. Preventive Medicine, Am. Coll. Healthcare Execs., Can. Coll. Health Svc. Execs., Coll. Family Physicians Can. Office: 1186 Eaglenest Pl Victoria BC V8Y 3C7 Canada Office Phone: 250-598-5158. Business E-Mail: rnuttall@shaw.ca.

NUTZLE, FUTZIE (BRUCE JOHN KLEINSMITH), artist, writer, animator; b. Lakewood, Ohio, Feb. 21, 1942; s. Adrian Ralph and Naomi Irene Kleinsmith; children: Adrian David, Ariel Justine and Tess Alexandra (twins); m. Halina Pochron Kleinsmith. Author: Modern Loafer, Thames and Hudson, 1981, (authobiography) Futzie Nutzle, 1983, Earthquake, 1989, Run the World: 50 Cents Chronicle Books, 1991; illustrator: The Armies Encamped Beyond Unfinished Avenues (Morton Marcus), 1977, Box of Nothing, 1982, The Duke of Chemical Birds (Howard McCord), 1989, Book of Solutions, 1990, Fact and Friction, 1990, Managing for the 90s, 1992, Soundbites for Success, 1994; feature cartoonist Rolling Stone, N.Y.C., 1975-80, The Japan Times, Tokyo and L.A., 1986-98, The Prague Post, Czechoslovakia, 1991-92; contbr. exhbns. include Inaugural, 1966, Cupola, 1967, Rolling Renaissance, San Francisco, 1968, 100 Acres, O.K. Harris 1971, N.Y.C., San Francisco Mus. Art, 1972, Indpls. and Cin. Mus. Art, 1975, Leica, L.A., 1978, Santa Barbara Mus. Annex, Calif., 1978, Swope, Santa Monica, West Beach Cafe, Venice, Calif., 1985, Les Oranges, Santa Monica, Correspondence Sch., NY Correspondence Sch., 1968-75, 1st Ann. Art-A-Thon, N.Y.C., 1985, Am. Epiphany with Phillip Hefferton, 1986, Polit. Cartoon Show, Braunstein, San Francisco, Komsomolskaya Pravda, 1988, retrospective Eloise Packard Smith, 1990, exemplary contemporary, Cowell, U. Calif. Santa Cruz, 1991, Silicon Graphics Inc., Computer Graphics for NAB, Las Vegas, 1993, Prague Eco-Fair, 1991; represented in pvt. and pub. collections (complete archives) Spl. Collections, McHenry Libr., U. Calif., Santa Cruz, Mus. Modern Art, N.Y.C., San Francisco Mus. Modern Art, Oakland Mus., San Francisco Mus. Cartoon Art, Whitney Mus. Am. Art, N.Y.C., Aromas (Calif.) Libr., San Juan Bautista Libr., contbr. The Redwood Coast Review, (bugle) Art Secundas Artists Periodical Scottsdale, Ariz. Address: Fools Gold 34A Polk St PO Box 1083 San Juan Bautista CA 95045 Office Phone: 831-623-9275. Personal E-mail: fnutzle@aol.com.

NYBAKKEN, JAMES WILLARD, marine biology educator; b. Warren, Minn., Sept. 16, 1936; s. Clarence G. and Effie Pearl (Knutson) N.; m. Bette Halvorsen, Aug. 20, 1960; children: Kent Edward, Scott Jordan. BA summa cum laude, St. Olaf Coll., Northfield, Minn., 1958; MS, U. Wis., 1961, PhD, 1965. Curator zool. museum U. Wis., 1961-62, 64-65; mem. faculty Calif. State U., Hayward, 1965—98, prof. marine ecology and invertebrate zoology, 1972—98; mem. staff Moss Landing Marine Lab., Calif., 1966—98; ret., 1998. Environ. cons., 1972— Author: Readings in Marine Ecology, 1971, 2d edit., 1986, Elements of Zoology, 4th edit, 1977, General Zoology, 6th edit, 1979, Guide to the Nudibranchs of California, 1980, Marine Biology: An Ecological Approach, 1982, 2d edit., 1987, 3d edit., 1992, 4th edit., 1996, 5th edit., 2001, 6th edit., 2005, Diversity of the Invertebrates: A Laboratory Manual, 1996; editor: Interdisciplinary Encyclopedia of Marine Science (3 vols.), 2003. Fellow Calif. Acad. Scis.; mem. AAAS, Am. Soc. Zoologists, Am. Malacological Union (pres. 1985-86), Ecol. Soc. Am., Malacological Soc. London, Western Soc. Malacologists (pres. 1974-75), Western Soc. Naturalists (pres.-elect 1985, pres. 1986, secretariat 1990-96), Sigma Xi.

NYCUM, SUSAN HUBBELL, lawyer; BA, Ohio Wesleyan U., 1956; JD, Duquesne U., 1960; postgrad., Stanford U., Calif. Bar: Pa. 1962, Calif. 1964, U.S. Supreme Ct. 1967. Pvt. practice, Pitts., 1962—65; designer, adminstr. legal rsch. sys. U. Pitts., Aspen Sys. Corp., Pitts., 1965-68; mgr. ops. Computer Ctr., Carnegie Mellon U., Pitts., 1968-69; dir. computer facility Computer Ctr., Stanford U., 1969-72, Stanford Law and Computer fellow, 1972-73; cons. in computers and law, 1973-74; sr. assoc. MacLeod, Fuller, Muir & Godwin, Los Altos, LA and London, 1974-75; ptnr. Chickering & Gregory, San Francisco, 1975-80; ptnr.-in-charge high tech. group Gaston Snow & Ely Bartlett, Boston, NYC, Phoenix, San Francisco, 1980-86; mng. ptnr. Palo Alto office Kadison, Pfaelzer, Woodard, Quinn & Rossi, LA, Washington, Newport Beach, Palo Alto, Calif., 1986-87; sr. ptnr., chmn. U.S. intellectual property/info. tech. practice group Baker & McKenzie, Palo Alto, 1987—2002, mem. U.S. leadership team, 1987-97, mem. Asia Pacific regional coun., 1995—2002; with Tech. Disputes Resolution Svcs. Inc., 2002—. Founder Tech. Disputes Resolution Svcs., Inc., 2002—; trustee EDUCOM, 1978-81; mem. adv. com. for high tech. Ariz. State U. Law Sch., Santa Clara U. Law Sch., Stanford Law Sch., U. So. Calif. Law Ctr., Harvard U. Law Sch., U. Calif.; U.S. State Dept. del. OECD Conf. on Nat. Vulnerabilities, Spain, 1981; invited spkr. Telecom., Geneva, 1983; lectr. N.Y. Law Jour., 1975—, Law & Bus., 1975—, Practicing Law Inst., 1975—; chmn. Office of Tech. Assessment Task Force on Nat. Info. Sys., 1979-80. Author:(with Bigelow) Your Computer and the Law, 1975, (with Bosworth) Legal Protection for Software, 1985, (with Collins and Gilbert) Women Leading, 1987; contbr. monographs, articles to profl. publs. Fellow Am. Bar Found.; mem. Town of Portola Valley Open Space Acquisition Com., Calif., 1977; mem. Jr. League of Palo Alto, chmn. evening div., 1975-76 NSF and Dept. Justice grantee for studies on computer abuse, 1972-. Fellow Am. Bar Found., Assn. Computer Machinery (mem. at large of coun. 1976-80, nat. lectr. 1977—, chmn. standing com. on legal issues 1975—, mem. blue ribbon com. on rationalization of internat. propr. rights protection on info. processing devel. in the '90s 1990—, Hall of Fame 2004), Coll. Law Practice Mgmt. (trustee 2002—), Coll. Comml. Arbitration; mem. ABA (chmn. sect. on sci. and tech. 1979-80), Computer Law Assn. (v.p. 1983-85, pres. 1986—, bd. dirs. 1975—), Calif. State Bar Assn. (founder first chmn. econs. of law sect., vice chmn. law and computers com.), Internat. Bar Assn. (U.S. mem. computer com. of corps. sect.), Nat. Conf. Lawyers and Scientists (rep. ABA), Strategic Forum on Intellectual Property Issues in Software of NAS, Internat. Coun. for Computer Comm. (gov. 1998). Office: 35 Granada Ct Portola Valley CA 94028-7736 Office Phone: 650-851-3304. Business E-Mail: susan@nycum.net.

NYE, DAN, Internet company executive; BA in Polit. Sci., Hamilton Coll., 1988; MBA, Harvard Bus. Sch., 1994. Mem. brand mgmt. Procter & Gamble, 1988—92; various positions including, v.p., gen. mgr. internat. divsn., dir. mktg. for small bus. products and svcs., v.p., gen. mgr., small bus. divsn. Intuit, Inc., 1995—2001; exec. v.p., gen. mgr., investment mgmt. Advent Software, 2002—07; CEO LinkedIn Corp., Moutain View, Calif., 2007—. Office: LinkedIn Corp 2029 Stierlin Ct Mountain View CA 94043

NYGREN, DAVID ROBERT, physicist, researcher; BA in Math., Whitman Coll., 1960; PhD in Physics, U. Wash., 1967. Rsch. assoc. Nevis Labs. Columbia U., NYC; assoc. prof. Physics Columbia U., 1969; divsn. fellow Lawrence Berkeley (Calif.) Nat. Lab., 1973-75, sr. physicist, 1975—. Distinguished visiting scientist Jet Propulsion Lab., Pasadena, Calif.; exec. com. mem. Am. Physical Soc. Divsn. Particles and Fields. Recipient E.O. Lawrence award, W.H.K. Panofsky prize in Experimental Particle Physics 1998. Fellow Am. Physicl Soc. Office: Lawrence Berkeley Nat Lab U Calif Mailstop 50B 6208 One Cyclotron Rd Berkeley CA 94720

NYHAN, WILLIAM LEO, pediatrician, educator; b. Boston, Mar. 13, 1926; s. W. Leo and Mary N.; m. Christine Murphy, Nov. 20, 1948; children: Christopher, Abigail. Student, Harvard U., 1943-45; MD, Columbia U., 1949; MS, U. Ill., 1956, PhD, 1958; doctorate (hon.), Tokushima U., Japan, 1981. Intern Yale U.-Grace-New Haven Hosp., 1949-50, resident, 1950-51, 53-55; asst. prof. pediatrics Johns Hopkins U., 1958-61, assoc. prof., 1961-63; prof. pediatrics, biochemistry U. Miami, 1963-69, chmn. dept. pediatrics, 1963-69; prof. U. Calif., San Diego, 1969—, chmn. dept. pediatrics, 1969-86. Mem. FDA adv. com. on Teratogenic Effects of Certain Drugs, 1964-70; mem. pediatric panel AMA Council on Drugs, 1964-70; mem. Nat. Adv. Child Health and Human Devel. Council, 1967-71; mem. research adv. com. Calif. Dept. Mental Hygiene, 1969-72; mem. med. and sci. adv. com. Leukemia Soc. Am., Inc., 1968-72; mem. basic adv. com. Nat. Found. March of Dimes, 1973-81; mem. Basil O'Connor Starter grants com., 1973-93; mem. clin. cancer program project rev. com. Nat. Cancer Inst., 1977-81; vis. prof. extraordinario U. del Salvador (Argentina), 1982. Author (with E. Edelson): The Heredity Factor, Genes, Chromosomes and You, 1976; author: Genetic & Malformation Syndromes in Clinical Medicine, 1976, Abnormalities in Amino Acid Metabolism in Clinical Medicine, 1984, Diagnostic Recognition of Genetic Diseases, 1987; author: (with P. Ozand) Atlas of Metabolic Diseases, 1998; author: (with B. Barshop and P. Ozand) 2d edit., 2005; author: (with G. Hoffmann, J. Zschocke, S.G. Kahler and E. Mayatepek) Inherited Metabolic Diseases, 2001; editor: Amino Acid Metabolism and Genetic Variation, 1967, Heritable Disorders of Amino Acid Metabolism, 1974; mem. editl. bd.: Jour. Pediat., 1964—78, Western Jour. Medicine, 1974—86, King Faisal Hosp. Med. Jour., 1981—85, Annals of Saudi Medicine, 1985—87, mem. editl. com.: Ann. Rev. Nutrition, 1982—86, mem. editl. staff: Med. and Pediat. Oncology, 1975—83. Served with U.S. Navy, 1944-46; U.S. Army, 1951-53. Nat. Found. Infantile Paralysis fellow, 1955-58; recipient Commemorative medallion Columbia U. Coll. Physicians and Surgeons, 1967, Guthrie award Am. Assn. Mental Retardation, 1998, Pool of Bethesda award Bethesda Luth. Homes and Svcs., 1999. Fellow: Inst. Medicine of Nat. Acad. Scis., Am. Acad. Pediat. (Borden award 1980, Lifetime Achievement award 1999, Leonard Tow Humanism Medicine award Arnold P. Gold Found. 2008); mem.: AAAS, Biochem. Soc., Am. Coll. Med. Genetics, Am. Assn. Clin. Chemists, Am. Soc. Human Genetics (dir. 1978—81), Am. Soc. Clin. Investigation, Soc. Exptl. Biology and Medicine, Am. Inst. Biol. Scis., Am. Pediatric Soc., South African Human Genetics (hon.), Nat. Acad. Scis. Inst. Medicine (hon.), Inst. Investigaciones Citologicas (Spain) (corr.), Soc. Francaise de Pediatrie (corr.), N.Y. Acad. Sci., Western Soc. Pediatric Rsch. (pres. 1976—77), Am. Soc. Pharmacology and Exptl. Therapeutics, Am. Assn. Cancer Rsch., Soc. Pediatric Rsch. (pres. 1970—71), Am. Chem. Soc., Am. Fedn. Clin. Rsch., Alpha Omega Alpha, Sigma Xi. Office: U Calif San Diego Dept Pediatrics # 0830 9500 Gilman Dr La Jolla CA 92093-0830 Office Phone: 619-543-5237. Business E-Mail: wnyhan@ucsd.edu.

NYMAN, MICHAEL S., marketing executive; BA, U. So. Calif., 1986. Prin. Bragman, Nyman, Cafarelli, Inc., Beverly Hills, Calif., 1990—. Office: Bragman Nyman Cafarelli 8687 Melrose Ave West Hollywood CA 90069-5701

OAKLAND, SUZANNE N.J. CHUN, state legislator; d. Philip S. and Mei-Chih Chun; m. Michael Sands Chun Oakland, June 11, 1994; children: Mailene Nohea Pua, Michael Sing Kamakaku, Lauren Suzanne LeRong. BA in Comm. and Psychology, U. Hawaii. Adminstrv. asst. Au's Plumbing and Metal Works, 1979—90; cmty. svcs. specialist Hawaii State Senate, 1984; adminstrv. asst. Smolenski & Woodell, Attys. at Law, 1984—86; rsch. asst., office mgr. City Coun. mem. Gary Gill, 1987—90; state rep. House Dist. 27, 1990—96; state senator Senate Dist. 13, 1996—. Vice chair com. on health State Senate, 2003—, chair com. on human svcs., 2003—, com. on edn. and mil. affairs, 2005—, com. on higher edn., 2005—. Mem. Hawaii State Youth Vol. Bd., 1978—; bd. dirs. Honolulu Neighborhood Housing Svcs., 1986—88, 1989—, McKinley H.S. Found. and McKinley Alumni Assn., 1989—; mem. adv. bd. Lanakila Milti-Purpose Sr. Ctr., 1991—; com. The CHOW Project, 1992—; mem. Chung Wah Chung Kung Hui, 1991—; adv. bd. Sex Abuse Treatment Ctr., 1993—; vol. Legal Svcs. Hawaii, 1994—; bd. dirs. Susannah Wesley Cmty. Ctr., 2001—, Hawaii Housing Devel. Corp., 1993—; mem. Children's Trust Fund Adv. Coun., 1993—; bd. dirs. Liliha-Palama Bus. Assn., 1994—; mem. Hawaii Kids Count Coun., 1994—; chair senate com. Human Svcs. Pub. Housing, 2006—, Human Svcs., 2003—06. Recipient Friend of Family award, Hawaii Assn. for Marriage and Family Therapy, 1998, Legislator of Yr. award, Mental Health Assn., 1999, Outstanding Legislator award, Hawaii Med. Assn., 1999, Legislator of Yr. award, Aloha State Assn. of Deaf, 1999, Hawaii State Chiropractic Assn., 2000, numerous other awards, Best Adv. Hawaii Children and Families, Children's Right Coun. Hawaii, 2005, Cert. Appreciation, MATAH, 2005, Child & Family Svc. award, Families Elders of Hawaii, 2007, Shining Light award, Hawaii Alliance Ret. Ams., 2008, 4-H Ali'i award, 2008; named Internat. Profl. of Yr., Internat. Biog. Ctr's., 2005, Woman of Yr., Am. Biog. Inst., Profl. of Yr., IBC Internat., 2006, Hawaii Cert. Appreciation, AARP, 2006. Mem.: Farrington HS Cmty. Based Mgmt., Bayanihan Clin. Without Walls (adv. bd. 2002—), Honolulu Cmty. Action Program (bd. dirs. 2002—), Hawaii Chinese Civic Assn., Chinese C. of C.

OAKLEY, CAROLYN LE, state legislator, city manager, director; b. Portland, Oreg., June 28, 1942; d. George Thomas and Ruth Alveta Victoria (Engberg) Penketh; children: Christine, Michelle. BS in Edn., Oreg. State U., 1965. Educator Linn County (Oreg.) Schs., 1965-76; owner Linn County Tractor, 1965-90; mem. Oreg. Legis. Assembly, Salem, 1989—, asst. majority leader, 1993—, majority whip, 1994; apptd. regional dir. region 10 Dept. Health and Human Svcs., Seattle, 2002—. Mem. exec. bd. Oreg. Retail Coun., 1987-90. Chmn. Linn County Rep. Ctrl. Com., 1982-84; chmn. bd. dirs. North Albany Svc. Dist., 1988-90; chair Salvation Army, Linn and Benton Counties, 1987—; vice chmn. bd. trustees Linn-Benton C.C. Found., 1987—; pres. Women for Agr., Linn and Benton Counties, 1984-86; mem. STRIDE Leadership Round Table, 1991—; state chair Am. Legis. Exch. Coun., 1991-96; nat. bd. dirs., 199-99, exec. com., 1995, 1st vice chair, 1998; mem. Edn. Commn. of the States, 1991—, com. policies and priorities, 1993—, steering com., 1998—, exec. com., 1998; mem. Leadership Coun. on Higher Edn., 1995—; mem. nat. policy bd. Danforth Found., 1995—; state dir., Women in Govt., 1996—; state dir., Nat. Order Women Legislators, 1993—; hon. mem. Linn-Benton Compact Bd., 1993—; active Linn County Criminal Justice Coun., 1994—; vol. Good Samaritan Hosp. Found., State Land Trust for Affordable Housing, Majestic Theater; bd. trustees Good Samaritan Found., 2006—; pres. Benton County Rep. Women, 2000-02. Named Woman of Yr. Albany chpt. Beta Sigma Phi, 1970. Mem. Nat Conf. State Legislators (chmn. edn. com. 1992—), Albany C. of C. (bd. dirs. 1986-93, 96—), Linn County Rep. Women (legis. chmn. 1982-91, pres. 2006—), Greater Corvallis Rotary Club (bd. dirs., 2004-), Delta Kappa Gamma Soc. Internat. Republican. Avocations: gardening, camping, volunteering. Home: 3197 NW Crest Loop Albany OR 97321-9627 Office Phone: 541-928-7745. Personal E-mail: cloakley@juno.com.

OAKS, DALLIN HARRIS, lawyer, church official; b. Provo, Utah, Aug. 12, 1932; s. Lloyd E. and Stella (Harris) Oaks; m. June Dixon, June 24, 1952 (dec. July 1998); children: Sharmon, Cheri Lyn, Lloyd D., Dallin D., TruAnn, Jenny June; m. Kristen McMain, Aug. 25, 2000. BA with high honors, Brigham Young U., 1954, LLD (hon.), 1980; JD cum laude, U. Chgo., 1957; LLD (hon.), Pepperdine U., 1982, So. Utah U., 1991. Bar: Ill. 1957, Utah 1971. Law clk. to Chief Justice Earl Warren U.S. Supreme Ct., 1957—58; with firm Kirkland, Ellis, Hodson, Chaffetz & Masters, Chgo., 1958—61; mem. faculty U. Chgo. Law Sch., 1961—71, assoc. dean and acting dean, 1962, prof., 1964—71, mem. vis. com., 1971—74; pres. Brigham Young U., Provo, Utah, 1971—80; also prof. law J. Reuben Clark Law Sch., 1974—80; justice Utah Supreme Ct., 1981—84; mem. Coun. of Twelve Apostles Ch. Jesus Christ of Latter Day Sts., 1984—, pres. Philippines area, 2002—04. Legal counsel Bill of Rights com. Ill. Constl. Conv., 1970. Author (with G.G. Bogert): Cases on Trusts, 1967, 1978; author: (with W. Lehman) A Criminal Justice System and The Indigent, 1968; author: The Criminal Justice Act in the Federal District Courts, 1969; author: (with M. Hill) Carthage Conspiracy, 1975; author: Trust Doctrines in Church Controversies, 1984, Pure in Heart, 1988, The Lord's Way, 1991, His Holy Name, 1998, With Full Purpose of Heart, 2002; editor: The Wall Between Church and State, 1963; contbr. Mem. adv. com. Nat. Inst. Law Enforcement and Criminal Justice, 1974—76; mem. Wilson coun. Woodrow Wilson Internat. Ctr. for Scholars, 1973—80; trustee Intermountain Health Care Inc., 1975—80; regional rep. Ch. of Jesus Christ of Latter-day Saints, 1974—80, past 1st counselor Chgo. South Stake; bd. dirs. Notre Dame Ctr. for Constl. Studies, 1977—80, Rockford Inst., 1980—2000, Pub. Broadcasting Svc., 1977—85, chmn., 1980—85; bd. dirs. Polynesian Cultural Ctr., 1987—96, chmn., 1988—96. Fellow: Am. Bar Found. (exec. dir. 1970—71); mem.: Am. Assn. Pres. Ind. Colls. and Univs. (pres. 1975—78, dir. 1971—78), Order of Coif. Lds Ch. Office: Quorum of Twelve 47 E South Temple Salt Lake City UT 84150-1200

O'BARA, KENNETH J., physician; b. Detroit, Feb. 27, 1947; s. John Joseph and Catherine (Levens) O'Bara; m. Marianne Schwartz, July 29, 1972; children: Thomas, Mickel. BSE, U. Mich., Ann Arbor, 1969, MD, 1976. Diplomate Am. Bd. Emergency Medicine. Resident Truman Med. Ctr., Kansas City, Mo., 1976-79; mem. staff St. Joseph Mercy Hosp., Ann Arbor, 1979-80, Centralia (Wash.) Gen. Hosp., 1980-81, St. Helen's Hosp., Chehalis, Wash., 1980-81, Valley Med. Ctr., Renton, Wash., 1981—. ACLS affiliate faculty Am. Heart Assn., Seattle, 1982-86; co-dir. Assn. Emergency Physicians, Seattle, 1983-85. Fellow Am. Coll. Emergency Physicians, Wash. State Med. Soc., King County Med. Soc. Office: 8009 S 180th St Ste 103 Kent WA 98032-1042

OBERG, LARRY REYNOLD, librarian; b. Midvale, Idaho; s. Gustav Wilhelm and Esther Marie (Watkins) O.; m. Marilyn Ann Gow, Jan. 1, 1964 (div. 1985); 1 child, Marc Aurelien. AB in Anthropology, U. Calif., Berkeley, 1977, MLS, 1978. Reference librarian Stanford (Calif.) U., 1979-80, U. Calif., Berkeley, 1981-82; dir. libr. Lewis-Clark State Coll., Lewiston, Idaho, 1984-86; dir. library Albion (Mich.) Coll., 1986-92; univ. libr. Willamette U., Salem, Oreg., 1992—. Author: Human Services in Postrevolutionary Cuba, 1985 (named a Choice Outstanding Acad. Book, Choice Editors 1984-85); mem. adv. bd. Jour. Info. Ethics; contbr. numerous articles to profl. jours. Mem. Am. Library Assn. (chair coll. librs. sect. 1997-98), Oreg. Library Assn., Phi Beta Kappa. Democrat. Office: Willamette U Mark O Hatfield Libr 900 State St Salem OR 97301-3931

O'BERRY, CARL GERALD, former military officer, electrical engineer; b. Lansing, Mich., Apr. 11, 1936; s. Gerald Ray and Edith Lenore (Watson) O'B.; m. Charlene Marice Bussche, June 21, 1958; children: Brian, Eileen, Kevin, Bradley, Kathleen. BSEE, N.Mex. State U., 1972; MS in Systems Mgmt., Air Force Inst. Tech., 1977. Commd. 2d lt. USAF, 1961, advanced through grades to lt. gen., 1993; comdr. 2019 Communications Squadron, Griffiss AFB, NY, 1974-76; project engr. Rome Air Devel. Ctr., Griffiss AFB, 1979-81; asst. dep. chief of staff requirements Air Force Systems Command, Andrews AFB, Md., 1982-84; comdr. Rome Air Devel. Ctr., Griffiss AFB, 1984-86; joint program mgr. WWMCCS info. system Hdqrs. USAF, Washington, 1986-88; dir. command, control and communications U.S. European Command, Stuttgart, Fed. Republic Germany, 1988-90; dir. command control systems and logistics U.S. Space Command, Peterson AFB, Colo., 1990-92; command control comm. and computers DCS, HQ USAF, Washington, 1992-95; v.p., dir. strategic planning Motorola Space and Sys. Tech. Group, Scottsdale, Ariz., 1995-98; tech. cons. Def. Sci. Bd., Washington, 1998—; v.p., gen. mgr. govt.

info. and comms. sys., space group The Boeing Co., Anaheim, Calif., 2000—05; ret. Exec. chair Network Centric Ops. Industry Consortium, 2004—. Mem. Air Force Assn., Armed Forces Communications-Electronics Assn., Soc. Logistics Engrs. Roman Catholic.

OBERSTEIN, NORMAN S., lawyer; b. Oskaloosa, Iowa, Nov. 5, 1940; BA magna cum laude, U. Iowa, 1962; JD, U. Calif., Berkeley, 1965. Bar: Calif. 1966, US Supreme Ct. 1996. Mng. mem. and sr. ptnr. Litig. Dept. Kaplan, Livingston, Goodwin, Berkowitz & Selvin, Beverly Hills, Calif.; of counsel Gipson Hoffman & Pancione, Calif., 2006—. Mem.: LA County Bar Assn., Beverly Hills County Bar Assn., State Calif. Bar Assn., Omicron Delta Kappa, Order of Coif, Phi Beta Kappa. Office: Gipson Hoffman & Pancione Floor 11 1901 Avenue of the Stars Los Angeles CA 90067 Office Phone: 310-556-4660. Office Fax: 310-556-8945. E-mail: noberstein@ghplaw.com.

O'BOYLE, MAUREEN, television show host; News prodr., anchor Sta. KREM-TV, Spokane, Wash.; reporter, prodr., writer, co-anchor Sta. WMAZ-TV, Macon, Ga.; nightside reporter, anchor Sta. WECT-TV, Wilmington, N.C.; morning news anchor Sta. WITN-TV, Washington, N.C.; anchor A Current Affair; anchor, sr. corr. Extra, Glendale, Calif., 1995-96, co-host, 1997—; host In Person With Maureen O'Boyle, 1996-97.

O'BRIEN, BARBARA, Lieutenant Governor of Colorado; b. Apr. 18, 1950; m. Rick O'Brien; children: Jared, Connor. BA, U. Calif., LA, 1972; PhD, Columbia U., NYC, 1981. Project asst. Inst. for Urban and Minority Edn., Columbia U., 1977—79; head speechwriter, dep. dir. Policy Office of Gov., Gov. Richard Lamm, 1983—85; dir., Campus Affairs U. Colo. Denver, 1985—88; exec. dir. Inst. Internat. Bus., Colo. U. Denver, 1988—90; pres. Colo. Children's Campaign, 1990—; lt. gov. State of Colo., 2007—. Mem. Mayor's Leadership Team on Early Edn., Governor's Commn. on Children and Families, Nat. Kids County Steering Com., Tony Grampsas Youth Services Fund; founder, co-chair Kids Caucus. Democrat. Office: Lieutenant Governor 130 State Capital Denver CO 80203 Office Phone: 303-866-2087. Office Fax: 303-866-5469. Business E-Mail: Ltgovernor.obrien@state.co.us.*

O'BRIEN, BRADFORD CARL, lawyer; b. Lafayette, Ind., Jan. 25, 1949; s. Hubbert L. and Jeane (Howard) O'Brien; m. Judith Mayer, June 19, 1971. AB magna cum laude, Princeton U., 1971; JD, UCLA, 1974. Bar: Calif. 1974. Assoc. Ruffo, Ferrari & McNeil, San Jose, Calif., 1975—81; ptnr. Wilson Sonsini Goodrich & Rosati, Palo Alto, Calif., 1981—, co-chmn. real estate/environ. practice group. Mem.: Santa Clara County Bar Assn., ABA. Office: Wilson Sonsini Goodrich & Rosati 650 Page Mill Rd Palo Alto CA 94304-1055 Office Phone: 650-320-4851. Office Fax: 650-493-6811. Business E-Mail: bobrien@wsgr.com.

O'BRIEN, DANIEL J., lawyer; b. Los Alamos, N.Mex., Nov. 18, 1951; BS, U. N.Mex., 1975, MBA, 1980, JD, 1983. Bar: N.Mex. 1983, Tex. 1993, U.S. Dist. Ct. N.Mex. 1984, U.S. Ct. Appeals (10th cir.) 1987. Ptnr. O'Brien & Ulibarri, P.C., Albuquerque, shareholder. Mem.: ABA, Albuquerque Bar Assn., N.Mex. Trial Lawyers Assn., N.Mex. Def. Lawyers Assn. (pres. 1999—2000), State Bar N.Mex. (bd. commrs. 1994—2000, v.p. 2002, pres. 2004). Office: O'Brien & Ulibarri PC 6000 Indian Sch NE Ste 200 Albuquerque NM 87110 Office Phone: 505-883-8181. Office Fax: 505-883-3232. Business E-Mail: dobrien@obrienlawoffice.com.

O'BRIEN, DAVID PETER, corporate director; b. Montreal, Que., Can., Sept. 9, 1941; m. Gail Baxter Cornell, June 1, 1968; children: Tara, Matthew, Shaun. BA in Econs. with honors, Loyola Coll., Montreal, 1962; BCL, McGill U., Montreal, 1965. Assoc. and ptnr. Ogilvy, Renault, Montreal, 1967-77; v.p., gen. counsel Petro-Can., Calgary, Alta., 1977-81, sr. v.p., 1982-85, sr. v.p. fin. and planning, 1982-85, exec. v.p., 1985-89; pres., CEO Noverco Inc., Montreal, 1989; chmn. bd., pres., CEO PanCan. Petroleum Ltd., Calgary, 1990—95; pres., COO Can. Pacific Ltd., Montreal, 1995—96, chmn., pres., CEO Calgary, 1996—2001; chmn., CEO PanCan. Energy Corp., 2001—02; chmn. EnCana Corp., 2002—. Chmn. Royal Bank Can., 2004—; bd. dirs. TransCan. PipeLines Ltd., Molson Coors Brewing Co., Focus Energy Trust. Mem.: Calgary Golf and Country Club, Calgary Petroleum Club, Glencoe Club.

O'BRIEN, EDWARD JOHN, musician, vocalist; b. Oxford, England, Apr. 15, 1968; Student in Econs., Manchester U., Eng. Barman; photographer's asst.; guitarist, vocalist Radiohead, 1992—. Musician (and vocalist): (albums) Pablo Honey, 1993, The Bends, 1995, OK Computer, 1997 (Grammy award for Best Alternative Music Performance, 1997), Kid A, 2000 (Grammy award for Best Alternative Music Performance, 2000), Amnesiac, 2001, I Might Be Wrong: Live Recordings, 2001, Hail to the Thief, 2003, In Rainbows, 2007 (Grammy award for Best Alternative Music Album, 2009). Office: Capital Records 1750 North Vine St 10th Fl Hollywood CA 90028*

O'BRIEN, ELMER JOHN, librarian, educator; b. Kemmerer, Wyo., Apr. 8, 1932; s. Ernest and Emily Catherine (Reinhart) O'B.; m. Betty Alice Peterson, July 2, 1966. AB, Birmingham So. Coll., 1954; Th.M., Iliff Sch. Theology, 1957; MA, U. Denver, 1961. Ordained to ministry Methodist Ch., 1957; pastor Meth. Ch., Pagosa Springs, Colo., 1957—60; circulation-reference librarian Boston U. Sch. Theology, 1961—65; asst. librarian Garrett-Evang. Theol. Sem., Evanston, Ill., 1965—69; librarian, prof. United Theol. Sem., Dayton, Ohio, 1969—96, prof. emeritus, 1996—; abstractor Am. Bibliog. Center, 1969—73; dir. Ctr. for Evang. United Brethren Heritage, 1979—96; acting libr. Iliff Sch. Theology, 2000—01. Chmn. div. exec. com. Dayton-Miami Valley Libr. Consortium, 1983-84; rsch. assoc. Am. Antiquarian Soc., 1990. Author: Bibliography of Festschriften in Religion Published Since 1960, 1972, Religion Index Two: Festschriften, 1960-69; contbg. author: Communication and Change in American Religious History, 1993, Essays in Celebration of the First Fifty Years, 1996; pub. Meth. Revs. Index, 1818-1985, 1989-91; contbr. articles to profl. jours. Recipient theol. and scholarship award Assn. Theol. Schs. in U.S. and Can., 1990-91; Libr. Staff Devel. grant Assn. Theol. Schs. in U.S. and Can., 1976-77, Rsch. grant United Meth. Ch. Bd. Higher Edn. and Ministry, 1984-85 Mem. ALA, Acad. Libr. Assn. Ohio, Am. Theol. Libr. Assn. (head bur. personnel and placement 1969-73, dir. 1973-76, v.p. 1977-78, pres. 1978-79), Am. Antiquarian Soc. (rsch. assoc. 1990), Delta Sigma Phi, Omicron Delta Kappa, Eta Sigma Phi, Kappa Phi Kappa. Clubs: Torch Internat. (v.p. Dayton club 1981-82, pres. 1982-83). Home: 4840 Thunderbird Dr Apt 281 Boulder CO 80303-3829 Personal E-mail: ejobr@aol.com.

O'BRIEN, JACK GEORGE, artistic director; b. Saginaw, Mich., June 18, 1939; s. J. George and Evelyn (MacArthur Martens) O'B. AB, U. Mich., 1961, MA, 1962. Asst. dir. APA Repertory Theatre, NYC, 1963-67, asso. dir., 1967-69; worked with San Diego Nat. Shakespeare Festival, 1969-82, A.C.T., 1970-80, Loretto Hilton, 1975, Ahmanson, Los Angeles, 1978-80, San Francisco Opera, Houston Grand Opera, Washington Opera Soc.; artistic dir. N.Y.C. Opera, 1982, Old Globe Theatre, San Diego, 1981—. Dir.: (Broadway plays) Cock-A-Doodle Dandy, 1969, The Time of Your Life, 1975, Porgy and Bess, 1976, 1983, The Most Happy Fella, 1979, Two Shakespearean Actors, 1992, Damn Yankees, 1994—95, Getting Away With Murder, 1996, The Little Foxes, 1997, More to Love, 1998, The Full Monty, 2000—02 (Tony nom. best dir. of a musical, 2001), Imaginary Friends, 2003, Hairspray, 2002 (Tony award best dir. of a musical, 2003), Henry IV, 2003—04 (Tony award best dir. of a play, 2004), The Coast of Utopia, 2006 (Outer Critics Cir. award outstanding dir. of a musical, 2007, Tony award best dir. of a play, 2007, Drama Desk award outstanding dir. of a play, 2007); art. dir. (Broadway plays) Into the Woods, 1987—89, Rumors, 1988—90, The Piano Lesson, 1990—91, Two Trains Running, 1992, Redwood Curtain, 1993, Play On!, 1997, Oldest Living Confederate Widow Tells All, 2003. Mem. Actors' Equity, Am. Soc. Composers and Performers, Soc. Stage Dirs. and Choreographers, Dirs. Guild Am. Office: Old Globe Theatre PO Box 122171 San Diego CA 92112-2171

O'BRIEN, JOHN CONWAY, economist, educator, writer; b. Hamilton, Lanarkshire, Scotland; s. Patrick and Mary (Hunt) O'B.; m. Jane Estelle Judd, Sept. 16, 1966; children: Kellie Marie, Kerry Patrick, Tracy Anne, Kristen Noël. B.Com., U. London, 1952, cert. in German lang., 1954; tchr.'s cert., Scottish Edn. Dept., 1954; AM, U. Notre Dame, 1959, PhD, 1961. Tchr. Scottish High Schs., Lanarkshire, 1952-56; instr. U. B.C., Can., 1961-62; asst. prof. U. Sask., Can., 1962-63, U. Dayton, Ohio, 1963-64; assoc. prof. Wilfrid Laurier U., Ont., Can., 1964-65; from asst. to full prof. Econs. and Ethics Calif. State U., Fresno, 1965—. Vis. prof. U. Pitts., 1969-70, U. Hawaii, Manoa, 1984, U. Queensland, Brisbane, Australia, 1994; keynote speaker Wageningen Agrl. U., The Netherlands, 1987; presenter papers 5th, 6th, 10th World Congress of Economists, Tokyo, 1977, Mexico City, 1980, Moscow, 1992; presenter Schmoller Symposium, Heilbronn am Neckar, Fed. Republic Germany, 1988, paper The China Confucius Found. and "2540" Conf., Beijing, 1989, 6th Internat. Conf. on Cultural Econs., Univ. Umeå, Sweden, 1990, Internat. Soc. Intercommunication New Ideas, Sorbonne, Paris, 1990, European Assn. for Evolutionary Polit. Economy, Vienna, Austria, 1991; active rsch. U. Göttingen, Fed. Republic Germany, 1987; acad. cons. Cath. Inst. Social Ethics, Oxford; presenter in field. Author: Karl Marx: The Social Theorist, 1981, The Economist in Search of Values, 1982, Beyond Marxism, 1985, The Social Economist Hankers After Values, 1992; editor: Internat. Rev. Econs. and Ethics, Internat. Jour. Social Econs., Ethical Values and Social Econs., 1981, Selected Topics in Social Econs., 1982, Festschrift in honor of George Rohrlich, 3 vols., 1984, Social Economics: A Pot=Pourri, 1985, The Social Economist on Nuclear Arms: Crime and Prisons, Health Care, 1986, Festschrift in honor of Anghel N. Rugina, Parts I and II, 1987, Gustav von Schmoller: Social Economist, 1989, The Eternal Path to Communism, 1990, (with Z. Wenxian) Essays from the People's Republic of China, 1991, Festschrift in Honor of John E. Elliott, Parts I and II, 1992, Communism Now and Then, 1993, The Evils of Soviet Communism, 1994, Ruminations on the USSR, 1994, The Future Without Marx, 1995, Essays in Honour of Clement Allan Tisdell, 1996, Essays in Honor of Clement Allan Tisdell, Part I, 1996, Part II and III, 1997, Part IV and V, 1998, Part VI, 1999, Part VII and VIII, 2000, Social Economists at Work, 1999, Our Fragile Civilization, 2001; translator econ. articles from French and German into English; contbr. numerous articles to profl. jours. With British Royal Army Service Corps, 1939-46, ETO, NATOUSA, prisoner of war, Germany. Recipient GE Corp. award Stanford U., 1966, Ludwig Mai Svc. award Assn. for Social Econs., Washington, 1994; named Disting. Fellow of Internat. Soc. for Intercomm. of New Ideas, Paris, 1990. Fellow Internat. Inst. Social Econs. (mem. coun., program dir. 3d World Cong. Social Econs. Fresno Calif. 1983, keynote spkr. 4th conf. Toronto 1986), Internat. Soc. for Intercomm. New Ideas (disting.); mem. Assn. Social Econs. (dir. west region 1977—, pres.-elect 1988-89, program dir. conf. 1989, pres. 1990, presdl. address Washington 1990, Thomas Divine award 1997), Western Econ. Assn. (organizer, presenter 1977-95), History Econs. Soc., Soc. Reduction Human Labor (exec. com.), European Assn. Evolutionary Polit. Econs., Ga. Acad. Econ. Scis. (Republic of Ga. fgn. mem.). Roman Catholic. Avocations: jogging, collecting miniature paintings, soccer, tennis, photography. Home: 11594 E Chama Rd Scottsdale AZ 85255-5790 Office Phone: 559-661-2121. Personal E-mail: johnconwayobrien@aol.com.

O'BRIEN, JOHN WILLIAM, JR., management consultant; b. Bronx, NY, Jan. 1, 1937; BS, MIT, 1958; MS, UCLA, 1964. Sr. assoc. Planning Rsch. Corp., LA, 1962—67; dir. fin. systems group Synergetic Scis., Inc., Tarzana, Calif., 1967—70; dir. analytical svcs. divsn. James H. Oliphant & Co., LA, 1970—72; chmn. bd., CEO, pres. Wilshire Assocs. (formerly O'Brien Assocs. Inc.), Santa Monica, Calif., 1972—75; v.p. A.G. Becker Inc., 1975—81; chmn., CEO Leland O'Brien Rubinstein Assocs., 1981—97; mng. dir. Credit Suisse Asset Mgmt., NYC, 1997—2000; adj. prof. fin. U. Calif. Berkeley Haas Sch. Bus., 2000—. Recipient Graham and Dodd award Fin. Analysts Fedn., 1970, Matthew McArthur award Investment Mgmt. Consultants Assn., 2004; named Businessman of Yr. Fortune Mag., 1987. Mem.: Delta Upsilon. Home: 119 Jasmine Creek Dr Corona Del Mar CA 92625-1418 Office Phone: 510-643-1396. Personal E-mail: obrien@jwobrien.com. Business E-Mail: obrien@haas.berkeley.edu.

O'BRIEN, KEVIN D., medical educator; BS summa cum laude, U. Idaho, 1980; MD honors, U. Wash., 1984. Diplomate Am. Bd. Internal Medicine, Cardiovascular Diseases Am. Bd. Internal Medicine. Intern, resident U. Wash., Seattle, 1984—87, chief med. resident, 1987—88, prof., medicine, 2008—; atteding physician U. Wash. Med. Ctr., Seattle, 1988—. Med. student rsch. fellow Fred Hutchinson Cancer rsch. Ctr., Seattle, 1981. Contbr. articles to profl. jours. Recipient Sheard-Sanford award, Am. Soc. Clin. Pathologists, 1983. Fellow: Am. Heart Assn.; mem.: Western Soc. Clin. Investigation (pres. 2007—, councilor 2003—06, Outstanding Investigator award 2003), Am. Fedn. Med. Rsch. (pres. 2001—02, found. pres. 2002—03). Office: Univ Wash Med Ctr Campus Box 356422 1959 NE Pacific St Seattle WA 98195-6422 Office Phone: 206-685-3930. Business E-Mail: cardiac@u.washington.edu.

O'BRIEN, KEVIN E., lawyer; b. Teaneck, NJ, Nov. 22, 1952; BA, U. Notre Dame, 1975; JD, U. Denver, 1977. Bar: Colo. 1980. Mem. Hall & Evans, L.L.C., Denver, 1984—. Instr. Nat. Inst. Trial Advocacy, 1987. With USAR, 1972-78. Office: Hall & Evans LLC 1125 17th St Ste 600 Denver CO 80202-5817

O'BRIEN, KRISTIANA, lawyer; b. Chapel Hill, NC, Aug. 12, 1973; BA, Bucknell Univ., Penn., 1995; MA, Columbia Univ., 1996; JD, Univ. Wash., 1999. Bar: Wash. 1999, U.S. Dist. Ct., Western Dist. Wash. 1999, U.S. Ct. Appeals Ninth Circuit 1999. Bus. atty. Montgomery Purdue Blankinship & Austin LLP, Seattle. Contbr. articles to numerous profl. jours. Named Wash. Rising Star, SuperLawyer Mag., 2006. Mem.: ABA, Wash. State Bar Assn. Office: Montgomery Purdue Blankinship and Austin LLP 55th Fl Bank of America Tower 701 Fifth Ave Seattle WA 98104-7096

O'BRIEN, PAT, television personality; b. Sioux Falls, SD, Feb. 14, 1948; m. Linda O'Brien, 1973; 1 child, Sean. Grad., U. SD, 1970; postgrad., Johns Hopkins U. Prodn. asst. The Huntley-Brinkley Report; reporter WMAQ-TV, Chgo., KNXT-TV (now KCBS-TV), LA; host The Krypton Factor, 1981; anchor CBS Sports, 1981—97; host Overtime...with Pat O'Brien, 1990, How'd They Do That?, 1993—94; host (TV spls.) The Road to Olympic Gold, 1996, 2000; host CNBC coverage of the Sydney Olympics, 2000; corr. NBC coverage of the Utah Olympics, 2002; co-anchor Access Hollywood, 1997—2004; host NBC coverage of the Athens Olympics, 2004, The Insider, 2004—08. Author: Talkin' Sports: A B.S.-er's Guide, 1998; columnist: N.Y. Daily News, Inside Sports, Live!, TV Guide, Ego, Men's Health, gadget editor: Gear Mag. Recipient newswriting award, L.A. Press Club, 1987. Office: ICM LA 10250 Constellation Blvd Los Angeles CA 90067

O'BRIEN, RAYMOND FRANCIS, transportation executive; b. Atchison, Kans., May 31, 1922; s. James C. and Anna M. (Wagner) O'B.; m. Mary Ann Baugher, Sept. 3, 1947; children: James B., William T., Kathleen A., Christopher R. BS in Bus. Adminstrn., U. Mo., 1948; grad., Advanced Mgmt. Program, Harvard, 1966. Accountant-auditor Peat, Marwick, Mitchell & Co., Kansas City, Mo., 1948-52; contr., treas. Riss & Co., Kansas City, Mo., 1952-58; regional contr. Consol. Freightways Corp. of Del., Indpls., also, Akron, Ohio, 1958-61; contr. Consol. Freightways, Inc., San Francisco, 1961—, v.p., treas., 1962-63, bd. dirs., 1966, v.p. fin., 1967-69, exec. v.p., 1969-75, pres., 1975—, chief exec. officer, 1977-88, 90-91, chmn., 1988—; now chmn. emeritus CNF Transportation. Pres. CF Motor Freight subs. Consol. Freightways, Inc., 1973; dir. Transam. Corp., Watkins-Johnson, Inc.; past chmn. WesternHwy. Inst., Champion Road Machinery, Ltd. Former mem. bus. adv. bd. Northwestern U., U. Calif., Berkeley; bd. dirs., regent, former chmn. bd. trustees St. Mary's Coll.; bd. dirs., regent Charles Armstrong Sch., 1991—; mem. Pres.'s Adv. Herbert Hoover Boys and Girls Club; dir. Boy Scouts Am. Bay Area Coun. Served to 1st lt. USAAF, 1942-45. Recipient Disting. Svc. Citation Automotive Hall Fame, 1991; named Outstanding Chief Exec. five times Financial World Mag. Mem. Am. Trucking Assn. (bd. dirs. Found., exec. com.), Pacific Union Club, World Trade Club, Commonwealth Club (San Francisco), Menlo Country Club.

O'BRIEN, RICHARD T., mining executive; BA in Economics, U. Chgo., 1976; JD, Lewis and Clark Coll., Northwestern Sch. Law, 1985. Joined PacifiCorp, 1983; CFO, sr. v.p. PacifiCorp, Portland, Oreg., 1995—98, CFO, exec. v.p., 1998; v.p. Mirant (formerly S. Energy, Inc.), 2000—01, pres., Mirant Capital Mgmt., 2000—01; sr. v.p., CFO AGL Resources, 2001, exec. v.p., CFO Atlanta, 2001—05; sr. v.p., CFO Newmont Mining Co., Denver, 2005—06, exec. v.p., CFO, 2006—07, pres., CEO, 2007—. Office: Newmont Mining 1700 Lincoln St Denver CO 80203

O'BRIEN, ROBERT CHARLES, lawyer; s. Robert Charles and Judith Lorie O'Brien; m. Louisa Maria Thuynsma, May 9, 1988; children: Margaret Elizabeth, Robert Christopher, Lauren Marie. BA, UCLA, 1988; JD, U. Calif., Berkeley, 1991. Bar: Calif. 1991. Legal officer UN Compensation Commn., Geneva, Vaud, 1996—98; ptnr. O'Brien Abeles LLP, LA, 1999—2006; US alt. rep. to UN Gen. Assembly US Dept. State, NYC, 2005—06; ptnr. Arent Fox LLP, LA, 2006—. Co-chmn. Lawyers Bush Cheney, Calif., 2004; co-chair US Dept. State Pub. Pvt. Ptnr. Justice Reform, Afghanistan, 2007—; mem. nat. steering com. Lawyers for Mitt Romney, Boston, 2007—, US Cultural Adv. Com., 2008—. Maj. US Army, 1992—2005. Mem.: State Bar Calif. (exec. com. 1999—2002), J. Reuben Clark Law Soc. (chmn. LA chpt. 2003—05). Mem. Lds Ch. Office: Arent Fox LLP 555 W 5th St 48th Floor Los Angeles CA 90013-1065 Office Fax: 213-629-7401. E-mail: obrien.robert@arentfox.com.

O'BRIEN, SEAN, chef; b. NY, 1968; B in Mktg., Santa Clara U. Chef Ritz-Carlton Dining Room, San Francisco, Fifth Floor, Viognier, San Mateo, Calif.; exec. sous chef Restaurant Gary Danko, San Francisco, 1999—2004; owner, exec. chef Myth, San Francisco, 2004—. Named Myth Best New Restaurant, Esquire mag., 2005, Rising Star Chef, San Francisco Mag., 2005; named one of Best New Chefs, Food and Wine Mag., 2007. Office: Myth 314 El Camino Real Redwood City CA 94062-1724 Office Phone: 415-677-8986. Office Fax: 415-677-8987. Business E-Mail: seanobrien@mythsf.com.

O'BRYANT, DANIEL R., consumer products company executive; BS in Mgmt. Sci., Calif. State Polytechnic U., Pomona, Calif.; MBA, U. So. Calif. Fin. mgmt. positions Baker Hughes; dir. cap. planning Avery Dennison, Pasadena, Calif., 1990—91, dir. fin. spl. tape div. Belgium, 1991—92, group fin. dir. Netherlands, 1992—94, v.p. fin. European ops., 1994—95, v.p. ops. planning Pasadena, Calif., 1995—96, v.p. ops. audit, 1996—97, v.p. gen. mgr. Fasson Roll div. Painesville, Ohio, 1997—2001, sr. v.p. fin., CFO, 2001—05, exec. v.p. fin., CFO, 2005—. Office: Avery Dennison Corp Ctr 150 North Orange Grove Blvd Pasadena CA 91103-3596

O'BYRNE, MICHAEL, retired management consultant; b. Butte, Mont., Dec. 26, 1938; s. Michael E. and Margaret F. (Turner) O'B.; m. Penny L. Graham, Nov. 14, 1964; children: Jennifer L. McLellan, Gregory M. O'Byrne, Andrew G. O'Byrne. BSME, U. Wash., 1961. Cert. engr., Wash. V.p. PACCAR, Inc., Bellevue, Wash., 1969-84; pres. Mobi-Dock, Inc., Mercer Island, Wash., 1985-86; ptnr. The Catalyst Group, Mercer Island, 1986-89; pres. Raima Corp., Bellevue, 1988-89, Pacific North Equipment Co., Kent, Wash., 1990-95; cons. Master Performance, Inc., Bellevue, 1995-2000, Vehicle Monitor Corp., Redmond, Va., 1996—2004; ret. Council mem. Hunts Point, Wash., 1980-97; mem. bd. dirs. Mcpl. League of King County, Seattle, 1994-95; dist. chmn. Boy Scouts Am., Seattle, 1994-98; pres. USO Puget Sound Area, 1997-2004. Lt. comdr. USN, 1961-69. Mem. Soc.

Automotive Engrs., Assoc. Equiptment Distributors (chpt. pres. 1994-95), Rotary Internat., Seattle Yacht Club. Republican. Avocations: sailing, skiing, fishing. E-mail: michael.obyrne@comcast.net.

OCKEY, RONALD J., lawyer; b. Green River, Wyo., June 12, 1934; s. Theron G. and Ruby O. (Sackett) O.; m. Arline M. Hawkins, Nov. 27, 1957; children: Carolyn S. Ockey Baggett, Deborah K. Ockey Christiansen, David, Kathleen M. Ockey Hellewell, Valerie Ockey Sachs, Robert. BA, U. Utah, Salt Lake City, 1959, postgrad., 1959-60; JD with honors, George Wash. U., Washington, DC, 1966. Bar: Colo. 1967, Utah 1968, US Dist. Ct. Colo. 1967, US Dist. Ct. Utah 1968, US Ct. Appeals (10th cir.) 1969, US Ct. Claims 1987. Missionary to France for Mormon Ch., 1954-57; law clk. to judge U.S. Dist. Ct. Colo., 1966-67; assoc. ptnr., shareholder, v.p., treas., dir. Jones, Waldo, Holbrook & McDonough, Salt Lake City, 1967-91; mem. Utah Ho. of Reps., 1988-90, Utah State Senate, 1991-94; of counsel Mackey Price & Williams, Salt Lake City, 1995-98; asst. atty. gen. Utah, 1998—. Trustee SmartUtah, Inc., 1995-2002; trustee Utah Tech. Fin. Corp., 1995-98; lectr. in securities, pub. fin. and bankruptcy law. Mem. editl. bd. Utah Bar Jour., 1973-75; mem. staff and bd. editors George Washington Law Rev., 1964-66; contbr. articles to profl. jours. State govtl. affairs chair Utah Jaycees, 1969; del. state Rep. Convs., 1972-74, 76-78, 80-82, 84-86, 94-96, del. Salt Lake County Rep. Conv., 1978-80, 88-92; sec. Wright for Gov. campaign, 1980; legis. dist. chmn. Utah Rep. Party, 1983-87; trustee Food for Poland, 1981-85, pres., trustee Unity to Assist Humanity Alliance, 1992-95; bd. dirs. Utah Opera Co., 1991-94; trustee Utah Info. Tech. Assn., 1991-2000. Lt. US Army, 1960-66, to capt. JAG, USAR, 1966-81. Mem. ABA, Utah State Bar Assn. (various coms.), Nat. Assn. Bond Lawyers (chmn. con. on state legislation 1982-85), George Washington U. Law Alumni Assn. (bd. dirs. 1981-85), Order of Coif, Phi Delta Phi. Home Phone: 801-278-3809; Office Phone: 801-366-0359. Business E-Mail: rockey@utah.gov.

O'CONNELL, HUGH MELLEN, JR., retired architect; b. Oak Park, Ill., Nov. 29, 1929; s. Hugh M. and Helen Mae (Evans) O'C.; m. Frances Ann Small, Apr. 13, 1957; children: Patricia Lynn, Susan Marie, Jeanette Maureen. Student mech. engring., Purdue U., 1948-50; BS in Archtl. Engring, U. Ill., 1953. Registered architect, Ariz., Calif., La., Nev., Nat. Council Archtl. Registration Bds. Designer John Mackel; structural engr. Los Angeles, 1955-57; architect Harnish & Morgan & Causey, Ontario, Calif., 1957-63; pvt. practice Ventura, Calif., 1963—69; architect Andrews/O'Connell, Ventura, 1970-78; dir. engring. div. Naval Constrn. Bn. Center, Port Hueneme, Calif., 1978-91, supervisory architect, 1991-93; ret., 1993. Mem. tech. adv. com. Ventura Coll., 1965-78; sec. Oxnard Citizens' Adv. Com., 1969-79, v.p., 1970-72, pres., 1972—; chmn. Oxnard Beautification Com., 1969, 74, Oxnard Cmty. Block Grant adv. com., 1975-76; mem. Oxnard Planning Commn., 1976-86, vice chmn., 1978-79, chmn., 1980-81. Mem. Oxnard Art-in-Pub. Places Commn., 1988-93, 2003—. Served with AUS, 1953-55. Mem. AIA (emeritus, pres. Ventura chpt. 1973), Am. Concrete Inst., Soc. Am. Registered Architects (Design award 1968, dir. 1970), Am. Legion, Soc. for Preservation and Encouragement of Barbershop Quartet Singing in Am. (chpt. pres. 1979, chpt. sec. 1980-83), Acad. Model Aeros. (#9190 1948—), Channel Islands Condors Club (treas. 1986-99), Sports Flyers Assn., Alpha Rho Chi (Anthemios chpt.). Presbyterian (elder 1963, deacon 1967). Lodges: Kiwanis (pres. 1969, div. sec. 1974-75), Elks. Home and Office: 520 Ivywood Dr Oxnard CA 93030-3527 Personal E-mail: hughoarch@msn.com.

O'CONNELL, JACK T., school system administrator; b. Glen Cove, NY, Oct. 8, 1951; m. Doree O'Connell; 1 child, Jennifer Lynn. Student, Ventura Coll.; BA in History, Calif. State U., Fullerton; cert. secondary tchr., Calif. State U., Long Beach, 1975. Tchr. various high schs.; mem. Calif. State Assembly, 1982—94, Calif. State Senate, 1994—2002; state supt. pub. instrn. State of Calif., 2002—. Mem. Santa Barbara County Sch. Bd. Democrat. Office: Calif Dept Edn Ste 5602 1430 N St Sacramento CA 95814 Office Phone: 916-319-0800.*

O'CONNELL, KEVIN, lawyer; s. Michael Frederick and Kathryn Agnes (Kelley) O'Connell; m. Mary Adams, July 14, 1990; children: Tiffany W., Elizabeth H., Dana A., Lisel E. AB, Harvard, 1955, JD, 1960. Bar: Calif. 1961. Assoc. firm O'Melveny & Myers, LA, 1960-63; asst. U.S. atty. criminal div. Ctrl. Dist. Calif., LA, 1963-65; staff counsel Gov. Calif. Commn. to Investigate Watts Riot, LA, 1965-66; ptnr. Tuttle & Taylor, LA, 1966-70, Coleman & O'Connell, LA, 1971-75; pvt. practice law LA, 1975-78; of counsel firm Simon & Sheridan, LA, 1978-89; ptnr. Manatt, Phelps & Phillips, LA, 1989—. Adj. prof. law U. So. Calif. Law Sch., 2002—. Bd. editors Harvard Law Rev., 1958—60. Bd. dirs. Calif. Supreme Ct. Hist. Soc.; mem. Los Angeles County Dem. Ctrl. Com., Calif., 1973—74. Lt. USMCR, 1955—57. Recipient Best Lawyers in Am. Mem.: Pacific Coun. on Internat. Policy, Am. Law Inst. Avocations: hiking, reading. Home: 426 N Mccadden Pl Los Angeles CA 90004-1026 Office: Manatt Phelps & Phillips Trident Ctr E Tower 11355 W Olympic Blvd Los Angeles CA 90064-1614 Home Phone: 323-935-2116; Office Phone: 310-312-4222. Business E-Mail: koconnell@manatt.com.

O'CONNELL, MARY ANN, state legislator, small business owner; b. Albuquerque, Aug. 3, 1934; d. James Aubrey and Dorothy Nell (Batsel) Gray; m. Robert Emmett O'Connell, Feb. 21, 1977; children: Jeffery Crampton, Gray Crampton. Student, U. N.Mex., Internat. Coun. Shopping Ctrs. Exec. dir. Blvd. Shopping Ctr., Las Vegas, Nev., 1968-76, Citizen Pvt. Enterprise, Las Vegas, 1976; media supr. Southwest Advt., Las Vegas, 1977—; owner, operator Meadows Inn, Las Vegas, 1985—99, 3 Christian bookstores, Las Vegas, 1985-99; mem. Nev. State Senate, 1985—, chmn. govtl. affairs com., vice chmn. commerce and labor com. Vice chmn. Legis. Commn., 1985—86, 1995—96, mem. edn. com. to rewrite standards; mem. Edn. Commn. of the States, 1997—; rep. Nat. Conf. State Legislators; past vice chair State Mental Hygiene and Mental Retardation Adv. Bd. Pres. explorer div. Boulder Dam Area coun. Boy Scouts Am., Las Vegas, 1979-80, former mem. exec. bd. mem. adv. bd. Boulder Dam chpt.; pres., bd. dirs. Citizens Pvt. Enterprise, Las Vegas, 1982-84, Secret Witness, Las Vegas, 1981-82; vice chmn. Gov.'s Mental Health-Mental Retardation, Nev., 1983-; past mem. community adv. bd. Care Unit Hosp., Las Vegas; past mem. adv. bd. Kidney Found., Milligan Coll., Charter Hosp.; tchr. Young Adult Sunday Sch.; 1st vice chmn. Clark County Rep. Party, 2001-03. Recipient Commendation award Mayor O. Grayson, Las Vegas, 1975, Outstanding Citizenship award Bd. Realtors, 1975, Silver Beaver award Boy Scouts Am., 1980, Free Enterprise award Greater Las Vegas C. of C., Federated Employers Assn., Downtown Breakfast Exch., 1988, Award of Excellence Women in Politics, 1989, Legislator Yr. award Bldg. and Trades, 1991, Legislator Yr. award Nat. ASA Trade Assn., 1991, 94, Guardian Liberty award Nev. Coalition Conservative Citizens, 1991, Internat. Maxi Awards Promotional Excellence, Guardian Small Bus. award Nat. Fedn. Ind. Bus., 1995-96, Legislator Yr. award Nev. Med. Polit. Com., 1999, Assoc. Builders and Contractors, New Mortgage Brokers, 2000, Nev. Ind. Check Cashing Assn., 2001, Nev. Phys. Therapists, 2002, Women's Role Model award Atty. Gen., 2002, Nicholas J. Horn award Nev. State Med. Assn., 2003, Liberty award Nev. Policy Rsch. Inst., 2004; named Nev. Public Health Assoc. Legislator Yr., Nev. Retail Assn., 1992, New Assn. Bldg. Contractors, 1999, Nev Polit. Med. Action Com., 1999; inducted into Nev. Vets. Citizens Hall Fame, 1999; named one of 25 Notable Las Vegas Women, 2004. Mem. Retail Mchts. Assn. (former pres., bd. dirs.), Taxpayers Assn. (bd. dirs.), Greater Las Vegas C. of C. (past pres., bd. dirs., Woman of Achievement Politics women's coun. 1988). Republican. Mem. Christian Ch. Avocations: china painting, reading.

O'CONNELL, TAAFFE CANNON, actress, publishing executive; b. Providence; d. Joseph Ceril and Edith Ethelyn (Dent) O'C. BA, MFA, U. Miss., University. Regional supr. Gloria Marshall Figure Salons, SC; v.p., co-founder Doc Sox Inc., Pacific Palisades, Calif., 1988-90; pres., founder Canoco Pub., LA, 1991—, 1-800-266-DYNE, LA, 1992-93. Founder Rising Star Distbn., Yes I Can Actor's Workshops, 2001—, Get Inside the Agent's Head Seminars, 2003, Actors Acing Hollywood Seminars, 2006; exec. prodr. Beanie/Twigg 1999—, Canoco Prodn. Appeared in films, including Men Without Dates, Dangerous, Hot Chili, Cheech & Chong Nice Dreams, Rocky II, Galaxy of Terror, New Years Evil, Rich Man Poor Man Book I, Caged Fury; TV appearances include Malubu Branch, General Hospital, Dangerous Women, Dallas, Knight and Daye, The New Gidget, Knight Rider, Three's Company, Dr. Joyce Brothers Show, Blansky's Beauties, Peter Lupus Show, Fix-It City, Happy Days, Laverne & Shirley, Wonder Woman, The Incredible Hulk; theater appearances include Too True to be Good, Damn Yankees, Anastasia, Star Spangled Girl, The Beaux Stratagem, The Canterbury Tales; founder, pub. The Caster, 1991, Power Agent, 1993; Jan. founder Rising Star Distbn. and Canoco Prodns., 1999—, Get Inside the Agents' Head Seminars, Yes I Can Actors Workshops, Actors Acing Hollywood Seminars, 2005—; exec prodr.: Beanie & Twigg, Paranormal Private Eyes, Inside the Industry, 2000. Mem. Screen Actors' Guild, Am. Fedn. TV Radio Artists, Actor's Equity, Actor's Forum (bd. dirs. 1985-94). Avocations: singing, spinning, sailing, travel. Office: Canoco Pub 11611 Chenault St Ste 118 Los Angeles CA 90049-4574 Office Phone: 310-471-2287. Personal E-mail: industryedge@adelphia.net.

O'CONNOR, EDWARD JOSEPH, neurologist; b. LA, Jan. 12, 1944; s. Edward Joseph and Claire Smith O'Connor; m. Laura Davidson Folks, Mar. 6, 1982; children: Charles, Kevin, Andrew. BS, U. Notre Dame, Ind., 1966; MD, UCLA, 1970. Diplomate Am. Bd. Neurology and Psychiatry, Am. Bd. Electrodiagnostic Medicine. Intern U. Calif. Affiliate Hosps., 1970—71; resident internal medicine Wadsworth VA Hosp., LA, 1971—72; resident neurology U. N.Mex., 1974—76; chief resident UCLA, 1976—77; registrar Inst. Neurology, London, 1977—78; chief section neurology White Meml. Hosp., LA, 1979—86; owner Nerol. Assocs. West LA, Santa Monica, Calif., 1986—. Assoc. prof. neurology USC & UCLA. Bd. dirs. UCLA Rugby. Recipient UCLA Ruger Hall of Fame, 2008. Fellow: Am. Acad. Neurology. Democrat. Roman Catholic. Office: Neurol Assocs West LA 2811 Wilshire Blvd # 790 Santa Monica CA 90403

O'CONNOR, JENNIFER L., lawyer, energy executive; BA cum laude, U. Calif., Los Angeles; JD, U. Calif. Hastings Coll. of Law. Atty. Tobin and Tobin, San Francisco, Squire, Sanders & Dempsey, Columbus, Ohio; counsel Honda of Am.; v.p., asst. gen. counsel Starbucks Corp., 1998—2001, sr. v.p., dep. gen. counsel, 2001—02, interim gen. counsel, 2002—03; v.p., gen. counsel Puget Energy/Puget Sound Energy, 2003—. Office: Puget Sound Energy PO Box 97034 10885 NE 4th St Bellevue WA 98009-9734

O'CONNOR, KEVIN, professional sports team executive; b. Bronx, NY; m. Linda O'Connor; children: Katie, Adam, Lindsay, Brian(dec.). Grad. in econs. and bus., Belmont Abbey Coll., NC, 1969. Asst. coach Va. Poly. Inst. and State U., 1972—74, Va. Mil. Inst., 1974—76, U. Colo., 1976—79, UCLA, 1979—84; scout LA Clippers, Portland Trail Blazers, NJ Nets, 1990—94, Utah Jazz, 1994—97, v.p. basketball ops., 1999—2002, sr. v.p. basketball ops., 2002—07, exec. v.p. basketball ops., gen. mgr., 2007—; dir. player pers. Phila. 76ers, 1997—99. Mem. Men's Sr. Nat. Team Com. USA Basketball. Served in US Army, 1969—71. Office: Utah Jazz 301 W South Temple Salt Lake City UT 84101

O'CONNOR, KEVIN JOHN, psychologist, educator; b. Jersey City, July 18, 1954; s. John Lanning and Marilyn (Reynolds) O'C.; m. Ryan Michael, Matthew Benham. BA, U. Mich., 1975; PhD, U. Toledo, 1981. Clin. psychologist Blythedale Children's Hosp., Valhalla, NY, 1980-83; dir. psychol. svcs. Walworth Barbour Am. Internat. Sch., Kfar Shmaryahu, Israel, 1983-84; adj. faculty dept. psychology Iona Coll., New Rochelle, NY, 1984; clin. psychologist No. Westchester Guidance Clinic, Mt. Kisco, NY, 1985; exec. dir., newsletter editor Assn. for Play Therapy, Fresno, Calif., 1982-97; cons. psychologist Fresno (Calif.) Treatment Ctr., 1986-87, Diagnostic Sch. for Neurologically Handicapped Children, Fresno, Calif., 1986-90; adj. faculty Pacific Grad. Sch. of Psychology, Palo Alto, Calif., 1997—2001, Calif. Sch. Profl. Psychology, Berkeley, Calif., 1988-89; prof. Alliant Internat. U., Calif. Sch. Profl. Psychology, Fresno, 1985—, dir. clinical PsyD and PhD programs, 1985—. Contbr. numerous publications and presentations in field. Named Psychologist of Yr. San Joaquin Psychol. Assn., 1994. Fellow APA; mem. Assn. for Play Therapy (dir. emeritus). Democrat. Avocations: travel, art, ceramics. Office: Calif Sch Profl Psych Alliant Internat U 5130 E Clinton Way Fresno CA 93727-2014 Office Phone: 559-253-2273. Business E-Mail: koconnor@alliant.edu.

O'CONNOR, PAUL DANIEL, lawyer; b. Paterson, NJ, Nov. 24, 1936; s. Paul Daniel and Anne Marie Christopher O'C.; children: Steven Paul, Sheryl Lynn, Laura Ann. BS in Engring, U.S. Naval Acad., 1959; LLB, U. Va., 1965. Bar: N.Y. 1965, Calif. 1995. Assoc. firm Winthrop, Stimson, Putnam & Roberts, NYC, 1965-72, partner, 1972-80; sr. v.p., gen. counsel Singer Co., Stamford, Conn., 1980-86; CEO Citation Builders, 1986—95; trustee Valley Trusts, Oakland, Calif., 1986—; gen. coun. Berg Holdings, Sausalito, Calif., 2007. 1st lt. USAF, 1959-62. Mem.: Assn. Bar City NY, Bar Assn. San Francisco. Office Phone: 510-874-4300. Personal E-mail: poconnor59@comcast.net.

O'CONNOR, THOMAS C., energy executive; b. 1955; m. Diane O'Connor; 3 children. BS cum laude in Biology, U. Mass., Lowell, 1977, MS in Environ. Studies, 1980. Dir. mktg. svcs., dir. bus. devel. Tex. Ea. Transmission Corp.; pres. PanEnergy Devel. Co.; supr. environ. compliance to mgr. environ. compliance to mgr. market devel. Algonquin Gas Transmission Duke Energy Corp., Charlotte, NC, 1987—89, sr. v.p. mktg. and capacity mgmt., v.p. mktg., v.p. east coast mktg. NE pipeline group, 1994—2002, pres., CEO Duke Energy Gas Transmission's US ops., 2002—05, group v.p. corp. strategy, 2005—06, group exec., COO US Franchised Electric and Gas, group exec., pres. comml. business, 2006—07; chmn., pres., CEO DCP Midstream, LLC, Denver, 2007—. Mem. sci. devel. bd. U. Mass Lowell Coll. Arts & Scis. Office: DCP Midstream LLC 370 17th St Ste 2500 Denver CO 80202

ODA, YOSHIO, physician, internist; b. Papaaloa, Hawaii, Jan. 14, 1933; s. Hakuai and Usako (Yamamoto) O.; AB, Cornell U., 1955; MD, U. Chgo., 1959. Diplomate Am. Bd. Internal Medicine. Intern U. Chgo. Clinics, 1959-60; resident in pathology U. Chgo., 1960-62, Queen's Hosp., Hawaii, 1962-63, Long Beach (Calif.) VA Hosp., 1963-65; resident in allergy, immunology U. Colo. Med. Center, 1966-67; pvt. practice, L.A., 1965-66; pvt. practice internal medicine, allergy and immunology, Honolulu, 1970—; asst. clin. prof. medicine U. Hawaii, Honolulu, 1970—. Maj., AUS, 1968-70. Mem. ACP, Am. Acad. Allergy. Office: Piikoi Med Bldg 1024 Piikoi St Honolulu HI 96814-1925

O'DEA, PATRICK J., food products executive; m. Holly O'Dea; 4 children. BS in bus. administration, U. Albany. With Procter & Gamble, 1984—95; v.p., gen. mgr. specialty cheese divsn. Stella Foods, 1995—97; CEO, pres. Mother's Specialty Foods Corp., 1997; CEO Archway, Mother's Cookies and Mother's Cake and Cookie Co., 1997—2001; CEO, pres. Peet's Coffee & Tea Inc., 2002—, dir., 2002—. Mem.: Nat. Coffee Assn. (bd. trustees), Calif. C. of C. (bd. trustees). Avocation: triathlon. Office: Peet's Coffee & Tea 1400 Park Ave Emeryville CA 94608

ODELL, JOHN H., construction executive; b. Toledo, Oct. 31, 1955; s. John H. and Doris Odell; m. Kathryn Lau, Oct. 1, 1988; children: Ceara, Heather, Victoria. B in Environ. Design, U. Miami, Oxford, Ohio, 1977. Staff arch. Richard Halford and Assocs., Santa Fe, 1978-79; ptnr. B.O.A. Constrn., Santa Fe, 1980-84; owner John H. Odell Constrn., Santa Fe, 1985—; v.p. Los Pintores Inc., Santa Fe, 1990-92; pres. Uncle Joey's Food Svcs. Inc., 1991—, John H. Odell Assocs. Inc., Santa Fe, 1995—. Musician: Huntington (W.Va.) Cmty. Orch., 1972—73, Santa Fe Cmty. Orch., 1982. Mem. citizen rev. com. Santa Fe Sch. Bd., chmn., 1999—, mem. bond and mil. levy com., 2000—; bd. mem. Santa Fe Area Home Builders Assn., Partners in Edn. Recipient Hist. Preservation award, City of Santa Fe, 1997. Mem.: AIA (assoc.; treas., bd. dirs. Santa Fe chpt. 1988—, mem. liaison com. design 1987—, Cmty. Svc. award 1993), Santa Fe Remodeler Coun., Nat. Assn. Home Builders, Vine and Wine Soc. (N.Mex No. Rio Grande chpt. pres., bd. dirs., v.p.). Avocations: skiing, scuba diving, handball, racquetball. Home: PO Box 2967 Santa Fe NM 87504-2967 Office: John H Odell Assn 1523 Taos St Santa Fe NM 87505-3835 E-mail: johnoinc@aol.com.

ODEN, GREG, professional basketball player; b. Buffalo, Jan. 22, 1988; s. Greg Oden, Sr. and Zoe Oden. Student in Bus. Adminstrn., Ohio State U., Columbus, 2006—07. Draft pick Portland Trail Blazers, Oreg., 2007. Mem. USA Basketball Men's Sr. Nat. Team, 2007—. Recipient Arthur L. Trester Mental Attitude award, Ind. Boy's Basketball Class 4A, 2005—06, Morgan Wootten award (McDonald's All-Am. Player of Yr.), 2006; named USA Today Player of Yr., 2005, 2006, Parade Mag. Player of Yr., 2005, 2006, Gatorade Ind. and Nat. Player of Yr., 2005, 2006, Gatorade Nat. HS Male Athlete of Yr., 2006, Player of Yr., Nat. HS Coaches Assn., 2006, Ind. Mr. Basketball, Indpls. Star, 2006, Atlanta Tipoff Club 2006 Naismith Prep Player of Yr.; named a McDonald's All-Am., 2006. Achievements include being the number one pick in the 2007 NBA Draft. Office: Portland Trail Blazers Rose Quarter One Center Ct Portland OR 97227

ODER, KENNETH WILLIAM, lawyer; b. Newport News, Va., July 9, 1947; s. Thomas William and Joy Reletta (McNeil) O.; m. Lucinda Ann Fox, July 20, 1969; children: Joshua, Devon, Chelsea. BA, U. Va., 1969, JD, 1975. Bar: Calif. 1975, U.S. Dist. Ct. (cen. dist.) Calif. 1975, U.S. Dist. Ct. (so. and no. dists.) Calif. 1977, U.S. Ct. Appeals (9th cir.) 1977, D.C. 1979. Assoc. Latham & Watkins, Los Angeles, 1975-77, 79-82, ptnr., 1982-94, assoc. Washington, 1978-79; exec. v.p. Safeway Inc., Oakland, 1994—. Exec. editor U. Va. Law Rev., 1973-74. Coach San Marino Little League, Calif., 1983—, Am. Youth Soccer Orgn., Rosemeade, Calif., 1984—. Mem. Calif. Bar Assn. (employment law sect.), Los Angeles County Bar Assn., D.C. Bar Assn. Republican. Methodist. Avocations: jogging, hiking, fishing. Office: Safeway Inc 5918 Stoneridge Mall Rd Pleasanton CA 94588-3229

ODERMAN, JEFFREY M., lawyer; b. Orange, NJ, Oct. 30, 1949; BA summa cum laude, UCLA, 1971; JD, Stanford U., 1974. Bar: Calif. 1975, U.S. Supreme Ct., U.S. Ct. Appeals (9th cir.), U.S. Dist. Ct. (ctrl. and no. dists.) Calif. Mem. Rutan & Tucker, Costa Mesa, Calif. Mem. State Bar Calif., Phi Beta Kappa, Order of Coif. Office: Rutan & Tucker PO Box 1950 611 Anton Blvd Ste 1400 Costa Mesa CA 92626-1931

ODERMATT, ROBERT ALLEN, architect; b. Oakland, Calif., Jan. 3, 1938; s. Clifford Allen and Margaret Louise (Budge) O.; m. Diana Birtwistle, June 9, 1960; children: Kristin Ann, Kyle David. BArch, U. Calif., Berkeley, 1960. Registered architect, Calif., Oreg., Nev., Colo., Hawaii; cert. Nat. Coun. Archtl. Registration Bds. Draftsman Anderson Simonds Dusel Campini, Oakland, 1960-61; architect James R. Lucas, Orinda, Calif., 1961-62, ROMA Architects, San Francisco, 1962-76, architect, pres., 1976-84; prin. ROMA Design Group, San Francisco, 1962-92; pres. The Odermatt Group, Berkeley, Calif., 1992—. Prin. spkr. Internat. Conf. on Rebuilding Cities, Pitts., 1988; mem. U.S. Design in Am. Program, Sofia, Bulgaria, Armenian Disaster Assn. Team, 1989, NA Collateral Internship Mgmt. Com.; prin. State of Calif. Bay Area Facilities Plan, 1992, Greece Resort Privatization Program, 1993. Prin. designer U.S. Embassy, Bahrain, Grand Canyon Nat. Park, 1977, Yosemite Nat. Park, 1987; prin. planner hotel complex Westin Hotel, Vail, Colo., 1982, Kaanapali Resort, 1987, Las Montanas Resort, San Diego; master plan U. Calif., Berkeley, 1988, Kohanaiki and Mauna Lani resorts, 1989, Calif. State Strategic Real Estate Plan, 1992, Greek Resort/Marina Privatization Program, 1993, Tektronix Strategic Plan, 1994, United Labs, Manila Master Plan, 1995, State of Calif. Real Estate Orgn. Plan, 1996, Ford Island Pearl Harbor Master Plan, 1996, Pearl Harbor Visitor Ctr. Plan, 1997, Albiano Resort Study, 1998; master plans include Trefethen Vineyards, Bell Garden, Napa Valley Expo. Bd. dirs. Nat. Archtl.

Accrediting Bd., 2003—, pres., 2005; mem. Koa Ridge Urban Design Plan, Santa Monica LRT Urban Design Plan, Santa Cruz Downtown Assessment, Eisenhower E. Plan, Alexandria, Va., Upper Potomac W. Plan, Alexandria, King St. Revitalization Study, Alexandria, 2004, Oakland Mayor's Com. on High Density Housing, 1982, Oakland Gen. Plan Congress, 1994; mem. waterfront plan adv. com. City of Oakland, 1996, Westpark Town Ctr., 2003, Koa Ridge Cmty., Oahu, Hawaii, King St. Retail Plan, Alexandria; mem. adv. com. Queen Emma Founds. Lands of Waikiki Plan, 2004—05; mem. adv. com. land use, circulation plan City of Santa Monica, 2007—08. Recipient Leslie M. Boney Spirit of Fellowship award. Fellow AIA (dir. East Bay chpt. 1969-71, pres. 1980-81, dir. Calif. coun. 1979-81, Disting. Svc. award Calif. chpt., 1991, nat. dir. 1983-86, nat. v.p. 1986-87, chair AIA internat. steering com. 1993-94, graphic stds. adv. com. 1991-92, U. Calif. archtl. review commn. 1992-96, exec. com. Coll. Fellows 1996-98, vice chancellor Coll. Fellows 1999, chancellor 2000, East Bay medal 1997, Edward C. Kemper medal for outstanding svc. 2004), Am. Archtl. Found. (regent, bd. dirs.), Nat. Archt. Accreditation Bd. (pres.). E-mail: raomatt@aol.com.

ODETTE, G. ROBERT, mechanical and environmental engineering educator; PhD, MIT, 1970. Prof. mech. & environ. engring. U. Calif., Santa Barbara. Office: U Calif Dept Mech & Environ Engring Santa Barbara CA 93106

ODGERS, RICHARD WILLIAM, lawyer; b. Detroit, Dec. 31, 1936; s. Richard Stanley and Elsie Maude (Trevarthen) O.; m. Gail C. Bassett, Aug. 29, 1959; children: Thomas R., Andrew B. AB, U. Mich., 1959, JD, 1961. Bar: Calif. 1962. Assoc. Pillsbury, Madison & Sutro, San Francisco, 1961—69, ptnr., 1969—87, 1998—2000; exec. v.p., gen. counsel Pacific Telesis Group, 1987-98; ptnr. Pillsbury Winthrop Shaw Pittman, San Francisco, 2001—. Mem. Calif. Task Force Lawyer Support for Legal Svcs. Dir. Legal Aid Soc. Employment Law Ctr.; dir. Legal Cmty. Against Violence; dir., sec. Van Loben Sels/RembeRock Charitable Found.; bd. dirs. Immigrant Legal Resource Ctr., Fed. Dist. Ct. Hist. Soc.; mem. Calif. Legal Svcs. Trust Fund Commn. With USNR. Fellow Am. Bar Found., Am. Judicature Soc., Am. Coll. Trial Lawyers; mem. ABA, Am. Law Inst., Am. Coll. Law Practice Mgmt., Bar Assn. San Francisco (past dir., co-chair task force charitable giving). Office: Pillsbury Winthrop Shaw Pittman 50 Fremont St San Francisco CA 94105 Office Phone: 415-983-1202. Office Fax: 415-983-1200. Business E-Mail: richard.odgers@pillsburylaw.com.

ODOM, LAMAR JOSEPH, professional basketball player; b. Jamaica, NY, Nov. 6, 1979; Student, UNLV; grad., U. Rhode Island, 2001. Player LA Clippers, 1999—2003, Miami Heat, 2003—04, LA Lakers, 2004—. Mem. US Olympics Basketball Team, Athens, Greece, 2004. Named to All-Rookie First Team, 2000. Office: c/o LA Lakers 555 N Nash St El Segundo CA 90245

O'DONNELL, PIERCE HENRY, lawyer; b. Troy, NY, Mar. 5, 1947; s. Harry J. and Mary (Kane) O'Donnell; m. Dawn Donley, Mar. 17, 1995; children: Meghan Maureen, Brendan Casey, Courtney Dawn, Pierce Dublin, Aidan Yeats. BA, Georgetown U., 1969, JD, 1972; LLM, Yale U., 1975. Bar: D.C. 1973, U.S. Supreme Ct. 1975, Calif. 1978. Law clk. to Justice Byron R. White U.S. Supreme Ct.; law clk. to Judge Shirley M. Hutstedler U.S. Ct. Appeals (9th cir.); assoc. Williams & Connolly, Washington, 1975-78; ptnr. Beardsley, Hufstedler & Kemble, LA, 1978-81, Hufstedler, Miller, Carlson & Beardsley, LA, 1981-82, O'Donnell & Gordon, LA, 1982-87, Kaye, Scholer, Fierman, Hays & Handler, LA, 1988-95, O'Donnell Shaeffer & Mortimer, L.L.P., LA, 1996—. Exec. asst. U.S. Sec. Edn., 1979; spl. counsel Commn. Jud. Performance, San Francisco, 1979; chmn. Nat. Media, Inc., 1984—92. Co-author: (book) Fatal Subtraction: The Inside Story of Buchwald v Paramount, 1992, Toward A Just and Effective Sentencing System: Agenda for Legislative Reform, 1976; author: Dawn's Early Light, 2001, Funny You Asked About That, 2005, In Time of War, 2005; contbr. articles to profl. jours. Chmn. Friends Cal Tech YMCA, 1983—84, Verdugo-San Rafael Urban Mountain Park Fund, 1980—84; bd. dirs. Foothill Family Svc., 1979—85, chmn., 1984—85; bd. dirs. Interfaith Ctr. To Reverse Arms Race, 1984—90, pres., 1987—88; mem. Econ. Round Table of L.A., 1979—, pres., 2000—01; chmn. Calif. Coast Baseball Acad., 2001—; mem. Santa Barbara Sheriff's Coun., 2003—; bd. dirs. Friends of Altadena Libr., 1979—81, Pasadena-Foothill Urban League, E. Altadena Little League, 1993—97. Fellow: Internat. Acad. Trial Lawyers; mem.: NAACP, PEN, Am. Coll. Trial Lawyers, Cal Tech Assocs., Am. Law Inst., Am. Bd. Trial Advocates, Sierra Club, Calif. Club, Gridiron Club (Georgetown U.), Bel Air Country Club. Episcopalian. Office: O'Donnell & Shaeffer LLP 550 S Hope 20th fl Los Angeles CA 90071-2027 Home: 3475 Marina Dr Santa Barbara CA 93110-2426 Home Phone: 805-565-2226; Office Phone: 213-532-2000. Business E-Mail: pod@oslaw.com.

O'DONNELL, ROSIE, television personality, actress, comedienne; b. Commack, NY, Mar. 21, 1962; m. Kelli Carpenter, Feb. 26, 2004; children: Parker Jaren, Chelsea Belle, Blake Christopher, Vivienne Rose. Student, Dickinson Coll., Boston U. Host The Rosie O'Donnell Show, 1995—2002; editor Rosie mag., 2000—02; co-host The View, 2006—07. Actress (films) A League of Their Own, 1992, Sleepless in Seattle, 1993 (American Comedy award nomination for best supporting female in a motion picture, 1994), Another Stakeout, 1993 (American Comedy award nomination for best actress in a motion picture, 1994), Car 54, Where Are You?, 1994, I'll Do Anything, 1994, The Flintstones, 1994, Exit to Eden, 1994, Now and Then, 1995, Beautiful Girls, 1996, Harriet the Spy, 1996, A Very Brady Sequel, 1996, Wide Awake, 1996, Get Bruce, 1999, Jackie's Back, 1999, Tarzan (voice only), 1999, Flintstones in Viva Rock Vegas, 2000, (TV films) The Twilight of the Golds, 1997, (TV series) Gimme A Break, 1986—87, Stand By Your Man, 1992, Women Aloud, 1992, (Broadway plays) Grease, 1994, Seussical the Musical, 2001, Fiddler on the Roof, 2005, host, comedienne (TV series) Stand-up Spotlight, VH-1, 1993 (American Comedy award nomination for best female performer in a TV special, 1994, Cable ACE award nomination for best entertainment host, 1994), actress, exec. prodr. (TV films) Riding the Bus with My Sister, 2005; exec. prodr.: (TV films) Kids are Punny, 1998; (films) Mina & the Family Treasure, 2004; (Broadway plays) Taboo, 2003—04; TV appearances include Ally McBeal, 1999, Third Watch, 2000, The Practice, 2000, Will & Grace, 2002, Judging Amy, 2003, Queer as Folk, 2005, Nip Tuck, 2006—07; author: Find Me, 2002, Celebrity Detox: (the fame game), 2007. Recipient Daytime Emmy awards for The Rosie O'Donnell Show, 1997—2001; named one of The World's Most Influential People, TIME mag., 2007.

O'DONNELL, WILLIAM RUSSELL, state legislator; b. Quincy, Mass., Jan. 16, 1951; s. Alfred Joseph and Ruth Irene (McCausland) O.; m. Mary Hogan, June 13, 1976; children: Meagan, Patrick, Kevin, Colleen, Kyle. BS in Bus. and Econs., U. Nev., Las Vegas, 1979. Patrolman Las Vegas Met. Police, 1973-74; realtor Coldwell-Banker, Las Vegas, 1988—; pres. Computer System Concepts, Las Vegas, 1980—; mem. Nev. Senate, Dist. 5 Clark County, Carson City, 1987—, Nevada Assembly, 1985-86. Nev. state assemblyman, Las Vegas, 1985-86; alt. legis. commn. Nev., 1987-89; majority Whip Rep. Party Nev., 1989; mem. Nev. Child Watch Adv. Bd., Assn. for the Handicapped, Pro-Life Nev., Citizens for Responsible Govt.; pres. Sect. 10 Homeowners Assn., Las Vegas, 1986—, Spring Valley Town Bd., 1984—; bd. dirs. Home of the Good Shepherd, St. Rose de Lima Hosp., 1985—. Mem. Las Vegas Bd. Realtors, Rotary, Nev. Assoc. of the Handicapped, St. Rose de Lima Hosp., Las Vegas Chamber of Commerce, Nev. Devel. Authority. Republican. Roman Catholic. Address: Nev Senate 401 S Carson St Rm 244 Carson City NV 89701-4747 Office: 2780 S Jones Blvd Las Vegas NV 89146-5625

O'DONNELL, WILLIAM THOMAS, management consultant; b. Latrobe, Pa., Feb. 22, 1939; s. William Regis and Kathryn Ann (Coneff) O'D; m. Judith Koetke, Oct. 1, 1965; children: William Thomas, William Patrick, Allison Rose, Kevin Raymond. Student Ea., N. Mex. U., 1961-65; student in mktg., John Carrol U., 1961-65; student, Inst. Tech., 1965-66; BSBA, U. Phoenix, 1982, MBA with distinction, 1984; PhD applied orgnl. mgmt. personel psychographics, Union Inst., 1999. Various positions Hickok Elec. Instrument Co., Cleveland, 1961-65; with Fairchild Semicondr., Mpls., 1965-67, Transitron Semicondr., Mpls., 1967-69; regional sales mgr. Burroughs Corp., Plainfield, N.J., 1967-71; mktg. mgr. Owens-Ill., Co., 1972-73; v.p. mktg. Pantek Co. subs. Owens-Ill. Co., Lewiston, Pa., 1973-75; v.p. mktg., nat. sales mgr. Toledo, 1975-76; mktg. mgr. Govt. Electronics divsn. group Motorola co., Scottsdale, Ariz., 1976-80, U.S. mktg.mgr. radar positioning syss., 1981; gen. mgr. J.K. Internat., Scottsdale, 1980-81; mgmt. cons., pres. Cambridge Grp., 1987—; v.p. mktg. Pinnacle Surg. Products, 1989, Kroy, Inc., 1992-94; mgmt. cons., 1994; v.p. mktg. and bus. devel. Kroy, inc., 1992. Adj. prof. Union Grad. Sch; guest lectr. U. Mich. Grad. Sch. Bus. Administn.; instr. U. Phoenix, 1984-88, chair strategic mgmt. 1988, pres. faculty, 1989—, area chair mktg., 1995—, area chair grad. mgmt., 1999-2003, mem. doctoral program coun., 2001-02, area chair orgnl. behavior doctoral program, 2002—, master faculty U. Phoenix, 2004; lectr. Scottsdale C.C., Paradise Valley C.C.; talk show host Sta. KFNN, 1992-95; area chmn gen. mgmt. Union Grad. Sch. Maricopa C.C., U. Phoenix Chmn., Rep. precinct, Burnsville, Minn., 1968-70; bd. dirs. Pacific Gateway. Chmn. City fin., Burnsville; dir. community devel. U.S. Jaycees, Mpls., 1968-69; mem. Scottsdale 2000 Com. Pres; bd. dirs. Winfield Home Owners Assn., 2004-. With USAF, 1957-61 With USAF, 1957—61. Recipient Outstanding Performance award Maricopa C.C. System, 1987, Faciliation award, Maricopa C.C.; Citation for Faciliation Ability, U. Phoenix, 1986, 90, 93, 99; named Hon. Citizen, Donaldsville, La., 1978. Mem. Am. Mktg. Assn., Afron-Am. Small Bus. Assn), Phoenix Indian Ctr., Inc. (bd. dirs. 1994), Amateur Athletic Union (swimming ofcl. 1980-82), Phoenix Execs. Club, U. Phoenix Faculty Club (bd. dirs., pres., 1988-91 recipient Presdl. Designation award, officer), North Cape Yacht Club, Scottsdale Racquet Club, Toftness country Club. Roman Catholic. Home: 33144 N 72d Way Scottsdale AZ 85266 Office Phone: 480-998-0197. Personal E-mail: wto@cox.net.

O'DOWD, DONALD DAVY, retired university president; b. Manchester, NH, Jan. 23, 1927; s. Hugh Davy and Laura (Morin) O'D.; m. Janet Louise Fithian, Aug. 23, 1953; children: Daniel D., Diane K., James E., John M. BA summa cum laude, Dartmouth Coll., 1951; postgrad. (Fulbright fellow), U. Edinburgh, Scotland, 1951-52; MA, Harvard U., 1955, PhD, 1957. Instr., asst. prof. psychology, dean freshmen Wesleyan U., Middletown, Conn., 1955-60; assoc. prof., prof. of psychology, dean Univ. Oakland Univ., Rochester, Mich., 1960-65, provost, 1965-70; pres. Oakland U., Rochester, Mich., 1970-80; exec. vice chancellor SUNY, Albany, 1980-84; pres. U. of Alaska Statewide System, 1984-90. Carnegie Corp. fellow, 1965—66. Mem. APA, AAAS, Phi Beta Kappa, Sigma Xi. Home and Office: 801 A Senda Verde Santa Barbara CA 93105

O'DOWD, SARAH A., lawyer; b. Manchester, NH, Sept. 7, 1949; AB, Immaculata Coll., 1971; MA, Stanford U., 1973, JD, 1977. Bar: Calif. 1978. Atty. Heller, Ehrman, White & McAuliffe, Palo Alto, Calif., 1978—, managing shareholder, Silicon Valley Office, 1995—99, firmwide practice chair, mem. exec. comm., 1999—2002. Mem. ABA.

OEHLER, RICHARD WILLIAM, lawyer; b. NYC, Nov. 24, 1950; s. John Montgomery and Florence Mae (Jahn) O.; m. Linda Tyson. BA, Dartmouth Coll., 1972; JD, Harvard U., 1976. Bar: Calif. 1976, Wash. 1987, D.C. 1988, U.S. Dist. Ct. (no. dist.) Calif. 1976, U.S. Dist. Ct. Wash. 1987, U.S. Claims Ct. 1979, U.S. Ct. Appeals (fed. cir.) 1982. Assoc. Pillsbury, Madison & Sutro, San Francisco, 1976-78; trial atty. U.S. Dept. Justice, Washington, 1978-87; of counsel Perkins Coie, Seattle, 1987-90, ptnr., 1990—. Mem. ABA, Nat. Contract Mgmt. Assn. (Spl. Achievement award 1990-92), Wash. State Bar Assn. Office: Perkins Coie 1201 3rd Ave Fl 40 Seattle WA 98101-3029 Office Phone: 206-359-8419. Business E-Mail: roehler@perkinscoie.com.

OEHLKE, JACK W., computer company executive; b. 1946; Dir. ops., dir. quality Microswitch divsn. Honeywell, Inc., 1968-93; v.p. mfg. ops. Key Tronic Corp., Spokane, Wash., 1993-95, sr. v.p. ops., 1995, COO, 1995-97, pres., CEO, 1997—. Office: Key Tronic Corp N 4424 Sullivan Rd Spokane WA 99216 Fax: 509-927-5248.

OESTING, DAVID W., lawyer; b. Chgo., Aug. 6, 1944; AB, Earlham Coll., 1967; JD, Wash. U., 1970. Bar: Wash. 1970, Alaska 1981. Ptnr. in charge of Anchorage Office Davis Wright Tremaine, Anchorage, 1980—. Editor-in-chief Wash. U. Law Quarterly, 1969-70. Mem. ABA, Am. Coll. Trial Lawyers, Wash. State Bar Assn., Alaska Bar Assn., Anchorage Bar Assn., Order of Coif. Office: Davis Wright Tremaine 701 W 8th Ave Ste 800 Anchorage AK 99501-3467 Home Phone: 907-248-3146; Office Phone: 907-257-5300. Business E-Mail: daveoesting@dwt.com.

OFFENBERGER, ALLAN ANTHONY, retired electrical engineering educator; b. Wadena, Sask., Can., Aug. 11, 1938; s. Ivy Viola (Hagglund) O. (dec.); m. Margaret Elizabeth Patterson, Apr. 12, 1963; children: Brian, Gary. BS, U. B.C., 1962, MS, 1963; PhD, MIT, 1968. Asst. prof. U. Alta., Edmonton, Canada, 1968—70, assoc. prof., 1970—75, prof., 1975—95, prof. emeritus, 1996—. Vis. prof. UK Atomic Energy Agy., Abingdon, Oxon, 1975-76, U. Oxford, UK, 1992, U. Osaka, Japan, 2000; project dir. Laser Fusion Project, Edmonton, 1984-91; mem. strategic adv. com. Nat. Fusion Program, Atomic Energy Can. Ltd., Chalk River, Ont., 1987-96; Cons. Lawrence Livermore Nat. Lab., Calif., 1996-2007; served on several execs. bds., sci. adv. and rsch. grant committees; hosted internat. scholars; invited lectr., cons. in field. Mem. editorial bd. Laser and Particle Beams, 1987-2004; contbr. over 150 sci. articles on lasers and plasma physics Killam Rsch. fellow Can. Coun., 1980-82. SERC rsch. fellow, Eng., 1992. Mem. Can. Assn. Physicists (exec. officer, v.p. elect 1987-88, pres. 1989-90), Am. Phys. Soc., Sigma Xi. Achievements include establishing a major center for high power laser research and development (particularly krypton fluoride lasers) for fusion energy and other applications. Home: 412 Lessard Dr Edmonton AB Canada T6M 1A7 Office: U Alta Dept Elec Computer Engring Edmonton AB Canada T6G 2V4 Office Phone: 780-492-3939. Business E-Mail: aao@ece.ualberta.ca.

OFFER, STUART JAY, lawyer; b. Seattle, June 2, 1943; m. Judith Spitzer, Aug. 29, 1970; children: Rebecca, Kathryn. BA, U. Wash., 1964; LLB, Columbia U., 1967. Bar: D.C. 1968, U.S. Tax Ct. 1968, Calif. 1972. Atty., advisor U.S. Tax Ct., Washington, 1967-68; assoc. Morrison & Foerster, LLP, San Francisco, 1972-76, ptnr., 1976—. Trustee Am. Tax Policy Inst. Served as capt. U.S. Army, 1968-72. Mem. ABA (chmn. taxation sect., corp. tax com. 1991-92, coun. dir. 1995-98, vice chmn. adminstrn. 1998-2000), Internat. Fiscal Assn. (regent), Am. Coll. Tax Counsel. Office: Morrison & Foerster LLP 425 Market St San Francisco CA 94105-2482 Office Phone: 415-268-7052. Business E-Mail: soffer@mofo.com.

OGDEN, VALERIA MUNSON, management consultant, state representative; b. Okanogan, Wash., Feb. 9, 1924; d. Ivan Bodwell and Pearle (Wilson) Munson; m. Daniel Miller Ogden Jr., Dec. 28, 1946; children: Janeth Lee Ogden Martin, Patricia Jo Ogden Hunter, Daniel Munson Ogden. BA magna cum laude, Wash. State U., 1946. Exec. dir. Potomac Coun. Camp Fire, Washington, 1964-68, Ft. Collins (Colo.) United Way, 1969-73, Designing Tomorrow Today, Ft. Collins, 1973-74, Poudre Valley Community Edn. Assn., Ft. Collins, 1977-78; pres. Valeria M. Ogden, Inc., Kensington, Md., 1978-81; nat. field cons. Camp Fire, Inc., Kansas City, Mo., 1980-81; exec. dir. Nat. Capital Area YWCA, Washington, 1981-84, Clark County YWCA, Vancouver, Wash., 1985-89; pvt. practice mgmt. cons. Vancouver, 1989—; mem. Wash. Ho. of Reps., 1990—2002, spkr. pro tempore, 1999—2002. Mem. adj. faculty pub. adminstrn. program Lewis and Clark Coll., Portland (Oreg.) State U., 1979-94; mem. Pvt. Industry Coun., Vancouver, 1986-95; mem. regional Svcs. Network Bd. Mental Health, 1993-03. Author: Camp Fire Membership, 1980. Mem. Wash. State Coun. Vol. Action, Olympia, 1986—90; county vice-chair Larimer County Dems., Ft. Collins, 1974—75; spkr. pro tem Wash. Ho. of Reps., 1999—2002; rep. Gov. Chris Gregoire S.W. Wash., 2005; mem. precinct com. Clark County Dems., Vancouver, 1986—88; treas. Mortar Bd. Nat. Found., Vancouver, 1987—96; bd. dirs. Clark County Coun. for Homeless, Vancouver, 1989—2004, chmn., 1994; bd. dirs. Wash. Wild Life and Recreation Coalition, 1995—2002, Human Svcs. Coun., 1996—2002, Wash. State Hist. Soc., 1996—2006, State Legis. Leaders Found., 2001—02, Columbia Springs Environ. Edn. Ctr. Found., 2003—06, Clark County Skill Ctr. Found., 2003—06; emeritus mem.; bd. dirs. S.W. Wash. Child Care Consortium, 2003—; chair arts and tourism com. Nat. Conf. State Legis., 1996—97; chair Affordable Cmty. Environments, 1998—, Wash. State Interagy. Com. for Outdoor Recreation, 2003—09, Wash. State Historic Preservation Fund, 2003—06, S.W. Wash. Ctr. for the Arts, 2003; pres. Nat. Order of Women Legislators, 1999—2001; mem. exec. com. Nat. Conf. State Legis., 2000—02; mem. adv. bd. Wash. State U., Vancouver, 2002—. Named Citizen of Yr. Ft. Collins Bd. of Realtors, 1975, State Legislator of Yr., Wash. State Labor Coun., 2000, Citizen of Yr., Vancouver, Wash., 2002, First Citizen, Clark County, 2006; recipient Gulick award Camp Fire Inc., 1956, Alumna Achievement award Wash. State U. Alumni Assn., 1988; named YWCA Woman of Achievement, 1991, 100 Most Powerful Women, Clark County, 2007, Caring Heart award, 2009. Mem. AAUW, Internat. Assn. Vol. Adminstrs. (pres. Boulder 1989-90), Nat. Assn. YWCA Exec. Dirs. (nat. bd. nominating com. 1988-90), Sci. and Soc. Assn. (bd. dirs. 1993-97), Women in Action, Philanthropic and Ednl. Orgn., Soroptimists, Phi Beta Kappa. Democrat. Avocations: hiking, travel. Home: 2916 NE 88th Ct Vancouver WA 98662-6836 Office Phone: 360-254-8886. Personal E-mail: repval@comcast.net.

OGILVIE, LLOYD JOHN, clergyman; b. Kenosha, Wis., Sept. 2, 1930; s. Vard Spencer and Katherine (Jacobson) O.; m. Mary Jane Jenkins, Mar. 25, 1951 (dec. Apr. 2003), Doris Kaiser (Somner), Apr. 19, 2005. BA, Lake Forest Coll., 1952, DD, 1997; MA, Garrett Theol. Sem., 1957; postgrad., New Coll., U. Edinburgh, Scotland, 1955-56; LHD, U. Redlands, 1974, Seattle Pacific U., 1995; DD, Whitworth Coll., 1973, Westmount Coll., 1997, Lehigh U., 1999, Azusa Pacific Coll., 2001, U. Edinburgh, 2003, Carthage Coll., 2004; LLD, Ea. U., 1988, George Fox U., 1997, Pepperdine U., 1998, Belhaven Coll., 2001; HHD, Moravian Coll., 1975, Dickinson Coll., 1998; DST, Roberts Wesleyan Coll., 2000; DD, Astory Coll., 2008; LittD, Kings Coll., 2002. Ordained to ministry Presbyn. Ch., 1956; student pastor Gurnee, Ill., 1952-56; first pastor Winnetka (Ill.) Presbyn. Ch., 1956-62; pastor 1st, Presbyn. Ch., Bethlehem, Pa., 1962-72, 1st Presbyn. Ch., Hollywood, Calif., 1972—95. Preacher Chgo. Sunday Evening Club, 1963—1989; frequent radio and TV personality weekly syndicated TV program Let God Love You. Chaplain US Senate, 1995-2003, ret. 2003. Author: A Life Full of Surprises, 1969, Let God Love You, 1974, If I Should Wake Before I Die, 1973, Lord of the Ups and Downs, 1974, You've Got Charisma, 1975, Cup of Wonder, 1976, Life Without Limits, 1976, Drumbeat of Love, 1977, When God First Thought of You, 1978, The Autobiography of God, 1979, The Bush Is Still Burning, 1980, The Radiance of the Inner Splendor, 1980, Congratulations, God Believes in You, 1981, Life as it Was Meant to Be, 1981, The Beauty of Love, The Beauty of Friendship, 1981, The Beauty of Caring, The Beauty of Sharing, 1981, God's Best for My Life, 1981, God's Will in Your Life, 1982, Ask Him Anything, 1982, Commentary on Book of Acts, 1983, Praying with Power, 1983, Falling into Greatness, 1983, Freedom in the Spirit, 1984, Making Stress Work For You, 1984, The Lord of the Impossible, 1984, Why Not Accept Christ's Healing and Wholeness, 1984, If God Cares, Why Do I Still Have Problems?, 1985, Understanding the Hard Sayings of Jesus, 1986, 12 Steps to Living Without Fear, 1987, A Future and a Hope, 1988, Enjoying God, 1990, Silent Strength, 1990, The Lord of the Loose Ends, 1991, Conversation with God, 1992, The Greatest Counselor in the World, 1994, Perfect Peace, 1997, Quiet Moments with God, 1998, The Red Ember In the White Ash, 2006, The Essence of His Presence, 2007, God: Best For Your Life, 2008; gen. editor: Communicator's Commentary of the Bible, 1982, TV, 1995, Radio, 1985-1995; host: (TV and radio program) Let God Love

You. Pres. Leadership Unlimited Fuller Theol. Sem., Lloyd John Ogilvie Inst. of Preaching. Recipient Disting. Svc. Citation, Lake Forest Coll., Silver Angel award, Gold Medallion Book award, 1985, Angel award, Religion in Media, 1986—. William Booth award, Salvation Army, 1992; named Preacher of Yr., Religion in Media, 1982; named one of 12 Most Effective Preachers in the English-Speaking World, Baylor U. Office: 10112 Empyrean Way Los Angeles CA 90067 Office Phone: 310-203-3085. Business E-Mail: logilvie@sbcglobal.net.

OGILVY, GEOFF, professional golfer; b. Adelaide, Australia, June 11, 1977; m. Juli Ogilvy. Profl. golfer Profl. Golf Assn., 2001—. Achievements include winner PGA Tour events: Chrysler Classic of Tucson, 2005, WGC Accenture Match Play Championship, 2006, 2009, WGC-CA Championship, 2008, Mercedes-Benz Championship, 2009; winner Major Championships: US Open, 2006. Office: Geoff Ogilvy Inc 8377 E Hartford Dr Ste 105 Scottsdale AZ 85255-5686 Office Fax: 61 3 9592 5633.*

OGREAN, DAVID WILLIAM, sports association executive; b. New Haven, Feb. 7, 1953; s. Richard Berton and Dorothy (Nystrom) O.; m. Maryellen Harvey, Aug. 10 1974; children: Matthew David, Tracy Erin, Dana Marie. BA in English cum laude, U Conn., 1974; MS in Film, Boston U., 1978. Asa S. Bushnell intern Ea. Coll. Athletic Conf., Centerville, Mass., 1977—78; dir. pub. rels. Amateur Hockey Assn. U.S., Colorado Springs, Colo., 1978—80; mng. editor Am. Hockey and Arena mag., 1979—80; comm. rep. ESPN, Inc., Bristol, Conn., 1980—83, program mgr., 1983—88; asst. exec. dir. for TV Coll. Football Assn., Boulder, Colo., 1988—90; dir. broadcasting US Olympic Com., Colorado Springs, 1990—93, dep. exec. dir. mktg., 1999—2000; exec. dir. USA Hockey, Colorado Springs, 1993—99, 2005—; chmn. Colorado Springs Sports Corp., 1996—97, pres., CEO, 2000—02; exec. dir. USA Football, 2002—05. Chmn. legis. com. US Olympic Com., 1997-99, 2000-04; chmn. Colo. Springs Sports Corp., 1996-97; bd. dirs. Colo. Springs World Arena, 1998-2002, 05-, Colo. Springs Conv. and Visitors Bur., 2000-02. Home: 4110 San Felice Pointe Colorado Springs CO 80906 Office: USA Hockey 1775 Bob Johnson Dr Colorado Springs CO 80906 Business E-Mail: daveo@usahockey.org.

OH, ANGELA E., lawyer; b. LA, Sept. 8, 1955; BA, UCLA, 1977, MPH, 1981; JD, U. Calif., Davis, 1986. Bar: Calif. 1986. Lawyer, 1987—. Lawyer del. 9th Cir. Jud. Conf., 1995-96, lawyer rep.; mem. Senator Boxer's Jud. Noms. Com. for Ctrl. Dist. Calif., 1994-95; bd. dirs. Calif. Women's Law Ctr., Lawyers Mut. Ins. Co.; mem. cmty. adv. bd. First Interstate Bank Calif.; spkr. in field. Contbr. articles to profl. jours. and newspapers. Spl. counsel to the Assembly Spl. Com. on the L.A. Crisis. Mem. ABA, State Bar Calif., Korean-Am. Bar Assn. So. Calif. (pres.), L.A. County Bar Assn. Office: 8th Fl 601 W Fifth St Los Angeles CA 90071 Office Phone: 213-225-5825.

OH, TAI KEUN, business educator, consultant; b. Seoul, Korea; came to U.S., 1958, naturalized, 1969; BA, Seijo U., 1957; MA, No. Ill. U., 1961; MLS, U. Wis., 1965, PhD, 1970; m. Gretchen Brenneke, Dec. 26, 1964; children: Erica, Elizabeth, Emily. Asst. prof. mgmt. Roosevelt U., Chgo., 1969-73; assoc. prof. Calif. State U., Fullerton, 1973-76, prof. mgmt., 1976—2001; prof. mgmt. emeritus, 2001—; vis. prof. U. Hawaii, 1983-84, 86, U. Nuertingen, Germany, 1996-97, 99; advisor Pacific Asian Mgmt. Inst., U. Hawaii; internat. referee Asia-Pacific Jour. Mgmt., 1990—; cons. Calty Design Rsch., Inc. subs. Toyota Motor Corp.; guest lectr. Chiba U. Commerce, Japan; cons., spkr. in field. Named Outstanding Prof., Sch. Bus. Adminstrn. and Econs., Calif. State U., Fullerton, 1976, 78. Tai Keun Oh received early tenure and jump promotion to full professor in 1976 before completing the regular probationary period at California State University Fullerton, which is regarded as one of the more rapid promotions in the California State University system. He helped over 100 organizations solve complex human resource and management problems over the course of his career and has served as consultant to Calty Design Research, one of Toyota Motor Corporation's think tanks, for over 25 years. Grandfather, Kung Sun Oh, was the first Western trained medical doctor in Korea; he came to the United States in 1902 to begin his education at Center College of Kentucky and completed his medical training at the University of Louisville in 1909. In Korea, he founded a Presbyterian church and high school in Kunsan and then pioneered in the area of social services by establishing Kyungsan orphanage in 1919 and a home for the elderly. In Seoul, he became associated with Severance Hospital and Yonsei University Medical School and eventually became its Korean president. He died at 85 as one of the most respected men in Korea. NSF grantee, 1968-69, recipient Exceptional Merit Svc. award Calif. State U., 1984, Meritorious Performance and Profl. Promise award Calif. State U., 1987. Editl. bd. Acad. Mgmt. Rev., 1978-81; contbg. author: Ency. Profl. Mgmt., 1978, Handbook of Management 1985; contbr. articles to profl. jours.; Mem. Acad. Mgmt Home: 2044 E Eucalyptus Ln Brea CA 92821-5911 E-mail: toh@fullerton.edu.

O'HARA, CATHERINE, actress, comedienne; b. Toronto, Mar. 4, 1954; m. Bo Welch, 1992; children: Dylan, Matthew. Actress: films include After Hours, 1985, Heartburn, 1986, Beetlejuice, 1988, Dick Tracy, 1990, Betsy's Wedding, 1990, Home Alone, 1990, Little Vegas, 1990, There Goes The Neighborhood, 1992, Home Alone II: Lost In New York, 1992, (voice) The Nightmare Before Christmas, 1993, The Paper, 1994, Wyatt Earp, 1994, A Simple Twist of Fate, 1994, Tall Tale, 1995, Waiting for Guffman, 1996, The Last of the high Kings, 1996, (voice) Pippi Longstocking, 1997, Home Fries, 1998, The Life Before This, 1999, Surviving Christmas, 2004, Lemony Snicket's A Series of Unfortunate Events, 2004, Game 6, 2005, (voice) Chicken Little, 2005, (voice) Over the Hedge, 2006, Monster House, 2006, Penelope, 2006, For Your Consideration, 2006 (Best Supporting Actress Nat. Bd. Review, 2006); (TV films) The Last Polka, 1985, Hope, 1997, Late Last Night, 1999, The Wool Cap, 2004, (TV series) SCTV, 1976-1979 (Emmy award), Coming Up Rosie, 1976-77, The Steve Allen Comedy Hour, 1980, SCTV Network 90, 1981-82, (voice) Committed, 2001; dir.: (TV series) Dream On, 1990-96; writer Really Weird Tales, 1987; TV guest appearances The Simpsons Show, The Larry Sanders Show, 1992, The Outer Limits, 1995.

OHASHI, JOAN M., legislative staff member; Chief of staff to Senator Daniel Akaka US Senate, Honolulu. Democrat. Office: Dist Office Prince Kuhio Fed Bldg 300 Ala Moana Blvd Rm 3-106 Honolulu HI 96850-4977 Office Phone: 808-522-8970.

O'HURLEY, JOHN, actor; b. Kittery, Maine, Oct. 9, 1954; m. Eva LaRue Callahan, 1992 (div. 1994); m. Lisa Mesloh, Aug. 14, 2004; 1 child, William Dylan. BA, Providence Coll., 1976, DFA, 2006. Co-owner J. Peterman Co., bd. dirs.; principal ptnr. Heritage Capitol Advisors, Atlanta, Round One Investments, Los Angeles. Actor: (TV series) The Edge of Night, 1983—84, Loving, 1984—86, All My Children, 1988, The Young & the Restless, 1989—91, Santa Barbara, 1990—91, Scorch, 1992, General Hospital, 1992, Valley of the Dolls, 1994, A Whole New Ballgame, 1995, Seinfeld, 1995—98, Lost on Earth, 1997, Over the Top, 1997, Cursed, 2000—01, The Mullets, 2003—04; (TV films) Something is Out There, 1988, Billy the Kid, 1989, White Hot: The Mysterious Murder of Thelma Todd, 1991, Seduction: 3 Tales from the "Inner Sanctum", 1992, My Son is Innocent, 1996, The Secret, 1997, Murder Live!, 1997, Blood on Her Hands, 1998, Tempting Fate, 1998, Life of the Party: The Pamela Harriman Story, 1998, Wild Grizzly, 1999, Three Secrets, 1999; (films) Night Eyes II, 1992, Mirror Images, 1992, The Power Within, 1995, Love Stinks, 1999, Slammed, 2001, Firetrap, 2001, Race to Space, 2001, Teddy Bears' Picnic, 2002, Buying the Cow, 2002, Knuckle Sandwich, 2004; voice actor: (TV series) Mickey Mouse Works, 1999—2000; Buzz Lightyear of Star Command, 2000; House of Mouse, 2001—02; Duck Dodgers, 2003—; Father of the Pride, 2004; (films) Tarzan & Jane, 2002; host: (TV series) Extraordinary World of Animals, 1999; Get Golf with the PGA Tour!, 2000; To Tell the Truth, 2000—01; NBC National Dog Show, 2001—; Family Feud, 2006—; contestant Dancing with the Stars, 2005; composer: (albums) Peace of Our Minds, 2005; author: It's Okay To Miss the Bed On The First Jump, 2006 (NY Times Bestseller), Before Your Dog Can Eat Your Homework, First You Have To Do It, 2007. Named one of sexiest men alive, People mag., 2005. Avocations: golf, tennis, carpentry, interior design, wine collection. Office: 11611 San Vicente Blvd #104 Los Angeles CA 90049

OJALVO, MORRIS, civil engineer, educator; b. NYC, Mar. 4, 1924; s. Nissim and (Fanny) O.; m. Anita Bedein, Dec. 26, 1948; children: Lynne, Joseph, Howard, Isobel. B.C.E., Rensselear Poly. Inst., Troy, NY, 1944, M.C.E., 1952; PhD, Lehigh U., Bethlehem, Pa., 1960; JD, Ohio State U., Columbus, 1978. Bar: Ohio 1979. Draftsman Am. Bridge Co., Elmira, N.Y., 1946-47; tutor civil engring. CCNY, 1947-49; instr. Rensselear Poly. Inst., 1949-51; asst. prof. Princeton U., 1951-58; research instr. Lehigh U., 1958-60; mem. faculty Ohio State U., 1960—, prof. civil engring., 1964-82, prof. emeritus, 1982—; vis. prof. U. Tex.-Austin, 1982-83. Author: Thin-Walled Bars With Open Profiles, 1990; contbr. papers in field; patentee warp restraining device. With USN, 1943—46. Mem.: ASCE, Structural Stability Rsch. Coun. Home and Office: 1024 Fairway Ln Estes Park CO 80517-7156 Office Phone: 970-577-0237. E-mail: morris_ojalvo@yahoo.com.

OKAMURA, ARTHUR SHINJI, artist, educator; b. Long Beach, Calif., Feb. 24, 1932; s. Frank Akira and Yuki O.; m. Elizabeth Tuomi, Aug. 7, 1953 (div.); children: Beth, Jonathan, Jane, Ethan; m. Kitty Wong, 1991. Student, Art Inst. Chgo., 1950-54, U. Chgo., 1951, 52, 57. Faculty Ctrl. YMCA Coll., Chgo., 1956, 57, Evanston (Ill.) Art Center, 1956-57, Art Inst. Chgo., North Shore Art League, Winnetka, Ill., Acad. Art, San Francisco, 1957, Calif. Sch. Fine Arts, 1958, Ox Bow Summer Art Sch., Saugatuck, Mich., 1963, Calif. Coll. Arts and Crafts, Oakland, 1958-59, prof. arts, 1966-97, prof. emeritus, 1997—. Instr. watercolor painting, 1987; dir. San Francisco Studio Art, 1958; tchr. watercolor workshops, Bali, Indonesia, 1989, 92; lectr. in field. Author (with Robert Creeley): 1, 2, 3, 4, 5, 6, 7, 8, 9, 0, 1971; author: (with Joel Weishaus) Ox-Herding, 1971; author: (with Robert Bly) Basho, 1972, Ten Poems by Issa, 1992; author: (with Steve Kowit) Passionate Journey, 1984; author: (with David Rosen and Joel Weishaus) The Healing Spirit of Haiku; author: Magic Rabbit, 1995, The Paper Propeller, 2000; one-man shows include Charles Feingarten Galleries, Chgo., 1956, 1958, 1959, San Francisco, 1957, Santa Barbara Mus. Art, 1958, Oakland Mus. Art, 1959, Legion Honor, San Francisco, 1961, Dallas, 1962, La Jolla (Calif.) Mus., 1963, U. Utah, 1964, San Francisco Mus. Art, 1968, Hanssen Gallery, 1968, 1971, Ruth Braunstein, San Francisco, 1981, 1982, 1984, 1986—88, 1990, 1994, 1997, 2000, 2003, 2006, Commonweal Gallery, Bolinas, Calif., 2001, Claudia Chapline Gallery, Stinson Beach, Calif., 2007, exhibited in group shows at Pa. Acad. Fine Art, U. Chgo., U. Wash., U. Ill., Art Inst. Chgo., L.A. County Mus., Am. Fedn. Art, Denver Mus., NAD, De Young Mus., San Francisco, Knoedler Gallery, N.Y.C., Feingarten Galleries, Whitney Mus. Art, others; retrospective at Bolinas Mus., 2002, Claudia Chapline Galleries, Stinson Beach, Calif., 1995; Represented in permanent collections Art Inst. Chgo., Borg-Warner Collections, Chgo., Whitney Mus. Art, Santa Barbara Mus. Art, San Francisco Mus. Art, Ill. State Normal, Corcoran Mus., Nat. Collection Fine Arts, Smithsonian Instn., many others. Served as pvt. AUS, 1955-56. Recipient 1st prize religious art U. Chgo., 1953; Ryerson travelling fellow, 1954; Martin Cahn award contemporary Am. paintings Art Inst. Chgo., 1957; purchase award U. Ill., 1959; purchase award Nat. Soc. Arts and Letters, N.Y.C., 1960; Neysa McMein purchase award Whitney Mus. Art, 1960; Schwabacher-Frey award 79th Ann. of San Francisco Mus. Art, 1960 Mem.: Commonweal (bd. dirs. 1993—2007). Home: 210 Kale Rd Bolinas CA 94924 E-mail: arthurokamura@earthlink.net.

OKARMA, THOMAS BERNARD, biotechnology company executive; b. 1946; AB, Dartmouth Coll., 1968; MD, Stanford U., 1972, PhD in Pharmacology, 1974; exec. MBA, Stanford Grad. Sch. Bus., 1997. Asst. prof., dept. medicine Stanford U. Sch. Medicine, 1980—85; scientific founder Applied Immune Sciences, Inc., 1985; v.p. R&D to, chmn., CEO, bd. dir. Applied Immune Sciences, Inc.(acquired by Rhone-Poulene Rorer in 1995); sr. v.p. Rhone-Poulenc Rorer, 1995—96; with Geron Corp., Menlo Park, Calif., 1997—, v.p., cell therapies, 1997—98, v.p. R&D, 1998—99, pres., CEO, 1999—, pres., oncology drug develop, 2008—. Bd. dirs. Geron Corp., Menlo Park, Calif., 1999—, Geron Bio-Med Ltd., TA Therapeutics, Ltd., BIO (Biotechnology Industry Orgn.); spkr. in field. Contbr. several articles to profl. jours. Chmn., bd. overseers Dartmouth Med. Sch., 2000—07. Achievements include patents in field. Avocations: scuba diving, water and snow skiing, fishing, anything outdoors. Office: Geron Corp 230 Constitution Dr Menlo Park CA 94025 Office Phone: 650-473-7700. Office Fax: 650-473-7750. E-mail: info@geron.com.*

O'KEEFE, EDWARD FRANKLIN, lawyer; b. SI, NY, June 9, 1937; s. Francis Franklin and Bertha (Hall) O'K.; m. Toni Lynne McGohan; children: Kira Kathleen, Douglas Franklin, Andrew Franklin, Alison Elizabeth, Theadore William, Nigel Francis. AB, U. N.C., 1959; JD, U. Denver, 1961. Bar: Colo. 1962, N.C. 2000. Law clk. Colo. Supreme Ct., Denver, 1962-63; assoc. gen. counsel Hamilton Mgmt. Corp., Denver, 1966-69, sec., 1968-76, v.p. legal, gen. counsel, 1969-76; ptnr. Moye White, Denver, 1976—2006; pvt. practice Southport, NC, 2006—. Assoc. gen. counsel, sec. ITT Variable Annuity Ins. Co., Denver, 1969, v.p. legal, gen. counsel, 1969-70; sec. Hamilton Funds Inc., Denver, 1968-76 With USNR, 1963—66. Mem. Nat. Assn. Security Dealers (dist. conduct com., chmn. 1976), Colo. Assn. Corporate Counsel (pres. 1974-75) Office Phone: 910-253-5040.

O'KEEFE, MARK DAVID, state official; b. Pittston, Pa., July 10, 1952; s. Gervase Frances and Anne Regina (Faltyn) O'K.; m. Lucy Bliss Dayton, Sept. 24, 1983; children: Margaret, Angus, Greer. BA in Environ. Studies, Calif. State U., Sacramento, 1977; MS in Environ. Studies, U. Mont., 1984. Mgr. adjudication program Mont. Dept. Nat. Resources, Helena, 1979-81, dir. water devel., 1981-83; owner, operator Glacier Wilderness Guides, West Glacier, Mont., 1983-89; mem. Mont. Ho. Reps., Helena, 1989-92; state auditor State of Mont., Helena, 1993—. Bd. dirs. Boyd Andrew Chem. Dependency Treatment Ctr., Helena, 1991—. With U.S. Army, 1971-73. Democrat. Avocations: backpacking, jogging, rafting, fly fishing. Home: 531 Power St Helena MT 59601-6115 Office: State Auditors Office PO Box 4009 Helena MT 59604-4009

OKERLUND, ARLENE NAYLOR, academic administrator, writer; b. Emmitsburg, Md., Oct. 13, 1938; d. George Wilbur and Ruth Opal (Sensenbaugh) Naylor; m. Michael Dennis Okerlund, June 6, 1959 (div. Apr. 1983); 1 dau., Linda Susan. BA, U. Md., 1960; PhD, U. Calif.-San Diego, 1969. Instr. sci. Mercy Hosp. Nursing Sch., Balt., 1959-63; prof. English San Jose (Calif.) State U., 1969—2005, dean humanities and arts, 1980-86, acad. v.p., 1986-93. Cons. Ednl. Testing Svc., Berkeley, Calif., 1976—80. Author: Elizabeth Wydeville: The Slandered Queen, 2005, Elizabeth Of York, 2009; editor San Jose Studies, 1975—80; contbr. articles on the humanities to profl. jours. Bd. dirs. World Forum Silicon Valley, Peninsula Banjo Band. Grantee NEH, 1979; grantee San Jose State U., 1971-72. Mem.: MLA (del. to assembly, west coast rep. 1976—77), Am. Beethoven Soc. (v.p. bd. dirs. 1983—2006), Calif. Coun. Fine Arts Deans (pres. 1984—86), Internat. Coun. Fine Arts Deans, Philol. Assn. Pacific Coast (sec.-treas. 1975—78). Democrat. Office: San Jose State U Dept English Washington Sq San Jose CA 95192-0090 Office Phone: 408-924-4425. Business E-Mail: okerlund@email.sjsu.edu.

OKERLUND, RALPH, state legislator; m. Cindy Okerlund; 3 children. AA, Dixie Coll., 1972; BS in Polit. Sci., U. Utah, 1973. Tchr. South Sevier High Sch. & Middle Sch., 1973—78; dairyman, 1978—2008; farmer, 1978—; commr. Sevier Co., 1995—; former coun. mem. Monroe City, former mayor; mem. Dist. 24 Utah State Senate, 2008—. Republican. Office: W115 State Capitol Complex Salt Lake City UT 84144 Mailing: 248 S 500 W Monroe UT 84754 Home Phone: 435-527-3370; Office Phone: 801-538-1035. Fax: 435-527-3370; Office Fax: 801-326-1475. Business E-Mail: rokerlund@utahsenate.org.

OKINAGA, LAWRENCE SHOJI, lawyer; m. Carolyn Hisako Uesugi, Nov. 26, 1966; children: Carrie, Caryn, Laurie. BA, U. Hawaii, 1963; JD, Georgetown U., 1972. Bar: Hawaii 1972, U.S. Dist. Ct. Hawaii 1972, U.S. Ct. Appeals (9th cir.) 1976. Adminstrv. asst. to Congressman Spark Matsunaga, Honolulu, 1964, 65-69; law clk. to chief judge U.S. Dist. Ct. Hawaii, Honolulu, 1972-73; assoc. Carlsmith Ball, Honolulu, 1973-76, ptnr., 1976—. Mem. Gov.'s Citizens Adv. Com. Coastal Zone Mgmt., 1974—79; sec. Hawaii Bicentennial Corp., 1975—77, vice chmn., 1983—85, chmn., 1985—87; mem. Jud. Selection Commn., State of Hawaii, 1979—87, vice chmn., 1986; mem. consumer adv. coun. Fed. Res. Bd., 1984—86; chmn. Jud. Conduct Commn., State of Hawaii, 1991—94; apptd. mem. Fed. Savs. and Loan Adv. Coun., Washington, 1988—89; mem. nat. adv. coun. U.S. SBA, 1994—2000; mem. adv. coun. Fed. Res. Bank, San Francisco, 1995—2002. Pres., bd. dirs. Moiliili Cmty. Ctr., Honolulu, 1965—68, 1973—86, trustee, 1993—; bd. dirs. Pub. Sch. Hawaii Found., 2004—; bd. visitors Georgetown U. Law Ctr., 1993—; trustee Kuakini Med. Ctr., 1984—88, 1989—96. Capt. USAFR, 1964—72, capt. USAFR, 1974—76. Mem.: ABA (ho. of dels. 1991—94, mem. standing com. jud. selection tenure and compensation 1993—96, mem. standing com. jud. independence 1999—2002), Am. Judicature Soc. (bd. dirs. 1986, treas. 1995—97, pres. 1997—99), Hawaii Bar Assn. (sec., bd. dirs. 1981), Georgetown U. Law Alumni Assn. (bd. dirs. 1986—91), Omicron Delta Kappa. Office: Carlsmith Ball PO Box 656 Honolulu HI 96809-0656 E-mail: lso@carlsmith.com.

OKUR, MEHMET, professional basketball player; b. Yalova, Turkey, May 26, 1979; s. Abdullah and Nimet Okur; m. Yeliz Caliska, 2004. Profl. basketball player Turkish League Oyak Renault, Turkey, 1997—98, Turkish League Tofas Bursa, Turkey, 1998—2000, Turkish League Efes Pilsen, Turkey, 2000—02; draft pick NBA Detroit Pistons, 2001, ctr./power forward, 2002—04, NBA Utah Jazz, 2004—. Named to Western Conf. All-Star Team, NBA, 2007. Achievements include winning an NBA Championship as a member of the Detroit Pistons in 2004; winner, Turkish National Cup as a member of Tofas Bursa in 1999. Mailing: Utah Jazz 301 W South Temple Salt Lake City UT 84101

OLAFSON, FREDERICK ARLAN, philosophy educator; b. Winnipeg, Man., Can., Sept. 1, 1924; s. Kristinn K. and Fredericka (Björnson) O.; m. Allie Lewis, June 20, 1952 (dec.); children— Peter Niel, Christopher Arlan, Thomas Andrew. AB, Harvard U., 1947, MA, 1948, PhD, 1951. Instr. philosophy and gen. edn. Harvard U., 1952-54; asst. prof. philosophy, then assoc. prof. Vassar Coll., 1954-60; assoc. prof. Johns Hopkins U., 1960-64; prof. edn. and philosophy Harvard Grad. Sch. Edn., 1964-71; prof. philosophy U. Calif., San Diego, 1971-91, chmn. dept., 1973-76, assoc. dean grad. studies and research, 1980-85. Author: Principles and Persons, 1967, Ethics and Twentieth Century Thought, 1973, The Dialectic of Action, 1979, Heidegger and the Philosophy of the Mind, 1987, What Is A Human Being?, 1995, Heidegger and the Ground of Ethics, 1998, Naturalism and the Human Condition, 2001. Served to lt. (j.g.) USNR, 1943-46. Mem. Nat. Acad. Edn. Home: 6081 Avenida Chamnez La Jolla CA 92037-7404 Business E-Mail: folafson@ucsd.edu.

OLAH, GEORGE ANDREW, chemist, educator; b. Budapest, Hungary, May 22, 1927; arrived in U.S., 1964, naturalized, 1970; s. Julius and Magda (Krasznai) Olah; m. Judith Agnes Lengyel, July 9, 1949; children: George John, Ronald Peter. PhD, Tech. U. Budapest, 1949, D (hon.), 1989; DSc (hon.), U. Durham, 1988, U. Munich, 1990, U. Crete, Greece, 1994, U. Szeged, Hungary, 1995, U. Veszprem, 1995, Case Western Res. U., Cleve., 1995, U. So. Calif., 1995, U. Montpellier, 1996, SUNY, 1998, U. Pecs, Hungary, 2001, U. Debrecen, 2003; DSc, U. We. Hungary, 2007. Mem. faculty Tech. U. Budapest, 1949—54; assoc. dir. Ctrl. Chem. Rsch. Inst., Hungarian Acad. Scis., 1954—56; rsch. scientist Dow Chem. Can. Ltd., 1957—64, Dow Chem. Co., Framingham, Mass., 1964—65; prof. chemistry Case Western Res. U., Cleve., 1965—69, C.F. Mabery prof.

rsch., 1969—77; Donald P. and Katherine B. Loker disting. prof. chemistry, dir. Hydrocarbon Rsch. Inst., U. So. Calif., LA, 1977—, dist. prof. engring., 2008—. Vis. prof. chemistry Ohio State U., 1963, U. Heidelberg, Germany, U. Colo., 1969, Swiss Fed. Inst. Tech., 1972, U. Munich, 1973, U. London, 1973—79, Louis Pasteur U., Strasbourg, France, 1974, U. Paris, 1981; hon. vis. lectr. U. London, 1981—95; cons. to industry. Author: Friedel-Crafts Reactions, Vols. I-IV, 1963—64; author: (with P. Schleyer) Carbonium Ions, Vols. I-V, 1969—76; author: Friedel-Crafts Chemistry, 1973, Carbocations and Electrophilic Reactions, 1973, Halonium Ions, 1975; author: (with Goeppertm Prakash and J. Sommer) Superacids, 1984; author: (with G. Prakash, R.E. Williams, L.D. Field and K. Wade) Hypercarbon Chemistry, 1987; author: (with R. Malthotra and S.C. Narang) Nitration, 1989; author: Cage Hydrocarbons, 1990; author: (with Wade and Williams) Electron Deficient Boron and Carbon Clusters, 1991; author: (with Chambers and Prakash) Synthetic Fluorine Chemistry, 1992; author: (with Molnar) Hydrocarbon Chemistry, 1995; author: (with Laali, Wang, Prakash) Onium Ions, 1998; author: A Life of Magic Chemistry, 2001; author: (with Prakash) Across Conventional Lines, 2003; author: (with Goeppert and Prakash) Beyond Oil and Gas: The Methanol Economy, 2006; author: (with Klumpp) Superelectrophiles and Their Chemistry, 2008; author: (with Prarash, Molnal an Somner) Superacid Chemistry, 2009; contbr. chapters to books, articles to profl. jours. Recipient Alexander von Humboldt Sr. US Scientist award, 1979, Calif. Scientist of Yr. award, 1989, Pioneer of Chemistry award, Am. Inst. Chemists, 1993, Mendeleev medal, Russian Acad. Scis., 1992, Nobel prize in Chemistry, 1994, Kapitsa medal, Russian Acad. Natural Scis., 1995, Order of the Hungarian Corvin-Chain, 2001, Albert Einstein medal, Russian Acad. Natural Scis., 2002, Bolyai prize, Hungarian Acad. Sci., 2002, Order of Merit with Cross of Star, Republic of Hungary, 2006, Hon. Citizen Budapest, Budapest; Guggenheim fellow, 1972, 1988. Fellow: AAAS, Chem. Inst. Can., Brit. Chem. Soc. (hon.; hon./centenary lectr. 1978, Centenary lectr. 1978); mem.: NAS, NAE, Indian Nat. Acad. Sci. (fgn.), Can. Royal Soc., Royal Soc. Sci. Arts Barcelona, Royal Acad. Sci. and Arts, Am. Acad. Arts and Sci., Chem. Soc. Japan (hon.), Italy Chem. Soc. (hon.), Royal Chem. Soc. (hon.), Hungarian Acad. Sci. (hon.), German Chem. Soc. (hon.), Am. Philos. Soc., Am. Chem. Soc. (award petroleum chemistry 1964, Leo Hendrik Baekeland award N.J. sect. 1966, Morley medal Cleve. sect. 1970, award Synthetic Organic Chemistry 1979, Roger Adams award in organic chemistry 1989, Arthur C. Cope award 2001, Priestley medal 2005), European Acad. Arts, Sci. and Humanities, Royal Soc. London (fgn. mem.), Italian Nat. Acad. Sci. Lincei, Grand Cordon of the Order of the Rising Sun (Japan). Achievements include patents in field. Office: U So Calif Loker Hydrocarbon Rsch Inst Los Angeles CA 90007 Business E-Mail: olah@usc.edu.

OLBRANTZ, JOHN PAUL, museum director, art historian; b. Tacoma, June 19, 1950; s. Walter John and Theresa Christine (Hill) O.; m. Pamela Ann Southas, Apr. 12, 1980; children: Aaron Michael, Sarah Jessica. BA, Western Wash. U., 1972; attended, U. Calif., Santa Barbara, 1973-74; MA, U. Wash., 1976. Cert. in arts adminstrn. and mgmt. U. Calif., Berkeley, 1984. Dirs. Bellevue Art Mus., Wash., 1976-85, San Jose Mus. Art, Calif., 1985-87; dep. dir. Whatcom Mus. History and Art, Bellingham, Wash., 1987-98; Maribeth Collins dir. Hallie Ford Mus. Art, Willamette U., Salem, 1998-. Adj. faculty, art dept., Western Wash. U., Bellingham, 1987-98; cons. City Everett, Wash., 1997-98; lectr. in field. Exhbns. arranged: Eye for Eye: Egyptian Art and Inscriptions, 1978; 5,000 Years of Faces, 1982; Dale Chihuly: A Decade of Glass, 1984, Two Centuries of Afro-American Art, 1985, Robert Colescott: A Retrospective, 1987, A Different War: Vietnam in Art, 1989, Clearly Art: Pilchuck's Glass Legacy, 1992, Jacob Lawrence: American Printmaker, 2000, In the Fullness of Time: Masterpieces of Egyptian Art from American Collections, 2002, others; contbr. articles to profl. publs. J. Paul Getty Trust scholar, 1984. Mem. Archaeol. Inst. Am. (v.p. 1978-79, pres. 1979-80), Am. Assn. Mus., We. Mus. Assn. (v.p. 1990-94). Independent. Ea. Orthodox. Office: Hallie Ford Mus Art Willamette Univ 900 State St Salem OR 97301 Office Phone: 503-370-6854. Business E-Mail: jolbrant@willamette.edu.

OLDFIELD, JAMES EDMUND, retired nutrition educator; b. Victoria, BC, Can., Aug. 30, 1921; came to U.S., 1949; s. Henry Clarence and Doris O. Oldfield; m. Mildred E. Atkinson, Sept. 4, 1942; children: Nancy E. Oldfield McLaren, Kathleen E. Oldfield Sansone, David J., Jane E. Oldfield, Richard A. BSA, U. B.C., 1941, MSA, 1949; PhD, Oreg. State U., 1951. Faculty Oreg. State U., Corvallis, 1951-90, head dept. animal sci., 1967-83, dir. Nutrition Rsch. Inst., 1986-90; ret., 1990. Mem. nat. tech. adv. com. on water supply U.S. Dept. Interior, Washington, 1967-68; bd. dirs. Coun. for Agrl. Sci. and Tech., Ames, Iowa, 1978-84; mem. nutrition study sect. NIH, Bethesda, Md., 1975-80, 85-87; cons. Selenium Tellurium Devel. Assn., Grimbergen, Belgium, 1990-2002. Editor: Selenium in Biomedicine, 1967, Sulphur in Nutrition, 1970, Selenium in Biology and Medicine, 1987; author: Selenium in Nutrition, 1971, Selenium World Atlas, 1999. Served to maj. Can. Army, 1942-46, ETO. Decorated Mil. Cross Can.; Fulbright Rsch. scholar U.S. Dept. State, 1974, Massey U., New Zealand; recipient Klaus Schwarz medal Internat. Assn. Bioinorganic Scientists, 1998. Fellow Am. Soc. Animal Sci. (pres. 1966-67, Morrison award 1972), Am. Inst. Nutrition; mem. Am. Chem. Soc., Am. Registry Profl. Animal Scientists (pres. 1990, editor: Profl. Animal Scientist 1993-96), Fedn. Am. Socs. Exptl. Biol., Pacific Fisheries Technologists (pres. 1966), Kiwanis (pres. 1964, lt. gov. 1986). Republican. Episcopalian. Office: Oreg State Univ Dept Animal Sci Corvallis OR 97331 Home: 4766 SW Birdsong Dr Corvallis OR 97333 Office Phone: 541-737-1894. Office Fax: 541-737-4174. Business E-Mail: james.e.oldfield@oregonstate.edu.

OLDHAM, WILLIAM GEORGE, electrical engineering and computer science educator; b. Detroit, May 5, 1938; m. Nancy Dereich; children: Katherine Ann, William James. BS, Carnegie Mellon Inst., 1960, MS, 1961, PhD, 1963. Staff scientist Siemens-Schuckert, Erlangen, W.Ger., 1963-64; mem. faculty elec. engring. and computer scis. dept. U. Calif., Berkeley, 1964—, prof., 1972—, dir. Electronics Research Lab., 1985-90; project mgr. Intel Corp., Santa Clara, Calif., 1974-75. Author: An Introduction to Electronics, 1972, Electrical Engineering, An Introduction, 1984. NSF fellow, 1970; Guggenheim fellow, 1985-86. Fellow IEEE; mem. NAE. Office: U Calif Berkeley Electronic Rsch Lab 509 Cory Berkeley CA 94720-0001

OLDSTONE, MICHAEL BEAUREGARD ALAN, immunologist, educator; b. NYC, Feb. 9, 1934; MD, U. Md., 1961. Fellow USPHS U. Md. Sch. Med., Balt., 1958; intern Medicine U. Hosp., Balt., 1961, resident, 1962-63, resident in Neurology, 1963-64, chief resident, 1964-66, fellow Dept. Pathology, 1966-69, assoc., 1969-71; head Neurology rsch. Scripps Rsch. Inst., 1969—; prof. Dept. Immunology and Neuropharmacology U. Calif., San Diego, 1978—, prof. Neurosci. and Pathology, 1988—. Adj. prof. Pathology U. Calif. San Diego, 1971—, adj. prof. Neurosci., 1972—; sci. coun. NIH, 1991-96; cons. WHO, 1992—. Recipient NIH-AID career devel. award, 1969, Maurice Pincoffs award, 1984, Cotzias award, 1986, Abraham Flexner Lectr. award for contributions in biomed. rsch., 1988, Rouse-Whipple award, 1993, Kakolin Sci. award, 1994. Mem. Inst. Med. Nat. Acad. Sci., Am. Assn. Immunology, Am. Soc. Neurology, Am. Soc. Virology, Am. Assn. Physicians, Am. Soc. Clin. Investigation, British Soc. Microbiology, Scandinavian Soc. Immunology, Office: Dept Neuropharm Scripps Mail Drop IMM6 10550 N Torrey Pines Rd La Jolla CA 92037-1000

O'LEARY, MARION HUGH, retired dean, chemist; b. Quincy, Ill., Mar. 24, 1941; s. J. Gilbert and Ruth Elizabeth (Kerr) O'L.; m. Sandra E. Eisemann, Sept. 5, 1964 (div. 1979); children—Catherine, Randall, Jessica; m. Elizabeth M. Kean, Jan. 24, 1981. BS, U. Ill., 1963; PhD, MIT, 1966. Asst. prof. chemistry U. Wis., Madison, 1967-73, assoc. prof., 1973-78, prof. chemistry and biochemistry, 1978-89; prof. and head dept. biochemistry U. Nebr., Lincoln, 1989-96; dean Coll. Natural Scis. and Math., Calif. State U., Sacramento, 1996—2006. Cons. Institut Pertanian Bogor, Indonesia, 1983-84; vis. prof. Universitas Andalas, Padang, Indonesia, 1984-85, Australian Nat. U., 1982-83. Author: Contemporary Organic Chemistry, 1976. Editor: Isotope Effects on Enzyme-Catalyzed Reactions, 1977. Contbr. articles to sci. publs. Grantee, NSF, U.S. Dept. Agr., Dept. Energy, NIH; Guggenheim Found. fellow, 1982-83; Sloan Found. fellow, 1972-74. Fellow AAAS; mem. Am. Chem. Soc., Am. Soc. Biochemistry and Molecular Biology.

O'LEARY, PRENTICE LEE, retired lawyer; b. LA, May 6, 1942; BA, UCLA, 1965, JD, 1968. Bar: Calif. 1969. Of counsel Sheppard, Mullin, Richter & Hampton, LA, 1974—2005; ret., 2005. Bd. dirs. Legal Aid Found. LA, 1987—93, Legal Aid Found. L.A., 2000—06. Mem. ABA (bus. bankruptcy com.), State Bar Calif., Los Angles County Bar Assn. (chmn. bankruptcy com., chmn. comml. law and bankrupt sect. 1985-86), Am. Coll. Bankruptcy Profls., Order of Coif. Office: Sheppard Mullin Richter & Hampton 333 S Hope St Fl 48 Los Angeles CA 90071-1406 Home Phone: 310-458-1357; Office Phone: 213-359-9094. E-mail: prenticeo@gmail.com.

O'LEARY, THOMAS MICHAEL, lawyer; b. NYC, Aug. 16, 1948; s. James and Julia Ann (Connolly) O'L.; m. Luise Ann Williams, Jan. 13, 1978; 1 child, Richard Meridith. BA, CUNY, 1974; JD, Seattle U., 1977. Bar: Wash. 1977, U.S. Ct. Mil. Appeals 1978, U.S. Ct. Appeals (9th cir.), U.S. Supreme Ct. 1983. Dep. pros. atty. Pierce County, Tacoma, 1978; commd. 1st lt. U.S. Army, 1978, advanced through grades to capt., 1978; chief trial counsel Office of Staff Judge Adv., Ft. Polk, La., 1978-79, trial def. counsel, trial def. svc., 1979-81; chief legal advisor Office Insp. Gen., Heidelberg, Fed. Republic of Germany, 1981-82; sr. def. counsel Trial Def. Svc., Giessen, Fed. Republic of Germany, 1982-84; asst. chief adminstrv. law U.S. Army Armor Ctr., Ft. Knox, Ky., 1984-85, chief adminstrv. law, 1985, chief legal asst., 1985-86; ret. U.S. Army, 1996; sr. trial atty. Immigration and naturalization Svc., Phoenix, 1987; sector counsel, spl. asst. U.S. atty., U.S. Border Patrol, Tucson, 1987-90; enforcement counsel U.S. Immigration and Naturalization Svc., Tucson, 1990-95, asst. dist. counsel Phoenix litigation, 1995-97. Apptd. U.S. Immigration Judge, U.S. Immigration Ct., Imperial, Calif., 1997-2000, apptd. sr. U.S. Immigration Judge, Tucson, 2000—; adj. prof. Embry-Riddle Aero. U., Tucson, 2002- Decorated Purple Heart, Cross of Gallantry (Vietnam). Mem. Judge Advs Assn., Wash. State Bar Assn., Order Ky. Cols. (commd. col. 1985). Home: 9080 E 25th St Tucson AZ 85710-8675 Office: US Immigration Ct 160 N Stone Ave Rm 300 Tucson AZ 85701 Office Phone: 520-670-5212. E-mail: thomas.o'leary@usdoj.gov.

OLEFSKY, JERROLD M., medical educator, researcher; MD, U. Ill. With Stanford U. Sch. Med., 1970—78; prof. med., chief div. endocrinology & metabolism U. Colo. Sch. Medicine, 1979—83; prof. medicine, rschr. U. Calif. San Diego, 1983—, chief, div. endocrinology & metabolism, VA San Diego Healthcare Sys.; assoc. dean U. Calif. San Diego Sch. Medicine. Pres. Metabolex, 1998—99; assoc. editor Jour. Biol. Chemistry, San Diego; sci. dir. Whittier Inst. for Diabetes, La Jolla, Calif.; editorial bd. Endocrinology & Diabetes; adv. bd. EthicAd. Recipient Banting medal, Am. Diabetes Assn., 1998; grantee MERIT award, Nat. Inst. Diabetes and Digestive and Kidney Diseases, 1994—97, 2001—06. Mem.: Inst. of Medicine.

OLIN, KENT OLIVER, banker; b. Chgo., July 27, 1930; s. Oliver Arthur and Beatrice Louise Olin; m. Marilyn Louise Wood, May 27, 1956. BS in Econs., Ripon Coll., 1955. Dist. sales rep. Speed Queen Corp., Ripon, Wis., 1955—57; v.p. United Bank, Denver, 1957—71; exec. v.p., pres. Bank One Boulder (formerly Affiliated First Nat. Bank), Boulder, 1971—74; pres., CEO Bank One Colorado Springs, 1971—86; CEO Bank One Colo. (formerly Affiliated Bankshares of Colo.), Denver, 1986—91, vice chmn. bd., 1992—94, also bd. dirs. Trustee Colo. Coll., Colorado Springs, 1983-89, Falcon Found., Colorado Springs, 1983—; trustee El Pomar Found., Colorado Springs, 1992—, chair investment com.; trustee Colorado Springs Fine Arts Ctr., 1992-95; sec. Air Force Acad. Found., Colorado Springs, 1988; dir., chair exec. com. Garden City (Kans.) Co.; bd. dirs. Rocky Mountain Arthritis Found., Denver, 1989-94, Goodwill Industries, Colorado Springs, 1993-99. Staff sgt. USAF, 1950-54. Mem. Broadmoor Golf Club (dir. 1975-88, 93-98). Office: El Pomar Found 10 Lake Cir Colorado Springs CO 80906-4201 Home: 2735 Springmede Ct Colorado Springs CO 80906-3716

OLIVER, DALE HUGH, lawyer; b. Lansing, Mich., June 26, 1947; s. Alvin Earl and Jean Elizabeth (Stanton) Oliver; m. Sarah Elyse Sanders, Mar. 18, 2001; children: Nathan Corey, John Franklin. BA, Mich. State U., 1969; JD cum laude, Harvard U., 1972. Bar: DC 1973, Calif. 1991, US Dist. Ct. (DC dist.) 1973, US Ct. Appeals (DC cir.) 1976, US Supreme Ct. 1980, US Ct. Appeals (fed. cir.) 1983, US Ct. Claims 1983. Assoc., ptnr. Jones, Day, Reavis & Pogue, Washington, 1975—79; ptnr. Crowell & Moring, Washington, 1979—84, Gibson, Dunn & Crutcher, Washington, 1984—87, Jones, Day, Reavis & Pogue, Washington, 1987—92, Quinn Emanuel Urquhart & Oliver, LA, 1992—. Editor: (jour.) Pub. Contracts Law, 1980—86; contbr. articles to profl. jours. Spl. counsel 1980 Presdl. Inaugural Com., Washington, 1980; bd. dirs. LA coun. Boy Scouts Am., 1991—; bd. dirs. Armory Ctr. for Arts, 2006—. Capt. USAF, 1973—75. Mem.: ABA (com. chmn. pub. contract sect. 1979—), Pasadena Arts and Cultural Commn. (commr. 2006—), Nat. Security Indsl. Assn., Nat. Contract Mgmt. Assn., Harvard Law Sch. Assn., Mich. State U. Alumni Club of Washington (pres., dir. 1984—88). Office: Quinn Emanuel Urquhart & Oliver & Hedges 865 S Figueroa St 10 Fl Los Angeles CA 90017-2543 Office Phone: 213-443-3154. E-mail: daleoliver@quinnemanuel.com.

OLIVER, DANIEL T., military education administrator, career officer, retired; b. Camden, SC, Apr. 22, 1945; BA, MA, U. Va.; student, Harvard U. Commd. ensign U.S. Navy, advanced through grades to vice admiral, 1996-2000, ret., 2000; pres. Naval Postgraduate Sch., Monterey, Calif., 2007—. Office: Naval Postgrad Sch Office of the President 1 University Cir Monterey CA 93943 Office Phone: 831-656-2023. Office Fax: 831-656-3238.

OLIVER, NURIA MARIA, computer science researcher; b. Alicante, Spain; BS, Tech. U. Madrid, 1992, MS, 1994; PhD in Media Arts & Scis., MIT, 2000. Rsch. asst. engr. Siemens F&E, 1992—93; software engr. Telefonica R&D, Spain, 1994—95; rsch. asst. Media Lab, MIT, 1995—2000; rschr. adaptive systems & interaction group Microsoft Rsch., 2000—. Named one of 40 Most Promising Young Spanish Persons, El Pais, 1999, Top 100 Young Innovators, MIT Tech. Review, 2004; fellow, La Caixa Found., 1995; Motorola fellow, 1997. Mem.: ACM, IEEE. Avocations: ballet, dance, yoga, swimming, art.

OLIVER, WILLIAM DONALD, orthodontist; b. Montreal, Ont., Can., Dec. 14, 1946; s. Austen William and Margaret Kay (Donald) O. BS in Physics, Mt. Allison U., 1964; DDS, McGill U., 1968; MSD in Orthodontics, U. Pa., 1970. Pres. Orthodontic Enterprises Internat., Geneva, 1973—78; orthodontist Barrington, RI, 1979—94; pvt. practice Everett, Wash., 1993—. Instr. Frankfurt Carolinium, 1972-74; witness Senate Armed Svcs. Com., 1975. Inventor Piezo Electric Bone Healing; contbr. articles to profl. jours. Mem. Olympic Ski Team, Squaw Valley, 1960. Served with USAF, 1970-73. Recipient Carter Meml. award, 1964, M.T. Dohan prize, 1966. Mem. ADA, Can. Assn. Orthodontists, Am. Assn. Orthodontists, European Orthodontic Soc., Can. Dental Assn., Fedn. Internat. d'Automobile, Wash. State Soc. Orthodontists, Royal Ocean Racing Club. Republican. Office: 10812 19th Ave SE Everett WA 98208-5153 Office Phone: 425-338-5414. Business E-Mail: braces@seanet.com.

OLIVERIO, PIERLUIGI, councilman; Degree, San José State U. With semiconductor and software industry; councilman, Dist. 6 San José City Coun., 2007—. Mgr. Libr. Measure E Campaign. Involved with Willow Glen Neighborhood Assn., Next Door Solutions Battered Women's Shelter, San Jose Anti-Litter Program, San Jose Downtown Assn., Joint Venture Silicon Valley Coun. on Tax & Fiscal Policy, Neighborhood Tree Planting. Office: San Jose City Coun 200 E Santa Clara St San Jose CA 95113-1905 Office Phone: 408-535-4906. Office Fax: 408-292-6465. Business E-Mail: Pierluigi.Oliverio@sanjoseca.gov.*

OLLER, THOMAS R., state senator; b. Fresno, Calif., July 16, 1958; m. Londa Oller; 4 children. BA, Stanislaus State U., 1980. Owner, entrepreneur Material Ventures, Inc., 1981—; Rep. rep. dist. 4 Calif. Ho. of Reps., 1996-2000; Rep. senator dist. 1 Calif. State Senate, 2000—. Mem. banking and fin., consumer protection, govtl. efficiency and econ. devel., transp. and water, pks. and wildlife coms. Calif. Ho. of Reps., vice chair ins., labor and employment and natural resources coms. Past chmn. Turner Pk. Com; past exec. bd. dirs. Progressive Club San Andreas; past mem. Calaveras County Fish and Game Commn.; sponsor Match-2 Prisoner Outreach, 1990; mem. bd. trustees Cmty. Covenant Ch., 1990-93, chmn., 1993. Mem. Calaveras County C. of C. Office: Calif State Senate State Capitol Rm 4208 Sacramento CA 95814 Fax: 916 774-4433; 916 319-2104. E-mail: ao4o@assembly.ca.gov.

OLLMAN, ARTHUR LEE, museum director, photographer; b. Milw., Mar. 6, 1947; s. Benn and Shirley O. BA, U. Wis., 1969; student, San Francisco Art Inst., 1974; M.F.A., Lone Mountain Coll., 1977. Mus. dir. Mus. Photog. Arts, San Diego. Founder, dir., producer Photo History Video Project; author: Samuel Bourne, Images of India, 1983, Arnold Newman, Five Decades, 1986, William Klein: An American in Paris, 1987, Revelaciones, The Art of Manuel Alvarez Bravo, 1990, Fata Morgana: The American Way of Life, 1992, Seduced by Life: The Art of Lou Stoumen, 1992, Points of Entry: A Nation of Strangers, 1995, The Model Wife, 1999; exhibited in one-man shows including Grapestake Gallery, San Francisco, 1979, Centre Georges Pompidou, Musee Nat. D'Art et De Culture, Paris, 1979, Inst. Contemporary Art, Boston, 1985, Night: Photograph Gallery, N.Y.C., 1981, Kodak Gallery, Tokyo, 1988; exhibited in group shows at Milw. Art Ctr., 1979, U. Hawaii, 1979-81, San Francisco Mus. Modern Art, 1980, Monas Heiroglyphicas, Milan, Italy, 1978, Mus. Modern Art, N.Y.C., 1978, Whitney Mus. Am. Art, N.Y.C., 1981, Detroit Inst. Arts, 1994, Mus. Contemporary Art, L.A., 1994, Tower of David Museum, Jerusalem, 1996; represented in permanent collections, including, Mus. Modern Art, N.Y.C, Centre Georges Pompidou, Bibliotheque Nationale, Paris, Tokyo Inst. Polytechnics, Met. Mus. Art, N.Y.C., Nat. Mus. Am. Art, Washington, Chase-Manhattan collection, N.Y.C., J. Paul Getty Mus., L.A. NEA fellow, 1979; Calif. Arts Council grantee, 1977-78, NEA grantee, 1978, exhbn. aid grantee, 1979-80. Mem. San Francisco CAMERAWORK (pres. bd. dirs. 1978-83), Am. Assn. Mus. Jewish. Address: 4310 Goldfinch St San Diego CA 92103-1315 also: Mus Photographic Arts MOPA Balboa Park 1649 El Prado San Diego CA 92101-1662

OLLSON, MICKEY LOUIS, zoo owner; b. Phoenix, May 12, 1941; s. William Archie and Edith Iris (Curnow) O.; m. Donna Marie Ollson, Dec. 5, 1965 (div. Feb. 1975); children: Micalin, Louis Michael. AA, Phoenix Coll., 1961; BS, Ariz. State U., 1963. Owner, dir. Ollson's Exotic Animal Farm, Glendale, Ariz., 1965-83, Wildlife World Zoo, Glendale, 1983—. Contbr. articles to profl. publs. Mem. Am. Assn. Zool. Parks and Aquariums (profl.), Am. Fedn. Aviculture (v.p. 1976-77), Am. Game Bird Fedn. (bd. dirs. 1988—, pres. 1984-89, Outstanding Mem. of Yr. award 1968), Internat. Soc. Zooculturists (charter; treas. 1987-88), Am. Pheasant and Waterfowl Soc. (bd. dirs. 1972-78), Avondale-Goodyear-Litchfield Park C. of C. (bd. dirs. 1985-88), Kappa Sigma (pres. Rho chpt. 1964). Republican. Office: Wildlife World Zoo 16501 W Northern Ave Litchfield Park AZ 85340-9466

OLMSTEAD, MARJORIE ANN, physics professor; b. Glen Ridge, NJ, Aug. 18, 1958; d. Blair E. and Elizabeth (Dempwolf) Olmstead. BA in Physics, Swarthmore Coll., 1979; MA in Physics, U. Calif., Berkeley, 1982, PhD, 1985. Rsch. staff Palo Alto (Calif.) Rsch. Ctr. Xerox Corp., 1985-86; asst. prof. physics U. Calif., Berkeley, 1986-90, U. Wash., Seattle, 1991-93, assoc. prof., 1993-97, prof., 1997—, dir. nanotech. PhD program, 2004—. Prin. investigator sci. materials divsn. Lawrence Berkeley Lab., 1988—93. Contbr. articles to profl.

jours. Recipient Devel. award, IBM, 1986, 1987, Rsch. award, A. von Humboldt Found., 2000; named Presdl. Young Investigator, NSF, 1987. Fellow: Am. Phys. Soc. (chair com. on status of women in physics 1999, Maria Goeppart-Mayer award 1996), Am. Vacuum Soc. (Peter Mark Meml. award 1994). Office: U Washington Dept Physics PO Box 351560 Seattle WA 98195-1560 Office Phone: 206-685-3031. E-mail: olmstd@u.washington.edu.

OLSCHWANG, ALAN PAUL, lawyer, crossword and variety puzzle author; b. Chgo., Jan. 30, 1942; s. Morton James and Ida (Ginsberg) O.; m. Barbara Claire Miller, Aug. 22, 1965; children: Elliot, Deborah, Jeffrey. BS, U. Ill., Champaign Urbana, 1963, JD, 1966. Bar: Ill. 1966, NY 1984, Calif. 1992. Law clk. Ill. Supreme Ct., Bloomington, 1966-67; assoc. Sidley & Austin and predecessor firm, Chgo., 1967-73; with Montgomery Ward & Co. Inc., Chgo., 1973-81, assoc. gen. counsel, asst. sec., 1979-81; ptnr. Seki, Jarvis & Lynch, Chgo., 1981-84, dir., mem. exec. com.; dir., exec. v.p., gen. counsel Mitsubishi Electric & Electronics USA, Inc. and predecessors, NYC, 1983-91, Cypress, Calif., 1991—. Mem. ABA, Am. Corp. Counsel Assn., Calif. Bar Assn., Ill. Bar Assn., Chgo. Bar Assn., NY State Bar Assn., Am. Arbitration Assn. (panel arbitrators). Office: Mitsubishi Elec & Electronics USA Inc PO Box 6007 5665 Plaza Dr Cypress CA 90630-0007 Business E-Mail: alan.olschwang@meus.mea.com.

OLSEN, ALFRED JON, lawyer; b. Phoenix, Oct. 5, 1940; s. William Hans and Vera (Bearden) O.; m. Susan K. Smith, Apr. 15, 1979. BA in History, U. Ariz., 1962; MS in Acctg., Ariz. State U., 1964; JD, Northwestern U., 1966. Bar: Ariz. 1966, Ill. 1966, U.S. Tax Ct. 1970, U.S. Supreme Ct. 1970; C.P.A., Ariz., Ill. cert. tax specialist. Acct. Arthur Young & Co., C.P.A.s, Chgo., 1966-68; dir. firm Ehmann, Olsen & Lane (P.C.), Phoenix, 1969-76; dir. Streich, Lang, Weeks & Cardon (P.C.), Phoenix, 1977-78; mgr. Olsen-Smith, Ltd., Phoenix, 1978—. Chmn. tax adv. commn. Bd. Legal Specialization, 1990-92. Bd. editors: Jour. Agrl. Law and Taxation, 1978-82, Practical Real Estate Lawyer, 1983-95. Mem. Phoenix adv. bd. Salvation Army., 1973-81. Fellow: Am. Coll. Tax Counsel, Am. Coll. Trust and Estate Counsel (state chair 2002—03, regent 2005—); mem.: ABA (chmn. com. on agr., sect. taxation 1976—78, chmn. CLE com. sect. taxation 1982—84), AICPA, Internat. Acad. Estate and Trust Law (exec. coun. 1994—99), Nat. Cattlemen's Assn. (tax com. 1979—88), Am. Law Inst. (life; chmn. tax planning for agr. 1971—82), Ctrl. Ariz. Estate Planning Coun. (pres. 1972—73), State Bar Ariz., Ariz. Soc. CPAs, Phi Beta Kappa, Phi Kappa Phi, Beta Gamma Sigma, Sigma Nu Internat. (pres. 1986—88). Office: 3300 Virginia Fin Pla 301 E Virginia Ave Phoenix AZ 85004-1218 Office Phone: 602-254-1040.

OLSEN, CLIFFORD WAYNE, retired physical chemist, consultant; b. Placerville, Calif., Jan. 15, 1936; s. Christian William and Elsie May (Bishop) O.; m. Margaret Clara Gobel, June 16, 1962 (div. 1986), remarried, Mar. 4, 2000; children: Anne K. Olsen Cordes Bothe, Charlotte M. Olsen Habecker; m. Nancy Mayhew Kruger, July 21, 1990 (div. 1993). AA, Grant Tech. Coll., Sacramento, 1955; BA, U. Calif.-Davis, 1957, PhD, 1962. Physicist, project leader, program leader, task leader Lawrence Livermore Nat. Lab., Calif., 1962-93; ret., 1993; lab. assoc., 1993—98; cons. Keystone Internat., 2000—09, Bechtel-Nevada, 2003—06, Nat. Security Tec, 2006—09. Mem. Containment Evaluation Panel, US Dept. Energy, 1984-07, mem. Cadre for Joint Nuclear Verification Tests, 1988; organizer, editor procs. for 2nd through 7th Symposiums on Containment of Underground Nuclear Detonations, 1983-93; cons. in field. Author: Containment of Underground Nuclear Explosions- A Source Book, 2006; contbr. articles to profl. jours. Mem. bd. convocators Calif. Luth. U., 1976-78. Recipient Chevalier Degree, Order of DeMolay, 1953, Eagle Scout, 1952. Mem. AAAS, Am. Radio Relay League, Seismol. Soc. Am., Livermore Amateur Radio Klub (pres. 1994-96), Sigma Xi, Alpha Gamma Sigma (life), Gamma Alpha (U. Calif.-Davis chpt. pres. 1960-61). Democrat. Lutheran. Avocations: photography, amateur radio, music, cooking, philately. Office Phone: 925-362-8236. Personal E-mail: kk6sj@comcast.net.

OLSEN, DONALD BERT, biomedical engineer, experimental surgeon, research facility director; b. Bingham, Utah, Apr. 2, 1930; s. Bertram Hansen and Doris (Bodel) O.; m. Joyce Cronquist; children: Craig, Kathy, Debbie, Jeff, Gary. BS, Utah State U., 1952; DVM, Colo. State U., 1956. Gen. practice vet. medicine, Smithfield, Utah, 1956-63; extension veterinarian U. Nev., Reno, 1963-65, researcher Deseret Rsch. Inst., 1965-68; postdoctoral fellow U. Colo. Med. Sch., Denver, 1968-72; researcher U. Utah, Salt Lake City, 1972—, rsch. prof. surgery, 1973—, dir. artificial heart lab., 1976—, rsch. prof. pharmaceutics, 1981—, rsch. prof. biomed. engring., 1986—, dir. Inst. Biomed. Engring., 1986—, prof. surgery, 1986—. Mem. sci. adv. bd. Link Resources, Inc., 1987 Contbr. articles to profl. jours.; patentee in field. Recipient Clemson award Soc. Biomaterials, N.Y.C., 1987, Centennial award for outstanding alumni Utah State U., Logan, 1988, Gov.'s medal for Sci. and Tech., 1988; named Alumnus of Yr. Colo. State U., 1986. Mem. Am. Soc. Artificial Internal Organs (trustee 1985—, mem. fellowship rev. com. 1983, chmn. program com. 1988-89, sec., treas. 1989-90, pres. elect. 1990-91, pres. 1991-92), Internat. Soc. Artificial Organs (v.p. 1987—), Am. Coll. Vet. Surgeons (hon.), Utah Vet. Med. Assn. (trustee 1985-88), Alpha Zeta Mem. Lds Ch. Avocations: fishing, hunting, camping, hiking. Office: U Utah Inst Biomed Engring 803 N 300 W Salt Lake City UT 84103-1414

OLSEN, FRANCES ELISABETH, law educator, theorist; b. Chgo., Feb. 4, 1945; d. Holger and Ruth Mathilda (Pfeifer) O.; m. Harold Irving Porter, June 8, 1984. Cert., Roskilde (Denmark) Højskole, 1967; BA, Goddard Coll., 1968; JD, U. Colo., 1971; SJD, Harvard U., 1984. Bar: Colo. 1972, U.S. Dist. Ct. Colo. 1972. Law clk. hon. Arraj U.S. Dist. Ct. Colo., Denver, 1972; lawyer Am. Indian Movement, Wounded Knee, S.D., 1973; pvt. practice Denver, 1973-74; law prof. U. Puget Sound, Tacoma, Wash., 1975-79, St. John's U., Jamaica, N.Y., 1982-83, UCLA, 1984—. Vis. fellow New Coll., Oxford (Eng.) U., 1987; vis. prof. U. Mich., Ann Arbor, 1988, Harvard U., Cambridge, Mass., 1990-91, U. Berlin, Germany, 1995, Ochanomizu U., Tokyo, 1997, U. Tokyo, 1997, Cornell U., 1997, French U. Reunion, 2000, Hebrew U. Jerusalem, 2001, Haifa U., 2001, Tel Aviv U., 2001, 2002, Addis Ababa U., 2002, Bar Ilan U., 2002, Alberto Hurtado U., Santiago, Chile, 2004; sr. Fulbright prof. U. Frankfurt, Germany, 1991-92; overseas fellow Churchill Coll., Cambridge, Eng., 1997-99; mem. faculty law Cambridge U., 1997-99; del. UN 4th World Conf. on Women, Beijing, China, 1995, NGO Forum, Huairou, China, 1995. Co-author: Cases and Materials on Family Law: Legal Concepts and Changing Human Relationships, 1994; editor: Feminist Legal Theory I: Foundations and Outlooks, 1995, Feminist Legal Theory II: Positioning Feminist Theory Within the Law, 1995; contbr. articles to law revs. Named Outstanding Alumnus U. Colo., 1989. Mem. Assn. Am. Law Schs. (chair jurisprudence sect. 1987-88, chair women in law tchg. sect. 1995-96), Conf. on Critical Legal Studies, European Conf. Critical Legal Studies, Internat. Bar Assn. Avocations: scuba diving, kayaking, hiking. Office: UCLA Sch Law 405 Hilgard Ave Los Angeles CA 90095-1476 Home Phone: 310-475-6225; Office Phone: 310-825-6083. E-mail: olsen@law.ucla.edu.

OLSEN, HAROLD FREMONT, lawyer; b. Davenport, Wash., Oct. 17, 1920; s. Oscar E. and Dorothy (Sprowls) O.; m. Jeanne L. Rounds, Aug. 30, 1942; children: Eric O., Ronald R., Margaret Ruth. BA, Wash. State U., 1942; LLB, Harvard U., 1948. Bar: Wash. 1948, U.S. Ct. Claims 1970, U.S. Supreme Ct. 1982; CPA, Wash. Instr. Oxford Bus. Sch., Cambridge, Mass., 1946-47; examiner Wash. State Dept. Pub. Utilities, 1948; with firm Perkins Coie (and predecessors), Seattle, 1949—, ptnr., 1954-88, of counsel, 1989—. Trustee Exec. Svcs. Corp. Wash., 1990-96. Bd. dirs. Northwest Hosp. Found., Northwest Hosp., 1980-90; trustee Wash. State U. Found., chmn. 1986-88; mem. adv. coun. Wash. State U. Sch. Bus. and Econs., 1978-90; trustee, mem. exec. com., pres. Mus. of Flight, 1991-92, chmn., 1993; trustee Horizon House, 1994-97. Maj. USAAF, 1942-45, NATOUSA, Mid. East, ETO. Decorated Silver Star. Mem. ABA, Wash. Bar Assn., Seattle Bar Assn., Aircraft Industry Assn. (chmn. legal com. 1957), Phi Beta Kappa, Phi Kappa Phi, Tau Kappa Epsilon, Rainier Club, Queenstown (New Zealand) Golf Club, Seattle Golf Club (pres. 1986-87), Sr. N.W. Golf Assn. Congregationalist. Office: 1201 3rd Ave Ste 4500 Seattle WA 98101-3029 Home: 900 University St Apt 501 Seattle WA 98101 Personal E-mail: h7olsen@comcast.net. Business E-Mail: holsen@perkinscoie.com.

OLSEN, RANDY J., university librarian; b. Logan, Utah; BA, Utah State U.; MLS, Brigham Young U., 1973, MPA, 1981. German cataloguer Harold B. Lee Libr. Brigham Young U., Provo, 1972, asst. univ. libr. collection devel. and pub. svcs., asst. univ. libr. budget and adminstrv. svcs., dep. univ. libr., univ. libr., 2002—. Mem.: Utah Academic Libr. Coun., Mountain Plains Libr. Assn., Am. Libr. Assn., Utah Libr. Assn. (past pres.). Office: Brigham Young U Harold B Lee Libr PO Box 26800 Provo UT 84602-6800 Office Phone: 801-422-2905. E-mail: randy_olsen@byu.edu.

OLSEN, STEVEN KENT, dentist; b. Spanish Fork, Utah, Nov. 20, 1944; s. Earl Clarence and Adela (Faux) O.; children: Curt, Christopher, Sara Kate, Vanessa BS, Brigham Young U., 1969; DDS, U. Pacific, 1974. Ptrn. practice dentistry in surg. and endodontics Brooks & Olsen, Salt Lake City, 1974—; gen. practice dentistry Steven K. Olsen, D.D.S., San Francisco, 1974-75; pres. S.K. Olsen, P.C., San Francisco, 1975—; ptnr. Olsen, H. & P., San Francisco, 1977-83; instr. U. Pacific, San Francisco, 1978—, Baylor U., 1978—. Chmn. bd. Am. Dentists Ins. Corp., Grand Cayman, W.I., 1978-81; instr. Stanford (Calif.) Inst., Chabot Coll. Inst., 1979-82; med. staff Latter-day Saints Hosp.; cons. Calif. Inst., San Francisco, 1981—; ptnr. J.B. Devel. Co., Russell Harris Restorations, Ryan Bott Restorations, Jason Herget Restorations, D.W. Mmgt. Co., Bob Steck Mgmt. Co., Dave Olsen & Co.; chmn. bd., pres. R.O.R., 1977-80; bd. dirs. Wilks & Topper, Inc., San Francisco, Curt Facchino Ltd., Woodside. Author: Accolade, 1963, (play) Lancer Ballade, 1963, (acad. course) World Religions, 1979; editor corr. course Calif. Inst., 1981. Recipient Good Citizenship medal SAR, 1963, Golden State award, 1988, others. Mem. Assn. Coll. of Physicians and Surgeons, ADA, Calif. Dental Assn., Utah Dental Assn., Physicians and Surgeons Club (San Francisco), Alpha Epsilon Delta. Home: 385 Old La Honda Rd Woodside CA 94062-2617 Office: 2 Embarcadero Ctr Promenade San Francisco CA 94111

OLSEN, STEVEN LLOYD, museum administrator, educator; b. Salt Lake City, Sept. 25, 1950; s. Lloyd V. and Mary (Jensen) O.; m. Kathi L. Brening, Apr. 6, 1979; children: Michael, Daniel, Emily, Sarah, Chelsea. BS summa cum laude, Brigham Young U., 1975; AM, U. Chgo., 1978, PhD, 1985. Sr. instr. Stanley H. Kaplan Ednl. Ctr., Salt Lake City, 1979—92; sr. researcher LDS Ch. Hist. Dept., Salt Lake City, 1979-82; supr. of rsch. Mus. Ch. History & Art, Salt Lake City, 1982-86, mgr. collections and rsch., 1986-89, mgr. ops., 1989—2003; adj. prof. dept. anthropology Brigham Young U., Salt Lake City, 1990—2004; assoc. mng. dir. family and ch. history dept. Ch. Jesus Christ of LDS, Salt Lake City, 2003—. Mem. spkrs. bur. Utah Endowment for Humanities, Salt Lake City, 1990; co-chair Gov.'s Initiative on Museums, 1991—92; mem. Gov.'s Task Force on History and Heritage, 1992—93; mem. adv. bd. Utah State Office Mus. Svcs., 1993—2000, Charles Redd Ctr. for Western Studies, Brigham Young U., 1997—2003; bd. mem. Utah Humanities Coun., 2007—. Contbr. articles to profl. jours. Bd. dirs. Salt Lake City Bd. of Edn., 1989. NSF fellow, 1976-79. Mem.: Am. Soc. Ch. History (coun. mem. 2008—), Nat. Alliance State Museums Associations (mem. steering com. 1998—2003), Western Museums Assn. (first v.p. 1994—96, pres. 1996—98, Directors Chair award 2007), Utah Museums Assn. (v.p. 1988—90, pres. 1990—92). Mem. Lds Ch. Avocations: reading, bicycling, photograhy. Office: Mus of Ch History & Art 45 N West Temple Salt Lake City UT 84150-3810 Office Phone: 801-240-4648. Office Fax: 801-240-5342. Business E-Mail: olsensl@ldschurch.org.

OLSON, A. CRAIG, foundation administrator, former retail executive; m. Cathy; 1 child, Sarah. BS in Acctg., U. Idaho, 1974. CPA, Idaho. From checker to sr. v.p., CFO Albertson's, Inc., Boise, Idaho, 1967-91, sr. v.p., CFO, 1991—2001; exec. dir. J.A. and Kathryn Albertson Found., Boise, Idaho, 2002—. Adv. bd. U. Idaho Coll. Bus. & Econs., bd. dirs. Bogus Basin Recreational Assn. Mem. Am. Inst. CPAs, Idaho Soc. CPAs, Financial Exec. Inst. Avocations: sailing, running, skiing. Office: JA & Kathryn Albertson Found PO Box 70002 Boise ID 83707-0102

OLSON, DALE C., public relations executive; b. Fargo, ND, Feb. 20, 1934; s. Arthur Edwin and Edith (Weight) Olson Neubauer. Sr. v.p., prin., pres. motion picture divsn. Rogers and Cowan, Inc., Beverly Hills, Calif., 1967-85; prin. Dale C. Olson & Assocs., Beverly Hills, 1985—; mktg. dir. Hollywood History Mus., 2003. Cons. Filmex, L.A., 1972-83; U.S. del. Manila Film Festival, 1982-83. Editor L.A. edit. Theatre ann. Best Plays, 1963-67, 2007; prodr. Rollesgesby. V.p. Diamond Cir. City of Hope, Duarte, Calif., 1980-83; mem. adv. bd. Calif. Mus. Sci. and Industry, L.A., 1975-81; mem. bd. govs. Film Industry Workshops, Inc., 1965-80; pres. Hollywood Press Club, 1963-66; assoc. Los Angeles County Art Mus., 1981-83; bd. trustees Hollywood Arts Coun.; chair 1999 jury USA Film Festival, Dallas; cons. L.A. 2000. Recipient Golden Key, Pub. Rels. News, 1982, Les Mason and pub. svc. awards Publicists Guild, Golden Satellite award for lifetime achievement Internat. Press Acad., 1999, Prism award for pub. svc. Entertainment Industries Coun., 2000, Named in his honor, Dale Olson Lobby, Actors' Fund L.A. Office, 2005. Mem. NATAS, Acad. Motion Picture Arts and Scis. (chmn. pub. rels. coordinating com. 1982—), Actors Fund Am. (chmn. Western coun. 1991, trustee 1992, exec. com. 1998), Hollywood Arts Coun. (bd. dirs.), Pres.'s Club, Thalians. Lutheran. Office Phone: 323-876-9331. Personal E-mail: dolson2000@earthlink.net.

OLSON, DAVID JOHN, political science professor; b. Brantford, ND, May 18, 1941; s. Lloyd and Alice Ingrid (Black) O.; m. Sandra Jean Crabb, June 11, 1966; 1 dau., Maia Kari. BA, Concordia Coll., Moorhead, Minn., 1963; Rockefeller fellow fellow, Union Theol. Sem, NYC, 1963-64; MA (Brooklings Instn. predoctoral rsch. fellow 1968-69), U. Wis., Madison, 1966, PhD (univ. fellow 1967), 1971. Cmty. planner Madison Redvel. Authority, 1965-66; lectr. U. Wis., 1966-67; from lectr. to asso. prof. polit. sci. Ind. U., Bloomington, 1969-76; prof. polit. sci. U. Wash., Seattle, 1976—2005, chmn. dept., 1983-88, Harry Bridges endowed chairlabor studies, 1992-94; bd. dirs. Harry Bridges Inst.; Disting. lectr. in labor studies San Francisco State U., 1994; dir. Ctr. Labor Studies U. Wash., Seattle, 1992-94, prof. emeritus polit. sci., 2005—. Vis. prof. U. Bergen, 1987, Harvard U., 1988-89, U. Hawaii, 1989, U. Calif., Berkeley, 1996, U. Wales, 2006. Co-author: Governing the United States, 1978, Commission Politics, 1977, To Keep the Republic, 1975, Black Politics, 1971; co-editor: Theft of the City, 1974. Recipient Disting. Tchg. award, Ind. U., 1973, Alumni Achievement award, Concordia Coll., 1998, S. Sterling Munro Disting. Tchg. award, 2005, Disting. Tchg. award, U. Wash., 2005, knight, Harold V of Norway, 2006, Outstanding Civic Educator award, Wash. State Senate, 2007; named faculty fellow, Ind. U., 1973. Mem. Am. Polit. Sci. Assn., Western Polit. Sci. Assn. (v.p. 1984, pres. 1985), Midwest Polit. Sci. Assn., So. Polit. Sci. Assn. Democrat. Lutheran. Home: 6512 E Green Lake Way N Seattle WA 98103-5418 Office: U Wash Dept Polit Sci Seattle WA 98195-0001 Office Phone: 206-543-7948. Business E-Mail: davidols@u.washington.edu.

OLSON, DONALD, state legislator; b. Nome, Alaska, June 18, 1953; BA in Chemistry, U. Minn., Deluth; MD, U. Alaska, Fairbanks. Lic. Airline Transport Pilot, Comml. Airplane & Helicopters, Airframe & Power Plant Mechanics, Inspector Authorization. App by Governor Knowles, Alaska State Medical Bd, 1995-; Alaska State Senator, District S, 2001-02; Alaska State Senator, District T, 2003-.Pres/Chief Exec Officer, Olson Air Serv, Inc, Donald Olson Enterprises, Olson Ventures LLC, currently. Alaska State Medical Association; Amundson Education Center; Missionary Aviation Repair Center-Advisory Bd; Explorers Club of New York; Aviation Medical Examiners Association. Democrat. Office: State Capitol Rm 514 Juneau AK 99801 also: Dist T 716 W 4th Ave Ste 560 Anchorage AK 99501 Office Phone: 907-465-3707, 907-269-0254. Office Fax: 907-465-4821, 907-465-4821. Business E-Mail: Senator_Donny_Olson@legis.state.ak.us.*

OLSON, GENE L., food products executive; Sr. v.p. fin. Golden State Foods, Irvine, Calif. Office: Golden State Foods 18301 Von Karman Ave Ste 1100 Irvine CA 92612-0133

OLSON, JAMES (JIM OLSON), telecommunications industry executive; BS in Elec. Engring., Univ. Calif., Davis; MS in Elec. Engring, Santa Clara Univ., MBA. Sr. mgmt., engring. mfg., mktg. Hewlett-Packard Co.; gen. mgr., Stanford Park Divsn. Hewlett-Packard, 1992; sr. v.p., gen. mgr., Wide Area Network Ops. 3Com Corp.; pres., CEO SkyStream Networks, 1997—. Spkr. in field. Office: SkyStream Networks 455 DeGuigne Dr Sunnyvale CA 94085-3890 Office Fax: 408-616-3404.

OLSON, JAMES WILLIAM PARK, architect; b. St. Louis, Oct. 6, 1940; s. James William Park; s. Louis Garfield and Gladys Helen (Schuh) O.; m. Katherine Fovargue, June 11, 1971; children: Park, Reed. BArch, U. Wash., 1963. Registered arch., Wash., Oreg., Calif., Ill., Colo., Hawaii, Ga., Fla. Ptnr. Olson Sundberg Kundig Allen Archs., Seattle, 1985—. Assoc. arch. New Seattle Art Mus., 1991. Prin. works include Pike and Virginia Bldg. (AIA Honor award 1980), Seattle's Best Coffee Retail Locations (AIA Honor award 1984), Hauberg Residence (AIA Honor award 1997), Mayer Lodo residence, Denver (AIA Honor award 1998, AIA NW and Pacific Regional Merit award 1999, AIA We. Internat. Design award 2000), St. Mark's Cathedral Renovation (AIA Commendation award), Seattle (IFFRA award 1998, AIA citation 1998, AIA and Pacific Regional Merit award 2000), numerous residences nationwide; (subject of monologue) Monacelli Press: Architecture, Art and Craft. Bd. dirs. Ctr. Contemporary Art, Seattle, 1982-86, Artist Trust, Seattle, 1986-90, U. Wash. Henry Art Gallery, Seattle, 1986-92, Seattle Art Mus., 1996—. Recipient Best Arch. award Seattle Mag., 1985. Fellow AIA; mem. NEA (juror). Avocation: art. Office: Olson Sundberg Kundig Allen Architects 159 South Jackson St Ste 600 Seattle WA 98104-2557 Office Phone: 206-624-5670. E-mail: jim@olsonsundberg.com.

OLSON, KRISTINE, prosecutor; b. NYC, Aug. 9, 1947; d. Harold John and Arline (Schneider) Olson; children: Karin, Tyler. BA, Wellesley Coll., 1969; JD, Yale U., 1972. Bar: Oreg. 1973, US Dist. Ct. Oreg. 1974, US Ct. Appeals (9th cir.) 1975. Asst. US atty. Dept. Justice, Portland, 1971—84, US atty., 1994—2001; vice chair State Indigent Def. Bd., Salem, Oreg., 1985—87; assoc. dean., prof. law Lewis & Clark Coll., 1989—94. Adj. prof. Northwestern Sch. Law, 1975—89, Lewis & Clark Coll., U. Oreg. Law Ctr., 1984—; bd. dirs. State Bd. Police Stds. and Tng., 1976—80; chmn. Cmty. Corrections Adv. Bd. Multnomah County, Portland, 1978—80; mem. 9th Cir. Task Force on Tribal Cts., World Affairs Coun., Oreg.; bd. dirs., chmn. bd. Oreg. Coun. on Crime and Delinquency, 1981—87; chmn. women's rights project ACLU, Oreg.; commr., mem. exec. com. Met. Human Rels. Commn., mayor's appointee, 1986—. Contbr. articles to profl. jours. Root Tilden fellow, 1969. Mem.: Nature Conservancy, Archaeol. Conservancy, Earthwatch, 1000 Friends of Oreg., Native Am. Rights Fund, Soc. Am. Archaeology, Multnomah Athletic Club, City Club Portland (bd. govs. 1984—, pres.-elect 1995), Early Keyboard Soc. Democrat. Home: 900 SW 83rd Ave Portland OR 97225-6308

OLSON, KURT, state legislator; b. Sacramento, Calif., Mar. 24, 1948; m to Barbara; children: Madelyn & Valerie. BA, Calif. State U., 1977. Alaska State Representative, District 33, 2004-; Alaska legislation aide, formerly. Commercial lines insurance broker, currently; member, chairman, serv area board director, Cent Emergency Serv, formerly. Served USAF, 1967—71. Rotary (Spenard, Kenai & Soldotna); Kenai & Soldotna Chamber of Commerce (board director). Republican. Avocations: fishing, photography, hiking. Office: State Capitol Rm 110 Juneau AK 99801 Mailing: 145 Main St Loop Ste 221 Kenai AK 99611 also: 120 4th St Juneau AK 99801-1182 Office Phone: 907-465-2693, 907-283-2690. Office Fax: 907-465-3835, 907-283-2763. Business E-Mail: Representative_Kurt_Olson@legis.state.ak.us.

OLSON, LUTE (ROBERT LUTHER OLSON), retired men's college basketball coach; b. Mayville, ND, Sept. 22, 1934; s. Albert E. and Alinda E. (Halvorson) O.; m. Roberta R. Russell, Nov. 27, 1953 (dec. 2001); children: Vicki, Jody, Gregory, Christi, Steven m. Christine Jack Toretti, 2003 (div., 2008) BA, Augsburg Coll., Mpls., 1956; MA, Chapman Coll., Orange, Calif., 1964. Cert. counselor. Head basketball coach Mahonomen HS, Minn., 1956-57, Two Harbors HS, Minn., 1957-61; dean of boys Baseline Jr. HS, Boulder, Colo., 1961-62; head basketball coach Loara HS, Anaheim, Calif., 1962-64, Marine HS, Huntington Beach, Calif., 1964-69, Long Beach City Coll., Calif., 1969-73, Long Beach State U., 1973-74, U. Iowa, Iowa City, 1974-83, U. Ariz. Wildcats, 1983—2008, head coach NCAA Men's Basketball Tournament champions, 1997; ret., 2008. Author: Passing Game Offense, 1980, Multiple Zone Attack, 1981, Pressure Defense, 1981, Match-up Zone, 1983. Crusade chmn. Am. Cancer Soc., Iowa, 1982. Named Coach of Yr. Orange League, 1964, Sunset League, 1968, Yr. Met. Conf. Calif., 1970-71, PCAA, 1974, Big Ten Conf., 1979, 80, PAC-10 Conf., 1986, 87, 89, 93, 94, 98, 2003; inducted to Naismith Meml. Basketball Hall of Fame, 2002. Mem. Nat. Assn. Basketball Coaches (Coach of Yr. 1980) Lutheran.

OLSON, ROBERT HOWARD, lawyer; b. July 6, 1944; s. Robert Howard and Jacquiline (Wells) O.; m. Diane Carol Thorsen, Aug. 13, 1966; children: Jeffrey, Christopher. BA in Govt. summa cum laude, Ind. U., 1966; JD cum laude, Harvard U., 1969. Bar: Ohio 1969, Fla. 1980, Ariz. 1985, Calif. 2001, U.S. Supreme Ct. 1973. Assoc. Squire, Sanders & Dempsey, L.L.P., Cleve., 1969, 70-71, 76-81, ptnr., 1981—, Phoenix, 1985—2002, Squire, Sanders & Dempsey, San Francisco, 2002—; sr. law clk. U.S. Dist. Ct., No. Dist., Ind., 1969-70; chief civil rights divsn. Ohio Atty. Gen.'s Office, Columbus, 1971-73, chief consumer protection, 1973-75, chief counsel, 1975, 1st asst. (chief of staff), 1975-76. Instr. Ohio State U. Law Sch., Columbus, 1974; Cen. Phoenix com. to advise city council and mayor City of Phoenix, 1987—89; bd. dirs. Orpheum Theater Found., 1989—2002, sec., 1989—90, pres., 1990—97, exec. com., 1997—99, The Ariz. Ctr. for Law in the Pub. Interest, 1989—2001, treas., 1992—93, 1997—2001, v.p., 1993—94; mem. Ariz. Ctr. for Disability Law, 1994—96, treas., 1994—95; mem. Valley Leadership Class XIV; rsch. com. Ariz. Town Hall, 1998—2002; mem. fin. com. Pub. Advs., Inc.; co-chair Calif. Pub. Fin. Conf., 2006. Contbr. articles to profl. jours. Bd. dirs. 1st Unitarian Ch. Phoenix, 1987-89, 98-2001, v.p., 1987-89, 2000-2001, pres. 1998-99; bd. dirs. 1st Unitarian Ch. Found., 1987-93, pres., 1990-93; exec. com. San Francisco (Calif.) Heartwalk, Am. Heart Assn., 2005. Named Arts Advocate of Yr. Bus. Vols. Arts/Phoenix, 1997, Super Lawyer, 2008. Mem. Ariz. State Bar Assn., Calif. Bar Assn., Pub. Adv. Inc. (mem. fin. com. 2007-), Phi Beta Kappa. Office: Squire Sanders & Dempsey LLP One Maritime Plaza Suite 300 San Francisco CA 94111-3492 Office Phone: 415-393-9819.

OLSON, RONALD LEROY, lawyer; b. Carroll, Iowa, July 9, 1941; s. Clyde L. and Delpha C. (Boyens) Olson; m. Jane Tenhulzen, June 21, 1964; children: Kristin, Steven, Amy. BS, Drake U., 1963; JD, U. Mich., 1966; Diploma Law, Oxford U., Eng., 1967. Bar: Wis. 1966, Calif. 1969, US Dist. Ct. (cen. dist.), Calif. 1969, US Dist. Ct. (so. dist.),Calif. 1973, US Ct. Appeals (9th cir.) 1974, US Ct. Appeals (10th cir.) 1980, US Ct. Appeals (5th cir.) 1982, US Supreme Ct. 1976, US Dist. Ct., Alaska 1983. Atty. civil rights divsn. US Dept. Justice, 1967; law clk. to chief judge David L. Bazelon US Ct. Appeals (DC cir.), Washington, 1967—68; ptnr. Munger, Tolles & Olson LLP, Los Angeles, Calif., 1968—; lawyer del. Ann. 9th Cir. Conf., 1984—89; lectr. in field; mem. editorial bd. Alternatives, 1983—. Mem. bd. dirs. The Wash. Post Co., 2003—. Contbr. articles legal jour. Recipient Burton scholar, U. Mich.; named one of 100 Most Influential Lawyers, Nat. Law Jour., 2006; fellow Am. Coll Trial Lawyers. Fellow: Am. Bar Found., Ford Found. Oxford U.; mem.: 9th Cir. Jud. Conf. (exec. com. 1984—89), Chancery, LA County Barristers (pres. 1976), Assn. Bus. Trial Lawyers (mem. adv. com. trial ct. improvement fund for Calif. jud. coun. 1988—), State Bar Calif. (bd. dir. 1985, v.p. 1986—87), LA County Bar Assn., Am. Arbitration Assn. (bd. dir. 1983, comml. panel 1983), LA Bar Found. (bd. dir. 1977), Am. Judicature Soc., Human Rights (editorial bd., publ. sect. ind. rights and responsibilities 1986—), Soviet Exchange Program (litig. sect. com. 1983—), ABA (litig. sect. council 1976, chmn. sp. com. on dispute resolution 1976—86, chmn. litig. section 1981—82, chmn. standing com. on fed. judiciary 1991—92), Skid Row Housing Trust of LA (mem. 1986—), U. Mich. Law Sch. (com. visitors 1986—), Salzburg Seminar (bd. dir.), Legal Aid Found. LA (bd. dir. 1975—86, pres. 1984—85), Claremont U. Ctr. and Grad. Sch. (chmn. bd. fellows 1984—94), Sequoia Nat. Pk. Natural History Assn., Drake U. (trustee 1977), Alternatives (mem. editorial bd. 1983—88), LA Arts Festival (sec. 1985), Lawyers Alliance for Nuclear Arms Control (adv. com. Los Angeles and Orange Counties chpt.), Frat. of Friends of Music Ctr. (bd. dir., pres. 1978), Omicron Delta Kappa, Phi Eta Sigma, Beta Gamma Sigma. Democrat. Episcopalian. Office: Munger Tolles & Olson LLP 355 S Grand Ave Fl 35 Los Angeles CA 90071-1560 E-mail: Ron.Olson@mto.com.

OLSON, STEVEN STANLEY, social service executive; b. Longview, Wash., Aug. 5, 1950; s. Robert Martin and Martha Virginia (Duffin) O.; 1 child, Derek Thomas Dailey. BA, Wash. State U., 1972; MEd, Auburn U., 1977; postgrad., Seattle U., 1981-83. Cert. rehabilitation mgmt. Agrl. extensionist Action/Peace Corps, Popayan, Colombia, 1972-73; supr. Stonebelt Ctr. for the Mentally Retarded, Bloomington, Ind., 1974; adjustment counselor Exceptional Industries, Bowling Green, Ky., 1974-75, vocat. evaluator, 1975-76; alcohol counselor E. Ala. Mental Health, Opelika, 1976; intern Auburn Univ./Ptnrs. of the Americas, Guatemala City, Guatemala, 1976; planner, rschr. Marion County Mental Health, Salem, Oreg., 1977-78; assoc. dir. Reliable Enterprises, Centralia, Wash., 1979-80, exec. dir., 1980-98, Olympia (Wash.) Child Care Ctr., 1999—. Cons. in field, 1998-99; v.p. govt. affairs Rehab. Enterprises Wash., Olympia, 1984-86, chmn. regional rep., 1986-89, pres., 1990-91; treas. Arc of Wash., Olympia, 1983-85, 1999-2002, 2003-05, govt. affairs chmn., 1983-89, v.p., 1989-90, sec., 1996-97, 2002-03; coun. Lewis/Mason/Thurston Area Agy. on Aging, 1993-99. Contbr. articles to Vocat. Evaluation and Work Adjustment Bull., 1976, Rehab. World, 1977. Treas. Cmtys. United Responsible Energy, Lewis County, Wash., 1979—; mem. statewide steering com. The Collaborative, 2005—; mem. adv. bd. Ptnrs. for Children, Youth and Families, Thurston County, 2001—; bd. dirs. Thurston County United Way, Olympia, 2002—04; vice chairperson Wash. Solar Coun., Olympia, Wash., 1980—83; co-chair Early Childhood Help Orgn., Olympia, 1988; mem. Thurston County Interagy. Coord. Coun., Olympia, 2000—. Home: 4333 Maytown Rd SW Olympia WA 98512-9239 Office: Olympia Child Care Ctr PO Box 7304 Olympia WA 98507

OLSON, WALTER GILBERT, lawyer; b. Stanton, Nebr., Feb. 2, 1924; s. O.E. Olson and Mabel A. Asplin; m. Gloria Helen Bennett, June 26, 1949; children: Clifford Warner, Karen Rae Olson. BS, U. Calif., Berkeley, 1947, JD, 1949. Bar: Calif. 1950, U.S. Dist. Ct. (no. dist.) Calif. 1950, U.S. Tax Ct. 1950, U.S. Ct. Appeals (9th cir.) 1950. Assoc. Orrick, Herrington and Sutcliffe (formerly Orrick, Dahlquist, Herrington and Sutcliffe), San Francisco, 1949-54, ptnr., 1954-88. Bd. dirs. Alltel Corp., Little Rock, 1988-94; mem. Commn. to Revise Calif. Corp. Securities Law, 1967-69, Securities Regulatory Reform Panel, 1978-80; mem. corp. security adv. com. Calif. Commr. of Corps, 1975-88. Editor-in-chief Calif. Law Review, 1948-49. Bd. dirs. Internat. Ho., Berkeley, 1981-86. With U.S. Army, 1943-46, ETO. Fellow Am. Bar Found.; mem. ABA (trust divsn. nat. conf. of lawyers and reps. of Am. Bankers Assn.), Calif. Bar Assn. (chmn. corps com. 1975-76, exec. com. bus. law sect. 1977-78), San Francisco Bar Assn., U. Calif. Alumni Assn., Boalt Hall Alumni Assn. (bd. dirs. 1982-90, sec. 1985, v.p. 1987, pres. 1988), Order of Coif, Menlo Country Club (Woodside, Calif.), Pacific-Union Club. Home: 501 Portola Rd #8162 Portola Valley CA 94028-8616

OLSSON, RONALD ARTHUR, computer science educator; b. Huntington, NY, Nov. 16, 1955; s. Ronald Alfred and Dorothy Gertrude (Hofmann) O. BA and MA, SUNY, 1977; MS, Cornell U., 1979; PhD, U. Ariz., 1986. Teaching asst. Cornell U., Ithaca, N.Y., 1977-79, rsch. asst., 1979; lectr. SUNY, Brockport, 1979-81; rsch. assoc. U. Ariz., Tucson, 1981-86; prof., vice chair Computer Sci. Dept. U. Calif., Davis, 1986—. Author (book) The SR Programming Language: Concurrency in Practice, 1993; contbr. articles to profl. jours. Grantee MICRO U. Calif., 1987, 92, NSF, 1988, 96, Dept. Energy, 1988-92, Advanced Rsch. Projects Agy., 1993—. Mem. Assn. for Computing Machinery. Avocations: bicycling, hiking, cross country skiing, movies. Office: U Calif Dept Computer Sci Davis CA 95616-8562

OLSTAD, ROGER GALE, science educator; b. Mpls., Jan. 16, 1934; s. Arnold William and Myra (Stroschein) O.; m. Constance Elizabeth Jackson, Aug. 20, 1955; children: Karen Louise, Kenneth Bradley. BS, U. Minn., 1955, MA, 1959, PhD, 1963. Instr. U. Minn., Mpls., 1956-63; asst. prof. U. Ill., Urbana, 1963-64; mem. faculty U. Wash., Seattle, 1964—, assoc. prof. sci. edn., 1967-71, prof., 1971-95, asso. dean grad. studies Coll. Edn., 1971-85; prof. emeritus, 1995—. Bd. trustees Shoreline C.C., 2006—. Chair environ. quality commn. City of Lake Forest Park, Wash., 1997-2000, city coun., 2000-2007, mayor pro tempore, 2006-2007. Fellow AAAS; mem. NSTA (bd. dirs.) Wash. Sci. Tchrs. Assn. (pres. 1973-74), Nat. Assn. Rsch. Sci. Teaching (pres. 1977-78, bd. dirs.), N.W. Sci. Assn. (chmn. 1966-68), Assn. Edn. Tchrs. in Sci. (regional pres. 1966-68, pres. 1991-92), Nat. Assn. Biology Tchrs., Biol. Scis. Curriculum Study (chmn., bd. dirs. 1989-94), U. Wash. Faculty Club, Phi Delta Kappa. Home: 20143 53rd Ave NE Seattle WA 98155-1801 Office: U Wash Coll Edn Seattle WA 98195-0001 Personal E-mail: rolstad@earthlink.net. Business E-Mail: rolstad@u.washington.edu.

O'MALLEY, EDWARD, psychiatrist, consultant; b. Hudson, NY, May 30, 1926; s. Thomas Patrick and Helen Mary (Cornell) O. BS, St. John's U., Bklyn., NY, 1949; MS, Loyola U., Chgo., 1952, PhD, 1954; MD, SUNY, Bklyn., 1958. Diplomate Am. Bd. Forensic Examiners, Am. Bd. Psychiatry and Neurology. Psychiat. cons. Corrections Dept., NYC, 1962—68; psychiatrist Cath. Charities, NYC, 1963—68; dir. mental health Suffolk County Govt., Hauppauge, NY, 1968—70; commr. mental health Orange County, Goshen, NY, 1970—72; dir. drug abuse svcs. State of N.Y., Bronx, 1972—78; lic. sch. psychiatrist N.Y.C. Bd. of Edn., 1962—82; chief psychiatry svcs. VA, Huntington, W.Va., 1982—86; med. cons. State of Calif., San Diego, 1986—. psychiat. cons. dept. of corrections, 1987—. Asst. prof. psychiatry N.J. Med. Sch., Newark, 1975—; examiner Am. Bd. of Psychiatry and Neurology, Los Angeles, 1980; assoc. prof. psychiatry U. Calif., San Diego, 1980—; prof. psychiatry Marshall U. Sch. of Medicine, Huntington, 1982-86; dir. com. on sea cadets Navy League, San Diego, 1987—; cons. HHS, Social Security Adminstrn., Office of Hearings and Appeals, 1989—. Contbr. articles to profl. jours. Bd. dirs. Suffolk Community Council, Hauppauge, 1968-70, United Fund of Long Island, Huntington, 1968-70. Capt. ret. USNR, 1960-86. Scholar N. Y. State Coll., 1946-49, SUNY Joseph Collins Med. Sch., 1955-58; Teaching and Research fellow Loyola U., 1952-54. Fellow Am. Psychiat. Assn.(disting., life); mem. San Diego Psychiat. Soc., Soc. of Med. Cons. to Armed Forces, Soc. of Mil. Surgeons U.S.A., N.Y. Celtic Med. Soc., Union Am. Physicians and Dentists (steward 1990—), State Employed Physicians Assn. (bd. dirs. 1993). Roman Catholic. Home: 3711 Alcott St San Diego CA 92106-1212 Personal E-mail: omalleyedwr@aol.com. Business E-Mail: edward.p.omalley.md@ssa.gov.

O'MALLEY, JAMES TERENCE (TERRY), lawyer; b. Omaha, Nov. 24, 1950; s. John Austin and Mayme Bernice (Zentner) O'M.; m. Colleen L. Kizer, May 22, 1972; children: Erin C., Michael B., Patrick J. BA magna cum laude, U. Notre Dame, 1972; JD, Stanford U., 1975. Bar: Calif. 1975, Tex. 1998. Ptnr. Gray, Cary, Ames & Frye, San Diego, 1975-87, of counsel, 1987-91, ptnr., 1991—94; vice chmn., exec. v.p., gen. counsel Noble Broadcast Group, Inc., San Diego, 1987-91; ptnr. Gray Cary Ware & Freidenrich LLP, San Diego, 1994—2004, chmn., CEO, 1996—2004; mng. ptnr. US DLA Piper Rudnick Gray Cary US LLP, San Diego, 2005—. Pres. San Diego Taxpayers Assn., 1986—87; co-chmn. Mayor's City of the Future Health Care Task Force, San Diego, 1994—95; mem. C. of C. CEO Roundtable, San Diego, 1997—2002; adv. bd. Hildebrandt Internat., Inc., 2001; bd. dirs. San Diego Regional Econ. Devel. Corp., 1997—2002. Mem. Order of Coif, Sorin Soc. Avocations: jogging, music. Office: DLA Piper Rudnick Ste 1700 401 B St San Diego CA 92101-4297 Office Fax: 858-677-1401. Business E-Mail: terry.omalley@dlapiper.com.

O'MALLEY, ROBERT EDMUND, JR., mathematics professor; b. Rochester, NH, May 23, 1939; s. Robert E. and Jeanette A. (Dubois) O'M.; m. Candace G. Hinz, Aug. 31, 1968; children: Patrick, Timothy, Daniel. BS in Elec. Engring., U. N.H., 1960, MS, 1961; PhD, Stanford U., 1966. Mathematician Bell Labs., Gen. Electric Research Co., RCA, summers 1961-63; asst. prof. U. N.C., Chapel Hill, 1965-66; vis. mem. Courant Inst., NYU, 1966-67; research mem. Math. Research Ctr., Madison, Wis., 1967-68; asst. prof., assoc. prof. NYU, NYC, 1968-73; prof. math. U. Ariz., Tucson, 1973-81, chmn. applied math. program, 1976-81; prof. math. Rensselaer Poly. Inst., Troy, N.Y., 1981-90, chmn. dept. math. scis., 1981-84, Ford Found. prof., 1989-90; prof., chair applied math. U. Wash., Seattle, 1990-93, prof., 1993—. Sr. vis. fellow U. Edinburgh, (Scotland), 1971-72; guest prof. Tech. U. Vienna, 1987-88; vis. Univ. Lyon I and Univ. of Cambridge, 1994-95, Fields Inst., 2002-03, U. Minn., 2002-03, Dublin City U., 2002-03. Author: Introduction to Singular Perturbations, 1974; editor: Asymptotic Methods and Singular Perturbations, 1976, Singular Perturbation Methods for Ordinary Differential Equations, 1991, Thinking About Ordinary Differential Equations, 1997; editor ICIAM 91 procs.; co-editor Multiscale Phenomena, 1999, Singular Perturbations and Hysteresis, 2005; contbr. numerous articles to profl. jours Mem. Soc. for Indsl. and Applied Math. (pres. 1991-92), Am. Math. Soc. Roman Catholic. Home: 3415 W Laurelhurst Dr NE Seattle WA 98105-5345 Office: U Wash Dept Applied Math Box 352420 Seattle WA 98195-2420 Office Phone: 206-685-1905. E-mail: omalley@amath.washington.edu.

OMAN, MARK C., bank executive; b. Cedar Falls, Iowa; B, U. No. Iowa. CPA. With Delooitte, Haskins & Sells, Des Moines, Norwest Corp., 1979; CEO Wells Fargo Home Mortgage, Inc., 1989—97, chmn., 1997—; exec. v.p. mortgage svcs. Norwest, 1997—98; group exec. v.p. home and consumer fin. Wells Fargo & Co., 2002—. Office: Wells Fargo & Co 420 Montgomery St San Francisco CA 94163

OMATSU, GLENN, Asian American studies professor; b. Cleve., 1947; Grad., East Los Angeles Coll., U. Calif., Santa Cruz. Assoc. editor Amerasia Jour., 1985—2002; editor CrossCurrents, 1985—2002; prof. Asian Am. studies UCLA, Calif. State U., Northridge, Pasadena City Coll. Co-editor: Asian Americans: The Movement and the Moment, 2001. Mem. New Otani Workers Support Com., Koreatown Restaurant Workers Support Com. Recipient Cmty. Svc. award, Japanese Am. Hist. Soc. of So. Calif., Cmty. Activism award, Korean Immigrant Workers Advocates of L.A. Office: CSUN EOP 18111 Nordhoff St Northridge CA 91330-8366 Business E-Mail: glenn.omatsu@csun.edu.

O'MEARA, SARA, non-profit organization executive; b. Knoxville, Tenn., Sept. 09; m. Robert O'Meara (dec.); children: John Hopkins, Charles Hopkins (dec.); m. Robert Sigholtz, Nov. 1986 (dec.); stepchildren: Taryn, Whitney. Attended, Briarcliff Jr. Coll.; BA, The Sorbonne, Paris; D (hon.), Endicott Coll. Co-founder, chmn. bd., CEO Childhelp USA (formerly Children's Village USA), Scottsdale, Ariz., 1960—. Bd. dirs. Nat. Soc. for Prevention of Child Abuse and Neglect of Gt. Britain, Children to Children, Inc.; hon. com. mem. The Dyslexia Found., Inc.; mem. Mayor's adv. bd., Defense for Children Internat., Nat. Soc. Prevention Cruelty to Children, World Affairs Coun., Ariz. Found. Women Charter 100; bd. dirs. Internat. Alliance on Child Abuse and Neglect; sustaining mem. Spastic Children's League, past pres.; mem., past recording sec. Assistance League So. Calif. Recipient Cross of Merit, Knightly Order of St. Brigitte, 1967, Victor M. Carter Diamond award Japan-Am. Soc., 1970, Dame Cross of Merit of Order of St. John of Denmark, 1980, Official Seal of 34th Gov. Calif., 1981, Woman of Achievement award Career Guild, 1982, Women Making History award Nat. Fedn. Bus. Profl. Women's Clubs, 1983, Disting. Am. award for svc., 1984, Humanitarian award Nat. Frat. Eagles, 1984, Nat. Recognition award outstanding leadership Am. Heritage Found., 1986, Notable Am. award svc. to Calif., 1986, Dove of Peace award Pacific Southwest and Ctrl. Pacific Regions B'nai B'rith, 1987, Paul Harris fellow award Rotary Found., 1989, Internat. Collaboration to Prevention Child Abuse award HRH Queen of Eng., 1989, Living Legacy award Women's Internat. Ctr., 1989, Love and Help the Children award, 1990, Presdl. award, 1990, Kiwanis World Svc. medal, 1991, Women Who Make a Difference award Family Circle Mag., 1992, Outstanding Woman from Tenn. award Nat. Mus. Women in Arts, 1993, Nat. Caring award Nat. Caring Inst., 1993, Hubert Humphrey award Touchdown Club Washington, 1993, Lifetime Achievement award Nat. Charity Awards Com., 2001, Champions of Children award Nat. Children's Alliance, Sandra Day O'Connor award Ariz. Found. Women, 2004, Nobel Peace Prize nominee, 2005, numerous others. Mem. SAG, AFTRA, Victory Awards (exec. com.), Am. Biographical Inst. (nat. bd. advisors), Alpha Delta Kappa (hon.). Office: Childhelp USA 15757 N 78th St Scottsdale AZ 85260-1629 Office Phone: 480-922-8212.

OMER, GEORGE ELBERT, JR., retired orthopaedic surgeon, educator; b. Kansas City, Kans., Dec. 23, 1922; s. George Elbert and Edith May (Hines) O.; m. Wendie Vilven, Nov. 6, 1949; children: George Eric, Michael Lee. BA, Ft. Hays Kans. State U., 1944; MD, Kans. U., 1950; MSc in Orthopaedic Surgery, Baylor U., Waco, Tex., 1955. Diplomate Am. Bd. Orthopaedic Surgery, 1959, (bd. dirs. 1983-92, pres. 1987-88), re-cert. orthopaedics and hand surgery, 1983, cert. surgery of the hand, 1989. 2nd lt. US Army, 1945, advanced through grades to col., 1967, ret., 1970; rotating intern Bethany Hosp., Kansas City, 1950-51; resident in orthopaedic surgery Brooke Army Hosp., San Antonio, 1952-55, William Beaumont Army Hosp., El Paso, Tex., 1955-56; chief surgery Irwin Army Hosp., Ft. Riley, Kans., 1957-59; cons. in orthopaedic surgery 8th Army, chief orthop. surgery 121st Evacuation Hosp. Republic of Korea, 1959-60; asst. chief orthopaedic surgery, chief hand surgeon Fitzsimons Army Med. Center, Denver, 1960-63; dir. orthopaedic residency tng. Armed Forces Inst. Pathology at Walter Reed Army Med. Ctr., Washington, 1963-65; chief orthopaedic surgery and chief Army Hand Surg. Center, Brooke Army Med. Center, 1965-70; cons. in orthopaedic and hand surgery Surgeon Gen. Army, 1967-70; prof. orthopaedics, surgery, and anatomy, chmn. dept. orthopaedic surgery, chief div. hand surgery U. N.Mex., 1970-90, med. dir. phys. therapy, 1972-90, acting asst. dean grad. edn. Sch. Medicine, 1980-81. Mem. active staff U. N.Mex. Hosp., Albuquerque, 1970—2005, chief of med. staff, 1984-86; cons. staff other Albuquerque hosps.; cons. orthopedic surgery USPHS, 1966-85, US Army, 1970-92, USAF, 1970-78, VA, 1970-2000; cons. Carrie Tingley Hosp. for Crippled Children, 1970-99, interim med. dir., 1970-72, 86-87, mem. bd. advisor 1972-76, chair, 1994-96. Mem. bd. editors Clin. Orthopaedics, 1973-90, Jour. AMA, 1973-74, Jour. Hand Surgery, 1976-81; trustee Jour. Bone and Joint Surgery, 1993-99, sec., 1993-96, chmn., 1997-99; contbr. more than 300 articles to profl. jours., numerous chpts. to books. Decorated Legion of Merit, Army Commendation medal with oak leaf cluster; recipient Alumni Achievement award Ft. Hays State U., 1973, Recognition plaque Am. Soc. Surgery Hand, 1989, Recognition plaque N.Mex. Orthopaedic Assn., 1991, Recognition award for hand surgery Am. Osteo. Acad. Orthopaedics, 1982, Pioneer award Internat. Socs. for Surgery Hand, 1995, Rodey award U. N.Mex. Alumni Assn., 1997, Cornerstone award U. N.Mex. Health Scis. Ctr., 1997; recognized with Endowed Professorship U. N.Mex. Sch. Medicine, 1995; recognized with named Annual Orthop. Seminar and Alumni Day Brooke Army Med. Ctr., 1999. Fellow ACS, Am. Orthopaedic Assn. (pres. 1988-89, exec. dir. 1989-93), Am. Acad. Orthopaedic Surgeons, Assn. Orthopaedic Chmn., N.Mex. Orthopaedic Assn. (pres. 1979-81, 1999-2000), La. Orthopaedic Assn. (hon.), Korean Orthopaedic Assn. (hon.), Peru Orthopaedic Soc. (hon.), Caribbean Hand Soc., Am. Soc. Surgery Hand (pres. 1978-79), Am. Assn. Surgery of Trauma, Assn. Bone and Joint Surgeons, Assn. Mil. Surgeons US, Riordan Hand Soc.

(pres. 1967-68), Sunderland Soc. (pres. 1981-83), Soc. Mil. Orthopaedic Surgeons, Brazilian Hand Soc. (hon.), S.Am. Hand Soc. (hon.), Groupe D'Etude de la Main, Brit. Hand Soc. (hon.), Venezuela Hand Soc. (hon.), South African Hand Soc. (hon.), Western Orthopaedic Assn. (pres. 1981-82), AAAS, Russell A. Hibbs Soc. (pres. 1977-78), 38th Parallel Med. Soc. (Korea) (sec. 1959-60); mem. AMA, Phi Kappa Phi, Phi Sigma, Alpha Omega Alpha, Phi Beta Pi. Achievements include pioneer work in hand surgery. Home: 316 Big Horn Ridge Rd NE Sandia Heights Albuquerque NM 87122 Personal E-mail: geoomer@juno.com.

OMER, ROBERT WENDELL, hospital administrator; b. Salt Lake City, Feb. 10, 1948; s. Wayne Albert and Melva Bernice (Thunell) O.; m. Deborah Jackson, May 4, 1972;children: Melinda, Carmen, Creighton, Preston, Allison. BS in Biology, U. Utah, 1972; MHA, Washington U., St. Louis, 1975. V.p. St. Luke's Hosp., Cedar Rapids, Iowa, 1974-80; asst. adminstr. Franciscan Med. Ctr., Rock Island, Ill., 1980-82, Latter Day Saints Hosp., Salt Lake City, 1982-85, Clarkson Hosp., Omaha, 1985-93, v.p., COO, 1993-97; CEO Creighton St. Joseph's Clinics, Omaha, 1998-99; pres., CEO MCH Health Sys., Blair, Nebr., 1999—2001; CEO Cooper County Hosp., Boonville, Mo., 2002—03; rural health advisor U. Mo. Health Care, 2003—; CEO Pioneers Hosp., Meeker, Colo., 2003—. Bd. dirs. ARC, Heartland chpt. Omaha; bd. dirs. Nebr. Scanning Svcs. Lt. col. USAR, 1972. Fellow Am. Coll. Healthcare Execs. (regent); mem. Nebr. Hosp. Assn., Omaha C. of C. (Leadership Omaha award 1978), Omaha Healthcare Execs. Group (pres. 1989-90), Rotary (bd. dirs. 1990). Republican. Mem. Lds Ch. Avocations: jogging, history, bicycling, backpacking, racquetball. Home: PO Box 333 Meeker CO 81641

OMIDYAR, PIERRE M., Internet company executive; b. Paris, June 21, 1967; arrived in U.S., 1973; m. Pam Kerr; 3 children. BS in Computer Sci., Tufts U., 1988. With developer rels. Gen. Magic, Inc.; software developer Claris (subsidiary of Apple Computer), 1988—91; co-founder Ink Devel. Corp., 1991; founder, chmn. eBay, Inc., 1995—. Trustee Tufts U., mem. adminstrn. and finance com., mem., com. on trusteeship.; trustee Santa Fe Inst. Co-founder, chair bd. dirs. Omidyar Found., 1998—; co-founder, CEO Omidyar Network; bd. dir. Meetup.com. Recipient Light on the Hill award (with Pam Omidyar), Tufts U.; named one of World's Richest People, Forbes, 1999—2007, 50 Most Generous Philanthropists, Fortune Mag., 2005, Forbes Richest Americans, 2006. Office: eBay Inc 2125 Hamilton Ave San Jose CA 95125-5905

ONAK, THOMAS PHILIP, chemistry educator; b. Omaha, July 30, 1932; s. Louis Albert and Louise Marie (Penner) O.; m. Sharon Colleen Neal, June 18, 1954. BA, Calif. State U., San Diego, 1954; PhD, U. Calif., Berkeley, 1957. Research chemist Olin Mathieson Chem. Corp., Pasadena, Calif., 1957-59; asst. prof. Calif. State U., Los Angeles, 1959-63, assoc. prof., 1963-66, prof. chemistry, 1966-99, prof. emeritus, 1999. Author: Organoborane Chemistry, 1975; Contbr. articles to profl. jours., chpts. to books. Recipient Rsch. Career award NIH, 1973-78, Nat. award Am. Chem. Soc., 1990, Outstanding Prof. award Calif. State U., System, 1993-94; named Calif. Prof. of Yr. Carnegie Found. and Coun. for the Advancement and Support of Edn., 1995; Fulbright Rsch. fellow U. Cambridge, Eng., 1965-66. Home: 230 E Highcourte Ln Tucson AZ 85737-6859 Office: Calif State U Dept Chemistry 5151 State U Dr Los Angeles CA 90032

O'NEAL, SHAQUILLE RASHAUN, professional basketball player; b. Newark, Mar. 6, 1972; s. Philip A. Harrison and Lucille O'Neal; m. Shaunie Nelson, Dec. 26, 2002 (separated 2007); children: Shareef Rashaun, Amira Sanaa, Shaquir Rashuan, Me'arah Sanaa. BS, La. State U., Baton Rouge, 2000; MBA, U. Phoenix, 2005. Ctr. Orlando Magic, Fla., 1992—96, LA Lakers, 1996—2004, Miami Heat, Fla., 2004—08, Phoenix Suns, 2008—. Mem. US men's basketball team World Championships, Toronto, Canada, 1994, Olympic Games, Atlanta, 1996; owner, clothing line and record label TWIsM. Actor: (films) Blue Chips, 1994, Kazaam, 1996, Steel, 1997, The Wash, 2001, After the Sunset, 2004, The Year of the Yao, 2004, Scary Movie 4, 2006; performer: (albums) Shaq Diesel, 1993, Shaq Fu: Da Return, 1994, You Can't Stop the Reign, 1995, The Best of Shaquille O'Neal, 1996, Shaquille O'Neal Presents his Superfriends, Vol. 1, 2002. Res. officer Miami Beach Police Dept., Fla.; vol. Tempe Police Dept., Ariz.; res. dep. officer Bedford County Sheriff's Dept., Va., 2004—07; spl. dep., col. Maricopa County Sheriff's Dept., Ariz., 2006—08. Recipient Gold medal, men's basketball, World Championships, 1994, Atlanta Olympic Games, 1996; named 1st Team All-Am., Sporting News, 1991, 1992, NBA Rookie of Yr., 1993, NBA All-Star Game MVP, 2000, 2004, NBA All-Star Game co-MVP, 2009, NBA MVP, 2000, NBA Finals MVP, 2001, 2002; named one of 50 Greatest Players in NBA History, 1996, The Most Influential People in the World of Sports, Bus. Week, 2007, 100 Most Powerful Celebrities, Forbes.com, 2008; named to Eastern Conf. All-Star Team, NBA, 1993—96, 2005—07, Western Conf. All-Star Team, 1997, 1998, 2000—04, 2009, All-NBA 2nd Team, 1995, 1999, All-NBA 1st Team, 1998, 2000—06, NJ Hall of Fame, 2008. Achievements include being first overall pick in the NBA Draft, 1992; member of NBA Championship winning: Los Angeles Lakers, 2000-2002; Miami Heat, 2006; leading the NBA in: field goals, 1994, 1995, 1999-2001; field goal attempts, 1995; field goal percentage, 1994, 1998-2002, 2004-06; free throw attempts, 1995, 1999-2002, 2004; points, 1995, 1999, 2000; points per game, 1995, 2000. Office: Phoenix Suns 201 E Jefferson St Phoenix AZ 85004*

O'NEAL, TATUM, actress; b. LA, Nov. 5, 1963; d. Ryan and Joanna (Moore) O'N.; m. John McEnroe, Aug. 1, 1986 (div. 1994); 3 children: Kevin, Sean, Emily. Student, pvt. schs. and tutors. Appearances include (films) Paper Moon, 1973 (Acad. award for best supporting actress), The Bad News Bears, 1976, Nickelodeon, 1976, International Velvet, 1978, Little Darlings, 1979, Circle of Two, 1981, Certain Fury, 1985, Prisioners, 1981, Certain Fury, 1985, Little Noises, 1992, Basquiat, 1996, The Scoundrel's Wife, 2002, The Technical Writer, 2003; (TV movies) 15 and Getting Straight, 1989, Woman on the Run: The Lawrencia Bambenek Story, 1993 (documentary) Award Show Awards Show, 2003; TV guest appearances include: Sex and the City, 2003, Celebrities Uncensored, 2003, 8 Simple Rules...for Dating My Teenage Daughter, 2004, Law & Order Criminal Intent, 2004, Rescue Me 2006-; performer, Dancing with the Stars, 2006; author: (book) A Paper Life: My Story, 2004. Office: c/o Untitled Entertainment 1801 Century Park E Ste 700 Los Angeles CA 90067

O'NEIL, HAROLD FRANCIS, psychologist, educator; b. Columbia, SC, Jan. 26, 1943; s. Harold Francis Sr. and Margaret Mary O'Neil; m. Eva L. Baker, Sept. 15, 1984; children: Tristan, Christopher. PhD, Fla. State U., 1969; MS, Hollins Coll., 1970. Asst., assoc. prof. U. Tex., Austin, 1971-75; program mgr. Def. Advanced Rsch. Projects Agy., Arlington, Va., 1975-78; from team chief to dir. tng. rsch. lab. sr. exec. svc. Army Rsch. Inst., Alexandria, Va., 1978—85; prof. U. So. Calif., LA, 1985—. Cons. Army Rsch., 1985—, Inst. Def. Analyses, Alexandria, 1985—, Army Sci. Bd., Washington, 1994—2001, Def. Sci. Bd. Task Force on Tng., Washington, 1999—2002. Editor: (book) Academic Press Education and Technology Series, 1977—92; editl. adviser Lawrence Erlbaum Assocs., Inc., Pubs., 1992—; contbr. chapters to books, articles to profl. jours.; founding editor Japanese Jour. Edn. Fellow: APA, Am. Psychol. Soc. Achievements include research in role of cognition and affect in computer-based instruction, role of motivation in testing, cross-cultural rsch. in Japan on the role of test anxiety and performance; Taiwan and Korea on the role of self-regulation anc achievement, games for tng; development of measures for metacognition, effort, and anxiety. Office: Univ So Calif 600 Wph University Park Los Angeles CA 90089-0001 Business E-Mail: honeil@usc.edu.

O'NEIL, JERRY, state legislator; Montana State Senator, District 3, 2001-, Montana State Senate; member Bills and Journal Committee; Public Health, Welfare and Safety Committee; Highways and Transportation Committee. Republican. Mailing: 985 Walsh Rd Columbia Falls MT 59912-9044 Office Phone: 406-892-7602.

O'NEIL, MICHAEL JOSEPH, opinion survey executive, marketing research consultant; b. Springfield, Mass., June 22, 1951; s. James Francis and Mary Helen (Apolis) O'N.; children: Heather Rose, Sean Michael, Ryan Joseph, Matthew James. BA, Brown U., 1974, MA, 1975; PhD, Northwestern U., 1977. Faculty Northwestern U., 1976-77, U. Ill., Chgo., 1977, U. Mich., Ann Arbor, Mich., 1977-79, fellow Survey Rsch. Ctr., Inst. Social Rsch., 1977-79; dir. Pub. Opinion Rsch. Ctr. Ariz. State U., Tempe, Ariz., 1979-81; pres. O'Neil Assoc., Tempe, Ariz., 1981—; ptnr. Social Venture Ptnrs., 2003—. Reviewer grant proposals NSF, Washington, 1977—; mem. mktg. com. Phoenix Art Mus., 1992-96; bd. dir. Phoenix Children's Hosp. Found., vice-chmn., 1999—. Manuscript reviewer Social Problems, 1977—, Pub. Opinion Quar., 1977—, Urban Affairs Quar., 1977—, Jour. Ofcl. Statistics, 1990—, Sociological Methods and Rsch., 1993; contbr. articles to profl. jours. Chmn. Tempe Union HS Dist. Bus. Edn. adv. com., 1986-88; mem. mktg. com. Mesa Assn. Retarded Citizens, 1985-87; bd. dirs. East Valley Camelback Hosp., Mesa, 1985-90, v.p., 1988-90; bd. dirs. Valley Leadership, Ariz., 1997-99; active Acad./Ariz. Town Halls, Maricopa County Citizens' Jud. Adv. Coun.; v.p. Ariz. Coalition for Tomorrow, 1998-99, pres., 1999-2001, 06—; mem. Phoenix Pride Commn., 1991-94. Mem. Am. Mktg. Assn., Am. Assn. Pub. Opinion Rsch., Alumni Assn. Brown U. (nat. bd. dirs. 1985-90, Ariz. pres. 1984-2005), Phoenix City Club (bd. dirs. 1987-93, pres. 1990-91), East Valley Partnership (mem. bd. dirs. 1993—), Phi Beta Kappa. Independent. Avocation: tennis. Office: O'Neil Assocs 412 E Southern Ave Tempe AZ 85282-5212 Personal E-mail: mike.oneil@alumni.brown.edu. Business E-Mail: oneil@oneilresearch.com.

O'NEIL, THOMAS MICHAEL, physicist, researcher; b. Hibbing, Minn., Sept. 2, 1940; married; 1 child. BS, Calif. State U., Long Beach, 1962; MS, U. Calif., San Diego, 1964, PhD in Physics, 1965. Rsch. physicist Gen. Atomic, 1965-67; prof. physics U. Calif., San Diego, 1967—. Mem. adv. bd. Inst. Fusion Studies, 1980-83, Inst. Theoretical Physics, 1983-86; mem. plasma sci. com. NRC, 1998—, chmn., 2001—, mem. bd. on physics and astronomy, 2001—. Assoc. editor Physics Review Letters, 1979-83; correspondent Comments Plasma Physics & Controlled Fusion, 1980-84. Alfred P. Sloan fellow, 1971; recipient Disting. Alumnus award Sch. Natural Sci. CSULB, 1985, Alumni Disting. Tchg. award UCSD, 1996. Fellow Am. Phys. Soc. (award for excellence in plasma physics 1991, James Clerk Maxwell prize 1996). Achievements include research in theoretical plasma physics with emphasis on nonlinear effects in plasmas and on non-neutral plasmas.

O'NEILL, BEVERLY LEWIS, former mayor, college president; b. Long Beach, Calif., Sept. 8, 1930; d. Clarence John and Flossie Rachel (Nicholson) Lewis; m. William F. O'Neill, Dec. 21, 1952 AA, Long Beach City Coll., 1950; BA, Calif. State U., Long Beach, 1952, MA, 1956; EdD, U. So. Calif., 1977. Elem. tchr. Long Beach Unified Sch. Dist., 1952-57; instr., counsellor Compton (Calif.) Coll., 1957-60; curriculum supr. Little Lake Sch. Dist., Santa Fe Springs, Calif., 1960-62; women's advisor, campus dean Long Beach City Coll., 1962-71, dir. Continuing Edn. Ctr. for Women, 1969-75, dean student affairs, 1971-77, v.p. student svcs., 1977-88, supt.-pres., 1988—93, exec. dir. LBCC Found.; mayor City of Long Beach, Calif., 1994—2006. Mem. New Commn. Skills Am. Workforce; bd. dirs. Internat. City Bank, 2007-. Advisor Jr. League, Long Beach, 1976—, Nat. Coun. on Alcoholism, Long Beach, 1979—; bd. dirs. NCCJ, Long Beach, 1976—; Meml. Hosp. Found., Long Beach, 1984-92, Met. YMCA, Long Beach, 1986-92, United Way, Long Beach, 1986-92. Named Woman of Yr., Long Beach Human Rels. Commn., 1976, to Hall of Fame, Long Beach City Coll., 1977, Disting. Alumni of Yr., Calif. State U., Long Beach, 1985, Long Beach Woman of Yr. Rick Rackers, 1987, Assistance League Aux., 1987, Woman of Yr., Calif. Legislature 54th Dist., 1995; recipient Hannah Solomon award Nat. Coun. Jewish Women, 1984, Outstanding Colleague award Long Beach City Coll., 1985, NCCJ Humanitarian award, 1991, Woman of Excellence award YWCA, 1990, Community Svc. award Community Svcs. Devel. Corp., 1991, Citizen of Yr. award Exch. Club, 1992, Pacific Regional CEO award Assn. Community Coll. Trustees, 1992, EDDY award, 1999, Long Beach Excellence in Leadership, 1999. Mem. Assn. Calif. Community Coll. Adminstrs. (pres. 1988-90, Harry Buttimer award 1991), Calif. Community Colls. Chief Exec. Officers Assn., Rotary, Soroptomists (Women Helping Women award 1981, Hall of Fame award 1984), U.S. Conf. Mayors (trustee, 2001-, pres. 2005-06), League Calif. Cities (pres. 2002-). Democrat.

O'NEILL, BRIAN, national recreation area administrator; b. Washington, 1942; s. John and Virgina O'Neill; m. Marti Hendricks; 2 children. Student, U. Md., 1964. Joined Bur. Outdoor Recreation, Dept. Interior, 1965, mgr. Heritage Conservation and Recreation Svc. Albuquerque, 1973—81, San Francisco, 1973—81; asst. supt. Golden Gate Nat. Recreation Area, San Francisco, 1981—86, supt., 1986—; acting assoc. dir. Nat. Pk. Svc. Bd. mem. San Francisco Planning and Urban Rsch. Assn.; instr. Dale Carnegie & Assocs., 1975—77. Recipient Exec. Leadership award, Dept. of the Interior, 2004. Avocations: gardening, glasswork, sailboarding, body surfing, hiking. Office: Golden Gate Nat Rec Area Fort Mason Bldg 201 San Francisco CA 94123

O'NEILL, LAWRENCE JOSEPH, federal judge; b. Oakland, Calif., 1952; BA, U. Calif. Berkeley, 1973; MPA, Golden Gate U., 1976; JD, U. Calif. Hastings Coll. Law, 1979. Bar: Calif. 1979. Police officer, San Leandro, Calif., 1973—76; law clk. Alameda County Dist. Atty.'s Office, 1976—78, Hon. Robert Francis Kane, Calif Ct. Appeal, 1st dist., 1978—79; assoc. McCormick, Barstow, Sheppard, Wayte & Caruth, Fresno, 1979—84, ptnr., 1984—90; judge Superior Ct. (Fresno County) Calif., 1990—98, presiding judge juvenile divsn., 1992—93, presiding judge, 1996—98; magistrate judge US Dist. Ct. (Ea. dist.) Calif., 1999—2007, dist. judge, 2007—. Adj. prof. San Joaquin Coll. Law, 1986—92. Mem. adv. bd. Fresno County Sch. Dist., 1983—; life mem. Calif. Scholarship Fedn., 1970; mem. adv. bd. United Way, 1992—; exec. mem. Fresno County Suspected Child Abuse & Neglect Com., 1992—93; mem. adv. bd. YWCA, 1993—, Drug Abuse Resistance Edn. Program (D.A.R.E.), 1993—, pres., 1993—. Recipient Outstanding Young Men in Am. award, Nat. Jr. C. of C., 1979, Prof. of Yr. award, San Joaquin Coll. Law, 1992, Ann. Mentor's award, Fresno County Bar Assn. Young Lawyers, 1992, Judy Andreen-Nilson award, 1993, Achievement in Juvenile Justice award, Fresno County Juvenile Justice Commn., 1993. Mem.: Assn. Bd. Trial Advocates, State Bar Calif., Calif. Judges' Assn. (state chmn. Com. Pub. Info & Edn. 1993—94, Com. Benchguide Pub. Rev. 1993—, Bench Bar Media 1992—93). Office: US Dist Ct Ea Calif 2500 Tulane St Fresno CA 93721 Office Phone: 559-499-5682. Office Fax: 559-494-3961.

OPEL, WILLIAM, medical research administrator; BA, Pepperdine U., 1968; MBA, U. So. Calif., 1993; PhD, Claremont Grad. U., 1998. Mem. staff Pasadena Found. Med. Rsch., Calif., 1961-63, rsch. assoc., 1964-70, asst. to dir., 1970-72, adminstr., 1972-76, exec. dir., 1976-82; acting exec. dir. Huntington Inst. Applied Med. Rsch., 1978-82; exec. dir. Huntington Med. Rsch. Inst., Pasadena, Calif., 1982—. Lectr. in technology, mgmt., Pepperdine U.; adj. prof. tech. mgmt. Claremont Grad. U. Mem. Beta Gamma Sigma, Phi Kappa Phi. Office: Huntington Med Rsch Insts 734 Fairmount Ave Pasadena CA 91105-3104

OPITZ, JOHN MARIUS, clinical geneticist, pediatrician; b. Hamburg, Germany, Aug. 15, 1935; came to the U.S., 1950, naturalized, 1957; s. Friedrich and Erica Maria (Quadt) O.; m. Susan O. Lewin, Marian C. Ohden; children: Lea, Teresa, John, Chrisanthi, Felix(dec.), Emma. BA, State U. Iowa, 1956, MD, 1959; DSc (hon.), Mont. State U., 1983, Ohio State U., 2007; MD (hon.), U. Kiel, Germany, 1986, U. Bologna, Italy, 1999, U. Copenhagen. Diplomate Am. Bd. Pediat., Am. Bd. Med. Genetics. Intern State U. Iowa Hosp., 1959-60, resident in pediat., 1960-61; resident, chief resident in pediat. U. Wis. Hosp., Madison, 1961-62; fellow in pediat. and med. genetics U. Wis., 1962-64, asst. prof. med. genetics and pediat., 1964-69, assoc. prof., 1969-72, prof., 1972-79; founder dir. Wis. Clin. Genetics Ctr., 1974-79; clin. prof. med. genetics and pediat. U. Wash., Seattle, 1979—; prof. pediat., human genetics, pathology and ob-gyn. U Utah, SLC, 1997—. Adj. prof. medicine, biology, history and philosophy, vet. rsch. and vet. sci. Mont. State U., Bozeman, 1979-94, McKay lectr., 1992, univ. prof. med. humanities, 1994—; adj. prof. pediat., med. genetics U. Wis., Madison, 1979—, Class of 1947 Disting. prof., 1992; coord. Shodair Mont. Regional Genetic Svcs. Program, Helena, 1979-82; chmn. dept. med. genetics Shodair Children's Hosp., Helena, 1983-94; dir. Found. Devel. and Med. Genetics, Helena, Mont., 1994-96; pres. Heritage Genetics P.C., Helena, 1996; Farber lectr. Soc. Pediat. Pathology, 1987; Joseph Garfunkel lectr. So. Ill. U., Springfield, 1987, McKay lectr. Mont. State U., 1992; Warren Wheeler vis. prof. Columbus (Ohio) Children's Hosp., 1987, 2001; Bea Fowlow lectr. in med. genetics U. Calgary, 1996; 1st vis. prof. Hanseatic U. Found. of Lübeck, 1996; Lew Barness lectr. U. South Fla., 2001; Enid Gilbert Barness lectr. U. Wis., 2001; vis. prof. U. Cattolica del Sacro Cuore, Rome, 2001-02. Editor, author 14 books; founder, editor in chief Am. Jour. Med. Genetics, 1977-2000, emeritus assoc. editor; mng. editor European Jour. Pediat., 1977-85; contbr. numerous articles on clin. genetics. Chair Mont. Com. for Humanities, 1991. Recipient Pool of Bethesda award for excellence in mental retardation rsch. Bethesda Luth. Home, 1988, Med. Alumni citation U. Wis., 1989, Col. Harlan Sanders Lifetime Achievement award for work in field of genetic scis. March of Dimes, Purkinje medal Czech Soc. Medicine, Mendel medal Czech Soc. Med. Genetics, 1996, Internat. prize Phoenix-Anni Verdi for Genetic Rsch., 1996. Fellow AAAS, Am. Coll. Med. Genetics (founder); mem. German Acad. Scis. (Leopoldina), Am. Soc. Human Genetics, Am. Pediat. Soc., Soc. Pediat. Rsch., Am. Bd. Med. Genetics, Am. Inst. Biol. Scis., Am. Soc. Zoologists, Teratology Soc., Genetic Soc. Am., European Soc. Human Genetics, Soc. Study Social Biology, Am. Acad. Pediat., German Soc. Pediat. (hon.), Western Soc. Pediat. Rsch. (emeritus), Italian Soc. Med. Genetics (hon.), Israel Soc. Med. Genetics (hon.), Russian Soc. Med. Genetics (Hon.), So. Africa Soc. Med. Genetics (hon.), Japanese Soc. Human Genetics (hon.), Sigma Xi, German Soc. Human Genetics(honor medal), Israeli Soc. Pediat. Pathol.(hon.) Democrat. Roman Catholic. Achievements include First Evangeline Heaton lectr. in human genetics, U. Colo. Med. Ctr. Home: 2930 E Craig Dr Salt Lake City UT 84109-3636 Office: U Utah Sch Medicine 50 N Mario Capecchi Dr Salt Lake City UT 84132 E-mail: john.opitz@hsc.utah.edu.

OPPEDAHL, JOHN FREDERICK, newspaper publisher, executive; b. Duluth, Minn., Nov. 9, 1944; s. Walter H. and Lucille (Hole) Oppedahl; m. Alison Owen, 1975 (div. 1983); m. Gillian Coyro, Feb. 14, 1987 (div. 2002); 1 child, Max. BA, U. Calif., Berkeley, 1967; MS, Columbia U., 1968. Reporter San Francisco Examiner, 1967; reporter, asst. city editor Detroit Free Press, 1968-75, city editor, 1975-80, exec. city editor, 1981, exec. news editor, 1981-82, asst. mng. editor, 1983; nat. and fgn. editor Dallas Times Herald, 1983-85, asst. mng. editor, 1985-87; mng. editor/news L.A. Herald Examiner, 1987-89; mng. editor Ariz. Republic, Phoenix, 1989-93; exec. editor Phoenix Newspapers, Inc., 1993-95; pub., CEO The Republic, 1996—2000; chmn., pub., CEO San Francisco Chronicle, 2000—03. Chmn. bd. The Daily Californian. Mem.: Am. Soc. Newspaper Editors. Personal E-mail: joppedahl@yahoo.com.

OPPENHEIM, CHARLES B., lawyer; b. NYC, Oct. 18, 1962; s. Barry J. and Jean Elizabeth (Reeve) O.; m. Lydia Vitlacil, July 25, 1992; children: Calvin, Dean. BA, Cornell U., 1984; JD, Fordham U., 1988. Bar: Calif. 1988. Assoc. Skadden Arps et al., San Francisco, 1988-90, McDermott & Trayner, Pasadena, Calif., 1991-93, Weissburg and Aronson, LA, 1993-95; ptnr. Weissburg & Aronson, LA, 1996, Foley, Lardner, Weissburg & Aronson, LA, 1996, Foley & Lardner LLP, LA, 1996—2009, Hooper, Lundy & Bookman, LA, 2009—. Co-editor: Health Care Law Sourcebook, 1995-2000; contbr. articles to profl. jours. Bd. trustees The Accelerated Sch., LA, 2000—. Recipient Nat. Philanthropy Day medallion, L.A., 2001. Mem. Am.

Health Lawyers Assn., Calif. Soc. Healthcare Attys. Office: Hooper Lundy & Bookman Inc 1875 Century Pk E Ste 1600 Los Angeles CA 90067 Office Phone: 310-551-8110. Business E-Mail: coppenheim@health-law.com.

OPPENHEIM, WILLIAM L., pediatric orthopedist; b. Bangor, Maine, Jan. 4, 1945; BS in Chemistry, U. Md., Coll. Park, 1966; MD magna cum laude, Georgetown U., Washington, DC, 1970. Cert. Am. Bd. Orthop., 1980. Intern in surgery San Francisco Gen. Hosp.; resident in orthop. surgery U. Wash., Seattle; fellow Nuffield Orthop. Ctr., Oxford, England, 1977; fellow in pediatric orthopedics LA Orthop. Hosp., 1979; dir. UCLA/Orthopaedic Hosp. Ctr. Cerebral Palsy; Margaret Jones Kanaar chair, cerebral palsy UCLA Sch. Medicine, prof., chief pediatric orthopedics; cons. LA Shriner's Hosp. Mem. bd. dirs. Temple Beth Shir Shalom, Santa Monica, LA Soc. for Prevention of Cruelty to Animals, 1990—2000. Recipient White Swan award, Abilities First/Jones Kennar Found., 2000; named to America's Best Doctors, 1999, 2004. Fellow: Am. Orthop. Foot and Ankle Soc., Am. Acad. Cerebral Palsy and Devel. Medicine (mem. bd. dirs., sec., webmaster), Am. Acad. Orthop. Surgery, Am. Acad. Pediat. (mem. bd. dirs.), Pediatric Orthop. Soc. North America; mem.: Am. Orthop. Assn., State Orthop. Soc., State Med. Soc., AMA, Western Orthop. Assn. LA Chpt. (pres.). Office: UCLA Sch Medicine Rm 76-134 CHS 10833 Le Conte Los Angeles CA 90095 Office Phone: 310-206-6345. Office Fax: 310-206-0063. Business E-Mail: woppenhe@ucla.edu.

OPPENHEIMER, PETER, computer company executive; BA with honors, Calif. Polytechnic U.; MBA with honors, U. Santa Clara. Former mgr. info. tech. cons. practice Coopers and Lybrand; former CFO automatic data processing Apple Computer Inc., controller Americas, 1996—97, v.p. worldwide sales controller to corp. controller, 1997—2004; sr. v.p. fin., CFO Apple Inc. (formerly Apple Computer Inc.), 2004—. Office: Apple Inc 1 Infinite Loop Cupertino CA 95014 Office Phone: 408-996-1010.

OPPENHEIMER, RANDY (MARK RANDALL OPPENHEIMER), lawyer; b. Balt., 1952; AB summa cum laude, Harvard U., 1974; JD, U. Chgo., 1977. Bar: Calif. 1977. Ptnr., co-chair Entertainment, Sports, and Media practice O'Melveny & Myers LLP, LA. Mem.: ABA. Office: O'Melveny & Myers LLP 1999 Ave of Stars, 7th Fl Los Angeles CA 90067-6035 Office Phone: 310-246-6722. Office Fax: 310-246-6779. E-mail: roppenheimer@omm.com.

OPRI, DEBRA ANN, lawyer; b. Paterson, NJ, June 10, 1960; BFA, NYU, 1982; JD, Whittier Coll., 1987. Bar: Calif. 1989, NJ 1991, DC 1991. Founder, ptnr. Opri & Assoc., Beverly Hills, Calif., 1989—. Legal/polit. analyst and commentator 97.1 FM Talk, LA, Fox News, Inside Edition; columnist The Opri Opinion, www.debraopri.com. Author: Video Rentals and the First Sale Doctrine: The Deficiency of Proposed Legislation, 1986. Mem.: ATLA, Calif. Trial Lawyers Assn., LA Trial Lawyers Assn. Office: Opri & Associates 8383 Wilshire Blvd Ste 830 Beverly Hills CA 90211 Office Phone: 213-658-6774. Office Fax: 213-658-5160.

ORCUTT, JOHN ARTHUR, geophysicist, researcher; b. Holyoke, Colo., Aug. 29, 1943; married, 1967; 2 children. BS, U.S. Naval Acad., 1966; MSc, U. Liverpool, 1968; PhD in Earth Scis., U. Calif., San Diego, 1976. Rsch. geophysicist Scripps Inst. Oceanography, La Jolla, Calif., 1977—, assoc. prof., 1982-84, prof. geophysics, 1984—, dir. Inst. Geophysics & Planetary Physics, 1984—. Recipient Newcomb Cleveland prize AAAS, 1980, Maurice Ewing medal Am. Geophys. Union, 1994 Mem. Am. Geophys. Union, Soc. Exploration Geophysicists, Seismological Soc. Am. Office: U Calif Inst Geophys & Planetary Physics 9500 Gilman Dr La Jolla CA 92093-5004

ORDIN, ANDREA SHERIDAN, lawyer; m. Robert Ordin; 1 child, M. Victoria; stepchildren: Allison, Richard. AB, UCLA, 1962, LLB, 1965. Bar: Calif. 1966. Dep. atty. gen. Calif., 1965-72; So. Calif. legal counsel Fair Employment Practices Commn., 1972-73; asst. dist. atty. L.A. County, 1975-77; U.S. atty. Central Dist. Calif. LA, 1977-81; adj. prof. UCLA Law Sch., 1982; chief asst. atty. gen. Calif. LA, 1983-90; sr. counsel Morgan, Lewis & Bockius, LA, 1993—. Mem. L.A. County Bar Assn. (past pres., past exec. dir.). Office: Morgan Lewis & Bockius 300 S Grand Ave Ste 2200 Los Angeles CA 90071-3109 Office Phone: 213-612-1090. Business E-Mail: aordin@morganlewis.com.

O'REILLY, DAVID J., oil industry executive; b. Dublin, Jan. 1947; BS ChemE, University Coll., Dublin, 1968, D (hon.) of Sci., 2002. Process engineer Chevron Corp., 1968—71, process engineer, operating assist., 1971—75, adviser, foreign operations, 1976—78, planning mgr., chemical div., 1979, mgr. agricultural chem., 1980—82, mgr. Salt Lake Refinery, 1983—85; mgr. manufacturing Chevron Chemical Co., 1985; gen. mgr. El Segundo Refinery, 1986—88; sr. v.p. Chevron Chemical Corp., 1989—90; v.p. Chevron Corp., 1991—94; pres. Chevron Products Co., San Francisco, 1994—98; dir., vice-chmn. Chevron Corp., San Francisco, 1998—2000, chmn. bd. dirs., CEO, 2000—01; CEO, chmn. ChevronTexaco Corp. (now Chevron Corp.), San Francisco, 2001—. Bd. govs. San Francisco Symphony, Bay Area Coun. Mem.: Am. Soc. Corp. Execs., Bus. Coun., Nat. Petroleum Coun., Am. Petroleum Inst. (treas., bd. dirs.). Office: Chevron Corp 6001 Bollinger Canyon Rd San Ramon CA 94583-2324*

O'REILLY, PATRICK JAMES, public relations executive; b. Riverside, Calif., Oct. 4, 1965; s. Patrick Gerard and Anne Mary (Caslin) O'R. BA in Internat. Rels., U. So. Calif., 1989. Account exec. Geogeson & Co., NYC, L.A., 1987-89; rsch. analyst Rep. Nat. Com., Washington, 1989; campaign mgr. Riverside (Calif.) County Supr. Norton Younglove Election, 1989-90; sr. account exec. Stoorza, Ziegaus & Metzger, Riverside, 1990—2001; pres. O'Reilly Pub. Rels., 2001—. Guest speaker in field. Republican. Roman Catholic. Office: O'Reilly Pub Rels 3403 10th St 110 Riverside CA 92501

O'REILLY, THOMAS EUGENE, retired human resources consultant; b. Wichita, Kans., Sept. 7, 1932; s. Eugene William and Florence Irene (Gustner) O'R.; m. Lorraine Bryant, Feb. 9, 1957; children: Thomas Jr., Patricia, Susan, Gregory, Pamela. BA, Iona Coll., 1954; MBA, NYU, 1958. Mem. human resources staff Chase Manhattan Bank, NYC, 1957-69, dir. employee rels., 1969-71, mgr. internat. personnel, 1971-75, dir. internal staffing, 1976-77, dir. mgmt. resources, 1978-80, dir. exec. resources NYC, 1980-87; v.p., sr. cons. Lee Hecht Harrison, Inc., NYC, 1988-93; ret. Spl. agt. counter-intelligence corps, U.S. Army, 1954-57. Mem. Nat. Fgn. Trade Coun., Exec. Issues Forum, Ariz. State Horseman's Assn. (1st v.p.). Republican. Roman Catholic. Home: 6200 E Cielo Run N Cave Creek AZ 85331-7645

O'REILLY, TIM, computer book publishing company executive, open sourcer advocate; b. Cork, Ireland, 1954; BA in Classics (cum laude, Harvard Coll., 1975. Founder, pres. O'Reilly & Associates (now called O'Reilly Media, Inc.), Sebastopol, Calif., 1978—. Former bd. dir. Macromedia; bd. dir. CollabNet; spkr. in field. Co-author UNIX Text Processing (with Dale Dougherty and Howard Sams), 1987, (with Grace Todino) Managing UUCP and USENET, (with Valerie Quercia) The X Window System Users' Guide, (with Adrian Nye) The X Toolkit Intrinsics Programming Manual, (with Jerry Peek and Mike Loukides) UNIX Power Tools, (with Troy Mott) Windows 98 in a Nutshell; editor, (with O'Reilly & Associates) major contbr. in the development of many of other titles, including UNIX in a Nutshell, Programming Perl, Sendmail, Essential System Administration, and The Cathedral and the Bazaar; O'Reilly Media Inc. published The Whole Internet User's Guide & Catalog (First popular book about the internet, selected by NY Pub. Libr. as one of the most signicant books of the 20th Century), 1992; introduced Safari Books Online (first web-native svc. for online book content), 2000; writer (web blog) radar.oreilly.com Recipient Industry Achievement award for advocacy on behalf of the open source community, InfoWorld, 1998; named one of 50 Who Matter Now, CNNMoney.com Bus. 2.0, 2006, 2007, 50 Most Important People on the Web, PC World, 2007. Mem.: Electronic Frontier Found. (bd. trustee), Internet Soc. (bd. trustee). Achievements include O'Reilly's Global Network Navigator site (GNN, sold to American Online in 1995) was the first web portal and the first true commerical site on the World Wide Web in 1993. Office: O Reilly Media Inc 1005 Gravenstein Hwy N Sebastopol CA 95472-2811 Office Phone: 707-827-7000. Office Fax: 707-829-0104.

ORESKES, NAOMI, science historian; b. NYC, Nov. 25, 1958; d. Irwin Oreskes and Susan Eileen Nagin Oreskes; m. Kenneth Belitz, Sept. 28, 1986; children: Hannah Oreskes Belitz, Clara Oreskes Belitz. BSc with honors, Imperial Coll., London, 1981; PhD, Stanford U., 1990. Geologist We. Mining Corp., Adelaide, Australia, 1981—84; rsch. and tng. asst. Stanford U., Calif., 1984—89; vis. asst. prof. Dartmouth Coll., Hanover, NH, 1990—91, asst. prof., 1991—96; assoc. prof. Gallatin Sch. NYU, 1996—98, U. Calif., San Diego, 1998—2005, prof., 2005—, provost, sixth coll., 2008—. Consulting geologist Western Mining Corp., 1984-90; consulting historian Am. Inst. Physics, N.Y.C., 1990-96. Author: The Rejection of Continental Drift, 1999, Theory and Method in American Earth Science, 1999; editor: Plate Tectonics: An Insider's History of the Modern Theory of the Earth, 2001; contbr. articles to profl. jours. Recipient Lindgren prize Soc. Econ. Geologists, 1993, Young Investigator award NSF, 1994-99, George Sarton Lectr. award AAAS, 2004; fellow NEH, 1993. Mem. Geol. Soc. Am., History Sci. Soc., History Earth Scis. Soc. (pres.). Jewish. Office: Univ Calif San Diego Sixth Coll 9500 Gilman Dr La Jolla CA 92093-0054 Office Phone: 858-822-5951. Business E-Mail: noreskes@ucsd.edu.

ORFALEA, PAUL JAMES, investment company executive, former printing company executive; b. L.A., Nov. 28, 1947; s. Al and Virginia Orfalea; m. Natalie Orfalea; children: Mason, Keenan. BS in Fin., U. So. Calif., 1971; LLD (hon.), Babson Coll., Mass., 2004; Ph.D (hon.), Lebanese Am. U., 2006, Cal Poly U., 2007. Founder, CEO, chmn. Kinko's, Santa Barbara, Calif., 1970—2000, chmn. emeritus, 2000—04; co-founder West Coast Asset Mgmt., Ventura, Calif., 2000—. Co-founder The Orfalea Foundations, Santa Barbara, Calif., 2000—; lectr. Univ. So. Calif., Univ. Calif., Davis, Santa Barbara; adv. bd. Stone Canyon Venture Ptnrs. LP; bd. dirs. Espresso Royale, DataProse. Co-author (with Ann Marsh): Copy This: Lessons from a Hyperactive Dyslexic Who Turned a Bright Idea into One of America's Best Companies, 2005; co-author: (with Lance Helfert, Atticus Lowe, & Dean Zatkowsky) The Entrepreneurial Investor: The Art, Science and Business of Value Investing, 2007. Bd. trustee Univ. Calif. Santa Barbara Found. Recipient Entrepreneur of Yr. award, Univ. So. Calif. Marshall Sch. Bus., 1998, Philanthropist of Yr., 2000, Conrad Hilton Entrepreneur award, 2001, Friend of Calif. Cmty. Colleges, 2003, R.O.S.E. award, Univ. So. Calif., 2003, Hello Friend award, Ennis William Cosby Found., 2003, Lifetime Achievement award, Santa Barbara News Press, 2005, Beta Gamma Sigma Medallion for Entrepreneurship, Sally award, Salvation Army, Ellis Island Medal of Honor; named Lifetime Philanthropist of Yr., Assn. Funding Professionals, 2005; named to CEO Hall of Fame. Office: The Orfalea Foundations 1283 Coast Village Cir Santa Barbara CA 93108 also: West Coast Asset Mgmt Ste 1000 1205 Coast Village Rd Santa Barbara CA 93108-2718 Office Phone: 805-653-5333. Office Fax: 805-648-6466.

ORFORD, ROBERT RAYMOND, physician, consultant; b. Winnipeg, Manitoba, Can., Apr. 18, 1948; came to U.S., 1988; s. Robert Raymond and Sarah Gloria L. (Gullden) O.; m. Dale Laura Stuart, June 2, 1972; children: Carolyn Tiffany, Andrew Craig, Loren Brent. BS, McGill U., 1969, MD, 1971; MS, U. Minn., 1975; MPH, U. Wash., 1976. Assoc. prof. cmty. medicine U. Alberta, Edmonton, Can., 1976-88; dir. med. svcs. Govt. of Alberta, Edmonton, Can., 1979-81, exec. dir. occupational health svcs., 1981-85, deputy min. cmty. occupational health, 1985-88; med. dir. employee health U. Alberta Hosp., Edmonton, Can., 1988; sr. assoc. cons. Mayo Clinic, Rochester, Minn., 1988-91, cons. preventive medicine, 1991-96, Scottsdale, Ariz., 1996—. Asst. prof. Mayo Med. Sch., Rochester, 1988—; mem. Alberta Energy Resource Conservation Bd., 1988-89; chmn. divsn. preventive and occupl. medicine, dir. exec. health program, Mayo Clinic, Scottsdale, 1999-2007, cons. exec. health program, 2008—. Contbr. articles to profl. jours. Mem. Olmsted County Environ. Commn., Rochester, 1991-96, chair, 1994. Govt. of Can. Nat. Health fellow, 1975-76. Fellow Royal Coll. Physicians and Surgeons Can., Am. Coll. Occupational and Environ. Medicine (pres. 2008-), Am. Coll. Preventive Medicine, Aerospace Med. Assn.; mem. Internat. Commn. Occupational Health Medicine (nat. sec. 2001—). Presbyterian. Avocations: languages, fitness, travel. Home: 15516 E Acacia Way Fountain Hills AZ 85268-3158 Office: Mayo Clinic Scottsdale Divsn Preventive Medicine 13400 E Shea Blvd Scottsdale AZ 85259-5499 Office Phone: 480-301-7379. Office Fax: 480-301-7569. Business E-Mail: rorford@mayo.edu.

ORGEL, STEPHEN KITAY, language educator; b. NYC, Apr. 11, 1933; s. Samuel Zachary and Esther (Kitay) O. AB, Columbia, 1954; PhD (Woodrow Wilson fellow), Harvard, 1959. Instr. in English Harvard, Cambridge, Mass., 1959-60; asst. prof. U. Calif., Berkeley, 1960-66, asso. prof., 1966-72, prof., 1972-76, Johns Hopkins U., Balt., 1976-82, Sir William Osler prof., 1982-85; Jackson Eli Reynolds prof. humanities Stanford (Calif.) U., 1987—. Bd. suprs. English Inst., 1974-77, chmn., 1976-77 Author: The Jonsonian Masque, 1965, (with Roy Strong) Inigo Jones, 1973, The Illusion of Power, 1975, Impersonations, 1996, The Authentic Shakespeare, 2002, Imagining Shakespeare, 2003; editor: Ben Jonson's Masques, 1969, Marlowe's Poems and Translations, 1971, The Renaissance Imagination, 1975, (with Guy Lytle) Patronage in the Renaissance, 1981, The Tempest, 1987, (with Jonathan Goldberg) John Milton, 1991; editor-in-chief: English Literary History, 1981-85. Am. Council Learned Socs. fellow, 1968, 73; NEH sr. fellow, 1982-83, 93-94, Guggenheim fellow, 2000-01; Getty scholar, 1986-87. Mem. Am. Acad. Arts and Scis., Modern Lang. Assn., Renaissance Soc. Am., Shakespeare Assn. Am. Office: Stanford U English Dept Stanford CA 94305

ORIANS, GORDON HOWELL, biology professor; b. Eau Claire, Wis., July 10, 1932; s. Howard Lester and Marion Meta (Senty) O.; m. Elizabeth Ann Newton, June 25, 1955; children: Carlyn Elizabeth, Kristin Jean, Colin Mark. BS, U. Wis., 1954; PhD, U. Calif., Berkeley, 1960. Asst. prof. zoology U. Wash., Seattle, 1960-64, assoc. prof., 1964-68, prof., 1968-95, prof. emeritus, 1995—. Active Wash. State Ecol. Commn., Olympia, 1970-75, ecology adv. com. EPA, Washington, 1974-79; assembly life scis. NAS/NRC, Washington, 1977-83, environ. studies and toxicology bd., 1991—2003. Author: Some Adaptations of Marsh Nesting Blackbirds, 1980, Blackbirds of the Americas, 1985, Life: The Science of Biology, 2003; editor: Biodiversity and Ecosystem Processes in Tropical Forests, 1996. 1st lt. U.S. Army, 1955-56. Mem. AAAS, NAS, Am. Inst. Biol. Scis. (Disting. Svc. award 1994), Am. Ornithologists Union (Brewster award 1976), Am. Soc. Naturalists, Animal Behavior Soc., Royal Netherlands Acad. Arts and Scis., Orgn. for Tropical Studies (pres. 1988-94), Ecol. Soc. Am. (v.p. 1975-76, pres. 1995-96, Eminent Ecologist award 1998). Avocations: hiking, opera. Office: U Wash Dept Biology PO Box 351800 Seattle WA 98195-1800 Home Phone: 206-364-5743. E-mail: blackbrd@serv.net.

ORMAN, JOHN LEO, software engineer, writer; b. San Antonio, Mar. 19, 1949; s. Alton Woodlee and Isabel Joan (Paproski) O. BS in Physics, N.Mex. Inst. Mining & Tech., 1971, BS Math., MS Physics, 1974. Rsch. asst. N.Mex. Inst. Mining & Tech., Socorro, 1967-74; computer programmer State of N.Mex., Santa Fe, 1974-76; computer analyst Dikewood Corp., Albuquerque, 1976-83; nuclear engr. Sandia Nat. Labs., Albuquerque, 1983-88, software engr., 1988—. Author numerous poems. NSF fellow, 1971-74; recipient 2d place award N.Mex. State Postry Soc., 1987. Mem. IEEE Computer Soc., Am. Assn. Physics Tchrs., Assn. for Computing Machinery, Nat. Writer's Club (poetry award 1987), Southwest Writers Workshop (3d place award non-fiction 1987), N.Mex. Mountain Club. Avocations: photography, travel, skiing, hiking, tennis. Home and Office: 9125 Copper Ave NE Apt 609 Albuquerque NM 87123-1071 Office: Sandia Nat Labs MS 0974 PO Box 5800 Albuquerque NM 87185-0100 Personal E-mail: john.orman@att.net.

ORMASA, JOHN, retired utilities executive; b. Richmond, Calif., May 30, 1925; s. Juan Hormaza and Maria Inocencia Olondo; m. Dorothy Helen Trmble, Feb. 17, 1952; children: Newton Lee, John Trumble, Nancy Jean Davies. BA, U. Calif., Berkeley, 1948; JD, Harvard U., Cambridge, Mass., 1951. Bar: Calif. 1952, US Supreme Ct. 1959. Assoc. Clifford C. Anglim, 1951—52, Richmond, Carlson, Collins, Gordon & Bold, 1952—56, ptnr., 1956—59; v.p. sys. gen. counsel Pacific Lighting Svc. Co., LA, 1966—72; gen. atty., v.p., gen. counsel So. Calif. Gas Co., LA, 1959—66; v.p. gen. counsel Pacific Lighting Corp., LA, 1973—75, v.p., sec., gen. counsel, 1975; ret., 1975. Acting city atty. El Cerrito, Calif., 1952. With USN, 1943—46. Mem.: ABA, Richmond Bar Assn. (pres. 1959), Calif. State Bar Assn., Kiwanis (v.p. 1959). Republican. Roman Catholic.

ORME, ANTONY RONALD, geography educator; b. Weston-Super-Mare, Somerset, Eng., May 28, 1936; came to U.S., 1968; s. Ronald Albert and Anne (Parry) O.; m. Amalie Jo Brown, Nov. 18, 1984; children: Mark Antony, Kevin Ronald, Devon Anne. BA with 1st class honors, U. Birmingham, 1957, PhD, 1961. Lectr. Univ. Coll., Dublin, Ireland, 1960-68; mem. faculty UCLA, 1968—, prof. geography, 1973—, dean social scis., 1977-83. Cons. in field. Editor-in-chief Phys. Geography. Recipient Award of Merit Am. Inst. Planners, 1975, Outstanding Svc. award USAF, 1977-80, Founders' medal Brit. Soc. for Geomorphology Mem. Geol. Soc. Am., Assn. Am. Geographers (Disting. Career award), Assn. Geography Tchrs. Ireland (pres. 1964-68), Inst. Brit. Geographers, Internat. Geog. Union. Home: 5128 Del Moreno Dr Woodland Hills CA 91364-2426 Office: UCLA Dept Geography Los Angeles CA 90095-1524 Business E-Mail: orme@geog.ucla.edu.

ORMES, JONATHAN FAIRFIELD, astrophysicist, researcher, educator; b. Colorado Springs, Colo., July 18, 1939; s. Robert Manly and Suzanne (Viertel) O.; m. Karen Lee Minnick, Dec. 26, 1960 (div.); 1 child, Laurie Kylee; m. Janet Carolyn Dahl, Sept. 12, 1964; children: Marina, Nicholas. BS, Stanford U., 1961; PhD, U. Minn., 1967. NRC assoc. Goddard Space Flight Ctr., NASA, Greenbelt, Md., 1967-69, astrophysicist, 1969, head cosmic radiations br., 1981-82, head nuclear astrophysics br., 1983-87, assoc. chief lab. for high energy astrophysics, 1987-90, chief lab. for high energy astrophysics, 1990-2000, project sci. for gamma ray astronomy obs., 1998—2004, dir. space scis., 2000—04; rsch. prof. U. Denver, 2004—; dir. Denver Rsch. Inst., 2005—. Acting head high energy astrophysics NASA hdqrs., Washington, 1982-83, mem. high energy astrophysics mgmt. ops. working group, 1975-83, cosmic ray program working group, 1984-91; com. on space and solar physics, com. on cosmic ray physics Nat. Acad. Sci., Washington, 1991-94; adj. prof. U. Md. Balt., 2000-, U. Utah, 2001—. Editor: Essays in Space Science, 1987; assoc. editor astrophysics Phys. Rev. Letters, 1991-93; contbr. Astrophysics Jour., Phys. Rev. Letters, Astronomy and Astrophysics. Trustee Paint Br. Unitarian Universalist Ch., Adelphi, Md., 1987-88, chair bd. trustees, 1989, numerous positions, 1972—. Recipient Meritorious Exec. Award (presdl. rank), 2001. Fellow: Am. Phys. Soc. (various divsn. offices); mem.: Am. Geophys. Union, Am. Astron. Soc. (sec.-treas. High Energy Astrophysics divsn. 1985—87), Internat. Astron. Union. Achievements include discovery of unusual isotopic abundance of Ne in galactic cosmic rays; research on composition and energy spectra of cosmic rays, antiprotons and gamma rays from the Milky Way galaxy. Office: U Denver Dept Physics & Astronomy Denver CO 80208-0001 Office Phone: 303-871-3552. Business E-Mail: jonathan.ormes@du.edu.

ORMOND, JULIA, actress; b. Surrey, Eng., Jan. 4, 1965; m. Rory Edwards, Apr. 1989 (div. 1994); m. Jon Rubin, 1999 (separated, 2007); 1 child, Sophie Grad., Webber Douglas Acad. Drama Art,

1988; attended, West Surrey Coll. Art and Design. Founder prodn. co. Indican. Actress: (films) The Baby of Macon, 1992, Legends of the Fall, 1994, Nostradamus, 1994, Captives, 1994, First Knight, 1995, Sabrina, 1995, Smilla's Sense of Snow, 1997, Sibirsky Tsiryulnik, 1998, The Prime Gig, 2000, Resistance, 2003, Inland Empire, 2006, The Way, 2006, I Know Who Killed Me, 2007, Kit Kittredge: An American Girl, 2008, The Curious Case of Benjamin Button, 2008; (TV movies) Young Catherine, 1991, Stalin, 1992, (voice only) Animal Farm, 1999, Varian's War, 2001, Iron Jawed Angels, 2004; (TV mini-series) Traffik, 1990, Beach Girls, 2005; (TV appearances) Ruth Rendall Mysteries, 1990; stage appearances include Faith, Hope and Charity, 1989 (London Critics best newcomer award); prodr.: Calling the Ghosts, 1996. Recipient Female Star of Tomorrow award Sho West Awards, 1995. Office: Endeavor Talent Agy 9601 Wilshire Blvd 10th Fl Beverly Hills CA 90210

ORMSBY, MICHAEL CHARLES, lawyer; b. Spokane, Wash., Jan. 6, 1957; m. Jeanette K. Ormsby, Oct. 6, 1979; children: Allison, Tyler, Zachary, Erin. BA, Gonzaga U., 1979, JD, 1981. Bar: Wash. 1981, Idaho 1990. From assoc. to prin. Lukins & Annis, PS, Spokane, 1981-88; ptnr. Preston, Gates & Ellis LLP, Spokane, Wash., Coeur d'Alene, Idaho, 1988—. Bd. dirs. United Way of Spokane, 1988—, Citizen League of Spokane, 1989; mem. City of Spokane Planning Commn., 1979; chair state adv. com. Wash. Dept. Social Svcs., Olympia, 1988—; bd. trustees Ea. Wash. U., Spokane, 1985-2002. Harry S. Truman fellow, 1977. Mem.: Spokane County Bar Assn. (chair, pro bono project 1984—88, bd. trustees 1988—92, pres. 1991—92). Home: 3620 S Ridgeview Dr Spokane WA 99206-9535 Office: Ste 315 1200 Ironwood Dr Coeur D' Alene ID 83814-2260 also: Preston Gates Ellis Llp 618 W Riverside Ave Ste 300 Spokane WA 99201-5102 Office Phone: 509-241-1507. Office Fax: 509-444-7868. E-mail: mormsby@prestongates.com.

ORNSTEIN, DONALD SAMUEL, mathematician, educator; b. NYC, July 30, 1934; s. Harry and Rose (Wisner) O.; m. Shari Richman, Dec. 20, 1964; children— David, Kara, Ethan. Student, Swarthmore Coll., 1950-52; PhD, U. Chgo., 1957. Fellow Inst. for Advanced Study, Princeton, N.J., 1955-57; faculty U. Wis., Madison, 1958-60, Stanford (Calif.) U., 1959—, prof. math., 1966—. Faculty Hebrew U., Jerusalem, 1975-76 Author: Ergodic Theory Randomness and Dynamical Systems, 1974. Recipient Bocher prize Am. Math. Soc., 1974 Mem. NAS, Am. Acad. Arts and Sci. Jewish. Office: Stanford U Dept Math Stanford CA 94305

OROPEZA, JENNY, state legislator; b. Montebello, Calif., Sept. 27, 1957; m Tom Mullins, 1977. BS in Bus. Adminstrn., Calif. State U., Long Beach. California State Assemblywoman, District 55, 2000-2006, co-vchmn, Select Committee on Title IV, chairman, Budget Committee, Transportation Jobs, Econ Develop & Economy Committees, vice chairman Joint Committee Legislature Budget, Transportation, Agriculture & Governor Org Committee, spec liaison to ofcl foreign visitors, Association Comn on Structural Challenges to Budgeting in California, formerly, California State Assembly; member, Long Beach City Coun, 94-2000; California State Senator, District 28, 2006-, Dem. caucus chair, currently. Member Long Beach Unified Sch District Bd Education, 88-94; Trustee, California State Univ Sys. Legislator of the Year, League of California City's Latino Caucus, 2005; Smith-Weiss Environ Champion Award, Los Angeles League of Conservation Voters, 2006. Democrat. Office: Dist 28 2512 Artesia Blvd Ste 200 Redondo Beach CA 90278 Office Phone: 310-318-6994. Office Fax: 310-318-6733. Business E-Mail: Senator.Oropeza@senate.ca.gov.*

O'ROURKE, C. LARRY, lawyer; b. Colusa, Calif., Dec. 10, 1937; s. James Harold and Elizabeth Janice (Jenkins) O'R.; m. Joy Marie Phillips, May 22, 1965; children: Ryan, Paula, Alina. BSEE, Stanford U., 1959, MBA, 1961; JD, George Washington U., 1972. Bar: Va. 1971, D.C. 1974, Calif. 2002, U.S. Ct. Appeals (fed. cir.) 1973, U.S. Patent and Trademark Office 1971, U.S. Supreme Ct. Patent atty. Westinghouse Elec., Washington, 1969-70, Pitts., 1970-73; assoc. Finnegan, Henderson, Farabow, Garrett & Dunner, Washington, 1974-79, ptnr., 1979—, mng. ptnr. Palo Alto, Calif. Dir. Zest Inc., Md., 1988, chmn. bd. dirs., 1990-95; mem. George Washington Law Sch. I.P. adv. coun., mem. bd. dirs. Stanford Bus. Sch. Alumni and mem. devel. coun. Stanford GSB. Mem. ABA, Am. Intellectual Property Law Assn., Inter-Pacific Bar Assn. Democrat. Presbyterian. Home Phone: 650-462-1889; Office Phone: 650-849-6640.

ORR, ETHAN, non-profit organization executive; b. 1974; BA in Hist., U. Ariz., BA in Polit. Sci., MPA. Empowerment Zone adminstr. Office of Econ. Devel., Tucson; coun. aid City of Tucson City Coun.; exec. dir. Linkages Inc. Adj. faculty Polit. Sci. dept., U. Ariz., Bus. dept., Pima Cmty. Coll.; faculty mentor Flinn Found. of Ariz. Mem. Faith Christian Ch. Make A Difference Day projects; mem Ariz. Joint Legis. Com. on Homelessness; mem. Fred G. Acosta Cmty. Rels. Coun. Named one of 40 Under 40, Tucson Bus. Edge, 2006. Mem.: Southern Ariz. Job Developers Assn. (co-chair). Office: Linkages Inc Goodwill Bldg Ste 201 1920 E Silverlake Rd Tucson AZ 85710 Office Phone: 520-571-8600.

ORR, FRANKLIN MATTES, JR., petroleum engineering educator; b. Baytown, Tex., Dec. 27, 1946; s. Franklin Mattes and Selwyn Sage (Huddleston) O.; m. Susan Packard, Aug. 30, 1970; children: David, Katherine. BSChemE, Stanford U., Calif., 1969; PhD in Chem. Engring., U. Minn., 1976; DEng (hon.), Heriot-Watt U., Edinburgh, Scotland, 2005. Asst. to dir. Office Fed. Activities EPA, Washington, 1970-72; rsch. engr. Bellaire Rsch. Ctr. Shell Devel. Co., Houston, 1976—77; head miscible flooding and gas injection N.Mex Petroleum Recovery Rsch. Ctr. N.Mex Inst. Mining and Tech., Socorro, 1978-84; assoc. prof. petroleum engring. Stanford U., Calif., 1985-87, prof., 1987—, prof. chem. engring., 1994—, Keleen and Carlton Beal prof. petroleum engring., 1994—; dir. Global Climate and Energy Project, 2002—. Bd. dirs. Monterey Bay Aquarium Rsch. Inst., 1987—, Am. Geol. Inst. Found., 1997—2002, David and Lucile Packard Found., 1999—; interim dean Stanford U. Sch. Earth Scis., 1994—95, dean, 1995—2002; mem. adv. bd. Princeton U. Carbon Mitigation Initiative, 2004—; sr. fellow Ctr. Environ. Sci. and Policy Stanford U. Inst. Internat. Studies, 2005—; mem. com. to visit Earth and planetary scis. Harvard U., 2006—. Contbr. articles to profl. jours. Bd. dirs. Wolf Trap Found. for Performing Arts, 1988-94 Recipient Robert Earll McConnell award, AIME, 2001. Mem.: Soc. Indsl. and Applied Math., Soc. Petroleum Engrs. (Disting. Lectr. award 1988—89, Disting. Achievement award, Petroleum Engring. Faculty 1993), AAAS, AIChE, NAE. Office: Stanford U Dept Petroleum Engring 074 Green Earth Scis Bldg 367 Panama Str Stanford CA 94305-2220 Home Phone: 650-853-3066. E-mail: fmorr@pangea.stanford.edu.

ORR, RONALD STEWART, lawyer; b. LA, Nov. 19, 1946; s. Ashley S. and Nancy (McKenna) O.; divorced; children: Justin, Hailey. BSEE, Leland Sanford Jr. U., 1968; JD, U. So. Calif., 1972, MBA, 1987. Bar: Calif. 1973, U.S. Dist. Ct. (so. dist.) Calif. 1973, U.S. Ct. Appeals (2nd, 3rd, 5th and 9th cirs.) 1974, U.S. Supreme Ct. 1983. Mem. tech. staff Hughes Aircraft Co., LA, 1968-72; ptnr. Shutan and Trost, LA, 1972-80, Gibson, Dunn and Crutcher, LA, 1980-97, Ron Orr & Profls., Inc., Marina Del Rey, Calif., 1997—. Commr. Calif. Law Revison Commn., 1998-99, Co-author: Secured Creditors Under the New Bankruptcy Code, 1979, Entertainment Contracts, 1986. Trustee U. So. Calif., L.A., 1986-91; exec. com. Nancy Reagan Ctr., L.A., 1988-89; chmn. Firestone for Lt. Gov. and Firestone for Congress, 1996-98. Mem. U. So. Calif. Alumni Assn. (bd. dirs. 1984-89), Order of Coif. Office: 520 Washington Blvd # 389 Marina Del Rey CA 90292-5442 Fax: 310 301-6549. E-mail: RonOrrEsq@aol.com.

ORRIS, DONALD C., freight transportation executive; BA, BS, Denver Univ. With Denver & Rio Grande We. Railroad; exec. positions, including pres., stacktrain and intermodal mktg. bus. APL; pres., COO So. Pacific R.R. (merged with Union Pacific R.R.); chmn., CEO Pacer Internat., Concord, Calif., 1997—2006. Named an Intermodal Founding Father, Univ. Denver Intermodal Transp. Inst. Office: Pacer Internat 2300 Clayton Rd Concord CA 94520 Office Phone: 887-917-2237.

ORSATTI, ALFRED KENDALL, organization executive; b. LA, Jan. 31, 1932; s. Alfredo and Margaret (Hayes) O.; m. Patricia Decker, Sept. 11, 1960; children: Scott, Christopher, Sean. BS, U. So. Calif., 1956. Assoc. prodr., v.p. Sabre Prodns., LA, 1957-58; assoc. prodr. Ror Vic Prodns., LA, 1958-59; bus. rep. AFTRA, LA, 1960-61; Hollywood exec., sec. SAG, LA, 1961-81, nat. exec. dir., 1981—, trustee Pension Welfare Plan, 1971—. Del. Los Angeles County Fedn. Labor, Los Angeles, Hollywood Film Council, Los Angeles; v.p., mem. exec. Calif. Fedn. Labor; pres. Calif. Theatrical Fedn.; chmn. arts, entertainment and media com. dept. profl. employees AFL-CIO Mem. Mayor's Film Devel. Com., Los Angeles. Mem. Actors and Artists Am. Assn. (1st v.p.) Office: SAG 5757 Wilshire Blvd Los Angeles CA 90036-3635

ORTIZ, DEBORAH V., state legislator; b. Sacramento, Mar. 19, 1957; Student, U. Calif., Davis, 1975-81; JD, U. of the Pacific, 1987. Mem. Calif. State Assembly, 1996-98, chair select com. on taxpayer's rights; mem. Calif. State Senate, 1998—. Mem. Sacramento City Coun., 1993-96; chair ad hoc com. Neighborhood Svcs. Dept., 1993. Recipent Sacramento Housing Alliance award. Democrat. Roman Catholic. Office: State Capital Rm 4032 Sacramento CA 95814 also: 1020 N St Ste 576 Sacramento CA 95814-5606 Home: 1020 N St Ste 576 Sacramento CA 95814-5664

ORTIZ, JOHN MICHAEL, provost; BS, U. N.Mex., 1970, MA, 1971; PhD, U. N.C., 1981. Spl. edn. tchr., Albuquerque, 1969-72; instr. Appalachian State U., Boone, N.C., 1972, asst. prof. dept. spl. edn., 1972-75, assoc. prof. grad. faculty dept. spl. edn., 1976-81, interim dept. chair, prof. grad. faculty, 1982-83, dept. chair, prof. grad. faculty, 1983-85, dir. Office Extension Instrn., prof. lang., 1985-90; prof. spl. edn., dean continuing edn., dir. summer sch. U. Southern Colo., 1990-93, assoc. provost, prof. spl. edn., 1993-95, interim provost, prof. spl. edn., 1995-96; assoc. provost, prof. spl. edn. Calif. State U., Fresno, 1996-97, provost, v.p. acad. affairs ad interim, prof. spl. edn., 1997-99, provost, v.p. acad. affairs, 1999—2003; pres. Calif. State Poly. U., Pomona, 2003—. Cons., evaluator North Ctrl. Assn. of Colls. and Schs., 1995-97; pres. N.C. Fedn. of the Coun. for Exceptional Children, 1984-85, state advisor 1979-80; spl. advisor Pres. Com. on Mental Retardation; presenter in field. Contbr. articles to profl. publs. Recipient numerous grants. Mem. ASCD, Am. Assn. of Higher Edn., Nat. U. Continuing Edn. Assn., Am. Assn. for Adult and Continuing Edn., Assn. of the Severely Handicapped, Coun. for Exceptional Children. Office: Calif State U 5241 N Maple Ave MSTA 54 Fresno CA 93740-0001 Fax: 559-278-7987.

ORTIZ, PABLO, composer; b. Buenos Aires; Grad., Cath. U. Argentina; Masters in music composition, PhD in music composition, Columbia U. Co-dir Electronic Music Studio, prof. composition U. Pitts., 1990—94; prof. music U. Calif. Davis, 1994—. Composer: numerous instrumental and vocal works, (plays) Dance of Death, 1983, El Campo, 1984, El sol naciente, 1984, (films) Gracias por el fuego, 1984, My Sin Was To Love You, 1988, (Operas) Parodia, 1997, Una voz en el viento, 1998. Recipient ASCAP award, 1994, Acad. award, AAAL, 2008; fellow Wellesley Composers Conf., 1986, Guggenheim Found., 1993; Charles Ives fellow, AAAL, 1996. Office: UC Davis Dept Music 1 Shields Ave Davis CA 95616 Office Phone: 530-752-7509. E-mail: pvortiz@ucdavis.edu.

ORTIZ, PATRICK T., lawyer; b. 1950; BA, Coll. Santa Fe; JD, Georgetown U. Bar: N.Mex. 1976. Dep. gen. counsel ins. dept. N.Mex. State Corp. Commn., gen. counsel; asst. atty. gen. energy and utilities sect. Atty. Gen.'s Office, N.Mex.; staff counsel N.Mex. Public Svc. Commn., chief commn. counsel, commr.; atty. Mountain States Telephone & Telegraph Co.; chief counsel US West Comm.; sr. v.p., gen. counsel, sec. PNM Resources, Albuquerque, 1991—. Bd. dirs. N.Mex. Bar Bus. Law Sect.; corp. exec. bd. Gen. Counsel Roundtable. Bd. trustees PNM Found.; pro bono counsel Challenge N.Mex.; bd. dirs. Archdiocese Santa Fe Catholic Found., Nat. Hispanic Cultural Ctr. Found.; mem. bd. visitors Coll. Santa Fe. Named one of Most Influential Hispanics, Hispanic Bus. Mag., Corp. Elite, 2007. Mem.: Chief Legal Officers Assn. (mem. exec. com.), Am. Law Inst., N.Mex Hispanic Bar Assn., Oliver Seth Am. Inn of Ct. (master of bench), Edison Elec. Inst. (mem. legal com.), Am. Gas Assn. (mem. legal com.). Office: PNM Resources Inc Alvarado Sq MS2822 Albuquerque NM 87158-0001

ORTIZ Y PINO, GERALD, state legislator; b. Santa Fe, N.Mex., Aug. 28, 1942; BA in Latin Am. Studies, U. N.Mex., 1965; MSW, Tulane U., 1968. Lic. N.Mex. Bd. Social Work Examiners. Social svcs. specialist Dona Ana and San Miguel Counties N.Mex. Health and Social Svc. Dept., Albuquerque, 1968-69, cmty. worker Taos Welfare Office, 1969-71; asst. prof. social work, dir. cmty. mental health tng. Coll. Santa Fe, 1971-75; chief program devel. bur. Social Svcs. divsn. N.Mex. Human Svcs. Dept., Albuquerque, 1975-78; assoc. dir. Albuquerque Tng. Svcs. Ctr., 1978-79; exec. dir. N.Mex. Youth Work Alliance, Albuquerque, 1979-82; chief maternal, child and adolescent health bur. N.Mex. State Dept. Health, Albuquerque, 1982-83; dir. Social Svcs. divsn. N.Mex. Human Svcs. Dept., Albuquerque, 1983-84, social worker V, 1984-87; social worker Vista Sandia Psychiat. Hosp., Children's Psychiat. Hosp., Albuquerque, 1987-88; dir. Human Affairs Internat., Albuquerque, 1988-91; pvt. practice Albuquerque, 1991-92; dir. planning and resource allocation United Way Ctrl. N.Mex., Albuquerque, 1992-95; exec. dir. N.Mex. Adv. for Children and Families, Albuquerque, 1995-97; dept. dir. family and cmty. svcs. City of Albuquerque, 1997—; mem. Dist. 12 N.Mex. State Senator, 2004—. Instr. Webster U., Albuquerque, 1984-89, Coll. St. Francis, Albuquerque, 1986-89, Chapman Coll., Albuquerque, 1986, U. N.Mex., Albuquerque, 1977; social worker La Familia, 1987—; cons. in field. Columnist Santa Fe Reporter, 1988—. Mem. NASW, Acad. Cert. Social Workers. Democrat. Catholic. Home: 400 12th St NW Albuquerque NM 87102-1820 Office: City Albuquerque Dept Family & Cmty Svcs 400 Marquette Ave NW Rm 504 Albuquerque NM 87102-2167 Office Phone: 505-986-4380. E-mail: jortizyp@msn.com.*

ORTOLANO, LEONARD, civil engineering educator, water resources planner; b. Bklyn., Sept. 26, 1941; s. Salvatore Thomas and Anna Ortolano. BSCE, Poly. Inst. Bklyn., 1963; MS in Engring., Harvard U., 1966, PhD, 1969. Sanitary engr. USPHS, Denver, 1963-65; rsch. scientist Ctr. for the Environment and Man, Hartford, Conn., 1969-70; prof. civil engring. Stanford U., Calif., 1970—, dir. program on urban studies Calif., 1980—2003, interim dir., Haas Ctr. for Pub. Svc., 2003—04, Peter E. Haas dir., Haas Ctr. for Pub. Svc., 2004—. Interim dir. Haas Ctr. Pub. Svc., 2003-; vis. prof. Inst. Ricerca sulle Acqua, Rome, 1979, South China Environ. Inst. Sci., Guanzhou, 1987, Ecole Nat. des Ponts et Chaussées, Paris, 1987-88, Inst. Universitario Architecture Venice, Italy, 1996, 98, Nat. Poly. Inst. of Toulouse, France, 2000; Univ. of Montpellier, France, 2002vis. scholar Kyoto (Japan) U., 1992; vis. lectr. Nat. Sci. Coun. China, 1991. Author: Environmental Planning and Decision Making, 1984 (Chinese edit. 1989), Environmental Regulation and Impact Assessment, 1997, co-author: Implementing Environmental Policy in China, 1995, Environmental Regulation in China, 2000, Ecologia dell' Impatto Ambientale, 2000. Resources for the Future Natural Resources fellow, 1968-69; Fulbright-Hays grantee, 1979, 87. Mem. Internat. Water Resources Assn., Internat. Assn. for Impact Assessment. Office: Haas Ctr for Pub Svc Stanford U 562 Salvatierra Walk Rm 114 Stanford CA 94305-8620 Office Fax: 650-723-4662. Business E-Mail: director@haas.stanford.edu.

ORTON, KYLE, professional football player; b. Altoona, Iowa, Nov. 14, 1982; s. Byron. BA in History, Purdue U., 2005. Quarterback Chgo. Bears, 2005—09, Denver Broncos, 2009—. Recipient Big Ten Offensive Player Yr, Sporting News, 2004. Office: Denver Broncos 13655 Broncos Pky Englewood CO 80112 Office Fax: 847-295-6600.*

ORULLIAN, B. LARAE, retired bank executive; b. Salt Lake City, May 15, 1933; d. Alma and Bessie (Bacon) O. Cert., Am. Inst. Banking, 1961, 63, 67; grad. Nat. Mortgage Sch., Ohio State U., 1969-71; DHL (hon.), Whittier Coll., Calif., 2004. With Tracy Collins Trust Co., Salt Lake City, 1951-54, Union Nat. Bank, Denver, 1954-57; exec. sec. Guaranty Bank, Denver, 1957-64, asst. cashier, 1964-67, asst. v.p., 1967-70, v.p., 1970-75, exec. v.p., 1975-77, also bd. dirs.; chair, CEO, pres. The Women's Bank N.A., Denver, 1977-97, Colo. Bus. Bankshares, Inc., 1980-97; pres. Guaranty Corp., Denver, 1998—2007, vice chair; ret. Pres., bd. dirs. Lange Golf Co., Holladay Bank, Utah; bd. dirs. World Found., NYC; chmn. bd. dirs. Frontier Airlines; bd. dirs. KBDI Channel 12TV; trustee Delta Dental Colo., 2005—, Women's Found. Colo.; vice-chair Fronteer Holdings Inc. Treas. Girl Scouts U.S., 1981-87, 1st nat. v.p., chair exec. com., 1987-90, nat. pres., 1990-96; 1st vice chair world bd. World Assn. Girl Guides Girl Scouts, London. Recipient Woman Who Made a Difference award Internat. Women's Forum, 1994, Ultimate Woman of Colo. award, 2005, Women Enterprise award U. Denver, 2005; named to Colo. Women Hall of Fame, 1988; named Colo. Entrepreneur of Yr., Inc. Mag. and Arthyr Young and Co., 1989, Woman of Yr., YWCA, 1989, Citizen of Yr., EMC Lions Club, 1995, laureate Colo. Bus. Hall of Fame, 1999. Mem. Bus. and Profl. Women Colo. (3d Century award 1977, Unique Woman of Colo. 2005, Colo. Woman of Enterprise 2005), Internat. Women's Forum, Com. of 200. Independent. Mem. Lds Ch. Home: 6650 W 10th Pl Lakewood CO 80214

OSBY, ROBERT EDWARD, protective services official; b. San Diego, Oct. 29, 1937; s. Jesse William and Susie Lillian (Campbell) O.; m. Clydette Deloris Mullen, Apr. 11, 1961; children: Daryl Lawrence, Gayle Lorraine. AA in Fire Sci., San Diego Jr. Coll., 1970; BA in Mgmt., Redlands U., 1985. Recreation leader San Diego Parks and Recreation Dept., 1955-58; postal carrier U.S. Postal Service, San Diego, 1958-59; fire fighter San Diego Fire Dept., 1959-67, fire engr., 1967-71, fire capt., 1971-76, fire bn. chief, 1976-79; fire chief Inglewood (Calif.) Fire Dept., 1979-84, San Jose (Calif.) Fire Dept., 1985—. Served to 2d lt. Calif. NG, 1960-65. Mem. Calif. Met. Fire Chiefs (chmn. 1987—), Internat. Assn. Black Firefighters (regional dir. 1974-77), Brothers United (pres. 1972-75). Democrat. Avocations: fishing, jogging, landscaping. Home: 28203 Engelmann Oak Trl Escondido CA 92026-6960 Office: San Diego Fire Dept 1010 2nd Ave Ste 400 San Diego CA 92101-4970

O'SCANNLAIN, DIARMUID FIONNTAIN, federal judge; b. NYC, Mar. 28, 1937; s. Sean Leo and Moira (Hegarty); m. Maura Nolan, Sept. 7, 1963; children: Sean, Jane, Brendan, Kevin, Megan, Christopher, Anne, Kate. BA, St. John's U., 1957; JD, Harvard U., 1963; LLM, U. Va., 1992; LLD (hon.), U. Notre Dame, 2002, Lewis & Clark Coll., 2003. Bar: Oreg. 1965, NY 1964. Tax atty. Standard Oil Co. (NJ), NYC, 1963—65; oassoc. Davies, Biggs, Strayer, Sotel & Boley, Portland, Oreg., 1965—69; dep. atty. gen. State of Oreg., 1969—71, pub. utility commr., 1971—73; dir. Oreg. Dept. Environ. Quality, 1973—74; sr. ptnr. Ragen, Roberts, O'Scannlain, Robertson & Neill, Portland, 1978—86; judge US Ct. Appeals (9th cir.), San Francisco, 1986—, mem. exec. com., 1988—89, 1993—94; mem. Jud. Coun. 9th Cir., 1991—93. Mem. US Jud. Conf. Com. on Automation and Tech., 1990—; cons. Office of Pres.-elect and mem. Dept. Energy Transition Team (Reagan Transition), Washington, 1980—81; chmn. com. adminstrv. law Oreg. State Bar, 1980—81; chmn. fed. jud. ctrs. adv. com. appellate edn., 2003. Bd. trustees James Madison Meml. Fellowship Found.; mem. coun. of legal advisors Rep. Nat. Com., 1981—83, mem., 1983—86; chmn. Oreg. Rep. Party, 1983—86; del. Rep. Nat. convs., 1976, 1980, chmn. Oreg. del., 1984; nominee US Ho. of Reps., 1st Congl. Dist., 1974; team leader energy task force Pres.'s Pvt. Sector Survey on Cost Control, 1982—83; trustee Jesuit H.S.; bd. visitors U. Oreg. Law Sch., 1988—; mem. citizens adv. bd. Providence Hosp., 1986—92. Maj. USAR, 1955—78. Mem.: ABA (sec. Appellate Judges Conf. 1989—90, exec. com. 1990—, chmn. 1994—95, chmn. jud. divsn. 2001—02), Fed. Judges Assn., Fed. Bar Assn., Multnomah Club. Roman Catholic. Office: US Ct Appeals Pioneer Courthouse 700 SW 6th Ave Ste 313

Portland OR 97204-1396 Home: 700 SW 6th Ave # 313 Portland OR 97204-1396 Office Phone: 503-833-5380. E-mail: Judge_O'Scannlain@ca9.uscourts.gov.

OSE, DOUGLAS, former congressman; b. Sacramento, June 27, 1955; m. Lynnda Ose; children: Erika, Emily. BS, U. Calif., Berkeley, 1977. Project mgr. Ose Properties, Sacramento, 1977-85; owner real estate devel. and investment co., 1986—; mem. U.S. Congress from 3d Calif. dist., 1999—2005; mem. agr., fin. svcs., and govt. reform coms., joint com. on printing. Former bd. dirs. Citrus Heights C. of C., Sacramento Housing and Redevel. Commn.; mem. Citrus Heights Incorporation Project. Republican.

OSENBAUGH, KIMBERLY W., lawyer; b. Mpls., Nov. 28, 1948; BA, U. Iowa, 1970, JD with distinction, 1973. Bar: Wash. 1973. Ptnr., chair Bankruptcy and Insolvency Practice, mem. exec. com. Preston Gates & Ellis LLP, Seattle. Trustee Seattle Ctr. Found. Mem.: ABA, Fed. Bar Assn., We. Dist. Wash., Am. Bankruptcy Inst., Wash. State Bar Assn., King County Bar Assn., Phi Alpha Delta. Office: Preston Gates & Ellis LLP Ste 2900 925 Fourth Ave Seattle WA 98104-1158 Office Phone: 206-370-8288. Office Fax: 206-370-6147. Business E-Mail: kimo@prestongates.com.

O'SHEA, ERIN K., biomedical researcher; m. Doug Jeffery O'Shea. AB in biochemistry, Smith Coll., 1988; PhD in chemistry, MIT, 1992. Asst. prof. biochemistry and biophysics U. Calif., San Francisco, 1993—97, assoc. prof. biochemistry and biophysics, 1997—2001, prof., vice chair biochemistry and biophysics, 2001—; asst. investigator Howard Hughes Med. Inst., 2000—. Chair sci. adv. bd. Boston U. Sch. Medicine, Dept. Genetics and Genomics, 2002—; mem. sci. adv. com. Helen Hay Whitney Found., 2002—; chair external review com. Bauer Ctr. Genomics Harvard U., 2004. Pub. Libr. Sci., 2003—. Recipient Promega Early Career Life Sci. award, Am. Soc. Cell Biology, 2000, Irving Sigal Young Investigator award, Protein Soc., 2004; fellow, David and Lucile Packard Found., 1994. Fellow: Am. Acad. Arts and Scis.; mem.: NAS (mem. NTC com. on standards and principles in biol. rsch. 2002—, award in molecular biology 2001). Office: Howard Hughes Med Inst Harvard U Dept Molecular & Cellular Biology Bauer 307 7 Divinity Ave Cambridge MA 02138 Office Phone: 617-495-4328. Office Fax: 617-496-5425. Business E-Mail: Erin_OShea@harvard.edu.

O'SHEA, JAMES E., former editor-in-chief; b. St. Louis, 1944; BA, MA, U. Mo. Reporter US Army; fin. editor The Des Moines Register, 1973—76, Washington corr., 1976—79; reporter The Chgo. Tribune, 1979—90, assoc. mng. editor for fgn. & nat. news, 1990—95, dep. mng. editor for news, 1995—2001, mng. editor, 2001—06; exec. v.p., editor LA Times, 2006—08. Bd. gov. Oversea Press Club Am. Author: The Daisy Chain, 1991; co-author (with Charles Madigan): Dangerous Company, 1997. Recipient Disting. Svc. award for Washington Correspondence, Sigma Delta Chi, 1985, 1989, Peter Lisagor award, Pub. Svc. award, AP Mng. Editors, Nat. Edn. Writers award, William Jones award, Chgo. Tribune, 1989. Mem.: Sigma Delta Chi.

OSHEROFF, DOUGLAS DEAN, physics professor, researcher; b. Aberdeen, Wash., Aug. 1, 1945; s. William and Bessie Anne (Ondov) Osheroff; m. Phyllis S.K. Liu, Aug. 14, 1970. BS in Physics, Calif. Inst. Tech., 1967; MS, Cornell U., 1969, PhD in Physics, 1973. Mem. tech. staff Bell Labs., Murray Hill, NJ, 1972—82, head solid state and low temperature physics research dept., 1982—87; prof. Stanford (Calif.) U., 1987—, J.G. Jackson and C.J. Wood prof. physics, 1992—, chair physics, 1993—96, 2001—. Mem. Columbia Accident Investigation Bd., 2003. Recipient Oliver E. Buckley Solid State Physics prize, 1981, Walter J. Gores award, 1991, Nobel prize in Physics, 1996; co-recipient Simon Meml. prize, Brit. Inst. Physics, 1976; fellow John D. and Catherine T. MacArthur prize, 1981. Fellow: Am. Acad. Arts and Scis., Am. Phys. Soc.; mem.: NAS. Achievements include research in properties of matter near absolute zero of temperature; co-discovery of nuclear antiferromagnetic resonance in solid 3He, superfluidity in helium-3. Office: Stanford U Rm 150 Varian Physics Bldg 382 Via Pueblo Mall Stanford CA 94305-4060 Fax: 650-725-6544. E-mail: osheroff@stanford.edu.

OSHEROW, JACQUELINE SUE, poet, English language educator; b. Phila., Aug. 15, 1956; d. Aaron and Evelyn (Victor) Osherow; m. Saul Korewa, June 16, 1965 (div. 2003); children: Magda, Dora, Mollie. AB Magna cum laude, Radcliffe Coll., Harvard U., 1978; postgrad., Trinity Coll., Cambridge U., 1978-79; PhD in English and Am. Lit., Princeton U., 1990. Prof. English C. Utah, Salt Lake City, 1989—. Author: (poetry) Looking for Angels in New York, 1988, Conversations with Survivors, 1994, With a Moon in Transit, 1996, Dead Men's Praise, 1999. Recipient Witter Bynner prize Am. Acad. and Inst. Arts and Letters, 1990; Ingram Merrill Found. grantee, 1990; Guggenheim fellow, 1997-98, Nat. Endowment for the Arts fellow, 1999—. Mem. Poetry Soc. Am. (John Masefield Meml. award 1993, Lucille Medwick Meml. award 1995, Cecil Hemley Meml. award 1997). Jewish. Office: U Utah Dept English 255 S Central Campus Dr Rm 3500 Salt Lake City UT 84112-0494 Home Phone: 801-355-7006; Office Phone: 801-581-7947, 801-581-6168. Business E-Mail: j.osherow@english.utah.edu.

OSHINS, STEVEN JEFFREY, lawyer; b. Washington, Oct. 21, 1969; BS in Actuarial Stats., U. Calif., Santa Barbara, 1991; JD, U. of the Pacific, 1994. Bar: Calif. 1994, Nev. 1995. Assoc. Law Offices of Oshins & Assocs., Las Vegas, Nev., 1994-98, lawyer, shareholder, 1998—; mem. CEO Law Offices of Oshins & Assocs. LLC, Las Vegas; co-founder Entertainment Direct TV Inc.; pres. Nev. Entity Svcs. LLC; mem. Trust Cons. LLC; owner, CEO The Lockett Oshins Collection; mem., pres. Steven J. Oshin Enterprises LLC; former shareholder Premier Trust of Nev. Inc. Tech. cons. Leimberg & LeChair, 2000-, mem. estate planning & Taxation Com. Trusts & Estates mag. 2001-02. Contbr. articles to profl. jours. and mags., and lectr. at various seminars, co-author: various legis. bills. Recipient EPIC award for Best Young Author, Trusts & Estates mag., 1998, Rated AV, Martindale-Hubbell Law Dir., 1999—; named Spl. Tax Counsel for Estates above $10 Million, Paleveda & Fantini LLC, 2000—, Super Lawyer in Nev., Nev. Bus. Jour., 2002; named one of Top 100 Attys., Worth mag., 2006; named to List of Best Lawyers in Am., 2005—06. Mem. So. Nev. Estate Planning Coun. (pres. 1998-99). designed software prog. Sale to Defective Trust Megaanalyzer. Office: Law Offices Oshins & Assocs LLC 1645 Village Center Cir Ste 170 Las Vegas NV 89134-6371 Office Phone: 702-341-6000. Office Fax: 702-341-6001. E-mail: soshins@oshins.com.

OSHMAN, M. KENNETH, computer company executive; Pres., CEO Rolm Corp.; pres., CEO, chmn. Echelon Corp., Palo Alto, Calif. Mem. NAE. Office: Echelon Corp 550 Meridian Ave San Jose CA 95126-3422

OSMAN, LEE R., lawyer; b. 1965; BS in Mech. Engring., Colo. State U., 1988; JD, U. Denver, 1993. Bar: Colo. 1993, registered: US Patent and Trademark Office. Engr. Honeywell, ATMEL Corp.; atty., intellectual property group Holland & Hart, Denver; ptnr. Dorsey & Whitney LLP, Denver, 2000—, and chair, worldwide patent group, 2003—06, head, intellectual property group, 2004—07, chair worldwide patent group, 2007—. Named one of 40 Under 40, Denver Bus. Jour., 2004. Mem.: Pi Tau Sigma. Office: Dorsey & Whitney LLP Ste 4700 Republic Plz Bldg 370 Seventeenth St Denver CO 80202-5647 Office Phone: 303-629-3434. Office Fax: 303-629-3450. Business E-Mail: osman.lee@dorsey.com.

OSMENT, HALEY JOEL, actor; b. LA, Apr. 10, 1988; s. Eugene Osment. Actor: (Broadway plays) American Buffalo, 2008; (films) Forrest Gump, 1994, Mixed Nuts, 1994, For Better or Worse, 1995, Bogus, 1996, I'll Remember April, 1999, The Sixth Sense, 1999 (Acad. award nomination, 2000, MTV Movie award for Breakthrough Male Performance, 2000), Pay it Forward, 2000, Artificial Intelligence: AI, 2001, Edges of the Lord, 2001, Secondhand Lions, 2003, Home of the Giants, 2007; (TV films) Lies of the Heart: The Story of Laurie Kellogg, 1994, Last Stand at Saber River, 1997, The Lake, 1998, The Ransom of Red Chief, 1998, Cab to Canada, 1998; (TV series) Thunder Alley, 1994—95, The Jeff Foxworthy Show, 1995—97, Murphy Brown, 1997—98, (voice actor): (films) Beauty and the Beast: The Enchanted Christmas, 1997, Edwurd Fudwupper Fibbed Big, 2000, Discover Spot, 2000, The Country Bears, 2002, The Hunchback of Notre Dame II, 2002, The Jungle Book 2, 2003, (video games) Kingdom Hearts, 2002, Kingdom Hearts II, 2005, Kingdom Hearts: Chain of Memories, 2007. Office: c/o Meredith Fine Coast to Coast Talent Group 3350 Barham Blvd Los Angeles CA 90068-1404

OSSERMAN, ROBERT, mathematician, educator, writer; b. NYC, Dec. 19, 1926; s. Herman Aaron and Charlotte (Adler) O.; m. Maria Anderson, June 15, 1952; 1 son, Paul; m. Janet Adelman, July 21, 1976; children— Brian, Stephen. BA, NYU, 1946; postgrad., U. Zurich, U. Paris; MA, Harvard U., 1948, PhD, 1955. Tchg. fellow Harvard U., 1949-52, vis. lectr., rsch. assoc., 1961-62; instr. U. Colo., 1952-53; mem. faculty Stanford U., 1955-94, prof. emeritus, 1994—, prof. math., 1966—, chmn. dept. math., 1973-79, Mellon Prof. Interdisciplinary Studies, 1987-90; dep. dir. Math. Scis. Rsch. Inst., Berkeley, Calif., 1990-95, dir. spl. projects, 1995—. Mem. NYU Inst. Math. Scis., 1957-58, Math. Scis. Rsch. Inst., Berkeley, 1983-84, head math. br. Office Naval Rsch., 1960-61; researcher and author publs. on differential geometry, complex variables, differential equations, astronomy, cosmology, especially minimal surfaces, isoperimetric inequalities. Author: Two-Dimensional Calculus, 1968, A Survey of Minimal Surfaces, 1969, 1986, Poetry of the Universe, 1995; author: (videos) Fermat's Last Theorem, 1994, Mathematics in Arcadia, 1999, Galileo: A Dialog, 2000; co-author (with Steve Martin): Funny Numbers, 2003; co-author: (with Michael Foale) (DVD) The Right Spin, 2005. Fulbright lectr. U. Paris, 1965-66; Guggenheim fellow, 1976-77; vis. fellow U. Warwick, Imperial Coll., U. London; recipient Comms. award Joint Policy Bd. for Math., 2003, Support of Sci. award Coun. Sci. Soc. Presidents, 2004. Fellow AAAS; mem. Am. Math. Soc. (Comm. award, 2003), Math. Assn. Am., Astron. Soc. Pacific. Office: Math Sci Rsch Inst 17 Gauss Way Berkeley CA 94720 Office Phone: 510-642-0143.

OSTER, GEORGE F., molecular biologist, environmental scientist; BS, US Merchant Marine Acad., 1961; PhD, Columbia U., 1967. Asst. prof. dept. mech. engring. U. Calif., Berkeley, 1972—73, prof. cell & devel. biology, dept. molecular & cellular biology, 1973—, prof. environ. sci., policy & mgmt., coll. natural resources, 1973—; prof. Miller Found., 1983—84, 2003; Oppenheimer prof. Los Alamos Nat. Lab., 1985. Mem. sci. adv. bd. Santa Fe Inst. Recipient Levy medal, Franklin Inst., 1971, 1974, Weldon Meml. prize, Oxford U., 1992—94; Postdoctoral Fellow, NIH, 1967—70, U. Calif. Berkeley & Weitzmann Inst. Sci., 1969—71, Guggenheim Fellow, 1975—76, MacArthur Found. Fellow, 1985—90. Fellow: Am. Acad. Arts & Sciences; mem.: NAS. Office: U Calif Berkeley Dept Molecular & Cellular Biology 201 Wellman Hall Berkeley CA 94720-3112 Office Phone: 510-642-5277. Office Fax: 510-642-7428. Business E-Mail: goster@nature.berkeley.edu.

OSTERGAARD, JONI HAMMERSLA, lawyer; b. Seattle, May 26, 1950; d. William Dudley and Carol Mae (Gillett) Hammersla; m. Gregory Lance Ostergaard, May 22, 1976 (div. 1985); 1 child, Bennett Gillett; m. William Howard Patton, Jan. 1, 1988; 1 child, Morgan Hollis; stepchildren: Colin W., Benjamin C. BS, U. Wash., 1972; MS, Purdue U., 1974; JD, U. Wash., 1980. Bar: Wash. 1980, U.S. Dist. Ct. (we. dist.) Wash. 1980, U.S. Ct. Appeals (9th cir.) 1981, U. S. Ct. Claims 1983. Clin. psychol. intern Yale Med. Sch., 1976-77; law clk. U.S. Ct. Appeals (9th cir.), Seattle, 1980-81; assoc. Roberts & Shefelman, Seattle, 1982-86, ptnr., 1987, Foster Pepper & Shefelman, Seattle, 1988-92; sole practitioner Seattle, 1996—2003; dep. pros. atty. Snohomish County Prosecuting Attys. Office Civil Divsn., Everett, Wash., 2004—. Contbr. articles to profl. jours.; notes and comments editor Wash. Law Rev., 1979-80. Recipient Sophia and Wilbur Albright scholarship U. Wash. Law Sch., 1979-80, law sch. alumni scholarship U. Wash. Law Sch., 1978-79; fellow NIMH. Avocations: gardening, reading. Office: Snohomish County Prosecuting Attys Office Civil Divsn 3000 Rockefeller Ave M/S 504 Everett WA 98201-4046 Home Phone: 425-697-3050; Office Phone: 425-388-6370. Office Fax: 425-388-6333. Business E-Mail: jostergaard@co.snohomish.wa.us.

OSTERHAUS, WILLIAM ERIC, broadcast executive; b. NYC, July 31, 1935; s. Eric Hugo and Helen (McAuliff) O.; m. Nancy Jean Heinemann, June 19, 1960 (dec.); children: Eric Frank, Marc Andrew; m. Annemarie Clark, Dec. 28, 1985 Student, Fordham U., 1953-54, Harvard U. Bus. Sch., summer 1970. Staff producer news and spl. events dept. Sta. WNBC-AM-TV, NYC, 1956-61; exec. producer Sta. KYW-TV, Cleve., 1961-64, Sta. KPIX, San Francisco, 1964-67, gen. mgr., 1969-73; program mgr. Sta. KYW-TV, Phila., 1967-69; pres., gen. mgr. Sta. KQED Inc., San Francisco, 1973-78; pres. SiteLine Comms., Inc., San Francisco, 1979—2004; chmn. bd. VariCom Inc., San Francisco, 1982-86. Chmn. TV adv. com. Calif. Pub. Broadcasting Commn., 1977-78; mem. joint com. on film and broadcasting Indo-U.S. Subcommn. on Edn. and Culture, 1975-85; chmn. TV com. San Rafael Redevel. Agy., Calif., 1977-78; mem. citizens adv. com. CATV, San Rafael, 1976-77, Dominican Coll., San Rafael, 1972-80; v.p., bd. dirs. Downtown Parking Corp. Bd. dirs. The Ctr. for the Arts, San Francisco, 1985-2003; bd. dirs. Zeum, 1995—2004. 1st lt. U.S. Army, 1958-60. Recipient Peabody award and Hillman award for One Nation Indivisible documentary, 1968.

OSTLER, CLYDE W., banker; b. 1947; BA, U. Calif. San Diego, 1968; MBA, U. Chgo., 1976. With Touche Ross & Co., San Diego, 1970-71; with Wells Fargo Bank NA, San Francisco, 1971, v.p., 1977-81, sr. v.p., 1981-83, gen. auditor, 1983-85, exec. v.p, 1985-86, CFO, from 1986; with Wells Fargo & Co., San Francisco, 1971—, exec. v.p., CFO, from 1986, vice chmn., now group exec. v.p. internet svcs. Office: Wells Fargo & Co 420 Montgomery St San Francisco CA 94104-1205

OSTRACH, MICHAEL SHERWOOD, lawyer, business executive; b. Providence, Nov. 7, 1951; s. Morris Louis and Marion Molly Ostrach. AB magna cum laude, Brown U., 1973; JD, Stanford U., 1976. Bar: N.Y. 1977, Calif. 1977, U.S. Dist. Ct. (so. and ea. dists.) N.Y. 1977. Assoc. Debevoise & Plimpton, N.Y.C., 1976-78, Pillsbury, Madison & Sutro, San Francisco, 1978-81; v.p., gen. counsel Cetus Corp., Emeryville, Calif., 1981-86, sr. v.p. legal affairs and gen. counsel, 1986-88, sr. v.p. law and adminstrn., gen. counsel, 1988—. Bd. editors Stanford Law Rev., 1976. Mem. ABA, Phi Beta Kappa. Office: Cetus Corp 1400 53rd St Emeryville CA 94608-2919

OSTROFF, PETER I., lawyer; b. Washington, Dec. 15, 1942; BA, Washington U., 1964; JD, U. Chgo., 1967. Bar: Ill. 1967, Calif. 1970. Teaching fellow in law Monash U., Melbourne, Australia, 1968—69; law clk. to Hon. Shirley M. Hufstedler US Ct. Appeals (9th cir.), 1969-70; ptnr. comml. trial and litig. practice Sidley Austin Brown & Wood LLP, LA, mem. exec. com. Named one of Best Lawyers in Am. for Bus. Litig., supplement to Am. Lawyer mag., 2003, LA's pit bull lawyers, LA mag. Mem. ABA (dir. divsn. substantive law 1982-83, chmn. comml. transations litigation com. 1976-80, coun. mem. 1980-83, chmn. computer litigation com. 1985—, dir. programs divsn. 1990—), State Bar Calif. (mem. exec. com. intellectual property sect. 1988-89, litig. sect. 1990—), LA County Bar Assn. (bd. trustees 1974-76, chair human rights sect. 1975-76, mem. ethics com. 1982-84), Assn. Bus. Trial Lawyers (pres. 1988-89, mem. exec. com. litig. sect. 1990—). Office: Sidley Austin Brown & Wood LLP Fl 40 555 W 5th St Los Angeles CA 90013-1010 Office Phone: 213-896-6612. Office Fax: 213-896-6600. Business E-Mail: postroff@sidley.com.

OSTROVSKY, LAWRENCE ZELIG, lawyer; b. Cleve., June 1, 1956; s. Peter and Yetta Ostrovsky. BA, St. John's Coll., Annapolis, Md., 1978; JD, Lewis and Clark Coll., 1982. Bar: Ohio 1982, Alaska 1983. Assoc. Berger & Kirschenbaum, Cleve., 1982, Birch, Horton, Bittner, Pestinger & Anderson, Anchorage, 1983—87; spl. asst. to the commr. of natural resources Alaska Dept. Natural Resources, Anchorage, 1987—91; assoc. dir. for energy and public lands Alaska Gov. Office, Washington, 1991—94; asst. atty. gen. oil, gas, and mining sect., Alaska Dept. Law, Anchorage, 1994—. Mem. Commonwealth North, Anchorage, 1986, Alaska Bar Assn.(bd. of governors, 1998—, pres. elect, 2003, pres. 2004). Business E-Mail: larry_ostrovsky@law.state.ak.us.

OSTROW, JAY DONALD, gastroenterology educator, researcher; b. NYC, Jan. 1, 1930; s. Herman and Anne Sylvia (Epstein) O.; m. Judith Fargo, Sept. 9, 1956; children: George Herman, Bruce Donald, Margaret Anne. BS in Chemistry, Yale U., 1950; MD, Harvard U., 1954; M.Sc. in Biochemistry, Univ. Coll., London, 1970. Diplomate Am. Bd. Internal Medicine, Am. Bd. Gastroenterology. Intern Johns Hopkins Hosp., Balt., 1954—55; resident Peter Bent Brigham Hosp., Boston, 1957—58; NIH trainee in gastroenterology, 1958—59; NIH trainee in liver disease Thorndike Meml. Lab. Boston City Hosp., 1959—62; instr. in medicine Harvard U., Boston, 1959—62; asst. prof. medicine Case-Western Res. U., Cleve., 1962—70; assoc. prof. U. Pa., Phila., 1970—76, prof., 1977—78; Sprague prof. medicine Northwestern U., Chgo., 1978—89, prof. medicine, 1989—95, prof. emeritus, 1995—, chief gastroenterology sect., 1978—87; vis. prof. gastroenterology and hepatology dept. Acad. Med. Ctr., U. Amsterdam, Netherlands, 1995—98; affiliated prof. medicine GI/Hepatology divsn. U. Wash., Seattle, 1999—. Med. investigator VA Hosp., Phila., 1973-78, VA Med. Ctr. Lakeside, Chgo., 1990-95. Editor, contbg. author: Bile Pigments and Jaundice, 1986. Asst. scoutmaster Valley Forge coun. Boy Scouts Am., Merion, Pa., 1972-78, asst. scoutmaster N.E. Ill. coun., 1978-81; vestryman St. Matthew's Episcopal Ch., Evanston, Ill., 1979-82, Christ Episcopal Ch., Seattle, 2004-07; treas. Classical Children's Chorale, Evanston, 1982; mem. Sacred Music Chorale, Seattle, 1999-, bd. dirs., sec. and editor, 2002-05, mng. dir., 2005—. Advanced from lt. j.g. to lt. comdr. med. corps. USN, 1955—57, with USNR, 1957—63. Recipient Gastroenterology Rsch. award Beaumont Soc., El Paso, 1979, Sr. Disting. Scientist award Alexander von Humboldt Found., Germany, 1989-90; NIH fellow, 1958-62, grantee, 1962-92; VA grantee, 1970-95. Mem. Am. Assn. Study Liver Diseases (councillor 1983-85, v.p. 1985-86, pres. 1987), Am. Gastroent. Assn. (chmn. exhibit com. 1969-72, mem. undergrad. tchg. project 1972-88), Am. Soc. Clin. Investigation, Am. Physiol. Soc. (asst. editor 1979-84), Internat. Assn. Study Liver, Seattle Audubon Soc. (co-chair membership com. 1999-2004). Avocations: birdwatching, singing. Office: GI/Hepatology Divsn HSB AA 103-F Box 356424 Univ Wash Sch Medicine 1959 NE Pacific St Seattle WA 98195-6424 Office Phone: 206-221-6147. Business E-Mail: jdostrow@medicine.washington.edu.

OTELLINI, PAUL S., electronics company executive; b. San Francisco, Oct. 12, 1950; s. David Otellini; m. Sandy Otellini; 2 children. BA in Econs., U. San Francisco, 1972; MBA, U. Calif., Berkeley, 1974. Joined Intel Corp., Santa Clara, Calif., 1974, managed Intel's bus. with IBM Corp., 1980—85, gen. mgr. peripheral components ops., 1985—87, gen. mgr., Folsom Microcomputer Divsn., 1987—89, v.p. operating group, 1988, asst. to pres. (Andrew S. Grove), 1989, gen. mgr., microprocessor products group, 1990, corp. officer, 1991, exec. v.p., sales and mktg., 1992—98, sr. v.p., 1993—96, exec. v.p., 1996—2002, exec. v.p., gen. mgr., architecture group, 1998—2002, pres., COO, 2002—05, pres., CEO, 2005—. Bd. dirs. Intel Corp., 2002—. Named one of 50 Who Matter Now, CNNMoney.com Bus. 2.0, 2006. Office: Intel Corp 2200 Mission College Blvd Santa Clara CA 95052-8119 Office Phone: 408-765-8080. Office Fax: 408-765-9904.

O'TOOLE, JAMES JOSEPH, business educator; b. San Francisco, Apr. 15, 1945; s. James Joseph and Irene (Nagy) O'T.; m. Marilyn Louise Burrill, June 17, 1967; children: Erin Kathleen, Kerry Louise. BA, U. So. Calif., LA, 1966; DPhil, Oxford U., Eng., 1970. Corr. Time-Life News Service, LA, 1967-68, Nairobi, Kenya, 1967-68; mgmt. cons. McKinsey & Co., San Francisco, 1969-70; coordinator field investigations Pres.'s Comm. on Campus Unrest, Washington,

1970; spl. asst. to sec. HEW, Washington, 1970-73; prof. mgmt. U. So. Calif., LA, 1973-93, Univ. Assocs. Chair of Bus., 1982-93; v.p. Aspen Inst., 1994-97; mng. dir. Booz-Allen & Hamilton Leadership Ctr., San Francisco, 1997—2005; rsch. prof. Ctr. for Effective Orgn., U. So. Calif., 1999—2007; Daniels disting. prof. bus. ethics Denver U., 2007—. Chmn. sec.'s com. work in Am. HEW, Washington, 1971-72; exec. dir. The Leadership Inst., 1990-93. Prin. author: Work in America, 1973, Energy and Social Change, 1976; author: Work, Learning and the American Future, 1977, Making America Work, 1982 (Phi Kappa Phi prize 1982), Vanguard Management, 1985, The Executive's Compass, 1993, Leading Change, 1995, Leadership A to Z, 1999, Creating the Good Life, 2005, The New American Workplace, 2006; bd. editors: Ency. Britannica, 1981-87; editor: New Management, 1983-89, The American Oxonian, 1996-98. Active Project Paideia, Chgo., 1981-83. Rhodes scholar, 1966; recipient Mitchell prize Woodlands Conf., 1979. Mem. Phi Beta Kappa. Office: Daniels Sch Bus Denver Univ 2101 S University Blvd Denver CO 80208 Business E-Mail: jim@jamesotoole.com.

OTOSHI, TOM YASUO, electrical engineer, consultant; b. Seattle, Sept. 4, 1931; s. Jitsuo and Shina O.; m. Haruko Shirley Yumiba, Oct. 13, 1963; children: John, Kathryn. BSEE, U. Wash., 1954, MSEE, 1957. Tech. staff Hughes Aircraft Co., Culver City, Calif., 1956-61; tech. sr. staff Jet Propulsion Lab. Calif. Inst. Tech., Pasadena, Calif., 1961—2004; ret. Cons. in field. Contbr. articles to profl. jours.; patentee in field. Treas. West LA United Meth. Ch., 1958-60; active Towne Singers, La Canada, Calif. Recipient New Tech. award, NASA, Space Act award, Exceptional Svc. medal, 1994. Fellow IEEE (life); mem. Sigma Xi, Tau Beta Pi. Home: 3551 Henrietta Ave La Crescenta CA 91214-1136

OTT, DAVID MICHAEL, engineering company executive; b. Glendale, Calif., Feb. 24, 1952; s. Frank Michael and Roberta (Michie) O.; m. Cynthia Dianne Bunce. BSEE, U. Calif., Berkeley, 1974. Electronic engr. Teknekron Inc., Berkeley, 1974-79; chief engr. TCI, Berkeley, 1979-83; div. mgr. Integrated Automation Inc., Alameda, Calif., 1983-87, Litton Indsl. Automation, Alameda, 1987-92; founder, chmn. Picture Elements Inc., Berkeley, 1992—. Inventor method for verifying denomination of currency, method for processing digited images, automatic document image revision. Mem. IEEE, AAAS, Assn. Computing Machinery, Union of Concerned Scientists. Office: Picture Elements Inc 777 Panoramic Way Berkeley CA 94704-2538

OTT, JASON E., banker; b. 1973; married; 1 child. Pub. affairs officer Citi Cards N.A. Campaign cabinet mem. United Way, services chair; bd. mem. Am. Heart Assn.; bd. chair March of Dimes; bd.mem. Art WORKS!; mem., publicity com. El Tour de Tucson. Named one of 40 Under 40, Tucson Bus. Edge, 2006.

OTTEN, ROBIN DOZIER, state agency administrator; Supt. regulation and licensing dept. State of N. Mex., Santa Fe. Office: Office Of The Super Reg Lic 2550 Cerrillos Rd Santa Fe NM 87505-3260

OTTER, BUTCH (C. L. OTTER, CLEMENT LEROY OTTER), Governor of Idaho, former United States Representative from Idaho; b. Caldwell, Idaho, May 3, 1942; s. Joseph Bernard and Regina Mary (Buser) O.; m. Gay Corinne Simplot, 1964 (div. 1992); children: John Simplot, Carolyn Lee, Kimberly Dawn, Corinne Marie; m. Lori Easley, Aug. 18, 2006 BA in Polit. Sci., Coll. Idaho, 1967; PhD (hon.), Mindanao State U., 1980. Mgr. J.R. Simplot Co., Caldwell, Idaho, 1971-76, asst. to v.p. adminstrn., 1976-78, v.p. adminstrn., 1978-82, internat. pres., 1982—93; mem. Idaho House Reps., 1973—77; lt. gov. State of Idaho, Boise, 1987—2001, gov., 2007—; mem. US Congress from 1st Idaho Dist., 2001—07. Mem. Presdl. Task Force-AID, Washington, 1982—84, U.S. C. of C., Washington, 1983—84; com. mem. invest tech. devel. State Adv. Council, Washington, 1983—84; mem. exec. council Bretton Woods Com., 1984—. With Nat. Guard, 1968—73. Mem. Young Pres.' Orgn., Sales and Mktg. Execs., Idaho Assn. Commerce and Industry, Idaho Agrl. Leadership Council, Idaho Ctr. for Arts, Idaho Internat. Trade Council, Pacific N.W. Waterways Assn., N.W. Food Producers, Ducks Unltd, Safari Club Internat. (life). Clubs: Arid, Hillcrest Country. Lodges: Moose, Elks. Republican. Roman Catholic. Avocations: jogging, music, art collecting, horse training, fishing. Office: Office of Gov PO Box 83720 Boise ID 83720

OTTERHOLT, BARRY L., technology management consultant; b. Richland, Wash., Aug. 15, 1953; s. Ernest D. and Jean T. Otterholt; m. Nancy L. Musgrave, Dec. 13, 1985; children: Casey J., Kris K., Cody M.E. BA in Computer Sci. Acctg., Western Wash. U., 1980; MBA in Bus. Adminstrn., Seattle Pacific U., 1982. Mgr. Robinson's, Wenatchee, Wash., 1971-75; purchasing agt. Sound Ctrs., Inc., Bellingham, Wash., 1975-79; chief oper. officer Speakerlab/Compulab, Seattle, 1979-82; mgmt. cons. Deloitte & Touche, Seattle, 1982-88; founder, prin. Solutions Consulting Group LLC, Bellevue, Wash., 1988—. Mem. Inst. Mgmt. Cons. (cert.). Office: Solutions Consulting Group 1400 112th Ave SE Bellevue WA 98004-6901

OTTO, FRED DOUGLAS, chemical engineering professor; b. Hardisty, Alta., Can., Jan. 12, 1935; BSc, U. Alta., 1957, MSc, 1959; PhD in Chem. Engring., U. Mich., Ann Arbor, 1963. From asst. prof. to assoc. prof. U. Alta., Edmonton, 1962-70, chmn., 1975-84, prof. chem. engring., 1970-96, dean engring., 1985-94, prof. emeritus, 1996—; pres., CEO DB Robinson & Assocs. Ltd., 1998—2002. Mem. governing coun. NRC, 1991-94. Recipient Donald L. Katz award, Gas Processors Assn., 1998. Fellow: Can. Acad. Engring.; mem.: AIChE, Can. Coun. Profl. Engrs. (bd. dirs. 1997—2003), Assn. Profl. Engrs., Geologists and Geophysicists of Alta. (1st v.p. 1995—96, pres. 1996—97, Centennial award 1993), Can. Soc. Chem. Engrs. (pres. 1986—87). Office: 12319 52d Ave Edmonton AB Canada T6H 0P5 Personal E-mail: fotto@interbaun.com.

OTUS, SIMONE, public relations executive; b. Walnut Creek, Calif., Jan. 10, 1960; d. Mahmut and Alexa (Artemenko) O. BA, U. Calif., Berkeley, 1981. Account exec. Marx-David Advt., San Francisco, 1981-82; freelance writer Mpls. and San Francisco, 1982-83; account exec. D'Arcy, MacManus & Masius, San Francisco, 1983; account supr. Ralph Silver Assocs., San Francisco, 1984-85; ptnr., co-founder Blanc & Otus Pub. Relations, San Francisco, 1985—.

OUSTERHOUT, DOUGLAS KENNETH, plastic surgeon; b. Bellaire, Mich., Aug. 30, 1935; s. Kenneth and Naomi Ousterhout; children from previous marriage: Donald, Susan, Oliver, Thomas. Student, U. Colo., 1953—55; DDS, U. Mich., 1961, MD, 1965. Resident gen. surgery U. Med.; resident in plastic surgery Stanford U., Palo Alto, Calif., 1969—72; craniofacial tng. Dr. Tessier, Paris, 1972—73; clin. instr. U. Calif., San Francisco, 1973—86, clin. prof., 1986—. Editor: Aesthetic Contouring of the Craniofacial Skeleton, 1991; author: Cocktails for Two (AKA: Death Gets a Facelift), 1993, A Guide to Feminization Male to Female Transsexual. Capt. US Army, 1966—68. Mem.: French Soc. Maxillofacial Surgeons, French Soc. Plastic, Reconstructive and Aesthetic Surgeons, Pan Pacific Surg. Assn. (pres. 1998—2000), Am. Soc. Maxillofacial Surgeons (pres. 1994—95), Internat. Soc. Craniofacial Surgeons, Am. Assn. Plastic Surgeons, Am. Soc. Plastic Surgeons, Equadorian Soc. Craniofacial Surgery (hon.), Japan Soc. Craniofacial Surgery (hon.). Avocations: piano, sculpting, gardening, travel. Home: 2640 Steiner St San Francisco CA 94115 Office: Ste 150 45 Castro St San Francisco CA 94114 Office Phone: 415-626-2888. E-mail: ousterht@cris.com.

OUZTS, EUGENE THOMAS, minister, secondary education educator; b. Thomasville, Ga., June 7, 1930; s. John Travis and Livie Mae (Strickland) O.; m. Mary Olive Vineyard, May 31, 1956. BA, Harding U., Searcy, AR, 1956, MA, 1957; postgrad., Murray State U., KY, U. Ark., U. Ariz., Ariz. State U., No. Ariz. U. Cert. secondary tchr., Ark., Mo., Ariz.; cert. c.c. tchr., Ariz.; ordained minister Church of Christ, 1956. Min. various chs., Ark., Tex., Mo., 1957—65; tchr. various pub. schs., 1959—92; min. Ch. of Christ, Ariz., 1965—; 1st lt. CAP/USAF, 1980, advanced through grades to lt. col., 1989, chaplain Ariz., 1982—, asst. wing chaplain, 1985—. Adviser student activities Clifton (Ariz.) Pub. Schs., 1965-92; bd. dirs. Ariz. Ch. of Christ Bible Camp, Tucson, 1966-2005. Mem. airport adv. bd. Greenlee County, Clifton, Ariz., 1992—. Recipient Meritorious Svc. award, 1994, Exceptional Svc. award, 1997, Civil Air Patrol; named Ariz. Wing Chaplain of Yr, 1984, Thomas C. Casaday Unit Chaplain of Yr., 1985, Ariz. Wing Safety Officer of Yr., 1989, Ariz. Wing Sr. Mem. of Yr., 1994, Southwest Region Sr. Mem. of Yr., 1995, Civil Air Patrol. Mem. Mil. Chaplains Assn., Air Force Assn., Disabled Am. Vets., Am. Legion, Elks. Democrat. Avocations: flying, building and flying model aircraft, reading. Home and Office: 739 E Cottonwood Rd Duncan AZ 85534-8108

OVENS, DAVID, food service executive, marketing professional; b. Australia; Various mktg. positions Unilever, Kimberly-Clark Corp., Johnson & Johnson; joined Yum! Brands Inc., 2001, chief mktg. officer Yum! Restaurants Internat. Australia, New Zealand, chief mktg. officer Taco Bell Corp. (subs.), 2007—. Named a Power Player, Advt. Age mag., 2008. Office: Taco Bell Corp 17901 Von Karman Irvine CA 92614 Office Phone: 949-863-4500. Office Fax: 949-863-2252.

OVERGAARD, WILLARD MICHELE, retired political scientist; b. Montpelier, Idaho, Oct. 16, 1925; s. Elias Nielsen and Myrtle LaVerne (Humphrey) O.; m. Lucia Clare Cochrane, June 14, 1946; children: Eric Willard, Mark Fredrik, Alisa Claire. BA, U. Oreg., 1949; MA, U. Wis., 1955; PhD in Polit. Sci., U. Minn., 1969. Instr., Soviet and internat. affairs Intelligence Sch., U.S. Army, Europe, 1956-62, dir. intelligence rsch. tng. program, 1958-61; asst. prof. internat. affairs George Washington U., 1964-67; sr. staff polit. scientist Ops. Rsch. Inst., U.S. Army Inst. Advanced Studies, Carlisle, Pa., 1967-70; assoc. prof. polit. sci., chmn. dept., dir. Internat. Studies Inst., Westminster Coll., New Wilmington, Pa., 1970-72; prof. polit. sci. and pub. law Boise (Idaho) State U., 1972-94, chmn. dept., 1972-87, acad. dir. M.P.A. degree program, pers. adminstr., mem. humanities coun. interdisciplinary studies in humanities, 1976-87, prof. of pub. law emeritus, 1994—, dir. Taft Inst. Seminars for Pub. Sch. Tchrs., 1985-87, coord. Legal Asst. Program, 1990-95. Mem. comml. panel Am. Arbitration Assn., 1974—; mem. Consortium for Idaho's Future, 1974-75; adv. com. Idaho Statewide Tng. Program Local Govt. Ofcls., 1974-78; adv. group Gov. Idaho Task Force Local Govt., 1977; co-dir. Idaho State Exec. Inst., Office of Gov., 1979-83; grievance hearing officer City of Boise, 1981-85; arbitrator U.S. Postal Svc., 1988-90; cons. in field. Author: The Schematic System of Soviet Totalitarianism, 3 vols, 1961, Legal Norms and Normative Bases for the Progressive Development of International Law as Defined in Soviet Treaty Relations, 1945-64, 1969; co-author: The Communist Bloc in Europe, 1959; editor: Continuity and Change in International Politics, 1972; chief editor: Idaho Jour. Politics, 1974-76. Served with USAAF, 1943-45; with AUS, 1951-54; ret. maj. USAR. Named Disting. Citizen of Idaho, Idaho Statesman, 1979; Fulbright scholar, U. Oslo, 1949—50, Non-resident scholar, U. Wis., 1954—55, Adminstrv. fellow, U. Minn., 1955—56, Rsch. fellow, 1962—64. Mem. ABA (assoc.), Res. Officers Assn. (life), Am. Legion. Home: 2023 S Five Mile Rd Boise ID 83709-2316 Personal E-mail: wgaard@velocitus.net.

OVERMAN, LARRY EUGENE, chemistry educator; b. Chgo., Mar. 9, 1943; s. Lemoine Emerson and Dorothy Jane Overman; m. Joanne Louise Dewey, June 5, 1966; children: Michael, Jackie. BA in Chemistry, Earlham Coll., 1965; PhD in Organic Chemistry, U. Wis., 1969. Asst. prof. chemistry U. Calif., Irvine, 1971-76, assoc. prof. chemistry, 1976-79, prof. chemistry, 1979-94, chair dept. chemistry, 1990-93, disting. prof. chemistry, 1994—. Mem. sci. adv. bd. Pharmacopeia, Inc., 1993—; co-chair bd. chem. scis. and tech. NRC, 1997-2000. Editor-in-chief Organic Reactions, 1999—; bd. editors Organic Reactions, 1984-97, Organic Syntheses, 1986-94; hon. mem. editl. adv. bd. Ann. Reports in Hetero Chem., 1989-95, Synlett, 1989—, Jour. Am. Chem. Soc., 1996-, Chem. Revs., 1996-2000, Accounts Chem. Rsch., 1996-99; mem. cons. editors Tetrahedron Publs., 1995—; mem. editl. bd. Procs. NAS, 1998-2000. Recipient Sr. Scientist award Alexander von Humboldt Found., 1985-87, Jacob Javits award Nat. Inst. Neurol. Sci., 1985-92, 92-99, Disting. Faculty award Earlham Coll., 1999, S.T. Li prize for achievements in sci. and tech., 1999, Yamada Prize, Japan Soc. for Promotion of Sci., 2000 & 2002; Internat. Soc. of Heterocyclic Chem. Sr. award, 2005; predoctoral fellow NIH, 1966-69, postdoctoral fellow, 1969-71; fellow A.P. Sloan Found., 1975-77, Guggenheim fellow, 1993-94, Japan Soc. Promotion Sci. fellow, 2000. Fellow NAS, AAAS, Am. Acad. Arts and Scis.; mem. Am. Chem. Soc. (exec. com. organic divsn., Cope Scholar award 1989, Creative Work in Synthetic Organic Chemistry award 1995, Arthur C. Cope award, 2003), Royal Soc. Chemistry (Centenary medal 1997). Achievements include research in new methods for organic synthesis, natural products synthesis, medicinal chemistry. Office: U Calif Irvine Dept Chemistry 516 Rowland Hl Irvine CA 92697-2025 E-mail: leoverma@uci.edu.

OVERMYER, DANIEL LEE, humanities educator; b. Columbus, Ohio, Aug. 20, 1935; s. Elmer Earl and Bernice Alma (Hesselbart) O.; m. Estella Velazquez, June 19, 1965; children: Rebecca Lynn, Mark Edward. BA, Westmar Coll., LeMars, Iowa, 1957; BD, Evang. Theol. Sem., Naperville, Ill., 1960; MA, U. Chgo., 1966, PhD, 1971. Pastor Evangel. United Brethren Ch., Chgo., 1960-64; asst. prof. dept. religion Oberlin (Ohio) Coll., 1970-73; prof. Asian studies U. B.C., Vancouver, Canada, 1973—2000, acting head religious studies, 1984-85, head Asian studies, 1986-91, prof. emeritus, 2000—. Vis. prof. Princeton (N.J.) U., 1983, U. Heidelberg, Heidelberg, Germany, 1993, Nat. Chengchi U., Taiwan, 2002; prof. Chinese U., Hong Kong, 1996—98; hon. prof. Shanghai Normal U., China, 1997—. Author: Folk Buddhist Religion, 1976, 2005, Religions of China, 1986; author: (with David Jordan) The Flying Phoenix, 1986, 2005; author: Precious Volumes: An Introduction to Chinese Sectarian Scriptures From the Sixteenth and Seventeenth Centuries, 1999; editor: Ethnography in China Today: A Critical Assessment of Methods and Results, 2002, Religion in China Today, 2003; editor spl. issue: The China Quar.; contbr. articles to encys. and profl. jours. Chmn. Sch. Consultative Com., Vancouver, 1976-77; coord. Vancouver Boys Soccer League, 1979-81; adult edn. coord. United Ch. Can., Vancouver, 1981-84; co-chmn. Endowment Lands Regional Park Com., 1987-90; co-chair China and Inner Asia Coun., Assn. Asian Studies, 1992—. With USNR, 1953-61. Recipient Killam faculty rsch. prize U. B.C., 1986, Killiam faculty tchg. prize, 2000; named Alumnus of Yr., U. Chgo. Divinity Sch., 2001; NEH fellow, 1978, 79, China Rsch. fellow, 1981, sr. fellow coun. humanities Princeton U., 1983, Wang Inst. Grad. Studies fellow, 1985-86. Fellow Royal Soc. Can.; mem. Am. Soc. Study Religion, Soc. Study Chinese Religions (pres. 1985-88), Assn. Asian Studies. Democrat. Avocations: photography, swimming, hiking, gardening, birdwatching. Home: 3393 W 26th Ave Vancouver BC Canada V6S 1N4 Office: UBC Ctr Chinese Rsch Vancouver BC Canada V6T 1Z2 E-mail: eodano@shaw.ca.

OVERSTREET, JAMES WILKINS, obstetrics and gynecology educator, administrator; BA in Biology magna cum laude, U. South, 1967; BA in Natural Scis., U. Cambridge, Eng., 1970, PhD in Reproductive Physiology, 1973, MA in Natural Scis., 1974; MD, Columbia U., 1974. Diplomate Nat. Bd. Med. Examiners; lic. physician, Calif. NIH Med. Scientist Tng. fellow dept. anatomy coll. physicians ans surgeons Columbia U., 1970-72, NIH Med. Scientist Tng. fellow Internat. Inst. for Study Human Reproduction, 1972-74; asst. resident in ob-gyn. Presbyn. Hosp., NYC, 1974; Ford Found. Postdoctoral Rsch. fellow dept. ob-gyn. Cornell U. Med. Coll., 1975-76; asst. prof. human anatomy and ob-gyn. sch. medicine U. Calif., Davis, 1976-80, assoc. prof. human anatomy, 1980-84, assoc. prof. ob-gyn. sch. medicine, 1980-85, prof. ob-gyn. sch. medicine, 1985—, chief divsn. reproductive biology and medicine dept. ob-gyn. sch. medicine, 1983-86, dir. lab. for energy-related health rsch., 1985-88, dir. Inst. Toxicology and Environ. Health, unit leader devel. and reproductive biology Primate Rsch. Ctr., 1988—. Mem. sci. rev. panel for health rsch., reviewer test rules dept. and reproductive abd devel. toxicology brs. U.S. EPA; mem. ad hoc study sect., cons. Nat. Inst. for Occupational Safety and Health; chair AIDS and related rsch. rev. group NIH; chmn. spl. study sect., mem. site visit team, mem. ad hoc reproductuve endocrinology study sect. Nat. Inst. Child Health and Human Devel.; reviewer, mem. site visit team Nat. Inst. Environ. Health Scis./NIH, Med. Rsch. Coun. Can.; mem. tech. adv. com. and site visit team contraceptive rsch. and devel. project Agy. for Internat. Devel./Ea. Va. Med. Sch.; temp. advisor spl. program rsch. devel. and rsch. tng. in human reproduction WHO; mem. reproductive and devel. toxicology program rev. panel Chem. Industry Inst. Toxicology; mem. exec. com. systemwide toxic substances rsch. and tng. program U. Calif.; reviewer NSF, Office Health and Environ. Rsch., U.S. Dept. Energy, March of Dimes Reproductive Hazards in the Workplace Rsch. Grants Program, Mt. Sinai Hosp., Alta. Heritage Cancer Grants, U.S.-Israel Binational Agrl. Rsch. and Devel. Fund; clin. cons. lab. surveys program Coll. Am. Pathologists; cons. Ctr. for Drugs and Biologics, U.S. FDA, Inst. for Internat. Studies in Natural Family Planning, Georgetown U., Internat. Devel. Rsch. Ctr. Assoc. editor Molecular Reproduction and Devel.; mem. editorial bd. Biology of Reproduction, 1983-86, Jour. In Vitro Fertilization and Embryo Transfer, 1984-89, Reproductive Toxicology, Fertilty and Sterility, 1984-92, Jour. Andrology, 1990-92; referee Jour. Reproduction and Fertilty, Jour. Exptl. Zoology, Am. Jour. Physiology, Am. Jour. Ob-Gyn., Jour. Urology, Science, Jour. Clin. Endocrinology and Metabolism, Archives Internal Medicine, Internat. Jour. Andrology, Reproduction, Nutrition, Devel., Western Jour. Medicine, Contraception, Human Reproduction, Proceedings Royal Soc. Series B.; invited lectr. in field. Georgia Fulbright scholar, 1967-68; recipient Rsch. Career Devel. award NIH, 1978-83, Disting. Career in Clin. Investigation award Columbia Presbyn. Med Ctr., 1992; grantee Syntex Rsch. Divsn., 1978-81, NIH, 1978-81, 78-83, 79-90, 81-90, 85-88, 86—, 87—, 88—, 89—, 90— (two grants), 91—, 92—, 93—, U. Calif., 1981-82, U.S. EPA, 1981-84, 82-84, Nat. Inst. for Occupational Safety and Health, 1982-84, U.S. Dept. Energy, 1985-88, Georgetown U., 1987-89, 92—, Merck Rsch. Labs., 1988-90, 92, 92—, March of Dimes, 1988-90, Semiconductor Industry Assn., 1989-92, Tobacco Related Disease Rsch. Program, 1990-93, Andrew W. Mellon Found., 1993—, Mem. Am. Fertility Soc., Am. Soc. Andrology (exec. coun. 1986-89), Soc. for Study Fertility, Soc. for Study Reproduction, Phi Beta Kappa. Achievements include research in physiology of mammalian spermatozoa, sperm transport in the female reproductive tract, in vivo and in vitro mammalian fertilization, diagnosis and therapy of human male infertility, reproductive toxicology, environmental and occupational hazards to male and female fertility, contraceptive development, reproductive endocrinology. Office: U Calif Davis Inst Toxicology & Enviro Health Rsch Office Davis CA 95616

OVERSTREET, KAREN A., federal bankruptcy judge; BA cum laude, Univ. of Wash., 1977; JD, Univ. of Oregon, 1982. Assoc. Duane, Morris & Heckscher, Phila., 1983-86; ptnr. Davis Wright Tremaine, Seattle, 1986-93; bankruptcy judge U.S. Bankruptcy Ct. (we. dist.) Wash., Seattle, 1994—. Assoc. editor Oregon Law Review; dir. People's Law Sch.; mem. advisory com. U.S. Bankruptcy Ct. (we. dist.) Wash. Mem. Nat. Conf. of Bankruptcy Judges, Wash. State Bar Assn. (creditor-debtor sec.), Seattle-King County Bar Assn. (bankruptcy sec.), Am. Bar Assn., Wash. Women Lawyers Assn. Office: US Bankruptcy Ct 700 Stewart St Rm 7216 Seattle WA 98101 Office Phone: 206-370-5330.

OVIATT, LARRY ANDREW, retired art educator; b. Boone, Iowa, Mar. 13, 1939; s. Eli Charles and T. Mae (Lathrop) O.; children: Julia, Vanessa, Dana. BA, Drake U., Des Moines, 1962; MS, San Diego State U., 1975. Tchr. art San Diego City Schs., 1969-96, mentor tchr., 1992-96; owner Perfect Travel of La Jolla, 1989-97; prof. art edn. Calif. State U., Northridge, 1998—2008; art cons. for Crayola. Prof. art edn. Calif. State U., Northridge; vol. art tchr. Vallejo Libr. San Diego dir. Anderson for Pres., 1976; dist. coord. Hedgecock for Mayor, San Diego, 1984; dir. elder Help Corp., San Diego, 1988; v.p. Afrian Am. Mus., 1989-92; pres. Sushi Gallery, 1980-82; bd. dirs. Mingei Internat. Mus., 1983-87; pres. Cmty. Svc. Assn., 1984-88; past pres. Diversionary Theatre, African Am. Mus.; dir. AIDS Walk for Life, 1988, 89; bd. dirs. AIDS Art Alive; com. mem. Long Beach AIDS Walk, 2007. Named 1986 Tchr. of Yr. Urban League, 1986, Sec.

Art Tchr. of Yr. Calif. Art Tchrs. Assn., 1988, Art Tchr. of Yr. Calif. Art Tchrs. Assn., 1992, Vol. of Yr. San Diego City Schs., 1993. Mem. So. Calif. Art Tchrs. Assn. (pres. 1984-89), Calif. Art Edn. Assn. (dir. 1984-89, conf. adminstr., Art Edn. Tchr. of Yr. award 1992), Nat. Art Edn. Assn. (dir. 1987-93). Avocations: reading, basketball, art. Home: 700 E Ocean Blvd Unit 2702 Long Beach CA 90802 Home Phone: 562-519-4516; Office Phone: 818-677-4540. Business E-Mail: larry.oviatt@csun.edu.

OVITSKY, STEVEN ALAN, musician, classical music executive; b. Chgo., Oct. 12, 1947; s. Martin N. and Ruth (Katz) O.; m. Camille Levy; 1 child, David Isaac. MusB, U. Mich., 1968; MusM, No. Ill. U., 1975. Fine arts dir. Sta. WNIU-FM Pub. Radio, Dekalb, Ill., 1972-76; program mgr. Sta. WMHT-FM Pub. Radio, Schenectady, NY, 1976-79; gen. mgr., artistic dir. Grant Park Concerts, Chgo., 1979-90; v.p., gen. mgr. Minn. Orch., Mpls., 1990-95; v.p., exec. dir. Milw. Symphony Orch., 1995-99, pres., exec. dir., 1999—2003; exec. dir. Santa Fe Chamber Music Festival, 2004—; owner Sotone Hist. Recordings. Panelist Ill. Arts Coun., Chgo. Artists Abroad, Nat. Endowment for the Arts; bd. dirs. Ill. Arts Alliance, Chamber Music Chgo.; hon. dir. Chgo. Sinfonietta. With U.S. Army, 1968-71, Korea. Mem. NARAS, Am. Symphony Orch. League. Jewish. Avocations: audio, record collecting, softball, scuba diving. Office: Santa Fe Chamber Music Festival PO Box 2227 Santa Fe NM 87504-2227 Office Phone: 505-231-8212.

OVITT, GARY C., mayor; b. May 3, 1947; BA, U. Redlands, 1969. Tchr. Chaffey H.S., Ontario, Calif.; mayor City of Ontario, Calif., 1998—. Chmn. dept. edn. Chaffey Joint Unified Sch. Dist., 1970—. Mem. Ontario (Calif.) City Coun., 1992-99. Office: City Hall 303 E B St Ontario CA 91764-4105

OVITZ, MICHAEL S., communications executive; b. Chgo., Dec. 14, 1946; m. Judy Reich, 1969; children Christopher, Kimberly, Eric. Grad., UCLA, 1968. With William Morris Agy., 1969—75; pres., bd. dir. Walt Disney Co., Burbank, Calif., 1995-97; co-founder, chmn. Creative Artists Agy., LA, 1975-95; principal Artists Mgmt. Group, 1998—2002; owner, principal CKE Assocs., Beverly Hills, Calif., 1998—. Chmn. exec. bd. dirs. UCLA Hosp. and Med. Ctr.; bd. advisors Sch. Theater, Film and TV UCLA; bd. dirs. Livent, Inc., Gulfstream Aero. Corp., J. Crew Group, Inc., Opsware, Inc., Yankee Candle Corp. Exec. prodr.: Gangs of NY, 2002; exec. prodr.: Timeline, 2003. Trustee Mus. Modern Art, N.Y.C.; bd. govs. Cedars-Sinai Hosp., L.A.; mem. exec. adv. bd. Pediatric AIDS Found.; bd. dir. D.A.R.E. America; nat. bd. advisors, Children's Scholarship Fund. Named one of Top 200 Collectors, ARTnews Mag., 2004—08. Mem. Coun. Fgn. Rels., Zeta Beta Tau. Avocation: art collector. Office: 2601 Colorado Ave Santa Monica CA 90404-3518

OWADES, RUTH MARKOWITZ, marketing company executive; b. LA, Sept. 2, 1944; d. David and Yonina (Graf) Markowitz; m. Joseph L. Owades, Sept. 7, 1969. BA with hon., Scripps Coll., Claremont, Calif., 1966; MBA, Harvard U., 1975; postgrad. U. Strasbourg, France, 1966-67. Exec. asst. LA Econ. Devel. Bd., NYC, 1968-69; copywriter D'Arcy Advt. Co., St. Louis, 1970-71; asst. program dir. KMOX-AM Radio, St. Louis, 1971-72; assoc. prodr. WCVB-TV, Boston, 1972-73; mktg. project mgr. United Brands Co., Boston, 1975; mktg. dir. CML Group Inc., Concord, Mass., 1975-78; founder, pres. Gardener's Eden Inc., Boston, 1978-82, Calyx & Carolla, Inc., 1988—; pres. Gardener's Eden, div. Williams-Sonoma Inc., Emeryville, Calif., 1982-87; bd. dirs. Hellenic Breweries S.A., Athens, Greece. Bd. of advisors An Income of Her Own; trustee Scripps Coll. Recipient Bausch & Lomb award, 1962, Disting. Alumna award Scripps Coll., 1989, Woman of Achievement award Woman's City Club Cleve., 1991, Woman Who Has Made a Difference award Internat. Women's Forum, 1991, Woman of Yr. award Woman's Direct Response Group NY, 1992, Cataloger of Yr. award Target Marketing Mag., 1992, Direct Marketer of Yr. award, No. Calif. Direct Mktg. Club, 1993; Fulbright scholar, 1966; named student Goodwill Ambassador to Nagoya, Japan, 1960. Mem. Direct Mktg. Assn., Phi Beta Kappa. Club: Harvard (NYC), Women's Forum West (v.p. and treas.), Com. of 200. Home: 2164 Hyde St San Francisco CA 94109-1788 also: 2700 Hyde St San Francisco CA 94109-1223

OWEN, AMY, library director; b. Brigham City, Utah, June 26, 1944; d. John Wallace and Bertha (Jensen) Owen. BA, Brigham Young U., 1966, MLS, 1968. Sys. libr. Utah State Libr., Salt Lake City, 1968—72, dir. reference svcs., 1972—74, dir. tech. svcs., 1974—81, dep. dir., 1981—87, dir., 1987—2003. Serials com. chmn. Utah Coll. Libr. Coun., Salt Lake City, 1975—77, exec. sec., 1978—84, mem. coun., 1987—2003; mem. staff Gov.'s Utah Sys. Planning Task Force, Salt Lake City, 1982; staff liaison Utah Gov.'s Conf. on Libr. and Info. Svcs., 1977—79, chmn. exec. planning com., 1990—91; mem. pres.'s adv. panel Baker & Taylor Co., Somerville, NJ, 1977—78; panelist U.S. Dept. Edn., 1992; mem. rsch. project adv. com. U. Wis. Sch. Libr. and Info., Madison, 1992—94; mem. adv. panel Nat. Commn. Libr. & Info. Svcs., 1985, bd. dirs.; Alumni Honor lectr. Coll. Humanities Brigham Young U., 1990; cons., trainer in field. Contbr. chpts. to books; contbg. author: various manuals. Presdl. apptd. mem. Nat. Mus. and Libr. Svcs. Bd., 2004; mem. coun. Utah Endowment for Humanities, 1986—91, vice chmn., 1987—88, chmn., 1988—90; trustee Bibliographic Ctr. for Rsch., 1987—2003, mem. pers. com., 1988—90, chmn. person com., 1989—90, mem. nominating com., 1984, v.p. bd. trustees, 1989—91, pres., 1991—93; active Chief Officers of State Libr. Agys., 1987—2003, mem. stats. com., 1988—93, mem. network com., 1993—97, mem. state info. policy workshop com., 1988, bd. dirs., 1992—96; mem. conf. program com. Fedn. of State Humanities Couns., 1988; mem. coop. pub. libr. data sys. task force Nat. Commn. on Libr. and Info. Svcs., 1988—90; grant rev. panelist NEH, 1988, 1992, panel mem. reading and discussion groups, 1988; regional project mgmt. bd. mem. Intermountain Cmty. Learning and Info. Ctr. Project, 1987—90; mem. midcontinental regional adv. com. Nat. Libr. Medicine, 1991—94; mem. adv. com. Brigham Young U. Sch. Libr. and Info. Svcs., 1989—92. Named Libr. of Yr., Libr. Jour., 1990. Mem.: ALA (planning, orgn. and bylaws com. 1981—85, LITA divsn. Satellite Conf. Task Force mem. 1982, bd. dirs. ASCLA divsn. 1984—86, clene roundtable mem. com. 1984—86, fin. com. 1984—86, SLAS program com. 1984—86, ALA Office for Rsch. coop. pub. libr. data sys. adv. com. 1985—89, pres. program com. 1986, nominations com. 1986—87, PLA divsn. editor column 1987—89, PLA divsn. goals, guidelines and stds. com. 1987—90, nat. adv. bd. office comms. svcs., voices and visions project 1988—89, exec. bd. mem. 1988—90, PLA pub. libr. data svc. adv. com. 1988—91, fin. com. 1989—92, chair 1990—91, PLA non MLS involvement com. 1990—91, PLA Kellogg Phase III EIC project adv. com. chmn. 1990—92, PLA strategic issues and directions com. 1991—92, exec. bd. mem. 1993—94, bd. dirs. ASCLA divsn. 1993—96, fin. com. 1993—96, pres. ASCLA divsn. 1994—95, ASCLA Divsn. Profl. Achievement award 2004), Utah Partnership Edn. and Econ. Devel. (rsch. com. 1995—95), Utah Edn. Network (steering com. 1996—2003), Dynix Snowbird Leadership Inst. (nat. adv. bd. 1990—2002), Mountain Plains Libr. Assn. (rec. sec. 1979—80, fin. com. 1982—84, Disting. Svc. award 1989), Utah Libr. Assn. (exec. bd. 1976—80, pres. 1978—79, Disting. Svc. award 2003, Spl. Svc. award 1989), Alpha Lambda Alpha, Phi Kappa Phi.

OWEN, BRADLEY SCOTT, Lieutenant Governor of Washington; b. Tacoma, May 23, 1950; s. Laural Willis; m. Linda Knoll, Jan. 20, 1983; children: Shanie, Dana, Mark, Sherrie, Adam, Royce. Student pub. sch., Germany. Mem. Wash. House of Reps., Olympia, 1976-82, Wash. State Senate, Olympia, 1983-96, pres., 1997—; lt. gov. State of Wash., Olympia, 1997—. Chmn. Legis. Com. on Economic Devel.; founder, pres. Strategies for Youth. Mem. Wash. State substance abuse coun., 1997—. Mem. Elks. Democrat. Office: Office Lt Governor 220 Legislative Bldg PO Box 40400 Olympia WA 98504-0400 Office Fax: 360-786-7749. Business E-Mail: ltgov@leg.wa.gov.*

OWEN, CLIVE, actor; b. Keresley, Warwickshire, Eng., Oct. 3, 1964; m. Sarah-Jane Fenton, Mar. 6, 1995; children: Hannah, Eve. Various stage roles including: Design for the Living, The Day in the Death of Joe Egg; actor: (films) Vroom, 1988, Close My Eyes, 1991, Century, 1993, The Turnaround, 1994, The Rich Man's Wife, 1996, Bent, 1997, Croupier, 1998, Greenfingers, 2000, Ambush, 2001, Chosen, 2001, Star, 2001, The Follow, 2001, Powder Keg, 2001, Godsford Park, 2001, The Bourne Identity, 2002, Hostage, 2002, Beat the Devil, 2002, Ticker, 2002, I'll Sleep When I'm Dead, 2003, Beyond Borders, 2003, King Arthur, 2004, Closer, 2004 (Golden Globe award for best supporting actor, 2005), Sin City, 2005, Derailed, 2005, The Pink Panther, 2006, Inside Man, 2006, Shoot 'Em Up, 2007, Elizabeth: The Golden Age, 2007, The International, 2009, Duplicity, 2009; (TV films) Precious Bane, 1989, Lorna Doone, 1990, Class of '61, 1993, The Magician, 1993, An Evening with Gary Lineker, 1994, Nobody's Children, 1994, Doomsday Gun, 1994, The Echo, 1998, Second Sight, 1999, Second Sight: Parasomnia, 2000, Second Sight: Kingdom of the Blind, 2000, Second Sight: Hide and Seek, 2000; (TV series) Capital City, 1989—90, Chancer, 1990, Sharman, 1996. Office: c/o 42 West 11400 W Olympic Blvd Los Angeles CA 90064

OWEN, DAVID TURNER, state legislator, owner, operator; b. NYC, June 9, 1931; s. William Myrou Owen and Cynthia Foster Wolf; m. Marilyn Laura Clarks BA, Colo. Coll., 1955; postgrad, Northern Va. Coll., 1978. With U.S. Army, Wash., 1955-79; owner, operator Greeley (Colo.) Tonis Sales, 1979—; mem. Colo. Ho. of Reps., 1988-98, Colo. Senate, Dist. 16, Denver, 1998—. Mem. Am. Legis. Exchange Council, Nat. Assn. Antique Collecters, Western Legis., Nat. Fed. Bus. Republican. Home: 2722 W Buena Vista Dr Greeley CO 80634-7717 Office: State Capitol 200 E Colfax Ave Denver CO 80203-1776

OWEN, JOHN, retired newspaper editor; b. Helena, Mont., June 10, 1929; s. John Earl and Ella Jean (McMillian) O.; m. Alice Winnifred Kesler, June 9, 1951; children— David Scott, Kathy Lynn. BA in Journalism, U. Mont., 1951. Sports editor Bismarck (N.D.) Tribune, 1953-55; wire editor Yakima (Wash.) Herald, 1956; with Seattle Post-Intelligencer, 1956-94, sports editor, 1968-80, assoc. editor, 1980-94, columnist, 1968-94. Author: Intermediate Eater Cookbook, 1974, Gourmand Gutbusters Cookbook, 1980, Seattle Cookbook, 1983, Great Grub Hunt Cookbook, 1989, Press Pass, 1994, Gluttony Without Guilt, 1997, Seattle Walks, 2000; also short stories. Served with AUS, 1951-52. Named Top Sports Writer in Wash. Nat. Sportswriters Orgn., 1966, 68, 69, 71, 74, 85, 88. Home: 611 Bell St Apt 4 Edmonds WA 98020-3065 E-mail: ieater@verizon.net.

OWEN, MARC E., health products executive; b. Wales; Grad., Oxford U.; MBA, Stanford U., Calif. Sr. ptnr. McKinsey and Co., 1988—2000; pres., CEO MindCrossing, 2000—01; sr. v.p. corp. strategy and bus. devel. McKesson Corp., San Francisco, 2001, exec. v.p. corp. strategy and bus. devel. Office: McKesson Corp One Post St San Francisco CA 94104

OWEN, MICHAEL LEE, lawyer; b. LA, Aug. 17, 1942; s. Richard M. Owen and Betty Hamilton; m. Espy Bolivar-Owen. AB in Econ. with distinction, Stanford U., Calif., 1964; LLB, Harvard U., Cambridge, Mass., 1967. Bar: Calif., 1968, NY 1968. Assoc. Reid & Priest, NYC, 1967—69; mem. legal dept. Bank of Am. NT&SA, San Francisco, 1969—81; corp. sec. BRE Properties, San Francisco, 1970—75; v.p., assoc. gen. counsel Bank of Am. NT&SA, LA, 1979—81; ptnr., past co-chair L.Am. practice group Paul, Hastings, Janofsky & Walker, LLP, LA, 1981—. Founder, vice chmn. adv. bd. Inst. for Internat. and Comparative Law Ctr. Am. and Internat. Law (formerly Southwestern Legal Found.). Contbr. articles to profl. jours. regarding legal issues affecting financing and investment in Latin Amer. Bd. dirs. Constnl. Rights Found. Mem. US-Mex. Law Inst. (mem. adv. bd.). Office: Paul Hastings Janofsky & Walker LLP 515 S Flower St 25th Fl Los Angeles CA 90071-2228 Office Phone: 213-683-6214. Office Fax: 213-627-0705. Business E-Mail: michaelowen@paulhastings.com.

OWEN, RAY DAVID, biology professor; b. Genesee, Wis., Oct. 30, 1915; s. Dave and Ida (Hoeft) O.; m. June J. Weissenberg, June 24, 1939; 1 son, David G. BS, Carroll Coll., Wis., 1937, ScD, 1962; PhD, U. Wis., 1941, ScD, 1979, U. of Pacific, 1965, Ohio State U., 2002. Asst. prof. genetics, zoology U. Wis., 1944-47; Gosney fellow Calif. Inst. Tech., Pasadena, 1946-47, assoc. prof. div. biology, 1947-53, prof. biology, 1953-83, also chmn., v.p. for student affairs, dean of students, prof. emeritus, 1983—. Research participant Oak Ridge Nat. Lab., 1957-58; Cons. Oak Ridge Inst. Nuclear Studies; mem. Pres.'s Cancer Panel. Author: (with A.M. Srb) General Genetics, 1952, 2d edit. (with A.M. Srb, R. Edgar), 1965; Contbr. articles to sci. jours. Recipient Gregor Mendel medal Czech Acad. Scis., 1965, Medawar prize The Transplantation Soc., 2000, President's Disting. Achievement award, Am. Soc. Transplantation, 2005. Fellow AAAS; mem. Genetics Soc. Am. (pres., Thomas Hunt Morgan medal 1993), Am. Assn. Immunologists (Excellence in Mentoring award 1999), Am. Soc. Human Genetics, Western Soc. Naturalists, Am. Soc. Zoologists, Am. Genetics Assn., Nat. Acad. Scis., Am. Acad. Arts and Scis., Am. Philos. Soc., Am. Acad. Allergy and Immunology (hon.), Internat. Soc. Animal Genetics (hon.), Sigma Xi. Home: 1583 Rose Villa St Pasadena CA 91106-3524 Office: Calif Inst Tech # 156-29 Pasadena CA 91125-0001 Home Phone: 626-796-0905; Office Phone: 626-395-4960.

OWENS, DOUGLAS K., physician, researcher; s. Richard C. and Dorothy D. Owens; m. Sara H. Cody. BS, Stanford U., Stanford, California, 1978; MS, Stanford U., Stanford, Calif., 1991; MD, U. Calif., San Francisco, 1982. Diplomate Am. Bd. of Internal Medicine, 1985. Prof. medicine Stanford U., 2006—, assoc. prof. medicine, 1997—2006, asst. prof. medicine, 1991—97. Trustee Soc. for Med. Decision Making, Phila., 1995—97, pres., 1998—99; chair, clin. efficacy assessment com. ACP, Phila., 2005—. Recipient Rsch. Assoc. Career Devel. Award, Dept. Vet. Affairs, 1992-1995, Sr. Rsch. Assoc. Career Devel. Award, 1995 to 1999, Under Secs. award for outstanding achievement in health svcs. rsch., Dept. Vet. Affairs, 2007; Fellowship Health Care Rsch. and Health Policy, Stanford U., 1998-1991. Mem.: Soc. for Med. Decision Making (pres. 1998—99, Lee Lusted Prize 1991), ACP (chair, clin. efficacy assessment com. 2005), Phi Beta Kappa. Office: Stanford U 117 Encina Commons Stanford CA 94305-6019

OWENS, JACK BYRON, lawyer; b. Orange, Calif., Oct. 14, 1944; s. Jack Byron and Lenna Mildred (Gobar) O.; children: John Byron, David Harold, James Paul, Alexandra Grace. AB, Stanford U., 1966, JD, 1969. Bar: Calif. 1970, D.C. 1970. Law clk. U.S. Ct. Appeals 9th Circuit, 1969-70; asso. firm Wilmer, Cutler & Pickering, Washington, 1970-71, 74-75; atty. adv. Dept. Air Force, 1971-73; law clk. U.S. Supreme Ct., 1973-74; prof. law Boalt Law Sch., U. Calif., Berkeley, 1975-79; partner firm Orrick, Herrington & Sutcliffe, San Francisco, 1978-81; exec. v.p., gen. counsel E & J Gallo Winery, 1981—. Adj. prof. Georgetown U. Law Sch. Contbr. articles legal publns. Served with USAF, 1971-73. Mem. Am. Law Inst., Am. Bar Assn., Phi Beta Kappa, Order of Coif. Office: E & J Gallo Winery PO Box 1130 600 Yosemite Blvd Modesto CA 95354-2760

OWENS, JAMES FRANKLIN, lawyer; b. Mar. 20, 1961; BA polit. sci., Emory U., 1983; JD, Stetson U. Coll. Law, 1986. Bar: Ga. 1986, Calif. 1989. Ptnr. Paul, Hastings, Janofsky & Walker LLP, LA, vice chmn. healthcare practice group, co-chmn.-atty. devel. Mem.: State Bar Calif. (health law com.), Calif. Soc. Healthcare Atty., Am. Health Lawyers Assn. (chmn. hosp. & health systems practice group 2000—03), L.A. County Bar Assn. (chmn. healthcare sect. 1997—98). Office: Paul Hastings Janofsky & Walker LLP 515 S Flower St Los Angeles CA 90071-2228 Office Phone: 213-683-6191. Office Fax: 213-627-0705. Business E-Mail: jamesowens@paulhastings.com.

OWENS, SUSAN, state supreme court justice; b. Kinston, NC, Aug. 19, 1949; d. Frank and Hazel Owens; children: Sunny Golden, Owen Golden. BA, Duke U., 1971; JD, U. N.C., Chapel Hill, 1975. Bar: Oreg. 1975, Wash. 1976. Judge Dist. Ct., Western Clallam County, 1981—2001; chief judge Quileute Tribe, Lower Elwha S'Klallam Tribe; justice Wash. Supreme Ct., 2001—. Co-founder, chair Rural Courts Com., 1990; lecturer Jud. Coll., Nat. Coll. of Prosecuting Attorneys' Domestic Violence Conference. Co-author: Northwest Tribal Judges Domestic Violence Manual. Mem.: Dist. and Mcpl. Ct. Judges' Assn. (bd. dirs., sec.-treas., v.p., pres.-elect). Avocation: baseball. Office: Wash Supreme Ct PO Box 40929 Olympia WA 98504-0929

OWEN-TOWLE, CAROLYN SHEETS, clergywoman; b. Upland, Calif., July 27, 1935; d. Millard Owen and Mary (Baskerville) Sheets; m. Charles Russell Chapman, June 29, 1957 (div. 1973); children: Christopher Charles, Jennifer Anne, Russell Owen; m. Thomas Allan Owen-Towle, Nov. 16, 1973. BS in Art and Art History, Scripps Coll., 1957; postgrad. in religion, U. Iowa, 1977; DD, Meadville/Lombard Theol. Sch., Chgo., 1994. Ordained to ministry Unitarian-Universalist Ch., 1978. Minister lst Unitarian Universalist Ch., San Diego, 1978—2004. Pres. Ministerial Sisterhood, Unitarian Universalist Ch., 1980-82; mem. Unitarian Universalist Svc. Com., 1979-85, pres., 1983-85. Bd. dirs. Planned Parenthood, San Diego, 1980-86; mem. clergy adv. com. to Hospice, San Diego, 1980-83; mem. U.S. Rep. Jim Bates Hunger Adv. Com., San Diego, 1983-87; chaplain Interfaith AIDS Task Force, San Diego, 1988—. Mem. Unitarian Universalist Ministers Assn. (exec. com. 1988, pres. 1989-91, African Am. minister's action com. 1995-98). Avocations: reading, walking, promoting human rights.

OWINGS, DONALD HENRY, psychologist, educator; b. Atlanta, Dec. 7, 1943; s. Markley James and Loyce Erin (White) O.; m. Sharon Elizabeth Calhoun, Jan. 29, 1966; children: Ragon Matthew, Anna Rebekah. BA in Psychology, U. Tex., 1965; PhD, U. Wash., 1972. Asst. prof. psychology U. Calif., Davis, 1971—78, assoc. prof., 1978—83, prof., 1983—, chair dept., 1989—93. Editor: (with M.D. Beecher & N.S. Thompson) Perspectives in Ethology, Vol. 12: Communication, 1997, (with R.G. Coss & K.R. Henry) Introduction to Psychobiol., 1998, 99 (2nd edit.), 2003 (3rd edit.), (with C.M. Greene, L.A. Hart and A.P. Klimley) Jour. Comparative Psychology, Special Issue: Revisiting the Unwelt: Environments of Animal Communication, 2002; author: (with E.P. Morton) Animal Vocal Communication: A New Approach, 1998; contbr. articles to profl. jours., book chpts. NSF rsch. grantee, 1978-80, 82-84. Fellow Animal Behavior Soc.; mem. Internat. Soc. for Comparative Psychology, Internat. Soc. for Behavioral Ecology. Democrat. Avocations: hiking, wildlife, travel, reading. Home: 815 Oeste Dr Davis CA 95616-1856 Office: U Calif Dept Psychology 1 Shields Ave Davis CA 95616-8686 Home Phone: 530-753-2839; Office Phone: 530-752-1673. Business E-Mail: dhowings@ucdavis.edu.

OWSLEY, JOHN QUINCY, IV, plastic surgeon, educator; b. Manila, Luzon, Philipines, Oct. 2, 1928; came to US, 1930; s. John Quincy Owsley III and Sara Christine Maxwell; m. Mary Leslie Marriott, Apr. 27, 1957 (div. 1969); children: John Quincy V, Sara Elizabeth; m. Sharon Theresa Anton, Jan. 2, 1971. BA, Vanderbilt U., 1950; MD, Vanderbilt U. Sch. Medicine, 1953. Intern, surgery U. Calif. Med. Ctr., San Francisco, 1953—54, asst. resident in surgery, 1956—58, asst. resident, chief resident plastic surgery, 1959—60, clin. instr. to asst. prof. to assoc. prof., clin. prof. surgery, 1960—80, disting. prof. emeritus surgery, 2008; resident Franklin Hosp., 1958—59; pvt. practice San Francisco, 1960—. Dir. Esthetic Surgery Inst. San Francisco Fellowship, 1989—; vis. prof. Columbia U. Coll. of Physicians and Surgeons, 1989, Divsn. of Plastic Surgery U. Pa., 1993; Donald P. Hause Meml. lectr. U. Calif., Davis Med. Ctr., 1993; guest reviewer Jour. of Plastic and Reconstructive Surgery; founder, dir. ann. aesthetic surgery symposium U. Calif., San Francisco, 1989-2002; past chmn., dept. plastic surgery, Davies Med. Ctr., San Francisco, Calif. Author: Aesthetic Facial Surgery, 1994; contbr. chpts. to books and articles to profl. publs. Fellow ACS; mem. Am. Soc. of Plastic Surgeons (chmn. ethics com. 1973-76, Plastic Surgery Ednl. Found. award for spl. recognition for innovation and excellence in edn., 2003), Am. Soc. for Aesthetic Plastic Surgery (gen. sec.

1975-77), Am. Assn. of Plastic Surgeons, Am. Soc. Plastic and Reconstructive Surgeons (past chmn. ethics com.), Am. Cleft Palate Assn. (pres. 1977-78), Internat. Soc. for Aesthetic Plastic Surgery, Bohemian Club, Pacific Union Club Avocations: sailing, bird hunting, travel. Office: 45 Castro St Ste 111 San Francisco CA 94114 Office Phone: 415-861-8040. Office Fax: 415-861-0626. Business E-Mail: owsley@drjohnowsley.com.

OXMAN, (RICKY) BRIAN, lawyer; b. Nov. 9, 1951; BS, U. So. Calif., 1973; JD, Loyola Law Sch., 1976. Bar: Calif. 1976. Atty. R. Brian Oxman Law Offices, Santa Fe Springs, Calif., 1976—. Law prof. Western State U., Calif.; bd. dirs. Recom Managed Systems Inc., 2002; mem. Michael Jackson def. team, 2004—05. Office: Oxman & Jaroscak 14126 E Rosecrans Blvd Santa Fe Springs CA 90670 Office Phone: 562-921-5058. Office Fax: 562-921-5058.

OXTOBY, DAVID WILLIAM, academic administrator, chemistry professor; b. Bryn Mawr, Pa., Oct. 17, 1951; s. John Corning and Jean (Shaffer) O., m. Claire Bennett, Dec. 17, 1977; children: Mary-Christina, John, Laura. BA, Harvard U., Cambridge, Mass., 1972; PhD, U. Calif., Berkeley, 1975; DHL (hon.), Occidental Coll., LA, 2005. Asst. prof. U. Chgo., 1977-82, assoc. prof., 1982-86, prof., 1986—2003, Mellon prof., 1987-92, dir. James Franck Inst., 1992-95, dean phys. scis. divsn., 1995—2003, William Rainey Harper prof., 1996—2003; pres., prof. chemistry Pomona Coll., Claremont, Calif., 2003—. Co-author: Principles of Modern Chemistry, 1986, Chemistry: Science of Change, 1990. Trustee Bryn Mawr Coll., 1989—, Tchrs. Acad. Math. and Sci., 1999-03, Toyota Technol. Inst., Chgo., 2002—, The Webb Schs., 2005-; mem. bd. govs. Argonne Nat. Lab., 1996-02, Astrophys. Rsch. Consortium, 1998-03; mem. bd. overseers Claremont Univ. Consortium, 2003-, Harvard U., 2008-. Recipient Quantrell award U. Chgo., 1986, Alumni award of merit William Penn Charter Sch., 2003; Alfred P. Sloan Found. fellow, 1979, John Simon Guggenheim Found. fellow, 1987; Camille and Henry Dreyfus Found. tchr.-scholar, 1980. Fellow AAAS, Am. Phys. Soc.; mem. Am. Chem. Soc., Am. Assn. Colls. and Univs. (bd. dirs. 2006—), Royal Soc. Chemistry (Marlow medal 1983), Phi Beta Kappa. Office: Office of the Pres Pomona Coll 550 N College Ave Claremont CA 91711 Home Phone: 909-624-0931; Office Phone: 909-621-8131.

OYER, PAUL, economist; b. Newark, Aug. 10, 1963; s. Calvin E. and Alice Cinader Oyer; m. Amy Friedman, July 25, 1992; children: David Friedman, Lucienne Friedman. BA, Middlebury Coll., Vt., 1985; MBA, Yale U., New Haven, Conn., 1989; PhD, Princeton U., NJ, 1996. Asst. prof. mgmt. and strategy Northwestern U., Kellogg Sch. Mgmt., Evanston, Ill., 1996—2000; assoc. prof. econs. Stanford U., Grad. Sch. Bus., Calif., 2000. Office: Stanford University Grad School of Bus 518 Memorial Way Stanford CA 94305

OYLER, DAVID L., real estate development executive; V.p., Melody Homes, Colo. divsn. Schuler Homes Inc., Honolulu, 1998—. Office: Schuler Homes Inc 828 4th St Mall Fl 4th Honolulu HI 96813-4321

OYLER, JAMES RUSSELL, JR., manufacturing executive; b. Gettysburg, Pa., Mar. 18, 1946; s. James Russell and Gail Louise (Dinwiddie) O.; m. Clare Marie Walther, Sept. 16, 1967; children: Catherine Meredith, Amanda Christine, Margaret Anne. BSEE magna cum laude, Lehigh U., 1967; MA in Econs. with honors, Cambridge U., Eng., 1969. Cert. mgmt. acct. Assoc. Booz, Allen & Hamilton, NYC, 1972-76; product dir. Harris Corp., Dallas, 1976-79, v.p. Ft. Lauderdale, Fla., 1979-82, gen. mgr. Melbourne, Fla., 1982-86, sr. v.p., 1986-90; also bd. dirs. Harris Iberica, Madrid; pres. Am. Mfg. Group Inc., Vero Beach, Fla., 1990-93, AMG Inc., Harvard, Mass., 1993-94; pres., CEO Evans & Sutherland Computer Corp., Salt Lake City, 1994—, also bd. dirs. Bd. dirs. Ikos Systems, Inc., sec. audit com., 1992—; bd. dirs. Silicon Light Machines. Bd. dirs. Utah Opera. 1st lt. U.S. Army, 1969-72. Fellow Am. Chem. Soc.; mem. IEEE, Nat. Am. Electronics Assn. (bd. dirs. Fla. chpt. 1984-87, nat. bd. dirs. 1988), Corp. for Open Systems (bd. dirs. 1986-88), Utah Info. Tech. Assn. (chmn.), Tau Beta Pi. Republican. Roman Catholic. Avocations: tennis, photography. Home: 1873 Carrigan Cir Salt Lake City UT 84109-1475 Office: PO Box 58700 600 Komas Dr Salt Lake City UT 84158

OZCAN, AYDOGAN, electrical engineer, educator; b. Sinop, Turkey, Sept. 24, 1978; BS in Elec. Engring., Bilkent U., Turkey, 2000; MS in Elec. Engring., Stanford U., Calif., 2002, PhD in Elec. Engring., 2005. Post-doctoral fellow Stanford U., 2005—06; instr. Med. Sch. Harvard U., Boston, 2006—07; prof. elec. engring. dept. UCLA, 2007—. Contbr. articles to profl. jours. Mem.: IEEE, OSA. Achievements include patents pending in field; patents in field; by adding a few off-the-shelf parts (cost less than $50) to a typical Sony Ericsson cell phone, has created LUCAS, which stands for lensless ultra-wide-field cell monitoring array platform based on shadow imaging. It uses a short wavelength blue light to illuminate a sample of liquid blood, saliva or another fluid on a laboratory slide. Office: Elec Engring Dept UCLA Los Angeles CA 90095 Home: 827 Levering Ave Los Angeles CA 90024 Business E-Mail: ozcan@ee.ucla.edu.*

OZIER, IRVING, physicist, researcher; b. Montreal, Que., Can., Sept. 7, 1938; s. Harry and Peppi (Schwartzwald) O.; m. Joyce Ruth Weinstein, July 4, 1963; children: Elizabeth, David, Douglas. BA, U. Toronto, 1960; AM, Harvard U., 1961, PhD, 1965. Rsch. fellow Harvard U., Cambridge, Mass., 1965-67, MIT, Cambridge, Mass., 1966-67; tech. staff Rockwell Internat. Sci. Ctr., Thousand Oaks, Calif., 1966-70; assoc. prof. physics U. B.C., Vancouver, Canada, 1970-77, prof., 1977—2003, prof. emeritus, 2003—. Vis. rsch. fellow Cath. U., Nijmegen, The Netherlands, 1976-77, U. Nijmegen, 1997; vis. rsch. officer Nat. Rsch. Coun. Can., Ottawa, 1982-83; vis. prof. Eidgenossische Technische Hochschule, Zurich, Switzerland, 1988-89, 98. Author research articles in molecular spectroscopy. Alfred P. Sloan research fellow, 1972-74; Izaak Walton Killiam Meml. Sr. fellow U. B.C., 1982-83 Office: U BC Dept Physics & Astron 6224 Agricultural Rd Vancouver BC Canada V6T 1Z1

OZZIE, RAY (RAYMOND E. OZZIE), computer software company executive; b. Nov. 20, 1955; B in Computer Sci., U. Ill., Urbana-Champaign, 1979. Sys. programmer Protection Mut. Ins. Co., 1972—73; technician dept. nuc. engring. U. Ill., 1974, sys. programmer PLATO project, 1974—79; co-founder Urbana Software Enterprises, 1978—79; with Data Gen. Corp., 1979—81; co-founder Microcosm Corp., 1981; with Software Arts, 1981—82, Lotus Devel., 1983—84; founder, pres. Iris Assocs., 1984—97; founder, chmn., CEO Groove Networks, Inc. (acquired by Microsoft Corp.), Beverly, Mass., 1997—2005; chief tech. officer Microsoft Corp., Redmond, Wash., 2005—06, chief software architect, 2006—. Adv. bd. mem., Live Labs (rsch. partnership between MSN and Microsoft Rsch.) Microsoft Corp., 2006—. Recipient W. Wallace McDowell award, IEEE Computer Soc., 2000; named Person of Yr., PC Mag., 1995, Disting. Alumnus, U. Ill., Urbana-Champaign; named one of Seven "Windows Pioneers", Microsoft Corp., Top Five Developers of the Century, Computer Reseller News, 50 Who Matter Now, CNNMoney.com Bus. 2.0, 2006, 50 Most Important People on the Web, PC World, 2007; named to Computer Mus. Industry Hall of Fame, InfoWorld Hall of Fame. Mem.: NRC (mem. computer sci. and telecom. bd.), World Econ. Forum (gov. IT and telecom., honored as technology pioneer 2001), NAE. Achievements include first to field of collaboration technology; creator, developer Lotus Notes, 1984; instrumental in development of Lotus Symphony, TK!Solver and VisiCalc. Office: Microsoft Corp 1 Microsoft Way Redmond WA 98052-6399

PACE, PETER, retired military officer, management consultant; b. Bklyn., Nov. 5, 1945; m. Lynne Ann Holden; children: Peter Jr., Tiffany Marie. BS, US Naval Acad., 1967; MBA, George Washington U., 1972; student, USMC Command & Staff Coll., 1979; grad., Nat. War Coll., 1986; student in Nat. and Internat. Security, Harvard U. Commd. lt. USMC, 1967, advanced through grades to gen., 2000, ret., 2007; served in 2d Bn., 5th Marines, 1st Marine Divsn., Vietnam, 1968-69; ops. officer, Security Element Marine Aircraft Group 15, 1st Marine Aircraft Wing, Nam Phong, Thailand, 1972, exec. officer, 1972; asst. majors' monitor Hdqs. Marine Corps, Washington, 1973-76; ops. officer, 2nd Bn., 5th Marines, exec. officer, 3rd Bn., & divsn. staff sec. 1st Marine Divsn., Camp Pendleton, Calif., 1976—79; commdg. officer Marine Corps Recruiting Sta., Buffalo, 1980-83, 2nd Bn, 1st Marine Divsn., Pendleton, Calif., 1983—85; chief, ground forces branch Combined/Joint Staff, Seoul, Republic of Korea, 1986-87, exec. officer to asst. chief of staff, 1987—88; commdg. officer Marine Barracks, Washington, 1988—91; chief of staff, 2nd Marine Divsn. USMC, Camp Lejeune, NC, 1991—92, pres. Marine Corps. U., commdg, gen. Marine Corps. Combat Devel. Command Quantico, Va., 1992—94, dep. comdr. Marine forces Somalia, 1992—93, dep. comdr. Joint Task Force, 1993—94; dep. comdr., chief of staff US Forces Japan, 1994—96; dir. ops. (J-3) Joint Staff, Washington, 1996—97; comdt. USMC, Washington, 1997—2000; comdr. US So. Command (USSOUTHCOM), Miami, 2000—01; vice chmn. Joint Chiefs of Staff, US Dept. Def., Washington, 2001—05, chmn., 2005—07; pres., CEO SM&A Strategic Advisors Inc., Newport Beach, Calif., 2008—; operating ptnr. Behrman Capital, NYC & San Francisco, 2008—; chmn. Pelican Products, Inc., 2008—. Bd. dir. SM&A Inc., 2008—, ILC Industries Inc., 2008—, Nephapsis Inc., 2008—; mem. Def. Policy Bd. Advisory Com., 2007—, Fgn. Intelligence Adv. Bd., Washington, 2008—. Decorated Def. DSM, Def. Legion of Merit, Def. Superior Service medal, Def. Meritorious Service medal, Navy Commendation medal, Navy Achievement medal, Combat Action medal; recipient Tongil Medal of Nat. Security, Govt. of South Korea, 2007, Presdl. Medal of Freedom, The White House, 2008. Office: SM&A Strategic Advisors 8th Fl 4695 MacArthur Ct Newport Beach CA 92660

PACE, SAL, state legislator; m. Marlene Valdez Pace; 1 child, Wyatt. BA in Polit. Sci., Fort Lewis Coll., Durango; MA in Am. Polit. Theory, LSU. Chief aide Colo. House of Reps., US Congress; dir. US Congressman John Salazar Dist. Offices; mem. Dist. 46 Colo. House of Reps., 2008—. Adj. prof. Colo. State U., Pueblo; former prof. Am. govt. Pueblo Cmty. Coll. Southwest. Former organizer Enable America; mem. Pueblo Chicano Dem. Caucus, Pueblo Latino C. of C., Pueblo City Schools Strategic Plan Core Team. Mem.: La Familia, Knights of Columbus, Sons of Italy of Southern Colo. Democrat. Office: State House 200 E Colfax Denver CO 80203 Office Phone: 303-866-2968. Business E-Mail: sal.pace.house@state.co.us.*

PACE, THOMAS M., lawyer; b. Mesa, Ariz., Feb. 5, 1952; s. Lemuel Max and Ann (Green) P.; m. Vi Garrett Pace, Jan. 24, 1981; children: Melanie, Brittany. BA, Stanford U., 1973; JD, U. Ariz., 1976. Bar: Ariz.; cert. real estate specialist. Assoc. Martin, Feldhacker & Freidl, Phoenix, 1976-77, Trew & Woodford, Phoenix, 1977-78; ptnr. Hecker, Phillips & Hooker, Tucson, 1978-88; sr. ptnr. O'Connor Cavanagh, Tucson, 1988-95; pvt. practice Law Office of Thomas M. Pace, Tucson, 1995—. Mem. Mayor's Housing Task Force, Tucson, 1993; bd. dirs. Tucson Urban League, 1986-96; chmn. So. Ariz. Homebuilders Polit. Action Com., 1995, 96. Mem. So. Ariz. Homebuilders (tech. com), Stanford Club So. Ariz. Democrat. Office: 1670 E River Rd Ste 124 Tucson AZ 85718-8900 Office Phone: 520-322-5511. Business E-Mail: tom@pacelawaz.com.

PACHECO-RANSANZ, ARSENIO, language educator, historian, educator; b. Barcelona, Feb. 8, 1932; s. Arsenio Pacheco and Jacoba Ransanz-Alvarez; m. Mercedes Olivella-Sole, Sept. 1, 1956; children: Arsenio-Andrew, David-George. MA, U. Barcelona, 1954, PhD, 1958. Tutor Colegio Mayor Hispanoamericano Fray Junipero Serra, Barcelona, 1954-56; lectr. Hochschüle für Wirtschaft und Sozialwissenschaften, Nurnberg, Germany, 1956; asst. lectr. U. Glasgow, Scotland, 1957-59; lectr. U. St. Andrews, Scotland, 1960-70; vis. prof. U. Pitts., 1966; prof. Hispanic and Italian studies U. B.C., Vancouver, Canada, 1970-97, prof. emeritus, 1997—. Editor: Historia de Xacob Xalabin, 1964, Testament de Bernat Serradell, 1971, Varia fortuna del soldado Pindaro, 1975, Obres de Francesc de la Via, 1997; contbr. articles to profl. jours. Bd. dirs. Can. Fedn. Humanities, 1981-84. Fellow Royal Soc. Can.; mem. Can. Assn. Hispanists (pres. 1978-81), Asociacion Internacional de Hispanists, MLA, Assn. Hispanists Gt. Britain and Ireland, N.Am. Catalan Soc. (v.p. 1984-87, pres. 1987-90), Anglo Catalan Soc., Associacio Internacional de Llengua i Literatura Catalana. Roman Catholic. Office: U BC Dept French Hispanic Ital Vancouver BC Canada V6T 1Z1 Home Phone: 604-263-8106. Business E-Mail: arp@interchange.ubc.ca.

PACHINO, BARTON P., lawyer; BA in Pol. Sci. magna cum laude, Duke U.; JD cum laude, Northwestern U. Law Sch. Assoc. corp. counsel KB Home, 1987-89, corp. counsel, 1989-91, v.p., 1991-93, sr. v.p., gen. counsel, 1993—. Bd. dirs. Bet Tzecek Legal Svcs., former chmn. corp. law dept. section Century City Bar Assn. Mem. Am. Bar Assoc., Ca. Bar Assoc., L.A. County Bar Assoc. Office: KB Home 10990 Wilshire Blvd Fl 7 Los Angeles CA 90024-3913 E-mail: bpachino@kbhome.com.

PACHOLSKI, RICHARD FRANCIS, securities trader, financial consultant; b. Seattle, June 18, 1947; s. Theodore Francis and Nellie (Tarabochia) P.; m. Dorothy Irene Nelson, May 25, 1974; children: Nicolas, Tara. BA cum laude, U. Wash., 1969, MBA summa cum laude, 1970. CPA Wash. Mgr. Arthur Andersen & Co., Seattle, 1970-76; v.p., contr. SNW Enterprises, Seattle, 1976-82; sr. v.p., treas., sec., dir. Seattle N.W. Securities, 1982-93; cons. Carl & Co., Portland, Oreg., 1984-88, Ellis & Carl Inc., Portland, Oreg., 1979-83; pres. R. Pacholski, P.C., Redmond, Wash., 1979—. Adj. prof. U. Wash., Seattle, 1976-80. Mem. AICPA, Nat. Assn. Securities Dealers (past bd. dirs. local dist.), Wash. Athletic Club (life), PacWest Club (Redmond, Wash.). Roman Catholic. Personal E-mail: pacholski@prodigy.net.

PACHON, HARRY PETER, politics educator; b. Miami, Fla., June 4, 1945; s. Juan and Rebeca (Perez) P.; children: Marc, Melissa, Nicholas. BA, Calif. State U., LA, 1967, MA, 1968; PhD, Claremont Grad. Sch., Calif., 1973. Adminstrv. aide U.S. Ho. of Reps., Washington, 1977-81; assoc. prof. CUNY, 1981-86; Kenan prof. politics Pitzer Coll., Claremont, 1987—. Pres. Tomas Rivera Ctr., 1993—; cons. Ford & Carnegie Founds., U.S. A.I.D. Co-author: Hispanics in the U.S., 1985, Americans by Choice, 1994; contbr. articles to profl. jours. NEH fellow, 1973-74, Nat. Assn. Schs. Pub. Affairs and Adminstrn. postdoctoral fellow, 1976-77. Mem. Am. Polit. Sci. Assn. (coun. fgn. rels.), Am. Soc. Pub. Adminstrs., Nat. Assn. Latino Elected and Appointed Ofcls. (chmn. ednl. found.). Democrat. Home: 404 Damien Ave La Verne CA 91750-4104 Office: Scripps Coll Steele Hall Toms River Ctr Claremont CA 91711

PACINO, AL (ALFREDO JAMES PACINO), actor; b. NYC, Apr. 25, 1940; s. Salvatore and Rose Pacino; 1 child (with Jan Tarrant) Julie Marie; children (with Beverly D'Angelo) Anton, Olivia. Student, High Sch. of Performing Arts, Actors Studio. Formerly mail deliverer editorial offices Commentary Mag.; formerly messenger, movie theatre usher, bldg. supt.; co-artistic dir. The Actors Studio, Inc., NYC, 1982-84. Actor: (films) Me, Natalie, 1969, The Panic in Needle Park, 1971, The Godfather, 1972 (Best Actor award Nat. Soc. Film Critics, Acad. award nominee), Scarecrow, 1973, Serpico, 1973 (Golden Globe for best actor), The Godfather, Part II, 1974 (BAFTA award for best actor), Dog Day Afternoon (BAFTA award for best actor), 1975, Bobby Deerfield, 1977, And Justice for All...., 1979, Cruising, 1980, Author! Author!, 1982, Scarface, 1983, Revolution, 1985, Sea of Love, 1989, Dick Tracy, 1990, The Godfather Part III, 1990, Frankie and Johnny, 1991, Glengarry Glen Ross, 1992, Scent of a Woman, 1992 (Acad. award for Best actor, Golden Globe award for Best Actor), Carlito's Way, 1993, Two Bits, 1995, Heat, 1995, City Hall, 1996, Donnie Brasco, 1997, Devil's Advocate, 1997, Chinese Coffee, 1999, The Insider, 1999, Any Given Sunday, 1999, People I Know, 2002, Simone, 2002, Insomnia, 2002, The Recruit, 2003, Gigli, 2003, The Merchant of Venice, 2004, Two for the Money, 2005, 88 Minutes, 2007, Ocean's Thirteen, 2007, Righteous Kill, 2008; actor, dir.: (films) Chinese Coffee, 2000; actor: (TV miniseries) Angels in America, 2003 (Golden Globe for best actor, Screen Actors Guild Award for best actor, 2004, Emmy award Outstanding Lead Actor in a Miniseries or a Movie, 2004); (short films) The Local Stigmatic, 1990; dir. (documentaries) Looking for Richard, 1996 (Dir. Guild of America award for Best Dir. of Documentary); appeared in a one-act play Off Broadway The Indian Wants the Bronx, opened Astor Pl. Theater on Jan. 17, 1968 (Obie as best actor in Off-Broadway prodn. 1967-68); Does A Tiger Wear A Necktie?, 1969 (Tony award as Best Dramatic Actor in a Supporting Role), The Basic Training of Pavlo Hummel, Boston Repertory Theater, 1972, Camino Real, Richard III, 1973, 79, Jungle of Cities, 1979, The Connection, Hello Out There, Tiger at the Gates, American Buffalo, 1980, Julius Caesar, 1988, Salome, Chinese Coffee, 2000, Circle in the Square, 1992; actor, dir.: (plays) Hughie, 1996 Recipient Lifetime Achievement award Ind. Feature Project Gotham awards, 1996, Cecil B. DeMille Award Hollywood Fgn. Press. Assn., 2001, Am. Cinematheque Lifetime Achievement award, 2006, Lifetime Achievement award, Am. Film Inst., 2007, Marcus Aurelius Lifetime Achievement award, Rome Film Festival, 2008, Internat award, Variety Club, 2008 Office: c/o Rick Nicita Creative Artists Agy 9830 Wilshire Blvd Beverly Hills CA 90212-1804

PACK, RUSSELL T., retired theoretical chemist; b. Grace, Idaho, Nov. 20, 1937; s. John Terrell and Mardean (Izatt) P.; m. Marion Myrth Hassell, Aug. 21, 1962; children: John R., Nathan H., Allen H., Miriam, Elizabeth, Quinn R., Howard H. BS, Brigham Young U., 1962; PhD, U. Wis., 1967. Postdoctoral fellow U. Minn., Mpls., 1966-67; asst. prof. Brigham Young U., Provo, 1967-71, assoc. prof., 1971-75, adj. prof., 1975-88; staff scientist Los Alamos (N.Mex.) Nat. Lab., 1975-83, fellow, 1983—2008, assoc. grp. leader, 1979-81. Vis. prof. Max Planck Institut, Gottingen, 1981; chmn. Gordon Rsch. Conf., 1982; lectr. in field. Contbr. articles to profl. jours. Named Sr. U.S. Scientist, Alexander Vol Humboldt Found., 1981. Fellow Am. Phys. Soc. (sec.-treas. div. Chem. Physics 1990-93); mem. Am. Chem. Soc., Sigma Xi. Mem. Ch. of Jesus Christ of Latter Day Saints. Home: 240 Kimberly Ln Los Alamos NM 87544-3526

PACKARD, JULIE, aquarium administrator; b. Los Altos Hills; d. David and Lucile Packard. Co-founder & exec. dir. Monterey Bay Aquarium, Monterey, Calif., 1984—, vice chair, bd of trustees, 1984—. Mem. Pew Oceans Commn. Bd. dirs. David and Lucile Packard Found., Monterey Bay Aquarium Rsch. Inst., Calif. Nature Conservancy. Recipient Audubon Medal for Conservation, 1998, Ted Danson Ocean Hero award, 2004. Office: Monterey Bay Aquarium 886 Cannery Row Monterey CA 93940-1023

PACKARD, ROBERT GOODALE, III, urban planner; b. Denver, Apr. 12, 1951; s. Robert and Mary Ann (Woodward) Packard; m. Jane Ann Collins, Aug. 25, 1973; children: Jessica Nelson, Robert Gregg. BA, Williamette U., 1973; M in Urban and Regional Planning/Cmty. Devel., U. Colo., 1976. Project mgr. Environ. Disciplines, Inc., Portland, 1973—75; asst. dir. planning Portland Pub. Schs., 1976—78; dir. planning Bur. Parks, 1978—79; dir. planninng and urban design Zimmer Gunsul Frasca, 1979—81, dir. project devel., 1981—84, mng. ptnr., 1984—. Mem. Mayor's Task Force for Joint Use of Schs., 1979—80, Waterfront Commn., Portland, 1982—83; mem. steering com. Washington Pk. Master Plan, 1980—81; dir., pres. Grant Park Neighborhood Assn., 1981—83. Co-author: The Baker Neighborhood/Denver, 1976; contbr. articles to profl. jours. Pres. New Rose Theatre, 1981—83, Arts Celebration Inc./Artquake, 1986—, Pioneer Square Bd., 1997—98; mem. Archtl. Found. Oreg., 1992; trustee Williamette U., 1994; bd. mem. Regional Arts and Cultural Coun.; mem. crafts bd. Oreg. Sch. Arts; bd. dirs. Washington Pk. Zoo, 1983—86. Recipient Spl. Citation, Nat. Sch. Bds. Assn., 1978, Meritorious Planning Project award, Nat. Am. Planning Assn., 1981, Meritorious Design award, Am. Soc. Landscape Architects, 1981, Honor award, Progressive Arch, 1983. Mem.: AIA (assoc. Architecture Firm award 1991), Young Pres. Assn., Am. Planning Assn. (Meritorious Planning Project award 1980), City Club, Arlington Club, Racquet Club. Office: Zimmer Gunsul Frasca Partnership 320 SW Oak St Ste 500 Portland OR 97204-2737 Home: PO Box 1775 Edwards CO 81632-1775

PACKARD, RONALD C., former congressman; b. Meridian, Idaho, Jan. 19, 1931; m. Jean Sorenson, 1952; children: Chris, Debbie, Jeff, Vicki, Scott, Lisa, Theresa. Student, Brigham Young U., 1948-50, Portland State U., 1952-53; D.MD, U. Oreg., Portland, 1953-57. Gen. practice dentistry, Carlsbad, Calif., 1959-82; mem. 98th-106th Congresses from 48th (formerly 43d) Calif. dist., 1983-2001; chmn. appropriations legis. com.; former mem. pub. works and transp. com., sci., space, tech.; also chmn. appropriations fgn. ops. and transp. subcoms.; prin. Dawson & Assoc., Washington, 2001—. Mem. Carlsbad Sch. Dist. Bd., 1962-74; bd. dirs. Carlsbad C. of C., 1972-76; mem. Carlsbad Planning Commn., 1974-76, Carlsbad City Coun., 1976-78; Carlsbad chmn. Boy Scouts Am., 1977-79; mayor City of Carlsbad, 1978-82; mem. North County Armed Svcs. YMCA, North County Transit Dist., San Diego Assn. Govts., Coastal Policy Com., Transp. Policy Com.; pres. San Diego div. Calif. League of Cities. Served with Dental Corps USN, 1957-59. Republican. Mem. Ch. Lds.

PACKARD BURNETT, NANCY, biologist; d. David Packard; m. Robin Burnett. BS in Biology, Stanford U., 1965; MS, San Francisco State. Former marine biologist Hopkins Marine Station; founder, marine biologist Monterey Bay Aquarium. Exec. prodr.: (TV films) The Shape of Life, 2002. Bd. dirs. Monterey Bay Aquarium Rsch. Inst.; adv. Whatcom Community Found.; vice chmn. David and Lucile Packard Found.; chmn. Sea Studios Found. Office: Sea Studios Found 810 Cannery Row Monterey CA 93940

PACKER, BOYD K., church official; s. Ira Wright and Emma Jensen Packer. BA, MA, U State; PhD, Brigham Young U. Asst. to Twelve Ch. of Jesus Christ of Latter-Day Saints, 1961—70, Apostle, Quorum of the Twelve, 1970—, former pres. New England Mission, former supr. of Seminaries, acting pres. Quorum of the Twelve, 1994, 1995. Pilot, PTO, WWII. Office: LDS Church 50 E South Temple Salt Lake City UT 84150-0001

PACKER, MARK BARRY, lawyer, financial consultant, foundation official; b. Phila., Sept. 18, 1944; s. Samuel and Eve (Devine) P.; m. Donna Elizabeth Ferguson (div. 1994); children: Daniel Joshua, Benjamin Dov, David Johannes; m. Helen Margaret (Jones) Klineinst, July, 1995. AB magna cum laude, Harvard U., 1965, LLB, 1968. Bar: Wash. 1969, Mass. 1971. Assoc. Ziontz, Pirtle & Fulle, Seattle, 1968-70; pvt. practice Bellingham, Wash., 1972—. Bd. dirs., corp. sec. BMJ Holdings (formerly No. Sales Co., Inc.), 1977—; trustee No. Sales Profit Sharing Plan, 1977—; bd. dirs. Whatcom State Bank, 1995-98. Mem. Bellingham Planning and Devel. Commn., 1975—84, chmn., 1977—81, mem. shoreline subcom., 1976—82, capital improvements adv. com., 1999—2001; mem. Bellingham Mcpl. Arts Commn., 1986—91, landmark rev. bd., 1987—91; chmn. Bellingham campaign United Jewish Appeal, 1979—90; trustee, chmn. program com. Bellingham Pub. Sch. Found., 1991—96, Heavy Culture classic lit. group, 1991—, Jewish studies group, 1993—; trustee Kenneth L. Kellar Found., 1995—; mng. trustee Bernard M. & Audrey Jaffe Found.; Torah reader, trustee Frederick S. & Emma Gartner Charitable Trust, 1996—2007; instr. Acad. Lifelong Learning, 2004—; pres. Congregation Eytz Chaim, Bellingham, 1998—2000; bd. dirs. Whatcom Cmty. Coll. Found., 1989—92. Recipient Blood Donor award ARC, 1979, 8-Gallon Pin, 1988, Mayor's Arts award City of Bellingham, 1993. Mem. Wash. State Bar Assn. (sec. real property, probate and trust, com. law examiners 1992-94). Office: PO Box 1151 Bellingham WA 98227-1151 Home Phone: 360-738-9788; Office Phone: 360-671-7500. Business E-Mail: Packer@nas.com.

PADIAN, NANCY, medical educator, epidemiologist; BA cum laude, Colgate U., 1974; MS in Reading Edn., Syracuse U., 1974; MPH, U. Calif., Berkeley, 1983, PhD in Epidemiology, 1987. Co-founder UZ-U. Calif. San Francisco Collaborative Rsch. Programme Women's Health, Zimbabwe, 1994; founder Women's Global Health Imperative, 2001; assoc. dir. rsch. U. Calif. San Francisco Global Health Scis., 2004; dir. AIDS Rsch. Inst. U. Calif. San Francisco; with Ob.-gyn. dept. U. Calif. San Francisco, co-dir. Ctr. Reproductive Health Rsch. and Policy, internat. expert heterosexual transmission HIV and other sexually transmitted infections, prof. dept. Ob.gyn. and reproductive scis., 2005—; with epidemiology dept. U. Calif. Berkeley. Mem.: Inst. Medicine. Achievements include research in developing and evaluating female-controlled methods for disease prevention, such as the diaphram and microbicides, along with alternative strategies for fostering young women's economic independence; thus reducing their susceptibility to HIV, STIs, and unwanted pregnancies.

PADILLA, STEPHEN, former mayor; 1 child, Ashleigh. AA in Liberal Arts, Southwestern Coll.; B in Pub. Adminstrn., Nat. U. Detective Coronado Police Dept.; educator Sweetwater Union H.S. Dist. Mem. Chula Vista (Calif.) City Coun., 1994—98, 1998—2002; mayor City of Chula Vista, 2003—06; active Chula Vista 2000 Cmty. Task Force; mem. bd. ethics, vice-chmn. Chula Vista Safety Commn.; rep. Internat. Coun. for Local Environ. Initiatives; active Police Facility Policy Oversight Com., Otay Valley Regional Park Policy Com.; alt. Met. Transit Devel. Bd.; bd. dirs. Svc. Authority for Freeway Emergencies, Automated Regional Justice INfo. Sys. Office: Mayor and City Council 276 Fourth Ave Chula Vista CA 91910

PADOVANI, ROBERTO, communications executive; Degree, U. Padova, Italy; MS in Elec. and Computer Engring., PhD in Elec. and Computer Engring., U. Mass. With M/A-COM Linkabit, 1984—86; from mem. staff to exec. v.p., chief tech. officer QUALCOMM Inc., San Diego, 1986—2002, exec. v.p., 2002—, chief tech. officer, 2002—. Contbr. articles to profl. jours. Mem.: NAE, IEEE (Best Paper award 1991). Achievements include holds over 50 patents on wireless CDMA systems. Office: QUALCOMM Inc 5775 Morehouse Dr San Diego CA 92121

PAEZ, RICHARD A., federal judge; b. 1947; BA, Brigham Young U., 1969; JD, U. Calif., Berkeley, 1972. Staff atty. Calif. Rural Legal Assistance, Delano, Calif., 1972—74, Western Ctr. on Law and Poverty, 1974—76; sr. counsel Legal Aid Found. of LA, 1976—78, dir. litigation, 1978—79, act. exec. dir., 1980—81; judge LA Mcpl. Ct., 1981—94, superior ct, Los Angeles, 1993—94, US Dist. Ct. (ctrl. dist.) Calif., LA, 1994—2000, US Dist. Ct. (9th cir.), Pasadena, Calif., 2000—. Active Hollywood-Los Feliz Jewish Cmty. Ctr. Mem.: Calif. Jud. Coun., Mex.-Am. Bar Assn. LA County, LA County Bar Assn., Calif. State Bar Assn. Office: US Ct Appeals Richard H Chambers US Courthouse 125 S Grand Ave Rm 204 Pasadena CA 91105-1652

PAGDEN, ANTHONY ROBIN, political science professor, historian, writer; b. Bexhill, Sussex, Eng., May 27, 1945; arrived in US, 1997; s. John Brian and Joan Elizabeth Pagden; m. Chantal Brotherton-Ratcliffe, 1991 (div. 1998); children: Felix Alexander Xavier, Sebastian George Aurelian. BA, U. Oxford, 1972, MA, 1975, DPhil, 1982. Fellow Merton Coll., Oxford, England, 1973-76, The Warburg Inst., London, 1976-79; reader Cambridge U., England, 1980-96; prof. European U. Inst., Florence, Italy, 1982-83; fellow King's Coll., Cambridge, 1985-96; Harry C. Black prof. history Johns Hopkins U., Balt., 1997—2002; disting. prof. polit. sci. and history UCLA, 2002—. Author: The Fall of Natural Man: The American Indian and the Origins of Comparative Ethnology, 1982, Spanish Imperialism and the Political Imagination: Studies in European and Spanish-American Social and Political Theory 1513-1830, 1990, European Encounters with the New World: From Renaissance to Romanticism, 1993, Lords of all the World: Ideologies of Empire in Spain, Britain and France c.1500-c.1800, 1995, Facing Each Other: The World's Perception of Europe and Europe's Perception of the World, 2000, Peoples and Empires: A Short History of European Migration, Exploration, and Conquest, from Greece to the Present, 2001, Imperialisms: Historical and Literary Investigations, 1500-1900, 2004, Worlds at War: The 2,500-Year Struggle Between East and West, 2008; editor: The Languages of Political Theory in Early-Modern Europe, 1987, The Idea of Europe: From Antiquity to the European Union, 2002; co-editor: Colonial Identity in the Atlantic World, 1500-1800, 1987. Grantee Guggenheim Found. Fellowship, 2006. Fellow: Real Acad. de Buenas Letras (corr. fellow), Royal Hist. Soc.; mem.: Athenaeum. Office: UCLA Dept Polit Sci 4289 Bunche Hall Box 951472 Los Angeles CA 90095-1475 Office Phone: 310-825-9984. Office Fax: 310-825-0778. E-mail: pagden@polisci.ucla.edu.

PAGE, ALBERT LEE, soil science educator, researcher; b. New Lenox, Ill., Mar. 19, 1927; m. Shirley L. Jessmore, Sept. 14, 1952; children: Nancy, Thomas. BA in Chemistry, U. Calif.-Riverside, 1956; PhD in Soil Sci., U. Calif.-Davis, 1960. Prof. soil sci. U. Calif.-Riverside, 1960—. Dir. Kearney Found., Univ. Calif.-Riverside, program of excellence in energy research Editor: Methods of Soil Analysis, 1983, Utilization of Municipal Wastewater and Sludge on Land, 1983, Heavy Metals in the Environment, 1977 With USN, 1944—52. Recipient Environ. Quality Research award Am. Soc. Agronomy, 1984, Disting. Teaching award U. Calif., Riverside, 1976, Disting. Svc. award USDA, 1991; Fullbright scholar, 1966-67; Guggenheim Meml. Found. fellow, 1966-67 Fellow AAAS, Am. Soc. Agronomy, Soil Sci. Soc. Am.; mem. Internat. Soil Sci. Soc., Western Soil Sci. Soc., Soc. Environ. Geochemistry and Health, Sigma Xi. Home: 5555 Canyon Crest Dr Apt 1F Riverside CA 92507-6443 Office: U Calif Dept Soil & Environ Sci Riverside CA 92521-0001 Home Phone: 951-682-1913; Office Phone: 951-827-3433, 951-787-3433. Business E-Mail: albert.page@ucr.edu.

PAGE, CHERYL MILLER, elementary school educator; BS in Social Sciences, Calif. Polytechnic State Univ., San Luis Obispo, Calif., 1975; MS in Ednl. Policy, Found. and Adminstrn., Portland State U., 2006. Cert. health edn. specialist Nat. Commn. for Health Edn. Credentialing, 1993, Edn. Certification Program Calif. Polytechnic State Univ., San Luis Obispo, Calif., 1976. Elem. educator The Dalles Pub. Schs., The Dalles, Oreg., 1980—86, Salem-Keizer Pub. Schs., Salem, Oreg., 1986—95, middle sch. health educator, 1995—2002, health educator, prevention curriculum resource specialist Salem-Keizer Pub. Schs. Mid Valley Partnership, prevention program assoc., 2006—. Recipient Tambrands award, Am. Assn. Health Edn., 1996, Health and Safety Educator of Year, NW Divsn. AAHPERD, 1996; named Oreg. Outstanding Elementary Health Educator, 1991, Oreg. Outstanding Secondary Health Educator of Yr., 1996, Vol. of Yr., Am. Cancer Soc., 1996. Mem.: Oreg. Alliance Health, Phys. Edn., Recreation and Dance (treas. 1992—96, pres. 2001—02), Oreg. Assn. for the Advancement of Health Edn. (sec./treas. 1990—92), Nat. Bd. for Profl. Tchg. Stds. (bd. mem.). Avocations: running, reading. Office: Salem-Keizer Sch Dist PO Box 12024 Salem OR 97309 Office Phone: 503-399-3101. E-mail: page_cheryl@salkerz.k12.or.us.

PAGE, LARRY (LAWRENCE E. PAGE), information technology executive; b. Ann Arbor, Mich., Mar. 26, 1973; s. Carl Victor and Gloria Page; m. Lucy Southworth, Dec. 8, 2007. BS in Computer Engring., U. Mich., 1995; student, Stanford U. Co-founder Google, Inc., Mountain View, Calif., 1998, CEO, 1998—2001, pres. products, 2001—. Spkr. in field; spkr. World Econ. Forum; bd. dirs. Google, Inc., 1998—. Mem. nat. adv. com. U. Mich. Coll. Engring., Ann Arbor, Mich.; bd. trustee X Prize, 2005—. Recipient Engring. Grad. award, U. Mich. Alumni Soc., Golden Plate award, Acad. Achievement, 2004, Bus. Leader of Yr. for Google, Inc., Sci. Am. 50, 2005; co-recipient (with Sergey Brin) Marconi prize, 2004; named Innovator of Yr., R&D Mag., 2002; named a Global Leader for Tomorrow, World Econ. Forum, 2002, Young Innovator Who Will Create the Future, MIT Tech. Rev. Mag.; named one of Persons of Week (with Sergey Brin), ABC World News Tonight, 2004, World's 100 Most Influential People, TIME mag., 2005, Forbes Richest Americans, 2006, 50 Who Matter Now, CNNMoney.com Bus. 2.0, 2006, 2007, World's Richest People, Forbes Mag., 2006, 2007, 2008, 50 Most Important People on the Web, PC World, 2007, 25 Most Powerful People in Bus., Fortune Mag., 2007. Mem.: NAE, Eta Kappa Nu. Office: 1600 Amphitheatre PKWY #41 Mountain View CA 94043-1351 Office Phone: 650-623-4000. Office Fax: 650-618-1499.

PAGE, ROY CHRISTOPHER, periodontist, scientist, educator; b. Campobello, SC, Feb. 7, 1932; s. Milton and Anny Mae (Eubanks) P. BA, Berea Coll., 1953; DDS, U. Md., 1957; PhD, U. Wash., 1967; ScD (hon.), Loyola U., Chgo., 1983. Cert. in periodontics. Pvt. practice periodontics, Seattle, 1963-98; asst. prof. U. Wash. Schs. Medicine and Dentistry, Seattle, 1967-70, prof., 1974—2002, Disting. prof. dentistry, 1996-98, dir. Ctr. Research in Oral Biology, 1976-96; dir. grad. edn. U. Wash. Sch. Dentistry, 1976-80, dir. rsch. Seattle, 1976-94, dir. Regional Clin. Dental Rsch. Ctr., 1990—2008, assoc. dean rsch., 1994-2000, prof. emeritus, 2003—. Vis. scientist MRC Labs., London, 1971-72; cons., lectr. in field; fellow Pierre Fauchard Acad. Author: Periodontal Disease, 1977, 2d edit., 1990, Periodontitis in Man and Other Animals, 1982. Recipient Gold Medal award U. Md., 1957; recipient Career Devel. award NIH, 1967-72, Disting. Alumnus award U. Wash. Sch. Dentistry, 2000. Fellow Internat. Coll. Dentists, Am. Coll. Dentists, Am. Acad. Periodontology (Gies award 1982, fellowship award 1989, spl. citation 1998); mem. ADA (Norton Rose award for clin. rsch. 1998), Am. Assn. Dental Rsch. (pres. 1982-83, disting. scientist award 2001), Am. Soc. Exptl. Pathology, Internat. Assn. Dental Rsch. (pres. 1987, basic periodontal rsch. award 1977). Home: 5583 171st Ave SE Bellevue WA 98006-5503 Office Phone: 206-543-5599. E-mail: roypage@u.washington.edu.

PAGET, JOHN ARTHUR, mechanical engineer; b. Ft. Frances, Ont., Can., Sept. 15, 1922; s. John and Ethel (Bishop) Paget; m. Vicenta Herrera Nunez, Dec. 16, 1963 (dec. Sept. 2004); children: Cynthia Ellen, Kevin Arthur, Keith William. B in Applied Sci., Toronto, 1946. Chief draftsman Gutta Percha & Rubber, Ltd., Toronto, Ont., 1946—49, Viceroy Mfg. Co., Toronto, 1949—52; supr., design engr. C.D. Howe Co. Ltd., Montreal, Que., Canada, 1952—58; sr. staff engr. Gen. Atomic, Inc., La Jolla, Calif., 1959—81; ret., 1981. Mem.: Brit. Nuc. Energy Soc., Inst. Mech. Engrs., Soc. History Tech., ASME. Achievements include patents in field. Home: 3183 Magellan St San Diego CA 92154-1515 Home Phone: 619-423-6723.

PAGNI, ALBERT FRANK, lawyer; b. Reno, Jan. 28, 1935; s. Bruno and Daisy Rose (Recami) Pagni; m. Nancy Lynne Thomas, Aug. 12, 1961; children: Elisa, Michelle, Melissa, Michael. AB, U. Nev., 1961; JD, U. Calif., 1964. Bar: Nev. 1964. Assoc. Vargas, Dillon, Bartlett & Dixon, Reno, 1965—70; ptnr. Vargas & Bartlett and Jones Vargas, Reno, 1970—. Adv. bd. 9th Cir. Ct., 2001—, chmn. adv. bd., 2006—07; ct.-apptd. arbitrator; dist. ct. judge pro tem. Mem. Nev. Dist. Appeal Bd.; mem. hospice coun. St. Mary's Hosp.; mem. adminstrv. coun. U. Nev., 1974—81; treas. U. Nev. Legis. Commn., 1973—74, pres., 1975; bd. dirs. Better Bus. Bur. With US Army, 1955—57. Recipient Outstanding Alumni award, U. Nev., 1978; named Mountain States Super Lawyer; named one of Best Lawyers in Am. Master: Am. Inns Ct.; fellow: Am. Bd. Trial Advocates (mem. nat. bd. 1991—2007), Nev. Law Found. (trustee, vice chair), Am. Coll. Barristers, Am. Coll. Trial Lawyers (state chair); mem.: ATLA, ABA, State Bar Nev. (bd. govs. 1976—87, v.p. 1984—85, pres.-elect 1985—86, pres. 1986—87, mediator, arbitrator 1990), Am. Judicature Assn. (mediator, arbitrator 1990), Assn. Def. Counsel Calif. and Nev. (state chmn. 1983—85), Def. Rsch. Inst., Nev. Trial Lawyers Assn., Washoe County Bar Assn., Am. Softball Found. (bd. dirs.), Wolf Club, Order of the Coif. Office: 12th Fl 100 W Liberty St Fl 12 Reno NV 89501-1962 Office Phone: 775-786-5000.

PAGNI, PATRICK JOHN, mechanical engineering science educator, safety engineer, researcher; b. Chgo., Nov. 28, 1942; s. Frank and Helen P.; m. Carol DeSantis, Dec. 26, 1970 (div. Jan. 2000); children: Christina Marie, Catherine Ann, Patrick John Jr; m. Feriel Palmer, Mar. 21, 2003. B in Aeronautical Engring. magna cum laude, U. Detroit, 1965; SM, MIT, 1967, ME, 1969, PhD, 1970. Registered profl. mechanical engr., Calif., fire protection engr., Calif. Rsch. asst. MIT, Cambridge, 1965-70; asst. prof. dept. mech. engring. U. Calif., Berkeley, 1970-76, assoc. prof., 1976-81, prof., 1981—2003, prof. emeritus, 2003—, vice chmn. grad. study, 1986-89; acting assoc. dean Coll. Engring. U. Calif., 1990; assoc. faculty scientist Lawrence Berkeley Lab., 1976—. Vis. scientist Factory Mut. Research Corp., Norwood, Mass., 1980; cons. on fire safety sci. various orgns., 1972—; affiliate prof. fire protection engring. dept. Worcester Poly. Inst., 2000-03; vis. rsch. scholar U. Ulster, No. Ireland, 2000-03. Editor: Fire Science for Fire Safety, 1984, Fire Safety Science--Procs. of the First Internat. Symposium, 1986, Procs. of the Second Internat. Symposium, 1989; contbr. articles to profl. jours. Grantee NSF, NASA, Nat. Bur. Standards, Nat. Inst. Standards and Tech., U.S. Forest Svc., 1971—; Applied Mechanics fellow Harvard U., 1974, 77; Pullman Found. scholar, 1960. Mem. ASME (life), Am. Phys. Soc. (life), Combustion Inst., Soc. Fire Protection Engrs. (hon., Bono award for best paper 1999), Internat. Assn. Fire Safety Sci. (life mem., exec. com.), Tau Beta Pi, Pi Tau Sigma, Alpha Sigma Nu Democrat. Roman Catholic. Home: 1901 Ascot Dr Moraga CA 94556-1412 Office: U Calif Coll Engring Mech Engring Dept Berkeley CA 94720-1740 Office Phone: 925-376-4288. Business E-Mail: pjpagni@me.berkeley.edu.

PAGON, ROBERTA ANDERSON, pediatrician, educator; b. Boston, Oct. 4, 1945; d. Donald Grigg and Erna Louise (Goettsch) Anderson; m. Garrett Dunn Pagon Jr., July 1, 1967; children: Katharine Blye, Garrett Dunn III, Alyssa Grigg, Alexander Goettsch. BA, Stanford U., 1967; MD, Harvard U., 1972. Diplomate Am. Bd. Pediat., Am. Bd. Med. Genetics. Pediatric intern U. Wash. Affiliated Hosp., Seattle, 1972-73, resident in pediat., 1973-75; fellow in med. genetics U. Wash. Sch. Medicine, Seattle, 1976-79, asst. prof. pediat., 1979-84, assoc. prof., 1984-92, prof., 1992—. Prin. investigator, editor in chief GeneTests (www.genetests.org), Seattle, 1992—; pres. Am. Bd. Med. Genetics, 2002, 03; bd. sci. counselors Nat. Human Genome Rsch. Inst., NIH, 2000—04. Sponsor N.W. region U.S. Pony Club, 1985-94. Mem. Am. Soc. Human Genetics (bd. dirs. 2005-2007, Excellence award in Edn. 2006), Am. Coll. Med. Genetics, Western Soc. Pediat. Rsch., Phi Beta Kappa. Avocations: hiking, backpacking, horseback riding. Office: Gene Tests 9725 Third Ave NE Ste 602 Seattle WA 98115 Office Phone: 206-221-4674. Business E-Mail: bpagon@u.washington.edu.

PAGTER, CARL RICHARD, lawyer; b. Balt., Feb. 13, 1934; s. Charles Ralph and Mina (Amelung) P.; m. Judith Elaine Cox, May 6, 1978; 1 child by previous marriage: Corbin Christopher. AA, Diablo Valley Coll., 1953; BA, San Jose State U., 1955; LLB, U. Calif., Berkeley, 1964. Bar: Calif. 1965, D.C. 1977, U.S. Supreme Ct. 1976. Law clk. Kaiser Industries Corp., Oakland, Calif., 1963-64, counsel, 1964-70, assoc. counsel Washington, 1970-73, counsel Oakland, Calif., 1973-75, dir. govt. affairs Washington, 1975-76; v.p., sec., gen. counsel Kaiser Cement Corp., Oakland, Calif., 1976-88, cons., gen. counsel San Ramon, 1988-98, cons., 1998—. Author: (with A. Dundes) Urban Folklore from the Paperwork Empire, 1975, More Urban Folklore from the Paperwork Empire, 1987, Never Try to Teach a Pig to Sing, 1991, Sometimes the Dragon Wins, 1996, Why Don't Sheep Shrink When It Rains, 2000. Trustee Internat. Bluegrass Music Mus., Owensboro, Ky.; bd. mem., treasurer Bluegrass Music Found., Nashville. With USNR, 1957—61, to comdr. USNR, 1978. Mem. Calif. Bar, Am. Folklore Soc., Calif. Folklore Soc., Calif. Bluegrass Assn. (founder, chmn. bd. emeritus), Mariners Square Athletic Club. Republican. Home and Office: 17 Julianne Ct Walnut Creek CA 94595-2610

PAISLEY, CHRISTOPHER B., business educator; BA in Econ., U. Calif., Santa Barbara; MBA, UCLA. Various acctg. and fin. positions Hewlett Packard Co.; v.p. fin. Ridge Computers, 1982-85; sr. v.p. fin., CFO 3Com Corp., Santa Clara, Calif., 1985-2000; prof. Santa Clara (Calif.) U. Leavey Sch. Bus., 2000—. Bd. dirs. Brocade Comm. Sys., Volterra, Electronics for Imaging, Fortinet Corp. Mem. Fin. Execs. Inst. Office: Santa Clara U Leavey Sch Bus 500 El Camino Real Santa Clara CA 95053

PAKULA, ANITA SUSAN, dermatologist; b. LA, Nov. 20, 1961; BA, Pomona Coll., 1983; BS, Calif. Luth. Coll., 1985; MD, U. Calif., Irvine, 1988. Diplomat Am. Bd. Dermatology, NAt. Bd. Med. Examiners. Intern Evanston (Ill.) Hosp., 1988-89; resident Northwestern U. Med. Sch., Chgo., 1989-92; asst. clin. prof. dermatology UCLA

MEd. Ctr., 1993—. Presenter in field. Contbr. articles to profl. jours. Fellow Am. Acad. Dermatology; mem. Soc. Pediatric Dermatology. Office: 267 W Hillcrest Dr Thousand Oaks CA 91360-4923

PAL, PRATAPADITYA, curator; b. Bangladesh, Sept. 1, 1935; came to U.S., 1967; s. Gopesh Chandra and Bidyut Kana (Dam) P.; m. Chitralekha Bose, Apr. 20, 1968; children: Shalmali, Lopamudra. MA, U. Calcutta, 1958, DPhil, 1962; PhD (UK Commonwealth Scholar), U. Cambridge, 1965. Rsch. assoc. Am. Acad. Benares, India, 1966—67; keeper Indian collections Mus. Fine Arts, Boston, 1967—69; sr. curator Indian and Southeast Asian art Los Angeles County Mus. Art, 1970—95, acting dir., 1979; vis. curator Indian and S.E. Asian art Art Inst. Chgo., 1995—2003; rsch. fellow Norton Simon Mus., Pasadena, Calif., 1995—2005. Gen. editor Marg Publs., Mumbai, 1993-; adj. prof. fine arts U. So. Calif., 1971-89; vis. prof. U. Calif., Santa Barbara, 1980, Irvine, 1994-95; Sir George Birdwood Meml. lectr., The Royal Asiatic Soc., London, 1973; William Cohn lectr. Oxford U., 1983; Catherine Mead meml. lectr. Pierpont Morgan Libr., NYC, 1986; Ananda K. Coomaraswamy meml. lectr. Prince of Wales Mus., Bombay, 1987; D.J. Sibley prehistoric art lectr. U. Tex., Austin, 1989; Anthony Gardner meml. lectr. Victoria and Albert Mus., London, 1993, keynote spkr. 1st Internat. Conf. on Tibetan Art, 1994; spkr. Chgo. Arts Festival, 2002, Aspen Ideas Festival, 2008; mem. commr.'s art adv. panel IRS, Washington, 1986-96. Author: Vaisnava Iconology in Nepal, 1970, The Arts of Nepal, vol. 1, 1974, vol. 2, 1979, The Sensuous Immortals, 1977, The Ideal Image: Gupta Sculptures and its Influence, 1978, The Classical Tradition in Rajput Painting, 1978, Elephants and Ivories, 1981, A Buddhist Paradise: Murals of Alchi, 1982, Art of Tibet, 1983, Tibetan Painting, 1984, Art of Nepal, 1985, From Merchants to Emperors, 1986, Indian Sculpture, vol. 1, 1986, Icons of Piety, Images of Whimsey, 1987, Indian Sculpture, vol. 2, 1988, Buddhist Book Illuminations, 1988, Romance of the Taj Mahal, 1989, Art of the Himalayas, 1991, Pleasure Gardens of the Mind, 1993; Indian Painting, vol. 1, 1993, The Peaceful Liberators: Jain Art from India, 1994, A Collecting Odyssey, 1997, Divine Images, Human Visions, 1997, Tibet Change and Tradition, 1997, Desire and Devotion, 2001, Himalayas: An Aesthetic Adventure, 2003, Asian Art in the Norton Simon Museum, vols. 1 and 2, 2003, vol. 3, 2004; Painted Poems, 2004, Durga: Avenging Goddess Nurturing Mother, 2005, The Arts of Kashmir, 2007; Sindh: Past Glory Present Nostalgia, 2008. Khaira Rsch. Scholar, Kolkata U. 1959-62, Commonwealth Scholar, UK, 1962-65, John D. Rockefeller III Fund fellow, 1964, 69, fellow NEA, 1974; Getty scholar, 1995-96; recipient Padma Shri award, India, 2009, U. Gold medal, 1959. Fellow Asia Soc. (Bombay, hon.); mem. Asiatic Soc. (Calcutta, B.C. Law gold medal 1993, R.P. Chanda Centenary medal, 2003)

PALACIO, JUNE ROSE PAYNE, nutritional science educator; b. Hove, Sussex, Eng., June 14, 1940; came to U.S., 1949; d. Alfred and Doris Winifred (Payne) P.; m. Moki Moses Palacio, Nov. 30, 1968 (wid. June 1999); m. Cliff Duboff, Dec. 22, 2002. AA, Orange Coast Coll., Costa Mesa, Calif., 1960; BS, U. Calif., Berkeley, 1963; PhD, Kans. State U., 1984. Registered dietitian. Asst. dir. food svc. and res. halls Mills Coll., Oakland, Calif., 1964-66; staff dietitian Servomation Bay Cities, Oakland, 1966-67; commissary mgr. Host Internat., Inc., Honolulu, 1967-73; dir. dietetics Straub Clinic and Hosp., Honolulu, 1973-80; instr. Kans. State U., Manhattan, 1980-84; prof. and program dir. Calif. State U., LA, 1984-85; prof., asst. dean Pepperdine U., Malibu, Calif., 1985—. Instr. Kapiolani C.C., Honolulu, 1973-79, U. Hawaii, Honolulu, 1975-80, Ctr. for Dietetic Edn., Woodland Hills, Calif., 1986—; cons. Clevenger Nutritional Svcs., Calabasas, Calif., 1985—, Calif. Mus. Sci. and Industry, L.A., 1989—, Calif. State Dept. Edn., Sacramento, 1985—. Author: Foodservice in Institutions, 1988, Introduction to Foodservice, 1992, 97, 2001, 05, The Profession of Dietetics, 1996, 2000, 05. Mem. Am. Dietetic Assn. (del. 1977-80, 86-89, commr. Commn. for Accreditation of Dietic Edn. 1997—), Calif. Dietetic Assn. (pres. 1992-93), L.A. Dist. Dietetic Assn., Foodsvc. Systems Mgmt. Edn. Coun., Dietetic Educators of Practitioners, Gamma Sigma Delta, Omicron Nu, Phi Upsilon Omicron. Republican. Episcopalian. Avocations: tennis, running, reading, travel. Office: Pepperdine U 24255 Pacific Coast Hwy Malibu CA 90263-0002 Business E-Mail: june.palacio@pepperdine.edu.

PALACIOS, CHRISTINA, academic administrator; With S.W. Gas, 1984—, former mgr. human resources, adminstrn., customer rels., ops. and support, v.p. So. Nev. divsn., 1995—97, v.p. in charge of So. Ariz. divsn., 1997—; mem., asst. sec. Ariz. Bd. Regents, Phoenix. Mem. Sch. Facilities Bd., Ariz. Office: Ariz Bd Regents Ste 230 2020 N Central Ave Phoenix AZ 85004

PALEN, TIM, film company executive; V.p. theatrical mktg. Lionsgate Films, 2001, exec. v.p. theatrical mktg., co-pres. film mktg., 2006—. Author: Guts, 2007. Named one of 50 Smartest People in Hollywood, Entertainment Weekly, 2007. Office: Lionsgate Entertainment Corp 2700 Colorado Ave Santa Monica CA 90404

PALFENIER, DAVID, food products executive; BBA, Ea. Wash. U., Cheney. Sales and mktg. assoc. Proctor & Gamble; dir. mktg., Famous Brands Chiquita Brands Internat., Cin., 1990—91, v.p. mktg., John Morell, 1990—91; mktg. and mgmt. positions including v.p. mktg. and gen. mgr. immediate consumption bus. Frito Lay Corp., Plano, Tex., 1991—2004; sr. v.p. mktg. frozen foods divsn. ConAgra Foods, Inc., 2004—05, gen. mgr. frozen foods divsn., 2005, pres. frozen foods divsn., pres. grocery foods, 2006—. Office: Conagra Foods 8101 E Kaiser Blvd Ste 160 Anaheim CA 92808-2256 Office Phone: 402-595-6000.

PALFREY, THOMAS ROSSMAN, economics professor, political science professor; b. Lafayette, Ind., Oct. 11, 1953; s. Thomas Rossman and Emily Skillings Palfrey; m. Cheryl Craig, July 9, 1976; 1 child, Rossman Craig. BA in Polit. Sci. magna cum laude, U. Mich., 1975, MA in Polit. Sci., 1976; PhD, Calif. Inst. Tech., 1981. Prof. politics and econs. Princeton U., NJ, 2004—06; prof. econs. and polit. economy Carnegie Mellon U., Pasadena, Pa., 1980—; prof. econs. and polit. sci. Calif. Inst. Tech., Pasadena, 1986—2005, Flintridge Found. prof. econs. and poliitcal sci., 2006—. Author: (book) Bayesian Implementation, 1993, Voting: What is, What Could Be, 2001; editor: Laboratory Research in Political Economy, 1991, Experimental Foundations of Political Science, 1993; contbr. over 100 scholarly articles to profl. jours. Dir. Caltech-MIT Voting Tech. Project, Pasadena, 2000—02. Fellow, Ctr. Advanced Study Behavioral Scis., 1986—87; grant, NSF, 1982—. Fellow: Am. Acad. Arts and Scis., Econometric Soc.; mem.: Pub. Choice Soc., Am. Econ. Assn., Game Theory Soc., Econ. Sci. Assn. (pres., v.p., exec. bd. 1988—99). Avocations: classical guitar, tennis, hiking. Office: Calif Inst Tech Mail Code 228-77 (HSS) Pasadena CA 91125

PALIN, SARAH HEATH, Governor of Alaska; b. Sandpoint, Idaho, Feb. 11, 1964; d. Chuck and Sally Heath; m. Todd Mitchell Palin, Aug. 29, 1988; children: Bristol, Piper, Track, Willow, Trig Paxon. BS in Journalism, U. Idaho, 1987. Mem. city council City of Wasila, Alaska, 1992—96, mayor, 1996—2002; chair Alaska Oil and Gas Conservation Commn., 2003—04; mem. Interstate Oil and Gas Compact Commn.; gov. State of Alaska, Juneau, 2006—; Rep. vice-presdl. nominee, 2008—. Mem. Alaska Resource Devel. Coun. Pres. Alaska Conf. Mayors; mem. steering com. Youth Ct.; bd. mem. Alaska Mcpl. League, Valley Hosp. Assn. Recipient Person of Yr. award, Am. Pub. Works Assn. (Alaska chpt.), Top 40 Under 40 award, Alaska State Chamber; named Miss Wasila, 1984; named one of The Ten Most Fascinating People of 2008, Barbara Walters, The World's Most Influential People, TIME mag., 2009. Mem.: Alaska Miner's Assn., Alaska Outdoor Coun., NRA (life), Rotary (hon.), Sigma Beta Delta. Republican. Achievements include being the youngest person and the first woman to hold the office of governor of Alaska, 2006. Avocations: hunting, fishing, running, history. Office: Office of the Gov State Capitol PO Box 110001 Juneau AK 99811*

PALKOVIC, MICHAEL W., broadcast executive; With Times Mirror Cable TV, DIRECTV Group, El Segundo, Calif., 1996—, sr. v.p., CFO US bus., 2001—04, exec. v.p., CFO US bus., 2004—, exec. v.p., CFO, 2005—07, exec. v.p. ops., 2007—. Office: DIRECTV Group 2230 E Imperial Hwy El Segundo CA 90245 Office Phone: 310-964-5000.

PALL, GURDEEP SINGH, computer software company executive; Grad., Birla Inst. Tech., India; MS in Computer Sci., U. Oreg., 1989. Software design engr. Microsoft Corp., Redmond, Wash., 1990, gen. mgr. Windows networking, 2001, gen. mgr. Windows real-time comm. efforts, 2002, corp. v.p. Unified Comm. Group, 2005—. Co-recipient Innovation of Yr. award, PC Magazine, 1996; named one of the 15 Innovators & Influencers Who Will Make A Difference in 2008, Info. Week. Office: Microsoft Corp One Microsoft Way Redmond WA 98052-6399

PALLIN, SAMUEL LEAR, ophthalmologist, educator, medical director; b. NYC, May 8, 1941; s. Irving and Gertrude (Lear) P.; children: Daniel Jay, Marla Jean, Laura Jane; m. Karen K. King, 2004. BA, Hofstra U., 1963; MD, SUNY, Bklyn., 1968. Diplomate Nat. Bd. Med. Examiners, Am. Bd. Ophthalmology. Intern L.I. Jewish Med. Ctr., 1968-69; resident Bklyn. Eye and Ear Hosp., 1972-75; prin. The Lear Eye Clinic, Ltd., Sun City, Ariz., 1975—, Phoenix, 1998—; asst. prof. dept. ophthalmology Sch. Medicine Midwestern U., 1997—; with White Dog Ranch, LLC, Tonopah, Ariz., 2005—; physician supr., med. dir. Arizona State Prison Complex, Perryville, 2005—. Mem. staff Walter O. Boswell Meml. Hosp., Del E. Webb Meml. Hosp., St. Luke's Med. Ctr., Thunderbird Samaritan Hosp.; presenter in field. Patentee in method of making self-sealing episcleral incision. Trustee Congr. Beth El Endowment Fund, 1987; mem. exec. bd. Ariz. chpt. Israel Bonds, 1988; lt. mounted unit cmty. svcs. posse Maricopa County Sheriff's Office, 1996—. With USAF, 1969-71. Mem. AMA, ACS, Am. Soc. Cataract and Refractive Surgery, Am. Acad. Ophthalmology, Ariz. Med. Assn., Ariz. Easter Seal Soc. (bd. dirs. 1989, life dir.), Maricopa County Med. Assn., Lions; hon. mem. Mex. Ophthalmology Soc. N.E., Mex. Intraocular Implant Soc., Ctrl. Mex. Ophthalmol. Soc.

PALLOTTI, MARIANNE MARGUERITE, foundation administrator; b. Hartford, Conn., Apr. 23, 1937; d. Rocco D. and Marguerite (Long) P. BA, NYU, 1968, MA, 1972. Asst. to pres. Wilson, Haight & Welch, Hartford, 1964-65; exec. asst. Ford Found., NYC, 1965-77; corp. sec. Hewlett Found., Menlo Park, Calif., 1977-84, v.p., 1985—. Bd. dirs. N.Y. Theatre Ballet, N.Y.C., 1986-98, Austin Montessori Sch., 1993, Djerassi Resident Artists Program, 1998—, Mexican Mus., 1999—; mem. women's adv. com., nat. coun.World Wildlife Fund, 1997—; mem. program com. Ind. Sector, Washington, 1998—. Mem. Women in Founds., No. Calif. Grantmakers. Office: William and Flora Hewlett Foundation 2121 Sand Hill Rd Menlo Park CA 94025-6903

PALM, CHARLES GILMAN, academic administrator; b. Havre, Mont., Apr. 25, 1944; s. Victor F. and Laura (McKinnie) P.; m. Miriam Willits, Sept. 15, 1968. AB, Stanford U., 1966; MA, U. Wyo., 1967; MLS, U. Oreg., 1970. From asst. archivist to dep. dir. Hoover Instn. Stanford (Calif.) U., Palo Alto, Calif., 1971—90; dep. dir. Hoover Instn. Stanford U., 1990—2001, dep. dir. emeritus, 2002—. Adv. bd. Calif. Hist. Records, 2006—. Co-author: Guide to Hoover Institution Archives, 1980, Herbert Hoover, Register of His Papers in the Hoover Institution Archives, 1983. Mem. Calif. Heritage Preservation Commn., Sacramento, 1988-2005, vice chmn., 1993-97, chmn., 1997-2004; mem. Nat. Hist. Records and Publs. Commn., Washington, 1990-96; mem. history and edn. ctr. adv. bd. ARC, 1994-2005; trustee Golden State Mus. Corp., 1997-2004. Fellow: Soc. Am. Archivists; mem.: Soc. Calif. Archivists (pres. 1983—84), Bohemian Club. Republican. Office: Hoover Instn Stanford CA 94305

PALMA, JACK D., lawyer; b. NYC, Sept. 15, 1946; BA, Allegheny Coll., 1968; JD with honors, U. Denver, 1974. Bar: Colo. 1975, Wyo. 1976. Ptnr. Holland & Hart, Cheyenne, Wyo., 1984—. Mem. ABA, Colo. Bar Assn., Wyo. State Bar, Order St. Ives. Office: Holland & Hart PO Box 1347 Cheyenne WY 82003-1347 Office Phone: 307-778-4200. E-mail: jpalma@hollandhart.com.

PALMER, BEVERLY BLAZEY, psychologist, educator; b. Cleve., Nov. 22, 1945; d. Lawrence E. and Mildred M. Blazey; m. Richard C. Palmer, June 24, 1967; 1 child, Ryan Richard. PhD in Counseling Psychology, Ohio State U., 1972. Lic. clin. psychologist, Calif. Adminstrv. assoc. Ohio State U., Columbus, 1969—70; rsch. psychologist Health Svcs. Rsch. Ctr. UCLA, 1971—77; commr. pub. health L.A. County, 1978—81; pvt. practice Torrance, Calif., 1985—; prof. psychology Calif. State U., Dominguez Hills, 1973—2006; faculty Saybrook Grad. Sch. and Rsch. Ctr., 2005—. Author: Interpersonal Skills for Helping Professionals Online Course, 2001, 04, reviewer manuscripts for numerous textbook pubs; contbr. articles to profl. jours. Recipient Proclamation, County of L.A., 1972, 1981, Outstanding Prof. award, Calif. State U., 1995; Fulbright scholar, Borneo, 2001, Fulbright Sr. scholar, Malaysia, 2004—05, Fulbright scholar, Barbados, 2005. Mem. APA. Office: Calif State U Dominguez Hills Dept Psychology Carson CA 90747-0001 Office Phone: 310-373-6691 2. Business E-Mail: bpalmer@csudh.edu.

PALMER, DAVID GILBERT, lawyer; b. Lakewood, NJ, Jan. 10, 1945; s. Robert Dayton and Lois (Gilbert) P.; m. Susan Edmundson Walsh, Aug. 17, 1968; children: Jonathan, Megan. AB, Johns Hopkins U., 1967; JD, U. Colo., 1970. Bar: Colo. 1970, U.S. Dist. Ct. Colo. 1970, U.S. Ct. Appeals (9th and 10th cirs.) 1970, U.S. Supreme Ct. 1970. Ptnr., mng. ptnr., chmn. litig. dept. Holland & Hart, Denver, 1970-87; ptnr., mng. ptnr. Gibson, Dunn & Crutcher, Denver, 1987-97; mng. ptnr. Zevnik, Horton, Palmer, Denver, 1997-2001; mng. shareholder Greenberg Traurig LLP, Denver, 2001—. Chmn. N.W. region Am. Heart Assn., Dallas, 1986—, bd. dirs., 1986—, sec., 1990—, nat. chmn., 1992-93; pres., bd. dirs. Colo. Heart Assn., Denver, 1974; bd. dirs. C.H. Kempe Nat. Ctr. for Prevention of Child Abuse, Denver, 1984-90, pres., 1989-90; bd. dirs. Goodwill Industries, Denver, 1981-84, Metro Denver Econ. Devel. Corp., 2004—; mem. coun. of advisors U. Colo. Med. Sch., 2004—. Mem. ABA, Colo. Bar Assn., Denver Law Club, Univ. Club of Denver (pres. 2004-05), Mile High Club. Office: Greenberg Traurig Tabor Ctr 1200 17th St Ste 2400 Denver CO 80202 Office Phone: 303-572-6539. Office Fax: 303-572-6540. Business E-Mail: palmerdg@gtlaw.com.

PALMER, DAVID J., library director, municipal official; BA, M, U. Mich. With City of Chula Vista, Calif., 1988—, asst. libr. dir., 1988—93, libr. dir., 1993—, head libr. and recreation dept., 1998—2000, dep. city mgr., 2000—03, asst. city mgr., 2003—. Office: Chula Vista Pub Libr 365 F St Chula Vista CA 91910 Office Phone: 619-691-5069.

PALMER, DOUGLAS S., JR., lawyer; b. Peoria, Ill., Mar. 15, 1945; AB cum laude, Yale U., 1966; JD cum laude, Harvard U., 1969. Bar: Wash. 1969. Mem. Foster Pepper & Shefelman PLLC, Seattle, 1975—2002, Hillis Clark Martin & Peterson, P.S., Seattle, 2002—. Office: Hillis Clark Martin & Peterson PS 500 Galland Bldg 1221 Second Ave Seattle WA 98101-2925 Office Phone: 206-623-1745.

PALMER, EARL A., ophthalmologist, educator; m. Carolyn Mary Clark. BA, Ohio State U., 1962; MD, Duke U., 1966. Diplomate Am. Bd. Pediat., Am. Bd. Ophthalmology. Resident in pediat. U. Colo. Med. Ctr., Denver, 1966-68; resident in ophthalmology Oreg. Health & Scis. U., Portland, 1971—74, prof., 1979—; fellow Baylor Coll. Medicine, Houston, 1974-75; asst. prof. Pa. State U., Hershey, 1975-79. Eye alignment specialist; expert in retinopathy of prematurity. Contbr. articles to profl. jours. Fellow: Am. Acad. Ophthalmology (Honor award); mem.: Am. Assn. Pediatric Ophthalmology and Strabismus (pres. 1996—97). Avocation: golf. Office: Casey Eye Inst 3375 SW Terwilliger Blvd Portland OR 97239-4197 Home Phone: 503-635-4004; Office Phone: 503-494-7675. Business E-Mail: palmere@ohsu.edu.

PALMER, GARY ANDREW, portfolio manager; b. Stamford, Conn., Dec. 30, 1953; s. Andrew and Edna Balz (Brogan) P.; m. Suzanne Branyon, Oct. 10, 1981; children: Gregory Allen, Kimberly Lynn. BS in Bus. Adminstrn., U. Vt., 1977; MBA, U. N.C., 1979. Sr. fin. analyst Carolina Power and Light Co., Raleigh, NC, 1979—80; dir. fin. planning and analysis Fed. Home Loan Mortgage Corp., Washington, 1980—85; sr. v.p. capital markets Imperial Corp. of Am., San Diego, 1985—90; sr. v.p., treas. Pacific 1st Fin. Corp., Seattle, 1990—92, Gentral Capital Corp., Seattle, 1993—95; CFO So. Pacific Funding Corp., Lake Oswego, Oreg., 1995—97; pvt. practice Lake Oswego, 1998—99; CFO FiNet.com, Inc., San Ramon, Calif., 1999—2000; exec. v.p. Capital Mkts., LoanCity.com, San Jose, 2001; sr. dir. product devel. Fannie Mae, Washington, 2002—04; pres. Winning Attitudes, LLC, 2004—.

PALMER, JAMES F., aerospace transportation executive; BS, Southeast Mo. State, 1971. Sr. v.p., CFO McDonnell Douglas Corp., 1995—97; pres., Boeing Shared Services Group The Boeing Co., 1997—2000, sr. v.p.; pres. Boeing Capital Corp., 2000—04; exec. v.p., CFO Visteon Corp., 2004—07; corp. v.p., CFO Northrop Grumman Corp., LA, 2007—. Office: Northrop Grumman Corp 1840 Century Park E Los Angeles CA 90067-2199 Office Phone: 734-710-2020.

PALMER, JERRY PHILIP, medical educator, researcher, internist; b. NYC, Apr. 5, 1944; BA in Biology, SUNY, 1966; MD cum laude, Upstate Med. Ctr., Syracuse, NY, 1970. Diplomate Am. Bd. Internal Medicine, Am. Bd. Endocrinology and Metabolism. Intern Dartmouth Affiliated Hosps., Hanover, N.H., 1970-71, resident, 1971-72; sr. rsch. fellow divsn. endocrinology dept. medicine U. Wash., Seattle, 1972-74, acting instr. dept. medicine, 1974-75, dir. adminstrn. core diabetes endocrinology ctr., 1975—; dir. clin. rsch. core Diabetes Endocrinology Rsch. Ctr. U. Wash., Seattle, 1975-88, 91—, dep. dir., 1977-96, dir., 1996—; acting asst. prof. dept. medicine U. Wash., Seattle, 1975-77, asst. prof. dept. medicine, 1977-80, assoc. prof. dept. medicine, 1980-86, prof. dept. medicine, 1986—; assoc. med. staff Univ. Hosp., Seattle, 1975—; attending physician Seattle Pub. Health Hosp., 1975-82, Pacific Med. Ctr., Seattle, 1982-89; mem. med. staff Providence Med. Ctr., Seattle, 1988-89, VA Med. Ctr., Seattle, 1989—; chief divsn. endocrinology, metabolism and nutrition Seattle VA Med. Ctr., 1989—; dir. diabetes care ctr. U. Wash. Med. Ctr., 1991—. Pfizer vis. prof. U. Tex., Houston, 1996. Assoc. editor: Diabetes, 1984, 85, 86. Mem. Am. Diabetes Assn. (Wash. affiliate bd. dirs. 1975-83, Wash. affiliate v.p. 1976, 77, Wash. affiliate chmn. peer rev. com. 1984, 85, 86, mem. rsch. com. 1985, 86, 87, 88, ad hoc expert com. on immunotherapy of IDDM 1990, chmn. task force on profl. membership 1991-92, mem. publs. policy com. 1993-95, bd. dirs. 1994-96, mem. scientific and med. meetings oversight com. 1995—, clin. rsch. grant 1996), Am. Fedn. for Clin. Rsch., Am. Soc. for Clin. Investigation, Endocrine Soc., King County Med., Assn. Am. Physicians, We. Assn. Physicians, We. Soc. for Clin. Rsch., Immunology Diabetes Soc. (pres. 1994-95), Alpha Omega Alpha. Office: VA Puget Sound Healthcare Sys 1660 S Columbian Way Seattle WA 98108-1532

PALMER, JOE, state legislator; m. Leslie Palmer; children: Page, Chase, Ty, Cord. Attended, Ricks Coll.; grad., Boise State U. Employee Pat Palmer Construction; owner Cherry's Built in Vacs, 1986—2002, Cherry's Consignment Home Furnishings, 2002—; mem. Dist. 20 Idaho House of Reps., 2008—. With Idaho Nat. Guard US Army. Republican. Office: Capitol Annex PO Box 83720 Boise ID 83720-0054 also: 1523 W First Meridian ID 83642 Office Phone: 208-334-2475, 208-887-9488. Office Fax: 208-334-2125, 208-884-0181. Business E-Mail: jpalmer@house.idaho.gov.*

PALMER, ROBERT ARTHUR, private investigator; b. St. Augustine, Fla., May 20, 1948; m. Christine Lynn Creger, May 14, 1974. AA, Glendale C.C., 1975; BS, U. Phoenix, 1981; MA, Prescott Coll., 1993; PhD, Union Inst., 1999. Lic. pvt. investigator, Ariz.; bd. cert. forensic examiner. Dep. sheriff Maricopa County Sheriff's Office, Phoenix, 1971-79; owner Palmer Investigative Svcs., Prescott, Ariz., 1980-90; pres. The Magnum Corp., Prescott, 1990—; deacon, 2006, V.p. Mountain Club Homeowners, Prescott, 1986-03, deacon Roman

Cath. Diocese Phoenix, 2006. Mem. Internat. Assn. Chem. Testing, World Assn. Detectives, Nat. Assn. Legal Investigators, Nat. Assn. Profl. Process Servers, Am. Coll. Forensic Examiners, Ariz. Assn. Lic. Pvt. Investigators (pres. 1984), Ariz. Process Servers Assn. (pres. 1985-86), Prescott C. of C. (v.p. 1987-90). Avocations: photography, collecting western art. Office: Palmer Investigative Svcs PO Box 10760 Prescott AZ 86304-0760 Office Phone: 928-778-2951. Business E-Mail: magnum@cableone.net.

PALMER, ROBERT BRIAN, physicist; b. London, Feb. 28, 1934; s. Reginald William and Beatrice M. (Carter) P.; m. Magdalena Wipf, Dec. 29, 1961; children: Susannah, Malcolm. BS, Imperial Coll., London, 1956, PhD, 1959. Research assoc. Imperial Coll., 1959-60; physicist Brookhaven Nat. Lab., Upton, N.Y., 1960—, assoc. dir. for high energy physics, 1983-86; physicist Stanford (Calif.) Linear Accelerator Corp., 1987—. Mem. high energy physics adv. panel Dept. Energy, Washington, 1983-86. 2 Patents in field; contbr. 71 articles on particle and accelerator physics. Mem. Am. Phys. Soc. (div. particles and fields). Democrat. Avocations: sailing, skiing, climbing. Office: Stanford Linear Accelerator Corp Sand Hill Walk Rd # 4349 Palo Alto CA 94304 also: Brookhaven Nat Lab Physics Dept Bldg 901A PO Box 5000 Upton NY 11973-5000 also: IRT Corp 6020 Cornerstone Ct W Ste 300 San Diego CA 92121-3707

PALMER, ROBERT L., lawyer; b. Bryn Mawr, Pa., Aug. 15, 1946; BA, Georgetown U., 1968; JD, Columbia U., 1971. Bar: D.C. 1972, Ariz. 1976. Law clerk to Hon. Harold Leventhal U.S. Ct. Appeals (D.C. cir.), 1971-72; with Covington & Burling, Washington, 1972-73, 75; asst. spec. prosecuter Watergate spec. prosecution force U.S. Dept. Justice, 1973-74; mem. Meyer, Hendricks, Victor, Osborn & Maledon, Phoenix, Ariz., 1976-95, Hennigan, Mercer & Bennett (name now Hennigan, Bennett & Dorman), LA, 1995—. Adj. prof. law U. Ariz., 1983.; bd. dirs. Ariz. Ctr. for Law in Pub. Interest, 1990-96, pres., 1990-92. Notes and comments editor Columbia Law Rev., 1970-71. Mem. ABA (assoc. editor litigation jour. sect. litigation 1979-82). Home: 865 S Figueroa St Ste 2900 Los Angeles CA 90017-2576

PALMER, VENRICE ROMITO, lawyer, educator; b. Springfield, Mass., Jan. 11, 1952; s. Venrice Wellesley and Mildred Adlay (Foster) P. Higher diploma, U. Besançon, France, 1973; AB maxima cum laude, King's Coll., Wilkes-Barre, Pa., 1974; JD, Harvard U., 1977. Bar: N.Y. 1978, U.S. Dist. Ct. (so. and ea. dists.) N.Y. 1979, Ill. 1986, Calif. 1997. Spl. asst. atty. gen. Office N.Y. Atty. Gen., NYC, 1977-79; staff atty. SEC, NYC, 1979-82, br. chief, 1982-83, spl. trial counsel, 1983-85, acting asst. regional adminstr., 1984-85; sr. counsel Sears, Roebuck and Co., Hoffman Estates, Ill., 1985-97, Bank of Am., San Francisco, 1997-99; counsel McCutchen, Doyle, Brown & Enersen, LLP, San Francisco, 1999—2002; of counsel Bingham McCutchen LLP, San Francisco, 2002—07; pvt. practice San Francisco, 2007—. Guest lectr. St. John's U. Bus. Sch., N.Y.C., 1984; lectr. Practicing Law Inst., N.Y.C., 1995—, Glasser LegalWorks, Little Falls, N.J., 1997—, Am. Soc. Corp. Secs., 1997-99, Nat. Bus. Inst., Eau Claire, Wis., 2000—. Contbr. articles to various law publs. Recipient cert. of appreciation N.Y. State Bar Assn., 1978, Benaglia award King's Coll., 1974. Mem.: ABA, Calif. State Bar Assn. (mem. fin. instns. com. 2000—03), Alpha Mu Gamma, Delta Epsilon Sigma. Avocations: opera, ballet, reading. Home and Office: 1200 Gough St Apt 7A San Francisco CA 94109-6616 E-mail: steveintel@aol.com.

PALMER, WILLIAM JOSEPH, accountant; b. Lansing, Mich., Sept. 3, 1934; s. Joseph Flammin Lacchia and Henrietta (Yagerman) P.; m. Judith Pollock, Aug. 20, 1960 (div. Nov. 1980); children: William W., Kathryn E., Leslie A., Emily J.; m. Kathleen Francis Booth, June 30, 1990; stepchildren: Blair T. Manwell, Lindsay H. Manwell. BS, U. Calif., Berkeley, 1963. CPA. With Coopers & Lybrand, 1963—80, mng. ptnr. Sacramento, 1976—80; ptnr. Arthur Young & Co., San Francisco, 1980—89, Ernst & Young, San Francisco, 1989—94; prof. U. Calif., Berkeley, 1994—. Bd. dirs. Dutra Group; chair constrn. industry group Coopers & Lybrand, 1973-80, Arthur Young, 1980-89, Ernst & Young, 1989-94; guest lectr. Engring. Sch. Stanford U., 1976; lectr. Golden Gate Coll., 1975. Author: Businessman's Guide to Constuction, 1981, Construction Management Book, 1984, Construction Accounting and Financial Management, 5th edit., 1994, Construction Litigation-Representing The Contractor, 1992, Construction Insurance, Bonding and Risk Management, 1996. Bd. dirs. Sacramento Met. YMCA, 1976-82, KXPR, Sacramento 1976-85, V.p., 1979-82; bd. dirs. Sacramento Symphony Found., 1977-80; asst. state fin. chmn. Calif. Reagan for Pres., 1980. Lt. USN naval aviator, 1953-59. Mem. AICPA (vice chmn. com. constrn. industry 1975-81), Nat. Assn. Accts. (pres. Oakland/East Bay chpt. 1972, Man of Yr. 1968), Calif. Soc. CPAs, Assn. Gen. Contractors Calif. (bd. dirs. 1971-74), World Trade Club, Del Paso Country Club, Sutter Club, Lambda Chi Alpha. Roman Catholic. Avocations: antique boats, golf, book collecting, pipe collecting. Home: PO Box 60405 Sacramento CA 95860-0405 Personal E-mail: kathpalm@hotmail.com.

PALOLA, HARRY JOEL, retired international affairs executive, consultant; b. Kaukola, Viipuri, Finland, May 13, 1943; came to U.S., 1961; s. Heikki and Mary Dagmar (Ahokas) P.; m. Rita Hannele Ahokas, Sept. 15, 1968 (div. July 1992); children: Christine, Kathy, Kimberly. AA, LA City Coll., 1966; BS in Mech. Engring., Calif. State U., Long Beach, 1971; MA in Internat. Affairs, Calif. State U., Sacramento, 1995. Registered engr.-in-tng., Calif. Design engr. Northrop Corp., Hawthorne, Calif., 1971-77, Ford Aerospace and Comm. Corp., Newport Beach, Calif., 1977-81, B&M Assocs., San Diego, 1982; mech. engr. Raytheon Corp., Goleta, Calif., 1982-84; electronic packaging engr. LPL Tech. Svc., Seattle, 1984-86; design/test engr. Boeing Co., Seattle and Vandenberg, Calif., 1986-92; CEO Internat. Consultancy Corp., Santa Ynez, Calif., 1993—2003, ret., 2003. Cons. in basic and applied rsch. in human comm., 1993—2003. Author: International Finnish Studies: Language, History and Culture, 1995, The Karjala Question-Thoughts on Religious Directions, 1997. Econ. devel. student intern City of Sacramento, 1992-93. Sgt. USNG, 1966-72. Republican. Lutheran. Avocations: ocean sailing, private flying, Finno-Urgic and Ural-Altaic languages.

PALTROW, GWYNETH, actress; b. LA, Sept. 28, 1972; d. Bruce Paltrow and Blythe Danner; m. Chris Martin, Dec. 5, 2003; children: Apple Blythe Alison Martin, Moses Martin. Student, U. Calif. Santa Barbara. Grad. Spence Sch., NYC, 1990. Spokesmodel Estee Lauder; designer ZOEtee's Loves Gwyneth, 2009—. Appeared in films: Shout, 1991, Hook, 1991, Malice, 1993, Flesh and Bone, 1993, Mrs. Parker and the Vicious Circle, 1994, Jefferson in Paris, 1995, Moonlight and Valentino, 1995, Seven, 1995, The Pallbearer, 1996, Emma, 1996, Hard Eight, 1996, Sliding Doors, 1998, Out of the Past, 1998 (voice), Great Expectations, 1998, Hush, 1998, A Perfect Murder, 1998, Shakespeare in Love, 1998 (Academy Award for Best Actress, Golden Globe for Best Actress), The Talented Mr. Ripley, 1999, Duets, 1999, The Intern, 2000, Bounce, 2000, The Anniversary Party, 2001, The Royal Tenenbaums, 2001, Shallow Hal, 2001, Possession, 2002, View From the Top, 2003, Sylvia, 2003, Sky Captain and the World of Tomorrow, 2004, Proof, 2005, Infamous, 2006, Love and Other Disasters, 2006, Running with Scissors, 2006, The Good Night, 2007, Two Lovers, 2008; TV films: Cruel Doubt, 1992, Deadly Relations, 1993; Theatre: Picnic, The Adventures of Huck Finn, Sweet Bye and Bye, The Seagull, Proof; co-host (TV Series) Spain...On the Road Again, 2008-. Named one of The 100 Most Powerful Celebrities, Forbes.com, 2008. Mem. Screen Actors Guild (Outstanding Performance with others). also: Screen Actors Guild 5757 Wilshire Blvd Los Angeles CA 90036-3635

PAMPLIN, ROBERT BOISSEAU, SR., retired textile manufacturing executive; b. Sutherland, Va., Nov. 25, 1911; s. John R. and Pauline P. (Beville); m. Mary K. Reese, June 15, 1940; 1 child, Robert Boisseau Jr. BBA, Va. Poly. Inst. & State U., 1933; postgrad., Northwestern U., 1933-34; LLD (hon.), U. Portland, Oreg., 1972; LHD (hon.), Warner Pacific Coll., 1976. With Ga.-Pacific Corp., Portland, 1934-76, sec., from 1936, adminstrv. v.p., 1952-55, exec. v.p., 1955-57, pres., 1957-67, chmn. bd., chief exec. officer, from 1967; ret., 1976; with R.B. Pamplin Corp., 1957—, chmn. bd., CEO, to 1996, Mt. Vernon Mills Inc. (subs. R.B. Pamplin Corp.), Greenville, S.C., retired, 1996. Office: R B Pamplin Corp Ste 2400 805 SW Broadway Portland OR 97205-3341

PAMPLIN, ROBERT BOISSEAU, JR., manufacturing company executive, minister, writer; b. Augusta, Ga., Aug. 3, 1941; s. Robert Boisseau and Mary Katherine (Reese) P.; m. Marilyn Joan Hooper; children: Amy Louise, Anne Boisseau. Student, Va. Poly. Inst., 1960-62, BSBA, 1964, BS in Acctg., 1965, BS in Econs., 1966; BS (hon.), Va. Tech., 2001; LHD (hon.), Va. Poly. Inst., 1995, Pacific U., 2001; DHL (hon.), Va. Poly. Inst., 1995; MBA, U. Portland, 1968, LLD (hon.), 1972, MEd, 1975; MA, Western Conservative Bapt. Sem. (name now Western Sem.), 1978, DMin, 1982, D (hon.) of Sacred Letter, 1991, MA, 2000; PhD, Calif. Coast U.; DHL (hon.), Warner Pacific Coll., 1988; LLD (hon.), Western Baptist Coll., 1989, George Fox U., 2005; cert. in wholesale mgmt., Ohio State U., 1970; cert. labor mgmt., U. Portland, 1982; cert. in advanced mgmt., U. Hawaii, 1975; DD (hon.), Judson Baptist Coll., 1984; DBA (hon.), Marquis Giuseppe Scicluna Internat. U. Found., 1986; LittD (hon.), Va. Tech. U., 1987, LHD (hon.), BS (hon.) in Bus. Adminstrn., 2001; LHD (hon.), Western Seminary, 1991; DD, Western Evang. Sem., 1994; DBA (hon.), U. S.C., 1996; D Pub. Svc., DHL (hon.), U. Puget Sound, Pacific U., 1999, 2001. Pres., CEO R.B. pamplin Corp., Portland, Oreg., 1964—. Chmn. bd., CEO Columbia Empire Farms Inc., Lake Oswego, Oreg., 1976—. Pamplin Comms.; chmn. bd., CEO Mt. Vernon Mills Inc.,; pres., CEO Ross Island Sand & Gravel; lectr. bus. adminstrn. Lewis and Clark Coll., 1968-69; adj. asst. prof. bus. adminstrn., U. Portland, 1973-76; pastor Christ Cmty. Ch., Lake Oswego; lectr. in bus. adminstrn. and econs. U. Costa Rica, 1968, Va. Tech. Found., 1986; chmn. bd. dirs. Christian Supplly Ctrs. Inc.; prof. with tenure U. Portland, 1999. Author: Everything is Just great, 1985, The Gift, 1986, Another Virginian: A Study of the Life and Beliefs of Robert Boisseau Pamplin, 1986; author: (with others) A Portrait of Colorado, 1976, Three in One, 1974, The Storybook Primer on Managing, 1974, One Who Believed, Vol. I, 1988, vol. II, 1991, Climbing the Centuries, 1993, Heritage the Making of an American Family, 1994, American Heroes, 1995, Prelude to Surrender, 1995, Alaska Gold, 1998, Robert Reese, 1998; editor: Oreg. Mus. Sci. and Industry Press, 1973; trustee Oreg. Mus. Sci. and Industry Press, 1971, 1974—; editor: Portrait of Oregon, 1973; editor: (with others) Oregon Underfoot, 1975. Trustee Lewis and Clark Coll., 1989—, chmn. bd. trustees, 1988-96, life trustee 1996-; hon. life pres. Western Conservative Bapt. Sem.; chmn. regents Western Sem., 1994; mem. nat. adv. coun. on vocat. Edn., 1975—; mem. Western Interstate Com. on Higher Edn., 1981-84; co-chmn. Va. Tech. $50 Million Campaign for Excellence, 1984-87, Va. Tech. Found., 1986—, Va.-Oreg. State Scholarship Commn., 1974—, chmn. 1976-78; mem. Portland dist. adv. coun. SBA, 1973-77; mem. rewards rev. com., City of Portland, 1973-78, chmn., 1973-78; bd. regents U. Portland, 1971-79, chmn. bd., 1975-79, regent emeritus, 1979—; trustee Oreg. Episc. Schs., 1979, Linfield Coll., U. Puget Sound, 1989—; dr. pub. svc., U. Puget Sound, 1999; chmn. bd. trustees Portland Art Mus., 2003-05. Recipient Disting. Alumnus award, Lewis and Clark Coll., 1974, ROTC Disting. Svc. award, USAF, 1974, bronze medal, Albert Einstein Acad., 1986, Disting. Leadership medal, Freedoms Found., Disting. Bus. Alumnus award, U. Portland, 1990, Nat. Caring award, Caring Inst., 1991, Pride of Portland award, Portland Lions Club, Hero Athlete award, 1994, Herman Lay Entrepreneurship award, 1995, Thomas Jefferson award, Oreg. Hist. Soc., 1998, Aubrey R. Watzek award, Lewis and Clark Coll., 1998, Leadership award, Portland Living Mag., 1998, Unique Contbns. to Comms. award, Portland Advt. Fedn., 2001, Oliver Wendell Holmes, Jr. award for Civil War Preservationalist of Yr., 2001, Govs. Arts award, 2001, Legacy award, Civil War Preservation Trust, 2003, Gov.'s Gold award as Oregonian of Achievement, 2003, Corp. Citizenship award, Woodrow Wilson Internat. Ctr. for Scholars, 2005, Nat. Vol. Outstanding Svc. award, Vol. Am., 2006; named Outstanding Philanthropist of Yr. award, Nat. Soc. Fund Raising Execs., 1997, Western Conservative Bapt. Sem. Lay Inst. for Leadership, Edn. Devel. and Rsch. named for R.B. Pamplin Jr., 1988, Textile World's Top 10, 1999, Portland First Citizen, Portland Met. Assn. Realtors, 1999, Parents of Yr., Juvenile Diabetes Found., 2001, Entrepreneur of Yr., Oreg. Entrepreneur Forum, 2001, Va. Tech. Coll. Bus. Adminstrn. renamed R.B. Pamplin Coll. Bus. Adminstrn. in his honor, U. Portland Sch. Bus. renamed Dr. Robert B. Pamplin, Jr. in his honor, Civil War Preservationalist of Yr., Civil War Preservation Trust, 2003, Nat. Vol. of Yr., Vols. of Am., 2006; named one of 20 Most Influential Execs. Past 20 Yrs., Bus. Jour. Mem. Acad. Mgmt., Delta Epsilon Sigma, Beta Gamma Sigma, Sigma Phi Epsilon, Waverley Country Club (pres. 2003-04), Arlington, Multnomah Athletic Club, Capitol Hill Club, Greenville Country Club, Poinsett Club, Eldorado Country Club, Thunderbird Country Club, Rotary. Republican. Episcopalian. Office: RB Pamplin Corp Inc Ste 2400 805 SW Broadway Portland OR 97205-3341

PANCRAZI, LYNNE, state legislator; Student, Ariz. Western Coll.; BA in Physical Edn., Point Loma Nazarene Coll., San Diego; MEd in Elem. Edn., Northern Ariz. U. Lic. realtor. Ret. tchr., athletic coach Yuma Elem. Sch. Dist. #1, Ariz.; mem. Dist. 24 Ariz. House of Reps., 2007—, mem. natural resources & rural affairs com.,pub. employees, retirement & entitlement reform com. Past. pres. Yuma Elem. Edn. Assn. Vol., coach Yuma Parks & Recreation Dept. Mem.: NEA, Nat. Assn. Realtors, Yuma Assn. Realtors. Democrat. Office: Ariz House Reps Capitol Complex 1700 W Washington Rm 324 Phoenix AZ 85007 Office Phone: 928-246-0846, 602-926-3004. Office Fax: 602-417-3179. Business E-Mail: lpancrazi@azleg.gov.*

PANELLI, EDWARD ALEXANDER, retired state supreme court justice; b. Santa Clara, Calif., Nov. 23, 1931; s. Pilade and Natalina (Della Maggiora) P.; m. Lorna Christine Mondora, Oct. 27, 1956; children: Thomas E., Jeffrey J., Michael P. BA cum laude, Santa Clara U., 1953, JD cum laude, 1955, LLD (hon.), 1986, Southwestern U., LA, 1988. Bar: Calif. 1955. Ptnr. Pasquinelli and Panelli, San Jose, Calif., 1955-72; judge Santa Clara County Superior Ct., 1972-83; assoc. justice 1st Dist. Ct. of Appeals, San Francisco, 1983-84; presiding justice 6th Dist. Ct. of Appeals, San Jose, 1984-85; assoc. justice Calif. Supreme Ct., San Francisco, 1985-94. Chief judicial officer JAMS/Endispute, 1995—; instr. Continuing Legal Edn., Santa Clara, 1976-78. Trustee West Valley Community Coll., 1963-72; trustee Santa Clara U., 1963—, chmn. bd. trustees, 1984—. Recipient Citation, Am. Com. Italian Migration, 1969, Community Legal Svcs. award, 1979, 84, Edwin J. Owens Lawyers of Yr. award Santa Clara Law Sch. Alumni, 1982, Merit award Republic of Italy, 1984, Gold medal in recognition of Italians who have honored Italy, Lucca, Italy, 1990, St Thomas More award, San Francisco, 1991, Filippo Mazzei Internat. award, Florence, Italy, 1992; Justice Edward A. Panelli Moot Courtroom named in his honor Santa Clara U., 1989. Mem. ABA, Nat. Italian Bar Assn. (inspiration award 1986), Calif. Trial Lawyers Assn. (Trial Judge of Yr. award Santa Clara County chpt. 1981), Calif. Judges Assn. (bd. dirs. 1982), Jud. Coun. Calif. (vice-chair 1989-93), Alpha Sigma Nu, Phi Alpha Delta Law Found. (hon. mem. Douglas Edmonds chpt.). Republican. Roman Catholic. Avocations: golf, jogging, sailing. Office: JAMS Endispute Inc 160 W Santa Clara St San Jose CA 95113-1701

PANICCIA, PATRICIA LYNN, journalist, writer, lawyer, educator; b. Glendale, Calif., Sept. 19, 1952; d. Valentino and Mary (Napoleon) P.; m. Jeffrey McDowell Mailes, Oct. 5, 1985; children: Alana Christine, Malia Noel. BA in Comm., U. Hawaii, 1977; JD, Pepperdine U., 1981. Bar: Hawaii 1981, Calif. 1982, U.S. Dist. Ct. Hawaii 1981. Extern law clk. hon. Samuel P. King U.S. Dist. Ct., Honolulu, 1980; reporter, anchor woman Sta. KEYT-TV, Santa Barbara, Calif., 1983-84; reporter Sta. KCOP-TV, LA, 1984-88; reporter CNN, LA, 1989-93. Adj. prof. comm. law Pepperdine Sch. Law, 1987, gender & the law, 1994—, adj. prof.; profl. surfer, 1977-81. Author: Worksmarts for Women: The Essential Sex Discrimination Survival Guide, 2000. Recipient Clarion award Women in Comm., Inc., 1988. Mem. ABA (chair of law and media com. young lawyers divsn. 1987-88, nat. conf. com. lawyers and reps. of media 1987-91), Calif. State Bar (mem. com. on fair trial and free press 1983-84, pub. affairs com. 1985-87), Hawaii Bar Assn., Phi Delta Phi (historian 1980-81). Office: PO Box 881 La Canada CA 91012-0881

PANISH, BRIAN JOSEPH, lawyer; b. LA, Apr. 19, 1958; s. Howard Raymond and Mary Patricia (Murphy) P. Student, Calif. State U., 1980; JD cum laude, Southwestern Sch. Law, 1984. Bar: Calif. 1984, U.S. Dist. Ct. (no., ea. and cen. dists.) Tex. 1984. Assoc. Engstrom, Lipscomb & Lack, LA, 1984-86, Greene, Broillet, Taylor & Wheeler and predecessor firm, LA, 1987—93, ptnr., 1993—2005, Panish, Shea & Boyle, LLP, LA, 2005—. Recipient American Jurisprudence Awards in Evidence, Wills and Trusts, Legal Ethics and Sales and Secured Transactions, Fresno State Scholar Athlete Award, 1980, Athletics Directors Award, 1980; named Trial Lawyer of the Yr., Trial Lawyers for Pub. Justice; named one of 100 Most Influential Lawyers, Nat. Law Jour., 2006. Mem. L.A. County Bar Assn., Am. Bar Assn., Assn. Trial Lawyers Am., Calif. Trial Lawyers Assn., L.A. Trial Lawyers Assn., Consumer Attorneys Assn. of Calif. (Bd. Govs.), Internat. Soc. of Barristers, Consumer Attorneys Assn. of L.A., Am. Bd. of Trial Advocates, Western Trial Lawyers Assn., Trial Lawyers for Pub. Justice, Eighth Street Lawyers, Am. Bd. Advocates, Inner Circle Advocates, Santa Monica Leaders Club. Home: 2527 3rd St Santa Monica CA 90405-3604 Office: Panish, Shea & Boyle, LLP 11111 Santa Monica Blvd Suite 700 Los Angeles CA 90025 Business E-Mail: panish@psandb.com.

PANKE, HELMUT, retired automotive executive; b. Storkow, Germany, Aug. 31, 1946; PhD in Physics, U. Munich, 1976. Tchr. U. Munich, 1976—78; with Swiss Inst. Nuclear Rsch., 1976—78, McKinsey & Co., Dusseldorf, Germany, 1978—82; from various positions to head N. American operations BMW AG, Munich, 1982—93, head N. American operations, 1993—96, mem. bd. mgmt. for Human Resources and Info. Technol., 1996—99, mem. bd. mgmt. for fin., 1999—2002, chmn. bd. mgmt., 2002—06. Bd. dirs. UBS AG, Switzerland, Microsoft Corp., 2003—; supr. bd. mem. Bayer AG; adv. bd. Global Strategic Equities Fund, Dubai Internat. Capital LLC. Office: Microsoft Bd Directors 1 Microsoft Way Redmond WA 98052

PANKOW, JAMES F., environmental science and engineering educator; BA in Chemistry with honors, SUNY, Binghamton, 1973; MS in Environ. Engring. Sci., Calif. Inst. Tech., 1976, PhD in Environ. Engring. Sci., 1979. Grad. rsch. and tchg. asst. Calif. Inst. Tech., Pasadena, 1973-78; prof., asst. head dept. environ. sci. and engring. Oreg. Grad. Inst. Sci. and Tech., Beaverton, 1978—. Mem. rev. panel Office and Sci. Tech. Policy; mem. adv. panel U.S. Geol. Survey. Author: Dense Chlorinated Solvents in Porous and Fractured Media, 1988, Aquatic Chemical Concepts, 1991, Aquatic Chemistry Problems, 1992, Dense Chlorinated Solvents..., 1995; co-editor: Dense Chlorinated Solvents and Other DNAPLs in Groundwater History, Behavior and Remediation; contbr. articles to profl. publs. Office: Oreg Grad Inst Sci and Tech Dept Environ Sci & Engring 20000 NW Walker Rd Beaverton OR 97006-8921

PANKRATZ, FRANK D., real estate company executive; B in Commerce, U. Sask., 1971; chartered accts. degree, McGill U., 1974. With Del Webb Corp., Phoenix, 1987—. Sr. v.p. Del Webb Corp., G.M. So. Nev. active adult ops. and regional v.p. Nev. and Calif. active adult ops., Henderson, Nev.

PANNER, OWEN M., federal judge; b. 1924; Student, U. Okla., 1941-43, LL.B., 1949. Atty. Panner, Johnson, Marceau, Karnopp, Kennedy & Nash, 1950-80; judge, now sr. judge U.S. Dist. Ct. Oreg., Portland, 1980—, sr. judge, 1992—. Recipient Am. Bd. Trial Advocates Trial Lawyer of Yr., 1973. Mem. Am. Coll. Trial Lawyers, Am. Bd. Trial Advs., Order of Coif. Office: US Courthouse 310 W 6th St Medford OR 97501

PANY, KURT JOSEPH, finance educator, consultant; b. St. Louis, Mar. 31, 1946; s. Joseph Francis and Ruth Elizabeth (Westerman) P.; m. Darlene Dee Zabish, June 3, 1971; children: Jeffrey, Michael. BSBA, U. Ariz., 1968; MBA in Mgmt., U. Minn., 1971; PhD in Accountancy, U. Ill., 1977. CPA, Ariz., cert. fraud examiner. Staff auditor Arthur Andersen & Co., Mpls., 1968-69, Touche Ross & Co., Phoenix, 1971-73; teaching asst. U. Minn., Mpls., 1969-71; teaching asst. auditing and acctg. U. Ill., Urbana, 1972-76; asst. prof. acctg. Ariz. State U., Tempe, 1977-81, assoc. prof., 1981-85, Arthur Andersen/Don Dupont prof. acctg., 1985-91. Mem. acctg. and auditing standards com. State of Ariz., Phoenix, 1989—; reviewer Jour. Acctg. and Pub. Policy, 1983—. Contbg. author: CPA Exam. Rev., 1983—; co-author: Principles of Auditing, 1988—, Auditing, 1993—; co-editor Auditing: A Jour. Practice and Theory, 1984-88; mem. editl. bd. Advances in Acctg., 1982—, Jour. Acctg. Edn., 1983—; reviewer Acctg. Rev., 1984—, ad hoc editor, 1989—; contbr. numerous articles to profl. jours. Active various child-related orgns. Peat, Marwick, Mitchell & Co. Found. grantee, 1985. Fellow AICPA (auditing stds. divsn. 1989-90, acctg. lit. selection com. 1989-90, acctg. lit. awards com. 1979-83, mem. auditing stds. bd. 1995—); mem. Am. Acctg. Assn. (tech. program com. 1980-81, chairperson Western region auditing sect. 1981-83, acctg. lit. nominating com. 1982-84, 88-89, acctg. lit. selection com. 1989-90, dir. auditing stds., chmn. auditing stds. com. 1989-90), Ariz. Soc. CPA's (auditing stds. com. 1978-81, ethics com. 1981-84). Avocation: baseball. Address: 7445 S Rita Ln Tempe AZ 85283-4792 Office: Ariz State U Sch Accountancy Tempe AZ 85287 Business E-Mail: kpany@cox.net, kurt.pany@asu.edu.

PAPADOPOULOS, GREGORY MICHAEL, information technology executive; b. Oakland, Calif., Apr. 30, 1958; s. Michael Nicholas and Imogen (Sherman) Papadopoulos; m. Elizabeth Ann Woellner, Nov. 26, 1982; children: Michael Gregory, Kathryn Elizabeth. BA in Systems Sci., U. Calif., San Diego, 1979; MS in Elec. Engring. and Computer Sci., MIT, Cambridge, 1983; PhD in Elec. Engring., MIT, 1988. Programmer Scripps Instn. Oceanography, La Jolla, Calif., 1977—79; devel. engr. Hewlett-Packard, Inc., San Diego, 1979—81; sr. rsch. scientist Honeywell, Inc., Mpls., 1981—84; co-founder, chief systems arch. PictureTel Corp., Danvers, Mass., 1984—86; co-founder, chief tech. officer A.I. Archs., Inc., Cambridge, 1985—88; project mgr. MIT Lab. Computer Sci., 1988—90; asst. prof. elec. engring. and computer sci. MIT, 1990—93, assoc. prof., 1993—95; sr. arch. Thinking Machines Corp., Cambridge, 1993—94; chief scientist server sys. engring. Sun Microsystems Computer Co. (now Sun Microsystems Inc.), Santa Clara, Calif., 1994—95, bd. dirs., 1994—, chief tech. officer enterprise servers and storage group, 1995—96, v.p. tech. and advanced devel., chief tech. officer, 1996—98, v.p., chief tech. officer, 1998—2000, sr. v.p., chief tech. officer, 2000—02, exec. v.p. R & D, chief tech. officer, 2002—. Rsch. fellow Charles Stark Draper Labs., Cambridge, 1981—83; dir. Ergo, Inc., 1989—90; co-founder Exa Corp.; vis. prof. elec. engring. and computer sci. MIT, 2002—03; mem. Pres.'s Bd. Sci. and Innovation U. Calif.; tech. advisor BP Alien Techs. Contbr. articles to profl. jours. Mem. Meml. chpt. Am. Field Svc., Houston, 1975—76; bd. trustees Anita Borg. Inst. Women and Tech. Recipient Spl. Distinction award, Forensic League, 1976, Presdl. Young Investigators award, NSF; U. Calif. Regents scholar, 1978. Mem.: AAAS, Search Extraterrestrial Intelligence (chmn. bd.), Sigma Xi, Phi Beta Kappa. Republican. Avocations: bicycling, soccer, diving. Office: Sun Microsystems 4150 Network Cir Santa Clara CA 95054 Office Phone: 650-960-1300. Office Fax: 408-276-3804.

PAPAKONSTANTINO, STACY, language educator; b. San Francisco, Feb. 27, 1967; d. Demetrios and Eugenia (Yiallely) P. AA, City. Coll. of San Francisco, 1987; BA in English Lit., San Francisco State U., 1989, MA in English Lang. Studies, 1991. Cert. in tchg. composition and postsecondary reading. English, ESL tutor City Coll. of San Francisco, 1986-87, instr. of English, 1991—; Greek instr. Holy Trinity Sch., 1988-90; program dir. Inst. Reading Devel., Novato, Calif., 2004; supr. Barnes and Noble Booksellers, Colma, Calif., 2004—; SAT scorer Pearson, Iowa, 2006—. Chair student grade and file rev. com., City Coll. of San Francisco, 1996-98, resource mem. student success com., 1997-98, mem. student complaint com., 1997-98, mem. composition/lit./reading com., 1996-98. Mem. Nat. Coun. Tchrs. of English. Democrat. Orthodox. Avocations: reading, movies and plays, helping needy people, spiritual worship, exercise. Home: 48 Westpark Dr Daly City CA 94015-1055 Office: Barnes & Noble Booksellers 280 Metro Mall Colma CA 94014 Personal E-mail: spapak@hotmail.com.

PAPE, REBECCA HOGAN, lawyer; b. Chgo., Feb. 2, 1972; PLDV, U. So. Calif., 1992; JD, U. Mont., 1997. Bar: Mont. Bar Assn. 1997, US Dist. Ct., Dist. Mont. 2002. Law clk. Dist. Ct. Judge McKittrick, 1997—2000; assoc. Sedivy, White and White, P.C., 2000—. Mem.: Mont. Trial Lawyers Assn. (chair new lawyers com. 2002—), State Bar Mont. Office: Sedivy White and White PC 2090 Stadium Dr PO Box 1906 Bozeman MT 59715-1906 Office Phone: 406-586-4311.

PAPERMASTER, MARK D., computer company executive; b. 1961; m. Kathy Papermaster. BS in Elec. Engring., U. Tex.; MS in Elec. Engring., U. Vt., 1988. With IBM Corp., 1983—2008, v.p. microprocessor & systems tech. devel., v.p. blade devel. unit; sr. v.p. devices hardware engring. Apple Inc., Cupertino, Calif., 2008—. Office: Apple Inc Hdqs 1 Infinite Loop Cupertino CA 95014 Office Phone: 408-996-1010. Office Fax: 408-974-2113.

PAPIANO, NEIL LEO, lawyer; b. Salt Lake City, Nov. 25, 1933; s. Leo and Ruth Ida (Cotten) P. BA, Stanford, 1956, MA in Polit. Sci, 1957; JD, Vanderbilt U., 1961. Bar: Calif. bar 1961. Partner Iverson, Yoakum, Papiano & Hatch (and predecessor firm), Los Angeles, 1961—. Bd. dirs. Nederlander Orgn. and related cos., SCOA Industries, Inc., Ocean Tech., Inc., King Nutronics, Inc. V.p. Los Angeles County Welfare Planning Coun., 1966-71; chmn. L.A. Forward, 1970-71; vice chmn. Cal. Com. for Welfare Reform, 1972; mem. Calif. Jud. Selection Com., 1972-74; co-finance chmn. Rep. State Central Com., 1975; treas. L.A. Opera Co., 1964, bd. dirs., 1965; treas. So. Calif. Choral Music Assn., 1964, bd. dirs., 1964-73; bd. dirs. Citizens Adv. Coun. on Pub. Transp., Orthopaedic Hosp., Stanford U. Athletic Bd., Nat. Athletic Health Inst., L.A. Music Ctr. Operating Co., L.A. Light Opera; bd. govs. USO, 1967-71, Performing Arts Coun. L.A. Music Ctr., 1981-87, Greater L.A. Homeless Partnership, 1985—, L.A. Olympic Com., 1986-88; bd. trustees The Am. U., 1981-95. Mem. Am., Calif. bar assns., Los Angeles Area C. of C. (pres. 1966, dir. 1964-67, 72-75), California Club, Los Angeles Country Club, Rotary, Phi Delta Theta. Office: Neil Papiano 515 S Flower St Ste 2900 Los Angeles CA 90071-2225

PARDEN, ROBERT JAMES, engineering educator, management consultant; b. Mason City, Iowa, Apr. 17, 1922; s. James Ambrose and Mary Ellen (Fahey) P.; m. Elizabeth Jane Taylor, June 15, 1955; children: Patricia Gale, James A., John R., Nancy Ann. BS in Mech. Engring, State U. Iowa, 1947, MS, 1951, PhD, 1953. Reg. profl. engr. Iowa, Calif.; lic. gen. contractor Calif. Indsl. engr. LaCrosse Rubber Mills, 1947-50; asso. dir. Iowa Mgmt. Course, 1951-53; asso. prof. indsl. engring. Ill. Inst. Tech., 1953-54; prof. engring. mgmt. Santa Clara U., 1955—, dean Sch. Engring., 1955-82; prin. Saratoga Cons. Group (Calif.), 1982—. Mem. Sec. Navy's Survey Bd. Grad. Edn., 1964 Mem. Saratoga Planning Commn., 1959-61. Served to 1st lt., Q.M.C. AUS, 1943-46. Named to Silicon Valley Engring. Hall of Fame Silicon Valley Engring. Coun., 1993. Mem. ASME (chmn. Santa Clara Valley sect. 1958), Am. Soc. Engring. Edn. (chmn. Pacific N.W. sect. 1960), Am. Inst. Indsl. Engrs. (edn. chmn. 1958-63, dir. ASEE-ECPD affairs 1963-68), Nat. Soc. Profl. Engrs., Engrs. Council Profl. Devel. (dir. 1964-65, 66-69), Soc. Advancement Mgmt., ASEM, Sigma Xi, Tau Beta Pi. Roman Catholic. Home: 19832 Bonnie Ridge Way Saratoga CA 95070-5010 Office: Santa Clara U Sch Engring Santa Clara CA 95053-0001 Business E-Mail: rparden@scu.edu.

PARDUE, A. MICHAEL, retired plastic and reconstructive surgeon; b. Nashville, June 23, 1931; s. Andrew Peyton and Ruby (Fly) P. BS, Sewanee U. of the South, 1953; MD, U. Tenn., 1957. Resident in gen. surgery Pittsfield (Mass.) Affiliated Hosps., 1966; resident in plastic surgery N.Y. Hosp./Cornell Med. Ctr., 1968; plastic surgeon A. Michael Pardue, M.D., Thousand Oaks, Calif., 1968-98; ret., 1995. Lt. comdr. USN, 1956-62. Fellow ACS; mem. Am. Soc. Plastic Surgeons, Am. Soc. Aesthetic Plastic Surgery, Calif. Soc. Plastic Surgeons. Episcopalian. Avocations: fly fishing, skiing, golf, horses, African safaris. Home: 3217 Augusta Dr Bozeman MT 59715-8792

PARENT, MARY CAMPBELL, film company executive; b. 1965; Agt. trainee ICM; dir. develop. to v.p. prodn. New Line Cinema, 1994—97; sr. v.p. prodn. Universal Pictures, Universal City, Calif., 1997—2000, exec. v.p. prodn., 2000—01, co-pres. prodn., 2001—03, vice chmn., worldwide prodn., 2003—05, prodr., 2006—08; chairperson worldwide motion picture group Metro-Goldwyn-Mayer Studios Inc., L.A., 2008—. Exec. prodr.: (films) Set It Off, 1996, Trial and Error, 1997, Pleasantville, 1998, The Kingdom, 2007; prodr.: You, Me and Dupree, 2006, Welcome Home, Roscoe Jenkins, 2008; prodn. mgr.: Dangerous Ground, 1997. Named one of The 100 Most Powerful Women in Entertainment, Hollywood Reporter, 2004. Office: Metro-Goldwyn-Mayer Studios Inc 10250 Constellation Blvd Los Angeles CA 90067

PARENTI, KATHY ANN, sales professional; b. Gary, Ind., Sept. 24, 1957; d. Lee Everett Huddleston and Barbara Elizabeth (Daves) Tilley; m. Michael A. Parenti, Mar. 31, 1979 (div. Sept. 1990); m. S. Curtis McCoy, Sept. 6, 1996. Student, Ind. U., Gary, 1977; cert., U. Nev., Las Vegas, 1978; diploma, Interior Design Inst., Las Vegas, 1984. Supr. Circus Circus Hotel, Las Vegas, 1980-87; owner Interior Views, Las Vegas, 1984-87; sales rep. Win-Glo Window Coverings, 1987-88; owner Dimension Design, 1988-90; sales rep. Sidney Goldberg & Assoc., Las Vegas, 1990-99, Parenti & Assocs., 1990—. Mem.: Archtl. Decorative Art Soc., Art and Design Archtl. Soc., Internat. Interior Design Assn., Network of Exec. Women in Hospitality, Am. Soc. Interior Designers. Avocations: exercise, reading, piano, guitar, singing.

PARISEAU, WILLIAM G., mining engineer, educator; Prof. dept. mining & engring. U. Utah, Salt Lake City. Recipient Rock Mechanics award Soc. Mining, Metallogy & Exploration, 1990. Office: U Utah Dept Mining & Engring 313 Browning Building Salt Lake City UT 84112-1118

PARISI, PAULA ELIZABETH, writer, photographer, editor; b. NYC, Feb. 27, 1960; d. Alfred John and Patricia Ann (Delucas) P. BA, Rutgers U., 1982; photography classes, Phila. Coll. Art, 1978-82. Reporter TVSM Inc./The Cable Guide, Horsham, Pa., 1982-84; assoc. editor Home Viewer Publs., Phila., 1984-85, mng. editor, 1985-87; home video cable TV, technology editor The Hollywood Reporter, Los Angeles, 1987—, editorial dir., 2000—. Contbr. articles to Billboard, Film & Video Prodn., Mix, Hollywood Reporter, Phila. Inquirer; photographs published in Phila. Inquirer, Washington Jour., Miami Herald, Circus, Us, Sixteen, others. Republican. Roman Catholic. Office: The Hollywood Reporter 5055 Wilshire Blvd Ste 600 Los Angeles CA 90036-4396

PARK, CHONG S., computer company executive; BA in Mgmt., Yonsei U.; MA in Mgmt., Seoul Nat. U.; MBA, U. Chgo.; PhD in Mgmt., Nova Southeastern U. Chmn., pres., CEO Axil Computer, Inc., 1993—95; pres., CEO Hynix Semiconductor Am., Inc., 1996—2000, chmn., 1996—2002; pres., CEO, chmn. Hynix Semiconductor, Inc., 2000—02; pres., CEO Maxtor Corp., Milipitas, Calif., 1995—96, chmn., 1998—2006, CEO, 2004—06. Chmn. MMC Tech. (Maxtor subs.), 1996—2000; bd. dir. Dot Hill Sys. Corp., ChipPAC, Seagate Tech., 2006—. Mailing: Seagate Technology Bd Directors 920 Disc Dr Scotts Valley CA 95066-4544

PARK, HYUN, lawyer, utilities executive; BA summa cum laude, Columbia U., NYC; MA, Oxford U.; JD cum laude, Harvard U., 1989. Ptnr. Latham & Watkins, LA, NYC, Hong Kong; sr. v.p., gen. counsel, sec. Sithe Energies Inc., 1998—2005; v.p., gen. counsel Allegheny Energy Inc., Greensburg, Pa., 2005—06; sr. v.p., gen. counsel PG&E Corp., San Francisco, 2006—. Office: PG&E Corp Ste 2400 One Market Spear Tower San Francisco CA 94105-1126 Office Phone: 415-367-7070. Office Fax: 415-267-7268.

PARK, JANIE C., provost; children: Christopher, Eric. BSN, Baylor U., 1968; MS in Cell and Molecular Biology, Fla. Inst. Tech., 1979, PhD in Cell and Molecular Biology, 1982. Nurse Holmes Regional Med. Ctr., Melbourne, Fla., 1968-69; grad. student tchg. asst. Fla. Inst. Tech., Melbourne, 1977-82, instr. biol. scis., 1982-84, asst. prof. biol. scis., 1984-89, chair preprofl./premed. program, 1986-93, assoc. prof. biol. scis., 1989-93, assoc. dean coll. sci. and liberal arts, 1990-93; dean coll. arts and scis., prof. biol. scis. Mont. State U., Billings, 1993-96, provost, acad. vice chancellor, prof. biol. scis., 1996—. Rsch. dir. Ctr. for Interdisciplinary Rsch. in Aging, 1988-90; rsch. dir. elctron microscopy svcs. Joint Ctr. Advanced Therapy and Biomed. Rsch. Fla. Inst. Tech. and Holmes Regional Med. Ctr., 1991-93; spkr. in field. Contbr. articles to profl. jours. Bd. dirs. St. Vincent's Regional Med. Ctr., Youth Dynamics, Inc.; mem. steering com. Billings Town and Gown; mem. Bldg. a Healthy Cmty. Task Force. Mem. Microscopy Soc. Am., Am. Assn. of State Colls. and Univs., Southeast Electron Microscopy (sessions chair ann. meeting 1991, 92), Soc. for Neurosci., Rocky Mountain Deans' Assn. (ann. meeting organizer 1995), Assn. for Rsch. in Otolaryngology (mem. membership com. 1991-97, chair membership com. 1993-97), Fla. Soc. for Electron Microscopy (v.p. 1983, bd. dirs. 1983-93, session chair ann. meeting 1989-92, pres.-elect 1989, pres. 1990-91, mem. local arrangements com. 1991, meeting registration chair 1990—), Coun. Colls. of Arts and Scis. (session chair ann. meeting 1995), Coun. Arts and Scis. of Urban Univs., Billings Rotary Internat., Leadership Billings Alumni Assn. Office: Mont State U Office Acad Vice Chancellor 1500 N 30th St Billings MT 59101-0245

PARK, LEE (LEE PARKLEE), artist; b. Seoul, Republic of Korea; s. Chung-Kun Park and Mil-Hwa Kim; m. Chai Kyung Lim, June 3, 1994. MA, Fla. State U., 1986. Prof. associated academician dept. arts Vinzaglio, Italy, 2002—. Group shows include Shinpara Gallery, LA, Up-Stairs Gallery, LA, Beverly Plz. Hotel, Pacific Mus., Pasadena, Calif., Barnsdall Art Gallery, Hollywood, Calif., Brand XXII The Assn. of Brand Art Ctr., Glendale, Calif., Asia Invitation Art Exhibn., Sejong Cultural Ctr., Seoul, la Peintre Moderne Coreend '93, Paris, Korea-Japan Interchange Exhbn., Tokyo, 1994, Downtown Lives '96 Art Exhbn., LA, City Hall of Paris, 4, Biennale Internat. de Paris, 1994, Musee d'Art Moderne de la Commanderie d'Unet, Paris, 1994, Bridgeport (NY) U., 1995, San Bernardino County Mus., 1995, Kong-Ja Culture Art Exhbn., China, 1995, His Majesty the King's 50th Anniversary Art Exhbn., Thailand, 1996, 1st Venice Ann. Internat. Open Art Exhbn., Venice, 1998, 1st Internat. Biennial Contemporary Art, Perugia, Italy, 1998, Heukyong-gangsung Internat. Art Exhbn., China, 1998, Ting Shao-Kuang Fine Art Ctr., Beverly Hills, Articulture Gallery, Hermosa Beach, Calif., 1998, '99 World Peace Art Exhbn., Sejong Cultural Ctr., Seoul, 1999, The Millennium Art Collection, 2000, Invitational Art Exhbn. Jin-Jiang Gen. Assn. Gallery, Philipines, 2001, Galerie Michelangelo, Las Vegas, 2002, Reasons to Love the Earth, Den Haag, Netherlands, 2002; 2 person shows include Cosmos Gallery, Honolulu, The City of LA Cultural Affairs Dept.; solo exhibits include Modern Art Gallery, LA, Olympic Gallery, LA, Sun Space Gallery, LA, Gallery Nuevo, Pusan, Republic of Korea, Westside Jewish Cmty. Ctr., LA, World Festival of Art Exhbn., Slovenia, Caesars Palace Hotel Michelangelo, Las Vegas, Nev., 49th Toyo Calligraphy Art Assn., Tokyo, Eloge du Petit Fermat Dans L'Art D'Aujourd' Hui, Paris, Singapore, Korea Art Exhbn., Ngee Annual Cultural Ctr., Rubicon Gallery, LA, 2007, LA Mcpl. Art Gallery, Hollywood, 2007, Rancho Palos Verdes Art Ctr., LA, 2007, Luoyang Mus. Art Invitational Exhbn., China, 2007, Bunam Gallery, Seoul, Republic of Korea, 2008, See and Sea Gallery, Pusan, Republic of Korea, 2008, Asia Expo, LA Convention Ctr., West Hall "A", 2008; publ. artwork in American References, Art of California mag., Artweek mag., The Biweekly Art Jour., Seoul, Artprint mag., Washington, Art Exposure mag., Calif., Ency. of Living Artists mag., Calif., Art 2000, Seoul, Mag. for World Art & Culture Vergil Quarterly, Seoul, 2004, Art Diary Internat. 1998—, Milan, Italy, Internat. Encyclopaedic Dictionary Modern and Contemporary Art, Ferrara, Italy, 2002-08, Dictionary Internat. Biography Ctr., Cambridge, Eng. (Top 100 artists 2005), Portraits d'Artistes (Regards), France, 2008. Recipient Bronze award Art of Calif., 1993, Gold award Art Addiction, Stockholm, 1997. Avocations: collecting stamps and antiques, music, jogging, playing tennis, reading. Home: 1935 S La Salle Ave Apt 31 Los Angeles CA 90018-1627 E-mail: park@b17.com.

PARK, MARINA H., lawyer; b. Pasadena, Calif., Nov. 6, 1956; BA with honors, Univ. Calif., Berkeley, 1978; JD, Univ. Mich., 1982. Bar: Calif. 1983. Mng. ptnr. Pillsbury Winthrop LLP, Palo Alto, Calif., 1999—2005; ptnr., Emerging Growth & Tech. practice & mng. ptnr. Pillsbury Winthrop Shaw Pittman, Palo Alto, Calif., 2005—. Office: Pillsbury Winthrop Shaw Pittman 2475 Hanover St Palo Alto CA 94304-1114 Office Phone: 650-233-4770. Office Fax: 650-233-4545. Business E-Mail: marina.park@pillsburylaw.com.

PARK, MICHAEL S., computer software company executive; married; 3 children. BA, U. Rochester; MBA, Harvard U. Sales and brand mgmt. Procter & Gamble; gen. mgr. Siebel Sys. Inc.; exec. Hire.com; sr. v.p. product mktg. SAP AG; joined Microsoft Corp., Redmond, Wash., 2005, corp. v.p. US Small and Midmarket Solutions & Ptnrs. Group. Avocations: golf, tennis, bicycling.

PARK, NO-HEE, dean, academic administrator; b. Jan. 30, 1944; m. Yu Bai Yuly, 1969; 1 child, Jennifer. DDS, Seoul Nat. U., 1968, MSD, 1970; PhD, Med. Coll. Ga., 1978; DMD, Harvard U., 1982. Postdoctoral fellow in oral biology and pharmacology Med. Coll. Ga., 1975—78; rsch. assoc., Eye Rsch. Inst. Harvard Med. Sch., Boston, 1978—80, instr., dept. ophthalmology, 1978—82, asst. scientist, Eye Rsch. Inst., 1980—82, assoc. scientist, Eye Rsch. Inst., 1982—83; asst. prof., oral biology and pathophysiology Harvard U. Sch. Dental Medicine, Boston, 1982—83; assoc. prof., oral biology UCLA Sch. Dentistry, LA, 1984—85, prof., 1985—, assoc. dean rsch., 1997—98, dean, 1998—; assoc. dir. UCLA Dental Rsch. Inst., LA, 1986—90, dir., 1995—, UCLA Wound Healing Rsch. Ctr., LA, 1997—. Contbr. articles to profl. jours.; ad-hoc reviewer for various publs., 1990—, editl. bd. Internat. Jour. Oncology, 1996—, Electronic Jour. Biotechnology, 1997—, editor-in-chief Internat. Jour. Oral Biology, assoc. editor Odontology, 2000—. Mem.: Internat. Assoc. for Dental Rsch. (Selection Com. for Distinguished Scientist in Oral Medicine 2001—), Friends of NIDCR (Exec. Com. 2001—), Am. Assn. for Dental Schools Coun. of Deans Exec. Com., Am. Dental Assn., Calif. Dental Assn., Tissue Culture Assn., Am. Assn. for Cancer Rsch., Am. Dental Edn. Assn., Am. Assn. for Dental Schools, Am. Soc. for Microbiology, Am. Assn. for the Advancement of Sci., Internat. Assn. for Dental Rsch., Internat. Coll. Dentistry, Omicron Kappa Upsilon Dental Soc. Achievements include research in the role of telomerase in oral carcinogenesis, gene therapy for oral cancer, molecular mechanism of replicative senescence in normal human oral keratinocytes and viral and chemical oncogenesis; cellular proto-oncogenes and tumor suppressor genes, cell cycle and DNA repair, and antiviral chemotherapy. Office: UCLA 10833 Leconte Ave Rm 53-038 Los Angeles CA 90095

PARK, ROGER COOK, law educator; b. Atlanta, Jan. 4, 1942; s. Hugh and Alice (Cook) Park; m. Rosemarie J. Lilliker, June 14, 1967 (div. 1979); 1 child, Matthew; m. Suzanne Nicole Howard, Feb. 18, 1984; stepchildren: Sophie Currier, Nicolas Currier. BA cum laude, Harvard U., 1964, JD magna cum laude, 1969. Bar: Mass. 1969, Minn. 1973. Law clk. to Hon. Bailey Aldrich U.S. Ct. Appeals (1st cir.), Boston, 1969-70; with Zalkind & Silverglate, Boston, 1970-73; prof. Law Sch. U. Minn., Mpls., 1973-95, Fredrikson and Byron prof. law, 1990-95; Disting. James Edgar Hervey prof. law Hastings Coll. Law U. Calif., San Francisco, 1995—. Vis. prof. Law Sch. Stanford U., Palo Alto, Calif., 1977, Sch. Law Boston U., 1981—82, Law Sch. U. Mich., Ann Arbor, 1984; bd. dirs. Ctr. Computer-Aided Legal Instrn., 1982—96; reporter adv. group Civil Justice Reform Act, Dist. Minn.; mem. evidence adv. com. Minn. Supreme Ct., 1988—95. Author: Computer Aided Exercises in Civil Procedure, 1979, 2d edit., 1995, Waltz and Park Casebook on Evidence, 8th edit., 1994; author: (with Leonard and Goldberg) 10th edit., 2005; author: Evidence Law, 1998, 2d edit., 2004; author: (with McFarland) Trial Objections

Handbook, 1991, 2d edit., 2001; contbr. articles to profl. jours. Lt. US Army, 1964—66, Vietnam. Mem.: ABA (mem. rules criminal procedure and evidence com. criminal justice sect. 1988—, mem. subcom. fed. rules evidence), Am. Assn. Law Schs. (chairperson evidence sect. 1994), Am. Law Inst. Office: Hastings Coll Law 200 Mcallister St San Francisco CA 94102-4707

PARK, SUSAN, lawyer; b. Guam; BA, Boston Coll., 1996; JD, Northeastern U., 1999. Atty. corp. dept. Goodwin Procter, Boston, 1999—2001; staff atty. j2 Global Comm. Inc., Hollywood, Calif., 2002—06; v.p. legal affairs Blackboard Connect Inc. (formerly NTI Group, Inc.), Sherman Oaks, Calif., 2006—. Avocation: golf. Office: Blackboard Connect Inc 15301 Ventura Blvd Bldg B, Ste 300 Sherman Oaks CA 91403 Office Phone: 877-684-4411.

PARK, WILLIAM ANTHONY (TONY PARK), lawyer; b. Blackfoot, Idaho, June 4, 1934; s. William Clair and Thelma Edelweiss (Shear) P.; m. Elizabeth Taylor, Aug. 26, 1961 (div.); children: Susan E., W. Adam, Patricia A.; m. Gail Chaloupka, Aug. 6, 1983. AA, Boise Jr. Coll., 1954; BA, U. Idaho, 1958; JD, U. Idaho, 1963. Bar: Idaho 1963. Sole practice, Boise, Idaho, 1963-70, 82-83; atty. gen. State of Idaho, 1971-75; ptnr. Park & Meuleman, Boise, 1975-81, Park & Burkett, Boise, 1983-84, Martin, Chapman, Park & Burkett, Boise, 1984-90, Park, Costello & Burkett, Boise, 1990-93, Park, Redford, Thomas & Burkett, Boise, 1994-97, Park, Thomas, Burkett & Williams, Boise, 1997-99; of counsel Huntley Park (formerly Huntley, Park, Thomas, Burkett, Olsen & Williams), Boise, 1999—2008, Thomas Williams Park, 2008—. Chmn. Idaho Bicentennial Commn., 1971—77; bd. dirs. ACLU, Idaho, 1996—2000, pres. Idaho, 1997—99; chmn. Idaho State Dem. Party, 1998—99; bd. dirs. Radio Free Europe/Radio Liberty, Inc., 1977—82, Am. Lung Assn., 1978—90, Am. Lung Assn. NW, 1976—96; pres. Am. Lung Assn. Northeast, 1991—95, 2002—04, bd. dirs., 1999—. With US Army, 1956—58. Recipient Disting. Svc. award. Home: 706 Warm Springs Ave Boise ID 83712-6420 Office: PO Box 1776 Boise ID 83701-1776 Office Phone: 208-345-7800. Personal E-mail: gchaloupka@msn.com. Business E-Mail: tpark@twplegal.com.

PARKE, MARILYN NEILS, writer; b. Libby, Mont., June 5, 1928; d. Walter and Alma M. Neils; m. Robert V. Parke, Aug. 25, 1951; children: Robert, Richard, Gayle Crawford, Lynn Parke Castle. BA, U. Mont., 1950; MEd, Colo. State U., 1973. Tchr. Poudre R-1, Fort Collins, 1973—. Co-author: (with Sharon Panik) A Quetzalcoatl Tale of Corn, 1992, A Quetzalcoatl Tale of the Ball Game, 1992 (Parent's Choice Gold award paperback of yr. 1992), A Quetzalcoatl Tale of Chocolate, 1994. Mem. Internat. Reading Assn., Soc. Children's Book Writers and Illustrators, Nat. Edn. Assn., Colo. Coun. Internat. Reading Assn. Avocations: gardening, cooking, sports, reading, travel.

PARKER, CANDACE NICOLE, professional basketball player; b. St. Louis, Apr. 19, 1986; d. Larry and Sara Parker. B in Sports Mgmt., Psychology, U. Tenn., 2008. Forward, center, guard U. Tenn. Lady Volunteers, 2005—08, LA Sparks, 2008—. Mem. USA Basketball Women's Sr. Nat. Team, Beijing, 2008. Recipient John R. Wooden award, 2007, 2008, Sports award, Honda, 2007, Wade Trophy, 2007, ESPY award, Best Female Athlete, ESPN, 2008, ESPY award, Best Female Coll. Athlete, 2008, Gold medal, women's basketball, Beijing Olympic Games, 2008; named Tournament MVP, Southeastern Conf., 2006, Freshman of Yr., 2006, Rookie of Yr., 2006, Freshman of Week, 2006, Player of Week, 2006, 2007, Player of Yr., 2007, US Basketball Writers Assn., 2007, Lady Vol Athlete of Week, U. Tenn., 2006, Lady Vol Athlete of Month, 2006, Most Outstanding Player, NCAA Women's Basketball Tournament, 2007; named a Kodak All-Am., 2006; named to, 2007, NCAA Cleve. Regional All-Regional Team, 2006, All-Southeastern Conf. First Team, 2006, 2007, All-Southeastern Conf. Freshman Team, 2006, Second Team All-Am., AP, 2006, 1st Team All-Am., 2007, John R. Wooden All-Am., 2007. Achievements include being a member of the NCAA Women's Basketball Championship winning University of Tennessee Lady Volunteers, 2007, 2008; being the first overall pick in the WNBA draft, 2008. Office: LA Sparks 1111 S Figueroa St Ste 3100 Los Angeles CA 90001

PARKER, DONALD FRED, dean, human resources specialist, educator; b. Oilton, Okla., Nov. 7, 1934; s. Robert Fred Parker and Georgia Marie (Culley) Meek; m. Jo Ellen Dunfee, Apr. 6, 1963; children: Margaret Elizabeth, Emily Lyle. BA in Sociology, U. Okla., 1957; MS in Personnel Adminstrn., George Washington U., 1966; PhD in Human Resource Mgmt., Cornell U., 1974. Commd. ensign USN, 1957, advanced through grades to capt., 1977, staff officer with chief naval ops. Washington, 1969-71, comdg. officer, exec. officer, Patrol Squadron Ten Brunswick, Maine, 1974-76, prof. Naval War Coll. Newport, RI, 1976-78, comdg. officer Navy Personnel Research & Devel. Ctr. San Diego, 1978-80, ret., 1980; asst. prof. Grad. Sch. Bus., U. Mich., Ann Arbor, 1980-84; prof., dean Coll. Commerce and Industry U. Wyo., Laramie, 1984-91; Sara Hart Kimball dean bus., prof. human resources mgmt. Oreg. State U., Corvallis, 1991—2001, dean emeritus, 2003—; lectr. Student Leadership Forum; vis. prof. St. Georges U., 2007—08. Advisor US West Wyo. State Bd. Advisors, Cheyenne, 1986-91; ex-officio dir. Wyo. Indsl. Devel. Corp., Casper, 1987; vis. prof. Acad. Internat. Econ. Affairs, Hsinchu, Taiwan, 1986-91, St. George's U., 2007, 08. Author numerous articles, book chpts., case studies. Mem. Acad. of Mgmt. (human resource mgmt. divsn. dir. 1983-85), Midwest Assn. Deans and Dept. Chairs in Bus. (pres.), Western Assn. Collegiate Schs. Bus. (bd. dirs., pres. 1999), Phi Kappa Phi, Beta Gamma Sigma (pres. 1998-2000, past pres. 2000—02). Avocations: skiing, hiking.

PARKER, DOUG (WILLIAM DOUGLAS PARKER, W. DOUGLAS PARKER), air transportation executive; m. Gwen Parker; 3 children. BA in Econ., Albion Coll., 1984; MBA, Vanderbilt U., 1986. Various fin. mgmt. positions Am. Airlines, 1986—91; v.p., fin. planning and analysis, v.p., asst. treas. Northwest Airlines; sr. v.p., CFO Am. West Holdings, 1995—99, exec. v.p., corp. group, 1999—2000, pres., COO, 2000—01, chmn., pres., CEO, 2001—05; interim pres. US Airways Group Inc., Tempe, Ariz., 2005, chmn., CEO, 2005—. Recipient Disting. Alumnus award, Vanderbilt U. Owen Grad. Sch. Mgmt., 2004. Methodist. Office: US Airways 111 W Rio Salado Pkwy Tempe AZ 85281*

PARKER, EDWIN BURKE, communications executive; b. Berwyn, Alta., Can., Jan. 19, 1932; m. Frances G. Spigai, 1976; children: David Kendall, Karen Liane. BA, U. B.C., Can., 1954; MA, Stanford U., 1958, PhD in Mass Comms., 1960. Staff reporter Vancouver (Can.) Sun., 1954-55; info. officer U. B.C., Vancouver, 1955-57; rsch. asst. Inst. Comms. Rsch. Stanford U., 1957-60, asst. prof., 1962-63, assoc. prof., 1963-71, prof., 1971-79; v.p. Equatorial Comms. Co., 1979-85, chmn. bd. dirs., 1986-87; pres. data networks divsn. CONTEL, 1987-88; pres. Parker Telecomm., Gleneden Beach, Oreg., 1989—. Asst. prof. Communications U. Ill., Urbana, 1960-62. Ctr. for Advanced Studies in Behavioral Sci. fellow, 1969-70; named Leader of Yr., Oreg. Local Econ. Devel., 1995, Man of Yr., Lincoln City, 2005. Avocation: bridge. Office: Parker Telecommunications PO Box 402 Gleneden Beach OR 97388-0402 Office Phone: 541-764-3058. Business E-Mail: edparker@teleport.com.

PARKER, ELIZABETH RINDSKOPF, dean, law educator; b. Detroit, Dec. 2, 1943; d. Arthur C. and Kathryn G. (Rodgers) Roediger; m. Peter E. Rindskopf, May 25, 1968; 1 child; m. Robert Parker. BA in Philosophy cum laude, U. Mich., 1964, JD, 1968. Bar: Ga. 1968, U.S. Dist. Ct. (no. dist.) Ga. 1969, U.S. Ct. Appeals (5th cir.) 1970, U.S. Supreme Ct. 1971, U.S. Ct. Appeals (6th cir.) 1972, U.S. Ct. Appeals (3rd cir.) 1974, U.S. Ct. Appeals (4th cir.) 1977, U.S. Ct. Appeals (9th cir.) 1978, D.C. 1979. Reginald Heber Smith fellow, mng. atty. Emory Legal Svcs., Atlanta, 1968-71; ptnr. Moore, Alexander & Rindskopf, Atlanta, 1971-74; dir. New Haven Legal Assistance Assn., Inc., 1974-76; dep. dir. Lawyers Com. Civil Rights Under Law, Washington, 1978-79; ptnr. Cohen, Vitt & Annand, Alexandria, Va., 1978-79; acting asst. dir. mergers and joint ventures, dep. asst. dir. health care Bur. of Competition, Fed. Trade Commn., 1979-81; of counsel Surrey & Morse, Washington, 1981-84; gen. counsel Nat. Security Agy., Washington, 1984-89; prin. dep. office of the legal adviser US Dept. State, Washington, 1989-90; gen. counsel CIA, Washington, 1990-95; of counsel Bryan Cave, LLP, 1995—99; gen. counsel U. Wis. Sys., 1999—2002; dean, prof. law U. Pacific McGeorge Sch. Law, Sacramento, 2002—. Co-operating atty. NAACP Legal Def. and Edn. Fund, Inc., 1971-74; trustee Monterey Inst. Internat. Studies. Contbr. articles to profl. jours. Mem. ABA (standing com. law and nat. security, counsel sect. internat. law and politics, adv. bd. Ctr. and Eastern European Law Initiative), Coun. Fgn. Rels, NAS (com. on sci. comm. and nat. security, com. on a new govt.-univ. partnership on sci. and security). Office: U of Pacific McGeorge Sch Law 3200 Fifth Ave Sacramento CA 95817 Office Phone: 916-739-7151. E-mail: elizabeth@pacific.edu.

PARKER, GERHARD H., communications professional; BSEE, Calif. Inst. Technology, 1965, MSEE, 1966, D Elec. Engring., 1969. Quality engr. to various positions Intel Corp., Santa Clara, Calif., 1969-99, exec. v.p., gen. mgr. New Bus. Group, 1999—. Office: 2200 Mission College Blvd 2200 Mission College Blvd Santa Clara CA 95054-1537

PARKER, JAMES AUBREY, federal judge; b. Houston, Jan. 8, 1937; s. Lewis Almeron and Emily Helen (Stuessy) P.; m. Florence Fisher, Aug. 26, 1960; children: Roger Alan, Pamela Elizabeth. BA, Rice U., 1959; LLB, U. Tex., 1962. Bar: Tex. 1962, N.Mex. 1963. With Modrall, Sperling, Roehl, Harris & Sisk, Albuquerque, 1962-87; judge U.S. Dist. Ct. N.Mex., Albuquerque, 1987—2000, chief judge, 2000—03. Mem. Standing Commn. on Rules of Practice and Procedures of U.S. Cts., 1993-99, N.Mex. Commn. on Professionalism, 1986-2004; bd. vis. U. N.Mex. Law Sch., 1996-2004; bd. dirs. Fed. Jud. Ctr., 2004-2007. Articles editor Tex. Law Rev., 1961-62. Mem. Fed. Judges Assn., Am. Judicature Soc., Am. Bd. Trial Advocates, N.Mex. Bar Assn. (Outstanding Judge award 1994), Albuquerque Bar Assn. (Outstanding Judge award 1993, 00), Law Dragon 500 Leading Judges in Am. 2006, Nat. Assn. Criminal Def. Lawyers (Courageous Judiciary award 2001), Order of Coif, Chancellors, Phi Delta Phi. Avocations: ranching, fly fishing, skiing. Office: US Dist Ct 421 Gold S W 6th Fl Albuquerque NM 87102-2277 Mailing: PO Box 669 Albuquerque NM 87103 Office Phone: 505-348-2220. Office Fax: 505-348-2225. Business E-Mail: jparker@nmcourt.fed.us.

PARKER, JOHN WILLIAM, retired pathology educator; b. Clifton, Ariz., Jan. 5, 1931; m. Barbara A. Atkinson; children: Ann Elizabeth, Joy Noelle, John David, Heidi Susan. BS, U. Ariz., 1953; MD, Harvard U., 1957. Diplomate Am. Bd. Pathology. Clin. instr. pathology U. Calif. Sch. Medicine, San Francisco, 1962-64; asst. prof. U. So. Calif. Sch. Medicine, LA, 1964-68, assoc. prof., 1968-75, prof., 1975-98, prof. emeritus, 1998—, dir. clin. labs., 1974-94, vice chmn. dept. pathology, 1985-97, dir. pathology reference labs., 1991-94, assoc. dean sci. affairs, 1987-89, prof. emeritus, 1998—. Co-chmn. 15th Internat. Leucocyte Culture Conf., Asilomar, Calif., 1982; chmn. 2d Internat. Lymphoma Conf., Athens, Greece, 1981; v.p. faculty senate U. So. Calif., 1991-92; bd. dirs. ann. meeting Clin. Applications of Cytometry, Charleston, S.C., 1988-97. Founding editor (jour.) Hematological Oncology, 1982-93; assoc. editor Jour. Clin. Lab. Analysis, 1985-98; co-editor: Intercellular Communication in Leucocyte Function, 1983; founding co-editor (jour.) Communications in Clin. Cytometry, 1993-97; contbr. over 200 articles to profl. jours., chpts. to books. Named sr. oncology fellow Am. Cancer Soc., U. So. Calif. Sch. Medicine, 1964-69, Nat. Cancer Inst. vis. fellow Walter and Eliza Hall Inst. for Med. Rsch., Melbourne, Australia, 1972-73. Fellow Coll. Am. Pathologists, Am. Soc. Clin. Pathologists; mem. Am. Assn. Pathologists, Am. Soc. Hematology, Internat. Acad. Pathology, Clin. Cytometry Soc. (v.p. 1994-95, pres. 1995-97), Phi Beta Kappa, Phi Kappa Phi. Avocations: gardening, reading, hiking.

PARKER, KEVIN, state legislator; m. Kerry Parker; children: Emelia, Eve. B in Polit. Sci., Whitworth U., Spokane, Wash.; M in Bus. Adminstrn., George Fox U., Newburg, Oreg.; cert. in Leadership, Harvard U., Cambridge, Mass. Cert. Leadership Harvard U. Served on staff former Congressman Smith, Oreg.; founder & former owner Parker & Assocs.; pres. GTG Ventures; asst. whip Wash. House of Reps., mem. Dist. 6, 2008—. Asst. minority whip. Bd. mem. YMCA, Boys and Girls Club. Republican. Office: 404 John L O'Brien Bldg PO Box 40600 Olympia WA 98504-0600 Office Phone: 360-786-7922. Business E-Mail: parker.kevin@leg.wa.gov.

PARKER, MARK G., apparel executive; b. Poughkeepsie, NY; BS in Polit. Sci., Pa. State U., 1977. With Nike, Inc., 1979—, designer, devel. mgr. Exeter, NH, 1979—80, mgr. advanced product design, 1980—81, dir. design concepts & engring. Beaverton, Oreg., 1981—82, dir. footwear design, 1982—83, mgr. footware mktg., 1983—85, head, spl. design project teams, 1985—87, divsn. v.p. footware rsch., design and devel., 1987—88, corp. v.p. rsch. design & devel., 1988—93, v.p. consumer product mktg., 1993—98, v.p., gen. mgr. global footware, 1998—2001, pres. Nike Brand, 2001—06, pres., CEO, 2006—. Named one of The Most Influential People in the World of Sports, Bus. Week, 2007, 2008. Avocations: running, rock climbing, mountain biking, sailing, kayaking, drawing, painting, collecting art. Office: Nike Inc One Bowerman Dr Beaverton OR 97005-6453 Office Phone: 503-671-6453.

PARKER, MARY-LOUISE, actress; b. Ft. Jackson, SC, Aug. 2, 1964; 1 child, William Atticus. Attended, Bard Coll. Actress: (plays) Hay Fever, 1987, The Miser, 1988, The Art of Success, 1989, The Importance of Being Earnest, 1989, Prelude to a Kiss, Broadway, 1990-91 (Theatre World award, Clarence Derwent Award, Tony nomination, 1990), Babylon Gardens, 1991, How I Learned to Drive, 1997 (Lucille Lortel Award for outstanding actress, OBIE Award, 1997), Proof, Broadway (Tony award for best actress in a play, 2001), Dead Man's Cell Phone, 2008, Hedda Gabler, 2009; (films) Signs of Life, 1989, Longtime Companion, 1990, Grand Canyon, 1991, Fried Green Tomatoes, 1991, Mr. Wonderful, 1993, Naked in New York, 1994, The Client, 1994, Bullets Over Broadway, 1994, Boys on the Side, 1995, A Portrait of a Lady, 1996, Reckless, 1995, Murder in Mind, 1997, The Maker, 1997, Let the Devil Wear Black, 1998, Goodbye, Lover, 1998, Five Senses, 1999, Pipe Dream, 2002, Red Dragan, 2002, The Best Thief in the World, 2004, Saved!, 2004, Romance & Cigarettes, 2005, The Assassination of Jesse James by the Coward Robert Ford, 2007, The Spiderwick Chronicles, 2008; (TV movies) Too Young the Hero, 1988, A Place for Annie, 1994, Sugartime, 1995, Legalese, 1998, Saint Maybe, 1998, The Simple Life of Noah Dearborn, 1999, Cupid & Cate, 2000, Master Spy: The Robert Hanssen Story, 2002, Miracle Run, 2004, Vinegar Hill, 2005, The Robber Bride, 2007; (TV miniseries) Angels in America, 2003 (Golden Globe for best supporting actress 2004, Emmy award, Outstanding Supporting Actress in a Miniseries or a Movie, 2004); (TV series) Ryan's Hope, 1975, West Wing, 2001-05,(Emmy nomination, 2002), Weeds, 2005- (Best Performance by an Actress in a TV Series-Musical or Comedy, Hollywood Fgn. Press Assn. (Golden Globe award), 2006. Named one of Top 25 Entertainers of Yr., Entertainment Weekly, 2007. Office: William Morris Agy care Scott Henderson 151 S El Camino Dr Beverly Hills CA 90212-2775

PARKER, PAM, apparel manufacturing company executive; b. San Francisco, 1960; BA, U. Calif., Berkeley; MBA, Stanford U., 1989. Cons. Bain and Co.; co-founder, co-pres. Ariat Internat., Inc., San Carlos, Calif., 1990—. Office: 26 Heritage Dr San Rafael CA 94901-8308 Home: 855 Worcester Rd Ste 18 Framingham MA 01701-5229

PARKER, PHILIP M., management science educator, writer; b. June 20, 1960; m. Regine Parker; children: Paul, Claire. BSc, Calif. Poly. U., 1981; DEA, U. Aix Marseille, France, 1982; PhD, U. Pa., 1988. Prof. internat. strategy and econs. U. Calif., San Diego; prof. bus. INSEAD, France, 1988—, now chaired prof. mgmt. sci.; owner Icon Group Internat., Inc., San Diego. Vis. scholar Hong Kong U. Sci. and Tech., 1993—94, 1995, U. Calif., 1996, MIT, 1996, Stanford U., 1997; former bd. mem. Rand Jour. Econs., Mktg. Sci., Jour. Internat. Bus. Studies, Internat. Jour. Forecasting. Author: Climatic Effects on Individual, Social and Economic Behaviour, 1995, Cross Cultural Encyclopedia of the World, 1997, 2007 Import and Export Market for Household Refrigerators in Czech Republic, 2006, 2007-2012 World Outlook for Automotive Aerosol Tire Inflators, 2006, 2007 Import and Export Market for Tempered or Laminated Safety Glass in Mexico, 2006, 2007-2012 Outlook for Lemon-Flavored Bottled Water in Japan, 2006, 2007-2012 World Outlook for Commercial and Industrial Floor Sanding and Scrubbing Machines, 2006, 2007-2012 World Outlook for Tufted Washable Scatter Rugs, Bathmats, and Sets That Measure 6-Feet by 9-Feet or Smaller, 2006, 2007 Import and Export Market for Electrical Relays Used with Circuits of Up to 1,000 Volts in Ireland, 2006, Webster's English to Zarma Crossword Puzzles: Level 1, 2007, and many others; co-editor: Official Patient's Sourcebook on Acne Rosacea: A Revised and Updated Directory for the Internet Age, 2002, Official Patient's Sourcebook on Hemochromatosis, 2002, Official Patient's Sourcebook on Reflex Sympathetic Dystrophy Syndrome, 2002. Named Rotary Exch. scholar, Académie de Dijon, 1979; Meml. scholar, Calif. Polystate U., 1981, Getting Oil scholar, U. Aix, France, 1982. Office: INSEAD Blvd de Constance 77305 Fontainebleau Cedex France also: ICON Group Internat, Inc 7404 Trade St San Diego CA 92121 Office Phone: 858-635-9414.

PARKER, ROBERT ALLAN RIDLEY, federal agency administrator, astronaut; b. NYC, Dec. 14, 1936; s. Allan Elwood and Alice (Heywood) P.; m. Joan Audrey Capers, June 14, 1958 (div. 1980); children: Kimberly Ellen, Brian David Capers; m. Judith S. Woodruff, Apr. 2, 1981. AB, Amherst Coll., 1958; PhD, Calif. Inst. Tech., 1962. NSF postdoctoral fellow U. Wis., 1962-63, asst. prof., then assoc. prof. astronomy, 1963-74; astronaut NASA, Johnson Space Ctr., 1967-91; dir. policy plan Office Space Flight, NASA Hdqs., Washington, 1991, dir. space ops. utilization program, 1992-97; dir. NASA Mgmt. Office, JPL, Pasadena, Calif., 1997—. Mem. support crew Apollo XV and XVII, mission scientist Apollo XVII, program scientist Skylab program, mission specialist for Spacelab 1, 1983, ASTRO-1, 1990. Mem. Am. Astron. Soc., Phi Beta Kappa. Office: NMO 180 801 JPL 4800 Oak Grove Dr Pasadena CA 91109-8001 Business E-Mail: rparker@nmo.jpl.nasa.gov.

PARKES, WALTER F., film company executive; b. Bakersfield, Calif. m. Laurie MacDonald; 2 children. AB in Anthropology, Yale U.; student, Grad. Sch. Comm., Stanford U. Pres. Amblin Entertainment, 1994; co-head, dir. motion pictures Dreamworks Pictures, 1995—. Prodr., dir.: (films) The California Reich, 1975 (nominated Acad. Award, spl. citation Cannes Film Festival); prodr.: Volunteers, 1985, True Believer, 1987, Awakenings, 1990 (nominated best picture, 1990), Men in Black, 1997, The Peace Maker, 1997, Gladiator, 2000, Artificial Intelligence, 2001; prodr.: (films) The Time Machine, 2002; prodr.: (films) Minority Report, 2002, Men in Black II, 2002, Road to Perdition, 2002, The Tuxedo, 2002, The Ring, 2002, Catch Me If You Can, 2002, The Terminal, 2004, Lemony Snicket's A Series of Unfortunate Events, 2004, The Ring Two, 2005, The Island, 2005, Just Like Heaven, 2005, The Legend of Zorro, 2005; prodr.: (films) The Lookout, 2007; exec. prodr.: (TV series) Birdland, 1994, Men in Black: The Series, 1997; (films) Littler Giants, 1994, Twister, 1996, The Trigger Effect, 1996, Amistad, 1997, Deep Impact, 1998, Small Soldiers, 1998, Mask of Zorro, 1998; writer: WarGames, 1983 (nominated best original screenplay, 1983); prodr., writer: (films) Sneakers, 1992 (nominated Acad. Award, spl. citation Cannes Film Festival). Named one of 50 Most Powerful People in Hollywood, Premiere mag., 2004—05. Office: DreamWorks SKG 1000 Flower St Glendale CA 91201 Office Phone: 818-733-7000. Office Fax: 818-695-7574.

PARKHURST, VIOLET KINNEY, artist; b. Derby Line, Vt., Apr. 26, 1926; d. Edson Frank and Rosa (Beauchiene) Kinney; student Sch. Practical Arts, Boston, 1941-42, Baylor U., Waco, Tex., 1943, Calif. State U., Los Angeles, 1950-51; m. Donald Winters Parkhurst, Apr. 10, 1948. Fgn. corr. 5 Brazilian mags., 1946-53; tech. illustrator, 1954-55; owner five galleries including Ports of Call, San Pedro,

Calif.; artist, specializing in seascapes; work included in permanent collection of Stockholm Mus., many pvt. collections including Presidents Richard M. Nixon, Ford, Reagan, Bush, Gov. Wilson, Mayor of Kobe, Japan, Mayor Yorty of L.A., Rory Calhoun, Barbara Rush, Jim Arness, David Rose, President Hu of China, 2005; one-shows shows at prominent galleries; numerous paintings published. Winner 30 blue ribbons for art. Fellow Am. Inst. Fine Arts. Mem. Ch. of Religious Sci. Author: How to Paint Books, 1966; Parkhurst on Seascapes, 1972. Paintings reproduced on covers South West Art, Arizona Living, Hollywood Bowl Easter Sunrise Service program; ltd. edit. prints published, also ltd. edit. plates. The first artist in the world invited to present a painting to Pres. Jiang Zemin, Beisin, China, 2002; the first western artist to have a painting in China Nat. Mus. of Fine Arts and the Hall of the People. Office: Parkhurst Gallery Ports of Call Village San Pedro CA 90731 E-mail: violet@parkhurstartgalleries.com.

PARKIN, JAMES LAMAR, retired otolaryngologist, educator; b. Salt Lake City, June 2, 1939; s. Elmer Lamar and Mary Ilene (Soffe) Parkin; m. Bonnie Dansie, July 1, 1963; children: Jeffrey, Brett, Matthew, David. BS, U. Utah, 1963, MD, 1966; MS, U. Wash., 1970. Diplomate Am. Bd. Otolaryngology. Resident in otolaryngology U. Wash., Seattle, 1968—72; practice medicine specializing in otolaryngology Salt Lake City, 1972—; chmn. divsn. otolaryngology U. Utah Sch. Medicine, Salt Lake City, 1974—93, prof. surgery, 1981—, acting chmn. dept. surgery, 1984—84, 1993—94, chmn., 1994—96, prof. emeritus, 2004—. Pres. med. bd. Univ. Med. Ctr., Salt Lake City, 1983—85, chmn. exec. com. faculty practice orgn., 1994—96, assoc. v.p. health scis., 1996—97, v.p. sch. medicine alumni, 2003—, v.p. med. alumni, 2003—, chmn. centennial com., 2005—; bd. govs. Utah Med. Ins. Assn., Salt Lake City, 1979—81. Guest editor Ear, Nose and Throat Jour., 1982, assoc. editor Archives of Otolaryngology. Leader Boy Scouts Am.; bishop Ch. of Jesus Christ of Latter-Day Saints, Salt Lake City, 1983—86, stake pres., 1986—96, pres. Eng. London South Mission, 1996—2000. Recipient Honor award, Am. Acad. Otolaryngology, 1980. Fellow: ACS, Am. Neurotology Soc., Am. Soc. Laser Medicine and Surgery, Am. Otol. Soc., Am. Plastic and Reconstructive Surgery, Am. Laryngol, Rhinol. and Otol. Soc.; mem.: Collegium Aesculapium (pres. 2005—), Soc. Otolaryngology-Maxillofacial Surgery (pres. Utah chpt. 1979), Am. Cancer Soc. (pres. Utah chpt. 1984—86), Soc. Univ. Otolaryngologists (pres. 1984—85), Assn. Acad. Depts. Otolaryngology (chmn. nat. faculty survey com. 1980—90, sec.-treas. 1982—84, pres. 1986—88).

PARKIN, STUART STEPHEN PAPWORTH, materials scientist, physicist; IBM fellow IBM Almaden Rsch. Ctr., San Jose, Calif., 1983—. Recipient Internat. prize for new materials Am. Phys. Soc., 1994, C.V. Boys prize Inst. Physics, London, 1991, Inaugural Outstanding Young Investigator award Materials Rsch. Soc., 1991, Europhysics prize Hewlett-Packard, 1997, Indsl. Applications of Physics prize Am. Inst. Physics, 1999-2000, Humbboldt award, 2005; named Innovator of Yr., R&D Mag., 2001. Fellow AAAS, NAS, IEEE (Daniel Noble award, 2008, Disting. Lecturer award, 2008), Am. Phys. Soc., Royal Soc. London, Inst. Physics (London), MRS. Office: IBM Almaden Rsch Ctr 650 Harry Rd San Jose CA 95120-6099 Office Phone: 408-927-2390. E-mail: parkin@almaden.ibm.com.

PARKINSON, BRADFORD WELLS, astronautical engineer, educator; b. Madison, Wis., Feb. 16, 1935; s. Herbert and Metta Tisdale (Smith) P.; m. Virginia Pinkham Wier, Nov. 26, 1977; children: Leslie, Bradford II, Eric, Ian, Bruce, Jared Bradford. BS, U.S. Naval Acad., 1957; MS, MIT, 1961; PhD, Stanford U., 1966; grad. (disting.), USAF Command and Staff Coll., 1969, Naval War Coll., 1972. Commd. 2d lt. USAF, 1957, advanced through grades to col., 1972; divsn. chief AF Test Pilot Sch., 1966-68; chair dept. astronautics and computer sci. USAF Acad., 1969-71; dir. engring. ABRES, 1972; program mgr. NAVSTAR GPS, 1972-78; ret. USAF, 1978; prof. mech. engring. Colo. State U., Ft. Collins, 1978-79; v.p. advanced engring. Rockwell Internat., Downey, Calif., 1979-80; gen. mgr., v.p. Intermetrics, Inc., Cambridge, Mass., 1980-84; prof. emeritus, assoc. dir. gravity probe-B Stanford (Calif.) U., 1984—; CEO, pres. Trimble Navigation Ltd., 1998-99. Chair adv. coun. JPL NASA; dir. Trimble Navigation Ltd., Sunnyvale, Calif., NTV, Cambridge; past chair bd. dirs. Aerospace Corp., El Segundo, Calif. Decorated Def. Superior Svc. medal, AF Commendation medal with oak leaf cluster, Meritorius Svc. medal, Presdl. Unit citation, Bronze Star, Legion of Merit, Air medal with oak leaf cluster; recipient Pub. Svc. award, Disting. Pub. Svc. award, NASA, 1984, Thurlow award Inst. Navigation, 1986, Burka award, 1987, Kepler award, 1991, Aerospace Contbn. to Soc. award, 1991, Goddard medal, von Karman Lectureship AIAA, 1996, Magellan Premium, Am. Philos. Soc., 1997, Gold medal Space Tech. Hall of Fame of U.S. Space Found., 1998, Williams Space medal Soc. Logistics Engrs., 1996, ASME medal, 2004; named to National Inventors Hall of Fame, 2004. Fellow AIAA, Royal Inst. Navigation (Gold medal 1983), Inst. Navigation, IEEE (Kirchner award 1986, Pioneer award 1994, Sperry award 1999, Simon Remo medal); mem. AAS, NAE (councillor, Charles Stark Draper Prize, 2003), Internat. Acad. Astronautics, Sigma Xi, Tau Beta Pi. Avocations: hiking, skiing, sailing. Office: Stanford U 4085 Mail Code Stanford CA 94305 Home: 2360 Camino Edna San Luis Obispo CA 93401

PARKS, BERNARD, councilman; s. Earl W. Parks; m. Bobbie Parks; children: Felicia, Michelle, Trudy, Bernard Jr. BS, Pepperdine U.; MPA, U. Southern Calif. Police officer LA Police Dept., police chief, 1997—2002; councilman, Dist. 8 LA City Coun., 2003—. Coach Baldwin Hills Youth Football. NAACP (life); Challengers Boys & Girls Club; LA Urban League; Brotherhood Crusade; Civil Rights Walk of Fame, Atlanta, Ga. Office: 200 N Spring St Rm 460 Los Angeles CA 90012 Office Phone: 213-473-7008. Office Fax: 213-485-7683. E-mail: councilmember.parks@lacity.org.*

PARKS, DEBORA ANN, retired principal; b. Homestead, Fla., July 23, 1954; d. Jack Wesley and Blanche Margaret (Shawver) Hardin; m. Lewis O'Dell Parks, Apr. 12, 1970 (div. May 1980); 1 child, Kerri Shane Parks. BS in Early Childhood Edn., U. Ala., Tuscaloosa, 1983, MA in Spl. Edn., 1984, MA in Early Childhood Edn., 1987, PhD in Elem. Edn., 1991. Kindergarten tchr. Martin Luther King Jr. Elem. Sch., Tuscaloosa, 1983-85; tchr. gifted grades 2-5 Martin Luther King Jr. Elem. Sch. and Univ. Place Elem. Sch., Tuscaloosa, 1985-86; early childhood edn. instr. Shelton State C.C., Tuscaloosa, 1985-88; instr. U. Ala., Tuscaloosa, 1987; elem. tchr. 1st grade Martin Luther King Jr. Elem. Sch., Tuscaloosa, 1988-89; tchr. gifted grades 3-6 Carthay Elem. Sch., L.A. Unified Sch. Dist., 1991; faculty-in-residence Sunset Village Residence Halls UCLA, 1991-95; tchr. gifted grades K-8 Maimonides Acad., LA, 1992-94; asst. rschr. So. Calif. Injury Prevention Rsch. Ctr. Sch. Pub. Health, UCLA, 1993-95; faculty liaison on campus housing darkroom UCLA, 1993-95, instr. dept. edn., 1994, 95, instr., rschr., 1989-95; tchr. gifted grades 2-8 Maimonides Acad., LA, 1995, gen. studies prin., 1995—2005. Chair Yom Iyun Citywide In-Svc. for Tchrs., L.A., 2000; grad. tchg. asst. elem. edn. U. Ala., Tuscaloosa, 1986-87; field coord., instr. Tchr. Edn. Lab., Grad. Sch. Edn., UCLA, 1989-93; enrichment tchr. grades 3-5 The Buckley Sch., Sherman Oaks, Calif., summer, 1991, 92, 93; evaluation coach/cons. Stanford Rsch. Inst., SB 620 Statewide Healthy Start Initiative Program, L.A., 1993-95; spl. faculty advisor UCLA Photographic Soc., 1993-95; evaluator lang. arts program, curriculum and tchrs. Maimonides Acad., L.A., 1994; enrichment tchr. grades 4-5 Buckley Sch., Sherman Oaks, Calif., summer 1994, enrichment tchr., summer 1995; evaluation coach, cons. Stanford Rsch. Inst., L.A., 1993-95; mem. governing bd. Nat. Assn. Creative Children and Adults, Ohio, 1992-94; rsch. adviser Phi Delta Kappa, UCLA chpt., 1992-94; mem. Adopt-A-Sch. Coun., L.A. Unified Sch. Dist., 1990-95; chairperson Tuscaloosa City Sch.'s Kindergarten Math. Com., 1984; presenter confs. and workshops. Author: The Newspaper Workbook, 1983, Pedestrian and Bicyclist Safety Curriculum for Grades K-5, 1994, Adopt-A-School Programs: A Guide for Pre-Service Teachers, 1995, Exercises and Tests in English Grammar, 2000, Contemporary American Slang, 2004; manuscript asst. editor Am. Mid. Sch. Edn., 1986-87; asst. editor Adopt-A-School Newsletter, 1993; contbr. articles to profl. jours; Photog. Exhib., Paralel 45 Pub. House, Pitesti, Romania, 2001/ Vol. Rebuild L.A., 1992-93 Recipient award NEA and Kodak, N.Y. and Ala., 1985, scholarships Am. Bus. Women's Assn., Ala., 1988, Beta Chi of Delta Kappa Gamma, 1983, Epsilon chpt. Alpha Delta Kappa, 1984, Yewell R. Thompson Endowed scholarship, 1988; designee Ala. Tchr. of Yr. Program, 1984-85, 85-86. Mem. Phi Delta Kappa. Democrat. Avocations: photography, calligraphy, graphic arts, genealogy. Home: 1015 Columbia St South Pasadena CA 91030 Personal E-mail: dparks555@yahoo.com.

PARKS, MICHAEL CHRISTOPHER, journalist, educator; b. Detroit, Nov. 17, 1943; s. Robert James and Rosalind (Smith) P.; m. Linda Katherine Durocher, Dec. 26, 1964; children: Danielle Anne (dec.), Christopher, Matthew. AB, U. Windsor, Ont., Can., 1965. Reporter Detroit News, 1962-65; corr. Time-Life News Service, NYC, 1965-66; asst. city editor Suffolk Sun, Long Island, NY, 1966-68; polit. reporter, foreign corr. The Balt. Sun, Saigon, Singapore, Moscow, Cairo, Hong Kong, Peking, 1968-80; fgn. corr. L.A. Times, L.A., Peking, Johannesburg, Moscow, Jerusalem, 1980-95, dpty. fgn. editor, 1995-96, mng. editor, 1996-97, editor, 1997-2000, v.p., 1996-97, sr. v.p., 1997-98, exec. v.p., 1998-2000; v.p. Times Mirror Co., 1998-2000; prof. Annenberg Sch. Comm. U. So. Calif., LA, 2000—02, dir. Annenberg Sch. Journalism, 2002—08, prof. journalism and internat. rels., 2002—. Disting. fellow Pacific Coun. Internat. Policy, 2000-02, dir. 1998-; dir. L.A. Jewish Jour., 2004-. Recipient Pulitzer prize, 1987. Mem. Am. Soc. Newspaper Editors, AP Mng. Editors, Pacific Coun. Internat. Policy, Radio-TV News Dirs., Soc. Profl. Journalists, Athenaeum (Pasadena, Calif.), Coun. on Fgn. Rels., Rsch. Pk. City Club (L.A.), Nat. Press Club. Office: Annenberg Sch U So Calif Los Angeles CA 90089-0281 Office Phone: 213-243-5324. E-mail: mparks@usc.edu.

PARKS, MICHAEL JAMES, editor; b. Spokane, Wash., June 3, 1944; s. Floyd Lewis and Marie (McHugh) Parks; m. Janet K. Holter, Aug. 12, 1967; children: Michael J., Gregory F., Sarah M. BA, Seattle U., 1966. Reporter The Seattle Times, 1966—74, fin. editor, 1974—77; pub., editor Marple's Pacific N.W. Letter, Seattle, 1977—. Bd. govs. Seattle U. Alumni Assn.; trustee Seattle Rotary Svc. Found. Fellow, Am. Press Inst., N.Y.C., 1973. Mem.: Rotary. Roman Catholic. Avocations: opera, reading, swimming, walking. Office: Marples NW Letter Ste 200 117 W Mercer St Seattle WA 98119-3960 Personal E-mail: michaeljparks@gmail.com. E-mail: info@marples.com.

PARKS, PATRICIA JEAN, lawyer; b. Portland, Oreg., Apr. 2, 1945; d. Robert and Marion (Crosby) Parks; m. David F. Jurca, Oct. 17, 1971 (div. 1976). BA in History, Stanford U., 1967; JD, U. Pa., Phila., 1970. Bar: N.Y. 1971, Wash. 1974. Assoc. Milbank, Tweed, Hadley & McCoy, NYC, 1970-73, Shidler, McBroom, Gates & Lucas, Seattle, 1974-81, ptnr., 1981-90, Preston, Thorgrimson, Shidler, Gates & Ellis, Seattle, 1990-93; pvt. practice Seattle, 1993-99; spl. counsel Karr Tuttle Campbell, Seattle, 1999—2007. Active Vashon Allied Arts; former bd. dirs. Seattle chpt. Western Pension and Benefits Conf. Mem.: ABA, Pension Roundtable, Seattle-King County Bar Assn., Wash. Women Tax, Wash. State Bar Assn. (past chair gift and estate tax com.), Wash. Native Plant Soc., Wash. Athletic Club. Avocations: kayaking, hiking, contra dancing, birdwatching. Personal E-mail: parkspat@comcast.net.

PARKS, ROBERT MYERS, appliance manufacturing company executive; b. Nevada, Mo., July 18, 1927; s. Cecil R. and Marcella (Myers) P.; m. Audrey Lenora Jones, June 18, 1955; children: John Robert, Janet M. Parks Huston. BS, U. Mo., 1949; MBA, Harvard U., 1952. Asst. dept. mgr. Jewett & Sherman Co., Kansas City, Mo., 1949-50; staff cons. Harbridge House, Inc., Boston, 1952; v.p. Electronic Splty. Co., Inc., Los Angeles, 1952-57; founder, chmn. bd. Parks Products, Inc., Hollywood, Calif., 1957—; pres. Generalist Industries, Inc., Hollywood, 1960-73. Chmn. bd. Shaver Corp. Am., LA, 1965—; lectr. mktg. UCLA Extension divsn., 1960-61. Contbr. articles to profl. jours.; patentee in field. Active YMCA; bd. dirs. Hollywood Presbyn. Med. Center Found., Presbyn. Homes Found.; mem. dean's adv. council U. Mo. Bus. Sch., mayor's task force on L.A. River Cahuenga Pass Coalition. With USNR, 1944-45. Named in his honor Grad. Bus. Sch., U. Mo. Mem. Sales and Marketing Execs. Assn., C. of C., Navy League, World Affairs Coun., Calif. Caballeros, Rangers, Vaqueros del Desierto, Los Caballeros, Rancheros Visitadores, E Clampus Vitus, Delta Sigma Pi, Sigma Chi. Clubs: Mason (Shriner), LA Breakfast, Braemar Country, Saddle and Sirloin. Presbyterian. Home: 7421 Woodrow Wilson Dr Los Angeles CA 90046-1322 Office: 3611 Cahuenga Blvd Hollywood CA 90068-1205 Office Phone: 323-876-5454.

PARLETTE, LINDA EVANS, state legislator; b. Wenatchee, Wash., Aug. 20, 1945; m to Bob. Washington State Representative, District 12, 1997-2001, member, Appropriations Committee, 1997-2001, co-chairwoman, Health Care Committee, 1997-2001, Washington House Representative; Washington State Senator, District 12, 2001-, Republican Dep Leader, currently, Washington State Senate.Member, Lake Chelan Sch Bd, formerly, N Center ESD Bd, formerly; board director, Washington State Ag-Forestry Leadership Found, currently. Margaret Chase Smith Award; Rural Healthcare Award, Washington State, 97-98. Rotary. Republican. Protestant. Mailing: 661-15 Wheeler Hill Rd Wenatchee WA 98801 Office: State Senate 415 Legislative Bldg, PO Box 40412 Olympia WA 98504 Office Phone: 360-786-7832.

PARMELEE, ARTHUR HAWLEY, JR., pediatric medical educator; b. Chgo., Oct. 29, 1917; s. Arthur Hawley and Ruth Frances (Brown) P.; m. Jean Kern Rheinfrank, Nov. 11, 1939; children: Arthur Hawley III, Ann (Mrs. John C. Minahan Jr.), Timothy, Ruth Ellen. BS, U. Chgo., 1940, MD, 1943. Diplomate Am. Bd. Pediatrics (examiner 1966—). Intern U.S. Naval Hosp., Bethesda, Md., 1943-44; extern Yale Inst. Child Devel., 1947, New Haven Hosp., 1947-48, L.A. Children's Hosp., 1948-49; mem. faculty UCLA Med. Sch., 1951—, prof. pediat., 1967-88, prof. emeritus, 1988, dir. divsn. child devel., 1964-88; mem. Brain Rsch. Inst., 1966-88, Mental Retardation Rsch. Ctr., 1970-88. Rsch. prof. pediat. U. Göttingen, Germany, 1967-68; mem. com. child devel. rsch. and pub. policy NRC, 1977-81; cons. Nat. Inst. Child Health and Human Devel., 1963-70, Holy Family Adoption Svc., 1949-80. Author articles, chpts. in books. Trustee Los Angeles Children's Mus., 1979. Served with USN, 1943-47. Recipient C. Anderson Aldrich award in child devel., 1975; Commonwealth fellow Centre de Recherches Biologiques Neonatales, Clinique Obstetricale Baudelocque, Paris, 1959-60; fellow Ctr. Advanced Study in Behavioral Scis., Stanford U., 1984-85; hon. lectr. Soc. for Developmental and Behavioral Pediat., 1996. Mem. AMA, Am. Pediat. Soc., Soc. Pediat. Rsch., Western Soc. Pediat. Rsch., Am. Acad. Pediat. (chmn. com. sect. child devel. 1966), Assn. Ambulatory Pediat. (mem. coun. 1966-69), Soc. Rsch. in Child Devel. (pres. 1983-85, Disting. Sci. Contbns. to Child Devel. award 1993), Assn. Psychophysiol. Study of Sleep, Los Angeles County Med. Soc., Phi Beta Kappa. Home: 764 Iliff St Pacific Palisades CA 90272-3927 Office: Univ Calif Dept Pediatrics Los Angeles CA 90024 Home Phone: 310-454-2618.

PARNAFES, ITZIK, Internet company executive; Co-founder, R&D mgr. Class Data Sys. (acquired by Cisco Networks, 1998); co-founder, v.p. products Kagoor Networks; sr. dir. product mgmt. Juniper Networks (formerly Kagoor Networks). Spkr. in field; consul. in field. Office: Juniper Networks 1194 No Mathilda Ave Sunnyvale CA 94089-1206 Office Fax: 408-745-2100.

PARNELL, FRANCIS WILLIAM, JR., otolaryngologist; b. Woonsocket, RI, May 22, 1940; s. Francis W. and Dorothy V. (Lalor) P.; m. Diana DeAngelis, Feb. 27, 1965; children: Cheryl Lynn, John Francis, Kathleen Diana, Alison Anne, Thomas William. Student, Coll. Holy Cross, 1957-58; AB, Clark U., 1961; MD, Georgetown U., 1965. Diplomate: Nat. Bd. Med. Examiners, Am. Bd. Otolaryngology. Intern Univ. Hosps., Madison, Wis., 1965-66, resident in gen. surgery, 1966-67, otolaryngology, 1967-70; pvt. practice medicine specializing in otolaryngology San Rafael, Calif., 1972-75, Greenbrae, Calif., 1978—2000; chmn., pres., CEO Parnell Pharms., Larkspur, Calif., 1982—. Cons. corp. med. affairs, 1978-82; corp. med. dir. Becton, Dickinson & Co., Rutherford, N.J., 1976-78; clin. instr. U. Calif. at San Francisco, 1972-75, asst. clin. prof., 1975-76; Alt. del., U.S. Del. 27th World Health Assembly WHO, Geneva, 1974. Contbr. articles to profl. jours. Candidate Calif. State Assembly, 1988; bd. dirs. Marin Coalition, 1980-96, 97-01, chmn., 1986-87; trustee Ross (Calif.) Sch. Dist., 1981-89; mem. governing bd. Marin Cmty. Coll. Dist., 1995-03, pres., 1999-00, 02-03; dir. Coll. Marin Found., 2004-, pres., 2006-. Maj. M.C. AUS, 1970-72, lt. col. M.C., USAR, 1985-93. Fellow ACS (gov. 1988-94), Am. Acad. Otolaryngology. Home: PO Box 998 Ross CA 94957-0998 Office: 1100 S Eliseo Dr Greenbrae CA 94904-2017 Office Phone: 415-256-1800.

PARNELL, SEAN, Lieutenant Governor of Alaska, former state legislator, lawyer; b. Hanford, Calif., Nov. 19, 1962; m. Sandy Parnell; children: Grace, Rachel. BBA, Pacific Luth. U., 1984; JD, U. Puget Sound, 1987. Comml. atty., 1987—; pvt. bus. owner, 1991—2000; mem. State House of Representatives, 1992—96, Alaska State Senate, 1996—2000, co-chair fin. com., mem. resources com., legis. budget and audit com.; ptnr. Patton Boggs, LLP, Anchorage; lt. gov. State of Alaska, 2007—. Vol. mentor for H.S. youth groups and orgns., 1988-91; mem. Telecom. Info. Coun., Energy Coun., Western Legis. Timber Task Force, Bayshore-Klatt Cmty. Coun., Uniform Code Revision Commn.; dissenting mem. Long Range Fin. Planning Commn. Mem. Nat. Fedn. Ind. Bus. Republican. Avocations: teaching and coaching high school youth, running, reading, softball. Office: 716 W 4th Ave Ste 530 Anchorage AK 99501-2107 also: Lieutenant Governor PO Box 110015 Juneau AK 99811-0015 Office Phone: 907-465-3520.

PARNES, ANDREW H., financial executive; V.p. fin., treas., CFO Standard Pacific Corp., Costa Mesa, Calif., 1996—. Office: Standard Pacific Corp 26 Technology Dr Irvine CA 92618-2301

PARODE, ANN, lawyer; b. LA, Mar. 3, 1947; d. Lowell Carr and Sabine Parode. BA, Pomona Coll., 1968; JD, UCLA, 1971. Bar: Calif. 1972, U.S. Dist. Ct. (so. dist.) Calif. 1972, U.S. Ct. Appeals (9th cir.) 1975, U.S. Supreme Ct. 2000. Assoc. Luce, Forward et al, San Diego, 1971-75; gen. counsel, exec. v.p., sec. San Diego Trust & Savs., 1975-94; with First Interstate Bank, 1994—97; campus counsel U. Calif., San Diego, 1997—. Judge pro tem San Diego Mcpl. Ct., 1978—84; campus counsel U. Calif., San Diego, 1997—. Bd. dirs. San Diego Cmty. Found., 1989-97, chmn., 1994-96; bd. dirs. The Burnham Inst., 1995-2001, Girard Found., 1990-. Mem. Calif. Bar Assn. (corp. law com. 1980-83, client trust fund commn. 1986-90, chmn. 1989-90), San Diego County Bar Found. (founder, bd. dirs. 1979-86, 98-2001, pres. 1980-83), San Diego Bar Assns. (bd. dirs. 1977-81, v.p. 1977-78, 80-81, treas. 1979-80), Law Libr. Justice Found. (pres. 1994). Office Phone: 858-822-1236. Business E-Mail: aparode@ucsd.edu.

PARRAGUIRRE, RONALD DAVID, state supreme court justice; b. Reno, July 8, 1959; s. Paul Charles and Iris Mae (Bleick) P.; m. Leslie, 2 children. BBA, San Diego State U., 1982; JD, U. San Diego, 1985. Bar: Pa. 1986, Nev. 1986, D.C. 1987. Legis. asst. U.S. Senator Paul Laxalt, Washington, 1985-86; counsel subcom. on criminal law, judiciary com. U.S. Senate, Washington, 1986-87; lawyer Parraguirre & Parraguirre, Las Vegas, Nev., 1987-91; mcpl. ct. judge Dept. 6 City of Las Vegas, 1991-99; dist. ct. judge Eighth Jud. Dist. Ct., Clark County, Nev., 1999—2004; justice Nev. Supreme Ct., 2004—. Mem. Nev. State-Federal Jud. Council, Nev. Supreme Ct. State Ct. Funding Com.; former mem. Nev. Supreme Ct. Jud. Election Practices Com. Mem. ABA, ATLA, Am. Judges Assn., Nev. Judges Assn., Nev. State Bar Assn. (mem. multi-jurisdictional task force com.), Clark County Bar Assn. (former exec. bd. mem.) Republican. Lutheran. Avocations: skiing, racquetball, hunting, fishing. Office: Nev Supreme Court 201 S Carson St Carson City NV 89701-4702

PARRIS, MARK S., lawyer, professional athletes consultant; b. Caldwell, Wash., Mar. 22, 1957; s. Wayne Wesley and Helen (Padgett) P. BA, Gonzaga U., 1980; JD, U. Wash., 1983. Bar: Wash. 1983, U.S.

Dist. Ct. (we. dist.) Wash. 1983, (ea. dist.) Wash. 1989, U.S. Dist. Ct. (ea. dist.) Wash. 1989, U.S. Ct. Appeals (9th cir.) 1990. Assoc. Syndal, Danelo, Seattle, 1983-88, Heller, Ehrman, White & McAuliffe, Seattle, 1988-90, ptnr., 1990—. Cons. Athlete Cons. Svcs., Seattle. Pres., Athletes That Care, Seattle; vol. Lake City Legal Clinic, Seattle, Children's Hosp., Seattle. Avocations: cricket, golf, squash, mountain climbing. Office: Heller Ehrman White & McAuliffe 721 5th Ave 6100 Columbia Ctr Seattle WA 98104-7043

PARRISH, JENNI, law librarian, educator; b. Houston; BA, Rice U.; MLS, JD, U. Tex., Austin. Assoc. law libr. U. Okla.; dir. Law Libr. U. Pitts., 1980; faculty mem. U. Calif., Hastings Coll. of Law, San Francisco, 1993—, prof. law, dir. Law Libr. Contbr. articles to profl. jours. Office: U Calif Hastings Coll of Law 200 McAllister St San Francisco CA 94102 Office Phone: 415-565-4881. E-mail: parrishj@uchastings.edu.

PARRISH, JILL NIEDERHAUSER, state supreme court justice; BA, Weber State U., 1982; JD, Yale U., 1985. Bar: Utah 1985, 10th Cir. Ct. Appeals 1987, U.S. Supreme Ct. 2000. Clk. Hon. David K. Winder U.S. Dist. Ct., Utah, 1985; atty. Parr, Waddoups, Brown, Gee & Loveless, Salt Lake City, 1986—90, shareholder, 1990—95; asst. U.S. atty. Civil Divsn. U.S. Dist. Ct., Utah, 1995—2003; justice Utah Supreme Ct., Salt Lake City, 2003—, mem. tech. com., judicial performance evaluation com., 2003—. Supr. Fin. Litigation Unit U.S. Attys. Office. Mem.: Fed. Bar Assn. (pres.). Office: Utah Supreme Ct PO Box 140210 Salt Lake City UT 84114-0210

PARROTT, DENNIS BEECHER, retired insurance industry executive; b. St. Louis, June 13, 1929; s. Maurice Ray and Mai Ledgerwood (Beecher) P.; m. Vivian Cleveland Miller, Mar. 24, 1952; children: Constance Beecher, Dennis Beecher, Anne Cleveland. BS in Econs., Fla. State U., Tallahassee, 1954; postgrad., Princeton U., NJ, 1964; MBA, Pepperdine U., Malibu, Calif., 1982. With Prudential Ins. Co. Am., 1954-74, v.p. group mktg. LA, 1971-74; sr. v.p. Frank B. Hall Cons. Co., LA, 1974—83; v.p. Johnson & Higgins, LA, 1983-95; exec. v.p. Arthur J. Gallagher & Co., LA, 1995-98; ret., 1998. Spkr. in field. Chmn. Weekend with the Stars Telethon, 1976-80; chmn. bd. dirs. United Cerebral Palsy/Spastic Children's Found., LA County, 1979-82, chmn. bd. govs., 1982-83; bd. dirs. Nat. United Cerebral Palsy Assn., 1977-82, pres., 1977-79; bd. dirs. LA Emergency Task Force, 1992; mem. cmty. adv. coun. Birmingham High Sch., Van Nuys, Calif., 1982-85; sect. chmn. United Way, LA, 1983-84; bd. dirs. The Betty Clooney Found. for Brain Injured, 1986-88; mem. com. to fund an endowed chair in cardiology at Cedars-Sinai Med. Ctr., 1986-88; adv. coun. Family Health Program, Inc., 1986-88; bd. deacons Bel Air Presbyn. Ch., 1990-92, chmn., 1991-92, elder, 1993-96; mem. adv. coun. Blue Cross Calif., 1996-98; chmn. Danny Arnold Meml. Golf Classic at Riviera Country Club benefitting John Wayne Cancer Inst., 1997. 1st lt. AUS, 1951-53. Named Tournament Champion, Sunkist Invitational Golf Tournament, 1995. Mem. Am. Soc. CLUs, Internat. Found. Employee Benefits, Mchts. and Mfrs. Assns. 44th Ann. Mgmt. Conf. (chmn. 1986), Employee Benefits Planning Assn. So. Calif., LA Club, Woodland Hills Country Club, Jonathan Club (LA). Republican. Presbyterian. Home: 17023 Encino Hills Dr Encino CA 91436-4009 Personal E-mail: CallParrott@aol.com.

PARROTT, JOEL J., zoo director; b. Lake George, NY, Aug. 21, 1952; married; 2 children. BS in Biology, Colo. State U., 1975, DVM, 1980. Intern Denver Zoo, 1979; veterinarian in pvt. practice Castro Valley, Calif., 1980-84; asst. dir. Oakland (Calif.) Zoo, 1984, exec. dir., 1985—. Office: The Oakland Zoo PO Box 5238 9777 Golf Links Rd Oakland CA 94605-4925

PARRY, CLINT, business coaching executive; b. 1970; Owner Action Internat. Bus. Coaching, Tucson. Involved with Northern Pima County Chamber of Commerce. Named one of 40 Under 40, Tucson Bus. Edge, 2006. Mem.: Ariz. Assn. Bus. Brokers, Ariz. Small Bus. Assn., Jr. Achievement of Ariz. (bd. mem.), Tucson Assn. of Executives (pres/). Office: Action International 5670 Wynn Rd Ste A & C Las Vegas NV 89118

PARRY, RICHARD D., lawyer, construction executive; b. LA, July 12, 1952; BA, Calif. State U., 1977; JD, Brigham Young U. J. Rueben Clark Law Sch., 1980. Bar: Utah 1980, Ohio 1983, U.S. Ct. of Appeals, 6th Circuit, U.S. Dist. Ct., Dist. of Utah, U.S. Ct. of Appeals, 10th Circuit. Atty. priv. practice; interim U.S. atty. State of Utah, asst. U.S. atty.; v.p., assoc. gen. counsel Wash. Group Internat., 1993—97, v.p., gen. counsel, 1997—2001, sr. v.p., gen. counsel, 2001—. Assoc. counsel U.S. Senate Select Com. on Iran-Contra, 1987. Mem.: ABA, Ohio State Bar Assn., Utah State Bar Assn. Office: Wash Group Internat PO Box 73 720 Park Blvd Boise ID 83729

PARSA, FEREYDOUN DON, plastic surgeon; b. Tehran, Iran, May 20, 1942; came to U.S., 1970; s. Issa and Zahra (Bisnark) P.; m. Touri Akhlaghi, June 17, 1972; children: Natalie, Alan, Sean. MD, Lausanne U., Switzerland, 1969. Diplomate Am. Bd. Plastic Surgery. Chief of plastic surgery, prof. surgery U. Hawaii, Honolulu, 1981—. Contbr. articles to profl. jours. Mem. AMA, Am. Soc. Plastic Surgeons, Hawaii Med. Assn. Avocation: painting. Office: U Hawaii Sch Med Surgery 1329 Lusitana St 807 Honolulu HI 96813-2421 Personal E-mail: hawaiiplasticsurgery@yahoo.com.

PARSKY, BARBARA J., utilities executive; BA, Rollins Coll., Winter Park, Fla. Various mgmt. positions in mktg. and strategic comm. GE, mgr. corp. advt.; gen. mgr. Porter Novelli, LA, ptnr.; prin., owner consulting bus.; v.p. corp. comm. Edison Internat., Rosemead, Calif., 2002—07, sr. v.p. corp. comm., 2007—, sr. v.p. corp. comm. So. Calif. Edison subs., 2007—. Office: Edison Internat 2244 Walnut Grove Ave Rosemead CA 91770-3714

PARSKY, GERALD LAWRENCE, lawyer; b. West Hartford, Conn., Oct. 18, 1942; s. Isadore and Nettie (Sanders) P.; m. Susan Haas, June 26, 1966; children: Laura, David; m. Robin Cleary, Jan. 27, 1980. AB, Princeton U., 1964; JD, U. Va., 1968. Bar: N.Y. 1969, D.C. 1974, Calif. 1983. Assoc. Mudge Rose Guthrie & Alexander, NYC, 1968-71; spl. asst. to under sec. U.S. Treasury Dept., Washington, 1971-73, exec. asst. to dep. sec. Fed. Energy Office, 1973-74, asst. sec. internat. affairs, 1974-77; sr. ptnr. Gibson, Dunn & Crutcher, LA, 1977-90; of counsel Gibson, Dunn & Cruther, 1990-92; chmn. Aurora Capital Ptnrs., 1990—. Bd. dirs. James A. Baker III Inst. Pub. Policy. Trustee George Bush Presdl. Libr. Found., 1993—, Ronald Reagan Presdl. Found., 1995—; bd. dirs. Music Ctr. Found., 1998—. Recipient Alexander Hamilton award U.S. Treasury, 1976, Woodrow Wilson award, 2000. Mem. ABA, Coun. Fgn. Rels., N.Y. Princeton Club, Calif. Club, Racquet Club N.Y., Rolling Rock Club, Rancho Santa Fe Golf Club. Office: Aurora Capital Group 10877 Wilshire Blvd Ste 2100 Los Angeles CA 90024-4376

PARSONS, A. PETER, lawyer; b. Norwood, Mass., May 29, 1945; s. Charles A.A. and Elizabeth P. (Coombs) P.; children: A. Peter, Christopher P.; m. Nimfa Pacayra, Dec. 13, 2003; 1 child Alex W. AA, Palm Beach Jr. Coll., 1968; BS Fla. Atlantic U., 1969; JD, Duke U., 1973. Bar: Wash. 1973, U.S. Dist. Ct. (ea. and we. dists.) Wash. 1974, U.S. Ct. Appeals (9th cir.) 1974; CPA, Fla., Wash. Acct., Haskins & Sells, Ft. Lauderdale, 1969-70; tax cons. Arthur, Young & Co., Portland, Oreg., 1972; law clk. Wash. Supreme Ct., 1973-74; atty. Perkins, Coie, Seattle, 1974-77; mem., mng. dir. Weinrich, Gilmore & Adolph, Seattle, 1978-87; ptnr. Davis Wright Tremaine LLP, 1988—; adj. prof. U. Puget Sound, 1974-75; lectr. U. Wash., 1978-81. Mem. editorial bd. Duke U. Law Jour., 1971-73. Contbr. articles to legal jours. Chmn. bd. dirs. PIVOT, non-profit corp., Seattle, 1975-78; Group Theater, Seattle, 1984-86; chmn. bd. dirs. MIT Enterprise Forum, Seattle, 1984-92; Wash. State Biotechnology Assn. 1991-94, Washington Software Alliance, Bellevue, 1996-98, 2000-2002, 2005—, Midisoft Corp., Issaquah, 1996-98, Info. Technol. World Congress N.Am., 1998—, BC Softworld Soc., 1998—. Bd. dirs. Animas Corp., Humane Soc. Seattle, 1998-2006, Kings County, 2004—. Served with USAF, 1963-67. Mem. ABA, Wash. Bar Assn., Am. Intellectual Property Law Assn., Computer Law Soc., Am. Inst. CPAs, Wash. Soc. CPAs, Seattle-King County Bar Assn., Am. Coll. of Mediators, Rainier Club, Seattle Yacht Club. Office: Davis Wright Tremaine LLP 2600 Century Sq 1501 4th Ave Seattle WA 98101-1688 Home: 8841 SE 60th St Mercer Island WA 98040 Office Phone: 206-628-7741. Business E-Mail: peterparsons@dwt.com.

PARSONS, ERIC E., insurance company executive; Degree, Lewis & Clark Coll., Northwestern U. V.p. Standard Ins. Co., pres. mortgage and real estate subs.; sr. v.p., CFO, then COO StanCorp Fin. Group/Standard Ins. Co., Portland, Oreg.; pres., CEO StanCorp Fin. Group, Portland, Oreg., 2003—04, chmn., pres., CEO, 2004—08, chmn., CEO, 2008—. Vice-chmn. Oreg. Health & Sci. Univ. Found.; chmn. OSHU Cancer Inst. Council; trustee Oreg. Zoo Found.; bd. dirs. Oreg. Bus. Council, Portland Opera, Portland Art Mus. Fellow: Life Mgmt. Inst. Office: StanCorp Fin Group Inc 1100 SW 6th Ave Portland OR 97204

PARTHASARATHY, SANJAY, computer software company executive; BS in Mech. Engring., Anna U., Madras, India; MS in Engring., MIT, MS in Mgmt. Product mgr. Windows multimedia group Microsoft Corp., Redmond, Wash., 1990, product unit mgr. internet security products, regional dir. South Asia Region, gen. mgr. worldwide customer sys., corp. v.p. Strategy & Bus. Devel. Group, corp. v.p. Developer and Platform Evangelism Group (D&PE), corp. v.p. Startup Bus. Accelerator, 2008—. Office: Microsoft Corp One Microsoft Way Redmond WA 98052-6399

PARTHEMORE, JACQUELINE GAIL, internist, educator, hospital administrator; b. Harrisburg, Pa., Dec. 21, 1940; d. Philip Mark and Emily (Buvit) Parthemore; m. Alan Morton Blank, Jan. 7, 1967; children: Stephen Eliot, Laura Elise. BA, Wellesley Coll., 1962; MD, Cornell U., 1966. Diplomate Am. Bd. Internal Medicine. Resident in internal medicine N.Y. Hosp./Cornell U., 1966-69; fellow in endocrinology Scripps Clinic and Rsch. Found., La Jolla, Calif., 1969-72; rsch. ednl. assoc. VA Hosp., San Diego, 1974-78; staff physician VA San Diego Health Care Sys., 1978-79, asst. chief, med. svc., 1979-83, acting chief, med. svc., 1980-81, chief of staff, 1984—; asst. prof. medicine U. Calif. Sch. Medicine, San Diego, 1974-80, assoc. prof. medicine, 1980-85, prof. medicine, assoc. dean, 1985—. Mem. nat. rsch. resources coun. NIH, Bethesda, Md., 1990—94; mem. VHA Performance Measures Work Group, 2006—, Blue Ribbon Panel Acad. Affiliations, 2007—. Contbr. chapters to books, articles to profl. jours. Mem. adv. bd. San Diego Opera, 1993—2007; mem. Roundtable and Channel 10 Focus Group, San Diego Millennium Project, 1999; v.p. bd. dirs. San Diego Vets. Med. Rsch. Found., 1989—. Recipient Bullock's 1st Annual Portfolio award, 1985, San Diego Pres.'s Coun. Woman of Yr. award, 1985, YWCA Tribute to Women in Industry award, 1987, San Diego Women Who Mean Bus. award, 1999, Excellence in Leadership award Am. Hosp. Assn., 2002, Local Legend award AMWA/Nat. Libr. Medicine, 2005. Fellow ACP (gov. 2005-, mem. edn. com. 2006-, vice-chair edn. com. 2008-), Am. Assn. Clin. Endocrinologists; mem. Endocrine Soc., Nat. Assn. VA Chiefs Staff/Physician Execs. (pres. 1989-91), Assn. Am. Med. Colls. (mem. steering group chief med. officers, 2005—), Wellesley Coll. Alumnae Assn. (1st v.p. 1992-95), San Diego Wellesley Club (pres. 1997-99), San Diego Herb Soc. (co-pres. 2003-04), Nat. Assn. VA Rsch. and Fedn. (bd. mem., 2003—). Avocations: gardening, reading, sailing, cooking, travel. Office: VA San Diego Healthcare Sys 3350 La Jolla Village Dr San Diego CA 92161-0002 Home Phone: 858-756-2917; Office Phone: 858-552-7419. Business E-Mail: jparthemore@ucsd.edu.

PARTIDA, GILBERT A., lawyer; b. Nogales, Ariz., July 27, 1962; s. Enrique Gilberto and Mary Lou (Flores) P.; m. Soncee Ray Brown, July 30, 1992. BA with distinction, U. Ariz., 1984; JD cum laude, Pepperdine U., 1987; LLD (hon.), Calif. Western Sch Law, San Diego, 1993. V.p., bd. mem. Partida Brokerage, Inc., Nogales, 1983-91; law clk. Office of Ariz. Atty. Gen., Tucson, 1985; assoc. Gray, Cary, Ames & Frye, San Diego, 1986-89, sr. assoc., 1990-92, chmn. Mex. Practice Group, 1992; pres. Greater San Diego C. of C., 1993-98; pres., CEO Price Smart, San Diego, 1998—. Corp. counsel San Diego Incubator Corp., 1990—. Contbr. articles to profl. jours. Mem. United Way Latino Future Scan Com., 1990; mentor Puente, 1991; leadership tng. mentor Chicano Fedn., 1992; dinner com. Young at Art, 1991; mem. Children's Initiative, 1993, Superbowl Task Force, 1993, San Diego Dialogue, 1993; hon. mem. Sister City, 1993, LEAD, 1993; hon. chair Easter Seals Telethon, 1994; vice chmn. Border Trade Alliance, 1989-91; mem. nat. gala com. HDI Ednl. Svcs., 1990; Calif. state del. U.S.-Mexico Border Govs.' Conf., 1990, 92; exec. com. San Diego Conv. and Visitors Bur. Mem. San Diego County Hispanic C. of C. (chmn. 1991, pres. 1990-91, v.p. 1989-90, internat. com. chair 1989-90, sec. 1989, founding bd. mem. 1988), Consejo Nacional de Maquiladoras, Calif. Hispanic C. of C. (state conv. joint venture com. 1991, spl. projects chair 1991), San Diego/Tijuana Sister Cities Soc. (adv. coun. 1993—), San Diego County Bar Assn. (U.S./Mexico liaison com.), ABA (U.S./Mexico bar liaison com.), Hispanic Alliance for Free Trade, Rotary Club San Diego. Avocations: tennis, running, creative writing.

PARTRIDGE, BRUCE JAMES, lawyer, educator, writer, parliamentarian; b. Syracuse, NY, June 4, 1926; arrived in Can., 1969; s. Bert James and Lida Marion (Rice) P.; m. Mary Janice Smith, June 13, 1948 (dec. 1986); children: Heather Leigh, Eric James, Brian Lloyd, Bonnie Joyce; m. May S. Archer, May 28, 1988; stepchildren: Sheila Archer, Laurel Archer. AB cum laude, Oberlin Coll., Ohio, 1946; LLB, Blackstone Coll., Chgo., 1950, JD, 1952; LLB, U. B.C., 1974. Bar: B.C. 1976, N.W.T. 1980. Rsch. physicist Am. Gas Assn., Cleve., 1946-48; bus. mgr. Cazenovia (N.Y.) Coll., 1948—51; bus. mgr., purchasing agt., asst. treas. Rochester Inst. Tech., NY, 1953—58; bus. adminstr. Baldwin-Wallace Coll., Berea, Ohio, 1951-53; v.p. bus. and mgmt. U. Del., Newark, 1958-63; v.p. adminstrn. Johns Hopkins U., Balt., 1963-69; pres. U. Victoria, B.C., Can., 1969-72; assoc. Clark, Wilson & Co., Vancouver, B.C., Can., 1975-78; successively solicitor, mng. solicitor, gen. solicitor, v.p. law and gen. counsel, sec. Cominco Ltd., Vancouver, 1978-88; exec. dir. Baker & McKenzie, Hong Kong, 1988-90; v.p. Pacific Creations, Inc., 1990-92; faculty Camosun Coll., 1992-99. Author: Management in Canada: The Competitive Challenges, 2000; co-author: College and University Business Administration, 1968; chmn. editl. com. Purchasing for Higher Education, 1962; contbr. numerous articles to profl. jours. Chmn. commn. on adminstrv. affairs Am. Coun. on Edn., Washington, 1966-69; mem. Pres.'s Com. on Employment of Handicapped, Washington, 1967-69; mem. adv. coun. Ctr. for Resource Studies, Queen's U., 1983-88; bd. dirs. L'Arche in the Americas, 1984-88; mem. adv. coun. Westwater Rsch. Ctr., U. B.C., 1982-88. Mem. Assn. Can. Gen. Counsel, Def. Rsch. Inst. (product liability com.), Am. Inst. Parliamentarians, Nat. Assn. Parliamentarians. Fair Vote Can. Party. Unitarian Universalist. Office Phone: 250 722-3081. Business E-Mail: brucepart@telus.net.

PARTRIDGE, LOREN WAYNE, art historian, educator; b. Raton, N.Mex., Apr. 11, 1936; s. Don F. and Ruth (Isaacson) P.; widowed; children: Wendy, Amy; married. BA in English Lit., Yale U., 1958; cert. in L.Am. lit., U. Buenos Aires, 1959; diploma in Russian, U.S. Army Lang. Sch., Monterey, Calif., 1961; MA in Fine Arts, Harvard U., 1965, PhD in Fine Arts, 1969. Tchg. fellow Harvard U., Cambridge, Mass., 1964-66; lectr. U. Calif., Berkeley, 1968, acting asst. prof., 1969-70, asst. prof., 1970-76, assoc. prof., 1976-80, prof., 1980—, chmn. Dept. Art History, 1978—87, 1990—93, 1999, chmn. Dept. Art Practice, 2002—03, 2004—08. Resident in art history Am. Acad. in Rome, 1985; reviewer Art Bull, 1972, 78, 80, 83, Renaissance Quar., 1984, 87, 90, 99, Design Book Rev., 1987, Master Drawings, 1987, Am. Hist. Rev., 1993, Apollo, 1996. Author: John Galen Howard and the Berkeley Campus: Beaux-Arts Architecture in the Athens of the West, 1978, Caprarola, Palazzo Farnese, 1988, (with Randolph Starn) A Renaissance Likeness: Art and Culture in Raphael's Julius II, 1980, (with Randolph Starn) Arts of Power: Three Halls of State in Italy 1300-1600, 1992, The Art of Renaissance Rome, 1400-1600, 1996, Michelangelo: The Sistine Chapel Ceiling, Rome, 1996, Michelangelo Last Judgement: A Glorious Restoration, 1997; contbr. author: Ency. of Italian Renaissance, 1981, Internat. Dictionary Art and Artists, 1990, Dictionary of Art, 1996; contbr. articles to profl. jours. With U.S. Army, 1960-63. Scholar Yale U., 1955-58, Harvard U., 1964-66; Fulbright fellow, 1958-59, 75, Am. Acad. in Rome fellow, 1966-68, Kress fellow Inst. for Advanced Studies, 1974-75, U. Calif., 1972, 77, 82, 85, 93-94, 99-2000, 2003-04, Guggenheim fellow, 1981-92; grantee Kress Found., 1968-69, 71-72, Getty. sr. rsch. grantee, 1988-89. Office: U Calif Dept Art History 6020 416 Doe Libr Berkeley CA 94720-6020 Office Phone: 510-643-6301. Business E-Mail: lpart@berkeley.edu.

PASAHOW, LYNN HAROLD, lawyer; s. Samuel and Cecelia (Newman) P.; m. Leslie Aileen Cobb, June 11, 1969; 1 child, Michael Alexander. AB, Stanford U., 1969; JD, U. Calif., Berkeley, 1972. Bar: Calif. 1972, U.S. Ct. Appeals (9th cir.) 1972, U.S. Dist. Ct. (no. dist.) Calif. 1973, U.S. Dist. Ct. (ctrl. dist.) Calif. 1974, U.S. Supreme Ct. 1976, U.S. Dist. Ct. (ea. dist.) Calif. 1977, U.S. Ct. Appeals (fed. cir.) 1990. Law clk. judge US Dist. Ct. (no. dist.) Calif., San Francisco, 1972—73; with McCutchen, Doyle, Brown & Enersen, 1973—2001; ptnr. Fenwick & West LLP, Mountain View, Calif., 2001—. Co-author: Civil Discovery and Mandatory Disclosure: A Guide to Effective Practice, 1994, Berkeley Center for Law & Technology Patent Case Management Judicial Guide, 2007; author: Pretrial and Settlement Conferences in Federal Court, 1983; contbr. articles to profl. jours. Bd. dirs. Bay Area Biosci. Ctr. Mem. ABA, Calif. Bar Assn. Democrat. Office: Fenwick & West LLP Silicon Valley Ctr 801 California St Mountain View CA 94041 Office Phone: 650-335-7225. Business E-Mail: lpasahow@fenwick.com.

PASCAL, AMY BETH, film company executive; b. LA, Mar. 1958; d. Tony and Barbara Pascal; m. Bernard Weinraub, Aug. 9, 1997; 1 adopted child, Anthony. BA in Internat. Rels., UCLA. With Kestral Films; v.p. prodn. 20th Century Fox, 1986—87, Columbia Pictures, 1987—89, exec. v.p. prodn., 1987—94; pres. prodn. Turner Pictures, 1994—96; pres. Columbia Pictures, Culver City, Calif., 1996-99, chmn., 1999—2002; vice chmn. Sony Pictures Entertainment, Culver City, Calif., 2002—06, co-chmn., 2006—; chmn. Sony Pictures Entertainment Motion Picture Group, Culver City, Calif., 2003—. Bd. trustees Rand Corp. Bd. trustees AFI; mem. UCLA Sch. Theater, Film & Television. Named one of 50 Most Powerful People in Hollywood, Premiere mag., 2004—06, 100 Most Powerful Women in Entertainment, Hollywood Reporter, 2004—07, 100 Most Powerful Women, Forbes mag., 2005—08, 50 Most Powerful Women in Bus., Fortune mag., 2006, 2007, 50 Smartest People in Hollywood, Entertainment Weekly, 2007. Office: Sony Pictures Entertainment 10202 Washington Blvd Culver City CA 90232

PASCAL, C(ECIL) BENNETT, classics educator; b. Chgo., May 4, 1926; s. Jack and Goldie (Zeff) P.; m. Ilene Joy Shulman, Feb. 1, 1959; 1 child, Keith Irwin. BA, UCLA, 1949, MA, 1950, Harvard U., 1953, PhD, 1956. Instr. U. Ill., Champaign, 1955-56, Cornell U., Ithaca, NY, 1957-60; asst. prof., then assoc. prof. U. Oreg., Eugene, 1960-75, prof. classics, 1975-96, prof. emeritus, 1996—, head dept., various years - 1965-85. Author: Cults of Cisalpine Gaul, 1964; contbr. articles to profl. jours. Active Eugene Bicycle Com., 1971-83. Wwith USN, 1944-46. Traveling fellow, Italy, Harvard U., 1956-57, Fulbright-Hays fellow, Rome, 1967-68. Mem. Am. Philol. Assn., Classical Assn. Pacific N.W. (pres. 1965-66), AAUP, Archeol. Inst. of Am. (past pres., sec. Eugene Soc.) Democrat. Jewish. Avocations: skiing, fly fishing, novel writing. Home: 330 Fulvue Dr Eugene OR 97405-2788 Office: U Oreg Dept Classics Eugene OR 97403 Business E-Mail: cbpasc@uoregon.edu.

PASCAL, NAOMI BRENNER, editor-at-large, publishing executive; b. Bklyn., Mar. 13, 1926; d. Mortimer and Sylvia (Freehof) Brenner; m. Paul Pascal, June 27, 1948; children: David Morris, Janet Brenner. BA, Wellesley Coll., 1946. Editor Vanguard Press, Inc., NYC, 1946-48, U. N.C. Press, Chapel Hill, N.C., 1948-50, 52-53, U. Wash. Press, 1953-75, editor-in-chief, 1976—2002, assoc. dir., 1985—2002. Dir. Assn. Am. Univ. Presses, 1976-78; cons. editor Scholarly Pub. jour., Toronto, Ont., Can., 1979—; del. Wash. State

Gov.'s Conf. on Library and Info. Services, Olympia, 1978-79. Co-author: Glossary Typesetting Terms, 1994; contbr. chpts. to books, articles to profl. jours. Durant scholar, 1945; recipient constituency award Assn. Am. Univ. Presses, 1991. Mem. Women in Scholarly Pub., Assn. Asian Am. Studies, Native Am. Art Studies Assn., Phi Beta Kappa (treas. Alpha of Wash. chpt. 1975-78). Office: U Wash Press PO Box 50096 Seattle WA 98145-5096

PASCOE, PATRICIA HILL, former state legislator; b. Sparta, Wis., June 1, 1935; d. Fred Kirk and Edith (Kilpatrick) Hill; m. D. Monte Pascoe, Aug. 3, 1957; children: Sarah, Edward, William. BA, U. Colo., 1957; MA, U. Denver, 1968, PhD, 1982. Tchr. Sequoia Union H.S. Dist., Redwood City, Calif. and Hayward (Calif.) Union H.S. Dist., 1957-60; instr. Met. State Coll., Denver, 1969-75, Denver U., 1975-77, 81, rsch. asst. bur. ednl. rsch., 1981-82; tchr. Kent Denver Country Day Sch., Englewood, Colo., 1982-84; freelance writer Denver, 1985—; mem. Colo. Senate, Dist. 32, Denver, 1989—93, Colo. Senate, Dist. 34, Denver, 1995—2003; chair minority caucus Colo. Senate, Denver, 1996-2000, chair policy and planning com., 2001, chair edn. com., 2002. Commr. Edn. Commn. of the States, Denver, 1975-82, 01-05. Contbr. articles to numerous publs. and jours. Bd. dirs. Samaritan House, 1990-94, Cystic Fibrosis Found., 1989-93, 2007—, chmn. legis. com.; pres. East HS Parent Tchr. and Student Assn., Denver, 1984-85; mem. Moore Budget Adv. Com., Denver, 1966-72; legis. chmn. alumni bd. U. Colo., Boulder, 1987-89; del. Dem. Nat. Conv., San Francisco, 1984, NYC, 1992; mem. Denver Woman's Press Club, 1986—, pres., 2005-06, Colo. Arts Coalition, 1988-97, Conflict Ctr. Bd., 2003-05; bd. dirs. Opera Colo., 1996-02; mem. bd. ACLU Colo., chair legis. com. Mem. Soc. Profl. Journalists, Common Cause (bd. dirs. Denver chpt. 1986-88), Lions Club (dir. 2003-05), Phi Beta Kappa. Democrat. Presbyterian.

PASCOTTO, ALVARO, lawyer; b. Rome, Mar. 8, 1949; came to U.S., 1984; s. Antonio and Anna Ludovica (Habig) P.; m. Linda Haldan, July 20, 1985. JD, U. Rome, 1973. Bar: Italy 1976, Calif. 1987, U.S. Dist. Ct. (cen. dist.) Calif. 1987, U.S. Ct. Appeals (9th cir.) 1987. Ptnr. Studio Legale Pascotto, Rome, 1976-86, Pascotto, Gallavotti & Gardner, LA and Rome, 1986-90, Pascotto & Gallavotti, LA, 1990—; of counsel Irell & Manella LLP, LA, 1994—2003, Morrison & Foerster, LLP, LA, 2003. Ofcl. counsel Consulate Gen. Italy, L.A., 1987—. Mem. ABA, Calif. Bar Assn., Italian-Am. Bar Assn., Am. Mgmt. Assn., Consiglio dell'Ordine Degli Avvocati e Procuratori di Roma. Clubs: Circolo del Golf (Rome); Malibu (Calif.) Racquet Club, Regency Club (L.A.), L.A. Country Club, Calif. Club. Home: 6116 Merritt Dr Malibu CA 90265-3847 Office: 555 W 5th St Ste 3500 Los Angeles CA 90013 Office Phone: 213-892-5635. Office Fax: 213-892-5637. Business E-Mail: apascotto@mofo.com.

PASHGIAN, MARGARET HELEN, artist; b. Pasadena, Calif., Nov. 7, 1934; d. Aram John and Margaret (Howell) P. BA, Pomona Coll., 1956; student, Columbia U., 1957; MA in Fine Arts, Boston Univ., 1958. Art instr. Harvard-Newton Program Occidental Coll., 1977-78; artist in residence Calif. Inst. Tech., 1970-71. Grants panelist Calif. Arts Coun., Sacramento, 1993. One-woman shows include Rex Evans Gallery, LA, 1965, 67, Occidental Coll., 1967, Kornblee Gallery, NYC, 1969-72, U. Calif., Irvine, 1975, U. Calif. Santa Barbara, 1976, Stella Polaries Gallery, LA, 1981-82, Kaufman Galleries, Houston, 1982, Modernism Gallery, San Francisco, 1983, Works Gallery, Long Beach, Costa Mesa, Calif., 1986-92, Malka Gallery, LA, 1997; exhibited in group shows at Pasadena Art Mus., 1965, Carson Pirie Scott, Chgo., 1965, Calif. Palace of Legion of Honor, San Francisco, 1967, Esther Bear Gallery, Santa Barbara, 1967, 69, Lytton Ctr. of the Visual Arts, LA, 1968, Salt Lake Art Inst., Salt Lake City, 1968, Mus. Contemporary Crafts, 1969, Second Flint (Mich.) Invitational, 1969, Milw. Art Ctr., 1969, U.S.I.S. Mus., NYC, Mus. Contemporary Art, Chgo., 1970, Studio Merconi, Milan, 1970, Calif. Inst. Tech., Baxter Art Galley, 1971, 1980, Calif. Innovations, Palm Springs Dessert Mus., 1981, Calif. Internat. Arts Found. Mus. Modern Art, Paris, 1982, LA Artists in Seoul, Donsangbang Gallery, 1982, An Artistic Conversation, 1931-82, Poland, USA, Ulster Mus., Belfast, Ireland, 1983, Madison Art Ctr., Wis., 1994, Calif. State U., Fullerton, 1995, Oakland Mus., Calif., 1995, Molly Barnes Gallery, LA, Calif., 2000, Pasadena Mus. Calif. Art, 2002, Patricia Faure Gallery, LA, 2006, Norton Simon Mus., Pasadena, Calif., 2006; represented in pub. collections at River Forest State Bank, Ill., Atlantic Richfield Co., Dallas, Frederic Weisman Collection, L., Security Pacific Bank, LA, Singapore, Andrew Dickson White Mus. Art, Cornell U., Ithaca, NY, LA County Mus. Art, Santa Barbara Art Mus., Laguna Beach Mus. Art, Portland Art Mus., Oreg., Palm Springs Art Mus., Calif. Trustee, Pomona Coll, Claremont, Calif., 1987—; parade judge Tournament of Roses Centennial Parade, Pasadena, 1987; bd. dirs. LA Master Chorale, 1992—, Ojai Music Festival, 2004— NEA grantee, 1986. Home: 731 S Grand Ave Pasadena CA 91105-2424

PASHLER, HAROLD E., psychologist, educator; AB in Logic and Philosophy of Sci., Brown U., 1980, ScB in Psychology magna cum laude, 1980; PhD in Psychology, U. Pa., 1985. Asst. prof. dept. psycholgoy U. Calif., San Diego, 1985-90, assoc. prof., 1990-93, prof. dept. psychology, 1993—. Mem. various coms. U. Calif. San Diego; ad hoc reviewer Hong Kong Rsch. Coun., Natural Sci. and Engring. Rsch. Coun., Can., NSF, Behavioral and Neural Scis., USAF Office Sci. Rsch. Life Scis. Program. Assoc. editor Psychonomic Bull. and Rev., 1998—; mem. editl. bd. Perception & Psychophysics, 1988—, Psychol. Rsch., 1989—, Cognitive Psychology, 1992-98, Visual Cognition, 1994—, Psychonomic Bull. and Rev., 1994-97, Am. Jour. Psychology, 1998—; ad hoc reviewer Am. Jour. Psychology, Attention and Performance XII, XIV, Cognition, Cognitive Psychology, Cognitive Sci., Current Directions in Psychol. Sci., Ency. Human Biology, Exptl. Brain Rsch., Jour. Exptl. Psychology: Human Perception and Performance, Jour. Exptl. Psychology: Learning, Memory and Cognition, Memory and Cognition, Nature, Nature Neurosci., Perception, Perception & Psychophysics, Psychol. Rsch., Psychol. Rev., Quarterly Jour. Exptl. Psychology, Spatial Vision, Vision Rsch. Recipient Troland Rsch. award NAS, 1999; NSF grad. fellow, 1981-84, IBM grad. fellow, 1984-85. Fellow Am. Psychol. Soc.; mem. Phi Beta Kappa, Sigma Xi. Office: Dept Psychology 0109 U Calif San Diego La Jolla CA 92093 E-mail: hpashler@ucsd.edu.

PASICH, KIRK ALAN, lawyer; b. La Jolla, Calif., May 26, 1955; s. Chris Nick and Iva Mae (Tormey) P.; m. Pamela Mary Woods, July 30, 1983; children: Christopher Thomas, Kelly Elizabeth, Connor Woods. BA in Polit. Sci., UCLA, 1977; JD, Loyola Law Sch., LA, 1980. Bar: Calif. 1980, U.S. Dist. Ct. (no., so., ea. and cen. dists.) Calif. 1981, Mich. (ea. dist.) 1997, Tex. (ea. dist.) 2001, U.S. Ct. Appeals (9th cir.) 1981, U.S. Ct. Appeals (1st cir.) 1992. Assoc. Paul, Hastings, Janofsky & Walker, LA, 1980-88, ptnr., 1988-89, Troop Steuber Pasich Reddick & Tobey, LLP, 1989-2000, Howrey Simon Arnold & White LLP, 2001—03, Pasich & Kornfeld LLP, 2003—05, Dickstein Shapiro LLP, 2005—. Author: Casualty and Liability Insurance, 1990, 2000, 03; co-author: Officers and Directors: Liabilities and Protections, 1996, 2000, 03, The Year 2000 and Beyond: Liability and Insurance for Computer Code Problems, 2000; contbg. editor: West's California Litigation Forms: Civil Procedure Before Trial, 2000; co-author, co-editor: ABA Manual for Complex Insurance Coverage Litigation, 1999, 2000, 04; entertainment law columnist, ins. law columnist L.A. and San Francisco Daily Jour., 1989—; contbr. articles to profl. jours. Active bd. dirs. Nat. Acad. Jazz, L.A., 1988-89, chmn. bd. dirs. Woody Herman Found., L.A., 1989-92, Constnl. Rights Found., 2000; active L.A. City Atty's. Task Force for Econ. Recovery, 1992-93. Named to Calif's. Legal Dream Team as 1 of state's top 25 litigators, Calif. Law Bus., 1992; named one of the nation's top 45 lawyers under age 45, Am. Lawyer, 1995, market leader for policyholder representation in California, Chambers Am. Leading Bus. Lawyers, 2003-07; named one of 500 Leading Lawyers in Am., Lawdragon, 2005, 06, Nation's Top 12 Leading Policyholder Lawyer, Chambers USA, 2007, 08. Mem. ABA (mem. Task Force on Complex Insurance Coverage Litigation), Risk & Insurance Mgmt. Soc., Def. Rsch. Inst. Democrat. Avocations: reading, music, basketball. Office: Dickstein Shapiro LLP 2049 Century Park East Ste 700 Los Angeles CA 90067 Home Phone: 310-476-2329; Office Phone: 310-772-8305. Business E-Mail: pasichk@dicksteinshapiro.com.

PASSMAN, PAMELA S., computer software company executive; b. NYC, Aug. 11, 1961; m. Frederick Guinee; children: Emily, Sarah. BA, Lafayette Coll., 1983; JD, U. Va., 1987. Bar: Va. & DC 1987. Articles editor Va. Jour. Internat. Law, 1985—87; with Covington & Burling, Washington, 1987—91, 1994—96, Nagashima & Ohno, Tokyo, 1991—93; spl. counsel Office of Polit. & Econ. Rsch., Itochu Corp., 1993; assoc. gen. counsel Microsoft Corp. Law & Corp. Affairs Dept., Tokyo, 1996—2002, dep. gen. counsel, v.p. Redmond, Wash., 2002—. Mem. Coun. Fgn. Rels. Mem. bd. Bus. for Social Responsibility, Seattle Art Mus., Nat. Bur. Asian Rsch., 2004—, Pacific Coun. Internat. Policy. Fellow Thomas J. Watson Found., 1983—84. Mem.: Info. Tech. Industry Council (exec. com.). Office: Microsoft Corp Law & Corp Affairs Dept 1 Microsoft Way Redmond WA 98052-6399 Office Phone: 425-882-8080. Office Fax: 425-936-7329.

PASTEGA, RICHARD LOUIS, retired retail specialist; b. Klamath Falls, Oreg., Mar. 25, 1936; s. Louie and Jennie (Borgialli) P. BS, So. Oreg. U., Ashland, 1960; MS, Mont. State U., Bozeman, 1961. Tchr. social studies Henley High Sch., Klamath Falls, Oreg., 1962-63, Juneau (Alaska) Douglas High Sch., 1964-67, Thessaloniki (Greece) Internat. High Sch., 1967-69; editor, pub. Breakdown Newspaper, Klamath Falls, Oreg., 1971-73; mgr. Pastega's Market, Klamath Falls, 1975-98, ret., 1998. Del. Dem. Nat. Conv., N.Y.C., 1976, Oreg. Dem. Platform conv., Eugene, Beaverton and Ashland, 1978-80, 82; councilor City of Klamath Falls, 1986-88; bd. dirs. Basin Transit Svc., Klamath Falls, 1981-87; chair Klamath County Dem. Ctrl. Com., 1983-86, 2008-, sec. 1992-94; Klamath County alt. del. Oreg. Dem. State Ctrl. Com., 1998—, 2004. Mem. Sons of Italy, Klamath Solar Assn. (bd. dirs. 1998—), Klamath Basin Peace Forum. Democrat. Home: 428 S 9th St Klamath Falls OR 97601-6126 Personal E-mail: pastega@hotmail.com.

PASTER, JANICE DUBINSKY, lawyer, former state legislator, state legislator; b. St. Louis, Aug. 4, 1942; BA, Northwestern U., 1964; MA, Tufts U., 1967; JD, U. N.Mex., 1984. Bar: N.Mex. 1984. Atty. in pvt. practice, 1984—; mem. N.Mex. State Senate from 10th dist., 1988-96. Democrat. Home and Office: 5553 Eakes Rd NW Albuquerque NM 87107-5529

PASTOR, EDWARD, United States Representative from Arizona; b. Claypool, Ariz., June 28, 1943; m. Verma Mendez; children: Yvonne, Laura. BA in chemistry, Ariz. State U., 1966, JD, 1974. Former chem. teacher N. High Sch.; former dep. dir. Guadalupe Org., Inc.; mem. Maricopa County Bd. Suprs., Phoenix, 1976-91, U.S. Congress from 4th Ariz. dist. (formerly 2nd), Washington, 1991—; mem. appropriations com., steering & policy com. Mem. Arts Caucus, Biotechnology Caucus, Border Caucus, Congressional Caucus on Women's Issues, Congressional Children's Caucus. Democrat. Office: US Ho Reps 2465 Rayburn Ho Office Bldg Washington DC 20515-0304

PATCHIN, REBECCA J., anesthesiologist, educator, administrator; b. Detroit, Dec. 8, 1949; d. Robert Ira and Doris J. (Hubert) P.; m. Carl W. Anderson, 1988 (dec.) ASN, Pacific Union Coll., 1969; BSN, Walla Walla Coll., 1971; MD, Loma Linda U., 1989. Diplomate in anesthesiology and pain mgmt. Am. Bd. Anesthesiology. Resident in internalmedicine Loma Linda U. Med. Ctr., Calif., 1989-90, resident in anesthesiology Calif., 1990-93, fellow in pain mgmt. dept. anesthesiology Calif., 1993-94, asst. prof. anesthesiology, 1994—; assoc. med. dir. Ctr. for Pain Mgmt., Loma Linda, 1995—; private practice Riverside, Calif. Appointed to Joint Commn. on Accreditation od Healthcare Organizations' Standards and Surveys Coms., 2006; mem. Accreditation Coun. Grad. Med. Edn. (mem. liaison com. med. edn., co-chair 2001-2002); presenter in field. Contbr. abstracts to profl. jours. Mem. AMA (mem. credentials com. 1986—, mem. bd. nominations and awards com. 1988-89, chair, Med. Liability Task Force, del. ho. of dels. 1990-99, mem. reference com. 1994—, mem. coun. on med. edn. 1996-2003, chair, 2002-03, mem. bd. trustee 2003-, sec. 2006-, liasion polit. action com., mem. young physician sect., chair, membership com., bd. audit, mem. orgn. and ops. com.), Internat. Anesthesiology Rsch. Soc., Internat. Assn. for Study of Pain, Am. Soc. Anesthesiology, Am. Pain Soc., Am. Soc. Regional Anesthesia, Am. Acad. Pain Medicine, Calif. Soc. Anesthesiology (del. resident component 1991-93, mem. com. on young physicians 1994—96, chair com. on young physicians 1996—), Calif. Med. Assn. (mem. reference com. 1988, trustee 1991-93, mem. com. on health professions and licensure 1992—, chair com. on health professions and licensure 1993-96, mem. coun. on legislation 1995-96, chair coun. on legislation, liaison com. on specialty bds., bd. dir.), So. Calif. Cancer Pain Initiative, Riverside County Med. Assn. (sec.-treas 2002, pres. 2004), San Bernardino County Med. Soc. Avocation: sailing. Home Phone: 951-780-8121; Office Phone: 951-413-0200.

PATÉ-CORNELL, MARIE-ELISABETH LUCIENNE, engineering educator; b. Dakar, Senegal, Aug. 17, 1948; (parents Am. citizens); d. Edouard Pierre Lucien and Madeleine (Tournissa) Paté; m. C. Allin Cornell, Jan. 3, 1981 (dec.); children: Phillip, Ariane. BS in Math. and Physics, 1968; MS in Engring., Inst. Polytechnique de Grenoble, France, 1970; MS in Ops. Rsch., Stanford U., Calif., 1972; PhD in Engring.-Econ. Sys., Stanford U., 1978. EIT Inst. Polytechnique de Grenoble, 1971. Asst. prof. civil engring. MIT, 1978-81; asst. prof. indsl. engring. Stanford U., 1981-84, assoc. prof. indsl. engring., 1984-91, prof. indsl. engring., 1991—99, chmn. dept. indsl. engring., 1997-99, Burt & Deedee McMurtry prof., chmn. dept. mgmt. sci. and engring., 1999—. Cons. SRI Internat., 1993, Electric Power Rsch. Inst., 1995, Atty. Gen. of N.Mex., 1995, Swiss Re, 2002, Boeing, 2003—; mem. Marine Bd. NRC, 1995—97; mem. adv. coun. NASA, 1995—98; mem. Army Sci. Bd., 1995—97, Air Force Sci. Bd., 1998—2002, Calif. Coun. Sci. & Tech., 2000—, Fgn. Intelligence Adv. Bd., Washington, 2001—; chmn. bd. advs. Naval-Postgrad. Sch., 2004—06. Contbr. articles to profl. jours. Fellow: Inst. Mgmt. Scis.; mem.: Nat. Acad. Engring. (councilor 2001—), Ops. Rsch. Soc. of America, Soc. Risk Analysis (councilor 1985—86, pres. 1995). Avocations: tennis, swimming, chess, music. Home: 110 Coquito Way Menlo Park CA 94028-7404 Office: Stanford U Dept Mgmt Sci and Engring Stanford CA 94305 E-mail: mep@leland.stanford.edu.*

PATEK, SHEILA N., biologist, educator; MA/AB with honors in Biology, Harvard U., Cambridge, Mass., 1994; PhD in Biology, Duke U., Durham, NC, 2001. Postdoctoral fellow Miller Inst. Basic Rsch. in Sci. U. Calif., Berkeley, 2001—04, asst. prof. dept. integrative biology, 2004—. Contbr. articles to sci. jours. Named one of Brilliant 10, Popular Sci. mag., 2004. Office: Dept Integrative Biology U Calif Berkeley 3060 Valley Life Scis Bldg Number 3140 Berkeley CA 94720-3140 Office Phone: 510-643-9159. Office Fax: 510-643-6264. E-mail: patek@berkeley.edu.

PATEL, CHANDRA KUMAR NARANBHAI, communications executive, educator, entrepreneur, researcher; b. Baramati, India, July 2, 1938; came to U.S., 1958, naturalized, 1970; s. Naranbhai Chaturbhai and Maniben P.; m. Shela Dixit, Aug. 20, 1961; children: Neela, Meena. BS in Engring., Poona U., 1958; MS, Stanford U., 1959, PhD, 1961. Mem. tech. staff Bell Telephone Labs., Murray Hill, NJ, 1961-93, head infrared physics and electronics rsch. dept., 1967-70, dir. electronics rsch. dept., 1970-76, dir. phys. rsch. lab., 1976-81, exec. dir. rsch. physics and acad. affairs div., 1981-87, exec. dir. rsch., materials sci., engring. and acad. affairs div., 1987-93; trustee Aerospace Corp., LA, 1979-88; vice chancellor rsch. UCLA, 1993-2000, prof. dept. physics and astronomy, dept. chemistry, 2000—, prof. dept. elec. engring., 2000—; chmn., CEO Pranalytica, Inc, Santa Monica, Calif., 2001—. Mem. governing bd. NRC, 1990-91; bd. dirs. Newport Corp.; chmn. bd. Calif. Accuwave Corp., 1994-98; founder, chmn. bd. Pranalytica, Inc., Santa Monica, Calif.; co-founder Photuris, Inc. Contbr. articles to tech. jours. Chmn. Calif. Biomed. Found., 1994-2000; mem. exec. bd. Calif. Healthcare Inst., 1995-2000; mem. LA Regional Tech. Alliance, 1997-2003. Recipient Ballantine medal Franklin Inst., 1968, Nat. Sci. medal 1996, Coblentz award Am. Chem. Soc., 1974, Honor award Assn. Indians in Am., 1975, Founders prize Tex. Instruments Found., 1978, award N.Y. sect. Soc. Applied Spectroscopy, 1982, Schawlow medal Laser Inst. Am., 1984, Thomas Alva Edison Sci. award N.J. Gov., 1987, William T. Ennor Manufacturing Technology award ASME, 1995, Nat. Medal of Sci., Pres. of US, 1996, prize Internat. Photoacoustic and Photothermal Assn. prize, 2007. Fellow AAAS, IEEE (Lamme medal 1976, medal of honor 1989, Millennium medal 2000), Am. Acad. Arts and Scis., Am. Phys. Soc. (coun. 1987-91, exec. com. 1987-90, George E. Pake prize 1988, pres. 1995), Optical Soc. Am. (Adolph Lomb medal 1966, Townes medal 1982, Ives medal 1989, Lifetime Achievement award Def. and Security Symposium 2006), Indian Nat. Sci. Acad. (fng.); mem. NAS (coun. 1988-91, exec. com. 1989-91), NAE (Zworykin award 1976), Def. and Security Symposium (Lifetime Achievement award 2006), Gynecol. Laser Surgery Soc. (hon.), Am. Soc. for Laser Medicine and Surgery (hon.), Third World Acad. Scis. (assoc.), Calif. Biomed. Found. (pres. 1994-00), Calif. Healthcare Inst. (exec. com. 1995-00), Fedn. Am. Scientists (bd. dirs. 2002-),Sigma Xi (pres. 1994-96). Achievements include invention of many lasers including the Carbon Dioxide laser. Office: Pranalytica Inc 1101 Colorado Ave Santa Monica CA 90401 Business E-Mail: patel@pranalytica.com.

PATEL, MARILYN HALL, judge; b. Amsterdam, NY, Sept. 2, 1938; d. Lloyd Manning and Nina J. (Thorpe) Hall; m. Magan C. Patel, Sept. 2, 1966; children: Brian, Gian. BA, Wheaton Coll., 1959; JD, Fordham U., 1963. Bar: N.Y. 1963, Calif. 1970. Mng. atty. Benson & Morris, Esq., NYC, 1962-64; sole practice NYC, 1964-67; atty. U.S. Immigration and Naturalization Svc., San Francisco, 1967-71; sole practive San Francisco, 1971-76; judge Alameda County Mcpl. Ct., Oakland, Calif., 1976-80, U.S. Dist. Ct. (no. dist.) Calif., San Francisco, 1980—; now chief judge U.S. Dist. Ct. for No. Dist. Calif., San Francisco, 1998—. Adj. prof. law Hastings Coll. of Law, San Francisco, 1974-76 Author: Immigration and Nationality Law, 1974; also numerous articles Mem. bd. visitors Fordham U. Sch. Law. Mem. ABA (litigation sect., jud. adminstrn. sect.), ACLU (former bd. dirs.), NOW (former bd. dirs.), Am. law Inst., Am. Judicature Soc. (bd. dirs.), Calif Conf. Judges, Nat. Assn. Women Judges (founding mem.), Internat. Inst. (bd. dirs.), Advs. for Women (co-founder), Assn. Bus. Trial Lawyers (bd. dirs.). Democrat. Avocations: piano, travel. Office: US Dist Ct PO Box 36060 450 Golden Gate Ave Ste 36052 San Francisco CA 94102-3482

PATEL, SUNIT, telecommunications industry executive; Treas. MFS Comm., Inc., 1994—97, MCI WorldCom, 1997—2000; CFO, co-founder Looking Glass Networks, Inc., 2000—03; group v.p., CFO Level 3 Comm., Inc., Broomfield, Colo., 2003—. Office: Level 3 Comm 1025 Eldorado Blvd Broomfield CO 80021

PATERSON, RICHARD DENIS, corporate financial executive; b. Ottawa, Ont., Can., Oct. 13, 1942; m. Antoinette Paterson; children: Christopher, Russell, Kathlyn, Victoria, Connor. B in Commerce, Concordia U., Montreal, Que., Can., 1964. Auditor Coopers & Lybrand, Montreal, 1964-67; acct. Genstar Corp., Montreal, 1967-69; dir. fin. and adminstrn. Industa Corp. (subs. Genstar Corp.), NYC, 1969-73; v.p., comptroller Genstar Corp., Montreal and San Francisco, 1973-83, sr. v.p., CFO San Francisco, 1983-87; exec. v.p. Genstar Investment Corp., San Francisco, 1987-95; mng. dir. Genstar Capital LP, San Francisco, 1996—. Bd. dirs. Installs Inc., Am. Pacific Enterprises, Inc., Propex Fabrics, Inc., Woods Equipment Co. Mem. Order Chartered Accts. Que. Office: Genstar Capital LP Four Embarcadero Ctr Ste 1900 San Francisco CA 94111-4191 E-mail: rpaterson@gencap.com.

PATINO, DOUGLAS XAVIER, academic foundation and government agency administrator; b. Calexico, Calif., Apr. 11, 1939; s. Jose Luis and Maria Teresa (Seymour) P.; m. Barbel Wilma Hoyer, Aug. 13, 1970; 1 child, Viktor Xavier. AA, Imperial Valley Coll., 1960; BA, Calif. State U., San Diego, 1962, MA, 1966; PhD, U.S. Internat. U., 1972. Deputy dir. Sacramento Concilio, Inc., Calif., 1968-69; v.p. student affairs U. So. Colo., Pueblo, 1973-75; dep. dir. for planning and rev. svc. br. to dir. Calif. Employment Devel. Dept., dir.; sec. Calif. Health & Welfare Agy., 1975-83; dir. Ariz. Dept. of Econ.

Security, Phoenix, 1983-87; pres., chief exec. officer Marin Community Found., Larkspur, Calif., 1987-91; vice chancellor Calif. State U. Sys., Long Beach, 1993—2002; prof. social welfare Calif. State U., LA, 1998—2004. Commr. W.T. Grand Found., 1986—88, Enterprize for the Ams., Washington, 1994—; trustee C.S. Mott Found., Flint, Mich., 1995—, Calif. Wellness Found., Woodland Hills, 1997—; chmn., treas. Hispanics in Philanthropy, 1993—2002. Mem. Sec. of U.S. Dept. of Labor Task Force, Ariz., 1985-86, Staff Adv. Com. of the Human Resource Com., Nat. Gov. Assn., Washington, 1983-86; bd. dirs. Calif. Leadership, Santa Cruz, Calif., 1985-95, No. Calif. Grantmakers, 1990-91, Ariz. Assn. Bus., 1984; chair U.S. Savs. Bond Dr. for State of Calif., 1982; trustee Nat. Hispanic U., Oakland, Calif., 1987-90, Hispanic Community Fund, San Francisco, 1989-95, bd. dirs. Calif. Sch. Profl. Psychology, 1989-94, Coun. on Found., Washington, 1990-96, Found. Ctr., N.Y., 1993; pres. Calif. State U. Found. Recipient Monty Disting. Alumni award San Diego State U., 1997, Simon Bolivar award Hispanic Cmty. Found. and Bay Area United Way, 1996, Azteca award Human Devel. Corp., 1991, Leadership award Nat. Concilors Am. and United Way of Bay Area, 1990, Disting. Performance award Nat. Alliance of Bus., Washington, 1985, Superior Svc. Mgmt. award Am. Soc. Pub. Adminstrn., 1985, Humanitarian award Los Padrinos, Inc., 1981, Small and Minority Bus. award for the State of Calif. 1982, Disting. Alumni award Calif. Jr. CC Assn., Sacramento, 1982, Silver Spur award Nat. Fedn. Charros in Guadalajaro, Jalisco, Mex., 1974, Calif. Cmty. Svc. award Former Gov. Ronald Reagan, Sacramento, 1973; named to 100 Most Influential Hispanics, Hispanic Bus., 1995, 1997, 1999; named one of 100 Most Influential Latinos, Latino Leaders Mag., 2005-07. Mem. Am. Pub. Welfare Assn. (bd. dirs., Leadership award 1987), Assn. Black Found. Execs. (dir. 2003-07), Rotary, 1987-93.

PATMORE, KIMBERLY S., financial services executive; BBA, U. Toledo. CPA Colo. With Ernst & Young, 1981—92; named contr. First Data Corp., Greenwood Village, Colo., 1992, exec. v.p., CFO, 2000—08. Mem. Colo. Econ. Futures Panel. Recipient CFO Excellence Award, CFO Mag., 2000, "Best Workplaces" Award, 2001, Woman of Distinction Award, Girl Scouts, 2001, Outstanding Woman in Bus. Award, Denver Bus. Jour., 2005. Mem.: AICPA, Colo. Soc. CPAs.

PATNAUDE, WILLIAM EUGENE, architect; b. Sanger, Calif., Sept. 24, 1937; s. Eugene Joseph Patnaude and Vera Mae (Giles) Patnaude Fagan; m. Mary Esther Simerly, Aug. 22, 1971 (div. 1987); children: Nathaniel, Matthew BArch, U. Calif., Berkeley, 1961; postgrad., Calif. State U., Fresno, 1968-72. Registered arch., Calif., Wash., Idaho, Nev., Colo., Utah, Ariz., Mont., Nebr. Draftsman, arch. Robert Stevens Assoc., Santa Cruz, Calif., 1963-66; arch. Llewelyn Davies, Weeks & Ptnrs., London, 1966, Allen Y. Lew, Fresno, Calif., 1967-69, assoc., 1969-74; v.p., arch. Lew & Patnaude, Inc., Fresno, Calif., 1978-84, pres., 1985—. Instr. Calif. State U., Fresno, 1968-81 Constn. arbitrator Am. Arbitration Assn., 1976-96; chair ctrl. area plan citizen's adv. com. City of Fresno, 1991-93, chair gen. plan update com., 1994-97; bd. dirs. Fresno Arts Ctr., 1971-74, Fresno County Alliance for the Arts, 1986-88, 91-94. With USNR, 1961-63. Recipient Merit award Calif. Hist. Preservation Conf., Orange County, 1983, Excellence award Woodwork Inst. Calif., 1982, Recognition cert. City Fresno, 2004, Calif. State Assembly commendation City Fresno, 2004. Fellow AIA (nat. dir. 1983-85, pres. Calif. Coun. 1982, San Joaquin chpt. 1978, Awards of Excellence, 1972-95); mem. Constrn. Specifications Inst. (pres. Fresno chpt. 1977). Democrat. Avocations: photography, fine wines. Home: 4190 N Van Ness Blvd Fresno CA 93704-4213 Office: Lew & Patnaude Inc 1050 S St Fresno CA 93721-1497 Personal E-mail: wp@lewpatnaude.com. Business E-Mail: billp@csufresno.edu.

PATON, JONATHAN L., state legislator; b. Tuscon; BA in German and Russian, summa cum laude, U. Ariz., 1996. Intern to Gov. Fife Symington State of Ariz., 1994, Ariz. State Senate, 1994; US Army Reserve German instr. U. Ariz., 1998—2000; founder, pres. Paton & Assocs., Tuscon, 2001—; mem. Dist. 30 Ariz. House of Reps., 2005—08, Ariz. State Senate, 2008—, chair judiciary com. Active US Army Reserve, 1998—, commd. as 2nd lt., 2002. Recipient Achievement Medal, US Army, 2000, Commendation Medal, 2000; named Soldier of Yr., US Army Reserve, 2000. Republican. Office: Ariz State Senate Capitol Complex 1700 W Washington Rm 304 Phoenix AZ 85007 Office Phone: 602-926-3235. Office Fax: 602-417-3030. Business E-Mail: jpaton@azleg.gov.*

PATRICK, DONALD LEE, sociologist, educator; b. Eugene, Oreg., Sept. 23, 1944; s. Lawrence Leonard and Marie Esther (Bell) P.; m. Shirley Anne Alexander Beresford, May 31, 1980; children: Alistair Lawrence Beresford, Mira Yvonne Bell. AB with distinction, Northwestern U., 1966; MSPH, Columbia U., 1968, PhD, 1972. Rsch. assoc. U. Calif., San Diego, 1970-72; lectr. Yale U., New Haven, 1972-76; sr. lectr. U. London, 1976-82; assoc. prof. U. N.C., Chapel Hill, 1982-87; prof. and dir. social and behavioral scis. program U. Wash., Seattle, 1987—. Adj. prof. sociology, U. Wash., 1988—, dept. rehab. medicine, 1987—. Author: Health Status and Health Policy, 1993; editor: Sociology as Applied to Medicine, 1976, Disablement in Community, 1989. Mem. APHA (mem. coun. 1993-96), Spina Bifida Assn. Am. (chair profl. adv. bd. 1990-93, Pres.' award 1995), Internat. Soc. for Quality of Life Rsch. (pres. 1994-96, Pres. award 2001), Inst. Medicine. Democrat. Unitarian Universalist. Avocations: gardening, music, travel. Home: 5427 43rd Ave W Seattle WA 98199-1061 Office: Univ Wash PO Box 358852 Seattle WA 98103 Office Phone: 206-685-7252. E-mail: donald@u.washington.edu.

PATRICK, H. HUNTER, retired judge, lawyer; b. Gasville, Ark., Aug. 19, 1939; s. H. Hunter Sr. and Nelle Frances (Robinson) P.; m. Charlotte Anne Wilson, July 9, 1966; children: Michael Hunter, Colleen Annette. BA, U. Wyo., 1961, JD, 1966. Bar: Wyo. 1966, U.S. Dist. Ct. Wyo. 1966, Colo. 1967, U.S. Supreme Ct. 1975. Mcpl. judge City of Powell, 1967-68; sole practice law Powell, 1966-88; atty. City of Powell, 1969-88; justice of the peace County of Park, Wyo., 1971-88; bus. law instr. Northwest C.C., Powell, 1968-98; dist. judge State of Wyo. 5th Jud. Dist., 1988—2006; drug ct. judge Park County, Wyo., 2001—06; ret. 2006; sole practice law Powell, 2006—. Mem. Wyo. Dist. Judges Conf., sec.-treas., 1993-94, vice chair, 1994-95, chair, 1995-96. Editor: Bench Book for Judges of Courts of Limited Jurisdiction in the State of Wyoming, 1980-90; author: (nonfiction essay) Visualize-Verbalize, 2007, 2008. Dir. cts. Wyo. Girls State, Powell, 1982—85, 1989—99, 2005—; mem. Wyo. Commn. Jud. Conduct and Ethics, 1997—2003; judge, chair mgmt. com. Park County Drug Ct., 2001—06; adv. bd. NW Coll. Nursing Program, 2007—08; elder, deacon, moderator of deacons Powell Presbyn. Ch., 1997; bd. dirs. Heart Mountain Vol. Med. Clinic, 2007—08. Recipient Wyo. Crime Victim Compensation Commn. Judicial award, 1995, Wyo. Criminal Justice Assn. Svc. award, 2005. Fellow Am. Bar Found. (life), Wyo. Jud. Adv. Coun.; mem. ABA (Wyo. state del. to ho. of dels. 1994-2001, Wyo. del. jud. adminstrn. divsn., exec. com. nat. conf. trial ct. judges representing Wyo., Colo., Kans., Nebr., N.Mex. 1996-2000, bd. govs. 2001-04, Pub. Svc. award for ct.-sponsored Law Day programs 1990, 92, standing com. judges adv. com. on ethics in profession 2004-07), Wyo. Bar Assn. (Cmty. Svc. award 1999, Ann. Pub. Svc. award 1999), Colo. Bar Assn., Park County Bar Assn. (sec. 1969-70, pres. 1970-71), Wyo. Assn. Cts. Ltd. Jurisdiction (pres. 1973-80), Wyo. Dist. Judges Conf. (chair 1996), Am. Judicature Soc. (mem. jud. adv. coun.). Avocations: photography, travel, fishing, reading, writing. Home: PO Box 941 Powell WY 82435-0941 Personal E-mail: hpatrick2778@msn.com.

PATRON, SUSAN HALL, librarian, writer; b. San Gabriel, Calif., Mar. 18, 1948; d. George Thomas and Rubye Denver Hall; m. René Albert Patron, July 27, 1969. BA, Pitzer Coll., 1969; MLS, Immaculate Heart Coll., 1972. Children's libr. LA Pub. Libr., 1972-79, sr. children's libr., 1980—, juvenile materials collections devel. Reviewer Sch. Libr. Jour., 1980-90, Pubs. Weekly, 1986-91, The Five Owls, 1987-95. Author: (with Christopher Weiman) Marbled Papers, 1979, Burgoo Stew, 1991, Five Bad Boys, Billy Que, and the Dustdobbin, 1992, Maybe Yes, Maybe No, Maybe Maybe, 1993 (ALA Notable Book 1994), Bobbin Dustdobbin, 1993, Dark Cloud Strong Breeze, 1994, The Higher Power of Lucky, 2006 (winner Newbery medal 2007.) Mem. ALA (Caldecott award com. 1988, Laura Ingalls Wilder award com. 2001), PEN (mem. West Lit. awards jury 1997, 2006), Calif. Libr. Assn. (Patricia Beatty award com. 1987-89, 91-92), Internat. Bd. on Books for Young Children, Soc. Children's Book Writers and Illustrators, So. Calif. Coun. on Lit. for Children and Young People (awards com. 1985), Authors Guild, Friends of Children and Lit. (mem. award com. 1984). Office: LA Pub Libr Childrens Svcs 630 W 5th St Los Angeles CA 90071-2002

PATTEN, DUNCAN THEUNISSEN, ecologist educator; b. Detroit, Oct. 13, 1934; s. Marc T. and Doris (Miller) P.; m. Eva Chittenden, July 27, 1957; children: Michael, Marc, Robin, Scott. BA, Amherst Coll., 1956; MS, U. Mass., Amherst, 1959; PhD, Duke U., 1962. Asst. prof. ecology Va. Poly. Inst., Blacksburg, 1962-65, Ariz. State U., Tempe, 1965-67, assoc. prof., 1967-73, prof., 1973-95, prof. emeritus, 1995—, dir. ctr. environ. studies, 1980-95. Rsch. prof. Mont. State U., 1995—. Contbr. articles to profl. jours. Fellow AAAS, Ariz.-Nev. Acad. Sci.; mem. Ecol. Soc. Am. (bus. mgr. 1979-95), Brit. Ecol. Soc., Soc. Range Mgmt., Am. Inst. Biol. Scis., Soc. Wetland Scientists (pres. 1996-97), Am. Water Resource Assn., Am. Geophys. Union, Sigma Xi Office: Mont State U Land Resources and Environ Scis Box 173120 Bozeman MT 59717-3120 Office Phone: 406-994-2784. Business E-Mail: dtpatten@montana.edu.

PATTEN, THOMAS HENRY, JR., retired educator, personnel director; b. Cambridge, Mass., Mar. 24, 1929; s. Thomas Henry and Lydia Mildred (Lindgren) Patten. AB, Brown U., 1953; MS, Cornell U., 1955, PhD, 1959. Dir. program planning Ford Motor Co., Dearborn, Mich., 1957-65; prof. mgmt. and sociology U. Detroit, 1965-67; prof. orgnl. behavior and personnel mgmt. Sch. Labor and Indsl. Relations, Mich. State U., E. Lansing, 1967-84; prof. mgmt. and human resources Calif. State Poly. U., Pomona, 1984—2003, prof. emeritus, 2003—07; ret., 2007. Cons. in field. Author: The Foreman: The Forgotten Man of Management, 1968, Manpower Planning and the Development of Human Resources, 1971, OD-Emerging Dimensions and Concepts, 1973, A Bibliography of Compensation Planning and Administration, 1960-1974, 2d rev. edit., 1981, 3d rev. edit., 1987, Pay: Employee Compensation and Incentive Plans, 1977, Classics of Personnel Management, 1979, Organizational Development Through Teambuilding, 1981, A Manager's Guide to Performance Appraisal, 1982, Fair Pay: The Managerial Challenge of Comparable Job Worth and Job Evaluation, 1988, Exercises for Developing Human Resources Management Skills, 1996. With USMC, 1946—51. Mem. ASTD (chmn. orgn. devel. div. 1972), Indsl. Rels. Rsch. Assn. (chpt. pres. 1970-71), Am. Sociol. Assn., Internat. Pers. Mgmt. Assn., Internat. Indsl. Rels. Assn., Inst. Applied Behavioral Sci., Am. Compensation Assn. Home: 407 Mossy Ct Lincoln CA 95648-8158 Home Phone: 916-408-2026.

PATTERSON, CARLY, singer, former Olympic gymnast; b. Baton Rouge, Feb. 4, 1988; d. Ricky and Natalie. Mem. TOPS Nat. Team, 1996, 1997, US Nat. Gymnastics Team, 2000—06; gymnast Team USA, Athens Olympic Games, 2004; singer Musicmind Records, 2008—. Contestant Celebrity Duets, 2006. Singer: Back to the Beginning, 2007. Achievements include member of US World Championships Gold medal team, 2003; winning silver medal, all-around, World Championships, 2003; won Visa Am. Cup Championship by winning all four events, 2004; winning gold medal, all-around, Athens Olympic games, 2004; member of US Women's Silver medal Gymnastics team, Athens Olympic games, 2004. Office: c/o MusicMind Records Chicago IL 60607 Office Phone: 312-733-2424. Office Fax: 312-733-2425.

PATTERSON, DANIEL, state legislator; married; 1 child. Grad., Mich. State U. Coll. Agr. & Natural Resources. Formerly with Bur. Land Mgmt. US Dept. Interior; Southwest dir. Pub. Employees Environ. Responsibility; mem. Dist. 29 Ariz. House of Reps., 2009—, mem. mil. affairs & pub. safety com., water & energy com. Democrat. Office: Ariz House Reps Capitol Complex 1700 W Washington Rm 123 Phoenix AZ 85007 Office Phone: 602-926-5342. Office Fax: 602-417-3169. Business E-Mail: dpatterson@azleg.gov.*

PATTERSON, DANIEL WILLIAM, retired dentist; s. Girdell William and Fern Lemay Patterson. DDS, Northwestern U., 1972; Alumnus degree (hon.), U. Colo., 1977; BS in Biology, U.N.Y., 1993; M in Healthcare, U. Denver, 1994. Cert. health industry orgn., ops. U.Denver, 1993, cert. gerontology, 1996. Dentist Dan L. Hansen, DDS, P.C., Lakewood, Colo., 1974-75; pvt. practice dentistry Littleton, Colo., 1975-88; clin. instr. dept. applied dentistry U. Colo., Denver, 1981-83, lectr., 1983, clin. asst. prof. depts. restorative and applied dentistry, 1989-91, dir. advanced dentistry program, 1989-90, asst. prof. clin. track dept. restorative dentistry, 1991—2000; ret., 2000. Mem. editorial adv. panel Dental Econs. Jour., 1981; also articles. Active Chatfield Jaycees, Littleton, 1976-81; vocal soloist, mem. Denver Concert Chorale, 1978-82; gospel singer Gospel Music Ministry, 2000-, (album) It Is No Secret, 2000, Hymns My Grandmother Loved, 2001. Lt. USN, 1968-74. Fellow Acad. Gen. Dentistry; bd. eligible Am. Bd. Gen. Dentistry; mem. ADA, Met. Denver Dental Soc., Colo. Dental Assn. (Pres.'s Honor Roll 1982-84), Mensa. Baptist. Avocations: reading, fishing, photography. Home: 6984 N Fargo Trl Littleton CO 80125-9270

PATTERSON, DAVID ANDREW, computer scientist, educator, consultant; b. Evergreen Park, Ill., Nov. 16, 1947; s. David Dwight and Lucie Jeanette (Ekstrom) P.; m. Linda Ann Crandall, Sept. 4, 1967; children: David Adam, Michael Andrew. BS in Math., UCLA, 1969, MS in Computer Sci., 1970, PhD, 1976. Mem. tech. staff Hughes Aircraft Co., LA, 1972-76, Thinking Machines Corp., Cambridge, Mass., 1979; prof. computer sci. divsn. U. Calif., Berkeley, 1977—, chmn., 1990-93, E.H. and M.E. Pardee chair computer sci., 1992—. Cons. Sun Microsystems, Inc., Mountain View, Calif., 1984—. Author: A Taste of Smalltalk, 1986, Computing Unbound, 1989, Computer Architecture: A Quantative Approach, 2d edit., 1996, 4th edit., 2007, Computer Organization & Design: The Hardware/Software Interface, 2d edit., 1998, 3rd edit., 2005. Recipient Disting. Tchg. award U. Calif., Berkeley, 1982, Diane S. McEntyre award, 1998, Outstanding Alumnus award UCLA Computer Sci. Dept.; named to Silicon Valley Engring. Hall of Fame, 2006. Fellow IEEE (undergrad. tchg. award 1996, tech. achievement award 1995, co-recipient Reynold B. Johnson Info. Storage award, John Von Neumann medal 2000, James H. Mulligan Edn. medal, 2000), Assn. Computer Machinery (Karl V. Karlstrom Outstanding Educator award, 1991, co-recipient, Sigmod Test of Time award 1998), Computer Soc., Am. Acad. Arts & Sciences; mem. NAE, AAAS, Computing Rsch. Assn. (bd. dirs. Washington 1991-2003, chair 1993-97, spl. interest group on computer architecture), Assn. Computer Machinery (bd. dirs. 1987-90, chair 1993-95, pres. 2004-2006), NAS (computer sci. and telecomm. bd.). Avocations: biking, soccer, weightlifting, body surfing. Office: Univ Calif Computer Sci Computer Sci Divsn 1776 465 Soda Hall Berkeley CA 94720-1776 Office Phone: 510-642-6587. Office Fax: 510-643-7352. Business E-Mail: patterson@cs.berkeley.edu.

PATTERSON, DENNIS JOSEPH, retired management consultant; b. Honolulu, Apr. 13, 1948; s. Joseph John and Dorothy Elizabeth (Snajkowski) P.; divorced; children: Valerie Jean, Christina Elizabeth. BA, Elmhurst Coll., Ill., 1970; MA, George Washington U., 1973. Asst. dir. Vancouver (B.C.) Gen. Hosp., 1973-76, dir., 1975-76; v.p. Shaugnessy Hosp., Vancouver, 1976-79; pres. Westcare, Vancouver, 1979-84; mgr. Ernst & Whinney, Chgo., 1984-86, sr. mgr., 1986-88, ptnr., 1988-93; pres. FHP Internat. Cons. Group, Inc., Fountain Valley, Calif., 1993-95; ptnr. KPMG Peat Marwick, 1996-97; sr. cons. Hay Group, 1997-98; chmn., CEO IMC Rsch. Inst. (now Healthcare Net); ptnr. Wellspring Ptnrs.; ret., 2007. Author: Indexing Managed Care, 1997; contbr. articles to profl. jours. Fin. mgr. Electoral Action Movement, Vancouver, 1978; trustee George Washington U., 1992-96, Calif. Sch. Profl. Psychology, 1993-96, Alliant U., 1999-2003, Elmhurst Coll., 2006—. Mem. Royal Vancouver Yacht Club, Union League Chgo., Chgo. Yacht Club, Phi Gamma Mu. Republican. Anglican. Avocations: sailboat racing, golf. Home Phone: 310-386-0995. Personal E-mail: djpdennis@yahoo.com.

PATTERSON, JAMES RANDOLPH, physician; b. Lancaster, Pa., Jan. 30, 1942; m. Linda Lewis Patterson, Nov. 22, 1969. AB, U. Pa., 1964; MD, Columbia U., 1968. Diplomate Nat. Bd. Med. Examiners, Am. Bd. Internal Medicine, Subsplty. of Pulmonary Disease. Pulmonary and critical care specialist The Oreg. Clinic, Portland, 1975—; clin. prof. medicine Oreg. Health Scis. U., Portland, 1978—. Mem. Am. Bd. Internal Medicine, Phila., 1995—, sec.-treas., 2002--; trustee Collins Med. Trust, Portland, Oreg., 1992—, chair subsplty. bd. pulmonary disease, 1998-2002. Contbr. numerous articles to profl. jours. Recipient Class of 1964 award U. Pa., Van Loan award Am. Lung Assn. Oreg., 1990, Meritorious Achievement award Oreg. Health Scis. U., 1991; named Class Pres. Coll. Physicians and Surgeons of Columbia U., 1968, Tchr. of Yr. Providence Med. Ctr., Portland, Oreg., 1976, Internist of Yr., 1983, Best Doctors in Am., 1992—, Consumers Guide to Top Doctors, 2002-. Mem. AMA, Am. Thoracic Soc., Am. Coll. Chest Physicians, Oreg. Lung Assn., North Pacific Soc. of Internal Medicine, Pacific Interurban Clin. Club, Multnomah County Med. Soc., Oreg. Med. Assn., Oreg. Soc. Critical Care Medicine. Office: The Oregon Clinic 1111 NE 99th St Ste 200N Portland OR 97220 Office Phone: 503-963-3030. Business E-Mail: jpatterson@orclinic.com.

PATTERSON, STEVE, former professional sports team executive; b. Beaver Dam, Wis., Sept. 21, 1957; BBA with honors, U. Tex., 1980, JD, 1984. Bar: Tex. 1984. Gen. mgr., profl. basketball team counsel Houston Rockets, NBA, 1984-89, profl. basketball mktg. exec. group ticket sales, mgr., bus. ops. exec., gen. mgr., 1989-94; pres. profl. hockey team Houston Aeros, 1994-97; pres. Arena Oper. Co., Houston, 1995-99; exec. v.p. Houston NFL Holdings, 1997—2003; pres. Portland Trail Blazers, NBA, Oreg., 2003—07, gen. mgr., 2006—07; pres. Pro Sports Consulting, 2007—. Office Phone: 503-680-3500. Personal E-mail: stevewpatterson@gmail.com. Business E-Mail: spatterson@prosportsconsulting.net.

PATTON, ANTWAN ANDRE (BIG BOI), rap artist, singer; b. Savannah, Ga., Feb. 1, 1975; children: Jordan Alexus, Bamboo. Performer Outkast, 1992—. Singer: (albums) Southernplayalisticadillacmuzik, 1994, ATLiens, 1996, Aquemini, 1998, Stankonia, 2000 (Grammy awards: Best Rap Album, 2001, Best Rap Performance By A Duo Or Group for song "Ms Jackson", 2001), Big Boi and Dre Present...Outkast, 2001 (Grammy award: (with Killer Mike) Best Rap Performance By A Duo Or Group for song "The Whole World", 2002), Speakerboxxx/The Love Below, 2003 (Grammy awards: Album Of The Yr., 2003, Best Urban/Alternative Performance for song "Hey Ya!", 2003, Best Rap Album, 2003, Am. Music Awards Favorite Album-Rap/Hip-Hop, 2004), Idlewild, 2006; actor: (films) ATL, 2006, Idlewild, 2006; performer: (with Atlanta Ballet) Big, 2008. Recipient Best New Rap Group of Yr., Source award, 1995, Favorite Band, Duo or Group-Pop or Rock, Am. Music Awards, 2004, Favorite Band, Duo or Group-Rap/Hip-Hop, 2004, Duo/Group Artist of Yr., Billboard Music Awards, 2004, Billboard 200 Duo/Group Album Artist of Yr., 2004, Hot 100 Duo/Group of Yr., 2004, R&B/Hip-Hop Duo/Group of Yr., 2004, Digital Track of Yr., 2004. Address: Arista Records Inc 8750 Wilshire Blvd Beverly Hills CA 90211-2713

PATTON, JACK THOMAS, family practice physician; b. Rogers, Ark., Feb. 18, 1941; s. Jack Marcus and Jewell Selah (Pense) P.; m. Lynette Anne Carr, Sept. 2, 1960; children: Robert, John, Mark, Christopher. BA in History, Calif. State U., Long Beach, 1963; MA in History, Calif. State U., Fresno, 1993; MD in Medicine, U. So. Calif., 1967; MA in Bibl. Studies, Mennonite Brethren Bib. Sem., Fresno, Calif., 1980. Cert. Bd. Med. Examiners, Calif., Hawaii. Intern Tripler Army Med. Ctr., Honolulu, 1967-68; resident in gen. practice Walson Army Hosp., Ft. Dix, NJ, 1968-70; med. supt. Nazarene Hosp., Papua New Guinea, 1973-80; chmn. family practice dept. Sharp Rees-Stealy, San Diego, 1981-86; chmn. occupational medicine Kaiser Permanent, Fresno, 1986-87; assoc. med. dir. Sharp Rees-Stealy, San Diego,

1987-92; med. dir. Summer Inst. Linguistics, Papua New Guinea, 1993-94; with family practice dept. Sharp Rees-Stealy Med. Group, San Diego, 1994-97, Northwest Med. Group, Fresno, Calif., 1997—2007; chmn. dept. family practice St. Agnes Med. Ctr., 2002—05. Family practice residency liaison Tripler Army Med. Ctr., Honolulu, 1972-73; chief medicine, dep. commr. Schofield Army Med. Clinics, Wahiawa, Hawaii, 1970-72; lectr. Calif. State U., Fresno, 1978-79, Pt. Loma Nazarene Coll., 1982-85, San Jose Christian Coll., 1997-2003; v.p. Patton Industries, Inc., 2005—. Mem. med. sch. support Salerni Collegium, U. So. Calif. Sch. Medicine, 1967-85; lectr. Ch.-Mission Inst., Mennonite Brethren Bib. Sem., 1984-92; sec. S.E. Asian task force Mennonite Brethren Ch. Fresno, 1990-93. Maj. U.S. Army, 1966-73. Mackenzie scholar U. So. Calif. Sch. Medicine, 1966-67; decorated Meritorious Svc. medal. Fellow Am. Acad. Family Physicians; mem. Am. Bd. Family Practice (diplomate), Calif. Acad. Family Physicians, Royal Soc. Medicine (assoc., London). Avocations: history, travel, hiking. Home: 847 Rosewood Ave Sanger CA 93657-5400 Office: 831 Rosewood Ave Sanger CA 93657-5400 Office Phone: 559-875-9791. E-mail: dr_jack@verizon.net.

PATTON, JODY, management company executive; With Pacific Northwest Ballet; pres., CEO Vulcan, Inc., Seattle; pres. Vulcan Prodns. Vice-chair First & Goal, Inc.; exec. dir. Experience Music Project, Seattle; co-founder Sci. Fiction Mus. and Hall of Fame, Seattle, Allen Inst. for Brain Sci., Wash.; bd. dir. Charter Comm. Exec. prodr.: The Blues. Exec. dir. Paul G. Allen Family Found.; bd. dir. U. Wash. Found., Internat. Glass Mus., Oreg. Shakespeare Festival, Theatre Comm. Group. Office: Vulcan Inc 505 Fifth Ave S Ste 900 Seattle WA 98104 Office Phone: 206-342-2000. Office Fax: 206-342-3000.

PATTON, JOHN, state legislator; m. Virginia Patton; 5 children. Mem. Dist. 29 Wyo. House of Reps., 2009—. Republican. Episcopalian. Office: 213 State Capitol Bldg Cheyenne WY 82002 also: 1623 Pond View Ct Sheridan WY 82801 Office Phone: 307-777-7881. Office Fax: 307-777-5466. Business E-Mail: johnpatton@wyoming.com.

PATTON, RICHARD WESTON, retired mortgage company executive; b. Evanston, Ill., Sept. 26, 1931; s. Robert Ferry and Sue Buckley P.; m. Lynda A. Kruse, Feb. 2, 1971; 1 child, Robert Weston BA, Amherst Coll., 1954. Sales engr. Thermo Fax Sales Corp., Chgo., 1958-60; account exec. Nat. Mortgage Investors, Inc., Chgo., 1960-61, sales mgr. Pasadena, Calif., 1962-66, asst. v.p., 1966-67, v.p., 1967-69, exec. v.p., 1969-73, pres., chief exec. officer, dir., 1973-84, vice-chmn. bd., 1984-90; pres. Richard W. Patton Enterprises, Pasadena, 1990—2004; ret., 2005. Pres., chmn. exec. com., dir. Ocean Park Restaurant Corp., Santa Monica, Calif., 1977-88; dir. Cenfed Bank, Cenfed Fin. Corp. Bd. dirs. Pasadena Boys' Club, 1963-66, Opera Assocs., 1984-90; mem. steering com. Amherst Coll. Capital Fund Drive, 1963-66; mem. citizens adv. com. L.A. County Sheriffs Dept. 1st lt. USMCR, 1955-58. Mem. Amherst Coll. Alumni Assn. (bd. dirs. 1963—2001, pres. 1977-79, 86-89), Kroenstadt Ski Club (past pres.). Office: Rich W Patton Enterprises 3644 San Pasqual St Pasadena CA 91107-5419

PATTON, STUART, biochemist, educator; b. Ebenezer, NY, Nov. 2, 1920; s. George and Ina (Neher) P.; m. Colleen Cecelia Lavelle, May 17, 1945; children: John, Richard, Gail, Thomas, Mary Catherine, Patricia, Joseph. BS, Pa. State U., 1943; MS, Ohio State U., 1947, PhD, 1948. Chemist Borden Co., 1943-44; rsch. fellow Ohio State U., Columbus, 1946-48; faculty Pa. State U., University Park, 1949-80, prof., 1959-80, Evan Pugh rsch. prof. agr., 1966-80; adj. prof. neurosci. Sch. Medicine U. Calif., San Diego, 1981—99; ret., 1999. Vis. scientist Scripps Instn. Oceanography; cons. in field. Author: (with Robert Jenness) Principles of Dairy Chemistry, 1959; (with Robert G. Jensen) Biomedical Aspects of Lactation, 1975; Milk: Its Remarkable Contribution to Human Health and Well-Being, 2004. Lt. (j.g.) USNR, 1944-46. Recipient Borden award chemistry milk Am. Chem. Soc., 1957, Agrl. and Food Chemistry award, 1975, Alexander von Humboldt sr. scientist award, 1981, Macy-Gyorgy award Internat. Soc. for Rsch. on Human Milk and Lactation, 1997, Distinguished Alumnus award, Pa. State U., 2002, Distinguished Svc. award Am. Dairy Sci. Assn., 1999, fellow Pa. State Alumni Assn., 2001. Fellow Am. Dairy Sci. Assn.; mem. Am. Chem. Soc., Am. Soc. Biochemistry and Molecular Biology, Am. Soc. Cell Biology. Home and Office: 6208 Avenida Cresta La Jolla CA 92037-6510

PAUL, CHARLES S., motion picture and television company executive; b. 1949; BA, Stanford U., 1971; JD, U. Santa Clara, 1975. Law clk. U.S. Supreme Ct., 1975-76; with Cooley Castro Huddleson & Tatum, 1976-79, Atari Inc., 1979-85, sr. v.p., gen. counsel, pres. coin-operated games div., 1983-85; with MCA, Inc., Universal City, Calif., 1985-96, v.p., pres. MCA Enterprises div., 1986-89, exec. v.p., 1989, also bd. dirs., 1985-96; chmn., founder Sega Game Works, Universal City, Calif., 1996—. Office: Universal Studios MCA 1024 N Orange Dr Los Angeles CA 90038-2318

PAUL, ELDOR ALVIN, agriculture, ecology educator; b. Lamont, Alta., Can., Nov. 23, 1931; s. Reinhold and Ida (Mohr) P.; m. Phyllis Ellen Furhop, Aug. 3, 1955; children: Lynette, Linda. BSc, U. Alta., 1954, MSc, 1956; PhD, U. Minn., 1958. Asst. prof. U. Saskatchewan, Saskatoon, Can., 1959-64, assoc. prof., 1964-70, prof., 1970-80; mem. faculty, chmn. dept. plant and soil biology U. Calif., Berkeley, 1980-85; mem. faculty, chairperson dept. of crop and soil sciences Mich. State U., East Lansing, 1985-94, prof. crop and soil sci., 1994—2000; rsch. scientist Nat. Resource Ecology Lab., Colo. State U., Ft. Collins, 2000—. Vis. prof. U. Ga., Athens, 1972-73, USDA, Ft. Collins, 1992-93. Author: Soil Microbiology and Biochemistry, 1988, 1996; editor: Soil Biochemistry, vols. 3-5, 1973-81; Soil Organic Matter in Temperate Agro Ecosystems, 1997; contbr. over 260 articles on microbial ecology, soil microbiology and soil organic matter to sci. publs. Fellow AAAS, Soil Sci. Soc. Am., Can. Soc. Soil Sci., Am. Soc. Agronomy (Soil Sci. Rsch. award 1995); mem. Internat. Soc. Soil Sci. Soil Biology (chmn. 1978-82), Am. Ecol. Soc. Home: 843 Rossum Dr Loveland CO 80537-7944 Office: Natural Resource Ecology Lab Colo State Univ Fort Collins CO 80521 Home Phone: 970-461-3034; Office Phone: 970-491-1990. E-mail: eldor@nrel.colostate.edu.

PAUL, MALCOLM DAVID, plastic and reconstructive surgeon; b. Balt., Nov. 8, 1943; s. William and Rose (Friedman) P.; m. Pamela Sisk Paul, May 15, 1981; children: Stephen, Scott, Jacquie, Matthew. BS, U. Md., 1965; MD, U. Md., Balt., 1969. Cert. Am. Bd. Platic Surgery, 1976. Intern Mt. Sinai Hosp., NYC, 1969-70, resident, 1970-71, George Washington U., Washington, 1971-75; practice medicine specializing in plastic surgery Fountain Valley, Calif., 1975—. Asst. clin. prof. to assoc. prof. clin. surgery, divsn. plastic surgery U. Calif., Irvine, 1976-; bd. dirs. CAP-MPT; adv. bd. mem., med. spa advisor Cosmetic Surgery Exposition Group; mem. adv. bd. Cosmetic Enhancement Expo. Named to Best Doctors in America, Orange County Top Doctors, Guide to Top Doctors. Mem. Am. Soc. Plastic and Reconstructive Surgery, Am. Soc. Aesthetic Plastic Surgery, Inc. (past pres., chmn. bd. trustees), Am. Bd. Plastic Surgery (past dir.), Orange County Soc. Plastic Surgeons, Inc. (past pres.), Am. Assn. Plastic Surgeons, Am. Soc. Plastic Surgery, Inc.(bd. trustee, 2009), Aesthetic Surgery Edn. and Rsch. Found., Internat. Soc. Aesthetic Plastic Surgery (past US Nat. sec.), Calif. Soc. Plastic Surgeons Republican. Jewish. Office: 1401 Avocado Ave Ste 810 Newport Beach CA 92660-8708 Office Phone: 949-760-5047.

PAULSON, CHESTER LEON FREDERICK, brokerage house executive; b. Portland, Oreg., Jan. 24, 1936; s. Charles August and Clara L. (Crann) P.; m. Jacqueline Marie Crawford, 1969; children: Charles, Erick. BS in Econs., U. Oreg., 1959; MBA, U. Portland, 1980. Trader June S. Jones Co., Portland, 1959-63; head trader May & Co., Portland, 1963-70; pres. Paulson Investment Co. subs. Paulson Capital Corp., Portland, 1970—, also bd. dirs. Chmn. bd. dirs. Regional Investment Brokers, Highland Park, Ill.; bd. dirs. Skolniks, Louisville. Mem. Mayor's Econ. Devel. Adv. Com., Portland, 1984. Avocations: reading, tennis, skiing. Office: Paulson Investment Co 811 SW Naito Pkwy, Ste 200 Portland OR 97204-3332

PAULSON, DONALD ROBERT, chemistry professor; b. Oak Park, Ill., Sept. 6, 1943; s. Robert Smith and Florence Teresa (Beese) P.; m. Elizabeth Anne Goodwin, Aug. 20, 1966; children: Matthew, Andrew. BA, Monmouth Coll., 1965; PhD, Ind. U., 1968. Asst. prof. chemistry Calif. State U., Los Angeles, 1970-74, assoc. prof., 1974-78, prof., 1979—, chmn. dept., 1982-90. Vis. prof. U. B.C., Vancouver, Can., 1977-78, U. Sussex, Brighton, Eng., 1984-85. Author: Alicyclic Chemistry, 1976; contbr. articles to profl. jours. Named Outstanding Prof., Calif. State U., Los Angeles, 1978, 84, 96. Mem. Am. Chem. Soc., Chem. Soc. (London), InterAm. Photochem. Soc., Nat. Assn. Sci. Tchrs., Sigma Xi. Democrat. Episcopalian. Avocations: photography, hiking, soccer. Office: Calif State U Dept Chemistry 5151 State University Dr Los Angeles CA 90032-4226 Home: PO Box 1168 Ouray CO 81427 Home Phone: 970-325-0931; Office Phone: 323-343-2300. Business E-Mail: dpaulso@calstatela.edu.

PAULSON, RICHARD JOHN, obstetrician, gynecologist, educator; b. Prague, Czech Republic, Feb. 2, 1955; came to U.S., 1966, naturalized citizen, 1972. m. Lorraine M. Cummings, Oct. 11, 1987; children: Jessica, Jennifer, Philip, Erika, Josef. BS in Physics magna cum laude, UCLA, 1976, MD, 1980; MS, U. So. Calif., 1998. Diplomate Am. Bd. Ob-Gyn., Reproductive Endocrinology and Infertility. Rotating intern Harbor-UCLA Med. Ctr., Torrance, 1980-81, resident in ob-gyn., 1981-84; clin. rsch. fellow dept. ob-gyn. Los Angeles County/U. So. Calif. Med. Ctr., LA, 1984-86, mem. staff, 1984—; clin. instr. ob-gyn. Sch. Medicine U. So. Calif., LA, 1984-86, asst. prof., 1986-91, assoc. prof., 1991-96, prof. clin. ob-gyn., 1996—; affiliate staff mem. Calif. Med. Ctr., LA, 1986—; staff mem. L.A. Clin. & U. So. Calif. Med. Ctr., 1986—, dir. clin. infertility program, 1986—; chief divsn. reproductive endocrinology and infertility Keck Sch. Medicine U. So. Calif., LA, 1996—; med. dir. U. So. Calif. Fertility. Vis. prof. in vitro fertilization lecture series Clinica Kennedy, Guayaquil, Ecuador, 1980; presenter at numerous profl. confs., symposia and grand rounds. Co-editor Infertility, Contraception and Reproductive Endocrinology, 4th edit., 1996; contbr. chpt. to Management of Common Problems in Obstetrics and Gynecology, 2nd. edit., 1988, 3rd edit., 1994, Infertility, Contraception and Reproductive Endocrinology, 1991; co-author several book chpts.; co-author (lay book) Rewinding Your Biological Clock: Motherhood Late in Life, 1998; technical reviewer for Infertility for Dummies, 2007; contbr. or co-contbr. several articles to sci. jours.; mem. editl. bd. Jour. of Assisted Reprodn. and Genetics, Jour. Soc. for Gynecologic Investigation; mem. ad hoc editl. bd. Fertility and Sterility, Am. Jour. Ob-Gyn., Jour. of AMA, Contraception, Am. Jour Reproductive Immunology, others. Co-recipient Wyeth award 1985, recipient, 1989; co-recipient Serono award, 1991, 92, 93, Poster award 1994, Excellence in Tchg. award-Keck Sch. Medicine U. So. Calif., Assn. Professors of Gynecology and Obstetrics, 2004; rsch. grantee Ortho Pharm. Corp., 1986-87, Tap Pharmas., 1989-91, Irvine Sci., 1990-91, Syntex, 1990-92, Serono, 1992-93; named one of Best Doctors in America, 1994-, America's Top Doctors, 2002-; named Best Doctors for Women, 1997. Fellow ACOG (mem. PROLOG task force for reproductive endocrinology 1993), L.A. Obstetrical and Gynecologic Soc.(bd. dirs.); mem. Pacific Coast Fertility Soc. (bd. dirs. 1992, past pres.), Am. Fertility Soc., Am. Fertility Assn. (bd. mem., Howard and Georgeanna Jones Lifetime Achievement award, 2005), Soc. Reproductive Surgeons, Soc. for Assisted Reproductive Tech., Soc. Reproductive Endocrinologists, Soc. for Reproductive Endocrinology and Infertility (past pres.), Am. Soc. Reproductive Medicine (past bd. mem.), Soc. for Gynecologic Investigation, Endocrine Soc. Office: USC Fertility 1127 Wilshire Blvd Ste 1400 & 1410 Los Angeles CA 90017*

PAULUS, NORMA JEAN PETERSEN, lawyer; b. Belgrade, Nebr., Mar. 13, 1933; d. Paul Emil and Ella Marie (Hellbusch) Petersen; m. William G. Paulus, Aug. 16, 1958; children: Elizabeth, William Frederick. LL.B., Willamette Law Sch., 1962; LL.D. (hon.), Linfield Coll., 1985; LittD (hon.), Whitman Coll., 1990; LHD (hon.), Lewis & Clark Coll., 1996. Bar: Oreg. 1962. Sec. to Harney County Dist. Atty., 1950-53; legal sec. Salem, Oreg., 1953-55; sec. to chief justice Oreg. Supreme Ct., 1955-61; of counsel Paulus and Callaghan, Salem; mem. Oreg. Ho. of Reps., 1971-77; sec. of state State of Oreg., Salem, 1977-85; supt. pub. instrn., 1990-99; of counsel Paulus, Rhoten & Lien, 1985-86. Mem. Oreg. exec. bd. U.S. West, 1985-97; adj. prof. Willamette U. Grad. Sch., 1985; mem. N.W. Power Planning Com., 1986-89. Mem. adv. com. Def. Adv. Com. for Women in the Svc., 1986, Nat. Trust for Hist. Preservation, 1988-90; trustee Willamette U., 1978-05; bd. dirs. Oreg. Grade Instn. Sci. and Tech., 1985-01, Edn. Commn. States, 1991-99, Coun. Chief State Sch. Officers, 1995-98, Nat. Assessment Governing Bd., 1996-99, Oreg. Garden Found., 1997—, Oreg. Coast Aquarium, 1999—; bd. dirs., adv. bd. World Affairs Coun. Oreg., 1997—; overseer Whitman Coll., 1985—; bd. cons. Marion-Polk Boundary Commn., 1970-71; mem. Presdl. Commn. to Monitor Philippines Election, 1986; dir. Oreg. Hist. Soc., Portland, 2000-03. Recipient Disting. Svc. award City of Salem, 1971, LWV, 1995, Path Breaker award Oreg. Women's Polit. Caucus, 1976, Statesman of Yr. award, 2005, Gold medal extraordinary achievement and contbn. to Oregon, 2003; named One of 10 Women of Future, Ladies Home Jour., 1979, Woman of Yr. Oreg. Inst. Managerial and Profl. Women, 1982, Oreg. Women Lawyers, 1982, Woman Who Made a Difference award Nat. Women's Forum, 1985; Eagleton Inst. Politics fellow Rutgers U. Mem. Oreg. State Bar, Nat. Order Women Legislators, Women Execs. in State Govt., High Desert Mus., Women's Polit. Caucus Bus. and Profl. Women's Club (Golden Torch award 1971), Delta Kappa Gamma. Home: 1209 SW 6th Ave Apt 201 Portland OR 97204-1023

PAUP, MARTIN ARNOLD, securities and real estate investor; b. Seattle, Aug. 30, 1930; s. Clarence Jacob and Emaline Ethel (Lodestein) P.; m. Mary Jean Iske, Apr. 4, 1959; children: Barbara Ann Paup Soriano, Jennifer Marie, Elizabeth Paup-Byrnes. BS, U. Wash., 1952. Indsl. engr. Boeing Airplane Co., Seattle, 1954—60; owner Coopers Unfinished Furniture, Seattle, 1960—63; claims rep. Unigard Ins., Seattle, 1963—66; asst. benefits mgr. Equitable Life Assurance, Seattle, 1966—85; owner Paup Ventures, Seattle, 1974—, Paup Investment Co., Seattle, 1963—, Ella Paup Properties, Seattle, 1963—. Bd. dirs. Denny Regrade Property Owners' Assn., Seattle, Denny Regrade Bus. Assn., Seattle, First Ave. Assn., Seattle. Grantee, Seattle Dept. Cmty. Devel., 1980. Mem. Greenwood C. of C., Seattle Opera Guild. Democrat. Avocations: opera, travel, literature, history.

PAUSA, CLEMENTS EDWARD, electronics company executive; b. South Gate, Calif., Oct. 18, 1930; s. Oscar Clements and Kathleen Patricia (O'Toole) P.; m. Janice Mary Hanson, Jan. 22, 1955; children: Geoffrey Clements, Ronald Edward. Student, UCLA, 1948-50; BS, U. Calif., Berkeley, 1953, MS, 1954, cert. in bus., 1960. Product mgr. Fairchild Semiconductor Corp., 1959-62, mgr. plant, 1962-64; gen. mgr. Fairchild Hong Kong Ltd., 1964-67, dir. plant group, 1967-68; dir. internat. mfg. Nat. Semiconductor Corp., Santa Clara, Calif., 1968-70, gen. mgr. Far East ops., 1970-73, v.p. internat. mfg., 1973-86, corp. v.p. internat. mfg., 1986-90, corp. v.p. internat. mfg. emeritus, 1991—. Dir. Price Waterhouse Coopers STS; v.p. ops. Power Integrations, Inc., 1997-99; bd. dirs. 8 subs. cos., 2 J.V. cos. Mem. internat. adv. bd. U. Santa Clara, 1984—. Capt. USNR, 1952-81. Mem. Naval Res. Assn., Res. Officer's Assn., Sons in Retirement, Calif. Alumni Assn., Delta Chi Alumni Assn. (v.p., pres. 1978-86). Republican. Roman Catholic. Office: Ste 1600 10 Almaden Blvd San Jose CA 95113 Office Phone: 408-817-5738. E-mail: clements.e.pausa@us.pwc.com.

PAVLATH, ATTILA ENDRE, chemist, researcher; b. Budapest, Hungary, Mar. 11, 1930; came to U.S., 1958; s. Eugene Rudolph and Yolanda Elizabeth (Hortobagyi) P.; m. Katalin Wappel, July 27, 1951; children: George, Grace. Diploma in chem. engring., Tech. U., Budapest, 1952; D in Chemistry, Hungarian Acad. of Sci., Budapest, 1955. Asst. prof. Tech. U., Budapest, 1952-56; group leader Cen. Chem. Rsch. Inst., Budapest, 1954-56; rsch. fellow McGill U., Montreal, Can., 1957-58; sr. group leader Stauffer Chem. Co., Richmond, Calif., 1958-67; project leader Western regional rsch. ctr. USDA, Albany, Calif., 1967-78, rsch. leader Western regional rsch. ctr., 1979—. Author three books; contbr. articles to profl. jours; patentee in field. Fellow Am. Inst. Chemists (councilor 1985-95, dir. 1993-95); mem. Am. Chem. Soc. (councilor 1973-90, dir. 1991-99, pres.-elect 2000, pres. 2001, immediate past pres. 2002), Royal Chem. Soc. Great Britain, Internat. Union of Pure and Applied Chemistry, German Chem. Soc., Hungarian Chem. Soc. Avocations: flying, bridge, tennis, ping pong/table tennis, computers. Office: USDA Western Regional Rsch Ctr 800 Buchanan St Berkeley CA 94710-1105 Office Phone: 510-559-5620. Business E-Mail: apavlath@pw.usda.gov.

PAVLEY, FRAN J., state legislator; b. LA, Nov. 11, 1948; m. Andy Pavley; children: Jennifer, David. BA, Calif. State U., Fresno, 1970; MA, Calif. State U., 1985. Cert. tchr. Calif. Tchr. Esparto Unified Sch. Dist., 1970—74, Moorpark Unified Sch. Dist., 1974—2000; mayor City of Agoura Hills, 1982—97; mem. Agoura Hills City Coun., 1982—97; coastal commr. Calif., 1995—2000; mem. Calif. Assembly, 2000—06; mem. Dist. 23 Calif. State Senate, 2008—. Founder Agoura Hills Disaster Response Team, 1987; mem. adv. com. Santa Monica Mountains Conservancy, 1990—; mem. Coastal Commn., State of Calif., 1995—2000; mem. coun., mayor Agoura Hills, Calif., 1982—97. Named one of Top Technology Leaders in Transportation, Scientific America, recipient 2006 Calif. League Conservation Voters Global Warming Leadership award. Democrat. Office: Dist 23 10951 West Pico Blvd Ste 202 Los Angeles CA 90064 Office Phone: 310-441-9084. Office Fax: 310-441-0724. Business E-Mail: senator.pavley@senate.ca.gov.*

PAXTON, JAY L., lawyer; b. Ft. Worth, Dec. 24, 1947; s. Carl C. Paxton and Mildred F. (Fawver) Shepherd; m. Carolyn P. Paxton, June 21, 1969; 1 child, Laura. BA, U. Calif., Berkeley, 1970, JD, 1973. Bar: Calif. 1973. Spl. asst. to chancellor U. Calif., 1973-74; ptnr., mng. ptnr. Bianchi, Paxton, Engel, Keegin & Sherwood, San Rafael, Calif., 1974—90; mem., mng. dir. Ellman, Burke, Hoffman & Johnson, San Francisco, 1990—. Bd. dirs., v.p. Internat. House, U. Calif., Berkeley, 1974—, mem. exec. com. Fisher Ctr. for Real Estate and Urban Econs., 2004—; trustee U. Calif. Berkeley Found., 1997—, Marin Cmty. Found., 2005—; mem., chair exec. com. San Francisco Dist. Coun., Urban Land Inst., 1976-; bd. dirs. Bay Area Coun., 1996—. Mem. ABA, Calif. Bar Assn., Urban Land Inst., Lambda Alpha. Office: Ellman Burke Hoffman Johnson 601 California St Ste 1900 San Francisco CA 94108-2824 Office Phone: 415-777-2727. Business E-Mail: jpaxton@ellman-burke.com.

PAYNE, ANITA HART, reproductive endocrinologist, researcher; b. Karlsruhe, Baden, Germany, Nov. 24, 1926; came to U.S., 1938; d. Frederick Michael and Erna Rose (Hirsch) Hart; widowed; children: Gregory Steven, Teresa Payne-Lyons. BA, U. Calif., Berkeley, 1949, PhD, 1952. From rsch. assoc. to prof. U. Mich., Ann Arbor, 1961-96, prof. emeritus, 1996—; assoc. dir. U. Mich. Ctr. for Study Reproduction, Ann Arbor, 1989-94; sr. rsch. scientist Stanford U. Med. Ctr., Calif., 1995—2007. Vis. scholar Stanford U., 1987-88; mem. reproductive biology study sect. NIH, Bethesda, Md., 1978-79, biochem. endocrinology study sect., 1979-83, population rsch. com. Nat. Inst. Child Health and Human Devel., 1989-93. Assoc. editor Steroids, 1987-93; contbr. book chpts., articles to profl. jours. Recipient award for cancer rsch., Calif. Inst. for Cancer Rsch., 1953, Acad. Women's Caucus award, U. Mich., 1986, Mentor award, Women in Endocrinology, 1999. Mem. Endocrine Soc. (chmn. awards com. 1983-84, mem. nominating com. 1985-87, coun. 1988-91), Am. Soc. Andrology (exec. coun. 1980-83), Soc. for Study of Reproduction (bd. dirs. 1982-85, sec. 1986-89, pres. 1990-91, Carl G. Hartman award 1998, Disting. Svc. award 2004).

PAYNE, DAVID L., bank executive; b. 1956; Chmn., pres., CEO Westamerica Bancorporation; gen. mgr. Gibson Publishing Co., Gibson Radio and Publishing Co., Vallejo, Calif. Office: Westamerica Bancorp 1108 5th Ave San Rafael CA 94901-2916

PAYNE, MARGARET ANNE, lawyer; b. Aug. 10, 1947; d. John Hilliard and Margaret Mary (Naughton) P. Student, Trinity Coll., Washington, 1965-66; BA magna cum laude, U. Cin., 1969; JD, Harvard U., 1972; LLM in Taxation, NYU, 1976. Bar: N.Y. 1975, U.S. Dist. Ct. (so. dist.) N.Y. 1975, Calif. 1979, U.S. Dist. Ct. (so. dist.) Calif. 1979. Assoc. Mudge, Rose, Guthrie, and Alexander, NYC, 1972-75, Davis, Polk and Wardwell, NYC, 1976-78, Seltzer, Caplan, Wilkins and McMahon, San Diego, 1978-79, Higgs, Fletcher and Mack, San Diego, 1980-82, ptnr., 1983-90, of counsel, 1991—. Adj. prof. grad. tax program U. San Diego Sch. Law, 1979-89, Calif. Western Sch. Law, San Diego, 1980-82; judge pro tem Mcpl. Ct., San Diego Jud. Dist., 1983, 92. Bd. dirs. Artist Chamber Ensemble, Inc., 1983-86, Libr. Assn. La Jolla, Calif., 1983-86, San Diego County Crimestoppers, Inc., 1993-95, San Diego Crime Commn., 1994-95, St. Augustine's H.S., 1994-95, San Diego Hist. Soc., 1993-95. Mem. ABA, Calif. State Bar Assn., San Diego County Bar Assn., Mortar Bd., Guidon Soc., Charter 100, Phi Beta Kappa. Office: Higgs Fletcher & Mack 401 W A St Ste 2600 San Diego CA 92101-7913

PAYNE, STANLEY E., mathematics professor; b. Chgo., Sept. 26, 1939; s. Don Ivan Payne and Agnes Eileen Craven - Payne; life ptnr. Angelika Adamic; m. Shirley Ann Ellison, Aug. 22, 1961 (div. Sept. 26, 1983); children: Tanya Marie Ker, Rahn Kenneth, Brian Curtis, Brett Ivan. MS in Math., Fla. State U., Tallahassee, 1963, PhD in Math., 1966. Prof. math. Miami U., Oxford, Ohio, 1966—84, U. Colo., Denver, 1984—. Contbr. articles to profl. jours. Mem.: Inst. Combinatorics and Its Applications, Am. Math. Soc. (life). Achievements include discovery of new examples of ovals and generalised quadrangles. Office: U Colo at Denver CB 170 POBox 173364 Denver CO 80217-3364 Office Fax: 303-556-8550. Business E-Mail: stanpayne@mac.com.

PAYTON, CYDNEY, museum director, curator; Owner Cydney Payton Artfolio, 1985—90; co-owner Payton-Rule Gallery, 1990—92; dir. Boulder Mus. Contemporary Art, Colo., 1992—2000; dir., curator Mus. Contemporary Art/Denver, 2001—08.

PAZNOKAS, LYNDA SYLVIA, elementary school educator; b. Portland, Oreg., Feb. 19, 1950; d. Marley Elmo and Undine Sylvia (Crockard) Sims. BA, Wash. State U., Pullman, 1972; MS, Portland State U., Oreg., 1975; EdD, Oreg. State U., Corvallis, 1984. Cert. tchr. Oreg. Tchr. 5th grade, outdoor sch. specialist Clover Park Sch. Dist. 400, Tacoma, 1971-72; tchr. 6th grade, outdoor sch. specialist Hillsboro Elem. Dist. 7, Oreg., 1972-78, Bend-La Pine Sch. Dist., Oreg., 1978-82, elem. curriculum specialist Oreg., 1983-85, tchr. 4th grade gifted and talented Oreg., 1985-90; grad. teaching asst. Oreg. State U., Corvallis, 1982-84; asst. prof., assoc. prof. No. Ariz. U., 1990-99, chair instnl. leadership, 1997-98; Boeing disting. prof. sci. edn. Wash. State U., Pullman, 1999—, assoc. dean sch. and cmty. collaboration, 2006—. Ednl. cons., tchr. workshops, 1973—; presenter workshop Soviet-Am. Joint Conf., Moscow State U., 1991, Meeting of Children's Culture Promoters, Guadalajara, Mex., 1994, internat. conf. Sci., Tech. and Math. Edn. for Human Devel., UNESCO, Panaji, India, 2001, Nishinomiya Joint Rsch. Conf., Japan, 2001, internat. workshop Promoting Sci. and Tech. Literacy Through Sci. Toys & Out-of-Sch. Sci. Activities, Pattaya, Thailand, 2005, Scientifically Literate Students as World Citizens, Singapore, 2006, World Environ. Edn. Congress, Durban, South Africa, 2007, Internat. Workshop Innovative Sci. Tchg., Guilin, China, 2007, regional coord., E3 Washington, State Environ. Planning Process, others; faculty Ariz. Journey Schs. for Math. and Sci. Tchg. Improvement; coord. Odyssey of the Mind, Bend, 1985-89, tchr. mentor program for 1st yr. tchrs., Beaverton, Oreg., 1982-83; reviewer Sci. Books and Films AAAS, 1992-2006; presenter Social Edn. Assn. of Australia, 1997, Nat. State Tchrs. of Yr., Guam, 2005; steering com. Wash. LASER (Leadership and Assistance for Sci. Edn. Reform), 2002—, mem. sci. drafting team sci. curriculum instml. frameworks; mem. Nat. Ecol. Obs. Network Design Consortium. Author: Pathways of America: Lewis and Clark, 1993, Pathways of America: The Oregon Trail, 1993, Pathways of America: The California Gold Rush Trail, 1994, Pathways of America: The Santa Fe Trail, 1995, Fifty States, 1997, U.S. Presidents, 1997, U.S. Map Skills, 1997, Human body, 1998, National Parks and Other Park Service Sites, 1999, Our National Parks, 1999, Pathways of America: The California Mission Trail, 2000, Circling the World: Festivals and Celebrations, 2000, Endangered Species, 2001; mem. adv. bd. (jour.) Sci. and Children; contbr. articles to profl. jours.; reviewer Turkish Jour. Sci. Edn. Vol., leader, bd. dirs. Girl Scouts US, 1957—; elder First Presbyn. Ch., Bend, 1980—; vol. hist. interpretation High Desert Mus., Bend, 1987-91; docent Mus. No. Ariz.; pres. bd. dirs. The Arboretum at Flagstaff; former sec. and v.p. bd. dirs. Palouse Discovery Sci. Ctr. (pres. bd. dirs.); past pres. Arboretum bd.; mem. Ptnrs. Achieving Leadership in Sci., Wash., DC, Leadership and Assistance for Sci. Edn. Reform, Wash., DC. Recipient Excellence in Teaching award Bend Found., 1985-86, 86-87; named Tchr. Yr. Oreg. Dept. Edn., 1982, Higher Edn. Tchr. Yr., Wash. Sci. Tchrs. Assn. (WSTA), 2003; Celebration Teaching grantee Geraldine Rockefeller Dodge Found., 1989, 90, 91, 92, 93, 94, 95, EPA grantee, 1997-99, 2006-, Eisenhower Math and Sci. Edn. Act grantee, 1997, 99, Grand Canyon Assn. grantee, 1996, 97, 98; commd. Ky. Col., 1993. Mem. NEA, Internat. Coun. Assns. Sci. Edn. (chair pre-secondary and informal sci. edn. of the exec. com. 2004—, editor Stepping Into Sci. Internat. Quar. jour. 2004—, jour/ advisor), Nat. Coun. Tchrs. Math., NSTA (past mem. nat. supervision com., internat. com., mem. sci. and children bd.), Nat. State Tchrs. of Yr. (nat. pres. 1988-90), Nat. Assn. Rsch. in Sci. Tchg., Oreg. Coun. Tchrs. Math. (bd. dirs. 1981-82), Oreg. Coun. Tchrs. English (bd. dirs. 1981-82), Ariz. Reading Assn. (bd. dirs.), Nat. Coun. for Social Studies, Coun. for Elem. Sci. Internat. (bd. dirs. 1995-98, 99—2003, chair informal edn. com.), Internat. Reading Assn., Oreg.-Calif. Trails Assn., Nat. Sci. Edn. Leadership Assn., Assn. for Sci. Tchr. Edn., Sch. Sci. and Math. Assn. (publs. com.), Nat. Assn. for Rsch. in Sci. Tchg., Assn. for Sci. Edn., Wash. Sci. Tchrs. Assn. (higher edn. rep. bd. dirs. 2004—, co-chair WSTA-Wash. Orgn. for Reading Devel. Joint Conf., 2006), N.W. Oreg.-Calif. Trails Assn., Lewis and Clark Trail Heritage Found., PEO (past corr. sec.), Delta Kappa Gamma (1st v.p.), Phi Delta Kappa (found. rep. 1991-92, v.p. programs 1992-93, historian 1993-94, v.p. membership 1994-95), Golden Key Hon., Pi Lambda Theta, Phi Kappa Phi, Kappa Delta Pi (chpt. counselor, mem. spkrs. bur., nat. Web com., sci. specialist), others. Avocations: cross country skiing, photography, hiking, researching immigrant trails, gardening. Home: 101 Enman-Kincaid Rd Pullman WA 99163

PEACE, STEVE, state legislator; b. San Diego; m. Cheryl Peace, 1974; children: Clint, Bret, Chad. Degree in Polit. Sci., U. Calif., San Diego. CFO, co-founder Four Square Prodns., National City, Calif., 1972; mem. Calif. State Assembly, 1982-93, chair fin., ins. and pub. investment com., 1993; mem. Calif. State Senate, 1993—, chair com. on energy, utilities and comm., mem. and chair budget and fiscal rev. com. Coach Pony and Little League; pres. Homeowner's Assn.; co-chair Citizens for Clean Water. Democrat. also: 430 Davidson St # E Chula Vista CA 91910-2411

PEALE, STANTON JERROLD, physics educator; b. Indpls., Jan. 23, 1937; s. Robert Frederick and Edith May (Murphy) P.; m. Priscilla Laing Cobb; June 25, 1960; children: Robert Edwin, Douglas Andrew. BSE, Purdue U., 1959; MS in Engring. Physics, Cornell U., 1962, PhD in Engring. Physics, 1965. Research asst. Cornell U., Ithaca, N.Y., 1962-64, research assoc., 1964-65; asst. research geophysicist, asst. prof. astronomy UCLA, 1965-68; asst. prof. physics U. Calif., Santa Barbara, 1968-70, assoc. prof., 1970-76, prof., 1976-94, prof. emeritus, rsch. prof., 1994—. Mem. com. lunar and planetary exploration NAS-NRC, Washington, 1980-84, lunar and planetary geosci. rev. panel, 1979-80, 86-89, 94-96, Planetary Sys. Sci. Working Group, 1988-93, Lunar and Planetary Sci. Coun., 1984-87, mem. com. astronomy and astrophysics, 1997—; lunar sci. adv. group NASA-JPL, Pasadena, Calif., 1970-72; mem. Keck time allocation com. NASA, 1996-98. Assoc. editor: Jour. Geophys. Research, 1987; contbr. articles to profl. jours. Recipient Exceptional Scientific Achievement medal NASA, 1980, James Craig Watson award Nat. Acad. Scis., 1982; vis. fellowships U. Colo., Boulder, 1972-73, 1979-80. Fellow AAAS (Newcomb Cleveland prize 1979), Am. Geophys. Union; mem. Am. Astron. Soc. (divsns. planet sci. and dynamic astronomy, Dirk Brouwer award 1992, chair dynamical astronomy 1999-2000), Internat. Astron. Union. Avocation: gardening. Office: U Calif Santa Barbara Dept Physics Santa Barbara CA 93106

PEARCE, DRUE, federal official, former state legislator; b. Fairfield, Ill., Apr. 2, 1951; d. H. Phil and Julia Detroy (Bannister) P.; m. Michael F.G. Williams; 1 child, Tate Hanna Pearce-Williams. BA in Biol. Scis., Ind. U., 1973; MPA, Harvard U., 1984; cert. exec. program Darden Sch. Bus., U. Va., 1989. Sch. tchr., Clark County, Ind., 1973-74; curator of edn. Louisville Zoo, 1974—76; dir. Summerscene, Louisville, 1976—77; asst. v.p., br. mgr. Alaska Nat. Bank of the North, 1977-82; legis. aide to Rep. John Ringstad Alaska Ho. of Reps., Juneau, 1983, mem., 1984-88, minority whip, 1987—88; mem. Alaska Senate, 1989—2001, chmn. com. oil and gas, mem. exec. com. energy coun., 1989-90, chmn. com. labor and commerce, mem. exec. coms. western state conf., coun. state govts., energy coun., 1991-92, co-chmn. senate fin., chmn. energy coun., vice chmn. com. energy, nat. coun. state govts., 1993-94, mem. select com. legis. ethics and legis. coun., pres. senate, mem. exec. com. energy coun., vice chmn. senate coms. resources and rules, 1995-96, co-chmn. com. senate fin., mem. exec. com. energy coun., vice chmn. com. senate judiciary, 1997—98; sr. adv. to sec. for Alaska affairs US Dept. Interior, 2001—; fed. coord. for Alaskan Natural Gas Transp. Projects Fed. Energy Regulatory Commn., 2006—. Senate pres., 1995-96, 1999-2000, senate rules chmn., 2001; ptnr. Cloverland N., Anchorage, 1993—; resources cons. Arctic Slope Regional Corp., Anchorage, 1987-91, 95-96; sr. adv. Sec. Interior for Alaska Affairs, 2001-. Former bd. dirs. Alaska Women's Aid in Crisis, Anchorage Econ. Devel. Coun., Alaska Aerospace Devel. Corp., Alaska Spl. Olympics, Gov.'s Bd. Mem. DAR, Commonwealth North, Resource Devel. Coun., Alaska Miners Assn., Alaska Fedn. Rep. Women, Aircraft Owners & Pilots Assn., U.S. Trotting Assn. Republican.

PEARCE, HARRY JONATHAN, lawyer, manufacturing executive; b. Bismarck, ND, Aug. 20, 1942; s. William R. and Jean Katherine (Murray) P.; m. Katherine B. Bruk, June 19, 1967; children: Shannon Pearce Baker, Susan J., Harry M. BS, USAF Acad., Colorado Springs, Colo., 1964; JD, Northwestern U., 1967; Degree in Engring. (hon.), Rose-Hulman Inst. Tech., 1997; LLD (hon.), Northwestern U., 1998. Bar: N.D. 1967, Mich. 1986. Mcpl. judge City of Bismarck, 1970-76, U.S. magistrate, 1970-76, police commr., 1976-80; sr. ptnr. Pearce & Durick, Bismarck, 1970-85; assoc. gen. counsel GM, Detroit, 1985-87, v.p., gen. counsel, 1987-92, exec. v.p., gen. counsel, 1992-94, exec. v.p., 1994-95, vice chmn., 1996—2001; chmn. Hughes Electronics, El Segundo, Calif., 2001—03; non exec. chmn. Nortel Networks Corp., Brampton, Ont., Canada, 2005—. Bd. dirs. GM Corp., Hughes Electronics Corp., GM Acceptance Corp., Delphi Automotive Sys. Corp., Alliance of Automobile Mfrs. of Am., Marriott Internat. Inc., Nortel Networks Corp., Econ. Strategy Inst., Theodore Roosevelt Medora Found., MDU Resources Group, Inc., Nat. Def. U. Found., Detroit Investment Fund. Mem. law bd. Sch. Law, Northwestern U.; mem. bd. visitors U.S. Air Force Acad.; chmn. Product Liability Adv. Coun. Found.; founding mem. minority counsel demonstration program Commn. on Opportunities for Minorities in the Profession, ABA; chmn. The Sabre Soc., USAF Acad.; trustee Howard U., U.S. Coun. for Internat. Bus., New Detroit, Inc.; mem. The Mentor's Group Forum for U.S.-European Union Legal-Econ. Affairs, The Conf. Bd., Network of Employers for Traffic Safety's Leadership Coun., Pres.'s Coun. on Sustainable Devel., World Bus. Coun. for Sustainable Devel., World Economic Forum Coun. Innovative Leaders in Globalization. Capt. USAF, 1964-70. Named Michiganian of Yr., The Detroit News, 1997; Hardy scholar Northwestern U., Chgo., 1964-67, recipient Alumni Merit award, 1991. Fellow Am. Coll. Trial Lawyers, Internat. Soc. Barristers; mem. Am. Law Inst. Avocations: amateur radio, woodworking, sailing. Office: Bowman and Brooke LLP 50 W Big Beaver Rd Ste 600 Troy MI 48084

PEARCE, RUSSELL, state legislator; b. Mesa, Ariz., June 23, 1947; m. LuAnne Pearce; children: Dodi, Sean, Colten, Justin, Joshua. BA in Mgmt., U. Phoenix, 1980; degree, Harvard U. John F. Kennedy Sch. Govt., 1997. Advanced exec. devel. degree Ariz. State U., 1993. Chief dep./under sheriff Maricopa County Sheriff's Office, Phoenix, 1970—93; judge North Mesa Justice Ct., 1991—92; dir. Ariz. Gov.'s Office Highway Safety, 1994; dir. motor vehicle divsn. Ariz. Dept. Transp., 1995; mem. Dist. 29 Ariz. House of Reps., 2001—02, mem. Dist. 18, 2003—08, Ariz. State Senate, 2008—, chair appropriations com., mem. fin. com., judiciary com. Mem. Multi-State Highway Transp. Assn., 1995—99, Transp. Users Leadership Nat. Alliance, 1996—99; v.p. bd. dirs. Am. Assn. Motor Vehicle Administrators, 1995—99; chair Arizona Auto Theft Authority, 1995—99. Exec. bd. mem. Mesa Sr. Ctr. Inc., 1991—99; mem. Heavy Vehicle Electronic License Plates, Inc., 1995—99; vol. Boy Scouts of America, Ariz. Police Olympics. Served with US Army Nat. Guard, 1965—72. Mem.: Nat. Sheriff's Assn., Maricopa County Deputies Assn., Internat. Assn. Chiefs of Police, Ariz. Chiefs of Police Assn., Ariz. Auto Theft Investigators Assn., Justice of Peace Assn., Fraternal Order of Police, Rotary Club. Republican. Office: Ariz State Senate Capitol Complex 1700 W Washington Rm 110 Phoenix AZ 85007-2890 Office Phone: 602-926-5760. Office Fax: 602-417-3118. Business E-Mail: rpearce@azleg.gov.*

PEARCE, WILLIAM D., marketing executive; b. 1963; BA in Econs., Syracuse U., NY, 1984; MBA, Cornell U. Johnson Sch. Mgmt., NY, 1992. Area mgr. Miller Brewing Co., 1984—88; acct. exec. Coca Cola Co., 1988—90; mktg. dir. Procter & Gamble Co., 1992—2003; v.p. mktg. Campbell Soup Co., 2003—04; chief mktg. officer Taco Bell Corp. Yum! Brands Inc., 2004—07; pres., CEO Foresight Med. Tech., LA, 2007—08; sr. v.p., chief mktg. officer Del Monte Foods Co., San Francisco, 2008—. Office: Del Monte Foods Hdqs Landmark at One Market PO Box 193575 San Francisco CA 94119 Office Phone: 415-247-3000.

PEARL, JUDEA, computer scientist, educator; b. Tel-Aviv, Sept. 4, 1936; U.S. citizen; m. Ruth Pearl; 3 children. BSc, Israel Inst. Tech., 1960; MSc, Newark Coll. Engring., 1961; PhD in Elec. Engring., Poly. Inst. Bklyn., 1965. Rsch. engr. Dental Sch., NYU, 1960-61; mem. tech. staff RCA Rsch. Labs., 1961-65; dir. advanced memory devices Electronic Memories, Inc., Calif., 1966-69; prof. Sch. of Engring./Dept. Computer Scis. UCLA, 1969—; co-founder, pres. Daniel Pearl Found., 2002—. Instr. Newark Coll. Engring., 1961; cons. Rand Corp., 1972, Integrated Sci. Corp., 1975, Hughes Aircraft, 1989.; dir. Cognitive Sys. Lab., UCLA. Author: Heuristics: Intelligent Search Strategies for Computer Problem Solving, 1984, Probabilistic Reasoning in Intelligent Systems: Networks of Plausible Inference, 1988, Casuality: Models, Reasoning, Inference, 2000. Recipient: Outstanding Achievement award RCA Labs., 1965, Rsch. Excellence award, Allen Newell award, Lakatos award in Philosophy Sci., Internat. Joint Confs. on Artificial Intelligence, 1999, Benjamin Franklin medal in computer and cognitive sci., Franklin Inst., 2008; co-recipient: Purpose prize, Civic Ventures, 2006. Fellow IEEE, ACM, Am. Assn. Artificial Intelligence (Classical Paper award 2000, Lakatos award 2001), Acad. Engring. (Allen Newell award, 2003), NAE; corr. mem. Spanish Acad. Engring. Office: UCLA Dept Computer Sci 4532 Boelter Hl Los Angeles CA 90095-0001

PEARL, MARIANE (MARIANE VAN NEYENHOFF PEARL), journalist, filmmaker; b. Clichy, Hauts-de-Seine, France, July 23, 1967; m. Daniel Pearl, Aug. 1999 (dec. Feb. 2002); 1 child, Adam Daniel. Journalist, documentary filmmaker; program host Radio France Internationale; reporter, monthly columnist Glamour mag., 2006—. Spkr. in field. Co-author (with Sarah Crichton): A Mighty Heart: The Brave Life and Death of My Husband Danny Pearl, 2003; author: In Search of Hope: The Global Diaries of Mariane Pearl, 2007; prodr.: (documentaries) Biological Memory (Sci. and Soc. Award); cons. (films) A Mighty Heart, 2007, contbr. NY Times, Conde Nast Traveler, Sunday Times of London. Co-founder, hon. bd. mem. Daniel Pearl Found. Recipient Jane Cunningham Croly Print Journalism Award for Excellence in Covering Issues of Concern to Women, Gen. Fedn. Women's Clubs, 2007; named one of the Women of Yr., Glamour mag., 2007. Mem.: Soka Gakkai Internat. Office: c/o Daniel Pearl Found 16161 Ventura Blvd #671 Encino CA 91436

PEARL, NANCY LINN, librarian; b. Detroit, Jan. 12, 1945; d. Sidney and Anne Linn; m. Joseph Harold Pearl; children: Eily Raman, Katie. Grad., U. Mich., 1965, MLS, 1967. Head collection devel. Tulsa City County Libr., Okla.; exec. dir. Washington Ctr. Book Seattle Pub. Lib., 1993—2004. Author: Now Read This: A Guide to Mainstream Fiction, 1978-1998, 1999, Now Read This II: A Guide to Mainstream Fiction, 1990-2001, 2002, Book Lust: Recommended Reading for Every Mood, Moment and Reason, 2003, More Book Lust: Recommended Reading for Every Mood, Moment and Reason, 2005. Recipient Open Book award, Pacific Northwest Writer's Conf., 1997, Allie Beth Martin award, Pub. Libr. Assn., 2001, Humanities Washington award, 2003, Ontario Library Assn. Media and Communications award, 2004, Louis Shores Greenwood Publishing award for Reviews, ALA, 2004, Women's Nat. Book Assn. award, 2004—05, Louis Shores Greenwood Publishing award for Reviews, ALA, 2004—05; named Fiction Reviewer of Yr., Libr. Jour. Magazine, 1998. Achievements include the shushing librarian action figure based on her likeness. Office: Sasquatch Books 119 S Main Ste 400 Seattle WA 98104

PEARMAN, RAVEN-SYMONÉ CHRISTINA See SYMONE, RAVEN

PEARSON, J. MICHAEL, pharmaceutical executive; b. Can. married; 4 children. BS, Duke U., Durham, NC, BSE summa cum laude; MBA, U. Va. Head pharm. practice McKinsey & Co., head mid.-Atlantic region; chmn., CEO Valaent Pharm. Internat., 2008—. Eagle scout Boy Scouts Am.; bd. overseers Whitehead Sch. Diplomacy Internat. Rels, Seton Hall U., 2002—. Recipient Shermet award, U. Va., Global Citizen award, Whitehead Sch. Diplomacy Internat. Rels, Seton Hall U., 2004. Office: Valeant Pharm Internat One Enterprise Aliso Viejo CA 92656-2606 Office Phone: 949-461-6000. Office Fax: 949-461-6609.

PEARSON, P. DAVID, dean; BA, U. Calif., Berkeley, 1963; PhD, U. Minn., 1969. Dean Coll. Edn. U. Ill., Urbana-Champaign, co-dir. Ctr. for Study of Reading; John A. Hannah Disting. prof. edn. Mich. State U., co-dir. Ctr. for Study of Reading; dean Grad. Sch. Edn. U. Calif., Berkeley, 2001—. Recipient Oscar Causey Award, Nat. Reading Conf., 1989, William S. Gray Citation of Merit, 1990. Mem.: Nat. Acad. Edn., Phi Beta Kappa. Office: Grad Sch Edn 1501 Tolman Hall #1670 Berkeley CA 94720-1670 Office Phone: 510-643-6644. Office Fax: 510-643-8904. E-mail: ppearson@berkeley.edu.

PEARSON, RICHARD JOSEPH, archaeologist, educator; b. Kitchener, Ont., Can., May 2, 1938; s. John Cecil and Henrietta Anne Pearson; m. Kazue Miyazaki, Dec. 12, 1964; 1 child, Sarina Riye. BA in Anthropology with honours, U. Toronto, 1960; PhD, Yale U., 1966. Asst. prof., then assoc. prof. archaeology U. Hawaii, 1966-71; mem. faculty U. B.C., Vancouver, 1971-2000. Sr. rsch. advisor Sainsbury Inst. Japanese Arts and Cultures, 2007. Author: The Archaeology of the Ryukyu Islands, 1969, Higashi Ajia no Kodai Shakai to Kokogaku, 1984, Windows on the Japanese Past, Studies in Archaeology and Prehistory, 1986, Ancient Japan, 1992; contbr. articles to profl. jours. Guggenheim fellow.

PEARSON, ROGER LEE, library director; b. Galesburg, Ill., Dec. 7, 1940; s. Clifford Emmanuel and Lillian Louise (Fisher) P. BA, Knox Coll., 1963; MA in Sociology, U. Nebr.-Omaha, 1968; MA in Library Sci., Rosary Coll., 1974. Vol. U.S. Peace Corps, Brazil, 1964-66; extension service supr. Brown County Libr., Green Bay,

Wis., 1974-75; system adminstr. Nicolet Libr. System, Green Bay, 1976-77; exec. dir. South Central Libr. System, Madison, Wis., 1977-81; dir. Corpus Christi Pub. Librs., Tex., 1981-84, Naperville (Ill.) Pub. Librs., 1984-95, Sonoma County Libr., Santa Rosa, Calif., 1996-2001; interim dir. Spokane (Wash.) Pub. Libr., 2001; interim libr. dir. Coll. of Marin, Kentfield, Calif., 2002; interim dist. libr. Dixon (Calif.) Pub. Libr., 2002—03; interim dir. Kans. City (Mo.) Pub. Libr., 2004—05, Sonoma County Libr., Santa Rosa, 2005, Berkeley Pub. Libr., Calif., 2006; interim county libr. Yolo County Libr., Calif., 2008; interim county libr. Colusa County Libr., Calif., 2008. Lectr. Grad. Sch. Libr. and Info. Sci., Dominican U., River Forest, Ill., 1991-95. Mem. ALA, Train Riders Assn. Calif., Calif. Libr. Assn., Wine Libr. Assocs. Sonoma County. Avocations: power walking, travel research, train travel.

PEASE, GERALD, state legislator; b. Hardin, Jan. 21, 1954; m to Maria; children: three. Montana State Representative, District 6, formerly; Montana State Senator, District 3, 2001-05, District 21, 2005-, Montana State Senate.Trustee, Lodge Grass Sch Bd, formerly; hwy construction & rancher, currently. Partners in Policy (advisor coun, currently); Parents Lets Unite for Kids. Democrat. Mailing: PO Box 556 Lodge Grass MT 59050 Office Phone: 406-444-4800.

PEASE, ROGER FABIAN WEDGWOOD, electrical engineering educator; b. Cambridge, Eng., Oct. 24, 1936; came to U.S., 1964; s. Michael Stewart and Helen Bowen (Wedgwood) P.; m. Caroline Ann Bowring, Sept. 17, 1960; children: Emma Ruth, Joseph Henry Bowring, James Edward. BA, Cambridge U., Eng., 1960, MA, PhD, Cambridge U., Eng., 1964. Rsch. fellow Trinity Coll., Cambridge, 1963-64; asst. prof. U. Calif., Berkeley, 1964-67; mem. tech. staff AT&T Bell Labs., Murray Hill, N.J., 1967-78; prof. elec. engring. Stanford (Calif.) U., 1978—. Cons. IBM, San Jose, Calif., 1964-67, Xerox Corp., Palo Alto, Calif., 1978-84, Perkin Elmer Co., Hayward, Calif., 1979-90, Lawrence Livermore (Calif.) Labs., 1984-92, Affymax Rsch. Inst., 1989-93, Affymetrix, 1993—; mem. tech. adv. bd. Ultratech. Stepper, 1993—; with Dept. of Def. Advanced Rsch. Project Agy., 1996-98. Contbr. more than 200 articles to profl. jours. Patentee (8) in field. Scoutmaster Boy Scouts Am., Holmdel, N.J., 1977-78. Pilot officer RAF, 1955-57. Fellow IEEE (Rappaport award 1982); mem. Nat. Acad. Engring., San Jose Sailing Club. Avocations: sailing, windsurfing. Office: Stanford U Dept Elec Engring Stanford CA 94305

PEASE-PRETTY ON TOP, JANINE B., community college administrator; b. Nespelam, Wash., Sept. 17, 1949; d. Benjamin and Margery Louise (Jordan) Pease; m. Sam Vernon Windy Boy, July 30, 1975 (div. Jan. 1983); children: Rosella L. Windy Boy, Sam Vernon Windy Boy; m. John Joseph Pretty On Top, Sept. 15, 1991. BA in Sociology, Anthropology, Ctrl. Wash. U., 1970; MEd, Mont. State U., 1987, EdD, 1994; HHD (hon.), Hood Coll., 1990; LLD (hon.), Gonzaga U., 1991; DHL (hon.), Teikyo/Marycrest U., 1992; EdD (hon.), Whitman Coll., 1993; HHD (hon.), Rocky Mountain Coll., 1998. Dep. dir. Wash. State Youth Commn., Olympia, 1971; tutor student svcs. Big Bend C.C., Moses Lake, Wash., 1971-72, upward bound dir., 1972-75; women's counselor Navajo C.C., Many Farms, Ariz., 1972; dir. adult & continuing edn. Crow Ctrl. Edn. Commn., Crow Agy., Mont., 1975-79; ednl. cons. Box Elder, Mont., 1979-81; dir. Indian career svc. Ea. Mont. Coll., Billings, 1981-82; pres. Little Big Horn Coll., Crow Agency, 1982—; with Rocky Mountain Coll., Billings, Mont. Exec. com. Am. Indian Higher Ednl. Consortium, Washington, 1983—; bd. dirs. Am. Indian Coll. Fund, N.Y.C., 1988—; sec. Indian Nations at Risk U.S. Dept. Edn., Washington, 1990-91, collaborator task force, 1990-91; 2d vice chmn. Nat. Adv. Coun. Indian Edn., Washington, 1994—. Chmn. Bighorn County Dem. Ctrl. Com., Hardin, Mont., 1983-88; mem. coun. First Crow Indian Bapt. Ch., 1989—; bd. dirs. Ctr. for Rocky Mountain West, 1998—; chmn. Mont. State Reappt. an Distructing Commn., 1999—. MacArthur fellow John D. & Catharine MacArthur Found., 1994. Mem. Nat. Indian Edn. Assn. (Indian educator of yr. 1990), Mont. Assn. Chs. (bd. dirs. 1997—), Crow Tribe Nighthawk Dance Soc.

PECK, ABRAHAM, editor, media consultant, educator; b. NYC, Jan. 18, 1945; s. Jacob and Lottie (Bell) Peckolick; m. Suzanne Wexler, Mar. 19, 1977; children: Douglas Benjamin, Robert Wexler. BA, NYU, 1965; postgrad., CUNY, 1965-67; cert. in advanced exec. program, Northwestern U., 1997. Engaged in cmty. organizing and tutoring, 1962-64; with NYC Welfare Dept., 1965—67; free-lance writer, 1967—; writer, organizer Chgo. Action Youth Internat. Party, 1968; editor Chgo. Seed, 1968-70; treas. Seed Pub., Inc., 1968-70; mem. coordinating com. Underground Press Syndicate, 1969; assoc. editor Rolling Stone mag., San Francisco, 1975-76, contbg. editor, 1976-2001; feature writer Chgo. Daily News, 1977-78; with features dept. Chgo. Sun-Times, 1978-81; from asst. prof. to prof. Northwestern U., Evanston, Ill., 1981—2001, Sills prof. journalism, 2001—06, Helen Gurley Brown prof. journalism, 2006—08, prof. emeritus svc., 2008—, chair mag. dept., 1981—2006, dir. mag. programs Media Mgmt. Ctr., 2002—, chair journalism and cross-media storytelling, 2006—08, dir., bus. to bus. communication, 2008—. Editor, cofounder Sidetracks, alt. newspaper supplement, Chgo. Daily News, 1977—78; critic at large Sta. WBBM, 1979—82; mem. exec. com. mag. divsn. Assn. Edn. Journalism and Mass Communication, 1987—89, 1992—96, 2003—04, pres., 1994—95; mem. adv. bd. Academe mag., AAUP, 1990—2000, Heartland Jour., 1990—2002, Technos, 1992—; editl. co-auditor Advanstar Comm., 1999—; mem. adv. bd. Chgo. chpt. Asian Am. Journalists Assn., 2002—08; chair ethics subcom. Am. Bus. Media, 2002; cons., lectr. in field. Editor: Dancing Madness, 1976; author: Uncovering the Sixties: The Life and Times of the Underground Press, 1985, 1991; contbg. editor: Satisfaction Mag., 2005—06, consulting editor, contbr.: The Sixties, 1977; contbr. chapters to books. With US Army, 1967. Recipient Lifetime Achievement award, Am. Soc. Bus. Press Editors, 2008; named Mag. Divsn. Educator of Yr., Assn. Edn. Journalism and Mass Comm., 2003—04; named to Hall of Fame, Chgo. Journalism, 2006. Home and Office: Northwestern Univ Medill Sch Journalism 1110 Via Bolzano Santa Barbara CA 93111 Office Phone: 805-681-1102. Business E-Mail: a.peck@northwestern.edu.

PECK, ART, retail executive; Grad., Occidental Coll., LA; MBA, Harvard Bus. Sch. Fin. and mktg. position Avery Denison, Pasadena, Calif.; sr. v.p. Boston Consulting Group, 1982—2005, dir., 1988—2005; exec. v.p. strategy and ops. Gap, Inc., San Francisco, 2005—, acting pres. Gap brand. Office: Gap Inc 2 Folsom St San Francisco CA 94105 Office Phone: 650-952-4400.

PECK, ERNEST JAMES, JR., academic administrator; b. Port Arthur, Tex., July 26, 1941; s. Ernest James and Karlton Maudean (Luttrell) P.; children: David Karl, John Walter, Michael R. Peck. BA in Biology with honors, Rice U., 1963, PhD in Biochemistry, 1966. Rsch. assoc. Purdue U., West Lafayette, Ind., 1966-68, asst. prof., 1968-73, Baylor Coll. Medicine, Houston, 1973-74, assoc. prof., 1974-80, prof., 1980-82; prof., chmn. biochemistry Sch. Med. Sci., U. Ark., Little Rock, 1982-89; dean sci. and math. U. Nev., Las Vegas, 1989-95; vice chancellor acad. affairs U. Nebr., Omaha, 1995-98; exec. dir. Coun. Colls. of Arts and Scis., rsch. prof. Ariz. State U., Tempe, 1998—. Adj. prof. U. Ark., Pine Bluff, 1986-88; program dir. NSF, Washington, 1988-89; mem. editl. bd. Jour. Neurosci. Rsch., N.Y.C., 1982-92. Co-author: Female Sex Steroids, 1979, Brain Peptides, 1979. Recipient Rsch. Career award NIH, Nat. Inst. of Child Health and Human Devel., 1975-80; NIH fellow, 1964-66. Fellow AAAS; mem. Am. Chem. Soc., Am. Soc. Biochemistry and Molecular Biology, Endocrine Soc., Sigma Xi. Avocations: fishing, hunting.

PECK, PAUL LACHLAN, minister; b. Glens Falls, NY, Sept. 11, 1928; s. Paul Lee and Caroline Jeannette (Stanton) Peck; children: Paul Barrett, Kathryn Elizabeth, Gretchen, Kole W. BS, U. Conn., 1952; ThD, Bernadean U., 1976; MEd, Westfield State Coll., 1983. Ordained to ministry Truth Ctr., 1972. With Proctor and Gamble Co., Watertown, NY, 1956-60; dir. deferred giving programs Syracuse (N.Y.) U., 1960-68, v.p., 1968-70, Fairleigh-Dickinson U., NJ, 1970-71, Manhattan Coll., Bronx, NY, 1971-75; founder, pastor Arete' Truth Ctr., San Diego, 1975—. Author: Footsteps Along the Path, 1978, Inherit the Kingdom, 1978, Milestones of the Way, 1978, Freeway to Health, 1980, Freeway to Work and Wealth, 1981, Freeway to Human Love, 1982, Freeway to Personal Growth, 1982, Your Dreams Count, 1990, Heroic Love Poems, 1990, Worth The Room: An Autobiography of Survival and Service, 2005 Bd. dirs. Girl Scouts U.S.A., Syracuse, 1967-70; trustee, bd. dirs. Erickson Ednl. Found., 1970-75; vol. chaplain Auburn (N.Y.) State Prison, 1967-68; mem. chaplains' coun. Syracuse U., 1960-70; co-founder suicide and drug abuse prevention program Syracuse U., 1968-71, Fairleigh-Dickinson U., 1970-71, Manhattan Coll., 1971-75. Staff sgt. USNG, 1947-50. Mem. Internat. New Thought Alliance, SAR, Rotary, Knights of Malta (svc. award 1973), Masons, Shriners, Spiritual Frontiers Fellowship. Avocations: golf, book collecting.

PECK, ROBERT DAVID, educational foundation administrator; b. Devil's Lake, ND, June 1, 1929; s. Lester David and Bernice Marie (Peterson) P.; m. Lylia June Smith, Sept. 6, 1953; children: David Allan, Kathleen Marie. BA, Whitworth Coll., 1951; MDiv, Berkeley (Calif.) Bapt. Div. Sch., 1958; ThD, Pacific Sch. Religion, 1964; postgrad., U. Calif., Berkeley, 1959-60, 62-63, Wadham Coll., Oxford U., Eng., 1963. Music tchr. pub. schs., Bridgeport, Wash., 1954-55; prof., registrar Linfield Coll., McMinnville, Oreg., 1963-69; asst. dir. Ednl. Coordinating Coun., Salem, Oreg., 1969-75; assoc. prof. Pacific Luth. U., Tacoma, 1976-79, U. Puget Sound, Tacoma, 1977; v.p. John Minter Assocs., Boulder, Colo., 1979-81, Coun. Ind. Colls., Washington, 1981-84; adminstrv. v.p. Alaska Pacific U., Anchorage, 1984-88; pres. Phillips U., Enid, Okla., 1988-94, chancellor, 1994-95; chmn. The Pres. Found. for Support of Higher Edn., Washington, 1995—; sr. assoc. InterEd, Phoenix, 1998—. Pres. Phillips U. Ednl. Enterprises Inc., 1994-95; cons. Higher Edn. Exec. Assocs., Denver, 1984—; owner Tyee Marina, Tacoma, 1975-77; yacht broker Seattle, 1977-79. Author: Future Focusing: An Alternative to Strategic Planning, 1983, also articles. Dem. county chmn., McMinnville, 1968, Dem. candidate for state Ho. of Reps., McMinnville, 1969; pres. McMinnville Kiwanis, 1965-69. Cpl. Signal Corps, U.S. Army, 1952-54. Carnegie Corp. grantee, 1982, 84. Mem. Okla. Ind. Coll. Assn. (sec. 1989—). Mem. Christian Ch. Avocations: sailing, sculpting. E-mail: robertpeckb@cs.com.

PEDEN, LYNN ELLEN, marketing executive; b. LA, 1946; d. Orlan Sidney and Erna Lou (Harris) Friedman; m. Ernest Peden, Aug. 1994. Student, UCLA, 1963-65, 71-72, Willis Bus. Coll., 1965-66, Fin. Schs. Am., 1982, Viewpoints Inst., 1970-71. Office mgr. Harleigh Sandler Co., LA, 1965-67; customer svc. Investors Diversified Svcs., West L.A., Calif., 1968-76; exec. sec. McCulloch Oil Corp., West L.A., 1976; mgr. publs. Security 1st Group, Century City, Calif., 1976-80; office mgr. Morehead & Co., Century City, 1980-81; dir. mktg., mgr. customer svc. Inst. Mktg. Svcs., Santa Monica, Calif., 1981-82; v.p. Decatur Petroleum Corp., Santa Monica, 1982-83; asst. v.p., broker svcs., dir. Angeles Corp., LA, 1984-87; asst. to pres. Pacific Ventures, Santa Monica, 1988-90, La Grange Group, West L.A., 1990-95; property mgmt. asst. Desert Resort Mgmt., Palm Desert, Calif., 1997-99, bus. mgr., 1999—. Fin. and ins. writer; contbr. poetry to UCLA Literacy Mag., 1964. Mem. Migi Car Am. Club (sec., newsletter editor). Home: 78580 Villeta Dr La Quinta CA 92253-3856

PEDERSEN, ARLENE, web design company executive; b. 1974; Creative dir., owner Pedersen Design Grp. Involved with Tanque Verde Sch. Dist.; mem. Leukemia and Lymphoma Soc. Team in Tng.; mentor Nike Women's Marathon. Named one of 40 Under 40, Tucson Bus. Edge, 2006. Office: Pedersen Design Group 12622 E Calle Tatita Tucson AZ 85749-8115 Office Phone: 520-270-7863. Office Fax: 520-270-7957.

PEDERSEN, BRYAN, state legislator; b. Cheyenne, Wyo., Jan. 27, 1975; m. Sara Pedersen; 2 children. BS, U. Wyo., 1998. Fin. cons. RBC Wealth Mgmt.; mem. Dist. 7 Wyo. House of Reps., 2009—. Republican. Lutheran. Office: 213 State Capitol Bldg Cheyenne WY 82002 also: 2572 Wind River Tr Cheyenne WY 82009 Office Phone: 307-777-7881. Office Fax: 307-777-5466, 307-432-2440. Business E-Mail: bpedersen@wyoming.com.

PEDERSEN, JAMIE D., state legislator, lawyer; b. Puyallup, Wash., Sept. 9, 1968; s. Douglas Kirk and Audrey Mary (Draheim) P. BA summa cum laude, Yale U., 1990, JD, 1994. Bar: Wash. 1994. Law clk. Hon. Stephen F. Williams US Ct. Appeals, DC Cir.; of counsel K & L Gates, Seattle; co-chair nat. bd. dirs Lambda Legal Defense & Edn. Fund, Inc., 2003—05; mem. Dist. 43 Wash. House Reps., 2007—. Outside gen. counsel McKinstry Co., Pacific Med. Ctr., Parametrix, Inc., Wash. Rsch. Found. Pres. Yale Russian Chorus, New Haven, 1992-94. Recipient Charles G. Albom prize Yale Law Sch., 1994; Nat. Merit scholar, 1986. Mem. Phi Beta Kappa. Democrat. Lutheran. Avocations: swimming, flute. Office: K&L Gates Ste 2900 925 Fourth Ave Seattle WA 98104-1158 also: 318 O'Brien Bldg PO Box 40600 Olympia WA 98504-0600 Office Phone: 206-370-7987, 360-786-7826. Office Fax: 206-370-6152. E-mail: jamiep@prestongates.com.*

PEDERSEN, NORMAN A., lawyer; b. Modesto, Calif., Dec. 29, 1946; s. Melvin R. and Hilda R. (Akenhead) P. BA, U. Calif., Berkeley, 1970, MA, 1972; JD, UCLA, 1975. Bar: Calif., D.C. Trial atty. Fed. Power Commn., Washington, 1975-77; asst. to commr. Fed. Regulatory Commn., Washington, 1977-79; ptnr. Kadison, Pfaelzer, Woodard, Quinn & Rossi, Washington, 1979-87, Graham & James, Washington, 1987-88, Jones, Day, Reavis & Pogue, Washington, 1988—. Office: Jones Day 555 S Flower St # 50 Los Angeles CA 90071-2300

PEDERSEN, PAUL BODHOLDT, psychologist, educator; b. Ringsted, Iowa, May 19, 1936; BA in History and Philosophy, U. Minn., 1958, MA in Am. Studies, 1959; ThM, Luth. Sch. Theology, Chgo., 1962; MA in Ednl. Psychology, U. Minn., 1966; PhD in Asian Studies, Claremont Grad. U., Calif., 1968. Asst. prof. dept. psychoednl. studies, psychologist U. Minn., Mpls., 1971-75; sr. fellow Culture Learning Inst. East-West Ctr., Honolulu, 1975-76, sr. fellow coord., 1975-76; assoc. prof. dept. psychoednl. studies, psychologist U. Minn., 1975-79, higher edn. coord., 1976-77; sr. fellow Culture Learning Inst. East-West Ctr., 1979-81; prof., chmn. dept. counselor edn. Syracuse (N.Y.) U., 1982-90, prof. edn. dept. counseling and human svcs., 1989—95, adj. prof. dept. internat. rels., 1993—95, prof. emeritus, 2000—; prof. counseling edn. U. Ala., Birmingham, 1996-2001. Vis. lectr. Nommensen U., Medan, Sumatra, Indonesia, 1962—65, U. Malaya, 1969—71; vis. prof. dept. psychology U. Hawaii, 1978—81, 2000—; spkr. in field. Author numerous books, chpts. in books, articles to profl. jours.; mem. editl. bd. Am. Jour. Multicultural Counseling and Devel.; editl. advisor Jour. Profl. Psychology, Jour. Simulation and Games, Internat. Jour. Intercultural Rels. Sr. Fulbright fellow Nat. Taiwan U., Taipei, 1999-2000. Mem. APA, Am. Assn. Counseling and Devel. Internat. (mem. rels. com., editl. bd. Jour. Counseling and Devel., editor Internationally Speaking newsletter, mentor media com.), Internat. Assn. for Cross Cultural Psychology, Internat. Coun. Psychologists, Soc. Intercultural Tng. and Rsch. (exec. com., program chairperson 1977, chairperson Pacific Com. 1977, pres. 1978-80, editl. bd. Jour. Intercultural Rels.). Home: 1330 Ala Moana Blvd Apt 1306 Honolulu HI 96814-4221 Home Phone: 808-721-1568; Office Phone: 808-589-2662.

PEDERSON, CON, animator; Grad., UCLA. Former writer, animator Walt Disney; animator Graphic Films Corp.; co-founder Abel & Assocs.; sr. animator MetroLight Studios, LA, 1987—. Animator for Redstone rocket project, also Explorer Satellite program, 1958. Spl. effects supr., animated models designer (film) 2001: A Space Odyssey.

PEDERSON, JIM, political party official; m. Roberta Pederson. B in Polit. Sci., 1965, M in Pub. Adminstrn., 1967. Intern City of Tucson, Ariz.; admin. asst. office of rsch. City of Phoenix; with US Senate campaign of Sam Grossman, 1970, Westcor; prin., owner Pederson Group, 1983—; chmn. State Dem. Party Ariz., 2001—05. Office: 2800 N Central Ave 15th Fl Phoenix AZ 85004-1046 Business E-Mail: jpederson@azdem.org.

PEEL, MARK, chef, restaurant owner; b. Calif. m. Daphne Brogdon; children: Vanessa, Benjamin, Oliver, Vivien Tiana. Student, Calif. Poly. U., Pomona; studied Agrl. Econ., U. Calif. Davis. Former apprentice Ma Maison, LA; former mem. staff La Tour d'Argents, Moulin de Mougins; former sous chef Michael's, Santa Monica, Calif., 1979; former mem. staff Chez Panisse, Berkeley, Calif.; head chef Spago, Hollywood, Calif., 1982—85; chef Maxwell's Plum, NYC, 1985—89; co-owner, chef Campanile, LA, 1989—, La Brea Bakery, LA, 1989—. Author (with Nancy Silverton): Mark Peel and Nancy Silverton at Home, Two Chefs Cook for Family and Friends, The Food of Campanile. Named Restaurateur of Yr., So. Calif. Restaurant Writers, 1995, Chef of Yr., Calif. Restaurant Assn., 2005; named one of Best New Chefs, Food & Wine Mag., 1990; nominee Best Am. Chef, Calif., James Beard Found., 1990, 1995, 1996, 2001, 2002, 2004. Office: Campanile 624 S La Brea Ave Los Angeles CA 90036

PEELER, STUART THORNE, oil industry executive, consultant; b. Los Angeles, Oct. 28, 1929; s. Joseph David and Elizabeth Fiske (Boggess) P.; m. Sylvia Frances Townley, Nov. 5, 1985. BA, Stanford U., 1950, JD, 1953. Bar: Calif. 1953. Ptnr. Musick, Peeler & Garrett, LA, 1958-73; with Santa Fe Internat. Corp., Orange, Calif., 1973-81, v.p., sec., assoc. gen. counsel, 1973-74, sr. v.p., gen. counsel, dir., 1975-81; vice-chmn. bd., chmn. exec. com. Supron Energy Corp., 1978-82; chmn. bd., CEO Statex Petroleum, Inc., 1982-89; chmn., pres., CEO Putumayo Prodn. Co., Tucson, 1989—. Bd. dirs. Chieftain Internat. Inc. Trustee J. Paul Getty Trust, 1963-99; mem. U.S. Tuna Team, 1957-67, capt., 1966. Served with U.S. Army, 1953-55. Decorated Army Commendation medal. Mem. AIME, State Bar Calif., Am. Judicature Soc., Theta Chi, Phi Delta Phi, Skyline Country Club. Republican. Congregationalist. Office: PO Box 35852 Tucson AZ 85740-5852 Office Phone: 520-575-0709. Office Fax: 520-544-0632.

PEER, LARRY HOWARD, literature educator; b. Ogden, Utah, Jan. 2, 1942; s. Howard Harvey and Edna Celina (Baron) P.; m. Janet Priday; 9 children. BA, Brigham Young U., 1963, MA, 1965; PhD, U. Md., 1969. From asst. to assoc. prof. U. Ga., Athens, 1968-75; assoc. prof. Brigham Young U., Provo, Utah, 1975-78, prof., 1978—. Acting head dept. comparative lit. U. Ga., Athens, 1973-74, Brigham Young U., Provo, 1978-81; pres. Western Regional Honors Coun., 1978-79; exec. dir. Am. Conf. on Romanticism, 1992—. Author: Beyond Haworth, 1984, The Reasonable Romantic, 1986, The Romantic Manifesto, 1988. Mem. MLA, Am. Comparative Lit. Assn. (exec. officer 1988-94), Am. Soc. for Aesthetics, Rocky Mountain Soc. for Aesthetics (pres. 1986-87), Internat. Byron Soc., Internat. Brontë Soc. Mem. Lds Ch. Avocation: travel. Office: Brigham Young U Comparative Lit Dept Provo UT 84602

PEET, AMANDA, actress; b. NYC, Jan. 11, 1972; d. Charles and Penny Peet; m. David Benioff, Sept. 30, 2006; 1 child, Frances Pen. BA in History, Columbia U., 1994. Actor: (films) Animal Room, 1995, Winterlude, 1996, She's the One, 1996, Virginity, 1996, Grind, 1997, Touch Me, 1997, One Fine Day, 1996, Sax and Violins, 1997, 1999, 1998, Southie, 1998, Playing by Heart, 1998, Origin of the Species, 1998, Simply Irresistible, 1999, Jump, 1999, Two Ninas, 1999, Body Shots, 1999, Isn't She Great?, 2000, The Whole Nine Yards, 2000, Takedown, 2000, Whipped, 2000, Saving Silverman, 2001, High Crimes, 2002, Changing Lanes, 2002, Igby Goes Down, 2002, Whatever We Do, 2003, Identity, 2003, Something's Gotta Give, 2003, The Whole Ten Yards, 2004, Melinda and Melinda, 2004, A Lot Like Love, 2005, Syriana, 2005, Griffin and Phoenix, 2006, The Ex, 2007, Martian Child, 2007, The X-Files: I Want to Believe, 2008, What Doesn't Kill You, 2008; (TV films) Ellen Foster, 1997, Date Squad, 2001; (TV series) Central Park West, 1995—96, Jack & Jill, 1999—2001, Partners, 1999, Studio 60 on the Sunset Strip, 2006—07, (TV appearances) Law & Order, 1995, The Single Guy, 1996, Spin City, 1997, Seinfeld, 1997; (plays) Whale Music, Winter Lies, 27

Sketches: Fear and Misery in the Third Reich, The Country Club, This Is How It Goes, 2005, Escape: 6 Ways to Get Away, 2005, Barefoot in the Park, 2006. Office: The Gersh Agy Ste 201 232 N Canon Dr Beverly Hills CA 90210

PEETS, TERRY R., retail executive; Chmn. bd. dirs. Bruno's Supermarkets, Inc., Birmingham, Ala., 1999—. Office: Brunos Supermarkets Inc 327 Coral Ave Newport Beach CA 92662

PELLEGRINI, ROBERT J., psychology educator; b. Worcester, Mass., Oct. 21, 1941; s. Felix and Teresa (Di Muro) P.; 1 child, Robert Jerome. BA in Psychology, Clark U., 1963; MA in Psychology, U. Denver, 1966, PhD in Social Psychology, 1968. Prof. San Jose (Calif.) State U., 1967—. Rsch. assoc. U. Calif., Santa Cruz, 1989-90; pres. Western Inst. for Human Devel., San Jose, 1985—. Author: Psychology for Correctional Education, Bringing Psychology to Life; contbr. articles to profl. jours. Recipient Warburton award for scholarly excellence, 1995, Disting. Tchr. of Yr. award Western Psychol. Assn., 1996. Mem. Phi Beta Kappa. Office: San Jose State U Dept Psychology 1 Washington Sq San Jose CA 95192-0001

PELOSI, NANCY PATRICIA, United States Representative from California; b. Balt., Mar. 26, 1940; d. Thomas J. D'Alesandro Jr. and Annunciata M. Lombardi; m. Paul Pelosi, 1963; children: Nancy Corinne, Christine, Jacqueline, Paul, Alexandra. AB in Polit. Sci., Trinity Coll., 1962. Chair No. Calif. Dem. Party, 1977—81; chmn. Calif. State Dem. Com., 1981—83; committeewoman Dem. Nat. Com., 1976, 1980, 1984; fin. chmn. Dem. Senatorial Campaign Com., 1987; mem. US Congress from 5th Calif. Dist., 1987-93, 1987—; asst. minority leader (minority whip), 2002—03; minority leader, 2003—07; spkr. of the House, 2007—. Co-author (with Amy Hill Hearth): Know Your Power: A Message to America's Daughters, 2008. Recipient Pub. Svc. award, Fedn. Am. Societies for Experimental Biology, 1997, Congl. Svc. award, Am. Coun. for Voluntary Internat. Action, 1999, Alan Cranston Peace award, Global Security Inst., 2003, Legacy award, Cesar E. Chavez Found., 2003, Nat. Legis. award, League of United Latin Am. Citizens, 2004, Golden Plate award, Acad. Achievement, 2006; named Barbara Walters Most Fascinating Person of 2006; named one of The 100 Most Powerful Women, Forbes mag., 2005—08, The World's Most Influential People, TIME mag., 2007, America's Best Leaders, US News & World Report, 2007, The 50 Most Powerful People in DC, GQ mag., 2007, The Global Elite, Newsweek mag., 2008. Democrat. Achievements include being the first woman in US history to be elected Speaker of the House, 2006. Office: US Congress 2371 Rayburn Ho Office Bldg Washington DC 20515-0508 also: 450 Golden Gate Ave 14th Fl San Francisco CA 94102

PELOTTE, DONALD EDMOND, bishop; b. Waterville, Maine, Apr. 13, 1945; s. Norris Albert and Margaret Yvonne (LaBrie) P. AA, Eymard Sem. and Jr. Coll., Hyde Park, NY, 1965; BA, John Carroll U., 1969; MA, Fordham U., 1971, PhD, 1975. Ordained priest Congregation of the Blessed Sacrament, 1972; provincial superior Blessed Sacrament, Cleve., from 1978; ordained bishop, 1986; coadjutor bishop Diocese of Gallup, N.Mex., 1986-90, bishop N.Mex., 1990—. Nat. bd. dirs. Maj. Superiors of Men, Silver Spring, Md., 1981-86, Tekakwitha Conf., Great Falls, Mont., 1981—. Author: John Courtney Murray: Theologian in Conflict, 1976. 1st native Am. bishop. Mem. Cath. Theol. Soc. Am., Am. Cath. Hist. Soc. Roman Catholic.

PELTASON, JACK WALTER, retired academic administrator; b. St. Louis, Aug. 29, 1923; s. Walter B. and Emma (Hartman) P.; m. Suzanne Toll, Dec. 21,1946; children: Nancy Hartman, Timothy Walter H., Jill K. BA, U. Mo., 1943, MA, 1944, LLD (hon.), 1978; AM, Princeton U., 1946, PhD, 1947; LLD (hon.), U. Md., 1979, Ill. Coll., 1979, Gannon U., 1980, U. Maine, 1980, Union Coll., 1981, Moorehead State U., ND, 1980; LHD (hon.), 1980, Ohio State U., 1980, Mont. Coll. Mineral Scis. and Tech., 1982, Buena Vista Coll., 1982, Assumption Coll., 1983, Chapman Coll., 1986, U. Ill., 1989. Asst. prof. Smith Coll., Mass., 1947-51; asst. prof. polit. sci. U. Ill., Urbana, 1951-52, assoc. prof., 1953-59, dean Coll. Liberal Arts and Scis., 1960-64, chancellor, 1967-77; vice chancellor acad. affairs U. Calif., Irvine, 1964-67, chancellor, 1984-92; pres. U. Calif. System, Oakland, 1992-95, Am. Coun. Edn., Washington, 1977-84; prof. emeritus dept. politics and soc. U. Calif., Irvine, 1995—2003; pres. Bren Found., 1997—2003; ret., 2003. Cons. Mass. Little Hoover Commn., 1950 Author: The Missouri Plan for the Selection of Judges, 1947, Federal Courts and the Political Process, 1957, Fifty-eight Lonely Men, 1961, Understanding the Constitution, 15th edit., 2000, orig. edition, 1949, (with James M. Burns) Government By the People, 1952, 20th edit., 2003; contbr. articles and revs. to profl. jours. Recipient James Madison medal Princeton U., 1982 Fellow Am. Acad. Arts and Scis.; mem. Am. Polit. Sci. Assn. (coun. 1952-54), Phi Beta Kappa, Phi Kappa Phi, Omicron Delta Kappa, Alpha Phi Omega, Beta Gamma Sigma. Home: 18 Whistler Ct Irvine CA 92612-4069 Office: U Calif Dept Politics & Society Social Sci Plz Irvine CA 92697-0001 E-mail: jwpeltas@uci.edu.

PELTON, HAROLD MARCEL, mortgage broker; b. Montreal, Que., Can., Jan. 24, 1922; s. Grover Cleveland and Denise (Pigeon) P.; m. Frances Farley, June 1947 (div. 1968); children: Mary Virginia Joyner, Diane Jean Slagowski; m. Virginia L. King, July 11, 1970. Student, L.A. City Coll., 1948-49, Anthony Schs., Van Nuys, Calif., 1966. Lic. real estate real broker, Calif. Stockbroker, agt. Mitchum, Jones, Templeton Assurance Co., LA, 1957-60; owner Assurance Investment Co., Van Nuys, Calif., 1960-65; sales syndicator TSI Investment Co., LA, 1965-69; pres., owner Univest Co., Beverly Hills, Calif., 1970-72, Am. Oil Recovery, LA, 1973-79; v.p. Newport Pacific Funding Co., Newport Beach, Calif., 1979-81; chmn. bd. dirs. TD Publs., El Toro, Calif., 1981-83; pres., broker HP Fin., Inc., Laguna Hills, Calif., 1983--. Contbg. editor Am. Oil Recovery newspaper, 1973-79; editor Trust Deed Jour., 1981-83. Served with U.S. Army, 1942-46, PTO. Mem. L. A. Mus. Art, Laguna Hills C. of C., Kiwanis, Toastmasters. Republican. Avocations: photography, travel, reading, computers. Office: HP Fin Inc 24942 Georgia Sue Laguna Hills CA 92653-4323

PELTON, M. LEE, academic administrator; B magna cum laude, Wichita U., 1974; D, Harvard U., 1984. Tchg. fellow, English instr. Harvard U., 1980—86; sr. tutor Winthrop Ho., 1986; dean of student to dean of coll. Colgate U., 1986—91; dean of coll., adj. prof. Dartmouth Coll., 1991—98; pres. Willamette U., 1998—. Mem. bd. Oregon Ind. Coll. Fund, 1998—, Oregon Ind. Coll. Assn., 1998—; bd. overseers Harvard U., 2000; mem. Commn. on Minorities in Higher Edn., 2000—02. Mem.: Governor's Commn. on Financing Higher Edn. (Ore.), President's Coun. of Nat. Collegiate Athletic Assn. (Div. III), Nat. Assn. of Ind. Colleges and Universities (com. on policy analysis and pub. rels. 2000—03), Am. Coun. on Edn., Am. Assn. of Higher Edn. Office: Willamette U Office of Pres 900 State St Salem OR 97301 Office Phone: 503-370-6300, 503-370-6209. E-mail: president@willamette.edu.

PEÑA, AMADO MAURILIO, JR., artist, curator, lecturer; b. Laredo, Tex., Oct. 1, 1943; s. Amado Maurilio and Maria Baldomera (Arambula) Peña; children: Marcos, Jose Luis, Amado Maurilio III. BA, Tex. A&I U., Kingsville, 1965, MA in Art, 1971. Tchr. Laredo Ind. Sch. Dist., 1965—70, Tex. A&I U., Kingsville, 1970—72, Crystal City Ind. Sch. Dist., Tex., 1972—74, Austin Ind. Sch. Dist., Tex., 1974—80; resident artist El Taller, Inc., Austin, 1985—. One-man shows include Squash Blossom, Denver, 1985, Lincoln Sq. Gallery, Arlington, Tex., 1985, Galeria Capistrano, San Juan Capistrano, Calif., 1985, Andrews Gallery, Albuquerque, 1985, Joy Tash Gallery, Scottsdale, Ariz., 1985, Byrne-Getz Gallery, Aspen, Colo., 1985, Parke Gallery, Vail, Colo., 1985, Am. West Gallery, Chgo., 1985, Adagio Gallery, Palm Springs, Calif., 1985, Houshang's Gallery, Dallas, 1985, Mus. Native Am. Art, Spokane, Wash., 1985, El Taller, Taos, N.Mex., 1985, Austin, 1985, Kauffman Gallery, Houston, 1985, Peña Studio Gallery, Santa Fe, Represented in permanent collections Palacio del Gobernador, Baja California, Mex., Hist. Creative Arts Ctr., Lufkin, Tex., Mus. Nuevo Santander, Laredo, Smithsonian Inst., Washington, Whitney Mus., San Antonio, various corps., univs. and pvt. collections. Comdr. civic and arts orgns. for fund-raising events and spl. presentations. Avocation: horseback riding. Office: Peña Studio Gallery 235 Don Gaspar Santa Fe NM 87501 Office Phone: 505-820-2286. Business E-Mail: penastudios@earthlink.net.

PENDERGHAST, THOMAS FREDERICK, business educator; b. Cin., Apr. 23, 1936; s. Elmer T. and Dolores C. (Huber) P.; m. Marjorie Craig, Aug. 12, 1983; children: Brian, Shawna, Steven, Dean, Maria. BS, Marquette U., Milw., 1958; MBA, Calif. State U., Long Beach, 1967; D in Bus. Adminstrn., Nova U., Ft. Lauderdale, Fla., 1987. Cert. in data processing. Sci. programmer Autonetics, Inc., Anaheim, Calif., 1960-64; bus. programmer Douglas Missile & Space Ctr., Huntington Beach, Calif., 1964-66; computer specialist N.Am. Rockwell Co., Huntington Beach, Calif., 1966-69; asst. prof. Calif. State U., Huntington Beach, Calif., 1969-72; prof. Sch. Bus. and Mgmt. Pepperdine U., Malibu, 1972—2002; spl. adviser Commn. on Engring. Edn., 1968; v.p. Visual Computing Co., 1969-71; founder, pres. Scoreboard Animation Systems, 1971-77; exec. v.p. Microfilm Identification Systems, 1977-79; pres. Data Processing Auditors, Inc., 1981—; prof. Grad. Sch. Edn. and Psychology Pepperdine U., Malibu, 2002—. Mem. Orange County Blue Ribbon Com. on Data Processing, 1973; mem. Orange County TEC Policy Bd., 1982-87; cons. in field. Author: Entrepreneurial Simulation Program, 1988, Journey to Couples' Conflict Resolution Using Game Theory, 1999. Served to lt. USNR, 1958-60. Mem. Users of Automatic Info. Display Equipment (pres. 1966). Home: 17867 Bay St Fountain Valley CA 92708-4443 Personal E-mail: tom@penderghast.com.

PENDLETON, OTHNIEL ALSOP, fundraiser, clergyman; b. Washington, Aug. 22, 1911; s. Othniel Alsop and Ingeborg (Berg) P.; m. Flordora Mellquist, May 15, 1935; children: John, James (dec.), Thomas, Ann, Susan. AB, Union Coll., Schenectady, NY, 1933; BD, Eastern Bapt. Theol. Sem., 1936; MA, U. Pa., 1936, PhD, 1945; postgrad., Columbia U., 1937-38. Ordained to ministry Bapt. Ch., 1936. Pastor chs., Jersey City, 1935-39, Phila., 1939-43; dean Sioux Falls Coll., S.D., 1943-45; fund raiser Am. Bapt. Ch., NYC, 1945-47; fund-raiser Mass. Bapt. Ch., Boston, 1947-54, Seattle, Chgo., Boston, Washington, NYC and Paris, France, 1955-64, Westwood, Mass., 1971-84; staff mem. Marts & Lundy, Inc., NYC, 1964-71. Lectr. Andover-Newton (Mass.) Sem., 1958, Boston U. Sch. Theology, 1958, Harvard U., Cambridge, Mass., 1977-84; cons. Grant MacEwan Coll., Edmonton, Alta., Can. Author: New Techniques for Church Fund Raising, 1955, Fund Raising: A Guide to Non-Profit Organizations, 1981; contbr. articles in field to profl. jours. Home: 389 Belmont St Apt 311 Oakland CA 94610-4870

PENG, STANFORD LEE-YU, physician; s. Syd and Felicia Peng; m. Andrea Jeanne Gerth, Sept. 8, 2001; children: Avery, Charlotte. PhD, Yale U., New Haven, Conn., 1991—96, MD, 1991—97. Cert. in internal medicine ACP, 2000, in rheumatology ACP, 2002, diplomate Am. Bd. Internal Medicine, Am. Bd. Rheumatology. Intern Hosp. U. Pa., Phila., 1997—98, resident in internal medicine, 1998—99; rsch. assoc. immunology and infectious diseases Harvard U. Sch. Pub. Health, Boston, 2002; clin. rsch. fellow in rheumatology Brigham and Women's Hosp., Boston, 1999—2002; asst. prof. Wash. U. Sch. Medicine, St. Louis, 2002—05; clin. asst. prof. U Calif., San Francisco, 2005—. Group leader Roche, Palo Alto, 2005, dir. arthritis rsch., 2005—07, sr. dir. translational med. leader, rheumatology, 2007—. Recipient Arthritis Investigator, Arthritis Found., 2003; named Keck Disting. Young Scholar, 2005. Mem.: Am. Assn. Immunologists, Am. Coll. Rheumatology. Office: 3431 Hillview Ave M/S A2-209 Palo Alto CA 94304 Business E-Mail: stanford.peng@roche.com.

PENHOET, EDWARD E., retired foundation administrator, former biochemicals company executive, former dean; b. Oakland, Calif., Dec. 11, 1940; AB in Biology, Stanford U., 1963; PhD in Biochem., U. Wash., 1968. Prof. biochem. U. Calif., Berkeley, 1971—81; co-founder, CEO Chiron Corp., 1981—98; dean Sch. Pub. Health U. Calif., Berkeley, 1998—2002, dean emeritus, 2002—; sr. dir., Sci. & Higher Education Gordon and Betty Moore Found., 2002—04, pres., 2004—08, bd. trustees. Bd. dirs., sr. adv. to CEO Chiron Corp. Recipient Outstanding Philanthropist award, Assn. of Fundraising Professionals, No. Calif. Entrepreneur of the Yr. award, Ernst & Young and Inc. Mag. Mem.: Am. Soc. of Biological Chemists, Nat. Acad. of Sci., Inst. Medicine. Office: Chiron Corp 4560 Horton St Emeryville CA 94608-2900 also: Gordon and Betty Moore Found Presidio of San Francisco 1661 Page Mill Rd Palo Alto CA 94304-1209

PENIKETT, TONY, mediator, negotiator, writer; b. Nov. 14, 1945; s. Erik John Keith and Sarah Ann (Colwell) P.; m. Lula Mary Johns, 1974 (div. 1997); children— John Tahmoh, Sarah Lahlil, Stephanie Yahsan Exec. asst. to nat. leader New Dem. Party, Ottawa, Ont., Canada, 1975-76, nat. pres., 1981-85, fed. councillor, 1973—, leader Whitehorse, Y.T., Canada, 1980—, campaign mgr. N.W.T., Canada, 1972; alderman City of Whitehorse, Y.T., Canada, 1977-79; elected mem. Yukon Legis. Assembly, 1978-95, opposition leader Y.T., Canada, 1982-85, 92-95, elected premier Yukon Terr., 1985-92; sr. policy advisor Govt. of Sask., 1995-97; dep. min. negotiations Ministry of Fin. and Corp. Rels., Govt. of B.C., Victoria, 1997-2000; dep. min. labor Ministry of Fin., Govt. of B.C., Victoria, 2000—01; propr. Tony Penikett Negotiations Inc., Vancouver, B.C., Canada, 2001—. Author (film): The Mad Trapper, 1972, La Patrouille Perdue, 1974, (books) Breaking Trail, 2004, Reconciliation: First Nations Treaty Making in British Columbia, 2006. Office: Tony Penikett Negotiations Inc 550 Beatty St Unit 7-8 Vancouver BC Canada V6B 2L3 Office Phone: 604-724-6720. E-mail: tony_penikett@telus.net.

PENLEY, LARRY EDWARD, academic administrator, finance educator; b. Bristol, Va., Feb. 9, 1949; s. William Edward and June (Caudill) P.; m. Yolanda Elva Sanchez, Nov. 25, 1977; children: Jonathan Andrew, Josephine Anna. BA, Wake Forest U., 1971, MA, 1972; PhD, U. Ga., 1976. Vis. prof. ITESM, Monterey, Mexico, 1977, Universidad de Carobobo, Valencia, Venezuela, 1978; assoc. dean U. Tex., San Antonio, 1980-85; prof., chmn. dept. Ariz. State U., Tempe, 1985—90, dean Coll. Bus., 1990—2003; pres. Colo. State U., 2003—; chancellor Colo. State U. Sys., 2003—. Contbr. articles to profl. jours. Mem. NCAA Task Force on Future of Athletics, Nat. Western Stock Show and Rodeo, Citizen of West Com.; mem. adv. counsel Group Ecole Superieure De Commerce de Toulouse, 1997; chmn. Assn. Advance Collegiate Sch. of Bus., 2000—01; bd. mem. dir. Greater Phoenix Econ. Coun., 1993—2003. Recipient Frank C. Carr Founders award, INROADS, 1997, Disting. Svc. award, Greater Phoenix Econ. Coun., 2002. Mem.: Assn. Advance Collegiate Schs. of Bus. (chmn. 2001—02), Rocky Mountain Bd., Inst. Internat. Edn., Mountain States Employers Coun. Bd., Greater Denver Metro Chamber Bd., Acad. Mgmt. (chmn. divsn. program 1986), Mountain West Conf. Bd., Colo. Inst. of Tech. Bd., Colo. Concern. Roman Catholic. Office: Colo State U Office of the Pres Fort Collins CO 80523-0100 Home: 4700 S Fulton Ranch Blvd Unit 75 Chandler AZ 85248-5037 Office Phone: 970-491-6211. E-mail: presofc@lamar.colostate.edu.

PENNER, STANFORD SOL, engineering educator; b. Unna, Germany, July 5, 1921; arrived in US, 1936, naturalized, 1943; s. Heinrich and Regina (Saal) P.; m. Beverly Preston, Dec. 28, 1942; children: Merilynn Jean, Robert Clark. BS, Union Coll., 1942; MS, U. Wis., 1943, PhD, 1946; Dr. rer. nat. (hon.), Technische Hochschule Aachen, Germany, 1981. Rsch. assoc. Allegany Ballistics Lab., Cumberland, Md., 1944-45; rsch. scientist Standard Oil Devel. Co., Esso Labs., Linden, NJ, 1946; sr. rsch. engr. Jet Propulsion Lab., Pasadena, Calif., 1947-50; mem. faculty Calif. Inst. Tech., 1950-63, prof. divsn. engring., jet propulsion, 1957-63; dir. rsch. and engring. divsn. Inst. Def. Analyses, Washington, 1962-64; prof. engring. physics, chmn. dept. aerospace and mech. engring. U. Calif., San Diego, 1964-68, vice chancellor for acad. affairs, 1968-69, dir. Inst. for Pure and Applied Phys. Scis., 1968-71, dir. Energy Ctr., 1973-91, disting. prof. engring. physics emeritus, 1991—. Bd. dirs. Optodyne Corp.; US mem. adv. group aero. rsch. and devel. NATO, 1952-68, chmn. combustion and propulsion panel, 1958-60; mem. adv. com. engring. scis. USAF-Office Sci. Rsch., 1961-65; mem. subcom. on combustion NACA, 1954-58; mem. rsch. adv. com. on air-breathing engines NASA, 1962-64; mem. coms. on gas dynamics and edn. Internat. Acad. Astronautics, 1969-80; nat. lectr. Sigma Xi, 1977-79; chmn. fossil energy rsch. working group Dept. Energy, 1978-82, chmn. advanced fuel cell commercialization working group, 1993-95; mem. assembly engring. NAE, 1978-82; chmn. NAS-NRC U.S. Nat. Com. IIASA, 1978-82; mem. commn. engring. tech. sys. NRC, 1982-84; spl. guest Internat. Coal Sci. Confs., 1983, 85, 87, 89, 91; mentor Def. Sci. Studies Group, 1985-93; chmn. studies mcpl. waste incineration NSF, 1988-89, Calif. Coun. Sci. Tech., 1992; pub. info. adv. com. Nat. Acad. Engring., 1994-98, Ind. Commn. on Environ. Edn., 1995-97, Environ. Literacy Coun., 1998-2005; sci. adv. bd., San Diego County, 1997—, chair, 2004-07. Author: Chemical Reactions in Flow Systems, 1955, Chemistry Problems in Jet Propulsion, 1957, Quantitative Molecular Spectroscopy and Gas Emissivities, 1959, Chemical Rocket Propulsion and Combustion Research, 1962, Thermodynamics, 1968, Radiation and Reentry, 1968; sr. author: Energy, Vol. I (Demands, Resources, Impact, Technology and Policy), 1974, 81, Energy, Vol. II (Non-nuclear Energy Technologies), 1975, 77, 84, Energy, Vol. III (Nuclear Energy and Energy Policies), 1976; editor: Chemistry of Propellants, 1960, Advanced Propulsion Techniques, 1961, Detonations and Two-Phase Flow, 1962, Combustion and Propulsion, 1963, Advances in Tactical Rocket Propulsion, 1968, In Situ Shale Oil Recovery, 1975, New Sources of Oil and Gas, 1982, Coal Combustion and Applications, 1984, Advanced Fuel Cells, 1986, Coal Gasification: Direct Applications and Syntheses of Chemicals and Fuels, 1987, CO2 Emissions and Climate Change, 1991, Commercialization of Fuel Cells, 1995, Advanced Nuclear Techs., 1998; assoc. editor Jour. Chem. Physics, 1953-56; founding editor Jour. Quantitative Spectroscopy and Radiative Transfer, 1960-92, Jour. Def. Rsch., 1963-67, Energy (The Internat. Jour.), 1975-98; sect. editor Energy and Power Systems, Ency. Phys. Sci. and Tech., 1998-2002. Recipient spl. award People-to-People Program, pub. svc. award U. Calif., San Diego, N. Manson medal Internat. Colloquia on Gasdynamics of Explosions and Reactive Systems, 1979, internat. Columbus award Internat. Inst. Comm., Genoa, Italy, 1981, disting. assoc. award US Dept. Energy, 1990, Edward Teller award for def. of freedom, 1997, Rockwell medal, 2003. Fellow Am. Phys. Soc., Optical Soc. Am., AAAS, NY Acad. Scis., AIAA (dir. 1964-66, past chmn. com., G. Edward Pendray award 1975, Thermophysics award 1983, Energy Systems award 1983), Am. Acad. Arts and Scis.; mem. NAE (Founders award, 2007), Internat. Acad. Astronautics, World Level Hall of Fame for Engring., Sci. and Tech., Am. Chem. Soc., Sigma Xi. Home: 5912 Avenida Chamnez La Jolla CA 92037-7402 Office: U Calif San Diego 9500 Gilman Dr La Jolla CA 92093-0411 Home Phone: 858-456-9421; Office Phone: 858-534-4284. Business E-Mail: spenner@ucsd.edu.

PENNIMAN, RICHARD WAYNE See LITTLE RICHARD

PENRY, JOSHUA P., state legislator; Mem. Dist. 54 Colo. House of Reps., Denver, 2004—06; mem. Dist. 7 Colo. State Senate, Denver, 2007—, minority leader. Republican. Office: Colo State Capitol 200 E Colfax Denver CO 80203 Office Phone: 303-866-3077. Business E-Mail: joshpenry@gmail.com.*

PENSKAR, MARK HOWARD, lawyer; b. Detroit, Mar. 4, 1953; s. Sol Leonard and Frances (Rosenthal) P.; m. Carol Ann Stewart, Aug. 7, 1977; children: David, Rebecca. BA, U. Mich., 1974, M in Pub. Policy, 1975, JD cum laude, 1977. Bar: Calif. 1977, U.S. Dist. Ct. (no. dist.) Calif. 1977, U.S. Dist. Ct. (ea. and ctrl. dists.) Calif. 1983, U.S. Dist. Ct. (so. dist.) Calif. 1988, U.S. Ct. Appeals (9th cir.) 1987, U.S. Tax Ct. 1993. Assoc. Pillsbury, Madison and Sutro, San Francisco, 1977-84, ptnr., 1985-96; sr. bus. litig. atty. Pacific Gas and Electric Co., San Francisco, 1996—, dir. and counsel, 2006—. Mediator Superior Ct. early settlement program, San Francisco; mediator and early neutral evaluator U.S. Dist. Ct. Alternative Dispute Resolution Program; bd. dirs. Legal Aid Soc. of San Francisco Employment Law

Ctr. Mem. ABA, San Francisco Bar Assn., Commonwealth Club, Phi Gamma Delta (past pres. Bay Area grad. chpt.). Avocations: camping, golf, wine collecting, fishing. Home: 29 E Altarinda Dr Orinda CA 94563-2415 Office: Pacific Gas & Electric Co Law Dept B30A PO Box 7442 San Francisco CA 94120-7442 E-mail: MHP5@pge.com.

PENZIAS, ARNO ALLAN, astrophysicist, information scientist, researcher; b. Munich, Apr. 26, 1933; arrived in U.S., 1940, naturalized, 1946; s. Karl and Justine (Eisenreich) Penzias; m. Sherry Chamove Levit, Aug. 2, 1996; children: David Simon, Mindy Gail, Laurie Shifra. BS in Physics, CCNY, 1954; MA in Physics, Columbia U., 1958, PhD in Physics, 1962; DHC (hon.), Observatoire de Paris, 1976; ScD (hon.), Rutgers U., 1979, Wilkes Coll., 1979, CCNY, 1979, Yeshiva U., 1979, Bar-Ilan U., 1983, Monmouth Coll., 1984, Technion-Israel Inst. Tech., 1986, U. Pitts., 1986, Ball State U., 1986, Kean Coll., 1986, U. Pa., 1992, Ohio State U., 1988, Iona Coll., 1988, Drew U., 1989, Lafayette Coll., 1990, Columbia U., 1990, George Wash. U., 1992, Rensselaer Univ., 1992, U. Pa., 1992, Bloomfield Coll., 1994, Rankin Tech. U., 1997, Hebrew Union Coll., 1997, Oxford U., 2002. Mem. tech. staff Bell Labs., Holmdel, NJ, 1961—72, head radiophysics rsch. dept., 1972—76, dir. radio rsch. lab., 1976—79, exec. dir. rsch., comm. scis. div., 1979—81, v.p. rsch., 1981—85; v.p., chief scientist Lucent Technologies, 1995—98, sr. tech. adv., 1998—2000; venture ptnr. New Enterprise Assocs., 1998—. Sr. advisor New Enterprise Assocs., 1997—98; adj. prof. earth and scis. SUNY, Stony Brook, 1974—84, Univ. Disting. lectr., 1990; lectr. dept. astrophys. Scis. Princeton U., 1967—72, vis. prof., 1972—85; rsch. assoc. Harvard Coll. Obs., 1968—80; Edison lectr. US Naval Rsch. Lab., 1979; Kompfner lectr. Stanford U., 1979; Gamow lectr. U. Colo., 1980; Jansky lectr. Nat. Radio Astronomy Obs.1983, 1983; Michelson Meml. lectr., 85; Grace Adams Tanner lectr., 87; Klopsteg lectr. Northwestern U., 1987; grad. faculties alumni Columbia U., 1987—89; Regents' lectr. U. Calif., Berkeley, 1990; Lee Kuan Yew Disting. vis. Nat. U. Singapore, 1991; mem. astronomy adv. panel NSF, 1978—79, mem. indsl. panel on sci. and tech., 1982—92, disting. lectr., 1987; affiliate Max-Planck Inst. for Radioastronomy, 1978—85; chmn. Fachbeirat, 1981—83; rschr. in astrophysics, info. tech., its applications and impacts; bd. dirs. Konarka Techs., Glacier Bay, Inc., Bloom Energy Corp. Patentee auction-based selection of telecom. carriers, participant tracking in conf. call, computer-based transp. sys., fraud prevention in calling cards, identifying telephone extensions in residence environment, double-encrypted identity verification sys.; author: Ideas and Information Managing in a High-Tech World, 1989, Harmony-Business, Technology and Life After Paperwork, 1995; editl. bd. Ann. Rev. Astronomy and Astrophysics, 1974—78, AT&T Bell Labs. Tech. Jour., 1978—84, chmn., 1981—84, assoc. editor Astrophys. Jour., 1978—82, contbr. over 100 articles to tech. jours. Bd. overseers U. Pa. Sch. Engring. and Applied Sci., 1983—86; mem. vis. com. Calif. Inst. Tech., 1977—77; mem. Com. Concerned Scientists, 1975—, vice chmn., 1976; mem. adv. bd. Union of Couns. for Soviet Jews, 1983—95; bd. dirs. Coun. on Competitiveness, 1989—92; bd. trustees Trenton (N.J.) State Coll., 1977—79. With US Army, 1954—56. Recipient Herschel medal, Royal Astron. Soc., 1977, Nobel prize in Physics, 1978, Townsend Harris medal, CCNY, 1979, Newman award, 1983, Joseph Handleman prize in the scis., 1983, Grad. Faculties Alumni award, Columbia U., 1984, Achievement in Sci. award, Big Bros. Inc., N.Y.C., 1985, Priestly award, Dickinson Coll., 1989, Pender award, U. Pa., 1992, N.J. Sci. and Tech. medal, 1996, Internat. Eng. Cons. Fell. award, 1997, Indsl. Rsch. Inst. medal, 1998; named to N.J. Lit. Hall of Fame, 1991. Mem.: AAAS, NAS (Henry Draper medal 1977), IEEE (hon.), NAE, World Acad. Arts and Sci., Internat. Astron. Union, Am. Phys. Soc. (Pake prize 1990), Am. Astron. Soc. Office: New Enterprises Assocs 2855 Sand Hill Rd Menlo Park CA 94025-7022

PENZIEN, JOSEPH, structural engineering educator; b. Philip, SD, Nov. 27, 1924; s. John Chris and Ella (Stebbins) Penzien; m. Jeanne Ellen Hunson, Apr. 29, 1950 (dec. 1985); children: Robert Joseph, Karen Estelle, Donna Marie, Charlene May. Student, Coll. Idaho, 1942—43; BS, U. Wash., Seattle, 1945; ScD, MIT, Cambridge, Mass., 1950. Staff Sandia Corp., 1950—51; sr. structures engr. Consol. Vultee Aircraft Corp., Fort Worth, 1951—53; asst. prof. U. Calif. at Berkeley, 1953—57, assoc. prof., 1957—62, prof. structural engring., 1962—88, prof. emeritus, 1988—; dir. Earthquake Engring. Rsch. Ctr., 1968—73, 1977—80. Cons. engring. firms; chief tech. adv. Internat. Inst. of Seismology and Earthquake Engring., Tokyo, Japan, 1964-65; chmn. bd. Ea. Internat. Engrs., Inc., 1980-90, Internat. Civil Engring. Cons., Inc., 1990—2007, chmn. emeritus, ICEC Divsn. Paul C. Rizzo Assoc. Inc., 2007-. NATO Sr. Sci. fellow, 1969. Fellow Am. Acad. Mechanics; hon. mem. ASCE (Walter Huber Rsch. award, Alfred M. Freudenthal medal, Nathan M. Newmark medal, Ernest E. Howard award), Earthquake Engring. Rsch. Inst. (hon., dist. lectr. 2000, Hausner medal), IAEE (hon.), EERI (Alfred E. Alquist award, 1996, Dist. Lectr. 2000); Applied Tech. Coun. (Top Seismic Engr. 2006), Chinese Taiwan Soc. Earthquake Engring. (Hon. award 2006), mem. Am. Concrete Inst., Structural Engrs. Assn. Calif., Seismol. Soc. Am., Nat. Acad. Engring. Home: 800 Solana Dr Lafayette CA 94549-5004 Office: Paul C Rizzo Assoc Inc 2201 Broadway Oakland CA 94612-3017 Office Phone: 510-286-0214. E-mail: josephpenzien@yahoo.com.

PEOPLES, DONALD R., research scientist; b. 1939; Athletic dir. Butte (Mont.) Ctrl. High Sch., 1967-69; dir. info. and evaluation Butte Model Cities Program, 1969-70; dir. pub. works, model cities and cmty. devel. Butte, 1970-77; dir. pub. works dept. Butte-Silver Bow City-County Govt., 1977-79, CEO, 1979-89; with Mont. Tech. Cos., Butte, 1989—, now pres., CEO. Office: Montana Tech Companies 220 N Alaska St Butte MT 59701-9212

PEPE, STEPHEN PHILLIP, lawyer; b. Paterson, NJ, Oct. 30, 1943; s. Vincent Attilio and Emma (Opletal) P.; m. Catherine B. Hagen, Dec. 8, 1990. BA, Montclair State U., NJ, 1965; JD, Duke U., 1968. Bar: Calif. 1969, J.S. Dist. Ct. (no., so., ea. and cen. dists.) Calif. 1975, U.S. Ct. Appeals (9th cir.) 1975, U.S. Sup. Ct. 1978. Assoc. O'Melveny & Myers, LA, 1968-75, ptnr., 1976—, chmn. lab. and employment law dept., 1989-92. Co-author: Avoiding and Defending Wrongful Discharge Claims, 1987, Privacy in the Work Place, 1993, Corporate Compliance Series: Designing an Effective Fair Hiring and Termination Compliance Program, 1993, The Law of Libel & Slander, 1994; co-editor: Guide to Acquiring and Managing a U.S. Business, 1992, Calif. Employment Law Letter, 1990-94. Bd. visitors Duke Law Sch., 1992-96; bd. trustees Montclair State U. Found., 1991; bd. govs. Coll. of Labor and Employment Law, 1996—, pres., 2000—; pres. Inst. Indsl. Rels. Assn., 1989-91; bd. advisors UCLA Sch. Medicine, 2001--. With USAR, 1969-75. Fellow Coll. of Labor and Employment Law, 1996—. Mem. Am. Hosp. Assn. (labor adv. com. 1975-90), The Employers Group (bd. dirs., chmn. legal com. 1989-93), Calif. Club (chmn. employee rels. com. 1980—). Democrat. Roman Catholic. Avocations: wine collecting, winemaking, vineyard owner. Office: O Melveny & Myers 610 Newport Center Dr Newport Beach CA 92660-6419

PEPICELLO, WILLIAM J., academic administrator; b. Erie, Pa., 1949; B in Classics, Gannon U.; M in Linguistics, PhD in Linguistics, Brown U. Faculty position U. Del., U. Pacific, Temple U., chair, classics dept.; regional dean Southern Calif., Nat. U.; dean, coll. gen. and profl. studies U. Phoenix, 1995—2000, v.p., academic affairs, 1995, dean, sch. adv. studies, 2002—03, vice provost, academic affairs, 2003—06, provost, 2006, acting pres., 2006, pres., 2006—, U. Sarasota, 2000—02. Commr. Ariz. Comm. Postsecondary Edn. Office: University of Phoenix 4615 E Elwood St Phoenix AZ 85040

PEPPER, DAVID M., scientist, educator; s. Harold and Edith Pepper; m. Denise D. Pepper, 1992. BS in Physics summa cum laude, UCLA, 1971; MS in Applied Physics, Calif. Inst. Tech., 1974, PhD in Applied Physics, 1980. Mem. tech. staff Hughes Rsch. Labs., Malibu, Calif., 1973—87, sr. staff physicist, 1987—91, head nonlinear and electro-optic devices sect., 1989—91, sr. scientist, 1991—94; sr. rsch. scientist HRL Labs. (formerly Hughes Rsch. Labs.), Malibu, 1994—2004; owner, tech. cons., scientist Malibu Sci. and Malibu Photonics, 2004—. Adj. prof. math. and physics Pepperdine U., Malibu, 1981—; adv. panel NSF, Washington, 1997; panel advanced signal processing U. Va., 1999; mem. Def. Sci. Rsch. Coun., US Govt., Washington, 1999; panel invitee US Govt. Jason, 2008; presenter in field. Author: Scientific American, 1986, 1990, Laser Handbook, Vol. 4, 1985; co-author: Optical Phase Conjugation, 1983, 1995, Spatial Light Modulator Technology, 1995, CRC Handbook of Laser Science and Technology, 1995; contbr. articles to profl. jours. Mem. Sons and Daughters of 1939 Club, 2d Generation of Martyrs Meml., Mus. Holocaust Recipient Rudolf Kingslake award Soc. Photo-Optical Instrumentation Engrs., 1982, Publ. of Yr. award Hughes Rsch. Lab., 1986, Inventor of Yr. award, 1997-2007, HRL Labs.; NSF trainee Calif. Inst. Tech., 1971; Howard Hughes fellow Hughes Aircraft Co., 1973-80 Fellow Optical Soc. Am. (conf. chair 1996-2001, adv. bd. topical conf. on nonlinear optics, Hawaii 1996, 98, 2000, invited tutorial meeting laser ultrasound 2001, Top 10 cited Paper award); mem. AAAS, IEEE (guest editor, assoc. editor, program com. US CLEO laser conf. 1997-2001, 2005, instr. laser tech. 1994-2000, invited tutorial laser tech. 2001, European CLEO laser conf. program com. 2003), SPIE (guest editor, conf. co-chmn. 1998-2000), NY Acad. Scis., Am. Phys. Soc., Laser Inst. Am., Internat. Coun. Sci. Unions (com. sci. and tech. in developing countries), Sigma Xi (v.p. 1986-87, chpt. pres. 1987-88, 90-92), Sigma Pi Sigma Jewish. Achievements include 59 patents in field; 12 patents pending in field. Avocations: classical music, travel, sports, astronomy, amateur radio. Office: Malibu Scientific P O Box 126 Malibu CA 90265-0126 Personal E-mail: dmpepper@charter.net.

PERA, RENEE REIJO, biology professor; BS, U. Wis., 1983; PhD, Cornell U., 1993; postdoc., Whitehead Inst. Biomed. Rsch. MIT, 1997. Damon-Runyan fellow Whitehead Inst. Biomed. Rsch. MIT, 1993—97, instr. biology, 1995; asst. prof. in residence U. Calif., San Francisco, 1997—2003, assoc. prof. in residence, 2003—, co-dir. program in human stem cell biology, 2004—, assoc. dir. ctr. reproductive scis., 2004—. Spkr. in field. Contbr. articles to profl. jours. Office: USCF 513 Parnassus Ave Rm HSE 1636 Box 0556 San Francisco CA 94143-0556 Office Phone: 415-476-3178. Office Fax: 415-476-3121.

PERACCA, ALAIN, computer software company executive; b. France; Grad., Ecole Superiere d'Ingenieurs, Marseille, 1980; MBA, Columbia U., 1985. Data processing mgr. Ministry Pub. Health, Doha, Qatar, 1980—84; with Hewlett-Packard, Geneva, 1985—93, contr. mfg. & devel. ops. Bergamo, Italy, 1993, fin. & adminstrv. dir., 1993—96, worldwide contr. Comml. Channel orgn. Calif., 1996, contr. Home PC divsn., CFO of PC & Appliance bus., contr. mobility & emerging technologies, 2002—03; CFO of Windows Client orgn. Microsoft Corp., 2003—06, corp. v.p. of Audit, 2006—. Mem.: Fin. Executives Internat. Assn. Office: Microsoft Corp Audit 1 Microsoft Way Redmond WA 98052-6399

PERCY, HELEN SYLVIA, physician; b. Atlanta, May 7, 1923; d. George L. and Sophia (Toulchin) P.; 1 child, Valentina Stewart-Wajjon. BS, U. San Francisco, 1951; MD, Med. Coll. Pa., 1958. Intern Harbor Gen. Hosp., Torrance, Calif., 1958-59, resident, 1959; physician Maui Med. Group, Lahaina, Hawaii, 1968—; asst. prof. medicine U. Hawaii, Honolulu, 1978—2000. Adv. bd. Maui Community Health Ctr., 1986-89; v.p. Maui AIDS Found., 1986-89. Mem. AMA, Maui County Med. Soc. (pres. 1988-1989), Hawaii Med. Assn. (Maui councilor). Democrat. Buddhist. Avocation: dance. Office: Maui Med Group 130 Prison St Lahaina HI 96761-1247 Office Phone: 808-661-0051.

PERENCHIO, ANDREW JERROLD, film and television executive; b. Fresno, Calif., Dec. 20, 1930; s. Andrew Joseph and Dorothea (Harvey) P.; m. Robin Green, July 16, 1954 (div.); children: Candace L., Catherine M., John Gardner; m. Jacquelyn Claire, Nov. 14, 1969 (div.); m. Margaret McHugh, 1987. BS, UCLA, 1954. V.p. Music Corp. Am., 1958-62, Gen. Artists Corp., 1962-64; pres., owner theatrical agy. Chartwell Artists, Ltd., LA, from 1964; chmn. bd. Tandem Prodns., Inc. and TAT Communications Co., LA, 1973-83; pres., CEO Embassy Pictures, LA, 1983—85; pres. Chartwell Partnerships Group, LA; chmn., CEO Univision Communications, 1992—2007. Promoter Muhammad Ali-Joe Frazier heavyweight fight, 1971, Bobby Riggs-Billie Jean King tennis match, 1973. Nat co-finance dir. McCain Presdl. Campaign, 2008. Served to 1st lt. USAF, 1954-57. Named one of Richest Americans, Forbes Mag., 1999—, World's Richest People, 2001—, 25 Most Influential Republicans, Newsmax Mag., 2008. Mem.: Bel-Air Country Club (LA); Westchester Country Club, NY; Friars Club, NYC.*

PEREZ, JOHN A, state legislator; Apptd. by three mayors to LA. City Commn.; mem. Dist. 46 Calif. State Assembly, 2008—, Dem. caucus chair. Apptd. to serve on a Blue Ribbon panel studying state initiative reform.; former mem. President's Adv. Coun. on HIV & AIDS; elected mem. Dem. Nat. Com.; former bd. mem. Calif. League of Conservation Voters, AIDS Project LA, Calif. Ctr. for Regional Leadership, LA Econ. Develop. Corp. Democrat. Office: PO Box 942849 Rm 3160 Sacramento CA 94249-0046 also: 320 W 4th St Rm 1050 Los Angeles CA 90013 Office Phone: 916-319-2046, 213-620-4646. Office Fax: 213-620-6319, 213-620-6319. E-mail: Assemblymember.John.Perez@assembly.ca.gov.*

PEREZ, MANUEL V., state legislator; b. Indio, CA; m. Gladis Perez. BA, U Calif., Riverside; EdM in Edn., Harvard U. Sch. tchr.; mem. Coachella Valley sch. bd., Coachella, Calif.; cmty. healthcare dir.; mem. Dist. 80 Calif. State Assembly, Calif., 2008—. Trustee Coachella sch. bd., Coachella, Calif. Democrat. Office: State Capital Room 4162 PO Box 942849 Sacramento CA 94249 also: 45-677 Oasis St Indio CA 92201 also: Imperial Valley Office 1450 South Imperial Ave El Centro CA 92243 Office Phone: 760-342-8047, 916-319-2080, 760-336-8912. Office Fax: 760-347-8704, 916-319-2180, 760-336-8914. E-mail: Assemblymember.Manuel.Perez@assembly.ca.gov.*

PEREZ, ROSIE, actress; b. Bklyn., Sept. 6, 1964; d. Ismael Serrano and Lydia Perez. Actor: (TV) 21 Jump Street, WIOU, Rosie Perez Presents Society's Ride, 1993, Happily Ever After: Fairy Tales for Every Child, 1995, House of Buggin, 1995, One World Jame, 2002, Copshop, 2004, Lackawanna Blues, 2005, Lolo's Cafe, 2006, (films) Do the Right Thing, 1989, White Men Can't Jump, 1992, Night on Earth, 1992, Untamed Heart, 1993, Fearless, 1993 (Acad. award nom. Best Supporting Actress 1994), It Could Happen To You, 1994, Somebody to Love, 1995, A Brother's Kiss, 1997, Perdita Durango, 1997, 24-Hour Woman, 1998, Louis and Frank, 1998, The Road to El Dorado, 2000, King of the Jungle, 2000, Human Nature, 2001, Riding in Cars with Boys, 2001, Exactly, 2004, Jesus Children of America, 2005, All the Invisible Children, 2005, Just Like the Sun, 2006, The Take, 2007, Pineapple Express, 2008; exec. prodr.: (TV films) Subway Stories: Tales From The Underground, 1997, I'm Boricua, Just So You Know!, 2006. Office: c/o Untitled Entertainment 1801 Century Park E Ste 700 Los Angeles CA 90067

PEREZ DE ALONSO, MARCELA, human resources specialist, information technology executive; b. Chile; Grad., Cath. U., Chile. Various sr. level positions in human resources and ops. Citigroup, global consumer head human resources, 1996—99; divsn. head Citigroup North L.Am. Consumer Bank, 1999—2004; exec. v.p. human resources and workforce devel. Hewlett-Packard Co., Palo Alto, Calif., 2004—. Mem. adv. bd. Marshall Bus. Sch. U. So. Calif.; spkr. in field; bd. dirs. Catalyst, NYC, Hewlett-Packard Co. Fin. Svcs. Mem. adv. bd. U. So. Calif. Marshall Bus. Sch.; bd. mem. Next Door Solutions to Domestic Violence. Named Corp. Exec. of Yr., Hispanic-Net, 2005; named one of 50 Most Important Hispanics in Tech. and Bus., Hispanic Engr. & Info. Tech. mag. Office: Hewlett Packard Co 3000 Hanover St Palo Alto CA 94304*

PERHAM, LEN, communications executive; BSEE, Northeastern U., 1968. Various mgmt. positions AMD, Western Digital; pres., CEO Optical Info. Systems, Inc. (divsn. Exxon Enterprise), IDT, Santa Clara, Calif., 1983-99, also bd. dirs. Bd. dirs. IDT.

PERKIN, GORDON WESLEY, international health executive; b. Toronto, Ont., Can., Apr. 25, 1935; came to U.S., 1962; s. Irvine Boyer and Jean (Laing) P.; m. Elizabeth Scott, Dec. 21, 1957; children: Scott, Stuart. MD, U. Toronto, 1959. Asst. dir. clin. rsch. Ortho Rsch. Found., Raritan, N.J., 1962-64; assoc. med. dir. Planned Parenthood Fedn. Am., NYC, 1964-66; program advisor Ford Found., NYC, 1966-67, regional program advisor Bangkok, 1967-69, Rio de Janeiro, 1973-76, program officer Mexico City, 1976-80; project specialist Ministry Fin. and Econ. Planning, Accra, Ghana, 1969-70; cons. WHO, Geneva, 1971-73; pres. Program for Appropriate Tech. in Health, Seattle, 1980-99; dir. reproductive and child health program Bill and Melinda Gates Found., 1999—2003, sr. fellow, 2003—. Affiliate prof. pub. health, U. Wash., Seattle; mem. Global Health Coun. Contbr. numerous articles to profl. jours. APHA fellow, 1970. Mem. Planned Parenthood Fedn. Am. (bd. dirs. 1983-89), Planned Parenthood Seattle-King County (bd. dirs. 1982-96, mem. exec. com. 1983-86), Planned Parenthood Western Wash. (bd. dirs. 1996—), NAS (com. mem. 1987-90), Alan Guttmacher Inst. (bd. dirs. 1985-90), Assn. Reproductive Health Profls., Alpha Omega Alpha. Office: Bill & Melinda Gates Found PO Box 23350 Seattle WA 98102-0650

PERKINS, FRANK OVERTON, academic administrator, marine biologist; b. Fork Union, Va., Feb. 14, 1938; s. Frank Otie and Mary Ella Perkins; m. Beverly Anne Weeks. BA, U. Va., 1960; MS, Fla. State U., Tallahassee, 1962, PhD, 1966. Marine scientist Va. Inst. Marine Sci., Coll. William and Mary, Gloucester Point, 1966-69, sr. marine scientist, 1969-77, asst. dir., 1977-81, dir., dean Sch. Marine Sci., 1981-91, prof. marine sci., 1991-97; asst. v.p. rsch. and grad. edn. U. Hawaii, Honolulu, 1997—. Baptist. Home: 7519 Olowalu Pl Honolulu HI 96825-2950 Office: U Hawaii 223 Crawford Hall Honolulu HI 96822 Office Phone: 808-956-6635. E-mail: fperkins@hawaii.edu.

PERKINS, HERBERT ASA, hematologist, educator; b. Boston, Oct. 5, 1918; s. Louis and Anna (Robinson) P.; m. Frances Snyder, Sept. 2, 1942; children: Susan, Deborah, Dale, Karen, Ronnie. AB cum laude, Harvard U., 1940; MD summa cum laude, Tufts U., 1943. Intern Boston City Hosp., 1944, resident, 1947-48; practice medicine specializing in transfusion medicine; clin. instr. Stanford Med. Sch., 1953-57, asst. clin. prof., 1957-58; hematologist Open Heart Surgery Team, Stanford Hosp., San Francisco, 1955-58, Jewish Hosp., St. Louis, 1958-59; dir. rsch. Irwin Meml. Blood Ctrs. (now Blood Ctrs. of the Pacific), San Francisco, 1959-78, med. and sci. dir., 1978-90, exec. dir., 1987-91, pres., 1991-93, sr. med. scientist, 1993—. Asst. prof. medicine Washington U., St. Louis, 1958-59, U. Calif., San Francisco, 1959-66, assoc. prof., 1966-71, clin. prof., 1971—. Co-editor: Hepatitis and Blood Transfusion, 1972. Maj. M.C., U.S. Army, 1944-47. Mem. AAAS, Am. Assn. Blood Banks (chmn. sci. adv. com. 1972-73, chmn. stds. com. 1968-71, chmn. com. on organ transplantation and tissue typing 1970-80, bd. dirs. 1982-86), Am. Soc. Hematology, Internat. Transfusion Soc., Am. Soc. Histocompatibility and Immunogenetics (pres. 1985-86), Nat. Marrow Donor Program (chair bd. dirs. 1995-96, chmn. com. on stds. 1987-94, chmn. fin. com. 1987-94). Office: Blood Ctrs of the Pacific 270 Masonic Ave San Francisco CA 94118-4417 Home: 10 Wolfback Ridge Rd Sausalito CA 94965-2052 E-mail: hperkins@bloodcenters.org.

PERKINS, JAN, municipal official; BA in sociology, U. Kans., 1974, MPA, 1976. Cert. Program for Sr. Execs. in State and Local Govt., John F. Kennedy Sch. Govt., Harvard U., 1987. Adminstrv. asst. City of Grand Rapids (Mich.), 1975-79, dep. city mgr., 1982-84; asst. city mgr. City of Adrian (Mich.), 1979-82; dep. city mgr. City of Santa Ana (Calif.), 1984-90; city mgr. City of Morgan Hill (Calif.), 1990-92; asst. city mgr. City of Fremont (Calif.), 1992-93, city mgr., 1993—. Mem. Internat. City/County Mgmt. Assn. (internat., awards, innovations adv., conf. planning coms.), City Mgr.'s Dept. League of Calif. Cities (exec. com., com. on the profession), Calif. Redevel. Assn., Pub. Adminstrn. Grad. Program Alumni Assn., Niles (Fremont) Rotary Club.

PERKINS, TOM (THOMAS JAMES PERKINS), venture capital company executive; b. Oak Park, Ill., Jan. 7, 1932; s. Harry H. and Elizabeth Perkins; m. Gerd Thune-Ellefsen, Dec. 9, 1961 (dec.); children: Tor Kristian, Elizabeth Siri; m. Danielle Steel, 1998 (div. 1999). BSEE, MIT, 1953; MBA, Harvard U., 1957. Founder Univ. Lab. (merged with Spectra Physics in 1960's); gen. mgr. computer div. Hewlett Packard Co., Cupertino, Calif., 1965-70, dir. corp. devel., 1970-72; co-founder, gen. partner Kleiner & Perkins, San Francisco, 1972-80; sr. ptnr. Kleiner Perkins Caufield & Byers, San Francisco, 1980—; chmn. bd. Tandem Computers, Inc., Cupertino, Calif., 1974—97. Founder, chmn. Genentech; bd. dirs. Spectra Physics., Symantec, Corning Glass Works, Collagen Corp., LSI Logic Corp., Hybritech Inc., Econics Corp., Vitalink Communications Corp., News Corp., Iolon, Philips Electronics NV, Compaq Computer, Hewlett Packard Co., 2002-04, 2005-06; chmn. Acuson, Tandem Computers. Author: Classic Supercharged Sports Cars, 1984, Sex and the Single Zillionaire, 2006, Valley Boy: The Education of Tom Perkins, 2007 Trustee San Francisco Ballet, 1980—. Mem. Nat. Venture Capital Assn. (chmn. 1981-82, pres. 1980-81) Clubs: N.Y. Yacht, Links, Am. Bugatti (pres. 1983—). Office: Kleiner Perkins Caufield & Byers 2750 Sand Hill Rd Menlo Park CA 94025

PERKINS, WILLIAM CLINTON, manufacturing executive; b. Decatur, Ill., Mar. 7, 1920; s. Glen Rupert and Frances Lola (Clinton) P.; m. Eunice Cagle, Sept. 7, 1939 (div. 1954); stepchildren: William Rea Cagle, Howard Christy Cagle; 1 child, Clinton Colcord; m. Lillian Wuollet, Sept. 7, 1955 (div. 1965); m. Shirley Thomas, Oct. 24, 1969. BS Mil. Sci. and Meteorology, U. Md., College Park, 1954; MS in Bus. and Pub. Adminstrn., Sussex Coll., Eng., 1975. Commd. USAF, 1943—73, advanced through grades to col.; with Ship Sys. divsn. Litton Ind., Culver City, Calif., 1973—75; dir. material Hughes Aircraft Co., Tehran, Iran, 1974—78; mgr. internat. s/c Northrop Corp., Dhahran, Saudi Arabia, 1979—81; dir. materiel CRS, Riyadh, Saudi Arabia, 1981—83; head major subcontracts Lear Ziegler Corp., Santa Monica, Calif., 1984—88; pres., chmn. bd., CEO Snowtech, Inc., LA, 1984—. Bd. dirs. Ice Village Ctrs., Inc., LA, Forefront Industries, Maywood, Calif. Bd. dirs. World Children's Transplant Fund, LA, 1987-95; mem. Mayor's Space Adv. Com., LA, 1970-74; mem. Aerospace Hist. Com. Aerospace Hist. Soc., LA, 1988-, CA Inst. Tech. Mem. AIAA (sec. chmn. 1970), Ret. Officers Assn. (pres. 1992-95), Military Officers Assn. of Am. (chpt. pres. 2003-2005), Soc. for Non-destructive Testing (program chmn. 1973), Aerospace Hist. Soc., Am. Soc. Quality Control, Am. Meterol. Soc., Sigma Alpha Epsilon (alumni chpt. pres. 1974-76). Avocations: golf, scuba diving, sailing, flying, gardening. Home: 8027 Hollywood Blvd Los Angeles CA 90046-2510 Personal E-mail: snowtech@pacbell.net.

PERKOWITZ, SIMON (SY), architect, architectural firm executive; AA in Architecture, L.A. City Coll., 1968; BS in Archtl. Engring., Calif. Polytech. State U., 1971. Registered architect Oreg., Nev., Ga.; lic. architect Calif., profl. engr., Calif. V.p. Mackel Assocs., LA, 1966-79; prin., exec. v.p. Musil Perkowitz Ruth, Inc., 1979—, pres., CEO, 1998—. Chmn. City of Palos Verdes Estates (Calif.) Planning Commn. Mem. AIA, NSPE, Internat. Coun. Shopping Ctrs. (so. Calif. planning com.), Nat. Soc. Archtl. Engrs., Calif. C. of C. Office: Perkowitz & Ruth Architects Inc 111 W Ocean Blvd Ste 2100 Long Beach CA 90802-4653

PERL, MARTIN LEWIS, physicist, educator, chemical engineer; b. NYC, June 24, 1927; children: Jed, Anne, Matthew, Joseph. B in Chem. Engring., Poly. Inst. Bklyn., 1948; PhD, Columbia U., 1955; ScD (hon.), U. Chgo., 1990. Chem. engr. Gen. Electric Co., 1948—50; asst. prof. physics U. Mich., 1955—58, assoc. prof., 1958—63; prof. Stanford U., 1963—. Author: High Energy Hadron Physics, 1975, Reflections on Experimental Science, 1996; contbr. articles on high energy physics and on relation of sci. to soc. to profl. jours. With U.S. Mcht. Marine, 1944—45, with US Army, 1946—47. Recipient Wolf prize in physics, Wolf Found., Israel, 1982, Nobel prize in physics, 1995. Fellow: Am. Phys. Soc.; mem.: NAS, Am. Acad. Arts and Scis. Home: 3737 El Centro St Palo Alto CA 94306-2642 Office Phone: 650-926-2652. Business E-Mail: martin@slac.stanford.edu.

PERLEGOS, GEORGE, electronics executive; b. Greece; BS Electrical Engring., 1972. With American Microsystems; design engr. Intel, 1974—81; co-founder, v.p., tech. Seeq Technology, 1981—84; founder, pres., CEO, chmn. Atmel Corp., San Jose, 1984—2006, bd. dirs., 1984—. Achievements include inventing EEPROM technology, the basic technology for flash memory. Office: Atmel Inc 2325 Orchard Pkwy San Jose CA 95131-1034

PERLIS, MICHAEL FREDRICK, lawyer; b. NYC, June 3, 1947; s. Leo and Betty F. (Gantz) Perlis; m. Colleen M. DeLee, Sept. 8, 2003; children: William Garrison, Grace Joanne;children from previous marriage: Amy Hannah, David Matthew. BS in Fgn. Svc., Georgetown U., 1968, JD, 1971. Bar: DC 1971, NY 1993, US Dist. Ct. 1971, US Ct. Appeals 1971, DC Ct. Appeals 1971, Calif. Ct. Appeals 1980, US Dist. Ct. (no. dist.) Calif. 1980, US Dist. Ct. (ctrl. dist.) Calif. 1985, US Ct. Appeals (9th cir.) 1980, US Supreme Ct. 1980, NY Supreme Ct. 1993. Law clk. DC Ct. Appeals, Washington, 1971—72, asst. corp. counsel, 1972—74; counsel divsn. enforcement US SEC, 1974—75, br. chief, 1975—77, asst. dir., 1977—80; ptnr. Pettit & Martin, San Francisco, 1980—89; ptnr. fedl. securities law litig. Stroock & Stroock & Lavan, LA, 1989—, mem. operating exec. com. Adj. prof. Cath. U. Am., 1979—80. Mem.: ABA (co-chmn. subcom. securities and commodities litig. 1982—83), Calif. State Bar Assn., DC Bar Assn. Office: Stroock & Stroock & Lavan 2029 Century Park E Ste 1800 Los Angeles CA 90067-3086 Office Phone: 310-556-5821. Business E-Mail: mperlis@stroock.com.

PERLMAN, DAVID, journalist; b. Balt., Dec. 30, 1918; s. Jess and Sara Perlman; m. Anne Salz, Oct. 15, 1941 (dec. 2002); children: Katherine, Eric, Thomas. AB, Columbia U., 1939; MS, Columbia U. Sch. Journalism, 1940. Reporter Bismarck Capital, ND, 1940, San Francisco Chronicle, 1940—41, reporter, sci. editor, 1952-77, city editor, 1977-79, assoc. editor, sci. editor, 1979—; reporter New York Herald Tribune, Paris, NYC, 1945-49; European corr. Colliers mag. and New York Post, 1949-51. Regents prof. human biology U. Calif., San Francisco, 1974; vis. lectr. China Assn. Sci. and Tech., Beijing, Chengdu, Shanghai; sci. writer-in-residence U. Wis., 1989. Contbr. articles to maj. mags. Founding dir. Squaw Valley (Calif.) Cmty. Writers; bd. dirs. Alan Guttmacher Inst., 1990—99; trustee Scientists Inst. Pub. Info., 1986—94; chmn. pub. svc. award com. Nat. Sci. Bd., 1998—2001. With inf. USAAF, 1941—45. Recipient Atomic Indsl. Forum award, 1975, Sci. Writing award, AAAS, 1976, Exploratorium award, 1977, Ralph Coates Roe medal, ASME, 1978, Margaret Sanger Cmty. Svc. award, 1981, Fellows' medal, Calif. Acad. Scis., 1984, Career Achievement award, Soc. Profl. Journalists, 1989, Glenn T. Seaborg award, Internat. Platform Assn., 1993, Sustained Achievement award for sci. journalism, Am. Geophys. Union, 1997, medal, U. Calif., San Francisco, 2000, Journalism award, Columbia U., 2000, award for disting. med. reporting, San Francisco Med. Soc., 2000, Grady-Stack award for sci. journalism, Am. Chem. Soc., 2001, John Wesley Powell award, U.S. Geol. Survey, 2004, Hearst Eagle award, 2004; Poynter Inst. fellow, Yale U., 1984, Carnegie Corp. fellow, Stanford U., 1987. Fellow: Calif. Acad. Scis.; mem.: AAAS (mem. com. Pub. Understanding Sci. 1985—90, adv. bd. Science-81-86 mag.), Astron. Soc. Pacific (bd. dirs. 1976—78), Nat. Assn. Sci. Writers (pres. 1970—71, Disting. Sci. Journalism award 1994), Coun. Advancement Sci. Writing (pres. 1976—80), Sigma Xi. Office: San Francisco Chronicle 901 Mission St San Francisco CA 94103-2905 Business E-Mail: dperlman@sfchronicle.com.

PERLMAN, RON (RONALD FRANCIS PERLMAN), actor; b. NYC, Apr. 13, 1950; s. Dorothy Perlman; m. Opal Stone, Feb. 14, 1981; children: Blake Amanda, Brandon Avery. BFA in Theatre, Lehman Coll., NYC, 1971; MFA, U. Minn., 1973. Actor: (films) Quest for Fire, 1981, The Ice Pirates, 1984, The Name of the Rose, 1986, Sleepwalkers, 1992, Double Exposure, 1993, When the Bough Breaks, 1993, The Adventures of Huck Finn, 1993, Cronos, 1993, Romeo Is Bleeding, 1993, Police Academy: Mission to Moscow, 1994, Sensation, 1995, The City of Lost Children, 1995, Fluke, 1995, The Last Supper, 1995, The Island of Dr. Moreau, 1996, Betty, 1997, Prince Valiant, 1997, Tinseltown, 1997, Alien: Resurrection, 1997, Frogs for Snakes, 1998, The Protector, 1998, I Woke Up Early the Day I Died, 1998, Happy, Texas, 1999, Price of Glory, 2000, The King's Guard, 2000, Stroke, 2000; actor, actor: (films) Enemy at the Gates, 2001, Down, 2001, Night Class, 2001, Boys on the Run, 2001, Blade II, 2002, Crime and Punishment, 2002, Star Trek: Nemesis, 2002, Rats, 2003, Absolon, 2003, Two Soldiers, 2003, Hoodlum & Son, 2003, Looney Tunes: Back in Action, 2003, Hellboy, 2004, Quiet Kill, 2004, The Second Front, 2005, Missing in America, 2005, Local Color, 2006, How to Go Out on a Date in Queens, 2006, The Last Winter, 2006, 5ive Girls, 2006, No. 6, 2006, In the Name of the King: A Dungeon Siege Tale, 2007, (voice) Terra, 2007, Acts of Violence, 2008, Outlander, 2008, Hellboy II: The Golden Army, 2008; (TV films) Our Family Honor, 1985, A Stoning in Fulham County, 1988, Blind Man's Bluff, 1992, Arly Hanks, 1993, Original Sins, 1995, (voice) Tiny Toon Adventures: Night Ghoulery, 1995, The Adventures of Captain Zoom in Outer Space, 1995, The Second Civil War, 1997, A Town Has Turned to Dust, 1998, Supreme Sanction, 1999, Primal Force, 1999, Operation Sandman, 2000, The Trial of Old Drum, 2000, Desperation, 2006, (voice) Hellboy Animated: Blood and Iron, 2007,; (TV series) Beauty and the Beast, 1987—90 (Golden Globe award for Best Performance by an Actor in a TV-Series - Drama, 1989, Best Actor in a Quality Drama Series, Viewers for Quality Television Awards, 1988, 1989), Picture Windows, 1994, Mortal Kombat: Defenders of the Realm, The Magnificent Seven, 1998—2000, Justice League, 2003, Teen Titans, 2003—06, Danny Phantom, 2004—06, (voice) The Batman, 2004—08. Recipient Acting award of Excellence, Big Bear Lake Internat. Film Festival, 2004; named Male Discovery of Yr., Golden Apple Awards, 1989. Avocations: golf, jazz, pool. Office: c/o Kritzer Levine Wilkins Entertainment Llc 8840 Wilshire Blvd Ste 100 Beverly Hills CA 90211

PERLMAN, SETH JOSEPH, political risk analyst; b. Newark, Dec. 4, 1960; s. Preston Leonard and Evelyn Ann (Binder) P.; m. Lisette Antonia Quinones, 1990 (div. May 1992); 1 child, Rachel Aleeza; m. Alexandria Melissa Molyneaux, Apr. 2, 1993; children: Grant, Rachel. BA in Internat. Rels., George Washington U., 1985; MA in Internat. Rels., Am. U., 1988; MPhil in Polit. Sci. 1st class honors, London Sch. Econs./Polit. Sci., 1986; PhD in Internat. Security Policies, U. Md., 1990. Cert. Spanish lang. translator U.S. Dept. of State. Rsch. analyst mid.-east program U.S. Dept. State, Washington, 1984-86; legis. asst. fgn. affairs U.S. Rep. Edward F. Feighan, Washington, 1986-88; sr. writer Def. & Fgn. Affairs mag. Internat. Media, Inc., Alexandria, Va., 1988-90; S.W. editor Pacific Shipper Mag., Long Beach, Calif., 1990-91; mng. dir. Polecon Resources, Inc., Huntington Beach, Calif., 1991—. Contbr. Knight-Ridder, Inc., El Segundo, Calif., 1990-91, Reuter's News Svc., L.A., 1990-91. Contbr. articles to profl. jours., periodicals, mags. Congl. Rsch. Svc. Def. and Fgn. Affairs rsch. grantee Libr. of Congress, 1988; Ctr. for Rsch. and Documentation of European Community grantee, 1989. Mem. Am. U. Alumni Assn. (v.p. 1989-90). Avocations: travel, woodworking, reading, skiing. Mailing: 5025 Martinez Bay Ave Las Vegas NV 89131 E-mail: c3iguy2002@yahoo.com.

PERLMUTTER, DAVID (DADI), computer company executive; BSc in Elec. Engring., Technion Israel Inst. Tech., 1980. Devel. team leader Intel Corp., Haifa, Israel, gen. mgr. microprocessor divsn., mgr. Israel devel. ctr. Haifa, gen. mgr. basic microprocessor divsn., v.p. microprocessor products group, gen. mgr. mobile platforms group, co-mgr. mobility group, v.p., gen. mgr. mobile platforms group, exec. v.p., gen. mgr. mobility group. Recipient Innovation award, Pres. of Israel, 1987. Achievements include patents for branch target buffers; multiprocessing cache coherency protocols. Office: Intel Corp 2200 Mission College Blvd Santa Clara CA 95054-1549 Office Phone: 408-765-8080.

PERLMUTTER, ED (EDWIN GEORGE PERLMUTTER), United States Representative from Colorado, former state legislator, lawyer; b. Denver, May 1, 1953; m. Deana M. Perlmutter; children: Alexis, Abbey, Zoey. BA, U. Colo., Boulder, 1975; JD, U. Colo. Sch. Law, 1978. Atty. Berenbaum, Weinshienk & Eason, P.C., Denver, 1978—; mem. dist. 20 Colo. State Senate, Denver, 1994—2002, pres. pro tempore, 2001—03, mem. pub. policy & planning com., joint legal svcs. com.; mem. US Congress from 7th Colo. dist., 2006—, mem. fin. svcs. com., homeland security com. Bd. trustees First Jud. & Jud. Performance Commn., 1989—91, chair, 1991—93; fin. chair Jefferson County Dems. Active Jefferson Found., Girl Scouts of America, Am. Heart Assn.; PTA mem. Maple Grove Elem. Sch., Golden, Colo.; trustee Midwest Rsch. Inst.; mem. Applewood Cmty. Ch.; past bd. dirs. Nat. Jewish Med. & Rsch. Ctr. Mem.: ABA, Comml. Law League America, U. Colo. Alumni Assn., Colo. Trial Lawyers Assn., Colo. Oil & Gas Assn., Associated Gen. Contractors Colo., Applewood Bus. Assn., Am. Judicature Soc., Am. Bankruptcy Inst., Golden C. of C., West C. of C., Northwest Metro C. of C., Denver Bar Assn., Colo. Bar. Assn. (bd. govs.), Arvada Soccer Assn., Table Mountain Soccer Assn., Wheat Ridge Soccer Assn. Democrat. Office: 415 Cannon House Office Bldg Washington DC 20515 also: 12600 W Colfax Ave Ste 8400 Lakewood CO 80215

PERLMUTTER, ROGER, medical products executive; Chmn. dept. immunology U. Wash., 1989—97, prof. depts. immunology, biochemistry and medicine, 1991—97; investigator Howard Hughes Med. Inst., 1991—97; various positions including exec. v.p. Worldwide Basic Rsch. and Preclinical Devel. Merck Rsch. Labs., 1997—2000; exec. v.p. R & D Amgen, Inc., 2001—. Bd. dirs. Stem Cells, Inc. Office: Amgen Inc One Amgen Center Dr Thousand Oaks CA 91320-1799 Office Phone: 805-447-1000. Office Fax: 805-447-1010.

PERLMUTTER, SAUL, astrophysicist, educator; AB in Physics (magna cum laude), Harvard U., 1981; PhD in Physics, U. Calif. Berkeley, 1986. Postdoctoral rschr. Space Sci. Lab., Lawrence Berkeley Nat. Lab., 1987—88; sr. staff scientist, astrophysicist Lawrence Berkeley Nat. Lab.; prof., physics dept. U. Calif. Berkeley, 2004—. Leader Internat. Supernova Cosmology Project, 1998—. Contbr. articles to profl. jours., to Sky and Telescope mag.; guest appearances Pub. Broadcasting Sys., BBC documentaries on astronomy and cosmology. Recipient Henri Chretien award, Am. Astronomical Soc., 1996, Breakthrough of Yr. award, Science Mag., 1998, E.O. Lawrence award in Physics, Dept. Energy, 2002, John Scott award, 2005, Padua prize, 2005, Feltrinelli Internat. prize, Phys. and Math. Scis., Lincei Acad., Rome, 2006; co-recipient Shaw prize in Astronomy, Shaw Found., Hong Kong, 2006, Gruber Cosmology prize, 2007; named Scientist of Yr., Calif., 2003. Fellow: Am. Acad. Arts & Scis. Achievements include discovery of the universe's accelerating expansion using supernovae as "standard candles" to measure the cosmic expansion rate. Office: Lawrence Berkeley Lab 50-232 Univ Calif 392 LeConte Berkeley CA 94720 Office Phone: 510-486-5203, 510-642-3596. Office Fax: 510-486-5401. Business E-Mail: saul@lbl.gov.

PERLOFF, JOSEPH KAYLE, cardiologist, educator; b. New Orleans, Dec. 21, 1924; s. Richard and Rose (Cohen) P.; m. Marjorie G. Mintz; children: Nancy L., Carey E. BA, Tulane U., 1945; postgrad., U. Chgo., 1946-47; MD, La. State U., New Orleans, 1951; MA (hon.), U. Pa., 1973. Diplomate Am. Bd. Internal Medicine, Am. Bd. Cardiovascular Disease. Intern Mt. Sinai Hosp., NYC, 1951-52, resident in pathology, 1952-53, resident in medicine, 1953-54; Fulbright fellow Inst. Cardiology, London, 1954-55; resident in medicine Georgetown U. Hosp., Washington, 1955-56, fellow in cardiology, 1956-57; from clin. instr. to prof. Georgetown U. Sch. Medicine, Washington, 1957-72, dir. cardiac diagnostic lab., 1959-68, asst. dir. divsn. cardiology, 1968-72; prof. medicine and pediat. U. Pa. Sch. Medicine, Phila., 1972-77, chief cardiovascular sect., 1972-77; prof. medicine and pediatrics UCLA Sch. Medicine, 1977—, Streisand/AHA chair in cardiology, 1983. Cons. Nat. Heart, Blood and Lung Inst.; dir. UCLA Adult Congenital Heart Disease Ctr. Author: The Cardiomyopathies, 1988, Physical Exam Heart and Circulation, 1990, 2d edit., 2000, Clinical Recognition of Congenital Heart Disease, 1994, 5th edit., 2003, Congenital Heart Disease in Adults, 1998. Ensign USN, 1943—46, PTO. Recipient The Best of UCLA award Chancellor's Selection, 1987; Residency Career Devel. award NIH, 1959-69, Sherman M. Mellinkoff award UCLA Med. Sch., 2000, Extraordinay Merit award, 2004, Fellow ACP, Am. Coll. Cardiology(Lifetime Achievement award 2008); mem. Am. Fedn. Clin. Rsch., Assn. Univ. Cardiologists, Alpha Omega Alpha. Office: UCLA Sch Medicine Cardiology 47 123 Chs Los Angeles CA 90024 Office Phone: 310-825-2019. Personal E-mail: josephperloff@earthlink.net.

PERLOFF, MARJORIE GABRIELLE, literature educator; b. Vienna, Sept. 28, 1931; arrived in U.S., 1998; d. Maximilian and Ilse (Schueller) Mintz; m. Joseph K. Perloff, July 31, 1953; children: Nancy Lynn, Carey Elizabeth. AB, Barnard Coll., 1953; MA, Cath. U., 1956, PhD, 1965; LittD (hon.), Bird Coll., 2008. Asst. prof. English and comparative lit. Cath. U., Washington, 1966-68, assoc. prof., 1969-71, U. Md., 1971-73, prof., 1973-76; Florence R. Scott prof. English U. So. Calif., LA, 1976—; prof. English and comparative lit. Stanford (Calif.) U., 1986—, Sadie Dernham prof. humanities, 1990—, prof. emerita, 2000. Vis. prof. U. Utah, 2002; scholar-in-residence U. So. Calif., 2004—; guest prof. Beijing Lang. and Culture U., 2004. Author: Rhyme and Meaning in the Poetry of Yeats, 1970, The Poetic Art of Robert Lowell, 1973, Frank O'Hara, Poet Among Painters, 1977, 2nd edit., 1998, The Poetics of Indeterminacy: Rimbaud to Cage, 1981, 2d edit., 1999, The Dance of the Intellect: Studies in the Poetry of the Pound Tradition, 1985, 2d edit., 1996, The Futurist Moment: Avant-Garde, Avant-Guerre and the Language of Rupture, 1986, 2d edit., 2003, Poetic License: Essays in Modern and Postmodern Lyric, 1990, Radical Artifice: Writing Poetry in the Age of Media, 1991, Wittgenstein's Ladder: Poetic Language and the Strangeness of the Ordinary, 1996, Frank O'Hara, 2d edit., 1998, Poetry On and Off the Page: Essays for Emergent Occasions, 1998, Twenty-first Century Modernism, 2001, The Vienna Paradox, 2004, Differentials, 2004; editor: Postmodern Genres, 1990; co-editor: John Cage: Composed in America, 1994; contbg. editor: Columbia Literary History of the U.S., 1987; contbr. preface to Contemporary Poets, 1980, A John Cage Reader, 1983. Guggenheim fellow, 1981-82, NEA fellow, 1985; Phi Beta Kappa scholar, 1994-95. Fellow Am. Acad. Arts and Scis.; mem. MLA (exec. coun. 1977-81, Am. lit. sect. 1993—, 1st v.p. 2005, pres. 2006), Comparative Lit. Assn. (pres. 1993-94, mem. adv. bd. Libr. of Am.), Lit. Studies Acad. Home: 1467 Amalfi Dr Pacific Palisades CA 90272-2752 Personal E-mail: mperloff@earthlink.net.

PEROCK, WAYNE R., state agency administrator; Adminstr. Conservation and Natural Resources Dept. State of Nev., divsn. State Parks, Carson City, 1995—.

PERRAULT, JACQUES, biology professor; b. Montreal, Quebec, Can., June 25, 1944; s. Jean-Paul and Irene (Girard) P.; m. Katherine Hampton Rhodes, May 4, 1996; 1 child, Juliette. BSc, McGill U., 1964; PhD, U. Calif., San Diego, 1972. Asst. prof. dept. microbiology and immunology Washington U. Sch. Medicine, St. Louis, 1977-84; assoc. prof. biology San Diego State U., 1984-87, prof. dept. of biology, 1987—. Contbr. articles to profl. jour. Recipient Research Career Devel. award, NIH, 1980-85; grantee, NIH, NSF, March of Dimes Defects Found., 1977—. Mem.: Gen. Soc. for Microbiology, Am. Soc. Virology, Am. Soc. Microbiology, AAAS. Avocation: karate (shotokan japanese style). Office: San Diego State U Dept Biology San Diego CA 92182 E-mail: jperrault@sunstroke.sdsu.edu.

PERRIN, EDWARD BURTON, biomedical researcher, public health educator; b. Greensboro, Vt., Sept. 19, 1931; s. J. Newton and Dorothy E. (Willey) P.; m. Carol Anne Hendricks, Aug. 18, 1956; children: Jenifer, Scott. BA, Middlebury Coll., 1953; student in Stats., Edinburgh U., Scotland, 1953—54; MA in Math. Stats., Columbia U., 1956; PhD, Stanford U., 1961. Asst. prof. dept. biostats. U. Pitts., 1959-62; asst. prof. dept. preventive medicine U. Wash., Seattle, 1962-65, assoc. prof., 1965-69, prof., 1969-70, prof., chmn. dept.

biostats., 1970-72, prof. dept. health svcs., adj. prof. dept. biostats., 1975-98, chmn. dept., 1983-94, prof. emeritus, 1999—; hon. prof. West China U. of Med. Scis., Szechwan, China, 1988-98; overseas fellow Churchill Coll., Cambridge U., 1991-92; sr. scientist Seattle Vets. Affairs Med. Ctr., 1994—2001. Biometrician VA Co-op Study on Treatment of Esophageal Varices, 1961—73; sr. cons. biostatistics Wash., Alaska regional med. programs, 1967—72; mem. epidemiology & disease control study sect. NIH, 1969—73; clin. prof. dept. cmty. medicine and internat. health Sch. Medicine, Georgetown U., Washington, 1972—75; dep. dir. Nat. Ctr. Health Stats. HEW, 1972—73, dir., 1973—75; rsch. scientist Health Care Study Ctr. Battelle Human Affairs Rsch. Ctr., Seattle, 1975—76, dir., 1976—78, Health & Population Study Ctr. Battelle Human Affairs Rsch. Ctr., 1978—83; chmn. health svcs. rsch. study sect. HEW, 1976—79; chmn. health svcs. R & D field program rev. panel VA, 1988—91; chmn. health svcs. info steering com. State of Wash., 1993—94; mem. nat. adv. coun. Agy. for Health Care Policy & Rsch. Dept. HHS U.S. Govt., 1994—97; mem. com. on nat. stats. NRC, NAS, 1994—2000; chmn. sci. adv. com. Med. Outcomes Trust, 1994—99; mem. report rev. com. NAS, 2005—; bd. dirs. Wash. State Acad. Scis., 2007—. Contbr. articles on biostats., health svcs. and population studies to profl. publs.; mem. editl. bd.: Jour. Family Practice, 1978-90, Pub. Health Nursing, 1992-98. Mem. tech. bd. Milbank Meml. Fund, 1974-76, Health Svcs. and Outcomes Rsch. Methodology, 1999-04. Recipient Outstanding Svc. citation HEW, 1975; Fulbright scholar 1953-54. Fellow AAAS, APHA (Spiegelman Health Stats. award 1970, program devel. bd. 1971, chmn. stats. sect. 1978-80, governing coun. 1983-85, stats. sect. recognition award 1989), Am. Statis. Assn. (mem. adv. com. to divsn. statis. policy 1975-77); mem. Assn. Health Svcs. Rsch. (pres. 1994-95, bd. dirs. 1991-2000), Inst. Medicine of NAS (chmn. membership com. 1984-86, mem. bd. on health care svcs. 1987-96, forum health stats. 1994-95, chmn. com. on clin. evaluation 1990-93), Biometrics Soc. (pres. Western N.Am. Region 1971), U. Wash. Retirement Assn. (bd. dirs. 2006—), Sigma Xi, Phi Beta Kappa. Home: 4900 NE 39th St Seattle WA 98105-5209 Office: Univ Wash Dept Health Svcs PO Box 359455 Seattle WA 98195 Office Phone: 206-524-9410. E-mail: perrin@u.washington.edu.

PERRINE, RICHARD LEROY, environmental engineer, educator; b. Mountain View, Calif., May 15, 1924; s. George Alexander and Marie (Axelson) P.; m. Barbara Jean Gale, Apr. 12, 1945; children: Cynthia Gale, Jeffrey Richard. AB, San Jose State Coll., 1949; MS, Stanford U., 1950, PhD in Chemistry, 1953. Cert. environ. profl., 1987. Research chemist Calif. Research Corp., La Habra, 1953-59; assoc. prof. UCLA, 1959-63, prof. engring. and applied sci., 1963-92, prof. emeritus, 1992—, chmn. environ. sci. and engring., 1971-82; prin. Aspen Environ. Group, 1990-93. V.p. Sage Resources, 1988-91; cons. environ. sci. and engring., energy resources, flow in porous media; mem. Los Angeles County Energy Commn., 1973-81; mem. adv. council South Coast Air Quality Mgmt. Dist., 1977-82; mem. air conservation com. Los Angeles County Lung Assn., 1970-84; mem. adv. com. energy div. Oak Ridge Nat. Lab., 1987-90; mem. policy bd. William D. Ruckelshaus Inst. Environ. and Natural Resources U. Wyo., 1994-2004. Editor in chief The Environ. Profl., 1985-90. Served with AUS, 1943-46. Recipient Outstanding Engr. Merit award in environ. engring. Inst. Advancement Engring., 1975; ACT-SO award in field of chemistry West Coast region NAACP, 1984. Fellow AAAS; mem. Am. Chem. Soc., Soc. Petroleum Engrs., Am. Inst. Chem. Engrs., Can. Inst. Mining and Metallurgy, N.Am. Assn. Environ. Edn., Nat. Assn. Environ. Profls. (cert.), Air and Waste Mgmt. Assn., Assn. Environ. Engring. and Sci. Profs., Sierra Club, Wilderness Soc., Audubon Soc., Sigma Xi, Tau Beta Pi, Phi Lambda Upsilon. Home: 22611 Kittridge St West Hills CA 91307-3609 Office: Univ Calif Engring Bldg I Rm 3066D Los Angeles CA 90095-0001 E-mail: rperrine@ucla.edu.

PERRINEAU, HAROLD, actor; b. Bklyn., Aug. 7, 1963; s. Harold Williams; m. Brittany Perrineau; children: Aurora, Wynter Aria. Studied, Shenandoah Conservatory. Actor: (films) Shakedown, 1988, King of NY, 1990, Smoke, 1995, Flirt, 1995, Blood and Wine, 1996, The Edge, 1997, Come To, 1998, Lulu On The Bridge, 1998, The Tempest, 1998, A Day in Black and White, 1998, The Best Man, 1999, Woman on Top, 2000, Overnight Sensation, 2000, Someone Like You, 2001, Prison Song, 2001, On Line, 2002, The Matrix Reloaded, 2003; (TV series) Fame, 1982, Oz, 1997, Lost, 2004—06 (Outstanding Performance by an Ensemble in a Drama Series, Screen Actors Guild award, 2006), 2008—. Office: c/o Agy for the Performing Arts LA 405 S Beverly Dr Beverly Hills CA 90212-4425

PERRON, EDWARD ADRIAN, lawyer; b. Washington, Jan. 19, 1954; s. Edward Joseph and Irene (Lum) P.; m. Julie Cornman, June 29, 1980; children: Kelly Elizabeth, Christopher Edward. BA in Economics and East Asian Studies, Harvard U., 1975, JD, 1979. Bar: Calif. 1979, US Dist. Ct. (ctrl. dist.) Calif. 1979, US Ct. Appeals (9th cir.) 1980, DC 1995, NY 1996. Assoc. Lillick & McHose, Los Angeles, 1979-85, ptnr., 1985-90; ptnr., mem. exec. com., chair office mgmt. com. Pillsbury Madison & Sutro, Los Angeles, 1991—2001, vice chmn., ptnr. compensation com., 1996, chmn., ptnr. compensation com., 1997—98; (Pillsbury Madison & Sutro merged with Winthrop, Stimson, Putnam, 2001); ptnr., mem. mng. bd. & ptnr. compensation com. Pillsbury Winthrop LLP, Los Angeles, 2001—06; (Pillsbury Winthrop LLP merged with Shaw Pittman LLP, 2005); ptnr., corp. & securities dept., mem. mng. bd. & ptnr. compensation com. Pillsbury Winthrop Shaw Pittman LLP, Los Angeles, 2005—06. Co-chmn. ptnr. compensation com. Pillsbury Winthrop LLP, 2004, chmn. ptnr. compensation com., 2007—08. Author: (book) Distributing Foreign Products in the United States, 2000. Mem. exec. adv. bd. Japan Am. Cmty. & Cultural Ctr., LA, 1990—, Asian Pacific-Am. Legal Ctr., LA, 1995—. Mem. Japan Am. Soc. So. Calif. (gen. counsel, dir. 1985-2006, chmn. 2007—), Japan Bus. Assn. So. Calif., ABA, Calif. Bar Assn., Los Angeles County Bar Assn. Office: Pillsbury Winthrop Shaw Pittman LLP 725 S Figueroa St Los Angeles CA 90017-5524 Office Phone: 213-488-7352. Office Fax: 213-629-1033. Business E-Mail: edward.perron@pillsburylaw.com.

PERRY, DALE LYNN, chemist; b. Greenville, Tex., May 12, 1947; s. Francis Leon and Violet (Inabinette) P. BS, Midwestern U., 1969; MS, Lamar U., 1972; PhD, U. Houston, 1974. NSF fellow dept. chemistry Rice U., Houston, 1976-77; Miller Research fellow dept. chemistry U. Calif.-Berkeley, 1977-79; prin. investigator solid state chemistry and spectroscopy Lawrence Berkeley Lab. U. Calif., 1979—, sr. scientist, 1987—. Lectr. Ana G. Mendez Ednl. Found., 1988; rsch. mem. G.T. Seaborg Inst. for Transactinium Sci. Author, editor: Instrumental Surface Analysis of Geologic Materials, 1990, Applications of Analytical Techniques to the Characterization of Materials, 1992, Applications of Synchrotron Radiation Techniques to Materials Science, 1993, II, 1995, III, 1996, IV, 1998, V, 2001, VI, 2002, Handbook of Inorganic Compounds, 1995, Materials Synthesis and Characterization, 1997; contbr. articles to profl. jours. Named Outstanding Mentor for Undergrad. Rsch., US Dept. Energy, 2002. Fellow AAAS, Royal Soc. Chemistry (London); mem. Am. Chem. Soc. (chmn. materials chemistry and engring. subdivsn., indsl. and engring. chemistry divsn., 1992-96), Soc. Applied Spectroscopy, Coblentz Soc., Materials Rsch. Soc. (corp. participation com. 1991-96), Sigma Xi (nat. rsch. award 1974). Achievements include research in chem. and materials. Office: U Calif Lawrence Berkeley Nat Lab Mail Stop 70A 1150 Berkeley CA 94720-0001 Personal E-mail: dlperry510@comcast.net.

PERRY, JACQUELIN, orthopedist, surgeon; b. Denver, May 31, 1918; d. John F. and Tirzah (Kuruptkat) P. BE, U. Calif., LA, 1940; MD, U. Calif., San Francisco, 1950; DSc (hon.), U. So. Calif., 1996. Intern Children's Hosp., San Francisco, 1950-57; resident in orthop. surgery U. Calif., San Francisco, 1951-55; orthop. surgeon Rancho Los Amigos Hosp., Downey, Calif., 1955—, chief stroke svc., 1972-75; chief pathokinesiology Rancho Los Amigos Med. Ctr., 1961—; mem. faculty U. Calif. Med. Sch., San Francisco, 1966—, clin. prof., 1973—; mem. faculty U. So. Calif. Med. Sch., 1969—, prof. orthop. surgery, 1972—, dir. polio and gait clinic, 1972—. Disting. lectr. for hosp. for spl. surgery and Cornell U. Med. Coll., NYC, 1977-78; Packard Meml. lectr. U. Colo. Med. Sch., 1970; Osgood lectr. Harvard Med. Sch., 1978; Summer lectr., Portland, 1977; Shands lectr.; cons. USAF; guest spkr. symposia; cons. Biomechanics Lab. Centinela Hosp., 1979—. Served as phys. therapist U.S. Army, 1941-46. Recipient Disting. Svc. award Assn. Rehab. Facilities, 1981, Pres.'s award, 1984, Isabelle and Lenard Goldensen award for tech. United Cerebral Palsy Assn., 1981, Jow Dowling award, 1985, Profl. Achievement award UCLA, 1988, Milton Cohen award Nat. Assn. Rehab., 1993, Tribute Pres. award Ruth Jackson Orthop. Soc., 2004; named Woman of Yr. for Medicine in So. Calif. LA Times, 1959, Alumnus of Yr. U. Calif. Med. Sch., 1980, Physician of Yr. Calif. Employment Devel. Dept., 1994; Jacquelin Perry Neuro Trauma Inst. Rancho Clin. Bldg. named in her honor, 1996. Mem. AMA, Am. Acad. Orthop. Surgeons (Kappa Delta award for rsch. 1977, orthop. rsch. svc., 1976), Am. Orthop. Assn. (Shands lectr. 1988), Western Orthop. Assn., Calif. Med. Soc., LA County Med. Soc., Am. Phys. Therapy Assn. (hon. Golden Pen award 1965), Am. Acad. Orthotists and Prosthetists (hon.), Scoliosis Rsch. Soc., LeRoy Abbott Soc., Am. Acad. Cerebral Palsy, Gait & Clin. Movement Analysis Soc. (mem. emeritus, Lifetime Achievement award 2000), Orthop. Rsch. Soc. (Shands award 1998, 99). Home: 12319 Brock Ave Downey CA 90242-3503 Office: Rancho Los Amigos Med Ctr 7601 Imperial Hwy Downey CA 90242-3456 Office Phone: 562-401-7177. E-mail: pklab@larei.org.

PERRY, JAN, Councilwoman; BA cum laude, U. Southern Calif., 1977, MPA, 1981. Cert.: UCLA Ext. (in Litig.) 1979. Chief of staff, Dist. 9 LA City Coun., with legis. dept., 10th Dist., with sr. planning dept., 13th Dist., asst. pres. pro tempore, chair energy and environ. com., chair ad hoc homeless com., vice chair arts, parks, health, and aging com., vice chair ad hoc com. on recovering energy, natural resources, and econ. benefit from waste for LA, mem. housing, cmty., and econ. devel. com., mem. ad hoc LA river com., mem. ad hoc stadium com., councilwoman, Dist. 9, 2001—. With Hollywood Cmty. Housing Corp., 1990—93, African-Am./Jewish Leadership Connection, 1997, Coro Found., 1997, Japanese America Nat Mus, Black-Korean Alliance; exec. dir. Census 2000 Outreach Project, 1998; mem. bd. dirs. Cmty. Fin. Resources Ctr., LA Edn. Partnership, South Coast Air Quality Mgmt. Dist.; chair Light Rail Authority. Mem. bd. dirs. Metro region Nat. Women's Polit. Caucus, League of Women Voters, Santa Monica Mountains Conservancy, William O Douglas Outdoor Classroom, Jennessee Ctr. Vocational Edn. Com., Angels Flight Railway Found., Jewish Cmty. Rels. Com., Jewish Fedn. Coun. Mailing: City Hall 200 N Spring St Rm 420 Los Angeles CA 90012 Office: Dist Office 4703 S Broadway Ave Los Angeles CA 90037 Office Phone: 213-473-7009, 323-846-2651. Office Fax: 213-473-5946, 323-846-2656. Business E-Mail: Jan.Perry@lacity.org.*

PERRY, JEAN LOUISE, academic administrator; b. Richland, Wash., May 13, 1950; d. Russell S. and Sue W. Perry. BS, Miami U., Oxford, Ohio, 1972; MS, U. Ill., Urbana, 1973, PhD, 1976. Cons. ednl. placement office U. Ill., 1973-75; adminstrv. intern Coll. Applied Life Studies, 1975-76, asst. dean, 1976-77, assoc. dean, 1978-81, asst. prof. dept. phys. edn., 1976-81; assoc. prof. phys. edn. San Francisco State U., 1981-84, prof., 1984-90, chair, 1981-90; dean Coll. Human and Cmty. Scis. U. Nev., Reno, 1990—2006, spl. asst. to pres. for athletics, academics and compliance, 2006—. Named to Excellent Tchr. List, U. Ill., 1973—79. Mem.: AAHPERD (fellow rsch. consortium, pres. 1988—89), Nat. Assn. Girls and Women in Sports (guide coord., pres.), Nat. Assn. Phys. Edn. in Higher Edn., Am. Edn. Rsch. Assn., Am. Assn. Higher Edn., Phi Delta Kappa, Delta Psi Kappa. Home: 3713 Ranchview Ct Reno NV 89509-7437 Office: U Nev Legacy Hal/ 232 Reno NV 89557-0001 Office Phone: 775-784-3505.

PERRY, JOHN RICHARD, philosophy educator; b. Lincoln, Nebr., Jan. 16, 1943; s. Ralph Robert and Ann (Roscow) P.; m. Louise Elizabeth French, Mar. 31, 1962; children: James Merton, Sarah Louise, Joseph Glenn. BA, Doane Coll., Crete, Nebr., 1964; PhD, Cornell U., Ithaca, NY, 1968; DLitt (hon.), Doane Coll., 1982. Asst. prof. philosophy UCLA, 1968-72; vis. asst. prof. U. Mich., Ann Arbor, 1971-72; assoc. prof. UCLA, 1972-74, Stanford (Calif.) U., 1974-77; prof. Stanford U., 1977-85, Henry Waldgrave Stuart prof., 1985—, chmn. dept. philosophy, 1976-82, 90-91, 2000-01, dir. ctr. study lang. and info., 1985-86, 93-99, resident fellow Soto House, 1985-91. Author: Dialogue on Identity and Immortality, 1978, (with Jon Barwise) Situations and Attitudes, 1983, The Problem of the Essential Indexical, 1993, Dialogue on Good, Evil and the Existence of God, 1999, Knowledge, Possibility and Consciousness, 2001, Reference and Reflexivity, 2001. Pres. Santa Monica Dem. Club, Calif., 1972-74. Woodrow Wilson fellow, 1964-65, Danforth fellow, 1964-68, Guggenheim fellow, 1975-76, NEH fellow, 1980-81. Mem. Am. Philos. Assn. (v.p. Pacific divsn. 1992-93, pres. 1993-94). Office: Stanford U Dept Philosophy Bldg 90 Inner Quad Stanford CA 94305 E-mail: john@csli.stanford.edu.

PERRY, L. TOM, religious organization administrator, merchant; b. Aug. 5, 1922; s. Tom and Nora Sonne Perry; m. Virginia Lee (dec. 1974); 3 children; m. Barbara Dayton, 1976. BS, Utah State U. Ass. to the Twelve, 1972—74; mem. Quorum of the Twelve Ch. of Jesus Christ of LDS, Salt Lake City, 1974—; chmn. ZCMI, Salt Lake City. With USMC, WWII, PTO. Office: LDS Ch 50 E North Temple Salt Lake City UT 84150-0002

PERRY, MARK L., medical products executive; b. 1955; AB, U. Calif.; JD, U. Calif., Davis. Bar: Calif. 1980. Assoc. Cooley Godward, San Francisco, 1981-87, ptnr., 1987-94; sec., v.p., gen. counsel Gilead Scis., Inc., Foster City, Calif., 1994-96, CFO, v.p., gen. counsel, sec., 1996-98, sr. v.p., 1998-2000, sr. v.p. ops., 2000—. Office: Gilead Scis Inc 333 Lakeside Dr Foster City CA 94404-1146 Fax: (650) 574-4800.

PERRY, MICHAEL C., theatre publisher, educator; b. Denver, Nov. 20, 1953; s. Maurice L. and Maryann Jane (Champlin) P.; m. Sharon Yvonne Ronson, June 26, 1981; children: Jessica, Janalynn, Joelle, Jon-Christopher. BA, Brigham Young U., 1982. Cert. tchr., Utah. Technician Osmond Studios, Orem, Utah, 1977-84; educator Pleasant Grove (Utah) H.S., 1986-87, Spanish Fork (Utah) H.S., 1989—2000; pres. Encore Performance Pub., Orem, 1979—. Author, composer (musical play) Tom Sawyer, 1987; composer (musical play) Turn the Gas Back On, 1989, Onstage, 1992; editor (scene books) For Teens and Child Actors, 1992. Recipient Best of West award Rocky Mountain Pub. Broadcasting, 1977, Emmy award Acad. of TV, 1977. Mem. Am. Soc. Composers, Authors and Pubs., Am. Alliance for Theatre and Edn. (Disting Play award 1995), Ednl. Theatre Assn., Christians In Theatre Arts, Utah Theatre Assn., Rocky Mountain Theatre Assn. Office Phone: 801-282-8159. E-mail: encoreplay@aol.com.

PERRY, MICHAEL W., former bank executive; BBA with honors, Calif. State U., Sacramento. CPA. With Commerce Security Bank, 1987—92, sr. exec. v.p. Mortgage Banking Divsn.; joined IndyMac Bancorp, Pasadena, Calif., 1993, COO, 1993—97, pres., 1997—99, bd. dirs., 1997—, CEO, 1997—, vice chmn. bd., 2000—03, chmn. bd., 2003—08. Bd. trustees, mem. acad. affairs com. Mayfield Jr. Sch.; bd. dirs. YMCA of Pasadena. Recipient Fin. Industry Leader of Yr. award, LA Bus. Jour., 2002, Entrepreneur of Yr., fin. services, LA Ernst & Young, 2002; named LA Bus. Jour. Hall of Fame. Mem.: Young Presidents' Org. (San Gabriel chpt.), Calif. Soc. CPAs, Am. Inst. CPAs.

PERRY, RALPH BARTON, III, lawyer; b. NYC, Mar. 17, 1936; s. Ralph Barton Jr. and Harriet Armington (Seelye) P.; m. Mary Elizabeth Colburn, Sept. 2, 1961; children: Katherine Suzanne, Daniel Berenson. AB, Harvard U., 1958; LLB, Stanford U., 1963. Bar: Calif. 1964. Assoc. and mem. Keatinge & Sterling, L.A., 1963—68; mem. firm Graven Perry Block Brody & Qualls, L.A., 1968—2006, Perry & Grossman, L.A., 2006—. Bd. dirs. Planning and Conservation League, 1968-2005, PLC Found., 2005—, Coalition for Clean Air, 1970-2007, pres. 1972-80, 85-88. Served with U.S. Army, 1956-58. Mem. ABA (ho. of dels. 1975-95), State Bar Calif., L.A. County Bar Assn., Lawyers Club L.A. County (gov. 1968-82), Nat. and Internat. Wildlife Fedns., Sierra Club, L.A. Athletic Club. Home: 296 Redwood Dr Pasadena CA 91105-1339 Office: Graven Perry 523 W 6th St Ste 723 Los Angeles CA 90014-1223 Office Phone: 213-680-9770. Personal E-mail: rbp3@earthlink.net.

PERRY, WILLIAM JAMES, engineering educator, former United States Secretary of Defense; b. Vandergrift, Pa., Oct. 11, 1927; s. Edward Martin and Mabelle Estelle (Dunlap) Perry; m. Leonilla Green, Dec. 29, 1947; children: David, William, Rebecca, Robin, Mark. BS in Math., Stanford U., 1949, MS, 1950; PhD, Pa. State U., 1957. Instr. math. Pa. State U., 1951—54; sr. mathematician HRB-Singer Co., State College, Pa., 1952—54; dir. electronic def. labs. GTE Sylvania Co., Mountain View, Calif., 1954—64; founder, pres. ESL, Inc., Sunnyvale, Calif., 1964—77; tech. cons. US Dept. Def., Washington, 1967—77, under sec. for rsch. & engring., 1977—81; mng. dir. Hambrecht & Quist, San Francisco, 1981—85; chmn. Tech. Strategies & Alliances, Menlo Park, Calif., 1985—93; prof., co-dir. Ctr. for Internat. Security and Arms Control Stanford U., Calif., 1989—93, prof. mgmt. sci. & engring., 1997—, sr. fellow, Hoover Inst., 1997—, Michael and Barbara Berberian prof., co-dir. Preventive Def. Project, 1997—; dep. sec. US Dept. Def., Washington, 1993—94, sec., 1994—97. Chmn. Global Tech. Ptnrs. LLC; mem. Iraq Study Group, 2006, Def. Policy Bd. Advisory Com., 2007—. Served in US Army, 1946—47. Recipient Def. Disting. Svc. medal, US Dept. Def., 1980, 1981, Achievement medal, Am. Electronics Assn., 1980, Forrestal medal, 1994, Henry Stimson medal, 1994, Arthur Bueche medal, NAE, 1996, Eisenhower award, 1996, Presdl. Medal Freedom, The White House, 1997, Outstanding Civilian Svc. medals, US. Army, 1997, USN, 1997, USAF, 1997, USCG, 1997, NASA, 1981, Def. Intelligence Agy., 1997; sr. fellow, Freeman Spogli Inst. Internat. Studies, Stanford U., 1997—. Office: Stanford Univ CISAC Encina Hall Rm C229 Stanford CA 94305-6165 Office Phone: 650-725-6501. Office Fax: 650-725-0920.

PERRYMAN, LANCE, dean; DVM, Wash. State U., 1970, PhD in Vet. Sci., 1975; MS, Ohio State U., 1973. Asst. prof. Wash. State U. Coll. Vet. Medicine, 1975—78, assoc. prof., 1978—84, assoc. dean for rsch. and grad. studies, 1989—94, dir. Animal Health Rsch. Ctr., 1989—94; head of dept., prof. dept. microbiology, pathology, and parasitology NC State U. Coll. Vet. Medicine, 1994—2001; dean coll. vet. med. and biomedical studies Colo. State U., 2001—. Named Disting. Vet. Immunologist of Yr., Am. Assn. Vet. Immunologists, 1999. Mem.: AAAS, Colo. Vet. Med. Assn. (President's award 2005), Am. Vet. Medicine Assn., Am. Soc. Microbiology, Am. Assn. Immunologists, Am. Coll. Vet. Pathologists. Office: Colo State U Coll Vet Medicine & Biomed Scis 1601 Campus Delivery Fort Collins CO 80523-1601 Office Phone: 970-491-7051. Office Fax: 970-491-2250. E-mail: lance.perryman@colostate.edu.

PERSCHBACHER, REX ROBERT, dean, law educator; b. Chgo., Aug. 31, 1946; s. Robert Ray and Nancy Ellen (Beach) P.; children: Julie Ann, Nancy Beatrice. AB in Philosophy, Stanford U., 1968; JD, U. Calif., Berkeley, 1972. Bar: Calif. 1972, U.S. Dist. Ct. (no. dist.) Calif. 1973, U.S. Dist. Ct. (so. dist.) Calif. 1979, U.S. Ct. Appeals (9th cir.) 1980, U.S. Dist. ct. (ea. dist.) Calif. 1985. Law clk. to judge U.S. Dist. Ct. (no. dist.) Calif., San Francisco, 1973-74; asst. prof. law U. Tex., Austin, 1974-75; assoc. Heller, Ehrman, White & McAuliffe, San Francisco, 1975-78; asst. prof. law U. San Diego, 1978-79, assoc. prof. law, 1980-81; mem. faculty Inst. on Internat. and Comparative Law, London, 1984—88; acting prof. law U. Calif., Davis, 1981-85, prof., 1988—, assoc. dean, 1993-98, dean Law Sch., 1998—. Dir. clin. edn. Univ. Calif., Davis, 1981-93, acad. senate, law sch. rep., 1989-91; vis. prof. law Univ. Santa Clara (Calif.), summer 1986. Co-author: California Civil Procedure and Practice, 1996, The United States Legal system-An Introduction, 2002, 2d edit., 2007, California Legal Ethics, 7th edit., 2007, Problems in Legal Ethics, 9th edit., 2007, Cases and Materials on Civil Procedure, 5th edit., 2005; contbr. articles to legal jours. Bd. dirs. Legal Svcs. of No. Calif., 1990-96. Recipient Disting. Teaching Award, 1992. Mem. ABA (Section of

Legal Edn. and Admissions to Bar, Accreditation Com., 2000-), Calif. Bar Assn., Am. Assn. Law Schs., Inn of Ct. Democrat. Avocation: travel. Office: UC Davis Sch Law Dean Office 400 Mrak Hall Dr Davis CA 95616 Office Phone: 530-752-0243. E-mail: rrperschbacher@ucdavis.edu.

PERSHING, DAVID WALTER, chemical engineering educator, researcher; b. Anderson, Ind., Oct. 2, 1948; s. Walter L. and Treva B. (Crane) P.; m. Lynn Marie Kennard, Apr. 9, 1977; 1 child, Nicole. BSChemE, Purdue U., 1970; PhDChemE, U. Ariz., 1976. Rsch. asst. Exxon Prodn. Rsch., Houston, 1969; project engr. EPA, 1970-73; asst. prof. chem. engring. U. Utah, Salt Lake City, 1977-82, assoc. prof., 1982-85, prof., 1985—, assoc. dean Grad. Sch., 1983-87, dean Coll. Engring., 1987-98, v.p., 1998-99, sr. v.p. acad. affairs, 2000—; asst. to pres. Reaction Engring. Inc., Salt Lake City, 1990—. Vis. scientist Internat. Flame Rsch. Found., Ijmuiden, The Netherlands, 1972-73; vis. assoc. prof. chem. engring. U. Ariz., Tuscon, 1976-77; cons. Energy and Environ. Rsch. Ctr., Irvine, Calif., 1974-90, Acurex Corp., Mountain View, Calif., 1974-79, Kennecott Corp., Salt Lake City, 1979-81, Nat. Bur. Standards, Washington, 1976-78, Geneva Steel, 1989-95; assoc. dir. Engring. Rsch. Ctr., NSF, 1986-97. Contbr. articles to profl. publs.; patentee in field. Maj. USPHS, 1970-73. Recipient Disting. Teaching award U. Utah, 1982, Disting. Rsch. award U. Utah, 1990; grantee NSF, PYI, 1984-90. Mem. Am. Inst. Chem. Engrs., Combustion Inst. Methodist. Office: U Utah Coll Engring 201 Presidents Cir Rm 205 Salt Lake City UT 84112-9007 Office Phone: 801-581-5057. Business E-Mail: david.pershing@utah.edu.

PERSHING, ROBERT GEORGE, retired telecommunications industry executive; b. Battle Creek, Mich., Aug. 10, 1941; s. James Arthur and Beulah Francis P.; m. Diana Kay Prill, Sept. 16, 1961 (div. Jan. 1989); children: Carolyn, Robert; m. Charlene Jean Reed Wallis, Mar. 18, 1989 (div. Dec. 1995); m. Luz F. Villalon Dreisbach, July 23, 2006. BSEE, Tri-State Coll., 1961. Comm. engr. Am. Elec. Power, Ind., NY, and Ohio, 1961-69; design supr. Wescom, Inc., Ill., 1969-74; dir. engring. Tellabs, Inc., Lisle, Ill., 1974-78; pres., CEO Teltrend, Inc., St. Charles, Ill., 1979-89, chmn. bd., 1979-88; CEO DKP Prodns., Inc., St. Charles, Ill., 1986-89; exec. cons. Teltrend, St. Charles, Ill., 1979-93; asst. treas. Magnekopy, inc., Villa Park, Ill. Bd. dirs. TI Investors, Inc.; advisor entrepreneurial studies U. Ill.; engring. cons. Recipient Chgo. Area Small Bus. award, 1986., INC 500 awards, 1987, 88. Mem. IEEE. Office: PO Box 3377 Show Low AZ 85902 Home Phone: 928-537-8952; Office Phone: 928-537-8952. E-mail: rpershing@frontiernet.net.

PERSON, EVERT BERTIL, retired newspaper and radio executive; b. Berkele, Calif., Apr. 6, 1914; s. Emil P. and Elida (Swanson) P.; m. Ruth Finley, Jan. 26, 1944 (dec. May 1985); m. 2d, Norma Joan Betz, Mar. 12, 1986. Student, U. Calif., Berkeley, 1937; LHD, Calif. State Univ., 1983, LHD, 1993, Sonoma State U., 1993. Co-publisher, sec.-treas. Press Democrat Pub. Co., Santa Rosa, Calif., 1945-72, editor, 1972-73, pres., pub., editor-in-chief, 1973-85; sec.-treas. Finley Broadcasting Co., Santa Rosa, 1945-72, pres., 1972-89, Kawana Pubs., 1975-85; pub. Healdsburg Tribune, 1975-85; prin. Evert B. Person Investments, Santa Rosa, 1985—. Pres. Person Properties Co., Santa Rosa, 1945-70; v.p. Finley Ranch & Land Co., Santa Rosa, 1947-72, pres., 1972-79; pres. Baker Pub. Co., Oreg., 1957-67, Sebastopol (Calif.) Times, 1978-81, Russian River News, Guerneville, Calif., 1978-81; pres. publ. Kawana Pubs., 1978-85; mem. nominating com. AP, 1982-84, mem. auditing com., 1984-85 Bd. dirs Empire Coll., Santa Rosa, 1972-98, Sonoma County Taxpayers Assn., 1966-69, San Francisco Spring Opera Assn., 1974-79; bd. dirs. San Francisco Opera, 1986-95, v.p., 1988-95; pres. Calif. Newspaperboy Found., 1957-58; chmn. Santa Rosa Civic Arts Commn., 1961-62; pres. Santa Rosa Sonoma County Symphony Assn., 1966-68, Luther Burbank Meml. Found., 1979, Santa Rosa Symphony Found., 1967-77; adv. bd. Santa Rosa Salvation Army, 1959-67; commodore 12th Coast Guard Dist. Aux., 1969-70; trustee Desert Mus., Palm Springs, 1987-92, v.p. Nat. Bd. Canine Companions, Inc., 1989-92. Decorated Knight of the Holy Sepulchre. Mem. Calif. Newspaper Pubs. Assn. (pres. 1981-82), Internat. Newspaper Fin. Execs. (pres. 1961-62), Bohemian Club, Sonoma County Press Club, Santa Rosa Golf and Country club, The Springs Club, Santa Rosa Rotary (past pres.), Masons (33 degree, Legion of Merit), Shriners. Roman Catholic. Home: 775 White Oak Dr Santa Rosa CA 95409-6155 Office: The Oaks 1400 N Dutton Ave Ste 12 Santa Rosa CA 95401-4644

PERTH, ROD, network entertainment executive; b. LA; s. Milford Robert Martinson and Phyllis (Hove) Perth; m. Jill Sunderland, Apr. 27, 1974; children: Chelseah, Lauren, Eric. BS in Mgmt., San Jose State U., 1966. V.p., gen. mgr. spot sales CBS TV, NYC, 1974—86; v.p., station mgr. WBBM-TV, Chgo., 1986—89; sr. v.p. late night non-network programming CBS-TV, LA, 1989—94; pres. entertainment USA Network, LA, 1994—95; pres. HRTS, LA, 1995—99, Jim Henson T.V.; programming dir. USA Network. Account exec. KNXT, LA, 1968—71; ea. mgr. spot sales CBS, NYC, 1971—74, dir. midwest spot sales, Chgo., 1974—76; dir. sales KMOX-TV, St. Louis, 1976—79; bd. dirs. HRTS. Contbr. L.E.A.R.N. program, LA, 1995, Alliance for Children, LA, 1996; bd. mem. State St. Coun., Chgo., 1988. Lt. j.g. USN, 1968—74. Named Man of Yr., Alliance for Children, L.A., 1996. Mem.: Hollywood (Calif.) Radio and TV Soc. (pres. 1995—). Avocations: skiing, motorcycling, photography. Office: Jim Henson Television 1416 N Labrea Ave Hollywood CA 90068

PERU, RAMEY (RAMIRO G. PERU), transportation executive; b. 1956; BSBA, U. Ariz., 1978; postgrad., Duke U. Acct. western contrs. dept. Phelps Dodge Corp., 1979, various positions in acctg. and fin., 1979-87, contr. Phelps Dodge Mining Co., 1987, asst. contr., 1987—93, v.p. Phelps Dodge Mining Co., 1993, v.p., treas., 1995, sr. v.p., 1997, sr. v.p. orgn. devel. and info. tech., CFO, 1999—2007, exec. v.p., 2004—07; exec. v.p., CFO Swift Transp. Corp., 2007, adv., 2007—. Bd. dirs. WellPoint, Inc., 2004—. Office: Swift Transp Corp 2200 S 75th Ave Phoenix AZ 85043

PESHKIN, SAMUEL DAVID, retired lawyer; b. Des Moines, Oct. 6, 1925; s. Louis and Mary (Grund) P.; m. Shirley R. Isenberg, Aug. 17, 1947; children: Lawrence Allen, Linda Ann. BA, State U. Iowa, 1948, JD, 1951. Bar: Iowa 1951. Ptnr. Bridges & Peshkin, Des Moines, 1953-66, Peshkin & Robinson, Des Moines, 1966-82. Mem. Iowa Bd. Law Examiners, 1970—. Bd. dir. State U. Iowa Found., 1957—, Old Gold Devel. Fund, 1956—, Sch. Religion U. Iowa, 1966—. Fellow Am. Bar Found., Internat. Soc. Barristers; mem. ABA (chmn. standing com. membership 1959—, ho. of dels. 1968—, bd. govs. 1973—), Iowa Bar Assn. (bd. govs. 1958—, pres. jr. bar sect. 1958-59, award of merit 1974), Inter-Am. Bar Assn., Internat. Bar Assn., Am. Judicature Soc., State U. Iowa Alumni Assn. (dir., pres. 1957) Home and Office: 14500 N Frank Lloyd Wright Blvd Apt 310 Scottsdale AZ 85260-8822 Office Phone: 480-607-3136.

PETAK, WILLIAM JOHN, systems management educator; b. Johnstown, Pa., June 23, 1932; s. Val Andrew and Lola Agatha (Boroski) P.; m. Ramona Janet Cayuela, Dec. 28, 1957; children: Elizabeth Ann Petak-Aaron, William Matthew, Michael David. BS in Mech. Engring., U. Pitts., 1956; MBA, U. So. Calif., 1963, DPA, 1969. Engr. Northrop Corp., Hawthorne, Calif., 1956-59; test engr. Wyle Labs., El Segundo, Calif., 1959-63; we. regional mgr. Instrument div. Budd Co., Phoenixville, Pa., 1963-69; v.p., dir. J.H. Wiggins Co., Redondo Beach, Calif., 1969-81; prof. systems mgmt. U. So. Calif., LA, 1982-98, exec. dir. Inst. Safety and Sys. Mgmt., 1987-98, prof. policy, planning and devel., 1998—2005, emeritus prof., 2006. Chmn. earthquake mitigation com. Nat. Com. on Property Ins., Boston, 1990-92; mem. com. on natural disasters NRC, Washington, 1985-91, mem. U.S. nat. com. for the decade for natural disaster reduction, 1989-92. Co-author: Natural Hazard Risk Assessment and Public Policy, 1982, Politics and Economics of Earthquake Hazard Reduction, 1986, Disabled Persons and Earthquake Hazards, 1988; editor spl. issue Pub. Adminstrn. Rev., 1985. Commr. County of Los Angeles, 1994—; mem. policy bd. So. Calif. Earthquake Prep. Project, L.A., 1986-92; trustee Marymount Coll., Palos Verdes, Calif., 1974-2009. Sgt. U.S. Army, 1950-52. Mem. Soc. for Risk Analysis, Earthquake Engring. Rsch. Inst., Am. Soc. for Pub. Adminstrn., Sigma Xi. Republican. Roman Catholic. Avocations: skiing, fishing, hiking. Office: 6044 Moss Bank Dr Rancho Palos Verdes CA 90275 Business E-Mail: petak@usc.edu.

PETERS, AULANA LOUISE, lawyer, former government agency commissioner; b. Shreveport, La., Nov. 30, 1941; d. Clyde A. and Eula Mae (Faulkner) Pharis; m. Bruce F. Peters, Oct. 6, 1967. BA in Philosophy, Coll. New Rochelle, 1963; JD, U. So. Calif., 1973. Bar: Calif., 1974. Sec., English corr. Publimondial, Spa, Milan, Italy, 1963-64, Fibramianto, Spa, Milan, 1964-65, Turkish del. to Office for Econ. Cooperation & Devel., Paris, 1965-66; adminstrv. asst. Office for Econ. Cooperation & Devel., Paris, 1966-67; assoc. Gibson, Dunn & Crutcher, LA, 1973-80, ptnr., 1980-84, 88—; commr. SEC, Washington, 1984-88. Bd. dirs. 3M Corp., Merrill Lynch & Co., Mobil Corp., Northrop Grumman, Callaway Golf Co. Recipient Disting. Alumnus award Econs. Club So. Calif., 1984, Washington Achiever award Nat. Assn. Bank Women, 1986, Critics Choice award nat. Women's Econ. Alliance, 1994, Women in Bus. award HOllywood C. of C., 1995. Mem. ABA, State Bar of Calif. (civil litigation cons. group 1983-84), Los Angeles County Bar Assn., Black Women Lawyers Assn. L.A., Assn. Bus. Trial Lawyers (panelist L.A. 1982), Women's Forum, Washington. Office: Gibson Dunn & Crutcher 333 S Grand Ave Ste 4400 Los Angeles CA 90071-3197

PETERS, CHARLES WILLIAM, nuclear energy industry executive; b. Pierceton, Ind., Dec. 9, 1927; s. Charles Frederick and Zelda May (Line) Peters; m. Katharine Louise Schuman, May 29, 1953; 1 child, Susan Kay; m. Patricia Ann Miles, Jan. 2, 1981; stepchildren: Bruce Miles Merkle, Leslie Ann Merkle Sanaie, Philip Frank Merkle, William Macneil Merkle. AB, Ind. U., 1950; postgrad., U. Md., 1952—58. Supervisory rsch. physicist Naval Rsch. Lab., Washington, 1950—71; physicist EPA, Washington, 1971—76; mgr. advanced sys. EATON-Consol. Controls Corp., Springfield, Va., 1976—89; v.p. Nuc. Diagnostic Sys., Inc., Springfield, Va., 1989—92; cons. Am. Tech. Inst., Memphis, 1993—. With US Army, 1945—47. Mem.: AAAS, IEEE, Am. Phys. Soc. Home and Office: 5235 N Whispering Hills Ln Tucson AZ 85704-2510

PETERS, JOSEPH DONALD, filmmaker; b. Montebello, Calif., Mar. 7, 1958; s. Donald Harry and Anna Lucia (Suarez) Peters; m. Cherrie Renea Peters. BA in Comm., U. So. Calif., LA, 1982. Filmmaker Renaissance Prodns., Ltd., San Dimas, Calif., 1986—. Writer, prodr., dir. films, TV, Seniors and Alcohol Abuse, 1986, Eskimo Ice Cream Shoes, 1990 (Gold award 1991), Rachel, 1994 (Silver and Bronze award 1995), Emotions, 1999 (Gold and Honorable Mention award 1999), When Autumn Comes, 2003. Mem. Am. Film Inst., Nat. Assn. Latino Independent Producers, The Writer's Table. Avocations: collecting dvd's, sporting events, reading. Office: Renaissance Prodns Ltd PO Box 582 San Dimas CA 91773-2734 Business E-Mail: jpeters@josephdpeters.com.

PETERS, RICHARD T., lawyer; b. La Mesa, Calif., Sept. 24, 1946; BA, Santa Clara U., 1968; JD, UCLA, 1971. Bar: Calif. 1972. Ptnr. Sidley & Austin, LA, 1995—. Mem. Am. Coll. Bankruptcy (regent; chair 9th civic admissions coun.), State Bar Calif. (mem. debtor-creditor rels. and bankruptcy subcom. bus. law sect. 1979-81, chmn. 1981-82, mem. exec. com. bus. law sect. 1982-85, vice chmn. 1984-85), Calif. Continuing Edn. Bar (cons. 1984, 95), L.A. Fin. Lawyers Conf. (bd. govs. 1976-80), L.A. County Bar Assn. (comml. law and bankruptcy sect., bankruptcy com. 1996—). Office: Sidley & Austin 555 W 5th St Fl 40 Los Angeles CA 90013-1010

PETERS, ROBERT WOOLSEY, retired architect; b. Mpls., Mar. 24, 1935; s. John Eugene and Adelaide Elizabeth (Woolsey) P. BArch., U. Minn., 1958; MArch., Yale U., 1964. Registered architect, N.Mex. Participating assoc. Skidmore Owings & Merrill, Chgo., 1961-74; dir. design Schaefer & Assocs., Wichita, Kans., 1975-76; ptnr. Addy & Peters, Albuquerque, 1979-82; owner, sole proprietor Robert W. Peters AIA Architect, 1982—2004, ret., 2004. Exhibited work Centre Georges Pompidou, Paris, 1980, U. Art Mus., Albuquerque, 1982, 92, Albuquerque Mus., 1988; contbr. articles to Century Mag., Progressive Architecture, House & Garden, House Beautiful, also others. Recipient honor awards N.Mex. Soc. Architects, 1980-83, 86, 87, 92, HUD, 1980; 5th Nat. Passive Solar Conf., Amherst, Mass., 1981. Fellow AIA; mem. Contemporary Art Soc. N.Mex. (bd. dirs., pres.), N.Mex. Arch. Found. (pres. 2004-), Yale N.Mex. Democrat. Roman Catholic.

PETERS, SCOTT, lawyer, former councilman; b. Springfield, Ohio, June 17, 1958; m. Lynn Peters; 2 children. BA in Econs. and Polit. Sci. magna cum laude, Duke U.; JD, NYU. Economist EPA, Washington; atty. Dorsey & Whitney, Mpls., Baker & McKenzie, San Diego; ptnr. Peters & Varco LLP, 1996—; dep. company counsel San Diego, 1991—96; councilman, Dist. 1 San Diego City Coun., 2000—08, pres., 2006—07, vice chmn. Natural Resources & Culture Com., 2002, chmn. Land Use and Housing Com. Lutheran. Office: 3368 Governor Dr, # 223 San Diego CA 92122 Office Phone: 619-236-6611. E-mail: ScottPeters@sandiego.gov.*

PETERS, STEPHEN C., lawyer; b. Kansas City, Mo., Apr. 8, 1957; BA cum laude, Kans. State U., 1979; JD, Duke U., 1983. Bar: Colo. 1983, US Dist. Ct. (dist. Colo.), US Ct. Appeals. Asst. US atty. Dist. Colo., 1987—94; instr. Nat. Inst. Trial Advocacy, 1990—2001; atty. Lindquist & Vennum, PLLP, Denver. Mem. criminal justice act panel US Dist. Ct. (dist. Colo.). Recipient Dir.'s award, US Dept. Justice, 1994; named a Colo. Super Lawyer, 2006. Mem.: N.W. Colo. Bar Assn., Colo. Trial Lawyers Assn., Colo. Bar Assn., ABA (criminal justice sect.), Phi Beta Kappa. Office: Lindquist & Vennum PLLP Ste 1800 S 600 17th St Denver CO 80202-5441 Office Phone: 303-454-0519. Office Fax: 303-573-1956. E-mail: speters@lindquist.com.

PETERS, THOMAS, foundation administrator; BA, San Francisco State U., 1966; PhD, U. Minn., 1973. Various positions including assoc. dir. of health Dept. of Public Health, San Francisco, 1974—90; dir. Health and Human Services, Marin County, 1991—98; pres., CEO Marin Community Found., 1998—. Mem. Cmty. Leadership Team Council on Foundations; bd. mem. Cmty. Foundations of Am., League of Calif. Cmty. Foundations; fellow NIH, 1968—71. Office: Marin Cmty Found 5 Hamilton Landing Novato CA 94949

PETERS, WILLIAM JAMES, lawyer; b. Washington, Jan. 12, 1967; s. Richard Jacob and Concepcion Valera Peters; m. Amy D. Peters, May 8, 2004; children: Matthew James, Natalie Christine. BA, UCLA, 1990; JD, Loyola U., 1994. Corp. counsel MCI Systemhouse, LA, 1994-96; assoc. Milbank, Tweed, Hadley & McCloy, LA, 1996-99; dir. legal Exult, Irvine, 1999—; ptnr. O'Melveny & Myers LLP, LA. Office: O'Melveny & Myers LLP 400 South Hope St Los Angeles CA 90071-2899 Office Phone: 213-430-7598. Office Fax: 213-430-6407. E-mail: wpeters@omm.com.

PETERSEN, CHRIS, college football coach; b. 1964; m. Barbara Petersen; children: Jack, Sam. BA in Psychology, U. Calif. Davis, 1988, M in Edn. & Psychology. Freshman football coach U. Calif. Davis, 1987—88, receivers coach, 1989—91; quarterbacks coach U. Pitts., 1992, Portland St. U., 1993—94; offensive coord. U. Oreg., 1995—2000, Boise State U., 2000—05, head football coach, 2006—. Recipient Paul "Bear" Bryant award, Nat. Sportscasters & Sportswriters Assn., 2006; named WAC Coach of Yr., Sporting News, 2008. Achievements include coaching Boise St. to a perfect 12-0 record, 2006. Office: Boise State U Dept Athletics Boise ID 83725*

PETERSEN, FINN BO, oncologist, educator; b. Copenhagen, Mar. 26, 1951; came to U.S., 1983; s. Jorgen and Ebba Gjeding (Jorgensen) P.; m. Merete Secher Lund, Mar. 7, 1979; children: Lars Secher, Thomas Secher, Andreas Secher. BA, Niels Steensen, Copenhagen, 1971; MD, U. Copenhagen, 1978. Intern U. Copenhagen, Copenhagen, 1978-79, resident in hematology, 1980-83; fellow oncology Fred Hutchinson Cancer Rsch. Ctr. U. Wash., Seattle, 1983-85, assoc. rschr. oncology, 1985-87, asst. mem. in clin. rsch., 1987-91, asst. prof., 1988-91, prof. medicine, 1992—; program dir. U. Utah Blood and Marrow Transplant, 1992—; med. dir. bone marrow transplant program LDS Hosp., 1997—. Author: Hematology, 1977; contbr. articles to profl. jours. Mem. AMA, AAAS, Internat. Soc. Exptl. Hematology, Am. Soc. Clin. Oncology, Am. Soc. Hematology, Assn. Gnotobiology. Office: U Utah Bone Marrow Transplant Program Div Hematology & Oncology Salt Lake City UT 84132-0001

PETERSEN, FREDERICK J., lawyer; b. 1975; Grad., Gonzaga U.; degree in law, U. Ariz. Atty. Mesch, Clark & Rothschild, 1999—. Bd. mem. Greater Tucson Leadership; mem. Vol. Lawyers Prog., Southern Ariz. Legal Aid; former pres. Handidogs Inc. Mem. Lawyers for Literacy. Named one of 40 Under 40, Tucson Bus. Edge, 2006. Mem.: Pima County Bar Assn. Young Lawyers Divsn. Office: Mesch, Clark & Rothschild 259 N Meyer Ave Tucson AZ 85701 Office Phone: 520-624-8886. Office Fax: 520-798-1037.

PETERSEN, KURT EDWARD, electrical engineer, researcher, entrepreneur; b. San Francisco, Feb. 13, 1948; s. William Ernest and Shirley Ann (Bailey) Petersen; m. Carol Tao, Sept. 24, 2000; children: Scott Edward, Brett William. BSEE cum laude, U. Calif., Berkeley, 1970; MS, MIT, 1972, PhD, 1975. Mem. rsch. staff IBM, San Jose, Calif., 1975-82; founder, v.p. tech. Transensory Devices, Inc., Fremont, Calif., 1982-85, NovaSensor, Fremont, Calif., 1985-95; founder, pres. Cepheid, Sunnyvale, Calif., 1996—2004; founder, CEO SiTime, Sunnyvale, Calif., 2004—. Cons. prof. Stanford (Calif.) U., 1994—. Fellow: IEEE (gen. chmn. solid state sensors workshop 1986, Simon Ramon medal 2001); mem.: Nat. Acad. Engring. Achievements include patents in micromachining technology. Avocations: skiing, travel. Office: SiTime 990 Almanor Dr Sunnyvale CA 94085 Office Phone: 408-328-4401. E-mail: kp@sitimecorp.com.

PETERSEN, MARTIN EUGENE, curator; b. Grafton, Iowa, Apr. 21, 1931; s. Martin S. and Martha Dorothea (Paulsen) P. AA, Mason City Jr. Coll., Iowa; BA, State U. Iowa, 1951, MA, 1957; postgrad., The Hague (Netherlands), 1964. Curator San Diego Mus. Art, 1957-96; advisor Olaf Wieghorst Mus., El Cajon, Calif., 1996—. Extension instr. U. Calif., 1958, lectr., 1960 Author art catalogues, books, articles in field. Served with AUS, 1952-54. Mem. So. Calif. Art Historians. Achievements include specialist in early southern California art.

PETERSEN, RICHARD HERMAN, federal agency administrator, aeronautical engineer; b. Quincy, Ill., Oct. 9, 1934; s. Herman Hiese and Nancy (Getty) P.; m. Joandra Windsor Shenk, Sept. 15, 1959; children: Eric Norman, Kristin. BS in Aero. Engring., Purdue U., 1956, Dr. Engring. (hon.), 1986; MS in Aeronautics, Calif. Inst. Tech., 1957; D in Pub. Service (hon.), George Washington U., 1987; DSc (hon.), Coll. of William and Mary, 1992. Rsch. engr. NASA Ames Rsch. Ctr., Moffett Field, Calif., 1957-63, aerospace engr., 1963-65, 66-70, br. chief, 1970-73, div. chief, 1975-80; aerospace engr. NASA, Washington, 1965-66; exec. Nielsen Engring. & Rsch. Inc., Mountain View, Calif., 1973-75; dep. dir. NASA Langley Research Ctr., Hampton, Va., 1980-85, dir., 1985-91; assoc. adminstr. Aeronautics and Space Tech. NASA Hdqrs., Washington, 1991-93, retired, 1993; aerospace cons., 1993—. 1st lt. USAF, 1957-60. Recipient Disting. Alumnus award Purdue U., 1980, Meritorious Exec. award U.S. Pres., 1982, Disting. Exec. award U.S. Pres., 1989; Sloan exec. fellow Stanford U., 1973. Fellow AIAA (bd. dirs. 1984-90, Sylvanus A. Reed Aeronautics award 1991), Nat. Acad. Engring. Republican. Avocations: golf, skiing. Home: 2245 Via Tabara La Jolla CA 92037-5842

PETERSEN, ROLAND, artist, printmaker; b. Endelave, Horsens, Denmark, 1926; came to US, 1928; m. Caryl Ritter, Mar. 4, 2003; children from previous marriage: Dana Mark, Maura Brooke, Julien Conrad, Karena Caia. BA, U. Calif., Berkeley, 1949, MA, 1950; postgrad., Han Hofmann's Sch. Fine Arts, 1950-51, S.W. Hayter's

Atelier 17, Paris, 1950, 63, 70, Islington Studio, London, 1976, The Print Workshop, 1980. Tchr. State Coll. Wash., Pullman, 1952-56; faculty U. Calif., Davis, 1956-91, prof. art, 1991; ret., 1991. Exhibited one-man shows: Oakland At Mus., 1954, Calif. Palace Legion of Honor, San Francisco, 1961, Gump's Gallery, San Francisco, 1962, Staempfli Gallery, N.Y.C., 1963, 65, 67, Adele Bednarz Gallery, Los Angeles, 1966, 69, 70, 72, 73, 75, 76, Crocker Art Gallery, Sacramento, 1965, de Young Mus., San Francisco, 1968, La Jolla Mus., 1971, Phoenix Mus., 1972, Santa Barbara Mus., 1973, U. Reading, Eng., 1977, 80, U. Calif., Davis, 1978, 92, Brubaker Gallery, Sarasota, Fla., 1979, Rorick Gallery, San Francisco, 1981, 82, 83, 84, 85, Himovitz-Salomon Gallery, Sacramento, 1987-88, 91, Vanderwoude Tananbaum Gallery, N.Y.C., 1987-89, Harcourts Gallery, San Francisco, 1989, 91, 93, U. Calif., Davis, 1992, Maxwell Galleries, San Francisco, 1995, Endelave (Denmark) Mus., 1996, John Natsoulas Gallery, Davis, Calif., 1998, Hackett-Freedman Gallery, San Francisco, 2002, 2004, 2008; group shows include Calif. Palace Legion of Honor, San Francisco Art Inst., 1962, Mus. Art, Carnegie Inst., Pitts., 1964, Obelisk Gallery, Washington, John Herron Art Inst., Indpls., 1964, Pa. Acad. Fine Arts, Phila., Crocker Art Gallery, Sacramento, 1965, 81, Art Inst. Chgo., 1965, Va. Mus. Fine Arts, Richmond, 1966, U. Ariz. Art Gallery, Tucson, 1967, Am. Cultural Center, Paris, 1971, Nat. Gallery, Washington, 1972, Otis Art Inst. Gallery, Los Angeles, 1974, Auerbach Fine Art Gallery, London, 1977, U. Wis., Madison, 1977, Bklyn. Mus., 1978, U. Ill., 1978, U. Nev., Las Vegas, 1980, Brubaker Gallery, Sarasota, Fla., 1983, U.S.A. World Print Council, San Francisco, Nat. Mus., Singapore, Nat. Gallery, Bangkok, Thailand, Amerika Haus, Berlin, Malmo Konsthall, Sweden, Museo Carrillo Gil, Mexico City, all 1984-86, Crocker Art Mus., 1991, Fresno Met. Mus., 1992, Hall of Pictures, Uman, Russia, 1992, Calif. State U., L.A., 1992, San Bernardino, 1993 Pence Gallery, Davis, Calif., 1993, Artists Contemporary Gallery, Sacramento, 1994, Andre Milan Gallery, Sao Paulo, Brazil, 1995; represented in permanent collections: de Young Mus., San Francisco, San Francisco Mus. Modern Art, Va. Mus. Fine Arts, Richmond, Mus. Modern Art, N.Y.C., Phila. Mus. Art, Whitney Mus. Am. Art, Phoenix Mus., Santa Barbara Mus., Musée Municipal, Brest, France, Smithsonian Instn. Nat. Collection Fine Arts & Archives of Am. Art, Hirschorn Coll., Washington, San Jose Mus. Art, Calif., others. With USN, 1944-46, PTO. Guggenheim fellow, 1963, U. Calif. creative arts fellow, 1967, 70, 77; Fulbright grant, 1970. Home: 1148 Crespi Dr Pacifica CA 94044-3539 Office: Hackett Freedman Gallery 250 Sutter St Fl 4 San Francisco CA 94108 Office Phone: 415-362-7152.

PETERSON, ANDREA, elementary school educator; b. BC, Canada; d. Victor and Darlene Rahn; m. Joel Peterson. BA in Music Edn., U. Wash., 1996. Cert. in early and mid. childhood music Nat. Bd. Tchg. Standards, 2002. Music tchr. to elem. music specialist Monte Cristo Elem. Sch., Granite Falls, Wash., 1997—. Named Wash. Tchr. of Yr., Coun. Chief State Sch. Officers, 2007, Nat. Tchr. of Yr., 2007. Avocations: saxophone, singing (mezzo soprano). Office: Monte Cristo Elem Sch 1201 100th St NE Granite Falls WA 98252 Business E-Mail: apeterso@gfalls.wednet.edu.

PETERSON, ANDREA LENORE, law educator; b. LA, July 21, 1952; d. Vincent Zetterberg and Elisabeth (Karlsson) P.; m. Michael Rubin, May 29, 1983; children: Peter Rubin, Eric Rubin, Emily Rubin. AB, Stanford U., 1974; JD, U. Calif., Berkeley, 1978. Bar: Calif., 1979, U.S. Dist. Ct. (no. dist.) Calif., 1979. Law clk. to Judge Charles B. Renfrew U.S. Dist. Ct. (no. dist.) Calif., San Francisco, 1978-79; lawyer Cooley, Godward, Castro, Huddleson & Tatum, San Francisco, 1979-80; law clk. to Justice Byron R. White U.S. Supreme Ct., Washington, 1980-81; lawyer Heller, Ehrman, White & McAuliffe, San Francisco, 1981-83; prof. law Boalt Hall U. Calif., Berkeley, 1983—. Contbr. articles to profl. jours. Office: U Calif Sch Law Boalt Hall Berkeley CA 94720

PETERSON, ARTHUR LAVERNE, foundation administrator; b. Glyndon, Minn., June 27, 1926; s. John M. and Hilda C. (Moline) P.; m. Connie Lucille Harr, June 14, 1952 (dec. July 26, 2002); children: Jon Martin, Rebecca Ruth, Donna Harr, Ingrid Bliss; m. Mary Kinum, Sept. 12, 2003. AB, Yale U., 1947; MSPA, U. So. Calif., 1949; postgrad., U. Chgo., 1949-50; PhD, U. Minn., 1962; LLD, Lebanon Valley Coll., 1988. Mem. Wis. State Legislature, 1951-55; from instr. to asst. prof. polit. sci. U. Wis., Eau Claire, 1954-60; assoc. prof. to prof. polit. sci. Ohio Wesleyan U., Delaware, 1961-65, 70-80; pres. Am. Grad. Sch. Internat. Mgmt., Phoenix, 1966-70; dean spl. programs Eckerd Coll., St. Petersburg, Fla., 1980-84, dir. Acad. Sr. Profls., 1987-94; pres. Lebanon Valley Coll., Annville, Pa., 1984-87; pres., CEO Ctr. for the Study of the Presidency, 1997-99; Scott prof. leadership Rocky Mountain Coll., Billings, Mont., 1999—2002; mem. Mont. Ho. Reps., 2001—; pres. Thomas Wathen Found. Acad., Riverside, Calif., 2002—. Bd. dirs. Arnold Industries; asst. to chmn. Rep. Nat. Com., Washington, 1960-61; founding dir. Ctr. Internat. Bus., L.A., 1969-70; cons. Novin Inst. Polit. Affairs, Tehran, Iran, 1973; exec. dir. Fla. Assn. Colls. and Univs., 1988—. Author: McCarthyism: Ideology and Foundations, 1962; co-author: Electing the President, 1968; contbr. articles to profl. jours. Chmn. Ohio Civil Rights Commn., 1963-65; dep. chmn. Republican Nat. Com., 1965-66; mem. Ohio Ethics Commn., 1976-80. Capt. USMC, 1951-52, Korea Citizenship Clearing House Nat. Faculty fellow, 1960; recipient citation for excellence Sigma Phi Epsilon, 1977, Marshall award Ohio Wesleyan Students, 1979. Mem. Am. Polit. Sci. Assn., Am. Judicature Soc. (dir. 1975—), Soc. Polit. Enquiries (pres. 1985—), Acad. Polit. Sci., Rotary, Masons, Pi Sigma Alpha (dir. 1972—), Phi Mu Alpha Sinfonia, Omicron Delta Kappa Republican. Mem. United Ch. of Christ. Avocations: sailing, flying, music. Home: 26555 Chambers Ave Sun City CA 92586-2132 Office: Wathen Found 4130 Mennes Ave Riverside CA 92509 E-mail: apeter333@aol.com.

PETERSON, CHASE N., university president; b. Logan, Utah, Dec. 27, 1929; s. E.G. and Phebe (Nebeker) P.; m. Grethe Ballif, 1956; children: Erika Elizabeth, Stuart Ballif, Edward Chase. AB, Harvard U., 1952, MD, 1956. Diplomate: Am. Bd. Internal Medicine. Asst. prof. medicine U. Utah Med. Sch., 1965-67; assoc. Salt Lake Clinic; dean admissions and fin. aids to students Harvard U., 1967-72, v.p. univ., 1972-78; v.p. health scis. U. Utah, Salt Lake City, 1978-83, prof. medicine, 1983—, pres., 1983-91, clin. prof. medicine, 1991—. Pres. emeritus U. Utah, Salt Lake City, 1992—; bd. dirs. First Security Corp., Utah Power & Light Co., D.C. Tanner Co., OEC Med. Systems. Mem. Nat. Assn. State Univs. and Land-Grant Colls. (chmn. 1988-89, chair U.S. Ofc. Tech. Assessment adv. bd. 1990-92). Home: 66 Thaynes Canyon Dr Park City UT 84060-6711 Office: U Utah Sch Medicine 50 N Medical Dr Rm 1c26 Salt Lake City UT 84132-0001

PETERSON, COURTLAND HARRY, law educator; b. Denver, June 28, 1930; s. Harry James and Courtney (Caple) P.; m. Susan Schwab, Gisvold, Jan. 28, 1966; children: Brooke, Linda, Patrick. BA, U. Colo., 1951, LLB, 1953; MCL, U. Chgo., 1959; JD, U. Freiburg, Germany, 1964. Bar: Colo. 1953. Mem. faculty U. Colo. Law Sch., 1959—, prof., 1963—, dean, 1974-79, Nicholas Rosenbaum prof., 1991-94, Nicholas Doman prof. emeritus, 1995—. Vis. prof. UCLA Law Sch., 1965, Max Planck Inst., Hamburg, Germany, 1969-70, U. Tex. Law Sch., Austin, 1973-74, Summer Program, Tulane U., Rodos, Greece, 1993, Summer Program, La. State U., Aix-en-Provence, France, 1996; bd. dirs. Continuing Legal Edn. in Colo., 1974-77. Author: Die Anerkennung Auslaendischer Urteile, 1964; Translator: (Bauer) An Introduction to German Law, 1965. Served to 1st lt. USAF, 1954-56. Fgn. Law fellow U. Chgo., 1957-59; Ford Found. Law Faculty fellow, 1964; Alexander von Humboldt Stiftung fellow, 1969-70. Mem. ABA, Colo. Bar Assn. (bd. govs. 1974-79), Boulder County Bar Assn., Am. Soc. Comparative Law (dir., bd. editors, treas. 1978-89, hon. pres. 1996-98), Internat. Acad. Comparative Law, Am. Law Inst., Boulder County Bar Found. (trustee 1995-2000), U. Colo. Ret. Faculty Assn. (pres. 1998-2000). Home: 4135 Caddo Pky Boulder CO 80303 Office: U Colo Law Sch Boulder CO 80309-0001 Personal E-mail: courtpeterson@comcast.net.

PETERSON, CRAIG ANTON, state legislator; b. Salt Lake City, May 23, 1947; m. Annette Langford, Nov. 15, 1972; 5 children. BS Mfg. Engring. Tech., Weber State U., 1966; postgrad., Tex. A&M U., Corpus Christi, 1968-72. Pres. Craig A. Peterson Cons. LLC, Orem, Utah; mem. Utah Ho. of Reps., 1986-88, Utah State Senate, 1988-98, majority whip, 1993-94, majority leader, 1995-98; owner Craig Peterson Cons., Orem, Utah, 1998—. Mem. various coms. including mgmt., retirement, and human svcs. Republican. Office: 6195 Dry Creek CIR Highland UT 84003-3008

PETERSON, EDWIN J., retired judge, mediator, educator; b. Gilmanton, Wis., Mar. 30, 1930; s. Edwin A. and Leora Grace (Kitelinger) P.; m. Anna Chadwick, Feb. 7, 1971; children: Patricia, Andrew, Sherry. BS, U. Oreg., 1951, LLB, 1957. Bar: Oreg. 1957. Assoc. firm Tooze, Kerr, Peterson, Marshall & Shenker, Portland, Oreg., 1957-61, mem. firm, 1961-79; assoc. justice Supreme Ct. Oreg., Salem, 1979-83, 91-93, chief justice, 1983—91; ret., 1993; disting. jurist-in-residence, adj. instr. Willamette Coll. of Law, Salem, 1994—. Chmn. Supreme Ct. Task Force on Racial Issues, 1992-94, Oreg. Law Enforcement Contacts Policy and Data Review Com., 2005-; standing com. on fed. rules of practice and procedure, 1987-93; bd. dirs. Conf. Chief Justices, 1985-87, 88-91; founder Understanding Racism Found., 1998; mem. Oreg. Joint Bench-Bar Commn. on Professionalism, 1996-, chair, 1996-97. Chmn. Portland Citizens Sch. Com., 1968-70; vice-chmn. Young Rep. Fedn. Oreg., 1951; bd. visitors U. Oreg. Law Sch., 1978-83, 87-93, chmn. bd. visitors, 1981-83; pres., bd. dirs. Understanding Racism Found., 1999-2002, bd. dirs., 2002—. 1st lt. USAF, 1952-54. Mem. Oreg. State Bar (bd. examiners 1963-66, gov. 1973-76, vice chmn. profl. liability fund 1977-78), Multnomah County Bar Assn. (pres. 1972-73), Phi Alpha Delta, Lambda Chi Alpha. Episcopalian. Office: Willamette Univ Coll Law 245 Winter St SE Salem OR 97301-3916 Home: 471 High St SE # 340 Salem OR 97301 Office Phone: 503-375-5399. Business E-Mail: epeterso@willamette.edu.

PETERSON, G. P. (BUD PETERSON), academic administrator; b. Prairie Village, Kans. BS in Mech. Engring. and Math., Kans. State U., 1975, MS in Engring., 1980; PhD, Tex. A&M U., 1985. Engring. prof. Tex. A&M U., College Station, 1981—2000; provost Rensselaer Poly. Inst., Troy, NY, 2000—06; chancellor U. Colo., Boulder, 2006—. Editor: Jour. Exptl. Thermal and Fluid Scis.; assoc. editor: ASME Jour. Heat Transfer, AIAA Jour. Thermophysics and Heat Transfer, Internat. Jour. Heat and Fluid Flow, Microscale Thermophysical Engring.; contbr. articles to profl. jours. Recipient Best Paper award, AIAA, 1990, award for outstanding mgmt., NSF, 1994, Ralph James and the O. L. (Andy) Lewis awards, ASME, Dow Outstanding Young Faculty award, ASEE, Pi Tau Sigma Gustus L. Larson Meml. award, ASME, Thermophysics award, AIAA, Meml. award, ASME, Sustained Svc. award, AIAA; fellow, Tex. Engring. Expt. Sta., 1986, 1988; sr. fellow, 1989. Fellow: Am. Inst. of Aeronautics and Astronautics, Am. Soc. of Mech. Engrs.; mem.: Phi Kappa Phi, Sigma Xi, Tau Beta Pi, Pi Tau Sigma. Office: U Colo Office of Chancellor 17 UCB, Regent 301 Boulder CO 80309 Office Phone: 303-492-8908. E-mail: chanchat@spot.colorado.edu.

PETERSON, GARY ANDREW, agronomics researcher; b. Holdrege, Nebr., Apr. 30, 1940; s. Walter Andrew and Evelyn Christine (Johnson) P.; m. Jacquelyn Charlene Flick, June 18, 1965; children: Kerstin, Ingrid. BS, U. Nebr., 1963, MS, 1965; PhD, Iowa State U., 1967. Research assoc. agronomy Iowa State U., Ames, 1964-67; prof. U. Nebr., Lincoln, 1967-84; prof. soil and crop scis. Colo. State U., Ft. Collins, 1984—, head dept. soil and crop scis., 2003—. Assoc. editor AGronomy Jour., 1979-81, tech. editor, 1981-83, editor, 1984-89, editor-in-chief, 1991-96; contbr. articles to profl. jours. Fellow Am. Soc. Agronomy (Ciba-Geigy Agr. Achievement award 1974, Agronomic Achievement award-Soils 1990), Soil Sci. Soc. Am. (prs. 2008, Applied Rsch. award 1987); mem. Soil Conservation Soc. Am. Republican. Avocations: reading, hiking, skiing. Office: Colo State U Dept Soil Crop Scis Fort Collins CO 80523-0001 Home Phone: 970-224-5752; Office Phone: 970-491-6501. Business E-Mail: gary.peterson@colostate.edu.

PETERSON, JANE WHITE, nursing educator, anthropologist; b. San Juan, Feb. 15, 1941; d. Jerome Sidney and Vera (Joseph) Peterson; 1 child, Claire Marie. BS, Boston U., 1968; M in Nursing, U. Wash., 1969, PhD, 1981. Staff nurse Visiting Nurse Assn., Boston, 1964-66; prof. Seattle U., 1969—, dir. nursing home project, 1990-92, chair pers. com., 1988-90; chair dept. Community Health and Psychiat. Mental Health Nursing, 1987-89. Sec. Coun. on Nursing and Anthropology, 1984-86; pres. Wash. League Nursing, Seattle, 1988-90; pres. bd. Vis. Nurses Svcs., Seattle, 1988-90; contbg. cons. CSI Prodn., Okla., 1987; cons. in nursing WHO/U. Indonesia, Jakarta, fall 1989, Myanmar (Burma), Yangon, winter 1995, Beijing, 1995. Contbr. articles to profl. jours., chptrs. to books. Co-owner (with Robert Colley) North End Train Ctr., Seattle; mem. Seattle Art Mus., 1986—. Fellow: Soc. for Applied Anthropology; mem. Am. Anthropological Assn., Soc. for Med. Anthropology, Nat. League for Nursing, Am. Ethological Soc. Office: Seattle U Sch Nursing Broadway and Madison Seattle WA 98122

PETERSON, JEFFREY V., construction executive; b. 1946; m. Eva Peterson; 3 children. BS, U. So. Calif.; MBA, Stanford U., 1971. Mng. dir. investment banking Kidder, Peabody & Co., 1987—92; mng. dir. pvt. client services Trust Co. of the West, 1992—2005; bd. dir. Standard Pacific Corp., 2000—, lead ind. dir., 2004—08, chmn., pres., CEO, 2008. Am. Heart Assn.; bd. mem. Am. Hosp. in Paris, Pitzer Coll., Lowe Inst., Claremont McKenna Coll. Office: Standard Pacific Corp 26 Technology Dr Irvine CA 92618-2301*

PETERSON, JOE, computer software company executive; Student, U. Wash., 1983—88. With Microsoft Corp., Redmond, Wash., 1995—, with Internet Explorer devel. group, 1995—99, with MSN customer experience group, 1999—2001, v.p. Windows Client Core Platform unit, corp. v.p. market expansion platform group, 2006—07, corp. v.p. software protection & commerce grp., 2007—. Avocations: snowboarding, skiing, hiking, scuba diving.

PETERSON, JOEL C., investment company executive; b. May 20, 1947; m. Diana J. Hulme; 7 children. BS, Brigham Young U.; MBA, Harvard U., 1973. Treas. Trammell Crow Co., 1973—77, CFO, 1977—85, CEO, 1988—91; founding ptnr. Peterson Ptnrs., LP, Salt Lake City, 1995—; vice chmn. JetBlue Airways Corp., 2007—08, chmn., 2008—. Lectr. entrepreneurial mgmt. Stanford U. Grad. Sch. Bus., 1992—; bd. dirs. Asurion, Dallas Market Ctr., Texas Commerce Bank, Dallas, Franklin Covey Co., 1997—, JetBlue Airways Corp., 1999—. Bd. dirs. Covey Leadership Ctr., 1993—97, vice chmn., 1994—97. Office: Peterson Ptnrs, LP 2825 E Cottonwood Parkway, St 400 Salt Lake City UT 84121 Office Phone: 801-365-0180. Office Fax: 801-365-0181. E-mail: joel@petersonpartnerslp.com.

PETERSON, JOHN LEONARD, lawyer, judge; b. Butte, Mont., Sept. 11, 1933; s. Roy victor and Lena Pauline (Umhang) P.; m. Jean Marie Hollingsworth, June 10, 1957; children: Michael R., John Robert, Carol Jean. BA in Bus., U. Mont., 1957, JD, 1957. Bar: Mont. 1957, U.S. Supreme Ct. 1964, U.S. Ct. Appeals (9th cir.) 1974, U.S. Tax Ct. 1978. Assoc. McCaffery, Roe, Kiely & Joyce, 1957-63; ptnr. McCaffery & Peterson, 1963-79; sole practice Butte, 1979-85. Part-time U.S. bankruptcy judge, 1963-85; U.S. bankruptcy judge, Mont., 1985—; bd. govs. Nat. Conf. Bankruptcy Judges, 1989-92. Mem. Mont. Bd. Regents Higher Edn., 1975-82; del. Dem. Nat. Conv., 1968. Mem. Nat. Conf. Bankruptcy Judges, Mont. Bar Assn., Silver bow County Bar Assn., Butte Country Club. Democrat. Lutheran. Office: US Dist Ct Chief Bankruptcy Judge 215 Fed Bldg Butte MT 59701

PETERSON, KURT C., lawyer; b. Salem, NJ, Mar. 31, 1953; BA in Econs. and Polit. Sci., Stanford U., 1975; JD, U. Calif. Hastings Coll. Law, 1978. Bar: Calif. 1978, US Dist. Ct. No. Dist. Calif., US Dist Ct. Ctrl. Dist. Calif. Law clk. to Hon. Robert Kane Calif. Ct. Appeal 1st Dist., 1978; with Crosby Heafey Roach & May (combined with Reed Smith in 2003), 1978—2003, opened L.A. office & served as first mng. ptnr., 1990, opened Century City office, 1997, mng. ptnr., 2000—03; ptnr., mem. exec. com. Reed Smith LLP, 2003—. Contbr. ABA Profl. Liability Litig. Newsletter. Bd. trustees Ctr. for Law in the Pub. Interest; bd. dirs. Music Ctr. of LA County and Techno. Named Alumnus of Yr., Hastings Alumni Assn. LA Chpt., 2001; named one of the top 25 lawyers under 45 in Calif., Calif. Law Bus., 1993. Mem.: ABA (vice chair litig. sect. legal malpractice subcom. 1989—92), Assn. Bus. Trial Lawyers, L.A. Bar Assn. Office: Reed Smith LLP 1901 Ave of the Stars, Ste 700 Los Angeles CA 90067-6078 Office Phone: 310-734-5201. Office Fax: 310-734-5299. Business E-Mail: kpeterson@reedsmith.com.

PETERSON, LAURENCE E., physics educator; b. Grantsburg, Wis., July 26, 1931; m. Joelle Dallancon, 1956; children: Mark L., Daniel F., Lynn M., Julianne. BS, U. Minn., 1954, PhD, 1960. Rsch. assoc. in physics U. Minn., Mpls., 1960-62; from resident physicist to prof. physics U. Calif., San Diego, 1962—. Physics subcom. NASA Space Sci. Steering Com., 1964—, assoc. dir. sci. astrophysics divsn., 1986-88; dir. Ctr. Astrophysics & Space Sci., U. Calif., San Diego, 1988—. Fellow NSF, 1958-59, Guggenheim Found., 1973-74. Fellow Am. Phys. Soc.; mem. AIAA (space sci. award 1978), AAAS, Am. Astron. Soc., Internat. Astronomical Union. Office: U Calif San Diego Ctr Astrophysics & Space Scis MC 0424 9500 Gilman Dr La Jolla CA 92093

PETERSON, LESLIE RAYMOND, barrister; b. Viking, Alta., Can., Oct. 6, 1923; s. Herman S. and Margaret (Karen) P.; m. Agnes Rose Hine, June 24, 1950; children: Raymond Erik, Karen Isabelle. Student, Camrose Luth. Coll., Alta., McGill, U., Can., London U.; LLB, U. B.C., Can., 1949; LLD (hon.), U. B.C., 1993; LLD, Simon Fraser U., Can., 1965; EdD, Notre Dame U., Nelson, Can., 1966; diploma tech. (hon.), B.C. Inst. Tech., 1994. Bar: B.C. 1949; called to Queens Counsel, 1960. Pvt. practice barrister, Vancouver, B.C., 1949-52; with Peterson & Anderson, 1952, Boughton & Co., 1953—55; mem. B.C. Legislature for Vancouver Centre, 1956—63, Vancouver-Little Mountain, 1966; min. of edn., 1956-68; min. of labour, 1960-71; atty. gen., 1968-72; bd. govs. U. B.C., Vancouver, 1979-83, chancellor, 1987-93. Bd. dirs. Can. Found. Econ. Edn., Inst. Corp. Dirs. Can., West Vancouver Found., Inst. for Pacific Ocean Sci. and Tech.; trustee Peter Wall Inst. for Advanced Studies; chmn. U. B.C. Found., 1990—96. Bd. dirs. Portland unit Shriners Hosp. for Children, 1994-96; past bd. dirs. Western Soc. of Rehab., YMCA, Victoria B.C.; past pres. Twenty Club; hon. mem. Vancouver Jr. C. of C.; former v.p. Normanna Old People's Home; founding mem. Convocation, Simon Fraser U. and U. Victoria; hon. dep. French Nat. Assembly, Paris; hon. commr. labor State of Okla.; gov. Downtown Vancouver Assn. With Can. Army, 1942-46, ETO. Recipient Disting. Alumnus award Camrose Luth. Coll., 1980. Fellow: Royal Soc. Arts; mem.: Internat. Assn. Govt. Labour Ofcls. (chmn. standing com., Can. mins. of edn. 1965—66), Law Soc. B.C., Vancouver Bar Assn., Wesbrook Soc. of U. B.C. (chmn. 1987), Union Club (Victoria), Terminal City Club (pres. 1991—92), Scandinavian Bus. Men's Club (past pres.), Order of Can., Venerable Order of Saint John (comdr.), Order of B.C., Freemason (potentate Gizeh Temple Shrine 1988), Order of St. Lazarus (knight comdr.). Avocations: skiing, golf, fishing, tennis. Home: 814 Highland West Vancouver BC Canada V7S 2G5 Office: Boughton Peterson Law Corp 595 Burrard St Ste 1000 PO Box 49290 Vancouver BC Canada V7X 1S8 Home Phone: 604-922-0667; Office Phone: 604-647-4156. Personal E-mail: lpeterson@bpya.com. Business E-Mail: lpeterson@boughton.ca.

PETERSON, LINDA S., lawyer; b. Grand Forks, ND, Mar. 15, 1952; BA summa cum laude, U. N.D., 1973; JD, Yale U., 1977. Bar: N.D. 1977, D.C. 1978, U.S. Dist. Ct. D.C. 1979, U.S. Ct. Appeals (D.C. cir.) 1979, U.S. Ct. Appeals (3d cir.) 1982, Calif. 1986, U.S. Ct. Appeals (fed. cir.) 1986. Law clk. Ct. of Appeals for D.C., Washington, 1977-78; ptnr. Sidley & Austin, LA, 1978—. Dep. counsel Webster Commn., 1992; mem. bd. trustees Southwestern U. Sch. Law, 1995. Recipient Dean Phillips Memorial Award, Vietnam Veterans of America. Mem. State Bar Calif. (rules of ct. com. 1988-91), L.A. County Bar Assn. (conf. dels. 1987-90, trustee 1998-99), Women

Lawyers Assn. L.A. (bd. dirs. 1989-99, pres. 1998-99), Phi Beta Kappa. Office: Sidley Austin Brown & Wood LLP 555 W 5th St Ste 4000 Los Angeles CA 90013-3000

PETERSON, MARISSA T., former computer systems network executive; b. Philippines, 1962; arrived in US, 1978; BS in Mech. Engring., Kettering U., 1983; MBA, Harvard U. Mgmt. cons. Booz, Allen and Hamilton; previously held mktg., fin., and engring. positions Saturn Corp., Gen. Motors Corp.; dir. US mfg. Sun Microsystems Inc., Santa Clara, Calif., 1993—95, v.p. worldwide ops., logistics, 1995—98, v.p. worldwide ops., 1998—99, exec. v.p. worldwide ops., 2000—02, exec. v.p. worldwide ops. & chief customer advocate, 2002—05. Bd. dirs. SuperValu Inc., 2003—, Humana Inc., 2008—. Bd. trustees Kettering U., Industry Advisory Coun., Alliance for Innovative Mfg., Stanford U.; bd. dirs. Lucille Packard Children's Hosp., Stanford. Recipient Silicon Valley Tribute to Women and Industry, Mgmt. Achievement award, Kettering U.; named to Top 100 in Bus., SF Bus. Times.

PETERSON, MARY L., state agency official; BA in English, Carleton Coll., 1972; MA in Tchg. in Edn. and English, Duke U., 1974; postgrad., U. Utah, 1977-80. Tchr. English, New Canaan (Conn.) Sch. Dist., from 1973, Brighton Ctrl. Sch. Dist., Rochester, N.Y., Davis County Sch. Dist., Kaysville, Utah, until 1977; rsch. asst. in cultural founds. and ednl. adminstrn. U. Utah, Salt Lake City, 1977-79; prin. St. Nicholas Elem. Sch., Rupert, Idaho, 1979-81; cons. Nev. Dept. Edn., Carson City, 1981-92, dep. supt. instrnl., rsch. and evaluative svcs., 1992-94, supt. pub. instrn., 1994—. Assessor Nev. Assessment Ctr., Nat. Assn. Secondary Sch. Prins.; mem. accreditation team N.W. Assn. Schs. and Colls.; trainer Tchr. Effectiveness for Student Achievement, Correlates Effective Schs.; facilitator Assisting Change in Edn.; mem. state team Nat. Coun. for Accreditation Tchr. Edn. Asst. editor: Work, Family and Careers (C. Brooklyn Derr), 1980; contbr. to profl. publs. Scholar Carleton Coll., Duke U. Mem. Phi Kappa Phi, Delta Kappa Gamma. Office: Nev Dept Edn Capitol Complex 700 E 5th St Carson City NV 89701-5096

PETERSON, MILLIE M., state senator; b. Merced, Calif., June 11, 1944; BS, U. Utah, 1979, MSW, 1984. Mem. Utah Senate Dist. 12, Salt Lake City, 1991—2002. Susa Young Gates Award, 1998. Mem. NASW. Democrat. Address: 7131 W 3800 S West Valley City UT 84128-3416 Office Phone: 801-566-4423. Personal E-mail: mpeter7131@aol.com.

PETERSON, RALPH RANDALL, engineering executive; b. Hayti, Mo., Oct. 12, 1944; s. James Tony and Helen Irene (Webb) P.; m. Betty Shoemaker, Nov. 7, 1964; children: Jamie Marie Jones, Jeffrey Scott. BSCE, Oreg. State U., 1969; MS in Environ. Engring., Stanford U., 1970; AMP in Bus., Harvard U., 1991. Registered profl. engr., Oreg., Wash., Colo. Engring. aide Johnson, Underkofler & Briggs, Boise, Idaho, 1962—63; surveyor Smith, Keyes, & Blakely, Caldwell, Idaho, 1963—64; with Chronic & Assocs., Boise, Idaho, 1964—65; various project devel. and dept. mng. roles CH2M Hill Cos., Corvallis, Oreg., 1965-78, v.p. indsl. process divsn., 1978-87, sr. v.p., tech. dir. Denver, 1987-90, CEO, 1990—, chmn., 2000—. Bd. dirs. Std. Ins. Co., Portland, Oreg.; bd. advisors Constrn. Industry Pres. Forum, Washington, 1994—; co-chair Nat. Congress Advancement of Minorities in Environ. Professions, Atlanta, 1993-94; industry co-chair tech. for sustainable future White House Office Sci. and Tech. Policy, 1995-96. Bd. dirs. Stapleton Devel. Corp., Denver, 1994—, World Trade Ctr., Denver, 1990—; corp. patron Smithsonian Instn. Corp. Patron. Recipient Colo. Gov.'s award for internat. trade devel., 1995. Mem. ASCE, Am. Water Works Assn., Water Environment Fedn., Colo. Environ. Bus. Assn. (co-chair 1993—), Oreg. State U. Alumni Assn. (bd. dirs. 1992—). Avocations: skiing, camping, fishing, performing arts. Office: CH2M Hill 9191 S Jamaica St Englewood CO 80112

PETERSON, ROBIN TUCKER, marketing educator; b. Casper, Wyo., July 31, 1937; s. Walfred Arthur and Mary Lurene Peterson; m. Marjorie K. Greenwald, June 25, 1963; children: Timothy, Kimberly. BS, U. Wyo., 1959, MS in Bus., 1961; PhD, U. Wash., 1967. Mem. faculty Idaho State U., Pocatello, 1963-73; prof. mktg., head mktg. dept. St. Cloud (Minn.) State U., 1973-76; prof. mktg. N.Mex. State U., Las Cruces, 1976—2007, head dept. mktg., 1976—, endowed disting. prof., 2007—. Fulbright lectr., Yugoslavia, 1973; vis. scholar Ea. Mont. State Coll., 1985; Sunwest Fin. Svcs. Disting. Centennial prof. N.Mex. State U., 1991, 92; Norwest Disting. prof. N.Mex. State U., 1999, Wells Fargo Disting. prof., 2002;endowed prof., 2008, en vis. lectr. Nirma Inst. Ahmedabad, India, 1999, Chiang Moi U., Thailand, 2000; Fulbright lectr. Kathmandu U., Nepal, 2001. Author: Marketing-A Contemporary Introduction, 1976, Forecasting, 1976, edit., 1983, Personal Selling, 1977, Marketing in Action, 1977, Lernbook Marketing, 1984, Marketing: Concepts and Decision Making, 1987, Principles of Marketing, 1989, Argentina, 1990, Managing the Distributor Sales Network, 1990, Business Forecasting, 1992, Getting New Products to Market Rapidly, 1994; exec. editor Bus. Forecaster, 1993-94; editor Jour. Bus. and Entrepreneurship, 1994-98; contbr. articles to profl. publs. Served with USAR, 1962-63. Fellow Assn. Small Bus. Entrepreneurship; mem. Am. Mktg. Assn., Sales and Mktg. Execs. Internat., Acad. Mktg. Sci. (pres. 1977-78, 80-82), Am. Arbitration Assn. (Outstanding Educators Am. award), S.W. Small Bus. Assn. (pres. 1983-84, Outstanding Mktg. Educators award, Outstanding Educator, Assn. of Small Bus., 2002), S.W. Mktg. Assn., Western Mktg. Educators, Las Cruces C. of C., Las Cruces Sales and Mktg. Club, Beta Gamma Sigma, Phi Kappa Psi, Alpha Kappa Psi, Alpha Mu Alpha. Republican. Presbyterian. Home: 4350 Diamondback Dr Las Cruces NM 88011-7539 Office: NMex State U PO Box 5280 Las Cruces NM 88003-5280 Office Phone: 505-646-5748. Business E-Mail: ropeters@nmsu.edu.

PETERSON, ROBYN GAYLE, museum director; b. San Francisco, Jan. 17, 1958; BA, UCLA, 1979; MA, U. Wis., 1982, PhD, 1987. Goldsmith, 1974-80; collections acquisition asst. social studies bibliographer Meml. Libr./U. Wis., 1984-86; curator of collections The Rockwell Mus., Corning, N.Y., 1988-99; sr. dir. exhbns. and programs Turtle Bay Exploration Park, Redding, Calif., 1999—2006; exec. dir. Yellowstone Art Mus., Billings, Mont., 2006—. Author: American Frontier Photography, 1993, Edward Borein, 1997, Warp and Weft: Cross-cultural Exchange in Navajo Weavings, 1997, Transforming Trash: Bay Area Fiber Art, 2000, Second Nature: the Art of Michael Haykin, 2006; co-author: Sudden and Solitary: Mount Shasta and Its Artistic Legacy, 2008; contbg. author: Allgemeines Künstlerlexikon, 1998—; editor/contbr.: Collector's Choice Review: Masterpieces of Glassmaking; Frederick Carder and the Steuben Glass Works, 1993, Brilliance in Glass: The Lost Wax Glass Sculpture of Frederick Carder, 1993, Journey to Justice: The Wintu People and the Salmon, 2002, The Other Side of the Looking Glass: The Glass Body and Its Metaphors, 2003, Bug-Eyed: Art, Culture, Insects, 2004; mng. editor: Frederick Carder and Steuben Glass: American Classics (Thomas P. Dimitroff), 1998; contbr. articles to profl. jours.; peer reviewer IMLS. Mem. Coll. Art Assn., Am. Assn. Mus. (peer reviewer accreditation). Office: Yellowstone Art Mus 401 N 27th St Billings MT 59101 Office Phone: 406-256-6804. Business E-Mail: director@artmuseum.org.

PETERSON, ROY JEROME, physicist, educator; b. Everett, Wash., Oct. 18, 1939; married; four children. BS, U. Wash., 1961, PhD, 1966. Instr. physics Princeton (N.J.) U., 1966-68; rsch. assoc. Yale U., New Haven, 1968-70; from rsch. assoc. to prof. physics U. Colo., Boulder, 1970—, asst. vice chancellor rsch., 1996—. Program dir. Intermediate Energy Physics NSF, 1978-79. Fellow Am. Phys. Soc.; mem. Pakistan Acad. Scis. Office: U Colo Box 446 Nuclear Physics Lab Boulder CO 80309

PETERSON, THOMAS W., engineering educator; b. Tucson, June 15, 1950; BS in Chem. Engring., Tufts U., 1972; MS in Chem. Engring., U. Ariz., 1973; PhD, Calif. Inst. Technology, Pasadena, 1977. From asst. prof. to prof., dean chem. engring. dept. U. Ariz., Tucson, 1977—, head dept. chem. and environ. engring., 1990—98, dean Coll. Engring. and Mines. Office: U Ariz Coll Engring Engring Rm 200 PO Box 210020 Tucson AZ 85721

PETICOLAS, WARNER LELAND, retired physical chemistry educator; b. Lubbock, Tex., July 29, 1929; s. Warner Marion and Beulah Francis (Lowe) P.; m. Virginia Marie Wolf, June 30, 1969; children— Laura M., Alicia B.; children by previous marriage— Cynthia M., Nina P., Phillip W. BS, Tex. Technol. Coll. (now Tex. Tech U.), 1950; PhD, Northwestern U., 1954; D (honoris causa), U. Lille, France, 1997. Research asso. DuPont Co., Wilmington, Del., 1954-60; research div. IBM, San Jose, Calif., 1960-67, cons., 1967-69, mgr. chem. physics group, 1965-67; prof. phys. chemistry U. Oreg., 1967-98; ret., 1998. Vis. prof. U. Paris-Pierre and Marie Curie, 1980-81; vis. prof. Weizmann Inst. Sci., Rahovat, Israel, 1991, vis. prof. U. Reims, 1996. Committeeman Democratic party, Eugene, Oreg., 1967-70. Served with USPHS, 1955-57. Recipient Alexander von Humboldt award, W. Ger., 1984-85. Guggenheim fellow Max von Laue-Paul Langevin Inst., Grenoble, France, 1973-74 Fellow Am. Phys. Soc.; mem. Am. Chem. Soc., Am. Phys. Soc., Sigma Xi, Alpha Chi Sigma, Tau Beta Pi. Episcopalian. Home: 2829 Arline Way Eugene OR 97403-2527 Office Phone: 541-687-0434. E-mail: peticola@oregon.uoregon.edu, peticolas@comcast.net.

PETKANICS, DONNA M., lawyer; BA, Northwestern U., 1980; JD, U. Calif., Boalt Hall Law Sch., 1985. Staff economist President Carter Administrn., Washington; with Wilson Sonsini Goodrich & Rosati, Palo Alto, Calif., 1985—, assoc. mng. ptnr., 1996—97, co-chmn., nominating com., 1997, 1998, mng. dir. ops., ptnr., mem. exec. mgmt. com. & policy com. Office: Wilson Sonsini Goodrich & Rosati 650 Page Mill Rd Palo Alto CA 94304-1050 Office Phone: 650-493-9300. Office Fax: 650-493-6811. Business E-Mail: dpetkanics@wsgr.com.

PETRAKIS, NICHOLAS LOUIS, epidemiologist, medical researcher, educator; b. San Francisco, Feb. 6, 1922; s. Louis Nicholas and Stamatina (Boosalis) P.; m. Patricia Elizabeth Kelly, June 24, 1947; children: Steven John, Susan Lynn, Sandra Kay. BA, Augustana Coll., 1943; BS in Medicine, U. S.D., 1944; MD, Washington U., St. Louis, 1946. Intern Mpls. Gen. Hosp., 1946-47; physician, researcher U.S. Naval Radiol. Def. Lab., San Francisco, 1947-49; resident physician Mpls. Gen. Hosp., 1949-50; sr. asst. surgeon Nat. Cancer Inst., USPHS, San Francisco, 1950-54; asst. research physician Cancer Research Inst., U. Calif., San Francisco, 1954-56; asst. prof. preventive medicine U. Calif. Sch. Medicine, San Francisco, 1956-60, assoc. prof., 1960-66, prof., 1966-91, chmn. dept. epidemiology and internat. health, 1978-88, prof. emeritus, 1991—; prof. epidemiology U. Calif. Sch. Pub. Health, Berkeley, 1981-91. Assoc. dir. G.W. Hooper Edn., U. Calif., San Francisco, 1970-74, acting dir., 1974-77, chmn. dept. epidemiology and internat. health, 1979-89; co-dir. Breast Screening Ctr. of No. Calif., Oakland, 1976-81; cons. Breast Cancer Task Force, Nat. Cancer Inst., Bethesda, Md., 1972-76; chmn. Biometry & Epidemiology Contract Rev. Com., Bethesda, 1977-81; bd. sci. counselors, divsn. cancer etiology Nat. Cancer Inst., Bethesda, 1982-86; scientific adv. com. Calif. State Tobacco-Related Disease Rsch. Program, 1991-93; cons. U. Crete Sch. Medicine, Heraklion, Greece, 1984. Contbr. articles to profl. jours. Eleanor Roosevelt Internat. Cancer fellow Am. Cancer Soc., Comitato Reserche Nucleari, Cassacia, Italy, 1962; U.S. Pub. Health Service Spl. fellow Galton Lab., U. London, 1969-70; recipient Alumni Achievement award Augustana Coll., Sioux Falls, S.D., 1979, Axion award Hellenic-Am. Profl. Soc. of Calif., San Francisco, 1984, Lewis C. Robbins award Soc. for Prospective Medicine, Indpls., 1985, Otto W. Sartorius, MD, award from Susan Love MD Breast Cancer Found., 2001. Mem. Am. Soc. Preventive Oncology (founding, pres. 1984-85, Disting. Achievement award 1992), Soc. for Prospective Medicine (founding), Am. Assn. Cancer Rsch., Am. Epidemiol. Soc., Am. Soc. Clin. Investigation, Am. Bd. Preventive Medicine (cert.). Achievements include research in breast cancer, med. oncology and hematology. Office: U Calif Sch Medicine Dept Epidemiology & Biostats Box 0560 MU420W San Francisco CA 94143-0001 Home: 1450 Post St Apt 415 San Francisco CA 94109

PETRICK, ALFRED, JR., economist, educator; b. Mt. Vernon, NY, Dec. 30, 1926; s. Alfred and Ruth (Updike) P.; m. Ruth Goodridge, Jan. 2, 1956; children: Elizabeth, Andrew Wayne. BS, BA, Columbia U., 1952, MS, 1962; MBA, Denver U., 1966; PhD, U. Colo., 1969. Registered profl. engr., Colo. Sales engr. Ingersoll Rand Co., NYC, 1953-54; project engr. U.S. AEC, Grand Junction, Colo., 1954-57; mining engr. Reynolds Metals Co., Bauxite, Ark., 1957-61, Guyana, 1957-61; mineral economist U.S. Bur. Mines, Denver, 1963-70; Coulter prof. Colo. Sch. Mines, Golden, 1970-84, emeritus prof., 1984—; dir. Petrick Assocs., Evergreen, Colo., 1974—2004; ret., 2004. Author: Economics International Development, 1977, Economics of Minerals, 1980, Preparacion y Evaluacion, 1982. Mem. com. tech. aspects strategic materials Nat. Acad. Sci., Washington, 1973-76, mem. com. surface mining and reclamation, 1979. Served with USAF, 1945-47, PTO. Fulbright research scholar U. Otago, Dunedin, New Zealand, 1986; recipient Edn. award Instituto Para Funcionarios De Las Industrias Minera y Siderurgica, Mexico City, 1981; recipient Service award Office Tech. Assessment, U.S. Congress, 1981. Mem. AIME (chmn. council econs. 1977-78, Henry Krumb lectr. 1986, service award), Profl. Engrs. Colo. Presbyterian. Home: 5544 S Hatch Dr Evergreen CO 80439-7233 Office: Colo Sch Mines Golden CO 80401 Personal E-mail: peta33@comcast.net.

PETRIE, GEOFFREY MICHAEL, professional sports team executive, retired professional basketball player; b. Darby, Pa., Apr. 17, 1948; m. Anne-Marie Petrie; children: Mike, Anne-Marie, Susanne. Grad., Princeton U., NJ, 1970. Player Portland Trail Blazers, 1970—76, exec., 1976—89, sr. v.p. ops., 1989—93; v.p. basketball ops. Sacramento Kings, 1994—2006, pres. basketball ops., 2006—. Named NBA Rookie of Yr., 1971, NBA Exec. of Yr., The Sporting News, 1999, 2001; named to NBA All-Star Team, 1971, 74, NBA All-Rookie Team, 1971. Avocations: golf, tennis, guitar. Office: Sacramento Kings One Sports Pky Sacramento CA 95834

PETRIE, GREGORY STEVEN, lawyer; b. Seattle, Feb. 25, 1951; s. George C. and Pauline P.; m. Margaret Fuhrman, Oct. 6, 1979; children: Kathryn Jean, Thomas George. AB in Polit. Sci and Econs., UCLA, 1973; JD, Boston U., 1976. Bar: Wash. 1976, U.S. Dist. Ct. (we. dist.) Wash. 1976. Adminstr. Action/Peace Corps, Washington, 1973, Fed. Power Commn., Washington, 1974; assoc. Oles Morrison et al, Seattle, 1976-80; ptnr. Schwabe Williamson Ferguson & Burdell, Seattle, 1981-94; mng. shareholder Krutch Lindell Bingham Jones & Petrie, Seattle, 1994—. Mem. Seattle-King County Bar Assn., Profl. Liability Architects and Engrs., Wash. Athletic Club. Avocations: woodworking, skiing. Office: Krutch Lindell Bingham Jones & Petrie 1420 Fifth Ave Ste 3150 Seattle WA 98101 Home Phone: 206-632-4555; Office Phone: 206-682-1505. Business E-Mail: gsp@krutchlindell.com.

PETRINOVICH, LEWIS FRANKLIN, psychologist, educator; b. Wallace, Idaho, June 12, 1930; s. John F. and Ollie (Steward) Petrinovich. BS, U. Idaho, 1952; PhD, U. Calif., Berkeley, 1962. Asst. prof. San Francisco State Coll., 1957—63; from assoc. to prof. SUNY, Stony Brook, 1963-68; prof. U. Calif., Riverside, 1968-91, chmn. psychology, 1968-71, 86-89, prof. emeritus, 1991—2009. Bd. dirs. Eastman Med. Products, Cymed Corp. Author: Understanding Research in Social Sciences, 1975, Introduction to Statistics, 1976, Human Evolution, Reproduction and Morality, 1995, Living and Dying Well, 1996, Darwinian Dominion: Animal Welfare and Human Interests, 1999, The Cannibal Within, 2000; editor: Behavioral Development, 1981, Habituation, Sensitization and Behavior, 1984; cons. editor Behavioral and Neural Biology, 1972-90, Jour. Physiol. and Comparative Psychology, 1980-82, Jour. Comparative Psychology, 1983-90. Bd. dirs. Friends of Big Band Jazz, 2001—07. Fellow APA, Am. Psychol. Soc., Calif. Acad. Scis., Human Behavior and Evolution Soc., Western Psychol. Assn.; mem. Am. Ornithol. Union, Animal Behavior Soc., Sigma Xi Home: 415 Boynton Ave Berkeley CA 94707-1701 Office: U Calif Riverside Psychology Dept Riverside CA 92521-0001 Personal E-mail: lpetrin@aol.com.

PETROCELLI, DANIEL M., lawyer; b. East Orange, NJ; m. Alison Petrocelli; 4 children. BS cum laude, U. Calif., Los Angeles, 1976; JD magna cum laude, Southwestern U., 1980. Bar: Calif. 1981, US Ct. Appeals (9th cir.) 1981, US Dist. Ct. (ctrl. and no. districts.) Calif. 1981, US Supreme Ct. 1981, US Dist. Ct. Colo. 1998. Ptnr. (Century City office) O'Melveny & Myers LLP, LA, mem. policy com. Mem. The American Lawyer's Litigation Dept. of Yr.; nat. commentator on trials and other legal issues; spkr. to bus. groups, bar and judges associations, and citizen groups. Mem. Southwestern U. Law Review, 1978—79, editor-in-chief, 1979—80; author: Triumph of Justice: The Final Judgement on the Simpson Saga, 1998; contbr. articles to profl. jours. Named Litigator of Yr., Century City Bar Assn., honoree, Columbus Citizens Found., Alumnus of Yr., Southwestern U., Trial Lawyer of Yr., Malibu Bar Assn., San Diego Trial Lawyers Assn., So. Calif. Super Lawyer, LA Mag.; named one of Los Angeles' Top 50 Litigators, LA Bus. Jour., Lawyers of Yr., Calif. Lawyer. Mem.: Assn. of Bus. Trial Lawyers, State Bar Calif. (antitrust and unfair competition sects.), ABA (litigation sect. and corp. counsel com.), LA County Bar (antitrust and unfair competition sects.). Office: O'Melveny & Myers LLP 1999 Avenue of Stars 7th Fl Los Angeles CA 90067-6035 Office Phone: 310-246-6850. Office Fax: 310-246-6779. Business E-Mail: dpetrocelli@omm.com.*

PETROFF, LAURA R., lawyer; b. Cleve., July 7, 1955; BA, Denison U., 1977; JD, Vanderbilt U., 1980. Bar: Ill. 1980, U.S. Dist. Ct. Ill. (No. dist.) 1980, Calif. 1986, U.S. Dist. Ct. Calif. (Ctrl. So. and No. dist.) 1986, U.S. Ct. Appeals (9th cir.). Ptnr. Winston & Strawn LLP, LA, 2000—, mng. ptnr. Chair, ptnr. compensation com. Winston & Strawn LLP, LA, mem. exec. com., mem. diversity com. Gen. counsel PIHRA Found.; founding mem. Women Rainmakers Roundtable. Mem.: ABA (bd. dirs. pub. counsel law ctr.), State Bar Calif., L.A. County Bar Assn. (co-chair edn. com. 1989—91, mem. exec-.com. 1990—92). Office: Winston & Strawn LLP 333 S Grand Ave Los Angeles CA 90071-1543 Office Phone: 213-615-1736. Office Fax: 213-615-1750. E-mail: lpetroff@winston.com.

PETROS, RAYMOND LOUIS, JR., lawyer; b. Pueblo, Colo., Sept. 19, 1950; BS, Colo. Coll., 1972; JD, U. Colo., 1975. Bar: Colo. 1975. Jud. clk. to Justice Paul V. Hodges Colo. Supreme Ct., Denver, 1975-77; assoc. Bermingham, White, Burke & Ipsen, Denver, 1977-78; from assoc. to ptnr. Hall & Evans, Denver, 1978-81; ptnr. Kirkland & Ellis, Denver, 1981-86; mem. Holme, Roberts & Owen, Denver, 1986-96, Petros & White, LLC, 1996—. Contbr. articles to profl. jours. Bd. dirs. Rocky Mountain Poison Control Found., Denver, 1988-94. Office: Petros White Llc 1999 Broadway Ste 3200 Denver CO 80202-5732

PETRY, DON D., educational association administrator; b. Grant City, Mo., Dec. 23, 1940; s. Harold and Mary R. (Barnett) P.; m. Peggy L. Luhrs, May 29, 1966; children: Clayton James, Heather Lynn. BSE, N.W. Mo. State U., 1962; MEd, U. Mo., 1966, EdD, 1969. Cert. elem. tchr., elem. prin., secondary prin., second English tchr., Mo. Elem. tchr. to HS prin. Rock Port Schs., Mo., 1961—66; instr. U. Mo., Columbia, 1966—69; assoc. dean adminstrn. to exec. v.p., prof. N.W. Mo. State U., Maryville, 1969—78; v.p. adminstrn., prof. to interim pres. CBN U., Virginia Beach, Va., 1978—84; founder, pres. Teled Internat., Virginia Beach, 1984; exec. dir. Nat. Coun. Pvt. Sch. Accreditation, Seattle. Cons. Oral Roberts U. Ednl. Fellowship and Internat. Christian Accrediting Assn., Tulsa, 1986—, Dominian Coll., Seattle, Graceland U., Ind.; adv., bd. dirs. Josue Internat. Ministries, El Salvador, 1991—; internat. vice chancellor Christian Faith U., Nigeria, 1989—; adj. prof. Oral Roberts U., Tulsa, 1990—. Author: Budgetary Guidelines for Higher Education, 1971. Mem. ASCD, Phi Delta Kappa (chpt. pres.), Rotary Club. Office: Nat Coun Pvt Sch Accreditation PO Box 13686 Seattle WA 98198-1010 Office Phone: 253-874-3408. Office Fax: 253-874-3409. E-mail: ncpsaexdr@aol.com.

PETTIGREW, EDWARD W., lawyer; b. Aurora, Ill., July 16, 1943; AB, Kenyon Coll., 1965; JD, U. Mich., 1968. Bar: Wash. 1970, Mich. 1971, U.S. Ct. Appeals (9th cir.) 1971, U.S. Dist. Ct. (we. and ea. dists.) Wash. 1971. Shareholder Graham & Dunn, Seattle, 1970—. Mem. Fed. Bar Assn. (pres. western dist. Wash. 1987-88). Office: Graham and Dunn PC 2801 Alaskan Way Ste 300 Seattle WA 98121-1128 Home Phone: 425-369-2467; Office Phone: 206-340-9621. Business E-Mail: epettigrew@grahamdunn.com.

PETTIS-ROBERSON, SHIRLEY MCCUMBER, Former US Repr, Calif; b. Mountain View, Calif. d. Harold Oliver and Dorothy Susan (O'Neil) McCumber; m. John J. McNulty (dec.); m. Jerry L. Pettis (dec. Feb. 1975); children: Peter Dwight Pettis, Deborah Pettis Moyer; m. Ben Roberson, Feb. 6, 1988. Student, Andrews U., Berrien Springs, Mich., 1942—43, student, 1945, U. Calif., Berkeley, 1944—45; PhD (hon.), Loma Linda U., Calif., 2002. Mgr. Audio-Digest Found., LA, Glendale, 1958—61; sec. treas. Pettis, Inc., Hollywood, Calif., 1958-68; mem. U.S. Congress, Calif., 1975—79. Pres. Women's Rsch. Edn. Inst., 1979—80; bd. dirs. Lumbermens Mut. Ins. Co., Kemper Corp., Am. Motors, Am. Mfg. Co., 1980—97. Mem. Former Mems. Congress, 1980—, Pres.'s Commn. Arms Control Disarmament, 1982—85, Commn. Presdl. Scholars, 1990—93; chair bd. Loma Linda U. Children's Hosp. Found.; trustee U. Redlands, Calif., 1980—83, Loma Linda U. Med. Ctr., Calif., 1990—95, bd. mem.

PETTIT, ERIN, glaciologist; Grad. student in Geophysics, U. Wash. Lead scientist Girls on Ice, 1999—; glaciologist U. Wash., instr., Exploration Seminar, 2005—; tchr. Portland State U., 2006—. Lead scientist studying glaciers and ice sheets in Antarctica, Wash., Alaska, 1999—; program co-instr. North Cascades Inst., 2000—. Recipient Women of Discovery, Earth award, Wings WorldQuest, 2007. Achievements include research in dynamics of ice flow with focus on the West Antarctic Ice Sheet; dynamic behaviors of ice divide, the movement of glaciers, and the formation of glacial ice cliffs; encouraging high school girls the opportunity to study the scientific method while gaining mountaineering and wilderness skills through the Girls on Ice program; with team camped beneath Blood Falls on Taylor Glacier (Antarctica), trekking up the Taylor Glacier, boring holes in the ice to place instruments to measure the strains & stresses in frozen ice.

PETTIT, GEORGE ROBERT, chemist, educator, cancer researcher; b. Long Branch, NJ, June 8, 1929; s. George Robert and Florence Elizabeth (Seymour) P.; m. Margaret Jean Benger, June 20, 1953; children: William Edward, Margaret Sharon, Robin Kathleen, Lynn Benger, George Robert III. BS, Wash. State U., 1952; MS, Wayne State U., 1954, PhD, 1956. Tchg. asst. Wash. State U., 1950-52, lecture demonstrator, 1952; rsch. chemist E.I. duPont de Nemours and Co., 1953; grad. tchg. asst. Wayne State U., 1952-53, rsch. fellow, 1954-56; sr. rsch. chemist Norwich Eaton Pharms., Inc., 1956-57; asst. prof. chemistry U. Maine, 1957-61, assoc. prof. chemistry, 1961-65, prof. chemistry, 1965; vis. prof. chemistry Stanford U., 1965; prof. chemistry Ariz. State U., 1965—, chmn. organic chemistry divsn., 1966-68, disting. rsch. prof., 1978-79, Dalton prof. medicinal chemistry and rsch., 1986—2005, Regent's prof. chemistry, 1990—. Vis. prof. So. African, Univs., 1978; dir. Cancer Rsch. Lab., 1974-75, 2005, Cancer Rsch. Inst., 1975-2005; co-dir. Ariz. Prostate Cancer Task Force, 2000-05; lectr. various colls. and univs.; cons. in field. Contbr. articles to profl. jours. Mem. adv. bd. Wash. State U. Found., 1981—85. With Res. USAF, 1949—53. Recipient Alumni Achievement award, Wash. State U., 1984. Fellow: Am. Inst. Chemists (Pioneer award 1989, Ariz. Gov.'s Excellence award 1993); mem.: Am. Soc. Oncology, Am. Assn. Cancer Rsch., Am. Soc. Pharmacognosy (Rsch. Achievement award 1995), Chem. Soc. London, Am. Chem. Soc. (mem. awards com. 1968—71, Guenther award in chemistry of natural products 1998), Phi Lambda Upsilon, Sigma Xi. Office: Ariz State U Dept Chemistry and Biochemistry Tempe AZ 85287-2404

PETTIT, GHERY ST. JOHN, electronics engineer; b. Woodland, Calif., Apr. 6, 1952; s. Ghery DeWitt and Frances Marie (Seitz) P.; m. Marilyn Jo Van Hoose, July 28, 1973; children: Ghery Christopher, Heather Kathleen. BS in Electrical Engring., Wash. State U., 1975. Cert. EMC engr., NARTE, EIT Wash., Colo. Nuclear engr. Mare Island Naval Shipyard, Vallejo, Calif., 1975-76; electronics engr. Naval Electronic Systems Engring. Ctr., Vallejo, 1976-79; sr. engr. Martin Marietta Denver Aerospace, 1979-83; staff engr. Tandem Computers Inc., Santa Clara, Calif., 1983-90, mgr. electromagnetic capability Cupertino, Calif., 1990-91, electromagnetic compatibility lead engr., 1991-95; electromagnetic compatibility engr. Intel Corp., Hillsboro, Oreg., 1995-96, Dupont, Wash., 1996—. Mem. U.S. tech. adv. group subcom. I, Spl. Com. on Radio Frequency Interferences subcom. Internat. Electrotechnical Commn.; mem. CISPR SC I, WG2, WG3 and WG4. Asst. cubmaster Boy Scouts Am., San Jose, Calif., 1985-86, cubmaster, 1986-88, ast. scoutmaster, 1988-90, scoutmaster, 1990-93. Mem. IEEE (sr.), Nat. Rsch. Coun. (bd. assessment of NIST programs 1999—2005), EMC Soc. (bd. dirs. 1999-2004, 2006—, v.p. commn. svcs. 2003—08, v.p. conferences, 2009-), Electromagnetic Capability Soc. (sec.-treas. Littleton, Colo. chpt. 1983, sec. Santa Clara Valley chpt. 1985-87, vice chmn. 1987-89, chmn. 1989-91, sec. Santa Clara Valley sect. 1991-92, treas. 1992-93, vice chmn. 1993-94, chmn. 1994-95), IEEE Electromagetic Capability Soc. (chmn. Seattle chpt. 1997-2000). Republican. Presbyterian. Avocations: flying, amateur radio, sailing. Office: Intel Corp 2800 Center Dr Dupont WA 98327-9773 Business E-Mail: ghery.pettit@intel.com.

PETTIT, JOHN W., health facility administrator; b. Detroit, Mar. 6, 1942; s. John W. and Clara (Schartz) P.; m. Kathleen Endres, Aug. 8, 1970; children: Julie, Andrew, Michael. BBA, U. Notre Dame, 1964; MBA, Mich. State U., 1974. CPA, Mich.; CFP, 2001. Acct. Ernst & Ernst, Detroit, 1964-67; chief acct. Detroit Inst. Tech., Detroit, 1967-69; controller, dir. adminstrn. & fin. Mich. Cancer Found., Detroit, 1969-80; chief adminstrv. officer Dana-Farber Cancer Inst., Boston, 1980-94; exec. v.p., chief oper. officer John Wayne Cancer Inst., Santa Monica, Calif., 1995-97; fin. cons. LA, 1998—. Grant reviewer Nat. Cancer Inst., Bethesda, Md., 1979-94. Pres. advanced mgmt. program Mich. State U., 1978-79; mem. adv. bd. Arthritis Found. So. Calif. chpt., 1999—2004; mem. Town Meeting, Wellesley, Mass., 1991-94. Avocations: sailing, woodworking, photography, music. Home and Office: 4518 Winnetka Ave Woodland Hills CA 91364 Office Phone: 818-226-3838. E-mail: john@jwpfinancial.com.

PETTY, GEORGE OLIVER, retired lawyer; b. LA, Mar. 31, 1939; s. Hugh Morton and May (Johnson) P.; m. Sandra Diane Kilpatrick, July 14, 1962; children: Ross Morton, Alison Lee, Christopher Henry. AB, U. Calif., Berkeley, 1961; LLB, U. Calif., 1964. Bar: Calif. 1965, Eng. and Wales 1986, U.S. Supreme Ct. 1976. Atty. Huovinen & White, Oakland, Calif., 1967-69; counsel Bechtel Power Corp., San Francisco, 1969-83; prin. counsel Bechtel Ltd., London, 1983-86; gen. counsel Sun-Diamond Growers of Calif., Pleasanton, Calif., 1987-95; pvt. practice, 1995—96; gen. counsel Tone Bros. Inc., 1997—2008. Leader Arlington Ave. Utilities Undergrounding Com., 1987—2001. Capt. US Army, 1965—67. Mem. Calif. State Bar Assn., Alameda County Bar Assn., Eng. and Wales Bar Assn., Middle Temple Inn. Office Phone: 415-477-2800, 510-528-1721. Personal E-mail: gopetty@aol.com.

PETTY, THOMAS LEE, internist, educator; b. Boulder, Colo., Dec. 24, 1932; s. Roy Stone and Eleanor Marie (Kudrna) P.; m. Carol Lee Piepho, Aug. 7, 1954; children: Caryn, Thomas, John. BA, U. Colo., 1955, MD, 1958. Intern Phila. Gen. Hosp., 1958-59; resident U. Mich., 1959-60, U. Colo., Denver, 1960-62, pulmonary fellow, 1962-63, chief resident medicine, 1963-64, instr. medicine, 1962-64, asst. prof., 1964-68, assoc. prof., 1968-74, prof. medicine, 1974—; pres. Presbyn./St. Luke's Ctr. for Health Scis. Edn., 1989-95; practice medicine, specializing in internal medicine, pulmonary medicine Denver, 1962—; prof. medicine Rush Univ., 1992—. Cons. Kindred Hosp., 1991-. Author: For Those Who Live and Breathe, 1967, 2d edit., 1972, Intensive and Rehabilitative Respiratory Care, 1971, 3d edit., 1982, Chronic Obstructive Pulmonary Disease, 1978, 2d edit., 1985, Principles and Practice of Pulmonary Rehabilitation, 1993, Enjoying Life With COPD, 1995, 3d edit., Pulmonary Disorders of the Elderly, 2007, others; contbr. articles to profl. jours. NIH and Found. grantee, 1966-88. Master ACP, Am. Coll. Chest Physicians (master, pres. 1982); mem. Assn. Am. Physicians, Assn. of Pulmonary Program Dirs. (founding pres. 1983-84, chmn. nat. lung health edn. program 1995—, co-chmn. 2000-04), Am. Bd. Internal Medicine (bd. govs. 1986-92), Am. Thoracic Soc. (Disting. Achievement award 1995), Phi Beta Kappa, Phi Delta Theta, Alpha Omega Alpha, Phi Rho Sigma (pres. 1976-78). Home: 1325 Clermont Street Denver CO 80220 Office: 899 Logan St Ste 103 Denver CO 80203 Home Phone: 303-717-0325. Personal E-mail: tlpdoc@aol.com.

PETTY, TOM (THOMAS EARL PETTY), musician, composer; b. Gainesville, Fla., Oct. 20, 1950; s. Earl and Katherine Petty; m. Jane Benyo, 1974 (div. Sept. 9, 1996); children: Adria, Kim; m. Dana York, June 3, 2001. With band the Sundowners (1964) which later was called the Epics (1965-69) and Mudcrutch (1970-74), Gainesville, Fla.; songwriter, musician for Leon Russell, 1974—75; lead singer, guitarist Tom Petty and the Heartbreakers, 1975—. Singer:(albums with the Heartbreakers) Tom Petty and the Heartbreakers, 1976, You're Gonna Get It, 1978, Damn the Torpedoes, 1979, Hard Promises, 1981, Long After Dark, 1982, Southern Accents, 1985, Pack Up the Plantation-Live!, 1986, Let Me Up (I've Had Enough), 1987, Into the Great Wide Open, 1991 (Grammy nomination for Best Rock Performance by a Duo or Group with Vocal, 1992), Tom Petty and the Heartbreakers' Greatest Hits, 1993, Playback, 1995, Echo, 1999 (Grammy nomination for Best Rock Album, 2000), Anthology: through the Years, 2000, The Last DJ, 2002, Live at the Olympic: The Last DJ and More, 2003; (soundtracks) She's The One, 1996; (with The Traveling Wilburys) Traveling Wilburys Vol. 1, 1989 (Grammy Award for Best Rock Performance by a Duo or Group with Vocal, 1990, Grammy nomination for Album of Yr., 1990), Traveling Wilburys Vol. 3, 1990; (albums with Mudcrutch) Mudcrutch, 2008; (solo albums) Full Moon Fever, 1989 (Grammy nomination for Album of Yr., 1990), Wildflowers, 1994 (Grammy nomination for Best Rock Album, 1996), Highway Companion, 2006; hit singles include Breakdown, 1978, Here Comes My Girl, 1979, Refugee, 1979, (duet with Stevie Nicks) Stop Dragging My Heart Around, 1981, The Waiting, 1981, You Got Lucky, 1982, Don't Come Around Here No More, 1985, Jammin' Me, 1987, Free Fallin', 1989, Running Down A Dream, 1989, I Won't Back Down, 1989, Into the Great Wide Open, Learning to Fly, 1991, Mary Jane's Last Dance, 1993, You Don't Know How It Feels, 1994, You Wreck Me, 1994, Walls, 1996, Free Girl Now, 1999, Swingin', 1999; Actor: (films) Made in Heaven, 1987, The Postman, 1997; (TV appearances) (voice only) The Simpsons, 2002, (voice only), King of the Hill, 2005; host (radio show) Buried Treasure, 2005—; subject of documentary: Tom Petty and the Heartbreakers: Runnin' Down a Dream, 2007 (Grammy award for Best Long Form Music Video, 2009). Grammy nomination for Best Rock Performance by a Duo or Group with Vocal (with Stevie Nicks for Stop Draggin' My Heart Around), 1982, Grammy nomination for Best Rock Song (Learning to Fly), 1992, Grammy nomination for Best Rock Performance by a Duo or Group with Vocal (with Bob Dylan, Roger McGuinn, Neil Young, Eric Clapton, and George Harrison for My Back Pages), 1994, Grammy nomination for Best Rock Song (with the Heartbreakers for Room At The Top), 2000, Grammy Award for Best Male Rock Vocal Performance (for You Don't Know Hot It Feels), 1996, MTV Video Music Award for Best Male Video (with the Heartbreakers for Mary Jane's Last Dance), 1994, Video Vanguard Award, MTV Video Music Awards, 1994, MTV Video Music Award for Best Male Video (for You Don't Know How It Feels), 1995, Songwriter Award, ASCAP, 1990, Golden Note Award, ASCAP, 1996, Nat. Veteran's Foundation Special Award of Recognition, 1995, UCLA George & Ira Gershwin Award, 1996, Bill Graham Lifetime Achievement Award, CA Music Awards, 1998, Hollywood Walk of Fame Star (with the Heartbreakers), 1999, inducted, Rock & Roll Hall of Fame (with the Heartbreakers), 2002, Legend Award, Radio Music Awards, 2003, Century award, Billboard Music Awards, 2005. Office: Warner Bros Records 3300 Warner Blvd Burbank CA 91505-4694

PEZZUTO, JOHN MICHAEL, dean, pharmacology educator; b. Hammonton, NJ, Aug. 29, 1950; s. Michael L. and Elizabeth (Brown) P.; m. Mimi Faith Rotstein, Aug. 29, 1986; children: John-Henry Albert, Elisabeth Lee, Michael Joseph Ivan; 1 child from previous marriage, Jennifer Anne. AB, Rutgers U., 1973; PhD, Coll. Medicine & DentistryN.J., 1977. Postdoctoral assoc. MIT, Cambridge, 1977-79; instr. chemistry U. Va., Charlottesville, 1979-80; asst. prof. U. Ill.-Chgo., 1980-84, assoc. prof., 1984-91, prof., 1991—2002, Disting. Univ. prof., 2002; dean Purdue U., Coll. Pharmacy, Nursing and Health Scis., West Lafayette, Ind., 2002—06, prof. medicinal chemistry and molecular pharmacology, 2002—06; founding dean, prof. chemistry Coll. Pharmacy, U. Hawaii, Hilo, 2006—. Assoc. dir. U. Ill. Cancer Ctr, 1991-95, dep. dir., 2000-02; interim head dept. med. chemistry and pharmacognosy, U. Ill., Chgo., 1992-95, 2000-01, head, 2001-02; dir. program for collaborative rsch. in pharm. scis. U. Ill., Chgo., 1995-98; pres., co-founder Internat. Therapeutics Inc., River Forest, Ill., 1996—; assoc. dean for rsch. and grad. edn. U. Ill., Chgo., 1998-2002. Editor-in-chief Internat. Jour. Pharmacognosy, 1991-95, Combinatory Chemistry and High Throughput Screening, 1996-97, Pharmaceutical Biology, 1997—; editor: Biotechnology and Pharmacy; contbr. articles to profl. jours. NIH fellow, 1977-80, Rsch. fellow Alexander von Humboldt Found., 1990-91; NIH Rsch. Career Devel. awardee, 1984-89, grantee NAt. Cancer Inst., 1984—, Nat. Inst. Dental Rsch., 1984-85. Mem. AAAS, Am. Chem. Soc., Am. Soc. Pharmacognosy, Am. Assn. Cancer Rsch., N.Y. Acad. Scis., Am. Soc. Biol. Chemists. Office: Univ Hawaii at Hilo Coll Pharmacy 60 Nowelo St Ste 101 Hilo HI 96720-4091 Office Phone: 808-443-5900. Business E-Mail: pezzuto@hawaii.edu.

PFAELZER, MARIANA R., federal judge; b. LA, Feb. 4, 1926; AB, U. Calif., 1947; LLB, UCLA, 1957. Bar: Calif. 1958. Assoc. Wyman, Bautzer, Rothman & Kuchel, 1957-69, ptnr., 1969-78; judge U.S. Dist. Ct. (ctrl. dist.) Calif., 1978—. Mem. Jud. Conf. Adv. Com. on Fed. Rules of Civil Procedure. Pres., v.p., dir. Bd. Police Commrs. City of L.A., 1974-78. UCLA Alumnus award for Profl. Achievement, 1979, named Alumna of Yr., UCLA Law Sch., 1980, U. Calif. Santa Barbara Disting. Alumnus award, 1983. Mem. ABA, Calif. Bar Assn. (local adminstrv. com., spl. com. study rules procedure 1972, joint subcom. profl. ethics and computers and the law coms. 1972, profl. ethics com. 1972-74, spl. com. juvenile justice, women's rights subcom. human rights sect.), L.A. County Bar Assn. (spl. com. study rules procedure state bar 1974), Ninth Cir. Dist. Judges Assn. (pres.). Office: US Dist Ct 312 N Spring St Ste 152 Los Angeles CA 90012-4703

PFAU, GEORGE HAROLD, JR., investment advisor; b. Milw., May 7, 1924; s. George Harold and Elisabeth C. (Hunter) P.; m. Anne Elizabeth Mayhew (dec.); 1 child, George Harold III; children by previous marriage: Mary D., Peter W., Elizabeth C.; m. Susan Colomb, Jan., 3, 2005. BS, Yale U., 1948. Tchr. Thacker Sch., 1948-49; with Fleishhacker Paper Box Co., San Francisco, 1952-54; salesman A.G. Becker & Co., San Francisco, 1954-55; v.p., sec., dir. Carl W. Stern & Co., San Francisco, 1955-57; with White Weld & Co. Inc., San Francisco, 1957-78; 1st v.p. corp. fin. dept. Blyth Eastman Dillon, San Francisco, 1978-79; sr. v.p. UBS Fin. Svcs., San Francisco, 1979—. Bd. dirs. 1 A Dist. Arg. Assn. Bd. dirs. The Guardsmen, 1966-67, Pathfinder Fund, 1974-82, San Francisco Zool. Soc., 1979-80; trustee Thacher Sch., Ojai, Calif., 1967-76, Town Sch., San Francisco, 1966-70; pres. Planned Parenthood San Francisco-Alameda County, 1968-69, bd. dirs., 1965—; chmn. Lincoln Club of No. Calif., 1993-95, mem., 1982—; chmn. Citizens for Better San Francisco. With C.E., 1942-44; with Am. Field Svc., 1944-45. Mem. Kappa Beta Phi, San Francisco Bond Club, Bohemian Club (San Francisco), Calif. Tennis Club, Villa Taverna. Office: UBS Fin Svcs 555 California St Fl 32D San Francisco CA 94104-1502 Home Phone: 415-931-3307. E-mail: george.ptau@ubs.com.

PFEFFER, JEFFREY, business educator; b. St. Louis, July 23, 1946; s. Newton Stuart and Shirlee (Krisman) P.; m. Kathleen Frances Fowler, July 23, 1986. BS, MS, Carnegie Mellon U., 1968; PhD, Stanford U., 1972. Tech. staff Rsch. Analysis Corp., McLean, Va., 1968-69; asst. prof. U. Ill., Champaign, 1971-73; from asst. prof. to assoc. prof. U. Calif., Berkeley, 1973-79; prof. Grad. Sch. Bus., Stanford (Calif.) U., 1979—. Dir. Audible Magic, Inc.; vis. prof. Harvard U. Sch. Bus., Boston, 1981—82, London Bus. Sch., 2005, IESE, Barcelona, 2006, Singapore Mgmt. U., 2006. Author: The External Control of Organizations, 1978, Organizational Design, 1978, Power in Organizations, 1981, Organizations and Organization Theory, 1982 (Terry Book award 1984), Managing with Power, 1992, Competitive Advantage Through People, 1994, New Directions for Organization Theory, 1997, The Human Equation, 1998, The Knowing-Doing Gap, 1999, Hidden Value, 2000, Hard Facts, Dangerous Half-Truths, and Total Nonsense, 2006, What Were They Thinking?, 2007. Bd. dir. San Francisco Playhouse. Fellow Acad. Mgmt. (bd. govs. 1984-86, New Concept award 1979, Richard D. Irwin award for scholarly contbns. to mgmt. 1989); mem. Labor and Employment Rels. Assn. Jewish. Avocations: cooking, music. Home: 425 Moseley Rd Hillsborough CA 94010-6715 Office: Stanford U Grad Sch Bus Stanford CA 94305 Home Phone: 650-340-7331; Office Phone: 650-723-2915. E-mail: pfeffer_jeffrey@gsb.stanford.edu.

PFEIFER, LARRY ALAN, public health service coordinator; b. Rock Springs, Wyo., July 20, 1958; s. Jack Albert and Betty Lee (Ethington) P.; m. Sandra Lynn, June 20, 1986. BS cum laude, So. Oreg. State Coll., 1983, MS in Health Edn., 1989; paramedic diploma, Rogue Community Coll., 1984; postgrad., Columbia Pacific U. Cert. paramedic, Oreg. Cpt., paramedic Tualatin Valley Fire and Rescue, Portland, Oreg., 1991—. Adj. faculty Oreg. Health Scis. U. Sch. of Medicine, Dept. of Emergency Medicine, 1995; lectr. in field. Author (text) Non-Verbal Pre-Hospital Assessment of the Trauma Patient. Mem. Oreg. Paramedic Assn., Phi Kappa Phi, Kappa Delta Pi. Home: 10026 NW Priscilla Ct Portland OR 97229-5273

PFEIFFER, PHYLLIS KRAMER, publishing executive; b. NYC, Feb. 11, 1949; d. Jacob N. and Estelle G. Rosenbaum-Pfeiffer; m. Stephen M. Pfeiffer, Dec. 21, 1969; children: Andrew Kramer, Elise Kramer. BS, Cornell U., 1970; postgrad., U. San Diego, 1976-78. Instr. Miss Porter's Sch., Farmington, Conn., 1970; tchr. Dewey Jr. HS NYC Bd. Edn., 1970—73; rschr. Hunter Coll., NYC, 1971—72; account exec. La Jolla (Calif.) Light, 1973—75, advt. dir., 1975—77, gen. mgr., 1977-78, pub., 1978-87; exec. v.p. Harte Hanks So. Calif. Newspapers, 1985—87; gen. mgr. San Diego edit. L.A. Times, 1987—93; pres., pub. Marin Ind. Jour., Novato, Calif., 1993—2000; v.p. advt. and mktg. Contra Costa Times, 2000—04; sr. v.p. advt. San Francisco Chronicle, 2005—07; pub. San Diego Suburban Newspapers, 2008—. Dir. comm. ctr. San Diego State U., 1980-93. Bd. dirs. La Jolla Cancer Rsch. Found., 1979-82, YMCA, San Diego Ballet, 1980, Dominican Coll., San Rafael, Calif, 1994—, Marin Theater Co., Alvarado Hosp., 1981-88, chmn. fin. com., 1986, sec. bd., 1986; co-chmn. Operation USS La Jolla, USN, 1980—; mem. mktg. com. United Way, 1979-81, chmn., 1983; trustee La Jollan's Inc., 1975-78, Nat. Pk. Trust, 2000-02, Dogs for the Blind, 2001-.; mem. Conv. and Visitors Bur. Blue Ribbon Com. on Future, 1983; mem. resource panel Child Abuse Prevention Found., 1983—; bd. overseers U. Calif., San Diego; mem. violent crimes task force San Diego Police Dept.; dir. Guide Dogs for the Blind, Oakland Mus. Grantee N.Y. Bd. Edn., 1971-72; named Pub. of Yr., Gannet Co., Inc., 1995. Mem. Newspaper Assn. Am., Calif. Newspaper Pubs. Assn. (bd. dirs., exec. com.), Chancellor's Assn. U. Calif.-San Diego, Clairemont Club. Home: 6333 La Jolla Blvd Unit 370 La Jolla CA 92037-6622 Office Phone: 858-875-5940. Business E-Mail: ppfeiffer@lajoualight.com. E-mail: ppfeiffer@sfchronicle.com.

PFENNINGER, KARL H., cell biology and neuroscience educator; b. Stafa, Switzerland, Dec. 17, 1944; came to U.S., 1971, naturalized, 1993; s. Hans Rudolf and Delie Maria (Zahn) P.; m. Marie-France Maylié, July 12, 1974; children: Jan Patrick, Alexandra Christina MD, U. Zurich, 1971. Rsch. instr. dept. anatomy Washington U., St. Louis, 1971-73; rsch. assoc. sect. cell biology Yale U., New Haven, 1973-76;

assoc. prof. dept. anatomy and cell biology Columbia U., NYC, 1976-81, prof., 1981-86; prof., chmn. Dept. Cellular and Devel. Biology U. Colo. Sch. Medicine, Denver, 1986—2005; prof. pediat. Mental Retardation and Devel. Disabilities Rsch. Ctr., 2005—. Dir. interdeptmental program in cell and molecular biology Columbia U. Coll. Physicians and Surgeons, N.Y.C., 1980-85; chmn. Given Biomed. Inst., Aspen, Colo., 1992-93. Author: Essential Cell Biology, 1990, The Origins of Creativity, 2001; contbr. articles to profl. jours. Recipient C.J. Herrick award Am. Assn. Anatomists, 1977; I.T. Hirschl Career Scientist award, 1977; Javits neurosci. investigator awards NIH, 1984, 91. Mem. AAAS, Am. Soc. for Cell Biology, Am. Soc. Biochemistry and Molecular Biology, Toxicology Forum (bd. dirs. 1995-01), Assn. Anatomy, Cell Biology and Neurosci. Chairpersons (pres. 1998), Harvey Soc., Soc. for Neurosci., Internat. Brain Rsch. Orgn., Internat. Soc. for Neurochemistry. Office: U Colo Health Scis Ctr Dept Pediat Men Retard Mail Stop 8313 12800 E 19th Ave PO Box 6511 Aurora CO 80045 E-mail: Karl.pfenninger@uchsc.edu.

PFEUFFER, ROGER, school system administrator; Teacher Tuscon Unified Sch. Dist., 1970—85; assoc. supt. to supt. Vail Elementary Sch. Dist., 1985—88; asst. supt. Tucson Unified Sch. Dist., 1988—2002; supt. Tucson Unified Sch. Dist., 2004—. Office: Tucson Unified School District 1010 E 10th St Tucson AZ 85719

PFISTER, TERRI, city official; Cert. stenographer, Stenotype Inst. of S.D., 1986. Police pension sec. City of Spokane, Wash., 1991-96, city clk. Wash., 1996—. Office: 808 W Spokane Falls Blvd Spokane WA 99201-3342

PFLAUMER, KATRINA C., lawyer; BA in English Lit. cum laude, Smith Coll.; MA in Tchg. English, Columbia U.; JD, NYU. Tchr. English and Am. Lit. Westtown Sch., Pa., 1970-72; staff atty. Seattle King County Defender Assn., 1975-77, Fed. Pub. Defender's Office, Seattle, 1977-80; pvt. practice, 1980-93; U.S. atty. Dept. Justice (we. dist.) Washington, 1993-01. Pro tem judge King County Superior Ct.; adj. prof. U. Puget Sound Sch. Law; guest lectr. U. Washington, Hastings, Cardozo, Nat. Inst. Trial Advocacy programs; lawyer rep. 9th Cir. Jud. Conf.; named to Atty. Gen. Adv. Com., 1994-95. Mem. Fire Brigade Emergency Response Team. Mem. FBA (pres. we. dist. Washington 1991, chair implementation of gender task force report com.), Nat. Assn. Criminal Def. Lawyers (mem. nominating com.), U.S. Sentencing Commn. (practitioners adv. group), Am. Civil Liberties Union (mem. legal com.), Seattle-King County Bar Assn. (mem. jud. conf. com.), Washington Assn. Criminal Def. Lawyers (pres. 1988-89), State Bench Bar (mem. press com.), Phi Beta Kappa. Office: Us Dept Of Justice 700 Stewart St Seattle WA 98101-1271

PHAIR, JOSEPH BASCHON, lawyer; b. NYC, Apr. 29, 1947; s. James Francis and Mary Elizabeth Phair; m. Bonnie Jean Hobbs, Sept. 04, 1971; children: Kelly I., Joseph B., Sean P. BA, U. San Francisco, 1970, JD, 1973. Bar: Calif., U.S. Dist. Ct. (no. dist.) Calif., U.S. Ct. Appeals (9th cir.). Assoc. Berry, Davis & McInerney, Oakland, Calif., 1974-76, Bronson, Bronson & McKinnon, San Francisco, 1976-79; staff atty. Varian Assocs., Inc., Palo Alto, Calif., 1979-83, corp. counsel, 1983-86, sr. corp. counsel, 1986-87, assoc. gen. counsel, 1987-90, v.p., gen. counsel, 1990-91, v.p., gen. counsel, sec., 1991-99; v.p. adminstrn., gen. counsel, sec. Varian Med. Sys., Inc., Palo Alto, Calif., 1999—2005. Mem. devel. bd. St. Vincent de Paul Devel. Coun., San Francisco, 1992—; mem. athletic devel. bd., U. San Francisco, 1999-, mem. athletic adv. bd., 2004-07. Mem. Bay Area Gen. Counsel, Silicon Valley Assn. Gen. Counsel, The Olympic Culb. Roman Catholic. Business E-Mail: joseph.phair@varian.com.

PHALEN, ROBERT FRANKLYNN, environmental scientist; b. Fairview, Okla., Oct. 18, 1940; married, 1966; 2 children. B in Physics, San Diego State U., 1964, M in Physics, 1966; PhD in Biophysics, U. Rochester, 1971. Engring. aide advanced space systems dept. Gen. Dynamics/Astronautics, San Diego, 1962-63; asst. to radiation safety officer, lab. teaching asst. San Diego State U., 1964-66, instr. physics dept., 1966; mem. summer faculty biology dept. Rochester (N.Y.) Inst. Tech., 1970-72; rsch. assoc. aerosol physics dept. Lovelace Found. for Med. Edn. and Rsch., Albuquerque, 1972-74; from adj. asst. prof. to assoc. prof. in residence dept. community and environ. medicine U. Calif., Irvine, 1974-84, prof., dir. Air Pollution Health Effects Lab., 1985—, faculty Ctr. for Occupl. Environ. Health, 1985—. Editor Aerosol Sci. and Tech., mem. editl. bd., 2002-05; reviewer Am. Rev. Respiratory Disease, Applied Indsl. Hygiene, Bull. Math. Biology, Exptl. Lung Rsch., Jour. Toxicology and Environ. Health, Jour. Toxicology and Applied Pharmacology, Jour. Aerosol Sci., Sci., Toxicol. Scis.; reviewer, mem. editl. bd. Fundamental and Applied Toxicology, 1986-92, Inhalation Toxicology, 1988-04, Jour. Aerosol Medicine, 1988-98; mem. safety and occupl. health study sect. NIH, 1988-01, mem. spl. study sects., 1980, 81, chmn. spl. study sects., 1982-84, 87, 88, 92, mem. site visit teams, 1980-01; mem. expert panel on sulfur oxides EPA, mem. inhalation toxicology divsn. peer rev. panel, 1982, session chmn., 1983, participant workshop on non-oncogenic lung disease, 1984, mem. grants rsch. sci. rev. panel on health rsch., EPA advisor, 1985-88, 93-98, 03; mem. com. animal models testing interventions against aerosol agts. Nat. Acad. Sci., 2005-06; mem. task group on respiratory tract kinetic model Nat. Coun. Radiation Protection, 1978-97; mem. adv. panel on asbestos APHA, 1978; chmn. atmospheric sampling com. Am. Coun. Govtl. Indsl. Hygienists, 1982-92; chmn. NIOSH spl. study sect., 1983; panelist workshop NHLBI, 1982; sci. advisor Prentice Day Sch., 1986-04; mem. Clean Air Sci. Adv. Ctr., EPA, 2007-; mem. bd. dirs. Calif. BioMed. Rsch. Assoc.; dir. four internat. confs. on health effects of particulate air pollution; dir. internat. conf. on inhaled aerosol doses. Author: Inhalation Studies: Foundations and Techniques, 1984, The Particulate Air Pollution Controversy, 2002, second edit., 2008, (with others) Advances in Air Sampling, 1988, Concepts in Inhalation Toxicology, 1989, Deposition, Retention and Dosimetry of Inhaled Radioactive Substances, 1997; editor: Methods in Inhalation Toxicology, 1997; contbr. numerous articles to profl. jours. Am. Legion scholar. Fellow Acad. Toxicol. Scis.; mem. Am. Assn. Aerosol Rsch. (charter, chmn. ann. meeting 1985), Am. Conf. Govtl. Indsl. Hygienists, Am. Indsl. Hygiene Assn. (jour. reviewer, chmn. ann. conf. 1981, 85, 86), Brit. Occupl. Hygiene Soc., Internat. Soc. Aerosols in Medicine, So. Calif. Acad. Scis., Soc. for Aerosol Rsch., Health Physics Soc., Internat. Hormesis Soc. (charter), Soc. Toxicology, Career Achievement award 2000). Achievements include research in nasal, tracheobronchial and pulmonary transport of inhaled deposited particles and effects of pollutant exposure on transport kinetics, laboratory simulation and characterization of airborne environmental pollutants, respiratory tract deposition and clearance models for inhaled particles, including species comparisons and body size effects, behavior of highly-concentrated aerosols with respect to deposition in the respiratory tract. Office: U Calif Air Pollution Health Effects Lab Cmty & Environ Medicine Irvine CA 92697-1825 Business E-Mail: rfphalen@uci.edu.

PHANSTIEL, HOWARD G., managed healthcare company executive; BA in Political Sci., Syracuse U., M in Pub. Adminstrn. Exec. budget officer Wis. Bureau of Planning and Budget; division chief, office of fiscal affairs Ill. Bureau of Budget; dir., office of mgmt. and budget, health care financing administration US Dept. of Health, Ed. and Welfare; exec./mgmt. Prudential Bache Internat. Bank/Securities, Marine Midland Banks, Sallie Mae; exec. v.p. fin./info. svcs. WellPoint Health Networks, Inc., Woodland Hills, Calif.; chmn., CEO ARV Assisted Living, Inc., Costa Mesa, Calif.; exec. v.p., CFO PacifiCare Health Sys., Inc., Calif., 2000, pres., CEO Calif., 2000—04, pres., CEO, chmn., 2004—06.

PHELPS, ARTHUR VAN RENSSELAER, physicist, consultant; b. Dover, NH, July 20, 1923; s. George Osborne and Helen (Ketchum) P.; m. Gertrude Kanzius, July 21, 1956 (dec. Jan. 3, 2003); children: Wayne Edward, Joan Susan. ScD in Physics, MIT, 1951. Cons. physicist rsch. labs. Westinghouse Elec. Corp., Pitts., 1951-70; sr. rsch. scientist Nat. Bur. Standards, Boulder, Colo., 1970-88; fellow Joint Inst. Lab. Astrophysics U. Colo., Boulder, 1970-88, adjoint fellow, 1988—, chmn., 1979-81. Chmn. Gordon Rsch. Conf., Plasma Chemistry, 1990. Recipient Silver Medal award Dept. Commerce, 1978. Fellow Am. Phys. Soc. (Will Allis prize 1990). Achievements include patent for Schulz-Phelps ionization gauge; research on electron and atomic collision processes involving low energy electrons, molecules, ions, metastable atoms and resonance radiation; on laser processes and modeling; on gaseous electronics. Office: U Colo JILA Campus Box 440 Boulder CO 80309-0440 Home: 1331 E Hecla Dr Unit 247 Louisville CO 80027-2341

PHELPS, BARTON CHASE, architect, educator; b. Bklyn., June 27, 1946; s. Julian Orville and Elizabeth Willis (Faulk) P.; m. Karen Joy Simonson; 1 child, Charlotte Simonson Phelps. BA in Art with honors, Williams Coll., 1968; MArch, Yale U., 1973. Registered architect, Calif. With Colin St. John Wilson & Ptnrs., London, 1972-73, Frank O. Gehry and Assocs., Inc., Santa Monica, Calif., 1973-76, Charles Moore/Urban Innovations Group, LA, 1976-78; dir. architecture Urban Innovations Group, LA, 1980-84; prin. Barton Phelps & Assocs., LA, 1984—; asst. prof. architecture Rice U. Sch. of Architecture, Houston, 1977-79; asst. dean Grad. Sch. Architecture and Urban Planning, UCLA, 1980-83; prof. architecture Sch. Arts and Architecture UCLA, 1979—2001. Faculty mem. Nat. Endowment Arts, Mayors Inst. for City Design, 1990, 92, 98. Author, editor Architecture California, 1988-92, mem. editl. bd., 1998; editor: Views From the River, 1998; mem. editl. bd. Archtl. Record, 1998-2000. Mem. design review com. U. Calif., Santa Barbara, Calif., 2000—06; jury mem. US Presdl. Design Awards, 2000, Nat. AIA Honor Awards, 2003; mem. mayor's advisory panel Cultural Affairs Commn., LA, 2001—06; mem. architectural advisory bd. for oversees bldg. ops. US State Dept., 2005—06; bd. dirs. U. Elem. Sch. UCLA, 2000—06. Fellow Graham Found. for Advanced Studies in the Fine Arts, 1989, 96, Nat. Endowment for the Arts, 1990, 98. Mem. AIA (Coll. of Fellows, chair nat. com. on design, design excellence program USGSA, recipient design awards for L.A. Pub. Libr., Los Feliz, Woodland Hills, Will & Ariel Durant Branch, Cabrillo Marine Aquarium, Royce Hall at UCLA, Arroyo House, Kranz House, Sinquefield Ho., North Range Clark Libr. UCLA, L.A. Dept. Water and Power Ctrl. Dist. Hdqrs., North Hollywood Pump Sta., East Bldg. Seeds U. Elem. Sch., UCLA, Inst. Honor for Collaborative Design, Games XXIII Olympiad L.A. 1984), L.A. Conservancy (bd. dirs.). Democrat. Home: 10256 Lelia Ln Los Angeles CA 90077-3144 Office: Barton Phelps & Assocs 5514 Wilshire Blvd Los Angeles CA 90036-3829 Office Phone: 323-934-8515. Business E-Mail: bphelps@bpala.com.

PHELPS, MARSHALL C., JR., computer software company executive; m. Eileen Phelps; 2 children. BA, Muskingum Coll.; MS, Stanford Grad. Sch. Bus.; Doctorate, Cornell Law Sch. With IBM Corp., 1972—2000, v.p. intellectual property & licensing, dir. govt. rels.; chmn., CEO Spencer Trask Intellectual Capital Co. LLC; dep. gen. counsel, Legal & Corp. Affairs group Microsoft Corp., 2003—06, corp. v.p. IP policy & strategy, 2006—. Exec.-in-residence Fuqua Sch. Bus., Duke U., bd. visitors; bd. dirs. Internat. Intellectual Property Inst. Recipient Career Achievement award, IBM Corp., 1999; named to Intellectual Property Hall of Fame, 2006. Office: Microsoft Corp 1 Microsoft Way Redmond WA 98052-6399 also: Fuqua Sch Bus Duke U 1 Towerview Dr Durham NC 27708

PHELPS, MICHAEL EDWARD, biophysics professor; b. Cleve., Aug. 24, 1939; s. Earl E. and Regina Bridget (Hines) P.; m. Patricia Emory, May 15, 1969; children: Patrick, Kaitlin. BA in Chemistry and Math., Western Wash. State U., 1965; PhD in Chemistry, Washington U., St. Louis, 1970. Asst. prof. Washington U. Sch. Medicine and Engring., 1970-73, assoc. prof., 1973-75; assoc. prof. dept. radiology U. Pa., Phila., 1975-76; prof. radiological sciences UCLA, 1976—92, prof. biomathematics, 1980—84, chief divsn. biophysics, 1981—84, Jennifer Jones Simon prof., 1983—86, Norton Simon prof., 1996—, chief div. nuclear medicine, 1984—92, dir. Crump Inst. for Biol. Imaging, 1989—, chmn., dept. molecular and med. pharmacology, 1992—, chief, divsn. nuclear medicine, dept. molecular and med. pharmacology, 1992—2000; assoc. dir. UCLA/DOE Lab. Structural Biology and Molecular Medicine, 1984—2002; dir. UCLA/DOE Inst. Molecular Medicine, 2002—. Mem. study sect. NIH, Bethesda, Md., 1974-78. Author: Reconstruction Tomography in Diagnostic Radiology and Nuclear Medicine, 1977, Physics in Nuclear Medicine, 1980, 1987, 2002, Principles of Tracer Kinetics, 1983, PET: Molecular Imaging and its Biological Applications, 2004; contbr. articles to profl. jours. Recipient Von Hevesy Found. award, 1975,George Von Hevesy prize Von Hevesy Found., Zurich, 1978, 82, Oldendorf award, Soc. for Computerized Tomography and Neurologicval Imaging, 1981, S. Weir Mitchell award, Am. Acad. of Neuology, 1981, Ernest O. Lawrence award US Dept. Energy, 1984, Spec. award for Individual Distinction, Am. Nuclear Soc., 1984, Landauer Mem. award, Am. Assn. for Physicists in Medicine, 1988, Robert J. and Claire Pasarow Found. award, 1992, Disting. Scientists award, Inst. for Clin. PET, 1995, Enrico Fermi Presdl. award, 1999, Charles F. Kettering prize, GM Cancer Rsch. Found., 2001; holder Norton Simon endowed chair, 1983-; named Disting. Alumnus Western Wash. State U., 1980 Fellow Am. Heart Assn.; mem. ACP (Richard and Hinda Rosenthal award 1987), Inst. Medicine NAS (elected), Nat. Acad. Scis. (elected 1999), Soc. Nuclear Medicine (Paul Aebersold award 1983, Ted Block Mem. award, 1989), Internat. Soc. Cerebral Blood Flow and Metabolism (Cert. Excellence award 1979), NY Acad. Scis. (Sarah L. Poiley award 1984), Soc. Neuroscis. Roman Catholic. Business E-Mail: mphelps@mednet.ucla.edu.

PHILBIN, ANN, art facility director; b. Boston, Mar. 21, 1952; d. Richard Moore and Ann Theresa (Muller) Philbin BA in art history, BFA in painting, U. NH, 1976; MA in mus. studies/arts adminstrn., NYU, 1982. Rschr. Frick Art Reference Libr., NYC, 1977-79; asst. to dir., program coord. Artists Space, NYC, 1979-80; asst. curatorial coord. The New Mus., NYC, 1980-81; curator Ian Woodner Family Collection, NYC, 1981-83; asst. dir. Grace Borgenicht Gallery, NYC, 1983-85; dir. Curt Marcus Gallery, NYC, 1985-88; account dir., dir. Art Against AIDS Livet Reichard Inc., NYC, 1988-90; dir. The Drawing Ctr., NYC, 1990—99, UCLA Hammer Museum, LA, 1999—. Bd. dirs. Elizabeth Streb, Ringside, NY, 1990, HIV Law Project, N.Y.C., 1993; founding mem. Women's Action Coalition, NYC, 1991. Recipient Best Monographic Mus. Show Nationally Award for exhibition Lee Bontecou: A Retrospective, Internat. Assn. Art Critics/USA, 2004. Address: UCLA Hammer Museum 10899 Wilshire Blvd at Westwood Blvd Los Angeles CA 90024

PHILIPPON, MARC JOSEPH, orthopaedic surgeon; b. Quebec City, Can., May 9, 1965; arrived in U.S., 1990; s. Pontien Aderville and Micheline (Lortie) P.; m. Senenne Catalina Reid, Mar. 25, 1995; children: Michèle, Marc-Christophe, Mia-Véronique. BA with honors, Fla. Atlantic U., 1987; MD, McMaster U., Hamilton, Ont., Can., 1990. Lic. physician, Fla., Pa.; diplomate Am. Bd. Orthopaedic Surgery. Orthop. surgery resident U. Miami, Jackson Meml. Hosp., 1995; orthopaedic surgeon Holy Cross Hosp., Ft. Lauderdale, Fla., 1995; chief orthopaedic surgery, 2000-01; chief orthopaedic surgeon humanitarian mission to Ukraine Kiev Orthopaedic Inst., 1997; orthopaedic surgeon Broward Gen. Hosp., Ft. Lauderdale, 1998—2002; dir. sports medicine/hip disorders dept. orthopaedic surgery U. Pitts. Med. Ctr.; dir. fellowship program U. Pitts. Med. Ctr. for Sports Medicine, dir. hip arthroscopy fellowship, dir. golf medicine program, dir. Fla. site; orthop. surgeon, ptnr. Steadman-Hawkins Clinic, Vail, Colo., 2005—. Cons. Howmedica Inc., Rutherford, N.J., 1996-97, Smith & Nephew Inc., Memphis, 1998-99, Zimmer (Bristol-Myers Squibb), NHL, NFL, NBA and MLB profl. teams and has treated PGA golfers; clin. adv. bd. Oratec Interventions, Inc., Menlo Park, Calif., 1998-2002; clin. asst. prof., U. Pitts. Med. Ctr.; med. cons. Ctr. for Sports Medicine; orthop. surgeon Nat. Hockey League Players Assn.; lectr. in field. Contbr. chapters to books, articles to profl. jours. Bd. dirs. Svc. Agy. for Sr. Citizens, Ft. Lauderdale, 1996-2000. Farquharson scholar Can. Med. Rsch. Coun., 1989. Fellow Internat. Coll. Surgeons, Am. Acad. Orthop. Surgeons; mem. AMA, Fla. Med. Assn., Am. Orthop. Soc. for Sports Medicine, Arthroscopy Assn. N.Am. (master instr.), Herodicus Soc., Phi Kappa Phi. Roman Catholic. Achievements include invention of orthopaedic surgery instrument and devices. Avocations: skiing, tennis, sailing, hockey, soccer, golf. Office: Steadman Hawkins Clinic 181 W Meadow Dr Ste 400 Vail CO 81657 Office Phone: 970-476-1100.

PHILIPS, SUZANNE MARGUERITE See CASEY, SUE

PHILLIPS, ANTHONY GEORGE, neurobiology researcher; b. Barrow, Cumbria, Eng., Jan. 30, 1943; came to Can., 1953; s. George William and Mabel Lilian (Wood) P. BA, U. Western Ont., London, Can., 1966, MA, 1967, PhD, 1970. Asst. prof. psychobiology U. B.C., Vancouver, Canada, 1970-75, assoc. prof., 1975-80, prof., 1980—, head dept. psychology, 1994-99, prof. dept. psychiatry, 1999—, founding dir. U. B.C. Inst. Mental Health. Founder Quadra Logic Tech., Inc., Vancouver. Contbr. numerous papers to sci. jours. Chair inst. adv. bd. CIHR Inst. for Neurosci. Mental Health & Addiction, 2001—; bd. dirs. Tibetian Refuge Aid Soc., 1980—; chmn. Can.-India Village Aid, Vancouver, 1981—86, 2003—05. Recipient Killam Rsch. prize Can. Coun., 1977, D.O. Hebb award Can. Psychol. Assn.; Steacie fellow Nat. Scis. and Engring. Rsch. Coun. Can., 1980. Fellow Royal Soc. Can.; mem. Soc. Neurosci., Can. Soc. for Neurosci., Can. Coll. Neuropsychopharmacology. Office: U BC Dept Psych 2255 Wesbrook Mall Vancouver BC Canada V6T 1Z4 Office Phone: 604-822-4624. Business E-Mail: aphillips@psych.ubc.ca.

PHILLIPS, CHARLES E., JR., computer software company executive; b. Little Rock, Ark., 1960; BS in Computer Sci., USAF Acad., 1981; MBA in Fin., Hampton U., Va.; JD, NY Law Sch. CFA; bar: Ga., DC. Prin. Morgan Stanley & Co., Inc., 1994—95, mng. dir., 1995—2003; exec. v.p. strategy, partnerships & bus. devel. Oracle Corp., Redwood City, Calif., 2003—04, pres., 2004—, co-pres. PeopleSoft Calif., 2004. Bd. dirs. Oracle Corp., 2004—, Viacom Corp., 2004—, Morgan Stanley, 2006—; mem. President's Econ. Recovery Advisory Bd., 2009—. Trustee Joint Ctr. for Polit. and Econ. Studies, Washington, NY Law Sch., bd. dirs., Jazz at Lincoln Ctr., NYC. Capt. USMC. Named one of 50 Black Profls. on Wall Street, Black Enterprise Mag., 50 Who Matter Now, Business 2.0, 2007. Office: Oracle Corp 500 Oracle Pky Redwood City CA 94065 Office Phone: 650-506-7000. Office Fax: 650-506-7200.*

PHILLIPS, JILL META, writer, critic, astrologer; b. Detroit, Oct. 22, 1952; d. Leyson Kirk and Leona Anna (Rasmussen) P. Student pub. schs., Calif. Lit. counselor Book Builders, Charter Oak, Calif., 1966-77; pres. Moon Dance Astro Graphics, Covina, Calif., 1994—. Author: (with Leona Phillips) A Directory of American Film Scholars, 1975, The Good Morning Cookbook, 1976, G.B. Shaw: A Review of the Literature, 1976, T.E. Lawrence: Portrait of the Artist as Hero, 1977, The Archaeology of the Collective East, 1977, The Occult, 1977, D.H. Lawrence: A Review of the Literature and Biographies, 1978, Film Appreciation: A College Guide Book, 1979, Annus Mirabilis: Europe in the Dark and Middle Centuries, 1979, (with Leona Rasmussen Phillips) The Dark Frame: Occult Cinema, 1979, Misfit: The Films of Montgomery Clift, 1979, Butterflies in the Mind: A Précis of Dreams and Dreamers, 1980; The Rain Maiden: A Novel of History, 1987, Walford's Oak: A Novel, 1990, The Fate Weaver: A Novel in Two Centuries, 1991, Saturn Falls: A Novel of the Apocalypse, 1993, Birthday Secrets, 1998, Your Luck is in the Stars, 2000; columnist Dell Horoscope Mag., Astrology Your Daily Horoscope Mag., 1998—; contbr. book revs. to New Guard mag., 1974-76; contbr. numerous articles to profl. jours. including Dell Horoscope, Midnight Horoscope, Astrology-Your Daily Horoscope, Am. Astrology. Mem. Young Ams. for Freedom, Am. Conservative Union, Elmer Bernstein's Film Music Collection, Ghost Club London, Count Dracula Soc., Dracula Soc. London, Richard III Soc. Republican. Personal E-mail: queenofwands52@aol.com.

PHILLIPS, JOHN EDWARD, zoologist, educator; b. Montréal, Que., Can., Dec. 20, 1934; s. William Charles and Violet Mildred (Lewis) P.; m. Eleanor Mae Richardson, Sept. 8, 1956; children: Heather Anne, Jayne Elizabeth, Jonathan David, Catherine Melinda, Wendy Susannah. BSc with honors, Dalhousie U., Halifax, NS, 1956, MSc, 1957; PhD, Cambridge U., Eng., 1961. Asst. prof. Dalhousie U., Halifax, N.S., 1960-64; assoc. prof. U. B.C., Vancouver, Canada, 1964-71, prof., 1971—, head dept. zoology, 1991-96. Vis. rschr. Cambridge (Eng.) U., 1972, 76, 81; chair grant selection com. Nat. Rsch. Coun. Can., Ottawa, Ont., 1969-71; mem. coun. Nat. Sci. and Engring. Rsch. Coun., Ottawa, 1983-87. Mem. editorial bd.: Can. Jour. Zoology, 1971-75, Am. Jour. Physiology, 1978-93, Jour. Experimental Biology, 1981-85, Am. Zool., 1996-01; contbr. articles to profl. jours. Mem. grant selection com. Can. Cystic Fibrosis Found., Toronto, 1989-91; active Vancouver Bach Choir. Named to James chair St. Francis Xavier U., Antigonish, N.S., 1993; recipient Killam Rsch. prize U. B.C. Fellow Royal Soc. Can.; mem. Can. Soc. Zoologists (sec. 1972-76, v.p. 1976-78, pres. 1979, Fry medal 2000), Am. Soc. Zoologists (exec. 1983-85, chair divsn. comp. physiol. biochemistry 1983-85). Avocations: music, singing. Home: 12908 22 B Ave White Rock BC Canada V4A 6Z3 Personal E-mail: jephillips@telus.net.

PHILLIPS, JOHN RICHARD, engineering educator; b. Albany, Calif., Jan. 30, 1934; s. Eric Lester and Adele Catherine (Rengel) P.; m. Joan Elizabeth Soyster, Mar. 23, 1957; children: Elizabeth Huntley, Sarah Rengel, Catherine Hale. BS, U. Calif., Berkeley, 1956; M in Engring., Yale U., 1958, PhD in Engring., 1960. Registered profl. engr., Calif. Chem. engr. Stanford Rsch. Inst., Menlo Park, Calif., 1960; rsch. engr. Chevron Rsch. Co., Richmond, Calif., 1962-66; mem. faculty Harvey Mudd Coll., Claremont, Calif., 1966—2002, James Howard Kindleberger prof. engring., 1991—2002, prof. engring., 1974—2002, prof. emeritus, 2002—, dir. engring. clinic, 1977-93, chmn. engring. dept., 1993-99. Vis. prof. U. Edinburgh, Scotland, 1975, Cambridge (Eng.) U., 1981, ESIEE, France, 1981, Naval Postgrad. Sch., 1984-85, Calif. Poly. U., San Luis Obispo, 1992, 99, U. Canterbury, New Zealand, 2000, Smith Coll., 2001; vis. scientist So. Calif. Edison Co., 1980; founder Claremont Engring., 1973; cons. in field. Contbr. articles to profl. jours. 1st lt. AUS, 1960-62. Mem. Am. Inst. Chem. Engrs., Am. Soc. Engring. Edn., Sigma Xi, Alpha Delta Phi, Tau Beta Pi. Home: 911 W Maryhurst Dr Claremont CA 91711-3320

PHILLIPS, KEITH WENDALL, minister; b. Portland, Oreg., Oct. 21, 1946; s. Frank Clark and Velma Georgina (Black) P.; m. Mary Katherine Garland, July 16, 1973; children: Joshua, Paul, David. BA, UCLA, 1968; MDiv, Fuller Theology Sem., 1971, D. of Ministries, 1972; LHD (hon.), John Brown U., 1990; LHD (hon.), Sterling Coll., 2002. Dir. Youth For Christ Clubs, LA, 1965-71; pres. World Impact, LA, 1971—. Commencement speaker Tabor Coll., 1969, 91, John Brown U., 1990, Sterling Coll., 2002. Author: Everybody's Afraid in the Ghetto, 1973, They Dare to Love the Ghetto, 1975, The Making of a Disciple, 1981, No Quick Fix, 1985, Out of Ashes, 1996. Chmn. L.A. Mayor's Prayer Breakfast Com., 1985—; bd. dirs. Christian Cmty. Devel. Assn., 1992—; founder/coord. Crowns of Beauty Confs.; spkr. Promise Keeper. Named Disting. Staley lectr., 1969. Mem. Evangelistic Com. of Newark (pres. 1976—), World Impact of Can. (pres. 1978—), The Oaks (pres. 1985—), Faith Works (pres. 1987—) Baptist. Office: World Impact 2001 S Vermont Ave Los Angeles CA 90007-1279

PHILLIPS, LAYN R., lawyer; b. Oklahoma City, Jan. 2, 1952; s. James Arthur Cole and Eloise (Gulick) P.; m. Kathryn Hale, Aug. 17, 1986; children: Amanda, Parker, Graham. BS, U. Tulsa, 1974, JD, 1977; postgrad., Georgetown U., 1978-79. Bar: Okla. 1977, D.C. 1978, Calif. 1981, Tex. 1991. Asst. U.S. atty., Miami, 1980-81, LA, 1980-83; trial atty. Bur. of Competition, Washington, 1977-80; U.S. atty. U.S. Dist. Ct. (no. dist.) Okla., Tulsa, 1983-87; judge U.S. Dist. Ct. (we. dist.) Okla., Oklahoma City, 1987-91; litigation ptnr. Irell & Manella, Newport Beach, Calif., 1991—. Tchr. trial practice U. Tulsa Coll. Law, Okla. City U. Law Sch.; lectr. Attys. Gen's. Adv. Inst., Washington. Pres. Am. Inn of Ct. XXIII, Sch. Law, Okla. U., 1989-90; pres. Am. Inn. of Ct. CVIII, Sch. Law., Okla. City U. 1990-91. Named one of Outstanding Young Ams., U.S. Jaycees, 1989. Fellow: ACTL; mem.: Fed. Bar Assn. (pres. Orange County chpt.). Office: Irell & Manella 840 Newport Center Dr Ste 400 Newport Beach CA 92660-6323

PHILLIPS, MICHELLE GILLIAM, actress, writer; b. Long Beach, Calif., June 4, 1944; d. Gardner Burnett and Joyce Leon (Poole) Gilliam; m. John Phillips, Dec. 31, 1962 (div. 1970); children: Gilliam Chynna Phillips, Austin D. Hines, Aron S. Wilson. Grad. high sch., Ft. Jones, Calif. Model Francis Gill Agy., NYC, 1962-64; singer Mamas and Papas, 1965-69. Guest appearances in TV shows include Vega$, 1980, The Fall Guy, 1983, Santa Barbara, 1984, Murder, She Wrote, 1984, Scene of the Crime, 1985, Alfred Hitchcock Presents, 1985, T.J. Hooker, 1985, Star Trek: The Next Generation, 1988, Herman's Head, 1994, Diagnsos Murder, 1994, 99, Burke's Law, 1994, Lois & Clark: The New Adventures of Superman, 1995, Too Something, 1996, Beverly Hills, 90210, 1997, 98, Pauly, 1997, The Magnificent Seven, 1998, 99, 2000, The Love Boat: The Next Wave, 1998, Rude Awakening, 1999, Providence, 1999, Twice in a Lifetime, 2000; appeared in tv movies The Death Squad, 1974, The California Kid, 1974, The Useres, 1978, Moonlight, 1982, Murder Me, Murder You, 1983, Secrets of a Married Man, 1984, Covenant, 1985, Paint Me a Murder, 1985, Stark: Mirror Image, 1986, Assault and Matrimony, 1987, Mike Hammer: Murder Takes All, 1989, Trenchcoat in Paradise, 1989, Appearances, 1990, Rubdown, 1993, Rock 'n' Roll Revolution: The British Invade America, 1995, 919 Fifth Avenue, 1995, No One Would Tell, 1996, Pretty Poison, 1996, Sweetwater, 1999; appeared in feature films Monterey Pop, 1969, The Last Movie, 1971, Dillinger, 1973, Valentino, 1977, Bloodline, 1979, The Man with Bogart's Face, 1980, Savage Harvest, 1981, American Anthem, 1986, Let It Ride, 1989, Flashing on the Sixties: A Tribal Document, 1990, Scissors, 1991, Army of One, 1993, Anna Petrovic, You Rock!, 1998, Lost in the Pershing Point Hotel, 2000, TV series Aspen, 1977, The French Atlantic Affair, 1979, Hotel, 1983, Knots Landing, 1979, Second Chances, 1993, Malibu Shores, 1996, Knots Landing: Back to the Cul-de-Sac, 1997; author: California Dreamin', 1986, Monday Monday (Grammy award). Recipient medal of Honor for Stop War Toys Campaign Alliance for Survival, 1987, Soap Opera Awards for Best Villainess, 1990.

PHILLIPS, RANDY, state legislator, marketing professional; b. Seattle, Aug. 30, 1950; m. Norma Banta; children: Christopher, Matthew. BA in Polit. Sci. and History, Alaska Meth. U., 1973. Contract adminstrv. asst.; mktg. rschr. Gamel Homes, 1982-84; pres., mng. ptnr. No. Family Home Video, 1985-87; pvt. practice mktg. and rsch., 1988—; mem. Alaska Ho. of Reps., 1976-92, Alaska Senate, Dist. L, Juneau, 1992—. Chmn. senate labor & commerce com., senate state affairs com., senate rules com., senate cmty. & regional affairs com., legis. budget & audit com., Alaska Senate., Anchorage. Named Outstanding Freshman Legislator, Tenth Legislature, 1977-78, Outstanding Rep., Standing Together Against Rape, 1987. Mem. Eagle River Fine Arts Acad., Elks. Republican. Avocations: family cabin, hockey, classic cars, coin collecting/numismatics. also: PO Box 142 Eagle River AK 99577 Fax: 907-465-4979. E-mail: senator_randy_phillips@legis.state.ak.us.

PHILLIPS, ROBERT, engineering educator, researcher; BS, U. Minn., 1986; PhD, Wash. U., 1989. Clark Millikan vis. asst. prof. Caltech, 1997—2000, prof. mech. engring. and applied physics, 2000—. Contbr. articles to profl. jour. Recipient Pioneer award, NIH, 2004. Achievements include research in exploring nanoscale mechanics in biol. systems; the way DNA binding proteins that control gene expression expert mechanical forces on DNA resulting in the formation of loops. Office: Calif Inst Tech 159 Broad MC 128-95 Office 221 Steele 1200 E Calif Blvd Pasadena CA 91125 Office Phone: 626-395-3374. Office Fax: 626-583-4963. Business E-Mail: phillips@aero.caltech.edu.

PHILLIPS, ROGER, retired steel company executive; b. Ottawa, Ont., Can., Dec. 17, 1939; s. Norman William Frederick and Elizabeth (Marshall) P.; m. Katherine Ann Wilson, June 9, 1962; 1 child, Andrée Claire. BSc, McGill U., Montreal, Can., 1960. V.p. mill products Alcan Can. Products Ltd., Toronto, Ont., 1969-70, exec. v.p., 1971-75; pres. Alcan Smelters and Chems. Ltd., Montreal, Que., 1976-79; v.p. tech. Alcan Aluminium Ltd., Montreal, 1980-81; pres. Alcan Internat. Ltd., Montreal, 1980-81; pres., CEO IPSCO Inc., Regina, Sask., Canada, 1982—2001. Sr. mem. Conf. Bd., Inc., NY, 1987—2002; bd. dirs. Toronto Dominion Bank, Can. Pacific Rlwy., Imperial Oil Ltd.; hon. dir. IPSCO Inc.; dir. Cleveland-Cliffs Inc. Bd. dirs. Conf. Bd. of Can., 1984-87; chmn. Coun. for Can. Unity, 1987-88. Fellow Inst. Physics UK (chartered physicist); mem. Can. Assn. Physicists, Am. Iron and Steel Inst. (bd. dirs. 1984-2001), Sask. C. of C. (bd. dirs. 1984-), Que. C. of C. (pres. 1981), Order of Can. (officer 1999), St. Denis Club, Univ. Club (Montreal), Calgary Petroleum Club. Home: 3220 Albert St Regina SK Canada S4S 3N9 Office: IPSCO Inc Armour Rd Regina SK Canada S4P 3C7 E-mail: rphillips@ipsco.com.

PHILLIPS, RONALD FRANK, academic administrator; b. Houston, Nov. 25, 1934; s. Franklin Jackson and Maudie Ethel (Merrill) P.; m. Jamie Jo Bottoms, Apr. 5, 1957 (dec. Sept. 1996); children: Barbara Celeste Phillips Oliveira, Joel Jackson, Phil Edward. BS, Abilene Christian U., 1955; JD, U. Tex., 1965. Bar: Tex. 1965, Calif. 1972. Bldg. contractor Phillips Homes, Abilene, Tex., 1955-56; br. mgr. Phillips Weatherstripping Co., Midland and Austin, Tex., 1957-65; corp. staff atty. McWood Corp., Abilene, 1965-67; sole practice law Abilene, 1967-70; mem. adj. faculty Abilene Christian U., 1967-70; prof. law Pepperdine U., Malibu, Calif., 1970—, dean Sch. Law, 1970-97, dean emeritus, 1997—, vice chancellor, 1995—. Mem. Nat. Conf. Commrs. on Uniform State Laws, 1988—2003. Deacon North A and Tenn. Ch. of Christ, Midland, 1959-62; deacon Highland Ch. of Christ, Abilene, 1965-70; elder Malibu Ch. of Christ, 1978-95; mgr., coach Little League Baseball, Abilene, Huntington Beach and Malibu, 1968-78, 90-95; coach Youth Soccer, Huntington Beach, Westlake Village and Malibu, 1972-80, 85-86, 91. Recipient Alumni citation Abilene Christian U., 1974 Fellow Am. Bar Found. (life); mem. ABA, State Bar Tex., State Bar Calif., Christian Legal Soc., L.A. Bar Assn., Assn. Am. Law Schs. (chmn. sect. on adminstrn. law schs. 1982, com. on cts. 1985-87), Am. Law Inst. Republican. Office: Pepperdine U 24255 Pacific Coast Hwy Malibu CA 90263-4951 Business E-Mail: ronald.phillips@pepperdine.edu.

PHILLIPS, STACY D., lawyer; b. NYC, Sept. 5, 1958; d. Gerald F. and Francine Anne (Kantor) Phillips. AB cum laude with high distinction, Dartmouth Coll., 1980; JD, Columbia U., 1983. Cert.: Family Law Specialist, bar: Calif. 1984, US Dist. Ct. Ctrl. and So. Districts Calif., US Ct. Appeals 9th Cir. Law clk. to Hon. Edward Rafeedie US Dist. Ct., LA, 1983-84; assoc. Wyman, Bautzer, Rothman, Kuchel & Silbert, LA, 1984-85, Jaffe & Clemens, Beverly Hills, Calif., 1986—90; founding ptnr. Mannis & Phillips, LA, 1995—2000, Phillips Lerner, Lauzon & Tamra LLP, LA, 2000—. Guest commentator various TV programs including Good Morning America, Hard Copy, Inside Edition; contbr. Divorce Mag., adv. bd.; bd. dirs. Legal Momentum (previously NOW Legal Def. and Edn. Fund); co-chair Calif. Leadership Coun. Author: Divorce: It's All About Control - How To Win the Emotional, Psychological and Legal Wars; co-author: Mother Knows Best-Family Law Practitioners Must Nurture, Not Wield Poison Pens; contbr. articles to profl. jours. Bd. dirs. Vista del Mar Child and Family Services, Levitt & Quinn Family Law Ctr., Bnai Zion Found. Inc.; bd. trustees Alternative Living for the Aging; bd. govs., bd. dirs. Legal Momentum; past chair, bd. dirs. ALA. Recipient Women of Action Award, Israel Cancer Rsch. Fund, 2000, Women of Achievement Award, Bnai Zion Found. Inc., 2001, Women Who Make a Difference Award, LA Bus. Jour., 2001, Patricia McClure Award, Asthma & Allergy Found. Am., 2001, Women of Achievement Award in Family Law and Mediation, Century City C. of C., 2001, 2002, Women to Watch award, Jewish Women Internat., 2005; named one of 50 Most Powerful Women in LA Law, LA Bus. Jour., 1998, Top 20 Attorneys Under 40 Years Old, LA Daily Jour., 1998, Top 50 Women Litigators in Calif., 2003; grantee Policy Study Internship, Dartmouth Coll., 1978. Mem.: ABA (mem. family law sect.), Beverly Hills Bar Assn. (mem. family law sect., mem. alternative dispute resolutions com.), LA Bar Assn. (mem. family law sect.), State Bar Calif. (mem. child custody and visitation com.), National Partnership of Women & Families, Chancery Club of LA. Avocations: cooking, tennis. Office: 2029 Century Park E Ste 1200 Los Angeles CA 90067 Office Phone: 310-277-7117. Business E-Mail: sdpdissoqueen@plljlaw.com.

PHILLIPS, STEVE, electronics executive; arrived in US, 2001; BSc with honors in Electronic Engring., U. Essex, Eng.; postgraduate diploma in Mgmt. Studies, Thames Valley U., Eng. Various leadership positions Thorn EMI, 1984—96; info. tech. dir. European foods divsn. Diageo, 1996—99; v.p. info. tech. to sr. v.p., chief info. officer Gateway, Dublin, 1999—2003, sr. v.p., chief info. officer, 2003—04, Memec, 2004—05, Avnet, Inc., Phoenix, 2005—. Bd. dirs. Ariz. Tech. Coun., 2007—. Named one of Top 100 Chief Info. Officers, eWeek, 2007. Fellow: Instn. Elec. Engrs. Office: Avnet Inc 2211 S 47th St Phoenix AZ 85034-6403 Office Phone: 480-643-2000.

PHILLIPS, TED RAY, advertising executive; b. Am. Falls, Idaho, Oct. 27, 1948; s. Virn E. and Jessie N. (Aldous) P.; m. Dianne Jacqulynne Walker, May 28, 1971; children: Scott, Russell, Stephen, Michael. BA, Brigham Young U., 1972, MA, 1975. Account exec. David W. Evans, Inc., Salt Lake City, 1972-75; dir. advt. divsn. continuing edn. U. Utah, Salt Lake City, 1975-78; sr. v.p. Evans/Lowe & Stevens, Inc., Atlanta, 1978, exec. v.p., 1979; pres., CEO David W. Evans/Atlanta, Inc., 1979-80; dir. advt. O.C. Tanner Co., Salt Lake City, 1980-82; pres. Thomas/Phillips/Clawson Advt., Inc., Salt Lake City, 1982-86, Hurst & Phillips, Salt Lake City, 1986-94; CEO, chmn. The Phillips Agy., Salt Lake City, 1994-2000; CEO Virtual Ad Agy., 2000—. Advt. instr. divsn. continuing edn. Brigham Young U., 1983-85. Dir. comms. Salt Lake County Mayor's Office, 2002-04. Recipient Silver Beaver award Boy Scouts Am., 1994, Spurgeon award, 1995. Mem. Am. Advt. Fedn. (8 Best-in-West awards, 2 nat. Addy awards, Clio finalist 1984, Telly award 1991, 92, 2002), Utah Advt. Fedn. (bd. dirs. 1976-78, 80-87, pres. 1984-85). Mem. Lds Ch. Home: 1792 Cornwall Ct Sandy UT 84092-5436 Office: 1792 E Cornwall Ct Ste A Sandy UT 84092 Office Phone: 801-550-1808. Personal E-mail: phillips66er@earthlink.net, ted@phillipsad.com.

PHILLIPS, THEODORE LOCKE, radiologist, educator; b. Phila., June 4, 1933; s. Harry Webster and Margaret Amy (Locke) Phillips; m. Joan Cappello, June 23, 1956; children: Margaret, John, Sally. BSc, Dickinson Coll., 1955; MD, U. Pa., 1959. Intern Western Res. U., Cleve., 1960; resident in therapeutic radiology U. Calif., San Francisco, 1963, clin. instr., 1963—65, asst. prof. radiation oncology, 1965—68, assoc. prof., 1968—70, prof., 1970—, chmn. dept. radiation oncology, 1973—98. Rsch. radiobiologist U.S. Naval Radiologic Def. Lab., San Francisco, 1963—65; rsch. physician Lawrence Berkeley Lab. Contbr. numerous articles to profl. publs. With USNR, 1963—65. Grantee, Nat. Cancer Inst., 1970—99. Mem.: Inst. Medicine, No. Calif. Radiation Oncology Assn., Radium Soc., Radiation Rsch. Soc. (pres. 1977), Am. Coll. Radiology, Calif. Med. Assn., Am. Assn. Cancer Rsch., N.Am. Hyperthermia Soc. (pres. 1994), Radiol. Soc. N.Am., Am. Soc. Clin. Oncology, Am. Soc. Therapeutic Radiology and Oncology (pres. 1984), Alpha Omega Alpha, Phi Beta Kappa. Republican. Office: U Calif San Francisco Dept Radiation Oncology 1600 Divisidero St ste H1031 San Francisco CA 94143-1708

PHILLIPS, VICKI L., school system administrator; b. Marion, Ind., Jan. 15, 1958; d. Denver Phillips and Vivian (Burnette) Fuqua. BS in Edn., Western Ky. U., 1980, MA in Psychology, 1987; doctoral student, U. Ky., 1988—; EdD in instrnl. leadership, U. of Lincoln, Eng., 2002. Dir. devel. tng. dept. Panorama, Bowling Green, Ky., 1978—80; tchr. learning and behavior disorders Simpson County Bd. Edn., 1981—85; exceptional child cons. Ky. Dept. Edn. Office Edn. for Exceptional Children, 1986—90; chief exec. asst. to edn. commr. Ky. Dept. of Edn., 1986—93; dep. dir./chief of staff Nat. Alliance for Restructuring Edn., Wash., DC, 1993—95; dir. Greater Phila. First Partnership for Reform; exec. dir. Children Achieving Challenge, 1995—98; supt. Sch. Dist. of Lancaster, 1998—2003; sec. of edn. Pa. Dept. Edn., Harrisburg, 2003—04; supt. Portland Pub. Schools, Oreg., 2004—. Mem. ASCD, Nat. Coun. for Exceptional Children, Coun. for Behavior Disorders, Nat. Assn. for Sch. Psychologists, Ky. Assn. Sch. Adminstrs., Ky. Assn. for Psychology in the Schs., Ky. Assn. for Family-Based Svcs., Ky. Families for Family-Based Svcs., Ky. Families as Allies. Office: 501 N Dixon St Portland OR 97227-1804

PHILLIPS, VIRGINIA A., judge; BA magna cum laude, U. Calif., Riverside, 1979; JD, Boalt Hall, 1982. Ct. commr. Calif. Superior Ct., Riverside, 1991-95; magistrate judge U.S. Dist. Ct., LA, 1995-99, dist. judge, 1999—. Office: US Courthouse 3470 Twelfth St Riverside CA 92501

PHILLIPS, WILLIAM ROBERT, physician; b. Wash., Apr. 26, 1950; BA, U. Wash., 1971, MD, MPH, U. Wash., 1975. Diplomate Nat. Bd. Med. Examiners, Am. Bd. Family Practice, Am. Bd. Preventive Medicine; lic. physician and surgeon, Wash. Resident family practice Providence Med. Ctr., Seattle, 1975-78; resident preventive medicine U. Wash. Sch. Pub. Health & Cmty. Medicine, Seattle, 1976-79; vis. prof. U. Auckland, New Zealand, 1979, U. Tasmania, Hobart, Australia, 1979, U. Zimbabwe, Harare, 1993; clin. prof. family medicine U. Wash., Seattle, 1994—. Chief staff Ballard Cmty. Hosp., Seattle, 1985, chief family practice, 1984. Sr. assoc. editor Annals of Family Medicine, 2001—; Contbr. articles to profl. jours. Bd. trustees Ballard Cmty. Hosp., Seattle, 1985. Recipient USPHS primary care policy fellowship, 1995; named Family Physician of the Yr. Wash. Acad. Family Physicians, 1999. Fellow Am. Acad. Family Physicians (Mead Johnson award 1976, Warner-Chilcott award 1979), Wash. Acad. Family Physicians (Family Physician of Yr. 1999), Am. Coll. Preventive Medicine; mem. N.Am. Primary Care Rsch. Group (pres., rsch. awards), Soc. Tchrs. of Family Medicine. Office: Univ Washington Dept Family Medicine Box 356390 Seattle WA 98195-6390

PHILLIPS, ZAIGA ALKSNIS, pediatrician; b. Riga, Latvia, Sept. 13, 1934; arrived in US, 1949; d. Adolfs and Alma (Ozols) Alksnis; (div. 1972); children: Albert L., Lisa K., Sintija. BS, U. Wash., 1956, MD, 1959. Fellow Colo. Med. Ctr., Denver, 1961-62; sch. physician Bellevue and Issaquah (Wash.) Sch. Dists., 1970-77; pvt. practice Bellevue, 1977—; staff pediatrician Overlake Med. Ctr., 1977—, Childrens Hosp. and Med. Ctr., Seattle, 1977—, Evergreen Med. Ctr., 1977—. Attending physician Allergy Clinic, Childrens Hosp., Seattle, 1988-2005; cons. and contact to pediatricians in Latvia, 1988—; team mem. to Latvia, Healing the Children Contact with Latvia, 1993-97; bd. mem. Bellevue's Stay in Sch. Program, 1994-97. Mem. Am. Latvian Assn., 1972—, Wash. Latvian Assn., Seattle, 1972—; pres. Latvian Sorority Gundega, Seattle, 1990-93; bd. dirs. Sister Cities Assn., Bellevue, 1992-98, Wash. Asthma Allergy Found. Am., 1992-99. Recipient Recognition award, City of Liepaja, 1995, Latvian Assn. Am., 2003, Recognition cross, Pres. of Latvia, 2005. Fellow Am. Acad. Pediat.; mem. Am. Latvian Physicians Assn. (bd. dirs. 1998—), Wash. State and Puget Sound Pediatric Assn. Office: Pediatric Assn 2700 Northup Way Bellevue WA 98004-1463 Office Phone: 425-827-4600. Personal E-mail: zap@u.washington.edu. Business E-Mail: zphillips@peds-associates.com.

PHILLIPSON, DONALD E., lawyer; b. Denver, July 22, 1942; BS, Stanford U., 1964, JD, 1968; MS, U. Calif., Berkeley, 1965. Former mem. Davis, Graham & Stubbs, Denver; now cons., writer. Mem. Nat. Soccer Hall of Fame (builder). Office: 14325 Braun Rd Golden CO 80401-1431 Office Phone: 303-279-1577.

PHILPOTT, LINDSEY, civil engineer, researcher, educator; b. Bridestowe, Devonshire, Eng., Aug. 2, 1948; came to U.S., 1983; s. George Anthony and Joyce Thirza (Teeling) P.; m. Christine May Pembury, Aug. 20, 1974 (div.); children: David, Elizabeth; m. Kathleen Linda Matson, Feb. 17, 1982 (div.); children: Nicholas, Benjamin; m. Kim Elaine Moore, Nov. 24, 1991. Higher Nat. Cert. in Civil Engring., Bristol Poly., Eng., 1973; BSCE, U. Ariz., 1986, MSCE, 1987, U. Norwich, 2008. Registered profl. engr., Calif.; lic. water treatment plant operator, Calif.; USCG lic. operator 100 ton master. Area structural engr. Dept. Environment (Property Svcs. Agy.), Bristol, 1971-73; civil engr. Webco Civil Engring., Exeter, Eng., 1973-75; tech. mgr. Devon & Cornwall Housing Assn., Plymouth, Eng., 1975-79; prin., architect S.W. Design, Plymouth, 1979-81; archtl. engr. United Bldg. Factories, Bahrain, 1981-83; jr. engr. Cheyne Owen, Tucson, 1983-87; civil engr. Engring. Sci. Inc., Pasadena, Calif., 1987-89; project engr. Black & Veatch, Santa Ana, Calif., 1989-90; sr. engr. Brown & Caldwell, Irvine, Calif., 1990-91; environ. engr. Met. Water Dist. So. Calif., LA, 1991—2002; instr. USCG and marlinespike seamanship Orange Coast Coll. Sailing Ctr., Newport Beach, Calif., 1999—; mgr. vol. support svcs. Ocean Inst., Dana Point, Calif., 2002—03; instr. Calif. Sailing Acad., Marina del Rey, 2003—. Adj. prof. hydraulics and instrumentation, San Antonio Coll., Walnut, Calif., 1995-2000, ACC instr., Calif. Sailing Acad., Marina del Rey, 2002—; cons. forensic specialist, Garrett Engrs., Inc., Long Beach, Calif., 2003—. Author: Knots-A Complete Guide, 2004, Pocket Guide to Knots, 2006, The Complete Book of Fishing Knots, Leaders and Lines, 2008. Foster parent Foster Parents Plan, Tucson, 1985-87; vol. reader tech. books Recording for the Blind, Hollywood, Calif., 1988-89, South Bay, Calif., 1990-91, Pomona, Calif., 1991—; vol. sailor/tchr. L.A. Maritime Inst. Topsail Youth Program, 1994—, Ocean Inst., 1998—; instr. Calif. Sailing Acad., Marina delRay, Calif., 2002—. Mem.: ASCE, Calif. Sailing Acad., ACCI, Am. Sailing Assn., Engrs. Soc. (pres. 1985—96), Water Environment Fedn., Am. Water Resources Assn. (water quality com. 1990—), Am. Water Works Assn., Santa Monica Bay Power Fleet (sec. Marina del Rey chpt. 2000—), Mensa, Internat. Guild of Knot Tyers (pres. Pacific Am. br. 2000—04, 2006—08, editor, J. Knotting Matters 2008—), Marina Venice Yacht Club (commodore 1999), South Bay Yacht Racing Club (Marina del Rey, Calif., commodore 1996), Internat. Order of Blue Gavel (treas. dist. 11 2002, sec. 2009). Avocations: hiking, bicycling, sailing, crosswords, knot-tying. Office: Garrett Engrs Inc Atlantic Ave Long Beach CA 90807 Home Phone: 562-595-8854; Office Phone: 800-229-3647. Personal E-mail: marline.man@verizon.net.

PHINNEY, E. STERL, III, astrophysicist; b. Berkeley, Calif., Jan. 27, 1960; s. Edward Sterl Jr. and Mary Catherine (Davis) P.; m. Lin Yan, June 20, 1993; 1 child, Isabelle. BS, Calif. Inst. Tech., 1980; PhD, Cambridge U., UK, 1983. Mem. Inst. Advanced Study, Princeton, N.J., 1983-85; asst. prof. Calif. Inst. Tech., Pasadena, 1985-90, assoc. prof., 1991-94, prof., 1995—. Adv. bd., steering com. NSF Inst. for Theoretical Physics, Santa Barbara, Calif., 1990-93; chair mission definition team Laser Interferometer Space Antenna, 1997—. Contbr. articles to profl. jours.; co-author: Pulsars as Physics Laboratories, 1993. Marshall scholar Marshall Aid Commemoration Comm., 1980-83; Presdl. Young Investigator, NSF, 1985-91; fellow A.P. Sloan Found., 1990-94. Fellow Royal Astron. Soc. (U.K.), Am. Phys. Soc.; mem. Am. Astron. Soc. (Helen B. Warner prize 1995). Achievements include contbn. to theory of: black hole magnetohydrodynamics, radiation from active galactic nuclei, and the physics of binary pulsars. Office: Theoretical Astrophysics 130 33 Caltech Pasadena CA 91125-0001

PHINNEY, JEAN SWIFT, psychology professor; b. Princeton, NJ, Mar. 12, 1933; d. Emerson H. and Anne (Davis) Swift; m. Bernard O. Phinney, Dec. 11, 1965; children: Peter, David. BA, Wellesley Coll., 1955; MA, UCLA, 1969, PhD, 1973. Asst. prof. psychology Calif. State U., LA, 1977-81, assoc. prof. psychology, 1981-86, prof. psychology, 1986—. Editor: Children's Ethnic Socialization, 1987; mem. editl. bd. Jour. Adolescent Rsch., Identity: An Internat. Jour.; contbr. articles to profl. jours. Grantee, NIH. Fellow APA; mem. Soc. for Rsch. in Child Devel., Soc. for Rsch. in Adolescence, Internat. Assn. Cross-Cultural Psychology; Soc. Study of Identity Formation (pres.-elect). Avocations: skiing, hiking, travel. Office: Calif State U Dept Psychology 5151 State University Dr Los Angeles CA 90032-4226

PI, EDMOND HSIN-TUNG, psychiatry educator; MD, Cath. U. Coll. Medicine, 1972. Cert. in subspecialty psychosomatic medicine, Am. Bd. Psychiatry and Neurology. Chief resident U. Ky. Med. Ctr., Lexington, 1977-78; instr. psychiatry U. So. Calif. Sch. Medicine, LA, 1978-80, asst. prof., 1980-83; assoc. prof. Med. Coll. Pa., Phila., 1983-85, U. So. Calif. Sch. Medicine, 1985-88, prof. clin. psychiatry, 1988—98; prof. Charles R. Drew U. Medicine and Sci., 1998—2003; clin. prof. psychiatry Sch. Medicine, UCLA, 1999—2005; prof. clin. psychiatry Sch. Medicine, U. So. Calif., 2005—, assoc. chair for clin. affairs, dept. psychiatry, 2006—. Asst. dir. psychopharmacology U. So. Calif. Sch. Medicine, 1978-80; asst. dir. adult psychiat. clinic L.A. County and U. So. Calif. Med. Ctr., 1980-83; dir. adult psychiat. clinic Med. Coll. Pa., Phila., 1983-85; dir. Adult Psychiat. Inpatient Svcs., L.A. County and U. So. Calif. Med. Ctr., 1985-91, dir. Adult Psychiat. Outpatient Svcs., 1995-97; dir. transcultural psychiatry U. So. Calif. Sch. Medicine, 1991-98; med. dir. State of Calif. Dept. Mental Health, 1997-98; dir. Consultation and Liaison Svcs., L.A. County and U. So. Calif. Med. Ctr., 1998; exec. vice-chmn., assoc. ctr. dir. Augustus F. Hawkins Mental Health Ctr., Martin Luther King. Jr./Charles R. Drew U. Med. Ctr., 1998-2003; dir. psychiat. inpatient svc. Harbor/UCLA Med. Ctr., 2003-05; dir. psychiat. consultation and liaison svcs. L.A. (Calif.) County and U. So. Calif. Med. Ctr., 2005—, assoc. chair clin. affairs, 2006—. Author: Reactions to Psychotropic Medications, 1987, (book chpts.) Transcultural Psychiatry, Clinical Psychopharmacology, 1985—; contbr. articles to profl. jours. Mem. Calif. Gov.'s Com. Employment Disabled Persons, Sacramento, 1993—2007; bd. dirs. Chinese Bus. Assn., LA, 1990—92, Com. of 100, NYC, 1993—98, San Gabriel chpt. ARC, Calif., 1994—97, Mental Health Assn., LA County, Calif., 1995—97, 1998—2001. Vis. scholar Com. on Scholarly Comm. with People's Republic of China U.S. Nat. Acad. Scis., Washington, 1987-88; Treval fellow Am. Coll. Neuropsychopharmacology, 1982. Fellow Am. Psychiat. Assn. (chair com. Asian-Am. psychiatrists 1998-2000), Am. Soc. Social Psychiatry, Pacific Rim Coll. Psychiatry (treas. 1991-97), Am. Coll. Psychiatrists; mem. Soc. Study Psychiatry and Culture, Pacific Rim Assn. Clin. Pharmogenetics, Assn. Chinese Am. Psychiatrists (pres. 1995—). Avocations: photography, writing, travel, tennis, media communications. Office: LAC & USC Med Ctr Dept Psychiatry 2020 Zonal Ave IRD 13 Los Angeles CA 90033 Office Phone: 323-226-7975. Business E-Mail: ehpi@usc.edu.

PICCININI, ROBERT M. (BOB PICCININI), grocery store chain executive; s. Mike Piccinini. Head, real estate dept. Save Mart Supermarkets, Modesto, Calif., 1971, pres., 1981, owner, 1985—, CEO, chmn. Former owner Fresno Giants. Mailing: Save Mart Supermarkets PO Box 4278 Modesto CA 95352-4278 Office: Save Mart Supermarkets 1800 Standiford Ave Modesto CA 95350

PICCOLO, RICHARD ANDREW, artist, educator; b. Hartford, Conn., Sept. 17, 1943; S. John D. and Lenore (Pasqual) P. BID, Pratt Inst., 1966; MFA, Bklyn. Coll., 1968. Instr. Pratt Inst., Bklyn., 1966-68, Rome, 1969—, dir., 1980—; instr. U. Notre Dame Rome Program, 1984—. Artist: solo exhibitions include: Robert Schoelkopf Gallery, N.Y.C., 1975, 79, 83, 89, Suffolk C.C., Long Island, N.Y., 1976, Am. Acad. in Rome, 1977, Galleria Temple, Rome 1979, Galleria Il Gabbiano, Rome. 1985, Contemporary Realist Gallery, San Francisco, 1989, 95; exhibited in group shows Six Americans in Italy, 1973, Metaphor in Painting, Fed. Hall Meml., N.Y., 1978, Realism and Metaphor, U. S. Fla. (traveling), 1980, Contemporary Figure Drawings, Robert Schoelkopf Gallery, 1981, Contemporary Arcadian Painting, 1982, Moravian Coll. Invitational, Bethlehem, Pa., 1981, Art on Paper, Weatherspoon Gallery of Art, N.C., 1981, Out of N.Y., Hamilton Coll., Clinton, N.Y., 1981, Galleria Gabbiano, Rome, FIAC, Paris, 1982, Contemporary Arts Mus., Houston, 1984, Umbria: Americans Painting in Italy, Gallery North, Setauket, N.Y., 1985, Storytellers, Contemporary Realist Gallery, San Francisco, Painted from Life, Bayly Mus., Charlottesville, Va., 1987; work in permanent collections Crown Am. Corp., Johnstown, Pa., Grosvenor Internat., Sacramento, Calif., Mrs. Lillian Cole, Sherman Oaks, Calif., Mr and Mrs. Robert Emery, San Francisco, Mr. Graham Gund, Boston, Dr. Robert Gutterman, San Francisco, Mr and Mrs. Joseph Jennings, San Francisco, Dr. and Mrs. Donald Innes, Jr., Charlottesville, Va., Mr. and Mrs. Alan Ovson, San Francisco, Mr. Frank Pasquerilla, Johnstown, Pa., Mr. Jon Roberts and Mr. John Boccardo, L.A. Recipient E. A. Abbey Meml. scholarship for mural painting, 1973-75; grantee NEA, 1989; mural commn. Simplicity Inspiring Invention: An Allegory of the Arts, Crown Am. Corp., Johnstown, Pa., 1989, Aer, Ignis, Terra, Aqua, U.S. Bank Plaz., Sacramento, Calif., 1991-94. Home: Piazza S Apollonia 3 Rome 00153 Italy Office: Hacket Freedman Gallery 250 Sutter St Fl 4 San Francisco CA 94108-4451

PICHETTE, PATRICK, information technology company executive; b. Can., 1962; BA in Bus. Adminstrn., U. du Québec à Montréal, Can., 1987; MA in Philosophy Politics and Econs., Oxford U., Eng., 1989. Assoc. McKinsey & Co., Toronto, Canada, 1989—94, ptnr., lead mem. N.Am. telecom practice Montréal, Canada, 1996—2000; v.p., CFO Call-Net Enterprises, 1994—96; exec. v.p., planning and performance mgmt. Bell Can. Enterprises, 2001—02, CFO, 2002—03, exec. v.p., Bell Can., 2003—04, pres. ops., Bell Can., 2004—08; sr. v.p., CFO Google, Inc., Mountain View, Calif., 2008—. Bd. mem. Engineers Without Borders, The Trudeau Found. Rhodes Scholar, 1987—89. Office: Google Inc 1600 Amphitheatre Pky Mountain View CA 94043 Office Phone: 650-253-0000. Office Fax: 650-253-0001.*

PICK, JAMES BLOCK, business professor, writer; b. Chgo., July 29, 1943; s. Grant Julius and Helen (Block) Pick. BA, Northwestern U., 1966; MS in Edn., No. Ill. U., 1969; PhD, U. Calif., Irvine, 1974. Cert. computer profl. Asst. rsch. statistician, lectr. Grad. Sch. Mgmt., U. Calif., Riverside, 1975-91, dir. computing, 1984-91; co-dir. U.S.-Mex. Database Project, 1988-91; assoc. prof. mgmt. and bus., dir. info. mgmt. program U. Redlands, Calif., 1991-95, 99-01, prof. bus., 1995—, chair dept. mgmt. and bus., 1995-97, 98-99, chair faculty assembly Sch. Bus., 2001—04. Vis. prof. U. Iberoam., Mexico City, 1997, Mexico City, 2001; cons. internat. divsn. U.S. Census Bur., 1978; mem. Univ. Commons. Bd., 1982—86; mem. nat. curriculum task force IS, 1997; mem. U. Commn. Future Bus. Programs, 1998—2000; pres. Orange County chpt. Assn. Sys. Mgmt., 1978—79; mem. bd. govs. PCCLAS, Assn. Borderlands Studies, 1989—92, v.p., 2000—01, pres., 2002—; bd. profls. advisors demographic analysis U. Calif, Irvine, 2002—; mem. exec. coun. Info. Resources Mgmt. Assn., 2003—07; vis. rschr. Ctr. for Rsch. on Immigration, Population, and Pub. Policy U. Calif., Irvine, 2005; external faculty rsch. assoc. CRITO, U. Calif., Irvine, 2006—; vis. rschr. dept. sociology U. Calif., Irvine, 2009. Author: Geothermal Energy Development, 1982, Micro-Manual, 1986, Computer Systems in Business, 1986, Atlas of Mexico, 1989, The Mexico Handbook, 1994, Mexico Megacity, 1997, Mexico and Mexico City in the World Economy, 2001, Geographic Systems in Business, 2004, Exploring the Urban Community: A GIS Approach, 2005, Geo-Business: GIS in the Digital Organization, 2008; mem. editl. bd. Jour. Borderlands Studies, 1999—, Jour. Info. Tech. Cases and Applications, 2002—, Frontera Norte, 2006; mem. editl. bd.: Jour. Info. Tech. for Devel., 2007, Revista Latinoamericana y del Caribe de la Asociación de Sistemas de Información, 2008; condr. rsch. info. sys., population, environ. studies; contbr. articles to profl. jours. Trustee Newport Harbor Art Mus., 1981—87, 1988—96, mem. acquisitions com., 1987—91, v.p., 1991—96; trustee, chmn. collection com. Orange County Mus. Art, 1996—; mem. com. Block Mus., 1999—2001, mem. bd. advisors, 2006—; trustee Berkeley Art Mus. and Pacific Film Archives, 2003—. Recipient Thunderbird award, Bus. Assn. L.Am. Studies, 1993, Outstanding Alumnus award, No. Ill. U., 2004; grantee co-principal investigator grant, US Small Bus. Adminstrn., 2006—08; vis. scholar, Lingnan U., Hongkong, 2009; Ford Found. grantee, 1998—99, Sr. Fulbright scholar, 2001. Mem.: AAAS, Assn. for Info. Sys., Assn. Am. Geographers, Sociedad de Demografia Mexicana, Internat. Union Sci. Study Population, Population Assn. Am., Am. Statis. Assn., Am. Sociol. Assn., Assn. for Info. Systems, Assn. Computing Machinery, Standard Club (Chgo.). Office: U Redlands Sch Bus 1200 E Colton Ave Redlands CA 92374-3755 Business E-Mail: james_pick@redlands.edu.

PICKENS, JAMES T., JR., actor; b. Cleve., Oct. 26, 1954; m. Gina Pickens; 2 children. Actor: (films) F/X, 1986, Trespass, 1992, Menace II Society, 1993, Hostile Intentions, 1994, Jimmy Hollywood, 1994, Dead Presidents, 1995, Nixon, 1995, Power 98, 1996, Sleepers, 1996, Ghosts of Mississippi, 1996, Gridlock'd, 1997, Rocketman, 1997, Sphere, 1998, Bulworth, 1998, How Stella Got Her Groove Back, 1998, Liberty Heights, 1999, Traffic, 2000, Home Room, 2002, White Rush, 2003, Venom, 2005; (TV series) Roseanne, 1990—96, Beverly Hills, 90210, 1991—92, The Practice, 1997—2000, The X-Files, 1998—2002, Grey's Anatomy, 2005— (Outstanding Performance by an Ensemble in a Drama Series, SAG, 2007); (TV films) Exclusive, 1992, Sodbusters, 1994, A Child's Cry for Help, 1994, Lily in Winter, 1994, Trial by Fire, 1995, Sharon's Secret, 1995, Bloodhound, 1996, The Uninvited, 1996, Little Girl Fly Away, 1998, A Slight Case of Murder, 1999. Avocation: horseback riding. Mailing: Grey's Anatomy Los Feliz Tower 4th Fl 4151 Prospect Ave Los Angeles CA 90027

PICKETT, DONN PHILIP, lawyer; b. Chgo., May 3, 1952; s. Philip Gordon and Gloria Joan (Hansen) P.; m. Janet Benson, Aug. 25, 1973; children: Jessica Kelly, William Benson. BA magna cum laude, Carleton Coll., Minn., 1973; JD, Yale U., 1976. Bar: Calif. 1976, US Dist. Ct. (no. dist.) Calif. 1976, US Dist. Ct. (ctrl. dist.) Calif. 1980, US Dist. Ct. (ea. dist.) Calif. 1983, US Ct. Appeals (9th cir.) Calif. 1979, US Ct. Appeals (5th cir.) Tex. 1994, US Supreme Ct. 1991, US Dist. Ct. Ariz. 1997, US Dist. Ct. Colo. 1997, US Ct. Appeals (fed. cir.) 1997, US Ct. Appeals (11th cir.) 1998, US Ct. Appeals (1st cir.) 2006. Assoc. McCutchen, Doyle, Brown & Enersen, San Francisco, 1976-83, ptnr., 1983—2002, chair, 2001—02; ptnr. Bingham McCutchen LLP, San Francisco, 2002—, vice chmn., 2002—08; co chair Bingham Litigation Area, 2008—. Mem. U.S. Dist. Ct. Civil Justice Reform Act adv. group, 1995-99; bd. dirs. Equal Justice Works, 2005—, Legal Aid Soc., San Francisco, 2006—. Bd. dirs. Bay Area Coun., 2003—. Mem. ABA (chmn. civil practice com. antitrust sect. 2001-04, vice chmn. trial practice com. 2004-), State Bar Calif. (com. on adminstrn. of justice 1988-91, vice chmn. 1992-93, chmn. 1993-94, legis. chmn. 1994-96), San Francisco Bar Assn. (judiciary com. 1988-92, exec. com. conf. of dels. 1993-96, 2000, bd. dirs. 1997-99), Phi Beta Kappa. Office: Bingham McCutchen LLP 3 Embarcadero Ctr San Francisco CA 94111 Home Phone: 415-435-2313; Office Phone: 415-393-2082. Business E-Mail: donn.pickett@bingham.com.

PICRAUX, SAMUEL THOMAS, physicist, researcher; b. St. Charles, Mo., Mar. 3, 1943; s. Samuel F. and Jeannette D. Picraux; m. Danice R. Kent, July 12, 1970; children: Jeanine, Laura, Samantha. BS in Elec. Engring., U. Mo., 1965; postgrad., Cambridge U., Eng., 1965-66; MS in Engring. Sci., Calif. Inst. Tech., 1967, PhD in Engring. Sci. and Physics, 1969. Mem. tech. staff Sandia Nat. Labs., Albuquerque, 1969-72, div. supr., 1972-86, dept. mgr., 1986-96, dir., 1996-2001; prof. materials engring., exec. dir. materials rsch. Ariz. State U., 2001—05; chief scientist Ctr. Integrated Nanotech., Los Alamos Nat. Lab., 2005—. Mem. solid state scis. com. NRC, 1996-98; vis. scientist dept. physics Aarhus U., Denmark, 1975; NATO lectr., 1979, 81, 83, 86.; NSF lectr. 1976, 81. Author: Materials Analysis by Ion Channeling, 1982; editor: Applications of Ion Beams to Metals, 1974, Metastable Materials Formation by Ion Implantation, 1982, Surface Alloying by Ion Electron and Laser Beams, 1986, Beam-Solid Interactions and Transient Processes, 1987; editor Nuclear Instruments and Methods International Jour. B, 1983-91; contbr. numerous articles to profl. jours. Recipient Ernest Orlando Lawrence Meml. award U.S. Dept. Energy, 1990, 3 Basic Energy Scis. Outstanding Rsch. awards U.S. Dept. Energy, 1985, 92, 94, Mo. Honor award disting. svc. in engring., 2006; Fulbright fellow, 1965-66. Fellow AAAS, Am. Phys. Soc. (chmn. materials physics divsn. 1990), Materials Rsch. Soc. (pres. 1993); mem. IEEE (sr.), Am. Vacuum Soc. Office: Los Alamos Nat Lab Ctr Integrated Nanotech MST-CINT MSK771 Los Alamos NM 87545 Home Phone: 505-232-2977; Office Phone: 505-665-8554. Business E-Mail: picraux@lanl.gov.

PIELS, WILLIAM B., lawyer; b. Richmond, Calif., Jan. 4, 1955; BA cum laude, Macalester Coll., 1977; JD, U. Oregon, 1980. Bar: Calif. 1980. Ptnr. Holland & Knight LLP, San Francisco. Contbr. professional journals on aviation law; frequent speaker on aviation law. Mem.: Inter-Pacific Bar Assn., ABA (mem. subcom. on aircraft finance and contracts), State Bar Calif., Bar Assn. San Francisco. Office: 50 California St Ste 2800 San Francisco CA 94111 Office Phone: 415-743-6930. Office Fax: 415-743-6910. Business E-Mail: william.piels@hklaw.com.

PIERCE, DANNY PARCEL, artist, educator; b. Woodlake, Calif., Sept. 10, 1920; s. Frank Lester and Letitia Frances (Parcel) P.; m. Julia Ann Rasmussen, July 19, 1943; children: Julia Ann, Mary L., Danny L., Duane Nels. Student, Art Ctr. Sch., LA, 1939, Chouinards Art Inst., 1940-41, 46-47, Am. Art Sch., NYC, 1947-48, Bklyn. Mus. Art Sch., 1950-53; BFA, U. Alaska, 1963. Instr. Hunter Coll., NYC, 1952-53, Burnley Sch. Art, Seattle, 1954-58, Seattle U., 1956-59; publ. Red Door Studio Press, Kent, Wash., 1959—; artist-in-res. U. Alaska, College, 1959-63; asst. prof. U. Wisc., Milw., 1964; head art dept. Cornish Sch. Allied Arts, Seattle, 1964-65; prof. art U. Wisc., Milw., 1965-84, prof. emeritus, 1984—. One-man shows include Contemporaries Gallery, N.Y.C., 1953, Handforth Gallery, Tacoma, Washington, 1958, U. Alaska, College, 1959, 63, 73, 74, Gonzaga U., Bradley Galleries, Milw., 1966, 68, 70, 72, 74, 76, 78-80, 82, Martin-Zambito Gallery, Seattle, 1997, 2002, Apple Blossom Time, 2000, Centennial Gallery, Kent, Wash., 2003, 04; father/son exhbn., 2002, Martin-Zambito Gallery, Seattle, 1999, 2007; represented in permanent collections Bibliothèque Nationale, Paris, Mus. Modern Art, N.Y.C., Libr. Congress, Washington, Smithsonian Instn., Washington, Seattle Art Mus., U. Washington Henry Art Gallery, Bklyn. Mus., Princeton U., U. Alaska, U. So. Calif., William and Mary Coll., Oostduinkerke (Belgium) Nat. Fishing Mus., Nat. Mus. Sweden, Stockholm, Johnson Wax Found., Racine, Wisc., Gen. Mills Collection Art, Mpls., Huntington Libr., San Marino, Calif., various pvt. collections; pub. 27 ltd. edit. books, 1959-98. Recipient Best Oil Landscape award Conn. Acad. Fine Arts, Hartford, 1st Prize oil Kohler Gallery, Seattle, 1974, others; chosen one of twelve artists to represent State Wash. Expo 70, Osaka, Japan, rep. U.S. Internat. São Paulo Biannual Art Exhbn.; established archives at Golda Meier Libr., U. Wis.-Mils. Mem. Artist Equity Assn. (charter, pres. Seattle chpt. 1958), Am. Colorprint Soc., Internat. Arts and Letters (life). Office: Red Door Studio 404 Summit Ave N Kent WA 98030-4712 Office Phone: 253-859-1504.

PIERCE, GARY L., Arizona Corp Commissioner; b. Ill., Jan. 1952; m Sherry Moore Pierce, 1973; children: four. Bd supervisers, Yuma County, Arizona; Arizona State Representative, District 19, 2003-07, majority whip, formerly, member, Committee on Judiciary, Committee on Public Instns & Counties, chairman, Committee on Transportation, 2003-04, Arizona House Representative; Arizona Corp Commissioner, 2007-. Tchr, Taft Elementary Sch, Mesa, Arizona, 1974-77; owner, Shell gas station, Budget Rent-A-Car franchise, formerly; Honda and Nissan new car dealer, Yuma, Arizona, formerly. Republican. Office: Ariz Corp Commission 1200 West Washington Phoenix AZ 85007-2996

PIERCE, STEVE, state legislator; b. Phoenix, 1950; m. Joan Reed; 4 children. BS in Animal Sci., U. Ariz., 1972. Owner Las Vegas Ranch, Prescott, Ariz., 1973—; mem. Dist. 1 Ariz. State Senate, 2008—, mem. appropriations com., fin. com. Chmn. Yavapai County Rep. Party; Gov. apptd. mem. Ariz. Beef Coun.; mem. Ctrl. Ariz. Partnership; past mem. US Beef Export Bd., Nat. Cattlemans' Beef Bd., US Meat Export Fedn. Bd. dirs. County Bank. Named Range Mgr. of Yr., Ariz. Soc. Range Mgmt., 1983. Mem.: Ariz. Angus Assn., Ariz. Hereford Assn., Ariz. Cattle Growers Assn. (past pres.), Yavapai

Cattle Growers Assn. (past pres.). Republican. Office: Ariz State Senate Capitol Complex 1700 W Washington Rm 304 Phoenix AZ 85007 Office Phone: 602-926-5584. Office Fax: 602-926-3429. Business E-Mail: spierce@azleg.gov.*

PIERCE, SUSAN RESNECK, academic administrator, literature educator, consultant; b. Janesville, Wis., Feb. 6, 1943; d. Elliott Jack and Dory (Block) Resneck; 1 child, Alexandra Siegel. BA, Wellesley Coll., 1965; MA, U. Chgo., 1966; PhD, U. Wis., 1972. Lectr. U. Wis., Rock County, 1970-71; from asst. prof. to prof. English Ithaca (N.Y.) Coll., 1973-82, chmn. dept., 1976-79; program officer Nat. Endowment for Humanities, 1982-83, asst. dir., 1983-84; dean Henry Kendall Coll. Arts and Scis. U. Tulsa, 1984-90; v.p. acad. affairs, prof. English Lewis and Clark Coll., Portland, Oreg., 1990-92; pres. U. Puget Sound, Tacoma, 1992—2003, Boca Raton Comty. Hosp. Found., 2004—05; pvt. practice, 2005—; sr. cons. Academic Search, 2006—. Vis. assoc. prof. Princeton (N.J.) U., 1979; bd. dirs. Janet Elson Scholarship Fund, 1984-1990, Tulsa Edn. Fund, Phillips Petroleum Scholarship Fund, 1985-90, Okla. Math. & Sci. High Sch., 1984-90, Hillcrest Med. Ctr., 1988-90, Portland Opera, 1990-92, St. Joseph's Hosp., 1992—, Seattle Symphony, 1993—; cons. U. Oreg., 1985, Drury Coll., Springfield, Mo., 1986; mem. Middle States and N. Cen. Accreditation Bds.; mem. adv. com. Fed. Women's Program, NEH, 1982-83; participant Summit Meeting on Higher Edn., Dept. Edn., Washington, 1985; speaker, participant numerous ednl. meetings, sems., commencements; chair Frederick Ness Book Award Com. Assn. Am. Colls., 1986; mem. award selection com. Dana Found., 1986, 87; mem. Acad. Affairs Council, Univ. Senate, dir. tchr. edn., chmn. adv. group for tchr. preparation, ex-officio mem. all Coll. Arts and Scis. coms. and Faculty Council on Internat. Studies, all U. Tulsa; bd. dirs. Am. Conf. Acad. Deans; bd. trustees Hillcrest Med. Ctr.; participant Aspen Inst. Md. 1999, Annapolis Group Media Roundtable, 1996, Harvard Seminar, 1992; former bd. dirs. Assn. Am. Colls. and Univs., 1989-92, Am. Conf. of Academic Deans, 1988-91, Am. Assn. Colls., 1989-92. Author: The Moral of the Story, 1982, also numerous essays, jour. articles, book sects., book revs.; co-editor: Approaches to Teaching "Invisible Man"; reader profl. jours. Bd. dirs. Arts and Humanities Coun., Tulsa, 1984-90, Mizener Pk., 2004-; trustee Hillcrest Hosp., Tulsa, 1986-90; mem. cultural series com., community rels. com. Jewish Fedn., Tulsa, 1986-90; bd. dirs. Tulsa chpt. NCCJ, 1986-90, Kemper Mus. 1996—, Seattle Symphony, 1993-96, St. Joseph Hosp., 1992-93, Portland Opera, 1990-92, Ctr. for Arts, Boca Raton, 2004—. Recipient Best Essay award Arix. Quar., 1979, Excellence in Teaching award N.Y. State Edn. Council, 1982, Superior Group Service award NEH, 1984, other teaching awards; Dana scholar, Ithaca Coll., 1980-81; Dana Research fellow, Ithaca Coll., 82-83; grantee Inst. for Ednl. Affairs, 1980, Ford Found., 1987, NEH, 1989. Mem. MLA (adv. com. on job market 1973-74), South Ctrl. MLA, NIH (subcom. on college drinking), Assn. Governing Bds. (coun. of pres.), Nat. Inst. on Alcohol Abuse (presl. advisory group), Soc. for Values in Higher Edn., Assn. Am. Colls. (bd. dirs.), Am. Conf. Acad. Deans (bd. dirs. 1988-91), Coun. of Presidents, Assn. Governing Bds., The Annapolis Group (mem. exec. com.), Phi Beta Kappa, Phi Kappa Phi, Phi Gamma Kappa. Office Phone: 561-212-5103. Business E-Mail: srpconsulting@adelphia.net.

PIERCY, GORDON CLAYTON, bank executive, educator; b. Takoma Park, Md., Nov. 23, 1944; s. Gordon Clayton and Dorothy Florence (Brummer) Piercy; m. Roberta Margaret Walton, 1985; children: Elizabeth Anne, Kenneth Charles, Virginia Walton, Zachary Taylor Walton. BS, Syracuse U., 1966; MBA, Pace U., 1973. Mgmt. trainee Suburban Bank, Bethesda, Md., 1962-66; mktg. planning assoc. Chemical Bank, NYC, 1966-70; sr. market devel. officer Seattle-First Nat. Bank, 1970-74; product expansion adminstr., mktg. planning mgr. VISA, Inc., San Francisco, 1974-76; v.p., dir. mktg. Wash. Mutual Bank, Seattle, 1976-82; v.p., mktg. dir. First Interstate Bank Wash. N.A., Seattle, 1983-86; sr. v.p., mktg., dir. Puget Sound Nat. Bank, Tacoma, 1986-92; sr. v.p., dir. mktg. and sales Key Bank, Tacoma, 1993-94; dir. corp. sales KIRO-TV, Seattle, 1994; sr. v.p., dir. mktg. and sales Pacific N.W. Bancorp, 1994—2004; pres. Whidbey Western R.R., 1995—; prin. Whidbey Mktg., 2004—; mktg. and fin. instr. Embry-Riddle U., Oak Harbor, Wash., 2005—. Bd. dirs., treas. Whidbey Gen. Hosp. Found.; chair, bd. trustee Skagit Valley Coll. Mem.: S.W. Railcar Ltd. (mem. exec. com.), Island County Econ. Devel. Assn. (bd. dirs.), Pacific Railcar Operators, Mktg. Comm. Exec. Internat. (v.p.), Ctrl Whidbey Lions, Delta Mu Delta, Alpha Kappa Psi, Sigma Nu (treas.). Episcopalian. Home and Office: 750 N Snowberry Ln Coupeville WA 98239-3110 Office Phone: 360-678-4488.

PIERIK, MARILYN ANNE, retired librarian, piano teacher; b. Bellingham, Wash., Nov. 12, 1939; d. Estell Leslie and Anna Margarethe (Onigkeit) Bowers; m. Robert Vincent Pierik, July 25, 1964; children: David Vincent, Donald Lesley. AA, Chaffey Jr. Coll., Ontario, Calif., 1959; BA, Upland Coll., Calif., 1962; cert. in teaching, Claremont Coll., Calif., 1963; MSLS, U. So. Calif., LA, 1973. Tchr. elem. Christ Episcopal Day Sch., Ontario, 1959-60; tchr. Bonita High Sch., La Verne, Calif., 1962-63; tchr., libr. Kettle Valley Sch. Dist. 14, Greenwood, Can., 1963-64; libr. asst. Monrovia (Calif.) Pub. Libr., 1964-67; with Mt. Hood C.C., Gresham, Oreg., 1972-98, reference libr., 1983-98, chair faculty scholarship com., 1987-98, campus archivist, 1994-98; ret., 1998; pvt. piano tchr. Gresham, 1998—. Pvt. piano tchr., 1998; mem. site selection com. Multnomah County (Oreg.) Libr., New Gresham br., 1987, adv. com. Multnomah County Libr., Portland, Oreg., 1988-89; bd. dirs. Oreg. Episcopal Conf. of Deaf, 1985-92. Bd. dirs. East County Arts Alliance, Gresham, 1987-91; vestry person, jr. warden St. Luke's Episc. Ch., 1989-92; vestry person St. Aidan's Episcopal. Ch., 2000—; founding pres. Mt. Hood Pops, 1983-88, orch. mgr., 1983-91, 93—, bd. dirs., 1983-88, 91—. Recipient Jeanette Parkhill Meml. award Chaffey Jr. Coll., 1959, Svc. award St. Luke's Episcopal Ch., 1983, 87, Edn. Svc. award Soroptimists, 1989. Mem. AAUW, NEA, Oreg. Edn. Assn., Oreg. Libr. Assn., ALA, Gresham Hist. Soc. Avocations: music, reading. E-mail: pierikm@teleport.com.

PIERNO, ANTHONY ROBERT, lawyer; s. Anthony M. and Mary Jane (Saporita) P.; m. Beverly Jean Kohn, 1954 (dec. 2008); children: Kathryn Ann, Robert Lawrence, Linda Jean Derengowski, Diane Marie Leonard. BA with highest honors, Whittier Coll., 1954; JD, Stanford U., 1959; LLD (hon.), Whittier Coll., 2000. Bar: Calif. 1960, DC 1979, Tex. 1994. Assoc. Adams, Duque & Hazeltine, LA; ptnr. Poindexter & Barger, LA; chief dep. commr. State of Calif., 1967-69, commr. of corps., 1969-71; ptnr. Wyman, Bautzer, Rothman & Kuchel, Beverly Hills, Calif.; sr. ptnr. Memel, Jacobs, Pierno & Gersh, LA, 1976-86, Pillsbury, Madison & Sutro, LA, 1986-89; sr. v.p., gen. counsel MAXXAM, Inc., L.A. and Houston, 1989-97. Author: Corporate Disaggregation, 1982; editor Stanford U. Law Rev. Trustee Whittier Coll., 1977-2000, chmn. bd. trustees, 1994-2000, chmn. presdl. selection com., 1989-90, trustee emeritus, 2005-; chmn. Marymount Coll., Palos Verdes, Calif., 1989-92, trustee, 1976-2000, trustee emeritus, 2006-; past mem. Los Angeles County Children's Svcs. Commn. With US Army, 1954-56. Recipient Emcalian award Marymount Palos Verdes Coll., 1983, Whittier Coll. Lancer Soc. Lifetime Achievement award, 1984—, Lifetime Svc. award, 2004. Mem. ABA, LA County Bar Assn., State Bar Calif. (chmn. com. on corps. 1971-75, advisor to com. on corps. 1975-76, mem. exec. com. bus. law sect. 1976-80, chmn. spl. com. on franchise law), Calif. Club (LA), Am. Inns of Ct. Republican. Roman Catholic. Office: 92 Avenida Lirio Blanco Rancho Mirage CA 92270 Office Phone: 760-341-7595. E-mail: arplaw@msn.com.

PIGFORD, THOMAS HARRINGTON, nuclear engineering educator; b. Meridian, Miss., Apr. 21, 1922; s. Lamar and Zula Vivian (Harrington) P.; m. Catherine Kennedy Cathey, Dec. 31, 1948 (dec. 1992); children: Cynthia Pigford Naylor, Julie Earnest; m. Elizabeth Hood Weekes, Nov. 12, 1994. BS in Chem. Engring., Ga. Inst. Tech., 1943; S.M. in Chem. Engring., M.I.T., 1948, Sc.D. in Chem. Engring., 1952. Asst. prof. chem. engring., dir. Sch. Engring. Practice, M.I.T., 1950-52, asst. prof. nuclear and chem. engring., 1952-55, assoc. prof., 1955-57; head engring., dir. nuclear reactor projects and asst. dir. research lab. Gen. Atomic Co., La Jolla, Calif., 1957-59; prof. nuclear engring., chmn. dept. nuclear engring. U. Calif., Berkeley, 1959—; sr. rsch. scientist Lawrence Berkeley Lab., 1959—. Mem. panel Nat. Atomic Safety Licensing Bd. AEC-Nuclear Regulatory Commn., 1963-77; mem. Pres.'s Commn. on accident at 3-Mile Island, 1979; mem. bd. radioactive waste mgmt. and energy engring. bd., NAS-NAE, chmn. waste isolation systems panel, waste isolation pilot plant panel, fusion hybrid panel, separations and transmutations panel, transmutation of military plutonium panel, panel on health standard for radioactive waste disposal, chmn. adv. coun. Inst. Nuclear Power Op.; mem. Sec. of Energy's expert cons. group on Chernobyl accident; chmn. nuclear oversight com. Sacramento Mcpl. Utility Dist.; chmn. nuclear safety com. Gulf States Utilities Co.; mem. expert cons. group Swedish Nuclear Power Inspectorate; mem. peer rev. group for waste isolation pilot plant; mem. corp. rev. com. Oak Ridge Nat. Lab; lectr. Taiwan Nat. Sci. Found., 1990; vis. prof. Kyoto U., 1975, Kuwait U., 1976; cons. in field. Author: (with Manson Benedict) Nuclear Chemical Engineering, 1958, 2d edit., 1981; contbr. numerous articles to profl. jours.; patentee in field. Served with USNR, 1944-46. Recipient John Wesley Powell award U.S. Geol. Survey, 1981; named Outstanding Young Man of Greater Boston, Boston Jaycees, 1955; E. I. DuPont DeNemours rsch. fellow, 1948-50; Berkeley citation U. Calif., 1987; Japan Soc. for Promotion Sci. fellow, 1974-75; grantee NSF, 1960-75, EPA, 1973-78, Dept. Energy, 1979-92, Ford Found., 1974-75, Electric Power Rsch. Inst., 1974-75, Mitsubishi Metals Corp., 1989-90; named to Ga. Tech. Hall of Fame, 1995. Fellow Am. Nuclear Soc. (bd. dirs., Arthur H. Compton award 1971); mem. AIME, NAE, Am. Chem. Soc., Am. Inst. Chem. Engrs. (Robert E. Wilson award 1980, Service to Society award 1985), Atomic Indsl. Forum (dir.), Sigma Xi, Phi Kappa Phi, Tau Beta Pi. Home: 166 Alpine Ter Oakland CA 94618-1823 Office: U Calif Dept Nuclear Engring Berkeley CA 94720-0001 Office Phone: 510-652-0393. Business E-Mail: pigford@nuc.berkeley.edu.

PIGLIUCCI, RICCARDO, pharmaceutical executive; B.Indsl. Chemistry, Chem. Inst. of Milan, Italy. With Perkin-Elmer Corp., pres., COO, 1993—95; CEO Life Scis. Internat. PLC, 1996—97; pres., CEO Discovery Ptnrs. Internat., Inc., San Diego, 1998—, chmn. bd. dirs., 1999—. Dir. BioSphere Med., Inc., Dionex Corp., Epoch BioScis., Inc.; adv. bd. Chem. & Engring. News. Bd. trustees Worcester Found. for Biomed. Rsch.

PIGOTT, CHARLES MCGEE, transportation equipment manufacturing executive; b. Seattle, Apr. 21, 1929; s. Paul and Theiline (McGee) P.; m. Yvonne Flood, Apr. 18, 1953. BS, Stanford U., 1951. With PACCAR Inc, Seattle, 1959—, exec. v.p., 1962-65, pres., 1965-86, chmn., pres., 1986-87, chmn., chief exec. officer, 1987-97, also bd. dirs., chmn. emeritus, 1997—. Pres. Nat. Boy Scouts Am., 1986-88, mem. exec. bd. Mem. Bus. Council. Office: Paccar Inc 777 106th Ave NE Bellevue WA 98004-5017

PIGOTT, MARK C., automotive executive; BS in Indsl. Engring., Stanford U., Calif., MBA. V.p. Paccar Inc., Bellevue, Wash., 1988—89, sr. v.p., 1990—93, exec. v.p., 1993—95, bd. dirs., 1994—, vice chmn., 1995—96, chmn., CEO, 1997—. Mem. exec. com. Washington Roundtable. Named Mgr. of Yr., Truck & Off-Hwy. Ledger, 2004; named a Top CEO, Instl. Investor mag., 2005. Office: PACCAR PO Box 1518 Bellevue WA 98009 Office Phone: 425-468-7400. Office Fax: 425-468-8216.

PIKE, MALCOLM CECIL, preventive medicine educator; b. Johannesburg, Republic of South Africa, May 2, 1935; m. Anne; 1 child. BS in Math. with honors, Witwatersrand U., Republic of South Africa, 1956; postgrad., London U., 1956; D Math. Stats., Cambridge U., Eng., 1958; PhD in Math. Stats., Aberdeen U., Scotland, 1963. Asst. lectr., lectr. stats. U. Aberdeen, 1959-62; mem. sci. staff statis. rsch. unit Med. Rsch. Coun., London, 1963-69; 1st asst. Regius dept. medicine U. Oxford, Eng., 1969-73, dir. ICRF Cancer Epidemiology and Clin. Trials Units, 1983-87; prof. preventive medicine U. So. Calif. Sch. Medicine, LA, 1973-83, 1987—, chair preventive medicine, 1989-99. Mem. coun. Royal Statis. Soc., 1972-73, chmn. med. sect., 1984-86; mem. devel. rsch. segment virus cancer program NCI, 1971-78; mem. pres.' biomed. rsch. panel Interdisciplinary Cluster in Epidemiology, Biostats. and Bioengring., 1976; mem. rev. group on analysis of case-control studies Internat. Agy. Cancer Rsch., 1977; mem. safe drinking water com. NAS, 1977-83, cons. to Radiation Effects Rsch. Found., Hiroshima, Japan, 1979, 81, mem. com. on Pyrenes, 1981-83, mem. commn. on life scis., 1992-95; mem. rev. com. Internat. Agy. Cancer Rsch., 1979; mem. adv. com. on breast cancer screening Internat. Union Against Cancer, 1982; mem. faculty Internat. Agy. for Cancer Rsch., 1985; mem. U.K. Coord. Com. on Cancer Rsch., 1985-86; mem. com. on immunology of leprosy WHO, 1986-87, mem. bd. sci. counselors tropical diseases rsch., 1989-93; mem. med. rsch. del. to USSR U.K. Dept. Health and Social Security, 1986; mem. adv. panel Nat. Cancer Inst., 1987; mem. coun. Nat. Inst. Environ. Health Scis., 1992-95; mem. sci. adv. com. Tobacco-Related Disease Rsch. program State of Calif., 1993-96; mem. adv. bd. GM Cancer Rsch. Found., 2004. Assoc. editr Med. Stats. and Epidemiology of Biometrics, 1972-76; editl. bd. Brit. Jour. Haematology, 1972-73, Brit. Jour. Cancer, 1972-73; contbr. articles to profl. publs. Recipient Guy Bronze medal Royal Statis. Soc., 1968, Brinker Internat. award of the Susan G. Komen Breast Cancer Found., 1994, Am. Cancer Soc. award for rsch. excellence in cancer epidemiology & prevention, 2004. Mem. NAS (mem. inst. medicine). Office: Mail Stop 44 1441 Eastlake Ave Los Angeles CA 90089-0112 E-mail: mcpike@hsc.usc.edu.

PILAND, NEILL FINNES, health services economist, researcher, educator; b. Pomona, Calif., Nov. 6, 1943; s. Finnes Elmer and Sylvia Beatrice (Renick) PiL.; m. Diane Lynn Fiedor, Aug. 12, 1977; children: Evan Neill, Spencer Lowell, Arden Geneva. BA, UCLA, 1965, MPH, 1970, PhD, 1979; MA, U. Calif., Davis, 1966. Rsch. assoc. Sch. Pub. Health UCLA, 1971-73, sr. rsch. assoc., 1973; health economist Stanford Rsch. Inst., Menlo Park, Calif., 1973-77, asst. mgr. health svcs. rsch., 1974-77; dir. health ctr. study Jicarilla Apache Tribe, Dulce, N.Mex., 1978-82; dir. health systems evaluation program Lovelace Med. Found., Albuquerque, 1982-83, dir. health svcs. rsch. and edn., 1983-91; dir. Ctr. Health & Population Rsch., Albuquerque, 1991-94, Lovelace Inst. for Health and Population Rsch., Albuquerque, 1994-96; rsch. dir. Ctr. Rsch. Med. Group Mgmt. Assn., Englewood, Colo., 1996—2002; prof. and dir. Inst. Rural Health, Idaho State U., Pocatello, 2002—, rsch. prof., 2005—; clin. assoc. prof. U. Colo. Sch. Medicine; rsch. prof. U. Denver; dir. policy and rsch. Colo. Health Inst., Denver, 2004—05; rsch. prof. Inst. Rural Health Idaho State U., 2005—. Clin. asst. prof. medicine U. N.Mex., Albuquerque, 1981, clin. assoc. prof., 1994—; vis. prof. U. N.H., Durham, 1989-90; mem. commn. tobacco control, Idaho, 2003-04 Co-author: Strategic Nursing Management: Power and Responsibility in a New Era; mem. editorial bd. Jour. Managerial Issues, 1991—; co-editor: Physician Profiling: A Sourcebook for Adminstrators, Chart Accounts for Healthcare Organizations, Reinventing Medical Practice; contbr. over 100 articles to profl. jours. Mem. rsch. com. N.Mex. HealthNet, 1986-88; chair econ. issues N.Mex. Com. on Pub. Health Impact of Smoking, 1988; bd. dirs. Am. Geriat. and Gerontology, 1984-87, Healthcare for Homeless, 1988-92; mem. exec. coun. N.Mex. ASSIST Com., 1992—, sci. adv. com. N.Mex. ASSIST Project, 1992—; mem. steering com. Group Practice Improvement Network, 1996—; mem. workgroup smoking control Colo. Dept. Health and Environment, 1999-2002; scholarship interviewer NHSC, 2003-04; mem. Idaho State Commn. Tobacco Control, 2004—; bd. dirs. Vets. Med. Rsch. Found., 2002—. Recipient traineeship, USPHS, 1968-70. Mem. APHA, Am. Econ. Assn., Soc. Rsch. Adminstrs., Assn. Health Svcs. Rsch. Avocations: tennis, hockey, hiking, biking. Home: 2 Rice Ave Pocatello ID 83201 Office: Inst Rural Health Idaho State U Graveley Hall 205 Campus Box 8174 Pocatello ID 83209-8174 Office Phone: 208-282-5021. Business E-Mail: pilaneil@isu.edu.

PILEGGI, JENNIFER WENDY, transportation services executive; b. NYC, July 27, 1964; d. Jerome E. Rosenfeld. BA in Art History, cum laude, Yale U., 1986; JD, NYU, 1990. Bar: Calif. 1990. Assoc. Heller, Ehrman, White & McAuliffe, San Francisco, Marron, Reid & Sheehy, San Francisco; joined CNF Inc., Palo Alto, Calif., 1996; corp. counsel Menlo Worldwide Logistics subs., Redwood City, Calif., 1996—99, v.p., corp. counsel, 1999—2003, Menlo Worldwide subs., Redwood City, Calif., 2003—04; sr. v.p., gen. counsel, corp. sec. Con-way Inc. (formerly CNF Inc.), 2004—. Mem.: ABA, Calif. State Bar Assn. Office: CNF Inc 2855 Campus Dr Ste 300 San Mateo CA 94403 Office Phone: 650-378-5200. Office Fax: 650-357-9160.

PILGERAM, LAURENCE OSCAR, biochemist; b. Great Falls, Mont., June 23, 1924; s. John Rudolph and Bertha Roslyn (Phillips) P.; m. Cynthia Ann Moore, Apr. 16, 1971; children: Karl Erich, Kurt John. AA, U. Calif., Berkeley, 1948, BA, 1949, PhD, 1953. Instr. dept. physiology U. Ill. Profl. Coll., Chgo., 1954-55; asst. prof. dept. biochemistry Stanford (Calif.) U. Sch. Medicine, 1955-57; dir. arteriosclerosis rsch. lab. U. Minn. Sch. Medicine, Mpls., 1957-65, Santa Barbara, Calif., 1965-71; dir. coagulation lab., assoc. dir. Cerebrovascular Rsch. Ctr., Baylor Coll. Medicine, Tex. Med. Ctr., Houston, 1971-75; dir. Thrombosis Control Labs., Palo Alto, Calif., 1975-79, Santa Barbara, 1979—; prof. dept. molecular biology U. Calif., Santa Barbara, 2004—. Cons. NIH, Bio-Sci. Labs., FDA; del. Coun. on Thrombosis and Coun. on Strokes, Am. Heart Assn. Assembly. Co-editor: Nutrition and Thrombosis for the Nat. Dairy Coun., 1973; contbr. sci. articles to profl. jours. Recipient CIBA award, London, 1958, Karl Thomae award, Germany, 1973; NIH grantee, 1954-75; Life Ins. Med. Rsch. Fund fellow, 1952-54. Mem. Am. Soc. for Biochemistry and Molecular Biology. Office: PO Box 1583 Goleta PO Santa Barbara CA 93116 Office Phone: 805-967-5994.

PILISUK, MARC, psychology educator; b. NYC, Jan. 19, 1934; s. Louis and Charlotte (Feferholtz) P.; m. Phyllis E. Kamen, June 16, 1956; children: Tammy, Jeff. BA, Queens Coll., 1955; MA, U. Mich., 1956, PhD, 1961. Asst. prof., assoc. rsch. psychologist U. Mich., Ann Arbor, 1961-65, founder teach-in, 1965; assoc. prof. Purdue U., West Lafayette, Ind., 1965-67; prof.-in-residence U. Calif., Berkeley, 1967-77, prof. cmty. psychology Davis, 1977—. Vis. prof. U. Calif., Wright Inst., 1991—93; cons. Ctr. for Self Help Rsch., Berkeley, Calif., 1991—93; prof. psychology Saybrook Grad. Sch. & Rsch. Ctr., San Francisco, 1993—. Author: (textbooks) International Conflict and Social Policy, 1972, The Healing Web: Social Networks and Human Survival, 1986, Who Benefits from Global Violence and War: Uncovering a Destructive System, 2008; editor: The Triple Revolution, 1969, Poor Americans, 1970, Triple Revolution Emerging, 1972, How We Lost the War on Poverty, 1973. Grantee, NSF, 1962—66;, NIMH fellow, 1959—60, tng. grantee, Nat. Inst. Alcoholism and Drug Abuse, 1973—77. Fellow: APA (pres. divsn. peace psychology 1996—97, cadre experts on violence, Presdl. award 2005, Lifetime Contbn. award 2005), Am. Orthopsychiat. Assn., Soc. for Psychol. Study Social Issues (coun., Sage award 2004—05); mem.: ACLU, APHA, Faculty for Human Rights in C.Am., Psychologists for Social Responsibility (adv. bd. mem., Disting. Svc. award 2001, Anthony Marsalla Peace and Justice award 2006), Am. Soc. on Aging, Soc. for Cmty. Rsch. and Action. Business E-Mail: mpilisuk@saybrook.edu.

PILLER, CHARLES LEON, journalist; b. Chgo., Jan. 9, 1955; s. Jack H. and Alice (Shakow) P.; m. Surry Piller Bunnell, Aug. 21, 1984; 1 child, Nathan Bunnell Piller. BA, Lone Mountain Coll., 1977. Editor, writer U. Calif., San Francisco, 1982-89; sr. editor Macworld mag., San Francisco, 1990-96; exec. editor PC World Mag., San Francisco, 1996—97; tech. writer L.A. Times, 1996—2002, science writer, computer tech. and biology, 2002—06, bus. & tech. reporter, 2006—. Chair Ctr. Pub. Integrity, Washington, 1988—, also bd. dirs.; cons. US Senate, Washington, 1989-92. Author: Gene Wars, 1988, The Fail-Safe Society, 1991; contbr. numerous articles to newspapers and mags. Recipient of the John Swett Journalism award, 1993, Benjamin Fine Journalism award, 1995, Runner-Up Lincoln Steffens

Journalism award, 1994, Am. Soc. of Business Press Editors (various awards). Office: LA Times 202 W First St Los Angeles CA 90012 Office Fax: 213-237-4712. Business E-Mail: charles.piller@latimes.com.

PIMENTEL, ALBERT A. (ROCKY PIMENTEL), computer software company executive; BS in Commerce, Santa Clara U., Calif. Founding mem. Conner Peripherals; mem. founding mgmt. team Seagate Tech.; v.p., CFO Momenta Corp.; sr. v.p., CFO SLI Logic, WebTV Networks; ptnr. Redpoint Ventures, Menlo Pk., Calif., 2001—03; exec. v.p., CFO Zone Labs, San Francisco, 2003—04, Sorrent, Inc., San Mateo, Calif., 2004, Glu Mobile, San Mateo, 2004—08; COO, CFO McAfee, Santa Clara. Bd. dirs. Livingston Comm., Crossworlds Software, Danger, Inc. Office: McAfee Corp Hdqs 3965 Freedom Cir Santa Clara CA 95054

PINCUS, HOWARD J., geologist, engineer, educator; b. NYC, June 24, 1922; s. Otto Max and Gertrude (Jankowsky) Pincus; m. Maud Lydia Roback, Sept. 6, 1953; children: Glenn David, Philip Ethan. BS, CCNY, 1942; PhD, Columbia U., 1949. Cert. profl. geol. scientist Ind., 1964, profl. engr. Wis., 1981, profl. geologist Am. Inst. Profl. Geologists, 1981. Rsch. assoc. Lamont Geol. Obs., Columbia U., 1949-51; geologist Ohio Dept. Natural Resources, summers 1950-61; faculty Ohio State U., 1949-67, from instr. to assoc. prof., 1949-59, prof., 1959-67, chmn. dept. geology, 1960-65; rsch. geologist U.S. Bur. Mines, 1963—67, geologist, rsch. supr., 1967-68; prof. geol. sci. and civil engring. U. Wis., Milw., 1968-87, prof. emeritus, 1987—, dean Coll. Letters and Sci., 1969-72; cons. geology and rock mechanics, 1954-67, 68—. Sr. postdoctoral fellow NSF, 1962; mem. U.S. nat. com. tunneling tech. NAE, 1972—74; mem. U.S. nat. com. rock mechanics NAS/NAE, 1975—78, 1980—89, chmn., 1985—87; mem. U.S. com. Internat. Assn. Engring. Geology/NAS, chmn., 1987—90. Tech. editor: Geotechnical Testing Jour., 1992—95; mem. editl. bd. Geotechnical Testing Jour., 1996—2007. Served to 1st lt. C.E. US Army, 1942—46. Recipient award for tchg. excellence, U. Wis.-Milw. Alumni Assn., 1978. Fellow: AAAS, ASTM (Frank W. Reinhart award 1987, Merit award 1989), Geol. Soc. Am. (chmn. engring. geology divsn. 1973—74); mem.: Am. Inst. Profl. Geologists (pres. Ohio sect. 1965—66), Assn. Engring. Geologists, Am. Rock Mechanics Assn., Internat. Soc. Rock Mechanics, Internat. Assn. Engring. Geology, Soc. Mining Engrs., Geol. Soc. Am., Am. Geophysical Union, Sigma Xi, Phi Beta Kappa (pres. Ohio State U. chpt. 1959—60, pres. U. Wis.-Milw. chpt. 1975—77). Home and Office: 17523 Plaza Marlena San Diego CA 92128-1807 Personal E-mail: hpincus@san.rr.com.

PINCUS, ROBERT LAWRENCE, art critic, historian; b. Bridgeport, Conn., June 5, 1953; s. Jules Robert and Carol Sylvia (Rosen) P.; m. Georgianna Manly, June 20, 1981; 1 child, Matthew Manly. BA, U. Calif., Irvine, 1976; MA, U. So. Calif., 1980, PhD, 1987. Instr. writing and Am. studies U. So. Calif., LA, 1978-83; art critic L.A. Times, 1981-85, San Diego Union, 1985-92, San Diego Union-Tribune, 1992—. Vis. prof. art history San Diego State U., 1985-86, 92, lectr. U. San Diego, 1998-. Author: On A Scale That Competes with the World: The Art of Edward and Nancy Reddin Kienholz, 1990; co-author West Coast Duchamp, 1991, But Is It Art: The Spirit of Art as Activism, 1994, Paradise, 1994, Anne Mudge: Traces, 1996, Introduction to W.D.'s Midnight Carnival, 1988, Kitchen: Liza Lou, 1996, Manuel Neri: Early Work, 1953-78, 97, Gordas: Paintings and Installations by Tania Candiani, 2002, Defining of Vision: The Museum of Photographic Arts, 2007; contbr. reviewer, Artweek, 79; corr. editor, Art in America, 1988-. Recipient Ring Truth Prizes, Best Art Story, 1986, 1987, 1988, Chem. Bank award for Disting. Newspaper Art Criticism, 1994, Mo. Lifestyles Journalism award, 2001, Best Critical Writing award, San Diego Press Club, 1994, 2004, 2006. Mem. Internat. Assn. Art Critics, Coll. Art Assn. Democrat. Office: San Diego Union Tribune PO Box 120191 350 Camino De La Reina San Diego CA 92108-3003 Office Phone: 619-293-1831. Business E-Mail: robert.pincus@uniontrib.com.

PINES, ALEXANDER, chemistry educator, researcher, consultant; b. Tel Aviv, June 22, 1945; came to US, 1968. US citizen in 1981. s. Michael and Neima (Ratner) P.; m. Ayala Malach, Aug. 31, 1967 (div. 1983); children: Itai, Shani; m. Ditsa Kafry, May 5, 1983; children: Noami, Jonathan, Talia. BSc, Hebrew U., Jerusalem, 1967; PhD in Chemical Physics, MIT, 1972; D (hon.), U. Paris "Pierre et Marie Curie", 1999, U. Rome "La Sapienza", 2001. Asst. prof. chemistry U. Calif., Berkeley, 1972-75, assoc. prof., 1975-80, prof., 1980—, Pres.'s chair, 1993-97, Chandellor's rsch. prof., 1997-99, Miller rsch. prof., 1998-99, Glenn T. Seaborg prof. chemistry, 1999—. Faculty sr. scientist materials scis. div. Lawrence Berkeley Nat. Lab., 1975—; cons. Mobil Oil Co., Princeton, N.J., 1980-84, Shell Oil Co., Houston, 1981—; chmn. Bytel Corp., Berkeley, Calif., 1981-85; vis. prof. Weizmann Inst. Sci., 1982; adv. prof. East China Normal U., Shanghai, People's Rep. of China, 1985; sci. dir. Naloracc, Martinez, Calif., 1986-92; Joliot-Curie prof. Ecole Superieure de Physique et Chemie, Paris, 1987; Walter J. Chute Disting. lectr. Dalhousie U., 1989, Charles A. McDowell lectr. U. B.C., 1989, E. Leon Watkins lectr. Wichita State U., 1990; Hinshelwood lectr., U. Oxford, 1990, A.R. Gordon Disting. lectr. U. Toronto, 1990, Venable lectr. U. N.C., 1990, Max Born lectr. Hebrew U. of Jerusalem, 1990; William Draper Harkins lectr. U. Chgo., 1991, Kolthoff lectr. U. Minn., 1991; Md.-Grace lectr. U. Md., 1992; mem. adv bd. Nat. High Magnetic Field Lab., Inst. Theoretical Physics, U. Calif. Santa Barbara, Ctr. Pure and Applied Math. U. Calif., Berkeley; mem. adv. panel chem. Nat. Sci. Found.; Randolph T. Major Disting. Lectr. U. Conn., 1992; mem. bd. sci. govs. Weizemann Inst. Sci., 1997—; Peter Smith lectr. Duke U., 1993, Arthur William Davidson lect. U. Kansas, 1992, Arthur Birch lect. Australian Nat. U., 1993, Richard C. Lord Meml. lectr. MIT, 1993, Steacie lectr. Nat. Rsch. Coun. Can., 1993, Morris Loeb lectr. Harvard U., 1994, Jesse Boot Found. lectr., U. Nottingham, 1994, Frontiers in Chemistry lectr. Tex. A&M U., 1995, Bergman lectr. Weizmann Inst. Sci., 1995, faculty rsch. lectr. U. Calif., Berkeley, 1996, Raymond & Beverly Sackler lectr. Tel Aviv U., 1996; Priestley lectr. Pa. State U., 1997; Amy Mellon lectr. Purdue U., 1997; Rsch. frontiers chemistry lectr. U. Iowa, 1998, Moses Gomberg lectr. U. Mich., 1998, J and N Max T. Rogers, Mich. State U., 1998, Frontiers in Chemistry lectr., Wayne State U., 1998, Lord Todd Prof., Cambridge U., 1999, Abbot lectr., U. N.D., 2000, John D. Roberts lectr., Calif. Tech. U., 2000, Willard lectr., U. Wis., 2000, Cliford lectr., U. Pitts., 2000, William Lloyd Evan lectr. Ohio State U., 2000, Jacob Bigeleisen lectr. Stony Brook U., 2001, Laird lectr. U. B.C., 2001; Alan S. Tetelman fellow Yale U., 2001, Regitze Vold Meml. lectr. U. Calif., San Diego, 2001, Sammet guest prof. Goëethe U., Frankfurt, 2001. Editor Molecular Physics, 1987-91; mem. bd. editors Chem. Physics, Chem. Physics Letters, Nmr: Basic Principles and Progress, Advances in Magnetic Resonance, Accounts Chemistry Research, Concepts in Magnetic Reson; adv. editor Oxford U. Press; contbr. articles to profl. jours.; patentee in field. Recipient Strait award North Calif. Spectroscopy Soc., Outstanding Achievement award U.S. Dept. of Energy, 1983, 87, 89, 97, 98, R & D 100 awards, 1987, 89, Disting. Teaching award U. Calif., Ernest O. Lawrence award, 1988, Pitts. Spectroscopy award, 1989, Wolf prize in chemistry, Wolf Found., Israel, 1991, Donald Noyce Undergrad. Teaching award U. Calif., 1992, Robert Foster Cherry award for Great Tchrs. Baylor U., 1995, F.A. Cotton Medal for Excellence in Chemical Rsch., 1998, Dickson prize Carnegie Mellon U., 2001; Guggenheim fellow, 1988, Christensen fellow St. Catherine's Coll., Oxford, 1990; named in honor of his 50th birthday, Ampere Advanced Inst., Varenna, Italy; named to Scientific American 50 List, 2002. Fellow Am. Phys. Soc. (chmn. divsn. chem. physics), Inst. Physics; foreign fellow Royal Soc.; mem. NAS, Am. Chem. Soc. (mem. exec. com. divsn. phys. chemistry, Nobel Signature award in Graduate Edu. 1982, Baekeland Medal for Pure Chemistry, 1985, Harrison Howe award 1991, Centennial Spkr., Jour. Physical Chemistry, 1997, Langmuir award in Chemical Physics, 1998, Remsen award (Md. sect.) 2000, Dickson prize 2001), Royal Soc. Chemistry (Bourke lectr., Bourke Medal, 1988, Centenary lectr. and medal 1994), Internat. Soc. Magnetic Resonance (v.p., pres. 1993-96), Lawrence Hall Sci. Outreach Com. Achievements include pioneering contributions to the development of nuclear magnetic resonance (NMR) spectroscopy; his techniques are widely used in chemistry and materials science. Office: U Calif Chemistry Dept D64A Hildebrand Hill Berkeley CA 94720-0001 Office Phone: 510-642-1220. Office Fax: 510-486-5744. Business E-Mail: pines@berkeley.edu.

PINGS, ANTHONY CLAUDE, architect; b. Fresno, Calif., Dec. 16, 1951; s. Clarence Hubert and Mary (Murray) P.; m. Carole Clements, June 25, 1983; children, Adam Reed, Rebecca Mary. AA, Fresno City Coll., 1972; BArch, Calif. Poly. State U., San Luis Obispo, 1976. Lic. architect, Calif.; cert. Nat. Council Archtl. Registration Bds. Architect Aubrey Moore Jr., Fresno, 1976-81; architect, prin. Pings & Assocs., Fresno, 1981-83, 86—, Pings-Taylor Assocs., Fresno, 1983-85. Prin. works include Gollaher Profl. Office (Masonry Merit award 1985, Best Office Bldg. award 1986), Fresno Imaging Ctr. (Best Instnl. Project award 1986, Nat. Healthcare award Modern Health Care mag. 1986), Orthopedic Facility (award of honor Masonry Inst. 1987, award of merit San Joaquin chpt. AIA 1987), Modesto Imaging Ctr. (award of merit San Joaquin chpt. AIA 1991), Peachwood Med. Ctr. (award of merit San Joaquin chpt. AIA). Mem. Calif. Indsl. Tech. Edn. Consortium Calif. State Dept. Edn., 1983, 84. Recipient Excellence in Bus. award Fresno, 1999. Mem. AIA (bd. dirs. Calif. chpt. 1983-84, v.p. San Joaquin chpt. 1982, pres. 1983, Calif. Coun. evaluation team 1983, team leader Coalinga Emergency Design Assistance team), Fresno Arts (bd. dirs., counsel 1989—, pres. 1990-93), Fig Gardens Home Owners Assn. (bd. dir. 1991—, pres. 1994—). Republican. Home: 4350 N Safford Ave Fresno CA 93704-3509

PINKEL, DONALD PAUL, pediatrician; b. Buffalo, Sept. 7, 1926; s. Lawrence William and Ann (Richardson) P.; m. Marita Donovan, Dec. 26, 1949 (div. 1981); children: Rebecca, Nancy, Christopher, Mary, Thomas, Anne, Sara, John, Ruth; m. Cathryn Barbara Howarth, May 16, 1981; 1 child, Michael. BS, Canisius Coll., 1947; MD, U. Buffalo, 1951. Diplomate Am. Bd. Pediatrics, Pediatric Hematology and Oncology, Nat. Bd. Med. Examiners. From intern to resident to chief resident Children's Hosp., Buffalo, 1951-54; research fellow Children's Hosp. Med. Ctr., Boston, 1955-56; chief. of pediatrics Roswell Park Meml. Inst., Buffalo, 1956-61; founding dir. St. Jude Children's Rsch. Hosp., Memphis, 1961-73; chmn. pediatrics Med. Coll. Wis., Milw., 1974-78; pediatrician-in-chief Milw. Children's Hosp., 1974-78; founding dir. Midwest Children's Cancer Ctr., Milw., 1974; chief. of pediatrics City of Hope Med. Ctr., Duarte, Calif., 1978-82; chmn. pediatrics Temple U. Sch. Medicine, Phila., 1982-85; prof., Kana Rsch. chair, dir. pediatric leukemia program M.D. Anderson Cancer Ctr. U. Tex., Houston, 1985-93; prof. pediat. U. Tex. Med. Sch., Houston, 1985-99; prof. emeritus U. Tex.-M.D. Anderson Cancer Ctr., Houston, 1994—. Clin. prof. pediats. U. So. Calif., LA, 2002—; adj. prof. biol. scis. Calif. Polytechnic State U., San Luis Obispo, Calif., 2001—. Contbr. articles to profl. jours. Bd. dirs. Lee County Coop. Clinic, Mariana, Ark., 1972-74. Served with USN, 1944-45, served to 1st lt. U.S. Army, 1954-55. Recipient Albert Lasker award for Med. Rsch., Lasker Found., 1972, Windermere Lectureship Brit. Pediatric Assn., 1974, David Karnofsky award Am. Soc. Clin. Oncology, 1978, Zimmerman prize for Cancer Rsch. Zimmerman Found., 1979, Charles Kettering prize Gen. Motors Cancer Rsch., 1986, Clin. Rsch. award Am. Cancer Soc., 1988, Return of the Child award Leukemia Soc. Am., 1992, Pollin prize in pediat. rsch. N.Y. Presbyn. Hosp., 2003. Mem. Am. Soc. Clin. Oncology, Am. Pediat. Soc., Am. Assn. Cancer Rsch., Soc. Exptl. Biology and Medicine, Am. Soc. Hematology. Democrat. Roman Catholic. Avocations: swimming, sailing. Home: 275 Marlene Dr San Luis Obispo CA 93405 E-mail: donpinkel@yahoo.com.

PINKERTON, STEVEN JAMES, city official; b. Madison, Wis., Jan. 21, 1960; BA, U. Mo., 1983; MPI in Urban Planning, U. So. Calif., 1988, MA in Econs., 1988. Mem. staff Econ. Devel. Assn. City of Redondo Beach, Calif., 1984-91; mem. redevel. adminstrn. City of Long Beach, Calif., 1991-94; dir. housing and redevel. City of Stockton, Calif., 1994—. Mem. Am. Planning Assn. (cert. city planner). Office: City Of Stockton Hrd 22 E Weber Ave Ste 305 Stockton CA 95202-2326

PINKETT-SMITH, JADA, actress; b. Balt., Sept. 18, 1971; m. Will Smith, Dec. 31, 1997; 2 children. Actor (films) Menace II Society, 1993, The Inkwell, 1994, Jason's Lyric, 1994, A Low Down Dirty Shame, 1994, Demon Knight, 1995, The Nutty Professor, 1996, Set It Off, 1996, Blossoms and Veils, 1997 (also exec. prodr.), Scream 2, 1997, Woo, 1998, Return to Paradise, 1998, Bamboozled, 2000, Kingdom Come, 2001, Ali, 2001, The Matrix Reloaded, 2003, The Matrix Revolutions, 2003, Collateral, 2004, (voice) Madagascar, 2005, Reign Over Me, 2007, The Women, 2008, (voice) Madagascar: Escape 2 Africa, 2008, (TV films) If These Walls Could Talk, 1996, Maniac Magee, 2003, (TV series) A Different World, 1992-93, exec. prodr. All of Us, 2003-; exec. prodr. (films) The Seat Filler, 2004; author (children's book): Girls Hold Up This World, 2004 (NY Times Bestseller list, NAACP Image award for outstanding lit. work-children's 2006). Office: c/o Overbrook Entertainment Inc 450 North Roxbury Dr 8th Fl Beverly Hills CA 90210

PINNELL, ROBERT PEYTON, chemistry educator; b. Fresno, Calif., Dec. 5, 1938; s. Paul Peyton and Iris Ione (Shepherd) P.; m. Sharron Lyne Gregory, Aug. 18, 1962; children: Jason Peyton, Sabrina Lyne. BS, Calif. State U., Fresno, 1960; PhD, U. Kansas, 1964. Postdoctoral fellow U. Tex., Austin, 1964-66; asst. prof. chemistry Claremont (Calif.) McKenna Coll., Scripps Coll. and Pitzer Coll., 1966-72, assoc. prof., 1972-78, prof., 1978—, chmn. joint sci. dept., 1974-77, 97—. Rsch. affilate Jet Propulsion Lab., 1986-88, vis. assoc. prof. chemistry Calif. Inst. Tech., 1973-74. Postdoctoral fellow U. Calif. at Santa Barbara, 1980-81; NASA-Am. Soc. for Engring. fellow, 1982, 83, 86, 87. Mem. Nat. Sci. Tchrs. Assn., Am. Chem. Soc., Calif. Assn. Chemistry Tchrs., Sigma Xi. Democrat. Avocation: reading. Office: Claremont McKenna Scripps & Pitzer Colls 925 N Mills Ave Claremont CA 91711-5916

PINNEY, THOMAS CLIVE, retired English language educator; b. Ottawa, Kans., Apr. 23, 1932; s. John James and Lorene Maude (Owen) P.; m. Sherrill Marie Ohman, Sept. 1, 1956; children— Anne, Jane, Sarah. BA, Beloit Coll., Wis., 1954; PhD, Yale U., 1960. Instr. Hamilton Coll., Clinton, NY, 1957-61; instr. English Yale U., New Haven, 1961-62; asst. prof. to prof., chmn. dept. English Pomona Coll., Claremont, Calif., 1962-97; ret., 1997. Editor: Essays of George Eliot, 1963, Selected Writings of Thomas Babington Macaulay, 1972, Letters of Macaulay, 1974-81, Kipling's India, 1986, A History of Wine in America, 1989, Kipling's Something of Myself, 1990, Letters of Rudyard Kipling, 1990,-2004 The Vineyards and Wine Cellars of California, 1994, The Wine of Santa Cruz Island, 1994, A History of Wine in America: From Prohibition to the Present, 2005. Guggenheim fellow, 1966, 84,Recipient Disting. Svc. citation Beloit Coll., 1984; fellow NEH, 1980; grantee Am. Coun. Learned Socs., 1974, 84, Am. Philos. Soc., 1968, 82, 94. Mem. MLA, Elizabethan Club (New Haven), Zamorano Club (L.A.), Phi Beta Kappa. Office: Pomona Coll Dept English Claremont CA 91711 Home: 890 E Harrison Ave 32 Pomona CA 91767

PINSKY, DREW (DAVID DREW PINSKY), television personality, psychotherapist; b. Pasadena, Calif., Sept. 4, 1958; s. Morton and Helene; m. Susan Pinsky, July 20, 1991; children: Jordan Davidson, Douglas Drew, Paulina Marie. BS in Biology, Amherst Coll., Mass., 1980; MD, U. Southern Calif., 1984. Chief resident Huntington Meml. Hosp.; med. dir. dept. chem. dependency svcs. Aurora Las Encinas Hosp., Pasadena, Calif.; pvt. practice; asst. clin. prof. psychiatry Keck U. Southern Calif. Sch. Medicine. Spokesperson Musicians Assistance Prog.; works with Advocates for Youth, Ind. Women's Forum, Media Project, Entertainment Industry Coun., Hillside Home for Children. Host (radio) Loveline, 1982—, (TV series), MTV, 1996—2000, Men Are from Mars, Women Are from Venus, 2000, Strictly Sex with Dr. Drew, 2005, Strictly Dr. Drew, 2006, host, prodr. Celebrity Rehab with Dr. Drew, 2008—, appearances on Dawson's Creek, 2003, Family Guy, 2005, The Adam Carolla Project, 2005, Minoriteam, 2006, Robot Chicken, 2006, Code Monkeys, 2007; actor: (films) New York Minute, 2004, Wild Hogs, 2007, Big Stan, 2007; author: Cracked: Putting Broken Lives Together Again, 2003, When Painkillers Become Dangerous, 2004. Recipient Kaiser Sexual Health in Entertainment award, Planned Parenthood of Am. award, PRISM award, Claire Found. award. Mem.: Am. Soc. Internal Medicine, Calif. Med. Assn., Am. Soc. Addiction Medicine, AMA, Am. Coll. Physicians. Avocations: opera, running, skiing, surfing. Office: Aurora Las Encinas Hospital 2900 E Del Mar Blvd Pasadena CA 91107

PINSON, LARRY LEE, pharmacist, state agency administrator; b. Van Nuys, Calif., Dec. 5, 1947; s. Leland J. and Audrey M. (Frett) Pinson; m. Margaret K. Pinson, Mar. 18, 1972; children: Scott C., Kelly E. Student, U. Calif., Davis, 1967—69; AA, Am. River Coll., Sacramento, 1969; PharmD, U. Calif., San Francisco, 1973. Lic. pharmacist Calif., Nev. Staff pharmacist/asst. dir. pharm. svcs. St. Mary's Hosp., Reno, 1973-77; chief pharmacist May Ang Base USAF, 1973-77; mng. pharmacist Scolari's Food & Drug, Reno, 2001—05; exec. sec. Nev. State Bd. Pharmacy, 2005—, pres., 1996—2004, exec. sec., 2005—; pharm., therapeutics com. State Nev., 2004—. Cons. pharmacist Physicians Hosp., 1974—93, Reno Med. Plz., 1973—2001, Rural Calif. Hosp. Assn., 1973—74, Ford Ctr. Foot Surgery, 1980—2007; pharmacy coord. Intensive Pharm. Svcs., 1986—87; cons. Calif. Dept. Health & Corrections, Susanville, 1975—76, Nev. Med. Care Adv. Bd., Carson City, 1984—87; provider, reviewer Nev. State Bd. Pharmacy, Reno, 1975—84; instr. Nev. CC, 1974—76; adj. prof. Idaho State U., Pocatello, 1989—. Coauthor: Care of Hickman Catheter, 1984. Softball coach Reno/Sparks Recreation Dept., 1973—92; bd. dirs. Am. Cancer Soc., 1986—90; mem. State of Nev. Pharmaceutics and Therapy Com., 2004—05, Nev. Arthritis Found.; cubmaster Pack 153 Boy Scouts Am., Verdi, Nev., scoutmaster com. chmn. Reno troop 1, 1988—92. Recipient Bowl of Hygeia award, Nev. Pharmacists Assn. and A. H. Robbins Co., 1984; named Pharmacist of the Yr., Nev. Pharm. Alliance, 1999. Mem.: Greater Nev. Heatlh Sys. Agy., Nev. Profl. Stds. Rev. Orgn., Nev. Pharmacists Assn. (pres. 1981—82), Am. Pharm. Assn., Nat. Assn. Bds. Pharmacy, Kappa Psi. Avocations: skiing, fishing, backpacking, softball, golf. Home: PO Box 478 Verdi NV 89439-0478 Office: 555 Double Eagle Ct Ste 1100 Reno NV 89521 Office Phone: 775-850-1440. Personal E-mail: Rx2005@aol.com.

PINTO, FREIDA, actress; b. Bombay, Oct. 18, 1984; Studied, St. Xaviers Coll., Mumbai, India. Model. Anchor (TV series) Full Circle, 2006—07, actress (films) Slumdog Millionaire, 2008 (Outstanding Performance by a Cast in a Motion Picture, SAG, 2009). Recipient Breakthrough Performance award, Palm Springs Internat. Film Festival, 2008, Best Actress award, Elle Mag., 2009. Office: c/o Creative Artists Agy 2000 Ave of the Stars Los Angeles CA 90067

PINTO, JOHN, state legislator; b. Lupton, Ariz., Dec. 15, 1924; son of Jim Pinto & Ellen Goodluck P; married 1953 to Joann Dennison; children: Flora Jean Dennison, Cecile B, Galen D & Karen. Secytreas, Red Rock Chap, District 16 Democratic Party, New Mexico, 70-; member, McKinley Co Bd Commissioners, New Mexico, 73-74, chairman, 75-76; member, Nat Transportation Committee, Washington, DC, 75-76; member, Nat Association Regional Coun, Washington, DC, 75-76; New Mexico State Senator, District 3, 77-, chairman, Indian & Cult Affairs Committee, currently, member, Education Committee, currently, New Mexico State Senate.Chairman, Eastern Navajo Agency Road Committee, New Mexico, 70-75; vice chairman, Gallup Inter-Agency Alcoholism, 73-76; member & treasurer, McKinley Area Governor Coun, 73-76; chairman, Gallup Indian Community Center, 73-; member, Tohatchi Planning Comn, 75-; teacher, currently. Democrat. Catholic. Address: PO Box 163 Tohatchi NM 87325 Mailing: State Capitol Rm 301 Santa Fe NM 87503

PINTO, MARK R., manufacturing executive; B, Rensselear Poly. Inst., Troy, NY; M, PhD, Stanford U., Calif. V.p., gen. mgr. network product IC divsn., chief tech. officer Bell Labs. and Lucent Microelectronics Group (later Agere Systems); sr. v.p., chief tech. officer, gen. mgr. New Bus. and New Products Group Applied Materials, Inc., 2004—, chmn. Venture Investment Com. Adj. prof. Yale U., New

Haven. Contbr. articles to sci. jours. Named a Bell Labs fellow. Fellow: IEEE. Achievements include patents in field. Office: Applied Materials Inc PO Box 58039 Santa Clara CA 95052-8039 Office Phone: 408-727-5555.

PIPES, SALLY C., think-tank executive; Asst. dir. Fraser Inst., Vancouver, B.C., Canada, 1974—91; pres., CEO Pacific Rsch. Inst. for Pub. Policy, San Francisco, 1991—. Co-author (with Spencer Star): Income and Taxation in Canada, (with Michael Walker) 7 editions of Tax Facts; has appeared nationally on TV programs such as 20/20 and Politically Incorrect, Dateline, Inside Politics and PBS's Think Tank; regularly asked to comment on timely issues by radio and print journalists; opinion editls. have been published in various newspapers including San Francisco Chronicle, L.A. Times, Investor's Business Daily, L.A. Daily News, The Orange County Register; writes a bi-monthly column in Chief Executive mag. Bd. dirs. Fin. Instns. Commn. (B.C.), 1980-84 (vice chmn. 1982-84, chmn. 1989-); mem. Vancouver City Planning Commn., 1982-84; trustee St. Luke's Hosp. Found. in San Francisco; bd. dirs. Ind. Women's Forum; mem. bd. advisors Western Jour. Ctr. and Citizens for Term Limits, San Francisco Lawyers chpt. of the Federalist Soc.; commr. Calif. Commn. on Transp. Investment, 1996; bd. govs. Donner-Can. Found. Mem. Mont Pelerin Soc., Nat. Assn. Bus. Economists, Can. Assn. for Bus. Econs. (pres. 2 terms), Assn. Profl. Economists of B.C. Office: Pacific Research Institute 1 Embarcadero Ctr Ste 350 San Francisco CA 94111-3631 Office Phone: 415-955-6100.

PIPPENGER, NICHOLAS JOHN, mathematician, Computer Scientist Researcher Educator; b. Abington, Pa., Mar. 14, 1947; s. Robert and Mary Emma Pippenger; m. Maria Margaret Klawe, May 12, 1980; children: Janek Evan Klawe, Sasha Kathleen. BS, Shimer Coll., 1965, MIT, 1967, MS, 1969, PhD, 1974. Mem. tech. staff Charles Stark Draper Lab., Cambridge, Mass., 1969—73; mem. rsch. staff IBM Corp., Yorktown Heights, NY, 1973—80, San Jose, Calif., 1980—87, fellow, 1987—89; prof. U. BC, Vancouver, Canada, 1988—2000, rsch. chair, 2000—03; prof. Princeton U., NJ, 2003—06, Harvey Mudd Coll, Claremont, Calif., 2006—. Fellow: IEEE, Assn. Computing Machinery, Acad. Sci., Royal Soc. Can.; mem.: Math. Assn. of Am., Am. Math. Soc., Soc. Indsl. and Applied Math. Office: Harvey Mudd Coll Dept Math 1250 N Dartmouth Ave Claremont CA 91711 Business E-Mail: njp@math.hmc.edu.

PIPPIN, DONALD FERRELL, musician, director, conductor; b. Raleigh, NC, Dec. 8, 1925; s. Raymond Edward and Dorothy (Law) Pippin. Pianist, producer Sunday Night Concerts, San Francisco, 1954-78; artistic dir. Pocket Opera, San Francisco, 1978. Translator, condr. over 60 operas including Marriage of Figaro, 1981, Belle Helene, 1981, Merry Wives, 1983, Merry Widow, 1987, Barber of Seville, 1991 among others. Democrat. Home: 34 Miley St San Francisco CA 94123-3266

PIRCHER, LEO JOSEPH, lawyer, director; b. Berkeley, Calif., Jan. 4, 1933; s. Leo Charles and Christine (Moore) P.; m. Phyllis McConnell, Aug. 4, 1956 (div. Apr. 1981); children: Christopher, David, Eric; m. Nina Silverman, June 14, 1987. BS, U. Calif., Berkeley, 1954, JD, 1957. Bar: Calif. 1958, (N.Y.) 1985, cert.: Calif. Bd. Legal Specialization (cert. specialist taxation law). Assoc. Lawler, Felix & Hall, L.A., 1957-62, ptnr., 1962-65, sr. ptnr., 1965-83, Pircher, Nichols & Meeks, L.A., 1983—. Adj. prof. Loyola U. Law Sch., LA, 1959—61; corp. sec. Am. Metal Bearing Co., Gardena, Calif., 1975—; dir. Varco Internat., Inc., Orange, Calif.; spkr. various law schs. and bar assns. edn. programs. Author (with others): (novels) Definition and Utility of Leases, 1968. Chmn. pub. fin. and taxation sect. Calif. Town Hall, LA, 1970—71. Mem.: ABA, Nat. Assn. Real Estate Investment Trusts Inc. (cert. specialist taxation law). L.A. County Bar Assn. (exec. com. comml. law sect.), N.Y. State Bar, Calif. State Bar, Regency (L.A.). Republican. Office: Pircher Nichols & Meeks Ste 1700 1925 Century Park E Los Angeles CA 90067-6022 Home Phone: 310-274-2455; Office Phone: 310-201-8901. Personal E-mail: lpircher@pircher.com.

PISANO, A. ROBERT, former actors guild executive, former film company executive; b. San Jose, Calif., Mar. 3, 1943; s. Anthony Edward and Carmen Jeanne (Morisoli) P.; m. Carolyn Joan Pollock, May 5, 1979; children: Catherine J., Anthony Daniel, Elizabeth A., Alexandra N. BA in Pub. Adminstrn., San Jose State U., 1965; JD, U. Calif.-Berkeley, 1968. Bar: Calif. Assoc. O'Melveny & Myers, LA, 1968-75, ptnr., 1976-85, 92-93; exec. v.p. office of chmn., gen. counsel Paramount Pictures, LA, 1985-91; exec. v.p. Metro-Goldwyn-Mayer Inc., Santa Monica, Calif., 1993-96; vice chmn. Metro-Goldwyn-Mayer, Inc., 1997-99; nat. exec. dir., CEO SAG, LA, 2001—05; pres., COO Motion Picture Assn. Am., 2005—. Bd. dirs. Resources Global Profls., 2002—, Fin. Planning Assn. Group of Funds, 2002—; cons. in field.

PISANO, JANE G., museum administrator; BA in Polit. Sci., Stanford U.; MA in Internat. Rels., PhD in Internat. Rels., John Hopkins U. White House fellow Nat. Security Coun.; faculty Sch. Fgn. Svc., Georgetown U.; head LA 2000, The 2000 Partnership; dean, Sch. Pub. Adminstrn. U. Southern Calif., v.p. external rels., sr. v.p. external rels., 1998—2001; pres., dir. Natural Hist. Mus. LA County, 2001—. Chair bd. govs. Calif. Cmty. Found.; pres. bd. trustees John Randolph Haynes and Dora Haynes Found.; bd. chair Nat. Acad. Pub. Adminstrn.; mem. Coun. Fgn. Rels.; bd. dirs. WellPoint, Inc. Office: Natural Hist Mus LA County 900 Exposition Blvd Los Angeles CA 90007

PISTER, KARL STARK, engineering educator; b. Stockton, Calif., June 27, 1925; s. Edwin LeRoy and Mary Kimball (Smith) P.; m. Rita Olsen, Nov. 18, 1950; children: Francis, Therese, Anita, Jacinta, Claire, Kristofer. BS with honors, U. Calif., Berkeley, 1945, MS, 1948; PhD, U. Ill., 1952; D of Pub. Policy (hon.), U. Fla., 2004; LHD (hon.), U. Colo., 2005. Instr. theoretical and applied mechanics U. Ill., 1949-52; faculty U. Calif., Berkeley, 1952-62, prof. engring. scis., 1962-96, Roy W. Carlson prof. engring., 1985-90, dean Coll. Engring., 1980-90, Roy W. Carlson prof. emeritus, chancellor Santa Cruz, 1991-96, pres., chancellor emeritus, 1996—, sr. assoc. to pres. Oakland, 1996-99, v.p. ednl. outreach, 1999-2000. Richard Merton guest prof. U. Stuttgart, Germany, 1978; cons. to govt. and industry; bd. dirs. Monterey Bay Aquarium Rsch. Inst.; trustee Am. U. Armenia, Grad. Theol. Union, Berkeley; chmn. bd. Calif. Coun. Sci. and Tech.; bd. dirs. Ctr. Future Tchg. and Learning. Contbr. articles to profl. jours.; mem. editl. bd. Jour. Optimization Theory and Applications, 1982, Ency. Phys. Sci. and Tech. With USNR, WWII. Fulbright scholar, Ireland, 1965, West Germany, 1973; recipient Wason Rsch. medal Am. Concrete Inst., 1960, Vincent Bendix Minorities in Engring. award Am. Soc. for Engring. Edn., 1988, Lamme medal, 1993, Alumni Honor award U. Ill. Coll. Engring., 1982, Disting. Engring. Alumnus award U. Calif. Berkeley Coll. Engring., 1992, Berkeley medal, 1996, U. Calif. Presdl. medal, 2000, World Tech. Network award for policy, World Tech. Coun., London, 2002 Alumnus of Yr. award Calif. Alumni Assn., Berkeley, 2006, Clark Kerr award U. Calif. Berkeley, 2007. Fellow: AAAS, ASME (Applied Mechanics award 1999, Internat. Pres.'s award 2000), Am. Acad. Arts and Scis., Am. Acad. Mechanics, Calif. Acad. Sci. (hon.); mem.: ASCE, NAE. Office: U Calif Dept Civil & Environ Engr Berkeley CA 94720 Office Phone: 510-642-3066. Business E-Mail: pister@ce.berkeley.edu.

PISZEL, ANTHONY S. (BUDDY PISZEL), mortgage company executive; b. 1954; BA in Economics, Rutgers U., NJ; MBA in Acctg., Golden Gate U., San Francisco. Practice fellow Fin. Acctg. Stds. Bd., 1988—90; audit ptnr. Deloitte & Touche, 1990—93; CFO individual life ins. Prudential Fin. Inc., 1993—95, CFO inst. life ins., 1995—97, corp. v.p., 1997—98, sr. v.p., contr., 1998—2004; exec. v.p., CFO Health Net, Inc., Woodland Hills, Calif., 2004—06, Freddie Mac (Fed. Home Loan Mortgage Corp.), McLean, Va., 2006—08; CFO, treas. The First Am. Corp., Santa Ana, Calif., 2009—. Bd. dirs. RehabCare Group, Inc., 2005—. Mem.: AICPA, NJ State Soc. CPAs. Office: The First American Corporation 1 First American Way Santa Ana CA 92707

PITKIN, ROY MACBETH, retired obstetrician, educator; b. Anthon, Iowa, May 24, 1934; s. Roy and Pauline Allie (McBeath) Pitkin; m. Marcia Alice Jenkins, Aug. 17, 1957; children: Barbara, Robert Macbeth, Kathryn, William Charles. BA with highest distinction, U. Iowa, 1956, MD, 1959. Diplomate Am. Bd. Ob-Gyn. Intern King County Hosp., Seattle, 1959—60; resident in ob-gyn U. Iowa Hosps. and Clinics, Iowa City, 1960—63; asst. prof. ob-gyn U. Ill., 1965—68; assoc. prof. ob-gyn U. Iowa, Iowa City, 1968—72, prof., 1972—87, head dept. ob-gyn, 1977—87; prof. UCLA, 1987—97, head dept. ob-gyn., 1987—95, prof. emeritus, 1997—. Mem. residency rev. com. ob-gyn., 1981—87; chmn., 1985—87. Author: The Green Journal 50 Years On, 2003; co-editor: The Best of After Office Hours, 2003; editor-in-chief Year Book of Obstetrics and Gynecology, 1975—86, Clinical Obstetrics and Gynecology, 1979—2000; editor: Obstetrics and Gynecology, 1985—2001; editor emeritus Obstetrics and Gynecology, 2001; contbr. articles to med. jours. Served to lt. comdr. M.C. USNR, 1963—65. Recipient NIH career awardee, 1972—77, Disting. Alumni Achievement award, U. Iowa, 2002. Fellow: Royal Ob-Gyn. (ad eundem); mem.: Coun. Sci. Editors (Dist. Svc. award 2002), Inst. Medicine, NAS, Soc. Perinatal Obstetricians (pres. 1978—79), Soc. Gynecol. Investigation (pres. 1985—86), German Soc. Gyn-Ob. (hon.), Ctrl. Assn. Ob-Gyn., Am. Gyn-Ob. Soc. (pres. 1994—95), Am. Coll. Ob-Gyns., AMA (Goldberger award in clin. nutrition 1982). Presbyterian. Home: 78900 Rancho La Quinta Dr La Quinta CA 92253-6252 E-mail: r.pitkin@earthlink.net.

PITMAN, JIM, professional sports team executive; m. Linda Pitman; children: Amy, Kyle. Grad. in Acctg., U. Ill., 1987. With audit divsn. Arthur Andersen, Phoenix, 1987—92; asst. contr. to corp. contr., v.p. fin. Phoenix Suns, 1992—99, exec. v.p. fin. and adminstrn., 1999—. Treas. Phoenix Suns Charities; bd. mem. US Airways Ctr. Edn. Found., Valley of the Sun YMCA. Avocations: basketball, softball, golf. Office: Phoenix Suns 201 E Jefferson St Phoenix AZ 85004

PIUZE, MICHAEL JOSEPH, lawyer; b. Worcester, Mass., July 31, 1944; s. Albert Charles Piuze and Pauline (Sadick); m. Marnie Smart, Apr. 24, 1971; children: Nicole, Stephanie, Kate. BA, Lake Forest Coll., 1967; JD, U. Tex., Austin, 1971. Bar: Calif. 1972. Atty. Gilbert, Kelly, Crowley & Jennett, LA, 1972—75; sr. mem. Law Offices Michael J. Piuze, LA, 1973—. Named LA Trial Lawyer of Yr., 1996, Southern Calif. Trial Lawyer of Yr., 1998, Calif. Lawyer of Yr., 2001, Winningest Lawyer in US, Nat. Law Jour., 2001, 2002; named one of Best Lawyers in Am., 1993—2006, Top 10 Super Lawyers, LA Mag., 2004, Top 100 LA County Super Lawyers, 2004, 2005, 2006, Top 100 Calif. Atty., Daily Jour., 2000—06, Top 10 Litigators, Nat. Law Jour., 2003. Mem.: LA Trial Lawyers Assn., Calif. Trial Lawyers Assn., Assn. Trial Lawyers Am. Office: 11755 Wilshire Blvd Ste 1170 Los Angeles CA 90025 Office Phone: 310-312-1102. Office Fax: 310-473-0708. Business E-Mail: mpiuze@mjplaw.net.

PIVEN, JEREMY, actor; b. New York, New York, July 26, 1965; s. Byrne and Joyce Piven. Student, Drake U. Actor: (films) Lucas, 1986, One Crazy Summer, 1986, Say Anything, 1989, Elvis Stories, 1989, The Grifters, 1990, White Palace, 1990, The Player, 1992, Body Chemistry II: The Voice of a Stranger, 1992, Bob Roberts, 1992, Singles, 1992, There Goes the Neighborhood, 1992, Judgement Night, 1993, Twenty Bucks, 1993, Car 54, Where Are You?, 1994, Floundering, 1994, PCU, 1994, Twogether, 1994, The Ticket, 1994, Miami Rhapsody, 1995, Dr. Jekyll and Ms. Hyde, 1995, Heat, 1995, Larger Than Life, 1996, Layin' Low, 1996, E=mc—2, 1996, Just Write, 1997, Grosse Pointe Blank, 1997, Livers Ain't Cheap, 1997, Kiss the Girls, 1997, Phoenix, 1998, Very Bad Things, 1998, Music From Another Room, 1998, Red Letters, 2000, The Crew, 2000, The Family Man, 2000, Rush Hour 2, 2001, Serendipity, 2001, Black Hawk Down, 2001, Highway, 2002, Me and Daphne, 2002, Old School, 2003, Runaway Jury, 2003, Scary Movie 3, 2003, Chasing Liberty, 2004, Two for the Money, 2005, Keeping Up with the Steins, 2006, Smokin' Aces, 2006, (voice) Cars, 2006, The Kingdom, 2007, RocknRolla, 2008; (TV films) 12:01, 1993, Don King: Only in America, 1997, Partners, 1999; (TV series) Carol & Company, 1990, Rugrats (voice), 1991, The Larry Sanders Show, 1992—93, Pride and Joy, 1995, Ellen, 1995—98, Cupid, 1998, Entourage, 2004— (Emmy award for Outstanding Supporting Actor in a comedy series, 2006, Primetime Emmy for Outstanding Supporting Actor in a Comedy Series, Acad. TV Art and Scis., 2007, 2008, Best Performance by an Actor in a Supporting Role in a Series, Mini-Series or Motion Picture Made for TV, Golden Globe award, 2008); (Broadway plays) Fat Pig, 2004, Speed-the-Plow, 2008; exec. prodr. Jeremy Piven's Journey of a Lifetime, 2006. Office: c/o Tracy Brennan Creative Artists Agy LCC 2000 Avenue of the Stars Los Angeles CA 90067

PIVEN, PETER ANTHONY, architect, management consultant; b. Bklyn., Jan. 3, 1939; s. William Meyer and Sylvia Lee (Greenberg) P.; m. Caroline Cooper, July 9, 1961; children: Leslie Ann, Joshua Lawrence. AB, Colgate U., Hamilton, NY, 1960; MArch, U. Pa., Phila., 1963; MS, Columbia U., NYC, 1964. Diplomate: cert. Nat. Coun. Archtl. Registration Bds.; registered arch., NY, Pa., NJ. Arch. Westermann-Miller Assocs., NYC, 1964-66, Bernard Rothzeid, A.I.A., NYC, 1967-68; v.p. Caudill Rowlett Scott, NYC, 1968-72; prin. Geddes Brecher Qualls Cunningham, Phila., 1972-87; pres. The Coxe Group, Inc., Phila., 1980-90, dir., prin. cons., 1980—. Adj. prof. U. Pa. Grad. Sch. Fine Arts, 1989—, Rensselaer Poly. Inst. Sch. Architecture, 1994—; vis. instr. Harvard U. Grad. Sch. Design.; lectr. U. Pa. Sch. Design, 2005; mem. 14th edit. com. Architects Handbook Profl. Practice; dir. PennPraxis, 2008. Author: Compensation Management: A Guideline for Small Firms, 1982, Architect's Essentials of Ownership Transition, 2002; co-author: Success Strategies for Design Professionals, 1987, Architect's Essentials of Starting a Design Firm, 2003, Architect's Essentials of Starting, Assessing and Transitioning a Design Firm, 2008; contbg. editor: Archtl. Record and Design Intelligence; author (contbg.): Architects Handbook of Professional Practice, 1994, 2001, 2008, Architects Handbook of Professional Practice Update, 2004, 2005, 2006. Mem. NYC Cmty. Planning Bd., 1969-72. Recipient Thomas U. Walter award, Phila., 2008. Fellow AIA (chmn. fin. mgmt. com. 1976-80, chmn. Fellows Jury 1998, mem. conv. task force 1998, mem. Nat. Ethics Coun. 1998-2004, chmn. 2004, pres. Phila. chpt. 1980); mem. Phila. C. of C. (dir. 1980-81), The Carpenters Co. of City and County of Phila. (mng. com. 1989-91). Home: Apt 10 201 Queen St Philadelphia PA 19147 Office: The Coxe Group Inc 1904 3rd Ave Seattle WA 98101-3097 Home Phone: 215-952-2780. Business E-Mail: ppiven@coxegroup.com.

PIZZO, PHILIP A., dean, pediatrician, educator; b. NYC, Dec. 6, 1944; BA, Fordham U., 1966; MD, U. Rochester, 1970. Diplomate Am. Bd. Pediat., Am. Bd. Hematology/Oncology. Intern Children's Hosp. Med. Ctr., Boston, 1970-71, jr. asst. resident, 1971-72, sr. resident, 1972-73; clin. assoc. Pediatric Oncology Br. of Nat. Cancer Inst., 1973-75, investigator, 1975-76, sr. investigator, 1976-80; head infectious disease sect. Pediatric Br. of Nat. Cancer Inst., 1980-96, chief pediat., 1982-96; sci. dir. divsn. clin. scis. Nat. Cancer Inst., 1994-96; prof. pediat. Sch. Medicine, Uniformed Svcs. U. Health Sci., 1987-96; Thomas Morgan Rotch prof., chmn. dept. pediat. Harvard U. Sch. Medicine, Boston, 1996—2001; dean Stanford U. Sch. Medicine, 2001—. Mem. Elizabeth Glaser Pediatric AIDS Found. (bd. dirs. 1996-2006), Internat. Immunocompromised Host Soc., IDSA (bd. dirs. 1996-99), Calif. Healthcare Inst. (bd. dirs. 2003-), NIH Blue Ribbon Panel, Admin Boal, HAMC, Ind. Citizen Oversight Com., AAHC (bd. dirs. 2006-), Inst. Medicine (coun. 2006-). Office: Stanford U Sch Med 300 Pasteur Dr, Ste M121 Palo Alto CA 94305 Office Phone: 650-724-5688. E-mail: philip.pizzo@stanford.edu.*

PLACENTI, FRANK MICHAEL, lawyer; b. Columbus, Ohio, Sept. 2, 1953; s. Anthony Joseph and Evelyn (Piteo) P.; m. Tobi M. Placenti, Apr. 29, 1971. BA cum laude, Ohio State U., 1975, JD summa cum laude, 1979. Bar: Ariz. 1979, U.S. Dist. Ct. Ariz. 1979, U.S. Ct. Appeals (9th cir.) 1979. Ptnr., transactions and corp. governance Squire, Sanders and Dempsey LLP, Phoenix. Chmn., Phoenix Childrens Hosp. Found. Chmn. Super Bowl Kick-Off Luncheon, 1996, NBA All Star Kick-Off Luncheonj, 1995, Phoenix C. of C., 1991—92, Boys & Girls Clubs Met. Phoenix, 1992—93; chmn. bd. dirs. Phoenix Children's Hosp. Found., 2005—. James K. Barton Meml. scholar Ohio State U., 1977-79; named one of Outstanding Young Men in Am., 1981. Mem. ABA (litigation, communication law and young lawyers sects.), Maricopa County Bar (chmn. com., lectr. on litigation 1985-86), Greater Phoenix Leadership, Phoenix C. of C., Order of Coif, Phi Kappa Theta, Phi Kappa Tau, Phi Eta Sigma. Avocations: golf, travel, wine. Office: Squire Sanders and Dempsey LLP 40 North Central Ave Phoenix AZ 85004-4498 Office Phone: 602-528-4000.

PLAISANCE, MELISSA C., consumer products company executive; b. Feb. 12, 1960; BSBA cum laude, Bucknell U., 1982; MBA, UCLA, 1990. With Bankers Trust Co. Corp. Fin., LA, 1982—90; dir., investor rels. Safeway Inc., 1990—93, v.p., investor rels., 1993—94, v.p., investor rels. & pub. affairs, 1994—95, sr. v.p. fin., investor rels. & pub. affairs Pleasanton, Calif., 1995—2000, sr. v.p., fin. & investor rels., 2000—03, 2004—; sr. v.p., fin. & corp. comm. Del Monte Foods Co., San Francisco, 2004. Office: Safeway Inc PO Box 99 5918 Stoneridge Mall Rd Pleasanton CA 94566-0009

PLAMANN, ALFRED A., wholesale distribution executive; Pres., CEO Cert. Grocers Calif., Unified Grocers Inc. (formerly Unified Western Grocers), Commerce, Calif., 2000—. Office: Unified Grocers Inc 5200 Sheila St City Of Commerce CA 90040

PLANCHON, HARRY PETER, JR., research development manager; b. Aurora, Mo., Aug. 28, 1941; s. Harry P. and Ruth Arminta (Eden) P.; m. Virginia Grace Sapp, June 13, 1964; children: Benjamin John, Matthew Brian. BSME, U. Mo., 1964; MS in Nuclear Engring., U. Ill., 1971, PhD in Nuclear Engring., 1974; MBA, U. Chgo., 1990. Cert. profl. engr. Rsch. assoc., asst. prof. U. Ill. Nuclear Engring. Dept., Urbana, 1970-74; sr. engr., mgr. Clinch River Breeder Reactor Plant Systems Westinghouse Advanced Reaction Div., Madison, Pa., 1974-84; mgr. reactor analysis Exptl. Breeder Reacter Div., Argonne (Ill.) Nat. Lab., 1984-90; assoc. dir. Reacter Analysis Div., Argonne Nat. Lab., 1990-91; assoc. dir. ENG divsn. Argonne Nat. Lab., Idaho Falls, Idaho, 1991-2000, dir. nuclear tech. divsn., 2000—. Contbr. articles to profl. jours. Lt. USN, 1964-70. Fellow Am. Nuc. Soc. (Seaborg medal 1996); mem. Am. Soc. Mech. Engrs., Beta Gamma Sigma, Tau Beta Pi, Pi Mu Epsilon, Pi Tau Sigma. Presbyterian. Avocations: hiking, skiing, photography, golf, reading. Office: Argonne National Laboratory PO Box 1625 Idaho Falls ID 83403-1625

PLANTS, WALTER DALE, retired elementary school educator, minister; b. Middlefield, Ohio, June 8, 1942; s. William E. and Hazel A. Plants; m. Sarah A. Gaddis, July 5, 1962; children: Dale Anthony, Jeanette Marie. BD, Azusa Pacific U., 1967; MEd, U. Nev., 1970. Cert. elem. tchr., ednl. adminstr. Elem. tchr. Churchill County Sch. Dist., Fallon, Nev., 1967—69, 1970—72, elem tchr., 1988—2001; grad. asst. U. Nev., Reno, 1969-70; tchr. Kingman (Ariz.) Elem. Sch. Dist. #4, 1972-77; head sci. program E. C. Best Elem. Sch., Fallon, 1988—2001; ret., 2007. Adj. instr. Ariz. State U., Tempe, 1973-77; cons. sci. Ariz. State Dept. Edn., 1975-77. Bd. dirs. Solar Energy Commn. Mohave County, Ariz., 1974; coord. County Sci. Fair, 1988-93; active Western Regional Sci. Fair Com.; sci. fair coord. Churchill County, 1989-94; mem. com. Regional Sci. Fair, 1992-94; min. non-demoninational ch., 1969-2005. HEW fellow, 1969; NSF grantee, 1973; AIMS Found. scholar, 1988; recipient Ariz. State PTA award, 1977, Ruth Neldon award Ariz. State Dept., 1977, Conservation award Big Sandy Natural Resources Conservation Dist. Ariz., 1976, Community Builder Svc. award Masons, Fallon, 1991, Disting. Leadership award, 1991-93; named State Tchr. of Yr. Nev. PTA, 1991, Conservation Tchr. of Yr., 1991; named to Congl. Select Edn. panel U.S. Congress, 1993. Mem. NEA, AAAS, Nat. Sci. Tchrs. Assn., Nat. Coun. Tchrs. Math., Internat. Reading Assn., Churchill County Edn. Assn. (Tchr. of Yr. 1989), Internat. Platform Assn., Nat. Arbor Day

Found., World Wildlife Fund, Nat. Parks and Conservation Assn., Nat. Audubon Soc., Nev. State Tchrs. of Yr. Assn. (pres. 1994-96, pres. 1996-97), Phi Delta Kappa. Personal E-mail: wpla@charter.net.

PLATE, THOMAS GORDON, columnist, educator; b. NYC, May 17, 1944; s. John William and Irene (Henry) P.; m. Andrea I. Margolis, Sept. 22, 1979; 1 child, Ashley Alexandra. AB, Amherst Coll., 1966; MPA, Princeton U., 1968. Writer Newsweek, NYC, 1968-70; editor Newsday, LI, N.Y., 1970-72; sr. editor N.Y. Mag., NYC, 1972-75; editor edit. page L.A. Herald Examiner, 1978-82; sr. editor Time Mag., NYC, 1982-83; editor in chief Family Weekly, NYC, 1984-85; editor edit. pages N.Y. Newsday, NYC, 1986-89, L.A. Times, 1989-95, Times Op-Ed Page columnist, contbg. editor, 1995—. Adj. prof. UCLA Pub. Policy Sch. and Letters and Scis.; mem. founders bd. UCLA Sch. Pub. Policy; founder Asia Pacific Media Network; participant World Econ. Forum, Davos. Author: Understanding Doomsday, 1971, Crime Pays!, 1975, Secret Police, 1981; co-author: Commissioner, 1978. Recipient Best Deadline Writing award Am. Soc. Newspaper Editors, 1981, Best Edit. awards L.A. Press Club, 1979, 80, 81, Best Edit. award Calif. Newspaper Pubs. Assn., 1991, 92, 94; media fellow Stanford U. Mem. Pacific Coun. on Internat. Rels., Century Assn. (N.Y.C.), Phi Beta Kappa. Avocations: tennis, photography, travel. Office: LA Times 405 Hilgard Ave Los Angeles CA 90095-9000

PLATT, OLIVER, actor; b. Windsor, Ont., Can., Jan. 12, 1960; s. Nicholas Platt and Sheila Maynard; m. Camilla Campbell, 1993; children: Lily, George, Claire. Attended, Tufts U. Actor: (films) Crusoe, 1988, Married to the Mob, 1988, Working Girl, 1988, Flatliners, 1990, Postcards from the Edge, 1990, Beethoven, 1992, Diggstown, 1992, Benny & Joon, 1993, Indecent Proposal, 1993, The Temp, 1993, The Three Musketeers, 1993, Tall Tale, 1995, Funny Bones, 1995, Executive Decision, 1996, A Time to Kill, 1996, Venice, 1997, Bulworth, 1997, Dangerous Beauty, 1998, Doctor Dolittle, 1998, A Small Miracle, 1998, The Impostors, 1998, Simon Birch, 1998, Three to Tango, 1999, Gun Shy, 1999, Lake Placid, 1999, Bicentennial Man, 1999, Gun Shy, 2000, Ready to Rumble, 2000, Don't Say a Word, 2001, Liberty Stands Still, 2002, ZigZag, 2002, Ash Wednesday, 2002, Pieces of April, 2003, Hope Springs, 2003, Kinsey, 2004, Loverboy, 2005, The Ice Harvest, 2005, Casonova, 2005, The Ten, 2007, Martian Child, 2007, Frost/Nixon, 2008, (TV films) The Infiltrator, 1995, Cinderelmo, 1999, (TV series) Deadline, 2000-01, Queens Supreme, 2003, Huff, 2004-, (Broadway plays) Shining City, 2006; assoc. prodr. (film) Big Night, 1996. Office: c/o William Morris Agy 151 S El Camino Dr Beverly Hills CA 90212-2704

PLATT, WARREN E., lawyer; b. McNary, Ariz., Aug. 5, 1943; BA, Mich. State U., 1965; JD, U. Ariz., 1969. Bar: Ariz. 1969, Calif. 1991, Texas 1993. Atty. Snell & Wilmer, Phoenix. Mng. editor Ariz. Law Rev., 1968—69. Fellow Am. Coll. Trial Lawyers; mem. Blue Key, Order of Coif, Phi Alpha Delta Office: Snell & Wilmer One Arizona Ctr Phoenix AZ 85004-0001 also: 6000 Anton Blvd Ste 1400 Costa Mesa CA 92626 Office Phone: 602-382-6292, 714-427-7475. Business E-Mail: wplatt@swlaw.com.

PLEASANTS, JOHN F., electronics executive; b. 1965; m. Jennifer Pleasants; children: Jack, James. BA in Polit. Sci., Yale U., 1987; MBA, Harvard U., 1993. With Frito-Lay divsn. PepsiCo; with Hygiene Industries; gen. mgr., new mkts. divsn. City Search IAC / InterActive Corp, 1996; exec. v.p. new markets Ticketmaster Online-CitySearch (divsn. IAC/InterActiveCorp), Pasadena, Calif., pres. ticketing & transactions; pres. info. sys., CEO Ticketmaster, Pasadena, Calif., 2000—03; pres., CEO Ticketmaster, Reserve Am., Ticketweb, Pasadena, 2003—05, Revolution Health Group, 2005—08; pres. global publishing, COO Electronic Arts, Inc., Redwood City, Calif., 2008—. Bd. dir. Ticketmaster7, Australia, The Active Network, La Jolla, Calif. Office: Electronic Arts Inc 209 Redwood Shores Pky Redwood City CA 94065

PLETSCH, MARIE ELEANOR, plastic surgeon; b. Walkerton, Ont., Can., May 3, 1938; came to U.S. 1962; d. Ernest John and Olive Wilhemina (Hossfeld) P.; m. Ludwig Philip Breiling, Aug. 25, 1967; children: John, Michael, Anne. MD, U. Toronto, 1962. Diplomate Am. Bd. Plastic Surgery. Intern Cook County Hosp., Chgo., 1962-63, resident, gen. surgery, 1963-64, St. Mary's Hosp., San Francisco, 1964-66; resident in plastic surgery St. Francis Hosp., San Francisco, 1966-69; practice med. specializing in plastic surgery Santa Cruz, Calif., 1969—; Monterey, Calif., 1990—; adminstr. Plasticenter, Inc., Santa Cruz, 1976-88, med. dir., 1987-88. Mem. AMA, Am. Soc. Plastic and Reconstructive Surgeons, Calif. Soc. Plastic Surgeons (mem. coun. 1986-89, sec. 1989-93, v.p. 1994-95, pres. elect 1995-96, pres. 1996-97), Am. Soc. Aesthetic Plastic Surgeons, Calif. Med. Assn., Assn. Calif. Surgery Ctrs. (pres. 1988-92), Santa Cruz County Med. Soc. (bd. govs. 1983-88, 1992-94), Santa Cruz Surgery Ctr. (bd. dirs. 1988-93, 2004—). Roman Catholic.: 24571 Silver Cloud Ct Monterey CA 93940 Office: Santa Cruz Can Am Medical 223A Mount Hermon Rd Scotts Valley CA 95066- Office Phone: 831-462-1000. Personal E-mail: pletsch@pacbell.net.

PLIMPTON, THOMAS E., automotive executive; BS in Acctg., U. Kans.; MBA, Rockhurst Coll. Asst. gen. mgr. Peterbilt, Newark, Calif., gen. mgr., 1992—96; with Foden Truck Co. PACCAR Inc., England, exec. v.p. Bellevue, Wash., 1998—2002, pres., 2002—08, vice-chmn., 2008—. Dir. PACCAR Fin. Corp. Avocations: golf, college football, basketball, reading. Office: Paccar Inc 777 106th Ave Bellevue WA 98004 Mailing: Paccar Inc PO Box 1518 Bellevue WA 98009

PLISHNER, MICHAEL JON, lawyer; b. Rockville Center, NY, Jan. 22, 1948; s. Meyer J. and Lillian (Gold) P.; m. Rosalind F. Schein, Jan. 26, 1969; children: Aaron, Alexander, Elias. BA summa cum laude, Yale U., 1969, JD, 1972. Bar: Calif. 1972, U.S. Dist. Ct. (no. dist.) Calif. 1972, U.S. Ct. Appeals (9th cir.) 1972. Assoc. McCutchen, Doyle, Brown & Enersen, San Francisco, 1972-79, ptnr., 1979—2001, Bingham McCutchen, San Francisco, 2001—, dep. chmn. litig. practice group. Mem. Phi Beta Kappa. Office: Bingham McCutchen LLP 3 Embarcadero Ctr San Francisco CA 94111-4003 Office Phone: 415-393-2240. Business E-Mail: michael.plishner@bingham.com.

PLISKOW, VITA SARI, anesthesiologist; b. Tel Aviv, Sept. 13, 1942; arrived in Can., 1951; came to U.S., 1967; d. Henry Norman and Renee (Mushkatel) Stahl; m. Raymond Joel Pliskow, June 30, 1968; children: Tia, Kami. MD, U. B.C., Vancouver, 1967. Diplomate Am. Bd. Anesthesiology. Ptnr. Olympic Anesthesia, Bremerton, Wash., 1971-84, pres., anesthesiologist, 1974-84; co-founder Olympic Ambulatory Surgery Ctr., Bremerton, 1977-83; ptnr., anesthesiologist Allenmore Anesthesia Assocs., Tacoma, 1983—. Staff anesthesiologist Harrison Meml. Hosp., Bremerton, 1971-95, Allenmore Hosp., Tacoma, 1983—. Trustee Tacoma Youth Symphony Assn., 1994—; active Nat. Coun. Jewish Women, 1972—. Fellow Am. Coll. Anesthesiologists, Am. Coll. Chest Physicians; mem. Am. Soc. Anesthesiologists (del. Wash. State 1987—), Wash. State Med. Assn. (del. Pierce County 1993-94), Wash. State Soc. Anesthesiologists (pres. 1985-87), Pierce County Med. Soc. (sec.-treas. 1992). Avocations: classical music, opera, singing (mezzo soprano). Office: Vita Pliskow Md Pc PO Box 97115 Lakewood WA 98497-0115

PLOMP, TEUNIS (TONY PLOMP), minister; b. Rotterdam, Netherlands, Jan. 28, 1938; arrived in Can., 1951; s. Teunis and Cornelia (Pietersma) P.; m. Margaret Louise Bone, July 21, 1962; children: Jennifer Anne, Deborah Adele. BA, U. B.C., Vancouver, Can., 1960; BD, Knox Coll., Toronto, Ont., Can., 1963, DD (hon.), 1988. Ordained to ministry Presbyn. Ch., 1963. Min. Goforth Meml. Presbyn. Ch., Saskatoon, Sask., Canada, 1963-68, Richmond (B.C.) Presbyn. Ch., 1968—2004. Clerk Presbytery of Westminster, Vancouver, 1969-2003; moderator 113th Gen. Assembly Presbyn. Ch. Can., 1987-88, dep. clk., 1988—; chaplain New Haven Correctional Centre, Burnaby, B.C., 1973-99. Contbr. mag. column You Were Asking, 1982-2002. Presbyterian. Avocations: record collecting, bicycling, swimming. Personal E-mail: tony_plomp@telus.net.

PLOPPER, CHARLES GEORGE, anatomist, cell biologist; b. Oakland, Calif., June 16, 1944; s. George Eli and Josephine Viola P.; m. Suzanne May, Nov. 9, 1969. AB, U. Calif., Davis, 1967, PhD, 1972. Chief. electron microscopy br. U.S. Army Med. Research Nutrition Lab., Denver, 1972-73; vis. scientist Calif. Primate Research Ctr., Davis, 1974-75; chief. electron microscopy div. Letterman Army Inst. Research, San Francisco, 1974-75; asst. prof. U. Hawaii Sch. Medicine, Honolulu, 1975-77; assoc. prof. Kuwait U. Sch. Medicine, 1977-78; sr. staff fellow Nat. Inst. Environ. Health Sci. Research, Triangle Park, N.C., 1978-79; from asst. to assoc. prof. U. Calif. Sch. Vet. Medicine, Davis, 1979-86, dept. chmn., 1984-88, 96—; prof. anatomy, physiology and cell biology, Sch. Vet. Medicine U. Calif., Davis, 1986—. Mem. study sect. NIH div. Research Grants, Bethesda, Md., 1986-90; Paley vis. prof. Boston U. Sch. Medicine, 1985; vis. pulmonary scholar Duke U., U. N.C., N.C. State U., 1991. Served to capt. U.S. Army, 1972-75. Recipient Norden Teaching award, Faculty Rsch. award. Mem. Am. Soc. Cell Biology, Am. Thoracic Soc., Am. Assn. Antomists, Am. Assn. Pathologists, Anat. Soc. Great Britain and Ireland, Davis Aquatic Masters (bd. dirs. 1993-95). Democrat. Avocations: swimming, hiking, tennis. Office: Univ Calif Sch Vet Medicine Dept Anatomy Physiol Cell Biology Davis CA 95616 Home: PO Box 395 Chester CA 96020-0395

PLOTKIN, ALLEN, aerospace engineer, educator; b. NYC, May 4, 1942; s. Oscar and Claire (Chasick) P.; m. Selena Berman, Dec. 18, 1966; children: Samantha Rose, Jennifer Anne. BS, Columbia U., 1963, MS, 1964; PhD, Stanford U., 1968. Asst. prof. aerospace engring. U. Md., College Park, 1968-72, assoc. prof., 1972-77, prof., 1977-85; prof. dept. aerospace engring. San Diego State U., 1985—, chmn. dept., 1985-90, 93-96, 2008—. Vis. assoc. Calif. Inst. Tech., Pasadena, 1975-76; cons. Naval Surface Weapons Ctr., White Oak, Md., 1981-84. Co-author: Low-Speed Aerodynamics, 1991, 2d edit., 2001. Recipient Engring. Sci. award Washington Acad. Scis., 1981; rsch. grantee NASA, NSF; NASA-Am. Soc. Engring. Edn. summer faculty fellow, 1969, 70. Fellow AIAA (assoc., assoc. editor jour. 1986—, Young Engr.-Scientist award Nat. Capital sect. 1976, Sustained Svc. award 2003, J. Leland Atwood award, 2005), ASME; mem. Soc. Naval Architects and Marine Engrs., Am. Soc. Engring. Edn., Aerospace Dept. Chairmen's Assn. (chmn. 1989-90), Sigma Xi, Tau Beta Pi. Democrat. Jewish. Avocations: jogging, reading, country music. Home: 17364 St Andrews Dr Poway CA 92064-1231 Office: San Diego State U Dept Aerospace Engring San Diego CA 92182 Office Phone: 619-594-7019.

PLOTNICK, ROBERT DAVID, economic consultant, educator; b. Washington, Aug. 3, 1949; s. Theodore and Jean (Hirshfeld) P.; m. Gay Lee (Jensen), Dec. 22, 1972. BA, Princeton U., 1971; MA, U. Calif., Berkeley, 1973, PhD, 1976. Rsch. assoc. Inst. Rsch. on Poverty, Madison, Wis., 1973—75; asst. prof. Bates Coll., Lewiston, Maine, 1975—77, Dartmouth Coll., Hanover, NH, 1977—84; assoc. prof. U. Wash., Seattle, 1984—90, prof., 1990, assoc. dean, 1990—95, acting dean, 1994—95. Vis. scholar Russell Sage Found., 1990, U. NSW, 1997, London Sch. Econs., 2004; rsch. affiliate Inst. Rsch. Poverty, 1989—, Nat. Poverty Ctr., 2004—; chmn. Population Leadership Program, 1999—2005; dir. Ctr. for Studies in Demography and Ecology, 1997—2002; adj. fellow Pub. Policy Inst. Calif., 1998—2000; cons. Wash. Dept. Social and Health Svcs., Olympia, 1984—86, 1990—96, 2000; cons. in field; rsch. affiliate West Coast Poverty Ctr., 2005—, assoc. dir., 2008—. Author: Progress Against Poverty, 1975; contbr. articles to profl. journals. Recipient Teaching Excellence Award U. Wash., 1985, 89. Mem. Am. Econ. Assn., Assn. Policy Analysis and Mgmt., Population Assn. Am. Avocations: hiking, birdwatching. Office: U Wash Evans Sch Pub Affairs PO Box 353055 Seattle WA 98195-3055 Office Phone: 206-685-2055. Business E-Mail: plotnick@u.washington.edu.

PLOTT, CHARLES RAYMOND, economics educator; b. Frederick, Okla., July 8, 1938; s. James Charles and Flossie Ann (Bowman) P.; m. Marianna Brown Cloninger, May 30, 1961; children: Rebecca Ann, Charles Hugh. BS in Prodn. Mgmt., Okla. State U., 1961, MS in Economics, 1964; PhD in Economics, U. Va., 1965; LHD (hon.), Purdue U., 1995; degree (hon.), L'université Pierre Mendès France, Grenoble, 1996. Asst. prof. economics Purdue U., 1965—67, assoc. prof. economics, 1968-70; Edward S. Harkness prof. econs. and polit. sci. Calif. Inst. Tech., Pasadena, 1971—, dir. Program for Study of Enterprise and Pub. Policy, 1979—, dir. Lab. for Exptl. Econs. and Polit. Sci., 1987—. Prin. investigator, NSF, 1972-; mem. Environ. Quality Lab., Calif. Inst. Tech., 1972, Resources for the Future, 1973; vis. prof. law U. So. Calif. Law Ctr., 1976; vis. prof. Stanford U., 1968-69, U. Chgo., 1980; Hooker Disting. prof., McMaster U., 1983; chmn. review bd. Calif. Inst. Tech.; mem. bd. on behavioral, cognitive and sensory scis., NRC Commn. on Behavioral and Social Scis. and Edn., 1997-2003; bd. dir. Lee Pharm., 1978-95. Author works in fields of econs., polit. sci., philosophy, exptl. methods, math. methods; contbr. articles to profl. jours.; mem. edit. bd. Social Sci. Rsch., 1976-77, Pub. Choice, 1973-90, Jour. Econ. Behavior, 1983-85, Econ. Theory, 1994-. Named to Coll. Bus. Hall of Fame Okla. State U., 1988; Ford Found. fellow, 1968, Guggenheim fellow, 1981-82, fellow Ctr. for Advanced Studies in Behavioral Scis., 1981-82, sr. rsch. fellow, Inst. for Policy Reform, 1992-93; Fulbright Scholar, 2006; NSF grantee, 1972, 74, 78, 79, 80, 83, 86, 88, 92, 95, 98, 2000; recipient Jour. of Finance Markets award, 1994, Best Paper award, 2003, GSAM Quant Best Paper prize, Review of Finance, 2004, Economic Inquiry 2006 Best Article award, GAIM Rsch. Paper of Yr. 2006 award. Fellow Am. Acad. Arts and Scis., Econometric Soc.; mem. Am. Econ. Assn., Econ. Sci. Assn. (pres. 1987-88), So. Econ. Assn. (mem. exec. com. 1977-78, v.p. 1985-87, pres. 1989-90, Georgescu-Roegen prize, 1995), Pub. Choice Soc. (pres. 1977-78), Western Econ. Assn. Internat. (v.p. 1996-97, pres. 1998-99), Consortium of Social Scis. Assns. (bd. dir. 1996-98), Royal Econ. Assn., Am. Polit. Sci. Assn., Econs. Sci. Assn. (pres. 1987-88), Mont Pelerin Soc., Pub. Choice Soc. (pres. 1976-78), The Mont Pèlerin Soc., NAS. Office: Calif Inst Tech Divsn Humanities & Social Scis 337 Baxter Hall MC 228-77 Pasadena CA 91125 Office Phone: 626-395-4209. Office Fax: 626-793-8580. Business E-Mail: cplott@hss.caltech.edu.

PLOUGH, ALONZO L., city health department administrator; BA in Biology, San Diego State U., 1973; MA in Sociology, Cornell U., 1975; MPH, Yale U. Sch. Medicine, 1977; PhD in Anthropology, Cornell U., 1978. Lectr., health policy and mgmt. Harvard U. Sch. Pub. Health, Cambridge, Mass., 1985—95; dep. commr., dir., pub. health Boston Dept. Health and Hosps., 1989—95; assoc. prof., health svcs. U. Wash. Sch. Pub. Health and Cmty. Medicine, 1995—; dir., health officer Seattle-King Co. Health Dept., 1995—. Mem., scientific adv. com. Nat. Ctr. for Health Statistics. Bd. dirs. Am. Lung Assn. of Wash., United Way of King Co., Wash. Dental Found.; chair, bd. Edn. Devel. Ctr., Inc.; chair, adv. com. King Co. Health Action Plan. Mem.: Nat. Assn. of City and County Health Officials. Office: Seattle-King Co Health Dept 999 Third Ave Ste 1200 Seattle WA 98104

PLOURD, CHRISTOPHER JOHN, lawyer, consultant; b. 1955; BA, Butler U., Indpls., 1977; JD, Thomas Jefferson Coll. Law, San Diego, 1980. Bar: Calif. 1981, US Dist. Ct. (so. dist. Calif.) 1981, cert.: State Bar Calif. (criminal law) 1991, bar: US Dist. Ct. (dist. Ariz.) 1995. Atty. Plourd, Blume, Scoville, Strickland & Breeze, P.C., El Centro, Calif., 1980—82; asst. pub. defender Imperial County Pub. Defenders Office, El Centro, 1983—86; staff atty. Defenders Inc., 1986—88; prin. Law Office of Christopher J. Plourd, San Diego, 1988—. Forensic sci. evidence cons. Mem.: San Diego Lawyers Club, Calif. Pub. Defenders Assn., NY Acad. Scis., Calif. Attys. for Criminal Justice, San Diego County Bar Assn., Am. Soc. Forensic Odontology, AAAS, Am. Acad. Forensic Scis. Office: Law Office of Christopher J Plourd 1168 Union St Ste 303 San Diego CA 92101 Office Phone: 619-615-6200. Office Fax: 619-615-6204. E-mail: dnacjp@flash.net.

PLOVNICK, MARK STEPHEN, business educator; b. NYC, June 8, 1946; s. Jacob and Dorothy Edith (Berger) Plovnick; m. Daisy Shulan Chan, Mar. 13, 1982. BSME, Union Coll., 1968; BA in Econs., Union Coll., 1968; MS in Mgmt., MIT, 1970, PhD in Mgmt., 1975. Instr., rschr. MIT, Cambridge, 1970—76; asst. prof. Clark Univ., Worcester, Mass., 1976—79, assoc. prof., 1979—89, chmn. dept. mgmt., 1979—82, assoc. dean Grad. Sch. Mgmt., 1982—89; prof. and dean Eberhardt Sch. Bus. U. Pacific, Stockton, Calif., 1989—2006, dir. economic devel., 2006—. Cons. to various orgns., 1970—; dir. Devel. Rsch. Assocs., Reston, Va., 1979—82; adj. assoc. prof. U. Mass. Med. Sch., Worcester, Mass., 1982—89; adj. asst. prof. Boston Univ. Sch. Medicine, 1974—75; clin. instr. Harvard Med. Sch., Boston, 1977—78. Author: 5 books; contbr. numerous articles to profl. jours. Mem. Civil Svc. Commn., San Joaquin County, 1989—94; mem. gen. plan action team City of Stockton, 2004—; editl. bd. Comstock's Mag., 2006—; bd. dirs. United Way, 1991—94, Goodwill Industries, 1992—, Stockton Symphony, 1995—2001, Stockton Rotary Endowment, 2005—, No. Calif. World Trade Ctr., 2006—, Bank of Agrl. and Commerce, 2006—. Mem.: San Joaquin Angels (bd. dirs. 2008—), San Joaquin County Pub. Facilities Financing Corp. (bd. dirs. 2006—), Greater Stockton C. of C. (bd. dirs. 1990—94, 2006—), Yosemite Club (bd. dirs. 2004—). Office: Univ Pacific Stockton CA 95211-0001 E-mail: mplovnic@pacific.edu.

PLUMMER, CHRISTOPHER (ARTHUR PLUMMER), actor; b. Toronto, Ont., Can., Dec. 13, 1929; s. John and Isabella Mary (Abbott) P.; m. Tammy Grimes, Aug. 19, 1956 (div. 1960); 1 child, Amanda; m. Particia Audrew Lewis, May 4, 1962 (div. 1967); m. Elaine Taylor, 1970. Student pub. and pvt. schs., Can.; pupil, Iris Warren, C. Herbertcasari; LLD (hon.), U. We. Ont., 2004; DFA (hon.), NY Julliard Sch.; PhD (hon.), U. Toronto, Ryerson and Western Ont. Stage debut in The Rivals with Can. Repertory Theatre, 1950; Broadway debut in Starcross Story, 1954, J.B.; London debut in Becket, 1961; leading actor Cymbeline, Am. Shakespeare Theatre, Stratford, Conn., 1955, Royal Shakespeare Co., London and Stratford, Avon, Eng., 1961-62, Stratford (Ont.) Shakespeare Festival, 1956, 57, 58, 60, 62, 67, Nat. Theatre Co., London; radio roles include Shakespeare, Canada; plays include Home is the Hero, 1954, Twelfth Night, 1954, 70-71, Dark is Light Enough, The Lark, Julius Caesar, The Tempest, 1955, (rearranger with Sir Neville Mariner) Henry VI, 1956, Hamlet, 1957, Winter's Tale, 1958, Much Ado About Nothing, 1958, J.B., 1958, King John, 1960, Romeo and Juliet, 1960, Richard III, 1961, Arturo Ui, 1963, The Royal Hunt of the Sun, 1965, Antony and Cleopatra, 1967, Danton's Death, 1971, Amphitryon 38, 1971, The Constant Wife, The Dark is Light Enough (Theatre World award), Medea, The Lark; (musicals) Cyrano, 1973 (Tony award for Best Actor in a Musical, 1974), The Good Doctor, 1973, Love and Master Will, 1975; performer (with Sir Neville Mariner and rearranged by Michael Lankester) A Midsummer's Night's Dream; Othello, 1982, Macbeth, 1988, No Man's Land, 1993, Barrymore, 1996 (Tony award for best actor in a play, 1997, Drama Desk, Outer Critics Cr. award, Edwin Booth award, Boston Critics' award, Chgo.'s Jefferson award, LA Ovation award best actor 1997-98), King Lear, 2004 (Tony nom. best actor in a play, 2004), Inherit the Wind, 2007; made TV debut 1953; TV prodns. include Little Moon of Alban, Johnny Belinda, 1958, Cyrano de Bergerac, 1962, Oedipus Rex, After the Fall, 1974, The Doll's House, The Prince and the Pauper, Prisoner of Zenda, Hamlet at Elsinore, BBC, 1964, Time Remembered, Capt. Brassbound's Conversion, The Shadow Box, 1981, The Thornbirds, 1983, Little Gloria-Happy at Last, A Hazard of Hearts, 1987, Crossings, 1986, Danielle Steele's Secrets, 1992, Liar's Edge, 1992, On Golden Pond, 2001, Night Flight, 2002; star TV series The Moneychangers, 1977, Harrison Bergeron, 1995, We the Jury, 1996, The Conspiracy of Fear, 1996; actor: (films) Stage Struck, 1957, Wind Across the Everglades, 1958, The Fall of the Roman Empire, 1963, Inside Daisy Clover, 1965, Sound of Music (Acad. award), 1965, Triple Cross, 1967, Nobody Runs Forever, 1969, The Battle of Britain, 1969, The Royal Hunt of the Sun, 1969, Lock up your Daughters, 1969, The Phyx, 1970, Waterloo, 1971, The Man Who Would Be King, 1975, The Return of the Pink Panther, 1975, Conduct Unbecoming, 1975, International Velvet, 1978, Murder By Decree, 1979, Starcrash, 1979, The Silent Partner, 1979, Hanover Street, 1979, Somewhere in Time,

1980, Eyewitness, 1981, The Disappearance, 1981, The Amateur, 1982, Dreamscape, 1984, Ordeal by Innocence, 1984, Lily in Love, 1985, The Boss' Wife, 1986, The Boy In Blue, 1986, An American Tail, 1986 (voice), Souvenir, 1987, Dragnet, 1987, Light Years (voice), 1988, Where the Heart Is, 1989, Fire Head, 1991, Star Trek: VI: The Undiscovered Country, 1991, Rock a Doodle, 1992 (voice), Malcolm X, 1992, Wolf, 1994, Dolores Claiborne, 1994, Twelve Monkeys, 1995, Skeletons, 1996, The Arrow, 1997, Hidden Agenda, 1998, The Clown at Midnight, 1998, Blackheart, The Insider (Boston, L.A., Chgo., Las Vegas and Nat. Critics's awards), 1999, All the Fine Lines, 1999, The Dinosaur Hunter, 2000, Dracula 2000, A Beautiful Mind, 2001, Nicholas Nickleby, 2002, Ararat, 2002, Blizzard, 2003, Cold Creek Manor, 2003, National Treasure, 2004, Alexander, 2004, Tma, 2005, Must Love Dogs, 2005,, Syriana, 2005, The New World, 2005, Inside Man, 2006, The Lake House, 2006; (TV movies) Winchell, 1998, Four Minute Mile, 2005, Our Fathers, 2005; (TV mini-series) Celebrate the Century, 1999, Nuremberg, 2000, American Tragedy, 2000; Author: In Spite of Myself: A Memoir, 2008 Decorated companion Order of Can., 1968; recipient Theatre World award, 1955, Evening Std. Theatre award, 1961, Delia Austrian medal, 1973, 2 Drama Desk awards, 1973, 82, Antoinette Perry award, 1974, Emmy award Nat. Acad. TV Arts and Scis., 1977, Genie award, Can., 1980, Golden Badge of Honor, Austria, 1982, Maple Leaf award Nat. Acad. Arts and Letters, many honors Eng., Austria, Can., Two Tony awards (seven nominations), Two Emmy awards (six nominations), Gt. Britain's Evening Std. award, Can.'s Genie award, Gov. Gen's Lifetime Achievement award, 2001, William Shakespeare award (Will award) classical theatre, Nat. Bd. Rev. Career Achievement award, NY., Jason Robard's award excellence in memory great friend, 2002; inducted in Am.'s Theatre's Hall of Fame, 1986, Can.'s Walk of Fame, 1997. Office: c/o Lou Pitt The Pitt Group 9465 Wilshire Blvd Ste 480 Beverly Hills CA 90212-2612

PLUMMER, JAMES D., electrical engineering educator, dean; BS in elec. engring., UCLA, 1966; MS in elec. engring., Stanford U., 1967, PhD in elec. engring., 1971. Rsch. assoc. Stanford U., 1971—74, sr. rsch. assoc., 1974—78, assoc. dir. integrated circuits lab., 1974—84, dir. integrated circuits lab., 1984—93, assoc. prof. elec. engring., 1978—83, prof. elec. engring., 1983—, John M. Fluke Prof. Elec. Engring., 1988—, prof. (by courtesy) materials sci. and engring., 1996—, sr. assoc. dean. Sch. Engring., 1993—96, Frederick Emmons Terman dean. Sch. Engring., 1999—, chmn. elec. engring. dept., 1997—99, dir. Stanford Nanofabrication Facility, 1994—2000; nat. dir. NSF Nat. Nanofabrication Users Network, 1995—2000. Cons. to numerous semiconductor and other companies, 1970—; mem. bd. dirs. Internat. Rectifier, 1995—; mem. Cypress Semiconductor Tech. Adv. Bd., 1995-; Herbert H. Johnson lectr. in materials sci. and engring. Cornell U., 1998. Author, co-author of over 300 publs.; patentee in field. Recipient Outstanding Paper Award, Internat. Solid-State Circuits Conf., 1970, 1976, 1978, Outstanding Svc. Award, Elec. Engring. Dept., Stanford U., 1988, 2 Inventor Recognition Awards, Semiconductor Rsch. Corp., Tau Beta Pi Undergrad. Tchg. Award, Sch. Engring., Stanford U., 1992, Best Tchr. Award, Soc. Women Engineers, 1995, J.J. Ebbers award, IEEE, 2003, Aldert Van der Ziel award, 2003, Jacob Millman award, McGraw/Hill, 2004. Fellow: Am. Acad. Arts and Sciences, IEEE (Third Millenium Medal 2000); mem.: NAE, Materials Rsch. Soc., Am. Phys. Soc., Electrochem. Soc. (Solid State Sci. and Tech. Award 1991), Sigma Xi, Tau Beta Pi. Office: Stanford U Sch Engring 380 Panama Mall, 214 Terman Stanford CA 94305-4027

PODBOY, JOHN WATTS, clinical, forensic psychologist; b. York, Pa., Sept. 27, 1943; s. August John and Harriett Virginia (Watts) P.; 1 son, Matthew John. B.A., Dickinson Coll., 1966; M.S., San Diego State Coll., 1971; Ph.D., U. Ariz., 1973. Dir., Vets. Counseling Center, U. Ariz., Tucson, 1972-73; project dir. San Mateo County (Calif.) Human Relations Dept., Redwood City, 1974; staff psychologist Sonoma State Hosp., Eldridge, Calif., 1975-81; cons. clin. psychologist Comprehensive Care Corp., Newport Beach, Calif., 1974-75, Sonoma County (Calif.) Probation Dept., 1976-88; pvt. practice, Kenwood, Calif., 1982—; cons. to Calif. Superior Cts., 1983-85; asst. prof. Sonoma State U., 1977-81; dir. Sonoma Diagnostic and Remedial Center, 1979-82. Chmn. San Mateo County Diabetes Assn., 1975. Served to lt. USNR, 1966-69. Fellow Am. Coll. Forensic Psychology, Am. Bd. Med. Psychotherapists (fellow); mem. APA, Western Psychol. Assn., Redwood Psychol. Assn. (pres. 1983), Nat. Council Alcoholism, Nat. Rehab. Assn. Home: PO Box 488 Kenwood CA 95452-0488 Office Phone: 707-833-6023. Personal E-mail: ikpod@yahoo.com.

POE, JERRY B., financial educator; b. Springfield, Mo., Oct. 3, 1931; s. Carlyle and Eunice P.; m. Carol J. Mussler, Sept. 9, 1959; children: Cheryl Marie, Jennifer Brenna. AB, Drury Coll., 1953; MBA (Weinheimer fellow), Washington U., St. Louis, 1957; DBA (Ford Found. fellow), Harvard U., 1963. Instr. U. Ark., spring 1957; indsl. engr. McDonnell Aircraft Corp., St. Louis, 1957; lectr. on fin. Boston U., 1959-61; asst. prof. bus. adminstrn. Drury Coll., 1961-64, assoc. prof., 1964-68, prof., 1968-74; dir. Breech Sch. Bus. Adminstrn., 1968-74; prof. emeritus Ariz. State U., 2000—, prof. fin., 1974—2000, chmn. dept. fin., 1974-82. Vis. prof. Fla. Tech. U., 1971; examiner, mem. Higher Learning Commn. of the North Cetrl. Assn. Colls. and Schs.; dir. NDEA Inst. Econs.; cons. in field Author: Essentials of Finance: An Integrated Approach, 1995, An Introduction to the American Business Enterprise, 1969, 7th rev. edit., 1989, Cases in Financial Management, 1977, 3d rev. edit., 1987. Mem. Regional Manpower Adv. Com.; mem. bus. and profl. adv. council Empire Bank. Served to lt. comdr. USNR, 1953-55. Recipient Hall Fame, Br. Sch. Bus. Adminstrn., 2006. Mem. Fin. Mgmt. Assn., Kappa Alpha, Beta Gamma Sigma, Omicron Delta Kappa. Methodist. Office: Ariz State U Coll Bus Dept Fin Tempe AZ 85287-3906

POE, LAURA, nursing educator, administrator; b. Salt Lake City, July 20, 1962; d. William D. and Laree Jardine (Birch) P. Grad., Utah Tech. Coll., 1980; A degree, Brigham Young U., 1984, B, 1986, MS, 1988. Asst. dir. Divsn. Occupl. and Profl. Licensing Utah Bd. Nursing, exec. dir. Author: (with others) Geri-Assistant Care Manual; contbr. articles to profl. jours. Mem. Utah Nurses Assn. (del., chair govt. rels. com.), Nightingale Soc., Phi Kappa Phi, Sigma Theta Tau.

POE, ROBERT ALAN, lawyer; b. Bracken County, Ky., Apr. 25, 1951; Student, U. Ky.; BA, Centre Coll., 1973; JD, U. Va., 1976. Bar: Colo. 1976. Mem. Holland & Hart, Denver, 1976—. Adj. prof. taxation U. Denver, 1986-88. Articles editor Va. Law Rev., 1974-76. Mem. ABA, Order of Coif, Phi Beta Kappa. Office: Holland & Hart 8390 E Crescent Pkwy Ste 400 Greenwood Village CO 80111-2822 Home Phone: 303-766-7694; Office Phone: 303-290-1616. E-mail: apoe@hollandhart.com.

POE, ROBERT GEORGE, JR., state official, management and finance consultant; b. St. Louis, July 27, 1954; s. Robert G. and Julie Ann (Deibel) P.; m. Cathy Annette August, Apr. 25, 1981 (div. Apr. 1984); m. Kelly Ann Cecil, Jan. 6, 1990. BSBA, U. Mo., St. Louis, 1977, MBA, 1979. Sr. cons. Price Waterhouse, St. Louis, 1979-83; mgr. Coopers & Lybrand, Anchorage, 1984-86; dep. commr. Alaska Dept. Transp. and Pub. Facilities, Juneau, 1987-88; dir. Alaska Gov.'s Office Internat. Trade, Anchorage, 1987—. Bd. dirs., advisor World Trade Ctr., Anchorage, 1989—; bd. dirs. Alaska Ctr. for Internat. Bus., Anchorage, 1990—; chmn. No. Regions Conf. Corp., Anchorage, 1990—. Treas. Cowper for Gov. Alaska, Anchorage, 1985-86. Roman Catholic. Avocations: mountain climbing, skiing, motorcycling. Office: Trade Link Inc 2712 Montana Ave Apt C Santa Monica CA 90403-2241

POEHLER, AMY, comedienne, actress; b. Burlington, Mass., Sept. 16, 1971; m. Will Arnett, Aug. 29, 2003; 1 child, Archie Arnett. Grad., Boston Coll. Performer Second City comedy troupe, Chgo., 1993—96, Improv Olympic, LA. Actor: (films) Saving Manhattan, 1998, Tomorrow Night, 1998, Deuce Bigalow: Male Gigolo, 1999, The Devil and Daniel Webster, 2001, Wet Hot American Summer, 2001, Martin & Orloff, 2002, Mean Girls, 2004, Envy, 2004, Southland Tales, 2006, Man of the Year, 2006, Blades of Glory, 2007, (voice) Horton Hears a Who!, 2008, Baby Mama, 2008, Hamlet 2, 2008, (voice) Monsters vs. Aliens, 2009; actor, writer, prodr. (films) Wild Girls Gone, 2005, actor, writer (TV series) Upright Citizens Brigade, 1998—2000; actor: (TV series) Saturday Night Live, 2001—08; appearances include (TV series) Late Night with Conan O'Brien, 1998—2000, Apt. 2F, 1997, Spin City, 1998, Undeclared, 2002, Arrested Development, 2004. Named a Maverick, Details mag., 2008; named one of The 50 Most Powerful Women in NYC, NY Post, 2008. Office: c/o 3 Arts Entertainment 9460 Wilshire Blvd 7th Fl Beverly Hills CA 90212

POINAR, GEORGE ORLO, JR., entomologist, science educator; b. Spokane, Wash., Apr. 25, 1936; s. George O. and Helen Louise (Ladd) P.; m. Eva I. Hecht; children: Hendrik, Maya; m. 2d, Roberta Theresa Heil; 1 child, Gregory. BS, Cornell U., 1958, MS, 1960, PhD, 1962. Prof. dept. entomology U. Calif., Berkeley, 1964—95; courtesy prof. dept. zoology Oreg. State U., Corvallis, 1995—. Author: Entomogenous Nematodes, 1975, Nematodes for Biological Control of Insects, 1979, The Natural History of Nematodes, 1983, co-author (with Roberta Poinar) The Quest for Life in Amber, (with Roberta Poinar) The Amber Forest, (with R. Milki) Lebanese Amber, 2001, (with G.M. Thomas) Diagnostic Manual for the Identification of Insect Pathogens, 1978, (with G.M. Thomas) Laboratory Guide to Insect Pathogens and Parasites, 1984, (with Hans-Börje Jansson) Diseases of Nematodes, Vols. 1, 2, 1988. Grantee NATO, NSF, NIH, 1962-72. Avocations: photography, piano, tennis. Office: Oreg State Univ Dept Zoology Corvallis OR 97331 Home Phone: 541-752-0917; Office Phone: 541-737-5366. Business E-Mail: poinarg@science.oregonstate.edu.

POLAK, ELIJAH, engineering educator, computer scientist; b. Bialystok, Poland, Aug. 11, 1931; came to US, 1958, naturalized, 1977; s. Isaac and Fruma (Friedman) P.; m. Virginia Ann Gray, June 11, 1961; children: Oren, Sharon. BSEE, U. Melbourne, Australia, 1957; MSEE, U. Calif., Berkeley, 1959, PhD in Elec. Engring., 1961. Instrument engr. ICIANZ, Melbourne, Australia, 1956-57; summer student IBM Rsch. Labs., San Jose, Calif., 1959-60; vis. asst. prof. MIT, fall 1964; assoc. dept. elec. engring. and computer scis. U. Calif., Berkeley, 1958-61, asst. prof. elec. engring. and computer scis., 1961-66, assoc. prof., 1966-69, prof., 1969-94, prof. grad. Sch., 1994—. Author: (with L.A. Zadeh) System Theory, 1969, (with E. Wong) Notes for a First Course on Linear Systems, 1970, (with others) Theory of Optimal Control and Mathematical Programming, 1970, Computational Methods in Optimization, 1971, Optimization: Algorithms and Consistent Approximations, 1997. Guggenheim fellow, 1968; UK Sci. Rsch. Coun. Sr. fellow, 1972, 76, 79, 82 Fellow IEEE; mem. Soc. Indsl. and Applied Math. (assoc. editor Jour. Theory and Applications Optimization 1972—), Soc. Math. Programming. Jewish. Avocation: cross country skiing. Home: 38 Fairlawn Dr Berkeley CA 94708-2106 Office: U Calif Dept Elec Engring Cp S Berkeley CA 94720-0001 Office Phone: 510-642-2644. Business E-Mail: polak@eecs.berkeley.edu.

POLAN, MARY LAKE, obstetrics and gynecology educator; b. Las Vegas, N.Mex., July 17, 1943; Student, Smith Coll., Paris, 1963—64; BA cum laude, Conn. Coll., 1965; PhD in Biophysics and Biochemistry, Yale U., 1965—70, MD, 1972—75. Diplomate Am. Bd. Ob-Gyn., Am. Bd. Reproductive Endocrinology, Nat. Bd. Med. Examiners. Clin. clk. in ob-gyn. and pediat. Radcliffe Infirmary, Oxford (Eng.) U. Med. Sch., 1974; instr. Pahlavi U., Shiraz, Iran, 1978; postdoctoral fellow dept. biology, NIH postdoctoral fellow Yale U., New Haven, 1970—72, resident dept. ob-gyn. Sch. Medicine, 1975—78, fellow in oncology, then fellow in endocrinology-infertility, 1978—80, asst. instr., then lectr. molecular biophysics-biochemistry, 1970—72, instr., then asst. prof. ob-gyn., 1978—79, 1980—85, assoc. prof., 1985—90; Katharine Dexter McCormick and Stanley McCormick Meml. prof. Stanford (Calif.) Sch. Medicine, 1990—, chair dept. gynecology and obstetrics, 1990—. Vis. prof. Hunan Med. Coll., Changsha, China, 1986; mem. med. bd. Yale-China Assn., 1987—90; liaison com. on ethics in modern world Conn. Coll., New London, 1988—90; mem. med. adv. bd. Ova-Med Corp., Palo Alto, Calif., 1992—95, Vivus, Menlo Park, Calif., 1993—97; bd. dirs. Metra Biosys., Mountain View, Quidel, San Diego, 1993—, Am. Home Products, Madison, NJ, 1994, Adiana Inc., Redwood City, Calif., 2002—; mem. reproductive endocrinology study sect. NIH, 1989—90, co-chmn. task force on opportunities for rsch. on woman's health, 1991, mem. dir. panel on clin. rsch., 1995—98; mem. sci. adv. bd. Apop Corp., Princeton, NJ, 2003—; mem. health adv. bd. DuPont, Wilmington, Del., 2003—. Author: Second Seed, 1987; guest editor: Seminars in Reproductive Endocrinology, 1984, Infertility and Reproductive Medicine Clinics of North America: GnRH Analogues, Vol. 4, 1993; editor, with DeCherney: Surgery in Reproductive Endocrinology, 1987; editor: (with DeCherney, S. Boyers and R. Lee) Decision Making in Infertility; ad hoc reviewer: Jour. Clin. Endocrinology and Metabolism, Fertility and Sterility, Ob-Gyn., others; contbr. chapters to books, articles to med. jours.; editl. bd. Jour. Women's Health, Rodale Health Bd. Adv., 1993—2002. Mem. bd. trustees Conn. Coll., New London, 2000—. Grantee, NIRA, 1982—85, HD, 1985—90, NRSA, 1987—88, Johnson & Johnson, 1993—96; fellow, NSRA, 1981—82; scholar, Assn. Acad. Health Ctrs., 1993—96. Fellow: ACOG (PROLOG task force for reproductive endocrinology and infertility 1988—89, rep. to CREOG coun. 1994—97); mem.: Bay Area Reproductive Endocrine Soc., San Francisco Gynecologic Soc., Inst. Medicine (com. on rsch. capabilities of acad. depts. ob-gyn. 1990—91, bd. on health scis. policy 1992—96, membership com. 1996—98, chair membership com. 1998—2001, mem. governing coun. 2002—05, coun. liaison to food and nutrition bd. 2002—, coun. mem. 2006—), Am. Gynecologic and Obstetric Soc., Soc. for Reproductive Endocrinologists, Soc. for Gynecologic Investigation, Am. Fertility Soc., Phi Beta Kappa. Achievements include patents for methods of diagnosing and treating urinary incontinence relating to collagen proteolysis in pelvic supporting tissue, US patent number 6,420,119; issued July 2002. Office: Stanford U Sch Medicine Dept Gyn OB 300 Pasteur Dr HH333 Stanford CA 94305-5317 Office Phone: 650-723-5533. Office Fax: 650-723-7737. E-mail: polan@stanford.edu.

POLANSKI, ROMAN, film director, writer, actor; b. Paris, Aug. 18, 1933; s. Ryszard and Bule (Katz-Przedborska) P.; m. Barbara Lass, Sept. 19, 1959 (div. 1962); m. Sharon Tate, Jan. 20, 1968 (dec. Aug. 9, 1969); m. Emmanuelle Seigner, Aug. 30, 1989 Student, Art Sch., Cracow, State Film Coll., Lodz. Appeared in (children's radio show) The Merry Gang, (stage prodn.) Son of the Regiment, When Angels Fall, 1958, Le Gros et le Maigre, 1960, Knife in the Water, 1962 (Venice Film Festival award), The Mammals, 1963 (Tours Film Festival award), Repulsion, 1965 (Berlin Film Festival award), Cul-de-Sac, 1966 (Berlin Film Festival award), Rosemary's Baby, 1968, Macbeth, 1971, Tess, 1980 (Cesar award), Pirates, 1986, Frantic, 1988, Bitter Moon, 1994, Death and the Maiden, 1994, The Ninth Gate, 1999, The Pianist, 2002 (Best Dir. Acad. award, 2003, Best Film, British Acad. Film Award (BAFTA), 2003, The David Lean Award for Achievement in Direction, 2003, 2003), Oliver Twist, 2005; actor, dir. (films) The Fearless Vampire Killers, 1967, Chinatown, 1974 (Best Dir. award Soc. Film and TV Arts, Priz Raoul-Levy, 1975), What?, 1972, The Tenant, 1976, appeared in (documentaries) Roman Polanski: Wanted and Desired, 2008; actor: (films) A Generation, 1955, End of the Night, 1957; dir., actor: (films) Two Men and a Wardrobe, 1958, See You Tomorrow, 1960, The Innocent Sorcerers, 1960, The Magic Christian and Andy Warhol's Death, 1969, Back in the U.S.S.R., 1992, A Pure Formality, 1994; actor, dir.: (plays) Amadeus; Warsaw, 1981; Paris, 1982; Amadeus/Italy, 1999; dir.: (Operas) Lulu, 1974, Rigoletto, 1976; (Operas, (musical comedy) Tales of Hoffman, Master Class, 1996—97; (Operas) Tanz der Vampire, 1997, 2000; author: (autobiography) Roman, 1984. Recipient Lifetime Achievement award, European Film Awards, 2006. Office: ICM 8942 Wilshire Blvd Beverly Hills CA 90211-1934

POLDEN, DONALD, dean, law educator; BBA, George Washington U.; JD cum laude, Ind. U. Sch. Law. Law clerk for Hon. William C. Hanson, Chief Justice U.S. Dist. Ct. for So. Dist. Iowa, 1975—76; of counsel Hawkins and Norris, 1978—90; prof. law Drake U. Sch. Law, 1976—93; assoc. dean U. Memphis Sch. Law, 1991—93, dean, prof law, 1993—2003, Santa Clara U. Sch. Law, 2003—. Vis. prof. U. Louisville Sch. Law, 1984. Co-author: Employment relationships: law and practice, 1998; contbr. articles to law jours. Fellow: Coll. Labor and Employment Lawyers; mem.: Am. Law Inst. (elected mem. 1993), ABA (life). Office: Santa Clara U Sch Law El Camino Real Santa Clara CA 95053 Office Phone: 408-554-4362. E-mail: dpolden@scu.edu.

POLESE, KIM, software company executive; BS, U. Calif., Berkeley, 1984; student, U. Wash. Product mgr. Sun Microsys., 1988—95; co-founder, pres., CEO Marimba, Inc. (acquired by BMC Software), 1996—2000; chmn. Marimba, Inc. (acquired by BMC Software), 1996—2004; CEO SpikeSource, Inc., Redwood City, Calif., 2004—. Exec. coun. TechNet; bd. dirs. Technorati, Inc., 2004—06. Bd. dirs. Do Something, Global Security Inst., Long Now Found., U. Calif. President's Bd. Sci. and Innovation, Carnegie Mellon Computer Sci. Advisory Coun. Named one of Time Mags. Most Influential Ams., Most Influential Women in Technology, Fast Company, 2009; Fellow at Carnegie Mellon University's Ctr. for Engineered Innovation. Mem.: Silicon Valley Mfg. Group. Achievements include a pivotal role in launching Java. Office: SpikeSource Inc 2000 Seaport Blvd 2nd Fl Redwood City CA 94063*

POLICANO, ANDREW J., dean, finance educator; b. July 4, 1949; m. Pamela Z. Policano; children: Emily, Keith. BS in math., SUNY, Stony Brook, 1971; MA in economics, Brown U., 1973, PhD in economics, 1976. Asst. prof. U. Iowa, Iowa City, 1975-79, assoc. prof. dept. economics, 1979-81, prof., chair dept. economics, 1984-87, sr. assoc. dean academic affairs, 1987-88; prof. dept. economics Fordham U., NYC, 1981-84, asst. chair, dir. grad. studies, 1982-83; rsch. assoc. Ctr. for Study of Futures Markets Columbia U., NYC, 1982-86; dean divsn. social & behavioral sci. SUNY, Stony Brook, 1988-91; dean Sch. Bus., U. Wis., Madison, 1991—2001, Kuechenmeister Prof. Bus., 2001—04; dean Pual Merage Sch. Bus., U. Calif., Irvine, 2004—, prof. economics/pub. policy, 2004—. Guest prof. Inst. Advanced Studies, Vienna, Austria, 1985; dir. Nat. Guardian Life, Madison, 1991-2004, PIC Wis., 1995-2002, Badger Meter, 1997—; mem. Wis. Glass Ceiling Commn., 1995-2000. Recipient Disting. Alumnus award SUNY, Stony Brook, 1994. Mem. Assn. to Advance Collegiate Schools of Bus. (bd. dirs., 1997-98). Office: U Calif Paul Merage Sch Bus 350 SB Irvine CA 92697-3125 Office Phone: 949-824-8470. Business E-Mail: dean@merage.uci.edu.

POLINSKY, A. MITCHELL, law and economics educator; b. Feb. 6, 1948; m. Joan Roberts, June 29, 1945; 2 children. AB in Econs. magna cum laude, Harvard U., 1970; PhD in Econs., MIT, 1973; MSL, Yale U., 1976. Asst. prof. econs. Harvard U., Cambridge, Mass., 1973—75, resident law and social sci. Law Sch., 1976—77, asst. prof. econs. and law, 1977—79; resident law and social sci. Russell Sage Found. Yale Law Sch., 1975—76; assoc. prof. econs. and law Stanford U., 1979—84, dir. John M. Olin program in law and econs., 1979—, Josephine Scott Crocker prof. law and econs., 1984—, nat. fellow domestic studies program Hoover Instn., 1985—86, co-dir. Ctr. for Law, Econs. and Bus., 2002—. Fellow Ctr. for Advanced Study in Behavioral Scis., Stanford, Calif., 1997—98; vis. prof. law and econs. Harvard Law Sch., 1992—93, 2000, 03; rsch. assoc. law and econs. program Nat. Bur. Econ. Rsch., 1978—. Mem. editl. bd.: Hour. Law, Econs. and Orgn., 1983—, Internat. Rev. Law and Econs., 1987—, Jour. Pub. Econs., 1999—, B.E. Jours. Econs., Analysis & Policy, 2001—, adv. editor: Jour. Risk and Uncertainty, 1987—. Fellow, John Simon Guggenheim Meml. Found., 1993—94. Mem.: Am. Law and Econs. Assn. (bd. dirs. 1991—93, sec.-treas. 1991—92, v.p. 1992—93, pres. 1993—94). Office: Stanford Law Sch Crown Quadrangle 559 Nathan Abbott Way Stanford CA 94305-8610 Office Phone: 650-723-0886. Office Fax: 650-723-3557. Business E-Mail: polinsky@stanford.edu.

POLIS, JARED SCHUTZ, United States Representative from Colorado, entrepreneur, philanthropist; b. Boulder, Colo., May 12, 1975; s. Stephen and Susan (Polis) Schutz. BA in Polit. Sci, Princeton U., NJ.

Sales mgr. Blue Mountain Arts; exec. dir. internet startups Bluemountain.com, FrogMagic, Dan's Chocolates; founder Proflowers.com/Proflowers Inc., San Diego, 1998, Sonora Entertainment Grp., 2001, TechStars, 2006; mem. US Congress from 2nd Colo. dist., 2009—. Mem. exec. com. Colo. Dem. Party, 2000—07, Boulder County Dems., 2000—07; former chmn. Colo. State Bd. Edn.; co-chair Colo. Commn. HS Improvement; chair fin. literacy study grp. Nat. Assn. Sate Bds. Edn.; bd. mem. Latin Am. Rsch. & Svc. Agy., Colo. Anti-Defamation League, Colo. Consumer Health Initiative, Colo. Conservation Voters. Founder Jared Polis Found., 2000, Cmty. Computer Connection, Aurora, Colo.; founder, superintendent New America Sch., Thornton, Colo., 2004; co-founder Acad. Urban Learning, Denver, 2005; bd. dirs. Watershed Sch., Boulder. Recipient Pacesetter award in edn., Boulder Daily Camera, 2007, Ohtli award, Denver consul gen. of Mex., Cmty. Builder award, Anti-Defamation League, Cmty. award, Kauffman Found., Martin Luther King, Jr. Humanitarian award; named an Ernst & Young Entrepreneur of Yr., 2000, Outstanding Philanthropist, State of Colo., 2006, Outstanding Young Coloradoan, Colo. Jaycees; named one of Forty Under 40, Denver Bus. Journal, 2000. Democrat. Office: US Congress 501 Cannon House Office Bldg Washington DC 20515-0602 also: Dist Office 4770 Baseline Dr Ste 220 Westminster CO 80303 Office Phone: 202-225-2161, 303-484-9596. Office Fax: 202-226-7840.*

POLITZER, HUGH DAVID, physicist, educator; b. NYC, Aug. 31, 1949; s. Alan A. and Valerie T. (Diamant) P. BS, U. Mich., 1969; PhD, Harvard U., 1974. Jr. fellow Harvard U. Soc. Fellows, 1974-77; mem. faculty Calif. Inst. Tech., 1975—, prof. theoretical physics, 1979—, exec. officer for physics, 1986-88. Author: Asymptotic Freedom: An Approach to String Interactions, 1974; appeared in Fat Man and Little Boy, 1989. Recipient J.J. Sakurai prize, 1986; fellow NSF, 1969-74, Sloan Found., 1977-81, Woodrow Wilson grad. fellow, 1969-74, Guggenheim fellow, 1997-98; co-recipient High Energy and Particle Physics prize European Phys. Soc., 2003, Nobel Prize in Physics, 2004. Mem. Am. Physical Soc., Harvard Soc. Fellows, Phi Beta Kappa. Achievements include discovery of asymptotic freedom in the theory of the strong interaction. Office: Calif Inst Tech High Energy Physics 1201 E California Blvd Mail Code 452-48 Pasadena CA 91106-3368 Business E-Mail: politzer@theory.caltech.edu.

POLK, DENNIS, electronics executive; BS acctg., Santa Clara Univ. CPA. Audit mgr. Grant Thornton LLP; fin. mgmt. positions from corp. contr. to sr. v.p., CFO Savoir Technology Group Inc., 1995—2000; v.p. fin. DoveBid Inc., 2000—01; sr. v.p. corp. fin., CFO SYNNEX Corp., Fremont, Calif., 2002—06, CFO, COO, 2006—07, COO, 2007—. Office: SYNNEX Corp 44201 Nobel Dr Fremont CA 94538-3178

POLLACE, PAMELA L., public relations executive; b. San Jose, Calif., May 1953; BA, U. Santa Clara, 1975. Acct. mgr. mktg. comm. Oxbridge, Inc.; acct. supr. Burson Marsteller; spokesperson, mgr., dir. Intel Corp, Santa Clara, Calif., 1987-96, v.p., dir. worldwide press rels., 1996—2000; v.p. dir. corp. comms. Intel Corp., Santa Clara, Calif., 2000—. Office: Intel Corp Worldwide Press Rels PO Box 58119 Santa Clara CA 95052-8119

POLLACK, BETTY GILLESPIE, retired health care services executive; b. Oak Park, Ill., Apr. 4, 1940; d. Leon H. and Elta F. Gillespie; m. David Pollack, Dec. 18, 1971; 1 son, Michael Alan. BA, Whittier Coll., 1962; MS, Columbia U., 1964. Cmty. organizer, Boston, 1964-66; faculty mem. Grad. Sch. Social Welfare, U. Calif., Berkeley, 1967-71; exec. dir. Calif. chpt. Nat. Assn. Social Workers, Millbrae, 1971-81; pres., CEO Vis. Nurse Assn., Santa Clara County, Calif., 1981-94; exec. dir. San Francisco Med. Soc., 1994—98, ret., 1998. Mem. exec. com. Assn. United Way Agencies, 1982-85, 91-93; chmn. bylaws commn. of San Mateo County Jr. Hockey Club, 1988-89. Mem. No. Calif. Soc. Assn. Execs. (sec.-treas. 1980-82, pres.-elect 1982-83, pres. 1983-84, program chmn. 1984-85, chmn. nominating com. 1985-86, chmn. publs. com. 1995), Peninsula Profl. Women's Network (sec. 1981-82, chmn. networking conf. 1981, pres. ednl. fund 1981-82), No. Calif. Coalition Vis. Nurse Assns. (v.p. 1983-85, pres. 1985, v.p. reorganized VNA Network No. Calif. 1993-94), Bay Area Profl. Women's Network (mem. newsletter com. 1980-81), Am. Soc. Assn. Execs., Peninsula Forum West, Rotary (San Jose chpt., chmn. program com. 1993-94, youth leadership com., internat. com. 1991-92, chmn. health programs subcom. 1992-94, co-chair Acad. Decatholon San Francisco chpt. 1996, mem. membership com., chmn. program com. 1997-98, bd. dirs. 1998-99), Automate RV Club (pres. 2003-2005), San Carlos Rotary Club. Democrat. Home: 316 Sycamore St San Carlos CA 94070-2020

POLLAN, MICHAEL, author, journalist, professor; b. LI, NY, Feb. 6, 1955; s. Stephen and Corky Pollan; m. Judith Belzer, Sept. 6, 1987; 1 child, Isaac. Student, Mansfield Coll., U. Oxford, Eng.; BA, Bennington Coll., Vt., 1977; MA in English, Columbia U., NYC, 1981. Former exec. editor Harper's Mag.; now Knight prof. journalism U. Calif., Berkeley, also dir. Knight Prog. Sci. & Environ. Journalism. Author: Second Nature: A Gardener's Education, 1991, Place of My Own: The Education of an Amateur Builder, 1997, The Botany of Desire: A Plant's-Eye View of the World, 2001, The Omnivore's Dilemma: A Natural History of Four Meals, 2006 (Named one of Five Best Nonfiction Books of Yr., NY Times, 2006, One of 10 Best Books of Yr., Washington Post, 2006, James Beard award for best food writing, 2007, Calif. Book award), In Defense of Food: An Eater's Manifesto, 2008 (Publishers Weekly bestseller); contbg. writer NY Times Mag., articles anthologized Norton Book of Nature Writing, 1990, Best American Essays, 1990, 2003, American Science Writing, 2004, The Animals: Practicing Complexity, 2006; contbr. numerous articles/essays to periodicals. Recipient Reuters World Conservation Union Global award for environ. journalism, 2000, James Beard award for best mag. series, 2003, Am. Humane Assn. Genesis award. Office: U Calif Grad Sch Journalism 121 N Gate Hall #5860 Berkeley CA 94720 Office Phone: 510-642-8240.*

POLLARD, HENRY, arbitrator, mediator; b. NYC, Jan. 10, 1931; s. Charles and Sarah (Lanster) P.; m. Adele Ruth Brodie, June 16, 1954; children: Paul A., Lydia S. AB, CCNY, 1953; JD, Columbia U., 1954. Bar: N.Y. 1954, Calif. 1962. Assoc. Sullivan & Cromwell, NYC, 1954, 56-61; ptnr. Kaplan, LIvingston, Goodwin, Berkowitz & Selvin, Beverly Hills, Calif., 1962-81, Pollard, Bauman, Slome & McIntosh, Beverly Hills, 1981-87, Seyfarth, Shaw, LA, 1987-95; of counsel Oberstein, Kibre & Horwitz, LA, 1995-99. Arbitrator/mediator, mem. large complex case program Am. Arbitration Assn.; arbitrator/mediator, N.Y. Stock Exch., Am. Stock Exch., Pacific Stock Exch., L.A. County Dispute Resolution Svcs.; settlement officer Beverly Hills Mcpl. Ct., L.A. County Superior Ct. Editor Columbia U. Law Rev., 1953-54. Served with U.S. Army, 1954-56. Harlan Fiske Stone scholar, 1953-54. Mem. ABA, Calif. Bar Assn., Beverly Hills Bar Assn. Home Phone: 310-457-4420; Office Phone: 310-457-1713. Office Fax: 310-457-1713. Business E-Mail: adrpollard@aol.com.

POLLARD, ROYCE, Mayor, Vancouver, Washington; Ret. comdr. US Army Vancouver Barracks, 1961—88; councilman City of Vancouver, Wash., 1988—96, mayor Wash., 1996—. Rep. Bi-State Transp. Com., SW Wash. Regional Transp. Coun., Columbia River Edn. Workforce Coun., Joint Policy Adv. Com. Transp., Growth Mgmt. Act Steering Com. of Countrywide Elected Officials; bd. mem. Vancouver Fire Pension Bd., Vancouver Police Pension Bd., CRESA Bd. Dirs. Mem.: Vietnam Veterans of America, Ret. Officers Assn. (Columbia River Chpt.), Am. Legion Post 14, La Societe des Quarante Hommes at Huit Chevaux (Forty & Eight). Mailing: PO Box 1995 Vancouver WA 98668-1995 Office: City Hall 210 E 13th St Vancouver WA 98668 Office Phone: 350-487-8629. Business E-Mail: mayor@ci.vancouver.wa.us.*

POLLITT, BYRON H., JR., finance company executive, former retail executive; b. 1951; BS in Bus. Econs., U. Calif.; MBA, Harvard U. Mgmt. cons. McKinsey & Co.; v.p. corp. ops. planning Walt Disney Co., 1990—92, v.p. bus. planning, 1992—94, CFO, 1994—95, sr. v.p., CFO Disneyland Resorts, 1995—99, exec. v.p., CFO Walt Disney Pks. and Resorts, 1999—2003; exec. v.p., CFO Gap, Inc., San Francisco, 2003—07; CFO Visa Inc., Foster City, Calif., 2007—. Bd. mem. ARC Bay Area Chpt. Office: Visa Inc 900 Metro Ctr Blvd Foster City CA 94404 Office Phone: 650-952-4400.

POLLOCK, GALE SUSAN, career military officer; b. Kearny, NJ, 1954; BS in Nursing, U. Md., Balt., 1976; MBA, Boston U., 1984; M in Healthcare Adminstrn., Baylor U., 1987; MA in Nat. Security & Strategy, Nat. Def. U., 1997; D in Pub. Svc. (hon.), U. Md., Balt., 2005; grad., US Dept. Def. CAPSTONE Program, Sr. Svc. Coll. at Idsl. Coll. Armed Forces, Air War Coll., Interagency Inst. Fed. Health Care Execs., Milt. Health Sys. CAPSTONE Program, Principles Advanced Nurse Adminstrs., NATO Staff Office Course. Cert. Registered Nurse Anesthetist. Enlisted US Army, advanced through grades to maj. gen., 2004, spl. asst. to surgeon gen. for info. mgmt. and health policy; comdr. Martin Army Cmty. Hosp., Ft. Benning, Ga., US Army Med. Activity, Ft. Drum, NY; staff officer Strategic Initiatives Command Group for Army Surgeon Gen.; healthcare advisor to Congl. Commn. to Svc. Mems. and Vets. Transition Assistance US Dept. Def.; health fitness advisor Nat. Def. U.; sr. policy analyst in health affairs US Dept. Def.; chief Anesthesia Nursing Svc., Walter Reed Army Med. Ctr., Washington, DC; lead agent TRICARE Pacific, Honolulu; commdg. gen. Tripler Army Med. Ctr. of Pacific Regional Med. Command, Honolulu; chief Army Nurse Corps, 2004—06; dep. surgeon gen. US Army, 2006—07, acting surgeon gen., 2007, dep. surgeon gen. for force mgmt., 2007—. Decorated Disting. Svc. medal US Army, Legion of Merit with 2 oak leaf clusters, Def. Meritorious Svc. medal, Meritorious Svc. medal with 4 oak leaf clusters, Joint Svc. Commendation medal, Army Commendation medal, Army Achievement medal, Expert Field Med. Badge, Parachutist Badge, Army Staff Identification Badge, German Armed Forces Milt. Efficiency Badge in Gold. Fellow: Am. Coll. Healthcare Execs. Office: Tripler Army Med Ctr 160 Krukowski Rd Honolulu HI 96859 Office Phone: 808-433-5716.

POLLOCK, JOHN PHLEGER, retired lawyer; b. Sacramento, Apr. 28, 1920; s. George Gordon and Irma (Phleger) P.; m. Juanita Irene Gossman, Oct. 26, 1945; children: Linda Pollock Harrison, Madeline Pollock Chiotti, John, Gordon. AB, Stanford U., 1942; JD, Harvard U., 1948. Bar: Calif. 1949, U.S. Supreme Ct. 1954. Ptnr. Musick, Peeler & Garrett, LA, 1953-60, Pollock, Williams & Berwanger, LA, 1960-80, Rodi, Pollock, Pettker, Christian & Pramov, LA, 1980—89, of counsel, 1989—. Contbr. articles to profl. publs. Trustee Pitzer Coll., Claremont, Calif., 1968-76, Fletcher Jones Found., 1969—, Good Hope Med. Found., 1980-2006, Pacific Legal Found., 1981-91; pres. LA area coun., Boy Scouts Am., 1970. Fellow Am. Coll. Trial Lawyers; mem. ABA, LA County Bar Assn. (trustee 1964-66). Home: 30602 Paseo Del Valle Laguna Niguel CA 92677-2317 Home Phone: 949-495-2948; Office Phone: 213-895-4900. Personal E-mail: phleger1@msn.com.

POLUMBUS, GARY M., lawyer; b. Tulsa, 1941; BS, U. Colo., 1964; JD, U. Denver, 1967. Bar: Colo. 1967, D.C. 1968. Mem. Dorsey & Whitney, Denver, 1996—. Mem. ABA, Am. Intellectual Property Law Assn. Office: Ste 4700 370 17th St Denver CO 80202-5687

POMBO, RICHARD WILLIAM, former congressman, rancher, farmer; b. Tracy, Calif., Jan. 8, 1961; s. Ralph and Onita Pombo; m. Annette Rina Cole, 1983; children: Richie, Rina, Rachel. Student, Calif. State U., Pomona, 1979—82. Councilman City of Tracy, 1991-92; mayor pro-tem Tracy City Coun., 1992; mem. US Congress from 11th Calif. dist., 1993—2007; mem. agrl. com., resources com., transp. and infrastructure com., chmn. subcom. on livestock and horticulture. Chmn. Pvt. Property Rights Task Force, 1993-94, Endangered Species Act Task Force, 1995-96; co-chmn. Spkr.'s Environ. Task Force, 1996. Author (with Joseph Farah) This Land Is Our Land: How to End the War on Private Property, 1996 Co-founder San Joaquin County Citizen's Land Alliance, Calif., 1986—; active San Joaquin County Econ. Devel. Assn., Tracy Bus. Improvement Dist., City Coun. (vice chmn. Cmty. Devel. Agy., Cmty. Parks Com., and Waste Mgmt. Com.), San Joaquin County Rep. Ctrl. Com. Mem. Rotary Club. Republican. Roman Catholic.

POMERANTZ, MARVIN, thoracic surgeon; b. Suffern, NY, June 16, 1934; s. Julius and Sophie (Luksin) Pomerantz; m. Margaret Twigg, Feb. 26, 1966; children: Ben, Julie. AB, Colgate U., 1955; MD, U. Rochester, 1959. Diplomate Nat. Bd. Med. Examiners, Am. Bd. Surgery, Am. Bd. Thoracic Surgery (bd. dirs. 1989-95). Intern Duke U. Med. Ctr., Durham, NC, 1959—60, resident, 1960—61, instr. surgery, 1966—67; asst. prof. surgery U. Colo. Med. Sch., Denver, 1967—71, assoc. prof. surgery, 1971—74, assoc. clin. prof. surgery, 1974—93, prof. surgery, chief gen. thoracic surgery, 1992—; chief thoracic and cardiovascular surgery Denver Gen. Hosp., 1967—73, asst. dir. surgery, 1967—70, assoc.dir. surgery, 1970—73; pvt. practice Arapahoe CV Assocs., Denver, 1974—92; prof., chief gen. thoracic surgery sect. U. Colo. Health Sci. Ctr., 1992—; resident Duke U. Med. Ctr., Durham, NC, 1963—67. Clin. assoc. surgery br. NCI, 1961—63; mem. staff Univ. Hosp., Denver, Denver Gen. Hosp., Rose Med. Ctr., Denver, Denver VA Med. Ctr., Children's Hosp., Denver, U. Coll. Health Sci. Ctr., 1992—, bd. dirs., 1990—96; vice chmn. Am. Bd. Thoracic Surgery, 1995—97, chmn., 1997—99. Guest editor Chest Surgery Clinics N.Am., 1993; contbr. numerous articles to profl. publs., chapters to books. Master: AMA; fellow: ACS, Am. Coll. Chest Surgeons; mem.: Soc. Vascular Surgeons, Soc. Thoracic Surgeons (nomenclature/coding com. 1991—95, standards and ethics com., govt. rels. com., chmn. program com. 1994—95), Rocky Mtgn. Traumatologic Soc., rgery Soc., Internat. Cardiovascular Soc., Denver Acad. Surgery (pres. 1980), Colo. Med. Soc., Am. Heart Assn. (bd. dirs. Colo. chpt. 1993), Am. Assn. Thoracic Surgeons (program com. 1991), Western Thoracic Surg. Assn. (v.p. 1992, pres. 1993—94, counselor-at-large 1988—90). Office: UCHSC Divsn CTS 4200 E 9th Ave # C310 Denver CO 80262-0001 Business E-Mail: marvin.pomerantz@uchsc.edu.

POMMER, JOHN (JACK POMMER), state legislator; m. Jane Pommer; children: Addie, Brock. BA in Philosophy, U. Colo., Boulder, 1986. TV/video prodr.; adj. prof. U. Colo. Sch. Journalism; mem. Dist. 11 Colo. House of Reps., Denver, 2002—. Active Big Brothers of Colo. Democrat. Office: Colo State Capitol 200 E Colfax Rm 271 Denver CO 80203 Office Phone: 303-866-2780. Business E-Mail: jack.pommer.house@state.co.us.*

POMPEO, ELLEN, actress; b. Everett, Mass., Nov. 10, 1969; d. Joseph and Kathleen Pompeo; m. Chris Ivery, Nov. 9, 2007. Actor: (films) 8 1/2 x 11, 1999, Coming Soon, 1999, Eventual Wife, 2000, In the Weeds, 2000, Moonlight Mile, 2002, Catch Me If You Can, 2002, Daredevil, 2003, Old School, 2003, Undermind, 2003, Nobody's Perfect, 2004, Art Heist, 2004; (TV series) Grey's Anatomy, 2005— (Outstanding Performance by an Ensemble in a Drama Series, SAG, 2007), (TV appearances) Strangers with Candy, 1999, Law and Order, 1996, 2000, Get Real, 2000, Strong Medicine, 2001, The Job, 2001. Office: c/o Creative Artists Agency 2000 Avenue of the Stars Los Angeles CA 90067

POND, RANDY, computer company executive; B in acctg. & fin., Ball State Univ. Fin. & mgmt. positions Versatec, David Systems, Xerox, Schlumberger, Arthur Andersen; v.p. fin., CFO, v.p. ops. Crescendo Comm.; joined Cisco Systems Inc., San Jose, Calif., 1993, dir. mfg. ops., 1994—95, v.p. mfg., 1995—2000, sr. v.p. We. Coast & Asia ops., 2000—01, sr. v.p. worldwide mfg. ops. & logistics, 2001—03, sr. v.p. ops. processes & systems, 2003—07, exec. v.p. ops. processes & systems, 2007—. Bd. mem. Islamic Networks Group, Am. Leadership Forum Silicon Valley; pres. Children's Discovery Mus., San Jose. Office: Cisco Systems Inc 170 W Tasman Dr San Jose CA 95134-1706

PONDER, CATHERINE, clergywoman; b. Hartsville, SC, Feb. 14, 1927; d. Roy Charles and Kathleen (Parrish) Cook; 1 child, Richard. Student, Worth Bus. Coll., 1948; BS in Edn., Unity Ministerial Sch., 1956; doctorate (hon.), Unity Sch., 1976. Ordained to ministry Unity Sch. Christianity, 1958. Min. Unity Ch., Birmingham, Ala., 1958-61, founder, min. Austin, Tex., 1961-69, San Antonio, 1969-73, Palm Desert, Calif., 1973—. Author: (books) The Dynamic Laws of Prosperity, 1962, The Prosperity Secret of the Ages, 1964, The Dynamic Laws of Healing, 1966, The Healing Secret of the Ages, 1967, Pray and Grow Rich, 1968, The Millionaires of Genesis, 1976, The Millionaire Moses, 1977, The Millionaire Joshua, 1978, The Millionaire from Nazareth, 1979, The Secret of Unlimited Prosperity, 1981, Open Your Mind To Receive, 1983, Dare To Prosper!: The Prospering Power of Prayer, 1983, The Prospering Power of Love, 1984, Open Your Mind to Prosperity, 1984, The Dynamic Laws of Prayer, 1987, (memoir) Prosperity Love Story, From Rags to Enrichment, 2003. Office: 73-669 US Hwy 111 Palm Desert CA 92260-4033

PONTUAL, ROMULO, broadcast executive; V.p. space tech. News Corp., 1996—98, sr. v.p., 1998—99, exec. v.p. news tech., 1999—2002, exec. v.p. TV platforms, 2002; with Hughes Electronics Corp.; exec. v.p., chief tech. officer DIRECTV Group, El Segundo, Calif., 2004—. Vice chmn. Innova S de RL, 2000; mem. mgmt. bd. Sky Brasil Servicos Ltd., 2001. Office: DIRECTV Group 2230 E Imperial Hwy El Segundo CA 90245 Office Phone: 310-964-5000.

POOLE, CHRISTOPHER K., arbitration services company executive; b. 1957; BA in Econ., Harvard U., 1979; MBA in Computers & Mktg., UCLA, 1984. Dir. tech. Latham & Watkins LLP, 1989—93, exec. dir., 1993—95; COO Elite Info. Group, Inc., 1995-97, pres., CEO, 1997—2006; chmn. Thompson Elite (formerly Elite Info. Group, Inc.), 2006—07; pres., CEO JAMS, The Resolution Experts, Irvine, Calif., 2008—. Recipient Ernst & Young Entrepreneur of Yr. award, 2002. Office: JAMS The Resolution Experts 1920 Main St at Gillette Ave Ste 300 Irvine CA 92614

POOLE, HENRY JOE, JR., business executive; b. Rocky Point, NC, July 5, 1957; s. Henry Joe Sr. and Marjorie (Morse) P.; m. Loretta Lynn Scott, Sept. 12, 1981; children: Robert Howard, Amanda Lynn. AA, Cypress Coll., 1977; student, San Diego State U., 1978, Calif. State U., Fullerton, 1978-79. Pres. Poole Ventura Inc., Ventura, Calif., 1979-92; gen. mgr. W.I.C. PVI systems divsn., Ventura, Calif., 1992-94; pres. PVI, Oxnard, Calif., 1995—. Inventor in field. Mem. ASME, Soc. Mfg. Engrs., Am. Vacuum Soc., Am. Welding Soc., Soc. Vacuum Coaters. Office Phone: 805-981-1784. E-mail: pvi@vcnet.com.

POOLE, WILL, computer software company executive, information technology executive; BS in Computer Sci., Brown U. Sr. mktg. & engring. mgmt. Sun Microsystems Inc., 1985—90; co-founder, pres., CEO eShop Inc., 1991—96; with Microsoft Corp., 1996—, corp. v.p. New Media Platforms divsn., sr. v.p. Windows Client bus., 2003—07, corp. v.p. Unlimited Potential group, 2007—. Avocations: bicycling, sailing, building furniture. Office: One Microsoft Way Redmond WA 98052-6399

POPE, C. ARDEN, III, economics professor; b. Logan, Utah, Sept. 30, 1955; s. Clive Arden Pope Jr. and Vivian Harper Pope; m. Ronda Lou Gneiting, Aug. 5, 1977; children: Jaren Clive, Devin Garret, Weston Arden, Nolan Gneiting, Bryson Ron, Dallin Kimball, Collin Harper. BS, Brigham Young U., Provo, Utah, 1978; MS, PhD, Iowa State U., Ames, 1981. Rsch. assoc., staff economist Iowa State U., 1980—82; asst. prof. Tex. A&M U., College Station, 1982—84; asst. to assoc. prof. Brigham Young U., 1984—94, prof. econs., 1994—. Vis. scientist Harvard Sch. Pub. Health, Boston, 1992—93. Author: (book chapter) Acute respiratory effects of particulate air pollution, Epidemiology of acute health effects, Epidemiology of chronic health effects, Outdoor Air: Particles, Epidemiology of Particle Effects, Effects of particulate air pollution exposures, Epidemiological evidence of relationship between particle exposure and cardiovascular outcomes, Air Pollution: Coronary Heart Disease Epidemiology; contbr. articles to numerous profl. jours. Recipient Creative Achievement award, Brigham Young U., 1986, Karl G. Maeser, Excellence in Rsch. and Creative Arts award, 1995, Karl G. Maeser Disting. Faculty Lectr., 2006, Mary Lou Fulton Professorship, 2005-, Clarence Olds

Sappington Meml. Lectr., Am. Coll. Occupl. and Environ. Medicine, 1997, Lectr. award, Sigma Xi, 2000, Thomas T. Mercer Joint prize, Am. Assn. Aerosol Rsch. and the Internat. Soc. Aerosols in Medicine, 2001, Governor's medal Sci. & Tech., Utah Governor's Office, 2004; fellow Interdisciplinary Programs in Health, Harvard U., 1992-1993, Honorary, Am. Coll. Chest Physicians, 2008. Avocations: running, backpacking, community and church youth leader. Office: Brigham Young Univ 130 Fob Provo UT 84602 E-mail: cap3@byu.edu.

POPE, CHARLES C., computer hardware company executive; BS in Acctg., U. Utah; MBA, Brigham Young U. With Hewlett Packard Co., Diasonics Corp.; dir. budgets and analysis Seagate Technology, Scotts Valley, Calif., 1985, dir. fin. for Thailand ops., v.p. fin. Far East ops., v.p. fin., treas. Scotts Valley; v.p., gen. mgr. Seagate Magnetics; sr. v.p. storage products Seagate Technologies, sr. v.p. fin., CFO, 1998—2008, sr. v.p. Seagate Services group. Office: Seagate Tech PO Box 66360 Scotts Valley CA 95067-0360

POPE, KATHERINE COLLINS, former broadcast executive; b. Glencoe, Ill., Oct. 15, 1972; d. Michael A. and Christine Pope; m. Richard A. Robbins, June 2, 2001. Grad., Sarah Lawrence Coll. Assoc. prodr. A&E; writer & prodr. documentaries CBS; writer & prodr. VH1, 1999—2000; mgr. primetime series NBC Studios, 2000—01, dir. primetime series, 2001—02, v.p. primetime series, 2002—04; v.p. drama devel. NBC Entertainment, 2003—04, exec. v.p., 2006—07; sr. v.p. drama series NBC Universal TV Studio (name changed to Universal Media Studios, 2007), 2004—06, pres., 2007—08. Assoc. prodr. (TV series) Biography, writer & prodr. Behind the Music, 1999—2000. Named one of The 100 Most Powerful Women in Entertainment, The Hollywood Reporter, 2006, 2007, 2008. E-mail: katherine.pope@nbcuni.com.

POPE, MARCIA L., lawyer; b. St. Petersburg, Fla., May 12, 1961; AB, Harvard Univ., 1983; JD, Univ. Va., 1986. Bar: Calif. 1986. Assoc. to ptnr., Employment & Labor practice Pillsbury Winthrop Shaw Pittman, San Francisco, 1986—, employment counsel. Office: Pillsbury Winthrop Shaw Pittman 50 Fremont St San Francisco CA 94105 Office Phone: 415-983-6487. Office Fax: 415-983-1200. Business E-Mail: marcia.pope@pillsburylaw.com.

POPOFSKY, MELVIN LAURENCE, lawyer; b. Oskaloosa, Iowa, Feb. 16, 1936; s. Samuel and Fannye Charlotte (Rosenthal) P.; m. Linda Jane Seltzer, Nov. 25, 1962; children: Mark Samuel, Kaye Sylvia. BA in History summa cum laude, U. Iowa, 1958; BA in Jurisprudence (first class honors), Oxford U., Eng., 1960; LLB cum laude, Harvard U., 1962. Bar: Calif. 1962. Assoc. Heller, Ehrman, White & McAuliffe, San Francisco, 1962-69, ptnr., 1969—2008, mem. exec. com., 1980-93, co-chair, 1988-93; sr. ptnr. Orrick, Herrington & Sutcliffe, LLP, 2008—. Contbr. articles to law jours. Bd. dirs. Mt. Zion Hosp., San Francisco, 1982-88, U.S. Dist. Ct. (no. dist.) Calif. Hist. Soc., 1988-2004, Jewish Home for Aged, San Francisco, 1989-96, Golden Gate U., 1997-2000, Jewish Cmty. Fedn., 1997-2001. Recipient Anti-Defamation League's Disting. Jurisprudence award, 2000; named State Bar of Calif. Antitrust Lawyer of the Yr., 2000, Best Lawyers in Am. Calif., 1988-2008, Sr. Statesman Antitrust, Chambers, 2007-2008; Rhodes scholar, 1958. Fellow Am. Bar Found., Am. Coll. Trial Lawyers; mem. ABA, Calif. Bar Assn., San Francisco Bar Assn., Bur. Nat. Affairs (adv. bd. antitrust sect.), Calif. Acad. Appellate Lawyers. Democrat. Jewish. Home: 1940 Broadway Apt 10 San Francisco CA 94109-2216 Office: Orrick Herrington & Sutcliffe LLP 405 Howard St San Francisco CA 94105 Office Phone: 415-773-4590. Business E-Mail: lpopofsky@orrick.com.

POPOV, EGOR PAUL, retired engineering educator; b. Kiev, Russia, Feb. 19, 1913; s. Paul T. and Zoe (Derabin) P.; m. Irene Zofia Jozefowski, Feb. 18, 1939; children: Katherine, Alexander. BS with honors, U. Calif., 1933; MS, MIT, 1934; PhD in Civil Engrng./Applied Mechs., Stanford U., 1946. Registered civil, structural and mech. engr., Calif. Structural engr., bldg. designer, LA, 1935-39; asst. prodn. engr. Southwestern Portland Cement Co., LA, 1939-42; machine designer Goodyear Tire & Rubber Co., LA, 1942-43; design engr. Aerojet Corp., Calif., 1943-45; asst. prof. civil engrng. U. Calif. at Berkeley, 1946-48, assoc. prof., 1948-53, prof., 1953-83, prof. emeritus, 1983—, chmn. structural engrng. and structural mechanics div., dir. structural engrng. lab., 1956-60. Miller rsch. prof. Miller Inst. Basic Rsch. in Sci., 1968-69. Author: Mechanics of Materials, 1952, 2d edit., 1976, Introduction to Mechanics of Solids, 1968, Engineering Mechanics of Solids, 1990, 2d edit., 1999; contbr. articles profl. jours. Recipient Disting. Tchr. award U. Calif.-Berkeley, 1976-77, Berkeley citation U. Calif.-Berkeley, 1983, Disting. Lectr. award Earthquake Engrng. Rsch. Inst., 1993, George W. Housner medal Earthquake Engrng. Rsch. Inst., 1999. Fellow AAAS (assoc.), Am. Concrete Inst.; mem. NAE, Am. Soc. Metals, Internat. Assn. Shell Structures (hon. mem.), ASCE (hon. mem., Ernest E. Howard award 1976, J. James R. Cross medal 1979, 82, Nathan M. Newmark medal 1981, Raymond C. Reese rsch. prize 1986, Norman medal 1987, von Karman medal 1989), Soc. Exptl. Stress Analysis (Hetenyi award 1967, William M. Murray medallion 1986), Am. Soc. Engrng. Edn. (Western Electric Fund award 1976-77, Disting. Educator award 1979), Soc. Engrng. Sci., Internat. Assn. Bridge and Structural Engrng., Am. Inst. Steel Constrn. (adv. com. specifications, Lifetime Achievement award 1999), Ukrainian Acad. Constrn. (fgn. mem.), Sigma Xi, Chi Epsilon, Tau Beta Pi. Office: Davis Hall Univ Calif Berkeley CA 94720 Home: 3967 Crater Lake Hwy Medford OR 97504-9742 E-mail: epp@uclinkA.berkeley.edu.

POPSON, LUCY (MARIA D. POPSON), elementary school educator; BS, Pacific Union Coll., MA in Edn. with Reading emphasis. Tchr. Walter Douglas Elem. Sch., Tucson, 1994—. Named Ariz. Tchr. of Yr., 2006. Office: Walter Douglas Elem Sch 3302 N Flowing Wells Tucson AZ 85705 Business E-Mail: popsonm@flowingwells.k12.az.us.

PORCELLO, LEONARD JOSEPH, engineering research and development executive; b. NYC, Mar. 1, 1934; s. Savior James and Mary Josephine (Bacchi) P.; m. Patricia Lucille Berger, July 7, 1962 (dec. Sept. 1991); children: John Joseph, Thomas Gregory; m. Victoria Roberta Smith, June 21, 1996. BA in Physics, Cornell U., 1955; MS in Physics, U. Mich., 1957, MSEE, 1959, PhD in Elec. Engring, 1963. Research asst. U. Mich., Ann Arbor, 1955-58, instr. elec. engring., 1958-61; research engr. Radar & Optics Lab., 1968-72; asso. dir. Willow Run Labs., 1970-72, asso. prof., 1969-72, prof., 1972-73, adj. prof., 1973-75. Dir. radar and optics divsn. Environ. Rsch. Inst. of Mich., Ann Arbor, 1973-76, v.p., 1973-76, trustee, 1975; asst. v.p., mgr. sensor sys. operation Sci. Applications Internat. Corp., Tucson, 1976-79, v.p., 1979-85, corp. v.p., 1985-87, mgr. def. sys. group, 1986-95, sr. v.p., 1987—, dep. mgr. tech. and advanced sys. sector, 1993-97, mgr. applied sys. group, 1995-2000, dep. mgr. space and tech. solutions sector, 1997-99; CFO TIAS ARMS, 2004-08, bd. dirs., 2004-. Bd. dirs. Tucson Jr. Strings, 1977-79, chmn., 1978-79 Fellow IEEE; mem. Optical Soc. Am., AAAS, Sigma Xi, Eta Kappa Nu. Roman Catholic. Achievements include research on imaging radar, synthetic aperture radar systems and radar remote sensing. Home: 5072 Grandview Ave Yorba Linda CA 92886-4216 Office: Sci Applications Internat Corp Attn LJ Porcello PO Box 820 Yorba Linda CA 92885-0820 Office Phone: 714-695-1465. Business E-Mail: leonard.j.porcello@saic.com.

PORFILIO, JOHN CARBONE, federal judge; b. Denver, Oct. 14, 1934; s. Edward Alphonso Porfilio and Caroline (Carbone) Moore; m. Joan West, Aug. 1, 1959 (div. 1983); children: Edward Miles, Joseph Arthur, Jeanne Kathrine; m. Theresa Louise Berger, Dec. 28, 1983; 1 stepchild, Katrina Ann Smith. Student, Stanford U., 1952—54; BA, U. Denver, 1956, LLB, 1959, LLD (hon.), 2000. Bar: Colo. 1959, US Supreme Ct. 1965. Asst. atty. gen. State of Colo., Denver, 1962—68, dep. atty. gen., 1968—72, atty. gen., 1972—74; US bankruptcy judge Dist. of Colo., Denver, 1975—82; judge US Dist. Ct. Colo., Denver, 1982—85, US Ct. Appeals (10th cir.), Denver, 1985—99, sr. judge, 1999—. Instr. Colo. Law Enforcement Acad., Denver, 1965—70, State Patrol Acad., Denver, 1968—70; guest lectr. U. Denver Coll. Law, 1978. Committeeman Arapahoe County Rep. Com., Aurora, Colo., 1968; mgr. Dunbar for Atty. Gen., Denver, 1970. Mem.: ABA. Roman Catholic. Office: US Ct Appeals Byron White US Courthouse 1825 Stout St Denver CO 80238

PORT, SIDNEY CHARLES, mathematician, educator; b. Chgo., Nov. 27, 1935; s. Isadore and Sarah (Landy) P.; m. Idelle Jackson, Mar. 24, 1957; children— Ethan, Jonathan, Daniel. AB, Northwestern U., 1957, MS, 1958, PhD, 1962. Staff mathematician Rand Corp., 1962-66; asso. prof. math. U. Calif. at Los Angeles, 1966-69, prof., 1969—. Author: (with P. Hoel and C. Stone) Probability, Statistics and Stochastic Processes, 1971, (with C. Stone) Brownian Motion and Classical Potential Theory, 1978, Theoretical Probability for Applications, 1993; contbr. articles to profl. jours. Fellow Inst. Math. Statistics; mem. Am. Math. Soc. Office: UCLA Dept Math Los Angeles CA 90024 Home: 680 Kingman Ave Santa Monica CA 90402 Home Phone: 310-454-0717; Office Phone: 310-825-4701.

PORTER, BLAINE ROBERT MILTON, sociology professor, psychology professor; b. Morgan, Utah, Feb. 24, 1922; s. Brigham Ernest and Edna (Brough) P.; m. Elizabeth Taylor, Sept 27, 1943 (dec.); children: Claudia Jackson, Roger B., David T., Patricia A. Hintze, Corinna; m. Myrna Katherine Kennedy, Feb. 26, 1988. Student, Utah State U., 1940-41; BS, Brigham Young U., 1947, MA, 1949; PhD (Grant Found. fellow family life edn. 1951-52), Cornell U., 1952. Instr. sociology Iowa State Coll., 1949-51; asst. prof. sociology and child devel. Iowa State U., 1952-55; prof., chmn. dept. human devel. and family relationships Brigham Young U., 1955-65, dean Coll. Family Living, 1966-80, univ. prof., 1980-87. Vis. prof. Fulbright rsch. scholar U. London, 1965-66; vis. prof. U. Wurzberg, 1980-81, 83; facilitator human rels. workshops for the Human Devel. Inst., Denver, 1988-98, pres., CEO Families for Children Internat., Inc., 2001—. Editor: The Latter-day Saint Family, 1963, rev. edit., 1966; editor quar. jour.: Family Perspective, 1966-82; contbr. articles to profl. jours. Pres. elect Iowa Coun. Family Rels., 1954-55; pres. Utah Coun. Family Rels. Coun., 1957-58; chmn. sect. marriage counseling Nat. Coun. Family Rels., 1958-59, bd. dirs., 1957-60, exec. com., 1958-72, pres., 1963-64; bd. dirs. Am. Family Soc., 1975-85. Pilot USAAF, 1942-45. Recipient Prof. of Yr. award Brigham Young U., 1964. Mem. Am. Home Econs. Assn. (vice chmn. sect. family relations and child devel. 1955-56), Am. Sociol. Assn. (sec. sect. on family 1964-67), Am. Assn. Marriage and Family Therapy, Am. Psychol. Assn., Soc. Research in Child Devel., Sigma Xi, Phi Kappa Phi (chpt. pres. 1969-71) Home: 1675 Pine Ln Provo UT 84604-2163 Office: 4505 HBLL Brigham Young U Provo UT 84602 Personal E-mail: porter22@comcast.net.

PORTER, BRUCE DOUGLAS, federal agency administrator, educator, writer; b. Albuquerque, Sept. 18, 1952; s. Lyle Kay and Wilma (Holmes) P.; m. Susan Elizabeth Holland, Feb. 2, 1977; children: David William, Christopher Jonathan, Lisa Jeanette, Jennifer Rachel. BA in History, Brigham Young U., 1976; AM in Soviet Studies, Harvard U., 1978, PhD in Polit. Sci., 1979. Sr. rsch. analyst Radio Free Europe/Radio Liberty, Inc., Munich, 1980-83; profl. staff mem. armed svcs. com. U.S. Senate, Washington, 1983-84; sr. analyst Northrop Corp. Analysis Ctr., Washington, 1984-86; exec. dir. Bd. for Internat. Broadcasting, Washington, 1986-90; Bradley sr. rsch. assoc. Harvard U., Cambridge, Mass., 1990-93; assoc. prof. Brigham Young U., Provo, Utah, 1993-95; min. LDS Ch., 1995—. Author: The USSR in Third World Conflicts, 1976, Red Armies in Crisis, 1991, War and the Rise of the State, 1994; co-author: The Polish Drama: 1980-82, 1983; contbr. articles to profl. jours. Lay min. Ch. Jesus Christ Latter-day Saints, bishop, 1985-90, missionary, Düsseldorf, Fed. Republic Germany, 1971-73. Post doctoral fellow Harvard Ctr. for Internat. Affairs, 1979-80, Danforth fellow, 1976-79, David O. McKay scholar Brigham Young U., 1970-71, 74-76; recipient Meritorious Svc. award Pres. of U.S., 1990. Mem. Am. Polit. Sci. Assn., Am. Assn. Advancement Slavic Studies, Internat. Studies Assn. Avocations: swimming, creative writing. Office: Quorum 70 47 E South Temple Salt Lake City UT 84150-0001

PORTER, JOHN E., lawyer; b. Cin., Oct. 23, 1958; s. Robert Carl Jr. and Joanne (Patterson) P.; children: Rebecca Sheyne, Robin Leigh. BSEE with distinction, Stanford U., 1980, JD, 1983. Bar: Calif. 1983, U.S. Ct. Appeals (9th cir.) 1983, U.S. Dist. Ct. (cen. dist.) Calif. 1984. Law clk. to Hon. Procter Hug U.S. Ct. Appeals, ninth cir., 1983—84; ptnr. Paul, Hastings, Janofsky & Walker LLP, LA, mem. policy com. Bd. visitors Stanford (Calif.) Law Sch., 1990-94. Mem. Stanford Law Soc. of So. Calif. (treas. 1990-95). Office: Paul Hastings Janofsky & Walker LLP 515 S Flower St Los Angeles CA 90071-2228 Office Phone: 213-683-6305. Office Fax: 213-996-3305. E-mail: johnporter@paulhastings.com.

PORTER, KEVIN, professional hockey player; b. Detroit, Mich., Mar. 12, 1986; s. John and Sue Porter. BA, U. Mich., 2008. Center U. Mich. Wolverines, 2004—08, capt., 2007—08; center Phoenix Coyotes, 2008—. Mem. Team USA, IIHF Under-18 Championship, 2003, 04, Team USA, IIHF World Jr. Championship, 2005, capt., 06. Recipient Hobey Baker Meml. Award, 2008, RBK West All-Am. First Team, 2008; named Ctrl. Collegiate Hockey Assn. (CCHA) Player of Yr., 2008, Hockey Commrs. January Nat. Player of Month, 2008; named to All-CCHA First Team, 2008. Office: c/o Phoenix Coyotes Hockey Club 6751 N Sunset Blvd, #200 Glendale AZ 85305

PORTER, LOUISA S., federal judge; Apptd. presiding magistrate judge so. dist. U.S. Dist. Ct. Calif., 1997—2002. Mem.: Fed. Magistrate Judges Assn. (pres. 2003—04). Office: 1140 US Courthouse 940 Front St San Diego CA 92101 Office Phone: 619-557-5383. Office Fax: 619-702-9925.

PORTER, STEPHEN CUMMINGS, geologist, educator; b. Santa Barbara, Calif., Apr. 18, 1934; s. Lawrence Johnson Porter Jr. and Frances (Cummings) Seger; m. Anne Mary Higgins, Apr. 2, 1959; children: John, Maria, Susannah. BS, Yale U., 1955, MS, 1958, PhD, 1962. Asst. prof. geology U. Wash., Seattle, 1962-66, assoc. prof., 1966-71, prof., 1971—2002, dir. Quaternary Research Ctr., 1982-98, prof. emeritus, 2002—. Bd. earth scis. Nat. Acad. Sci., Washington, 1983-85; adv. com. divsn. polar programs NSF, Washington, 1983-84; vis. fellow Clare Hall Cambridge (Eng.) U., 1980-81; guest prof. Chinese Acad. Scis., People's Republic of China, 1987—; v.p. Internat. Union Quaternary Rsch., 1992-95, pres., 1995-99. Co-author: Physical Geology, 1987, The Dynamic Earth, 1989, 5th edit., 2004, The Blue Planet, 1995, 2d edit., 1999, Environmental Geology, 1996, Dangerous Earth, 1997; editor: Late Quaternary Environments of the United States, 1983, Quaternary Rsch., 1976—2000; co-editor: The Quaternary Period in the U.S., 2004; assoc. editor Radiocarbon, 1982—89, Am. Jour. Sci., 1997—, mem. editl. bd. Quaternary Sci. Revs., 1988—, Quaternary Internat., 1989—2005. Served to lt. USNR, 1955-57. Recipient Benjamin Silliman prize Yale U., 1962; Willis M. Tale lectr. So. Meth. U., 1984, S.F. Emmons lectr. Colo. Sci. Soc., 1996; Fulbright Hays sr. rsch. fellow, New Zealand, 1973-74; Einstein Professorship Chinese Acad. Scis., 2007. Fellow Geol. Soc. Am. (Kirk Bryan award 2004, Disting. Career award 2005), Arctic Inst. N.Am. (bd. govs.), AAAS; mem. Am. Quaternary Assn. (coun., pres. 1992-94, Disting. Career award 2004). Avocations: photography, genealogy. Home: 18034 15th Ave NW Shoreline WA 98177-3305 Office: U Wash Dept Earth and Space Scis Seattle WA 98195-1310

PORTER, VERNA LOUISE, lawyer; b. May 31, 1941; BA, Calif. State U., 1963; JD, Southwestern U., 1977. Bar: Calif. 1977, U.S. Dist. Ct. (ctrl. dist.) Calif. 1978, U.S. Ct. Appeals (9th cir.) 1978; cert. Dispute Resolutions Programs Act Mediator, L.A. County Bar Assn., 2005. Ptnr. Eisler & Porter, LA, 1978-79, mng. ptnr., 1979-86; pvt. practice, 1986—. Judge pro-tempore LA Mcpl. Ct., 1983—, LA Superior Ct., 1989—, Beverly Hills Mcpl. Ct., 1992—; mem. subcom. landlord tenant law, State Calif., panelist conv.; mem. real property law sect. Calif. State Bar, 1983; mem. client rels. panel, vol. LA County Bar Dispute Resolution; ct. appointed arbitrator civil cases, fee arbitrator LA Superior Ct.; mem. BBB Abitrator Automobile Lemon Laws, 2000—. Editl. asst., contbr. Apt. Bus. Outlook, Real Property News, Apt. Age. Mem. adv. coun. Freddie Mac Vendor, 1995—; mem. World Affairs Coun. Mem. ABA, LA County Bar Assn. (client-rels. vol. dispute resolution fee arbitration 1981—; arbitrator lemon law claims), LA Trial Lawyers Assn., Wilshire Bar Assn. Women Lawyers' Assn., Landlord Trial Lawyers Assn. (founding, pres.), Da Camera Soc. Republican. Office: 2500 Wilshire Blvd Ste 1226 Los Angeles CA 90057-4365 Office Phone: 213-385-1568. Business E-Mail: vlporter@vlpesq.com.

PORTIS, ALAN MARK, physicist, researcher; b. Chgo., July 17, 1926; s. Lyon and Ruth P.; m. Beverly Portis, Sept. 5, 1948; children: Jonathan, Stephen, Sara, Eliyahu. Ph.B., U. Chgo., 1948; AB, U. Calif., Berkeley, 1949, PhD, 1953. Mem. faculty U. Pitts., 1953-56, U. Calif.-Berkeley, 1956—, prof. physics, 1964-95, prof. emeritus, 1995—, asst. to chancellor for research, 1966-67, asso. dean grad. div., 1967-68, dir. Lawrence Hall Sci., 1969-72, univ. ombudsman, 1981-83, 92-94, assoc. dean Coll. Engring., 1983-87, 94-95. Author: Electromagnetic Fields/Sources and Media, 1978, Electrodynamics of High-Temperature Superconductors, 1993; contbg. author: Berkeley Physics Laboratory, 1964, 65, 66, 71. Fulbright fellow, 1961, 67, Guggenheim fellow, 1965, SERC sr. fellow, U.K., 1991-92. Fellow Am. Phys. Soc.; mem. Am. Assn. Physics Tchrs. (Robert Andrews Millikan award 1966). Personal E-mail: amportis@sbcglobal.net.

PORZAK, GLENN E., lawyer; b. Ill., Aug. 22, 1948; m. Judy Lea McGinnis, Dec. 19, 1970; children: Lindsay and Austin. BA with distinction, U. Colo., 1970, JD, 1973. Bar: Colo. 1973. Assoc. Holme Roberts & Owen, Denver, 1973-80, ptnr., 1980-85, mng. ptnr. Boulder office, 1985-95; mng. ptnr. Porzak Browning & Bushong LLP, Boulder, 1996—. Bd. dirs. Wells Fargo Bank Boulder, Ctr. of Am. West, U. Colo. Mus., U. Colo., presdl. search com., 2005-06. Contbr. articles to profl. jours. Bd. dirs. Manor Vail Resorts Condominium Assn., 2001, pres., 2003—07; bd. dirs. U. Colo. Found., 2002—, vice chmn., 2004—06, chmn., 2006—. Named Disting. Alumnus U. Colo., 1991, U. Colo. Sch. Law, 2006. Fellow Explorers Club (bd. dirs. 1995-96, Citation of Merit 1998); mem. Am. Alpine Club (pres. 1988-91), Colo. Mtn. Club (pres. 1983, hon. mem. 1983—), Colo. Outward Bound (trustee 1992-2002, vice chmn. 1997-99, chmn. 1999-2001), Phi Beta Kappa. Achievements include reaching summit of Mt. Everest, climbing highest peak on all seven continents. Home: 405 Baseline Rd Boulder CO 80302 Office: Porzak Browning & Bushong 929 Pearl St Ste 300 Boulder CO 80302-5108 Office Phone: 303-443-6800. Business E-Mail: gporzak@pbblaw.com.

POSEY, PARKER, actress; b. Balt., Nov. 8, 1968; d. Chris Posey. Student, SUNY, Purchase. Actor (films) Joey Breaker, 1993, Description of a Struggle, 1993, The Wake, 1993, Sleepless in Seattle, 1993, Dazed & Confused, 1993, Coneheads, 1993, Flirt, 1993, Dead Connection, 1994, Opera No. 1, 1994, Iris, 1994, Mixed Nuts, 1994, Amateur, 1994, Sleep With Me, 1994, Drunks, 1995, Frisk, 1995, An Eviction Notice, 1995, Party Girl, 1995, Kicking and Screaming, 1995, The doom Generation, 1995, The Daytrippers, 1996, Basquiat, 1996, Waiting for Guffman, 1996, SubUrbia, 1997, The House of Yes, 1997, Clockwatchers, 1997, Henry Fool, 1997, What Rats Won't Do, 1998, You've Got Mail, 1998, The Misadventures of Margaret, 1998, The Venice Project, 1999, Dinner at Fred's, 1999, Scream 3, 2000, Best in Show, 2000, Josie and the Pussycats, 2001, The Anniversary Party, 2001, Personal Velocity: Three Portraits, 2002, The Sweetest Thing, 2002, The Event, 2003, A Mighty Wind, 2003, Laws of Attraction, 2004, The Sisters of Mercy, 2004, Blade: Trinity, The OH in Ohio, 2006, Superman Returns, 2006, For Your Consideration, 2006, Fay Grim, 2006, Broken English, 2007, Broken English, 2007, The Eye, 2008; (TV series) As The World Turns, 1991-92; (TV films) First Love, Fatal Love, 1991, Tracey Takes on New York, 1993, Hell on Heels: The Battle of Mary Kay, 2002, Frankenstein, 2004; (TV miniseries) Armistead Maupin's Tales of the City, 1993, More Tales of the City, 1998, Further Tales of the City, 2001; (TV appearances) (voice only) Futurama, 2000, (voice only) The Simpsons, 2000, Will & Grace, 2001, Boston Legal, 2006; (stage) Hurlyburly, 2005, (Lucille Lortel awards, outstanding featured acress, 2005); screenwriter (with Rory Kelly) Dumb in Love, 1995; contributing editor,

Open City literary mag. Recipient Spl. Jury prize Sundance Film Festival, 1997; named Queen of Indies by TIME Mag. Office: William Morris Agy 151 S El Camino Dr Beverly Hills CA 90212-2775

POSNER, HARRIET S., lawyer; b. Chgo., 1960; BA, Harvard U., 1980; JD, UCLA, 1984. Ptnr. Skadden, Arps, Slate, Meagher & Flom LLP. Bd. dirs. Legal Aid Found., LA, 2002—, NOW Legal Defense, 2004—. Pres., bd. dirs. CityLife, 2000—; bd. trustees Ctr. Early Edn., 2001—. Office: Skadden, Arps, Slate, Meagher & Flom LLP 300 S Grand Ave Ste 3400 Los Angeles CA 90071 Office Phone: 213-687-5237. E-mail: hposner@skadden.com.

POST, DENNY MARIE, telecommunications industry executive, marketing professional; BA in Journalism and Social Scis., cum laude, Trinity U.; student, So. Meth. U. Cox Sch. Bus. Chief mktg. officer Tricon Global Restaurants Inc., 2000—02; chief food innovation officer KFC USA Yum! Brands Inc., 2002; sr. v.p. global food/beverage Starbucks Corp.; sr. v.p., chief mktg. officer T-Mobile USA Inc., 2008—. Chief concept officer, sr. v.p., mem. exec. leadership team Burger King Holdings Inc., 2004—. Named a Power Player, Advt. Age mag., 2008. Office: T Mobile USA Inc Hdqs 12920 SE 38th St Bellevue WA 98006 Office Phone: 425-378-4000. Office Fax: 425-378-4040.

POST, GERALD V., business educator; b. Chippewa Falls, Wis., Nov. 27, 1955; s. Vernon Otto and Doris Post; m. Sarah S. Post, Aug. 14, 1982. BA, U. Wis., Eau Claire, 1978; PhD, Iowa State U., 1983. Asst. prof. Oakland U., Rochester Hills, Mich., 1982-89; prof. Western Ky. U., Bowling Green, 1989-99; prof. dept. bus. U. of the Pacific, Stockton, Calif., 1999—. Cons. analyst/programmer The Wala Group, Arden Hills, Minn., 1985-99. Author: Management Information Systems, 2009, Database Management Systems, 2007; contbr. articles to profl. jours. Office: Univ of the Pacific 3601 Pacific Ave Stockton CA 95211-0197

POST, WILLIAM JOSEPH, utility executive; b. Salem, Ohio, Oct. 13, 1950; s. John Joseph and Barbara Louise (Walton) P.; m. Mary Kay Lane, May 2, 1987; children: Kathryn Leigh, Carly Nancy. BS, Ariz. State U., 1972. Budget mgr. Ariz. Pub. Svc., Phoenix, 1978-82, contr., 1982-85, v.p., contr., 1985-87, v.p. fin. and rates, 1987—; chmn., CEO Pinnacle West Capital Corp., 2001—. Mem. exec. com. Nuclear Energy Inst. Bd. dir. Tumbleweed, Phoenix, Tempe Leadership, 1987, YMCA, Phoenix, 1989. Staff sgt. U.S. Army, 1969-75. Republican. Presbyterian. Office: Pinnacle West Capital 400 N Fifth St Phoenix AZ 85004 Home: 4235 E Claremont St Paradise Valley AZ 85253-3948

POSTAER, LARRY, advertising executive; b. Chgo. Grad., U. Mo. Sch. Journalism, 1959. Catalog copywriter Sears; with Stern, Walters & Simmons, Chgo., 1962-64, creative dir., 1964-76; sr. v.p., group creative dir. Needham Harper & Steers, Chgo., 1976-81, exec. v.p., dir. creative svcs. LA, 1981-86; co-founder, exec. v.p., dir. creative svcs. Rubin Postaer and Assoc., Santa Monica, 1986—. Named Co-leader of Yr. for 1990, Western States Advt. Agys. Assn., 1991. Office: 2525 Colorado Ave Santa Monica CA 90404

POSTE, GEORGE HENRY, biology professor, former pharmaceutical company executive; b. Polegate, Sussex, Eng., Apr. 30, 1944; came to U.S., 1972; s. John H. and Kathleen B. (Brooke) P.; 1 child, Eleanor Kathy; m. Linda C. Suhler Lopez, Nov. 21, 1992; stepchildren: John Robert, Lisa Carolyn. DVM, U. Bristol, 1966, PhD, 1969, DSc, 1987, LLD (hon.), 1995. Lectr. U. London, 1969-72; assoc. prof. SUNY, Buffalo, 1972-76; prof. pathology Roswell Park Meml. Inst., Buffalo, 1976-80; v.p. rsch. SmithKline Beckman, Phila., 1980-82, v.p. R & D, 1982-86, v.p. worldwide rsch. and pre-clin. devel., 1987-88, pres. R & D, 1988-89; pres. R & D techs. SmithKline Beecham, King of Prussia, Pa., 1989-90, vice-chmn., exec. v.p. R & D, 1990-91, pres. and chmn. R & D, 1992-97; chief sci. and tech. officer SmithKline Beecham Corp. PLC, King of Prussia, Pa., 1997-99; CEO Health Tech. Networks, Scottsdale, Ariz., 2000—; non-exec. chmn. OrchidBioSciences Inc., Princeton, NJ, 2002—; Del E. Webb Disting. prof biology Ariz. State U., Tempe, 2003—, dir. Biodesign Inst., 2003—. Mem. pathology B study sect. NIH, Bethesda, Md., 1978-82; chmn. Gordon Conf., N.H., 1985-86, diaDeXus, 1997-2003, Cerebrus, 1997; pres. coun. U. Tex. M.D. Anderson Cancer Ctr.; bd. dirs. Monsanto, Exelixis, SmithKline Beecham Corp. PLC, Orchid BioSciences Inc., 2000-; mem. adv. coun. Beckman Ctr. for Molecular and Genetic Medicine, Stanford U.; mem. coun. Oxford Internat. Biomedical Centre; chmn. task force on bioterrorism, U.S. Dept. of Defense, 2001-04. Editor: Cell Surface Revs., New Horizons in Therapeutics, Cancer Metastasis Revs., Advanced Drug Delivery Revs., 15 books; contbr. articles to profl. jours. Mem. governing bd. UCLA Symposia, Life Sci. Rsch. Found.; mem. bd. Overseers Sch. Vet. Medicine, U. Penn., Gov.'s adv. com. Sci. and Tech., Pa.; mem. adv. bd. Natural Sci. Assn., U. Pa. Fleming fellow U. Oxford, Eng., 1995, Pitt fellow U. Cambridge, Eng., 1995; named Comdr. of British for svcs. in devel. of bioscis., 1999, Scientist of the Year, R&D mag., 2004. Fellow Royal Soc., Royal Coll. Vet. Surgeons, Royal Coll. Pathologists, Ins. Biology (London), Acad. Med. Scis. (London); mem. AAAS, Am. Soc. Cell Biology, Pathol. Soc., Nat. Assn. Biomed. Rsch. (bd. govs. 1984), Univ. Assn. Space Rsch. (mem. coun. 1984), Pharm. Mfrs. Assn. (former chmn. rsch. and devel. section 1988). Avocations: military history, foreign affairs, photography, auto racing. Office: Biodesign Inst Ariz State Univ PO Box 875001 Tempe AZ 85287-5001 Office Phone: 480-727-8662. Business E-Mail: george.poste@asu.edu.

POSTEL, MITCHELL PAUL, association administrator; b. Chgo., May 27, 1952; s. Bernard and Rosalin P.; m. Kristie McCune, Mar. 29, 1981. BA, U. Calif.-Berkeley, 1974; MA, U. Calif.-Santa Barbara, 1977. Devel. officer San Mateo County Hist. Mus., San Mateo, Calif., 1977-81; exec. dir. Ft. Point and Army Mus. Assn., San Francisco, 1981-84, San Mateo County Hist. Assn., 1984—. Faculty Coll. San Mateo. Author: History of the Burlingame Country Club, 1982, Peninsula Portrait: A Pictorial History of San Mateo County, San Mateo: A Centennial History; Seventy-five Years in San Francisco, History of Rotary Club No. 2. Mem. San Mateo County Hist. Resources, Presidio Hist. Soc. (bd. dirs.). Office: San Mateo County Hist Assn 777 Hamilton St Redwood City CA 94063-1618

POSTER, STEVEN B., cinematographer, photographer, publisher, digital imaging consultant; b. Chgo., Mar. 1, 1944; s. David and Lillian Violet (Diamondstone) P. Student, So. Ill. U., 1962-64, LA Art Ctr. Coll. Design, 1964-66; BS, Ill. Inst. Tech., 1967. Pres. Posters Internat. Ltd., LA, 1980. Dir.(photography): (films) Strange Brew, 1983, Testament, 1984, Heavenly Kid, 1985, Blue City, 1986, The Boy Who Could Fly, 1986, Someone to Watch Over Me, 1986 (Am. Soc. Cinematographers nomination, 1987), Big Top Pee Wee, 1987, Next of Kin, 1988, Opportunity Knocks, 1989, Rocky V, 1990, Life Stinks, 1991, Cemetery Club, 1993, Roswell, 1994, A Midwife's Tale, 1996, The Color of Justice, 1996, Rocket Man, 1997, Une Chance Sur Deux, 1997, Donnie Darko, 2001, Stuart Little II, 2002, Daddy Day Care, 2003, Mrs. Harris, 2004, Southland Tales, 2005. Mem.: Internat. Alliance of Theatrical & Stage Employees (bd. dir.), Can. Soc. Cinematographers, Acad. Motion Picture Arst & Sci., Am. Soc. Cinematographers (past pres.). Democrat. Jewish. Avocations: still photography, computers.

POTASH, JEREMY WARNER, public relations executive; b. Monrovia, Calif., June 30, 1946; d. Fenwick Bryson and Joan Antony (Blair) Warner; m. Stephen Jon Potash; 1 son, Aaron Warner. AA, Citrus Coll., 1965; BA, Pomona Coll., 1967. With Forbes Mag., NYC, 1967-69, JETRO, San Francisco, 1970-75; v.p., co-founder, pres. Potash & Co. Pub. Rels., Oakland, Calif., 1980—. Founding exec. dir. Calif.-Asia Bus. Coun., Alameda, 1991—; editor Cal-Asia Member Alert, 1991—; exec. dir. Customs Brokers and Forwarders Assn., San Francisco, 1990—; adv. bd. Asia Pacific Econ. Rev., 1996—; mem. No. Calif. Dist. Export Coun., 2000—, Pacific Coun. Internat. Policy, 2000—; mem. adv. bd. Ctr. Pacific Rim U. San Francisco, 2005—; mem. adv. bd. China-Am. Bus. and Edn. Ctr., Calif. State U. East Bay, 2005. Editor: Southeast Asia Environmental Directory, 1994, Southeast Asia Infrastructure Directory, 1995-96. Co-founder J.L. Magnes docent program, 1980; pres. NorCal WAORT, 1985—86; bd. dirs. Judah L. Magnes Mus., Berkeley, 1981—94. Named Export Citizen of Yr., U.S. Dept. Commerce, 1998. Mem. Oakland Women's Lit. Soc., Book Club Calif. Office: Potash & Co Pub Rels 1050 Marina Village Pkwy Alameda CA 94501

POTASH, STEPHEN JON, public relations executive; b. Houston, Feb. 25, 1945; s. Melvin L. and Petrice (Edelstein) P.; m. Jeremy Warner, Oct. 19, 1969; 1 child, Aaron Warner. BA in Internat. Rels., Pomona Coll., 1967. Account exec. Charles von Loewenfeldt, Inc., San Francisco, 1969-74, v.p., 1974-80; founder, pres. Potash & Co., Pub. Rels., Oakland, Calif., 1980-87, 1990—. Exec. dir. Calif. Coun. Internat. Trade, 1970-87; v.p. corp. communications APL Ltd., Oakland, 1987-90; chmn. Potash & Co., Oakland, 1990-2007, dir., 1990-. Co-author (with Robert J. Chandler): Gold, Silk, Pioneers & Mail: The Story of Pacific Mail Steamship Company, 2007. Bd. dir. Calif. Coun. Internat. Trade, 1987-94, Calif.-Asia Bus. Coun., 1992—, Temple Sinai, Oakland, 1979-81; adv. com. Old Mint, San Francisco Mus., Clampers-Yerba Buena. Mem.: Pub. Rels. Soc. Am. E-mail: steve@potashco.com.

POTTENGER, MARK MCCLELLAND, computer programmer; b. Tucson, Feb. 9, 1955; s. Henry Farmer and Zipporah Herrick (Pottenger) Dobyns. BA, UCLA, 1976, DDiv (hon.), 1998. Data entry operator Astro Computing, Pelham, NY, 1976-77; programmer/analyst LA-CCRS, LA, 1977-80; programmer/analyst cons. LA and San Diego, 1977—, R. Gonzalez Mgmt., LA, 1980—. Rsch. dir. Internat. Soc. Astrol. Rsch., LA, 1985-95. Editor: Astrological Research Methods, 1995; co-author: Tables for Aspect Research, 1986; editor The Mutable Dilemma, 1977-99; author: (computer programs) CCRS Horoscope program, 1977-92, Frequencies for Aspect Rsch., 1986-92. Recipient Jansky award Aquarius Workshops, LA, 1989. Mem. Internat. Soc. Astrol. Rsch., Nat. Coun. Geocosmic Rsch. Democrat. Mem. Religious Sci. Ch. Avocation: reading. Home and Office: 3808 49th St San Diego CA 92105-2101 Office Phone: 619-284-2919. Personal E-mail: markpott@pacbell.net.

POTTER, JAMES G., lawyer, food products executive; s. Maxine Potter. BS in Philosophy and Psychology, U. Chicago; JD, Harvard Law Sch. Assoc. Keck, Mahin & Cate, Morgan, Lewis and Bockius; chief legal officer Prudential Bank and Trust Co. & Prudential Savings Bank (subsidiaries of Prudential Insurance Co.), 1989—97; exec. v.p., gen. counsel, sec. Provident Mutual Life Insurance Co., 1997—2000; v.p., gen. counsel, sec. Del Monte Foods Co., 2001—02, sr. v.p., gen. counsel, sec., 2002—. Office: Del Monte Foods Co One Market St San Francisco CA 94105

POTTER, MYRTLE STEPHENS, healthcare consulting company executive, retired pharmaceutical executive; b. Las Cruces, N Mex., Sept. 28, 1958; d. Albert and Allene (Baker) Stephens; m. James Potter; children: Jamison, Lauren Elizabeth. BA in Polit. Sci., U. Chgo., 1980. Mktg. intern IBM, 1979—80; sales rep. Proctor & Gamble, 1980—81, dist. sales training mgr., 1981—82; sales rep. Merck and Co., 1982—84, mktg. analyst, 1984—85, training & planning mgr., 1985—86, field meeting svc. mgr., 1986—87, dist. sales mgr., 1987—89, product mgr., 1989—90, dir. Astra/Merck affairs, 1990—92, sr. dir market planning, 1992—93, v.p. N.E. Region Bus. Group, 1993—96; v.p. strategy and econ. US Pharmaceuticals Group Bristol-Myers Squibb, 1996—97, group v.p. Worldwide Medicine Group, 1997—98, sr. v.p. sales, US Cardiovascular/Metabolics, 1998, pres. US Cardiovascular/Metabolics, 1998—2000; exec. v.p. Genetech, Inc., South San Francisco, 2000—01, exec. v.p. comml. ops., COO, 2001, pres., comml. ops., co-chmn., product portfolio com., cons., 2004—; founder Myrtle Potter Consulting, LLC, Woodside, Calif., 2005—. Bd. dirs. Calif. Healthcare Inst., 2001—, Amazon.com, 2004—, Medco Health Solutions Inc., 2007—. Mem. Phila. Urban League, 1988—96; mem. bd. trustees Del. Valley Boys & Girls Club, 1996—2000; co-founder Chapman Devel. Group; mem. adv. bd. Healthcare Bus. Women's Assn., 2003—. Recipient National Woman of Distinction award, Girl Scouts of the USA, 2004; named Woman of Yr., Healthcare Bus. Women's Assn., 2000, Top 50 Most Powerful Women In Business, Fortune mag., 2003, Most Powerful Black Executives in America, 15 Young Global Business Influentials, TIME mag.; named one of 50 Women to Watch, Wall St. Jour., 2005. One of the architects of the Astra/Merck joint venture and led the work that set Prilosec on pace to be one of the biggest pharmaceutical products in the world; Won the Merck Chairman's Award for work on the Astra/Merck joint venture. Office: Myrtle Potter Consulting LLC 2995 Woodside Rd Ste 400 Woodside CA 94062 E-mail: myrtle@myrtlepotter.com.

POTTRUCK, DAVID STEVEN, private equity firm executive; b. 1948; m. Emily Pottruck; 2 children. BA, U. Pa., 1970, MBA with honors, 1972. With Arthur Young & Co., 1974-76, sr. cons.; with Citibank N.Am., 1976-81, v.p.; with Shearson/American Express, 1981-84, sr. v.p. consumer mktg. & advt.; with Charles Schwab & Co., San Francisco, 1984—; exec. v.p. mktg., br. adminstr. Charles Schwab and Co., Inc.; pres. Charles Schwab & Co., 1992—94; pres., COO The Charles Schwab Corp., 1994—98, pres., co-CEO, 1998—2003, pres., CEO, 2003—04; chmn., CEO Red Eagle Ventures Inc. (formerly Pottruck Group), 2004—. Apptd. commr. by Congress The Advisory Commn. on Internet Commerce; bd. dirs. Intel Corp., 1998—, US Trust Co., N.A., DoveBid, Inc.; chmn. Eos Airlines. Co-author: Clicks and Mortar: Passion Driven Growth in an Internet Driven World. Bd.dirs. US Ski and Snowboard Team Found.; pres. Pottruck Family Found.; trustee U. Penn. Recipient Torch of Liberty award, Anti-Defamation League, 2000; named Exec. of the Year, San Francisco Bus. Times, CEO of the Year, Morningstar; named one of The Top 15 CEOs, Worth mag. Office: Red Eagle Ventures Inc 201 Spear St San Francisco CA 94105 also: Pottruck Family Foundation 1016 Lincoln Blvd #221 San Francisco CA 94129*

POTTS, DAVID MALCOLM, family planning specialist, educator; b. Sunderland, Durham, England, Jan. 8, 1935; came to the U.S., 1978; s. Ronald Windle and Kathleen Annie (Cole) P.; m. Marcia Jaffe (dec.); children: Oliver, Henry; m. Martha Madison Campbell, Mar. 25, 1995. MA, Cambridge U., Eng., 1960, MB, BChir, 1962, PhD, 1965. Med. dir. Internat. Planned Parenthood Fedn., London, 1969-78; pres., CEO Family Health Internat., Research Triangle Park, N.C., 1978-90; Bixby prof. population and family planning U. Calif. Sch. Pub. Health, Berkeley, 1990—. Fellow and dir. med. studies Sidney Sussex Coll. U. Cambridge., Cambridge, England; Cosgrove lectr. Am. Coll. Ob-gyn, 2005. Author: Textbook of Contraceptive Practice, 1967, 2nd edit., 1983, Abortion, 1977, Victoria's Gene: Haemophilia & the Royal Family, 1997, Ever Since Adam and Eve: The Evolution of Human Sexuality, 1999. Recipient Hugh Moore award Population Action Internat., Washington, 1972, Citizen award The Ind., Durham, N.C., 1987, Charles Schultz Lifetime Achievement award. Fellow AAAS, Royal Coll. Ob-gyn.; mem. Internat. Union Study Population, Population Assn. Am. Achievements include developments in contraception condoms, spermicides and manual vacuum aspiration; studies in breastfeeding, maternal mortality and contraceptive safety. Office: Sch Pub Health Warren Hall Univ Calif Hl Berkeley CA 94720-0001 Office Phone: 510-642-6915. Business E-Mail: potts@berkeley.edu.

POTTS, DENNIS WALKER, lawyer; b. Santa Monica, Calif., Dec. 17, 1945; s. James Longworth and Donna (Neely) P.; children: Brandon Earl Woodward, Trevor Shipley. BA, U. Calif., Santa Barbara, 1967; JD, U. Calif., 1970. Bar: Hawaii 1971, Calif. 1971, U.S. Dist. Ct. Hawaii 1971, U.S. Ct. Appeals (9th cir.) 1973, U.S. Supreme Ct. 1978, U.S. Dist. Ct. (cen. dist.) Calif. 1983. Assoc. Chuck Mau, Honolulu, 1971-74; sole practice Honolulu, 1974—. Mem. litigation com. ACLU Hawaii, 1977-82; former mem. Hawaii Acad. Plaintiff's Attys. Disting. Svc. Cert. ACLU Hawaii. Fellow Internat. Napoleonic Soc.; mem. AAJ (sustaining), Consumer Lawyers Hawaii (treas., bd. govs., Outstanding Lawyers in America). Office: 2755 ASB Tower 1001 Bishop St Honolulu HI 96813-3429 Office Phone: 808-537-4575. Business E-Mail: dennispotts@hawaii.rr.com.

POULTER, CHARLES DALE, chemist, educator, consultant; b. Monroe, La., Aug. 29, 1942; s. Erwin and Mary Helen Poulter; m. Susan Raetzsch, Aug. 24, 1964; children: Mary Christa, Gregory Thomas. BS, La. State U., Baton Rouge, 1964; PhD, U. Calif., Berkeley, 1967. NIH postdoctoral fellow UCLA, 1967-68; asst. prof. chemistry U. Utah, Salt Lake City, 1969-75, assoc. prof., 1975-78, prof., 1978-94, John A. Widtsoe prof. chemistry, 1994—, chair dept. chemistry, 1995-2000; editor-in-chief Jour. Organic Chemistry, 2001—. Fellow AAAS, Am. Acad. Arts and Scis.; mem. Am. Chem. Soc. (organic exec. com. 1983-86, biol. divsn. councillor 1993-98, chair organic divsn. 1998, Ernest Guenther award 1991, Utah award 1992, Arthur C. Cope scholar 1998, Repligen award 2002, James Flack Norris award 2004). Office: U Utah Dept Chemistry 340 S 1500 E Rm 2020 Salt Lake City UT 84112

POULTON, L. STEVEN, state legislator; b. Salt Lake City, Jan. 10, 1950; m. Andrea Robins. BA in Bus. Mgmt., U. Utah. Lic. property and casualty ins. agt./broker, Utah; cert. ins. counselor. Formerly in ins. bus.; mem. Utah Senate, Dist. 9, Salt Lake City, 1994—; mem. bus., labor and econ. devel. com., human svcs. com.; mem. health and human svcs. appropriations; chair rules com., asst. majority whip. Treas., Salt Lake County Rep. Party. Mem. Salt Lake C. of C., Salt Lake Rotary Club. Republican. Home: 4524 Briarcreek Dr Salt Lake City UT 84117-4573 Fax: 801-486-7541.

POUND, JOHN BENNETT, lawyer; b. Champaign, Ill., Nov. 17, 1946; s. William R. and Louise Catherine (Kelly) P.; m. Mary Ann Hanson, June 19, 1971; children: Meghan Elizabeth, Matthew Fitzgerald. BA, U. N. Mex., 1968; JD, Boston Coll., 1971. Bar: N. Mex. 1971, U.S. Dist. Ct. N. Mex. 1971, U.S. Ct. Appeals (10th cir.) 1972, U.S. Supreme Ct., 1993. Law clk. to Hon. Oliver Seth, US Ct. Appeals, 10th Cir., Santa Fe, 1971-72. Asst. counsel Supreme Ct. Disciplinary Bd., 1977-83, dist. rev. officer, 1984—; mem. Supreme Ct. Com. on Jud. Performance Evaluation, 1983-85; bd. dirs. Archdiocese Santa Fe Cath. Social Svcs., 1995—. Contbr. articles to profl. jours. Pres. bd. dirs. N.Mex. Ind. Coll. Fund, Santa Fe; chmn. N.Mex. Dem. Leadership Coun., 1991—; bd. dirs. Santa Fe Boys Club, 1989-92; rules com. N.Mex. Dem. Party, 1982—; v.p. Los Alamos Nat. Lab. Comm. Coun., 1985-90; fin. chmn. N.Mex. Clinton for Pres. campaign, 1992; co-chmn. Clinton-Gore Re-election Campaign, N.Mex., 1996, 2000; co-chmn. Gore for Pres., N.Mex., 2000; co-chmn. Kerry for Pres., N.Mex., 2004. Fellow Am. Bar Found., Am. Coll. Trial Lawyers, N.Mex. Bar Found.; mem. ABA, Am. Bd. Trial Advocates, N.Mex. Bar Assn. (health law sect. 1987—), Santa Fe County Bar Assn. Democrat. Roman Catholic. Avocations: history, languages, literature, swimming, baseball. Office: Long Pound Komer PA PO Box 5098 2200 Brothers Rd Santa Fe NM 87505-6903 Office Phone: 505-982-8405. Personal E-mail: lpk@nm.net, jmpound@comcast.net.

POWDRELL-CULBERT, JANE, state legislator; New Mexico State Representative, District 44, 2003-.Public relations training consultant, currently. Republican. Office: Capitol Add NMex State Capitol, Rm 203GCN Santa Fe NM 87503

POWELL, AMY RUTH, film company executive; d. William T. and Phyllis Powell; m. Douglas Keith Chernack, June 12, 2004. BA in Art Hist. and Lit., Emory U., Atlanta; MBA, UCLA. With CNN, Sony Pictures, LA; v.p. interactive mktg. Paramount Studios, LA, 2004—. Recipient Key Art award, 2005, London Internat. award, 2005; named Media Maven, Ad Age, 2006; named a Next Gen Exec., Hollywood Reporter, 2005; named one of 50 Smartest People in Hollywood, Entertainment Weekly, 2007. Office: Paramount Pictures Corp 5555 Melrose Ave Ste 121 West Hollywood CA 90038

POWELL, DENNIS D., retired computer company executive; BBA in Acctg., Oreg. State U. Former sr. ptnr. Coopers & Lybrand LLP; v.p., corp. contr. Cisco Systems, Inc., San Jose, Calif., 1997—2002, sr. v.p. corp. fin., 2002—03, sr. v.p., CFO, 2003—08. Mem. FDIC Adv.

Com. on Banking Policy; expert witness on fin. reporting Senate Banking Com. and Ho. Fin. Subcom. Mem.: AICPA (task force for in-process R&D 2000), Fin. Execs. Internat.

POWELL, JAMES LAWRENCE, educational association administrator, museum director, geologist; b. Berea, Ky., July 17, 1936; s. Robert Lain and Lizena (Davis) P.; m. Joan Hartmann; children: Marla, Dirk, Joanna. AB, Berea Coll., 1958; PhD, MIT, 1962; DSc (hon.), Oberlin Coll., 1983; LHD (hon.), Tohoku Gakuin U., 1986; DSc (hon.), Beaver Coll., 1992. Asst. prof., assoc. prof., prof. Oberlin Coll., Ohio, 1962-83, chmn. geol. dept., 1965—73, v.p., provost, 1975—81, assoc. dean, 1973—75, acting pres., 1981—83; pres. Franklin and Marshall Coll., Lancaster, Pa., 1983-88, Reed Coll., Portland, Oreg., 1988-91; pres., chief exec. officer The Franklin Inst., Phila., 1991-94; pres., dir. Los Angeles County Mus. Natural History, LA, 1994—2001; exec. dir. Nat. Physical Sci. Consortium, LA, 2001—. Mem. Nat. Sci. Bd., 1986-98; adj. prof. Univ. So. Calif., 1995-2001 Author: Strontium Isotope Geology, 1972, Pathways to Leadership: Achieving and Sustaining Success: A Guide for Nonprofit Executives, 1995, Night Comes to the Coctzcems; Dinosaur Extinction and the Transformation of Modern Geology, 1998; Mysteries of Terra Firma: Age and Evolution of the Earth, 2001, Grand Canyon: Solving Earth's Grandest Puzzle, 2005. Fellow: Geol. Soc. Am.; mem.: Phi Beta Kappa, Phi Kappa Phi, Sigma Xi. Office: Nat Physical Science Consortium Ste 348 3716 S Hope Los Angeles CA 90007-4344 Business E-Mail: jpowell@usc.edu.

POWELL, KRAIG, state legislator; b. Tacoma, Wash., Mar. 18, 1966; m. Kim Powell; children: Kristopher, Benjamin, Jessica, Sarah. BA, Willamette U., 1989; MA, U. Va., 1992; JD, U. Va. Law Sch., 1995; PhD in Govt., U. Va., 2000. Former legis. intern US Senator Orrin Hatch; briefing atty. Tex. Law Ct., 1995; sr. law clk. Ill. Supreme Ct., 1996—2000; atty. Tesch Law Offices, 2001—; mem. Dist. 54 Utah House of Reps., 2009—. Named an Eagle Scout, Boy Scouts of Am. Republican. Mormon. Office: W030 State Capitol Complex Salt Lake City UT 84114 Mailing: 943 E 530 N Heber City UT 84032 Office Phone: 801-538-1029, 435-654-1550. Office Fax: 801-538-1908. Business E-Mail: kraigpowell@utah.gov.

POWELL, TREVOR JOHN DAVID, archivist; b. Hamilton, Ont., Can., Feb. 3, 1948; s. David Albert and Morvydd Ann May (Williams) P.; m. Marian Jean McKillop, May 1, 1976. BA, U. Sask., Regina, 1971; MA, U. Regina, Sask., Can., 1980. Staff archivist Sask. Archives Bd., Regina, Sask., 1973-80, dir., 1980-86, acting provincial archivist, 1986-87, provincial archivist, 1988—. Co-author: Living Faith: A Pictorial History of Diocese of Qu'Appelle; author: From Tent to Cathedral: A History of St. Paul's Cathedral, Regina. Archivist Diocese of Qu'Appelle, Regina, Sask., 1971—, registrar, 1979—; archivist, eccles. Province of Rupert's Land, Winnipeg, Man., 1988—; mem. adv. coun. Sask. Order of Merit, 1988-95, Sask Honours, 1995—; chair selection com. Sask Vol. medal, 1995-96, Can. 125 medal, 1992. Recipient Queen's Golden Jubilee medal, 2002, Sask. Centennial medal, 2005. Mem. Soc. Am. Archivists, Can. Hist. Assn., Commonwealth Archivists Assn., Sask. Coun. Archives (sec.-treas. 1987-88, 90-92, pres. 1994-96, Can. Coun. Archives rep. 1994-96), Assn. Can. Archivists (bd. dirs. 1979-81). Anglican. Avocations: gardening, walking, reading, music, birdwatching. Home: 241 Orchard Cres Regina SK Canada S4S 5B9 Office: Sask Archives Bd 3303 Hillsdale St Univ Regina Regina SK Canada S4S 0A2 E-mail: tpowell@archives.gov.sk.ca.

POWER, FRANCIS WILLIAM, newspaper publisher; b. Webster, SD, Aug. 12, 1925; s. Frank B. and Esther C. (Fowler) P.; m. Margaret Jean Atkinson, Mar. 24, 1951; children: Patricia Ann, John Michael, Kerry Jean. BBA, U. N.Mex., 1948. Display advt. sales rep. The Register, Santa Ana, Calif., 1948-51; advt. mgr. Valley Morning Star, Harlingen, Tex., 1951-62; gen. mgr. Pampa (Tex.) Daily News, 1962-69; bus. mgr. Brownsville (Tex.) Herald, 1969-75; pub. The Lima (Ohio) News, 1975-91; v.p. Freedom Comm., Inc., until 1991; ret., 1991. Served with USNR, 1943-46. Mem.: Shawnee Country Club, Elks, Rotary. Roman Catholic. Office: Freedom Comm Inc 17666 Fitch Irvine CA 92614-6022

POWER, J.D., III, (JAMES DAVID POWER III), marketing executive; b. Worcester, Mass., May 30, 1931; m. Julie Power (dec. 2002); 4 children; m. Joan Power, 2003. BA in English, Coll. of the Holy Cross, Worcester, Mass., 1953; MBA, U. Penn., 1959; PhD (hon.), Coll. of the Holy Cross, Calif. Lutheran U., Calif. State U. Northridge, Coll. Misericordia. Financial analyst Ford; mktg. rsch. cons. Marplan GM; mktg. rsch. exec. J.I. Case; dir. corp. planning McCulloch Motors Inc., Los Angeles, Calif.; founder, pres. J.D. Power & Assocs., Calif., 1968—, chmn., 1996—. Adj. prof. mktg. Calif. State U. Northridge. Line officer duty U.S. Coast Guard, Arctic and Antarctica. Recipient Disting. Service Citation, Automotive Hall of Fame, 1992. Office: J D Power & Assocs 2625 Townsgate Rd Westlake Village CA 91361

POWER, JOHN BRUCE, lawyer; b. Glendale, Calif., Nov. 11, 1936; m. Sandra Garfield, Apr. 27, 1998; children by previous marriage: Grant, Mark, Boyd. AB magna cum laude, Occidental Coll., 1958; JD, NYU, 1961; postdoctoral, Columbia U., 1972. Bar: Calif. 1962. Assoc. O'Melveny & Myers, LA, 1961—70, ptnr., 1970—97, resident ptnr. Paris, 1973—75; Sheffelman disting. lectr. Sch. Law, U. Wash., Seattle, 1997. Mem. Social Svcs. Commn. City of L.A., 1993, pres., 1993; pres. circle, exec. com. Occidental Coll., 1979-82, 91-94, chair, 1993-94; adj. prof. UCLA Sch. Law, 1999; mem. Tri-Bar Opinion Com., 2005-. Contbr. articles to jours. Bd. dirs. Met. L.A. YMCA, 1988—, treas., 1998-2001; steering com. Working Group Legal Opinions, 2005-; bd. mgrs. Stuart Ketchum Downtown YMCA, 1985-92, pres., 1989-90; mem. L.A. County Rep. Ctrl. Com., 1962-63; trustee Occidental Coll., 1992—, chmn., 2001-03, acting gen. counsel, 1998-2000. Recipient YMCA Golden Book of Disting. Svc. award, 2002, Alumni Seal award Occidental Coll., 2003; Root Tilden scholar. Fellow Am. Coll. Comml. Fin. Lawyers (bd. regents 1999-03); mem. ABA (comml. fin. svcs. com., com. legal opinions, vice chair 2005-07, chair 2007—, UCC com., bus. law sect.), Am. Bar Found., Calif. Bar Assn. (chmn. partnerships and unincorporated assns. com. 1982-83, chmn. uniform commn. code com. 1984-85, chmn. opinions com. 2000-05, exec. com. 1987-91, chmn. bus. law sect. 1990-91, chmn. coun. sect. chairs 1992-93, liaison to state bar commn. on future of legal profession and state bar 1993-95, advisor to exec. com. 1997—, Bus. Law Sect. Lifetime Achievement award 2004), LA County Bar Assn. (exec. com. comml. law and bankruptcy sect. 1970-73, 86-89), Fin. Lawyers Conf. (bd. govs. 1982—, pres. 1984-85), Exec. Svc. Corps (sec. 1985-00, dir. 1994-2007, vice-chmn. 2000-07), Occidental Coll. Alumni Assn. (bd. govs. 1965-68, pres. 1967-68), Phi Beta Kappa (councilor 1982—, pres. 1990-92). Office: O Melveny & Myers 400 S Hope St Los Angeles CA 90071-2899 Personal E-mail: johnpower@earthlink.net.

POWER, THOMAS MICHAEL, economist, educator; b. Milw., May 12, 1940; s. Paul C. and Edith (Thomas) P.; m. Pamela Shore, June 13, 1977; children: Donovan, Kate. BA, Lehigh U., 1962; MA, Princeton U., 1965, PhD, 1971. Instr. Lehigh U., Bethlehem, Pa., 1966-67, Princeton (N.J.) U., 1967-68; from asst. to assoc. prof. U. Mont., Missoula, 1968-78, prof. econ., chmn., 1978—. Author: Economic Value of Quality of Life, 1980, The Economic Pursuit of Quality, 1987, Lost Landscapes and Failed Economies: The Search for an Economic Value of Place, 1996, Environmental Protection and Local Economic Well-Being: The Economic Pursuit of Quality, 1996, Post-Cowboy Economics: Pay and Prosperity in the New American West, 2001. Chmn. bd. dirs. Sussex Sch. Bd., Missoula, 1984-93. Woodrow Wilson Nat. fellow, 1963. Mem. Phi Beta Kappa. Avocations: mountain climbing, bicycling, skiing. Office: U Montana Dept Econs Missoula MT 59812-0001 E-mail: tom.power@mso.umt.edu.

POWERS, JOHN T., JR., former mayor; Mayor City of Spokane, Wash., 2001—03. Bd. dirs. Assn. Wash. Cities, Inland Northwest Tech. Edn. Ctr., Spokane Regional Econ. Devel. Coun.; co-chair Spokane Task Force on Race Rels., U.S. Conf. Mayors; mem. Gas & Elec. Utility Restruction Task Force, Wash. State Competitiveness Coun., Assn. Northeast Wash. Mayors.

POWERS, LINDA SUE, biophysicist, educator, biomedical engineer; b. Pitts., Feb. 8, 1948; d. Luther Thurston and Helen Grace (Currence) Powers. BS in Physics and Chemistry, Va. Poly. Inst. and State U., 1970; MA in Physics, Harvard U., 1972, PhD in Biophysics, 1976. Mem. tech. staff AT&T Bell Labs., Murray Hill, N.J., 1976-88; dir. bio-catalysis sci. ctr., prof. chemistry & biochemistry Utah State U., Logan, 1988-91, prof. elec. engring., biol. & irrigation engring., 1991—2006; dir. Nat. Ctr. for the Design of Molecular Function, 1991—; Thomas R. Brown prof. bioengring., prof. elec. and computer engring. U. Ariz., Tucson, 2007—. Adj. prof. U. Pa. Med. Sch., Phila., 1978-2000; vis. fellow Princeton U., 1981-82. Mem. editl. corr. Comments Molecular Cellular Biophysics, 1980-89; editl. bd. Biophysics Jour., 1989-96, editl. bd. Am. Inst. of Physics Internat. Series Basic and Applied Biol. Physics, 1993—, Wiley Encyclopedia of Biomedical Engineering, 2002-05; contbr. numerous articles to profl. jours. and books. Recipient 1st U.S. Bioenergetics award, 1982, State of Utah Gov.'s medal for sci. and tech., 1994. Fellow Am. Phys. Soc. (divsn. biol. physics 1988-92, exec. bd. 1977-83, chmn. 1984-85, fellow com. mem.), Am. Inst. Chemists, IEEE (steering com. 2002-03), AAAS, NAS (com. chem. and biol. terrorism, 1997-98, com. countering agr. bioterrorism 2001-02), Biophys. Soc., Soc. Applied Spectroscopy, Sigma Pi Sigma, Phi Lambda Upsilon. Avocations: breeding and showing horses, writing music, windsurfing, snowboarding. Office: Univ Ariz Dept Elec and Computer Engring PO Box 210104 Tucson AZ 85721-0104 Business E-Mail: lsp@ece.arizona.edu.

POWERS, MATTHEW DOUGLAS, lawyer; b. San Francisco, July 7, 1959; BS, Northwestern U., 1979; JD cum laude, Harvard Law Sch., 1982. Bar: Calif. 1982, Dist. Ariz., US Dist. Ct. (no. dist. Calif.) 1982, US Dist. Ct. (ctrl. dist. Calif.) 1983, US Ct. Appeals (9th cir.) 1983, US Dist. Ct. (ea. dist. Calif.) 1985, US Ct. Appeals (fed. cir.) 1986, US Supreme Ct. 1988, US Ct. Internat. Trade 1990, US Dist. Ct. (so. dist. Tex.) 1990, US Dist. Ct. (no. dist. Ind.) 1991, US Dist. Ct. (ea. dist. Mich.) 2003, US Ct. Appeals (2nd, 5th, and 7th cirs.) 1991, US Dist. Ct. (ea. dist. Mich.) 2003. Head, mng. ptnr., global patent litig. grp. Weil, Gotshal & Manges, LLP, Redwood City, Calif., mem. mgmt. com. Lectr. in field; tchr. patent litig. U. Calif. Boalt Hall Sch. Law, Berkeley; lectr. patent law Stanford U., Santa Clara U.; mem. adv. bd. Inst. Transitional Arbitration; mem. exec. com. Boalt Hall, Berkeley Ctr. for Law & Tech., Santa Clara U. Sch. Law, High Tech. Law Inst.; mem. No. Dist. Calif. Patent Rules Com., No. Dist. Calif. Patent Jury Instrn. Com.; chmn. Internat. Patent Law Subcommittee, 1989; mem. ICC Commn. on Intellectual and Indsl. Property, 1990. Editor-in-chief Intellectual Property & Tech. Law Jour., co-editor-in-chief Jour. of Propriety Rights, mem. editl. bd. Mealey's Litig. Reports: Intellectual Property, Internat. Litig. Quarterly, 1991, published (numerous articles). Mem. leadership coun. Am. Diabetes Assn., San Francisco; bd. dirs. Greater Bay Area Make-A-Wish Found.; mem. exec. com. Orientation in In USA Law Prog., U. Calif. Named The "Go To" Patent Litigator in No. Calif., The Recorder, 2003, Father of Yr., Father's Day Coun. San Francisco, 2004, Trial Lawyer of Yr., Santa Clara County Trial Lawyers Assn., 2005, Calif. Lawyer Atty. of Yr. in Intellectual Property, Calif. Lawyer mag., 2005; named a Leading Lawyer, PLC Which Lawyer?, 2006; named one of 8 Star Attys. in all fields in the US, Chambers Global Guide, 2001, Top 10 Attys. in Silicon Valley, The Lawyer (London), 2001, Top 100 Attys. in the World, 2001, 7 Top IP Trial Lawyers in the Country, IP Worldwide, 2002, Top 25 IP Lawyers in Calif., San Francisco Daily Jour., 2003, Top 25 Attys. in All Fields in the San Francisco Bay Area, San Francisco Chronicle, 2003, Top 45 Attys. Under 45, Am. Lawyer mag., 2003, Top 10 Trial Lawyers in Am., Nat. Law Jour., 2006. Mem.: ABA. Office: Weil Gothal & Manges LLP 201 Redwood Shores Pky Redwood City CA 94065 Office Phone: 650-802-3200. Office Fax: 650-802-3100. E-mail: matthew.powers@weil.com.

POWERS, RAY LLOYD, former state senator, dairy farmer, rancher; b. Colorado Springs, Colo., June 27, 1929; s. Guy and Cora (Hill) P.; m. Dorothy Parrish, Dec. 14, 1975; 1 child, Janet. Student, Pub. Schs. Dairy farmer, Colo. Springs, 1947—; v.p. bus. devel., dir. The Capitol Pulse Inc., Washington, 2000—. Mem. Colo. Ho. of Reps., 1978-80; mem. Colo. Senate, 1981-2000, senate pres., 1998-2000; bd. dirs. Mountain Empire Dairyments Coop., Denver, 1967-81. Mem. Colo. Cattlemen, Republican Men's Club, Lions. Republican.

POWERS, REBECCA ANN, psychiatrist, health facility administrator; b. Portland, Oreg., Sept. 28, 1955; m. Gary A. Gusewitch. B in Tech. and Med. Tech., Oreg. Inst. Tech., 1977; M in Pub. Health, Loma Linda U., 1983, MD, 1990. Cert. Am. Bd. Psychiatry and Neurology. Receptionist and vet. asst. Gresham (Oreg.) Vet. Clinic, 1969-77; micobiologist clin. lab. Portland Adventist Med. Ctr., 1977-86; rsch. asst. dept. microbiology Loma Linda (Calif.) U. Med. Ctr., 1987, residency gen. psychiatry, 1990-93; cons. psychiatrist arrowhead home Geriatric Psychiat. Home, San Bernardino, Calif., 1992-93; gen. psychiat. review instr. nat. med. bds. Arc Ventures, Pasadena, Calif., 1992-93; fellowship child and adolescent psychiatry Stanford (Calif.) U. Hosp., 1993-95; psychiat. disability evaluations state Calif. Sunnybrook, Amberstone and Stanford Med. Groups, 1994-95; cons. child and adolescent psychiatry Seneca Ctr. Day Treatment, Fremont, Calif., 1994—; attending staff physician comprehensive pediatric care unit, med. psychiat. unit Stanford U. Hosp., 1995-97, developer and med. dir. clin. faculty co. Terminus Adolescent Alcohol and Drug Treatment Program, 1995-96; pvt. practice physician Child, Adolescent, Adult and Family Psychiatry, Los Gatos, Calif., 1995—; attending for eating disorders clin., clin. faculty co. Terminus Lucile Salter Packard Children's Hosp. at Stanford, 1995—. Founder and pres. Art Soc., 1976-77; planning com. Portland Adventist Med. Ctr., 1982-83, team capt. fund raising program, 1984, cmty svc., 1983-86, instr. clin. lab, 1977-86; cons. pub. health Clackamas County Health Dept., 1983; pub. rels. officer Med. Sch. Class 1990, 1987-90; PULSE rep. Loma Linda U. Sch. Med., 1988-90; rsch. aid, schizophrenia dopamine receptor rsch. Jerry L. Pettis VA Meml. Hosp., Loma Linda, 1991; lecturer Am. Lupus Soc., 1991, Loma Linda U. Med. Ctr., 1992; mem. com. Treatment Improvement Group for anxiety and personality disorders Behavioral Medicine Ctr. Loma Linda U. Med. Ctr., 1991-92;psychiat. evaluations smoking cessation Wellburtin Study Jerry L. Pettis Va Meml. Hosp., Loma Linda, 1992-93; co-founder, pres. elect L.A. Preventive Psychiatry Tak Force So. Calif. Psychiat. Soc., 1992-93; del. Calif. Med. Assn. Calif. House Officer Med. Soc.; developer and coord. Pediatric Psychiatry Lecture Series for pediatricians and other primary care physicians Lucile Salter Packard Children's Hosp. at Stanford, 1994-95; com. Forensic Cmty. Project for Oakland Neighborhood Steering and Oakland Planning Commn., 1994; dir. Pediatric Psychiatry Screening Stanford U., 1994; appointment prevention com. Am. Acad. Child and Adolescent Psychiatry, 1994-97, com. Well Being Physicians Calif. Med. Assn., 1995—, adv. bd. Adult and Adolescent Alcohol and Drug Treatment Program, Stanford U. Hosp, 1995-96; assoc. mem. Consortium Med. Educators in Substance Abuse, 1994; program development adolescent alcohol and drug treatment Stanford U. Med. Ctr., 1995-96; vol. clin. instr. and supervisor Stanford U. Hosp., 1995—. Asst. editor newsletter Lab Lines, 1984-86; planned and presented symposium Everything you always wanted to know about Mediacl Practice, San Bernardino County Med. Soc., 1989; contbr. chpts. to books. Recipient Janssen Clin. Scholar award U.S. Psychiat. and Mental Health Congress, 1994, Presdl. Scholar award Am. Acad. Child and Adolescent Psychiatry, 1995. Mem. AMA, Am. Acad. Child and Adolescent Psychiatry, Am. Assn. Orthopsychiatry, Am. Lupus Soc., Am. Psychiatric Assn., Calif. Acad. Preventive Medicine, Calif. Med. Assn. (com. for Well Being of Physicians), Calif. Soc. Addiction Medicine, Healthy Young 2000, No. Calif. Psychiat. Soc., No. Calif. Region Child and Adolescent Psychiat. Home: 36275 Easterday Way Fremont CA 94536-1671 Office: Stanford U Child Psychiatry 401 Quarry Rd MC 5540 Stanford CA 94305-5540 also: 14651 S Bascom Ave Ste 225 Los Gatos CA 95032-2005

POYNTER, DAN, author, publisher, speaker; b. NYC, Sept. 17, 1938; s. William Frank and Josephine E. (Thompson) P BA, Calif. State U., Chico, 1960; postgrad., San Francisco Law Sch., 1961—63. federally lic. master parachute rigger; lic. pilot. Pub., prin. Para Pub., Santa Barbara, Calif., 1969—. Expert witness Nat. Forensic Ctr., Tech. Adv. Svc. for Attys., Consultants and Consulting Orgns. Directory, Lawyer's Guide to Legal Consultants, Expert Witnesses, Svcs., Books and Products Author: The Parachute Manual, Parachuting, The Skydiver's Handbook, 2006, Parachuting Manual with Log, Hang Gliding, Manned Kiting, The Self-Publishing Manual, 2006, How to Write, Print & Sell Your Own Book, Publishing Short Run Books, Business Letters For Publishers, Computer Selection Guide, Word Processing and Information Processing, Publishing Forms, Parachuting Manual for Square/Piggyback Equipment, Frisbee Players' Handbook, Toobee Players' Handbook, Writing Nonfiction, Successful Nonfiction, 115 others, some translated in fgn. languages; past editor news mag. Spotter; monthly columnist Parachute mag., 1963—; contbr. over 500 articles and photographs to mags; patentee parachute pack, POP TOP Recipient numerous certs. of appreciation for directing parachuting competitions Mem. U.S. Parachute Assn. (life, chmn. bd., exec. com. 12 yrs., nat. and internat. del., Achievement award, 1981, Cert. 40 yr., awarded Gold Parachute Wings, 1972), Parachute Industry Assn. (pres. 1985, 86), AIAA, Soc. Automotive Engrs., Nat. Aeronautic Assn., Aviation Space Writers Assn. (internat. conf. 1978, 79, 82), Calistoga Skydivers (past sec.), No. Calif. Parachute Coun. (past sec.), U.S. Hang Gliding Assn. (life, past dir., del.), Internat. Assn. Ind. Pubs. (past bd. dirs., pres. Santa Barbara chpt. 1979-82), Assn. Am. Pubs., Pub. Mktg. Assn. (bd. dirs., v.p.), Book Pubs. So. Calif., Am. Booksellers Assn., Commn. Internat. de Vol Libre of Fedn. Aero. Internat. in Paris (U.S. del., past pres., lifetime Pres. d'Honneur award 1979, recipient Paul Tissander diploma, 1984), Nat. Spkrs. Assn Home: RR 1 Santa Barbara CA 93117-1047 Office: Para Publishing PO Box 8206 Santa Barbara CA 93118-8206 Office Phone: 805-968-7277. E-mail: danpoynter@parapublishing.com.

POZNER, LARRY S., lawyer, educator; b. Indpls., Nov. 13, 1947; BS in Bus. Adminstrn., U. Colo., 1969; JD, U. Calif., 1973. Bar: Colo. 1973. Dep. state pub. defender, 1973—77; pub. defender Colo. Springs, 1973—77, Denver, 1973—77; former lead counsel Broncos Football Club; ptnr. Reilly Pozner & Connelly, Denver. Adj. prof. law U. Denver, 1983—92, lectr., 1981—82, adj. asst. prof., 1982—85; with faculty Nat. Criminal Def. Coll., 1985—95; legal analyst NBC News, 1998—2000; lectr. on cross examination more than 200 times in 47 states & Canada. TV appearances include: NBC Nightly News; The Today Show; Fox News; CNN; NPR; Court TV; co-author (with Roger Dodd): Cross Examination: Science & Techniques, 2nd edit., 2005; contbr. articles to profl. jours. Mem.: Criminal Def. Bar (pres. 1985—86), Nat. Assn. Criminal Def. Lawyers (officer 1992, pres. 1998—99, immediate past pres. 1999—2000). Office: Reilly Pozner & Connelly The Kittredge Bldg 511 16th St Ste 700 Denver CO 80202 Office Phone: 303-893-6100. Office Fax: 303-893-6110. E-mail: lpozner@litigationcoloradox.com.

PRAGER, ELLIOT DAVID, surgeon, educator; b. NYC, Sept. 10, 1941; s. Benjamin and Sadye Zelda (Newman) P.; m. Phyllis Damon Warner, July 1, 1967; children: Rebecca, Sarah, Katherine. AB, Dartmouth Coll., 1962; MD, Harvard U., 1966. Diplomate Am. Bd. Surgery, Am. Bd. Colon and Rectal Surgery. Surg. resident Roosevelt Hosp., NYC, 1966-71; colon-rectal fellow Lahey Clinic, Boston, 1971-72; staff surgeon Sansum Clinic, Santa Barbara, Calif., 1974—, dir. colorectal fellowship, 1982-97, chief of surgery, 1986-94; dir. surg. edn. Cottage Hosp., Santa Barbara, 1994-96. Mem., vice chair Residency Rev. Com., 1992—. Author: (with others) Operative Colorectal Surgery, 1994, Current Therapy in Colon and Rectal Surgery, 1990; contbr. articles to profl. jours. Lt. comdr. USN, 1972-74. Fellow Am. Coll. Surgeons (adv. coun. 1992—), Am. Soc. of Colon and Rectal Surgeons (v.p. 1992, sec. of program dirs., 1990—). Achievements include 5 patents for colostomy control devices. Office: Sansum Clinic 317 W Pueblo St Santa Barbara CA 93105-4365

PRATER, MARY ANNE, special education educator, researcher; d. Herman Bates and Barbara M. Prater. MusB, U. Utah, Salt Lake City, 1975, MS, 1982; PhD, Utah State U., Logan, 1987. Asst. prof. So. Ill. U., Carbondale, 1987—90; prof., dept. chair, assoc. dean U. Hawaii at Manoa, Honolulu, 1990—2001; prof., dept. chair Brigham Young U., Provo, Utah, 2001—. Author: Developmental Disabilities in Children's Literature: Issues and Annotated Bibliography, 2000, Teaching Strategies for Students with Mild to Moderate Disabilities, 2007, Teaching About Disabilities Through Children's Literature, 2008, Making Accommodations and Adaptations for Students with Mild to Moderate Disabilities, 2009. Active Ch. of Jesus Christ of Latter-day Saints. Recipient Disting. Paper award, Hawaii Edn. Rsch. Assn., 1996, 2002, 2009, Spl. Recognition award, Devel. Disabilities Divsn. of the Coun. for Exceptional Children, 2000; Rsch. grantee, U.S. Dept. Edn., 1986—87, 2000—01, Pers. Preparation grantee, 1987—90, 2004—08, Leadership Preparation grantee, 1996—2001, Post-Doctoral fellow, U. Ky., 1997. Mem.: ASCD, Coun. for Learning Disabilities, Am. Assn. Colls. Tchr. Edn., Coun. for Exceptional Children (various coms.). Office: Brigham Young Univ 340 MCKB Provo UT 84602

PRATKANIS, ANTHONY RICHARD, social psychologist, educator; b. Portsmouth, Va., Apr. 2, 1957; s. Tony R. and Rosemarie (Gray) P. BS summa cum laude, Ea. Menonite Coll., 1979; MA, Ohio State U., 1981, PhD, 1984. Rsch. assoc. Ohio State U., Columbus, 1981-83; asst. prof. indsl. adminstrn. & psychology Carnegie Mellon, 1984—87; asst. prof., then assoc. prof. psychology U. Calif., Santa Cruz, 1987-95, prof., 1995—. Expert legal witness; reviewer acad. jours. Co-author: (with E. Aronson) The Age of Propaganda, 1992, (with D. Shadel) Weapons of Fraud, 2005; co-editor: (with A. Greenwald and S. Breckler) Attitude Structure and Function; contbr. articles to profl. papers, book chpts Postdoctor fellow Carnegie-Mellon U., Pitts., 1983-84; J.B. Smith scholar Ea. Mennonite Coll., Harristonburg, Va., 1975-79. Fellow APA, Soc. Personality and Social Psychology; mem. Midwestern Psychol. Assn., Soc. Exptl. Social Psychology. Democrat. Research includes attitudes, persuasion, social influence. Home: 166 Montclair Dr Santa Cruz CA 95060-1025 Office: U Calif Bd Psychology Santa Cruz CA 95064 Business E-Mail: peitho@cats.ucsc.edu.

PRATT, DAVID TERRY, engineering consultant; b. Shelley, Idaho, Sept. 14, 1934; s. Eugene Francis and Bernice (Montague) P.; m. Marilyn Jean Thackston, Dec. 22, 1956; children: Douglas Montague, Elizabeth Joann, Brian Stephens. BSc in Mech. Engring., U. Wash., 1956; MSc, U. Calif., Berkeley, 1962, PhD, 1968. Asst. prof. marine engring. U.S. Naval Acad., Annapolis, Md., 1961-64; prof. mech. engring., asst. dean Wash. State U., Pullman, 1968-76; prof. mech. engring. U. Utah, Salt Lake City, 1976-78; prof., chmn. mech. engring. and applied mechanics U. Mich., Ann Arbor, 1978-81; prof., chmn. mech. engring. U. Wash., Seattle, 1981-86, prof. mech. engring., 1987-96, prof. emeritus; engring. cons. Rsch. dir. supercomputing Aerojet Propulsion Rsch. Inst., Sacramento, 1986-87. Author (with W.H. Heiser) Hypersonic Airbreathing Propulsion, 1994, (with J.D. Mattingly and W.H. Heiser) Aircraft Engine Design, 2002; editor (with L.D. Smoot) Combustion and Gasification of Pulverized Coal, 1976; contbr. articles to profl. jours. Served to 1st lt. USMC, 1956-60. NSF sci. faculty fellow, 1965-66; Fulbright-Hays sr. research fellow Imperial Coll., 1974-75; David Pierpont Gardner faculty fellow U. Utah, 1976. Fellow AIAA (assoc., Summerfield award 1999, 2005); mem. ASME, Combustion Inst. Lutheran. Home and Office: 2304 Cascade Ct Anacortes WA 98221 Personal E-mail: pratt@combustion.com.

PRATT, FRANK, state legislator; b. Florence, Ariz, Aug. 27, 1942; m. Janice Pratt; 1 child, Bryan. Attended, Central Ariz. Coll., Ariz. Western Coll., Northern Ariz. Coll. Owner Frank Pratt Farms; pres. & owner Pratt Pools Inc., 1986—, Casa Grande Dive Shop Inc., 1996—; precinct committeeman Ariz. House of Reps., 2004—, mem. Dist. 23, 2008—. Chmn. County Sheriff Election Com., 1992, 2000; campaign co-chmn. Pinal County Sheriff Election Com., 2000. Mem. Pub. Safety Retirement Bd., 1994—, Casa Grande C. of C., Project CNTRL Rural Leadership Program; vol. United Way, 2004; chmn. Pinal County Merrit Commn. Mem.: Profl. Assn. Diving Instrs. (instr. & owner), Rotary Club (pres.). Republican. Office: Capitol Complex 1700 W Washington Rm 115 Phoenix AZ 85007-2890 Office Phone: 602-926-5761. Office Fax: 602-417-3023. Business E-Mail: fpratt@azleg.gov.*

PRATT, GEORGE JANES, JR., psychologist author; b. Mpls., May 3, 1948; s. George Janes and Sally Elvina (Hanson) P.; m. Vonda Pratt; 1 child, Whitney Beth. BA cum laude, U. Minn., 1970, MA, 1973; PhD with spl. commendation, Calif. Sch. Profl. Psychology, San Diego, 1976. Diplomate Am. Acad. Pain Mgmt., Assn. Comprehensive Energy Psychology; lic. psychologist, Calif., 1976. Psychology trainee Ctr. for Behavior Modification, Mpls., 1971—72, U.Minn. Student Counseling Bur., 1972—73; predoctoral clin. psychology intern San Bernardino County Mental Health Svcs., Calif., 1973—74, San Diego County Mental Health Services, 1974—76; mem. staff San Louis Rey Hosp., 1977—78; postdoctoral clin. psychology intern Mesa Vista Hosp., San Diego, 1976; clin psychologist, dir. Psychology and Cons. Assocs. of San Diego, 1976—90; chmn. Psychology and Cons. Assocs. Press, 1977—94. Bd. dirs. Optimax, Inc., 1985-94; pres. George Pratt Ph.D., Psychol. Corp., 1979—; chmn. Pratt, Korn & Assocs., Inc., 1984-94; mem. staff Scripps Meml. Hosp., La Jolla, Calif., 1986—, chmn. psychology, 1993-95, 2000—; founder La Jolla Profl. Workshops, 1977-81; clin. psychologist El Camino Psychology Ctr., San Clemente, Calif., 1977-78; grad. teaching asst. U. Minn. Psychology and Family Studies divsn., 1971; teaching assoc. U. Minn. Psychology and Family Studies divsn., Mpls., 1972-73; instr. U. Minn. Extension divsn., Mpls., 1971-73; faculty Calif. Sch. Profl. Psychology, 1974-83, San Diego Evening Coll., 1975-77, Nat. U., 1978-79, Chapman Coll., 1978, San Diego State U., 1979-80; vis. prof. Pepperdine U., L.A., 1976-78; cons. U. Calif. at San Diego Med. Sch., 1976-78, also instr. univ., 1978—; psychology chmn. Workshops in Clin. Hypnosis, 1980-84; cons. Calif. Health Dept., 1974, Naval Regional Med. Ctr., 1978-82, ABC-TV; also speaker. Author: Sensory/Progressive Relaxation, 1979, Effective Stress Management, 1979, Clinical Hypnosis: Techniques and Applications, 1985, Rx for Stress, 1994; co-author: A Clinical Hypnosis Primer, 1984, 88, 2009, HyperPerformance, 1987, 2009, Release Your Business Potential, 1988, Instant Emotional Healing, 2000, Emotional Self-Management, 2000; contbr.: Hypnosis: Questions and Answers, 1986, Handbook for Hypnotic Suggestions and Metaphors, 1990, Imagery in Sports and Physical Performance, 1994. With USAR, 1970-76. Fellow Am. Soc. Clin. Hypnosis (cert., approved cons.); mem. APA, Nat. Register of Health Svc. Providers in Psychology, San Diego Soc. Sex. Therapy and Edn. (past pres.), San Diego Soc. Clin. Hypnosis (past pres.), San Diego Psychol. Assn., Grammy (voting mem.), U. Minn. Alumni Assn., Beta Theta Pi. Office: Scripps Meml Hosp Campus 9834 Genesee Ave Ste 321 La Jolla CA 92037-1216 Home: 1127 Muirlands Vista Way La Jolla CA 92037-6210 Office Phone: 858-457-3900.

PRAUSNITZ, JOHN MICHAEL, chemical engineer, educator; b. Berlin, Jan. 7, 1928; arrived in U.S., 1937, naturalized, 1944; s. Paul Georg and Susi Prausnitz; m. Susan Prausnitz, June 10, 1956; children: Stephanie, Mark Robert. B Chem. Engring., Cornell U., 1950; MS, U. Rochester, 1951; PhD, Princeton, 1955; Dr. Ing., U. L'Aquila, 1983, Tech. U. Berlin, 1989, U. Padova, 2004; DSc, Princeton U., 1995. Mem. faculty U. Calif., Berkeley, 1955—, prof. chem. engring., 1963—. Cons. to cyrogenic, polymer, petroleum and petrochem. industries; Miller rsch. prof., 1966, 78; sr. investigator Lawrence Berkeley Nat. Lab., Berkeley; Wilhelm lectr. Princeton U., 1980; W.K. Lewis lectr. MIT, 1993; Edward Mason lectr. Brown U., 1999; Danckwerts lectr. Royal Acad. Engring., London, 2000; hon. prof. Tech. U. Shanghai, 2001; Dodge lectr. Yale U., 2004. Author: (with others) Computer Calculations for Multicomponent Vapor-Liquid Equilibria, 1967, (Computer Calculations for High-Pressure Vapor-Liquid Equilibria, 1968, Molecular Thermodynamics of Fluid-Phase Equilibria, 1969, 2d edit., 1986, 3d edit., 1999, Regular and Related Solutions, 1970, Properties of Gases and Liquids, 3d edit., 1977, 4th edit., 1987, 5th edit., 2000, Computer Calculations for Multicomponent Vapor-Liquid and Liquid-Liquid Equilibria, 1980; contbr. to profl. jours. Recipient Alexander von Humboldt Sr. Scientist award, 1976, Carl von Linde Gold Meml. medal, German Inst. for Cryogenics, 1987, Solvay prize, Solvay Found. for Chem. Scis., 1990, Corcoran award, Am. Soc. for Engring. Edn., 1991, 1999, D.L. Katz award, Gas Processors Assn., 1992, Waterman award, Tech. U. Delft, 1998, Rossini award, Internat. Union of Pure and Applied Chemistry, 2002, Nat. medal of Sci., 2005; Guggenheim fellow, 1962, 1973, fellow, Inst. Advanced Study, Berlin, 1985, Christensen fellow, St. Catherine's Coll. Oxford U., 1994, Erskine fellow, U. Canterbury, Christchurch, New Zealand, 1996. Mem.: NAS, NAE, AIChE (Colburn award 1962, Walker award 1967, Inst. Lectr. award 1994), Am. Acad. Arts and Scis., Am. Chem. Soc. (E.V. Murphee award 1979, Petroleum Chemistry Rsch. award 1995). Office: U Calif 308 Gilman Hl Berkeley CA 94720-1462 Office Phone: 510-642-3592. Business E-Mail: prausnit@cchem.berkeley.edu.

PRAY, DONALD EUGENE, lawyer; b. Tulsa, Jan. 16, 1932; s. Clyde Elmer and Ruth Annette (Frank) P.; m. Margaret Morrow, June 12, 1953; children: Melissa, Susan; m. Lana J. Dobson, Nov. 18, 1985. BS n Petroleum Engring., U. Tulsa, 1955; LLB with honors, U. Okla., 1963. Bar: Okla. 1963, U.S. Dist. Ct. (no. dist.) Okla. 1965, U.S. Supreme Ct. 1965. Assoc. firm Fuller, Smith, Mosberg, Davis & Bowen, Tulsa, 1963-65; ptnr. firm Schuman, Deas, Pray & Doyle, Tulsa, 1965-68, Pray, Scott & Livingston, and predecessor firm, Tulsa, 1968-79; chmn., mem. exec. com. firm Pray Walker, Jackman, Williamson & Marlar (merger), Tulsa, 1979-95; exec. dir. Donald W. Reynolds Found., Tulsa, 1993-99, trustee, 2000—. Bd. dirs. Grace and Franklin Bernsen Found., U. Tulsa, St. Johns Med. Ctr., Philbrook Art Mus.; bd. dirs., exec. v.p. Tulsa Ballet Theater. Served to capt. USAF, 1955-57. Fellow Am. Bar Found.; mem. ABA (econs. com.), Tulsa Estate Planning Forum (pres.), Tulsa Mineral Lawyers Sect. (pres.), Summit Club (pres.). Republican. Presbyterian. Office: 1701 Village Center Cir Las Vegas NV 89134-6303

PRAY, RALPH MARBLE, III, lawyer; b. San Diego, June 7, 1938; s. Ralph Marble, Jr. and Doris (Thomson) Pray; m. Karen L. Pray (div. May 1988); children: Matthew Thomson, Kristen Leigh; m. Sandra Anne Shaw, June 7, 1988. BS, U. Redlands, 1960; JD, U. Calif., San Francisco, 1967. Bar: Calif. 1967, US Dist. Ct. (so. dist.) Calif. 1968, US Supreme Ct. 1972, US Dist. Ct. (ea. dist.) Calif. 1985, US Dist. Ct. (ctrl. dist.) Calif. 1989, US Dist. Ct. (no. dist.) Calif. 1992. Assoc. Gray, Cary, Ware & Friedenrich and predecessor, San Diego, 1967-73, ptnr., 1973—; mem. mgmt. com. Gary, Cary, Ames & Frye, San Diego, 1975-80. Arbiter Superior Ct., San Diego, 1984—. Lt. USN, 1960—64. Mem.: NRA, SAR, ABA, Am. Arbitration Soc. (arbiter), Calif. Bar Assn., Thurston Soc., San Diego Zool. Soc., Ducks Unltd., Club of Coronado, Rotary, Order of Coif. Republican. Episcopalian. Home: 535 C Ave Coronado CA 92118-1824 Office: DLA Piper US LLP 4365 Exec Dr Ste 1100 San Diego CA 92121-2133 Office Phone: 858-638-6890.

PREBLE, LAURENCE GEORGE, lawyer; b. Denver, Apr. 24, 1939; s. George Enos and Ruth (Jewett) Preble; m. Deborah Joan Horton, Aug. 24, 1963; children: Robin Lee, Randall Laurence. B in Petroleum Refining Engring., Colo. Sch. Mines, 1961; JD cum laude, Loyola U., Los Angeles, 1968. Bar: Calif. 1969, D.C. 1983, N.Y. 1987, U.S. Dist. Ct. (cen. dist.) Calif. 1969. Assoc. firm O'Melveny & Myers, Los Angeles, 1968-76, ptnr. LA, 1976—2000; dir. devel. KUD Internat. LLC, 2001—. Adj. prof. law Southwestern U., 1970-75, Loyola U. of L.A. Sch. Law, 1984-92, 99-2000, Fordham U. Sch. Law, 1992-98, Calif. Continuing Edn. of the Bar; lectr., author Practicing Law Inst. Trustee Harvey Mudd Coll., 1991-94, Citizens Bidget Commn. N.Y.C., 1994-98, Ho. Ear Inst., 1998—, vice-chmn., 2001—. Recipient Disting. Achievement medal, Colo. Sch. Mines, 1998. Mem. Los Angeles County Bar Assn. (chmn. real property sect. 1979-80, Outstanding Leadership award 1999), Assn. Bar City of N.Y. (real property sect. exec. com. 1993-96), N.Y. State Bar Assn. (exec. com. real property sect. 1996—), Calif. Bar Assn. (mem. exec. com. real property sect.), ABA, Am. Coll. Real Estate Lawyers (bd. govs. 1986—), Anglo-Am. Real Property Inst., La Canada-Flintridge C. of C. (pres. 1974-75), Loyola Law Sch. Alumni Assn. (pres. 1978). Office: KUD Internat LLC STE 950 100 Wilshire Blvd Santa Monica CA 90401-1145

PREGERSON, HARRY, federal judge; b. LA, Oct. 13, 1923; s. Abraham and Bessie (Rubin) P.; m. Bernardine Seyma Chapkis, June 28, 1947; children: Dean Douglas, Kathryn Ann. BA, UCLA, 1947; LL.B., U. Calif.-Berkeley, 1950. Bar: Calif. 1951. Pvt. practice, Los Angeles, 1951—53; Assoc. Morris D. Coppersmith, 1952; ptnr. Pregerson & Costley, Van Nuys, 1953—65; judge Los Angeles Mcpl. Ct., 1965—66, Los Angeles Superior Ct., 1966—67, US Dist. Ct. Central Dist. Calif., 1967—79, US Ct. Appeals (9th cir.), Woodland Hills, 1979—. Faculty mem., seminar for newly appointed distr. Judges Fed. Jud. Center, Washington, 1970—72; mem. faculty Am. Soc. Pub. Adminstrn., Inst. for Ct. Mgmt., Denver, 1973—; panelist LA chpt. FBA, 1989, Calif. Continuing Edn. of Bar, 9th Ann. Fed. Practice Inst., San Francisco, 1986, Internat. Acad. Trial Lawyers, LA, 1983; lectr. seminars for newly-appointed Fed. judges, 1970—71. Author: over 450 published legal opinions. Mem. Community Rels. Com., Jewish Fedn. Coun., 1984—, Temple Judea, Encino, 1955—; bd. trustees Devil Pups Inc., 1988—; adv. bd. Internat. Orphans Inc., 1966—, Jewish Big Brothers Assn., 1970, Salvation Army, LA Met. area, 1988—; worked with US Govt. Gen. Svcs. to establish the Bell Shelter for the homeless Child Day Care Ctr., the Food Partnership and Westwood Transitional Village; bd. dirs. Marine Corps Res. Toys for Tots Program, 1965—, Greater LA Partnership for the Homeless, 1988—. 1st lt. USMCR, 1944—46. Decorated Purple Heart, Medal of Valor Apache Tribe; recipient Promotion of Justice Civic award, City of San Fernando, 1965, award, San Fernando Valley Jewish Fedn. Coun., 1966, Profl. Achievement award, Los Angeles Athletic Club, 1980, Profl. Achievement award UCLA Alumni Assn., 1985, Louis D. Brandeis award, Am. Friends of Hebrew U., 1987, award of merit, Inner City Law Ctr., 1987, Appreciation award, Navajo Nation and USMC for Toys for Tots program, 1987, Humanitarian award, Los Angeles Fed. Exec. Bd., 1987—88, Grateful Acknowledgement award, Bet Tzedek Legal Svcs., 1988, Commendation award, Bd. Suprs. Los Angeles County, 1988, Others award, Salvation Army, 1988. Mem.: ABA, Marines Corps Res. Officers Assn., State Bar Calif., San Fernando Valley Bar Assn., L.A. County Bar Assn., Am. Legion (Van Nuys Post), DAV (Birmingham chpt.). Office: US Ct Appeals 9th Cir 21800 Oxnard St Ste 1140 Woodland Hills CA 91367-7919

PREMO, PAUL MARK, oil industry executive; b. Syracuse, NY, Nov. 20, 1942; s. Matthias George and Kathryn (Whitbread) P.; m. Mary Catherine Hennessy, June 19, 1965; children: Deborah, Mark. BSChemE, Manhattan Coll., Riverdale, NY, 1964; MS in Chem. Engring., MIT, 1965. Chem. engr. Chevron Rsch., Richmond, Calif., 1965-69; fin. analyst Chevron Corp., San Francisco, 1969-72, coord., mgr. supply and distbn., 1972-79; mgr. petroleum regulations Chevron USA, San Francisco, 1979-81, sec.-treas., 1981-85, mgr. property tax adminstrn., 1985-86, mgr. natural gas regulatory affairs, 1986-92; exec. cons. Resource Mgmt. Internat., San Rafael, Calif., 1992-95; v.p. Foster Assoc., Inc., San Francisco, 1995—98; prin. Energy Econs. Consulting, Mill Valley, Calif., 1998—. Dir. Ky. Agrl. Energy Corp., Franklin. Trustee Calif. Tax Found., 1985-. Mem. Calif. State C. of C. (tax com.), Western Oil and Gas Assn., Am. Petroleum Inst. (property tax com.), Natural Gas Supply Assn., Inst. Property Taxation, Calif. Taxpayers Assn. (bd. dirs. 1985-), MIT Alumni Assn., Commonwealth (San Francisco), Sigma Xi, Tau Beta Pi. Avocations: investments, carpentry, travel. Home: 310 Hazel Ave Mill Valley CA 94941-5054 Personal E-mail: paulpremo@msn.com.

PRENTICE, MARGARITA, state legislator; b. San Bernardino, Calif., Feb. 22, 1931; m to Bill; children: Kathy, Christy,(Mrs Burton) & Bill, III, five grandchildren. Washington State Representative, District 11, 88-93; Washington State Senator, District 11, 93-, vchairwoman, Majority Caucus, 93-94, member, Democratic Nat Committee, Commerce, Financial Serv, Housing & Ins Committee, Hwys & Transportation Committee, ranking minority member, currently, Washington State Senate.Registered nurse, currently; board trustees, Mus Indust & Hist, currently; member, Renton Sch Bd, formerly. Legislator of Year, Retail Association & Mortgage Brokers Association, Washington Health Care Association, Washington State Labor Coun, Washington State Nurses Association, Home Health Care Association & Washington State Hygienists' Association; Nurse of Year, King Co; Champion of Health Care, Valley Med Center; Distinguished Serv Award, Washington Association Homes for Aging. America Civil Liberties Union; Amnesty Int; Renton Hist Soc; Humane Soc United States. Democrat. Roman Catholic. Mailing: 419 John A Cherberg Bldg PO Box 40482 Olympia WA 98504-0482 Fax: 360-786-1999. E-mail: prentice_ma@leg.wa.gov.

PRENTKE, RICHARD OTTESEN, lawyer; b. Cleve., Sept. 8, 1945; s. Herbert E. and Melva B. P.; m. Susan Ottesen, June 9, 1974; children: Catherine, Elizabeth. BSE, Princeton U., 1967; JD, Harvard U., 1974. Assoc. Perkins Coie, Seattle, 1974-80, ptnr., 1981—, CFO, 1989-94. Author: School Construction Law Deskbook, 1989, rev. 2d edit. 1998; contbr. articles to profl. jours. Pres., trustee Seattle County Day Sch., 1990-95; trustee Pocock Rowing Found., 1996-02. Lt. USN, 1967—70. Fellow Leadership Tomorrow, Seattle, 1985-86. Mem. ABA, Wash. State Bar Assn. (mem. jud. screening com. 1985-91, chmn. 1987-91), Seattle-King County Bar Assn. (chmn. jud. task force 1990-93), Am. Arbitration Assn. (arbitrator 1988—2000), Princeton U. Rowing Assn. (pres. 1993-02, trustee 1976—), Rainier Club, Princeton Varsity Club (trustee 2003-), Princeton Club Wash. (trustee 1986-95, pres. 1990-92), Seattle Tennis Club. Avocations: art, carpentry, travel, rowing, sports. Office: Perkins Coie 1201 3rd Ave Fl 40 Seattle WA 98101-3029 Office Phone: 206-359-8000. Business E-Mail: rprentke@perkinscoie.com.

PREONAS, GEORGE ELIAS, lawyer; b. Dayton, Ohio, Oct. 5, 1943; s. Louis D. and Mary (Drakos) P.; m. Aileen Strike, June 1, 1944; children: Annemarie, Michael, Stephen. BA, Stanford U., 1965; JD, U. Mich., 1968. Bar: Ill. 1968, Nev. 1969, Calif. 1974. Ptnr. Seyfarth, Shaw, Fairweather & Geraldson, LA, 1968—. Mem. ABA, L.A. County Bar Assn., Calif. Bar Assn., Ill. Bar Assn., Nev. Bar Assn. Office: Seyfarth Shaw 2029 Century Park E Ste 3300 Los Angeles CA 90067-3019

PRESANT, SANFORD CALVIN, lawyer, educator, writer, tax specialist; b. Buffalo, Nov. 15, 1952; s. Allen and Reeta Presant; children: Jarrett, Danny, Lauren; m. Nancy Loeb. BA, Cornell U., 1973; JD cum laude, SUNY, Buffalo, 1976; LLM in Taxation, Georgetown U., NYU, 1981. Bar: N.Y. 1977, D.C. 1977, U.S. Tax Ct. 1977, U.S. Ct. Claims 1978, Calif. 1992, U.S. Supreme Ct. 1982. Staff atty. SEC Options Task Force, Washington, 1976-78; assoc. Barrett Smith Schapiro, NYC, 1978-80, Trubin Sillcocks, NYC, 1980-81; ptnr. Carro, Spanbock, Fass, Geller, Kaster, NYC, 1981-86, Finley, Kumble, Wagner, Heine, Underberg, Manley, Myerson & Casey, NYC, 1987, Kaye, Scholer, Fierman, Hays & Handler, NYC, 1987-95, Battle Fowler LLP, LA, 1995-2000, Ernst & Young, LA, 2000; nat. dir. real estate tax strategies, opportunity funds Ernst & Young LLP, LA, 2000; ptnr. DLA Piper Rudnick Gray Cary US LLP, LA, 2005—. Adj. assoc. prof. real estate NYU, 1984-00; frequest lectr. in tax law; regular TV appearances Nightly Bus. Report, PBS, 1986-88; co-chmn. NYU Conf. Fed. Taxation Real Estate Trans., 1987, PLI Advanced Tax Planning Real Estate, 1987, PLI Ann. Real Estate Tax Forum, 1999—; program dir. Nareit Law and Acctg. Conf., 2003; conf. chmn. various confs. in field. Author: Realty Joint Ventures, 1980-86, Tax Sheltered Investments Handbook-Special Update on Tax Reform Act of 1984, Real Estate Syndication Handbook, 1986, The Tax Reform Act of 1986, 1987, Real Estate Syndication Tax Handbook, 1987, Understanding Partnership Tax Allocations, 1987, The Final Partnership Nonrecourse Debt Allocation Regulations, 1987, Taxation of Real Estate Investments, 1987, Understanding Partnership Tax Allocations, 1987, Tax Aspects of Environmental (Superfund) Settlements, 1994, The Proposed Publicly Traded Partnership Regulations, 1995, (with others) Tax Aspects of Real Investments, 2002, Structuring Real

Estate Private Equity Funds, 2005, Joint Ventures With Tax-Exempt Entities, 2005, others. Kripke Securities Law fellow NYU, 1976. Mem. ABA (nat. chmn. audit subcom. of tax sect. partnership com. 1984-86, partnership tax allocation subcom. chmn. 1986-90, nat. chmn. partnership com. 1992-94, chmn. task force publicly traded partnerships 1995—, others), N.Y. State Bar Assn. (tax sect. partnership com. 1980—), Assn. Bar City of N.Y. Republican. Jewish. Office: Real Estate Capital Markets DLA Piper Rudnick Gray Cary US LLP 1999 Avenue of the Stars Fourth Fl Los Angeles CA 90067-5403 Office Phone: 213-977-3303, 310-595-3190. Office Fax: 866-222-9401, 310-595-3490. Business E-Mail: sanford.presant@ey.com, susan.teague@dlapiper.com.

PRESCOTT, DAVID MARSHALL, biology professor; b. Clearwater, Fla., Aug. 3, 1926; s. Clifford Raymond and Lillian (Moore) P.; m. Gayle Edna Demery; children: Lavonne, Jason, Ryan. BA, Wesleyan U., 1950; PhD, U. Calif., Berkeley, 1954. Asst. prof. UCLA Med. Sch., 1955-59; biologist Oak Ridge (Tenn.) Nat. Lab., 1959-63; prof. U. Colo. Sch. Medicine, Denver, 1963-66; prof. molecular, cell and devel. biology U. Colo., Boulder, 1966-80, Disting. prof. molecular, cell and devel. biology, 1980—2002, Disting. prof. emeritus, 2002—. Pres. Am. Soc. Cell Biology, 1966. Author: Cell Reproduction, 1976, Cancer: The Misguided Cell, 1986, Cells, 1988; also numerous rsch. reports; editor: Methods in Cell Biology, 15 vols., 1963-78. Adv. com. March of Dimes, 1979-90. Recipient von Humboldt prize Fed. Republic Germany, 1979; grantee NIH, 1985-95, 97-2002, Nat. Found. Cancer Rsch., 1985-89, NSF, 1990-91, 95—; John Simon Guggenheim Meml. Found. fellow, 1990-91. Fellow Am. Acad. Arts and Scis.; mem. NAS, Soc. Protozoologists (pres. 1995-96). Avocations: coin collecting/numismatics, gardening. Home: 285 Brook Pl Boulder CO 80302-8031 Office: Univ Colo Campus Box 347 MCDB Biology Boulder CO 80309-0347

PRESCOTT, EDWARD C., economist, educator; b. 1940; BA in Math., Swarthmore Coll., 1962; MS in Ops. Rsch., Case Western Res. U., 1963; PhD in Econs., Carnegie Mellon U., 1967. Lectr. U. Penn, 1966—67; asst. prof. econs. dept. U. Penn., 1967—71; asst. prof. Grad. Sch. Indsl. Admin., Carnegie Mellon U., 1971—72, assoc. prof., 1972—75, prof. econs., 1975—80, U. Minn., 1980—98, 1999—2003; vis. prof. econs. Norweigan Sch. Bus. and Econs., 1974—75, Northwestern U., 1979—80, vis. prof. fin., Kellogg Grad. Sch. Mgmt., 1980—82; Ford vis. rsch. prof. U. Chgo., 1978—79, prof. econs., 1998—99; sr. advisor rsch. dept. Fed. Reserve Bank, Mpls., 1980—2003; prof. dept. econs. Ariz. State U., 2003—; sr. monetary advisor Fed. Res. Bank, Mpls., 2003—. Leader NBER/NSF Workshop in Indsl. Orgn., 1977—84; rsch. assoc. Nat. Bureau of Economic Rsch., 1988—; spkr. in field. Author (with S.L. Parente): Barriers to Riches, 2000; co-editor: Economic Theory, 1991; assoc. editor: Jour. Econometrics, 1976—82, Internat. Economic Review, 1980—90, Jour. Economic Theory, 1990—92; contbr. articles to profl. jours. Recipient Erwin Plein Nemmers prize in Econ., Northwestern U., 2002, Laurea Honoris Causa in Economica, U. Rome, 2002, Nobel Prize for Econ. Sciences, 2004; named Regents' Prof., U. Minn., 1996, McKnight Presidential Chair in Economics, 2003, W.P. Carey Chair, U. Ariz., 2003; fellow, Econometric Society, 1980, Am. Acad. Arts & Scis., 1992; Brookings Economic Policy Fellow, 1969—70, Guggenheim Fellow, 1974—75. Mem.: Soc. Advancement of Econ. Theory (pres. 1992—94), Soc. Econ. Dynamics and Control (pres. 1992—95). Office: Ariz State U Dept Econs Tempe AZ 85287-3806

PRESKILL, JOHN PHILLIP, physics professor; b. Highland Park, Ill., Jan. 19, 1953; m. Roberta M. Gross, June 22, 1975; children: Carina Lou, Micaela Marie. AB in Physics, Princeton U., 1975; AM in Physics, Harvard U., 1976, PhD in Physics, 1980. Jr. fellow Harvard Soc. Fellows, 1980-81; asst. prof. physics Harvard U., Cambridge, Mass., 1981-82, assoc. prof., 1982-83; assoc. prof. theoretical physics Calif. Inst. Tech., Pasadena, 1983-90, prof., 1990—; dir. Inst. Quantum Info., 2000—; John D. MacArthur prof., 2002—; dir. Ctr. for Physics of Info., 2003—. Andrejewski lectr. Humbolt U., Berlin, 2001; Lorentz chair U. Leiden, 2002; Rouse Ball lectr. U. Cambridge, 2005. Recipient Presdl. Young Investigator award NSF, 1984-89; fellow NSF, 1975-78, Alfred P. Sloan Found., 1982-86. Fellow Am. Phys. Soc. Office: Calif Inst Tech 452-48 Div Physics Math & Astronomy Pasadena CA 91125-0001 Office Phone: 626-395-6691. Office Fax: 626-568-8473. E-mail: preskill@theory.caltech.edu, preskill@iqi.caltech.edu.

PRESLEY, PRISCILLA (PRICILLA ANN WAGNER, PRISCILLA BEAULIEU PRESLEY), actress; b. Bklyn., May 24, 1945; m. Elvis Presley, 1967 (div. 1973); 1 child, Lisa Marie; 1 child (with Marco Garibaldi), Navarone. Studied with Milton Katselas; student, Steven Peck Theatre Art Sch., Chuck Norris Karate Sch.; HHD (hon.), Rhodes Coll., Memphis, 1998. Co-owner Bis and Beau Boutique, 1973—76; co-executor, pres. Elvis Presley Enterprise, Inc. (acquired by CKX, Inc.), Memphis, 1979—2005, founder, 1980—2005, exec. cons., 2005—; bd. dir. CKX, Inc., Las Vegas, Nev., 2005—. Launched & developed internat. fragrance line, 1988—, Moments, 1990, Experiences, 1994, Indian Summer, 1996; designer of jewelry line; launched website, 2005—; bd. dir. Metro-Goldwyn-Mayer Inc., 2000—; lectr. SMART TALK. Appearances include (films) The Naked Gun: From the Files of Police Squad!, 1988, The Adventures of Ford Fairlaine, 1990, The Naked Gun 2 1/2, 1991, The Naked Gun 33 1/3: The Final Insult, 1994, (TV series) Those Amazing Animals, 1980-81, Dallas, 1983-88, Melrose Place, 1996, (TV movies) Love Is Forever, 1983, Breakfast With Einstein, 1998 (also exec. prodr.), Hayley Wagner, Star, 1999, After Dallas, 2002; performer (TV series) Dancing with the Stars, 2008; exec. prodr. (TV movie) Elvis and Me, 1988, The Road to Graceland, 1998, Finding Graceland, 1998; co-prodr.(TV mini series) Elvis, 1990; host, Elvis: The Great Performances, 1992; featured in (TV) Elvis 85, 1984, Elvis: Life and Times, 1997, After Dallas, 2002, Elvis by the Presleys, 2005, (TV mini series) Between the Lines, 2004; guest appearances include The Fall Guy, 1983, Tales from the Crypt, 1993, Touched by an Angel, 1997, Spin City, 1999, After They Were Famous, 2002, Oprah Winfrey Show, 2005; author: Elvis and Me, 1987. Amb. Dream Found., 2000—; mem. Citizen's Commn. on Human Rights. Named one of 50 Most Beautiful People in the World, People Mag., 1992. Office: Paul Bloch & Michelle Bega c/o Rogers & Cowan 8687 Melrose Ave 7th Fl West Hollywood CA 90069 Address: Norman Brokaw c/o William Morris Agency 151 El Camino Beverly Hills CA 90212 Office Phone: 310-850-4206, 310-854-8100.

PRESS, ANTHONY L., lawyer; BA in Economics and Polit. Sci., Yale U., 1981; JD, UCLA, 1986. Bar: Calif. 1986. Dep. gen. counsel Kolts Commn.; asst. to dep. gen. counsel Christopher Commn.; ptnr. Morrison & Foerster LLP, LA, chmn. litig. dept.-LA office, chmn. pro bono com., mng. ptnr.-Century City, CA office. Mem.: LA County Bar Assn., ABA (mem. litig. sect.).

PRESS, WILLIAM HENRY, physicist, computer scientist; b. NYC, May 23, 1948; s. Frank and Billie (Kallick) P.; m. Margaret Ann Lauritsen, 1969 (div. 1982); 1 dau., Sara Linda; m. Jeffrey Foden Howell, Apr. 19, 1991; 1 son, James Howell. AB, Harvard Coll., 1969; MS, Calif. Inst. Tech., 1971, PhD, 1972. Asst. prof. theoretical physics Calif. Inst. Tech., 1973-74; asst. prof. physics Princeton (N.J.) U., NJ, 1974—76; prof. astronomy and physics Harvard U., Cambridge, Mass., 1976-98, chmn. dept. astronomy, 1982-85; dep. lab. dir. Los Alamos Nat. Lab., N.Mex., 1998—2004, sr. fellow, 2004—; Raymer prof. computer scis. and integrative biology U. Tex., Austin, 2007—. Mem. numerous adv. coms. and panels NSF, NASA, NAS, NRC; vis. mem. Inst. Advanced Study, 1983-94; mem. Def. Sci. Bd., 1985-89, sci. adv. com. Packard Found., 1988—, program com. Sloan Found., 1985-91; chmn. adv. bd. NSF Inst. Theoretical Physics, 1986-87; mem. Computer Sci. and Telecomm. Bd., 1991-96; U.S. del. IUPAP Gen. Assembly, 1996; cons. MITRE Corp., 1977—; trustee Inst. Def. Analysis, 1988—, exec. com., 1990—; chief naval ops. Exec. Panel, 1994-2000. Author: Numerical Recipes, 1986; contbr. articles to profl. jours. Sloan Found. research fellow, 1974-78 Fellow: Am. Phys. Soc., Am. Acad. Arts and Scis.; mem.: NAS, Coun. on Fgn. Rels., Assn. for Computing Machinery, Internat. Soc. Relativity and Gravitation, Internat. Astron. Union, Am. Astron. Soc. (Helen B. Warner prize 1981). Office: Los Alamos Nat Lab MS F 600 Los Alamos NM 87545-0001

PRESSLER, PAUL S., former retail executive; b. 1956; m. Mindy Pressler; 2 children. BS in Bus. Economics, SUNY, Oneonta, 1978. V.p. mktg. & design Kenner-Parker Toys, The Walt Disney Co., 1987—90, sr. v.p. licensing, 1990—92, sr. v.p. consumer products, 1992—94, exec. v.p., gen. mgr. Disneyland Parks & Hotels, 1994—98, pres. Walt Disney Parks & Resorts, 1998—2002; pres., CEO Gap, Inc., San Francisco, 2002—07. Dir. Avon Products Inc. Adv. bd. Children Affected by AIDS Found.; bd. dirs. Resources Children with Spl. Needs, Big Bros. Big Sisters Greater LA, Disney GOALS, Anaheim, Calif.

PRESSLY, JAIME ELIZABETH, actress; b. Kinston, NC, July 30, 1977; m. Eric Cubiche; 1 child, Dezzi James. Spokesmodel Liz Claiborne Cosmetics, 2000. Actress (films) Against the Law, 1997, The Journey: Absolution, 1997, Poison Ivy: The New Seduction, 1997, Can't Hardly Wait, 1998, Ringmaster, 1998, Trash, 1999, Inferno, 1999, Poor White Trash, 2000, 100 Girls, 2000, Tomcats, 2001, Joe Dirt, 2001, Ticker, 2001, Not Another Teen Movie, 2001, Footprints, 2002, Demon Island, 2002, Torque, 2004, The Karate Dog, 2004, Cruel World, 2005, Death to the Supermodels, 2005, DOA, 2006, I Love You, Man, 2009, Venus & Vegas, 2007, actress (voice) Horton Hears a Who!, 2008, actress (TV films) Mercenary, 1997, Best Actress, 2000, The Johnny Chronicles, 2002, Alligator Point, 2003, (TV series) Push, 1998, Mortal Kombat: Conquest, 1998—99, Jack & Jill, 1999—2001, My Name Is Earl, 2005— (Primetime Emmy for Outstanding Supporting Actress in a Comedy Series, Acad. TV Arts and Scis., 2007), guest appearences include Silk Stalkings, 1998, Going to California, 2001, Charmed, 2002, The Twilight Zone, 2002, Fastlane, 2003, Becker, 2003, Happy Family, 2004, Las Vegas, 2006. Avocations: hiking, horseback riding, swimming, kickboxing, dance. Office: c/o Dar Rollins Internat Creative Mgmt 10250 Constellation Blvd Los Angeles CA 90067

PRESSLY, THOMAS JAMES, history professor; b. Troy, Tenn., Jan. 18, 1919; s. James Wallace and Martha Belle (Bittick) P.; m. Lillian Cameron, Apr. 30, 1943; children: Thomas James II, Stephanie Suzuki. AB, Harvard U., 1940, AM, 1941, PhD, 1950; LLD (hon.), Whitman Coll., 1981. Instr. history Princeton (NJ) U., 1946-49; asst. prof. U. Wash., 1949-54, assoc. prof., 1954-60, prof., 1960-87, prof. emeritus, 1987—. Vis. assoc. prof. Princeton U., 1953-54, Johns Hopkins U., 1969-70. Author: Americans Interpret Their Civil War, 1954; editor: (with W. H. Scofield) Farm Real Estate Values in the United States, 1965, (with others) American Political Behavior, 1974, Diary of George Templeton Strong (abridged), 1988, (with Glenn M. Linden) Voices From the House Divided, 1995, (with Maclyn P. Burg) The Great War At Home and Abroad, 1999; contr. articles to profl. jours., Free Black Shareholders, Journal of African American History, 2006. With US Army, 1941—45. Ford Found. Faculty fellow, 1951-52; Ctr. for Advanced Study in Behavioral Scis. fellow, 1955-56. Mem. Am. Hist. Assn., So. Hist. Assn. (editl. bd. Jour. So. History 1973-77), Orgn. Am. Historians. Home and Office: 4545 E Laurel Dr NE Seattle WA 98105-3838 Home Phone: 206-525-4655.

PRESZLER, SHARON MARIE, psychiatric home health nurse; b. LA; d. Rudolph Edward Wirth and Bertha Marie (Thornton) Paddock; m. Alan Preszler, Aug. 31, 1966; children: Brent, Alison. BS in Nursing, Loma Linda U., Calif., 1963, MS in Marriage and Family Counseling, 1978. RN, Calif., Idaho; cert. pub. health nurse. Team leader med. fl. Loma Linda U. Hosp., 1963-64; office nurse Dr. Lowell Johnson, Redlands, Calif., 1964-65, Dr. H. Glenn Stevens, Loma Linda, 1965-72; team leader women's oncology Loma Linda U. Hosp., 1974-75; pub. health nurse Riverside County Pub. Health, Hemet, Calif., 1975-78; nurse, staff psychologist Dept. Health and Welfare, Idaho Falls, Idaho, 1989-91, Boise, Idaho, 1991-92; psychiat. nurse Cmty. Home Health, Boise, 1992-94, Mercy Home Health & Hospice, Nampa, Idaho, 1995-99; hospice nurse, home health nurse Mercy Med. Ctr., 1995-99, personal care supr. nurse for medicaid, 1996—; case mgr. Ada Can, 2001—05; supervising nurse A Full Life, 2005—. Instr. YWCA, Bartlesville, Okla., 1984-88; tchr. Bartlesville Pub. Sch., 1984-88, Heritage Retirement, Boise, 1994. Contbr. to Focus, 1986. Mem. Am. Assn. Marriage and Family Therapy, Sigma Theta Tau. Avocations: reading, tennis.

PREUSS, CHARLES FREDERICK, lawyer; b. Santa Barbara, Calif., Feb. 27, 1941; BA, Dartmouth Coll., 1962; JD, Stanford U., 1969. Bar: Calif. 1970. Atty. Bronson, Bronson & McKinnon, 1969—93; ptnr. Preuss Walker & Shanagher, San Francisco, 1993-98, Preuss, Shanagher, Zvoleff & Zimmer, San Francisco, 1998; mng. ptnr., head West Coast offices Drinker Biddle & Reath LLP, San Francisco, and ptnr., products liability practice group. Mem. Product Liability Adv. Coun., Inc., bd. dir., Def. Rsch. Inst., 1996-99. Mem. Am. Bd. Trial Advocates, Internat. Assn. Def. Counsel. Office: Drinker Biddle & Reath LLP 50 Fremont St San Francisco CA 94105-2235 Office Phone: 415-591-7566. Office Fax: 415-591-7510. Business E-Mail: charles.preuss@dbr.com.

PREVITTI, JAMES P., real estate executive; Founder Forecast Group, Rancho Cucamonga, Calif., 1971—, pres., CEO, 1989—. Recipient Fair Housing award L.A. Times; named Builder of Yr., Real Estate Entrepreneur of Yr. Mem. Calif. Bldg. Industry Assn. (pres., Medal of Honor). Office: James L 9331 Mariposa Rd Hesperia CA 92344-8086

PREWITT, CHARLES THOMPSON, geochemist; b. Lexington, Ky., Mar. 3, 1933; s. John Burton and Margaret (Thompson) P.; m. Gretchen B. Hansen, Jan. 31, 1958; children: Daniel Hansen. SB, MIT, 1955, SM, 1960, PhD, 1962. Rsch. scientist E.I. DuPont De Nemours & Co. Inc., Wilmington, Del., 1962-69; assoc. prof. SUNY, Stony Brook, 1969-71, prof., 1971-86, chmn. dept. earth and space scis., 1977-80; dir. Geophys. Lab., Carnegie Inst. of Washington, 1986-98, mem. rsch. staff, 1998—2003; adj. prof. Dept. Geoscis. U. Ariz., Tucson, 2003—. Sec.-treas. U.S. Nat. Com. for Crystallography, Washington, 1983-85, 99—; gen. chmn. 14th Meeting of Internat. Mineral Assn., Stanford, Calif., 1986; chmn. NRC/NAS com. on physics and chemistry of earth materials, 1985-87; mem. bd. govs. Consortium for Advanced Radiation Svcs.; co-dir. NSF Ctr. for High Pressure Rsch., 1991—; disting. vis. prof. chemistry Ariz. State U., 1983. Editor: (jour.) Physics and Chemistry of Minerals, 1976-85; contbr. more than 190 articles to profl. jours. Bd. dirs. Internat. Ctr. for Diffraction Data, 1998-2002. Capt. USAR, 1956-65. NATO sr. postdoctoral fellow, 1975, Churchill overseas fellow, 1975, Japan Soc. for Promotion of Sci. fellow, 1983, Ernst Cloos Meml. scholar Johns Hopkins U., 2002-. Fellow AAAS, Mineral. Soc. Am. (pres. 1983-84, Roebling medal 2003), Am. Geophys. Union, Internat. Centre Diffraction Data; mem. Geol. Soc. Am., Am. Crystallographic Assn., Materials Rsch. Soc., Mineral. Soc. Gt. Britain and Ireland, Cosmos Club. Office: Dept Geoscis Univ Arizona Tucson AZ 85721-0077 Office Phone: 520-621-9993.

PREWITT, JEAN, not-for-profit organization executive; b. Oklahoma City; Degree, Harvard U.; degree in law, Georgetown U. Formerly lawyer Donovan Leisure Newton & Irvine; sr. v.p., gen. counsel United Internat. Pictures, 1982—89; with Nat. Telecomm. and Info. Adminstrn. U.S. Dept. Commerce, 1989—94; prin. Podesta Assocs., Washington DC, 1994—99; pres. Ind. Film & TV Alliance, LA, 2000—01, CEO, 2001—; bd. mem. Film LA, 2004—. Pres. Casa De Los Amigos, LA, 2003—. Adv. bd. Friends of Cancer Rsch., Washington DC, 2003—. Named one of The 100 Most Powerful Women in Entertainment, Hollywood Reporter, 2007. Office: Ind Film and TV Alliance 10850 Wilshire Blvd 9th Fl Los Angeles CA 90024-4321 Business E-Mail: jprewitt@ifta-online.org.

PRICE, B. BYRON, historian; BS, U.S. Mil. Acad., 1970; MA in Mus. Sci., Tex. Tech. U., 1977; postgrad., Am. U., Washington, 1975. Tchg. asst. Tex. Tech. U., Lubbock, 1975, rsch. coord. Ranching Heritage Ctr./Mus., 1976-77; curator of history Panhandle-Plains Hist. Mus., Canyon, Tex., 1977-82, exec. dir., 1982-86, Nat. Cowboy Hall of Fame and Western Heritage Ctr., Oklahoma City, 1987-96, Buffalo Bill Hist. Ctr., Cody, Wyo., 1996—. Lectr. in field; condr. seminars in field; cons. in field. Advisory editor: The Handbook of Texas, 1986-96; editl. bd. N.Mex. Hist. Rev., 1990-93, Jour. Ariz. History, 1993-95; assoc. editor The Ency. of the West, 1996; author: Cowboys of the American West, 1996, Crafting a Southwestern Masterpiece, 1986, Imagining the Open Range: Erwin E. Smith, Cowboy Photographer, 1997, Longheed: A Painter's Painter, 1991, The National Cowboy Hall of Fame Chuck Wagon Cook Book, 1995, She Doesn't Write Like a Woman: Mari Sandoz and the Cattlemen, 1996, Fine Art of the West, 2004; co-author: The Golden Spread: An Illustrated History of Amarillo and the Texas Panhandle, 1986; co-editor: Cowboy Justice, 1997, Adventuring with the Old-Timers: Trails Traveled and Tales Told, 1979; contbr. articles to profl. jours. Mem. tourism task force Okla. Dept. Commerce, 1987; mem. Okla. Film Adv. Commn., 1988-90; bd. dirs. Okla. Ctr. for the Book, 1990—; judge Arts for the Parks Ann. Exhbn., 1992-93; mem. cultural opportunities work group Okla. Futures, 1993; mem. Oklahoma City Conv. and Visitors Commn., 1996—. Recipient Gov.'s Arts award State of Okla., 1994. Mem. Tex. Assn. Mus. (exec. coun. 1985-86), Okla. Mus. Assn. (v.p. 1993-95), Mus. West Consortium (pres. 1996—), Western History Assn. (mem. program com. 1997), Am. Assn. Mus., Tex. State Hist. Assn., Western Writers of Am., Panhandle Plains Hist. Soc. Office: Buffalo Bill Hist Ctr 720 Sheridan Ave Cody WY 82414-3428

PRICE, CURREN D., state legislator; BA in Polit. Sci., Stanford U., 1972; JD, U. Santa Clara, 1976. California State Assemblyman, District 51, 2006-;chair, Committee on Elections and Redistricting; exec. prodr. Political Empowerment: The Black Vote & Implications for the Future; dep., LA City Coun.; councilman, Inglewood City Coun., 1993-97, 2001-2006. Democrat. Office: Dist 51 One Manchester Blvd Suite 601 Inglewood CA 90301 Office Phone: 310-412-6400. Office Fax: 310-412-6354. Business E-Mail: Assemblymember.Price@assembly.ca.gov.

PRICE, DAVID WILLIAM, physician, educator, researcher; MD, U. Medicine and Denistry NJ, Piscataway, 1985. Diplomate Am. Bd. of Family Medicine, 1988, Fellow Am. Acad. of Family Physicians, 1992. Dir. med. edn. Kaiser Permanente, Denver, 1997—, clin. lead, edn. and depression Care Mgmt. Inst. Oakland, Calif., 2001—; prof. family medicine Denver Health Scis. Ctr. U. Colo., 2007—. Bd. chair Am. Bd. Family Medicine, Lexington, Ky., 2007—08. Recipient Colo. Family Medicine Tchr. of the Yr., Colo. Acad. Family Physicians, 1991; co-recipient Superhero of Family Medicine, 1998. Fellow: Am. Acad. Family Physicians (life). Office: Kaiser Permanente Colo 10065 E Harvard Ave Denver CO 80231 Business E-Mail: david.price@uchsc.edu.

PRICE, HUMPHREY WALLACE, aerospace engineer; b. San Antonio, Sept. 25, 1954; s. Humphrey Rodes and Ruth (Wallace) P. BS in Engring., U. Tex., 1976, MS in Engring., 1978. Rsch. asst. nuc. reactor lab. U. Tex., Austin, 1976; nuc. engr. EDS Nuc., Inc., San Francisco, 1977-78; engr. Jet Propulsion Lab., Pasadena, Calif., 1978-82; rsch. engr. SW Rsch. Inst., San Antonio, 1982-84; tech. group leader Jet Propulsion Lab., Pasadena, Calif., 1984-89; configuration engr. Cassini spacecraft NASA, 1989-93; sys. engr. Pluto Spacecraft, 1994-97, Mars Sample Return Mission, 1998-2000; mgr. Solar Sail Tech. Devel., 2000—03; engr. space sys. Jupiter Icy Moons Orbiter, 2003—05, Constellation Requirements Engring., 2005—07, sys. engr. GRAIL project, 2008—. Cons. Am. Rocket Co., Camarillo, Calif., 1986-87; mem. tech. staff World Space Found., Pasadena, 1980-97. Patentee in field; contbr. to tech. papers in field. Mem. AIAA (sr.). Avocations: wind surfing, skiing, scuba diving. Office: HW Price Cons PO Box 454 La Canada Flintridge CA 91012-0454 Personal E-mail: hoppyprice@netscape.net.

PRICE, JOHN, former ambassador; m to Marcia; children: three. United States Ambassador, Mauritius, Seychelles & Comoros, 2002-05.Chairman, Chief Exec Officer, JP Realty Inc, Salt Lake City, formerly; director, exec com member, Alta Industries LTD, formerly; trustee, Univ Utah, 1992-99; member, Small Bus Admin Advisor Bd, Industry Sector Advisor Council on Small & Minority Bus for Trade/Policy Matters, formerly; member management com & trustees, 2002 Winter Olympics, Salt Lake City.

PRICE, JOHN R., lawyer, educator; b. Indpls., Nov. 28, 1934; s. Carl Lee and Agnes I. P.; m. Suzanne A. Leslie, June 22, 1963; children: John D., Steven V. BA with high honors, U. Fla., 1958; LL.B. with honors, NYU, 1961. Bar: Wash. 1977, U.S. Ct. Appeals (9th cir.), U.S. Dist. Ct. (we. dist.) Wash. Assoc. McCutchen, Doyle, Brown & Enersen, San Francisco, 1961-69; prof. law U. Wash., Seattle, 1969-97, dean, 1982-88; of counsel Perkins Coie, Seattle, 1976—2004. Author: Contemporary Estate Planning, 1983, Price on Contemporary Estate Planning, 1992, 2d edit., 2000, (with Samuel A. Donaldson), 2007, 2008, 2009, Conflicts, Confidentiality and Other Ethical Issues, 2000, 2d edit., 2007. Served with U.S. Army, 1953-55 Root-Tilden fellow NYU Sch. Law, 1958-61 Fellow Am. Coll. Trust and Estate Counsel (former regent); mem. ABA, Am. Law Inst., Order of Coif, Phi Beta Kappa. Congregationalist. Home: 3794 NE 97th St Seattle WA 98115-2564 Office: 1201 3rd Ave Ste 4800 Seattle WA 98101-3099 E-mail: jprice@perkinscoie.com.

PRICE, JONATHAN G., geologist; b. Danville, Pa., Feb. 1, 1950; s. A. Barney and Flora (Best) P.; m. Elisabeth McKinley, June 3, 1972; children: Alexander D., Argenta M. BA in Geology and German, Lehigh U., 1972; MA, U. Calif., Berkeley, 1975, PhD, 1977. Cert. profl. geologist. Geologist Anaconda Copper Co., Yerington, Nev., 1974-75, U.S. Steel Corp., Salt Lake City, 1977, Corpus Christi, 1978-81; rsch. assoc. Bur. Econ. Geology, U. Tex., Austin, 1981-85, rsch. sci., 1984-88, program dir., 1987-88; dir. Tex. Mining & Mineral Resources Rsch. Inst., Austin, 1984-88; dir., state geologist Nev. Bur. Mines & Geology, U. Nev., Reno, 1988-92, 95—. Staff dir. Bd. on Earth Scis. & Resources Nat. Rsch. Coun., Washington, 1993-95; asst. prof. Bucknell U., Lewisburg, 1977-78; chair We. States Seismic Policy coun., 1998-2002. Author, editor: Igneous Geology of Trans-Pecos Texas, 1986. Vol. instr. CPR and first aid ARC, 1983-95, bd. dirs. Sierra Nev. chpt., 1991-92. German Acad. Exch. Svc. fellow U. Heidelberg, 1972-73; recipient Explorer award Am. Geol. Inst., 1995. Fellow Geol. Soc. Am., Soc. Econ. Geologists (nat. pres. 2003); mem. Am. Inst. Profl. Geologists (Nev. sect. pres. 1992, nat. pres. 1997, John T. Galey Sr. Meml. pub. Svc. award 1999), Assn. Am. State Geologists (pres. 2000-01), Mineral. Soc. Am., Phi Beta Kappa. Office: Nev Bur Mines & Geology UNR Ms 178 Reno NV 89557-0088 Office Phone: 775-784-6691 15. Business E-Mail: jprice@unr.edu.

PRICE, KATHLEEN MCCORMICK, editor, writer; b. Topeka, Dec. 25, 1932; d. Raymond Chesley and Kathleen (Shoffner) McCormick; m. William Faulkner Black, Aug. 25, 1956 (div. 1961); 1 child, Kathleen Serena; m. William Hillard Price, Aug. 13, 1976. BA, U. Colo., Denver, 1971. Book reviewer Denver Post, 1971-78; book editor San Diego Mag., 1978-92. Cons. editor St. John's Cathedral, Denver, 1985-95. Author: There's a Dactyl Under My Foot, 1986, The Lady and the Unicorn, 1994, From Vision to Vestment, 2001. Dir. Colo. Episcopal Vestment Guild, 1991-2008. Fellow Phi Beta Kappa; mem. Denver County Club, La Garita Club, Nat. Soc. Colonial Dames America. Episcopalian. Home: 27 Crestmoor Dr Denver CO 80220-5853 Personal E-mail: kmccp@msn.com.

PRICE, PETER WILFRID, ecology educator, researcher; b. London, Apr. 17, 1938; arrived in U.S., 1966; BSc with honors, U. Wales, Bangor, 1958-62; MSc, U. New Brunswick, Fredericton, 1964; PhD, Cornell U., 1970. Asst. prof. U. Ill., Urbana, 1971-75, assoc. prof., 1975-79; research ecologist Mus. No. Ariz., Flagstaff, 1979-80; assoc. prof. No. Ariz. U., 1980-85, prof. ecology, 1985-94, Regents' prof., 1994—2002, Regents' prof. emeritus, 2002—. Author: Evolutionary Biology of Parasites, 1980, Biological Evolution, 1996, Insect Ecology, 3d edit., 1997, Macroevolutionary Theory on Macroecological Patterns, 2003; editor: Evolutionary Strategies of Parasitic Insects, 1975, A New Ecology, 1984, Plant-Animal Interactions, 1991, Effects of Resource Distribution on Plant-Animal Interactions, 1992, The Ecology and Evolution of Gall-Forming Insects, 1994, Population Dynamics, 1995, Population Dynamics: New Approaches and Synthesis, 1995. Guggenheim fellow, 1977—78, Fulbright Sr. scholar, 1993—94. Fellow: NSF (panel mem. 1978—81, 1991—93), Entomol. Soc. Am. (Founders award 1993), Brit. Ecol. Soc., Ecol. Soc. Am. (bd. editors 1973—76), Royal Entomol. Soc. (hon.). Office: No Ariz U PO Box 5640 Flagstaff AZ 86011-5640

PRICE, ROBERT E., manufacturing executive; b. 1942; BA, Pomona Coll., 1964. V.p. Fed-Mart Corp., 1964-75; pres., chief exec. officer Price Corp., San Diego, 1976-89; pres., chmn. bd., chief exec. officer Price Enterprises, San Diego, 1989-91, chmn. bd., chief exec. officer, 1991—, also bd. dirs. Office: Excel Legacy Corp 17140 Bernardo Ctr Dr San Diego CA 92128

PRICE, ROBERT OTIS, former mayor; b. Abilene, Kans., Jan. 4, 1932; s. Iru Paul and Irene Isabel (Parrish) P.; m. Dorothy Faye Price, Jan. 26, 1951 (dec. 1996); m. Sondra Boyd, Mar. 28, 1997; children: Fred Dennis, Donald Eugene. BA, U. Redlands, 1978. Patrolman, sgt., lt., capt. Bakersfield Police Dept., 1956-73, chief police, 1973-88; cons., troubleshooter, various cities, 1988-92; mayor City of Bakersfield, 1993—2001. Pres. Secret Witness Bd., 1980-83. Mem. Calif. Coun. on Criminal Justice, Sacramento, 1983-93; chmn. State Adv. Group on Juvenile Justice, Sacramento, 1988-93, Citizens Adv. Com., Fresno, Calif., 1993—, Youth Devel. Coalition, Bakersfield, 1993—, Econ. Devel. Discussion Group, Bakersfield, 1993—; chmn. western region Nat. Coalition Juvenile Justice and Delinquency Prevention, 1988-93; founder, cons. Youth Adv. Coun., Bakersfield, 1993—; founder Bakersfield Action Team, 1994. Sgt. U.S. Army, 1952-54. Recipient John W. Doubenmier award Am. Soc. Pub. Admins., 1978, Califf Morris award Calif. Probation, Parole and Corrections Officers Assn., 1982. Mem. Internat. Assn. Chiefs Police, Calif. Police Chiefs Assn., Calif. Peace Officers Assn., Calif. Council Criminal Justice, Kern County Police Chiefs Assn. (pres. 1979), Kern County Law Enforcement Admin. Assn. (pres. 1974). Republican. Avocations: photography, fishing, travel.

PRICE, ROBERT WILLIAM, school superintendent, consultant; b. Ogden, Utah, May 13, 1950; s. William Robert and Eileen Louise (Rabe) P.; m. Sally Sandman, Sept. 20, 1975; children: Geoffrey Thomas, Caitlin Elizabeth. BS in Child Devel., Calif. State U., Hayward, 1973, MS in Sch. Adminstrn., 1986; EdD, U. Pacific, 1998. Cert. elem. tchr., Calif. Tchr. Turlock (Calif.) Sch. Dist., 1974-81; asst. prin. Monte Vista Mid. Sch., Tracy, Calif., 1981-82, prin., 1982-87; asst. supt. instrn. Tracy Pub. Schs., 1987-90, 91-93, interim supt., 1990-91; supt. Empire Union Sch. Dist., Modesto, Calif., 1993—. Cons. Campfire, Tracy, 1983; founding mem. Tracy Exch. Club, 1985; co-founder Project Bus. & Edn. Together, Tracy, 1985; bd. dirs. Boys and Girls Club of Tracy, 1987-93. Recipient Adminstrv. Leadership award Calif. Media & Libr. Educators Assn., 1994. Mem. Assn. Calif. Sch. Adminstrs. (planning com. supts. symposium 1995—, v.p. programs Region 7 1994—), Calif. League Mid. Schs. (adv. panel Region 6 1993—, chair legis. action 1994-95, Region 6 Educator of Yr. 1991). Democrat. Office: Empire Union Sch Dist 116 N Mcclure Rd Modesto CA 95357-1329 E-mail: bprice@empire.k12.ca.us.

PRICE, THOMAS MUNRO, computer consultant, retired; b. Madison, Wis., Oct. 2, 1937; s. John Edward and Georgia Winifred (Day) P.; m. Judith Ann Holm, Aug. 8, 1959; children: Scott Michael, Andrea Lynn. BS, Carroll Coll., Waukesha, Wis., 1959; MS, U. Wis., 1961, PhD, 1964. Prof. math. U. Iowa, 1964-77, U. Wyo., Laramie, 1978-79, computer user cons., 1979-85, MIS prof., 1985-89; computer cons., 1989—; home rebuilder Pecos, N.Mex., 1994-97; historic home renovator Yerington, Nev., 1997—. Contbr. articles to profl. jours. Mem.: Yerington Rotary (pres. 2006—07, co-pres. 2008—). Home: Nordyke House 727 State Rt 339 Yerington NV 89447

PRICE, WILLIAM CHARLIE, lawyer; b. Bristol, Va., Oct. 28, 1956; BA, Duke U., 1978; JD, Yale U., 1981. Bar: Calif. 1983. Law clk. to Hon. Stanley A. Weigel US Dist. Ct. (no. dist. Calif.), 1981—82; asst. US atty. major crimes unit and pub. fraud and corruption unit, Dist. Oreg. US Dept. Justice, 1985—88; ptnr. Quinn, Emanuel, Urquhart, Oliver & Hedges, LLP, LA, 1988—. Instr. Nat. Inst. Trial Advocacy. Recipient John Fletcher Caskey prize, 1981; named one of Top 10 Trial Lawyers in Am., Nat. Law Jour., 2004, 2006. Mem.: State Bar Calif., Phi Beta Kappa. Office: Quinn Emanuel Urquhart Oliver & Hedges LLP 865 S Figueroa St 10th Fl Los Angeles CA 90017 Office Phone: 213-443-3000. E-mail: williamprice@quinnemanuel.com.

PRICKETT, DAVID CLINTON, physician; b. Fairmont, W.Va., Nov. 26, 1918; s. Clinton Everett and Mary Anna (Gottschalk) Prickett; m. Mary Ellen Holt, June 29, 1940 (dec. Feb. 1987); children: David C., Rebecca Ellen, William Radcliffe, Mary Anne, James Thomas, Sara Elizabeth; m. Pamela S. Blackstone, Nov. 17, 1991 (dec. Mar. 2002). Student, Fairmont State Coll., 1940—42; AB, W.Va. U., 1944; MD, U. Louisville, 1946; MPH, U. Pitts., 1955. Pres. Prickett Chem. Co., 1938-43; acct. W.Va. Conservation Commn. and Fed. Works Agy., 1941, 42; lab. asst., instr. chemistry W.Va. U., 1943; intern Louisville Gen. Hosp., 1947; surg. resident St. Joseph's Hosp., Parkersburg, W.Va., 1948-49; gen. practice W.Va., 1948-50, 55-61; mem. staff Fairmont (W.Va.) Gen. Hosp., 1955-60, Fairmont Emergency Hosp., 1955-60; physician USAF, N.Mex. and Calif., 1961-62, U.S. Army, Fort Ord, Calif., 1963-64; resident physician San Luis Obispo County Hosp., 1965-66; pvt. practice LA, 1967—; mem. staff St. Francis Hosp., LA, 1970-71; physician So. Calif. Edison Co., 1981-84. Physician Bethlehem Mines Corp., Idamay, W.Va., 1956; resident physician Sedgwick County Hosp., Wichita, Kans., 1964-65; med. dir. South Gate auto assembly plant GM, 1969-71; staff physician City of LA, 1971-76; relief med. practice Appalachia summer seasons, W.Va. and Ky., 1977, 86, 88-97. Author: The Newer Epidemiology, 1962, rev., 1990, Public Health, A Science Resolvable by Mathematics, 1965; contbr. articles to profl. jours. Sr. counsellor, US Commercial Travelers, Fairmont, W.Va., 1939-40; med. officer USPHS, Navajo Indian Reservation, Tohatchi (N.Mex.) Health Ctr., 1953-55, surgeon, res. officer, 1957-59; pres. W.Va. Pub. Health Assn., 1951-52; sec. indsl. and pub. health sect. W.Va. Med. Assn., 1956; W.Va. dist. 4 health officer; health officer Marion County, W.Va., 1951-53; dist. health officer Allegheny County, Pa., 1957; officer Aux. Civil Def. Police, W.Va., 1942; med. adviser Boy Scouts Am., W.Va., 1956-57, N.Mex., 1954; mem. Med. Rsv. Corps of LA, 2005—. 2d lt. AUS, 1943-46. Dr. Thomas Parran fellow U. Pitts. Sch. Pub. Health, 1955; named to Hon. Order Ky. Cols. Fellow APHA; mem. AMA, Am. Occupl. Med. Assn., Am. Acad. Family Physicians, Western Occupl. Med. Assn., Calif. Med. Assn., Los Angeles County Med. Assn., SR, W.Va., Am. Legion, Elks, Sierra Club Calif., Rio Hondo Symphony Guild, Phi Chi. Avocations: photography, amateur radio, square and round dancing, history, choir. Address: PO Box 4032 Whittier CA 90607-4032 Office Phone: 626-330-4106.

PRIEBE, LANCE, Internet company executive, application developer; Founder, owner RocketSnail Games, 1999—2007; with New Horizon Prodns., Kelowna, BC, New Horizons Interactive Ltd., 2005—; co-founder, chief tech. officer & lead designer ClubPenguin-.com, 2005—07; sr. mgr. Club Penguin unit Walt Disney Internet Grp., Burbank, Calif., 2007—. Office: Club Penguin/NHI 410-1620 Dickson Ave Kelowna BC V1Y 9Y2 Canada E-mail: info@nhinteractive.com.

PRIEM, RICHARD GREGORY, writer, executive; b. Munich, Sept. 18, 1949; arrived in U.S., 1953; s. Richard Stanley and Elizabeth Teresa (Thompson) Priem; m. Janice Lynne Holland, July 27, 1976; children: Michael John, Matthew Warren(dec.), Kathryn Elizabeth Guthrie. BS in Radio-TV-Film, U. Tex., 1970; MEd in Ednl. Tech., U. Ga., 1979; postgrad., Coll. William and Mary, 1981-82. Cert. fraud examiner. Radio personality, sales exec. KOKE, Inc., Austin, Tex., 1968-73; numerous positions including asst. prof. dept. behavioral scis. and leadership U.S. Mil. Acad., anti-terorism staff officer and insp. gen. U.S. Army, 1973-94; dep. divsn. mgr. Sci. Applications Internat. Corp., Vienna, Va., 1994-97; asst. v.p. SAIC, 2003—. Cons. Dallas Cowboys Football Club, 1981; scouting coord. Army Football, 1983-85; cons. in field of anti-terrorism. Contbr. articles to profl. jours. Mem. Assn. Cert. Fraud Examiners, Internat. Soc. for Performance Improvement, Phi Kappa Phi, Kappa Delta Pi, Internat. Assn. Bomb Technicians and Investigators. Home: 13505 Trail Vista Ct NE Albuquerque NM 87111-9248 Personal E-mail: rpriem@earthlink.net.

PRIMM, RICHARD KIRBY, physician; b. Thomasville, NC, May 23, 1944; s. Richard Wesley and Gertrude (Berrier) P.; m. Sharon Kay Lucas, Dec. 28, 1968; children: Heather, Lucas. BA, Duke U., 1966; postgrad., Baylor U., 1966-67; MD, U. N.C., 1970. Intern internal medicine Vanderbilt U. Hosp., Nashville, 1970-71, resident in internal medicine, 1973-75, chief resident, 1975-76; fellow cardiovascular diseases U. Ala., Birmingham, 1976-78, chief fellow, instr. medicine, 1978-79; asst. prof. medicine Vanderbilt U. Sch. Medicine, Nashville, 1979-84; staff cardiologist Wenatchee Valley Med. Ctr., 1984—. Clin. asst. prof. medicine U. Wash., Seattle, 1985-91, clin. assoc. prof. medicine, 1991-2003, clin. prof. medicine, 2003—; adminstrv. lead dept. cardiology Wenatchee Valley Clinic, 1987-91, 1997-2006. Contbr. articles to profl. jours. Capt. U.S. Army, 1971-73. Recipient Heusner Pupil award U. N.C., 1969, Hillman Teaching Excellence award Vanderbilt U., 1976. Fellow: Am. Coll. Cardiology (gov. Wash. chpt. 2002—05); mem.: AHA, Wash. Heart Assn. (trustee 1990—94), North Pacific Soc. Internal Medicine (pres. 2007), Physicians for Social Responsibility, Alpha Omega Alpha. Avocations: downhill skiing, backpacking. Office: Wenatchee Valley Med Ctr 820 N Chelan Ave Wenatchee WA 98801-2028 Home Phone: 509-662-3789; Office Phone: 509-663-8711. Business E-Mail: rprimm@wvclinic.com.

PRINCE, FAITH, actress, singer; b. Augusta, Ga., Aug. 5, 1957; m. Larry Lunetta, 1986; 1 child, Henry. Performer: (Broadway plays) Jerome Robbins' Broadway, 1989—90, Nick & Nora, 1991, Guys and Dolls, 1992 (Drama Desk award, Outstanding Actress in a Musical, Tony award, Best Actress in a Musical, 1992), What's Wrong With This Picture?, 1994, The King and I, 1996—98, Little Me, 1998—99, James Joyce's The Dead, 2000, Bells Are Ringing, 2001, Noises Off, 2001—02, A Catered Affair, 2008, The Little Mermaid, 2009; actor: (films) The Last Dragon, 1985, Dave, 1993, My Father, the Hero, 1994, Big Bully, 1996, Picture Perfect, 1997, It Had to Be You, 2000, Our Very Own, 2005, Material Girls, 2006; (TV series) Encyclopedia, 1986, High Society, 1995, Spin City, 1997—2000, Now and Again, 2000, Huff, 2004—06; (TV films) Friends at Last, 1995, A Season for Miracles, 1999, Sweet Potato Queens, 2003.

PRINCE, THOMAS E., bank executive; b. 1947; With Security Pacific Corp., LA, 1968-92, sr. v.p., controller, 1984—92; exec. v.p., treas. Downey Savs Loan Assn., Newport Beach, Calif., 1992—2004, CFO, 1992, COO, 2004—08, interim CEO, 2008, sr. exec. v.p., CEO office, 2008—. Office: Downey Savs Loan Assn 3501 Jamboree Rd Ste 5000 Newport Beach CA 92660-2980 Mailing: Downey Savings Loan Assn PO Box 6000 Newport Beach CA 92658-6000 Office Phone: 949-509-4440. Office Fax: 949-854-8162.*

PRINCE, TIMOTHY PETER, lawyer; b. San Bernardino, Calif., July 11, 1965; s. Ralph H. and Alexine C. Prince; m. Luci Prince; children: Annelise, Justin. BA in Polit. Sci., U. Calif., Berkeley, 1987; JD, U. Calif. Hastings Coll. Law, San Francisco, 1990. Bar: Calif., US Dist. Ct. (ctrl. dist.) Calif. Extern Justice Marcus Kaufman Calif. Supreme Ct., 1989; asoc. Wilson, Borror, Dunn & Scott, San Bernardino, Calif., 1990-98; ptnr. Tomlinson, Nydam & Prince LLP, San Bernardino, 1998—. Judge pro tem San Bernardino County Superior Ct.; founder, chair San Bernardino Summit; elected parliamentarian Dem. Ctrl. Com., 2004—; treas. 63d Assembly Dist. Dem. Com., 2004—. Editor: Hastings Constnl. Law Quar., 1989—90; contbr. articles to profl jours. Chmn. Citizens Accountable City Govt., San Bernardino, 1997; bd. dirs. Downtown Bus. Assn., Am. Lung Assn. Inland Counties, 1993—96, sec., 1994—96; v.p. North End Neighborhood Assn., 1998—2000. Grantee Gannett Found., 1983—87. Mem.: San Bernardino County Bar Assn. (chmn. resolutions com. 2001—03), Native Sons of Golden West (trustee), San Bernardino Cmty. Scholarship Assn. (pres. 2006—07), Inland C's U. Calif. Berkeley Alumni Club (pres. 1995), Dem. Luncheon Club San Bernardino (pres. 2002—03), Rotary Club (bd. dirs. 2001—03, v.p. 2005—, pres. 2007—). Democrat. Presbyterian. Avocations: hiking, jogging, music, travel, politics. Office: Tomlinson Nydam & Prince 290 N D St Ste 807 San Bernardino CA 92401-1704 Office Phone: 909-888-1000.

PRINCE, WILLIAM B., lawyer; b. Albuquerque, Feb. 7, 1949; BS cum laude, Brigham Young U., 1973; JD, U. Utah, 1978. Bar: Utah 1978. Ptnr. Holme Roberts & Owen, Salt Lake City; ptnr.-in-charge, co-chmn., environ., natural resources, energy practice Dorsey & Whitney LLP, Salt Lake City, 1996—. Mem. Office of Exception and Appeals Fed. Energy Adminstrn., 1974-75. Co-author: Utah Environmental and Land Use Permits Manual, 1981; assoc. editor Jour. Contemporary Law U. Utah, 1977-78. Mem. ABA (natural resources, energy and environ. law sect., chmn. hard minerals com. 1991—), Utah State Bar (past chmn. energy, natural resources and environ. law 1986-87), Northwest Mining Assn., Air and Waste Mgmt. Assn. (Rocky Mountain sect., treas. Great Basin chpt. 1991—). Office: Dorsey & Whitney LLP Ste 925 Wells Fargo Plz 170 S Main St Salt Lake City UT 84101-1655 Office Phone: 801-933-7370. Office Fax: 801-933-7373. Business E-Mail: prince.william@dorsey.com.

PRINDLE, WILLIAM ROSCOE, retired glass company executive; b. San Francisco, Dec. 19, 1926; s. Vivian Arthur and Harriette Alnora (Nickerson) P.; m. June Laverne Anderson, June 20, 1947; children—Carol Susan, William Alastair. BS, U. Calif., Berkeley, 1948, MS, 1950; Sc.D., M.I.T., 1955. Asst. tech. dir. Hazel-Atlas Glass Co., 1954-56; mgr. research Hazel-Atlas Glass div. Continental Can Co., Wheeling, W.Va., 1956-58, gen. mgr. research and devel., 1959-62; mgr. materials research Am. Optical Co., Southbridge, Mass., 1962-65; v.p. research Southbridge and Framingham, Mass., 1971-76; dir; research Ferro Corp., Cleve., 1966-67, v.p. research, 1967-71; exec. dir. Nat. Materials Adv. Bd., NRC-NAS, Washington, 1976-80; dir. adminstrv. and tech. svcs. R & D div. Corning Glass Works, NY, 1980-85, dir. materials rsch. NY, 1985-87; assoc. dir. R & D, Engring. div. Corning Glass Works (now Corning, Inc.), NY, 1987-90; div. v.p., assoc. dir. tech. group Corning Inc., NY, 1990-92; ret. Pres. XII Internat. Glass Congress, 1980, Internat. Commn. on Glass, 1985-88. Served with U.S. Navy, 1944-46. Named Disting. Ceramist of New Eng., New Eng. sect. Am. Ceramic Soc., 1974, Toledo Glass and Ceramic award NW Ohio sect., 1986, Albert Victor Bleininger Meml. award Pitts. sect., 1989, Phoenix award as Glass Industry Man of Yr., 1983; Friedberg Meml. lecture Nat. Inst. Ceramic Engrs., 1990, Greaves-Walker award, 2004. Fellow Am. Ceramic Soc. (disting. life, pres. 1980-81), Soc. Glass Tech., Am. Soc. for Metals Internat.; mem. NAE, AAAS, World Acad. of Ceramics, Cosmos Club (Washington), Sigma Xi, Phi Gamma Delta. Home: 1556 Crestline Dr Santa Barbara CA 93105-4611 Personal E-mail: wprindle@aol.com.

PRINGLE, CURT, Mayor, Anaheim, California; m. Alexis Pringle; children: Katie, Kyle. BBA, MPA, Calif. State U., Long Beach. Pres. Curt Pringle and Associates, LLC, Irvine, Calif.; mem. Calif. State Assembly, 1988—90, 1992—98; mayor City of Anaheim, Calif., 2003—. Rep. leader, Rep. Caucus chair, chmn. appropriations com., chmn. rules com., vice chmn. budget com. Calif. State Assembly, spkr. house, 1996; vis. faculty mem. U. Calif., Irvine. Bd. dirs. Tiger Woods Learning Ctr. Found., John Burton Found. for Children Without Homes; bd. mem. Leadership Traq; mem. Calif. Film Commn., 1996—99; nominee Calif. State Treas., 1998; Calif. del. Nat. Rep. Conv., 1996; active Calif. Rep. Ctrl. Com.; mem. Calif. High Speed Rail Authority, 2008—, Commn. on 21st Century Economy, 2008—; served on Pub. Employees Post-Employment Benefit Commn., 2007, 2008; dir. Orange County Transportation Authority; governing bd. mem. Ukleja Ctr. for Ethical Leadership, Calif. State U. Named Best

Problem Solver and as the Most Influential Leader of the Calif. State Assembly, Calif. Jour. Office: Anaheim City Hall 200 S Anaheim Blvd Anaheim CA 92805 Office Phone: 714-765-5247.*

PRINGLE, PAUL C., lawyer; b. 1943; AB, Dartmouth Coll., 1965; JD, U. Mich., 1968. Bar: NY 1969, Calif. 1972. Ptnr. corp. securities Sidley Austin Brown & Wood LLP, San Francisco and LA. Office: Sidley Austin Brown & Wood Ste 2000 555 California St San Francisco CA 94104-1715 Office Phone: 415-772-1249. Office Fax: 415-772-7400. Business E-Mail: ppringle@sidley.com.

PRINGLE, ROBERT BERNARD, lawyer; b. Summit, NJ, Jan. 2, 1944; s. Edward Harvey and Caroline (Mazuco) P.; m. Rebecca Winslow, June 29, 1974; children: Robin Stevens, Parker Winslow, Edward Sterling. BS, U. NC, 1966; JD, Duke U., 1969. Bar: Pa. 1970, Calif. 1971, US Dist. Ct. (no. dist.) Calif. 1971, US Ct. Appeals (9th cir.) Calif. 1970, US Dist. Ct. (cen. dist.) Calif. 1975, Supreme Ct. of US, US Ct. of Appeals (fed. cir.), bar assn. of City & County of San Francisco. Assoc. Thelen, Marrin, Johnson & Bridges, San Francisco, 1971-77, ptnr., 1978—2004, Thelen Reid Brown Raysman & Steiner LLP, San Francisco, 2004—08, Winston & Strawn LLP, San Francisco, 2008—. Spl. litig. coun. to bd. dir. of major software co. Contbr. articles to prof. journs., co-author numerous books on law. Mem. Tiburon Planning Commn., 1980-83, chmn., 1984; mem. bd. visitors Duke U. Sch. Law. Best Lawyers in US, Chambers USA's America's Leading Lawyers for Bus., Super Lawyer (San Francisco magazine). Mem. ABA (anti-trust sect., civil practice and procedure com. 1977—, litigation sect., chair intellectual property litigation com.), Olympic Club (San Francisco), San Francisco Yacht Club (Belvedere, Calif.), litig. sect. (past chair of various com. chair ann. meeting) 1992, State Bar Calif., mem. exec. com. Unfair Competition & Antitrust sect. 2001-2003, bd. of advisors 2003, Utility, Communications & Transp. Law (chair, antitrust com.), Tiburon Peninsula Club. Avocations: sailing, skiing, tennis, golf. Office: Winston & Strawn LLP 101 California St San Francisco CA 94111 Office Phone: 415-491-1420. Office Fax: 415-591-4000. Business E-Mail: rpringle@winston.com.

PRINZ, PATRICIA A., retired psychiatry educator, researcher; b. Huntington, W.Va., July 17, 1942; d. Fred and Ruth (Samons) Nasser; m. Rudolph A. Prinz, Dec. 20, 1963 (div. 1976); 1 child, Alyssa Ann; m. Hugh MacMahon, Sept. 9, 2001. BS, Duke U., 1963; PhD, Stanford U., 1968. Rsch. career scientist VA, Tacoma, 1982—97; prof psychiatry U. Wash., Seattle, 1986—97, rsch. prof. physiol. nursing, 1997—2005. Dir. Sleep and Aging Rsch. prog., U. Wash., 1976—. Contbr. articles to profl. jours., chpts. to books. Rsch. grantee, Nat. Inst. Aging, 1994-97, NIMH, 1980-99, VA, 1978-97. Fellow Am. Gerontol. Soc. Avocations: biking, singing, travel. Business E-Mail: prinz@uwashington.edu.

PRIOLA, KEVIN, state legislator; m. Michelle Priola, 1996; 2 children. BS in Fin., Acctg., U. Colo., Boulder. V.p., treas. CAP Land Co., Henderson, Colo., Priola Greenhouses, Henderson; mem. Dist. 30 Colo. House of Reps., Denver, 2009—. Mem.: Commerce City Rotary Club. Republican. Office: Colo State Capitol 200 E Colfax Denver CO 80203 Office Phone: 303-866-2912. Business E-Mail: kpriola@gmail.com.*

PRISELAC, THOMAS M., health facility executive, educator; BA in Biology, Washington & Jefferson Coll.; MPH Health Svcs. Adminstrn. and Planning, U. Pitts. Asst. adminstr. Cedars-Sinai Med. Ctr., LA, 1979—81, assoc. adminstr., 1981—82, sr. assoc. adminstr., 1982—83, v.p. adminstrn., 1983—85, sr. v.p. ops., 1985—91, exec. v.p., COO, 1988—94, pres., CEO, 1994—. Adj. prof. UCLA Sch. Pub. Health; tchr., principles of orgn. leadership Master of Pub. Health for Health Professionals; past chmn. Coun. of Teaching Hosp. of Assn. of Am. Med. Coll.; chmn. Calif. Healthcare Assn., Healthcare Assn. of Southern Calif.; bd. dirs. Am. Hosp. Assn., VHA, Inc., Nat. Com. for Quality Healthcare, Calif. Healthcare Found.; lectr. in field. Bd. dirs. Blue Cross Calif. Office: Cedars Sinai Med Ctr 8700 Beverly Blvd Rm 2628 Los Angeles CA 90048 Address: UCLA Sch Pub Health Dept Health Services Box 951772 Los Angeles CA 90095-1772 Office Phone: 310-423-5711, 310-206-3435. Office Fax: 310-423-0120, 310-206-4722. Business E-Mail: tmp@cshs.org.

PRITCHARD, KEVIN, professional sports team executive; b. Bloomington, Ind., July 17, 1967; Grad., U. Kans., 1990. Player Golden State Warriors, 1990—91, Boston Celtics, 1991—92, Phila. 76ers, 1994, Miami Heat, 1995, Washington Bullets, 1995—96; scout San Antonio Spurs; coach, gen. mgr., dir. player pers. Am. Basketball Assn. Kans. City Knights; dir. player pers. Portland Trail Blazers, 2004—05, interim head coach, 2005, asst. gen. mgr., 2006—07, gen. mgr., 2007—. Office: Portland Trail Blazers Rose Garden One Center Ct Portland OR 97227

PRITCHARD, LLEWELYN GEORGE, lawyer; b. NYC, Aug. 13, 1937; s. Llewelyn and Anne Mary (Streib) P.; m. Joan Ashby, June 20, 1959; children: David Ashby, Jennifer Pritchard Vick, Andrew Harrison, William Llewellyn. AB with honors, Drew U., 1958; LLB, Duke U., 1961. Ptnr. Helsell & Fetterman, Seattle. Trustee Allied Arts Found., pres. 2005-07; pres., trustee, corp. counsel Allied Arts Seattle, 1973-76; dir. Fifth Ave. Theatre, 2005-; trustee Meth. Ednl. Found., 1970-85, pres., 1991-92; life trustee PONCHO Patrons of Pacific N.W. Civil, Cultural and Charitable Orgns., pres., 1972-73; bd. dirs. Planned Parenthood of Western Wash., 1972-78, 2007-; trustee Seattle Symphony Orch., 1979-83, chmn. bd., 1980-82, life trustee; trustee U. Puget Sound., 1972-99, exec. com., 1973-96, chmn. bd. visitors to Law Sch., 1984-88; trustee Mus. of Glass, 2000-07, Betty Bowen com. Seattle Art Mus., 2007; chancellor Pacific N.W. Ann. conf. United Meth. Ch., 1969—. Fellow Am. Bar Found. (life, state chmn. 1988-98); mem. ABA (state del. 1982-86, bd. govs. 1986-89, chmn. program com. 1988-89, exec. com. 1988-89, Ho. of Dels. 1979—, nat. dir. young lawyers divsn. 1971, chmn. sect. of individual rights and responsibilities 1975-76, exec. coun. family law sect. 2002-05, chair standing com. on legal aid and indigent defendants 1973-75, chair legal needs study 1995-98, chair adv. com. to pro bono immigration project 1991-01, dir. Ctr. for Human Rights 2001-), Commn. Rule of Law Initiatives, World Justice Project Commn., Wash. State Bar Assn. (chair young lawyers com., bd. govs. King County 1972-75), King County Bar Assn. (chair young lawyers sect. 1970). Avocations: reading, art collector. Home: 5229 140th Ave NE Bellevue WA 98005-1024 Office: Helsell & Fetterman 1001 Fourth Ave Ste 4200 Seattle WA 98154 Office Phone: 206-292-1144.

PRITT, FRANK W., III, computer company executive; b. Charleston, W. Va. m. Julia Pritt (div.); 3 children. BS, Northrop Inst. Tech., Inglewood, Ca. With sales IBM; product mgr. Harris Corp., 1972—82; founder Attachmate Corp., Bellevue, Wash., 1982, chmn., CEO, 1982—2005. Avocations: racing vintage sports cars, boating.

PRITZKER, JOHN A., leisure services executive; s. Robert Pritzker; m. Lisa S. Pritzker; 3 children. Grad., Menlo Coll., U. Denver Coll. Hotel and Restaurant Mgmt. Various positions to divisional v.p. Calif. Hyatt; pres. Hyatt Ventures, Inc.; founder, pres. Red Sail Sports, Inc., 1988—. Exec. v.p. bus. devel. Key3Media Events, Inc., 2000; bd. dirs. Zoomedia Inc. Trustee San Francisco Mus. Modern Art; dir. Pritzker Found., Pritzker Cousins Found., Children Now; bd. dirs. U. Calif. San Francisco Found. Named one of Forbes Richest Americans, 2006, Top 200 Collectors, ARTnews mag., 2005—08. Office: Red Sail Sports 5 Pier 102 San Francisco CA 94111-2027

PRIVETT, STEPHEN A., academic administrator, priest; b. San Francisco; BA in Philosophy and Classics, Gonzaga U., 1966; MDiv, U. Calif., Berkeley, 1972; postgrad., U. Calif., Santa Barbara, 1973—74; MA in Catechetics/Religious Edn., Cath. U. Am., 1982, PhD in Catechetics, 1985. Entered Soc. of Jesus, 1960. Instr. Latin, western civilization and religion Jesuit H.S., Sacramento, 1966—69; dir. Project 50 Santa Clara U., 1970—71; asst. dir. novices Coll. Queen of Peace, Santa Barbara, 1972—73; instr. modern European history, Latin and English Bellarmine Coll. Preparatory, San Jose, Calif., 1974—80, prin., 1975—80; asst. prof. religious studies dept. Santa Clara U., 1985—90, assoc. prof. religious studies dept., 1990—2000, co-dir. The Eastside Project, 1985—91, dir. Voice of the Voiceless: Inst. on Human Rights and Social Justice, 1989—91, v.p. acad. affairs, 1991—97, provost, v.p. acad. affairs, 1997—2000; pres. U. San Francisco, 2000—. Mem. U.S. Cath. Conf. on Certification and Accreditation, 1990—99; mem. Strategic Planning Commn. Calif. Province of the Soc. of Jesus, 1996—2002; mem. Nat. Seminar on Jesuit Higher Edn. U. Scranton, 1999—. Contbr. articles to profl. jours.; author: The U.S. Catholic Church and Its Hispanic Members: The Pastoral Vision of Robert E. Lucey, 1988. Vol. pastoral worker Jesuit Refugee Svc., El Salvador, 1988; bd. dirs. Jesuit Vol. Corps S.W., 1987—95, chair, 1988—91; bd. dirs. Christians for Peace in El Salvador, 1997—2000, Fromm Inst. for Lifelong Learning, U. San Francisco, 2000—; trustee Brophy Coll. Preparatory, Phoenix, 1996—, Seattle U., 2000—, U. Iberoamericana, Mexico City, 2001—; hon. mem. San Francisco Host Com., 2000—. Mem.: Assn. Grad. Programs in Ministry, Assn. Profs. and Rschrs. in Religious Edn. (mem. Cath. Assembly), Religious Edn. Assn., Assn. Cath. Colls. and Univs. (bd. dirs. 2002—), Assn. Jesuit Colls. and Univs. (bd. dirs. 2000—), Commonwealth Club Calif. (bd. govs.). Office: U San Francisco Office of Pres 2130 Fulton St San Francisco CA 94117 Office Phone: 415-422-6762. E-mail: president@usfca.edu.

PRO, PHILIP MARTIN, judge; b. Richmond, Calif., Dec. 12, 1946; s. Leo Martin and Mildred Louise (Beck) P.; m. Dori Sue Hallas, Nov. 13, 1982; 1 child, Brenda Kay. BA, San Francisco State U., 1968; JD, Golden Gate U., 1972. Bar: Calif. 1972, Nev. 1973, U.S. Ct. Appeals (9th cir.) 1973, U.S. Dist. Ct. Nev. 1973, U.S. Supreme Ct. 1976. Pub. defender, Las Vegas, 1973-75; asst. U.S. atty. Dist. Nev., Las Vegas, 1975-78; dep. atty. gen. State of Nev., Carson City, 1979-80; magistrate US Dist. Ct. Nev., Las Vegas, 1980-87, judge, 1987—, chief judge, 2002—07. Instr. Atty. Gen.'s Advocacy Inst., Nat. Inst. Trial Advocacy, 1992; chmn. com. adminstrn. of magistrate judge system Jud. Conf. U.S., 1993—; bd. dirs. Fed. Jud. Cts. Program com. and issues in justice com. NCCJ, Las Vegas, 1982—. Mem. ABA, Fed. Judges Assn. (bd. dirs. 1992—, v.p. 1997-2001), Nev. State Bar Assn., Calif. State Bar Assn., Nev. Judges Assn. (instr.), Assn. Trial Lawyers Am., Nev. Am. Inn Ct. (pres. 1989-91), Ninth Cir. Jury (instructions com.), Nat. Conf. U.S. Magistrates (sec.). Republican. Office: US Dist Ct 7015 Fed Bldg 333 Las Vegas Blvd S Ste 7015 Las Vegas NV 89101-5883 Office Phone: 702-464-5510. Business E-Mail: philip_pro@nvd.uscourts.gov.

PROBASCO, CALVIN HENRY CHARLES, clergyman, college administrator; b. Petaluma, Calif., Apr. 5, 1926; s. Calvin Warren and Ruth Charlene (Winans) P.; m. Nixie June Farnsworth, Feb. 14, 1947; children— Calvin, Carol, David, Ruth BA cum laude, Biola Bible Coll., La Mirada, Calif., 1953; D.D. (hon.), Talbot Theol. Sem., La Mirada, 1983. Ordained to ministry, 1950. Pastor Sharon Baptist Ch., El Monte, Calif., 1951-58, Carmichael Bible Ch., Calif., 1958-97, pastor emeritus, 1997—; pres. Sacramento Bible Inst., Carmichael, Calif., 1968—86. Mem. Ind. Fundamental Chs. Am. (rec. sec. 1978-81, pres. 1981-84, 1st v.p. 1987-88), Delta Epsilon Chi. Republican.

PROBST, JEFF LEE, television personality; b. Wichita, Kans., Nov. 4, 1961; m. Shelley Wright, 1961 (div. 2001). Actor: (films) Face of a Stranger, 1991, The A-List, 2001; (TV series) Fillmore!, 2002; host (TV series) Backchat, 1996, Rock & Roll Jeopardy!, VH1, 1998—2001, host, writer Survivor, 2000— (Emmy Award for Outstanding Non-Fiction Program, 2001, Primetime Emmy for Outstanding Host for a Reality or Reality-Competition Program, Acad. TV Arts and Scis., 2008), co-host The 60th Primetime Emmy Awards, 2008; dir.: (films) Finder's Fee, 2001. Office: c/o Endeavor Agency 9601 Wilshire Blvd, 3rd Fl Beverly Hills CA 90212

PROBST, LAWRENCE F., III, interactive software/gaming executive; b. 1950; BS, U. Del., 1972. Dist. sales mgr. Johnson & Johnson, 1972-80; nat. accounts mgr. The Clorox Co., 1980-82, Mediagenic (formerly Activision Inc.), 1982-84; v.p. sales Electronic Arts, Inc., 1984—86, sr. v.p., distbn., 1987—91, pres., 1991—98, CEO Redwood City, Calif., 1991—2007, exec. chmn., 1994—. Bd. dirs. Electronic Arts, Inc., 1991—, MP3.com, Inc., 1999—. Office: Electronic Arts Inc 209 Redwood Shores Pkwy Redwood City CA 94065

PROBST, TIM, state legislator; m. Tahira Probst; children: Alli, Charlotte, Aaron, Ginny. Degree in Govt. & Internat. Rels. with honors, U. Notre Dame, Notre Dame, Ind.; studied Politics & Economics of EU, U. Innsbruck, Austria. Former state budget analyst; former legis. liaison; former asst. Gov. of Ill., Welfare Reform & Workforce Devel.; mem. Dist. 17 Wash. House of Reps., 2008—. Democrat. Office: 325 John L O'Brien Bldg PO Box 40600 Olympia WA 98504-0600 Office Phone: 360-786-7994. Business E-Mail: probst.tim@leg.wa.gov.

PROCHNOW, JAMES R., lawyer; b. Hutchinson, Minn., Sept. 22, 1943; BA, Hamline U., 1965; JD, William Mitchell Law Sch., 1969. Bar: Minn. 1969, U.S. Supreme Ct. 1973, Colo. 1975. Staff civil divsn. Dept. Justice, Washington, 1973-74; legal counsel to Pres. The White House, Washington, 1974; ptnr. Baker & Hostetler, Denver, 1974—94, Patton Boggs, Denver, 1994—2003, Greenberg Traurig LLP, Denver, 2003—. Mem.: Direct Selling Assn., Am. Herbal Products Assn., Colo. Bar Assn., Denver Bar Assn. Office: Greenberg Traurig LLP 1200 17th St Ste 2400 Denver CO 80202

PROCTER, EMILY MALLORY, actress; b. Raleigh, NC, Oct. 8, 1968; d. William Procter and Barbara. Grad., East Carolina U. Weather girl CBS affiliate, Greenville. Actress (TV films) Fast Company, 1995, The Dukes of Hazzard: Reunion!, 1997, Submerged, 2001, (films) Leaving Las Vegas, 1995, Crosscut, 1996, Jerry Maguire, 1996, The Girl Gets Moe, 1997, Breast Men, 1997, Family Plan, 1998, Kingdom Come, 1999, Guinevere, 1999, Forever Fabulous, 1999, Body Shots, 1999, The Big Tease, 1999, Big Momma's House 2, 2006, (TV series) The West Wing, 2000—06, CSI: Miami, 2002—07. Vol. All Saints' Episcopal Ch. soup kitchen, Beverly Hills. Office: c/o William Morris Agy 1 William Morris Pl Beverly Hills CA 90212

PROCTOR, RICHARD JAMES, geologist, consultant; b. LA, Aug. 2, 1931; s. George Arthur and Margaret Y. (Goodman) P.; m. Ena McLaren, Feb. 12, 1955; children: Mitchell, Jill, Randall. BA, Calif. State U., LA, 1954; MA, UCLA, 1958. Engring. geologist, Calif.; cert. profl. geologist Am. Inst. Profl. Geologists. Chief geologist Met. Water Dist., LA, 1958-80; pres., cons. geologist Richard J. Proctor, Inc., Arcadia, Calif., 1980-95. Vis. assoc. prof. Calif. Inst. Tech., Pasadena, 1975-78. Author: History of AIPG, 2003; co-author: Citizens Guide to Geologic Hazards, 1993; editor: Professional Practice Guidelines, 1985, Engineering Geology Practice in Southern California, 1992, (screenplays) My Friend Tom Horn, 2005, Stopping by Woods, 2006. Pres., dir. Arcadia Hist. Soc., 1993-96. Fellow Geol. Soc. Am. (Burwell Meml. award 1972); mem. Assn. Engring. Geologists (hon., pres. 1979), Am. Inst. Profl. Geologists (hon., pres. 1989, Van Couvering Meml. award 1990, Parker Meml. medal 2003), Am. Geol. Inst. (sec.-treas. 1979-83), Conf. Calif. Hist. Socs. (pres. 2004-06).

PRONGER, CHRIS, professional hockey player; b. Dryden, Ont., Can., Oct. 10, 1974; m. Lauren Pronger, 2001. Defenseman Hartford Whalers, 1993—95, St. Louis Blues, 1995—2005, Edmonton Oilers, 2005—06, Anaheim Ducks, 2006—, capt., 2007—08; mem. Can. Nat. Hockey Team, 1992—93, 1996—97, 1997—98, 2001—02. Recipient Gold medal, Can. Under 18 Team, Phoenix Cup, 1991, World Jr. Hockey Championship, 1993, World Championship, 1997, Bud Ice Plus-Minus award, 1997—98, Norris Trophy, 2000, Hart Trophy, 2000; named to All-Rookie Team, NHL, 1994, Second All-Star Team, 2007, NHL All-Star Game, 1999, 2000, 2002, 2004, 2008; finalist Lester B. Pearson award, 2000. Achievements include being a member of gold medal Canadian Hockey team, Salt Lake City Olympic Games, 2002; being a member of Stanley Cup Champion Anaheim Ducks, 2007. Office: Anaheim Ducks 2695 E Katella Ave Anaheim CA 92806

PRONGER, SEAN JAMES, coach, former professional hockey player; b. Thunder Bay, Ont., Can., Nov. 30, 1972; Grad., Bowling Green State U., 1994. Center Mighty Ducks of Anaheim, Calif., 1995—98, Pitts. Penguins, 1998, NY Rangers, 1998, LA Kings, 1999, Boston Bruins, 1999—2000, Columbus Blue Jackets, 2001—03, Vancouver Canucks, 2003—04; asst. coach Anaheim Jr. Ducks. Office: Anaheim Ice 300 W Lincoln Ave Anaheim CA 92850

PRONZINI, BILL JOHN (WILLIAM PRONZINI), writer; b. Petaluma, Calif., Apr. 13, 1943; s. Joseph and Helene (Guder) P.; m. Marcia Muller. Author: 67 novels (including under pseudonyms), 4 books of non-fiction, 20 collections of short stories, 1971—; first novel, The Stalker, 1971, novel, Hoodwink, 1981 (Best Novel), Boobytrap, 1998 (Best Novel); editor 80 anthologies; contbr. numerous short stories to publs. Recipient 6 scroll awards Mystery Writers Am., Named Grand Master, 2008; recipient Life Achievement award Pvt. Eye Writers Am., 1987. Office: PO Box 2536 Petaluma CA 94953-2536 E-mail: pronhack@comcast.net.

PROTAS, JOSH, non-profit organization director; b. 1975; Grad., Wesleyan U.; M in Pub. Hist., Ariz. State U. Exec. dir. Stone Ave. Temple; dir., Jewish Cmty. Rels. Coun. Jewish Fedn. Southern Ariz. Mem. Pima Coun. on Aging and Jewish Family & Children's Svc. Involved with Salvation Army, Cmty. Food Bank, Southern Ariz. Cmty. Diaper Bank, YWCA, Tucson Save Darfur Coalition; men's shelter meal team Primavera Svc. Named one of 40 Under 40, Tucson Bus. Edge, 2006. Office: Jewish Cmty Relations Council 3822 E River Rd Tucson AZ 85718 Office Phone: 520-577-9393. Office Fax: 520-577-0734.

PROTZMAN, GRANT DALE, university administrator, state legislator, state legislator; b. Ogden, Utah, May 3, 1950; s. Paul L. and Maxine E. (Nelson) P.; m. Linda Sue Gerasta, Mar. 30, 1985; children: Heather Sue, Kristen Marie, Erin Elizabeth. BA, Utah. State U., 1976; MS, Calif. Am. U., 1979; MA, U. No. Colo., 1987, EdD, 1988. Coord. student activities Weber State U., Ogden, 1976-81, coord. student govt., 1981-82, assoc. dir. student life, 1982-84, dir. co-curricular learning, 1984-87, planning and devel. officer, dir. drug and alcohol program, 1987-91, asst. to v.p., 1991—; mem., asst. minority whip Utah State Ho. of Reps., Salt Lake City, 1986-97. Sr. cons. Inst. for Leadership Devel., Ogden, 1978—. Author: An Examination of Select Motivational Variables of Members in Three Different Types of Volunteer Organizations in a Collegiate Setting, 1988, An Investigation of the State of Motivation Management and Assessment in Volunteer Organizations, 1988; contbr. articles to profl. jours. Mem. adv. bd. Wasatch Care Ctr., Ogden, 1986-93, Families in Edn., 1992, Weber Sch. Dist., 1992; mem. Weber Area Emergency Planning Com., Ogden, 1988-93, critical workplace skills adv. bd. Applied Tech. Ctr., 1991—, mem. adv. bd. Pvt. Industry Coun./Local Community Coun., 1994—, State of Utah Region II Dept. Corrections, 1992—; mem. bd. dirs. Hospice No. Utah, 1994—. Named Outstanding Young Man of the Year, Jay Cees; Recipient Ptnrs. in Edn. Recognition award Weber Sch. Dist., 1987, Appreciation award Utah Vocat. Leadership Orgns., 1987, Extended Svc. award Ogden Sch. Dist., 1988, Outstanding Legislator award Utah Democratic Party Chmn's. award, 1988, Utah Sch. Employees Assn. Scroll of Honor award as Outstanding legislator, 1990, Weber State U. Student Svcs. Soar award, 1991, Utah Edn. Assn. Honor Roll award as Outstanding legislator, 1991, Utah Ednl. Libr. Media Assn. award for Outstanding Dedication and Svc. to Utah Lib. Media programs, 1992, Utah Assn. of Rehabilitative Facilities award for Svc. to Persons with disabilities, 1992, U.B.A.T.C. award for Support of Vocational Edn., 1992, Golden Key award, 1993, Utah Govt. Coun. for People with Disabilities award State Legis. Coalition, 1994. Mem. Nat. Assn. Campus Activities (regional coord. 1982-85, conf. educator 1980-83, Nat. Outstanding Unit of Yr. 1986, Regional

Outstanding Unit of Yr. 1985), Utah Edn. Assn. (honor roll award 1991), Rotary (pres. Ogden chpt.), Kappa Delta Pi, Phi Sigma Alpha, Phi Delta Kappa. Democrat. Mem. Lds Ch. Avocations: auto restoration, water-skiing, hiking. Home: 3073 N 575 E Ogden UT 84414-2077 Office: Weber State U 3750 Harrison Blvd Ogden UT 84408-0001

PROULX, (EDNA) ANNIE, writer; b. Norwich, Conn., Aug. 22, 1935; d. George Napolean and Lois Nellie (Gill) Proulx; m. James Hamilton Lang, June 22, 1969 (div. 1990); children: Sylvia Marion, Jonathan Edward, Gillis Crowell, Morgan Hamilton. BA cum laude, U. Vt., 1969; MA, Sir George Williams U., Montreal, Can., 1973; DHL (hon.), U. Maine, 1994; DLitt (hon.), U. Toronto, 2000; LLD, Concordia U., Montreal, 2002. Author: Sweet and Hard Cider: Making It, Using It and Enjoying It, 1980, Heart Songs and Other Stories, 1988, Postcards, 1991 (PEN/Faulkner award for fiction, 1993), The Shipping News, 1993 (Irish Times Internat. Fiction award, 1993, Nat. Book award for fiction, 1994, Pulitzer Prize for fiction, 1994), Accordion Crimes, 1996 (Dos Passos prize for lit., 1996), Brokeback Mountain (later adapted to film), 1998 (Nat. Mag. award, 1998), Close Range: Wyoming Stories, 1999, That Old Ace in the Hole, 2002, Bad Dirt: Wyoming Stories 2, 2004, Fine Just the Way It Is: Wyoming Stories 3, 2008; editor: Best American Short Stories, 1997; contbr. articles to mags. Recipient Amb. Book award, English Speaking Union, 2000. Mem.: PEN Am. Ctr., Phi Alpha Theta, Phi Beta Kappa. Avocations: canoeing, reading, fishing.*

PROZANSKI, FLOYD, state legislator; b. Lubbock, Tex., 1954; m to Susan. Oregon State Representative, District 40, 94-2001, vice chairman, Judiciary Committee, currently, member, Ways & Means Subcomt on Public Safety/Regulation, formerly, Oregon House Representative; member, United States Department Interior Bureau Land Mgt-Eugene District Timber Sales Advisor Bd, formerly; member, Lane Co Federal Emer Management Agency Bd, 89-96, chairman, 91-93; Oregon State Representative, District 8, formerly; Oregon State Senator, District 4, 2004-.Atty, currently; advisor, Sch Law Client Counseling Team, Univ Oregon, 87-; student conduct hearings officer, Univ Oregon, currently; board director, BRING Recycling, currently. Lane Co Bar Association; City Club of Eugene; Lane Co Domestic Violence Coun. Democrat. Office: 900 Court St NE, S-417 Salem OR 97301 Address: PO Box 11511 Eugene OR 97440 Home Phone: 541-342-2447; Office Phone: 503-986-1704. Business E-Mail: sen.floydprozanski@state.or.us. E-mail: floydp@darkwing.uoregon.edu.

PRUEITT, ELISABETH, pastry chef; m. Chad Robertson, 1994. Grad., Culinary Inst. America, Hyde Park, NY. With Montrachet restaurant, NY; pastry chef Canyon Ranch, Lenox, Mass.; baker, dessert cons.; co-owner, pastry chef Bay Village Bakery, Point Reyes Station, Calif., Tartine Bakery, San Francisco, 2002—. Contbr. Canyon Ranch Spa Cookboo; guest appearances on (TV series) Martha Stewart, local San Francisco TV. Recipient Outstanding Pastry Chef award (with Chad Robertson), James Beard Found., 2008; named Pasty Chef of Yr., San Francisco Mag., 2003; nominee Outstanding Pastry Chef award (with Chad Robertson), James Beard Found., 2006. Office: Tartine Bakery 600 Guerrero St San Francisco CA 94110 Office Phone: 415-487-2600.

PRUETZ, ADRIAN MARY, lawyer; Student, U. Wis., 1966—69; BA, Loyola U., Chgo., 1972, postgrad., 1972—73; JD magna cum laude, Marquette U., 1982. Bar: Wis. 1982, Calif. 1985. Assoc. Whyte and Hirschboeck, SC, 1982—84, Morrison and Foerster, 1984—88, ptnr., 1988—94, Quinn Emanuel Urquhart Oliver & Hedges, LLP, LA, 1994—2007, co-chair intellectual property litigation group; with Pruetz Law Group LLP, El Segundo, Calif., 2007—. Spkr., lectr. Price Waterhouse Intellectual Property Forum, Licensing Execs. Soc., Am. Soc. Indsl. Security. Named Top Patent, Corp. Counsel, 2007—08, Rank I in Copyright, Trademark and Trade Secret, Chambers USA, 2008; named one of Calif. Top 50 Litigators, LA Daily Jour., 2001—07, Most Influential Trial Lawyers in Calif., 2002—07, State's Top 25 Intellectual Property Lawyers, 2003—05, Calif.'s Most Successful Lawyers, Calif. Law Bus., Top 10 trademark Litigators, Chambers USA, 2008. Mem.: ABA (past chair com. U.S. lit. affecting internat. patent problems, past chair com. impact 1991 amendments), LA County Bar, State Bar Calif., Fed. Bar Assn. (spkr., lectr.). Office: Pruetz Law Group LLP 200 N Sepulveda Blvd Ste 1525 El Segundo CA 90245-4399 Office Phone: 310-765-7655. Business E-Mail: ampruetz@pruetzlaw.com.

PRUITT, GARY B., publishing company executive; b. 1957; m. Abby Pruitt; children: Katherine, Allison. BA summa cum laude, U. Fla., 1978; MA in Pub. Policy, U. Calif. Berkeley, 1981, JD, 1982. Counsel The McClatchy Co., 1984—87, gen. counsel, corp. sec., 1987—91, v.p. ops. & tech., 1994-95, pres., 1995—, COO, 1995—96, CEO, 1996—, chmn., 2001—; pub. The Fresno Bee, 1991-94. Bd. dirs. The McClatchy Co., 1995—. Mem. chancellors com. U. Calif., Berkeley, mem. bd. advisors Goldman Sch. Pub. Policy. Mem.: James Irvine Found. (bd. dirs. 1999—, vice chmn. 2003—05, chmn. 2006—), Newspaper Assn. Am, Phi Betta Kappa. Office: The McClatchy Co 2100 Q St Sacramento CA 95816-6816

PRUNES, FERNANDO, plastic surgeon, educator; b. Chihuahua, Mex. m. Linda R. Underwood; children: Alexander, Ariadne, Anthony. MD, U. Chihuahua, Mex., 1968. Surg. intern Booth Meml. Med. Ctr., Flushing, NY, 1971-72; resident in gen. surgery Tucson Hosps. Med. Edn. Program, 1972-76; resident in plastic surgery Mayo Grad. Sch. Medicine, 1979-81; chief divsn. plastic surgery Kern Med. Ctr., Bakersfield, Calif., 1983—. Asst. clin. prof. surgery U. Calif., San Diego, 1983-98. Mem. Am. Soc. Plastic Surgeons, Mayo Alumni Assn. Avocations: golf, computers. Office: Kern Med Ctr 1830 Flower St Bakersfield CA 93305-4186 Office Phone: 661-326-2274.

PRUSINER, STANLEY BEN, neurologist, biochemist, virologist, educator; b. Des Moines, May 28, 1942; s. Lawrence Albert and Miriam (Spiegel) Prusiner; children: Helen Chloe, Leah Anne. AB cum laude, U. Pa., Phila., 1964, MD, 1968, DS (hon.), 1998; PhD (hon.), Hebrew U., Jerusalem, 1995, René Descartes U., Paris, 1996; DS (hon.), Dartmouth Coll., Hanover, NH, 1999, U. Liege, 2000; MD (hon.), U. Bologna, Italy, 2000; DSc (hon.), Pa. State U., 2001; DVM (hon.), U. Cardenal Herrera, 2005; PhD (hon.), Claremont Grad. U., Calif., 2007. Diplomate Am. Bd. Neurology. Intern in medicine U. Calif., San Francisco, 1968—69, resident in neurology, 1972—74, asst. prof. neurology, 1974—80, assoc. prof., 1980—84, prof., 1984—, prof. biochemistry, 1988—2008, acad. senate faculty rsch. lectr., 1989—90, prof. virology Berkeley, 1984—, dir. Inst. for Neurodegenerative Diseases, 1999—, Imperial Coll., London, 2007—08; Leverhulme vis. prof., founder, chmn. bd. dirs. InPro Biotech. Inc., South San Francisco, Calif., 2001—08. Mem. neurology rev. com. Nat. Inst. for Neurodegenerative Diseases, NIH, Bethesda, Md., 1982—86, Bethesda, 1990—92; mem. Coun. Nat. Inst. Aging, NIH, Bethesda, Md., 2001—04; mem. sci. adv. bd. French Found., LA, 1985—, chmn. sci. adv. bd., 1996—; mem. sci. rev. com. Alzheimer's Disease Diagnosic Ctr. & Rsch Grant Program, State of Calif., 1985—89; chmn. sci. adv. bd. Am. Health Assistance Found., Rockville, Md., 1986—2000, hon. mem. bd. dirs., 2001—; mem. spongiform encephalopathy adv. com. FDA, 1997—2001; mem. adv. bd. Family Survival Project for Adults with Chronic Brain Disorders, San Francisco, 1982—90; mem. adv. bd. San Francisco chpt. Alzheimer's Disease and Related Disorders Found., 1985—91; mem. bd. dirs. Fromm Inst. for Lifelong Learning, San Francisco, 2002—; cons. Inst. of Medicine Com. on Advancing Prion Sci., Washington, 2002—03; mem. bd. govs. Found. for Biomed. Rsch., Washington, 2002—; bd. dirs. Internat. Longevity Ctr., NYC, 2003—. Editor: The Enzymes of Glutamine Metabolism, 1973, Slow Transmissible Diseases of the Nervous System, 2 vols., 1979, Prions--Novel Infectious Pathogens Causing Scrapie and CJD, 1987, Prion Diseases of Humans and Animals, 1992, Prions Prions Prions, 1996, Molecular and Genetic Basis of Neurologic Disease, 3d edit., 2003, Prion Biology and Diseases, 2d edit., 2004; contbr. more than 350 articles to profl. jours. Trustee U. Pa., 2000—05, Congregation Sherith Israel, San Francisco, 1999—2002. Lt. comdr. USPHS, 1969—72. Recipient Leadership and Excellence Alzheimer's Disease award, NIH, 1990—97, Potamkin prize Alzheimer's Disease Rsch., 1991, Disting. Med. Grad. award, U. Pa. Sch. Medicine, 1991, Med. Rsch. award, Met. Life Found., 1992, Christopher Columbus Discovery award, NIH and Med. Soc. Genoa, Italy, 1992, Charles A. Dana award, 1992, Dickson prize, U. Pitts., 1992, Max Planck Rsch. award, Alexander von Humboldt Found. and Max Planck Soc., 1992, Gairdner Found. Internat. award, 1993, Disting. Achievement in Neurosci. Rsch. award, Bristol-Myers Squibb, 1994, Albert Lasker award Basic Med. Rsch., 1994, Caledonian Rsch. Found. prize, Royal Soc. Edinburgh, 1995, Paul Ehrlich and Ludwig Darmstaedter award, Germany, 1995, Paul Hoch award, Am. Psychopathol. Assn., 1995, Wolf prize in medicine, 1996, ICN Virology prize, 1996, Victor and Clara Soriano award, World Fedn. Neurology, 1996, Pasarow Found. prize, 1996, Charles Leopole Mayer prize, French Acad. Scis., 1996, Keio Internat. prize, 1996, Baxter award, Am. Assn. Med. Colls., 1996, Louisa Gross Horwitz prize, Columbia U., 1997, Nobel prize Medicine, 1997, K.J. Zulch prize, Gertrude Reemtsma Found., 1997, Benjamin Franklin medal, Franklin Inst., 1998, Jubilee medal, Swedish Med. Soc., 1998, Prize Lecture medal, U. Coll. London, 1999, Sir Hans Krebs medal, Fedn. European Biochem. Socs., 1999, Ellen Browning Scripps medal, 2000, Disting. Alumni award, Coll. Arts and Scis., U. of Pa., 2003, Commonwealth award, 2004, William Beaumont medal, 2005, T.S. Srinivasan Gold Medal, Srinivasan Trust, Chennai, India, 2007; grantee Med. Investigator grantee, Howard Hughes Med. Inst., 1976—81, excellence in neurosci., Senator Jacob Javits Ctr., NIH, 1985—90; fellow Alfred P. Sloan Rsch. fellow, U. Calif., 1976—78. Fellow: AAAS, Royal Coll. Physicians, Am. Acad. Arts & Scis., Am. Soc. Microbiology; mem.: NAS (councilor 2007—, Inst. Medicine, Richard Lounsbery award extraordinary achievements biology and medicine 1993), NRC (governing bd. mem. 2008—), World Jewish Acad. Scis., Serbian Acad. Scis., Protein Soc. (Amgen award 1997), Royal Soc. London, Am. Philos. Soc., Am. Soc. Molecular Biol. Biochemistry, Am. Soc. Cellular Biology, Am. Soc. Cell Biology, Genetics Soc. Am., Am. Soc. Human Genetics, Soc. Neurosci., Am. Chem. Soc., Am. Soc. Biochemistry and Molecular Biology, Am. Soc. Clin. Investigation, Am. Neurol. Assn., Am. Soc. Virology, Am. Soc. Neurochemistry, Am. Soc. Neurochemistry, Am. Assn. Physicians, Am. Acad. Neurology (George Cotzias award outstanding rsch. 1987, Presdl. award 1993, Disting. Achievement award 1998), Bohemian Club, Concordia Argonaut Club (bd. dirs. 1997—2005).

PRYOR, JAY R., oil industry executive; b. Miss. BSc in Petroleum Engring., Miss. State U., 1979. Petroleum engr. to mgmt. positions with increasing responsibilities in Asia, US, Europe and the former Soviet Union Chevron USA Prodn. Co., 1979—92; mgr. petroleum engring. Chevron Overseas Petroleum Inc., Kazakhstan, 1992—96; sponsor career devel. for ops. pers., gen. mgr. human resources, worldwide ops. Chevron Corp., San Ramon, Calif., 1996—99; mng. dir. Chevron Offshore Ltd., Thailand, 1999—2002, Chevron Nigeria Ltd., 2002—06; v.p. corp. bus. devel. Chevron Corp., 2006—. Co-chair Nigerian Bus. Coalition Against HIV/AIDS. Mem.: Soc. Petroleum Engrs., Kazakhstan Br. Office: Chevron Corp Hdqs 6001 Bollinger Canyon Rd San Ramon CA 94583

PRYPCHAN, LIDA D., psychiatrist; b. Caracas, DF, Venezuela, July 8, 1960; arrived in USA, 1989; d. Roman Orestes Prypchan Hryculak and Edel Sayagues Sanchez. MD, U. Carabobo, Venezuela, 1986. Cert. physician Ednl. Commn. Fgn. Med. Grads., USA, Venezuela, adult psychiatrist U. Ctrl. Venezuela, Venezuelan Psychiatric Assn. Physician Clinica Residencia Carabobo, Valencia, Venezuela, 1986—89; rsch. assoc., the Schizophrenia Project at We. Psychiatric Inst. and Clinic U. Pitts. Med. Ctr., 1989—90, rsch. assoc., the Anxiety Disorders Project at Pitts. Adolescent Alcohol Rsch. Ctr., 1990—92, sr. rsch. assoc. World Psychiatric Assn., 1990—94; adult psychiatric resident Hosp. U. Caracas, U. Ctrl. de Venezuela, 1996—99, Elmhurst Hosp. Ctr., NY, 2001—05; fellow Child and Adolescent Psychiatry Elmhurst Hosp. Ctr., Mt. Sinai Sch. Medicine, 2005—07; attending adult, child and adolescent psychiatrist Wyo. Behavioral Inst., 2007—. Sr. rsch. assoc. Elmhurst Hosp. Ctr./World Psychiatric Assn., 2003—05; founder ppphusa.org, 2008. Contbr. articles to profl. jours. Active mem. Soka Gakkai Internat.-USA, 1989—. Recipient Nat. Sci. Journalism award, Venezuela, 1987, 1988, 1989. Mem.: AMA, Nat. Assn. Mental Illness, Wyo. Psychiatric Assn., Wyo. Med. Assn., Acad. Child and Adolescent Psychiatry, Am. Psychiatric Assn. Democrat. Buddhist. Avocations: movies, theater, travel, walking, reading. Home: 2661 East 15th St Unit 204 Casper WY 82609 Office: Wyo Behavioral Inst 2417 East 15th St Casper WY 82609 Office Phone: 307-472-2271. Personal E-mail: lidaprypchan@hotmail.com.

PTACEK, LOUIS JOHN, medical educator, medical researcher; b. Madison, Wis., May 14, 1961; married. BS in Math., U. Wis., Madison, 1982, MD, 1986. Lic. Utah, 1987, cert. Am. Bd. Neurology and Psychiatry, 1993, lic. Calif., 2006. Intern in medicine U. Wash., 1986—87; resident in neurology U. Utah, 1987—90, chief neurology resident, 1989—90, Muscular Dystrophy Assn. neuromuscular fellow, 1990—91, postdoc in molecular biology, 1991—94, instr. neurology, 1990—92, asst. prof. neurology, 1992—96, assoc. prof. neurology and human genetics, 1996—2002, dir. neurogenetics divsn., 2000—03, prof. neurology and human genetics, 2002—03; prof. neurology U. Calif., San Francisco, 2003—, dir. neurogenetics divsn., 2003—, John C. Coleman disting. prof. neurogenerative diseases, 2004—. Assoc. investigator Howard Hughes Med. Inst., 1997—2003, investigator, 2003—. Assoc. editor Annals of Neurology, 1997—, Neurogenetics, 1997—, Neuromuscular Disorders, 2000—04, Jour. Neuroscience, 2005—. Fellow: Am. Acad. Arts and Sciences, Am. Soc. for Clin. Investigation; mem.: Am. Acad. Neurology, NAS Inst. Medicine. Office: U Calif San Francisco Fu & Ptacek Labs 1550 4th St San Francisco CA 94158-2324 Office Phone: 415-502-5614. Office Fax: 415-502-5641. E-mail: ljp@ucsf.edu.*

PTACEK, WILLIAM H., library director; BA in English and Psychology, U. Ill., 1972; MLS, SUNY, Geneseo, 1974; cert. of advanced study, U. Ill., Chgo., 1979. Reference libr. South Br. Chgo. Pub. Libr., 1974-75, head libr. Mt. Greenwood br., 1975-76, head system-wide circulation, 1976-77, asst. dir. pers., 1977-78, chief NE dist., 1978-79; dir. Idaho Falls Pub. Libr., 1979-83, Louisville Free Pub. Libr., 1984-89, King County Libr. Sys., Wash., 1989—. Co-author: (with Peggy Sullivan) Public Libraries: Smart Practices in Personnel, 1982; contbr. articles to profl. jours. Mem.: Pub. Libr. Assn., Bellevue Rotary Club (pres. 2002—03). Office: King County Libr Sys 960 Newport Way NW Issaquah WA 98027-2702 Office Phone: 425-369-3232. E-mail: billp@kcls.org.

PTAK, JOHN, talent agent; b. San Diego, Sept. 23, 1942; s. John and Doris Elizabeth P.; m. Margaret Elizabeth Black, May 21, 1981; 1 child, Hillary Elizabeth. BA, UCLA, 1967. Theatre mgr., booker Walter Reade Orgn., Beverly Hills, Calif., 1967-69; adminstrv. exec. Am. Film Inst., Beverly Hills, 1968-70; talent agent Internat. Famous Agy. (now ICM), LA, 1971-75, William Morris Agy., Beverly Hills, 1976-91, Creative Artists Agy., Beverly Hills, 1991—2006; ptnr. Arsenal, 2006—. Co-chmn. Am. Film Inst. Ctr. for Film & Video Preservation, L.A., 1991—; mem. Nat. Film Preservation Bd., Washington, 1992—. Bd. dirs. Motion Pictures and T.V. Fund Found., 1996—, Nat. Film Preservation Found., 1997—. Avocations: tennis, travel.

PUCCINELLI, ANDREW JAMES, lawyer; b. Elko, Nev., July 21, 1953; BA cum laude, U. of the Pacific, 1975, JD, 1978. Bar: Nev. 1978. Ptnr. Puccinelli & Puccinelli, Elko, Nev., 1978—2002; dist. judge 4th Judicial Dist. Ct., 2002—. Bus. law adj. prof. No. Nev. C.C., 1982-93; legal advisor Nev. Home Health Svcs., 1980-88. Bd. dirs. Nev. Legal Svcs., 1986-93. Mem. ATLA, Nev. Trial Lawyers Assn., Nev. State Bar Assn. (bd. govs. 1993-2000, v.p. 1996-97, pres.-elect 1997-98, pres. 1998-99, No. Nev. disciplinary bd. 1988-93, CLE com. 1981-85), Elko County Bar Assn. (pres. 1985-86), Phi Delta Phi. Office: 4th Jud Dist Ct Elko County Cthse 571 Idaho St Elko NV 89801 Office Phone: 775-753-4602.

PUCK, WOLFGANG, chef; b. St. Veit, Austria, July 8, 1949; m. Marie France, 1976 (div. 1979); m. Barbara Lazaroff, 1984 (div. Nov. 27, 2002); children: Cameron, Bryon; m. Gelila Assefa, July 2008; children: Oliver Wolfgang, Alexander. Doctor of Culinary Arts (hon.), Johnson & Wales U., Providence, RI, 1998. Former chef Hotel de Paris, Monaco, Maxim's, Paris, L'Oustau de Baumanière, Provence; chef, part owner Ma Maison, LA, 1975—; exec. chef, ptnr. Spago, 1982—, Chinois on Main, Santa Monica, 1983—, Postrio, San Francisco, 1989—, Trattoria del Lupo, Las Vegas, 1989—, Granita, Malibu, Calif., 1991—, Spago Las Vegas, 1992—, Chinois Las Vegas, 1998—, Postrio Las Vegas, 1998—, Wolfgang Puck Bar & Grill, Las Vegas, 2004—, 20 21, Mpls., 2005—, Vert, Hollywood, Calif., CUT, Beverly Hills, Calif., 2006—; owner Wolfgang Puck Express, Wolfgang Puck Cafes, 1993—; owner, chef Wolfgang Puck Catering, 1998—; ptnr. Wolfgang Puck Worldwide, Inc., 2000—. Fund raising Meals on Wheels, A. Cancer Soc. LA; exec. chef Governor's Ball, The Oscars, 1995-, ptnr. with Humane Soc. US, factory farming animal welfare prog., 2007- Author: (cookbooks) Modern French Cooking for the American Kitchen, 1982, The Wolfgang Puck Cookbook: Recipes from Spago and Chinois, 1986, Adventures in the Kitchen with Wolfgang Puck, 1991, Pizza, Pasta and More!, 2000, Live, Love, Eat! The Best of Wolfgang Puck, 2002, Wolfgang Puck Makes It Easy, 2004, (newspaper columns) Wolfgang Puck's Kitchen, 2003-; producer (instructional cooking video) Spago Cooking with Wolfgang Puck; appeared in TV series Wolfgang Puck, 2001 (Daytime Emmy for Outstanding Service Show, 2004), Wolfgang Puck's Cooking Class, 2003-; actor: (guest appearances) (films) The Weather Man, 2005, (TV series) Who's the Boss?, 1987, Blossom, 1991, Tales from the Crypt, 1992, Ellen, 1996, Frasier, 2000, 2002, Good Morning Am., Late Night with David Letterman, Tonight Show with Jay Leno, Entertainment Tonight, Hollywood Squares, Wheel of Fortune, ABC News, CBS News, Politically Incorrect with Bill Maher, Las Vegas, 2006, (voice) The Simpsons, 2002. Founder Puck-Lazaroff Charitable Found., 1982—. Recipient Humanitarian of Yr. award, James Beard Found., 1994, Bus. Statesman of Yr. award, Harvard Bus. Sch. of So. Calif., 2001, Smithfield Foods Outstanding Service award, James Beard Found., 2005; named Outstanding Chef of the Yr., 1991; named one of The 100 Most Powerful Celebrities, Forbes.com, 2008.

PUGH, DONALD E., industry executive; Pres. Cummins Northwest, Inc. Office: Cummins Northwest Inc 811 SW Grady Way Renton WA 98055-2900

PUGH, JOHN ROBERT, academic administrator, educator, retired state official; b. New Orleans, Dec. 20, 1945; s. Edward Nicholls and Yvonne Marie (Duplantier) P.; m. Margaret Louise McMullen, Aug. 26, 1975; children— Margaret Elizabeth, John Robert. BA in Philosophy, Baylor U., 1967; M. in Social Work, U. Tex.-Austin, 1970. Program dir. McLaughlin Youth Ctr., Anchorage, Alaska, 1973-78; dep. dir. Alaska Div. Social Services, Juneau, 1978-80; dir. Alaska Family and Youth Services, Juneau, 1980-83; dep. commr. Alaska Dept. Health and Social Services, Juneau, 1983, commr., 1983-86; dean, Sch. of Education Univ. Alaska Southeast, Juneau, 1986-95, chancellor, 1995—. Cons., lectr. in field Mem., Blue Ribbon Commn. for Revision of Children's Code, 1975-77; supt. Sunday Sch., No. Light United Ch., Juneau, 1979—; mem. Gov.'s Council for Handicapped and Gifted, 1980-84; mem. precinct com. Greater Juneau Democratic Com., 1983—; bd. dirs. Alaska State Fin. Corp., 1985—; coach Juneau Little League, 1984—. Served to capt. USAF, 1969-73 Mem. Nat. Assn. Social Workers (pres. 1975-76), Am. Pub. Welfare Assn., Am. Correctional Assn., Alaska Pub. Employees Assn. (pres. 1977-79), Acad. Cert. Social Workers (cert.) Methodist. Avocations: fishing, sports. Office: U Alaska Southeast 11120 Glacier Hwy Juneau AK 99801

PUGH, RICHARD CRAWFORD, lawyer, educator; b. Phila., Apr. 28, 1929; s. William and Myrtle P.; m. Nanette Bannen, Feb. 27, 1954; children: Richard Crawford, Andrew Lembert, Catherine Elizabeth. AB summa cum laude, Dartmouth Coll., 1951; BA in Jurisprudence, Oxford U., Eng., 1953; LLB, Columbia U., 1958. Bar: N.Y. 1958.

Assoc. firm Cleary, Gottlieb, Steen & Hamilton, NYC, 1958—61, ptnr., 1969—89; disting. prof. law U. San Diego, 1989—, univ. prof., 1998—99. Mem. faculty Law Sch. Columbia U., 1961-89, prof., 1964-69, adj. prof., 1969-89; lectr. Columbia-Amsterdam-Leyden (Netherlands) summer program Am. law, 1963, 79; dep. asst. atty. gen. tax div. U.S. Dept. Justice, 1966-68; Cons. fiscal and fin. br. UN Secretariat, 1962, 64. Editor: Columbia Law Rev., 1957—58; co-editor: Legal Aspects of Foreign Investment, 1959; co-author: International Law, 2001, Taxation of Business Enterprises, 2002, Taxation of International Transactions, 2006. With USNR, 1954—56. Rhodes scholar, 1951-53. Mem. ABA, Am. Law Inst., Am. Coll. Tax Counsel, Internat. Fiscal Assn. (pres. U.S. br. 1978-79). Home: 7335 Encelia Dr La Jolla CA 92037-5729 Office: U San Diego Sch Law Alcala Park San Diego CA 92110-2429 Office Phone: 619-260-2322. Business E-Mail: rpugh@sandiego.edu.

PUGLISI, RICHARD LAWRENCE, federal judge; b. Apr. 30, 1953; BA, U. N.Mex., 1975, JD, 1979. Bar: N.Mex. 1980, Hawaii, 1981. U.S. Navy judge adv. gen. corp., 1979-82; asst. U.S. atty. Honolulu, 1982-84; with Montgomery & Andrews, P.A., 1984-91, Madison, Harbour, Mroz & Puglisi, P.A., 1991-96; magistrate judge for N.Mex. U.S. Dist. Ct., Albuquerque, 1996—. Office: US Magistrate Judge US Courthouse 333 Lomas Blvd NW Albuquerque NM 87102-2272

PUGSLEY, ROBERT ADRIAN, law educator; b. Mineola, NY, Dec. 27, 1946; s. Irvin Harold and Mary Catherine P. BA, SUNY-Stony Brook, 1968; JD, NYU, 1975, LLM in Criminal Justice, 1977. Instr. sociology New Sch. Social Rsch., NYC, 1969-71; coord. Peace Edn. programs The Christophers, NYC, 1971-78; assoc. prof. law Southwestern U., LA, 1978-81, prof., 1981—, Paul E. Treusch prof. law, 2000-01. Adj. asst. prof. criminology and criminal justice Southampton Coll.-Long Island U., 1975-76; acting dep. dir. Criminal Law Edn. and Rsch. Ctr., NYU, 1983-86; bd. advisors Ctr. Legal Edn. CCNY-CUNY, 1978, Sta. KPFK-FM, 1985-86; founder, coord. The Wednesday Evening Soc., L.A., 1979-86; vis. prof. Jacob D. Fuchsberg Law Ctr. Touro Coll., L.I., N.Y., summers, 1988, 89; lectr. in criminal law and procedure Legal Edn. Conf. Ctr., L.A., 1982-96; prof., dir. Comparative Criminal Law and Procedure Program U. B.C., Vancouver, summers, 1994, 98-2003; chair pub. interest law com. Southwestern U., 1990-2001; lectr. legal profl. responsibility West Bar Rev. Faculty, Calif., 1996-98; legal analyst/commentator for print and electronic media, 1992—. Creative advisor (syndicated TV program) Christopher Closeup, 1975-83; host (cable TV) Earth Alert, 1983-87; prodr., moderator (TV program) Inside L.A., Sta. KPFK-FM, 1979-86, Open Jour. program, Sta. KPFK-FM, 1991-94; contbr. articles to profl. jours. Founding mem. Southwestern U. Pub. Interest Law com., 1992—; mem. L.A. County Bar Assn. Adv. Com. on Alcohol & Drug Abuse, 1991-95, co-chair, 1993-95; mem. exec. com. non-govtl. orgns. UN Office Pub. Info., 1977; mem. issues task force L.A. Conservancy, 1980-81, seminar for law tchrs. NEH UCLA, 1979; co-convenor So. Calif. Coalition Against Death Penalty, 1981-83, convener, 1983-84; mem. death penalty com. Lawyer's Support Group, Amnesty Internat., U.S.A.; founding mem. Ch.-State Coun., L.A., 1984-88; bd. dirs. Equal Rights Sentencing Found., 1983-85, Earth Alert, Inc., 1984-87; mem. adv. bd. First Amendment Info. Resources Ctr., Grad. Sch. Libr. and Info. Scis., UCLA, 1990—; mem. coun. Friends UCLA Libr., 1993—, pres., 1996-2002; mem. adv. bd. Project Prevention, 1998-. Robert Marshall fellow Criminal Law Edn. and Rsch. Ctr., NYU Sch. Law, 1976-78. Mem. ABA (sect. criminal justice 1978-, Ctr. Profl. Responsibility 1995-), Am. Legal Studies Assn., Am. Soc. Polit. and Legal Philosophy, Assn. Am. Law Schs., Inst. Soc. Ethics and Life Scis., Soc. Am. Law Tchrs., Internat. Platform Assn., Internat. Soc. Reform of Criminal Law, The Scribes. Democrat. Roman Catholic. Office: Southwestern U Sch Law 675 S Westmoreland Ave Los Angeles CA 90005-3905 Office Phone: 213-738-6757. Business E-Mail: rpugsley@swlaw.edu.

PULATIE, DAVID L., metal products executive; BS in Psychology and Personnel Mgmt., Ariz. State U.; MEd, No. Ariz. U. Sr. v.p., corp. dir. change mgmt. Motorola Inc., sr. v.p., dir. human resources semiconductor products sector, v.p., regional dir. Europe, Mid. E., S. Africa, sr. v.p., corp. dir. govt. rels. human resources; sr. v.p. human resources Phelps Dodge Corp., Phoenix, 1999—. Office: Phelps Dodge Corp 1 N Central Ave Phoenix AZ 85004-4414

PULIAFITO, CARMEN ANTHONY, ophthalmologist, healthcare executive; b. Buffalo, Jan. 5, 1951; s. Dominic F. and Marie A. (Nigro) P.; m. Janet H. Pine, May 19, 1979 AB cum laude, Harvard Coll., 1973, MD magna cum laude, 1978; MBA, U. Pa., 1997. Diplomate Am. Bd. Ophthalmology. Intern Faulkner Hosp., Tufts U. Sch. Medicine, 1978-79; resident Mass. Eye and Ear Infirmary, Boston, 1979-82, retina fellow, 1982-83; instr. Harvard Med. Sch., Boston, 1983-85, asst. prof., 1985-89, assoc. prof., 1989-91, dir. divsn. continuing edn. dept. ophthalmology, 1989-91; dir. Bascon Palmer Eye Inst., Miami, 2001—; dean Keck Sch. Medicine, U. Southern Calif, LA, 2007—. Vis. scientist MIT Regional Laser Ctr., Cambridge, 1982—, asst. prof. health scis. and tech. program, 1987-89, assoc. prof., 1989-91; mem. staff Mass. Eye and Ear Infirmary, Boston, 1983; dir. Morse Laser Ctr., Mass. Eye and Ear Infirmary, 1986-91, dir. New Eng. Eye Ctr., 1991-2001; prof., chmn. dept. ophthalmology Tufts U. Sch. Medicine, 1991-2001, prof. ophthalmology and health mgmt., 1997-2001; adj. prof. biomed. engring. Tufts U., 1991—; chmn. med. bd. New Eng. Med. Ctr. Hosps., 1994-95, ophthalmologist in chief, 1991-2001; assoc. examiner Am. Bd. Ophthalmology, 1990—; sr. v.p. for network devel. Lifespan, 1997-2001; prof., chmn. dept. ophthalmology U. Miami Sch. Medicine, 2001—; med. dir. Anne Bates Leach Eye Hosp., 2001—. Author: (with D. Albert) Foundations of Ophthalmic Pathology, 1979, (with R. Steinert) Principles and Practice of Ophthalmic YAG Laser Surgery, 1984, Lasers in Surgery and Medicine: Principles and Practice, 1996, (with M.R. Hee, J.S. Schuman and J.G. Fujimoto) Optical Coherence Tomography of Ocular Diseases, 1996, (with E. Reichel) Atlas of Indocyanine Green Angiography, 1996; editor-in-chief Lasers in Surgery and Medicine, 1987-95, Ophthalmic Surgery and Lasers, 1995—; contbr. about 120 articles to profl. jours. Pres. Am. Soc. for Laser Medicine and Surgery, 1994-95; v.p. Mass. Soc. Eye Physicians and Surgeons, 1994-96; assoc. examiner Am. Bd. Ophthalmology, 1990—; retina trustee Assn. Rsch. in Vision and Ophthalmology, 1995-99, pres., 2000-01. Recipient Richard and Hinda Rosenthal award in visual scis., 1994, Man of Vision award Boston Aid to the Blind, 1993, Leon Goldman award Biomed. Optics Soc., 1993, I Migliori award Pirandello Lyceum of Mass., 1994. Fellow Am. Acad. Ophthalmology, Am. Soc. for Laser Medicine and Surgery (pres. 1994-95); mem. Assn. Rsch. in Vision and Ophthalmology (pres.-elect 1998-99, pres. 1999-2000, immediate past pres. 2000-2001), Mass. Soc. Eye Physicians and Surgeons (v.p. 1994-96). Roman Catholic. Home: 1365 S Los Robles Ave Pasadena CA 91106 Office Phone: 323-442-1900. Office Fax: 323-442-2724. Business E-Mail: deanksom@usc.edu.

PULIDO, MIGUEL ANGEL, Mayor, Santa Ana, California; b. Mex. City, 1956; m. Laura Pulido; children: Miguel Robert, David Andrew, Isabel. BSME, Calif. State U., Fullerton. V.p. McCaughey & Smith Energy Assocs., dir. computer program; mayor City of Santa Ana, Calif., 1986—. Mem. Santa Ana Redevel. Agy.; bd. dirs. Orange County Transp. Authority, mem. 1st dist. Santa Ana rep. Orange County Transp. Authority; bd. dir. Calif. Workforce Investment, Bowers Mus., Discovery Sci. Ctr. Orange County, Pacific Symphony Orch., UCI Found., Fed. Inter-Govtl. Policy Adv. Com. Trade, Fullerton Cmty. Bank, Great Park Corp., South Coast Air Quality Mgmt. Dist. Achievements include becoming the first Latino mayor in the city's history; development of the Mayor's Task Force on Arts and Culture. Avocations: chess, backgammon, tennis, music, guitar. Office: Office Mayor & City Coun 20 Civic Ctr Plaza PO Box 1988 M31 Santa Ana CA 92702-1988 Address: Pulido for Mayor 401 E 1st St Santa Ana CA 92701 Fax: 714-647-6954. Business E-Mail: mpulido@santa-ana.org. E-mail: mpulido@ci.santa-ana.ca.us, pulidoformayor@gmail.com.*

PULLEN, RANDY, political organization administrator; MBA, Ariz. State U. CPA Calif., Ariz. Founder Charleston Marina and Shipbuilding, 1979—88; ptnr. Deloitte & Touche, 1988—92; pres. ILX Resorts, Inc., 1992—99; dir. Oasis Partners, LLC; chmn, CEO WageWatch, Inc., 1999—. Co-founder Ariz. Pachyderm Coalition; pres. Rosie's House Music Acad. for Children; chmn. First Class Edn. for Ariz.; bd. dirs. ePropety Tax, Inc. Chmn. Yes On Proposition 200; mem.-at-large Maricopa County Rep. Com.; co-chair fin. com. Ariz. Rep. Party, 2000, chmn., 2007—; nat. committeeman Ariz. Rep. Assembly. Republican. Office: Ariz Rep Party 3501 N 24th St Phoenix AZ 85061 Office Phone: 602-957-7770. Office Fax: 602-224-0932.*

PULLIAM, FRANCINE SARNO, real estate broker, developer; b. San Francisco, Sept. 14, 1937; d. Ralph C. Stevens and Frances I. (Wilson) Sarno; m. John Donald Pulliam, Aug. 14, 1957 (div. Mar. 1965); 1 child, Wendy; m. Terry Kent Graves, Dec. 14, 1974. Student, U. Ariz., 1955—56, U. Nev., Las Vegas, 1957. Airline stewardess Bonanza Airlines, Las Vegas, 1957; real estate agt. The Pulliam Co., Las Vegas, 1958-68, Levy Realty, Las Vegas, 1968—76; real estate broker, owner Prestige Properties, Las Vegas, 1976—. Importer, exporter Exports Internat., Las Vegas, 1984—; bd. dirs. Citicorp Bank of Nev.; mem. adv. bd. to Amb. to Bahamas Chic Hect.; property mgr. Prestigo Properties, 1992—. Bd. dirs. Las Vegas Bd. Realtors, Fedn. Internat. Realtors, Nat. Kidney Found., Assistance League, Cancer Soc., Easter Seals, Econ. Rsch. Bd., Children's Discovery Mus., New Horizons Ctr. for Children with Learning Disabilities, Girl Scouts, Home of the Good Shepard, St. Jude's Ranch for Homeless Children; pres., bd. dirs. Better Bus. Bur.; chmn. Las Vegas Taxi Cab Authority; pres. Citizens for Pvt. Enterprises. Mem. Las Vegas C. of C. (bd. dirs., developer). Republican. Roman Catholic. Office: 2340 Paseo Del Prado Ste D202 Las Vegas NV 89102-4341 Office Phone: 702-382-0770.

PULLMAN, BILL, actor; b. Hornell, NY, Dec. 17, 1953; m. Tamara Hurwitz, 1987; children: Maesa, Jack, Louis. BFA, SUNY, Oneonta; MFA, U. Mass., Amherst. Theatre instr. Mont. State U., Bozeman. Actor: (plays) The Rover, 1981, Ah, Wilderness!, 1983, The Old Flag, 1983, Dramathon '84, 1984, Curse of the Starving Class, 1985, All My Sons, 1986, Barabbas, 1986, Nanawatai, 1986, Demon Wine, 1988, Control Freaks, 1993, The Subject Was Roses, 2006, Peter and Jerry, 2007; (Broadway plays) The Goat, or Who Is Sylvia?, 2002; (films) Ruthless People, 1986, Spaceballs, 1987, The Serpent and the Rainbow, 1988, Rocket Gibraltar, 1988, The Accidental Tourist, 1989, Cold Feet, 1989, Brain Dead, 1989, Sibling Rivalry, 1990, Going Under, 1991, Bright Angel, 1991, Newsies, 1992, A League of Their Own, 1992, Singles, 1992, Sommersby, 1993, Sleepless in Seattle, 1993, Malice, 1993, Mr. Jones, 1993, The Favor, 1994, Wyatt Earp, 1994, While You Were Sleeping, 1995, Casper, 1995, Mr. Wrong, 1996, Independence Day, 1996, Lost Highway, 1997, The End of Violence, 1997, The Thin Red Line, 1998, Brokedown Palace, 1998, Zero Effect, 1998, A Man is Mostly Water, 1999, History Is Made at Night, 1999, The Guilt, 1999, Brokedown Palace, 1999, Lake Placid, 1999, (voice) Coming to Light: Edward S. Curtis and the North American Indians, 2000, (voice) Titan A.E., 2000, Numbers, 2000, Ignition, 2001, Igby Goes Down, 2002, 29 Palms, 2002, Rick, 2003, The Grudge, 2004, The Orphan King, 2005, Dear Wendy, 2005, Scary Movie 4, 2006, You Kill Me, 2007, Nobel Son, 2007, Bottle Shock, 2008, Phoebe in Wonderland, 2008, Surveillance, 2008; (TV movies) Home Fires Burning, 1989, Crazy in Love, 1992, The Last Seduction, 1994, Mistrial, 1996, Merry Christmas George Bailey, 1997, The Virginian, 2000, Tiger Cruise, 2004; (TV series) Revelations, 2005-. Office: Big Town Prodns Ste 80 6201 Sunset Blvd Los Angeles CA 90028-8704

PURCELL, CYNTHIA D., bank executive; married; 4 children. Controller First Am. Banking Co.; sr. v.p. pres., CFO Inland Empire Bank; exec. v.p., COO Banner Bank, Walla Walla, Wash., 2000—. Mgmt. asset com. Inland Empire Bank, chair, asset and liability mgmt. com.; mem. exec. com. Banner Bank; prof. Am. Banker's Assn. Grad. Sch. Bank Investments and Fin. Mgmt. Active YWCA, Walla Walla; chair, bd. dirs. BancSource, 2005—. Named one of 25 Women to Watch, US Banker, 2007. Mem.: Oreg. Banker's Assn., Am. Banker's Assn. (bd. advisors, exec. com., funds mgmt. and capital markets divsn., exec. acctg. com.). Office: Banner Corp 10 S First Ave PO Box 907 Walla Walla WA 99362-0265 Office Phone: 509-527-3636. Office Fax: 509-526-8898.

PURCELL, JOHN F., lawyer; b. Bellingham, Wash., Apr. 25, 1954; AB with honors, Stanford U., 1976; JD, Lewis and Clark Coll., 1980. Bar: Oreg. 1980. Ptnr. Miller Nash LLP, Portland, 1987—. Mem. Oreg. State Bar. Office: Miller Nash LLP 111 SW 5th Ave Ste 3500 Portland OR 97204-3638 Office Phone: 503-224-5858.

PURCELL, SCOTT, Internet company executive, publishing executive; b. Deerfield, Mass., Feb. 8, 1967; married. Grad., Univ. So. Calif., Sloan Sch. Bus., MIT. Founder, pres., CEO Epoch Networks, Irvine, Calif., 1994—99; pres., CEO OnAir Streaming Networks Inc. (originally www.com), 1999; pres. Browsercast, 2002—; founder, pres. WebBiographies, Denver, 2005—; publisher Kasidie Mag., 2007—. Mem.: Big Brothers. Office: WebBiographies PO Box 17409 Denver CO 80217

PURCELL, STEVEN RICHARD, international management consultant, engineer, economist; B in Mech. and Indsl. Engring., NYU Coll. Engring., 1950; MS in Indsl. Engring., Columbia U., 1951; EdM, Harvard U., 1968. Registered profl. engr., Can. Lectr. engring. NYU Coll. Engring., NYC, 1948-50; gen. mgr. Dapol Plastics Co., Inc., Boston, 1956-58; gen. div. mgr. Am. Cyanamid Co., Sanford, Maine, 1958-61; sr. prin., mgmt. cons. investment banking Purcell & Assocs., NYC, 1961-66; prof., chmn. Bristol Coll., Fall River, Mass., 1966-68; assoc. dean grad. faculty adminstrv. studies York U., Toronto, Ont., Can., 1969-71; chief economist Dept. Manpower and Immigration, Ottawa, Ont., Can., 1970-71; cons. Treasury Bd., Ottawa, 1971-72; dir. urban and internat. environ. policy Ministry of State for Urban Affairs Internat. Activities, Ottawa, 1973-74; mem. com. on challenges of modern soc. NATO, Ottawa, 1973-74; mem. sci., econ. policy com. OECD UN, Ottawa, 1973-74; prof. Grad. Sch. Bus. Adminstrn. and Econs. Algonquin Coll., Ottawa, 1974-76; advisor, cons. House of Commons, 1976-77; sr. prin. Purcell & Assocs., Internat. Mgmt. Cons., Washington, 1977-80, chmn., CEO, 1981—, Phoenix Internat. Capital Associates, Washington, 1981—; exec. dir. nat. coastal zone mgmt. adv. com. NOAA U.S. Dept. Commerce, Washington, 1980-81. Profl. lectr. Northeastern U. Grad. Sch. Bus. Adminstrn., Boston, 1953-56, U. Toronto, 1968-69, George Washington U. Grad. Sch. Bus. Adminstrn., Washington, 1979; vis. prof. Rensselaer Poly. Inst. Advanced Mgmt. Program, 1967, U. Ottawa Grad. Sch. Bus. Adminstrn., 1971-74; lectr. Council for Internat. Progress in Mgmt., N.Y.C., 1960, Royal Bank Can. Mgmt. Assn., Toronto, Ont., 1970; corp. appointment cons. Harvard U., Cambridge, Mass., 1967-68; cons. Govt. Venezuela, 1967-68, Can. Inst. Bankers, Toronto, 1969-70; internat. sr. adviser NASA, 1985-86, mem. nat. adv. bd. Ctr. for Nat. Policy; dir. Rental Resource Corp., 1986-89. Contbr. articles on indsl. orgn., sci. policy and fin. to profl. jours. Lt. AC, USNR, 1943-46. Mem. UN Assn., Soc. for Advancement of Mgmt. (pres. 1949-50, leadership award 1950), Tau Beta Pi, Alpha Pi Mu (v.p. 1949-50), Columbia Univ. Club (Washington, trustee 1982-84, chmn., sr. trustee 1984-85), Harvard Univ. Club.

PURDY, ALAN HARRIS, biomedical engineer; b. Mt. Clemens, Mich., Dec. 13, 1923; s. Harry Martin and Elinor (Harris) P.; m. Anna Elizabeth Sohn, Aug. 16, 1968 (dec.); children: Catherine, Charles, Susan, Harry; m. Margaret Josephine Kelley, Mar. 5, 1997. BSME, U. Miami, 1954; MS in Physiology, UCLA, 1967; PhD in Engring., U. Mo., 1970. Cert. clin. engr., Washington. Project engr. in acoustics Arvin Industries, Columbus, Ind., 1954-56, AC Spark Plug Co., Flint, Mich., 1956-60; asst. prof. engring. Calif. Poly. U., Pomona, 1960-62; assoc. dir. biomed. engring. U. Mo., Columbia, 1967-71; dep. assoc. dir., assoc. dir. Nat. Inst. for Occupational Safety and Health, Rockville, Md., 1971-81, scientist, biomed. engr. Cin., 1983-86; asst. dir. Fla. Inst. Oceanography, St. Petersburg, 1981-83; pres. Alpha Beta R & D Corp., San Marcos, Calif., 1986—. Cons. Smithy Muffler Corp., L.A., 1961-62, Statham Instruments, L.A., 1966; cons. faculty, Tex. Tech. U., Lubbock, 1972-73; lectr. U. Cin., 1980. Patentee in diving, acoustical and occupational safety fields. Pilot CG Aux., 1989-98. With USAF, 1942-43. Nat. Heart Inst. spl. fellow, 1963-67; Fulbright scholar, Yugoslavia, 1984. Mem. Acoustical Soc. Am., Biomed. Engring. Soc., Am. Inst. Physics, Exptl. Aircraft Assn., Aircraft Owners and Pilots Assn., DAV, FAA (Inspection Authorization 1983, Designated airaworthiness Rep., 2003). Democrat. Home and Office: 941 Cycad Dr San Marcos CA 92078-5013 E-mail: ahpurdy@nethere.com.

PURDY, ALAN MACGREGOR, financial executive; b. Iowa City, Apr. 23, 1940; s. Rob Roy MacGregor and Frances (Edwards) P.; m. Sarah Lane Robins, June 13, 1964; children— William Wallace, John Alan, Tammi Ann. AB, Duke U., 1962; MBA, Wharton Sch. Fin. and Commerce, U. Pa., 1968. Bus. analyst Gen. Mills, Inc., Mpls., 1968-71; sr. fin. analyst Dayton Hudson Corp. (now Target Corp.), Mpls., 1972-73; mgr. capital expenditure analysis Dayton Hudson Corp., Mpls., 1973, dir. corp. analysis, 1973-75, dir. planning and analysis, 1975-77; v.p., treas. Fleming Cos., Inc., Oklahoma City, 1977-81; v.p. fin., chief fin. officer John A. Brown Co. (subs. Target Corp.), Oklahoma City, 1981-83; sr. v.p., chief fin. officer B. Dalton Co. (subs. Target Corp.), Mpls., 1983-86, Robinson's of Fla.(subs. May Co.), St. Petersburg, 1986-87, Miller's Outpost (subs. Am. Retail Group), Ontario, Calif., 1988-92, Builders Emporium (subs. Collins and Aikman Group), Irvine, Calif., 1993, RemedyTemp, Aliso Viejo, Calif., 1994—2002. Served with USN, 1962-66. Office: Remedy Temp 101 Enterprise Aliso Viejo CA 92656-2604 Home: 93 Ambroise Newport Coast CA 92657-0122 also: 31111 Almara Ln Laguna Niguel CA 92677 Home Phone: 949-376-9604. Personal E-mail: sallyalan@gmail.com.

PURDY, JAMES AARON, medical physics professor; b. Tyler, Tex., July 16, 1941; s. Walter Bethel and Florence (Hardy) P.; m. Marilyn Janette Coers, Jan. 29, 1965; children: Katherine, Laura. BS, Lamar U., 1967; MA, U. Tex., 1968, PhD, 1971. Asst. rsch. scientist U. Tex., Austin, 1969-71; rsch. asst. M.D. Anderson Hosp. and Tumor Inst., Houston, 1968-69, fellow in med. physics, 1972-73; from instr. physics to prof. Sch. of Medicine, Washington U., St. Louis, 1973—83, chief physics sect., 1976—2004, prof., 1983—2004, assoc. dir. Radiation Oncology Ctr., 1987—2004; prof., vice chmn. Med. Ctr. Dept. Radiology Oncology U. Calif., Davis, 2004—. Mem. NIH Radiaton Study sect. Divsn. Rsch. Grantes, 1991-95; Landauer lectr., Oakland, Calif., 1991. Editor: Three Dimensional Treatment Planning, 1991, Advances in Radiation Oncology, 1992, 3D Radiation Treatment Planning and Conformal Therapy, 1995, A Practical Guide to 3D Planning and Conformal Radiation Therapy, 1999, 3-D Conformal and Intensity Modulated Radiation Therapy: Physics and Clinical Applications, 2001, Technical Basis of Radiation Therapy, 2006; sr. physics editor: Internat. Jour. Radiation Oncology, Biology, and Physics, 1996—2003. With USMC, 1961-64. Fellow Am. Assn. Physicists in Medicine (pres. 1985, William D. Coolidge award 1997), Am. Coll. Radiology (ACR Gold Medal 2002), Am. Coll. Med. Physics (chmn. bd. chancellors 1990, Marvin M.D. Williams award 1996); mem. Am. Inst. Physics, Am. Bd. Med. Physics (vice chmn. 1988-92), Am. Bd. Radiology, Am. Soc. Therapeutic Radiology and Oncology (ASTRO Gold medal 2000). Methodist. Avocation: travel. Home: 918 Eucalyptus St Davis CA 95616 Office: Univ Calif Davis Med Ctr Dept Rad Oncology 4501 X St Ste G126 Sacramento CA 95817 Home Phone: 530-758-9149; Office Phone: 916-734-3932. Business E-Mail: james.purdy@ucdmc.ucdavis.edu.

PURE, PAMELA J., former health products executive; B in Health Adminstrn., U. NC. Various mgmt., product devel. and mktg. positions Shared Med. Sys. (now divsn. Siemens); COO Channel Health Subs. IDX Systems, 1999—2001; grp. pres. product devel. and support McKesson Corp., San Francisco, 2001—02, COO McKesson Info. Solutions, 2002—04, exec. v.p., pres. McKesson Technology Solutions, 2004—09. Named Woman of Yr. Tech. (enterprise bus.), (WIT) Women in Tech., 2005.

PURKIS, LEONARD C., media executive; b. Cardiff, Wales; Grad., Inst. Chartered Accts., Eng., Wales. Audit mgr. Coopers & Lybrand; sr. v.p. fin. GE Capital Fleet Svcs.; CFO Iomega Corp., 1995-98; CFO, exec. v.p. fin. and adminstrn. E Trade Group Inc., Palo Alto, Calif., 1998—. Office: E Trade Group Inc 4500 Bohannon Dr Menlo Park CA 94025

PURVES, WILLIAM KIRKWOOD, biologist, educator; b. Sacramento, Oct. 28, 1934; s. William Kirkwood and Dorothy (Brandenburger) P.; m. Jean McCauley, June 9, 1959; 1 son, David William. BS, Calif. Inst. Tech., 1956; MS, Yale U., 1957, PhD, 1959. NSF postdoctoral fellow U. Tubingen, Germany, 1959-60; Nat. Cancer Inst. postdoctoral fellow UCLA, 1960-61; asst. prof. botany U. Calif., Santa Barbara, 1961-65, assoc. prof. biochemistry, 1965-70, prof. biology, 1970-73, chmn. dept. biol. scis., 1972-73; prof. biology, head biol. sci. group U. Conn., Storrs, 1973-77; Stuart Mudd prof. biology Harvey Mudd Coll., Claremont, Calif., 1977-95, prof. emeritus, 1996—, chmn. dept. biol., 1985-95, chmn. dept. computer sci., 1985-90; adj. prof. plant physiology U. Calif., Riverside, 1979-85. V.p., sci. dir. The Mona Group LLC, 1996-2004. Author: Life, the Science of Biology, 1983, 8th edit., 2007. NSF sr. postdoctoral fellow U. London, 1967, Harvard U., 1968; vis. fellow computer sci. Yale U., 1983-84; vis. scholar Northwestern U., 1991; NSF rsch. grantee, 1962-83, 97-2001. Fellow AAAS; mem. Sigma Xi. E-mail: Bill_Purves@hmc.edu.

PUTMAN, ROBERT DEAN, retired golf course architect; b. Wallace, Idaho, Dec. 18, 1924; m. Sally Harmon, 1945; 3 children. Grad., Fresno State Coll. Art dir. Sta. KJEO-TV, Fresno, Calif., 1950's; ret., 2000. Prin. works include Arvin Mcpl. Golf Course, Wasco, Calif., Madera (Calif.) Mcpl. Golf Course, Rancho Canada Golf Course, Carmel Valley, Calif., La Manga Golf Course, Costa Blanca, Spain, Monterey (Calif.) Country Club Shore Course, San Joaquin Country Club, Fresno, Visalia (Calif.) Mcpl. Golf Course, River Island Golf Course, Poterville, Calif., Kings River Country Club, Kingsburg, Calif. Office: Robert Dean Putman GCA 5644 N Briarwood Ave Fresno CA 93711-2501

PUZDER, ANDREW F., food service executive, lawyer; b. Cleve., July 11, 1950; s. Andrew F. and Winifried M. Puzder; m. Deanna L. Descher, Sept. 26, 1987. BA, Cleve. State U., 1975; JD, Washington U., 1978. Atty. Offices of Morris A. Shenker, 1978—84, Stolar Partnership, 1984—91; ptnr. Lewis, D'Amato, Brisbois, & Bisgaard, 1991—94, Yocca, Carlson & Rauth, 1994—95; exec. v.p., gen. counsel Fidelity Nat. Fin., Inc., 1995—97; CEO Santa Barbara Restaurant Group, 1997—2000; gen. counsel, exec. v.p. CKE Restaurants, Inc., Carpinteria, Calif., 1997-99; CEO Hardee's Food Systems, Inc., 2000—; pres., CEO CKE Restaurants, Inc., Carpinteria, Calif., 2000—. Editor Washington U. Law Quarterly, 1977-78. Mem. State Bar Nev., The Mo. Bar, State Bar Calif., Phi Alpha Theta. Office: CKE Restaurants Inc Ste A 6307 Carpinteria Ave Carpinteria CA 93013

PYATT, KEDAR DAVIS, JR., research and development company executive; b. Wadesboro, NC, May 20, 1933; s. Kedar D. and Frances (Hales) P.; m. Mary Mackenzie, June 2, 1956; children: Geoffrey, Kira, David, Rebecca. BS in Physics, Duke U., 1955; PhD in Physics, Yale U., 1960. With Gen. Atomic, San Diego, 1959-67; sr. v.p. Fed. sys. divsn. Maxwell Techs., San Diego, 1967—2001; chief scientist CAIC, San Diego, 2001—. Recipient Exceptional Pub. Svc. medal Dept. Def., 1985, Lifetime Achievement medal DSWA, 1997. Office Phone: 858-826-1629. Personal E-mail: bud-mary@att.net. Business E-Mail: kedar.d.pyatt@saic.com.

PYLE, KENNETH BIRGER, historian, educator; b. Bellefonte, Pa., Apr. 20, 1936; s. Hugh Gillespie and Beatrice Ingeborg (Petterson) P.; m. Anne Hamilton Henszey, Dec. 22, 1960; children: William Henszey, Anne Hamilton. AB magna cum laude, Harvard U., 1958; PhD, Johns Hopkins U., 1965. Asst. prof. U. Wash., 1965-69, assoc. prof., 1969-75, prof. history and Asian studies, 1975—, dir. Henry M. Jackson Sch. Internat. Studies, 1978-88; pres. Nat. Bur. Asian Rsch., 1988—; vice chmn. Japan-U.S. Friendship Commn., 1989-92, chmn., 1992-95. Co-chmn. Joint Com. on U.S.-Japan Cultural and Ednl. Coop., 1992-95; vis. lectr. history Stanford U., 1964-65; vis. assoc. prof. history Yale U., 1969-70, Edwin O. Reischauer Meml. Lectr., 1997; Mansfield Freeman lectr. Wesleyan U., 2002. Author: The New Generation in Meiji, Japan, 1969, The Making of Modern Japan, 1978, rev. edit., 1996; editor: The Trade Crisis: How Will Japan Respond?, 1987, The Japanese Question: Power and Purpose in a New Era, 1992, rev. edit., 1996, From APEC to Xanadu, 1997; founding editor Jour. Japanese Studies, 1974-86, chmn. editl. bd., 1987-89, assoc. editor, 1989—. Bd. dirs. Maure and Mike Mansfield Found., 1979-88; bd. govs. Henry M. Jackson Found., 1983—; adv. bd. Japan Found., 1989-99, Japan-Am. Student Conf., 1991—. Recipient Japanese Imperial award 3d Class, Order of Rising Sun, 1999, The Henry M. Jackson award for disting. pub. svc., 2000; Ford Found. fellow, 1961-64; Fulbright-Hays fellow, 1970-71; Social Sci. Research Council-Am. Council Learned Socs. fellow, 1970-73, 77, 83-84 Mem. Assn. Asian Studies, Am. Hist. Assn., Coun. Fgn. Rels. Presbyterian. Home: 8416 Midland Rd Medina WA 98039-5336 Office: Henry M Jackson Sch Internat Studies U Wash Seattle WA 98195-0001

PYLE, NANCY, Councilwoman; m. Roger Pyle; 2 children. BS, LeMoyne Coll., Syracuse; M in Ednl. Adminstrn., US Internat. U., San Diego. Tchr. San José Unified Sch. Dist., cmty. rels. mgr., legis. analyst; councilwoman, Dist. 10 San José City Coun., 2005—. Bd. trustee San Jose/Evergreen Cmty. Coll. Dist., 1997—. Mem. San José Small Bus. Commn.; bd. mem. Notre Dame High Sch., YWCA. Mem.: Almaden Valley Cmty. Assn. (bd. mem.). Democrat. Office: San Jose City Coun 200 E Santa Clara St San Jose CA 95113 Office Phone: 408-535-4910. Office Fax: 408-292-6478. Business E-Mail: district10@sanjoseca.gov.*

PYM, BRUCE MICHAEL, lawyer; b. Alameda, Calif., Sept. 29, 1942; s. Leonard A. and Willamay (Strandberg) Pym. BBA, U. Wash., 1964, JD, 1967. Bar: Wash. 1967, US Dist. Ct. (we. dist.) Wash. 1968, US Ct. Appeals (9th cir.) 1968, US Tax Ct. 1969, US Supreme Ct. 1971. Law clk. Wash. State Supreme Ct., Olympia, 1967—68; assoc. Graham & Dunn, Seattle, 1968—73, shareholder, 1973—92; ptnr. Heller Ehrman LLP, 1992—, mng. ptnr. Northwest Offices, 1994—99. Bd. dirs. United Way King County, 1986—92, chmn., 1990. Mem.: ABA, King County Bar Assn. (pres. 1984—85), Wash. State Bar Assn. Office: Heller Ehrman LLP 701 5th Ave Ste 6100 Seattle WA 98104-7098 Business E-Mail: bruce.pym@hellerehrman.com.

PYOTT, DAVID EDMUND IAN, pharmaceutical executive; b. London, Eng., Oct. 13, 1953; married; 4 children. MA, U. Edinburgh, 1975; diploma in German and European Law, U. Amsterdam, 1976; MBA, London Bus. Sch., 1980. Numerous positions Sandoz Nutrition, Barcelona, 1980-90, gen. mgr., 1990-92; pres., CEO Sandoz Nutrition Corp., Mpls., 1992-95; head divsn. nutrition Sandoz Internat. AG, 1995—97; mem., exec. com. Novartis AG (merger Sandoz and Ciba), 1995—97; pres. Allergan, Inc., Irvine, Calif., 1998—2006, CEO, 1998—, chmn., 2001—. Bd. dirs. PhRMA, Avery Dennison Corp., Edwards Lifescis. Corp., Advanced Med. Optics, Inc.; chmn. Calif. Healthcare Inst.; mem. bd. dirs. U. Calif. (Irvine) Grad. Sch. Mgmt.; mem.LA Bus. Advisors; vice-chair Chief Exec. Roundtable for UCI Bd. dirs. Internat. Coun. of Ophthalmology Found., Eyecare Am.; pres. Pan-Am. Ophthalmological Found. Mem. Pharm. Rsch. and Mfrs. Am. (bd. dirs., Allergan rep.), Pan Am. Assn. Ophthalmology (bd. dirs.), L.A. Bus. Advisors. Achievements include transforming Botox, an obsure treatment for rare muscular diseases, into a cultural and medical phenomenon. Office: Allergan Inc 2525 Dupont Dr Irvine CA 92612-1531 Address: Allergan Inc PO Box 19534 Irvine CA 92623

QUACKENBUSH, JUSTIN LOWE, federal judge; b. Spokane, Wash., Oct. 3, 1929; s. Carl Clifford and Marian Huldah (Lowe) Q.; m. Marie McAtee; children: Karl Justin, Kathleen Marie, Robert Craig. Student, U. Ill., 1947-49; BA, U. Idaho, 1951; LLB, Gonzaga U., Spokane, 1957. Bar: Wash. 1957. Dep. pros. atty., Spokane County, 1957-59; ptnr. Quackenbush, Dean, Bailey & Henderson, Spokane, 1959-80; dist. judge U.S. Dist. Ct. (ea. dist.) Wash., Spokane, 1980—, now sr. judge. Part-time instr. Gonzaga U. Law Sch., 1960-67 Chmn. Spokane County Planning Commn., 1969-73. Served with USN, 1951-54. Mem. Wash. Bar Assn., Spokane County Bar Assn. (trustee 1976-78), Internat. Footprint Assn. (nat. pres. 1967), Shriners. Episcopalian. Office: US Dist Ct PO Box 1432 Spokane WA 99210-1432 Office Phone: 509-458-5280.

QUAID, DENNIS, actor; b. Houston, Apr. 9, 1954; s. William Rudy and Juanita B.; m. P.J. Soles, Nov. 25, 1978 (div. Jan. 23, 1983); m. Meg Ryan, Feb. 14, 1991 (div. July 16, 2001); 1 child, Jack Henry; m. Kimberly Buffington, July 4, 2004; children: Thomas Boone, Zoe Grace. Student, U. Houston, 1972-75. Actor (films) Crazy Mama, 1975, I Never Promised You A Rosegarden, 1977, Sept. 30, 1955, 1977, Our Winning Season, 1978, The Seniors, 1978, Breaking Away, 1979, G.O.R.P., 1980, The Long Riders, 1980, Caveman, 1981, All Night Long, 1981, The Night the Lights Went Out in Georgia, 1981, Tough Enough, 1983, Jaws 3-D, 1983, The Right Stuff, 1983, Dreamscape, 1984, Enemy Mine, 1985, Innerspace, 1987, The Big Easy, 1987, Suspect, 1987, D.O.A., 1988, Everybody's All-American, 1988, Great Balls of Fire, 1989, Postcards from the Edge, 1990, Come See the Paradise, 1990, Undercover Blues, 1993, Wilder Napalm, 1993, Flesh and Bone, 1993, Wyatt Earp, 1994, Something to Talk About, 1995, Dragonheart, 1996, Criminal Element, 1997, Going West, 1997, Gang Related, 1997, Savior, 1997, Switchback, 1997, The Parent Trap, 1998, On Any Given Sunday, 1999, Frequency, 2000, Traffic, 2000, The Rookie, 2002, Far From Heaven, 2002, Cold Creek Manor, 2003, The Alamo, 2004, The Day After Tomorrow, 2004, Flight of the Phoenix, 2004, In Good Company, 2004, Yours, Mine and Ours, 2005, Am. Dreamz, 2006, Vantage Point, 2008, Smart People, 2008, The Express, 2008, The Horsemen, 2009; (theatre) The Last of the Knucklemen, 1983, True West, 1984; (TV movies) Are You In the House Alone?, 1978, Amateur Night at the Dixie Bar and Grill, 1979, Bill, 1981, Johnny Belinda, 1982, Bill: On His Own, 1983, Everything That Rises (also dir, prod.), 1998, Dinner with Friends, 2001; (TV appearances) Baretta, 1977. Named Hollywood Walk of Fame, 2005. Office: The William Morris Agy One William Morris Pl Beverly Hills CA 90212

QUAIL, BEVERLY J., lawyer; b. Glendale, Calif., June 19, 1949; d. John Henry and Dorothy Marie Q.; m. Timothy D. Roble; children: Benjamin W., Elizabeth L. BA magna cum laude, U. So. Calif., 1971; JD, U. Denver, 1974. Bar: Colo. 1974. Dir. Dufford & Brown, P.C., Denver, 1975-95; ptnr. Ballard Spahr Andrews & Ingersoll, Denver, 1996—. Broker Colo. Assn. Realtors, 1982—; lectr. CLE, Colo.; past mem. adv. com. John Marshall Law Sch. Author Colo. Real Estate Forms-Practice, Real Property Practice & Litigation; editor newsletter The Colo. Lawyer, 1983-87; contbr. articles to profl. jours. Bd. dirs., v.p. Girls Club Denver, 1984-87; bd. dirs. Swedish Hosp. Found., Legal Aid of Colo. Found., 1994-97, Ctrl. City Opera House Assn Bd., 1996—. Mem. ABA (real property, probate and trust law sect. 1990-95, co-chair membership com. 1993-95, sec. 1995-96, vice chmn. 1996-98, chair elect 1998-99, chair 1999-2000), Am. Coll. Real Estate Lawyers (bd. govs. 1990-95, treas. 1995-96), Am. Coll. Mortgage Attys., Anglo Am. Real Property Inst., Colo. Real Estate Coun., Castle Pines Golf Club, Cherry Hills Country Club (Denver), Phi Beta Kappa. Office: Ballard Spahr Andrews & Ingersoll 1225 17th St Ste 2300 Denver CO 80202-5535 Office Phone: 303-292-2400. Business E-Mail: quaib@ballardspahr.com.

QUAIL, PETER HUGH, biologist, educator; b. Australia, Feb. 4, 1944; BSc, U. Sydney, 1964, PhD, 1968. Rsch. assoc. Mich. State U/AEC Plant Rsch. Lab., East Lansing, 1968—71, U. Freiburg, Biologisches Inst., Germany, 1971—73; rsch. fellow, group leader photobiology lab. Australian Nat. U., Sch. Biol. Scis., Canberra, Australia, 1973—77; sr. fellow dept. biology Stanford (Calif.) U., Carnegie Instn., 1977—79; assoc. prof. botany U. Wis., Madison, 1979—84, prof. botany and genetics, 1984—87; rsch. dir., prof. molecular plant biology U. Calif.-Berkeley, Plant Gene Expression Ctr., 1987—89, rsch. dir., prof. dept. plant biology, 1989—. Cons. Resources Devel. Found., 1988, Rockefeller Found. Internat. Rice Rsch. Program, 1988—89; vis. scientist plant genetics Weizmann Inst. Sci., Rehovot, Israel, 1977; mem. NSF Oversight Panel, 1982; mem. rev. com. dept. energy U. Ga., Complex Carbohydrate Ctr., 1986; mem. NSF Grant Rev. Panel, 1988; mem. biochem. genetics program NSF, 1993; ad hoc mem. Biochem. Genetics/Mechanisms of Gene Expression Program, NSF Panel, 1996—2000; mem. sci. adv. com. Rockefeller Found. Biotech., Breeding and Seed Sys. for African Crops Program, 2001—. Reviewer: Dept. Energy, Plant Molecular Biology, Genes and Devel., others, mem. editl. bd.: Planta, 1980—87, Plant Physiology, 1980—87, Plant Molecular Biology, 1980—87. Recipient Commonwealth scholarship, 1961—64, Sibella MacArthur Onslow Meml. prize, 1964, Commonwealth Rsch. studentship, 1965—68, Fulbright-Hays travel grantee, 1968, Alexander von Humboldt stipend, 1971—73, Romnes Faculty fellow, U. Wis., 1984, Am. Soc. Photobiologists Rsch. award, 1988, award for disting. contbns. to photochemistry/photobiology, LI-COR Inc., 1995, Anton Lang Meml. award, Australian Soc. Plant Physiologists, 2000. Mem.: NAS, Internat. Soc. Plant Molecular Biology (bd. dirs. 1992—96), Am. Soc. Plant Physiologists (chmn. phytochrome session 1977).

QUAKE, STEPHEN R., physics professor, researcher; BS in Physics, Stanford U., 1991, MS in Math., 1991; PhD in Physics, U. Oxford, 1994. Asst. prof. applied physics Calif. Inst. Tech., 1996—99, assoc. prof., 1999—2002, assoc. prof. applied physics and physics, 2002—03, prof., 2003—04, Thomas E. and Doris Everhard prof., 2004; prof. dept. bioengineering Stanford U. Mem. Quake Group, Calif. Inst. Tech., Pasadena, CSULA-Calif. Inst. Tech. Partnerships for Rsch. and Edn. in Materials (PREM) Collaborative, 2004—; co-founder Fluidigm Corp. Contbr. articles to profl. jours. Recipient Career award, 1997, R29 "First" award, NIH, 1997, Pioneer award, 2004; named one of Brilliant 10, Popular Sci. mag., 2003; named to TR100 "Young Innovators that will create the Future", MIT Tech. Rev., 2002; Packard fellow, 1999. Achievements include research in fundamental and applied topics in biophysics, specifically single molecule science. Office: Stanford U Dept Bioengineering James H Clark Ctr Rm E300 318 Campus Dr Stanford CA 94305 Office Phone: 650-736-7890. E-mail: quake@stanford.edu.

QUALL, DAVE, state legislator; b. Bellingham, Wash., Jan. 26, 1936; m to Allene; children: Kim (Mrs Brown) & Kay (Mrs Witt), six grandchildren. Washington State Representative, District 40, 1992-, member, Financial Inst & Rules Committees, currently, co-chmn, Education Committee. Teacher history & counselor, Mt Vernon High Sch, formerly; counselor & basketball coach Skagit Valley Col, formerly; president, Skagit Improvement Inc, formerly; vice president, Skagit Valley YMCA, formerly. Legislature Friend of Housing, Washington State Housing Authorities, 94. Democrat. Address: 1330 A S Second St Ste 103 Mount Vernon WA 98273 Office: State House Repr 301 John L O'Brien Bldg PO Box 40600 Olympia WA 98504 Office Phone: Olympia Off: 360-786-7800; Dist: 360-428-1023. E-mail: quall_da@leg.wa.gov.

QUALLEY, CHARLES ALBERT, art educator; b. Creston, Iowa, Mar. 19, 1930; s. Albert Olaf and Cleora (Dietrick) Q.; m. Betty Jean Griffith, Nov. 26, 1954; children: Janet Lynn, John Stuart. BFA, Drake U., 1952; MA, U. Iowa, 1956, MFA, 1958; EdD, Ill. State U., 1967. Art tchr. Des Moines Pub. Schs., 1952, 1954—55; critic art tchr. U. Iowa, 1955-57; prof. fine arts U. Colo., Boulder, 1958-90, prof. emeritus, 1990—, chmn. dept. fine arts, 1968-71, assoc. chmn., 1981-82. Vis. prof. Inst. for Shipboard Edn., semester at sea, 1979, vis. disting. prof. Ill. State U., 1985. Author: Safety in the Art Room, 1986, rev. edit., 2005; contbg. editor Sch. Arts, 1978-85, mem. editl. adv. bd., 1985-87; author column Safetypoint, 1981-85. Served with AUS, 1952-54, Korea. Fellow Nat. Art Edn. Assn. (v.p. 1980-82, pres. 1987-89, dir. conv. svcs. 1990-99, Art Educator of Yr. 1993); mem. Nat. Art Edn. Found. (trustee 1987—, chair bd. trustees 1996-2004), Colo. Art Edn. Assn. (editor 1965-67, 75, pres. 1976- 78), Delta Phi Delta, Omicron Delta Kappa, Pi Kappa Delta. Home: 9025 Natalie Ave NE Albuquerque NM 87111-3131

QUALSET, CALVIN O., agronomist, educator; b. Newman Grove, Nebr., Apr. 24, 1937; s. Herman Qualset and Adeline (Hanson) Vakoc; m. Kathleen Boehler; children: Douglas, Cheryl, Gary. BS, U. Nebr., 1958; MS, U. Calif., Davis, 1960, PhD, 1964. Asst. prof. U. Tenn., Knoxville, 1964-67; from asst. prof. to assoc. prof. U. Calif., Davis, 1967, prof., 1973-94, prof. emeritus, 1994—, chmn. dept. agronomy and range sci., 1975-81, 91-94, assoc. dean Coll. Agrl. and Environ. Sci., 1981-86, dir. Genetic Resources Conservation Program, 1985—2002, dir., found. seed and plant materials svc., 1991—93, dir. Agrl. Sustainability Inst., 2005—06. Sci. liaison officer U.S. AID, Washington, 1985-93, rsch. adv. com., 1989-92; nat. plant genetic resources bd. USDA, Washington, 1982-88; trustee Am. Type Culture Collection, 1993-99, Internat. Rice Rsch. Inst., 1999-2004, Agronomic Sci. Found., 1999—2008, chmn., 2006—08. Contbr. over 300 articles to profl. jours. and tech. publs. Bd. dirs. Calif. Crop Improvement Assn., 1975—85, Auksuciai Found., 1999—; contbr. to wheat improvement in Mex. citation, 1988. Fulbright fellow, Australia, 1976, Yugoslavia, 1984; recipient Pub. Plant Breeding award U.S. Coun. Comml. Plant Breeders, 1996, Master Alumni award U. Nebr., 1997, Charles Black award Coun. Agrl. Sci. and Tech., 2002, William L. Brown award Mo. Bot. Garden, 2002, Citation for Excellence, U. Calif., Calif. Aggie Alumni Assn., 2003, Citation for contbns. to Calif. agr. State Calif. Senate, 2003, award of excellence Coll. Agrl. and Environ. Sci., U. Calif., Davis, 2003, Citation for contbns. to agr. in Lithuania, 2004, 06. Fellow AAAS (chmn. agr. sect. 1992), Am. Soc. Agronomy (pres. 1994, agronomy honoree Calif. sect. 2001), Crop Sci. Soc. Am. (pres. 1989, editor-in-chief 1980-84, Frank N. Meyer medal for plant genetic resources 2006); mem. Soc. Conservation Biology, Soc. Econ. Botany, Genetic Soc. Am., Internat. Union Biol. Scis. (mem. U.S. nat. com. 2000-06), Am. Genetic Assn., U. Nebr. Alumni Assn. Achievements include development of more than 18 cultivars of wheat, oat, triticale. Office: Dept Plant Sci U Calif One Shields Ave Davis CA 95616 Office Phone: 530-754-8502.

QUATE, CALVIN FORREST, engineering educator; b. Baker, Nev., Dec. 7, 1923; s. Graham Shepard and Margie (Lake) Quate; m. Dorothy Marshall, June 28, 1945 (div. 1985); children: Robin, Claudia, Holly, Rhodalee; m. Arnice Streit, Jan. 1987; children: Christine, Carol, Richard. BS in Elec. Engring, U. Utah, 1944; PhD, Stanford U., 1950. Mem. tech. staff Bell Telephone Labs., Murray Hill, NJ, 1949-58; dir. research Sandia Corp., Albuquerque, 1959—60, v.p. research, 1960-61; prof. dept. applied physics and elec. engring. Stanford U., Calif., 1961-95, chmn. applied physics Calif., 1969-72, 78-81, Leland T. Edwards prof. sch. engring. Calif., 1986—, assoc. dean Sch. Humanities and Scis. Calif., 1972-74, 82-83, rsch. prof. dept. elec. engring. Calif., 1995—. Sr. rsch. fellow Xerox Rsch. Ctr., Palo Alto, Calif., 1984—94. Contbr. several articles to profl. jours. Served as lt. (j.g.) USNR, 1944—46. Recipient Pres.'s Nat. medal of Sci., 1992; named Scientist of Yr., R&D Mag., 1995; Guggenheim Fellow and Fulbright Scholar, Faculty Sci., Montpellier, France, 1968—69. Fellow: World Tech. Network (co-recipient, World Tech. award for IT Hardware 2006), Am. Phys. Soc. (Joseph F. Keithley award for Advances in Measurement Sci. 2000), Am. Acad. Arts and Scis., Acoustical Soc. Am., IEEE (Morris N. Liebmann award 1981, IEEE medal of honor 1988, Third Millennium award 2000, Ultrasonics Rayleigh award 2002), Royal Microscop. Soc. (hon.); mem.: Royal Soc. London (fgn.) (Rank prize for Optoelectronics 1982), NAS, NAE, Tau Beta Pi, Sigma Xi. Achievements include being one of the inventors of the the scanning acoustic microscope. Avocations: skiing, hiking, jogging, kayaking, sailboarding. Office: Stanford U Ginzton Laboratory Room 12 Palo Alto CA 94305-4085 Office Phone: 650-723-0213. Business E-Mail: quate@stanford.edu.

QUATTRONE, FRANK P., investment company executive; b. Phila., 1955; m. Denise Quattrone. BA in Econs. with honors, U. Pa. Wharton Sch. Bus., 1977; MBA, Stanford U., Calif., 1981. Investment banker Morgan Stanley, Deutsche Bank, Credit Suisse First Boston; co-founder, CEO Qatalyst Group, San Francisco, 2008—. Fundraiser The Innocent Project, 2004—. Office: Qatalyst Group c/o JMP Securities 600 Montgomery St San Francisco CA 94111

QUAYLE, DAN (JAMES DANFORTH QUAYLE), former Vice President of the United States; b. Indpls., Feb. 4, 1947; s. James C. and Corinne (Pulliam) Q.; m. Marilyn Tucker, Nov. 18, 1972; children: Tucker Danforth, Benjamin Eugene, Mary Corinne Berger. BS in Polit. Sci., DePauw U., Greencastle, Ind., 1969; JD, Ind. U., 1974. Bar: Ind. 1974. Ct. reporter, pressman Huntington (Ind.) Herald-Press, 1965-69, assoc. pub., gen. mgr., 1974-76; with consumer protection divsn. Office Atty. Gen., State of Ind., 1970-71; adminstrv. asst. to Gov. State of Ind., 1971-73; dir. Ind. Inheritance Tax Div., 1973-74; tchr. bus. law Huntington Coll., 1975; mem. US Congress from 4th Ind. dist., Washington, 1977—81; US Senator from Ind. Washington, 1981-89; v.p. US, Washington, 1989-93; founder BTC, 1994; chmn. global investments Cerberus Capital Mgmt., LP, 2000—; pres. Quayle & Associates, Phoenix. Disting. vis. prof. Am. Grad. Sch. Internat. Mgmt., 1997-99; bd. mem. IAP Worldwide Svcs., Inc., K2, Inc., Aozora Bank Ltd., 2000—; cons. in field. Author: Standing Firm: A Vice-Presidential Memoir, 1994, Worth Fighting For, 1999; co-author (with Diane Medved) The American Family: Discovering the Values that Make Us Strong, 1996 Chmn. Campaign Am., 1995-99; hon. trustee emeriti Hudson Inst. With Ind. Army N.G., 1970-76. Republican. Office: Cerberus Investments 7001 N Scottsdale Rd Ste 2010 Scottsdale AZ 85253-3644

QUAYLE, MARILYN TUCKER, wife of former United States Vice President, lawyer; b. 1949; d. Warren S. and Mary Alice (Craig) Tucker; m. J. Danforth Quayle, Nov. 18, 1972; children: Tucker Danforth, Benjamin Eugene, Mary Corinne. BA in Polit. Sci., Purdue U., 1971; JD, Ind. U., 1974. Pvt. practice atty., Huntington, Ind., 1974—77; ptnr. Krieg, DeVault, Alexander & Capehart, Indpls., 1993—2001; pres. BTC Inc., Phoenix, 2001—. Author (with Nancy T. Northcott): Embrace the Serpent, 1992; author: The Campaign, 1996. Nat. adv. bd. The Salvation Army. Office: Quayle and Associates Ste 2010 7001 N Scottsdale Rd Scottsdale AZ 85253-3644

QUEALLY, HYLDA, agent; b. Ireland; Talent agent Triad Artists, 1989; head ind. divsn. William Morris Agy., sr. v.p. motion picture dept., 2000—04; motion picture talent agent Creative Artists Agy, 2004—. Named one of The 100 Most Powerful Women in Entertainment, Hollywood Reporter, 2003, 2004, 2005, 2006, 2007.

QUEHL, GARY HOWARD, educational association administrator, consultant; b. Green Bay, Wis., Mar. 25, 1938; s. Howard and Virginia Babcock (Dunning) Q.; children: Scott Boyer, Catherine Mary. BA, Carroll Coll., 1960; MS, Ind. U., 1962, EdD, 1965; LHD, Buena Vista Coll., 1977, Davis and Elkins Coll., 1979; EdD (hon.), Columbia., SC, 1987. Asst. dean students Wis. State U., 1962; asst. dean coll. Wittenberg U., 1965-67; v.p., dean coll. Lindenwood Colls., St. Charles, Mo., 1967-70; exec. dir. Coll. Ctr. of the Finger Lakes, Corning, NY, 1970-74; pres. Coun. of Ind. Colls., Washington, 1974-86, Coun. for Advancement and Support of Edn., Washington, 1986-90, Quehl Assocs., 1990—. Cons. in field, 1990—. Editor, author books in field. Mem. secretariat Nat. Ctr. for Higher Edn.; bd. dirs. St. Norbert Coll., Carroll Coll., Muskingum Coll., Elmira Coll., Nat. Assn. Ind. Colls. and Univs., ind. sector, Cornell Coll. Mem. Am. Coun. Edn., Am. Conf. Acad. Deans, Nat. Panel for Women in Higher Edn., North Ctrl. Assn. Acad. Deans (past pres.) Mem. United Ch. Christ. Office Phone: 530-265-3956. E-mail: quehl@queasso.com.

QUELLAND, DOUG, state legislator; b. La Jolla, Calif., June 16, 1948; m. Donna Quelland; 3 children. BS, Iowa State U., 1970; attended, Am. Grad. Sch. Internat. Mgmt. Owner Bell Lawnmower, 1980—, Thank-Q Rentals, 1980—; mem. Dist. 10 Ariz. House of Reps., 2003—06, 2008—. Elem. & high sch. tchr. Mem.: YMCA (bd. mem.). Republican. Office: Capitol Complex 1700 W Washington Rm 128 Phoenix AZ 85007-2890 Office Phone: 602-926-3024. Office Fax: 602-417-3110. Business E-Mail: dquelland@azleg.gov.*

QUIAT, GERALD M., lawyer; b. Denver, Jan. 9, 1924; s. Ira L. and Esther (Greenblatt) Q.; m. Roberta M. Nicholson, Sept. 26, 1962; children: James M., Audrey R., Melinda A., Daniel P., Ilana L., Leonard E. AA, U. Calif., Berkeley, 1942; AB, LLB, U. Denver, 1948, changed to JD, 1970. Bar: Colo. 1948, Fed. Ct. 1948, U.S. Dist. Ct. Colo. 1948, U.S. Ct. Appeals (10th cir.) 1948, U.S. Surpeme Ct. 1970. Dep. dist. atty. City and Co. of Denver, Colo., 1949-52; partner firm Quiat, Seeman & Quiat, Denver, 1952-67, Quiat & Quiat (later changed to Quiat, Bucholtz & Bull, P.C.), 1968; pres. Quiat, Bucholtz & Bull & Laff, P.C. (and predecessors), Denver, 1968-85; pvt. practice Denver, 1985—. Bd. dirs., past chmn. audit com. Guaranty Bank & Trust Co., Denver. Past trustee Holding Co.; pres., chmn. bd. dirs. Rose Med. Ctr., Denver, 1976—79; mem. Colo. Civil Rights Com., 1963—71, chmn., 1966—67, 1969—70, hearing officer, 1963—71; bd. dirs. AMC Cancer Rsch. Ctr., Denver, 1971—2004, chmn. bd., 1991—93, sec. treas., 2000—04; chmn. bd. Am. Med. Ctr., 1993—95; hon. mem. nat. civil rights com. Anti-Defamation League, hon. mem. nat. exec. com., hon. nat. commr.; chmn. Mountain State region, 1980—82; mem. exec. com., bd. mem. Mountain States region Anti-Defamation League. With inf. US Army, 1942—45. Decorated Combat Infantry Badge, Bronze Star. Mem. ABA, Colo. Bar Assn., Am. Legion (comdr. Leyden-Chiles-Wickersham post 1 1955-56, past judge adv. Colo. dept.). Home: 5361 Nassau Cir E Englewood CO 80110-5100 Office: 1873 S Bellaire St Ste 900 Denver CO 80222-4304 Home Phone: 303-300-0722; Office Phone: 303-759-1000 ext. 102. E-mail: gqph@aol.com.

QUICK, JAMES S., geneticist, plant breeder; b. Devils Lake, ND, Oct. 20, 1940; s. James R. and Anne (Sather) Q.; children: Alissa, Kathryn, Jeanette; m. Jacklynn Panuska, June 13, 1994. BS, N.D. State U., 1962; MS, Purdue U., 1965, PhD, 1966. Asst. geneticist Rockefeller Found. India, NYC, 1966-69; from assoc. prof. to prof. N.D State U., Fargo, 1969-81; prof. Colo. State U., Ft. Collins, 1981—, head, 1998—. Cons. USDA, ARS, Spain, 1977-81, Morocco, 1985—; advisor Australian Wheat Rsch. Coun., Toowoomba, Queensland, 1987-88. Editor Annual Wheat Newsletter, 1983-94; contbr. articles to profl. jours. Recipient Achievement award U.S. Durum Growers, 1978, Disting. Toastmaster award Toastmasters Internat., 1985; grantee U.S. Pasta Industry, 1977-78. Fellow Am. Soc. Agronomy (Achievement award-crops 1996), Crop Sci. Soc. Am.; mem. Coun. Agrl. Sci. and Technology, Sigma Xi. Achievements include development of 13 durum wheat cultivars, 13 hard red winter wheat cultivars, 1 soft white spring wheat cultivar; discovered new resistance to Russian wheat aphid. Office: Colo State U Dept Agronomy Fort Collins CO 80523-0001

QUICKSILVER, WILLIAM TODD, lawyer; b. St. Louis, July 26, 1952; AB magna cum laude, Princeton U., NJ, 1974; JD, U. Chgo., 1978. Bar: Calif. 1978. COO, dep. mng. ptnr. Manatt, Phelps & Phillips, LLP, LA, 2003—06, chief exec., mng. ptnr., bd. dirs., co-chair bus. and transactions divsn., 2007—. Dir. Pub. Counsel Law Ctr.; spkr. in field. Assoc. editor: U. Chgo. Law Rev. Mem.: ABA, Century City Bar Assn. Office: Manatt Phelps & Phillips LLP 11355 W Olympic Blvd Los Angeles CA 90064-1614 Office Phone: 310-312-4210. Office Fax: 310-312-4224. E-mail: wquicksilver@manatt.com.

QUIGLEY, JOHN MICHAEL, economist, educator; b. NYC, Feb. 12, 1942; BS with distinction, U.S. Air Force Acad., 1964; MSc with honors, U. Stockholm, Sweden, 1965; AM, Harvard U., 1971, PhD, 1972; TekD (hon.), Royal Inst. Tech., 2007. Commd. 2d lt. USAF, 1964, advanced through grades to capt., 1968; asst. prof. econs. Yale U., 1972-74, assoc. prof., 1974-81; prof. pub. policy U. Calif., Berkeley, 1979—, prof. econs., 1981—, Chancellor's prof., 1997—, prof. bus., 1999—, I. Donald Terner disting. prof., 1999—, chmn. dept. econs., 1992-95; vis. prof. econs. and stats. U. Gothenberg, 1978. Cons. numerous govt. agys. and pvt. firms; econometrician Hdqrs. U.S. Air Force, Pentagon, 1965-68; research assoc. Nat. Bur. Econ. Research, N.Y.C., 1968-78; mem. com. on nat. urban policy NAS, 1985-93. Author, editor, contbr. articles to profl. jours.; editor in chief Reg. Sci. and Urban Econs., 1987-2003; mem. editl. bd. many sci. and scholarly jours. Fulbright scholar, 1964-65; fellow NSF, 1968-69, Woodrow Wilson, 1968-71, Harvard IBM, 1969-71, NDEA, 1969-71, Thord-Gray Am. Scandinavian Found. 1971-72, Social Sci. Research Council, 1971-72. Mem. Am. Econ. Assn., Econometric Soc., Regional Sci. Assn. (bd. dirs. 1986—), Nat. Tax Assn., Assn. for Pub. Policy and Mgmt. (bd. dirs. 1986-89, v.p. 1987-89), Am. Real Estate and Urban Econs. Assn. (bd. dirs. 1987-2001, pres. 1995-97), Royal Swedish Acad. Engring. Scis. (fgn.). Office: U Calif 2607 Hearst Ave Berkeley CA 94720-7305 Business E-Mail: quigley@econ.berkeley.edu.

QUIGLEY, KEVIN WALSH, state legislator, lawyer; b. Everett, Wash., Feb. 23, 1961; s. David W. Quigley and Mary (Cernetig) Thoreson; m. Suzanne Marion Bakke. BA with spl. honors, George Washington U., 1983; JD cum laude, NYU, 1986; LLM, Harvard U., 1992. Bar: Wash. 1988. Jr. fellow ctr. internat. studies NYU Law Sch., NYC, 1986; assoc. Perkins Coie, Seattle, 1987-94; of counsel Perkins Cole, Seattle, 1995-97; mem. Wash. State Senate, Olympia, 1993-97. Chmn. health and long-term care com., mem., vice chmn. ways and means com.; dir. bus. affairs Teledesic Corp. Grad. fellow Harvard Law Sch., 1987. Mem. Rotary, Phi Beta Kappa. Democrat. Avocations: mountain climbing, architecture, carpentry. Home: 1029 Springbrook Rd Lake Stevens WA 98258-9425

QUIGLEY, PHILIP J., retired telecommunications industry executive; b. 1943; With Advanced Mobile Phone Svc. Inc., 1982-84, v.p., gen. mgr., Pacific region; with Pac Tel Mobile Access, 1984-86, pres., chief exec. officer; with Pac Tel Personal Communications, 1986-87, pres., chief exec. officer; exec. v.p., chief oper. officer Pac Tel Corp., 1987; ret. chmn., pres., chief exec. officer Pacific Telesis Group, San Francisco, 1997; pres. Pacific Bell, 1987-94. Bd. dir. Wells Fargo & Co., Sienna Holdings, Thomas Weisel Partnership, SRI International, Luminous Networks and Nuance Comm. Mailing: Bd Dir Wells Fargo Co PO Box 63750 San Francisco CA 94163

QUIGLEY, ROB WELLINGTON, architect; b. Calif., 1945; B, Univ. Utah, 1969. Registered Architect, Calif., 1976. Architect Peace Corps, Chile; prin. Quigley Architects, San Diego, Palo Alto, 1974—. Adj. prof. arch. Univ. Calif., San Diego; vis. design prof. Harvard Univ. Grad. Sch. Design, 1991, Univ. Tex., Austin, 1994, Univ. Calif., Berkeley, 1997, 98; spkr. in field; invited juror and advisor. Prin. works include San Diego New Main Libr. (Honor award, AIA San Diego, 1998), Sherman Heights Cmty. Ctr. (Citation, AIA San Diego, 1990, Orchid, San Diego Chpt. AIA, 1992, Merit award, AIA San Diego, 1996), Golden Hill Community Ctr., Baltic Inn, San Diego (Honor award, AIA San Diego, 1987, Panda award, City of San Diego, 1988), 202 Island Inn (One of "Ten Best Designs of 1992," Time Mag., 1993, Nat. AIA Honor award, 1993, Merit award, AIA San Diego, 1993, Honor award with Distinction, AIA Calif. Coun., 1994), Solana Beach Transit Sta. (Orchid, San Diego Chpt., AIA, 1996, Honor award, AIA Calif. Coun., 1998), Escondido Transit Sta. (Citation, AIA San Diego, 1990, Orchid,AIA San Diego, 1991, Beautification award, City of Escondido, 1990), San Diego Children's Mus., Calif., Student Academic Services Facility, U. Calif. San Diego, San Diego Historic Harbor Front, West Valley Branch Libr. (Divine Detail, AIA San Diego, 2003, Merit award, AIA Santa Clara, 2004), Leslie Shao-ming Sun Field Station, Stanford U. (Merit award, AIA San Diego, 2003, Honor award, AIA Santa Clara, 2004, COTE Top Ten Green Buildings, Nat. AIA, 2005), Opportunity Ctr. for the Midpeninsula (Advocacy Planning award, Northern Sect. Am. Planning Assn., 2003), Shaw Lopez Park, Casa Feliz, and several others, solo exhibitions, Retrospective, So. Calif. Inst. of Architecture, Santa Monica, 1982, Exhibit of Recent Work, UCLA, 1984, Recent Work, Portland State U., 1991, exhibitions include Visual Communication Towards Architecture, Installation Gallery, San Diego, 1982, Don Clos Pegase Competition, San Francisco Mus. Contemporary Art, 1985, The Emerging Generation in the USA, Global Architecture Gallery, Tokyo, Japan, 1987, Five Choose Five, Nat. AIA Conf., St. Louis, 1989, Fabrications, San Francisco Mus. Modern Art, 1998, Books, Bytes and Mortar, Mus. Contemporary Art, San Diego, 2001, Modern Trains and Splendid Stations, Art Inst. Chgo., 2002, and several others; co-author: (monograph) Buildings & Projects, 1996. Recipient Presdl. Commendation for Exemplary Cmty. Svc., 1988, Firm award, AIA Calif. Coun., 1995, Maybeck award, 2005, The Irving Gill award, AIA San Diego, 1997, several mag. and cmty. program awards, several awards for design excellence from the Nat. AIA, AIA Santa Clara, AIA San Diego, and AIA Calif. Coun.; named Headliner of Yr. in Architecture, San Diego Press Club, 1995; named one of 100 Foremost Architects of the World, AD 100, Architectural Digest, 1991, 88 San Diegans to Watch in '88', San Diego Mag., 1988, The San Diego 50 People to Watch in 1997, 1997; fellow Inst. for Urban Design, 1996. Fellow: AIA; mem.: NAD. Office: Quigley Architects 434 W Cedar St San Diego CA 92101 also: 210 High St Palo Alto CA 94301 Office Phone: 619-232-0888, 650-328-8030. E-mail: office@robquigley.com.

QUILLIGAN, EDWARD JAMES, retired obstetrician, gynecologist, educator; b. Cleve., June 18, 1925; s. James Joseph and Maude Elvira (Ryan) Q.; m. Betty Jane Cleaton, Dec. 14, 1946; children: Bruce, Jay, Carol, Christopher, Linda, Ted. BA, MD, Ohio State U., 1951; MA (hon.), Yale, 1967. Intern Ohio State U. Hosp., 1951-52, resident, 1952-54, Western Res. U. Hosps., 1954-56; asst. prof. obstetrics and gynecology Western Res. U., 1957-63, prof., 1963-65; prof. obstetrics and gynecology UCLA, 1965-66; prof., chmn. dept. Ob-Gyn Yale U., 1966-69, U. So. Calif., 1969-78, asso. v.p. med. affairs, 1978-79; prof. Ob-Gyn. U. Calif., Irvine, 1980-83, vice chancellor health affairs, dean Sch. Medicine, 1987-89; prof., chmn. ob.-gyn. dept. U. Wis., 1983-85; prof., chmn. Ob-Gyn Davis Med. Ctr. U. Calif., Sacramento, 1985-87, vice chancellor Health Scis., dean Coll. Med. Irvine, 1987-89, prof. ob-gyn, 1987-94, prof. emeritus ob-gyn., 1994; exec. dir. med. edn. Long Beach (Calif.) Meml. Health Svcs., 1995—2005; ret., 2005. Contbr. articles to med. jours.; editor-in-chief emeritus: Am. Jour. Obstetrics and Gynecology. Served to 2d lt. AUS, 1944—46. Recipient Centennial award Ohio State U., 1970 Mem. Soc. Gynecologic Investigation, Am. Gynecol. Soc., Am. Coll. Ob-Gyn., Sigma Xi. Home: 1 Goldenglow Irvine CA 92612-4077 E-mail: equilligan@cox.net.

QUINBY, WILLIAM ALBERT, lawyer, arbitrator, mediator; b. Oakland, Calif., May 28, 1941; s. George W. and Marge (Diaz) Q.; m. Marion Bach, Nov. 27, 1964; 1 child, Michelle Kathleen. BA, Harvard U., 1963; JD, U. Calif., San Francisco, 1967. Bar: Calif. 1967. V.p., dir., shareholder Crosby, Heafey, Roach & May, Oakland, 1967-96; mediator, arbitrator Am. Arbitration Assn. and AAA Ctr. for Mediation, San Francisco, 1996—; ptnr. Wulff, Quinby & Sochynsky, 2001—. Bd. dirs. Haws Drinking Faucet Co., Berkeley, Calif.; mem. faculty Hastings Coll. Advocacy, San Francisco, 1980, instr. Boalt Hall Sch. Law, 1997; co-moderator Counsel Connect's Calif. ADR Discussion Group; lectr. currents devels. in banking arbitration and mediation; mem. fellowship rev. com. HEW; mem. mediation panel Nat. Assn. Securities Dealers; trustee Nat. Pre-Suit Mediation Program; adj. prof. Hastings Coll. of the Law, U. Calif., 1998, 99. Author: Six Reasons--Besides Time and Money--to Mediate Rather Than Litigate, Why Health Care Parties Should Mediate Rather Than Litigate, Starting an ADR Practice Group in a Law Firm, Mediation Process Can Amicably Solve Business Disputes and Not a Gold Rush (But Silver, Maybe), ADR Practice in a Large Law Firm Produces No Overnight Bonanzas, Making The Most of Mediation (Effective Mediation Advocacy). Bd. dirs. Big Bros. East Bay, Oakland, 1983-87, Easter Seals Soc. East Bay, 1973; past bd. dirs. Oakland East Bay Symphony, Oakland Pub. Libr. Found.;past chmn. bd. dirs. Bay Area Tumor Inst. Scholar Harvard U., 1962-63. Fellow Coll. Comml. Arbitrators; mem. ABA (sect. on dispute resolution, chair programs, mediation coms.), Calif. Bar Assn., Alameda County Bar Assn., San Francisco Bar Assn., Contra Costa County Bar Assn., Calif. Bus. Trial Lawyers Assn., Am. Arbitration Assn. (large, complex case panel, internat., employment, constrn., and comml. mediation and arbitration panels), Oakland C. of C. (past bd. dirs., exec. com.), Alameda County Barristers Club (bd. dirs., pres. 1972), Harvard Club, San Francisco Calimari Club. Republican. Avocations: running, skiing, tennis, travel, gardening. Office: Wulff Quinby & Sochynsky Dispute Resolution 1901 Harrison St Ste 1420 Oakland CA 94612-3582 Office Phone: 510-663-5220. Personal E-mail: wquinby@aol.com.

QUINLAN, CATHERINE, library director; MusB, Queens U.; MLS, Dalhousie U.; MBA, Meml. U. Newfoundland. Dir. librs., chief libr. U. Western Ontario; univ. libr. U. BC, 1997—2007, dir. Irving K. Barber Learning Ctr., 2004—07; dean librs. U. So. Calif., 2007—. Mem.: Harry Hawthorne Found., Canadian Libr. Assn., Canadian Assn. Rsch. Libraries, Assn. Rsch. Libraries, Golden Key Soc., Coalition for Networked Info. Avocations: playing chamber music, opera, queuing theory, running. Office: U So Calif Dean Libr Los Angeles CA 90089 Office Phone: 213-821-2344. Business E-Mail: cquinlan@usc.edu.

QUINN, EDWARD J., broadcasting company executive; BS in Speech, U. Wis. Gen. sales mgr. WTMJ-TV, Milw.; v.p., gen. mgr. KTNV-TV, Las Vegas, WVUE-TV, New Orleans; gen. mgr. KGTV, v.p. McGraw-Hill Broadcasting Co., San Diego, 1986-96, pres., 1996—. Bd. govs. ABC TV Affiliates Assn.; pres.'s adv. bd. San Diego State U.; chmn. San Diego Baha Comms. Coun. Recipient George Walker Smith humanitarian award San Diego Coalition for Equality, medal of honor DAR, disting. svc. award Soc. Profl. Journalists, golden mike award Radio and TV News Dirs. Assn. So. Calif., Emmy award NATAS. Home: 4600 Air Way San Diego CA 92102-2528

QUINN, FRANCIS ANTHONY, bishop emeritus; b. LA, Sept. 11, 1921; Attended, St. Joseph's Coll., Mountain View, Calif., St. Patrick's Sem., Menlo Park, Calif., Cath. U., Washington, U. Calif., Berkeley. Ordained priest Archdiocese of San Francisco, 1946, aux. bishop, 1978—79; ordained bishop, 1978; bishop Diocese of Sacramento, 1979—94, bishop emeritus, 1994—. Roman Catholic. Office: 2110 Broadway Sacramento CA 95818-2518 Office Phone: 916-733-0200.

QUINN, HELEN RHODA ARNOLD, physicist; b. Melbourne, Victoria, Australia, May 19, 1943; came to U.S. 1961; d. Ted Adamson and Helen Ruth (Down) Arnold; m. Daniel James Quinn, Oct. 8, 1966; children: Elizabeth Helen, James Arnold. BS in Physics, Stanford U., 1963, MS in Physics, 1964, PhD in Physics, 1967; DSc (hon.), Notre Dame U., 2002, U. Melbourne, 2005. Rsch. assoc. Stanford Linear Accelerator Ctr., 1967—68, 1978—79, mem. permanent sci. staff, 1979—2003, edn. coord., 1988—93, asst. to dir. edn. and pub. outreach, 1998—2003, prof. physics, 2003—; hon. rsch. fellow Harvard U., 1971, rsch. fellow, 1971—72, asst. prof. physics, 1972—76, assoc. prof. physics, 1976—77. Guest scientist (non German postdoctoral rschr.) Deutsches Elektronen Sychrotron, Hamburg, 1968—70; vis. assoc. prof. Stanford U., 1976—78; vis. scientist Stanford Linear Accelerator Ctr., 1977—78. Contbr. articles to profl. jours. Pres. Contemporary Physics Edn. Project, Portola Valley, Calif., 1989-95; vol., chair Town of Portola Valley Trails Com., 1988-98; pres. Am. Phys. Soc., 2004. Decorated Hon. officer Order of Australia, 2005; recipient DIRAC medal Internat. Ctr. Theoretical Physics, Trieste, Italy, 2000; fellow Alfred Sloan Found., 1975-79. Fellow AAAS, Am. Phys. Soc. (pres. 2004); mem. Nat. Acad. Sci. Avocations: hiking, native plants. Business E-Mail: quinn@slac.stanford.edu.

QUINN, JOHN J., lawyer; b. Sept. 19, 1932; BA, Univ. So. Calif., 1954, JD, 1959. Bar: Calif. 1959, US Supreme Ct. 1965. Ptnr., LA Office Mgmt. Arnold & Porter, LA. Past chmn. US Senator Barbara Boxer Fed. Judicial Selection Com.; chmn., Disciplinary Com. US Dist. Ct., Ctrl. Calif., 1995—2001. Recipient Learned Hand award, Am. Jewish Com., Disting. Svc. award, U.S. Ct. Appeals, Ninth Cir. Fellow: Am. Col. Trial Lawyers; mem.: ABA (mem. Ho. of Dels. 1977—82), L.A. County Bar Assn. (pres. 1976—77, Shattuck-Price award), Am. Bd. Trial Advocates, Order of the Coif. Office: Arnold & Porter 777 S Figueroa St Los Angeles CA 90017-2513 Office Phone: 213-243-4080. Office Fax: 213-243-4199. Business E-Mail: john.j.quinn@aporter.com.

QUINN, MARK T., medical educator; b. San Jose, Calif., June 11, 1958; BA in Biology and Chemistry, Point Loma Coll., 1982; PhD in Physiology and Pharmacology, U. Calif., San Diego, 1987. Postdoctoral rsch. assoc. Rsch. Inst. Scripps Clinic, La Jolla, Calif., 1988-89; sr. rsch. assoc. Mont. State U., Bozeman, 1989-90, asst., assoc. rsch. prof., 1991-95, asst. prof., 1995—, assoc. prof., 1998. Contbr. articles to profl. jours. Recipient Investigator award Arthritis Found., 1991, Health FIRST award NIH, 1992—, Charles and Nora Wiley Meritorious Rsch. award, 1993; grantee Am. Cancer Soc., 1989, Am. Lung Assn., 1991-93, Arthritis Found., 1994—, USDA, 1995—; U. Calif. Regents fellow, 1981, Point Loma Coll. Rsch. Assocs. fellow, 1981, San Diego & Grad. Opportunity Rsch. fellow, 1986-87, Arthritis Found. Postdoctoral fellow, 1989-91. Mem. Am. Soc. Cell Biology, Am. Heart Assn. (coun. basic rsch., Established Investigator award 1996—), Soc. Leukocyte Biology. Office: Mont State U Dept Vet Molecular Biology Bozeman MT 59717-0001

QUINN, PATRICIA K., international television consultant, coproducer; b. Chico, Calif. d. Donald Joseph and Kathleen (Alexander) Q. BA, Bennington Coll.; MFA in Drama, Yale U. Prodr., devel. exec. various Off-Broadway and regional theatres, 1976-84; devel. cons. Sundance Film Inst., Utah, 1983—85; theatrical agt. I.C.M., LA, 1985-90; v.p. comedy devel. Warner Bros. TV, Burbank, Calif., 1990-92; lit. and packaging agt. various agys. LA, 1995—2006; cons. Quinn Media, 2006—. Instr. UCLA Ext., 1995—; spkr., lectr. Nat. Assn. of TV Programming Execs., Fla. Bar, NATAS, Media Xchange (Internat.); mem. TV com. Brit. Acad. Film and TV Arts, 2002-; adj. faculty Dodge Coll. Film and Media Arts, Chapman U., 2007-; ptnr., mgr. Quinn Media Mgmt., 2006-. Founding mem. N.Y. Theatre Workshop, NYC, 1980—86. Mem.: Women in Film (v.p. 1995—2001, bd. dirs. 2005—). Office: 330 S Spalding Dr #403 Beverly Hills CA 90212 Office Phone: 310-656-5141, 310-228-8720. Personal E-mail: pat@patquinnmedia.com. E-mail: p_quinn@sbcglobal.net.

QUIRK, KATHLEEN L., mining executive; BS in Acctg., La. State U. With Mobil Oil Corp., Dallas; from mem. staff to treas. Freeport-McMoRan Copper & Gold Inc., New Orleans, 1989—2000, v.p., treas., 2000—03, sr. v.p., CFO, treas., 2003—07, exec. v.p., CFO, treas., 2007—. Office: Freeport McMoRan 1 N Central Ave Phoenix AZ 85004-4414

QUREISHI, A. SALAM, computer company executive; b. Aligarh, India, July 1, 1936; s. M.A. Jabbar and Saira (Sattar) Q.; m. Naheed Fatima; children: Lubna, Leila. BS in Physics and Math., Aligarth U., India, 1954; MS in Stats., Patna U., India, 1957. Mgr. applications IBM Corp., Palo Alto, Calif., 1961-67; founder, pres., chmn. bd. Optimum Sys., Inc., Palo Alto, Calif., 1967-71; CEO Sysorex Internat., Inc., Mountain View, Calif., 1972—. Republican. Home: 925 Mountain Home Rd Woodside CA 94062-2519 Office: A Salam Qureishi 506 Clyde Ave Mountain View CA 94043-2212

RAB, GEORGE T., pediatric orthopedic surgeon; b. Cleve., Nov. 11, 1946; s. Thomas P. and Patricia S. Rab; m. Wendy Andereson Rab, Aug. 31, 1968; children: Geoffrey W., Nicholas A. BS, Northwestern U., Chgo., 1968; MD, Northwestern U., 1970; MS, U. Minn., Mpls., 1975. Lic. physician Calif., diplomate Am. Bd. Orthop. Surgery, Nat. Bd. Med. Examiners. Intern in surgery Chgo. Wesley Meml. Hosp., 1970—71; resident in orthop surgery Mayo Clinic, Rochester, Minn., 1971—75; resident in pediat. orthop. surgery Gillette Children's Hosp., St. Paul, 1974; asst. prof. dept. orthop. surgery Sch. Medicine, U. Calif., Davis, 1977—82, assoc. prof. dept. orthop. surgery, 1982—88, prof. dept. orthop., 1988—, Ben Ali chair in pediat. orthop., 1998—, chair dept. orthop. surgery, 2000—06. Guest lectr. Shriners Hosp. for Crippled Children and Sch. Medicine Oreg. Health Scis. U., Portland, 1985, Duncan Seminar Children's Orthop. Hosp. and Med. Ctr., Seattle, 1987; vis. prof., guest lectr. dept. orthop. Children's Hosp. Med. Ctr., Cin., 1986; vis. prof., guest lectr. Carrie Tingley Hosp. Annual Meeting, Albuquerque, 1992; vis. prof., guest lectr., Robert Samilson lectr., San Francisco, 96; vis. prof. U. Calif., Irvine, 1998, U. Colo., 1999, New Eng. Med. Ctr., 1999, Children's Hosp. Med. Ctr. of Akron, Ohio, 2001; Arthur A. Thibodeau vis. prof. Tufts U. Sch. Medicine, 1999; John M. Roberts vis. prof. Children's Hosp. of New Orleans, 2000; vis. prof., Leslie Meyers lectr. Shriners Hosp., Greenville, SC, 2001; Charles LeRoy Lowman vis. prof. Orthop. Hosp., LA, 2002; orthop. surgeon, med. dir. motion analysis lab. Shriners Hosp. for Children, 1995—; pediat. orthop. specialist Sutter Cmty. Hosps., Sacramento, 1987—; vis. assoc. prof. dept. orthop. Harvard Med. Sch., Boston, 1983—84; rsch. fellow gait lab. Children's Hosp., Boston, 1983—84; editl. cons. Am. Jour. Diseases of Children, 1990—93; cons., rev. com. Orthop. Rsch. and Edn. Found., 1994—99; civilian cons. med. specialist in pediat. orthop. surgery Oakland Naval Hosp., Calif., 1990—95; pediat. orthop. cons. Kaiser Permanente Hosp., Sacramento, 1977—98. Mem. editl. bd. Gait and Posture, 1992—97, bd. editors Jour. Pediat. Orthopedics, 1992—, Jour. Children's Orthopedics, 2006—. Bd. dirs. Sacramento Make-A-Wish Found., Inc., 1988—92. Maj. US Army, 1975—77. Recipient Goldsmith Intern Humanitarian award, Chgo. Wesley Meml. Hosp., 1971, Frank Stitchfield award, Hip Soc., 1976, annual award for excellence in tchg. clin. scis., Kaiser Found. Hosp., 1978, Best Poster award, Gait and Clin. Analysis Soc. Meeting, 2000; named Outstanding Clin. Instr., U. Calif. Davis Sch. Medicine, 1980, Outstanding Tchr. of Yr. in Orthop. Surgery, 1991, 1996; named one of Best Drs. in Am., 2005—06; Berg-Sloat Traveling fellow, 1977. Fellow: Am. Acad. Pediat., Am. Acad. Orthop. Surgeons (com. on biomed. engring. 1980—82, com. on psychomotor skills 1980—87, com. ednl. content 1981—82, sec. com. on biomed. engring. 1982—85, subcom. on pediat. of com. on exams. and evaluations 1985—91, chmn. com. on biomed. engring. 1986—87); mem.: Sierra Sacramento Valley Med. Soc., Sacramento Pediat. Soc., Paul R. Lipscomb Soc., West Coast Gait Lab. Group, Western Orthop. Assn., Calif. Med. Assn., Am. Orthop. Assn., Pediat. Orthop. Soc. N.Am. (com. on computer applications in pediat. orthop. 1985—90), Orthop. Rsch. Soc., Internat. Soc. Electrophysiol. Kinesiology, Internat. Pediat. Orthop. Think Tank (site selection com. 1998—2000), Gait and Clin. Movement Analysis Soc. (awards com. 2001—02), Am. Soc. Biomechanics (arrangements com. annual meeting 1987, pres.-elect 1989—90, exec. com. 1989—93, pres. 1990—91), Am. Bd. Orthop. Surgery (certifying examiner 1984—92), Am. Acad. Cerebral Palsy and Devel. Medicine (nominating com. 1990—94). Avocations: bicycling, sailing, hiking, cooking. Office: Dept Orthop Surgery U Calif-Davis 4860 Y St # 3800 Sacramento CA 95817 Office Phone: 916-734-5770. Office Fax: 916-734-7904. E-mail: george.rab@ucdmc.ucdavis.edu.

RABBAT, GUY, electronics executive, consultant; b. Cairo, Jan. 30, 1943; arrived in U.S., 1972; s. Victor and Alice R.; m. Elfriede Freitag, Aug. 3, 1968; children: Ralph, Shirley; m. Nadia Kobinger, Feb. 8, 1992; children: Richard, Jacques, Laurent. Baccalaureate, France; BS, Queens U., Eng., 1967; MS, Queens U., 1969, PhD Elec. Engring. honors, 1971. Design supr. Siemens AG, Germany, 1964—68; asst. lectr. Queens U., England, 1968—72; dir. ops. IBM, 1972—84; v.p. Austin ops., CAE sys. divsn. Tektronix, 1984—86; head elec. engring. GM Corp., Mich., 1986—87; pres., CEO Modular Computer Sys., Inc., Ft. Lauderdale, Fla., 1987—92; mng. dir., exec. bd. dirs. Rank Xerox, Ltd., Welwyn Garden City, Herts, England, 1992—96; corp. v.p. GE, Milw., 1996—98; chief tech. officer, chief info. officer Gen. Elec. Med. Sys., Milw., 1996—98; sr. v.p. Solectron Corp., 1998—2004; chmn., gen. ptnr. Corcica Tech. Ventures, 2001—05; pres., CEO HTC Corp., Sunnyvale, Calif., 2004—; CEO Nest Group Cos., Foster City, Calif., 2005—. Chmn. Internat. IEEE Conf. on Circuits and Computers, 1980, Internat. IEEE Conf. on Computer Design, 1983; bd. dirs. indsl. affiliates Mich. State U., 1986-88; pres. Am. Automation Assn., 1984-86; chmn., founder High Tech. Consortium Yr. 2000 and Beyond, 1998-02 Author: Hardware and Software Concepts in VLSI, 1983, Advanced Semiconductor Technology and Computer Systems, 1988; contbr. numerous scis. tech. papers; patentee in field Fellow: IEEE (Eng. chpt., editor-in-chief, chmn. editl. bd. Circuits and Devices Mag. 1984—86, invention and outstanding contbn. awards), Royal Engring. Coun. (London). Avocations: history, archaeology, poetry, jogging. Home: 360 Saint Andrews Ln Half Moon Bay CA 94019 Office: Nest Group Cos 373E Vintage Park Dr Foster City CA 94404 Office Phone: 408-218-4393. Business E-Mail: guy.rabbat@nestgroup.net.

RABENSTEIN, DALLAS LEROY, chemistry professor; b. Portland, Oreg., June 13, 1942; s. Melvin Leroy and Rose Marie (Nelson) R.; m. Gloria Carolyn Duncan, Aug. 30, 1964; children: Mark, Lisa. BS, U. Wash., 1964; PhD, U. Wis., 1968. Lectr. U. Wis., Madison, 1967-68; research chemist Chevron Research Co., Richmond, Calif., 1968-69; from asst. prof. to prof. chemistry U. Alta., Edmonton, Can., 1969-85; prof. U. Calif., Riverside, 1985-97, chmn. dept. chemistry, 1989—92, 1998—2000, 2002—03, dean Coll. Natural and Agrl. Scis., 1993-94, disting. prof. chemistry, 1997—, dean, grad. divsn., 2003—08, exec. vice chancellor & provost, 2009—. Vis. prof. U. Oxford, 1976-77, U. Western Ont., 1982; McElvain lectr. U. Wis., 1981; Dow lectr. U. B.C., 1983; Eli Lilly lectr., Ind. U., 1993; faculty rsch. lectr. U. Calif., Riverside, 2000; cons. in field. Contbr. articles to profl. jours. NIH and NSF grantee. Fellow AAAS, Chem. Inst. Can. (Fisher Sci. Lecture award 1984); mem. Am. Chem. Soc., Internat. Soc. Magnetic Resource. Avocations: reading, gardening, music. Home: 5162 Palisade Cir Riverside CA 92506-1521 Office: U Calif Dept Chemistry Riverside CA 92521-0001 Office Phone: 951-827-5649. Business E-Mail: dallas.rabenstein@ucr.edu.

RABIN, ROBERT L., law educator; b. 1939; BS, Northwestern U., 1960, JD, 1963, PhD in Polit. Sci., 1967. Bar: Ill. 1963. Asst. prof. law U. Wis., Madison, 1966-69, assoc. prof., 1969-70; vis. assoc. prof. Stanford Law Sch., Calif., 1970-71, assoc. prof. Calif., 1971-73, prof. Calif., 1973-84, A. Calder Mackay prof. Calif., 1984—. Sr. environ. fellow EPA, 1979—80; vis. fellow Centre Sociolegal Studies Wolfson Coll., Oxford U., 1982; vis. prof. Harvard Law Sch., 1987—88, NYU Law Sch., 1999—2000; Jack N. Pritzker disting. vis. prof. Northwestern Sch. Law., 1994. Author: Perspectives on the Administrative Process, 1979, Perspective on Tort Law, 1995; co-author: Smoking Policy: Law, Politics and Culture, 1993, Cases and Materials on Tort Law and Alternatives, 2001, Regulating Tobacco, 2001, Torts Stories, 2006. Fellow, Ctr. Advanced Study Behavioral Scis., 1982—83. Office: Stanford Law Sch Crown Quadrangle 559 Nathan Abbott Way Stanford CA 94305-8610 Office Phone: 650-723-3073. Business E-Mail: rrabin@stanford.edu.

RABINOVITCH, BENTON SEYMOUR, chemist, educator emeritus; b. Montreal, Que., Can., Feb. 19, 1919; came to U.S., 1946; s. Samuel and Rachel (Schachter) R.; m. Marilyn Werby, Sept. 18, 1949; children: Peter Samuel, Ruth Anne, Judith Nancy, Frank Benjamin; m. Flora Reitman, 1980. BSc, McGill U., 1939, PhD, 1942; DSc (hon.), Technion Inst., Haifa, 1991. Postdoctoral fellow Harvard, 1946-48; Milton fellow, 1949—50; mem. faculty U. Wash., Seattle, 1948—, prof. chemistry, 1957—, prof. chemistry emeritus, 1985—. Cons. and/or mem. sci. adv. panels, coms. NSF, Nat. Acad. Scis.-NRC; adv. com. phys. chemistry Nat. Bur. Standards. Author Antique Silver Servers, 1991, Contemporary Silver, 2000, Contemporary Silver Part II, 2005; co-author: Physical Chemistry, 1964; former editor: Ann. Rev. Phys. Chemistry; mem. editorial bd.: Internat. Jour. Chem. Kinetics, Rev. of Chem. Intermediates, Jour. Phys. Chemistry, Jour. Am. Chem. Soc. Served to capt. Canadian Army, 1942-46, ETO. Nat. Research Council Can. fellow, 1940-42; Royal Soc. Can. Research fellow, 1946-47; Milton Research fellow Harvard, 1948; Guggenheim fellow, 1961; vis. fellow Trinity Coll., Oxford, 1971; recipient Sigma Xi award for original research, Debye award in phys. chemistry, 1984, Polanyi medal Royal Soc. Chemistry; named hon. liveryman Worshipful Co. of Goldsmiths, London, 2000. Fellow Am. Phys. Soc., Am. Acad. Arts and Scis., Royal Soc. London; mem. Am. Chem. Soc. (past chmn. Puget Sound sect., past chmn. phys. chemistry divsn., assoc. editor jour.), Faraday Soc. Achievements include rsch. in Unimolecular gas phase reaction and history and design of silver implements. Home: 12530 42nd Ave NE Seattle WA 98125-4621 Office: Univ Washington Chemistry Box 351700 Seattle WA 98195 Office Fax: 206-285-8665.

RABINOVITZ, JOEL, lawyer, educator; b. 1939; AB, Cornell U., 1960; LLB, Harvard U., 1963. Bar: N.Y. 1963, Calif. 1981. Asst. prof. U. Fla., Gainesville, Fla., 1966—68; vis. assoc. prof. UCLA, 1968—69, acting prof., 1969—72, prof., 1972—79; vis. prof. NYU, 1976; dep. Internat. Tax Counsel, Dept. Treasury, 1980—81; ptnr. with Irell & Manella LLP, LA, 1981—. Office: Irell & Manella LLP 1800 Avenue Of The Stars Los Angeles CA 90067-4212

RABOW, MICHAEL WARREN, physician, educator; b. June 30, 1965; BA, Harvard U., 1987; MD, U. Calif., San Francisco, 1993. Diplomate Am. Bd. Internal Medicine. Resident in primary care U. Calif., San Francisco, 1993-96, fellow in gen. medicine, 1996-97, asst. prof. medicine, 1997—. Author: (with others) Current Medical Diagnosis and Treatment, 1998; contbr. articles to profl. jours. Office: U Calif San Francisco 1701 Divisadero St Ste 500 San Francisco CA 94115-3011

RABUCK, DONNA FONTANAROSE, English writing educator; b. Edison, NJ, Aug. 2, 1954; d. Arthur Thomas and Shirley Gertrude (Golub) Fontanarose; m. John Frederick Rabuck, July, 28, 1973; 1 child, Miranda Rose. BA in Eng., Rutgers U., 1976, MA in Eng. Lit., 1980, PhD in Eng. Lit., 1990. Prof. writing Pima C. C., Tucson, 1981-86; asst. dir. writing skills program U. Ariz., Tucson, 1983—. Asst. dir. summer inst. writing U. Ariz., Tucson, 1985—, dir. grad. writing inst., 1996—; adj. faculty Pima C. C., Tucson, 1992-95. Author: The Other Side of Silence: Performing Heroinism in the Victorian Novel, 1990, Writing Ctr. Perspectives, 1995; editor: Writing is Thinking: Collected Writings of the Summer Inst., 1985—. Founder, pres. Miles East-West Neighborhood Assn., Tucson, 1983—; dir. Ctr. for Sacred Feminine, Tucson, 1995—; program coord. U. Ariz. Arts and Scis. Minority Retention Program, 1988-93. Rutgers Alumni scholar, 1972-76; Bevier fellow Rutgers U., 1976-78. Mem. Intercollegiate Writing Com. (task force), Commn. Cultural Thinking (task force), Nat. Coun. Tchrs. Eng. Avocations: feminist scholarship, women's rituals, yoga, hiking, meditation. Home: 1115 N Camino Miraflores Tucson AZ 85745-1612 Office: Univ Ariz Writing Skills Program 1201 E Helen St Tucson AZ 85719-4407 E-mail: drabuck@u.arizona.edu.

RABY, WILLIAM LOUIS, writer, consultant; b. Chgo., July 16, 1927; s. Gustave E. and Helen (Burgess) R.; m. Norma Claire Schreiner, Sept. 8, 1956 (dec. Feb. 2006); children: Burgess, Marianne, Marlene. BSBA, Northwestern U., 1949; MBA, U. Ariz., 1961, PhD, 1971. Ptnr. VAR CPA Firms, 1950-76, Touche Ross & Co., NYC, 1977-87; ret. ptnr. Deloitte & Touche, NYC. Pres. Ariz. State Bd. Accountancy, 1993-94; mem. Ariz. State Bd. Tax Appeals, 1994-2006, chmn., 1997-99, 2003-05; prof. acctg. emeritus Ariz. State U.; columnist Tax Notes mag., Arlington, Va., 1990—; cons. on video and audio tax edn. tapes Bisk Pub. Co., 1992—. Author: The Income Tax and Business Decisions, 1964, Building and Maintaining a Successful Tax Practice, 1964, The Reluctant Taxpayer, 1970, Tax Practice Management, 1974, Introduction to Federal Taxation, annually, 1980-91, Tax Practice Management: Client Servicing, 1986; editor: Raby Report on Tax Practice, 1986-96, PPC Guide To Successful Tax Practice, 1991; mem. editorial adv. bd. Practical Tax Strategies; contbr. articles to profl. jours. Mem. AICPA (chmn. fed. tax divsn. 1980-83, v.p. 1983-84, coun. 1983-90), Tax Ct. Bar. Presbyterian (elder, United Presbyn. Ch. chmn. adv. coun. on ch. and soc. 1979-81). Office: PO Box 26846 Tempe AZ 85285-6846 Home Phone: 480-756-4333; Office Phone: 480-967-1501. Personal E-mail: rabyw@aol.com.

RACHELEFSKY, GARY STUART, medical educator; b. NYC, 1942; BS, Columbia Coll., 1963. Intern Bellevue Hosp. Ctr., NYC, 1967-68; resident in pediatrics Johns Hopkins Hosp., 1968-70, Ctr. Disease Control, 1970-72; fellow UCLA Med. Ctr., 1972-74; prof. allergy and immunology, dir. exec. care UCLA, Ctr. Asthma, Allergy and Immunology. Fellow Am. Acad. Allergy, Asthma and Immunology (bd. dirs., past pres.). Mailing: 14933 Alva Dr Pacific Palisades CA 90272 Office Phone: 310-754-6884. Personal E-mail: rachruss@ix.netcom.com.

RACINE, SCOTT H., lawyer; b. Chgo. BA, Bradley U., 1972; JD cum laude, Pepperdine U., 1978; LLM in Tax., NYU, 1979. Bar: Calif. 1978, US Dist. Ct. (ctrl., so. districts) Calif., US Ct. of Appeals (9th cir.), US Tax Ct., US Ct. of Claims. Law clk. Judge William M. Drennen US Tax Ct., 1979—80; shareholder tax specialty firm, LA; ptnr., chair, tax practice group LA Akin Gump Strauss Hauer & Feld LLP, LA. Adj. prof. law Pepperdine Univ., 1980—, Univ. San Diego, 1983—87, Loyola Univ., 2000—. Student writings editor Pepperdine Law Rev., 1976—78; author: numerous articles for profl. publs. Bd. visitors Pepperdine Univ. Sch. Law; bd. adv. Loyola Univ. Sch. Law; planning com. Univ. So. Calif. Tax Inst. Mem.: ABA (sect. on tax.), Calif. Bar Assn. (sect. on tax.), LA County Bar Assn. (sect. on tax.). Office: Akin Gump Strauss Hauer & Feld LLP Ste 2400 2029 Century Pk E Los Angeles CA 90067-3012 Office Phone: 310-229-1059. Office Fax: 310-229-1001. Business E-Mail: sracine@akingump.com.

RACITI, CHERIE, artist; b. Chgo., June 17, 1942; d. Russell J. and Jacque (Crimmins) R. Student, Memphis Coll. Art, 1963-65; BA in Art, San Francisco State U., 1968; M.F.A., Mills Coll., 1979. Assoc. prof. art San Francisco State U., 1984—89, prof., 1989—2007, prof. emeritus, 2007—. Lectr. Calif. State U., Hayward, 1974, San Francisco Art Inst., 1978; mem. artist com. San Francisco Art Inst., 1974-85, sec., 1980-81. One woman shows include U. Calif., Berkeley, 1972, Nicholas Wilder Gallery, L.A., 1975, San Francisco Art Inst., 1977, Marianne Deson Gallery, Chgo., 1980, Site 375, San Francisco, 1989, Reese Bullen Gallery, Humboldt State U., Arcata, Calif., 1990, Mills Coll. Art Mus., Oakland, Calif., 1998; group shows include Whitney Mus. Art, 1975, San Francisco Sci. Fiction, The Clocktower, N.Y.C., Otis-Parsons Gallery, Los Angeles, 1984-85, San Francisco Art Inst., 1985, Artists Space, N.Y.C., 1988, Angles Gallery, Santa Monica, 1987, Terrain Gallery, San Francisco, 1992, Ctr. for the Arts, San Francisco, 1993, Santa Monica Coll., 1998, 25/25 25th Anniversary Exhbn., So. Exposure Gallery, San Francisco, 1999, Santa Cruz Mus., 2003, Thacher Gallery U. San Francisco, 2004. Bd. dirs. New Langton Arts, 1988-92. Eureka fellow Fleishhacker Found., San Francisco, Va.Ctr. for Creative Arts fellow, Amherst, Va., 2005; recipient Adaline Kent award San Francisco Art Inst., 1976, Djerassi resident, 1994, Tyrone Guthrie Ctr. resident, Ireland, 1995, Millay Colony for Arts resident 1999, Juror's award Artadia San Francisco.

RADANOVICH, GEORGE P., United States Representative from California; b. Mariposa, Calif., June 20, 1955; s. George F. and Joan Radanovich; m. Ethie Weaver; 1 child, George King. BS in Agr. Bus. Mgmt., Calif. State Polytechnic U., San Luis Obispo, 1978. Owner Radanovich Winery, 1986—2004; mem. Mariposa County Bd. Suprs., 1989—92, US Congress from 19th Calif. dist., Washington, 1994—, asst. whip, 1994—, mem. energy & commerce com., chmn. natural parks subcom., water/power subcom. Vice chair Congl. Competitiveness Caucus; mem. Scouting Caucus, Nat. Guard & Reserve Components Caucus, Nat. Environment Policy Act Task Force, Methamphetamine Caucus, Ho. Energy Action Team, Horticulture Caucus, Heart & Stroke Caucus, Forest Task Force, Forest Caucus, Fire Services Caucus, Diabetes Caucus, Courthouse Caucus, Armenian Caucus,

Western Caucus, 1997—2005; co-chair Congl. Wine Caucus, 1997—2005, Congl. Croatian Caucus, 2005. Mem. Calif. Agrl. Leadership Found., 1990—92. Mem.: Mariposa C. of C., Calif. Farm Bureau, Calif. Assn. Wine Grape Growers, Wine Inst., Mariposa Rotary. Republican. Roman Catholic. Office: US Ho Reps 438 Cannon Ho Office Bldg Washington DC 20515-0519 Office Phone: 202-225-4540.

RADCLIFFE, ALBERT E., judge; b. 1947; BA in History, U. Oreg., 1969, JD, 1972. Bar: Oreg. 1972, U.S. Dist. Ct. Oreg. 1973, U.S. Ct. Appeals (9th cir.) 1983. Pvt. practice, 1973-86; judge U.S. Bankruptcy Ct. Oreg., Eugene, 1986—2001, chief bankruptcy judge, 2001—. Vis. bankruptcy judge Western Dist. Wash., 1992; pro-tem bankruptcy judge Bankruptcy Appellate Panel for 9th Cir., 1998, 96, 93. Mem. Fed. Bar Assn. (hon.), N.W. Bankruptcy Inst. Planning Com., Lane County Bar Assn. (bankruptcy subcom. chmn. 1993-94), Tau Kappa Epsilon. Office: Us Bankruptcy Court 405 E 8th Ave Ste 2600 Eugene OR 97401-2725

RADCLIFFE, MARK FLOHN, lawyer; b. Dayton, Ohio, Mar. 11, 1952; Cert. of completion, Sorbonne, Paris, 1972; BS in Chem. magna cum laude, U. Mich., 1974; JD, Harvard U., 1981. Bar: Calif. 1982. Law clk. to chief judge U.S. Dist. Ct. (so. dist.) Calif., San Diego, 1981-82; assoc. Brobeck, Phleger & Harrison, San Francisco, 1982-86; assoc. to ptnr. Gray Cary Ware & Freidenrich, Palo Alto, Calif., 1986—2004; ptnr. DLA Piper, 2004—, co-chmn. Technology and Sourcing Group Ea. Palo Alto, Calif., 2005—. Gen. counsel The Open Source Initiative; chair com. C for reviewing GPLv3. Mem. editorial bd.: Computer Lawyer, 1988—, Cyberspace Lawyer; mem. adv. bd. BNA Electronic Commerce & Law Report, Global Intellectual Property Asset Mgmt. Report; country corr. European Intellectual Property Rev.; editor-in-chief Jour. Internet Law; co-author Multimedia Law, Internet Law and Business; contbr. articles to profl. law jours. Lt. (j.g.) USNR, 1974-77. Recipient Disting. Alumni award, Harvard Univ., 1998; named one of Am. 100 Most Influential Lawyers, Nat. Law Jour., 1997, World's Leading Trademark Lawyers, Expert Guide, 2003, No. Calif Super Lawyer & one of Top 100 No. Calif. IP Lawyers, San Francisco mag., 2004, Best Lawyers in Am., 2005—06, Am. Leading Lawyers for Bus., Chanbers USA, 2006. Mem. ABA (chmn. subcom. 1985-88), Am. Intellectual Property Law Assn., Internat. Trademark Assn., San Francisco Bar Assn. (chmn. computer law sect. 1985-86), Computer Law Assn. (dir.), Licensing Exec. Soc., South Bay Trademark Lawyers Assn. (founder), Harvard Club. Office: DLA Piper 2000 University Ave Palo Alto CA 94303 Office Phone: 650-833-2266. Office Fax: 650-833-2001. Business E-Mail: mark.radcliffe@dlapiper.com.

RADEBAUGH, ALAN PAINE, artist; b. Boston, May 2, 1952; s. John Franklin and Dorothy (Paine) R.; m. Ann Harrison Craig, Feb. 13, 1981 (div. 1987); m. Karen Rae Olson, Dec. 3, 1991. Student, Coll. Wooster, 1970-72; BFA, U. N.Mex., 1996. Visual artist, Albuquerque, 1981—. Juror N.Mex. Ann. Woodworkers Show, Santa Fe, 1984, U. N.Mex Fine Arts Alumni Show, 2000; cons. Albuquerque Conv. and Visitors Bur., 1992; curator 22 exhbns. Outpost Performance Space, Albuquerque, 1997-98. One-man shows include Artichoke/Dartmouth St. Gallery, Albuquerque, 1991, St. Michael Episcopal. Ch., Albuquerque, 1993, 1st Unitarian Ch., Albuquerque, 1994, Firehouse Gallery, Del Rio, Tex., 1997, Outpost Performance Space Albuquerque, 1998, Peter Eller Gallery, Albuquerque, 1998, James Reid Ltd., Santa Fe, 1997, 1999, 2004, U. N.Mex., 1999, 2007, Coleman Gallery, Albuquerque, 2001, 05-06, 516 Magnifico Artspace, Albuquerque, 2002, U. N.Mex., 2007, Open Mind Space, Albuquerque, 2009; group shows include McNeese State U., 1991, Mus. Albuquerque, 1991, 2002, 04-05, Ctrl. Mo. State U., 1991, Cork Gallery, Avery Fisher Hall, Lincoln Ctr., 1992, EMU Gallery, U. Oreg., 1992, San Francisco State U., 1992, Coll. Santa Fe, 1993, 95, Museo Regional U., Chihuahua City, Mex., 1994, San Bernardino County Mus., 1995, Kanagawa Kenmin Gallery, Yokohama, Japan, 1995, 97, Washington & Jefferson Coll., 1996, SITE, Santa Fe 1997, U. N.Mex., 1997, 2000, Coos Art Mus., 1998, San Diego Art Inst., 1999, William Rainey Harper Coll., Ill., 2000, Delaware Ctr. for Contemporary Art, 2002, Butler Inst. Am. Art, 2003, Internat. Mus. Art, Tex., 2004, Holter Mus. of Art, Mont., 2004, Hi Desert Mus. Calif., 2005, Portland Mus. of Art, Maine, 2005; represented in permanent collections including Albuquerque Mus. Fine Arts, Mus. N.Mex., N.Mex. State Capitol Art Collection, U. N.Mex. Mus., Washington & Jefferson Coll., Coll. Wooster, Ohio State U., Portland Mus. Art; prin. works include model of mus. and exhibition spaces N.Mex. Mus. Natural History, 1983, clay miniatures Archeol. Mus. Andros, Greece, 1983, graphic image Nat. Med. Assn. Dartmouth Med. Sch., 1993; appeared in Fine Woodworking Design Book III, 1983, Capitol Art Foundation Collection: New Mexico, 1998, Abstract Art: New Mexico Artist Series, 2003, American Art Collector, 2006, Alan paine radebaugh Mass: Of our World, Catalog of Work, 1977. Mem. U. N.Mex. Coll. Fine Arts Alumni Bd., 1998-, Institutional Review Bd. Presby Terian Hosp., 2005-. Artist's grantee, Vt. Studio Ctr., 1997, Gushul Studio, U. Lethbridge, Alberta, Canada, 2001, 2002; recipient 1st pl. in design N.Mex. Ann. Woodworkers Show, Santa Fe, 1982, Merit award Paxton Co., Albuquerque, 1983, Albuquerque United Artists, 1983, Purchase award Albuquerque Mus. Fine Arts, 1984, hon. mention award Art Ctr., Los Alamos, N.Mex., 1993, Oliver Meml. award, 1994, Albuquerque Bravos award, 2008. Avocations: music, squash, golf. Office: PO Box 37112 Albuquerque NM 87176 Office Phone: 505-268-1647. E-mail: alan@radebaughfineart.com.

RADLO, EDWARD JOHN, lawyer, mathematician; b. Pawtucket, RI, Mar. 7, 1946; s. Edward Zygmund and Sue Mary (Borek) Radlo; m. Patricia Jackson, Feb. 22, 1989; children: Heather Sue, Graeme Michael, Connor Andrew. BS, MIT, 1967; JD, Harvard U., 1972. Bar: Calif. 1972, U.S. Dist. Ct. (no. dist.) Calif. 1972, R.I. 1973, U.S. Patent Office 1973, Can. Patent Office 1974. Staff. dir. Atty. Gen.'s Adv. Commn. on Juvenile Code Revision, Boston, 1970—72; law clk. R.I. Supreme Ct., 1972—73; patent atty. Honeywell Info. Systems, Waltham, Mass., 1973—74, Varian Assoc., Palo Alto, Calif., 1974—78, Ford Aerospace Corp., 1978—83, patent counsel, 1983—90; ptnr. Fenwick & West LLP, Mountain View, Calif., 1991—2004, Sonnenschein Nath & Rosenthal LLP, San Francisco, 2004—. Lectr. U. Calif., San Jose State U., U. Santa Clara, 1975—78. Organizer So. Peninsula Emergency Comm. Sys., 1970; mem. Los Altos Hills (Calif.) Emergency Comm. Com, Lawyers' Alliance for Nuclear Arms Control, 1982—83, Environ. Def. Fund, 1979—; bd. dir. Tomahawks Lacrosse Club, Menlo Park, Calif., 2002—05; bd. dirs. No. Calif. Jr. Lacrosse Assn., Corte Madera, Calif., 2004—05. Lt. (jg.) USPHS, 1967—69. Mem.: ABA, Calif. Bar (intellectual property sect.), Silicon Valley Intellectual Property Law Assn., Assn. Radio Amateurs of So. New England Inc. (sec. 1962—63), No. Calif. Contest Club (pres. 1984—85), Sigma Xi. Home: 28040 Elena Rd Los Altos Hills CA 94022-2454 Office: Sonnenschein Nath & Rosenthal LLP 525 Market St San Francisco CA 94105

RADZIK, ALBIN F., federal analyst, military consultant; b. Berwyn, Ill., Oct. 21, 1947; s. Albin F. and Evelyn Clara Radzik; children: Melanie Rose, Amy Marie. BS, Northwestern U.; MBA, Georgetown U., 1994; HHD (hon.), Kalinin U., St. Petersburg, 1995. Analyst U.S. Govt., Washington, 1976—, mil. cons., 1978—2001. Author: (poetry) Love and Distance, 1967 (Hole Creative Writing award, 1967). Mem. and vol. Cambodian Land Mine Relief Org.; vol. Chechnya Refugee Org.; open space com. City of Redlands, Calif., 1985—86. Served to capt. US Army, 1966—82. Decorated Bronze Star for Valor, Purple Heart, Disting. Svc. Cross, Army Commendation medal for valor, Air medal for valor, Combat Inf. badge, Rnager badge Spl. Forces Grad., Parachutist badge, hon. capt. Russian Army; recipient Cold War Recognition cert., U.S. Sec. Def., 2003, cert. Special Merit, City Police Dept., Redwood City, Calif., Cert. Appreciation, Belmont, Calif., Police Dept. Mem.: MENSA, VFW, Royal Order of the Purple Heart. Roman Catholic. Personal E-mail: aradzik@netzero.net.

RAEBER, JOHN ARTHUR, architect, construction consultant; b. St. Louis, Nov. 24, 1947; s. Arthur William and Marie (Laux) R. AA, Jefferson Coll., 1968; AB, Washington U., 1970, MArch, 1973. Registered architect, Calif., Mo.; cert. constrn. specifier; cert. Nat. Coun. Arch. Specification writer Hellmuth, Obata & Kassabaum, St. Louis, 1973-78, constrn. administr., 1978-79; mgr. of specifications Gensler & Assocs., San Francisco, 1979-82; ind. constrn. specifier San Francisco, 1982—. Adj. prof. architecture Calif. Coll. Arts and Crafts, San Francisco, 1986—; access code advisor Constrn. Industry & Owners, 1982—; spkr., instr. seminars orgns., univs., 1982—; mem. Calif. State Bldg. Standards Commn. Accessibility Adv. Panel, Sacramento, 1981, Calif. Subcom. Rights of Disabled Adv. Panel, Sacramento, 1993; cons. Nat. Inst. Bldg. Scis., 1996—. Author: CAL/ABL: Interpretative Manual to California's Access Barriers Laws, 1982; co-author: (with Peter S. Hopf) Access for the Handicapped, 1984; columnist Constrn. Specifier Mag., 1988-95. Vol. Calif. Office Emergency Svcs. Safety Assessment, Sacramento, 1991—. Fellow AIA (San Francisco chpt. codes com., Calif. coun. codes and standards com., nat. masterspec rev. com. 1982-84, nat. codes com. corr.), Contrns. Specifications Inst. (cert., columnist newsletter San Francisco chpt. 1984-95, Ben John Small award for Outstanding Stature as practicing specifications writer 1994, pres. St. Louis chpt. 1978-79, pres. San Francisco chpt. 1993-94, tech. com., edn. com., publs. com., Specifications Proficiency award San Francisco chpt. 1989, Tech. Commendation award 1987); mem. Specifications Cons. in Ind. Practice (nat. pres. 1990-92, nat. sec./treas. 1988-90), Internat. Conf. Bldg. Officials, Phi Theta Kappa. Avocations: history, anthropology, science fiction. Home and Office: 3962 26th St San Francisco CA 94131-2002

RAEBURN, ANDREW HARVEY, performing arts consultant; b. London, July 22, 1933; arrived in Canada, 1993, permanent resident, 2007; s. Walter Augustus Leopold and Dora Adelaide Harvey (Williams) Raeburn. BA in History, King's Coll., Cambridge U., 1958, MA, 1962; diploma in music performance (hon.), Mt. Royal Coll., 1998; LLD (hon.), U. Calgary, 2005. Mus. dir. Argo Record Co., London, 1959—64; asst. to music dir., program editor Boston Symphony Orch., 1964—73; dir. artists and repertory New World Records, NYC, 1975—79; artistic adminstr. Detroit Symphony Orch., 1979—82; exec. dir. Van Cliburn Found. Inc., Ft. Worth, 1982—85; performing arts cons., 1985—93; exec. v.p. The Peter Pan Children's Fund, 1990—91; exec. dir. Esther Honens Internat. Piano Competition Found., 1993—95, pres., 1995—99, vice chmn., artistic dir., 1999—2001, pres., artistic dir., 2001—04; freelance cons., recording prodr. Calgary, Canada, 2004—. Cons. music; radio and TV commentator; mem. faculty Boston U., 1966-67; condr. New World String Orch., 1978; v.p. World Fedn. Internat. Music Competitions, 2003-06. Author record liner notes, Argo, RCA, Time-Life records, 1960-79, program notes, Boston Symphony Orch., 1968-73. Served with Royal Arty. Brit. Army, 1952-55; founding dean Prague Mozart Acad. 1992-93. Recipient Lifetime Achievement award, World Fedn. Internat. Music Competitions, 2006. Home and Office: 702 235 15th Ave SW Calgary AB Canada T2R 0P6 Office Phone: 403-263-9939. Personal E-mail: araeburn@telus.net, ar@andrewraeburn.com.

RAEDER, MYRNA SHARON, lawyer, educator; b. NYC, Feb. 4, 1947; d. Samuel and Estelle (Auslander) R.; m. Terry Oliver Kelly, July 13, 1975; children: Thomas Oliver, Michael Lawrence. BA, Hunter Coll., 1968; JD, NYU, 1971; LLM, Georgetown U., 1975. Bar: N.Y. 1972, D.C. 1972, Calif. 1972. Spl. asst. U.S. atty. U.S. Atty's Office, Washington, 1972-73; asst. prof. U. San Fransisco Sch. Law, 1973-75; assoc. O'Melveny & Myers, LA, 1975-79; assoc. prof. Southwestern U. Sch. Law., LA, 1979-82, prof., 1983—, Irwin R. Buchalter prof. law, 1990, Paul E. Treusch prof. law, 2002; mem. faculty Nat. Judicial Coll., 1993—. Prettyman fellow Georgetown Law Ctr., Washington, 1971—73. Author: Federal Pretrial Practice, 3d edit., 2000; co-author: Evidence, State and Federal Rules in a Nutshell, 4th edit., 2003, Evidence, Cases, Materials and Problems, 3d edit., 2006; co-editor: Acheiveing Justice: Freeing the Innocent, Convicting the Guilty, 2006. Named to Alumni Hall of Fame, Hunter Coll., 2005. Mem.: ABA (trial evidence com. 1980—, criminal justice sect. 1994—97, adv. to nat. conf. commrs. uniform state laws drafting com. 1996—99, vice-chair planning 1997—98, chair elect 1997—98, chair 1998—99, mem. mag. bd. 2000—, co-chair ad hoc innocence com. 2002—, mem. youth at risk commn. 2006—07, mem. litig. sect. 1980—, Margaret Brent Women Lawyers of Achievement award 2002), Am. Law Inst., Assn. Am. Law Schs. (chair women in legal edn. sect. 1982, com. on sects. 1984—87, chair elect evidence sect. 1996, chair 1997), Nat. Assn. Women Lawyers (bd. dirs. 1991—98, pres.-elect 1993, pres. 1994—96), Women Lawyers Assn. LA (coord. mothers support group 1987—96, bd. dirs., Ernestine Stallhutt award 2003), Am. Bar Found. (life), Order of Coif, Phi Beta Kappa. Office: Southwestern U Sch Law 675 S Westmoreland Ave Los Angeles CA 90005-3905 Business E-Mail: mraeder@swlaw.edu.

RAESE, DAVID SENNA, aerospace and mass properties engineer, consultant; b. Morgantown, W.Va. s. John Thomas and Joan Marie (Keeney) Raese. BSCE, Washington State U., Pullman, 1981, BS in Gen. Sci., 1981; attended, U. Bonn, Germany, 1978—79. Cert. profl. engr., Wash., 1995. Engr. Boeing Comml. Airplanes, Everett, Wash., 1981—85, Renton, 1981—85, Boeing Space and Comm., Huntsville, Ala., 1985—87; engring. team leader Boeing Missile Sys. Divsn., Kent, Wash., 1987—91, Boeing Comml. Space Co., Tukwila, 1997—99; engr., auditor, cons. Boeing Helicopters Divsn., Ridley Park, Pa., 1991—93; engring. team leader, cons. Boeing Def. and Space Divsn., Kent, Wash., 1993—97, Boeing Integrated Def. Sys., Kent, 1999—. Mass properties engring. mentor Boeing Ed Wells Mentoring Program NW Region, 2005—; tech. focal cons., Boeing assoc. tech. fellow N.W. Region, 2006. Contbr. chapters to books. Mem.: SAR, Soc. Automotive Engrs., Soc. Allied Weight Engrs., Inc., Am. Inst. Aeronautics and Astronautics (sr.), Descendants of Knights of Garter, Friends of St. George's, Nat. Hugenot Soc. Wash., Nat. Soc. Magna Charta Dames and Barons. Independent. Presbyterian. Avocations: travel, hiking, art, history. Office: The Boeing Co PO Box 3999 Seattle WA 98124-2499 Business E-Mail: david.s.raese@boeing.com.

RAFFIN, THOMAS ALFRED, physician, educator, venture capitalist; b. San Francisco, Jan. 25, 1947; s. Bennett L. and Carolyn M. Raffin; m. Michele Raffin, June 19, 1987; children: Ross Daniel, Jason Bennett, Nicholas Ethan; m. Margaret Raffin, June 23, 1969; 1 child, Elizabeth S. AB in Biol. Sci., Stanford Med. Sch., 1968, MD, 1973. Cert. Am. Bd. Internal Medicine, diplomate Am. Bd. Pulmonary Medicine, Am. Bd. Critical Care Medicine. Med. resident Peter Bent Brigham Hosp., 1973-75; fellow in respiratory medicine sch. medicine Stanford U., Stanford, Calif., 1975-78, med. fiberoptic bronchoscopy service dir. med. ctr., 1978—, acting asst. prof. sch. medicine, 1978-80, assoc. dir. med. ctr. intensive care units, med. dir. dept. respiratory therapy hosp., 1978—, assoc. prof. medicine sch. medicine, 1986-95, chief divsn. pulmonary and critical care, 1990—2004, prof. medicine sch. of medicine, 1995—, Colleen and Robert Haas emeritus prof. medicine/biomed. ethics, 1999—; dir. emeritus Stanford U. Ctr. for Biomed. Ethics, 1989—; co-founder Rigel Pharms., Inc. Co-founder, gen. ptnr. Telegraph Hill Ptnrs., San Francisco, 2002—; bd. dirs. New Link Genetics, BioProtection Services, AngioScore, Pneum Rx, LDR Holding, Confirma, Freedom Innovations. Author: Intensive Care: Facing the Critical Choices, 1988; contbr. articles to profl. jours. V.p. lung cancer com. No. Calif. Oncology Group, 1983—85; com. mem. NIH Workshop, 1984; pres. Raffin Family Found., San Francisco. Recipient award, Henry J. Kaiser Found., 1981, 1984, 1988, 1997, Arthur L. Bloomfield award, 1981. Fellow: ACP (rep. coun. subspecialty socs. 1986), Am. Coll. Chest Physicians (program com. mem. 1985—86); mem.: AAAS, Calif. Thoracic Soc., Soc. Critical Care Medicine, Calif. Med. Assn. (chmn. sect. chest diseases 1984—85), Santa Clara County Med. Soc., Santa Clara County Lung Assn., Am. Thoracic Soc., Am. Fedn. Clin. Rsch. Independent. Jewish. Avocations: painting, gardening, raising miniature donkeys, Nigerian dwarf goats. Office: Telegraph Hill Ptnrs 360 Post Ste 601 San Francisco CA 94108 also: Ctr Biomed Ethics Stanford U 701 Welch Rd Ste A1105 Palo Alto CA 94304-1709 Office Phone: 415-765-6980, 415-765-6985. Business E-Mail: tar@stanford.edu.

RAGAN, CHARLES RANSOM, lawyer; b. NYC, Aug. 13, 1947; s. Charles Alexander Jr.; children: Alexandra Watson, Madeline McCue. AB, Princeton U., 1969; JD, Fordham U., 1974. Bar: N.Y. 1975, U.S. Ct. Appeals (3d cir.) 1975, Calif. 1976, U.S. Ct. Appeals (9th cir.) 1976, U.S. Dist. Ct. (no. dist.) Calif. 1976, U.S. Supreme Ct. 1981, U.S. Dist. Ct. (so. dist.) N.Y. 1982, U.S. Ct. Appeals (2d cir.) 1984. Law clk. to Hon. R.J. Aldisert U.S. Ct. Appeals (3rd cir.), 1974-76; assoc. Pillsbury, Madison & Sutro, San Francisco, 1976-81, ptnr., 1982-97, Palo Alto, 1997-2000, Pillsbury Winthrop, Palo Alto, San Francisco, 2001—05; founder, ptnr. Redgrave Daley Ragan & Wagner, 2005—. Mem. exec. com. 9th Cir. Judicial Conf., 1987-91. Avocations: bicycling, swimming, sports. Office: Redgrave Daley Ragan & Wagner LLP 1750 Montgomery St San Francisco CA 94111 Home Phone: 415-264-1319; Office Phone: 612-455-4403, 415-954-7113. Business E-Mail: cragan@rdrw.com.

RAGAN, JAMES THOMAS, communications executive; b. San Diego, Mar. 15, 1929; m. Susan Held, Nov. 9, 1957; children: James, Maria, Carey, Andrew. BA, Oxford U., Eng., 1951, MA, 1955; elect. engring. vocat. cert., U. State of N.Y., 1954. With Gen. Electric Co., 1954-69; pres., chief operating officer Athena Communications Corp. subs. Gulf & Western Industries, Inc., NYC, 1969-74; v.p. broadcast services Western Union Telegraph Co., 1974-76, v.p. satellite services, 1976-82, pres. Western Union personal communications corp., v.p. communication systems group, 1982-85; pres. Associated Info. Services Corp., 1985-86; pres., dir. Bunting, Inc., 1985-88; ptnr. Pierce Kennedy Hearth, 1988-91; CEO Nat. Lang. Assocs. Lanarea Pub., Green Valley, Ariz., 1990—. Patentee recreational sports equipment; author: The Ultimate Diet, The First Alaskans, A Guide to the Geography of the Native Languages, Cultures, Their Communities, and Populations, 1996. Pres. Wilton Pop Warner Football League, Wilton, Conn., 1972—73. Maj. USMCR, 1952—54, Korea. Home: PO Box 1112 Green Valley AZ 85622 Office: Nat Lang Assocs PO Box 1112 Green Valley AZ 85622 Office Phone: 520-399-2294. Personal E-mail: jtragan@gmail.com.

RAGENT, BORIS, physicist; b. Cleve., Mar. 2, 1924; s. Samuel and Bertha (Lev) R.; m. Dorothy Kohn, Sept. 11, 1949; children: David Stefan, Lawrence Stanton, Jesse Ron. Student, Ohio State U., 1941—44; BSEE, Marquette U., 1944; PhD in Physics, U. Calif., Berkeley, 1953. Registered profl. engr., Calif. Engr. Victoreen Instrument Co., Cleve., 1946-48; engr., physicist Radiation Lab., U. Calif., Berkeley, 1948-53; physicist Livermore, Calif., 1953-56, Broadview Rsch. Corp., Burlingame, Calif., 1956-59, Vidya divsn. Itek Corp., Palo Alto, Calif., 1959-66, Ames Rsch. Ctr., NASA, Moffett Field, Calif., 1966-87, San Jose (Calif.) State U. Found., 1987-98. Lectr. Stanford U., U. Calif. Ext. Served in USNR, 1944-46. Mem. AAAS, Am. Phys. Soc., Optical Soc. Am., Am. Geophys. Union, Sigma Xi.

RAGGIO, WILLIAM JOHN, state legislator, lawyer; b. Reno, Oct. 30, 1926; s. William John and Clara M. (Cardelli) R.; m. Dorothy Brigman, August 15, 1948 (dec. Apr. 1998); children: Leslie Ann, Tracy Lynn, Mark William (dec.); m. Dale Checket, Apr. 27, 2003. Student, La. Poly. Inst., 1944-45, U. Okla., 1945-46; BA, U. Nev., 1948; JD, Boalt Hall Sch. Law, U. Calif., Berkeley, 1951. Bar: Nev. 1951, U.S. Supreme Ct. 1959. Atty., Reno and Las Vegas; asst. dist. atty. Washoe County, Nev., 1952-58; dist. atty., 1958—70; ptnr. Wiener, Goldwater, Galatz & Raggio, Ltd., 1971-72, Raggio, Walker & Wooster, Reno and Las Vegas, 1974-78, Raggio, Wooster & Lindell, 1978-92; sr. ptnr. Vargas & Bartlett, 1992-98, Jones-Vargas (formerly Vargas & Bartlett), 1998—. Coun. State Govts., 1972-75; v.p., dir. Archon Corp.; mem. legis. commn., Nev. State Senate, vice chmn. criminal law and adminstrn. com., majority fl. leader, 1987-07, minority fl. leader, 1977-81, 82-87, 91, 2009, mem. Dist. Washoe 3, 1973—. Mem. Nev. Am. Revolutionary Bicentennial Commn., 1975-81; mem. Republican State Cen. Com.; past nat. chmn., current dir. Am. Legislative Exchange Council, dir. Sierra Health Svcs., 1983-2006; republican candidate for U.S. Senate, 1970. Served with USNR, 1944-46; to 2d lt. USMCR, 1946-47. Named Young Man of Yr., Reno-Sparks Jr. C. of C., 1959, Alumnus of Yr., U. Nev. Reno, 1999, Civic Leader of Yr., Greater Reno C. of C., Disting. Eagle Scout,

1989; named to Jr. Achievement of Nev. Hall of Fame, 1999, Reg. Trans. Commn. Hall of Fame; recipient Disting. Nevadan award, 1968, Fellows award The Salvation Army, Torch of Liberty award The Anti-Defamation League, SIR award Assoc. Gen. Contractors, 1995, Outstanding Svc. award Airport Authority of Washoe County, Pres.'s medal UNLV, 2000. Fellow Am. Bd. Criminal Lawyers; mem. ABA (state chmn. jr. bar conf. 1957-60, ho. dels.) Am. Judicature Soc., Am. Coll. Trail Lawyers, Am. Bd. Trial Advocates, Am. Inns of Ct., Nat. (nat. pres. 1967-68; named Outstanding Prosecutor 1965), Nev. State (sec. 1959, pres. 1960-63) Dist. Attys. Assn., NCJ (Brotherhood award 1965), Nev. Peace Officers Assn., Internat. Assn. Chiefs Police, Am. Leg. Exch. Coun. (nat. chmn. 1991-92, The William J. Raggio Excellence in Leadership Outstanding award 2007), Coll. of Edn. U. Nev. (life), Am. Legion, Elks, Lion Club, Prospectors Club, Alpha Tau Omega, Phi Alpha Delta. Republican. Roman Catholic. Office: Nevada State Senate 401 South Carson St Rm 2160 Carson City NV 89701 Home Phone: 775-786-5000; Office Phone: 775-684-1419. Office Fax: 775-786-1177. Business E-Mail: wraggio@sen.state.nv.us. E-mail: wjr@jonesvargas.com.*

RAGINSKY, NINA, artist; d. Bernard Boris and Helen Theresa R.; 1 child, Sofya Katrina. BA, Rutgers U., 1962; studied painting with, Roy Lichtenstein; studied sculpture with, George Segal; studied Art History with Allan Kaprow, Rutgers U. Freelance photographer Nat. Film Bd., Ottawa, Ont., Canada, 1963-81; instr. metaphysics Emily Car Coll. Art, Vancouver, B.C., Canada, 1973-81; painter Salt Spring Island, B.C., 1989—. Sr. artist, jury Can. Coun.; selected Can. rep. in Sweden for Sweden Now Mag., 1979; tchr., lectr. in field, 1973—. One woman shows include Vancouver Art Gallery, Victoria Art Gallery, Edmonton Art Gallery, Art Gallery Ont., San Francisco Mus. Art, Acadia U., Nancy Hoffman Gallery, N.Y.C., Meml. U. Newfoundland Art Gallery; exhibited in group shows at Rutgers U., 1962, Montreal Mus. Fine Arts, 1963, Nat. Film Bd., Ottawa, 1964, 65, 67, 70, 71, 76, 77, Internat. Salon Photography, Bordeaux, France, 1968, Nat. Gallery Ottawa, 1968, Eastman House, Rochester, N.Y., 1969, Vancouver Art Gallery, 1973, 80, Mural for Conf. Ctr. Ottawa, 1973, Field Mus., Chgo., 1976, Edmonton Art Gallery, 1978, 79, Walter Philips Gallery, 1979, Glenbow Mus. Gallery, 1979, Harbour Front Community Gallery, 1980, Hamilton Art Gallery, 1980, Musée Maisil de St. Lambert, 1981, Mendel Art Gallery, 1981, Dunlop Art Gallery, Regina, Can., 1981, Vancouver Art Gallery, 2001; represented in permanent collections Nat. Film Bd. Stills divsn., Ottawa, Ont., Banff (Alta.) Sch. Fine Arts, Nat Gallery Ottawa, Can., George Eastman House, Rochester, NY, Wadsworth Atheneum, Conn., Edmonton Art Gallery, U. Victoria, B.C., various pvt. collections. Bd. dirs. Island Watch, Salt Spring Island, B.C., 1993; founder, coord. Salt Spring Island Ecosys. Stewardship Project, 1993; founder, coord. Salt Spring Island Waterbird Watch Collective, 1994—. Decorated officer Order of Can., 1984; recipient Kees Vermeer award for edn. and conservation Simon Fraser U., 1997, Burns Bog award for environ. excellence, Vancouver, 2005. Mem.: Soc. for Advancement of Slow, Royal Can. Acad. Arts. Avocations: gardening, birding, subject of numerous publs. Home and Office: 272 Beddis Rd Salt Spring Island BC Canada V8K 2J1

RAHMAN, YUEH-ERH, biologist; b. Kwangtung, China, June 10, 1928; came to U.S., 1960; d. Khon and Kwei-Phan (Chan) Li; m. Aneesur Rahman, Nov. 3, 1956; 1 dau., Aneesa. BS, U. Paris, 1950; MD magna cum laude, U. Louvain, Belgium, 1956. Clin. and postdoctoral research fellow Louvain U., 1956-60; mem. staff Argonne (Ill.) Nat. Lab., 1960-72, biologist, 1972-81, sr. biologist, 1981-85; prof. pharmaceutics Coll. Pharmacy, U. Minn., Mpls., 1985—2002, prof. emeritus, 2002—, dir. grad. studies, pharmaceutics, 1989-92, head dept. pharmaceutics, 1991-96, 97-98. Vis. scientist State U. Utrecht, Netherlands, 1968-69; adj. prof. No. Ill. U., DeKalb, 1971-85; cons. NIH.; Mem. com. of rev. group, div. research grants NIH, 1979-83 Author; patentee in field. Recipient IR-100 award, 1976; grantee Nat. Cancer Inst., Nat. Inst. Arthritis, Metabolic and Digestive Diseases. Fellow Am. Assn. Pharm. Scientists; mem. AAAS, Am. Soc. Cell Biology, N.Y. Acad. Scis., Radiation Rsch. Soc., Assn. for Women in Sci. (1st pres. Chgo. area chpt. 1978-79). Unitarian Universalist. Home: 939 Coast Blvd Unit 6G La Jolla CA 92037-4115

RAICHLEN, FREDRIC, civil engineering educator, consultant; b. Balt., Oct. 12, 1932; s. Samuel Israel and Ethel Lee (Fribush) R.; m. Judith Kurschner, May 29, 1968; children: Robert, David. B of Engring., Johns Hopkins U., 1953; MSc, MIT, 1955, DSc, 1962. Registered profl. engr., Calif., N.J. Asst. prof., assoc. prof. civil engring. Calif. Inst. Tech., Pasadena, 1962-72, prof. civil engring., 1972—. Fellow, asst. prof. civil engring. MIT, 1962; consulting engr., Pasadena, 1962—. 1st lt. USAF, 1956-59. Fellow ASCE (recipient John C. Moffatt and Frank E. Nichol Harbor and Coastal Engring. award 1994); mem. NAE, Internat. Assn. Hydraluic Rschrs., Sigma Xi. Home: 2157 Homet Rd San Marino CA 91108-1325 Office: Calif Inst Tech Dept Civil Engring 138-78 1200 E California Blvd Pasadena CA 91125-0001

RAIKES, JEFFREY SCOTT, foundation administrator, former computer software company executive; b. Nebr., May 29, 1958; m. Tricia Raikes. BS in Engring. & Econ. Systems, Stanford U., 1980. Software devel. mgr. Apple Computer Inc., 1980—81; product mgr. Microsoft Corp., Redmond, Wash., 1981—84, dir., applications mktg., 1984, chief strategist, v.p. office sys., sr. v.p., Microsoft N.Am., 1993—98, group v.p. worldwide sales and support group, 1998—2000, group v.p. productivity & bus. services, 2000—04, group v.p., information worker bus. Redmond, Wash., 2004—05, pres., bus. software divsn., 2005—08; CEO The Bill & Melinda Gates Found., 2008—. Ptnr. Seattle Mariners Baseball Club, 1992—; mem. Sr. Leadership Team, Bus. Leadership Team, Microsoft Corp.; bd. dirs. Software publishers Assn., 1987—93, XO Comm. Inc., Washington Technology Ctr.; co-founder Raikes Family Found., 1997—. Trustee U. Nebr. Found., Wash. State U. Found.; leader Online Wash. State U. Initiative. Named to Computer Industry Hall of Fame, Computer Reseller News Mag., 2003. Mem.: Software Publishers Assn. (bd. dir. 1987—93, chmn. bd. (twice)). Office: The Bill & Melinda Gates Found PO Box 23350 Seattle WA 98102

RAILSBACK, SHERRIE LEE, management consultant, educator; b. Phila., Mar. 12, 1942; children: Ricky, Cindy. BBA, U. Ky., 1981. Sales mgr. Marjo Cosmetics, Ft. Wayne, Ind.; asst. dir. patient fin. svcs. Riverside Meth. Hosp., Columbus, Ohio; cons. Railsback and Assocs., Long Beach, Calif.; adoption search/reunion cons., educator Spirited Comm., L.A. Mem.: ASTD, NAFE, Book Publicists So. Calif., Nat. Spkrs. Assn. Office Phone: 562-822-3671. Personal E-mail: sherrierailsback@yahoo.com.

RAINER, WILLIAM GERALD, cardiac surgeon; b. Gordo, Ala., Nov. 13, 1927; s. Jamie Fleurnoy and Lula (Davis) R.; m. Lois Sayre, Oct. 7, 1950; children: Vickie, Bill, Julia, Leslie. Student, Emory U., Atlanta, Ga., 1943-44, U. Ala., 1944-45; MD, U. Tenn., Memphis, 1948; MS in Surgery, U. Colo., Denver, 1958. Diplomate Am. Bd. Surgery, Am. Bd. Thoracic Surgery. Intern Wesley Hosp., Chgo., 1949; gen. practice medicine Blue Island, Ill., 1950-52; resident Denver VA Hosp., 1954-59; practice medicine specializing in cardiac surgery Denver, 1960—. Bd. dirs. St. Joseph Hosp. Found., Denver; disting. clin. prof. surgery U. Colo. Health Sci. Ctr. Contbr. articles to profl. jours. Active Colo. Symphony Assn.; dir. emeritus St. Joseph Hosp. Found. Bd. Lt. U.S. Army, 1952-54. Decorated Bronze Star; recipient Disting. Alumnus award U. Tenn. Health Sci. Ctr., 1992, Florence Sabin award U. Colo. Health Sci. Ctr., 1998, Disting. Svc. award U. Colo., 2004, Outstanding Clin. Vol., U. Colo. Health Sci. Ctr., 2006, Disting. Svc. award We. Thoracic Surg. Assn., 2007. Mem. Soc. Thoracic Surgeons (sec. 1980-85, pres. 1989, historian 1992—, Disting. Svc. award 1998), Colo. Med. Soc. (pres. 1984-85), Denver Med. Soc. (pres. 1984), Denver Clin. and Pathology Soc. (pres. 1997), Am. Coll. Chest Physicians (pres. 1984), Am. Bd. Thoracic Surgeons (bd. dirs. 1982-88), Am. Surg. Assn., Am. Assn. Thoracic Surgery, Societé Internationale de Chirugie, Cactus Club. Avocations: photography, travel. Office: 2552 E Alameda 48 Denver CO 80209 Office Phone: 303-601-0532. Personal E-mail: wrainer@qwest.net.

RAINEY, RICHARD K., state legislator; b. Medford, Oreg. m. Sue McNulty; seven children. B in Adminstn. of Justice, Calif. State U., Sacramento; MPA, Golden Gate U. Police officer City of Compton, 1962; various positions ending with sheriff Contra Costa County Sheriff's Dept., 1978-92; mem. Calif. State Assembly, 1992-96, Calif. State Senate, 1996—, mem. local govt. com., vice chair pub. safety com. With USN. Recipient Policy award Calif. Child Devel. Adv. Com., Cornucopia award for legis. excellence Calif. Women for Agr., 1997, award for outstanding achievement in policy for children and youth Calif. Child Devel. Adv. Com., 1998; named Legislator of Yr., Calif. Probation, Parole and Correctional Assn., 1995, Legislator of Yr. award Calif. Child Devel. Adminstrs. Assn., 1997. Republican. Office: State Capitol Sacramento CA 95814 also: 1948 Mt Diablo Blvd Walnut Creek CA 94596-4412 also: Antioch City Hall 3rd and H Sts Antioch CA 94509 Fax: 925-280-0299.

RAINEY, WILLIAM JOEL, lawyer; b. Flint, Mich., Oct. 11, 1946; s. Ralph Jefferson and Elsie Matilda (Erickson) R.; m. Cynthia Hetsko, June 15, 1968; children: Joel Michael, Allison Elizabeth. AB, Harvard U., 1968; JD, U. Mich., 1971. Bar: NY 1973, Wash. 1977, Ariz. 1987, Mass. 1992, Oreg. 2007, US Dist. Ct. (so. and ea. dists.) NY 1973, US Ct. Appeals (2nd cir.) NY 1973, US Dist. Ct. (we. dist.) Wash. 1977, US Supreme Ct. 1976, US Ct. Appeals (9th cir.) Wash. 1978, US Dist. Ct. Ariz. 1987, US Dist. Ct. Mass. 1992; registered in-house counsel, Calif., 2005. Assoc. atty. Curtis, Mallet-Prevost, Colt & Mosle, NYC, 1971-76; atty., asst. corp. sec. Weyerhaeuser Co., Tacoma, 1976-85; v.p., corp. sec., gen. counsel Southwest Forest Industries Inc., Phoenix, 1985-87; sr. v.p., corp. sec., gen. counsel Valley Nat. Corp. and Valley Nat. Bank, Phoenix, 1987-91; v.p., gen. counsel Cabot Corp., Boston, 1991-93; exec. v.p., gen. counsel, corp. sec. Fourth Fin. Corp., Wichita, Kans., 1994-96; sr. v.p., gen. counsel, corp. sec. Payless ShoeSource, Inc., Topeka, 1996—2003, Longs Drug Stores Corp., Walnut Creek, Calif., 2003—. Editor U. Mich. Jour. Law Reform, 1970-71. Bd. dirs. Big Bros./Big Sisters, 1994—96. Maj. USAR, 1970—91. Mem. ABA (chmn. task force 1984-91, com. of corp. gen. counsel, 1993—), Wash. State Bar Assn., State Bar of Ariz., Assn. Bank Holding Cos. (steering com. 1989-91, chmn. lawyers com. 1990-91), Assn. Corp. Coun., Soc. Corp. Secs. and Governance Profls., Harvard Club of Phoenix (bd. dirs. 1989-91). Avocations: hiking, running, bicycling. Home: 1208 Bridlewood Ct Clayton CA 94517 Office: Longs Drug Stores Corp 141 N Civic Dr Walnut Creek CA 94596 Office Phone: 925-210-6720. Business E-Mail: brainey@longs.com.

RAINS, CAMERON JAY, lawyer; BA cum laude, Coll. Holy Cross, 1978; JD summa cum laude, Notre Dame U., 1981. Bar: Calif. 1981, US Dist. Ct. (so. dist. Calif.) 1981. Ptnr., co-chmn. Corp. & Securities practice group DLA Piper US LLP, San Diego, 1981—. Editor (assoc.): Notre Dame Lawyer. Mem.: State Bar Calif., San Diego County Bar Assn., US Golf Assn. (mem. exec. com., chmn. 2008 US Open Com., v.p.), Century Club San Diego (past pres., gen. chmn. 2000 Buick Invitational), Phi Alpha Delta. Office: DLA Piper US LLP 4365 Executive Dr Ste 1100 San Diego CA 92121 Office Phone: 858-677-1476. Office Fax: 858-677-1401. Business E-Mail: jay.rains@dlapiper.com.

RAISBECK, JAMES DAVID, engineering company executive; b. Milw., Sept. 29, 1936; m. Sherry Raisbeck; 1 child, Jennifer Lee; stepchildren: Eric Valpey, Laura Valpey. BS in Aerodynamics, Purdue U., 1961. Rsch. aerodynamist Boeing Comml. Airplane Co., Seattle, 1961-66; new airplane and rsch. outplant mgr. Boeing Airplane Co., Wright-Patterson AFB, Ohio, 1966-68; program mgr. comml. STOL airplane programs Boeing Co., 1968-69; pres., CEO Robertson Aircraft Corp., Seattle, 1969-73; v.p., tech. Am. Jet Industries, Van Nuys, Calif., 1973-74; CEO Raisbeck Group, San Antonio and Seattle, 1974-80, Raisbeck Engring., Inc., Seattle, 1980—, Raisbeck Comml. Air Grp., Inc., Seattle, 1996—. Recipient Outstanding Engr. award Purdue U., 1999; named Disting. Engring. Alumnus 1979, Purdue U. Fellow AIAA (assoc.); mem. Soc. Automotive Engrs., NBAA, Purdue U. Alumni Assn., Tau Beta Pi, Phi Eta Sigma, Sigma Gamma Tau. Achievements include numerous patents in aircraft design. Office: Raisbeck Engring Inc 4411 S Ryan Way Seattle WA 98178-2021 Fax: 206-722-1892.

RAISIAN, JOHN, think-tank executive, economist; b. Conneaut, Ohio, July 30, 1949; s. Ernest James and Ruby Lee (Owens) Raisian; m. Joyce Ann Klak, Aug. 17, 1984; children: Alison Kathleen, Sarah Elizabeth. BA, Ohio U., 1971; PhD, UCLA, 1978; LLD (hon.), Albertson Coll. Idaho, 1995. Rsch. assoc. Human Resources Rsch. Ctr., U. So. Calif., LA, 1972—73; cons. Rand Corp., Santa Monica, Calif., 1974—75; vis. asst. prof. econs. U. Wash., Seattle, 1975—76; asst. prof. econs. U. Houston, 1976—80; sr. economist Office Rsch. and Evaluation, US Bur. Labor Stats., Washington, 1980—81; spl. asst. for econ. policy Office Asst. Sec. for Policy, US Dept. Labor, Washington, 1981—83, dir. rsch. and tech. support, 1981—84; pres. Unicon Rsch. Corp., LA, 1984-86; sr. fellow Hoover Instn., Stanford, Calif., 1986—, assoc. dir., dep. dir., 1986—90, dir., 1989—. Advisor Nat. Coun. on Handicapped, Washington, 1985—86, Nat. Commn. on Employment Policy, Washington, 1987—88; chmn. minimum wage bd. Calif. Indsl. Welfare Commn., 1987; mem. nat. adv. com. Student Fin. Assistance, Washington, 1987—89; corp. mem. Blue Shield Calif., 1994—96; bd. dirs. Sentinel Groups Fund, Inc., 1997—; mem. Pacific Coun. Internat. Policy; nat. adv. bd. City Innovation. Editor (editl. bd.): (jour.) Jour. Labor Rsch., 1983—; contbr. articles to profl. jours. Exec. dir. Presdl. Task Force on Food Assistance, Washington, 1983—84. Recipient Best Publ. of Yr. award, Econ. Inquiry, Western Econ. Assn., 1979, Disting. Tchg. award, U. Houston Coll. Social Scis., 1980, Disting. Svc. award, U.S. Dept. Labor, 1983; fellow predoctoral fellow, Rand Corp., 1976. Mem.: Nat. Assn. Scholars, Coun. on Fgn. Rels., Mont Pelerin Soc., World Affairs Coun., Commonwealth Club of Calif., We. Econs. Assn., Am. Econs. Assn., Phi Beta Kappa. Republican. Avocation: wine collecting, sports enthusiast. Office: Hoover Instn Stanford Univ 434 Galvez Mall Stanford CA 94305-6010 Office Phone: 650-723-1198. Office Fax: 650-725-8990.*

RAKOW, JAY, lawyer, film company executive; AB, NYU, 1974; JD, Cornell U., 1977. Bar: Calif. 1980, DC 1980. Assoc. Dewey, Ballantine, 1977—80, Wyman, Bautzer, Christensen, Kuchel & Silbert; ptnr. Christensen, Miller, Fink, Jacobs, Glaser, Weil & Shapiro, LLP, 1988—93, 1996—2000; sr. v.p., gen. counsel Paramount Pictures Corp., 1993—96; sr. exec. v.p., gen. counsel Metro-Goldwyn-Mayer Inc., LA, 2000—05, mediator, arbitrator, 2005—. Office: 1925 Century Park East Ste 1975 Los Angeles CA 90067 Office Phone: 310-277-3669.

RALEIGH, CECIL BARING, geophysicist; b. Little Rock, Aug. 11, 1934; s. Cecil Baring and Lucile Nell (Stewart) R.; m. Diane Lauster, July 17, 1982; children: Alison, Marianne, Lawrence, David. BA, Pomona Coll., Calif., 1956; MA, Claremont Grad. Sch., Calif., 1958; PhD, UCLA, 1963. Fellow Research Sch. Phys. Sci., Australian Nat. U., Canberra, 1963-66; geophysicist U.S. Geol. Survey, Menlo Park, Calif., 1966-80, program mgr. for earthquake prediction research program, 1980-81; dir. Lamont-Doherty Geol. Obs. and prof. geol. scis. Columbia U., Palisades, NY, 1981-89; dean Sch. Ocean and Earth Sci. and Tech. U. Hawaii, Honolulu, 1989—2003; rschr. Hawaii Nat. Energy Inst. U. Hawaii, 2003—. CEO Ctr. for a Sustainable Future, Inc., 1996-2005, pres., chmn., HR Biopetroleum, 2004—; mem. Gov.'s Task Force on Sci. Tech., 1996-98; mem. NAS/NRC Ocean Studies Bd.; chmn. NAS/NRC Yucca Mountain Panel. Author papers control earthquakes, rheology of the mantle, mechanics of faulting, crystal plasticity. Trustee Bishop Mus., 1997—2003. Recipient Interdisciplinary award U.S. Nat. Com. Rock Mechanics, 1969, 74; Meritorious Service award Dept. Interior, 1974; Barrows Centennial Dist. Alumnus award Pomona Coll. Fellow Am. Geophys. Union, Geol. Soc. Am. Democrat. Inventor formation fracturing method. Business E-Mail: cbraleigh@att.net.

RALSTON, BARBARA JO, bank executive; b. Youngstown, Ohio, Apr. 11, 1940; d. Fred Kenneth and Juanita Ruth (Welch) Roof; m. Donald Gene Ralston, Jan. 9, 1960; children: Mark David, Lori Sue. Cert., Pacific Coast Banking Sch. U. Wash., Seattle, 1981; AA in fin., Maricopa County CC. Sec. Bank of Scottsdale, Ariz., 1962-66; adminstrv. asst. Talley Industries, Mesa, Ariz., 1966-73; asst. mgr. Continental Bank, Phoenix, 1973-77; exec. v.p. Continental Bank Service Corp., Phoenix, 1977-85, pres., dir., 1985—86; chmn., pres. to sr. v.p. electronic and convenience banking to exec. v.p. personal banking group Chase Bank of Ariz., exec. v.p., COO; exec. v.p., mgr. northeast Ariz. retail area First Interstate Bank, 1994—95, Phoenix area pres., 1995—96; sr. v.p., mgr. in-store banking Wells Fargo Bank, Ariz., 1996—97; founder, pres., CEO Camelback Cmty. Bank, Phoenix, 1998—. Pres. Ariz. Bus. Leadership. Bd. dirs. Valley Big Bros.-Big Sisters, Phoenix, 1986; mem. Ariz. Acad., Phoenix, 1984; treas. Phoenix Together Town Hall, 1986; chair Am. West Airlines Edn. Found.; immediate past chair, Fresh State Women's Found.; past chair Ariz. Town Hall; past internat. pres. Financial Women Internat. Recipient You Too Can Make A Difference award Valley Christian Ctrs., Phoenix, 1985. Mem. Nat. Assn. Bank Women (state pres. 1981-82), Am. Inst. Banking (state edn. chmn. Ariz. chpt. 1984), Tumbleweed (pres. 1983); Am. Bankers Assn. (state membership chair for Ariz., chair ABA Edn. Found, 2003-), Ariz Bankers Assn. (bd. dirs., 2001-03, pres., 2001-02. Lodges: Soroptimists (pres. 1982, Women Helping Women award 1984). Republican. Methodist. Avocations: reading, travel, sewing. Office: Camelback Cmty Bank 2777 E Camelback Rd Ste 100 Phoenix AZ 85016

RALSTON, HENRY JAMES, III, neurobiologist, anatomist, educator; b. Berkeley, Calif., Mar. 12, 1935; s. Henry James and Sue Harris (Mahnke) R.; m. Diane Cornelia Daly, Oct. 29, 1960; children: Rachel Anne, Amy Sue. BA, U. Calif., Berkeley, 1956, MD, 1959. Intern Mt. Sinai Hosp., NYC, 1959-60; resident in medicine U. Calif., San Francisco, 1960-61, prof., 1973—, chmn. dept. anatomy, 1973-97, chmn. acad. senate, 1986-88; spl. postdoctoral fellow U. Coll., London, 1963-65, lectr., 1981; asst. prof. anatomy Stanford (Calif.) U., 1965-69; assoc. prof. U. Wis., Madison, 1969-73; prof. anatomy U. Calif., San Francisco, 1973—, assoc. dean admissions, 2001—. Cons. NIH; mem. com. for future of anat. scis., Macy Found., 1977-80; vis. prof. French Med. Rsch. Inst.-INSERM, Paris, 1981-82; chair step I U.S. med. lic. examination com. Nat. Bd. Med. Examiners, 1992-96. With M.C. U.S. Army, 1961-63. Recipient Henry J. Kaiser award for excellence in tchg., 1978, Jacob Javits Neurosci. Investigator award NIH, 1988-95; USPHS grant, 1966—. Mem. AAAS, Soc. Neurosci., Soc. Study Pain, Am. Pain Soc., Am. Assn. Anatomists (pres. 1987-88, chmn. publs. com. 1989-91, Henry Gray award 1997), Am. Assn. Med. Colls. (adv. panel on biomed. rsch. 1996-99), Anat. Assn. Gt. Britain, Alpha Omega Alpha. Achievements include research in field of organization of mammalian nervous system studied by electron microscopy, mechanisms subserving pain in animals and humans. Office: U Calif Dept Anatomy PO Box 0452 San Francisco CA 94143-0452 E-mail: hjr@phy.ucsf.edu.

RALSTON, JOANNE SMOOT, public relations executive; b. Phoenix, May 13, 1939; d. A. Glen and Virginia (Lee) Smoot; m. W. Hamilton Weigelt, Aug. 15, 1991 (dec.). BA in Journalism, Ariz. State U., 1960. Reporter The Ariz. Rep., Phoenix, 1960-62; co-owner, pub. rels. dir. The Patton Agy., Phoenix, 1962-71; founder, pres., owner Joanne Ralston & Assocs., Inc., Phoenix, 1971-87, 92—. Pres. Nelson Ralston Robb Comm., Phoenix, 1987—91, Joanne Ralston & Assocs., Inc., Scottsdale, 1991—, Kapaau, Hawaii, 2000—. Contbr. articles to profl. jours. Bd. dirs. Ariz. Parklands Found. 1984-86, Gov.'s Coun. on Health, Phys. Fitness and Sports, 1984-86; mem. task force Water and Natural Resources Coun., Phoenix, 1984-86; mem. Hawaii Gov.'s Adv. Bd., 2003-05, Hawaii Gov.'s Coun. Advisors, 2005—, others. Recipient Lulu awards (36) L.A. Advt. Women, 1964—, Gold Quill (2) Internat. Assn. Bus. Communicators, Excellence awards Fin. World mag., 1982-93, others; named to Walter Cronkite Sch. Journalism Hall of Fame, Coll. Pub. Programs Ariz. State U., 1987; named one of 25 Most Influential Arizonians, Phoenix Mag., 1991. Mem. Pub. Rels. Soc. Am. (counselor sect.), Internat. Assn. Bus. Communicators, Phoenix Press Club (pres. bd.), Investor Rels. Inst., Phoenix Met. C. of C. (bd. dirs. 1977-84, 85-91), Governor's Adv. Coun., Norway, Rotary Internat. Republican. Avocations: horses, dog training. Address: PO Box 808 Kapaau HI 96755-0808 Office Phone: 808-889-6433. Personal E-mail: joanne-ralston@juno.com.

RALSTON, LENORE DALE, academic policy and program analyst; b. Oakland, Calif., Feb. 21, 1949; d. Leonard Earnest and Emily Allison (Hudnut) R. BA in Anthropology, U. Calif., Berkeley, 1971, MPH in Behavioral Sci., 1981; MA in Anthropology, Bryn Mawr Coll., 1973, PhD in Anthropology, 1980. Asst. rschr. anthropology inst. internat. studies U. Calif., Berkeley, 1979-82, rsch. assoc. Latin Am. Study Ctr., 1982-83, acad. asst. to dean Sch. of Optometry, 1990-95, prin. policy analyst, chancellor's office, 1995—; assoc. scientist, rsch. adminstr. Med. Rsch. Inst., San Francisco, 1982-85; cons. health sci. Berkeley, 1986-90. Mem. fin. bd. Med. Rsch. Inst., 1983-84; speaker in field. Co-author: Voluntary Effects in Decentralized Management, 1983; contbr. articles to profl. jours. Commr. Cmty. Health Adv. Com., Berkeley, 1988-90; vice chair, commr. Cmty. Health Commn., Berkeley, 1990-93; mem. bd. safety com. Miles, Inc., Berkeley, 1992-94. Grantee Nat. Rsch. Svc. Award, WHO, NIMH, NSF. Fellow Applied Anthropology Assn.; mem. APHA, Am. Anthropology Assn., Sigma Xi. Home: 1232 Carlotta Ave Berkeley CA 94707-2707 Office Phone: 510-642-5746. Business E-Mail: ralston@berkeley.edu.

RAMER, BRUCE M., lawyer; b. Teaneck, NJ, Aug. 2, 1933; s. Sidney and Anne S. (Strassman) R.; children: Gregg B., Marc K., Neal I. BA, Princeton U., 1955; LLB, Harvard U., 1958. Bar: Calif. 1963, NJ 1958. Assoc., Morrison, Lloyd & Griggs, Hackensack, NJ, 1959-60; ptnr. Gang, Tyre, Ramer & Brown, Inc., LA, 1963—. Exec. dir. Entertainment Law Inst., Law Ctr. U. So. Calif., bd. councilors; chmn., nat. bd. govs. Am. Jewish Com., 1995-98, nat. v.p., 1982-88, pres., 1998—, LA chpt., 1980-83, chair Western region, 1984-86, Cmty. Svc. award, 1987, nat. pres., 1998—, adv. bd. Skirball Inst. on Am. Values, 1998—; chmn. Asia Pacific Rim Inst., 1989-98; trustee Loyola Marymount U., LA Children's Mus., 1986-89; vice chair United Way, 1991-93, corp. bd. dirs., 1981-93, chair coun. pres. 1989-90, mem. cmty. issues coun., 1989-90, chair discretionary fund distbn. com., 1987-89; bd. dirs., chair Geffen Playhouse, 1995-98, founding chair, 1998—; bd. dirs. LA Urban League, 1987-93, 96—, Jewish Fedn. Coun. of Greater LA (mem. Cmty. Rels. com., bd. dirs., exec. com.), Jewish TV Network, Sta. KCET-TV; mem., bd. dirs. Rebuild LA, 1992-96; mem. bd. govs. Calif. Cmty. Found., 1988-98; recipient Ann. Brotherhood award NCCJs, 1990; mem. Fellows of Am. Bar Found.; mem. econ. strategy panel State Calif., 1997—; bd. dirs. Shoah Visual History Found., Righteous Persons Found., LA 2012 Bid Com. for So. Calif. Olympic Games; bd. dirs. Jewish Fedn. Coun. Greater LA, mem. exec. com., cmty. rels. com. Pvt. US Army, 1958-59, 2d lt., 1961-62. Mem. ABA (mem. spl. com. jud. ind.), LA County Bar Assn., Calif. Bar Assn., Beverly Hills Bar Assn. (Exec. Dirs. award 1988, Entertainment Lawyer of Yr. award 1996), LA Copyright Soc. (pres. 1974-75), Calif. Copyright Conf. (pres. 1973-74), Princeton Club (pres. 1975-78). Office: Gang Tyre Ramer & Brown Inc 132 S Rodeo Dr Beverly Hills CA 90212-2415

RAMER, LAWRENCE JEROME, corporation executive; b. Bayonne, NJ, July 29, 1928; s. Sidney and Anne (Strassman) R.; m. Ina Lee Brown, June 30, 1957; children: Stephanie Beryl, Susan Meredith, Douglas Strassman. BA in Econs, Lafayette Coll., 1950; MBA, Harvard U., 1957; LLD (hon.), Lafayette Coll., 1992. Sales rep., then v.p. United Sheet Metal Co., Bayonne, 1953-55; with Am. Cement Corp., 1957-64; v.p. mktg. div. Riverside Cement Co., 1960-62, v.p. mktg. parent co., 1962-64; vice chmn. bd., chief exec. officer Clavier Corp., NYC, 1965-66; exec. v.p., vice chmn. bd. Pacific Western Industries, LA, 1966-70; pres., chief exec. officer Nat. Portland Cement Co. Fla., 1975-89; chmn. bd. Sutro Partners, Inc., LA, 1977-89, Somerset Mgmt. Group, 1975-92, Luminall Paints Inc., LA, 1972-95; chmn. bd., CEO Bruning Paint Co., Balt., 1979—2000; chmn. bd., chief exec. officer Pacific Coast Cement Co., LA, 1979-90; pres., CEO Ramer Equities, Inc., 1990—2000, chmn., 2000—; chmn. bd. Scott Paint Co., Sarasota, Fla., 2000—. Chmn. Lee and Lawrence J. Ramer Family Found., 1986—; bd. dirs. The Music Ctr., LA, Canyon Ranch, Tucson; bd. dirs. Ctr. Theatre Group-Mark Taper Ahmanson Theatres, LA, pres. and chmn., 1987-97. Mem. Coun. on Fgn. Rels., NYC; chmn. bd. trustees Lafayette Coll., Easton, Pa., 1992—2001, bd. trustees, 1976—2001, Helen Keller Internat., NYC, Calif. Inst. Arts, Valencia, 2000—, chmn. bd. trustees, 1995—2006; nat. bd. govs. Am. Jewish Com., NY, treas. NY; bd. dirs. LA World Affairs Coun., Pacific Coun. Internat. Policy; bd. govs. Hebrew Union Coll.; trustee Leo Baeck Inst., NY; bd. dirs. RAND Corp. Ctr. on Mid. East Policy. Mem.: Geffen Theatre (bd. dirs.). Office: Ramer Equities Inc 10900 Wilshire Blvd Ste 550 Los Angeles CA 90024-6501 Office Phone: 310-209-0442.

RAMIREZ, ARCHIMEDES, neurosurgeon, educator; b. Binakayan, The Philippines, Nov. 26, 1938; came to U.S., 1947; s. Francisco Mendoza and Mercedes (Parales) R.; m. Carol Domush, Mar. 19, 1944. BS in Chemistry, Va. Mil. Inst., 1961; MD, U. Va., 1966. Diplomate Am. Bd. Neurol. Surgery. Intern Saginaw (Mich.) Gen. Hosp., 1967; resident in gen. surgery Saginaw Coop. Hosps., Inc., 1971-72; resident in neurosurgery Walter Reed Army Med. Ctr., Washington, 1972-76; commd. 2d lt. U.S. Army, 1961, advanced through grades to col., 1984, gen. med. officer Vietnam, 1968-69, Ft. Story, Va., 1969-70; chief neurol. surgery Letterman Army Med. Ctr., San Francisco, 1976-79; chief neurosurgery svc. Marin Gen. Hosp., Greensbrae, Calif., 1981—; neurosurgeon "Desert Storm", Letterman Army Med. Ctr., San Francisco, 1990—91; ret. U.S. Army M.C., 1991. Cons. Letterman Army Med. Ctr., 1979-92; mem. admission com. U. Calif.-San Francisco Med. Sch., 1978-79; mem. clin. faculty dept. neurosurgery U. Calif.-San Francisco Med. Ctr., 1978—; cons. neurosurgeon Kaiser Hosp. Terra Linda, San Rafael, Calif., 2000—. Mem. Am. Assn. Neurol. Surgeons, Congress Neurol. Surgeons, Pan Pacific Neurosurgery Congress (adv. coun. 1986—), Calif. Assn. Neurologist Surgeons (dist. dir. 2004-08). Avocation: golf. Office: Archimedes ramirez Md PO Box 10386 San Rafael CA 94912-0386 Office Phone: 415-464-7511. Personal E-mail: abackdoc@gmail.com.

RAMIREZ, MICHAEL P., editorial cartoonist; b. Tokyo; s. Ireneo Edward and Fumiko Maria R. Degree, Univ. Calif., Irvine. Cartoonist Baker Comm./Palos Verdes Peninsula News, Calif., 1982—89, The Daily Sun/Post, San Clemente, Calif., 1989—90, The Comml. Appeal, Memphis, 1990—97, LA Times, 1997—2005; syndicated cartoonist Copley News Svc., 1986—; sr. editor, cartoonist Investor's Bus. Daily, 2005—. Recipient Pulitzer prize for editorial cartooning, 1994, Soc. Profl.Journalism award for editorial cartooning, 1996, Nat. Journalism award for editorial cartooning, Scripps Howard Found., 2006, Pulitzer prize for editorial cartooning, 2008. Office: Copley News Service 7776 Ivanhoe Ave La Jolla CA 92037-4520

RAMO, SIMON, retired engineering executive; b. Salt Lake City, May 7, 1913; s. Benjamin and Clara (Trestman) Ramo; m. Virgina Smith, July 25, 1937; children: James Brian, Alan Martin. BS, U. Utah, 1933, DSc (hon.), 1961; PhD, Calif. Inst. Tech., 1936; DEng (hon.), Case Western Res. U., 1960, U. Mich., 1966, Poly. Inst. NY, 1971; DSc (hon.), Union Coll., 1963, Worcester Polytechnic Inst., 1968, U. Akron, 1969, Cleve. State U., 1976; LLD (hon.), Carnegie-Mellon U., 1970, U. So. Calif., 1972, Gonzaga U., 1983, Occidental Coll., 1984, Claremont U., 1985. With Gen. Electric Co., 1936—46; v.p. ops. Hughes Aircraft Co., 1946—53; with Ramo-Woolridge Corp., 1953—58; dir. U.S. Intercontinental Ballistic Missile Program, 1954—58, TRW Inc., 1954—85, exec. v.p., 1958—61, vice chmn. bd., 1961—78, chmn. exec. com., 1969—78, cons., 1978—; pres. The Bunker-Ramo Corp., 1964—66; chmn. bd. TRW-Fujitsu Co., 1980—83. Vis. prof. mgmt. sci. Calif. Inst. Tech., 1978—; Regents lectr. UCLA, 1981—82, U. Calif. at Santa Cruz, 1978—79; chmn. Ctr. for Study Am. Experience, U. So. Calif., 1978—80; Faculty fellow John F. Kennedy Sch. Govt., Harvard U., 1980—84; mem. White House Energy Rsch. and Devel. Adv. Coun., 1973—75; chmn. Pres.'s Com. on Sci. and Tech., 1976—77; bd. advisors for sci. and tech. Repu. of China, 1981—84; chmn. bd. Aetna, Jacobs & Ramo Venture Capital, 1987—90, Allenwood Ventures, Inc., 1987—. Author: The Business of Science, 1988, other sci., engring. and mgmt. books, (non-fiction) Meetings, Meetings and More Meetings, 2005. Life trustee Calif. Inst. Tech., Nat. Symphony Orch. Assn., 1973—83; trustee emeritus Calif. State U.; bd. govs., pres. Performing Arts Coun. Mus. Ctr. LA, 1976—77; co-chair bd. overseers Keck Sch. Medicine, U. So. Calif., 1999—; bd. dirs. W. M. Keck Found., 1983—, LA World Affairs Coun., 1973—85, Mus. Ctr. Found., LA, LA Philharm. Assn., 1981—84. Recipient IAS, 1956, award, Am. Inst. Elec. Engrs., 1959, Am. Iron and Steel Inst., 1968, Medal of Achievement, AEA, 1970, DSM, Armed Forces Comm. and Electronics Assn., 1970, medal of achievement, WEMA, 1970, Kayan medal, Columbia U., 1972, award, Am. Cons. Engrs. Coun., 1974, Nat. Medal of Sci., Pres. of US, 1976, 1979, medal, Franklin Inst., 1978, awards, U. So. Calif., 1979, Pres. medal Sci., 1981, UCLA medal, 1982, Presdl. Medal of Freedom, Pres. of US, 1983, Aesculapian award, UCLA, 1984, Durand medal, AAIA, 1984, John Fritz medal, 1986, Henry Townley Heald award, Ill. Inst. Tech., 1988, Nat. Engring. award, Am. Assn. Engring. Socs., 1988, Franklin-Jefferson medal, 1988, Howard Hughes meml. award, 1989, Air Force Space and Missile Pioneers award, 1989, Pioneer award, Internat. Coun. on Sys. Engring., 1997, Disting. pub. Svc. medal, NASA, 1999, Lifetime Achievement trophy, Smithsonian Inst., 1999, John F. Kennedy Astronautics award, Am. Astronautical Soc., 2000, John R. Alison award for indsl. leadership, Air Force Assn., 2000, Presdl. Medallion, U. So. Calif., 2002, Founders award, USC Thornton Sch. of Music, 2003, Lifetime Space Achievement award, Space Found., 2007; named to Bus. Hall of Fame, 1984. Fellow: IEEE (Electronic Achievement award 1953, Golden Omega award 1975, Founders medal 1980, Centennial medal 1984), Am. Acad. Polit. Sci., Am. Acad. Arts and Scis.; mem.: NAS, Nat. Acad. Engring. (founder, coun. mem. Bueche award), Internat. Acad. Astronautics, Pacific Coun. Internat. Policy, Coun. Fgn. Rels., Inst. advancement Engring., Am. Philos. Soc., Am. Phys. Soc., NY Acad. Scis., Theta Tau (Hall of Fame laureate), Eta Kappa Nu (eminent mem. award 1966). Office: 9200 W Sunset Blvd Ste 801 Los Angeles CA 90069-3603

RAMO, VIRGINIA M. SMITH, civic worker; b. Yonkers, NY; d. Abraham Harold and Freda (Kasnetz) Smith; m. Simon Ramo; children: James Brian, Alan Martin. BS in Edn., U. So. Calif., DHL (hon.), 1978. Nat. co-chmn., ann. giving U. So. Calif., 1968-70, vice chmn., trustee, 1971—, co-chmn. bd. councilors Sch. Performing Arts, 1975-76, co-chmn. bd. councillors Schs. Med. and Engring. Vice-chmn. bd. overseers Hebrew Union Coll., 1972-75; bd. dirs. The Muses of Calif. Mus. Sci. and Industry, UCLA Affiliates, Estelle Doheny Eye Found., U. So. Calif. Sch. Medicine; mem. adv. coun. L.A. County Heart Assn., chmn. com. to endow Chair in cardiology at U. So. Calif.; vice chmn., bd. dirs. Friends of Libr. U. So. Calif.; bd. dirs., nat. pres. Achievement Rewards for Coll. Scientists Found., 1975-77; bd. dirs. Les Dames L.A., Cmty. TV So. Calif.; bd. dirs., v.p. Founders L.A. Music Ctr.; v.p. L.A. Music Ctr. Opera Assn.; v.p. corp. bd. United Way; v.p. Blue Ribbon-400 Performing Arts Coun.; chmn. com. to endow chair in gerontology U. So. Calif.; vice chmn. campaign Doheny Eye Inst. 1986; co-chair, bd. overseers Keck Sch. Medicine U. So. Calif., 1999—. Recipient Svc. award Friends of Librs., 1974, Nat. Cmty. Svc. award Alpha Epsilon Phi, 1975, Disting. Svc. award Am. Heart Assn., 1978, Svc. award U. So. Calif., Spl. award U. So. Calif. Music Alumni Assn., 1979, Life Achievement award Mannequins of L.A. Assistance League, 1979, Woman of Yr. award Pan Hellenic Assn., 1981, Disting. Svc. award U. So. Calif. Sch. Medicine, 1981, U. So. Calif. Town and Gown Recognition award, 1986, Asa V. Call Achievement award U. So. Calif., 1986, Phi Kappa Phi scholarship award U. So. Calif., 1986, Vision award Luminaires of Doheny Eye Inst., 1994, Presdl. medallion U. So. Calif., 2002, USC Thornton Sch. of Music Founder's award, 2003. Mem. UCLA Med. Aux., U. So. Calif. Pres.'s Cir., Commerce Assocs. U. So. Calif., Cedars of Lebanon Hosp. Women's Guild (dir. 1967-68), Blue Key, Skull and Dagger.

RAMOS, JORGE, newscaster; b. Mex. City, Mar. 16, 1958; arrived in U.S., 1983; 2 children. Grad. in Comm., Ibero-Am. U., Mex. City; M in Internat. Studies, U. Miami. News reporter Univision, LA, 1984—86; host Mundo Latino, Univision TV prog., 1986; anchorman Noticiero Univision, 1986—. Founder Wake Up Reading book club, 2002—. Author: (autobiography) No Borders: a Journalist's Search for Home, Behind the Mask, The Other Face of America, What I Saw, Hunting the Lion, The Latino Wave, Dying to Cross; contbr. weekly column, NY Times Syndicate. Recipient Maria Moors Cabot award, Columbia Univ., 2001, Ruben Salazar award, Nat. Council La Raza, 2002, Ron Brown award, Nat. Child Labor Com., 2002, David Brinkley award for Journalistic Excellence, Barry Univ., 2003, 8 Emmy awards, Nat. Acad. Television Arts & Sci.; named one of Ten Most Admired Latinos, Latino Leaders mag., 2004, 25 Most Influential Hispanics, Time Mag., 2005. Office: Univision Communications Ste 3050 1999 Ave of the Stars Los Angeles CA 90067 Studio: WNJU-TV Noticiero 47 6th Fl 2200 Fletcher Ave Fort Lee NJ 07024 Office Phone: 201-969-4247. Office Fax: 201-969-4120. E-mail: jramos@univision.net, jorge.ramos@nbcuni.com.

RAMPINO, LOUIS J., bank executive; Pres., CEO Fremont Gen. Corp., 1998—. Office: Ste 600 2020 Santa Monica Blvd Santa Monica CA 90404

RAMSAY, MICHAEL, communications company executive; BSEE, U. Edinburgh, Scotland. Sr. v.p., gen. mgr., visual systems group Silicon Graphics, Inc., 1991—94, pres. Silicon Studio, Inc, 1994—96, sr. v.p. Silicon Desktop Group, 1996—97; CEO TiVo Inc., 1997—2005, chmn., 1997—2005; mem. adv. group Pentech Ventures, London, 2006; venture ptnr. New Enterprise Associates, 2007—. Bd. dir. Netflix. Office: NEA 2855 Sand Hill Rd Menlo Park CA 94025-7022

RAMSBY, MARK DELIVAN, lighting designer, consultant; b. Portland, Oreg., Nov. 20, 1947; s. Marshall Delivan and Verna Pansy (Culver) R.; married; children: Aaron Delivan, Venessa Mercedes. Student, Portland State U., Oreg., 1966-67. With C.E.D., Portland, 1970-75; minority ptnr. The Light Source, Portland, 1975-78, pres., 1978-87; prin. Illume Lighting Design, Portland, 1987-90; ptnr. Ramsby, Dupuy & Seats, Inc., Portland, 1990-91; dir. lighting design PAE Cons. Engrs., Inc., Portland, 1991—2001; dir. design LUMA, Portland, 2001—. Pvt. practice cons. Portland, 1979—. Recipient Top 100 Outstanding Achievement award Metalux Lighting, 1981-85, 100% award, 1985, Edwin F. Guth award of merit, 1990, 95, 96, 99, 2001, 03, Edison award of excellence, 1990, Edwin F. Guth award of excellence, 1993, 94, Paul Waterbury award of Merit, 1995. Mem. Illuminating Engring. Soc. Am. (sec.-treas. Oreg. sect. 1978-79, Oreg. sect. pres. 2002-03, Oreg. Section and Regional and Internat. awards 1989, 90, 93, 94, Lighting Design awards), Internat. Assn. Lighting Designers. Lutheran. Avocations: lighting design, historical restoration, fly fishing, downhill skiing. Office: LUMA 808 SW 3d Ave Ste 450 Portland OR 97204-2426 Office Phone: 503-226-3905.

RAMSEY, JERRY A., lawyer; b. Jan. 9, 1936; BA in philosophy, Calif. State U., LA; LLB, U. Calif., LA, 1964. Bar: Calif. 1965, US Dist. Ct., Central Dist. Calif., US Ct. Appeals, Ninth Circuit, US Dist. Ct., No. Dist. Calif. 1987. Assoc. Engstrom, Lipscomb & Lack, 1993—. Mem.: Am. Bd. Trial Atty. (diplomat, mem. LA bd. dir., mem. nat. bd. dir.), Am. Bd. Trial Advocates (pres. LA chpt. 1997), Nat. Inst. Trial Advocacy, Consumer Atty. Assn. Calif., Consumer Atty. Assn. LA, Calif. State Bar Assn., LA County Bar Assn., ABA. Office: Engstrom Lipscomb Lack 10100 Santa Monica Blvd Los Angeles CA 90067-4003 Office Phone: 310-552-3880. Business E-Mail: jramsey@elllaw.com.

RAMSEY, JOHN ARTHUR, lawyer; b. Apr. 1, 1942; s. Wilbert Lewis and Lillian (Anderson) R.; m. Nikki Ann Ramsey, Feb. 9, 1943; children: John William, Bret Anderson, Heather Nichole. AB, San Diego State U., 1965; JD, Calif. Western Sch. Law, 1969. Bar: Colo. 1969, Tex. 1978. Assoc. Henry, Cockrell, Quinn & Creighton, 1969-72; atty. Texaco Inc., 1972-80; asst. to pres. Texaco U.S.A., 1980-81, asst. to divsn. v.p. Houston, 1981-82, divsn. atty. Denver, 1982-88; ptnr. Holland & Hart, 1989—. Editor-in-chief: Calif. Western Law Rev., 1969. Bd. dirs. Selective Svc., Englewood, Colo., 1972-76; chmn. coun. Bethany Luth. Ch., Englewood, 1976; mem. exec. bd. Denver Area coun. Boy Scouts Am., 1999—. Mem. ABA (vice-chmn. oil, natural gas exploration and prodn. com. sect. natural resource law 1983-88, chmn. 1989, coun. sect. natural resources, energy and environ. law 1990-93). Republican. Office: Holland & Hart 8390 E Crescent Pkwy Ste 400 Greenwood Village CO 80111-2822 Office Phone: 303-290-1600.

RAMSEY, PAUL GLENN, dean, internist; b. Pitts., 1949; MD, Harvard U., 1975. Diplomate Am. Bd. Internal Medicine. Intern Cambridge Hosp., 1975-76; resident in medicine Mass. Gen. Hosp., Boston, 1976-78, U. Wash., Seattle, 1980-81, fellow infectious diseases, 1978-80, prof., 1991—, chmn. dept. medicine, 1992-97; physician-in-chief U. Wash. Med. Ctr., 1992-97; v.p. for med. affairs, dean Sch. Medicine U. Wash., Seattle, 1997—2006; CEO U. Wash Sch. Medicine, 2006—, exec. v.p., Med. Affairs, 2006—, dean, 2006—. Mem.: Inst. Medicine, AAAS, Assn. Am. Physicians, Am. Fedn. Clin. Rsch., ACP. Office: U Wash Sch Medicine PO Box 356350 Seattle WA 98195-6350*

RANCE, QUENTIN E., interior designer; b. St. Albans, Eng., Mar. 22, 1935; came to U.S., 1981. s. Herbert Leonard and Irene Ann (Haynes) R.; m. India Adams, May 17, 1974. Grad., Eastbourne Sch. Art, Eng., 1960. Soft furnishings buyer Dickeson & French Ltd., Eastbourne, 1960-61, outside sales mgr., 1961-62; design dir. Laszlo Hoenig, Ltd., London, 1962-73; mng. dir. Quentin Rance Interiors Ltd., London, 1973-81; pres. Quentin Rance Enterprises, Inc., Encino, Calif., 1981—. Works featured in Designers West, 1983, Design House Rev., 1983, Profiles mag., 1987, Nat. Assn. Mirror Mfrs. Jour., 1988, Designer Specifier, 1990, Los Angeles Homes, 2005, SpectacularHomes of Calif., 2006, Visions of Design, 2008. Mem. Founders for Diabetic Research/City of Hope. Served with RAF, 1953-55. Recipient Hon. Mention award Nat. Assn. Mirror Mfrs., 1987, 1st Pl. Nat. Pub. Svc. award, Designer Specifier, 1990. Fellow Chartered Soc. Designers (Eng.); mem. Am. Soc. Interior Designers (profl., chpt. bd. dirs. 1983-87, 89-91, chmn. Avanti 1983-85, admissions chmn. 1985—2005, Presdl. citations 1984, 87, 91, 95, 97). Knights of Vine. Avocations: bicycling, antiques, fine wines, stamp collecting/philately, theater. Home and Office: 18005 Rancho St Encino CA 91316-4214 Office Phone: 818-705-8111. Business E-Mail: quentin@quentinrance.com.

RAND, DUNCAN DAWSON, retired librarian; b. Biggar, Sask., Can., Oct. 28, 1940; s. Dawson Ellis and Elizabeth Edna (Gabie) R.; m. Nancy Jean Daugherty, Sept. 7, 1963; children: Jacqueline Nancy, Duncan Dawson, Thomas Nelson, John David, Jennifer Nancy. BA, U. Sask., 1963; B.L.S., McGill U., 1964. Young adult librarian Regina Pub. Library, Sask., 1964-65; coordinator library services Regina Separate Sch. Bd., 1965-68; asst. chief librarian Regina Pub. Library, 1968-71; dep. dir. London Pub. Library and Art Mus., 1971-73, acting dir., 1973-74; chief librarian Lethbridge Pub. Library, Alta., 1974-2000, ret. Alta., 2001. Dir. So. Alta. Art Gallery, Alberta Libr., 1996—. Editor: Sask. Geneal. Soc. Bull, 1968-71. Vice pres. Alta. council Boy Scouts. Mem. Libr. Assn. Alta (dir., pres. 1986-87), Can. Libr. Assn. (dir.), Can. Assn. Pub. Librs. (chair 1976-77), Sask. Geneal. Soc. (pres.), Assn. Profl. Librs. of Lethbridge (chmn. 1982-84), So. Alta. Regional Info. Network (chmn. 1996-2000), Samaritans (pres. 1998-2001), Allied Arts Coun. (bd. dirs. 1993-98), Southern Alberta Regional Info. Network (chmn.), Rotary, Ipalosh (archivist, sec. 1980-94). Office: 810 5th Ave S Lethbridge AB Canada T1J 4C4

RANDALL, JANET ANN, biology professor, researcher; b. Twin Falls, Idaho, July 3, 1943; d. William Franklin and Bertha Silvia Orr; m. Bruce H. MacEvoy, BS, U. Idaho, Moscow, 1965; MEd, U. Wash., Seattle, 1969; PhD, Wash. State U., Pullman, 1977. Postdoctoral fellow U. Texas, Austin, 1977-79; from asst. to assoc. prof. biology Ctrl. Mo. State U., Warrensburg, 1979-87; assoc. prof. biology San

Francisco State U., 1987-92, prof., 1992—2004, emeritus, 2004—. Vis. prof. Cornell U., Ithaca, N.Y., 1984-85. Contbr. articles to profl. jours. Rsch. grantee Nat. Geog. Soc., 1982, 86, 94, 96, NSF, 1984, 87, 88-89, 89-91, 91-93, 93-95, 97-00; Civilian R&D Found., 2000, 02, Alumni Achieve. award U. Idaho. Fellow Calif. Acad. Sci.; mem. Animal Behavior Soc. (mem. at large 1986-89, sec. 2005-08, editor 2008-), Am. Soc. Zoologists (program officer), Am. Soc. Mammalogists, Internat. Soc. Behavioral Ecology, Soc. Behavioral Neurobiology, Endangered Species Coalition (bd. mem.). Avocations: opera, travel, hiking. Office: San Francisco State U Dept Biology San Francisco CA 94132 Home: 862 Jonive Rd Sebastopol CA 95472-9567 Business E-Mail: jrandall@sfsu.edu.

RANDALL, JEFFREY G., lawyer; BS in Fin., U. Oreg.; JD, U. Calif. Ptnr. Skadden, Arps, Slate, Meagher & Flom LLP, Palo Alto, Calif. Named one of California's Top 30 IP Attorneys, Daily Jour., Litigation's Rising Stars, The Am. Lawyer, 2007. Office: Skadden Arps Slate Meagher & Flom LLP 525 University Ave Ste 1100 Palo Alto CA 94301 Office Phone: 650-470-4500. Office Fax: 650-470-4570.

RANDERSON, JAMES T., geophysicist, educator; s. Tremper and Laurie Randerson. BS in Chemistry, Stanford U., Calif., 1992, PhD in Biol. Scis., 1998. Postdoctoral scholar U. Calif. Berkeley and U. Alaska, 1998—2000; asst. prof. biogeochemistry and environ. sci. and engring. Calif. Inst. Tech., Pasadena, 2000—03; assoc. prof. dept. earth sys. sci. U. Calif., Irvine, 2003—. Contbr. articles to sci. jours. Fellow: Am. Geophys. Union (James B. Macelwane medal 2005); mem.: AAAS, Ecol. Soc. Am., Sigma Xi. Office: Dept Earth Sys Sci U Calif Irvine 3212 Croul Hall Irvine CA 92697 Office Phone: 949-824-9030. Office Fax: 949-824-3874. E-mail: jranders@uci.edu.

RANDHAWA, BIKKAR SINGH, retired psychologist, educator; b. Jullundur, India, June 14, 1933; came to Can., 1961, naturalized, 1966; s. Pritam S. and Sawaran K. (Basakhi) R.; m. Leona Emily Bujnowski, Oct. 8, 1966; children: Jason, Lisa. BA in Math., Panjab U., India, 1954, BT in Edn., 1955, MA in History, 1959; BEd, U. Alta., Can., 1963; MEd in Measurement and Evaluation, U. Toronto, 1967, PhD, 1969. Tchr. secondary sch. math., Panjab, 1955-61; asst. headmaster, then headmaster, 1955-61; tchr. h.s. math. and sci. Camrose County, Canada, 1961—64, Beaver County, 1964—65, Edmonton (Alta.) Pub. Schs., 1965-67; tutor in math. for social sci. Ont. Inst. Studies in Edn., Toronto, 1968-69; mem. faculty U. Sask., Saskatoon, Canada, 1969—76, 1977—, prof. ednl. psychology, 1977-2000, prof. emeritus, 2000—, asst. dean rsch. and field svcs., 1982-87. Prof., coord. Visual Scholars' Program, U. Iowa, 1976-77; adj. prof. edu. psychology, U. Alta., 2002-; cons. in field. Contbr. articles to profl. jours. Treas. St. Albert Crime Stoppers, 2002—05. Fellow APA, Am. Psychol. Soc. (charter), Can. Psychol. Assn.; mem. Can. Ednl. Rsch. Assn. (pres. 1997-99), Can. Soc. Study Edn., St. Albert Rotary Club (treas. 2003-05), Phi Delta Kappa (pres. Saskatoon chpt. 1971, 85). Home: 14 Harwood Dr Saint Albert AB Canada T8N 5V5 Home Phone: 780-419-2547; Office Phone: 780-419-2549. Personal E-mail: randy.randhawa@shaw.ca.

RANDISI, ELAINE MARIE, accountant, educator, writer; b. Racine, Wis., Dec. 19, 1926; d. John Dewey and Alveta Irene (Raffety) Fehd; m. John Paul Randisi, Oct. 12, 1946 (div. July 1972); children: Jeanine Randisi Manson, Martha Randisi Chaney (dec.), Joseph, Paula, Catherine Randisi Carvalho, George, Anthony (dec.); m. John R. Woodfin, June 18, 1994 (div. Nov. 2006). AA, Pasadena Jr. Coll., 1946; BS cum laude (Giannini scholar), Golden Gate U., 1978. With Raymond Kaiser Engrs., Inc., Oakland, Calif., 1969-75, 77-86, corp. acct., 1978-79, sr. corp. acct., 1979-82, sr. payroll acct., 1983-86; accts. payable coord. Crosby, Heasfey, Roach & May, Oakland, Calif., 1989—96; acctg. mgr. Lilli Ann Corp., San Francisco, 1986-89; accounts payable coord. Crosby, Heafy, Roach & May, Oakland, 1989—96, ret., 1996. Initiated Minority Vendor Purchasing Program for Kaiser Engrs., Inc., 1975-76; corp. buyer Kaiser Industries Corp., Oakland, 1975-77; lectr. on astrology Theosophical Soc., San Francisco, 1979-99; mem. faculty Am. Fedn. Astrologers Internat. Conv., Chgo., 1982, 84. Mem. Speakers Bur., Calif. Assn. for Neurologically Handicapped Children, 1964-70, v.p., 1969; bd. dirs. Ravenwood Homeowners Assn., 1979-82, v.p., 1979-80, sec., 1980-81, mem. organizing com. Minority Bus. Fair, San Francisco, 1976; pres., bd. dirs. Lakewood Condominium Assn., 1984-87; mem. trustee Ch. of Religious Sci., 1992-95; treas. First Ch. Religious Sci., 1994-98, lic. practitioner, pres., 1990-91, sec., 1989-90. Mem. Am. Fedn. Astrologers, Calif. Scholarship Fedn. (life), Alpha Gamma Sigma (life). Home: 1200 Russell Way Hayward CA 94541 also: 1200 Russell Way Apt 303 Hayward CA 94541-2892

RANDLE, CAMMON C., filmmaker; b. Provo, Utah, 1981; m. Lorri Randle. Student in Multi-media, Utah Valley State Coll.; B in Comm., Brigham Young U., Provo, Utah. Founder, dir. photography CopperRain Prodns., Provo, Utah, 2004—. Attendee Provo Labs, Utah. Lighting technician intern: The Work and the Glory: Pillar of Light, 2005. Named one of Best Entrepreneurs Under 25, BusinessWeek mag., 2006. Office: CopperRain Prodns 2419 W 180 South Provo UT 84601-3678 Office Phone: 801-836-0182. E-mail: cammon@copperrain.com.

RANDLE, ELLEN EUGENIA FOSTER, opera and classical singer, educator; b. New Haven, Oct. 2, 1948; d. Richard A.G. and Thelma Lousie (Brooks) Foster; m. Ira James William, 1967 (div. 1972); m. John Willis Randle, Dec. 24, 1983. Student, Calif. State Coll., Sonoma, 1970; studied with Boris Goldovsky, 1970; student, Grad. Sch. Fine Arts, Florence, Italy, 1974; studied with Tito Gobbi, Florence, 1974; student, U. Calif., Berkeley, 1977; BA in World History, Lone Mountain Coll., 1976, MA in Performing Arts, 1978; studied with Madam Eleanor Steber, Graz, Austria, 1979; studied with Patricia Goehl, Munich, Germany, 1979; MA in Counseling and Psychology, U. San Francisco, 1990, MA in Marriage and Family Therapy, 1994, EdD in Internat. Multicultural Edn., 1998. Asst. artistic dir. Opera Piccola, Oakland, Calif., 1990—92; instr. African Am. culture and humanities Mission C.C., Santa Clara, Calif., 1997—; instr. Peralta C.C. Dist., Oakland, 1998—; psychotherapy intern, sr. peer counseling program City of Fremont, Calif., 1999—2000; psychotherapist, marriage family therapist intern Portia Bell Human Behavioral Health and Tng. Ctr., Concord, Calif., 2000—01; family facilitator EMQ Family and Children Svcs., Sacramento, 2002; family cons. Positive Options Family Svcs., Sacramento, 2002—; pvt. practice (with Dr. Harmesh Kumar), dir. residential svcs. Therapeutic Residential Svc., Inc., Concord, 2004—. Instr. East Bay Performing Art Ctr., Richmond, 1986, Chapman Coll., 1986, Las Positas C.C., Livermore, Calif., 1999—; adj. prof. U. Phoenix, 1999-2000, adj. prof. U. Pheonix, Northern Calif., 2001-. Singer opera prodns. Porgy & Bess, Oakland, Calif., 1980-81, LaTraviata, Oakland, Calif., 1981-82, Aida, Oakland, 1981-82, Madame Butterfly, Oakland, 1982-83, The Magic Flute, Oakland, 1984, numerous others; performances include TV specials, religous concerts, musicals; music dir. Natural Man, Berkeley, 1986; asst. artistic dir. Opera Piccola, Oakland, Calif., 1990—. Art commr. City of Richmond, Calif. Recipient Black Am. Achievement award. Mem. Music Tchrs. Assn., Internat. Black Writers and Artists Inc. (life, local #5), Nat. Coun. Negro Women, Nat. Assn. Negro Musicians, Calif. Arts Fedn., Calif. Assn. for Counseling and Devel. (black caucus), Nat. Black Child Devel. Inst., The Calif.-Nebraskan Orgn., Inc., Calif. Marital & Family Therapist Assn. (San Francisco chpt.), Black Psychotherpist of San Francisco and East Bay Area, San Francisco Commonwealth Club, Gamma Phi Delta. Democrat. Mem. A.M.E. Zion Ch. Avocations: cooking, entertaining. Home: 5314 Boyd Ave Oakland CA 94618 Office: Therapeutic Residential Svc Inc 2063 Pacheco St Concord CA 94520 Office Phone: 925-356-0122. E-mail: ellenefoster@comcast.net.

RANK, LARRY GENE, retired bank executive; b. Auburn, Ind., July 14, 1935; s. Lloyd R. Rank and Elizabeth M. (Williamson) Jackson; m. Bette Whitehurst, May 2, 1959; children: Kevin, Karen Grad., Am. Inst. Banking, 1962, U. Balt., 1969, Grad. Sch. Banking, Brown U., 1975, Nat. Council Savs. Instns., 1985. Exec. v.p. Provident Bank Md., Balt., 1982-85, pres., COO, 1985-90, dir., 1984-90; mng. dir. Jannotta, Bray & Assocs. Inc., Balt., 1991-92; exec. dir. Big Bros. and Big Sisters Ctrl. Md. Inc., 1993-96. Assoc. cons. Drake, Beam, Morin, 1997-98. Bd. dirs. ARC, Ctrl. Md. chpt., 1984-98, chmn. bd., 1990-92, bd. dirs. Ctrl. Ariz. chpt., 1998—, nat. com. on nominations; bd. dirs. United Way of Ctrl. Md., Balt., 1990-92; chair Gov.'s Vol. Awards Selection com., 1989; chmn. Am. Heart Assn.-Heart Ball, 1989-98, bd. dirs. Am. Heart Assn.; chmn. bd. Neighborhood Housing Svcs.; bd. dirs. Goodwill Industries, 1989-98; vol. Valley Big Bros./Big Sisters, Phoenix; bd. dirs. N.W. Hosp. Ctr., 1985-98, chair sys. bd., 1997-98; bd. dirs. Big Bros./Big Sisters Ctrl. Md. Mem.: Wildcat Club Villanova U., Foothills Golf Club (Phoenix), Deacon Club Wake Forest. Lutheran. Avocations: golf, sports, books, travel. Personal E-mail: rank37@msn.com.

RANKAITIS, SUSAN, artist; b. Cambridge, Mass., Sept. 10, 1949; d. Alfred Edward and Isabel (Shimkus) Rankaitis; m. Robbert Flick, June 5, 1976. BFA in Painting, U. Ill., 1971; MFA in Visual Arts, U. So. Calif., 1977. Rsch. asst., art dir. Plato Lab., U. Ill., Urbana, 1971-75; art instr. Orange Coast Coll., Costa Mesa, Calif., 1977-83; chair dept. art Chapman Coll., Orange, Calif., 1983-90; Fletcher Jones chair art Scripps Coll., Claremont, Calif., 1990—. Represented by Robert Mann Gallery, NYC; overview panelist visual arts Nat. Endowment for Arts, 1983, 84; selector Bingham Ednl. Trust, 1997—2002; scholar-in-residence Borchard Found., Missillac, France, 2004; artist-in-residence Europos Parkus, 2005. One-woman shows include LA County Mus. Art, 1983, Internat. Mus. Photography, George Eastman House, 1983, Gallery Min. Tokyo, 1988, Ruth Bloom Gallery, Santa Monica, 1989-90, 92, Schneider Mus., Portland, Ore., 1990; Ctr. Creative Photography, 1991, Robert Mann Gallery, NYC, 1994, 97, 2007, Mus. Contemporary Photography, Chgo., 1994, Mus. Photog. Arts, 2000, Europos Parkas, Vilnius, 2005; represented in permanent collections MOCA, LA, U. N.Mex Art, Ctr. Creative Photography, Mus. Contemporary Photography, Chgo., Santa Barbara Mus. Art, LA County Mus. Art, Mpls. Inst. Arts, St. Louis Art Mus., San Francisco Mus. Modern Art, Art Inst. Chgo., Mus. Modern Art, Lodz, Poland, Princeton U. Art Mus., Stanford U. Art Mus., Contemporary Art Mus., Honolulu, Mus. Contemporary Photography, Art Inst. Chgo., St. Louis Art Mus., others. Active art auction Venice Family Clinic, 1980-2005. Recipient Graves award in Humanities, 1985; fellow NEA, 1980, 88, US Annapolis Found. French, 1989, Agnes Bourne fellow Djerassi Found., 1989, Award in the Visual Arts, Flintridge Found., 2004; Durfee Chinese/Am. grantee, 2000-2001, Cultural Affairs grantee City L.A., 2001, grantee Mellon Found., 2005, 06; Borchard Found. scholar-in-residence, France, 2004. Mem. Mus. of Photographic Arts, Coll. Art Assn., LA County Mus. Art, Mus. Contemporary Art. Home: 3117 N Lansbury Ave Claremont CA 91711-4146 Office Phone: 909-607-4439, 909-920-5969. Business E-Mail: srankait@scrippscollege.edu.

RANKER, KEVIN, state legislator; b. Orcas Island, Wash. married; 1 child. BS in Coastal Ecol. & Cmty. Devel., Evergreen State Coll., Olympia, Wash. Former student counselor; former chair Bd. County Commrs., Wash. Counties Transp. Com., Wash. Coastal Counties Caucus, Puget Sound Salmon Recovery Coun.; former bd. mem. Puget Sound Partnership; former mem. Wash. State Shoreline Hearings Bd.; councilmember San Juan County, 2004—08; mem. Dist. 40 Wash. State Senate, 2008—. Former chmn. Wash. Counties Transp. Com., Wash. Coastal Counties Caucus. Democrat. Office: 402 Legislative Bldg PO Box 40440 Olympia WA 98504-0440 Office Phone: 360-786-7678.

RANKIN, ALEX C., management executive; B in Commerce, BA in Psychology, MBA. With Agra Industries, Ltd., 1976-94; pres., CEO NexCycle, Inc., Irving, Tex., 1994—. Office: Nexcycle 26021 Business Center Dr Redlands CA 92374-4553 E-mail: arankin@nexcycle.com.

RANNEY, HELEN MARGARET, retired internist, hematologist, educator; b. Summer Hill, NY, Apr. 12, 1920; d. Arthur C. and Alesia (Toolan) Ranney. AB, Barnard Coll., 1941; MD, Columbia U., 1947; ScD, U. S.C., 1979, SUNY, Buffalo, 1996. Diplomate Am. Bd. Internal Medicine. Intern Presbyn. Hosp., NYC, 1947—48, resident, 1948—50, asst. physician, 1954—60; practice medicine specializing in internal medicine, hematology NYC, 1954—70; instr. Coll. Phys. and Surg. Columbia, NYC, 1954—60; from assoc. prof. to prof. medicine Albert Einstein Coll. Medicine, NYC, 1960—70; prof. medicine SUNY, Buffalo, 1970—73, U. Calif., San Diego, 1973—90, chmn. dept. medicine, 1973—86. Disting. physician vet. adminstr., 1986—91; cons. Alliance Pharm. Corp., San Diego, 1991—2004; ret., 2004. Master: ACP; fellow: AAAS; mem.: NAS, Am. Acad. Arts and Scis., Am. Assn. Physicians, Harvey Soc., Am. Soc. Hematology, Am. Soc. for Clin. Investigation, Inst. Medicine, Alpha Omega Alpha, Sigma Xi, Phi Beta Kappa. Personal E-mail: hranney@ucsd.edu.

RANSLOW, PAUL B., former academic administrator; BA, Pacific Univ., 1971; MA, Springfield Coll.; PhD, Harvard Univ. Dean admissions, v.p. admissions, exec. v.p., interim pres. Pitzer Coll., Calif., 1984—95; pres. Ripon Coll., Wis., 1995—2002; cons. College Board, Assoc. Ind. Calif. Coll. & Univ., 2002—05; pres. Sierra Nevada Coll., N.Mex., 2005—06.

RAO, NARSING A., ophthalmologist, pathologist, educator; arrived in U.S., 1968; MD, Osmania U., Hyderabad, India, 1967. Cert. Am. Bd. Ophthalmology, Am. Bd. Pathology. Prof. ophthalmology and pathology U. So. Calif., LA, 1983—; dir. uveitis and ophthalmic pathology Doheny Eye Inst., LA, 1983—. Contbr. articles to profl. jours. Pres. Internat. Uveitis Soc., Bethesda, Md., 2000—05. Recipient Zimmerman Gold (Bietti) medal, Am. Acad. Ophthalmology, 2003; grantee, NIH, 1985—2008. Mem.: Am. Ophthal. Soc. Achievements include research in free radical biology. Office: Doheny Eye Inst 1450 San Pablo St Los Angeles CA 90033 Office Fax: 323-442-6634. Business E-Mail: nrao@usc.edu.

RAPADAS, LEONARDO M., prosecutor; b. 1960; BS, Pacific Univ.; JD, Williamette Univ. Coll of Law. Pros. Guam Atty. Gen. office, 1989—97, chief pros., 1997—99; US Atty. dist. Guam & Mariana Islands US Dept. Justice, Saipan, 2003—. Office: US Attys Office Sirena Plz Ste 500 108 Hernan Cortez PO Box 500377 Saipan MP 96950-0377

RAPAPORT, MICHAEL, actor; b. Bronx, NY, Mar. 20, 1970; m. Nichole Beattie, Jan. 2000 (separated); 2 children. Founder Release Entertainment. Actor: (films) Zebrahead, 1992, Point of No Return, 1993, Poetic Justice, 1993, Money for Nothing, 1993, True Romance, 1993, The Scout, 1994, Higher Learning, 1994, Kiss of Death, 1995, Mighty Aphrodite, 1995, The Basketball Diaries, 1995, Ill Town, 1996, Beautiful Girls, 1996, The Pallbearer, 1996, Copland, 1997, Kicked in the Head, 1997, Metro, 1997, A Brother's Kiss, 1997, Subway Stories: Tales from the Underground, 1997, The Naked Man, 1998, Men, 1998, Palmetto, 1998, King of the Jungle, 1999, Deep Blue Sea, 1999, Kiss Toledo Goodbye, 1999, Small Time Crooks, 2000, Men of Honor, 2000, Bamboozled, 2000, Chain of Fools, 2000, Lucky Numbers, 2000, The 6th Day, 2000, (voice) Dr. Doolittle 2, 2001, King of the Jungle, 2001, Paper Soldiers, 2002, Triggermen, 2002, A Good Night to Die, 2003, This Girl's Life, 2003, America Brown, 2004, Scrambled Eggs, 2004, Hitch, 2005, Special, 2006, (TV series) Boston Public, 2001-04, The War at Home, 2005, (TV films) Subway Stories: Tales from the Underground, 1997, Rescuers: Stories of Courage: Two Families, 1998; actor, exec. prodr. (films) 29 Palms, 2002; TV appearances include China Beach, 1990, Murphy Brown, 1992, The Fresh Prince of Bel-Air, 1993, NYPD Blue, 1993, ER, 1998, Rude Awakening, 1998, Friends, 1999.

RAPHAEL, MOLLY (MARY E. RAPHAEL), retired library director; b. Columbus, Ohio; d. Paul and Dorothy Osborn Horst; m. Ted Raphael. B in Psychology, Oberlin Coll., Ohio, 1967; MLS, Simmons Coll., Boston, 1969. Various positions starting with asst. children's libr. DC Pub. Libr., 1970—98, dir., 1998—2003; dir. librs. Multnomah County Libr., Portland, Oreg., 2003—09, ret., 2009. Mem. Freedom to Read Found., Friends of Librs. USA. Recipient Alumni Achievement award, Simmons Coll. Grad. Sch. Libr. and Info. Sci., 2007, Arthur Flemming Civil Rights award, 2008. Mem.: ALA (mem. governing bd.), Urban Librs. Coun.*

RAPHAEL, STEVEN P., dean, political science professor; BA in Econs., San Diego State U., 1990; PhD in Econs., U. Calif., Berkeley, 1996. Asst. prof. econs. U. Calif., San Diego, 1996—99, asst. prof. pub. policy Berkeley, 1999—2002, assoc. prof., 2002—06, chancellors prof., 2002—07, prof. pub. policy, 2006—; assoc. dean Goldman Sch. Pub. Policy, U. Calif., Berkeley, 2003—06, now interim dean. Rsch. affiliate Nat. Poverty Ctr., U. Mich., 2004—; co-dir., co-prin. investigator Berkeley Integrated Grad. Edn., Rsch., and Training (IGERT) Program in Politics, Economics, Psychology, and Public Policy, 2005—. Contbr. articles to profl. jours. Office: Richard & Rhoda Goldman Sch Pub Policy U Calif, Berkeley 2604 Hearst Ave Berkeley CA 94720-7320 Office Phone: 540-643-0536. Office Fax: 510-643-9657. E-mail: stevenraphael@berkeley.edu.*

RAPINO, MICHAEL, music company executive; b. Can. Grad. in Bus., Lakehead U., Thunder Bay, Ont. Dir. entertainment and sports Labatt's Breweries Can., head mktg. brands; ptnr. Core Audience Entertainment (acquired by SFX in 1999), Canada; head Internat. Music divsn. Clear Channel Entertainment (formerly SFX), London; CEO, pres. Global Music Clear Channel Music Group; CEO Live Nation, 2005—. Named a Maverick, Details mag., 2008. Office: Live Nation 9348 Civic Ctr Dr Beverly Hills CA 90210 Office Phone: 310-867-7000.

RAPOPORT, NANCY B., law educator; m. Jeffrey D. Van Niel, Oct. 13, 1996. BA in Legal Studies, Psychology with hon., summa cum laude, Rice U., 1982; JD, Stanford Law Sch., 1985. Bar: Calif. 1987, Ohio 1993, Nebr. 1999, Calif. Supreme Ct. 1987, Ohio Supreme Ct. 1993, Nebr. Supreme Ct. 1999, US Dist. Ct. Hawaii 1988, US Dist. Ct. (no., ea., ctrl., and so. dists.) Calif. 1987, US Dist. Ct. (no. dist.) Tex. 2003, US Ct. Appeals (9th cir.) 1987, US Supreme Ct. 2000. Jud. clk. Hon. Joseph T. Sneed, U.S. Ct. Appeals (9th cir.), San Francisco, 1985—86; assoc. bus.dept. of bankruptcy and workouts group Morrison & Foerster, San Francisco, 1986—91; asst. prof. Ohio State U. Coll. Law, Columbus, 1991—95, tenured assoc. prof., 1995—98, assoc. dean student affairs, 1996—98, prof., 1998; dean, prof. law U. Nebr. Coll. Law, Lincoln, 1998—2000; dean U. Houston Law Ctr., 2000—06, prof. law, 2000—06; with Gordon & Silver Ltd., 2006—07; prof. law. William S. Boyd Sch. Law, U. Nev., Las Vegas, 2007—. Invited spkr., panelist, and presenter in field. Co-editor (with Bala G. Dharan): Enron: Corporate Fiascos and Their Implications, 2004. Bd. trustees Law Sch. Admissions Coun., 2001—04; bd. dir. ADL Southwest Regional Bd., 2001—, Houston Area Women's Ctr., 2003—; bd. mem. Mayor's Adv. Bd. of World Energy Cities Partnership, 2001—04, Houston Disaster Relief Adv. Bd., 2001—04, Houston Chpt. Tex. Gen. Counsel Forum, 2001—05, Anti-Defamation League Southwest Regional Bd., 2001—06, Advisory Coun., WWW United Inc., 2002—06, Tex. Environ. Health Inst., 2002—04, Houston Hillel, 2002—07, Vinson & Elkins Women's Initiative Adv. Bd., 2003—, Houston Area Women's Ctr., 2003—06, Tex. Ctr. for Legal Ethics, 2004—06, Tex. Supreme Ct. Hist. Soc. Adv. Bd., 2004—06, Houston World Affairs Coun., 2002—05, NALP Found. for Law Career Rsch. and Edn., 2005—, Assn. Rice Alumni Bd., 2006—, Am. Bd. Cert., 2007—. Recipient Rice U. Dist. Alumna award; named Outstanding Prof. of Yr., Ohio State U. Coll. Law., 1997, fellow, Am. Bankruptcy Law Jour., 1998. Fellow: Am. Coll. Bankruptcy, Am. Bar Found., Houston Bar Found. (selection com. 2000—, Best Article award); mem.: ABA (task force atty. discipline 2005—, commn. legal debt and forgiveness), Assn. Am. Law Sch.'s Profl. Develop. Com., Ohio State Bar Assn. (legal edn. com. 1997—98), Am. Bankruptcy Inst. (law sch. com. 1994—), Bar Assn. San Francisco, Nat. Assn. Coll. and U. Attys., Nebr. State Bar Assn. (Named Legal Pioneer for Women in Law 1999), Houston Bar Assn., Am. Law Inst. Democrat.

Jewish. Avocations: dance, photography, music, movies, history. Office: Univ Nev Las Vegas William Boyd Sch Law Box 451003 4505 S Maryland Pkwy Las Vegas NV 89154-1003 Business E-Mail: nrapoport@money-law.org.

RAPPAPORT, LAWRENCE, plant physiology and horticulture educator; b. NYC, May 28, 1928; s. Aaron and Elsie R.; m. Norma, Nov. 21, 1953; children: Meryl, Debra Kramer, Craig. BS in Horticulture, U. Idaho, 1950; MS in Horticulture, Mich. State Coll., 1951; PhD in Horticulture, Mich. State U., 1956. Lectr. U. Calif., Davis, 1956-67, jr. olericulturist, dept. vegetable crops, 1956-58, asst. olericulturist, 1958-63, assoc. olericulturist, 1963-67, prof., 1968—, prof. emeritus, 1991—, dir. plant growth lab., 1975-78, chairperson dept. vegetable crops, 1978-84. Vis. scientist Calif. Inst. Tech., 1958; co-dir. Horticulture Subproject, Calif./Egypt project, 1978-82. Contbr. articles to profl. jours. 1st pres. Davis Human Rels. Coun., 1964-66; v.p. Jewish Fedn. Sacramento, 1969; pres. Jewish Fellowship, Davis, 1985-89; founder, 1st dir. Hillel Counselership at Davis, 1965-76. Decorated Bronze star; Guggenheim Found. fellow, 1963, Fulbright fellow, 1964, USPHS Spl. fellow, 1970, Am. Soc. Horticulture Sci. fellow, 1987, Sir Frederick McMaster fellow, 1991. Achievements include discovery of evidence for gibberellin-binding protein in plants; evidence for the signal hypothesis operating in plants, positive evidence for phytochrome-mediated gibberellin metabolism and stem growth; isolation of somaclonal variants of celery bearing stable resistance to Fusarium oxysporum f. sp. apii. Home: 637 Elmwood Dr Davis CA 95616-3514 Office: Dept Plant Environ Sci One Shields Ave Davis CA 95616 Business E-Mail: lrappaport@ucdavis.edu.

RAPPEPORT, IRA J., lawyer; b. Phila., Jan. 13, 1954; BA with honors, Washington U., 1975; JD with honors, Villanova U., 1978. Bar: Calif. 1978. Assoc. Pillstory Madison & Sutro, 1978-83, Memel, Jacobs, Pietro & Gersh, 1983-85, ptnr., 1985-87, McDermott, Will & Emery, LA, 1987—. Mng. editor Villanova Law Rev., 1977-78. Recipient Scribes award Villanova Sch. Law, 1978. Mem. Am. Acad. Hosp. Attys., L.A. County Bar Assn. (mem. healthcare law sect.), Beverly Hills Bar Assn. (mem. healthcare law sect.), Century City Bar Assn. (mem. healthcare law sect.), Nat. Health Lawyers Assn., Calif. Soc. Healthcare Attys. Office: McDermott Will & Emery 2049 Century Park E Fl 34 Los Angeles CA 90067-3101

RAPSON, RICHARD L., history professor; b. NYC, Mar. 8, 1937; s. Louis and Grace Lillian (Levenkind) R.; m. Susan Burns, Feb. 22, 1975 (div. June 1981); m. Elaine Catherine Hatfield, June 15, 1982; 1 child, Kim Elizabeth. BA, Amherst Coll., 1958; PhD, Columbia U., 1966. Asst. prof. Amherst (Mass.) Coll., 1960-61, Stanford (Calif.) U., 1961-65, U. Calif., Santa Barbara, 1965-66; from assoc. prof. to prof. history U. Hawaii, Honolulu, 1966—, founder, dir. New Coll., 1968-73. Bd. dirs. Semester at Sea, U. Pitts.; psychotherapist, Honolulu, 1982—. Author: Individualism and Conformity in the American Character, 1967, Britons View America, 1971, The Cult of Youth, 1972, Major Interpretations of the American Past, 1978, Denials of Doubt, 1980, Cultural Pluralism in Hawaii, 1981, American Yearnings, 1989, Amazed By Life: Confessions of a Non-Religious Believer, 2003, Magical Thinking and The Decline of America, 2007; co-author: (with Elaine Hatfield) Love, Sex and Intimacy: Their Psychology, Biology and History, 1993, Emotional Contagion, 1994, Love and Sex: Cross-Cultural Perspectives, 1995, Rosie, 2000, Recovered Memories, 2002, Darwin's Law, 2003; mem. editl. bd. Univ. Press Am., 1981—. Woodrow Wilson fellow Wilson Found., Princeton, 1960; Edward Perkins scholar, Columbia U., 1961; Danforth tchr. Danforth Found., St. Louis, 1965; recipient E. Harris Harbison for Gifted Tchg. award Danforth Found., 1973, Outstanding Tchr. award Stanford U. 25th Reunion Class, 1992. Mem. Am. Hist. Assn., Orgn. Am. Hist., Nat. Womens Hist. Project, Phi Beta Kappa, Outrigger Canoe Club, Honolulu Club. Avocations: squash, travel, classical music. Office: U Hawaii Dept History 2530 Dole St Honolulu HI 96822-2303 Office Phone: 808-956-6801.

RASGON, NATALIE LUZINA, psychiatry and behavioral sciences professor, director; b. Odessa, Russia, Sept. 9, 1957; d. Lev Lazarevich and Nadejda Abramovna (Vainstein) Luzin; m. Dave Rasgon, Sept. 1, 1989; 1 child, Alexander. MD, Odessa Med. Inst., 1980; PhD in Obstetrics and Gynecology, Acad. Med. Scis., Moscow, 1988, PhD in Path. Physiology, 1988. Assoc. prof. psychiatry and behavioral sciences, obstetrics and gynecology Stanford U., Palo Alto, Calif., 2002—06, prof., 2006—. Dir. Behavior Neuroendocrinology Program, Palo Alto, 2003—07, Ctr. for Neuroscience in Women's Health, Stanford, Calif., 2007—. Recipient Leo G. Rigler, M.D. award for academic achievement, Cedars-Sinai Med. Ctr., 1995. Fellow: Am. Psychiat. Assn.; mem.: AAAS, Soc. Biol. Psychiatry, Internat. Assn. on Women's Mental Health, North Am. Menopause Soc., No. Calif. Psychiat. Soc., Am. Coll. Neuropsychopharmacology (assoc.), Endocrine Soc., NY Acad. Scis., Internat. Soc. Psychoneuroendocrinology, Soc. Neuroscience. Democrat. Achievements include patents for method of dysmenorrhea treatment; improved method of mitochondrial destruction; substance for the reduction of side effects during physical medicine treatment. Avocations: music, theater, tennis. Office: Stanford Dept Psychiatry 401 Quarry Rd Ste 2368 Palo Alto CA 94305 Office Fax: 650-724-3144; Home Fax: 650-724-3144. Business E-Mail: nrasgon@stanford.edu.

RASHID, KAMAL A., university administrator, research educator; b. Sulaimania, Kurdistan, Iraq, Sept. 11, 1944; came to U.S., 1972; s. Ahmad Rashid and Habiba M. Muhiedin; m. Afifa B. Sabir, May 23, 1970; children: Niaz K., Neian K., Suzanne K. BS, U. Baghdad, Iraq, 1965; MS, Pa. State U., 1974, PhD, 1978. Lab. instr. U. Baghdad, Iraq, 1966-72; mem. faculty U. Basrah, Iraq, 1978-80, U. Sulaimania, Iraq, 1980-83; sr. rsch. assoc., vis. prof. Pa. State U., University Park, 1983-86, rsch. assoc. prof. dept. biochemistry and molecular biology, 1992-2000; assoc. dir., prof. biotechnology ctr. Utah State U., Logan, 2000—. Dir. Biotech. Tng. Program program Pa. State U., 1989-2000, dir. summer symposium molecular biology, 1991-92; v.p. Cogenic Inc., State College, Pa., 1989-90; cons., spkr. biotech. tng. program developer. Contbr. articles to profl. jours. Iraqi Ministry Higher Edn. scholar. Mem. AAAS, Soc. for Indsl. Microbiology, Am. Soc. Microbiology, Am. Chem. Soc., Environ. Mutagen Soc., Rotary. Avocations: travel, swimming, reading. Home: 2835 N 2050 E Logan UT 84341-8327 E-mail: krashid@cc.usu.edu.

RASHID, RICHARD F., computer software company executive; B math. & comp. literature, with hon., Stanford U., 1974; MSc in Computer Sci., U. Rochester, 1977, PhD in Computer Sci., 1980. Prof. computer sci. Carnegie Mellon U., Pitts., 1979—91; with Microsoft Corp., Redmond, Wash., 1991—, from mem. staff to v.p. rsch., 1991—94, v.p. rsch., 1994—2000, sr. v.p. rsch., 2000—. Mem. computer directorate adv. com. Nat. Sci. Found.; bd. trustees Anita Borg Inst. Women and Technology, 2004—. Contbr. articles to profl. jours. Fellow: Am. Acad. Arts and Sciences; mem.: IEEE (sr. Emanuel R. Piore award 2008), Assn. Computing Machinery, Nat. Acad. Engring. Achievements include development of one of earliest networked computer games, Alto Trek. Office: One Microsoft Way Redmond WA 98052-6399

RASMUSON, EDWARD BERNARD, banker; b. Aug. 27, 1940; s. Elmer Edwin and Lile Vivian Rasmuson; m. Cathryn Elaine Robertson, Sept. 11, 1969; children: Natasha Ann, Laura Lile, David Edward. BA, Harvard U., 1962. Mgmt. trainee Brown Brothers Harriman, 1963, Chem. NY, 1964; asst. cashier Nat. Bank Alaska, Anchorage, 1964—66, asst. v.p., 1966—68, v.p., 1968—73, pres., 1973—85, chmn. bd. dirs., 1986—2001; chmn. adv. bd. Wells Fargo Bank, Anchorage, 2001—02. Bd. regents U. Alaska, 1975—89; mem. Rasmuson Found., 1973—; past trustee Sheldon Jackson Coll.; past pres. Anchorage United Way; Hon. Consul of Sweden State of Alaska. Mem.: World Bus. Coun., Young Pres.'s Orgn., Harvard Club (N.Y.C.), Rainier Club, Seattle Yacht Club, Wash. Athletic Club, Metropolitan Club, Pioneers Club Am., Explorers Club, Elks, Rotary. Office: Wells Fargo K3212-051 PO Box 196127 Anchorage AK 99519 Home Phone: 907-243-1155; Office Phone: 907-265-2927. Personal E-mail: erasmuson@gci.net.

RASMUSSEN, HARRY PAUL, horticulture and landscape educator; b. Tremonton, Utah, July 18, 1939; s. Peter Y. and Lorna (Nielsen) R.; m. Mary Jane Dalley, Sept. 4, 1959; children: Randy Paul, Lorianne, Trent Dalley, Rachelle. AS, Coll. of So. Utah, 1959; BS, Utah State U., 1961; MS, Mich. State U., 1962, PhD, 1965. Rsch. scientist Conn. Agr. Expt. Sta., New Haven, 1965-66; rschr., instr. Mich. State U., East Lansing, 1966-81; chmn. dept. horticulture and landscape architecture Wash. State U., Pullman, 1981-88; dir. Utah Agrl. Expt. Sta. Utah State U., 1988—, assoc. v.p., 1992—99, 2002—06. Contbr. articles to profl. jours., chpts. to books. Mem. bd. control YMCA, Lansing, Mich., 1976; mem. coun. Boy Scouts Am., Lansing, 1980; stake pres. Ch. of Jesus Christ of Latter Day Saints, Lansing, 1973-81. NDEA fellow, 1961-65. Fellow Am. Soc. Horticulture Sci.; mem. AAAS, Scanning Electron Microscopy (chmn. plant sect. 1976-83, chmn. exptl. sta. com. on orgn. and policy 1996-97). Home: 1949 N 950 E Logan UT 84341-1813 Office: Utah State U 225 Agr Sci Bldg Logan UT 84322-0001

RASMUSSEN, JOHN OSCAR, nuclear research scientist; b. St. Petersburg, Fla., Aug. 8, 1926; s. John Oscar and Hazel R.; m. Louise Brooks, Aug. 27, 1950; children: Nancy, Jane, David, Stephen. BS, Calif. Inst. Tech., 1948; PhD, U. Calif., Berkeley, 1952; MA (hon.), Yale U., 1969. Mem. faculty dept. chemistry U. Calif., Berkeley, 1952-68, 73-91, prof. chemistry, 1971-91, ret., 1991, mem. research staff, 1952-68; sr. rsch. assoc. Lawrence Berkeley Nat. Lab., 1972—91, participating retiree, 1991—; cons., mem. panel nuclear isomer energy project U.S. Dept. Energy, 2004—06. Prof. chemistry Yale U. 1969-73; assoc. dir. Yale Heavy Ion Accelerator Lab., 1970-73; vis. research prof. Nobel Inst. Physics, Stockholm, 1953; vis. prof. Inst. Nuclear Sci. U. Tokyo, 1974, Fudan U., Shanghai, 1979, hon. prof., 1984. Contbr. articles to profl. jours. Served with USN, 1944-46. Recipient E.O. Lawrence Meml. award AEC, 1967; NSF sr. postdoctoral fellow Niels Bohr Inst., Copenhagen, 1961-62, NORDITA fellow, 1979, Guggenheim Meml. fellow, 1973, Alexander von Humboldt sr. rsch. fellow Tech. U. Munich, 1991. Fellow Am. Phys. Soc., AAAS; mem. Am. Chem. Soc. (Nuclear Applications in Chemistry award 1976), Fedn. Am. Scientists (chmn. 1969). Office: Lawrence Berkeley Nat Lab MS 70 319 Berkeley CA 94720-0001

RASMUSSEN, MARILYN, state legislator; b. Seattle, Mar. 10, 1939; m to Don Rasmussen; children: seven, twelve grandchildren. Washington State Representative, 86-92; member, Sch Bd, formerly; Washington State Senator, District 2, 92-, chairwoman, Agriculture & Rural Econ Develop Committee, member, Transportation, Commerce, Trade, Housing & Financial Inst, Education, Ways & Means Committees, State Patrol & Capital Subcomt, currently, Washington State Senate; member, State-Fed Assembly Agriculture & Forestry; member, Women of Vision Advisor Committee & Governor's Prayer Breakfast Committee, currently; member, Nat Conf State Legislature, currently.Farmer, currently; member, Eatonville Sch Bd, 80-87; member, board director, Nisqually Regional Arts Coun & Harborview Visitor's Advisor Committee, currently; member, board director, Good Samaritan Mental Health Bd & Pierce Co Community Action Bd, currently. Marymount Association Sr Housing (board director, currently); Rocky Mountain Elk Found; Sparaway-Parkland Kiwanis; Washington State Dairy Fedn; America Agri-Women; Ohop Grange; Washington Women for Survival Agriculture; Washington Cattlemen's Association; Washington Cattlewoman's Association; America Tree Farm Syst; Tacoma Sportsmen's Club; Nisqually River Interpretive Center Found (board director, currently); South Pierce Chamber of Commerce; Greater Graham Bus Association; Vladivostok Sister City Association. Democrat. Catholic. Address: 33419 Mountain Hwy E Eatonville WA 98328 Mailing: 409 Legis Bldg PO Box 40482 Olympia WA 98504-0482 Office Phone: Legis: 360-786-7602; 800-562-6000; Off: 253-847-2168; Dist: 206-847-3276. Fax: 360-786-7524. E-mail: rasmusse_ma@leg.wa.gov, senrasmussen@msn.com.

RASMUSSEN, ROBERT KENNETH, dean, law educator; b. Brunswick, Ga., Mar. 13, 1960; s. Robert Edward and Marlene Joan (Kus) Rasmussen; m. Rebecca Brown. BA magna cum laude, Loyola U., Chgo., 1982; JD cum laude, U. Chgo., 1985. Bar: Calif. 1987, US Ct. Appeals (1st, 2nd, 5th, 9th cirs.) 1987, US Ct. Appeals (DC, 4th cirs.) 1988. Law clk. for Hon. John C. Godbold US Ct. Appeals (11th cir.), Montgomery, Ala., 1985-86; atty. US Dept. Justice, Washington, 1986-89; asst. prof. law Vanderbilt U. Law Sch., Nashville, 1989—92, assoc. prof., 1992—94, prof., 1994—2007, dir. law and econs. program, 1998—2006, assoc. dean academic affairs, 2002—04, Fed Ex rsch. prof., 2004—05, Milton Underwood prof. law, 2004—07, dir. Ctr. Law and Human Behavior, 2006—07; dean Gould Sch. Law, U. So. Calif., LA, 2007—. Vis. prof. law U. Mich. Law Sch., 1994, U. Chgo. Law Sch., 2004. Contbr. articles to law jours. Mem.: ABA, Order of the Coif. Democrat. Roman Catholic. Avocations: softball, astronomy, cooking. Office: Gould Sch Law U So Calif Los Angeles CA 90089-0071 Office Phone: 213-740-6473.

RASOR, DINA LYNN, journalist, private investigator; b. Downey, Calif., Mar. 21, 1956; d. Ned Shaurer and Genevieve Mercia (Eads) R.; m. Thomas Taylor Lawson, Oct. 4, 1980. BA in Polit. Sci., U. Calif., Berkeley, 1978. Editorial asst. ABC News, Washington, 1978-79; researcher Pres.'s Commn. on Coal, Washington, 1979; legis. asst. Nat. Taxpayers Union, Washington, 1979-81; founder, dir. Project on Mil. Procurement, Washington, 1981-89; investigative reporter Lawson-Rasor Assocs., El Cerrito, Calif., 1990-92; pres., CEO, investigator Bauman & Rasor Group, El Cerrito, Calif., 1993—; chief investigator Follow the Money Project, 2005—. Author: The Pentagon Underground, 1985, Betraying Our Troops, 2007; editor: More Bucks, Less Bang, 1983; contbr. articles to profl. jours. Recipient Sigma Delta Chi Outstanding Leadership award Soc. Profl. Journalists, 1986; named to register Esquire Mag., 1986, Nat. Jour., 1986. Mem. United Ch. Christ. Office Phone: 510-235-5021.

RASTETTER, WILLIAM H., biotechnology company executive; BS in Chemistry, MIT; MA, Harvard U., PhD in Chemistry. Faculty MIT, Cambridge, Mass., 1975—82; scientist/rschr. biocatalysis and chem. scis. groups Genentech, 1982—84, dir. corp. ventures, 1984—86; pres. & CEO IDEC Pharms. Corp., San Diego, 1986—2002, CFO, 1988—93; dir. IDEC Pharms. Corp. (now Biogen IDEC), 1986—; chmn. bd. dirs. IDEC Pharms. Corp., 1996—2002; CEO Biogen IDEC, 2002—03, exec. chmn., 2003—. Bd. dir. Argonaut Technologies, Inc., Illumina, Inc., 1998—, non-exec. chmn., 2005—; mem. Calif. Healthcare Inst.; R.B. Woodward vis. scholar, dept. chem. and chem. biology Harvard U. Office: Biogen IDEC 5200 Research Pl San Diego CA 92122 also: Biogen IDEC 14 Cambridge Ctr Cambridge MA 02142

RATH, ALAN T., sculptor; b. Cin., Nov. 25, 1959; s. George and Carolyn R. BSEE, MIT, 1982. One-man exhbns. include San Jose (Calif.) Art Mus., 1990, Dorothy Goldeen Gallery, Santa Monica, Calif., 1990, 92, Walker Art Ctr., Mpls., 1991, Mus. Contemporary Art, Chgo., 1991, Carl Solway Gallery, Cin., 1991, Inst. Contemporary Mus., Honolulu, 1992, Ctr. Fine Art, Miami, Fla., 1992, Galerie Hans Mayer, Dusseldorf, Germany, 1992, Hiroshima (Japan) City Mus. Contemporary Art, 1994, Worcester (Mass.) Art Mus., 1994, John Weber Gallery, N.Y.C., 1994, Haines Gallery, San Francisco, 1995, 96, 98, Contemporary Art Mus., Houston, 1995, Aspen Art Mus., Colo., 1996, Dorfman Projects, N.Y.C., 1998, Yerba Buena Ctr. for the Arts, San Francisco, 1998, Site Santa Fe (N.Mex.), 1998, Mus. of Art, Austin, Tex., 1999, Scottsdale Mus. of Contemporary Art, 1999; group exhbns. include Visiona, Zurich, 1989, Ars Electronica, Linz, Austria, 1989, L.A. Contemporary Exhbns., 1989, Mus. Folkwang, Essen, Germany, 1989, Cite des Arts et des Nouvelles Technologies, Montreal, 1990, Stadtmuseum Siegburg, Siegburg, Germany, 1990, San Francisco Mus. Modern Art, 1990, 95, 98, Denver ArtMus., 1991, Whitney Am. Art, N.Y.C., 1991, Alvar Alto Mus., Jyvaskyla, Finland, 1992, Internat. Ctr. Photography, N.Y.C., 1992, Padigilione d'Arte Contemporanea, Ferrara, Italy, 1992, John Weber Gallery, N.Y.C., 1993, Spiral Art Ctr., Tokyo, 1994, Aldrich Mus. of Contemporary Art, Ridgefield, Conn., 1995, Otso Gallery, Espo Finland, 1996, LaLonja, Palma de Malloren, Spain, 1996, Kunsthalle, Vienna, 1998, L.A. Mus. Contemporary Art, 1999, Taipei ICA, Taiwan, 2001, Bienal de Valencia, Spain, 2001. Grantee NEA, 1988; Guggenheim fellow, 1994. Office: IKON 830 E 15th St Oakland CA 94606-3631

RATH, HOWARD GRANT, JR., lawyer; b. LA, Sept. 2, 1931; s. Howard Grant and Helen (Cowell) R.; m. Peyton McComb, Sept. 13, 1958 (dec. Apr. 1984); children: Parthenia Peyton, Francis Cowell; m. Dorothy Moser, Aug. 29, 1986. BS, U. Calif., 1953; JD, U. So. Calif., 1958. Bar: Calif. 1959, US Dist. Ct. (cen. dist.) Calif., 1959, US Ct. Claims 1974, US Tax Ct. 1960. Assoc. O'Melveny & Myers, LA, 1959-66; tax counsel, dir. tax adminstrn., asst. treas. Northrop Corp. LA, 1966-74; sr. tax ptnr. Macdonald, Halsted & Laybourne, LA, 1974-86, Hill & Weiss, LA, 1986-90; ptnr. Lewis Brisbois Bisgaard & Smith, LA, 1990—; dir. Rath Packing Co., Waterloo, Iowa, 1966-81. 1st lt. US Army, 1953-55. Mem. State Bar Calif., LA County Bar Assn., LA Yacht Club, The Athenaeum, Order of Coif, Phi Beta Kappa. Republican. Episcopalian. Office: Lewis Brisbois Bisgaard & Smith 221 N Figueroa St Ste 1200 Los Angeles CA 90012-2646 Business E-Mail: rath@lbbslaw.com.

RATHMANN, GEORGE BLATZ, genetic engineering company executive; b. Milw., Dec. 25, 1927; s. Louis and Edna Lorle (Blatz) R.; m. Frances Joy Anderson, June 24, 1950; children: James, Margaret, Laura, Sally, Richard. BS in Phys. Chemistry, Northwestern U., 1948; MS, Princeton U., 1950, PhD in Phys. Chemistry, 1952. With 3M Co., St. Paul, 1951-72, various positions including rsch. chemist, rsch. dir., group tech. dir., mgr. X-ray products; with Litton Med. Systems, Des Plaines, Ill., 1972-75; v.p. R & D diagnostics div. Abbott Labs., North Chicago, Ill., 1975-80; pres., chief exec. officer Amgen Inc., Thousand Oaks, Calif., 1980-88, chmn. Newbury Park, Calif., 1980—90, chmn. emeritus; founder, chmn. ICOS Corp., 1990-2000; pres & CEO Hyseq, Inc., Sunnyvale, Calif., 2000—01, chmn., 2000—; chmn. bd. dir. ZymoGenetics Inc., Seattle, 2000—05. Bd. dirs. ZymoGenetics Inc., Seattle. Mem. NAE, AAAS, Am. Chem. Soc., Indsl. Biotech. Assn. (bd. dirs.), Nat. Sci. and Tech. Medals Found. (bd. dir., pres.), Phi Beta Kappa, Sigma Xi. Office: Hyseq Inc 201 Industrial Rd # 310 San Carlos CA 94070-6211

RATHWELL, PETER JOHN, lawyer; b. Windsor, Ont., Can., Aug. 20, 1943; came to U.S., 1947; s. Harold Wilfred and Jean Isabel (Lucas) R.; m. Ann Wickstrom Williams, Sept. 10, 1977; 1 child, James Michael. BA, U. Ariz., 1965, JD, 1968. Bar: Ariz. 1968. Assoc. Boettcher, Crowder & Schoolitz, Scottsdale, Ariz., 1972-73; ptnr. Snell & Wilmer, Phoenix, 1978—. Lectr. in field. Mem. exec. com. Jr. Achievement Ariz., Phoenix, 1980—92, 2000—, bd. advisors, 1980—, chmn. bd. advisors, 2006—; chmn. scholarship fund St. Mary H.S., 1982—91; mem., chmn. Phoenix Pks. Bd., 1982—87; trustee Orme Sch., 1991—, chair devel. com., 1994—, mem. exec. com., 2006—; treas., trustee Smith Scholarship Trust U. Ariz. Law Sch., 1985—; bd. advisors ABI S.W. Bankruptcy Conf., 1995—, co-chair, 2003—04. Capt. JAGC USAF, 1969—72. Fellow State Bar Ariz. Found. (founding mem.), Maricopa County Bar Found. (founding mem.); mem. Am. Bankruptcy Inst., Ariz. Bar Assn. (bar counsel 1982-87, 97, chmn. discipline hearing com. 1987-93, mem. bankruptcy sect.), Maricopa County Bar Assn. (seminar lectr. 1987), Comml. Law League Am., Phoenix Zoo Wildest Club in Town (founding mem. 1972). Republican. Avocations: fishing, raising cattle. Home: 4523 E Mountain View Rd Phoenix AZ 85028-5213 Office: Snell & Wilmer 1 Arizona Ctr Phoenix AZ 85004 Home Phone: 480-948-5154; Office Phone: 602-382-6203. Business E-Mail: prathwell@swlaw.com.

RATKOWSKI, DONALD J., mechanical engineer, consultant; b. Cleve., July 29, 1938; m. Joyce Ellen Kotlarczyk, July 15, 1961; children: Rhonda, Tamyra, Cheryl, Randall. Student, Ariz. State U.; AAS, Alliance Coll., 1959, DSc (hon.), 1986. Sr. project engr. semiconductor products div. Motorola, 1960-70, 75-77; v.p. engring. Danker & Wohlk, 1970-75; founder, pres. Paragon Optical Inc., 1976-90; exec. v.p. Pilkinton Vision Care, 1987-90, cons., 1990-91; pres. DJR Resources Inc., Paradise Valley, Ariz., 1990—. Mem. adv.

bd. Am. Sec. Coun., 1988-89; mem. steering com. Optometry Coll., Marcinkowski Acad. Medicine, Poland, 1989-91; founder Rigid Gas Permeable Lens Inst., 1985; speaker Nat. Contact Lens Examiners, 1984-91. Contbr. articles to profl. jours.; patentee in field. Sustaining mem. Rep. Nat. Com., 1983-90; mem. U.S. Congl. Adv. Bd., 1990. Recipient Alumnus of Yr. award Alliance Coll., 1985. Mem. Opticians Assn. Am. (assoc. mem. adv. coun. 1987-88), Contact Lens Soc. Am. (bd. dirs. 1986-88, founder scholarship program 1988, hon. chmn. steering com. edn. fund 1989-91), Contact Lens Mfrs. Assn. chmn. external communication com. 1981-90, bd. dirs. 1982-84, Trailblazer award 1987, program chmn. 1989-90, Leonardo DaVinci award 1990), Ariz. Soc. Plastic Engrs. bd. dirs. 1976-78, 83, v.p. 1980-81, pres. 1981-82), Sigma Tau Gamma (Outstanding Alumni award 1985). Home and Office: DJR Resources Inc 8105 N 47th St Paradise Valley AZ 85253

RATLIFF, LOUIS JACKSON, JR., mathematics professor; b. Cedar Rapids, Iowa, Sept. 1, 1931; s. Louis Jackson and Ruth Sara (Sidlinger) R.; m. Georgia Lee Smith, May 9, 1996. BA, State U. Iowa, 1953, MA, 1958, PhD, 1961. Lectr. Ind. U., Bloomington, 1961-63, U. Calif., Riverside, 1963-64, asst. prof. math., 1964-67, assoc. prof., 1967-69, prof., 1969—. Author: Chain Conjectures in Ring Theory, 1978; assoc. editor Procs. of AMS, 1987-92, Comm. in Algebra, 1990-95; contbr. articles to profl. jours. 1st lt. USAF, 1953-57. NSF fellow, 1960-62, grantee, 1965-69, 71-88; recipient Disting. Teaching award, U. Calif.-Riverside, 1983. Mem. Am. Math. Soc., Phi Beta Kappa. Democrat. Seventh Day Adventist. Home: 26660 Ridgemoor Rd Sun City CA 92586 Office: U Calif Dept Math Riverside CA 92521-0001 Office Phone: 951-827-5020. Business E-Mail: ratliff@math.ucr.edu.

RATNER, BUDDY DENNIS, biomedical engineer, educator; b. Bklyn., Jan. 19, 1947; s. Philip and Ruth Ratner; m. Cheryl Cromer; 1 child, Daniel Martin. BS in Chemistry, Bklyn. Coll., 1967; PhD in Polymer Chemistry, Bklyn. Poly. U., 1972. From fellow to prof. U. Wash., Seattle, 1972—86, prof., 1986—, Darland prof. bioengring., 2005—. Dir. U. Wash. Engineered Biomaterials Engring. Ctr.; founder Asemblon, Inc., Healionics, Inc. Editor: Surface Characterization of Biomaterials, 1989, Plasmas and Polymers, 1994-99, Biomaterials Science: An Introduction to Materials in Medicine, 2d edit., 2004, Characterization of Polymeric Biomaterials, 1997; mem. editl. bds. 9 jours. and book series; editor Jour. Undergrad. Rsch. in Bioengring., 1998—; contbr. over 400 articles to profl. jours. Recipient Faculty Achievement/Outstanding Rsch. award, Burlington Resources Found., 1990, Perkin Elmer Phys. Electronics award for excellence in surface sci. Fellow AAAS, Internat. Acad. Med. and Biol. Engring., Am. Inst. Med. Biol. Engring. (founder, pres. 2002-03), AVS Sci. Technol. Soc. (Medard Welsh medal 2002); mem. AIChE (C.M.A. Stine award 1998), Nat. Acad. Engring., Am. Chem. Soc., Internat. Soc. Contact Lens Rsch., Materials Rsch. Soc., Soc. for Biomaterials (pres. 1991-92, Clemson award 1989, fellow 1994, Founders award 2004, C.W. Hall award 2006), Biomed. Engring. Soc. Achievements include patents in field. Home Phone: 206-286-0969; Office Phone: 206-685-1005. E-mail: ratner@uweb.engr.washington.edu.

RATNER, DAVID LOUIS, retired law educator; b. London, Sept. 2, 1931; AB magna cum laude, Harvard U., 1952, LLB magna cum laude, 1955. Bar: N.Y. 1955. Assoc. Sullivan & Cromwell, NYC, 1955-64; assoc. prof. Cornell Law Sch., Ithaca, NY, 1964-68, prof., 1968-82; prof. law U. San Francisco Law Sch., 1982-99, dean, 1982-89, prof. emeritus, 1999—. Exec. asst. to chmn. SEC, Washington, 1966-68; chief counsel Securities Industry Study, Senate Banking Com., Washington, 1971-73; vis. prof. Stanford (Calif.) U., 1974, Ariz. State U., Tempe, 1974, U. San Francisco, 1980, Georgetown U., Washington, 1989-90, U. Calif., Hastings, San Francisco, 1992, U. Ariz., 2004; mem. Larkspur (Calif.) Planning Commn., 1992-2004. Author: Institutional Investors: Teaching Materials, 1978, Securities Regulation: Cases and Materials, 6th edit., 2002, Securities Regulation in a Nutshell, 9th edit., 2006. Fulbright scholar Monash U., Australia, 1981. Mem. Harvard Club of San Francisco (pres. 1999-2000), Phi Beta Kappa. Home and Office: 84 Polhemus Way Larkspur CA 94939-1928 E-mail: dlratner@aol.com.

RATTIE, KEITH O., gas industry executive; Sr. v.p. The Coastal Corp., 1996—2001; pres. Questar Corp., 2001—02, pres., CEO, 2002—03, chmn., pres., CEO, 2003—. Dir. Zions First Nat. Bank, Gas Technology Institute, U. Wyo. Energy Resources Coun. Mem.: Salt Lake C. of C. Office: c/o Questar 180 E 100 S Salt Lake City UT 84111*

RATTO, DOUGLAS C., protective services official; b. Feb. 19, 1939; m. Katty Ratto; children: Brian, Chris, Julie. With Lincoln Fire Dist., North Stockton, Calif., 1961-65; firefighter City of Stockton, 1965-73, capt., 1973-80, bn. chief, 1980-82, dep. fire chief, 1982-88, fire chief, 1988—. Mem. Local 1229 (pres.). Office: City of Stockton Fire Dept 425 N Eldorado St Stockton CA 95202-1997

RATZENBERGER, JOHN DESZO, actor, writer, film director; b. Bridgeport, Conn., Apr. 6, 1947; s. Dezso Alexander and Bertha (Grohowski) R.; m. Elizabeth Georgia Stiny, Sept. 9, 1984 (div. May 27, 2004); children: James John, Nina Katherine. Grad. high sch., Bridgeport, Conn.; PhD, Sacred Heart U., 1992, LHD (hon.), 2002. Actor, writer, dir. own theater troupe Sal's Meat Market, 1971-75; touring actor, 1971-81. Owner, pres., founder Eco-Pack Industries, Kent, Wash. Performed various one-man shows and directed, Stowe Playhouse, Vermont; appeared in plays Curse of the Starving Class, The Connection; films include The Ritz, 1974, Twilight's Last Gleaming, 1977, A Bridge Too Far, 1977, Valentino, 1977, Warlords of Atlantis, 1978, Superman, 1978, The Bitch, 1979, Arabian Adventure, 1979, Yanks, 1979, Star Wars: Episode V-The Empire Strikes Back, 1980, Motel Hell, 1980, Superman II, 1980, Outland, 1981, Ragtime, 1981, Warlords of the 21st Century, 1982, Firefox, 1982, Gandhi, 1982, House II: The Second Story, 1987, Going to the Chapel, 1988, Toy Story (voice), 1995, That Darn Cat, 1997, One Night Stand, 1997, Bad Day on the Block, 1997, A Fare to Remember, 1998, A Bug's Life (voice), 1998, Toy Story 2 (voice), 1999, Tic Tock, 2000, Determination of Death, 2001, Monsters, Inc., 2002, Finding Nemo (voice), 2003, The Incredibles (voice), 2004, All In, 2005, Something New, 2006, (voice) Cars, 2006, Superman II (voice), 2006, Ratatouille (voice), 2007, WALL-E (voice), 2008; (TV films) The Good Soldier, 1981, Goliath Awaits, 1981, Combat High, 1986, Timestalkers, 1987, Friends in Space, 1990 (also writer), Camp Cucamonga, 1990, Dog's Best Friend, 1997, The Pennsylvania Miners' Story, 2002, Mystery Woman: Redemption, 2006; video (voice) Toy Racer, 2001, Extreme Skate Adventure, 2003, The Incredibles: Rise of the Underminer, 2005; TV performances include Songs of a Sourdough, Secret Amy, 1979, (series) Cheers, 1982-1993 (also dir. several episodes 1988-93); guest appearences include Hill Street Blues, 1982, Wizards and Warriors, 1983, Magnum P.I., 1984, St. Elsewhere, 1985, The Love Boat, 1985, The Tortellis, 1987, Mickey's 60th Birthday, 1988, Disneyland, 1990, Wings, 1990, Captain Planet and the Planeteers, 1990, Nurses, 1992, Bill Nye, the Science Guy, 1993, Moon Over Miami, 1993, (voice) The Simpsons, 1994, Murphy Brown, 1995, Caroline in the City, 1996, Sabrina, The Teenage Witch, 1997, The Detectives, 1997, Remember WENN, 1998, Touched by an Angel, 2000, (voice) Pigs Next Door, 2000, That '70's Show, 2001, Fraiser, 2002, 8 Simple Rules for Dating My Teenage Daughter, 2003; (TV mini series) Small World, 1988; dir. (TV series) Sister, Sister, 1994, (1 episode) Evening Shade, 1994, Pearl, 1996; prodr., screenwriter BBC, Paravision, Royal Court Theater, Hampstead Theater Club, Royal Acad. Dramatic Arts, and Granada TV; co-author TV plays: Friends in Space, 1978, Scalped, 1979; exec. prodr., creator, (TV) Locals, 1994; host Pixar's 20th Anniversary Special, 2006; performer Dancing with the Stars, 2007; co-author with Joel Engel We've Got It Made In America: A Common Man's Salute to an Uncommon Country, 2006. Chmn., largest internet venture connecting diabetes info. & rsch. www.childrenwithdiabetes.com; nat. walk chmn. Juvenile Diabetes Found.; actively involved with other various diabetes organizations; founder, actively involved Nuts, Bolts and Thingamajigs Found.: road trip (Travel Channel) Made in America. Recipient cash award Arts Council of Great Britain, Father of Yr. award, Father's Day Coun. Am., 1996, Outstanding Role Model award, Am. Diabetes Assn., for writing, directing and producing, awarded Cleo and 3 Aegis awards. Mem. AFTRA, SAG, Writers Guild Am., Dirs. Guild, Am. Farmland Trust, Brit. Actors Equity Assn., Greenpeace, Wilderness Soc., Nat. Resources Def. Coun., Sierra Club (San Francisco). Achievements include development of packaging alternatives in 1989 made from biodegradable and non-toxic recycled paper; rowed a boat non-stop for more than 36 miles around Vashon Island, Wash. State to raise money for Special Olympics, 1993. Holds record as only person to make this 16 hour trip non-stop; drove Harley Davidson cross-country from NY to Las Vegas to raise awareness for Juvenile Diabetes, 1998. Avocations: sailing, reading, woodworking. Mailing: c/o Schachter Entertainment 1157 S Beverly Dr Los Angeles CA 90035

RATZLAFF, CORDELL R., application developer; b. Mar. 1960; m. Karen Ratzlaff. BA in Psychology, U. Nebr.; grad. studies in Industrial Engring., Ohio State U. With NASA Ames Rsch. Ctr.; joined Apple, Inc., 1990, mgr. Human Interface Group, Macintosh Sys. Software, 1994—99; head design and devel. of online travel reservation sites GetThere.com; creative dir. Digital Media Group Frog Design, San Francisco; dir. user-centered design Cisco Sys., Inc., San Jose, Calif., 2007—. Office: Cisco Sys, Inc 170 W Tasman Dr San Jose CA 95134 Office Phone: 408-526-4000.

RAUCH, BILL, performing company executive, theater director; BA, Harvard Coll. Co-founder, artistic dir. Cornerstone Theater Co., LA, 1986—2006; artistic dir. Oreg. Shakespeare Festival, Ashland, 2007—. Assoc. artist Yale Repertory Theater, South Coast Repertory Theater; bd. dirs. Theater Comm. Group, 1992—98; Claire Trevor prof. drama U. Calif., Irvine, 2005—07. US Artists Prudential fellow, 2008. Office: Oreg Shakespeare Festival 15 S Pioneer St Ashland OR 97520*

RAUCH, IRMENGARD, linguist, educator; b. Dayton, Ohio, Apr. 17, 1933; d. Konrad and Elsa (Knott) R.; m. Gerald F. Carr, June 12, 1965; children: Christopher, Gregory. Student, Nat. U. Mex., summer 1954; BS with honors, U. Dayton, 1955; MA, Ohio State U., 1957; postgrad. (Fulbright fellow), U. Munich, Fed. Republic Germany, 1957-58; PhD, U. Mich., 1962. Instr., German and linguistics U. Wis., Madison, 1962-63, asst. prof., 1963-66; assoc. prof. German U. Pitts., 1966-68; assoc. prof. German and linguistics U. Ill., Urbana, 1968-72, prof., 1972-79, U. Calif., Berkeley, 1979—. Author: The Old High German Diphthongization: A Description of a Phonemic Change, 1967, The Old Saxon Language: Grammar, Epic Narrative, Linguistic Interference, 1992, Semiotic Insights: The Data Do the Talking, 1998, The Gothic Language: Genetic Provenance and Typology, Readings, 2002, The Phonology/ Paraphonology Interface and the Sounds of German Across Time, 2008; editor (with others): Approaches in Linguistic Methodology, 1967; editor: Spanish edit., 1974, Der Heliand, 1974, Linguistic Method: Essays in Honor of Herbert Penzl, 1979, The Signifying Animal: The Grammar of Language and Experience, 1980, Language Change, 1983, The Semiotic Bridge: Trends from California, 1989, On Germanic Linguistics: Issues and Methods, 1992, Insights in Germanic Linguistics I: Methodology in Transition, 1995, Across the Oceans: Studies from East to West in Honor of Richard K. Seymour, 1995, Insights in Germanic Linguistics II: Classic and Contemporary, 1996, Synthesis in Diversity: Semiotics Around the World, 1997, New Insights in Germanic Linguistics I, 1999, II, 2001, III, 2002; editor of three series: Berkeley Insights in Linguistics and Semiotics, Berkeley Models of Grammars, Studies in Old Germanic Languages and Literatures; founder, co-editor Interdisciplinary Jour. for Germanic Linguistics and Semiotic Analysis; contbr. articles to profl. jours. Named outstanding woman on campus U. Ill. Sta. WILL, 1975; recipient Disting. Alumnus award U. Dayton, 1985; research grantee U. Wis., summer 1966, U. Ill., 1975-79, Eastern Ill. U., 1976, Nat. Endowment Humanities, 1978, U. Calif., Berkeley, 1979—; travel grantee NSF, Linguistics Soc. Am., 1972; Guggenheim fellow, 1982-83; IBM Distributed Acad. Computing Environment, 1986; NEH grantee, 1988; Festschrift: Interdigitations: Essays for Irmengard Rauch, 1999. Mem. Linguistics Soc. Am., MLA, Am. Assn. Tchrs. German (hon.), Society for Germanic Philogy, Philogical Assn. of the West Coast, Phonetics Assn., Semiotic Soc. Am. (pres. 1982-83), Semiotic Circle of Calif. (founder), Internat. Assn. for Semiotic Studies (pres., dir. 5th congress 1994), Alpha Sigma Tau, Delta Phi Alpha. Home: 852 Camden Ct Benicia CA 94510-3633 Office: U Calif Dept German Berkeley CA 94720-0001

RAUE, JORG EMIL, electrical engineer; b. Stettin, Germany, June 13, 1936; came to U.S., 1952; s. Ludwig and Liselotte (Barth) R.; m. Anke Volkmann, June 29, 1957; children: Monika Kay, Jennifer Faye. BSEE, Milw. Sch. Engring., 1961; MSEE, Marquette U., 1965, PhDEE, 1968. Mem. faculty Milw. Sch. Engring., 1961-68, chmn. dept., 1968-69; research engr. TRW Systems, Redondo Beach, Calif., 1969-76, mgr. dept., 1976-79; sr. research scientist TRW Electronic Systems, Redondo Beach, advanced systems mgr., 1980-93; tech. cons. Calif., 1993—; chmn. dept. elec. engring. Calif. Poly. State U., San Luis Opispo, 1979-80. Mem. faculty Marquette U., Milw., 1968-69, Loyola U., L.A., 1970-72, U. So. Calif., L.A., 1983—. Contbr. articles to profl. jours. Served with U.S. Army, 1955-58. Recipient Disting. Tchr. award Milw. Sch. Engring., 1968; named Outstanding Alumnus Milw. Sch. Engring., 1985. Fellow IEEE; mem. Microwave Soc. of IEEE (sec. adminstrn. com. 1985—), Sigma Xi. Avocations: tennis, bicycling, flying, bridge. Home and Office: 28813 Rothrock Dr Palos Verdes Estates CA 90275-3060

RAULINAITIS, PRANAS ALGIS, electronics executive, consultant; b. Kaunas, Lithuania, May 13, 1927; came to U.S., 1954, naturalized, 1960; s. Pranas Viktoras and Paulina (Gervaite) R.; m. Angele Staugaityte, Oct. 4, 1952; 1 son, Pranas Darius. With Commonwealth Rys. of Australia, Melbourne, 1949-53; asst. to fin. acct. Kitchen & Sons, Pty. Ltd., Melbourne, 1953-54; v.p. photo divsn. Interphoto Corp., LA, 1954-71; sr. v.p. fin., sec. Craig Corp., LA, 1971-87; pres. PAR Enterprises, Burbank, Calif., 1987—. Adviser Ministry Fgn. Affairs Republic of Lithuania, 1992; asst. sec. M & F Corp. Enterprises, Ltd., Chgo., 2004-07. Former pres. Lithuanian Am. Coun., Inc. of Calif.; bd. dirs. Lithuanian-Am. Assns.; founder, former dir., v.p. Baltic Am. Freedom League; former mem. Am. Soc. Internat. Law. Home and Office: PAR Enterprises 1501 W Riverside Dr Burbank CA 91506-3027

RAUSSER, GORDON C(LYDE), agricultural and resource economics educator; b. Lodi, Calif., July 21, 1943; s. Elmer A. and Doyve Ester (Meyers) R.; children: Sloan, Stephanie, Paige. BS summa cum laude, Calif. State U., 1965; MS with highest honors, U. Calif., Davis, 1968, PhD with highest honors, 1971. Prof. econs. and agrl. econs. U. Calif., Davis, 1969-74; vis. prof. U. Chgo., 1972-74; prof. econs. and stats. Iowa State U., 1974-75; prof. bus. adminstrn. Harvard U., 1975-78; prof., chmn. dept. agrl. and resource econs. U. Calif., Berkeley, 1979-85, 93-94, Robert Gordon Sproul disting. prof., 1985—, dean nat. resources, 1994-2000; dir. Giannini Found., Berkeley, 1984-86. Vis. prof. Hebrew U. and Ben-Gurion U., Israel, 1978; Ford Found. vis. prof., Argentina, 72; spl. cons. and sr. economist Coun. Econ. Advisors, 1986—87; chief economist AID, 1988—90; advisor econ. rsch. svc. USDA, 1978—80, 1986—88, Agr. Can., 1977—79, Bur. Agrl. Econs., Australia, 1987, U.S. Office Mgmt. and Budget, 1986; mem., chmn. planning com. Sch. Bus. Adminstrn. U. Calif., Berkeley, 1986—87, mem. adv. com. Agrl. Issues Ctr., 1984—85, mem. planning com. Agrl. and Natural Resources Program, 1986, mem. econs. programs evaluation com., 1987—88; mem. Citrus Planning Commn., Brazil, 1984; pres. Inst. for Policy Reform, Washington, 1989—94; prin., founder Law & Econ. Cons. Group, Berkeley, Washington, Chgo., NYC, 1990—2000; sr. cons. CRA Internat., 2000—06. Author: Macroeconomic Environment for U.S. Agricultural Policy, Alternative Agricultural and Food Policies and the 1985 Farm Bill, The Emergence of Market Economies in Eastern Europe, New Directions in Econometric Modeling and Forecasting, Dynamics of Agricultural Systems: Economic Prediction and Control, Quantitative Methods in Agricultural Economics, GATT Negotiations and the Political Economy of Policy Reform; co-editor: Handbook of Agricultural Economics, Vol. 2A, 2002, Vol. 2B, 2002, Vol. 1A, 2001, Vol. 1B, 2001; editor Decision-Making in Business and Economics, 1977-79, Am. Jour. Agrl. Econs., 1983-86, Ann. Rev. Resource Econs., 2006. Mem. western nutrition ctr. coordinating com. USDA, 1980-83; mem. Arab-Am. Coun. for Cultural and Econ. Exch., 1979-81; bd. dirs. Giannini Found. Agrl. Econs., 1979-84, mem. exec. com., 1979-84; mem. planning com. Berkeley Food Coop., 1980-83, planning com. for food policy Resources for the Future, 1984-85; mem. adv. com. Calif. State Dept. Agr., 1982-84; bd. dirs. Am. Agrl. Econs. Awards. Grantee USDA, NSF, World Bank, Chgo. Merc. Exch., U.S. Bur. Mines; Fulbright scholar, Australia, 1987; Sr. fellow Resources for Future, 1984-85. Fellow: AAAS, Am. Agrl. Econs. Assn. (oustanding enduring rsch. contbn. com. 1982—84, outstanding PhD dissertation com. 1974—76, chmn. outstanding article com. 1983—86, rsch. awards of merit 1976, 1978, 1980, 1982, 1986, 1989, 1992, Pub. Enduring quality award 1993, rsch. awards of merit 1993, Disting. Policy Contbn. award 1993, rsch. awards of merit 1994, 2000, 2001), Am. Statis. Assn.; mem.: Coll. Natural Resources Citation, Western Agrl. Econ. Assn. (Best Pub. Rsch. award 1978, Outstanding Pub. Rsch. award 1994), Ops. Rsch. Soc., Math. Assn. Am., Econometric Soc., Am. Acad. Polit. and Social Sci., Am. Econ. Assn., Commonwealth Club (dir. agr. study group 1983—84), Alpha Zeta, Alpha Gamma Rho. Home: 661 San Luis Rd Berkeley CA 94707-1725 Office: U Calif Berkeley ARE 230 Giannini Hall Berkeley CA 94720-3310 Business E-Mail: rausser@are.berkeley.edu.

RAVEN, BERTRAM H(ERBERT), psychology professor; b. Youngstown, Ohio, Sept. 26, 1926; s. Morris and Lillian R.; m. Celia Cutler, Jan. 21, 1961; children: Michelle G., Jonathan H. BA in psychology summa cum laude with great distinction, Ohio State U., 1949, MA in psychology, 1950; PhD in social psychology, U. Mich., 1953. Rsch. assoc. Rsch. Ctr. for Group Dynamics, Ann Arbor, Mich., 1952-54; lectr. psychology U. Mich., Ann Arbor, 1953-54; vis. prof. U. Nijmegen, U. Utrecht, Netherlands, 1954-55; psychologist RAND Corp., Santa Monica, Calif., 1955-56; prof. UCLA, 1956—, chair dept. psychology, 1983-88, prof. emeritus, 1991—. Vis. prof. Hebrew U., Jerusalem, 1962-63, U. Wash., Seattle, 1965, U. Hawaii, Honolulu, 1968, London Sch. Econs. and Polit. Sci., 1969-70; external examiner U. of the W.I., Trinidad and Jamaica, 1980—, rsch. assoc. Psychol. Rsch. Ctr., 1993—; participant Internat. Expert Conf. on Health Psychology, Tilburg, Netherlands, 1986; cons., expert witness in field, 1979—; mem. internat. adv. bd. Acad. Freedom, Bar-Ilan U., 2005—; mem. sci. bd. Kurt Lewin Ctr. Psychol. Rsch. Kazimierza Wielkiego U., Poland; affiliate prof. U. Haifa, 2006—. Author: (with others) People in Groups, 1976, Discovering Psychology, 1977, Social Psychology, 1983, Social Psychology: People in Groups (Chinese edit.), 1994; editor: (with others) Contemporary Health Services, 1982, Policy Studies Rev. Ann., 1980; editor: (with others) Lewinian Psychology, 2006; editor: Jour. Social Issues, 1969-74; mem. editl. bd. Jour. of Criminology and Social Psychology, 2001-, Revista de Psicologia de la Salud, 1995-; mem. adv. bd. Jour. Entrepreneurship, 2004-; contbr. articles to profl. jours. Co-dir. Tng. Program in Health Psychology, UCLA, 1979-88; cons. WHO, Manila, 1985-86; cons., expert witness various Calif. cts., 1978—; mem. bd. dir., UCLA Emeriti Assn., 2007-. Guggenheim fellow, Israel, 1962-63; Fulbright scholar Netherlands, 1954-55, Israel, 1962-63, Britain, 1969-70; recipient Citation from L.A. City Coun., 1966, 2006, Rsch. on Soc. power by Calif. Sch. of profl. psychology, L.A., 1991; NATO sr. fellow, Italy, 1989. Fellow APA (chair bd. social and ethical responsibility 1978-82, ethics com. 2003-06), Assn. Psychol. Sci., Soc. for Psychol. Study of Social Issues (pres. 1973-74, coun. 1995-97, Kurt Lewin award 1998), Soc. for Personality and Social Psychology; mem. AAAS, Am. Sociol. Assn., Internat. Assn. Applied Psychology, Soc. Exptl. Social Psychology, Assn. Advancement of Psychology (founding, bd. dirs. 1974-81), Internat. Soc. Polit. Psychology (governing coun. 1996-98), Interam. Psychol. Soc., Am. Psychology-Law Soc. Democrat. Jewish. Avocations: guitar, travel, international studies. Home: 2212 Camden Ave Los Angeles CA 90064-1906 Office: UCLA Dept Psychology Los Angeles CA 90095-1563 Office Phone: 310-825-2296.

RAVENHOLT, REIMERT THOROLF, epidemiologist, researcher; b. Milltown, Wis., Mar. 9, 1925; s. Ansgar Benedikt and Kristine Henriette (Petersen) R.; divorced; children: Janna, Mark, Lisa, Dane; m. Betty Butler Howell, Sept. 26, 1981. BS, U. Minn., 1948, MB, 1951, MD, 1952; MPH, U. Calif., Berkeley, 1956. Bd. cert. preventive medicine. Intern USPHS Hosp., San Francisco, 1951-52; epidemic intelligence service officer USPHS Communicable Disease Ctr., Atlanta, 1952-54; dir. epidemiology and communicable disease div. Seattle-King County Health Dept., 1954-61; epidemiology cons. European area USPHS, Paris, 1961-63; assoc. prof. preventive medicine U. Wash. Med. Sch., Seattle, 1963-66; dir. Office of Population, AID, Washington, 1966-79, World Health Surveys, Ctrs. for Disease Control, 1980-82; asst. dir. epidemiology and research Nat. Inst. Drug Abuse, Rockville, Md., 1982-84; chief epidemiology br. FDA, Rockville, Md., 1984-87; dir. World Health Surveys, Inc., Seattle, 1987-93; pres. Population Health Imperatives, Seattle, 1993—. Author/designer website Adventures in Epidemiology. Served with USPHS, 1951-54, 61-63. Recipient Disting Honor award AID, 1973, Hugh Moore Meml. award IPPF and Population Crisis Com., 1974. Fellow Am. Coll. Epidemiology, APHA (Carl Schultz award 1978), mem. Am. Coun. on Sci. and Health (bd. dirs.); mem. Cosmos Club (Washington). Independent. Achievements include discovery of cause of Meriwether Lewis' death of progressive neurosyphilis. Home: 3156 E Laurelhurst Dr NE Seattle WA 98105-5333 Personal E-mail: ravenrt@oz.net.

RAVISHANKARA, AKKIHEBAL R., chemist; PhD, U. Fla., 1975. Chief atmospheric chem. kinetics group NOAA, Boulder, Colo. Adj. prof. dept. chemistry U. Colo., Boulder; postdoctoral rsch. assoc. U. Md., 1976. Named Robertson Meml. lectr., NAS, 1999. Office: DSRC Rm 1A123 325 Broadway Boulder CO 80305-3328

RAWITCH, ROBERT JOE, journalist, educator; b. LA, Oct. 11, 1945; s. Sam and Jean (Reifman) R.; m. Cynthia Z. Knee, Oct. 27, 1968; children: Dana Leigh, Jeremy Aaron, Joshua Eric. BA in Journalism, Calif. State U., Northridge, 1967; MS in Journalism, Northwestern U., 1968. Reporter L.A. Times, 1968-80, asst. met. editor, 1980-82, editor Valley sect., 1982-83, suburban editor, 1983-89, exec. editor Valley and Ventura County edits., 1989-93; dir. editl. ops. Valley and Ventura County edits., 1993-95; sr. v.p. Winner and Assocs., 1996—. Lectr. Calif. State U., Northridge, 1971-83, 95-96, 03-. Co-author: Adat Ari El, The First Fifty Years, 1988. Chmn. Calif. Freedom of Info. Com., 1978-79; pres. Calif. First Amendment coalition, 1991-93; bd. dirs. Temple Adat Ari El, 1987-92, Calif. State U. Northridge Found., 1999-, Univ. Corp., 2000-. Recipient Greater L.A. Press Club award, 1973, 75, 79, L.A. Jewish Youth of Yr. award United Jewish Fund, 1963, Clarence Darrow Found. award, 1979, Heitz award outstanding vol. Calif. State U. Northridge, 2003. Mem. Soc. Profl. Journalists (nat. bd. dirs. 1979-82), Calif. Soc. Newspaper Editors (pres. 1995-96), Medill Alumni Assn. (bd. dirs. 1994-2000), CSUN Journalism Alumni Assn. (bd. dirs. 2002—). Office: Winner & Assocs 2029 Century Park E Ste 1750 Los Angeles CA 90067-3036 Office Phone: 818-385-1900. Business E-Mail: brawitch@winnr.com.

RAWLINGS, ROBERT HOAG, newspaper publisher; b. Pueblo, Colo., Aug. 3, 1924; s. John W. and Dorothy (Hoag) R.; m. Mary Alexandra Graham, Oct. 18, 1947; children: Jane Louise, John Graham, Carolyn Anne, Robert Hoag II. Student, Colo. Coll., 1942—44, Colo. U., 1944—45; BA, Colo. Coll., 1947. Reporter Pueblo Chieftain and Pueblo Star-Jour., 1947-51, advt. rep., 1951-62, gen. mgr., 1962-79, pub., editor, 1980—. Sec. Star-Jour. Pub. Corp., 1962-84, pres., 1984—; past chmn. bd. dirs. Colo. Nat. Bank, Pueblo; mem. adv. bd. U.S. Bank. Bd. dirs. U.S. Air Force Acad. Found., Colo. State U.-Pueblo Found.; pres. Robert Hoag Rawlings Found., So. Colo. Cmty. Found., Medal of Honor Meml. Com. With USNR, 1945-47. Named Colo. Newspaper Person of Yr., 1989, Disting. Univ. Fellow Pres. Club U. So. Colo., 1993, Outstanding Citizen of Yr. Pueblo C. of C. 1994, Colo. Bus. Leader of Yr., Colo. Assn. of Commerce and Industry, 1994; recipient Outstanding Svc. to Univ. award U. So. Colo. Alumni Assn., 1993, Colo. Corp. Philanthropy award Nat. Philanthropy Assn., 1993, Louis T. Benezet award Colo. Coll. Alumni Assn., 1996, Living Legend award U. Colo., 1997, Outstanding Am. Achievement award U. So. Colo., 1997, Outstanding Svc. to Hispanic Cmty. award, U. So. Colo. and Pueblo Hispanic Edn. Found., 1999, Creative Spirit award Pueblo United Way, 1998, Lifetime Svc. award Colo. Bd. Vet. Affairs, 2000, Medal of Valur, Congl. Medal Honor Soc., 2000, Libr. Benefactor award Pueblo Libr. Assn., 2001, Vol. of Yr. award Coun. for Advancement and Support Edn., 2004, Voice award Nat. Alliance for Mentally Ill, 2002, Vol. of Yr. award Dist. VI of Coun. for Advancement and Support of Edn., 2004; named to Pueblo Hall of Fame, 1999, The Pueblo Greater Sports Assn. Hall of Fame, 1999; named Donor of Yr. Nat. Assn. Univ. Athletic Devel. dirs., 1995. Mem. Colo. Press Assn. (dir. 1963-66, 76-78, pres. 1985, chmn. bd. dirs. 1986, Golden Rule Makeup award 1998), Rocky Mountain Ad Mgrs. (past pres.), Colo. Forum (past pres.), U. So. Colo. Found. (trustee emeritus), Colo. Mental Health Inst., Rotary. Presbyterian. Home: 1401 Rancho Del Sol Pueblo CO 81008-2043 Office: The Pueblo Chieftain Star Jour Pub Corp PO Box 4040 Pueblo CO 81003-0040

RAWLINS, V. LANE, economics professor, retired academic administrator; b. Rigby, Idaho, Nov. 30, 1937; m. Mary Jo Rawlins, three children. BA in Economics, Brigham Young U., 1963; PhD in Economics, U of Calif., Berkeley, 1969. Faculty Wash. State U., Pullman, 1968-86, chair. economics, 1977-82, vice provost, 1982—86; vice chancellor, academic affairs U. of Alabama, 1986-91; pres. Memphis St. U., Memphis, 1991-00, Wash. State U., Pullman, 2000—07, prof. econs.; mem. William D. Ruckelshaus Ctr. Office: Washington State U Hulbert 121C Pullman WA 99164-1048 Office Phone: 509-335-6666. E-mail: rawlins@wsu.edu.

RAWLINSON, DENNIS PATRICK, lawyer; b. Portland, Oreg., Mar. 1, 1947; s. Thomas F. and Betty (Price) R.; m. M. Diane Schatz, Apr. 26, 1980. BA, U. Notre Dame, 1969; MBA, JD, Cornell U., 1976. Bar: Oreg. 1976, U.S. Dist. Ct. Oreg. 1976; cert. civil trial lawyer Nat. Inst. Trial Advocacy. Assoc. Miller, Nash, Wiener, Hager & Carlsen, Portland, Oreg., 1976-82, ptnr., 1982—. Contbr. articles to profl. jours. Pres., bd. dirs. Portland Opera Assn., 1990-96. 1st lt. Army Med. Svc. Corps, 1970-72, Korea. Mem. ABA (chair creditor's rights subsection and task force on discovery guidelines litigation sect.), Oreg. State Bar Assn. (mem. exec. com. debtor/creditor sect. 1988-91, chair-elect and mem. exec. com. litigation sect. 1992—, mng. editor litigation jour. 1992—, mng. editor Oreg. Comml. Practice manual 1988—), Owen Panner Inn of Ct. (master), Arlington Club Toastmasters (pres.), Rotary Club Portland (pres., bd. dirs.), Multnomah Athletic Club (pres., trustee). Avocations: running, backpacking, white-water rafting, wine collecting. Office: Miller Nash Wiener Hager & Carlsen 111 SW 5th Ave Ste 3500 Portland OR 97204-3699

RAWLINSON, JOHNNIE BLAKENEY, federal judge; b. Concord, NC, Dec. 16, 1952; BS in Psychology summa cum laude, NC A&T State U., 1974; JD, U. of Pacific, 1979. Private practice, Las Vegas, 1979—80; staff atty. Nevada Legal Services, 1980; from dep. dist. atty. to asst. dist. atty. Clark County Dist. Atty.'s Office, 1980—98; judge US Dist. Ct. Nev., 1998—2000, US Ct. Appeals (9th cir.), 2000—. Office: 333 Las Vegas Blvd S Rm 7072 Las Vegas NV 89101 Office Phone: 702-464-5670.

RAWLINSON, JOSEPH ELI, foundation administrator, lawyer; b. Delta, Utah, May 9, 1915; s. Eli Wilford and Dora Pearl (Day) Rawlinson; m. Elaine Millicent Andersen, June 2, 1947; children: James, Jolene, Nancy, Rex, Anina, Cheryl, Mark, Lisa, David. BS, U. Utah, 1936; JD, Loyola U., 1958. CPA Calif.; bar: Calif. 1959. Agt. IRS, Wichita, Kans., 1938—52; acct. Serene Koster, Barbour, Calif., 1952—62; pvt. practice Calif., 1959; pres., CEO Fritz B. Burns Found., Burbank, Calif., 1980—. Recipient Silver medal, Am. Inst. Accts., 1942. Office: Fritz B Burns Found 4001 W Alameda Ave Ste 203 Burbank CA 91505-4338 Home Phone: 818-886-3142. Personal E-mail: josepheli@sbcglobal.net.

RAWSON, ERIC GORDON, optical engineer; b. Saskatoon, Sask., Can., Mar. 4, 1937; s. Donald Strathern and Hildred Iantha (Patton) R.; m. Zivile Anne Nalivaika, May 5, 1966; children: Carol, Dalia, Cliff. BA, U. Saskatchewan, 1959, MA, 1960; PhD, U. Toronto, Ont., 1966. Mem. tech. staff Bell Telephone Labs., Murray Hill, N.J., 1966-73; mem. rsch. staff Xerox PARC, Palo Alto, Calif., 1973-78, area mgr., 1978-94; prin. Rawson Optics, Inc., Brentwood, Calif., 1994-99, pres., CEO, 1999—. Bd. dirs., sec. Alamed. Corp., Palo Alto, 1991—. Editor: Book of Milestones Fiber Optics Local Area Networks, 1994; contbr. over 65 articles to profl. jours. Fellow Optical Soc. Am. (mem. engring. coun. 1995—, Engring. Excellence award 1990), Soc. Photo-Instrumentation Engrs.; mem. IEEE (sr.). Achievements include over 30 patents for optics and biomedical monitoring. Office: 763 Franklin Dr Brentwood CA 94513-6463 E-mail: ericrawson@rawsonoptics.com.

RAWSON, LEONARD LEE, state legislator; b. Albuquerque, Oct. 19, 1954; son of Carl Bernard Rawson & Joan Marion Raitt R; married 1980 to Moira Susan Phillips; children: Philip Mark, Simon Andrew, Benjamin Luke & Caleb. New Mexico State Representative, 1987-1992; New Mexico State Senator, District 37, 1992-, Minority Whip, currently, member, Fin Committee, currently, New Mexico State Senate.President, Rawson Inc Builders Supply, 1973-2000. Eagle Scout, Boy Scouts of America, 68; 1st Pl Aluminum & 2nd Pl Fiberglass, Nat Canoe Champion, 72; Assoc of Year, Las Cruces Home Builders Association, 79, Bldg Contractors Association New Mexico, 80. The Navigators; Cub & Boy Scouts; Nat Home Builders Association (spike member, 73-); New Mexico State Univ Alumni Association; Synod of the Southwest Mission Committee; Las Cruces & Alamogordo Chamber of Commerce; Mothers Against Drunk Driving; New Mexico Right to Life; Bldg Contractors Association New Mexico; Mesilla Valley People in Action; Las Cruces Citizens Against Pornography; Assoc Locksmiths of America, Nat Rifle Association; Order of the Arrow; Explorers. Republican. Presbyterian. Address: PO Box 996 Las Cruces NM 88004 Mailing: State Capitol Rm 109 Santa Fe NM 87503 Home Phone: 505-522-8289. E-mail: lrawson@state.nm.us.

RAWSON, RAYMOND D., dentist, state legislator; b. Sandy, Utah, Nov. 2, 1940; s. James D. and Mable (Beckstead) R.; m. Linda Downey, July 23, 1959; children: Raymond Blaine, Mark Daniel, Pamela Ann, David James, Kristi Lynn, Kenneth Glenn, Richard Allen. BS, U. Nev. at Las Vegas, 1964; DDS, Loma Linda U., 1968; MA, U. Nev., 1978. Diplomate Am. Bd. Forensic Odontology (pres. 1984), Am. Bd. Oral Medicine. Gen. practice dentistry, Las Vegas, 1968—. Instr. dental hygiene, dental dir. Clark County Community Coll., 1977—, dep. coroner, chief dental examiner, 1977—; adj. prof. U. Nev., 1977—, adj. assoc. prof. oral diagnosis and forensic dentistry Northwestern U., Chgo., 1985—. Contbr. articles to profl. jours. Active Boy Scouts Am., 1968—; chmn. youth and family health comm. assembly on fed. issues, Nat. Conf. State Legislators, mem. steering comm. Reforming STates Group, coun. of State Govts.; pres. Red Rock Stake; bishop Ch. Jesus Christ Latter-day Saints, 1978-84; asst. majority leader Nev. State senator. Recipient Cmty. Heroes award Nat. Conf. Christians and Jews, Las Vegas, 1994. Fellowo Am. Acad. Forensic Scis. (pres., chmn.), ADA (editl. rev. bd. jour.), Fedn. Dentaire Internat., Omicron Kappa Upsilon (commr. edn. commn. of the states). Republican. Office: 6375 W Charleston Blvd Las Vegas NV 89146-1139 Address: Nev Senate 401 S Carson St Rm 213A Carson City NV 89701-4747

RAY, ALBERT, physician, educator; b. NYC, Aug. 8, 1948; s. Herman and Stella (Meritz) R.; m. Cheryl Antecol, Oct. 8, 1977; children: Heather, Erin, Samantha. BA, Bklyn. Coll., 1969; MD, Cath. U. Louvain, Belgium, 1976. Diplomate Am. Bd. Family Practice, Can. Coll. Family Physicians, cert. profl. coder AAPC. Intern Meml. U. of Nfld., St. John's, Can., 1976; resident McGill U., Montreal, 1978; family physician SCPMG, San Diego, 1978—. Clin. prof. U. Calif., San Diego, 1978—; cmty. faculty UCLA, USD, U. Calif., Davis, USC; clerkship cmty. adv. bd. U. Calif., San Diego, 1995—; pres. profl. staff Kaiser Found. Hosp.; bd. dirs. So. Calif. Permanente Med Group; asst. chief family medicine Kaiser Permanente, San Diego; physician coord. health promotion and preventive care Kaiser Permanente. Author: Lecons d'Histologie, 1973; contbr. to profl. jours. Program chair adult edn. Congregation Beth Israel, 1995; bd. dirs. Temple Emanuel, San Diego, 1990, Agy. for Jewish Edn.; expert reviewer Med. Bd. Calif., 1995; spl. med. cons. Calif. Dept. of Corps., 1996; hon. chmn. physician's adv. bd. Nat. Rep. Congl. Com. Named Family Physician of Yr., Calif. Acad. Family Physicians, 2002. Fellow: Am. Acad. Family Physicians; mem.: Calif. Acad. Family Physicians, San Diego Acad. Family Physicians, San Diego County Med. Soc. (councilor 2002—03, treas. 2004—06, pres.-elect 2006—07, pres. 2007—08), Calif. Med. Assn. (ho. of dels.), AMA (alt. del.). Avocations: golf, tennis, travel, antiques, gardening. Office: Kaiser Permanente 4405 Vandever Ave San Diego CA 92120-3315 Office Phone: 619-516-7400.

RAY, EDWARD JOHN, economics professor, academic administrator; b. Jackson Heights, NY, Sept. 10, 1944; s. Thomas Paul and Cecelia Francis (Hiney) R.; m. Virginia Beth Phelps, June 14, 1969; children: Stephanie Elizabeth, Katherine Rebecca, Michael Edward. BA, CUNY, 1966; MA, Stanford U., 1969, PhD, 1971. Asst. prof. econs. Ohio State U., Columbus, 1970-74, assoc. prof., 1974-77, prof., 1977—2003, chmn. dept. econs., 1976-92, assoc. provost acad. affairs Office Acad. Affairs, 1992-93, sr. vice provost, chief info. officer Office Acad. Affairs, 1993-98, acting sr. v.p. and provost, 1997-98, exec. v.p., provost, 1998—2003; pres. Oreg. State U., 2003—, prof., 2003—. Mem. bd. dirs. Com. Instl. Cooperation Net, 1994—97, Midwest Universities Consortium for Internat. Activities, 1994—95, Columbus Coun. World Affairs, 1994—, Ohio State U. Rsch. Found., 1998—, John Glenn Inst. Pub. Svc. and Pub. Policy, 1998—; provost Consortium Instl. Cooperation, 1998—, Ohio Inter-U. Coun., 1999—; bd. chair Ohio Principals Leadership Acad., 2000—; mem. Ohio Tchr. Edn. and Certification Adv. Commn., 2000—03, Ohio Higher Edn. Funding Commn., 2002—. Contbr. articles to profl. jours. Active Upper Arlington Civic Assn., Columbus, 1983—, Wexner Ctr. Found. Bd., 1998-. Recipient Chairperson's Recognition award, Ohio State U., 1989, Disting. Svc. award, 2006. Mem. Am. Econs. Assn., Western Econ. Assn., Econ. Hist. Assn., Internat. Trade and Fin. Assn., Phi Beta Kappa Home: 3700 SW Brooklane Dr Corvallis OR 97333 Office: Office of Pres Oreg State U Corvallis OR 97331-2128

RAY, GENE WELLS, industrial executive; b. Murray, Ky., Apr. 23, 1938; s. Terry Lee and Loreen (Lovett) R.; m. Becky Huie, Mar. 5, 1956 (dec. 1976); m. Taffin Ray; children: Don Dickerson, Kathy Pratt, Nancy Solomon. BS in Math., Physics and Chemistry, Murray State U., 1956; MS in Physics, U. Tenn., 1962, PhD in Theoretical Physics, 1965. With tech. staff Aerospace Corp., San Bernardino, Calif., 1965-68; mgr. strategic div. USAF (OA), Washington, 1968-70; scientist, sr. v.p., systems group mgr. Sci. Applications Inc., La Jolla, Calif., 1970-81, also bd. dirs.; pres., chief exec. officer Titan Systems Inc., San Diego, 1981-85, CEO, 1985—, CEO, pres., chmn.; assoc. prof. Carson Newman Coll., Tenn., 1964-65. Inventor mass flow meter. 1st lt. USAR, 1963-68. Republican. Avocations: tennis, wine collecting. Home: PO Box 2464 Rancho Santa Fe CA 92067-2464 Office: Titan Corp 3033 Science Park Rd San Diego CA 92121-1199

RAY, GILBERT T., lawyer; b. Mansfield, Ohio, Sept. 18, 1944; s. Robert Lee Ray and Renatha (Goldie) Washington; m. Valerie J. Reynolds, June 14, 1969; children: Tanika, Tarlin. BA, Ashland Coll., 1966; MBA, U. Toledo, 1968; JD, Howard U., 1972. Assoc. O'Melveny & Myers, LA, 1972-79, ptnr., 1980-2000, ret. ptnr., 2000—. Bd. dirs. Sierra Monolithics, Inc., IHOP Corp., Watson, Wyatt & Co., Advance Auto Parts, Automobile Club of So. Calif., Haynes Found., DiamondRock Hospitality, Inc., Seasons Series Fund, SunAmerica Series Trust. Mem. The Calif. Club, L.A. Country Club. Democrat. Office: 400 S Hope St Ste 1900 Los Angeles CA 90071-2899

RAYMOND, DOROTHY GILL, lawyer; b. Greeley, Colo., June 2, 1954; d. Robert Marshall and Roberta (McClure) Gill; m. Peter J. Raymond, June 8, 1974. BA summa cum laude, U. Denver, 1975; JD, U. Colo., 1978. Bar: Conn. 1978, Colo. 1981. Assoc. Dworkin, Minogue & Bucci, Bridgeport, Conn., 1978-80; counsel Tele-Communications, Inc., Englewood, Colo., 1981-88; v.p., gen. counsel WestMarc Communications, Inc., Denver, 1988-91, Cable Television Labs., Inc., Boulder, Colo., 1991-96, sr. v.p., gen. counsel, 1996—. Mem. Am. Corp. Counsel Assn. (pres. 1990-91, Colo. chpt. dir. 1988-94), Colo. Assn. Corp. Counsel (pres. 1987), Sports Car Club Am. (nat. champion ladies stock competition 1981, 85, 86, 88). Avocations: sewing, reading, outdoor activities. Office: Cablelabs 858 Coal Creek Cir Louisville CO 80027-9750

RAYMOND, KENNETH NORMAN, chemistry professor, researcher; b. Astoria, Oreg., Jan. 7, 1942; s. George Norman and Helen May (Dunn) R.; m. Jane Galbraith Shell, June 19, 1965 (div. 1976); children: Mary Katherine, Alan Norman; m. Barbara Gabriele Sternitzke, June 17, 1977; children: Gabriella Petra, Christopher Norman. BA, Reed Coll., 1964; PhD, Northwestern U., 1968. Asst. prof. chemistry U. Calif.-Berkeley, 1967-74, assoc. prof., 1974-78, prof., 1978—; vice chmn. dept. U. Calif. Berkeley, 1982-84, 1999—2000, chmn., 1993-96; faculty sr. scientist Lawrence Berkeley Lab., 1996—; dir. Seaborg Ctr., 2002—. Mem. study sect. NIH, 1983—86, 2006—; adv. com. NSF, 1985—87; co-chmn. bd. chem. scis. & tech. NRC, 2000—; co-founder Lumiphore, Inc., 2001; Chancellor's prof. U. Calif., Berkeley, 2007—. Editor: Bioinorganic Chemistry II, 1977; assoc. editor Biology of Metals, 1987-91; editl. bd. Inorganic Chemistry, 1976-86, Accounts Chem. Rsch., 1982-90, Inorganica Chemica Acta f-Block Elements, 1984-90, Jour. Coordination Chemistry, 1981-2003, Jour. Inorganic and Nuclear Chemistry, 1974-81, Jour. Am. Chem. Soc., 1983-95, Topics in Current Chemistry, 1981-97, Metals in Biology, 1993—, Jour. Supramolecular Chemistry, 1992—, Jour. Biol. Inorganic Chemistry, 1996-2004, Procs. NAS USA, 2002-04, Accts. Chem. Rsch., 1982-88, 2005—; US editl. advisor Springer-Verlag in Chemistry, 1972-91; contbr. articles to profl. jours.; author more than 400 papers. Alfred P. Sloan rsch. fellow, 1971-73; Miller rsch. prof., 1977-78, 96, 2004; Guggenheim fellow, 1980-81; recipient E.O. Lawrence award Dept. Energy, 1984, Humboldt Rsch. award for U.S. Scientists, 1992, 2000, Alfred R. Bader award Am. Chem. Soc., 1994, Vollum award Reed Coll., 2002, Izatt/Christensen award, 2005. Mem. NAS, Am. Acad. Arts and Scis., Am. Chem. Soc. (chair divsn. inorganic chemistry 1996, Inorganic Chemistry award, 2008), Am. Crystallographic Soc., Sigma Xi. Democrat. Achievements include 15 patents in field. Office: U Calif Berkeley Dept Chemistry Berkeley CA 94720-1460 E-mail: raymond@socrates.berkeley.edu.

RAZZOUK, ANEES JACOB, surgeon; s. Yacoub and Mona Razzouk; m. Teri Thompson; children: Jacob, Gabrielle. BA, Mid. East Coll., 1975; MA, Andrews U., 1977; MD, Loma Linda U., 1982. Medical Examiner Nat. Bd. of Med. Examiners, General Surgery Am. Bd. of Surgery, Thoracic Surgery Am. Bd. of Surgery, Surgical Critical Care Am. Bd. of Surgery, Md State of Calif. Lectr. of math. Loma Linda U., Calif., 1978; asst. prof. of surgery Loma Linda U., Sch. of Medicine, 1990—99, prof. of surgery, 2000—, dir. of thoracic surgery residency program, 2001—, chief, divsn. of cardiothoracic surgery, 2002—, chmn. dept. cardiovascular and thoracic surgery, 2007—. Fellowship Hosp. for Sick Children, Toronto, Canada, 1990—91. Recipient Humanitarian award, Hosp. for Sick Children, Toronto Can., 2000; Albert Starr scholar, 1990. Fellow: ACS, Am. Coll. of Cardiology; mem.: The Western Thoracic Surg. Assn., Internat. Soc. for Heart & Lung Transplantation, Soc. of Thoracic Surgeons, Congenital Heart Surgeons' Soc., Internat. Soc. for Minimally Invasive Cardiac Surgery, Western Soc. for Pediatric Rsch., Pacific Coast Surg. Assn., Am. Assn. for Thoracic Surgery, Calif. Soc. of Thoracic Surgeons, Am. Soc. for Artificial Internal Organs, The

Nat. Honor Med. Soc. (life), The Nat. Honor Math. Soc. (life), Alpha Omega Alpha (life), Pi Mu Epsilon (life). Office: Loma Linda U Med Ctr 11175 Campus St Ste 21121 Loma Linda CA 92354 E-mail: arazzouk@llu.edu.

RE, DONALD MAURICE, lawyer; b. 1946; AB, Princeton U.; JD, U. Calif. Bar: Calif. 1971. Atty. Law Offices of Donald Re, PC. Named one of Top 10 Trial Lawyers in Am., Nat. Law Jour., 2000. Office: 624 S Grand Ave 22 Fl Los Angeles CA 90017 Office Phone: 213-623-4234. E-mail: donaldmre@yahoo.com.

READ, DWIGHT, anthropologist, researcher; b. Oakland, Calif., July 25, 1943; s. Wilma and Paul Read; m. Fadwa El Guindi, June 21, 1980; children: Magda El Guindi-Rosenbaum, Khalid Rosenbaum. BA, Reed Coll., Portland, Oreg., 1964; MA, U. Wis., Madison, 1965; PhD, UCLA, 1970. Vis. prof. IBM Rsch. Ctr., LA, 1985—89, U. Kent, Canterbury, England, 1999—99; asst. prof. UCLA, 1970—76, assoc. prof., 1976—85, prof., 1985—. Cons. Am. Rsch. Inst., Santa Barbara, Calif., 1982—84, Archeol. Rsch. Labs., Las Cruces, N.Mex., 1989—92. Author: Archaeological Classification; contbr. articles to numerous profl. jours. Chair, com. academic freedom UCLA Academic Senate, 1973—74, chair, com. privilege and tenure, 1991—94, chair, coun. planning and budget, 1995—96, U. Calif. Academic Senate, Oakland, 1998—99, chair, com. privilege and tenure (statewide), 1994—95. Mem.: AAAS, Soc. Am. Archaeology, Am. Math. Assn., Am. Anthrop. Assn. Liberal. Avocations: travel, hiking. Office: Dept Anthropology UCLA 405 Hilgard Los Angeles CA 90095 Office Fax: 310-206-7833. Business E-Mail: dread@anthro.ucla.edu.

READ, RICHARD EATON, newspaper reporter; b. St. Andrews, Scotland, Sept. 3, 1957; s. Arthur H. and Katharine (Eaton) R.; m. Kim R. Kunkle, July 26, 1986; 1 child, Nehalem Kunkle-Read. BA in English, Amherst Coll., 1980; postgrad., Harvard U., 1996—97; LHD (hon.), Williamette U., 2003. Press sec. Mass. Commn. on State and County Bldgs., 1980; staff writer The Oregonian, 1981-86; fellow The Henry Luce Found./The Nation, Bangkok, 1986-87; freelance writer Tokyo, 1987-89; Asia bur. chief The Oregonian, Tokyo, 1989-94; sec., 1st dir., 1st v.p. Fgn. Corrs. Club of Japan, 1990-93; internat. bus. writer The Oregonian, Portland, 1994-99, sr. writer internat. affairs, 1999—. V.p., pres., bd. dirs. The Internat. Sch., Portland, 2007—08. Recipient Pulitzer prize for explanatory reporting, 1999, Overseas Press Club award for bus. reporting from abroad, 1999, Scripps Howard Found. award for bus. reporting, 1999, Blethen award for enterprise reporting Pacific Northwest Newspaper Assn., 1999, 2001, Pacific Northwest Soc. Prof. Journalists first place award for social issues, 2001, 05, bus. 1998, 2004, spot news 1997, edn. 1990, Oreg. Gov.'s award for achievement in internat. bus., 2000, Pulitzer prize for pub. svc., 2001, Unity award in media investigative reporting, Lincoln U., 2001, Blethen award, 2001, Bruce Baer award, 2001, Media Leadership award Am. Immigration Lawyers Assn., 2001; named Internat. Citizen of Yr. 1999 World Affairs Coun. Oreg., named Internat. Citizen of Yr. 2002 Oreg. Assn. Consuls Gen. Eisenhower Exch. fellow, Peru, 1997; Nieman fellow, 1996-97; U. Md. CASE fellow, 2002.

REAGAN, GARY DON, state legislator, lawyer; b. Amarillo, Tex., Aug. 23, 1941; s. Hester and Lois Irene (Marcum) R.; m. Nedra Ann Nash, Sept. 12, 1964; children: Marc Kristi, Kari, Brent. BA, Stanford U., 1963, JD, 1965. Bar: N.Mex. 1965, US Dist. Ct. N.Mex. 1965, US Supreme Ct. 1986. Assoc. Smith & Ransom, Albuquerque, 1965—67; ptnr. Smith, Ransom, Deaton & Reagan, Albuquerque, 1967—68, Williams, Johnson, Houston, Reagan & Porter, Hobbs, N.Mex., 1968—77, Williams, Johnson, Reagan, Porter & Love, Hobbs, 1977—82; pvt. practice Hobbs, 1982—; city atty. City of Hobbs, 1978—80, 1997—2004, City of Eunice, N.Mex., 1980—2004; mem. N.Mex. State Senate, 1993—96. Instr. N.Mex. Jr. Coll. and Coll. of S.W., Hobbs, 1978-84; N.Mex. commr. Nat. Conf. Commrs. Uniform State Laws, 1993-96; adv. mem. N.Mex. Constl. Revision Commn., 1993-95. Mayor City of Hobbs, 1972-73, 76-77, 2008-, city commr., 1970-78; pres., dir. Jr. Achievement of Hobbs, 1974-85; pres., trustee Landsun Homes, Inc., Carlsbad, N.Mex., 1972-84; trustee Lydia Patterson Inst., El Paso, Tex., 1972-84, N.Mex. Conf. United Meth. Ch., 1988—, Coll. SW Hobbs, 1989-2001. Mem. ABA, State Bar N.Mex. (coms. 1989-96, v.p. 1992-93, pres. 1994-95), Lea County Bar Assn. (pres. 1976-77), Hobbs C. of C. (pres. 1989-90), Rotary (pres. Hobbs 1985-86), Hobbs Tennis Club (pres. 1974-75). Home: 200 E Eagle Dr Hobbs NM 88240-5323 Office: 1819 N Turner Ste G Hobbs NM 88240-3834 Home Phone: 575-393-9072; Office Phone: 575-397-6551. Business E-Mail: lglregan@nm.net.

REAGAN, HARRY EDWIN, III, lawyer; b. Wichita, Kans., Sept. 9, 1940; s. Harry E. II and Mary Elizabeth (O'Steen) R.; m. Marvene R. Rogers, June 17, 1965; children: Kathleen, Leigh, Mairen. BS, U. Pa., 1962, JD, 1965. Bar: Pa. 1965, U.S. Dist. Ct. (ea. dist.) Pa. 1965, U.S. Ct. Appeals (3d cir.) 1965. From assoc. to ptnr. Morgan, Lewis & Bockius, Phila., 1965-98. Chmn. Northhampton Twp. Planning Commn., Bucks County, Pa., 1974-79; mem. Warwick Twp. Planning Commn., 1980-95, chmn., 1994; supr. Warwick Twp., 1996-98; mem. San Miguel County (Colo.) Open Space Commn., 1998—, chmn., 2001-05; mem. Town of Telluride Open Space Commn., 1999-2002, San Miguel County Planning Commn., 2002—. Mem. ABA (labor sect.), Pa. Bar Assn. (labor sect.), Phila. Bar Assn. (labor sect.), Indsl. Rels. Assn. (pres. Phila. chpt. 1990-91). Republican. Presbyterian. Avocations: rugby, skiing, raising horses, bicycling. Home and Office: Box 190 Norwood CO 81423

REAGAN, JANET THOMPSON, psychologist, educator; b. Sept. 15, 1945; d. Virgil Joe and Carrie (Alexander) Thompson; children: Natalia Alexandria, Robert Barry. BA in Psychology, Berea Coll., 1967; PhD in Psychology, Vanderbilt U., 1972. Mgr. rsch. and eval. Nashville Mental Health Ctr., 1971-72; mgr. eval. Family Health Found., New Orleans, 1973-74; asst. prof. dept. health systems mgmt. Tulane U., New Orleans, 1974-77; dir. eval. Project Heavy West, LA, 1977-78; asst. prof. health adminstrn. Calif. State U.-Northridge, 1978-83; assoc. prof., dir. health adminstrn., 1983-87; prof., dir. health adminstrn., 1987—. Cons. in field. Contbr. articles to profl. jours., chpts. to books; mem. editl. bd. Jour. Long Term Care Adminstrn., Healthcare Papers. Mem. Am. Pub. Health Assn., Am. Coll. Health Care Adminstrn., Am. Coll. Health Care Execs. (com. on higher edn. 1987, chmn. 1991), Assn. Univ. Programs in Health Adminstrn. (task force on undergrad. edn. 1985-90, chmn. 1988-90, mem. bd. dirs. 1995, chmn. bd. dirs. 1998-99), Psi Chi, Phi Kappa Phi. Office: Calif State U Dept Health Sci Northridge CA 91330-0001 Office Phone: 818-677-2298. Business E-Mail: janet.reagan@csun.edu.

REAGAN, JOSEPH BERNARD, retired aerospace executive, management consultant; b. Somerville, Mass., Nov. 26, 1934; s. Joseph B. and Helen Lowry R.; m. Dorothy Hughes; children: Patrick, Michael, Kevin, Kathleen, Brian, John, Maureen. BS in Physics, Boston Coll., 1956, MS in Physics, 1959; PhD in Space Sci., Stanford U., 1975; postgrad. exec. mgmt., Pa. State U., State College, 1981. Staff scientist, rsch. scientist, sr. scientist, scientist Lockheed Rsch. & Devel. Div., Palo Alto, Calif., 1959-75, mgr., 1975-84, dir., 1984-86, dep. gen. mgr., 1986-88, v.p., asst. gen. mgr., 1988-90; v.p. gen. mgr. Lockheed Missle and Space Co., 1991-96. Contbr. articles to profl. jours. Capt. U.S. Army, 1956-64. Recipient Career Achievement in Sci. award Boston Coll. Alumni Assn., 1993. Fellow AIAA (outstanding engr. San Francisco chpt. 1988); mem. Am. Geophys. Union, Nat. Acad. of Engring., Nat. Rsch. Coun. Republican. Roman Catholic. Avocation: computer and woodworking hobbies. Home and Office: 13554 Mandarin Way Saratoga CA 95070-4847 Home Phone: 408-867-0557. Personal E-mail: jbr733@comcast.net.

REAGAN, MICHELE, state legislator; BA in Comm., Ill. State U. With FASTSIGNS Ctrl. Ave., Phoenix, 1991—2001; mng. ptnr. Reagan Properties, 2001—; mem. Dist. 8 Ariz. House of Reps., 2003—, chair commerce com., mem. ways & means com. Active Valley Presbyn. Ch.; bd. dirs. Scottsdale Found. for Handicapped (STARS), Ariz. Econ. Resource Orgn. Mem.: Women of Scottsdale, Nat. Fedn. Ind. Bus., Las Rancheras Rep. Women, Fountain Hills C. of C., Ariz. Young Rep. League, Ariz. Small Bus. Assn., Delta Delta Delta. Republican. Presbyterian. Office: Ariz House Reps Capitol Complex 1700 W Washington Rm 220 Phoenix AZ 85007 Office Phone: 602-926-5828. Fax: 602-417-3008. Business E-Mail: mreagan@azleg.gov.*

REAGAN, NANCY DAVIS (ANNE FRANCIS ROBBINS), former First Lady of the United States, volunteer; b. NYC, July 6, 1921; d. Kenneth and Edith (Luckett) Robbins, Loyal Davis (Stepfather); m. Ronald Reagan, Mar. 4, 1952 (dec. June 5, 2004); children: Patricia Ann, Ronald Prescott stepchildren: Maureen(dec.), Michael. BA in Theatre, Smith Coll., 1943; LLD (hon.), Pepperdine U., 1983; LHD (hon.), Georgetown U., 1987. Sales clk. Marshall Fields Dept. Store, Chgo.; First Lady of the US Washington, 1981—89. Contract actress, MGM, 1949-56; films include Portrait of Jennie, 1948, East Side, West Side, 1949, Doctor and the Girl, 1949, Shadow on the Wall, 1950, The Next Voice You Hear, 1950, Night into Morning, 1951, It's a Big Country, 1951, Shadow in the Sky, 1952, Talk About a Stranger, 1952, Donovan's Brain, 1953, Hellcats of the Navy, 1957, Crash Landing, 1958, You Can't Hurry Love, 1988, Lunar: Silver Star Story, 1992; TV credits include Schlitz Playhouse of Stars, 1951, Climax, 1954, General Electric Theater, 1953, Zane Grey Theater, 1956, The Tall Man, 1960, 87th Precint, 1961, Wagon Train, 1957, Different Strokes, 1978, Dynasty, 1981; Broadway: Lute Song, 1946; formerly author syndicated column on prisoner-of-war and missing-in-action soldiers and their families; author: Nancy, 1980; (with Jane Wilkie) To Love a Child, 1982, (with William Novak) My Turn: The Memoirs of Nancy Reagan, 1989. Civic worker, visited wounded Viet Nam vets., sr. citizens, hosps. and schs. for physically and emotionally handicapped children, active in furthering foster grandparents for handicapped children program; hon. nat. chmn. Aid to Adoption of Spl. Kids, 1977; spl. interest in fighting alcohol and drug abuse among youth: hosted first ladies from around the world for 2d Internat. Drug Conf., 1985; hon. chmn. Just Say No Found., Nat. Fedn. of Parents for Drug-Free Youth, Nat. Child Watch Campaign, President's Com. on the Arts and Humanities, Wolf Trap Found. bd. of trustees, Nat. Trust for Historic Preservation, Cystic Fibrosis Found., Nat. Republican Women's Club; hon. pres. Girl Scouts of Am. Named one of Ten Most Admired Am. Women, Good Housekeeping mag., ranking #1 in poll, 1984, 85, 86; Woman of Yr. Los Angeles Times, 1977; permanent mem. Hall of Fame of Ten Best Dressed Women in U.S.; recipient humanitarian awards from Am. Camping Assn., Nat. Council on Alcoholism, United Cerebral Palsy Assn., Internat. Ctr. for Disabled; Boys Town Father Flanagan award; 1986 Kiwanis World Service medal; Variety Clubs Internat. Lifeline award; numerous awards for her role in fight against drug abuse. Republican. Presbyterian.

REAL, MANUEL LAWRENCE, federal judge; b. San Pedro, Calif., Jan. 27, 1924; s. Francisco Jose and Maria (Mansano) R.; m. Stella Emilia Michalik, Oct. 15, 1955; children: Michael, Melanie Marie, Timothy, John Robert. BS, U. So. Calif., 1944, student fgn. trade, 1946-48; LL.B., Loyola Sch. Law, Los Angeles, 1951. Bar: Calif. 1952. Asst. U.S. Atty.'s Office, Los Angeles, 1952-55; pvt. practice law San Pedro, Calif., 1955-64; U.S. atty. So. Dist. Calif., 1964-66; judge U.S. Dist. Ct. (cen. dist.) Calif., LA, 1966—. Served to ensign USNR, 1943-46. Mem. Am., Fed., Los Angeles County bar assns., State Bar Calif., Am. Judicature Soc., Chief Spl. Agts. Assn., Phi Delta Phi, Sigma Chi. Clubs: Anchor (Los Angeles). Roman Catholic. Office: US Dist Ct 312 N Spring St Ste 217P Los Angeles CA 90012-4704

REAM, JAMES TERRILL, architect, sculptor; b. Summit, NJ, Sept. 8, 1929; s. Merrill Jay and Catherine Ada (Terrill) R.; m. Joyce Kimball Johnson, June 9, 1953 (div. Dec. 1976); children— Claudia, Sarah, Benjamin, m. Nancy Ann Buford, Jan. 1, 1980; stepchildren— Kathleen, Ann Maguire BArch, Cornell U., 1953; postgrad., Pratt Inst., 1953-54, U. Rome, 1956-57. Registered architect. Assoc. W. C. Muchow Assocs., Denver, 1959-62; prin. Ream, Quinn & Assocs., Denver, 1962-66; v.p. design John Carl Warnecke & Assocs., San Francisco, 1966-69; prin., pres. James Ream & Assocs., Inc., San Francisco, 1969-78, Robbins and Ream Inc., San Francisco, 1978-83; prin. James Ream Architect, San Francisco, 1983—. Prin. archtl. works include Denver Convention Ctr., Currigan Hall, Pasadena Conf. Ctr., Stapleton Plaza Hotel, Vail Transp. Ctr. Bd. dirs. San Francisco Planning and Urban Rsch. Assn., 1977—; chmn. bd. dirs. San Francisco Heritage, 1984-91, pres., 1983-84. Served to 1st lt. USAF, 1954-56. Recipient citation for design in steel Am. Iron and Steel Inst., 1975; Honor award Am. Concrete Inst., 1975; Nat. Design award Prestressed Concrete Inst., 1983; Honor award for design in steel Am. Inst. Steel Constrn., 1970 Fellow AIA (honor award western region 1969, fellowship in design 1979, honor award for design excellence 1983, design cons. San Jose Arena). Democrat. Avocations: opera, theater, hiking, tennis. Office: 3385 Clay St San Francisco CA 94118-2006

REARDEN, CAROLE ANN, clinical pathologist, educator; b. Belleville, Ont., Can., June 11, 1946; d. Joseph Brady and Honora Patricia (O'Halloran) R. BSc, McGill U., 1969, MSc, MDCM, 1971. Diplomate Am. Bd. Pathology, Am. Bd. Immunohematology and Blood Banking, Am. Bd. Histocompatibility and Immunogenetics. Resident and fellow Children's Meml. Hosp., Chgo., 1971-73; resident in pediatrics U. Calif., San Diego, 1974, resident then fellow, 1975-79, asst. prof. pathology, 1979-86, dir. histocompatability and immunogenetics lab., 1979-94, assoc. prof., 1986-92, prof., 1992—, head divsn. lab. medicine, 1989-94; dir. med. ctr. U. Calif. Thornton Hosp. Clin. Labs., San Diego, 1993—. Prin. investigator devel. monoclonal antibodies to erythroid antigens, recombinant autoantigens; dir. lab. exam. com. Am. Bd. Histocompatibility and Immunogenetics. Contbr. articles to profl. jours.; patentee autoantigen pinch. Mem. Mayor's Task Force on AIDS, San Diego, 1983. Recipient Young Investigator Rsch. award NIH, 1979; grantee U. Calif. Cancer Rsch. Coordinating Com., 1982, NIH, 1983; scholar Nat. Blood Found. Mem. Am. Soc. Investigative Pathology, Am. Soc. Hematology, Am. Assn. Blood Banks (com. organ transplantation and tissue typing 1982-87, tech. com. 13 and 14 edit. tech. manual 1996-2002). Office: U Calif San Diego Dept Pathology 0612 9500 Gilman Dr La Jolla CA 92093-0612 E-mail: arearden@ucsd.edu.

REBER, DAVID JAMES, lawyer; b. Las Vegas, Mar. 1, 1944; s. James Rice and Helen Ruth (Cusick) R.; m. Jacqueline Yee, Aug. 31, 1968; children: Emily, Brad, Cecily BA, Occidental Coll., LA, 1965; JD, Harvard U., 1968. Bar: Calif. 1969, Hawaii 1975, U.S. Dist. Ct. Hawaii, U.S. Ct. Appeals (9th cir.), U.S. Supreme Ct. Asst. prof. law U. Iowa, Iowa City, 1968-70; assoc. Sheppard Mullin Richter & Hampton, LA, 1970-75, Goodsill Anderson Quinn & Stifel, Honolulu, 1975-76, ptnr., 1976—. Bd. dirs. Enterprise Honolulu, Legal Aid Soc. Hawaii, Lawyers Equal Justice. Mem. ABA (bus. and pub. utilities sects.), Hawaii Bar Assn. Avocations: golf, tennis, softball, travel. Office: Goodsill Anderson Et Al 1099 Alakea St Ste 1800 Honolulu HI 96813-4511 Office Phone: 808-547-5611. E-mail: dreber@goodsill.com.

REBHUN, JOSEPH, allergist, immunologist, medical educator; b. Przemysl, Poland, Oct. 7, 1921; came to U.S., 1950; s. Baruch and Serel R.; m. Maria Birkenhejm, Aug. 10, 1945; children: Lillian Friedland, Richard B.R., Donald. MD, U. Innsbruck, Austria, 1950; MS in Medicine, Northwestern U., 1954. Diplomate Am. Bd. Allergy and Immunology. Intern Barnert Meml. Hosp., Patterson, NJ; resident in internal medicine Tompkins County Meml. Hosp. and Cornell U., NY, 1951-52; fellow in allergy Northwestern U. Med. Sch./Chidlren's Meml. Hosp., Chgo., 1952-54; fellow instr. Northwestern U. Med. Sch., 1954; asst. clin. prof. medicine Loma Linda U., 1957-93; clin. prof. medicine U. So. Calif., LA, 1965-91, ret., 1998. Chief allergy Chgo. Eye, Ear, Nose and Throat Hosp., 1953-55; cons. Pacific State Hosp., Spadra Pomona Valley Cmty. Hosp., Pomona Casa Colina Hosp. Author: SOS, 1946, The Cry of Democracy for Help, God and Man in Two Worlds, 1985, The Embers of Michael, 1993, Crisis of Morality and Reaction to the Holocaust, 1998, Leap to Life: Triumph Over Nazi Evil, 2000, Why Me?, 2004; contbr. numerous articles to med. jours. Pres. Am. Congress Jews from Poland, 1969—70. Capt. U.S. Mil., San Francisco, capt. med. reserve corps., L.A. Recipient honors City and County of L.A., L.A. Office Dist. Atty., Senate of State of Calif., all 1985. Fellow Am. Acad. Allergy (rsch. coun. 1960-65), Am. Coll. Allergy, Assn. Clin. Allergy and Immunology; mem. West Coast Allergy Soc., Calif. Allergy Assn., L.A. Soc. Allergy, L.A. Med. Assn., Calif. Med. Assn, Pomona Valley (head of Med. Reserve Corp). Office Phone: 909-624-1792. Personal E-mail: joerebhun@yahoo.com.

RECHARD, PAUL ALBERT, retired civil engineering company executive, consultant; b. Laramie, Wyo., June 4, 1927; s. Ottis H. and Mary R. (Bird) R.; m. Mary Lou Roper, June 26, 1949; children: Robert Paul, Karen Ann. BS, U. Wyo., 1948, MS, 1949, CE, 1955. Registered land surveyor, Wyo.; registered profl. engr., Wyo.; cert. profl. hydrologist Am. Inst. Hydrology. Hydraulic engr. U.S. Bur. Reclamation, Cody, Wyo. and Billings, Mont., 1949-54; dir. water resources Natural Resource Bd., Cheyenne, Wyo., 1954-58; prin. hydraulic engr. Upper Colorado River Commn., Salt Lake City, 1958-64; dir. Water Resources Rsch. Inst. U. Wyo., Laramie, 1964-81, mem. faculty dept. civil engring., 1964-82, prof., 1964-82; pres. Western Water Cons., Laramie, 1980-2001, Hydrology Assocs., Laramie, 1978-80; ret. Western Water Consults., Inc., 2001. Owner Paul A. Rechard, P.E., Laramie, 1964-1978, 2001-. Editor: Compacts, Treaties and Court Decrees Affecting Wyoming Water, 1956; contbr. articles to tech. publs. Pres., Thayer Sch. PTA, Laramie, 1965; mem. Laramie City Planning Commn., 1974-80. Served with USNR, 1945-46. Recipient Wyo. Eminent Engr. award Tau Beta Pi, 1993; named Disting. Alumnus U. Wyo., 1998; named Outstanding Engr. Wyo. Engring. Soc., 1999. Fellow ASCE (life mem., pres. Wyo. sect. 1968); mem. NSPE (life), Am. Geophys. Union, Wyo. Engring. Soc. (pres. 1976, hon.), U.S. Com. on Irrigation and Drainage, Lions (pres. Laramie 1968), Masons, Sigma Xi (pres. Wyo. chpt. 1973), Phi Kappa Phi (pres. Wyo. chpt. 1969), Gamma Sigma Delta, Sigma Tau (pres. Wyo. chpt. 1948, selected Wyo. Eminent Engr. 1993). Republican. Presbyterian. Home and Office: 316 Stuart St Laramie WY 82070-4866 Office Phone: 307-745-7477. Personal E-mail: prechard@msn.com.

RECKTENWALD, MARK E., state supreme court justice; AB magna cum laude, Harvard Univ.; JD with honors, Univ. Chgo. Bar: Hawaii 1986. Reporter United Press Internat., Honolulu; comm. clk. Hawaii State legis.; law. clk. US Dist. Ct. Chief Judge Harold M. Fong., 1986—87; assoc. Goodsill Anderson Quinn & Stifel, 1988—91; asst. US atty. US Dept. Justice Hawaii Dist., 1991—97; ptnr. Marr Hipp Jones & Pepper, 1997—99; asst. US atty. US Dept. Justice Hawaii Dist., 1999—2003; dir. Hawaii Dept. Commerce & Consumer Affairs, 2003—07; chief judge Hawaii Intermediate Ct. Appeals, 2007—09; assoc. justice Hawaii Supreme Ct., 2009—. Office: Hawaii Supreme Ct 417 S King St Honolulu HI 96813 Office Phone: 808-539-4735.*

REDD, F. BENNION, federal magistrate; b. 1921; BS, U. Utah, 1949, JD, 1951. County atty. Office of County Atty., 1951-78; magistrate judge U.S. Dist. Ct. Utah, Monticello, 1979—. Served with U.S. Army, 1944-46 N.G., 1947-49. Office: PO Box 157 132 S Main St Monticello UT 84535 Home Phone: 435-587-2244; Office Phone: 435-587-2424. E-mail: fbr1921@yahoo.com.

REDDEN, JAMES ANTHONY, federal judge; b. Springfield, Mass., Mar. 13, 1929; s. James A. and Alma (Cheek) R.; m. Joan Ida Johnson, July 13, 1950; children: James A., William F. Student, Boston U., 1951; LL.B., Boston Coll., 1954. Bar: Mass., 1954, Oreg., 1955. Pvt. practice, Mass., 1954-55; title examiner Title & Trust Ins. Co., Oreg., 1955; claims adjuster Allstate Ins. Co., 1956; mem. firm Collins, Redden, Ferris & Velure, Medford, Oreg., 1957-73; treas. Oreg., 1973-77; atty. gen., 1977-80; U.S. dist. judge, now sr. judge U.S. Dist. Ct. Oreg., Portland, 1980—. Chmn. Oreg. Pub. Employee Relations Bd.; mem. Oreg. Ho. of Reps., 1963-69, minority leader, 1967-69.

With AUS, 1946-48. Mem. ABA, Mass. Bar Assn., Oreg. State Bar. Office: US Dist Ct 1527 US Courthouse 1000 SW 3d Ave Portland OR 97204-2902 Office Phone: 503-326-8370.

REDDICK, C.N. (FRANK)LIN, III, lawyer; b. Quantico, Va. BA with high honors, Calif. State Univ., San Jose, 1977; JD, Univ. Calif., 1980. Bar: Calif. 1980. Mng. ptnr., chair, corp. practice group Troop Steuber Pasich Reddick & Tobey LLP, LA; ptnr., chair corp. and securities practice group and mem. mgmt. com. Akin Gump Strauss Hauer & Feld LLP, LA, 2001—. Bd. dir. VCA Antech Inc., LA, 2002—. Mem. Hastings Law Jour., 1978—79, note and comment editor, 1979—80. Mem.: ABA, Thurston Soc., Order of Coif. Office: Akin Gump Strauss Hauer & Feld LLP Ste 2400 2029 Century Pk E Los Angeles CA 90067-3012 Office Phone: 310-728-3204. Office Fax: 310-229-1001. Business E-Mail: freddick@akingump.com.

REDING, JOHN ANTHONY, JR., lawyer; b. Orange, Calif., May 26, 1944; AB, U. Calif., Berkeley, 1966, JD, 1969. Bar: Calif. 1970, U.S. Dist. Ct. (no., ctrl., ea. and so. dists.) Calif., U.S. Claims Ct., U.S. Supreme Ct. Formerly mem. Crosby, Heafey, Roach & May P.C., Oakland, Calif.; ptnr. Paul, Hastings, Janofsky & Walker, LLP, San Francisco, global chmn. litig. dept. Mem. ABA (sects. on litigation, intellectual property, and natural resources, energy and eviron. law, coms. on bus. torts, internat. law, trial practice and torts and insurance), Am. Intellectual Property Law Assn., State Bar Calif. (sect. on litigation), Bar Assn. San Francisco, Assn. Bus. Trial Lawyers. Office: Paul Hastings Janofsky & Walker LLP 55 Second St 24th Floor San Francisco CA 94105-3441 Office Phone: 415-856-7004. Office Fax: 415-856-7100. Business E-Mail: jackreding@paulhastings.com.

REDMAN, ERIC, lawyer; b. Seattle, June 3, 1948; s. M. Chandler and Marjorie Jane (Sachs) R.; children: Ian Michael, Graham James, Jing, Amanda; m. Heather Bell, 1996. AB, Harvard U., 1970, JD, 1975; BA, Oxford U., 1972, MA, 1980. Bar: Wash. 1975, U.S. Dist. Ct. (we. dist.) Wash. 1975, D.C. 1979, U.S. Ct. Appeals (9th cir.) 1981, U.S. Supreme Ct. 1983. Asst. U.S. senator W.G. Magnuson, Washington and Seattle, 1968-71, 74-75; assoc. Preston, Thorgrimson et al, Seattle, 1975-78, ptnr., 1979-82, Heller, Ehrman, White & McAuliffe, Seattle, 1983—. Author: Dance of Legislation, 1973; also book revs., articles. Home: Heller Ehrman LLP 10477 Maplewood Pl SW Seattle WA 98146-1076 Home Phone: 206-935-5205. E-mail: eric.redman@hellerehrman.com.

REDMOND, JOHN T., hotel and recreational facility executive; Sr. agt. audit divsn. Nev. Gaming Control Bd., 1980-85; with Caesars Palace, 1985-95, sr. v.p., CFO, 1995-96; with MGM Grand Devel., 1996-99; pres., COO Primadonna Resorts, 1999—; co-CEO MGM Grand, Inc., 1999—. Office: MGM Grand 3799 Las Vegas Blvd S Las Vegas NV 89109

REECE, PARIS G., real estate company executive; V.p. Richmond Amer Home, 1988-90, sect., 1990-96, CFO, 1990-93, treas., 1993-96, sr. v.p., 1994-99, exec. v.p., 1999—. Office: Richmond Amer Homes 6550 Greenwood Plaza Blvd Centennial CO 80111-4934

REED, CHARLES BASS, chief academic administrator; b. Harrisburg, Pa., Sept. 29, 1941; s. Samuel Ross and Elizabeth (Johnson) R.; m. Catherine A. Sayers, Aug. 22, 1964; children: Charles B. Jr., Susan Allison. BS, George Washington U., 1963, MS, 1964, EdD, 1970; postgrad. Summer Inst. for Chief State Sch. Officers, Harvard U. Grad Sch. Edn., 1977; D of Pub. Svc. (hon.), George Washington U., 1987; LLD (hon.), Stetson U., 1987; LHD (hon.), St. Thomas U., 1988; LittD (hon.), Waynesburg Coll., 1990; LHD, Fla. State Univ., 1997; d of the U. (hon.), British Open U., 2000. From asst. prof. to assoc. prof. George Washington U., Washington, 1963—70; asst. dir. Nat. Performance-Based Tchr. Edn. Project, Am. Assn. Colls. for Tchr. Edn., Washington, 1970—71; assoc. for planning and coordination Fla. Dept. Edn., Tallahassee, 1971—75, dir. Office Ednl. Planning, Budgeting, and Evaluation, 1975—79; edn. policy coord. Exec. Office of Gov., Tallahassee, 1979—80, dir. legis. affairs, 1980—81, dep. chief of staff, 1981—84, chief of staff, 1984—85; chancellor State Univ. System Fla., Tallahassee, 1985—98, Calif. State U. Sys., Long Beach, 1988—. Mem. Nat. Commn. on H.S. Sr. Yr., Pres. Leadership Group, Higher Edn. Ctr. for Alcohol and Other Drug Prevention, Coll. Edn. Nat. Bd., Policy Bd., EdVoice; mem. Rand Edn. Adv. Bd; bd. dirs. Nat. Ctr. for Ednl. Accountability, Mem. Coun. for Advancement and Support of Edn., Coun. on Fgn. Rels., Bus.-Higher Edn. Forum. Disting. fellow,Fullbright Commn. 50th Anniversary, Peru, 1996, Lamar R. Plunkett Award, So. Regional Edn. Bd., 2001. Mem. Am. Assn. State Colls. and Univs., Am. Assn. for Higher Edn., Am. Coun. on Edn., Assn. Governing Bds. of Univs. and Colls., Nat. Assn. State Univs. and Land-Grant Colls., Nat. Assn. Sys. Heads, Internat. Assn. Univ. Presidents, Hispanic Assn. Colls. and Univs. Democrat. Roman Catholic. Office: Calif State U Office Chancellor 401 Golden Shore St Fl 6 Long Beach CA 90802-4210 E-mail: creed@calstate.edu.

REED, CHARLES RUFUS (CHUCK REED), Mayor, San Jose, California, lawyer; b. Garden City, Kans., Aug. 16, 1948; s. Ambers Reed and Estelle (Robinson) Sinclair; m. Paula Marie Weeg; children: Kim Nicole, Alexander Ryan. BS, USAF Acad., 1970; M in Pub. Affairs, Princeton U., 1972; JD, Stanford U., 1978. Bar: Calif. 1978. Assoc. Campbell, Warburton et al, San Jose, Calif., 1978-80; ptnr. Glaspy, Elliott et al, San Jose, 1981-85; mng. ptnr. Reed, Elliott, Creech & Roth, San Jose, 1985-96; pres. Reed & Roth, San Jose, 1996—99; mem. San Jose City Council, San Jose, 2000—07; mayor City of San Jose, San Jose, 2007—. Mem. Berryessa Citizens Adv. Coun., 1984—, Friends of the Guadalupe River Park, 1986-88, Horizon 2000 Task Force, 1983-84, Sm. Bus. Assn., 1981-83, Enterprise Zone Design Com., 1983, fund raising com. Vinci Park Sch. Site Coun., 1981-82, Bay Area Lawyers for the Arts, 1981-82, Urban Svcs. and Constn. and Conveyance Tax Task Force, 1982, Citizens for Park Improvements, 1982, Mayor's Com. on Ballot Measures, 1982, Berryessa Union Sch. Dist. Human Rels. Task Force, 1980-81, chmn. community rels. subcom., 1981; mem. San Jose Planning Commn., 1982-90, vice chmn., 1985-86, chmn., 1986-87; mem. Mayor's Task Force on Homeless, 1987; mem. site coun. Piedmont Mid. Sch., 1986-88; bd. dirs. San Jose Repertory Co., 1981-83, bd. counsel, 1982-83; mem. adv. bd. San Jose Shelter Found., 1988—; chmn. Destination Downtown steering com., 1988; San Jose Symphony Chmn.'s Coun., 1989; mem. adv. bd. Community Leadership San Jose, 1989—; v.p. Friends of Edn. for Berryessa Students, 1991—; mem. Santa Clara County Planning Commn., 1994—, chair, 1995-96; chair Santa Clara County Charter Rev. Com., 1997—; co-chair San Jose Gen. Plan Task Force GP 2020, 1991-93; mem. Land Trust for Santa Clara County, 1997-98; mem. Walden West Outdoor Sch. Found., 1997—. Served to capt. USAF, 1970-75. Mem. ABA, NAACP, Calif. Bar Assn., Santa Clara County Bar Assn. (mem. exec. com. bus law com., pub. edn. com.), San Jose C. of C. (v.p., bd. dirs. 1985—, chmn. 1990, chmn. high tech. com. 1983-85, participant leadership San Jose program, chmn. cen. bus. dist. com. 1981-83, chmn. downtown roundtable 1987-88) San Jose Downtown Assn. (1987—, pres. 1989, downtown working rev. com 1989-90, urban design rev. bd. 1989-90, mayor's earthquake relief com. 1989-90), USAF Acad. Assn. of Grads. (founder No. Calif. chpt. 1987, pres. 1987-88). Democrat. Avocations: skiing, jogging, boating. Office: Office of Mayor 200 E Santa Clara St San Jose CA 95113 Office Phone: 408-535-4800. Office Fax: 408-292-6422. Business E-Mail: mayoremail@sanjoseca.gov.*

REED, DOUG, Internet company executive; BS in Computer Engring., Ohio State U. Rsch. engr. Ohio State U., 1992—94; software engr. Sun Microsystems, 1994—96; sr. engr. Iona Technologies, 1996—97; sr. software engr. Avolent, 1997—99; architect of info. retrieval Digital Insight/1View Network, 2000—02; cons. internet commerce engring. Wells Fargo Bank, 2002—05; prin. Circular Bin Software, 2002—05; engring. mgr. Intuit, 2005—06; founder, chief info. officer Cake Fin. Corp., San Francisco, 2006—. Office: Cake Fin Corp 500 Third St, Ste 260 San Francisco CA 94107

REED, EDWARD CORNELIUS, JR., federal judge; b. Mason, Nev., July 8, 1924; s. Edward Cornelius Sr. and Evelyn (Walker) R.; m. Sally Torrance, June 14, 1952; children: Edward T., William W., John A., Mary E. BA, U. Nev., 1949; JD, Harvard U., 1952. Bar: Nev. 1952, U.S. Dist Ct. Nev. 1957, U.S. Supreme Ct. 1974. Atty. Arthur Andersen & Co., 1952-53; spl. dep. atty. gen. State of Nev., 1967-79; judge U.S. Dist. Ct. Nev., Reno, 1979—, chief judge, now sr. judge. Former vol. atty. Girl Scouts Am., Sierra Nevada Council, U. Nev., Nev. Agrl. Found., Nev. State Sch. Adminstrs. Assn., Nev. Congress of Parents and Teachers; mem. Washoe County Sch. Bd., 1956-72, pres. 1959, 63, 69; chmn. Gov.'s Sch. Survey Com., 1958-61; mem. Washoe County Bd. Tax Equalization, 1957-58, Washoe County Annexation Commn., 1968-72, Washoe County Personnel Com., 1973-77, chmn. 1973; mem. citizens adv. com. Washoe County Sch. Bond Issue, 1977-78, Sun Valley, Nev., Swimming Pool Com., 1978, Washoe County Blue Ribbon Task Force Com. on Growth, Nev. PTA (life); chmn. profl. div. United Way, 1978; bd. dirs. Reno Siver Sox, 1962-65. Served as staff sgt. U.S. Army, 1943-46, ETO, PTO. Mem. ABA (jud. adminstn. sect.), Nev. State Bar Assn. (adminstrv. com. dist. 5, 1967-79, lien law com. 1965-78, chmn. 1965-72, probate law com. 1963-66, tax law com. 1962-65), Am. Judicature Soc. Democrat. Baptist. Named in his honor Edward C. Reed H.S., Sparks, Nev., 1972. Office: US Dist Ct 400 S Virginia St Ste 606 Reno NV 89501-2182 Office Phone: 775-686-5919.

REED, IRVING STOY, electrical engineer; BS in Math., Cal. Inst. Tech., 1944, PhD in Math., 1949. With Northrop Aircraft Co., 1949-50, Computer Rsch. Corp., 1950-51; with Lincoln Lab. MIT, 1951-60; with Rand Corp., 1960-63; prof. dept. elec. engring. and computer sci. U. So. Calif., LA, 1963—. Cons. Jet Propulsion Lab., Hughes Aircraft Co., Rand Corp., Mitre Corp.; Shannon lectr. Internat. Symposium Info. Theory, Les Arcs, France, 1982. Co-author: Theory and Design of Digital Machines, 1962, Error—Control Coding for Data Networks, 1994; contbr. articles to profl. jours. Recipient Roy Carlton award for Outstanding Paper 1985, Disting. Alumni award Calif. Inst. Tech., 1992. Fellow IEEE (life, Charles Babbage Outstanding Sci. award 1986, Richard W. Hamming medal 1989, Masaru Ibuka Consumer Electronics award 1995, Warren White Radar medal 2001); mem. NAE. Office: U So Calif Dept Elec Engring Sys Los Angeles CA 90089-2560 Office Phone: 213-740-7335.

REED, JOHN C., physician, researcher; b. NYC, Oct. 11, 1958; s. Anthony J. and Patricia A. (Brown) R.; m. Martha Walker, June 7, 1986; children: Hunter Ashley, Tyler Austin. BA in Biochemistry, U. Va., 1980; MD, PhD, U. Pa., 1986. Resident, pathology and lab. medicine Hosp. U. of Pa., Phila., 1986-90; asst. dir. lab. molecular diagnosis U. Pa., Phila., 1990—; postdoctoral rsch. fellow, molecular biology Wistar Inst., Phila., 1986-88; asst. prof. U. Pa., Phila., 1990—92, dir., Lab. for Molecular Diagnosis; joined Burnham Inst., La Jolla, Calif., 1992—, scientific dir., 1995—2002, dep. dir., NCI-sponsored Cancer Ctr., 1994—2002, interim dir., NCI-sponsored Cancer Ctr., 2002, pres., CEO, 2002—, current bd. trustee. Mem. grant rev. com. Am. Cancer Soc., Atlanta, 1990—; cons. Genta, Inc., La Jolla, Calif., 1991—.; adj. prof. U. Calif.-San Diego, San Diego State U.; advisor nat. Cancer Inst., Am. Cancer Soc., Am. Assn. for Cancer Rsch.; advisor and cons. to numerous biotechnology and pharm. cos.; sci. co-founder, scientific adv. bd., (current) bd. dir. IDUN Pharm., Inc.; sci. co-founder, sci. adv. bd. GMP/Diagnostics; current bd. dir. ISIS Pharm., Inc. (also sci. adv. bd.), STRATAGENE, Inc. (also sci. adv. bd.), and BIOCOM; sci. adv. bds. Abbott Lab., Bristol-Myers-Squibb, Genta, Structural Bioinformatics, Genome Biosciences, Entropia, global Life-sciences Information Tech. initiative. Author 50 book chpts.; contbr. over 600 articles to profl. jours.; serves on editl. bds. of over 12 scientific jours. Leukemia Soc. Am. fellow, 1988-91, recipient scholar award, 1991—, Rsch. award Am. Cancer Soc., 1989—; grantee NIH, Nat. Cancer, Inst., Am. Cancer Soc., Leukemia Soc. Am., CaP-CURE, ABC2, and the Susan B. Komen Breast Cancer Found. Mem. AAAS, Am. Assn. Cancer Rsch., Am. Soc. Human Genetics, Am. Assn. Immunology. Republican. Episcopalian. Achievements include patent for DNA therapeutic strategy for treating cancer; research on cancer causing genes (oncogenes), on mechanism of action of immunomodulator Interleukin 2; his inventions have resulted in over 40 US Patents or Patent applications, and have spawn drug-discovery programs at several biopharmaceutical cos.; pioneer in delineating the fundamental mechanisms that regulate programmed cell death; has the distinction of having published more papers on programmed cell death (known as "apoptosis") during the past decade than any other scientist worldwide; recognized by the Institute for Scientific Information as the world's most cited scientist in all areas of research from 1997-99. Office: Burnham Inst 10901 N Torrey Pines Rd La Jolla CA 92037 Office Phone: 858-646-3132. Fax: 858-646-3199. Business E-Mail: president@burnham.org.

REED, JOHN THEODORE, writer; b. Camden, NJ, July 5, 1946; s. Theodore and Marion Theresa (Simonsick) R.; m. Margaret Ogden Tunnell, May 31, 1975; children: Daniel Tunnell, Steven Tunnell, Michael Tunnell. BS, U.S. Mil. Acad., West Point, NY, 1968; MBA, Harvard U., 1977. Salesman Pritchett & Co., Pine Hill and Collingswood, NJ, 1972-74; property mgr. Fox & Lazo Inc., Cherry Hill, NJ, 1974-75; writer Harcourt Brace Jovanovich, Boston, 1976-86; bank exec. Crocker Nat. Bank, San Francisco, 1977-78; writer, pub. Alamo, Calif., 1977—. Author: Apartment Investing Check Lists, 1978, Aggressive Tax Avoidance for Real Estate Investors, 1981, Aggressive Tax Avoidance for Real Estate Investors, 16th edit., 1998, How to Manage Residential Property for Maximum Cash Flow and Resale Value, 1995, How to Manage Residential Property for Maximum Cash Flow and Resale Value, 5th edit., 1998, How to Use Leverage to Maximize Your Real Estate Investment Return, 1984, 1986, How to Increase the Value of Real Estate, 1986, Office Building Acquisition Handbook, 1982, 1985, 1987, Residential Property Acquisition Handbook, 1991, How to Buy Real Estate for at Least 20% Below Market Value, 1993, How to Buy Real Estate for at Least 20% Below Market Value, 2d edit., 1996, Coaching Youth Football Defense, 1994, Coaching Youth Football Defense, 2d edit., 1996, John T. Reed's Real Estate Investor's Monthly Newsletter, 1986—, Coaching Youth Football, 1995—, Coaching Youth Football, 3d edit., 2000—, Football Clock Management, 1997—, Football Clock Management, 2d edit., 2001—, Aggressive Tax Avoidance for Real Estate Investors, 17th edit., 2001—, Youth Baseball Coaching, 2000—, How to Get Started in Real Estate Investment, 2000—, Gap-Air-Mirror Defense for Youth Football, 2000—, How to Buy Real Estate for Little or No Money Down, 2001—, Single-Wing Offense for Youth Football, 2001—, Fixers, 2002, Succeeding, 2003. Coach Youth Flag Football, 1999. 1st lt. U.S. Army, 1968-72, Vietnam. Mem. Nat. Assn. Real Estate Editors, Am. Baseball Coaches Assn., Am. Football Coaches Assn., Nat. Youth Sports Coaches Assn., Nat. Fedn. Interscholastic Coaches Assn., Calif. Coaches Assn., Football Writers Assn., Profl. Football Rschrs. Assn., Nat. Single-Wing Coaches Assn. Avocations: reading, activities with family. Home and Office: 342 Bryan Dr Alamo CA 94507-2858 Office Phone: 925-820-6292. E-mail: johnreed@johntreed.com.

REED, KATHLEEN RAND, manufacturer, marketing consultant, sociologist; b. Chgo., Feb. 6, 1947; d. Kirkland James Reed and Johnnie Viola Rand. Student, San Jose State U. Investigator, research cons. Ill. Supreme Ct., Chgo., 1970; account exec. ETA Pub. Relations, Chgo., 1970-72; pub. relations and promotion dir. Sta. WTVS TV, Detroit, 1972; pub. affairs dir. Sta. WJLB Radio, Detroit, 1972-74; pvt. practice bus. resource and research cons. K.H. Arnold, San Francisco, 1974-80; spl. projects coordinator The Hdqrs. Co. subs. United Techs., San Francisco, 1980-81; adminstrn. mgr. Nat. Alliance of Bus.-Region IX, San Francisco, 1981-83; pres. Michael St. Michael/Corp. Leather and Leather Goods Mfr., Menlo Park, Calif., 1983—. Pres. Necronomics, Stanford, Calif., cons. organ transplantation, 1989—. Mem. Am. Sociol. Assn., Pacific Sociol. Assn., Sociologists for Women in Society, Women in Communications, Western Social Sci. Assn., Nat. Assn. Sci. Writers, Acad. Ind. Scholars, Soc. for Study of Women in Legal History, Inst. for Hist. Study, NOW, Women's Inst. for Freedom, Am. Women in Radio and TV Inc., San Francisco C. of C. (com. mem. 1984—), World Trade Assn., Bay Area Purchasing Council (com. mem. 1986—), Urban Coalition West, (bd. dirs. Phoenix chpt. 1986—), San Francisco Convention and Visitors Bur. (bd. dirs. 1986—). Office: 181 Santa Margarita Ave Menlo Park CA 94025 also: 1923 Second St NW Washington DC 20001-1667

REED, KENNETH G., petroleum company executive; b. 1917; married. Student, U. Tex. With Amerada Petroleum Corp., Tulsa, 1948-70, sr. v.p., 1967-70; exec. v.p. internat. operations Amerada Hess Corp., NYC, 1970; pres., chief exec. officer APEXCO, Inc., Tulsa, 1971-77, Natomas Internat. Corp., 1977, also dir.; exec. v.p. energy, dir. Natomas Co., San Francisco, 1977-83, vice chmn., pres., 1983—; pres., dir. Natomas Energy Co., 1979—; chmn., chief exec. officer Overseas Petroleum Ltd., San Francisco, 1984—. Dir. Natomas N.Am. Inc., 1st Nat. Bank & Trust Co., Tulsa, Oneok Inc., Tulsa. Office: Apt 1518 3840 Rimrock RD Billings MT 59102-0107

REED, SAM, Secretary of State, Washington; b. Portland, Oreg. m. Margie Reed, 1963; children: David, Kristen. BA, MA, Wash. State U. Cert. profl. elections officer. Exec. dir. Gov. Evans' Urban Affairs Coun.; asst. sec. state State of Wash., Olympia, 1969—75; dir. State Constl. Reform Commn., 1975—77; auditor Thurston County, 1978—2000; sec. state State of Wash., Olympia, 2001—. Exec. dir. Gov. 's Urban Affairs Coun., 1967—69; sec. Nat. Assn. Secretaries State (NASS), 2004; bd. mem. Fed. Election Commn. Voting System; internat. election observer, Uganda; mem. Americorps Adv. Coun., Wash. State Election Admin. & Cert. Bd. Recipient Gov.'s Disting. Vol. award, Thurston County Citizen of the Year Disting. Svc. award. Mem.: Mainstream Reps. of Wash., Wash. State Assn. County Auditors, Olympia Kiwanis. Republican. Avocations: running, piano, arts, tennis. Office: Office Sec of State Legislative Bldg 2nd Floor PO Box 40220 Olympia WA 98504 Office Phone: 360-902-4151. Office Fax: 360-586-5629. E-mail: sreed@secstate.wa.gov.

REED, WALLACE ALLISON, anesthesiologist; b. Covina, Calif., May 19, 1916; s. Wallace Allison and Mary Julia (Birdsall) Reed; m. Maria Eva Wiemers, Jan. 20, 1938; children: Ellen E., Barbara R., Wallace J., Michael E., Kathryn L., Vikki T. AB, UCLA, 1937; postgrad., U. Cologne, 1937-38, U. Freiburg, 1938-39; MD, U. So. Calif., 1944. Diplomate Am. Bd. Anesthesiology. Intern Santa Fe Coast Lines Hosp., Los Angeles, 1943—44; resident Precept Sanders-Valley Forge Hosp., 1944—46, Los Angeles County Gen. Hosp., 1946-47; asst. to head dept. anesthesiology Precept Dillon-Los Angeles County Gen. Hosp., 1946-47; clin. instr. surgery U. So. Calif. Sch. Medicine, 1946-47; practice medicine, specializing in anesthesiology Phoenix, 1948-89; ret., 1989. Hon. staff mem. Good Samaritan Hosp., St. Joseph Hosp., Maricopa County Gen. Hosp.; mem. hon. staff Children's Hosp.; co-founder John L. Ford, M.D., Surgicenter, 1970; vice pres. Maricopa Found. for Med. Care, 1970-74, pres., 1975-76; mem. House Ways and Means Adv. Com.; adv. coun. Nat. Health Inst., 1975-76; mem. accreditation coun. for ambulatory health care Joint Commn. on Accreditation of Hosps., 1975-79; vice-chmn. Accreditation Assn. for Ambulatory Health Care, 1979-81, pres., 1981-83; mem. panel for study Nat. Health Ins., Congl. GAO; chmn. bd. Alterna Care Corp., 1984-87, now chmn. bd. emeritus; mem. adv. bd. Kino Inst., 1994-95. Bd. dirs. South Phoenix Montessori Sch., pres. bd., 1971—75; bd. dirs. Alzheimer's Assn., Greater Phoenix chpt., 1998—2000, co-v.p., 2000; co-chmn. med. and sci. adv. com. Desert S.W. chpt. Alzheimer's Assn., 2004—05; bd. dirs. Ctrl. Ariz. Health Sys. Agy., 1975—78; exec. dir. Surgictr. of Phoenix, 1987—97. Capt. M.C. AUS, 1944—46. Recipient Pinal award Ariz. Psychiat. Soc., 1967-68, Gerard B. Lambert Merit award for innovative ideas that improve patient care; John L. Ford M.D., 1972; recipient spirit of philanthropy award Alzheimer's Assn., 1996, Samba Disting. Svc. award, 2000; Disting. Svc. award Ariz. Soc. Anesthesiology, 2003. Fellow: Am. Coll. Anesthesiologists; mem.: AMA, Alzheimer's Assn. (co-chmn. med. and sci. adv. com. Desert S.W. chpt. 2004—05, co-v.p. Greater Phoenix (Ariz.) chpt. 2000), Soc. for Advancement Geriatric Anesthesia (charter mem.), Guedel Assn. (pres. 1972), Am. Assn. Founds. for Med. Care (dir. 1970—74),

Central Ariz. Physicians Svc. Assn. (pres. 1982—83), Maricopa County Med. Soc. (pres. 1964, dir., Salsbury medal 1967, 1971, Thomas Dooley medal 1970), Internat. Assn. Amb. Surgery (hon.), Soc. for Ambulatory Anesthesia (bd. dirs. 1985—87), Federated Amb. Surgery Assn. (pres. 1974—75, dir.), Acad. Anesthesiology (dir. 1966—72, pres. 1969), Ariz., Maricopa County Socs. Anesthesiologists, Am. Soc. Anesthesiologists, WarMer Rsch. Found., Seed Money for Growth Found. (pres. 1984—). Methodist. Home: 4716 N Dromedary Rd Phoenix AZ 85018-2939 Office: 1040 E Mcdowell Rd Phoenix AZ 85006-2622 Home Phone: 602-840-6349; Office Phone: 602-258-1521. Personal E-mail: somnus4@cox.net.

REEDER, F. ROBERT, lawyer; b. Brigham City, Utah, Jan. 23, 1943; s. Frank O. and Helen H. (Heninger) R.; m. Joannie Anderson, May 4, 1974; children: David, Kristina, Adam. JD, U. Utah, 1967. Bar: Utah 1967, U.S. Ct. Appeals (10th cir.) 1967, U.S. Ct. Appeals (D.C. and 5th cirs.) 1979, U.S. Ct. Mil. Appeals 1968, U.S. Supreme Ct. 1972. Shareholder Parsons, Behle & Latimer, Salt Lake City, 1968—, bd. dirs., 1974—92. Bd. dir. Holy Cross Found., 1981-90, chmn., 1987-90; bd. dir. Holy Cross Hosp., 1990-93, treas., 1986-87, vice chmn., 1987-93; bd. dirs. Holy Cross Health Svcs. Utah, 1993-94, treas., 1993-94; bd. dir. Salt Lake Regional Med. Ctr., 1995—, vice chmn., 1995-2000, chmn., 2000-07; trustee Univ. Hosp. Found.; hon. col. Salt Lake City Police, Salt Lake County Sheriff; bd. dir. Utah Hosp. and Health Sys. Assn., 2005—, This is the Place Found., 2006-, Utah Facility Com., 2006-. With USAR, 1967—73. Mem. ABA, Utah Hosp. Health Sys. Assn. (bd. dir. 2006—), Utah State Bar, Salt Lake County Bar (ethics adv. com. 1989-94), Cottonwood Country Club (bd. dir. 1978-82, 83-86, pres. 1981-82), The Country Club (Salt Lake), Rotary. Office: Parsons Behle & Latimer PO Box 45898 Salt Lake City UT 84145-0898 Office Phone: 801-536-6769. Business E-Mail: bobreeder@parsonsbehle.com.

REED-GRAHAM, LOIS L., counseling administrator, writer, management consultant; b. Muscogee, Okla., Jan. 19, 1933; d. Louis G. and Bonnie (Hill) Reed; children: Harold Gibson, Kathryn Ann Graham. RN, San Diego County Hosp., 1957; BA, Calif. State U., Sacramento, 1972, MPA, 1978; postgrad., Calif. State U., Sacremento; EdD, U. Laverne. Tchr., adminstr., job developer CETA, Sacramento, 1972-78; bus. instr. Los Rios Community Coll., Sacramento, 1978-84; tchr. grade 6 Mark Hopkins Sch., Sacramento, 1984-89; acting adminstr. Fern Bacon Sch., Sacramento; adminstr. Sacramento City Schs.; tchr. grades 7,8, mentor tchr. Fern Bacon Sch., Sacramento; asst. prin. secondary edn. Sacramento City Schs., 1989-93; elem. sch. prin. Theodore Judah Elem. Sch., Sacramento, 1993—; asst. supt. secondary, middle and K-8 schs. Sacramento City Unified Sch.; prin. Hubert Bancroft Elem. Sch., Sacramento; ret., 2003; edn. cons., author, mgmt. organizer, 2003—. Cons. Prentice Hall Pub. Co. Contbr. articles to profl. publs. Mem. Calif. State Fair Employment and Housing Commn. Mem. AAUW (bd. dirs., pres. Sacramento chpt. 1990), Nat. Assn. Univ. Women (pres.) Home: 7408 Toulon Ln Sacramento CA 95828-4641 Personal E-mail: loisreed@comcast.net.

REES, NORMA S., academic administrator; b. NYC, Dec. 27, 1929; d. Benjamin and Lottie (Schwartz) D.; m. Raymond R. Rees, Mar. 19, 1960; children— Evan Lloyd, Raymond Arthur BA, Queens Coll., 1952; Ma, Bklyn. Coll., 1954; PhD, NYU, 1959; D of Arts and Letters honoris causa, John F. Kennedy U., 2001. Cert. speech-language pathology, audiology. Prof. communicative disorders Hunter Coll., NYC, 1967-72; exec. officer, speech and hearing scis. grad. sch. CUNY, NYC, 1972-74, assoc. dean for grad. studies, 1974-76, dean grad. studies, 1976-82; vice chancellor for acad. affairs U. Wis., Milw., 1982-85, from 1986, acting chancellor, 1985-86; vice chancellor for acad. policy and planning Mass. Bd. Regents for Higher Edn., Boston, 1987-90; pres. Calif. State U. East Bay, Hayward, 1990—. Chmn. Commn. Recognition of Postsecondary Accreditation, 1994-96; mem. adv. com. quality and integrity U.S. Dept. Edn., commn. on internat. edn. Coun. on Higher Edn. Accreditation, 2003—. Contbr. articles to profl. jours. Trustee Citizens Govtl. Rsch. Bur., Milw., 1985-87; active Task Force on Wis. World Trade Ctr., 1985-87; bd. dirs. Am. Assn. State Colls. and Univs., 1995-97, Coun. of Postsecondary Accreditation, Washington, 1985-94, Greater Boston YWCA, 1987-90; mem. Calif. Sch. to Career Coun.; bd. dir. Econ. Devel. Alliance for Bus., Alameda County, 1995—; sec. edn. Nat. Adv. Com. Institutional Quality and Integrity, 1998-2002; bd. dirs. Bay Area World Trade Ctr., 2001—, Alameda County Health Care Found., 2002-. Fellow Am. Speech-Lang-Hearing Assn. (honors); mem. Am. Coun. Edn. (com. internat. edn. 1991-93), Am. Assn. Colls. and Univs. (chair task force on quality assessment 1991-92), Nat. Assn. State Univs. and Land Grant Colls. (exec. com. divsn. urban affairs 1985-87, com. accreditation 1987-90), Hayward C. of C. (bd. dirs. 1995-98), Oakland C. of C. (bd. dirs. 1997-2004). Office: Calif State Univ East Bay 25800 Carlos Bee Blvd Hayward CA 94542-3001 Home Phone: 510-889-8069; Office Phone: 510-885-3877. E-mail: norma.rees@csueastbay.edu.

REES, RAYMOND F., military officer; b. Pendleton, Oreg., Sept. 29, 1944; s. Raymond Emmett and Lorna Doone (Gemmell) R.; m. Karen Kristine Young, Nov. 1966 (div. Mar. 1974); children: Raymond Gordon, Christian Frederick; m. Mary Len Middleton, Dec. 30, 1977; 1 child, Carrie Evelyn. BS, U.S. Mil. Acad., 1966; JD, U. Oreg., 1976. Commd. 2d lt. U.S. Army, 1966, 2005—; platoon leader, troop exec. officer, co. comdr. 2d Armored Cavalry Regiment, Bamberg, Fed. Republic Germany; troop comdr. 2-17 Cavalry 101 Airborn divsn., Camp Eagle, Vietnam, 1969; troop exec. officer 1-17 Cavalry 82 Airborn divsn., Ft. Bragg, N.C., 1972; resigned U.S. Army, 1973; with Oreg. Army Nat. Guard, 1973—, advanced through grades to maj. gen., 1990; asst. ops. officer Infantry Brigade; co. comdr. 2d Battalion, 162d Infantry, Corvallis, Oreg.; with 116th Armored Calvary Regiment, 1976-87; comdr. 116th cavalry regiment, adjutant gen. Oreg. Army Nat. Guard, 1987-91; dir. Army N.G., 1991-92; vice chief N.G. Bur., Washington, 1992-94; adjutant gen. Oreg. N.G., 1994-99; vice chief N.G. Bur., Washington, 1999—2002, acting chief, 2002—03; chief of staff Hdqrs. NORAD and U.S. No. Command, 2003—05. Decorated Bronze Star, Legion of Merit, D.S.M., Def. Disting. Svc. medal. Mem. VFW, Adjutant Gen. Assn. U.S., Nat. Guart Assn. U.S., Assn. of U.S. Army, Oreg. Nat. Guard Assn., U.S. Armor Assn., Oreg. Bar Assn., Am. Legion, Mil. Order World Wars, West Point Soc. Oreg., 101st Airborne Div. Assn., 116th Armored Cavalry Assn., 41st Infantry Div. Assn., Elks. Office Phone: 503-584-3991.

REESE, JOHN ROBERT, lawyer; b. Salt Lake City, Nov. 3, 1939; s. Robert McCann and Glade (Stauffer) R.; m. Francesca Marroquin Gardner, Sept. 5, 1964 (div.); children: Jennifer Marie, Justine Francesca; m. Robin Ann Gunsul, June 18, 1988. AB cum laude, Harvard U., 1962; LLB, Stanford U., 1965. Bar: Calif. 1966, U.S. Dist. Ct. (no. dist.) Calif. 1966, U.S. Ct. Appeals (9th cir.) 1966, U.S. Dist. Ct. (ctrl. dist.) Calif. 1974, U.S. Supreme Ct. 1976, U.S. Dist. Ct. (ea. dist.) Calif. 1977, U.S. Ct. Appeals (6th cir.) 1982, U.S. Ct. Appeals (8th cir.) 1985, U.S. Ct. Appeals (10th cir.) 1992, U.S. Ct. Appeals (Fed. cir.) 1994. Assoc. McCutchen, Doyle, Brown & Enersen, San Francisco, 1965—74, ptnr., 1974—2002, Bingham McCutchen, San Francisco, 2002—06, of counsel, 2007—. Adj. asst. prof. law Hastings Coll. of Law, 1991; lectr. U. Calif., Berkeley, 1987, Berkeley, 92. Mem. editl. and adv. bds.: Antitrust Bull., Jour. Reprints for Antitrust Law and Econs., 1981—99. Bd. dirs. Friends of San Francisco Pub. Libr., 1981-87; bd. vis. Stanford U. Law Sch., 1983-86. Capt. U.S. Army, 1966-68. Decorated Bronze Star. Mem. ABA, Am. Acad. Appellate Lawyers, State Bar Calif., San Francisco Bar Assn., U.S. Supreme Ct. Hist. Soc., Ninth Jud. Cir. Hist. Soc., Calif. Acad. Appellate Lawyers, Order of Coif. Avocation: gardening. Home: 9 Morning Sun Dr Petaluma CA 94952-4780 Office: Bingham McCutchen 3 Embarcadero Ctr San Francisco CA 94111-4003 Home Phone: 707-765-1941; Office Phone: 415-393-2225. Business E-Mail: john.reese@bingham.com.

REESE, MONTE NELSON, agricultural association executive; b. Mooreland, Okla., Mar. 31, 1947; s. James Nelson and Ruby Edith (Bond) R.; m. Treisa Lou Bartow, May 25, 1968; children: Bartow Allan, Monica Lynnelle. BS in Agrl. Econs., Okla. State U., 1969. Staff asst. Wilson Cert. Foods, Oklahoma City, 1969-71; assoc. farm dir. Sta. WKY Radio and TV, Oklahoma City, 1971-73; radio-TV specialist Tex. A&M U., College Station, 1973; dir. agrl. devel. Oklahoma City C. of C., 1973-76; asst. exec. dir. Am. Morgan Horse Assn., Westmoreland, N.Y., 1976-77; v.p. pub. affairs Farm Credit Banks of Wichita, Kans., 1977-87; exec. dir. Coffey County Econ. Devel., Burlington, Kans., 1987-88; farm dir. Mid-Am. Ag Network, Wichita, 1988-89; CEO Cattlemen's Beef Promotion and Rsch. Bd., Englewood, Colo., 1989-96; exec. dir. Cattlemen's Beef Promotion & Rsch. Bd., Englewood, CO, 1996-98, COO, 1998—. Lt. col. USAR, 1969—. Office: Cattlenens Beef Board 9000 E Nichols Ave Ste 215 Centennial CO 80112-3406

REESE, PAUL WAYNE, state representative; b. Dallas, Sept. 19, 1953; m. Sandra Reese; 4 children. Mgr. Shakey's Inc., 1975—76; asst. signalman Union Pacific R.R., 1976—77, cond., locomotive engr., 1977; state rep. dist. 11 Wyo. State Legis., Cheyenne, 1997. Com. Wyo. State Legis., Cheyenne; coun. State Govt. Nest Exec. Com. Mem.: United Transp. Union Engrs. Democrat. Home: 716 E 20th St Cheyenne WY 82001 Office: Capitol Bldg Wyo State Legis Cheyenne WY 82002

REEVES, BARBARA ANN, lawyer; b. Buffalo, Mar. 29, 1949; d. Prentice W. and Doris Reeves; m. Richard C. Neal; children: Timothy R. Neal, Stephen S. Neal (dec.), Robert S. Neal, Richard R. Neal. Student, Wellesley Coll., Mass., 1967-68; BA (NSF fellow, Lehman fellow), New Coll., Sarasota, Fla., 1970; JD cum laude, Harvard U., 1973. Bar: Calif. 1973, D.C. 1977. Law clk. U.S. Ct. Appeals, 9th Circuit, Portland, Oreg., 1973—74; assoc. firm Munger, Tolles and Rickershauser, LA, 1977—78; trial atty. spl. trial sect. Dept. Justice (Antitrust div.), 1974—75; spl. asst. to asst. atty. gen. Antitrust div. Dept. Justice, Washington, 1976—77; chief antitrust div. L.A. field office, 1978—81; ptnr. Morrison & Foerster, LA, 1981—94, Fried, Frank, Harris, Shriver & Jacobson, LA, 1995—97, Paul, Hastings, Janofsky & Walker, LA, 1997—99; assoc. gen. counsel So. Calif. Edison, 1999—2004, v.p. shared svcs., 2004—06; mediator, arbitrator JAMS, 2006—. Mem. exec. com. state bar conf. of dels. L.A. Delegation, 1982-91; del. 9th Cir. Jud. Conf., 1984-88; mem. Fed. Ct. Magistrate Selection Com., 1989; bd. dirs. Pub. Counsel, 1988-92, Western Ctr. Law and Poverty, 1992-98; lectr. in field. Editor: Federal Criminal Litigation, 1994; contbg. author: World Antitrust Law, 1995; contbr. articles to profl. jours. Mem. ABA (litigation sect., antitrust sect.), Fed. Bar Assn. (officer 1998—), Assn. Bus. Trial Lawyers (officer 1997—), Am. Arbitration Assn. (arbitrator, mediator, mem. adv. panel large complex case program), L.A. County Bar Assn. (antitrust sect. officer 1980-81, litigation sect. officer 1988-93 trustee 1990-92, chair alternative dispute resolution sec. 1992-95, L.A. County Ct. ADR com.). Home: 1410 Hillcrest Ave Pasadena CA 91106-4503 Office: 46th Fl 707 Wilshire Blvd Los Angeles CA 90017 Home Phone: 626-449-5809; Office Phone: 213-620-1133. Business E-Mail: breeves@jamsadr.com.

REEVES, JAMES N., lawyer; b. Albert Lea, Minn., Oct. 14, 1945; AB, Dartmouth Coll., 1967; student, George Washington U.; JD, U. Minn., 1970. Bar: Minn. 1970, Alaska 1972, U.S. Ct. Appeals (9th cir.), U.S. Supreme Ct. Law clk. U.S. Dist. Ct. Minn., 1970-71; asst. atty. gen. State of Alaska, 1971-78; mem. Bogle & Gates (now Dorsey & Whitney), Anchorage; ptnr.-in-charge, Anchorage; mem. trial dept., environ. and natural resources practice groups Dorsey & Whitney LLP, Anchorage. Sr. fellow East-West Ctr., Honolulu, 1977. Mem. ABA, Alaska Bar Assn. Office: Dorsey & Whitney 1031 W 4th Ave Ste 600 Anchorage AK 99501-5907 Office Phone: 907-276-4557. Office Fax: 907-276-4152. Business E-Mail: reeves.jim@dorsey.com.

REEVES, KEANU, actor; b. Beirut, Sept. 2, 1964; s. Samuel Nowlin Reeves and Patricia Taylor. Stage appearances: Wolf Boy (debut), For Adults Only, Romeo and Juliet; films: Flying, 1986, Youngblood, 1986, River's Edge, 1987, Permanent Record, 1988, The Night Before, 1988, The Prince of Pennsylvania, 1988, Dangerous Liaisons, 1988, Bill and Ted's Excellent Adventure, 1989, Parenthood, 1989, I Love You to Death, 1990, Tune in Tomorrow, 1990, Bill and Ted's Bogus Journey, 1991, Point Break, 1991, My Own Private Idaho, 1991, Bram Stoker's Dracula, 1992, Much Ado About Nothing, 1993, Little Buddha, 1994, Even Cowgirls Get the Blues, 1994, Speed, 1994, Johnny Mnemonic, 1995, A Walk in the Clouds, 1995, Feeling Minnesota, 1996, Chain Reaction, 1996, Devil's Advocate, 1997, The Last Time I Committed Suicide, 1997, The Matrix, 1999, The Replacements, 2000, The Watcher, 2000, The Gift, 2000, Hard Ball, 2001, Sweet November, 2001, The Matrix Reloaded, 2003, The Matrix Revolutions, 2003, Something's Gotta Give, 2003, Thumbsucker, 2005, Constantine, 2005, A Scanner Darkly, 2006, The Lake House, 2006 (with Sandra Bullock Movie Choice Liplock, Teen Choice Awards, 2006), Street Kings, 2008, The Day the Earth Stood Still, 2008, The Private Lives of Pippa Lee, 2009; TV films: Letting Go, 1985, Act of Vengeance, 1986, Young Again, 1986, Babes in Toyland, 1986, Under the Influence, 1986, Brotherhood of Justice, 1986, Life Under Water, 1989, Children Remember the Holocaust, 1995, (narrator) The Great Warning, 2003. Named one of 50 Most Powerful People in Hollywood, Premiere mag., 2004—06.

REFO, PATRICIA LEE, lawyer; b. Alexandria, Va., Dec. 31, 1958; m. Don Bivens; 1 child, Andrew stepchildren: Jody, Lisa. BA with high honors and high distinction, U. Mich., 1980, JD cum laude, 1983. Bar: Ill. 1983, US Dist. Ct. (no. dist.) Ill. 1983, US Ct. Appeals (7th cir.) 1988, US Ct. Appeals (11th cir.) 1989, US Ct. Appeals (5th cir.) 1993, Ariz. 1996, US Dist. Ct., Ariz. 1997, US Ct. Appeals (9th cir.) 1998, US Tax Ct. Assoc. Jenner & Block, Chgo., 1983—90, ptnr., 1990—96, Snell & Wilmer LLP, Phoenix, 1996—. Mem. bd. advisors Comml. Lending Liability News, 1989—, Nat. Law Jour., 2005—; mem. faculty Nat. Inst. Trial Advocacy, 1989—; adv. com. on fed. rules of evidence US Jud. Conf., 2000—06; lectr. ALI/ABA and Practicing Law Inst.; William Reese Smith Jr. disting. lectr. litig. ethics Stetson Law Sch., 2006. Chancellor Episcopal Parish St. Barnabas Desert, 1999—2008; bd. dirs. Ariz. Academic Decathlon Assn., 1997—2001, bd. advisors, 2001—; bd. dirs. Ariz. Found. for Women, 1999—2005; dir. Greater Phoenix C. of C., 2005—; sr. warden Episcopal Parish St. Barnabas Desert, 2008—. Recipient Disting. Achievement Medal, Sandra Day O'Connor Coll. Law at Ariz. State U., 2007; named Southwest Super Lawyer, Law & Politics Mag., 2007; named one of The 50 Most Influential Women Lawyers in Am., Nat. Law Jour., 2007. Fellow: Ariz. Found. for Legal Services and Edn., Am. Bar Found.; mem.: ABA (sec. sect. litig. 1994—98, exec. com. sect. litig. 1994—, ho. delegates 1998—2001, standing com. on membership 2000—03, chmn. sect. litig. 2003—04, chair Am. Jury Project 2004—05, ho. delegates 2005—), Women Lawyers Honoring Justice O'Connor, Nat. Assn. Women Lawyers. Office: Snell & Wilmer LLP One Arizona Ctr Phoenix AZ 85004-2202

REGALA, DEBBIE, state legislator; b. Tacoma, Apr. 27, 1945; m to Leo; children: Alisa (Mrs O'Hanlon), Tim & Jonathan. Commissioner, Metrop Park District, Tacoma, 86-92, president, 89 & 91; member, Puyallup River Watershed Coun, currently; Washington State Representative, District 27, 94-2001, co-chairwoman, Natural Resources Committee, formerly, member, Appropriations & Joint Legislature Audit & Rev Committees, Govt Coun on Natural Resources, formerly, Washington House Representative; Washington State Senator, District 27, 2001-.Work site coordinator for environmental restoration project in our community, formerly; volunteer, McCarver Elem, 14 years; docent, Tacoma Art Museum, 8 years, member, Activities Coun, 3 years; board director, Pt Defience Zoological Soc, 6 years. Point Defiance Zoological Soc (board director, currently); Tacoma Recreation Found (board director, currently); Literacy Center for Tacoma/Pierce Co (member, steering comt, formerly). Democrat. Catholic. Address: 1802 N Puget Sound Ave Tacoma WA 98406 Office: State Senate 417 John A Cherberg Bldg, PO Box 40427 Olympia WA 98504 Home Phone: 253-759-9674; Office Phone: 360-786-7974. E-mail: regala_de@leg.wa.gov.

REGAN, WILLIAM JOSEPH, JR., energy company executive; b. Bronx, NY, Mar. 7, 1946; s. William Joseph and Eleanor F. (Malone) R.; m. Mary Lee Wynn; children— Katrina Lee, Thomas Wynn, James William BS, U.S. Air Force Acad., 1967; MBA, U. Wis.-Madison, 1969, PhD, 1972. Asst. prof. Wayne State U., Detroit, 1971-75; with Nat. Bank Detroit, 1975-77; sr. bus. planner Am. Natural Resources Co., Detroit, 1977-78, dir. fin. planning, 1978-82, v.p., treas., 1982-85; v.p. corp. fin. United Svcs. Automobile Assn., San Antonio, 1986-88, sr. v.p., treas., 1988-95; v.p., treas. Entergy Corp., New Orleans, 1995-99; CFO Calif. Ind. Sys. Operator Corp., Folsom, Calif., 1999—. Office: 151 Blue Ravine Rd Folsom CA 95630 Home: 8624 FAIRWAY GREEN DR Fair Oaks TX 78015-4480 Office Phone: 916-351-4437. E-mail: wregan37@earthlink.net.

REGAN GOSSAGE, MURIEL, librarian; b. NYC, July 15, 1930; d. William and Matilda (Riebel) Blome; m. Robert Regan, 1966 (div. 1976); 1 child, Jeanne Booth; m. Wayne Gossage, 2003 (dec. 2006). BA, Hunter Coll., NYC, 1950; MLS, Columbia U., 1952; MBA, Pace U., NYC, 1982. Post libr. US Army, Okinawa, 1952-53; researcher P.F. Collier, NYC, 1953-57; asst. libr. to libr. Rockefeller Found., NYC, 1957-67; dep. chief libr. Manhattan Community Coll., NYC, 1967-68; libr. Booz Allen & Hamilton, NYC, 1968-69, Rockefeller Found., NYC, 1969-82; prin. Gossage Regan Assocs., Inc., NYC, 1980-95; pub. svcs. libr. Carlsbad (N.Mex.) Pub. Libr., 1995-2000. Dir. N.Y. Met. Reference and Rsch. Libr. Agy., 1988-95, Coun. Nat. Libr. and Info. Assns., 1991-95; cons. Librs. Info. Ctrs., Gossage Sager Assocs., 2001-05. Elder First Presbyn. Ch. of Carlsbad, 1997-99, 2006—, Stephen min., 2000-05, deacon, 2002-03. Mem. Spl. Librs. Assn. (pres. 1989-90), Archons of Colophon. Avocations: cats, reading, playing piano, travel. Home: 702 Lakeside Dr Carlsbad NM 88220-5209 Personal E-mail: murielregan@zianet.com.

REGIER, KEITH, state legislator; Mem. Dist. 5 Mont. House of Reps., 2008—. Republican. Office: Montana House of Representatives PO Box 200400 Helena MT 59620-0400 Mailing: 1078 Stillwater Rd Kalispell MT 59901-6902 Home Phone: 406-756-6141; Office Phone: 406-444-4800. Office Fax: 406-444-4825. Personal E-mail: kregier@centurytel.net.

REGNI, JOHN F., academic administrator, career military officer; BS in Biology, USAF Acad., 1973; MS in Systems Mgmt., St. Mary's U., 1981; attended, Air Command and Staff Coll., Maxwell AFB, 1984, Air War College, 1990, Nat. Defense U., Fort Lesley J. McNair, 1997. Commd. 2d lt. USAF, 1973, advanced through grades to lt. gen., 2004; pers. officer Ogden Air Logistics Ctr., Hill AFB, Utah, 1973-76; chief, pers. utilization 40th Tactical Group, Aviano AB, Italy, 1976-78; chief force anlysis and asst., col. assignments Air Force Manpower and Pers. Ctr., Randolph AFB, Tex., 1978-81; asst. exec., dep. chief of staff for manpower and pers. Hdqrs. USAF, The Pentagon, Washington, 1981-83; asst. chief of staff Hdqrs. Air Tng. Command, Randolph AFB, Tex., 1984-87; dep. base comdr. 3380th Air Base Group, Keesler AFB, Miss., 1987-89; base comdr. 8th Combat Support Group, Kunsan AB, Republic of Korea, 1990-91; dir. manpower, pers. and support Hdqrs. U.S. Pacific Command, Camp H.M. Smith, Hawaii, 1991-94; dir. pers. Hdqrs. Air Mobility Command, Scott AFB, Ill., 1994-96; dir., mil. pers. policy, dep. chief of staff for pers. Hdqrs. USAF, the Pentagon, Washington, 1996-98, dir. pers. resources, dep. chief of staff for pers., 1998—2000; dir. Air Force Pers. Ops. Agy., Washington, 1998-2000; comdr. 2nd Air Force, Keesler AFB, Miss., 2000—04, Air Univ., Maxwell AFB, Ala., 2004—05; supt. USAF Acad., Colorado Springs, 2005—. Decorated Legion of Merit, Air Force Commendation Medal, Meritorious Svc. Medal with silver oak leaf cluster, Defense Superior Svc. Medal, Disting. Svc. Medal with oak leaf cluster. Office: Supt 2304 Cadet Dr, Ste 342 U S A F Academy CO 80840-5001

REHBERG, DENNIS R., United States Representative from Montana; b. Billings, Mont., Oct. 5, 1955; m. Janice Rehberg; 3 children. Student, Mont. State U., 1974; BA in Pub. Adminstrn. and Polit. Sci., Wash. State U., Pullman, 1977. Tchr. gymnastics, Billings, Mont., 1973—74; with Green Giant Co., Dayton, Wash., 1975—76, Ramada Inn, Billings, 1977; ditch digger Lockrem Constrn., Billings, 1977; real estate salesman Billings, 1977—79; legis. aide Staffs of State

Senator Bill Mathers and State Senator Sonny Lockrem, 1977; legis. asst. Staff of US Rep. Ron Marlenee, Mont., 1979—82; mgr. Rehberg Ranch, Billings, 1982—2000; mem. Mont. State Ho. Reps. from Dist. 88, 1985—89; state dir. Staff of US Senator Conrad Burns, Mont., 1989—91; lt. gov. Mont., 1991—97; mem. US Congress from Mont. at large, 2001—, mem. appropriations com. Recipient Guardian of Senior's Rights award, 60 Plus Assn., 2002, Presdl. award, for leadership, Nat. Farmers Union, 2003; named a Champion of Small Bus., Small Bus. Survival Com., 2001, 2002, Hero of Taxpayer, Americans for Tax Reform, 2002. Republican. Episcopalian. Office: US House Reps 2448 Rayburn House Office Bldg Washington DC 20515-2601 Office Phone: 202-225-3211. Office Fax: 202-225-5687.

REHM, SUSAN J., social services professional; b. Yorktown, Va., May 17, 1945; d. Gilbert F. and Jeradean Dolly (Field) R. BA, U. Redlands, 1967; MSW, San Diego State U., 1969. Diplomate in clin. social work; lic. social worker, Calif.; cert. tchr., Calif. Dir. clin. social work home health care and child devel. depts. UCLA Med. Ctr.; dir. social work svcs. Mercy Hosp. and Med. Ctr., San Diego, Calif.; lectr. Sch. Social Work San Diego State U.; exec. dir. Family Svc. Agy., Santa Barbara, Calif. Named state scholar, Calif., 1963-67, U.S. Children's Bur. Fellow, 1968-69. Mem. NASW, Family Svc. Am. (exec. coun.), Santa Barbara Sunrise Rotary, Nat. Found. Infectious Diseases (pres.). Office: Family Svc Agy 123 W Gutierrez St Santa Barbara CA 93101-3424

REHMUS, CHARLES MARTIN, arbitrator; b. Ann Arbor, Mich., June 27, 1926; s. Paul A. and Amy D. (Martin) R.; m. Carolyn Brown, Dec. 21, 1948 (div. July 1982); children— Paul, James, Jon, David; m. Laura Carlson, Sept. 4, 1982 AB, Kenyon Coll., 1947; MA, Stanford U., 1951, PhD, 1955. Commr. Fed. Mediation and Conciliation Service, San Francisco, 1952-58; staff dir. Presdl. R.R. Commn., Washington, 1959-61; prof. polit. sci. U. Mich., Ann Arbor, 1962-80, dir. Inst. Labor and Indsl. Relations, 1962-76; chmn. Mich. Employment Relations Commn., Detroit, 1976-80; dean N.Y. State Sch. Indsl. and Labor Relations, Cornell U., Ithaca, 1980-86; prof. law U. San Diego, 1988-97. Author: Final-Offer Arbitration, 1975, The Railway Labor Act at Fifty, 1977, Labor and American Politics, 1967, rev. edit., 1978, The National Mediation Board, 1984, Emergency Strikes Revisited, 1990. Chmn. 4 Presdl. emergency bds. at various times. Served to lt. USNR, 1943-45; PTO Mem. Internat. Inst. Labor Studies (bd. govs. 1984-92), Indsl. Rels. Rsch. Assn. (exec. bd. 1984-88), Nat. Acad. Arbitrators (hon. life mem. 2008). Home: 18755 W Bernardo Dr Apt 1027 San Diego CA 92127-3011

REICH, MICHAEL, economics professor; b. Poland, Oct. 18, 1945; came to U.S., 1949; s. Melvin and Betty (Mandelbaum) R.; children: Rachel, Gabriel. BA, Swarthmore Coll., 1966; PhD, Harvard U., 1974. Asst. prof. Boston U., 1971-74, U. Calif., Berkeley, 1974-81, acting assoc. prof., 1981-82, assoc. prof., 1982-89, prof., 1989—. Rsch. dir. Nat. Ctr. for the Workplace, 1993-96, Inst. Labor and Employment, 2001-04; dir. Inst. Indsl. Rels., 2004-. Author: Segmented Work, Divided Workers, 1982, Racial Inequality, 1981, The Capitalist System, 1986, Social Structures of Accumulation, 1994, Work and Pay in the U.S. and Japan, 1997; editor: Indsl. Rels. Jour., 1986-94; contbr. articles to profl. jours. Mem. Am. Econ. Assn., Indsl. Rels. Rsch. Assn., Phi Beta Kappa, Sigma Xi. Office: Dept of Econs U Calif 611 Evans Hl Berkeley CA 94720-0001

REICH, ROBERT BERNARD, political economics educator, former United States Secretary of Labor; b. Scranton, Pa., June 24, 1946; s. Edwin Saul and Mildred Dorf (Freshman) R.; m. Clare Dalton, July 7, 1973. BA, Dartmouth Coll., 1968, MA (hon.), 1988; MA, Oxford U., Eng., 1970; JD, Yale U., 1973. Asst. solicitor gen. US Dept. Justice, Washington, 1974-76; dir. policy planning FTC, Washington, 1976-81; mem. faculty John F. Kennedy Sch. Govt. Harvard U., Cambridge, Mass., 1981-92; sec. US Dept. Labor, Washington, 1993-97; Maurice B. Hexter prof. econ. & social policy Brandeis U., Waltham, 1997—2006; prof. pub. policy Richard & Rhoda Goldman Sch. Pub. Policy, U. Calif, Berkely, 2006—. Chmn. biotech. sect. U.S. Office Tech. Assessment, Washington, 1990-91; vis. prof., Richard & Rhoda Goldman Sch. Pub. Policy, U. Calif, 2004, 2005 Author: The Next American Frontier, 1983, New Deals: The Chrysler Revival and the American System, 1986, Tales of a New America: The Anxious Liberals's Guide to the Future, 1987, The Resurgent Liberal: And Other Unfashionable Prophecies, 1989, The Work of Nations: Preparing Ourselves for 21st Century Capitalism, 1991, Locked in the Cabinet, 1997, The Future of Success: Working and Living in the New Economy, 2001, I'll Be Short: Essentials for a Decent Working Society, 2002, Reason: Why Liberals Will Win the Battle for America, 2004, Supercapitalism: The Transformation of Business, Democracy, and Everyday Life, 2007; editor: The Power of Public Ideas, 1987; contbg. editor The New Republic, Washington, 1982-93; co-founder, nat. editor, chmn. editl. bd. The Am. Prospect, 1990—; playwright Public Exposure, 2005. Mem. governing bd. Common Cause, Washington, 1981-85; bd. dirs. Bus. Enterprise Trust, Palo Alto, Calif., 1989-93; trustee Dartmouth Coll., Hanover, N.H., 1989-93. Rhodes scholar, 1968; recipient Louis Brownlow award ASPA, 1983, Vaclev Havel Found. prize, 2003 Democrat. Office: Richard & Rhoda Goldman School Pub Policy U Calif Berkeley 2607 Hearst Ave Berkeley CA 94720 E-mail: rreich@berkeley.edu.

REICHERT, DAVID G. (DAVE REICHERT), United States Representative from Washington; b. Detroit Lakes, Minn., Aug. 29, 1950; m. Julie Reichert; children: Angela, Tabitha, Daniel. AA, Concordia Lutheran Coll., Portland, Oreg., 1970. Police officer Sheriff's Office King County, Wash., 1972—97, sheriff Wash., 1997—2004; mem. US Congress from 8th Wash. dist., 2005—, mem. sci. com., mem. transp. and infrastructure com., vice chmn. Coast Guard and maritime transp. subcommittee, mem. homeland security com., chmn. emergency preparedness, sci. and tech. Author: Chasing the Devil: My Twenty Year Quest to Capture the Green River Killer, 2004. Co-chmn. Wash. State Ptnrs. in Crisis; mem. adv. bd. Criminal Justice Coun., King County, Wash., Domestic Violence Coun., King County, Wash. Served in USAFR, 1971—76, served in USAF, 1976. Recipient Champion of Freedom award, Wash. Policy Ctr., 2 Medal of Valor awards, King County Sheriff's Office; named Sheriff of Yr., Nat. Sheriffs Assn., 2004. Mem.: Wash. Assn. Sheriffs & Police Chiefs (mem. exec. bd.), Wash. State Sheriffs Assn. (past pres.). Republican. Lutheran. Office: US Ho Reps 1223 Longworth Ho Office Bldg Washington DC 20515-4708 Office Phone: 202-225-7761.

REICHNER, SCOTT M., state legislator; Mem. Dist. 9 Mont. House of Reps., 2008—. Republican. Office: Montana House of Representatives PO Box 200400 Helena MT 59620-0400 Mailing: 78 Redtail Rdg Bigfork MT 59911-6283 Home Phone: 406-837-3929; Office Phone: 406-444-4800. Office Fax: 406-444-4825. Personal E-mail: sreichner@centurytel.net.

REID, CHARLES CLARK, artist; b. Cambridge, NY, Aug. 12, 1937; s. David Gordon and Peggy (Van Kirk) Reid; m. Judith Hendrickson, July 1, 1961; children: Peter Van Kirk, Sarah Worth. Student, U. Vt., 1955-57, Art Students League, NYC, 1957-59. Assoc. Nat. Acad., NYC, 1980-83, academician, 1983—. Group shows include Am. Watercolor Soc., Nat. Acad. Design., Am. Inst. Arts and Letters; exhbns. include Govt. House, Madeira, Portugal, 1961, Roko Gallery, N.Y.C., 1973-74, FAR Gallery, N.Y.C., 1975-79, Munson Gallery, Santa Fe-Chatham, 1980-91, Gallery Fair, Mendocino, Calif., 1991-92, Susan Conway Gallery, Washington, 1992, Stremmel Gallery, 2005; pub. collections include: Smith Coll., Brigham Young U., Yellowstone Art Ctr., The Century Assn., Roche Corp., Mktg. Corp. Am., The Nat. Acad. Design; author: Figure Painting in Watercolor, 1972, Portrait Painting in Watercolor, 1973, Flower Painting in Oil, 1975, Flower Painting in Watercolor, 1981, Painting What You Want to See, 1983, Pulling Your Paintings Together, Painting by Design, Painting Flowers in Watercolor with Charles Reid, 2001. Recipient Child Hassem Purchase Fund award Am. Acad. Arts and Letters, 1976, 77, Sam Bluenthal Meml. award Am. Watercolor Soc., 1978, High Winds award Am. Watercolor Soc., 1977, Silver medal Soc. Illustrators, 1983. Mem. NAD (assoc., 1st Altman prize, 2nd Altman prize, Julius Hulgarten award, Clark prize, Salmagundi award 1975, Ranger fund., Emil Dines award, Obrig prize), Nat. Watercolor Soc, Century Assn. Office: Munson Gallery 800 Main St Chatham MA 02633-2735 also: Munson Gallery 225 Canyon Rd Santa Fe NM 87501

REID, E. LEWIS, lawyer; Grad., Princeton U.; JD, Harvard Law Sch. Former minority counsel U.S. Senate Interior Comm.; former gen. counsel Calif. Endowment, exec. dir., 1999—2001; founding ptnr. Marron, Reid, LLP. Former pres., trustee Am. Trust for Wolfson Coll.; adv. dir. U. So. Calif. Ctr. for Nonprofit Mgmt.; chmn., pres. Am. Soc. for Royal Botanic Gardens, Joseph Banks Soc.; mem. legal adv. comm. Counsel on Environmental Quality; lecturer U. Calif. Berkeley. Bd. dirs. Calif. Endowment, 2000—, Sonoma Land Trust, Larry Hillblom Found., CSR Am.; adv. dir. Am. Land Conservancy. Office: Calif Endowment 1000 N Alameda St Los Angeles CA 90012

REID, FRANCES EVELYN KROLL, freelance/self-employed cinematographer, film director, communications executive; b. Oakland, Calif., Mar. 25, 1944; d. William Farnham and Marion Storm (Teller) Kroll. BA, U. Oreg., 1966. Tchr. secondary sch., Los Angeles, 1968-69; sound recordist Churchill Films, Los Angeles, 1971; freelance sound recordist Los Angeles, 1972-75; freelance dir., prodr., 1975—; freelance cinematographer Berkeley, Calif., 1978—; dir. Iris Films, Berkeley, 1977—; lectr. U. Calif. Grad. Sch. Journalism, 2005. Vol. Peace Corps, Malawi, Africa, 1969-70. Producer/dir. Long Night's Journey Into Day, 2000 (Grand Jury award Sundance 2000, Acad. award nominee 2001); dir. (film) In The Best Interests of the Children, 1977 (Blue Ribbon Am. Film Festival 1978), The Changer: A Record of the Times, 1991, The Faces of AIDS, 1992, Skin Deep, 1995, Talking About Race, 1994, Straight from the Heart, 1994 (Acad. award nominee 1995); cinematographer: (film) The Times of Harvey Milk, 1984 (Oscar 1985), Living with AIDS, 1986 (Student Acad. award 1987), Common Threads: Stories from the Quilt, 1989 (Oscar award 1990), Complaints of a Dutiful Daughter, 1994 (Acad. award nominee 1995). Mem. Film Arts Found., Assn. Ind. Video and Filmmakers, Acad. Motion Picture Arts and Scis. Office: Iris Films 2600 10th St Ste 607 Berkeley CA 94710-2522 Office Phone: 510-845-5414.

REID, HARRY MASON, United States Senator from Nevada; b. Searchlight, Nev., Dec. 2, 1939; s. Harry and Inez Jaynes Reid; m. Landra Joy Gould; children: Lana, Rory, Leif, Josh, Key AS, Southern Utah State U., 1959; BS in Hist. and Polit. Sci., Utah State U., 1961; JD, George Washington U., 1964; LLD (hon.), U. So. Utah, 1984. Bar: Nev. Bar 1963. Police officer US Capitol, Washington, 1961—64; city atty. City of Henderson, Henderson, Nev., 1964—66; mem. Nev. State Assembly, 1969—70; lt. gov. State of Nev., 1971—75; chmn. Nev. Gaming Commn., 1977—81; mem. US Congress from 1st. Nev. Dist., Washington, 1983—87; US Senator from Nev. Washington, 1987—; asst. minority leader (minority whip), 1999—2001, 2001, 2003—05; asst. majority leader (majority whip), 2001—03; minority leader, 2004—07; majority leader, 2007—; chmn. US Senate Select Com. on Ethics, 2001—03, US Senate Com. on Environment & Pub. Works, 2001. Chmn. US Senate Democratic Conf., 2005—. Author: Searchlight: The Camp that Didn't Fail, 1998. Bd. dirs. Am. Cancer Soc., Legal Aid Soc., Young Men's Christian Assn.; bd. trustees So. Nev. Meml. Hosp., 1967—69. Recipient Humanitarian award, Nat. Asthma Ctr. and Nat. Jewish Hosp., 1984, Public Svc. award, Am. Found. Suicide Prevention, 1999, Friend of Zion award, The Jerusalem Fund, 2000, MLA award disting. public svc., 2002, Award of Merit, The Military Coalition, 2002, Arthur T. Marix award, Military Officers Assn. Am., 2003, Disting. Svc. award, Am. Public Works Assn., 2003, Inspirational Leadership award, Military Order of Purple Heart, 2003, Nat. Landscape Conservation Sys. Champion award, NLCS Coalition, 2004, Pick and Gravel award, Assn. Am. State Geologists, 2004, TechNet Founders Cir. award, 2005; named one of The 50 Most Powerful People in DC, GQ Mag., 2007. Mem.: Nev. Athletic Commn., Nat. Conf. Lt. Governors, Am. Bd. Trial Advocates, Clark County Bar Assn., Nev. Bar Assn., ABA. Democrat. Lds Ch. Office: US Senate 528 Hart Senate Office Bldg Washington DC 20510-0001 also: Lloyd D George Bldg Ste 8016 333 Las Vegas Blvd South Las Vegas NV 89101 Office Phone: 202-224-3542, 702-388-5020. Office Fax: 202-224-7327, 702-388-5030. E-mail: senator_reid@reid.senate.gov.*

REID, ROBERT TILDEN, medical association administrator, internist; b. Dallas, Feb. 20, 1931; s. Robert Tilden and Gldays Tressy (King) R.; divorced; children: Robert Tilden, Richard Thomas, Annette Marie, Randolph Young. BS, So. Meth. U., Dallas, 1957; MD, U. Tex.-Southwestern, Dallas, 1959. Diplomate Am. Bd. Internal Medicine, Am. Bd. Rheumatology, Am. Bd. Allergy and Immunology. Intern Parkland Meml. Hosp., Dallas, 1959-60, resident, 1960-63; with Scripps Clinic and Rsch., La Jollla, Calif., 1963-70; pvt. practice La Jollla, Calif., 1970—; chief staff Scripps Meml. Hosp., La Jollla, Calif., 1976-78; scientific dir. Erik and Ese Banck Clinical Rsch. Ctr., San Diego, 1994—. Mem. San Diego County Med. Soc. (pres. 1991), Calif. Med. Assn. (trustee 1992-95). Office: 8716 Production Ave San Diego CA 92121 Home Phone: 858-481-2910; Office Phone: 858-271-0049. Personal E-mail: banckcrc@pacbell.net.

REIDEL, ARTHUR, health products executive, semiconductor company executive; BS in Math., MIT. Held mgmt. and exec. positions, including v.p. engring. and ops. Interactive Tng. Systems, 1973—84; v.p. tech. Schlumberger Computer-Aided Systems, 1973—84; gen. ptnr. ABS Ventures Ltd. Partnerships; several exec. positions including v.p. and gen. mgr. user interface products divsn. Weitek Corp., 1991—92; pres., CEO Sunrise Test Systems, Inc. (acquired by Viewlogic Systems), 1992—94; v.p. bus. devel. Viewlogic Systems, Inc., 1994—95; pvt. investor, cons., 1995—96; founder, dir. Pharsight Corp., Mountain View, Calif., 1995, pres., 1995—2002, CEO, 1995—2002, chmn. bd. dirs., 1995—; CEO Scintera Networks, Inc., San Jose, Calif., 2006—. Dir. Insightful Corp. Office: Pharsight Corp 321 E Evelyn Ave # 3 Mountain View CA 94041-1530 also: Scintera Networks Inc 1154 Sonora Ct Sunnyvale CA 94086-5308

REIF, (FRANK) DAVID, artist, educator; b. Cin., Dec. 14, 1941; s. Carl A. and Rachel L. (Clifton) R.; m. Ilona Jekabsons, July 30, 1966; 1 child, Megan Elizabeth. BFA, Art Inst. Chgo., 1968; MFA, Yale U., 1970. Asst. prof. art U. Wyo., Laramie, 1970-74, assoc. prof., 1974-81, U. Mich., Ann Arbor, 1980-81; prof. U. Wyo., Laramie, 1981—2004, acting head dept. art, 1986—87, Disting. prof. emeritus, 2004—; prin., owner Reif Artworks & Design Consulting, Laramie, Wyo., 2005—. Selection cons. Ucross Found. Residency Program, Wyo., 1983—; exhibit juror Artwest Nat., Jackson, Wyo., 1986; panelist Colo. State U., Ft. Collins, 1981; lectr. U. Mich., 1980; apptd. Wyo. Arts Coun., 1993-96; vis. artist lectr. Colo. State U., 1996; vis. artist Colo. State U., Ft. Collins, 1996; 3-D juror, art exhbn. Colo. State Fair, Pueblo, 2001. One-man shows include U. Wyo. Art Mus., 1993, Dorsky Galleries, NYC, 1980, No. Ariz. U., 1977, 87, U. Mich., 1980-81, One West Ctr. Contemporary Art, Ft. Collins, 1991, West Wyo. C.C., Rock Springs, 1999, Casper Coll. Goldstein Gallery, 2003; exhibited in group shows at First, Second and Third Wyo. Biennial Tour, 1984-88, U.S. Olympics Art Exhbn., LA, 1984, Miss. Mus. Art and NEA Tour, 1981-83, LA Invitational Sculpture Tour Exhbn., 1991-92, Nicolaysen Art Mus., Casper, Wyo., 1994, Jackson Hole Ctr. Arts, Wyo., 2006, Gene Siskel Film Ctr. Gall, Art Inst. Chgo., 2006. Apptd. chair Wyo. Arts Coun., 1995-96. With USAR, 1963-69. Recipient F.D. Pardee award Yale U., 1970; Best Sculpture award Joslyn Art Mus. Omaha, 1978; grantee Nat. Endowment Arts, 1978-79, Wyo. Basic Rsch., 1983-84, 86-87; Tchg. Excellence grantee U. Wyo., 1996-97. Mem. Coll. Art Assn., Internat. Sculpture Ctr. Democrat. Home: 3340 Aspen Ln Laramie WY 82070-5702 Office: U Wyo Dept Art PO Box 3138 Laramie WY 82071-3138 Office Phone: 307-745-3110.

REIF, JOHN STEVEN, epidemiologist, veterinarian; b. NYC, Sept. 18, 1940; s. Hans V. and Anne (Marie) R. DVM, Cornell U., 1963; MSc in Epidemiology, U. Pa., 1966. NIH postdoctoral fellow U. Pa., Phila., 1966-68, asst. prof., 1969-73, assoc. prof., 1974-78; prof., chief comparative medicine sect. Inst. Rural Environ. Colo. State U., Ft. Collins, 1979-95, chmn. dept. environ. health, 1995—. Prof. U. Otago Sch. Medicine, Wellington, N.Z., 1987-88. Contbr. numerous articles to profl. jours. Mem., pres. Larimer County Bd. Health, Ft. Collins, 1980-85; mem. Colo. Bd. Health, Denver, 1982-87. Fogarty fellow NIH, 1987-88; recipient Recognition award Tchrs. Preventive Medicine, 1989. Fellow Am. Coll. Epidemiology; mem. Internat. Epidemiology Assn., Internat. Soc. Environ. Epidemiology, Soc. for Epidemiologic Rsch. Office: Colo State U Dept Environ Health Fort Collins CO 80523-0001 E-mail: jreif@cvmbs.colostate.edu.

REIJO PERA, RENEE A., reproductive science director, educator; BS in Biology, U. Wis., 1983; PhD in Molecular and Cell Biology, Cornell U., 1993. Damon-Runyan/Walter Winchell postdoctoral fellow Whitehead Inst. for Biomedical Rsch. Lab., 1993—97; instr., human genetics, dept. biology MIT, 1995; asst. prof. in residence, dept. ob-gyn. & reproductive scis., physiology & urology, programs in human & cancer genetics, develop. & stem cell biology U. Calif., San Francisco, 1997—2003, assoc. prof. in residence dept. ob-gyn. & reproductive scis., physiology & urology, programs in human & cancer genetics, develop. & stem cell biology, 2003—, co-dir., program in human stem cell biology, 2004—, assoc. dir., Ctr. for Reproductive Scis., 2004—. Invited participant, chair German Am. Frontiers of Sci., NAS, 2000—03. Contbr. several articles to profl. jours. Scholar Searle Found., 1998—2001; DuPont Tchg. Fellow, 1989, US Army Biotechnology Grad. Fellowship, 1991—93. Office: U Calif Dept Obstetrics Gynecology & Reproductive Sciences 513 Parnassus Ave Rm HSE 1634 Box 0556 San Francisco CA 94143-0556 Office Phone: 415-476-3178. Office Fax: 415-476-3121. Business E-Mail: reijoperar@obgyn.ucsf.edu.*

REILLY, JOAN, nursing educator; b. Johnson, Wash., May 2, 1931; d. Jacob and Vernice Althea (Marine) Steiner; m. Robert Joseph Reilly, June 20, 1960; children— Sean Michael, Patrick Joseph, Bridget Colleen. B.S.N., Wash. State U., 1953; M.S.N., St. Louis U., 1970; EdD, Seattle U., 1989. R.N. Staff nurse VA Hosp., Spokane, 1953-55, 1962-63; office nurse pediatrician's office, Spokane, 1955-56; nursing supr. Bakersfield Meml. Hosp. (Calif.), 1956-58; instr. St. Luke's Sch. Nursing, Spokane, 1958-60; staff nurse Ireland Army Hosp., Ft. Knox, Ky., 1961-62; instr. St. Joseph Sch. Nursing, Tacoma, 1964-65, 66-67, nursing svc. staff asst. St. Joseph Hosp., Tacoma, 1970; charge nurse St. Peter Hosp., Olympia, Wash., 1973-74; vis. nurse Tacoma Gen. Hosp., 1974-77; instr. Tacoma Community Coll., 1977—92, ret., 1992; with Wash. State Nursing Commn., 1992-99. Unit service chmn. ACS, Tacoma, 1977; mem. corp. Hospice of Tacoma, 1981—; vol. ARC, Karlsruhe, Germany, 1971; mem. Tacoma Zool. Soc., 1983; mem. Friends of Libr., Steilacoom, Wash., 1983; mem. Steilacoom Hist. Mus. Soc., 1983; key person United Way, Tacoma, 1983-84; parish nurse St. Luke's Episc. Ch., 2004—, group facilitator Good Grief Ctr., 2004—, chmn. Christian edn. com. 2006—, ch. vestry mem.; 2005-08. Named to Phi Delta Kappa, 1997, Sigma Theta Tau Internat., 1998. Mem. Wash. State Nurses' Assn. (chmn. Ways and Means Com. 1982-83, bd. dirs. 1981-84), Nat. Assn. Alcohol and Drug Abuse Counselors, NW Nurses Soc. on Chem. Dependency, Alcoholism Profl. Staff Soc. Wash., Ft. Steilacoom Running, Irish Cultural (pub. com. Tacoma 1982-83), Phi Kappa Phi, Tacoma Musical Playhouse (bd. mem. 1997-2000). Home: 1521 Willow Pl Wenatchee WA 98801-8005

REILLY, PAUL V., printing company executive; CPA. Various positions Polychrome Corp.; with Saddle River Capital, 1994-95; sr. v.p. fin., CFO Mail-Well Inc., Englewood, Colo., 1995-98, pres., COO, 1998—, also bd. dirs. Office: Mail Well Inc Ste 400 8310 S Valley Hwy Englewood CO 80112-5815

REILLY, WILLIAM KANE, investment company executive, preservationist, former federal agency administrator; b. Decatur, Ill., Jan. 26, 1940; s. George P. and Margaret (Kane) M.; m. Elizabeth Bennett Buxton; children: Katherine, Megan. BA in History, Yale U., 1962; JD, Harvard U., 1965; MS in Urban Planning, Columbia U., 1971. Bar: Ill., Mass. 1965. Atty. firm Ross & Hardies, Chgo., 1965; assoc. dir. Urban Policy Center, Urban Am., Inc., also Nat. Urban Coalition, Washington, 1969-70; sr. staff mem. Pres.'s Council Environ. Quality, 1970-72; exec. dir. Task Force Land Use and Urban Growth, 1972-73; pres. Conservation Found., Washington, 1973-89, World Wildlife Fund, Washington, 1985-89; adminstr. EPA, Washington, 1989-93; Payne vis. prof. Stanford U., 1993-94, vis. prof., 1994-97; pres., CEO Aqua Internat. Ptnrs., Tex. Pacific Group, San Francisco, 1997—. Chmn. Natural Resources Coun. Am., 1982-83; head U.S. del. Earth Summit, 1992; head U.S. del. to negotiate Amendments to Montreal Protocol on the Ozone Layer, 1990, 92; bd. dirs. E.I. DuPont de Nemours and Co., 1993-, ConocoPhillips Co., 1997-, Royal Caribbean Internat., 1998-, Am. Acad. in Rome, Evergreen Holdings, Inc., Ionics Inc., Enviance, 2006-, Nat. Geog. Soc., World Wildlife Fund, Presidio Trust; mem. internat. adv. bd., Lafarge; chair adv. bd. Goldman Sch. Pub. Policy U. Calif. at Berkeley. Editor: The Use of Land, 1973, Environment Strategy America, 1994-96; author articles in field, chpts. in books. Served to capt., CIC U.S. Army, 1966-67; bd. dirs. David and Lucile Packard Found. Fellow: Am. Acad. Arts & Scis.; mem.: University (Washington), Univ. (N.Y.C.).

REINGLASS, MICHELLE ANNETTE, lawyer, mediator, arbitrator; b. LA, Dec. 9, 1954; d. Darwin and Shirley (Steiner) R. Student, U. Calif., Irvine, 1972-75; BSL, Western State U., 1977; JD, Western State U., Coll. Law, 1978. Bar: Calif. 1979, U.S. Dist. Ct. (ctrl. dist.) Calif. 1979, U.S. Ct. Appeals (9th cir.) 1981, U.S. Dist. Ct. (so. dist.) Calif. 1990. Pvt. practice employee litig., Laguna Hills, Calif., 1979—, Instr. Calif. Continuing Edn. of Bar, 1990—, Western State Coll., 1991, Rutter Group, 1994—; chmn. magistrate selection com. ctrl. dist. US Dist. Ct.,Calif., LA, 1991, 93-95, com. mem., 1994-97, 2003-06, lawyer rep. to 9th cir. jud. conf.; lectr. in field. Contbr. articles to profl. jours. Pres., bd. dirs. Child or Parental Emergency Svcs., Santa Ana, Calif., 1982-92; bd. dirs. Pub. Law Ctr., Santa Ana, Coalition for Justice, Working Wardrobes; mem. exec. com. and cast CHOC Follies. Recipient Jurisprudence award Anti-Defamation League, 1997; named to Western State U. Hall of Fame, 1993; named one of Top 100 Most Influential Lawyers in Calif., LA Daily Jour., 2001; one of Top 30 Female Litigators in Calif., LA Daily Jour., 2002; one of Top 50 Female Litigators, LA Daily Jour., 2003-04; named to Super Lawyers, LA Mag., 2004-07. Fellow Coll. Labor and Employee Lawyers; mem. State Bar Calif., Assn. Bus. Trial Lawyers (bd. dirs.), Orange County Bar Assn. (del. to state conv. 1980-94, bd. dirs. 1983-94, chmn. bus. litigation sect. 1989, sec. 1990, treas. 1991, pres.-elect 1992, pres. 1993), Nat. Employee Lawyers Assn., Calif. Employee Lawyers Assn. (com. mem., chair 2005-07), Orange County Trial Lawyers Assn. (bd. dirs. 1987-89, Bus. Trial Lawyer of Yr. award 1995, Employee Trial Lawyer of Yr. 2004), So. Calif. Mediation Assn., Orange County Women Lawyers (Lawyer of Yr. award 1996), Vols. in Parole (chmn. adv. com. 1990-91), Peter Elliot Inns Ct. (master), Am. Bd. of Trial Advocates. Avocations: distance running, skiing. Office: 23161 Mill Creek Dr Ste 170 Laguna Hills CA 92653-1650 E-mail: michelle@reinglasslaw.com.

REINHARD, CHRISTOPHER JOHN, merchant banker, venture capitalist, biotechnologist, director; b. Bridgeport, Conn., Nov. 11, 1953; s. Warren John and Marian Louise (Dutter) R.; m. Maureen Francis, Sept. 24, 1977; 1 child, Griffin John. BS, Babson Coll., 1976, MBA, 1977. Sr. fin. analyst Gen. Motors Corp., Detroit and NYC, 1977-81; asst. sec. Wheelabrator-Frye Inc., NH, 1981-83; asst. sec., asst. treas. The Signal Cos., Inc., La Jolla, Calif., 1983-86; mng. dir., v.p. The Henley Group, Inc., La Jolla, 1986-90; mng. dir. Fisher Sci. Group, Inc., La Jolla, 1986-90; mng. dir., v.p. Wheelabrator Tech. Inc., Henley Mfg. Corp., 1987-90; founder, pres. Colony Group Inc., Rancho Santa Fe, 1990—, Reinhard Assocs., Rancho Santa Fe, 1990-95; founder, v.p., CFO Advanced Access, Inc., San Diego, 1995-97. Pres. Direct Feedback, Inc., 1990, Dairy Queen Ventures, 1990-94, Winsor Sport Fencing, 1993—; CEO, founder, pres. Collateral Therapeutics Inc., 1995-2005; gen. ptnr. Cabrillo Ventures, 1995-96; founder, pres. ihumon, 2000—; exec. chmn. Artes Med., Inc., 2004—; exec. chmn., CEO, founder Cardium Therapeutics Inc., 2003—. Mem. Boston Athenaeum, N.Y. Athletic Club, San Diego Polo Club, Rancho Santa Fe Polo Club. Office: Cardium Therapeutics 12255 El Camino Real Ste 250 San Diego CA 92130-4090

REINHARDT, STEPHEN ROY, federal judge; b. NYC, Mar. 27, 1931; s. Gottfried and Silvia (Hanlon) Reinhardt; children: Mark, Justin, Dana. BA cum laude, Pomona Coll., 1951; LLB, Yale, 1954. Bar: Calif. 1958. Law clk. to Hon. Luther W. Youngdahl US Dist. Ct., Washington, 1956—57; atty. O'Melveny & Myers, LA, 1957—59; ptnr. Fogel Julber Reinhardt Rothschild & Feldman LC, LA, 1959—80; judge US Ct. Appeals (9th cir.), LA, 1980—. Adj. prof. Loyola Law Sch., LA, 1988—90. Pres. LA Recreation and Parks Commn., 1974—75; active Coliseum Commn., 1974—75, LA Police Commn., 1974—78, pres., 1978—80; sec., exec. organizing com. LA Olympics, 1980—84; exec. com. Dem. Nat. Com., 1969—72; nat. Dem. committeeman State of Calif., 1976—80; bd. dirs. Amateur Athletic Found. LA, 1984—92. 1st lt. USAF, 1954—56. Mem.: ABA (labor law coun. 1975—77), Calif. Bar Assn., LA County Bar Assn. Office Phone: 213-894-3639.

REINHARDT, WILLIAM PARKER, chemical physicist, educator; b. San Francisco, May 22, 1942; s. William Oscar and Elizabeth Ellen (Parker) R.; m. Katrina Hawley Currens, Mar. 14, 1979; children: James William, Alexander Hawley. BS in Basic Chemistry, U. Calif., Berkeley, 1964; AM in Chemistry, Harvard U., 1966, PhD in Chem. Physics, 1968; MA (hon.), U. Pa., 1985. Instr. chemistry Harvard U., 1967-69, asst. prof. chemistry, 1969-72, assoc. prof., 1972-74; prof. U. Colo., Boulder, 1974-84, chmn. dept. chemistry, 1977-80; prof. chemistry U. Pa., Phila., 1984-91, chmn. dept., 1985-88, D. Michael Crow prof., 1987-91; prof. chemistry U.Wash., Seattle, 1991—, assoc. chmn. undergrad. program, 1993-96. Adj. prof. physics U. Wash., Seattle, 1998—; vis. fellow Joint Inst. for Lab. Astrophysics of Nat. Bur. Stds. and U. Colo., 1972, 74, fellow, 1974-84; dir. Telluride Summer Rsch. Ctr., 1986-89, treas., 1989-93; com. on atomic, molecular and optical scis. NRC, 1988-90; sub com. Internat. Union Pure and Applied Physics, Atomic Molecular Physics, 2002—05; vis. scientist Nat. Inst. Stds. and Tech., summers 1993—, Harvard-MIT Ctr. Ultra-Cold Atoms, 2005; vis. prof. chemistry U. Paris VI, 1991, U. Melbourne, Australia, 1997, Harvard U., 1998, Davidson lectr. U. Kans., 2000; Kohler lectr. U. Calif., Riverside, 2002; R.S. Berry pub. lectr. Telluride, Colo., 2004, Bertman Meml. lectr. Wesleyan U., Middletown, Conn., 2005. Mem. editl. bd. Phys. Rev. A., 1979-81, 05-, Chem. Physics, 1985-94, Jour. Chem. Physics, 1987-89, Jour. Physics B. (U.K.), 1992-2004, Internat. Adv. Bd., 2004-; Internat. Jour. Quantum Chemistry, 1994-2001, Digital Libr. of Math. Functions, 1999-; rschr. theoretical chem. physics, theoretical atomic and molecular physics for numerous publs Recipient Camille and Henry Dreyfus Tchr. Scholar award, 1972; Alfred P. Sloan fellow, 1972; J.S. Guggenheim Meml. fellow, 1978; Coun. on Rsch. and Creative Work faculty fellow, 1978; Wilsmore fellow U. Melbourne (Australia), 1997; J.W. Fulbright sr. scholar, Australia, 1997. Fellow AAAS, Am. Phys. Soc., Inst. Physics (U.K.), Phi Beta Kappa; mem. Am. Chem. Soc., Sigma Xi (nat. lectr. 1980-82), Phi Lambda Upsilon (Fresenius award 1977), Phi Beta Kappa (vis. scholar 2002-03, disting. fellow lectr., 2004-, Cooper lectr. 2006-07, mem. nat. nominating com. 2006-). Office: U Wash Dept Chemistry Box 351700 Seattle WA 98195-1700 Office Phone: 206-543-0578. Business E-Mail: rein@chem.washington.edu.

REINHOLD, JUDGE (EDWARD ERNEST REINHOLD JR.), actor; b. Wilmington, Del., May 21, 1957; m. Carrie Frazier, 1986 (div.); m. Amy Miller, Jan. 8, 2000. Student, Mary Washington Coll., N.C. Sch. of the Arts. Actor: (feature films) Running Scared, 1979, Stripes, 1981, Thursday the Twelfth, 1982, Pandemonium, 1982, Fast Times at Ridgemont High, 1982, Gremlins, 1984, Beverly Hills Cop, 1984, Roadhouse, 1985, Ruthless People, 1986, Head Office, 1986, Off Beat, 1986, Beverly Hills Cop II, 1987, Vice-Versa, 1988, Rosalee Goes Shopping, 1990, Daddy's Dyin'...Who's Got the Will, 1990, Zandalee, 1991, Beverly Hills Cop III, 1994, The Santa Clause, 1994, Last Lives, 1997, Homegrown, 1998, Floating Away, 1998, Big Monster on Campus, 1998, Wild Blue, 1999, (voice) Robots of Mars, 1999, Redemption High, 1999, Puss in Boots, 1999, My Brother the Pig, 1999, Walking Across Egypt, 1999, NewsBreak, 2000, Ping!, 2000, Wild Blue, 2000, Betaville, 2001, No Place Like Home, 2001, Hollywood Palms, 2001, Whacked!, 2002, The Santa Clause 2, 2002, (voice) Clifford's Really Big Movie, 2004, The Hollow, 2004, Checking Out, 2005, Crab Orchard, 2006, The Santa Clause 3: The Escape Clause, 2006, Swing Vote 2008; (TV episodes) Wonder Woman, Magnum P.I., Seinfeld, 1993 (Emmy nomination, Guest Actor - Comedy Series, 1994); (TV films) The Survival of Dana, 1979, Brothers and Sisters, A Step Too Slow, The Wilmar Eight, Booker, Promised a Miracle, Dad, the Angel, and Me, 1995, Right to Remain Silent, 1996, Runaway Car, 1997, Coming Unglued, 1999, NetForce, 1999, Dead in a Heartbeat, 2002, Thanksgiving Family Reunion, 2003; (TV series) Secret Service Guy, 1997. Mem. Screen Actors Guild, AFTRA. Office: c/o Evolution Entertainment Inc 901 N Highland Ave Los Angeles CA 90038

REINOLD, CHRISTY DIANE, school counselor, consultant; b. Neodasha, Kans., July 21, 1942; d. Ernest Sherman and Faye Etta (Herbert) Wild; m. William Owen Reinold, Dec. 20, 1964; children: Elizabeth, Rebecca. BA Edn., Calif. State U., Fresno, 1964, MA in Edn. and Psychology, 1964. Cert. counselor, Family Wellness instr.; lic. mental health counselor, Fla. Tchr. Clovis (Calif.) Unified Sch. Dist., 1965-66, Santa Clara (Calif.) Unified Sch. Dist., 1966-67, Inst. Internat. Chateaubriand, Cannes, France, 1968-69; tchr., vice prin. Internat. Sch., Sliema, Malta, 1969-70; elem. sch. counselor Duval City Schs., Jacksonville, Fla., 1977-82, Lodi (Calif.) Unified Sch. Dist., 1982—2004. Cons. Calif. Dept. Edn.; mem. Calif. Commn. on Tchr. Credentialing, Sacramento, 1986—2004, mem. adv. panel, 1998—2004; mem. stds. rev. com. Nat. Bd. Cert. Sch. Counselors, 2002—. Co-author: The Best for Our Kids; Counseling in the 21st Century; contbr. articles. Chmn. bd. dirs. Oak Crest Child Care Ctr., Jacksonville, 1979-81. Recipient H.B. McDaniel Individual award, 1986, James Saum Legis. award, Calif. Sch. Counselor's Assn., 1991, Donald Hayes Lifetime Achievement award, Assn. Calif. Sch. Counselors, 2002; named Anne Upton Sch. Counselor of Yr. for Calif., Calif. Sch. Counselor's Assn., 1995; named to H.B. McDaniel Hall of Fame, Stanford U., 2003. Mem.: AAUW (3rd v.p. 1974, 1st v.p. 1980, by-laws chmn. 1990, chmn. pub. policy 1991—93, pres. 1993), Lodi Pupil Pers. Assn. (pres. 1986—87), Calif. Alliance Pupil Svcs. Orgns. (bd. dirs. 1988—95), Fla. Sch. Counselors Assn., Calif. Assn. Counseling and Devel., Calif. Sch. Counselor Assn. (legis. chmn. 1985—90, pres. 1991), Am. Sch. Counselor Assn. (govt. rels. specialist 1993—94). Republican. Avocations: history, travel, politics. Home: 1772 Le Bec Ct Lodi CA 95240 Personal E-mail: creinold@earthlink.net.

REISBERG, LEON ELTON, education educator; b. Dallas, Sept. 1, 1949; s. Morris Abraham and Gertrude (Turner) R.; m. Iris Fudell, July 3, 1973 (div. 1986); children: Joshua Fudell, Leah Fudell; m. Donna Brodigan, July 11, 1993. BS in Edn., U. Tex., Austin, 1971; MEd, U. Ark., Fayetteville, 1972; EdD, U. Kans., Lawrence, 1981. Tchr. Oklahoma City Sch. Dist., 1972-75, Putnam City Sch. Dist., Oklahoma City, 1975-78, U. Kans. Med. Ctr., Kansas City, 1978-79; asst. prof. Pacific Luth. U., Tacoma, 1981-88; tchr. Tacoma (Wash.) Sch. Dist., 1989-90; assoc. prof. edn. Pacific Luth. U., 1988-94, chmn. dept. spl. edn. Tacoma, 1986-93, chmn. profl. edn. adv. bd., 1992-94, assoc. dean sch. edn., 1993-98, prof., 1995—, assoc. dean info. resources, 1999, dean info. resources, 2000—01. Project dir., Consulting Spl. Edn. Personnel Tng. Project, Tacoma, 1983-86; chmn. Profl. Edn. Adv. Bd. Cons. editor Learning Disability Quar., 1981-89, Acad. Therapy, 1988-90, Intervention, 1990—; contbr. articles to profl. publs. Bd. trustees First Place for Children; pres. Temple Beth El, 2002—04. Mem. Coun. Exceptional Children, Coun. Learning Disabilities (Pacific Rim region rep. 1993-96), Assn. Trainer Spl. Edn. Pers. (chmn. 1991), Phi Kappa Phi. Democrat. Jewish. Office: Pacific Luth U Sch Edn Tacoma WA 98447-0001 Home Phone: 253-756-9752; Office Phone: 253-535-7280. Business E-Mail: reisberg@plu.edu.

REISER, PAUL, actor, comedian, film critic, writer; b. NYC, Mar. 30, 1957; m. Paula Reiser; 2 children. BFA in Music, SUNY, Binghampton, 1977. Comedian various nightclubs and venues including Catch a Rising Star, N.Y.C., The Comic Strip, N.Y.C., The Improv, N.Y.C., 1977-; current founder, prodr. Nuance Productions. Performances include (feature films) Diner, 1982, Odd Jobs, 1984, Beverly Hills Cop, 1984, Aliens, 1986, Beverly Hills Cop II, 1987, Cross My Heart, 1987, Crazy People, 1990, The Marrying Man, 1991, Family Prayers, 1993, Mr. Write, 1994, Bye Bye, Love, 1995, Pros and Cons, 1999, The Story of Us, 1999, Get Bruce, 1999, One Night at McCool's, 2001, Purpose, 2002, The Things About My Folks, 2005 (also writer, prodr.); (TV series) The Investigator, HBO, The Comedy Zone, (TV spls.) Paul Reiser: Out on a Whim, HBO, 1987, (TV pilots) Diner, CBS, Just Married, ABC, (TV movies) Sunset Limousine, 1987, Diner, 1983, From Here to Maternity, 1985, You Ruined My Life, 1987, The Tower, 1993, Now That's Funny!, 2001, My Beautiful Son, 2001, Strange Relations, 2001, Women vs. Men, 2002; regular (TV series) My Two Dads, NBC, 1987-1991, Mad About You, NBC, 1992-99 (Emmy nomination, Lead Actor - Comedy Series, 1994)(also creator, writer for several episodes)(exec. prodr., prodr., 1995-96); co-creator, writer, exec. prodr. (TV) Paul Reiser Out on a Whim, 1988, Untitled NY Pilot, 2003, (film) 3 1/2 Blocks from Home, 1992,(video) Popeye's Voyage: The Quest for Pappy, 2004; writer (TV Series) Loved By You, 1997, Loco por ti, 2004; guest star various talk shows including The Tonight Show, Late Night with David Letterman, Curb Your Enthusiasm, 2002, Ellen: The Ellen DeGeneres Show, 2005 and several others; author: Couplehood, 1994, Babyhood; co-writer (with Don Was), The Final Frontier (theme song from Mad About You). Office: care William Morris Agency 151 S El Camino Dr Beverly Hills CA 90212-2704

REISMAN, ELLEN KELLY, lawyer; b. Oct. 24, 1959; BA summa cum laude, Boston Coll., 1981; JD cum laude, U. Chgo., 1984. Bar: DC 1984, US Dist. Ct., DC 1985, Calif. 1996. Assoc. Arnold & Porter LLP, Washington, 1984, ptnr., 1992—99; assoc. gen. counsel, v.p. legal divsn. Wyeth-Ayerst Pharmaceuticals, 1999—2001; ptnr., Product Liability Practice Group Arnold & Porter LLP, LA, 2001—. Named one of Top 50 Women Litigators, The Nat. Law Jour., 2001, The Top 45 Under 45, The Am. Lawyer, 2003. Office: Arnold & Porter 777 S Figueroa St 44th Flr Los Angeles CA 90017-2513 Office Phone: 213-243-4111. Office Fax: 213-243-4199.

REISMAN, JUDITH ANN GELERNTER, media communications executive, educator; b. Hillside, NJ, Apr. 11, 1935; MA in Speech Comm., Case Western Res. U., 1976, PhD in Speech Comm., 1980. Faculty dept. anthropology and sociology Haifa U., Israel, 1981—83; rsch. prof. sch. edn. Am. U., Washington, 1983—85; founder, pres. Inst. Media Edn., 1985—. Cons., reviewer grant proposals audio-visual drug programs for youth Dept. Edn., 1987; rsch. design cons. Alcohol and Tobacco Media Analysis in Mainstream Mags., Dept. HHS, 1987—90; cons., field reviewer Drug Free Youth Sch. Candidates Dept. Edn., 1988; lectr., adj. prof. George Mason U., Va., 1990; expert witness Pres.'s Commn. on Assignment of Women in Armed Forces, 1992, U.S. Atty. Gen. Commn. on Pornography, 1985—86, U.S. Atty. Gen. Task Force on Domestic Violence, Washington, 1985, Mapplethorpe Trial, Cin., 1990, Australian Parliament, 1992, Ga. State Senate, 1992; nominated to panel on sex harassment in the Air Force U.S. Inspector Gen., 2003; sci. advisor Protective Parents Assn.; subcom. junk sci. Am. Legis. Exchange Coun. Edn. Task Force, 1999—2004. Author: Images of Children, Crime and Violence in Playboy, Penthouse and Hustler, 1989, Kinsey, Sex and Fraud, 1990, Softport Plays Hardball, 1991, Kinsey, Crimes and Consequences, 1998, 2003; contbr. preme Ct. cases to profl. jours. Recipient Gold Camera award, 1982, Silver Screen award, 1982, Filmstrip of Yr. award, 1981—82, Silver Plaque award, 1982, Family Svc. Assn. Am. 1st pl. award local TV series, 1974, Best of 1965 award, 1965, Scientist of Yr. for Children award, 1993; co-recipient Scholastic Mag. awards, Dukane award, 1982; U.S. Dept. Justice grantee. Mem.: AAAS, World Net Daily.Com (columnist 1998—), Women in Neurosci., Nat. Black Child Devel. Inst., Soc. Sci. Study Sex, N.Y. Acad. Scis., Internat. Comm. Assn., Am. Statis. Assn., Am. Assn. Composers, Authors and Pubs., Nat. Assn. Scholars. E-mail: jareisman@cox.net.

REISS, HOWARD, chemistry professor; b. NYC, Apr. 5, 1922; s. Isidor and Jean (Goldstein) R.; m. Phyllis Kohn, July 25, 1945; children: Gloria, Steven. AB in Chemistry, NYU, 1943; PhD in Chemistry, Columbia U., 1949. With Manhattan Project, 1944-46; instr., then asst. prof. chemistry Boston U., 1949-51; with Ctrl. Rsch. Lab., Celanese Corp. Am., 1951-52, Edgar C. Bain Lab. Fundamental Rsch., U.S. Steel Corp., 1957, Bell Telephone Labs., 1952-60; asso. dir., then dir. rsch. div. Atomics Internat., div. N.Am. Aviation, Inc., 1960-62; dir. N.Am. Aviation Sci. Ctr., 1962-67, v.p. co., 1963-67; v.p. rsch. aerospace systems group N.Am. Rockwell Corp., 1967-68; vis. lectr. chemistry U. Calif. at Berkeley, summer 1957; vis. prof. chemistry UCLA, 1961, 62, 64, 67, prof., 1968-91, prof. emeritus, 1991—2003, disting. prof. emeritus, 2003—; vis. prof. U. Louis Pasteur, Strasbourg, France, 1986, U. Pa., 1989; vis. fellow Victoria U., Wellington, New Zealand, 1989. Vis. fellow Princeton (N.J.) Materials Inst., 1996; vis. sci., Hebrew U., Jerusalem, 1998; cons. to chem.-physics program USAF Cambridge Rsch. Labs., 1950-52; chmn. editor Procs. Internat. Conf. Nucleation and Interfacial Phenomena, Boston; mem. USAF Office Sci. Rsch. Physics and Chemistry Rsch. Evaluation Groups, 1966—, Oak Ridge Nat. Lab. Reactor Chemistry Adv. Com., 1966-68; adv. com. math. and phys. scis. NSF, 1970-72, ARPA Materials Rsch. Coun., 1968—; chmn. site rev. com. NRC Associateships Program, Naval Rsch. Lab., 1989. Author: Methods of Thermodynamics, 1965, republished, 1996; author articles; editor in field.; editor: Progress in Solid State Chemistry, 1962-71, Jour. Statis. Physics, 1968-75, Jour. Colloid Interface Sci; mem. editorial adv. bd. Internat. Jour. Physics and Chemistry of Solids, 1955, Progress in Solid State Chemistry, 1962-73, Jour. Solid State Chemistry, 1969, Jour. Phys. Chemistry, 1970-73, Ency. of Solid State, 1970, Jour. Nonmetals, 1971—, Jour. Colloid and Interface Sci., 1976-79, Langmuir, 1985—. Guggenheim Meml. fellow, 1978; Howard Reiss chair in chemistry and biochemistry established named in his honor, UCLA, 1999. Fellow AAAS, Am. Phys. Soc. (exec. com. div. chem. physics 1966-69); mem. NAS, Am. Chem. Soc. (chmn. phys. chemistry sect. N.J. sect. 1957, Richard C. Tolman medal 1973, Kendall award in colloid and surface chemistry 1980, J.H. Hildebrand award in theoretical and exptl. phys. chemistry of liquids 1991, Van Arkel hon. chair in chemistry U. Leiden, The Netherlands, 1994), Am. Assn. for Aerosol Rsch. (David Sinclair award 1997), Phi Beta Kappa, Sigma Xi, Phi Lambda Upsilon. Office: U Calif Dept Chemistry And Biochemis Los Angeles CA 90095-0001 Office Phone: 310-825-3029. Business E-Mail: reiss@chem.ucla.edu.

REITAN, HAROLD THEODORE, management consultant; b. Max, ND, Nov. 3, 1928; s. Walter Rudolph and Anna Helga (Glesne) R.; m. Margaret Lucille Bonsac, Dec. 29, 1954 (div.); children: Eric, Karen, Chris, Jon. BA, St. Olaf Coll., 1950; MA in Social Psychology, U. Fla., 1962, PhD, 1967. Commd. officer USAF, 1951, advanced through grades to col., 1971; comdr. USAF Spl. Treatment Ctr., Lackland, Tex., 1971-74, USAF Corrections and Rehab. Group, Lowry, Colo., 1974-76, USAF Tech. Tng. Wing, 1976-78; ret., 1978; mgr. health svcs. Coors Industries, Golden, Colo., 1978-84, mgr. tng. and orgnl. devel., 1984—89, cons. mgmt. assessment, tng. and devel., 1989—. Contbr. articles to profl. jours. Decorated D.F.C. with oak leaf cluster, Bronze Star, Legion of Merit with oak leaf cluster, Air medal with 5 oak leaf clusters. Mem. APA, Phi Kappa Phi. Republican. Lutheran. Home and Office: 116 S Nome St Aurora CO 80012-1242 Personal E-mail: htr1@earthlink.net.

REITEN, RICHARD G., natural gas industry executive; b. 1939; BA, U. Wash., 1962. With Simpson Timber Co., Seattle, 1962-64, St. Regis Paper Co., Tacoma, 1964-66, Hearin Products, Inc., Portland, Oreg., 1966-71, Di Giorgio Corp., San Francisco, 1971-79, pres. bldg. material group; with Nicoli Co., Portland, 1979-87; dir. Oreg. Econ. Devel. Dept., Salem, 1987-89; pres. Portland Gen. Corp., 1989-92, Portland Gen. Electric Co., 1992-95, pres., COO, 1996-97, pres., CEO, 1997—. Office: Richard G Reiten 1211 SW 5th Ave Ste 1600 Portland OR 97204-3716

REITSEMA, HAROLD JAMES, aerospace engineer; b. Kalamazoo, Jan. 19, 1948; s. Robert Harold and Bernice Jean (Hoogsteen) R.; m. Mary Jo Gunnink, Aug. 6, 1970; children: Ellen Celeste, Laurie Jean. BA, Calvin Coll., 1972; PhD, N.Mex. State U., 1977. Rsch. assoc. U. Ariz., Tucson, 1977-79, sr. rsch. assoc., 1979-82, vis. scientist, 1987—; sr. mem. tech. staff Ball Aerospace, Boulder, Colo., 1982-85, prin. systems engr., 1985-88, program mgr., 1988-89, staff cons., 1989-96, dir., 1996—2008. Cons. Aerospace Tech., 1987—. Contbr. articles to profl. jours. including Astrophys. Jour., Aston. Jour., Nature, Sci., Icarus. Bd. dirs. EE Barnard Obs., Golden, Colo., 1984-91, Space Sci. Inst., 2005-; adv. bds. N.Mex. State U. Arts & Scis., U. Colorado Dept. Astrophysics, Planetary Scis. Fellow AIAA (assoc., tech. com. chair 1991, Engr. of Yr. Colo. region 1990); mem. Am. Astron. Soc. (planetary sci. com. 1991-94), Internat. Astron. Union. Achievements include discovery of Larissa, fifth satellite of Neptune; co-discovery of Telesto, seventeenth satellite of Saturn; patents for Optically-coupled Shaft Angle Encoder. Home: 4795 Hancock Dr Boulder CO 80303-1103 Personal E-mail: hreitsema@aol.com.

REITZ, BRUCE ARNOLD, cardiac surgeon, educator; b. Seattle, Sept. 14, 1944; BS, Stanford U., 1966; MD, Yale U., 1970. Diplomate: Am. Bd. Surgery, Am. Bd. Thoracic Surgery. Intern Johns Hopkins Hosp., Balt., 1970-71, cardiac surgeon-in-charge, 1982-92; resident Stanford U. Hosp., Calif., 1971-72, 74-78; clin. assoc. Nat. Heart Lung Blood Inst., NIH, Bethesda, Md., 1972-74; asst. prof. Stanford U. Sch. Medicine, 1977-81, assoc. prof., 1981-82; prof. surgery Johns Hopkins U. Sch. Medicine, Balt., 1982-92; prof., chmn. Sch Medicine Stanford (Calif.) U., 1992—2005; prof. Stanford U. Sch. Medicine, 2005—. Developer heart-lung transplant technique, 1981. Office: Stanford U Sch Medicine Dept Cardiothoracic Surgery Stanford CA 94305-5407 Office Phone: 650-725-4497. Business E-Mail: breitz@stanford.edu.

REMBE, TONI, lawyer, director; b. Seattle, Apr. 23, 1936; d. Armin and Doris (McVay) R.; m. Arthur Rock, July 19, 1975. Cert. in French Studies, U. Geneva, 1956; LL.B., U. Wash., 1960; LLM in Taxation, NYU, 1961. Bar: N.Y., Wash., Calif. Assoc. Chadbourne, Parke, Whiteside & Wolff, NYC, 1961-63, Pillsbury, Madison & Sutro, San Francisco, 1964-71, ptnr., 1971—. Bd dirs. Aegon N.V., The Netherlands, Potlatch Corp., Spokane, Wash., SBC Comms., Inc., San Antonio. Pres. VanLobenSels/RembeRock Charitable Found., San Francisco; trustee Am. Conservatory Theatre, San Francisco. Fellow Am. Bar Found.; mem. ABA, Am. Judicature Soc., State Bar Calif., Bar Assn. San Francisco, Commonwealth Club of Calif. Office: Pillsbury Winthrop LLP 50 Fremont St San Francisco CA 94105-2230

REMER, DONALD SHERWOOD, engineering educator, economist, cost estimator, management consultant; b. Detroit, Mich., Feb. 16, 1943; s. Nathan and Harriet R.; m. Louise Collen, Dec. 21, 1969; children: Tanya, Candace, Miles. BS, U. Mich., 1965; MS, Calif. Inst. Tech., 1966, PhD, 1970. Registered profl. engr., Calif., Mich., La. Tech. service engr., chem. raw materials div. coordinator, sr. running plan coordinator, task team mgr. Exxon, Baton Rouge, 1970-75; assoc. prof. engring. Harvey Mudd Coll., Claremont, Calif., 1975-79, prof., 1980—, Oliver C. Field prof. engring., dir. Energy Inst., 1981-83; cons., mem. tech. staff, mgr. planning analysis Jet Propulsion Lab., Calif. Inst. Tech., 1976-98; co-founder, ptnr. Claremont Cons. Group, 1979—2006, pres., 2007—. Mem. adv. coun. Nat. Energy Found., 1981—85; mem. Inst. Mgmt. Cons., 1988—89; presenter short courses Calif. Inst. Indsl. Rels. Ctr., 1994—, UCLA Engring. and Tech. Mgmt. Program, 1994—; Lyceum spkr. St. Jude Med., 2001. Case study editor Am. Soc. Engring. Edn., Inst. Indsl. Engrs., Engring. Economist, 1977-89; mem. editorial bd. Jour. Engring. Costs and Prodn. Econs., 1985-91, Internat. Jour. Prodn. Econs., 1992—; contbr. articles to profl. jours. Shelter mgr. ARC, Baton Rouge, 1970-75. Recipient Outstanding Chem. Engr. award U. Mich., 1965, First Place Pub. Relations award Am. Inst. Chem. Engring., 1975, Outstanding Alumni Fund Achievement award Calif. Inst. Tech., 1976, Outstanding Young Man of Am. award, 1976, NASA award, 1983, Best Paper of the Year in Jour. Parametrics, Internat. Soc. Parametric Analysts, 1991-92, Centennial award certificate Am. Soc. Engring. Edn., 1993; named Outstanding Research Seminar Speaker Occidental Research Corp., 1976. Mem. Am. Soc. Engring. Mgmt. (bd. dirs. 1981-83), Toastmasters Club (pres. Claremont-Pomona chpt. 1978).

REMINGTON, BRUCE A., physics researcher; Hydrodynamics group leader Lawrence Livermore Nat. Lab., 1986—. Recipient Excellence in Plasma Physics award Am. Phys. Soc., 1995. Fellow Am. Physical Soc. (pub. rels. coord. divsn. plasma physics). Office: Lawrence Livermore Nat Lab PO Box 808 Livermore CA 94551-0808

REN, XING JIAN, physician; b. Shanghai, June 27, 1961; s. Yun Feng Ren and Xin Yi Zhang; m. Bei Xie, June 27, 1990; 1 child, Oriana Leigh. MD, Shanghai First Med. Coll., 1984. Diplomate internal medicine and geriatric medicine Am. Bd. Internal Medicine. Resident in surgery Shanghai Ruhui Hosp., China, 1984-85; resident Ft. Wayne (Ind.) Med. Edn. Program, 1993-94; resident, intern in medicine Loyola U. of Chgo., Maywood, Ill., 1994-97; fellow in medicine Harvard Med. Sch., Boston, 1997-99; staff physician Scripps Clinic Found., La Jolla, Calif., 1999—; asst. clin. prof. medicine U. Calif. Sch. Medicine, 2003—. Co-author: Virology, 1986; contbr. articles to profl. jours. Fellow Harvard Med. Sch., 1998; recipient 1st prize Nat. Med. Student Competition for Knowledge of Med. Lit., 1983, grad. student scholarship U. N.C., Chapel Hill, scholarship Carolina Biotechnolgoy Ctr., others. Fellow ACP; mem. AMA, Mass. Med. Soc., Am. Geriatrics Soc., Fell. Am. Coll. Physician. Home Phone: 858-794-9284; Office Phone: 858-268-9500, 858-554-8077, 619-245-2830.

RENARD, RONALD LEE, allergist; b. Chgo., July 31, 1949; s. Robert James and Dorothy Mae (Fruik) R.; m. Maureen Ann Gilmore, Aug. 5, 1972 (div. Mar. 1992); children: Jeffrey, Stephen, Justin, Leigh Ellen; m. Catherine L. Walker, Apr. 1, 1992; children: Morgan, Michal, Luke. Degrees in Lang., U. de Montepellier, France, 1970; BS in French, U. San Francisco, 1971; MD, Creighton U., 1976. Dir. med. ICU, lt. U.S. Army Hosp., Ft. Leonard Wood, Md., 1980-81; dir. respiratory therapy, asst. chief allergy svc. Walter Reed Med. Ctr., Washington, 1981-84; staff allergist Chico (Calif.) Med. Group, 1984-86; allergist pvt. practice Redding, Calif., 1986—. Dir. ACLS program Enloe Hosp., Chico, 1988-91; bd. dirs. Am. Lung Assn. Calif., 1989-91, med. dir. asthma camp, Chico, Redding, 1986-95; asst. prof. medicine USPHS, Bethesda, Md., 1982-84; asst. prof. family medicine U. Calif. Davis Med. Sch., Redding, 1990-94; Shasta County Planning Commr., 1994-95. Contbr. articles to profl. jours. Fellow Am. Acad. Allergy and Immunology, Am. Coll. Allergists; mem. Assn. Mil. Allergists, Calif. Thoracic Soc., Alpha Omega Alpha. Republican. Roman Catholic. Avocations: hunting, biking. Office: 1505 Victor Ave Redding CA 96003 Home Fax: 530-246-8856. Personal E-mail: rrenard@juno.com.

RENCHER, NATALIE R., library director; married; 2 children. BS in Child Devel., San Diego State U.; MLS, San Jose State U., Calif. Libr. technician San Diego County Libr., 1978, libr. capital projects mgr., dep. dir., interim dir., 2005; with San Diego Pub. Libr., San Jose Pub. Libr.; dir. libr. svcs. Stockton-San Joaquin County Pub. Libr., Calif., 2005—. Office: Stockton San Joaquin County Pub Libr 605 N El Dorado St Stockton CA 95202 Office Phone: 209-937-8365. Office Fax: 209-937-8683. E-mail: nrencher@ci.stockton.ca.us.

RENDA, LARREE M., retail executive; Joined Safeway, Inc., 1974, exec. v.p. retail ops., human resources, pub. affairs, labor and govtl. rels. Pleasanton, Calif., 1999—. Office: Safeway Inc 5918 Stoneridge Mall Rd Pleasanton CA 94588

RENDU, JEAN-MICHEL MARIE, mining executive; b. Tunis, Tunisia, Feb. 25, 1944; s. Paul C. and Solange M. (Krebs) R.; m. Karla M. Meyer, Aug. 18, 1973; children: Yannick P., Mikaël P. Ingénieur des Mines, Ecole des Mines St. Etienne, France, 1966; MS, Columbia U., 1968, D of Engring. Sci., 1971. Mgr. ops. rsch. Anglovaal, Johannesburg, 1972-76; assoc. prof. U. Wis., Madison, 1976-79; assoc. Golder Assocs., Denver, 1979-84; dir. tech. and sci. systems Newmont Mining Corp., Danbury, Conn., 1984-88; v.p. Newmont Gold Co., Denver, 1988-93, Newmont Mining Corp., Denver, 1993-2001; ind. cons. Denver, 2001—. Author: An Introduction to Geostatistical Methods of Mineral Evaluation, 1978, 81; contbr. tech. papers to profl. jours. Fellow South African Inst. Mining and Metallurgy (corr. mem. of coun.), Australasian Inst. Mining and Metallurgy; mem. NAE, Soc. Mining, Metallurgy and Exploration (bd. dirs. 1998—2005, Jackling award 1994, Pres.'s citation 1993, 2004), Sigma Xi. Roman Catholic. E-mail: JMRendu@aol.com.

RENEKER, MAXINE HOHMAN, librarian; b. Chgo., Dec. 2, 1942; d. Roy Max and Helen Anna Christina (Anacker) Hohman; m. David Lee Reneker, June 20, 1964 (dec. Dec. 1979); children: Sarah Roeder, Amy Johannah, Benjamin Congdon. BA, Carleton Coll., 1964; MA, U. Chgo., 1970; DLS, Columbia U., 1992. Asst. reference libr. U. Chgo. Libraries, 1965-66; classics libr. U. Chgo. Libr., 1967-70, asst. head acquisitions, 1970-71, personnel libr., 1971-73; personnel/bus. libr. U. Colo. Libr., Boulder, 1978-80; asst. dir. sci. and engring. div. Columbia U., NYC, 1981-85; assoc. dean of univ. librs. for pub. svcs. Ariz. State U. Libr., Tempe, 1985-89; dir. instrnl. and rsch. svcs. Stanford (Calif.) Univ. Librs., 1989-90; assoc. provost for libr. and info. resources Naval Postgrad. Sch., Monterey, Calif., 1993—2005, prof. emerita, 2005—. Acad. libr. mgmt. intern Coun. on Libr. Resources, 1980-81; chmn. univ. librs. sect. Assn. Coll. and Rsch. Librs., 1989-90. Contbr. articles to profl. jours. Trustee Monterey Pub. Libr. Rsch. grantee Coun. on Library Resources, Columbia U., 1970-71, fellow, 1990-92. Mem. ALA, Am. Soc. Info. Sci., Sherlockian Scion Soc., Phi Beta Kappa, Beta Phi Mu. Home: 740 Dry Creek Rd Monterey CA 93940-4208 Personal E-mail: mreneker@pacbell.net.

RENFREW, CHARLES BYRON, lawyer; b. Detroit, Oct. 31, 1928; s. Charles Warren and Louise (McGuire) R.; m. Susan Wheelock, June 28, 1952 (div. June 1984); children: Taylor Allison Ingham, Charles Robin, Todd Wheelock, James Bartlett; m. Barbara Jones Orser, Oct. 6, 1984; 5 stepchildren. AB, Princeton U., 1952; JD, U. Mich., 1956. Bar: Calif. 1956. Assoc. Pillsbury, Madison & Sutro, San Francisco, 1956-65, ptnr., 1965-72, 81-82; U.S. dist. judge No. Dist. Calif., San Francisco, 1972-80; dep. atty. gen. U.S. Washington, 1980-81; instr. U. Calif. Boalt Hall Sch. Law, 1977-80; v.p. law Chevron Corp. (formerly Standard Oil Co. Calif.), San Francisco, 1983-93, also bd. dirs.; ptnr. LeBoeuf, Lamb, Greene & McRae, San Francisco, 1994-97; pvt. practice San Francisco, 1998—. Mem. exec. com. 9th Cir. Jud. Conf., 1976-78, congl. liaison com. 9th Cir. Jud. Council, 1976-79, spl. com. to propose standards for admission to practice in fed. cts. U.S. Jud. Conf., 1976-79; chmn. spl. com. to study problems of discovery Fed. Jud. Ctr., 1978-79; mem. council on role of cts. U.S. Dept. Justice, 1978-83; mem. jud. panel Ctr. for Pub. Resources, 1981—; head U.S. del. to 6th UN Congress on Prevention of Crime and Treatment of Offenders, 1980; co-chmn. San Francisco Lawyers Com. for Urban Affairs, 1971-72, mem., 1983—; bd. dirs. Internat. Hospitality Ctr., 1961-74, pres., 1967-70; mem. adv. bd. Internat. Comparative Law Ctr., Southwestern Legal Found., 1983-93; trustee World Affairs Council No. Calif., 1984-87, 94—, Nat. Jud. Coll., 1985-91, Grace Cathedral, 1986-89. Contbr. articles to profl. jours. Bd. fellow Claremont U., 1986-94; bd. dirs. San Francisco Symphony Found., 1964-80, pres., 1971-72; bd. dirs. Coun. Civic Unity, 1962-73, pres., 1971-72; bd. dirs. Opportunity Through Ownership, 1969-72, Marin County Day Sch., 1972-74, No. Calif. Svc. League, 1975-76, Am. Petroleum Inst., 1984—, Nat. Crime Prevention Coun., 1982—; alumni trustee Princeton U., 1976-80; mem. vis. com. u. chgo. Law Sch., 1977-79, u.Mich. Law Sch., 1977-81; bd. visitors J. Reuben Clark Law Sch., Brigham Young U., 1981-83, Stanford Law Sch., 1983-86; trustee Town Sch. for Boys, 1972-80,pres. 1975-80; gov. San Fransciso Symphony Assn., 1974—; mem. nat. adv. bd. Ctr. for Nat. Policy, 1982—; bd. dirs. Nat. Coun. Crime and Deliquency, 1981-82,NAACP Legal Def. and Edn. Fund, 1982—; parish chancellor St. Luke's Episcopal Ch., 1968-71, sr. warden, 1974-76; mem. exec. coun. San Francisco Deanery, 1969-70; mem. diocesan coun. Episcopal Diocese of Calif., 1970; chmn. Diocesan Conv., 1977, 78, 79. Served with USN, 1946-48, 1st lt. U.S. Army, 1952-53. Fellow Am. Bar Found.; mem. ABA (coun. mem. sect. antitrust law 19778-82, vice c hmn. sect. antitrust law 1982-83), San Francisco Bar Assn. (past bd. dirs.), Assn. Gen. Counsel, State Bar Calif., Am. Judicature Soc., Am. Coll. Trial Lawyers (pres. 1995-96), Am. Law Inst., Coun. Fgn. Rels., Order of Coif, Phi Beta Kappa, Phi Delta Phi. Office: 710 Sansome St San Francisco CA 94111-1704

RENFRO, JOHN M., human resources specialist; b. Collinsville, Ill., Dec. 31, 1959; BS, So. Ill. U., 1982. V.p. human resources A.C. Nielson Internat.; v.p. human resources consumer mktg. info. group Asia-Pacific, Latin Am. and Africa ops. Dun & Bradstreet; v.p. human resources and adminstrn. small bus. svcs. divsn. Ameritech, Chgo.; sr. v.p. human resources and adminstrn. Zenith Electronics Corp., Chgo.; v.p. corp. human resources to sr. v.p. human resources Gateway, San Diego, 1998—2002; sr. v.p., chief human resources officer Walt Disney Co., Burbank, Calif., 2002—06; v.p. human resources HP Imaging and Printing Group (IPG) Hewlett-Packard, 2006—. Mem. external adv. bd. coll. bus. adminstrn. So. Ill. U.; bd. dirs. LA Urban League; mem. external adv. bd. So. Ill. U., Carbondale. Mem. exec. com. United Way, San Diego, mem. Alexis de Tocqueville Soc. Office: HP Imaging and Printing Group 3000 Hanover St Palo Alto CA 94304 Office Phone: 818-560-1000. Office Fax: 818-560-1930.

RENFROE, SCOTT, state legislator; b. Greeley, Colo., Dec. 7, 1966; m. Pamela; children: Olivia, Sylvia, Vivian, Derek, Spencer. B, Colo. State U., Ft. Collins, 1989. Co-owner, v.p. Found. Builders, Inc.; mem. Dist. 13 Colo. State Senate, 2007—. Mem. Eaton Sch. Dist. Bd. Edn., 1997, 2001; trustee, chmn. Evangelical Free Ch. Eaton, mem. deacon bd. Mem. Weld County Builders Assn. (past pres.), Northern Colo. Home Builders, Nat. Fedn. Ind. Bus. Republican. Office: Colo State Senate 200 E Colfax Denver CO 80203 Office Phone: 303-866-4451. Business E-Mail: scott.renfroe.senate@state.co.us.*

RENGER, MARILYN HANSON, elementary school educator; b. Shelly, Idaho, July 17, 1949; d. Merril H. and Betty Jean (Hendricksen) Hanson; m. Robert Carl Renger, Sept. 11, 1971; children: Katherine, James. BA in History, U. Calif., Santa Barbara, 1971; postgrad., Calif. Luth. U., 1973-74. Tchr. Ventura (Calif.) Unified Schs., 1974-79, 85-98, asst. prin., 1998—. Cons. State of Calif., 1989-93. Recipient Disting. Tchr. K-12 award Nat. Coun. for Geog. Edn., 1992. Mem. Nat. Coun. Geographic Edn. (Nat. Disting. Teaching award 1992), Calif. Geographic Soc. (steering com. 1989-93, co-dir. summer inst. 1992), Nat. Coun. Social Studies. Office: Balboa Mid Sch 247 S Hill Rd Ventura CA 93003-4401

RENKES, GREGG D., former state attorney general; b. 1958; m. Maureen Renkes; 2 children. BA, Vassar Coll.; MS, Yale U.; JD, U. Colo. Bar: Alaska 1987. Law clk., magistrate State Alaska Ct. Sys.; chief of staff, chief counsel to U.S. Senator Frank Murkowski; majority staff dir. U.S. Senate Com. on Energy and Natural Resources, 1995—98; pres. The Renkes Group, Ltd.; atty. gen. State of Alaska, Juneau, 2002—05. Spkr. in field. Contbr. articles to profl. jours. Mem. Campaign to Re-elect Senator Frank Murkowski, 1992, 1998, Murkowski 2002 Alaska Gubernatorial Campaign; active Rep. Nat. Conv. Platform Com., 1996. Republican.

RENNE, PAUL A., lawyer; b. Mpls., Nov. 2, 1930; AB, Univ. Minn., 1956; JD, Harvard Univ., 1959. Bar: DC 1959, NY 1961, Calif. 1964, US Supreme Ct. 1964. Law clk. Judge Edwin D. Steel, Jr., US Dist Ct. (Del.), 1959—60; assoc. Haight Gardner Poor & Havens, NYC, 1960—61; atty. U.S. Dept. Justice, civil rights div., Washington, 1961—62; asst. U.S. atty. U.S. Dept. Justice, DC dist., 1962—64; sr. counsel, litigation dept. Cooley Godward LLP, San Francisco, 1964—. Adj. prof. Golden Gate Univ.; lectr. Calif. CLE; mediator Assn. San Francisco, US Dist. Ct. Contbr. articles to profl. jours. Pilot USAF, 1951—56. Mem.: ABA, Am. Coll. Trial Lawyers (state chmn., no. Calif.), Am. Arbitration Assn. (mem. com. panel), Bar Assn. San Francisco. Office: Cooley Godward Llp 101 California St Fl 5 San Francisco CA 94111-5800 Office Phone: 415-693-2073. Office Fax: 415-951-3699. Business E-Mail: prenne@cooley.com.

RENNER, ANDREW IHOR, surgeon; b. Buenos Aires, Aug. 1, 1951; came to U.S., 1956; s. Vladimir and Emelia R.; m. Cristina Sasyk, Apr. 17, 1982. MD, Albert Einstein Coll. Medicine, 1975. Diplomate Am. Bd. Surgery. Pvt. practice gen. surgery, Burbank, Calif.; chief of staff Providence-St. Joseph Med. Ctr., 2005, 2006; chief of quality assurance Providence St. Joseph Hosp., 2007—08. Chmn. dept. surgery St. Joseph Hosp., Burbank, 1995-97, vice chief of staff Providence St. Joseph Med. Ctr., Burbank, 2003-04, chief of staff, 2005-06. Fellow ACS, Internat. Coll. Surgeons; mem. Am. Soc. Gen. Surgeons, L.A. Surg. Soc. Office: 2701 W Alameda Ave Ste 300 Burbank CA 91505-4408 Office Phone: 818-843-1492. Office Fax: 818-843-5283.

RENNIE, I. DRUMMOND, periodical editor, medical educator; Dep. editor Jour. AMA; nephrologist Rush-Presbyn. St. Lukes Hosp. and Rush Med. Sch., Chgo., 1967-77; assoc. prof. medicine Harvard (Brigham and Women's Hosp.); dep. editor New England Jour. of Medicine. Adv. com. on scientific integrity to Pub. Health Svc.; adj. prof. of medicine U. Calif. San Francisco; co-dir. San Francisco Cochrane Ctr.; proposal rev. adv. team Nat. Sci. Found.; founder CONSORT, QUOROM coms. Contbr. numerous articles to profl. publs. Fellow ACP; mem. New World Assn. of Med. Editors (pres. coun. of biology editors, past pres., exec. bd.). Office: Inst for Health Policy Studies Adjunct Prof UCSF School of Medicine San Francisco CA 94118 E-mail: rennie@itsa.ucsf.edu.

RENNIE, PAUL STEVEN, research scientist, surgeon; b. Toronto, Ont., Can., Feb. 9, 1946; m. Carol Andrews, 1968; 1 child, Jan. BSc, U. Western Ont., 1969; PhD in Biochemistry, U. Alta., Can., 1973. Rsch. assoc. U. Alta., 1975-76, asst. prof. medicine, 1976-79, assoc. prof., 1979; rsch. scientist B.C. Cancer Agy., Canada, 1979-92, dir. rsch., 1992-97; prof. surgery U. B.C., 1986—, dir. prostate rsch. lab., 1998—. Med. Rsch. Coun. rsch. fellow Imperial Cancer Rsch. Fund, 1973-75; rsch. scholar Nat. Cancer Inst. Can., 1976-79. Achievements include research on biochemical control of growth in androgen responsive organs and neoplasms; genetic markers in prostate cancer. Office: Prostate Ctr Jack Bell Rsch Ctr 2660 Oak St Vancouver BC Canada V6H 3Z6 Home Phone: 604-275-5030. Business E-Mail: prennie@interchange.ubc.ca.

RENTON, HOLLINGS C., health products executive; BS Maths., Colo. State U.; MBA, U. Mich. Pres., COO Cetus Corp., 1981—91; pres., Chiron Corp., 1991—92; chmn., pres., CEO Onyx Pharms. Inc., Emeryville, Calif., 1993—. Office: Onyx Pharms Inc 2100 Powell St Emeryville CA 94608

RENUART, VICTOR EUGENE, JR., (GENE RENUART), career military officer; b. Nov. 26, 1949; s. Victor Eugene and Ruthann Wigglesworth Renuart; m. Jill Colleen Jenner; children: Ryan Victor, Andrew John. BS in Prodn. and Indsl. Mgmt., Ind. U., 1971; MA in Psychology, Troy State U., 1975; Disting. grad., Squadron Officer Sch., Maxwell AFB, Ala., 1977; Grad., Air Command & Staff Coll., 1979, Army War Coll., 1992, Sr. Officers in Nat. Security Program, 1997. Commd. 2d. lt. USAF, 1973, advanced through grades to gen., 2007; instr., pilot Craig AFB, 1973-76; asst. prof. aerospace studies U. Notre Dame, South Bend, Ind., 1976-79; A-10 instr. pilot, flight comdr. to ops. officer 81st Tactical Fighter Wing, RAF Bentwaters, Eng., 1980-84; ops. inspector Office of the Inspector Gen. Hdqrs. USAF Europe, Ramstein AB, West Germany, 1984-85, exec. officer to inspector gen., 1985-86; chief wing inspections 23rd Tactical Fighter Wing, England AFB, La., 1986-91, ops. officer to comdr., 1986-91, dir. assignments, 1992-93; comdr. support group Allied Air Forces Ctrl. Europe, England AFB, 1993-94, asst. chief of staff, ops., sr. U.S. rep., 1994-95; dir. ops. plans NATO Combined Air Ops. Ctr. 5th Allied Tactical AF, Vicenza, Italy, 1994-95; asst. dir. ops. Hdqrs. USAF Europe, Ramstein, Germany, 1995-96; comdr. 52nd Fighter Wing, Spangdahlem AB, Germany, 1996-98, 347th Wing, Moody AFB, Ga., 1998—2000; comdr. Joint Task Force-Southwest Asia, comdr. 9th Air & Space Expeditionary Task Force-Southwest Asia US Ctrl. Command, Riyadh, Saudi Arabia, 2000—01; dir. ops. (J-3) US Ctrl Command, MacDill AFB, Fla., 2001—03; vice comdr. Pacific Air Forces, Hickam AFB, Hawaii, 2003—05; dir. strategic plans & policy (J-5) Joint Staff, The Pentagon, Washington, 2005—06; sr. mil. asst. to sec. US Dept. Def., Washington, 2006—07; comdr. N.Am. Aerospace Def. Command (NORAD), Peterson AFB, Colo., 2007—, US No. Command, Peterson AFB, 2007—. Decorated Def. Disting. Svc. medal with oak leaf cluster, Disting. Svc. medal, Def Superior Svc. medal with oak leaf cluster, Meritorious Svc. medal with four oak leaf clusters, Aerial Achievement medal with three oak leaf clusters, Air Force Commendation medal with oak leaf cluster, Air Force Achievement medal with oak leaf cluster, Legion of Merit with oak leaf cluster, Air medal with two oak leaf clusters. Office: US Northern Command 250 Vandenberg Ste B016 Colorado Springs CO 80914

RENWICK, EDWARD S., lawyer; b. LA, May 10, 1934; AB, Stanford U., 1956, LLB, 1958. Bar: Calif. 1959, U.S. Dist. Ct. (cen. dist.) Calif. 1959, U.S. Ct. Appeals (9th cir.) 1963, U.S. Dist. Ct. (so. dist.) Calif. 1973, U.S. Dist. Ct. (no. dist.) Calif. 1977, U.S. Dist. Ct. (ea. dist.) Calif. 1981, U.S. Supreme Ct. 1985. Ptnr. Hanna and Morton LLP, LA. Mem., bd. vis. Stanford Law Sch., 1967-69; mem. environ. and natural resources adv. bd. Stanford Law Sch. Bd. dirs. Calif. Supreme Ct. Hist. Soc. Fellow Am. Coll. Trial Lawyers, Am. Bar Found.; mem. ABA (mem. sect. on litigation, antitrust law, bus. law, chmn. sect. of nat. resources, energy and environ. law 1987-88, mem. at large coord. group energy law 1989-92, sect. rep. coord. group energy law 1995-97, Calif. del. legal com., interstate oil compact com.), Calif. Arboretum Assn. (trustee 1986-92), L.A. County Bar Assn. (chmn. natural resources law sect. 1974-75), The State Bar of Calif., Chancery Club (pres. 1992-93), Phi Delta Phi. Office: Hanna and Morton LLP 444 S Flower St Ste 1500 Los Angeles CA 90071-2922 Office Phone: 213-628-7131. Business E-Mail: erenwick@hanmor.com.

RENZI, RICK (RICHARD GEORGE RENZI), former United States Representative from Arizona; b. Sierra Vista, Ariz., June 11, 1958; s. Eugene Carmen and Faye Marie Renzi; m. Roberta Renzi; 12 children. BS in Criminal Justice, No. Ariz. U., 1980; JD, Cath. U., 2002. Owner Renzi & Co.; staff mem. to Senator Jon Kyl US Senate; mem. US Congress from 1st Ariz. Dist., 2003—09. Indicted on federal charges (conspiracy, money laundering, wire and insurance fraud and extortion) on Feb. 22, 2008. Recipient Friends of Affordable Housing award, Fed. Home Loan Bank San Francisco, 2004, Unsung Hero award, Ariz. Am. Legion, 2004; named to No. Ariz. U. Hall of Fame, 1998. Republican. Roman Catholic.*

REPINE, JOHN EDWARD, internist, educator; b. Rock Island, Ill., Dec. 26, 1944; married, 1969, 88; 6 children. BS, U. Wis., 1967; MD, U. Minn., 1971. Instr., then assoc. prof. internal medicine U. Minn., Mpls., 1974-79; asst. dir divsn. exptl. medicine Webb-Waring Inst. Biomedical Rsch., Denver, 1979-89; prof. medicine, pres. and dir. Webb-Waring Inst. Cancer, Aging & Antioxidant Rsch., Denver, 1989—; prof. medicine U. Colo., Denver, 1979—, James J. Waring prof. medicine, 1996—, prof. pediatrics, 1981-96. Mem. rsch. com., co-chmn. steering com. Aspen Lung Conf., 1980, chmn., 1981; assoc. dean for student advocacy Nat. Heart and Lung Inst., 1990—. Young Pulmonary Investigator grantee Nat. Heart & Lung Inst., 1974-75; recipient Basil O'Connor Starter Rsch. award Nat. Found. March of Dimes, 1975-77. Mem. AAAS, Am. Assn. Immunologists, Am. Soc. Clin. Investigation, Am. Heart Assn. (established investigator award 1976-81), Am. Thoracic Soc., Assn. Am. Physicians. Achievements include research in role of phagocytes and oxygen radicals in lung injury and host defense (ARDS). Office: Webb Waring Inst Cancer Aging & Antioxidant Rsch Box C322 4200 E 9th Ave Denver CO 80220-3706

REPP, PAGE W., JR., construction executive; b. 1974; Owner, pres. Repp Enterprises Inc., Tucson, 1995—. Steering com. vice-chair West Side Weed and Seed. Pres. Barrio Blue Moon Neighborhood Assn. Named one of 40 Under 40, Tucson Bus. Edge, 2006. Office: Repp Design & Construction 422 W Speedway Tucson AZ 85705 Office Phone: 520-791-7035. Office Fax: 520-791-7075.

RESCH, CHARLOTTE SUSANNA, plastic surgeon; b. Charlottesville, Va., Sept. 24, 1957; d. Johann Heinrich and Eleonore Susanne (Stenzel) R.; m. John Arthur Niero, Jan. 31, 1990. Student, Dalhousie U., Halifax, Nova Scotia, Can., 1974-76; MD with distinction, Dalhousie U. Med. Sch., Halifax, Nova Scotia, Can., 1980. Diplomate Dalhousie U., Am. Bd. Plastic Surgery; licentiate Med. Coun. Can.; cert. Bd. Med. Quality Assurance Calif. Intern Ottawa Gen. Hosp., Ont., Can., 1980-81; gen. surgery resident Dalhousie U., Halifax, Nova Scotia, Can., 1981-85; plastic surgery resident Wayne State U., Detroit, 1985-87; pvt. practice San Francisco, 1988-89; pre-ptnr. Southern Calif. Permanente Physicians Group, Fontana, 1989-92, ptnr., 1992—. Contbr. articles to profl. jours. Fellow ACS; mem. Am. Soc. Plastic and Reconstructive Surgeons, Calif. Med. Soc., San Bernardino Med. Soc., Alpha Omega Alpha. Avocations: travel, skiing, bicycling, gardening, gourmet cooking. Office: Kaiser Found Hosp Dept Plastic Surgery 9985 Sierra Ave Fontana CA 92335-6720

RESHOTKO, ELI, aerospace engineer, educator; b. NYC, Nov. 18, 1930; s. Max and Sarah (Kalisky) R.; m. Adina Venit, June 7, 1953; children: Deborah, Naomi, Miriam Ruth. BS, Cooper Union, 1950; MS, Cornell U., 1951; PhD, Calif. Inst. Tech., 1960. Aero. research engr. NASA-Lewis Flight Propulsion Lab., Cleve., 1951-56, head fluid mechanics sect., 1956-57; head high temperature plasma sect. NASA-Lewis Research Center, 1960-61, chief plasma physics br., 1961-64; asso. prof. engring. Case Inst. Tech., Cleve., 1964-66, dean, 1986-87; prof. engring. Case Western Res. U., Cleve., 1966-88, chmn. dept. fluid thermal and aerospace scis., 1970-76, chmn. dept. mech. and aerospace engring., 1976-79, Kent H. Smith prof. engring., 1989-98, Kent H. Smith prof. emeritus, 1999—. Susman vis. prof. dept. aero. engring. Technion-Israel Inst. Tech., Haifa, Israel, 1969-70; cons. Inst. Def. Analyses, Dynamics Tech. Inc., Aerion Corp., Rockwell Sci. Ctr.; adv. com. fluid dynamics NASA, 1961-64; aero. adv. com. NASA, 1980-87, chmn. adv. subcom. on aerodynamics, 1983-85; chmn. U.S. Boundary Layer Transition Study Group, NASA/USAF, 1970—2001, steering com., 2001-; US mem. fluid dynamics panel AGARD-NATO, 1981-88; chmn. steering com. Symposium on Engring. Aspects of Magneto-hydro-dynamics, 1966, Case-NASA Inst. for Computational Mechanics in Propulsion, 1985-92, USRA/NASA ICASE Sci. Coun., 1992; Joseph Wunsch lectr. Technion-Israel Inst. Tech., 1990. Contbr. articles to tech. jours. Chmn. bd. govs. Cleve. Coll. Jewish Studies, 1981-84 (life trustee); bd. govs. Technion-Israel Inst. Tech., Haifa, Israel, 1999-2005; mem. NRC Air Force Studies bd., 2000-06, NRC Aeronautics & Space Engring. Bd., 2008-. Guggenheim fellow Calif. Inst. Tech., 1957-59. Fellow ASME, AAAS, AIAA (Fluid and Plasma Dynamics award 1980, Dryden lectr. in rsch. 1994), Am. Phys. Soc. (vice-chmn. divsn. fluid dynamics 1998, chair-elect 1999, chair 2000, Otto Laporte award in fluid dynamics 1999), Am. Acad. Mechanics (pres. 1986-87); mem. NAE, Ohio Sci. and Engring. Roundtable, Sigma Xi, Tau Beta Pi, Pi Tau Sigma. Home: 1200 Humboldt St Apt 601 Denver CO 80218-2454

RESNECK, JACK SELWYN, JR., dermatologist, medical educator; b. Shreveport, La., Oct. 16, 1970; BA in Pub. Policy, Brown Univ.; MD, Univ. Calif., San Francisco, 1997. Cert. Dermatology. Resident in dermatology Univ. Calif., San Francisco, 1997—98; fellow Inst. Health Policy Studies, Univ. Calif., San Francisco, 1998—2001; asst. prof. dermatology and health policy Univ. Calif., San Francisco, 2001—. Dir., dermatology faculty practice clinics U. Calif., San Francisco, dir., dermatology residency tng. program; co-dir., health policy curriculum U. Calif. Med. Sch., San Francisco. Contbr. articles to profl. jours. Recipient Clinical Career Devel. award in health care policy, Dermatology Found., 2003, 2004, 2005, Excellence in Medicine Leadership award, AMA Found., 2004. Mem.: AMA (mem. coun. legis.), Am. Acad. Dermatology (resident bd. dirs.), Calif. Med. Assn. (mem. coun. legis.), Calif. Soc. Dermatology and Dermatologic Surgery (past pres.). Office: Dept Dermatology Univ Calif San Francisco 1701 Divisadero St 4th Fl San Francisco CA 94115 Office Phone: 415-476-9350, 415-353-7880. Office Fax: 415-476-3686, 415-353-9654.

RESNICK, JEFFREY I., plastic surgeon; b. Jersey City, Mar. 2, 1954; s. Victor and Regina (Bistritz) R.; m. Michele Gail Zinger, July 12, 1981; children: Andrew Gregory, Daniel Zachary. BS, Yale U., 1975; MD, U. Pa., 1980. Diplomate Am. Bd. Surgery, Am. Bd. Plastic Surgery. Resident in surgery Mass. Gen. Hosp., Boston, 1980—85, resident in plastic surgery, 1985—87; asst. clin. prof. plastic surgery UCLA, 1987—, fellow in craniofacial surgery, 1987—88; asst. prof. clin. surgery U. So. Calif, Santa Monica, 1998—. Contbr. articles to profl. jours. Surgeon Interplast, Vietnam, Nepal, Myanmar. Mem. Am. Assn. Plastic Surgeons, Am. Soc. Plastic Surgeons, Am. Soc. Maxillofacial Surgeons, Am. Cleft Palate-Craniofacial Assn., Plastic Surgery Ednl. Found., Sigma Xi, Alpha Omega Alpha. Office: 1301 20th St Ste 470 Santa Monica CA 90404-2082 Home Phone: 310-471-3532; Office Phone: 310-315-0222. Business E-Mail: jresnick@ucla.edu.

RESNICK, LYNDA, corporate financial executive; Co-owner, vice chmn. Franklin Mint; co-owner Roll Internat. Chmn. Teleflora. Chmn. mktg. com. Conservation Internat.; bd. dirs. Assn. for Cure of Cancer of the Prostate, CaP CURE, Milken Family Found.; mem. exec. com., trustee, chmn. acquisitions com. LA County Mus. Art; mem. com. on sculpture and decorative arts Met. Mus. Art; trustee Phila. Mus. Art. Recipient Gold Effie award, 1983; named one of Top 50 US Women Bus. Owners, Working Women, Top 100 US art collectors Art & Antiques mag., Top 200 Collectors, ARTnews mag., 2008 #1 L.A.-based woman Bus. Owner, LA bus. Jour. Avocation: collecting Old Masters. Office: Roll Internat Ctr 11444 W Olympic Blvd Los Angeles CA 90064-1549

RESNICK, STEWART ALLEN, diversified company executive; b. Jersey City, Dec. 24, 1936; s. David and Yetta (Goldmaker) R.; children from previous marriage: Jeffrey Brian, Ilene Sue, William Jay; m. Lynda Rae Harris, Nov. 26, 1972; children: Jonathan Charles Sinay, Jason Daniel Sinay. BS, UCLA, 1959, LLB, 1962. Co-chmn., CEO, pres. Roll Internat. Corp., LA; chmn., CEO The Franklin Mint, Aston, Pa., 1985—; co-chmn., CEO Teleflora, LA; pres. Paramount Farms, Inc., LA; other subsidiaries of Roll Internat. Corp. include Paramount Citrus, Fiji Water, POM Wonderful. Bd. trustees J. Paul Getty Trust, LA, 2005—; mem. bd. Caltech, Bard Coll., Conservation Internat. Named one of Top 200 Collectors, ARTnews, 2008. Avocations: health and fitness related activities, collecting Old Masters. Office: Roll Internat Corp 10th Fl 11444 W Olympic Blvd Los Angeles CA 90064 Office Phone: 310-966-5700. Office Fax: 310-914-4747.

RESNIK, ROBERT, medical educator; b. New Haven, Dec. 7, 1938; s. Nathan Alfred and Elsie (Hershman) R.; m. Lauren Brahms, Oct. 29, 1966; children: Andrew Scott, Jamie Layne. BA, Yale U., 1960; MD, Case Western Res. U., 1965. Intern in internal medicine Mt. Sinai Hosp., Cleve., 1965-66; resident in ob-gyn. Yale U. Sch. Medicine, 1966-70; asst. prof. Sch. Medicine U. Calif., San Diego, 1974-78, assoc. prof., 1978-82, prof. reproductive medicine, 1982—, chmn. dept., 1982-95, dean clin. affairs, 1988-90, dean admissions, 1995—2003. Cons. Nat. Heart, Lung and Blood Inst. NIH, Washington, 1987; mem. exec. com. Coun. Residency Edn. Ob-Gyn, Washington, 1988-94, residency rev. com., 1988-94. Editor: (textbook) Maternal-Fetal Medicine: Principles and Practice, 1984, 5th edit., 2004; contbr. numerous articles to profl. jours. Major U.S. Army, 1970-72. Recipient Lifetime Achievement award, Soc. Maternal Fetal Medicine, 2004, Mentor of Yr., U. Calif. San Diego, 2005; Rsch. grantee, Nat. Found., NIH. Fellow: Royal Coll. Obstet. Gynecologists (ad eundem), N.W. Obstet. Gynecological Soc., Pacific Coast Obstet. and Gynecol. Soc., Am. Coll. Ob-Gyn. (vice chmn. obs. practice com. 1998—2000), New England Obstet. Gynecological Soc.; mem.: San Diego Gynecol. Soc. (pres. 1982), Am. Gynecologic and Obstet. Soc. (pres. 2009—), Perinatal Rsch. Soc. (pres. 1985), Soc. Gynecologic Investigation (coun. 1983—88), Yale Club, Am. Gynecol. Club (pres. 2002—03). Office: UCSD Med Ctr 200 W Arbor Dr 8433 San Diego CA 92103-8433 Business E-Mail: rresnik@ucsd.edu.

RESSLER, ALISON S., lawyer; b. NYC, 1958; AB, Brown U., 1980; JD, Columbia U., 1983. Bar: NY 1984, Calif. 1985. Ptnr., corp. fin. Sullivan & Cromwell, LA, and mem., mgmt. com. Deans coun. Columbia Law Sch.; trustee Brown Univ., Harvard Westlake. Office: Sullivan & Cromwell LLP 1888 Century Park E Los Angeles CA 90067-1725 Office Phone: 310-712-6600. Office Fax: 310-712-8800.

RETALLACK, GREGORY JOHN, geologist, educator; b. Hobart, Australia, Nov. 8, 1951; arrived in U.S., 1977; s. Kenneth John Retallack and Moira Wynn (Dean) Gollan; m. Diane Alice Retallack, May 31, 1981; children: Nicholas John, Jeremy Douglas. BA, Macquarie U., Sydney, 1973; BSc with honors, U. New Eng., 1974, PhD, 1978. Vis. asst. prof. No. Ill. U., DeKalb, 1977—78; vis. scholar Ind. U., Bloomington, 1978—81; asst. prof. U. Oreg., Eugene, 1981—86, assoc. prof., 1986—92, prof., 1992—. Author: Late Eocene and Oligocene Paleosols from Badlands National Park, South Dakota, 1983, Soils of the Past, 1990, 2d edit., 2001, Miocene Paleosols and Ape Habitats in Pakistan and Kenya, 1991, Colour Guide to Paleosols, 1997; contbr. articles to profl. jours. Grantee, NSF, 1979—, Wenner-Gren Found., 1983. Fellow: AAAS, Geol. Soc. Am.; mem.: Soc. Econ. Paleontologists and Mineralogists, Oreg. Acad. Sci. (pres. 1986), Paleontology Soc. (pres. Pacific sect. 1986), Bot. Soc. Am., Geol. Soc. Australia, Sigma Xi (pres. U. Oreg. chpt. 1983—84). Home: 2715 Elinor St Eugene OR 97403-2513 Office Phone: 541-346-4558. Business E-Mail: gregr@uoregon.edu.

RETHORE, BERNARD GABRIEL, manufacturing and mining company executive, consultant; b. May 22, 1941; s. Francis Joseph and Katharine Eunice (MacDwyer) Rethore; m. Marilyn Irene Watt, Dec. 1, 1962 (div. Apr. 2002); m. Shirley Ann Michels, July 7, 2007; children: Bernard Michael, Tara Jean, Kevin Watt, Alexandra Marie, Rebecca Ann, Christopher Philip, Abigail Lyn, Ryan Victor (Michels). BA, Yale U., 1962; MBA, U. Pa., 1967. Assoc. McKinsey & Co., Inc., Washington, 1967—73, sr. assoc., 1973; v.p., gen. mgr. Greer div. Microdot, Inc., Darien, Conn., 1973—77, v.p. ops. connector group, 1977—78, pres. bus. devel. group, 1978—82, pres. fastening sys. and sealing devices groups, 1982—84; pres. Microdot Industries, Darien, Conn., 1984—87, pres., CEO, 1988; pres. Microdot Europe Ltd., Darien, Conn., 1984—88; sr. v.p. Phelps Dodge Corp., Phoenix, 1989—95; group exec. Phelps Dodge Industries, Phoenix, 1989—90, pres., 1990—95; pres., CEO, bd. dirs. BW/IP Internat., Inc., Long Beach, Calif., 1995—97, chmn., 1997; CEO, chmn. bd. dirs. Flowserve Corp., Dallas, 1997—2000, chmn. emeritus, 2000—; chmn. McDyre & Spendley, Ltd., 2000—. Bd. dirs. Belden, Inc., Dover Corp., Walter Industries, Inc., Mueller Water Products, Inc.; cons. U.S. Govt., UN; dean's adv. bd. Wharton Sch. Bus., U. Pa., 1972—80. Elected mem. bd. fin. Town of Westport, Conn., 1986-90; trustee Ballet Ariz., 1989-95, vice chmn., 1991-95; bd. dirs. Boys Hope of Phoenix, 1989-95, Franciscan Renewal Ctr., 2005—, vice chair 2006—; trustee Phoenix Country Day Sch., 1992-2003, adv. trustee, 2003-; mem. global coun. Thunderbird Sch. Global Mgmt., 1990—, chmn., 1991-94, trustee, 1994—, vice chmn., 2004—. Served to capt. inf. US Army, 1962—65. Decorated Bronze Star; named Outstanding Dir., Outstanding Dirs.' Exchange, 2008. Mem. Nat. Assn. Mfrs. (bd. dirs. 1994-95, 96-99), Yale Club (NYC), Union League (Chgo.), Nat. Assn. Corp. Dirs. (blue ribbon com. on bd. role in strategic plan 2000), Gainey Ranch Club (Scottsdale, Ariz.). Home: 7010 East Avenida El Alba Paradise Valley AZ 85253 Office: McDyre & Spendley Ltd 6929 N Hayden Rd Ste 4C-401 Scottsdale AZ 85250 Office Phone: 480-368-8033. Personal E-mail: bgreth@aol.com.

RETHORE, BERNARD M., lawyer; b. Ft. Bragg, NC; BA, LeMoyne Coll., 1985; JD, Pa. State U. Dickinson Sch. Law, 1988. Bar: Conn. 1988, Pa. 1988, Ariz. 1993. Founding ptnr., mem. estate planning grp. Graves & Rethore, P.C., Phoenix. Named one of Top 100 Attys., Worth mag., 2005. Mem.: Esperti Peterson Inst. Advanced Studies for Estate and Wealth Planning, Pa. State Bar Assn., Conn. State Bar Assn., Maricopa County Bar Assn., Ariz. State Bar Assn. Office: Graves & Rethore PC 5060 N 40th St Ste 112 Phoenix AZ 85018 Office Phone: 602-381-6253. Office Fax: 602-381-6260.

REUBEN, DON, lawyer; s. Michael B. and Sally (Colucci) R.; m. Evelyn Long, Aug. 27, 1948 (div.); children: Hope Reuben Boland, Michael Barrett, Timothy Don, Jeffrey Long, Howard Ellis; m. Jeannette Hurley Haywood, Dec. 13, 1971; stepchildren: Harris Hurley Haywood, Edward Gregory Haywood. BS, Northwestern U., 1949, JD, 1952. Bar: Ill. 1952, Calif. 1996, U.S. Supreme Ct. 1957. With firm Kirkland & Ellis, Chgo., 1952-78, sr. ptnr., Reuben & Proctor, Chgo., 1978-86, Isham, Lincoln & Beale, Chgo., 1986-88; sr. counsel Winston & Strawn, Chgo., 1988-94; of counsel Altheimer & Gray, Chgo., 1994—2003, Fioretti, Lower & Carbonara, Ltd., Chgo., 2007—08, 2008—. Spl. asst. atty. gen. State of Ill., 1963—64, 1969, 84; gen. counsel Tribune Co., 1965—88, Chgo. Bears Football Club, 1965—88, Cath. Archdiocese of Chgo., 1975—88; counsel spl. session Ill. Ho. of Reps., 1964, for Ill. treas. for congl., state legis. and jud. reapportionment, 1963; spl. fed. ct. master, 1968—70; mem. citizens adv. bd. to sheriff County of Cook, 1962—66, jury instrn. com., 1963—73; past mem. pub. rules com. Ill. Supreme Ct., 1963—73; past mem. pub. rels. com. Nat. Conf. State Trial Judges; com. study caseflow mgmt. in law divsn. Cook County Cir. Ct., 1979—88; adv. implementation com. U.S. Dist. Ct. No. Dist. Ill., 1981—82; mem. Chgo. Better Sch. Com., 1968—69, Chgo. Crime Commn., 1970—80; supervisory panel Fed. Defender Program, 1971—78; sec. gen. counsel, chair audit com. Palm Springs Air Mus., 1998—. Bd. dirs. Lincoln Pk. Zool. Soc., 1972—84; trustee Northwestern U., 1977—; mem. vis. com. U. Chgo. Law Sch., 1976—79; bd. dirs. Blood Bank of the Desert, 1999—2004, vice-chmn., 2003—04; chmn. gen. plan adv. com. City of Rancho Mirage, 1994—; dir., sec. Friends of the Animal Campos, 2004—. Recipient Northwestern U. Law Sch. Alumni Merit award, 2002. Fellow: Am. Bar Found., Internat. Acad. Trial Lawyers; mem.: ABA (standing com. on fed. judiciary 1973—79, standing com. on jud. selection, tenure and compensation 1982—85), ADR Sys. America, Desert Bar Assn., Calif. Bar Assn., Am. Arbitration Assn. (nat. panel arbitrators 1998—2008), Am. Coll. Trial Lawyers (Rule 23 com. 1975—82, judiciary com. 1987—91), Am. Law Inst., Chgo. Bar Assn. (chmn. subcom. propriety and regulation of contingent fees com. devel. 1966—69, subcom. on media liaison 1980—82, com. on profl. info. 1980—82), Ill. Bar Assn., Casino Club, Chgo. Club, Mid-Am. Club, Tamarisk Country Club (hon.), Order of Coif, Beta Gamma Sigma, Beta Alpha Psi, Phi Eta Sigma. Roman Catholic. Office: 74-900 Hwy 111 Ste 222 Indian Wells CA 92210 also: 1100 Glendon Ave 10th fl Los Angeles CA 90024 also: 222 S Riverside Plz Ste 1550 Chicago IL 60606-6000 also: 333 W Wacker Dr Ste 1800 Chicago IL 60604 Business E-Mail: dreuben456@yahoo.com.

REULING, MICHAEL FREDERICK, supermarket company, real estate executive; b. Peoria, Ill., May 11, 1946; s. F.H. and Doris (Salzenstein) R.; m. Susan Ruth Morgan, Aug. 10, 1968; children—Jessica Sue, Jeremy Michael BA in Econs., Carleton Coll.; JD, U. Mich. Bar: Utah, Idaho, Tex., Fla. Assoc. Van Cott, Bagley, Cornwall & McCarthy, Salt Lake City, 1971-73; assoc. real estate Skaggs-Albertson's, Richardson, Tex., 1974-78; assoc. contracts Albertson's,

Inc., Boise, Idaho, 1973-74, sr. v.p., gen. counsel, 1978-81, sr. v.p. real estate, 1981-86, exec. v.p. store devel., 1986-99, vice chmn., 1999—. Mem. Idaho State Bar Assn., Utah State Bar Assn., Fla. State Bar Assn., Tex. State Bar Assn.

REVEAL, ERNEST IRA, III, retired lawyer; b. Chgo., Oct. 19, 1948; s. Ernest Ira Jr. and Hazel (Holt) R.; m. Katherine Trennerry, Nov. 24, 1979; children: Genevieve, Adrienne, Danielle. BA, Cornell U., 1970; JD cum laude, U. Mich., 1973. Bar: Minn. 1973, U.S. Dist. Ct. Minn. 1973, U.S. Ct. Appeals (8th cir.) 1974, U.S. Dist. Ct. S.D. 1976, U.S. Ct. Claims 1976, U.S. Ct. Appeals (7th cir.) 1984, U.S. Dist. Ct. (ctrl. dist.) Calif. 1991, U.S. Ct. Appeals (9th cir.) 1991, U.S. Supreme Ct., 1991, U.S. Cir. Ct. Appeals (fed. cir.)2001. Assoc. Robins, Kaplan, Miller & Ciresi, Mpls., 1973—79, ptnr., 1979—2002, mediator, arbitrator, 2003—; temp. judge Orange County Superior Ct., 2007—. Panel mem. Am. Arbitration Assn., Nat. Arbitration Forum, Internat. Inst. Conflict Preservation & Resolution. Author: Public Sector Labor Law, 1983. Pro tem mem. Civil Svc. Commn., St. Paul, 1976; chmn. regional adv. com. So. Calif. Pub. Radio. Mem. ABA, Minn. Bar Assn. (past chair labor and employment law sect.), Calif. State Bar Assn. (adv., past exec. com., antitrust and unfair competition sect.), Cornell Club of Minn. (past pres.). Democrat. Presbyterian. Avocations: history, travel. Office Phone: 949-589-1276. Personal E-mail: ernest.reveal@cox.net.

REVEL, JEAN-PAUL, biology professor; b. Strasbourg, France, Dec. 7, 1930; arrived in U.S., 1953; s. Gaston Benjamin and Suzanne (Neher) Revel; m. Helen Ruth Bowser, July 27, 1957 (div. 1986); children: David, Daniel Neher, Steven Robert; m. Galina Avdeeva Moller, Dec. 24, 1986 (dec. 2004); 1 stepchild, Karen (dec.). BS, U. Strasbourg, 1949; PhD, Harvard U., 1957. Rsch. fellow Cornell U. Med. Sch., NYC, 1958-59; from instr. to prof. Harvard Med. Sch., Boston, 1959-71; prof. Calif. Inst. Tech., Pasadena, 1971—, emeritus, 2006—, AB Ruddock chair in biology, 1978—2006, dean of students, 1996—2005, emeritus, 2006—. Mem. sch. advisors bd. Nat. Insts. Aging, Balt., 1977-80; mem. ad hoc adv. biology NSF, Washington, 1982-83; mem. Nat. High Voltage Microscopy Adv. Group, Bethesda, Md., 1983, Nat. Rsch. Resources Adv. Coun., 1986-90. Author: (with E.D. Hay) Fine Structure of Developing Avian Cornea, 1969, over 150 publs., 1952-99; editor: Cell Shape and Surface Architecture, 1977, Science of Biological Specimen Preparation, 1986; mem. editl. bd. Jour. Cell Biology, 1969-72, Internat. Rev. Cytology, 1970, Cell and Tissue Rsch., 1979—, Molecular and Cell Biology, 1983-91; editor in chief Jour. Microscopy Soc. Am., 1994-96. Fellow AAAS (leader biol. scis. sect. 1991-92, Gordon conf. cell adhesion); mem. Am. Soc. Cell Biology (pres. 1972-73), Electron Micros. Soc. Am. (pres. 1988, Disting. Scientist award 1993), Soc. Devel. Biology. Avocations: watercolors, photography. Office: Calif Inst Tech # 114-96 Pasadena CA 91125-0001 Home Phone: 626-796-0701; Office Phone: 626-395-4986. Business E-Mail: revelj@caltech.edu.

REVILLE, ROBERT T., economist; PhD, Brown U. Economist RAND Inst. Civil Justice, 1995—99, rsch. dir., 1999—2003, dir., 2003—; co-dir. RAND Ctr. for Terrorism Risk Mgmt. Policy. Author of books & articles on workers compensation issues. Mem.: Nat. Acad. Social Insurance (mem. Workers' Compensation Steering Com.). Office: RAND Institute for Civil Justice 1776 Main St PO Box 2138 Santa Monica CA 90407-2138 Office Phone: 310-393-0411. E-mail: reville@rand.org.

REW, LAWRENCE BOYD, lawyer; b. Eugene, Oreg., June 22, 1936; BA, Whitman Coll., 1958; JD, Willamette U., 1961. Bar: Oreg. 1961. Ptnr., of counsel Corey, Byler, Rew, Lorenzen & Hojem, LLP, Pendleton, Oreg., 1965—2005; ret., 2005. Fellow Am. Bar Found.; mem. ABA, Oreg. State Bar Assn. (pres. 2000, Pub. Svc. award 1991, bd. bar examiners 1975-79, bd. govs. 1996-2000).

REWCASTLE, NEILL BARRY, neuropathologist; b. Sunderland, Eng., Dec. 12, 1931; arrived in Can., 1955; s. William Alexander and Eva R.; m. Eleanor Elizabeth Barton Boyd, Sept. 27, 1958 (dec. Jan. 1999); 4 children. MB, BChir cum laude, U. St. Andrews, Scotland, 1955; MA, U. Toronto, 1962. Licentiate Med. Coun. Can., 1957; cert. in gen. pathology, 1962, cert. in neuropathology. Rotating intern Vancouver Gen. Hosp., 1955-56; resident in pathology Shaughnessy Hosp., Vancouver, 1956-57, U. Toronto, Ont., Canada, 1957-60, demonstrator dept. pathology, 1964-65, lectr., acting head divsn. neuropathology, dept. pathology, 1965—69, assoc. prof., 1969-70, prof., head divsn. neuropathology, 1970—81; fellow Med. Rsch. Coun. Can., 1960-64; prof. & head dept. pathology U. Calgary, 1981-91, prof., 1981-2000, prof. emeritus pathology, lab. medicine, clin. neuroscis., 2000—, mem. neurosci. rsch. group, 1982—2003; sr. pathologist Toronto Gen. Hosp., 1970—81. Dir. dept. histopathology Foothills Hosp., Calgary, 1981-91, pathologist, 1981—2003, cons. neuropathology, 1981-2003; spl. acad. adv. to dean faculty medicine U. Calgary, 1995-97; presenter in field. Contbr. over 146 articles to profl. jour., chpts. to books. Recipient Queen Elizabeth Silver Jubilee medal, 1977. Fellow: Royal Coll. Physicians & Surgeons Can.; mem. Can. Assn. Neuropathologists (ret. mem., sec. 1965-69, pres. 1976-79), Am. Assn. Neuropathologists (sr.), Sunshine Coast Power and Sail Squadron (bd. dirs., comdr. 2007-), Gibsons Curling Club (bd. dirs.) Sunshinre Cost Golf and Country Club. Avocations: gardening, philately, golf, curling, sailing. Personal E-mail: rewcastb@telus.net.

REYES, ED P., councilman; b. LA; m to Martha Reyes; children: Natalie, Eddie Jr., Adan & Angel. BA, M, UCLA. Planner, econ. development specialist, legislation dep., & chief of staff to LA City Coun. Mem. Mike Hernandez; councilman, Dist. 1 LA City Coun., 2001—, chmn. planning & land use mgmt. com., vice chmn. transp. com., vice chmn. public safety com., mem. housing and cmty. development com.; vice chmn. Pasadena Blue Line Transit Authority. Office: City Hall 200 N Spring St Rm 410 Los Angeles CA 90012 also: Dist Office Rm 202 163 S Ave 24 Los Angeles CA 90031 Office Phone: 213-473-7001, 213-485-0763. Office Fax: 213-485-8907, 213-485-8908. Business E-Mail: councilmember.reyes@lacity.org.*

REYES, GEORGE, retired information technology executive; b. 1954; BA in Acctg., U. South Fla.; MBA, Santa Clara U., 1979. V.p., corp. contr. Sun Microsystems Inc., Santa Clara, Calif., 1994—99, v.p., treas., 1999—2001; interim CFO ONI Systems, 2002; v.p., CFO Google Inc., Mountain View, Calif., 2002—06, sr. v.p., CFO, 2006—08. Bd. dirs. Informix Corp., 1998—, Symantec Corp., 2000—, Chordiant Software, Inc., 2001—04, BEA Systems Inc., 2003—, LifeLock, Inc., 2008—.

REYES, GREGORY L., former communications executive; V.p. sales and support Convergent Techs., Banyan Sys.; divsn. v.p. Norand Data Sys.; pres., CEO Wireless Access, Inc., Brocade Comm. Sys., Inc., San Jose, Calif., 1998—2005. Charged in 2006 with falsifying documents such as meeting minutes and financial documents.; Found guilty, including charges of securities fraud, conspiracy, and of falsifying financial records on August 7, 2007.; Sentenced to 21 months in prison for orchestrating a scheme to tamper with financial records of stock options the company offered on Jan. 16, 2008.

REYES ROBBINS, ANN MARIE, lawyer, researcher, educator, former magistrate judge; b. LA, Mar. 9, 1966; d. Raymond Alexander and Flora (Sanchez) Reyes; m. Jeffrey Warren Schroeder, Sept. 20, 1986 (div. July 22, 1997); 1 child, Andrew Nicholas Reyes Schroeder; m. Bruce Anthony Robbins, Nov. 7, 1997. BA in Am. Lit. and Bus. minor with honors, U. So. Calif., LA, 1994; attending, U. So. Calif., 2005—; JD, U. Mich., Ann Arbor, 1998; AA in Social and Behavioral Scis., Mt. San Antonio Coll., Walnut, Calif., 2004, AA in Fine Arts and Humanities, 2004, AA in Lang. Arts and Communication, 2005; grad. cert. in Pub. Policy, U. So. Calif., LA, 2007. Bar: Ind. 1999, US Dist. Ct. (so and no. dists.) Ind. 1999, cert.: Ind. Jud. Ctr. (probation officer) 1998, Ind. (domestic rels. mediator) 1999, Ind. Bar Assn. (family law specialist) 2002. Edn. track liaison, title IV-E waiver coord. Allen Superior Ct. Family Rels. Divsn., Fort Wayne, Ind., 1998, asst. chief juvenile probation officer, adminstrv. divsn., 1999—99; assoc. atty. Avery & Van Gilder, Fort Wayne, Ind., 1999—2000; assoc. atty., jr. ptnr. Blume Connelly Jordan & Stucky, LLP, Fort Wayne, Ind., 2000—01, ptnr., 2002; magistrate judge Allen Superior Ct. Family Rels. Divsn., Fort Wayne, Ind., 2003; family law specialist Mallor, Clendening, Grodner & Bohrer LLP, Bloomington, Ind., 2003—04; tchr. Elite Ednl. Inst., Rowland Heights, Calif., 2004—05; sr. pub. adminstrv. analyst, dept. social welfare Children and Families Rsch. Consortium, Inter-U. Consortium Social Work Schs., U. Calif., LA, 2006; rsch. asst., ctr. rsch. crime and social control U. So. Calif., 2006—07, rsch. asst., Gould School of Law, 2007—; rsch. asst. U. So. Calif. Sch. Social Work, 2005—07; tchg. asst., part-time faculty U. So. Calif. Sch. Policy, Planning, Devel., 2007—. Trial atty. Allen County Divsn. Children and Family Svcs., Ft. Wayne, 1999—2000; continuing legal edn. tchr., Ind., 2000—04; gen. counsel Allen County Apptd. Spl. Advs., 2001—02; com. mem. Ind. 3rd Dist. Pro Bono Commn., Fort Wayne, 2002—03; lectr. in field; cons. in field. Latino/Hispanic liaison Allen County Dem. Party, Fort Wayne, Ind., 2001, vice chair, 2002; bd. dirs. Assn. Hispanic Profls. Edn., LA, 1992—95, vice chair fin., 1994—95; v.p. League of United Latin Am. Citizens, Fort Wayne, Ind., 1999—2000; bd. dirs. United Hispanic Ams., Fort Wayne, 1999—2001, Ind. Minority Health Coalition, 2001—02, Vol. Lawyers Program, Fort Wayne, 2002—04; pres. Allen County Minority Health Coalition, Fort Wayne, 2001—02; mem. parent adv. com. Diabetech, Inc., Dallas, 2003—. Fellow Kellogg/Bergstom Child Welfare Law Summer Fellow, U. Mich. Law Sch., 1997, Mexican Am. Legal Def. and Edn. Fund, Pub. Interest Law Initiative (PILI), 1997, Hispanic Lawyers Assn., 1997; scholar Juan Luis Tienda scholarship, U. Mich. Law Sch., 1996. Fellow: Ind. Bar Found.; mem.: Juvenile Diabetes Rsch. Found. Internat., Am. Diabetes Assn., Soc. Social Work and Rsch., Coun. Social Work Edn., Nat. Ct. Apptd. Spl. Advs., Nat. Assn. of Counsel for Children, Ind. State Bar Assn., Hispanic Nat. Bar Assn., U. Mich. Alumni Assn., UCLA Anderson Sch. Mgmt. Riordan Fellows Alumni Assn., U. So. Calif. Mexican Am. Alumni Assn. Democrat. Office: U Southern Calif Sch Policy Planning and Devel CUB 313 Univ Pk Los Angeles CA 90089 Office Fax: 213-743-1581. Personal E-mail: childlaw@charter.net. Business E-Mail: reyesrob@usc.edu.

REYNDERS, JOHN VAN WICHEREN, computational physicist; b. NYC, May 24, 1964; s. Charlton Jr. and Knowlton (Ames) R.; m. Mary Frances Neven, Oct. 8, 1994; 1 child, Rebecca. BS, Rensselaer Poly. Inst., 1986; PhD, Princeton U., 1992. Team leader Los Alamos (N.Mex.) Nat. Lab., 1992-93, mem. staff, 1993-94, postdoctoral rsch. assoc., 1994—. Mem. Am. Phys. Soc. Methodist. Office: Los Alamos Nat Lab Mail Stop B287 Los Alamos NM 87545-0001 Home: 49 Adams Ave West Newton MA 02465-1001

REYNOLDS, BURT, actor, film director; b. Waycross, Ga., Feb. 11, 1936; s. Burt R.; m. Judy Carne (div. 1965); m. Loni Anderson, Apr. 29, 1988 (div. 1994). Ed., Fla. State U., Palm Beach Jr. Coll. Owner ranch, Jupiter, Fla. Actor numerous stage prodns. including The Rainmaker; movie appearances include: Angel Baby, 1961, Armored Command, 1961, Operation CIA, 1965, Navajo Joe, 1967, Impasse, 1969, 100 Rifles, 1969, Sam Whiskey, 1969, Skullduggery, 1970, Shark, 1970, Deliverance, 1972, Fuzz, 1972, Everything You've Always Wanted to Know about Sex But Were Afraid to Ask, 1972, Shamus, 1973, The Man Who Loved Cat Dancing, 1973, White Lightning, 1973, The Longest Yard, 1974, At Long Last Love, 1975, W.W. and the Dixie Dance Kings, 1975, Hustle, 1975, Lucky Lady, 1975, Silent Movie, 1976, Nickelodeon, 1976, Smokey and the Bandit, 1977, Semi-Tough, 1977, Hooper, 1978, Starting Over, 1979, Rough Cut, 1980, Smokey and the Bandit II, 1980, Cannonball Run, 1981, Paternity, 1981, The Best Little Whorehouse in Texas, 1982, Best Friends, 1982, Stroker Ace, 1983, The Man Who Loved Women, 1983, City Heat, 1984, Cannonball Run II, 1984, Stick, 1985, Uphill All The Way, 1986, Rent A Cop, 1987, Heat, 1987, Malone, 1987, Switching Channels, 1988, Physical Evidence, 1989, Breaking In, 1989, Modern Love, 1990, Cop and a Half, 1993, also voice in All Dogs Go To Heaven, 1989, The Maddening, 1996, Striptease, 1996, Ravin, 1996, Mad Dog Time, 1996, Frankenstein and Me, 1996, Citizen Ruth, 1996, Meet Wally Sparks, 1997, Crazy Six, 1997, Boogie Nights, 1997, Raven, 1997, Waterproof, 1998, Mystery Alaska, 1998, The Hunter's Moon, 1998, Without a Paddle, 2004, The Librarians, 2004, Grilled, 2005, Forget About It, 2005, The Longest Yard, 2005, The Dukes of Hazzard, 2005, Broken Bridges, 2006, Deal, 2008, In the Name of the King: A Dungeon Siege Tale, 2008, (voice) Delgo, 2008; dir., actor: Gator, 1976, The End, 1978, Sharkey's Machine, 1981; TV appearances include: M Squad, 1959, Alfred Hitchcock Presents, 1960, Zane Grey Theater, 1961, Route 66, 1962, Perry Mason, 1962, The Twilight Zone, 1963, Branded, 1965, Flipper, 1965, Twelve O'Clock High, 1965, The Carol Burnett Show, 1967, The FBI, 1968, Love American Style, 1970, The Golden Girls, 1986, Dolly, 1987, Beverly Hills, 90210, 1993, The Larry Sanders Show, 1993, Hope & Gloria, 1995, Cybill, 1995, (voice) King of the Hill, 1997, The X Files, 2002, Hollywood Squares, 2002, Ed, 2003, Dinner for Five, 2004, The King of Queens, 2005; regular appearances on Gunsmoke, 1962-65; star series Hawk, 1966, Dan August, 1970-71, B.L. Stryker, 1989, ABC Saturday Mystery Movie, 1988, Evening Shade, 1990-94, (TV movie) The Cherokee Kid, 1996. Recipient Emmy award as Outstanding Lead Actor in a Comedy Series ("Evening Shade") Nat. Acad. TV Arts and Scis., 1991. Mem. Dirs. Guild Am. Office: Jeffrey Lane & Associates 155 N Crescent Dr Apt 416 Beverly Hills CA 90210-5430

REYNOLDS, JAMES FRANCIS, JR., physician; b. St. Albans, Vt., June 20, 1947; s. James F. Sr. and Eleanor (Paquette) R.; married; children: Matthew, Katelyn, Aaron. BS, U.S. Mil. Acad., West Point, NY, 1969; MD, U. Louisville, 1978. Diplomate Am. Bd. Pediatrics, Am. Bd. Med. Genetics. Commd. U.S. Army, 1969, advanced through grades to brig. gen., 2003; pediatrics resident U. Va., Charlottesville, 1978-81, genetics fellow, 1981-83; clin. geneticist dept. med. genetics Shodair Hosp., Helena, Mont., 1983—. Assoc. editor Am. Jour. Med. Genetics, 1983-95; editor various books on med. genetics; contbr. articles to profl. jours. Mem. health profl. adv. com. Mont. March of Dimes, 1987—; mem. Mont. Coun. for Maternal and Child Health, 1987—. Fellow Am. Acad. Pediatrics, Am. Coll. Med. Genetics; mem. Am. Soc. Human Genetics. Avocations: hiking, skiing. Office: Shodair Hosp PO Box 5539 Helena MT 59604-5539

REYNOLDS, JERRY OWEN, professional sports team executive; b. French Lick, Ind., Jan. 29, 1944; m. Dodie Reynolds; children: Danielle, Jay. Student, Vincennes U.; grad., Oakland City Coll., Ind., 1966; student, Ind. U.; M in Phys. Edn., Ind. State U., 1970. Coach Rockhurst Coll., Kansas City, Mo., 1975—84, Pittsburg State U., Kans., 1984—85; asst. coach Sacramento Kings, 1985—88, head coach, 1987, 1988—89, dir. player pers., 1990—92, dir. player pers., TV color analyst, 1994—, gen. mgr., 1992—93; gen. mgr, v.p. WNBA Sacramento Monarchs, 1998—2003. Mem. USA Basketball Women's Sr. Nat. Team Com., 2001—04. Office: Sacramento Kings 1 Sports Pkwy Sacramento CA 95834-2300

REYNOLDS, JOHN FRANCIS, insurance company executive; b. Escanaba, Mich., Mar. 29, 1921; s. Edward Peter and Lillian (Harris) R.; m. Dorothy Gustafson, May 1, 1946; children: Lois, Margaret, Michael. BS, Mich. State U., 1942. Claims and assoc. surety mgr. Hartford Ins. Co., Escanaba, Mich. and Chgo., 1946-55; asst. v.p., bond mgr. Wolverine Ins. Co., Battle Creek, Mich., 1955-64, v.p. underwriting, 1964-69; Midwest zone underwriting mgr. Transamerica Ins. Co. (Wolverine Ins. Co.), Battle Creek, Mich., 1969-74; pres., gen. mgr. Can. Surety Co. subs. Transamerica Ins. Co., Toronto, Ont., Canada, 1974-75; v.p. midwestern zone mgr. Transamerica Ins. Group, Battle Creek, Mich., 1975-83, pres., chief operating officer Los Angeles, 1983-84, chmn., chief exec. officer, 1984-85; apptd. spl. dep. ins. commr., dep. conservator Cadillac Inc. Co., 1989. Pres. Underwriting Exec. Council Midwest, 1967; dir. Underwriters Adjustment Bur., Toronto, 1974, Underwriters Labs. of Canada, Montreal, 1974; chmn. Mich. Assn. Ins. Cos., Lansing, 1976, Mich. Basic Property Ins. Assn., Detroit, 1973. Commr. City of Battle Creek, 1967-69; dir. Urban League, Battle Creek, 1969, 70, dir. Mich. Ins. Fedn., Lansing, 1975-83. Served to sgt. U.S. Army, 1942-45; New Guinea Roman Catholic. Avocations: golf, fishing. Home: 14037 N Cameo Dr Sun City AZ 85351-2903 Personal E-mail: reynolds213@yahoo.com.

REYNOLDS, ROGER LEE, composer, educator; b. Detroit, July 18, 1934; s. George Arthur and Katherine Adelaide (Butler) Reynolds; m. Karen Jeanne Hill, Apr. 11, 1964; children: Erika Lynn, Wendy Claire. BSE in Physics, U. Mich., 1957, MusB in Music Lit., 1960, MusM in Composition, 1961. Assoc. prof. U. Calif. San Diego, La Jolla, 1969—73, founding dir. Ctr. Music Expt. and Related Rsch., 1972—77, prof., 1973—; George Miller prof. U. Ill., 1971—. Vis. prof. Yale U., New Haven, 1981; sr. rsch. fellow ISAM Bklyn. Coll., 1985; Valentine prof. Amherst (Mass.) Coll., 1988; Rothschild composer in residence Peabody Conservatory of Music, 1992—93; pub. Peters Music Pubs.; mgr. Graham Hayter, Contemporary Music Promotions. Author: MIND MODELS: New Forms of Musical Experience, 1975, A Searcher's Path: A Composer's Ways, 1987, A Jostled Silence: Contemporary Japanese Musical Thought, 1992—93, Form and Method: Composing Music, 2002; first Dolby Digital 5.1 DVD release of custom-designed, multichannel classical compositions: WATERSHED, Mode Records, 1998; contbr. numerous articles and revs. to profl. jours. Mem. bd. govs. Inst. Current World Affairs; co-founder ONCE festivals, 1960; bd. dirs. Am. Music Ctr., Meet the Composer; bd. dirs. Fromm Found. Harvard U. Recipient Koussevitzky Internat. Rec. Award, 1970, Nat. Inst. Arts and Letters award, 1971, NEA awards, 1975, 1978, 1979, 1986, Pulitzer prize for music, 1989; named sr. fellow, Inst. Studies in Am. Music, 1985, fellow, Inst. Current World Affairs, Rockefeller Found., Guggenheim Found., Fulbright scholar. Office: U Calif San Diego Dept Music 0326 La Jolla CA 92093 Office Phone: 858-534-3230.

REYNOLDS, RYAN RODNEY, actor; b. Vancouver, BC, Can., Oct. 23, 1976; s. Jim and Tammy Reynolds; m. Scarlett Johansson, Sept. 27, 2008. Actor: (TV series) Hillside, 1990, The Odyssey, 1993—94, The Outer Limits, 1995—98, Two Guys, a Girl and a Pizza Place, 1998—2001; (films) Ordinary Magic, 1993, Life During Wartime, 1997, Coming Soon, 1999, Dick, 1999, Big Monster on Campus, 2000, We All Fall Down, 2000, Finder's Fee, 2001, Van Wilder, 2002, Buying the Cow, 2002, The In-Laws, 2003, Foolproof, 2003, Harold & Kumar Go to White Castle, 2004, Blade: Trinity, 2004, The Amityville Horror, 2005, Waiting, 2005, Smokin' Aces, 2006, The Nines, 2007, Chaos Theory, 2007, Definitely, Maybe, 2008, Fireflies in the Garden, 2008, X-Men Origins: Wolverine, 2009. Office: c/o United Talent Agy 9560 Wilshire Blvd Ste 500 Beverly Hills CA 90212-6700

REYNOLDS, STEPHEN PHILIP, utility company executive; b. Berkeley, Calif., Jan. 5, 1948; s. Philip Elmore and Annette (Medefind) R.; m. Sharon Ann Rudd, Sept. 6, 1969; 1 child, Matthew. BA in Econs., U. Calif., Berkeley, 1970; MBA in Prodn. Mgmt., U. Oreg., 1972. Various mktg./rate positions Pacific Gas and Electric Co., San Francisco, 1967-75, sr. rate engr., 1975-77, supervising rate engr., 1977-80, mgr. rate dept., 1980-84, v.p. rates, 1984-87; pres., CEO Pacific Gas Transmission Co. (subs. Pacific Gas and Electric), 1987—98, Reynolds Energy Internat., 1998—2002; chmn., pres., CEO Puget Energy, Bellevue, Wash., 2002—. Bd. dirs. UNOVA Inc., Oregon Steel Mills Inc., InfrastruX Group., Interstate Gas of Am., Interstate Gas of Am. Found., Assn. of Northwest Gas Utilities. Contbr. numerous articles to trade publs. and profl. symposiums on rate issues. Served with Calif. Army N.G., 1970-76. Mem. Pacific Coast Gas Assn., Nat. Planning Assn. (Canadian-American Com.), Calif. Found. on Environment & Economy, San Francisco World Affairs Coun., San Francisco Engrs. Club, Commonwealth Club, World Trade Club. Office: Puget Energy 10885 NE 4th St PO Box 97034 Bellevue WA 98009-9734

REYNVAAN, MICHAEL THOMAS, lawyer; b. Bremerton, Wash., Sept. 26, 1953; s. Theodore Thomas Reynvaan and Clara Anne (Malinowski) Reynvaan-Graves; m. Gale Arlene Beegle; children: Amanda, Angela, Matthew. Student, Whitman Coll., 1971-73; BA in Polit. Sci, Lewis and Clark Coll., 1976; JD, U. Puget Sound, 1982. Bar: Wash. 1982, US Dist. Ct. (We. Dist.) Wash. 1983, US Ct. Appeals

(9th Cir.) 1983, US Dist. Ct. (Ea. Dist.) Wash. 1985. Mill worker Internat. Telephone & Telegraph/Rayonier Inc., Hoquiam, Wash., 1976-77, 79; legal asst. Bogle & Gates, Seattle, 1979; law clk. to chief justice Wash. State Supreme Ct., Olympia, 1982-83; assoc. Perkins Coie, Seattle, 1983—, ptnr., mem. mgmt. com. & exec. com. Active Alki Found., Seattle, 1988, Leadership Tomorrow, 1988—; campaign treas. Callow for Supreme Ct., Seattle, 1984; del. Kitsap County Dem. Conv. Mem. ABA (YLD labor law com., vice-chair 1988-89, chmn. 1989—), Seattle-King County Bar Assn. (young lawyers div., bd. trustees), Wash. State Bar Assn., Wash. Athletic Club. Episcopalian. Office: Perkins Coie LLP 1201 3rd Ave Fl 40 Seattle WA 98101-3029 Office Phone: 206-359-8469. Office Fax: 206-359-9000. Business E-Mail: mreynvaan@perkinscoie.com.

REZNICK, RICHARD HOWARD, pediatrician; b. Chgo., Oct. 31, 1939; s. Louis and Mae Reznick; m. Barbara Ann Glantz, June 20, 1965; children: Steven L., Alicia T., Scott M., Stacey R. BS, U. Ill., 1961; MD, Loyola U., Chgo., 1965. Diplomate Am. Bd. Pediatrics. Resident in pediat. Michael Reese Hosp., Chgo., 1966-68; pediatrician USAF, Homestead AFB, Fla., 1968-70; pediatrician pvt. practice Winnetka, Ill., 1970—71, Scottsdale, Ariz., 1971—. Pres. med. staff Phoenix Children's Hosp., 1990-93, bd. dirs. 1990-94. Capt. USAF, 1968-70. Fellow Am. Acad. Pediatrics (treas. Ariz. chpt. 1982-84); mem. Ariz. Med. Assn., Phoenix Pediatric Soc. (treas. 1976-77), Maricopa County Med. Soc. Avocations: aerobics, bicycling, gardening, classical music, collecting stamps. Office: Papago Buttes Pediatric Ctr 8573 E San Alberto Ste E100 Scottsdale AZ 85258-4318 Office Phone: 480-778-1732.

RHEAULT, KEITH W., school system administrator; m. Denise Rheault; 4 children. BS, ND State U., 1976, MS in Agrl. Edn., 1980; PhD in Agrl. Edn., Iowa State U., 1985. With Nev. Dept. Edn., 1986—, agriculture edn. cons., state FFA adv., asst. dir. to dir. Office of Occupational and Continuing Edn., dep. supt. for Instructional, Rsch. and Evaluative Svcs., supt. pub. instrn., 2004—. Adj. prof. Agrl. Engring. Dept. Iowa State U. Officer USAR, 1977—85. Office: Nev Dept Edn 700 E Fifth St Carson City NV 89701-5096 Office Phone: 775-687-9217. Office Fax: 775-687-5660, 775-687-9101. E-mail: krheault@doe.nv.gov.

RHEIN, TIMOTHY J., retired transportation company executive; b. 1941; BS, U. Santa Clara, 1962. Mil. contract and revenue analyst Am. Pres. Lines Ltd., Oakland, Calif., 1967-71, sr. analyst, 1971-72, mgr. mktg. planning, 1972-73, dir. traffic systems and adminstrn., 1973-75, dir. mktg. adminstrn., 1975-76, dir. worldwide sales, 1976-78, v.p. N.Am., 1978-80, v.p. traffic, 1980-84, sr. v.p., 1984-87, pres., also chief oper. officer, 1987-90; pres., chief exec. officer APL Ltd., Oakland, Calif., 1990-2000, retired, 2000. With U.S. Army, 1962-67. Office: APL Ltd 1111 Broadway Fl 25 Oakland CA 94607-4036

RHEINGOLD, TED, Internet company executive; BA in Internat. Rels., U. Penn., 1992. Adminstrv. dir. Calif. Coun. Internat. Trade, San Francisco; web designer, software engr. Preview Travel (now Travelocity.com); sr. web application developer Voquette, Inc. (now Semagix); founder OneMatchFire.com, San Francisco, 2002; founder, CEO Dogster.com, San Francisco, 2004—, Catster.com, 2004—. Fellow Internat. Devel. Exch. Office: Dogster Inc Ste 350 555 De Haro St San Francisco CA 94107 Office Phone: 415-934-0400. Office Fax: 415-864-6261. E-mail: ted@dogster.com.

RHEINISH, ROBERT KENT, university administrator; b. Mt. Vernon, NY, Oct. 27, 1934; s. Walter Washington and Doris Elizabeth (Standard) R.; m. Dorothy Ellen Steadman, May 3, 1957 (div. 1975); children: Deborah Marie, Robert Scott, Joel Nelson; m. Shirley Marie Suter, Aug. 1, 1976. BA, U. South Fla., 1963; MS, Ind. U., 1969, EdD, 1971. Staff engr. Armed Forces Radio & TV Svc., Anchorage, 1960-61; trainee Nat. Park Svc. Tng. Ctr., Grand Canyon, Ariz., 1965; historian Home of F.D.R., Nat. Historic Site, Hyde Park, N.Y., 1964-65, Sagamore Hill Nat. Hist. Site, Oyster Bay, N.Y., 1965-66; asst. coord. nat. environ. edn. devel. program Dept. of Interior, Washington, 1968; supervisory historian Lincoln Boyhood Nat. Meml., Lincoln City, Ind., 1966-68; dir. learning resources ctr. Whittier (Calif.) Coll., 1971-73; dir. media and learning resources Calif. State U., Long Beach, 1973-88. Chmn. media dirs. The Calif. State Univs., Long Beach, 1975-76; radio announcer Sta. WTCX-FM, St. Petersburg, Fla., 1961-63; co-host with David Horowitz (2 broadcasts) On Campus, Sta. KNBC-TV, L.A., 1972-73; guest lectr. 6th Army Intelligence Sch., Los Alamitos Armed Forces Res. Ctr., 1987; founder Rheino Ltd., 1997. Coord. multi-media program: In Search of Yourself, 1975 (Silver award Internat. Film and TV Festival of N.Y.), The House that Memory Built, 1981 (Cindy award Info. Film Producers of Am.), The Indochinese and Their Cultures, 1985 (Silver award Internat. Film & TV Festival of N.Y.); holder 2 patents. With RCAF, 1954-55, USAF, 1957-61. U.S. Office of Edn. grad. fellow, 1969-71; recipient Learning Resources Ctr. Devel. Fund award Pepsico, Sears, Prentice-Hall, et al, 1973; Nat. Def. Edn. Act grantee, 1974-76. Mem. NRA, VFW, Am. Legion (life). Republican. Avocations: collecting militaria, boating, political writing. Home: 380 Long Br W Prescott AZ 86303-5306 E-mail: rheino@commspeed.net.

RHENEY, SUSAN O., paper company executive; MBA, Harvard Univ. CPA. Public acctg. auditor Deloitte & Touche; prin. Sterling Group LP (parent co., Mail-Well), 1992—2001; dir. Mail-Well, 1993—97; interim chmn. Cenveo (formerly Mail-Well), 2005—. Bd. dir. Genesis Energy LP, Cenveo, 2003—. Office Phone: 303-790-8023. Office Fax: 303-566-7466.

RHIMES, SHONDA, producer, director, writer; b. Chgo., Jan. 13, 1970; 1 adopted child. Harper. BA in English, Dartmouth Coll., Hanover, NH, 1991; MFA, U. So. Calif., 1994. Dir., writer: (films) Blossoms and Veils, 1998; writer Crossroads, 2002; The Princess Diaries 2: Royal Engagement, 2004; exec. prodr., writer: (TV series) Grey's Anatomy, 2005— (Norman Felton Prodr. of Yr. award in Episodic TV, Prodrs. Guild of America, 2007, NAACP Image award for Outstanding Writing in Drama Series, 2007, 2008, Golden Globe award, Best Drama TV Series, 2007). Named one of The World's Most Influential People, TIME mag., 2007, 40 Under 40, Advt. Age, 2007; named to Power 150, Ebony mag., 2008. Office: c/o ABC TV 500 S Buena Vista St Burbank CA 91521-4551

RHINES, PETER BROOMELL, oceanographer, atmospheric scientist; b. Hartford, Conn., July 23, 1942; s. Thomas B. and Olive (Symonds) R.; m. Marie Louise Lenos, Oct. 12, 1968; (div. 1983); m. Linda Jean Mattson; 1 child, Andrew Nelson BS, MS, M.I.T., Cambridge U., 1964; PhD, Trinity Coll., Cambridge U., Eng., 1967. Asst. prof. oceanography M.I.T., Cambridge, 1968-71; rsch. asst. dept. applied math. and theoretical physics Cambridge U., Eng., 1971-72; scientist Woods Hole Oceanographic Inst., Woods Hole, Mass., 1972-84; prof. oceanography and atmospheric scis. U. Wash., Seattle, 1984—. Vis. fellow Christ's Coll., Cambridge, Eng., 1979-80, 1983 Recipient de Florez research award MIT, 1963; NSF fellow, 1963-64; Guggenheim fellow, 1979-80; Queen's fellow in marine scis., Australia, 1988; A.E. Sloan Research scholar MIT, 1960-63; Marshall scholar Cambridge, 1964-67; Green scholar U. Calif., San Diego, 1981. Fellow Am. Geophys. Union, Am. Meteorol. Soc. (Henry Stommel award 1999); mem. Am. Acad. Arts and Scis., Nat. Acad. Scis. Avocations: guitar, walking, studying global environment. Home: 5753 61st Ave NE Seattle WA 98105-2037 Office: U Wash Sch Oceanography Dept Oceanography Seattle WA 98195-0001

RHOADS, DEAN A., state legislator; b. Tonasket, Wash., Oct. 5, 1935; m to Sharon Packer; children: Shammy & Chandra. Nevada State Assemblyman, District 33, 1977-81; president, Elko Co Fair Bd, formerly; president, Public Lands Coun, formerly; member, President Reagan's Federalism Advisor Committee, formerly; member, Nevada Bureau Land Management District Grazing Bd, currently; Nevada State Senator, Rural Nevada Senatorial District, 1985—, Majority Whip, 2003-2006, chairman, Committee on Transportation, 1985, Committee on Taxation, 1993, Committee on Nat Resources, from 1995, Legislature Committee on Public Lands, 1985-, member, Interim Finance Committee, 1979-82, 1987-90, 1992-96 & 1998-2006, Committee on Finance, 2003-06, Legislature Comn, 1993-94 & 1999-2000, Nevada State Senate. Rancher, currently; member, Bureau Land Management District Grazing Bd, currently. Nevada Taxpayers Association (director, currently); Nevada Cattlemens Association (director, currently); Nat & Nevada Cattlemens Association; Rotary; America Legislature Exchange Coun (director, currently). Republican. Presbyterian. Mailing: Box 8 Tuscarora NV 89834-0008 E-mail: drhoads@sen.state.nv.us.

RHODE, DEBORAH LYNN, law educator; b. Jan. 29, 1952; BA, Yale U., 1974, JD, 1977. Bar: D.C. 1977, Calif. 1981. Law clk. to judge U.S. Ct. Appeals (2d cir.), NYC, 1977-78; law clk. to Hon. Justice Thurgood Marshall U.S. Supreme Ct., Washington, 1978-79; asst. prof. law Stanford U., Calif., 1979-82, assoc. prof. Calif., 1982-85, prof. Calif., 1985—; dir. Inst. for Rsch. on Women and Gender, 1986-90, Keck Ctr. of Legal Ethics and The Legal Profession, 1994—2003; sr. counsel jud. com. Ho. of Reps., Washington, 1998. Trustee Yale U., 1983-89; pres. Assn. Am. Law Schs., 1998; Ernest W. McFarland prof. Stanford Law Sch., 1997—; sr. counsel com. on the jud. U.S. Ho. of Reps., 1998; dir. Stanford Ctr. Legal Profession, 2008-. Author: Justice and Gender, 1989, (with Geoffrey Hazard) the Legal Profession: Responsibility and Regulation, 3d edit., 1993, (with Annette Lawson) The Politics of Pregnancy: Adolescent Sexuality and Public Policy, 1993, (with David Luban) Legal Ethics, 2005, 4th edit., 2004, Speaking of Sex, 1997, Professional Responsibility: Ethics by the Pervasive Method, 1998, In the Interests of Justice, 2000 (with Geoffrey Hazard, Jr.) Professional Responsibility and Regulation, 2002; editor: Theoretical Perspectives on Sexual Difference, 1990, Ethics in Practice, 2000, The Difference Difference Makes: Women and Leadership, 2002, Access to Justice, 2004, Pro Bono in Principle and in Practice, 2005, (with Katherine Bartlett) Gender and Law, 2005, (with Carol Sanger) Gender and Rights, 2005, Moral Leadership: The Theory and Practice of Power, Judgment and Policy, 2006, In Pursuit of Knowledge: Scholars, Status, and Academic Culture, 2006, Women and Leadership: The State of Play and Strategies for Change, 2007; contbr. articles to profl. jours. Mem.: ABA (chmn. commn. on women 2000—02). Office: Stanford U Law Sch Crown Quadrangle Stanford CA 94305

RHODE, EDWARD ALBERT, veterinary medicine educator, veterinary cardiologist; b. Amsterdam, NY, July 25, 1926; s. Edward A. and Katherine (Webb) R.; m. Dolores Bangert, 1955; children: David E., Peter R., Paul W., Robert M., Catherine E. DVM, Cornell U., 1947. Diplomate Am. Coll. Veterinary Internal Medicine. Prof. emeritus vet. medicine U. Calif., Davis, 1964—, chmn. dept. vet. medicine, 1968-71; assoc. dean instrn. U. Calif. Sch. Vet. Medicine, Davis, 1971-81, dean, 1982-91. Mem. AAAS, Nat. Acad. Practices, Am. Coll. Vet. Internal Medicine, Am. Vet. Medicine Assn., Basic Sci. Coun., Am. Heart Assn., Am. Acad. Vet. Cardiology, Am. Physiol. Soc., Calif. Vet. Medicine Assn. Office: U Calif Sch Vet Med Davis CA 95616 E-mail: earhode@ucdavis.edu.

RHODY, RONALD EDWARD, bank, communications executive; b. Frankfort, Ky., Jan. 27, 1932; s. James B. and Mary M. (Clark) R.; m. Patricia Schupp, Apr. 23, 1955; children: Leslie K., Mary M., Virginia K., Ronald C. Student, Georgetown Coll., Ky., 1950-52, U. Ky., 1953-55. Pub. rels. dir. Kaiser Aluminum & Chem. Corp., Ravenswood, W.Va., 1959-62, NYC, 1962-67, corp. v.p. Oakland, Calif., 1967-83; sr. v.p. corp comm. Bank of Am. NT&SA, San Francisco, 1983—, exec. v.p., 1992-94; CEO Rhody, Inc., 1994—. Author: The CEO's Playbook, 1999, Wordsor Thing, 2006, Theos Story, 2009; contbr. articles to profl. jours. Founding chmn. adv. bd. San Francisco Acad. Named Pub. Rels. Profl. of Yr., Pub. Rels. News, 1981; recipient Hall of Fame award Page Soc., 1997. Fellow Pub. Rels. Soc. Am.; mem. Pub. Rels. Soc. Am. (accredited, pres.'s adv. coun. Rex Harlow award), Internat. Assn. Bus. Communicators (Gold Quill award 1980), Pub. Rels. Roundtable San Francisco (mem. bd. govs., awards 1980, 85). Home: 187 Juniper Creek Blvd Pinehurst NC 28374-6993 E-mail: ron.rhody@yahoo.com.

RHYNE, JAMES JENNINGS, condensed matter physicist; b. Oklahoma City, Nov. 14, 1938; s. Jennings Jefferson and Clyde Margaret (Russell) R.; m. Susan Margaret Watson, May 26, 1990; children: Nancy Marie, Edward Paxton. BS in Physics, U. Okla., 1959; MS in Physics, U. Ill., 1961; PhD in Physics, Iowa State U., 1965. Rsch. scientist Naval Ordnance Lab., White Oak, Md., 1965-75; rsch. physicist Nat. Inst. of Stds. and Tech., Gaithersburg, Md., 1975-90; prof. physics U. Mo., Columbia, 1991—2003, dir. Rsch. Reactor Ctr., 1991-96; dep. group leader Lujan Ctr., Los Alamos Nat. Lab., 2003—. Adv. editor Jour. of Magnetism and Mag. Materials, 1990—; editl. bd. Jour. Applied Physics, 1986-89; co-editor procs. Fellow: Neutron Scattering Soc. Am. (pres. 1999—2002), Am. Phys. Soc. Home Phone: 505-661-8629; Office Phone: 505-665-0071. Personal E-mail: jrhyne@los-alamos.net. Business E-Mail: rhyne@lanl.gov.

RIASANOVSKY, NICHOLAS VALENTINE, retired historian, educator; b. Harbin, China, Dec. 21, 1923; arrived in U.S., 1938, naturalized, 1943; m. Arlene Ruth Schlegel, Feb. 15, 1955; children: John, Nicholas, Maria. BA, U. Oreg., 1942; AM, Harvard U., 1947; DPhil, Oxford U., Eng., 1949. Mem. faculty U. Iowa, 1949-57, U. Calif., Berkeley, 1957—, prof. history, 1961—, Sidney Hellman Ehrman prof. European history, 1969—2003, ret., 2003. Vis. rsch. prof. USSR Acad. Scis., Moscow, 1969, Moscow and Leningrad, 1974, 79. Author: Russia and the West in the Teaching of the Slavophiles: A Study of Romantic Ideology, 1952, Nicholas I and Official Nationality in Russia, 1825-1855, 1959, A History of Russia, 1963, 7th edit. (with Prof. Mark Steinberg), 2005, The Teaching of Charles Fourier, 1969, A Parting of Ways: Government and the Educated Public in Russia, 1801-1855, 1976, The Image of Peter the Great in Russian History and Thought, 1985, The Emergence of Romanticism, 1992, Collected Writings 1947-94, 1993, Russian Identities, a Historical Survey, 2005; co-editor: California Slavic Studies, 1960—; editl. bd. Russian rev., Zarubezhnaia Periodicheskaia Pechat' na Russkom Iazyke, Simvol; contbr. articles to profl. jours. Trustee Nat. Coun. Soviet and East European Rsch., 1978—82; mem. Kennan Inst. Acad. Coun., 1986—89. 2d lt. AUS, 1943—46. Decorated Bronze Star; recipient Silver medal Commonwealth Club Calif., 1964; Rhodes scholar, 1947-49; Fulbright grantee, 1954-55, 74, 79; Guggenheim fellow, 1969; sr. fellow NEH, 1975; Fulbright sr. scholar, sr. fellow Ctr. Advanced Studies in Behavioral Scis., 1984-85; sr. fellow Woodrow Wilson Internat. Ctr. for Scholars, 1989-90. Mem. Am. Assn. Advancement Slavic Studies (pres. 1973-76, Disting. Contbr. award 1993), Am. Hist. Assn. (award for Scholarly Distinction 1995), Am. Acad. Arts and Scis.

RIBAK, CHARLES ERIC, neuroscientist, educator; b. July 19, 1950; s. Marcus and Adele (Blank) R.; m. Julia Marianne Wendruck, Jan. 2, 1977; children: Marc Aaron, William Michael. BS, SUNY, Albany, 1971; PhD, Boston U., 1975. Assoc. rsch. scientist City of Hope Med. Ctr., Duarte, Calif., 1975-78; from asst. prof. to full prof. U. Calif., Irvine, 1978-90, prof., 1990—. NIH NLS-2 Study Sect., 1989-92. Assoc. editor Jour. Neurocytology, London, 1984-88, Epilepsy Rsch., 1986-2006, Brain Rsch., 1988-, Jour. Mind and Behavior, 1988-, Anatomy and Embryology, 1992-96, Jour. Hirnforschung, 1993-99, Archives of Med. Rsch., 1993-, Epilepsia, 1995-2004, Hippocampus, 2000-, Acta Histochemica et Cytochemica, 2005-; contbr. over 150 articles on brain rsch. to profl. jours. Recipient Michael prize, 1987, Citation Classic award, 1987, Javits award, 1990; NSF grantee, Washington, 1981-84, 87-91, 96-98, rsch. grantee NIH, 1979, 83, 86, 90, 99, 2005; Klingenstein fellow, 1983. Fellow AAAS; mem. Am. Assn. Anatomists, Soc. Neurosci., Internat. Brain Rsch. Orgn., Cajal Club (pres. 2000-02). Office: U Calif Dept Of Anatomy Neurob Irvine CA 92697-1275 Home Phone: 949-388-7090; Office Phone: 949-824-5494. E-mail: ribak@uci.edu.

RICARDO-CAMPBELL, RITA, retired economist educator; b. Boston, Mar. 16, 1920; d. David and Elizabeth (Jones) Ricardo; m. Wesley Glenn Campbell, Sept. 15, 1946; children: Barbara Lee, Diane Rita, Nancy Elizabeth. BS, Simmons Coll., 1941; MA, Harvard U., 1945, PhD, 1946. Instr. Harvard U., Cambridge, Mass., 1946—48; asst. prof. Tufts U., Medford, Mass., 1948—51; labor economist U.S. Wage Stabilization Bd., 1951—53; economist Ways and Means Com. U.S. Ho. of Reps., 1954; economist, 1957—60; prof. San Jose (Calif.) State U., 1960—61; sr. fellow Hoover Instn. on War, Revolution, and Peace, Stanford, Calif., 1968—95, sr. fellow emerita, 1995—2008. Lectr. health Stanford U. Med. Sch., 1973—78; bd. dirs. Watkins-Johnson Co., Palo Alto, Calif., Gillette Co., Boston; mgmt. bd. Samaritan Med. Ctr., San Jose. Author: Voluntary Health Insurance in the U.S., 1960, Economics of Health and Public Policy, 1971, Food Safety Regulation: Use and Limitations of Cost-Benefit Analysis, 1974, Drug Lag: Federal Government Decision Making, 1976, Social Security: Promise and Reality, 1977, The Economics and Politics of Health, 1982, 2d edit., 1985, Resisting Hostile Takeovers: The Case of Gillette, 1997, Chinese transl., 2004; co-editor: Below-Replacement Fertility in Industrial Societies, 1987, Issues in Contemporary Retirement, 1988; contbr. articles to profl. jours. Mem. Western Interstate Commn. for Higher Edn. Calif., 1967-75, chmn., 1970-71; mem. Pres. Nixon's Adv. Coun. on Status of Women, 1969-76; mem. Pres. Ford's Adv. Coun. on Status of Women, 1976-79; mem. task force on taxation Pres.'s Coun. on Environ. Quality, 1970-72; mem. Pres.'s Com. Health Svcs. Industry, 1971-73, FDA Nat. Adv. Drug Com., 1972-75; mem. Pres. Reagan's Econ. Policy Adv. Bd., 1981-90, Pres. Reagan's Nat. Coun. on Humanities, 1982-89, Pres. Reagan's Nat. Medal of Sci. com., 1988-91, Pres. Bush's Nat. Medal of Sci. com., 1991-94; bd. dirs. Ind. Colls. No. Calif., 1971-87; mem. com. assessment of safety, benefits, risks Citizens Commn. Sci., Law and Food, Rockefeller U., 1973-75; mem. adv. com. Ctr. Health Policy Rsch., Am. Enterprise Inst. Pub. Policy Rsch., Washington, 1974-80; mem. adv. coun. on social security Quadrennial Health and Human Svcs., 1974-75; bd. dirs. Simmons Coll. Corp., Boston, 1975-80; mem. adv. coun. bd. assocs. Stanford Librs., 1975-78; mem. coun. SRI Internat., Menlo Park, Calif., 1977-90. Mem. Am. Econ. Assn., Mont Pelerin Soc. (bd. dirs. 1988-92, v.p. 1992-94), Harvard Grad. Soc. (coun. 1991-94), Phi Beta Kappa. Home: Classic Residence Hyatt 620 Sand Hill Rd Apt 308D Palo Alto CA 94304 Home Phone: 650-325-7038. Personal E-mail: rricardocampbell@sbcglobal.net.

RICCARDI, VINCENT MICHAEL, pediatrician, educator, entrepreneur; b. Bklyn., Oct. 14, 1940; s. Gabriel John and Frances Mary (Novak) R.; m. Susan Leona Bogda, July 27, 1967; children: Angela M., Ursula M., Mikah F. AB, UCLA, 1962; MD, Georgetown U., 1966; MBA, U. LaVerne, 1993. Intern, resident in medicine U. Pitts., 1966-68; fellow in genetics Harvard Med. Sch., Boston, 1968-70, 72; asst. prof. medicine U. Colo. Med. Ctr., Denver, 1973-75; assoc. prof. medicine, pediatrics Med. Coll. Wis., Milw., 1975-77; prof. medicine, pediatrics Baylor Coll. Medicine, Houston, 1977-90; med. dir. The Genetics Inst., Pasadena, Calif., 1990-92; clin. prof. pediatrics UCLA, 1991—; founder, CEO Am. Med. Consumers, La Crescenta, 1992. Dir. The Neurofibromatosis Inst., La Crescenta, Calif., 1985—. Author: Genetic Approach to Human Disease, 1977, Communication and Counseling in Health Care, 1983, Neurofibromatosis, 1986, rev. edit., 1992, 99. Maj. U.S. Army, 1970-71. Fellow ACP, AAAS, Am. Coll. Med. Genetics; mem. Am. Soc. Human Genetics, Am. Coll. Physician Execs. Avocations: creative writing, acting. Office: Am Med Consumers 5415 Briggs Ave La Crescenta CA 91214-2205 Home Phone: 818-957-4926; Office Phone: 818-957-3508. Business E-Mail: riccardi@medconsumer.com.

RICCI, CHRISTINA, actress; b. Santa Monica, Calif., Feb. 12, 1980; Actress: (films) Mermaids, 1990, The Hard Way, 1991, The Addams Family, 1991, The Cemetery Club, 1993, Addams Family Values, 1993, Casper, 1995, Now and Then, 1995, Gold Diggers: The Secret of Bear Mountain, 1995, Bastard Out of Carolina, 1996, The Last of the High Kings, 1996, That Darn Cat, 1996, Ice Storm, 1997, Little Red Riding Hood, 1997, (voice only) Souvenir, 1998, Pecker, 1999, I Woke Up Early When I Died, 1998, Fear and Loathing in Las Vegas, 1998, Desert Blue, 1998, Buffalo 66, 1998, The Opposite of Sex, 1998, Small Soldiers, 1998, (voice only) Souvenir, 1998, 200 Cigarettes, 1999, No Vacancy, 1999, Sleepy Hollow, 1999, Bless the Child, 2000, The Man Who Cried, 2000, All Over the Guy, 2001,

Prozac Nation, 2001, The Laramie Project, 2002, The Gathering, 2002, Anything Else, 2003, I Love Your Work, 2003, Monster, 2003, Cursed, 2005, Penelope, 2006, Black Snake Moan, 2006, Home of the Brave, 2006; actress, prodr.(films) Pumpkin, 2002; actress (TV appearances) H.E.L.P., 1990, (voice only) The Simpsons, 1996, Ally McBeal, 2002, Malcolm in the Middle, 2002, Joey, 2005, Grey's Anatomy, 2006. Office: c/o ICM 8942 Wilshire Blvd Beverly Hills CA 90211-1934

RICCITIELLO, JOHN S., interactive software/gaming executive, venture capitalist; b. Erie, Pa., Aug. 3, 1959; BS cum laude in Mktg., Economics and Finance, U. Calif. Berkeley, 1981. Brand mgr. The Clorox Co., Oakland, Calif., 1981—84; mktg. mgr. Henkel GmbH, Germany, 1984—85; mktg. & sales dir. 17 country Middle East/Greece regions Pepsi-Cola Co., Cyprus, 1985—89, group mktg. dir. then bus. devel. dir.; joined Hagen-Dazs, 1989, London, mng. dir. internat. divisions Paris; pres., CEO Wilson Sporting Goods Co., Chgo., 1993—96; pres., CEO Sara Lee bakery worldwide divsn. Sara Lee Corp., Chgo., 1996—97; pres., COO Electronic Arts, Inc., Redwood City, Calif., 1997—2004, CEO, 2007—; co-founder Elevation Partners, Menlo Park, Calif., 2004—. Bd. dirs. Hyperion Solutions, Forbes Media LLC. Named one of Most Influential People in the World of Sports, Bus. Week, 2008. Office: Electronic Arts Inc 209 Redwood Shores Pkwy Redwood City CA 94065

RICCO, EDWARD ROBERT, lawyer; b. Teaneck, NJ, Jan. 17, 1950; s. Leopold Joseph and Rose Mary (Lotito) R.; m. Mary Ann Sweeney, Feb. 2, 1974; children: Alanna Catherine, Susanna Maria. BS, Stevens Inst. Tech., 1971; MA, Columbia U., 1973; JD, U. N.M., 1980. Bar: N.Mex. 1980, U.S. Dist. Ct. N.Mex. 1980, U.S. Ct. Appeals (10th cir.) 1981, U.S. Supreme Ct. 1984, U.S. Ct. Appeals (D.C. cir.) 1992, U.S. Ct. Appeals (9th cir.) 2004. Law clk. to chief judge U.S. Dist. Ct., Albuquerque, 1980-81; assoc. Rodey, Dickason, Sloan, Akin & Robb P.A., Albuquerque, 1981-87, ptnr., 1987—. Mem. com. uniform jury instrns. in civil cases N.Mex. Supreme Ct., Albuquerque, 1986-98, mem. com. rules of appellate procedure, 1999-04; adj. prof. law U. N.Mex. Lead articles editor Natural Resources Jour., 1979-80. Served to capt. USAF, 1973-77. Mem. ABA (sect. antitrust law, sect. litigation), Am. Acad. Appellate Lawyers, Albuquerque Bar Assn., State Bar Assn. N.Mex. (chmn. health law sect. 1987-88, chmn. appellate practice sect. 1997-98). Office: Rodey Dickason Sloan Akin & Robb PA PO Box 1888 201 3rd St NW Ste 2200 Albuquerque NM 87103-1888 Office Phone: 505-768-7314. Business E-Mail: ericco@rodey.com.

RICCOBONO, RICHARD M., bank executive, former federal administrator; b. Bklyn., Sept. 15, 1957; Grad., SUNY, Albany; JD, Western New Eng. Sch. Law; postgrad., Boston U. With Deloitte & Touche, Fed. Home Loan Bank Boston; regional dep. dir. Office of Thrift Supervision, US Dept. Treasury, Washington, 1990-98, dep. dir., 1998—2005, acting dir., 2005; exec. v.p., COO Fed. Loan Bank Seattle, 2005—07, pres., CEO, 2007—. Bd. dirs. FDIC, 2005. Office: Fed Home Loan Bank 1501 4th Ave Ste 1800 Seattle WA 98101-1693

RICE, CONDOLEEZZA, political science professor, former United States Secretary of State; b. Birmingham, Ala., Nov. 14, 1954; d. John Wesley and Angelena Ray Rice. BA cum laude in Polit. Sci., U. Denver, 1974; PhD in Polit. Sci., U. Denver Josef Korbel Sch. Internat. Studies, 1981; MA in Polit. Sci., U. Notre Dame, 1975; PhD (hon.), Morehouse Coll., 1991, U. Ala., 1994, U. Notre Dame, 1995, Nat. Def. U., 2002, Miss. Coll. Sch. of Law, 2003, U. Louisville, 2004, Mich. St. U., 2004; degree (hon.), Boston Coll., 2006. Intern, Bur. Ednl. & Cultural Affairs US Dept. State, Washington, 1977; intern The Rand Corp., Santa Monica, Calif., 1978; polit. sci. cons. Stanford U., 1980—81, asst. prof. polit. sci., 1981—87, assoc. prof., 1987—93, prof., 1993—99, 2009—; provost Stanford U., 1993-99; spl. asst. to dir. of the Joint Chiefs of Staff US Dept. Def., Washington, 1986; spl. asst. to the Pres. for nat. security affairs NSC, 1989-91, dir. to sr. dir. Soviet & East European Affairs, 1989—91; sr. fellow The Hoover Instn., Stanford, Calif., 1991—93, 1999—2001, Thomas & Barbara Stephenson sr. fellow on pub. policy, 2009—; nat. security cons. George W. Bush Presdl. Campaign, Washington, 2000; asst. to the Pres. for nat. security affairs NSC, Washington, 2001—05; sec. US Dept. State, Washington, 2005—09. Cons. ABC News, Washington; mem. spl. advisory panel to comdr. and chief strategic air commd.; mem. gov. ind. adv. redistricting state of Calif.; mem. US Delegation to 2+4 talks on German Unification; bd. dirs. Chevron Corp., 1991—2001, Transamerica Corp., 1991—2001, Charles Schwab Corp., 1999—2001; internat. adv. coun. J.P. Morgan & Co., William & Flora Hewlett Found., U. Notre Dame. Author: Uncertain Allegiance: The Soviet Union and the Czechoslovak Army, 1984; co-author (with Alexander Dallin): The Gorbachev Era, 1986; co-author: (with Philip Zelikow) Germany Unified and Europe Transformed, 1995. Ex officio trustee Nat. Gallery Art; trustee John F. Kennedy Ctr. for the Performing Arts. Recipient Dean's award for Disting. Tchg., Stanford U. Sch. Humanities and Scis., 1993, Walter J. Gores award for Excellence in Tchg., Stanford U., 1984, Pres. award, NAACP Image Awards, 2002; named one of The World's Most Influential People, TIME mag., 2005—07, The 100 Most Powerful Women, Forbes mag., 2005—08, The 10 Most Fascinating People of 2005, Barbara Walters Special, The Most Influential Black Americans, Ebony mag., 2006—08, The 50 Most Powerful People in DC, GQ Mag., 2007, Glamour's Women of the Yr., 2008. Fellow: AAAS; mem.: Coun. Fgn. Rels. Republican. Office: Hoover Memorial Stanford University Stanford CA 94305-6010 Office Phone: 650-723-6867, 202-647-4000. Office Fax: 650-723-9376. E-mail: condi@stanford.edu.*

RICE, DENIS TIMLIN, lawyer; b. Milw., July 11, 1932; s. Cyrus Francis and Kathleen (Timlin) R.; m. Pamela Stefania Rice, May 8, 2007; children: James Connelly, Tracy Ellen. AB, Princeton U., 1954; JD, U. Mich., 1959. Bar: Calif. 1960. Practiced in, San Francisco, 1959—; assoc. firm Pillsbury, Madison & Sutro, 1959-61, Howard & Prim, 1961-63; prin. firm Howard, Rice, Nemerovski, Canady, Falk & Rabkin, 1964—. Bd. dirs. Anabas, Inc.; chmn., mng. com. San Francisco Inst. Fin. Svcs., 1983—92. Councilman, City of Tiburon, Calif., 1968-72, mayor, 1970-72; dir. Marin County Transit Dist., 1970-72, 77-81, chmn., 1979-81; supr. Marin County, 1977-81, chmn., 1979-80; commr. Marin Housing Authority, 1977-81; mem. San Francisco Bay Conservation and Devel. Commn., 1977-83; bd. dirs. Planning and Conservation League, 1981-2006, Marin Symphony, 1984-92, Marin Theatre Co., 1987-97, Marin Conservation League, 1995-2000, Digital Village Found., 1995—, pres., 1997—; mem. Met. Transp. Commn., 1980-83; mem. bd. visitors U. Mich. Law Sch. 1st lt. AUS, 1955-57. Recipient Freedom Found. medal, 1956 Fellow Am. Bar Found.; mem. ABA (fed. regulation of securities com., chair Asia-Pacific Bus. Law Com., chmn. subcom. on internat. venture law), State Bar Calif. (editor 1978-80, vice-chair sect. bus. law 1978-80, chair com. adminstrn. justice 1997-98, chair com. cyberspace law 1997-2001), San Francisco Bar Assn., Am. Judicature Soc., Internat. Tech. Law Assn. (bd. dirs.), Am. Internat. Property Law Assn., Inter-Pacific Bar Assn. (vice-chmn. securities com.). South End Rowing Club, Tiburon Peninsula Club, Pacific Union Club, Olympic Club, Order of Coif, Phi Beta Kappa, Phi Delta Phi. Office: 3 Embarcadero Ctr Ste 700 San Francisco CA 94111-4003 Office Phone: 415-434-1600. Business E-Mail: drice@hrice.com, brice@howardrice.com.

RICE, DONALD BLESSING, corporate executive, former federal official; b. Frederick, Md., June 4, 1939; s. Donald Blessing and Mary Celia (Santangelo) R.; m. Susan Fitzgerald, Aug. 25, 1962; children: Donald Blessing III, Joseph John, Matthew Fitzgerald. BSChemE, U. Notre Dame, 1961, DEng (hon.), 1975; MS in Indsl. Mgmt., Purdue U., 1962, PhD in Econs., 1965, D (hon.) in Mgmt., 1985; LLD (hon.), Pepperdine U., 1989; LHD (hon.), West Coast U., 1993; D in Pub. Policy (hon.), Rand Grad. Sch., 1995. Dir. cost analysis US Dept. Def., Washington, 1967-69, dep. asst. sec. for resource analysis, 1969-70; asst. dir. Office Mgmt. and Budget, Exec. Office of the Pres., Washington, 1970-72; pres., CEO The Rand Corp., Calif., 1972-89; sec. USAF, Washington, 1989-93; pres., COO Teledyne, Inc., LA, 1993-96; chmn. Scios, Inc., Sunnyvale, Calif., 1998—2003; chmn., pres., CEO Agensys, Inc., Santa Monica, Calif., 1996—. Bd. dirs. Vulcan Materials Co., Wells Fargo & Co., Chevron Corp.; mem. nat. adv. com. oceans and atmosphere Dept. Commerce, 1972-75; mem. Nat. Sci. Bd., 1974-86; mem. adv. coun. Coll. Engring., U. Notre Dame, 1974-88; chmn. Nat. Commn. Supplies and Shortages, 1975-77; mem. adv. panel Office Tech. Assessment, 1976-79; mem. Def. Sci. Bd., 1977-83, sr. cons., 1984-88; dir. for sec. def. and Pres. Def. Resource Mgmt. Study, 1977-79; mem. U.S. Commn. Nat. Security/21st Century, 1998-2001; trustee RAND, 2001-, chmn. grad. sch. bd. govs., 1999—. Author articles. Served to capt. AUS, 1965-67. Recipient Sec. Def. Meritorious Civilian Svc. medal, 1970, Def. Exceptional Civilian Svc. medal, 1993, Forrestal award, 1992; Ford Found. fellow, 1962-65. Fellow AAAS, Nat. Acad. of Pub. Adminstrn.; mem. Inst. Mgmt. Scis. (past pres.), Tau Beta Pi. Home: 2225 Colorado Ave Santa Monica CA 90404-3505 Office Phone: 310-820-8029 ext. 210. Business E-Mail: drice@agensys.com.

RICE, DOROTHY PECHMAN, medical economist; b. Bklyn., June 11, 1922; d. Gershon and Lena (Schiff) Pechman; m. John Donald Rice, Apr. 3, 1943; children: Kenneth D., Donald B., Thomas H. Student, Bklyn. Coll., 1938—39; BA, U. Wis., 1941; DSc (hon.), Coll. Medicine and Dentistry N.J., 1979. With hosp., and med. facilities USPHS, Washington, 1960—61; med. econs. studies Social Security Adminstrn., 1962—63; health econs. br. Community Health Svc., USPHS, 1964—65; chief health ins. rsch. br. Social Security Adminstrn., 1966—72, dep. asst. commr. for rsch. and statistics, 1972—75; dir. Nat. Ctr. for Health Stats., Rockville, Md., 1976—82; prof. Inst. Health & Aging U. Calif., San Francisco, 1982—94, prof. emeritus, 1994—. Developer, mgr. nationwide health info. svcs.; expert on aging, health care costs, disability, and cost-of-illness. Contbr. articles to profl. jours. Recipient Social Security Adminstrn. citation, 1968, DSM, HEW, 1974, Jack C. Massey Found. award, 1978, UCSF medal, 2002. Fellow: Am. Statis. Assn.; mem.: LWV, APHA (domestic award for excellence 1978, Sedgwick Meml. medal 1988), Assn. Health Svc. Rsch. (President's award 1988), Inst. Medicine. Office: Univ Calif Sch Nursing 3333 California St Ste 340 San Francisco CA 94118 Office Phone: 415-476-5685. Business E-Mail: dorothy.rice@ucsf.edu.

RICE, EARLE, JR., (EARLE WILMONT RICE JR.), writer; b. Lynn, Mass., Oct. 21, 1928; s. Earle Wilmont and Grace Elizabeth (Nottingham) Rice; m. Georgia Joy Black Wood, Nov. 1, 1958; children: Ellen Jean, Earle Wilmont, III. Student, Sch. Practical Art, Boston, 1947, San Jose City Coll., Calif., 1959, Foothill Coll., Los Altos, Calif., 1971. Product engr. ISS/Sperry Univac, Cupertino, Calif., 1973-74; sr. design specialist GTE/Sylvania, Mountain View, Calif., 1974; sr. design checker Westinghouse Corp., Sunnyvale, Calif., 1974; tech. writer Nuclear Svcs. Corp., Campbell, Calif., 1974; lead checker, tech. writer ESL, Inc., Sunnyvale, 1975; sr. E/M designer Finnigan Corp., Sunnyvale, 1975-76, Advanced Devices Labs., Inc., Santa Clara, Calif., 1976, Argosys., Inc., Palo Alto, Calif., 1976; equipment designer Raytheon Co., Goleta, Calif., 1976-78; sr. staff specialist Vitro Labs./Automation Ind., Oxnard, Calif., 1978-79; engring. drawing checker Gen. Dynamics, San Diego, 1979, 87-89; sr. E/M designer GE Co., Lompoc, Calif., 1980; sr. field engr. Martin Marietta Corp., Vandenberg AFB, Calif., 1980-84; engring. pub. specialist Lockheed Austin Divsn., Austin, Tex., 1984-85; design engr. Sundstrand Turbomach, San Diego, 1985-87; sr. design engr. ROHR, INC., Chula Vista, 1989-93. Author (fiction) Tiger, Lion, Hawk, 1977, The Animals, 1979, Fear on Ice, 1981, More Than Macho, 1981, Death Angel, 1981, The Gringo Dies at Dawn, 1993, (chpt.) The Secret of Barking Dog Bayou, 1993 (Second Pl. award Fla. Freelance Writers Assn.), White Sun and Blue Sky, 1994 (Third Place award Fla. Freelance Writers Assn.), So Long, Slimeball!, 1994, (non-fiction) The Cuban Revolution, 1995, The Battle of Britain, 1996, The Battle of Midway, 1996, The Inchon Invasion, 1996, The Battle of Belleau Wood, 1996, The Attack on Pearl Harbor, 1996, The Tet Offensive, 1996, The Nuremberg Trials, 1996, The Salem Witch Trials, 1996, The O.J. Simpson Trial, 1996, The Final Solution, 1997, Nazi War Criminals, 1997, The Battle of the Little Bighorn, 1997, Life Among the Great Plains Indians, 1997, Life During the Crusades, 1997, Life During the Middle Ages, 1998, Kamikazes, 1999, The Third Reich, 2000, The Bombing of Pearl Harbor, 2000, The Cold War, 2000, Strategic Battles in Europe, 2000, Strategic Battles in the Pacific, 2000, Sir Francis Drake, 2003, Normandy, 2002, First Battle of the Marne, 2002, Gettysburg, 2002, Claire Chennault, Flying Tiger, 2003, Manfred von Richthofen, The Red Baron, 2003, Point of No Return: Tonkin Gulf and the Vietnam War, George S. Patton 2004, Erwin J.E. Rommel, 2004, Douglas MacArthur, 2004, Korea 1950, 2004, Alexandra David-Néel: Explorer at the Roof of the World, 2004, Ulysses S. Grant, 2005, Robert E. Lee, 2005, Enpire in the East: The Story of Genghis Khan, 2005, Adolf Hitler and Nazi Germany, 2006, The US Army and Military Careers, 2006, The Life and Times of Sir Walter Raleigh, 2007, The Life and Times of John Cabot, 2007, A Brief Political and Geographic History of Latin America, 2008, Canaletto, 2008, Blitzkrieg! Hitler's Lightning War, 2008, Overview of the Korean War, 2009, Overview of the Persian Gulf War, 2009, The Life and Times of Erik the Red, 2009, The Life and Times of Lief Eriksson, 2009, The Brothers Custer: Galloing to Glory, 2009; series cons. editor: Great Military Leaders; adaptor: Dracula, 1995, All Quiet on the Western Front, 1995, The Grapes of Wrath, 1996; contbr. articles to mags. With USMC, 1948-57. Mem. Soc. Children's Book Writers Illustrators, League WW I Aviation Historians, Air Force Assn. Avocations: reading, spectator sports. Home and Office: PO Box 2131 Julian CA 92036-2131 Personal E-mail: ericejr@sbcglobal.net.

RICE, JERRY LEE, retired professional football player; b. Starkville, Miss., Oct. 13, 1962; s. Joe Nathan and Eddie Rice; m. Jackie Rice; children: Jaqui, Jerry Jr. Student, Miss. Valley State U., 1981—84. Wide receiver San Francisco 49ers, 1985—2000, Oakland Raiders, 2001—04, Seattle Seahawks, 2004—05, Denver Broncos, 2005. Celebrity dancer Dancing With the Stars, 2006; co-author (with Brian Curtis): Go Long!: My Journey Beyond Fame and the Game, 2007. Recipient Pro Bowl MVP, 1995; named MVP, NFL, 1987, Super Bowl XXIII, 1989, AP/NFL/Sports Illustrated Offensive Player of Yr., 1993; named to Sporting News Coll. All-Am. team, 1984, Pro Bowl team, 1986—96, 1998, 2002. Achievements include holds NFL career records for most touchdowns, receptions, touchdown receptions; having the most consecutive games with one or more touchdowns (13), 1987; holds the NFL single-season record for most touchdown receptions (22), 1987; shares NFL single-game record for most touchdown receptions (5), 1990; holds NFL record of 274 consecutive games with a reception, 1985-2004; led NFL in receptions, 1990, 1996; led NFL in recieving touchdowns, 1986, 1987, 1989-1991, 1993; led NFL in recieving yards, 1986, 1989, 1990, 1993-1995; being a member of SuperBowl XIX, XXIII, XXIV, XXIX Champion San Francisco 49ers.

RICE, JIM, state supreme court justice; b. Ramore AFB, Ont., Canada, Nov. 15, 1957; (parents Am. citizens); BA in Polit. Sci., Mont. State U., 1979; JD U. Mont., 1982. Former firefighter Mont. Dept. of Natural Resources & Conservation; former legal intern Missoula City Atty. Office, Lewis and Clark County Atty. Office; former pub. defender Lewis and Clark County; mem. Mont. House Reps., 1989—95, house majority whip, 1993; ptnr. Jackson & Rice, Helena, Mont., 1985—2001; assoc. justice Mont. Supreme Ct., 2001—. Active in Montana Hope Project, Kiwanis; mem. Governor's Council on Food and Nutrition. Recipient Thomas McHugh Disting. Community Service award, Helena Jaycees, 1993. Mem.: Mont. Bar Assn. Office: Justice Bldg Rm 323 PO Box 203003 Helena MT 59620-3003

RICE, JOE, state legislator; m. Kendall; children: Harrison, Alexandria, Dalton. Mayor City of Glendale, 1996—2003; mem. Dist. 38 Colo. House of Reps., Denver, 2007—. Exec. com. mem. Denver Regional Coun. Govts.; former vice chair Metro Mayors Caucus. Served with US Army, 2003—06, Bosnia-Herzegovina, Iraq, lt. col. USAR. Decorated Combat Action Badge, Expert Infantryman's Badge, Bronze Star; recipient John V. Christensen award, Denver Regional Coun. Govts., 2004. Democrat. Office: Colo State Capitol 200 E Colfax Denver CO 80203 Office Phone: 303-866-2953. Business E-Mail: joe.rice.house@state.co.us.*

RICE, NANCY E., state supreme court justice; b. Denver, June 2, 1950; 1 child. BA cum laude, Tufts U., 1972; JD, U. Utah, 1975. Law clerk U.S. Dist. Ct. of Colo., 1975-76, dep. state pub. defender, appellate divn., 1976-77; asst. U.S. atty. Dist. of Colo., 1977-87; dep. chief civil divn. U.S. Attorney's Office, 1985-88; judge Denver Dist. Ct., 1988-98; justice Colo. Supreme Ct., 1998—. Adjunct prof. law, trial advocacy U. Colo. Sch. of Law, 1987—. Contbr. articles to profl. jours. Mem. Denver Bar Assn. (Judicial Excellence award 1993), Colo. Bar Assn. (bd. govs. 1990-92, exec. coun., 1991-92), Women's Bar Assn., Rhone-Brackett Inn of Ct. (master 1993-97), Women Judges Assn. (co-chair nat. conf. 1990). Office: Colo Supreme Ct Colo State Jud Bldg 2 E 14th Ave Fl 4 Denver CO 80203-2115

RICE, NORMAN B., bank executive, former mayor; b. Denver, May 4, 1943; m. Constance Rice; 1 child, Mian. BA in Comm., U. Wash., MPA. Past mgr. corp. contbns. and soc. policy Rainier Nat. Bank; past dir. govt. svcs. Puget Sound Coun. Govts.; past asst. dir. Seattle Urban League; past reporter KIXI Radio; past editor, writer KOMO TV; with govt. City of Seattle, 1978—, city councilman, 1978-89, mayor, 1990-97; pres., chief exec. officer Fed. Home Loan Bank of Seattle, 1999—. Pres. U.S. Conf. of Mayors, 1995; bd. dirs. Safeco Corp. Office: Fed Home Loan Bank 1501 4th Ave Ste 1900 Seattle WA 98101-1693

RICE, PETER, broadcast executive; Degree, U. Nottingham, England, 1989. Dir. acquisitions Twentieth Century Fox, 1994, dir. prodn., v.p. prodn., sr. v.p. prodn.; pres. prodn. Fox Searchlight Pictures, 2000—09; chmn. Fox Entertainment Group, 2009—. Named one of The 50 Smartest People in Hollywood, Entertainment Weekly, 2007. Office: Fox Entertainment Group 10201 W Pico Blvd Ste 100 Los Angeles CA 90035*

RICE, REGINA KELLY, marketing executive; b. Yonkers, NY, July 11, 1955; d. Howard Adrian and Lucy Virginia (Butler) Kelly; m. Mark Christopher Rice, Sept. 11, 1981; children: Amanda Kelly, Jaime Brannen. BS in Cmty. Nutrition, Cornell U., 1978. Account exec. J. Walter Thompson Co., NYC, 1978—79; sr. account exec. Ketchum, MacLeod & Grove, NYC, 1979—80; supr. Burson Marstellar, Hong Kong, 1981—83; v.p., dep. dir. food and beverage unit, creative dir. N.Y. office Hill and Knowlton, NYC, 1983—91; mktg. cons. Rice & Rohr, NYC, 1991—93; sr. v.p., dir. consumer mktg. practice Manning, Selvage & Lee, NYC, 1993—97, sr. v.p global tng. dir., 1999—; chief inspiration officer, dir. corp. devel. Internat. Pub. Rels. Assn., 1999—2001. Writer Fast and Healthy Mag., 1991-2000. Mem. Pub. Rels. Soc. Am. Roman Catholic. Avocation: collecting Provence pottery. Home: 31 Wrangler Ln Bell Canyon CA 91307 Office: Manning Selvage & Lee 6500 Wilshire Blvd Los Angeles CA 90048-4920 Office Phone: 323-866-6023.

RICE, ROD W., corporate executive; b. 1964; BSBA in Acctg. and Econs., Portland State U. CPA. Former acct. Deloitte & Touche; controller Direct Focus Inc., Vancouver, Wash., 1994-95, chief fin. officer, treas., sec., 1995—.

RICE, SUSAN F., fundraising consultant; b. Chgo., Dec. 10, 1939; BA, St. Mary's Coll., 1961; MPA, UCLA, 1976; EdD, Pepperdine U., 1986. Pres. YWCA, Santa Monica, Calif., 1978, League of Women Voters Calif., San Francisco, 1979-81; sr. fundraising profl. adminstr., instr. Santa Monica (Calif.) Coll., 1978-81; dir. govtl. rels. UCLA Alumni Assn., 1981-82; dir. devel. UCLA Grad. Sch. Mgmt., 1982-89; dep. dir. mktg. and devel., dir. major gifts Spl. Olympics Internat., Washington, 1989-90; v.p. devel. Bus. Exec. Nat. Security, Washington, 1991-92; pres., CEO Greater L.A. Zoo Assn., 1992-96; prin. SFR Consulting, LA, 1996—. Co-author: Women, Money and Political Clout in Women as Donors, Woman as Philanthropists, 1994, Fund Raising in Crisis Mode in Advancing Philanthropy, 1997. Bd. dirs. St.

Mary's Coll. Alumnae Assn., Notre Dame, Ind., 1982-84, Santa Monica Coll. Assocs., 1984-94, Internat. Human Rights Law Group, 1990-92; trustee, chair pers. compensation com. L.A. Mus. Nat. History Found., 1982-89; treas. Women's Commn. Refugee Women, 1990-96; vice chmn. pers. commn. Santa Monica Coll. Dist., 1985-89. Recipient Disting. Alumna award St. Mary's Coll., 1986, Humanitarian award, NCCJ-L.A., 1995. Mem. Nat. Soc. Fundraising Execs. (bd. dirs. 1995-97, v.p. Greater L.A. chpt.).

RICE, THOMAS HILARY (SPEEDY RICE), lawyer; b. Richmond, Va., Apr. 10, 1954; s. Spencer Victor and Kathleen Francis (Reney) R.; m. Judy Clare Clarke, Dec. 31, 1975. BA in Sociology, Furman U., Greenville, SC, 1976; JD summa cum laude, Calif. Western Sch. Law, San Diego, 1986. Bar: Calif. 1986, Wash. 1994, US Supreme Ct., US Ct. Appeals (9th cir.). Travel cons. TMT Travel, La Jolla, Calif., 1977; mgr. TLC Travel, San Diego, 1977-80; mgr. passenger/interline sales Pinehurst Airlines, Greenville, SC, 1980-81; gen. mgr. Mission Airlines, El Cajon, Calif., 1981-82; customer svc. and pub. rels. coord. Balboa Travel, San Diego, 1982-83; assoc. Luce, Foreward, Hamilton & Scripps, San Diego, 1983-89; of counsel Robinson & Phillips, San Diego, 1989—90; pvt. practice atty. Law Office of Speedy Rice, San Diego, 1989—95. Aviation cons. Calif. Air Express, Marina del Ray, 1982; instr. Nat. U., San Diego, 1982-83, San Diego Cmty. Coll. Dist., 1979-80; dir. externship prog., trial advocacy instr. Gonzaga U. Sch. Law, 1993-2002. Contbr. articles to profl. publs. Trustee Calif. Western Sch. Law; mem., sec. Internat. Aerospace Hall of Fame; bd. dirs. US-USSR Hist. Aircraft Search. Mem. NACDL, Am. Trial Lawyers Assn., ABA, San Diego Trial Lawyers Assn., Calif. Trial Lawyers Assn. Democrat. Roman Catholic. Avocations: flying, photography, bicycling. Mailing: PO Box 80188 San Diego CA 92138

RICH, ANDREA LOUISE, former museum administrator; BA, UCLA, 1965, MA, 1966, PhD, 1968. Asst. prof. comms. studies UCLA, LA, 1976, asst. dir. office learning resources, 1976, acting dir. Media Ctr., 1977, dir. office of instructional devel., 1978-80, asst. vice chancellor office of instructional devel., 1980-86, asst. exec. vice chancellor, 1986-87, vice chancellor acad. adminstrn., 1987-91, exec. vice chancellor, 1991-95; pres., CEO L.A. County Mus. of Art, 1995—2006, pres., Wallis Annenberg dir., 2003—06.

RICH, MICHAEL DAVID, think-tank executive, lawyer; b. LA, Jan. 23, 1953; s. Ben Robert and Faye (Mayer) Rich; m. Debra Paige Granfield, Jan. 12, 1980; children: Matthew, William. AB, U. Calif., Berkeley, 1973; JD, UCLA, 1976. Bar: Calif. 1976. Extern law clk. to judge U.S. Dist. Ct., Boston, 1975; staff mem. RAND, Santa Monica, Calif., 1976—85, dir. resource mgmt. program, 1980—85, dep. v.p., 1986, v.p. nat. security rsch. and dir. Nat. Def. Rsch. Inst., 1986—93, sr. v.p., 1993—95, exec. v.p., 1995—. Co-chmn. bd. overseers Rand-Qatar Policy Inst., 2003—. Author: numerous classified and unclassified reports and articles. Bd. dirs. WISE & Healthy Aging, Coun. Aid to Edn., chmn., 1996—2005; mem. bd. councillors UCLA Found., 2000—; mem. fin. oversight com. Santa Monica-Malibu Unified Sch. Dist., 2000—04; bd. advisers Santa Monica-UCLA Med. Ctr.; mem. adv. coun. Everychild Found.; chmn. bd. trustees The Comm. Inst., 2003—. Mem.: Internat. Inst. Strategic Studies (mem. governing coun. 2001—07, chmn. bd. trustees IISS-US 2004—), Coun. Fgn. Rels. Office: RAND PO Box 2138 1776 Main St Santa Monica CA 90407-2138 Office Phone: 310-451-6934. E-mail: mrich@rand.org.

RICH, ROBERT STEPHEN, lawyer; b. NYC, Apr. 30, 1938; s. Maurice H. and Natalie (Priess) R.; m. Myra N. Lakoff, May 31, 1964; children: David, Rebecca, Sarah. AB, Cornell U., 1959; JD, Yale U., 1963. Bar: N.Y. 1964, Colo. 1973, U.S. Tax Ct. 1966, U.S. Supreme Ct. 1967, U.S. Ct. Claims 1968, U.S. Dist. Ct. (so. dist.) N.Y. 1965, U.S. Dist. Ct. (ea. dist.) N.Y. 1965, U.S. Dist. Ct. Colo. 1980, U.S. Ct. Appeals (10th cir.) 1978; conseil juridique, Paris, 1968. Assoc. Shearman & Sterling, NYC, Paris, London, 1963-72; ptnr. Davis, Graham & Stubbs, Denver, 1973—. Adj. faculty U. Denver Law Sch., 1977—; mem. adv. bd. U. Denver Ann. Tax Inst., 1985—, global bus. and culture divsn., U. Denver, 1992—, Denver World Affairs Coun., 1993—; mem. Colo. Internat. Trade Coun., 1985—; mem. Rocky Mt. Dist. Export Coun., US Dept. Commerce, 1993—; tax adv. com. US Senator Hank Brown; bd. dirs. Clos du Val Wine Co. Ltd., Danskin Cattle Co., Ouray Ranch, Areti Wines, Ltd., Taltarni Vineyards, Christy Sports, others. Contbr. articles to profl. jours. Actor, musician N.Y. Shakespeare Festival, 1960; sponsor Am. Tax Policy Inst., 1991—; adv. bd. Middle Park Land Trust, Granby, Colo., 2003—; pres. So. Boulder Park Ecol. Assn., 1999—; sec. Bhutan Found.; sec., treas. Citizens for Arts to Zoo; bd. dirs. Alliance Francaise, 1977—, Copper Valley Assn., Denver Internat. Film Festival, 1978—79, Anschutz Family Found.; trustee, sec. Denver Art Mus., 1982—; pres., bd. dirs. Ouray Ranch, Granby, Colo., 2001—; bd. dirs. Aspen Music Festival and Sch., 2004—. Capt. US Army, 1959—60. Fellow Am. Coll. Tax. Coun. (bd. regents 10th cir. 1992—), Soc. Fellows Aspen Inst.; mem. ABA, Internat. Bar Assn., Colo. Bar Assn., NY State Bar Assn., Assn. Bar City of NY, Asia-Pacific Lawyers Assn., Union Internat. des Avocats, Internat. Fiscal Assn. (pres. Rocky Mt. br. 1992—, US regional v.p. 1988—), Japan-Am. Soc. Colo. (bd. dirs. 1989—, pres. 1991-93), Confrerie des Chavaliers du Tastevin, Rocky Mt. Wine and Food Soc., Meadowood Club, Denver Club, City Club Denver, Mile High Club, Cactus Club Denver, Yale Club, Denver Tennis Club. also: Antelope Co 555 17th St Ste 2400 Denver CO 80202-3941 Home Phone: 303-321-4965; Office Phone: 303-299-1230. Personal E-mail: robertrich@tac-denver.com. Business E-Mail: robertrich@aya.yale.edu.

RICHARD, EDWARD H., manufacturing executive, retired municipal official; b. Mar. 15, 1937; s. Henry and Ida Richard. BA, Antioch Coll., 1959. Pres., chmn., bd. dirs. Magnetics Internat. Inc., Maple Heights, Ohio, 1967-86; exec. v.p. Stearns Magnetics S.A., Brussels, Belgium, 1974-77; prin. Edward H. Richard & Assocs., Cleve., 1967-96; pres., treas. David Round & Son, Inc., Cleve. Chmn. Cleve. dist. adv. council Small Bus. Adminstrn., 1975-79; past nat. adv. council Dept. Treasury; cons. and advisor in field; del. world trade fairs. Former trustee Regional Econ. Devel. Coun., Met. Cleve. Jobs. Coun., Cleve. Devel. Found., Cleve. BBB; former trustee Hiram House, Antioch U., former treas., 1972-77; N.E. Ohio Regional Sewer Dist., Greater Cleve. Domed Stadium Corp., Greater Cleve. Conv. and Visitor Bur.; former trustee, vice-chmn. Cleve. Ctr. Econ. Edn.; former pres. Bratenahl Condominium Assn.; chmn. fin. com. Bratenahl Bd. Edn., 1971-75; former trustee, chmn. nominating com., exec. com. La Jolla Playhouse; CFO Mainly Mozart Festival, 1998—; CFO, chmn. bd. orch. rels. com., exec. com., fin. com., trustee San Diego Symphony Orch. Mailing: 1811 Englewood Rd Ste 217 Englewood FL 34223

RICHARD, ROBERT JOHN, library director; b. Oakland, Calif., Sept. 20, 1947; s. John Argyle and Vern Elizabeth (Bauer) R.; m. Anne Elizabeth Terrell, June 8, 1968 (div. 1982); children: Jennifer Lynn, Laura Ellen, Constance Anne, Andrea Lee. Student, Fullerton Coll., 1965—67; BA in Biology, Chapman Coll., Orange, Calif., 1972; MLS, Calif. State U., Fullerton, 1973. Cert. county libr., Calif. Audiovisual specialist Fullerton Pub. Libr., 1969-72, asst. to city libr., 1972-73, libr., 1973-76; br. libr. Orange County Pub. Libr., 1976-78, regional adminstr., 1979-80; assoc. dir. Long Beach Pub. Libr., Calif., 1980-81; dir. Sacramento Pub. Libr., 1981-86, Santa Ana Pub. Libr., Calif., 1986—. Mem. ALA, Pub. Libr. Execs. Assn So. Calif., Calif. Libr. Assn., Libr. Adminstrn. and Mgmt. Assn., Libr. Info. and Tech. Assn., Pub. Libr. Assn. Office: Santa Ana Pub Libr 26 Civic Center Plz Santa Ana CA 92701-4078 Office Phone: 714-647-5250.

RICHARDS, ERIC ALBERT STEPHAN, lawyer; b. Detroit, Jan. 1, 1965; s. June Hill. BA, Yale Coll., 1986; JD cum laude, Harvard U., 1989. Bar: Calif. 1989, US Ct. Appeals (9th Cir.) 1989, US Dist. Ct. (Ctrl. Dist. Calif.) 1989. With O'Melveny & Myers, LA, 1989—, assoc., ptnr., mem. policy com., mem. project development practice group, mem., 1940 Act Practice group, active with joint venture and corp. combinations. Mem.: LA County Bar Assn., Nat. Bar. Assn., ABA. Office: O'Melveny & Myers LLP 400 S Hope St Los Angeles CA 90071-2899

RICHARDS, NORMAN BLANCHARD, lawyer; b. Melrose, Mass., May 27, 1924; s. Henry Edward and Annie Jane (Blanchard) R.; m. Diane Maionchi, July 9, 1977; children— Terri, Jeffrey. BS, Bowdoin Coll., 1945; JD, Stanford U., 1951. Bar: Calif. bar 1951. Mem. firm McCutchen Doyle Brown & Enersen, San Francisco, 1951—, partner, 1960—. Mem. faculty Tulane Admiralty Law Inst., Hastings Coll. Advocacy. Bd. visitors Stanford Law Sch. With USN, 1943-46. Fellow Am. Coll. Trial Lawyers; mem. ABA, Calif. State Bar, San Francisco Bar Assn., Maritime Law Assn. U.S. Home: 85 Platt Ave Sausalito CA 94965-1897 Office: Bingham McCutchen 3 Embarcadero Ctr San Francisco CA 94111-4003 Home Phone: 415-332-0894.

RICHARDS, PAUL LINFORD, physics educator, researcher; b. Ithaca, NY, June 4, 1934; s. Lorenzo Adolph and Zilla (Linford) R.; m. Audrey Jarratt, Aug. 24, 1965; children: Elizabeth Anne, Mary-Ann. AB, Harvard U., 1956; PhD, U. Calif., Berkeley, 1960. Postdoctoral fellow U. Cambridge, England, 1959-60; mem. tech. staff Bell Telephone Labs., Murray Hill, NJ, 1960-66; prof. physics U. Calif., Berkeley, 1966—, prof. emeritus. Faculty sr. scientist Lawrence Berkeley Lab., 1966-2001; advisor NASA, 1975-92, 98-2000; hon. prof. Miller Inst. Rsch. in Phys. Scis., Berkeley, 1969-70, 87-88, 2001; vis. prof. Ecole Normale Superieure, Paris, 1984, 92; vis. astronomer Paris Obs., 1984. Contbr. over 350 articles to profl. jours. Guggenheim Meml. Found. fellow, Cambridge, Eng., 1973-74; named Calif. Scientist of Yr. Mus. Sci., LA, 1981; recipient sr. scientist award Alexander von Humboldt Found., Stuttgart, Fed. Republic Germany, 1982, Button medal, British Inst. of Physics, 1997, Frank Isakson prize for optical effects in solids, Am. Physical Soc., 2000; Berkeley Faculty Rsch. lectr. 1991. Mem. NAS, Am. Acad. Arts and Sciences; fellow Am. Phys. Soc. (Isakson prize 2000). Avocations: vineyardist, wine making. Office Phone: 510-642-3027, 510-642-4359. Office Fax: 510-643-5204. E-mail: richards@physics.berkeley.edu.

RICHARDS, STEPHEN C., corporate development executive; BA in Stats. and Econs., U. Calif., Davis; MBA in Fin., U. Calif., LA. CPA, Calif. V.p., contr. Jefferies and Co., Inc.; v.p., dep. contr. Becker Paribas; mng. dir., CFO corr. clearing Bear Stearns and Co.; sr. v.p. corp. devel. and new ventures E*TRADE, Palo Alto, Calif., 1996—, chief online trading officer Menlo Park, Calif. Office: E*Trade Group Inc 4500 Bohannon Dr Menlo Park CA 94025

RICHARDS, THOMAS E., telecommunications industry executive; m. Mary Beth Richards; 2 children. BA in Econs., U. Pitts.; MS in Mgmt., MIT, Cambridge. Various mgmt. positions Bell of Pa., 1976—83, Bell Atlantic, 1983—95; exec. v.p. comm. & info. products Ameritech, 1995—99; chmn., pres., CEO Clear Comm., 1999—2003; exec. v.p. bus. markets group Qwest Comm. Internat., Inc., Denver, 2005—08, COO, 2008—. Bd. dirs. Nat. Alliance Bus., Tele Danmark (TDK). Mem. Pitts. coun. Boy Scouts Am.; bd. dirs. Pa. Econ. League, Pa. SW Econ. Devel. Assn., Pitts. C. of C. Alfred P. Sloan Fellow. Office: Qwest Comm Internat Inc 1801 California St Denver CO 80202 Office Phone: 303-992-1400. Office Fax: 303-896-8515.

RICHARDS, VINCENT PHILIP HASLEWOOD, librarian; b. Sutton Bonington, Nottinghamshire, Eng., Aug. 1, 1933; arrived in Can., 1956, naturalized, 1961; s. Philip Haslewood and Alice Hilda (Moore) R.; m. Ann Beardshall, Apr. 3, 1961; children: Mark, Christopher, Erika. ALA, Ealing Coll., London, 1954; BLS with distinction, U. Okla., 1966. Cert. profl. libr., B.C. Joined Third Order Mt. Carmel, Roman Cath. Ch., 1976; with Brentford and Chiswick Pub. Librs., London, 1949-56; asst. librarian B.C. (Can.) Pub. Libr. Commn., Dawson Creek, 1956-57; asst. dir. Fraser Valley Regional Libr., Abbotsford, B.C., 1957-67; chief librarian Red Deer Coll., Alta., Canada, 1967-77; dir. librs. Edmonton (Alta.) Pub. Libr., Edmonton, 1977-89; libr. and book industry cons. Victoria, Canada, 1990—. Pres. Faculty Assn. Red Deer Coll., 1971-72, bd. govs., 1972-73; pres. Libr. Assn. Alta., 1984-85. Contbr. articles to profl. jours. V.p. Jeunesses Musicales, Red Deer, 1969-70; bd. dirs. Red Deer TV Authority, 1975-76; dir. Alta. Found. Lit. Arts, 1984-86. Served with Royal Army Ednl. Corps, 1951-53. Home and Office: 105 1049 Costin Ave Victoria BC Canada V9B 2T4 Home Phone: 250-391-9892; Office Phone: 250-391-9892. Personal E-mail: v.p.h.richards@gmail.com.

RICHARDSON, BETTY H., lawyer, former prosecutor; b. Oct. 3, 1953; BA, U. Idaho, 1976; JD, Hastings Coll. Law, 1982. Staff aide U.S. Senator Frank Church, 1976-77; tchg. asst. Hastings Coll. Law, 1980-82, 1980-82; legal rsch. asst. criminal divsn. San Francisco Superior Ct., 1982-84; jud. law clk. Chamber of Idaho Supreme Ct. Justice Robert C. Huntley Jr., 1984-86; atty. U.S. Dept. Justice, Boise, Idaho, 1993-2001, Richardson & O'Leary, Eagle, Idaho, 2001—; jud. law clk. Chamber of Chief U.S. Dist. Ct. Judge B. Lynn Winmill, Idaho, 2003—. Instr. Boise State U., 1987, 89; mem. U.S. Atty. Gen.'s Adv. Com. subcoms. on environ., civil rights and native Am. issues, others, 1993-2001; mem. hon. adv. bd. for Crime Victims Amendment in Idaho, 1994; mem. Dist. of Idaho Judges and Lawyer Reps. com., gender fairness com., Civil Justice Reform Act com. and criminal adv. com., 1993-2001; Dem. nominee Dist 1 Idaho, U.S. Ho. of Reps., 2003; adj. prof. constnl. law Boise State U., 2004; program planner Idaho State Bar and Law Found., 2004—. Mem. Idaho Indsl. Commn., 1991-93, chmn., 1993; mem. adv. bd. Family and Workplace Consortium, 1995-2001; bd. dirs. Tony Patino Fellowship. Recipient Harold E. Hughes Exceptional Svc. award Nat. Rural Inst. on Alcohol and Drug Abuse, 1999; Tony Patino fellow Hastings Coll. Law, 1982. Mem. FBA, Idaho Bar Assn. (governing coun. govt. and pub. sectors lawyers sect. 1999-01, Pro Bono Svc. award 1988), Idaho State Bar (alt. dispute resolution sect.), Idaho Women Lawyers (Kate Feltham award 2006), Idaho Legal Hist. Soc. Ptnrs. for Justice, Assistance League Boise, YMCA, City Club Boise. Office: Richardson & O'Leary 515 N 27th Boise ID 83702 Office Phone: 208-938-7900.

RICHARDSON, BILL (WILLIAM BLAINE RICHARDSON III), Governor of New Mexico, former United States Secretary of Energy; b. Pasadena, Calif., Nov. 15, 1947; s. William Blaine & María Luisa López-Collada Márquez Richardson; m. Barbara Flavin, 1972. BA, Tufts U., Medford, Mass., 1970; MA, Fletcher Sch. Law and Diplomacy, 1971. Mem. staff US Congress, 1971-72, US Dept. State, 1973-75; mem. staff fgn. relations com. US Senate, 1975-78; exec. dir. N. Mex. State Democratic Com., 1978, Bernalillo County Democratic Com., 1978; businessman Santa Fe, 1978-82; mem. US Congress from 3rd N.Mex. Dist., Washington, 1982-96; permanent US rep. to UN US Dept. State, NYC, 1997-98; sec. US Dept. Energy, Washington, 1998-2001; sr. mng. dir. Kissinger McLarty, Washington, 2001—02; gov. State of N. Mex., Santa Fe, 2003—. Ranking minority mem. Resources Com. on Nat. Pks., Forests and Lands; mem. Select Com. on intelligence, Helsinki Commn.; adj. prof. pub. policy Harvard U., 2001; cons. Salomon Smith Barney; chair Democratic Governor's Assoc.; Western Governors Assoc. Author (with Michael Ruby): Between Worlds: The Making of an American Life, 2005; author: Leading By Example: How We Can Inspire an Energy and Security Revolution, 2007. Vice chair Dem. Nat. Com.; active Big Bros.-Big Sisters, Santa Fe. Named one of 25 Most Influential Hispanics, Time Mag., 2005. Mem. Santa Fe Hispanic C. of C., Santa Fe C. of C., Council Fgn. Relations, NATO 2000 Bd., Congl. Hispanic Caucus, Am. G.I. Forum Democrat. Catholic. Office: Office of the Gov State Capitol Rm 400 Santa Fe NM 87501 Office Phone: 505-476-2200. Office Fax: 505-476-2226.

RICHARDSON, CAMPBELL, retired lawyer; b. Woodland, Calif., June 18, 1930; s. George Arthur and Mary (Hall) R.; m. Patricia Packwood, Sept. 3, 1957 (dec. Oct. 1971); children: Catherine, Sarah, Thomas; m. Carol Tamblyn, June 1975 (div. Dec. 1977); m. Susan J. Lienhart, May 3, 1980; 1 child, Laura. AB, Dartmouth Coll., 1952; JD, NYU, 1955. Bar: Oreg. 1955, U.S. Dist. Ct. Oreg. 1957. Ptnr. Stoel Rives LLP, Portland, 1964-2000; ret., 2000—. Co-author: Contemporary Trust and Will Forms for Oregon Attorneys, 2003, and for Idaho Attorneys, 2001; contbr. articles to profl. jours. Mem. Portland/Metro Govt. Boundary Commn., 1976; mem. Oreg. Adv. Com. to U.S. Commn. on Civil Rights, 1976-84; bd. dirs. Ctr. for Urban Edn., Portland, 1980-84, Dorchester Conf., Inc., 1982, Oreg. Zoo Found., 1993-2003; chmn. planned giving com. St. Vincent Med. Found., 1988-98; mem. planned giving coun. Oreg. Health Scis. Found., 1994-2003; trustee Met. Family Svc. Found., 1990-98; bd. dirs. Elders in Action, Portland, 2000-06. Served with U.S. Army, 1955-57. Mem. ABA, Oreg. Bar Assn., Multnomah County Bar Assn., Estate Planning Coun. Portland (pres. 1978), Am. Coll. Trust and Estate Counsel, City Club, Multnomah Athletic Club (Portland). Republican. Home: 1500 SW 5th Ave Unit 1701 Portland OR 97201-5430 Office: Stoel Rives LLP 900 SW 5th Ave Ste 2300 Portland OR 97204-1229 Office Phone: 503-294-9337. E-mail: crichardson@stoel.com.

RICHARDSON, CHARLES H., lawyer; b. Sept. 25, 1951; Student, Univ. Calif., 1973; LLB, Denver Coll. Law, 1976. City atty., Aurora, Colo., 1986—.

RICHARDSON, DENNIS MICHAEL, lawyer, educator; b. LA, July 30, 1949; s. Ralph Lee and Eva Catherine (McGuire) R.; 1 child from previous marriage, Scott Randol; m. Catherine Jean Coyl, July 27, 1973; children: Jennifer Eve, Valerie Jean, Rachel Catherine, Nicole Marie, Mary Rose, Marie Christina, Laura Michelle, Alyssa Rose. BA, Brigham Young U., 1976, JD, 1979. Bar: Oreg. 1979. Owner Law Firm of Dennis Richardson, P.C., Central Point, Oreg., 1979—; pvt. practice law Central Point, Oreg., 1979—; mem. Oreg. House of Reps., 2003—, spkr. pro tem, 2005—07. Guest lectr. in field. Contbr. articles to profl. jours. Bd. dirs. Oreg. Lung Assn., 1980, Shakespearean Festival, Ashland, 1981, Jackson County Legal Services, 1982; chmn. GOP Oreg. 2d. Congl. Dist., 1996-2000, treas. GOP Oreg. Exec. Com., 1996-2002; councilman Ctrl. Point City, 2001-2002. Served as helicopter pilot U.S. Army, 1969-71, Vietnam. Decorated Vietnamese Cross Gallantry. Republican. Office: Law Firm of Dennis Richardson PC 55 S 5th St Central Point OR 97502-2474 Office Phone: 541-664-6622. Business E-Mail: dennis@justiceonline.com.

RICHARDSON, EVERETT VERN, hydraulic engineer, educator, administrator, consultant; b. Scottsbluff, Nebr., Jan. 5, 1924; s. Thomas Otis and Jean Marie (Everett) R.; m. Billie Ann Kleckner, June 23, 1948; children: Gail Lee, Thomas Everett, Jerry Ray. BS, Colo. State U., 1949, MS, 1960, PhD, 1965. Registered profl. engr., Colo. From hydraulic engr. to project chief US Geol. Survey, Wyo., 1949—52, Iowa, 1952—56, rsch. hydraulic engr., 1956—63, project chief Ft. Collins, Colo., 1963—68; adminstr. Engring. Rsch. Ctr. Colo. State U., Ft. Collins, 1968—88, dir. Egypt water use project, 1977-84, prof. in charge of hydraulic program, 1982-88, dir. hydraulic lab. Engring. Rsch. Ctr., 1982-88, prof. emeritus, 1988—, dir. Egypt irrigation improvement project, 1985-90; dir. Egypt Water Rsch. Ctr. Project, Ft. Collins, 1988-89; sr. assoc. Ayers Assocs. Inc. (formerly Resource Cons./Engr., Inc.), Ft. Collins, 1989—. Dir. Consortium for Internat. Devel., Tucson, 1972-87; developer stream stability and scour at hwy. bridges course for State Dept. Transps. for NHI, FHWA; investigator for NTSB 1987 I-90 bridge failure, NY, 1997, railroad bridge failure, Ariz., CALTRAN 1995 I-5 bridge failure; chmn. peer rev. panel Turnefairbanks Rsch. Ctr. Hydraulics Lab., 2004; cons. in field; lectr. in field. Sr. author Highways in the River Environment: Hydraulic and Environmental Considerations, FHWA, 1975, 1990, Evaluating Scour at Bridge, FHWA, 1991, 1993, 1995, 2001, FHWA Hydr. Design Series No. 6: River Engineering for Highway Encroachments, 2001, Civil Engring. Handbook, 1995; co-author: Engring. Handbook, 1995, 2003; contbr. Handbook of Fluid Dynamics and Fluid Machinery, 1996, Water Resources-Environmental Planning, Management and Development, 1996, more than 200 articles to profl. jours. Mem. Ft. Collins Water Bd., 1969-84; mem. NY State Bridge Safety Assurance Task Force, 1988-91. Decorated Bronze Star, Purple Heart, Combat Infantry Badge; named hon. diplomate Am. Acad. Water Resources Engring. 2005; U.S. Govt. fellow MIT, 1962-63. Fellow: ASCE (chair task com., bridge scour rsch. 1990—96, editor Compendium of Stream Stability and Scour Papers 1991—98, vice chair 1997—2002, J.S. Stevens award 1961, hydraulics divsn. task com. excellence award 1993, Hans Albert Einstein award 1996); mem.: Am. Acad. Water Resource Engrs. (hon. diplomate 2005), Internat. Congress for Irrigation and Drainage, Sigma Xi, Sigma Tau, Chi Epsilon. Home: 824 Gregory Rd Fort Collins CO 80524-1504 Office: Ayres Assocs PO Box 270460 Fort Collins CO 80527-0460 Office Phone: 970-223-5556. Personal E-mail: mudih2o@aol.com. Business E-Mail: richardsone@ayresassociates.com.

RICHARDSON, JOHN VINSON, JR., library and information science professor; b. Columbus, Ohio, Dec. 27, 1949; s. John Vinson Sr. and Hope Irene (Smith) R.; m. Nancy Lee Brown, Aug. 22, 1971. BA, Ohio State U., 1971; MLS, Peabody Coll., 1972; PhD, Ind. U., 1978. Asst. prof. UCLA, 1978-83, assoc. prof., 1983-98, editor The Libr. Quar., 1994—2003, editor emeritus, 2003—, prof., 1998—, assoc. dean grad. divsn., 2002—07, mem. editl. bd., The Libr. Quar., 2004—08. Faculty coord. UCLA-St. Petersburg State Acad. of Culture Exch. Program, 1996—; fellow advanced rsch. Inst. U. Ill., 1991; pres. Info. Transfer, Inglewood, Calif., 1988—; vis. fellow Charles Sturt U. NSW Australia, 1990; vis. scholar ALISE Russia Project, St. Petersburg and Moscow, 1996; vis. disting. scholar OCLC Inc., Dublin, Ohio, 1996-97; presidential scholar, Libr. Sys. & Svcs., LLC, 2002—03; chmn. Calif. Pacific Ann. Conf. Com. on Archives and History, 1992-96; Henderson lectr. U. N.C., Chapel Hill, 1997; mem. UCLA Privilege and Tenure, 1999-2000, chair, 2000-02; Fulbright sr. specialist Vladivostok State U. Econ. and Svc., Russia, 2005.; cons. to U.S. Dept of State, Vladivostok, 2000, Uganda and Zambia, 2001, Eritrea, 2003, Turkmenistan, 2005. Author: Spirit of Inquiry, 1982, Government Information, 1987, Gospel of Scholarship, 1992, Knowledge-based Systems for General Reference Work, 1995, Understanding Reference Transactions, 2002; mem. editl. bd. Ref. Svcs. Rev., Ann Arbor, Mich., 1991—, Jour. Govt. Info., Oxford, Eng., 1975-2005, Index to Current Urban Documents, Westport, Conn., 1987—, U. Calif. Press Catalogues and Bibliographies series, 1994-97, Jour. Edn. for Libr. and Info. Sci., 2005-07. Mem. UCLA Grad. Coun., 1992-96, chair, 1995-96; mem. U. Calif. systemwide coord. com. on grad. affairs, 1993-96; pres. Wesley Found., L.A., 1981-87; lay del. Cal-Pac Conf. United Meth. Ch., 1985, 86, 92-96, chair conf. commn. on archives and history, 1992—96. Rsch. grantee Coun. on Libr. Resources, 1985, 90, Assn. Libr. and Info. Sci. Educators rsch. grantee, 1984, 87, 98, Online Computer Libr. Ctr. Libr. and Info. Sci. rsch. grantee, 1999; Harold Lancour scholar Beta Phi Mu, 1986, 99, Kaliper Sr. scholar U. Mich., 1998-99, Presdl. scholar Libr. Systems and Svcs. LLC, 2002—03; recipient Louise Maxwell award Ind. U. Alumni Assn., 1995. Mem. ALA (Justin Winsor prize 1990, Ref. and Adult Svcs. divsn. Outstanding Paper award 1992), AAAS, Assn. Libr. and Info. Sci. Educators (rsch. paper prize 1986, 91, rsch. grants 1984, 87, 98), Am. Soc. for Info. Sci. (Best Info. Sci. book 1995), Am. Assn. Adv. Slavic Studies, Sigma Xi. Democrat. Avocations: wine tasting, bread baking, reading, foreign travel. Office: UCLA GSE&IS DIS Campus Box 951520 Los Angeles CA 90095-1520 Office Phone: 310-206-9369. Business E-Mail: jrichard@ucla.edu.

RICHARDSON, JOHN W., telecommunications industry executive; m. Rose Richardson; children: Anne Marie, Jake. BBA, Ohio U., Athens, 1967. CPA Ohio. Mgmt. positions through v.p. fin. N.Am. tire bus. Goodyear Tire & Rubber Co., 1967—2002; sr. v.p., contr. Qwest Comm. Internat., Inc., Denver, 2003—04, sr. v.p., chief acctg. officer, 2004—07, exec. v.p., CFO, 2007—. Bd. dirs. Ashworth, Inc. Mem. adv. bd. Ohio U. Sch. Accountancy. Office: Qwest Comm Internat Inc 1801 California St Denver CO 80202 Office Phone: 303-992-1400. Office Fax: 303-896-8515.

RICHARDSON, JUDY MCEWEN, investment banker, consultant; b. Appleton, Wis., June 3, 1947; d. John Mitchell and Isabel Annette (Ruble) McEwen; m. Larry Leroy Richardson, Mar. 19, 1972 (div. Oct. 1983). BA in English, Stanford U., 1968, MA in Edn., 1969; PhD in Higher Edn., U. Wash., 1975. Dir. ednl. rsch. St. Olaf Coll., Northfield, Minn., 1975-79; evaluation specialist Northwest Regional Ednl. Laboratory, Portland, 1980-82; legis. rsch. analyst Ariz. State Sen., Phoenix, 1982-87; dir. sch. fin. Ariz. Dept. Edn., Phoenix, 1987-92, assoc. supt., 1992-94; ednl. cons. Scottsdale, Ariz., 1994-96; exec. dir. Ariz. State Bd. for Sch. Capital Facilities, Phoenix, 1996-98; sch. fin. cons. Peacock, Hislop, Staley & Given, Phoenix, 1998—2002; v.p. Stone & Youngberg, Phoenix, 2002—. Cartoonist for the Ariz. Capitol Times, 1995-96. Office: Stone & Youngberg LLC 2555 E Camelback Rd Ste 280 Phoenix AZ 85016 Office Phone: 602-794-4012. Business E-Mail: jrichardson@syllc.com.

RICHARDSON, LAURA A., United States Representative from California; b. LA, Apr. 14, 1962; m. Anthony W. Batts (div.). BA in Polit. Sci., UCLA, 1984; MBA, U. So. Calif., 1996. With Xerox Corp., 1987—2001; So. Calif. dir. office Lt. Gov. Cruz Bustamante State of Calif., 2001—06; mem. Calif. State Assembly from Dist. 55, 2006—07, asst. spkr. Pro Tempore Leadership Team, 2006—, mem. budget, human svcs., utilities & commerce, govt. orgn., and joint legis. budget coms.; mem. US Congress from 37th Calif. Dist., 2007—, mem. sci. & tech. com., transp. & infrastructure com. Field dep. to congresswoman Juanita Millender-McDonald US Congress, 1997; mem. Long Beach City Coun., 2000—06. Named to Power 150, Ebony mag., 2008. Mem.: Calif. Mfg. & Tech. Assn. (bd. mem.). Democrat. Methodist. Office: US Congress 2233 Rayburn House Office Bldg Washington DC 20515 also: PO Box 50080 Long Beach CA 90815

RICHARDSON, MELVIN MARK, state legislator, broadcast executive; b. Salt Lake City, Apr. 29, 1928; s. Mark and Mary (Lundquist) R.; m. Dixie Joyce Gordon, 1952; children: Pamela, Mark, Lance, Todd, Kristi. Grad., Radio Operational Engring. Sch., Burbank, Calif., 1951. Radio announcer, program dir. Sta. KBUH, Brigham City, Utah, 1951-54; mgr. Sta. KLGN, Logan, Utah, 1954-58; announcer, sports dir. Sta. KID Radio/TV, Idaho Falls, Idaho, 1958-86; mgr., program dir. Sta. KID-FM/AM, Idaho Falls, 1986; mem. Idaho Ho. of Reps., 1988-92, Idaho Senate, Dist. 32, Boise, 1992—. Cons., dir. INEL Scholastic Tournament, Idaho Nat. Engring. Lab.; speaker in field. Host: Mel's Sports Scene, Thirty Minutes, Channel Three Reports, Probes, Probing America. Dir. Assn. Idaho Cities, Ricks Coll. Booster Club, Bonneville County Crime Stoppers, Idaho Falls Child Devel. Ctr.; active Idaho Centennial Commn., Anti-Lottery Com., Gov.'s Conf. on Children; commr. Bonneville County Parks and Recreation Commn.; mayor City of Ammon, Idaho, 1966-72; candidate from Idaho Dist. # 2 for U.S. Congress. Sgt. USAR, 1951-57. Named Man of Yr., Ricks Coll., 1980. Mem. Idaho Broadcasters Assn. (bd. dirs.). Republican. Mem. Lds Ch. Home and Office: 3725 Brookfield Ln Idaho Falls ID 83406-6803 Address: State Capitol PO Box 83720 Boise ID 83720-3720

RICHARDSON, WALTER JOHN, architect; b. Long Beach, Calif., Nov. 14, 1926; s. Walter Francis and Ava Elizabeth (Brown) R.; m. Marilyn Joyce Brown, June 26, 1949 (div. 1982); children: Mark Steven, Glenn Stewart; m. Mary Sue Sutton, Dec. 4, 1982. Student, UCLA, 1944—45, Long Beach City Coll., 1946; BA, U. Calif., Berkeley, 1950. Registered arch., Ala., Ariz., Calif., Colo., Fla., Hawaii, Ill., Kans., Md., Mass., Nev., N.J., N.Y., Okla., Oreg., Tex., Utah, Vt., Va., Wash. Draftsman Wurster, Bernardi, Emmons, San Francisco, 1950-51, Skidmore, Owings & Merrill, San Francisco, 1951; designer Hugh Gibbs Arch., Long Beach, 1952-58; ptnr. Thomas & Richardson Archs., Long Beach, Costa Mesa, 1958-70; pres. Walter Richardson Assocs. Archs., Newport Beach, Calif., 1970-74; chmn. bd. Richardson, Nagy, Martin Archs. and Planners, Newport Beach, 1974—2000, RNM Architecture-Planning, Newport Beach, 2000—. Co-author: The Architect and the Shelter Industry, 1975. Chmn. Planning Commn., City of Orange, Calif., 1967-68. With USAF, 1945. Recipient over 200 Gold Nugget Design awards Pacific Coast Builders Conf., San Francisco, 1969-96, 12 Builders Choice Design awards Builder Mag.; named Arch. of Yr. Profl. Builder mag., 1986; named to Hall of Fame Builder Mag., 2005 Fellow AIA (pres. Orange County chpt. 1970, chmn. nat. housing com. 1976, 77 design awards); mem. Nat. Assn. Home Builders, Nat. Coun. Archtl. Registration Bds., Urban Land Inst., Alpha Tau Omega. Republican. Avocations: photography, downhill skiing, travel. Home: RNM Design 2 Corporate Park Ste 100 Irvine CA 92606-5103 Office Phone: 949-752-1800.

RICHEY, MARY ELLEN, lawyer; b. Boston, Mar. 16, 1949; BA summa cum laude, Radcliffe Coll., 1970; JD, Stanford U., 1977. Bar: Calif. 1978. Law clk. to Hon. Charles B. Renfrew U.S. Dist. Ct. (no. dist.) Calif., 1977-78; law clk. to Hon. Lewis F. Powell, Jr., assoc. justice U.S. Supreme Ct., 1979-80; with Farella, Braun & Martel, San Francisco; assoc. Providian Fin. Corp., San Francisco, 1980—85, ptnr., v.p., sec., 1985—93, gen. counsel, 1985—, vice chmn., 2001—. Symposium editor Stanford Law Rev., 1976-77. Mem. ABA (bus. law sect., real property probate and trust law sect.), State Bar Calif. (bus. law sect., real property law sect.), Bar Assn. San Francisco, Phi Beta Kappa, Order of Coif.

RICHIE, LIONEL B., JR., singer, lyricist, theater producer; b. Tuskegee, Ala., June 20, 1949; s. Lionel and Alberta Richie; m. Brenda Harvey, 1975 (div.); 1 child, Nicole; m. Diane Alexander, 1996; children: Miles, Sofia. BS in Econs., Tuskegee U., 1971, MusD (hon.), 1985, Boston Coll., 1986. Pres. Brockman Music, LA. Mem. group The Mystics (name changed to The Commodores), 1969-81; writer, producer songs for Commodores including: Easy, Three Times a Lady (Am. Music award 1979, People's Choice award for best song 1979), Still (People's Choice award for best song 1980), Sail On, Lady (Nat. Music Pubs. award 1980, 81, People's Choice award for best composer 1981); songwriter, producer album for Kenny Rogers; albums (with The Commodores) include Midnight Magic, Machine Gun, Movin' On, Commodores, Caught in the Act, Hot on the Tracks, Natural High, Heroes, (solo albums) Lionel Richie, 1982, Can't Slow Down, 1983 (Grammy award Album of Yr. 1985), Dancing on the Ceiling, 1986, Back to Front, 1992, Louder Than Words, 1996, Truly-The Love Songs, 1997, Time, 1998, Renaissance, 2001 (Grammy nomination for Angel); prodr., composer: (songs) Truly (Grammy award 1982, 2 Am. Music awards 1983, People's Choice award Best Song, 1983), All Night Long (Nat. Music Pubs. award 1984, 3 Black Gold awards 1984, Am. Music award 1984, Hello (2 Am. Music awards 1985), Say You, Say Me (ASCAP Pop award 1987, Am. Music award 1987, Oscar award Best Song 1986, Golden Globe award Best Song 1986), Dancing on the Ceiling (3 Am. Music awards 1987), (duet with Diana Ross) Endless Love (Grammy award 1982, 2 Am. Music awards 1982, Am. Movie award 1982, Rojo award Gold Status in Hong Kong 1982, People's Choice award Best Song 1982), (sung by Kenny Rogers) Lady, (with Michael Jackson) We Are The World, 1985 (Grammy awards Best Song, Record of Yr. 1986, People's Choice award Best Song 1986); actor (film) The Preacher's Wife, 1996. Recipient Best Young Artist in Film award, 1980, 2 NAACP image awards, 1983, Favorite Male Vocalist Pop/Rock award Am. Music Acad., 1987, Favorite Male Vocalist Soul/R&B award Am. Music Acad., 1987, Lifetime Achievement award San Remo Festival, Italy, 1996, Lifetime Achievement award World Music Awards, Golden Note award, ASCAP, 2008; inductee Ala. Music Hall of Fame, 1997; named Man of Yr. Children's Diabetes Found., 1984, Alumnus of Yr. United Negro Coll. Fund, 1984, Favorite Male Singer People mag. Readers Poll, 1985, Entertainer of Yr., NAACP, 1987. Mem. ASCAP (Writer of Yr. 1984, 85, 86, Pub. of Yr. 1985).

RICHIE, NICOLE, television personality; b. Berkeley, Calif., Sept. 21, 1981; d. Lionel and Brenda Harvey Richie; 1 child (with Joel Madden), Harlow Winter Kate Madden Co-star: (TV series) The Simple Life, 2003; The Simple Life 2: Road Trip, 2004; The Simple Life 3: Interns, 2005; The Simple Life 4: 'Til Death Do Us Part, 2006; The Simple Life 5: Goes to Camp, 2007; guest appearance Punk'd, 2003; Mad TV, 2004; Rock Me Baby, 2004; Six Feet Under, 2004; actor: (films) Kids in America, 2005; author: The Truth About Diamonds, 2005 (Publishers Weekly hardcover fiction bestseller list). Office: Creative Artists Agency 2000 Avenue Of The Stars Los Angeles CA 90067-4700

RICHLAND, KENT LEWIS, lawyer; b. Nov. 1946; m. Barbara Sue Circle, 1969; children: Justin Blake, Sara Circle. AB, U. Calif., Berkeley, 1968; JD, UCLA, 1971. Bar: Calif. 1972, US Supreme Ct. 1975, US Ct. Appeals (9th cir.) 1972, US Dist. Ct. (ctrl. dist.) Calif. 1972. Supervising dep. atty. gen. Calif. State, 1972—76; supervising atty. for Calif. State Pub. Defender, 1976—78; sr. rsch. atty. to Presiding Justice Otto M. Kaus Calif. Ct. Appeals, 1978—79; atty. Horvitz & Greines, 1980—83; founding mem. Greines, Martin, Stein & Richland LLP, LA, 1983—. Trustee state appellate jud. evaluation com., 1998—2000; chair appellate cts. com., 1985—88, Calif. jud. sys. com., 1988—90, jud. appts. com., 2001—03; adj. prof. law Southwestern Sch. Law, 1986—87; guest lectr. U. So. Calif. Law Ctr., UCLA Sch. Law, U. West LA Sch. Law. Bd. editors LA Bar Jour. and LA Lawyer, 1973—78, articles editor and mng. editor, 1977—78, bd. advisors Hastings Constl. Law Quarterly, 1978—88; contbr. articles to law jours. Fellow: Am. Acad. Appellate Lawyers; mem.: ABA (co-chair Nat. Inst. on Med. Malpractice 1989—90, mem. appellate adv. com. 2001—, mem. torts and ins. practice sect. appellate advocacy com.), Calif. Judicial Coun., LA County Bar Assn. (trustee 1998—2000), Calif. Acad. Appellate Lawyers (pres. 1995—96), Calif. Supreme Ct. Hist. Soc. (bd. dirs. 1998—, pres. 1999—2005). Achievements include successful arguing Marshall versus Marshall (Anna Nicole Smith case) in the United States Supreme Court, 2006. Office: Greines Martin Stein Richland Llp 5900 Wilshire Blvd Ste 1200 Los Angeles CA 90036-5009 Office Phone: 310-859-7811. Office Fax: 310-276-5261. Business E-Mail: krichland@gmsr.com.

RICHMAN, ANTHONY E., textile rental industry association executive; b. Dec. 13, 1941; s. Irving M. and Helen V. (Muchnic) R.; Judy Harriet Richman, Dec. 19, 1964; children: Lisa Michele, Jennifer Beth. BS, U. So. Calif., 1964. With Reliable Textile Rental Svcs., LA, 1964—; svc. mgr., 1969; sales and svc. mgr., 1970-73; plant mgr., 1973-75; gen. mgr., bd. dirs., 1975-78; v.p., sec.-treas., 1975-82; exec. v.p., CEO, 1982-84; pres., CEO, 1984—. Bd. dirs. Guild for Children, 1979—, Valley Guild for Cystic Fibrosis, 1974—, Cystic Fibrosis Found. of L.A. and Orange Counties, 1989—; pres. Textile Rental/Svc. Assn. Am., 1993-95; exec. dir. Western Textile Svcs. Assn., Studio City, Calif., 1996—. Office: Western Textile Svcs Assn 12031 Ventura Blvd #4 Studio City CA 91604-2409 Office Phone: 818-399-5408.

RICHMAN, DAVID PAUL, neurologist, educator, researcher; b. Boston, June 9, 1943; s. Harry S. and Anne (Goodkin) R.; m. Carol Mae von Bastian, Aug. 31, 1969; children: Sarah Ann, Jacob Charles. AB, Princeton U., 1965; MD, Johns Hopkins U., 1969. Diplomate Am. Bd. Psychiatry and Neurology. Intern, then asst. resident in medicine Albert Einstein Coll. Medicine, NYC, 1969-71; resident in neurology Mass. Gen. Hosp., Boston, 1971-73, chief resident, 1973-74; instr. neurology Harvard U. Med. Sch., Boston, 1975-76; asst. prof. neurology U. Chgo., 1976-80, assoc. prof., 1981-85, prof., 1985-91, Straus prof. neurol. Scis., 1988-91; prof. neurology U. Calif., Davis, 1991—, chmn. dept., 1991-97. Mem. com. Nat. Inst. Aging, NIH, 1984-85, mem. immunological scis. study sect., 1986-90. Mem. AAAS, Am. Assn. Immunologists, Am. Acad. Neurology, Am. Neurol. Assn., Phi Beta Kappa, Sigma Xi. Office: U Calif Davis Dept Neurology 1515 Newton Ct Davis CA 95616-4859 Office Phone: 530-752-5013. Business E-Mail: dprichman@ucdavis.edu.

RICHMAN, DOUGLAS DANIEL, medical virologist, educator, internist; b. NYC, Feb. 15, 1943; s. Daniel Powell and Louise Kohnstamm (Woolf) R.; m. Eva Acquino, June 21, 1965; children: Sara, Matthew. AB cum laude, Dartmouth Coll., 1965; MD, Stanford U., 1970. Diplomate Am. Bd. Internal Medicine, Am. Bd. Infectious Diseases, Am. Bd. Med. Examiners. Intern Stanford Med. Sch., Calif., 1970—71, resident, 1971—72; rsch. assoc. LID/NIAID NIH, Bethesda, Md., 1972—75; fellow Beth Israel and Children's Hosps., Harvard Med. Ctr., Boston, 1975—76; asst. prof. depts. pathology and medicine U. Calif., San Diego, 1976—82, assoc. prof., 1982—88, prof., 1988—, Florence Seeley Riford chair in AIDS rsch., 2004—. Vis. prof. Hubei Med. Coll., Wuhan, People's Republic of China, 1987, Tokyo Med. and Dental U., Kumamoto U. Sch. Medicine, Inst. for Virus Rsch. at Kyoto U., St. Marianna U., Tokyo, Inst. Med. Rsch., Tokyo, Fukishima Prefecture Med. Sch., Japan, 1990; vis. fellow Clare Hall, U. Cambridge, 1984-85; mem. U. Calif. Pres.'s Cancer Rsch. Coord. Com., 1984-89, NIH AIDS Rsch. Rev. Com., 1987-90; cons. FDA Ctr. for Drugs and Biologics, 1986-89; dir. U. Calif.-San Diego Ctr. for AIDS Rsch., AIDS Rsch. Inst. Co-editor: Clin. Virology, —; mem. editl. bd.: Antimicrobial Agts. and Chemotherapy, 1987—, Jour. of AIDS, 1988—, Antiviral Agts., 1988—, AIDS, 1990—, AIDS Alert, 1990—, Antiviral Drug Resistance, 1996—, Virology, 1997—, others; contbr. more than 550 articles to profl. jours. Recipient Lowell Rantz award in infectious diseases, 1970, AMA Physicians Recognition award, 1976, 79, 82, 85, 88, William S. Middleton award Dept. Vet. Affairs, 2002; John Simon Guggenheim fellow, 1984. Fellow: ACP, AAAS, We. Assn. Physicians, Am. Assn. Physicians, Infectious Diseases Soc. Am.; mem.: Am. Clin. and Climatologic Assn., VA Soc. for Physicians in Infectious Diseases, Internat. AIDS Soc., Internat. Soc. Antiviral Rsch., Am. Soc. for Virology, Am. Fedn. for Clin. Rsch., Am. Soc. for Microbiology. Office: U Calif San Diego Dept Pathology & Medicine 9500 Gilman Dr La Jolla CA 92093-0679

RICHMAN, KEITH, communications executive; b. 1973; married. BA in Internat. Policy Studies, MA in Internat. Policy Studies, Stanford. Dir., Corp. Planning Walt Disney Co.; mgr. Excite, Classifieds2000; dir., Bus. Devel. Billpoint Inc.; co-founder, CEO Break.com. Named one of 40 Executives Under 40, Multichannel News, 2006. Office: Break.com 311 N Robertson Blvd Ste 917 Beverly Hills CA 90211

RICHMAN, PETER MARK, actor, painter, film producer; b. Phila., Apr. 16, 1927; s. Benjamin and Yetta Dora (Peck) Richman; m. Theodora Helen Landess, May 10, 1953; children: Howard Bennett, Kelly Allyn, Lucas Dion, Orien, Roger Lloyd. BS in Pharmacy, U. of the Scis., 1951; student of Lee Strasberg, NYC, 1952-54; mem., Actors' Studio, NYC, 1954—. Registered pharmacist Pa., NY. Actor: (plays), 1946—51, Have I Got a Girl for You, 1963, Ctr. Theater Group, 1965, Grove Theater, 1952, Westchester Playhouse, 1953, Drury Ln., 1957, Strand, 1957, Capri, 1959, Ongonquit Playhouse, 1955—62, 1955, 1953—55, 1955, 1962, 1955—62, Phila. Playhouse in Pk., 1962—63; (Broadway plays) End as a Man, 1953, Hatful of Rain, 1956—57, Masquerade, 1959; (plays) End as a Man, 1953, The Dybbuk, 1954, The Zoo Story, 1960—61, Rainmaker, Private Lives, Angel Street, Arms and the Man, Rose Tattoo, Liliom, Funny Girl, Owl and the Pussycat, Hold Me, Equus, Night of the Iguana, Blithe Spirit, Twelve Angry Men, 1985, Babes in Toyland, 1988, Ray Bradbury's Next in Line, 1992, numerous others, stage, radio, TV, 1948—65; writer, performer: 4 Faces, 1995 (Drama-Logue Critics Performance award, 1996), 1996; The Actors Studio, 1996; others; narrator 7 Circles of Life: A Subud Cantata, 1997, Inssbruck, Austria, 2005, A Lincoln Portrait, 2004, 2007; actor: (films) Friendly Persuasion, 1956, The Strange One, 1956, Black Orchid, 1958, The Dark Intruder, 1965, Agent for HARM, 1965, For Singles Only, 1967, Judgement Day (formerly The Third Hand), 1988, Friday the 13th, Part 8: Jason Takes Manhattan, 1989, Naked Gun 2 1/2: The Smell of Fear, 1991, Pool Hall Junkies, 2003; prodr., writer, actor: 4 Faces, 2000; actor: (TV series) Cain's Hundred, 1961—62, David Chapter III, 1966, Longstreet, 1971—72, Three's Company, 1978—79, Heroes of the Bible, 1979, Dynasty, 1981—84, Santa Barbara, 1984, Defenders of the Earth, 1986, My Secret Summer (formerly Mystery of the Keys), 1991; guest actor: Hotel; Dallas; Hart to Hart; Fantasy Island; Murder She Wrote; Nothing Sacred; Three's Company; Knight Rider; Star Trek: The Next Generation; Matlock; Beverly Hills 90210; Over 500 Shows; actor: (TV films) House on Greenapple Road, 1968, McCloud, 1969, Yuma, 1970, Nightmare at 43 Hillcrest, 1974, Mallory, 1975, The Islander, 1978, Greatest Heroes of the Bible, 1979, Blind Ambition, 1979, The PSI Factor, 1981, Dynasty, 1981, Dempsey, 1983, City Killer, 1984, Bonanza: The Next Generation, 1988; one-man shows include Am. Masters Gallery, LA, 1967, Orlando Gallery, 1966, McKenzie Gallery, 1969, 1973, Hopkins Gallery, 1971,

Goldfield Gallery, 1979, Galerie des Stars, 1968, Crocker Mus., Sacramento, 1967, Parkhurst Gallery, Seal Beach, Calif., 1991, Henley Gallery, Chapman U., Orange, Calif, 1996, exhibited in group shows at Bednarz Gallery, LA, 1968, Dohan Gallery, 1966, Celebrity Art Exhibits, 1964—65; author: (plays) Heavy, Heavy What Hangs Over?, 1971, A Medal for Murray, 1991, 2008, 4 Faces, 1995 (Commendation award Prism Film Festival, 2002); dir.: (plays) Apple of His Eyes, 1954, Glass Menagerie, 1954; author: Hollander's Deal, 2000, The Rebirth of Ira Masters, 2001; performer: (albums) Twilight Zone, 2005. Trustee Motion Picture and TV Fund. With USN, 1945—46. Recipient Silver medallion, Motion Picture TV Fund, 1990, Sybil Brand Humanitarian award, Jeffrey Found., 1990, Spl. award, 1997, Golde Halo Eagle award, So. Calif. Motion Picture Coun., 1997, Lifetime Achievement award, 2004. Mem.: AFTRA, SAG, Dramatists Guild America, Acad. TV Arts and Scis., Acad. Motion Picture Arts and Scis., Assn. Can. TV and Radio Artists, Actors Equity Assn. Office: 4 Faces Prodns 19528 Ventura Blvd Ste 385 Tarzana CA 91356 Office Phone: 818-623-6476. Personal E-mail: office@petermarkrichman.com.

RICHMOND, GERALDINE LEE, chemist, educator; BS in Chemistry magna cum laude, Kansas State U., 1975; PhD in Phys. Chemistry, U. Calif., Berkeley, 1980. Rsch. and teaching asst. Kans. State U., 1973-76, U. Calif., Berkeley, 1976-80; asst. prof. chemistry Bryn Mawr Coll., 1980-85; assoc. prof. chemistry U. Oreg., Eugene, 1985-91, dir. rsch. experience for undergrad. program, 1987—2004, dir. chem. phys. inst., 1991-95, prof. chemistry, 1991—, Knight prof. liberal arts and sci., 1998—2001, Richard M. and Patricia H. Noyes prof. chemistry, 2001—. Mem. adv. bd. Chemistry, NSF, 1986-89, Materials Sci., 1989-92; mem. adv. bd. Accounts of Chem. Rsch., 1991-94, Analytical Chemistry, 1992-95; chair, founder Com. Advancement Women Chemists (COACh), 1998-2005; mem. governor's sci. adv. bd., State of Oreg., 1986-89; mem., Basic Energy Sci. Adv. Com. Dept. Energy, 1995-2003, chair, 1998-2003; regent Oregon State Bd. Higher Edn. (Gov. Kitzhabor appointee), 1999-2003, system atrategic planning com., 1999-2000, Budget and Fin. Com., 2000-03, regent, v.p. (Gov. Kulongoski appointee), 2002-, mem. exec. com., 2003-05, v.p. and interim pres., 2004, chair, chancellor's office reorganization com., 2004-05; mem. Coun. on Chem. Sciences, Dept. Energy 1996-2001; mem. bd. chem. sci. and tech. matter, NAS/NRC, 1989-92, mem.bd. on solid state sciences, 1991-94, mem. chem. sci. roundtable 2003-;chair, NAS Frontiers in Sci. Symposium, 1993-94, Women Faculty Resource Network, U. Oreg., 1992-2004;lectr. in field. Mem. editl. bd. Critical Reviews and Surface Anatomy, 1991-95, Analytical Chemistry, 1992-95, Accounts of Chemical Research, 1991-94, Vibrational Spectroscopy, 1990-94, Jour. Physical Chemistry, 1989-1994, Applied Spectroscopy, 1993-96, Langmuir, 2001-03; adv. bd. mem. Chemical and Engineering News, 2002-04; assoc. editor, Annual Review of Physical Chemistry, 2005-; contbr. articles to profl. jours. King Meml. scholar, 1973-75; Alfred P. Sloan rsch. fellow, 1985-89; recipient Rosalyn Schwartz award, 1982, NSF Presdl. Young Investigator award, 1985-90, Camile and Henry Dreyfus Tchr. award, 1986-90, Chemistry Dept. Alumni award, Kansas State U., 1986, Women Scientists and Engrs. Faculty award, NSF, 1991-96, Rsch. Creativity award, NSF, 1991, Agnes Faye Morgan Rsch. award, 1993, Coll. Arts & Sciences Alumni award, Kansas State U., 1997, Presdl. award Excellence Sci. and Engring. Mentoring White House, 1997, Women Helping Women award Soroptomist Internat., 1998, Rsch. Creativity award, NSF, 2000, Advance Leadership award, NSF, 2001, Oregon Outstanding Sci. award Oregon Acad. Sci., 2001, Spiers medal, Royal Soc. Chemistry (UK) Faraday divsn., 2004 Fellow AAAS, Am. Phys. Soc.(mem. adv. com. laser sci. topical group, 1990-95), Am. Acad. Arts & Sciences; mem. Am. Chem. Soc. (Analytical Chemistry award 1973, Francis P. Garvan medal, 1996, Women Chemist Com. Regional award Diversity, 2002, Spectrochemical Analysis award, 2002, award for Encouraging Women into Careers in Chem. Sci. 2005), Assn. Women in Sci., Coblentz Spectroscopy Soc. (mem. exec. com., 1988-91, award 1989), Electrochem. Soc., Soc. Applied Spectroscopy, Western Spectroscopy Assn. (exec. bd. mem. 1986-1989) Office: Dept Chemistry 1274 Univ Oregon Eugene OR 97403 Office Phone: 541-346-4635. Office Fax: 541-346-5859. Business E-Mail: richmond@uoregon.edu.

RICHMOND, ROCSAN, television executive producer, investigative reporter, small business owner; b. Chgo., Jan. 30; d. Alphonso and Annie Lou (Combest) Richmond; 1 child from previous marriage, Tina S. Student, Wilson Jr. Coll., 1963, 2d City Theatre, Chgo., 1969, Alice Liddel Theatre, 1970; cert. fingerprint classifier, LA City Coll., 1996. Lic. 3d class radio/tel. operator FCC. Vegetarian editor Aware mag., Chgo., 1977—78; investigative reporter, film critic Chgo. Metro News, 1975—81; prodr., talk show host Sta. WSSD, Chgo., 1980—81; dir. pub. rels. IRMCO Corp., Chgo., 1981—82; dir. pub. rels., newsletter editor Hollywood (Calif.) Reporter, 1985—86; exec. prodr. Donald Descendent's Prodns., Hollywood, 1983—. Future News, TV show, 1983—86; pres. Richmond Estates; tchr. TV prodn. Profl. Bus. Acad., Hollywood, 1998—2000; founder, pres. Richmond Acad. Fine Manners, 2000—; v.p. adminstrv. svcs. S.G. Mgmt. Co., Manhattan Beach, Calif., 2000—06; pres. Integrity Mgmt. Co. Invention invisible drapery tieback. Jehovah's Witness. Achievements include invention of invisible drapery tieback. Personal E-mail: estateofrichmond@aol.com.

RICHTER, BURTON, physicist, educator; b. NYC, Mar. 22, 1931; s. Abraham and Fanny (Pollack) Richter; m. Laurose Becker, July 1, 1960; children: Elizabeth, Matthew. BS, MIT, 1952, PhD, 1956; degree in physics (hon.), U. Pisa, 2001. Research assoc. Stanford U., 1956—60, asst. prof. physics, 1960—63, assoc. prof., 1963—67, prof., 1967—2006, Paul Pigott prof. phys. sci., 1980—2005, tech. dir. Linear Accelerator Ctr., 1982—84, dir. Linear Accelerator Ctr., 1984—99; dir. emeritus, 1999—2006. Loeb lectr. Harvard U., 1974; DeShalit lectr. Weizmann Inst., 1975; pres. Internat. Union of Pure and Applied Physics, 1997; Astor vis. lectr. Oxford U., 2000; cons. NSF, 1999—2002, advisor, chair NERAC subcom. adv. nuc. transmutation tech., 2002—; sec., bd. dirs. AREVA Enterprises, Inc., Litel Instruments. Contbr. over 300 articles to profl. publs. Recipient E.O. Lawrence medal, Dept. Energy, 1976, Nobel prize in Physics, 1976. Fellow: AAAS, Am. Acad. Arts and Scis., Am. Phys. Soc. (pres. 1994, chmn. energy efficiency study group); mem.: NAS, Nat. Rsch. Coun. (mem. bd. physics and astronomy, chair 2003—), Internat. Coun. Sci. (mem. exec. bd. 2002—05), Regents Mercersburg Acad. (hon.), Nat. Climate Change Assessment (PCAST rev. panel), Am. Phil. Soc. (bd. dirs.). Achievements include research in elementary particle physics. Office: SLAC 2575 Sand Hill Rd Menlo Park CA 94025

RICHTER, PETER CHRISTIAN, lawyer; b. Opava, Czechoslovakia, June 13, 1944; came to U.S., 1951; s. Hanus and Alzbeta (Kindlarova) R.; m. Leslie Diane Rousseau, Nov. 25, 1967; children: Timothy Jason, Lindsey Berta. BS, U. Oreg., 1967, JD, 1971. Bar: Oreg. 1971, U.S. Dist. Ct. 1972, U.S. Ct. Appeals (9th cir.) 1972, U.S. Supreme Ct. 1983. Assoc. Veatch, Lovett & Stiner, Portland, Oreg., 1971-73; ptnr. Miller Nash LLP, Portland, 1978—. Adj. prof. law trial advocacy Northwestern Sch. of Law, Lewis and Clark Coll., Portland, 1986—; pro tempore judge Multnomah County Cir. Ct., Portland, 1985—1998, Oreg. State Bar Trial Advocacy Seminars, 1988—; trial advocacy coll. planner, instr. Oreg. State Bar, 1998—. Author: (handbook) Oregon State Bar, 1987, 88, 89; co-author: (chpt. in book) Oregon State Bar Damage Manual, 1985, 90; editor, program planner Sales: The Oregon Experience, 1989. Trustee, bd. dirs. Parry Ctr. for Children, Portland, 1990; former bd. dir. Boy Scouts of Am., Columbia Pacific Coun., Portland, Nat. Conf. Christians and Jews, Portland, 1983; bd. advisers Pacific Crest Outward Bound, 2000. With Oreg. Army N.G., 1967-75. Recipient Cert. of Appreciation Northwestern Sch. of Law, 1990; named one of ten Best Litigators in Oreg, Nat. Bar Jour. Fellow Am. Bar Found.; mem. ABA (trial techniques com.), Fed. Bar Assn. (Oreg. chpt.), Am. Bd. Trial Advocates (advocate), Internat. Assn. of Def. Counsel, Oreg. Bar Assn. (lectr. trial advocacy seminars 1988—, mem. jud. adminstn. com, bus. lit. sec. exec. comm.), Multnomah Bar Assn. (former bd dirs.), Oreg. Assn. Def. Counsel (cert. of appreciation 1987, 89) Inns of Ct., Multnomah Athletic Club (trustee, pres.), Arlington Club. Avocations: squash, tennis, skiing, golf, reading, motorcycling riding. Office: Miller Nash LLP 111 SW 5th Ave Ste 3500 Portland OR 97204-3699 Office Phone: 503-224-5858. Business E-Mail: peter.richter@millernash.com.

RICKARD, MARGARET LYNN, library director, consultant; b. Detroit, July 31, 1944; d. Frank Mathias and Betty Louise (Lee) Sieger; m. Cyriac Thannikary, Nov. 13, 1965 (div. Feb. 1973); 1 child, Luke Anthony Thannikary; m. Marcos T. Perez, Mar. 1973 (dec. Oct. 1973); m. Lui Gotti, Dec. 23, 1984 (dec. Aug. 1997); m. William A. Rickard, Aug. 22, 1998 (dec. Aug. 21, 2005). AB, U. Detroit, Mich., 1968; MLS, Pratt Inst., Bklyn., 1969; postgrad., NYU, 1976—77. Cert. libr. N.Y. Sr. libr. Queens Pub. Libr., Jamaica, NY, 1969-77; libr. dir. El Centro (Calif.) Pub. Libr., 1977-99; ret., 1999. Vice chmn., chmn. Serra Coop. Libr. Sys., San Diego, 1980—82, libr. cons., 1998—; county libr./cons. Imperial County Free Libr., 1993—99. Pres. Hist. Site Found., El Centro, 1988—99, 1992, sec., 1989, trustee, 1989—99, v.p., 1991—92; mem. Downton El Centro Assn., mem. arches bus. improvement dist.; mem. comm. and arts task force Imperial County Arts Coun.; coord. arts and culture com. City of El Centro Strategic Plan; fin. sec. St. Elizabeth Luth. Ch., El Centro, 1988. Recipient Disting. Svc. award, El Dorado County ACSA, 2004, El Dorado County Disting. Employee Svc. award, ACSA, 2004; Title IIB fellow, Pratt Inst., 1968—69. Mem.: AAUW (v.p. El Centro 1988), ALA, Calif. County Librs. Assn., Calif. Libr. Assn., Toastmasters, El Centro C. of C., Women of Moose (sr. regent El Centro 1988—89, ednl. advancment chmn. 1999—2000), Soroptomists (life; v.p. El Centro 1978, corr. sec. 1990—91, 1st v.p. 1991—92, pres. 1992—93, 2d v.p. 1995—96, 1998—99, rec. sec. 1997—98). Democrat. Lutheran. Home and Office: 6169 Terrace Dr PO Box 232 Pollock Pines CA 95726 E-mail: rickmeg@worldnet.att.net.

RICKETSON, MARY E., former dean, lawyer; m. Nathan Ben Coats. JD, U. Denver, 1978. Asst. atty gen., Colo.; dep. dist. atty. Colo.; pvt. practice specializing in employment dispute mediation, arbitration; exec. dir. Colo. Lawyer's Com.; dean, univ. prof. U. Denver Sturm Coll. Law, 2000—06. Affiliated Jud. Arbitrators and Mediators. Trustee Dian Fossey Found. Internat.; co-chair Mayor Wellington Webb's 2025 Commn., 2002. Recipient Women of Distinction award, Mill High Girl Scouts, 2004, Edwin Wolf award, Lawyers Com. Civil Rights Under Law, 2004, Mile High Coun. Girl Scouts award, 2004. Mem.: Am. Bar Found., Am. Law Inst., Colo. Hispanic Bar Assn. (Cmty. Svc. award 2003), Colo. Profl. Soc. on Abuse of Children (former pres.), Colo. Women's Bar Found. (former pres.), Colo. Women's Bar Assn. (former pres., Mary Lathrop award 2003).

RICKLES, DONALD JAY, comedian, actor; b. LI, NY, May 8, 1926; s. Max S. and Etta (Feldman) R.; m. Barbara Sklar, Mar. 14, 1965; children: Mindy Beth, Lawrence Corey. Grad., Am. Acad. Dramatic Arts, NYC. Appeared in TV shows The Don Rickles Show, 1971-72, C.P.O. Sharkey, 1976-77, Foul-Ups, Bleeps and Blunders, 1984, Daddy Dearest, 1993; appeared in movies Run Silent, Run Deep, 1958, The Rat Race, 1960, Kelly's Heroes, 1992, Casino, 1995, Toy Story, 1995, Quest for Camelot, 1998, Toy Story 2, 1999, The Wool Cap, 2004, others; Reno and Lake Tahoe, Nev., Orleans, Lasvegas, Tropicana, Atlantic City, numerous other nightclubs; numerous appearances TV variety shows, (HBO documentary) Mr. Warmth: The Don Rickles Project, 2007 (Primetime Emmy for Outstanding Individual Performance in a Variety or Music Program, Acad. TV Arts and Scis., 2008), DVD, 2008; rec. albums include Don Rickles Speaks, Hello Dummy; author: Rickles Book, 2007 (NY Times Bestseller). With USN, 1943—45. Named Entertainer of Yr. Friars Club, 1974, Entertainer of Yr., Am. Gaming Assn., 2004, Las Vegas Comedian of Yr., Las Vegas Conv. and Visitor's Authority, 2004; awarded star on Hollywood Walk of Fame, 2000; recipient Pinnacle award US Comedy and Arts Festival, 2007. Office: care Shefrin Co 808 S Ridgeley Dr Los Angeles CA 90036-4727

RICKS, MARK G., former lieutenant governor, state senator; b. Rexburg, Idaho, July 4, 1924; s. Peter J. and Emily E. (Arnold) Ricks; m. Evelyn Tonks, Aug. 9, 1944; children: Michael T., Gary M., Alan D., Adele Ricks Nielson, Glen L., Kathie Ricks Tensmeyer, Grant H., Merle K., Douglas T. AS in Agrl., Ricks Coll. Mem. Idaho State Senate, 1979—94, chmn. senate commerce and labor commn., 1981—82, chmn. reapportionment com., 1982, 1990—94, majority leader, 1983—88, vice chmn. senate fin. com., 1989—94, mem. state affairs com., chmn., 1989—94, chmn. revenue and projection com., 1989—94; lt. gov. State of Idaho, 2006—07. Mem. exec. and adv. bd. coun. Boy Scouts Am. Recipient Cmty. Svc. Prodn. and Example award, Rexburg C. of C., 1976, Outstanding Svc. award, Madison Sch. Dist., 1987, Disting. Alumni award, Ricks Coll., 1988; named one of Ten Outstanding Legislators, Nat. Rep. Legislators Assn., 1987; named to, Eastern Idaho Agrl. Hall of Fame, 1989, Idaho Blue Ribbon Task Force, 2002. Mem.: Rexburg C. of C. (maj. gifts com. Ricks Coll.), Nat. Fedn. Ind. Bus., Idaho Wheat Growers, Counc. State Govts. (chmn. western legis. conf. 1988—89, chmn. ann. meeting com. 1988—90, mem. budget com. 1989—90, mem. exec. com.), Nat. Conf. State Legis. (mem. exec. com. 1985—87, chmn. nom. com. 1988, mem. rsch. and grants com., vice chmn. fed. taxation com., vice chmn. trade and econ. devel. com., mem. budget and rules com., co-chmn. reapportionment com. 1989, vice chmn. state fed. assembly 1988). Republican. Mem. Lds Ch.

RIDD, BRIAN V., chemicals executive; With Huntsman Corp., Salt Lake City, 1984—, v.p. purchasing Huntsman Chem. Corp. subs., v.p. purchasing Huntsman Petrochemical Corp. subs., v.p. Olympus Oil subs., v.p. purchasing, 1995—2000, sr. v.p. purchasing, 2000—. Office: Huntsman Corp 500 Huntsman Way Salt Lake City UT 84108 Office Phone: 801-584-5700.

RIDDER, P(AUL) ANTHONY, newspaper company executive; b. Duluth, Minn., Sept. 22, 1940; s. Bernard H. and Jane (Delano) Ridder; m. Constance Louise Meach, Nov. 6, 1960; children: Katherine Lee Pennoyer, Linda Jane, Susan Delano Cobb, Paul Anthony Jr. BA in Econs., U. Mich., 1962. With Aberdeen Am. News, SD, 1962—63; With Pasadena Star News, Calif., 1963—64; with San Jose Mercury News, Calif., 1964—86, bus. mgr., 1968—75, gen. mgr., 1975—77, pub., 1977—86, pres., 1979—86, Knight-Ridder Inc., Miami, Fla., 1989—95, pres., chmn., CEO, 1995—. Bd. dirs. Seattle Times, Knight-Ridder, Inc.; adv. bd. Stanford U. Grad. Sch. Bus. Bd. trustees Santa Clara U. Named Calif. Pub. of Yr., 1983, Newspaper Exec. of Yr., Ad Week, 1991. Mem.: San Francisco Golf Club, Pine Valley Golf Club, Cypress Point Club. Office: Knight-Ridder Inc Ste 1500 50 W San Fernando St San Jose CA 95113-2413

RIDE, SALLY KRISTEN, physics professor, research scientist, retired astronaut; b. L.A., May 26, 1951; d. Dale Burdell and Carol Joyce (Anderson) R.; m. Steven Alan Hawley, July 26, 1982 (div.). BA in English, Stanford U., 1973, BS in Physics, 1973, PhD in Physics, 1978. Tchg. asst. Stanford U., Palo Alto, Calif., rschr. dept. physics, sci. fellow, 1987-89; astronaut candidate, trainee NASA, 1978-79, astronaut, 1979-87, on-orbit capsule communicator STS-2 mission Johnson Space Ctr. Houston, on-orbit capsule communicator STS-3 mission, mission specialist STS-7, 1983, mission specialist STS-41G, 1984; dir. Calif. Space Inst. U. Calif. San Diego, La Jolla, 1989—96, pres. space com., 1999-2000; prof. dept. physics U. Calif. San Diego, 1989—. Pres., CEO Space web site, 1999—2000, Imaginary Lines, Inc., 2001—; mem. Presdl. Commn. on Space Shuttle Challenger Accident, 1986, World Resources Inst. Global Coun., 1993—, Presdl. Com. Advisors on Sci. and Tech., 1994—, U. Calif. Oversight Com. for Nat. Labs, Pacific Coun. on Internat. Policy; intiated NASA EarthKAM project; bd. dir. Nat. Rsch. Coun. Space Studies, Congressional Office of Tech. Assessment, Carnegie Instn. Washington; past bd. dir. NCAA Found.; bd. trustee Caltech; lectr. in field. Author: (with Susan Okie) To Space and Back, 1986, (with T.O'Shaughnessy) Voyager: An Adventure to the Edge of the Solar System, 1992, The Third Planet: Exploring the Earth From Space, 1994, (revised 2004), The Mystery of Mars, 1999, Exploring Our Solar System, 2003. Recipient Jefferson award for Pub. Svc., Nat. Spaceflight medal (twice), Von Braun award, Lindbergh Eagle award, Silver Anniversary award, NCAA, 1998, Golden Plate award, Acad. Achievement, 2004, Theodore Roosevelt award, NCAA, 2005; named to The Nat. Women Hall of Fame, 1988, Astronaut Hall of Fame, Kennedy Space Center, 2003, Nat. Aviation Hall of Fame, 2007. Fellow: Am. Physical Soc. Achievements include becoming the first American woman to orbit Earth when she flew aboard Space Shuttle Challenger, June, 18 1983. Avocations: tennis, running, volleyball, softball, stamp collecting. Office: U Calif San Diego Dept Physics 0426 La Jolla CA 92093-0426 Address: Sally Ride Science 9191 Towne Centre Dr San Diego CA 92122*

RIDENOUR, JIM, Mayor, Modesto, California; b. Modesto, CA; m. Renee Ridenour; 3 children. Paramedic Santa Barbara County, 1974; dep. sheriff Stanislaus & Santa Barbara County; ops. exec. Central Valley Ops. Am. Med. Response; mayor City of Modesto, 2003. Chmn. Calif. Ambulance Assoc. With Nat. Guard US Army. Office: 1010 10th St Modesto CA 95354 Mailing: PO Box 642 Modesto CA 95353 Office Phone: 209-571-5597. Office Fax: 209-571-5586. Business E-Mail: mayor@modestogov.com. E-mail: jridenour@modestogov.com.*

RIDINGER, TIM, state representative; b. Sacramento, May 24, 1956; m. Penny Ridinger; children: Tristan, Tara Jo, Tara Renae, Jordan. BBA in Real Estate and Bus. Mgmt., Boise State U. Hay hauler, trucker, rancher; councilman Shoshone City Coun., 1982—85; mayor Shoshone, 1986—; state rep. dist. 25B Idaho Ho. of Reps., Boise, 1996—, mem. commerce and human resources, and revenue and taxation coms., vice chair, transp. and def. com. Mem.: Assn. Idaho Cities (pres.), Shoshone C. of C., Dietrich Grange. Republican. Office: State Capitol PO Box 83720 Boise ID 83720-0038

RIECKE, HANS HEINRICH, architect; b. Münster, Westfalia, Germany, Mar. 30, 1929; came to U.S., 1955; s. Hans Joachim and Hildegard (Schwarze) R.; m. Elvira Maria Magdalena Kaatz, Nov. 30, 1954; children: Christine, Annette, Monica, Ralph, Heidi. Student architecture, Technische Hochschule, Hannover, Fed. Republic. Germany, 1953; BA in Architecture, U. Calif., Berkeley, 1957. Registered architect, Calif., Hawaii, Ind. Draftsman Orinoco Mining Co., Puerto Ordaz, Venezuela, 1954-55, H.K. Ferguson Co., San Francisco, 1956-57; architect, ptnr. Hammarberg and Herman, Oakland, Calif., 1957-74; prin. Hans Riecke, Architect Inc., Kahului, Maui, Hawaii, 1974-78, Riecke Sunnland Kono Architects Ltd, Kahului, Maui, Hawaii, 1978-96; pres. HR Architect Inc., Maui, 1996—. Bd. dirs. Kihei Community Assn., Maui, Hawaii, 1975-77, Seabury Hall, Makawao, Maui, 1980-82; chmn. Mayor's Com. on Housing, County of Maui, 1984. Recipient Merit award Pacific Coast Builders Con., Kahului, Hawaii, 1990. Fellow AIA (pres. Maui chpt. 1990); mem. Am. Arbitration Assn. (panel of arbitrators 1980). Avocations: bicycling, gardening. Office: HR Arch Inc 77 Apalapani Ln Haiku HI 96708-5625

RIEDEL, BERNARD EDWARD, retired pharmaceutical sciences educator; b. Provost, Alta., Can., Sept. 25, 1919; s. Martin and Naomi E. (Klingaman) R.; m. Julia C. McClurg, Mar. 5, 1944 (dec. Mar. 1992); children: Gail Lynne, Dwain Edward, Barry Robert; m. Della Williams, Sept. 2, 2000. BS in Pharmacy, U. Alta., Edmonton, 1943, MS in Pharmacology, 1949, DSc (hon.), 1990; PhD in Biochemistry, U. Western Ont., 1953. Lectr., asst. prof. Faculty of Pharmacy U. Alta., Edmonton, 1946-49, asst. prof. then assoc. prof., 1953-58, prof., 1959-67, exec. asst. to v.p., 1961-67; dean, prof. Faculty Pharm. Scis. U. B.C., Vancouver, Canada, 1967-84, coord. Health Scis. Centre, 1977-84. Mem. sci. adv. com. Health Rsch. Found. of B.C., 1991-95. Contbr. numerous articles on pharmacology to profl. jours. Elder Ryerson United Ch.; mem. exec. bd. Boy Scouts Can., Edmonton Region, Alta.; mem. Cancer Control Agy. of B.C., trustee 1979-86, v.p., 1984, pres. 1985-86; bd. dirs. B.C. Lung Assn., 1988-2000, v.p., 1989, pres., 1990-91; chmn., bd. dirs. B.C. Organ Transplant Soc., 1986-89, hon. bd. dirs., 2000. Wing comdr. RCAF, 1943-46, 49-67. Decorated mem. Order of Can.; recipient Gold medal in Pharmacy, 1943; Centennial medal, 1967, 75th Anniversary medal U. B.C., 1990;

Can Forces decoration, 1965; Commemorative medal for 125th Anniversary of the Confedn. of Can., 1992, Spl. Svcs. award Assn. Faculties of Pharmacy of Can., 2001, Queen Elizabeth II Golden Jubilee medal, 2002. Mem. Alta. Pharm. Assn. (hon. life), Can. Pharm. Assn. (hon. life), Assn. of Faculties of Pharmacy of Can. (hon. life, chmn. 1959, 69, Spl. Svc. award 2001), Can. Biochem. Soc., Pharmacol. Soc. Can., Can. Assn. of Univ. Tchrs., Can. Soc. Hosp. Pharmacists, B.C. Coll. Pharmacists (hon. life), U. B.C. Profs. Emeriti Divsn. Alumni Assn. (pres. 1993-95). Home: 8394 Angus Dr Vancouver BC Canada V6P 5L2 E-mail: briedel@interchange.ubc.ca.

RIEDY, MARK JOSEPH, finance educator; b. Aurora, Ill., July 9, 1942; s. Paul Bernard and Kathryn Veronica R.; m. Erin Jeanne Lynch, Aug. 29, 1964; children: Jennifer Erin, John Mark. BA in Econs. maxima cum laude, Loras Coll., 1964; MBA, Washington U., St. Louis, 1966; PhD, U. Mich., 1971. Asst. prof. bus. adminstrn. U. Colo., Boulder, 1969-71; sr. staff economist Council of Econ. Advisers, Washington, 1971-72; spl. asst. to chmn. Fed. Home Loan Bank Bd., Washington, 1972; v.p., dir. research PMI Investment Corp., San Francisco, 1973; v.p., chief economist Fed. Home Loan Bank of San Francisco, 1973-77; exec. v.p., chief operating officer Mortgage Bankers Assn. of Am., Washington, 1978-84; pres., chief operating officer Fed. Nat. Mortgage Assn., Washington, 1985-86, cons., 1986-87; pres., chief operating officer J.E. Robert Cos., Alexandria, Va., 1987-88; pres., chief exec. officer Nat. Coun. Community Bankers, Washington, 1988-92, also bd. dirs.; prof. real estate fin. U. San Diego, 1993—, exec. dir. Burnham-Moores Ctr. Real Estate, 1993—. Mem. adv. coun. Credit Rsch. Ctr., Purdue U., 1981-82; bd. dirs. Fed. Nat. Mortgage Assn., Continental Savs. Bank, AccuBanc Mortgage Corp., Pan Pacific Retail Properties, Inc., Am. Mortgage Network, Inc., Bio-Med. Realty Trust, Noble Broadcast Group, Drayton Ins. Cos., Perpetual Savs. Bank, Ctr. for Fin. Studies; chmn., bd. dirs., Neighborhood Bancorp; mem. San Diego Mayor's Renaissance Commn. Bd. dirs. Lambda Alpha Internat. Woodrow Wilson scholar, 1964; Nat. Def. scholar, 1964-66; U.S. Steel Found. fellow, 1966-68; Robert G. Rodkey Found. fellow, 1966-69; Earhart Found. fellow, 1968-69 Mem. Am. Econ. Assn., Am. Fin. Assn., Nat. Assn. Bus. Economists, Am. Soc. Assn. Execs., Urban Land Inst. Office: U San Diego Sch Bus Adminstrn 5998 Alcala Park San Diego CA 92110-2492 Business E-Mail: mriedy@sandiego.edu.

RIEKE, PAUL VICTOR, lawyer; b. Seattle, Apr. 1, 1949; s. Luvern Victor and Anna Jane (Bierstedt) R.; m. Judy Vivian Farr, Jan. 24, 1974; children: anna Katharina, Peter Johann. BA, Oberlin Coll., 1971; postgrad., U. Wash., 1971, Shoreline C.C., 1972-73; JD, Case Western Res. U., 1976. Bar: Wash. 1976, U.S. Dist. Ct. (we. dist.) Wash. 1976, U.S. Tax Ct. 1978. Assoc. Hatch & Leslie, Seattle, 1976-82, ptnr., 1982-91, Foster, Pepper & Shefelman, PLLC, 1991—. Exec. notes editor Case Western Res. U. Law Rev., 1975-76. Mem. exec. bd. dist. coun. N. Pacific dist. Am. Luth Ch., Seattle, 1978-83, coun. pres., 1983, Am. Luth. Ch. pub bd., 1984-87; v.p. Northwest Wash. Synod of Evangelical Luth. Ch. Am., Seattle, 1988-90, mem. Synod Coun., 1990-92, del. ELCA Nat. Assembly, 1991, ELCA Northwest Synod Regional Rep., 1992-96, region one coun. pres., 1994-96. Mem. ABA, Wash. State Bar Assn., Seattle-King County Bar Assn., Order of Coif. Lodges: Seattle Downtown Central Lions. Democrat. Home: 321 NE 161st St Shoreline WA 98155-5741 Office: Foster Pepper & Shefelman PLLC 34th Fl 1111 3rd Ave Seattle WA 98101 E-mail: RiekP@Foster.com.

RIEMENSCHNEIDER, PAUL ARTHUR, retired physician, retired radiologist; b. Cleve., Apr. 17, 1920; s. Albert and Selma (Marting) R.; m. Mildred McCarthy, May 12, 1945; children: Barbara Anne, Nancy Emelia, David Andrew, Paul Albert, Mary Elizabeth, Sarah Bache. BS magna cum laude, Baldwin-Wallace Coll., 1941; MD, Harvard U., 1944. Diplomate Am. Bd. Radiology (trustee 1973-85), Nat. Bd. Med. Examiners. Prof., chmn. dept. radiology SUNY, Syracuse, 1950—64; chief diagnostic radiology Santa Barbara Cottage Hosp., Calif., 1964—89, bd. dirs., 1984—90; ret., 1990. Vis. prof. in residence SUNY, Syracuse, 1983-98; vis. prof. of Radiology, U. Malaya, 1990-91. Co-editor: N.Y. State Jour. Medicine, 1960-64; mem. editorial adv. bd. Yearbook of Cancer, 1960-64; contbr. articles to profl. jours. Mem. appropriations com. Santa Barbara Found., 1984-93; vestryman All Saints Episc. Ch., 1970-76, sr. warden, 1973; bd. dirs. ARC, Santa Barbara, 1968-72, Am. cancer Soc., Santa Barbara, 1967-70, Casa Dorinda Retirement Residence, 1975-76, 89-96, pres., 1993-96; bd. dirs. Wood Glen Hall Retirement Residence, sec., 1987, v.p. 1998, pres. 2000; bd. dirs. Cancer Found. Santa Barbara, 1966-82, 89-95, chmn. equipment com., 1973-82; bd. dirs. Direct Relief Internat., 1997-2003, sec., 1999. Lt. comdr. USNR, 1945-46, 54-56. Recipient Alumni Merit award Baldwin-Wallace Coll., 1985. Fellow Am. Coll. Radiology (cancer com. 1952-54, coun. 1956-64, bd. chancellors 1967-73, chmn. commn. stds. in radiologic practice 1968-71, v.p. 1972, pres. 1974, chmn. com. manpower 1972-86, chmn. com. manpower in armed svcs. 1975-86, Gold medal 1982); mem. AMA, Calif. Med. Assn., Santa Barbara County Med. Soc. (chmn. med. sch. com. 1967-71), Am. Roentgen Ray Soc. (publs. com. 1965-75, chmn. 1970-75, exec. coun. 1970-75, 77-82, chmn. program com. 1977-79, pres.-elect 1977-79, pres. 1979, Gold medal award 1986), South Coast Radiol. Soc. (pres. 1967), Assn. U. Radiologists (sec. 1960, pres. 1961, com. resident tng. 1984-88), Radiol. Soc. N.Am. (vis. prof., Gold medal award 1990), Am. Soc. Neuroradiology, Soc. Pediat. Radiology, Ea. Radiol. Soc. (pres.-elect 1987, pres. 1988-89), Calif. Radiol. Soc., So. Calif. Radiol. Soc., Detroit Roentgen Soc. (hon.), Bluegrass Radiol. Soc. (hon.), Pacific N.W. Radiol. Soc. (hon.), Birnam Wood Golf Club (bd. dirs. 1996-98), Skaneateles Country Club, Cosmopolitan Club (sec. 1996), Alpha Omega Alpha. Republican. Avocations: tennis, swimming. Home: 300 Hot Springs Rd Santa Barbara CA 93108-2038

RIEMKE, RICHARD ALLAN, nuclear engineer; b. Vallejo, Calif., Oct. 11, 1944; s. Allan Frederick and Frances Jewell (O'Brien) R. BA in Physiology, U. Calif., Berkeley, 1967, MA in Physiology, 1971, PhD in Engring. Sci., 1977. Postdoctoral fellow U. So. Calif., LA, 1977-78; rsch. engr. Del Mar Avionics, Irvine, Calif., 1979; staff fellow NIH, Bethesda, Md., 1980; nuc. engr. Battelle Energy Alliance, Idaho Nat. Lab., Idaho Falls, 1980—. With USAR, 1969—75. Mem. AAAS, ANS, ASME, Biomed. Engring. Soc., Soc. Computer Simulation, Soc. Math. Biology, Soc. Engring. Sci., Order of Golden Bear, Alpha Sigma Phi. Republican. Roman Catholic. Avocations: swimming, surfing. Home: 1727 Grandview Dr # 4 Idaho Falls ID 83402-5016 Office: Battelle Energy Alliance Idaho Nat Lab Idaho Falls ID 83415-3870

RIENNER, LYNNE CAROL, publishing executive; b. Pitts., Aug. 3, 1945; d. David and Molly (Rice) R. BA, U. Pa., 1967. Exec. v.p., assoc. publisher, editorial dir. Westview Press Inc., Boulder, Colo., 1975-84; pub., owner Lynne Rienner Pub. Inc., Boulder, Colo., 1984—. Pub. cons. various orgns.; lectr. U. Denver Pub. Inst., 1981-84, 93—; panelist nat. meetings Bd. dirs. Boulder Breast Cancer Coalition, 1993-95. Mem. Assn. Am. Pubs. (bd. dirs. 1992-96, 99—, exec. coun. of profl. and scholarly pub. divsn. 1996—). Office: Lynne Rienner Pub Inc 1800 30th St Ste 314 Boulder CO 80301-1026

RIESBERG, JAMES L., state legislator; b. Denver, Apr. 4, 1942; BA, U. No. Colo., Greeley, 1964, MA, 1992. Owner, cons., gerontologist JLR Co., 1992—; mem. Dist. 50 Colo. House of Reps., Denver, 2004—. Democrat. Lutheran. Office: Colo State Capitol 200 E Colfax Denver CO 80203 Office Phone: 303-866-2929. Business E-Mail: jim.riesberg.house@state.co.us.*

RIESS, GORDON SANDERSON, management consultant; b. Thessaloniki, Greece, Feb. 25, 1928; came to U.S., 1932; s. Lewis William and Dorothy Onward Riess; m. Priscilla Rich, June 2, 1951; children: Mark C., Kimberly A., Blake G. AB with highest honors, Whitman Coll., 1949; MBA cum laude, Harvard U., 1951. Cert. mgmt. cons.; registered profl. cons.; accredited profl. cons. With Ford Internat. Div., NYC, 1951-53; asst. fin. mgr. Ford Motor Co., Mid. East, Alexandria, Egypt, 1953-57; gen. sales mgr. Ford Motor Co., Rome, Italy, 1957-60; regional fin. mgr. Ford Motor Co., Scandinavia, Copenhagen, Denmark, 1960-62; gen. mgr. Ford Motor Co., European, Brussels, Belgium, 1962-67; v.p. Internat. Paper Co., Zurich, Switzerland, 1967-71; exec. v.p. Cinema Internat. Corp., London, 1971-75; chmn., pres. Stewart-Riess Labs. Inc., Tarzana, Calif., 1976-83; pres., CEO Intercontinental Enterprises Ltd., Beverly Hills, Calif., 1983—. Chmn. Vis. Nurse Found., L.A., 1985-87; bd. dirs., chmn. Vis. Nurse Assn., L.A., 1976-97; bd. dirs. Beverly Found., Pasadena, Calif., 1990-97; vice-chmn. of bd. Witman Coll., Walla Walla, Wash., 1985-96. Author: Confessions of a Corporate Centurion--Tales of International Adventures, 2000, From Communism to Capitalism, 2001, Passports to Adventure, 2005; inventor/patentee pre-fillable hypodermic syringe. Chmn. Inter-Community Sch. Zurich, 1968-71; trustee Am. Sch. London, 1972-75; vice chmn. Krafterliner Mfgs. Assn., Zurich, 1968-71; bd. dirs. Vols. in Tech. Assistance, Arlington, Va., 1986-93; bd. overseers Muhlenberg Coll., 1993—; internat. bd. Czechoslovak Mgmt. Ctr., 1992—. Sgt. U.S. Army, 1946-47. R.H. Macy scholar, Harvard Bus. Sch., 1949. Mem. Am. Assn. Profl. Cons., Am. Cons. League, Asia Acad. Mgmt., Hollywood Radio & Television Soc., Inst. Mgmt. Cons., Lic. Execs. Soc. Avocations: skiing, scuba diving. Home: PO Box 2912 Beverly Hills CA 90213-2912 Personal E-mail: g.riess@sbcglobal.net.

RIFF, LAWRENCE P., lawyer; BA in History with highest honors and high distinction, U. Mich., 1978; JD, U. Oreg., 1982. Bar: Calif. 1982, Oreg. 1985, Washington 1987. Lawyer So. Pacific Transp. Co., San Francisco, 1982—86; mng. ptnr., toxic tort, transp. & litig. depts. Steptoe & Johnson LLP, LA, 1997—. John Williams Fellowship. Mem.: Am. Bd. Trial Advocacy, LA County Bar Assn. (Litig. Sect.), Internat. Moot Ct. Team, Jessup Competition. Office: Steptoe & Johnson LLP 633 W 5th St Ste700 Los Angeles CA 90071 Office Phone: 213-439-9494. Office Fax: 213-439-9599. Business E-Mail: lriff@steptoe.com.

RIFFENBURGH, ROBERT HARRY, biostatistician, researcher; b. Christiansburg, Va., June 19, 1931; s. Harry Buchholz and Ada Swallow Riffenburgh; m. Gerrye Harlow, Nov. 22, 1952; children: Robin, Scott, Marc, Karen, Douglas. BS, Coll. William and Mary, Richmond, Va., 1951, MS, 1953; PhD, Va. Poly. Inst., Blacksburg, 1957. Asst. prof. math. Va. Poly. Inst., Blacksburg, 1955—57, U. Hawaii, Honolulu, 1957—61; prof., head dept. stats. U. Conn., Storrs, 1962—70; prof. stats. San Diego State U., 1968—74, 1979—82, 1990—93, 2006—; head, biomedical program Naval Undersea Ctr., San Diego, 1970—73; scientist Naval Facility, Brawdy, Wales, 1974—77; math. statistician Naval Ocean Systems Ctr., San Diego, 1977—82; leader, naval ops. rsch. NATO SHAPE Tech. Centre, The Hague, Netherlands, 1982—86; head, ops. rsch. NATO SACLANT Undersea Rsch. Centre, La Spezia, Italy, 1986—90; chief biostats. Naval Med. Ctr. San Diego, San Diego, 1991—. Pres. and ceo Gen. Systems Analysis Co., Storrs, Conn., 1963—70. Author: Statistics in Medicine; contbr. articles to profl. jours. Capt. NATO, 1982—89. Decorated Navy Commendation Medal; Predoctoral fellow, NIH, 1954-1956. Fellow: Am. Statis. Assoc., Royal Statis. Soc. (life); mem.: Internat. Biometrics Soc., Phi Kappa Phi, Sigma Xi.

RIFKIN, ARNOLD, film company executive; b. Bklyn. m. Nikki MacGregor five children. BA, U. Cin. Founder Rifkin-David, 1974-80; merged to form Rifkin/David/Kimble/Parseghian, 1980-81, DH-KPR, 1981-84; head motion picture dept. Triad Artists, Inc., 1984-92, founding ptnr.; exec. v.p., worldwide head motion picture divsn. William Morris Agy., Beverly Hills, Calif., 1992-96; pres. William Morris Talent and Lit. Agy., Beverly Hills, Calif., 1996-2000; CEO Cheyenne Enterprises, LLC, Santa Monica, Calif., 2000—06; co-CEO Rifkin/Eberts LLC, 2007—. Bd. dirs. Am. Cinematheque; faculty, co-chair UCLA Sch. Theatre, Film & TV; lecturer Yale Law Sch., Harvard Sch. Bus., 2002-. Bd. councillors U. So. Calif. Office: Rifkin/Eberts LLC 406 Wilshire Blvd Santa Monica CA 90401-1410

RIGBY, RANDY, professional sports team executive; m. Sandra Rigby; 5 children. Grad. in bus. mgmt., Brigham Young U., 1979. Sr. v.p. CFS Financial Corp.; sr. v.p. sales, CMO Larry H. Miller Sports & Entertainment Group, gen. mgr., Sta. KJZZ-TV, sr. v.p. broadcasting, pres., COO, 2007—. Alt. NBA Bd. Govs. Mem. NBA Broadcasting Adv. Bd.; past pres., bd. mem. Utah Broadcasters Assn. Avocations: golf, scuba diving, fly fishing. Office: Larry H Miller Group 9350 S 150 E Rte 1000 Sandy UT 84070 also: Utah Jazz 301 W South Temple Salt Lake City UT 84101 Office Phone: 801-563-4100. Office Fax: 801-563-4191.

RIGGS, GEORGE E., newspaper publishing executive; m. Elise Riggs. With Contra Costa (Calif.) Times, 1985—2004, pub., CEO, 1991—2004; chmn., pub. San Jose Mercury News, Calif., 2004—07; pres. & CEO Calif. Newspaper Partnership, 2006—. Bd. dir. Tony LaRussa's Animal Rescue Found., John Muir Hosp. Found., Calif. Symphony; corp. adv. com. St. Mary's Coll. Mem.: Calif. Newspaper Pub. Assn. (past pres.). Office: San Jose Mercury News 750 Ridder Pk Dr San Jose CA 95190 Office Phone: 650-688-7500.

RIGGS, HENRY EARLE, academic administrator, engineering educator; b. Chgo., Feb. 25, 1935; s. Joseph Agnew and Gretchen (Walser) Riggs; m. Gayle Carson, May 17, 1958; children: Elizabeth, Peter, Catharine. BS, Stanford U., 1957; MBA, Harvard U., 1960; Doctorate (hon.), Harvey Mudd Coll., 2006, Kech Grad. Inst., 2007. Indsl. economist SRI Internat., Menlo Park, Calif., 1960—63; v.p. Icore Industries, Sunnyvale, Calif., 1963—67, pres., 1967—70; v.p. fin. Measurex Corp., Cupertino, Calif., 1970—74; prof. engring. mgmt. Stanford U., Calif., 1974—88, Ford prof. Calif., 1986—88, Ford prof. emeritus Calif., 1990, v.p. for devel. Calif., 1983—88; pres. Harvey Mudd Coll., Claremont, Calif., 1988—97, pres. emeritus, 1997; pres. Keck Grad. Inst., Claremont, 1997—2003, pres., trustee emeritus, 2003—. Bd. dirs. Capital Rsch. Group, 1989—; dir. Inst. for Sys. Biology, 2006—. Author: Accounting: A Survey, 1981, Managing High-Tech Companies, 1983, Financial and Economic Analysis, 1994, 2d edit., 2004, Understanding the Financial Score, 2007; contbr. articles to profl. jours. Recipient Gores Tchg. award, Stanford U., 1980; Baker scholar, Harvard Bus. Sch., 1959. Mem.: Stanford U. Alumni Assn. (bd. dirs. 1990—94, chmn. 1993), Palo Alto Club, Sunset Club, Calif. Club, Tau Beta Pi, Phi Beta Kappa. Home: 24 Peter Coutts Circle Stanford CA 94305 Personal E-mail: henryriggs@comcast.net.

RIGGS, JACK TIMOTHY, emergency physician, retired lieutenant governor; b. Coeur d'Alene, Idaho, Oct. 1, 1954; BS summa cum laude, U. Idaho, 1976; MD, U. Wash., 1980. Diplomate Am. Bd. Emergency Medicine. Intern Deaconess Med. Ctr., Spokane, Wash., 1980-81; mem. Idaho Senate, Dist. 4, Boise, 1996-2000; owner North Idaho Immediate Car Ctrs., 1985—; lt. gov. State of Idaho, 2001—03. Fellow Am. Coll. Emergency Physicians; mem. AMA, Am. Coll. Physician Execs., Idaho Med. Assn., Am. Coll. Occupl. and Environ. Medicine. Address: 927 E Polston Post Falls ID 83854

RIGGS, R. WILLIAM, retired state supreme court justice; Grad., Portland State U., 1961; JD, U. Oreg., 1968. Atty. Willner Bennett & Leonard, 1968—78; judge circuit ct. 4th Jud. Dist., 1978—88; judge Oreg. Ct. of Appeals, 1988—98, presiding judge, 1995—98; judge Oreg. Supreme Ct., 1998—2006. Vice-chair exec. com. Oreg. Jud. Conference, 1996—98; mem. Council on Ct. Procedures, 1986—89; founder Oreg. Acad. of Family Law Practitioners. Active mem. Cmty. Law Project; founder Integra Corp. Capt. USNR. Mem.: Oreg. Trial Lawyers Assn. (pres. 1973—74), Oreg. Appellate Judges Assn. (pres. 1993—94, 2001—02), Oreg. State Bar Assn. (founding mem., chair Family Law Section 1979). Office: Lewis & Clark Law Sch 10015 SW Terwilliger Blvd Portland OR 97219

RIGHETTI, DAVID ALLEN (DAVE RIGHETTI), professional baseball coach, retired professional baseball player; b. San Jose, Calif., Nov. 28, 1958; s. Leo Righetti; m. Kandice Righetti, Feb. 11, 1989; children: Nicolette, Natalee, Wesley. Pitcher NY Yankees, 1981-90, San Francisco Giants, 1990—93, minor league pitching instr., 1999, pitching coach, 2000—; pitcher Oakland Athletics, 1994, Toronto Blue Jays, 1994, Chgo. White Sox, 1995. Active Boys and Girls Clubs America, Leukemia Soc.; bd. dirs. Jean Weingarten Peninsula Oral Sch. for the Deaf. Named Am. League Rookie of Yr., Maj. League Baseball, 1981, Am. League Rolaids Relief Man of Yr., 1986, 1987; named to Am. League All-Star Team, Maj. League Baseball, 1986, 1987. Achievements include leading the American League in: ERA (2.05), 1981; saves (46), 1986; throwing a no-hitter, July 4, 1983. Office: San Francisco Giants AT&T Pk 24 Willie Mays Plz San Francisco CA 94107

RILEY, CARROLL LAVERN, anthropology educator; b. Summersville, Mo., Apr. 18, 1923; s. Benjamin F. and Minnie B. (Smith) R.; m. Brent Robinson Locke, Mar. 25, 1948; children: Benjamin Locke, Victoria Smith Evans, Cynthia Winningham AB, U. N.Mex., 1948, PhD, 1952; MA, UCLA, 1950. Instr. U. Colo., Boulder, 1953-54; asst. prof. U. N.C., Chapel Hill, 1954-55, So. Ill. U., Carbondale, 1955-60, assoc. prof., 1960-67, prof., 1967-86, Disting. prof., 1986-87, Disting. prof. emeritus, 1987—, chmn. dept., 1979-82, dir. mus., 1972-74; rsch. assoc. lab. anthropology Mus. N.Mex., 1987—. Rsch. collaborator Smithsonian Instn., 1988—; adj. prof. N.Mex. Highlands U., 1989—. Author: The Origins of Civilization, 1969, The Frontier People, 1982, expanded edit., 1987, Rio del Norte, 1995, Bandelier, 1996, The Kachina and Cross, 1999, 2003, Becoming Aztlan, 2005; editor: American Historical Anthropology, 1967, Man Across the Sea, 1971, Southwestern Journals of Adolph F. Bandelier, 4 vols., 1966, 70, 75, 84, Across the Chichimec Sea, 1978, A Zuni Life, 1998, The Casas Grandes World, 1999, others; contbr. numerous articles to profl. jours. Served in USAAF, 1942-45 Decorated 4 battle stars; grantee Social Sci. Rsch. Coun., NIH, Am. Philos. Soc., Am. Council Learned Socs., NEH, others. Home and Office: 1106 6th St Las Vegas NM 87701 E-mail: criley@desertgate.com.

RILEY, GRANNAN, performing company executive; Studied with Doreen Gilday, Eugene, Oreg.; BFA, US Internat. U., San Diego; postgrad., Academie des Grand Ballets Canadiens, Montreal. Cofounder Eugene (Oreg.) Ballet Co, 1978—, mng. dir., 1984—. Mem. dance touring panel Western States Arts Found.; mem. selection panel Arts N.W., Individual Artist Fellowship, Oreg. and Idaho. Dancer (ballets) Petrushka, the Firebird, Coppelia, others, worldwide tours. Active outreach programs Young Audiences Oreg., Wash. State Cultural Enrichment Program. Co-recipient Gov.'s Arts award, 1996. Office: Eugene Ballet Co PO Box 11200 Eugene OR 97440-3400

RILEY, JACK, actor, writer; b. Cleve., Dec. 30, 1935; s. John A. and Agnes C. (Corrigan) R.; m. Ginger Lawrence, May 18, 1975; children: Jamie, Bryan. BS in English, John Carroll U., 1961. Mem. Rolling Along of 1960, Dept. Army Travelling Show; co-host: Baxter & Riley, Sta.-WERE, Cleve., 1961-65; numerous TV appearances, including: as Mr. Carlin on Bob Newhart Show, CBS-TV, 1972-78; Occasional Wife, 1966, Mary Tyler Moore, 1972, Barney Miller, 1979, Diff'rent Strokes, 1979, Hart to Hart, 1980, Love Boat, 1984, Night Court, 1985-91, St. Elsewhere, 1986, Evening Shade, 1992, Family Matters, 1993, Married with Children, 1994, Coach, 1996, The Drew Carey Show, 1996, Seinfeld, 1997, Working, 1998, Son of the Beach, 1999-2002, Lucky, 2003, Yes, Dear, 2004, That 70's Show, 2004, numerous appearances on Tonight Show with Jay Leno, 1997-99; appeared in feature films including Catch-22, 1969, McCabe and Mrs. Miller, 1970, Long Goodbye, 1972, Calif. Split, 1974, World's Greatest Lover, 1978, High Anxiety, 1978, Butch and Sundance: The Early Years, 1979, History of the World, Part I, 1981, Frances, 1983, To Be or Not To Be, 1983, Finders Keepers, 1984, Spaceballs, 1987, Rented Lips, 1987, Gleaming the Cube, 1988, The Player, 1992, T-Rex, 1995, (voice) The Rugrat's Movie, 1998, Boogie Nights, 1997, Rugrats in Paris, 2000, Rugrats Go Wild, 2003, (TV movie) McBride, 2005, (feature film) Room 6; plays West Coast premier of Small Craft Warnings, 1975, Los Angeles revival of 12 Angry Men, 1985, Zeitgeist, 1990, House of Blue Leaves, at Cleve. Playhouse and tour Ea. Europe, 1993, The Odd Couple, Beck Ctr., Cleve., 1999, Do I Hear a Waltz? at Pasadena playhouse, 2001; TV writer: Mort Sahl Show, 1967, Don Rickles Show, 1968; writer commls. for, Blore & Richman Inc., Los Angeles, 1966-84; numerous radio commls. and TV voice-overs, Rugrats (cartoon series), 1993. With US Army,

1958—61. Named to, Ohio Broadcasters' Hall of Fame, 2002. Mem.: AFTRA, Acad. TV Arts and Scis., Acad. Motion Picture Arts and Scis., Writers Guild Am., Actor's Equity, Screen Actors Guild. Office: care Ho of Reps 400 S Beverly Dr Beverly Hills CA 90212-4424 Personal E-mail: jackriley2005@aol.com.

RILEY, MICHAEL, college football coach; b. Wallace, Idaho, July 6, 1953; m. Dee Riley; children: Matthew, Kate. BS in Soc. Sci., U. Ala., 1975; MS, Whitworth Coll., 1976. Defensive back Crimson Tide U. Ala., 1971-74; grad. asst. coach U. Calif. Golden Bears, 1975; def. coord., secondary coach, asst. athletic dir. Linfield Coll. Wildcats, McMinnville, Oreg., 1977-82; secondary coach Winnipeg Blue Bombers, CFL, 1983-84, head coach, 1987-90; defensive coord., sec. coach U. No. Colo. Bears, 1986; head coach San Antonio Riders, World League Am. Football, 1991-92; asst. head coach, offensive coord./quarterbacks coach U. So. Calif. Trojans, 1993-96; head coach Oreg. State U. Beavers, 1997-98, 2003—, San Diego Chargers, 1999—2001; asst. coach New Orleans Saints, 2002. Named Coach of Yr., Canadian Football League, 1988, 1990; named to Winnipeg Blue Bombers Hall of Fame, 2007. Achievements include being a member of the Grey Cup Championship winning Winnepeg Blue Bombers, 1988, 1990. Office: c/o Oreg State U Athletics Comm 104 Gill Coliseum Corvallis OR 97331 Office Phone: 541-737-2614. Business E-Mail: kelly.harness@oregonstate.edu.

RILEY, WILLIAM L., lawyer; b. Bay Shore, NY, 1942; BA, Williams Coll., 1964; JD, Duke U., 1967. Bar: N.Y. 1967, Calif. 1970. Mem. Orrick, Herrington & Sutcliffe, San Francisco, 1972-95, ptnr., 1975—. Contbr. to profl. jours. Office: Orrick Herrington Sutcliffe 405 Howard St Fl 11 San Francisco CA 94105-2680

RIMES, LEANN, country music singer; b. Jackson, Miss., Aug. 28, 1982; m. Dean Sheremet, Feb. 23, 2002. Singer: (albums) Blue, 1996, Unchained Melody: The Early Years, 1997, You Light Up My Life: Inspirational Songs, 1997 (Contemporary Christian Album of Yr., 1998), Sittin' on Top of the World, 1998, LeAnn Rimes, 1999, I Need You, 2001, God Bless America, 2001, Twisted Angel, 2002, Greatest Hits, 2003, What a Wonderful World, 2004, This Woman, 2005, Whatever We Wanna, 2006, Family, 2007; co-writer: (TV films) Holiday in Your Heart, 1997; guest appearance (TV films) Holiday in Your Heart, 1997, (TV series) American Dreams, 2003, (TV) Days of Our Lives, 1998, Moesha, 1999, MadTV, 2000, Tinseltown TV, 2003, and several others, (films) Coyote Ugly, 2000, host (TV series) Nashville Star, 2003—; performer: (TV) LeAnn Rimes Live, 2003, LeAnn Rimes: Custom Concert, 2004; author: (children's books) Jag, 2003, Jag's New Friend, 2004; singer: (soundtrack) Can't Fight The Moonlight for Coyote Ugly (Favorite Song, Blockbuster award, 2001), Looking Through Your Eyes for Quest for Camelot, (soundtrack-TV miniseries) I Need You for Jesus, 2000. Internat. spokesperson Children's Miracle Network; established LeAnn Rimes Adventure Gym (Vanderbilt Children's Hosp.), Nashville. Nominated Best Country Singer award, Country Music Assn., 1996; recipient Best New Artist,(youngest person to win a top award) & Best Female Country Vocal Performance, Grammy award, 1997, Song of Yr. & Single Record of Yr., Blue, Top New Female Vocalist, Acad. Country Music, 1997, Home Depot Humanitarian award, 2009, Horizon award, Country Music Assn., 1997, Favorite Female Artist, Blockbuster award, 1998; named Female Rising Video Star of Yr., Country Music TV, 1997, New Country Act of Yr., Internat. Touring Talent Pub., Internat. Rising Star, British Country Music Awards, Artist of Yr., North Tex. Music Festival, Country Single Sale Artist of Yr., Female Country Artist of Yr., Contemporary Christian Artist of Yr., Billboard, 1998, and others. Office: c/o Alix Gucovsky Special Artists Agy 9465 Wilshire Blvd Ste 890 Beverly Hills CA 90212 also: c/o Curb Records 2d Fl 3907 W Alameda Ave Burbank CA 91505-4332

RIMOIN, DAVID LAWRENCE, medical geneticist; b. Montreal, Nov. 9, 1936; s. Michael and Fay (Lecker) Rimoin; m. Mary Ann Singleton, 1962 (div. 1979); 1 child, Anne; m. Ann Piilani Garber, July 27, 1980; children: Michael, Lauren. BSc, McGill U., Montreal, 1957, MSc, MD, CM, 1961; PhD, Johns Hopkins U., 1967; LHD (hon.), Finch U., 1997. Asst. prof. medicine, pediat. Washington U., St. Louis, 1967—70; assoc. prof. UCLA, 1970—73, prof., 1973—, chief med. genetics, Harbor-UCLA Med. Ctr., 1970—86; chair dept. pediat., dir. Med. Genetics and Birth Defects Ctr. Cedars-Sinai Med. Ctr., LA, 1986—2004, Steven Spielberg chair, 1989—, dir. Med. Genetics Inst., 2004—. Chmn. coun. Med. Genetics Orgn., 1993. Co-editor: Emory and Rimoin's Principles and Practice of Medical Genetics, 1983, 5th edit., 2007; contbr. chapters to books, articles to profl. jours. Recipient E. Mead Johnson award, Am. Acad. Pediat., 1976, Col. Harland Saunders award, March of Dimes, 1997, Pioneer in Medicine award, Cedars Sinai Med. Ctr., 2001, Extraordinary Merit award, UCLA Med. Alumni Assn., 2005, Legends Harbor award, LA Biomed. Found., 2006, Leadership award, Am. Soc. Human Genetics, 2006. Fellow: Am. Coll. Med. Genetics (pres. 1991—96, bd. dirs. 1996—2000), AAAS, ACP; mem.: Inst. of Medicine, Assn. Am. Physicians, Am. Pediat. Soc., Am. Soc. Human Genetics (pres. 1984, Leadership award 2006), Am. Bd. Med. Genetics (pres. 1979—83), Western Soc. Pediat. Rsch. (pres. 1995, Ross Outstanding Young Investigator award 1976), Western Soc. Clin. Rsch. (pres. 1978), Am. Fedn. Clin. Rsch. (sec.-treas. 1972—75), Am. Coll. Med. Genetics Found. (pres. 1999—2002, bd. dirs. 2002—), Johns Hopkins Soc. Scholars. Office: Cedars Sinai Med Ctr 8700 Beverly Blvd Los Angeles CA 90048-1865 Office Phone: 310-423-4461. Business E-Mail: david.rimoin@cshs.org.

RIMSZA, SKIP, former mayor; b. Chgo. m. Kim Gill; children: Brian, Jenny, Alexander, Taylor, Nicole. Mem. Phoenix City Coun., 1990-94; vice mayor City of Phoenix, 1993, mayor, 1994—2003. Former pres. Bd. Realtors. Mem. several cmty. bds.

RINDER, LAWRENCE R., museum director, curator; Curator 20th-century art & contemporary projects Berkeley Art Museum; found. dir. Wattis Inst. Calif. Coll. of Arts, San Francisco; curator contemporary art Whitney Museum of Am. Art, NYC, 2000—04, adjunct curator, 2004—; dean grad. studies California Coll. of Arts, San Francisco, 2004—; dir. Berkeley Art Mus./Pacific Film Archive, Berkeley, Calif., 2008—. Office: California Coll of Arts 1111 Eighth St San Francisco CA 94107-2247

RINDONE, JOSEPH PATRICK, clinical pharmacist, educator; b. Santa Fe, Oct. 4, 1954; s. Guido Salvatore and Elizabeth Ann (Murphy) R.; m. Diane Marie Rollins, June 23, 1991; children: Jacqueline, Alexandra. BS, U. Nebr., 1977; PharmD, Creighton U., 1978. Lic. pharmacist, Nebr., Calif. Staff pharmacist Bergan Mercy Hosp., Omaha, 1978, Phoenix (Ariz.) VA Med. Ctr., 1978-81, clin. resident, 1981; clin. pharmacist Tucson VA Med. Ctr., 1982-93; assoc. prof. U. Ariz., Tucson, 1982—; clin. pharmacist Prescott (Ariz.) VA Med. Ctr., 1993—, rsch. coord., 1994—. Author: Therapeutic Monitoring of Antibiotics, 1991; contbr. articles to Arch. Internal Medicine, Pharmacotherapy, Clin. Therapeutics, Am. Jour. Cardiology, Am. Jour. Therapeutics, Chest, West Jour. Medicine, Am. Jour. Health Sys. Pharm., Federal Practioner, Jour. AMA. Regents scholar U. Nebr., 1976. Avocations: sports, photography, bridge, astronomy. E-mail: JosephRindone@med.va.gov.

RINE, JASPER, geneticist, educator; BS, SUNY Albany, 1975; PhD in molecular genetics, U. Oreg., 1979. Prof. genetics, genomics and devel. U. Calif., Berkeley, dir. Ctr. Computational Biology; prof. Howard Hughes Med. Inst., 2006—. Recipient Disting. Tchg. award, U. Calif. Berkeley, 1997. Fellow: Am. Acad. Arts and Sciences, Am. Soc. Miocrobiology; mem.: NAS, AAAS. Office: Rine Lab 176 Stanley Hall #3220 U Calif Berkeley Berkeley CA 94720-3220 Office Phone: 510-642-7047. Office Fax: 510-642-6420. E-mail: jrine@berkeley.edu.

RINEARSON, PETER MARK, journalist, writer, software executive; b. Seattle, Aug. 4, 1954; s. Peter Morley and Jeannette Irene (Love) R.; m. Jill Chan, Sept. 15, 1991. Student, U. Wash., 1972-78. Editor Sammamish Valley News, Redmond, Wash., 1975-76; reporter Seattle Times, 1976-78, govt. and polit. reporter, 1979-81, aerospace reporter, 1982-84, Asian corr., 1985-86; pres. Alki Software Corp., Seattle, 1990—, Raster Ranch, Ltd., 1995-99; sr. v.p. Oxygen Media, 1999-2000; corp. pres. Microsoft Corp., 2002—. Mem. vis. com. Sch. Comm., U. Wash., 1996—; mem. nat. adv. bd. Poynter Inst. for Media Studies, 2000—. Author: Word Processing Power with Microsoft Word, 4th edit., 1991, Microsoft Word Style Sheets, 1987, Quick Reference Guide to Microsoft Word, 1988, Microsoft Word Companion Disk, 1988, Masterword, 1990, 91, 92, (with Bill Gates and Nathan Myhrvold) The Road Ahead, 1995, rev. edit., 1996, Babynamer.com, 1977-79, To The Day, 2001. Recipient Spl. Paul Myhre award-series Penney-Mo. Newspaper awards, 1983, Disting. Writing award Am. Soc. Newspaper Editors, 1984, Pulitzer prize for feature writing, 1984, Lowell Thomas Travel Writing award, 1984, John Hancock award,1985, semi-finalist NASA Journalist-in-Space Project, 1986; U.S.-Japan Leadership Program fellow Japan Soc., 1988.

RING, ALICE RUTH BISHOP, retired preventive medicine physician; b. Ft. Collins, Colo., Oct. 11, 1931; d. Ernest Otto and Mary Frances Bishop; m. Wallace Harold Ring, July 26, 1956 (div. 1969); children: Rebecca, Eric, Mark; m. Robert Charles Diefenbach, Sept. 10, 1977. BS, Colo. State U., 1953; MD, U. Colo., 1956; MPH, U. Calif., Berkeley, 1971. Diplomate Am. Bd. Preventive Medicine. Physician cons. Utah State Divsn. Health, Salt Lake City, 1960—65; med. dir., project head start Salt Lake City Cmty. Action Program, 1965—70; resident Utah State Divsn. Health, 1969—71; asst. assoc. regional health dir. USPHS, San Francisco, 1971—75, med. cons. Atlanta, 1975—77, dir. primary care, 1977—84; dir. divsn. diabetes control Ctrs. Disease Control, Atlanta, 1984—88; dir. WHO Collabor Ctr., Atlanta, 1986—91; dir. preventive medicine residency Ctrs. Disease Control, Atlanta, 1988—93; exec. dir. Am. Bd. Preventive Medicine, 1993—98. Trustee Am. Bd. Preventive Medicine, 1990—92; lectr. Emory U. Sch. Pub. Health, 1988—94; bd. dirs. Redwood Coast Med. Svcs., v.p., 1994—2004; mem. adv. com. Shamli Hospice, Gualala, Calif.; mem. adv. coun. Sonoma County Area Agy. on Aging, Santa Rosa, Calif., 2001—07, sec., 2004—06, v.p., 2006—07; bd. dirs. Alliance Rural Cmty. Health, Calif., 2002—04. Co-author: Clinical Diabetes, 1991; author: History of the American Board of Preventive Medicine, 2002. Bd. dirs. Diabetes Assn. Atlanta, 1985—90. Recipient Disting. Svc. award, Am. Bd. Med. Splties, 2004. Fellow: Am. Coll. Preventive Medicine (bd. dirs. 1990—94, Spl. Recognition award 1998); mem.: AMA (grad. med. edn. adv. com. 1993—97), Steering Com. Environ. Commons, Am. Bd. Med. Specialists (Disting. Svc. award 2004), Am. Acad. Pediat., Assn. Tchrs. Preventive Medicine. Office: PO Box 364 Gualala CA 95445-0364 Business E-Mail: ard@mcn.org.

RING, CAMERON, Internet company executive; BS, MS, Stanford Univ. Co-founder, chief server engr. netElement, 1999—2001; co-founder, chief architect Plaxo Inc., Mountain View, Calif., 2001—. Named a President's Scholar, Stanford Univ. Office: Plaxo Inc 203 Ravendale Dr Mountain View CA 94043 Office Phone: 650-254-5400.

RING, RAY, editor; No. Rockies editor High Country News, Colo. Author: (novels) Telluride Smile, 1988, Peregrine Dream, 1990, Arizona Kiss, 1991. Recipient Journalism award, Investigative Reporters and Editors Scroll, 1982, Am. Planning Assn., 2006, award, Soc. Environ. Journalists, 2003, 2004, 2005, George Polk award for Political Reporting, 2007. Office: High Country News 119 Grand Ave PO Box 1090 Paonia CO 81428 Office Phone: 970-527-4898. E-mail: rayring@hcn.org.

RING, TERRY WILLIAM, company executive, environmentalist; b. Lewiston, Idaho, Nov. 11, 1955; s. Robert L. and Irene M. (Sullivan) R. BA, Boise State U., 1979. Pres. Silver Creek Outfitters, Inc., Ketchum, Idaho, 1980—. Bd. dirs. Idaho Nature Conservancy, Ketchum, 1982—, chmn., 1986-2; bd. dirs. The Peregrine Fund, Boise, Idaho, 1994—. Mem. Nature Conservancy (Oak Leaf Awd. 1993) Home: PO Box 1096 Sun Valley ID 83353-1096

RINSKY, ARTHUR C., lawyer; b. Cin., July 10, 1944; AB with honors, U. Cin., 1966; JD cum laude, U. Mich., 1969; LLM in Taxation, NYU, 1974. Bar: Fla. 1969, Calif. 1975, US Tax Ct. 1974, Tex. 2004; cert. tax specialist, Calif. Ptr. DLA Piper US LLP, Palo Alto, Calif., 1975—. Mem. ABA, State Bar Calif., Phi Beta Kappa, Phi Eta Sigma. Office: DLA Piper US LLP 2000 University Ave East Palo Alto CA 94303

RIORDAN, GEORGE NICKERSON, investment banker; b. Patchogue, NY, May 16, 1933; s. E. Arthur and Constance E. (Whelden) R.; m. Ann Wiggins, Jan. 4, 1958; children— Susan M., Peter G. BS, Cornell U., 1955; MBA, Harvard U., 1960. Vice-pres. Lehman Bros., NYC, 1960-71; mng. dir. Blyth Eastman Paine Webber, Los Angeles and NYC, 1971-81, Prudential-Bache Securities, Los Angeles, 1981-88, Bear Stearns & Co., Inc., LA, 1988-89, Dean Witter Reynolds Inc., 1989-91. Chmn. bd. MSC Software, Inc., 1997-99; bd. dirs. MSC Software, Inc., L.A. Served to capt. USAF, 1955-57 Mem. Calif. Club, Quoque Field Club (L.I., N.Y.), Athenaeum Club, Valley Hunt Club (Pasadena, Calif.). Office: 815 Colorado Blvd Ste 104 Los Angeles CA 90041-1720 Business E-Mail: george.riordan@mscsoftware.com.

RIORDAN, RICHARD J., former state official, former mayor; b. Flushing, NY, 1930; m. Eugenia Riordan; 6 children (2 dec.); m. Jill Riordan; m. Nancy Daly Riordan; 3 children. Attended, U. Calif., Santa Clara; grad., Princeton U., 1952; JD, U. Mich., 1956. With O'Melveny & Myers, LA; owner, operator Original Pantry Cafe; founder Total Pharmaceutical Care, Tetra Tech; atty. Riordan & McKinzie, 1970—2003; mayor LA, 1993—2001; sec. of edn. State of Calif., Sacramento, 2003—05. Co-founder LEARN, 1991; sponsor Writing to Read computer labs Riordan Found.; active Eastside Boys and Girls Club. Lt. U.S. Army, Korea.

RIOS, REBECCA ANGELA, state legislator; b. Hayden, June 4, 1967; d. Peter Duarte and Gloria Ann (Mendoza) Rios; m. Steve Leal (div.); children: Diego Esteban, Milan Sophia. AA, Ctrl. Ariz. Coll., 1987; BSW, Ariz. State U., 1989, MSW, 2003. Child/family counselor Wayland Family Ctr., Phoenix, 1988-90; children's case mgr. Cmty. Care Network, Phoenix, 1990-92; case mgr., dir. children's behavioral health svcs. Pinal Gila Behavioral Health Assn., Apache Junction, Ariz., 1992—2005; mem. Dist. 7 Ariz. House of Reps., 1995—2000; mem. Dist. 23 Ariz. State Senate, 2005—, mem. pub. safety & human svcs. com., appropriations com., retirement & rural devel. com., asst. minority leader. Mem. adv. bd. Ariz. State U. Sch. Social Work, 2006—; bd. dirs. Cmty. Alliance Against Family Abuse, 2007—. Mem.: Nat. Assn. Social Workers (mem. adv. bd. 2007—), Ariz. Rural Health Assn. (bd. dirs. 2007—). Democrat. Roman Catholic. Office: Ariz State Senate Capitol Complex 1700 W Washington St Rm 213 Phoenix AZ 85007-2812 Office Phone: 602-926-5685. Office Fax: 602-417-3167. Business E-Mail: rrios@azleg.gov.*

RIPLEY, AFA, JR., (FEPULEA'I A. RIPLEY JR.), attorney general; b. 1949; BBA, MBA, Kans. State Teachers Coll., Emporia, Kans.; JD, Calif. Western Sch. Law, San Diego, 1978. Dep. atty. gen. Atty. Gen. Office, Hawaii, 1978; dep. pros. atty. City and County of Honolulu, 1979—80, dep. corp. counsel, trial divsn., 1980—82; atty. Minn & Ripley, Hawaii, 1982—89; chmn., bd. mem. Am. Samoa Power Authority; lawyer pvt. practice; atty. gen. Am. Samoa, 2007—. Office: American Samoa Govt Exec Office Bldg Utulei Territory of American Samoa Pago Pago AS 96799 Office Phone: 684-633-4163.*

RIPLEY, STUART MCKINNON, real estate consultant; b. July 28, 1930; s. Rob Roy and Nina Pearl (Young) R.; m. Marilyn Haerr MacDiarmid, Dec. 28, 1964; children: Jill, Bruce, Kent. BA, U. Redlands, 1952; MBA, U. Calif., Berkeley, 1959. V.p., dir. J.H. Hedrick & Co., Santa Barbara/San Diego, 1958-63; v.p. mktg. Cavanaugh Devel. Co., San Gabriel, Calif., 1963-65; v.p. mktg. dir. Calabasas Park, Bechtel Corp., Calabasas, Calif., 1967-69; v.p. mktg. Avco Cmty. Developers, Inc., La Jolla, Calif., 1969-74; mktg. dir. U.S. Home Corp., Fla. Divsn., Clearwater, 1974-75; pres., dir. Howard's Camper Country, Inc., National City, Calif., 1975-77; v.p., mktg. dir. Valcas Internat. Corp., San Diego, 1976-77, pres., 1977-79, Stuart M. Ripley, Inc., 1977-79, Sunview Realty, Inc., Watt Industries Co., Santa Monica, Calif., 1979-80; owner Everett Stunz Co., Ltd., La Jolla, 1981—84. Exec. v.p. Harriman-Ripley Co., Fallbrook, Calif., 1982-1984; avocado, floraculture rancher, subdivider, Fallbrook, 1978—; lectr. UCLA, 1961; pres. Century 21 Coastal, Century 21 Bajamar, Baja Calif., Mex., 1994-97. Lt. comdr. USNR, 1952-55, ret. U. Redlands fellow, 1960—. Mem. Nat. Assn. Homebuilders, Sales and Mktg. Coun., Sales and Mktg. Execs., Elks, Pi Chi. Republican. Episcopalian. Office Phone: 916-316-7499.

RIPPEL, CLARENCE W., academic administrator; Acting pres. Lincoln U., to 1998, pres., 1998—. Office: Lincoln U Office of President 401 15th St Oakland CA 94612-2801

RIPPEN, HELGA EDITH, pharmaceutical company administrator; b. Tripoli, Libya, Mar. 10, 1959; BSME, Fla. Atlantic U., 1981; PhD, Duke U., 1986; MD, U. Fla.; MPH, Johns Hopkins U., Baltimore. Diplomate in pub. health and gen. preventive medicine Am. Bd. Preventive Medicine. DAAD postdoctoral fellow Max Planck Inst. for Biochemistry, Martinsried, Fed. Republic Germany, 1986-87; NATO postoctoral fellow U. B.C., Vancouver, Can., 1987-88; AAAS sci. engring. diplomacy fellow U.S. AID, Arlington, Va., 1991-96; residency preventive medicine Johns Hopkins U., 1996; dir. Health Info. Tech. Inst., 1996-99; chmn. Internet Healthcare Coalition, 1998—; co-chmn. eHeath Ethics Initiative, 2000; dir. med. informatics Pfizer Health Solutions, Santa Monica, Calif., 2001—. Chair IEEE-USA Med. Tech. Policy Com., 1998-2000. Co-creator, initiator Equal Access Student Run Clinic, Gainesville, Fla., 1991. Wimberly scholar, 1980; Am. Heart Assn. grantee, 1985-86. Mem. AMA, AAAS, Am. Coll. Preventive Medicine, Am. Tchrs. Preventive Medicine, Sigma Xi, Phi Kappa Phi, Tau Beta Pi. Avocations: painting, bicycling, hiking, cooking, travel. Home: 8305 Summerwood Dr Mc Lean VA 22102 E-mail: helga.rippen@pfizer.com.

RIPPON, THOMAS MICHAEL, art educator, artist; b. Sacramento, Apr. 1, 1954; s. Samuel Joseph Jr. and June Evelyn (Garnet) R.; m. Sarah Sterrett, Dec. 22, 1980; children: Adam Michael, Peter Thomas. MFA, Art Inst. Chgo., 1979. Instr. Columbia Coll., Chgo., 1978-79; asst. prof. Montana State U., Bozeman, 1980, Calif. State U., Sacramento, 1981; assoc. prof. Tenn. Tech. U., Cookeville, 1982-87; asst. prof. U. Nev., Reno, 1987-89; assoc. prof. U. Montana, Missoula, 1989—, chair dept. art, 1990-96. Artist in residence U. Nevada, Reno, 1988; vis. prof. U. Calif., Davis, 1989; lectr. in field, 1973—. Solo exhbns. include Quay Gallery, San Francisco, 1975, 77, 81, 85, Rochester (Minn.) Art Ctr., 1979, Betsy Rosenfield Gallery, Chgo., 1980, 82, 84, Drake U., Des Moine, Iowa, 1985, Cross Creek Gallery, Malibu, Calif., 1987, 88, Judith Weintraub Gallery, Sacramento, 1990, 91, Huntington (W.Va.) Mus. Art, 1991, Kohler Art Ctr., Sheboygan, Wis., 1992, Yellowstone Art Ctr., Billings, Mont., 1993, Missoula Mus. Arts, 1994, Holter Mus. Art, Helena, Mont., 1995, John Natsovlas Gallery, 1995, 97, Mobila Gallery, Cambridge, Mass., 1999, others; group exhbns. include San Francisco Mus. Modern Art, 1972, Davis (Calif.) Art Ctr., 1973, Oakland Mus., 1974, Evanston (Ill.) Art Ctr., 1974, Fendrick Gallery, Washington, 1975, Campbell Mus., Camden, N.J., 1976, Montana State U., Bozeman, 1976, De Young Mus., San Francisco, 1978, Am. Craft Mus., N.Y.C., 1978, 81, Phila. Mus. Modern Art, 1980, Craft and Folk Mus., L.A., 1980, Indpls. Mus. Art, 1982, Impressions Today Gallery, Boston, 1982, Elements Gallery, N.Y.C., 1983, Tampa (Fla.) Mus., 1983, Hyde Park Art Ctr., Chgo., 1983, 85, Traver-Sutton Gallery, Seattle, 1984, Erie (Pa.) Art Mus., 1985, Fay Gold Gallery, Atlanta, 1986, Seattle Art Mus., 1987, Candy Store Art Gallery, Folsom, Calif., 1987, Crocker Art Mus., Sacramento, 1988, Lang Gallery Scripps Coll., Claremont, Calif., 1988, Sherley Koteen & Assoc., Washington, 1989, 90, Eve Mannes Gallery, Atlanta, 1989, Art Gallery Western Australia, 1989, Joanne Rapp Gallery, Scottsdale, 1990, Missoula Mus. of Arts, 1991, 92, Sutton West Gallery, Missoula, 1992, Yellowstone Art Ctr., 1992,

Natsoulas Gallery, Davis, Calif., 1993, Mus. Internat. del Ceramiche, Faenza, Italy, 1997, John Elder Gallery, N.Y.C., 1998, M.H. De Young Mus., San Francisco, 1999, many others; represented in pvt. collections; pub. collections include San Francisco Mus. Art, L.A. County Mus. Art, Sheldon Meml. Collection U. Nebr., Mus. Fine Arts, Salt Lake City, Ch. Fine Arts Collection U. Nev., Reno, Kanzawa-Shi, Hokkoku Shinbun, Kyoto, Japan, Renwick Gallery Smithsonian Institution, Contemporary Art Mus., Honolulu, J.B. Speed Art Mus., Louisville, Ky., U. Iowa, Ames, Missoula Mus. Arts, others. Recipient Kingsley Art Club award Crocker Art Mus., Sacramento, 1971, Crocker-Kingsley award, 1972; NEA fellow, 1974, 81, Nelson Raymond fellow Art Inst. Chgo., 1979. Office: U Montana Dept Art Missoula MT 59812-0001

RISCH, JIM (JAMES ELROY RISCH), United States Senator from Idaho, former Governor of Idaho; b. Milw., May 3, 1943; s. Elroy A. and Helen B. (Levi) R.; m. Vicki L. Choborda, June 8, 1968; children: James E., Jason S., Jordan D. BS in Forestry, U. Idaho, 1965, JD, 1968. Dep. pros. atty. Ada County, Idaho, 1968-69, chief dep. pros. atty. Idaho, 1969-70, pros. atty. Idaho, 1971-75; mem. Idaho Senate from Dist. 18, Boise, 1974—88, 1995—2002, majority leader, 1977—82, 1997—2002, pres. pro tem, 1983-88; ind. counsel to Gov. State of Idaho, Boise, 1996; ptnr. Risch Goss & Insinger, Boise, 1975—; lt. gov. State of Idaho, Boise, 2003—06, 2007—09, gov., 2006—07; US Senator from Idaho, 2009—; mem. US Senate Fgn. Rels. Com., 2009—, US Senate Energy & Nat. Resources Com., 2009—, US Senate Select Com. on Ethics, 2009—, US Senate Select Com. on Intelligence, 2009—, US Senate Joint Econ. Com., 2009—. Prof. law Boise State U., 1972-75. Bd. dirs. Nat. Dist. Attys. Assn., 1973, Idaho Co., 1992-94, State Legis. Leaders Found., 2002; chmn. bd. dirs. Am. Trailer Mfg. Co., 1995—; pres. Idaho Pros. Attys., 1970-74; chmn. George Bush Presdl. Campaign, Idaho, 1988; gen. counsel Idaho Rep. Party, 1991-2002. Mem. ABA, Idaho Bar Assn., Boise Bar Assn., Ducks Unlimited, Nat. Rifle Assn., Nat. Cattlemans Assn., Idaho Cattlemans Assn., Am. Angus Assn., Idaho Angus Assn., Am. Legis. Exch. Coun., Boise Valley Angus Assn., Phi Delta Theta, Xi Sigma Pi Republican. Roman Catholic. Avocations: hunting, fishing, skiing. Office: US Congress 2 Russell Courtyard Washington DC 20510 also: 350 N 9th St Ste 302 Boise ID 83702 Office Phone: 202-224-2752, 208-342-7985. Office Fax: 208-343-2458, 202-224-2573.

RISHWAIN, JAMES MICHAEL, JR., lawyer; b. Stockton, Calif., Apr. 28, 1959; BA with honors, UCLA, 1981; JD cum laude, Pepperdine U., 1984. Bar: Calif. Firm chair and CEO Pillsbury Winthrop Shaw Pittman LLP, LA, 2006—, leader real estate group, 1995—2006. Editor (Note & Comment): Pepperdine Law Rev. Mem. adv. bd. LA City Coun. for Holmby Pk., Calif. Coalition for Adequate Sch. Housing, Jonathan Club; bd. mem. Bldg. Owners and Mgrs. Assn.; bd. experts Internat. Real Estate Trade Orgn., mem. pres.'s cir. Recipient Calif. Lawyer of Yr. award, 2004, 2005; named Best Lawyer Am., 2005—06; named one of Calif. Super Lawyers, 2004, 2005, 2006—08. Mem.: ABA, State Calif. Bar Assn., LA County Bar Assn., Urban Land Inst. Office: Pillsbury Winthrop Shaw Pittman LLP Ste 2800 725 S Figueroa St Los Angeles CA 90017-5406 Office Phone: 213-488-7111. Office Fax: 213-488-7400. E-mail: jrishwain@pillsburylaw.com.

RISSE, GUENTER BERNHARD, physician, historian, educator; b. Buenos Aires, Apr. 28, 1932; s. Francisco B. and Kaete A. R.; m. Alexandra G. Paradzinski, Oct. 14, 1961; children— Heidi, Monica, Alisa. MD, U. Buenos Aires, 1958; PhD, U. Chgo., 1971. Intern Mercy Hosp., Buffalo, 1958-59; resident in medicine Henry Ford Hosp., Detroit, 1960-61, Mt. Carmel Hosp., Columbus, Ohio, 1962-63; asst. dept. medicine U. Chgo., 1963-67; asst. prof. dept. history of medicine U. Minn., 1969-71; asso. prof. dept. history of medicine and dept. history of sci. U. Wis., Madison, 1971-76, prof., 1976-85, chmn. dept. history of medicine, 1971-77; prof. dept. history health scis. U. Calif., San Francisco, 1985-99, prof. dept. anthropology, history and social medicine, 1999-2001, prof. emeritus, 2001—, dept. chair, 1985—99; affiliate prof. dept. bioethics and humanities U. Wash. Sch. Medicine, Seattle, 2002—. Mem. project com. Ctr. for Photog. Images in Medicine and Health Care, San Francisco's Plaque: The View from China Forum. Author: Paleopathology of Ancient Egypt, 1964, Hospital Life in Enlightenment Scotland, 1986, Mending Bodies-Saving Souls: A History of Hospitals, 1999, New Medical Challenges During the Scottish Enlightenment, 2005; editor: Modern China and Traditional Chinese Medicine, 1973, History of Physiology, 1973, Medicine Without Doctors, 1977, AIDS and the Historian, 1991, Culture, Knowledge and Healing, Historical Perspectives of Homeopathic Medicine in Europe and North America, 1998; mem. editl. bd. Jour. History of Medicine, 1971-74, 90-93, Clio Medica, 1973-88, Bull. History of Medicine, 1980-94, Medizinhistorisches Jour., 1981—, Med. History, 1989-95, NTM Internat. Jour. of History, Ethics, Medicine, 1992—, History of Philos. Life Scis., 1993—, Asclepio, 1995—, Health and History, 1998—. With Argentine Armed Forces, 1955. Recipient NIH grants, 1971-73, 82-84, WHO grant, 1979, named Logan Campbell Disting. Lectr., New Zealand, 1994, Karl Sudhoff Meml. Lectr., Germany, 2000; grantee Nat. Lib. Medicine, 2006—. Mem. Am. Assn. History of Medicine (pres. 1988-90, William H. Welch medal 1988, Lifetime Achievement award 2005), History Sci. Soc., Deutsche Gesellschaft fur Geschichte der Medizin, European Assn. History of Medicine and Health, Internat. Network for History of Pub. Health, Mex. Soc. History and Philosophy of Medicine, Peruvian Assn. Med. Ethnology and History, Brit. Soc. for Social History of Medicine, Argentine Ateneo de Historia de la Medicina, AIDS History Group (co-chair 1988-94), Internat. Network for History of Hosps. (convenor 1995—), Bay Area Med. Hist. Club (pres. 1994-96). Home: 2612 SW 167th St Burien WA 98166-3228 Business E-Mail: risseg@u.washington.edu.

RISTOW, BRUNNO, plastic surgeon; b. Brusque, Brazil, Oct. 18, 1940; s. Arno and Ally Odette (von Bruettner) Ristow; m. Urannia Carrasquilla Gutierrez, Nov. 10, 1979; children from previous marriage: Christian Kilian, Trevor Roland. Student, Coll. Sinodal, Brazil, 1956—57; MD magna cum laude, U. Brazil, 1966. Diplomate Am. Bd. Plastic and Reconstructive Surgery. Intern in surgery Hosp. dos Estrangeiros, Rio de Janeiro, 1965, Hosp. Estuadual Miguel Couto, Brazil, 1965—66, Instituto Aposentadoria Pensao Comerciarios Hosp. for Gen. Surgery, 1966; resident in plastic and reconstructive surgery Dr. Ivo Pltanguy Hosp. Santa Casa de Misericordia, Rio de Janeiro, 1967; fellow Inst. Reconstructive Plastic Surgery NYU Med. Ctr., NYC, 1967—68, jr. resident, 1971—72, sr. and chief resident, 1972—73; practice medicine specializing in plastic surgery Rio de Janeiro, 1967, NYC, 1968—73, San Francisco, 1973—; asst. surgeon NY Hosp., Cornell Med. Ctr., NYC, 1968—71. Clin. instr. surgery NYU Sch. Medicine, 1972—73; chmn. plastic and reconstructive surgery divsn. Presbyn. Hosp., Pacific Med. Ctr., San Francisco, 1974—92, chmn. emeritus, 1992—. Contbg. author: Cancer of the Hand, 1975, Current Therapy in Plastic and Reconstructive Surgery, 1988, Male Aesthetic Surgery, 1989, How They Do It: Procedures in Plastic and Reconstructive Surgery, 1990, Middle Crus: The Missing Link in Alar Cratilage Anatomy, 1991, Surgical Technology International, 1992, Aesthetic Plastic Surgery, 1993, Mastery of Surgery: Plastic and Reconstructive Surgery, 1993, Reoperative Aesthetic Plastic Surgery of the Face and Breast, 1994; contbr. articles to profl. jours. With M.C. Brazilian Army Res., 1959—70. Decorated knight Venerable Order of St. Hubertus, Knight Order St. John of Jerusalem; fellow in surgery, Cornell Med. Sch., 1968—71. Fellow: ACS, Internat.Coll. Surgeons; mem.: AMA (Physician's Recognition award 1971—83), San Francisco Med. Assn., Calif. Med. Assn., Calif. Soc. Plastic Surgeons, Internat. Soc. Aesthetic Plastic Surgeons, Am. Soc. Plastic and Reconstructive Surgeons, Am. Soc. Aesthetic Plastic Surgery (chmn. edn.), San Francisco Olympic Club. Republican. Evangelical. Office: Calif Pacific Med Ctr 2100 Webster St Ste 501 San Francisco CA 94115-2373 Home Phone: 415-346-0465; Office Phone: 415-202-1507. Office Fax: 415-202-0131. Personal E-mail: info@brunnoristow.com.

RITCHEY, SAMUEL DONLEY, JR., retired retail executive; b. Derry Twp., Pa., July 16, 1933; s. Samuel Donley and Florence Catherine (Litsch) R.; m. Sharon Marie Anderson, Apr. 6, 1956; children: Michael Donley, Tamara Louise, Shawn Christopher. BS, San Diego State U., 1955, MS, 1963; postgrad., Stanford U., 1964. With Lucky Stores Inc., 1951-61, 64-86, pres., chief operating officer, 1978-80, pres., chief exec. officer, 1980-81, chmn., chief exec. officer, 1981-85, chmn. bd., 1981-86. Bd. dirs. The McClatchy Co., De La Salle Inst., John Muir Health; chair Coll. Bus., San Diego State U.; grad. mgr. San Diego State U., 1961-63; lectr. in field; past chmn. Calif. Power Exch., mem. AT&T bd. adv. coun. Grad. Sch. Bus., Stanford U. Sloan Found. fellow, audit comm. chair. Mem. Mex. Am. Legal Def. and Edn. Fund, Western Assn. Food Chains (bd. dirs., pres.), Food Mktg. Inst. (bd. dirs., vice chmn.), Sloan Alumni Assn. (adv. bd., pres.).

RITCHIE, DANIEL LEE, former academic administrator; b. Springfield, Ill., Sept. 19, 1931; s. Daniel Felix and Jessie Dee (Binney) R. BA, Harvard U., 1954, MBA, 1956. Exec. v.p., CFO MCA, Inc., LA, 1962—70; pres. Archon Pure Products Co., LA, 1970-73; exec. v.p. Westinghouse Electric Corp., Pitts., 1975-78; pres. corp. staff and strategic planning Westinghouse Broadcasting Co., 1978-79, pres., CEO, 1979-81; chmn., CEO Westinghouse Broadcasting & Cable, Inc., 1981-87; owner Rancho Cielo, Montecito, Colo., 1977—; chancellor U. Denver, Colo., 1989—2005, chancellor emeritus, 2005—, chmn. bd. trustees. Mem. Nat. Assn. Univ. Pres., Nat. Assn. Ind. Coll & Univ., Internat. Assn of Univ. Pres.; pres. Ind. Higher Edn. of Colo. Trustee, vice chmn., chmn. of bd., U. Denver, 1983-89; pres., Temple Hoyne Buell Found., Denver; chmn. Ctrl. City Opera; mem., adv. bd. Nat. Park Sys. With U.S. Army, 1956-58. Office: Chmn Bd U Denver 270 Saint Paul St, Ste 300 Denver CO 80206 Office Phone: 303-871-2122. Office Fax: 303-871-3770. E-mail: dritchie@du.edu.

RITCHIE, GUY STUART, film director, film producer, scriptwriter; b. Hatfield, Hertfordshire, England, Sept. 10, 1968; m. Madonna Ritchie, Dec. 22, 2000 (separated 2008); 1 adopted child, David Banda Mwale Ciccone 1 child, Rocco John 1 stepchild, Lourdes. Writer, dir. (films) The Hard Case, 1995, Lock, Stock and Two Smoking Barrels, 1998 (Best Motion Picture Edgar Allen Poe Awards, 2000, Best New Filmmaker MTV Movie award, 1999, Brit. Screenwriter of Yr. London Critics Cir. Film award, 1999, Best Dir. award Tokyo Internat. Film Festival, 1998), Snatch, 2000 (Most Promising Newcomer Evening Standard Brit. Film award, 1999, Best Brit. Dir. Empire Award, 2001), Star, 2001, Swept Away, 2002, Revolver, 2005; exec. prodr.: (films) Mean Machine, 2001; dir., writer, prodr. (films) RocknRolla, 2008, exec. prodr., writer (TV series) Lock, Stock..., 2000, exec. prodr., dir. (TV films) Suspect, 2007. Office: c/o Anonymous Content 3532 Hayden Ave Culver City CA 90232

RITCHIE, JAMES L., cardiologist; BA, Yale U., 1963. Chief divsn. of cardiology U. Wash. Sch. Medicine. Recipient Disting. Achievement award Am. Heart Assn., 1996. Office: U Wash Sch Medicine Box 356422 1959 NE Pacific St Seattle WA 98195-0001

RITCHIE, ROBERT OLIVER, materials science educator, department chairman; b. Plymouth, Devon, Eng., Jan. 2, 1948; arrived in US, 1974, naturalized, 1990; s. Kenneth Ian and Kathleen Joyce (Sims) Ritchie; m. Connie Olesen (div. 1978); 1 child, James Oliver; m. HaiYing Soong, 1991; 1 child, Duncan Soong. BA with honors, U. Cambridge, Eng., 1969, MA, PhD, 1973, ScD, 1990. Cert. engr., UK. Goldsmith's rsch. fellow Churchill Coll. U. Cambridge, 1972-74; Miller fellow in basic rsch. sci. U. Calif., Berkeley, 1974-76, prof., 1981—, chair Materials Sci. and Engring. Dept., 2005—; assoc. prof. mech. engring. MIT, Cambridge, 1977-81; dep. dir. Materials Scis. Divsn. Lawrence Berkeley Nat. Lab., Cambridge, 1990-94, dir. Ctr. for Advanced Materials, 1987-95, head structural Materials Dept., Materials Scis. Divsn., 1995—. Cons. Alcan, Allison, Applied Materials, Boeing, Chevron, Cordis, Exxon, GE, GM, Grumman, Guidant, Instron, Northrop, Rockwell, Westinghouse, Baxter, Carbomedics, Med. Inc., Shiley, St. Jude Med.; Van Horn Disting. lectr. Case Western U., 1997. Editor: 19 books; contbr. more than 580 articles to profl. jours. Recipient G. R. Irwin medal, ASTM, 1985, Mathewson gold medal, TMS-AME, 1985, Curtis W. McGraw Rsch. award, Am. Soc. Engring. Educators, 1987, Rosenhain medal, Inst. Materials London, 1992, Wohler medal, European Structural Integrity Soc., 2006, Van Horn Disting. Lectr. award, Case Western U., 1997; named one of Top 100 Scientists, Sci. Digest mag., 1984. Fellow: Royal Acad. Engring. (London), Minerals, Materials and Metals Soc. (Mathewson Gold medal 1985, Disting. Structural Materials Scientist/Engr. award 1996), Am. Soc. Metals Internat. (Marcus A. Grossman award 1980), Internat. Congress on Fracture (pres. 1997—2001), Inst. Materials (London, AA Griffith medal 2007); mem.: NAE, ASME (NADAI medal 2004), Am. Acad. Arts and Scis., Am. Ceramic Soc., Materials Rsch. Soc. Avocations: skiing, hiking, antiques, orchids. Home: 590 Grizzly Peak Blvd Berkeley CA 94708-1238 Office: U Calif Dept Materials Sci and Engring Berkeley CA 94720-1760 Office Phone: 510-486-5798. Business E-Mail: roritchie@lbl.gov.

RITONDARO, GARY H., printing company executive; With Diamond Shamrock Corp.; v.p., CFO Ferro Corp.; sr. v.p. fin., CFO Mail-Well Inc, Englewood, Colo., 1999—. Office: Mail-Well Inc Ste 400 8310 S Valley Hwy Englewood CO 80112-5815

RITSEMA, FREDRIC A., lawyer; b. Kansas City, Mo., Feb. 12, 1951; AB, Calvin Coll., 1973; JD, U. Colo., 1976. Bar: Colo. 1976. Ptnr. Ritsema & Lyon PC, 1993—. Subcoms. Workers' Compensation. Mem. Denver Bar Assn., Colo. Def. Lawyers Assn. Office: Ritsema & Lyon PC 999 18th St Ste 3100 Denver CO 80202-2499

RITTER, BILL (AUGUST WILLIAM RITTER JR.), Governor of Colorado, former prosecutor; b. Aurora, Colo., Sept. 6, 1956; s. August William and Ethel Ritter; m. Jeannie L. Ritter; children: August, Abe, Sam, Tally. BA, Colo. State U., 1978; JD, U. Colo. Sch. Law, 1981. Dep. dist. atty. City of Denver, 1981—84, chief dep. dist. atty., 1984—87, 1992—93, dist. atty. Denver, 1993—2005; asst. US atty. criminal divsn. Dist. Colo. US Dept. Justice, Denver, 1990—91; coord. Mongu Nutrition Grp., Zambia, 1987—90; gov. State of Colo., Denver, 2006—. Bd. mem. Nat. Assn. Drug Ct. Profls., 1995—2002; v.p. Nat. Dist. Attys. Assn., 1995—2004; chmn. Am. Prosecutors Rsch. Inst., 1998—2004; pres. Colo. Dist. Attys. Coun., 1999—2000, 2003—04. Bd. chair Project PAVE (Promoting Alternatives to Violence through Edn.), 1992—2003; bd. mem. Mile High United Way, 1999—2004. Democrat. Roman Catholic. Office: Office Gov 136 State Capitol Denver CO 80203-1792

RITTER, DANIEL BENJAMIN, lawyer; b. Wilmington, Del., Apr. 6, 1937; s. David Moore and Bernice Elizabeth (Carlson) R.; m. Shirley F. Sether, Jan. 29, 1971 (dec. Jan. 1998); 1 child, Roxane Elise. AB with honors, U. Chgo., 1957; LLB, U. Wash., 1963. Bar: Wash. 1963, U.S. Dist. Ct. (we. dist.) Wash. 1963, U.S. Tax Ct. 1965, U.S. Ct. Appeals (9th cir.) 1963. Assoc. Davis, Wright Tremaine LLP (formerly Davis, Wright and Jones), 1963-69, ptnr., 1969—2006; ret., 2006. Lectr. Bar Rev. Assocs. Wash., Seattle, 1964—86; chmn. internat. dept. Davis, Wright and Jones, Seattle, 1984—85, chmn. banking dept., 1986—89. Casenote editor U. Wash. Law Rev., 1962-63; editor-in-chief, contbg. author Washington Revised Article 9 Deskbook, 2003; contbg. author: Washington Commercial Law Desk Book, 1982, rev. edit., 1987, Washington Community Property Desk Book, 1977. Trustee Cathedral Assoc., Seattle, 1980-86; legal counsel Wash. State Reps., Bellevue, 1983-92; bd. dirs. U. Chgo. Club Puget Sound, Seattle, 1982-95, pres., 1984-86; bd. dirs. Am. Lung Assn. Wash., Seattle, 1983-92; mem. vis. com. U. Wash. Law Sch., 1984-88; trustee U. Wash. Law Sch. Found., 1989-92; chmn. alumni rels. coun. U. Chgo., 1986-88; mem. statute law com. State of Wash., 1978-87; bd. dirs. Seattle Camerata, 1991-93; bd. dirs. Early Music Guild, Seattle, 1993-96. Mem. ABA (bus. law sect.), Wash. State Bar Assn. (chmn. bus. law sect. 1988-89, uniform comml. code com. 1980—, chmn. 1980-86, chmn. internat. law com. 1979-81, jud. recommendations com. 1991-93), Seattle-King County Bar Assn. (chmn. internat. and comparative law sect. 1980-82), Rainier Club, Order of Coif. Republican. Lutheran. Avocations: reading, theater, early music. Home: 907 Warren Ave N Apt 202 Seattle WA 98109-5635 Personal E-mail: dan.b.ritter@gmail.com.

RITVO, EDWARD ROSS, psychiatrist; b. Boston, June 1, 1930; s. Max Ritvo; m. Riva Golan, Sept. 11, 1989; children: Deborah, Eva, Anne, Matthew, Victoria, Skylre, Max. BA, Harvard U., 1951; MD, Boston U. Sch. Medicine, 1955. Diplomate Am. Bd. Psychiatry and Neurology, Am. Bd. Child Psychiatry. Prof. UCLA Sch. Medicine, 1963—. Author 4 books; contbr. over 150 articles to profl. jours. Capt. U.S. Army, 1959-61. Recipient Blanche F. Ittleson award Am. Psychiat. Assn., 1990. Mem. Nat. Soc. for Autistic Children, Profl. Adv. Bd. (chmn.). Office: UCLA Sch Medicine Dept Psychiatry 760 Westwood Plz Los Angeles CA 90095-8353

RIVARA, FREDERICK PETER, pediatrician, educator; b. Far Rockaway, NY, May 17, 1949; s. Frederick P. and Mary Lillian (Caparelli) R.; m. J'May Bertrand, May 17, 1975; children: Matthew, Maggie. BA, Holy Cross Coll., 1970; MD, U. Pa., 1974; MPH, U. Wash., 1980. Diplomate Am. Bd. Pediatrics. Intern Children's Hosp. and Med. Ctr., Boston, 1974-75, resident, 1975-76, Seattle, 1978-80; RWJ clin. scholar U. Wash., Seattle, 1978-80, assoc. prof. pediatrics, 1984-89, prof. pediatrics, head divsn. gen. pediatrics, 1994—; mem. staff Nat. Health Svc. Corps, Hazard, Ky., 1976-78; asst. prof. pediatrics U. Tenn., Memphis, 1981-84. Editor Archives of Pedatrics and Adolescent Medicine. Fellow Am. Acad. Pediatrics; mem. Ambulatory Pediatrics Assn., SPR, Am. Radiation Soc., Internat. Assn. Child, Adolescent and Injury Prevention (pres. 1993-2000), Inst. Medicine (Washington), Acad. Sci. Office: Harborview Med Ctr 325 9th Ave PO Box 359960 Seattle WA 98195-9960 Business E-Mail: fpr@uwashington.edu.

RIVELUNI, TOMASSO P., engineer; Engr. Jet Propulsion Lab., Pasadena, Calif. Recipient Engring. of Yr. award, 1998. Mem. AIAA. Office: Jet Propulsion Lab 4800 Oak Grove Dr Bldg 180 Pasadena CA 91109-8001

RIVERA, JOSE DE JESUS, lawyer; b. Zacatecas, Mex., 1950; m. Nina Rivera; 5 children. BA, No. Ariz. U.; JD, Ariz. State U. Atty. civil rights divsn. Dept. of Justice, 1976—77; asst. U.S. atty. Dist. Ariz., 1977—81; with Langerman, Begam, Lewis and Marks, 1981—84; ptnr. Rivera, Scales and Kizer, 1984—98; atty. City of El Mirage, U.S. Atty., Dist. of Ariz., 1998—2001; with Haralson, Miller, Pitt & McAnally PLC, Phoenix, 2001—. Vice-chair adv. com. civil rights Atty. Gen. Ariz. dist., 1998-2001, adv. com. Native Am. issues, domestic terrorism subcom., 1998-2001, chair subcom. no Mem. com. Los Abogados; bd. dirs. Inst. for County Initiatives, 1996-98; with N.G. Mem. Ariz. State Bar. (bd. govs. 1995-98, bd. officer, sec. treas. 1996, 2d v.p. 1997-98, exec. dir. search com. 1996-97, chair appointments com. 1997-98), Hispanic Bar Assn., Los Abogados Bar Assn. (bd. dirs. 1981-83). Democrat. Avocation: reading. Office: Haralson Miller Pitt Feldman & McAnally PLC 2800 N Ctrl Ste 840 Phoenix AZ 85004 Home Phone: 602-279-5687; Office Phone: 602-266-5557. Business E-Mail: jrivera@hmpmlaw.com.

RIVERA, LIONEL, Mayor, Colorado Springs, Colorado; b. El Paso, Tex. B in Microbiology, Tex. Tech. U.; MBA, Jacksonville State U., 1986. V.p. investments UBS Fin. Svc.; mem. Colorado Springs City Coun., Colo., 1997—2001; vice mayor City of Colorado Springs, Colo., 2001—03, mayor Colo., 2003—; ret., 2009. Founder, past pres. Colorado Springs Hispanic C. of C.; trustee United Way; mem. exec. com., co-chair The Springs Cmty. Action Plan; mentor Big Bros.-Big Sisters. Capt. US Army, 1979—87. Office: PO Box 1575 Colorado Springs CO 80901 Office Phone: 719-385-5986. Office Fax: 719-385-5495. E-mail: lrivera@springsgov.com.*

RIVERS, PHILIP, professional football player; b. Decatur, Ala., Dec. 8, 1981; s. Steve Rivers. B in Bus., NC State U., Raleigh. Quarterback San Diego Chargers, 2004—. Named to Am. Football

Conf. Pro Bowl Team, NFL, 2006. Achievements include leading the NFL in: quarterback rating, passing touchdowns, 2008. Office: San Diego Chargers PO Box 609609 San Diego CA 92160-9609*

RIVET, ROBERT J., semiconductor company executive; b. Chgo., Mar. 23, 1954; s. Robert F. and Lucille E. (Fazy) R.; m. Cynthia J. Moderhack, June 11, 1977; children: Scott M., Lauren N. BS, No. Ill. U., 1976; MBA, U. Tex., 1985. CPA, Ill. Sr. acct. Motorola Corp. Hdqs., Schaumburg, Ill., 1976-79, fin. analyst, 1979-81; group contr. Motorola Microprocessor Group, Austin, Tex., 1981-90, v.p., contr., 1990-92, Motorola Semicondr. Europe, Geneva, 1992; CFO Advanced Micro Devices, Sunnyvale, Calif., 2000—01, exec. v.p., CFO, 2001—08, chief ops. & adminstrv. officer, 2008—. Mem. Nat. Assn. Accts. Avocations: tennis, golf, travel. Office: AMD 1 AMD Pl Sunnyvale CA 94088

RIVKIND, PERRY ABBOT, federal railroad agency administrator; b. Boston, Jan. 22, 1930; s. Samuel Alexander and Mae Edna (Polisnor) R.; m. Dolores Russo; children: Robert Douglas, Valerie Jean, Jeff Pettit; m. Kathleen Marie Lysher, Aug. 14, 1989. AA, Columbia U., 1948, Miami CC, Fla., 1963; BA, Fla. State U., 1965; MA, Fla. Atlantic U., 1966; postgrad., Nat. War Coll., Washington, 1981. Comml. charter pilot, 1956-58; police officer Met. Police Dept., Miami, 1958-61; chief investigator Dade County State Atty. Office, Miami, 1961-67; prof., dir. dept. Cen. Piedmont Coll., Charlotte, NC, 1967-68; asst. dir. Fed. Bur. Narcotics, Washington, 1968-74; asst. adminstr. Law Enforcement Assistance Adminstrn., Washington, 1974-81; assoc. commr. U.S. Immigration and Naturalization Svc., Washington, 1981-84, dist. dir. Miami, 1984-88; safety mgr. Miami Herald Pub. Co., 1988-89; dep. adminstr. Fed. R.R. Adminstrn., Washington, 1989—. Chmn. com. on tng. Pres.'s Coun. on Drug Abuse, Washington, 1971-74, chmn. com. on rsch. Working Group on Terrorism Nat. Security Coun., Washington, 1978-81. Capt. Cadet Program USAF, 1943-45, With U.S. Army, 1951-53. Perry A. Rivkind Day established in his honor City of Miami/Dade County/City of Miami Beach, 1985-89. Republican. Avocations: boating, hunting, fishing, motorcycling, camping. Home Phone: 704-992-5675.

RIZZO, ALBERT SKIP, research scientist, educator; b. Hartford, Conn., Aug. 31, 1954; s. Virginia Wood and Albert Rizzo. MS in Exptl. Psychology, U. New Orleans, 1979; PhD in Clin. Psychology, SUNY, Binghamton, 1985. Dir. virtual reality psychology lab. U. Southern Calif. Inst. Creative Techs., Marina del Rey, 1996—, rsch. scientist, 2004—. Independent. Achievements include development of virtual reality exposure therapy system for treating Iraq war PSTD. Avocations: rugby, motorcycling, travel. Office: Univ Southern California 13274 Fiji Way Marina Del Rey CA 90292 Business E-Mail: arizzo@usc.edu.

ROACH, CHARLES T., real estate company executive; Sr. v.p., gen. mgr. Sun City West and Sun City Grand Del Webb Corp., Phoenix, 1998—. Office: Del Webb Corp 15333 N Pima Rd Ste 300 Scottsdale AZ 85260-2782

ROACH, PAM, state legislator; b. San Diego, Apr. 26, 1948; m 1970 to James Larry (Jim) Roach; children: 5. Member, Washington State Elec Rev Bd, formerly; Washington State Senator, District 31, 91-, member state & local gov, Judiciary, Ways & Means Committees, Econ Develop Finance Authority, Sentencing Guidelines Comn & Statute Law Committees, Senator Financial Serv Committee, Washington State Senator; legislation aide King Co Coun. Legislator of Year, Washington Coun Police & Sheriffs, 95, 96, 97, 98 & 99; Guardian of Small Bus Award, Nat Fedn Ind Business, 95, 96, 97 & 98; Outstanding Legislator, Washington State Department Vets Affairs, 98; Defender of Justice Award; Washington State Mothers Against Drunk Driving Award, 97; Farm Bureau Awards. Auburn Food Bank (board director, currently). Republican. Address: Auburn WA Mailing: State Senate 202 Irving R Newhouse Bldg PO Box 40431 Olympia WA 98504-0482 E-mail: roach_pa@leg.wa.gov.

ROARK, KEITH (R. KEITH ROARK), lawyer, political organization administrator; b. Salt Lake City, Apr. 10, 1949; BA, U. Utah, 1974, JD, 1977. Dep. prosecuting atty. Blaine County, Idaho, 1977—78, prosecuting atty. Idaho, 1979—85; founder, sr. & mng. ptnr. The Roark Law Firm, Twin Falls and Hailey, Idaho, 1985—; mayor City of Hailey, Idaho, 1990—93; chmn. Idaho Dem. Party, 2008—. With US Army, 1969—71. Mem.: ABA, Am. Inns of Ct., Criminal Justice Advisory Com., Idaho Supreme Ct. Civil Rules Com., Am. Trial Lawyers' Assn., Idaho Trial Lawyers Assn., Nat. Assn. of Criminal Defense Attys., Idaho State Bar Assn., Nat. Dist. Attys. Assn. (former mem. bd. dirs.), Idaho Prosecuting Attys. Assn. (past pres.). Democrat. Office: The Roark Law Firm 409 N Main St Hailey ID 83333 also: Idaho Dem Party PO Box 445 Boise ID 83701 Office Phone: 208-788-2427, 208-788-2427. Office Fax: 208-788-3918. E-mail: keith@roarklaw.com, keith@idaho-democrats.org.*

ROARK, TERRY PAUL, astronomer, educator; b. Okeene, Okla., June 11, 1938; s. Paul J. and Erma K. (Morrison) R.; m. Beverly Brown, Sept. 7, 1963; 1 child, David. C. BA in Physics, Oklahoma City U., 1960; MS in Astronomy, Rensselaer Poly. Inst., 1962, PhD in Astronomy, 1966. Asst. provost for curricula Ohio State U., Columbus, 1977-79, assoc. provost for instrn., 1979-83; prof. physics Kent (Ohio) State U., 1983-87, v.p. acad. and student affairs, 1983-87, provost, 1985-87; pres. U. Wyo., Laramie, 1987-97, prof. physics and astronomy, 1987-2001; interim pres. Mont. State U., Bozeman, 2000. Bd. dirs. Rocky Mountain Fed. Savs. Bank, chmn. audit com., 1989-93; commr. Western Interstate Commn. for Higher Edn., 1987-97, chmn., 1991; bd. dirs. Associated Western Univs., 1987-94, chmn., 1991, bd. trustees, 1994-97, chmn. 1996; adv. bd. Wyo. Geol. Survey, 1987-97; mem. Warren AFB Civilian Adv. Coun., 1987-97; bd. dirs. First Interstate Bank of Wyo.; bd. dirs. Albany County Hosp. Dist., chmn. 2006. Mem., treas. Ctr. for Pub. Edn., Columbus, 1980-83; mem. fin. adv. com. LWV, Kent, 1986; mem. long range planning com. Cleve. Urban League, 1985-86; mem. adv. com. Battelle youth sci. program Columbus and Ohio Pub. Schs., 1982; bd. dirs. Ivinson Hosp. Found., 1987-97, 2005—. Mem. Am. Astron. Soc., Internat. Astron. Union, Nat. Assn. State Univs. and Land Grant Colls. (bd. dirs. 1994-96, chair commn. on internat. affairs 1995), Astron. Soc. Pacific, Sigma Xi, Phi Kappa Phi, Omicron Delta Kappa. Avocations: photography, music, hiking. Office: U Wyo Dept Physics & Astronomy Dept No 3905 1000 E University Ave Laramie WY 82071-3905

ROARKE, MICHAEL CHARLES, medical educator, nuclear medicine physician; b. Albany, NY, May 8, 1959; s. Charles Augustus and Joan Ann Roarke; m. Maria Giuliani, June 25, 1988; 1 child, Michael Andrew. BS, SUNY, Albany, 1981, MS, 1982; MD, U. Rochester Sch. Medicine, NYC, 1990. Cert. Am. Bd. Radiology, 1995, Am. Bd. Nuc. Medicine, 1996. Chemistry tchr. Albany Acad. Boys, NY, 1982—86; intern internal medicine St. Mary's Hosp., Rochester, 1990—91; resident diagnostic radiology Mallinckrodt Inst. Radiology, St. Louis, 1991—95, fellow nuc. medicine, 1995—96; asst. prof. radiology U. Tex. Med. Ctr., Houston, 1996—97, Mayo Med. Sch., Scottdale, 1997—. Sect. head nuc. radiology Mayo Clinic Ariz., Scottsdale, Ariz., 1997—2007, med. dir. nuc. radiology, 1997—2007. Recipient Best Intern award, St. Mary's Hosp. Internal Medicine Program, 1991, Tchr. Recognition award, White House Commn. on Presdl. Scholars, 1985; named one of Best Doctors in Am., 2003—08, America's Top Physicians, Consumer's Rsch. Coun., 2005—08; Klingenstein Summer Tchg. fellow, Columbia U., 1983. Mem.: AAAS, Am. Roentgen Ray Soc., Acad. Molecular Imaging (assoc.), Soc. Nuc. Medicine (assoc.), Radiol. Soc. N.Am. (assoc.), Beta Beta Beta, Alpha Omega Alpha (life). Avocations: music, composing, mineral photography, coin collecting/numismatics. Office: Mayo Clinic Ariz 13400 East Shea Blvd Scottsdale AZ 85259 Personal E-mail: mroarke@aol.com.

ROATH, STEPHEN D., retired pharmaceutical company executive; b. 1941; With Long's Drug Stores Corp., 1964—2002, exec. v.p. store ops., 1988-91, pres., CEO, 1991—2001, retired, 2002. Mem.: bd. dirs., Calif. Symphony.

ROBART, JAMES LOUIS, federal judge, lawyer; AB, Whitman Coll., 1969; JD, Georgetown U., 1973. Bar: Wash. 1973, U.S. Dist. Ct. (we. dist.) Wash. 1973, U.S. Supreme Ct. 1977, U.S. Ct. Appeals (9th cir.) 1978, U.S. Dist. Ct. (ea. dist.) Wash. 1981, Alaska 1985, U.S. Dist. Ct. Alaska 1985, U.S. Ct. Appeals (fed. cir.) 1985. Assoc. Lane Powell Moss Miller LLP, Seattle, 1973—79, ptnr., 1980—90, Lane Powell Spears Lubersky LLP, 1990—98; co-mng. ptnr. Lane Powel Spears Lubersky, 1998—2002, mng. ptnr., 2003—04; judge US Dist. Ct. (we. dist.) Wash., 2004—. Trustee Children's Home Soc., 1991-92, Seattle Children's Home, pres., 1984, Whitman Coll., bd trustees, 2000-, bd. overseers, 1988-2000. Mem. Fed. Cir. Bar Assn. (trustee 1985-88). Office Phone: 206-370-8920.

ROBB, JOHN DONALD, JR., lawyer; b. NYC, Jan. 11, 1924; s. John D. and Harriett (Block) R.; m. Peggy Hight, Feb. 8, 1946; children: John D., Celeste Robb Nicholson, Ellen, Bradford, George G., David. Student, Yale U., 1941—42, N.Mex.; BSL, U. Minn., 1948, LLB, 1949. Bar: N.Mex. 1950, U.S. Dist. Ct. N.Mex. 1950, U.S. Ct. Appeals (10th cir.) 1955, U.S. Supreme Ct. 1961. Pvt. practice, Albuquerque, 1950-51; assoc. Rodey, Dickason, Sloan, Akin & Robb PA, Albuquerque, 1951-56, ptnr., 1956-65, sr. dir., 1965-97, of counsel, 1997—. Nat. adv. com. legal svcs. program OEO, 1966-73; bd. dir. Christian Legal Soc., 1980-99, dir. legal aid, 1997-. Contbr. articles to profl. jours. Pres. Albuquerque Legal Aid Soc., 1957, bd. dirs., 1960-74; bd. dirs. Navajo Legal Svcs., 1967-68, United Cmty. Fund, 1962-64; chmn. Albuquerque Christian Legal Aid and Referral Svc., 1982-88; pres. Albuquerque Cmty. Coun., 1958-60, Family Consultation Svc. Albuquerque, 1955-57; chmn. bd. Drug Addicts Recovery Enterprises, 1974-79; bd. dirs. Pub. Ministries, 1997—; bd. dirs. N.Mex. Christian Legal Aid Inc., chmn., 1998—. Named Outstanding Man of Yr., Albuquerque Jr. C. of C., 1956; recipient Disting. Svc. award Albuquerque United Cmty. Fund, 1960, Hatton W. Sumners award Southwestern Legal Found., 1971. Fellow Am. Bar Found.; mem. ABA (nat. chmn. standing com. on legal aid and indigent defendants 1966-73), Nat. Legal Aid and Defendants Assn. (v.p. 1966-72), Albuquerque Bar Assn. (chmn. legal aid com. 1962-65), N.Mex. Bar Assn. (chmn. legal aid com.), Internat. Legal Aid Assn., Christian Legal Soc. (bd. dirs. 1982-2000), Albuquerque Christian Lawyers Assn. (chmn. 1979-2000), Am. Judicature Soc., Am. Bd. Trial Advs. Office: Rodey Dickason Sloan Akin & Robb PA PO Box 1888 Albuquerque NM 87103-1888 Home: 7200 Rio Grande Blvd NW Albuquerque NM 87107-6428 also: 201 3rd St NW Ste 2200 Albuquerque NM 87102-3380 Business E-Mail: jrobb@rodey.com.

ROBBINS, ANNE FRANCIS See REAGAN, NANCY

ROBBINS, DARREN J., lawyer; b. San Bernardino, Calif., 1966; BS in Economics, MS in Economics, U. Southern Calif., 1990; JD, Vanderbilt U., 1993. Bar: Calif. 1993, US Dist. Ct., Ctrl. Dist. Calif. 1994, US Dist. Ct., Northern Dist. Calif. 1994, US Dist. Ct., Southern Dist. Calif. 1994. Co-founder, ptnr. Lerach Coughlin Stoia Geller Rudman & Robbins LLP, San Diego, 2003—. Named one of Litigation's Rising Stars, The Am. Lawyer, 2007. Office: Lerach Coughlin Stoia Geller Rudman & Robbins LLP 655 W Broadway Ste 1900 San Diego CA 92101-4297 Office Phone: 619-231-1058. Office Fax: 619-231-7423.

ROBBINS, JAMES EDWARD, electrical engineer; b. Renovo, Pa., May 11, 1931; s. James Edward and Marguerite Neva (Cleary) Robbins; m. Elizabeth Anne Caton, 1959 (div. July 1971); children: James, Katherine, Ellen; m. Dorothy Raye Bell, July 23, 1971; stepchildren: Mark, Lori. BEE, Pa. State U., 1958; MS in Math., San Diego State U., 1961. Registered profl. engr., Calif., Ariz. Rsch. engr. Astronautics divsn. Gen. Dynamics Co., San Diego, 1961-62; sr. engr. Kearfott divsn. Gen. Precision Co., San Marcos, Calif., 1962-65; sys. engrng. specialist Teledyne Ryan Aerospace Co., San Diego, 1965—76; mgr. tech. ops. Electronics divsn. Gen. Dynamics Co., Yuma, Ariz., 1976—82; v.p. Cibola Info. Sys., Yuma, 1982-84; cons. engr. Robbins Engring. Co., Yuma, 1984-85; sr. engring. specialist Gen. Dynamics Svcs. Co., Yuma, 1985-90; sys. engr. Trimble Nav., Sunnyvale, Calif., 1990—2004; sr. system engr. Sci. Applications Internat. Corp., 2004—08; cons. Robbins Engring. Co., Los Alamitos, Calif., 2008—. Contbr. articles to profl. jours. With USN, 1951—55, Korea. Mem.: VFW (post comdr. 1963—65), Ariz. Soc. Profl. Engrs. (pres. western divsn. 1986), Nat. Soc. Profl. Engrs., Inst. Navigation, Am. Legion, Tau Beta Pi. Home: 2952 Yellowtal Dr Los Alamitos CA 90720 Office: Sci Applications Internat Corp 21151 Western Ave Torrance CA 90501 Office Phone: 562-230-8245. Business E-Mail: jim_robbins@earthlink.net.

ROBBINS, NANCY LOUISE See MANN, NANCY

ROBBINS, ROBERT CLAYTON, surgeon; b. Laurel, Miss., Nov. 20, 1957; AA in Chemistry, Jones Jr. Coll., Ellisville, Miss., 1977; BS in Chemistry, Millsaps Coll., Jackson, Miss., 1979; MD, U. Miss. Med. Ctr., Jackson, Miss., 1983. Cert. cardiothoracic surgery Am. Bd. Thoracic Surgery, gen. surgery Am. Bd. Surgery. Intern, gen. surgery U. Miss. Med. Ctr., Jackson, 1983—84, resident, gen. surgery, 1984—85, chief resident, gen. surgery, 1988—89; postdoctoral fellow, cardiothoracic transplantation, dept. surgery Columbia-Presbyn. Med. Ctr., 1986; clin. assoc., cardiothoracic surgery, surgery br., Nat. Heart Lung Blood Inst. NIH, Bethesda, Md., 1986—88; resident, cardiothoracic surgery Stanford U. Hosp., Calif., 1989—91, chief resident, cardiothoracic surgery Calif., 1991—92, co-dir., Cardiac Clin. Ctr. Calif., 2002—, dir., Stanford Inst. for Cardiovascular Medicine Calif., 2004; pediat. fellow, congenital heart surgery Emory U. Sch. Medicine, Atlanta, 1992, Royal Children's Hosp., Melbourne, Australia, 1993; dir., cardiothoracic transplantation lab. Stanford U. Sch. Medicine, 1993—, acting asst. prof., cardiothoracic surgery, 1993—95, asst. prof., cardiothoracic surgery, 1995—2001, dir., heart, heart-lung, and lung transplant program, 1998—, assoc. prof., cardiothoracic surgery, 2001—05, chmn., dept. cardiothoracic surgery, 2005, prof., cardiothoracic surgery, 2005—. Dir., clin. cardiothoracic surgery tchg. conf., 1993—2006; mem. expert panel on minimally invasive surgery Health Tech. Ctr., 2001; bd. dirs. Calif. Transplant Donor Network, 1997—2005, Cohesion Technologies, Palo Alto, 2000—; mem. scientific adv. bd. Cardica, Inc., Menlo Park, Calif., 1997—, bd. dirs., 2000—; mem. scientific adv. bd. Cytograft Tissue Engrng. Inc., Novato, Calif., 2000—, bd. dirs., 2003—; mem. scientific adv. bd. Transvascular, Inc., Menlo Park, Calif., 1995—2000, Embol-X, Inc., Sunnyvale, Calif., 1995—98, Arthro-Care, Corp., Sunnyvale, Calif., 1997—2000, Cardio Vention, Inc., Palo Alto, 1997—99, A-med, Inc., Sacramento, 1997—2000, Micro-heart, Inc., Sunnyvale, Calif., 1999—2001, Radiant Med., Redwood City, Calif., 2000—, Curis, Inc., Cambridge, Mass., 2001—, Paracor Surgical, Inc., Sunnyvale, Calif., 2001—; mem. clin. adv. bd. Xoma, LLC, Berkeley, Calif., 2002—, Afmedica, Inc., Kalamazoo, 2005, Theregen, Corp., San Francisco, 2005—; mem. physician adv. panel Cardiac Surgery Technologies, Medtronic, Inc., Mpls., 2001—. Ad hoc reviewer Nat. Inst. Neurological Disorders and Stroke Study Sect., NIH, 1996, manuscript reviewer Jour. Thoracic and Cardiovascular Surgery, 1996—, mem. editl. bd., 2001—, manuscript reviewer Annals Thoracic Surgery, 1995—, New Eng. Jour. Medicine, 1996—, abstract reviewer Internat. Soc. Heart and Lung Transplantation, 1996—, mem. editl. bd. Cardiac Surgery Digest, 2001—, Jour. Heart and Lung Transplantation, 2003—, Innovations, 2005—, guest editor, surgical supplement Circulation, 2002—05; contbr. several articles to peer-reviewed jours. Mem. Thoracic Organ Transplantation Com. United Network for Organ Sharing, 1999—2002, Region 5 Thoracic Organ Rep. and Review Bd. Chamn., 1999—2002; rsch. com. mem. Thoracic Surgery Found. for Rsch. and Edn., 2000—; mem. Calif. Transplant Donor Network-Med. Affairs Com., 1996—. Fellow: Am. Coll. Cardiology, Am. Heart Assn. (Vivien Thomas Young Investigator award selection com. 1997—, mem. exec. com., coun. on cardiothoracic and vascular surgery 1997—, mem. program com. 1999—), ACS; mem.: Bay Area Soc. Thoracic Surgeons (founding mem.) (pres. 2006, bd. dirs. 2000—), Soc. U. Surgeons, Am. Soc. Transplantation, Am. Soc. Transplant Surgeons, 21st Century Cardiac Surgical Soc., Transplantation Soc., AAAS, Internat. Soc. Heart and Lung Transplantation (co-chair, ventricular assist device coun. 2000—02, bd. dirs. 2000—, program chair 2001—02, mem. program com. 2003, pres. 2006), San Francisco Surgical Soc., Assn. Academic Surgeons (vice-chair, cardiovascular surgery and anesthesia coun. 2005—, mem. strategic planning com. 2006), Soc. Thoracic Surgeons (mem. workforce on clin. edn. 2004—, workforce on surgical treatment end-stage cardiopulmonary disease 2004—), Western Thoracic Surgical Assn., Am. Assn. Thoracic Surgery (membership com. 2003—06, mem. edn. com. 2003—, chair. membership com. 2005—06), Cardiothoracic Surgery Network, James D. Hardy Soc., Andrew G. Morrow Soc., Alpha Omega Alpha (Resident award 1989). Achievements include patents in field. Office: Dept Cardiothoracic Surgery Falk Cardiovasc Rsch Ctr Stanford U Sch Medicine 300 Pasteur Dr CVRB MC 5407 Stanford CA 94305-5407 Office Phone: 650-725-3828, 650-723-5771. Fax: 650-725-3846. E-mail: robbins@stanford.edu.

ROBBINS, STEPHEN J. M., lawyer; b. Seattle, Apr. 13, 1942; s. Robert Mads and Aneita Elberta (West) R.; m. Nina Winifred Tanner, Aug. 11, 1967; children: Sarah E.T., Alicia S.T. AB, UCLA, 1964; JD, Yale U., 1971. Bar: D.C. 1973, U.S. Dist. Ct. D.C. 1973, U.S. Ct. Appeals (D.C. cir.) 1973, U.S. Ct. Appeals (3d cir.) 1973, U.S. Dist. Ct. (ea. and no. dists.) Calif. 1982, U.S. Dist. Ct. (cen. dist.) Calif. 1983, Supreme Ct. of Republic of Palau, 1994. Pres. U.S. Nat. Student Assn., Washington, 1964-65; dir. scheduling McGovern for Pres., Washington, 1971-72; assoc. Steptoe & Johnson, Washington, 1972-75; chief counsel spl. inquiry on food prices, com. on nutrition and human needs U.S. Senate, Washington, 1975; v.p., gen. counsel Straight Arrow Pubs., San Francisco, 1975-77; dep. dist. atty. City and County of San Francisco, 1977-78; regional counsel U.S. SBA, San Francisco, 1978-80; spl. counsel Warner-Amex Cable Communications, Sacramento, 1981-82; ptnr. McDonough, Holland and Allen, Sacramento, 1982-84; v.p. Straight Arrow Pubs., NYC, 1984-86; gen. legal counsel Govt. State of Koror, Rep. of Palau, Western Caroline Islands, 1994-95; pvt. practice law, 1986—. Adj. prof. govt. Calif. State U., Sacramento, 1999-05. Staff sgt. U.S. Army, 1966-68. Fellow Acad. Polit. Sci.; mem. ABA (sect. urban, state and local govt.), DC Bar, State Bar Calif., Am. Hist. Assn., Supreme Ct. Hist. Soc. Democrat. Unitarian. Avocations: theater, art, hiking. Office: PO Box 85567 Seattle WA 98145

ROBBINS, THOMAS EUGENE, writer; b. Blowing Rock, NC, 1936; m. Terrie Hemingway (div.); m. Alexa d'Avalon, 1995; 1 child, Fleetwood Starr. Student, Washington and Lee U., 1954-56, U. Wash., 1963; degree in social sci., Va. Commonwealth U., 1959. Former copy editor Richmond (Va.) Times-Dispatch, 1959—62, Seattle Post-Intelligencer, 1967—69; art critic Seattle Times, 1962—65. Author: Guy Anderson, 1965, Another Roadside Attraction, 1971, Even Cowgirls Get the Blues, 1976 (Best Am. Short Story 1977), Still Life with Woodpecker, 1980, Jitterbug Perfume, 1984, Skinny Legs and All, 1990, Half Asleep in Frog Pajamas, 1994, Fierce Invalids Home from Hot Climates, 2000, Villa Incognito, 2003, Wild Ducks Flying Backward, 2005. With USAF. Named one of 100 Best Writers of 20th Century, Writer's Digest. Office: PO Box 338 La Conner WA 98257-0338

ROBBINS, TIM (TIMOTHY FRANCIS ROBBINS), actor, film director; b. West Covina, Calif., Oct. 16, 1958; s. Gil Robbins; life ptnr. Susan Sarandon; children: John Henry, Miles 1 stepchild, Eva Maria. BA with honors, UCLA, 1981. Founder, artistic dir. The Actor's Gang, 1981—. Actor: (films) No Small Affair, 1984, Toy Soldiers, 1984, Fraternity Vacation, 1985, The Sure Thing, 1985, Howard the Duck, 1986, Top Gun, 1986, Five Corners, 1987, Bill Durham, 1988, Tapeheads, 1989, Eric The Viking, 1989, Miss Firecracker, 1989, Cadillac Man, 1990, Twister, 1990, Jacob's Ladder, 1990, Jungle Fever, 1991, The Player, 1992 (Best Actor award Cannes Film Festival 1992), Short Cuts, 1993, The Hudsucker Proxy, 1994, The Shawshank Redemption, 1994, Ready to Wear (Prêt-à-Porter), 1994, I.Q., 1994, Nothing to Lose, 1997, Arlington Road, 1999, Austin Powers: The Spy Who Shagged Me, 1999, Mission to Mars, 2000, High Fidelity, 2000, Antitrust, 2001, Human Nature, 2001, The

Truth About Charlie, 2002, The Day My God Died (voice), 2003, Mystic River, 2003 (Golden Globe for best supporting actor in a drama, 2004, Screen Actors Guild Award for best supporting actor, 2004, Acad. Award for best supporting actor in a drama, 2004), Code 46, 2004, Anchorman: The Legend of Ron Burgundy, 2004, War of the Worlds, 2005, The Secret Life of Words, 2005, Zathura: A Space Adventure, 2005, Catch a Fire, 2006, Tenacious D: The Pick of Destiny, 2006, The Lucky Ones, 2008, City of Ember, 2008; (TV movies) Quarterback Princess, 1983, Malice in Wonderland, 1985; (TV appearances) St. Elsewhere, 1982, Legmen, 1984, Hardcastle and McCormick, 1984, Hill Street Blues, 1984, Moonlighting, 1985, Amazing Stories, 1986, (voice) The Simpsons, 1999, Jack & Bobby, 2005; actor, dir., writer, composer: Bob Roberts, 1992; dir., writer, prodr.: Dead Man Walking, 1995 (Golden Globe nomination for best dir. of film 1996, Acad. Award nomination for best dir. 1996), The Cradle Will Rock, 1999; exec. prodr., The Typewriter, the Rifle, and the Movie Camera, 1994, The Spectre of Hope, 2000; dir. (plays) Ubu Roi (L.A. Weekly Dir. award), A Midsummer's Night Dream, Methusalem, the Eternal Bourgeois, The Good Woman of Setzuan (L.A. Drama Critics Circle nominee), and others, (TV series) Queen's Supreme, 2003; co-writer: (plays) Alagazam...After the Dog Wars, Violence: The Misadventures of Spike Spangle, Farmer, Carnage, a Comedy, Embedded, and others. Recipient Tribute to Ind. Vision Award, Sundance Film Festival, 1997, Star on Hollywood Walk of Fame, 2008. Office: ICM c/o Elaine Goldsmith Thomas 40 W 57th St New York NY 10019

ROBERTS, DENNIS WILLIAM, construction executive; b. Chgo., Jan. 7, 1943; s. William Owen and Florence Harriet (Denman) R. BA in Journalism, U. N.Mex., 1968; MA in Legal Studies, Antioch U., 1982; MA, St. John's Coll., 1984. Gen. assignment reporter Albuquerque Pub. Co., 1964, sports writer, 1960-64, advt. and display salesman, 1967-68; dir. info. N.Mex. bldg. br. Asso. Gen. Contractors Am., Albuquerque, 1968-79, asst. exec. dir., 1979-82, dir., 1982—. Adj. prof. civil engring. U. N.Mex., 2004—08. Active United Way, Albuquerque, 1969-78; chmn. Albuquerque Crime Prevention Coun., 1982; bd. dirs. Rio Grande chpt. ARC, 1992-95, Albuquerque Lit. Coun., 1998-2004, Luth. Campus Ministry, U. N.Mex., 2003—; mem. cmty. adv. coun. Albuquerque Jobs Corps. Recipient Pub. Rels. Achievement award Assoc. Gen. Contractors Am., 1975, 78. Mem. N.Mex. Pub. Rels. Conf. (chmn. 1975, 82-83), Pub. Rels. Soc. Am. (accredited, pres. N.Mex. chpt. 1981, chmn. S.W. dist. 1984, chmn. sect. 1988), Constrn. Specifications Inst. (Outstanding Industry Mem. 1974, Outstanding Com. Chmn. 1978), Am. Soc. Safety Engrs., Toastmasters Club (dist. gov. 1977-78, Disting. Dist. award 1978, Toastmaster of Yr. 1979-80), Masons, Shriners, Sigma Delta Chi (pres. N.Mex. chpt. 1969). Republican. Lutheran. Office: Assn Gen Contractors 1615 University Blvd NE Albuquerque NM 87102-1717 Home: Apt 1-B 3700 Aspan Ave NE Albuquerque NM 87110 Office Phone: 505-842-1462. Business E-Mail: dennisr@agcnm.org.

ROBERTS, DONALD FRANK, JR., communications educator; b. Seattle, Mar. 30, 1939; s. Donald Frank Sr. and Ruth Amalia (Geiger) R.; m. Karlene Hahn, 1963 (div. 1981): 1 child, Donald Brett; m. Wendy G. Roberts, Aug. 26, 1983; stepchildren: Richard L., David L., Katherine M. AB, Columbia U., 1961; MA, U. Calif., Berkeley, 1963; PhD, Stanford U., 1968. Instr., dept. English U. Hawaii, Honolulu, 1963-64; asst. dir. ednl. svc. bur. The Wall Street Jour., Princeton, NJ, 1964-65; asst. prof., rsch. assoc. dept. Comm., Inst. Comm. Rsch. Stanford (Calif.) U., 1970-76, assoc. prof., 1976-84, prof. Comm., 1984—, dir. Inst. Comm. Rsch., 1985-90, chmn. dept. Comm., 1990-96, Thomas More Storke Prof., 1991—. Cons. NIMH, 1970—71, Rand Corp., 1972—74, Sta. KQED-TV, 1975—77, Far West Lab. Ednl. Rsch. and Devel., 1978—79, FTC, 1978—80, Westinghouse Broadcasting, 1983—86, Soc. Nutrition Edn., 1984—86, The Disney Channel, 1986—87, WHO, 1988—89, SRI Internat., 1988—89, Carnegie Coun. Adolescence, 1989—90, NBC, 1992, Ctr. Disease Control, 1992, Children Now, 1992—2004, Software Pubs. Assn., 1994, Nickelodeon, 1994, JP Kids, 1995—97, MGM Animation, 1996—98, DIC Entertainment, 1997—, Planet Lingo, 1997—2001, Sunbow Entertainment, 1999—2000, ABC/Disney TV Animation, 2000—02, Disney Online, 2000—02, Nelvana, Ltd., 2000—01; bd. advisors Media Scope, 1992—94; proposal reviewer NIMH, NSF, U.S. Agy. Internat. Devel., Can. Coun., John and Mary R. Markle Found., W.T. Grant Found.; spkr. numerous seminars, confs., symposia. Co-author: Process and Effects of Mass Communication, 1971, Television and Human Behavior, 1978, It's not ONLY Rock and Roll, 1998, Kids and Media at the New Millennium, 1999, Kids and Media in America, 2004, Generation M: Media in the Lives of 8-18 Year-olds, 2005; mem. editl. bd. Jour. Broadcasting, 1980—88, Pub. Opinion Quarterly, 1981—86, Communicare, 1986—2004, editl. reviewer Commn. Rsch., —, Comm. Monograph, Comm. Yearbook, Human Comm. Rsch., Jour. Comm., Jour. Quarterly, Child Devel., Jour. Applied Psychology, Jour. Ednl. Psychology, Psychology Bull., Jour. Adolescent Health; contbr. articles, chapters to books. Fellow Human Scis. Rsch. Coun., Pretoria. South Africa, 1985, 1987, Fullbright Teaching fellow Inst. for Unterrichtstechnologie Und Medienpadagogic, Austria, 1987. Mem. APA, Internat. Comm. Assn., Assn. Edn. in Journalism and Mass Comm., Soc. Rsch. Child Devel., Soc. Personality and Soc. Psychology. Office: Stanford U Dept Comm McClatchy Hall Stanford CA 94305-2050 Office Phone: 650-723-0780. Business E-Mail: droberts@stanford.edu.

ROBERTS, DONALD JOHN, economics, business professor, consultant; b. Winnipeg, Man., Can., Feb. 11, 1945; came to U.S., 1967; s. Donald Victor and Margaret Mabel R.; m. Kathleen Eleanor Taylor, Aug. 26, 1967 (dec. 2006). BA with honors, U. Man., 1967; PhD, U. Minn., 1972; LLD honoris causa, U. Winnipeg, 2007. Instr. dept. managerial econs. and decision scis. J.L. Kellogg Grad. Sch. Mgmt., Northwestern U., Evanston, Ill., 1971—72, asst. prof., 1972—74; assoc. prof. J. L. Kellogg Grad. Sch. Mgmt., Northwestern U., Evanston, Ill., 1974—77; prof. J.L. Kellogg Grad. Sch. Mgmt., Northwestern U., Evanston, Ill., 1977—80, Grad. Sch. Bus., Stanford (Calif.) U., 1980, Jonathan B. Lovelace prof., 1980—2001, assoc. dean, dir. rsch., 1987—90, dir. exec. program in strategy and orgn., 1992—, dir. global mgmt. program, 1994—, sr. assoc. dean, 2000—, John H. Scully prof., 2001—; dir. Ctr. for Global Bus. and the Economy, 2003—. Prof. (by courtesy) dept. econs. Stanford U., 1986—; vis. rsch. faculty U. Catholique de Louvain, Belgium, 1974-75; inaugural Clarendon lectr. mgmt. studies Oxford U., 1997; cons. bus., econs. and antitrust, 1976—; vis. fellow All Souls Coll., Oxford U., 1995, Nuffield Coll., Oxford U., 1999-00; vis. acad. fellow in leadership and orgn. McKinsey & Co., London, 1999-00. Author The Modern Firm: Organizational Design for Performance and Growth, 2004; co-author: Economics, Organization and Management, 1992; assoc. editor Jour. Econ. Theory, 1977-92, Econometrica, 1985-87, Games and Economic Behavior, 1988-; mem. editl. bd. Am. Econ. Rev., 1991-95, Jour. Econs. and Mgmt. Strategy, 1991-98, Orgns. and Markets Abstracts, 1996-; contbr. articles to profl. jours. NSF grantee, 1973-93; rsch. fellow Ctr. Ops. Rsch. and Econometrics, Heverlee, Belgium, 1974, fellow Ctr. for Advanced Study in the Behavioral Scis., 1991-92. Fellow Am. Acad. Arts and Scis., Econometric Soc. (coun. 1994-96); mem. Am. Econ. Assn., Beta Gamma Sigma. Home: 835 Santa Fe Ave Stanford CA 94305-1022 E-mail: roberts_john@gsb.stanford.edu.

ROBERTS, DONALD L., state legislator; b. Great Falls, Mont., July 18, 1948; m. Carol Roberts; children: Sara, Michelle, Melissa. DMD, Wash. U., St. Louis; DMD/MS Oral Surgery, U. Iowa Hosps. & Clinics, 1979. CEO Riverstone Oral Surgery & Implants, LLC, 2005—08; mem. Mont. House of Reps., 2003—07, mem. Dist. 56, 2008—. Republican. Protestant. Office: Montana House of Representatives PO Box 200400 Helena MT 59620-0400 Mailing: 5414 Walter Hagen Dr Billings MT 59106-1007 Home Phone: 406-652-3536; Office Phone: 406-444-4800. Office Fax: 406-444-4825.

ROBERTS, ELLEN, state legislator; m. Rick Roberts; 2 children. B, Cornell U., Ithaca, NY, 1981; JD, U. Colo. Law Sch., Boulder, 1986. Park ranger Nat. Pk. Svc., Rocky Mt. Nat. Pk.; practicing ind. atty.; mem. Dist. 59 Colo. House of Reps., 2007—. Bd. mem. Mercy Med. Ctr.; mem. Citizens Health Adv. Coun., First Presbyn. Ch. Recipient Athena award Durango C. of C., 2003; named a Four Corners Leader Four Corners Bus. Jour., 2003. Mem. Southwest Colo. Bar Assn. (Professionalism award, 2001), Club 20, High Noon Rotary. Republican. Presbyterian. Office: Colo State Capitol 200 E Colfax Denver CO 80203 Office Phone: 303-866-2914. Business E-Mail: ellen.roberts.house@state.co.us.*

ROBERTS, GEORGE P., computer company executive; Chmn., CEO P-Com, Campbell, Calif. Office: P Com 2146 Bering Dr San Jose CA 95131-2013

ROBERTS, GEORGE R., investment banker; b. Houston, Tex., 1945; m. Leanne Bovet Roberts (dec.); children: Eric, Mark, Courtney. BA, Claremont McKenna Coll., 1966; JD, U. Calif. Hastings Law Sch., San Francisco, 1969; LLD (hon.), Claremont McKenna Coll., 2003. Joined corp. fin. dept. to partner Bear Stearns & Co., New York, 1969—79; founding sr. ptnr. Kohlberg, Kravis, Roberts, San Francisco, 1976—. Dir. Accel-KKR, Safeway, Inc., DPL, Inc., KinderCare Learning Centers, Inc., Owens-Illinois, Inc. and PRIMEDIA Inc. Bd. San Francisco Symphony, San Francisco Ballet, Fine Arts Mus., San Francisco, Claremont McKenna Coll. Recipient Man of Yr. award, Culver Ednl. Found., 2006; named one of Forbes' Richest Americans, 2006. Achievements include historic billion dollar buyout of Wometco Companies in 1984; $25 billion RJR Nabisco buyout in 1989. Office: Kohlberg Kravis Roberts & Co 2800 Sand Hill Rd Ste 200 Menlo Park CA 94025-7055

ROBERTS, HARRY, beverage service company executive, marketing executive; b. Kingston, NY, June 27, 1942; s. Theresa Grace (Salanitro) Roberts; m. Lynda M. Hamilton; children: Christina, Robin, Becky, Melissa, Serra. New products mgr. J.C. Penney Co., NYC, 1965-71; pres. Everfast Inc., NYC, 1971-75; founder, pres. Kitchen Kaboodle, Portland, Oreg., 1975-82, The Roberts Group, Portland, Oreg., 1982; pres., CEO EvansGroup Portland, 1990—93; v.p. merchandising Starbucks Corp., Seattle, 1993—96; pres., COO Chart House Enterprises Inc., 1996—97; founder, pres., CEO Pallino Pastaria Co., 1999—; sr. v.p., chief creative officer Starbucks Corp., Seattle, 2008—. Cons. Support Techs. Inc., Portland, 1985; bd. dirs. Inter-Lock Inc., Ramagon Toys, Inc., Chart House Enterprises Inc., 1993. Inventor workshop tools. Active March of Dimes Gourmet Gala, Portland, 1984, chmn., 1980. Named one of Top Ten Retail Execs. in US, entree mag., NYC, 1981 Mem.: Portland Yacht. Avocations: boating, photography. Office: Starbucks Corp 2401 Utah Ave S Seattle WA 98134 Office Phone: 206-447-1575. Office Fax: 206-682-7570.

ROBERTS, JERRY, newspaper editor; Polit. editor city desk San Francisco Chronicle, editl. pg. editor, 1995-98, mng. editor, 1998—2002; exec. editor Santa Barbara News-Press, 2002—06. Mailing: PO Box 1359 Santa Barbara CA 93102 E-mail: jroberts@newspress.com.

ROBERTS, JOHN D., chemist, educator; b. LA, June 8, 1918; s. Allen Andrew and Flora (Dombrowski) Roberts; m. Edith Mary Johnson, July 11, 1942; children: Anne Christine, Donald William, John Paul, Allen Walter. AB, UCLA, 1941, PhD, 1944; D in Natural Scis. (hon.), U. Munich, 1962; DSc (hon.), Temple U., 1964, Notre Dame U., 1993, U. Wales, 1993, Scripps Rsch. Inst., 1996. Instr. chemistry UCLA, 1944—45; NRC fellow chemistry Harvard U., 1945—46, instr. chemistry, 1946, MIT, 1946, asst. prof., 1947—50, assoc. prof., 1950—52; vis. prof. Ohio State U., 1952, Stanford U., 1973—74; prof. organic chemistry Calif. Inst. Tech., 1953—72, inst. prof. chemistry, 1972—88, inst. prof. chemistry emeritus, lectr., 1988—, dean of faculty, v.p., provost, 1980—83, lectr., 1988—, chmn. divsn. chemistry and chem. engring., 1963—68, acting chmn., 1972—73. Bd. dirs. Huntington Med. Rsch. Insts., 1984—99, Organic Syntheses Inc.; Robert Noyce vis. prof. sci. Grinnell Coll., 2001. Author: Basic Organic Chemistry Part I, 1955, Nuclear Magnetic Resonance, 1958, Spin-Spin Splitting in High-Resolution Nuclear Magnetic Resonance Spectra, 1961, Molecular Orbital Calculations, 1961; author: (with M.C. Caserio) Basic Principles of Organic Chemistry, 1964, 2d edit., 1977, Modern Organic Chemistry, 1967; author: (with R. Stewart and M.C. Caserio) Organic Chemistry-Methane To Macromolecules, 1971; author: At The Right Place at the Right Time, 1990, ABCs of FT-NMR, 2000; contbg. editor: McGraw-Hill Series in Advanced Chemistry, 1957—60; editor: Organic Syntheses, Vol. 41, 1961; Spectroscopy, mem. editl. bd.: Organic Magnetic Resonance in Chemistry. Trustee L.S.B. Leakey Found., 1983—92; bd. dirs. Coleman Chamber Music Assn.; adv. com. Calif. Competitive Tech., 1989—92. Recipient Alumni Profl. Achievement award, UCLA, 1967, Nichols medal, 1972, Tolman medal, 1975, Michelson-Morley award, 1976, Norris award, 1978, Pauling award, 1980, Theodore Wm. Richards medal, 1982, Willard Gibbs Gold medal, 1983, Golden Plate award, Am. Acad. Achievement, 1983, Priestley medal, 1987, Madison Marshall award, 1989, Nat. Medal Sci., NSF, 1990, Glenn T. Seaborg medal, 1991, Award in nuclear magnetic resource, 1991, Svc. to Chemistry award, 1991, History Maker award, Pasadena Hist. Soc., 1994, Pauling Legacy award, 2006; co-recipient Robert A. Welch award, 1990; named Hon. Alumnus, Calif. Inst. Tech., 1990, SURF dedicatee, 1992; named one of Most Influential Chemists of Last 75 yrs., Chem. and Engring. News, 1998;, Guggenheim fellow, 1952—53, 1955—56. Mem.: AAAS (councillor 1992—95), NAS (councillor 1980—83, com. on sci. and engring. pub. policy 1983—87, Chem. Scis. award 1999, award for chemistry in svc. to soc. 2009), Royal Soc. Chemistry, Am. Acad. Arts and Scis., Am. Philos. Soc. (coun. mem. 1983—86), Am. Chem. Soc. (chmn. organic chemistry divsn. 1956—57, award pure chemistry 1954, Harrison Howe award 1957, Roger Adams award in organic chemistry 1967, Arthur C. Cope award 1994, Chem. Pioneer award 1994, Nakanishi prize 2001, Auburn Kosolapoff award 2003), Phi Lambda Upsilon, Sigma Xi. Office: Calif Inst Tech 358 Crellin Lab Mail Code 164-30 Pasadena CA 91125-0001 Office Phone: 626-395-6036. Business E-Mail: robertsj@caltech.edu.*

ROBERTS, JOHN DERHAM, lawyer; 1 child. Cert., Richmond Coll., Va., 1960; BS, Hampden-Sydney Coll., Va., 1964; LLB, Washington & Lee U., 1968. Bar: Va. 1968, Fla. 1969, U.S. Supreme Ct. 1969, U.S. Ct. Customs and Patent Appeals 1970, U.S. Tax Ct. 1970, U.S. Ct. Appeals (5th cir.) 1970, U.S. Ct. Appeals (9th cir.) 1974, U.S. Supreme Ct. 1969. Law clk. U.S. Dist. Ct., Jacksonville, Fla., 1968-69; assoc. Phillips, Kendrick, Gearhart & Aylor, Arlington, Va., 1969-70; asst. U.S. Atty. mid. dist. Fla. U.S. Dept. Justice, Jacksonville, 1970-74, Dist. of Alaska, Anchorage, 1974-77, U.S. magistrate judge, 1977—. Bd. dirs. Teen Challenge Alaska, Anchorage, 1984-93; chmn. Eagle Scout Rev. Bd., 1993—; bd. dirs. Alaska Youth for Christ, 1993-96; govs.'s Prayer Breakfast Com., 1994—, vice-chair, 1998—. Recipient Citizenship award DAR, Anchorage, 1984, plaque, U.S. Navy, Citizen Day, Adak, Alaska, 1980, Silver Beaver award, 2004. Mem. ABA, Nat. Conf. Spl. Ct. Judges (exec. bd. 1985-92), 9th Cir. Conf. Magistrate Judges (exec. bd. 1982-85, chmn. 1984-85, 2005-07), Alaska Bar Assn., Anchorage Bar Assn., Chi Phi, Psi Chi, Phi Alpha Delta. Republican. Office: US Magistrate Judge 222 W 7th Ave Unit 46 Anchorage AK 99513-7504 Office Phone: 907-677-6255.

ROBERTS, JOHN PETER LEE, cultural advisor, administrator, educator, writer; b. Sydney, Oct. 21, 1930; s. Noel Lee and Myrtle Winifred (Reid) R.; m. Christina Van Oordt, July 28, 1962; children—Noel, Christina, Olga. Student, State Conservatorium Music, New South Wales; MA, Carleton U., 1988; DFA (hon.), U. Victoria, 1992; LLD (hon.), U. Man., 1997. With CBC Radio, Toronto, Can., 1955—, producer, 1955—, head music and variety, 1971—, spl. adv. music and arts, 1975; sr. advisor cultural devel., head office Ottawa, 1983-87; mem. exec. bd. Internat. Music Centre, Vienna, 1968-80, first chmn. radio and comml. rec. group, 1969-70, hon. mem., 1980; mem. exec. bd. Internat. Inst. Music Dance and Theatre, Vienna, 1969-75; bd. govs. Can. Conf. Arts, 1970-76; exec. bd. Internat. Music Coun., Paris, 1973-79; v.p. Internat. Music Council, 1975, pres., 1978-79, Can. Music Centre, Toronto, 1971-77, dir. gen., 1977-81; pres. Can. Music Council, 1968-71, 75-77; dir. Festival Singers of Can., 1965-78, Elmer Iseler Singers, 1979-81, Toronto Mendelssohn Choir, 1969-81, Nat. Youth Orch. Can., 1973-80; chmn. 1st World Music Week, 1975, Internat. Music Day, 1975-82; v.p. Internat. Inst. Audio-Visual Communication and Cultural Devel. (Mediacult), Vienna, 1976-87, pres., 1987-93, Internat. Rsch. Inst. for Media, Communication, Cultural Devel., Vienna, 1993-95. V.p. Musicians Internat. Mus. Aid Fund, Geneva, 1978—79; pres. Les Jeunesses Musicales du Can., 1979—83; jury chmn. Internat. Vocal Competition, Rio de Janeiro, 1979; spl. advisor to chmn. Can. Radio-TV and Telecomm. Commn., 1981—83; sr. advisor cultural devel. CBC, 1983—87; dean Faculty of Fine Arts, U. Calgary, 1987—95; bd. dirs. Esther Honen's Internat. Piano Competition, 1994, chmn., 96, 2000, 03; adj. prof. U. Calgary, 1995—; vis. fellow McGill Inst. Study of Can., McGill U., Montreal, 1995—96. Mem. editorial bd. Can. Music Book, 1970-77; author: Glenn Gould: Selected Letters, 1992, The Art of Glenn Gould, 1999. Mem. exec. bd. dirs. Can. Nat. Commn. for UNESCO, 1976-80; founding pres. Glenn Gould Found., Toronto, 1983—. Decorated Order of Can. (mem., 1981, officer, 1996); Cross of Honour for Sci. and the Arts (Austria, 1981). Mem. Can. assn. Fine Arts Deans (chmn. 1989-93), Internat. Coun. Fine Arts Deans (bd. dirs. 1992-94). Office: U Calgary Faculty Fine Arts 2500 University Dr NW Calgary AB Canada T2N 1N4

ROBERTS, JULIA FIONA, actress; b. Smyrna, Ga., Oct. 28, 1967; d. Betty and Walter Roberts; m. Lyle Lovett, Jun. 25, 1993 (div. March 22, 1995); m. Daniel Moder, July 4, 2002; children: Hazel Patricia, Phinnaeus Walter, Henry Daniel. Actress: (films) Blood Red, 1986, Satisfaction, 1987, Mystic Pizza, 1988, Steel Magnolias, 1989 (Acad. Award nominee, Golden Globe award), Pretty Woman, 1990 (Acad. Award nominee, Golden Globe Award), Flatliners, 1990, Sleeping With the Enemy, 1991, Hook, 1991, Dying Young, 1991, The Player, 1992, The Pelican Brief, 1993, I Love Trouble, 1994, Ready to Wear (Prêt-à-Porter), 1994, Something To Talk About, 1995, Mary Reilly, 1996, Everybody Says I Love You, 1996, Michael Collins, 1996, My Best Friend's Wedding, 1997, Conspiracy Theory, 1997, Stepmom, 1998, Notting Hill, 1999, Runaway Bride, 1999, Erin Brockovich, 2000 (Acad. award for Best Actress, Golden Globe for Best Performance by an Actress), The Mexican, 2001, America's Sweethearts, 2001, Ocean's Eleven, 2001, Full Frontal, 2002, Confessions of a Dangerous Mind, 2002, Mona Lisa Smile, 2003, Closer, 2004, Ocean's Twelve, 2004, (voice only) The Ant Bully, 2006, (voice only) Charlotte's Web, 2006, Charlie Wilson's War, 2007, Fireflies in the Garden, 2008, Duplicity, 2009; (TV films) Baja Oklahoma, 1988, (narrator) Before Your Eyes: Angelie's Secret, 1995; (TV appearances) Crime Story, 1987, Miami Vice, 1988, Friends, 1996, Murphy Brown, 1998, Sesame Street, 1998, AFI's 100 Years...100 Movies, 1998, In the Wild, 1998, Law & Order, 1999; Broadway plays include Three Days of Rain, 2006; exec. prodr. (films) Kit Kittredge: An American Girl, 2008 Involved with UNICEF; lent celebrity name to help raise money for research to develop a cure for Rett Syndrome. Recipient People's Choice awards Favorite Motion Picture Actress, 1991, 98, Favorite Comedy/Dramatic Motion Picture Actress, 1992, Favorite Dramatic Motion Picture Actres, 1994; recipient Woman of Yr. award Hasty Pudding Theatricals, 1997, Spl. award Internat. Star of Yr., ShoWest Conv., 1998,; Named Female Star of the Yr., Nat. Assn. Theatre Owners, 1991, Am. Cinematheque award, 2007; named one of '50 Most Beautiful People in the World, People Mag., 1990, 1991, 50 Most Beautiful List', People Mag.(USA), 2000, 2002, '25 Most Intriguing People, People Mag., 2001, Top Entertainers, E!, 2001.; named one of 50 Most Powerful People in Hollywood Premiere mag., 2002-06, 100 Most Powerful Celebrities, Forbes.com, 2007. One of the most popular and sought-after talents in Hollywood; highest paid actress in film history. Office: c/o Hirsch Wallerstein Matlof and Fishman LLP 10100 Santa Monica Blvd Los Angeles CA 90067-1722

ROBERTS, KEN A., state legislator; b. Cascade, Idaho, May 5, 1963; m. Mary Jo Roberts; 3 children. Attended, Boise State U., 1984, Moody Bible Inst., Spokane, 1985, U. Idaho, 1986. Farmer, 1983—; chmn. McCall Donnelly Sch. Dist. 421, 1998—; mem. Dist. 8 Idaho

House of Reps., 2000—, majority caucus chmn. Republican. Baptist. Office: State Capitol Bldg PO Box 83720 Boise ID 83720-0081 Office Phone: 208-332-1000. Office Fax: 208-334-5397. Business E-Mail: kroberts@house.idaho.gov.*

ROBERTS, LAWRENCE GILMAN, telecommunications industry executive; b. Conn., Dec. 21, 1937; s. Elliott John and Elizabeth (Gilman) R.; m. June Ellen Stuller, 1959 (div. 1973); children: Paul, Kenny. BSEE, MIT, 1959, MSEE, 1960, PhD, 1963. Dir. info. proc. Advanced Rsch. Projects Agy. U.S. Dept. Def., Arlington, Va., 1969-73; pres., CEO, GTE Telenet Corp., Vienna, Va., 1973-82; pres. DHL, Redwood City, Calif., 1982-83; chmn., CEO, NetExpress, Inc., Foster City, Calif., 1983-93; pres. ATM Systems, Santa Clara, Calif., 1993-98; founder, chief tech. officer Caspian Networks, San Jose, Calif., 1998—2004; founder, CEO Anagran Inc., Woodside, Calif., 2004—. Recipient L.M. Ericsson award for comms., 1981, Prince of Asturias award, 2002, NEC Computer Comms. award, 2005. Mem.: AAAS, IEEE (W. Wallace McDowell award 1992, Internet award 2000), NAE (Draper award 2001), Assn. Computing Machinery (SIGCOM award 1998), Am. Fedn. Info. Processing, IEEE Computer Soc., Sigma Xi. Office Phone: 408-701-0880. E-mail: lroberts@packet.cc.

ROBERTS, MICHAEL FOSTER, biology professor; b. Guatemala City, Guatemala, Aug. 8, 1943; s. Ralph Jackson and Arleda (Allen) R.; m. Mary Sherill Noe, Dec. 27, 1966; children: Rosemary, Amelia. BA, U. Calif., Berkeley, 1966; MA, U. Wis., Madison, 1968, PhD, 1972. Fellow John B. Pierce Found. Lab., Yale U., New Haven, Conn., 1972-76; asst. prof. Yale U., New Haven, 1976-81, Linfield Coll., McMinnville, oreg., 1981-84, assoc. prof., 1984-90, prof. biology, 1990—. Guest referee editor Am. Physiol. Soc., Bethesda, Md., 1974—; peer rev. com. Am. Heart Assn., Portland, Oreg., 1982-87. Contbr. articles to profl. jours. Program dir. Murdock Trust. Named NIH Predoctoral Fellow, 1969-72, Postdoctoral fellow, 1972-76; recipient NIH Rsch. grant, 1982-85, Am. Heart Assn. rsch. grant, 1985-86, 99—; grantee Murdock Trust. Mem. Am. Physiol. Soc., Sigma Xi. Office: Linfield Coll Dept Biology Mcminnville OR 97128 Business E-Mail: mrobert@linfield.edu.

ROBERTS, PAUL HARRY, mathematics professor; b. Aberystwyth, Wales, Eng., Sept. 13, 1929; s. Percy Harry and Ethel Frances (Mann) R.; m. Maureen Frances Tabrett, Dec. 16, 1989. BA, Cambridge U., Eng., 1951, MA, PhD, 1954, ScD, 1966. Rsch. assoc. U. Chgo., 1954-55, assoc. prof., 1961-63; scientific officer Atomic Weapons Rsch. Establisment, Aldermaston, U.K., 1955-56; rsch. fellow U. Durham, Newcastle, U.K., 1956-59, lectr., 1959-61; prof. math. U. Newcastle upon Tyne, Eng., 1963-86; prof. math. and geophysical scis. U. Calif., LA, 1986—. Author: (book) An Introduction to Magnetohydrodynamics, 1967; co-editor: (book) Rotating Fluids in Geophysics, 1979; editor: Geophysical and Astrophysical Fluid Dynamics, 1976—. Mem. Royal Astronomical Soc., Royal Soc. London, Am. Geophysical Union (John Adam Fleming medal, 1999. Office: UCLA Inst of Geophysics & Planetary Physics Los Angeles CA 90095-1567

ROBERTS, PAUL V., civil and environmental engineering educator; BS, Princeton U., 1960; PhD in Chem. Engring., Cornell U., 1966; MS, Stanford U., 1971. Process engr. Chevron Rsch. Co., 1966-68; rsch. engr. Stanford (Calif.) Rsch. Inst., 1968-71; sr. rsch. scientist and group leader process engring. Swiss Fed. Inst. Water Supply and Water Pollution Control, Dubendorf, Switzerland, 1972, head engring. dept., 1973-76; from adj. prof. to assoc. prof. Stanford (Calif.) U., 1976-84, assoc. dept. chmn., 1985-90, prof. environ. engring. dept. civil engring., 1984—, C.L. Peck prof. engring., 1989—. Prin. investigator 25 sponsored projects at Stanford U., 1976— Mem. Nat. Acad. Engring., Am. Water Works Assn. (Rsch. Achievement award 1983, 85-87, 91). Achievements include rsch. projects including chemical process and environmental engineering with emphasis on trace contaminants, water reuse, unit operations of water treatment and advanced waste treatment; transfer of volatile organic pollutants to the atmosphere; transformation and fates of trace contaminants in the ground-water environment; hazardous waste remediation, sorption and mass transfer phenomena. Office: Stanford U Dept Civil & Environ Engrg Stanford CA 94305-4020

ROBERTS, RICHARD N., psychologist; AB in Govt., Columbia U., 1968; MSW, U. Hawaii, 1974, PhD in Psychology, 1977. Asst. prof. dept. psychology U. N.C., Greensboro, 1978-82; dir. pre-kindergarten edn. program Ctr. Devel. Early Edn. Kamehameha Schs., Honolulu, 1983-89; assoc. prof. dept. psychology Utah State U., Logan, 1989—, co-dir. Early Intervention Rsch. Inst., 1989—, dir. rsch. and evaluation Ctr. for Persons with Disabilities, 1989—. Cons. to Hawaii State Hosp., 1977, Hawaii Job Corps, 1977, USAF, 1976, others. Editor: Coming home to preschool: The sociocultural context of early education, 1993; author monograph and workbook; contbr. chpts. to books, articles to profl. jours.; presenter in field. Served as lt. USN, 1968-72. Recipient numerous grants. Mem. APA, APHA, Utah Pub. Health Assn., Assn. Maternal and Child Health Programs, Soc. for Rsch. in Child Devel., Coun. for Exceptional Children. Office: Utah State U Early Intervention Rsch Logan UT 84322-0001

ROBERTS, ROBERT WINSTON, social worker, educator, dean; b. Balt., July 23, 1932; s. Kelmer Swan Roberts and Lettie Mae (Collins) Johnston; m. Helen Elizabeth Perpich, Mar. 4, 1964 (div. Aug. 1997); life ptnr. Paul Edwards. BA with high honors, San Francisco State U., 1957; MSW, U. Calif., Berkeley, 1959; D in Social Welfare, Columbia U., 1970. Caseworker Edgewood Protestant Orphanage, San Francisco, 1959-62, Jewish Family Service, San Francisco, 1962-63; research assoc. U. Calif., Berkeley, 1963-65; research analyst Family Service Assn. Am., NYC, 1965-69; asst. prof. U. Chgo., 1967-70; prof. U. So. Calif., Los Angeles, 1970-90, dean sch. social work, 1980-88, dean emeritus, prof. emeritus, 1990—. Vis. prof. Western Australia Inst. Tech. (now Curtin U.), Perth, 1976-77, Chinese U. Hong Kong and U. Hong Kong, 1980; cons. Crittenton Services, Los Angeles, 1970-72, James Weldon Johnson Community Ctr., N.Y., 1966-67; bd. dirs. El Centro, Los Angeles. Editor: The Unwed Mother, 1966; co-editor: Theories of Social Casework, 1970, Child Caring: Social Policy and the Institution, 1973, Theories of Social Work with Groups, 1976, Theory and Practice of Community Social Work, 1980; editorial bd. Social Work Jour.; contbr. articles to profl. jours. Staff sgt. USAF, 1950-54; sgt. 1st class USAR, 1956-59. Fellow NIMH, 1957-58, 65-67, Crown Zellerbach Found., 1958-59; recipient Outstanding Educator award Los Amigos de la Humanidad, 1979; named Disting. Assoc., Nat. Acad. Practice in Social Work, 1985; decorated Commendation ribbon USAF, Korean Svc. ribbon USAF, Svc. medal UN, Good Conduct medal USAF, Nat. Def. Svc. medal, Ribbon medal, USAF. Mem. ACLU, NASW (chmn. social action com. 1960-61), Coun. on Social Work Edn. (bd. dirs. 1970-73, del. to assembly 1971-72, commn. minority groups 1972-73). Avocations: cooking, reading, travel, photography. Office: U So Calif Montgomery Ross Fisher Rm 21 Los Angeles CA 90089-0001 Personal E-mail: winstonr@cox.net.

ROBERTS, SIDNEY, biological chemist; b. Boston, Mar. 11, 1918; s. Samuel Richard and Elizabeth (Gilbert) R.; m. Clara Marian Szego, Sept. 14, 1943. BS, MIT, 1939; postgrad., Harvard U., 1939-41; MS, U. Minn., 1942, PhD, 1943. Instr. physiology U. Minn. Med. Sch., 1943-44, George Washington U. Med. Sch., 1944-45; rsch. assoc. Worcester Found. Exptl. Biology, Shrewsbury, Mass., 1945-47; asst. prof. physiol. chemistry Yale U. Med. Sch., 1947-48; mem. faculty U. Calif. Med. Sch., Los Angeles, 1948—, prof. biol. chemistry, 1957—; chmn. acad. senate UCLA, 1989-90; mem. adv. panel regulatory biology NSF, 1955-57, adv. panel metabolic biology, 1957-59; mem. metabolism study sect. NIH, 1960-63; basic sci. study sect. Los Angeles County Heart Assn., 1958-63. Cons. VA Hosp., Long Beach, Calif., 1951-55, Los Angeles, 1958-62, Pew Fin. Biomed. Scholar Program, 1992-; air conservation tech. adv. com. Los Angeles County Lung Assn., 1972-76 Author articles, revs.; editor med. jours. Served to 2d lt. AUS, 1944-48. MIT Nat. Entrance scholar, 1935; Guggenheim fellow, 1957-58. Fellow AAAS; mem. Am. Physiol. Soc., Endocrine Soc. (v.p. 1968-69, Ciba award 1953), Brit. Biochem. Soc., Soc. Neurosci., Am. Chem. Soc. (exec. com. div. biol. chemistry 1956-59), Am. Soc. Biol. Chemists, Am. Soc. Neurochemistry, Internat. Soc. Neurochemistry, Phi Beta Kappa, Sigma Xi (pres. UCLA chpt. 1959-60). Home: 1371 Marinette Rd Pacific Palisades CA 90272-2627 Office: UCLA Sch Med Dept Biol Chemistry Los Angeles CA 90095-1737 Office Phone: 310-825-6997. Business E-Mail: sr@ucla.edu.

ROBERTS, VIRGIL PATRICK, lawyer, judge; b. Ventura, Calif., Jan. 4, 1947; s. Julius and Emma D. (Haley) R.; m. Brenda Cecilia Banks, Nov. 10, 1979; children: Gisele Simone, Hayley Tasha. AA, Ventura Coll., 1966; BA, UCLA, 1968; JD, Harvard U., 1972. Bar: Calif. 1972. Assoc. Pacht, Ross, Warne Bernhardt & Sears, LA, 1972-76; ptnr. Manning, Reynolds & Roberts, LA, 1976-79, Manning & Roberts, 1980-81; mng. ptnr. Bobbitt & Roberts, 1995—; exec. v.p., gen. counsel Solar Records, LA, 1981—; pres. Dick Griffey Prodns., LA, 1982—, Solar Records, 1988—; judge pro tem L.A., Beverly Hills Mcpl. Cts., 1975—. Bd. mem. The Bridgespan Consulting Group, 2004—, Broadway Fed. Bank, 2003—. Past bd. dirs. LA Black Leadership Coalition, LA Mus. African Am. Art, Beverly Hills Bar Assn., LA Legal Aid Found.; bd. dirs. Coro Found., 1984-90, LA Edn. Alliance Restructuring Now, Cmty. Build; bd. dirs. Calif. Cmty. Found., 1991-99, chmn. bd., 1999-02; past pres. Beverly Hills Bar Scholarship Found.; commr. Calif. Commn. Tchr. Credentialing, 1980-83; chmn. LA Ednl. Partnership, 1989—, v.p. 1983-89; vice-chmn. Nat. Pub. Edn. Fund Network; chmn. bd. dirs. LA Annenberg Met. Project; trustee Com. Econ. Devel., 1991—, Occidental Coll., Marlborough Sch. (trustee 1994-03); mem. bd. councillors UCLA; trustee Claremont Grad. Sch., 2006-. Recipient NAACP Legal Def. Fund Equal Justice award, 1988, Rose award U. So. Calif., 1998. Mem. Recording Industry Assn. Am., Black Entertainment and Sports Lawyers (treas., bd. dirs. 1982—). Lead atty. for NAACP in Crawford vs. Bd. Edn. desegregation case, L.A., 1979-80. Address: 4820 Vista De Oro Ave Los Angeles CA 90043-1611 Office: Bobbitt & Roberts 6100 Center Dr Ste 910 Los Angeles CA 90404 Office Phone: 310-645-4100. Business E-Mail: vroberts@bobroblaw.com.

ROBERTS, WALTER HERBERT BEATTY, anatomist, educator; b. Field, BC, Can., Jan. 24, 1915; came to U.S., 1956, naturalized, 1965; s. Walter McWilliam and Sarah Caroline (Orr) R.; m. Olive Louise O'Neal, Sept. 1, 1937; children: Gayle, Sharon, David. MD, Coll. Med. Evangelists (nowLoma Linda U.), 1939. Intern St. Paul's Hosp., Vancouver, Canada, 1938-40; med. dir. Rest Haven Hosp. Sanitarium and Hosp., Sidney, Vancouver Island, Canada, 1940-53; post doctoral tng. White Meml. Hosp., LA, 1946-47, Edinburgh (Scotland) Hosp., 1953-55; instr. in anatomy Loma Linda U., 1955-58, asst. prof. anatomy, 1959-62, assoc. prof., 1962-70, prof., 1971—, chmn. dept. anatomy, 1974-81, prof. emeritus. Mem. Alpha Omega Alpha. Adventist. Home: 11366 Campus St Loma Linda CA 92354-3302 Office: Loma Linda Univ Dept Path & Human Anatomy Divsn Human Anatomy Loma Linda CA 92350-0001 Office Phone: 909-558-7602.

ROBERTS, WILLIAM R., lawyer; b. Wray, Colo., Nov. 8, 1951; BA phi beta kappa, U. Colo., 1973; JD cum laude, Harvard U., 1976. Bar: Colo. 1976. Mng. ptnr. Hogan & Hartson LLP, Boulder, Colo. Office: Hogan & Hartson LLP 1470 Walnut St Ste 200 Boulder CO 80302 Office Phone: 720-406-5310. Office Fax: 720-406-5301. Business E-Mail: wrroberts@hhlaw.com.

ROBERTS-DEMPSEY, PATRICIA E., secondary school educator; Tchr. Challenger High Sch., Spanaway, Wash., 1969—. Recipient Wash. State Tchr. of Yr. award, 1991-91. Office: Challenger HS 18020 B St E Spanaway WA 98387-8316

ROBERTSON, ARMAND JAMES, II, judge; b. San Diego, Sept. 23, 1937; s. Armand James and Muriel H. R.; m. Marion Sperry, Aug. 11, 1962; children: Armand James, Laura Marie. A.M. in Econs, Stanford U., 1960; LL.B., Harvard U., 1965. Bar: Calif. 1966. Law clk. to Charles M. Merrill, U.S. Ct. Appeals (9th cir.), 1965-66; assoc. firm Howard, Prim, Rice, Nemerovski, Canady & Pollak, San Francisco, 1966-71, ptnr., 1971-77; dir. Howard, Rice, Nemerovski, Canady, Robertson & Falk (P.C.), San Francisco, 1977-95; judge of the Superior Ct. City and County of San Francisco, 1995—. Bd. dirs. St. Francis Found., 1996—, chmn., 1999—. Lt. (j.g.) USN, 1960-62. Mem. Am. Law Inst., ABA (antitrust sect.), CPR Inst. for Dispute Resolution, Phi Beta Kappa. Office: San Francisco Superior Ct 400 Mcallister St Rm 210 San Francisco CA 94102-4512

ROBERTSON, CAREY JANE, musician, educator; b. Culver City, Calif., Apr. 18, 1955; d. Robert Bruce and Marjorie Ellen (Greenleaf) Coker;l m. Brian Collins Robertson, June 28, 1975 (div. July 1985); 1 child, Sean Kalen. BMus, Calif. State U., Northridge, 1977; MMus, U. So. Calif., LA, 1979, PhD of Mus. Arts, 1987. Organist/choir dir. Village Meth. Ch., North Hollywood, Calif., 1972-75, St. Bede's Episcopal Ch., Mar Vista, Calif., 1975-79; organist interim St. Alban's Episcopal Ch., Westwood, Calif., 1985; organist Covenant Presbyn. Ch., Westchester, Calif., 1985-90; organist/choir dir. St. David's United Ch., West Vancouver, B.C., Can., 1990-91; prin. organist Claremont United Ch. of Christ, Calif., 1991—; music educator Fontana Unified Sch. Dist. Prof. organ Claremont Grad. U., 1991—, New Calif. Conservatory, Buena Park, Calif., 2002—; concert organist Am. Guild of Organists, throughout U.S. and Can., 1974—; cons. Sch. Theology, U. B.C., 1990. Bd. dirs. Ruth and Clarence Mader Found., Pasadena, Calif., 1993—. Recipient Music Tchrs. Nat. Assn. Wurlitzer Collegiate Artist award, 1980; Irene Robertson scholar, 1977, 78. Mem. Am. Guild Organists (historian, sec. 1985-92, exec. com. 1983-85, sub-dean Pasadena chpt., 1998-99), Pi Kappa Lambda (Scholastic award 1987). Avocation: scuba diving instructor. Home: 3319 N Live Oak Ave Rialto CA 92377 Business E-Mail: carey.robertson@cgu.edu.

ROBERTSON, CLIFF, actor, writer, director; b. La Jolla, Calif., Sept. 9, 1925; s. Clifford Parker and Audrey (Willingham) R.; m. Cynthia Stone, 1957 (div. 1959); 1 child, Stephanie; m. Dina Merrill, Dec. 22, 1966 (div. 1986); 1 child, Heather. DFA (hon.), Bradford Coll., 1981, MacMurray Coll., 1986, Susquehanna U., 1988. Contbr. articles to various publs.; stage appearances include Late Love, Wisteria Trees, Orpheus Descending; films include Picnic, 1956, Autumn Leaves, 1956, The Naked and the Dead, 1958, The Girl Most Likely, 1958, Gidget, 1959, All in a Nights Work, 1961, The Big Show, 1961, Under-World, U.S.A., 1961, As the Sea Rages, 1961, The Interns, 1962, PT 109, 1963, Sunday in New York, 1964, The Best Man, 1964, 633 Squadron, 1964, Love Has Many Faces, 1965, Masquerade, 1965, Up From the Beach, 1965, The Honey Pot, 1967, The Devil's Brigade, 1968, Charly, 1968, (Academy award for Best Actor 1969), The Great Northfield Minnesota Raid, 1972, Ace Eli and Rodger of the Skies, 1973, Too Late the Hero, 1970, Man on a Swing, 1974, 3 Days of the Condor, 1975, Out of Season, Obsession, 1976, Shoot, 1976, Star 80, 1983, Brainstorm, 1983, Malone, 1987, Wild Hearts Can't Be Broken, 1991, Wind, 1992, The Sunset Boys, 1995, Escape from L.A., 1996, Assignment Berlin, 1997, Family Tree, 1999, (star, co writer) Curse of the 13th Child, 2002, Spider-Man, Spider-Man 2, 2004, Riding the Bullet, 2004, Spider-Man 3, 2007; TV films and miniseries appearances include The Days of Wine and Roses, 1958, The Sunshine Patriot, 1968, The Game, 1968 (Emmy award) The Man Without a Country, 1973, A Tree Grows in Brooklyn, 1974, My Father's House, 1975, Return to Earth, 1976, Washington: Behind Closed Doors, 1977, Overboard, 1978, Two of a Kind, 1982, The Key to Rebecca, 1985, Dreams of Gold, 1986, Ford: The Man and The Machine, 1987, Dead Reckoning, 1990, Dazzle, 1995, Pakten, 1995, Melting Pot, 1997, Assignment Berlin, 1998, "With God on Our Side: the Rise of the Religious Right in America," (T.V. Mini Series), 1996, The Last Best Place, Outer Limits, 1998; appeared in TV series Falcon Crest; writer, dir.: play The V.I.P.'s, 1981; J. W. Coop. Served to lt. (j.g.) USNR. Recipient Wallace award Am. Scottish Found., 1984, Sharples aviation award AOPA, 1983, Theatre World award, 1970, award Advt. Age, 1985, E.A.A. Freedom of Flight award, 1986, USAF Outstanding Supporter award, 1997, Nat. Aviation Henderson award, 1995 World Aviation Conf., India, Nat. Soaring Mus. award Expts. Aviation Assn., 1996, I.C.A.S. Aviation award, 1998; holder of Nev. state distance soaring record, 1996. Mem. SAG (bd. dirs. N.Y. chpt. 1980—), Dirs. Guild, Writers Guild Am., Bath & Tennis Club Palm Beach, Maidstone Club (East Hampton), River Club (N.Y.C.), Brook Club (N.Y.C.), Players (N.Y.C.), River Club, Wings Club. Presbyterian. Avocations: flying, skiing, soaring, tennis.

ROBERTSON, HUGH DUFF, lawyer; b. Grosse Pointe, Mich., Mar. 14, 1957; BBA in Fin., U. Wis., Whitewater, 1978; JD, Whittier Coll., 1982. Bar: Calif. 1983, U.S. Tax Ct. 1984, U.S. Supreme Court, 1999. Pres., CEO, A. Morgan Maree Jr. & Assocs., Inc., LA, 1979—. Mem. State Calif., L.A. County Bar Assn., Beverly Hills Bar Assn., Acad. TV Arts and Scis., Am. Film Inst., Phi Alpha Delta. Avocation: sports. Office: 1125 Gayley Ave Los Angeles CA 90024-3403

ROBERTSON, JOSEPH E., JR., academic administrator, ophthalmologist, educator; b. Jackson County, Ind., July 24, 1952; s. Joseph E. and Virginia Faye (Baxter) R.; children: Kathryn Faye, Charles Joseph. BS in Neuroscience, cum laude, Yale U., 1974; MD, Ind. U., 1978; MBA, U. Oreg., 1997. Diplomate Am. Bd. Ophthalmology. Intern Bapt. Med. Ctr., Birmingham, Ala., 1978-79; resident Oreg. Health Sci. U., Portland, 1979-82; pvt. practice Vancouver, Wash., 1982-83; fellow Oreg. Health Sci. U./Devers Hosp./Good Samaritan Hosp., Portland, 1983-84; vitreous surgery fellow Steve Charles, M.D., Memphis, 1984-85; asst. prof. Oreg. Health Sci. U., Portland, 1985-92, assoc. prof., 1992-97, prof., chmn. dept. ophthalmology, 1997—, dir. Casey Eye Inst., 1998—2003, interim dean, 2001—02, dean Sch. Medicine, 2003—06, pres., 2006—. Contbr. articles to profl. jours., chpts. to books; editor videotapes. Apptd. mem. Oreg. Commn. for the Blind, 1988-94. Mem. Am. Acad. Ophthalmology (Oreg. rep. to coun. 1992-95, COVE com. 1988-93, skills transfer adv. com. 1994-98, nat. chair and state coord. Diabetes 2000), Oreg. Acad. Ophthalmology (pres. 1990-91), Univ. Med. Group (exec. com. 1997—, v.p. 1998—), Oreg. Med. Assn. Democrat. Presbyterian. Avocations: skiing, windsurfing, snowboarding, hiking, jogging. Office: OHSU Office of Pres 3181 SW Sam Jackson Park Rd Portland OR 97239-3098 also: Casey Eye Inst OHSU 3375 SW Terwilliger Blvd Portland OR 97239 Office Phone: 503-494-3056.

ROBERTSON, MARY LOUISE, archivist, historian; b. LA, May 19, 1945; d. Snell and Dorothy (Tregoning) R. BA, UCLA, 1966, MA, 1968, PhD, 1975. Teaching asst. dept. history UCLA, 1967-70; acting instr. UCLA Extension, 1973-74; acting instr. dept. history Pepperdine U., LA, 1970, Calif. State U., Northridge, 1972-73; asst. curator manuscripts Huntington Libr., San Marino, Calif., 1975, assoc. curator, 1977, chief curator, 1979—. Adj. prof. English Claremont Grad. Sch., 1994. Author: Guide to British Historical Manuscripts in the Huntington Library, 1982; co-author, editor: Guide to American Historical Manuscripts in the Huntington Library, 1979; co-editor: State, Sovereigns & Society in Early Modern England, 1998; contbr. articles on Tudor history to profl. jours. Mabel Wilson Richards dissertation fellow, 1970-72. Mem. Am. Hist. Assn., Soc. Calif. Archivists, N.Am. Conf. on Brit. Studies, Pacific Coast Conf. on Brit. Studies (treas. 1986-88, pres. 1988-90), Phi Beta Kappa. Office: Huntington Libr 1151 Oxford Rd San Marino CA 91108-1299

ROBERTSON, PAUL B., dean, dental educator; Dean dentistry U. Wash., Seattle. Office: U Wash Sch Dentistry PO Box 356365 Seattle WA 98195-6365

ROBERTSON, PIEDAD F., academic administrator; b. Cuba; BA, MA, U. Miami. V.p. pub. affairs, pres. Miami-Dade CC, Miami, 1980—88; pres. Bunker Hill C.C., 1988-91; sec. edn. State of Mass., Boston, 1991-95; pres., supt. Santa Monica (Calif.) Coll., 1995—2005; pres. Edn. Commn. of the States, Denver, 2005—07. Bd. dir. Ednl. Testing Svc., Gates Millennium Scholarship, Tomas Rivera Policy Inst., Inst. for Higher Edn. Policy. Named Named Woman of Yr., Santa Monica YMCA, 1999.

ROBERTSON, RICHARD TRAFTON, entertainment company executive; b. Tacoma Park, Md., Aug. 23, 1945; s. Collins Trafton and Sigrid (Bergman) R.; m. Beverly Wise, Dec. 20, 1969 (div. Jan. 1984). BS, Va. Commonwealth U., 1967. Field rep. D. Van Nostrand Pub. Co., Princeton, N.J., 1968-69; account exec., sales mgr. NBC, Washington, San Francisco, Cleve. and NYC, 1969-73; account exec., v.p. sports mktg. CBS TV Network, Chgo. and NYC, 1973-78; exec. v.p., v.p. mktg. Office of Pres., Lorimar Telepictures, Culver City, Calif., 1978—; now pres. domestic TV distbn. Warner Bros., Burbank. Mem.: Bel-Air (Calif.) Country; Monterrey Country (Palm Desert, Calif). Lutheran. Avocations: golf, skiing, tennis. Office: Warner Bros Domestic TV Distbn 4001 W Olive Ave Burbank CA 91505-4272

ROBERTSON, ROBERT GRAHAM HAMISH, physicist; b. Ottawa, Ont., Can., Oct. 3, 1943; arrived in US, 1971, naturalized, 1993; s. Hugh Douglas and Alice Madeleine (Bell) R.; m. Peggy Lynn Dyer, July 4, 1980; 1 child, Ian. BA, Oxford U., Eng., 1965, MA, 1969; PhD, McMaster U., Can., 1971. Rsch. assoc. Mich. State U., East Lansing, 1971-72, asst. rsch. prof., 1972-73, asst. prof., 1973-78, assoc. prof., 1978-81, prof., 1981-82; mem. staff Los Alamos (N.Mex.) Nat. Lab., 1981—, fellow, 1988—; prof. U. Washington, Seattle, 1994—; sci. dir. Ctr. for Exptl. Nuc. Physics and Astrophysics, 2000—, Boeing disting. prof., 2008—. Rsch. assoc. Princeton U., NJ, 1975—76; vis. scientist Argonne Nat. Lab, Ill., 1979, Chalk River Nuc. Labs., Ont., Canada, 1980; dir. Sudbur Neutrino Obs., 2003. Contbr. over 80 articles to profl. jours. Alfred P. Sloan Found. fellow Mich. State U., 1976; Trevelyan scholar Eng., 1962-65, NRC scholar McMaster U., 1965-69, Oriel Coll. scholar, 1962-65. Fellow Am. Phys. Soc. (chair divsn. nuclear physics 2000, Tom W. Bonner prize 1997), Inst. Physics of Eng., Am. Acad. Arts and Scis.; mem. NAS, Can. Assn. Physicists. Achievements include first observation of nuclear isobaric quintet; development of technique for precise measurement of neutrino mass; determination of Lithium-6 synthesis in early universe; demonstration of neutrino mass, oscillations with Sudbury Neutrino Obs. Home Phone: 425-743-7468. E-mail: rghr@u.washington.eu.

ROBINO, DAVID J., computer company executive; b. Ft. Collins, Colo., Nov. 16, 1959; BS, Graceland Coll.; MS in Indsl. Rels., Iowa State U. With Maytag Co., Iowa, Pepsi-Cola., NY and Ind., AC Nielsen, sr. v.p. internat. bus., 1993; v.p. bus. markets divsn. AT&T; with Gateway, Inc., San Diego, 1998—, vice chmn., 2000—. Bd. dirs. San Diego Regional Econ. Devel. Corp. Bd. dirs. San Diego Sci. and Tech. Commn., U. Calif. San Diego Found.; chmn. bd. trustees Graceland U., Lamoni, Iowa; exec. com. bd. dirs. Iowa Coll. Found. Office: Gateway Inc 7565 Irvine Ctr Dr Irvine CA 92618-2930

ROBINOV, JEFF (JEFFREY STEPHEN ROBINOV), film company executive; b. Portland, ME, Nov. 8, 1958; s. Gerald Scott and Jacqueline (Bookbinder) Robinov; m. Sharon Morrill; 1 child, Reece Charles. Agent Writers & Artists; literary agent Internat. Creative Mgmt., 1992—97; sr. v.p. prodn. Warner Bros. Pictures, 1997—2000, exec. v.p. prodn., 2000—02, pres. domestic prodn., 2002—08; pres. Warner Bros. Pictures Group, 2008—. Exec. prodr.: (films) On Deadly Ground, 1994. Office: Warner Bros Pictures Group 4000 Warner Blvd Burbank CA 91522

ROBINSON, BERNARD LEO, lawyer; b. Kalamazoo, Feb. 13, 1924; s. Louis Harvey and Sue Mary (Starr) R.; m. Betsy Nadell, May 30, 1947; children: Robert Bruce, Patricia Anne, Jean Carol. BS, U. Ill., 1947, MS, 1958; JD, U. N.Mex., 1973. Bar: N.Mex. 1973, U.S. Supreme Ct. 1976. Rsch. engr. Assn. Am. Railroads, 1947-49; instr. architecture Rensselaer Poly. Inst., 1949-51; commd. 2d lt. U.S. Army, 1945, advanced through grades to lt. col., 1965, ret., 1968; engr. Nuclear Def. Rsch. Corp., Albuquerque, 1968-71; pvt. practice Albuquerque, 1973—91, Silver City, N.Mex., 1985-89, Green Valley, Ariz., 1989-90, Sierra Vista, Ariz., 1990-91; ret., 1990; pres. Robinson Fin. Svcs., Tucson, 1993-95, Belro Co., Tucson, 2004—07. Dist. commr. Boy Scouts Am., 1960-62. Decorated Air medal, Combat Inf. Badge. Mem. ASCE, ABA, Mil. Officers Assn., DAV, Assn. U.S. Army, VFW. Home: 3300 Paseo De Los Rios 13103 Tucson AZ 85712 Address: PO Box 30250 Tucson AZ 85751-0250 Business E-Mail: brobinson1924@cox.net.

ROBINSON, CHARLES FURLONGE, lawyer; b. Phila., 1957; married; 1 child. BA, Harvard U., Cambridge, Mass., 1979; JD, Yale Law Sch., New Haven, Conn., 1982. Bar: US Ct. Appeals, 9th Cir., US Dist. Courts, Calif. Law clk. to Hon. William Orrick US Dist. Ct. (no. dist.) Calif., San Francisco, 1982—83; assoc. Heller Ehrman White & McAuliffe, San Francisco, 1983—88, ptnr., 1989—95; divsn. counsel Raychem Corp., Menlo Park, Calif., 1995—99; asst. gen. counsel, dir. litig. Packard Bell NEC, Sacramento, 1999—2000; acting chief adminstrv. officer Calif. Ind. System Operator Corp., Folsom, Calif., 2004—05, v.p. gen. counsel, corp. sec., 2000—06; gen. counsel U. Calif., Oakland, 2006—. Mem.: Nat. Assn. Corp. Lawyers, Energy Bar Assn., ABA, NAACP Legal Def. Fund (NAACP Legal Def. Fund award 1994), Legal Services Trust Fund Commn. (bd. mem., vice chmn. 1994—97), Pub. Interest Clearinghouse (bd. mem., treasurer, pres. 1990—95), Bar Assn. San Francisco (co-chmn., Com. on Minority Employment 1989—95), La Raza Centro Legal (bd. mem., treasurer 1987—90), Calif. Bd. of Legal Specialization (bd. mem. 1985—88). Avocations: running, photography, music, travel, architecture. Office: Office of General Counsel of The Regents University of California 1111 Franklin St Oakland CA 94607 Office Phone: 510-987-9800. Business E-Mail: charles.robinson@ucop.edu.

ROBINSON, CHARLES PAUL, nuclear energy industry executive, diplomat; b. Detroit, Oct. 9, 1941; s. Edward Leonard and Mary Opal (Edmondson) R.; m. Barbara Thomas Woodard; children by previous marriage: Paula S., Colin C. BS in Physics, Christian Bros. U., 1963; PhD in Physics, Fla. State U., 1967; doctorate (hon.), Christian Brothers U. Mem. nuclear test staff Los Alamos (N.Mex.) Nat. Lab., 1967-69, chief test operator, 1969-70, mem. advanced concepts staff, 1971-72, assoc. div. leader, lasers, 1972-76, div. leader, 1976-79, assoc. dir., 1980-85; sr. v.p., bd. dirs. Ebasco Services Inc. subs. Enserch Corp., NYC, 1985-88; ambass. to nuclear testing talks U.S. Dept. State, Geneva, 1988-90; v.p. Sandia Nat. Labs., Albuquerque, 1990-95, pres., 1995—2005; capture exec. Lockheed Martin Corp., 2005—. Instr. U. N.Mex., Los Alamos, 1974-76; mem. sci. adv. group Def. Nuclear Agy., Washington, 1981-86; mem. nat. security bd. Los Alamos Nat. Lab., 1985-88; chmn. Presdl. Tech. Adv. Bd., 1991; mem. U.S. Strategic Command Adv. Bd.; bd. dirs. Wells Fargo Bank, Tech. Ventures Corp., Fla. State U. Rsch. Found.; trustee Kazakhstan Nonproliferation Inst. Mem. strategic adv. group for comdr. U.S. Strategic Command; chmn. policy panel, tech. adv. group Verification of Warhead Dismantlement and Spl. Nuc. Materials Controls; mem. threat reduction adv. com. Dept. Def., exec. bd. Boy Scouts of N.Mex. Recipient Outstanding Pub. Svc. medal Joint Chiefs of Staff, 1996. Mem. Am. Phys. Soc. (Pake Prize 2003), Am. Nuclear Soc., NAE. Achievements include testifing before Congress more than 80 times. Avocation: choral singing. Office: Lockheed Martin 2100 Airpark Rd SE Ste 150 Albuquerque NM 87106-3242 Home Phone: 505-856-5311, 505-856-5311; Office Phone: 505-843-4153. Business E-Mail: c.p.robinson@lmco.com, c.probinson@lmco.com.

ROBINSON, CHARLES WESLEY, boat design company executive; b. Long Beach, Calif., Sept. 7, 1919; s. Franklin Willard and Anna Hope (Gould) R.; m. Tamara Lindovna, Mar. 8, 1957; children: Heather Lynne, Lisa Anne, Wendy Paige. BA in Econs. cum laude, U. Calif., Berkeley, 1941; MBA, Stanford U., 1947. Asst. mgr. mfg. Golden State Dairy Products Co., San Francisco, 1947-49; v.p., then pres. Marcona Corp., San Francisco, 1952-74; undersec. of state for econ. affairs Dept. State, Washington, 1974-75; dep. sec. of state, 1976-77; sr. mng. ptnr. Kuhn Loeb & Co., NYC, 1977-78; vice chmn. Blyth Eastman Dillon & Co., NYC, 1978-79; chmn. Energy Transition Corp., Santa Fe and Washington, 1979-82; pres. Robinson & Assocs., Inc., Santa Fe, 1982—. Pres. CBTF Co., San Diego, 1992—, M Ship Co., San Diego, 1998; dir. emeritus NIKE, Inc. Patentee slurry transport and both sail and power boat designs, boat engr. Brookings Instn., Washington, 1977—; mem. Pres.'s Cir. NAS. Lt. USN, 1941-46. Recipient Disting. Honor award Dept. State, 1977, Lifetime Achievement award, N.Mex., 2007. Republican. Methodist. Office: Robinson & Assocs Inc PO Box 2224 Santa Fe NM 87504-2224 Office Phone: 505-988-5589.

ROBINSON, CRAIG, men's college basketball coach; b. 1962; s. Fraser and Marian Robinson; m. Kelly Robinson; children: Avery, Leslie. AB in Sociology, Princeton U., NJ, 1983; MBA in Fin., U. Chgo., 1992. Player Manchester Giants, England, gen. mgr., pub. rels. officer; asst. coach Illinois Inst. Tech. Scarlet Hawks, 1988—90; v.p. Continental Bank, 1990—92, Morgan Stanley Dean Witter, 1992—99; mng. dir. Loop Capital Markets, 1999; head coach U. Chgo. HS, 1999—2000; asst. coach Northwestern U. Wildcats, 2000—06; head coach Brown U. Bears, 2006—08, Oreg. State U. Beavers, 2008—. Named Ivy League Men's Basketball Coach of Yr., Basketball U., 2007. Office: Oreg State Beavers c/o Dept Athletics Corvallis OR 97331 Office Phone: 541-737-2076.

ROBINSON, CURTIS JOHN, writer, educator, marketing professional, consultant; b. NYC, Dec. 13, 1951; s. Herschel Edward and Delores Viola (Westberg) R.; children: Thomas Samuel, William Frederick. BA in History with honors, U. Calif., Davis, 1974, MA in Geography, 1981; PhD in Geography, U. Calif., 1995. Editor in chief The Calif. Aggie, Davis, 1973-74; teaching asst. U. Tex., Austin, 1974-75; acct., auditor Internat. Telephone, Fairbanks, Alaska, 1975-76; asst. to dean Cosumnes River Coll., Sacramento, 1976-77; editor, asst. editor U. Calif., Davis, 1977-80, mgr. data processing, 1982-85, mgr. promotional comm., 1980-85, dir. mktg., 1985-94; dep. to state supt. Calif. Dept. Edn., Sacramento, 1994—2002; asst. dir. Dept. Water Res., Sacramento, 2002—04; asst. v.p. Calif. State U., Hayward, Calif., 2004—. Dir. alumni assn. bd. U. Calif., Davis, 1986-90. Author, editor: Handbook Small and Specialty Crops, 1991, Market Share, 1994, (video) Bringing the World to UC Davis, 1992; author articles. Mem. Cmty. Cable TV Bd., Davis, 1984-86; chair Cmty. Devel. Block Grant, Davis, 1980-84; mem. Yolo County Devel. Com., Davis, 1983-85. Mem. Nat. Univ. Continuing Edn. Assn. (chair Region VI Profl. Devel. 1991-94, mem. nat. mktg. adv. com. 1992-95, mem. Region VI exec. com. 1993-94, Silver award for Mktd. Excellence 1994, Gold award 1994), Assn. Am. Geographers, Assn. Pacific Coast Geographers (Pres.'s award 1991). Democrat. Methodist. Avocations: gardening, guitar, writing, travel, maps. Office: Calif State Univ East Bay 25976 Carles Bee Blvd Hayward CA 94542 Office Phone: 510-885-3501. Personal E-mail: curt_robinson@yahoo.com.

ROBINSON, GAIL PATRICIA, retired mental health counselor; b. Medford, Oreg., Dec. 31, 1936; d. Ivan T. and Evelyn H. (Hamilton) Skyrman; m. Douglas L. Smith; children: Shauna J., James D. BS in Edn., Oreg. State U., 1958, PhD in Counseling, 1978; MS in Counseling, Western Oreg. State Coll., 1974. Tchr. Monterey (Calif.) Pub. Schs., 1958-59, Corvallis (Oreg.) Pub. Schs., 1959-62, 69-75, counselor, 1977-81; pvt. practice Corvallis, 1977-95. Vol. therapist Children's Svcs. divsn., Linn and Benton Counties, 1982-83; asst. prof. Western Oreg. State coll., 1977, counselor, 1982-83; mem. grad. faculty Oreg. State U., Corvallis, 1978-95; presenter workshops, lectr. in field. Contbr. articles to profl. jours. Mem. Benton County Mental Health Citizens Adv. Bd., 1979-85, chair, 1982-83; trustee WCTU Children's Farm Home, 1978-84, chair child welfare com., 1982-83, pres., 1984; adv. bd. Old Mill Sch., 1979-85, chair, 1979-81; bd. dirs. Cmty. Outreach, 1979-83; mem. Benton Com. for Prevention of Child Abuse, 1979-85, v.p., 1982; mem. Oreg. Bd. Lic. Profl. Counselors and Therapists, 1989-95, chair, 1989-90, Aurora Colony Historical Soc., vol., 2000-, bd. dirs., 2005-, sec., 2006—08, pres. 2008-. Mem. ACA (govt. rels. com. 1988-91, professionalization com. 1988-92, pres. 1996-97), Am. Mental Health Counselors Assn. (chair consumer and pub. rels. com. 1988-91, bd. dirs. Western region 1989-91, chair strategic planning com. 1994-95, pres. 1992-93), Oreg. Counseling Assn. (chair licensure liaison com. 1985-91, exec. bd. 1985-88, steering com. 1986-87, register editorial com. 1985-86, Disting. Svc. award 1985, 87, Leona Tyler award 1989), Oreg. Mental Health Counselors Assn. Personal E-mail: robinsgp@comcast.net.

ROBINSON, HERBERT HENRY, III, psychotherapist, educator; b. Leavenworth, Wash., Mar. 31, 1933; s. Herbert Henry II and Alberta (Sperber) R.; m. Georgia Murial Jones, Nov. 24, 1954 (div. 1974); children: Cheri Dean Asbury, David Keith, Peri Elizabeth Layton, Tanda Rene Graff, Gaila Daire. Grad. of Theology, Bapt. Bible Coll., 1959; BA in Philosophy/Greek, Whitworth Coll., 1968; MA in Coll. Teaching, Ea. Wash. U., 1976; PhD, Gonzaga U., 2002. Cert. psychotherapist, perpetrator treatment program supervision; nat. bd. cert. counselor. Choir dir. Twin City Bapt. Temple, Mishawaka, Ind., 1959-61; min. Inland Empire Bapt. Ch., Spokane, Wash., 1961-73; tchr. philosophy Spokane C.C., 1969-72; dir. Alternatives to Violence, Women in Crisis, Fairbanks, Alaska, 1985-87; tchr. pub. rels. U. Alaska, Fairbanks, 1986-87; dir. Alternatives to Violence Men Inc., Juneau, 1988-89; tchr. leadership mgmt. U. Alaska S.E., Juneau, 1988-89; min. Sci. of Mind Ctr., Sandpoint, Idaho, 1989-92; dir., therapist Tapio Counseling Ctr., Spokane, 1991—; cert. psychotherapist, supr. perpetrator treatment program Wash. Cons. Lilac Blind/Alpha Inc./Marshall Coll., Spokane, 1975-85, Alaska Placer Mining Co., Fairbanks, 1987; tchr. Spokane Falls C.C., Spokane, 1979-85; seminar, presenter Human Resource Devel., Spokane and Seattle, Wash., Pa., 1980; guest trainer United Way/Kellogg Found. Inst. for Volunteerism, Spokane, 1983. 1st trombone San Diego Marine Band, 1953-56, Spokane Symphony, 1961; bd. dirs. Tanani Learning Ctr., Fairbanks, 1987; mem. consensus bldg. team Sci. of Mind Ctr., Sandpoint, 1989-92. Cpl. USMC, 1953-56. Mem. ACA, Assn. for Humanistic Edn. and Devel., Assn. for Religious Values in Counseling, Internat. Assn. Addictions and Offender Counselors, Internat. Assn. Marriage and Family Counselors, Am. Assn. Profl. Hypnotherapists, Masterson Inst. Office: Tapio Counseling 5325 E Sprague Ave Spokane WA 99212-0820 Home Phone: 509-927-9825; Office Phone: 509-534-5028. E-mail: peace@herb-robinson.com.

ROBINSON, JEFFERY P., lawyer; b. Memphis, Aug. 30, 1956; BA cum laude, Marquette U., 1978; JD, Harvard U., 1981. Bar: Wash. 1981, US Dist. Ct. (we. dist. Wash.) 1981, US Ct. Appeals (9th cir.) 1986. Pub. defender state, fed. courts, 1981—88; atty. criminal def. Schroeter, Goldmark & Bender, P.S., Seattle. Instr. trial advocacy prog. U. Wash. Sch. Law, 1988—; faculty Nat. Criminal Def. Coll., Macon, Ga.; mem. trial advocacy workshop Harvard Law Sch., 1990—. Contbr. articles to law jours. Named Lawyer of Yr., King County Bar Assn., 2003; named one of Am. Top Black Lawyers, Black Enterprise Mag., 2003. Fellow: Am. Coll. Trial Lawyers; mem.: Nat. Inst. Trial Advocacy, NACDL (former mem. bd. dirs.), Wash. Assn. Criminal Def. Lawyers (past pres.), Wash. State Trial Lawyers Assn., Wash. State Bar Assn. (mem. criminal law exec. com. 1989). Office: Schroeter Goldmark & Bender PS 810 Third Ave Ste 500 Seattle WA 98104 Office Phone: 206-622-8000. Office Fax: 206-682-2305.

ROBINSON, JOHN LEWIS, geography educator; b. Leamington, Ont., Can., July 9, 1918; s. William John and Emily Laverne (Dunphy) R.; m. Josephine Rowan, Oct. 14, 1944; children: David, Jo-Anne, Patricia. BA, Western Ont. U., 1940; MA, Syracuse U., 1942; PhD, Clark U., 1946; LLD (hon.), Western Ont. U., 1984; DSc (hon.), U. B.C., 1994. Geographer N.W.T. Adminstrn., Ottawa, Ont., 1943-46; prof., head dept. geography U. B.C., Vancouver, 1946-68, prof. geography, 1968-85, prof. emeritus, 1985—. Author 14 books on aspects of regional geography of Can., including British Columbia: 100 Years of Geographical Change, 1973, Themes in the Regional Geography of Canada, 1983, 2d edit., 1989; contbr. articles to profl. jours. Recipient citation of merit Assn. Am. Geographers, 1966; Massey medal Canadian Geog. Soc., 1971 Mem. Canadian Assn. Geographers (pres. 1956, citation for service to profession 1976)

ROBINSON, PAUL ARNOLD, historian, educator, writer; b. San Diego, Oct. 1, 1940; s. Joseph Cook and Beryl Marie (Lippincott) R.; m. Ute Brosche, Aug. 3, 1964 (div. Aug. 1967); 1 child, Susan Marie; life ptnr. Stephen Dunatov. BA, Yale U., 1962; postgrad., Free U. Berlin, 1962-63; PhD, Harvard U., 1968. Asst. prof. history Stanford U. (Calif.), 1967-73, assoc. prof., 1973-80, prof. history, 1980—2007, Richard W. Lyman prof. in the humanities, 1994—2007; Lyman prof. emeritus, 2007—. Author: The Freudian Left, 1969, The Modernization of Sex, 1976, Opera and Ideas: From Mozart to Strauss, 1985, Freud and His Critics, 1993, Ludwig van Beethoven: Fidelio, 1996, Gay Lives: Homosexual Autobiography from John Addington Symonds to Paul Monette, 1999, Opera, Sex, and Other Vital Matters, 2002, Queer Wars: The New Gay Right and Its Critics, 2005; editor: Social Thought in America and Europe, 1970; contbg. editor The New Republic, 1979—85. Guggenheim fellow, 1970-71, Stanford Humanities Ctr. fellow, 1984-85, 96-97, Inst. for Advanced Study fellow, 1990-91, Ctr. for Advanced Study in the Behavioral Scis. fellow, 2002-03. Mem. Am. Acad. Arts and Scis., Am. Hist. Assn. Home: 671 Santa Ynez St Stanford CA 94305-8542 Office: Stanford Univ Dept History Stanford CA 94305 Business E-Mail: paulr@stanford.edu.

ROBINSON, PETER, retired paleontology educator, consultant; b. NYC, July 19, 1932; s. Edward and Carol Nye (Rhoades) R.; m. Patricia Ellen Fisher, Sept. 11, 1954 (div. Mar. 1980); children: Diane Elizabeth, Nathan; m. Paola D'Amelio Villa, Dec. 8, 1984 BS, Yale U., 1954, MS, 1958, PhD, 1960. Instr. Harpur Coll. SUNY, Binghamton, 1955-57; rsch. assoc. Yale Peabody Mus., New Haven, 1960-61; curator geology U. Colo. Mus., Boulder, 1961—2002, asst. prof. natural history, 1961-67, assoc. prof., 1967-71, prof., 1971—2002, dir. mus., 1971-82, prof. geol. sci., 1971—2002; ret., 2002. Geologist Colo. Nubian Expdn., Sudan, 1962-66; chief Colo. Paleontol. Expdn., Tunisia, 1967-81; mem. geol. adv. group Colo. Bur. Land Mgmt., Denver, 1983-91. Mem. AAAS, Soc. Vertebrate Paleontology (pres. 1977-78), Australian Mammal Soc., Soc. Española Paleontologia, Sigma Xi Democrat. Home: 912 Hover Ridge Cir Longmont CO 80501-4141 Office: Mus U Colo Campus Box 265 Boulder CO 80309 E-mail: peter.robinson@colorado.edu.

ROBINSON, RALPH W., lawyer; b. San Francisco, Mar. 26, 1947; BA, U. Calif., Berkeley, 1968; JD, Golden Gate U., 1971. Bar: Calif. 1972, US Supreme Ct., Supreme Ct. Calif. Mng ptnr. San Francisco office Wilson, Elser, Moskowitz, Edelman & Dicker LLP, head San Francisco trial practice area. Mem.: ABA, Alameda County Bar Assn., Bar Assn. San Francisco. Office: Wilson Elser Moskowitz Et Al Sten 1700 525 Market St San Francisco CA 94105-2725 Office Phone: 415-433-0990 ext. 3001. Office Fax: 415-434-1370. Business E-Mail: robinsonr@wemed.com.

ROBINSON, RICH, musician; b. Atlanta, May 24, 1969; s. Stan and Nancy Robinson. Co-founder & band mem. Mr. Crowe's Garden (name changed to Black Crowes), 1985—; founder Hookah Brown, 2003. Musician (albums): Shake Your Money Maker, 1990 (Album of Yr. Internat. Rock Awards 1991, double platinum record 1991), The Southern Harmony and Musical Companion, 1992, Amorica, 1994, Three Snakes and One Charm, 1996, Souled Out Live, 1998, By Your Side, 1999, Armorica, 2000, Lions, 2001, Live, 2002, Freak 'n' Roll...Into the Fog, 2006, Warpaint, 2008, (solo albums) Paper, 2004. Recipient (with Black Crowes) Grammy award nomination for Best New Artist; voted Best New Am. Band, Rolling Stone readers and critics polls; named Artist of Yr., 1991.

ROBINSON, ROBERT BLACQUE, foundation administrator; b. Long Beach, Calif., Apr. 24, 1927; s. Joseph LeRoi and Frances Hansel R.; m. Susan Amelia Thomas, Jan. 21, 1960; children: Victoria, Shelly, Blake, Sarah. Student, Oreg. State Coll., 1946; BA, UCLA, 1950; student, U. Hawaii. Partner, Pritchard Assocs. (Mgmt. Cons.), Honolulu, 1956-58; asst. dir. Econ. Planning and Coordination Authority, Hawaii, 1959; dep. dir. dept. econ. devel. State of Hawaii, 1960-63; asst. mgr. Pacific Concrete and Rock Co., Ltd., Honolulu, 1963-66, exec. v.p. and gen. mgr., 1966-68, pres. and gen. mgr., 1968-75, chmn., 1976-77; pres. C. of C. of Hawaii, Honolulu, 1977—. Bd. govs. Hawaii Employers Coun., 1969-74, mem. exec. com., 1969-74, vice chmn., 1973-74; bd. dirs. Pacific Aerospace Mus., 1982-86; mem. Hawaii Tourism Conf., 1977, chmn., 1981-82; bd. dirs. Aloha United Fund, 1970-76, sec., 1972, v.p., 1973-76; bd. dirs.

Oahu Devel. Conf., 1970-75; treas., bd. dirs. Crime Stoppers Hawaii, 1981—; mem. Hawaii Joint Coun. on Econ. Edn., 1985—; bd. dirs. Jr. Achievement Hawaii, 1967-73, pres., 1969; bd. dirs. Hawaii Ednl. Coun., 1974-75, Health and Community Services Coun. Hawaii, 1982-84; mem. exec. com. Hawaii Conv. Ctr. Coun., 1984—, Inter-agency Energy Conservation Coun., State of Hawaii, 1978—; trustee Cen. Union Ch., 1983-86; bd. dirs. Waikiki Improvement Assn. Inc., 1986—; mem. Ctr. for Tropical and Subtropical Aquacultute industry Adv. Coun., 1987—; chmn. Mayor's Adv. Com. on Pacific Nations Ctr., 1988-89. Lt. comdr. USNR, 1945-46, ret. Mem. Japan-Am. Conf. of Mayors and C. of C. Pres. (mem. Am. exec. com. 1974—), Am. Soc. Assn. Execs. (past dir. Hawaii chpt.), Hawaii Execs. Coun. (found., Young Pres. Assn. (past mem.), Aloha Soc. Assn. Execs., C. of C. Hawaii (dir. 1972-75, chmn. 1975), Coun. of Profit Sharing Industries (past dir. Hawaii sect.), Cement and Concrete Products Industry of Hawaii (pres. 1968), Hawaii Mfrs. Assn. (past dir.), Navy League of U.S. (Hawaii council), Engring. Assn. Hawaii, Pacific Club, Rotary, Sigma Chi. Home: 1437 Kalaepohaku St Honolulu HI 96816-1804 Office: C of C Hawaii 735 Bishop St Ste 220 Honolulu HI 96813-4816 Business E-Mail: robinson@hawaii.rr.com.

ROBINSON, WALTER J., III, lawyer; b. Seattle, Apr. 24, 1941; BA magna cum laude, Univ. Wash., 1963; JD magna cum laude, Univ. Chgo., 1966. Bar: Calif. 1967, Wash. 1967. Ptnr., chmn. Securities Litigation group Pillsbury Winthrop Shaw Pittman, Palo Alto, Calif. Contbr. articles to profl. jours. Mem.: ABA, San Francisco Bar Assn. Office: Pillsbury Winthrop Shaw Pittman 2475 Hanover St Palo Alto CA 94304-1114 Office Phone: 650-233-4792. Office Fax: 650-233-4545. Business E-Mail: walter.robinson@pillsburylaw.com.

ROBINSON, WILLIAM P., academic administrator, consultant, speaker; b. Elmhurst, Ill., Sept. 30, 1949; s. Paul Frederick and Lillian (Horton) R.; m. Bonnie Van Laan, Aug. 10, 1974; children: Brenna Kay, Benjamin Paul, Bailley Kay. Student, Moody Bible Inst., Chgo., 1967-70; AB, U. No. Iowa, 1972; postgrad., Princeton Theol. Sem., NJ, 1972-73; MA, Wheaton Coll., 1975; PhD, U. Pitts., 1979. Assoc. minister First Presbyn. Ch., Pitts., 1975-77; instr. U. Pitts., 1977-79; asst. prof. sch. continuing studies Nat. Coll. Edn., Evanston, Ill., 1979-80, dean sch. continuing studies, 1980-84, sr. v.p., 1984-86; pres. Manchester Coll., North Manchester, Ind., 1986-93, Whitworth Coll., Spokane, Wash., 1993—. Bd. dirs. Coun. Indep. Colls., Ind. Colls. Wash., ING Educators Adv. Bd., Whitworth Coll., Whitworth Found.; founding co-chmn. Higher Edn. Leadership Group of Spokane; cons., speaker for U.S. corps. and svc. orgns. Author: Leading People from the Middle: The Universal Mission of Mind and Heart, 2002. Bd. dirs. Wash. Friends of Higher Edn., Princeton Theol. Sem., Spokane Regional C. of C. (past chmn.), Spokane Symphony; vol. various orgns., especially prion work and hunger projects. Recipient various acad. awards. Mem. Nat. Assn. Ind. Colls. and Univs., Coun. Ind. Colls., Spokane Country Club, Spokane Club. Avocation: sports. Office: Whitworth Coll Office of Pres 300 W Hawthorne Rd Spokane WA 99218-2515

ROBINSON-ZAÑARTU, CAROL A., psychology professor, department chairman; d. Montgomery Scott and Doris Little Robinson; m. Juan Pablo Zanartu, July 1989; children: Felipe Reymundo Robinson-Zanartu, Federico Lautaro Robinson-Zanartu. BA, W.Va. Wesleyan U., 1966; MS, Boston U., 1967; PhD, U. Pitts., 1981. Cert. sch. psychologist Calif. Counselor Allegheny County CC, Pitts., 1968—70; dir. Learning Founds., Inc., San Diego, 1971—74; prin. Found. Elem. Sch., San Diego, 1973—74; sch. psychologist Grossmont Union HS Dist., La Mesa, Calif., 1977—79; edn. specialist Nat. Coun. Alcoholism, San Diego, 1974—75; co-director Interdisciplinary Devel. Ctr., La Mesa, 1975—77; sch. psychologist Lakeside Union Sch. Dist., Calif., 1979—80; prof., chair Dept. Counseling & Sch. Psychology San Diego State U., 1980—. Prin. investigator San Diego State U. Found., 1990—; pres. Calif. Assn. Mediated Learning, San Diego, 1996—97; standing panel reviewer Office Spl. Edn. U.S. Dept. Edn., DC, 2000—; panel reviewer U.S. Office Indian Edn., DC, 2000; dir., Native Am. Scholars & Collaborators Project Office Spl. Edn. U.S. Dept. Edn., DC, 2003—. Author: (book) Handbook of Psychological Assessment, Dynamic Assessment: Prevailing Models and Applications, (textbook) Manual de Evaluacion Psicologica, Handbook of Psychological Evaluation, The Psychology of Multiculturisation In the Schools. Grantee Tchg. fellow, U. Pitts., 1978-1979. Mem.: NASP (folio reviewer 1992—), APA, Calif. Assn. Sch. Psychologists, Calif. U. Educators Sch. Psychologists (chair, tng. standards & innovations com. 1992—98), Calif. Assn. Mediated Learning (pres. 1996—97). D-Liberal. Avocations: sailing, reading, writing. Office: San Diego State U 5500 Campanille Dr San Diego CA 92182-1179

ROBISON, SHANE V., computer company executive; BS in Computer Sci., MS in Computer Sci., U. Utah. With Apple Computer Co., 1988, v.p., gen.mgr., 1994—95; exec. v.p. rsch. & develop., pres. design productivity grp. Cadence Design Systems; exec. v.p. AT&T, 1995—97, pres. design productivity grp., 1997—99, pres. internet tech. and devel., 1999—2000; sr. v.p., chief tech. officer strategy and tech. Compaq Computer Corp., 2000—02; exec. v.p., chief strategy and tech. officer Hewlett-Packard Co., Palo Alto, Calif., 2002—. Cons. database systems architecture U. Utah. Office: Hewlett-Packard Co 3000 Hanover St Palo Alto CA 94304*

ROBITAILLE, LUC, sports team executive, retired professional hockey player; b. Montreal, Que., Can., Feb. 17, 1966; Left wing Hull Olympiques Major Jr. Hockey League, Que., 1983—84, LA Kings, 1984—94, 1997—2001, 2003—06, Pitts. Penguins, 1994—95, NY Rangers, 1995—97, Detroit Red Wings, 2001—03; owner, pres. Omaha Lancers, US Hockey League, 2006; asst. to gov. and alt. gov. LA Kings, 2006—07, pres. bus. ops., 2007—. Guest appearance (films) D2: The Mighty Ducks, 1994, Sudden Death, 1995, H-E Double Hockey Sticks, 1999. Recipient Guy LaFlleur Trophy, 1985—86, Can. Hockey Player of Yr. award, 1985—86, Calder Meml. Trophy; named NHL Rookie of Yr., 1986—87; named to NHL All-Star Team, 1987, 1988, 1990—91, 1992—93, Quebec Major Junior Hockey League Hall of Fame, 2007. Achievements include scoring the winning goal for the national team of Canada at the 1994 World Hockey Championship; being a member of Stanley Cup Champion Detroit Red Wings, 2002; having his number, 20, retired by LA Kings, 2007. Office: LA Kings Suite 3100 1111 S Figueroa St Los Angeles CA 90015 also: Omaha Lancers Mid-Am Ctr One Arena Way Council Bluffs IA 51501

ROBLE, RAYMOND GERALD, science administrator; b. Mar. 14, 1935; BS in Engring. Physics, U. Mich., 1957, BS in Engring. Math., 1957, MSME, 1961, PhD in Aeronomy, 1969. Engr. Bendix Rsch. Labs., Southfield, Mich., 1961-64; rsch. sci. Space Physics Rsch. Lab., U. Mich., 1964-69; postdoctoral fellow advanced study program Nat. Ctr. Atmospheric Rsch., 1969-70, scientist lab. for atmospheric scis., 1970-73, scientist atmospheric quality and modification div., 1973-77, project leader thermospheric dynamics and aeronomy project atmosphericchem. and aeronomy div., 1977-81, sr. scientist atmospheric chem. and aeronomy div., 1978-84, sr. scientist high altitude obs., 1984—, head, terrestrial impact of solar output sect. high altitude obs., 1986—2001, dep. dir. high altitude obs., 1993-95, acting dir. high altitude obs., 1995—. Commn. URSI III Working Group 8 Incoherent Scatter, 1975-77; guest investigator OSO-8 Satellite Team Occultation Studes, 1975-79, NASA Atmospheric Explorer Satelite Team, 1975-80; panel mem. USRA Sci. Definition for Atmosphere, Magnetosphere and Plasmas in Space Payload, 1976-78, Upper Atmoshpere Geophysics, Geophysics Study com., Geophysical Rsch. bd., NAS, 1976-77, USRA Computer Simulation in Space Physics, 1977-79, NASA Sci. Definition Panel UARS Satellite Program, 1977-78, Sun, Weather and Climate Geophysics Study com., Geophysical Rsch. bd., NAS, 1977-82, Survey on Solar-Terrestrial Rsch. in the 1980's, com. on Solar-Terrstrial Rsch. Geophysical Rsch. bd., NAS program, 1979-81, Mid. Atmosphere Program Panel, NAS, 1981-86; theoretician NASA Dynamics Explorer Satellite Team, 1977—; mem. AGU com. for Pub., 1977-84, Atmospheric and Space Physics Mgmt. Ops. Working Group, NASA Solar-Terrestrial Physics Program, 1978-81, Space Power Sys. Overviewcom. Inst. Telecomms., 1978-82; lecturer Dept. Astrophysical, Planetary and Atmospheric Scis. U. Colo., 1978—; com. Solar and Space Physics, Space Sci. bd. NAS, 1980-83, Geophysics Study com. Geophysical Rsch. bd. NAS, 1980-84, IUGG on Atmospheric Electricity, 1981—, AGU for Pub. Affairs, 1982-84, IUGG com. Solar-Terrestrial film Planet earth, 1984-86; sec. Aeronomy Div. Solar-Planetary Relationships Sect. AGU, 1982-84; mem. Earth Scis. Task Group Study Major Dirs. for Space Scis.: 1995-, Space Sci. bd., 1984-88; chmn. Am. Geophysical Union com. on Atmospheric and Space Electricity, 1984-88; co-investigator, prin. investigator, NASA; mem. Arecibo Observatory vis. com. Cornell U., 1997-2001; mem. rev. bd. Geophys. Inst. U. Alaska, 1984-. Contbr. over 250 articles to profl. jours. With USN, 1957-60. Recipient CEDAR Prize Lecture, 1994; grantee NASA, USAF. Fellow Am. Geophys. Union (chmn. space physics and aeronomy fellows com. 1996-98); mem. NAS (Arctowski medal, 1996), Am. Inst. Aeronautics and Astronautics. Office: Nat Ctr Atmospheric Rsch High Altitude Obs PO Box 3000 Boulder CO 80307-3000 Business E-Mail: roble@ncar.ucar.edu.

ROBLES, MARICELA, architect; b. 1975; Sr. designer D.R. Horton Homes. Mem. Tucson Xicano Mexicano Com. for Self-determination, Access Tucson Cnty. TV, National Chicano Moratorium Com.; co-founder Radio Chicana. Named one of 40 Under 40, Tucson Bus. Edge, 2006. Mem.: Am. Diabetes Assn., La Raza Unida Club (co-founder). Avocations: kickboxing, bikram yoga, mariachi music. Office: D R Horton Homes 3580 W Ina Rd Ste 100 Tucson AZ 85741-2270

ROBOTTOM, DAVID T., lawyer, energy executive; m. Bonnie Robottom; 2 children. B of Commerce with distinction, MBA; LLB, U. Alta., 1979. Bar: Alta. 1980. Nat. mng. ptnr., CEO Fraser Milner Casgrain LLP; sr. ptnr. Stikeman Elliott LLP, Calgary, Alta., Canada, 2004—06; grp. v.p. corp. law Enbridge Inc., 2006—. Bd. trustees Enbridge Comml. Trust; dir. Noverco, Inc., Gaz Métro Inc. Office: Enbridge Inc 3000 5th Ave Pl 425 1st St SW Calgary AB T2P 3L8 Canada Business E-Mail: david.robottom@enbridge.com.

ROCCO, NIKKI, film company executive; m. Joseph Rocco. Sales dept. Universal Pictures, 1967, asst. to gen. sales mgr., 1981—84, v.p. distbn., 1984—90, sr. v.p. distbn. and mktg., 1990—95, exec. v.p., distbn., 1995—96, pres., distbn., 1996—. Bd. dirs. Will Rogers Motion Picture Pioneers Found. Recipient Crystal award, Women in Film, 2000; named one of The 100 Most Powerful Women in Entertainment, Hollywood Reporter, 2004, 2005, 2006, 2007. Office: Universal Pictures 100 Universal City Plaza Universal City CA 91608

ROCHA, GUY LOUIS, archivist, consultant, historian; b. Long Beach, Calif., Sept. 23, 1951; s. Ernest Louis and Charlotte (Sobus) R. BA in Social Studies and Edn., Syracuse U., 1973; MA in Am. Studies, San Diego State U., 1975; postgrad., U. Nev., 1975—. Cert. archivist Am. Acad. Cert. Archivists. Tchr. Washoe County Sch. Dist., Reno, 1975-76; history instr. Western Nev. C.C., Carson City, 1976; curator manuscripts Nev. Hist. Soc., Reno, 1976-81, interim asst. dir., 1980, interim dir., 1980-81; state adminstr. archives and records Nev. State Libr. and Archives, Carson City, 1981—, interim divsn. adminstr., 2006—. Hist. cons. Janus Assocs., Tempe, Ariz., 1980, Rainshadow Assocs., Carson City, 1983—. Co-author: The Ignoble Conspiracy: Radicalism on Trial in Nevada, 1986, The Earp's Last Frontier: Wyatt and Virgil Earp in Nevada 1902-1905, 1988; contbr. to books and govt. study; host weekly radio talk show Sta. KPTL, Carson City, 1988-2000, KUNR/NPR, Reno, 2001-; hist. cons. to documentary Las Vegas, A&E Network, 1996, documentary Truckee and Carson Rivers, PBS Network, 1997, documentary Hoover Dam, PBS Network, 1999, documentary Lake Tahoe, PBS Network, 2001; dir. documentary Comstock Miners Union, 2003, Goldfield, 2004, They Died to Make the Desert Bloom, 2005, Whose Right to Work?, 2006, Nev. AFL-CIO; mem. editl. bd. Nev. Hist. Soc., 1983-2003. Mem. Washoe Heritage Coun., Reno, 1983—85; ex-officio mem. Nev. Commn. Bicentennial U.S. Constn., 1986—91; mem. Washoe County Dem. Ctrl. Com., Reno, 1984—87. Mem. Conf. Intermountain Archivists (coun. mem. 1979-87, v.p. 1984-85, pres. 1985-86), No. Nev. Pub. Adminstrs. Group (pres. 1986-87), S.W. Labor Studies Assn., State Hist. Records Adv. Bd. (dep. coord. 1984-86, coord. 1986—), Westerners Internat. Nev. Corral (dep. sheriff 1980-81, sheriff 1984-85, mem. state coords. steering com. 1985-87, vice chmn. 1986-87), Soc. Am. Archivists, Western History Assn., Nat. Assn. Govt. Archives and Records Adminstrs., Orgn. Am. Historians. Office: Nev State Libr & Archives 100 N Stewart St Carson City NV 89701-4285 Office Phone: 775-684-3317.

ROCK, ARTHUR, venture capitalist; b. Rochester, NY, Aug. 19, 1926; s. Hyman A. and Reva (Cohen) Rock; m. Toni Rembe, July 19, 1975. BS, Syracuse U., 1948; MBA, Harvard U., 1951. Gen. ptnr. Davis & Rock, San Francisco, 1961-68, Arthur Rock & Assocs., San Francisco, 1969-80. Mem. exec. com. Teledyne, Inc., L.A., 1961-94; dir. emeritus, founder, past chmn., chmn. exec. com., lead dir. Intel Corp., Santa Clara, Calif.; bd. dirs. Echelon Corp., San Jose, Calif.; bd. govs. Nasdaq Stock Market, Inc. Trustee Calif. Inst. Tech.; pres. Basic Fund; bd. dirs. San Francisco Opera Assn., 1970-92, San Francisco Mus. Modern Art; mem. vis. com. Harvard U. Bus. Sch., 1982-88. Recipient Medal of Achievement Am. Electronics Assn., 1987, Am. Acad. Achievement, 1989, Lifetime Achievement in Entrepreneurship and Innovation award U. Calif., 1999; named to Jr. Achievement Hall of Fame, 1990, Calif. Bus. Hall of Fame, 1990, Bay Area Bus. Coun. Hall of Fame, 1995, Arents Pioneer medal Syracuse U., 1997, Outstanding Dir., Corp. Am., 1999, SDForum Visionary award, 2001, Bus. Leader of Yr. award Harvard Bus. Sch. Assn. No. Calif., 2002. Fellow Am. Acad. Arts & Scis. Office: 1 Maritime Plz Ste 1220 San Francisco CA 94111-3502

ROCK, CHRIS, actor, comedian; b. Bklyn., Feb. 7, 1965; s. Julius and Rose Rock; m. Malaak Compton, Nov. 23, 1996; children: Lola Simone, Zahra Savannah. Actor: (films) Beverly Hills Cop II, 1987, I'm Gonna Git You Sucka, 1988, New Jack City, 1991, Boomerang, 1992, Panther, 1995, The Immortals, 1995, Sgt. Bilko, 1996, Beverly Hills Ninja, 1997, (voice) Doctor Dolittle, 1998, Lethal Weapon 4, 1998, Dogma, 1999, Torrance Rises, 1999, Spin Doctor, 1999, Nurse Betty, 2000, (voice) Artificial Intelligence, 2001, Pootie Tang, 2001, (voice) Osmosis Jones, 2001, Jay and Silent Bob Strike Back, 2001, Bad Company, 2002, Paparazzi, 2004, (voice) Madagascar, 2005, The Longest Yard, 2005, (voice) Bee Movie, 2007, You Don't Mess with the Zohan, 2008, (voice) Madagascar: Escape 2 Africa, 2008, actor, writer, dir. I Think I Love My Wife, 2007, actor, writer, exec. prodr. Down to Earth, 2001, actor, dir., prodr. Head of State, 2003, actor, writer, prodr. (with Nelson George) CB4, 1993; actor: (TV series) Saturday Night Live, 1990-93, Def Comedy Jam, 1992, In Living Color, 1993-94; (TV appearances) Miami Vice, 1987, The Fresh Prince of Bel-Air, 1995, Martin, 1996, Homicide: Life on the Street, 1996, (voice) King of the Hill, 1998, Chappelle's Show, 2003; actor, writer, exec. prodr. (TV series) The Chris Rock Show, 1997-2000 (Emmy for Outstanding Writing for a Variety or Music Program, 1998), Everybody Hates Chris, 2005-09; exec. prodr. (TV series) The Hughleys, 1998; writer, exec. prodr. (comedy specials) Chris Rock: Big Ass Jokes, 1993, Chris Rock: Bring the Pain, 1996 (Emmy for Outstanding Variety, Music or Comedy Special), Chris Rock: Bigger and Blacker, 1999 (American Comedy award for Funniest Male Performer in a TV Special, 2000), Chris Rock: Never Scared, 2004 (Grammy award, Best Comedy Album, 2006), Chris Rock: Kill The Messenger, 2008, writer, prodr. Best of Chris Rock, 1999; (voice) Whatever Happened to Michael Ray?, 2000; performer (comedy albums) Born Suspect, 1991, Roll with the New, 1997 (Grammy award for Best Spoken Comedy Album, 1997), Bigger & Blacker, 1999 (Grammy award for Best Spoken Comedy Album, 1999), Never Scared, 2004; Author Rock This!, 1998. Recipient Star, Hollywood Walk of Fame, 2003; named one of The 100 Most Influential People in the World, TIME mag., 2008. Office: c/o Mosaic Media Group 9200 West Sunset Blvd 10th Fl Los Angeles CA 90069

ROCKEFELLER, PHIL, state legislator; b. Rhinebeck, NY, Nov. 20, 1938; m to Anita; children: Rebecca, Melissa & Erika. Legislature spec asst, United States House Representative, formerly; education aide, Governor John Spellman, formerly, United States Department Education, ret, 94; Washington State Representative, District 23, 99-2004, member, Appropriations, Education & Natural Resources Committees, 99-2004, Washington House Representative; Washington State Senator, District 23, Washington State Senate, 2004-, Majority Assistant Floor Leader, Washington State Senate. Officer, Island Land Trust, formerly; board member, Bainbridge Public Library & Bainbridge Performing Arts, formerly. Democrat. Office: State Senate 419 John A Cherberg Bldg, PO Box 40423 Olympia WA 98504 Office Phone: 360-786-7934. E-mail: rockefel_ph@leg.wa.gov.

ROCKFORD, MARV, television executive; b. Chgo., Mar. 1, 1950; BS in Journalism, Northwestern U., 1972, MA in Sci. Journalism, 1973. News dir. KCNC TV, 1987-95, v.p., gen. mgr. Denver, 1995—. Bd. dirs. Denver Meml. C. of C., Colo. Bus. Com. Arts. Mem. RTNDA. Office: KCNC TV 1044 Lincoln St Denver CO 80203-2717

ROCKSTROH, DENNIS JOHN, journalist; b. Hermosa Beach, Calif., Feb. 1, 1942; s. Philip Herman and Alicia (Rubio) R.; m. Le Thi Que Huong, May 2, 1970; children: Bryan Benjamin, Paula Kim-Mai. Student, San Luis Rey Coll., 1960-61, El Camino Coll., 1961-62, San Fernando Valley State Coll., 1965-67. Reporter Thousand Oaks (Calif.) News Chronicle, 1966-67; tchr. Girls' High Sch., Qui Nhon, Vietnam, 1967-70; instr. Dalat U./Vietnamese Mil. Acad., 1970-71, Ohlone Coll., Fremont, Calif., 1984—; freelance war corr. Dispatch News Svc., Vietnam, 1967-71; city editor Santa Paula (Calif.) Daily Chronicle, 1972-73; reporter San Jose (Calif.) Mercury News, 1973-90, columnist, 1990—. Guest lectr. U. Calif., Berkeley, 1987-91. Vol. Internat. Vol. Svcs., Vietnam, 1967-71; bd. dirs. San Jose unit ARC, 1978, Hope Rehab., San Jose, 1976-77. With U.S. Army, 1962-65, Vietnam. Co-recipient Pulitzer prize for Loma Prieta earthquake coverage, 1989; decorated Army Commendation Medal for Valor, 1965. Mem. Soc. Profl. Journalists, St. Anthony's Sem. Alumni Assn., Nat. Soc. Newspaper Columnists. Roman Catholic. Home: 3573 Tankerland Ct San Jose CA 95121-1244 Office: San Jose Mercury News 750 Ridder Park Dr San Jose CA 95190 Personal E-mail: drockstroh@yahoo.com. Business E-Mail: drockstroh@mercurynews.com.

RODARTE, ARTHUR H., state legislator; b. Ojo Caliente, N.Mex., May 2, 1948; BBA, N.Mex. State U. Owner Oliver's Grocery Store; mem. N.Mex. Legislature, Santa Fe, 1996—, mem. conservation com., mem. rules com. Democrat. Office: PO Box 132 Ojo Caliente NM 87549-0132

RODEFER, BENJAMIN H., state legislator; married; 2 children. Attended, Cornell U. Founder and owner GoBox Software; mem. Dist. 23 N. Mex. House of Reps., 2009—. Democrat. Home: 147 Via Oreada Corrales NM 87048 Office: House of Representatives State Capitol Rm 203ECN Santa Fe NM 87501 Home Phone: 505-699-9803; Office Phone: 505-986-4211. E-mail: benrodefer@gmail.com.

RODEKOHR, DIANE E., state official; A in Bus. Mgmt., Nat. Bus. Inst., 1958. Asst. exec. dir. Associated Gen. Contractors of Wyo., 1963-78; field rep. to Sen. Alan Simpson Wyo., 1978-84; state dir. to Sen. Alan Simpson Wyo., 1984-96; state dir. to Sen. Michael Enzi, 1997—. Mem. PEO, Cheyenne C. of C., Rotary (sec. 1995-99). Office: Office Sen Michael Enzi 2120 Capitol Ave Ste 2007 Cheyenne WY 82001-3631

RODELLA, DEBBIE A., state legislator; b. Española, NM, Nov. 28, 1961; m to Thomas R Rodella; children: Thomas, Jr & Kara. New Mexico State Representative, District 41, 1992-, vice chairman, Bus & Indust, Voters & Elections, Rules & Order of Bus Committees, Revenue, Stabilization, Tax Policy, Legislature Coun Committees & Technology Oversight, Indian Affairs, Land Grant, Los Alamos Nat Laboratory Oversight, Econ Rural Develop, Telecommuncation, currently, New Mexico House Representative. Secretary, formerly; materials sci technician, 1998-. Democrat. Roman Catholic. Mailing: PO Box 1074 San Juan Pueblo NM 87566 Home Phone: 505-753-8247.

RODES, DAVID STUART, college program director; b. 1939; BA in Comparative Lit. summa cum laude, So. Meth. U., 1961; PhD in English, Stanford U., 1968. Asst. prof. English UCLA, 1966-74, lectr., 1974-79, sr. lectr. in English, 1980—, acting dir. Grunwald Ctr. for the Graphic Arts, 1989-92, dir. Grunwald Ctr. for the Graphic Arts, 1992—. Founder chancellor's adv. com. Office of Instrnl. Devel., 1974, chair, 1980-89; acad. advisor BBC-TV Shakespeare series, 1978-84; artistic dir. Shakespeare Santa Cruz, 1981—. Gen. editor Augustan Reprint Soc. Clark Libr., 1969-91; contbr. articles to profl. jours. Mem. Phi Beta Kappa (sec. 1979-72, treas. 1978-80). Office: Armand Hammer Mus Art Culture Ctr Grunwald Ctr Graphic Arts UCLA 10899 Wilshire Blvd Fl 3 Los Angeles CA 90024-4201

RODGERS, FREDERIC BARKER, judge; b. Albany, NY, Sept. 29, 1940; s. Prentice Johnson and Jane (Weed) R.; m. Valerie McNaughton, Oct. 8, 1988; 1 child: Gabriel Moore. AB in Polit. Sci., Amherst Coll., Mass., 1963; JD, Union U., Albany, 1966. Bar: NY 1966, US Ct. Mil. Appeals 1968, Colo. 1972, US Supreme Ct. 1974, US Ct. Appeals (10th cir.) 1981, US Ct. Appeals (fed. cir.) 2001. Chief dep. dist. atty., Denver, 1972-73; magistrate Denver Juvenile Ct., 1973—79; mem. Mulligan Reeves Teasley & Joyce, P.C., Denver, 1979-80; pres. Frederic B. Rodgers, P.C., Breckenridge, Colo., 1980-89; ptnr. McNaughton & Rodgers, Central City, Colo., 1989-91; county ct. judge Gilpin County Combined Cts., Colo., 1987—; probate judge Jefferson County Dist. Ct., 2005—07. Presiding mcpl. judge cities of Breckenridge, Blue River, Black Hawk, Central City, Edgewater, Empire, Idaho Springs, Silver Plume and Westminster, Colo., 1978-96; chmn. com. on mcpl. ct. rules of procedure Colo. Supreme Ct., 1984-96; mem. Colo. Supreme Ct. Task Force Probate Protective Procs., 2006—; mem. Colo. Supreme Ct. jud. Conf. Planning Com., 2007—; mem. gen faculty Nat. Jud. Coll. U. Nev., Reno, 1990—, mem. faculty coun., 1993-99, chair 1999, trustee, 2004—, sec., 2007-, chair of bd. elect for 2009-10, 2008. Author (with Dilweg, Fretz, Murphy and Wicker): Modern Judicial Ethics, 1992; contbr. articles to profl. jours., chapters to books; author: The Improvement of The Administration of Justice 7th edit., 2001. Mem. Colo. Commn. on Children, 1982-85, Colo. Youth Devel. Coun., 1989-98, Colo. Family Peace Task Force, 1994-96. Served with JAGC, US Army, 1967-72; to maj. USAR, 1972-88. Decorated Bronze Star with oak leaf cluster, 1969, 1970, Air medal, 1969, Army Commendation medal with silver oak leaf cluster, 1969-1972; recipient USAR Achievement Medal, 1986, Am. Spirit Honor medal, 1966, Outstanding County Judge award Colo. 17th Judicial Dist. Victim Adv. Coalition, 1991; Spl. Cmty. Svc. award Colo. Am. Legion, 1979, Lifetime Achievement award Denver Law Club, 2003; USAID grant, 2002-2003. Fellow Am. Bar Found. (life, Colo. state chair 2005—, Outstanding State Chair award 2009), Colo. Bar. Found. (life); mem. ABA (jud. div. exec. coun. 1989-2000, vice-chair 1996-97, chair-elect 1997, chair 1998-99, mem. House of Dels. 1993-2004, jud. divsn. del. to ABA nominating com. 2000-01, bd. govs. Dist. 11 2001-04, chair traffic ct. program com. 2005-06), Colo. Bar Assn. (bd. govs. 1986-88, 90-92, 93-99, 2002-05, 2007-, sr. v.p. 2004-05), Continental Divide Bar Assn., Denver Bar Assn. (trustee 1979-82), First Jud. Dist. Bar Assn. (trustee 2000-02), Nat. Conf. Spl. Ct. Judges (chmn. 1989-90), Colo. County Judges Assn. (pres. 1995-96, Anthony Greco award 2008), Colo. Mcpl. Judges Assn. (pres. 1986-87), Colo. Trial Judges Coun. (v.p. 1994-95, sec. 1996-97, 2006-07), Denver Law Club (pres. 1981-82), Colo. Women's Bar Assn., Am. Judicature Soc. (bd. dirs. 2003—), Nat. Coun. Juvenile and Family Ct. Judges, Nat. Coll. Probate Judges, Federalist Soc. for Law and Pub. Policy Studies, Judge Advs. Assn., Univ. Club (Denver), Arlberg Club (Winter Park), Marines Meml. Club (San Francisco), Rotary (charter pres. Peak to Peak 2000-01, Paul Harris fellow 1996). Episcopalian. Avocations: bicycling, skiing, hiking, music, writing. Office: First Judicial Dist Courts Gilpin County Justice Ctr 2960 Dory Hill Rd Black Hawk CO 80422 Office Phone: 303-582-5323 ext. 16. Personal E-mail: fbr@q.com. Business E-Mail: frederic.rodgers@judicial.state.co.us.

RODGERS, LOIS EVE, secondary school educator; BA, U. So. Miss.; MEd, William Carey Coll.; student, Bread Loaf Sch. English. Tchr. Hattiesburg (Miss.) High Sch. Named Miss. State English Tchr. of Yr., 1993.

RODGERS, T(HURMAN) J., semiconductor company executive; AB in physics and chemistry, Dartmouth Coll., 1970; MS in electrical engring., Stanford U., 1973, PhD in electrical engring., 1975. Managed MOS memory design group Am. Microsystems Inc., 1975—80; managed static RAM product group Advanced Micro Devices, 1980—82; founder, pres., CEO Cypress Semiconductor Corp., San Jose, Calif., 1982—. Bd. dirs. Silicon Light Machines, Bloom Energy (formerly Ion Am.), SunPower Corp., Cypress MicroSystems, Provina. Bd. trustees Dartmouth Coll., 2004—. Recipient Encore award entrepreneurial company of the year, Stanford U. Bus. Sch., 1988, Entrepreneur of the Year award, Ernst & Young, 1991; named CEO of the Year, Financial World mag., 1996; named one of 100 People Who Changed Our World, Upside mag., 2001, Top 100 Chief Executives, Chief Executive mag., 2002, 100 Best Corporate Citizens, Business Ethics mag., 2005. Mem.: Semiconductor Industry Assn. Achievements include patents in field. Avocations: cooking, movies, collecting wines, jogging. Office: Cypress Semiconductor Corp 198 Champion Ct San Jose CA 95134

RODMAN, ALPINE C., arts and crafts company executive, photographer; b. Roswell, N. Mex., June 23, 1952; s. Robert Elsworth and Verna Mae (Means) R.; m. Sue Arlene Lawson, Dec. 13, 1970; 1 child, Connie Lynn; m. Graham L. Jackson. Student, Colo. State U., 1970—71, U. No. Colo. Ptnr. Pinel Silver Shop, Loveland, Colo., 1965-68, salesman, 1968-71; real estate salesman Loveland, 1971-73; mgr. Traveling Traders, Phoenix, 1974-75; co-owner Deer Track Traders, Loveland, 1975-85; pres. Deer Track Traders, Ltd., Loveland, 1985—. Spkr., lectrs. at seminars in field, 2004—. Author: The Vanishing Indian: Fact or Fiction?, 1985. Mem. Civil Air Patrol, 1965-72, 87-92, dep. comdr. for cadets Greeley, Colo., 1988-90; cadet comdr. Ft. Collins, Colo., 1968, 70, Colo. rep. to youth tng. program, 1969, U.S. youth rep. to Japan, 1970. Mem. We. and English Salesmen's Assn. (bd. dirs. 1990), Indian Arts and Crafts Assn. (bd. dirs. 1988-94, exec. com. 1989-92, v.p. 1990, pres. 1991, market chmn. 1992), Compassion Internat.(sponsor), Crazy Horse Grass Roots Club, Crazy Horse Dreamkeepers Soc. Office: Deer Track Traders Ltd PO Box 448 Loveland CO 80539-0448

RODMAN, SUE A., wholesale company executive, artist, writer; b. Ft. Collins, Colo., Oct. 1, 1951; d. Marvin F. Lawson and Barbara I. (Miller) Lawson Shue; m. Alpine C. Rodman, Dec. 13, 1970; 1 child, Connie L. Rodman; m. Graham L. Jackson. Student, Woodbury Bus./Arts Coll., Calif., 1969, Colo. State U., 1970—73. Silversmith Pinel Silver Shop, Loveland, Colo., 1970-71; asst. mgr. Traveling Traders, Phoenix, 1974-75; co-owner, co-mgr. Native Am. arts and crafts company Deer Track Traders, Loveland, 1975-85; v.p. Deer Track Traders, Ltd., Loveland, 1985—. Author: The Book of Contemporary Indian Arts and Crafts, 1985, short stories; contbr. articles to popular mags. Mem. U.S. Senatorial Club, 1982-87, Rep. Presdl. Task Force, 1984-90; mem. Civil Air Patrol, 1969-73, 87-90, pers. officer, 1988-90. Mem.: Arbor Day Found., Indian Arts and Crafts Assn., Western and English Sales Assn., Compassion Internat. (sponsor), Nat. Wildlife Fedn., Crazy Horse Grass Roots Club. Mem. Am. Baptist Ch. Avocations: museums, piano, recreation research, fashion design.

RODRIGUE, GEORGE P., newspaper executive; Grad., U. Va., 1978. City hall reporter to city editor, European bur. chief, Washington corr. Dallas Morning News (Belo Corp.), Dallas, 1982—98, v.p., mng. editor, 2004—; exec. editor, v.p. news The Press Enterprise (Belo Corp.), Riverside, Calif., 1998; v.p. Capital Bur. Belo Corp., Washington. Co-recipient Two Pulitzer Prizes.

RODRIGUEZ, ARTURO SALVADOR, labor union official; b. San Antonio, June 23, 1949; s. Arthur Salvador and Felice (Quintero) Rodriguez; m. Linda Fabela Chavez (dec.); children: Olivia, Julie, Arthur; m. Sonia Rodriguez. BA in Sociology, St. Mary's U., 1971; MSW, U. Mich., 1973. Various positions United Farm Workers of Am., Keene, Calif., 1973-90, v.p., 1981-93, organizer, 1990-92; pres. United Farm Workers Am. AFL-CIO, Keene, 1993—. Chief instr. UFW Sch., Keene, 1978-79; coord. Edward Kennedy Presdl. Dr., San Antonio, 1980. Office: United Farm Workers Am AFL CIO PO Box 62 La Paz 29700 Woodford Tehachapi Rd Keene CA 93531*

RODRIGUEZ, DANIEL B., dean, law educator; b. 1962; BA, Calif. State U., Long Beach, 1984; JD, Harvard U., 1987. Law clk. to Hon. Alex Kozinski U.S. Ct. Appeals (9th cir.), Pasadena, Calif., 1987-88; acting prof. U. Calif., Boalt Hall Sch. Law, Berkeley, 1988—94, prof., 1994—98; dean, prof. law U. San Diego Sch. Law, 1998—2005, Warren Disting. prof. law, 2005—. Vis. scholar Hoover Inst., Stanford U.; vis. prof. McGeorge Sch. Law-Govt. Affairs Program, U. So. Calif., U. Tex., Austin, U. Ill.; John M. Olin Fellow in Law and Econs. U. Va.; adj. prof. U. Calif., San Diego Sch. Internat. Rels. and Pacific Studies. Contbr. articles to profl. jours. Mem.: Am. Bar Found., Am. Law Inst. Office: U San Diego Sch Law 5998 Alcalá Park San Diego CA 92110-2492

RODRIGUEZ, DENISE RIOS, lawyer; b. Detroit, Apr. 5, 1951; AA, Henry Ford Cmty. Coll., 1971; BA with distinction, Wayne State U., 1975; JD cum laude, U. Mich., 1979. Bar: Mich. 1979, Calif. 1988, U.S. Dist. Ct., Ctrl. Dist. Calif. 1988. Gen. counsel to Health Care Fin. Admin. U.S. Dept. Health & Human Svc.; ptnr. Foley & Lardner LLP, LA, chairperson health payments/compliance practice group. Mem.: ABA (health law sect.), Am. Health Lawyers Assn., Healthcare Fin. Mgmt. Assn., Mex.-Am. Bar Assn., Hispanic Nat. Bar Assn. Fluent in spanish. Office: Foley & Lardner LLP 2029 Century Park E Ste 3500 Los Angeles CA 90067 Office Phone: 310-277-2223. Office Fax: 310-557-8475. Business E-Mail: drodriguez@foley.com.

RODRIGUEZ, ENRIQUE, computer software company executive; BS, Tech. Inst. Monterrey, Mex., 1982. Exec. v.p. broadband access products Thomson/RCA, sr. v.p. multimedia products; v.p. Xbox Partnerships Microsoft Corp., 2003—06, corp. v.p. Microsoft TV divsn., 2006—. Office: Microsoft Corp Microsoft TV Divsn 1 Microsoft Way Redmond WA 98052-6399

RODRIGUEZ, JAI, television personality; b. Brentwood, NY, June 22, 1977; Actor: (films) The New Guy, 2002; (Broadway plays) Rent, Spinning into Butter, (off broadway plays) Zanna, Don't!, 2003; co-author: (books) Queer Eye for the Straight Guy: The Fab 5's Guide to Looking Better, Cooking Better, Dressing Better, Behaving Better, and Living Better, 2004; culture specialist (TV series) Queer Eye for the Straight Guy, 2003, host Groomer Has It, 2008; actor, actor: (Broadway plays) The Producers, 2005.

RODRIGUEZ, JUAN ALFONSO, information technology executive; b. Santiago, Cuba, Feb. 10, 1941; came to U.S., 1953; s. Alfonso and Marie Madeleine (Hourcadette) R. BEE, CCNY, 1962; MEE, NYU, 1963. Engr. IBM, Poughkeepsie, NY, 1963—66, Boulder, Colo., 1966—69, engring. mgr., 1968-69; dir. tech. Storage Tech. Corp., Louisville, Colo., 1969-74, v.p. engring., 1974—76, v.p., gen. mgr. disk, 1976—80, v.p., gen. mgr. optical disk Longmont, Colo., 1980—85; pres., CEO Exabyte Corp., Boulder, 1985-87, CEO, 1987-90, chmn., 1987-92; pres. Sweetwater Corp., 1992-93, chmn., 1992-95, also bd. dirs.; prof. elec. and computer engring. and engring. mgmt. U. Colo., 1992—2001, co-exec. dir. Deming Ctr. Entrepreneurship, 1994-2000; mem. adv. coun., 1994—; chmn. Datasonix, 1992-96, Vixel, 1995-99; chmn., CEO Ecrix Corp., 1996—2001; chief technologist, bd. dirs. Exabyte Corp., 2001—03, interim CEO, pres., 2002, chmn., 2003—06; connectivity ptnr. Appian Ventures, 2002—. Mem. devel. coun. Coll. Engring. U. Colo., 1990-92, mem. tech. transfer office adv. bd., 2000-, adv. bd. Boulder grad. sch., 2007-; Decisionism Corp.; bd. dirs. Maxtor Corp., 1992-94, HiveLive Corp., 2005-; mem. engring. adv. bd. CCNY, bd. dirs. Colo. Advanced Tech. Enterprise, 1994-98; Robert J. Appel Disting. lectr. law and tech. Law Sch. U. Denver, 1990. Patentee in field. Bd. dir. Boulder YMCA, 1982-87, U. Colo. Artist Series, 1988-92; mem. bd. govs. Boulder County United Way, 1989-93, chairperson campaign, 1992; commr. Colo. Advance Tech. Inst., 1988-92; co-chmn. Colo. Innovation Coun., 2008-. Recipient Ind. Quality award, Am. Soc. Quality Control (Rocky Mountain sect.), 1990, Gen. Palmer award Outstanding Engr. in Industry, Am. Cons. Engrs. Coun. Colo., 1995, Career Achievement award, Engring. Sch. Alumni CCNY, 2002, Townsend Harris medal, Alumni Assn. CCNY, 2003, Sprit Visionary award, Boulder C. of C., 2004, Hispanic Engr. of Yr., Entrepreneur Hispanic Engr. Nat. Achievement Awards Coun., 1995; named Boulder Spirit Entrepreneur of Yr., 1989, Entrepreneur of the Decade, 1994; named one of Top 50 Tech. Innovators, VAR Bus., 2004; finalist Entrepreneur of Yr., Arthur Young & Inc Mag., 1989. Fellow IEEE (life); mem. Computer Soc. of IEEE (mem. steering com. on mass storage 1981-93), Soc. Photo-Optical Instrumentation Engrs., Boulder C. of C. (chmn. entrepreneurs support program 1989), Greater Denver C. of C. (bd. dirs. 1990-91); mem. Beta Gamma Sigma (medallion of Entrepreneurship 2003). Office: Appian Ventures 1512 Larimer St Ste 200 Denver CO 80202 Personal E-mail: jar@ieee.org.

RODRIGUEZ, KATY, apparel designer; b. San Francisco; Co-founder Resurrection vintage store, LA, 1996, NYC; co-designer caitie et marc; designer Katy Rodriguez collection. Participating designer Calif. Design Biennial, 2007, NY Fashion Week, Gen Art Show, LA Fashion Week, 2006. Office: 8008 Melrose Ave Ste 2 Los Angeles CA 90046

RODRIGUEZ, (MAYTE) MICHELLE, actress; b. Bexar County, Tex., July 12, 1978; Actor: (films) Girlfight, 2000, 3 A.M., 2001, The Fast and the Furious, 2001, Resident Evil, 2002, Blue Crush, 2003, S.W.A.T., 2003, Control, 2004, Sian Ka'an (voice), 2005, Blood-Rayne, 2005, Battle in Seattle, 2007; (TV series) Lost, 2005— (Outstanding Performance by an Ensemble in a Drama Series, Screen Actors Guild award, 2006, Outstanding Supporting Actress in a TV Series, Nat. Coun. La Raza ALMA award (Am. Latin Media Arts), 2006); voice over: (video game) True Crime: Streets of L.A., 2003; Driv3r, 2004; Halo 2, 2004. Office: c/o True Pub Rels 6725 Sunset Blvd Los Angeles CA 90028

RODRIGUEZ, RICK, former executive editor; b. Salinas, Calif., Apr. 5, 1954; m. Emelyn Cruz Lat Rodriguez, July 25, 1998. Grad., Stanford U., 1976, Guadalajara, Mex. Newspaper intern Salinas Californian; reporter Fresno Bee, Sacramento Bee, asst. mng. editor, mng. editor, 1993—98, exec. editor & sr. v.p., 1998—2007. Mem. Pulitzer Prize juries 1994, 95. Mem. Am. Soc. Newspaper Editors (bd. dirs. 1997-2001, treas. designate 2001-02, treas. 2002-03, sec. 2003-04, v.p. 2004-2005, pres. 2005-06), Calif. Chicano News Media Assn. (co-founder Sacramento chpt., past bd. dirs.). Office Phone: 916-321-1007. E-mail: rrodriguez@sacbee.com.

RODRIGUEZ, ROBERT, filmmaker; b. San Antonio, June 20, 1968; s. Cecilio and Rebecca Rodriguez; m. Elizabeth Avellan, July 9, 1990 (separated), 5 children. Student, U. Tex. Dir. (films) Bedhead, 1991 El Mariachi, 1992, Desperado, 1995, Four Rooms (segment The Misbehaviors), 1995, From Dusk Till Dawn, 1995, The Faculty, 1998, Spy Kids, 2001, Spy Kids II: Island of Lost Dreams, 2002, Spy Kids 3-D: Game Over, Once Upon A Time in Mexico, 2003, Sin City (co-directed with Frank Miller & Quentin Tarantino), 2005, The Adventures of Shark Boy & Lava Girl in 3-D, 2005, Grindhouse, 2007; TV films: Roadracers (also wrote), 1994; wrote and prod-.(films), From Dusk Til Dawn 3: The Hangman's Daughter, 2000, Once Upon A Time in Mexico, 2003; prodr. only (films), From Dusk Til Dawn II: Texas Blood Money, 1999; TV appearances: Nash Bridges, 1997, Deadline, 2000. Named one of 25 Most Influential Hispanics, Time Mag., 2005, 50 Most Powerful People in Hollywood, Premiere mag., 2005.

ROE, CHARLES RICHARD, baritone; b. Cleve., May 24, 1940; s. Andrews Rogers and Margaret (Dalton) R.; children by previous marriage— Charles Andrews, Richard Nevins, Robert Arthur; m. Jo Ann Marie Belli, May 21, 1988. B.Mus., Baldwin-Wallace Coll., 1963; M.Mus., U. Ill., 1964. Instr. in music Tex. Tech. U., 1964-68; asst. prof. music Eastern Mich. U., 1968-74; vis. assoc. prof. U. So. Calif., LA, 1976-77, assoc. prof., 1979-84, prof., 1984-89, U. Ariz., Tucson, 1989—. Vis. prof. and artist in residence Western Mich. U., 1978-79; faculty Music Acad. of the West, 1981, 82 Leading singer, N.Y.C. Opera, 1974-81; appeared in leading roles with, Mich. Opera Theater, Sacramento Opera, San Antonio Opera, Ft. Worth Opera, Ky. Opera, Conn. Opera, Utah Opera, Cleve. Opera, Miss. Opera, Lake George Opera, Shreveport Opera, Toledo Opera; appeared with, symphonies: Phila., Cleve., Detroit, Toledo, Wichita, Duluth. Mem. Am. Guild Musical Artists, Actors Equity, Nat. Assn. Tchrs. Singing (S.W. region Singer of Year 1966), AAUP. Office: U Ariz Sch Music PO Box 210004 Tucson AZ 85721-0004

ROE, THOMAS LEROY WILLIS, retired pediatrician; b. Bend, Oreg., Sept. 1, 1936; MD, U. Oregon Health Scis. U., Portland, 1961. Diplomate Am. Bd. Pediatrics. Intern U. Calif., San Francisco, 1961-62, resident, 1962-64; physician Sacred Heart Med. Ctr., Eugene, Oreg.; pvt. practice Peace Health Med. Group, Eugene, 1969—2006; clin prof. pediatrics U. Oreg., Portland, 1985—2006; ret., 2006. Fellow Am. Acad. Pediatricians; mem. AMA, North Pacific Pediatrics Soc. Office: Peace Health Med Clinic 1162 Willamette St Eugene OR 97401-3568 Office Phone: 541-687-6061. Business E-Mail: troe@peacehealth.org.

ROEDEL, RICHARD W., video game developing company executive; b. Nov. 1949; BS in Acctg. & Econ., Ohio State U. CPA. Audit ptnr. BDO Seidman LLP, NYC, 1985—90, mng. ptnr. Chgo., 1990—94, NYC, 1994—99, chmn. & CEO, 1999—2000; co-founder & prin. Pinnacle Ventures LLC, Menlo Park, Calif., 2000—; CEO Take2Interactive, NYC, 2004—05, non-exec. chmn., 2004—. Bd. dir. Take2Interactive, NYC, 2002—, Brightpoint Inc., Dade Behring Holdings Inc. Office: Non-exec Chmn & CEO Take-Two Interactive Software 622 Broadway New York NY 10012 also: Co-Founder and Principal Pinnacle Ventures LLP Ste 125 2882 Sand Hill Rd Menlo Park CA 94025

ROEDER, RICHARD KENNETH, business owner, lawyer; b. Phila., Oct. 11, 1948; s. Walter August and Gloria (Miller) R.; 1 child, William Frederick; m. Allison Nunn Roeder, June 12, 1999. AB, Amherst Coll., 1970; JD, U. Calif., Berkeley, 1973, Cambridge U., 1973-74. Assoc. Paul, Hastings, Janofky & Walker, LA, 1974-81, ptnr., 1981-90; founding ptnr. Aurora Capital Group, LA, 1990—2007; ptnr. Vance St. Capital, 2007—. Office: Vance Street Capital Ste 750 11150 Santa Monica Blvd Los Angeles CA 90025 Business E-Mail: rroeder@vancestreetcapital.com.

ROEDERER, JUAN GUALTERIO, retired physics professor; b. Trieste, Italy, Sept. 2, 1929; came to US, 1967, naturalized, 1972; s. Ludwig Alexander and Anna Rafaela (Lohr) R.; m. Beatriz Susana Cougnet, Dec. 20, 1952; children: Ernesto, Irene, Silvia, Mario. PhD, U. Buenos Aires, 1952. Research scientist Max Planck Inst., Gottingen, W.Ger., 1952-55; group leader Argentine Atomic Energy Commn., Buenos Aires, 1953-59; prof. physics U. Buenos Aires, 1959-66, U. Denver, 1967-77, U. Alaska, Fairbanks, 1977-93, prof. emeritus, 1993—, dir. Geophys. Inst., 1977-86, dean Coll. Environ. Scis., 1978-82. Vis. staff Los Alamos Nat. Lab., 1969-81; chmn. US Arctic Research Com., 1987-91; sr. adviser Internat. Ctr. Theoretical Physics, Trieste, Italy, 1998—2002. Author: Dynamics of Geomagnetically Trapped Radiation, 1970, Physics and Psychophysics of Music, 1973, 4th edit., 2008, Mecanica Elemental, 2002, Information and Its Role in Nature, 2005; contbr. articles to profl. jours Nat. Acad. Sci. NASA sr. rsch. fellow, 1964—66. Fellow AAAS, Am. Geophys. Union (Edward A. Flinn III award, 2000); mem. Assn. Argentina de Geodestas y Geofisicos (hon.), Nat. Acad. Sci. Argentina (corr.), Nat. Acad. Sci. Austria (corr.), Third World Acad. Scis. (assoc.), Internat.

Assn. Geomagnetism and Aeronomy (hon.), Sci. Com. on Solar-Terrestrial Physics (hon.). Lutheran. Achievements include research in plasma and energetic particles in earth's and Jupiter's magnetosphere, policy issues for Arctic, perception of music, information theory. Office: Univ Alaska Geophys Inst Fairbanks AK 99775-7320 Business E-Mail: jgr@gi.alaska.edu.

ROEHL, JERRALD J., lawyer; b. Austin, Dec. 6, 1945; s. Joseph E. and Jeanne Foster (Scott) R.; m. Nancy J. Meyers, Jan. 15, 1977; children: Daniel J., Katherine C., J. Ryan, J. Taylor. BA, U. N.Mex., 1968; JD, Washington and Lee U., 1971. Bar: N.Mex. 1972, U.S. Ct. Appeals (10th cir.) 1972, U.S. Supreme Ct. 1977. Practice of law, Albuquerque, 1972—; pres. Roehl Law Firm P.C. and predecessors, Albuquerque, 1976—. Lectr. to profl. groups; real estate developer, Albuquerque. Bd. advs. ABA Jour. 1981-83; bd. editors Washington and Lee Law Rev., 1970-71. Bd. dirs. Rehab. Ctr. of Albuquerque, 1974-78; mem. assocs. Presbyn. Hosp. Ctr., Albuquerque, 1974-82; incorporator, then treas. exec. com. Ctr. City Coun., 1991-98, law coun. Washington & Lee U. Law Sch., 2002—08; founder Roehl Cir. Honor Trial Lawyers, State Bar N. Mex., 1996-, Concours du Soleil, 2004-, founder Roehl Cir. Honor Trial Lawyers, State bar of N.Mex., 1996-, Concours Du Soleil, Albuquerque, 2005-. Recipient award of recognition State Bar N.Mex., 1975-77. Mem. ABA (award of achievement Young Lawyers divsn. 1975, coun. econs. of law practice sect. 1978-80, exec. coun. Young Lawyers divsn. 1979-81, fellow divsn. 1984—, coun. tort and ins. practice sect. 1981-83), N.Mex. Bar Assn. (pres. young lawyers sect. 1975-76), Albuquerque Bar Assn. (bd. dirs. 1976-79), N.Mex. Def. Lawyers Assn. (pres. 1983-84), Albuquerque Country Club, Albuquerque Petroleum Club, Sigma Alpha Epsilon, Sigma Delta Chi, Phi Delta Phi. Roman Catholic. Office: 300 Central Ave SW Ste 2500e Albuquerque NM 87102-2320 Office Phone: 505-242-6900.

ROEHRIG, JOHN T., immunologist, educator; BS in Microbiology, U. Ill., 1973; PhD in Microbiology, U. Mo.-Columbia, 1977. Rsch. microbiologist divsn. vector-borne infectious diseases Ctr. Disease Control and Prevention, Fort Collins, Colo., 1981-84, supervisory rsch. microbiologist, 1984—, chief immunochemistry br./sect., 1985-98; chief arbovirus diseases br. Colo. State U., Fort Collins, 1981—, biosafety com. mem., 1981—, affiliate faculty mem. dept. microbiology, 1981—. Presenter in field. Ad hoc reviewer Am. Jour. of Tropical Medicine and Hygiene, Archives of Virology, Infectio and Immunity, Jour. of Gen. Virology, Jour. of Infectious Diseases, Jour. of Med. Virology, Jour. of Virology, Virology and Virus Rsch.; contbr. chpts. to books and numerous articles to profl. jours. Grantee U.S. Army, 1987-90, NATO, 1987-90, WHO, 1989-91. Mem. AAAS, Am. Soc. for Virology, Am. Soc. for Microbiology, Am. Com. for Arthropod-Borne Viruses, Protein Soc., Am. Peptide Soc., Am. Soc. for Tropical Medicine and Hygiene, U. Ill. Alumni Assn., U. Mo. Alumni Assn., Sigma Xi. Office: Divsn Vector Borne Infectious Diseases Ctrs Disease Control PO Box 2087 Fort Collins CO 80522-2087

ROELANDTS, WILLEM P., data processing executive; b. Jan. 4, 1945; came to U.S., 1982; BEE, Rijks Hogere Technische Sch., Belgium, 1965. Various position including sr. v.p. Hewlett-Packard, 1966—96; CEO, pres. Xilinx Inc., San Jose, 1996—2008, chmn., 2003—. Spkr. in field. Mem.: Fabless Semiconductor Assn. (pres.), Tech. Network (bd. dirs.), Semiconductor Industry Assn. (bd. dirs.). Office: Xilinx Inc 2100 Logic Dr San Jose CA 95124-3400

ROELLER, HERBERT ALFRED, biology professor; b. Magdeburg, Germany, Aug. 2, 1927; came to U.S., 1962; s. Alfred H. and Elfriede (Wartner) R.; m. Manuela R. Buresch, Dec. 20, 1957. Abiturium, Christian Thomasius Schule, Halle/Saale, 1946; PhD, Georg August U., Goettingen, 1962; MD, U. Muenster, 1955. Project assoc. zoology U. Wis., Madison, 1962-65, asst. prof. pharmacology, 1965-66, rsch. assoc. zoology, 1966-67, assoc. prof. zoology, 1967-68; prof. biology Tex. A&M U., 1968-83, prof. biochemistry and biophysics, 1974-83, dir. Inst. Devel. Biology, 1973-83, Disting. prof., 1977—, Alumni prof., 1980-85. V.p. rsch. Zoecon Corp., Palo Alto, Calif., 1968-72, sci. adv., 1972-85, chief scientist, Zoecon Rsch. Inst., Palo Alto, 1985-88; sci. advisor Syntex Rsch., Palo Alto, 1966-68, European Cmty., 1988—, Affymax Rsch. Inst., Palo Alto, 1989-96; corp. advisor Symyx Techs., Sunnyvale, Calif., 1996—; mem. adv. panel regulatory biology, divsn. biol. and med. scis. NSF, 1969-72; mem. Internat. Centre Insect Physiology and Ecology, Nairobi, Kenya, 1970—, dir. rsch., 1970-75. Mem. editl. bd. Jour. Chem. Ecology, 1974—; Contbr. articles to profl. jours. Recipient Disting. Achievement award for research Tex. A&M U., 1976. Fellow Tex. Acad. Sci.; mem. German Acad. Naturforscher Leopoldina, AAAS, Am. Soc. Zoologists, Entomol. Soc. Am., Am. Soc. Devel. Biology, Sigma Xi.

ROELLIG, LEONARD OSCAR, physics professor; b. Detroit, May 17, 1927; s. Oscar Otto and Laura K. (Rutz) R.; m. B. Pauline Cowdin, June 20, 1952; children: Thomas Leonard, Mark Douglas, Paul David. AB, U. Mich., 1950, MS, 1956, PhD, 1959. From asst. prof. to prof. physics Wayne State U., Detroit, 1958-78, dean, 1971-72, asso. provost, 1972-76; pres. Central Solar Energy Research Corp., Detroit, 1977; prof. physics CCNY, 1978-96, prof. emeritus, 1996—; vice chancellor acad. affairs CUNY, 1978-83. Vis. prof. Univ. Coll., London, 1968-69, Tata Inst. Fundamental Rsch., Bombay, India, 1973, Paul Scherrer Inst., Villigen, Switzerland, 1991-92; chmn. bd. advisers Midwest Regional Solar Energy Planning Venture, 1977. Co-author: Positron Annihilation, 1967; contbr. articles to profl. jours. Bd. dirs. Luth. Publicity Bur., 1981-91, v.p., 1984-85, pres., 1985-89; v.p. Grosse Pointe (Mich.) Human Rels. Coun., 1969-70. With USN, 1945-46, U.S. Army, 1950-52. Recipient Wayne State U. Fund Research Recognition award, 1963, Probus Club award for acad. achievement, 1968, Probus Club award for acad. leadership, 1977 Mem. Am. Phys. Soc. Home: 4520 Sioux Dr Boulder CO 80303-3733 Office: U Colo Dept Physics Boulder CO 80302 Office Phone: 303-492-8707. Personal E-mail: loroellig@aol.com.

ROEMER, ELIZABETH, retired astronomer, educator; b. Calif., 1929; d. Richard Quirin and Elsie Roemer. BA with honors, U. Calif., Berkeley, 1950, PhD (Lick Obs. fellow), 1955. Tchr. adult class Oakland pub. schs., 1950-52; lab technician U. Calif. at Mt. Hamilton, 1954-55; grad. research astronomer U. Calif. at Berkeley, 1955-56; research asso. Yerkes Obs. U. Chgo., 1956; astronomer US Naval Obs., Flagstaff, Ariz., 1957-66; asso. prof. dept. astronomy, also in lunar and planetary lab. U. Ariz., Tucson, 1966-69, prof., 1969-97; prof. emerita, 1997—; astronomer Steward Obs., 1980-97, astronomer emerita, 1997—. Chmn. working group on orbits and ephemerides of comets commn. 20 Internat. Astron. Union, 1964-79, 85-88, v.p. comm. 20, 1979-82, pres., 1982-85, v.p. commn. 6, 1973-76, 85-88, pres., 1976-79, 88-91; adv. panel Office Naval Rsch., Nat. Acad. Scis.-NRC, NASA. Recipient Dorothea Klumpke Roberts prize U. Calif., Berkeley, 1950, Mademoiselle Merit award, 1959; asteroid (1657) named Roemera, 1965; Benjamin Apthorp Gould prize Nat. Acad. Scis., 1971, NASA Spl. award, 1986. Fellow AAAS (council 1966-69, 72-73), Royal Astron. Soc. (London); mem. Am. Astron. Soc. (program vis. profs. astronomy 1960-75, council 1967-70, chmn. div. dynamical astronomy 1974), Astron. Soc. Pacific (publs. com. 1962-73, Comet medal com. 1968-74, Donohoe lectr. 1962), Internat. Astron. Union, Am. Geophys. Union, Brit. Astron. Assn., Phi Beta Kappa, Sigma Xi. Achievements include research in astrometry and astrophysics of comets and minor planets including 79 recoveries of returning periodic comets, visual and spectroscopic binary stars, computation of orbits of comets and minor planets. Office: U Ariz PO Box 210092 Lunar & Planetary Lab Tucson AZ 85721-0092

ROENICK, JEREMY, professional hockey player; b. Boston, Jan. 17, 1970; m. Tracy Roenick; children: Brandi, Brett. Center Chgo. Blackhawks, 1988—96, Phoenix Coyotes, 1996—2001, Pheonix Coyotes, 2006—07, Phila. Flyers, 2001—05, LA Kings, 2005—06, San Jose Sharks, 2007—; hockey analyst TSN, Canada, 2007. Mem. US Olympic Hockey Team, Nagano, Japan, 1998, Salt Lake City, 2002; player NHL All-Star Game, 1991—94, 1999, 2000, 2002—04. Named NHL Rookie of Yr., The Sporting News, 1989—90. Achievements include being a member of silver medal winning USA Hockey Team, Salt Lake City Olympics, 2002. Office: San Jose Sharks 525 W Santa Clara St San Jose CA 95113

ROESER, ANDY, professional sports team executive; m. Anne Roeser; 2 children. Grad., Mich. State U., East Lansing. Assoc. LA Clippers, 1981—84, exec. v.p., 1986—2007, NBA alt. gov., pres., 2007—. Mem. adv. com. Grad. Prog. Sport Mgmt. Calif. State U., Long Beach; bd. dirs. LA Sports Coun. Pres., CEO LA Clippers Found. Office: LA Clippers 1111 S Figueroa St Ste 1100 Los Angeles CA 90015

ROESNER, LARRY AUGUST, civil engineer; b. Denver, Mar. 14, 1941; s. Walter George and Sarah Jane (Merrick) R.; m. Kathleen Ann Fahrenbruch, Dec. 13, 1964; children: David John, Kevin Walter, Nathan August, Melissa Jane. BS in Civil Engring, Valparaiso U., Ind., 1959—63; MS in Civil Engring, Hydrology, Colo. State U., 1963—65; PhD, U. Wash., Seattle, 1969. Registered profl. engr., Calif., Colo., hydrologist. From assoc. engr. to prin. engr. Water Resources Engrs., Inc., Walnut Creek, Calif., 1968-77; from assoc. to v.p. Camp Dresser & McKee Inc., Annandale, Va., 1977-85, sr. v.p., dir. water resources Maitland, Fla., 1985-92, chief tech. officer, 1992-98; dean Camp Dresser & McKee Corp. U., 1998-99; Harold H. Short prof. urban water infrastructure systems Colo. State U., Ft. Collins, 1999—, interim head dept. civil engring., 2000. Guest lectr., cons. urban hydrology and surface water quality; NRC exec. com. Wastewater Mgmt. in Urban Coastal Areas, 1992; chair Engring. Found. Conf. Stormwater Mgmt.-Sustainable Urban Water Resources in the 21st Century, 1997, NRC study panel Oil in the Sea, 2001; urban wet weather adv. Water Environ. Rsch. Found. Contbr. articles to profl. jours. Recipient Water Resource Planning and Mgmt. Divsn. Svc. to the Profession award 1999. Fellow ASCE (life, chmn. 1995 water resources planning and mgmt. divsn. splty. conf., nat. Walter L. Huber civil engring. rsch. prize 1975); mem. NAE (elected mem. 1990), Am. Acad. Water Resource Engrs. (diplomate), Am. Water Resources Assn., Water Environ. Fedn., Tau Beta Pi (eminent engr.). Democrat. Lutheran. Achievements include development of mathematical models for U.S. government agencies including QUAL-II stream quality model for the EPA; an urban stormwater management model, the dynamic hydraulics model SWMMEXTRAN for storm drainage and sewer systems. Home: 5926 Huntington Hills Dr Fort Collins CO 80525-7118 Office: Colo State U Dept Civil Engring Fort Collins CO 80523-1372 Business E-Mail: larry.roesner@colostate.edu.

ROETHE, JAMES NORTON, lawyer; b. Milw., Jan. 27, 1942; s. Arthur Frantz and Bess Irma (Norton) R.; m. Nita May Dorris, July 15, 1967; children: Melissa Dorris, Sarah Rebacca. BBA, U. Wis., Madison, 1964, JD, 1967. Bar: Wis. 1967, Calif. 1968, U.S. Dist. Ct. (we. dist.) Wis. 1967, U.S. Dist. Ct. (no. dist.) Calif. 1972, U.S. Ct. Claims 1975, U.S. Ct. Appeals (9th cir.) 1980, U.S. Dist. Ct. (ea. dist.) Calif. 1982, U.S. Dist. Ct. (ctrl. dist.) Calif. 1986), U.S. Ct. Appeals (4th cir.) 1988, U.S. Ct. Appeals (2d cir.) 1989. Assoc. Pillsbury, Madison & Sutro, San Francisco, 1971-77, ptnr., 1978-92; sr. v.p., dir. litigation Bank of Am., San Francisco, 1992-96, exec. v.p., gen. counsel, 1996-98, dep. gen. counsel, 1998-99; ptnr. Litigation, Corp. & Securities practices Pillsbury Winthrop LLP (now Pillsbury Winthrop Shaw Pittman), San Francisco, 2000—. Staff atty. Commn. on CIA Activities within U.S., Washington, 1975. Editor: Africa, 1967; editor-in-chief Wis. Law Rev., 1966-67. Bd. dirs. Orinda (Calif.) Assn., 1984-85, pres., 1986; active City of Orinda Planning Commn., 1988-94, chmn., 1990, 93; bd. dirs. Calif. Shakespeare Festival, 1993—, pres., 2001-06; bd. vis. U. Wis. Law Sch., 1994-99. Lt. USNR, 1967-71 Fellow Am. Bar Found.; mem. ABA, Wis. Bar Assn., Calif. Bar Assn., Bar Assn. San Francisco, Wis. Law Alumni Assn. (bd. dirs. 2000—), Legal Aid Soc. (bd. dirs.), Orinda Country Club (pres. 2003-04), Order of Coif, Phi Kappa Phi Office: Pillsbury Winthrop Shaw Pittman 50 Fremont St San Francisco CA 94105 Office Phone: 415-983-1414. Office Fax: 415-983-1200. Business E-Mail: james.roethe@pillsburylaw.com.

ROFFMAN, HOWARD, motion picture company executive; b. Phila. Student, U. Pa.; JD, U. Fla. Assoc. Morgan, Lewis & Bockius, Washington; from legal counsel to gen. counsel Lucasfilm, Ltd., San Rafael, Calif., 1980-84, acting COO, 1984-85, v.p. licensing, 1986-99; pres. Lucas Licensing, San Rafael, Calif., 1999—. Author: Presumed Guilty, 1974, Understanding the Cold War, 1976, The Edge of Desire, 1995, Three, 1996, Tales, 1997, Pictures of Fred, 1998, Jagged Youth, 2000, Johan Paulik, 2001, Pictures of Kris, 2002. Mem. Calif. Bar Assn., Washington Bar Assn., Licensing Industry Merchandising Assn. Office: Lucas Licensing Ltd PO Box 29905 San Francisco CA 94129-0905

ROGAN, RICHARD A., lawyer; b. LA, Sept. 6, 1950; AB with honors, Hamilton Coll., 1972; JD, U. Calif., 1975. Bar: Calif. 1975. Ptnr. Broad, Schulz, Larson & Hastings Wineberg, 1978-94; chmn. Broad, Schulz, Larson & Wineberg, 1991-93; ptnr. Jeffer, Mangels, Butler & Marmaro, San Francisco, 1994—, mng. ptnr., San Francisco office, 2002—. Editorial assoc. Hastings Law Jour., 1974-75. Trustee Bentley Sch., 1989-92. Mem. ABA (mem. corp., banking, and bus. sect.), Bar Assn. of San Francisco (mem. comml. law and bankruptcy sect.), Calif. Receivers Forum (bd. dirs. Bay Area chpt.), Delta Sigma Rho. Office: Jeffer Mangels Butler Marmaro-JMBM 2 Embarcadero Ctr 5th Fl San Francisco CA 94111-3823 Office Phone: 415-398-8080. E-mail: rrogan@jmbm.com.

ROGEL, STEVEN R., paper company executive; b. Ritzville, Wash., Oct. 25, 1942; m. Connie Schuler, 1964; 3 children. BS in Chem. Engring., U. Wash., 1965. With St. Regis Paper Co., 1965—70; asst. mgr. St. Anne-Nackawic Pulp and Paper, Nackawic, N.B., Canada, 1970—72; tech. dir. Willamette Industries, Inc., Albany, Oreg., 1972—95, pres., CEO, 1995—97, Weyerhaeuser Co., Tacoma, 1997—99, chmn., pres., CEO, 1999—2007, chmn., CEO, 2008, non-exec. chmn., 2008—. Bd. dirs. Weyerhaeuser Co., 1997—, Kroger Co., 1999—, Union Pacific Corp., 2000—; co-chair Wood Promotion Network; bd. mem. World Forestry Ctr. V.p. adminstrn., western region Boy Scouts Am.; trustee Pacific U. Mem.: Am. Forest and Paper Assn. (bd. dirs.). Office: Weyerhaeuser Co 33663 Weyerhaeuser Way S Federal Way WA 98003-9620 Office Phone: 253-924-2345.

ROGER, KENT M., lawyer; b. San Francisco, May 8, 1955; s. Alberto Vasquez del Mercado and LaVerne Annette (Stadler) Newcombe; m. Margaret Ann Murphy, Aug. 10, 1985; children: Nicole, Lauren. AB, U. Calif., Berkeley, 1977; JD, U. Calif., San Francisco, 1980. Bar: Calif. 1980. Assoc. Brobeck, Phleger & Harrison, San Francisco, 1980-87, ptnr., 1987—2003; ptnr., leader litig. practice group Morgan, Lewis & Bockius LLP, San Francisco. Mem. ABA, Bar Assn. San Francisco, San Francisco Bank Atty. Assn Roman Catholic. Office: Morgan Lewis & Bockius LLP Spear St Tower 1 Market Plz San Francisco CA 94105-1420

ROGERS, HOWARD H., retired chemist; b. NYC, Dec. 26, 1926; s. Julian Herbert and Minnie (Jaffa) R.; m. Barbara Kniaz, Mar. 27, 1954 (div. 1978); children: Lynne, Mark David, Susan; m. Maureen Dohn, Dec. 28, 1978. BS in Chemistry, U. Ill., 1949; PhD in Inorganic Chemistry, MIT, 1953. Research group leader Allis-Chalmers Mfg. Co., West Allis, Wis., 1952-61; sr. tech. specialist Rocketdyne div., Rockwell, Canoga Park, Calif., 1961-70; chief research scientist Martek Instruments, Newport Beach, Calif., 1970-73; scientist Boeing Satellite Systems, Torrance, Calif., 1973—2002; ret., 2002. Contbr. sci. papers to profl. publs. in field. Vol. LA County Disaster Comm. Svc., 1998—. With USN, 1944—46. Recipient Lawrence A. Hyland Patent award Hughes Aircraft Co., 1987. Mem. Electrochem. Soc. (chmn. So. Calif./Nev. sect. 1976-78), Am. Chem. Soc. Achievements include development of nickel-hydrogen battery; 27 US patents. Avocation: amateur radio. Home: 18361 Van Ness Ave Torrance CA 90504-5309 Personal E-mail: howard.rogers@alum.mit.edu.

ROGERS, JACK DAVID, plant pathologist, educator; b. Point Pleasant, W.Va., Sept. 3, 1937; s. Jack and Thelma Grace R.; m. Belle C. Spencer, June 7, 1958. BS in Biology, Davis and Elkins Coll., 1960; MF, Duke U., 1960; PhD, U. Wis., 1963. From asst. prof. to prof. Wash. State U., Pullman, 1963-72, chmn. dept. plant pathology, 1986-99, Regents prof., 2007—. Contbr. articles to profl. jours. Recipient Eminent Faculty award, Wash. State U., 2006. Mem. Mycol. Soc. Am. (pres. 1977-78, William H. Weston Tchg. Excellence award 1992, Disting. Mycologist award 2004), Am. Phytopathol. Soc., Bot. Soc. Am., Brit. Mycol. Soc. Office Phone: 509-335-9541.

ROGERS, JERRY L., federal agency administrator; b. Tex., Dec. 22, 1938; s. Ancell Robert and Grace Evalena (Coin) R.; m. Peggy Floretta Sifford, Apr. 6, 1963; children: Tiana Lynne Conklin, Elvin Houston, Jeffrey Martin. BA in History, Tex. Tech, 1962, MA, 1965. Historian Nat. Park Svc., Ft. Davis, Tex., 1965-66, historian Nat. Register Washington, 1967-69, chief registration, 1972-73, chief grants divsn., 1973-75, chief archeology and hist. preservation, 1975-79, assoc. dir. cultural programs, 1981-83, assoc. dir. cultural resources, 1983-94; regional dir. S.W. region, 1994-95; supt. S.W. office, 1995-99; dir. Ranching Heritage Ctr. Tex. Tech Mus., Lubbock, 1969-72; dep. assoc. dir. Heritage Conservation Svc., Washington, 1979-81; nat. conf. chairperson NPS, 1998—. Internat. cons. in hist. preservation to Italy, Russia, Spain, China, India, Egypt. Contbr. articles to prof. jours. Mem. adv. com. on cemeteries and memls. VA, Washington, 1987-94. Recipient Meritorious Svc. award Dept. Interior, 1992. Mem. AIA (mem. com. hist. resources, ex-officio mem. 1979-94), Nat. Trust Hist. Preservation (trustee 1981-94), Civil War Trust. N.Mex. Heritage Preservation Alliance (bd. dirs. 1996—), Coun. on Am.'s Mil. Past (bd. dirs. 1997—). Avocations: genealogy, classic automobiles. Office: Nat Park Svc 1100 Old Santa Fe Trail PO Box 728 Santa Fe NM 87504-0728 Home: 107 Calle Galisteo Santa Fe NM 87508-1545

ROGERS, LEE FRANK, radiologist; b. Colchester, Vt., Sept. 24, 1934; s. Watson Frank and Marguerite Mortimer (Cole) R.; m. Donna Mae Brinker, June 20, 1956; children: Michelle, Cynthia, Christopher, Matthew. BS, Northwestern U., 1956, MD, 1959. Commd. 2d lt. U.S. Army, 1959, advanced through grades to maj., 1967; rotating intern Walter Reed Gen. Hosp., 1959-60; resident radiology Fitzsimons Gen. Hosp., 1960-63; ret., 1967; radiologist Bapt. Meml. Hosp., San Antonio, 1967-68, U. Tex. Med. Sch., San Antonio, 1968-71, dir. residency tng., radiologist Houston, 1972-74; prof., chmn. dept. radiology Northwestern U. Med. Sch., Chgo., 1974-95; editor-in-chief Am. Jour. Roentgenology, Winston-Salem, NC, 1995—2003; prof. radiology U. Ariz. Health Scis. Ctr., 2003—. Fellow Am. Coll. Radiology (past pres.), Am. Roentgen Ray Soc. (past pres.); mem. Assn. Univ. Radiologists (past pres.), Radiol. Soc. N.Am., Am. Bd. Radiology (past pres.), Alpha Omega Alpha. Episcopalian. Home: 8235 N Fairway View Dr Tucson AZ 85742 Office Phone: 520-626-6794. Personal E-mail: lfrogers@comcast.net.

ROGERS, MARK NICHOLL, lawyer; b. Rochester, NY, June 21, 1965; s. Howard James and Nancy Ellen (Nicholl) R.; m. Karen Marie Rettig, Mar. 14, 1992. BA, Brown U., 1987; JD, NYU, 1992. Bar: Ariz. 1992, U.S. Dist. Ct. Ariz. 1993. Assoc. Fennemore Craig, P.C., Phoenix, 1992-95, Quarles & Brady, Phoenix, 1996-99; v.p., gen. counsel Excell Global Svcs., Inc., Tempe, Ariz., 1999—2001; gen. counsel Integrated Info. Sys., Inc., Tempe, Ariz., 2001—03; corp. counsel Insight Enterprises Inc., Tempe, Ariz., 2003—. Com. mem. Childrens Cancer Ctr. Card Project, Phoenix, 1993—. Mem. ABA (bus. law sect., fed. regulation of securities com. and corp. practice com.), Ariz. State Bar, Maricopa County Bar Assn., Brown Club of Phoenix, Phi Beta Kappa. Avocations: golf, photography, travel. Office: Insight Enterprises Inc 1305 W Auto Dr Tempe AZ 85284 Office Phone: 480-333-3000. Office Fax: 480-760-9068.

ROGERS, SAMUEL SHEPARD See SHEPARD, SAM

ROGERS, T. GARY, apparel company executive, former food products company executive; b. 1943; BSME, U. Calif., 1963; MBA, Harvard U., 1968. Assoc. McKinsey & Co., San Francisco; founder, pres. Vintage Ho. Restaurants, Calif. and Tex.; chmn., CEO Dreyer's Grand Ice Cream, Inc., Oakland, Calif., 1977—2007; chmn. Levi Strauss & Co., 2008—. Bd. dirs. Levi Strauss & Co., 1998-, Shorenstein Co., L.P., Stanislaus Food Products, Gardonjim Farms, The Friends of Calif. Crew, Fed. Res. Bank San Francisco, 2004-, dep. chmn., 2006- Mem. Bay Area Coun. Mem. Internat. Dairy Foods Assn. (bd. dirs.). Office: Levi Strauss & Co 1155 Battery St San Francisco CA 94111

ROGERS, THOMAS SYDNEY, communications company executive; b. New Rochelle, NY, Aug. 19, 1954; s. Sydney Michael Rogers Jr. and Alice Steinhardt; m. Sylvia Texon, Oct. 9, 1983; children: Robert, Jessica, Jason. BA, Wesleyan U., 1975; JD, Columbia U., 1979. Bar: N.Y. 1980, U.S. Dist. Ct. (so. and ea. dists.) N.Y. 1980, U.S. Ct. Appeals (D.C. cir.) 1981. Legis. aide to Congressman Richard Ottinger U.S. Ho. Reps., Washington, 1975-76, sr. counsel subcom. telecommunications, 1981-86; assoc. Lord, Day & Lord, NYC, 1979-81; v.p. policy planning and bus. devel. Nat. Broadcasting Co., Inc., NYC, 1987-88; pres. NBC Cable, 1988-89, NBC Cable & Bus. Devel., 1989-99; exec. v.p. NBC, NYC, 1992-99; pres., CEO internat. coun. NATAS, 1994—97, chmn., 1998—99; vice chmn. NBC Internet, NYC, 1999; chmn., CEO Primedia, Inc., NYC, 1999—2003; chmn. TRget Media, NYC, 2003—; sr. oper. exec., media and entertainment exec. Censerus Capital, 2004—05; vice chmn. Tivo, Inc., Alviso, Calif., 2003—05, pres., CEO, 2005—; chmn. Teleglobe, Inc., 2004—06. Named one of Outstanding Young Men in Am., 1985. Mem. N.Y. State Bar Assn., Internat. Radio and TV Soc. Office: TiVo Inc 2160 Gold St PO Box 2160 Alviso CA 95002

ROHDE, JAMES VINCENT, software systems company executive; b. O'Neill, Nebr., Jan. 25, 1939; s. Ambrose Vincent and Loretta Cecillia Rohde; children: Maria, Sonja, Daniele, Olga. B of Comml. Sci., Seattle U., 1962. Chmn. bd. dirs., pres. Applied Telephone Tech., Oakland, Calif., 1974; v.p. sales and mktg. Automation Electronics Corp., Oakland, 1975-82; founder, pres., CEO, chmn. Am. Telecorp, Inc., Redwood City, Calif., 1982-99; founder, vice-chmn., bd. dirs. Ceon Corp., Redwood City, 1999—2008. Chmn. exec. com., chmn. emeritus Pres.'s Coun. Heritage Coll., Toppenish, Wash., 1985—; chmn. bd. dirs. Calif. chpt. Coun. Growing Cos., 1990—93; founder, CEO Greenpony Inc., Novato, Calif., 2009—; co-founder & CEO Birth Buddies, Inc., 2009—. Bd. dirs. Ind. Colls. No. Calif., 1991—93. With aux. USCG, 2005—. Republican. Roman Catholic. Personal E-mail: jvrohde@aol.com.

ROHDE, KURT, composer, music educator, musician; life ptnr. Tim Allen. BA, Peabody Inst., Johns Hopkins U.; diploma in viola and composition, Curtis Inst. Music, Phila.; MA, SUNY Stony Brook. Asst. prof. composition and theory U. Calif. Davis, 2006—, co-dir. Empyrean Emsemble; co-founder, artistic dir. Left Coast Chamber Ensemble, San Francisco. Composer: SLAM!, Oculus for String Orch., 1996, Music for String Quartet, 1997 (First prize, Lydian String Quartet Composition Contest, 1998), Concerto for Violin, Viola and Orch., 1998, Six Character Pieces for Viola and Piano, 2000, Three Fantasy Pieces for Viola, Cello and Double Bass, 2000, Five Pieces for Orch., 2001, Play Things, 2002, Strong Motion, 2002, Equinox, 2002, Double Trouble, 2002, Under the Influence, 2003, Plain and Simple, 2005, Bitter Harvest, 2005, Seeing Things, 2006, Endless, 2007, Gravities, 2008, F(o)UR, 2008. Recipient Hinrichsen award, AAAL, 2001, Berlin Prize, Am. Acad. in Berlin, 2002, Elliott Carter Rome Prize, Am. Acad. in Rome, 2008; fellow Guggenheim Found., 1999—2000; Commn. award, Barlow Endowment for Music Composition, 1999, 2003, Hanson Inst. Am. Music, 2001, Nat. Endowment Arts, 2003, Libr. Congress Koussevitsky Found., Harvard U. Fromm Found., Charles Ives fellowship, AAAL, 2005. Office: UC Davis Dept Music 220 Music Bldg One Shields Ave Davis CA 95616 E-mail: kefohde@ucdavis.edu, kurtrohde@dslextreme.com.

ROHLFING, FREDERICK WILLIAM, lawyer, retired judge, political scientist; b. Honolulu, Nov. 2, 1928; s. Romayne Raymond and Kathryn (Coe) R.; m. Joan Halford, July 15, 1952 (div. Sept. 1982); children: Frederick W., Karl A., Brad (dec.); m. Patricia Ann Santos, Aug. 23, 1983. BA, Yale U., 1950; JD, George Washington U., 1955. Bar: Hawaii 1955, Am. Samoa 1978. Assoc. Moore, Torkildson & Rice, Honolulu, 1955-60; ptnr. Rohlfing, Nakamura & Low, Honolulu, 1963-68, Hughes, Steiner & Rohlfing, Honolulu, 1968-71, Rohlfing, Smith & Coates, Honolulu, 1981-84; pvt. practice Honolulu, 1960-63, 71-81, Maui County, Hawaii, 1988—; dep. corp. counsel County of Maui, Wailuku, Hawaii, 1984-87, corp. counsel, 1987-88; land and legal counsel Maui Open Space Trust, 1992-97, also bd. dirs. Polit. cons., 1996, 98, 2002; magistrate judge U.S. Dist. Ct. Hawaii, 1991-96. Active Hawaii Ho. Reps., 1959-65, 80-84, Hawaii State Senate, 1966-75; US alt. rep. So. Pacific Commn., Noumea, New Caledonia, 1975-77, 1982-84; mem. adv. coun. State Reapportionment Commn., Maui, Hawaii, 2001, mem. salary commn. Maui (Hawaii) County, 2005-08, Statewide Health Coordinating Coun., 2008-; hon. chmn. Maui coms. George W. Bush for Pres., 2000, 2004, Maui coord., John McCain for pres., 2008. Mem. Hawaii Bar Assn., Maui Country Club, Naval Intelligence Profls. Avocations: golf, swimming. Home: 2807 Kekaulike Ave Kula HI 96790

ROHRABACHER, DANA T., United States Representative from California; b. Coronado, Calif., June 21, 1947; s. Donald and Doris Rohrabacher; m. Rhonda Carmony, Aug. 1997; 3 children. Student, LA Harbor Coll.; BA in Hist., Long Beach State Coll., 1969; MA in Am. Studies, U. So. Calif., 1976. Reporter City News Svc./Radio News West, LA; editl. writer Orange County Register, 1979-80; asst. press. sec. Reagan/Bush Com., 1980; speechwriter, spl. asst. to Pres. Reagan White House, Washington, 1981-88; mem. US Congress from 46th Calif. dist., Washington, 1988—, mem. fgn. affairs com., internat. rels. com., sci. & tech. com. US del Young Polit. Leaders Conf., Russia; disting. lectr. Internat. Terrorism Conf., Paris, 1985. Recipient Disting. Alumnus award, LA Harbor Coll., 1987. Republican. Baptist. Avocations: surfing, white water rafting. Office: US House Reps 2300 Rayburn House Office Bldg Washington DC 20515-0546 Office Phone: 202-225-2415.

ROHRER, SUSAN EARLEY, film producer, director, scriptwriter; b. Richmond, Va., Mar. 24; d. Charles Marion Jr. and Gloria Jean (Ripley) Earley; m. Mark Brooks Rohrer. BA in Art cum laude, James Madison U. Prodr., dir., co-story writer (tv shows) Never Say Goodbye, 1988 (Emmy award, Humanitas Prize finalist), Terrible Things My Mother Told Me, 1988 (Emmy nomination, Gold award Nat. Ednl. Film Festival); prodr., dir. (TV movies) For Jenny With Love (TV Movie award), Mother's Day, 1989 (3 Image award nominations), prodr., dir., writer (TV show) The Emancipation of Lizzie Stern, 1991 (Angel award, Bronze award Nat. Ednl. Film Festival, Emmy nomination, Monitor award finalist, TV Movie award), If I Die Before I Wake, 1993 (Emmy nomination, Humanitas Prize finalist, Cine Golden Eagle, TV Movie award); dir. (TV show) Sweet Valley High, 1996; dir. TV pilot Dojo Kids, 1996; prodr., dir., co-writer About Sarah, TV movie, 1998 (award of excellence Film Adv. Bd., Best of Festival award Breckenridge Film Festival, The Christopher award, Angel award, N.Y. Festivals finalist); writer (TV movies) Another Pretty Face, 2002, Book of Days, 2003. Recipient Resolution of Recognition Virginia Beach City Coun., 1988. Mem. ATAS, SAG, Writers Guild Am., Dirs. Guild Am. Office: Josh Schechter IPG 9200 Sunset Blvd Ste 820 Los Angeles CA 90069

ROIZEN, MICHAEL F., anesthesiologist, medical educator, writer; b. NY, Jan. 7, 1946; m. Nancy J. Roizen; children: Jeffery, Jennifer. AB in Chemistry with honors, Williams Coll., Williamstown, Mass., 1967; MD, U. Calif. Sch. Medicine, San Francisco, 1971. Cert. Am. Bd. Internal Medicine, Am. Bd. Anesthesiology. Intern, medicine Beth Israel Hosp., Boston, 1971—72, resident, medicine, 1972—73; rsch. assoc. in pharmacology NIH, Bethesda, Md., 1973-75; resident, anesthesia U. Calif., San Francisco, 1975—77, asst. prof., 1977-81, assoc. prof., 1981-85; prof. internal medicine U. Chgo., 1985, prof. and chair dept. anesthesia and critical care, 1985; prof., anesthesiology SUNY Upstate Med. Ctr. and Univ., Syracuse, NY; chmn., divsn. anesthiology, critical care medicine and comprehensive pain mgmt. Cleve. Clinic. Panel mem. FDA, past chmn. adv. com.; co-founder RealAge,Inc., chmn. scientific adv. bd; invited lectr. in field. Author: Essence of Anesthesia Practice, 1997, RealAge: Are You As Young as You Can Be?, 1999(#1 NY Times bestseller, Best Wellness Book, Books for a Better Life awards, 1999); co-author (with John La Puma) The RealAge Diet: Make Yourself Younger with What You Eat (NY Times bestseller), RealAge Way, The RealAge Makeover, 2004, (with Tracy Hafen) The RealAge Workout, (with Mehmet C. Oz) YOU: The Owner's Manual: An Insider's Guide to the Body That Will Make You Healthier and Younger (#1 Publishers Weekly bestseller, NY Times bestseller), 2005, YOU: The Smart Patient: An Insider's Handbook for Getting the Best Treatment, 2006, YOU: On a Diet-The Owner's Manual for Waist Management, 2006, YOU: Staying Young: The Owner's Manual for Extending Your Warranty, 2007(Publishers Weekly bestseller), YOU: Being Beautiful: The Owner's Manual to Inner and Outer Beauty, 2008, (compact disc) YOU: On a Walk, 2007, YOU: Breathing Easy: Meditation and Breathing Techniques to Help You Relax, Refresh and Revitalize, 2008; former editor of several med. jours.; reviewer numerous anesthesia and med. jours.; contbr. of articles to peer-reviewed jours., chpt. to books, med. books; guest appearances on Oprah Winfrey Show, Today Show, 20/20, CBN, CNN, CBS, Good Morning America, Montel Williams Show and PBS; featured in magazines including Fortune, Glamourm Cosmopolitan, Good Housekeeping, Ladies' Home Journal, Reader's Digest, Men's Health and Prevention. Named an Best Doctors in Am., 1989—. Mem. Am. Bd. Anesthesiology (assoc.), Am. Bd. Internal Medicine (assoc.), Am. Soc. Anesthesiologists, Soc. of Cardiovascular Anesthesiologists (pres. 1995-97), U.S. Squash Racquets Assn., Alpha Omega Alpha, Phi Beta Kappa. 12 US patents and several fgn. patents. Office: RealAge Inc 10675 Sorrento Valley Rd Ste 200 San Diego CA 92121 also: RealAge Inc 555 Fifth Ave 14th Fl New York NY 10017 Office Phone: 858-812-3800. Office Fax: 858-812-3801. Business E-Mail: roizenm@upstate.edu. E-mail: mrzz@airway2.bsd.uchicago.edu.

ROKKE, ERVIN JEROME, military officer, academic administrator; b. Warren, Minn., Dec. 12, 1939; s. Edwin K. and Joan (Ivery) R.; m. Pamela Mae Patterson, June 6, 1962; children: Lisa Mae, Eric Scott. Student, St. Olaf Coll., 1957-58; BS, USAF Acad., 1962; MPA, Harvard U., 1964, PhD in Polit. Sci., 1970. Commd. 2d lt. USAF, 1962, advanced through grades to lt. gen., 1994; intelligence officer Pacific Air Forces, Hawaii, Japan, 1965-68; assoc. prof. dept. polit. sci. USAF Acad., Colorado Springs, Colo., 1968-73, permanent prof., 1976-80, dean of faculty, 1982-86, chmn. characterand leadership devel., 2007—; plans officer NATO Hdqrs., Brussels, 1973-76; air attache Am. Embassy, London, 1980-82, def. attache Moscow, 1987-89; sr. staff Nat. Security Agy., Ft. Meade, Md., 1989-91; dir. intelligence Hdqrs. European Command, Stuttgart, Fed. Republic Germany, 1991-93; assigned to Hdqs. USAF, Washington, 1993-94; pres. Nat. Def. U., Ft. Lesley J. McNair, DC, 1994-97, Moravian Coll. and Moravian Theol. Sem., 1997—2006; pres. emeritus Moravian Coll., Bethlehem, Pa., 2007—. Cons. Dept. State, 1969. Editor: American Defense Policy, 1973. Chair character and leadership devel. USAF Acad., Colo. Decorated Def. Disting. Svc. medal, Disting. Svc. medal, Def. Superior Svc. medal, Legion of Merit. Mem. Coun. on Fgn. Rels., Falcon Found. Lutheran. Avocations: reading, skiing, squash. Home: 810 Dolan Dr Monument CO 80132-2219 Office Phone: 719-333-4510. Personal E-mail: chaos01@comcast.net.

ROKNALDIN, FARZAM, mechanical engineer, educator; b. Tehran, Iran, Jan. 17, 1965; arrived in US, 1991, naturalized, 2003; s. Hassan Roknaldin and Alye Tohidi; m. Maria Valera; 1 child, Aleyeh. PhD in Mechanical Engring., Stanford U., Calif., 2001. Sr. thermal analyst Applied Thermal Technologies, Santa Clara, Calif., 2000—. Faculty San Jose State U., Calif., 2002—, graduate degree advisor, 2004—. Mem.: ASME (assoc. Recognition award 2001), Planetary Soc. (assoc.), Pars FC Soccer Club (co-founder). Democrat. Achievements include development of over 150 different thermal designs for electronic devices ranging from routers, switches, servers, high-definition mediums to notebook computers and hand-held devices. Avocations: soccer, snowboarding, guitar, cars. Office: Applied Thermal Technologies 3255 Kifer Road Santa Clara CA 95051 Office Fax: 408-522-8729; Home Fax: 408-522-8729. Business E-Mail: roknaldi@athermal.com.

ROLL, JOHN MCCARTHY, judge; s. Paul Herbert and Esther Marie (McCarthy) Roll; m. Maureen O'Connor; 3 children. BA, U. Ariz., 1969, JD, 1972; LLM, U. Va., 1990. Bar: Ariz. 1972, U.S. Dist. Ct. Ariz. 1974, U.S. Ct. Appeals (9th cir.) 1980, U.S. Supreme Ct. 1977. Asst. pros. atty. City of Tucson, 1973; dep. county atty. Pima County (Ariz.), 1973-80; asst. U.S. Atty. U.S. Attys. Office, Tucson, 1980-87; judge Ariz. Ct. Appeals, 1987-91, U.S. Dist. Ct. Ariz., 1991—2006, chief judge, 2006—. Mem. criminal justice mental health standards project ABA, 1980—83, mem. com. model jury instrns. 9th cir., 1994—2001, chair com. model jury instrns. 9th circ., 1998—2001; mem. panel workshop criminal law CEELI Program, Moscow, 1997; mem. U.S. Jud. Conf. Adv. Com. Criminal Rules, 1997—2003. Contbr. Merit Selection: the Arizona Experience, Ariz. State Law Jour., 1991, The Rules Have Changed: Amendments ot the Rules of Civil procedure, Defense Law Jour., 1994, Ninth Cir. Judges' Benchbook on Pretrial Proceedings, 1998, 00, 02, 04. Recipient Disting. Faculty award Nat. Coll. Dist. Attys., U. Houston, 1979, Outstanding Alumnus award U. Ariz. Coll. Law, 1992. Mem. Fed. Judges Assn., KC (adv. coun. 1991). Republican. Office: US Dist Ct 405 W Congress Tucson AZ 85701

ROLLANS, JAMES O., service company executive; b. Glendale, Calif., July 7, 1942; s. Henry Leo and Geraldine Ada (Berg) R.; children: Jodie Helene, Thomas James, Daniel Joseph. BS, Calif. State U., Northridge, 1967. Vice pres., dir. Chase Manhattan Bank, 1976-78; v.p. corp. communications Dart Industries, Los Angeles, 1978-80; v.p. bus. analysis and investor relations Dart & Kraft, Chgo., 1980-82; sr. v.p., CFO Fluor Corp., Irvine, Calif., 1982-99, also bd. dirs., 1998—; pres., group exec. Bus. Svcs., Aliso Viego, Calif., 1999. Bd. dirs. Cupertino Elec.; mem. Flowserve Corp. Bd. dirs. Irvine Med. Ctr. Episcopalian. Avocations: boating, skiing, fishing, hunting. Home: 8152 Scholarship Irvine CA 92612-5698

ROLLE, ANDREW, historian, writer; b. Providence, Apr. 12, 1922; m. Frances Squires, Dec. 1945 (div.); children: John Warren, Alexander Frederick, Julia Elisabeth.; m. Myra Moss, Nov. 1983. BA, Occidental Coll., 1943; MA, UCLA, 1949, PhD, 1953; grad., So. Calif. Psychoanalytic Inst., 1976. Am. vice consul, Genoa, Italy, 1945-48; editorial asso. Pacific Hist. Rev., 1952-53; from asst. prof. to Cleland prof. history Occidental Coll., 1953-88; rsch. scholar Huntington Libr., San Marino, Calif., 1988—. Author: Riviera Path, 1946, An American in California, 1956, reprinted, 1982, The Road to Virginia City, 1960, reprinted, 1989, Lincoln: A Contemporary Portrait, 1961, (with Allan Nevins, Irving Stone) California: A History, 1963, rev. edits., 1963, 69, 78, 87, 98, 2002, 08, Occidental College: The First Seventy-Five Years, 1963, The Lost Cause: Confederate Exiles in Mexico, 1965, 1992, The Golden State, 1967, rev. edit., 1978, 1989, 2000, California, A Student Guide, 1965, Los Angeles, A Student Guide, 1965; Editor: A Century of Dishonor (Helen Hunt Jackson), 1964, Life in California (Alfred Robinson), 1971, Voyage to California (Jour. of Lucy Herrick), 1998; The Immigrant Upraised, 1968, The American Italians: Their History and Culture, 1972, Gli Emigrati Vittoriosi, 1973, reprinted, 2003; (with George Knoles others) Essays and Assays, 1973, (with others) Studies in Italian American Social History, 1975, (with others) Los Angeles: The Biography of a City, 1976, 2d edit., 1991; (with Allan Weinstein and others) Crisis in America, 1977, The Italian Americans: Troubled Roots, 1980, 2d edit. 1985, Los Angeles: From Pueblo to Tomorrow's City, 1981, 2nd edit., 1995, Occidental College: A Centennial History, 1986, John Charles Frémont: Character as Destiny, 1991, Henry Mayo Newhall and His Times, 1992, Westward the Immigrants, 1999, The Victorious Immigrants, 2005. Served to 1st lt. M.I. AUS, 1943-45, 51-52. Decorated Cavaliere Ordine Merito Italy; recipient silver medal Italian Ministry Fgn. Affairs; Commonwealth award for nonfiction; Huntington Libr.-Rockefeller Found. fellow; resident scholar Rockefeller Found. Ctr., Bellagio, Italy. Fellow Calif. Hist. Soc.; mem. Phi Beta Kappa.

ROLLE, MYRA MOSS **See MOSS, MYRA**

ROLLO, F. DAVID, healthcare company executive, cardiologist; b. Endicott, NY, Apr. 15, 1939; s. Frank C. and Augustine L. (Dumont) R.; m. Linda Wood, June 1, 1991; children: Mindee, Alex. BA, Harpur Coll., 1959; MS, U. Miami, 1965; PhD, Johns Hopkins U., 1968; MD, Upstate Med. Ctr., Syracuse, NY, 1972. Diplomate Am. Bd. Nuc. Medicine. Asst. chief nuc. medicine svcs. VA Hosp., San Francisco, 1974-77, chief nuc. medicine Nashville, 1977-79; sr. v.p. med. affairs Humana Inc., Louisville, 1980-92; dir. nuc. medicine div. Vanderbilt U. Med. Ctr., Nashville, 1977-81; prof. radiology Vanderbilt U., Nashville, 1979—; pres., CEO Metricor Inc., Louisville, 1992-95; sr. v.p. med. affairs HCIA, Louisville, 1995-96; sr. v.p. med. affairs, med. dir. Raytel Med. Corp., San Mateo, Calif., 1996-99; chief med. officer ADAC Labs., Milpitas, Calif., 1999—2002; internat. chief med. officer Philips Med. Sys., 2003—. Mem. med. adv. com. IBT, Washington, 1984—; mem. pvt. sector liaison panel Inst. of Medicine, Washington, 1983—; bd. dirs. ADAC Labs. Editor: Nuclear Medicine Physics, Instruments and Agents, 1977; co-editor: Physical Basis of Medical Imaging, 1980, Digital Radiology: Focus on Clinical Utility, 1982, Nuclear Medicine Resonance Imaging, 1983; mem. editorial adv. bd. ECRI, 1981—. Pres. bd. dirs. Youth Performing Arts Coun., Louisville, 1984-85; bd. dirs. Louisville-Jefferson County Youth Orch., 1983-85; sr. v.p., exec. com. USA Internat. Harp Competition, 1992-, chmn., 1994-. Fellow Am. Coll. Cardiology, Am. Coll. Nuc. Physicians (profl. Am. Coll. Radiology com. 1982-84, chmn. 1984); mem. AMA, Soc. Nuc. Medicine (trustee 1979-83, 84—, Cassen Meml. lectr. western region 1980, 84), Radiol. Soc. N.Am., NEMA (chmn. nuc. medicine sect., 2002-, bd. mem., 2002-, testimony medicine expert, 2003-), Am. Coll. Radiology, Ky. Sci. Tech. Coun. (exec. bd. 1987—), Advancement Med. Instrumentation (bd. dirs. 1986—), Louisville C. of C. (chmn. MIC com. 1987—). Avocations: racquetball, squash, golf. Home: 15735 Peach Hill Rd Saratoga CA 95070-6447

ROLSTON, HOLMES, III, theology studies educator, philosopher; b. Staunton, Va., Nov. 19, 1932; s. Holmes and Mary Winifred (Long) R.; m. Jane Irving Wilson, June 1, 1956; children: Shonny Hunter, Giles Campbell. BS, Davidson Coll., 1953; BD, Union Theol. Sem., Richmond, Va., 1956; MA in Philosophy of Sci., U. Pitts., 1968; PhD in Theology, U. Edinburgh, Scotland, 1958. Ordained ministry Presbyn. Ch. (USA), 1956. Asst. prof. philosophy Colo. State U., Ft. Collins, 1968-71, assoc. prof., 1971-76, prof., 1976—. Vis. scholar Ctr. Study World Religions, Harvard U., 1974-75; ofcl. observer UN Conf. on Environ. and Devel., Rio de Janiero, 1992; vis. prof. bioethics Yale U., 2005-06. Author: Religious Inquiry: Participation and Detachment, 1985, Philosophy Gone Wild, 1986, Science and Religion: A Critical Survey, 1987, new edit., 2006, Environmental Ethics, 1988, Conserving Natural Value, 1994, Genes, Genesis and God, 1999, Biography: Saving Creation, Christopher J. Preston, 2009; assoc. editor Environ. Ethics, 1979—; mem. editl. bd. Zygon: Jour. of Religion and Sci.; contbr. chpts. to books, articles to profl. jours. Recipient Univ. Disting. Prof., 1992; Disting. Lectr., Chinese Acad. of Social Scis., 1991, Disting. Lectr., Nobel Conf. XXVII, Gifford Lectr., U. Edinburgh, 1997; featured in Fifty Key Thinkers on the Environment, 2001, Templeton Prize in Religion, 2003, Gregor Mendel medal, Villanova Univ., 2005 Mem. AAAS, Am. Acad. Religion, Am. Philos. Assn., Internat. Soc. Environ. Ethics (pres. 1989-94), Phi Beta Kappa. Avocation: bryology. Home: 1712 Concord Dr Fort Collins CO 80526-1602 Office: Colo State U Dept Philosophy Fort Collins CO 80523-0001 Home Phone: 970-484-5883; Office Phone: 970-491-6315. Business E-Mail: rolston@lamar.colostate.edu.

ROMAN, STAN G., lawyer; b. Athens, Ga., Dec. 31, 1954; s. Costic and Marilyn (Gracey) R.; m. Elizabeth Ann Whelan, Sept. 18, 1982; 3 children. BA, U. N.C., 1976; JD with honors, U. Tex., 1979. Bar: Calif. 1979, U.S. Dist. Ct. (no., so., ctrl. and ea.) Calif. 1979, U.S. Ct. Appeals (9th cir.) 1979. Congl. intern Honorable John Buchanan, Washington, 1977; summer assoc. Bradley, Arant, Rose & White, Birmingham, Ala., 1978; assoc. Bronson, Bronson & McKinnon, San Francisco, 1979-85, ptnr., 1985-99, Krieg, Keller, Sloan, Reilley & Roman, San Francisco, 1999—. Judge pro tem, arbitrator, mediator Calif. Superior Ct., San Francisco, 1989—. Mem. ABA, Assn. Bus. Trial Lawyers, Def. Rsch. Inst., Calif. Bar Assn., San Francisco Bar Assn. San Francisco Com. Urban Affairs, Phi Beta Kappa, Phi Eta Sigma. Avocations: running, golf, skiing, swimming. E-mail: sroman@kksrr.com.

ROMANOFF, ANDREW, state legislator; b. Washington, Aug. 24, 1966; son of Marvin Romanoff & Gayle Caplan; State repr, District 9, Colorado, 2000-2002, member, Criminal Justice, Health, Environ, Welfare & Institurions Committees, formerly; policy advisor, Ken Gordon & Governor Roy Romer, formerly; Colorado State Representative, District 6, 2003-, vice chairman, Exec Committee of Legislature Coun and Legislature Coun Committees, currently, Colorado House Representative; speaker, currently, Colorado House Representative.Adj professor, Red Rocks Community Col, 97-; senior associate, Greenberg Baron Simon & Miller, formerly, consultant, Great Outdoors Colorado & Western Slope Head Start, currently; president, Washington St Community Center & Washington Park East Neighborhood Association, formerly, director, Center Women's Employment & Education & Colorado Common Cause, formerly. Democrat. Mailing: 200 E Colfax Room 305 Denver CO 80203 Office Phone: 303-866-2967. E-mail: romanoff@coloradohouse.org.

ROMANOV, VOLODYMYR ALEXEEVICH, computer science educator, researcher, computer science educator, researcher; b. Kamynino, Kursk, Russia, Jan. 23, 1960; s. Alexey Filippovich and Olga Sergeevna Romanov; m. Svitlana Chystova, Oct. 16, 1981; children: Olga Volodymyrivna, Volodymyr Volodymyrovych. MD, Nat. U., Kharkov, Ukraine, 1983, PhD, 1987. Cert. computer scis. and nuc. physics. Rschr. Nuc. Phys. Lab., Kharkiv, Ukraine, 1983-88; prof. State Tech. Univ. Agr., Kharkiv, 1988—2000, head Info. Tech. Ctr., 1996—2000; prof. Newton Coll., Montreal, Canada, 2000—05; sr. rsch. assoc. 3D Digital Corp., Newtown, Conn., 2005—06; rsch. assoc. Concordia U., Montreal, 2006—07; sr. rsch. scientist, project mgr. Phys. Optics Corp., Torrance, Calif., 2007—. Vice-head Coun. Young Rschrs., Kharkiv, 1984-91; editor Regional TV, Kharkiv, 1985-87 Author: (with S. Troubnikov) Nuclear Forces, 1992, (with I. Furman) Programmed Microcontrollers, 2000; contbr. articles to profl. jours. Mem. Can. Info. Processing Soc. Russian Orthodox. Avocations: russian literature, history, music. Office: 20600 Gramercy Pl Bldg 100 Torrance CA 90501-1821 Office Phone: 310-320-3088. Personal E-mail: volodymyr_romanov@yahoo.com. Business E-Mail: vromanov@poc.com.

ROMANOWSKI, BILL (WILLIAM THOMAS ROMANOWSKI), nutrition company executive, retired professional football player, actor; b. Vernon, Conn., Apr. 2, 1966; m. Julie Romanowski; 2 children. BA, Boston Coll. Linebacker San Francisco 49ers, 1988—93, Phila. Eagles, 1994—95, Denver Broncos, 1996—2001, Oakland Raiders, 2002—03; founder, pres., CEO Nutrition 53, 2006—. Author: (autobiography) Romo, 2005; actor: The Longest Yard, 2005, Shooting Gallery, 2005, The Benchwarmers, 2006, Wieners, 2008, Get Smart, 2008, Bedtime Stories, 2008. Named to Am. Football Conf. Pro Bowl Team, NFL, 1996, 1998. Achievements include member of the Super Bowl Championship winning San Francisco 49ers, 1989, 1990; Denver Broncos, 1998, 1999. Office: Nutrition 53 3706 Mt Diablo Blvd Ste 200 Lafayette CA 94549*

ROMAR, LORENZO, men's college basketball coach; b. Compton, Calif. m. Leona Romar; children: Terra, Tavia, Taylor. A. Cerritos CC, Calif., 1978; attended, U. Wash., Seattle, 1978—80; B in Criminal Justice, U. Cin., 1992. Guard Golden State Warriors, 1981—84, Milw. Bucks, 1984, Detroit Pistons, 1984—85; player, coach Athletes in Action, 1984—92; asst. coach UCLA Bruins, 1992—96; head basketball coach Pepperdine U. Waves, Malibu, Calif., 1996—99, St. Louis U. Billikens, Mo., 1999—2002, U. Wash. Huskies, 2002—. Asst. coach, USA under-22 nat. team World Championships, Melbourne, Australia, 1997; asst. coach, Team USA Pan Am. Games, 2003; head coach, USA under-18 nat. team FIBA Americas Championship, 2006. Named Coach of Yr., PAC-10 Conf., 2005, 2009. Office: Dept Intercollegiate Athletics Univ Wash Box 354070 Graves Bldg Seattle WA 98195*

ROMER, CHRIS, state legislator; b. Denver, 1959; m. Laurie Romer; children: Rachel, Paige, Grace. BA, Stanford U., Calif. Pres. KIPP Schools; mem. Dist. 32 Colo. State Senate, Denver, 2007—. Founder, past pres. Colo. I Have a Dream Found.; former chair Colo. Children's Campaign; co-founder Great Edn. Colo.; vol. supt. New Am. Sch.; youth coach, girls soccer & lacrosse. Democrat. Office: Colo State Capitol 200 E Colfax Denver CO 80203 Office Phone: 303-866-4852. Business E-Mail: chris.romer.senate@state.co.us.*

ROMER, PAUL MICHAEL, economics professor; b. Denver, Nov. 7, 1955; s. Roy R. and Beatrice A. (Miller) R.; m. Virginia K. Langmuir, Feb. 28, 1980; children: Geoffrey M., Amy J. BA in Math., U. Chgo., 1977, PhD in Econs., 1983. Asst. prof. economics U. Rochester, NY, 1982-88; prof. economics U. Chgo., 1988-90; fellow Ctr. for Advanced Study in Behavioral Sciences, Stanford, Calif., 1989-90; prof. economics U. Calif., Berkeley, 1990—; prof. Stanford U. Grad. Sch. Bus., 1996—; founder Aplia, Inc., 2000—; sr. fellow Hoover Instn.; Ralph Landau sr. fellow Stanford Inst. for Econ. Policy Rsch. (SIEPR). Recipient Disting. Teaching award, Stanford U., 1999, Horst Claus Rectenwald prize in Economics, 2002; named one of America's 25 Most Influential People, TIME mag., 1997. Fellow Econometric Soc.; mem. Am. Econs. Assn., Nat. Bur. Econ. Rsch., Am. Acad. Arts & Sciences Office: Stanford Institute for Economic Policy Research (SIEPR) Landau Economic Bldg 579 Serra Mall @ Galvez St Stanford CA 94305 Office Phone: 650-725-1874. Office Fax: 650-723-8611.*

ROMERO, GLORIA, state legislator; c Soledad Romero Ursua. Attended, Calif. State U., Long Beach, Barstow Cmty. Coll.; PhD, U. Calif., Riverside. Chairwoman, Los Angeles Charter Reform Comn, 97; California State Assemblywoman, District 49, 1999-2001, Majority Whip,1999-2001; California State Senator, District 24, 2001-, majority leader, currently, member, Transportation, Health, Housing & Community Develop, Labor & Industrial Relations, Public Employees Retirement Syst Committee, currently, California State Senate.Chairwoman, Hispanic advisor coun, Los Angeles Police Comn, formerly, cofound, Women's advisor coun; domestic violence task force, City Los Angeles, formerly; teach, California col system, 18 years; professor psychology, California State Univ, Los Angeles, formerly. Auth, The Prevalence and Circumstances of Child Sexual Abuse Among Latina Women, 99. Honored Faculty Award, Assoc Student Govt; Community Serv Award, Comn Femenil, Mexican-Am Los Angeles Co Bar Association & San Gabriel Valley League United Latin-Am Citizens; Community Award, Labor Coun for Latin-Am Advancement Education; Incredible Women Making Hist Award, YWCA; Women Pioneer, Los Angeles City Coun; Legislator of Year Award, California State Student Association, 2000. America Civil Liberties Union; Nat Organization Women; Nat Women's Polit Caucus; California Faculty Association; AFL-CIO. Democrat. Office: State Capitol Rm 313 Sacramento CA 94248 Office Phone: 916-651-4024. Office Fax: 916-445-0845. Business E-Mail: Senator.Romero@sen.ca.gov.*

ROMERO, RICHARD M., state legislator; b. Oakland, July 21, 1944; divorced. BS in Edn., U. Albuquerque, 1967; MA in Edn. Adminstrn., N.Mex. State U., 1971. Ednl. adminstr.; mem. N. Mex. Senate, Dist. 12, Santa Fe, 1992—; mem. rules com.; vice chair ways and means com.; pres. N. Mex. Senate, Dist. 12, Santa Fe, 2002—. Mem. Metro bd. YMCA. With USAF, 1968-69. Democrat. Office: 907 Silver Ave SW Albuquerque NM 87102-3002

ROMERO, TONY, information technology executive; Mgr. tech. svc. Western Airlines; tech. support specialist Mitsubishi Motors No. Am., Cypress, Calif., 1982, chief info. officer, 2001—, and sr. v.p. info. tech., 2003—. Named one of the Premier 100 IT Leaders, Computerworld mag., 2004. Office: SVP & CIO Mitsubishi Motors No Am 6400 Katella Ave Cypress CA 90630-0064

ROMERO-RAINEY, REBECA, bank executive; d. Martin and Cheryl Romero; m. John Rainey. Degree, Wellesley Coll. Pres., CEO Centinal Bank Taos, N.Mex., 1999—, bd. dir., 1999—. Bd. admissions Wellesley Coll. V.p. Taos Chpt. Habitat for Humanity; sec., treas. Bridges Project Edn. Taos; mem. Leadership N.Mex.; treas. N.Mex. Cmty. Found.; bd. dir. Taos (N.Mex.) Feeds Taos; treas. bd. dirs. Rocky Mountain Youth Corps. Named One of 25 Women to Watch, U.S. Banker Mag., 2003. Mem.: Ind. Cmty. Bankers Assn. N.Mex. (bd. dir. 2003—).

ROMIJN, REBECCA, actress, model; b. Berkeley, Calif., Nov. 6, 1972; d. Jaap Romijn and Elizabeth Kuizenga; m. John Stamos, Sept. 19, 1998 (div. Mar. 1, 2005); m. Jerry O'Connell, July 14, 2007; children: Dolly Rebecca Rose, Charlie Tamara Tulip. Attended, U. Calif., Santa Cruz. Model Sports Illustrated, Christian Dior, Victoria's Secret, Biotherm, Clarins, Dillards, Escada, Furla, Got Milk?, J.Crew, La Senza, Liz Claiborne, Matrix Essentials, Maybelline, Pantene Pro V, Tommy Hilfiger, various others. Actor: (films) Dirty Work, 1998, X-Men, 2000, Rollerball, 2002, Femme Fatale, 2002, X2, 2003, The Punisher, 2004, Godsend, 2004, The Alibi, 2006, Man About Town, 2006, X-Men: The Last Stand, 2006; (TV films) Hefner: Unauthorized, 1999; (TV series) Just Shoot Me, 1999—2000, Pepper Dennis, 2006, Ugly Betty, 2007—, (TV appearances) Friends, 1997, Jack & Jill, 2000. Office: Bragman Nyman Cafarelli 8687 Melrose Ave West Hollywood CA 90069-5701

RONALD, PAMELA C., plant pathologist, educator; m. Ronald Adamchak. Diploma in French Lang. Studies, U. Strasbourg, France, 1981; BA in Biology, Reed Coll., Portland, Oreg., 1982; MA in Biology, Stanford U., Calif., 1984; MS in Plant Physiology, U. Uppsala, Sweden, 1985; PhD in Molecular and Physiol. Plant Biology, U. Calif., Berkeley, 1985. Rsch. asst. dept. biology Stanford U., Calif., 1983—84; Fulbright fellow Inst. Botany U. Uppsala, Sweden, 1984—85; postdoctoral fellow dept. plant breeding Cornell U., 1990—92; asst. prof. dept. plant pathology U. Calif., Davis, 1992—97, assoc. prof., 1997—2002, prof. plant pathology, 2002—. Founder, CEO Tellus Genetics, Davis, Calif., 1998—2000; Guggenheim fellow Lab. Molecular Biology of Plant-Microorganism Interactions Nat. Ctr. Sci. Rsch., Nat. Inst. Agronomic Rsch., Castanet-Tolosan, France, 2000; hon. scientist Nat. Inst. Agrl. Biotechnology, Rural Develop. Adminstrn., Republic of Korea, 2002—05; chair plant genomics prog. U. Calif., Davis, 2004—, faculty asst. to Provost, 2004—07; external adv. Zhejiang U. Agrl. Inst., 2005—; dir., grass genetics Joint Bioenergy Rsch. Inst., Emeryville; chair U. Calif. David Disting. Women in Sci. seminar series; founder Genetics Resources Recognition Fund, U. Calif., Davis, 1996. Contbr. articles to sci. jours., including Nature and Science; also featured in New York Times, Wall Street Journal, Le Monde and on Nat. Pub. Radio; mem. editl. bd.: Planta, 1997—2002, Plant Molecular Pathology, 2002—; mem. editl. bd. Plant Physiology; assoc. editor: Transgenic Rsch., 2003—, sr. editor: Molecular Plant Microbe Interactions, 2003—; co-author (with husband): Tomorrow's Table: Organic Farming, Genetic and the Future of Food, 2008 (voted one of the best books of 2008, Seed Mag.). Co-recipient Consultative Group on Internat. Agrl. Rsch. Sci. award, 2007, USDA Nat. Rsch. Initiative Discovery award for work on submergence tolerant rice, 2008; fellow Davis Humanities Inst., Japan Soc. for the Promotion of Sci.; Fulbright Fellow, 1984—85, Guggenheim Fellow, 2000. Mem.: AAAS, Internat. Soc. Molecular Plant-Microbe Interactions, Am. Soc. Plant Biologists (chair, pub. affairs com. 2003—06), Am. Phytopathological Soc. Achievements include with colleagues genetically engineering rice for resistance to diseases and flooding. Office: Genome and Biomedical Scis Facility U Calif Davis 451 Health Sciences Dr Davis CA 95616-8816 Office Phone: 530-752-1654. Fax: 530-754-6940. E-mail: pcronald@ucdavis.edu.*

RONEY, RAYMOND G., dean, educator, writer; b. Phila., July 26, 1941; s. Wallace and Rosezell (Harris) R.; m. Ruth Agnes Westgaph, May 2, 1970; 1 child, Andre. BA in Polit. Sci., Cen. State U., Wilberforce, Ohio, 1963; MLS, Pratt Inst., Bklyn., 1965. Head reference dept. Howard U., Washington, 1965-66; dir. libr. and info. svcs. Nat. League of Cities/U.S. Conf. Mayors, Washington, 1967-70; dir. libr. svcs. Washington Tech. Inst., 1970-78; deputy dir. learning resources U. D.C., 1978-84; dean instnl. svcs. El Camino Coll., Torrance, Calif., 1984—; pub. Libr. Mosaics Mag., Culver City, Calif., 1989—. Pres. Yenor, Inc., Culver City, Calif., 1989—. Author: (books) Introduction to AV for Technical Assistants, 1981, AV Tech. Primer, 1988. Pres. Shepard Park Citizens Assn., Washington, 1973-83; chmn. Friends of Libr., L.A. Southwest Coll., 1993—; bond com. El Camino Coll., 2003. Recipient Adminstrv. Excellence award INTELECOM, Pasadena, Calif., 1993, Outstanding Adminstr. of Yr. award Calif. Assn. Postsecondary Adminstrs., 1997. Mem. ALA, Coun. on Libr. Media Technology (officer, bd. dirs., Outstanding Leadership award 1994), Calif. Acad. and Rsch. Librs. (program chmn.), Learning Resources Assn. of Calif. C.C. (bd. dirs.). Avocations: music, reading, travel. Office: El Camino Coll 16007 Crenshaw Blvd Torrance CA 90506-0001 Home Phone: 310-410-1573; Office Phone: 310-645-4998. Business E-Mail: rroney@librarymosaics.com.

ROOD, DAVID S., linguistics educator; b. Albany, NY, Sept. 14, 1940; s. J. Henry and Pearl B. (Stanley) R.; m. Juliette A. Victor; 1 child, Jennifer. AB, Cornell U., 1963; MA, U. Calif., Berkeley, 1965; PhD, U. Calif., 1969. Instr. U. Colo., Boulder, 1967-69, asst. prof., 1969-77, assoc. prof., 1977-82, prof., 1982—; vis. prof. U. Köln, Germany, 1998-99. Author: Wichita Grammar, 1975, Siouan Languages Archive, 1982; (with others) Beginning Lakhota, 1976; editor Internat. Jour. of Am. Linguistics, 1981-2002, (with others) Linguistic Diversity and Language Theories, 2005; contbr. articles to profl. jours. Grantee, NSF, 1972—96, 2006—, NEH, 1972—96, Volkswagen Stiftung, 2000—05. Mem.: Tchrs. English to Speakers Other Langs., Soc. for Study Indigenous Langs. Am. (pres. 2004), Linguistic Soc. Am. Office: U Colo Dept Linguistics 295 UCB Boulder CO 80309-0295 Home Phone: 303-494-0558; Office Phone: 303-492-2747. Business E-Mail: rood@colorado.edu.

ROOKLIDGE, WILLIAM CHARLES, lawyer; b. Portland, Oreg., Aug. 10, 1957; s. Chester Herbert and Barbara Kathryn (Dodson) R.; m. Kathryn Elaine Roosa, Aug. 20, 1983; children: Elizabeth Jill, Matthew Joseph. BS, U. Portland, 1979; JD, Lewis & Clark, 1984; LLM, George Wash. U., 1985. Bar: Oreg. 1985, US Patent Office 1985, US Ct. Appeals (fed. cir.) 1985, Calif. 1988, US Ct. Appeals (9th cir.) 1988, US Supreme Ct. 1993. Engr. Tube Forgings Am., Inc., Portland, 1978-82; jud. clk. US Ct. Appeals (fed. cir.), Washington DC, 1985-87; assoc. Knobbe, Martens, Olson & Bear, Newport Beach, Calif., 1987-89, ptnr., 1990-94; dir. Howard, Rice, Nemerovski, Canady, Falk & Rabkin, Newport Beach, Calif., 1995—2000. Contbr. articles to profl. jours. Recipient Joseph Rossman Meml. award Patent & Trademark Office Soc., 1988, Gerald Rose Meml. award John Marshall Law Sch., 1993. Mem. ABA (sect. intellectual property law, com. chair 1992-96), Am. Intellectual Property Law Assn. (com. chair 1988-93, dir. 1995-98, pres. 2005, Robert C. Watson award 1987), Orange County Patent Law Assn. (bd. dirs. 1990-93, pres. 1994). Republican. Presbyterian. Office: Howrey LLP 4 Park Plz Ste 1700 Irvine CA 92614-8557 Office Phone: 949-759-3904. Office Fax: 949-721-6910. Business E-Mail: rooklidgew@howrey.com.

ROOKS, CHARLES S., foundation administrator; b. Whiteville, NC, June 29, 1937; BA in English, Wake Forest Coll., 1959; Rockefeller Brothers fellow, Harvard U., 1959-60; MA in Polit. Sci., Duke U., 1964, PhD in Polit. Sci., 1968. Rsch. assoc. Voter Edn. Project, Atlanta, 1969-70, dir. tech. assistance programs, 1970-71, dep. dir., 1971-72; exec. dir. Southeastern Coun. of Founds., Atlanta, 1972-78; dir. mem. svcs. Coun. on Founds., Washington, 1979-80, v.p., 1981-82, acting CEO, 1981-82; exec. dir. Meyer Meml. Trust, Portland, Oreg., 1982—2002, Miller Found., 2007. Instr. polit. sci. Duke U., Durham, N.C., 1963, 65-67; asst. prof. of govt. Lake Forest Coll., Ill., 1967-69; asst. prof. polit. sci. Clark Coll., Atlanta, 1969-71; bd. dirs. Pacific Northwest Grantmakers Forum, Forum of Regional Assns. of Grantmakers; mem. adv. bd. Neighborhood Partnership Fund (Oreg. Cmty. Found.); mem., adv. bd. Giving in Oreg. Coun.; co-chair Northwest Giving Project; bd. mem. Oreg. Coll. Art and Craft; spl. advisor Oreg. Cultural Trust. Contbr. articles to profl. jours. Home: 2706 SW English Ct Portland OR 97201-1622 Personal E-mail: charlesrookspdx@hotmail.com.

ROOKS, JUDITH PENCE, nurse midwife, consultant; b. Spokane, Wash., Aug. 18, 1941; d. Lawrence Cyrus and Christine Atrice (Snow) Pence; m. Peter Geoffrey Bourne, Mar. 1972 (div.); m. Charles Stanley Rooks, Sept. 21, 1975; 1 child, Christopher Robert. BS, U. Wash., 1963; MS, Cath. U. Am., 1967; MPH, Johns Hopkins U., 1974. Cert. edpidemiology, nursing, nurse-midwifery, mediation. Staff nurse King County Harborview Hosp., Seattle, 1963—64, The Clin. Ctr., NIH, Bethesda, Md., 1965; asst. prof. nursing dept. San Jose (Calif.) State Coll., 1967-69; epidemiologist Ctrs. for Disease Control, Atlanta, 1970-78; asst. prof. dept. ob-gyn. Oreg. Health Sci. U., Portland, 1978-79; expert Office of the Surgeon Gen., Dept. HHS, Washington, 1979-80; project officer U.S. AID, Washington, 1980-82; prin. investigator Sch. Pub. Health Columbia U., NYC, 1988-89, assoc. Pacific Inst. for Women's Health, 1993-2001; cons. Portland, 1982—. Mem. tech. adv. com. Family Health Internat., Research Triangle Park, N.C., 1986-97; mem. midwifery adv. com. Frontier Nursing Svc., Hyden, Ky., 1997-2002; mem. com. Inst. of Medicine NAS, Washington, 1983-85; academic faculty cmty.-based nurse-midwifery edn. program Frontier Sch. Midwifery and Family Nursing, Hyden, Ky., 1993-95; dir. N.Y. Acad. Medicine/Maternity Ctr. Assn. evidence-based symposium on The Nature and Management of Labor Pain, 1999-01. Author: Midwifery and Childbirth in America, 1997; co-author: Nurse-Midwifery in America, 1986, Reproductive Risk in Maternity Care and Family Planning Services, 1992; mem. editl. bd. Birth, 1996—; editl. cons. Jour. Nurse Midwifery, 1992-2000, Jour. Midwifery and Women's Health, 2002--; contbr. articles to profl. jours. Mem bd. advisors World Affairs Coun. Oreg., Portland, 1987-90; bd. dirs. Planned Parenthood of the Columbia/Willamette, Portland, 1987-90; chm. Ga. Citizens for Hosp. Abortion, Atlanta, 1969-70; assoc. Pacific Coun. on Internat. Policy, 1995-97. Recipient nat. award Nat. Perintal Assn., 1999. Mem. APHA (chair com. on women's rights 1982-83, mem. governing coun. 1976-77, 79-82, Martha May Eliot award for svc. to mothers and children 1993, Hattie Hemschemeyer award for cont. outstanding contbns. to nurse-midwifery and maternal and child health care 1998), Am. Coll. Nurse-Midwives (life, pres. 1983-85). Avocations: gardening, walking, reading, travel, cooking. Home and Office: 2706 SW English Ct Portland OR 97201-1622 Office Phone: 503-243-2253. E-mail: jprooks1@comcast.net.

ROONEY, MARSHA, curator, museum staff member; BA in History & French, Albion Coll., Albion, Mich.; MA in History/Mus. Studies, SUNY Oneonta, Cooperstown Grad. Prog. Sr. curator of history Northwest Mus. Arts & Culture, Spokane, Wash. Mem.: Wash. Mus. Assn. (bd. dirs. 2002—, pres. 2007—08). Office: Northwest Mus Arts & Culture 2316 W 1st Ave Spokane WA 99201 also: Wash Mus Assn PO Box 10633 Yakima WA 98909 Office Phone: 509-363-5309. Office Fax: 509-363-5303. E-mail: marshar@northwestmuseum.org, contact@washingtonstatemuseums.org.

ROOP, OPHELIA GEORGIEV, library director; b. Kyustendil, Bulgaria; came to US, 1961; d. Boris Vangev and Raina Georgiev; m. Edward Donald Roop, May 8, 1973; 1 child, Zachary Andrei. BA in Russian and Slavic Studies, Ind. U., 1969, M Libr. and Info. Sci., 1982. Reference libr. arts divsn. Indpls.-Marion County Pub. Libr., 1970-81, asst. mgr. adult svcs., 1982-91; libr. dir. Herron Sch. Art

Ind.-Purdue U., Indpls., 1992-96; libr. dir. San Bernardino Pub. Libr., Calif., 1997—. Contbr. book revs. to profl. publs., chpt. to book, entries to Ency. of Indpls. Mem. ALA, Calif. Libr. Assn. (mgmt. svcs. sect. 1998—, pres.-elect, pres.). Avocations: skiing, travel, writing, reading, foreign films. Office: San Bernardino Pub Libr 555 W 6th St San Bernardino CA 92410-3094 Office Phone: 909-381-8215. E-mail: oroop@sbpl.org.

ROOS, ERIC EUGENE, plant physiologist; b. Charleroi, Pa., May 23, 1941; s. Carl F. and Isabelle (McPherson) R.; m. Lois Bonita Bruno, Aug. 24, 1964; children: Michael, Erin. BS, Waynesburg Coll., 1963; PhD, W.Va. U., 1967. Supr. plant physiologist, rsch. leader Nat. Seed Storage Lab, Agrl. Research Service of USDA, Ft. Collins, Colo., 1967—, now asst. area dir. Fellow Am. Soc. Agronomy, Am. Soc. Hort. Sci., Crop Sci. Soc. Am.; mem. Sigma Xi, Gamma Sigma Delta. Office: USDA AG Research Service 2150 Centre Ave Bldg D Fort Collins CO 80526-8119

ROOS, JOHN VICTOR, lawyer; b. San Francisco, Feb. 14, 1955; AB, Stanford U., 1977, JD, 1980. Bar: Calif. 1980. Ptnr. Wilson, Sonsini Goodrich & Rosati, San Francisco, 1988—, mng. dir. profl. services, CEO, 2005—, mem. exec. mgmt. com. & policy com. Mem.: Calif. Bar Assn., Order of the Coif. Office: Wilson Sonsini Goodrich & Rosati 650 Page Mill Rd Palo Alto CA 94304 Office Phone: 650-493-9300. Office Fax: 650-493-6811. E-mail: jroos@wsgr.com.

ROOSEVELT, MICHAEL A., lawyer; b. LA, Dec. 7, 1946; BA, Harvard U., 1969; JD, Columbia U., 1972. Bar: Calif. 1973. Shareholder Friedman, Olive, mcCabbin, Spalding, Bilter Roosevelt et al, San Franciso, 1996—. Mem. ABA. Office: Friedman McCubbin Spalding 425 California St Fl 22 San Francisco CA 94104-2102

ROOT, GEORGE LINCOLN, JR., lawyer; b. 1947; BA, Syracuse U.; JD cum laude, U. San Diego. Ptnr. Procopio, Cory, Hargreaves & Savitch LLP, San Diego, 2007—. Guest lectr. U. Calif., San Diego Nat. U.; adj. prof. San Diego State U. Mem. San Diego County Bar Assn. (chmn. mental health com. 1983, task force on children at risk 1995), Calif. Soc. Healthcare Attys., Healthcare Fin. Mgmt. Assn., Healthy San Diego (past vice-chmn. provider adv. com.). Office: Procopio Cory Hargreaves & Savitch LLP 530 B St Ste 2100 San Diego CA 92101-4469 Office Phone: 619-238-1900. Business E-Mail: jr@procopio.com.

ROOT, WAYNE ALLYN, entrepreneur, television producer, writer; b. Mt. Vernon, NY, July 20, 1961; s. David and Stella (Reis) R.; m. Victoria Payne, Sept. 9, 1986 (div. 1990); m. Debra Parks, Aug. 3, 1991; children: Dakota Skye, Hudson, Remington Reagan, Contessa Churchill. BA, Columbia U., 1983. Pres. Wayne A. Root & Assocs., Real Estate, White Plains, NY, 1983-86; account exec. Bixler Real Estate, Katonah, NY, 1986-88; owner Pure Profit Sport Analysis & Handicapping, White Plains, 1987-89; radio host NBC Source Radio Network, NYC, 1988; TV anchorman Fin. News Network, LA, 1989-91; author, pres. The Universal Frontier (renamed Power Principles), Las Vegas, Nev., 1991; pres., CEO WinningEDGE Internat., Las Vegas, Cool Hand ROOT Prodns., Las Vegas. Author: Root on Risk, 1989, Betting to Win on Sports, 1989, The Joy of Failure!: How to Turn Failure, Rejection, and Pain into Extraordinary Success, 1997, The Zen of Gambling: The Ultimate Guide to Risking It All and Winning at Life, 2004, Millionaire Republican, 2005, The King of Vegas' Guide to Gambling: How to Win Big at Poker, Casino Gambling & Life! The Zen of Gambling, 2006, The Conscience of a Libertarian: Empowering the Citizen Revolution with God, Guns, Gambling, & Tax Cuts!, 2009; contbg. sports editor: Robb Report Mag., 1989—91; creator, exec. prodr., host: (TV and radio series) Wayne Root's WinningEDGE, 2000—; (TV series) King of Vegas, 2006; prodr.: Extreme Ghost Adventures, 2008; (documentaries) Entebbe. US vice presdl. candidate Libertarian Party, 2008. Named to Las Vegas Walk of Stars, 2006. Libertarian. Avocations: tennis, running, football, weightlifting, skiing, horseback riding. Office: Winning Edge Internat 5052 S Jones Blvd Ste 100 Las Vegas NV 89118 Office Phone: 702-967-6000. Office Fax: 702-967-6002.*

ROPER, WILLIAM ALFORD, JR., Internet company executive; b. Birmingham, Ala., Mar. 14, 1946; BA in Math., U. Miss., 1968; grad., Southwestern Grad. Sch. So. Meth. U., 1974; grad. fin. mgmt. program, Stanford U., 1986. Owner, gen. mgr. real estate devel. and wholesale distbn. cos.; loan officer, br. mgr. Deposit Guaranty Nt. Bank, until 1981; various positions, including corp. v.p., treas. Bell & Howell Co., 1981-87; exec. v.p., CFO, Intelogic Trace, Inc., 1987-90; sr. v.p., CFO, Sci. Applications Internat. Corp., San Diego, 1990-2000, exec. v.p. strategic investments, 2000—07; lead independent dir. VeriSign, Inc., Mountain View, Calif., 2003—, pres., CEO, 2007—. Mem. adv. bd. Allendale Mut. Ins. Co., Johnston, R.I.; mng. dir. Carlisle Enterprises, LLC, La Jolla, Calif.; bd. dirs. Factory Mutual Ins. Co., Regents Bank, N.A., SkinMedica, Inc., Cush Automotive Group, San Diego, Network Solutions, Inc., Herndon, Va., Holiday Bowl, San Diego, San Diego Regional Econ. Develop. Corp. Chmn. bd. ACCION San Diego; bd. dirs. Alvarado Hosp. Med. Ctr., San Diego; vice chmn. bd. San Diego Conv. Ctr. Corp. Mem. CEO Roundtable, Calif. C. of C. (bd. dir.), Greater San Diego C. of C. (bd. dirs., exec. com., chmn. fin. com.). Office: VeriSign Inc 487 E Middlefield Rd Mountain View CA 94043

ROSE, AXL (WILLIAM BRUCE BAILEY, W. AXL ROSE), singer; b. Lafayette, Ind., Feb. 6, 1962; s. L. Stephen (stepfather) and Sharon Bailey; m. Erin Everly, 1991 (div. 1992). Lead singer Guns N' Roses, 1985—. Albums include Live Like A Suicide, 1986, Appetite For Destruction, 1987 (Am. Music award for Favorite Hard Rock Album, 1990), The Lies, the Sex, the Violence, 1988, GN'R Lies, 1989, Use Your Illusion I, 1991, Use Your Illusion II, 1991, The Spaghetti Incident?, 1993, Appetite for Destruction, 2001, Chinese Democracy, 2008; songs include Sweet Child O' Mine (Am. Music award for Favorite Rock Single, 1989, MTV Video Music award for Best Heavy Metal Video, 1989), November Rain. Co-recipient (with Guns N' Roses) Best New Artist award, MTV Video Music Awards, 1988, (with Guns N' Roses) Favorite Hard Rock Artist award, Am. Music Awards, 1990, 1992, (with Guns N' Roses) Video Vanguard award, MTV Video Music Awards, 1992, (with Guns N' Roses) World's Best-selling Hard Rock Artist of Yr. award, World Music Awards, 1993; named one of 100 Greatest Artists of Hard Rock (with Guns N' Roses), VH1, 2000. Office: care of David Geffen Co 9130 W Sunset Blvd West Hollywood CA 90069-3110

ROSE, CAROL MARGUERITE, law educator; b. Washington, Apr. 12, 1940; d. J. Hugh and Marie (Meenehan) R. BA, Antioch Coll., 1962; MA, U. Chgo., 1963, JD, 1977; PhD, Cornell U., 1970. Bar: Ill. 1977, Calif. 1978, D.C. 1978. Instr. history Ohio St. U., Columbus, 1969-73; assoc. dir. So. Govtl. Monitor Project, Atlanta, 1975-76; law clk. to judge U.S. Ct. Appeals (5th cir.), Austin, Tex., 1977-78; asst. prof. law Stanford U., 1978-80; acting prof. law U. Calif., Berkeley, 1980-82; prof. law Northwestern U., Chgo., 1982-88, Yale U., 1989—90, Fred A. Johnston prof. New Haven, 1990—94, Gordon Bradford Tweedy prof. of law and orgn., 1994—2005; emerita, 2005—06; Lohse prof. water and natural resource law U. Ariz., 2006—. Bd. editors Found. Press, Mineola, N.Y., 1986—. Mem. Am. Assn. Law Schs., Am. Acad. Arts and Scis., Order of Coif. Office: U Ariz Coll of Law PO Box 210176 Tucson AZ 85721-0176 Office Phone: 520-621-5544. E-mail: carol.rose@yale.edu.

ROSE, DAVE, men's college basketball coach; b. Houston; m. Cheryl Rose; 3 children. Attended, Dixie State Coll., St. George, Utah; B, U. Houston, 1983. Full-time mission The Church of Jesus Christ of Latter-day Saints, Manchester, England, 1977—79; head basketball coach Millard HS, 1983—86; asst. coach Pine View HS, 1986—87, Dixie State Coll. Rebels, 1987—90, head basketball coach, 1990—97; asst. coach Brigham Young U. Cougars, Utah, 1997—2005, head basketball coach, 2005—. Active Coaches vs. Cancer; hon. chmn. Children with Cancer Christmas Found.; youth group vol. coach. Recipient Game Pillar award, Nat. Assn. Basketball Coaches, 2008, Dale Rex Meml. award, 2008; named Dist. VIII Coach of Yr., US Basketball Writers Assn., 2006, Coach of Yr., Mountain West Conf., 2006, 2007, Citizen of Yr., St. George C. of C. Mem. Lds Church. Office: Brigham Young Univ Dept Athletics 2112 MC Provo UT 84602 Office Phone: 801-422-3612. Business E-Mail: dave_rose@byu.edu.*

ROSE, DEBRA FIELDS See FIELDS, DEBBI

ROSE, ERIC, physician, consultant; s. Israel and Susan Rose; m. Eleni Ledesma, 1997. BSc, Brown U., 1988; MD, Albert Einstein Coll. Medicine, 1993. Diplomate Am. Bd. Family Medicine. Physician U. Wash. Physicians, Seattle, 1997—2004; physician cons. IDX Sys. Corp., Seattle, 2004—05; product mgr. Practice Ptnr., Inc., Seattle, 2005—. Work group on functionality Cert. Commn. for Health Info. Tech., 2004—. Bd. dirs. Queen Anne Helpline, Seattle, 2005—. Fellow: Am. Acad. Family Physicians; mem.: Am. Med. Informatics Assn. (pub. policy com. 2004—). Avocations: homebrewing, cycling. Office: Practice Ptnr Inc 2401 4th Ave Ste 700 Seattle WA 98121

ROSE, I. NELSON, lawyer, educator; b. LA, May 23, 1950; s. Bernard and Helen Mae (Nelson) Rose. BA, UCLA, 1973; JD, Harvard U., 1979. Bar: Hawaii 79, U.S. Dist. Ct. Hawaii 79, Calif. 80, U.S. Supreme Ct. 91. Pvt. practice, Honolulu, 1979—82; asst. prof. law Whittier Coll., LA, 1982—85, assoc. prof., 1985—89, tenured prof. law, 1989—2007, disting. sr. prof., 2007—. Cons. legal gaming; vis. scholar Inst. for Study of Gambling and Comml. Gaming, U. Nev., Reno. Author: Gambling and the Law, 1986; author: (with Robert A. Loeb) Blackjack and the Law, 1998; co-author (with Robert M. Jarvis, J. Wesley Cochran, Ronald J. Rychlak): Gaming Law: Cases and Materials, 2003; co-author: (with Martin D. Owens) Internet Gaming Law, 2005, 2nd edit., 2009; contbr. articles profl. jour. and books. Founder, counsel Hawaii Lions Eye Bank, Honolulu; founder, v.p., counsel Calif. Coun. on Compulsive Gambling; mem. Calif. Gambling Policy Adv. Com., 2002—04. Mem.: ABA, Internat. Masters Gaming Law, Internat. Assn. Gaming Advisors., Hawaii Bar Assn., Calif. State Bar Assn. Democrat. Jewish. Home and Office: 17031 Encino Hills Dr Encino CA 91436-4009 Office Phone: 818-788-8509. Personal E-mail: rose@sprintmail.com. Business E-Mail: rose@gamblingandthelaw.com.

ROSE, IRWIN A. (ERNIE), biochemist, educator; b. Bklyn., July 16, 1926; s. Harry and Ella Greenwald Royze; m. Zelda Budenstein; 4 children. BS, U. Chgo., 1948, PhD in biochemistry, 1952. Researcher Fox Chase Cancer Ctr., Phila., 1963—95; ret., 1995; specialist, Dept. Physiology and Biophysics, Sch. Med. U. Calif., Irvine, Calif., 1997—. Contbr. articles to profl. jour. Served with USN, World War II. Co-recipient Nobel Prize in Chemistry, 2004. Mem.: NAS. Achievements include discovery of ubiquitin-mediated protein degradation. Office: U Calif Dept Physiology and Biophysics Coll Medicine Irvine CA 92697

ROSE, (ROBERT) KEVIN, Internet company executive, blogger; b. Calif., Feb. 21, 1977; Grad. in Computer Sci., U. Nev., Las Vegas. Tech. advisor Dept. Energy, Nev.; tech. prodn. asst. TechTV; co-founder Revision3 Corp., 2005, Megatechtronium, 2007; founder Digg.com, 2004, chief arch., 2004—. Contbr. (TV series) The Screen Savers, 2000—04, co-host, 2004—05, host (podcast) Diggnation, 2005—, blog writer: kevinrose.com, digg.com. Named a Maverick, Details mag., 2008; named one of Most Important People on the Web, PC World, 2007, Top 25 Web Celebs, Forbes mag., 2007. Avocation: rock climbing.

ROSE, MARGARETE ERIKA, pathologist; b. Esslingen, Germany, Feb. 12, 1945; came to U.S., 1967; d. Wilhelm Ernst and Lina (Schurr) Pfisterer; m. Arthur Caughey Rose, Feb. 3, 1967; children: Victoria Anne, Alexandra Julia, Frederica Isabella. MD, U. So. Calif., LA, 1972. Diplomate Am. Bd. Anatomic and Clin. Pathology. Pathologist St. Joseph Med. Ctr., Burbank, Calif., 1977-78, Glenview Pathology Med. Group, Culver City, Calif., 1979—. Dir. anatomic pathology Glenview Meml. Pathology, Culver City, 1988—; dir. Life Chem. Lab., Woodland Hills, Calif.; co-dir., lab. Holy Cross Med. Ctr., Mission Hills, Calif., 1994-95, chmn. dept. pathology, Brotman Med. Ctr., Culver City, Calif., 2002—; med. dir. Lab., City of Angels Med. Ctr., L.A., 2002—; bd. dirs. Women in Recovery, Inc. Mem. Because I Love You, L.A., 1994. Fellow Am. Soc. Pathology, Coll. Am. Pathology. Avocations: cross stitch, gardening, travel. Office: Brotman Med Ctr Dept Pathology 3828 Hughes Ave Culver City CA 90232-2716

ROSE, MARK ALLEN, humanities educator; b. NYC, Aug. 4, 1939; s. Sydney Aaron and Rose (Shapiro) R.; m. Ann (Bermingham); 1 son, Edward Gordon. AB (hon.), Princeton U., NJ, 1961; LittB, Merton Coll., Oxford, Eng., 1963; PhD, Harvard U., Cambridge, Mass., 1967. Instr. to assoc. prof. in English Yale U., 1967-74; prof. English U. Ill., 1974-77; prof. U. Calif., Santa Barbara, 1977—2008, emeritus prof., 2008—, chmn. dept. English, 1987-89; dir. U. Calif., Humanities Rsch. Inst., Santa Barbara, 1989-94, chmn. dept. English, 1997—2001, assoc. vice chancellor, 2002—06. Author: Heroic Love, 1968; (fiction) Golding's Tale, 1972; Shakespearean Design, 1972; Spenser's Art, 1975; Alien Encounters, 1981; Authors and Owners, 1993; editor: Twentieth Century Views of Science Fiction, 1976; Twentieth Century Interpretations of Antony and Cleopatra, 1977, (with Slusser and Guffey); Bridges to Science Fiction, 1980; Shakespeare's Early Tragedies, 1994; (CD-ROM) Norton Shakespeare Workshops. Woodrow Wilson Fellow, 1961; Henry Fellow, 1961-62; Dexter Fellow, 1966; Morse Fellow, 1970-71; NEH Fellow, 1979-80, 90-91. Mem. MLA, Renaissance Soc. Am., Shakespeare Soc. Am., Phi Beta Kappa. Office: U Calif English Dept Santa Barbara CA 93106 Business E-Mail: mrose@english.ucsb.edu.

ROSE, PETER J., delivery service executive; V.p. air divsn. The Harper Group, San Francisco, 1969-81; exec. v.p. Expeditors Internat. Wash. Inc., Seattle, 1981-88, pres., CEO, 1988—, chmn., 1996—. Office: Expeditors Internat Wash Inc 1015 3rd Ave Seattle WA 98104

ROSE, RAY, state legislator; m Donna Rose; children: Tina, one grandchild. Senior advisor, Jr Achievement, member Montrose Sheriff's Posse; Colorado State Representative, District 58, 2002-, member, Agriculture, Livestock, & Natural Resources and Education Committees, currently, Colorado House Representative.Cent office operation mgr-Southwestern Colorado, United States West/Qwest Communications, ret 2001; owner, Chief Exec Officer, Colorado Shooting Inst. Montrose Chamber of Commerce; NRA (benefactor member); Montrose Rod & Gun Club (life); Montrose Christian Church; Colorado Skeet Shooting Association; Colorado State Shooting Association. Republican. Mailing: State Capitol 200 E Colfax Rm 271 Denver CO 80203 Office Phone: 303-866-2955. E-mail: ray.rose.house@state.co.us.

ROSE, ROBERT EDGAR, retired state supreme court justice; b. Orange, NJ, Oct. 7, 1939; BA, Juniata Coll., Huntingdon, Pa., 1961; LL.B., NYU, 1964. Bar: Nev. 1965. Dist. atty. Washoe County, 1971-75; lt. gov. State of Nev., 1975-79; judge Nev. Dist. Ct., 8th Jud. Dist., Las Vegas, 1986-88; justice Nev. Supreme Ct., Carson City, 1989—2006, chief justice, 1993-94, 1999—2000, 2006, sr. justice, 2007—. Office Phone: 775-684-1540.

ROSE, SCOTT A., lawyer; b. Flint, Mich., Feb. 10, 1953; BS with distinction, Ariz. State U., 1975, JD cum laude, 1979. Bar: Ariz. 1979. Chmn. bd. The Cavanagh Law Firm, Phoenix, Ariz. Articles editor Ariz. State Law Jour., 1978-79. Ariz. Govt. Affairs chmn. Internat. Coun. Shopping Ctrs. Mem. ABA, State Bar Ariz., Maricopa County Bar Assn., Downtown Phoenix Rotary Club 100 (bd. dirs.). Office: The Cavanagh Law Firm 1850 N Central Ave Ste 2400 Phoenix AZ 85004

ROSEANNE, (ROSEANNE BARR), actress, comedienne, television producer, writer; b. Salt Lake City, Nov. 3, 1952; d. Jerry and Helen Barr; m. Bill Pentland, 1974 (div. 1989); children: Jessica, Jennifer, Brandi, Buck, Jake; m. Tom Arnold, 1990 (div. 1994); m. Ben Thomas, 1994. Former window dresser, cocktail waitress; prin. Full Moon & High Tide Prodns., Inc. As comic, worked in bars, church coffeehouse, Denver; produced showcase for women performers Take Back the Mike, U. Boulder (Colo.); performer The Comedy Store, L.A.; showcased on TV special Funny, 1986, also The Tonight Show; featured in HBO-TV spl. On Location: The Roseanne Barr Show, 1987 (Am. comedy award Funniest Female Performer in TV spl., 1987, Ace award Funniest Female in Comedy, 1987, Ace award Best Comedy Spl. 1987); writer, dir., star of TV series Roseanne ABC, 1988-97 (U.S. Mag. 2nd Ann. Readers Poll Best Actress in Comedy Series, 1989, Golden Globe nomination Outstanding Lead Actress in Comedy Series 1988, Emmy award Outstanding Lead Actress in Comedy Series, 1993), The Real Roseanne Show, 2003; actress: (motion pictures) She-Devil, 1989, Look Who's Talking Too (voice), 1990, Freddy's Dead, 1991, Even Cowgirls Get the Blues, 1994, Blue in the Face, 1995, Unzipped, 1995, Meet Wally Sparks, 1997, Home on the Range (voice), 2004; TV movies: Backfield in Motion, The Woman Who Loved Elvis, 1993; appeared in TV spl. Sinatra: 80 Years My Way, 1995; exec. prodr. Saturday Night Spl., Fox-TV; author: Roseanne: My Life as a Woman, 1989, My Lives, 1994; (host) Roseanne Show, 1998-2000, I am Your Child, 1997 (TV), Get Bruce, 1999. Active various child advocate orgns. Recipient Peabody award, People's Choice award (4), Golden Globe award (2), Am. Comedy award, Humanitas award, Nickelodeon Kids Choice award, 1990, Eleanor Roosevelt award for Outstanding Am. Women, Emmy award, 1993.

ROSEDALE, PHILIP E., computer software company executive; b. San Diego, 1968; m. Yvette Rosedale. BS in Physics, U. Calif., San Diego. V.p., chief tech. officer RealNetworks; entrepreneur-in-residence Accel Partners, San Francisco, 1999; founder, CEO Linden Lab, San Francisco, 1999—2008, chmn., 1999—. Recipient Rave award for bus., WIRED mag., 2006; named one of The World's Most Influential People, TIME mag., 2007, 50 Who Matter Now, Business 2.0, 2007, 50 Most Important People on the Web, PC World, 2007. Achievements include development of Second Life computer game software. Office: Linden Lab 945 Battery St San Francisco CA 94111-1305

ROSELL, SHARON LYNN, physics and chemistry professor; b. Wichita, Kans., Jan. 6, 1948; d. John E. and Mildred C. (Binder) Rosell. BA, Loretto Heights Coll., 1970; postgrad., Marshall U., 1973; MS in Edn., Ind. U., 1977; MS, U. Wash., 1988. Cert. profl. educator, Wash. Assoc. instr. Ind. U., Bloomington, 1973-74; instr. Pierce Coll. (name formerly Ft. Steilacoom CC), Wash., 1976-79, 82, Olympic Coll., Bremerton, Wash., 1977-78; instr. physics, math. and chemistry Tacoma CC, Wash., 1979—89; instr. physics and chemistry Green River CC, Auburn, Wash., 1983—86; rschr. Nuc. Physics Lab., U. Wash., Seattle, 1986-88; asst. prof. physics Cen. Wash. U., Ellensburg, 1989—. Faculty senate Ctrl. Washington U., 1992-98. Senator St. Andrew's Ch., Ellensburg, Wash., 1992—98, alternate senator 2006-09, mem. parish coun., 1995-2000. Mem.: Soc. Physics Students (councilor zone 17 1998—2004, com. judging Nat. Outreach and Rsch. awards 2000—01, 2003—05, nat. nominating com. 2005—07), Pacific NW Assn. Coll. Physics (bd. dirs. 1997—99, 2001—, treas. 2002—, pres. 2009—), Internat. Union Pure and Applied Chemistry (affiliate), Am. Chem. Soc., Am. Assn. Physics Tchrs. (rep. com. on physics for 2-yr. colls. Wash. chpt. 1986—87, v.p. 1987—88, pres. 1988—89, v.p. 1994—95, pres. 1995—96, past pres. 1996—97), Am. Phys. Soc. Democrat. Roman Catholic. Avocations: leading scripture discussion groups, reading, poetry, needlecrafts. Home: 1100 N B St Apt 7 Ellensburg WA 98926-2570 Office: Ctrl Wash U Physics Dept Ellensburg WA 98926 Office Phone: 509-963-2757. Business E-Mail: rosells@cwu.edu.

ROSELLINI, ALBERT D., former governor; b. Tacoma, Wash., Jan. 21, 1910; s. John and Annunziata Pagni Rosellini; m. Ethel McNeill, 1937 (dec. 2002); children: John M., Janey, Sue, Lynn, Albert D. Jr. Student, U. Wash., U. Wash. Law Sch. Dep. prosecutor King County, Wash., 1935—41; mem. Wash. State Senate from 33rd dist.,

1939—57; spl. asst. atty. gen. State of Wash., 1941—46, gov., 1957—65; atty., polit. consultant Seattle. Del. Dem. Nat. Conv., 1968; chmn. US Olympic Com., Wash., Wash. State Transp. Commn.; bd. dirs. Wash. State Conv. Ctr. Mem.: Wash. Bar Assn., Sons of Italy, Italian Club, K. of C., Eagles, Kiwanis, Moose, Elks, Tau Kappa Epsilon, Phi Alpha Delta. Democrat. Roman Catholic. Office: 5930 6th Ave S Seattle WA 98108-3318 Office Phone: 206-763-7110. Office Fax: 206-762-9367. Personal E-mail: govadr@nwlink.com.

ROSEMAN, KIM, gallery director; b. 1970; BFA, Monmouth U., NJ. Owner Karin Newby Gallery and Sculpture Garden, Tubac chpt. founder Hearts and Hooves; mem. Tubac Mus. of Arts, Tubac Ctr. for Arts, Tucson Plein Air Painters Soc. Named one of 40 Under 40, Tucson Bus. Edge, 2006.

ROSEN, JUDAH BEN, computer scientist; b. Phila., May 5, 1922; s. Benjamin and Susan (Hurwich) R.; children: Susan Beth, Lynn Ruth. BSEE, Johns Hopkins U., 1943; PhD in Applied Math., Columbia U., 1952. Rschr. Manhattan (N.Y.) Project, 1944—46, Brookhaven (N.Y.) Nat. Lab., 1946—48; rsch. assoc. Princeton (N.J.) U., 1952-54; head applied math. dept. Shell Devel. Co., 1954-62; vis. prof. computer sci. dept. Stanford (Calif.) U., 1962-64; prof. dept. computer sci. and math. rsch. ctr. U. Wis., Madison, 1964-71; prof., head dept. computer sci. U. Minn., Mpls., 1971-92, fellow Supercomputer Inst., 1985—2007; sr. fellow Supercomputer Ctr., San Diego, 1993—2007; adj. rsch. prof. dept. computer sci. and engrin. U. Calif. San Diego, La Jolla, 1992—2007, bioinformatics grad. program faculty, 2001—07; ret. Fulbright prof. Technion, Israel, 1968-69, Davis vis. prof. 1980; invited lectr. Chinese Acad. Sci., Peking, 1980, Guilin, 1996, Samos, Greece, 2000; lectr., cons. Argonne (Ill.) Nat. Lab.; mem. Nat. Computer Sci. Bd. Author: Topics in Parallel Computing, 1992; editor: Nonlinear Programming, 1970, Supercomputers and Large-Scale Optimization, 1988; assoc. editor Global Optimization, 1990—, Annals of Ops. Rsch., 1984—; contbr. articles to profl. jours. and procs. Grantee, NSF, 1995—, ARPA/NIST, 1994—97. Mem. Assn. Computing Machinery, Soc. Indsl. and Applied Math., Math. Programming Soc., European Acad. Scis. Achievements include research in supercomputers and parallel algorithms for optimization, computation of molecular structure and drug design by energy minimization and homology models, algorithms for structured approximation in signal processing. Business E-Mail: jbenr55@yahoo.com.

ROSEN, LOUIS, physicist; b. NYC, June 10, 1918; s. Jacob and Rose (Lipionski) R.; m. Mary Terry, Sept. 4, 1941; 1 son, Terry Leon. BA, U. Ala., 1939, MS, 1941; PhD, Pa. State U., 1944; DSc (hon.), U. N.Mex., 1979, U. Colo., 1987. Instr. physics U. Ala., 1940-41, Pa. State U., 1943-44; mem. staff Los Alamos Sci. Lab., 1944-90, group leader nuclear plate lab., 1949-65, alt. div. leader exptl. physics div., 1962-65, dir. meson physics facility, 1965-85, div. leader medium energy physics div., 1965-86, sr. lab. fellow, 1985-90, sr. fellow emeritus, 1990—; Sesquicentennial hon. prof. U. Ala., 1981. Panel on future of nuclear sci., chmn. subpanel on accelerators NRC of NAS, 1976, panel on instnl. arrangements for orbiting space telescope, 1976; mem. U.S.A.-USSR Coordinating Com. on Fundamental Properties of Matter, 1971-90 Mem. editl. bd. Applications of Nuclear Physics; co-editor Climate Change and Energy Policy, 1992; contbr. articles to profl. jours. Mem. Los Alamos Town Planning Bd., 1962-64; mem. Gov.'s Com. on Tech. Excellence in N.Mex.; mem. N.Mex. Cancer Control Bd., 1976-80, v.p., 1979-81; co-chmn. Los Alamos Vols. for Stevenson, 1956; Dem. candidate for county commr., 1962; bd. dirs. Los Alamos Med. Ctr., 1977-83, chmn., 1983; bd. govs. Tel Aviv U., 1986; bd. dirs. Sombillo Nursing and Rehab. Facility, 2004. Recipient E.O. Lawrence award AEC, 1963, Golden Plate award Am. Acad. Achievement, 1964, N.Mex. Disting. Pub. Svc. award, 1978; named Citizen of Yr., N.Mex. Realtors Assn., 1973; Guggenheim fellow, 1959-60; alumni fellow Pa. State U., 1978; Louis Rosen prize established in his honor by bd. dirs. Meson Facility Users Group, 1984; Louis Rosen Auditorium dedicated, 1995; recipient Los Alamos Nat. Lab. medal, 2002. Fellow AAAS (coun. 1989), Am. Phys. Soc. (coun. 1975-78, chmn. panel on pub. affairs 1980, div. nuclear physics 1985, mem. subcom. on internat. sci. affairs 1988). Achievements include research in nuc. sci. and applications of particle accelerators. Home: 1170 41st St Los Alamos NM 87544-1913 Office: Los Alamos Sci Lab PO Box 1663 Los Alamos NM 87544-0600 Office Phone: 505-667-4361.

ROSEN, MOISHE, religious organization founder; b. Kansas City, Mo., Apr. 12, 1932; s. Ben and Rose (Baker) R.; m. Ceil Starr, Aug. 27, 1950; children: Lyn Rosen Bond, Ruth. Diploma, Northeastern Bible Coll., 1957; DD, Western Conservative Bapt. Sem., 1986. Ordained to ministry Bapt. Ch., 1957. Missionary Am. Bd. Missions to the Jews, NYC, 1956, minister in charge Beth Sar Shalom Los Angeles, 1957-67, dir. recruiting and tng. NYC, 1967-70; leader Jews for Jesus Movement, San Francisco, 1970-73, exec. dir., 1973-96, founder, 1973—. Speaker in field. Author: Sayings of Chairman Moishe, 1972, Jews for Jesus, 1974, Share the New Life with a Jew, 1976, Christ in the Passover, 1977, Y'shua, The Jewish Way to Say Jesus, 1982, Overture to Armageddon, 1991, The Universe is Broken: Who on Earth Can Fix It?, 1991, Demystifying Personal Evangelism, 1992, Witnessing to Jews, 1998. Trustee Western Conservative Bapt. Sem., Portland, Oreg., 1979-85, 86-91, Bibl. Internat. Coun. on Bibl. Inerrancy, Oakland, Calif., 1979-89; bd. dirs. Christian Advs. Serving Evangelism, 1987-91. Named Hero of the Faith, Conservative Bapt. Assn. Am., 1997. Office: Jews for Jesus 90 Miraloma Dr San Francisco CA 94127-1641 Office Phone: 415-661-2263. Personal E-mail: MityMo@aol.com, moishe.rosen@gmail.com.

ROSEN, PETER, health facility administrator, emergency physician, educator; b. Bklyn., Aug. 3, 1935; s. Isadore Theodore and Jessie Olga (Solomon) R.; m. Ann Helen Rosen, May 16, 1959; children: Henry, Monte, Curt, Ted. BA, U. Chgo., 1955; MD, Washington U., St. Louis, 1960. Diplomate Am. Bd. Surgery, Nat. Bd. Med. Examiners, Am. Bd. Emergency Medicine; cert. Advanced Cardiac Life Support Instr., Advanced Trauma Life Support Provider. Intern U. Chgo. Hosps. & Clinics, 1960-61; resident Highland County Hosp., Oakland, Calif., 1961-65; assoc. prof. divsn. emergency medicine U. Chgo. Hosps. & Clinics, 1971-73, prof. divsn. emergency medicine, 1973-77; dir. divsn. emergency medicine Denver City Health & Hosps., 1977-86, 87-89; asst. dir. dept. emergency medicine U. Calif., San Diego Med. Ctr., 1989—, dir. edn. dept. emergency medicine, 1989—, dir. emergency medicine residency program, 1991-2000, dir. emeritus, 2000—. Attending physician Hot Springs Meml. Hosp., Thermopolis, Wyo., Worland (Wyo.) County Hosp., Basin-Graybull Hosp., Basin, Wyo., 1968-71, U. Chgo. Hosps. & Clinics, 1971-77; dir. emergency medicine residency program, divsn. emergency medicine U. Chgo. Hosps. & Clinics, 1971-77; emergency medicine med. advisor State of Colo., 1977-85; dir. emergency medicine residency program Denver Gen. Hosp., St. Anthony Hosp. Systems, St. Joseph Hosp., 1977-88; clin. prof. divsn. emergency medicine Oreg. Health Scis. U., Portland, 1978-89; prof. sect. emergency medicine, dept. surgery U. Colo. Health Scis. Ctr., 1984-89; dep. mgr. med. affairs Denver Dept. Health & Hosps., 1986-87; med. dir. life flight air med. svc. U. Calif., San Diego Med. Ctr., 1989-91; mem. hosp. staff U. Calif., San Diego Med. Ctr., Tri-City Med. Ctr., Oceanside, Calif., 1989—; base hosp. physician, adj. prof. medicine & surgery U. Calif., San Diego Med. Ctr., 1989—; chair med. ethics com., mem. ethics consult team U. Calif., San Diego Med. Ctr., 1990—, mem. recruitment and admissions com., 1992—; lectr. in field; cons. in field. Author: (with others) Case Reports in Emergency Medicine: 1974-76, 1977, Encyclopedia Brittannica, 1978, 85, Principles and Practice of Emergency Medicine, 1978, 86, Protocols for Prehospital Emergency Care, 1980, 84, Cardiopulmonary Resuscitation, 1982, An Atlas of Emergency Medicine Procedures, 1984, Critical Decisions in Trauma, 1984, Emergency Pediatrics, 1984, 86, 90, Controversies in Trauma Management, 1985, Standardized Nursing Care Plans for Emergency Department, 1986, Emergency Medicine: Concepts and Clinical Practice, 1988, 92, The Clinical Practice of Emergency Medicine, 1991, Essentials of Emergency Medicine, 1991, Current Practice of Emergency Medicine, 1991, Care of the Surgical Patient, 1991, Diagnostic Radiology in Emergency Medicine, 1992, Pediatric Emergency Care Systems: Planning and Management, 1992, The Airway: Emergency Management, 1992; contbg. editor, editor abstracts sect. Jour. Am. Coll. Emergency Physicians, Annals of Emergency Medicine, 1976-83; mem. editorial bd. Topics in Emergency Medicine, 1979-82, ER Reports, 1981-83; consulting editor Emergindex Microindex, 1980—; editor in chief Jour. Emergency Medicine, 1983—; contbr. articles to profl. jours. Capt. USMC, 1965-68, lt. col. Res. inactive. Recipient AMA award, 1970, Am. Hosp. Assn. award, 1973. Fellow Am. Coll. Surgeons, Am. Burn Assn., Am. Coll. Emergency Physicians (chmn. edn. com. 1977-79, bd. dirs. Colo. chpt. 1977-80, pres. Colo. chpt. 1981-82, N.C. chpt. award 1976, Outstanding Contbns. and Leadership in Emergency Medicine award 1977, Silver Tongue Debater award 1980, John. D. Mills Outstanding Contbn. to Emergency Medicine award 1984); mem. Am. Trauma Soc. (founding), Soc. Acad. Emergency Medicine (Leadership award 1990), Alpha Omega Alpha Honor Med. Soc. (grad.), Coun. Emergency Medicine Dirs. Office: U Calif 200 W Arbor Dr San Diego CA 92103-1911

ROSEN, STEVEN O., lawyer; b. NYC, Jan. 11, 1949; s. Albert I. and Yvette (Sterenbuch) R. BS Aerospace Engring., SUNY, 1970; MS System and Control Engring., Case Western Reserve, 1975; JD, Lewis & Clark Coll., 1977. Bar: Ill. 1977, Oreg. 1978, Wash. 2004. Assoc. Lord, Bissell & Brook, Chgo., 1977-79, Miller, Nash, Wiener, Hager & Carlsen, Portland, Oreg., 1979-84, ptnr., 1984-97; pvt. practice Rosen Law Firm, 1997—. Disting. adj. prof. Lewis & Clark Law Sch., 1986. Mem. ABA (dir. divsns. sect. of litigation 1996-97, chmn. aviation litigation com. 1990-93), Am. Bd. Trial Advocates, Oreg. State Bar Assn. (exec. com. aviation sect. 1984-2001, chmn. 1994-95), Washington State Bar Assn. Avocations: skiing, bicycling. Address: The Rosen Law Firm 620 SW Main St Ste 702 Portland OR 97205-3030 Home: 1330 SW 3rd Ave Apt Portland OR 97201 Office Phone: 503-525-2525. Business E-Mail: rosen@rosenlawfirm.com.

ROSENBAUM, DIANE M., state legislator; b. Berkeley, Calif., Nov. 26, 1949; m. Jas Adams. Attended, Reed Coll. Legis. rep. Comm. Workers Am., 1989; consumer adv. US West Comm., 1993—97; pres. Oreg. State Indust Union Coun, 1994; chmn. Oreg. Commn. for Women, 1993—, Minimum Wage Coalition, 1995—97; Dem. precinct committeewoman, 1993—; exec. bd. Northwest Oreg. Labor Coun. & Oreg. AFL-CIO; mem. Dist. 14 Oreg. House of Reps., 1999—2002, mem. Dist. 42, 2003—08, former Spkr. Pro-Tem., former Dem. Whip; mem. Dist. 21 Oreg. State Senate, 2008—. Mem. ACLU, Coalition of Labor Union Women, Basic Rights Oreg. Democrat. Office: 900 Court St NE S-405 Salem OR 97301 Mailing: 1125 SE Madison St Ste 100B Portland OR 97214 Office Phone: 503-231-9970, 503-986-1721. Fax: 503-239-9670. Business E-Mail: sen.dianerosenbaum@state.or.us.

ROSENBAUM, LOIS OMENN, lawyer; b. Newark, Apr. 10, 1950; d. Edward and Ruth (Peretz) Omenn; m. Richard B. Rosenbaum, Apr. 4, 1971; children: Steven, Laura. AB, Wellesley Coll., 1971; JD, Stanford U., 1974. Bar: Calif. 1974, Oreg. 1977, D.C. 1974, U.S. Supreme Ct. 1990, Wash. 2001. Assoc. Fried, Frank, Harris, Shriver & Kampelman, Washington, 1974-75, Orrick, Herrington, Rowley & Sutcliffe, San Francisco, 1975-77, Stoel Rives LLP (formerly Stoel, Rives, Boley, Jones & Grey), Portland, Oreg., 1977-81, ptnr., 1981—. Lawyer rep. 9th Cir. Jud. Conf.; mem. U.S. Dist. Ct. Mediation Panel. Bd. dirs. Providence Med. Found., 1990-95, Robison Jewish Home, 1994-97, Jewish Family & Child Svc., 1997-2000, Am. Jewish Commn., 2000-04; past mem. Nat. Legal Com. Am. Jewish Com. Wellesley Coll. scholar, 1971. Mem. ABA, Multnomah County Bar Assn. (arbitration panel), Wellesley Club (pres. 1987-88). Office: Stoel Rives LLP 900 SW 5th Ave Ste 2600 Portland OR 97204-1268 Office Phone: 503-294-9293. Business E-Mail: lorosenbaum@stoel.com.

ROSENBERG, DONALD JAY, communications company executive, lawyer; b. Feb. 19, 1951; BS in Math., SUNY, Stony Brook, 1972; JD, St. John's U. Sch. Law, 1975. Bar: NY 1976. Atty. CHQ IBM Corp., 1976—80, lab counsel data systems divsn., 1981—83, sr. atty., 1983—85, sr. counsel, 1985—86, divsn. counsel DSD, 1986—92, assoc. gen. counsel CHQ/L, 1992—97, asst. gen. counsel, 1997—98, v.p., asst. gen. counsel litig., 1998—2006, sr. v.p., gen. counsel, 2006; sr. v.p., gen. counsel, sec. Apple Inc. (formerly Apple Computer Inc.), Cupertino, Calif., 2006—07; exec. v.p., gen. counsel, corp. sec. Qualcomm Inc., San Diego, 2007—. Adj. prof. law Pace U. Sch. Law, NY. Contbr. chapters to books; editor: St. John's Law Rev. Chmn. bd. visitors Pace U. Sch. Law. Office: Qualcomm Inc 5775 Morehouse Dr San Diego CA 92121

ROSENBERG, HOWARD ANTHONY, journalist; b. Kansas City, Mo., June 10, 1942; s. Sherman Rosenberg and Claire (Kanchuk) Rosenberg Magady; m. Carol Finkel; 1 child, Kirsten. Journalist Los Angeles Times, TV critic, columnist, 1988—. Recipient Editorial award Los Angeles Times, 1981; Headliner award Atlantic City Press Club, 1984; Pulitzer prize Columbia U., 1985. Office: Los Angeles Times Times Mirror Sq Los Angeles CA 90053

ROSENBERG, JONATHAN, information technology executive; BA in Econ. (hon.), Claremont McKenna Coll.; MBA, U. Chgo. Former mgr. eWorld product line Apple Computer Inc.; former dir. product mktg. Knight-Ridder Info. Svcs., Palo Alto, Calif.; former sr. v.p. online products and svcs. Excite@Home, Redwood City, Calif.; founder @Home Product Group, Redwood City; v.p. product mgmt. Google Inc., Mountain View, Calif., 2002—. Office: Google Inc 1600 Amphitheatre Pky Mountain View CA 94043 Office Phone: 650-623-4000. Office Fax: 650-618-1499.

ROSENBERG, PAMELA, opera director, conductor; b. LA, 1945; m. Wolf Rosenberg (dec. 1996); 2 children. Diploma, London Opera Ctr.; B, U. Calif. at Berkely, 1966; M in Russian hist., Ohio State U. Various positions Frankfurt Opera, 1974—87; dir. of ops. Deutscher Schauspielhaus, Hamburg, Germany, 1987—88; mgr., artistic affairs Netherlands Opera, 1988—90; co-gen. dir. Stuggart Opera, 1990—2000; gen. dir. San Francisco Opera, 2001—06, exec. adv., 2006. Office: San Francisco Opera 301 VanNess Ave San Francisco CA 94102

ROSENBERG, PHILIP, production designer; Prodn. designer: (films) The Anderson Tapes, 1971, Child's Play, 1972, The Gambler, 1974, Network, 1976, Next Stop, Greenwich Village, 1976, The Sentinel, 1977, (with Tony Walton) The Wiz, 1978 (Academy award nomination best art direction 1978), (with Tony Walton) All the Jazz, 1979 (Academy award best art direction 1979), Eyewitness, 1981, Soup for One, 1982, Lovesick, 1983, Daniel, 1983, Garbo Talks, 1984, The Manhattan Project, 1986, Moonstruck, 1987, Running on Empty, 1988, The January Man, 1989, Family Business, 1989, Q & A, 1990, Other People's Money, 1992, A Stranger Among Us, 1993, Guilty as Sin, 1993, The Pelican Brief, 1993, Night Falls on Manhattan, 1995, Critical Care, 1996, A Perfect Murder, 1997, The Hurricane, 1998.

ROSENBERG, RAND L., utilities executive; B, Whitman Coll., Walla Walla, Wash.; MBA, U. Chgo. Engagement mgr. Marakon Assocs.; head corp. devel. Pacific Telesis Group; ptnr., founder media and telecom. group Montgomery Securities; sr. positions Goldman Sachs & Co.; mng. dir., head global telecom. investment banking Salomon Bros.; exec. v.p., CFO Infospace; sr. v.p. corp. strategy and devel. PG&E Corp., San Francisco. Office: PG&E Corp One Market Spear Tower Ste 2400 San Francisco CA 94105-1126 Office Phone: 415-267-7070. Office Fax: 415-267-7268.

ROSENBERG, SAUL ALLEN, oncologist, educator; b. Cleve., Aug. 2, 1927; BS, Western Res. U., 1948, MD, 1953. Diplomate Am. Bd. Internal Medicine, Am. Bd. Oncology. Intern Univ. Hosps., Cleve., 1953—54; resident in internal medicine Peter Bent Brigham Hosp., Boston, 1954—61; research asst. toxicology AEC Med. Research Project, Western Res. U., 1948—53; asst. prof. medicine and radiology Stanford (Calif.) U., 1961—65, assoc. prof., 1965—79, chief divsn. oncology, 1965—93, prof., 1970—95; prof. emeritus, 1995—; Am. Cancer Soc. prof. Stanford (Calif.) U., 1983—89, assoc. dean, 1989—92. Chmn. bd. No. Calif. Cancer Program, 1974—80. Contbr. articles to profl. jours. Served to lt. M.C. USNR, 1954—56. Master: ACP; fellow: Am. Coll. Radiology (hon.); mem.: Western Assn. Physicians, Western Soc. Clin. Rsch., Radiation Rsch. Soc., Calif. Acad. Medicine, Assn. Am. Physicians, Am. Soc. Clin. Oncology (pres. 1982—83), Inst. Medicine NAS, Am. Assn. Cancer Rsch., Am. Soc. Therapeutic Radiotherapy Oncology (hon.). Office: Stanford U Sch Medicine Div Oncology 269 Campus Dr Stanford CA 94305

ROSENBLATT, GERD MATTHEW, chemist; b. Leipzig, Germany, July 6, 1933; came to U.S., 1935, naturalized, 1940; s. Edgar Fritz and Herta (Fisher) R.; m. Nancy Ann Kaltreider, June 29, 1957 (dec. Jan. 1982); children: Rachel, Paul; m. Susan Frances Barnett, Nov. 23, 1990. BA, Swarthmore Coll., 1955; PhD, Princeton U., 1960; Doctorate in Physics (hon.), Vrije U. Brussel, 1989. Chemist Lawrence Radiation Lab., U. Calif., 1960-63, cons., guest scientist, 1968-84; from asst. to assoc. prof. chemistry Pa. State U., University Park, 1963-70, prof., 1970-81; assoc. div. leader Los Alamos (N.Mex.) Nat. Lab., 1981-82, chemistry div. leader, 1982-85; dep. dir. Lawrence Berkeley (Calif.) Lab., 1985-89, sr. chemist, 1985—. Lectr. U. Calif., Berkeley, 1962-63; vis. prof. Vrije U. Brussels, 1973; vis. fellow Southampton U., 1980, King's Coll., Cambridge, 1980; adj. prof. chemistry U. N.Mex., 1981-85; cons. Aerospace Corp., 1979-85, Solar Energy Rsch. Inst., 1980-81, Xerox Corp., 1977-78, Hooker Chem. Co., 1976-78, Los Alamos Nat. Lab., 1978, 1996—; mem. external adv. com. Ctr. for Materials Sci., Los Alamos Nat. Lab. 1985-93; mem. rev. com. chemistry divsn., 1985; mem. rev. com. for chem. engring. divsn. Arbonne Univ. Assn., 1974-80, chmn., 1977-78; mem. rev. com. for chem. sci. Lawrence Berkeley Lab., 1984; chmn. rev. com. for chem. and materials sci. Lawrence Livermore Nat. Lab., 1984-91; mem. bd. advs. Combustion Rsch. Facility, Sandia Nat. Lab., 1985-89; mem. bd. advs. R&D divsn. Lockheed Missiles & Space Co., 1985-87; chmn. chemistry III panel Nat. Com., Com. on Date for Sci. and Tech., 1986-92, Internat. Union of Pure and Applied Chemistry, 1986-92; mem. basic scis. lab. program panel energy, 1985-89; sec. IUPAC Commn. on High Temperature and Solid State Chemistry, 1992-95, chmn., 1996-97. Editor: (jour.) Progress in Solid State Chemistry, 1977—; mem. editorial bd. High Temperature Sci., 1979—; contbr. articles to profl. jours. Du Pont grad. fellow, Princeton U., 1957-58; fellow Solvay Inst., 1973, U.K. Rsch. Coun., 1980. Fellow AAAS; mem. Am. Chem. Soc., Am. Phys. Soc., Electrochem. Soc., Nat. Rsch. Coun. (chmn. high temperature sci. and tech. com. 1977-79, 84-85, panel on exploration of materials sci. and tech. for nat. welfare 1986-88, sci. and tech. info. bd. 1990-91, chmn. numerical data adv. bd. 1986-90, solid state scis. com. 1988-91, chmn. western regional materials sci. and engring. meeting 1990, panel on long-term retention of selected sci. and tech. records of fed. govt. 1993). Achievements include first use of imaging detectors to obtain Raman compositional profiles and two-dimensional maps of chemical compositions, of rotational Raman scattering as a temperature and state-population probe in high temperature and combustion systems; elucidation of role of crystal defects and molecular structure in the evaporation of solid materials; first experimental determination of how molecular polarizability anisotrophies change with internuclear distance; estimation of thermodynamic properties and molecular structures for gaseous molecules. Home: 1177 Miller Ave Berkeley CA 94708-1754 Office: Lawrence Berkely Nat Lab Berkeley CA 94720-0001

ROSENBLATT, PAUL GERHARDT, judge; b. 1928; AB, U. Ariz., 1958, JD, 1963. Asst. atty. gen. State of Ariz., 1963-66; adminstrv. asst. to U.S. Rep., 1967-72; soel practice Prescott, Ariz., 1971-73; judge Yavapai County Superior Ct., Prescott, Ariz., 1973-84, U.S. Dist. Ct. Ariz., Phoenix, 1984—. Office: US Dist Ct Sandra Day O'Connor Ct Ste 621 401 W Washington St SPC 56 Phoenix AZ 85003-2156

ROSENBLATT, ROGER ALAN, physician, educator; b. Denver, Aug. 8, 1945; s. Alfred Dreyfus and Judith Ann (Ginsburg) R.; m. Fernne Schnitzer, Sept. 23, 1942; children: Eli Samuel, Benjamin. BA magna cum laude, Harvard U., 1967, MD cum laude, M in Pub. Health, 1971. Diplomate Am. Bd. Family Practice, Nat. Bd. Med. Examiners. Intern internal medicine U. Wash., Seattle, 1971-72, resident in family medicine, 1974; regional med. cons. region X Pub. Health Service, Seattle, 1974-76, dir. Nat. Health Services Corps., 1976-77; asst. prof. dept. family medicine U. Wash., Seattle, 1977-81, assoc. prof. dept. family medicine, 1981-85, prof., vice chmn. dept. family medicine, 1985—. Cons. U.S. Agy. for Internat. Devel., 1978, Western Interstate Commn. Higher Edn., 1981-82; vis. prof. medicine U. Auckland, New Zealand, 1983-84, Royal Australia Coll. Gen. Practitioners, Victoria, 1984, U. Calgary, 1988, U. Mo., 1988; vis. prof., Fogarty Ctr. Sr. Internat. fellow dept. ob-gyn. NIH, Coll. Medicine, U. Wales, Cardiff, 1992-93. Author: Rural Health Care, 1982; contbr. numerous articles on healthcare to profl. jours. Mem. Beyond War, Physicians for Social Responsiblity. Served with USPHS, 1974-77. Recipient Hanes Rsch. award North Am. Primary Care Rsch. Group, 1996. Mem. Am. Acad. Family Physicians (Hanes Rsch. award 1996), Am. Pub. Health Assn., Soc. Tchrs. Family Medicine (Hanes Rsch. award 1996), Nat. Rural Health Assn., Nat. Council Internat. Health, Nat. Acad. Sci. (elected inst. medicine 1987), Am. Rural Health Assn. (Research award 1985), Phi Beta Kappa. Office: U Wash Dept Family Medicine PO Box 354696 Seattle WA 98195-4696

ROSENBLUM, ELLEN F., judge; b. 1951; m. Richard Meeker. BS, Sociol., U. Oreg., 1971, JD, 1975. Bar: Oreg. 1975. Atty. priv. practice, Eugene, Oreg., 1975—80; asst. U.S. atty. Eugene, Oreg., 1981—89; circuit ct. judge Multnomah County Ct., Portland, Oreg., 1989—. Trustee Nat. Jud. Coll.; past chmn., Jud. Conduct Comm. Oreg. Jud. Conf.; chmn. Gov. Adv. Comm. Corrections, Oreg. Citizens Just. Conf., 2000. Chmn. Oreg. Citizen's Justice Conf. Recipient Pres. Public Svc. award, Oreg. State Bar, Andrea Swanner Redding Mentoring award, Lewis & Clark Law Sch., Honorary Alumna award, Merit. Svc. award, Univ. Oreg. Law Sch.; Alumni Fellow, Univ. Oreg. Coll. Arts & Sci., 1990. Fellow: Am. Bar Found. (life); mem.: U.S. Dist. Ct. Oreg. Hist. Soc. (past pres.), Owen M. Panner Am. Inn of Ct. (past pres.), Oreg. Women Lawyers (founding bd. mem. 1989, Justice Betty Roberts award 2000), ABA (bd. govs., sec. 2002—06, mem. Comm. Racial & Ethnic Diversity).

ROSENDAHL, BILL, councilman; BA in Polit. Sci. and Economics, St. Vincent Coll., Latrobe, Pa.; MSW, U. Pitts. Psychiatric social worker US Army, spl. asst. to commanding gen., Ft. Carson Colo.; assoc. in philanthropic work for John D. Rockefeller, III; chief ops. US trade and devel. program US Dept. State; disting. prof. Cal State Dominguez Hills. Chair Southern Calif. Regional Airport Authority; mem. Santa Monica Bay Restoration Commn., Exposition Light Rail Constrn. Authority; councilman, Dist. 11 LA City Coun., 2005—. Prodr., host (TV series) Local Talk, Week in Review, Beyond the Beltway. Chair Calif. Commn. on Tax Policy in the New Economy. Served in US Army, 1969—71. Recipient Cable Ace award, Diamond award, Freedom of Info. award, Pub. Svc. award, LA League of Women Voters, Beacon award for Cable's Free Air Time Project. Mem.: Cable and Telecom. Assn. (chmn.), The Am. Legion, Post 283, LA Press Club (pres.). Office: Dist Office 1645 Corinth Ave Los Angeles CA 90025 also: City Hall 200 N Spring St Rm 415 Los Angeles CA 90012 Office Phone: 213-473-7011, 310-575-8461. Office Fax: 213-476-6926, 310-575-8305. Business E-Mail: councilman.rosendahl@lacity.org.*

ROSENDIN, RAYMOND JOSEPH, electrical contracting company executive; b. San Jose, Calif., Feb. 14, 1929; s. Moses Louis and Bertha C. (Pinedo) R.; m. Jeanette Marie Bucher, June 30, 1951 (dec. Feb. 1967); children: Mark R., Patricia A., Debra M., Cynthia C., David R.; m. Nancy Ann Burke, July 6, 1984; children: Raymond M., Callie R., Blake W. Student engring., San Jose State U., 1947-48; BSE.E., Heald's Engring. Coll., San Francisco, 1950. V.p., CEO Rosendin Electric, Inc., San Jose, Calif., 1953-59, exec. v.p., CEO, 1969-75, pres., CEO, 1975-94, chmn., CEO, 1995-2000, chmn., 2000—, former dir. Former dir. Community Bank, San Jose Bd. fellows U. Santa Clara, Calif., 1966-93, pres. bd., 1969-72, bd. regents, 1972-82; bd. dirs. United Way, Santa Clara, 1970-74; O'Connor's Hosp., San Jose, 1979-85, Community Hosp., Los Gatos, Calif., 1968-74. Recipient Man of Yr. award Santa Clara Valley Youth Village, 1963, Optimist of Yr. award Optimist Club, San Jose, 1970 Mem. C. of C. Greater San Jose (past dir.), Nat. Elec. Contractors Assn. (past pres., gov., dir.) Clubs: St. Claire (San Jose). Republican. Roman Catholic. Avocation: boating. Office: Rosendin Electric Inc 880 Mabury Rd San Jose CA 95133-1021

ROSENFELD, ARTHUR H., physics professor, researcher; b. Birmingham, Ala., June 22, 1926; BS in Physics, Va. Poly. Inst., 1944; PhD in Physics, U. Chgo., 1954; DSc (hon.), U. Durham, Eng., 1983. Rsch. assoc. Inst. Nuclear Studies U. Chgo., 1954-55; rsch. assoc. Lawrence Berkeley Lab. U. Calif., Berkeley, 1955-57; asst. prof. to assoc. prof. U. Chgo., 1957-63; prof. physics U. Calif., Berkeley, 1963-94, dir. particle data group Lawrence Berkeley Lab., 1964-75, acting chmn. dept. computer sci., 1967-68, leader rsch. group A Lawrence Berkeley Lab., 1971-73, leader energy-efficient bldgs. rsch program Lawrence Berkeley Lab., 1975-83, vice chmn. energy and resources grad. program, 1986-94, dir. Ctr. Bldg. Sci. Lawrence Berkeley Lab., 1986-94, founder, acting dir. Calif. Inst. for Energy Efficiency, 1988-90, prof. emeritus, 1994—; sr. advisor to asst. sec. energy efficiency U.S. Dept. Energy, Washington, 1994-99; commr. Calif. Energy Commn., Sacramento, Calif., 2000—. Vis. prof. Coll. de France, Paris, 1978; co-founder Am. Coun. Energy-Efficient Econ., 1979, chmn., 1981-83, pres., 1984-90, bd. dirs., 1990-94; mem. steering com. advanced customer tech. test maximum energy efficiency Pacific Gas & Electric Co., 1989-98; mem. tech. adv. panel joint com. on energy regulation and environ. State of Calif., 1990-91; mem. Nat. Sci. and Tech. Coun., 1994—, civilian indsl. tech. com, 1994—, co-chmn. subcom. constrn. and bldg., 1994—. Author: (with E. Fermi and others) Nuclear Physics, 1949, Experimental Meson Spectroscopy, 1968, 3d edit., 1972, Supplying Energy Through Greater Efficiency: The Potential for Conservation in California's Residential Sector, 1983, A New Prosperity: The SERI Solar/Conservation Study, 1991, Scenarios of U.S. Carbon Reductions, Interlaboratory Working Group, 1997; contbr. articles, seminars to profl. jours., confs.; assoc. editor Jour. Computational Physics, 1964-73, Energy and Bldgs., 1979—, Energy, the Internat. Jour., 1985-91; editl. cons. Ency. of Applied Physics, 1988—. Mem. governing bd. Am. Inst. Physics, 1974-77; co-founder Am. Coun. for an Energy Efficient Economy, 1979, Ctr. for Energy and Climate Solution, Washington, DC; chmn. 1981-83, pres. 1984—, mem. adv. com. Calif. Legis. Joint Com. on Energy Regulation and Environ., 1990-91. Recipient Leo Szilard award for Physics in Pub. Interest, 1986, Sadi Carnot award for Energy Efficiency, US Dept. Energy, 1993, Star Energy Efficiency for outstanding contbn. in promoting energy efficiency Alliance to Save Energy, 1995, 2005 Enrico Fermi award, US Dept. Energy. Fellow Am. Physical Soc. (sec., treas. divsn. particles and fields 1967-71, Leo Szilard award for physics in the pub. interest 1986); mem. NAS (panel on policy implications of greenhouse warm 1990—), Fedn. Am. Sci. (coun. 1964-72, 77-81, 83-87, 94-98, 2004—), Am. Inst. Physics (mem. governing bd. 1974-77). Achievements include co-developement of Ultra-Violet Water Works to purify water in villages and slums, 1996; studied under Enrico Fermi at U. Chgo. Office: Calif Energy Commn 1516 9th St Sacramento CA 95814 Office Phone: 916-654-4930. Business E-Mail: AHRosenfeld@LBL.gov.

ROSENFELD, LAWRENCE J. (LARRY), lawyer; b. Bronx, NY, Aug. 25, 1950; BA magna cum laude, Queens Coll., CUNY, 1972; JD, Yale, 1975. Bar: Ariz. 1976, US Supreme Ct. 1981. Named one of Leading Lawyers, Ariz. Bus. Jour., 2006; named to Best Lawyers in Am., 2003—06, Chambers USA (Labor and Employment Law), 2005—06. Mem.: ABA, Maricopa County Bar Assn., Ariz. State Bar Assn. Office: Greenberg Traurig LLP Ste 700 2375 E Camelback Rd Phoenix AZ 85016-9000 Office Phone: 602-445-8502. Office Fax: 602-445-8100. Business E-Mail: rosenfeldl@gtlaw.com.

ROSENFELD, MICHAEL GEOFFREY, medical educator; BS, Johns Hopkins Univ.; MD, Univ. Rochester; postdoctoral study, NIH, Washington Univ., St. Louis, Univ. Calif., San Diego. Prof. dept. medicine U. Calif. Med. Sch., La Jolla, 1996—; and medical investigator Howard Hughes Medical Inst., San Diego, 1985—. Recipient Ernst Oppenheimer Young Investigator award, Conrad Koch award. Mem.: AAAS, NAS. Office: U Calif San Diego Sch Medicine Howard Hughes Med Inst MC 0648 9500 Gilman Dr Room 345 La Jolla CA 92093-0648

ROSENFELD, ROBERT A., lawyer; BA in Pub. Affairs with highest distinction, George Wash. U., 1971; BA with first class honors, Oxford U., 1973; JD cum laude, Harvard U., 1976. Bar: Calif., US Ct. Appeals (7th and 9th cirs.), US Ct. Fed. Claims, US Supreme Ct. Law clerk for Honorable Marvin Frankel, 1976—77, Honorable Warren E. Burger, US Supreme Ct., 1977—78; atty., shareholder Heller Ehrmaer LLP, San Francisco, 1979—. Bd. dirs. Calif. Pacific Med. Ctr. Rhodes scholar, 1973. Office: Heller Ehrman 333 Bush St San Francisco CA 94104 Office Phone: 415-772-6609. Office Fax: 415-772-6268. Business E-Mail: bob.rosenfeld@hellerehrman.com.

ROSENFIELD, LORNE KING, plastic surgeon; b. Winnipeg, Man., Can., Jan. 24, 1956; children: Lauren, Ian, Michael. BS in Medicine, U. Man., Winnipeg, 1976; MD, U. Man., 1980. Diplomate Am. Bd. Surgery, Am. Bd. Plastic Surgery. Resident in gen. surgery St. Mary's Hosp., San Francisco, 1985-87; intern. Mt. Zion, San Francisco; fellow in plastic surgery Baylor Coll. Medicine, 1987; tchr. U. Calif. San Francisco Med. Ctr., Stanford U. Hosps.; chmn. dept. plastic surgery Mills-Peninsula Hosp., Burlingame, Calif., 1995—, vice chmn. dept. surgery, 1997—. Past chmn. St. Mary's Hosp., San Francisco, 1992-95; expert cons. Med. Bd. Calif., 1997—. Mem. Burlingame/San Mateo C. of C. Fellow Am. Coll. Surgeons; mem. San Francisco Med. Soc. (mem. ethics com. bd. 1990-95), Rotary. Avocations: writing, photography, cooking. Office: Peninsula Plastic Surgery Inc 1750 El Camino Real Ste 405 Burlingame CA 94010-3217 Office Phone: 650-692-0467. Office Fax: 650-692-0110.

ROSENHEIM, DANIEL EDWARD, journalist, television news director; b. Chgo., Aug. 12, 1949; s. Edward W. and Margaret Morton (Keeney) R.; m. Christina J. Adachi, May 10, 1974 (div. 1979); m. Cindy Catherine Salans, June 20, 1980; children: Joseph Michael, James Salans, Nicholas Edward. BA, Wesleyan U., 1971. Factory worker, Pitts. and Chgo., 1972-77; reporter Sun-Jour., Lansing, Ill., 1977; bus./labor editor Hammond (Ind.) Times, 1977-80; bus. writer Chgo. Sun Times, 1980-82, spl. writer, 1982-84; bus. writer Chgo. Tribune, 1984-85; econs. editor San Francisco Chronicle, 1985-87, city editor, 1987-94, mng. editor, 1994-96; news dir. KRON-TV, San Francisco, 1996-2000, KPIX-TV, San Francisco, 2000—05, v.p. news, 2005—. Mem. adv. bd. News Lab, Project for Excellence in Journalism. Recipient Peabody award, 1997, James Batten award, 1997, RTNDA Regional award for Overall News Excellence, 2003. Mem. Soc. Profl. Journalists, Radio and TV News Dirs. Assn., San Francisco Tennis Club. Avocations: tennis, golf, book collecting. Office: KPIX-TV 855 Battery St San Francisco CA 94127 Office Phone: 415-765-8618. Personal E-mail: drosen7777@hotmail.com. Business E-Mail: rosenheim@kpix.cbs.com.

ROSENKILDE, CARL EDWARD, retired physicist; b. Yakima, Wash., Mar. 16, 1937; s. Elmer Edward and Doris Edith R.; m. Bernadine Doris Blumenstine, June 22, 1963 (div. Apr. 1991); children: Karen Louise, Paul Eric; m. Wendy Maureen Ellison, May 24, 1992. BS in Physics, Wash. State Coll., 1959; MS in Physics, U. Chgo., 1960, PhD in Physics, 1966. Fellow Argonne (Ill.) Nat. Lab., 1966-68; asst. prof. math. NYU, 1968-70; asst. prof. physics Kans. State U., Manhattan, 1970-76, assoc. prof., 1976-79; physicist Lawrence Livermore (Calif.) Nat. Lab., 1979-93, lab. assoc., 1994-95, participating guest, 1995-97; chief scientist C.R. Sci., 1993-98; ret. Cons. Lawrence Livermore Nat. Lab., 1974-79; astronomy instr. Los Positas Coll., 1997; part-time instr. physics Bellarmine Coll. Prep., 1999-2000; full-time instr., 2000-04, Tchg. Opportunities Ptnrs. Sci., 2004—. Contbr. articles to profl. jours. Woodrow Wilson fellow, 1959-60. Mem.: NSTA, Math. Assn. Am., Accoustical Soc. Am., Am. Geophys. Union, Soc. Indsl. and Applied Math., Am. Astron. Soc., Calif. Math. Coun. C.C., Am. Assn. Physics Tchrs., Am. Phys. Soc., Sigma Xi, Phi Eta Sigma, Phi Kappa Phi, Phi Beta Kappa. Republican. Presbyterian. Achievements include research in nonlinear wave propagation in complex media, theoretical physics, fluid dynamics. Personal E-mail: carlrosenkilde@comcast.net.

ROSENSWEIG, DANIEL L., video gaming company executive; b. 1961; BA in Polit. Sci., Hobart Coll., NY, 1983. Assoc. pub. PC Mag., 1992—94, v.p., pub. NYC, 1994—96; pres. Ziff-Davis Internet Pub. Group, 1996-97; pres., CEO ZDNet, Inc., NYC, 1997—2000; pres. CNET Networks, 2000—02; COO Yahoo!, Inc., Calif., 2002—06; operating principal Quadrangle Capital Partners, 2007—09; pres., CEO Guitar Hero unit Activision Blizzard Inc., Santa Monica, Calif., 2009—. Bd. dir. Adobe Systems Inc., San Jose, Calif., 2009—. Mem. adv. bd. DonorsChoose.org. Office: Activision Blizzard Inc 3100 Ocean Park Blvd Santa Monica CA 90405*

ROSENTHAL, ARNON, science association director; PhD, Hebrew U., Jerusalem. Staff scientist Genentech, Inc.; pres., chief tech. officer Rinat Neurosci. Corp., Palo Alto, Calif., 2001—. Mem. NIH Adv. Com. on Parkinson's Disease and Neuronal Repair. Contbr. articles to profl. jours. Achievements include patents for neuronal factors and receptors. Office: Rinat Neruoscience Corporation 230 E Grand Ave South San Francisco CA 94080-4811

ROSENTHAL, GABRIEL, lawyer; b. Pomona, Calif., May 13, 1972; BA magna cum laude, Claremont McKenna Coll., 1994; JD, Univ. Wash., 1997. Bar: Wash. 1997. Prin. atty., corp. law Hillis Clark Martin & Peterson, Seattle. Contbr. articles to numerous profl. jours. Named Wash. Rising Star, SuperLawyer Mag., 2006. Office: Hillis Clark Martin & Peterson Ste 500 1221 Second Ave Seattle WA 98101

ROSENTHAL, J. THOMAS, hospital administrator, medical educator; b. Richmond, 1949; BA, Johns Hopkins U.; MD, Duke U., 1974. Intern Johns Hopkins U., Balt., 1970; resident U. Va. Hosp., Charlottesville, Va., 1976, Lahey Clinic Found., Boston, 1980; exec. vice chmn. dept. surgery UCLA Sch. Medicine, 1991, prof. surgery/urology, 1993—, assoc. vice chancellor, 2003—; dir., vice provost UCLA Med. Group, 1996—; chief med. officer UCLA Health Sys., 1999—; vice provost UCLA Med. Group Affairs. Office: UCLA Urology/David Geffen Sch Medicine Box 951731 14-214R CHS Los Angeles CA 90095-1731 Office Phone: 310-825-4686.

ROSENTHAL, ROBERT, psychology professor; b. Giessen, Germany, Mar. 2, 1933; came to U.S., 1940, naturalized, 1946. s. Julius and Hermine (Kahn) R.; m. Mary Lu Clayton, Apr. 20, 1951; children: Roberta, David C., Virginia. AB, UCLA, 1953, PhD, 1956; PhD (hon.), U. Giessen, 2003. Diplomate clin. psychology Am. Bd. Examiners Profl. Psychology. Clin. psychology trainee Los Angeles Area VA, 1954-57; lectr. U. So. Calif., 1956-57; acting instr. UCLA, 1957; from asst. to assoc. prof., coordinator clin. tng. U. N.D., 1957-62; vis. assoc. prof. Ohio State U., 1960-61; lectr. Boston U., 1965-66; lectr. clin. psychology Harvard U., Cambridge, Mass., 1962-67, prof. social psychology, 1967-95, chmn. dept. psychology, 1992-95, Edgar Pierce prof. psychology, 1995-99, Edgar Pierce prof. emeritus, 1999—; disting. prof. U. Calif., Riverside, 1999—, prof. univ. sys. wide, 2008—. Author: Experimenter Effects in Behavioral Research, 1966, enlarged edit., 1976; (with Lenore Jacobson) Pygmalion in the Classroom, 1968, expanded edit., 1992, Meta-analytic Procedures for Social Research, 1984, rev. edit., 1991, Judgment Studies, 1987; (with others) New Directions in Psychology 4, 1970, Sensitivity to Nonverbal Communication: The Pons Test, 1979; (with Ralph L. Rosnow) The Volunteer Subject, 1975, Primer of Methods for the Behavioral Sciences, 1975, Essentials of Behavioral Research, 1984, 3d edit., 2008, Understanding Behavioral Science, 1984, Contrast Analysis, 1985, Beginning Behavioral Research, 1993, 6th edit., 2008, People Studying People: Artifact and Ethics in Behavioral Research, 1997, (with Ralph L. Rosnow and Donald B. Rubin) Contrasts and Effect Sizes in Behavioral Research: A Correlational Approach, 2000; (with Brian Mullen) BASIC Meta-analysis, 1985; editor: (with Ralph L. Rosnow) Artifact in Behavioral Research, 1969, Skill in Nonverbal Communication, 1979, Quantitative Assessment of Research Domains, 1980, (with Thomas A. Sebeok) The Clever Hans Phenomenon: Communication With Horses, Whales, Apes and People, 1981, (with Blanck and Buck) Nonverbal Communication in the Clinical Context, 1986, (with Gheorghiu, Netter and Eysenck) Suggestion and Suggestibility: Theory and Research, 1989, (with Harrigan and Scherer) The New Handbook of Methods in Nonverbal Behavior Research, 2005. Recipient Donald Campbell award Soc. for Personality and Social Psychology, 1988, James McKeen Cattell Sabbatical award, 1995-96; co-recipient Golden Anniversary Monograph award Speech Comm. Assn., 1996; named Watson lectr. U. N.H., Lanzetta Meml. lectr. Dartmouth Coll., Bayer lectr. Yale Sch. Medicine, Foa lectr. Temple U., Disting. Alumni lectr. UCLA, Marschak lectr. UCLA; Guggenheim fellow, 1973-74, fellow Ctr. for Advanced Study in Behavioral Scis., 1988-89; sr. Fulbright scholar, 1972; recipient Gold Medal for Life Achievement in Sci. of Psychology Am. Psychol. Found., 2003. Fellow AAAS (co-recipient Sociopsychol. prize 1960, co-recipient Behavioral Sci. Rsch. prize 1993), APA (divsn. evaluation, measurement, and stats., co-recipient Cattell Fund award 1967, co-chmn. Task Force on Statis. Inference, Disting. Sci. award for applications of psychology, 2002, Disting. Sci. Contbns. award, 2002, divsn. evaluation, measurement and stats., others), Am. Psychol. Soc. (charter, James McKeen Cattell award 2001); mem. Soc. Exptl. Social Psychology (Disting. Scientist award 1996), Ea. Psychol. Assn. (Disting. lectr. 1989), Mid-we. Psychol. Assn., Mass. Psychol. Assn. (Disting. Career Contbn. award 1979), Soc. Projective Techniques (past treas.), Phi Beta Kappa, Sigma Xi. Office: U Calif Olmsted Hall Riverside CA 92521-0001 Office Phone: 951-827-4503.

ROSENTHAL, ROBERT JON, newspaper editor, journalist; b. NYC, Aug. 5, 1948; s. Irving and Ruth (Moss) R.; m. Inez Katherina von Sternenfels, Nov. 22, 1985; children: Adam, Benjamin, Ariella. BA, U. Vt., 1970. News asst. N.Y. Times, NYC, 1970-73; reporter Boston Globe, 1974-79, Phila. Inquirer, 1979-82, Africa corr., Nairobi, Kenya, 1982-86, fgn. editor, Phila., 1986-91, city editor, 1991-93, asst. mng. editor, daily, 1993-94, assoc. mng. editor, 1994-96, exec. editor, 1996-98, editor, exec. v.p., 1998—2001; mng. editor, v.p. San Francisco (Calif.) Chronicle, 2002—07; exec. dir. Ctr. Investigative Reporting, 2008—. Recipient Third World Reporting award Nat. Assn. Black Journalists, 1983, Mag. award Overseas Press Club, 1985, Disting. Fgn. Corr. award Sigma Delta Chi, 1985, Mag. Writing award World Population Inst., 1986. Avocations: ice hockey, gardening, fishing, cooking. Office: 1 Stevens Ct Belvedere Tiburon CA 94920-1549 Office Phone: 510-809-3162.

ROSENTHAL, SOL, lawyer; b. Balt., Oct. 17, 1934; s. Louis and Hattie (Getz) R.; m. Diane Myra Sackler, June 11, 1961; children: Karen Abby, Pamela Margaret, Robert Joel. AB, Princeton U., 1956; JD, Harvard U., 1959. Bar: Md. 1959, Calif. 1961. Law clk. to chief judge U.S. Ct. Appeals, 4th cir., Balt., 1959-60; assoc. Kaplan, Livingston, Goodwin, Berkowitz & Selvin, Beverly Hills, Calif., 1960-66, ptnr., 1966-74, Buchalter Nemer, LA, 1974—96; of counsel Blanc, Williams, Johnston & Kronstadt, LA, 1996-2000, Arnold & Porter, 2000—. Bd. dirs. Playboy Enterprises, Inc., Chgo.; arbitrator Dirs. Guild Am., LA, 1976—, Writers Guild Am., LA, 1976—, Ind. Film and TV Alliance, 1989—, SAG, LA, 1992—; negotiator Writers Guild-Assn. Talent Agts., LA, 1978—; mem. entertainment and large complex case panels Am. Arbitration Assn., 1997—. Founder Camp Ronald McDonald for Good Times, LA, 1985; charter founder Mus. Contemporary Art, LA, 1988. Fellow: Coll. Comml. Arbitrators, Am. Bar Found.; mem.: ABA, Beverly Hills Bar Assn. (pres. 1982—83), Acad. TV Arts and Scis. (bd. govs. 1990—92), LA Copyright Soc. (pres. 1973—74), LA County Bar Assn. (trustee 1981—82), Calif. Bar Assn., Phi Beta Kappa. Office: Arnold & Porter 777 S Figueroa St Ste 4400 Los Angeles CA 90017-5844 Office Phone: 213-243-4000. Business E-Mail: sol_rosenthal@aporter.com.

ROSENWASSER, LANNY JEFFREY, allergist, immunologist; b. NYC, Mar. 3, 1948; MD, NYU, 1972. Cert. in allergy and immunology; cert. in internal medicine. Intern U. Calif.-HC Moffitt Hosp., San Francisco, 1972-73; resident U. Calif. Affiliated Hosps., San Francisco, 1973-74; head Allergy Immunology Nat. Jewish Med. Rsch. Ctr., Denver, 1998—. Mem. Alpha Omega Alpha, Sigma Xi. Office: Nat Jewish Med & Rsch Ctr 1400 Jackson St Denver CO 80206-2761

ROSENZWEIG, MARK RICHARD, psychologist, neuroscientist, educator; b. Rochester, NY, Sept. 12, 1922; s. Jacob and Pearl (Grossman) R.; m. Janine S.A. Chappat, Aug. 1, 1947; children: Anne Janine, Suzanne Jacqueline, Philip Mark. BA, U. Rochester, 1943, MA, 1944; PhD, Harvard U., 1949; doctorate (hon.), U. René Descartes, Sorbonne, 1980, U. Louis Pasteur, Strasbourg, France, 1998, U. Montreal, Can., 2006. Postdoctoral rsch. fellow Harvard U., 1949-51; asst. prof. U. Calif., Berkeley, 1951-56, assoc. prof., 1956-60, prof. psychology, 1960-91, assoc. rsch. prof., 1958-59, rsch. prof., 1965-66, prof. emeritus, 1991—, prof. grad. studies, 1994—. Vis. prof. biology U. Sorbonne, Paris, 1973-74; mem. U.S. nat. com. for Internat. Union Psychol. Sci., NRC and NAS, 1984-96. Author: Biologie de la Mémoire, 1976, (with A.L. Leiman) Physiological Psychology, 1982, 2nd edit., 1989, (with M.J. Renner) Enriched and Impoverished Environments: Effects on Brain and Behavior, 1987, (with D. Sinha) La Recherche en Psychologie Scientifique, 1988, (with W.H. Holtzman, M. Sabourin and D. Bélanger) History of the International Union of Psychological Science, 2000; editor: (with P. Mussen) Psychology: An Introduction, 1973, 2nd edit., 1977, International Psychological Science: Progress, Problems, and Prospects, 1992, (with A.L. Leiman and S.M. Breedlove) Biological Psychology, 1996, 3d edit., 2002, (with S.M. Breedlove and N.V. Watson) 5th edit., 2007; co-editor: (with E.L. Bennett) Neural Mechanisms of Learning and Memory, 1976, (with L. Porter) Ann. Rev. of Psychology, 1968-94, (with K. Pawlik) International Handbook of Psychology, 2000; contbr. articles to profl. jours. Served with USN, 1944-46. Recipient Disting. Alumnus award U. Rochester; Fulbright Rsch. fellow; faculty Rsch. fellow Social Sci. Rsch. Coun., 1960-61; Rsch. grant NSF, USPHS, Easter Seal Found., Nat. Inst. Drug Abuse. Fellow AAAS, APA (Disting. Sci. Contbn. award 1982, Disting. Contbn. award for Internat. Advancement of Psychology 1997), Am. Psychol. Soc.; mem. NAS, NAACP (life), Am. Physiol. Soc., Internat. Union Psychol. Sci. (hon. life, mem. exec. com. 1996—, v.p. 1980-84, pres. 1988-92, past pres. 1992-96), Internat. Brain Rsch. Orgn., Soc. Exptl. Psychologists, Soc. for Neurosci., Société Française de Psychologie, Sierra Club (life), Common Cause, Fulbright Assn. (life), Phi Beta Kappa, Sigma Xi. Office: U Calif Dept Psychology 3210 Tolman Hall Berkeley CA 94720-1650 Office Phone: 510-642-5292.

ROSENZWEIG, RICHARD STUART, publishing company executive; b. Appleton, Wis., Aug. 8, 1935; s. Walter J. and Rose (Bahcall) R. BS, Northwestern U., 1957; Advanced Mgmt. Program, Harvard U., 1975. Credit rep. Dun & Bradstreet, Inc., 1958; with Playboy Enterprises, Inc., 1958—, exec. asst. to pres., 1963-73, sr. v.p., dir., 1973-82, dir. mktg., 1974-82, exec. v.p. pubs. group, 1975-77, exec. v.p., head West Coast ops., 1977-80, exec. v.p. corp. affairs Los Angeles, 1980-82, exec. v.p., chmn. emeritus, 1982—; pres. Playboy Jazz Festivals, 1989—. Dir. I. Bahcall Industries, Appleton; exec. v.p. (dir. 1973—) Playboy Enterprises; chmn. Alta Loma Entertainment, 2000—. Trustee L.A. Film Expn.; mem. 2d decade coun. Am. Film Inst.; bd. dirs. Mus. Contemporary Art, Chgo., Periodical and Book Assn. Am., Internat. Inst. Kidney Diseases of UCLA, Children of Night, Maple Ctr. Beverly Hills; mem., chmn. bd. UCLA Legis. Network, Town Hall of Calif.; adv. bd. West Hollywood Mktg. Corp., 1985—; bd. dirs. So. Calif. ACLU, 1985—; mem. Los Angeles County Mus.; apptd. to blue ribbon com. project West Coast Gateway. With AUS, 1957; chmn. Modern and Contemporary Art Coun. L.A. County Mus. of Art.; pres. Beverly Hills Cultural Ctr.; exec. com. Henry Mancini Inst.; v.p. Fraternity of Friends music Ctr.; dir. Variety Club So. Calif., West Hollywood C. of C; mem. UCLA Chancellor's Assocs., UCLA Royce 270; offcl. amb. Govt. Beverly Hills. Recipient Do-ers award, 1988, Beverly Hills medal Beverly Hills City Coun., 1993. Mem. Am. Mktg. Aslsn., L.A. Pub. Affairs Officers Assn., Pres.'s Cir., Beverly Hills C. of C. (bd. dirs., visitors' bur., v.p.), Beverly Hills Fine Art Commn. (chmn.), Beverly Hills Econ. Devel. Coun., Founders Circle of Music Ctr., Pub. Affairs Coun., Craft and Folk Art Mus., Pres.' Coun. and Contemporary Arts Coun. L.A. Mus. Contemporary Art, The Am. Cinematheque (groundbreaker), Beverly Hills Rotary Club, Acad. TV Arts and Scis. Office: Playboy Enterprises Inc 2706 Media Center Dr Los Angeles CA 90065-1733

ROSETT, ARTHUR IRWIN, lawyer, educator; b. NYC, July 5, 1934; s. Milton B. and Bertha (Werner) R.; m. Rhonda K. Lawrence; children: David Benjamin, Martha Jean, Daniel Joseph. AB, Columbia U., 1955, LL.B., 1959. Bar: Calif. 1968, N.Y. State 1960, U.S. Supreme Ct. 1963. Law clk. U.S. Supreme Ct., 1959-60; asst. U.S. atty. So. Dist. N.Y., 1960-63; practice law NYC, 1963-65; assoc. dir. Pres.'s Commn. on Law Enforcement and Adminstrn. Justice, 1965-67; acting prof. law UCLA, 1967-70, prof., 1970—. Author: Contract Law and Its Application, 1971, 6th edit. (with D.J. Bussell), 1999, (with D. Cressey) Justice by Consent, 1976, (with E. Dorff) A Living Tree, 1987. Served with USN, 1956-58. Mem. Am. Law Inst. Home: 641 S Saltair Ave Los Angeles CA 90049-4134 Office: UCLA Law Sch 405 Hilgard Ave Los Angeles CA 90095-1476 Business E-Mail: rosett@law.ucla.edu.

ROSETT, DANIEL J., film company executive; b. 1962; BS in bus. and econ., U. Calif., Santa Barbara, 1984. CPA. Mgr. KPMG Peat Marwick; with Walt Disney Co., exec. dir. studio ops.; v.p., corp. controller MGM Studios, 1994—95, sr. v.p. fin. ops., 1995—98, exec. v.p. studio fin. and ops., 1998—2001, exec. v.p. mktg. and distribution, 2001—04; pres. United Artists Corp., 2004—05; COO Overture Films, 2006—. Exec. prodr.: (films) Capote, 2005.

ROSHKO, ANATOL, aeronautical engineer; b. Bellevue, Alta., Can., July 15, 1923; arrived in U.S., 1950, arrived in U.S., 1950; married, 1957; 2 children. BSc, U. Alta, 1945; MS, Calif. Inst. Tech., 1947, PhD in Aero. Engring., 1952. Instr. math. U. Alta., 1945—46, lectr. engring., 1949—50; rsch. fellow Calif. Inst. Tech., Pasadena, 1952—55, asst. prof. to prof., 1955—85; acting. dir. Grad Aero. Labs, Pasadena, 1985—87; Theodore Von Karman prof. aeronautics Calif. Inst. Tech., Pasadena, 1985—, prof. emeritus, 1994—. Sci. liaison officer Office Naval Rsch., London, 1961-62; cons. McDonnell Douglas Corp., 1954-90, Rocketdyne Corp. Divsn., Rockwell Internat., 1984-90; founding dir. Wind Engring. Rsch. Inc., 1970; mem. Aero. & Space Engring. Bd., 1988-93. Recipient Timoshenko medal ASME, 1999; named to U. Alta. Alumni Wall of Recognition, 1998. Fellow AAAS, AIAA (Dryden Rsch. lectr. 1976, Fluid Dynamics award 1998), Am. Phys. Soc. (Fluid Dynamics prize 1987), Indian Acad. Scis. (hon.), Can. Aeronautics and Space Inst.; mem. NAS, ASME, NAE. Office: Calif Inst Tech Mail Sta 105-50 1201 E California Blvd Pasadena CA 91125-0001 Office Phone: 626-395-4484. E-mail: roshko@caltech.edu.

ROSINI, EDUARDO B., computer software company executive; b. 1968; married; 2 children. With Microsoft Corp., 1992—, gen. mgr. Microsoft Argentina, 1997—99, gen. mgr. Worldwide Enterprise group Redmond, Wash., 1999, regional v.p. Home & Office divsn. for Europe, Middle East & Africa, 2003—04, v.p. Microsoft Asia-Pacific Singapore, 2004—06, corp. v.p. Worldwide Small & Midmarket Solutions & Partners group Redmond, 2006—. Office: Microsoft Corp SMS&P Group 1 Microsoft Way Redmond WA 98052-6399

ROSKI, EDWARD P., JR., real estate developer, professional sports team executive; s. Edward P. Roski, III; m. Gayle Roski. BS in Fin. and Real Estate, U. So. Calif., 1962. Joined Majestic Realty Co., 1966, chmn., CEO; part owner Staples Ctr., LA Kings, LA Lakers; owner Silverton Hotel & Casino, Las Vegas, Nev. Bd. dirs. Comerica Bank, Calif., LA Sports & Entertainment Commn. Dir. Big Bros. of Greater L.A.; bd. govs. Natural History Mus. of L.A. County, Bowers Museum of Cultural Art; bd. trustees Loyola Marymount U., U. So. Calif.; bd. regents Loyola High School; founder Majestic Realty Found., 2002-. Served USMC, 1962—66. Recipient Partners with Youth award, Big Sisters of Greater Los Angeles and the Inland Empire, 2004, Woodrow Wilson award for Public Service, 2006; named a Champions of Industry, Calif. Bus. Properties Assn., 2004; named one of Forbes' Richest Americans, 2006. Mem. Explorers Club, Soc. Indsl. Realtors. Avocations: bicycling, mountain climbing. Office: Majestic Realty 13191 Crossroads Pkwy N 6th Fl City Of Industry CA 91746-3497 Office Phone: 562-948-4301. Business E-Mail: eroski@majesticrealty.com.

ROSKILL, JON, computer software company executive; m. Jennifer S. Roskill. BSS, U. Mass., Amherst, 1985; MBA, Boston U. Mktg. mgr. Digital Equipment Corp.; with Microsoft Corp., 1993—, gen. mgr. devel. & .NET enterprise server mktg., corp. v.p. US bus. & mktg., 2006—. Office: Microsoft Corp 1 Microsoft Way Redmond WA 98052-6399

ROSKY, BURTON SEYMOUR, lawyer; b. Chgo., May 28, 1927; s. David T. and Mary W. (Zelkin) R.; m. Leatrice J. Darrow, June 16, 1951; children: David Scott, Bruce Alan. Student, Ill. Inst. Tech., 1944-45; BS, UCLA, 1948; JD, Loyola U., LA, 1953. Bar: Calif. 1954, U.S. Supreme Ct 1964, U.S. Tax Ct 1964; C.P.A., Calif. Auditor City of L.A., 1948- 51; with Beidner, Temkin & Ziskin (C.P.A.s), LA, 1951-52; supervising auditor Army Audit Agy., 1952-53; practiced law L.A., Beverly Hills, 1954—; ptnr. Duskin & Rosky, 1972-82, Rosky, Landau & Fox, 1982-93, Rosky, Landau & Stahl, Beverly Hills, 1993-99; pvt. practice Beverly Hills, 1999—. Lectr. on tax and bus. problems; judge pro tem Beverly Hills Mcpl. Ct., L.A. Superior Ct.; mem. L.A. Mayor's Community Adv. Council. Contbr. profl. publs. Charter supporting mem. Los Angeles County Mus. Arts; contbg. mem. Assocs. of Smithsonian Instn.; charter mem. Air and Space Mus; mem. Am. Mus. Natural History, L.A. Zoo; supporting mem. L.A. Mus. Natural History; mem. exec. bd. So. Calif. coun. Nat. Fedn. Temple Brotherhoods, mem. nat. exec. bd.; mem. bd. govs. Loyola Sch. Law, L.A.; regent Coll. Am. Assn. Atty.-CPAs. With USNR, 1945-46. Walter Henry Cook fellow Loyola Law Sch. Bd. Govs. Fellow Jewish Chautauqua Soc. (life mem.); mem. Am. Arbitration Assn. (nat. panel arbitrators), Am. Assn. Attys.-CPAs (charter mem. pres. 1968), Calif. Assn. Attys.-CPAs (charter mem., pres. 1963), Calif. Soc. CPAs, Calif., Beverly Hills, Century City, Los Angeles County bar assns., Am. Judicature Soc., Chancellors Assocs. UCLA, B'nai B'rith, Tau Delta Phi, Phi Alpha Delta. Jewish (mem. exec. bd., pres. temple, pres. brotherhood). Club: Mason. Office Phone: 323-655-9757.

ROSS, BRUCE SHIELDS, lawyer; b. LA, Feb. 1, 1947; s. Floyd and Mary Louise (Shields) R.; m. Janet G. Ross, Jan 27, 1968 (div. Jan. 1977); 1 child, Stephanie; m. Carol Burlingame, Apr. 2, 1977; children: Andrew, Tiffany. AB cum laude, Oberlin Coll., 1968; JD, U. Calif., Berkeley, 1971. Bar: Calif. 1971, US Tax Ct. 1973, US Dist. Ct. (ctrl. dist. Calif.) 1977; cert. specialist in estate planning, trust, probate law, Calif. Assoc. Nossman & Krueger, LA, 1971-73; assoc. to ptnr. Poindexter & Doutre, LA, 1973-78; assoc. Alschuler & Grossman, LA, 1978, ptnr., 1979-84, Morrison & Foerster, LA, 1984—90, Ross, Sacks & Glazier, LA, 1991—2001; exec. ptnr. Holland & Knight, LLP, LA and Rancho Santa Fe, Calif., 2001—06; ptnr.-in-charge Luce, Forward, Hamilton & Scripps, LLP, LA, 2006—. Participant Temp. Judge Prog. LA Mcpl. Ct., 1989—95; mem. adv. bd. Philip E. Heckerling Inst. Estate Planning U. Miami, 2000—, adj. prof. law grad. prog. in estate planning, 2000—03; academician Internat. Acad. Estate and Trust Law; mem. panels, lectr. in field. Mem. U. Calif. Law Rev., 1969-71, note and comment editor 1970-71; author: Calif. Practice Guide: Probate, 1986-2004 (updated annually); co-editor Guidebook to the Calif. Rules of Profl. Conduct for Estate Planning, Trust and Probate Counsel, 1997; contbr. articles to profl. jours. Trustee Pacific Asia Mus., Pasadena, Calif., 1983-1991, pres., 1988-1991; fin. chmn. Boy Scouts Am., Glendale, Calif., 1984-85; gov. The Webb Schs. of Calif., Claremont, 1987—. Named one of Top 100 Attys., Worth mag., 2006. Fellow Am. Coll. Trust and Estate Counsel (sec., treas., v.p. and pres.-elect 2001-05, pres, 2005, mem. bd. regents 1995-2001, 02, mem. bd. exec. com. 2000-01, 02-).Mem. ABA (chair task force on state and local regulation, com. on exempt orgns., sect. taxation 1984-88, chair estate and trust litig. com. 1991-93, group chair litig. and controversy com. 1996-, mem. supervisory coun. 1997-2003, co-chair multijurisdictional practice com. 2000-02, sect. liasion to ethics 2000 commn. 1998-2000, real property, probate and trust law sect.), LA County Bar Assn. (exec. com. tax. sect. 1984-85, exec. com. estates and trusts sect. 1994-97, exec. com. alternative dispute resolution sect. 1996-97), State Bar Calif. (mem. 1987-89, vice-chair 1989-90, chair 1990-91, adv. 1991- 1994. Democrat. Unitarian Universalist. Avocations: music, opera, swimming, stamp collecting/philately. Office: Luce Forward Hamilton & Scripps 601 S Figueroa Ste 3900 Los Angeles CA 90017 Office Phone: 213-896-2400, 213-892-4962. Office Fax: 213-452-8042. Business E-Mail: bruce.ross@hklaw.com. E-mail: bruce@luce.com.

ROSS, CHARLES R., state legislator; Washington State Representative, District 14, 2007-; member, Public Safety and Emergency Preparedness Committee, Judiciary Committee, Local Govt Committee, currently, Washington State Assembly. Republican. Office: 418 John L O'Brien Bldg PO Box 40600 Olympia WA 98504-0600 Office Phone: 360-786-7856.

ROSS, CHARLOTTE PACK, social services administrator; b. Oklahoma City, Oct. 21, 1932; d. Joseph and Rose P. (Traibich) Pack; m. Roland S. Ross, May 6, 1951 (div. July 1964); children: Beverly Jo, Sandra Gail; m. Stanley Fisher, Mar. 17, 1991. Student U. Okla., 1949-52, New Sch. Social Rsch., 1953. Cert. tchr. Exec. dir. Suicide Prevention and Crisis Ctr. San Mateo County, Burlingame, Calif., 1966-88; pres., exec. dir. Youth Suicide Nat. Ctr., Washington, 1985-93; exec. dir. Death with Dignity Edn. Ctr., San Mateo, Calif., 1994—; pres. Calif. Senate Adv. Com. Youth Suicide Prevention, 1982-84; speaker Menninger Found., 1983, 84; instr. San Francisco State U., 1981-83; conf. coord. U. Calif., San Francisco, 1971—; cons. univs. and health svcs. throughout world. Contbg. author: Group Counseling for Suicidal Adolescents, 1984, Teaching Children the Facts of Life and Death, 1985; mem. editorial bd. Suicide and Life Threatening Behavior, 1976-89. Mem. regional selection panel Pres.'s Commn. on White House Fellows, 1975-78; mem. CIRCLON Svc. Club, 1979—, Com. on Child Abuse, 1981-85; founding mem. Women for Responsible Govt., co-chmn., 1974-79. Recipient Outstanding Exec. award San Mateo County Coordinating Com., 1971, Koshland award San Francisco Found., 1984. Fellow Wash. Acad. Scis.; mem. Internat. Assn. Suicide Prevention (v.p. 1985—), Am. Assn. Suicidology (sec. 1972-74, svc. award 1990), bd. govs. 1976-78, accreditation com. 1975—, chair region IX, 1975-82), Assn. United Way Agy. Execs. (pres. 1974), Assn. County Contract Agys. (pres. 1982), Peninsula Press Club.

ROSS, DAVID A., art museum director; b. Malverne, NY, Apr. 26, 1949; s. Joshua and Grayce R.; m. Margaret Gronner; children: Lindsay, Emily. BA, Syracuse U.; postgrad., Grad. Sch. Fine Arts, Syracuse. Curator video art Everson Mus. Art, Syracuse, N.Y., 1971-74; dep. dir. program devel. and TV Long Beach Mus. Art, Calif., 1974-77; chief curator Univ. Art Mus., Berkeley, Calif., 1977-82; dir. Inst. of Contemporary Art, Boston, 1982-91; dir., CEO Whitney Mus. Am. Art, 1991-98; dir. San Francisco Mus. Modern Art, 1998—. Active Fed. Adv. Com. om Internat. Exbns., 1990—. Contbr. articles to profl. jours. Mem. Assn. Art Mus. Dirs. Office: San Francisco Mus Modern Art 151 3rd St San Francisco CA 94103-3107

ROSS, DELMER GERRARD, historian, educator; b. Los Banos, Calif., Nov. 5, 1942; s. Elmer G. and Orva Beth (Dickinson) R.; m. Karen Ann Gibson, June 17, 1977; children: Michelle, Richard. BA, Pacific Union Coll., 1965; MA, U. Calif., Santa Barbara, 1967, PhD, 1970. Instr. Pacific Union Coll., Angwin, Calif., 1968-69; from asst. to assoc. prof. Oakwood Coll., Huntsville, Ala., 1970-76; from assoc. prof. to prof. history Loma Linda U., Riverside, Calif., 1976-91, chmn. dept. history and polit. sci., 1986-90; prof. history and polit. sci. La Sierra U., Riverside, 1991—. Author: Visionaries and Swindlers, 1975, Rails Across Costa Rica, 1976, Rails in Paradise, 1991, Gold Road to La Paz, 1992, Development of Railroads in Guatemala and El Salvador, 1849-1929, 2001, To End a Crooked Trail, 2002, Rockhounding the Wiley's Well District of California, 2006 Iner S. Ritchie, Medical Evangelist, 2007; co-author: Hope...Not Ashamed, 2002, Reminiscences of Walter D. Scott, Desert Entrepreneur of the American West, 2003; mem. editl. bd. Adventist Heritage mag., 1987-90. Bd. dirs. Inst. for Research in Latin Am., Mobile, Ala., 1968-82. Mem. Am. Hist. Assn., Assn. 7th Day Adventist Historians (exec. sec. 1973-74, sec.-treas. 1974-75, pres. 1981-82), Assn. Western Adventist Historians, Nat. Railway Hist. Soc., Colo. Railroad Hist. Found. (life), Railway and Locomotive Hist. Soc. Republican. Avocations: reading, retracing historical trails and railroad routes, faceting gemstones. Office: La Sierra U Dept History Riverside CA 92515 Home Phone: 951-789-9384; Office Phone: 951-785-2067. E-mail: dross@lasierra.edu.

ROSS, HUGH COURTNEY, electrical engineer; b. Dec. 31, 1923; s. Clare W. and Jeanne F. Ross; m. Sarah A. Gordon (dec.); m. Patricia A. Malloy; children: John C., James G., Robert W. Student, Calif. Inst. Tech., 1942, San Jose State U., 1946-47; BSEE, Stanford U., 1950, postgrad., 1954. Registered profl. elec. engr., Calif. Instr. San Benito (Calif.) High Sch. and Jr. Coll., 1950-51; chief engr. vacuum power switches Jennings Radio Mfg. Corp., San Jose, Calif., 1951-62; chief engr. ITT Jennings, San Jose, Calif., 1962-64; pres. Ross Engring. Corp., Campbell, Calif., 1964—. Contbr. articles to profl. jours. Fellow IEEE (life) (chmn. Santa Clara Valley subsect. 1960-61); mem. Am. Vacuum Soc., Am. Soc. Metals. Achievements include patents in field. Avocations: electronics, electric autos, camping, ranching, solar power. Office: 540 Westchester Dr Campbell CA 95008-5012 Office Phone: 408-377-4621. Office Fax: 408-377-5182.

ROSS, JEFFREY S., lawyer; b. NYC, Mar. 7, 1951; AB with highest honors, U. Mich., 1972; JD, Stanford U., 1975. Bar: Calif. 1975, US Dist. Ct. (no. Calif. dist.), US Ct. Appeals (9th cir.), US Supreme Ct. Atty., pres. Friedman Ross & Hersh PC; ptnr. Pillsbury Winthrop Shaw Pittman, San Francisco. Mem.: San Francisco Barrister Club (bd. dirs. 1981—83, pres. 1983), Nat. Assn. Bar Presidents, Bar Assn. San Francisco (bd. dirs. 1986—88, pres. 1997, Award of Merit 1990, 1998), Phi Beta Kappa, Phi Eta Sigma. Office: Pillsbury Winthrop Shaw Pittman 50 Fremont St San Francisco CA 94105 Office Phone: 415-983-1730. Office Fax: 415-983-1200. Business E-Mail: jeff.ross@pillsburylaw.com.

ROSS, JOHN, physical chemist, educator; b. Vienna, Oct. 2, 1926; arrived in U.S., 1940; s. Mark and Anna (Krcmar) Ross; m. Virginia Franklin (div.); 1 child, Robert K.; m. Eva Madarasz. BS, Queens Coll., 1948; PhD, MIT, 1951; D (hon.), Weizmann Inst. Sci., Rehovot, Israel, 1984, Queens Coll., SUNY, 1987, U. Bordeaux, France, 1987. Prof. chemistry Brown U., Providence, 1953—66, MIT, Cambridge, 1966—80, chmn. dept., 1966—71, chmn. faculty of Inst., 1975—77; prof. Stanford (Calif.) U., 1980—2001, chmn. dept., 1983—89, prof. emeritus, 2001—. Cons. to industries; mem. emeritus bd. govs. Weizmann Inst., 1971—. Author: Physical Chemistry, 1980, 2d edit., 2000; editor: Molecular Beams, 1966;: Determination of Complex Reaction Mechanisms, 2006, Thermodynamics and Fluctuations Far from Equilibrium, 2008; contbr. articles to profl. jours. 2nd lt. US Army, 1944—46. Recipient medal, Coll. de France, Paris, Presdl. Nat. Medal of Sci., 1999, Austrian Cross of Honor for Sci. and Art, 1st class, 2002. Fellow: AAAS, Am. Phys. Soc.; mem.: NAS, Am. Chem. Soc. (Irving Langmuir Chem. Physics prize 1992, Peter Debye award in phys. chemistry 2001, Theodore William Richards medal 2004), Am. Acad. Arts and Sci. Office: Stanford U Dept Chemistry Stanford CA 94305-5080 Home Phone: 650-858-2203; Office Phone: 650-723-9203. Business E-Mail: john.ross@stanford.edu.

ROSS, JOHN, JR., cardiologist, educator; b. NYC, Dec. 1, 1928; s. John and Janet (Moulder) R.; children: Sydnie, John, Duncan; m. Lola Romanucci, Aug. 26, 1972; children: Adan, Deborah Lee. AB, Dartmouth Coll., 1951; MD, Cornell U., 1955. Intern Johns Hopkins

Hosp., 1955—56; resident Columbia-Presbyn. Med. Center, NYC, 1960—61, NY. Hosp.-Cornell U. Med. center, 1961—62; chief sect. cardiovascular diagnosis cardiology br. Nat. Heart Inst., Bethesda, Md., 1962—68; prof. medicine U. Calif., San Diego, 1968—2000, also dir. cardiovascular div., 1968—91, rsch. prof. medicine, 2000—, disting. prof. medicine, 2003—; prof. cardiovascular research Am. Heart Assn. Western States Affiliate, 1984—99. Mem. cardiology adv. com. Nat. Heart, Lung and Blood Inst., 1975-78, task force on arteriosclerosis, 1978-80, adv. council, 1980-84; bd. dirs. San Diego Heart Assn.; vis. prof. Brit. Heart Assn., 1990. Author: Mechanisms of Contraction of the Normal and Failing Heart, 1968, 76, Understanding the Heart and Its Diseases, 1976; mem. editorial bd. Circulation, 1967-75, 80-88, editor in chief 1988-93, Circulation Research, 1971-75, Am. Jour. Physiology, 1968-73, Annals of Internal Medicine, 1974-78, Am. Jour. Cardiology, 1974-79, 83-88, Jour. Clin. Investigation, 1992-97, Italian Heart Jour., 1998-99, Jour. Cardiac Failure, 2000-05, Circulation Jour. Japan, 2000—; cons. editor Circulation, 1993-03; contbr. chpts. to books, sci. articles to profl. jours. Served as surgeon USPHS, 1956—63. Decorated grande ufficiale Order of Merit of Republic of Italy, 1998; recipient Ing. Enzo Ferrari prize for Enzo Ferrari, Modena, Italy, 1989, James B. Herrick award Coun. Clin. Cardiology Am. Heart Assn., 1990, Academic Mentorship award Am. Heart Assn., 2004. Master Am. Coll. Cardiology (v.p. trustee, pres. 1986-87, Disting. Scientist award 1990); fellow ACP; mem. Am. Soc. Clin. Investigation (councillor), Am. Physiol. Soc., Assn. Am. Physicians, Cardiac Muscle Soc., Assn. Univ. Cardiologists, Assn. West. Physicians (councillor), Japanese Circulation Soc. (hon.). Achievements include development of and application of transseptal left heart catherization for the diagnosis of heart disease; conceptualized "afterload mismatch" in the left ventricle of the heart and its application in the diagnosis and treatment of valvular heart disease and heart failure; demonstrated experimentally that reperfusion of a coronary artery after prolonged occlusion salvages heart muscle and partially restores heart function. Home: 8599 Prestwick Dr La Jolla CA 92037 Office: U Calif Dept Med M # 0613B San Diego CA 92093

ROSS, JUNE ROSA PITT, biologist, educator; b. Taree, NSW, Australia, May 2, 1931; came to U.S., 1957; d. Bernard and Adeline Phillips; m. Charles Alexander, June 27, 1959. BSc with honors, U. Sydney, New S. Wales, Australia, 1953, PhD, 1959, DSc, 1974. Rsch. assoc. Yale U., New Haven, 1959—60, U. Ill., Urbana, 1960—65, Western Wash. U., Bellingham, 1965—67, assoc. prof., 1967—70, prof. biology, 1970—2003, prof. emeritus, 2004—, chair dept. biology, 1989—90. Pres. Western Wash. U. Faculty Senate, Bellingham, 1984-85; conf. host Internat. Bryozoology Assn., 1986. Author (with others): A Textbook of Entomology, 1982, Geology of Coal, 1984; editor (assoc.): Palaios, 1985—89; contbr. 165 articles to profl. jours. Recipient J. Wolfensohn Award of Excellence Sydney U. Grad. Union of N.Am., 1995, P. and R. Olscamp Outstanding Rsch. award Western Wash. U., 1986; NSF grantee. Mem.: Internat. Bryozoology Assn. (pres. 1992—95), The Paleontol. Soc. (councillor 1984—86, treas. 1987—93), Australian Marine Scis. Assn., U.K. Marine Biol. Assn. (life). Avocations: hiking, classical music. Office: Western Wash U Dept Biology Bellingham WA 98225-9160 Office Phone: 360-650-3634. E-mail: ross@fire.biol.wwu.edu.

ROSS, KATHLEEN ANNE, academic administrator; b. Palo Alto, Calif., July 1, 1941; d. William Andrew and Mary Alberta (Wilburn) Ross. BA, Ft. Wright Coll., 1964; MA, Georgetown U., 1971; PhD, Claremont Grad. U., 1979; LLD (hon.), Alverno Coll. Milw., 1990, Dartmouth Coll., 1991, Seattle U., 1992, Pomona Coll., 1993, U. Notre Dame, 1999, Gonzaga U., 1999; LHD (hon.), Whitworth Coll., 1992, Coll. New Rochelle, 1998, Carroll Coll., 2003, Pacific Luth. U., 2004, U. Portland, Oreg., 2006, U. Puget Sound, 2007. Cert. tchr. Wash. Secondary tchr. Holy Names Acad., Spokane, Wash., 1964-70; dir. rsch. and planning Province Holy Names, Wash. State, 1972-73; v.p. acads. Ft. Wright Coll., Spokane, 1973-81; rsch. asst. to dean Claremont Grad. Sch., Calif., 1977-78; assoc. faculty mem. Harvard U., Cambridge, Mass., 1981; pres. Heritage U., Toppenish, Wash., 1981—. Cons. Wash. State Holy Names Schs., 1971-73; coll. accrediting assn. evaluator N.W. Assn. Schs. and Colls., Seattle, 1975—; dir. Holy Names U., Oakland, Calif., 1979—; cons. Yakama Indian Nation, Toppenish, 1975—; speaker, cons. in field. Author: (with others) Multicultural Pre-School Curriculum, 1977, A Crucial Agenda: Improving Minority Student Success, 1989; Cultural Factors in Success of American Indian Students in Higher Education, 1978. Chmn. Internat. 5-Yr. Convocation of Sisters of Holy Names, Montreal, 1981, 96; TV Talk show host Spokane Coun. of Chs., 1974-76; mem. Nat. Congl. Adv. Com. on Student Fin. Assistance, 2002-06. Recipient E.K. and Lillian F. Bishop Founds. Youth Leader of Yr. award, 1986, Disting. Citizenship Alumna award, Claremont Grad. Sch., 1986, Golden Aztec award, Wash. Human Devel., 1989, Harold W. McGraw Edn. prize, 1989, John Carroll awrd, Georgetown U., 1991, Holy Names medal, Ft. Wright Coll., 1981, Pres.'s medal, Estern Wash. U., 1994, First Ann. Leadership award, Region VIII Coun. Advancement and Support Edn., 1993, Wash. State Medal of Merit, 1995, Lifetime Achievement award, Yakima YWCA, 2001, numerous grants for projects in multicultural higher edn., 1974—; named Yakima Herald Rep. Person of Yr., 1987, MacArthur fellow, 1997. Mem. Nat. Assn. Ind. Colls. and Univs., Soc. Intercultural Edn., Tng. and Rsch., Sisters of Holy Names of Jesus and Mary-SNJM. Roman Catholic. Office: Heritage U Office of Pres 3240 Fort Rd Toppenish WA 98948-9562 Office Phone: 509-865-8600.

ROSS, RICH, broadcast executive; b. NYC, Oct. 7, 1961; BA in internat. rels. and English, U. Pa., 1983; JD, Fordham U., 1986. Mgr. talent rels. Nickelodeon, 1986—90, v.p. talent rels., 1990—92, v.p. program enterprises, 1992—93; sr. v.p. devel. and prodn. FX Networks, 1993—96; sr. v.p. programming and prodn. Disney Channel, 1996—99, exec. v.p., gen. mgr. programming and prodn., 1999—2002, pres., 2002—04, Disney Channel Worldwide, 2004—. Bd. dirs. Cable in the Classroom. Office: Disney Channel 500 S Buena Vista St Burbank CA 91521

ROSS, RICHARD FREDERICK, lawyer; b. Coral Gables, Fla., May 12, 1952; s. Norman and Jeanne (Gustafson) Ross; m. Carolyn Ross, June 30, 1985. BA magna cum laude, Mich. State U., 1974; JD, U. Detroit, 1977. Bar: Ariz. 1977; cert. real estate specialist Ariz. Bd. Legal Specialization. Atty. Cunningham, Goodson & Tiffany, Phoenix, 1977-81; founding ptnr. Storey & Ross, Phoenix, 1981-89; ptnr. Squire, Sanders & Dempsey LLP, Phoenix, 1989—, co-chmn., Real Estate & Hospitality Practice Group. Former bd. dirs. dean's coun. of 100 Ariz. State U. Coll. Bus., Tempe; former bd. dirs. Ctrl. Ariz. chpt. Am. Heart Assn., Phoenix; former bd. dirs. Phoenix Symphony, HomeBase Cmty. Youth Shelter, Phoenix, Terraco Properties (subs. Phoenix Meml. Hosp.), Phoenix. Mem. ABA (mem. hospitality com., mem. real property, probate and trust law), Internat. Soc. Hospitality Cons., Am. Hotel and Motel Assn., Urban Land Inst., Internat. Coun. Shopping Ctr., Valley Partnership. Office: Squire Sanders & Dempsey LLP Two Renaissance Sq 40 N Central Ave Ste 2700 Phoenix AZ 85004-4424 Office Phone: 602-528-4018. Office Fax: 216-479-8780. Business E-Mail: rross@ssd.com.

ROSS, ROBERT K., foundation administrator, physician; BA in Public Administration, M in Public Administration, MD, U. Penn. Clinical scholar U. Penn. Sch. of Medicine, 1988—90; former dir. Phila. Dept. of Health; former pediatrician Nat. Health Services Corps, Camden; former dir. Health and Human Services Agy., San Diego County, 1999—2000; pres., CEO Calif. Endowment, 2000—. Consultant Phila. Sch. Dist. Children's Health Initiative; mem. NJ Governor's Commn. on Health Care Costs, Nat. Vaccine Advisory Comm.; bd. mem. Nat. Marrow Donor Program; mem. President's Summit for America's Future. Bd. dirs. San Diego United Way, Jackie Robinson YMCA, Calif. Endowment. Recipient Youth Advocacy Humanitarian of Yr. award, Outstanding Community Svc. award, Volunteers of Am., Leadership award, Hosp. Council of San Diego, Health Administrator of Yr. Citation, Nat. Assn. of Health Svc. Exec. Mem.: Am. Acad. of Pediatrics. Office: Calif Endowment 1000 N Alameda St Los Angeles CA 90012 Office Phone: 800-449-4149.

ROSS, STEVEN CHARLES, business administration educator, consultant; b. Salem, Oreg., Jan. 14, 1947; s. Charles Reed and Edythe Marie (Calvin) R.; m. Meredith Lynn Buholts, June 15, 1969; children: Kelly Lynn, Shannon Marie. BS, Oreg. State U., 1969; MS, U. Utah, 1976, PhD, 1980. Cons. IRS Tng. Staff, Ogden, Utah, 1977-80; asst. prof. Marquette U., Milw., 1980-88; assoc. prof. Mont. State U., Bozeman, 1988-89; prof. bus. adminstrn. Western Wash. U., Bellingham, 1989—. Chmn. acad. coord. commn., Western Wash. U., 1997-2002, mem. faculty senate 2000-02, chmn. dept. decision scis., 2008-; govt. and industry cons.; cons. editor microcomputing series West Pub. Co. Author 35 books and several articles in computer systems field. Mem. adv. com. Milwaukee County Mgmt., 1981-85, Port of Bellingham, 1990-2000; chmn. 1998 U.S. Sailing Jr. Championships. Capt. U.S. Army, 1969-75. Rsch. fellow U. Utah, 1977-79, Marquette U., 1981-84, Western Wash. U., 1998, 2002, 04. Mem. Internat. Assn. Computer Info. Sys., Assn. for Computing Machinery, Bellingham Yacht Club (trustee 1992-93, sec. 1993-94, rear commodore, 1994-95, vice commodore 1995-96, commodore 1996-97). Office: Western Wash U Coll Bus and Econs Bellingham WA 98225

ROSSER, EDWIN MICHAEL, mortgage company executive; b. Denver, Oct. 11, 1940; s. Edwin Michael and Anne (Ratliff) R.; m. Keren Call, July 17, 1969; children: Kevin, William. BS, Colo. State U., 1964; MA, U. No. Colo., 1974. Cert. mortgage banker. Mktg. officer United Bank Mortgage, Denver, 1968-74; dir. nat. accounts PMI Mortgage Ins. Co., Denver, 1974-85; v.p. Moore Mortgage Co., Denver, 1985-87, Pacific First Mortgage Corp., Englewood, Colo., 1987-89; 1st v.p. 1st Nat. Bank, San Francisco, 1990-93; v.p. nat. accounts United Guaranty Corp., 1993—. Bd. dirs. Rocky Mtn. Women's Inst. Photographer represented in Denver Art Mus., The Buffalo in Winter, (1st place award 1981). Steering com. Blueprint for Colo., Govs. Unified Housing Task Force; mem. Colo. Housing Coun. (chmn. 1986-87); bd. dirs. Colo. State U. Found.; mem. adv. bd. Arapahoe County Open Space and Trails, 1999-; mem. Colo. Land Use Commn., 1999, Colo. State Housing Bd., 2003; bd. dirs. The Conservation Campaign, 2004. Fellow Soc. Mortgage Bankers; mem. Am. Planning Assn., Soc. of Cert. Mortage Bankers (chmn.). Mortgage Bankers Assn. Am. (cert., bd. govs. 1986-90, state and local achievement award 1986, Ernest P. Schumacher award 1988, disting. svc. award 2003, Burton Wood Legis. Svc. award), Colo. Mortgage Bankers Assn. (bd. dirs. 1979-88, pres. 1986, adv. bd. trust for pub. land, E.C. Spelman award 1978, Lifetime Achievement award 1998), Colo. Assn. Commerce and Industry, Denver Nat. Soc. Real Estate Fin., Mus. Natural History, Denver C. of C., Rocky Mtn. Mutual Housing Assn. (bd. dirs.), Ctr. of Fin. Real Estate (bd. dirs.), Colo. State U. Alumni Assn. (nat. pres. 1985, bd. dirs. 1979-87, mem. found. bd. 1987-91, 93-2000, Honor Alumnus 1984, ha Sasso award Dept. Athletics 1993), Univ. Club, City Club Denver, Nat. Soc. for Real Estate Fin. (CRF designation 1997), Colo. State U. Henry Alumni (Svc. award 2000), Univ. Club, Alpha Sigma Gamma Republican. Roman Catholic. Avocations: photography, fly fishing. Home: 12478 E Amherst Cir Aurora CO 80014-3306 Office: United Guaranty Residential Ins Co 6312 S Fiddlers Green Cir Englewood CO 80111-4943 Personal E-mail: emrcmb@aol.com.

ROSSI, DINO J., former state legislator; b. Seattle, Oct. 15, 1959; s. John and Eve Rossi; m. Terry Rossi, 1987; children: Juliauna, Jake, Joseph, Jillian. BA in Bus. Mgmtr., Seattle U., 1982. Mem. Wash. Senate, Dist. 5, Olympia, 1996—2003; mem. energy, tech., and telecom. com. Wash. Senate; mem. natural resources, parks and recreation com.; mem. ways and means com.; chmn., 2003; mem. capital budget subcom.; mem. joint com. on pension policy. Vol. Sr. Ctr.; co-founder Operation Homefront; past bd. dirs. Boys and Girls Club, Mountains to Sound Greenway Bd. Mem. Rotary (Issaquah). Republican.

ROSSI, MARIO ALEXANDER, architect; b. Chgo., Apr. 9, 1931; s. Gastone J. and Irma (Giorgi) R.; m. Jo Ann Therese Kneip, Apr. 12, 1958; children: John Vincent, Lyn Ann, Paul Alexander, Mara Ann. BArch, Ill. Inst. Tech., 1955. Architect Omnimetrics, LA, 1967-78; pvt. practice Seal Beach, Calif., 1975—. Prin. works include fin. models for Calif. Fed. Bank, L.A., First Nat. City Bank, N.Y.C., Glendale (Calif.) Fed. Bank, Wailea, Alexander and Baldwin, Hawaii. Lt. (j.g.) USN, 1955-58. Achievements include research computerized techniques in architecture and economic feasibility land development. Home and Office: 1721 Catalina Ave Seal Beach CA 90740-5710

ROSSING, THOMAS D., physics professor; b. Madison, SD, Mar. 27, 1929; s. Torstein H. and Luella E. Rossing; children: Karen, Barbara, Erik, Jane, Mary. BA, Luther Coll., 1950; MS, Iowa State U., 1952, PhD, 1954. Rsch. physicist Univac div. Sperry Rand, 1954-57; prof. physics St. Olaf Coll., 1957-71, chmn. physics dept., 1963-69; prof. physics No. Ill. U., DeKalb, 1971—2003, prof. Emeritus, 2000—, disting. rsch. prof., chmn. dept., 1971-73. Rschr. Microwave Lab., Stanford (Calif.) U., 1961-62, Lincoln Lab., MIT, Cambridge, Mass., summer 1963, Clarendon Lab., Oxford (Eng.) U., 1966-67, physics dept. MIT, 1976-77; rsch. assoc. Argonne (Ill.) Nat Lab., 1974-76, scientist-in-residence, 1990-95; vis. lectr. U. New Eng., Armidale, Australia, 1980-81; vis. exch. scholar to China, 1988; guest rschr. Royal Inst. Tech., Stockholm, 1983, 84, 85, Inst. Perception Rsch., Eindhoven, The Netherlands, 1984, 85, Physikalisch-Technische Bundesanstalt, Braunschweig, Germany, 1988-89; guest rschr. Ecole Nat. Superíeure des Telecomm., Paris, 1996, Luleå U. Tech., Sweden, 1996, U. Calif., San Diego, 1998, Fraunhofer Inst., Stuttgart, Germany, 1998; vis. prof. U. Edinburgh, Scotland, 2003, Stanford U., 2005, Seoul Nat. U., 2006. Contbr. articles to profl. jours.; author: (book) Heat Capacity Lag of Gaseous Mixtures, 1956, Musical Acoustics, 1976, Control of Environmental Noise, 1977, Environmental Noise Control, 1979, Science of Sound, 1982, 1990, 2002, Acoustical Laboratory Experiments, 1982, 2002, Acoustics of Bells, 1984, Acoustics and You, 1985, Musical Acoustics, 1988, Physics of Musical Instruments, 1991, 1998, Principles of Vibration and Sound, 1995, 2004, Light Science, 1998, Science of Percussion Instruments, 2000, Teaching Light and Color, 2002, Springer Handbook of Acoustics, 2007. Recipient Robert Millikan medal, 2000. Fellow AAAS, IEEE, Am. Phys. Soc., Acoustical Soc. Am. (Silver medal in mus. acoustics 1992), Acoustical Soc. India (hon.); mem. Am. Assn. Physics Tchrs. (pres. 1991, Robert A. Milliken medal 2000), Sigma Xi (nat. lectr. 1984-87), Sigma Pi Sigma. Achievements include research in musical acoustics, psychoacoustics, speech and singing, vibration analysis, magnetic levitation, environmental noise conrol, surface effects in fusion reactors, spin waves in metals, physics education; 9 U.S. and 11 foreign patents in field. Office: Univ Stanford CCRMA Dept Music Stanford CA 94305 Business E-Mail: rossing@ccrma.stanford.edu.

ROSSITER, BRYANT WILLIAM, chemistry consultant; b. Ogden, Utah, Mar. 10, 1931; s. Bryant B. and Christine (Peterson) R.; m. Betty Jean Anderson, Apr. 16, 1951; children: Bryant, Mark, Diane, Steven, Linda, Karen, Matthew, Gregory. BA, U. Utah, 1954, PhD, 1957. Researcher Eastman-Kodak Co., Rochester, NY, 1957-63, head color phys. chem. lab., 1963-70, dir. chemistry div., 1970-84, dir. sci., tech. devel., 1984-86; pres. Viratek Inc., Costa Mesa, Calif., 1986-89; sr. v.p. ICN Pharms., Costa Mesa, 1989-90; ret., 1990; pres., CEO WRECON, Inc., Laguna Hills, Calif., 1991-96, ret., 1996. Sr. editor John Wiley & Sons, N.Y.C., 1970—; chmn. bd. Nucleic Acid Rsch. Inst., Costa Mesa, 1987-88; trustee Eastman Dental Ctr., Rochester, 1973-93 (bd. pres. 1982-85); bd. dirs. Verax & Corp. Editor: (chem. treatises) Physical Methods of Chemistry (11 vols.), 1970-76, Physical Methods, (12 vols.), 1986—, Chemical Experimentation Under Extreme Conditions, 1979. Mem. rsch. adv. com. U.S. Agy. for Internat. Devel., Washington, chmn. rsch. adv. com., 1989-92; mem. panel on biosci. Pres.' Coun. Advisors on Sci. and Tech., 1991; mem. adv com. Cornell Internat. Inst. for Food, Agr. and Devel., 1991; presiding officer Ch. Jesus Christ Latter Day Saints, Ea. U.S. and Can., 1959-86, dir. cmty. rels. Orange County, 2004—; counselor presidency San Diego temple, 1998-2002, dir. cmty. rels. Orange county pub. affairs coun., 2005—. 1st lt. USAFR, 1951-58. Named Hon. Alumni Brigham Young U., Provo, Utah, 1982. Fellow AAAS, Am. Inst. Chemists (lectr., Fellows award 1988, Will Judy award Juanita Coll. 1978); mem. Internat. Union Pure and Applied Chemistry (chmn. U.S. nat. com., orignator, chmn. Chemical Rsch. Applied to World Needs com. 1975-87, chmn. Chemical Rsch. Applied to World Needs II The Internat. Conf. on Chemistry and World Food Supplies, 1982), Am. Chem. Soc. (chmn. internat. activities). Avocations: horseback riding, reading, fishing. Home and Office: 25662 Dillon Rd Laguna Hills CA 92653-5800 E-mail: bwr@rossitess.com.

ROSSUM, RALPH ARTHUR, political science professor; b. Alexandria, Minn., Dec. 17, 1946; s. Floyd Arthur and June Marion (Carlson) R.; m. Constance Mary Brazina, Aug. 19, 1972; children: Kristin, Brent, Pierce. BA summa cum laude, Concordia Coll., 1968; MA, U. Chgo., 1971, PhD, 1973. Instr. Grinnell (Iowa) Coll., 1972-73; asst. prof. Memphis State U., 1973-77, assoc. prof., 1977-80, Loyola U., Chgo., 1980-83, assoc. dean grad. sch., 1981-82; dep. dir. bur. justice stats. U.S. Dept. Justice, Washington, 1983-84; Alice Tweed Tuohy prof. govt. Claremont (Calif.) McKenna Coll., 1984-88, v.p. and dean of faculty, 1988-91; pres. Hampden-Sydney (Va.) Coll., 1991-92; Salvatori Vis. prof. Claremont (Calif.) McKenna Coll., 1992-93, Salvatori prof. Am. Constitutionalism, 1994—; Fletcher Jones Prof. of Am. Politics U. Redlands, Redlands, Calif., 1993-94. Mem. adv. bd. Nat. Inst. Corrections, U.S. Dept. Justice, 1988-91; mem. Robert Presley Inst. Corrections Rsch. and Tng., State of Calif., 1988-91; dir. Rose Inst. of State and Local Govt., 2000—; mem. nat. bd. dirs. FIPSE, U.S. Dept. Edn., 2002—. Author: Federalism, the Supreme Court and the Seventeenth Amendment, 2001, others, Antonin Scalia's Jurisprudence: Text and Tradition, 2006; co-author: The American Founding, 1981, American Constitutional Law, 1983, 1987, 1991, 1995, 1999, 2003—07, 2009—, others; editor (sr.): Benchmark, 1983—86; book rev. editor:, 1986—91; contbr. 65 articles to profl. jours., chapters to books. Trustee Episcopal Theol. Sch., Claremont, 1987-91. Ford Found. fellow, 1968—72. Mem.: Am. Polit. Sci. Assn. Episcopalian. Office: Claremont McKenna Coll Dept Govt 850 Columbia Ave Claremont CA 91711-3901 Home Phone: 909-625-3802; Office Phone: 909-607-3392. Business E-Mail: ralph.rossum@claremontmckenna.edu.

ROST, THOMAS LOWELL, retired botany educator; b. St. Paul, Dec. 28, 1941; m. Ann Marie Ruhland, Aug. 31, 1963. BS, St. John's U., Collegeville, Minn., 1963; MA, Minn. State U., 1965; PhD, Iowa State U., 1971. Postdoctoral fellow Brookhaven Nat. Lab., Upton, NY, 1970-72; asst. to full prof. dept. botany U. Calif., Davis, 1972-82, faculty asst. to chancellor, 1982-83, prof., chmn. plant biology sect., 1994-96, assoc. dean divsn. biol. sci., 1996—2003, exec. assoc. dean, 2003—05, prof. emeritus, 2006—. Cons. faculty of agronomy U. Uruguay, 1979, 89, 2005; vis. fellow Rsch. Soc. Biol. Sci., Canberra, Australia, 1979-80; vis. prof. U. Wroclaw, Poland, 1987, U. Exeter, Eng., 1993, Copenhagen U., 2003, Aristotle U., Thessalaniki, Greece, 2005. Co-author: Botany: A Brief Introduction to Plant Biology, 1979, Botany: An Introduction on Plant Biology, 1982; co-editor: Mechanisms and Control of Cell Division, 1977, Plant Biology, 1998, 2d edit., 2005; contbr. articles to profl. jours. Internat. pres. Gamma Sigma Delta, 2004—06. Served to capt. US Army, 1965—67. Fellow Japan Soc. Promotion of Sci.; mem. Bot. Soc. Am. (Edwin E. Bossen award 2007, Merit award, 2008, Soc. Exptl. Biology, Am. Inst. Biol. Sci. Democrat. Roman Catholic. Avocation: community theatre. Office: U Calif Sect Plant Biology Davis CA 95616-8537

ROSTER, MICHAEL, lawyer; b. Chgo., May 7, 1945; AB, Stanford U., 1967, JD, 1973. Bar: Calif. 1973, DC 1980. Ptnr. McKenna, Conner & Cuneo, LA, Washington, 1973—87, Morrison & Foerster, LA, Washington, 1987—93; gen. counsel Stanford (Calif.) U., 1993—2000; exec. v.p., gen. counsel Golden West Fin. Corp., Oakland, Calif., 2000—07. Bd. dirs. Silicon Valley Bancshares, vice chmn., 1995—98; chmn. Encirq, 1998—2000, Insert Therapeutics, 2000—04, Fed. Home Loan Bank, San Francisco, 2005—07. Contbr. articles to profl. jours. Bd. dirs. Pasadena Heritage, 1986—87. Lt. (j.g.) USN, 1969—71. Mem.: ABA (fin. svcs. com. 1981—, chmn. com. savs. instns. 1985—89, banking com. 1989—, vice chmn. 2005—08), Assn. Corp. Counsel Value Challenge (chmn. 2008—),

Calif. Bankers Assn., Am. Corp. Counsel Assn. (chmn. 2000—01), Calif. Bar Assn. (chmn. banking com. 1978—79), Stanford U. Alumni Assn. (chmn. 1992), LA Athletic Club.

ROSTOKER, GORDON, physicist, researcher; b. Toronto, Ont., Can., July 15, 1940; s. Louis and Fanny (Silbert) R.; m. Gillian Patricia Farr, June 29, 1966; children: Gary David, Susan Birgitta, Daniel Mark. BSc in Physics, U. Toronto, 1962, MA in Physics, 1963; PhD in Geophysics, U. B.C., Can., 1966. Postdoctoral fellow Royal Inst. Tech., Stockholm, 1966-68; asst. prof. physics U. Alta., B.C., 1968-73, assoc. prof. B.C., 1973-79, prof. B.C., 1979-97, McCalla Rsch. Prof. B.C., 1983-84, prof. emeritus B.C., 1997—, ann. Killam prof. B.C., 1991-92, dir. Inst. Earth and Planetary Physics B.C., 1985-91. Assoc. chmn. dept. physics U. Alta., 1976-79, univ. rep. to bd. dirs. Can. Network for Space Rsch., 1992-94, mem. univ. rsch. policy com., 1987-91; cons. TRW Sys. Group, 1973, Dome Petroleum Ltd., 1981, U. Western Ont., 1983, York U., 1986; contract rschr. Energy, Mines and Resources, Can., Hydro-Québec; mem. assoc. com. space rsch. Nat. Rsch. Coun. Can., 1975-80, mem. com. on internat. sci. exchgs., 1977-79, others; mem. physics and astronomy com. Natural Scis. and Engring. Rsch. Coun., 1979-82, mem. spl. ad hoc com. on physics and astronomy, 1987-91, mem. grant selection com. for sci. publs., 1988-92; prin. investigator CANOPUS, 1989-1999; chmn. divsn. III Internat. Assn. Geomagnetism and Aeronomy, 1979-83; chmn. working group on data analysis phase of Internat. Magnetospheric Study Sci. Com. on Solar Terrestrial Physics of Internat. Coun. Sci. Unions, 1980-86, co-chmn. steering com. for Solar-Terrestrial Energy Program, 1987-89, chmn., 1989-97. Editor Can. Jour. Physics, 1980-86, mem. edtl. adv. bd., 1986-96; assoc. editor Jour. Geomagnetism and Geoelectricity, 1993-96; contbr. over 250 articles to profl. publs. Mem. pub. adv. com. Govtl. Environ. Conservation Authority of Province of Alta., Edmonton, 1973-74. Recipient Steacie prize EWR Steacie Meml. Fund, 1979, Geophys. Centenary medal Acad. Scis. USSR, 1984. Fellow Royal Soc. Can.; mem. Am. Geophys. Union (assoc. editor Jour. Geophys. Rsch. 1976-79, 92-94, internat. sec. 1998-2002), Can. Assn. Physicists (sec.-treas. Can. Geophys. Union 1973-74, chmn. divsn. aeronomy and space physics 1977-78, publs. com. 1980-86), Internat. Assn. Geomagnetism and Aeronomy (v.p. 1995-99). Achievements include use of ground magnetometer arrays to discover stepwise evolution of electric current systems which flow in the ionosphere and magnetosphere during episodes of strong auroral disturbance. Office: U Alta Dept Physics Edmonton AB Canada T6G 2J1 Home Phone: 780-434-4277; Office Phone: 780-492-5286. E-mail: rostoker@space.ualberta.ca.

ROSTOKER, MICHAEL DAVID, retired micro-electronics company executive; b. Quincy, Mass., Mar. 15, 1958; s. David and E. Louise (Berleue) R. Student, Carnegie-Mellon U., 1976-78; BS in Indsl. Engring., U. Pitts., 1980; JD, Franklin Pierce Law Ctr., 1984; PhD in Indsl. Engring., City U., LA, 1992; JSM, Stanford U., 1997; PhD in Econs., Moscow State U., 1999. Bar: U.S. Patent and Trademark Office 1983, N.H. 1984, U.S. Dist. Ct. N.H. 1984, Mass. 1985, Pa. 1985, U.S. Dist. Ct. D.C. 1985, U.S. Ct. Appeals (D.C. cir.) 1985. Lectr. in computer sci. Point Park Coll., Pitts., 1979-80; sys. analyst GE, Fitchburg, Mass., 1980-81; patent atty. Rines and Rines, Boston and Concord, N.H., 1983-85; patent counsel Schlumberger Well Svcs., Houston, 1985-87; sr. counsel intellectual property Intel Corp., Santa Clara, Calif., 1987-88; v.p. strategic alliances LSI Logic Corp., Milpitas, Calif., 1988-96; pres., CEO Microelectronics Rsch. Inc. subs. Kawasaki, San Jose, Calif., 1996-99; ret., 1999. Cons. in field, Concord, 1981-85; mem. faculty computer sci. and math. Franklin Pierce Coll., Rindge, N.H., 1981-85; mem. adj. faculty law Franklin Pierce Law Ctr., 1983-85; edtl. bd. Software Protection Reporter, 1984-94; lectr. seminars in field. Author: Computer Jurisprudence: Legal Responses to the Information Revolution, 1985, Technology Management: Licensing and Protection for Computers in the World Market, 1993; contbr. articles to profl. jours.; patentee in field. Mem. ABA (patents, sci. and tech., litigation sects.), Am. Trial Lawyers Assn., Am. Intellectual Property Assn. Republican. Jewish. Avocations: volleyball, racquetball, weightlifting, theater, music. Office: Microelectronics Rsch Inc 2570 N 1st St Ste 301 San Jose CA 95131-1018 Home: PO Box 685 Nevada City CA 95959-0685

ROSZTOCZY, FERENC ERNO, construction and agricultural machinery executive; b. Aug. 16, 1932; came to U.S., 1957; naturalized, 1962; s. Ferenc Lipot and Edith Jolan (Kunzl) R.; m. Diane Elder, Dec. 21, 1963; children: Tthomas Ferenc, Robert Anthony, Stephanie R. McGeorge, Edward Joseph. MS, U. Szeged, 1955; PhD, U. Calif., Berkeley, 1961. Phys. chemnist Stanford Rsch. Inst., Menlo Park, Calif., 1961-64; mem. tech. staff Bell Labs., Murray Hill, N.J., 1964-68; mgr. semicondr. materials Bell & Howell, Pasadena, Calif., 1968-69; mgr. semicondr. crystal growth and device engring. Varian Assocs., Palo Alto, Calif., 1969-75; mgr. Ariz. Machinery, 1975—. Bd. dirs. Ariz. Machinery Co., Avondale, 1974—, pres., 1975-98, chmn. bd., 1976—; pres. Stotz Farms, Inc., 1979—; dir. Ariz. Indsl. Machinery Co., 1975-91; cons. Siltec Corp., Menlo Park, Calif., 1971-72; mem. agribusiness adv. bd. 1st Interstate Bank Ariz., 1995-96. Contbr. articles to profl. jours.; patentee in field. Trustee Agua Fria H.s., 1981-89, pres., 1986-87. Mem. United Dairymen Ariz. (bd. dirs. 1985-98), Wigwam Country. Roman Catholic. Home: 1010 E Acacia Cir Litchfield Park AZ 85340-4529 Office: Ariz Machinery Co 11111 W Mcdowell Rd Avondale AZ 85323-5000

ROTELLA, STEPHEN J., former bank executive; BA, SUNY, Stony Brook, 1975; MBA, SUNY, Albany, 1978. Dir. mortgage products Shearson Lehman Bros.; with JP Morgan Chase, 1987—2005, COO Chase Home Fin., 1998—2001, exec. v.p., mem. exec. com., CEO Chase Home Fin., 2001—04; pres., COO Washington Mutual Inc., Seattle, 2005—08. Mem. exec. com. Housing Policy Council Fin. Services Roundtable; bd. dir., mem. residential bd. gov. Mortgage Bankers Assn. Bd. dir. St. Barnabas Med. Ctr., NJ. Office: Washington Mutual Inc Washington Mutual Tower 1201 Third Ave Seattle WA 98101

ROTELLINI, FELECIA A., state agency administrator; b. Sheridan, Wyo., 1957; Grad. magna cum laude in Hist. and Polit. Sci., Rocky Mountain Coll., Billings, Mont., 1981; grad., Notre Dame Law Sch., 1986. Bar: Ariz. 1986, Wyo. Pvt. practice atty., Ariz., 1986—92; asst. atty. gen. State of Ariz., 1992—2005; asst. supt. Ariz. Dept. Fin. Instns., 2005—06, supt., 2006—. Trustee Boys and Girls Clubs Met. Phoenix Found., 1990—2002. Mem.: Wyo. State Bar, Ariz. State Bar (mem. adminstrv. law sect.). Office: Ariz Dept Fin Instns 2910 N 44th St Ste 310 Phoenix AZ 85018 Office Phone: 602-255-4421. Office Fax: 602-381-1225. E-mail: frotellini@azdfi.gov.

ROTENBERG, MANUEL, physics professor; b. Toronto, Ont., Can., Mar. 12, 1930; came to U.S., 1946; s. Peter and Rose (Plonzker) R.; m. Paula Weissbrod, June 22, 1952; children: Joel, Victor. BS, MIT, 1952, PhD, 1956. Staff Los Alamos (N.Mex.) Nat. Lab., 1955-58; instr. physics Princeton (N.J.) U., 1958-59; asst. prof. U. Chgo., 1959-61; prof. applied physics U. Calif., San Diego, 1961-93, dean grad. studies and research, 1975-84, chmn. dept. elec. engring. and computer sci., 1988-93, rsch. prof., 1993—. Author: The 3-j and 6-j Symbols, 1959; founding editor: Methods of Computational Physics, 1963, Jour. of Computational Physics, 1962; editor: Biomathematics and Cell Kinetics, 1981. Fellow Am. Phys. Soc.; mem. AAAS, Sigma Xi. Office: U Calif San Diego La Jolla CA 92093-0407 Home Phone: 858-552-0415; Office Phone: 858-534-2726. Business E-Mail: rote@ucsd.edu.

ROTH, BERNARD, mechanical engineering educator, researcher; b. NYC, May 28, 1933; s. Morris Michael and Sara (Goldfarb) R.; m. Ruth Ochs, June 24, 1954; children: Steven Howard, Elliot Marc. BS, CCNY, 1956; MS, Columbia U., 1958, PhD, 1962. Engr. Ford Instrument Co., LI, N.Y., 1955, Lockheed Aircraft Co., Van Nuys, Calif., 1956, Atlantic Design Co., Newark, 1958; lectr. CCNY, 1956-59; rsch. asst. Columbia U., NYC, 1959-62; prof. Stanford (Calif.) U., 1962—. Guest prof. U. Paris, 1988-90; expert, team leader UN Devel. Orgn., Vienna, Austria, 1986-88; hon. prof. IIT, Kanpur, 2005—; mem. adv. bd. Ctr. for Econ. Conversion, Mountain View, Calif., 1988—98; bd. dirs. Peace Rev. Jour., Palo Alto., Calif., 1988-93. Co-author: Theoretical Kinematics, 1979, 2d edit., 1990; contbr. numerous articles on kinematics, robotics and design to profl. jours. Recipient Joseph F. Engelberger award Robotics Industries Assn., 1986. Fellow ASME (Melville medal 1967, Best Papers award mechanism conf. 1978, 80, 82, 92, 94, chair design engring. divsn. 1981-82, Mechanisms Com. award 1982, Machine Design award 1984, Outstanding Design Educator award 2000), Japanese Soc. for Promotion Sci., IEEE (Pioneer in Robotics award 2000), Internat. Fedn. for Theory of Machines and Mechanisms (pres. 1980-83, hon. chmn. 7th World Congress 1987). Office: Stanford U Dept Mech Engring Stanford CA 94305

ROTH, DUANE J., pharmaceutical executive; Grad., Iowa Wesleyan Coll. Chmn., CEO Alliance Pharm. Corp. Chmn. San Diego Regional Econ. Devel. Corp.; mem. bd. dir. Biotechnology Industry Org., CA Healthcare Inst. Chmn. Am. Heart Assn. Heart Walk; co-chair Children's Hosp. Found.'s Ann. Miracles Weekend. Recipient AT & T Internat. Bus. Leadership award, San Diego Press Club's Headliner of Yr. award, Making a Difference award, San Diego Citizens Against Lawsuit Abuse, Price Waterhouse Svc. to the Biotechnology Cmty. award, James McGraw Disting. Contbn. award for svc. to San Diego biomed. industry; named IFCD Dir. of Yr. for Corp. Citizenship.

ROTH, ERIC, screenwriter; b. NYC, Mar. 22, 1945; 6 children. Student, Columbia U., UCLA. Screenplays include: The Stranger in 7A, 1972, The Nickel Ride, 1975, The Concorde - Airport '79, 1979, Suspect, 1987, Memories of Me, 1988 (with Billy Crystal), Mr. Jones, 1993, Forrest Gump, 1994 (Acad. award Best Adapted Screenplay), the Postman, 1997, The Horse Whisperer, 1998, The Insider (nominated for Acad., Golden Globe 1999), Munich, 2005, The Good Shepherd, 2006, Lucky You, 2007, The Curious Case of Benjamin Button, 2008 (Best Adapted Screenplay, Nat. Bd. Review, 2008); co-writer: (with Michael Mann) Ali, 2001. Office: care Creative Artists Agy 9830 Wilshire Blvd Beverly Hills CA 90212-1804

ROTH, JOE, motion picture company executive; b. NYC, June 13, 1948; m. Donna Roth. BA, Boston U. Prodn. assistant various commls. and feature films, San Francisco; also lighting dir. Pitchel Players, San Francisco, then producer LA; co-founder Morgan Creek Prodns., LA, 1987-89; chmn. 20th Century Fox Film Corp., LA, 1989-92; founder Caravan Pictures, LA, 1992-94; chmn. Walt Disney Motion Pictures Group, Burbank, 1994—96, Walt Disney Studios, Burbank, 1996—2000; founder Revolution Pictures, 2000—. Bd. dirs. Pixar Studios, 2000—. Prodr. (films) Tunnel Vision, 1976, Our Winning Season, 1978, Americathon, 1979, Ladies and Gentlemen, the Fabulous Stains, 1981, Final Terror, 1983, The Stone Boy, 1984, Moving Violations, 1985, Off Beat, 1986, Where the River Runs Black, 1986, Streets of Gold, 1986, P.K. and the Kid, 1987, Young Guns, 1988, Skin Deep, 1989, Major League, 1989, Nightbreed, 1990, The Three Musketeers, 1993, Angels in the Outfield, 1994, Low Down Dirty Shame, 1994, Houseguest, 1995, The Jerky Boys, 1995, Heavyweights, 1995, Tall Tale, 1995, While You Were Sleeping, 1995, The Forgotten, 2004; exec. prodr. (films) Cracking Up, 1977, Bachelor Party, 1984, Revenge of the Nerds II: Nerds in Paradise, 1987, Dead Ringers, 1988, Renegades, 1989, Enemies: A Love Story, 1989, The Exorcist III, 1990, Pacific Heights, 1990, Angie, 1994, Before and After, 1996, Tears of the Sun, 2003, Daddy Day Care, 2003, Hollywood Homicide, 2003, Mona Lisa Smile, 2003, An Unfinished Life, 2005; dir. Streets of Gold, 1986, Coupe de Ville, 1990, America's Sweethearts, 2001, Christmas with the Kranks, 2004, Freedomland, 2006. Named one of 50 Most Powerful People in Hollywood, Premiere mag., 2002—05. Office: Pixar 1200 Park Ave Emeryville CA 94608

ROTH, JOHN KING, philosopher, educator; b. Grand Haven, Mich., Sept. 3, 1940; s. Josiah V. and Doris Irene (King) R.; m. Evelyn Lillian Austin, June 25, 1964; children: Andrew Lee, Sarah Austin. BA, Pomona Coll., 1962; student, Yale U., 1962-63, MA, 1965, PhD, 1966; LHD, Ind. U., 1990, Grand Valley State U., 1998, Hebrew Union Coll., 1999, We. U. Health Scis., 1999. Asst. prof. philosophy Claremont McKenna Coll., Calif., 1966-71, assoc. prof., 1971-76, Russell K. Pitzer prof. philosophy, 1976—2003; vis. prof. philosophy Franklin Coll., Lugano, Switzerland, 1973; Edward J. Sexton prof. philosophy Claremont McKenna Coll., 2003—; dir. Center for the Study of the Holocaust, Genocide, and Human Rights, 2003. Fulbright lectr. in Am. studies U. Innsbruck, Austria, 1973-74, Royal Norwegian Ministry of Edn., Oslo, Norway, 1995-96; vis. prof. philosophy Doshisha U., Kyoto, Japan, 1981-82; vis. prof. Holocaust studies U. Haifa, Israel, 1982. Author: Freedom and the Moral Life, 1969, Problems of the Philosophy of Religion, 1971, American Dreams, 1976, A Consuming Fire, 1979; (with Richard L. Rubenstein) Approaches to Auschwitz, 1987, rev. ed., 2003; (with Frederick Sontag) The American Religious Experience, 1972, The Questions of Philosophy, 1988; (with Robert H. Fossum) The American Dream, 1981, American Ground, 1988; (with Rubenstein) The Politics of Latin American Liberation Theology, 1988; (with Michael Berenbaum) Holocaust: Religious and Philosophical Implications, 1989, Ethics, 1991; (with Carol Rittner) Memory Offended, 1991; (with Creighton Peden) Rights, Justice, and Community, 1992; (with Carol Rittner) Different Voices, 1993, American Diversity, American Identity, 1995, Inspiring Teaching, 1997, From the Unthinkable to the Unavoidable, 1997, Encyclopedia of Social Issues, 1997, Private Needs, Public Selves: Talk About Religion in American, 1997, (with Stephen R. Haynes) The Death of God Movement and the Holocaust, 1999, Ethics After the Holocaust, 1999, Holocaust Politics, 2001, (with Elisabeth Maxwell) Remembering for the Future, 2001, Pope Pius XII and the Holocaust, 2002, Will Genocide Ever End?, 2002, After-Words, (with David Patterson), 2004. Spl. advisor U.S. Holocaust Meml. Coun., Washington, 1980-85, mem., 1995-98. Danforth grad. fellow, 1962-66; Graves fellow, 1970-71; NEH fellow, 1976-77, Koerner fellow Oxford Ctr. for Hebrew and Jewish Studies, Eng., 2001; Ina Levine Scholar-in-residence, US Holocaust Meml. Mus., 2004-2005; Faculty Pairing grantee Japan-U.S. Friendship Commn., 1981-83; named U.S. Prof. of Yr. Coun. Advancement and Support of Edn. and Carnegie Found. Advancement of Tchg., 1988. Mem Am. Philos. Assn., Am. Acad. Religion, Am. Studies Assn., Calif. Coun. for Humanities, Phi Beta Kappa. Presbyterian. Office: Claremont McKenna Coll 850 Columbia Ave Claremont CA 91711-3901 Home: PO Box 1254 Winthrop WA 98862-1220 Office Phone: 909-607-2891. E-mail: John.Roth@claremontmckenna.edu.

ROTH, JOHN ROGER, geneticist, biology educator; b. Winona, Minn., Mar. 14, 1939; s. Frederick Daniel and Louise Mae (Wirt) R.; m. Uta Goetz (div.); children: Katherine Louise, Frederick Phillip; m. Sherylynne Harris, Jan. 4, 1986. BA, Harvard U., 1961; PhD, John Hopkins U., 1965. From asst. prof. molecular biology to prof. molecular biology U. Calif., Berkeley, 1967-76; prof. biology U. Utah, Salt Lake City, 1976—2002; prof. sect. microbiology U. Calif., Davis, 2002—, chair sect. microbiology, 2003—. Recipient Disting. Prof. award, 1990, Rosenblatt award, 1990. Mem. NAS, Am. Soc. for Microbiology, Genetics Soc. Am. Office: Univ Calif Microbiology 314 Briggs Hall One Shields Ave Davis CA 95616

ROTH, PAUL BARRY, dean, educator, emergency medicine physician; b. Glen Ridge, NJ, Oct. 7, 1947; s. Jerome M. and Selma (Leitner) R. BS, Fairleigh Dickinson U., 1969, MS, 1972; MD, George Washington U., 1976; postgrad., U. N.Mex., Albuquerque, 1976-79. Resident in family practice U. N.Mex. Sch. Medicine, Albuquerque, 1976—79; owner, pres. EMS of N.Mex., Albuquerque, 1978-82; owner, mem. of bd. Heights Urgent Care Ctr., Albuquerque, 1980-82; dir. divsn. emergency medicine dept. family, cmty. and emergency medicine U. N.Mex. Sch. Medicine, Albuquerque, 1982-91, prof. emerg. med., 1991—, chair dept. emergency medicine, 1991-93, interim chief med. officer, 1992—93, interim dean, 1994—95, dean, 1994—; interim dir. U. N.Mex. Med. Ctr., Albuquerque, 1994—95; med. dir. disaster medicine Nat. Disaster Med. Sys.; exec. v.p. U. N.Mex. Health Sci. Ctr., 2005—. Chair disaster com. U. N.Mex. Med. Ctr. Contbr. articles to Annals of EM, Current Practice of EM-Disaster Medicine, Jour. of AMA. Recipient Outstanding Individual Svc. award Nat. Disaster Med. Sys., 1986. Fellow Am. Coll. Emergency Physicians (chair sect. on disaster medicine, 1991-92), Am. Acad. Family Practice; mem. AMA, Soc. for Acad. Emergency Medicine, Am. Coll. Physician Execs., Am. Acad. Family Physicians.

ROTH, PETER, broadcast executive; b. Larchmont, NY; m. Andrea Roth; 2 children. Student, U. Pa.; grad., Tufts U., 1972. From mgr. to dir. children's programs ABC TV Network, 1976, dir. current programs, 1979, v.p. current prime-time series, 1981; past pres. Stephen J. Cannell Prodns.; pres. prodn. Twentieth Network TV, 1992, pres., 1993, 20th Century Fox TV, 1994, Fox Entertainment Group, LA, 1996—98, Warner Bros. TV Production, Burbank, Calif., 1999—. Office: Office of President Warner Bros TV Production 400 Warner Blvd Burbank CA 91522

ROTH, RANDALL W., lawyer; b. Ellinwood, Kans., May 14, 1948; BS summa cum laude, Regis Coll., 1970; LLM, U. Miami, 1975. Bar: Colo. 1975, Kans. 1980, Hawaii 1983. Of counsel Goodsill Anderson Quinn & Stifel, Honolulu. Prof. law U. Hawaii, 1982—. Mem. ABA, Am. Coll. Trust and Estate Counsel, Hawaii State Bar Assn. (pres. 1999), Alpha Sigma Nu. Office: Goodsill Anderson Quinn & Stifel 1099 Alakea St Honolulu HI 96813-4511 E-mail: rroth@hawaii.edu.

ROTH, RONALD LEE, engineering educator; b. Oakland, Calif., May 20, 1947; s. Howard Benjamin and Lillian Roth; m. Alma Hayes, July 7, 1984; children: Owen Howard, Adam Ronald. BS in Engring., Harvey Mudd Coll., Claremont, Calif., 1969; MS in Mech. Engring., Stanford U., Calif., 1971, PhD, 1976; MD, St. Georges U., Grenada, 1986. Engr. Westinghouse Corp., LA, 1969—70; lectr. Calif. State U., Fresno, Calif., 1975—76, U. Calif., Berkeley, 1977, 1979; vis. prof. U. Auckland, New Zealand, 1992—93, lectr., 1980—82, San Jose State U., Calif., 1979; postdoctoral rsch. affiliate Stanford U., 1976—77, lectr., 1973, 1980; assoc. prof. Calif. State U., Chico, 1986—90, prof., 1990—. Dept. chair Calif. State U., Chico, 2001—04, Chico, 2007—. Contbr. articles to profl. jours. Recipient Profl. Promise award, Calif. State U., 1987; John F O'Connell fellow, 1998—2000, NSF Traineeship fellow, Stanford U., 1970—74. Mem.: Am. Soc. Engring. Edn., Tau Beta Pi. Office: Calif State Univ Mech Engring and Mfg Tech Dept Chico CA 95929-0789 Office Fax: 530-898-4070.

ROTHBLATT, DONALD NOAH, urban and regional planner, educator; b. NYC, Apr. 28, 1935; s. Harry and Sophie (Chernofsky) Rothblatt; m. Ann S. Vogel, June 16, 1957; children: Joel Michael, Steven Saul. BCE, CUNY, 1957; MS in Urban Planning, Columbia U., 1963; diploma in comprehensive planning, Inst. Social Studies, The Hague, 1964; PhD in City and Regional Planning, Harvard U., 1969. Cert. Am. Inst. Cert. Planners; registered prof. engr., NY. Planner NYC Planning Commn., 1960-62, NY Housing and Redevel. Bd., 1963-66; research fellow Ctr. for Environ. Design Studies, Harvard U., Cambridge, Mass., 1965-71; tchg. fellow, instr., then asst. prof. city and regional planning Harvard U., 1967-71; prof. urban and regional planning, chmn. dept. San Jose (Calif.) State U., 1971—. Lady Davis vis. prof. urban and regional planning Hebrew U., Jerusalem, 1978, Tel-Aviv U., 1978; vis. scholar Indian Inst. Architects, 1979, Shandong Province, China, 1996, U. Lodz, Poland, 2000, Paris Transp. Authority, 2002, Greater London Authority, 2003, Sydney Regional Orgn. Councils, 2004, Toronto Urban Devel. Svcs., 2005, NY Met. Transp. Coun., 2006, Phila., Del. Valley Regional Planning Commn., 2007, Guatemala City TransMetro Agy., 2008; cons. to pvt. industry and govt. agys. Mpls.-St. Paul Met. Coun., 2009. Author: Human Needs and Public Housing, 1964, Thailand's Northeast, 1967, Regional Planning: The Appalachian Experience, 1971, Allocation of Resources for Regional Planning, 1972, The Suburban Environment and Women, 1979, Regional-Local Development Policy Making, 1981, Planning the Metropolis: The Multiple Advocacy Approach, 1982, Comparative Suburban Data, 1983, Suburbia: An International Assessment, 1986, Metropolitan Dispute Resolution in

Silicon Valley, 1989, Good Practices for the Congestion Management Program, 1994, Activity-Based Travel Survey and Analysis of Responses to Increased Congestion, 1995, An Experiment in Sub-Regional Planning: California's Congestion Management Policy, 1995, Estimating the Origins and Destinations of Transit Passengers from On/Off Counts, 1995, Changes in Property Values Induced by Light Transit, 1996, Comparative Study of Statewide Transportation Planning Under ISTEA, 1997, North American Metropolitan Planning Reexamined, 1999; actor: Government Performance Measures Linking Urban Mass Transportation with Land Use and Accessibility Factors, 2000, Best Practices in Developing Regional Transportation Plans, 2001, Comparative Study of U.S. Metropolitan Transportation Planning, 2004; editor: National Policy for Urban and Regional Development, 1974, Regional Advocacy Planning: Expanding Air Transport Facilities for the San Jose Metropolitan Area, 1975, Metropolitan-wide Advocacy Planning: Dispersion of Low and Moderate Cost Housing the San Jose Metropolitan Area, 1976, Multiple Advocacy Planning: Public Surface Transportation in the San Jose Metropolitan Area, 1977, A Multiple Advocacy Approach to Regional Planning: Open Space and Recreational Facilities for the San Jose Metropolitan Area, 1979, Regional Transportation Planning for the San Jose Metropolitan Area, 1981, Planning for Open Space and Recreational Facilities in the San Jose Metropolitan Area, 1982, Regional Economic Development Planning for the San Jose Metropolitan Area, 1984, Planning for Surface Transportation in the San Jose Metropolitan Area, 1986, Expansion for Air Transportation Facilities in the San Jose Metropolitan Area, 1987, Provision of Economic Development in the San Jose Metropolitan Area, 1989, Metropolitan Governance: American/Canadian Intergovernmental Perspectives, 1993, Metropolitan Governance Revisited, 1998; contbr. articles to profl. jours.; dir.: (TV series) Sta. KTEH, 1976. Mem. adv. coun. Bay Area Met. Transp. Commn., 1995—. Served to 1st lt. C.E. US Army Corps of Engrs., 1957—59. Recipient Innovative Tchg. award, Calif. State U. and Coll., 1975—79, award, Internat. Festival Films Architecture and Planning, 1983, Meritorious Performance award, San Jose State U., 1986, 1988, 1990, 1996—2001; co-recipient Best of West award, Western Ednl. Soc. Telecom., 1976; grantee, Nat. Inst. Dispute Resolution, 1987—88, Can. Studies Enrichment Program, 1992—93; Rsch. fellow, Harvard U., 1967—69, William F. Milton Rsch. fellow, 1970—71, Faculty Rsch. grantee, NSF, 1972—82, Calif. State U., 1977—78, Univ. Rsch. and Tng. Program grantee, Calif. Dept. Transp., 1993—97. Fellow: Am. Inst. Cert. Planners (inducted 2006); mem.: AAUP, Architecture and Urban and Regional Planning (chmn. 1973—75), Calif. Edn. Com. Architecture and Landscape, Internat. Fedn. Housing and Planning, Planners Equal Opportunity, Am. Planning Assn., Assn. Collegiate Schs. Planning (pres. 1975—76). Office: San Jose State U Dept Urban & Regional Planning San Jose CA 95192-0185

ROTHENBERG, ALAN I., lawyer, professional sports association executive; b. Detroit, Apr. 10, 1939; m. Georgina Rothenberg; 3 children. BA, U. Mich., 1960, JD, 1963. Bar: Calif. 1964. Assoc. O'Melveny & Myers, LA, 1963—66; ptnr. Manatt Phelps Rothenberg & Phillips, LA, 1968—90, Latham & Watkins, LA, 1990—2000; instr. sports law U. So. Calif., 1969, 1976, 1984, Whittier Coll. Law, 1980, 1984; pres., gen. counsel LA Lakers and LA Kings, 1967—79, LA Clippers Basketball Team, 1982—89; pres. U.S. Soccer Fedn., Chgo., 1990—98; founder, past chmn., trustee Maj. League Soccer, 1993—; chmn. Premier Partnerships, 1st Century Bank, LA, 2002—. Bd. dir. Calif. Pizza Kitchen Inc., 2006—, Arden Realty Inc., Zenith Nat. Corp.; mem. exec. com. CONCACAF. Bd. dirs., pres. Constl. Rights Found., 1987—90; soccer commr. 1984 Olympic Games; chmn., pres., CEO 1994 World Cup Organizing Com., 1990—94. Named to U.S. Nat. Soccer Hall of Fame, 2007. Mem.: NBA (bd. govs. 1971—79, 1982—89), ABA, N.Am. Soccer League (bd. govs. 1977—80, Major League Soccer mgmt. com. 1994—), LA Bar Assn., LA County Bar Assn., State Bar Calif. (pres. 1989—90), Order of Coif. Office: 1st Century Bank Ste 1400 1875 Century Park E Los Angeles CA 90067

ROTHENBERG, HARVEY DAVID, educational administrator; b. May 31, 1937; s. Max and Cecelia Rothenberg; m. Audrey Darlynne Roseman, July 5, 1964; children: David Michael, Mark Daniel. BBA, State U. Iowa, 1960; MA, U. No. Colo., Greeley, 1961; postgrad., Harris Tchrs. Coll., 1962-63; PhD, Colo. State U., Ft. Collins, 1972. Distributive edn. tchr. Roosevelt H.S., St. Louis, 1961-63, Proviso West H.S., Hillside, Ill., 1963-64, Longmont (Colo.) Sr. H.S., 1964-69, 70-71; supr. rsch. and spl. programs St. Vrain Valley Sch. Dist., Longmont, 1971-72; chmn. bus. divsn. Arapahoe C.C., Littleton, Colo., 1972-75; dir. vocat., career and adult edn. Arapahoe County Sch. Dist. 6, Littleton, 1975-96; part-time instr. Met. State Coll., Denver, 1975-85, Arapahoe C.C., Littleton, 1975-80, Regis U., 1980—. Dir. faculty, curriculum Sch. Profl. Studies, Regis U., 1996-98, instr., facilitator, 1998—; owner HDR Bus. and Ednl. Consulting, 1988—; owner Shreveport Bombers Indoor Football Team of Indoor Profl. Football League, 1999-2001; vis. prof. U. Ala., Tuscaloosa, summer 1972; dir. Chatfield Bank, Littleton, 1974-83, Yaak River Mines Ltd., Amusement Personified Inc.; pres. Kuytia Inc., Littleton, 1975—; co-owner Albuquerque Lasers. Author: Conducting Successful Business Research, 1996. Mem. City of Longmont Long-Range Planning Commn., 1971-72, pres. Homeowners Bd., 1978-80; mem. Denver Union Sta. renovation com., 2002—; mem. Jefferson County Cmty. Devel. Com., 2003—. Recipient Outstanding Young Educator award, St. Vrain Valley Sch. Dist., 1967, Outstanding Vocat. Educator, Colo., 1992, Western Region U.S., 1993. Mem. Am. Vocat. Assn., Nat. Assn. Local Sch. Adminstrs., Colo. Vocat. Assn. (mem. exec. com. 1966-68, treas. 1972-73), Littleton C. of C., Colo. Assn. Vocat. Adminstrs., Colo. Educators for and About Bus., Elks, Masons, Delta Sigma Pi, Delta Pi Epsilon. Home: 7461 S Sheridan Ct Littleton CO 80128-7084 Personal E-mail: rothenbergs@msn.com.

ROTHERHAM, LARRY CHARLES, insurance executive; b. Coun. Bluffs, Iowa, Oct. 22, 1940; s. Charles Sylvester and Edna Mary (Sylvanus) R.; m. Florene F. Black, May 29, 1965; children: Christopher Charles, Phillip Larry, Kathleen Florene. Student, Creighton U., 1959-61; BSBA, U. Nebr., 1965; postgrad., Am. Coll., Bryn Mawr, Pa., 1985-87. CPCU, CLU, ARM. Claims rep. and underwriter Safeco Ins. Co., Albuquerque, 1965-69; br. mgr. Ohio Casualty Group, Albuquerque, 1969-99, resident v.p. Denver, 1997-99. Assoc. in risk mgmt. Ins. Inst. Am., 1976—. Mem. PTA Collet Park Elem. Sch., Albuquerque, 1963-82, Freedom H.S., Albuquerque, 1982-86; bd. chmn. N.Mex. Property Ins. Program; mem. N.Mex. Workers compensation Appeals Bd.; bd. dirs. Friends of Hist. Ft. Logan. Mem. New Mex. Soc. Chartered Property & Casualty Underwriters (charter mem., pres. 1975-77), New Mex. Soc. Chartered Life Underwriters, New Mex. Ins. Assn. Democrat. Roman Catholic. Avocations: race walking, swimming, hiking, camping. Home: 10677 W Parkhill Pl Littleton CO 80127-5547

ROTHERHAM, THOMAS G., diversified financial services company executive; BA, U. Iowa. CPA. From mem. staff to exec. ptnr. McGladrey & Pullen LLP, Davenport, Iowa, 1971-88, exec. ptnr., 1988—97, COO, 1997—2000; pres., CEO RSM McGladrey Inc., 2000—03. Bd. dir. Peerless Systems Corp., 2004—. Mem. AICPA (SEC regulations com., SEC practice section exec. com.), Minn. Soc. CPAs. Mailing: Peerless Systems Corp Bd Directors 2381 Rosecrans Ave El Segundo CA 90245

ROTHFUSS, CHRISTOPHER J., political science professor; b. Ann Arbor, Mich., Oct. 21, 1972; m. Heather Hoveland; children: Connor, Zane. BA in Internat. Studies, U. Wyo., Laramie, 1994, MSChemE, 1996; PhD, U. Wash., 2002, MSc in Applied Physics, 2002. Tech. advisor US State Dept., 2003—06; instr., dept. polit. sci. and internat. studies U. Wyo., 2006—. US del. UN Com. on the Peaceful Uses of Outer Space. Recipient McCarthy Outstanding Tchg. Asst. award, U. Wash., 2002; Sci. and Tech. Diplomacy fellow, AAAS, 2003. Democrat. Office: c/o U Wyo Dept Polit Sci and Internat Studies 1000 E University Ave Laramie WY 82071

ROTHMAN, ELLIOTT, Mayor, Pomona, California; m. Pam Rothman; 1 child, Jason. Grad., U. La Verne. Councilman City of Pomona from Dist. 5, 1996—2008; mayor City of Pomona, 2008—. Rep. San Gabriel Valley Mosquito & Vector Control. Vol. Cat in the Hat Read Across America Program, Pomona Unified Sch. Dist. Reading Ranger Program, Boys & Girls Scouts America. Mailing: PO Box 660 Pomona CA 91769 Office: City Hall 505 South Garey Ave 2nd Fl Pomona CA 91766 Office Phone: 909-620-2376. Office Fax: 909-620-3707.*

ROTHMAN, PAUL A., publishing executive; b. Bklyn., June 26, 1940; s. Fred B. and Dorothy (Regosin) R.; m. Mary Ann Dalson, July 28, 1966 (div. 1992); m. Carol Ann Liske, Sept. 17, 1999; children: Deborah, Diana. BA, Swarthmore Coll., 1962; JD, U. Mich., 1965; LLM in Taxation, NYU, 1967. Bar: NY 1965. Assoc. Dewey, Ballentine, Busby, Palmer & Wood, NYC, 1965-67; v.p. Fred B. Rothman & Co., Littleton, Colo., 1967-85, pres., 1985-2000; chmn. bd. Colo. Plasticard, Littleton, 1983-95; owner LoDo Law Books, Denver, 1998—. Editor: Mich. Law Rev., 1963—65. Home: 1801 Wynkoop St Apt 708 Denver CO 80202-1196 Office: LoDo Law Books 1701 Wynkoop St Union Sta # 300 Denver CO 80202 Office Phone: 720-904-5145. E-mail: parothman@yahoo.com.

ROTHMAN, TOM (THOMAS EDGAR ROTHMAN), film company executive; b. Balt., Nov. 21, 1954; s. Donald and Elizabeth (Davidson) R.; m. Jessica Randolph Harper, Mar. 11, 1989; children: Elizabeth, Nora. BA, Brown U., 1976; JD, Columbia U., 1980. Ptnr. Frankfurt, Garbus, Klein, NYC, 1982-87; exec. v.p. prodn. Columbia Pictures, Burbank, Calif., 1987-89; sr. v.p. prodn. Samuel Goldwyn Co., LA, 1989-91, pres. worldwide prodn., 1991—94; founder, pres. Fox Searchlight Pictures, 1994; pres. Twentieth Century Fox, Beverly Hills, 1995—99, Twentieth Century Fox Film Group, 1999—2000; co-chmn. Fox Filmed Entertainment, Inc., L.A., 2000—. Exec. prodr.: (films) The Program, 1993; co-prodr.: Down By Law, 1986. Trustee Sundance (Utah) Inst. Recipient Arthur B. Krim award, Columbia U.; named one of The 50 Most Powerful People in Hollywood, Premiere mag., 2004—06, The 50 Smartest People in Hollywood, Entertainment Weekly, 2007. Office: Fox Filmed Entertainment Inc 10201 W Pico Blvd Los Angeles CA 90035*

ROTTER, JEROME ISRAEL, medical geneticist; b. LA, Feb. 24, 1949; s. Leonard L. and Jeanette (Kronenfeld) R.; m. Deborah Tofield, July 14, 1970; children: Jonathan Moshe, Amy Esther, Samuel Alexander. BS, UCLA, 1969, MD, 1973. Intern Harbor-UCLA Med. Ctr., Torrance, Calif., 1973-74, fellow in med. genetics, 1975-78, asst. research pediatrician, 1978-79, faculty div. med. genetics, 1978-86; resident in medicine Wadsworth VA Hosp., Los Angeles, 1974-75; asst. prof. medicine and pediatrics Sch. Medicine UCLA, 1979-83, assoc. prof. Sch. Medicine, 1983-87, prof. Sch. Medicine, 1987—; dir. divsn. med. genetics and co. dir. med. genetics birth defect ctr. Cedars-Sinai Med. Ctr., 1986—, assoc. dir. hypertension ctr., 1996—. Key investigator Ctr. for Ulcer Rsch. and Edn., L.A., 1980-89; dir. genetic epidemiology core Ctr. for Study of Inflammatory Bowel Disease, Torrance, 1985-91; assoc. dir. Cedars-Sinai Inflammatory Bowel Disease Ctr., L.A., 1992—; dir. Stuart Found. CSMC Common Disease Risk Assessment Ctr., 1986-96; dir. genetic epidemiology core project molecular biology of arteriosclerosis UCLA, 1987—. Bd. govs. Cedars-Sinai, chair med. genetics, 1990—. Recipient Regents scholarship UCLA, 1966-73; recipient Richard Weitzman award Harbor-UCLA, 1983, Ross award Western Soc. for Pediatric Rsch., 1985. Mem. Am. Heart Assn., Am. Soc. Human Genetics, Am. Gastroent. Assn., Am. Diabetes Assn., Soc. for Pediatric Research, Western Soc. for Clin. Investigation (mem. council 1985-88), Am. Fedn. for Med. Rsch., Western Assn. Physicians, Am. Soc. for Clin. Investigation, Am. Assn. Physicians. Jewish. Avocations: reading, racquetball. Office: Cedars Sinai Med Ctr Divsn Med Genetics 8700 Beverly Blvd Los Angeles CA 90048-1865

ROTTLER, JUERGEN, computer software company executive; Grad. in Computer Sci. and Bus. Adminstrn., Fachhochschule Furtwangen, Germany; MBA, Bentley Coll., Waltham, Mass. Mng. dir. Delphi Consulting Group; various positions up to sr. v.p. pub. sector, healthcare and edn. customer segment Hewlett-Packard, 1986—2004; exec. v.p. Oracle customer svcs. Oracle Corp., Redwood City, Calif., 2004. Office: Oracle Corp 500 Oracle Pky Redwood City CA 94065 Office Phone: 650-506-0024.

ROULAC, STEPHEN E., real estate consultant; b. San Francisco, Aug. 15, 1945; s. Phil Williams and Elizabeth (Young) R.; children: Arthur, Fiona. BA, Pomona Coll., 1967; MBA with distinction, Harvard Grad. Sch. Bus. Adminstrn., 1970; JD, U. Calif., Berkeley, 1976; PhD, Stanford U., 1978. CPA, Hawaii. Asst. constrn. supt., foreman, adminstr. Roulac Constrn. Co., Pasadena, Calif., 1963-66; rsch. asst. Econs. Rsch. Assocs., LA, 1966-67; assoc. economist Urbanomics Rsch. Assocs., Claremont, Calif., 1967; acquisition auditor Litton Industries Inc., Chgo., Beverly Hills, 1967-68; tax cons. Lybrand, Ross Bros. and Montgomery, LA, 1968; cons. to constrn. group and corp. planning dept. Owens-Corning Fiberglas Corp., Toledo, 1969-70; CEO Questor Assocs., San Francisco, 1972-83; chmn. nat. mgmt. adv. svcs. Kenneth Leventhal & Co., 1983-84; pres. Stephen E. Roulac & Co., 1985-86; mng. ptnr. Roulac Group of Deloitte Haskins & Sells (Deloitte & Touche), 1987-91; CEO The Roulac Group, Larkspur, Calif., 1992—. Strategic fin. econ. and transactions cons. Roulac Capitol Mkt. Strategies, Roulac Capitol Flows; expert witness, preparer econ. analyses for legal matters including civil trial of Irvine Co., Jewell et. al. vs. Bank of Am., Tchrs. vs. Olympia & York, Calif. Legis., Calif. Corps. Dept., Midwest Securities Commrs. Assn., Nat. Assn. Securities Dealers, SEC, Dept. of Labor, HUD; advisor to investment arm of Asian country, Calif. Pub. Employees Retirement System, U.S. Dept. Labor, numerous others; adj. prof. Tex. A&M U., 1986, U. Chgo., 1985, UCLA, 1983-84, Stanford Grad. Sch. Bus., 1970-79, Pacific Coast Banking Sch., 1978, Hastings Coll. Law, 1977-78, U. Calif., Berkeley, 1972-77, Calif. State U., 1970-71, Northeastern U., 1969-70; keynote speaker, instr. continuing edn. sessions, program chmn., corps., orgns. Author: Real Estate Syndications Digest: Principles and Applications, 1972, Case Studies in Property Development, 1973, Syndication Landmarks, 1974, Tax Shelter Sale-Leaseback Financing: The Economic Realities, 1976, Modern Real Estate Investment: An Institutional Approach, 1976, (with Sherman Maisel) Real Estate Investment and Finance, 1976 (1976 Bus. Book of Yr. The Libr. Jour.); editor-in-chief, pub. Calif. Bicyclist, 1988-95, Tex. Bicyclist, 1989-94, Roulac's Strategic Real Estate, 1979-89; columnist Forbes, 1983, 84, 87, 92, 93, Intuition Network, Ctr Real Estate Rsch. Nortwestern U., Nat. Bureau Real Estate Rsch., New Leaders, World 2000, NACORE/ARES Corp. Rsch. Found., Mystery Sch.; mem. editorial adv. bd. Am. Real Estate and Urban Econs. Assn. Jour., 1977-81, Housing Devel. Reporter, 1978-80, Fin. Edn. Jour., 1976-70, Jour. Housing Rsch., 1996—, Jour. Real Estated Edn. and Practice, 1996—, Jour. Real Estate Lit., 1996—, Jour. Property Valuation and Investment, 1992—, Real Estate Workouts and Asset Mgmt., 1992—; assoc. editor Real Estate Rev., 1993—; editor Jour. Real Estate Rsch., 1992—; contbg. editor Real Estate Law Jour., 1973-78, Real Estate Rev., 1973-75; spl. issue editor Calif. Mgmt. Rev., 1976; editor: Real Estate Syndication Digest, 1971-72, Notable Syndications Sourcebook, 1972, Real Estate Securities and Syndication: A Workbook, 1973, Due Diligence in Real Estate Transactions, 1974, Real Estate Venture Analysis, 1974, Real Estate Securities Regulation Sourcebook, 1975, Questor Real Estate Investment Manager Profiles, 1982, Questor Real Estate Securities Yearbook, 1980-85, Retail Giants and Real Estate, 1986, Roulac's Top Real Estate Brokers, 1984-88, (monograph) Ethics in Real Estate; contbr. articles to profl. jours., newspapers; cassettes; frequent appearer on TV shows including MacNeil/Lehrer Newshour, 1986, Cable News Network, 1987, ABC TV, 1987, KCBS Radio, 1986, WABC Radio, Dallas, 1986. Mem. real estate adv. com. to Calif. Commr. Corps., 1973, Calif. Corp. Commr.'s Blue Ribbon Com. on Projections and Track Records, 1973-74; mem. adv. bd. Nat. Bicycle Month, League of Am. Wheelmen, Ctr. for Real Estate Rsch. Kellogg Grad. Sch. Mgmt., Northwestern U. Named Highest Instr. Student Teaching Evaluations, Schs. Bus. Adminstrn., U. Calif., Berkeley, 1975-76; named to Pomona Coll. Athletic Hall of Fame, 1981; W.T. Grant fellow Harvard U., 1969-70,; George F. Baker scholar Harvard Grad. Sch. Bus. Adminstrn., 1970; Stanford U. Grad. Sch. Bus. fellow, 1970-71. Mem. Strategic Mgmt. Soc., Am. Acad. Mgmt., Am. Fin. Assn., Am. Planning Assn, European Real Estate Soc., Internat. Real Estate Soc., Inst. Mgmt. Cons., ISSSEEM, Soc. Sci. Exploration, Am. Real Estate and Urban Econs. Assn., Intuition Network (bd. dirs.), World Future Soc. (exec. com. and adv. bd. World 2000), Am. Econ. Assn., Am. Real Estate Soc. (pres. 1995-96, award for best paper presented in ann. meeting, 1995, 96), Noetic Soc., Nat. Bur. Real Estate Rsch. (founder, bd. dirs.), Harvard Club N.Y., L.A. Adventures Club. Avocations: art, antiquarian books, reading, bicycling. Office: The Roulac Group 709 5th Ave San Rafael CA 94901-3202

ROUNDS, BARBARA LYNN, psychiatrist; b. LA, Mar. 17, 1934; d. Ralph Arthur and Florene V. (Heyer) Behrend; divorced 1962; children: Steve, Mike, Pamela, Ronald, Thomas. BA, Stanford U., 1964, MD, 1966; postgrad., San Francisco Psychoanalytic, 1973-81. Diplomate Am. Bd. Psychiatry and Neurology; cert. psychoanalyst. Intern New Orleans Pub. Health Svc., 1966-67; resident psychiat. Mendocino State Hosp., 1967-69, U. Calif. Davis, 1969-70; staff psychiatrist U. Calif. Davis Med. Sch., Sacramento, 1970-77, clin. instr., 1970-76; psychiatrist pvt. practice, Sacramento, 1971—; asst. clin. prof. U. Calif. Davis, Sacramento, 1976-84, assoc. clin. prof., 1984-94. Mem. Am. Psychiat. Assn., Am. Psychoanalytic Assn., AMA, Cen. Calif. Psychiat. Soc. (pres.-elect 1990-91, pres. 1991-92). Democrat. Home: 8910 Leatham Ave Fair Oaks CA 95628-6506 Office: 1317 H St Sacramento CA 95814-1928

ROUNSAVILLE, GUY, JR., lawyer; b. 1943; BA, Stanford U., 1965; JD, U. Calif., San Francisco, 1968. Bar: Calif. 1969. Atty. Wells Fargo, 1969-73, v.p., counsel, 1974-77, v.p., chief counsel, 1977-78, sr. v.p., chief counsel, sec., 1980-85, exec. v.p., chief counsel, sec., 1985-98; ptnr. Allen, Matkins, Leck, Gamble & Mallory, San Francisco, 1999—.

ROURKE, MICKEY (PHILIP ANDRE ROURKE JR.), actor; b. Schenectady, NY, Sept. 16, 1956; m. Debra Feuer, 1981 (div. 1989); m. Carre Otis, June 26, 1992 (div. Dec. 1998). Profl. boxer, 1991—95; gym owner Shapiro, West Hollywood. Actor: (films) Nineteen Forty-One, 1979, Heaven's Gate, 1980, Fade to Black, 1980, Body Heat, 1981, Diner, 1982 (Nat. Soc. of Film Critics award best supporting actor 1982), Rumblefish, 1983, The Pope of Greenwich Village, 1984, Year of the Dragon, 1985, Eureka, 1985, 9 1/2 Weeks, 1985, Angel Heart, 1987, A Prayer for the Dying, 1987, Barfly, 1987, Homeboy, 1988, Johnny Handsome, 1989, Wild Orchid, 1990, Desperate Hours, 1990, Harley Davidson and the Marlboro Man, 1991, White Sands, 1992, F.T.W., 1994, Fall Time, 1995, Exit in Red, 1996, Bullets, 1996, The Rainmaker, 1997, Love in Paris, 1997, Double Team, 1997, Buffalo '66, 1997, Thursday, 1998, Shergar, 1999, Shades, 1999, Out in Fifty, 1999, The Animal Factory, 2000, Get Carter, 2000, The Pledge, 2001, Spun, 2002, Masked and Anonymous, 2003, Once Upon a Time in Mexico, 2003, Man on Fire, 2004, Sin City, 2005, Domino, 2005, Stormbreaker, 2006, The Wrestler, 2008 (Best Actor Boston Soc. Film Critics, 2008, Best Performance by an Actor in a Motion Picture - Drama, Golden Globe award, Hollywood Fgn. Press Assn., 2009, Best Actor, Brit. Acad. Film and TV Arts, 2009, Ind. Spirit award for Best Male Lead, Film Ind., 2009), The Informers, 2009, Killshot, 2009; (TV movies) Act of Love, 1980, City in Fear, 1980, Rape and Marriage: The Rideout Case, 1980, Thicker Than Blood, 1998. Recipient Best Actor award, Elle Mag., 2009. Avocation: motorcycling. Office: c/o ICM LA 10250 Constellation Blvd Los Angeles CA 90067

ROUSE, RICHARD HUNTER, historian, educator; b. Boston, Aug. 14, 1933; s. Hunter and Dorothee (Hüsmert) R.; m. Mary L. Ames, Sept. 7, 1959; children: Thomas, Andrew, Jonathan. BA, State U. Iowa, 1955; MA, U. Chgo., 1957; PhD, Cornell U., 1963. Mem. faculty UCLA, 1963—, prof. history, 1975—. Assoc. dir. Ctr. Medieval and Renaissance Studies, 1966-67, acting dir., 1967-68; dir. Summer Inst. in Paleography, 1978, chair grad. coun., 1989-90; adv. bd. Hill Monastic Microfilm Libr., St. John's U., Collegeville, Minn., Ambrosiana Microfilm Library, Notre Dame (Ind.) U., Corpus of Brit.

Medieval Libr. Catalogues, Brit. Acad. Beinecke, 2009; vis. prof. paleography Dept. Classics, Yale U. Author: Serial Bibliographies for Medieval Studies, 1969, (with M.A. Rouse) Preachers, Florilegia and Sermons: Studies on the Manipulus Florum of Thomas of Ireland, 1979; (with others) Texts and Transmission, 1983; (with C.W. Dutschke) Medieval and Renaissance Manuscripts in the Claremont Libraries, 1986; (with M.A. Rouse) Cartolai, Illuminators and Printers in Fifteenth-Century Italy, 1988; (with L. Bataillon and B. Guyot) La Production du livre universitaire au moyen age, exemplar et pecia, 1988; (with others) Guide to Medieval and Renaissance Manuscripts in the Huntington Library, 1989; (with M. Ferrari) Medieval and Renaissance Manuscripts at the University of California, Los Angeles, 1991; (with M.A. Rouse and R.A.B. Mynors) Registrum de libris doctorum et auctorum veterum, 1991; (with M.A. Rouse) Authentic Witnesses: Approaches to Medieval Texts and Manuscripts, 1991; (with M.A. Rouse) Manuscripts and Their Makers: Commercial Book Producers in Medieval Paris 1200-1500, 2 vols., 2000, (with M.A. Rouse) Henry of Kirkestede, Catalogus de libris autenticis et apocrifis, 2004; co-editor: Viator: Medieval and Renaissance Studies, 1970-; mem. editorial bd. Medieval and renaissance manuscripts in Calif. libraries, Medieval Texts, Toronto; Medieval Texts, Binghamton, Library Quar., 1984-88, Speculum, 1981-85, Revue d'histoire des Textes, 1986-, Cambridge Studies in Paleography and Codicology, 1990-96, Catalogue of Medieval and Renaissance Manuscripts in the Beinecke Rare Book and Manuscript Library Yale University, 1984-92, Filologia MedioLatina, 1994-, Manuscripta, 2000—, Utrecht Studies in Medieval Literacy, 2000—, Litterae Caelestes, 2005— Am. Coun. Learned Socs. fellow, 1972-73, vis. fellow All Souls Coll., Oxford, 1978-79, Guggenheim fellow, 1975-76, Rosenbach fellow in bibliography U. Pa., 1976, NEH fellow, 1981-82, 84-85, 94-96, Inst. for Advanced Studies fellow Jerusalem, 1991; J.R. Lyell reader in bibliogrpahy U. Oxford, 1991-92; vis. fellow Pembroke Coll., U. Oxford, 1992, Pembroke Coll., U. Cambridge, 2000-01. Fellow Royal Hist. Soc., Medieval Acad. Am.; mem. Medieval Assn. Pacific (councillor 1965-68, pres. 1968-70), Medieval Acad. Am. (councillor 1977-80), Comité international de paléographie (treas. 1985-90), Comité international du vocabulaire des institutions et de la communication intellectuelles au moyen age, 1987—, Societa internazionale per lo studio del medioevo latino, 1988—. Home: 11444 Berwick St Los Angeles CA 90049-3416 Office: Dept History U Calif Los Angeles CA 90024 Office Phone: 310-825-4168. Business E-Mail: rouse@history.ucla.edu.

ROVEN, ALFRED NATHAN, surgeon; came to the U.S., 1949. BA in Psychology, Calif. State U., Northridge, 1969; MD, U. So. Calif., 1977. Diplomate Am. Bd. Plastic and Reconstructive Surgery, Am. Bd. Otolaryngology. Resident in otolaryngology U. So. Calif., 1977-82; clin. chief plastic surgery Cedars Sinai Med. Ctr., LA, 1989-91; resident in plastic and reconstructive surgery U. N.C., 1982-84; clin. chief burns Cedars Sinai Med. Ctr., LA, 1990-92, clin. chief hands, 1990-92. Qualified med. examiner State of Calif., 1985. Contbr. articles to jours. Avocation: reading. Office: 5757 Wishire Blvd 6 Los Angeles CA 90036 Office Phone: 323-937-7733.

ROVIRA, LUIS DARIO, state supreme court justice; b. San Juan, Sept. 8, 1923; s. Peter S. and Mae (Morris) R.; m. Lois Ann Thau, June 25, 1966; children: Douglas, Merilyn. BA, U. Colo., 1948, LL.B., 1950. Bar: Colo. 1950. Justice Colo. Supreme Ct., Denver, 1979-95, chief justice, 1990-95, ret., 1995. Mem. Pres.'s Com. on Mental Retardation, 1970-71; chmn. State Health Facilities Council, 1967-76; arbiter and mediator Jud. Arbiter Group, Denver. Trustee Temple Buell Found. With AUS, 1943-46. Mem. ABA, Colo. Bar Assn., Denver Bar Assn. (pres. 1970-71), Colo. Assn. Retarded Children (pres. 1968-70), Alpha Tau Omega, Phi Alpha Delta. Clubs: Athletic (Denver), Country (Denver). Home: 4810 E 6th Ave Denver CO 80220-5137 Office: Judicial Arbiter Group 1601 Blake St Denver CO 80202 Office Phone: 303-572-1919.

ROWE, PETER A., columnist; b. Walnut Creek, Calif., Sept. 7, 1955; s. Raymond Alan and Marion (Green) R.; m. Lynn Hanson, Aug. 13, 1977; children: Kyle, Reid, Alec. BA in History, U. Calif., Berkeley, 1977, BA in Journalism, 1977; MSJ, Northwestern U., 1981. Reporter Argus, Fremont, Calif., 1977-80, Va.-Pilot, Norfolk, 1981-84, San Diego Union, 1984-87, asst. features editor, 1987-88, features editor, 1988-92; columnist San Diego Union-Tribune, 1992—. Gannett fellow Northwestern U., 1980-81, Jefferson fellow, 2006; Fulbright scholar, 2003. Mem.: Nat. Soc. Newspaper Columnists (pres. 2000—02). Roman Catholic. Office: San Diego Union Tribune PO Box 120191 San Diego CA 92112-0191 Office Phone: 619-293-1227. Business E-Mail: peter.rowe@uniontrib.com.

ROWE, SANDRA MIMS, editor; b. Charlotte, NC, May 26, 1948; d. David Lathan and Shirley (Stovall) Mims; m. Gerard Paul Rowe, June 5, 1971; children: Mims Elizabeth, Sarah Stovall. BA, East Carolina U., Greenville, NC, 1970; postgrad., Harvard U., 1991. Reporter to asst. mng. editor The Ledger-Star, Norfolk, Va., 1971-80, mng. editor, 1980-82, The Virginian-Pilot and The Ledger Star, Norfolk, Va., 1982-84, exec. editor, 1984-86, v.p., exec. editor, 1986-93; editor The Oregonian, Portland, 1993—. Mem. Pulitzer Prize Bd., 1994-2003, chair, 2003. Bd. visitors James Madison U., Harrisonburg, VA., 1991-95; chair journalism adv. bd. Knight Found.; mem. adv. bd. The Poynter Inst., Medill Sch. Journalism, Northwestern U.; chair bd. visitors Knight Fellowships, Stanford U. Recipient George Beveridge Editor of Yr. award Nat. Press Found., 2003; named Woman of Yr. Outstanding Profl. Women of Hampton Rds., 1987; inducted into Va. Journalism Hall of Fame, 2000; named editor of yr. Edit. Pub. Mag., 2008. Mem. Am. Soc. Newspaper Editors (pres., bd. dirs. 1992-99), Va. Press Assn. (bd. dirs. 1985-93). Episcopalian. Office: The Oregonian 1320 SW Broadway Portland OR 97201-3499 Office Phone: 503-221-8400. Office Fax: 503-294-4175. E-mail: srowe@news.oregonian.com.

ROWE, TINA L., government official; b. Griffin, Ga., July 22, 1946; 1 child. Student, FBI Nat. Acad., 1981; AA, Aurora CC, Colo., 1991; BA, Colo. Christian U., 1999. From patrol officer to comdr. patrol dist. 2 Denver Police Dept., 1969-94; U.S. marshal for Dist. Colo., U.S. Marshals Svc., Dept. Justice, Denver, 1994—. Trainer, spkr. cons. operational planning, motivation, leadership. Recipient various awards, including Woman of Yr. award Bus. and Profl. Women's Club, 1994; named Outstanding Law Enforcement officer, Am. Legion, 1999. Mem. FBI Nat. Acad. Assocs., Nat. Sheriffs Assn., Colo. Assn. Chiefs Police, Intenat. Assn. Chiefs of Police, Am. Coll. Forensic Examiners, Am. Bd. Law Enforcement Experts. Baptist. Office: US Marshals Svc Dept Justice 1929 Stout St Rm 324C Denver CO 80294-1929

ROWELL, ROBERT, professional sports team executive; B in Broadcast Journalism, Calif. Poly. State U., San Luis Obispo, 1989, M in Bus. Adminstrn., 1993. Bus. mgr. intercollegiate athletics dept. Calif. Poly. State U., 1989—91, asst. athletics dir., 1992—94, assoc. athletics dir., 1994—95; asst. contr. Golden State Warriors, 1995—96, dir. fin., contr., 1996—98, v.p. bus. ops., 1998—2001, NBA chief mktg. officer, COO, 2001—03, pres., 2003—. Golden State Warriors rep. NBA Bd. Govs. Recipient Forty Under 40 award, St. & Smith's Sports Bus. Jour., 2001. Office: Golden State Warriors 1011 Broadway Oakland CA 94607

ROWEN, HENRY STANISLAUS, retired economist, former federal agency administrator; b. Boston, Mass., Oct. 11, 1925; s. Henry S. and Margaret ISabelle (Maher) Rowen; m. Beverly Camille Griffiths, Apr. 18, 1951; children: Hilary, Michael, Michael, Christopher, Sheila Jennifer, Diana Louise, Nicholas. BS, MIT, 1949; M in Philosophy, Oxford U., Eng., 1955. Economist Rand Corp., Santa Monica, Calif., 1950—61, pres., 1967—72; dep. asst. sec. internat. security affairs US Dept. Def., Washington, 1961—64; asst. dir. Bur. Budget, 1965—66; prof. pub. policy Stanford (Calif.) U., 1972—95, prof. emeritus, 1995—, dir. pub. policy program, 1972—75; sr. fellow Hoover Inst., Stanford, Calif., 1983—; Edwin B. Rust prof. pub. policy Stanford (Calif.) U., 1986—95, dir. Asia/Pacific Rsch. Ctr., 1997—2001; asst. sec. internat. security affairs US Dept. Def., Washington, 1989—91. Chmn. nat. intelligence coun. CIA, Washington, 1981—83; chmn. US Dept. Energy Task Force on the Future of Sci. Programs, 2002—03; mem. Commn. on the Intelligence Capabilities of the US Regarding Weapons of Mass Destruction, 2004. Co-author (with R. Imai): Nuclear Energy and Nuclear Proliferation, 1980; co-author: (with C. Wolf Jr.) The Future of the Soviet Empire, 1987; editor: Options for U.S. Energy Policy, 1977, Behind East Asian Growth, 1998; co-editor (with C. Wolf Jr.): The Impoverished Superpower, 1990; co-editor: (with C. Lee, W. Miller, M. Hancock) The Silicon Valley Edge, 2001; contbr. articles to profl. jours. Chmn. chief naval ops. exec. panel USN, Washington, 1972—81, mem. exec. panel, 1983—89, 1991—93; mem. Def. Sci. Bd. US Dept. Def., 1983—89; chmn. Def. Policy Bd., 1991—94. With USN, 1943—46, PTO. Mem.: Internat. Inst. Strategic Studies. Republican. Roman Catholic.

ROWEN, MARSHALL, radiologist; b. Chgo. s. Harry and Dorothy (Kasnow) R.; m. Helen Lee Friedman, Apr. 5, 1952; children: Eric, Scott, Mark. AB in Chemistry with highest honors, U. Ill., Urbana, 1951; MD with honors, U. Ill., Chgo., 1954, MS in Internal Medicine, 1954. Diplomate Am. Bd. Radiology. Intern Long Beach (Calif.) VA Hosp., 1955; resident in radiology Los Angeles VA Hosp., 1955-58; practice medicine specializing in radiology Orange, Calif., 1960—. Chmn. bd. dirs. Moran, Rowen and Dorsey, Inc., Radiologists, 1969—2002; asst. radiologist L.A. Children's Hosp., 1958; assoc. radiologist Valley Presbyn. Hosp., Van Nuys, Calif., 1960; dir. dept. radiology St. Joseph Hosp., Orange, 1961—2004, v.p. staff, 1972; dir. dept. radiology Children's Hosp. Orange County, 1964—2002, chief staff, 1977—78, v.p., 1978—83, v.p., trustee, 2008—09, 1993—98, 2000—06; asst. clin. prof. radiology U. Calif., Irvine, 1967—70, assoc. clin. prof., 1979—82, clin. prof. radiology and pediat., 1976—, pres. clin. faculty assn., 1980—81; trustee Choc. Padrinos; sec. Choco Health Svcs., 1987—89, v.p., 1990—93, trustee, 1995—, Found. Med. Care Orange County, 1972—76, Calif. Commn. Adminstrn. Svcs. Hosp., 1975—79, Profl. Practice Systems, 1990—92, Med. Splty. Mgrs., 1990—2004, St. Joseph Med. Corp., 1993—98; v.p. Found. Med. Care Children's Hosp., 1988—89; v.p., sr. v.p. St. Joseph Med. Corp. IPA, 1995—98; sr. v.p. Orange Coast Managed Care Svcs., 1995—98, Paragon Med. Imaging, 1993—2003, Calif. Managed Imaging, 1994—2009, Alliance Premier Hosps., 1995—96; chmn. bd. dirs. Children's Healthcare Calif., 1995—2002, hon. chmn., bd. dirs., 2003—09; corp. mem. Blue Shield Calif., 1995—2006; mem. physician's rev. com. Blue Cross Calif., 1996—2009, mem. Blue Shield coun. advisors, 2001—07; trustee Children's Hosp. at Mission, 2004—09, sec. bd. dir., 2008—09, vice chair, 2009; cons. Imaging Adminstrn., 2005—09; Calif. dept. med. health care adv. com. mem. Patient Advocate Improvement Program, 2008—09. Mem. editl. bd. Western Jour. Medicine; contbr. articles to med. jours. Founder Orange County Performing Arts Ctr., mem. Laguna Art Mus., Laguna Festival of Arts, Opera Pacific, South Coast Reportory, Am. Ballet Theater, World Affairs Coun. Served to capt. M.C., U.S. Army, 1958-60. Recipient Rea sr. med. prize U. Ill. 1953; William Cook scholar U. Ill., 1951, Friend of Children award Children's Hosp. Guild, 1995, Charley award Children's Hosp., 1996. Fellow Am. Coll. Radiology; mem. AMA, Am. Heart Assn., Soc. Nuclear Medicine (trustee 1961-62), Orange County Radiol. Soc. (pres. 1968-69), Calif. Radiol. Soc. (pres. 1978-79), Radiol. Soc. So. Calif. (pres. 1976), Pacific Coast Pediatric Radiologists Assn. (pres. 1971), Soc. Pediatric Radiology, Calif. Med. Assn. (chmn. sect. on radiology 1978-79), Orange County Med. Assn. (chmn. UCI liaison com. 1976-78), Cardioradiology Soc. So. Calif., Radiol. Soc. N.Am., Am. Roentgen Ray Soc., Am. Coll. Physician Execs., Soc. Chmn. Radiologists Children Hosp., Center Club, Sports Club (Irvine), Phi Beta Kappa, Phi Eta Sigma, Omega Beta Phi, Alpha Omega Alpha. Office: St Joseph Hosp 1100 W Stewart Dr Orange CA 92868 Home Phone: 714-349-8667. Personal E-mail: romarsh@aol.com.

ROWLAND, FRANK SHERWOOD, chemistry professor; b. Del., Ohio, June 28, 1927; m. Joan Lundberg, 1952; children: Ingrid Drake, Jeffrey Sherwood. AB, Ohio Wesleyan U., 1948; MS, U. Chgo., 1951, PhD, 1952, DSc (hon.), 1989, Duke U., 1989, Whittier Coll., 1989, Princeton U., 1990, Haverford Coll., 1992, Clark U., 1996, U. East Anglia, 1996; LLD (hon.), Ohio Wesleyan U., 1989, Simon Fraser U., 1991, U. Calgary, 1997; laurea honoris causa, U. Urbino, Italy, 1998; DSc, Carleton Coll., 1998, Gustavus Adolphus Coll., 1997, Occidental Coll., 1998, Kanagawa U., Japan, 1999, LaTrobe U., Australia, 2000, U. Waterloo, Can., 2001, Ohio State U., 2002. Instr. chemistry Princeton (N.J.) U., 1952—56; asst. prof. chemistry U. Kans., 1956—58, assoc. prof. chemistry, 1958—63, prof. chemistry, 1963—64, U. Calif., Irvine, 1964—, dept. chmn., 1964—70, Aldrich prof. chemistry, 1985—89, Bren prof. chemistry, 1989—94, Donald Bren rsch. prof., chemistry, 1994—. Humboldt sr. scientist Fed. Republic Germany, 1981; chmn. Dahlem (Germany) Conf. on Changing Atmosphere, 1987; vis. scientist Japan Soc. for Promotion Sci., 1980; co-dir. western region Nat. Inst. Global Environ. Change, 1989—93; del. Internat. Coun. Sci. Unions, 1993—98; fgn. sec. NAS, 1994—2002; lectr., cons. in field; mem. ozone commn. Internat. Assn. Meteorology and Atmospheric Physics, 1980—88, hon. life mem., 1996, mem. commn. on atmospheric chemistry and global pollution, 1979—91; mem. acid rain peer rev. panel U.S. Office of Sci. and Tech., Exec. Office of White House, 1982—84; mem. vis. com. Max Planck Inst., Heidelberg and Mainz, Germany, 1982—96; ozone trends panel mem. NASA, 1986—88; chmn. Gordon Conf. Environ. Scis.-Air, 1987; mem. Calif. Coun. Sci. Tech., 1989—95; mem. exec. com. Tyler Prize, 1992—. Contbr. articles to profl. jours. Recipient numerous awards including, John Wiley Jones award, Rochester Inst. Tech., 1975, Disting. Faculty Rsch. award, U. Calif., Irvine, 1976, Profl. Achievement award, U. Chgo., 1977, Billard award, N.Y. Acad. Sci., 1977, Tyler World Prize in Environ. Achievement, 1983, Global 500 Roll of Honor for Environ. Achievement, UN Environment Program, 1988, Dana award for Pioneering Achievements in Health, 1987, Silver medal, Royal Inst. Chemistry U.K., 1989, Wadsworth award, N.Y. State Dept. Health, 1989, medal, U. Calif. Irvine, 1989, Japan prize in Environ. Sci., 1989, Dickson prize, Carnegie-Mellon U., 1991, Albert Einstein prize, World Cultural Coun., 1994, Nobel Prize in chemistry, 1995, Alumni medal, U. Chgo., 1997, Nevada medal, 1997, Gold medal, Acad. Athens, 2003; named to, GTE Acad. All-Am. Hall of Fame, 2000; fellow Guggenheim Found., 1962, 1974. Fellow: AAAS (pres.-elect 1991, pres. 1992, chmn. bd. dirs. 1993), Am. Geophys. Union (Roger Revelle medal 1994), Am. Phys. Soc. (Leo Szilard award for physics in pub. interest 1979); mem.: NAS (co-DATA com. 1977—82, com. atmospheric scis., solar-terrestial com. 1979—83, sci. com. on problems environment 1986—89, bd. environ. studies and toxicology 1986—91, com. on atmospheric chemistry 1987—89, Infinite Voyage film com. 1988—92, Robertson Meml. lectr. 1993, chmn. com. on internat. orgns. and programs 1993—2002, chmn. office of internat. affairs 1994—2002, coun. 1994—2002, co-chmn. interacad. panel 1995—2000, mem. exec. com. 2000—02, chair bd. atmospheric scis. and climate 2007—), Royal Soc. U.K. (fgn.), Academia Bibliotheca Alexandrinae, Inst. Medicine, Am. Philos. Soc., Am. Meteorol. Soc. (hon.), Korean Acad. Sci. Tech. (fgn. sec.), European Acad. Arts, Scis. and Humanities, Am. Chem. Soc. (chmn. divsn. nuclear sci. and tech. 1973—74, chmn. divsn. phys. chemistry 1974—75, E.F. Smith lectureship 1980, Orange County award 1975, Tolman medal 1976, Zimmerman award 1980, Environ. Sci. and Tech. award 1983, Esselen award 1987, Peter Debye Phys. Chem. award 1993), Am. Acad. Arts and Scis., Sigma Xi, Phi Beta Kappa. Office: Dept Chemistry U Calif Irvine 571 Rowland Hall Irvine CA 92697-2025 E-mail: rowland@uci.edu.

ROWLAND, JOHN ARTHUR, lawyer; b. Joliet, Ill., Mar. 6, 1943; s. John Fornof and Grace Ada (Baskerville) R.; children: Sean B., Keira L. BA, U. Notre Dame, 1965; JD, U. San Francisco, 1968. Bar: Calif. 1969, US Dist. Ct. (no. dist.) Calif. 1982, US Dist. Ct. (ctrl. dist.) Calif. 1998, US Dist. Ct. (so. dist.) Calif. 2006. Asst. dist. atty. San Francisco Dist. Atty.'s Office, 1971-81; assoc. Ropers, Majeski, Kohn and Bentley, San Francisco, 1982—, ptnr., 1985—. Pres., South of Market Boys, San Francisco, 1981. Served to capt. U.S. Army, 1969-70, Korea. Recipient Commendation San Francisco Bd. Suprs., 1981, Merit award Mayor of San Francisco, 1982. Mem.: Am. Bd. Trial Advocates. Roman Catholic. Office: Ropers Majeski Kohn and Bentley 201 Spear St Ste 1000 San Francisco CA 94105 Home Phone: 415-359-1204; Office Phone: 415-972-6311. Business E-Mail: jrowland@ropers.com.

ROWLEY, BEVERLEY DAVIES, sociologist; b. Antioch, Calif., July 28, 1941; d. George M. and Eloise Davies; m. Richard B. Rowley, Apr. 1, 1966 (div. 1983). BS, Colo. State U., 1963; MA, U. Nev., 1975; PhD, Union Inst., 1983. Social worker Nev. Dept. Pub. Welfare, Reno, 1963—65, Santa Clara County Dept. Welfare, San Jose, Calif., 1965—66; field dir. Sierra Sage coun. Camp Fire Girls, Sparks, Nev., 1966—70; program coord. divsn. health scis. Sch. Medicine U. Nev., 1976—78, program coord., health analyst office rural health, 1978—84, acting dir. office rural health, 1982—84; exec. asst. to pres. Med. Coll. of Hampton Rds., Norfolk, Va., 1984—87; rsch. mgr. Office Med. Edn. Info. AMA, Chgo., 1987—88, dir. dept. data systems, 1988-91; dir. med. edn. Maricopa Med. Ctr., Phoenix, 1991—99; pres. Med. Edn. and Rsch. Assocs., Inc., Phoenix, Chgo., 1999—, Med. Edn. & Rsch. Assocs., Tempe, Ariz., 1999—; vis. prof. Ariz. State U. East, Mesa, 1999—2000, profl. and personal coach, 2004—; pres., exec. dir. Maricopa Med. Found., Phoenix, 2004—. Various positions as adj. prof. and lectr. in health scis. U. Nev. Sch. of Medicine, 1972-75; lectr. dept. family and cmty. medicine U. Nev., 1978-84, asst. dir., evaluator Health Careers for Am. Indians Programs, 1978-84; cons. Nev. Statewide Health Survey, 1979-84; interim dir. Health Max, 1985-86; asst. prof. dept. family and cmty. medicine Med. Coll. of Hampton Rds., Norfolk, Va., 1985-87. Editor of five books; contbr. numerous articles to profl. jours. Mem. Am. Sociol. Assn., Nat. Rural Health Assn. (bd. dirs. 1986-88), Assn. Behavioral Sci. and Med. Edn. (pres. 1986), Assn. Am. Med. Colls. (exec. coun. 1993-95), Coun. Acad. Scis. (adminstrv. bd. 1992-97), Assn. Hosp. Med. Edn. (bd. dirs. 1997—), Delta Delta Delta. Achievements include development of three computer systems including AMA-FREIDA; four internet-based educational programs for physicians. Avocations: hiking, skiing, gardening, sewing, ceramics. Office: MERA Inc 1903 E Sarah Ln Tempe AZ 85284-3430 E-mail: BDR@MERAInc.com.

ROY, BRANDON DAWAYNE, professional basketball player; b. Seattle, July 23, 1984; Student in Am. ethnic studies, U. Wash., Seattle, 2002—06. Guard Portland Trail Blazers, Oreg., 2006—. Founder Brandon Roy Found., 2008—. Recipient Sportsmanship award, NBA, 2008; named Player of Yr., Pacific-10 Conf., 2006, 1st Team All-Conf., 2006, 1st Team All-Am., AP, 2006, NBA Rookie of Yr., 2007; named to All-Rookie First Team, NBA, 2007, Western Conf. All-Star Team, 2008, 2009. Office: Portland Trail Blazers Rose Quarter One Center Court Portland OR 97227*

ROYBAL-ALLARD, LUCILLE, United States Representative from California; b. Boyle Heights, Calif., June 12, 1941; d. Edward Roybal; m. Edward T. Allard; 4 children. BA in Speech, Calif. State U., LA, 1965. Former employee United Way; asst. dir. Alcoholism Coun. East LA; mem. Calif. State Assembly, 1987—92, US Congress from 34th Calif. dist., 1993—; mem. appropriations com., standards of ofcl. conduct com. Mem. Livable Communities Task Force, Homeland Security Task Force, Congl. Children's Working Grp.; chair Congl. Hispanic Caucus, 1999—2000. Recipient Madre y Mujer award, Kimberly-Clark, 2006. Democrat. Roman Catholic. Office: Ho of Reps 2330 Rayburn Bldg Washington DC 20515-0534 also: 225 E Temple St Ste 1860 Los Angeles CA 90012 Office Phone: 202-225-1766, 213-628-9230. Office Fax: 202-226-0350, 213-628-8578.

ROYCE, ED (EDWARD RANDALL ROYCE), United States Representative from California; b. LA, Oct. 12, 1951; m. Marie Therese Porter. BA in Bus. Adminstrn., Calif. State U., Fullerton, 1977. Tax mgr. Southwestern Portland Cement Co.; mem. Calif. State Senate from Dist. 32, 1983—92, US Congress from 40th Calif. Dist. (formerly 39th), 1993—, asst. whip, 1993—, mem. fin. svcs. com., internat. rels. com., fgn. affairs com. Legis. author, campaign co-chmn. Proposition 15 Crime Victims/Speedy Trial Initiative; mem. Stop Corporate Welfare Coalition; co-chair Porkbusters Coalition. Bd. dirs. Calif. Interscholastic Athletic Found. Recipient Medal of Commendation, Veterans of Fgn. Wars, 1985, Taxpayers Friend award, Nat. Taxpayers Union, 1994, Taxpayers Hero award, Citizens Against Govt. Waste, 1994, Visionaries for Africa award, Africa Soc. (Nat. Summit on Africa), 2004; named Legislator of Yr., Orange County Republican Com., 1986, Child Adv. of Yr., Calif. Assn. Svc. for Children, 1987. Mem.: Anaheim C. of C., Fullerton C. of C., Literacy Volunteers of America. Republican. Roman Catholic. Achievements include writing nation's 1st felony stalking law; writing bill for Foster Family Home Insurance Fund, creating foster parent recruitment and training programs. Office: US Congress 2202 Rayburn Ho Office Bldg Washington DC 20515 also: 305 N Harbor Blvd Ste 300 Fullerton CA 92832 Office Phone: 202-225-4111, 714-992-8081. Office Fax: 714-992-1668.*

ROYCHOWDHURY, JAIJEET, professor; BEE, Indian Inst. Tech., Kanpur, 1987; PhD, U. Calif., Berkeley, 1992. Mem. tech. staff Bell Labs., Murray Hill, NJ, 1992—2000; prof. elec. and computer engring. U. Minn., Mpls., 2001—08; prof. elec. engring. and computer sciences U. Calif., Berkeley, 2008—. Fellow: IEEE. Office: 545 E Cory Hall U Calif Berkeley CA 94720 Office Phone: 510-643-5664. E-mail: jr@eecs.berkeley.edu.

ROYER, KATHLEEN ROSE, pilot; b. Pitts., Nov. 4, 1949; d. Victor Cedric and Lisetta Emma (Smith) Salway; m. Michael Lee Royer, June 6, 1971 (div. Aug. 1975). Student, Newbold Coll., 1968-69; BS, Columbia Union Coll., 1971; MEd, Shippensburg U., 1974; student, Lehigh U., 1974-75. Cert. tchr. Pa. Music. Music tchr. Harrisburg Sch. Dist., Pa., 1971-77; flight instr. Penn-Air, Inc., Altoona, Pa., 1977; capt., asst. chief pilot Air Atlantic Airlines, Centre Hall, Pa., 1977-80; capt., chief pilot Lycoming Air Svc., Williamsport, Pa., 1980-81; govs. pilot Commonwealth of Pa., Harrisburg, 1981-87; flight engr. Pan-Am, NYC, 1987-91; pilot, 1st officer B737 United Airlines, Chgo., 1992-96, 1st officer B767 NYC, until 1996, Washington, 1996-99; flight officer B747-400 JFK Internat. Airport, Jamaica, NY, 1999—2001, capt. Airbus 320, 2001—, airbus line check airman, 2005—. Frist woman pilot/engr. crew mem. on 747 Pan Am. Airlines, 1989—91, chief pilot, cons. Mem.: UAL-Airline Pilot Assn. (coord. critical incident stress program 1994—96), Flight Engrs. Internat. Assn. (scheduling rep. 1989, scheduling dir. 1990, 1st vice chmn., mem. bd. adjustments 1989, v.p. dir. scheduling 1991—92), Internat. Soc. Women Airline Pilots, Whirley Girls (Washington), 99's (local chair Ctrl. Pa. chpt. 1987—92). Republican. Avocations: owner/flying 1965 Cessna 180, golf, music, reading. Home: 34 Lazy Eight Dr Daytona Beach FL 32128 Office: San Francisco Intl Airport San Francisco CA Personal E-mail: royer17@bellsouth.net.

ROZELL, WILLIAM BARCLAY, lawyer; b. Ossining, NY, Mar. 30, 1943; s. William M. and Doris M. (Mittenmaier) R.; m. Susan Kai Wylie, Oct. 4, 1969; m. Susan Marie Walker, Dec. 5, 1975; children: Rebecca, Mariah. BSc in Engring., Brown U., 1965; JD, Cornell U., 1968. Bar: Ohio 1969, N.Y. 1969, U.S. Dist. Ct. (so. dist.) N.Y. 1970, U.S. Dist. Ct. (ea. dist.) N.Y. 1971, Alaska 1972, U.S. Dist. Ct. Alaska 1972, U.S. Supreme Ct. 1976, U.S. Ct. Appeals (9th cir.) 1977. VISTA atty. Office Econ. Opportunity, Chgo. and Columbus, Ohio, 1968—69; assoc. White & Case, NYC, 1969—72, Faulkner, Banfield, Doogan & Holmes, Juneau, Alaska, 1972—74, ptnr., 1975—81, mem. firm, 1981—98; pvt. practice Juneau, 1998—. Bd. dirs. Alaska Legal Services Corp., 1974-77. Fellow Am. Bar Found.; mem. ABA, Alaska Bar Assn. (gov. 1976-82, pres. 1980-81), Alaska Bar Found. (trustee 1984-2001), Juneau Bar Assn., Order of Coif. Office: PO Box 20730 Juneau AK 99802-0730 Office Phone: 907-586-0142.

ROZWAT, CHARLES, computer software company executive; B in Fin. and Info. Systems, Marquette U., Milw. Mgmt. staff mem. Digital Equipment Corp.; with Oracle Corp., 1994—, v.p. New Eng. Devel. Ctr., exec. v.p. server techs. divsn. Redwood City, Calif. Office: Oracle Corp 500 Oracle Pky Redwood City CA 94085 Office Phone: 650-506-7000. Office Fax: 650-506-7200.

RUBEN, RICHARD S., lawyer; b. Bklyn., Jan. 21, 1950; BS magna cum laude, U. So. Calif., 1972; JD, UCLA, 1975. Bar: Calif. 1975. Ptnr. Pillsbury Winthrop Shaw Pittman LLP, Costa Mesa, Calif., mem. mng. bd., 1999—2003, ptnr. Litigation practice, sr. So. Calif. trial atty., 2005—. Adj. prof. Whittier Coll. Law Sch. Mem.: Order of the Coif. Office: Pillsbury Winthrop Shaw Pittman 7th Fl 650 Town Center Dr Costa Mesa CA 92626 Office Phone: 714-436-6800. Office Fax: 714-436-2800. Business E-Mail: richard.ruben@pillsburylaw.com.

RUBENSTEIN, BERNARD, orchestra conductor; b. Springfield, Mo., Oct. 30, 1937; s. Milton and Evelyn Marion (Friedman) R.; m. Ann Warren Little, Aug. 28, 1961; children: Tanya, Stefan Alexei. B.Mus. with distinction, Eastman Sch. Music, U. Rochester, 1958; M.Mus., Yale U., 1961. Assoc. prof. conducting, dir. orch. orgns. Northwestern U., Evanston, Ill., 1968-80; music dir. San Juan Symphony, Durango, Colo., 1997—2001, Farmington, N.Mex., 1997—2001, Fargo-Moorhead Symphony, 2003—. Asst. condr. R.I. Philharm. Orch., 1961-62; condr. music dir. Santa Fe Symphony Orch., 1962-64; condr. Greenwood Chamber Orch., Cummington, Mass., 1968-79; asst. condr. Stuttgart Opera, 1966-68; condr., music dir. Music for Youth, Milw., 1970-80; assoc. condr. Cin. Symphony Orch., 1980-86; music dir. Tulsa Philharm., 1984-96, condr. laureate, 1996—; music dir. San Juan Symphony, 1997-2001; guest condr. numerous orchs. including Milw. Symphony Orch., St. Paul Chamber Orch., Guadalajara Symphony Orch., Berlin Radio Orch., Frankfurt Radio Orch., Grant Park Orch., Chgo., die reihe, Vienna, Austrian Radio Orch., Eastman Philharm., Halle Symphony Orch., E. Ger., Warsaw Philharm., St. Louis Little Symphony, W. German Radio Orch., Palazzo Pitti Orch. Florence, Italy, Frankfurt Opera, Tonkuenstler Orch., Vienna, S.W. German Radio Orch., Baden-Baden, Jerusalem Symphony, Anchorage, Hamilton, Ont., Hartford Conn., L.A. Chamber Orch., Austin (Tex.) Symphony, Am. Composers Orch. N.Y.C., Nat. Opera of Mongolia, Cuban Nat. Symphony, Havana, Orquesta de Oriente, Santiago de Cuba. Winner internat. conducting competition Serate Musicale Fiorentine, 1965; Fulbright scholar, 1964-66; recipient Charles Ditson award Yale U., 1961, Martha Baird Rockefeller award, 1966-68 Mem. Am. Symphony Orch. League, Condrs. Guild. Office: 1070 Governor Dempsey Dr Santa Fe NM 87501-1078 E-mail: baton@ix.netcom.com.

RUBENSTEIN, EDWARD, physician, educator; b. Cin., Dec. 5, 1924; s. Louis and Nettie Rubenstein; m. Nancy Ellen Millman, June 20, 1954; children: John, William, James. MD, U. Cin., 1947. House staff Cin. Gen. Hosp., 1947—50; fellow May Inst., Cin., 1950; sr. asst. resident Ward Med. Svc., Barnes Hosp., St. Louis, 1953—54; chief of medicine San Mateo County Hosp., Calif., 1960—70; assoc. dean postgrad. med. edn., prof. medicine Stanford (Calif.) U., 1971—, emeritus, active. Faculty Stanford Photon Rsch. Lab.; affiliated faculty Stanford Synchortron Radiation Lab., 1971—; maj. materials facilities com. NRC, 1984—85, Nat. Steering Com. 6 GeV Electron Storage Ring, 1986—. Author (textbook): Intensive Medical Care; editor: Synchotron Radiation Handbook, 1988, vol. 4, 1991, Synchotron Radiation in the Biosciences, Molecular Medicine; mem. editorial bd.: Sci. Am., Inc., 1991—94; editor (textbook): Sci. Am. Medicine, 1978—94; editor: (series) Molecular Cardiovascular Disease, 1995, Molecular Oncology, 1996, Molecular Neuroscience, 1998. With USAF, 1950—52. Recipient Kaiser award for outstanding and innovative contbns. to med. edn., 1989, Albion Walter Hewlett award, 1993; named Disting. Scientist, SvrroMed, Inc., 2003. Master: ACP (Laureate 2002); fellow: AAAS, Royal Soc. Medicine; mem.: Am. Clin. and Climatol. Assn., Soc. Photo-Optical Engrs., Western Assn. Physicians, Calif. Acad. Medicine, Inst. Medicine, APS, Alpha Omega Alpha. Achievements include research in mechanisms of autoimmunity, dysfunction of the choroid plexus and cerebrospinal fluid circulatory system, synchrotron radiation, nonprotein amino acids, autoimmunity, and molecular chirality. Office: Stanford Med Ctr Dept Medicine Stanford CA 94305

RUBENSTEIN, STEVEN PAUL, newspaper columnist; b. LA, Oct. 31, 1951; s. Victor Gerald and Florence (Fox) R.; m. Caroline Moira Grannan, Jan. 1, 1989; children: William Laurence, Anna Katherine. BA, U. Calif., Berkeley, 1977. Reporter L.A. Herald Examiner, 1974-76, San Francisco Chronicle, 1976-81, columnist, 1981—. Office: San Francisco Chronicle 901 Mission St San Francisco CA 94103-2905

RUBIN, ANDREW E. (ANDREW E. RUBIN), technology product developer; b. Chappaqua, NY, 1963; BS in Computer Sci., Syracuse U. Develop. engr. Carl Zeiss, Inc., Thornwood, NY, 1985—88; software pyrotechnician Apple Computer, Inc., Cupertino, Calif., 1988—90, various positions, 1990—92; mnr., enterprise magic cup General Magic, Sunnyvale, Calif., 1992—95; with Artemis (acquired by Microsoft, Inc. in 1997); mgr., comm. engring. WebTV Networks, Palo Alto, Calif., 1995—99; co-founder, pres., CEO Danger, Inc., Palo Alto, Calif., 1999—2004; entrepreneur-in-residence Redpoint Ventures, 2004; founder, pres., CEO Android, Inc. (acquired by Google, Inc.), Palo Alto, Calif., 2005; dir., mobile platforms Google, Inc., Mountain View, Calif., 2005—. Adv. bd. Reatrix Media Systems, Inc. Named a Maverick, Details mag., 2008. Achievements include development of Google Phone. Office: Google Inc 1600 Amphitheatre Pkwy Mountain View CA 94043 E-mail: arubin@robot.net.

RUBIN, BRUCE ALAN, lawyer; b. Pitts., Sept. 12, 1951; s. Stanley and Elaine (Roth) R.; m. Suzanne Kay Boss, Aug. 23, 1975; children: Daniel, Jay. BA, Yale U., 1973; JD, Stanford U., 1976. Bar: Oreg. 1976, U.S. Dist. Ct. Oreg. 1976, U.S. Ct. Appeals (9th cir.) 1976. Atty. Miller, Nash LLP, Portland, 1976—, chair corp. governance litigation dept. Exec. com. Oreg. Task Force on Close Corps. and Shareholder Rights, 1999-2000. Author: Wrongful Discharge in Oregon, 1988. Mem. ABA (com. on corp. counsel, subcom. chair), Oreg. State Bar (disciplinary coun. 1990—), Multnomah Bar Assn. (ct. liaison com.). Avocation: running. Office: Miller Nash LLP 111 SW 5th Ave Ste 3500 Portland OR 97204-3638

RUBIN, BRUCE JOEL, screenwriter, director, producer; b. Detroit, Mar. 10, 1943; s. Jim and Sondra R.; m. Blanche Mallins; children: Joshua, Ari. Student, Wayne State U., 1960-62; grad. film sch., NYU, 1965; MA, Ind. U., 1980. Former asst. film editor NBC News; mem. film dept. Whitney Mus., assoc. curator; screenwriter Sanford-Gross, LA. Screenwriter: (with Robert Statzel and Phillip Frank Messina) Brainstorm, 1983, Deadly Friend, 1986, Ghost, 1990 (Academy award best original screenplay 1990), Jacob's Ladder, 1990, Deceived, 1991, Stewart Little, 2002, The Last Mimzy, 2007; writer, dir., prodr. My Life, 1993; filmmaker (with Brian de Palma and Robert Fiore) Dionysus in '69, 1970; screenwriter (with Michael Tolkin) Deep Impact, 1998.

RUBIN, GARY ANDREW, entrepreneur, computer engineer; s. Budd Email and Joanne Lee Rubin. BA in Math., U. Calif., Berkeley, 1978; MS in Computer Sci. & Engring., Stanford U., Palo Alto, Calif., 1982. Cert. instr. Cisco Sys., 1993, network assoc. Cisco Sys., 1996. Software engr., fed. sys. divsn. IBM, Houston, 1978—80, software engr., comm. products divsn. Palo Alto, Calif., 1982—86; software engr., network engr., competitive analyst ROLM Comm., Santa Clara, Calif., 1986—91; pres., founder Advanced Network Info., Inc., Santa Clara, 1992—. Mem.: Inst. Nautical Archaeology, ROLMan Forum Toastmasters (forum v.p. 1990—91, Competent Toastmaster award 1992), Young Entrepreneurs' Orgn. (chpt. mentorship chair, forum moderator 2005—07), Mensa. Achievements include development of the digital auto-pilot for the NASA space shuttle; design of General Motors' manufacturing automation protocol, common application service elements. Avocations: travel, archaeology, scuba diving. Home: 3567 Benton St #248 Santa Clara CA 95051 Office: Advanced Network Info Inc 530 Lakeside Dr Ste 200 Sunnyvale CA 94085 Business E-Mail: grubin@ani-training.com.

RUBIN, GERROLD ROBERT, advertising executive; b. Evanston, Ill., Mar. 31, 1940; s. Bennie George and Anita (Perich) R.; m. Barbara Ann Nieman, Sept. 5, 1962; children: John, Ann. BS in Radio, TV, Film, Northwestern U., 1962. Account exec. Leo Burnett Advt., Chgo., 1962-67, account supr. Toronto, Ont., 1967-68, Needham, Harper Steers, Chgo., 1968-73, account dir. Los Angeles, 1973-78; mgmt. rep. Needham, Harper & Steers, Chgo., 1978-81, pres., CEO Los Angeles, 1981-86, Rubin, Postaer & Assocs., Santa Monica, Calif., 1986—. Bd. dirs. Country Music Assn., Nashville, 1983—. Presbyterian. Office: Rubin Postaer & Assocs 2525 Colorado Ave Santa Monica CA 90404

RUBIN, KARL COOPER, mathematics educator; b. Urbana, Ill., Jan. 27, 1956; s. Robert J. and Vera (Cooper) R. AB, Princeton U., 1976; MA, Harvard U., 1977, PhD, 1981. Instr. Princeton (N.J.) U., 1982-83; mem. Inst. Advanced Study, Princeton, 1983-84; prof. Columbia U., NYC, 1988-89; asst. prof. math. Ohio State U., Columbus, 1984-87, prof., 1987-97; prof. math. Stanford (Calif.) U., 1997—. Contbr. articles to Inventiones Math. Recipient Presdl. Young Investigator award NSF, 1988; NSF postdoctoral fellow, 1981, Sloan fellow, 1985, Guggenheim fellow, 1994. Mem. Am. Math. Soc. (recipient Cole Prize, 1992), Phi Beta Kappa. Achievements include rsch. on elliptic curves, Tate-Shafarevich groups, Birch and Swinnerton-Dyer conjecture, Iwasawa theory and p-adic L-functions. Office: Stanford U Dept Math Stanford CA 94305-2125

RUBIN, MICHAEL, lawyer; b. Boston, July 19, 1952; m. Andrea L. Peterson, May 29, 1983; children: Peter, Eric, Emily. AB, Brandeis U., 1973; JD, Georgetown U., 1977. Bar: Calif. 1978, U.S. Dist. Ct. (no. dist.) Calif. 1978, U.S. Ct. Appeals (9th cir.) 1978, U.S. Ct. Appeals (5th, 7th, 10th cirs.) 1982, U.S. Supreme Ct. 1984, U.S. Ct. Appeals (D.C. cir.) 1984, U.S. Ct. Appeals (11th cir.) 1987. Teaching fellow Law Sch. Stanford (Calif.) U., 1977-78; law clerk to Hon. Charles B. Renfrew U.S. Dist. Ct. (no. dist.) Calif., San Francisco, 1978-79; law clerk to Hon. James R. Browning U.S. Ct. Appeals (9th cir.), San Francisco, 1979-80; law clerk to Hon. William J. Brennan, Jr. U.S. Supreme Ct., Washington, 1980-81; assoc. Altshuler & Berzon, San Francisco, 1981-85, ptnr., 1985-89, Altshuler, Berzon, Nussbaum, Berzon & Rubin, 1989-2000, Altshuler, Berzon, Nussbaum, Rubin & Demain, 2000—06, Altshuler Berzon LLP, 2007—. Office: Altshuler Berzon LLP 177 Post St Ste 300 San Francisco CA 94108-4700 Office Phone: 415-421-7151. E-mail: mrubin@altshulerberzon.com.

RUBIN, ROBERT TERRY, psychiatrist, researcher, educator; b. LA, Aug. 26, 1936; s. Joseph Salem and Lorraine Grace (Baum) R.; m. Lynne Esther Mathews, Mar. 10, 1962 (div. Dec. 1980); children: Deborah, Sharon, Rachel; m. Ada Joan Mickas, Jan. 18, 1985. AB in premedical studies, UCLA, 1957; MD, U. Calif., San Francisco, 1961; PhD in physiology, U. So. Calif., 1977. Diplomate Am. Bd. Psychiatry and Neurology. Intern Phila. Gen. Hosp., 1961-62; resident in psychiatry Sch. Medicine UCLA, 1962-65, asst. prof. psychiatry, 1965-71, prof. psychiatry, 1972; prof. Pa. State U., Hershey, 1972-93; prof. neuroscis. Coll. Medicine Drexel U., Pitts., 1992—2006, prof. psychiatry, dir. Ctr. Neurosci. Rsch. Allegheny Campus, 1992—2005; prof. psychiatry UCLA Sch. Medicine, 2005—; chief dept. psychiatry & mental health VA Greater LA Healthcare System, 2005—. Cons. Naval Health Rsch. Ctr., San Diego, 1969-70; mem. Brain Rsch. Inst. UCLA, 1969—89; assoc. dir. Pitts. Tissue Engring. Initiative, 1994-2004; trustee Kinsey Inst. Sex Rsch., Ind. U., 1986-90. Contbr. articles to profl. jours. With USNR, 1967—69. Recipient Rsch. Sci. Devel. awards NIMH, 1972-77, Rsch. Scientist award, 1982, 87, 93. Fellow: AAAS, Am. Coll. Psychiatrists, Am. Psychiat. Assn.; mem.: Internat. Soc. Psychoneuroendocrinology (pres. 1984—87). Avocations: swimming, bagpiping. Office: VA Greater LA Healthcare System Dept of Psychiatry 116A 11301 Wilshire Blvd Los Angeles CA 90073 Home Phone: 310-231-0380; Office Phone: 310-268-3319. Business E-Mail: robert.rubin@va.gov.

RUBINSTEIN, JONATHAN J., communications executive, former computer company executive; b. NYC, 1956; BSEE, Cornell U., 1978, MSEE, 1979; MS in Computer Sci., Colo. State U. Arch. HP 9000 series, mem. design team HP 9836 workstation Hewlett-Packard; mgr. processor devel. Titan graphics supercomputer family Stardent Computer, designer, arch. 3000 and 2000 computer sys.; v.p., gen. mgr. hardware, v.p. hardware engring. NeXT Computer; exec. v.p., COO FirePower Sys.; sr. v.p. hardware engring. Apple Computer, Inc., Cupertino, Calif., 1997—2004, sr. v.p. iPod divsn., 2004—06, cons., 2006—07; exec. chmn. Palm, Inc., 2007—. Owner, cons. J.R. Ruby Consulting Corp. Patentee in field; contbr. articles to profl. jours. Mem. IEEE, NAE, Assn. for Computing Machinery. Office: Palm Inc 950 W Maude Ave Sunnyvale CA 94085

RUBINSTEIN, MOSHE FAJWEL, engineering educator; b. Miechow, Poland, Aug. 13, 1930; came to US, 1950, naturalized, 1965; s. Shlomo and Sarah (Rosen) Rubinstein; m. Zafrira Gorstein, Feb. 3, 1953; children: Iris, Dorit. BS, UCLA, 1954, MS, 1957, PhD, 1961. Designer Murray Erick Assos. (engrs. and archs.), LA, 1954-56; structural designer Victor Gruen Assos., LA, 1956-61; asst. prof. UCLA, 1961-64, assoc. prof. dept. engring., 1964-69, prof., 1969—, chmn. engring. sys. dept., 1970-75, program dir. modern engring. for execs. program, 1965-70. Cons. Pacific Power & Light Co., Portland, Oreg., Northrop Corp., US Army, NASA Rsch. Ctr., Langley, Tex. Instruments Co., Hughes Space System Divsn., US Army Sci. Adv. Com., Kaiser Aluminum and Chem. Corp., IBM Corp., TRW. Author: (with W.C. Hurty) Dynamics of Structures, 1964 (Yugoslavian transl. 1973), Matrix Computer Analysis of Structures, 1966 (Japanese transl. 1974), Structural Systems, Statics Dynamics and Stability, 1970 (Japanese transl. 1979), Patterns of Problem Solving, 1975, (with K. Pfeiffer) Concepts in Problem Solving, 1980, Tools for Thinking and Problem Solving, 1986; IEEE Press Videotapes; Models for People Driven Quality, 1991, Quality through Innovation, 1991, Creativity for Ongoing Total Quality, 1993, Relentless Improvement, 1993, (with I.R. Firstenberg) Patterns of Problem Solving, 2d edit., 1995, (with I.R. Firstenberg) The Minding Organization, 1999 (Portuguese/Japanese transl. 2000, Spanish/Chinese/Russian transls. 2001). Recipient Disting. Tchr. award UCLA Acad. Senate, 1964, Western Electric Fund award Am. Soc. Engring. Edn., 1965, Disting. Tchr. trophy Engring. Student Soc., UCLA, 1966; Sussman prof. for disting. visitor Technion-Israel Inst. Tech., 1967-68; named Outstanding Faculty Mem., UCLA Engring. Alumni award, 1979, Outstanding UCLA Civil Engring. Alumni award, 1990, Outstanding Faculty Mem., State of Calif. Command Coll., 1987-89, 94-95; Fulbright-Hays fellow, Yugoslavia and Eng., 1975-76; named one of UCLA's Top 20 Profs. of the Century. Mem. ASCE, Am. Soc. Engring. Edn., Seismol. Soc. Am., Sigma Xi, Tau Beta Phi. Achievements include research in use of computers in structural systems, analysis and synthesis; problem solving and decision theory; creativity and innovation in the orgn. Home: 10488 Charing Cross Rd Los Angeles CA 90024-2646 Office: UCLA Sch Engring and Applied Sci Los Angeles CA 90024 Home Phone: 310-475-5198; Office Phone: 310-825-7731. Business E-Mail: mrubinst@ucla.edu.

RUCH, CHARLES P., academic administrator; b. Long Branch, NJ, Mar. 25, 1938; s. Claud C. and Marcella (Pierce) R.; m. Sally Joan Brandenburg, June 18, 1960; children: Cheryl, Charles, Christopher, Cathleen. BA, Coll. of Wooster, 1959; MA, Northwestern U., 1960, PhD, 1966. Counselor, tchr. Evanston (Ill.) Twp. High Sch., 1960-66; asst. prof. U. Pitts., 1966-70, assoc. prof., dept. chmn., 1970-74; assoc. dean sch. edn. Va. Commonwealth U., Richmond, 1974-76, dean sch. edn., 1976-85, interim provost, v.p., 1985-86, provost, v.p., 1986-93; pres. Boise (Idaho) State U., 1993—. Cons. various univs., govtl. agys., ednl. founds. Author or co-author over 50 articles, revs., tech. reports. Mem. Am. Psychol. Assn., Am. Ednl. Research Assn., Phi Delta Kappa. Office: Boise State U 1910 University Dr Boise ID 83725-0399 E-mail: cruch@boisestate.edu.

RUCKELSHAUS, WILLIAM DOYLE, investment company executive, former federal agency administrator; b. Indpls., July 24, 1932; s. John K. and Marion (Doyle) R.; m. Jill Elizabeth Strickland, May 11, 1962; children: Catherine Kiley, Mary Hughes, Jennifer Lea, William Justice, Robin Elizabeth. BA cum laude, Princeton U., 1957; LL.B., Harvard U., 1960. Bar: Ind. 1960. Atty. Ruckelshaus, Bobbitt & O'Connor, Indpls., 1960-68; dep. atty. gen. State of Ind., 1960-65, chief counsel Office of Atty. Gen., 1963-65; minority atty. Ind. State Senate, 1965-67; mem. Ind. Ho. of Reps., 1967-69, majority leader, 1967-69; asst. atty. gen. civil divsn. US Dept. Justice, Washington, 1969-70; adminstr. EPA, Washington, 1970-73, 1983-85; acting dir. FBI, Washington, 1973; dep. atty. gen. US Dept. Justice, Washington, 1973; ptnr. Ruckelshaus, Beveridge, Fairbanks & Diamond, Washington, 1974-76; sr. v.p. law & corp. affairs Weyerhaeuser Co., Tacoma, 1976-83; pres. William D. Ruckelshaus Assocs., 1985-88; ptnr. Perkins Coie, Seattle, 1985-88; chmn. bd., CEO Browning-Ferris Industries, Inc., Houston, 1988-95, chmn., 1995—99; founder, prin. Madrona Investment Group, LLC, 1996—; strategic dir. Madrona Venture Group, Seattle, 1999—; chmn. World Resources Inst., Washington D.C., 1999—. Bd. dirs. Cummins Engine Co., Nordstrom, Inc., Weyerhaeuser Co., Inc., Vykor, Inc. Rep. nominee for U.S. Senate, Ind., 1968; apptd. by Pres. Clinton to serve as U.S. envoy to Pacific Salmon Treaty with Can., 1997-98; mem., Pres. Council on Sustainable Devel., 1993-97; chmn. Salmon Recovery Funding Bd., Wash., 1999-, commr. Commn. on Ocean Policy, 2001-04 Recipient Outstanding First Year Legislator in House award, Ind. Broadcasters Assn., 1967; named Man of Yr., Indpls. Jaycess; named an Outstanding Republican Legislator in Ind. Ho. Representatives, Working Press, 1967. Mem. World Resource Inst. (chmn. 1998—), Fed. Bar Assn., Ind. Bar Assn., D.C. Bar Assn., Indpls. Bar Assn. Republican. Roman Catholic. Office: Madrona Investment Group LLC 1000 2nd Ave Ste 3700 Seattle WA 98104-1053 Office Phone: 206-674-3008. E-mail: bill@madrona.com.*

RUCKER, GABRIEL, chef; b. 1981; Sous chef Paley's Place, Gotham Building Tavern; owner, exec. chef Le Pigeon, Portland, Oreg., 2006—. Named Chef of Yr., Portland Mag., 2006; named one of Best New Chefs, Food and Wine Mag., 2007. Office: Le Pigeon 738 E Burnside St Portland OR 97214 Office Phone: 503-546-8796.

RUDD, PAUL, actor; b. Passaic, NJ, Apr. 6, 1969; m. Julie Yaeger, Feb. 23, 2003; 1 child. BA, U. Kans.; Grad., Am. Acad. Dramatic Arts, Los Angeles. Actor: (films) A Question of Ethics, 1992, Clueless, 1995, Halloween: The Curse of Michael Myers, 1995, The Size of Watermelons, 1996, Romeo + Juliet, 1996, The Locusts, 1997, Overnight Delivery, 1998, The Object of My Affection, 1998, 200 Cigarettes, 1999, The Cider House Rules, 1999, Wet Hot American Summer, 2001, The Château, 2001, Reaching Normal, 2001, The Shapes of Things, 2003, Two Days, 2003, House Hunting, 2003, Anchorman: The Legend of Ron Burgundy, 2004, P.S., 2004, Tennis, Anyone...?, 2005, The Baxter, 2005, The 40 Year Old Virgin, 2005, The OH in Ohio, 2006, Diggers, 2006, Night at the Museum, 2006, The Ex, 2007, Reno 911!: Miami, 2007, Knocked Up, 2007, I Could Never Be Your Woman, 2007, Over Her Dead Body, 2008, Forgetting Sarah Marshall, 2008, I Love You, Man, 2009, (voice) Monsters vs. Aliens, 2009; actor, prodr. (films) The Ten, 2007, actor, writer Role Models, 2008; actor: (TV films) The Fire Next Time, 1993, Moment of Truth: Stalking Back, 1993, Runaway Daughters, 1994, Twelfth Night, or What You Will, 1998, The Great Gatsby, 2000; (TV series) Wild Oats, 1994, Sisters, 1993—95, Friends, 2002—04, Reno 911, 2006—07, (TV appearances) Deadline, 2000, Strangers with Candy, 2000, Cheap Seats: Without Ron Parker, 2004, Stella, 2005, Robot Chicken, 2006, The Naked Trucker and T-Bones Show, 2007, Veronica Mars, 2007. Named one of Top 25 Entertainers of Yr. (with Apatow Gang), Entertainment Weekly, 2007. Office: United Talent Agy 9560 Wilshire Blvd Ste 500 Beverly Hills CA 90212-2401

RUDDER, ERIC D., computer company executive, information technology executive; married; 2 children. Grad. with honors, Brown U., 1988. With Microsoft Corp., Redmond, Wash., 1988—, gen. mgr. visual studio, v.p. tech. strategy, sr. v.p. developer and platform evangelism, 2001—03, sr. v.p. servers and tools to sr. v.p. tech. strategy, 2003—, work directly for chmn., chief software architect, Bill Gates, 2005—. Spkr. in field. Office: Microsoft One Microsoft Way Redmond WA 98052-6399

RUDEE, MERVYN LEA, engineering educator, researcher; s. Mervyn C. and Hannah Rudee; m. Elizabeth Eager, 1958; children: Elizabeth Diane, David Benjamin. BS, Stanford U., 1958, MS, 1962, PhD, 1965. Asst. prof. materials sci. Rice U., Houston, 1964-68, assoc. prof., 1968-72, prof. materials sci., 1972-74; prof. U. Calif. San Diego, La Jolla, 1974—, founding provost Warren Coll., 1974-82, founding dean Sch. Engring., 1982-93, coord. grad. program on materials sci., 1994-99, faculty athletic rep., 1999—2007; interim dean engring. U. Calif., Riverside, 1995-97. Vis. scholar Corpus Christi Coll., Cambridge, Eng., 1971-72; vis. scientist IBM Thomas J. Watson Rsch. Ctr., Yorktown Heights, N.Y., 1987; dir. fellows program Calif. Coun. on Sci. and Tech., 1999-2000. Pres., bd. trustees Mus. Photographic Art, San Diego, 1995-96; trustee The Burnham Inst., 1998—2004, The Glen Canyon Inst., 1999—, The San Diego River Park Found., 2003-. Lt. (j.g.) USN, 1958-61. Guggenheim fellow, 1971-72. Fellow AAAS; mem. Microscopy Soc. Am., Materials Rsch. Soc., Tex. Soc. Electron Microscopy (hon., pres. 1966), Sigma Xi, Tau Beta Pi. Office: U Calif San Diego Dept Elec & Computer Engring La Jolla CA 92093-0407 Office Phone: 858-534-8998. Business E-Mail: rudee@ucsd.edu.

RUDIN, ANNE, retired mayor, nursing educator; b. Passaic, NJ, Jan. 27, 1924; m. Edward Rudin, June 6, 1948; 4 children. BS in Edn., Temple U., 1945, RN, 1946; MPA, U. So. Calif., 1983; LLD (hon.), Golden Gate U., 1990. RN, Calif. Mem. faculty Temple U. Sch. Nursing, Phila., 1946-48; mem. nursing faculty Mt. Zion Hosp., San Francisco, 1948-49; mem. Sacramento City Council, 1971-83; mayor City of Sacramento, 1983-92; ind. pub. policy cons. Pres. LWV, Riverside, 1957, Sacramento, 1961, Calif., 1969-71, Calif. Elected Women's Assn., 1973—; trustee Golden Gate U., 1993-96; mem. adv. bd. U. So. Calif., Army Depot Reuse Commn., 1992-94; bd. dirs. Sacramento Theatre Co., 1992-99, Japan Soc. No. Calif., Sacramento Symphony, 1993-96, Calif. Common Cause, 1993 -96, Sacramento Edn. Found., 1993-2006; v.p. Sacramento Traditional Jazz Soc. Found.; pres. bd. dirs. Natomas Basin Conservancy; foreman Sacramento County Grand Jury, 2000-01. Recipient Women in Govt. award U.S. Jaycee Women, 1984, Woman of Distinction award Sacramento Area Soroptimist Clubs, 1985, Civic Contbn. award LWV Sacramento, 1989, Woman of Courage award Sacramento History Ctr., 1989, Peacemaker of Yr. award Sacramento Mediation Ctr., 1992, Regional Pride award Sacramento Mag., 1993, Humanitarian award Japanese Am. Citizen's League, 1993, Outstanding Pub. Svc. award Am. Soc. Pub. Adminstrn., 1994, Cmty. Svc. Recognition award, Japanese Am. Citizens League, 1999, Contbr. to Pub. Art award Am. Soc. for Pub. Admin., 2004, Robert T. Matsui award Pub. Svc., Town & Country Dem. Club, 2005; named Girl Scouts Am. Role model, 1989; named to Sacramento Traditional Jazz Soc. Hall of Fame, 2000. Mem.: Calif. Med. Alliance (Mem. of Yr. 2005).

RUDOLPH, ABRAHAM MORRIS, pediatrician, educator; b. Johannesburg, Republic of South Africa, Feb. 3, 1924; s. Chone and Sarah (Feinstein) Rudolph; m. Rhona Sax, Nov. 2, 1949; children: Linda, Colin, Jeffrey. MBBCh summa cum laude, U. Witwatersrand, Johannesburg, 1946, MD, 1951; MD (hon.), U. Witwatersrand, Johannesburg, S. Africa, 2006; D (hon.), Rene Descartes U., Paris, 1996. Instr. Harvard Med. Sch., 1955—57, assoc. pediat., 1957—60; assoc. cardiologist in charge cardiopulmonary lab. Children's Hosp., Boston, 1955—60; dir. pediatric cardiology Albert Einstein Coll. Medicine, 1960—66, prof. pediat., assoc. prof. physiology NYC, 1962—66; vis. pediatrician Bronx Mcpl. Hosp. Ctr., NYC, 1960—66; prof. pediat. U. Calif., San Francisco, 1966—94, prof. physiology, 1974—88, Neider prof. pediatric cardiology, prof. ob-gyn and reproductive scis., 1974—94, chmn. dept. pediat., 1987—91, prof. pediatr. emeritus, 1994—; practice medicine, specializing in pediatric cardiology San Francisco. Mem. cardiovasc. study sect. NIH, 1961—65; mem. nat. adv. heart coun., 1968—72; established investigator Am. Heart Assn., 1958—62; career scientist Health Rsch. Coun., NYC, 1962—66; Harvey lectr. Oxford (Eng.) U., 1984; inaugural lectr. 1st Nat. Congress Italian Soc. Perinatal Medicine, 1985. Editl. bd. Pediat., 1964—70, Circulation, 1966—74, 1983—88, assoc. editor Circulation Rsch., 1970, Pediatric Rsch., 1970—77; editor: Rudolph's Pediatrics, Congenital Diseases of the Heart: Clinical-Physiological Considerations, 2001, Rudolph's Fundamentals of Pediatrics; contbr. articles to profl. jours. Recipient Merit award, Nat. Heart, Lung and Blood Inst., 1986, Arvo Ylppo medal, Helsinki (Finland) U., 1987, Jonxis medal, Children's Hosp. Groningen, 1993, Nils Rosen von Rosenstein award, Swedish Pediat. Soc., 1999, Pollin prize for pediat. rsch., N.Y. Presbyn. Hosp., Columbia U. Coll. Physicians and Surgeons, 2005, award, FRCP(Edin.), 1965, FRCP(Lond.), 1985, E. Mead Johnson award, 1964, Borden Award, Am. Acad. Pediat., 1979, Howland award, Am. Ped. Soc., 1999, Arvo Ylipo award, U. Helsinki, 1987, JMP Jonxis Medal, U. Groningen, 1992, Rosen Von Rosentein award, U. Uppsala; named Disting. Scientist, Am. Heart Assoc., 2003. Fellow: AAAS, Am. Assn. Adv. Sci., Royal Coll. Physicians (London), Royal Coll. Physicians (Edinburgh); mem.: Am. Heart Assn. (Rsch. Achievement award 1991, Founding Disting. Scientist award 2003), Am. Pediatric Soc. (coun. 1985—92, v.p. 1992—93, pres. 1993—94, Howland award 1999), Soc. for Pediatric Rsch. (coun. 1961—64), Soc. for Clin. Investigation, Am. Phys. Soc., Am. Acad. Pediat. (past chmn. sect. on cardiology, E. Mead Johnson award for rsch. in pediat. 1964, Borden award 1979, Lifetime Med. Edn. award 1992, Joseph St. Geme leadership award Pediat. 1993, Founder award, cardiology sect. 2001, Pollin Pediatric Rsch. prize 2005), NAS Inst. Medicine. Office: U Calif Cardiovascular Rsch Inst Calif Rm HSE 1424 Box 0544 San Francisco CA 94143-0544 Home Phone: 415-665-6841. Business E-Mail: abraham.rudolph@ucsf.edu.

RUDOLPH, GILBERT LAWRENCE, lawyer; b. LA, Aug. 23, 1946; BA, Ariz. State U., 1967; postgrad., Am. U., Washington, 1967-69; JD, U. Cin., 1973. Bar: D.C. 1973, U.S. Dist. Ct. D.C. 1974, U.S. Ct. Appeals (D.C. cir.) 1974, Ariz. 1975, U.S. Dist. Ct. Ariz. 1975, Calif. 1979. Assoc. Streich, Lang, Weeks & Cardon, P.A., Phoenix, 1975-78; ptnr. Gilbert L. Rudolph, P.C., Phoenix, 1978-87; sr. mem. O'Connor, Cavanagh, Anderson, Killingsworth & Beshears, P.A., Phoenix, 1987-99; shareholder, co-chair fin. instn. practice group Greenberg Traurig LLP, Phoenix, 1999—. Lectr. on lending issues. Bd. dirs. Temple Chai, 2002—08, pres., 2008; bd. dirs. Make-A-Wish Found. of Am., 1984—89, Aid to Adoption of Spl. Kids, Ariz., 1995—2003. Fellow Am. Coll. Consumer Fin. Svcs. Lawyers; mem. ABA (com. on consumer fin. svcs. bus. law sect. 1981—, com. on comml. fin. svcs. 1989—, mem. com. on uniform comml. code 1992—), Conf. on Consumer Fin. Law (governing com. 1986-, v.p. 2007-). Republican. Jewish. Office: Greenberg Traurig LLP Ste 700 2375 E Camelback Rd Phoenix AZ 85016 Office Phone: 602-445-8206. E-mail: rudolphg@gtlaw.com.

RUDOLPH, JEFFREY N., museum director; Exec. dir. Calif. Sci. Ctr., LA. Office: Calif Sci Ctr 700 State Dr Expn Pk Los Angeles CA 90037-1210

RUDOLPH, RONALD ALVIN, human resources specialist; b. Berwyn, Ill., May 12, 1949; s. Alvin J. and Gloria S. (Nicoletti) Rudolph. BA, U. Calif., Santa Cruz, 1971; D in Psychology, Calif. Coast U., 2003. Sr. cons. De Anza Assocs., San Jose, Calif., 1971-73; pers. adminstr. McDonnell Douglas Corp., Cupertino, Calif., 1974-75; employment rep. Fairchild Semiconductor, Mountain View, Calif., 1973-74, 75; compensation analyst Sperry Univac, Santa Clara, Calif., 1975-78; mgr. exempt compensation div. Intel Corp., Santa Clara, 1978-79, compensation mgr., 1979-82, dir. corp. compensation, 1982-85; v.p. human resources UNISYS Corp., San Jose, 1985-91, ASK Group Inc., Mountain View, 1991-94, 3 Com Corp., Santa Clara, 1994-98; v.p. adminstrn. Wyse Tech. Inc., San Jose, 1999—2000; with Infogrames Inc., 2000—01, Netmanage Inc., 2003—. Cons. Rudolph Assocs., Cupertino, 1982—; bd. dirs. Dynamic Temp. Svcs., Sunnyvale, Calif. Mem. spl. com. parolee employment, Sacramento, 1973—75; bd. dirs. Jr. Achievement, San Jose, 1978—88. Mem.: No. Calif. Human Resources Coun., Am. Compensation Assn., Am. Soc. Pers. Adminstrs. Avocations: sailing, reading, running, camping. Office: 3 Com Corp Santa Clara CA 95050 Office Phone: 408-342-7674.

RUDOLPH, WALTER PAUL, engineering research company executive; b. Binghamton, NY, Aug. 17, 1937; s. Walter Paul and Frieda Lena (Hennemann) R.; m. Leila Ortencia Romero, Dec. 18, 1960; children: Jonathan, Jana, Catherine. BEE, Rensselaer Poly. Inst., 1959; MSBA, San Diego State U., 1964. Elec. engr. Gen. Dynamics/Astronautics, San Diego, 1959-62; ops. research analyst Navy Electronics Lab., San Diego, 1962-64; mem. profl. staff Gen. Electric Tempo, Honolulu, 1964-70, Ctr. for Naval Analysis, Arlington, Va., 1970-77; pres. La Jolla (Calif.) Rsch. Corp., 1977—. Capt. USNR. Republican. Presbyterian. Home: 1559 El Paso Real La Jolla CA 92037-6303 E-mail: rudolphw@sbcglobal.net.

RUEDRICH, RANDY, political organization administrator; BS, Tex. A&M U., M in Engring., PhD. Commr., formerly Alaska Oil & Gas Conservation Commn., 2003—; gen. mgr. Doyon Drilling; sr. drilling engr. Arco's Alaska; pres. Arctic E&P Advisors; fin. chmn. Alaska Rep. Party, 1986—88, rules chmn., 1998—2000, asst. treas., 1999—2000, vice chmn., 2000, chmn., 2000—. Republican. Office: Alaska Rep Com 1001 W Fireweed Ln Anchorage AK 99503*

RUFE, LAURIE J., museum director; b. Pa. m. Mike Rufe. BA in Art History, Va. Commonwealth U., 1972. Intern Valentine Mus., Hist. Ho. Mus.; with Mercer Mus., Doylestown, Pa., 1973—80; Big Horn Basin Project Wyo., 1981—85; with Douglas County Coun. for the Arts and Humanities, Castle Rock; dir. Custer County Art Ctr., Mont., 1986—87; asst. dir. Roswell Mus. and Art Ctr., Roswell, 1987—98, dir., 1998—2002, exec. dir., 2005—; dir. Tucson Mus. Art, 2002—05. Office: Roswell Mus and Art Ctr 100 W 11th St Roswell NM 88201 Office Phone: 575-624-6744. Business E-Mail: rufe@roswellmuseum.org.

RUFF, DOYLE C., airport manager; b. Orlando, Fla., Apr. 26, 1938; m. Lu R., 5 children. BS, Fla. State U., 1959. cert. airport exec. Commd. 2d. lt. USAF, 1959; advanced through grades to Col., 1980; retired, 1980; airport mgr. Fairbanks (AK) Internat. Airport, 1983-87; airport dir. Anchorage (AK) Internat. Airport, 1987-89; dir. of airports City of Redding (Calif.), 1989-93; airport mgr. Fairbanks (AK) Internat. Airport, 1993—. Mem. Rotary Club of Fairbanks. Recipient Airport Mgr. of the Year for Calif. and the Southwestern U.S. 1992-93. Mem. Am. Assn. of Airpot Execs., Airports Coun. Internat., Aircraft Owners and Pilots Assn., USAF Assn., USAF thunderbird Alumni Assn. Office: Fairbanks Internat Airport 6450 Airport Way Ste 1 Fairbanks AK 99709-4671

RUFFALO, MARK, actor; b. Kenosha, Wis., Nov. 22, 1967; s. Frank Lawrence and Marie Rose Ruffalo; m. Sunrise Coigney, June 2000; children: Keen, Bella, Odette. Actor: (films) Rough Trade, 1993, A Song For You, 1993, There Goes My Baby, 1994, Mirror, Mirror 2:Raven Dance, 1994, A Gift From Heaven, 1994, Mirror, Mirror III: The Voyeur, 1995, The Dentist, 1996, The Last Big Thing, 1996, Blood Money, 1996, Safe Men, 1998, 54, 1998, A Fish in the Bathtub, 1999, Ride with the Devil, 1999, You Can Count on Me, 2000, Committed, 2000, Life/Drawing, 2001, The Last Castle, 2001, XX/XY, 2002, Windtalkers, 2002, My Life Without Me, 2003, View From the Top, 2003, In the Cut, 2003, Eternal Sunshine of the Spotless Mind, 2004, 13 Going On 30, 2004, Collateral, 2004, Just Like Heaven, 2005, Rumor Has It..., 2005, All the King's Men, 2006, Zodiac, 2007; actor, actor: (films) Reservation Road, 2007, Blindness, 2008, What Doesn't Kill You, 2008; (TV films) On the 2nd Day of Christmas, 1997, Houdini, 1998; (TV series) The Beat, 2000; (films) The Destiny of Marty Fine, 1996; writer: films The Destiny of Marty Fine, 1996; exec. prodr., actor: (films) We Don't Live Here Anymore, 2004, Chicago, 2008; (Broadway plays) Awake and Sing!, 2006. Office: c/o Robert Stein 345 N Maple Dr Ste 317 Beverly Hills CA 90210 Office Phone: 310-550-2176. Business E-Mail: robertadamstein@aol.com.

RUIZ, HECTOR DE JESUS, information technology executive; b. Piedras Negras, Mex. BS in Elec. Engring., MS in Elec. Engring., U. Tex., Austin; D in Electronics, Rice U., 1973. Various positions Tex. Instruments, Dallas; pres. Motorola's Semiconductor Products Sector; COO Advanced Micro Devices, Inc., Sunnyvale, Calif., 2000—02, pres., 2000—06, CEO, 2000—08, chmn., 2004—. Bd. dirs. Eastman Kodak Co., Semiconductor Indus. Assn. Apptd. by Pres. Adv. Com. Trade Policy and Negotiations; mem. Govs. Task Force Econ. Growth; apptd. by Gov. G.W. Bush Tex. Higher Edn. Coord. Bd.; mem. adv. coun. Coll. Engring. U. Tex.; mem. adv. bd. Tsinghua Sch. of Econ. and Mgmt.; Nat. Sec. Telecommunications Adv. Com. Named one of 50 Most Important Hispanics in Tech. & Bus., Hispanic Engr. & Info. Tech. mag., 2005; named to, Hispanic Engr. Nat. Awards Conf. Hall of Fame, 2000; fellow, Internat. Engring. Consortium, 2002. Mem.: Hispanic Profl. Engrs. (apptd. bd. dirs.). Office: Advanced Micro Devices Inc 1 AMD Pl Sunnyvale CA 94088

RUIZ, VICKI LYNN, history professor, department chairman; b. Atlanta, May 21, 1955; d. Robert Paul and Erminia Pablita (Ruiz) Mercer; m. Jerry Joseph Ruiz, Sept. 1, 1979 (div. Jan. 1990); children: Miguel, Daniel; m. Victor Becerra, Aug. 14, 1992. AS in Social Studies, Gulf Coast Community Coll., 1975; BA in Social Sci., Fla. State, 1977; MA in History, Stanford U., 1978, PhD in History, 1982. Asst. prof. U. Tex., El Paso, 1982-85, U. Calif., Davis, 1985-87, assoc. prof., 1987-92; Andrew W. Mellon prof. Claremont Grad. Sch., Calif., 1992-95, chmn. history dept. Calif., 1993-95; prof. history Ariz. State U., Tempe, 1995—, chair dept. Chicano studies, 1997—; prof. history and chicano/latino studies U. Calif., Irvine. Dir. Inst. of Oral History, U. Tex., El Paso, 1983-85, minority undergrad. rsch. program U. Calif., Davis, 1988-92. Author: Cannery Women, Cannery Lives, 1987, From Out of the Shadows, 1998 (Choice Outstanding Book of 1998); editor: Chicana Politics of Work and Family, 2000; co-editor: Women on U.S.-Mexican Border, 1987, Western Women, 1988, Unequal Sisters, 1990, 3d edit., 1999. Mem. Calif. Coun. for Humanities, 1990-94, vice chmn., 1991-93. Fellow Univ. Calif. Davis Humanities Inst., 1990-91, Am. Coun. of Learned Socs., 1986, Danforth Found., 1977. Mem. Orgn. Am. Historians (chmn. com. on status of minority history 1989-91, nominating com. 1987-88, exec. bd. 1995-98, pres. 2005-06), Immigration History Soc. (exec. bd. 1989-91), Am. Hist. Assn. (nat. coun. 1999—), Am. Studies Assn. (nominating bd. 1992-94, nat. coun. 1996-99), Western History (nominating bd. 1993-95). Democrat. Roman Catholic. Avocations: walking, needlecrafts. Office: U Calif Irvine History Dept 269 Murray Krieger Hall Irvine CA 92697-3275

RUMMAGE, STEPHEN MICHAEL, lawyer; b. Massillon, Ohio, Dec. 27, 1955; s. Robert Everett and Kathleen Patricia (Newman) R.; m. Elizabeth Anne Seivert, Mar. 24, 1979; children: Everett Martin, Carter Kevin. BA in History and English, Stanford U., 1977; JD, U. Calif., Berkeley, 1980. Bar: Wash. 1980, U.S. Dist. Ct. (we. dist.) 1980, U.S. Ct. Appeals (9th cir.) 1983, U.S. Supreme Ct. 1985. Assoc. Davis, Wright et al, Seattle, 1980-85; ptnr. Davis Wright Tremaine, Seattle, 1986—. Co-author: Employer's Guide to Strike Planning and Prevention, 1985. Mem. Wash. Athletic Club. Democrat. Roman Catholic. Office: Davis Wright Tremaine 1201 Third Ave Ste 2200 Seattle WA 98101-3045 Home Phone: 206-726-8433; Office Phone: 206-622-3150. Business E-Mail: steverummage@dwt.com.

RUMMEL, ROBERT WILAND, aeronautical engineer, writer; b. Dakota, Ill., Aug. 4, 1915; s. William Howard and Dora (Ely) R.; m. Marjorie B. Cox, Sept. 30, 1939; children: Linda Kay, Sharon Lee, Marjorie Susan, Robert Wiland, Diana Beth. Diploma in Aero. Engring., Curtiss Wright Tech. Inst. Aerosci., 1935. Stress analyst Hughes Aircraft Co., Burbank, Calif., 1935-36, Lockheed Aircraft Corp., Burbank, 1936; draftsman Aero Engring. Corp., Long Beach, Calif., 1936, Nat. Aircraft Co., Alhambra, Calif., 1936-37; chief engr. Rearwin A/C & Engines, Inc., Kansas City, Kans., 1937-42; chief design engr. Commonwealth A/C, Inc., Kansas City, 1942-43; v.p. engring. Trans World Airlines, Inc., Kansas City, Mo., 1943-59, v.p. planning and rsch., 1959-69, v.p. tech. devel., 1969-78; pres. Robert W. Rummel Assocs., Inc., Mesa, Ariz., 1978-87; aerospace cons., 1987—. Commnr. Presdl. Commn. Space Shuttle Challenger Accident, 1986; chmn. nat. rsch. coun. Aero Space Engring. Bd. Fellow

Inst. Aero. Scis., Soc. Automotive Engrs.; mem. NAE, Masons (32 deg.), Shriners. Home and Office: 1189 Leisure World Mesa AZ 85206-3067 Office Phone: 480-396-9030. Personal E-mail: rwrummel@aol.com.

RUNNER, GEORGE CYRIL, JR., minister, educational administrator; b. Scotia, NY, Mar. 25, 1952; s. George Cyril and Kay Carol (Cooper) R.; m. Sharon Yvonne Oden, Jan. 13, 1973; children: Micah Stephen, Rebekah Kay. Student, Antelope Valley Coll., Lancaster, Calif., 1970-88; grad. mgmt. cert., Azusa Pacific U., 1988; student, U. Redlands. Lic. to ministry Am. Bapt. Chs. in USA, 1977. Exec. pastor 1st Bapt. Ch. Lancaster, 1973—; founder, exec. dir. Desert Christian Schs., Lancaster, 1977—; founder, internat. dir. Supporting Ptnrs. in Christian Edn., Lancaster, Guatemala City, Guatemala, 1989—. Seminar leader Internat. Ctr. for Learning, Ventura, Calif., 1972-82; curriculum cons. Gospel Light Publs., Glendale, Calif., 1974-80; bd. dirs. Greater L.A. Sunday Sch. Assn., 1978-79. Assemblyman State of Calif., 36th Dist., Lancaster, 1996; bd. dirs. Lancaster Econ. Devel. Corp.; mem. Salvation Army, Lancaster. Mem. Internat. Fellowship Ch. Sch. Adminstrs., Assn. Christian Schs. Internat., Christian Mgmt. Assn., Lancaster Ministerial Assn. Republican. Office: Desert Christian Schs 1st Bapt Ch 44648 15th St W Lancaster CA 93534-2806

RUNNICLES, DONALD, conductor; b. Edinburgh, Nov. 16, 1954; Student, Edinburgh U., Cambridge U., London Opera Ctr.; DMus (hon.), U. Edinburgh, 1995. Music dir., prin. condr. San Francisco Opera, 1992—; prin. condr. NY Orch. of St. Luke's. Prin. guest condr. Atlanta Symphony Orch., 2005—06. Repetiteur Nat. Theatre, Mannheim, Germany, 1980—, Kapellmeister, 1984—, prin. condr., Hanover, 1987—, numerous appearances with Hamburg Staatsoper, former gen. music dir. Stadtische Buhnen, Freiburg/Breisgau, appearances with Met. Opera include Lulu, 1988, The Flying Dutchman, 1990, The Magic Flute, condr. Vienna Staatsoper, 1990—91, Sonome, 1996, debut Don Giovanni, Glyndebourne, 1991, Salzburg Festival, 1996, condr. London Symphony Orch., La Scale Milan Freischutz, Orch. Paris, Israel Philharm., Rotterdam Philharm., Seattle Symphony, Pitts. Symphony, St. Louis Symphony, Chgo. Symphony, San Francisco Symphony, Cleve. Orch., New World Symphony, Bavarian Radio Symphony, Billy Budd and the Ring, Vienna State Opera, 2001, Katya Kabanova, San Francisco, 2002, Schoenberg's Gurrelieder, London Proms, 2002, Tristan und Isolde, BBC Symphony Orch., 2002—03, (world premier) Doctor Atomic, John Adams, 2005, rec. artist Hansel and Gretel, Gluck's Orphée with San Francisco Opera Orch., 1995, Tannhäuser-Bayreuth Festspick, 1995, Harvey Milk with San Francisco Opera, 1996, Mozart Requiem, 2005—, opened Edinburgh Festival, 1994, 1996. Recipient Officer of Brit. Empire. Office: San Francisco Opera War Meml Opera House 301 Van Ness Ave San Francisco CA 94102-4509

RUNQUIST, LISA A., lawyer; b. Mpls., Sept. 22, 1952; d. Ralf E. and Violet R. BA, Hamline U., 1973; JD, U. Minn., 1976. Bar: Minn. 1977, Calif. 1978, U.S. Dist. Ct. (ctrl. dist.) Calif. 1985, U.S. Supreme Ct. 1995. Assoc. Caldwell & Toms, LA, 1978-82; ptnr. Runquist & Flagg, LA, 1982-85; pvt. practice Runquist & Assocs., LA, 1985-99, 2005—, Runquist & Zybach LLP, LA, 1999—2005. Mem. adv. bd. Exempt Orgn. Tax Rev., 1990—, Calif. State U. L.A. Continuing Edn. Acctg. and Tax Program, 1995—. Mem. editl. bd.: ABA Bus. Law Today, 1994—2002; author: The ABCs of Nonprofits, 2005; editor: Nonprofit Resources, 2007; editor (prin. author) Guide to Representing Religious Organizations, 2009; contbr. chapters to books. Recipient Outstanding Lawyer award, ABA Bus. Law Sect., 1999. Mem. ABA (bus. law sect. counsel 1995-99, com. on nonprofit corps. 1986—, chair 1991-95, subcom. current devels. in nonprofit corp. law 1989—, chair 1989-91, subcom. rels. orgns. 1989—, chair 1987-91, 95-98, subcom. legal guidebook for dirs. 1986—, partnerships and unincorp. bus. orgns. com. 1987—, state regulation of securities com. 1988-99, ad hoc com. info. tech. 1997-2003, chmn., 1997-98, co-chmn. 1998-2002, sect. liaison to tech. coun. 1997-2000, sec. of taxation exempt orgns. com. 1987—, subcom. religious orgns. 1989—, chair 1995-97, 2005—, subcom. model nonprofit corp. act, co-chmn. subcom. non-exempt orgns. 1997-2003, co-chair state and local regulation subcom. 2003-05, corp. laws com. 1999-2005, subcom. guidebook for dirs. of closely held corps. chair 2000-04, liaison ALI/ABA principles of law of nonprofit orgns. project 2003—, standing com. solo and small firm practitioners 2004-05, ABA liason to NCCUSL project to create legal framework for Unicorp. NP Assn. in N. Am., 2005-), Calif. Bar Assn. (bus. law sect., nonprofit and unincorp. orgns. com. 1985-92, 93-96, 97—, chair 1989-91, 2006—, exec. com. mem. 2008-), Christian Legal Soc., Ctr. Law and Religious Freedom, Christian Mgmt. Assn. (dir. 1983-89). Office: 17554 Community St Northridge CA 91325 Office Phone: 818-609-7761. Business E-Mail: lisa@runquist.com.

RUSCH, THOMAS WILLIAM, manufacturing executive; b. Alliance, Nebr., Oct. 3, 1946; s. Oscar William and Gwen Falerne (Middleswart) R.; m. Gloria Ann Sutton, June 20, 1968 (div. Oct. 1979); children: Alicia Catherine, Colin William; m. Lynn Biebighauser, Jan. 17, 1981. BEE, U. of Minn., 1968, MSEE, 1970, PhD, 1973; MS in Mgmt. of Tech., U. Minn., 1993. Sr. physicist cen. rsch. 3M Co., St. Paul, 1973-77, rsch. specialist cen. rsch., 1977-79; project scientist phys. electronics div. Perkin Elmer Corp., Eden Prairie, Minn., 1979-83, sr. project scientist phys. electronics div., 1983-85, lab mgr. phys. electronics div., 1985-87, product mgr. phys. electronics div., 1987-88, sr. product mgr. phys. electronics div., 1988-93; v.p. product devel. Chorus Corp., St. Paul, 1993-94; pres. Creekside Techs. Corp., Plymouth, Minn., 1994—; co-founder Xoft, Inc., Plymouth, 1998, chief tech. officer Fremont, Calif., 2001—02, prin. engr., 2002—07, chair, advanced tech., 2007—. Editor: X-rays in Materials Analysis, 1986; co-author: Oscillatory Ion Yields, 1977; patentee in field. Recipient IR100 award for transfer vessel Rsch. and Devel. mag., 1981, IR100 award for energy analyser, 1985. Office: 49000 Milmont Dr Fremont CA 94538 also: 345 P Potrero Ave Sunnyvale CA 94085 Office Phone: 408-419-2300.

RUSCHA, EDWARD, artist; b. Omaha, Dec. 16, 1937; m. Danna Knego, 1967; children: Edward Joseph. Studied at, Chouinard Art Inst., Los Angeles, 1956-60. Numerous vis. artist positions including UCLA, 1969-70; US Rep., Venice Biennale, 2005. Author: Twentysix Gasoline Stations, 1962, Various Small Fires, 1964, Some Los Angeles Apartments, 1965, The Sunset Strip, 1966, Thirtyfour Parking Lots, 1967, Royal Road Test, 1967, Business Cards, 1968, Nine Swimming Pools, 1968, Crackers, 1969, Real Estate Opportunities, 1970, Records, 1971, A Few Palm Trees, 1971, Colored People, 1972, Hard Light, 1978; noted for numerous graphite, gunpowder and pastel drawings, over 200 limited-edit. prints; producer, dir.: films Premium, 1970, Miracle, 1974; began showing works, Ferus Gallery, LA, 1963; first internat. show Galerie Rudolf Zwirner, Cologne, Germany, 1968; works include (paintings) Standard Station, Amarillo, Tex., 1963; Annie, 1963, Smash, 1963, Electric, 1964, (mural) Miami-Dade Pub. Library, Fla., 1985; one-man exhbns. include Minn. Inst. Arts, 1972, Nigel Greenwood Ltd., London, 1970, 73, 80, Leo Castelli Gallery, N.Y.C., (10 shows) 1973—, Albright-Knox Art Gallery, Buffalo, 1976, Stedelijk Mus., Amsterdam, 1976, Ft. Worth Art Mus., 1977, San Francisco Mus. Modern Art, 1982, Whitney Mus. Am. Art, 1982, Vancouver Art Gallery, 1982, Contemporary Arts Mus., Houston, 1983, Los Angeles County Mus. Art, 1983, James Corcoran Gallery, Los Angeles, 1985, Gagosian Galleries, Chelsea, 2002, Beverly Hills, 2003, also others; exhibited in group shows at 64th Whitney Biennial, 1987, Centre Pompidou, Paris, 1989, Mus. Boymans—van Beuningen, Rotterdam, The Netherlands, 1990, Ghislaine Hussenot, Paris, 1990, Fundacio Caixa, Barcelona, Spain, 1990, Serpentine Gallery, London, 1990, Mus. Contemporary Art, L.A., 1990-91, Robert Miller Gallery, N.Y.C., 1992, Thaddaeus Ropac, Salzburg, Austria, 1992; represented in permanent collections including Mus. Modern Art, Los Angeles County Mus. Art, Whitney Mus., Hirshhorn, Washington, Miami-Dade Pub. Libr., Denver Pub. Libr., J. Paul Getty Mus., L.A., also others; restrospective of works on paper J. Paul Getty Mus., L.A., 1998; paintings exhibited, Gagosian Gallery, Beverly Hills, 1999, Metro Plots, N.Y., 1999; retrospective of career Hirshhorn Mus., 2000, Sculpture Garden, Washington, D.C., 2000, Mus. Contemporary Art, Chgo., Miami Art Mus., Modern Art Mus., Ft. Worth, Tex. Trustee Mus. Contemporary Art, LA. Guggenheim fellow; Nat. Endowment Arts grantee. Fellow: Am. Acad. Arts & Sci.; mem.: Am. Acad. Arts and Letters (mem. dept. art). Office: Gagosian Gallery 980 Madison Ave New York NY 10021-1848 also: 35 S Venice Blvd Venice CA 90291

RUSH, DOMENICA MARIE, health facilities administrator; b. Gallup, N.Mex., Apr. 10, 1937; d. Bernardo G. and Guadalupe (Milan) Iorio; m. W. E. Rush, Jan. 5, 1967. Diploma, Regina Sch. Nursing, Albuquerque, 1958. RN N.Mex.; lic. nursing home adminstr.; cert. legal nurse cons., 2004. Charge nurse, house supr. St. Joseph Hosp., Albuquerque, 1958-63; dir. nursing Cibola Hosp., Grants, 1960-64; supr. operating room, dir. med. seminars Carrie Tingley Crippled Children's Hosp., Truth or Consequences, N.Mex., 1964-73; adminstr. Sierra Vista Hosp., Truth or Consequences, 1974-88, pres., 1989—90, adminstr., 1995—2003, CEO, 2008—; clin. nursing mgr. U. N.Mex. Hosp., 1990—94; adminstr. Nor-Lea Hosp., Lovington, N.Mex., 1990-94; with regional ops. divsn. Presbyn. Healthcare Svcs., Albuquerque, 1994—, regional ops., 1994—2003, regional adminstr., 2003—04, intern adminstrn. and spl. projects, 2004—06; founder Rush Health Consulting Svc., 2004—; CEO Trans Health, Inc., Balt., 2006—08. Bd. dirs. N.Mex. Blue Cross/Blue Shield, 1977-88, chmn. hosp. relations com., 1983-85, exec. com. 1983—; bd. dirs. Region II Emergency Med. Svcs. Originating bd. SW Mental Health Ctr., Sierra County, N.Mex., 1975; chmn. Sierra County Personnel Bd., 1983—. Recipient Frank Gabriel award N.Mex. Hosp. Health Sys. Assn., 2003, Govenor's award Emergency Med. Svcs., 2003, Govs.award for Outstanding Woman, N. Mex., 2004; Named Lea County Outstanding Woman, N.Mex. Commn. on Status of Women, Woman of Yr. for Lea County, N.Mex.; 1993. Mem. Am. Coll. Health Care Adminstrs., Sierra County C. of C. (bd. dirs. 1972, 75-76, svc. award 1973, Businesswoman of the Yr. 1973-74), N.Mex. Hosp. Assn. (bd. dirs., sec.-treas., pres.-elect, com. chmn., 1977-88, pres. 1980-81, exec. com., 1980-83, 84-85, recipient meritorius svc. award 1988), N.Mex. So. Hosp. Coun. (sec. 1980-81, pres. 1981-82), Am. Hosp. Assn. (N.Mex. del. 1984-88, regional adv. bd. 1984-88). Republican. Roman Catholic. Avocations: raising thoroughbred horses, cooking. Home: 1100 N Riverside Dr Truth Or Consequences NM 87901-9789 Office Phone: 575-740-2334. Personal E-mail: domrush@gmail.com.

RUSH, GEOFFREY, actor; b. Toowomba, Queensland, Australia, July 6, 1951; m. Jane Menelaus, 1988; children: Angelica, James. diploma, LittD, U. Queensland. Actor: (plays) Wrong Side of the Moon, 1971, Lock Up Your Daughters, 1972, Assault With a Deadly Weapon, 1972, Twelfth Night, 1972, 1983, 1984, Ruling Class, 1972, You're a Good Man Charlie Brown, 1972, Puss in Boots, 1972, Juno and the Paycock, 1973, Expresso Bongo, 1973, National Health, 1973, The Imaginary Invalid, 1973, Suddenly at Home, 1973, Aladdin, 1973, Hamlet on Ice, 1973, Godspell, 1974, The Rivals, 1974, The Philanthropist, 1974, Present Laughter, 1974, Jack and the Beanstalk, 1975—77, King Lear, 1978, 1988, Point of Departure, 1978, Clowneroonies, 1978, Waiting for Godot, 1979, On Our Selection, 1979, Teeth and Smiles, 1980, Revenger's Tragedy, 1981, No End of Blame, 1982, You Can't Take It With You, 1981, A Midsummer Night's Dream, 1982, 1983, Mother Courage, 1982, Silver Lining, 1982, The Prince of Homburg, 1982, Royal Show, 1983, Blood Wedding, 1983, Netherwood, 1983, 1984, The Marriage of Figaro, 1983, Pal Joey, 1983, The Blind Giant is Dancing, 1983, Sunrise, 1983, Benefactors, 1986, On Parliament Hill, 1987, Shepherd on the Rocks, 1987, The Winter's Tale, 1987, Tristram Shandy-Gent, 1988, Les Enfants du Paradis, 1988, The Importance of Being Earnest, 1988, 1990—91, 1992, Troilus & Cressida, 1989, The Diary of a Madman, 1989, 1990, 1992 (Variety Club award for Stage Actor of Yr., 1989, Sydney Theatre Critics Cir. award for Most Outstanding Performance, 1989, Victorian Green Rm. award for Best Actor, 1990), Marat/Sade, 1990, The Comedy of Errors, 1990, The Government Inspector, 1991, Uncle Vanya, 1992, The Dutch Courtesan, 1993, Oleanna, 1993, Hamlet, 1994, 1995; (films) Hoodwink, 1980, Starstruck, 1981, Twelfth Night, 1985, On Our Selection, 1994, Five Easy Pizzas, 1994, Children of the Revolution, 1996, Shine, 1996 (BAFTA award Best Actor, 1997, Golden Globe award for Best Performance in Motion Picture, 1997, Screen Actors Guild award for Outstanding Performance, 1997, Oscar award for Best Actor, 1997), Oscar & Lucinda, 1997, Shakespeare in Love, 1998 (BAFTA award Best Supporting Actor, 1999), Elizabeth, 1998, Mystery Men, 1999, House on Haunted Hill, 1999, Quills, 2000 (NY Film Critics Online award for best actor, 2000), The Tailor of Panama, 2001, Lantana, 2001, Frida, 2002, The Banger Sisters, 2002, Swimming Upstream, 2003, Ned Kelly, 2003, Finding Nemo (voice), 2003, Pirates of the Caribbean: The Curse of the Black Pearl, 2003, Intolerable Cruelty, 2003, The Life and Death of Peter Sellers, 2004 (Golden Globe award for best actor miniseries or TV movie, 2005, Screen Actors Guild Award for best actor in a TV movie or miniseries, 2005, Emmy award for outstanding lead actor in a miniseries or a movie, 2005), Munich, 2005, Candy, 2006, Pirates of the Caribbean: Dead Man's Chest, 2006, Pirates of the Caribbean: At World's End, 2007, Elizabeth: The Golden Age, 2007; (TV series) Consumer Capers, 1979—81, Menotti, 1980—81, The Burning Piano, 1992, Mercury, 1996; dir.: (plays) Clowneroonies, 1978—80, Animal Acts, 1984—86, Teen Ages, 1984—86, Carols-By-Lazerlight, 1984—86, The 1985 Scandals, 1986, Pearls Before Swine, 1986, Pell Mell, 1986, 1987, 1988, The Merry Wives of Windsor, 1987, The Popular Mechanicals, 1987, 1988, 1992, Les Enfants du Paradis, 1989, The Wolf's Banquet, 1989, Popular Mechanicals 2, 1992, Aristophane's Frogs, 1992; co-translator The Government Inspector, 1991, writer (with George Whaley) (TV film) Clowning Around, 1992, (with John Clarke) (play) Aristophane's Frogs, 1992, Call Me Sal, 1996, Children of the Revolution, 1997, Les Misérables, 1998. Office: c/o Creative Artists Agy 9830 Wilshire Blvd Beverly Hills CA 90212-1804

RUSH, HERMAN E., television executive; b. Phila., June 20, 1929; s. Eugene and Bella (Sacks) R.; m. Joan Silberman, Mar. 18, 1951; children: James Harrison, Mandie Susan. BBA, Temple U., 1950. With Ofcl. Films, 1951-57; owner Flamingo Films, 1957-60; with Creative Mgmt. Assocs., NYC, 1960-71, pres. TV divsn., 1964-71, exec. v.p. parent co., dir., 1964-71; ind. prodr., 1971-75; prodr. Wolper Orgn., 1975-76; pres. Herman Rush Assocs., Inc. (Rush-Flaherty Agy. subs.), 1977-78; CEO Marble Arch TV, LA, 1979—80; pres. Columbia Pictures TV, Burbank, Calif., 1980-87; chmn., CEO Coca-Cola Telecom., 1987-88, Rush Assocs., Inc., Burbank, 1988—, Katz/Rush Entertainment Group, Beverly Hills, Calif., 1990-96, New Tech. Entertainment, LLC, Beverly Hills, 1996—, Internet Content Provider Cap. Fin. Corp., chmn. emeritus; mng. ptnr. Media Consulting Assocs. CEO Infotainment Internat., Inc.; pres., chmn. Royal Animated Art, Inc.; Entertainment Industries Coun.; co-owner, exec. prodr. The Montel Williams Talk Show, 1991-; mem. bd. advisors Smart Video Techs., Inc.; CEO Creative Content Providers, LLC Trustee Sugar Ray Robinson Youth Found., 1967-75; pres. Retarded Infant Svcs., N.Y.C., 1957-63; bd. dirs. U.S. Marshall's Svc. Found., Just Say No Found.; conferee White House Conf. for a Drug Free America, 1987, 88. Mem. Acad. TV Arts and Scis., Hollywood Radio and TV Soc., Producers Caucus. Clubs: Friars, Filmex. Office: 8871 Burton Way 305 Los Angeles CA 90048 Office Phone: 310-553-6145. Personal E-mail: hermanrush@aol.com.

RUSH, RICHARD R., academic administrator; Pres. Calif. State U. Channel Islands, Camarillo. Office: Calif State U Channel Islands 1 University Dr Camarillo CA 93012 Business E-Mail: richard.rush@csuci.edu.

RUSHER, WILLIAM ALLEN, writer, commentator, columnist; b. Chgo., July 19, 1923; s. Evan Singleton and Verna (Self) R. AB, Princeton U., 1943; JD, Harvard U., 1948; DLit (hon.), Nathaniel Hawthorne Coll., 1973. Bar: N.Y. 1949. Assoc. Shearman & Sterling & Wright, NYC, 1948-56; spl. counsel fin. com. N.Y. Senate, 1955; assoc. counsel internal security subcom. U.S. Senate, 1956-57; pub., v.p. Nat. Review mag., NYC, 1957-88, also bd. dirs.; Disting. fellow The Claremont Inst., 1989—. Mem. Adv. Task Force on Civil Disorders, 1972. Author: Special Counsel, 1968, (with Mark Hatfield and Arlie Schardt) Amnesty?, 1973, The Making of the New Majority Party, 1975, How to Win Arguments, 1981, The Rise of the Right, 1984, The Coming Battle for the Media, 1988; editor: The Ambiguous Legacy of the Enlightenment, 1995; columnist Universal Press Syndicate, 1973-82, Newspaper Enterprise Assn., 1982—; played role of Advocate in TV program The Advocates, 1970-74. Chmn.,bd. mem., bd. dirs. Media Rsch. Ctr., Washington, 2001-2008, Nat. Rev. Bd., 1957-88, 90-2008; bd. advisors Ashbrook Ctr., Ashland, Ohio, past chmn.; past vice chmn. Am. Conservative Union; past trustee Pacific Legal Found., Sacramento. Served as 2d lt. to capt., USAAF, 1943-45, India-Burma Theater. Recipient Disting. Citizen award NYU Sch. Law, 1973. Mem. ABA, Univ. Club (NYC), Met. Club (Washington). Anglican. Home and Office: 1661 Pine St Apt 933 San Francisco CA 94109

RUSKELL, TIM, professional sports team executive; m. Linda Ruskell; children: Samantha, Jack. B in Comm., U. South Fla., Tampa. Scout Saskatchewan Roughriders, Can. Football League, 1983—85; dir. scouting Tampa Bay Bandits, US Football League, 1985—86; regional scout Tampa Bay Buccaneers, 1987—92, dir. coll. scouting, 1992—2000, dir. player pers., 2001—03; asst. gen. mgr. Atlanta Falcons, 2004; pres. football ops., gen. mgr. Seattle Seahawks, 2005—. Office: Seattle Seahawks 12 Seahawks Way Renton WA 98056*

RUSKIN, IRA, state legislator; b. NYC, Nov. 12, 1943; m Cheryl. BA in History, U. Calif., Berkeley, 1968; MA in Comm., Stanford U., 1983. California State Assemblyman, District 21, 2005-; chairman, Association Environ Safety & Toxic Materials; member, Bank & Finance, Higher Education, Public Safety comts, currently; Redwood City CA, Mayor, 1999-2001. Ruskins Coomunications, 1993-. Democrat. Jewish. Office: Dist 21 5050 El Camino Real Ste 117 Los Altos CA 94022 Office Phone: 916-319-2021, 650-691-2121. Office Fax: 650-691-2120. Business E-Mail: Assemblymember.Ruskin@assembly.ca.gov.

RUSSELL, ANNE M., editor-in-chief; BA in Brit. Lit. magna cum laude, Yale U. Editor book divsn. Billboard Publ.; editor Photo Dist. News; reporter Adweek; assoc. editor Am. Photographer; sr. editor Working Women; exec. editor Folio: Pub. News, editor-in-chief, 1992—97, Living Fit, 1997—99, Vegetarian Times, 1999; editl. dir. Fox TV's Health Network; editl. dir. Shape mag. Am. Media Inc., 2001—03, editor-in-chief, 2003—06, Viv Mag. online, 2006—. Office: VIV Pub LLC El Cajon CA 92019 Office Phone: 858-832-1874.

RUSSELL, BARRY, federal judge; b. 1940; BS, UCLA, 1962, JD, 1966. Estate and gift tax examiner U.S. Treasury Dept., 1966-67; dep. pub. defender L.A. County, 1967-70; asst. U.S. atty. LA, 1970-74; apptd. bankruptcy judge ctrl. dist. U.S. Dist. Ct. Calif., 1974; apptd. to Ninth Cir. Bankruptcy Appellate Panel, 1988—2002, presiding judge, 1999—2002, chief judge, 2003—. Author: Bankruptcy Evidence Manual, 1987—. Recipient So. Calif. Mediation Assn. Judges award, 1997. Fellow Am. Coll. Bankruptcy; mem. ABA (Franklin N. Flaschner Jud. award as outstanding judge 1987), FBA (nat. pres. 1990-91), Nat. Conf. Bankruptcy Judges, L.A. County Bar Assn. (Dispute Resolution Svcs. Emil Gumpert Jud. ADR award, Outstanding Jurist award 2004), Phi Alpha Delta. Office: Roybal Fed Bldg 255 E Temple St Los Angeles CA 90012-3334 Office Phone: 213-894-6091.

RUSSELL, DAVID E., judge; b. Chgo. Heights, Mar. 19, 1935; s. Robert W. and Nellie Russell; m. Denise A. Hurst, Apr. 1, 1968 (div. 1978); children: Dirk, Kent, Laura, Rachel; m. Sandra M. Niemeyer, Oct. 31, 1982. BS in Acctg., U. Calif., Berkeley, 1957, LLB, 1960. Bar: Calif. 1961, U.S. Dist. Ct. (no. dist.) Calif. 1961, U.S. Tax Ct. 1967; CPA, Calif. Staff acct. Lybrand, Ross Bros. & Montgomery, San Francisco, 1960-64; assoc. Robert C. Burnstein, Esquire, Oakland, Calif., 1964-65; ptnr. Russell & Humphreys, Sacramento, 1965, Russell, Humphreys & Estabrook, Sacramento, 1966-70, prin., 1971-

73; shareholder Russell, Jarvis, Estabrook & Dashiell, Sacramento, 1974-86; bankruptcy judge U.S. Bankruptcy Ct. for Ea. Dist. Calif., Sacramento, 1986—. Office: US Bankruptcy Ct 501 I St Sacramento CA 95814-7300

RUSSELL, FINDLAY EWING, physician; b. San Francisco, Sept. 1, 1919; s. William and Mary Jane (Findlay) R.; m. Janet Louise Thiel, Feb. 14, 1950; children: Christa Ann, Sharon Jane, Robin Emily, Constance Susan, Mark Findlay. BA, Walla Walla Coll., Wash., 1941; MD, Loma Linda U., Calif., 1950; postgrad. (fellow), Calif. Inst. Tech., 1951-53; postgrad., U. Cambridge, Eng., 1962—63; PhD, U. Santa Barbara, Calif., 1974, LLD (hon.), 1989. Intern White Meml. Hosp., Los Angeles, 1950-51; practice medicine specializing in toxinology and toxicology Los Angeles, 1953—; mem. staff Los Angeles County-U. So. Calif. Med. Center, Loma Linda U. Med. Center, U. Ariz. Med. Ctr.; physiologist Huntington Inst. Med. Research, 1953-55; dir. lab. neurol. research Los Angeles County-U. So. Calif. Med. Center, 1955-80; mem. faculty Loma Linda U. Med. Sch., 1955—2007; prof. neurology, physiology and biology U. So. Calif. Med. Sch., 1966-81; prof. pharmacology and toxicology U. Ariz. Health Scis. Coll. Pharmacy, 1981—. Cons. USPHS, NSF, Office Naval Rsch., WHO, U.S. Army, Walter Reed, USAF, Brooks AFB. Author: Marine Toxins and Venomous and Poisonous Marine Animals, 1965, Poisonous Marine Animals, 1971, Snake Venom Poisoning, 1980; co-author: Bibliography of Snake Venoms and Venomous Snakes, 1964, Animal Toxins, 1967, Poisonous Snakes of The World, 1968, Snake Venom Poisoning, 1983, Bibliography of Venomous and Poisonous Marine Animals and Their Toxins, 1984, Venomous and Poisonous Marine Invertebrates of the Indian Ocean, 1996; editor: Toxicon, 1962-70. Served with AUS, 1942-46. Decorated Purple Heart, Bronze Star; recipient award Los Angeles County Bd. Suprs., 1960; award Acad. Medicine Buenos Aires, 1966; Skylab Achievement award, 1974; Jozef Stefan medal Yugoslavia, 1978; U.S. State Dept. medallion, 2006, Disting. Citizen award, 1992. Fellow A.C.P., Am. Coll. Cardiology, Royal Soc. Tropical Medicine, N.Y. Acad. Scis.; mem. Internat. Soc. Toxinology (pres. 1962-66, Francisco Redi medal 1967), Royal Soc. Medicine, Am. Soc. Physiology, Western Soc. Pharmacology (pres. 1973) Office: U Ariz Health Scis Coll Pharmacy Pharm/Tox Tucson AZ 85721 Office Phone: 520-626-4047.

RUSSELL, FRANCIA, retired ballet director, educator; b. LA, Jan. 10, 1938; d. W. Frank and Marion (Whitney) R.; m. Kent Stowell, Nov. 19, 1965; children: Christopher, Darren, Ethan. Studies with, George Balanchine, Vera Volkova, Felia Doubrouska, Antonina Tumkovsky, Benjamin Harkarvy; student, NYU, Columbia U.; degree (hon.), Seattle U., 2003. Dancer, soloist NYC Ballet, 1956-62, ballet mistress, 1965-70; dancer Ballets USA/Jerome Robbins, NYC, 1962; tchr. ballet Sch. Am. Ballet, NYC, 1963-64; co-dir. Frankfurt (Fed. Republic Germany) Opera Ballet, 1976-77; dir., co-artistic dir. Pacific N.W. Ballet, Seattle, 1977—2005; dir. Pacific N.W. Ballet Sch., Seattle, 1977—2005; ret., 2005. Affiliate prof. of dance U. Wash. Dir. staging over 100 George Balanchine ballet prodns. throughout world, including Russia and China, 1964—. Named Woman of Achievement, Matrix Table, Women in Comm., Seattle, 1987, Gov.'s Arts award, 1989, Dance Mag. award, 1996, Brava award Women's U. Club, 2003, ArtsFund Lifetime Achievement in the Arts award, 2004, Ernst & Young Entrepreneur of Yr. award, 2004, Seattle Mayor's Arts award for Lifetime Achievement, 2004. Mem. Internat. Women's Forum. Home: 2833 Broadway E Seattle WA 98102-3935 Office: Pacific NW Ballet 301 Mercer St Seattle WA 98109-4600

RUSSELL, JAMARCUS, professional football player; b. Mobile, Ala., Aug. 9, 1985; s. Bobby Lloyd and Zina Russell-Anderson. Attended, La. St. U., 2003—07. Quarterback Oakland Raiders, 2007—. Recipient Manning award, 2006; named Sugar Bowl MVP, 2007; named to First Team All-Southeastern Conference, 2006. Achievements include being the first overall selection in the NFL Draft, 2007. Office: Oakland Raiders 1220 Harbor Bay Pkwy Alameda CA 94502

RUSSELL, JEFFREY BURTON, historian, educator; b. Fresno, Calif., Aug. 1, 1934; s. Lewis Henry and Ieda Velma (Ogborn) R.; m. Diana Emily Mansfield, June 30, 1956; children: Jennifer, Mark, William, Penelope. AB, U. Calif., Berkeley, 1955, A.M., 1957; PhD, Emory U., 1960. Asst. prof. U. N.Mex., Albuquerque, 1960-61; jr. fellow Soc. of Fellows, Harvard U., Cambridge, Mass., 1961-62; mem. faculty U. Calif., Riverside, 1962-75, prof. dept. history, 1969-75, assoc. dean grad. div., 1967-72; dir. Medieval Inst.; Michael P. Grace prof. medieval studies U. Notre Dame, South Bend, Ind., 1975-77; dean grad. studies Calif. State U., Sacramento, 1977-79; prof. history U. Calif., Santa Barbara, 1979—, prof. religious studies, 1994—. Author: Dissent and Reform in the Early Middle Ages, 1965, Medieval Civilization, 1968, A History of Medieval Christianity: Prophecy and Order, 1968, Religious Dissent in the Middle Ages, 1971, Witchcraft in the Middle Ages, 1972, The Devil: Perceptions of Evil from Antiquity to Primitive Christianity, 1977, A History of Witchcraft: Sorcerers, Heretics, and Pagans, 1980, Medieval Heresies: a Bibliography, 1981, Satan: The Early Christian Tradition, 1981, Lucifer: The Devil in the Middle Ages, 1984, Mephistopheles: The Devil in the Modern World, 1986, The Prince of Darkness, 1988, Ruga in Aevis, 1990, Inventing the Flat Earth: Columbus and the Historians, 1991, Dissent and Order in the Middle Ages, 1992, A History of Heaven: The Singing Silence, 1997, Essays in Honor of Jeffrey B. Russell, 1998, Paradise Mislaid: How We Lost Heaven and How We Can Regain It, 2006, A New History of Witchcraft, 2007; contbr. articles to profl. jours. Fulbright fellow, 1959-60; Am. Council Learned Socs. grantee, 1965, 70; Social Sci. Research Council grantee, 1968; Guggenheim fellow, 1968-69; Nat. Endowment for Humanities sr. fellow, 1972-73 Fellow Medieval Acad. Am.; mem. Am. Soc. Ch. Histor Am. Acad. Religion, Astron. Soc. Pacific. Home: 4798 Calle Camarada Santa Barbara CA 93110-2053 Office: U Calif Dept History Santa Barbara CA 93106 Business E-Mail: russell@history.ucsb.edu.

RUSSELL, KURT, actor; b. Springfield, Mass., Mar. 17, 1951; s. Bing Oliver and Louise Julia (Crone) R.; m. Season Hubley, Mar. 17, 1979 (div. 1984), 1 child, Boston; 1 child (with Goldie Hawn), Wyatt Russell. Student, pub. schs. Profl. baseball player Calif. Angels-AA, 1971-73; co-head (with Goldie Hawn, Kate Hudson, Oliver Hudson) Cosmic Entertainment, 2003—. Actor: (films) The Absent Minded Professor, 1961, It Happened at the World's Fair, 1963, Guns of Diablo, 1964, Follow Me Boys!, 1966, Mosby's Marauders, 1967, The One and Only Genuine Original Family Band, 1968, The Horse in the Grey Flannel Suit, 1968, Guns in the Heather, 1969, The Computer Wore Tennis Shoes, 1970, The Barefoot Executive, 1971, Fools' Parade, 1971, Now You See Him Now You Don't, 1972, Charley and the Angel, 1972, Superdad, 1974, The Strongest Man in the World, 1975, Used Cars, 1980, (voice only) The Fox and the Hound, 1981, Escape from New York, 1981, The Thing, 1982, Silkwood, 1983, Swing Shift, 1984, The Mean Season, 1985, The Best of Times, 1986, Big Trouble in Little China, 1986, Overboard, 1987, Tequila Sunrise, 1988, Winter People, 1989, Tango and Cash, 1989, Backdraft, 1991, Unlawful Entry, 1992, Captain Ron, 1992, Tombstone, 1993, (voice only) Forrest Gump, 1994, Stargate, 1994, Executive Decision, 1996, Breakdown, 1997, Soldier, 1998, 3000 Miles To Graceland, 2001, Vanilla Sky, 2001, Interstate 60, 2002, Dark Blue, 2002, Miracle, 2004, Sky High, 2005, Dreamer: Inspired by a True Story, 2005, Poseidon, 2006, Grindhouse (Death Proof segment), 2007; actor, prodr., writer (films) Escape from L.A., 1996; actor (TV series) Travels with Jamie McPheeters, 1963-64, The New Land, 1974, The Quest, 1976; (TV movies) Dad, Can I Borrow the Car?, 1970, Search for the Gods, 1975, The Deadly Tower, The Quest, 1975, Christmas Miracle in Caulfield U.S.A., 1977, Elvis, 1979, Amber Waves, 1980; (TV appearences) Sam Benedict, 1963, The Eleventh Hour, 1963, Our Man Higgins, 1963, The Man from U.N.C.L.E., 1964, Gilligan's Island, 1965, The Virginian, 1964-65, The Legend of Jesse James, 1966, Laredo, 1966, Lost in Space, 1966, The F.B.I., 1966, The Fugitive, 1964-66, Daniel Boone, 1965-69, Then Came Bronson, 1969, Love, American Style, 1970, The High Cahaparral, 1970, Storefront Lawyers, 1970, The Road West, 1967, Room 222, 1971, Disneyland, 1967-72, Love Story, 1973, Gunsmoke, 1964, 1974, Hec Ramsey, 1974, The New Land, 1974, Harry O, 1975, Police Story, 1974-75, Hawaii Five-O, 1977; exec. prodr. (TV films) 14 Hours, 2005 Served with Calif. Air N.G. Recipient The Disney Legends award, 1998 Mem. Profl. Baseball Players Assn., Stuntman's Assn. Achievements include being the World championship Class Modified Stock, 1959 Race of Champions, Las Vegas.

RUSSELL, PAUL EDGAR, electrical engineering educator; b. Roswell, N.Mex., Oct. 10, 1924; s. Rueben Matthias and Mary (Parsons) R.; m. Lorna Margaret Clayshulte, Aug. 29, 1943; children: Carol Potter, Janice Russell Cook, Gregory. BSEE, N.Mex. State U., 1946, BSME, 1947; MSEE, U. Wis., 1950, PhDEE, 1951. Registered elec. engr., Ariz. From instr. to asst. prof. elec. engring. U. Wis., Madison, 1947-52; sr. engr., design specialist Gen. Dynamics Corp., San Diego, 1952-54; from prof. to chmn. elec. engring. dept. U. Ariz., Tucson, 1954-63; dean engring. Kans. State U., Manhattan, 1963-67; prof. Ariz. State U., Tempe, 1967-90; dir. engring. Ariz. State U. West, Phoenix, 1985-88; dir. Sch. Constrn. and Tech. Ariz. State U., Tempe, 1988-90. Cons. in field, 1954—; programs evaluator, mem. engring. commn. Accreditation Bd. for Engring. and Tech., N.Y.C., 1968-81. Contbr. articles to jours. and chpts. to books. Served as sgt. U.S. Army, 1944-46. Recipient Disting. Service award N.Mex. State U., 1965. Fellow IEEE (life, chmn. Ariz. sect. 1960), Accreditation Bd. Engring. and Tech.; mem. Am. Soc. Engring. Educators. Home: 5902 E Caballo Ln Paradise Valley AZ 85253 Office Phone: 480-948-0716.

RUSSELL, RICHARD DONCASTER, geophysics educator, academic administrator; b. Toronto, Ont., Can., Feb. 27, 1929; s. Richard Douglas and Ada Gwennola (Doncaster) R.; m. Virginia Ann Reid Clippingdale, Aug. 11, 1951; children: Linda Jean, Morna Ann, Mary Joyce. BA, U. Toronto, 1951, MA, 1952, PhD, 1954. Asst. prof. physics U. Toronto, 1956-58, prof., 1962-63; assoc. prof. physics U. B.C., Vancouver, Canada, 1958-62, prof. geophysics, 1963-91, prof. emeritus, 1991—, head dept. geophysics, 1968-72, head dept. geophysics and astronomy, 1972-79, bd. govs., 1978-81, assoc. dean sci., 1980-83, assoc. v.p. acad., 1983-86. Sec.-gen. Inter-Union Commn. on Geodynamics, 1976—80; profl. geoscientist. Author (with John Arthur Jacobs and J. Tuzo Wilson): Physics and Geology International Series in the Earth Sciences, first edit., 1959, Physics and Geology McGraw-Hill International Series in the Earth and Planetary Science, 2d edit., 1973; author: (with Ronald McCunn Farquhar) Lead Isotopes in Geology Interscience, 1960. Fellow Royal Soc. Can.; mem. Am. Geophys. Union, Can. Geophys. Union (J. Tuzo Wilson medal 1992). Home: 226-4955 River Rd Delta BC Canada V4K 4V9

RUSSELL, SABIN, newswriter; m. Ashley Wolff; 2 children. Grad., Yale U., 1974. Writer Venture Mag., Electronic News, various cmty. newspapers Vermont and NH; med. writer San Francisco Chronicle, 1988—. Recipient Sci. in Soc. Journalism award, Nat. Assn. Sci. Writers, Inc., 2001; grantee Kaiser mini-fellowship, Kaiser Family Found., 2004. Primary responsibilities include coverage of science and health policy, focusing on topics such as HIV/AIDS, bioterrorism, SARS, West Nile virus, mad cow, and other infectious diseases. Office: San Francisco Chronicle 901 Mission St San Francisco CA 94103-2988 Office Phone: 415-777-8447. Office Fax: 415-896-1107. Business E-Mail: srussell@sfchronicle.com.

RUSSIANO, JOHN See MILES, JACK

RUSSONIELLO, JOSEPH PASCAL, prosecutor, lawyer; b. Jersey City, Oct. 12, 1941; s. Sabin G. and Justine B. (Terraciano) Russoniello; m. Moira F. Ward, Aug. 29, 1969. B in Social Sci., Fairfield U., 1963; JD, NYU, 1966. Bar: N.J. 1967, Calif. 1969. Spl. agt. FBI, Washington, 1966—67; dep. dist. atty. City and County San Francisco Dist. Atty. Offices, 1969—75; assoc. Cooley Godward Castro Huddleson & Tatum, San Francisco, 1975—78; ptnr. Cooley Godward L.L.P., San Francisco, 1978—82, 1990—2001; sr. counsel Cooley Godward Kronish L.L.P., San Francisco, 2002—08; US atty. US Dept. Justice (no. dist.) Calif., San Francisco, 1982—90, 2008—. Pres., bd. dirs. San Francisco Law Sch., 1996—2001, dean, 2002—07; analyst Sta. KTVU-Ch. 2, Oakland, 1994—2007. Pres. Northgate Cottages, Napa, Calif., 1988—; chmn. Silverado Property Owners Assn., 2004—07; v.p. Mid-Pacific region Nat. Italian Am. Fedn., 1996—99; mem. nat. rev. bd. U.S. Conf. Cath. Bishops, 2004—07; chmn. Caths. Truth and Justice, San Francisco, 1991—. Recipient Man of the Yr. award, NIAF, 1986, St. Thomas More Soc., San Francisco, 2000, Italian Am. Cmty. Svc. Agy., San Francisco, 2004, Assumpta award, Trustees St. Mary's Cathedral, 2000, Papal Pro Ecclesia medal, 2000, Landsman award, 2005; named Alumni of the Yr., Pub. Sector, NYU Law Sch., 1991. Fellow: Am. Coll. Trial Lawyers; mem.: Am. Law Inst., Am. Bd. Trial Lawyers (adv.), McFetridge Inn of Ct. (barrister). Republican. Avocations: tennis, golf, reading, saxophone. Office: US Atty Office 450 Golden Gate Ave Box 36055 San Francisco CA 94102

RUSTAND, KAY, lawyer; Ptnr. Lawler, Felix & Hall, Arter & Hadden LLP, 1989—2001; v.p., gen counsel Reliance Steel & Aluminum Co., LA, 2001—. Office: Reliance Steel & Aluminum Co 350 S Grand Ave Ste 5100 Los Angeles CA 90071 Office Phone: 213-687-8792.

RUSZKIEWICZ, CAROLYN MAE, newspaper editor; b. Tucson, Nov. 10, 1946; d. Robert Frank and Charlotte Ruth (Hadley) Knapton; m. Joseph Charles Ruszkiewicz, July 11, 1969. BA, Calif. State U., Long Beach, 1971, MA, 1973. Reporter Long Beach (Calif.) Press-Telegram, 1968-85, consumer editor, 1985-86, lifestyle editor, 1986-89, regional news editor, 1989-91, city editor, 1991-95, asst. mng. editor, 1995-97, mng. editor, 1997—. Avocations: swimming, walking, reading. Office: Long Beach Press Telegram 604 Pine Ave Long Beach CA 90844-0003

RUTAN, BURT (ELBERT LEANDER RUTAN), aircraft designer, aircraft company executive; b. Portland, Oreg., June 17, 1943; s. George and Irene R. BS in Aero. Engring., Calif. State Polytech. U., 1965; attended, Space Tech. Inst., Calif. Inst. Tech.; attended academic portion of Aerospace Rsch. Pilots Sch., Edwards Air Force Base. Flight test project engr. Air Force Flight Test Ctr., Edwards AFB, Calif., 1965-72; dir. Bede Test Ctr., Kans., 1972-74; pres. Rutan Aircraft Factory, Mojave, Calif., 1974—; founder, CEO Scaled Composites Inc., Mojave, Calif., 1982—; v.p. Beech Aircraft, 1985. Designer more than 100 aircraft including BD-5J jet (world's smallest private jet aircraft), VariViggen, VariEze (a stall-proof kit airplane with a propeller at the back and winglets on the nose), Solitaire, Defiant, Raytheon Beechcraft Starship, Proteus (high altitude long endurance aircraft being used for everything from cellular communications to suborbital space launches), Boomerang, Virgin Atlantic GlobalFlyer (set a world record for the first solo, non-stop, non-refueled circumnavigation of the world, piloted by Steven Fossett, 2005), White Knight (an airborne launch aircraft) and other kits; designer Voyager aircraft (a superlight plane that could carry 10 times its weight in fuel, first to fly around-the-world without stopping, refueling in 1986); company made history with first private manned mission to space in SpaceShipOne (a two-passenger, high altitude research rocket); SpaceShipOne achieved two record flights (broke 62.5-mile barrier) and won the Ansari X prize on October 4, 2004; SpaceShipOne donated to Smithsonian Inst. on October 6, 2005; pilot for EZ-Rocket (XCOR), which made a record-setting point-to-point flight, departing from Mojave California Spaceport and gliding onto a neighboring airport in California City in 2005. Recip. Spirit of St. Louis medal, Am. Soc. Mech. Engrs., 1987, Best Design award, Exptl. Aircraft Assn.; Air medal, 1970, Stan Szik design contbn. trophy, 1972, EAA Outstanding New Design, 1975-76, 78; Dr. August Raspet Meml. award, 1976, ABC World News Tonight Person of the Week, 1986, Collier trophy for ingenious design and devel., Nat. Aeronautic Assn., 1986, Presdl. Citizens medal for design/develop. of the voyager "around-the-world" aircraft, 1986, FAI gold medal for Voyager Constrn., 1987, medal for the City of Paris, 1987, NASA langley Rsch. Ctr. dirs. award, 1987, Soc. of NASA Flight Surgeons, W. Randolph Lovelace award 1987, medal of Outstanding Achievement and disting. leadership, 1987, Soc. of exptl. test pilots, 1987, Aviation Man of the Yr, 1987, Lindbergh Eagle award, 1987, USAF 40th anniversary award, 1987, The City of Genoa, Italy, Christopher Columbus Internat. Communications medal, 1987, British gold medal, 1987, Outstanding Engring. achievement awards, 1988, Franklin medal, 1987, Disting. inventor award 1988, Meritorious Svc. award, 1988, Internat. Aerospace Hall of Fame Honoree, 1988, medal of achievement, 1989, Crystal Eagle award, 1989, Meritorious Civilian Svc. medal, 1989, Leroy Randle Grumman medal, 1989, Structures, Structural Dynamics and Materials award AIAA, 1991, Bus. Leader in Aerospace, Scientific Am., 2003, Ansari X prize, 2004, NAS Award in Aero. Engring., 2005, Breakthrough Leadership award, Popular Mechanics Breakthrough Awards, 2006; co-recipient with Paul Allen, Smithsonian's Nat. Air and Space Mus. Trophy, 2005; named Innovator of Yr., R&D Mag., 2004; named one of 100 Most Influential People of 2005, Time mag., Rave award in indsl. design, WIRED, 2005. Mem. NAE, Exptl. Aircraft Assn., Soc. Exptl. Test Pilots, Am. Inst. Aeronautics & Astronautics (recipient Reed Aeronautics award, 2001), Soc. Flight Test Engrs., Acad. Model Aeronautics, Internat. Order Characters, Aircraft Owners and Pilots Assn.; Fellow Am. Acad. Arts & Sciences Holds 3 US patents: Grizzly wide-chord flap suspension system; variable geometry high lift system incorporated in the Beech Starship (foreign patents also held); Rutan Model 115 Starship configuration (foreign patents also held). Office: Scaled Composites Inc Mojave Airport 1624 Flight Line Mojave CA 93501-1663 Office Phone: 661-824-4541. Office Fax: 661-824-4174.

RUTES, WALTER ALAN, architect; b. NYC, Sept. 21, 1928; s. Jack and Sarah (Ogur) R.; m. Helene Darville, Apr. 2, 1952; children: Daniel J., Linda Lee. B.Arch. (Sands Meml. medal 1950), Cornell U., 1950; fellow city planning, MIT, 1951; postgrad., Harvard U. Grad. Sch. Design, 1978. Cert. Nat. Council Archtl. Registration Bds. Assoc. ptnr. Skidmore, Owings & Merrill, NYC, 1951-72; v.p. John Carl Warnecke & Assocs., NYC, 1972-74; staff v.p. Intercontinental Hotels Corp., NYC, 1974-80; dir. architecture Holiday Inns, Inc., Memphis, 1980-83; dir. design The Sheraton Corp., Boston, 1983-85; chmn 9 Tek Ltd. Devel. Cons., 1985—. Chmn. adv. bd. Hult Fellowships for Constrn. Industry, 1968-75, Architects and Engrs. Com. New Bldg. Code, 1968; mem. zoning adv. com. N.Y.C. Planning Commn., 1970; lectr. in field, 1968—; mem. steering com. UNESCO Council Tall Bldgs. and Urban Habitat, 1980; vis. prof. Cornell-Essec Grad. Program; vis. prof. Nova U. Author: Hotel Planning and Design, 1985, Hotel Design, Planning and Development, 2001; (software) SHAPE, Megatrends and Marketecture; contbr. articles to profl. jours.; prin. works include Lincoln Center Library for Performing Arts, N.Y.C., 1967, Am. Republic Ins. Co. Nat. Hdqrs., Des Moines, 1967, HUD Apts., Jersey City, 1972, Merrill Lynch Bldg., N.Y.C., 1973, Tour Fiat, Paris, 1974, Aid Assn. for Luths. Nat. Hdqrs., Appleton, Wis., 1976, Semiramis Intercontinental Hotel, Cairo, 1985, Intercontinental, Jeddah, 1983, Embassy Suites Internat., 1985, Universal City Hotel Complex, L.A., 1986, TechWorld Conv. Hotel, Washington, 1986, Sheraton Fairplex Conv. Ctr., L.A., 1992, Orlando Conv. Ctr. Hotel, 1993, Winter Olympiad Media Complex, Norway, 1993, Ephesus Resort Complex, Turkey, 1986, Royal Christiania Hotel, Oslo, Norway, 1991, EuroFrance Leisure Park Complex, Cannes, 1993, Kuna Hills Multi Resort, Guam, 1994. Recipient Platinum Circle award Hotel Design Industry, 1988. Fellow AIA; mem. Ethical Culture Soc. Office: 8501 N 84th Pl Scottsdale AZ 85258-2419 also: 25 Richbell Rd White Plains NY 10605-4110

RUTHBERG, MILES N., lawyer; BA summa cum laude, Yale Univ., 1973; JD magna cum laude, Harvard Univ., 1976. Bar: DC 1979, Calif. 1979, NY 2006. Law clk. Judge Carl McGowan, US Ct. of Appeals, DC Cir., 1976—77, Justice Thurgood Marshall, US Supreme Ct., 1977—78; securities litigation and profl. liability practice group Latham & Watkins, 1998—99, nat. chair, 1999—2004, global dept. chair, litigation dept., 1999—2004, exec. com. mem., 2004—08. Bd. governors Assn. Bus. Trial Lawyers, 1994—98. Developments editor

Harvard Law Rev., 1976; author: numerous articles in profl. publications. Mem.: ABA, NY State Bar Assn., DC Bar Assn., Calif. State Bar Assn. Office: Latham Watkins 355 S Grand Ave Los Angeles CA 90071-1560

RUTHERFORD, GEORGE WILLIAMS, III, preventive medicine physician; b. San Diego, Apr. 6, 1952; s. G. Williams and Anna Gwyn (Dearing) R.; m. Lisa Anderson, Aug. 24, 1974 (div. 1984); children: Alicia Gwyn, George Williams IV; m. Mary Workman, Feb. 23, 1985; children: Alexandra Catherine, Anne Elizabeth Martha, Hugh Thomas Gwyn, Amanda Frances Julia. AB in Classics, Stanford U., 1974, BS in Chemistry, 1975, AM in History, 1975; MD, Duke U., 1978. Diplomate Am. Bd. Pediat., Am. Bd. Preventive Medicine, Nat. Bd. Med. Examiners. Intern in pediat. U. Calif. Med. Ctr., San Diego, 1978-79; resident in pediat. U. Calif. Med. Ctr., Hosp. for Children, San Diego, 1979-80; resident Hosp. for Sick Children, Toronto, 1980-81; chief resident Children's Hosp. and Health Ctr., San Diego, 1981-82; EIS officer divsn. viral diseases, divsn. field svcs Epidemology Office Ctrs. for Disease Control, Atlanta, 1982-84; dir. divsn. immunization, acting dir. divsn. tropical disease NYC Dept. Health, 1983-85; med. epidemologist AIDS program Ctrs. for Disease Control, San Francisco Dept. Pub. Health, 1985-87; from med. dir. to dir. AIDS office San Francisco Dept. Pub. Health, 1986-90; chief, infectious disease br. and state epidemiologist Calif. Dept Health, Berkeley, 1990-92, dep. dir. prevention svcs. and state epidemologist, 1992-95, state health officer, 1993-95; assoc. dean adminstrn., prof. epidemiology/health adminstrn. Sch. Pub. Health, U. Calif., Berkeley, 1995-97; prof. epidemiology and preventive medicine U. Calif., San Francisco, 1997—, dir. Inst. Global Health, 2004—. Transport physician Children's Hosp. and Health Ctr., San Diego, 1981; clin. asst. prof. pediatrics Emory U., Atlanta, 1982-83, Cornell U., N.Y.C., 1984-85, U. Calif., San Francisco, 1986-92, asst. clin. prof. epidemiology and biostats., 1987-92, family and cmty. medicine, 1988-90; assoc. adj. prof. epidemiology, biostats. and pediatrics, 1992-95, adj. prof., 1996—; assoc. clin. prof. cmty. health u. Calif., Davis, 1991-95; cons. Pan-Am. Health Orgn., S.Am., 1986-89, Ctrs. Disease Control, Atlanta, 1987—, WHO, 1988-90. Contbr. numerous articles to profl. jours., chpts. to books; co-translator cardiology teaching manual, other Spanish med. articles; editor in chief Calif. Morbidity, 1990-92; mem. editl. bd. Calif. AIDS Update, 1988—, Current Issues in Pub. Health, 1993-97; referee: AIDS, 1988—, Am. Jour. Pub. Health, 1989—, Brit. Med. Jour., 1994—, Internat. Jour. Epidemology, 1991—, Jour. Acquired Immune Deficiency Syndrome, 1989—, New Eng. Jour. Medicine, 1989—, Western Jour. Medicine, 1989—. Mem. numerous profl. adv. coms., task forces, etc. which aid govt. and charitable orgns. in work against infectious disease, especially AIDS. Capt. USPHSR, 1982—. Fellow Am. Acad. Pediatrics; mem. APHA, Am. Assn. for History of Medicine, Am. Soc. Tropical Medicine and Hygiene, Bay Area Communicable Disease Exch., Calif. Med. Assn., Infectious Diseases Soc. Am., No. Calif. Pub. Health Assn., Internat. AIDS Soc., Soc. for Epidemiol. Rsch., Assn. State and Territorial Health Ofcls. Republican. Episcopalian. Avocation: tennis. Office: U Calif San Francisco Global Health Inst Ste 1200 50 Beale St San Francisco CA 94105 Office Phone: 415-597-8200. E-mail: grutherford@psg.ucsf.edu.

RUTHERFORD, THOMAS TRUXTUN, II, state legislator, municipal official; b. Columbus, Ohio, Mar. 3, 1947; s. James William and Elizabeth Whiting (Colby) R.; m. Linda Sue Rogers, Aug. 28, 1965 (div.); 1 child, Jeremy Todd; m. Charlene Beth Smith, July 22, 2007. BBA, U. N.Mex., 1970, JD, 1982. Page, reading clk. N.Mex. State Legislature, 1960-65; mem. N.Mex. Atty. Gen. Environ. Adv. Commn., 1972; radio broadcaster Sta. KOB Radio and TV, 1963-72; mem. N.Mex. Senate, Albuquerque, 1972-96, majority whip, 1978-88. Chmn. rules com. N.Mex. State Senate, chmn. econ. devel. and new tech. interim. com., mem. sci. and new tech. oversight com., majority fl. leader, 1996; pres. Rutherford & Assocs., Albuquerque, 1978—83; pvt. practice, Albuquerque, 1983—; gen. counsel Nat. Fraternal Order of Police, 1996—2001; commr., chair Bernalillo County Commn., 1996—2004; lobbyist The Rutherford Group, 1996—; bd. dirs. Hispano C. of C., Kirtland Partnership Com., Albuquerque Econ. Devel., Camp Sierra Blanca Youth Detention Ctr., N. Mex. Bus. Weekly Top 100 Power Brokers, 1996—2004; past chmn. Albuquerque Cable TV Adv. Bd.; mem. S.W. Regional Energy Coun., N.Mex. Gov.'s Commn. on Pub. Broadcasting; bd. dirs., v.p. Rocky Mountain Corp. for Pub. Broadcasting; mem. Am. Coun. Young Polit. Leaders; del. mission to Hungary, Austria, Greece, 1983; mem. Fgn. Trade Adv. Com. Bd. Econ. Devel. and Tourism; trade del. People's Republic of China, 1985; local govt. del. Switzerland, 2001. Mem. Leadership N.Mex. Class of 2004; bd. dirs. Nat. Assn. Counties, N.Mex. Assn. Counties. N.Mex. Broadcasting Assn. scholar, 1970. Office: 1016 monroe NE Albuquerque NM 87110-5822

RUTHERFORD, WILLIAM DRAKE, investment executive; b. Marshalltown, Iowa, Jan. 14, 1939; s. William Donald and Lois Esther (Drake) R.; m. Janice W. Rutherford, Feb. 4, 1965 (div. Mar. 1982); children: Wayne Donald, Melissa Drake; m. Karen Anderegg, Jan. 2, 1994. BS, U. Oreg., 1961; LLB, Harvard U., 1964. Bar: Oreg. 1964, U.S. Dist. Ct. Oreg. 1966. Assoc. Maguire, Kester & Cosgrave, Portland, Oreg., 1966-69; house counsel May & Co., Portland, 1969-70, pvt. practice, 1970-71, McMinnville, Oreg., 1971-84; mem. Oreg. Ho. of Reps., Salem, 1977-84; state treas. State of Oreg., Salem, 1984-87; chmn. Oreg. Investment Coun., Salem, 1986-87; exec. v.p., dir. U.S. and Australia ops. ABD Internat. Mgmt. Corp., NYC, 1987-88, pres., chief exec. officer, bd. dirs., 1988-89; pres., bd. dirs. Societé Gen. Touche Remnant, 1990-93; dir. spl. projects Metallgesellschaft Corp., NYC, 1994-95; mng. dir. Macadam Capital Ptnrs., Portland, 1995-96; CEO Fiberboard Asbestos Compensation Trust, Portland, 1997; prin. Rutherford Investment Mgmt. LLC, 1998—. Past chmn. bd. dirs. Metro One Telecomms. Author: Who Shot Goldilocks?, 2006. Trustee The Nature Conservancy, 2005—; bd. dirs. Portland Opera Assn., 1995—99; mem. investment bd. Oreg. Cmty. Found., 2006—. Recipient Contbn. to Individual Freedom award ACLU, 1981 Mem. Nat. Assn. State Treas. (exec. v.p. 1985, 86, pres. western region 1985, 86), Nat. Assn. State Auditors, Comptr. and Treas. (exec. com. 1987). Office: 10300 S W Greenburg Rd Ste 115 Portland OR 97223 Business E-Mail: WRutherford@rutherfordinvestment.com.

RUTSALA, VERN A., poet, writer, language educator; b. Feb. 5, 1934; s. Ray Edwin and Virginia Mae (Brady) R.; m. Joan Merle Colby, Apr. 6, 1957; children: Matthew, David, Kirsten. BA, Reed Coll., Portland, 1956; MFA, U. Iowa, Iowa City, 1960. Instr. Lewis and Clark Coll., Portland, 1961-64, asst. prof., 1964-69, assoc. prof., 1969-76, prof., 1976—2004. Vis. prof. U. Minn., Mpls., 1968-69, Bowling Green State U., Ohio, 1970; vis. writer Idaho, Moscow, 1988, Redlands U., Calif., 1979; chmn. English dept. Lewis and Clark, Portland, 1986-89, MWC/Pacific MFA program, 2005. Author: The Window, 1964, Laments, 1975, The Journey Begins, 1976, Paragraphs, 1978, Walking Home from the Icehouse, 1981, Backtracking, 1985, Ruined Cities, 1987, Selected Poems, 1991, Little-Known Sports, 1994, Greatest Hits: 1964-02, 2002, A Handbook for Writers, 2004, The Moment's Equation, 2004, How We Spent Our Time, 2006. With U.S. Army, 1956-58. Guggenheim Found. fellow, 1982-83, NEA fellow, 1975, 79, Masters fellow Oreg. Arts Commn., 1990; recipient Carolyn Kizer prize Western Oreg. State Coll., 1988, N.W. Poets prize N.W. Rev., 1975, Hazel Hall award Oreg. Inst. Lit. Arts, 1992, Juniper prize U. Mass. Press, 1993, Duncan Lawrie prize Arvon Found., 1994, Carolyn Kizer prize, 1997, Richard Snyder prize, 2004, Akron Poetry prize, 2004, Kenneth O. Hanson award, 2005; finalist Nat. Book award, 2005, Missisippi Review Poetry prize, 2009. Mem. AAUP, AWP, PEN, Acad. Am. Poets. Avocations: drawing, painting, sports.

RUTTER, NATHANIEL WESTLUND, geologist, educator; b. Omaha, Nov. 22, 1932; s. John Elliot and Karleen (Ludden) R.; m. Mary Marie Munson, Sept. 11, 1961; children: Todd, Christopher. BS, Tufts U., 1955; MS, U. Alaska, 1962; PhD, U. Alta., 1965, DSc honoris causa, 2001, U. Córdoba, Argentina, 2006. Geologist Venezuelan Atlantic Refining Co., 1955-58; research scientist Geol. Survey Can., Calgary, Alta., 1965-74, head urban projects sect. Ottawa, Ont., 1974; environ. advisor Nat. Energy Bd., Ottawa, 1974-75; assoc. prof. dept. geology U. Alta., Edmonton, 1975-77, 77-80, prof., chmn. dept., 1980-89, 77-96, prof. dept. atmospheric scis., 1996-97, univ. prof., 1997—, assoc. dean. faculty sci.; pres. Can. nat. com. Internat. Geol. Correlation Program, UNESCO, 1996-97. Pres. Internat. Union Quaternary Rsch. Congress, 1982-87; mem. Internat. Geosphere-Biosphere Program: A Study of Global Change, 1988-94; mem. rsch. com. Can. Global Change Program, 1992-94; chmn. global change com. INUQA, 1991-95; hon. prof. Chinese Acad. Sci., Beijing, 1994—; disting. lectr. Sigma Xi, 1995-97; mem. sci. bd. Internat. Union of Geol. Scis.-UNESCO, 1997—. Contbr. numerous articles to profl. jours.; assoc. editor Arctic, Geosci. Can. Quaternary Rsch.; mem. editl. bd. Quaternary Sci. Revs., Quaternary Rsch., Estonia Jour. Sci., Arctic; editor-in-chief Quaternary Internat. Named Officer Order of Can., 2001; recipient Queen's Golden Jubilee medal, 2003, Alberta Centennial medal, 2005, Disting. Alumni award U. Alberta, 2007; grantee Natural Scis. and Engring. Rsch. Coun. Can., grantee Energy, Mines and Resources. Fellow Royal Soc. Can.; mem. Assn. Profl. Engrs., Geologists and Geophysicists of Alta., Internat. Union Quaternary Rsch. (v.p. 1982-87, pres. 1987-91, hon. 1999), Can. Quaternary Assn. (v.p. 1981-82, Johnston medal 1997), Geol. Soc. Am. (mgmt. bd. dirs. quaternary geol. and geomorphology divsn. 1982-84, Disting. Career award 2003), Geol. Assn. of Can. (J. Willis Ambrose medal 1998), Internat. Union Quaternary Rsch. (hon.), Explorer's Club, Cosmos Club. Home: Rural Route 3 Stony Plain AB Canada T7Z 1X3 Office: U Alta Dept Earth & Atmospheric Scis Edmonton AB Canada T6G 2E3 E-mail: nat.rutter@ualberta.ca.

RUUD, CLAYTON OLAF, engineering educator; b. Glassgow, Mont., July 31, 1934; s. Asle and Myrtle (Bleken) Ruud; m. Paula Kay Mannino, Feb. 24, 1990; children: Kelley Astrid, Kirsten Anne. BS in Metallurgy, Wash. State U., Pullman, 1957; MS in Materials Sci., San Jose State U., 1967; PhD in Materials Sci., U. Denver, 1970. Registered profl. engr., Calif., Colo. Asst. remelt metallurgist Kaiser Aluminum & Chem. Corp., Trentwood, Wash., 1957-58; devel. engr. Boeing Airplane Co., Seattle, 1958-60; mfg. rsch. engr. Lockheed Missiles & Space Corp., Sunnyvale, Calif., 1960-63; rsch. engr. FMC Corp., San Jose, 1963-67; sr. rsch. scientist U. Denver, 1967-79; prof. indsl. engring. Pa. State U., University Park, 1979—. Founder, developer, and co-director of quality and manufacturing management masters degree Pa. State U.; cons. in field; bd. dirs. Denver X-Ray Inst. Inc., Altoona, Pa. Editor series: Advances in X-Ray Analysis, Vol. 12-22, 1970-80, Nondestructive Character of Materials, Vol. 1-6, 1983-1996; editor X-Ray Spectometry, 1975-87; editl. com. Nondestructive Testing and Evaluation, 1991-1995; contbr. chpts. to books. Chmn. Nat. Acad. Sci. Safe Drinking Water Com., Washington, 1976-78. Recipient IR 100 award, 1983, Gov.'s New Product Award, Pa. Soc. Profl. Engrs., 1988. Fellow ASM Internat. (chmn. Resid. Stress Conf. 1989-91); mem. Internat. Ctr. for Diffraction Data, Soc. Mfg. Engrs., Metall. Soc. of AIME. Achievements include patents in x-ray analysis and residual stress measurement; invention of fiber optic based position sensitive scintillation X-ray detector, instrument for simultaneous stress and phase composition measurement; development of an X-ray diffraction instrument for manufacturing process quality control. Business E-Mail: corl@psu.edu.

RUYTER, NANCY LEE CHALFA, dance educator; b. Phila., May 23, 1933; d. Andrew Benedict Chalfa and Lois Elizabeth (Strode) McClary; m. Ralph Markson (div.); m. Hans C. Ruyter, Dec. 7, 1968 (dec. Jan. 1998). BA in History, U. Calif., Riverside, 1964; PhD in History, Claremont Grad. Sch., 1970. Tchr. theater dept. Pomona Coll., 1965-72; instr. dance program U. Calif., Riverside, 1972-76, acting chair dance program, 1974-75; instr. dance dept. UCLA, 1976; instr. phys. edn. dept. Orange Coast Coll., 1976-77; asst. prof. dept. phys. edn. and dance Tufts U., 1977-78; asst. prof. phys. edn. dept. Calif. State U., Northridge, 1978-82; from asst. prof. to full prof. dance dept. U. Calif., Irvine, 1982—, assoc. dean Sch. Fine Arts, 1984-88, 95-96, chair dept. dance, 1989-91. Presenter in field. Appeared with Jasna Planina Folk Ensemble, 1972-77, 78-79, Di Falco and Co., 1955-57; choreographer, dir. numerous coll. dance prodns.; contbr. articles, revs. to profl. publs.; author: Reformers and Visionaries: The Americanization of the Art of Dance, 1979, The Cultivation of Body and Mind in Nineteenth-Century American Delsartism, 1999. Mem. Am. Soc. Theatre Rsch., Bulgarian Studies Assn., Congress on Rsch. in Dance (bd. dirs. 1977-80, 2003-08, pres. 1981-85), Folk Dance Fedn., Internat. Fedn. Theatre Rsch., Soc. Dance Rsch., Soc. Ethnomusicology, Soc. Dance History Scholars (steering com. 1980-81), Spanish Dance Soc., Theatre Libr. Assn. Office: U Calif Dept Dance Irvine CA 92697-2775 Office Phone: 949-824-7284. Business E-Mail: nlruyter@uci.edu.

RYAN, AMY, actress; b. Queens, NY, Nov. 30, 1969; Actress (TV films) In the Deep Woods, 1992, Remembering Sex, 1998, Baseball Wives, 2002, (TV series) I'll Fly Away, 1992, The Naked Truth, 1995, The Wire, 2003—06, 100 Centre Street, 2001—02, (films) Roberta, 1999, A Pork Chop for Larry, 2000, You Can Count on Me, 2000, Keane, 2004, War of the Worlds, 2005, Capote, 2005, Looking for Comedy in the Muslim World, 2005, Marvelous, 2006, Shiner, 2006, Forward, 2007, Gone Baby Gone, 2007 (Best Supporting Actress, Wash., DC Area Film Critics Assn., 2007, Best Actress in a Supporting Role, Satellite Awards, 2007, Best Supporting Actress, San Francisco Film Critics Circle, 2007, Best Performance by an Actress in a Supporting Role, Phoenix Film Critics Soc. Awards, 2007, Best Supporting Actress, NY Film Critics Circle, 2007, Best Supporting Actress, Natinal Bd. Review, 2007, Best Supporting Actress, LA Film Critics Assn., 2007, Best Supporting Actress, Boston Soc. Film Critics, 2007, 2007 Best Supporting Actress, Critics Choice award, Broadcast Film Critics Assn., 2008), Before the Devil Knows You're Dead, 2007, Neal Cassady, 2007, Dan in Real Life, 2007, (TV miniseries) A Will of Their Own, 1998, (Broadway plays) Uncle Vanya, A Streetcar Named Desire. Office: Framework Entertainment Ste C 9057 Nemo St West Hollywood CA 90069

RYAN, DON, state legislator; Montana State Senator, District 10, 2005-, Montana State Senate. Democrat. Mailing: 2101 7th Ave S Great Falls MT 59405-2821

RYAN, FRANK HARRY, plastic surgeon; b. May 21, 1960; BS, U. Mich., Ann Arbor, 1982; MD, Ohio State U. Coll. Medicine, Columbus, 1986. Surgical residency Cedars-Sinai Med. Ctr., U. Mo. & UCLA Med. Ctr., 1986—94; plastic surgeon priv. practice, Beverly Hills, 1994—. Mem. adv. bd. A. Craig Matthias Found. Founder Bony Pony Ranch Found., Malibu. Avocations: boating, fishing, golf, skiing, tennis. Office: 9675 Brighton Wy Ste 340 Beverly Hills CA 90210 also: Bony Pony Ranch Found 9663 Santa Monica Blvd Ste 785 Beverly Hills CA 90210 Office Phone: 310-275-1075. Personal E-mail: drryand@drfrankryan.com.

RYAN, JANE FRANCES, corporate communications executive; b. Bronxville, NY, Nov. 1, 1950; d. Bernard M. and Margaret M. (Griffith) R.; m. Kevin Horan, Dec. 26, 1982; 1 child, Kevin. BS in Journalism, Ohio U., 1972; MBA in Mktg., Golden Gate U., 1990. Asst. promotion mgr. Fawcett Publs., Greenwich, Conn., 1972-75; mktg. coordinator Fawcett Mktg. Services div. CBS, Greenwich, Conn., 1975-78; dist. sales mgr. CBS Publs., San Francisco, 1978; prodn. mgr. Cato Inst., San Francisco, 1979-81; account supr. Bus. Media Resources, Mill Valley, Calif., 1981-90, dir. mktg. svcs., 1990-93; dir. publs. RAND Corp., Santa Monica, Calif., 1993—. Office: RAND 1700 Main St Santa Monica CA 90401-3297

RYAN, JOAN, columnist; b. Sept. 20, 1959; m. Barry Tompkins; 1 child. BS in Journalism with honors, U. Fla., 1981. Copy editor Orlando (Fla.) Sentinel, 1981-82, copy editor sports, 1982-83, sports writer, 1983-85; sports columnist San Francisco Examiner, 1985—2000; columnist San Francisco Chronicle, 2000—06, features writer, 2006—. Author: Little Girls in Pretty Boxes: The Making & Breaking of Elite Gymnasts & Figure Skaters; co-author: Shooting from the Outside: How a Coach & her Olympic Team Transformed Women's Basketball. Recipient Fla. Sports Columnist of Yr. award, 1984, numerous AP Sports Editors awards, AP 1st place enterprise reporting award, 1993, Nat. Headliner award for sports writing, 1990, Women's Sports Found. Journalism award, 1992, Excellence in Journalism award for Feature Writing, Northern Calif. ch. Soc. Profl. Journalists, 2004, 2007, Gideon Equal Justice award, San Francisco Pub. Defender's Office, 2004, AP News Execs. Coun. award for Feature Writing, 2007, Edgar A. Poe award, White House Corrs. Assn., 2007. Office: San Francisco Chronicle 901 Mission St San Francisco CA 94103 Office Phone: 415-777-1111. E-mail: jryan@sfchronicle.com.

RYAN, JOHN DUNCAN, lawyer; b. Portland, Oreg., Dec. 20, 1920; s. Thomas Gough and Virginia Abigail (Hadley) R.; m. Florence A. Ryan, Jan. 30, 1970 (dec. 1987); m. Virginia Kane Wilson, June 15, 1996 BS, Fordham U., Bronx, NY, 1943; JD, Lewis & Clark Coll., Portland, 1950. Bar: Oreg. 1950. Pvt. practice, Portland, 1950—. Adj. instr. Northwestern Sch. Law Lewis & Clark Coll., 1953-70 Author: (poems) Expressions, 1993, Expressions II, 1995, No Road without a Turning, 2005, (book) Expressions, 1988, 1999, Cooking with John Ryan, 2002, More Cooking with John Ryan, 2008 Sgt. Air Corps, U.S. Army, 1942-46, ETO Recipient St. Thomas More award Catholic Lawyers for Social Justice, 1993 Mem. ABA (Oreg. del. 1985-93, chmn. spl. com. on law & literacy 1991-93), ATLA, Am. Coll. Trial Lawyers, Oreg. State Bar (bd. govs. 1963-67), Oreg. Trial Lawyers Assn. (Trial Lawyer of Yr. 1993), Multnomah County Bar Assn. (Professionalism award 1997), Washington County Bar Assn, Londer Learning Ctr. Multnomah County, Oregon (co-founder) Home and Office: 503 SW Colony Dr Portland OR 97219-7763 Office Phone: 503-293-2207. Personal E-mail: v.ryan@comcast.net.

RYAN, JOHN EDWARD, federal judge; b. Boston, Jan. 22, 1941; s. Howard Frederick and Mary (Burke) R.; m. Terri Reynolds; children: Valerie, Jennifer, Keely. BSEE, U.S. Naval Acad., 1963; LLB, Georgetown U., 1972; MS, Pacific Christian U., 1979. Assoc. Hale and Dorr, Boston, 1972-76, C.F. Braun, Alhambra, Calif., 1976-77; gen. counsel Altec Corp., Anaheim, Calif., 1977-79; v.p., sr. atty. Oak Industries, San Diego, 1979-82; sr. v.p. Oak Media, San Diego, 1982-84; ptnr. Dale and Lloyd, La Jolla, Calif., 1984-85, Jennings, Engstrand and Henrikson, San Diego, 1985-86; bankruptcy judge U.S. Bankruptcy Ct., Santa Ana, Calif., 1986—. Ex officio dir. Orange County Bankruptcy Forum; mem. Ninth Cir. Bankruptcy Apellate Panel, 1996—, chief justice, 2000—. With USN, 1963-69. Fellow Am. Coll. Bankruptcy; mem. Mass. Bar Assn., Calif. Bar Assn., Orange County Bar Assn., Bankruptcy Judges Assn. Roman Catholic. Avocations: tennis, camping, kayaking. Home: 3155 Summit Dr Escondido CA 92025-7529 Office: US Bankruptcy Ct PO Box 22026 Santa Ana CA 92702-2026

RYAN, KEVIN VINCENT, lawyer, former prosecutor; b. 1957; m. Anne Ryan; 2 children. BA in History, Dartmouth Coll.; JD, U. San Francisco. Prosecutor Alameda County Dist. Atty.'s Office; judge San Francisco Mcpl. Ct., 1996—98; mem. San Francisco Superior Ct., 1999, presiding judge criminal divsn.; US atty. (no. dist.) Calif. US Dept. Justice, San Francisco, 2002—07; ptnr. Allen Matkins Leck Gamble Mallory & Natsis LLP, San Francisco, 2007—. Bd. dirs. No. Calif. High Intensity Drug Trafficking Area Working Group; mem. Pres. Bush's Corp. Fraud Task Force; apptd. mem. subcom. Controlled Substances and Terrorism and Nat. Security, appointed to Jud. Coun.'s Exec. Legis. Action Network, Chief Justice of Calif. Supreme Ct.; appointed to Criminal Law Planning Com. of Calif. Continuing Jud. Studies Program, Governing Com. of Calif. Ctr. for Jud. Edn. and Rsch.; appointed to Adult Probation Dept.'s Oversight Com., Presiding Judge for Cts.; mem. exec. com. San Francisco Superior Ct.; mem. exec. com. Am. Inn of Cts., U. San Francisco Sch. Law; bd. govs. U. San Francisco Law Soc.; bd. trustees Schs. of Sacred Heart, San Francisco; mem. faculty Intensive Trial Advocacy Program, U. San Francisco Sch. Law; lectr. in field. Recipient Mcpl. Ct. Trial Judge of Yr., San Francisco Trial Lawyers' Assn., 1998. Office: Allen Matkins 3 Embarcadero Ctr 12th Fl San Francisco CA 94111-4074

RYAN, LUCILLE FRANCIS See LAWLESS, LUCY

RYAN, MICHAEL D., state supreme court justice; BA, St. John's U., Collegeville, Minn., 1967; JD, Ariz. State U., 1977. Dep. county atty. Maricopa County Atty.'s Office, 1977—85; judge pro tempore Superior Ct. State of Ariz., Maricopa County, 1985—86, judge Maricopa County, 1986—96, assoc. criminal presiding judge Maricopa County, 1993—96; judge Ariz. Ct. Appeals, Divsn. 1, 1996—2002, vice chief judge, 2001—02; justice Ariz. Supreme Ct., 2002—. Chair Scottsdale Jud. Appts. Adv. Bd., 1999—2002; vice chair Ariz. State Bar Task Force on Persons with Disabilities, 2002—; mem. Maricopa County Resource Site Team for Ctr. for Sex Offender Mgmt., 1996—2000, Ariz. Atty. Gen.'s Capital Case Commn., 2000—02; mem. adv. com. Nat. Ctr. for State Cts., Ctr. for Effective Pub. Policy, also State Justice Inst.'s Nat. Solutions Project, 2003—; chair Ariz. Supreme Ct. Com. on Keeping Record, 2004—. Infantry platoon comdr. USMC, 1968, Vietnam. Recipient Semper Fi award, First Marine Divsn. Assn., Phoenix chpt., 2001, Outstanding Alumnus award, Ariz. State Univ. Coll. Law, 2003, Disting. Achievement award, 2003, James A. Walsh Outstanding Jurist award, State Bar Ariz., 2005. Mem.: State Bar of Arizona (Judicial award of Excellence 2001), Maricopa County Bar Assn. (bd. dirs. 1987—91, 1997—2002, chair task force recruitment and retention of women and minorities 1997—2004, Henry S. Stevens Judge of the Yr. award 2001). Office: Ariz Supreme Ct 1501 W Washington Phoenix AZ 85007-3231

RYAN, RAYMOND D., retired steel and insurance company executive; b. Big Timber, Mont., Feb. 7, 1922; s. Robert Allen and Elsie (Beery) R.; m. Dale Burnett, Jan. 17, 1943; children: Raymond Brant, Brenda Ruth, Ronald Dale. BA, U. Mont., Missoula, 1948, JD (hon.), 1970; LLM, NYU, 1949. Bar: Mont. 1948. Various fin. officer positions U.S. Steel and subsidiaries in U.S. and Venezuela, 1949-75; v.p., treas. U.S. Steel, 1975-83; pres. The Evergreen Group Inc., Stamford, Conn., 1984-94, chmn., 1995-96, Evergreen Benefits Inc., 1996-99, The Money Suite Co., Missoula, Mont., 1999—. With mil. police AUS, 1943-45, ETO. Mem. ABA, Met. Club (N.Y.C.), Phi Sigma Kappa, Phi Delta Phi. Home: PO Box 160601 Big Sky MT 59716-0601 Office Phone: 406-995-3397. Personal E-mail: raydryan@gmail.com.

RYAN, STEPHEN JOSEPH, JR., ophthalmologist, educator; b. Honolulu, Hawaii, Mar. 20, 1940; s. S.J. and Mildred Elizabeth (Farrer) Ryan; m. Anne Christine Mullady, Sept. 25, 1965; 1 child, Patricia Anne. AB, Providence Coll., 1961; MD, Johns Hopkins U., 1965. Intern Bellevue Hosp., NYC, 1965—66; resident Wilmer Inst. Ophthalmology, Johns Hopkins Hosp., Balt., 1966—69, chief resident, 1969—70; fellow Armed Forces Inst. Pathology, Washington, 1970—71; instr. ophthalmology Johns Hopkins U., Balt., 1970—71, asst. prof., 1971—72, assoc. prof., 1972—74; Grace and Emery Beardsley prof. ophthalmology Keck Sch. Medicine, U. So. Calif., LA, 1974—, chmn. dept. ophthalmology, 1974—95, dean, 1991—2004, sr. v.p. for med. care, 1993—2004, Grace and Emery Beardsley Chair in Ophthalmology, med. dir. Doheny Eye Inst. (formerly Estelle Doheny Eye Found.), 1977—86, pres. Doheny Eye Inst., 1987—, chief of staff Doheny Eye Hosp., 1985—88; acting head ophthalmology divsn. dept. surgery Children's Hosp., 1975—77. Mem. adv. panel Calif. Med. Assn., 1975—. Editor (with M.D. Andrews): A Survey of Ophthalmology—Manual for Medical Students, 1970; editor: (with R.E. Smith) Selected Topics on the Eye in Systemic Disease, 1974; editor: (with Dawson and Little) Retinal Diseases, 1985; editor: (with others) Retina, 1989; editor:, 2000, 4t edit., 2005; assoc. editor: Ophthalmol. Surgery, 1974—85, mem. editl. bd.: Am. Jour. Ophthalmology, 1981—, Internat. Ophthalmology, 1982—, Retina, 1983—, Graefes Archives, 1984—; contbr. articles to med. jours. Recipient cert. of merit, AMA, 1971, Louis B. Mayer Scholar award, Rsch. to Prevent Blindness, 1973, Rear Adm. William Campbell Chambliss USN award, 1982, Mildred Weisenfeld Award for Lifetime Achievement in Vision Rsch., Fight for Sight, 2000. Mem.: AMA, Inst. Medicine NAS (home sec. 2006), Jules Gonin Club, Rsch. Study Club, Nat. Eye Care Project, Retina Soc., Macula Soc., Pan-Am. Assn. Microsurgery, L.A. Acad. Medicine, Pacific Coast Oto-Ophthal. Soc., Los Angeles County Med. Assn., Calif. Med. Assn., L.A. Soc. Ophthalmology, Assn. Univ. Profs. of Ophthalmology, Pan-Am. Assn. Ophthalmology, Am. Ophthal. Soc., Am. Acad. Ophthalmology and Otolaryngology (award of Merit 1975), Wilmer Ophthal. Inst. Residents Assn., Soc. Scholars of Johns Hopkins U. (life). Office: 1450 San Pablo St Los Angeles CA 90033 Business E-Mail: sryan@doheny.org.

RYAN, SYLVESTER DONOVAN, bishop emeritus; b. Catalina Island, Calif., Sept. 3, 1930; Grad., St. John's Sem., Camarillo, Calif. Ordained priest Archdiocese of LA, Calif., 1957, aux. bishop, 1990—92; ordained bishop, 1990; bishop Diocese of Monterey, Calif., 1992—2006, bishop emeritus, 2006—. Roman Catholic. Office: Chancery Office PO Box 2048 631 Abrego St Monterey CA 93940-3203 Office Phone: 831-373-4345. Office Fax: 831-373-1175.

RYAN, THOMAS W., treasurer manufacturing company; b. Detroit, Jan. 28, 1947; m. Barbara L. Schembri, Sept. 6, 1968; children: Thomas III, Kristie, Kelly, Stephanie, Michael. BSBA, Wayne State U., 1969. Contr. Leader Internat. Industries, 1973; contr. Kenosha mfg. complex Am. Motors Corp., Wis., 1974-78, contr. mktg., 1978-80, dir. fin. planning, 1981-82, dir. internat. operations Southfield, Mich., 1982-85; v.p. A.O. Smith Corp., Milw., 1985—, treas., 1987-95, treas., contr., 1990-95; v.p. and CFO Tenneco Automotive Inc., Lake Forest, Ill.; exec. v.p. & CFO Federal-Mogul Corp., Southfield, Mich., 1997-2000, Allied Waste Industries, Inc., Scottsdale, Ariz., 2000—03, exec. v.p., chmn., 2003—04. Trustee Wis. Nat. Multiple Sclerosis Soc., Milw., 1986; mem. Zoning Bd. of Appeals, Whitefish Bay, Wis., 1987; bd. dir., treas. A.O. Smith Found., 1987. Mem.: Nat. Assn. Accts., Fin. Exec. Inst.

RYAN, TOM, reporting applications platform company executive; BS in Computer Sci., San Francisco State U.; MBA in Internat. Bus., U. Notre Dame de Namur. Sr. mgmt. positions at Informix, Illustra, Oracle and Amdahl; dir. customer support Actuate Corp., South San Francisco, Calif., 1997—2002, CIO, sr. v.p. customer svc., 2002—. Mem. adv. bd. AppMail, San Mateo County Cmty. Coll. Dist. Computer Sci. Divsn. Office: Actuate Corp 701 Gateway Blvd South San Francisco CA 94080-7084 Office Phone: 650-837-2000. Office Fax: 650-827-1560.

RYBERG, WILLIAM A., orchestra executive; BMus, Western Wash. State U., 1980; MMus, Ind. U., 1983. Teller, loan officer, br. mgr., regional mgr. Ranier Nat. Bank; v.p., area mgr. West One Bank, Tacoma; v.p., dist. mgr. Key Bank, Wash., 1993-96; exec. dir. Bellingham (Wash.) Festival of Music, 1996-98; pres. Grand Rapids (Mich.) Symphony, 1998—2004, Oreg. Symphony Orch., Portland, 2004—. Office: 921 SW Wahington Ste 200 Portland OR 97205

RYCHNOVSKY, SCOTT DOUGLAS, chemist, educator; b. Albuquerque, May 26, 1959; s. Raymond E. and Sheila Lee (Irish) R. BS, U. Calif., Berkeley, 1981; PhD, Columbia U., 1986; postgrad., Harvard U., 1986-87, Yale U., 1987-88. Asst. prof. U. Minn., 1988-94, assoc. prof., 1994-95; prof. U. Calif., Irvine, 1995-96. Contbr. articles to Jour. Am. Chem. Soc. Recipient Research award Pfizer Inc., 1992, Pres. Young Investigator award NSF, 1991; scholar Searle Found., 1989. Mem. Am. Chem. Soc. Achievements include research in new synthetic methods, and studies with ent-cholesterol.

RYDALCH, ANN, federal agency administrator, former state senator; b. 1935; m. Vernal Rydalch. BS in Bus. Edn., Idaho State U. Mem. Idaho Senate, 1983—90; chmn. Feb. Lab. Consortium Tech. Transfer, 2001—; state rep. Idaho, 2004—. Past mem. Idaho Bicentennial Commn.; former vice chmn. Idaho Rep. Com. Republican. Office: ID Natl Energy & Envrn Lab PO Box 1625 MS 3810 2525 N Fremont Ave Idaho Falls ID 83415-3810

RYDER, SUSAN R., elementary school educator; b. Ala. m. David Ryder. Lang. arts tchr. Estes Park (Colo.) Middle Sch., 2001—. Named Colo. Tchr. of Yr., 2007; grantee Nat. Writing Project Fellow, Dept. Edn., 2006. Office: Estes Park Middle Sch 1500 Manford Ave Estes Park CO 80517 Office Phone: 970-586-4439 ext 3278. Business E-Mail: susan_ryder@psdr3.k12.co.us.

RYLES, GERALD FAY, investor, finance company executive; b. Walla Walla, Wash., Apr. 3, 1936; s. L. F. and Janie Geraldine (Bassett) R.; m. Ann Jane Birkenmeyer, June 12, 1959; children—Grant, Mark, Kelly. BA, U. Wash., 1958; MBA, Harvard U., 1962. With Gen. Foods Corp., White Plains, NY, 1962—66, Purex Corp., Ltd., Lakewood, Calif., 1966-68; cons. McKinsey & Co., Inc., Los Angeles, 1968-71; with Fibreboard Corp., San Francisco, 1971-79, v.p., 1973-75, group v.p., 1975-79; with Consol. Fibres, Inc., San Francisco, 1979-88, exec. v.p., 1979-81, pres., dir., 1981-86, chief exec. officer, 1986-88; cons. Orinda, Calif., 1988-90; with Interchecks Inc., 1990-92, pres., CEO, 1990-92; bus. exec., pvt. investor, 1992-94; chmn. bd., CEO Microserv, Inc., Kirkland, Wash., 1994—2001, chmn. bd., 2001—03. Bd. dirs. Giant Campus, Inc., Zumiez, Inc., Wash. State Bd. Accountancy. Capt. U.S. Army, 1958-66. Mem.: Harvard Bus. Sch. Assn., U. Wash. Alumni Assn. Republican. Episcopalian. Home: 127 3rd Ave Apt 301 Kirkland WA 98033-6177 Home Phone: 425-827-3519. Personal E-mail: g.ryles@verizon.net.

RYMER, PAMELA ANN, federal judge; b. Knoxville, Tenn., Jan. 6, 1941; AB, Vassar Coll., 1961; LLB, Stanford U., 1964; LLD (hon.), Pepperdine U., 1988. Bar: Calif. 1966, US Ct. Appeals (9th cir.) 1966, US Ct. Appeals (10th cir.), US Supreme Ct. Dir., polit. rsch. and analysis Goldwater for President Com., 1964; v.p. Rus Walton & Assoc., Los Altos, Calif., 1965—66; assoc. Lillick McHose & Charles, LA, 1966—75, ptnr., 1973—75, Toy and Rymer, LA, 1975—83; judge US Dist. Ct. (ctrl. dist.) Calif., LA, 1983—89, US Ct. Appeals (9th cir.), LA, 1989—. Faculty The Nat. Jud. Coll., 1986-88; mem. com. summer edml. programs Fed. Jud. Ctr., 1987-88, mem. com. appellate judge edn., 1996-99; chair exec. com. 9th Cir. Jud. Conf., 1990; mem. com. criminal law Jud. Conf. US, 1988-93, Ad Hoc com. gender-based violence, 1991-94, fed.-state jurisdiction com., 1993-96; mem. commn. on structural alternatives Fed. Cts. Appeals, 1997-98. Mem. editorial bd. The Judges' jour., 1989-91; contbr. articles to profl. jours. and newsletters. Mem. Calif. Postsecondary Edn. Commn., 1974-84, chmn., 1980-84; mem. LA Olympic Citizens Adv. Commn.; bd. visitors Stanford U. Law Sch., 1986-99, trustee, 1991-2001, chair, 1993-96, exec. com., chmn. bd. trustees com. acad. policy, planning and mgmt. and its ad. hoc. com. athletics., chmn. bd. visitors Sch. Law, 1987—; bd. visitors Pepperdine U. Law Sch., 1987—; mem. Edn. Commn. of States Task Force on State Policy and Ind. Higher Edn., 1987-89, Carnegie Commn. Task Force Sci. and Tech. Jud. and Regulatory Decisionmaking, 1990-93, Commn. Substance Abuse Coll. and Univ. Campuses, 1992-94, commn. substance abuse high schs. Ctr. Addiction and Substance Abube Columbia U.; bd. dirs. Constnl. Rights Found., 1985-97, Pacific Coun. Internat. Policy, 1995—, Calif. Higher Edn. Policy Ctr., 1992-97; Jud. Conf. US Com. Fed.-State Jurisdiction, 1993, Com. Criminal Law, 1988-93, ad hoc com. gender based violence, 1991-94; chair exec. com. 9th cir. jud. conf., 1990-94. Recipient Outstanding Trial Jurist award LA County Bar Assn., 1988; named David T. Lewis Disting. Jurist-in-Residence U. Utah, 1992. Mem. ABA (task force on civil justice reform 1991-93, mem. coord. com. agenda civil justice reform in Am. 1991), State Bar Calif. (antitrust and trade regulation sect., exec. com. 1990-92), LA County Bar Assn. (chmn. antitrust sect. 1981-82, mem. editl. bd. The Judges Jour. 1989-91, mem. com. professionalism 1988—, numerous other coms.), Assn. of Bus. Trial Lawyers (bd. govs. 1990-92), Stanford Alumni Assn., Stanford Law Soc. So. Calif., Vassar Club So. Calif. (past pres.). Office: US Ct Appeals 9th Cir US Court of Appeals Bldg 125 S Grand Ave Rm 600 Pasadena CA 91105-1621

RYNN, NATHAN, physics professor, consultant; b. NYC, Dec. 2, 1923; s. Meyer and Rose (Wolkerwiczer) Rynkowsky; m. Glenda Brown, June 24, 1989; children by previous marriage: Jonathan, Margaret, David. BSEE, CCNY, 1944; MS, U. Ill., 1947; PhD, Stanford U., 1956. Rsch. engr. RCA Labs., Princeton, NJ, 1947-52; rsch. asst. Stanford U., Palo Alto, Calif., 1952-56, rsch. assoc., 1958; mem. tech. staff Ramo-Wooldridge, LA, 1956-57; supr. Huggins Labs., Menlo Park, Calif., 1957-58; rsch. staff physicist Princeton U., 1958-65; prof. physics U. Calif.-Irvine, 1965-94, prof. physics emeritus, rsch. prof. physics, 1994—. Vis. prof. Ecole Polytechnique Fed. of Lausanne, Switzerland, 1984-90, Ecole Polytechnique, Paris, and other European univs. and labs., 1973-80; indsl. sci. advisor/cons., 1964—; com. mem. Plasma Sci. Com. Nat. Rsch. Coun.; founder and leader plasma physics rsch. facility (the Q-Machine). Contbr. articles and revs. to profl. jours. With USN, 1944-46. Grantee NSF, U.S. Dept. Energy, Air Force Geophys. Lab.; Fulbright sr. fellow, 1978. Fellow Am. Phys. Soc., IEEE, AAAS; mem. Sigma Xi. Avocation: woodworking. Office: U Calif Dept Physics & Astronomy Irvine CA 92697-4575 Office Phone: 949-824-5944. Business E-Mail: nrynn@uci.edu.

SAARI, DONALD GENE, mathematician, department chairman, economist; b. Ironwood, Mich., Mar. 9, 1940; s. Gene August and Martha Mary (Jackson) S.; m. Lillian Joy Kalinen, June 11, 1966; children: Katri, Anneli. BS, Mich. Technol. U., 1962; PhD, Purdue U., 1967, DSc (hon.), 1989, U. Caen, France, 1998, Mich. Tech. U., 1999. Research astronomer Yale U., New Haven, 1967-68; prof. dept. math. Northwestern U., Evanston, Ill., 1968-2000, prof. econs., 1988-2000, Pancoe prof. math., 1995-2000, chmn. dept., 1981-84; prof. U. Nanjing (China), 1995; disting. prof. econ., math U. Calif., Irvine, 2000—, dir. Ctr. for Decision Analysis, 2002—05, dir. Inst. Math. Behavioral Sci., 2003—. Cons. Nat. Bur. Standards, Gaithersburg, Md., 1979-86, Commn. 9, Internat. Astron. Union, 1985-91; nat. com. math. Nat. Rsch. Coun., 1997-2003, chair 2001-03, math./sci. edn. bd., 2001-07, Bd. Internat. Sci. Orgns., 2001-03, NRC com. on Internat. Inst. Applied Sys. Analysis, 2004-; chair trustees Math. Sci. Rsch. Inst., 2004-07. Assoc. editor Jour. Econ. Behavior and Orgn., 1988-94, Celestial Mechanics and Dynamical Astronomy. 1989-97, Econ. Theory, 1990-2007, Social Choice and Welfare, 1997—, Qualitative Theory of Dynamical Sys., 1999—, Positivity, 2000—. Recipient Duncan Black award, Pub. Choice Soc., 1991, Chauvenet prize Math. Assn. Am., 1995, Ford prize Math. Assn. Am., 1985, Allendorfer award Math. Assn. Am., 1999; Guggenheim fellow, 1988-89. Fellow AAAS, Am. Acad. Arts and Scis.; mem. NAS, Am. Math. Soc. (chief editor bull. 1999-2005, mem. coun. 1999-2005), Am. Astron. Soc., Soc. Indsl. and Applied Math. (editor jour. 1981-88), Econometric Soc. Office: U Calif Inst Math Behavorial Scis SSPA 2119 Irvine CA 92697-5100 Office Phone: 949-824-5894. Business E-Mail: dsaari@uci.edu.

SAAVEDRA, HENRY (KIKI), state legislator; b. 1938; New Mexico State Representative, District 10, 1976-, vice chairman, Appropriations & Finance Committee, currently, member, Consumer & Public Affairs Committee, formerly, member, Govt & Urban Affairs Committee, currently, New Mexico House Representative Representative. Supt recreation, Albuquerque, formerly; Dep Director, Community Servs, Albuquerque, currently. Democrat. Address: 2838 Second SW Albuquerque NM 87102 Mailing: State Capitol Rm 304 Santa Fe NM 87503

SAAVEDRA, MAURA, legislative staff member; Press sec. and scheduler to Rep. Ed Pastor US House of Reps., Washington, 1991—. Office: Office of Rep Ed Pastor 2465 Rayburn House Office Bldg Washington DC 20515-0304 also: 411 N Central Ave Ste 150 Phoenix AZ 85004-2120 Office Phone: 202-225-4065, 602-256-0551. Office Fax: 202-225-1655, 602-257-9103. E-mail: maura.saavedra@mail.house.gov.

SABAN, HAIM, investment company executive, television producer; b. Alexandria, Egypt, 1944; arrived in Israel, 1952, arrived in France, 1975, arrived in USA, 1983; m. Cheryl Saban, 1987; children: Ness, Tanya. TV series composer, 1975—95; chmn., CEO Saban Entertainment, LA, 1988—97, Fox Family Worldwide, LA, 1997—2001, Saban Capital Group, Inc., LA, 2001—; founder Saban Music Group, LA, 2002—. Bd. dirs. DirectTV Group, Inc., El Segundo, Calif., Societe TV Francaise 1, France, Univision, 2007—; bd. regents U. Calif., 2002—; founder Saban Ctr. Middle East Policy Brookings Inst., Washington, 2002, chair internat. adv. coun., trustee; chmn. supervisory bd. ProSiebenSat.1, Germany, 2003—07. Composer: (TV series) Heathcliff, He-Man & the Masters of the Universe, The Littles, Inspector Gadget, Mister T, Punky Brewster, Kissyfur, Rainbow Brite, She-Ra: Princess of Power, MASK, Popples, The Real Ghost Busters, Zoobilee Zoo, Dennis the Menace, Maxie's World, Beverly Hills Teens, C.O.P.S., Dragon Quest, The Super Mario Bros. Super Show!, Samurai Pizza Cats; exec. prodr.: (TV series) Kidd Video, 1984—87, Rambo, 1986, Mighty Morphin' Power Rangers, 1993—96, V.R. Troopers, 1994, Sweet Valley High, 1994—98, Power Rangers Zeo, 1996—97, Big Bad Beetleborgs, 1997, Breaker High, 1997—98, Power Rangers Turbo, 1997, Beetleborgs Metallix, 1997, Diabolik, 1997, Power Rangers in Space, 1998, Mystic Knights of Tir Na Nog, 1998, Power Rangers Lost Galaxy, 1999, Power Rangers Lightspeed Rescue, 2000, Power Rangers Time Force, 2001; (films) Mighty Morphin' Power Rangers: The Movie, 1995, Turbo: A Power Rangers Movie, 1997, Rusty: A Dog's Tale, 1998, Addams Family Reunion, 1998; (TV films) The Phantom of the Opera, 1990, Casper: A Spirited Beginning, 1997, Casper Meets Wendy, 1998; writer (TV series) Around the World in 80 Dreams, 1992. Advisor Pres.'s Export Coun. The White House; founder Saban Family Found., 1999—; active in Israeli Cancer Rsch. Fund, John Wayne Cancer Inst., U. Tel Aviv, Nat. Park Found., United Friends of the Children, William Jefferson Clinton Found., Motion Picture and Television Fund, Soroka Children's Hosp., Israel, Children's Hosp. LA, Milken Cmty. High Sch. Served in Israeli Def. Force. Named one of Forbes' Richest Americans, 2006, 50 Most Generous Philanthropists in the US, BusinessWeek. Democrat. Office: Saban Capital Group Ste 1050 10100 Santa Monica Blvd Los Angeles CA 90067 Office Phone: 310-557-5100.

SABATINI, WILLIAM QUINN, architect; b. Pitts. s. William L. and Lydia M. (Contento) S.; m. Carol Anne Christoffel, Feb. 26, 1972; children: Quinn, Jay, Jillian. BA, Franklin & Marshall Coll., 1971; MArch, U. N.Mex., 1978. Registered arch., N.Mex., Nev.; cert. Nat. Coun. Archtl. Registration Bds. Intern Jess Holmes, Arch., Albuquerque, 1974-78; project mgr. Jack Miller & Assocs., Las Vegas, 1978-81; sr. design arch. HNTB, Kansas City, Mo., 1981-84; prin. Holmes Sabatini Assocs. Arch. (now Dekker Perich Sabatini), Albuquerque, 1984—. Prin. works include Ctrl. Campus Bookstore U. N.Mex. (Merit award N.Mex. Soc. Archs. 1977), Luna County Courthouse, Deming, N.Mex. (Honor award N.Mex. Hist. Preservation Soc. 1978), James R. Dickinson Libr. U. Nev., Las Vegas (Merit award AIA 1981, Honor award Nev. Soc. Arch. 1981), Reno Conv. Ctr. (Merit award Nev. Soc. Archs. 1983), Corp. Hdqs. Nev. Power Co., Las Vegas (Honor award Nev. Soc. Archs. 1983), YMCA, Las Vegas (Honor award Nev. Soc. Archs. 1983), Sanctuary Remodel St. Johns United Meth. Ch., Albuquerque (Best Interiors award N.Mex. Bus. Jour. 1986), The Presidio Office Bldg., Albuquerque (Best Bldgs. award and Best Interiors award N.Mex. Bus. Jour. 1987, Project of Yr. award Assoc. Gen. Contractors N.Mex. 1987), Suarez Residence, Albuquerque (Merit award N.Mex. Soc. Am. 1988), Fire Sta. Number 13 and Fire Marshall's Office, Albuquerque (Merit award Albuquerque Conservation Soc. 1987, Best Bldgs. award N.Mex. Bus. Jour. 1988), Santa Fe Imaging Ctr. (Citation of Excellence, Modern Health Care Mag., AIA com. on healthcare 1989, Best Bldgs. award N.Mex. Bus. Jour. 1989), Health Scis. Bldg. U. N.Mex. (Best Bldgs. award N.Mex. Bus. Jour. 1989), U.S. Port of Entry, Columbus, N.Mex. (Best Bldgs. award N.Mex. Bus. Jour. 1989, Honor award N.Mex. Soc. Archs. 1990, GSA Design award U.S. Gen. Svcs. Adminstrn. 1990), Student Svcs. Bldg., Albuquerque TVI (Best Bldgs. award N.Mex. Bus. Jour. 1989, Merit award Albuquerque Conservation Soc. 1990), Expansion and Renovation Albuquerque Conv. Ctr. (Best Bldgs. award N.Mex. Bus. Jour. 1990), Lovelace Multi-Specialty Clinic Facility, Albuquerque (Merit award N.Mex. Soc. Archs. 1991), Pete's Playground U. N.Mex. Hosp. (Honor award N.Mex. Soc. Archs. 1992, Best Bldgs. Spl. award N.Mex. Bus. Jour. 1993), Nursing Unit Remodel U. N.Mex. Hosp. (Excellence award Am. Soc. Interior Designers 1992), 3.5 Meter Telescope Kirtland AFB, N.Mex. (Honor award AIA 1993). Bd. dirs. Albuquerque Chamber Orch., 1988, Hospice Rio Grande, 1992-94; mem. adv. bd. Balloon Mus., 1989-91;

mem. adv. bd. St. Pius High Sch., 1993-96. With USAR, 1971-78. Mem. AIA (bd. dirs. Albuquerque chpt. 1986-87). Roman Catholic. Office: Dekker Perich Sabatini 6801 Jefferson St NE Albuquerque NM 87109-4379

SABEAN, BRIAN R., professional baseball team executive; m. Barbara Sabean; childrne: Colin, Sean, Brendan, Darren. Grad., Eckerd Coll., St. Petersburg, Fla., 1978. Asst. baseball coach St. Leo (Fla.) Coll., 1978-79, Tampa (Fla.) U., 1980-82, head baseball coach, 1983-85; dir. scouting N.Y. Yankees farm sys., 1986-90, v.p. player devel./scouting, 1990-92; asst. to gen. mgr., v.p. scouting/player pers. San Francisco Giants, 1993-95, sr. v.p., player pers., 1995-96, sr. v.p., gen. mgr., 1996—. Achievement: San Francisco Giants won divisional flag in 1997. Office: c/o San Francisco Giants 24 Willie Mays Plz San Francisco CA 94107-2134

SABERSKY, ROLF HEINRICH, mechanical engineer; b. Berlin, Oct. 20, 1920; came to U.S., 1938, naturalized, 1944; s. Fritz and Berta (Eisner) S.; m. Bettina Sofie Schuster, June 16, 1946; children—Carol, Sandra. BS, Calif. Inst. Tech., 1942, MS, 1943, PhD, 1949. Devel. engr. Aerojet Gen. Co., 1943-46, regular cons., 1949-70; asst. prof. Calif. Inst. Tech., Pasadena, 1949-55, asso. prof., 1955-61, prof. mech. engring., 1961-88, prof. emeritus, 1988—. Cons. various indsl. orgns. Author: Engineering Thermodynamics, 1957, Fluid Flow, 4th edit., 1999; contbr. articles to profl. jours. Fellow ASME (Heat Transfer Meml. award 1977, 50th anniversary award Heat Transfer Div 1988); mem. Sigma Xi, Tau Beta Pi. Home: 1135 Calle De Los Amigos Santa Barbara CA 93105-5467 Office: Calif Inst Tech Divsn Engring & Applied Sci Pasadena CA 91125-0001 E-mail: sabersky@cox.net.

SABEY, J(OHN) WAYNE, academic administrator, consultant; b. Murray, Utah, Dec. 10, 1939; s. Alfred John and Bertha (Lind) Sabey; m. Marie Bringhurst, Sept. 10, 1964; children: Clark Wayne, Colleen, Carolyn, Natasha Lynne. BA in Asian Studies, Brigham Young U., 1964, MA in Asian History, 1965; PhD in E. Asian History, U. Mich., 1972. Tchg. asst. Brigham Young U., Provo, Utah, 1964-65, rsch. asst., 1965, adj. prof. history, 1988-89, 2002—; rsch. asst. U. Mich., Ann Arbor, 1966; from instr. to asst. prof. history U. Utah, Salt Lake City, 1970-80; v.p. Western Am. Lang. Inst., Salt Lake City, 1980-84, dir., 1984-86, pres., 1986—; exec. v.p. Pacific Rim Bus. Coords., Salt Lake City, 1993—, also bd. dirs., 1993—; dir. Japan Ops. E'OLA Products, Inc., St. George, Utah, 1996-99; MBA program dir. Walden U., Mpls., 1999—2001. Assoc. dir. exch. program U. Utah and Nagoya Broadcasting Network Japan, 1973—79; lectr. in field. Contbr. articles to ency. Sec. to bd. trustees We. Am. Lang. Inst., 1980—86, chmn. bd. trustees, 1986—, Found. Internat. Understanding, 1982—; internat. adv. coun. Salt Lake CC, 1988—94; bd. advisors Consortium Internat. Edn., 1972—77. Recipient Superior award in extemporaneous speaking, 1956; U.S. Nat. Def. Fgn. Lang. fellow, 1965—68, Fulbright-Hays Rsch. fellow, Japan, 1968—69, Horace H. Rackham Sch. Grad. Studies fellow, 1969—70. Mem.: Assn. Asian Studies (gen. chairperson, chairperson arrangements we. conf. 1970—72), Phi Kappa Phi. Avocations: piano, hiking, basketball, stamp collecting/philately, tennis. Home and Office: 8710 Oakwood Park Cir Sandy UT 84094-1800 Home Phone: 801-566-7181; Office Phone: 801-566-7181. Business E-Mail: wayne.sabey@gmail.com.

SABIN, GARY B., real estate executive; b. Provo, Utah, 1954; Degree, Brigham Young U., 1977, Stanford U., 1985. Chmn. bd. dirs., CEO, pres. Excel Legacy Corp., San Diego. Office: Excel Legacy Corporation 23 Mauchly Ste 100 Irvine CA 92618-2330

SABLE, BARBARA KINSEY, retired music educator; b. Astoria, NY, Oct. 6, 1927; d. Albert and Verna (Rowe) Kinsey; m. Arthur J. Sable, Nov. 3, 1973. BA, Coll. Wooster, 1949; MA, Tchrs. Coll. Columbia U., NYC, 1950; DMus, U. Ind., 1966. Office mgr., music dir. Sta. WCAX, Burlington, Vt., 1954; instr. Cottey Coll., 1959-60; asst. prof. N.E. Mo. State U., Kirksville, 1962-64, U. Calif., Santa Barbara, 1964-69; prof. music U. Colo., Boulder, 1969—, prof. emeritus, 1992—. Author: (novels) The Vocal Sound, 1982; contbr. poetry and short stories to lit. jours. Mem.: Colo. Music Tchrs. Assn., AAUP, Nat. Assn. Tchrs. Singing (past state gov., assoc. editor bull.). Democrat. Avocation: poetry. Home: 3430 Ash Ave Boulder CO 80305-3432 Business E-Mail: bks@sable-boulder.com.

SABSAY, DAVID, library director, consultant; b. Waltham, Mass., Sept. 12, 1931; s. Wiegard Isaac and Ruth (Weinstein) S.; m. Helen Glenna Tolliver, Sept. 24,1 966. AB, Harvard U., 1953; BLS, U. Calif., Berkeley, 1955. Circulation dept. supr. Richmond (Calif.) Pub. Library, 1955-56; city libr. Santa Rosa (Calif.) Pub. Library, 1956-65; dir. Sonoma County Library, Santa Rosa, 1965-92; libr. cons., 1992—. Coordinator North Bay Coop. Library System, Santa Rosa, 1960-64; cons. in field, Sebastopol, Calif., 1968—. Contbr. articles to profl. jours. Commendation, Calif. Assn. Library Trustees and Commrs., 1984. Mem. Calif. Library Assn. (pres. 1971, cert. appreciation 1971, 80), ALA. Clubs: Harvard (San Francisco). Home: 667 Montgomery Rd Sebastopol CA 95472-3020 E-mail: dsabsay@sonic.net.

SACCHI, JOHN, film company executive; b. Feb. 14, 1971; m. Suzanne Fritz; 1 child, Owen Bennett. Student, Pepperdine U., Malibu, Calif. Intern with prodr. Chuck Gordon Universal; sr. v.p. prodn. and devel. Lionsgate. Co-prodr.: (films) Confidence, 2003, See No Evil, 2006; prodr.: In The Mix, 2005; exec. prodr.: The Cookout, 2004, Employee of the Month, 2006, Pride, 2007, Rogue, 2007, Lionsgate World Wrestling Entertainment films. Office: Lionsgate 2700 Colorado Ave Santa Monica CA 90404

SACCO, TONY, cinematographer, television director, film director; Prin. ABS Prodns., North Hollywood, Calif. Cinematographer: (TV series) Dream Builders, 1997, Treasures in Your Home, 1999, The Bachelor, 2002, EX-treme Dating, 2002, Last Comic Standing, 2003, Project Runway, 2004—, Project Greenlight 3, 2005; (documentaries) Behind the Action: Stuntmen in the Movies, 2002, Posse, 2003, Great White Shark Uncaged, 2004, Shark Hunter: Chasing the Great White, 2005, Air Guitar Nation, 2006; (films) Save the Mavericks, 2005; dir.: (TV series) R U the Girl, 2005, Tuesday Night Book Club, 2006, Last Comic Standing 4, 2006, Get This Party Started, 2006; prodr.: Project Runway, 2006; dir., prodr.: (TV series) Treasure Hunters, 2006. Office: ABS Prodns 5756 Craner Ave North Hollywood CA 91601-2015 Office Phone: 310-614-6473.

SACK, EDGAR ALBERT, electronics company executive; b. Pitts., Jan. 31, 1930; s. Edgar Albert and Margaret Valentine (Engelmohr) S.; m. Eugenia Ferris, June 7, 1952; children: Elaine Kimberley, Richard Warren. BS, Carnegie-Mellon U., 1951, MS, 1952, PhD, 1954. Dept. mgr. Westinghouse Rsch. Lab., Pitts., 1960-63; engring. mgr. Westinghouse Microelectronics, Balt., 1963-65, ops. mgr., 1965-67, divsn. mgr., 1967-69; div. v.p. Gen. Instrument Corp., Hicksville, NY, 1969-73, group v.p., 1973-77, sr. v.p., 1977-84; pres., CEO Zilog Inc., Campbell, Calif., 1984-98, also chmn. bd. dirs.; pres. Productivity Assocs., Coronado, Calif.; founder, chmn. CDT, Inc., San Jose, Calif., 1998-99. Bd. dirs. Enfo-Web, Inc., Mountainview, Calif., LXi, Inc., Mountainview; vis. com. elec. engring. dept. Carnegie-Mellon U., 1969-74; mem. indsl. adv. coun. SUNY, Stony Brook, 1979-83; mem. adv. com. on solid state electronics Poly. Inst. Tech., 1981-83. Author: Forward Controllership Business Management System, 1989, 2nd edit., 1993, Development of the Coronado Shores-A History, 2005; patentee in field. Mem. Action Com. L.I, 1982-84; bd. dir. Coronado Shores Assn. # 7, 2000-, landscaping and recreational com., 2000-, chair, 2002-03, treas., 2004-09; mem. Sharp Coronado Hosp. Aux.; sec. San Diego Imperial Coun. of Vols., 2002; bd. dirs. Coronado Hosp. Found., 2003-04, chair projects and allocations com., 2004. Recipient 2nd Ann. Hammerschlag Disting. Lectr. award Carnegie Mellon U., 1995. Fellow IEEE, Poly. Inst. Tech.; mem. Semicondr. Industry Assn. (dir. 1982-85), Carnegie Mellon Alumni Assn. (Merit award 1981), Eta Kappa Nu (Outstanding Young Elec. Engr. 1959), Huntington Yacht Club (vice comdr. 1977), Tau Beta Pi (finalist San Francisco Entrepreneur of Yr. award 1991), Phi Kappa Phi, Satern & Cero Emergency Svcs. Orgns. Home and Office: 1780 Avenida Del Mundo Unit 404 Coronado CA 92118-4011 Personal E-mail: esack@pacbell.net.

SACK, SEYMOUR, nuclear scientist; b. 1929; BS in Physics, MS in Physics, PhD in Physics, Yale U. Scientist Lawrence Livermore Nat. Lab., 1955—90, lab. assoc., 1990—. Specialist in nuclear weapon design; participant JASON (study on maintaining nuclear stockpile under a comprehensive test ban), 1995. Recipient Fleet Ballistic Missile Achievement award, Strategic Sys. Program, US Navy, 1997, Enrico Fermi award, US Dept. Energy, 2003. Office: Lawrence Livermore Nat Lab 7000 East Ave Livermore CA 94550

SACKETT, JOHN IRVIN, nuclear engineer; b. Spokane, Wash., May 5, 1943; s. Melvin and Mary Sackett; m. Karen King, June 15, 1965; children: Brent, Erik. BSME, U. Idaho, 1965; PhD in Nuclear Engring., U. Ariz., 1970. Registered profl. engr., Idaho. Asst. nuclear engr. EBR-II ops. Argonne Nat. Lab., Idaho Falls, Idaho, 1970-72, nuclear engr., 1973-74, sect. mgr. EBR-II ops. analysis, 1974-82, assoc. divsn. dir., 1982-89, sr. nuclear engr., 1983, mgr. EBR-II plant testing in support of IFR program, 1986, IFR divsn. dir., 1989-91, dep. assoc. lab. dir., 1991—. Bd. dirs. United Way, Bonneville County, Idaho, CHC Found., 1996; past squadron comdr. Civil Air Patrol. Recipient U. Chgo. award for Disting. Performance at Argonne Nat. Lab., 1976, 78, U. Idaho Outstanding Alumni award "Silver and Gold," 1996, ANA Spl. award for Pioneering Work in Passive Reactor Safety, Am. Nuclear Soc., 1991, Walker Cisler award for Disting. Work in Breeder Reactor Design and Operation, 1996. Fellow Am. Nuc. Soc. (asst. to nat. pres. 1989-90, chmn. Idaho sect. 1986-87, nat. bd. dirs. 1986-88, nat. chmn. profl. divsns. com. 1988-89, nat. chmn. planning com. 1987-88). Home: 4762 Aspen Ln Bozeman MT 59715-9601 Office: Argonne National Laboratory PO Box 1625 Idaho Falls ID 83403-1625

SACKETT, SUSAN DEANNA, writer; b. NYC, Dec. 18, 1943; adopted d. Maxwell and Gertrude Selma (Kugel) S. BA in Edn., U. Fla., 1964, MEd, 1965. Tchr. Dade County Schs., Miami, Fla., 1966-68, L.A. City Schs., 1968-69; asst. publicist, comml. coord. NBC-TV, Burbank, Calif., 1970-73; asst. to Gene Roddenberry, creator Star Trek, 1974-91; prodn. assoc. TV series Star Trek: The Next Generation, 1987-91, writer, 1990-91. Lectr. and guest spkr. Star Trek convs. in U.S., Eng., Australia, 1974-. Author, editor: Letters to Star Trek, 1977; co-author: Star Trek Speaks, The Making of Star Trek--The Motion Picture, 1979, You Can Be a Game Show Contestant and Win, 1982, Say Goodnight Gracie, 1986; author: The Hollywood Reporter Book of Box Office Hits, 1990, 2d edit., 1996, Prime Time Hits, 1993, Hollywood Sings, 1995, Inside Trek: My Secret Life with Star Trek Creator Gene Roddenberry, 2002. Mem. ACLU, Writers Guild Am., Am. Humanist Assn., Humanist Soc. Greater Phoenix (pres. 2000—), Mensa, Sierra Club, Am. Humanist Assn. (bd. dir., 2005—). Democrat.

SACKS, DAVID O., Internet company executive, film production company executive; m. Jacqueline Tortorice, 2007. Grad., Stanford U., 1990—94; JD, U. Chgo., 1995—98. Mgmt. cons. McKinsey, 1999; COO PayPal, 1999—2002; founder, CEO Room 9 Entertainment LLC, 2002—; co-founder, CEO Geni, Inc., LA, 2006—. Named one of 10 Producers to Watch, Variety, 2005. Office: Geni Inc 9255 Sunset Blvd Ste 727 West Hollywood CA 90069

SACKS, ROBERT A., lawyer; b. Long Beach, NY, 1957; AB, Harvard U., 1979; JD, U. Tex., 1982. Bar: NY 1983, Calif. 1990. Assoc. Sullivan & Cromwell, NYC, 1984—90, ptnr. litig. LA, 1990—, now ptnr.-in-charge LA office. Mem.: ABA. Office: Sullivan & Cromwell 1888 Century Pk E Los Angeles CA 90067-1725 Office Phone: 310-712-6600. Office Fax: 310-712-8800. Business E-Mail: sacksr@sullcrom.com.

SACKTON, FRANK JOSEPH, public affairs educator; b. Chgo., Aug. 11, 1912; m. June Dorothy Raymond, Sept. 21, 1940. Student, Northwestern U., Evanston, Ill., 1936, Yale U., New Haven, Conn., 1946, U. Md., College Park, 1951—52; BS, U. Md., 1970; grad., Command and Gen. Staff Coll., 1942, Armed Forces Staff Coll., 1949, Nat. War Coll., 1954; MPA, Ariz. State U., 1976, DHL (hon.), 1996. Mem. 131st Inf. Regt., Ill. N.G., 1929-40; commd. 2d lt. U.S. Army, 1934, advanced through grades to lt. gen., 1967; brigade plans and ops. officer (33d Inf. Div.), 1941, PTO, 1943-45; div. signal officer, 1942-43; div. intelligence officer, 1944; div. plans and ops. officer, 1945; sec. to gen. staff for Gen. MacArthur Tokyo, 1947-48; bn. comdr. 30th Inf. Regt., 1949-50; mem. spl. staff Dept. Army, 1951; plans and ops. officer Joint Task Force 132, PTO, 1952; comdr. Joint Task Force 7, Marshall Islands, 1953; mem. gen. staff Dept. Army, 1954-55; with Office Sec. Def., 1956; comdr. 18th Inf. Regt., 1957-58; chief staff 1st Inf. Div., 1959; chief army Mil. Mission to Turkey, 1960-62; comdr. XIV Army Corps, 1963; dep. dir. plans Joint Chiefs Staff, 1964-66; army general staff mil. ops., 1966-67; comptroller of the army, 1967-70; ret., 1970; spl. asst. for fed./state relations Gov. Ariz., 1971-75; chmn. Ariz. Programming and Coordinating Com. for Fed. Programs, 1971-75; lectr. Am. Grad. Sch. Internat. Mgmt., 1973-77; vis. asst. prof., lectr. public affairs Ariz. State U., Tempe, 1976-78; founding dean Ariz. State U. Coll. Public Programs, 1979-80; prof. public affairs Ariz. State U., 1980—, finance educator, v.p. bus. affairs, 1981-83, dep. dir. intercollegiate athletics, 1984-85, dir. strategic planning, 1987-88. Contbr. articles to public affairs and mil. jours. Mem. Ariz. Steering Com. for Restoration of the State Capitol, 1974-75, Ariz. State Personnel Bd., 1978-83, Ariz. Regulatory Coun., 1981-93. Decorated D.S.M., Silver Star, also Legion of Merit with 4 oak leaf clusters, Bronze Star with 2 oak leaf clusters, Air medal, Army Commendation medal with 1 oak leaf cluster, Combat Inf. badge. Mem.: Ariz. Acad. Public Adminstrn., Army-Navy Club (Washington), Arizona Country Club (Phoenix), Pi Alpha Alpha (pres. chpt. 1976—82). Home: 12000 N 90th St Unit 3072 Scottsdale AZ 85260-8643 Office: Ariz State U Sch Pub Affairs Tempe AZ 85287-0603 Business E-Mail: frank-sackton@asu.edu.

SADOWSKI, RAYMOND, electronics executive; married. BS in Acctg., Hunter Coll., NY, 1976. Acct. F. Schumacher; corp. acctg. supr. Avnet, Inc., 1978, acctg. mgr., asst. contr., contr., 1986, v.p., 1987—92, sr. v.p., 1992—, CFO, 1993—, asst. sec. Office: Avnet Inc 2211 S 47th St Phoenix AZ 85034-6403 Office Phone: 480-643-2000. Office Fax: 480-643-7370.

SADUN, ALFREDO ARRIGO, neuro-ophthalmologist, scientist, educator; b. New Orleans, Oct. 23, 1950; s. Elvio H. and Lina (Ottoleghi) S.; m. Debra Leigh Rice, Mar. 18, 1978; children: Rebecca Eli, Elvio Aaron, Benjamin Maxwell. BS, MIT, 1972; PhD, Albert Einstein Med. Sch., Bronx, NY, 1976, MD, 1978. Intern Huntington Meml. Hosp. U. So. Calif., Pasadena, 1978—79; resident Harvard U. Med. Sch., Boston, 1979—82, HEED Found. fellow in neuro-ophthalmology Mass. Eye and Ear Inst., 1982—83, instr. ophthalmology, 1983, asst. prof. ophthalmology, 1984; dir. residential tng. U. So. Calif. Dept. Ophthalmology, LA, 1984-85, 90—; asst. prof. ophthalmology and neurosurgery U. So. Calif., LA, 1984—87, assoc. prof., 1987—90, full prof., 1990—, mem. internal review bd., F. Thornton endowed chair, prof. vision rsch., 2000—. Prin. investigator Howe Lab. Harvard U., Boston, 1981-84, E. Doheny Eye Inst., L.A., 1984—; examiner Am. Bd. Ophthalmology; mem. Nat. Residency Rev. Com. for Accreditations, 1993—, chmn., 1998—; mem. internal rev. bd. U. So. Calif.; mem. sci. exec. bd. K. Rasmussen Found.; mem. sci. adv. bd. Internat. Found. for Optic Nerve Diseases. Author: Optics for Ophthalmologists, 1988, New Methods of Sensory Visual Testing, 1989, 4 books; editor: Ophthalmology, 2000, Neuroprotection: Implications for Eye Disease, 2001; contbr. 230 articles to profl. jours., 70 chpts. to books. Recipient Pecan D. award, 1988—92, Rsch. to Prevent Blindness Sr. Investigator award, 1996—97, 1996, Lighthouse Internat. Pizart award, 1999, James Adams scholar, 1990—91, sr. investigator award, 1999—2000, Decade medal, Cuban Nat. Acad. Scis., Bradley Straatsma award, Am. Acad. Ophthalmology, 2003, Silver Fellow award, Assn. Rsch. Vision & Ophthalmogy, 2009. Fellow Am. Acad. Ophthalmology Neuro-Ophthalmologists, Assn. Rsch. in Vision and Ophthalmology; mem. NIH (Med. Scientists Tng. award 1972-78), Am. Assn. Anatomists, Assn. Univ. Prof. Ophthalmology (assoc.), Am. Bd. Ophthalmology (rep. to residency rev. com. 1994-2001), Soc. to Prevent Blindness, Nat. Eye Inst. (New Investigator Rsch. award 1983-86, rsch. grants 1988-91, 93-2002), Soc. Neuroscis., N.Am. Neuro-Ophthal. Soc. (chmn. membership com. 1990—, v.p. 1994—). Avocation: writing. Home: 2478 Adair St San Marino CA 91108-2610

SAEGER, REBECCA, advertising executive; B in Psychology and Polit. Sci., Muhlenberg Coll., 1976; MBA, U. Pa., 1980. Various positions including sr. v.p., group dir. for Lever Bros. and Am. Express Ogilvy & Mather, NY, 1980—91; sr. v.p., group mgmt. supr., dir. account mgmt. Foote, Cone & Belding, San Francisco, 1991—97; exec. v.p. advt. and brand mktg. svcs. Visa USA, 1997—2001; exec. v.p. brand mgmt. and mktg. comm. Charles Schwab Corp., San Francisco, 2004—06, exec. v.p., chief mktg. officer, 2006—. Mem. exec. mgmt. com. Visa USA. Mem. mktg. com. San Francisco Symphony; mem. adv. bd. World Congress Sports. Mem.: Assn. Nat. Advertisers (bd. dirs.). Office: The Charles Schwab Corp 101 Montgomery St San Francisco CA 94104

SAFKA, JIM, information technology executive, investment services company executive; m. Mandy Safka; 2 children. BS in Acctg., U. So. Ca.; MBA, J.L. Kellogg School of Management, Northwestern U. Brand and product mgmt. positions Alberto-Culver, Inc., Warner Bros., Paramount Pictures; product mgr., Quicken Financial Planner and Quicken.com Intuit; positions up to v.p., mktg. E*Trade Fin. Corp., 1997—2002; v.p., gen. mgr. e-commerce AT&T Wireless, 2002—04; CEO Match.com, 2004—07, Primal Ventures, San Francisco, 2007—, IAC/InterActive Corp. (Ask.com), 2008—. Office: IAC Search & Media 555 12th St Ste 500 Oakland CA 94607

SAFONOV, MICHAEL GEORGE, electrical engineering educator, consultant; b. Pasadena, Calif., Nov. 1, 1948; s. George Michael and Ruth Garnet (Ware) S.; m. Nancy Kelshaw Schorn, Aug. 31, 1968 (div. Oct. 1983); 1 child, Alexander; m. Janet Sunderland, Feb. 25, 1985; 1 child, Peter. BSEE, MSEE, MIT, 1971, EE, 1976, PhDEE, 1977. Electronic engr. Air Force Cambridge Rsch. Lab., Hanscom AFB, Mass., 1968-71; rsch. asst. MIT, Cambridge, 1975-77; prof. elec. engring. U. So. Calif., LA, 1977—, assoc. chmn. dept., 1989-93, vice chmn. engring. faculty coun., 2001—02, chmn. engring. faculty coun., 2003—04, Vis. scholar Cambridge (Eng.) U., 1983-84, Imperial Coll., London, 1987, Calif. Inst. Tech., Pasadena, 1990-91; cons. Honeywell Systems and Rsch. Ctr., Mpls., 1978-83, Space Systems div. TRW, Redondo Beach, Calif., 1984, Northrop Aircraft, Hawthorne, Calif., 1985-91, also numerous others. Author: Stability and Robustness of Multivariable Feedback Systems (hon. mention Phi Beta Kappa 1981); co-author: (book and software) Robust-Control Toolbox, 1988; assoc. editor IEEE Trans. on Automatic Control, 1985-87, Internat. Jour. Robust and Nonlinear Control, 1989-93, Sys. and Control Letters, 1995—. Awards com. chair Am. Automatic Control Coun., 1993-95. Lt. (j.g.) USNR, 1972-75. Rsch. grantee Air Force Office Sci. Rsch., 1978—, NSF, 1982-84. Fellow IEEE, IFAC; mem. AIAA (sr.), Common Cause. Republican. Office: U So Calif Dept EE Sys MC 2563 3740 McClintock Ave # 310 Los Angeles CA 90089-2563 Home Phone: 310-551-0517; Office Phone: 213-740-4455. Business E-Mail: msafonov@usc.edu.

SAGAWA, YONEO, horticulturist, educator; b. Olaa, Hawaii, Oct. 11, 1926; s. Chikatada and Mume (Kuno) S.; m. Masayo Yamamoto, May 24, 1962 (dec. Apr. 1988); children: Penelope Toshiko, Irene Teruko. AB, Washington U., St. Louis, 1950, MA, 1952; PhD, U. Conn., Storrs, 1956. Postdoctoral rsch. assoc. biology Brookhaven Nat. Lab., Upton, NY, 1955—57, guest in biology, 1958; asst. prof., then assoc. prof. U. Fla., 1957—64; dir. undergrad. sci. ednl. rsch. participation program NSF, 1964; cons. biosatellite project NASA, 1966—67; prof. horticulture U. Hawaii, 1964—; dir. Lyon Arboretum, 1967—91; assoc. dir. Hawaiian Sci. Fair, 1966—67, dir., 1967—68; rsch. assoc. in biology U. Calif., Berkeley, 1970—71; rsch. assoc. Bot. Rsch. Inst. of Tex., 1993—, Hawaii Tropical Bot. Garden, 1995—;

external assessor U. Pertanian, Malaysia, 1994—; rsch. affiliate Bishop Mus., Honolulu, 2007—. Mem. Internat. Orchid Commn. on Classification, Nomenclature and Registration; fellow Inst. voor Toepassing van Atoomenergerie in de Landbouw, U. Agr., Wageningen, The Netherlands, 1979-80; mem. sci. adv. bd. Nat. Tropical Bot. Garden, Kauai, Hawaii; councilor Las Cruces Bot. Garden, Costa Rica; cons. FAO, Singapore, 1971, USAID-Agribus. Assistance Program, Vols. in Overseas Coop. Assistance, UN Devel. Program-UN Internat. Short Term Adv. Resources; dir. Hawaii Tropical Bot. Garden; hon. scientist Rural Devel. Adminstrn., Republic of Korea, 1998—; cons. Fiji-N.Z. Bus. Coun., 1996, 97, 98, 99, 2000; cons. IRETA, Samoa, 1997, 98, 2003, 06, 08; cons. Nat. Hort. Rsch. Inst., Suwon, Republic of Korea, 1998, 2000, UN FAO, 2008 Editor: Hawaii Orchid Jour., 1972-99, Pacific Orchid Soc. Bull., 1966-71; mem. editl. bd. Allertonia, 1976; mem. editl. adv. bd. Jour. Orchid Soc. India, 2002—; contbr. numerous articles to profl. jours. Trustee Friends of Honolulu Bot. Gardens, 1973-99. Recipient Disting. Svc. award South Fla. Orchid Soc., 1968, Grand prize for Poster, 1st Nagoya Internat. Orchid Show, 1990, Cert. of Achievement Garden Club Am., 1995, Digest Doer's Profile, 2000, Gold award Hawaii Orchid Growers Assn., 1996; grantee Am. Orchid Soc., Atomic Energy Commn., NIH, HEW, Inst. Mus. Svcs., Stanley Smith Hort. Trust, Honolulu Orchid Soc. Fellow Am. Orchid Soc. (hon. life, Achievement Gold medal 1999); mem. AAAS, Internat. Assn. Hort. Sci., Am. Assn. Hort. Sci., Am. Inst. for Biol. Scis., Bot. Soc. Am., Hawn Bot. Soc. (past v.p.), Internat. Assn. Plant Tissue Culture, Internat. Palm Soc., Am. Anthurium Soc. (hon. life), Pacific Orchid Soc. (trustee 1994), Kaimuki Orchid Soc. (hon. life), Orchid Growers Hawaii (hon. life), Honolulu Orchid Soc. (hon., life), Lyon Arboretum Assn. (trustee 1974-91), Garden Club Honolulu (hon., life), Aloha Bonsai Club, Sigma Xi, Gamma Sigma Delta, Phi Kappa Phi (past pres., v.p., councillor U. Hawaii chpt.). Democrat. Office: U Hawaii TPSS St John Rm 102 3190 Maile Way Honolulu HI 96822-2279 Fax: 808-956-3894. Business E-Mail: yoneo@hawaii.edu.

SAGE-GAVIN, EVA MARIE, retail executive; b. Boston, Sept. 26, 1958; d. Ross Francis and Theresa Veronica (Bufalo) S.; m. Dennis Gavin. BS in Indsl. and Labor Rels., Cornell U., Ithaca, NY, 1980. Affirmative action pers. specialist Xerox Corp., Washington, 1980-81, compensation analyst Rochester, NY, 1981-82, sales recruiter Boston, 1982, employment mgr., 1983, systems mktg. rep., 1983-85, pers. mgr. LA, 1985—86, human resources mgr. Irvine, Calif., 1986; dir. human resources PepsiCo, 1991, v.p. corp. human resources Taco Bell; sr. v.p. human resources Disney Consumer Products, 1997—2000, Sun Microsystems, Inc., 2000—03; exec. v.p. human resources and corp. comm. Gap Inc., 2003—. Mem. career adv. bd. Emmanuel Coll., Boston, 1983-85. Named one of Top 25 Most Powerful Women in HR, HR Exec. mag., 2005. Mem. Am. Soc. Pers. Adminstrn., Women in Mgmt., Xerox Women's Network (edn. com. 1988), Kappa Kappa Gamma. Democrat. Roman Catholic. Avocations: skiing, travel, boating, sailing, aerobics. Office: Gap Inc 2 Folsom St San Francisco CA 94105 Office Phone: 650-952-4400. Office Fax: 415-427-2553.

SAGER, KELLI L., lawyer; b. 1960; Attended, U. Southern Calif., 1977—81; BA in Polit. Sci. and Journalism, West Ga. Coll., 1981; JD, U. Utah Sch. Law, 1985. Bar: Calf. 1985. Adj. prof. U. Southern Calif. Law Sch., 2002; ptnr. Davis Wright Tremaine LLP, LA. Mem. adv. com. Donald W. Reynolds Nat. Ctr. for Courts and Media, Nat. Jud. Coll., 2000—; mem. internat. adv. bd. Nat. Inst. Entertainment and Media Law, Southwestern U. Law, 2001—; mem. bd. dirs. Pub. Counsel, 2001—; mem. atty. com. Nat. Ctr. for State Courts, 2002—; bd. mem. LA Copyright Soc., 2002—, treas., 2005—. Bd. dirs. LA Youth News, 1995—2001. Recipient ACLU First Amendment award, 1996, adv. award, Calif. First Amendment Coalition, 1996, Freedom of Info. award, Soc. Prof. Journalists, 1996, First Amendment award, LA Youth/LA Times, 1998; named one of 45 Lawyers Under 45, Am. Lawyer mag., 1995, 40 Professionals Under 40, LA Bus. Jour., 1996, 50 Top Lawyers in LA, 1997, Lawyers of Yr., Calif. Lawyer mag., 1997, The 100 Most Influential Lawyers in Calif., LA Daily Jour., 1998—99, 2001—04, Top 50 Women Litigators in Country, Nat. Law Jour., 2001, 500 Leading Lawyers in Am., Lawdragon, 2005, 500 Leading Litigators in Am., 2006, America's Leading Bus. Lawyers, Chambers USA, 2005—06, Top 75 Women Litigators in Calif., Daily Jour., 2005—07, Southern Calif. Super Lawyers, 2007, The 50 Most Influential Women Lawyers in Am., Nat. Law Jour., 2007, 100 Power Lawyers, Hollywood Reporter, 2007; named to Best Lawyers in Am., 1997—99, 2000, 2003, 2005—07. Mem.: ABA (western divsn. chair Forum on Comm. Law 2002—, co-chair litig. sect., 1st amendment com. 2005—), Order of the Coif. Office: Davis Wright Tremaine LLP Ste 2400 865 S Figueroa St Los Angeles CA 90017-2566 Office Phone: 213-633-6800. Office Fax: 213-633-6899. Business E-Mail: kellisager@dwt.com.

SAGER, PHILIP TRAVIS, pharmaceutical executive, cardiologist, researcher; b. NYC, Jan. 23, 1956; s. Clifford Julius and Ruth (Levy) Sager; m. Linda Sager. BS in Chemistry and Biology, MIT, 1977; MD, Yale U., 1982. Diplomate Am. Bd. Internal Medicine, Am. Bd. Cardiology, Am. Bd. Cardiac Electrophysiology. Resident, fellow in cardiology and cardiac electrophysiology Yale U., New Haven, 1982—88; asst. prof. medicine Sch. Medicine, U. So. Calif., LA, 1988-90, asst. dir. electrophysiology, 1988-90, dir. Pacemaker Ctr., 1988-90; asst. prof. medicine Sch. Medicine, UCLA, 1990-96, assoc. tenured prof. medicine, 1996—2001; dir. cardiac electrophysiology UCLA/West LA VA Med. Ctr., 1990—2001; dir. cardiac rsch. Schering-Plough Rsch. Inst., 2001—04; clin. prof. medicine UMDNJ Med. Sch., 2002—07; sr. dir., U.S. lead physician Astrazeneca Inc., Wilmington, Del., 2004—, med. sci. sr. dir., 2006—08, exec. dir., CV rsch., 2006—08, global QT strategy leader, 2006—08; chief med. officer CardioDX, 2008—. Mem. cardiology adv. com. VA, Washington, 1990-94; cons. electrophysiology ACGME, Chgo., 1995-01; vis. prof. Kern Med. Ctr., Bakersfield, Calif., 1991, 94, U. Iowa Sch. Medicine, 1994, Northwestern U. Sch. Medicine, 1994, Yale U. Sch. Medicine, 1995, U. Calif., San Francisco, 1996; PhRMA topic leader, ICH E14 Expert Working Group 2002-05; PhRMA lead ICH E14 Implementation Group, 2005-; co-chair sci. com., mem. exec. com. FDA CV Safety Rsch. Consortium, 2005-06; chair Internat. DIA-FDA-HRS-QT/CV Safety Conf., 2006-08, FDA PhRMA Evidentiary Standards Biomarkers, 2007—; cons. pharm. cos.; lectr. in field. Contbr. chpts. to books, numerous articles to profl. jours.; reviewer sci. jours. and sci. mags. Recipient many rsch. grants, including Am. Heart Assn., 1996. Fellow ACP, Am. Heart Assn., Am. Coll. Cardiology, Heart Rhythm Soc.; mem. Am. Fedn. Clin. Rsch., Nat. Assn. Pacing and Electrophysiology (program dirs. com. 1992-01, govt. com. 1994-01, co-chair program dirs. com. 1997-01), Phi Beta Kappa, Alpha Omega Alpha. Avocations: travel, bicycling, scuba diving, reading, movies. Office: CardioDX Inc 2500 Faber Pl Palo Alto CA 94303 Office Phone: 650-475-2744. Personal E-mail: psager@alum.mit.edu. Business E-Mail: psager@cardiodx.com.

SAGNESS, RICHARD LEE, education educator, former academic dean; b. Rock Rapids, Iowa, Jan. 9, 1937; s. David Harold and Joyce Morrow (Carlson) S.; m. Donna Jayne Lanxon, Feb. 18, 1956; children: Debbi Van Vooren, Becky Hardy, Beth Sagness Higbee. BA, U. No. Iowa, 1961; MS, Emporia State U., 1965; PhD, Ohio State U., 1970; grad. Inst. for Higher Edn. Mgmt., Harvard U., 1977. Tchr. biology Cen. High Sch., Sioux City, Iowa, 1961-66; lectr. biology Emporia (Kans.) State U., 1966-67; info. analyst Ohio State U., 1967-70; asst. prof. sci. edn. U. S.D., Vermillion, 1970-72, assoc. prof., 1972-75, coord. sci. edn., 1970-75; prof. sci. edn., assoc. dean Sch. Edn. U. S.D., Vermillion, 1975-79; prof. edn. Coll. Edn. Idaho State U., Pocatello, 1979-99, dean Coll. Edn., 1979-89, dir. clin. experiences and student svcs., 1993-99, prof. emeritus, 1999—; substitute mem. for Senator Edgar Malepeal Idaho State Senate, 2009—. Past mem. Idaho Profl. Stds. Commn.; faculty rep. to bd. dirs. Idaho State U. Found., 1992-97; mem. Idaho Sch.-to-Work Collaborative Team, 1994-97. Contbr. articles to profl. jours. Bd. dirs. Vermillion Devel. Corp., 1974-78, pres., 1976-77; bd. dirs. Pocatello United Fund, 1976-79, 82-83, v.p., 1982-83, pres., 1985-86, Bannock Meml. Hosp. Found., v. chmn. 1999—. With U.S. Army, 1955-57. Mem. Idaho Assn. Colls. Tchr. Edn. (pres. 1984-88), Am. Assn. Colls. of Tchr. Edn. (rep., chairperson govtl. rels. com. 1988-89, bd. dirs. 1988-92), Pocatello C. of C. (bd. dirs. 1983-89, pres. 1987-88), Tchr. Edn. Coun. State Colls. and Univs. (exec. coun. 1988-90), N.W. Assn. Schs. and Colls. (commn. on schs. 1995—, bd. trustees 1997—), Rotary (bd. dirs. local club 1988-89, team leader study exch. team to Sweden 1991, pres.-elect 1997-98), Masons, Order Eastern Star (past patron), Rotary (pres. Pocatello club 1998-99, dist. 5400 found. scholarship com. 1997—), Phi Delta Kappa (past pres.). Democrat. Office: Idaho State U PO Box 8059 Pocatello ID 83209-0001

SAHATJIAN, MANIK, retired nurse, retired psychologist; b. Tabris, Iran, July 24, 1921; came to U.S., 1951; d. Dicran and Shushanig (Der-Galustian) Mnatzaganian; m. George Sahatjian, Jan. 21, 1954; children: Robert, Edwin. Nursing Cert., Am. Mission Hosps.-Boston U., 1954; BA in Psychology, San Jose State U., 1974, MA in Psychology, 1979. RN Calif. Head nurse Am. Mission Hosp., Tabris, 1945-46; charge nurse Banke-Melli Hosp., Tehran, 1946-51; vis. nurse Vis. Nurse Assn., Oakland, Calif., 1956-57; research asst. Stanford U., 1979-81, Palo Alto (Calif.) Med. Research Found., 1981-84; documentation supr. Bethesda Convalescent Ctr., Los Gatos, Calif., 1985-86; sr. outreach worker City of Fremont (Calif.) Human Svcs., 1987-90, case mgr., 1990-97; ret., 1997. Guest rsch. asst. NASA Ames Lab., Mountain View, Calif., summers 1978, 79. Author (with others) psychol. research reports. Mentor elem. sch. children, 1997-2002; pro bono tchg./counseling for srs. who are home bound, Bay Area, Calif., 1999—; pro bono tchr. peer counseling trainers for srs. Armenian Cmty. Santa Clara, Calif., St. Andrew Ch. Fulbright scholar, 1951; Iran Found. scholar, 1953; Morgan-Segal scholar for peer counseling tng., 1998. Mem. AAUW, Western Psychol. Assn., Am. Assn. Sr. Counseling. Democrat. Mem. St. Andrew Armenian Church. Achievements include fluency in Armenian, Farsi, Turkish; familiarity in Spanish, Russian, French langs. Avocations: painting, classic dance. Home: 2 Crestline Dr Apt 3 San Francisco CA 94131-1422

SAIFER, MARK GARY PIERCE, pharmaceutical executive; b. Phila., Sept. 16, 1938; s. Albert and Sylvia (Jolles) S.; m. Phyllis Lynne Trommer, Jan. 28, 1961 (dec.); children: Scott David, Alandria Gail; m. Merry R. Sherman, June 26, 1994. AB, U. Pa., 1960; PhD, U. Calif., Berkeley, 1966. Acting asst. prof. zoology U. Calif., Berkeley, 1966, fellow, 1967-68; sr. cancer rsch. scientist Roswell Park Meml. Inst., Buffalo, 1968-70; lab. dir. Diagnostic Data Inc., Palo Alto, Calif., 1970-78; v.p. DDI Pharms., Inc., Mountain View, Calif., 1978-94, Oxis Internat., Inc., 1994-95; v.p., sci. dir. Mountain View Pharms., Inc., Menlo Park, Calif., 1996—, also bd. dirs. Lectr., expert witness in field. Author, patentee in field:, mem. editl. bd.: Current Pharm. Biotechnology Jour. Mem. AAAS (life), Am. Assn. Pharm. Scientists, Parenteral Drug Assn. Office: Mountain View Pharms Inc 3475 Edison Way Ste S Menlo Park CA 94025-1821 E-mail: saifer@mvpharm.com.

ST. GEORGE, WILLIAM ROSS, lawyer, retired naval officer, consultant; b. Southport, NC, Nov. 19, 1924; s. William B. and Ila (Ross) St. G.; m. Emma Louise Bridger, June 10, 1950; children—Victoria Butler, William Ross, Susan Bridger. BS, U.S. Naval Acad., 1946; JD, George Washington U., 1953. Bar: D.C. 1953, U.S. Supreme Ct. 1964, Calif. 1980. Commd. ensign U.S. Navy, 1946, advanced through grades to vice adm., 1973; comdg. officer U.S.S. Josephus Daniels, 1969-70; comdr. Cruiser-Destroyer Flotilla 11, also comdr. Cruiser-Destroyer Flotilla 3, 1973; dep. and chief staff to comdr.-in-chief U.S. Pacific Fleet, 1973-76; comdr. Naval Surface Force, U.S. Pacific Fleet, 1976-79, ret., 1979; sole practice San Diego, 1980—. Decorated D.S.M. with oak leaf cluster, Legion of Merit, Bronze Star. Presbyterian. Home: 862 San Antonio Pl San Diego CA 92106-3057 E-mail: williamstgeorge@aol.com.

SAINT-JACQUES, BERNARD, linguistics educator; b. Montreal, Que., Can., Apr. 26, 1928; s. Albert and Germaine (Lefebvre) Saint-J.; m. Marguerite Fauquenoy. MA, Sophia U., Tokyo, 1962; MS, Georgetown U., 1964; Doctorat es Lettres and Scis. Humaines, Paris U., 1975. Asst. prof. linguistics U. B.C., Vancouver, Canada, 1967—69, assoc. prof., 1969-78, prof., 1978-90, prof. emeritus, 1991—; prof. Aichi U., Japan, 1990—2003. Mem. U.S. Citizen Amb. Program, Order of the Rising Sun Author: Structural Analysis of Modern Japanese, 1971, Aspects sociolinguistiques du bilinguisme canadien, 1976, Language and Ethnic Relations, 1979, Japanese Studies in Canada, 1985, Studies in Language and Culture, 1995; editor: Intercultural Communication Studies, 1998; co-editor: Contrasting Political Institutions, 1997, (with M. Iwasaki) Democratic Viability in Politics, 2000. Leave fellow Can. Council, 1974; profl. fellow Japan Found., 1981; research fellow French Govt., 1982, Ohira Programme, Japan, 1983 Fellow Royal Soc. Can. Acad., Internat. Acad. Intercultural Rsch.; mem. Linguistic Soc. Am., Can. Soc. Asian Studies, Can. Linguistics Assn., Sietar Japan. Office Phone: 604-987-6319. Personal E-mail: bsaintj@telus.net.

ST. JOHN, KRISTOFF, actor; b. NYC, July 15, 1966; s. Christopher Kristoff and Maria St. John; m. Mia St. John, 1991 (div. 1995); children: Julian, Paris; m. Allana Nadal, Nov. 24, 2001; 1 child, Lola. Studied, Actor's Studio, LA. Owner Moonboy Inc. prodn. com. Actor: (TV series) The Young and the Restless, 1991— (Outstanding Younger Actor in Drama Series, Daytime Emmys, 1992, Outstanding Actor in Daytime Drama Series, NAACP Image Awards, 1994, 1995, 1996, 1997, 2003, 2004, Outstanding Actor in Daytime Drama Series, NAACP Image award, 2007, 2008); guest appearances (TV series) Happy Days, 1976, The Cosby Show, 1984, A Different World, 1988, Jake and the Fatman, Diagnosis Murder, 1994, Hanging with Mr. Cooper, 1994—95, Martin, 1996, Suddenly Susan, 1998, Family Matters, 1998, For Your Love, 1999, Get Real, 1999; actor: (TV films) Roots II: The Next Generation, 1979, Beulah Land, 1980, Atlanta Child Murders, 1985, Finish Line, 1989; (films) The Champ, 1979, Avatar; dir.: (TV series) CBS Soap Break; host (fitness video) Kick Butt, 1999, host, prodr. (video) Backstage Pass. Avocations: movies, guitar.

ST. JOHN, ROBERT M., lawyer; b. Jackson, Mich., July 16, 1932; BA, Yale U., 1954, LLB, 1959. Bar: N.Mex. 1959. Ptnr. Rodey, Dickason, Sloan, Akin & Robb PA, Albuquerque. Named one of best lawyers in Am., 2003—06. Fellow: Am. Coll. Mortgage Atty. 1995, American College of Real Estate Lawyers 1989 (state chmn. 1987—92, state chmn. fiduciary litig. com. 1987—92), Am. Coll. Trust & Estate Counsel; mem.: State Bar N.Mex. (chmn. adv. opinions com. 1983—96, com. women & the profession 1991—2000, chmn. lawyers care pro bono adv. com. 1996—99, com. legal svc. & programs 1996—, com. Supreme Ct. code profl. conduct 1997—2002, Supreme Ct. self represented litigants working group 2000, chmn. elder law com. 2006—, Outstanding Contribution Award 1984, Distinguished Svc. Award 1990, Outstanding Contribution Award 1992, Distinguished Svc. Award 1994, Outstanding Contribution Award 1996, Pro Bono Project Award 1998), Albuquerque Bar Assn. 1968, ABA. Office: Rodey Dickason Sloan Akin & Robb PA 201 Third St NW Ste 2200 PO Box 1888 Albuquerque NM 87103 Office Fax: 505-768-7395, 505-765-5900. Business E-Mail: rstjohn@rodey.com.

SAITTA, NANCY M., state supreme court justice; b. Detroit; married; 4 children. BS magna cum laude, Wayne State U., 1983, JD, 1986. Criminal def. atty., Detroit; atty. Pearson & Patton, Las Vegas; assoc. Gentile & Porter, Las Vegas; sr. dep. atty. gen., Children's Adv. State of Nev.; judge Las Vegas Mcpl. Ct., 1996—98, 8th Jud. Dist. Ct., 1998—2006; assoc. justice Nev. Supreme Ct., 2007—. Mem. Nev. State Juvenile Justice Commn.; founder Clark County Missing & Exploited Children Comprehensive Action Program (M/CAP), So. Nev. Fatality Rev. Team, Complex Litig. Divsn.; instr. Wayne State U., Criminal Justice Dept.; litig. instr. Am. Inst. Paralegal Studies; instr. U. Phoenix, Criminal Justice Dept. Mem. Clark County Pub. Edn. Found. Recipient For the Children award, Nev. Dist. Atty.'s Office, Dist. Atty. Outstanding Svc. award, Angels in Adoption award, US Congress, 2000, Child Advocate of Yr. award, 2001; named one of Top 500 Judges in Am., Law Dragon, 2005. Mem.: Clark County Bar Assn. (exec. com.), Ct. Apptd. Spl. Advocate (CASA) Found. Office: Nev Supreme Ct 201 S Carson St Ste 300 Carson City NV 89701-4702

SAJAK, PAT, television game show host; b. Chgo., Oct. 26, 1946; m. Lesly Brown, Dec. 31, 1989, 2 children. Student, Columbia Coll., Chgo. Newscaster WEDC-Radio, Chicago, IL; disk jockey WNBS-Radio, Murray, Ky., 1971—72; staff announcer, public affairs program host, weatherman WSM-TV, Nashville, 1972—77; weatherman, host The Sunday Show, LA, 1977-81; host Wheel of Fortune, 1981—, The Pat Sajak Show, 1989-90, Pat Sajak Weekend, 2003—. Film appearances include: Airplane II: The Sequel, 1982, Jack Paar is Alive and Well, 1987; NBC television specials, host, The Thanksgiving Day Parade, The Rose Parade. Served with U.S. Army, Vietnam. Recipient 3 Emmys, People's Choice award, star on Hollywood Walk of Fame.

SAKAMOTO, KATSUYUKI, retired academic administrator, psychologist, educator; b. LA, Oct. 24, 1938; m. Edna Christine Sakamoto; children: David Katsu, Bryce Yoshio. BA in Psychology, Calif. State U., Fresno, 1961, MA in Psychology, 1968; PhD in Exptl. Social Psychology, So. Ill. U., Carbondale, 1971; postgrad., Carnegie Mellon U., 1984. Acting dir. Army Edn. Ctr., Munich, 1962-63; dir. social svcs. Salvation Army, Fresno, Calif., 1964-66; assoc. prof. psychology Keuka Coll., Keyka Park, N.Y., 1971-78; prof. social psychology Ea. Oreg. State Coll., La Grande, 1978-85, assoc. dean, then acting dean, 1980-82, 84, assoc. dean acad. affairs, 1982-85; prof. psychology Ind. U. East, Richmond, 1985-91, vice chancellor for acad. affairs, 1985-90, spl. asst. to chancellor, 1990-91; prof., chancellor Calif. Sch. Profl. Psychology, Alameda, 1991-98, ret., 1998. Lectr. So. Ill. U., 1970-71; vis. prof. SUNY, Binghamton, 1973; adj. prof. Alfred (N.Y.) U., 1972-76, Nazareth Coll. Rochester, N.Y., 1975-78, Eisenhower Coll., Seneca Falls, N.Y., 1975-77; evaluator Western Assn. Schs. and Colls., 1991—; commr.-at-large North Ctrl. Assn. Colls. and Schs., 1989-91, educator, cons., 1986-91; mem. exec. bd. for study ctrs. in Japan, China and Korea, campus dir. Oreg. Sys. Higher Edn., 1980-85; bd. visitors Newark (N.Y.) Devel. Ctr., 1975-77; presenter in field. Contbr. articles to profl. jours. Bd. dirs. troop 119 Boy Scouts Am., Richmond, 1986-91, Project 100001, Townsend Cmty. Ctr., Richmond, 1987-89, Alameda Girls Club, Inc., 1992—, Asian Cmty. Mental Health Svcs., 1991—, Found. for Ednl. Excellence, Alameda, 1993—; pres., bd. dirs. Whitewater Opera Co., Richmond, 1987-91, Leadership Wayne County, Richmond, 1988-91; cons. teaching minigrant program Richmond Cmty. Schs., 1988-91; mem. citizens adv. bd. Wayne County Sheriff's Dept., 1989-91. Mem. APA, Am. Assn. for Higher Edn., Am. Assn. State Colls. and Univs., Am. Assn. Univ. Adminstrs. (nat. v.p. 1990-92, bd. dirs. Found. 1991—), Am. Assn. for Higher Edn. (founding mem. Asian Am. caucus), Asian Am. Psychol. Assn. (treas., membership officer 1983-91, pres. 1988-91), Calif. Psychol. Assn., Nat. Assn. Acad. Affairs Adminstrs., Nat. Coun. Schs. Profl. Psychology, Rotary (bd. dirs. Alameda 1993—). Office: Calif School Of Prof Psychology 1 Beach St Ste 100 San Francisco CA 94133-1221 Home: 1650 Polo Park DR Reno NV 89523-7169

SAKAMOTO, NORMAN LLOYD, state legislator, civil engineer; b. Honolulu, May 22, 1947; s. Shuichi and Fusa (Hayashi) S.; m. Penelope A. Hayasaka, July 12, 1970; children: David H., Gregory F., Katherine E. BSCE, U. Hawaii, 1969; MSCE, U. Ill., 1970. Registered profl. engr., Calif., Hawaii; lic. spl. inspector, Hawaii; lic. contractor, Hawaii. Pres. Sundance Cir., Inc., Hwn Emporium, Inc.; engr. storm drain City of L.A., 1970-71, engr. streets and frwys., 1972-73; engr. hydrology C.E., 1971-72; v.p. S & M Sakamoto, Inc., Honolulu, 1973-85; pres. SC Pacific Corp., Honolulu, 1985—; mem. Dist. 15 Hawaii State Senate, Honolulu, 1996—. Bd. dirs. Bldg. Industry Assn., Honolulu, spl. appointee, 1991-92, pres.-elect, 1993, pres., 1994; bd. dirs. City Contractors Assn., Honolulu; trustee Home Builders Inst., 1993-96; del. White House Conf. on Small Bus., 1995; co-chair Hawaii Congress on Small Bus. Scoutmaster Honolulu area Boy Scouts America, 1989-92, asst. scoutmaster, 1993; mem. Aliamanu Clubhouse adv. bd. Boys and Girls Club; exec. com. Edn.

Commn. of the States, 2006—. Named Remodeler of Month Bldg. Industry Assn., 1990, 91, 96, Remodeler of Yr., 1991, Legislator of Yr., Bldg. Industry Assn., 2003, Legislator of Yr., Friends of the Libr., 2004; recipient Excellence award U. Hawaii, 2005, Charles Dick Medal of Merit, Nat. Guard Assn. US, 2005, State Dirs. award, Career and Tech. Edn. U. Hawaii, 2006, Legis. Yr. award, Am. Sch. Health Assn., 2007. Mem. ASCE, Nat. Assn. Home Builders, Internat. Fellowship Christian Businessmen, Nat. Fedn. Ind. Bus. (Guardian of Small Bus. award 1999), Constrn. Industry Legis. Assn., C. of C., Nat. Fedn. Ind. Bus. (leadership coun., 2007, Leadership Coun. Emeritus award, 2007). Democrat. Evangelical. Office: SC Pacific Corp 3210-A Koapaka St Honolulu HI 96819 also: Hawaii State Capitol 415 South Beretania St Rm 230 Honolulu HI 96813 Office Phone: 808-586-8585. Business E-Mail: sensakamoto@Capitol.hawaii.gov.*

SAKIC, JOE (JOSEPH STEVE), professional hockey player; b. Burnaby, BC, Canada, July 7, 1969; m. Debbie Sakic. Center Colo. Avalanche (formerly Que. Nordiques), 1991—, capt., 1992—. Mem. Team Can., World Cup of Hockey, 1996, 2004, Team Can., Olympic Games, Nagano, Japan, 1998, Salt Lake City, 2002. Recipient Conn Smythe Trophy, 1996, Hart Trophy, 2001, Lester B. Pearson Award, 2001, Lady Byng Trophy, 2001, MVP Award, NHL All-Star game, 2004; named to NHL All-Star game, 1990—94, 1996, 1998, 2000—02, 2004, 2007. Achievements include being a member of Stanley Cup Champion Colorado Avalanche, 1996, 2001; being a member of gold medal winning Canadian Hockey Team, Salt Lake City Olympic Games, 2002; being a member of World Cup Champion Team Canada, 2004; becoming the 11th player in NHL history to record 1000 career assists, 2008. Office: c/o Colo Avalanche 1000 Chopper Cir Denver CO 80204-5809

SALAMANCA-RIBA, SUSANA ALICIA, mathematics professor; BA, U. Autonoma Metropolitana, Mexico City; PhD, MIT. Assoc. prof. math NM State Univ., Las Cruces. Achievements include being one of 18 top mathematicians and computer scientists (Atlas of Lie Groups Project) from the US to successfully map E8, one of the largest and most complicated structures in mathematics. Office: Dept Math SH260 NMSU PO Box 30001 Las Cruces NM 88003-8001 Office Phone: 505-646-2305. Business E-Mail: ssalaman@nmsu.edu.

SALAMON, PETER, mathematics professor, researcher; b. Budapest, Hungary, Nov. 5, 1950; s. Zoltan and Anna Salamon; m. Sarah Welling Sullivan, June 29, 1976; children: Anna Welling, David Lowy. BA in Math., Lindenwood Coll., St. Charles, Mo., 1971; MS in Math., Drexel U., Phila., 1972; PhD in Chemistry, U. Chgo., 1978. Math. prof. San Diego State U., 1980—. Contbr. articles to profl. sci. jours. Office: San Diego State Univ Dept Math & Stats 5500 Campanile Dr San Diego CA 92182-7720

SALAMONE, GARY P. (PIKE), newspaper editor-in-chief, cartoonist; b. Rochester, NY, Aug. 26, 1950; BA, St. John Fisher Coll., 1972; MA, San Diego State U., 1979. Editor, pub. Inkslinger's Review, San Diego, 1981—; founder, news dir. Continental News Svc., San Diego, 1985—; pub., columnist Continental Newstime, San Diego, 1987—; founder, editor-in-chief Continental Features/Continental News Svc., San Diego, 1988—; pub., cartoonist Kids' Newstime, San Diego, 1992—. Author: An Examination of Alexander Hamilton's Views on Civil Liberty, 1979, Valley in the Hollow of His Hand, 1999, 2d edit., 2000. Vol. radio announcer, reader Nat. Pub. Radio Affiliate Sta. KPBS, San Diego, 1977-82; founder Fisher Recycling, Rochester, N.Y., 1971; pres. Young People's Conservation Com., Webster-Penfield, N.Y., 1971; high sch. coord. Ecology Centre, San Diego, 1976; vol. pub. info. asst. Cleve. Nat. Forest, San Diego. Mem. Phi Alpha Theta, Pi Sigma Alpha. Democrat. Office: Continental Features/News Svc PMB 265 501 W Broadway Plaza A San Diego CA 92101-3562

SALAND, LINDA CAROL, anatomist, neuroscientist, educator; b. NYC, Oct. 24, 1942; d. Charles and Esther (Weingarten) Gewirtz; m. Joel S. Saland, Aug. 16, 1964; children: Kenneth, Jeffrey. BS, CCNY, 1963, PhD in Biology, 1968; MA in Zoology, Columbia U., 1965. Rsch. assoc. dept. anatomy Columbia U. Coll. Physicians and Surgeons, NYC, 1968-69; sr. rsch. assoc. dept. anatomy Sch. Medicine U. N.Mex., Albuquerque, 1971-78, asst. prof. anatomy, 1978-83, assoc. prof., 1983-89, prof., 1989-97, prof. dept. neurosci., 1997—. Ad hoc reviewer study sect. NIH, 1994, 1995, 1997, 2000, 2005, 2006, mem. site visit team. Mem. editl. bd. Anat. Record, 1980-98; contbr. articles to profl. jours. Recipient Khatali Tchg. Excellence award, U. N.Mex. Med. Class of 2001; fellow NDEA, 1966—68. Mem. AAAS, Soc. for Neurosci., Women in Neurosci. (chmn. steering com. 1991-93). Office: U New Mex Sch Medicine Dept Neurosci MSC 084740 Albuquerque NM 87131-0001 Business E-Mail: lsaland@salud.unm.edu.

SALAT, CRISTINA, writer; b. NYC; Student, L.I. U. Founder Shark Prodns., 1998—, Kulana Affordable Artists Sanctuary, Hawaii, 1999—. Freelance editor, 1987—; author, editor, manuscript cons., workshop facilitator, 1985—. Author: Living in Secret, 1993, Alias Diamond Jones, 1993, Min Mors Koereste hedder Janey, 1995, Peanut's Emergency, 2002; contbr. to anthologies including Sister/Stranger, 1993, Am I Blue, 1994, Once Upon A Time, 1996, Higher Learning, 2001; contbr. to popular publ. Office Phone: 808-985-9055. E-mail: discoverkulana@yahoo.com.

SALAZAR, ALEXANDER, bishop; b. San Jose, Costa Rica, Nov. 28, 1949; AA, East LA Coll., 1969; BA, Immaculate Heart Coll., LA, 1980; M. Div., St. John's Sem., 1984. Ordained priest Archdiocese of LA, Calif., 1984; assoc. pastor St. Gregory the Great parish, Whittier, Calif., Assumption of the Blessed Virgin Mary parish, Pasadena, Calif., St. Vibiana Cathedral; pastor St. Teresa of Avila parish, Silverlake, Calif.; vice-chancellor Archdiocese of LA, 2003—04; ordained bishop, 2004; aux. bishop Archdiocese of LA, 2004—. Roman Catholic. Office: Archdiocese of LA 3424 Wilshire Blvd Los Angeles CA 90010-2202

SALAZAR, JOHN PAUL, lawyer; b. Albuquerque, Feb. 6, 1943; s. Henry Houghton and Anita Salazar; m. Terri J. Bestgen, June 12, 1967; children: Monique Michelle, John Paul, Stephen Houghton. BA, U. N.Mex., 1965; JD, Stanford U., 1968. Bar: N.Mex. 1968, U.S. Dist. Ct. N.Mex. 1968, U.S. Ct. Appeals (10th cir.) 1968, U.S. Supreme Ct. 1979. Dir. Rodey, Dickason, Sloan, Akin & Robb, P.A., Albuquerque, 1968—, mem. exec. com., 1984—86, mng. dir., west side office, 1985—88, chmn., environ. law sect., 1989—92, mem. exec. com., 1992—93, chair, environ. and natural resources dept., 1992—95, mem. exec. com., 1999—2007, chair, bus. dept., 2000—. Bd. visitors Stanford U. Law Sch., Calif., 1973—76; state campaign chmn. Jeff Bingaman for Atty. Gen., 1978, Jeff Bingaman for U.S. Sen., 1982, 88, 94, 2000; mem. presdl. search com. U. N.Mex., 1989—90; co-chmn. Governor's Task Force on Responsible Use of Eminent Domain, 2006; mem. Albuquerque Econ. Forum, past chmn., gov. affairs com., 1990—96, past mem. bd. dirs., 1991—94, past vice chair, 1992—93; past hon. cmdr. Field Command Def. Nuc. Agy., Kirtland AFB. Sr. editor N.Mex. Environ. Law Handbook, 1990, 2d edit., 1991, 3d edit., 1993. Former bd. dirs. N.Mex. Symphony Orch.; vice chmn. City of Albuquerque Charter Revision com., 1970—71; active Albuquerque Unity, 1971—73; chmn. N.Mex. Disting. Pub. Svc. Awards Coun., 1986, 1987; chmn. city affairs com. Greater Albuquerque C. of C., 1972, v.p. govtl. affairs, 1973, pres.-elect, 1974, pres., 1975; active Presbyn. Hosp. Ctr. Assocs.; bd. dirs. Albuquerque Hispano C. of C., 2000—, vice-chair, 2001—04, chair, 2005; bd. dirs. Inter-Am. Found., 2007—. Mem.: ABA (environ. aspects of real estate transactions com., land use regulation com., real property, probate & trust law sect., land use planning & zoning com., state & local govt. sect.), Albuquerque Armed Forces Adv. Assn., U. N.Mex. Alumni Assn. (bd. dirs. 1979—85, exec. com. 1982—85, pres. 1983—84), Nat. Assn. Indsl. and Office Parks (govs. bus. adv. coun. 1991—94, past mem. N.Mex. border commn., past chair com. border devel. and internat. trade, mem. exec. com.), N.Mex. State Bar Assn. (former mem. jud. selection com., mem. Real Property, Probate and Trust sect., mem. Pub. Law sect., mem. Natural Resources, Energy and Environ. Law sect., former sec., treas. Young Lawyers sect.), Albuquerque Bar Assn. (former mem. jud. selection com., former dir.). Roman Catholic. Office: Rodey Dickason Sloan Akin & Robb PA PO Box 1888 Albuquerque NM 87103-1888 Office Phone: 505-768-7220. Office Fax: 505-768-7395. Business E-Mail: jsalazar@rodey.com.

SALAZAR, JOHN TONY, United States Representative from Colorado; b. Alamosa, Colo., July 21, 1953; s. Henry and Emma Salazar; m. Mary Lou Salazar; children: Jesus, Esteban, Miguel. Attended, Colo. State U., 1971—72; BS in Bus. Adminstrn., Adams State Coll., Colo., 1981; grad., Colo. Agrl. Leadership Prog., 1993, Rapport Leadership Prog., 1997. Owner & operator El Rancho Salazar; chmn., CEO Spudseed.com; state rep. dist. 62 Colo. Ho. of Reps., Denver, 2002—04, mem. agrl., livestock & natural resources com., info. & tech. com.; mem. US Congress from 3d Colo. dist., 2004—, mem. agrl. com., transp. & infrastructure com., vets. affairs com. Bd. dirs. Rio Grande Water Conservation Dist., 1990—94, Gov.'s Econ. Devel. Adv. Bd.; mem. Colo. State Agrl Commn. Youth group co-coord. Dr. Michael P. Espinoza Challenge for Success; chair seed export com. Colo Cert. Seed Growers; youth leadership athletic dir. Manasa Elem. Sch., St. Joseph's Parish. Served with Criminal Investigations Divsn. US Army, 1973—76. Named Colo. Seed Grower of Yr., 1995—96; named an Outstanding Colo. Legislator, Colo. Bd. Veterans Affairs, 2006. Democrat. Roman Catholic. Office: US House Reps 326 Cannon House Office Bldg Washington DC 20515-0603 also: Dist Office Ste 702 225 N 5th St Grand Junction CO 81501 Office Phone: 202-225-4761. Office Fax: 202-226-9669. E-mail: john.salazar.house@state.co.us.

SALAZAR, NICK L., state legislator; b. Chamita, NM, Apr. 18, 1929; married; children: Three. New Mexico State Representative, District 40, 1972-, vice chairman, Energy & Natural Resources Committee, currently, member, Appropriations & Finance Committee, currently, New Mexico House Representative. Fusion Research, currently. Democrat. Roman Catholic. Address: PO Box 1076 San Juan Pueblo NM 87566 Mailing: State Capitol Rm 413 Santa Fe NM 87503 Office Phone: 505-667-0362.

SALCUDEAN, MARTHA EVA, mechanical engineer, educator; b. Cluj, Romania, Feb. 26, 1934; arrived in Can., 1976, naturalized, 1979; d. Edmund and Sarolta (Hirsch) Abel; m. George Salcudean, May 28, 1955; 1 child, Septimiu E. BEng, U. Cluj, 1956, postgrad., 1962; PhD, U. Brasov, Romania, 1969; DSc (hon.), U. Ottawa, Ont., Can., 1992, U. B.C., Can., 2001. Mech. engr. Armatura, Cluj, 1956-63; sr. rsch. officer Nat. Rsch. Inst. Metallurgy, Bucharest, 1963-75; part-time lectr. Inst. Poly., Bucharest, 1967-75; sessional lectr. U. Ottawa, 1976-77, from asst. prof. to assoc. prof. to prof., 1977-85; prof., head dept. mech. engring. U. B.C., Vancouver, 1985-93, assoc. v.p. rsch., 1993-96, acting v.p. rsch. pro-tem, 1995, Weyerhaeuser Indsl. Rsch. chair computational fluid dynamics, 1996—2002, prof., Weyerhaeuser indsl. chair emerita dept. mech. engring., 2002—. Mem. grant selection com. for mech. engring. Natural Scis. and Engring. Rsch. Coun. Can.; mem. Nat. Adv. Panel to Min. Sci. and Tech. on advanced indsl. materials, Can., 1990; mem. governing coun. NRC; mem. def. sci.e adv. bd. Dept. Nat. Def.; chair Sci. Coun. B.C. Contbr. numerous articles to profl. jours. Decorated Order of BC, 1998; recipient Gold medal BC Sci. Coun., Killam Rsch. prize U. BC; Rsch. Coun. Can. grantee, 1978—, Commemorative medal 125th anniversary Can. Confederation, 1993, Julian C. Smith medal Engring. Inst. Can., 1994-95, Meritorious Achievement award Assn. Profl. Engrs. & Geoscientists BC, 1996, Killam Meml. prize engring., 1998, Innovation award NSERC Synergy, 2007. Fellow CSME, Can. Acad. Engring., Royal Soc. Can.; mem. ASME, Assn. Profl. Engrs. Ont., Order of Can. (apptd. officer 2004). Home: 1938 Western Pkwy Vancouver BC Canada V6T 1W5 Office Phone: 604-822-2732. Business E-Mail: msal@interchange.ubc.ca.

SALEM, KAREN E., information technology executive; BS in Indsl. Engring., Pa. State U.; MBA, U. Cin. Sr. cons. Anderson Consulting; dir. bus. solutions Burger King; v.p. info. tech. Rexall Sundown; IT head AFC Enterprises; sr. v.p. and CIO Corning Cable Sys.; former sr. v.p. and CIO Winn-Dixie Stores, Inc., Jacksonville, Fla., 2002; sr. v.p. and CIO Ingram Micro, Santa Ana, Calif., 2005—. Office: Ingram Micro PO Box 25125 1600 E St Andrew Pl Santa Ana CA 92799-5125

SALERNO, THOMAS JAMES, lawyer; b. Jersey City, Aug. 30, 1957; s. Thomas E. and Imelda (Gyurik) Salerno; m. Tricia Joan Neary, Feb. 14, 1982; children: Alissa Lee, Lauren Mae, Thomas James Jr., Laina Hope. BA summa cum laude, Rutgers U., 1979; JD cum laude, U. Notre Dame, 1982. Bar: Ariz. 1982, US Dist. Ct. Ariz. 1982, US Ct. Appeals (9th cir.) 1982. Ptnr. Streich Lang, Phoenix, 1982-94, Meyer, Hendricks, Victor, Osborn & Maledon, Phoenix, 1994-95, Squire, Sanders & Dempsey LLP, Phoenix, 1995—, chmn., Bankruptcy & Restructuring Practice Group. Lectr. Profl. Edn. Sys. INc., Eau Claire, Wis., 1984—, Robert Morris Assn., Phoenix, 1984—, Comml. Law League of Am., 1986, Am. Law Inst., 1990—, ABA, 1990—, Nat. Conf. Bankruptcy Judges, 1991—, Continuing Legal Edn. Satellite Network, 1991; adj. prof. London Inst. Internat. Bus. & Comml. Law, Inns of Ct. Sch. Law, London, 1994—, Salzburg U., Austria, 1995, 96, 97. Co-author: Arizona's New Exemption Statute, 1983, Bankruptcy Litigation & Practice: A Practitioner's Guide, 1988, 1995, Bankruptcy Law & Procedure: A Fundamental Guide for Law Office Professionals, 1989, Ins and Outs of Foreclosure, 1989, Troubled Construction Loans: Law & Practice, 1990, Advanced Chapter 11 Bankruptcy Practice, 1990, 1996, Norton Bankruptcy Law & Practice, 1993, Chapter 11 Theory & Practice: A Guide to Reorganizations, 1994; author: Executive Guide to Corporate Bankruptcy, 2001. Mem. Vol. Legal Svcs. Program. Mem.: Comml. Law League, Am. Bankruptcy Inst. (editor jour. 1991—, bd. dir. 1993—), Ariz. State Bar Assn. (co-chmn. bankruptcy sect. of continuing legal edn. com. 1988—89, chmn. bankruptcy sect. 1988—90, bankruptcy adv. commn. 1992—96), Am. Bankruptcy Bd. of Certification (bd. dir. 1994—), ATLA, ABA (bankruptcy com. 1990—, mem. working group prepackaged plans bus. bankruptcy com. 1991), Pi Sigma Alpha, Phi Beta Kappa. Fluent in German. Office: Squire Sanders & Dempsey Two Renaissance Sq 40 N Central Ave Ste 2700 Phoenix AZ 85004-4498 Office Phone: 602-528-4043. Office Fax: 602-253-8129. Business E-Mail: tsalerno@ssd.com.

SALESKY, WILLIAM JEFFREY, corporate executive; b. Boston, June 12, 1957; s. Harry Michael Salesky and Eleanor Faith (Stutman) Spater Bloch; m. Cherri Lynne DeGreek, Nov. 27, 1982; 1 child, Joshua Steven. BS, U. Calif., Davis, 1978; MS, U. Calif., Berkeley, 1980, PhD, 1982. Co-op engr. Bechtel Corp. Inc., San Francisco, 1977—78; engr. U. Calif., Davis, 1978—79; rsch. assoc. Lawrence Berkeley Lab., 1979—82; project mgr. Smith Internat., Irvine, Calif., 1982—89; dir. engring. & quality assurance Mark Controls, Long Beach, Calif., 1989—94; v.p. engring. Stamet Inc., Gardena, Calif., 1994—97; pres., founder Skytron Corp., Irvine, 1997—2002; founder VTMG, Inc., Irvine, 2002—; founder, CEO Sherlock Healthy Homes, Inc., Irvine, 2003—; founder, bd. mem. Internat. Environ. Mold Found., 2005—. Chmn. LA Conf. on Fugitive Emissions from Valves, 1993; mem exec. coun Calif. State U., Fullerton, 2004-05; chmn. program com. Inst. Real Estate Mgmt., LA, 2007-. Patentee in field. Mgr. Irvine Baseball Assn., 1990; grad. assembly rep. U. Calif., Berkeley, 1980-81; mem. race com. Internat. Am.'s Cup Class World Championship; mem. San Diego Crew Classic Race Com., 1992-2004; mem. Am.'s Cup Race Com., 1992, 95 Recipient Meritorious award Petroleum Engr. mag., 1988, award for outstanding contbns. Valve Mfrs. Assn. Am., 1993 Mem. ASTM, Am. Soc. Metals Internat. (bd. dirs. 1988-90, Earl Parker fellow 1981), Soc. Petroleum Engrs., Am. Petroleum Inst., Am. Assn. Sr. Execs. (bd. dirs. 2003-06), Assn. Profl. Consultants, Irvine C. of C., South Shore Yacht Club (CFO 1989-91, bd. dirs. 1991-93), Internat. Facility Mgrs. Assn Avocations: yacht racing, golf. Office: VTMG INC 5405 Alton Pkwy Ste 5A 165 Irvine CA 92604 Business E-Mail: info@vtmg.com.

SALI, ANDREJ, chemistry professor; BSc in Chemistry, U. Ljubljana, Slovenia, 1987; PhD in Molecular Biophysics, U. London, 1991. Postdoctoral fellow dept. chemistry Harvard U., Cambridge, Mass., 1991—94; asst. prof. Rockefeller U., 1995—2000, assoc. prof., 2000—03; prof. step V depts. biopharmaceutical scis. and pharm. chemistry Calif. Inst. Quantitative Biomedical Rsch. U. Calif., San Francisco, 2003—. Cons. Accelrys Inc., San Diego, 1994—, Biogen Inc., Cambridge, Mass., 2000—02, Millennium Inc., Cambridge, Mass., 2001—02; founder, cons. Structural Genomix, Inc. (formerly Prospect Genomics, Inc.), Calif., 1999—2004; vice chair computational biology dept. biopharmaceutical scis. U. Calif., San Francisco, 2003—; mem. adv. com. Protein Data Bank, 2005—; co-founder Tropical Disease Initiative. Contbr. articles to profl. jours.; editor: Structure; mem. editl. bd.: Pub. Libr. Sci. Computational Biology, Jour. Computer Aided Molecular Design, Molecular and Cellular Proteomics, Protein Engring., Design and Selection. Recipient Irma T. Hirschl Career award, 2000—03; named one of 50 Who Matter Now, CNNMoney.com Bus. 2.0, 2006; Alfred P. Sloan Rsch. fellow, 1998—2000. Mem.: AAAS, Protein Soc. (mem. exec. com. 2005—). Office: Dept Biopharmaceutical Scis U Calif San Francisco 1700 4th St Byers Hall Ste 503B San Francisco CA 94158-2330 Office Phone: 415-514-4227. Office Fax: 415-514-4231. E-mail: sali@salilab.org.

SALI, BILL (WILLIAM THOMAS SALI), former United States Representative from Idaho; b. Portsmouth, Ohio, Feb. 17, 1954; s. Gregory and Dorothy Hazel (Wilkinson) Sali; m. Terry Sue Petersen, Aug. 20, 1976; children: Jennifer, Levi, Micah, Anna, Rachel, Christina. BBA, Boise State U., 1981; JD, U. Idaho, 1984. Bar: Idaho, US Ct. Appeals (9th cir.). Pvt. law practice, Meridian, Idaho, 1984—2006; mem. Idaho House Reps. from Dist. 21A, Boise, 1990—2006, vice chmn. health & welfare com., 1993—2006; mem. US Congress from 1st Idaho dist., 2007—09, mem. oversight & govt. reform, nat. resources com. Named Champion of Family, Idaho Family Forum, 1992. Mem.: Idaho Bar Assn. Republican. Avocation: country music.*

SALINGER, CHARLES, dermatologist; b. NYC; s. Ernest and Mae (Brenner) S.; m. Donna Marcia Gafford, May 14, 1974 (div. 1992); children: Jennifer, Jeffrey. BS, U. Wis., 1965; MD, SUNY, Syracuse, 1968. Lic. M.D., Calif. Intern Charity Hosp., La. State U., New Orleans, 1968-69, resident in dermatology, 1969-72; chief of dermatology USAF Maxwell Hosp., Montgomery, Ala., 1972-74; pvt. practice, dermatology La Mirada, Calif., 1974—. Chief med. staff La Mirada (Calif.) Cmty. Hosp., 1987-88; clin. assoc. prof. dermatology, Coll. Osteo. Medicine, Pomona, Calif., 1977—; trustee Med. Ctr. La Mirada, 1985-90. Major USAF, 1972-74. Fellow Am. Acad. Dermatology, Am. Soc. Dermatologic Surgery, Internat. Soc. Dermatologic Surgery, Pacific Dermatologic Assn., L.A. Met. Dermatologic Soc. (pres. 1994-95, bd. dirs. 1987-90); mem. AMA, Calif. Med. Assn., L.A. County Med. Assn. Jewish. Avocations: downhill skiing, managing little league baseball. Home: 5440 Emerywood Dr Buena Park CA 90621-1635 Office: 12675 La Mirada Blvd La Mirada CA 90638-2200

SALLER, RICHARD PAUL, classics educator; b. Ft. Bragg, NC, Oct. 18, 1952; s. George E. and Arthea E. (North) S.; m. Carol Joann Fisher, Jan. 12, 1974 (div. Apr. 18, 2002; children: John E., Benjamin T.; m. Tanya M. Luhrmann, Jan. 4, 2003. BA in Greek and History, U. Ill., 1974; PhD in Classics, U. Cambridge, Eng., 1978. Asst. prof. Swarthmore (Pa.) Coll., 1979-84; assoc. prof. U. Chgo., 1984-89, prof., 1990—, dean of social scis., 1994—2001, provost, 2002—06; dean Sch. Humanities and Sci. Stanford U., 2007—. Author: Personal Patronage, 1982, Patriarchy, Property and Death in the Roman Family, 1994; co-editor: Economy and Society in Ancient Greece, 1981; co-author: Roman Empire, 1987; editor Classical Philology, 1991-93. Rsch. fellow Jesus Coll., U. Cambridge, 1978-79; Ctr. for Adv. Study fellow, Stanford U., 1986-87; Trinity Coll., U. Cambridge fellow commoner, 1991. Mem. Am. Philol. Assn., Am. Hist. Assn., Am. Acad. Arts and Scis. Office: Sch Humanities and Scis Stanford Univ Stanford CA 94305 Home: 441 Gerona Rd Stanford CA 94305-8448 Office Phone: 650-723-9784.

SALMON, BETH ANN, magazine editor-in-chief; b. Syracuse, NY, Oct. 1, 1969; d. Richard George and Sharon Dian (Clark) S. BFA, Emerson Coll., 1991. Editl. asst. Let's Live mag., LA, 1994, asst. editor, 1994-95, editor in chief, 1995—. Author: (screenplays) Postcards, 1994, Watch Me, 1995. Office: Lets Live Magazine 11050 Santa Monica Blvd Los Angeles CA 90025-3594

SALMON, DENIS R., lawyer; b. St. Paul, Sept. 20, 1951; BA magna cum laude, Hamline U., 1973; JD magna cum laude, U. Minn., 1976. Bar: Calif. 1976. Assoc. Brobeck, Phleger & Harrison, Palo Alto, Calif., 1976—83, ptnr., 1983—95; ptnr., co-chair intellectual property group Gibson Dunn & Crutcher LLP, Palo Alto, Calif., 1995—, and ptnr.-in-charge Palo Alto office. Mem.: ABA (litig. section), Fed. Cir. Bar Assn., State Bar of Calif. (intellectual property section), Am. Intellectual Property Law Assn. Office: Gibson Dunn & Crutcher LLP 1881 Page Mill Rd Palo Alto CA 94304 Office Phone: 650-849-5301. Office Fax: 650-849-5001. Business E-Mail: dsalmon@gibsondunn.com.

SALMON, MATT, Former United States Representative, Arizona, communications executive; b. Salt Lake City, Jan. 21, 1958; s. Robert James and Gloria (Aagard) S.; m. Nancy Huish, June, 1979; children: Lara, Jacob, Katie, Matthew. BA in English Lit., Ariz. State U., 1981; MA in Pub. Adminstrn., Brigham Young U., 1986. Mgr. pub. affairs U.S. West, Phoenix, 1988-94; mem. Ariz. State Senate, Mesa, 1990-94, U.S. Congress from 1st Ariz. dist., Washington, 1995-2001; mem. internat. rels. and sci. coms., asst. major whip; exec. v.p. APCO Worldwide, Scottsdale, Ariz., 2001—; chmn. Ariz. State Republican Party, 2006—. Bd. dirs. Mesa United Way, 1990—, Ariz. Sci. Mus., 1992—. Recipient Outstanding Svc. award Ariz. Citizens with Disabilities, 1991, Excellence in Govt. award Tempe Ctr. for Handicapped, 1992; named Outstanding Young Phoenician, Phelps Dodge/Phoenix Jaycees, 1990, Outstanding Legislator, Mesa United Way, 1991. Republican. Mem. Lds Ch. Avocations: tennis, racquetball, bicycling. Office: 3501 N 24th St Phoenix AZ 85016

SALOMON, DARRELL JOSEPH, lawyer; b. Feb. 16, 1939; s. Joseph and Rosalie Rita (Pool) S.; m. Christine Mariscal, Apr. 25, 1992; 1 child, Camilla Lind Mariscal. Student, Georgetown U., 1957-59; BS, U. San Francisco, 1965, JD, 1966. Bar: Calif. 1970, U.S. Dist. Ct. (cen. and no. dists.) Calif. 1970, U.S. Supreme Ct. 1971. Assoc. Offices of Joseph L. Alioto, San Francisco, 1970, 1973; dep. city atty. City of San Francisco, 1972; pvt. prac., 1973—84; ptnr. Hill, Farrer & Burrill, LA, 1984-87, Arter & Hadden, LA, 1987-94; dir. of litigation Keck, Mahin & Cate, San Francisco, 1994-96; chmn. Commerce Law Group A Profl. Corp., 1996-99; chief asst. dist. atty. City of San Francisco, 2000; gen. counsel San Francisco Examiner, 2001—03; chmn. Salomon & Assoc., PC, 2004—. Lectr. law Santa Clara U. Polit. columnist San Francisco Ind., 1999—2003. Mem. Human Rights Commn. City and County of San Francisco, 1975; mem., past pres. Civil Svc. Commn., San Francisco, 1976-84; trustee San Francisco War Meml. and Performing Arts Ctr., 1984-88; bd. dirs. L.A. Symphony Master Chorale, 1985-87, Marin Symphony Assn., 1995-97. Recipient Disting. Svc. citation United Negro Coll. Fund, 1975; D'alton-Power scholar Georgetown U., 1957. Mem. ABA, Consumer Attys. of Calif. (bd. govs. 1977), Soc. Calif. Pioneers, Chit Chat Club, San Francisco Lawyers Club.

SALTZ, HOWARD JOEL, newspaper editor; b. Bronx, NY, Apr. 11, 1960; s. Fred Raymond and Sheila Lois (Goldberg) S. BA in Liberal Arts, SUNY, Stony Brook, 1983. Reporter Greenwich Time, So. Conn. Newspapers divsn. Times Mirror, 1983-85; with MediaNews Group, 1985—, N.J. Advance, Dover, 1985-87, editor, 1987-88, Hamilton (Ohio) Jour.-News, 1988-89, Fremont (Calif.) Argus, 1989-91, Johnstown Tribune-Democrat, 1991; dep. bus. editor Denver Post, 1996-98, dep. mng. editor features, 1998-2000, multimedia editor, 2000—02, assoc. editor/new media & strategic devel., 2002—06; v.p. content develop. Media News Group Interactive, 2006—. Adv. com. dept. journalism Ohlone Coll., Fremont, Calif., 1990-91. Bd. dirs. YMCA, Fremont-Newark, Calif., 1990-91, Johnstown Area Heritage Assn., 1991-93. Mem. Greater Johnstown C. of C. (bd. dirs. 1991-96), Soc. Profl. Journalists (bd. dirs. Northern Calif. chpt. 1990-91). Avocations: skiing, travel, scuba. Address: 535 Garfield St Denver CO 80206-4513 Office: Media News Group Interactive 101 W Colfax Ave Ste 950 Denver CO 80202 Business E-Mail: hsaltz@medianewsgroup.com.

SALTZMAN, JOSEPH, journalist, educator, television producer; b. LA, Oct. 28, 1939; s. Morris and Ruth (Weiss) S.; m. Barbara Dale Epstein, July 1, 1962; children: Michael Stephen Ulysses, David Charles Laertes. BA, U. So. Calif., 1961; MS, Columbia U., 1962. Freelance writer, reporter, prodr., 1960—; reporter Valley Times Today, LA, 1962-64; editor Pacific Palisades Palisadian Post, 1964; sr. writer, prodr. CBS-TV, LA, 1964-74; freelance broadcast cons. LA, 1974—; prof. journalism U. So. Calif., LA, 1974—, acting dir. Sch. Journalism, 1999; assoc. dir. Sch. Journalism U. So. Calif. Annenberg, 1996-99; assoc. dean Annenberg Sch. Comm., 1999—2003; sr. prodr. investigative unit Entertainment Tonight, 1983; dir. Image of the Journalist in Popular Culture project Norman Lear Ctr., Annenberg Sch. Comm., U. So. Calif., 2001—. CFO The Jester & Pharley Phund. Author: Frank Capra and the Image of the Journalist in American Film, 2002; prodr.(writer): (documentaries) Black on Black, 1968, The Unhappy Hunting Ground, 1971, The Junior High School, 1971, The Very Personal: Death of Elizabeth Schell-Holt-Hartford, 1972, Rape, 1972, Why Me?, 1974, Entertainment Tonight, 1983; editor (columnist): USA Today Mag., 1983—; King Features Syndicate, 1983—92; contbg. editor: Emmy Mag., 1986—90, Roberts Reviewing Svc., 1964—95, others. Recipient AP cert. of excellence and merit, 1968, 72, 73, 74, 75, Edward R. Murrow awards for disting. achievements in broadcast journalism, 1969, 72, Alfred I. duPont-Columbia U. award in broadcast journalism, 1973-74, Silver Gavel award ABA, 1973, Ohio State award Am. Exhbn. Ednl. Radio-TV Programs and Inst. for Edn. by Radio-TV Telecom. Ctr., 1974, Broadcast Media awards San Francisco State U., 1974, 75, Media award for excellence in comm. Am. Cancer Soc., 1976, Disting. Alumni award U. So. Calif., 1992, Alumni award Columbia U. Grad. Sch. Journalism, 2005; Seymour Berkson fellow, 1961; Robert E. Sherwood fellow, 1962; alt. Pulitzer traveling fellow, 1962-63. Mem. NATAS (regional Emmy awards 1965, 68, 74, 75), Radio-TV News Assn. (Golden Mike awards 1969, 71, 73, 75), Writers Guild Am., Greater LA Press Club (awards 1968, 74, 75), Columbia U. Alumni Assn., U. So. Calif. Alumni Assn., Skull and Dagger, Blue Key, Phi Beta Kappa, Sigma Delta Chi, Pi Sigma Alpha, Alpha Epsilon Rho. Home: 2116 Via Estudillo Palos Verdes Peninsula CA 90274-1931 Office: U So Calif Annenberg Sch Journalism Univ Park Los Angeles CA 90089-0001 Office Phone: 310-377-8883. Business E-Mail: saltzman@usc.edu.

SALUSKY, ISIDRO B., pediatric nephrologist, educator; b. Buenos Aires, Sept. 3, 1948; MD, U. Buenos Aires, 1971. Diplomate Am. Bd. Pediat., cert. in Pediat. Nephrology. Intern pediat. Pedro de Elizalde Hosp., Buenos Aires, 1972—73, resident pediat., 1973—75; fellowship pediat. nephrology Hosp. Enfants Malades, Paris, 1976—79; advanced rsch. fellow nutritional metabolism V.A. Wadsworth Med. Ctr., LA, 1979—81; fellowship pediat. nephrology UCLA Med. Ctr., 1981—82, prof. pediat. nephrology, 1982—; attending physician Mattel Children's Hosp./UCLA Med. Ctr. Dir. pediat. dialysis prog. UCLA Med. Ctr., 1984—, assoc. dir. dialysis prog., 1989—, prog. dir. gen. clin. rsch. ctr., 1991—. Contbr. articles to profl. jours. Dir. summer urban health rsch. prog. UCLA/Drew U. Ctr. of Excellence for Minorities, 1995—98; chair edn. com. USA Olympic Transplant Games, LA, 1992. Mem.: Nat. Kidney Found. (pres. elect medical adv. bd. 1991—92, pres. medical adv. bd. 1992—94), Am. Soc. Pediat. Nephrology, Internat. Pediat. Nephrology Assn., Internat. Soc. Peritoneal Dialysis, Soc. Bone and Mineral Rsch. Office: UCLA Med Ctr Dept Pediat Nephrology 10833 Le Conte Ave Los Angeles CA 90095 Office Phone: 310-206-6987. Business E-Mail: isalusky@pediatrics.medsch.ucla.edu.

SALVESON, MELVIN ERWIN, management sciences company executive, educator; b. Brea, Calif., Jan. 16, 1919; s. John T. and Elizabeth (Green) S.; m. Joan Y. Stipek, Aug. 22, 1944; children: Eric C., Kent Erwin BS in Edn., U. Calif. Berkeley, 1941; MS, MIT, Cambridge, 1947; PhD, U. Chgo., 1952. Cons. McKinsey & Co., NYC, 1947—48; asst. prof., dir. mgmt. sci. rsch. UCLA, 1948—54; mgr. advanced data sys., cons. strategic planning GE, Louisville and NYC, 1954—57; pres. Mgmt. Scis. Corp., LA, 1957—67; group v.p. Control Data/CEIR, Inc., 1967—68; pres. Electronic Currency Corp., 1964—; chmn. OneCard Internat., Inc., 1983—92, UniCard Sys. Inc., 1992—. Bd. dirs. Diversified Earth Scis., Inc., Eco Rx Inc., Excel Enterprise Inc., Veritas et Justus Inc., Algeran, Inc., Electronic Currency Corp., So. Calif. Econ. Alliance, founder, pres., 1992-96; bd. dirs. Am. Soc. for Edn. and Econ. Devel., founding chair, 1996-98; exec. dir. Am. Found. for Edn. and Econ. Devel.; founder MasterCard Sys., LA, 1966; chmn. Corp. Strategies Internat.; prof. bus. Pepperdine U. 1972-85; adj. prof. U. So. Calif., Webster U., U. Phoenix, 1972-2008; adviser data processing City of LA, 1962-64; futures forecasting IBM, 1957-61; adviser strategic sys. planning USAF, 1961-67; info. sys. Calif. Dept. Human Resources, 1972-73, City of LA Automated Urban Data Base, 1962-67; tech. transfer NASA, 1965-70; mem. bd. trustees, Long Beach City Coll., 1990-95 Contbr. articles to profl. jours. Served to lt. comdr. submarine engring. USNR, 1941—46. Named to Long Beach City Coll. Hall of Fame; recipient Dist. Alumnus award Calif. Coll. Sys., 1992 Fellow: AAAS, Inst. Mgmt. Sci. (founder, past pres.), Inst. for Ops. Rsch. and Mgmt. Scis.; mem.: CSSP Alumnus, Calif. Yacht Club, Founders Club (LA Philharm. Orch.). Republican. Office: 515 Ocean Ave # 405 S Santa Monica CA 90402-2623 Office Phone: 310-917-1911. Personal E-mail: mesalveson@aol.com.

SALZMAN, DAVID ELLIOT, entertainment industry executive; b. Bklyn., Dec. 1, 1943; s. Benjamin and Rose Harriet (Touby) S.; m. Sonia Camelia Gonsalves, Oct. 19, 1968; children: Daniel Mark, Andrea Jessica, Adam Gabriel. BA, Bklyn. Coll., 1965; MA, Wayne State U., 1967. Dir. TV ops. Wayne State U., 1966-67; producer Lou Gordon Program, 1967-70; program mgr. Sta. WKBD-TV, Detroit, 1970-71, Sta. KDKA-TV, Pitts., 1971-72, gen. mgr., 1973-75; program mgr. Sta. KYW-TV, Phila., 1972-73; chmn. bd. Group W Prodns., NYC and Los Angeles, 1975—; founder, pres. United Software Assocs., 1980-81; creator News Info. Weekly Service, 1981; exec. v.p. Telepictures Corp., 1980-84, vice chmn., 1984; pres. Lorimar Telepictures Corp. (merger Telepictures and Lorimar, Inc.), 1985-90, Lorimar TV, 1986-90; creator Newscope: Nat. TV News Cooperative, 1983; pres., CEO David Salzman Entertainment, Burbank, Calif., 1990-93; co-CEO Quincy Jones-David Salzman Entertainment (QDE), 1993—; exec. prodr. Jenny Jones Show, 1991—2003. Exec. prodr. Mad-TV, 1995—, The Rerun Show, Jumble, In the House, 68th Ann. Acad. awards, Concert of the Americas, 1995, Vibe-TV, 1997-98, Steel, 1997, Their Eyes Were Watching God, 2005; CEO David Salzman Enterprises, 1998—; co-owner Vibe Mag., 1995-2006, Spin Mag., 1995-2006, Sta. WNOL-TV, 1995, Sta. WATL-TV, 1995, Sta. KCWE-TV, 1995-2006, Sta. WGRB-TV, 1998; guest lectr. at schs.; bd. govs. Films of Coll. and Univ. Students; co-prodr. (Broadway shows) Urinetown, The Dinner Party, 2001, Into the Woods, 2002. Contbr. articles to profl. jours. Bd. dirs. Pitts. Civic Light Opera, Am. Blood Bank, Pitts., Hebrew Inst., Jewish Community Ctr., Harrison, NY, Temple Etz Chaim, USC Sch. Cinema-TV, Emory U. Ctr. Leadership, Emory Bus. Sch., Bklyn. Coll. Found., HELP group; co-founding bd. mem. AMGEN Tour Calif., Tour Calif. Cycling Race, 2006, 07, 08. Recipient award Detroit chpt. Am. Women in Radio and TV, 1969, award Golden Quill, 1971, award Golden Gavel, 1971, local Emmy award, 1972, award AP, 1974, Gold medal Broadcast Promotion Assn., 1983, Lifetime Achievement award Bklyn. Coll., 1990, Disting. Alumnus award, Golden Plate award Am. Acad. Achievement, 1995, Ovation award, Wayne State U.; BPME Gold medal San Francisco Film Festival, 1984, N.Y., 1985, Chgo., 1986, Tree of Life award Jewish Nat. Fund, 1988. Mem. Acad. TV Arts and Scis., Nat. Assn. TV Program Execs., Radio-TV News Dirs. Assn., Am. Mgmt. Assn., Am. Film Inst., Brooklyn Coll. Found. Office: Sunset Bronson Studio 5800 sunset Blvd Bldg 10 2nd Fl Hollywood CA 90028 Office Phone: 323-762-8116. Business E-Mail: davids@madtv.com.

SAM, DAVID, federal judge; b. Hobart, Ind., Aug. 12, 1933; s. Andrew and Flora (Toma) S.; m. Betty Jean Brennan, Feb. 1, 1957 (dec. Aug. 2000); children: Betty Jean, David Dwight, Daniel Scott, Tamara Lynn, Pamela Rae, Daryl Paul, Angie, Sheyla; m. Bennie Lynn Malnar, Jan. 5, 2005. BS, Brigham Young U., 1957; JD, Utah U., 1960. Bar: Utah 1960, U.S. Dist. Ct. Utah 1966. Sole practice and ptnr., Duchesne, Utah, 1963-76; dist. judge State of Utah, 1976-85; judge U.S. Dist. Ct. Utah, Salt Lake City, 1985-97; chief judge U.S. Dist. Ct., Salt Lake City, 1997—99, sr. judge, 1999—. Atty. City of Duchesne, 1963-72; Duchesne County atty., 1966-72; commr. Duchesne, 1972-74; adv. com. Codes of Conduct of Jud. Conf. US, 1987-91, Jud. Coun. of 10th Cir., 1991-93; mem. US Del. to Romania, Aug. 1991. Chmn. Jud. Nomination Com. for Cir. Ct. Judge, Provo, Utah, 1983; bd. dirs. Water Resources, Salt Lake City, 1973-76. Served to capt. JAGC, USAF, 1961-63. Named Judge of Yr., Utah State Bar, 1999. Avocations: beekeeping, reading, sports. Office: US Dist Ct US Courthouse 350 S Main St Ste 441 Salt Lake City UT 84101-2180 Office Phone: 801-524-6190. Business E-Mail: david_sam@utd.uscourts.gov.

SAMBERG, ANDY, actor; b. Berkeley, Calif., Aug. 18, 1978; Grad., U. Calif., Santa Cruz, NYU Film School. Co-founder, mem. The Lonely Island, NYC, 2001—. Writer G-Phoria, 2004, MTV Movie Awards, 2004, 2005; actor: (TV special) Comedy Central Laughs for Life Telethon, 2004; (TV series) Saturday Night Live, 2005—; (films) Hot Rod, 2007, (voice) Space Chimps, 2008, I Love You, Man, 2009; guest appearances (TV series) 40 Most Awesomely Bad Dirrty Songs...Ever, 2004, Arrested Development, 2005, Premium Blend, 2005, The Late Show with David Letterman, 2006, Conan O'Brien, 2006. Recipient WIRED Rave Award - TV, 2006. Office: United Talent Agency Inc 9560 Wilshire Blvd Ste 500 Beverly Hills CA 90212 Office Phone: 310-273-6700. Office Fax: 310-247-1111.

SAMET, DEE-DEE, lawyer; BA, U. Ariz., 1962, JD, 1963. Bar: Ariz. 1964. Pvt. practice, Tucson, 1974—. Arbitrator U.S. Dist. Ct. Ariz., Gender Equality Task Force, 1993; judge pro tem Pima County Superior Ct., 1985—; Ninth Cir. Lawyer rep., 1990-93; mem. Jud. Performance Rev. Commn., 1996-99; pres. Casa de los Ninos, 2003-05. Mem. Fed. Bar Assn. (pres. Tucson chpt. 2004—), State Bar Ariz. (family law sect., workers compensation sect., trial law sect., co-chair workers compensation sect. 1988-89, gender bias task force, bd. govs. 1994-97, pres. 1999-2000, chair workers compensation sect. 2004, chair alternative dispute resolution sect. 2005-06), Am. Arbitration Assn. (nat. panel arbitrators, com. on exams., supreme ct. state Ariz. 1984-91), Pima County Bar Assn. (bd. dirs. 1994—, pres. 2007-), Nat. Assn. Counsel for Children, Ariz. Assn. Counsel for Children, So. Ariz. Women Lawyers Assn. (bd. dirs. 1990, pres. 1994-95, treas. alt. dispute resolution sect. 2003-04), Nat. Orgn. Social Security Claimants' Reps., Inn of Cts. Office: Dee-Dee Samet PC 717 N 6th Ave Tucson AZ 85705-8304 Office Phone: 520-624-8595. Business E-Mail: dee-dee@samet.psemoil.com.

SAMET, JACK I., lawyer; b. NYC, Aug. 6, 1940; s. William and Tillie (Katz) Samet; m. Helen Ray, Feb. 12, 1967; 1 child, Peter Lawrence. BA, Columbia U., 1961; JD, Harvard U., 1964. Bar: N.Y. 1964, Calif. 1973. Assoc. Whitman & Ransom, NYC, 1966-69, Hall, Casey, Dickler & Howley, NYC, 1969-73; ptnr. Ball, Hunt, Hart, Brown & Baerwitz, LA, 1973-81, Buchalter, Nemer, Fields & Younger, LA, 1981-94, Baker & Hostetler, LA, 1994—2006, active ret. ptnr., 2007—, mem. policy com., 1997-98, ptnr.-in-charge, 1997-98. Arbitrator Nat. Assn. Securities Dealers, LA, 1976—; spkr., panelist Calif. Continuing Edn. Bar, 1988. Actor: Playhouse W., 2005—07, Beverly Hills Playhouse, 2007—, Good Time Max, Amour, It's Another Beautiful Day, Empty Apartment, Welcome Home Soldier, A Midsummer Night's Dream. Named a So. Calif. Superlawyer, 2004—07. Mem.: ABA, NY Bar Assn., Calif. Bar Assn., Screen Actor's Guild, Am. Bd. Trial Advs., Million Dollar Advs. Forum, Sport Club/LA. Avocations: exercise, reading, acting. Home: 2741 Aqua Verde Cir Los Angeles CA 90077-1502 Office: Baker Hostetler 600 Anton Blvd Ste 900 Costa Mesa CA 92626 Personal E-mail: jsamet@belairmail.com. Business E-Mail: jsamet@bakerlaw.com.

SAMILJAN, KATRIANA, lawyer; b. Sacramento, Oct. 11, 1969; BA magna cum laude, Harvard Coll., Cambridge, Mass., 1991; JD, Harvard Law Sch., 1998. Former bankruptcy atty., Seattle; pvt. practice atty. Bush Strout & Kornfield, Seattle. Named Wash. Rising Star, SuperLawyer Mag., 2001—08. Mem.: ABA, Turnaround Mgmt. Assn., Am. Bankruptcy Inst., King Co. Bar Assn., Wash. State Bar Assn., Fed. Bar Assn. Office: Bush Strout and Kornfield 5000 Two Union Sq 601 Union St Seattle WA 98101-2373 Office Phone: 206-521-3857. Business E-Mail: ksamiljan@bskd.com.

SAMPLE, JOSEPH SCANLON, foundation executive; b. Chgo., Mar. 15, 1923; s. John Glen and Helen (Scanlon) S.; m. Patricia M. Law, Dec. 22, 1942 (div.); children: Michael Scanlon, David Forrest, Patrick Glen; m. Miriam Tyler Willing, Nov. 19, 1965 (dec.). BA, Yale U., 1947. Trainee, media analyst, media dir. Dancer-Fitzgerald-Sample, Inc., advt. agy., Chgo., 1947-50, v.p., media dir., 1952-53; pres. Mont. Television Network KTVQ, Billings, KXLF-AM-TV, Butte, Mont., KRTV, Great Falls, Mont., KPAX-TV, Missoula, Mont., 1955-84; dir., prodr. Yellowstone Pub. Radio KEMC, Billings, 1993—. Chmn. Wheeler Ctr. Mont State U., 1988—. Served with AUS, 1943-46. With U.S. Army, 1950-52. Mem. Rotary, Yellowstone Country Club, Port Royal Club, Hole in The Wall Golf Club, Hilands Golf Club, Naples Yacht Club. Home: 606 Highland Park Dr Billings MT 59102-1909 Office: 14 N 24th St Billings MT 59101-2422 Office Phone: 406-256-5667. Personal E-mail: scatman01@msn.com.

SAMPLE, STEVEN BROWNING, academic administrator; b. St. Louis, Nov. 29, 1940; s. Howard and Dorothy (Cunningham) Sample; m. Kathryn Brunkow, Jan. 28, 1961; children: Michelle Sample Smith, Elizabeth Ann. BS, U. Ill., 1962, MS, 1963, PhD, 1965; DHL (hon.), Canisius Coll., 1989, Hebrew Union Coll., 1994, Northeastern U., 2004; LLD (hon.), U. Sheffield, Eng., 1991; EdD (hon.), Purdue U., 1994; EdD, Northwestern U., 2004; DL (hon.), U. Nebr., 1995; DSc, U. Notre Dame, 2005; DSc (hon.), SUNY, 2006. Sr. scientist Melpar Inc., Falls Ch., Va., 1965—66; assoc. prof. elec. engring. Purdue U., Lafayette, Ind., 1966—73; dep. dir. Ill. Bd. Higher Edn., Springfield, 1971—74; exec. v.p. acad. affairs, dean Grad. Coll., prof. elec. engring. U. Nebr., Lincoln, 1974—82; prof. elec. and computer engring. SUNY, Buffalo, 1982—91; pres. U. So. Calif., LA, 1991—, prof. elec. engring., 1991—, Robert C. Packard pres.'s chair, 1995—. Bd. dirs. Santa Catalina Id. Co., Intermec, William Wrigley Jr. Co., Advanced Bionics, AMCAP/Am. Mut. Fund, Inc., Keck Sch. Medicine; vice-chmn. Western NY Tech. Devel. Ctr., Buffalo, 1982—91; chmn. bd. dirs. Calspan-UB Rsch. Ctr., Inc., Buffalo, 1983—91; mem. Calif. Coun. Sci. and Tech., Irvine, Calif., 1998—2003, L.A. Bus. Advisors, Nat. Acad. of Engring., 1998—; cons. in field; chmn. Pacific-10 Conf., 1997—. Author: Contrarian's Guide to Leadership, 2001, (ref. book) New Dictionary of the History of Ideas, 2004; contbr. articles to profl. jour. Timpanist St. Louis Philharm. Orch., 1955—58; chmn. Western NY Regional Econ. Devel. Coun., 1984—91; trustee U. at Buffalo Found., 1982—91, Studio Arena Theatre, Buffalo, 1983—91, Western NY Pub. Broadcasting Assn., 1985—91; chmn. Gov.'s Conf. on Sci. and Engring. Edn., Rsch. and Devel, 1989—91; sr. warden Ch. of Our Savior, 1996—98; mem. Calif. Bus.-Higher Edn. Forum (CBHEF), 1995—97; trustee LEARN, 1991—96; mem. bd. dir. 1st Interstate Bancorp, 1991—96, Galaxy Inst. Edn., 1991—94, Niagara Mohawk Power Corp., 1988—91; vestry Ch. of Our Savior, 1996—2001; mem. bd. gov. LA Annenberg Met. Project (LAAMP), 1994—2000; mem. bd. dir. Western Atlas, Inc., 1994—97, The Presley Co., 1991—; bd. dir. Buffalo Philharm. Orch., 1982—91, Regenstrief Med. Found., Indpls., 1982—, Rsch. Found. SUNY, 1987—91; bd. dir. LA chpt. World Affairs Coun.; bd. dir. Rebuild LA Com., Coalition of 100 Club, LA; mem. bd. dir. Dunlop Tire Corp., 1987—91, Greater Buffalo C.

of C., 1985—91, United Way Buffalo and Erie County, 1985—91; bd. dir. U. So. Calif. Keck Sch. Medicine; bd. trustees J. Paul Getty Trust, 2004—06; mem. leadership coun. Literacy Network of Greater L.A., 2004—; mem. Calif. Commn. for Jobs and Econ. Growth, 2004—. Recipient Disting. Alumnus award, U. Ill., 1980, Alumni Honor award, U. Ill. Coll. Engring., 1985, citation award, Buffalo Coun. on World Affairs, 1986, Outstanding Elec. Engr. award, Purdue U., 1993, Humanitarian award, Nat. Conf. Christians and Jews, 1994, Hollzer Meml. award, Jewish Fedn. Coun. Greater L.A, 1994, Eddy award, LA County Econ. Devel. Corp., 2000, Norton medal, SUNY, 2004, Humanitarian award, Alfred Mann Found., 2004, Heart of City award, Ctrl. City Assn. LA, 2005, KCET Visionary award, 2005, Disting. Bus. Leader award, LA Area C. of C., 2006; named Engr. of Yr., NY State Soc. Profl. Engrs., 1985; fellow, Sloan Found., 1962—63, Grad. fellow, NSF, 1963—65, Am. Coun. Edn. fellow, Purdue U., 1970—71. Mem.: NAE, IEEE (Outstanding Paper award 1976, Founders medal 2008), Am. Acad. Arts and Sci., Assn. Pacific Rim Univ. (co-founder, chmn. 1997—2002), Coun. on Fgn. Rels., Nat. Assn. State Univ. and Land-Grant Coll. (ednl. telecomms. com. 1982—83, chmn. coun. of pres. 1985—86, edn. and tech. com. 1986—87, exec. com. 1987—89), Assn. Am. Univ. (exec. com. 1995—2000, vice-chmn. 1997—98, tenure com. 1997—2001, chmn. 1998—99, assessing quality of univ. edn. and rsch. com. 2000—05, co-chair task force on rsch. accountability 2001—02, internationalization com. 2002—). Episcopalian. Achievements include patents in field. Office: U So Calif Office of Pres University Park Adm 110 Los Angeles CA 90089-0012 Office Phone: 213-740-2111.

SAMPSEL, HUNTER, mortgage company executive; b. 1971; Pres., owner Am. Home Mortgage. Involved with Casa de los Ni-os, U. Ariz. Disability Resource Ctr., El Rio Health Ctr., World Care, Salvation Army Adopt-A-Family. Named one of 40 Under 40, Tucson Bus. Edge, 2006. Mem.: Pan Asian Cmty. Alliance, Ariz. Medical Assn., Continental Ranch Little League, AYSO Soccer Teams, Southern Ariz. Golf. Office: American Home Mortgage 5401 N Oracle Rd Tucson AZ 85704 Office Phone: 877-581-9035. Office Fax: 520-531-9468.

SAMPSON, ROGER, school system administrator; M in Edn. Adminstrn., U. Mont., Missoula. Prin., sch. adminstr. Annette Island Sch. Dist., Metlakatia, Alaska, 1979—84; prin. Kenai Peninsula Borough Sch. Dist., Alaska, 1984—94; supt. Chugach Sch. Dist., Alaska, 1994—99; commr. edn. and early devel. State of Alaska, 2003—. Mem. standards based edn. com. State of Alaska. Named Alaska Prin. of Yr., 1987, Nat. Rural Supt. of Yr., 1997. Office: Dept Edn & Early Devel 801 W 10th St Ste 200 PO Box 110500 Juneau AK 99801 Office Phone: 907-465-2802. Business E-Mail: roger_sampson@eed.state.ak.us.

SAMS, JOHN B., JR., career officer; BA, The Citadel, 1967; MA in Personnel Mgmt., Ctrl. Mich. U., 1977. Commd. 2d. lt. USAF, 1967, advanced through grades to lt. gen., 1996; pilot Mather AFB, 1969-71; squadron ops. officer Cam Ranh Bay Air Base, South Vietnam, 1971-72; instr. pilot Kincheloe AFB, Mich., 1972-74; inspection plans officer Norton AFB, Calif., 1974-76; various assignments Offutt AFB, Nebr., 1977-80, 82-84, 1987-88, The Pentagon, Washington, 1981-82, 94-95; asst. dep. comdr. Minot AFB, N.C., 1985-87; comdr. Carswell AFB, Tex., 1988-90, Maxwell AFB, Ala., 1990-91, Travis AFB, Calif., 1991-93, 98—, Scott AFB, Ill., 1993-94, 96-98; dir. plans and policy U.S. Atlantic Command, Norfolk, Va., 1995-96. Decorated DFC, Legion of Merit with two oak leaf clusters, Meritorious Svc. medal with oak leaf cluster, Air Medal with two oak leaf clusters.

SAMUELI, HENRY, electrical engineer, educator, professional sports team executive; b. Buffalo, Sept. 20, 1954; s. Aron and Sala (Traubman) S.; m. Susan Faye Eisenberg, Aug. 22, 1982; children: Leslie Pamela, Jillian Meryl, Erin Sydney. BSEE, UCLA, 1975, MSEE, 1976, PhD in Elec. Engring., 1980. Staff engr. TRW Inc., Redondo Beach, Calif., 1980-83, section mgr., 1983-85, cons., 1985—89; co-founder, chief scientist PairGain Techs., Inc., Tustin, Calif., 1988—94; co-founder, chief tech. officer Broadcom Corp., Irvine, Calif., 1991—, v.p. rsch. & devel. & co-chmn., 1991—2003, chmn., 2003—08; asst. prof. UCLA, 1985-90, assoc. prof., 1990-94, prof., 1994—95, disting. adj. prof., elec. engring. and computer sci., 2003—. Co-owner Anaheim Ducks (formerly Mighty Ducks of Anaheim, 2005—. Named one of Top 20 Entrepreneurs of 1997, The Red Herring Mag., 1997, one of Top 50 Cyber Elite, Time Digital Mag., 1997; Schs. Engring. at both U. Calif. Irvine and UCLA named in honor of; recipient Presdl. award, U. Calif., 2000, Irvine medal, 2000, Alumnus of Yr. award, UCLA Sch. of Engring. and Applied Sci., 2000, Golden Plate award, Acad. Achievement, 2006. Fellow: IEEE (Circuits and Systems Soc. Indsl. Pioneer award 2000), Am. Acad. Arts & Sci.; mem.: NAE. Republican. Jewish. Holder of 22 US patents. Address: U Calif Irvine Henry Samueli Sch Engring Elec Engring and Computer Sci 325 Engineering Tower Irvine CA 92697-2625 Office: Broadcom Corporation 5300 California Ave Irvine CA 92617-3038

SAMUELIAN, STEVEN NEIL, state legislator; b. Arcadia, Calif., Aug. 26, 1969; m. Houry Chaderjian; children: Shant, Nicholas. BA, Calif. Poly. U., 1991. Vol. coord. Calif. Rep. Party, Burbank; vol. dir. Congressman Huffington; dist. dir. Congressman George Radanovich; mem. Calif. Ho. of Reps., 2002—. Bd. dirs. Fresno County United Way, FSU Armenian Studies Bd; state bd. dirs. Young Rep. Fedn.; state ctrl. com. Calif. Rep. Party, apptd. to exec. com., 2001. Named 2000 Class Pres., Fresno C. of C. Leadership Fresno Program; recipient United Way of Fresno County Outstanding Achievement award, 2001, Founders award Young Rep. Fedn. Calif., 2001. Mem. Clovis C. of C. (bd. dirs.), Crimestoppers (bd. dirs.). Office: PO Box 942849 Sacramento CA 94249 Office Phone: 916-319-2029.

SAMUELS, DONALD L., lawyer; b. Washington, May 8, 1961; s. Jack Donald Samuels and Francis Diane (Katcher) Yeoman; m. Sherri Tobin Samuels. AB, Brown U., 1983; JD, Columbia U., 1986. Bar: Calif. 1986, Calif. 1988, Tex. 1998, U.S. Dist. Ct. (cen., no., ea. and so. dists.), U.S. Dist. Ct. Colo. 1997, U.S. Ct. Appeals (9th cir.) 1989, Colo. 1996, U.S. Ct. Appeals (7th cir.) 1996, U.S. Ct. Appeals (10th cir.) 1997, U.S. Supreme Ct. 2004. Law clk. Hon. William D. Keller, LA, 1986-87; assoc. Sidley & Austin, LA, 1987-94, ptnr., 1994-95, Samuels & Samuels, LA, 1995-97; officer, dir., shareholder Ireland & Stapleton, Denver, 1997—2002; ptnr. Holme, Roberts & Owen, LLP, Denver, 2002—. Mem. ABA, Calif. Bar Assn., Colo. Bar Assn., Tex. Bar Assn., Phi Beta Kappa. Home: 5692 S Florence St Greenwood Village CO 80111-3713 Office: Holme Roberts & Owen LLP Ste 4100 1700 Lincoln St Denver CO 80203-4541 Home Phone: 303-770-9119; Office Phone: 303-866-0548. Business E-Mail: donald.samuels@hro.com.

SAMUELS, MARK A., lawyer; b. LA, 1957; BA, U. Calif., Berkeley, 1979; JD, U. Calif., LA, 1982. Bar: Calif. 1982, US Dist. Ct., Ctrl. Dist. Calif. 1982, US Ct. Appeals, 9th Cir. 1983, US Dist. Ct., So. and No. Districts of Calif. 1984, US Dist. Ct., Ea. Dist. Calif. 1987, US Ct. Appeals, Fed. Cir. 1991. Ptnr. O'Melveny & Myers LLP, LA, chair, intellectual property & technology dept. Mem. LA Superior Ct. Arbitration Panel. Mem. U. Calif LA Law Review, 1980—81, chief mng. editor, 1981—82. Bd. dir. U. Calif. LA Sch. Law Alumni Assn. Named one of Top 25 Intellectual Property Lawyers, LA Daily Jour. Mem.: Calif. State Bar (mem. intellectual property sect.), Assn. of Bus. Trial Lawyers, Fed. Cir. Bar Assn., Am. Intellectual Property Law Assn., LA County Bar Assn., ABA (liaison, lawyers conf. task force on reduction of litig. cost & delay 1993), Order of the Coif, Flintridge Riding Club (bd. dir., treas.), Phi Beta Kappa. Office: O'Melveny & Myers LLP 400 S Hope St Los Angeles CA 90071-2899 Office Phone: 213-430-6340. Office Fax: 213-430-6407. Business E-Mail: msamuels@omm.com.

SAMUELS, RALPH, state legislator; b. Anchorage, 1961; Alaska State Representative, District 29, 2003-,Chairman, board director, Anchorage Chamber of Commerce, 1999-2000; Bd director, Anchorage Chamber of Commerce, 1995-; board director, State Chamber of Commerce, formerly; Airline exec, businessman. Climbed Mt McKinley three times. Mcpl Budge Advisor Comm (2000-); Public Safety Advisor Comm; Alaska Air Carriers Association. Republican. Mailing: State Capitol Rm 126 Juneau AK 99801-1182 Fax: 907-465-3810. E-mail: representative_ralph_samuels@legis.state.ak.us.

SAMUELS, SANDOR ELI, lawyer, diversified financial services company executive; b. LA, Aug. 22, 1952; m. Claudia Wallack; 3 children. AB summa cum laude, Princeton U., NJ, 1974; JD, UCLA, 1977. Bar: Calif. 1977, US Dist. Ct. (ctrl. dist. Calif.) 1977. Law clk. to Hon. Irving Hill US Dist. Ct. (ctrl. dist. Calif.), 1977—79; atty. Munger, Tolles & Olson, 1979—83, First Interstate Bancorp, 1984—88, sr. v.p., asst. gen. counsel, 1988; sr. v.p., gen. counsel Fox Inc., 1989—90; sr. v.p., gen. counsel, sec. Countrywide Fin. Corp., Calabasas, Calif., 1990—91, mng. dir., legal, gen. counsel. sec., 1991—2000, sr. mng. dir., legal, gen. counsel, sec., 2001—03, sr. mng. dir., chief legal adv., sec., 2003, exec. mng. dir., chief legal adv., asst. sec. Bd. dirs. U. Judaism, Ziegler Sch. Rabbinic Studies, Shalhevet Sch., Bet Tzedek Legal Svcs., Adat Ari El Synagogue. Mem.: Mortgage Bankers Assn. Am. (chmn. legal services com. 1995—96), State Bar Calif., LA County Bar Assn., ABA, Order of the Coif. Office: Countrywide Fin Corp 4500 Park Granada Calabasas CA 91302-1613

SAMUELSON, CECIL O., JR., academic administrator; b. 1942; m. Sharon Giauque; 5 children. BS, MS, MD, U. Utah. V.p. health scis. U. Utah, Salt Lake City, 1970-90; sr. v.p. Intermountain Health Care, Inc., Salt Lake City, 1990—94; dean IHC Hosps. Inc., Salt Lake City, 1990—; pres. Brigham Young U., Provo, Utah, 2003—. Pres. LDS Ch. No. Area, Utah; Pres. LDS Ch. Europe No. Area; mem. First Quorum of the Seventy, Ch. of LDS, 1994—2003. Office: Office of the Pres Brigham Young U Provo UT 84602 Office Phone: 801-422-2521.

SAMUELSON, PAMELA ANN, law educator; b. Seattle, Aug. 4, 1948; d. Peter David and Margaret Susanne (Green) S.; m. Robert J. Glushko, May 7, 1988; 1 child, Robert M. BA in History, U. Hawaii, 1971, MA in Polit. Sci., 1972; JD, Yale U., 1976. Bar: NY 1977, US Dist. Ct. (so. dist.) NY 1977. Rsch. assoc. Vera Inst. of Justice, NYC, 1976-77; assoc. Willkie Farr & Gallagher, NYC, 1977-81; prin. investigator Software Engring. Inst., Pitts., 1985-86; asst. prof. Law Sch. U. Pitts., 1981-84, assoc. prof. Law Sch., 1984-87, prof. Law Sch., 1987-96; prof. law and info. mgmt. U. Calif. Law Sch./Sch. Info. Mgmt. and Sys., Berkeley, 1996—, chancellor's prof. info. mgmt. & law, 2001—06, Richard M. Sherman prof. law & info. mgmt., 2005—. Dir. Berkeley Ctr. for Law & Tech./U. Calif. Berkeley, 1997-; advisor Samuelson High Tech. Law & Pub. Policy Clinic, U. Calif. Berkeley; mem. adv. bd. Electronic Privacy Info. Ctr.; vis. prof. Emory Law Sch., Atlanta, 1989-90, Cornell Law Sch., Ithaca, 1995-96; hon. prof. U. Amsterdam, Netherlands, 2002-; mem. Nat. Rsch. Coun. Study Com. on Intellectual Property Rights and Info. Infrastructure, 1998-2000. Contbr.: articles to profl. jours, chapters to books; co-author: Software & Internet Law, 2000; author: The Future of the Information Society & the Role of Copyright In It, 1998. Bd. dirs. ACLU Greater Pitts., 1983-88, Electronic Frontier Found., 2000—. John D. and Catherine T. MacArthur Found. fellow, 1997-2002, Pub. Policy fellow Electronic Frontier Found., 1997—; recipient Pioneer award, Berkeley Tech. Law Jour., 1999, Disting. Alumni award U. Hawaii, 2000, World Tech. Network award for Law, 2004, Women of Vision award for Social Impact, Anita Borg Inst., 2005. Mem. ABA (sci. and tech. sect.), Am. Intellectual Property Law Assn. (subcom. chair 1988-89), Assn. Am. Law Schs. (intellectual property sect.), Am. Law Inst., Assn. Computing Machinery (contbg. editor comm.), Open Source Application Found. (bd. dirs., 2002-). Democrat. Avocations: gardening, reading. Office: U Calif Berkeley Sch Info Mgmt and Sys 102 South Hall #4600 Berkeley CA 94720-4600 E-mail: pam@sims.berkeley.edu.

SANCHEZ, BERNADETTE M., state legislator; New Mexico State Senator, District 26, 2000-, Bernalillo Co, vchairwoman, Corps & Transportation Committee, member, Public Affairs Committee, interim member, Corrections Oversight & Justice Committee, Econ & Rural Develop & Telecommunications Committee, Legislature Health & Human Servs Committee, Redistricting Committee, Revenue Stabilization & Tax Policy Committee, New Mexico State Senate.Sch counselor, currently. Democrat. Office: 1704 Avenida Rael NW Albuquerque NM 87105 Office Phone: 505-986-4267. E-mail: Bernadette.Sanchez@state.nm.us.

SÁNCHEZ, LINDA T., United States Representative from California; b. Orange, Calif., Jan. 28, 1969; m. Mark Valentine. BA in Spanish Lit., U. Calif., Berkeley, 1991; JD, UCLA, 1995. Bar: Calif. 1995. Clk. to hon. Chief Justice Terry Hatter, Jr. Ctrl. Dist. Ct., Calif.; compliance officer Internat. Brotherhood Elec. Workers Nat. Elec. Contractors Assn., 1998—2002; mem. US Congress from 39th Calif. dist., 2003—, mem. judiciary com., govt. reform com., small bus. com. Campaign aide Loretta Sanchez for US Congress, 1996, 1998; mem. Congl. Hispanic Caucus; co-founder Congl. Labor & Working Families Caucus; exec. sec.-treas. Orange County ctrl. labor coun. AFL-CIO; lectr. Nat. Assn. Elected & Apptd. Ofcls., 1998—. Mem.: Internat. Brotherhood Elec. Workers (Local 441). Democrat. Roman Catholic. Office: US Ho Reps 1007 Longworth Office Bldg Washington DC 20515-0539 also: Dist Office Ste 106 4007 Paramount Lakewood CA 90712 Office Phone: 562-429-8499, 202-225-6676. Office Fax: 562-938-1948, 202-226-1012.

SANCHEZ, LORETTA, United States Representative from California; b. Lynnwood, Calif., Jan. 7, 1960; BA in Econs., Chapman U., Orange, Calif., 1982; MBA in Fin., Am. U., 1984. Fin. mgr. Orange County Transp. Authority, 1984-87; asst. v.p. Fieldman Rolapp & Assocs., 1987-90; strategic mgmt. cons. Booz, Allen & Hamilton Inc., 1990—93; owner, operator AMIGA Advisors Inc., 1993—96; mem. US Congress from 47th Calif. dist., 1997—, mem. armed svcs. com., fgn. affairs com., edn. & labor com., homeland security com., judiciary com., joint econ. com. Mem. Blue Dog Dems., New Dem. Coalition, Older Americans Caucus, Women's Congl. Caucus, Law Enforcement Caucus, Hispanic Caucus, Congl. Sportsman's Caucus, Congl. Human Rights Caucus. Mem. Hispanic adv. coun. Pepperdine U., Malibu, Calif.; pres. Nat. Soc. Hispanic MBAs, 1993; mem. Anaheim Assistance League, 1995—; bd. dirs. Providence Speech & Hearing Ctr., Orange, 1985—; trustee Chapman U., 2001—. Mem.: Am. Assn. Univ. Women, Anaheim Rotary Club, Los Amigos Orange County. Democrat. Roman Catholic. Office: US Ho Reps 1230 Longworth Ho Office Bldg Washington DC 20515-0547 also: Dist Office Ste 101 12397 Lewis St Garden Grove CA 92840 Office Phone: 202-225-2965. Office Fax: 714-621-0401. E-mail: loretta@mail.house.gov.

SANCHEZ, MARLA RENA, communications executive; d. Tomas Guillermo and Rose Sanchez; m. Bradley D. Gaiser. BS, MS, Stanford U., 1979; MBA, Santa Clara U., 1983. Rsch. biologist Syntex, Palo Alto, Calif., 1980-81; fin. analyst Advanced Micro Devices, Sunnyvale, Calif., 1983-85; fin. mgr. ultrasound divsn. Diasonics, Inc., Milpitas, Calif., 1985-86, contr. therapeutic products divsn., 1989-93, contr. internat. divsn., 1992-93; contr. Ridge Computers, Santa Clara, Calif., 1986-88; dir. fin. VLSI Tech., Inc., San Jose, Calif., 1993-98; corp. contr. SDL, Inc., San Jose, 1999—2001, interim CFO, 2005; sr. v.p., CFO Avanex Corp., Fremont, Calif., 2006—. Office: Avanex Corp 40919 Encyclopedia Cir Fremont CA 94538

SANCHEZ, MICHAEL S., state legislator; b. Belen, N.Mex., Aug. 3, 1950; m. Lynn Sanchez, 1969; children: Joshua, Nolan, Katrina. BA, U. N.Mex., 1973, JD, 1978. Atty. Raymond G. Sanchez, 1972—82, Michael G. Sanchez, 1982—; mem. Dist. 29 N.Mex. State Senate, 1992—, majority leader; Grant county clk., 1993—. Chair Valencia County Dem. Party, 1986—92; co-dir. Best of the West; mem. bd. dirs. Gila Regional Found., U. N.Mex. Oncology Bd. Vol. Big Brothers Big Sisters; bd. mem. Habitat for Humanity, La Vida Felicidad. Mem.: U. N.Mex. Alumni Assn., Trial Lawyers Assn., N.Mex. Bar Assn., Loyal Order of the Moose, Los Lunas C. of C., Belen C. of C., Rotary, Silver City Moose Lodge Men's Fall Hardball League, Elks Lodge. Democrat. Catholic. Office: Dist 29 3 Bunton Rd Belen NM 87002 Office Phone: 505-865-0688. Business E-Mail: senatormssanchez@aol.com.*

SANCHEZ, RAYMOND G., former state legislator; b. Albuquerque, Sept. 22, 1941; s. Gillie and Priscilla S.; 1 child, Raymond Michael. BA, U. N.Mex., 1964, JD, 1967. Bar: N. Mex. 1967. Ptnr. Sanchez, Mowrer & Desiderio, P.C., Albuquerque; mem. N.Mex. Ho. of Reps., 1970—; speaker N. Mex. Ho. of Reps., 1983—84, 1987—88, 1992—2000; mem. judiciary com., rules and order of bus. com., voters and elections com.; interim mem. workers compensation, legis. reform study coms., legis. coun.; pres. Naleo Educational Fund, Albuquerque, 2001. Bd. dirs. New Mex. Amigos, N.Mex. Diamond Jubilee/U.S. Constl. Bicentennial Commn., New Mex. First, Albuquerque Com. Fgn. Rels., N. Valley Neighborhood Assn.; bd. regents U. N. Mex. Mem. Nat. Assn. Latino Elected and Apptd. Ofcls. (bd. dirs.), Alameda Optimist Club (bd. dirs., charter mem.), U. N.Mex. Sch. Law Alumni Assn. (bd. dirs.), Elks Club, Sigma Xi. Democrat. Avocations: handball, scuba diving, swimming, sports. also: PO Box 1966 Albuquerque NM 87103-1966 Office Phone: 505-247-4321.

SANCHEZ-KENNEDY, MARIA, museum director; b. Pueblo, Colo. BA in Anthropology, U. N.Mex.; MA in Mus. Sci., Texas Tech U. Curator edn. Nev. State Railroad Mus., Carson City, Nev.; exec. dir. Bessemer Hist. Soc., Pueblo, Colo., 2001—08, Steelworks Mus. Industry & Culture, 2001—08, Colo. Fuel & Iron Corp. Archives, 2001—08; mgr. Robert Hoag Rawlings Pub. Libr. Infozone News Mus., Pueblo, Colo., 2008—. Mem.: Colo.-Wyo. Assn. Museums (chair 2006—07, 2007—08). E-mail: maria.sanchez@cfisteel.org.

SAND, THOMAS CHARLES, lawyer; b. Portland, Oreg., June 4, 1952; s. Harold Eugene and Marian Anette (Thomas) S.; children: Kendall, Taylor, Justin. Student, Centro des Artes y Lenguas, Cuernavaca, Mex., 1972; BA in English, U. Oreg., 1974; JD, Lewis and Clark Coll., 1977. Bar: Oreg. 1977, U.S. Dist. Ct. Oreg. 1977, U.S. Ct. Appeals (9th cir.) 1984. Assoc. Miller, Nash, LLP, Portland, 1977-84, ptnr., 1984—, mng. ptnr., 1999—. Mem. Oreg. State Bar Com. on Professionalism, 1989, chmn., 1990; dir. young lawyers divsn. Multnomah County Bar Assn., 1980; spl. asst. atty. gen. Wasco County 1983 Gen. Election; spkr. in field. Contbr. articles to legal jours. Mem. U.S. Dist. Ct. of Oreg. Hist. Soc., 1990—; bd. dirs. Portland Area coun. Camp Fire, Inc., 1978-90, pres., 1984-86; bd. dirs. Oreg. Indoor Invitational Track Meet, Inc., 1982-84. Recipient Boss of the Yr. award Portland Legal Secs. Assn., 1989, Disting. Grad. award Lewis and Clark Law Sch., 2004. Mem. ABA (securities litig. com., subcom. on broker-dealer litig.), Oreg. Bar Assn., Multnomah Bar Assn. (bd. dirs. task force on structure and orgn. 1989, chmn. com. on professionalism 1988, nominating com. 1986, participating atty. in N.E. legal clin. Vol Lawyers project, award of merit for svc. to profession 1988), Securities Industry Assn. (compliance and legal divsn.), Northwestern Sch. of Law, Lewis and Clark Coll. Alumni Assn. (bd. dirs. 1992, pres. 1997, law sch. bd. visitors 2004-), Valley Comm. Presbyterian Ch., Multnomah Athletic Club, Portland Golf Club. Avocations: golf, guitar, camping, river rafting, children's sports. Office: Miller Nash LLP 111 SW 5th Ave Ste 3500 Portland OR 97204-3699 Office Phone: 503-224-5858. Business E-Mail: tom.sand@millernash.com.

SANDAGE, ALLAN REX, astronomer; b. Iowa City, June 18, 1926; s. Charles Harold and Dorothy (Briggs) S.; m. Mary Lois Connelley, June 8, 1959; children: David Allan, John Howard. AB, U. Ill., 1948, DSc (hon.), 1967; PhD, Calif. Inst. Tech., Pasadena, 1953; DSc (hon.), Yale U., New Haven, Conn., 1966, U. Chgo., 1967, Miami U., Oxford, Ohio, 1974, Graceland Coll., Iowa, 1985; LLD (hon.), U. So. Calif., 1971; D (hon.), U. Chile, 1992. Astronomer Mt. Wilson Obs., Palomar Obs., Carnegie Instn., Washington, 1952—; Peyton fellow Princeton U., 1952; asst. astronomer Hale Obs., Pasadena, Calif., 1952-56; astronomer Obs. Carnegie Instn., Pasadena, Calif., 1956—; sr. rsch. astronomer Space Telescope Sci. Inst. NASA, Balt., 1986—; Homewood Prof. of physics Johns Hopkins U., Balt., 1987-89. Vis. lectr. Harvard U., 1957; mem. astron. expdn. to South Africa, 58; cons. NSF, 1961—64; Sigma Xi nat. astronomer U. Basel, 1985, 92, lectr., vis. prof., 94; vis. rsch. astornomer U. Calif., San Diego, 1985—86; vis. astronomer U. Hawaii, 1986; Lindsey lectr. NASA Goddard Space, Durham, England, 1992; Grubb-Parsons lectr. U. Durham, England, 1992. Assoc. editor: Ann. Rev. Astronomy and Astrophysics, 1990—2005. Served USN, 1945—46. Recipient Helen Warner prize, Am. Astron. Soc., 1960, Pope Pius XI Gold medal, Pontifical Acad. Sci., 1966, Rittenhouse medal, 1968, US Pres. medal of Sci., 1971, Russell prize, 1973, Adon medal, Obs. Nice, 1988, Crafoord prize, Swedish Royal Acad. Scis., 1991, Tomalla Gravity prize, Swiss Phys. Soc., 1993, Peter Gruber Found. prize for cosmology, 2000; Fulbright-Hays scholar, Australia, 1972. Mem.: Astron. Soc. Pacific (Gold medal 1975), Royal Soc. London (fgn.), Franklin Inst. (Elliott Cresson medal 1973, Gruber Cosmology prize 2000), Royal Astron. Soc. Can., Royal Astron. Soc. (Eddington medal 1963, Gold medal 1967), Lincei Nat. Acad. (Rome), Phi Beta Kappa. Home: 8319 Josard Rd San Gabriel CA 91775-1003 Office: 813 Santa Barbara St Pasadena CA 91101-1232 Office Phone: 626-304-0246.

SANDBERG, ARLENE, elementary school educator; BS in Elem. Edn., Kans. State Univ.; MS in Spl. Edn., Fitchburg State Univ., Mass. Tchr. Mass., Va., NY, Hawaii, Pa., 1979—98; ESL tchr. Mountain View Elem. Sch., Anchorage, 1998—. Named Alaska Tchr. of Yr., 2006. Office: Mountain View Elem Sch 4005 McPhee Ave Anchorage AK 99508 Office Phone: 907-742-3926 ext. 3013. Business E-Mail: sandberg_arlene@asdk12.org.

SANDBERG, SHERYL KARA, Internet company executive; b. 1969; d. Adele and Joel Sandberg; m. David Bruce Goldberg, Apr. 17, 2004; 2 children. BA in Economics, summa cum laude, Harvard U., 1991, MBA, 1995. Economist The World Bank; mgmt cons. McKinsey & Co.; chief of staff to sec. US Dept. Treasury, Washington, 1999—2001; joined Google Inc., Mountain View, Calif., 2001, v.p. global online sales & ops.; COO Facebook, Inc., Palo Alto, Calif., 2008—. Bd. dirs. eHealthInsurance Services, Inc., 2006—. Recipient John H. Williams prize, Harvard U.; named one of 50 Most Powerful Women in Bus., Fortune mag., 2007, 2008, Most Influential Women in Technology, Fast Company, 2009. Office: Facebook Inc 151 University Ave Ste 200 Palo Alto CA 94301-1675*

SANDERS, ADRIAN LIONEL, retired educational consultant; b. Paragould, Ark., Aug. 3, 1938; s. Herbert Charles and Florence Theresa (Becherer) S.; m. Molly Jean Zecher, Dec. 20, 1961. AA, Bakersfield Coll., 1959; BA, San Francisco State U., 1961; MA, San Jose State U., 1967. 7th grade tchr. Sharp Park Sch., Pacifica, Calif., 1961-62; 5th grade tchr. Mowry Sch., Fremont, Calif., 1962-64; sci. tchr. Blacow Sch., Fremont, Calif., 1964-76; 5th grade tchr. Warm Springs Sch., Fremont, 1977-87, 5th grade gifted and talented edn. tchr., 1987-94; ret., 2006; edn. cons., 1994—2006. Mem. San Diego Hist. Soc., 1999, Mingei Internat. Mus., Balboa Park-San Diego; vol. 7 km. Race for Alzheimer's Disease Willow Glen Founders Day, San Jose, 1988-92. Named Outstanding Young Educator, Jr. C. of C., Fremont, Calif., 1965. Mem. Zoolog. Soc. San Diego, Calif. Ctr. for the Arts (Escondido), Calif. Retired Tchrs. Assn., 1994-, San Jose State U. Alumni Assn., 2006-. Avocations: photography, travel, collecting license plates. Home and Office: 1437 Stoneridge Cir Escondido CA 92029-5514

SANDERS, CHARLES FRANKLIN, energy executive, consultant; b. Louisville, Dec. 22, 1931; s. Charles Franklin and Maragret Rhea (Timmons) S.; m. Marie Audrey Galuppo, Dec. 29, 1956; children: Karen Lynn, Craig Joseph, Keith Franklin. B.Chem. Engring., U. Louisville, 1954, M.Chem. Engring., 1958; PhD, U. So. Calif., 1970. Rsch. engr. Exxon Rsch. and Engring. Co., Linden, NJ, 1955-62; asst. prof. engring. Calif. State U., Northridge, 1962-68, assoc. prof., 1968-71, prof., 1971-82, chmn. dept., 1969-72, dean Coll. Engring. and Computer Sci., 1972-81; pres., chief exec. officer, dir. Rusco Industries, Los Angeles, 1981-82; exec. v.p. Energy Systems Assocs., Tustin, Calif., 1982-89, Energeo, San Francisco, 1989-95, also bd. dirs.; v.p. tech. Smith-Bellingham Capital, San Francisco, 1989-91. Bd. dirs. Catalyst Air Tech., Inc. Bd. dirs. San Fernando Valley Child Guidance Clinic, 1979-81. Served to 1st lt. U.S. Army, 1956-57. NSF fellow, 1965-67 Mem. AIChE, NSPE, Calif. Soc. Profl. Engrs., Am. Soc. for Engring. Edn., Combustion Inst. Republican. Office Phone: 949-362-6585. Personal E-mail: cfs@cox.net.

SANDERS, ELIZABETH ANNE WEAVER (BETSY SANDERS), management consultant, coach, writer; b. Gettysburg, Pa., July 25, 1945; Student, Gettysburg Coll., 1963—65; BA in German Lang. and Linguistics, Wayne State U., 1967; MEd, Boston U., 1970; postgrad., U. Wash., 1976—78. With Nordstrom, 1971—90, v.p., gen. mgr., 1978—90; prin. The Sanders Partnership, Sutter Creek, Calif., 1971-90, prin., owner, 1990—; founder, dir. Nat. Bank So. Calif., 1971-90. Bd. dirs. Wal Mart Stores, Inc., Washington Mut., Wellpoint Health Sys., Inc., Wolverine Worldwide, Inc., Denny's Inc., H.F. Ahmanson Co., Carl Karcher Enterprises, Sport Chalet, St. Joseph Health Sys., spkr. in field, mgmt. cons., exec. coach, life coach, mentor, facilitator in leadership, svc., creating cultures. Author: Fabled Service, 1995. Trustee Gettysburg Coll.; regent U. Pacific; adv. bd. mem. Bimbo Bakeries USA. Recipient Woman of Achievement in Bus. award YWCA South Orange County, Director's Choice award, 1997; named Woman of Yr. Bus. and Industry YWCA North Orange County, Humanitarian of Yr. NCCJ, Author of Yr., 1996, Dir. of Yr., Corp. Gov. Forum for Corp. Dirs., 2002. Mem. Internat. Women's Forum. Home: 12835 Sutter Creek Rd Sutter Creek CA 95685-9733 Office: The Sanders Partnership PO Box 14 Sutter Creek CA 95685-0014 Office Phone: 209-267-5400. E-mail: betsanders@aol.com.

SANDERS, JACK THOMAS, religious studies educator; b. Grand Prairie, Tex., Feb. 28, 1935; s. Eula Thomas and Mildred Madge (Parish) S.; m. M. Patricia Chism, Aug. 9, 1959 (dec. Oct. 1973); 1 son, Collin Thomas; m. Susan Elizabeth Plass, Mar. 3, 1979. BA, Tex. Wesleyan Coll., 1956; M.Div., Emory U., 1960; PhD, Claremont Grad. Sch., 1963; postgrad., Eberhard-Karls U., Tuebingen, Germany, 1963-64. Asst. prof. Emory U., Atlanta, 1964-67, Garrett Theol Sem., Evanston, Ill., 1967-68, McCormick Theol. Sem., Chgo., 1968-69; assoc. prof. U. Oreg., Eugene, 1969-75, prof., 1975-97, head dept. religious studies, 1973-80, 85-90, prof. emeritus, 1997—. Author: The New Testament Christological Hymns, 1971, Ethics in the New Testament, 1975, 2d edit., 1986, Ben Sira and Demotic Wisdom, 1983, The Jews in Luke-Acts, 1987, Schismatics, Sectarians, Dissidents, Deviants: The First One Hundred Years of Jewish-Christian Relations, 1993, Charisma, Converts, Competitors: Societal and Sociological Factors in the Success of Early Christianity, 2000; editor: Gospel Origins and Christian Beginnings, 1990, Gnosticism and the Early Christian World, 1990; mem. edit. bd. Jour. Bibl. Lit., 1977-83. Mem. policy bd. Dept. Higher Edn. Nat. Council Chs., N.Y.C., 1971-73. NDEA grad. study fellow, 1960-63; Fulbright Commn. fellow, 1963-64; Am. Coun. Learned Socs. travel grantee, 1981; NEH fellow, 1983-84. Mem. Assn. for Jewish Studies, Soc. Bibl. Lit. (regional sec. 1969-76, sabbatical rsch. award 1976-77). Democrat. Home: 704 NW 3d Dr Pendleton OR 97801-1411 Office: U Oregon Dept Religious Studies Eugene OR 97403 E-mail: jsands@oregontrail.net.

SANDERS, JAMES ALVIN, retired minister, retired religious studies educator; b. Memphis, Nov. 28, 1927; s. Robert E. and Sue (Black) S.; m. Dora Cargille, June 30, 1951; 1 son, Robin David. BA magna cum laude, Vanderbilt U., 1948, BD with honors, 1951; student, U. Paris, 1950-51; PhD, Hebrew Union Coll., 1955; DLitt, Acadia U., 1973; STD, U. Glasgow, 1975; DHL, Coe Coll., 1988, Hebrew Union Coll., 1988, Hastings Coll., 1996, Calif. Luth. U., 2000. Ordained teacher Presbyn. Ch., 1955; instr. French Vanderbilt U., 1948-49; faculty Colgate Rochester Div. Sch., 1954-65, assoc. prof., 1957-60, Joseph B. Hoyt prof. O.T. interpretation, 1960-65; prof. O.T. Union Theol. Sem., NYC, 1965-70, Auburn prof. Bibl. studies, 1970-77; adj. prof. Columbia, NYC, 1966-77; prof. Bibl. studies Sch. Theology and Grad. Sch., Claremont, Calif., 1977-97, ret., 1997; vis. prof. Union Theol. Seminary and Columbia U., 1997-98. Ann. prof. Jerusalem Sch. of Am. Schs. Oriental Rsch., 1961-62; fellow Ecumenical Isnt., Jerusalem, 1972-73, 85; vis. prof. U. N.Mex., 1992, Southwestern U., 1992, Calif. Luth. U., 1992, 94, Willamette U., 1993, U. So. Ariz., 1993, Jewish Theol. Sem., 2001—; session chair, Internat. Congress for Fiftieth Anniversary of Dead Sea Scrolls, Jerusalem, 1997; mem. internat. O.T. text critical com. United Bible Socs., 1969—; mem. nat. adv. acad. bd. Hebrew Union Coll., 1997—; co-founder, exec. officer Ancient Bibl. Manuscript Ctr. for Preservation and Rsch., 1977-80, pres., 1980-2003, pres. emeritus, 2003—; chmn. bd. Shepherd U., L.A., 2002—, bd. mem. Early Manuscripts Electronic Literacy, 2005-, bd. adv. Mus. of Archeology and the Bible, 2006-,; vis. prof. Yale Divinity Sch., 1998, Jewish Theol. Seminary, 2001; lectr. in field Author: Suffering as Divine Discipline in the Old Testament and Post-Biblical Judaism, 1955, The Old Testament in the Cross, 1961, The Psalms Scroll of Qumran Cave 11, 1965, The Dead Sea Psalms Scroll, 1967, Near Eastern Archaeology in the Twentieth Century, 1970, Torah and Canon, 1972, 1974, 2d edit., 2005, Identité de la Bible, 1975, God Has a Story Too, 1979, Canon and Community, 1984, From Sacred Story to Sacred Text, 1987, Luke and Scripture, 1993; editor: Paul and the Scriptures of Israel, 1993, Early Christian Interpretation of the Scriptures of Israel, 1993, The Function of Scripture in Early Jewish and Christian Tradition, 1998, The Canon Debate, 2002; contbr. over 280 articles to profl. jours.; mem. editl. bd. Jour. Bibl. Lit., 1970—76, Jour. for Study Judaism, Bibl. Theology Bull., Interpretation, 1973—78, New Rev. Std. Version Bible Com., A Gift of God in Due Season, 1996, The Quest for Context and Meaning, 1997. Trustee Am. Schs. Oriental Research. Fulbright grantee, 1950-51, Lilly Endowment grantee, 1981, NEH grantee, 1980, 91-92; Lefkowitz and Rabinowitz interfaith fellow, 1951-53, Rockefeller fellow, 1953-54, 85, Guggenheim fellow, 1961-62, 72-73, Human Scis. Rsch. fellow, 1989. Mem. Soc. Bibl. Lit. and Exegesis (pres. 1977-78), Phi Beta Kappa, Phi Sigma Iota, Theta Chi Beta. Home: PO Box 593 Claremont CA 91711-0593 Personal E-mail: sandersja@aol.com.

SANDERS, JERRY, Mayor, San Diego, former social services executive; b. San Pedro, Calif., July 14, 1950; m. Rana Sampson; children: Jamie, Lisa. AA, Long Beach City Coll., 1970; BA in Pub. Adminstrn., Nat. U., 1988; student, San Diego State U. Cert. P.O.S.T mgmt. Police officer San Diego Police Dept., 1973-93, chief of police, 1993-99; CEO United Way San Diego, 1999—2005; mayor City of San Diego, 2005—. Bd. dirs. The Nat. Conf., San Diego State U. Cmty. Adv. Bd., Children's Initiative, Youth Econ. Enterprise Zones, Am. Red Cross San Diego; mem. cmty. leaders adv. bd. ElderHelp of San Diego. Recipient Headliner of Yr. award San Diego Press Club, 1984, 93, Exceptional Performance citation for SWAT leadership, 1986. Office: Office of Mayor 202 C St 11th Fl San Diego CA 92101 Office Phone: 619-236-6330. Office Fax: 619-236-7228. Business E-Mail: JerrySanders@sandiego.gov.*

SANDERS, JOEL STEVEN, lawyer; b. Mpls., Mar. 25, 1955; s. David M. and Miriam (Gelfand) S.; m. Carol G. Bieri, May 25, 1984; children: Daniel, Elizabeth. BA, Antioch Coll., 1976; JD, U. Calif., Berkeley, 1982. Bar: Calif. 1982, US Dist. Ct. (no. dist.) Calif. 1982, US Dist. Ct. (cen. dist.) Calif. 1984, US Ct. Appeals (9th cir.) 1983. Law clk. to Hon. Procter R. Hug Jr. US Ct. Appeals (9th cir.), 1982-83; atty. antitrust div. US Dept. Justice, San Francisco, 1983-87; assoc. Gibson, Dunn & Crutcher, San Francisco, 1987-91; ptnr. Gibson, Dunn & Crutcher LLP, San Francisco, 1992—, ptnr.-in-charge, Bay Area offices, 1995—2000. Former adj. asst. prof. law Univ. Calif. Hastings Coll. of Law; mem. exec. com. Gibson Dunn & Crutcher. Assoc. editor Calif. Law Rev., 1980-82. Mem. ABA, State Bar of Calif., Bar Assn. of San Francisco, Order of Coif. Office: Gibson Dunn & Crutcher Ste 3100 555 Mission St San Francisco CA 94105-2933 Office Phone: 415-393-8200. Office Fax: 415-374-8439. Business E-Mail: jsanders@gibsondunn.com.

SANDERS, LUCINDA (LUCY SANDERS), information technology organization executive; BS in Computer Sci. summa cum laude, La. State U., 1975; MS in Computer Sci., U. Colo., 1978. Mem. technical staff AT&T Bell Labs, 1977—82, R&D develop. mgr., 1982—95; R&D dir. Lucent Bell Labs, 1995—96; chief tech. officer Lucent Customer Care Solutions Bell Labs, 1996—99; v.p. R&D, chief tech. officer Avaya, Inc. CRM Solutions: Avaya Labs, 1999—2001; exec. in residence, Alliance for Tech., Learning, and Soc. (ATLAS) U. Colo., Boulder, 2001—, co-founder, CEO, Nat. Ctr. for Women & Info. Tech. (NCWIT), 2004—. Bd. dir. Gold Systems and Solidware Technologies; bd. trustee, Math. Scis. Rsch. Inst. U. Calif., Berkeley; mem., Info. Tech. Rsch. and Develop. Ecosystem Comm. Nat. Academies; mem. adv. bd. U. Col., ATLAS, 1999—2001, U. Denver Women's Coll. Applied Computing Program, 2001—, Denver Pub. Sch. Sys. Computer Magnet, 2002—; mem. sci. adv. bd., Dept. Computer Sci. U. Colo., 2002—; mem. Colo. Inst. Tech. Telecommunications Study, 2002, NSF Planning Grant for the Nat. Ctr. for Women and Info. Tech., 2003, Colo. Inst. Tech. Planning Grant for the Nat. Ctr. for Women and Info. Tech., 2003, Colo. Inst. Tech. Digital Currents Summer Camp, 2004, NSF Extension Svcs. Grant for Implementing effective practices across the country, 2005; CIO panelist, VoIP, Silicon Flatirons Telecommunications Program, 05; mem. adv. coun. U. Colo. Engring., 2005—; program chair Grace Hopper Celebration of Women in Computing, 2006, conf. chair, 07; panelist Google Faculty Summit, 2006, Dept. Edn. Summit on Math and Sci., 2006; plenary panelist Microsoft Faculty Summit, 2006; panelist Google Faculty Summit, 2006; independent cons. for customer svc. (call ctr.) industry, 2001—; invited spkr. in field. Contbr. articles to profl. jours.; guest expert Voice Over IP (VoIP), mem. queue editl. bd. Assn. for Computing Machinery, 2004, guest Nat. Pub. Radio, The Best of Our Knowledge Show, 2004, IT conversations interview VoIP & Women in Innovation, 2004, VoIP Panelist Haas Bus. Sch., U. Calif., Berkeley, 2004, guest Nat. Pub. Radio, Market Place, 2005. Bell Labs program leader, NSF/Colo. Sch. Mines Native Am. Math Camp, 1989—2000; mem. Crest View Habitat Wetlands Environ, Restoration Project, 1990—. Recipient Silicon Valley Tribute to Women in Industry award, 2000, U. Colo. at Boulder Disting. Engring. Alumni award for Industry and Commerce, 2004, Soroptimist Internat. LA Women of Vision award, 2006; named to Women in Tech. Internat. Hall of Fame, 2007; Bell Labs Fellow award, 1996, Aspen Inst. Exec. Seminar Academic Scholarship, 2005. Achievements include patents in field. Mailing: U Colo Campus Box 322 Boulder CO 80309-0322 Office: Nat Ctr for Women & Info Tech 231 ATLAS Bldg U Colo 1125 18th St Boulder CO 80309 Office Phone: 303-735-5108, 303-735-6671. Office Fax: 303-735-6606. E-mail: Lucinda.Sanders@colorado.edu.

SANDERS, RICHARD BROWNING, state supreme court justice; b. Tacoma; 1 child: Laura. BA, U. Wash., 1966, JD, 1969. Assoc. Murray, Scott, McGavick & Graves, Tacoma, Wash., 1969, Caplinger & Munn, Seattle, 1971; hearing examiner State Wash., Olympia, 1970; pvt. practice Wash., 1971-95; justice Wash. Supreme Ct., Olympia, 1995—. Adj. prof. U. Wash. Sch. Law; lectr. in field. Contbr. articles to profl. jours. Office: Supreme Court of Washington Temple of Justice PO Box 40929 Olympia WA 98504-0929 Fax: (360) 357-2092. E-mail: j_r.sanders@courts.wa.gov.

SANDERS, RICHARD KINARD, actor; b. Harrisburg, Pa., Aug. 23, 1940; s. Henry Irvine and Thelma S. BFA, Carnegie Inst. Tech., 1962; postgrad. (Fulbright scholar), London Acad. Music and Dramatic Art, 1962-63. Pres. Blood Star, Inc. Mem. various acting cos., Front St., Memphis, Champlain Shakespeare Festival, Vt., Center Stage, Balt., N.Y. Shakespeare Festival, N.Y.C., Chelsea Theater Center, N.Y.C., Mark Taper Forum, Los Angeles, Arena Stage, Washington; appeared on: (Broadway) Raisin; (TV series) Les Nessman on WKRP in Cincinnati and The New WKRP in Cincinnati, Paul Sycamore in You Can't Take It With You, Mr. Beanley in Spenser; writer of many episodes of WKRP and other situation comedies; writer NBC movie Max and Sam; numerous TV and film appearances. Vol. Peace Corps, Northeastern Brazil, 1966-69. Recipient Buckeye Newshawk award, 1974-79, Silver Sow award, 1979 Mem. Writers Guild Am., Screen Actors Guild, AFTRA, Actors Equity Assn. Office: PO Box 1644 Woodinville WA 98072-1644

SANDERS, W. J., III, information technology executive; BSEE, U. Ill., 1958. Various positions with engring. dept Douglas Aircraft Co.; sales and mktg. positions Motorola Semicondr.; various positions with semicondr. divsn., including sales mgr., area sales mgr., dept. head, dir. mktg., group dir. mktg. worldwide Fairchild Camera and Instrument Corp., 1967—69; chmn. bd., founder Advanced Micro Devices, Sunnydale, Calif., 1969—, CEO, 1969—2002. Co-founder Semicondr. Industry Assn., Santa Clara Mfg. Group, Semicondr. Rsch. Corp., Microelectronics and Computer Tech. Corp. Recipient Robert N. Noyce award, Semiconductor Industry Assn., 1998, Medal of Achievement, AeA, 2001, Lifetime Achievement award, PC Mag., 2002; named Best CEO in Semiconductor Industry, Wall Street Transcript, 1983, 1984, 1985; named to CRN Industry Hall of Fame, 2002. Office: AMD 1 AMD Pl Sunnyvale CA 94086 Office Phone: 408-749-4000. Office Fax: 408-749-4291.

SANDERSON, DAVID R., physician; b. South Bend, Ind., Dec. 26, 1933; s. Robert Burns and Alpha (Rodenberger) S.; divorced, 1978; children: David, Kathryn, Robert, Lisa; m. Evelyn Louise Klunder, Sept. 20, 1980. BA, Northwestern U., 1955, MD, 1958. Cons. in medicine Mayo Clinic, Rochester, Minn., 1965—87, chmn. dept. thoracic disease, 1977—87, cons. in medicine Scottsdale, Ariz., 1987—2000, chmn. dept. internal medicine, 1988—96, vice chmn. bd. govs., 1987—94. Assoc. dir. Mayo Lung Project, Nat. Cancer Inst., Rochester. Contbr. articles to profl. jours. Recipient Noble award Mayo Found., Rochester, Chevalier Jackson award Am. Bronchoesophagologic Assn., 1990. Fellow ACP, Am. Coll. Chest Physicians (gov. for Minn. 1981-87); mem. Am. Bronchoesophagologic Assn. (pres. 1986-87), World Assn. for Bronchology, Internat. Bronchoesophagologic Soc., Internat. Assn. Study of Lung Cancer, AMA, Sigma Xi, Sigma Chi (Significant Sig award 1989). Presbyterian. Home: 10676 E Bella Vista Dr Scottsdale AZ 85258-6086 Office: Mayo Clinic Arizona 13400 E Shea Blvd Scottsdale AZ 85259-5499 Personal E-mail: dsanderson958@cox.net.

SANDITZ, LISA, painter; b. St. Louis, 1973; Student, Studio Art Ctr. Internat., Florence, Italy, 1994; BA, MacAlester Coll., Minn., 1995; MFA, Pratt Inst., Bklyn., 2001. One-woman shows include The Rite Spot, San Francisco, 1998, Pratt Inst., Bklyn., 2001, Onefront Gallery, NYC, 2001, P.S. 122, NYC, 2003, CRG Gallery, NYC, 2003, 2005, Rodolphe Jansen Gallery, Brussels, 2004, Kemper Mus. Contemporary Art, Kansas City, 2006, ACME, LA, 2006, exhibited in group shows at Filler, Three Blue Lights, San Francisco, 1998, Pier Show, Bklyn. Working Artist Coalition, 2000, No Comment, Blake-Sherlock Gallery, NYC, 2000, Six Artists Drawings, im n il Gallery, Bklyn., 2000, Hello Franklin, 2003, Need to Know Basis, Geoff Young Gallery, Great Barrington, Mass., 2002, Sugarfree, The Puffin Room, NYC, 2002, Singing My Song, ACME, LA, 2004, Tugboat, 2007, Galerie Tanit, Munich, 2004, No Man's Land, Shoshana Wayne Gallery, LA, 2005, Landscape Confection, Wexner Ctr. Arts, Ohio, 2005, Orange County Mus. Art, Newport Beach, Calif., 2006, New Prints, Internat. Print Ctr., NYC, 2005, Ridykeulous, Participant Inc., NYC, 2006, Grounds for Progress, Ctr. Curatorial Studies, Bard Coll., NY, 2008, Beware of the Wolf II, Am. Acad. Rome, 2008. Fellow Guggenheim Found., 2008. Office: ACME Spaces 1&2 6150 Wilshire Blvd Los Angeles CA 90048

SANDLER, ADAM, actor; b. Bklyn., Sept. 9, 1966; m. Jackie Titone, June 22, 2003; children: Sadie Madison, Sunny Madeline. Grad., NYU. Actor: (films) Remote Control (also writer), 1987, Shakes the Clown, 1992, Coneheads, 1993, Airheads, 1994, Bullet Proof, 1996, Punch Drunk Love, 2002, Spanglish, 2004, Reign Over Me, 2007; actor, writer: Billy Madison, 1995 (also composer), Happy Gilmore, 1996, Bulletproof, 1996; actor, exec. prodr.: The Animal, 2001, Mr. Deeds, 2002, Anger Management, 2003, The Longest Yard, 2005, Bedtime Stories, 2008; actor, exec. prodr., writer: The Waterboy, 1998, Big Daddy, 1999, Little Nicky, 2000; actor (voice), prodr., writer, also writer (songs) soundtrack: Eight Crazy Nights, 2002; actor, soundtrack song(s) Going Overboard, 1989, Mixed Nuts, 1994, The Wedding Singer, 1998, 50 First Dates, 2004; actor, prodr., Click, 2006, I Now Pronounce You Chuck and Larry, 2007; writer, actor, prodr.: Deuce Bigalow: European Gigolo, 2005, You Don't Mess with the Zohan, 2008; prodr.: Benchwarmers, 2006; exec. prodr. (films)

Deuce Bigalow: Male Gigolo, 1999, Joe Dirt, 2001, The Master of Disguise, 2002, Hot Chick, 2002, Dickie Roberts: Former Child Star, 2003, Grandma's Boy, 2006, Strange Wilderness, 2007; exec. prodr. (TV) The Mayor, 2003, The Dana & Julia Show, 2004, Gay Robot, 2006; TV appearances include Saturday Night Live: The Best of Chris Farley, 1998, Saturday Night Live: The Best of Mike Myers, 1998, Saturday Night Live: The Best of Phil Hartman, 1998, The Cosby Show, 1987-1988, Couch, 2003; actor, writer Saturday Night Live (Emmy award nomination for writing 1991, 92), 1990-95; appeared on TV programs ABC Afterschool Special, Testing Dirty, 1990, Saturday Night Live Mother's Day Special, 1992, MTV Music Video Awards, 1994, Saturday Night Live Presents President Bill Clinton's All-Time Favorites, 1994, The 37th Annual Grammy Awards, 1995, The ESPY Awards, 1996; rec. artist (albums) They're All Gonna Laught at You!, 1993, What the Hell Happened to Me?, 1996 (also exec. prodr.), What's Your Name, 1997, Stan and Judy's Kid, 1999 (set record for most comedy albums sold in first week released), Shhh...Don't Tell, 2004; exec. prodr. (TV series) Rules of Engagement, 2007-. Named Funny Male Star, People's Choice Awards, 2000, 2006, 2009, Choice Comedian, Teen Choice Awards, 2006, 2008; recipient Generation award, MTV Movie Awards, 2008; named one of 50 Most Powerful People in Hollywood, 2004-06, 100 Most Powerful Celebrities, Forbes.com, 2007. Office: c/o Baker-Winouker-Ryder 9100 Wilshire Blvd 6th Fl Beverly Hills CA 90212

SANDLER, MICHAEL DAVID, lawyer; b. LA, Feb. 27, 1946; AB, Stanford U., 1967; JD, Yale U., 1972. Bar: Calif. 1973, DC 1973, Wash. 1985. Assoc. Steptoe & Johnson, Washington, 1972-75, 77-79, ptnr., 1980-85; spl. asst. to legal adviser Dept. of State, Washington, 1975-77; ptnr. Foster, Pepper & Shefelman, Seattle, 1985-97, Sandler Ahern & McConaughy PLLC, Seattle, 1997—, chair (former sect.). Adj. prof. law Georgetown U., Washington, 1979, 81-82, U. Wash., Seattle, 1985-92. Vol. Peace Corps, Ethiopia and Ghana, 1968-70. Mem. ABA (chair 1995-96 sect. internat. law and practice). Home: 9311 SE 36th St Ste 220 Mercer Island WA 98040-3741 Office Phone: 206-346-1751. E-mail: mike@sandlaw.com.

SANDLER, THOMAS R., accountant, director; b. Mt. Kisco, NY, Dec. 16, 1946; s. Louis and Susan (Rosen) S.; m. Alison G. Corneau, Aug. 26, 1972; children: Justin C., Shawn A. BS summa cum laude, Ithaca Coll., 1968; MS, SUNY-Binghamton, 1972. C.P.A., NY, Colo. 1982. Asst. acct. KPMG Peat Marwick, White Plains, N.Y., 1972, mgr. Phoenix, 1975, sr. mgr. NYC, 1978, ptnr. Denver, 1981-92, ptnr. in-charge corp. recovery svcs. NYC, 1993-94; mng. ptnr. BDO Seidman, Denver, 1994-95; CFO, treas., sec. Samsonite Corp., Denver, 1995-98; pres. Samsonite Am., 1998—2004; CEO Case Logic, Inc., Longmont, Colo., 2004—. Contbr. articles to profl. jours. Past trustee, past pres. Colo. Children's Chorale; treas., past pres., gov., mem. exec. com., committeeman Colo. Golf Assn.; committeeman US Golf Assn. bd. dirs. Pacific Coast Golf Assn.; chmn. Travel Goods Assn. Mem. AICPA, Colo. Soc. CPAs (chmn. real estate and govt. acctg. com.), Bear Creek Golf Club, Country Club at Castle Pines, Colo. Golf Club. Home: 896 Anaconda Ct Castle Rock CO 80108-9044 Office: Case Logic Inc 6303 Dry Creek Pkwy Longmont CO 80503

SANDMAN, IRVIN W(ILLIS), lawyer; b. Seattle, Mar. 19, 1954; BA summa cum laude, U. Wash., 1976; JD, UCLA, 1980. Bar: U.S. Dist. Ct. (we. and ea. dists.) Wash. 1980. Prin. Graham & Dunn, Seattle, 1980—. Staff mem. UCLA Law Rev. Mem. ABA (hotel resorts and tourism com. 1996-2001, co-chair 2001-04, chair hospitality industry liaison subcom. 2002—), Acad. Hospitality Attys. (charter), Wash. State Bar Assn. (chmn. creditor/debtor sect. 1988-90, editor newsletter 1983—, spkr. continuing legal edn.). Office: Graham & Dunn PC 2801 Alaskan Way Ste 300 Seattle WA 98121-1128 Office Phone: 206-340-9641. Business E-Mail: isandman@grahamdunn.com.

SANDMEYER, E. E., toxicologist, consultant; b. Winterthur, Zurich, Switzerland, Aug. 9, 1929; came to U.S., 1955; BSChemE, Technikum, Winterthur, 1951; MS in Organic Chemistry, Ohio State U., 1960, PhD in Biochemistry, 1965. Cert. civil svc. chemist II, Nev., biochemist II, Pa., clin. lab. dir. Ctrs. for Disease Control. Asst. prof. sci., gen. chemistry, organic chemistry Friends U., Wichita, 1965-66; asst. prof. biochemistry, labs., and rsch. U. Nev., Reno, 1966-71; head corp. toxicology Gulf Oil Corp., Pitts., 1971-76; divsn. head organic analysis Barringer Labs., Denver, 1987-88; pres., toxicologist, owner Transcontec, Inc., Kelseyville, Calif., 1976—. Div. head organic analysis Barringer Labs., Denver, 1986-88. Contbg. author: Patty's Industrial Hygiene and Toxicology, 1981, A Guide to General Toxicology, 1983. Mem. AAAS, Am. Chem. Soc., Soc. Environ. Health, Sigma Xi, Sigma Delta Epsilon. Home: PO Box 982 Ukiah CA 95482-0982

SANDOVAL, BRIAN EDWARD, federal judge, former state attorney general; b. Redding, Calif., Aug. 5, 1963; s. Ronald L. and Gloria Sandoval; m. Kathleen T. Sandoval; children: James, Madeline, Marisa. B in English & Econ., U. Nev., 1986; JD, Ohio State U., 1989. Bar: Nev., Calif., DC. Mem. Nev. State Assembly, 1995—97; atty. McDonald, Carano, Wilson, McCune Bergin, Frankovich & Hicks, Reno, 1989—91, Robinson, Belaustegui, Robb & Sharp, Reno, 1991—95, Gamboa, Sandoval & Stovall, Reno, 1995—99, Sandoval Law Office, Reno, 1999—2003; atty. gen. State of Nev., Carson City, 2003—05; judge US Dist. Ct. Dist. Nev., Reno, 2005—. Mem. Nev. Gaming Commn., 1998—2001, chmn., 1999—2001; mem. State and Local Officials' Adv. Com. US Dept. Homeland Security. Bd. trustees Children's Cabinet, Reno, St. Jude's Ranch for Children, Washoe County Law Libr., Nev. Recipient Torch of Liberty, Anti-Defamation League, 2003; named Public Lawyer of the Yr., Nevada St. Bar Assoc., 2004. Republican. Office: US Dist Ct 400 S Virginia St Reno NV 89501

SANDOVAL, PAULA E., state legislator; m. Paul Sandoval; 5 stepchildren. Mem. Dist. 34 Colo. State Senate, Denver, 2002—. Bd. govs. Colo. State Univ Sys.; sec. Denver County Dems.; mem. Denver Civil Svc. Commn., Denver Welfare Reform Bd., Greenway Found., Hispanic Edn. Adv. Coun., Colo. Healthy Kids Coalition. Democrat. Office: Colo State Capitol 200 E Colfax Denver CO 80203 Office Phone: 303-866-4862. Business E-Mail: paula.sandoval.senate@state.co.us.*

SANDQUIST, GARY MARLIN, engineering educator, researcher, consultant, writer, military officer; b. Salt Lake City, Apr. 19, 1936; s. Donald August Sandquist and Lillian (Evaline) Dunn; m. Kristine Powell, Jan. 17, 1992; children from previous marriage: Titia, Julia, Taunia, Cynthia, Carl; stepchildren: David, Michael, Scott, Diane, Jeff. BSME in Mech. Engring., U. Utah, 1956—60; MS in Engring. Sci., U. Calif., Berkeley, 1960—61; PhD in Mech. Nuclear Engring., U. Utah, 1961—64, MBA Exec. MS, 1993—95. Registered profl. engr., Utah, N.Y., Minn., Calif.; cert health physicist, quality auditor; diplomate Am. Acad. Environ. Engring. Staff mem. Los Alamos (N.Mex.) Sci. Lab., 1966; postdoctoral fellow MIT, 1969-70; rsch. prof. surgery Med. Sch., U. Utah, Salt Lake City, 1974—85, prof., dir. nuc. engring. dept. mech. engring., 1975—2007, acting chmn. dept., 1984-85, adj. prof. civil engring., 1996—2007; expert in nuc. sci. Internat. Atomic Energy Agy., UN, 1980—; chief scientist Rogers and Assocs. Engring. Corp., Salt Lake City, 1980—90, sr. nuclear engr., 1998—; sr. health physicist URS Corp., 1990—; mgr., owner Applied Sci. Profls., LLC, Salt Lake City, 1998—. Vis. scientist MIT, Cambridge, Mass., 1969-70; advisor rocket design Hercules, Inc., Bachus, Utah, 1962; sr. nuc. engr. Idaho Nat. Engring. Lab., Idaho Falls, 1963-65; cons. nuc. sci. State of Utah, 1982—; vis. prof. Ben Gurion U., Beer Sheva, Israel, 1985, disting. vis. prof. U.S. Mil. Acad., West Point, N.Y., 2003-05; affiliate faculty Idaho State U., 1998-; cons. various cos.; spkr. Nuc. Energy Inst., 1990—; mem. radiation adv com., EPA. Author: Geothermal Energy, 1973, Introduction to System Science, 1985, over 700 pub. presentations, reports in sci. and tech. Comdr. USNR, 1954-56, Korea; ret. Comdr. USNR, 1954—56, Intel officer USNR. Recipient Glen Murphy award in nuc. engring. Am. Soc. Engring. Edn., 1984. Fellow ASME, Am. Nuc. Soc.; mem. Am. Soc. Quality (sr.), Am. Health Physics Soc., Am. Soc. Engring. Edn., Alpha Nu Sigma, Sigma Xi, Tau Beta Pi, Pi Tau Sigma. Republican. Mem. Lds Ch. Achievements include development of 17 major computer codes; participated in 200 technical meetings, conferences, Government hearings. Home: 2564 E Neffs Cir Salt Lake City UT 84109 Office: U Utah 2232 Merrill Engring Bldg Salt Lake City UT 84112 Home Phone: 801-273-0200; Office Phone: 801-904-4125.

SANDRICH, JAY H., television director; b. LA, Feb. 24, 1932; s. Mark R. and Freda (Wirtschafter) S.; m. Nina Kramer, Feb. 11, 1952 (div.); children: Eric, Tony, Wendy; m. Linda Green Silverstein, Oct. 4, 1984. BA, UCLA, 1953. Prodr. (TV show) Get Smart, 1965; dir. (TV shows) He and She, 1967, Mary Tyler Moore Show, 1970-88, Soap, 1977-79, Cosby Show, 1984-92; dir. (films) Seems Like Old Times, 1980, For Richer, For Poorer (HBO), 1992, Neil Simon's London Suite (NBC), 1996. Served to 1st lt. Signal Corps U.S. Army, 1952-55. Mem. Dirs. Guild Am. (award 1975, 85, 86), TV Acad. Arts and Scis. (Emmy award 1971, 73, 85, 86). Office: care Andy Elkin Creative Artists Agy 9830 Wilshire Blvd Beverly Hills CA 90212

SANDS, KEVIN B., cosmetic dentist; Grad., U. Southern Calif. Sch. Dentistry; grad. Advanced Anterior Aesthetic Dentistry, Las Vegas Institute for Advanced Dental Studies. Pvt. practice, Beverly Hills. Featured in Life & Style, InTouch, US, In Style Weddings, Item and others, featured on E! and TLC. Mem. Beverly Hills C. of C., Calif. Mem.: ADA, Acad. Cosmetic Dentistry, Calif. State Dental Assn. Office: 414 N Camden Dr Ste 940 Beverly Hills CA 90210 Office Phone: 310-273-0111. Office Fax: 310-271-0584.

SANDS, RICK (RICHARD SANDS), former film company executive; BA with honors in Economics and Film, Syracuse U. Regional sales mem. Columbia Pictures, v.p. domestic distbn. divsn., 1978; exec. v.p., CFO Miramax Films, 1990—93, RHI Entertainment (sold to Hallmark Entertainment), 1993—95; pres. internat. Miramax Films, 1995—97, chmn. worldwide distbn., 1997—2002, COO, 2002—04; pres., COO DreamWorks SKG, 2005—06; COO Metro-Goldwyn-Mayer Inc., LA, 2006—08. Trustee Will Rogers Motion Pictures Pioneers Found. Recipient Humanitarian award, Variety Boys and Girls Club of Queens, 2003.

SANDWELL, DAVID, geophysicist, educator; BS in Physics, U. Conn., 1975; MS in Geophysics, UCLA, 1978, PhD in Geophysics and Space Physics, 1981. Rsch. geophysicist Nat. Geodetic Survey, 1982—85; rsch. scientist U. Tex., Austin, 1985—89; assoc. prof. geophysics Scripps Inst. Oceanography, La Jolla, Calif., 1989—93, prof. geophysics, 1993—. Fellow: Am. Acad. Arts and Sciences, Geol. Soc. America (George P. Woollard award 2004), Am. Geophys. Union (pres. elect geodesy sect. 2008, Bowie lecture 1995); mem.: Soc. Exploration Geophysics, Internat. Assn. Geodesy. Office: Scripps Inst Oceanography UC San Diego 9500 Gilman Dr La Jolla CA 92093-0225 Office Phone: 858-534-7109. E-mail: dsandwell@ucsd.edu.

SANGER, PRIYA SESHACHARI, lawyer; d. Candadai Seshachari and Neila C. S. BA in Classics, Smith Coll., Northampton, Mass.; JD, Univ. Utah, 1990. Bar: NY, Calif., Utah, US Ct. Appeals (9th cir.), US Supreme Ct. Former litigator; now sr. counsel Wells Fargo Bank NA, San Francisco. Staff: Utah Law Rev. Apptd. to San Francisco Human Rights Commn. Disadvantaged Bus. Com.; adv. com. Minority/Women/Local Bus. Enterprise Cmty. Named one of Best Lawyers Under 40, Nat. Asian Pacific Am. Bar Assn., 2004. Mem.: Lawyers for One Am. (founding mem.), Korean Am. Bar Assn., San Francisco Bank Attys. Assn. (pres.-elect 2004), Bar Assn. San Francisco (bd. dir. 2003—04), Barristers Club San Francisco (past pres.). Office: Sr Counsel Wells Fargo Bank NA 5th Fl 633 Folsom St San Francisco CA 94107 Office Phone: 415-396-4113. Office Fax: 415-975-7861. Business E-Mail: sangerps@wellsfargo.com.

SANI, ROBERT LEROY, chemical engineering professor; b. Antioch, Calif., Apr. 20, 1935; m. Martha Jo Marr, May 28, 1966; children: Cynthia Kay, Elizabeth Ann, Jeffrey Paul. BS, U. Calif.-Berkeley, 1958, MS, 1960; PhD, U. Minn., 1963. Postdoctoral researcher dept. math Rensselaer Poly. Inst., Troy, NY, 1963-64; asst. prof. U. Ill., Urbana, 1964-70, assoc. prof., 1970-76; prof. chem. engring. U. Colo., Boulder, 1976—, assoc. dept. chair, 2007—; co-dir. Ctr. for Low-g Fluid Mechanics and Transport Phenomena, U. Colo., Boulder, 1986-89, dir., 1989—. Assoc. prof. French Ministry Edn., 1982, 84, 86, 92, 94, 95, 96, 97; cons. Lawrence Livermore Nat. Lab., Calif., 1974-84. Contbr. numerous chpts. to profl. publs.; co-author three books; mem. editorial bd. Internat. Jour. Numerical Methods in Fluids, 1981—, Revue Européenne des Éléments Finis, 1990—, Internat. Jour. Computational Engring. Sci., 1998—, Internat. Jour. Computational & Numerical Analysis & Applications, 2000-. Guggenheim fellow, 1970 Mem. AICE, Soc. for Applied and Indsl. Math., World User Assn. in Applied Computational Fluid Dynamics (bd. dirs.). Democrat. Office: U Colo Dept Chem & Biol Engring UCB 424 Boulder CO 80309-0424 Office Phone: 303-492-5517. Business E-Mail: robert.sani@colorado.edu.

SANKEY, LAURA L., telecommunications industry executive; b. Sept. 6, 1964; m. Kevin B. Sankey. B in Psychology, Dartmouth Coll., Hanover, NH; M in Mktg. and Strategy, Northwestern U. Mktg. cons. Mktg. Corp. Am.; brand mgmt. position Procter & Gamble; v.p. mktg. Coors Brewing Co.; v.p. mktg. comm. and advt. Qwest Comm. Internat., Inc., 2006, exec. v.p. mktg. and comm., 2006—. Bd. dirs. Denver Metro Convention and Visitors Bur., Greenhouse Scholars, Warren Village. Office: Qwest Comm Internat Inc 1801 California St Denver CO 80202 Office Phone: 303-992-1400. Office Fax: 303-992-1724.

SANKS, ROBERT LELAND, environmental engineer, retired educator; b. Pomona, Calif., Feb. 19, 1916; s. John B. and Nellie G. (Church) Sanks; m. Mary Louise Clement, May 16, 1946 (dec. Oct. 1994); children: Margaret Russell, John Clement; m. Edith Millen Harrington, Dec. 2, 1999. AA, Fullerton Jr. Coll., Calif., 1936; BS, U. Calif., Berkeley, 1940; MS, Iowa State Coll., Ames, 1949; PhD, U. Calif., Berkeley, 1965. Registered profl. engr., Mont. Draftsman City of La Habra Calif., 1940; asst. engr. Alex Morrison cons. engr., Fullerton, Calif., 1941; jr. engr. US Army Engrs., LA, 1941-42; asst. rsch. engr. dept. civil engring. U. Calif.-Berkeley, 1942-45; structural engr. The Austin Co., Oakland, Calif., 1945-46; instr. dept. civil engring. U. Utah, Salt Lake City, 1946-49, asst. prof., 1949-55, assoc. prof., 1955-58; structural engr. The Lang Co., Salt Lake City, 1950; instrument man Patti McDonald Co., Anchorage, 1951; checker Western Steel Co., Salt Lake City, 1952; structural engr. Moran, Proctor, Meuser and Rutledge, NYC, 1953, F.C. Torkelson Co., Salt Lake City, 1955; soils engr. R.L. Sloane & Assocs., Salt Lake City, 1956; prof., chmn. dept. civil engring. Gonzaga U., Spokane, Wash., 1958-61; prof. dept. civil engring. Mont. State U., Bozeman, 1966-82, prof. emeritus, 1982—; vis. prof. U. Tex.-Austin, 1974-75; part-time sr. engr. Christian, Spring, Sielbach & Assocs., Billings, Mont., 1974-82. Cons. engr., 1945—; lectr. at pumping sta. design workshops, 1988—; assoc. specialist San. Engring. Research Lab., 1963-65, research engr., 1966. Author: Statically Indeterminate Structural Analysis, 1961; co-author: (with Takashi Asano) Land Treatment and Disposal of Municipal and Industrial Wastewaters, 1976, Water Treatment Plant Design for the Practicing Engineer, 1978; editor-in-chief: Pumping Station Design, 1989 (award Excellence profl. & scholarly pub. div. Assn. Am. Pubs. 1989), 2d edit., 1998, co-editor 3d edit., 2006; contbr. articles on civil engring. to profl. publs. Mem. Wall of Fame, Fullerton H.S., 1987, Hall of Fame, Mont. Profl. Engrs., 2005; NSF fellow, 1961-63 Mem. ASCE (life, chmn. local qualifications com. intermountain sect. 1950-56, pres. intermountain sect. 1957-58), Am. Water Works Assn. (pres. Mont. sect. 1981-82, George Warren Fuller award), Mont. Water Environ. Fedn., Assn. Environ. Engring. Profs., Rotary, Sigma Xi, Chi Epsilon. Home: 1201 Highland Blvd Apt D309 Bozeman MT 59715 Office Phone: 406-599-9615. Personal E-mail: bsanks@mcn.net.

SANNWALD, WILLIAM WALTER, librarian; b. Chgo., Sept. 12, 1940; s. William Frederick and Irene Virginia (Stanish) S.; children: Sara Ann, William Howard. BA, Beloit Coll., 1963; MAL.S., Rosary Coll., River Forest, Ill., 1966; MBA, Loyola U., Chgo., 1974. Mktg. mgr. Xerox Univ. Microfilms, 1972-75; assoc. dir. Detroit Public Library, 1975-77; dir. Ventura (Calif.) County Library, 1977-79; city libr. San Diego Public Libr., 1979-97; asst. to city mgr. for libr. design and devel. City of San Diego, 1997—. Vis. instr. mktg. San Diego State U. Author: Checklist of Library Building Design Considerations, 3d edit., 1997; chairperson editorial adv. bd. Pub. Librs. Pres. Met. Libraries Sect., 1989. Recipient Outstanding Prof. award and Outstanding Mktg. Prof. award, 1985; Award of Merit AIA San Diego chpt., 1988, Irving Gill award for Architecture and Mgmt., 1995. Mem. ALA, Online Computer Libr. Ctr. (mem. users coun. 1996), Calif. Library Authority for Systems and Services (pres. congress of mems. 1980), Calif. Library Assn., Libr. Admintrn. and Mgmt. Assn. (pres. 1995-96). Roman Catholic. Home: 3538 Paseo Salamoner La Mesa CA 91941-7329 Office: San Diego Pub Libr 820 E St San Diego CA 92101-6478

SANO, EMILY JOY, former museum director; b. Santa Ana, Calif., Feb. 17, 1942; d. Masao and Lois Kikue (Inokuchi) S. BA, Ind. U., 1967; MA, Columbia U., 1970, MPhil, 1976, PhD, 1983. Lectr. Oriental Art Vassar Coll., Poughkeepsie, NY, 1974-79; curator Asian Art, asst. dir. programs Kimbell Art Mus., Ft. Worth, 1979-89; dep. dir. collections and exhbns. Dallas Mus. Art, 1989-92; dep. dir., chief curator Asian Art Mus., San Francisco, 1993-95, dir., 1995—2007. Author: Great Age of Japanese Buddhist Sculpture, 1982; editor: The Blood of Kings, 1986, Weavers, Merchants and Kings, 1984, Painters of the Great Ming, 1993. Active Assn. Art Mus. Dirs.; vis. com. Harvard U. Art Mus. Woodrow Wilson Fellow, 1966-67; grantee Carnegie, 1963-64, Fulbright-Hays, 1977-78.

SANSONETTI, THOMAS L., lawyer, former federal agency administrator; b. Hinsdale, IL, May 18, 1949; BA in Fgn. Affairs, with distinction, U. Va., 1971, MBA, 1973; JD, Washington and Lee U., 1976. Chief of staff, legis. dir. to Congressman Craig Thomas US Ho. Reps; assoc. solicitor on energy and natural resources US Dept. Interior, 1987—89, solicitor, 1990—93; ptnr. Holland & Hart LLP, Cheyenne, Wyo., 1993—2001, 2005—; asst. atty. gen. for environment & natural resources US Dept. Justice, Washington, 2001—05. Founder Wyo. Tennis Assn., 1978; mem. Wyo. Rep. Nat. Com., 1996—2002; chmn. Wyo. Rep. Party, 1983—87; gen. counsel Rep. Nat. Com., 2001; leader Bush-Cheney transition team Interior Dept., 2001. Republican. Office: Holland & Hart LLP 2515 Warren Ave Cheyenne WY 82001-3162 Office Phone: 307-778-4200. Office Fax: 307-778-8175. E-mail: tlsansonetti@hollandhart.com.

SANSWEET, STEPHEN JAY, journalist, writer, marketing executive; b. Phila., June 14, 1945; s. Jack Morris and Fannie (Axelrod) S. BS, Temple U., Phila., 1966. Reporter Phila. Inquirer, 1966-69; reporter Wall Street Jour., Phila., 1969-71, Montreal, Que., Canada, 1971-73, LA, 1973-84, dep. bur. chief, 1984-87, bur. chief, 1987-96; dir. specialty mktg. Lucasfilm Ltd., San Francisco, 1996—97, dir. content mgmt. and fan rels., 1997—; sr. editor Star Wars Galaxy Mag., 1996-2000; columnist Star Wars Insider, 1994—. Lectr. bus. journalism U. So. Calif., LA, 1984-87. Author: The Punishment Cure, 1976, Science Fiction Toys and Models, 1981, Star Wars: From Concept to Screen to Collectible, 1992, Tomart's Price Guide to Worldwide Star Wars Collectibles, 1994, 2d edit., 1997, The Quotable Star Wars, 1996, Star Wars Scrapbook: The Essential Collection, 1998, Star Wars Encyclopedia, 1998, Star Wars Collectibles: A Pocket Manual, 1998, Anakin Skywalker: The Story of Darth Vader, 1998, Star Wars: The Action Figure Archive, 1999, The Star Wars Vault, 2007; co-author: The Star Wars Poster Book, 2005, Star Wars Chronicles: The Prequels, 2005; cons. editor: Star Wars Galaxy card sets, 1993, 2d series, 1994, 3d series, 1995; editor: Star Wars Trilogy Spl. Edn. card sets, 1997. Recipient award for best fire story Phila. Fire Dept., 1968, Pub. Svc.-Team Mem. award Sigma Delta Chi, 1977; finalist Loeb award, 1990. Mem. Soc. Profl. Journalists. Avocation: collecting toys and movie memorabilia. Office: Lucasfilm Ltd PO Box 29901 San Francisco CA 94129

SANTANA, RONNY, real estate agent, small business owner; m. Daniela Santana; 2 children. Real estate license 1981. Agent Coldwell Banker Real Estate LLC; owner Santana Realty Grp. Founder CAPSTONE Found. Republican. Office: Coldwell Banker 12029 Saratoga Sunnyvale Rd Saratoga CA 95070 Mailing: Campaign Address PO Box 3684 Saratoga CA 95070 Personal E-mail: Jxlkz@yahoo.com.

SANTER, BENJAMIN DAVID, atmospheric scientist; b. Washington, June 3, 1955; BS Environ. Scis. with 1st class honors, U. East Anglia, Norwich, Eng., 1976; NATO Rsch. Studentship, U. East Anglia, 1977, PhD in Climatology, 1987. Jr. rsch. assoc. Sch. Environ. Scis. U. East Anglia, Norwich, Eng., 1978-79, rsch. assoc. climatic rsch. unit, 1983-87; project engr. dept. new techs., air pollution and Dornier Sys. GmbH, Friedrichshafen, Germany, 1980-83; postdoct., rsch. scientist Max-Planck Inst. Meteorologie, Hamburg, Germany, 1987-92; physicist earth and environ. scis. directorate Lawrence Livermore Nat. Lab., Livermore, Calif., 1992—. Expert witness German Bundestag Enquete Commn. Hearings on Greenhouse-Gas-Induced Climate Change, Bonn, Germany, 1992; cons. Battelle Pacific Northwest Lab., 1992-93, mem. sci. adv. panel climate change, data and detection program NOAA, 1995—; mem. Climate Variability and Predictability Numerical Experimentation Group, 1995—; participant numerous confs., workshops; lectr. in field. Co-author: Proceedings of NATO Advanced Study Institute on Physically-Based Modelling and Simulation of Climate and Climatic Change, 1988, Science and Engineering on Supercomputers, 1990, Supercomputer '90, Greenhouse-Gas-Induced Climate Change: A Critical Appraisal of Simulations and Observations, 1991, Global Warming: Concern for Tomorrow, 1993, Agricultural Dimensions of Global Climate Change, 1993, Dahlem Workshop on Global Changes in the Perspective of the Past, 1993, Climate Change int the Intra-American Sea, 1993, Communicating About Climate: the Story of the Model Evaluation Consortium for Climate Assessment, 1997; mem. editl. bd. Climatic Change, 1996—; contbr. numerous articles to profl. jours., chpts. to books. MacArthur fellow John D. and Catherine T. MacArthur Found., 1998; Ford Travel scholar, 1974; recipient Outstanding Scientific Paper award U.S. Dept. Commerce Environ. Rsch. Lab. Nat. Oceanic and Atmospheric Adminstrn., 1997, Norbert Gerbier-MUMM Internat. award World Meteorol. Orgn., 1998, E.O. Lawrence award U.S. Dept. Energy, 2002. Mem. Am. Geophys. Union. Achievements include research in climate modeling and greenhouse-gas effects supporting the hypothesis that human activity contributes to global warming. Office: Lawrence Livermore Nat Lab PCMDI PO Box 808 L-264 Livermore CA 94551-0808 Home: 2160 Goldenrod Ln San Ramon CA 94583-5555 Fax: (925) 422-7675. E-mail: santer1@llnl.gov.

SANTILLAN, ANTONIO, financial company executive; b. Buenos Aires, May 8, 1936; naturalized, 1966; s. Guillermo Spika and Raphaella C. (Abaladejo) S.; children: Andrea, Miguel, Marcos. Grad., Morgan Park Mil. Acad., Chgo., 1954; BS in Psychology, Coll. of William and Mary, 1958. Cert. real estate broker. Asst. in charge of prodn. Wilding Studios, Chgo., 1964; pres. Adams Fin. Services, Los Angeles, 1965—. Writer, producer, dir. (motion pictures) The Glass Cage, co-writer Dirty Mary/Crazy Harry, Viva Knievel; contbg. writer Once Upon a Time in America; TV panelist Window on Wall Street; contbr. articles to profl. fin. and real estate jours. Served with USNR, 1959. Recipient Am. Rep. award San Francisco Film Festival, Cork Ireland Film Fest, 1961. Mem. Writer's Guild Am., L.A. Bd. Realtors, Beverly Hills Bd. Realtors (income/investment divsn. steering com.), Westside Realty Bd. (bd. dirs.), L.A. Ventures Assn. (bd. dirs.), Jonathan Club (L.A.), Rotary, Roundtable, Toastmasters Internat. Avocations: golf, tennis, skiing. Office: Adams Fin Svcs Inc 425 N Alfred St West Hollywood CA 90048-2504 Office Phone: 323-852-0444 ext. 204. E-mail: antonio@adamsfinancial.net.

SANTOS, SHARON TOMIKO, state legislator; b. San Francisco, Jan. 5, 1961; m to Bob; children: six. Washington State Representative, District 37, 99-, Majority Whip, currently, member, Education, Finance & Financial Inst & Ins Committees, 99-, Washington House Representative.Bd trustees, Wing Luke Asian Mus, 93-, World Affairs Coun, 94-; advisor board, KUOW 94.9 FM Public Radio, Univ Washington, 96-. Martin Luther King, Jr, Keeping the Dream Alive Award, 93; Celebrating Women's Leadership, Washington State Women's Polit Caucus, 96. Women's Int League for Peace & Freedom (treasurer, 96-). Democrat. Protestant . Office: State House Repr 436B Legislative Bldg PO Box 40600 Olympia WA 98504 Address: 1265 S Main St Ste 203 Seattle WA 98144 Office Phone: 360-786-7944. E-mail: santos_sh@leg.wa.gov.

SANTOSUOSSO, PATRICK See SMITH, PATRICK

SARASON, IRWIN G., psychology professor; b. Newark, Sept. 15, 1929; s. Max and Anna Sarason; m. Barbara June Ryrholm, Sept. 19, 1953; children: Suzanne, Jane, Donald. BA, Rutgers U., Newark, 1951; MS, U. Iowa, 1953; PhD, Ind. U., 1955. Intern clin. psychology VA Hosp., West Haven, Conn., 1955-56; from asst. prof. psychology to prof. emeritus U. Wash., Seattle, 1956—2003, prof. emeritus, 2003—. Co-author: Abnormal Psychology, 1972, 11th edit., 2005; editor: Jour. Personality and Social Psychology, 1985-91; author over 300 articles. The Netherlands Inst. for Advanced Study fellow, Wassenaar, 1975, 85. Fellow APA, Japan Soc. for Promotion of Sci., AAAS, Western Psychol. Assn. (pres. 1978-79), Wash. State Psychol. Assn. (pres. 1965). Avocations: travel, music, reading. Home: 13516 42nd Ave NE Seattle WA 98125-3826 Office: U Wash Dept Psychology Box 351525 Seattle WA 98195-0001 Business E-Mail: isarason@u.washington.edu.

SARASWAT, KRISHNA, electrical engineering educator; married; 2 children. BE in Electronics, Birla Inst. Tech. and Sci., India, 1968; MSEE, Stanford U., 1969, PhD in Elec. Engring., 1974. Product engr. Tex. Instruments, Dallas, 1963—70; rsch. assoc. Integrated Cirs. Lab. Stanford (Calif.) U., 1974—78, sr. rsch. assoc. Integrated Cirs. Lab., 1978—83, dir. rsch. program on mfg. sci. for VLSI, CIS, 1985—93, prof. elec. engring., 1983—. Dir. Integrated Cirs. Lab. Stanford U., 1996—97, dir. NSF/SRC Engring. Rsch. Ctr. for Environmentally Benign Semicondr. Mfg., 1999—; mem. tech. com. Internat. Workshop on Statis. Metrology, 1995—97; mem. Joint Indo/U.S. Com. on Microelectronics to Advise Govt. of India, 1986—88; sec. Internat. Symposium on Physics of VLSI, 1984. Contbr. numerous tech. papers to profl. jours. Recipient Inventor Recognition award, Semicondr. Rsch. Corp., 1987. Fellow: IEEE (mem. tech. com. internat. reliability physics symposium 1997—98, mem. tech. com. internat. interconnect tech. conf. 1997, mem. fellow evaluation com. 1994—, assoc. editor Transactions on Electron Device 1988—90, mem. tech. com. internat. device rsch. conf. 1985—88, chmn. device tech. group internat. electron devices meeting 1984, Best Paper award 1984, 1985, 1990); mem.: Materials Rsch. Soc., Electrochem. Soc. (Thomas D. Callinan award 2000). Achievements include research in physics and technology of silicon VLSI devices and interconnects. Office: Stanford U Elec Engring CISX 326 Stanford CA 94305

SARDELLA, EDWARD JOSEPH, television news anchor; b. Buffalo, June 2, 1940; s. Joseph Edward and Josephine Jenny (D'Amico) S.; m. Sandra K. Lorenzen, Jan. 17, 1975. BA in Speech Arts, Occidental Coll., LA, 1962. Radio disc jockey, newsman KWIN/KTIL/KHRG, Ashland/Tillamook/Eugene, Oreg., 1966-69; reporter KVAL-TV, Eugene, 1969-70; reporter/anchor KOIN-TV, Portland, Oreg., 1970-72, KMGH-TV, Denver, 1972-74; news anchor/sr. editor KUSA-TV, Denver, 1974—. Adj. instr. journalism U. Colo., Boulder, 1984-92. Author: Write Like You Talk, 1984; co-author: The Producing Strategy, 1995. Olympic torchbearer, 1996. Capt. USMC, 1962-66. Recipient Emmy award Nat. Assn. TV Arts and Scis., 1992, 93, 94, 95, 96, also Silver Circle Career Achievement award, 1999; named Colo. Broadcaster of Yr., 1997, Journalist of Yr. Colo. chpt. Soc. Profl. Journalists, 2000; inducted into Denver Press Club Hall of Fame, 2002.

SARGENT, ARLENE ANNE, nursing educator; b. Little Falls, Minn. Jan. 11, 1944; d. Anton Clarence and Eleanor Anne (Buerman) Hondl; m. Ken William Sargent, June 16, 1972; children: Lisa, Michelle. BSN, Coll. St. Catherine, 1969; MSN, U. Minn., 1972; EdD, No. Ill. U., 1980. Staff nurse U. Wash., Seattle, 1969-70, U. Minn. Hosp., Mpls., 1970-72; instr. Loyola U., Chgo., 1972-75; asst. prof. U. Dubuque, Iowa, 1975-76, assoc. prof., chairperson, 1976-79; assoc. prof. No. Ill. U., DeKalb, 1979-83; prof., chairperson Holy Names Coll., Oakland, Calif., 1983-98; assoc. dean St. Mary's-Samuel Merritt Intercollegiate Nursing Program, Oakland, Calif., 1999—2004, dean nursing program, 2000—04; mng. dir. for edn. and workforce Kaiser Permanente, Oakland, Calif., 2004—. Bd. mem. Calif. Strategic Planning Commn., 1993—. Mem. Sigma Theta Tau (mem. heritage com. 1994—), Pi Lambda Theta, Kappa Delta Pi. Presbyterian. Avocations: playing piano, hiking. Office: Samuel Merritt Coll 435 Hawthorne Ave Oakland CA 94609 E-mail: asargent@samuelmerritt.edu, sargentak@earthlink.net.

SARGENT, JOSEPH DANIEL, motion picture and television director; b. Jersey City, July 22, 1925; s. Domenico and Maria (Noviello) Sargente; m. Carolyn Nelson, Nov. 22, 1970; children: Athena, Lia. Student in Theatre Arts, New Sch. for Social Rsch., 1946—49. Pres. Joseph Sargent Prodns. Inc. Dir.: (films) Street-Fighter, 1959, The Spy in the Green Hat, 1966, One Spy Too Many, 1966, The Hell with Heroes, 1968, Colossus: The Forbin Project, 1970, The Man, 1972, White Lightning, 1973, The Taking of Pelham One Two Three, 1974 (Best Dir. award San Sebastian Film Festival), MacArthur, 1977, Goldengirl, 1979, Coast to Coast, 1980, Nightmares, 1983, Jaws: The Revenge, 1987; (TV films) The Sunshine Patriot, 1968, The Immortal, 1969, Tribes, 1970 (Outstanding Directorial Achievement award Dirs. Guild Am.), Maybe I'll Come Home in the Spring, 1971, Longstreet, 1971, Man on a String, 1972, The Marcus-Nelson Murders, 1973 (Emmy award, Dirs. Guild Am. award), The Man Who Died Twice, 1973, Wheeler and Murdoch, 1973, Sunshine, 1973, Hustling, 1975, Friendly Persuasion, 1975, The Night That Panicked America, 1975, Amber Waves, 1980, Freedom, 1981, Tomorrow's Child, 1982, Memorial Day, 1983, Choices of the Heart, 1983, Terrible Joe Moran, 1984, Sunday Night Live, 1984, Love Is Never Silent, 1985 (Emmy award), Passion Flower, 1986, The Must Be A Pony, 1986, Of Pure Blood, 1986, The Karen Carpenter Story, 1989, Day One, 1989, The Incident, 1990, Miss Rose White, 1992, Somebody's Daughter, 1992, Skylark, 1993, Abraham, 1994, World War II: When Lions Roared, 1994, My Antonia, 1995, Mandela and de Klerk, 1997, Miss Evers' Boys, 1997, The Long Island Incident, 1998, The Wall, 1998, Crime and Punishment, 1998, A Lesson Before Dying, 1999, Vola Sciusciu, 2000, For Love or Country, 2000, Bojangles, 2001, Out of the Ashes, 2003, Something the Lord Made, 2004, Warm Springs, 2005 (Outstanding Directorial Achievement in Movies for TV Dirs. Guild Am., 2005); (TV series) Gunsmoke, 1962—65, The Man From UNCLE, 1964, The Girl From UNCLE, 1966, Star Trek, 1966, Gallegher Goes West, 1966, The Invaders, 1967, Garrison's Gorillas, 1967, It Takes A Thief, 1968, The Manions of America, 1981, Space, 1985, Streets of Laredo, 1995, Salem Witch Trials, 2002; dir. & actor (TV films) Caroline?, 1990, Ivory Hunters, 1990, The Love She Sought, 1990. With US Army, 1943—46. Mem.: Actors Equity Assn., AFTRA, Screen Actors Guild, Dirs. Guild Am.

SARGENT, WALLACE LESLIE WILLIAM, astronomer, educator; b. Elsham, Eng., Feb. 15, 1935; naturalized, 2004; s. Leslie William and Eleanor (Denniss) S.; m. Anneila Isabel Cassells, Aug. 5, 1964; children: Lindsay Eleanor, Alison Clare. B.Sc., Manchester U., 1956, M.Sc., 1957, PhD, 1959. Research fellow Calif. Inst. Tech., Pasadena, 1959-62; sr. research fellow Royal Greenwich Obs., 1962-64; asst. prof. physics U. Calif., San Diego, 1964-66; mem. faculty dept. astronomy Calif. Inst. Tech., 1966—, prof., 1971-81, Ira S. Bowen prof. astronomy, 1981—, dir. Palomar Obs., 1997-2000. Miller prof. U. Calif., Berkeley, 1993; Thomas Gold lectr. Cornell U., Ithaca, NY, 1995; Sackler lectr. Harvard U., Cambridge, Mass., 1995, U. Calif., Berkeley, 1996; Icko Iben lectr. U. Ill., 2002. Contbr. articles to profl. jours. Alfred P. Sloan fellow, 1968-70. Fellow Am. Acad. Arts and Scis., NAS, Royal Soc. (London); mem Am. Astron. Soc. (v.p. 2004-07, Helen B. Warner prize 1969, Dannie Heineman prize 1991, Henry Norris Russell Lectureship, 2001), Royal Astron. Soc. (George Darwin lectr. 1987, assoc. 1998), Astron. Soc. Pacific (Bruce Gold medal 1994), Internat. Astron. Union. Clubs: Athenaeum (Pasadena). Home: 400 S Berkeley Ave Pasadena CA 91107-5062 Office: Calif Inst Tech Astronomy Dept 105-24 Pasadena CA 91125-0001 Office Phone: 626-395-4055.

SARGENT, WALTER HARRIMAN, II, lawyer; b. Norfolk, Va., Aug. 26, 1958; s. Richard E. and Martha F. (Bassett) S. BS in Philosophy, MIT, 1980, BS in Computer Sci. and Engring., 1980; JD, Harvard U., 1987. Bar: Colo. 1987, U.S. Dist. Ct. Colo. 1988, U.S. Ct. Appeals (3d, 6th, 9th and 10 cirs.), U.S. Supreme Ct. 1992. Assoc. Holme Roberts & Owen, Colorado Springs, 1987-95; pvt. practice Colorado Springs, 1995—; bd. trustees Colorado Legal Aid Found., 1998—2004. Bd. dirs. ARC of the Pikes Peak Region, 1991-97, Coalition for Adult Literacy, Colorado Springs, 1989-93. Recipient John M. Olin prize in law and econs. Harvard Law Sch., 1987, John M. Olin fellow, 1987, fellow Am. Acad. Appellate Lawyers, 2004—. Mem. ABA (appellate practice com.), Colo. Bar Assn. (appellate practice subcom.), Am. Acad. Appellate Lawyers. Avocation: distance running. Home: 1632 N Cascade Ave Colorado Springs CO 80907-7409 Office: Walter H Sargent A Profl Corp 1632 N Cascade Ave Colorado Springs CO 80907-7409 Home Phone: 719-632-2319; Office Phone: 719-577-4510. Personal E-mail: wsargent@wsargent.com.

SARICH, VINCENT M., anthropologist, educator; b. Chgo., Dec. 13, 1934; s. Matt and Manda Saric; m. Jorjan Snyder; children: Kevin, Tamsin. BS, Ill. Inst. Tech., 1955; PhD, U. Calif., Berkeley, 1967. Instr. anthropology Stanford U., Berkeley, Calif., 1965; from asst. prof. to assoc. prof. anthropology U. Calif., Berkeley, 1967-81, prof., 1981-94, prof. emeritus, 1994—; vis. faculty U. Auckland, New Zealand, 1999—. Office: U Calif Dept Anthropology 232 Kroeber Hall Berkeley CA 94720-3710

SARKISIAN, CHERILYN See CHER

SARNOFF, THOMAS WARREN, television executive; b. NYC, Feb. 23, 1927; s. David and Lizette (Hermant) S.; m. Janyce Lundon, May 21, 1955; children: Daniel, Timothy, Cynthia. Grad., Phillips Acad., 1939-43; student, Princeton, 1943-45; BS in Elec. Engring., Stanford U., 1948, postgrad. Sch. Bus. Adminstrn., 1948-49; D.H.L., Columbia Coll. Engaged in prodn. and sales with ABC, Inc., 1949-51; prodn. Metro-Goldwyn-Mayer, 1951-52; with NBC, 1952-77; v.p. prodn. and bus. affairs NBC (Pacific div.), 1956-60, v.p. adminstrn. West Coast, 1960-62, v.p. charge West Coast, 1962-65, staff exec. v.p. West Coast, 1965-77; pres. NBC Entertainment Corp., 1972-77, Sarnoff Internat. Enterprises, 1977-81, Sarnoff Entertainment Corp., 1981—; exec. v.p. Venturetainment Corp., 1981-87, pres., 1987—96. Bd. dirs. Multimedia Games, Inc., 1998-2006, chmn. bd., 2004-06, cons., 2006-08. Exec. producer Bonanza: The Next Generation, 1987, Bonanza: The Return, 1993, Back to Bonanza Retrospective, 1993, Bonanza: Under Attack, 1995. Mem. Calif. Commn. for Reform Intermediate and Secondary Edn. Pres., Research Found., St. Joseph Hosp., Burbank, 1965-73, Permanant Charities Com. of Entertainment Industries, 1971-72; nat. trustee Nat. Conf. Christians and Jews. Served with Signal Corps AUS, World War II. Mem. Acad. TV Arts and Scis. (chmn. bd. trustees 1972-74, chmn. past pres.'s coun. 1989-92), Acad. TV Arts and Scis. Found. (pres. 1990-99, chmn., CEO 1999—2005, chmn. emeritus 2005-), The Caucus for Prodrs., Writers and Dirs. Office: 2451 Century Hl Los Angeles CA 90067-3510 Office Phone: 310-203-9234. Personal E-mail: tsarnoff@aol.com.

SARPKAYA, TURGUT, mechanical engineering educator; b. Aydin, Turkey, May 7, 1928; came to U.S., 1951, naturalized, 1962; s. Hasip and Huriye (Fetil) S.; m. Gunel Ataisik, Aug. 26, 1963. BS in Mech. Engring, Tech. U. Istanbul, 1950, MS, 1951; PhD in Engring, U. Iowa, 1954. Research engr. MIT, Cambridge, 1954-55; asst. prof. U. Nebr., 1957-59, assoc. prof., 1959-62, prof. mech. engring., 1962, distinguished prof., 1962-66; research prof. U. Manchester, Eng., 1966-67, U. Gottingen, Fed. Republic of Germany, 1971-72; prof. mech. engring., chmn. dept. mech. engring. U.S. Naval Postgrad. Sch., Monterey, Calif., 1967-71, 72—, Disting. prof. mech. engring., 1975—. Cons. aerospace industry, 1967—, petroleum industry, 1976— Author: Mechanics of Wave Forces on Offshore Structures, 1981; mem. editorial bd.; Zentralbaltt fur Mathematik; editor: Procs. Heat Transfer and FLuid Mechanics Inst., 1970; contbr. chpts. to many books and over 200 papers on fluid dynamics. Served with C.E. AUS, 1955-57. Fellow Royal Instn. Naval Architects, AIAA, ASME (Lewis F. Moody award 1967, exec. bd. fluids engring. fivsn., chmn. review com., Freeman Scholar award 1988, Engring. award 1991, Fluids Engring. award 1990, Collingwood prize 1957, Offshore Mechanics and Arctic Engring. award 1993, Turning Goals into Reality award, NASA, 2002); mem. Heat Transfer and Fluid Mechanics Inst. (chmn., Am. Inst. Aeros. and Astronautics, Am. Soc. Engring. Edn. Achievements include patent for fluidic elements. Home: 25330 Vista Del Pinos Carmel CA 93923-8804 Office: Naval Postgrad Sch Mech Engring Code ME SL 700 Dyer Rd Monterey CA 93943-5000 E-mail: sarp@nps.navy.mil.

SARSGAARD, PETER, actor; b. Scott AFB, IL, Mar. 7, 1971; m. Maggie Gyllenhaal, May 2, 2009; 1 child, Ramona. BA in History, Washington U., 1994. Actor: (off-Broadway plays) Kingdom of Earth, Laura Dennis; (Broadway plays) The Seagull, 2008; (films) Dead Man Walking, 1995, Minor Details, 1998, The Man in the Iron Mask, 1998, Desert Blue, 1998, Another Day in Paradise, 1998, Boys Don't Cry, 1999, The Cell, 2000, Housebound, 2000, The Center of the World, 2001, Bacon Wagon: The Movie, 2001, Empire, 2002, The Salton Sea, 2002, K-19: The Widowmaker, 2002, Unconditional Love, 2002, Death of a Dynasty, 2003, Shattered Glass, 2003, Garden State, 2004, Kinsey, 2004, The Dying Gaul, 2005, The Skeleton Key, 2005, Flightplan, 2005, Jarhead, 2005, Rendition, 2007, The Mysteries of Pittsburgh, 2008, Elegy, 2008, An Education, 2009, In the Electric Mist, 2009; (TV films) Freak City, 1999.*

SARSON, JOHN CHRISTOPHER, television producer, director, writer; b. London, Jan. 19, 1935; s. Arnold Wilfred and Annie Elizabeth (Wright) S.; m. Evelyn Patricia Kaye, Mar. 25, 1963 (div. 2005); children: Katrina May, David Arnold BA with honors, Trinity Coll., Cambridge, Eng., 1960, MA, 1963. Dir. Granada TV, Manchester, Eng., 1960-63; producer, dir. Sta. WGBH-TV, Boston, 1963-73; pres. Blue Penguin, Inc., Boulder, Colo., 1974—; v.p. TV programming Sta. WYNC-TV, NYC, 1989-90. Dir. Pub. Broadcasting Assocs., Newton, Mass.; cons. to numerous pub. TV stations Creator, producer MAsterpiece Theatre, PBS, 1970-73, Zoom, PBS, 1971-73; producer Live From the Met, PBS, 1977-79, Kid's Writes, Nickelodeon, 1982-83, American Treasure, a Smithsonian Journey, 1986, Spotlight Colorado, 1991, Parenting Works, 1993, 95-97, Club 303, 1994, Videographer Roots of Empathy, 1999—, Coo, 2004-2005. Served with Royal Navy, 1956-57 Recipient Emmy award, 1973, 74, Peabody award Ohio State U., 1978, Internat. Emmy award, 1983, Nat. Acad. TV Arts and Scis. Gov.'s award, 1991. Mem. Dirs. Guild Am., Nat. acad. TV Arts and Scis. (gov. Heartland chpt.), Windows on the Rockies User Group (pres.). Avocations: music, cooking, gardening, travel, computers. Home and Office: 2515 7th St Boulder CO 80304 Office Phone: 303-352-1959, 303-447-6457.

SARTAIN, LIBBY, Internet company executive; married; 1 child. BA, So. Methodist U.; MBA, U. North Tex. Various positions Southwest Airlines, 1988—98, v.p. people, 1998—2001; sr. v.p. human resources, chief people Yahoo Yahoo!, Inc., Sunnyvale, Calif., 2001—. Bd. dirs. Peet's Coffee & Tea Inc., 2007—. Fellow: Nat. Acad. Human Resources; mem.: Soc. Human Resource Mgmt. (former chmn.). Office: Yahoo Inc 701 1st Ave Sunnyvale CA 94089 Office Phone: 408-349-3300. Office Fax: 408-349-3301.

SARTORIS, JOSEPH MARTIN, bishop emeritus; b. LA, July 1, 1927; Ordained priest Archdiocese of LA, 1953, aux. bishop, 1994—2002, aux.bishop emeritus, 2002—; ordained bishop, 1994. Roman Catholic. Home: 1988 Rolling Vista Dr Unit 21 Lomita CA 90717-3761

SARVER, ROBERT G., professional sports team owner; s. Jack Sarver; m. Penny Sanders, Nov. 2, 1996; 3 children. BBA, U. Ariz., 1982. CPA 1983. Founder, pres. Nat. Bank Ariz., 1984—94; lead investor, CEO GB Bancorporation, 1995—97; chmn., CEO Calif. Bank and Trust (formerly Grossmont Bank), San Diego, 1995—2002; dir., mem. credit com. Zions Bancorporation, 1995—2001, exec. v.p., 1998—2001; pres., chmn., CEO Western Alliance Bancorporation, 2002—; chmn., CEO Torrey Pines Bank, 2003—; co-founder S.W. Value Ptnrs.; mng. ptnr. Phoenix Suns, Ariz., 2004—. Bd. dirs. SkyWest Airlines, Meritage Corp., Phoenix. Mem. adv. bd. U. Ariz. Sarver Heart Ctr.; bd. trustees Japanese Am. Nat. Mus., LA. Avocations: golf, tennis, volleyball. Office: Alliance Bank Ariz 2701 E Camelback Rd Ste 110 Phoenix AZ 85016

SASAKI, TSUTOMU (TOM SASAKI), eco products trading company executive; b. Tokyo, July 28, 1945; came to US, 1979; s. Tsuneshiro and Kimiko (Fujiwara) S.; m. Yoko Katsura, Feb. 21, 1971; children: Mari, Tomoko. BA, Sophia U., Tokyo, 1969. Plant export adminstrn. Ataka & Co., Ltd., Osaka, Japan, 1969-76; officer Seattle-First Nat. Bank, Tokyo, 1976-79, AVP bus. mgr., 1982-84, AVP Japan mgr. Seattle, 1979-82, v.p. Japan mgr., 1984-90; owner, pres. BBS Internat., Inc., Seattle, 1990—2008, USJ Internat. Inc., 2008—; chmn. ECORE Global Inc., 2009—. Bd. dirs. Japanese Cmty. Svccs. Seattle, Adopt-a-Stream Found., Everett, Wash., 1987—2002; trustee NW Sch., Seattle, 1987—2002, internat. advisor to bd. trustees, 2002—04. Am. Field Svc. scholar, 1963-64. Mem. Japan Am. Soc. Wash. (chmn. membership com. 1988, 2008-09, bd. dir. 1997—, chmn. bd. 2006-07), British Am. Bus. Coun., Fairwood Golf & Country Club Avocations: golf, gardening, music, photography. Home: 4625 136th Ave SE Bellevue WA 98006-3007 Office: ECORE Global Inc 2819 Elliot Ave #201 Seattle WA 98121 Office Phone: 206-623-5714. Business E-Mail: sasaki@bbsint.com, sasaki@usjinvest.com.

SASENICK, JOSEPH ANTHONY, health care company executive; b. Chgo., May 18, 1940; s. Anthony E. and Caroline E. (Smicklas) S.; m. Betty Cheung, Dec. 22, 2007; children: Richard Allen, Susan Marie, Michael Joseph. BA, DePaul U., 1962; MA, U. Okla., 1966. With Miles Labs., Inc., Elkhart, Ind., 1963-70; product mgr. Alka-Seltzer, 1966-68, dir. mktg. grocery products divsn., 1968-70; with Gillette Corp., Boston, 1970-79, dir. new products/new ventures, personal care divsn., 1977; v.p. diversified cos. and pres. Jafra Cosmetics Worldwide, 1977-79; mktg. dir. Braun AG, Kronberg, W. Ger., 1970-73; chmn. mng. dir. Braun U.K. Ltd., 1973-77; with Abbott Labs., North Chicago, 1979-84, corp. v.p., pres. consumer products divsn., 1979-84; pres., CEO, Moxie Industries, 1984-87; pres., CEO Personal Monitoring Technologies, Rochester, NY, 1987; pres. Bioline Labs., Ft. Lauderdale, Fla., 1988; mng. dir., ptnr. Vista Resource Group, Newport Beach, Calif., 1988-90; pres., CEO, Alcide Corp., Redmond, Wash., 1991-92, chmn., CEO, 1992—2004; founder Board Romm Ltd., 2004; life sci. commercialization cons. Washington Biotech. & Biomed. Assn., Seattle. Mem. Columbia Tower Club, Wash. Athletic Club. Home and Office: Board Room Ltd 1301 Spring St # 24J Seattle WA 98104 Office Phone: 206-732-6703. Personal E-mail: jasasenick@msn.com.

SASTRY, SOSALE SHANKARA, electrical engineer, computer scientist, dean, educator; B, Indian Inst. Tech., Bombay, 1977; MS, U. Calif., Berkeley, 1979, MA in Math., 1980, PhD, 1981; MA (hon.), Harvard U., 1994. Asst. prof. MIT, 1980—82, U. Calif., Berkeley, 1983—84, assoc. prof., 1984—88, prof., 1988—, dir. Electronics Rsch. Lab., 1996—99, chmn. dept. elec. engring. and computer scis., 2001—04, dir. Ctr. Info. Tech. Rsch. in Interest of Soc., 2005—, dean, Coll. Engring., 2007—; dir. info. tech. office DARPA, 1999—2001. Vis. fellow Australian Nat. U., 1985; prof. U. Rome, 1990, 91, U. Pisa, 1995, 98; vis. Vinton Hayes prof. MIT, 1992; Gordon McKay prof. Harvard U., 1994; mem. Air Force Sci. Adv. Bd., 2002—; bd. mem. Fedn. Am. Scientists, 2002—; mem. bd. trustees Internat. Computer Sci. Inst., Berkeley, 2003—, bd. chmn., 2004—. Co-author: (books) A Mathematical Introduction to Robotic Manipulation, 1994, An Invitation to 3-D Vision From Images to Models; co-editor: Hybrid Systems II: Lecture Notes in Computer Science, 1995, Hybrid Systems IV: Lecture Notes in Computer Science, 1997, Hybrid Systems: Computation and Control, 1998, Essays in Mathematical Robotics, 1998; author: Nonlinear Systems: Analysis, Stability, and Control, 1999; co-author: over 250 technical papers. Recipient Gold medal, Pres. India, 1977, Presdl. Young Investigator award, NSF, 1985, David Marr prize, Internat. Conf. in Computer Vision, 1999, Disting. Alumnus award, Indian Inst. Tech., 1999, Ragazzini award, Am. Control Coun., 2005; Faculty Devel. grant, IBM, 1983. Fellow: IEEE, Am. Acad. Arts & Sciences; mem.: NAE. Office: U Calif Deans Office 320 McLaughlin Hall # 1700 Berkeley CA 94720

SATCHLER, GEORGE RAYMOND, physicist, researcher; b. London, June 14, 1926; came to U.S., 1959; s. George Cecil and Georgina Lillie (Strange) S.; m. Margaret Patricia Gibson, Mar. 27, 1948; children: Patricia Ann, Jacqueline Helen. BA, MA, Oxford U., 1951, D Phil., 1955, DSc, 1989. Rsch. fellow Clarendon Lab., Oxford U., 1954-59, 71; rsch. assoc. physics dept. U. Mich., 1956-57; physicist Oak Ridge (Tenn.) Nat. Lab., 1959-94, assoc. dir. physics div., 1967-74, dir. theoretical physics, 1974-76, mem. disting. rsch. staff, 1976-94; rsch. prof. U. Tenn., 1994—. Author: (with D.M. Brink) Angular Momentum, 1962, Introduction to Nuclear Reactions, 1980, Direct Nuclear Reactions, 1983; contbr. research articles to profl. jours. Served with RAF, 1944-48. Corp. rsch. fellow, 1976-94. Fellow Am. Phys. Soc. (mem. exec. com. nuclear physics div. 1974-75, T.W. Bonner prize 1977) Home: 171 E Aspley Ln Shelton WA 98584-8489

SATO, RICHARD MICHIO, consulting engineering company executive; b. Paia, Maui, Hawaii, Dec. 30, 1934; s. Shinichi and Namie (Hanazawa) S.; m. Althea Reiko Ouye; children: Janice Muraoka, Kelvin. BSCE, U. Hawaii, 1956. Registered civil/structural engr., Calif., Hawaii, Guam. Civil and structural engr. Dalton Dalton Assocs., LA, 1960-62; structural engr. William M. Taggart, SE, LA, 1962-67; project coord. Office of Univ. Planning U. Hawaii, Honolulu, 1967-69; project engr. T.Y. Lin Hawaii, Honolulu, 1969; pres. Sato & Assocs., Inc. (formerly Richard M. Sato & Assoc. & Sato & Kuniyoshi, Inc.), Honolulu, 1969—. 1st lt. U.S. Army, 1957-59. Mem. Am. Concrete Inst., Prestressed Concrete Inst., Structural Engrs. Assn. Hawaii (pres. 1976), Consulting Engrs. Coun. Hawaii, Hui Kokua Kinipopo (pres. 1993—), U. Hawaii Pres.'s Club, U. Hawaii Alumni Assn., Chi Epsilon. Avocations: golf, sports. Office: Sato & Assocs Inc 2046 S King St Honolulu HI 96826-2219

SATRE, PHILIP GLEN, casino entertainment executive, lawyer; b. Palo Alto, Calif., Apr. 30, 1949; s. Selmer Kenneth and Georgia June (Sterling) S.; m. Jennifer Patricia Arnold, June 30, 1973; children: Malena Anne, Allison Neal, Jessica Lilly, Peter Sterling. BA, Stanford U., 1971; JD, U. Calif.-Davis, 1975; postgrad. sr. exec. program, MIT, 1982. Bar: Nev. 1975, Calif. 1976. Assoc. Vargas & Bartlett, Reno, 1975-79; v.p., gen. counsel, sec. Harrah's, Reno, 1980-83, sr. v.p., 1983-84; pres. Harrah's East, Atlantic City, 1984; pres., CEO Harrah's Hotels and Casinos, Reno, 1984-91; dir., sr. v.p. Gaming Group The Promus Cos., Inc., Memphis, 1988-91, dir., pres., COO, 1991-94, dir., pres. CEO, 1994-95; pres., CEO Harrah's Entertainment, Inc., Memphis, 1995—97, chmn., pres., CEO, 1997—2005; dir. JDN Realty Co., Memphis, 1999—; chmn. NV Energy Inc., Reno, 2008—. Bd. dirs. Rite Aid Corp., 2005—, Nordstrom, Inc., 2006—. Active The Stanford Athletic Bd., 1996—; dir., treas. Nat. Jud. Coll., Reno; bd. dirs. Nat. Ctr. for Responsible Gaming, Nat. WWII Mus., Nev. Cancer Inst., and Sierra Pacific Resources; trustee Stanford U. Mem. ABA, Nev. Bar Assn., Calif. Bar Assn., Order of Coif, Phi Kappa Phi, Stanford Alumni Assn. (pres. Reno chpt. 1976-77), Young Pres. Orgn., The Bus. Roundtable. Office: PO Box 29526 Las Vegas NV 89126-9526*

SATTERWHITE, R. SCOTT, technology company executive; b. Albuquerque, Aug. 5, 1962; s. Ramon Stewart and Katherine Pricilla S. BSEE, Tex. A&M U., 1984; MBA, U. Houston, Clear Lake, 1991. Technician So. Avionics Co., Beaumont, Tex., 1976-80; engr. Fairchild Aircraft, San Antonio, 1982-83, IBM, Austin, Tex., 1983-84, program mgr. fed. sys. divsn. Houston, 1985-91; CEO, bd. dirs. Ecologics Engring., Inc., Houston, 1991—2000; regional, sr. account mgr. Wind River, 2000—07; CEO Device Tech., DeviceWare Inc., 2007—. Editor, author: Spirit of Apollo, 1989; contbr. articles to profl. jours. Chmn. com. Clear Lake Econ. Devel. Found., Houston, 1982-00; vol. Krug Internat. Space Med. Rsch., Houston, 1987-89. Mem. AIAA (sr. mem., exec. councillor 1988-89, chmn. 1987-89, treas. 1987-88, numerous awards), Students for Exploration and Devel. of Space (treas. 1990-91), World Futures Soc., Nat. Space Soc. Avocations: investing, skiing.

SATTLER, BRUCE WEIMER, lawyer; b. South Gate, Calif., July 30, 1944; s. LeRoy Edward and Mary Beth (Weimer) S.; m. Earle Martha Ross, July 22, 1972. BA, Stanford U., 1966, JD, 1969. Bar: Colo. 1969, U.S. Dist. Ct. Colo. 1969, U.S. Dist. Ct. Mont. 1982, U.S. Dist. Ct. (no. dist.) Tex. 1989, U.S. Ct. Appeals (10th cir.) 1969, U.S. Ct. Appeals (9th cir.) 1984. Assoc. Holland & Hart, Denver, 1969-75, ptnr., 1975-87; supervising trial atty. Equal Employment Opportunity Commn., Denver, 1973; ptnr. Morris, Lower & Sattler, Denver, 1987-90, Faegre & Benson, Denver, 1990—2004. Bd. dirs. ACLU of Colo., Denver, 1975-80, 88-94, 2003-, Colo. Legal Svcs., Legal Aid Soc. of Metro Denver, 1976—, Colo. Lawyers Com., Denver, 1990-94, Children's Legal Clinic, Denver, 1989-91, Colo. Women's Employment and Edn., Denver, 1986-89. Fellow Coll. Labor and Employment Lawyers; mem. Denver Bar Assn., Colo. Bar Assn. Office Phone: 303-321-5837. Business E-Mail: bruce@mesattler.com.

SATZ, LOUIS K., publishing executive; b. Chgo., Ill., Apr. 28, 1927; s. Harry Addison and Faye Satz; m. Janet Maas, Jan. 2, 1952 children: Jay, Jonathan BS in Mktg, U. Ill., 1949. Circulation dir. Pubs. Devel. Corp., Chgo., 1953, Guns mag., Jr. Arts and Activities, 1961; wholesaler sales mgr., then v.p., dir. sales Bantam Books, Inc., NYC, 1962-80, sr. v.p., dir. diversified markets, 1980-84; pub. Passport Books, Lincolnwood, Ill., 1985-88; pres. Louis K. Satz Assocs., Pub. Cons., NYC, 1988-91; ptnr. Scott/Satz Group, Pub. Cons., Walnut Creek, Calif., 1991—. Guest lectr. Sarah Lawrence Coll.Pub. Sch., Pace U.; faculty Hofstra U., Denver Pub. Inst.; cons. World Book Encyclopedia; bd. dirs. NY is Book Country, Brandeis U. Pub. Scholarship Fund, Oscar Dystel Fellowship NYU. Served with AUS, World War II, ETO. Mem. Am. Assn. Pubs. (chmn. small books mktg. div. 1975) Personal E-mail: louksatz@comcast.net.

SAUCIER, BONNIE L., dean, pediatrics nurse; b. Alton, Ill., Oct. 12, 1945; d. Robert E. and Laura L. (Rice) Powers; children: Michelle Marie, Kent Lawrence. Diploma, St. Johns Hosp. Sch. Nursing, Springfield, Ill., 1966; BA, Stephens Coll., 1976; MEd, U. Mo., 1977; MSN, U. Mo., Kansas City, 1983; PhD in nursing, Tex. Womans U., 1986. RN, Calif., Tex. Pediatric staff nurse St. Johns Hosp., St Louis, 1966-69; asst. head nurse pediatrics North Kansas City (Mo.) Meml. Hosp., 1969-71; instr. nursing Trenton (Mo.) Jr. Coll., 1974-81; asst. prof. Mo. Western State Coll., St. Joseph, Mo., 1981-84; Inst. Cook County Coll., Gainesville, Tex., 1984-85; dir. health scis. Midwestern State U., Wichita Falls, Tex., 1986-92; prof., chair dept. nursing Calif. State U., Bakersfield, 1992—. Adj. inst. U. Tex., Arlington, 1985-86; bd. dirs. ARC. Wichita Falls, 1988-92; adv. bd., cons. Vernon (Tex.) Regional Jr. Coll., 1987-92; trustee Red River Hosp. Wichita Falls, 1989-92. Contbr. articles to profl. jours. Adv. bd. Care Team Healtha Care Svcs. Wichita Falls, 1991-92; bd. dirs. March of Dimes, 1989, Nat. Kidney Found., 1989-90; mem. Midwestern Div. Tex. Hosp., 1987-92; Tex. Orgn. of Baccalaureate Nursing Programs, 1989-92, Tex. Outstanding Rural Scholars Adv., 1989-92, Tex. Nurses Edn. Adv., 1989-90. Profl. Nursing Shortage grant, Office of Gov., 1991, Profl. Nursing Retention grantee Coordinating Bd., 1991; named to Women's Hall of Fame, Mayors Commn., 1991. Mem. Tex. Nurses Assn. (coun. edn. 1991-92), Tex. Nurses Assn. #11 (pres. 1990-91, bd. dirs. 1991-92), Calif. Nurses Assn. (state adv. com. for nursing manpower study 1992), Calif. Assn. Colls. of Nursing (health care adv. com., MSA program 1992-93, acad. senator), Tex. League for Nursing (bd. dirs. 1985-92), So. Coun. on Collegiate Edn., Sigma Theta Tau. Republican. Roman Catholic. Avocations: walking, travel, racquetball, reading.

SAUER, DAVID ANDREW, librarian, writer; b. Urbana, Ill., Feb. 25, 1948; s. Elmer Louis and Frances (Hill) S. BA, Northwestern U., 1970; MS, Simmons Coll., 1975. Reference libr. Boston U., 1976-78, bibliographer, 1978-84, sci. bibliographer, 1984-88, founder and head libr. Stone Sci. Libr., 1988-94; v.p. info. svcs. CyberHelp, Inc., 1995-98; sr. tech. editor Qualcomm, Inc., 1997-2000, 2003—04, sr. tech. writer, 2004—06, staff tech. writer, 2006—; tech. pubs. supr. QCP Inc., 2000—01, staff tech. writer/libr., 2001—02; librarian San Diego Maritime Mus., 2002—03. Co-author of 12 books including: Access for Windows 95: The Visual Learning Guide, 1995, Windows NT 4.0 Visual Desk Reference, 1997, Discover Netscape Communicator, 1997. Mem. S.W. Corridor Project, Boston, 1977-87, Forest Hills Neighborhood Improvement Assn., Boston, 1977-90, Forest Hills/Woodbourne Neighorhood Group, 1991-94. Mem. ALA, IEEE, Spl. Librs. Assn., Soc. Tech. Comm. Democrat. Home: 2340 29th St San Diego CA 92104

SAUNDERS, DEBRA J., columnist; b. Newton, Mass., Dec. 8, 1954; BA in Latin and Greek, U. Mass., Boston, 1980. Asst. dir. Arnold Zenker Assocs., 1982-83; writer/rschr., account exec. Todd Domke Assocs., Sacramento, 1983-84, Russo Watts & Rollins, Sacramento, 1985-86; asst. to Rep. Leader Calif. Assembly, Sacramento, 1987-88; columnist, editl. writer L.A. Daily News, 1988-92; columnist San Francisco Chronicle, 1992—. Leader study group on polit. speechmaking Harvard U., Cambridge, Mass., 1984; tchr. editl. and column writing UCLA Ext., 1992. Published in Wall St. Jour., Nat. Review, Weekly Std., Reason mag.; syndicated nationally via Creators Syndicate; appeared on Politically Incorrect, CNN and BBC radio. Office: San Francisco Chronicle 901 Mission St San Francisco CA 94103-2905

SAUNDERS, JOSEPH W., finance company executive; BS, U. Denver, 1967, MBA, 1968. V.p., credit card ops. Bank of Am., 1984—85; with Household Fin. Corp., 1985—97; chmn., CEO Fleet Credit Card Services L.P., 1997—2001; chmn. bd, CEO & pres. Providian Fin. Corp., 2001—05; pres. card services divsn. Washington Mutual, Inc., Seattle, 2005—07; exec. chmn., CEO Visa Inc., 2007—. Office: PO Box 8999 San Francisco CA 94128-8999

SAUNDERS, PETER PAUL, investor; b. Budapest, Hungary, July 21, 1928; emigrated to Can., 1941, naturalized, 1946; s. Peter Paul and Elizabeth (Halom) Szende; m. Nancy Louise McDonald, Feb. 11, 1956; children: Christine Elizabeth McBride, Paula Marie McMullen. Student, Vancouver Coll., 1941-44; B.Com., U. B.C., 1948. Acct. Canadian Pacific Rly. Co., 1948-50; founder, pres. Laurentide Fin. Corp., Ltd., 1950-66, vice chmn., 1966-67; chmn., pres. Coronation Credit Corp. Ltd., Vancouver, B.C., Canada, 1968-78, Versatile Corp. (formerly Coronation Credit Corp. and Cornat Industries Ltd.), Vancouver, B.C., Canada, 1978-87; prin., pres. Saunders Investment Ltd., Vancouver, 1987—. Past pres. Vancouver Symphony Soc., 1968-70, Can. Cancer Soc., B.C. and Yukon Region, 1975-77, Vancouver Art Gallery Assn., 1981-83; chmn. Vancouver Opera Round Table, 1984-92; chmn. Arthritis Rsch. Ctr. of Can. Mem. Vancouver Club, Shaughnessy Golf and Country Club, Royal Vancouver Yacht Club, Thunderbird Country Club (Rancho Mirage, Calif.). Avocations: golf, skiing, hunting, boating. Home: 3620 Alexandra St Vancouver BC Canada V6J 4B9 Office: Saunders Investment Ltd PO Box 49352 Bentall Ctr Vancouver BC Canada V7X 1L4

SAUNDERS, RAYMOND JENNINGS, artist, educator; b. Pitts., Oct. 28, 1934; Student (Nat. Scholastic scholar), Pa. Acad. Fine Arts, U. Pa., Barnes Found.; B.F.A., Carnegie Inst. Tech., 1960; M.F.A., Calif. Coll. Arts and Crafts. Teaching asst. Calif. Coll. Arts and Crafts, 1960-61; resident Am. Acad. in Rome, 1964-66; art and urban affairs cons. N.Y.C. Bd. Edn. and Human Resources Adminstrn., 1967; art faculty Calif. State Univ., Hayward, 1968—88; prof. painting, drawing Calif. Coll. Arts and Crafts, Oakland, 1988—. Vis. artist, R.I. Sch. Design, 1968, artist-in-residence, vis. artist and critic at various art schs., univs., 1968—; subject of profl. articles.; one-man shows include San Francisco Mus. Modern Art, 1971, Seattle Art Mus., 1981, Pa. Acad. Fine Arts, 1990, Tampa Mus. Art, 1992, Stephen Wirtz Gallery, San Francisco, 1979, 1980, 1982, 1989, 1993, 1996, 1999, 2001, 2003, Galerie Resche, Paris, 1993, Oakland Mus., 1994, M.H. de Young Meml. Mus., San Francisco, 1995, Carnegie Mus. of Art, 1996, Galerie Resche, Paris, 1998, Hunsaker/Schlesinger Fine Art, 2001, Centre Jerome Cuzin, France, 2002, Schneider Mus. Art, So. Ore. Univ, 2004; represented in permanent collections, Mus. Modern Art, N.Y.C., Whitney Mus. Am. Art, N.Y.C., Phila. Mus. Art, Chrysler Mus., Va.; author: Black is a Color, 1968. Served with U.S. Army, 1957-59. Recipient Cresson European traveling scholar, 1956, Thomas Eakins prize, Schwabacher-Frey award San Francisco Mus. Art Ann., 1961, award Nat. Inst. Arts and Letters, 1963, Prix de Rome Am. Acad. in Rome, 1964-66, Ford Found. Purchase award, 1964, award City of Phila., Atwater Kent award Soc. Four Arts, 1970, Granger Meml. award Pa. Acad. Fine Arts, 1972, Art award KQED, 1975, Guggenheim Fellow, 1976, Nat. Endowment for Arts award, 1977, 84, Visual Arts award So. Ea. Ctr. for Contemporary Art, 1989. Office: Painting & Drawing Dept Calif Coll Arts & Crafts 5212 Broadway Oakland CA 94618-1426 Office Phone: 510-594-3600.

SAUSMAN, KAREN, zoological park administrator; b. Chgo., Nov. 26, 1945; d. William and Annabell (Lofaso) S. BS, Loyola U., 1966; student, Redlands U., 1968. Keeper Lincoln Park Zoo, Chgo., 1964-66; tchr. Palm Springs (Calif.) Unified Sch., 1968-70; ranger Nat. Park Svc., Joshua Tree, Calif., 1968-70; zoo dir. The Living Desert, Palm Desert, Calif., 1970—. Natural history study tour leader internat., 1974—; part-time instr. Coll. Desert Natural History Calif. Desert, 1975-78; field reviewer conservation grants Inst. Mus. Svcs., 1987—, MAP cons., 1987—, panelist, 1992—; internat. studbook keeper for Sand Cats, 1988-2001, for Cuvier's Gazelle, Mhorr Gazelle, 1990-2000; co-chair Arabian Oryx species survival plan propogation group, 1986-95; spkr. in field. Author Survival Captive Bighorn Sheep, 1982, Small Facilities- Opportunities and Obligations, 1983; wildlife illustrator books, mags, 1970—; editor Fox Paws newsletter Living Desert, 1970—, ann. reports, 1976—; natural sci. editor Desert Mag., 1979-82; compiler Conservation and Management Plan for Antelope, 1992; contbr. articles to profl. jours. Past bd. dirs., sec. Desert Protective Coun.; adv. coun. Desert Bighorn Rsch. Inst., 1981-85; bd. dirs. Palm Springs Desert Resorts Convention and Visitors Bur., 1988-94; bd. dirs., treas. Coachella Valley Mountain Trust, 1989-92. Named Woman Making a Difference Soroptomist Internat., 1989, 93, 97, Woman of Distinction, Riverside Bus. Press, 2000. Fellow Am. Assn. Zool. Parks and Aquariums (bd. dirs., accredation field reviewer, desert antelope taxon adv. group, caprid taxon adv. group, felid taxon adv. group, small population mgmt. adv. group, wildlife conservation and mgmt. com., chmn. ethics com. 1987, mem. com., internat. rels. com., ethics task force, pres'. award 1972-77, outstanding svc. award 1983, 88, editor newsletter, Zool. Parks and Aquarium Fundamentals 1982); mem. Internat. Species Inventory System (mgmt. com., policy adv. group 1980-96, trustee 1997-2004), Calif. Assn. Mus. (v.p. 1992-96), Calif. Assn. Zoos and Aquariums, World Assn. Zoos and Aquariums (coun. 2002-, governing coun. 2000-, pres. 2005-07), Western Interpretive Assn. (so. Calif. chpt.), Am. Assn. Mus., Arboreta and Bot. Gardens So. Calif. (coun. dirs.), Soc. Conservation Biology, Nat. Audubon. Soc., Jersey Wildlife Preservation Trust Internat., Nature Conservancy, East African Wildlife Soc., African Wildlife Found., Kennel Club Palm Springs (past bd. dirs., treas. 1978-80), Scottish Deerhound Club Am. (editor Scottish

Deerhounds in N.A., 1983, life mem. U.K. chpt.), Internat. Bengal Cat Soc. (pres. 1994-96). Avocations: pure bred dogs, cats, dressage, painting, photography. Office: The Living Desert 47 900 Portola Ave Palm Desert CA 92260 E-mail: kastld@aol.com.

SAUTE, ROBERT EMILE, drug and cosmetic consultant; b. West Warwick, RI, Aug. 18, 1929; s. Camille T. and Lea E. (Goffinet) S.; m. Anda T. Darnell, May 18, 1957; children: Richard R., Steven N., Allen K. BS, RI Coll. Pharmacy, 1950; MS, Purdue U., 1952, PhD, 1953. Registered pharmacist. Tech. asst. to pres. Lafayette (Ind.) Pharmacal, 1955-56; sr. rsch. and devel. chemist H.K. Wampole Denver Chem. Co., Phila., 1956-57; supt. Murray Hill (NJ) plant Strong Cobb Arner Inc., 1957-60; adminstrv. dir. rsch. and devel. Avon Products Inc., Suffern, NY, 1960-68; dir. rsch. and devel. toiletries divsn. Gillette Co., Boston, 1968-71; group v.p. Dart Industries, LA, 1972-75; pres. Saute Cons., Inc., LA, 1975—. Bd. dirs. Joico Labs., Inc., Cosmetics Enterprises, Ltd. Contbr. to books; patentee in field. With U.S. Army, 1953-55. Named Old Master, Disting. Alumnus, Purdue U. Fellow Soc. Cosmetic Chemists (bd. dirs. 1987-89, 94-96, chmn. Calif. chpt. 1986); mem. AAAS, N.Y. Acad. Scis., Soc. Investigative Dermatology, Am. Assn. Pharm. Scientists, Purdue U. Alumni Assn. (old master, disting. alumnus), Sigma Xi, Rho Chi. Avocations: travel, art, music, cooking, wine. Office Phone: 818-896-1444.

SAUVEY, RAYMOND ANDREW, museum director; b. Green Bay, Wisc., Aug. 6, 1953; s. Raymond Norbert and Joan Florence (Smits) S. BA Comm., U. Wisc., Green Bay, 1980. Gen. mgr. Nat. R.R. Museum, Green Bay, Wis., 1990; dir. Calif. St. Railroad Museum, Sacramento. With U.S. Army, 1971-74, USN, 1984-89. Mem. Nat. Railway Hist. Soc., Railway and Locomotive Hist. Soc., Rotary.

SAVAGE, DAVID WILLIAM, lawyer; b. Seattle, Nov. 14, 1944; s. Kenneth and Mary Savage; m. Sally Savage, Aug. 1, 1982; children: Jesse, Erin, Kathryn. BA in Polit. Sci., Wash. State U.; JD, U. Idaho. Bar: Wash. 1973, U.S. Dist. Ct. (ea. dist.) Wash. 1977, Idaho 1991, U.S. Dist. Ct. Idaho 1991, Mont. 1996, U.S. Ct. Appeals (9th cir.) 1997, U.S. Supreme Ct. 1999. Shareholder, pres. Irwin, Myklebust, Savage & Brown, P.S., Pullman, Wash., 1973—. Mem.: ABA, Wash. State Bar Assn. (pres.-elect 2002—03, pres. 2003—04), Idaho State Bar Assn. Office: Irwin Myklebust Savage & Brown PS 1230 SE Bishop Blvd Pullman WA 99163 Business E-Mail: savage@imsblaw.com.

SAVAGE, ELDON PAUL, retired environmental health educator; b. Bedford, Iowa, Apr. 4, 1926; s. Paul and Nora (Arthur) S.; m. Ella May, June 5, 1948; children: Steven P., Michael D. BS, U. Kans., 1950; MPH, Tulane U., 1958; PhD, Okla. U., 1968. Coord. environ. sanitation demonstration projects USPHS, Kans., Iowa and Pa., 1950-64; chief state aids sect. pesticide ctr. Ctr. for Disease Control, Atlanta, 1964-70; chief chem. epidemiology sect. Inst. Rural Environ. Health, Colo. State U., Ft. Collins, 1970-84, prof., dir. environ. health divsn., 1984-85, head dept. environ. health, 1985-90, dir. environ. health svcs., 1987-93, prof. emeritus, 1993—. Contbr. articles to profl. jours. Mem. Am. Acad. Sanitarians (sec., treas., diplomate), Nat. Environ. Health Assn., Sigma Xi, Gamma Sigma Delta. Home: Savage EE Arabian Horses 5220 Apple Dr Fort Collins CO 80526-4302 Office: Colo State U Inst Rural Envrion Health Fort Collins CO 80523-0001

SAVAGE, MARK RANDALL, lawyer; b. Chicopee, Mass., Mar. 10, 1959; m. Lucia Clara Savage; children: David, Ryan. BA, U. Calif., Berkeley, 1982; JD, Stanford U., 1988. Bar: Calif. Jud. law clk. to Judge James Holden, North Bennington, Vt., 1988-89; mng. atty. Pub. Advs., Inc., San Francisco, 1989—2003; sr. atty. Consumers Union of U.S., Inc., San Francisco, 2003—. Gen. counsel Cmty. Tech. Found. Calif., San Francisco, 1998—; bd. dirs. Family Bridges, Inc., Oakland, Calif. Contbr. articles to profl. jours. Bd. dirs. Unitarian Ch., Oakland, Calif., 2006—. Inst. for Civic Arts and Pub. Spaces, Inc., Albuquerque, 1996—2001. Recipient Drum Maj. award So. Christian Leadership Conf., 1998, Diversity, Innovation and Reform in Edn. award, 1995, El Fuego Nuevo award Assn. Mex. Am. Educators, 1999, Leadership Recognition award Calif. Primary Care Assn., 1999, Screaming Eagle award Calif. Reinvestment Coalition, 2004, Calif. Lawyer Attys. of Yr. award, 2007. Office: Consumers Union 1535 Mission St San Francisco CA 94103-2566 Home Phone: 510-261-8263; Office Phone: 415-431-6747. Business E-Mail: Mark.Savage@pacbell.net.

SAVAGE, MICHAEL (MICHAEL ALAN WEINER), radio personality, commentator; b. Bronx, NY, Mar. 31, 1942; m. Janet A. Savage (div.); children: Russell, Rebecca; m. Sheila Weiner-Rozzo, 1964 (div. 1967). BA in Sociology and Edn., CUNY Queens Coll., 1963; MS in Ethnobotany, U. Hawaii, 1970, MA in Medical Anthropology, 1972; PhD in Nutritional Ethnomedicine, U. Calif., Berkeley, 1978. HS tchr., NYC; fill-in talk show host Sta.KGO, San Francisco, 1994—95; talk radio host Sta.KSFO, San Francisco, 1995—2003; host (nationally-syndicated) The Savage Nation, Talk Radio Network, 1999—; host (TV) The Savage Nation MSNBC, 2003. Author: (books) The Death of the White Male, 1991, The Savage Nation: Saving America from the Liberal Assault on Our Borders, Language, and Culture, 2003 (#1 NY Times bestseller), The Enemy Within: Saving America from the Liberal Assault on Our Schools, Faith, and Military, 2004, Liberalism is a Mental Disorder, 2005, The Political Zoo, 2006, Psychological Nudity, 2008; author: (as Michael A. Weiner, Ph.D.) Plant a Tree, 1975, Bugs in Peanut Butter, 1976, Man's Useful Plants, 1976, The Taster's Guide to Beer: Brews and Breweries of the World, 1977, Earth Medicine, Earth Food, 1980, The Way of the Skeptical Nutritionist, 1981, The Art of Feeding Children Well, 1982, Nutrition Against Aging, 1983, Secrets of Fijian Medicine, 1983, Vital Signs, 1983, Getting Off Cocaine, 1984, Dr. Weiner's High Fiber Counter, 1984, Maximum Immunity, 1986, Reducing the Risk of Alzheimer's, 1987, The Complete Book of Homeopathy, 1989, The Herbal Bible, 1992, Healing Children Naturally, 1993, Herbs That Heal: Prescription for Herbal Healing, 1994, The Antioxidant Cookbook, 1995. Recipient Freedom of Speech award, Talkers Mag., 2007. Mem.: Paul Revere Soc. (founding mem.). Jewish. Address: Talk 910 KNEW 340 Townsend St San Francisco CA 94107 Office: c/o Talk Radio Network PO Box 3775 Central Point OR 97502 Office Phone: 800-449-8255. E-mail: michaelsavage@paulreveresociety.com.*

SAVAGE, STEPHEN MICHAEL, lawyer, department chairman; b. Norwich, Conn., Apr. 23, 1946; s. Alfred and Iva (Allen) S.; m. Lois Palestine, July 4, 1968; children: Meredith, William, Sam. BA, U. Pa., 1972; JD, Harvard U., 1973. Bar: Ariz. 1973, U.S. Dist. Ct. Ariz. 1973. With Fennemore Craig, Phoenix, 1973—, chmn. mgmt. com., 1988—2005. Bd. dirs. Ariz. Diabetes Assn., Phoenix, 1983-87, Verde Vaqueros; chmn. bd. trustees Ariz. Sci. Ctr., Phoenix; chmn. bd. dirs. All Saints' Episcopal Day Sch., Phoenix, 1988; comdr., pres. Mounted Sheriff's Posse Maricopa County, Phoenix, 1992-93. Mem. ABA, State Bar Ariz. (chmn. sect. corp., banking and bus. law 1983-84), Maricopa County Bar Assn., Phoenix Country Club, Forest Highlands Country Club. Avocation: team roping. Office: Fennemore Craig 3003 N Central Ave Ste 2600 Phoenix AZ 85012-2913

SAVAGEAU, MICHAEL ANTONIO, science educator, engineering educator; b. Fargo, ND, Dec. 3, 1940; s. Antonio Daniel and Jennie Ethelwin (Kaushagen) S.; m. Ann Elisa Birky, July 22, 1967; children— Mark Edward, Patrick Daniel, Elisa Marie BS, U. Minn., 1962; MS, U. Iowa, 1963; PhD, Stanford U., 1967, postgrad., 1968-70, UCLA, 1967-68. Rsch. fellow UCLA, 1967-68; lectr. Stanford U., Calif., 1968-69; from asst. to full prof. U. Mich., Ann Arbor, 1970—78, prof. microbiology and immunology, 1978—2003, chmn. dept., 1982—85, 1992—2003, prof. chem. engring., dir. cellular biotech. labs., 1988—91, dir. NIH tng. program in cellular biotechnology, 1991—92, dir. bioinformatics program, 1998—2001, Nicolas Rashevsky disting. univ. prof., 2002—03, Nicolas Rashevsky disting. univ. prof. emeritus, 2003—; Moore disting. scholar Calif. Inst. Tech., 2003; disting. prof. biomed. engring. U. Calif., Davis, 2003—, chmn. dept., 2005—. Cons. Upjohn Co., Kalamazoo, 1979—81, NIH, Bethesda, Md., 1981—82, 1994—95, 1997—2000, 2005, Synergen, Boulder, Colo., 1985—87, NRC/Howard Hughes Med. Inst., 1997—2001, NSF, 1999—, NAS, 2001—, Swedish Found. for Strategic Rsch., Stockholm, 2001—02; sr. rsch. fellow Max Planck Inst., Gottingen, Germany, 1976—77; fellow Australian Nat. U., Canberra, Australia, 1983—84; lectr. CIGENE Ctr. for Integrated Genetics, Agrl. U. Norway, Aas, 2001—; vis. prof. dept. biochemistry U. Ariz., Tucson, 1994; vis. prof. Institut des Hautes Etudes Scientifiques, Bures-Sur-Yvette, France, 2002. Author: Biochemical Systems Analysis, 1976; mem. editl. bd. Math. Scis., 1976-95, 2005—, editor, 1995-2005; mem. editl. bd. Jour. Theoretical Biology, 1989-96, 2004—, mem. adv. bd., 1996-2004; mem. editl. bd. Nonlinear World, 1992—, Nonlinear Digest, 1992—, inScight, 1998—, BioComplexity, 2000—; co-editor Math. Ecology, 1986—. Guggenheim fellow, 1976—77, sr. rsch. fellow, Fulbright Found., 1976—77, sr. fellow, Mich. Soc. Fellows, 1990—94. Fellow: AAAS; mem.: IEEE (sr.), Biomed. Engring. Soc., Inst. Medicine of Nat. Acad. Scis. (lectr. found for microbiology 1993—95, lectr. Am. Math. Soc. Josiah Willard Gibbs 2006), Internat. Fedn. Nonlinear Analysts (bd. dirs. 1997—), Soc. Math. Biology (bd. dirs. 1987—90), Soc. Gen. Physiologists, Biophys. Soc., Soc. Indsl. and Applied Math., Am. Soc. Microbiology, Am. Chem. Soc. Office: U Calif Dept Biomed Engring One Shields Ave Davis CA 95616

SAVITZ, MAXINE LAZARUS, retired aerospace transportation executive; b. Balt., Feb. 13, 1937; d. Samuel and Harriette (Miller) Lazarus; m. Sumner Alan Savitz, Jan. 1, 1961; children: Adam Jonathan, Alison Carrie. BA in Chemistry magna cum laude, Bryn Mawr Coll., 1958; PhD in Organic Chemistry, MIT, 1961. Instr. chemistry Hunter Coll., NYC, 1962-63; sr. electrochemist Mobility Equipment Rsch. and Devel. Ctr., Ft. Belvoir, Va., 1963-68; prof. chemistry Federal City Coll., Washington, 1968-72; program mgr. NSF, Washington, 1972-74; dir. FEA Office Bldgs. Policy Rshc. U.S. Dept. Energy, Washington, 1974-75, dir. div. indsl. conservation, 1975-76, from dir. div. bldgs. and community systems to dep asst sec., 1975-83; pres. Lighting Rsch. Inst., 1983-85; asst. to v.p. engring. Ceramic Components div. The Garrett Corp., 1985-87; gen. mgr. ceramic components divsn. AlliedSignal Inc., Torrance, Calif., 1987-99; gen. mgr. tech. partnerships Honeywell, Torrance, Calif., 1999—2001, ret., 2001; prin. Washington Adv. Group. Bd. dirs. Am. Coun. Energy Efficient Economy, Draper Corp., Fedn. Am. Scientists, Energetics, Inc.; cons. State Mich. Dept. Commerce, 1983, NC Alternative Energy Corp., 1983, Garrett Corp., 1983, Energy Engring. Bd., Nat. Rsch. Bd., 1986—93, Office Tech. Assessment, U.S. Congress Energy Demand Panel, 1987—91; nat. materials adv. bd. NRC, 1989—94, mem. bd. energy and environ. sys., 2002—, bd. dirs. divsn. engring. and phys. sci., 2003—06; chmn. US Advanced Ceramic Assn., 1992; adv. com. divsn. ceramics/materials ORNL, 1989—92, adv. com. dir., 1992—96; mem. lab. adv. com. Pacific NW Nat. Lab., 2000—07; adv. bd. Sec. Energy, 1992—2002; mem. Def. Sci. Bd., 1993—96; vis. com. adv. tech. Nat. Inst. Stds. and Tech., 1993—98, Nat. Sci. Bd., 1999—2004; mem. adv. bd. Sandia Sci., 2006—. Contbr. articles to profl. jours. Mem. policy com. NAE, 1994—98. NSF postdoctoral fellow, 1961, 62, NIH predoctoral fellow, 1960, 61. Mem. NAE (v.p. 2006-), AAAS.

SAWDEI, MILAN A., lawyer; b. Bakersfield, Calif., Aug. 23, 1946; BA, U. Calif., Long Beach, 1969; JD, W.S.U., 1975. Bar: Calif. 1975, U.S. Dist. Ct. (ctrl. dist.) Calif. 1975. House counsel Sanyo Electric, Inc., 1975-77; assoc. counsel Brown Co. (Gulf & Western), 1978-80; divsn. counsel Petrolane, Inc., 1980-83; sr. counsel Bergen Brunswig Corp., Orange, Calif., 1983-90, v.p., chief legal officer, 1990-92, exec. v.p., chief legal officer, sec., 1992—. Mem. ABA, Am. Corp. Counsel Assn., Am. Soc. Corp. Secs., L.A. County Bar Assn.

SAWYER, SANDRA MCCOMMAS, retired lawyer, former judge; b. Tulsa, Sept. 1, 1937; d. Franklin Delmar and Irene (Adams) McCommas; student Tex. Tech. Coll., Draughon Bus. Sch., LL.B., Oklahoma City U., 1967; m. L.L. Sawyer, Mar. 6, 1981; children—Lise Dyann, Richard Owen, Whitney Michelle. Legal sec., 1956-64; admitted to Okla. bar, 1967, Oreg. bar, 1983; legal asst. to U.S. Ct. Appeals judge, 1964-67, law clk., 1967-68; bill drafter Okla. Legislature, 1969-70; chief traffic ct. project Okla. Supreme Ct., 1970-75; individual practice law, Oklahoma City, from 1967; partner firm Moran & Johnson, Oklahoma City; referee juvenile div. Okla. County Dist. Ct., 1977-78, spl. dist. judge, 1978-80; assoc. Grant, Ferguson & Carter, P.C., 1981-90; pvt. practice, 1990-99; asst. CEO, gen. counsel KOGAP Enterprises, Inc., 2001-04; adj. prof. So. Oreg. State Coll.; lectr. Okla. Center Continuing Legal Edn., 1969-75, Okla. Bar Found. Legal Secs. Ednl. Series, 1974; mem. Okla. Legislature Interim. Com. Municipal Cts. Revision, 1973-74. Sunday Sch. tchr., supt. Resurrection Episcopal Ch., Oklahoma City; pres. regional adv. com. So. Oreg. State Coll., chancellor higher edn. bd. com. academic productivity; mem. So. Oreg. Drug Awareness Com.; pres. adv. bd. So. Oregon U., 1988-89; bd. dirs. Planned Parenthood So. Oreg., 2005—; vol. legal svcs. Jackson County. Recipient Outstanding Civic Contbn. award Modern Woodmen Am., 1977. Mem. Am. (nat. v.p. law student divsn. 1966; Gold Key award 1965, 66), Okla. (Outstanding Grad. Law Student award 1967, grievance com. 1977-78), Okla. County, Oreg. bar assns., Oklahoma City U. Law Sch. Alumni Assn. (sec. 1971), Iota Tau Tau, Zeta Tau Alpha. Author, editor in field; spl. cts. reporter Am. Judicature Soc., 1974-78, Athy Jackson County Legal Svcs., Medford, OR (vol.). Home: 585 Thornton Way Ashland OR 97520-1529 Home Phone: 541-488-2405; Office Phone: 541-488-2405. E-mail: slsaw@aol.com.

SAWYER, THOMAS WILLIAM, career officer; b. Turlock, Calif., Nov. 19, 1933; s. Everett Edward and Marie Georgine (Gunderson) S.; m. Faith Barry Martin, Feb. 16, 1957; children: William Everet, John Martin, Susan Quincy BS in Mil. Sci., U. Nebr., 1965; MS in Internat. Rels., George Washington U., 1974. Enlisted U.S. Air Force, 1952, commd. and advanced through grades to maj. gen., 1983; comdr. 57th Fighter Squadron, Keflavik, Iceland, 1971-73; chief internat. relations div. Hdqrs. U.S. Air Force, Washington, 1974-77; vice comdr. 20th Air Div., Fort Lee, Va., 1977-78; mil. asst. to Sec. Air Force, 1978-80; comdr. 26th Air Div., Luke AFB, Ariz., 1980-82; dep. ops. NORAD and Space Command, Colorado Springs, Colo., 1982-86; retired USAF, 1986; founder, pres. Aerospace Network Inc., 1986-98; pres. Pathfinder Tech., Inc., 1998—. Bd. dirs. Pikes Peak chpt. ARC, Colo./Wyo. chpt. Am. Def. Preparedness Assn. Decorated Disting. Service medal, Def. Disting. Service medal, Legion of Merit with 2 oak leaf clusters, Silver Star (2) Mem. Phoenix C. of C. (bd. dirs. 1980-82), Colorado Springs C. of C. Avocations: nat. security affairs, woodworking, automobile bldg. Office: Pathfinder Technology Inc PO Box 7640 Colorado Springs CO 80933-7640

SAX, JOSEPH LAWRENCE, lawyer, educator; b. Chgo., Feb. 3, 1936; s. Benjamin Harry and Mary (Silverman) S.; m. Eleanor Charlotte Gettes, June 17, 1958; children: Katherine Elaine Dennett, Valerie Beth Sax, Amber Sax Rosen. AB, Harvard U., 1957; JD, U. Chgo., 1959; LLD (hon.), Ill. Inst. Tech., 1992; LLD (hon.), Columbia U., 2009. Bar: D.C. 1960, Mich., 1966, U.S. Supreme Ct. 1969, US Ct. Appeals (Fed. cir.), 2008. Atty. U.S. Dept. Justice, Washington, 1959-60; pvt. practice law Washington, 1960-62; prof. U. Colo., 1962-65, U. Mich., Ann Arbor, 1966-86; dep. asst. sec. and counselor U.S. Sec. Interior, Washington, 1994-96; prof. U. Calif. Law Sch., Berkeley, 1986—. Fellow Ctr. Advanced Study in Behavioral Scis., 1977-78, Order of the Coif Disting. Visitor, 2004. Author: Waters and Water Rights, 1967, Water Law, Planning and Policy, 1968, Defending the Environment, 1971, Mountains Without Handrails, 1980, Legal Control of Water Resources, 4th edit., 2006, Playing Darts with a Rembrandt, 1999. Recipient Blue Planet prize, 2007. Fellow: AAAS. Office Phone: 510-642-1831. Business E-Mail: saxj@law.berkeley.edu.

SAX, PAUL J., lawyer; b. Sacramento, 1944; AB, Calif. State U., Sacramento, 1965; JD, U. Calif., San Francisco, 1968; LLM in Taxation, NYU, 1969. Bar: Calif. 1969. Mem. Orrick, Herrington & Sutcliffe, San Francisco, ptnr., chmn. tax group. Vice chair pubs. sect. of taxation ABA, 1990—, chair, vice chair standards tax practice com., 1984-88, coun. dir., 1988-90, dept. editor Jour. Taxation, 1990—. Grad. editor Tax Law Rev., 1968-69. Fellow Am. Bar Found.; Am. Coll. Tax Counsel, Am. Tax Policy Inst.; mem. Order of Coif, Thurston Honor Soc., ABA- Sect. Taxation (chmn. 1999-2000, House Delegates 2001-), ABA-Standard Tax Practice Com. (vice chmn./chmn. 1984-1988, coun. dir. 1988-1990), ABA (vice chmn. publ.), Calif. Bd. Legal Specialization (cert. specialist taxation 1975-), Am. Law Inst. (tax adv. group), Office: Orrick Herrington & Sutcliffe LLP The Orrick Building 405 Howard St San Francisco CA 94105 Office Phone: 415-773-5949. Office Fax: 415-773-5759. Business E-Mail: pjsax@orrick.com.

SAXE, DEBORAH CRANDALL, lawyer; b. Lima, Ohio, July 23, 1949; d. Robert Gordon and Lois Barker (Taylor) Crandall; m. Robert Saxe, June 3, 1989; children: Elizabeth Sara, Emily Jane. BA, Pa. State U., 1971; MA, UCLA, 1973, JD, 1978. Bar: Calif. 1978, D.C. 1979, U.S. Dist. Ct. D.C. 1979, U.S. Dist. Ct. (ea. dist.) Calif. 1981, U.S. Dist. Ct. (ctrl. dist.) Calif. 1982, U.S. Dist. Ct. (no. and so. dists.) Calif. 1987, U.S. Ct. Appeals (4th and D.C. cirs.) 1979, U.S. Ct. Appeals (6th cir.) 1985, U.S. Ct. Appeals (8th and 9th cirs.) 1987, U.S. Ct. Appeals (2nd cir.) 1990, U.S. Supreme Ct. 1982, U.S. Dist. Ct. (no. dist.) Ill. 2001, U.S. Ct. Appeals (7th cir.) 2001. Assoc. Seyfarth, Shaw, Fairweather & Geraldson, Washington, 1978-83, Jones, Day, Reavis & Pogue, Washington, 1983-85, LA, 1985-87, ptnr., 1988-97; shareholder Heller Ehrman LLP, 1997—2005; ptnr. Jones Day, LA, 2006—. Judge pro tem, Small Claims Ct., L.A., 1985-88. Co-author: Advising California Employers, 1990, 3d edit., 2007; contbg. editor Employment Discrimination Law, 1989. Bd. dirs. Constitutional Rights Found., 1997—2002; chair Eisner Pediatric and Family Med. Ctr., LA, 1996—98, bd. dirs., 1990—2003, Los Angeles County Bar Found., 1997—99. Fellow: Coll. Labor and Employment Lawyers; mem.: ABA (labor law sect. 1978—, Chamber Ptnr. 2004—08, Best Lawyers Am. 2006, 2007, 2008), L.A. County Bar Assn. (labor and employment law sect. 1985—, mem. exec. com. 1988—, chair 2002—03, trustee 2005—08), Calif. Bar Assn. (labor law sect. 1985—), Phi Beta Kappa, Pi Lambda Theta. Office: Jones Day 555 S Flower St 50th Fl Los Angeles CA 90071 Office Phone: 213-489-3939. Office Fax: 213-243-2539. Business E-Mail: dsaxe@jonesday.com.

SAXE, STEVEN LOUIS, lawyer; b. San Francisco, May 28, 1942; s. Jules Irving and Marian (Adams) S.; m. Joanne Saxe, July 12, 1964; children: Julie Ann, Jeffrey Scott. BS, U. Calif., Berkeley, 1964; JD, U. San Francisco, 1967. Bar: Calif. 1967, U.S. Dist. Ct. (no. and ea. dist.) Calif. 1967. Clk. Calif. Ct. Appeals, San Francisco, 1967-68; assoc. Farella, Braun & Martel, San Francisco, 1968-69; sr. counsel Bank Am., San Francisco, 1969-80; ptnr. Boyden, Cooluris, Hauser & Saxe, San Francisco, 1980-91, Pillsbury, Madison & Sutro, San Francisco, 1991-2000, Boyden Cooluris Livingston & Saxe PC, Larkspur, Calif., 2000—. Dir. Ecumenical Assn. Housing, San Rafael, Calif., 1985-92; pres. Congregation Rodef Sholom, San Rafael, 1992-94; dir., pres. Fair Housing Marin, San Rafael, 1995—. Mem. ABA, Consumer Bankers Assn., Coll. Am. Consumer Fin. Svcs. Lawyers (regent). Office: Boyden Cooluris Livingston Saxe 300 Tamal Plz Ste 180 Corte Madera CA 94925-1131 E-mail: ssaxe@bclslaw.com.

SAY, CALVIN KWAI YEN, state legislator; b. Honolulu, Feb. 1, 1952; s. Hugh Sun Chung and Clara Jim Say; m. Cora Kotake; children: Geoffrey, Jared. EdB, U. Hawaii, Manoa, 1974. Faculty Hawaii Dept. Edn., 1974—76; office mgr. to v.p., than pres. Kotake Shokai, Ltd., 1980—2006; mem. Dist. 25 Hawaii House of Reps., 1976—92, mem. Dist. 18, 1993—2002, mem. Dist. 20, 2003—, spkr. of house, 1999—. Bd. dirs. Internat. Savings & Loan Co., 1975—76, State Legis. Leaders Found., 2003—; pres., mem. exec. com. Nat. Speaker's Conf., 1999—. Bd. dirs. Hawaii Sports Hall of Fame & Mus., Pacific Rim Found. Mem.: Hong Kong Bus. Assn., Kaimuki Profl. & Bus. Assn., Hawaii Youth Symphony Assn., Honolulu Symphony Soc., St. Louis Heights Cmty. Assn., Kaimuki High Athletic Club, Palolo Lions Club. Democrat. Mailing: 1822 10th Ave Honolulu HI 96816 also: State Capitol Bldg 415 S Beretania St Rm 431 Honolulu HI 96813 Office Phone: 808-586-6100. Fax: 808-586-6101. E-mail: rep.say@capitol.hawaii.gov.

SAYKALLY, RICHARD JAMES, chemistry professor; b. Rhinelander, Wis., Sept. 10, 1947; s. Edwin L. and Helen M. S. BS, U. Wis., Eau Claire, 1970; PhD, U. Wis., Madison, 1977. Postdoctoral Nat. Bur. Standards, Boulder, Colo., 1977-79; asst. prof. U. Calif., Berkeley, 1979-83, assoc. prof., 1983-86, prof., 1986—, vice chmn. dept. chemistry, 1988-91, Miller Rsch. Prof., 1996, Class of 1932 chair prof., 1999—. Bergman lectr. Yale U., 1987; Merck-Frost lectr. U. B.C., 1988; Bourke lectr. Royal Soc. Chemistry, 1992; Samuel M. McElvain lectr. U. Wis., Madison, 1995; Harry Emmett Gunning lectr. U. Alta., 1995; U. Calif., Berkley, Miller Rsch. prof., 1997-98; Bryce Crawford lectr., U. Minn., 1999; prin. investigator Lawrence Berkeley Lab., 1983-91; prin. investigator Sci. for Sci. Tchrs., NSF; mem. Laser Sci. Topical Group Fellowship Com., 1993—; mem. internat. steering com. 12th Internat. Conf. on Laser Spectroscopy, 1995; mem. exec. com. Divsn. Chem. Physics, 1995—; vis. prof. U. Nijmegen, 1991, Max-Planck Inst. for Fluid Dynamics, Göttingen, 1991, Cambridge U., 1995, U. Montpellier, 1996, Tech. U. Munich, 1996-97, Max-Planck Inst. for Solid State Physics-Stuttgart, 1999, Physics Inst., U. Cologne, 2000, Fritz Haber Inst.-Berlin, 2001, Max-Planck Inst. for Extraterrestrial Physics-Munich, 2002-05, Max-Planck Inst. for Biochem.-Martinsried, 2002, Oxford U., 2006. Contbr. over 200 articles to profl. jours.; editl. rev. bd. Jour. Chem. Physics, 1993-95, Molecular Physics, 1983—, Chem. Physics Letters, 1987—, Spectroscopy Mag., 1986—, Rev. of Sci. Instruments, 1987-90, Jour. Molecular Spectroscopy, 1995—. Recipient Presdl. Young Investigator award NSF, 1984-88, Disting. Alumnus award U. Wis., Eau Claire, 1987, Bomen Michelson prize for spectroscopy, 1989, E.K. Plyler prize for molecular spectroscopy, 1989, E.R. Lippincott medal OSA, SAS, 1992, Disting. Tchg. award U. Calif. Berkeley, 1992, Humboldt sr. scientist award, 1995, Irving Langmuir awar in Chemical Physics, 2000, Centenary medal of the UK, Royal Soc. of Chemistry, 2001, E.O. Lawrence award, US Dept. Energy, 2004, Joannes Markus Marci medal, Acad. Scis. of the Czech Republic, 2004; fellow Dreyfuss Found., 1979, Churchill fellow Cambridge U., 1995, Christensen fellow, Oxford U., 2006. Fellow Royal Soc. Chemistry, 1986, Am. Phys. Soc., 1989, Am. Acad. Arts and Scis., 1995; mem. NAS, 1999, AAAS, 2001, AAUP, Optical Soc. Am., 1994, Am. Chem. Soc. (Harrison Howe award 1992, Irving Langmuir award 1999). Office: U Calif Dept Chemistry 419 Latimer Hall # 1460 Berkeley CA 94720-1460

SAYLER, GEORGE C., state legislator; b. Missoula, Mont., June 14, 1944; m. Kathleen; children: Heather & Michelle. BA, U. Montana, 1967; MA, Hartford Sem., 1973. Millworker Diamond Internat., 1972—74; tchr. Coeur d'Alene HS, Idaho, 1974—2002; mem. Dist. 4 Idaho House of Reps., Boise, 2003—. Mem., chmn. Couer d'Alene Edn. Assn. Ins. Com., 1990—2002. Democrat. Protestant. Office: Dist Office 1102 Ash Ave Coeur D' Alene ID 83814 also: Legis Services Office PO Box 83720 Boise ID 83720 Office Phone: 208-664-2787. Office Fax: 208-665-9704.*

SAYLES, JOHN THOMAS, film director, writer, actor; b. Schenectady, NY, Sept. 28, 1950; s. Donald John and Mary (Rausch) S. BS, Williams Coll., 1972. Film dir., writer, actor Paradigm, LA, 1994—. Author: Pride of the Bimbos, 1975, Union Dues, 1979, Thinking in Pictures: The Making of the Movie "Matewan," 1987, The Anarchists Convention, 1979, Los Gusanos, 1991; short stories I-80 Nebraska, M.490 - M.205, 1975 (O Henry award), Breed, Golden State, 1977 (O Henry award), Hoop; writer, dir. plays: New Hope for the Dead, 1981, Turnbuckle; screenwriter (films) Piranha, 1978, The Lady in Red, 1979, Battle Beyond the Stars, 1980, Alligator, 1981, The Challenge, 1982, Enormous Changes at the Last Minute, 1985, Wild Thing, 1987, The Clan of the Cave Bear, 1988, Breaking In, 1989; actor, screenwriter (films) The Howling, 1981; dir., screenwriter (films) Baby, It's You, 1983, Passion Fish, 1992; dir., screenwriter, actor (films) Return of the Secaucus Seven, 1980 (Los Angeles Film Critcs award, 1980), Lianna, 1983, The Brother From Another Planet, 1984, Matewan, 1987, Eight Men Out, 1988, City of Hope, 1991; dir., screenwriter; dir., writer (film) Lone Star, 1996, Limbo, 1999, Sunshine State, 2002, Casa de los babys, 2003, Silver City, 2004; actor(films) Hard Choices, 1986, Something Wild, 1986, Little Vegas, 1990, Straight Talk, 1992, Malcolm X, 1992, Matinee, 1993, My Life's in Turnaround, 1994; dir. Bruce Springsteen music videos Born in the U.S.A., I'm on Fire, Glory Days; TV work includes A Perfect Match, Unnatural Causes, Shannon's Deal, spl. Mountain View. MacArthur Found. grantee. Office: Paradigm c/o Lucy Stille 360 N Crescent Dr Beverly Hills CA 90210

SAYLOR, MARK JULIAN, newspaper editor; b. Wellsville, NY, Mar. 19, 1954; s. Richard Samuel and Naomi (Roth) S.; children: Samuel, Benjamin, Katie. BA cum laude, Harvard Coll., 1976. Staff writer Ark. Democrat, Little Rock, 1976-77, San Jose (Calif.) Mercury News, 1977-81, asst. met. editor, 1981-82, govt. and politics editor, 1982-85; asst. city editor San Diego County edit. LA Times, LA, 1985-89, city editor San Diego edit., 1989-91, Calif. polit. editor, 1991-95; entertainment editor Business, 1995—. Avocation: chess. Office: LA Times Times Mirror Sq Los Angeles CA 90053

SAYWELL, WILLIAM GEORGE GABRIEL, business development and management consultant; b. Regina, Sask., Can., Dec. 1, 1936; s. John Ferdinand Tupper and Vera Marguerite S.; m. Helen Jane Larmer; children: Shelley Jayne, William James Tupper, Patricia Lynn. BA, U. Toronto, 1960, MA, 1961, PhD, 1968; LLD (hon.), U. B.C., 1994, Simon Fraser U., 1997. Asst. prof. dept. East Asian studies U. Toronto, 1963-69, asst. prof., 1969-71, assoc. prof. RDt., 1971-82, prof., 1982-83, chmn. dept., 1971-76; prof. dept. history, pres., vice chancellor Simon Fraser U., Burnaby, B.C., Can., 1983-93; pres., chief exec. officer Asia Pacific Found. of Can., Vancouver, B.C., 1993-99; vice chmn. Intercedent Ltd., 1999—; pres. William Saywell & Assocs., Vancouver, 1999—. Cons. in higher edn.; sinologist and 1st sec. Can. Embassy, Beijing, 1972-73; dir. U. Toronto-York U. Ctr. Modern East Asia, 1974-75; prin. Innis Coll., 1976-79; vice provost U. Toronto, 1979-83; dir. Tokyo-Mitsubishi Bank (Can.), VLinx Ltd. Author articles and revs. on Chinese affairs to profl. jours. Decorated Order of Can., Order of BC.

SCAGLIONE, CECIL FRANK, marketing, publishing executive; b. North Bay, Ont., Can., Dec. 2, 1934; came to U.S., 1967, naturalized, 1982; s. Frank and Rose (Aubin) S.; m. Mary Margaret Stewart, Nov. 11, 1954 (div. 1982); children: Cris Ann, Michael Andrew, Patrick Andrew (dec.); m. Beverly Louise Rahn, Mar. 25, 1983. Student, North Bay Coll., 1947—52, Ryerson Tech. Inst., 1955—56, San Diego State U. Inst. on World Affairs, 1979. Accredited Pub. Rels. Soc. Am. Fin. Writer Toronto Telegram, 1955; reporter Sarnia Observer, Sarnia, Ont., 1956—57; reporter, editor Kitchener-Waterloo Record, Ont., 1957—61; reporter, editor, analyst Windsor Star, Ont., 1961—67; writer, editor, photo editor Detroit News, 1967—71; reporter, assoc. bus. editor San Diego Union, 1971—80; mgr. corp. comm. Pacific Southwest Airlines, San Diego, 1981—83; sr. v.p. media rels. Berkman & Daniels, Inc., San Diego, 1984—87; prin. Scaglione Mktg. Comm., 1987—. Pres., CEO, editor in chief Mature Life Features, 1990—. Founding editor-in-chief Aeromexico Mag., 1973; contbr. articles, columns and photographs to various publs. Mem. San Diego County Crime Commn. Recipient award B. F. Goodrich Can., Ltd., 1962, 66, San Diego Pub. Rels. Profl. of the Yr., 1995, Spl. Achievement award Nat. Assn. Recycling Industries, 1978; named Nat. Media Adv. SBA, 1980; Herbert J. Davenport fellow, 1977 U. Mo.; Can. Centennial grantee, 1966. Mem. San Diego Press Club (hon. life, past pres., awards 1978, 80, 84, 2008), Airline Editors Forum (awards 1982, 83), Soc. Profl. Journalists. Roman Catholic.

SCALA, JAMES, health facility administrator, consultant, writer; b. Ramsey, NJ, Sept. 16, 1934; s. Edvigi and Lorene (Hendricksen) Scala; m. Nancy Peters, June 15, 1957; children: James, Gregory, Nancy, Kimberly. BA, Columbia U., 1960; PhD, Cornell U., 1964; postgrad., Harvard U., 1968; LHD (hon.), Hofstra U., 1998. Cert. nutrition specialist. Staff scientist Miami Valley Labs., Procter and Gamble Co., 1964-66; head life scis., dir. fundamental rsch. Owens Ill. Corp., 1966-71; dir. nutrition T.J. Lipton Inc., 1971-75; dir. health scis. Gen. Foods Corp., 1975-78; v.p. sci. and tech. Shaklee Corp., San Francisco, 1978-85, sr. v.p. sci. affairs, 1986-87. Lectr. Georgetown U. Med. Sch.; instr. U. Calif., Berkeley; nutritionist U.S. Olympic Ski Team, 1981—87. Author: Making the Vitamin Connection, 1985, The Arthritis Relief Diet, 1987, 2d edit., 1989, Eating Right for a Bad Gut, 1990, 2d edit., 1992, Eating Right for a Bad Gut, new edit., 1999, The High Blood Pressure Relief Diet, 1988, 2d edit., 1990, Look 10 Years Younger, Feel 10 Years Better, 1991, 2d edit., 1993, Prescription for Longevity, 1992, 2d edit., 1994, If You Can't/Won't Stop Smoking, 1993, The New Arthritis Relief Diet, 1998, 25 Natural Ways to Manage Stress and Avoid Burnout, 2000, 25 Natural Ways to Relieve Irritable Bowel Syndrome, 2000, 20 Natural Ways to Reduce the Risk of Prostate Cancer, 2001, 25 Natural Ways to Lower Blood Pressure, 2002; editor: Nutritional Determinants in Athletic Performance, 1981, New Protective Roles for Selected Nutrients, 1989; columnist: Dance mag.; contbr. articles to profl. jours. With USAF, 1953—56. Disting. scholar, U. Miami, Fla., 1977, Atlantic U., 1977. Fellow: Am. Coll. Nutrition; mem.: AAAS, Am. Diabetic Assn., Mt. Diablo Astron. Soc., Eastbay Astron. Soc., Astron. Soc. Pacific (bd. dirs., chmn. devel. coun.), Inst. Food Technologists, Am. Soc. Cell Biology, Sports Medicine Coun., Brit. Nutrition Soc., Am. Inst. Nutrition, Oakland Yacht Club, Olympic Club (San Francisco), Sigma Xi. Libertarian. Avocations: astronomy, photography. Office Phone: 925-283-2753. Personal E-mail: jscala2@comcast.net.

SCALAPINO, DOUGLAS JAMES, physics educator; b. San Francisco, Dec. 10, 1933; s. John and Marie Constance (Pederson) S.; m. Diane Holmes Lappe, June 19, 1955; children: Lisa, Leigh, Kenneth, Lynne, Anne. BS, Yale U., 1955; PhD, Stanford U., 1961. Rsch. assoc. Washington U., St. Louis, 1961-62, U. Pa., Phila., 1962-64, asst. prof., 1964-66, assoc. prof., 1966-68, prof., 1968-69; vis. prof. U. Calif., Santa Barbara, 1968-69, prof. physics, 1969—; prin. investigator Inst. for Theoretical Physics, Santa Barbara, 1979—. Cons. E.I. Du Pont De Nemours & Co. Inc., Wilmington, Del., 1963-88; Faculty Rsch. lectr., U. Calif., Santa Barbara, 1983; IBM Almaden Rsch. Ctr., San Jose, Calif., 1989—; mem. sci. adv. bd. Superconductor Techs.Inc., Santa Barbara, 1987—; fellow Los Alamos Nat. Lab., 1992—. Contbr. articles to profl. jours. Fellow Alfred P. Sloan Found., 1964-66, fellowship, Guggenheim Found., 1976-77.; grantee NSF, U.S. Dept. Energy, pvt. corps., 1965—. Fellow Am. Phys. Soc. (Julius Edgar Lilienfeld prize 1998); mem. NAS, Am. Acad. Arts and Scis., Phi Beta Kappa, Sigma Xi. Office: U Calif Santa Barbara Dept Physics 552 University Ave Santa Barbara CA 93106-0002

SCALING, SAM T., obstetrician, gynecologist; b. Fort Monmouth, NJ, Aug. 16, 1945; s. Sam T. and Helen Louise Scaling; m. Lisa Janine Peck, Aug. 6, 1988; 1 child, Micah;children from previous marriage: Traci, Craig, Chad, Chris, Cory, Tiffany. BS, U. N.Mex., Albuquerque, 1967; MD, U. Tenn., Memphis, 1971. Diplomate Am. Bd. Ob/Gyn. Intern Confederate Meml. Med. Ctr., Shreveport, La., 1971—72; resident in ob-gyn. Baylor Coll. Medicine, Houston, 1975—78, chief resident ob/gyn., 1977—78; pvt. practice Obstetrics, Gynecology and Infertility Casper, Wyo., 1978—; founder, pres. Women's Health Assocs. Wyo., Casper, 2001—; med. staff Wyo. Med. Ctr., 1978—; chmn. dept. ob/gyn. Wyo. Med. Ctr., Meml. Hosp. Natrona County, 1981—83, 1986—88, 2001, 2002—05, sec. med. staff, 1989—91, vice chief of staff, 1991—93, chief of staff, 1993—95. Clin. asst. prof., instr. ob/gyn. Wyo. Family Practice Program, Casper, 1978—; v.p. Wyo. State Bd. Med. Examiners, 1984—92, 1989—90, pres., 1990—92; presenter in field; med. dir. Casper Family-Centered League Lamaze Prepared Childbirth, 1980—84, Christ-Centered Childbirth, 1984—87, Caring Ctr., Casper, 1986—90, Wyo. Med. Ctr. PMS Clinic, 1987—90. Author childrens book. Mem. Little Dilly Golf Tournament com. Casper Country Club, 1994—96; mem. adv. bd. Caring Ctr., 2001—; mem. Healing Pl. Counseling Ctr. adv. bd. Highland Park Cmty. Ch., 1994—95; v.p. bd. dirs. Casper Children's Chorale, 1981—82; bd. dirs. Wyo. Cmty. Health Care Alliance, 1997—, Christian Solidarity Worldwide-USA, 1997—2000. Maj. USAF, 1972—75. Named to Am.'s Top Obstetricians and Gynecologists, Consumers Rsch. Coun. Am., 2002—03, 2007; NSF summer scholar, N.Mex. Highlands U., 1962. Fellow: ACS, ACOG, Am. Fertility Soc.; mem.: Am. Soc. Reproductive Medicine (mem. nat. adv. coun. 1997), Natrona County Med. Soc., Am. Assn. Pro Life Obstetricians and Gynecologists, Am. Coll. Physician Execs., Soc. Reproductive Surgeons, Am. Assn. Gynecologic Laparascopists, Wyo. State Med. Soc., Ctrl. Assn. Obstetricians and Gynecologists, Found. N.Am. Wild Sheep (life), Alaska Profl. Hunters Assn., Bass Anglers Sportsman Soc. (life), N.Am. Hunting Club (life), Boone and Crockett Club (life), Safari Club Internat. (life), Rocky Mountain Elk Found., Alpha Omega Alpha. Republican. Mem. Ch. Of God. Avocations: hunting, fishing, hiking, gun collecting, coin collecting/numismatics. Office: Women's Health Assocs Wyo 1125 E 2d Casper WY 82601

SCANLAN, CHRISTINE, state legislator; m. Tim Scanlan; 3 children. BA in History, Regis U., Denver, MA in Nonprofit Orgn. Mgmt. Sr. v.p., COO The Keystone Ctr., devel. officer; mem. Dist. 56 Colo. House of Reps., Denver, 2008—. Pres. Summit Sch. Dist. Bd. Edn., Mountain BOCES Bd.; mem. Colo. Tourism Bd. Dirs. Democrat. Office: Colo State Capitol 200 E Colfax Denver CO 80203 Office Phone: 303-866-2952. Business E-Mail: christine.scanlan.house@state.co.us.*

SCANLON, JOHN M., fiber optics company executive; BSEE, U. Toronto; MSEE, Cornell U. Group v.p. AT&T and Bell Labs. until 1990; v.p. cellular infrastructure group Motorola; chief oper. officer Cambridge Tech. Group; CEO Global Crossings Ltd., Beverly Hills, Calif., vice chair, CEO Asia. Pres. emeritus Cornell U. Engring. Bd. Patentee in field. Bd. dirs. Outward Bound. Mem. IEEE (sr.), Nat. Acad. Scis.

SCARBOROUGH, DEAN A., consumer product company executive; b. Chester, Pa., Oct. 14, 1955; BA, Hiram Coll., 1977; MBA, U. Chgo., 1979. Mktg. mgr. Avery Dennison, Pasadena, Calif., 1985, v.p., gen. mgr. Follson Roll. divsn., 1990-95, mgr. Fosson Roll Europe The Netherlands, 1995-97, group v.p. Fosson Roll Worldwide Pasadena, Calif., 1999-2000, pres., COO, 2000—. Bd. dirs. United Way, Lake County, Ohio; mem. adv. com. Greater Western Res. coun. Boy Scouts Am., Ohio; bd. visitors Hiram Coll. Office: Avery Dennison Corp 150 N Orange Grove Blvd Pasadena CA 91103

SCATES, ALLEN EDWARD, coach; BA, UCLA, 1961, MS, 1962. Coach volleyball UCLA, 1970—. Coached UCLA to 18 NCAA championships. Recipient All Time Great Coach awrd USA Volleyball, 1995, Alumnas of Yr. in Profl. Devel., UCLA, 2003; inducted Volleyball Hall of Fame, 1993, Calif. Beach Volleyball Hall of Fame, 1998, UCLA Hall of Fame, 2003; named Coach of Yr., 5 times, U.S. Olympic Com. Coach Yr., 1998. Office: UCLA Morgan Ctr PO Box 24044 Los Angeles CA 90024-0044 E-mail: ascates@athletics.ucla.edu.

SCHAAF, DOUGLAS ALLAN, lawyer; b. Green Bay, Wis., Nov. 18, 1955; s. Carlton Otto and Fern (Brunette) S.; m. Kathlyn T. Bielke, Feb. 23, 1988. BBA magna cum laude in Internat. Bus., St. Norbert Coll., DePere, Wis., 1978; JD, U. Notre Dame, 1981. Bar: Ill. 1981, Calif. 1987. Assoc. McDermott, Will & Emery, Chgo., 1981-84, Skadden, Arps, Slate, Meagher & Flom, 1984-89; ptnr. Paul Hastings, Janofsky & Walker, LA, 1989—, chair tax dept., 2006—. Adj. faculty mem. John Marshall Law Sch., 1984-87. Atty. Chgo. Vol. Legal Services, 1984-87; bd. dirs. Orange County Alzheimer's Assn., 1993-2008. Mem. Orange County Bar Assn. (chair tax sect. 1994-96). Office: Paul Hastings Janofsky & Walker 695 Town Center Dr Ste 1700 Costa Mesa CA 92626-7191 Office Phone: 714-668-6221. Office Fax: 714-668-6441. Business E-Mail: dougschaaf@paulhastings.com.

SCHACHMAN, HOWARD KAPNEK, molecular biologist, educator; b. Phila., Dec. 5, 1918; s. Morris H. and Rose (Kapnek) S.; m. Ethel H. Lazarus, Oct. 20, 1945; children— Marc, David. BSChemE, Mass. Inst. Tech., 1939; PhD in Phys. Chemistry, Princeton, 1948; DSc (hon.), Northwestern U., 1974; MD (hon.), U. Naples, 1990. Fellow NIH, 1946-48; from instr. to asst. prof. U. Calif., Berkeley, 1948-54, assoc. prof. biochemistry, 1954-59, prof. biochemistry and molecular biology, 1959-91, chmn. dept. molecular biology, dir. virus lab., 1969-76, prof. emeritus, dept. molecular and cell biology, 1991-94, prof. grad. sch., 1994—. Mem. sci. coun. and sci. adv. bd. Stazione Zoologica, Naples, Italy, 1988—; cons. bd. sci. Meml. Sloan-Kettering Cancer Ctr., 1988—97; mem. sci. adv. com. Rsch. ! Am., 1990—; William Lloyd Evans lectr. Ohio State U., 1988; Carl and Gerty Cori lectr. Washington U. Sch. Medicine, 1993; faculty rsch. lectr. U. Calif., Berkeley, 1994; Alta. Heritage Found. for Med. Rsch. vis. prof. U. Alta., 1996; Wellcome vis. prof. in basic med. scis., 1999—2000; Walter C. MacKenzie lectr. Sch. Medicine U. Alta., Edmonton, Canada, 2001. Author: Ultracentrifugation in Biochemistry, 1959. Mem. bd. sci. counselors Cancer Biology and Diagnosis divsn. Nat. Cancer Inst., 1989-92; ombudsman in basic scis. NIH, 1994—2002. Lt. USNR, 1945-47. Recipient John Scott award, 1964, Warren Triennial prize Mass. Gen. Hosp., 1965, Alexander von Humboldt award, 1990, Berkeley citation for disting. achievement and notable svc. U. Calif., 1993, Theodor Svedberg award, 1998; Guggenheim Meml. fellow, 1956. Mem.: NAS (chmn. biochemistry sect. 1990—93, panelist sci. responsibility and conduct of rsch. 1990—92), AAAS (mem. com. on sci. freedom and responsibility 1998—, Sci. Freedom and Responsibility award 2000), Acad. Nat. Dei Lincei (fgn. mem.), Fedn. Am. Socs. for Exptl. Biology (pres. 1988—89, pub. affairs exec. com. 1989—, pub. svc. award 1994), Am. Soc. Biochemistry and Molecular Biology (pres. 1987—88, chmn. pub. affairs com. 1989—2000, Merck award 1986, Herbert A. Sober award 1994, pub. svc. award established in his name 2001 2001), Am. Chem. Soc. (Calif. sect. award 1958, award in chem. instrumentation 1962). Achievements include development of the ultracentrifuge as a tool for studying macromolecules of biological interest; studies on structure and function of a regulatory enzyme: Aspartate transcarbamylase. Office: U Calif Berkeley Dept Molecular Cell Bio 229 Stanley Hall # 3206 Berkeley CA 94720-3206

SCHADE, WILBERT CURTIS, education administrator; b. St. Louis, Jan. 4, 1945; s. Wilbert Curtis and Florence Mary (Allen) S.; m. Jacqueline Siewert, May 14, 1977; children: Benjamin Allen Siewert, Timothy Knorr Siewert. BA, U. Pa., 1967; AM, Washington U., St. Louis, 1970; PhD, Ind. U., 1986. Tchg. asst. dept. romance lang. Washington U., St. Louis, 1967-68; tchr. French St. Louis Priory Sch., 1970-71; assoc. instr. dept. French and Italian Ind. U., Bloomington, 1972-74, 76-80; tchr. French Webster Groves (Mo.) H.S., 1975-76; asst. dir. admissions Beloit (Wis.) Coll., 1980-83, assoc. dir. admissions, 1983-84; dir. coll. placement and dir. admissions Westover Sch., Middlebury, Conn., 1984-90; head upper sch. The Key Sch., Annapolis, Md., 1990-94, interim dir. devel., 1994-95; tchr. French, head lang. dept. Wasatch Acad., Mt. Pleasant, Utah, 1995-96, asst. headmaster for acad. affairs, 1996-2000; tchr., dir. of studies Internat. Seminar Series, Paris, 1999—. Lectr. in field. Co-editor: African Literature in its Social and Political Dimensions, 1983; mem. editl. bd. Jour. Coll. Admission, 2000—; contbr. articles to profl. jours. including World Lit. Written in English, Studies in 20th Century Lit. Active Anne Arundel County (Md.) Task Force on Year Round Edn., 1994-95, Utah State Office of Edn.'s Fgn. Lang. Instrl. Materials and Texbook Adv. Com., 1996-98. NEH Summer Inst. on African Am. Lit. and Film grant, 1994. Mem. Nat. Assn. Coll. Admission Counseling (presenter nat. conf. 1985), Rocky Mountain Assn. for Coll. Admission Counseling (exec. bd., chief assembly del. to Nat. Assn.), African Lit. Assn. (exec. com. 1979), Phi Delta Kappa. Mem. Soc. Of Friends. Avocation: tennis. Home: PO Box 3549 20 Malheur Ln Sunriver OR 97707

SCHAECHTER, MOSELIO, microbiology educator; b. Apr. 26, 1928; children: Judy, John. Student, Cen. U., Ecuador, 1947-49; MA, U. Kans., 1952; PhD, U. Pa., 1954. Postdoctoral fellow State Serum Inst., Copenhagen, 1956-58; from instr. to asst. prof. to assoc. prof. U. Fla., Gainesville, 1958-62; from assoc. prof. to disting. prof. dept. microbiology Tufts U., Boston, 1962-95, prof. emeritus, 1995—. Adj. prof. San Diego State U., 1995—, U. Calif., San Diego, 2004—. Editor: Molecular Biology Bacterial Growth, 1985, Escherichia coli and Salmonella Typhimurium, 1987, 95, Mechanisms of Microbiol. Disease, 1989, 92; author: In the Company of Mushrooms, 1997, Microbe, 2005. Mem. Am. Soc. Microbiology (pres. 1985-86, chmn.

internat. activities), Am. Soc. Med. Sch. Microbiology Chmn. (pres. 1984-85), Soc. Gen. Microbiology, Boston Mycol. Club, Sigma Xi. Avocation: field mycology. Home: 8515 Costa Verde Blvd Apt 554 San Diego CA 92122 Business E-Mail: mschaech@sunstroke.sdsu.edu.

SCHAEFER, KIM, music educator; married; 2 children. Student, Utah State Univ., Colo. State Univ., SD State Univ. Cert. Nat. Bd. Tchg. Standards. Music tchr. Whitehorse HS, Navajo Reservation, Montezuma Creek, Utah, 1998—. Dist. arts coord., 2004—. Named Utah Tchr. of Yr., 2007. Mem.: Music Educator's Nat. Conf., Utah Music Educator's Assn. (Superior Accomplishment award 2004), Tri-M Honor Soc. (chair). Achievements include being fluent in Navajo. Office: Whitehorse High Sch PO Box 660 Montezuma Creek UT 84534 Home Phone: 801-633-6755; Office Phone: 435-678-1887.

SCHAEFER, WILLIAM DAVID, language educator; b. Dighton, Mass., May 11, 1928; s. Louis and Elsie K. (Otterbein) S.; m. Josephine R. Lamprecht, Aug. 8, 1958; 1 dau., Kimberly. BA, NYU, 1957; MS, U. Wis., 1958, PhD, 1962. Mem. faculty UCLA, 1962-90, prof. English, 1970-90, chmn. dept., 1969-71, exec. vice chancellor, 1978-87. Author: James (BV) Thomson: Beyond the City, 1965, Speedy Extinction of Evil and Misery, 1967, Education Without Compromise: From Chaos to Coherence in Higher Education, 1990; contbr. articles to profl. jours., short stories to literary mags. Served with AUS, 1954-56. Fulbright fellow Eng., 1961-62 Mem. MLA (exec. dir. 1971-78). Home: 164 Stagecoach Rd Bell Canyon CA 91307-1044 Office: UCLA 405 Hilgard Ave Los Angeles CA 90095-9000 Personal E-mail: wschae444@aol.com.

SCHAEFFER, GLENN WILLIAM, casino corporate financial executive; b. Pomona, Calif., Oct. 11, 1953; s. William Donald and Mary Louise (Miller) S.; m. Deborah Lynn Helfer, Sept. 6, 1974 (div. Apr. 1981); m. Renee Sue Riebel, May 25, 1985 AB summa cum laude, U. Calif., Irvine, 1974, MA, 1975; MFA, U. Iowa, 1977. Fin. cons. Dean Witter, Los Angeles, 1977-78; assoc. Hill and Knowlton, Inc., Los Angeles, 1978-81; v.p. Ramada Inns, Inc., Phoenix, 1981-84; exec. v.p., chief fin. officer Circus Circus Enterprises, Inc., Las Vegas, Nev., 1984-91, pres., 1991-93, also bd. dirs. Las Vegas; ptnr. Gold Strike Resorts, Jean, Nev., 1993-95; pres. Mandalay Resort Group, 1995—. Wine grower and estate bottler, N.Z. Founder and patron Internat. Inst. Modern Letters. Pres. Hitch fellow U. Calif.-Irvine, 1973-74 Mem. Phi Beta Kappa. Avocations: reading, bicycling. Office: Mandalay Resort Group 3950 Las Vegas Blvd S Las Vegas NV 89119

SCHAEFFER, LEONARD DAVID, health insurance company executive; b. Chgo., July 28, 1945; s. David and Sarah (Levin) Schaeffer; m. Pamela Lee Sidford, Aug. 11, 1968; children: David, Jacqueline. BA, Princeton U., 1969. Mgmt. cons. Arthur Andersen & Co., 1969—73; dep. dir. mgmt. Ill. Mental Health/Devel. Disability, Springfield, 1973—75; dir. Ill. Bur. of Budget, Springfield, 1975—76; v.p. Citibank, N.A., NYC, 1976—78; asst. sec. mgmt. and budget HHS, Washington, 1978, adminstr. HCFA, 1978—80; exec. v.p., COO Student Loan Mktg. Assn., Washington, 1980—82; pres., CEO Group Health, Inc., Mpls., 1983—86; chmn., CEO Blue Cross of Calif., Woodland Hills, 1986—96, WellPoint Health Networks Inc., Thousand Oaks, Calif., 1992—2004; chmn. WellPoint Inc., 2004—05; sr. advisor Tex. Pacific Group, 2006—. Bd. dirs. Allergan, Inc., Irvine, Calif., Amgen, Inc., Thousand Oaks, Quintiles Transnational Corp., 2008; bd. councilors U. So. Calif. Sch. Policy, Planning & Devel., 1988—; bd. dirs., exec. com. Blue Cross-Blue Shield Assn., Chgo., 1986—2004; mem. Congl. Prospective Payment Assessment Commn., 1987—93, Pew Health Professions Com., Phila., 1990—93; chmn. bd. trustees Nat. Health Found., LA, 1992—2001; chmn. bd. dirs. Nat. Inst. Health Care Mgmt., 1993—2006; mem. Coun. on the Econ. Impact of Health Sys. Change, 1996—; co-chair adv. coun. dept. of health care policy Harvard Med. Sch., 1998—; founding chmn. Coalition for Affordable and Quality Healthcare, 2000; regents lectr. U. Calif., Berkeley, Calif., 2005—06; sr. advisor Tex. Pacific Group, 2006—; chmn. Surg. Care Affiliates, Birmingham, Ala., 2007—; Judge Robert Maclay Widney chair and prof. U. Southern Calif., 2008. Bd. govs. Town Hall, LA, 1989—2006; trustee The Brookings Inst., Nat. Health Mus., 2000—; adv. coun. Dept. Econs. Princeton U., NJ; adv. group Coun. on Health Care Econs. and Policy. Recipient Citation for Outstanding Svc., Am. Acad. Pediat., 1981, Disting. Pub. Svc. award, HEW, Washington, 1980; fellow, Kellogg Found., 1981—89; Internat. fellow, King's Fund Coll., London, 1990—. Mem.: Am. Assn. Health Plans (bd. dirs. 2001—04), Health Ins. Assn. Am. (chmn. 1999), Inst. Medicine NAS, Regency Club, Princeton Club, Cosmos Club. Office: 1733 Ocean Ave Ste 325 Santa Monica CA 90404 E-mail: lds@northbp.com.

SCHAEFFER, REINER HORST, military officer, foreign language professional; b. Berlin, Lichterfelde, Fed. Republic Germany, Jan. 13, 1938; arrived in U.S., 1958; s. Immanuel Emil and Wilhelmine (Fahrni) Frei-Schaeffer; m. Cathy Anne Cormack, Apr. 6, 1966; 1 child, Brian Reiner. Nat. cert., Bus. Sch., Thun, Switzerland, 1957; BGS in Bus., U. Nebr., 1970; MPA in Orgnl. Behavior, U. Mo., 1972; PhD in Fgn. Lang. Edn., Ohio State U., 1979. Commd. officer USAF, 1958, advanced through grades to lt. col.; instr. German, French USAF Acad., Colorado Springs, Colo., 1975-77, assoc. prof., 1979-81, chmn. German, 1981, dir. librs., 1982-86, prof., 1986-92, dir. Acad. Librs., 1986-92. Bd. dirs. Friends of AF Acad. Librs.; pres. Fgn. Lang. Ctr., Inc., 1999—2001; cons. Fgn. Langs., 2001—. Recipient 5 Meritorious Svc. medals, 5 Air Force Commendation medals; named Disting. Grad., Air Force Inst. Tech., 1979. Mem.: Am. Assn. Tchrs. German, Aspen Creek Meadows Homeowners Assn. (pres. 2004—), Swiss Club (pres. Colorado Springs chpt. 1990—96, chmn.), Alpha Sigma Alpha, Pi Alpha Alpha. Republican. Avocations: skiing, golf, hiking, soccer. Home: 848 Spring Trl Prescott AZ 86303-5901 Personal E-mail: swiss13@juno.com.

SCHAFER, RONALD WILLIAM, electrical engineering educator; b. Tecumseh, Nebr., Feb. 17, 1938; s. William Henry and Esther Sophia Schafer; m. Dorothy Margaret Hall, June 2, 1960; children: William R., John C. (dec.), Katherine L., Barbara Anne. Student, Doane Coll., Crete, Nebr., 1956-59; BEE, U. Nebr., 1961, MEE, 1962; PhD in Elec. Engring., MIT, 1968. Tech. staff Bell Labs., Murray Hill, NJ, 1968-74; John and Marilu McCarty prof. elec. engring. Ga. Inst. Tech., Atlanta, 1974—2004, Inst. prof., 1991—2004, emeritus prof., 2004—; HP fellow Hewlett-Packard Labs., Palo Alto, Calif., 2004—. Chmn. bd. Atlanta Signal Processors Inc., 1983-2001. Co-author: Digital Signal Processing, 1974, Digital Processing of Speech Signals, 1979, Speech Analysis, 1979, Discrete-Time Signal Processing, 1989, 2d edit., 1999, Computer-Based Exercises for Signal Processing Using Matlab, 1995, DSP First: A Multimedia Approach, 1998, Signal Processing First, 2003. Recipient Class of 34 Disting. Prof. award Ga. Inst. Tech., 1985. Fellow IEEE (Emanuel R. Piore award 1980, Edn. medal 1992, 3d millennium award 2000), Acoustical Soc. Am.; mem. IEEE Processing Soc. (soc. award 1982, edn. award 2000), Nat. Acad. Engring. Democrat. Office: Hewlett-Packard Labs 1501 Page Mill Rd Palo Alto CA 94304 Office Phone: 650-857-4142.

SCHAFER, SUE, state legislator; b. Portland, Maine; 2 children. BS in Secondary Edn., U. Nebr., Lincoln; MA in Counseling & Psychol., U. Colo., Boulder; EdD., U. Northern Colo. Lic. Principal. Social studies & French tchr. Denver Pub. Schools; high sch. & cmty. coll. counselor Omaha Pub. Schs., Skagit Valley Cmty. Coll., Mt. Vernon, Wash.; curriculum dir. & accreditation mgr. Colo. Dept. Edn.; mem. Dist. 24 Colo. House of Reps, Denver, 2008—. Sec. Wheat Ridge Sr & Cmty. Ctr. Adv. Com. Recipient Contribution award, Colo. Congress of Foreign Language Teachers, Leadership award, Order of Kentucky Colonels, Disting. Svc. award, Colo. Art Edn. Assn. Mem.: Colo. High Sch. Activities Assn. (exec. bd. mem.), League of Women Voters, Colo. Tennis Assn. Democrat. Office: State House 200 E Colfax Denver CO 80203 Office Phone: 303-866-5522. Business E-Mail: sue.schafer.house@state.co.us.*

SCHAFFER, JEFFREY L., lawyer; b. LA, Aug. 21, 1952; AB, U. Calif., Berkeley, 1974; JD, U. Calif., 1979. Bar: Calif. 1979, U.S. Dist. Ct. (no. dist.) Calif., U.S. Ct. Appeals (9th cir.) 1985. Mem. Howard, Rice, Nemerovski, Canady, Falk & Rabkin, San Francisco, 1988—. Panelist Continuing Edn. Bar, 1983-92, computer law inst. U. So. Calif., 1986. Assoc. editor Calif. Law REv., 1977-79. Mem. ABA (bus. law sect.), Am. Bankruptcy Inst., State Bar Calif. (bus. law sect., mem. debtor/creditor and bankruptcy com. 1987-90, 96-98, UCC com. 1998—), Bar Assn. San Francisco (comml. law and bankruptcy sect., co-chair barristers club's bankruptcy and comml. law com. 1984-85), Berkeley Law Found., Order of Coif, Phi Beta Kappa. Office: Howard Rice Nemerovski Canady Falk & Rabkin 3 Embarcadero Ctr Fl 7 San Francisco CA 94111-4074

SCHAFFER, JOEL LANCE, dentist; b. Bklyn., Oct. 18, 1945; s. Martin Alter and Irene Natalie Schaffer; m. Susan Anne Swearingen, Feb. 14, 1980 (div.); 1 child, Jericho Katherine. BS, L.I. U., 1967; DDS, Howard U., 1971. Diplomate Am. Bd. Aesthetic Dentistry. Dental intern Eastman Dental Ctr., Rochester, NY, 1971—72; gen. practice dentistry Boulder, Colo., 1973—. Evaluator Clin. Rsch. Assocs.; lectr. in field, 1972—. Contbr. articles to profl. jours.; patentee in field. Advisor Boulder Meals on Wheels; mem. Boulder County Com. for Persons with Disabilities. Fellow: Am. Soc. Dental Aesthetics; mem.: ADA, Alpha Omega, Boulder County Dental Soc., Am. Acad. Oral Implantology, Tau Epsilon Phi. Jewish. Home: 4171 S Hampton Cir Boulder CO 80301-6017 Office: 2880 Folsom St Boulder CO 80304-3739 Office Phone: 303-449-1792. Personal E-mail: joels64790@aol.com.

SCHAFFER, ROBERT W. (BOB SCHAFFER), former congressman; b. Cin., July 24, 1962; s. Robert James and Florence Ann (Bednar) Schaffer; m. Maureen Elizabeth Menke, Feb. 8, 1986; children: Jennifer, Emily, Justin, Sarah, Mary. BA in Polit. Sci., U. Dayton, 1984; doctorate (hon.), Colo. Tech. U. Rep. caucus speechwriter Ohio Gen. Assembly, 1984-85; legis. asst. State of Ohio, Columbus, 1985; majority adminstrv. asst. Colo. State Senate, Denver, 1985-87, mem., 1987-96, US Congress from 4th Colo. dist., Washington, 1997—2003, mem. agr. com., edn. & workforce com., resources com. Owner No. Front Range Mktg. & Distbn. Inc., 1990—94; mem. Rep. Policy Com., GOP Theme Team, Ukraine Caucus, Nat. Rep. Hispanic Assembly; human svcs. com. mem. Nat. Conf. State Legislatures; chmn. Jud. Confirmation Network, State Vets. & Mil. Affairs Com., Senate Fin. Com.; vice-chmn. Senate Edn. Com., Colo. State Bd. Edn.; commr. Eighth Jud. Dist. Nominating Commn., Colo. Advanced Tech. Inst. Mem. Mental Health Bd. Larimer County, 1986—87; chmn. Leadership Prog. of Rockies. Recipient Spirit of Enterprise award, US C. of C.; named Nat. Legislator of Yr., Rep. Nat. Legislators Assn., 1995, Bus. Legislator of Yr., Colo. Assn. Commerce & Industry; named a Taxpayer Champion, Colo. Union Taxpayers, 1995. Mem.: Air Force Assn., Nat. Fedn. Ind. Bus., KC, Jaycees (Mover and Shaker award 1989). Republican. Roman Catholic. Avocations: backpacking, skiing, baseball, painting, reading. Home: 5027 Alder Ct Fort Collins CO 80525-5588

SCHAIE, K(LAUS) WARNER, human development and psychology educator; b. Stettin, Germany (now Poland), Feb. 1, 1928; came to U.S., 1947, naturalized, 1953; s. Sally and Lottie Luise (Gabriel) S.; m. Coloma J. Harrison, Aug. 9, 1953 (div. 1973); 1 child, Stephan; m. Sherry L. Willis, Nov. 20, 1981. AA, City Coll., San Francisco, 1951; BA, U. Calif., Berkeley, 1952; MS, U. Wash., 1953, PhD, 1956; DPhil (hon.), Friedrich-Schiller U., Jena, Germany, 1997; ScD (hon.), W.Va. U., 2002. Lic. psychologist, Calif., Pa. Fellow Washington U., St. Louis, 1956-57; asst. prof. psychology U. Nebr., Lincoln, Nebr., 1957-64, assoc. prof., 1964-68; prof. chmn. dept. psychology W.Va. U., Morgantown, W.Va., 1964-73; prof. psychology, dir. Gerontology Rsch. Inst., U. So. Calif., 1973-81; Evan Pugh prof. human devel. and psychology Pa. State U., University Park, 1981—2008, Evan Pugh prof. emeritus, 2008—, dir. Gerontology Ctr., 1985—2003; affiliate prof. psychiatry and behavioral scis. U. Wash., 1991—. Devel. behavior study sect. NIH, Bethesda, Md., 1970-72, chmn., 1972-74, chmn. human devel. and aging study sect., 1979-84, expert panel in comml. airline pilot retirement, 1981, data and safety bd. shep project, 1984-91. Author: Developmental Psychology: A Life Span Approach, 1981, Adult Development and Aging, 1982, 5th rev. edit., 2002, Japanese, Chinese and Spanish edits., 2003, Intellectual Development in Adulthood: The Seattle Longitudinal Study, 1996, Developmental Influences on Adult Intelligence, 2005; editor: Handbook of Psychology of Aging, 1977, 6th rev. edit., 2006, Longitudinal Studies of Adult Development, 1983, Cognitive Functioning and Social Structure over the Life Course, 1987, Methodological Issues in Research on Aging, 1988, Social Structure and Aging: Psychological Processes, 1989, Age Structuring in Comparative Perspective, 1989, The Course of Later Life, 1989, Self-Directedness: Cause and Effects Throughout the Life Course, 1990, Aging, Health Behaviors and Health Outcomes, 1992, Caregiving Systems: Formal and Informal Helpers, 1993, Societal Impact on Aging: Historical Perspectives, 1993, Adult Intergenerational Relations: Effects of Societal Change, 1995, Older Adults Decision Making and the Law, 1996, Impact of Social Structures on Decision Making in the Elderly, 1997, Impact of the Workplace on Older Persons, 1998, Handbook of Theories of Aging, 1999, Mobility and Aging, 2000, Evolution of the Aging Self, 2000, Effective Health Behavior in the Elderly, 2002, Mastery and Control in the Elderly, 2003, Influence of Technology on Successful Aging, 2003; Independent Aging: Living Arrangements and Mobility, 2003, Religious Influences on Health and Wellbeing in the Elderly, 2004, Historical Influences on Lives and Aging, 2005, Social Structures, Self-Regulation and Aging, 2006, Demographic Influences on Health and Wellbeing in the Elderly, 2007, Social Structures and Aging Individuals, 2008; editor Ann. Rev. Gerontology and Geriat., vol. 7, 1987, vol. 11, 1991, vol. 17, 1997, series editor, 1996—; contbr. articles to profl. jours. Fellow APA (coun. reps. 1976-79, 83-86, Disting. Contbn. award, 1992), Am. Psychol. Soc., Gerontol. Soc. (Kleemeier award 1987, Disting. Mentorship award 1996); mem. Psychometric Soc., Internat. Soc. Study Behavioral Devel., Mensa (Lifetime Achievement award, 2000). Unitarian Universalist. Avocations: hiking, stamps. Home: 2500 6th Ave North Apt 1 Seattle WA 98109 Office Phone: 206-281-4050. Business E-Mail: schaie@u.washington.edu.

SCHALLER, ANTHONY JOSEF, technology management executive; b. Pitts., Nov. 17, 1957; s. Josef and Ruth Bridgette (Petschick) S.; m. Anna Marie Johnson (div. Nov. 1997); children: Kristofer, Derek. BS in Computer Sci. and Bus. Mgmt., U. Pitts., 1982; grad. degree computer sci., Carnegie-Mellon U., 1987. Mgr. sys. devel. Carnegie-Mellon U., Pitts., 1980-87; sr. mgr. applications engring. Ingres Corp., Alameda, Calif., 1988-91; dir. tech. mktg. MTI/SF2 Corp., Sunnyvale, Calif., 1991-92; dir. multidatabase sys. devel. MDL Info. Sys., Inc., San Leandro, Calif., 1992-93, dir. intersect project, 1993-94; pres., founder Intersect Software, Inc., Alameda, 1994-97; v.p. engring., chief tech. officer Open Object/Electric Classifieds, Inc., San Francisco, 1997-98; v.p. tech. Ticketmaster Online-CitySearch, Inc., Pasadena, Calif., 1998-99; sr. v.p. tech., chief tech. officer, COO RioPort.com, San Jose, Calif., 1999—2003; sr. v.p. tech. strategy Yahoo, Sunnyvale, Calif., 2003—. Bd. dirs. Altenheim Assn., Oakland, Calif., ZealMedia, Inc., L.A.; tech./mgmt. cons. Turnaround Mgmt. Assn., Alameda, 1998-2004. Mem. Assn. for Computing Machinery (program devel. and spkr. liason/coord. Pitts. chpt. 1983-84, vice-chmn. Pitts. chpt. 1984-85, chmn. Pitts. chpt. 1985-86, Svc. Recognition award 1985, 86). Achievements include patent for system and methods for performing multi-source searches over heterogeneous databases; coinventor of worlds first mp3 music player; creator of first music download service. Home: 211 Encounter Bay Alameda CA 94502-7909 Office: RioPort com 2895 Zanker Rd San Jose CA 95134-2101 Office Phone: 510-541-5480. Office Fax: 866-210-3108. E-mail: tony@schaller.net.

SCHALLER, GORDON A., lawyer; b. Aug. 27, 1949; BS with distinction, Iowa State U., 1970; JD magna cum laude, U. Minn., 1973. Bar: Calif. 1973, Washington 1980, US Tax Ct. Ptnr. Gibson, Dunn & Crutcher, Irvine, Calif.; nat. mng. dir. estate, philanthropy and ins. svcs. myCFO, Inc.; mng. dir. WealthAdvisors, LLC; of counsel Greenberg Traurig, LLP, 2003—04, mng. shareholder Costa Mesa, Calif., 2004—. Contbr. articles to profl. publs.; editor: Minn. Law Rev. 1971-73. Named one of Top 100 Attys., Worth mag., 2006. Fellow Am. Coll. Trust and Estate Counsel; mem. Order of the Coif, Wash. State Bar Assn., Calif. Bar Assn.

SCHALLER, JANE GREEN, pediatrician; b. Cleve., June 26, 1934; d. George and May Alice (Wing) Green; children: Robert Thomas, George Charles, Margaret May. AB, Hiram Coll., Ohio, 1956; MD cum laude, Harvard U., 1960. Diplomate Am. Bd. Pediat., Am. Bd. Med. Examiners. Resident in pediat. Children's Hosp.-U. Wash., Seattle, 1960-63; fellow immunology Children's Hosp. U. Wash., 1963-65; faculty U. Wash. Med. Sch., 1965-83, prof. pediat., 1975-83; head divsn. rheumatic diseases Children's Hosp., Seattle, 1968-83; prof., chmn. dept. pediat., pediatrician-in-chief Tufts U. Sch. Medicine/New Eng. Med. Ctr., 1983-98; Karp prof. pediat. Tufts U. Sch. Medicine, Boston, 1983—, disting. prof., 1995—. Vis. physician Med. Rsch. Coun., Taplow, Eng., 1971-72; adj. prof. diplomacy The Fletcher Sch. Law and Diplomacy, Tufts U., 1998-2000. Contbr. articles to profl. jours. Bd. dirs. Seattle Chamber Music Festival, 1982-85; trustee Boston Chamber Music Soc., 1985—; mem. Boston adv. coun. UNICEF, tech. advisor UN Study on the Impact of Armed Conflict on Children, 1995-97; chmn., adv. com. children's rights divsn. Human Rights Watch, 1995—; mem. adv. com. Middle East divsn., 1998—; exec. com. Women's Commn. for Refugee Women and Children Internat. Rescue com., 1989-94, adv. coun. 1994—. Mem.: AAAS, Royal Coll. Pediats. U.K., Internat. Women's Forum, Mass. Women's Forum, Harvard U. Med. Sch. Alumni Coun. (v.p. 1977—80, pres. 1982—83), Physicians for Human Rights (founding pres. 1986—89, exec. com. 1986—), Com. Health in So. Africa (exec. com. 1986—92), Assn. Med. Sch. Pediat. Chmn. (exec. com. 1986—89, rep. to coun. on govt. affairs and coun. acad. socs.), New Eng. Pediat. Soc. (pres. 1991—93), Am. Coll. Rheumatology, Internat. Pediat. Assn. (pres.-elect 1998—2001, pres. 2001—04, exec. dir. 2004—), Am. Acad. Pediat. (exec. com. sect. on internat. child health, head children's rights program, rep. to UNICEF), Am. Pediat. Soc., Soc. Pediat. Rsch., Inst. Medicine of NAS, Saturday Club, Tavern Club, Aesculapian Club (pres. 1988—89). Office: International Pediatric Association Executive Director 4480 Oak Street, Room 2D 14 Vancouver BC V6H 3V4 Canada Business E-Mail: jschaller@tufts-nemc.org.

SCHALLERT, WILLIAM JOSEPH, actor; b. LA, July 6, 1922; s. Edwin Francis and Elza Emily (Baumgarten) S.; m. Rosemarie Diann Waggner, Feb. 26, 1949; children: William Joseph, Edwin G., Mark M., Brendan C. BA, UCLA, 1946. Co-founder, owner Circle Theatre, Hollywood, Calif., 1947-50. Appeared in motion pictures, TV, stage, radio, 1947—; movies include Lonely Are the Brave, Heat of the Night, Charley Varrick, Red Badge of Courage, Teachers; starred in TV series Patty Duke Show, 1963-66, Nancy Drew Mysteries, 1977-78, Little Women, 1979, The New Gidget, 1986-88, The Torkelson's, 1991-92, Recount Justice Stevens, 2008; starred as judge in stage play and film The Trial of the Catonsville Nine, N.Y.C., Los Angeles, 1971 (Obie award 1971); starred as Dr. Pangloss in Candide, L.A., 1995; recorded voice of Abraham Lincoln for permanent installation at Lincoln Mus., Springfield, Ill., 2004. Trustee Motion Picture and TV Fund, 1977—. With AUS, 1942-44; with USAAC, 1944-45. Fulbright fellow Brit. Repertory Theatre, 1952-53. Mem. ASCAP, SAG (pres. 1979-81, trustee pension and health plan 1983—, founder Com. for Performers with Disabilities 1981—, Ralph Morgan award 1993). Personal E-mail: schlrt80@yahoo.com.

SCHAPIRA, DAVID, state legislator; b. Mesa, Ariz., Feb. 17, 1980; Student, Northern Ariz. U., Ariz. State U.; BA in Polit. Sci., George Washington U., 2001. Former aide to US Senator Tom Daschle, Washington; campaign mgr. Terry Goddard for Atty. Gen., Ariz., 2002; owner consulting bus. Democracy Online Campaigns, 2003—; mem. Dist. 17 Ariz. House of Reps., 2007—, mem. appropriations, com., edn. com. Vol. Am. Cancer Soc. Mem.: Kiwainis Youth Group, Key Club. Democrat. Jewish. Office: Ariz House Reps Capitol Complex 1700 W Washington Rm 332 Phoenix AZ 85007 Office Phone: 602-926-3028. Office Fax: 602-417-3038. Business E-Mail: dschapira@azleg.gov.*

SCHAPIRO, GEORGE A., electronics executive; b. Richmond, Va., Mar. 21, 1946; s. Irwin Abraham and Jeanne (Goldman) S.; m. Jo Ann Katzman, Aug. 6, 1978; children: Rebecca Jeanne, Amy Elizabeth. BA, U. Va., 1967; MS in Indsl. Adminstrn., Carnegie-Mellon U., 1969. Fin. analyst data processing group IBM, Harrison, N.Y., 1968; product mktg. mgr. data sys. divns. Hewlett-Packard Co., Cupertino, Calif., 1969-74, med. electronics divsn. Waltham, Mass., 1974-76; pres., CEO Andros Inc., Berkeley, Calif., 1976-80, 90-91, Andros Analyzers, Inc., Berkeley, 1979-90, chmn. profl. bd. dirs., 1991—. Pres., CEO Hepatix Inc., Houston, Tex., 1992-93; pres., CEO U.S. Med. Instruments, Inc., San Diego, Calif., 1992-93; CEO Sonic Force, LLC, Burlingame, Calif., 1993-98; CEO Megabios, Inc., Burlingame, 1994; pres. Cardiac Mariners, Inc., Los Gatos, Calif., 1999-2000; guest lectr. Stanford U. Sch. Bus., U. Calif. at Berkeley Coll. Engring. and Extension Sch., Am. Mgmt. Assn. Seminar Series. Bd. dirs. Anesthesia Patient Safety Found. Mem. Assn. Computing Machinery, Assn. Advancement Med. Instrumentation, World Pres.'s Orgn. Democrat. Jewish. Home and Office: 3880 Ralston Ave Hillsborough CA 94010-6743

SCHAPP, REBECCA MARIA, museum director; b. Stuttgart, Fed. Republic Germany, Dec. 12, 1956; came to U.S., 1957; d. Randall Todd and Elfriede Carolina (Scheppan) Spradlin; m. Thomas James Schapp, May 29, 1979. AA, DeAnza Coll., 1977; BA in Art, San Jose State U., 1979, MA in Art Adminstrn., 1985. Adminstrv. dir. Union Gallery, San Jose, Calif., 1979-82; from mus. coordinator to dep. dir. de Saisset Mus. Santa Clara (Calif.) U., 1982-92, dir., 1993—. Mem. San Francisco Mus. Modern Art; bd. dirs. Works of San Jose, v.p. 1983-85. Mem. Non-Profit Gallery Assn. (bd. dirs.). Democrat. Avocations: racquetball, walking, bicycling, camping. Office: De Saisset Mus Santa Clara U 500 El Camino Real Santa Clara CA 95050-4345

SCHAPPERT, JOHN CONRAD, computer software company executive; b. North Miami, Fla., July 14, 1970; s. John and Barbara Ann (Nash) S.; m. Kelly Elizabeth Johnson, May 4, 1996. AA with honors, Miami Dade C.C., Fla., 1990. Programmer Visual Concepts, San Mateo, Calif., 1991-94; pres. Tiburon Entertainment, Maitland, Fla., 1994—98; with Electronic Arts, Inc., Redwood City, Calif., 1998—2007, gen. mgr. Electronic Arts Tiburon, 1998—2002, gen. mgr. Electronic Arts Can., 2002, group gen. mgr., COO worldwide studios, sr. v.p., COO worldwide studios; corp. v.p. LIVE, Software & Services, Interactive Entertainment Bus. divsn. Microsoft Corp., Redmond, Wash., 2007—. Programmer (video games) Desert Strike, 1992, John Madden Football 94, 1993-94; programmer, project leader Bill Walsh College Football, 1993; developer, dir. John Madden Football 97, 1996, others. Named Programmer of the Yr. Electronic Arts, 1994; named one of 40 Under 40, Bus. in Vancouver, 2005. Office: Microsoft Corp 1 Microsoft Way Redmond WA 98052-6399

SCHATZ, BRIAN E., political organization administrator, environmentalist, former state legislator; b. Oct. 20, 1972; m. Linda Kwok Kai Yun; 1 child, Tyler. BA in Philosophy, Pomona Coll. Tchr. Punahou Sch.; mem. Dist. 25 Hawaii House of Reps., 1999—2006; CEO Helping Hands Hawaii; chmn. Dem. Party of Hawaii, 2008—. Dir. Makiki Cmty. Libr., Ctr. for a Sustainable Future. Recipient Pres.'s Award, Hawaii Audubon Soc., Bank of Hawaii Cmty. Leader of the Yr., 2004, NOAA's Environ. Hero Award. Democrat. Office: Dem Party of Hawaii 1050 Ala Moana Blvd, #26 Honolulu HI 96814 Office Phone: 808-596-2980.*

SCHATZ, IRWIN JACOB, cardiologist, educator; b. St. Boniface, Man., Can., Oct. 16, 1931; came to US, 1956, naturalized, 1966; s. Jacob and Reva S.; m. Barbara Jane Binder, Nov. 12, 1967; children: Jacob, Edward, Stephen and Brian (twins). Student, U. Man., Winnipeg, 1951, MD with honors, 1956. Diplomate: Am. Bd. Internal Medicine. Intern Vancouver (B.C.) Gen. Hosp., 1955-56; resident Hammersmith Hosp., U. London, 1957, Mayo Clinic, Rochester, Minn., 1958-61; head sec. peripheral vascular disease Henry Ford Hosp., Detroit, 1961-68; asso. prof. medicine Wayne State U., 1968-71, chief sect. cardiovascular disease, 1969-71; assoc. prof., asso. dir. sect. cardiology U. Mich., 1972-73, prof. internal medicine, 1973-75; prof. medicine John A. Burns Sch. Medicine, U. Hawaii, 1975—, chmn. dept. medicine, 1975-90, interim chmn. dept. medicine, 2003—05. Author: Orthostatic Hypotension, 1986; contbr. numerous articles to med. jour. Mem. jud. coun. State of Hawaii Supreme Ct., 2000—. Rockefeller Found. scholar, 1991. Master ACP (bd. gov. 1984-89, Laureate award Hawaii chpt. 1992); fellow Am. Coll. Cardiology (bd. gov. 1980-84); mem. Am. Heart Assn. (fellow coun. cardiology), Am. Fedn. Clin. Rsch., Asian-Pacific Soc. Cardiology (v.p. 1987-91), Accreditation Coun. for Grad. Med. Edn. (chmn. residence rev. com. internal medicine 1989-95), Hawaii Heart Assn. (pres.), Western Assn. Physicians, Am. Autonomic Soc. (chmn. bd. gov., pres. 1996-98), Pacific Interurban Club. Jewish. Office: 1356 Lusitana St Honolulu HI 96813-2421

SCHATZ, MONA CLAIRE STRUHSAKER, social worker, educator, consultant, researcher; b. Phila., Jan. 4, 1950; d. Milton and Josephine (Kivo) S.; m. James Fredrick Struhsaker, Dec. 31, 1979 (div.); 1 child, Thain Mackenzie. BA, Metro State Coll., 1976; postgrad., U. Minn., 1976; MSW, U. Denver, 1979; D Social Work/Social Welfare, U. Pa., 1986. Tchg. fellow U. Pa., 1981—82; asst. prof. S.W. Mo. State U., Springfield, 1982—85; prof. Colo. State U., Ft. Collins, 1985—2006; dir. social work divsn. Wyo. Edn. and Rsch. Inst., 2006—. Cons. Mgmt. and Behavioral Sci. Ctr., Wharton Sch. U. Pa., 1981-82; field coord. Colo. State U., 1986-88, dir. non-profit agy. adminstrn. program, 1995-97, dir. project Edn. and Rsch. Inst. Fostering Families, 1987—, dir. youth agy. adminstrn. program Am. Humanics, 1988-90; mem. coun. foster care cert. program We. Gov.'s U., 1998—; resource specialist South N.J. Health Sys. Agy., 1982; adj. faculty mem. U. Mo., Springfield, 1994; med. social worker Rehab. and Vis. Nurse Assn., 1985-90; mem. Colo. Child Welfare Adv. Com., Family Conservation Initiative; internat. cons. and trainer Inst. for Internat. Connections, Azerbaijan, Russia, Latvia, Albania, U.S., Hungary, Ukraine, Romania, Australia, Republic of Korea., Australia, China, New Zealand, 1992—; vis. prof. U. Canberra, Australia, 2006; scholar vis. prof. Mokwon U. Korea. Contbr. articles to profl. jours. including Jour. Social Work Edn., Jour. Baccalaureate Social Work, Internat. Jour. Social Work, New Social Worker, Chosen Child: Internat. Adoption Mag., others. Cons., field rep. Big Bros./Big Sisters Am., Phila., 1979-83; acting dir., asst. dir. Big Sisters Colo., 1971-78; owner Polit. Cons. Colo., Denver, 1978-79; active Food Co-op, Ft. Collins, Foster Parent, Denver, Capital Hill United Neighbors, Adams County (Denver) Social Planning Coun., Colo. Justice Coun., Denver, Regional Girls Shelter, Springfield; bd. dirs. Crisis Helpline and Info. Svc Scholar Lilly Endowment, Inc., 1976, Piton Found., 1978; recipient Spl. Recognition award Big Bros./Big Sisters Am., 1983, Recognition award Am. Humanics Mgmt. Inst., 1990, Innovative Tchg. award, Ctr. for Tchg. and Learning/Colo. State U., Jack Cermak Adv. award, 2003. Mem. Inst. Internat. Connections (bd. dirs., adv. bd.), Coun. Social Work Edn., Nat. Assn. Deans and Dirs. (bd. dirs), SWE Commn. Profl. Devel., Group for Study of Generalist Social Work, Social Welfare History Group, NASW (nominating com. Springfield chpt., state bd. dirs., No. Colo. rep.), Student Social Work Assn. Colo. State U. (adv. 1986-89), Permanency Planning Coun. for Children and Youth, NOW (treas. Springfield chpt. 1984-85), Student Nuc. Awareness Group (advisor), Har Shalom (tchr. youth edn. program), Alpha Delta Mu. Democrat. Avocations: cooking, travel, reading, bicycling, sewing. Office: Univ Wyoming Divsn Social Work 1000 E Univ Ave Dept 3632 Laramie WY 82071 Office Phone: 307-766-4933. Business E-Mail: mschatz@uwyo.edu.

SCHATZBERG, ALAN FREDERIC, psychiatrist, researcher; b. NYC, Oct. 17, 1944; s. Emanuel and Cila (Diamand) S.; m. Nancy R. Silverman, Aug. 27, 1972; children: Melissa Ann, Lindsey Diamand. BS, NYU, 1965, MD, 1968; MA (hon.), Harvard U., 1989. Diplomate Nat. Bd. Med. Examiners, Am. Bd. Psychiatry and Neurology. Intern Lenox Hill Hosp., NYC, 1968-69; resident in psychiatry Mass. Mental Health Ctr., Boston, 1969-72; clin. fellow in psychiatry Harvard Med. Sch., Boston, 1969-72, asst. prof. psychiatry, 1977-82, assoc. prof., 1982-88, prof., 1988-91; interim psychiatrist-in-chief McLean Hosp., Belmont, Mass., 1984-86, dir. depression rsch. facility, 1985—, svc. chief, 1982-84, 86-88; psychiatrist adv. panel Eli Lilly & Co., Indpls., 1986-93; clin. dir. Mass. Mental Health Ctr., Boston, 1988-91; Kenneth T. Norris, Jr. prof. psychiatry and behavioral scis. Stanford (Calif.) U., 1991—, chmn. dept. psychiatry and behavioral scis. Sch. Medicine, 1991—. Cons. AMA Videoclinics, Chgo., 1979-83; mem. AMA/FAA panel on health regulations, Chgo., 1984-86; mem. NIH Biol. Psychopathology and Clin. Neuroscis. Intitial Rev. Group, 1991-95, chmn., 1993-94, ITMA Rev. Group, 2007-09. Co-author: Manual of Clinical Psychopharmacology, 1986, 6th edit., 2007; co-editor: Depression: Biology, Psychodynamics and Treatment, 1978, Hypothalamic-Pituitary-Adrenal Axis, 1988, Textbook of Psychopharmacology, 1996, 2d edit., 1998, 4th edit., 2009; mem. editl. bd. McLean Hosp. Jour., 1975—88, Jour. Psychiat. Rsch., 1988—, co-editor-in-chief, 2000—, mem. editl. bd. Harvard Rev. Psychiatry, 1992—, Anxiety, 1993, Jour. Clin. Psychopharmacology, 1993—, Archives of Gen. Psychiatry, 1995—, Psychoneuroendocrinology, 1995—, Am. Jour. Psychiatry, 2002—05, assoc. editor-in-chief Depression and Anxiety, 1992—2007, translational field editor Neuropsychopharmacology, 2002—07; contbr. more than 400 articles to profl. publs., chapters to books. Maj. USAF, 1972-74. Rsch. grantee NIMH, 1984-87, 94—, Poitras Charitable Found., 1985-93, Pritzker Found., 1997—; recipient Mood Disorders Rsch. award Am. Coll. Psychiatrists, 2002, Klerman Lifetime Rsch. award Nat. Depressive and Manic Depressive Assn., 1998, Strecker award U. Pa., 2002, Falcone award Nat. Alliance Rsch. in Schizophrenia and Affective Diseases, 2005. Fellow: APA (Rsch. award 2002), Soc. Biol. Psychiatry (pres. 2005—06), Am. Coll. Psychiatrists (Disting. Svc. award in psychiatry 2005), Am. Coll. Neuropsychopharmacology (coun. 1994—97, pres. 2000—01), Am. Psychopathol. Assn.; mem.: NAS, Am. Psychiat. Assn. (pres. elect 2009—), Inst. Medicine, No. Calif. Psychiat. Soc. (v.p. 1997—99), Mass. Psychiat. Soc. (coun. 1987—90). Avocations: travel, swimming, fine arts, theater. Office: Stanford U Sch Medicine 401 Quarry Rd Rm 300 Stanford CA 94305-5717 Office Phone: 650-723-6811. Business E-Mail: afschatz@stanford.edu.

SCHAUF, VICTORIA, pediatrician, educator; b. NYC, Feb. 17, 1943; d. Maurice J. and Ruth H. (Baker) Bisson; m. Michael Delaney; 2 children. BS in Microbiology with honors, U. Chgo., 1965, MD with honors, 1969. Intern in pediat. U. Chgo. Hosp., 1969—70; resident in pediat. Sinai Hosp. of Balt., 1970—71; chief resident pediat. Children's Hosp. Nat. Med. Ctr., Washington, 1971—72; rsch. trainee NIH, Bethesda, Md., 1972; adj. asst. prof. microbiology Rush Med. Coll., Chgo., 1972—74; prof. pediat., head pediatric infectious diseases U. Ill., Chgo., 1974—84; med. officer FDA, Rockville, Md., 1984—86; chmn. dept. pediat. Nassau County Med. Ctr., East Meadow, NY, 1986—90; prof. pediat. SUNY, Stony Brook, 1987—94; pvt. practice, 1995—; chief pediatric svcs. Ridgecrest Regional Hosp., 2005—. Vis. prof. Rockefeller U., 1990-92; mem. vis. faculty Chiang Mai (Thailand) U., 1978; mem. ad hoc com. study sects. NIH, Bethesda, 1981-82; bd. dirs. Pearl Stetler Rsch. Found., Chgo., 1982-84; cons. FDA, 1987-88, 93-95, Can. Bur. Human Prescription Drugs, Ottawa, 1990-2004, Biotech. Investors, 1993-95, Calif. Children's Svcs., 2005—; course dir. pediat. infectious diseases rev. course Cornell U. Med. Coll., N.Y.C., 1994, faculty, 1995. Co-author: Pediatric Infectious Diseases: A Comprehensive Guide to the Subspecialty, 1997; prodr. radio and TV programs in field; contbr. articles to profl. jours., chpts. to books. Vol. physician Cook County Hosp., Chgo., 1974-84; mem. adv. com. Nat. Hansen's Disease Ctr., La., 1986, Nassau County Day Care Coun., N.Y., 1988-90; mem. adv. bd. Surg. Aid to Children of World, N.Y., 1986-90; commr., sec. Kern County Children and Families Commn., 1999-2002; sec., bd. dirs. Indian Wells Valley Cmty. Found., 2001-. Am. Lung Assn. grantee U. Ill., 1977; recipient contract NIH, U. Ill., 1978-81, grantee, 1979-84. Fellow Infectious Diseases Soc. Am.; mem. Pediatric Infectious Diseases Soc. (exec. bd.), Soc. Pediatric Rsch., Am. Pediatric Soc., AAAS, Am. Soc. Microbiology, Am. Acad. Pediat., Phi Beta Kappa, Alpha Omega Alpha. Avocation: walking. Home Phone: 760-384-2399; Office Phone: 760-371-2128. Business E-Mail: vschauf@pol.net.

SCHAUFLER, MICHAEL, state legislator; Member, Happy Valley Transportation Advisor Committee, 1996, Happy Valley City Coun, 1997-2000; Oregon State Representative, District 48, 2003-, member, Committee on Bus, Labor & Consumer Affairs & Committee on Water, currently.Member, rank & file, Laborer's Union, 1988-1996; contractor, 1996-2002. Democrat. Mailing: 900 Court St NE H-382 Salem OR 97301 Office Phone: 503-986-1448. E-mail: rep.MikeSchaufler@state.or.us.

SCHEFF, JONATHAN H., health and medical products executive; B, Amherst Coll., Mass.; MD, Tufts U., Boston; MBA, U. San Diego; grad. Advanced Mgmt. Program, Harvard Bus. Sch. Cert. internal medicine. Med. dir. Southbay NavCare Clinic; cons. Milliman & Robertson, San Diego; regional med. dir. CHAMPUS divsn. Aetna Health Plans, San Diego; various positions including v.p. govt. health affairs and sr. v.p. health care ops. Found. Health Corp.; pres., chmn. bd. dirs. Found. Health Med. Group, Inc., Sacramento; chmn. bd. dirs. Thomas Davis Med. Ctrs., Tucson; chief med. officer, sr. v.p. TRICARE Med. Mgmt. for Health Net Fed. Svcs., Inc. Health Net, Inc., sr. v.p., chief med. officer, 2003—07, 2008—. Office: Health Net Inc 21650 Oxnard St Woodland Hills CA 91367 Office Phone: 818-676-6000.

SCHEFFEL, MARK, state legislator; m. Chen Scheffel; 4 children. BS in Fin., U. Denver, 1982; JD with distinction, John Marshall Law Sch., Chgo., 1987; LLM in Taxation, NYU Law Sch., NYC, 1998. Bar: Colo. 1988, US Tax Ct. 1989, US Dist. Ct., Colo. 1990, US Ct. Appeals (10th cir.), DC Ct. Appeals 1991, US Supreme Ct. 1992. Founding incorporator, charter dir. Champion Bank; atty. Reid and Scheffel, PC, Parker, Colo., 1993—; mem. Dist. 4 Colo. State Senate, Denver, 2009—. Former chmn. & dist. capt. Douglas County Rep. Party, former coord., GOTV effort, precinct person; former chmn. bylaws com. Colo. Rep. Party; mem. citizen adv. bd. Wilflife Mus.; bd. dirs. Skycliff Stroke Ctr. Republican. Office: Colo State Capitiol 200 E Colfax Denver CO 80203 Office Phone: 303-866-4869. Business E-Mail: mark.scheffel.senate@state.co.us.*

SCHEFFLER, SAMUEL, philosophy educator; b. NYC, Oct. 20, 1951; s. Israel and Rosalind (Zuckerbrod) S.; m. Kathryn Granzow, Jan. 16, 1983; children: Adam Nathaniel, Gabriel Alexander. BA, Harvard U., 1973; PhD, Princeton U., 1977. Asst. prof. philosophy U. Calif., Berkeley, 1977-79, assoc. prof., 1979-85, prof., 1985—, chmn. dept., 1985-89, Class of 1941 World War II Meml. prof. Vis. fellow All Souls Coll., Oxford, 1990; chmn. adv. bd. Kadish Ctr for Morality Law & Public Affairs. Author: The Rejection of Consequentialism, 1982 (Franklin J. Machette prize Am. Philos. Assn. 1983), Human Morality, 1992, Boundaries and Allegiances; editor: Consequentialism and Its Critics, 1988; adv. editor Philosophy and Public Affairs; contbr. articles to profl. jours. U. Calif. Humanities Research fellow, 1982, Guggenheim Found. fellow, 1984, Pres.'s fellow U. Calif. 1989, NEH fellow, 1989. Fellow Am. Acad. Arts & Sci.; mem. Am. Philos. Assn. Office: Department of Philosophy 314 Moses Hall 2390 University of California Berkeley CA 94720-2390 Business E-Mail: scheffler@berkeley.edu.

SCHEIBEL, ARNOLD BERNARD, psychiatrist, educator, research director; b. NYC, Jan. 18, 1923; s. William and Ethel (Greenberg) Scheibel; m. Madge Mila Ragland, Mar. 3, 1950 (dec. Jan. 1977); m. Marian Diamond, Sept. 1982. BA, Columbia U., NYC, 1944, MD, 1946; MS, U. Ill., 1952. Intern Mt. Sinai Hosp., NYC, 1946-47; resident in psychiatry Barnes and McMillan Hosp., St. Louis, 1947-48, Ill. Neuropsychiat. Inst., Chgo., 1950-52; asst. prof. psychiatry and anatomy U. Tenn. Med. Sch., 1952-53, assoc. prof., 1953-55, UCLA Med. Ctr., 1955-67, prof., 1967—, mem. Brain Rsch. Inst., 1960—, acting dir. Brain Rsch. Inst., 1987-90, dir., 1990-95. Cons. in field. Contbr. numerous articles to tech. jours, chpts. to books.; mem. editl. bd. Brain Rsch., 1967-77, Developmental Psychobiology, 1968—, Internat. Jour. Neurosci., 1969—, Jour. Biol. Psychiatry, 1968—, Jour. Theoretical Biology, 1980—; assoc. editor News Report, 1989—. Mem. Pres.'s Commn. on Aging, Nat. Inst. Aging, 1980—. Served with AUS, 1943-46; from lt. to capt. M.C. AUS, 1948-50. Guggenheim fellow (with wife), 1953-54, 59; recipient Disting. Svc. award Calif. Soc. Biomed. Rsch., 1998. Fellow Am. Acad. Arts and Scis., Norwegian Acad. Scis., Am. Psychiat. Assn. (life, Harriet and Charles Luckman Disting. Tchg. award 1997) AAAS; mem. Am. Neurol. Assn., Soc. Neuorosci., Pyschiat. Rsch. Assn., Soc. Biol. Psychiatry, So. Calif. Psychiat. Assn. Home: 16231 Morrison St Encino CA 91436-1331 Office: UCLA Dept Neurobiology Los Angeles CA 90024 Business E-Mail: scheibel@mednet.ucla.edu.

SCHEIBER, HARRY N., law educator, historian; b. 1935; BA, Columbia U., 1955; MA, Cornell U., 1957, PhD, 1961; MA (hon.), Dartmouth Coll., 1965; D.Jur.Hon., Uppsala U., Sweden, 1998. Instr. to assoc. prof. history Dartmouth Coll., 1960-68, prof., 1968-71; prof. Am. history U. Calif., San Diego, 1971-80; prof. law Boalt Hall, U. Calif., Berkeley, 1980—. Chmn. jurisprudence and social policy program, 1982-84, 90-93, assoc. dean, 1990-93, 96-99; The Stefan Riesenfeld prof., 1991—; vice chair Univ. Academic Senate, 1993-94, chair 1994-95; dir. Earl Warren Legal Inst., 2002-05, Inst. for Legal Rsch., 2005—, Sho Sato Program, 1993—; co-dir. Law of the Sea Inst., 2002-; Fulbright disting. sr. lectr., Australia, 1983, marine affairs coord. Calif. Sea Grant Coll. Program, 1989-2000; vis. rsch. prof. Law Inst. U. Uppsala, Sweden, 1995, hon. prof. DiTella U., Buenos Aires, 1999; cons. Calif. Jud. Coun., 1992-93; acting dir. Ctr. for Study of Law and Soc., 1999-2001; Cassel lectr., Stockholm U., 2003. Author: The Wilson Administration and Civil Liberties, 1960, Ohio Canal Era, 1970, Inter-Allied Conflicts and Ocean Law (1945-1953), 2001; co-author: American Law and the Constitutional Order, 1988, The State and Freedom of Contract, 1998, American Law and the Constitutional Order, 1978, Law of the Sea: The Common Heritage and Emerging Challenges, 2000, Bringing New Law to Ocean Waters, 2004, Earl Warren and the Warren Court, 2006, Emerging Concepts of Rights in Japanese Law, 2007, Frontier Issues in Ocean Law, 2009; editor: Yearbook of the California Supreme Court Historical Society, 1994—2006; contbr. articles to profl. jours. Chmn. Littleton Griswold Prize Legal History, 1985-88, 2006-07, pres. NH Civil Liberties Union, 1969-70; chmn. Project '87 Task Force on Pub. Programs, Washington, 1982-85; dir. Berkeley Seminar on Federalism, 1986-95; cons. judiciary study U.S. Adv. Commn. Intergovernmental Rels., 1985-88, Pew Oceans Commn., 2002-03, Nat. Rsch. Coun., 2002-03, Joint Ocean Commn. Initiative, 2006-, sci. adv. bd. couns., 2007-, Pew oceans Cmty. State Calif.; dir. NEH Inst. Constitutionalism, U. Calif., Berkeley, 1986-87, 88-91; state corp. Ocean Protection Coun., 2008-. Recipient Sea Grant Colls. award, 1981-83, 84-85, 86-2002; fellow Ctr. Advanced Study in Behavioral Scis., Stanford Calif., 1967, 71; Guggenheim fellow, 1971, 88; Rockefeller Found. humanities fellow, 1979, NEH fellow, 1985-86; NSF grantee 1979, 80, 88-89. Fellow AAAS, Am. Acad. Arts and Scis., U. Calif. Humanities Rsch. Inst., Am. Soc. for Legal History (hon.; pres. 2003—), Japan Soc. for Promotion of Sci. (invitational fellow); mem. Am. Hist. Assn., Orgn. Am. Historians, Agrl. History Soc. (pres. 1978), Econ. History Assn. (trustee 1978-80), Law and Soc. Assn. (trustee 1979-81, 96-99), Nat. Assessment History and Citizenship Edn. (chmn. nat. acad. bd. 1986-87), Marine Affairs and Policy Assn. (bd. dirs. 1991-96), Ocean Governance Study Group (steering com. 1991-2004), Internat. Coun. Environ. Law, Calif. Supreme Ct. Hist. Soc. (bd. dirs. 1993—, v.p. 1997-98). Office: U Calif Berkeley Law Sch Boalt Hall Berkeley CA 94720-7200 Office Phone: 510-643-9788. E-mail: scheiber@law.berkeley.edu.

SCHEID, STEVEN L., investment company executive; 3 children. BS in acctg., Michigan St. U. CFO The Charles Schwab & Co. Inc., 1996—99, vice-chmn. San Francisco, 1999—2002; CEO Charles Schwab Investment Mgmt., 1999—2002; pres. Schwab Retail Group, 2000—02; chmn. Janus Capital Group, Denver, 2004—, CEO,

2004—06. Fed. Reserve Bank of San Francisco's representative Fed. Advisory Coun., 2001—02; bd. dirs. The PMI Group Inc., Auto Desk Inc. Avocations: piano, clarinet, running, wine collecting. Office: Janus Capital Group Inc 151 Detroit St Denver CO 80206-4923

SCHEITHAUER, CHRISTOPHER C., lawyer; JD, Univ. So. Calif., 1996. Bar: Calif., US Dist. Ct. No., Ea., Ctrl., So. Calif. Ptnr., employment litigation McDermott Will & Emory, Irvine, Calif. Author (contrib.): Employee Benefits Law. Named a Rising Star, So. Calif. Super Lawyers, 2005—06. Mem.: ABA, State Bar Calif. Office: McDermott Will & Emery Ste 500 18191 Von Karman Ave Irvine CA 92612-7108 Office Phone: 949-757-7163. Office Fax: 949-851-9348. Business E-Mail: cscheithauer@mwe.com.

SCHEKMAN, RANDY W., molecular biology administrator, biochemist; b. St. Paul, Dec. 30, 1948; married, 1973; 1 child. BA, UCLA, 1970; PhD in Biochemistry, Stanford U., 1975; PhD (hon.), U. Geneva, 1997. Fellow U. Calif., San Diego, 1974-76, from asst. to assoc. prof. Berkeley, 1976-83, prof., 1983—, head divsn. biochemistry and molecular biology, 1990-97, co-chair dept. molecular and cellular biology, 1997—. Fellow Woodrow Wilson Found., 1970, Cystic Fibrosis Found., 1974, John S. Guggenheim Found., 1982-83; recipient Research award in microbiology & immunology, Eli Lilly, 1987, Lewis S. Rosenstiel award in basic biomedical sci., 1994, Gairdner Found. Internat. award, 1996, Albert Lasker award for basic med. rsch., Albert and Mary Lasker Found., 2002, Louisa Gross Horwtiz prize, Columbia U., 2002; named Amgen award lecturer, Protein Soc., 1999, Berkeley Faculty Rsch. lecturer, U. Calif., 1999. Mem. Am. Soc. Microbiology, Am. Soc. Biochemists & Molecular Biologists, Am. Acad. of Arts & Sciences (elected 2000), NAS (elected 1992); hon. mem. Japanese Biochemical Soc.; foreign assoc. EMBO. Achievements include research on molecular mechanism of secretion and membrane assembly in eucaryotic cells. Office: U Calif Dept Molecular Cell Bio 401 Barker Hall Spc 3202 Berkeley CA 94720-3202 Office Phone: 510-642-5686. E-mail: schekman@uclink4.berkeley.edu.

SCHELBERT, HEINRICH RUEDIGER, nuclear medicine physician; b. Wuerzburg, Germany, Nov. 5, 1939; MD, U. Würzburg, Germany, 1964. Diplomate Am. Bd. Nuclear Medicine. Intern Mercy Med. Ctr., Phila., 1966-67, resident, 1967-68, 70-71; resident in cardiology U. Dusseldorf, Germany, 1971-72; fellow in cardiology, resident in nuclear medicine U. Calif., San Diego, 1968-69, asst. rsch. cardiologist, 1972-75, assoc. rsch. radiologist, 1975-76; hosp. assoc. UCLA Med. Ctr., 1977—; prof. radiol. scis. UCLA Sch. Medicine, 1980-90, prof. pharmacol. and radiol. scis., 1993—. Editor-in-chief: Jour. Nuc. Medicine, 2004. Recipient Georg von Hevesy prize 2d Internat. Congress World Fedn. Nuclear Medicine and Radiation Biology, 1978, 3d Internat. Congress World Fedn. Nuclear Medicine and Radiation Biology, 1982, Disting. Sci. award, Acad. Molecular Imaging, 2006. Fellow Am. Coll. Cardiology; mem. Am. Heart Assn. (disting. scientific achievement award 1989), Soc. Nuclear Medicine (Herrman L. Blumgart pioneer lectr. award 1989, George De Hevesy Nuclear Medicine Pioneer award 1998), German Soc. Nuc. Med. (hon.), Swiss Soc. Nuc. Medicine (hon.)(editor-in-chief). Office: UCLA Sch Medicine Dept Molecular Med B2 085J Box 956948 Los Angeles CA 90095-6948 Office Phone: 310-825-3076. Business E-Mail: hschelbert@mednet.ucla.edu.

SCHELL, ORVILLE, former dean; BA magna cum laude, Harvard Univ., 1964; MA, Univ. Calif., 1967, PhD, 1968. Co-producer WGBH-TV, Boston, 1984; rsch. assoc. U. Calif., Berkeley, 1986; con. NBC Nightly News, 1987; cons. CBS 60 Minutes, 1991; dean Grad. Sch. Journalism, U. Calif., Berkeley, 1996—2007. Co-dir. The Bay Area Inst., 1968-71; founder, editor-in-chief Pacific News Svc., 1970-96; corespondent New Yorker Mag., 1975, WGBH-TV Boston Frontline, 1994; rsch. assoc. Ctr. for Chinese Studies Univ. Calif,; cons. in field. Editorial bd. mem. Frontline, 1996. Bd. dirs. Yale-China Assn., Nat. Com. on U.S. China Rels., vice chmn. Human Rights Watch/Asia, 1989; pres. China Symposium, 1988-89; mem. coun. on fgn. rels. Recipient Best Magazine Article on Fgn. Subject award, 1992, Alfred I. Dupont-Columbia Univ. Silver Baton award, 1993, Emmy award, 1992, Page One award Bay Area Book Reviewers Assn., 1985; numerous rsch. grants; Guggenheim Found. fellow, 1981. Mem. Author's Guild, PEN, Coun. on Fgn. Rels. Office: U Calif Grad Sch Journalism 121 Northgate Hall Berkeley CA 94720-5860

SCHELLER, RICHARD H., physiologist, science educator; b. Milw., Oct. 30, 1953; BA in Biochemistry with honors, U. Wis., Madison, 1975; PhD in Chemistry, Calif. Inst. Tech., 1980. Postdoctoral fellow divsn. biology Calif. Inst. Tech., 1980—81; postdoctoral fellow in molecular neurobiology Columbia U. Coll. Physicians and Surgeons, 1981—82; asst. prof. dept. biol. scis. Stanford (Calif.) U., 1982—87, assoc. prof. dept. biol. scis., 1987—90, assoc. prof. dept. molecular and cellular physiology, 1990—93, assoc. prof. dept. biol. scis. by courtesy, 1990—93, prof. dept. molecular and cellular physiology, 1993—, prof. dept. biol. scis., 1993; assoc. investigator Howard Hughes Med. Inst., Stanford U. Med. Ctr., 1990—94, investigator, 1994—2001; sr. v.p., research Genentech, Inc., South San Francisco, 2001—03, exec. v.p., research, 2003—. Mem. molecular, cellular and devel. neurobiology rev. com. NIMH, 1993—96; mem. sci. adv. bd. Hereditary Disease Found., 1995—96; mem. neurobiology adv. bd. Cold Spring Harbor Lab., 1995; mem. sr. rev. com. McKnight Endowment Fund, 1995; mem. adv. bd. Nat. Adv. Mental Health Coun., NIH, 1996. Mem. editl. bd. Jour. Neurosci., 1984—90, DNA, 1984—, Ann. Rev. Neurosci., 1985—90, Molecular Brain Rsch., 1985, Cellular and Molecular Neurobiology, 1986, Synapse, 1989—91, Neuron, 1990, Current Opinion in Neurobiology, 1990, sect. editor Jour. Neurosci., 1991—95, monitoring editor Jour. Cell Biology, 1991, assoc. editor Genes to Cells, 1995; contbr. articles to profl. jours. Recipient Basil O'Connor award, March of Dimes Found., 1983, Presdl. Young Investigator award, 1985, Alan T. Waterman award, NSF, 1989, Merit award, NIMH, 1992, W. Alden Spencer award, Columbia U., 1993; fellow, NIH, 1976—80, 1981—82, Alfred P. Sloan Found., 1984, Klingstein fellow in Neuroscis., 1985; scholar, McKnight Found., 1983, Pew scholar in biomed. scis., 1986, Camile and Henry Dreyfus Tchr. scholar, 1986. Mem.: Acad. of Arts and Sciences, NAS (award in Molecular Biology 1997), Soc. for Neurosci. (young investigator award selection com. 1996). Office: Genentech Inc 1 DNA Way South San Francisco CA 94080 Office Phone: 650-225-1000.

SCHELLMAN, JOHN A., chemistry professor; b. Phila., Oct. 24, 1924; s. John and Mary (Mason) S.; m. Charlotte Green, Feb. 10, 1954; children: Heidi M., Lise C. AB, Temple U., 1948; MS, Princeton U., 1949, PhD, 1951; PhD (hon.), Chalmers U., Sweden, 1983. USPHS postdoctoral fellow U. Utah, 1951-52, Carlsberg Lab., Copenhagen, 1953-55; DuPont fellow U. Minn., Mpls., 1955-56, asst. prof. chemistry, 1956-58; assoc. prof. chemistry Inst. Molecular Biology, U. Oreg., Eugene, 1958-63, prof. chemistry, rsch. assoc., 1963—. Vis. Lab. Chem. Physics, Nat. Inst. Arthritis and Metabolic Diseases, NIH, Bethesda, Md., 1980; vis. prof. Chalmers U., 1986, U. Padua, 1987. Contbr. articles to profl. jours. Served with U.S. Army, 1943-46. Fellow Rask-Oersted Found., 1954, Sloan Found., 1959-63, Guggenheim Found., 1969-70. Fellow Am. Phys. Soc., Biophys. Soc.; mem. NAS, Am. Chem. Soc., Am. Soc. Biochemistry and Molecular Biology, Am. Acad. Arts and Scis., Phi Beta Kappa, Sigma Xi. Democrat. Business E-Mail: john@molbio.uoregon.edu.

SCHEMBRI, DAVID CHARLES, automotive company executive; b. Detroit, June 9, 1953; s. Anthony Joseph and Mary (Barbara) S.; m. Michele Ann Dunn, May 10, 1974; children: Anthony Joseph, Dana Marie. BSBA, U. Detroit, 1974, MBA, 1977. Accounts payable auditor, acct. Am. Motors Corp., Southfield, Mich., 1975-77, sr. analyst fgn. investments, 1977-78, sr. analyst profit planning, 1978-79; supr. investment analysis Volkswagen U.S. Inc., Troy, Mich., 1979-80, mgr. adminstrv. budgets, 1980-81, mgr. capital investments, 1981-84, mgr. nat. bus. mgmt., 1984-85, mgr. field sales, 1985-86, mgr. region sales Culver City, Calif., 1987-88, mgr. field ops. Troy, Mich., 1988—91, dir. sales mktg., 1991—94; gen. mgr. NY region Mercedes Benz-USA Inc., 1994—99, gen. mgr. LA region, 1999—2001, v.p mktg., 2001—05; exec. v.p. sales & mktg. Mitsubishi Motors N. Am., Inc., Cypress, Calif., 2005—. Ambassador United Found. United Way, Detroit, 1983. Roman Catholic. Office: Mitsubishi Motors N Am Inc 6400 Katella Ave Cypress CA 90630

SCHENDEL, STEPHEN ALFRED, surgeon, educator; b. Mpls., Oct. 10, 1947; s. Alfred Reck and Jeanne Shirley (Hagquist) S.; children: Elliott, Mélisande. BA, St. Olaf Coll., Northfield, Minn., 1969; BS with high distinction, U. Minn., 1971, DDS, 1973; diplome asst. etranger with high honors, U. Nantes, France, 1980; MD, U. Hawaii, 1983. Diplomate Am. Bd. Plastic Surgery, Nat. Bd. Med. Examiners, Nat. Bd. Dental Examiners, Am. Bd. Oral and Maxillofacial Surgery (adv. com., bd. examiner 1991-95). Intern, then resident in oral and maxillofacial surgery Parkland Meml. Hosp., Dallas, 1975-79; resident in gen. surgery Baylor U. Med. Ctr., Dallas, 1983-84, Stanford (Calif.) U. Med. Ctr., 1984-86, resident in plastic surgery, 1986-89, acting assoc. prof. surgery, 1989-91, assoc. prof., 1991-95, head divsn. plastic and reconstructive surgery, 1992—2002, dir. residency tng., 1992-98, chmn. dept. functional restoration, 1994—2001, prof. surgery, 1995—2002, prof. emeritus surgery, 2007; head plastic surgery, dir. Craniofacial Ctr. Lucile Salter Packard Children's Hosp., Stanford, 1991—2007, chief pediat. surgery, 1997—2002. Asst. to Dr. Paul Tessier, Paris, 1987-88; asst. dept. stomatology and maxillofacial surgery Centre Hospitalier Regional Nantes, 1979-80; med. bd. Lucile Salter Packard Children's Hosp. at Stanford, 1991—. Assoc. editor Selected Readings in Oral and Maxillofacial Surgery, 1989—; mem. editl. bd. Jour. Cranio-Maxillofacial Surgery; contbr. articles to profl. jours., chpts. to books. Recipient Disting. Alumnus award St. Olaf Coll., 1993; Fulbright fellow, Nantes, 1979-80, Chateaubriand fellow Govt. of France, 1987-88. Fellow ACS, Am. Acad. Pediat.; mem. Internat. Soc. Craniofacial Surgeons, European Assn. Cranio-Maxillofacial Surgeons, Am. Soc. Pediat. Plastic Surgeons, Am. Assn. Plastic Surgery, Soc. Baylor Surgeons (founding), Am. Cleft Palate-Craniofacial Assn., Am. Soc. Plastic Surgeons (sec. 1996—), Am. Soc. Maxillofacial Surgeons (sec., pres. 2000-01), Assn. Acad. Chairmen Plastic Surgery, Zedplast (bd. dirs. 1993—), Omicron Kappa Upsilon. Avocations: fly fishing, painting and sculpture. Office: Stanford U Med Ctr Divsn Plastic Reconstr Surg 770 Welch Rd Ste 400 Palo Alto CA 94304 Home Phone: 650-261-1081; Office Phone: 650-723-5824, 650-328-0511. Business E-Mail: sschendel@stanford.edu.

SCHENDEL, WINFRIED GEORGE, insurance company executive; b. June 19, 1931; arrived in US, 1952, naturalized, 1956; s. Willi Rudolf Max and Anna Margarete (Sassen) S.; m. Joanne Wiiest, Aug. 24, 1953; children: Victor Winfried, Bruce Lawrence, Rachelle Laureen. BS in Elec. and Indsl. Engring., Hannover-Stadthagen U., Hannover, Fed. Republic of Germany, 1952. Elec. draftsman Houston Lighting & Power Co., 1954-57; elec. draftsman, corrosion technician Transcontinental Gas Pipeline Co., Houston, 1957-59; elec. engr. Ken R. White Cons. Engrs., Denver, 1959-61; sales engr. Weco divsn. Food Machinery & Chem. Corp., various locations, 1961-64; ins. field underwriter N.Y. Life Ins. Co., Denver, 1964-66, asst. mgr., 1966-70, mgmt. asst., 1970-71, gen. mgr., 1971-77, mgr., 1979-85, field underwriter, 1985—; gen. agt. Woodmen Accident and Life Ins. Co., Ft. Collins, Colo., 1993—, Assurity Life, Inc., 2001—. Ind. gen. agt., Denver, 1978-79; ins. broker and adviser, 1979—; gen. agent Assurity Life Ins., Lincoln, Nebr.; spkr. and presenter in field. Instnl. rep., advancement chmn. Denver Area coun. Boy Scouts Am., Lakewood, Colo., 1968-72; precinct chmn. Rep. party, Jefferson County, Colo., 1976, 78; founder, life mem. Sister City Program, Lakewood, Colo.; chmn. adv. bd. ARC, Jefferson County, Colo., 1987-89; elder Presbyn. Ch.; lay min. First United Meth. Ch., Ft. Collins, Colo., 1999—, fin. com.; bd. of character City Fort Collins, 2003—. Recipient Centurion award, 1966, Salesman of Yr. award Jefferson County Salesman with a Purpose Club, 1983, Top awards ARC, 1988-89. Mem. Nat. Asn. Life Underwriters, Gen. Agts. and Mgrs. Assn. (Conf. Nat. Mgmt. award 1975), Colo. Life Underwriters Assn. (reg. v.p. Denver met. area 1989-90), Mile High Assn. Life Underwriters (pres. 1986-87, nat. com. 1988, 91), Lakewood C. of C. (pres. people-to-people, Trailblazer of Yr. award 1982-83, Trail Boss of Yr. 1983), Lions, Edelweiss Club, Internat. Order Rocky Mountain Goats, N.Y. Life Star, Masons, Rotary (bd. dirs. Foothills chpt. 2002—, Ft. Collins bd. dirs. 1999-2005, Rotary Found., Paul Harris award 1995), Shriners. Home and Office: 925 Deerhurst Cir Fort Collins CO 80525-6919 Home Fax: 970-206-9082. Personal E-mail: winschendel@aol.com.

SCHENK, LYNN, lawyer, former congresswoman; b. Bronx, NY, Jan. 5, 1945; m. C. Hugh Friedman, 1972 BA, UCLA, 1967; JD, U. San Diego, 1970; postgrad, London Sch. Econs., Eng., 1970—71. Dep. atty. gen. State of Calif., 1971—72; atty. San Diego Gas & Electric Co., 1972—76; spl. asst. v.ps. Nelson Rockefeller and Walter Mondale The White House, Washington, 1976-77; dep. sec. bus., transp. & housing State of Calif., 1977—80, sec., 1980-83; pvt. law practice, 1983—93, 2003—; mem. US Congress from 49th Calif. dist., 1993—95; chief of staff to Gov. Gray Davis State of Calif., 1999—2003. Founder San Diego Urban Corp, The Women's Bank, The Lawyer's Club; bd. dirs. Sempra Energy, 2008- Co-chair Presdl. Campaign of Michael S. Dukakis, 1988, Vice chair, San Diego Unified Port Dist, 1990-93, commr., Ctr. for Nat. Policy, Washington; bd dirs. Edmund G "Pat" Brown Inst. Govt. Affairs, Calif. State U., L.A.; trustee Claremont U. Ctr. & Grad. Sch. Recipient Israel Peace medal, Author E. Hughes award for Career Achievement, I. San Diegom 2002, Disting. Alumni award; named Outstanding Young Citizen San Diego Jaycees. Democrat. Jewish.

SCHENKEL, BARBARA ANN, minister, nurse, social worker; b. Albuquerque, Mar. 17, 1951; d. Richard Henry and Mildred (Voth) S. BSN, U. N.Mex., 1972; MDiv, Iliff Sch. Theology, 1978; MSW, Ariz. State U., 1988. RN, N.Mex.; ordained to ministry Meth. Ch., 1979. Minister intern Christ Ch. U. Meth. Ch., Denver, 1975-77; parish minister Herman (Nebr.) Federated and Riverside Bapt. Ch., 1978-82, Cambridge (Nebr.) Bartley U. Meth. Ch., 1982-85; family minister Red Mountain U.M.C., Mesa, Ariz., 1988-94; nurse Ariz. Health Cost Containment Sys., Phoenix, 1994—; minister Life in the Spirit Ministry, Crossroads, Ariz., 1999—2003; prayer coord., life in spirit leader Sunrise United Meth. Ch., Phoenix, 2005—. Christ Ch. Caring Community Coordinator, Denver, 1975-77; advisor alcohol treatment program Immanuel Hosp., Washington County, Nebr., 1980-82; mem. task group to study Ministry Effectiveness in Nebr., 1981; vis. del. to World Meth. Conf., Honolulu, 1981; registrar for candidacy Bd. or Ordained Ministry, 1980-84, strategy com., 1984-85; drug and alcohol cons. Salvation Army Adult Rehab. Ctr., Phoenix, 1987-88, Adult Protective Svcs., 1988—. Chaplain Jackson-Peck Am. Legion Post, Herman, 1980—82; prayer coord., spiritual life min. Sunrise United Meth. Ch., Phoenix, 2005—. Served to 1st lt. USAF Nurse Corps, 1973—75. Mem. Nebr. Ann. Conf. United Meth. Chs., Cambridge Ministerial Assn. (pres. 1984), Tekamah-Herman Ministerial Assn. (pres. 1981), S.W. Dist. Coun. Ministries (past com. memberships). Avocations: horseback riding, bowling, crochet, needlepoint, crewel. Office: Ariz Health Cost Containment Sys 2830 W Glendale Ave Phoenix AZ 85051-8400 Home: Unit 1134 2150 E Bell Rd Phoenix AZ 85022

SCHENKER, MARC BENET, preventive medicine physician, medical educator, department chairman; b. LA, Aug. 25, 1947; s. Steve and Dosella Schenker; m. Heath Massey; children: Yael, Phoebe, Hilary. BA, U. Calif., Berkeley, 1969; MD, U. Calif., San Francisco, 1973; MPH, Harvard U., Boston, 1980. Instr. medicine Harvard U., Boston, 1980-82; asst. prof. medicine U. Calif., Davis, 1982-86, assoc. prof., 1986-92, prof., 1992—, chmn. dept. pub. health scis., 1995—. Fellow ACP; mem. Am. Thoracic Soc., Am. Pub. Health Assn., Soc. Epidemiologic Rsch., Am. Coll. Epidemiology, Soc. Occupl. Environ. Health, Internat. Commn. Occupl. Health, Assn. Tchrs. Preventive Medicine, Phi Beta Kappa, Alpha Omega Alpha. Office Phone: 530-752-5676.

SCHENKKAN, DIRK MCKENZIE, lawyer; b. Durham, NC, Aug. 9, 1949; s. Robert Fredric and Jean (McKenzie) S.; m. Patricia Sinnott, Nov. 11, 1979; children: Jean, Penelope, Victoria. AB highest honors, U. Tex., 1971; JD, Yale U., 1975. Bar: Calif. 1976, U.S. Dist. Ct. (no. dist.) Calif. 1976, U.S. Ct. Appeals (9th cir.) 1978, U.S. Dist. Ct. (ea. dist.) Calif. 1987. Rsch. assoc., tutor Law Sch. Yale U., New Haven, 1975-76; arbitrator Fed. & State Cts. No. Dist., Calif., mediator San Francisco; prin. Howard, Rice, Nemerovski, Canady, Falk & Rabkin, San Francisco, 1976, dir. Contbr. articles to profl. jours. Bd. dirs. San Francisco Neighborhood Legal Assistance Found., 1984—, Assn. Bus. Trial Lawyers, 1994—, San Francisco Girls Chorus, 1994—, Pacific Primary Sch., San Francisco, 1985-88. Named No. Calif. Super Lawyer, by Law & Politics., 2004—06. Mem. ABA, Calif. Bar Assn., Bar Assn. San Francisco, Assn. Bus. Trial Lawyers, Rotary Internat. fellow U. Kent Canterbury, England 1972-1973, Phi Beta Kappa. Office: Howard Rice Nemerovski Canady Robertson & Falk 3 Embarcadero Ctr 7th Fl Ste 7 San Francisco CA 94111-4074 Office Phone: 415-434-1600, 415-399-3055. Office Fax: 415-217-5910. Business E-Mail: dschenkkan@hrice.com. E-mail: dschenkkan@howardrice.com.

SCHENKKAN, ROBERT FREDERIC, playwright, screenwriter; b. Chapel Hill, Mar. 19, 1953; s. Robert Frederic Sr. and Jean (McKenzie) Schenkkan; m. Maria Dahvana Headley; children: Sarah Victoria, Joshua McHenry. BA in Theatre Arts, U. Tex., 1975; MFA in Acting, Cornell U., 1977. Author: (plays) Final Passages, 1981, The Survivalist, 1982 (best of the fringe award Edinburgh Festival, 1984), Tachinoki, 1987, Tall Tales, 1988 (Playwrights Forum award, 1988, Best One Act Plays, 1993), Heaven on Earth, 1989 (Julie Harris Playwright award Beverly Hills Theatre Guild, 1989), The Kentucky Cycle, 1991 (Pulitzer prize for drama, 1992, L.A. Drama Critics Circle Best Play award, 1992, Penn Ctr. West award, 1993, Best Play Tony award nominee, 1993, Best Play Drama Desk award nominee, 1993), Conversations with the Spanish Lady and Other One-Act Plays, 1993, The Dream Thief, 1998, Handler, 1999, The Marriage of Miss Hollywood and King Neptune,The Devil and Daniel Webster, 2002, By the Waters of Babylon, 2004, Lewis and Clark Reach the Euphrates, 2005, (TV) Crazy Horse, (Miniseries) The Andromeda Strain, The Pacific, (Mous) Spartacus, (films) The Quiet American, 2002. Grantee Vogelstein Found., 1982, Arthur Found., 1988, Fund for New Am. Plays, 1990, Calif. Arts Coun., 1991. Mem.: SAG, Actors Equity, Writers Guild, Ensemble Studio Theatre, Dramatists Guild.

SCHEPPKE, JIM, library director; MLS, U. Tex., Austin. Ind. bookseller; with West Tex. Libr. Sys., Tex. State Libr.; adminstr. libr. devel. Oreg. State Libr., Portland, 1986—91, interim dir., 1991, state libr., 1991—. Bd. dirs. Bibliographical Ctr. Rsch., Colo. Mem.: Oreg. Libr. Assn. (pres. 1991, Libr. of Yr. award 1996). Office: Oreg State Libr 250 Winter St NE Salem OR 97301-3950 Office Phone: 503-378-4367. E-mail: jim.b.scheppke@state.or.us.

SCHER, LAURA SUSAN, financial company executive; b. Passaic, NJ, Jan. 18, 1959; d. Alan E. and Frances Scher; m. Ian H. Altman, May 28, 1984. BA in Econs., Yale U., 1980; MBA, Harvard U., 1985. Assoc. cons. Bain & Co., Boston, 1981-83; chief exec. officer Working Assets Funding Service, San Francisco, 1985—. Named Baker Scholar, Harvard U., 1985.

SCHERF, DIETMAR, publishing executive, artist, minister; b. Graz, Austria, June 12, 1961; came to US, 1990; s. Friedrich and Maria S.; m. Patricia Michaela Rech, Apr. 9, 1987; children: Alexander, Deborah, Daniel, David. Diploma, trade sch., Graz, 1979. CEO Handelshaus D. Scherf, Vienna, 1987-90; CEO, pres. Scherf, Inc., Las Vegas, Nev., 1990-2000, creative dir., 2001—03; pastor, founder Megagrace Christian Ctr., Las Vegas, 2003—05; chief designer Cascada Design Studies, Creative Consultant, Cascada Resorts, 1997—2005; CEO, pres. Cascada Corp., 2006—. Author: Short Term Trading, 1990, (booklet) Ross Perot, 1992, I Love Me: Avoiding and Overcoming Depressions, 1998, (as Alec Donzi) The Consultant, 2000; composer, producer, performer (CD) Nice to Meet Ya!, 1994.

Avocations: movies, reading, contemporary architecture, bible studies, music. Home and Office: Cascada Corp PO Box 80180 Las Vegas NV 89180-0180 Business E-Mail: ds@scherf.com.

SCHERGER, JOSEPH EDWARD, family physician, educator; b. Delphos, Ohio, Aug. 29, 1950; m. Carol M. Scherger, Aug. 7, 1973; children: Adrian, Gabriel. BS summa cum laude, U. Dayton, 1971; MD, UCLA, 1975. Family practice residency U. Wash., Seattle, 1975-78; clin. instr. U. Calif. Sch. Medicine, Davis, 1978-80, asst. clin. prof., 1980-84, assoc. clin. prof., 1984-90, clin. prof., 1990—, dir. predoctoral program, 1991-92; med. dir. family practice and community medicine Sharp Healthcare, San Diego, 1992-96; assoc. dean primary care, chair dept. family medicine U. Calif., Irvine, 1996—2001, prof. dept. family medicine, 1996—2001, prof. family and preventive medicine San Diego, 2003—; dean Fla. State U., Coll. Medicine, Tallahassee, 2001—03. Med. dir. AmeriChoice, 2006—; consulting med. dir. Lumetra, 2007—. Editor (in chief): (med. jour.) Hippocrates. Recipeient Hippocratic Oath award UCLA, Calif. Physician of Yr. award Am. Acad. Family Physicians. Mem. NAS (mem. Inst. Medicine), Am. Acad. Family Physicians, Soc. Tchrs. Family Medicine. Office Phone: 858-495-1371. Business E-Mail: jscherger@ucsd.edu.

SCHERMAN, CAROL E., human resources professional; married; three children. BS in Orgnl. Behavior, U. San Francisco. With Bergen Brunswig Corp., exec. v.p. human resources. CEO Medi-Mail, Inc. subs. Bergen Brunswig Corp., Las Vegas. Active Human Resources Exec. Forum of Orange County; mem. human resources adv. com. Chapman U., Orange.

SCHERR, JAMES EDWIN, sports association executive; m. April Vigil; 1 child, Evan. BS, U. Nebr.; MBA, Northwestern U. Exec. dir., treas. USA Wrestling, Colorado Springs, Colo., 1990—. Bd. dirs. USA Wrestling, Athlete Adv. Com., U.S. Olympic Com.; trustee U.S. Olympic Found.; mem. TV and mktg. commn. Internat. Fedn. Assoc. Wrestling Styles. Placed 5th in freestyle wrestling, Seoul Olympics, 1988; recipient silver medal World Championship, 1987, 89, bronze medal 1986 World meet, three U.S. Nationals titles, 2 World Cup gold medals, NCAA Championship, Outstanding Freestyle Wrestler, U.S. Nationals, 1989. Mem. USOC (exec. com.). Office: USA Wrestling 6155 Lehman Dr Colorado Springs CO 80918-3439

SCHEUER, RALPH H., lawyer; b. Albuquerque, Feb. 23, 1946; BA, U. Colo., 1967; JD, U. Va., 1970. Bar: N.Mex. 1970, US Tax Ct. 1982, US Dist. Ct. (dist. N.Mex.) 1982, US Ct. Appeals (10th cir.) 1982. Ptnr. Scheuer, Yost & Patterson, Santa Fe. Named one of Top 100 Attys., Worth mag., 2005. Mem.: ABA, First Jud. Dist. Bar Assn., Phi Alpha Delta, Pi Sigma Alpha. Office: Scheuer Yost & Patterson PC PO Drawer 9570 125 Lincoln Ave Ste 223 Santa Fe NM 87504 Office Phone: 505-982-9911. Office Fax: 505-982-1621.

SCHEUNEMAN, CHRISTINE A., lawyer; b. Kansas City, Mo., Dec. 30, 1950; BA, Univ. Kansas, 1972; JD, DePaul Univ., 1981. Bar: Ill. 1981, Calif. 1984. Ptnr., chmn. Orange County Litigation group Pillsbury Winthrop Shaw Pittman, Costa Mesa, Calif. Mem. nat. panel of arbitrators Am. Arbitration Assn. Pres. bd. dir. Orange County Chamber Orch. Mem.: Order of the Barristers. Office: Pillsbury Winthrop Shaw Pittman 7th Fl 650 Town Ctr Dr Costa Mesa CA 92626 Office Phone: 714-436-6814. Office Fax: 714-436-2800. Business E-Mail: christine.scheuneman@pillsburylaw.com.

SCHIFF, ADAM BENNETT, United States Representative from California, lawyer; b. Framingham, Mass., June 22, 1960; s. Edward Maurice and Sherrill Ann (Glovsky) Schiff; m. Eve Schiff; children: Alexa Marion, Elijah Harris. BA, Stanford U., 1982; JD cum laude, Harvard U., 1985. Bar: Calif. 1986. Assoc. Gibson, Dunn & Crutcher, LA, 1986; criminal prosecutor US Atty.'s Office, LA, 1987—93; mem. Calif. Senate, 1996—2000, chmn. judiciary com.; mem. US Congress from 29th Calif. dist., Washington, 2000—, mem. judiciary com., internat. rels. com., appropriations com. Spl. assignment to Czechoslovakia Justice Dept., Bratislava, 1992; mem. New Dem. Coalition, Dem. Homeland Security Task Force, Safe Neighborhoods Task Force, Ho. Edn. Caucus, Congl. Caucus Armenian Issues, Arts Caucus, Ho. Democracy Assistance Commn., 2005—; co-founder Freshman for Reform, Dem. Study Grp. Nat. Security, Congl. Internat. Anti-Piracy Caucus, 2003. Mock trial coach Burbank HS; nat. bd. mem. Big Brothers Big Sisters of America. Mem.: Glendale C. of C., Burbank C. of C. Democrat. Jewish. Avocation: creative writing. Office: US House of Reps 2447 Rayburn House Office Bldg Washington DC 20515-0529 Office Phone: 202-225-4176. Business E-Mail: congressman.schiff@mail.house.gov.

SCHIFF, DONALD WILFRED, pediatrician, educator; b. Detroit, Sept. 11, 1925; s. Henry and Kate (Boesky) S.; m. Rosalie Pergament; children: Stephen, Jeffrey, Susan, Douglas. Student, Wayne State U., 1943-44, Oberlin Coll., 1944-45; MD, Wayne State U., 1949. Diplomate Am. Bd. Pediatrics. Intern Detroit Receiving Hosp., 1949-50; resident in pediatrics U. Colo., 1954-55, chief resident in pediatrics, 1955-56; instr. U. Colo. Health Scis. Ctr., Denver, 1956-59, asst. clin. prof., 1959-69, assoc. clin. prof., 1969-78, clin. prof., 1978-87, prof., 1987—; pvt. practice Littleton (Colo.) Clinic, 1956-86, chmn. bd., 1973-79; med. dir. HMO Colo., Denver, 1980-86; med. dir. Child Health Clinic The Children's Hosp., Denver. Contbr. articles to profl. jours. Bd. dirs. Sch. Dist. VI, Colo., 1962; pres. Arapahoe Mental Health Clinic, Denver, 1968-70, bd. dirs., 1964-70; adv. coun. State of Colo. Medicaid, Denver, 1981—. With USN, 1944-46, USPHS, 1952-54, Turtle Mountain Indian Reservation, N.D. Recipient 25 Yrs. Teaching award U. Colo. Sch. Medicine, 1981. Mem. Am. Acad. Pediatrics (chmn. Colo. chpt. 1973-79, alternate dist. chmn. 1977-81, chmn. dist. 8 1981-86, nat. pres. 1988-89), Rocky Mountain Pediatric Soc., Colo. Med. Soc. Home: 600 Front Range Rd Littleton CO 80120-4052 Office: The Childrens Hospital 13123 E 16th Ave Aurora CO 80045-7106

SCHIFF, GUNTHER HANS, lawyer; b. Cologne, Germany, Aug. 19, 1927; came to U.S., 1936; s. Hans and Alice (Goldstein) S.; m. Katharine MacMillan, Jan. 27, 1950 (div. 1957); children: Eric Alan, Mary Alice; m. JoAnn R. Schiff; children: Jage, Hans Judson. BSFS., Georgetown U., 1949, JD, 1952. Bar: D.C. 1952, Calif. 1953. Assoc., ptnr., of counsel various firms, Beverly Hills, Calif., 1954-94; pvt. practice Beverly Hills, Calif., 1994—. Sec. Los Angeles Copyright Soc., Beverly Hills, 1975-76 Contbr. articles to profl. jours. Pres. Beverly Hills Civil Svc. Commn., 1984-85, 88-89; pres. Free Arts for Abused Children, 1993-94, dir.; chmn. Rent Control Rev. Bd., Beverly Hills, 1980-84; trustee Young Musicians Found. With USNR, 1945-46. Mem. ABA, Beverly Hills Bar Assn. (chmn. Resolutions Com. 1977-78), Los Angeles County Bar Assn., Los Angeles Copyright Soc., USCG Aux., Calif. Yacht Club. Avocations: sailing, skiing, golf. Office: 9430 W Olympic Blvd Beverly Hills CA 90212-4552 Home Phone: 310-271-7770; Office Phone: 310-557-9081. Personal E-mail: hgschiff@pacbell.net.

SCHIFF, MARTIN, physician, surgeon; b. Phila., July 16, 1922; s. Isidore and Cecelia (Miller) S.; m. Mildred Tepley, Jan. 5, 1946; children: Denise Schiff Simon, Michael, David BS, Pa. State U., 1943; MD, U. Calif.-Irvine, 1951. Intern L.A. County Gen. Hosp., 1950-51; gen. practice medicine specializing in bariatrics LA, 1951—. Lectr. L.A. area community colls. Author: Eat & Stay Slim, 1972, Miracle Weight-Loss Guide, 1976, One-Day-At-A-Time Weight Loss Plan, 1980, (5 tapes) Weight Loss Plan for Health, Happiness & A Longer Life Span, 1982, The Thin Connection, 1986, Lose Unwanted Pounds Permanently Without Dieting/Trying/Playing Games, 1998, Weight Control-Fact or Fiction?, 1999, The Power of Your Will, 1999, Connections: Feelings and Emotions, 2000, YOU: A Guide to Yourself and a Mental Roadmap to Your Inner Being, 2002, Mental Conditions and Situations-Fact or Fiction?, 2006, An Overview and Understanding of Mental Activity and Action, Conditions and Situations, 2006, Weight Thinkers, 2006. Lt. USN, 1943-45, PTO Mem. AMA, Calif. Med. Assn., L.A. Med. Assn., Am. Soc. Weight Control Specialists. Office Phone: 310-454-6172.

SCHIFFER, JOHN C., state legislator; b. Chadron, Nebr., Aug. 17, 1945; m. Nancy Schiffer; children: Ben, Wynne. BA, Colo. Coll., 1967. Rancher The Hat Ranch, 1971—87, 48 Ranch, 1987—; mem. Johnson Co. Sch. Bd., 1978—87, Johnson Co. ASCS Bd., Wyoming Environ Quality Coun; dir. Inst. Environ. & Natural Resources, 1997—; mem. Dist. 22 Wyo. State Senate, 1993—, former Majority Fl. Leader, Pres. Served USN, 1967—70. Wyoming & Nat Stockgrowers; North Fork Water Users. Republican. Episcopal. Mailing: 561 Sussex Rte Kaycee WY 82639 Office: 213 State Capitol Bldg Cheyenne WY 82002 Home Phone: 307-738-2232; Office Phone: 307-777-7881. Office Fax: 307-777-5466. Business E-Mail: jschiffe@wyoming.com.*

SCHIFFNER, CHARLES ROBERT, architect; b. Reno, Sept. 2, 1948; Robert Charles and Evelyn (Keck) S.; m. Iovanna Lloyd Wright, Nov. 1971 (div. Sept. 1981); m. Adrienne Anita McAndrews, Jan. 22, 1983. Student, Sacramento Jr. Coll., 1967-68, Frank Lloyd Wright Sch. Architecture, 1968-77. Registered architect, Ariz., Nev., Wis. Architect Taliesin Associated Architects, Scottsdale, Ariz., 1977-83; pvt. practice architecture Phoenix, 1983—. Lectr. The Frank Lloyd Wright Sch. of Architecture, 1994, 95. Named one of 25 Most Promising Young Americans Under 35, U.S. mag., 1979; recipient AIA Honor award Western Mountain Region, 1993, Western Home awards Sunset Mag., 1989, 91, AIA Ariz. Merit award, 1993 and numerous others. Home: 5202 E Osborn Rd Phoenix AZ 85018-6137 Office: 2944 N 44th St Ste 101 Phoenix AZ 85018

SCHILL, MICHAEL H., dean, law educator; b. Schenectady, NY, 1958; AB, Princeton U., 1980; JD, Yale Law Sch., 1984. Law clerk Hon. Marvin Katz Ea. Dist. Pa., 1984—85; assoc. Fried, Frank, Harris, Shriver & Jacobson, 1985—87; vis. lectr. Yale Law Sch., 1987; asst. prof. law U. Pa. Law Sch., 1987—91, assoc. prof., 1991—92; prof. law and real estate U. Pa. Law Sch. and Wharton Sch., 1993—95; vis. prof. Harvard Law Sch., 1999; dir. Furman Ctr. for Real Estate and Urban Policy, NYU, 1994—2004; prof. law and urban planning NYU Sch. Law and Robert F. Wagner Grad. Sch. Pub. Svc., 1995—2003, Wilf Family Prof. in property law and prof. urban planning, 2003—04; dean, prof. law UCLA Sch. Law, 2004—. Asst. counsel N.Y. State Assembly, Com. Housing, 1979; dir. Study of Neighborhood Reinvestment Princeton Urban and Regional Rsch. Ctr., 1980—81; vis. faculty U. Miami Law Sch., Grad. Prog. in Real Estate, 1994. Co-author: Revitalizing America's Cities: Neighborhood Reinvestment and Displacement, 1983, Reducing the Cost of New Housing Construction in New York City, 1999, The State of New York City's Housing and Neighborhoods, 2001; author: Housing and Community Development in New York City: Facing the Future, 1999; contbr. articles to law jours. Office: UCLA Sch Law Box 951476 Los Angeles CA 90095-1476 E-mail: schill@law.ucla.edu.

SCHILLER, PHILIP W., computer company executive; b. 1960; BS in Biology, Boston Coll., 1982. Former programmer, sys. analyst Mass. Gen. Hosp.; former IT mgr. Nolan, Norton & Co., Lexington, Mass.; various mktg. positions Apple Computer Inc., 1986—93; dir. product mktg. FirePower Sys., Menlo Park, Calif., 1993—95; v.p. product mktg. Macromedia, Inc., San Francisco, 1995—97; sr. v.p. worldwide product mktg. Apple Inc. (formerly Apple Computer Inc.), Cupertino, Calif., 1997—, interim v.p. mktg., 2006. Delivered keynote address MacWorld Conf. & Expo, San Francisco, 2009. Achievements include having been instrumental in the development and marketing of iMac, iBook, PowerBook G4, iPod, Mac OS X, and subsequent products. Office: Apple Inc 1 Infinite Loop Cupertino CA 95014 Office Phone: 408-996-1010.*

SCHIMMEL, PAUL REINHARD, biochemist, biophysicist, educator; b. Hartford, Conn., Aug. 4, 1940; s. Alfred E. and Doris (Hudson) S.; m. Judith F. Ritz, Dec. 30, 1961; children: Kirsten, Katherine. AB, Ohio Wesleyan U., 1962; postgrad., Tufts U. Sch. Medicine, 1962-63, Mass. Inst. Tech., 1963-65, Cornell U., 1965-66, Stanford U., 1966-67, U. Calif., Santa Barbara, 1975-76; PhD, Mass. Inst. Tech., 1966; DSc (hon.), Ohio Wesleyan U., 1996. Asst. prof. biology and chemistry MIT, 1967-71, assoc. prof., 1971-76, prof. biochemistry and biophysics, 1976-92, John D. and Catherine T. MacArthur prof. biochemistry and biophysics, 1992-97; prof. Scripps Rsch. Inst. and The Skaggs Inst. for Chem. Biology, 1997-2001, Ernest and Jean Hahn prof. molecular biology and chemistry, 2001—. Mem. study sect. on physiol. chemistry NIH, 1975-79; indsl. cons. on enzymes and recombinant DNA; bd. dirs. Cubist Pharms., 1993-2002, Repligen Corp., Alkermes, Inc., Alaylam, Inc. Author: (with C. Cantor) Biophysical Chemistry, 3 vols., 1980; mem. editl. bd. Archives Biochemistry, Biophysics, 1976-80, Nucleic Acids Rsch., 1976-80, Jour. Biol. Chemistry, 1977-82, Biopolymers, 1979-88, Internat. Jour. Biol. Macromolecules, 1983-89, Trends in Biochem. Scis., 1984—, Biochemistry, 1989—, Accounts of Chem. Rsch., 1989-94, European Jour. Biochemistry, 1991-96, Protein Sci., 1991-94, Proc. Nat. Acad. Scis., 1993-99. Alfred P. Sloan fellow, 1970-72; recipient Emily M. Gray award Biophys. Soc., 2000. Fellow AAAS, Am. Acad. Arts and Scis. (chmn. Amory prize com. 1995-96); mem. NAS (class II biochemistry sect. rep. 1995-96), Am. Philos. Soc., Am. Chem. Soc. (Pfizer award 1978, chmn. divsn. biol. chemistry 1984-85) Am. Soc. for Biochemistry and Molecular Biology (chmn. nominating com. 1990, awards com. 1995-97), Inst. Medicine, Ribonucleic Acid Soc. Office: The Scripps Rsch Inst 10550 N Torrey Pines Rd La Jolla CA 92037-1000

SCHIMMENTI, JOHN JOSEPH, lawyer; b. NYC, Mar. 21, 1938; s. John Marcus and Mae M. (Miranti) S.; m. Mary Elizabeth Sleep, Apr. 18, 1964. BA, Columbia Coll., 1959; JD, Georgetown U., Washington, DC, 1962, LLM, 1964. Bar: DC 1962, NY 1964, Calif. 1965, US Dist. Ct. (ctrl. dist.) Calif. 1965, US Ct. Appeals (9th cir.) 1966, US Supreme Ct. 1971. Trial atty. Anti-Trust divsn. US Dept. Justice, Washington, 1962-64, Lands divsn., LA, 1965-67; trial atty. Santa Fe R.R., LA, 1968-70; ptnr. Schimmenti, Mullins & Berberian, El Segundo, Calif., 1971-. Mem. S.W. Dist. Bar Assn. (pres. 1983), LA Bar Assn. (condemnation com. 1983), Columbia U. Alumni of So. Calif. (pres. 1978). Republican. Roman Catholic. Club: El Segundo Rotary (pres. 1977). Office: Schimmenti Mullins & Berberian Unit 303 5630 Ravenspur Dr Rancho Palos Verdes CA 90275-3535 Home Phone: 310-541-4906; Office Phone: 310-874-4801.

SCHINDLER, DAVID J., lawyer; b. 1962; BA, U. Calif., Berkeley, 1983; JD, U. Calif., LA, 1987. Bar: Calif. Clerk US Dist. Ct., Ctrl. Dist. Calif., US Ct. of Appeals, Ninth Cir.; sr. litig. counsel US Attorney's Office, LA, computer fraud, telecom. coord.; spl. atty. to US Atty. Gen.; ptnr. Latham & Watkins, LA. Recipient Atty. Gen. award for Disting. Svc., Director's award for Superior Performance; named one of Top Lawyers, Calif. Lawyer, 1997, Top 40 Lawyers, Daily Jour., Litigation's Rising Stars, The Am. Lawyer, 2007. Office: Latham Watkins 355 S Grand Ave Los Angeles CA 90071-1560 Office Phone: 213-485-1234. Office Fax: 213-891-8763.

SCHIRMER, HOWARD AUGUST, JR., civil engineer; b. Oakland, Calif., Apr. 21, 1942; s. Howard August and Amy (Freuler) S.; m. Leslie May Mecum, Jan. 29, 1965; children: Christine Nani, Amy Kiana, Patricia Leolani. BS, U. Calif., Berkeley, 1964, MS, 1965. Registered profl. engr., Hawaii, Guam. Engr. in tng. materials and research dept. Calif. Div. Hwys., Sacramento, 1960-64; engring. analyst Dames & Moore, San Francisco, 1964-67, asst. staff engr., 1967-68, chief engr., 1969-72, asso. Honolulu, 1972-75, partner, mng. prin. in charge, 1975-78, regional mgr. Pacific Far East and Australia, 1978-81, chief operating officer Los Angeles, 1981-83; mng. dir. Dames & Moore Internat., Los Angeles, 1983-89; mgr.-dir. CH2M Hill Internat. Ltd., Denver, 1989-90, pres., 1991-96; president Transnational Assocs., Englewood, Colo., 1996—. Chmn. geotech. engring. com. Am. Cons. Engrs. Council, 1976-78, prof. liability com. 1984—; past chmn. adv. com. for engring. tech. Honolulu Community Coll. Important works include AFDM Berthing Wharf, Pearl Harbor, Aloha Stadium, Hawaii, Century Ctr., Honolulu, Manila Internat. Airport, Philippines. Past mem. intable UCLA Grad. Sch. Mgmt.; chmn. engring. sect., mem. budget com. Aloha United Way, 1974; founder Mauna Kea Ski Patrol, 1969. Fellow ASCE (Past chmn. engring. mgmt. exec. com. 1986-87, Edmund Friedman Young Engr. award for profl. achievement 1974, pres. Hawaii sect., internat. actifities com., internat. dir. 1989-92; mem. Fedn. Internationale des Ingenieures-Conseils (chmn. standing com. on profl. liability 1986-89, U.S. rep to com., mem. task com. on constrn. ins. and law Environmental com., 1994—; Cons. Engrs. Coun. Hawaii (pres. 1972), Engring. Assn. Hawaii (past dir., 2d v.p.), Internat. Soc. Soil Mechanics and Found. Engring., Am. Public Works Assn. (sec. 1977-78, dir. 1979-0), Soc. Am. Mil. Engrs., Environmental Technologies Trade Advisory com. (vice chmn, 1994—), Market Access Subcom. (chmn. 1998), adv. com. to Internat. Trade Office, State of Colo., 1994-1998, Outrigger Canoe Club, Met. Club (Denver), Chi Epsilon (Hon. mem. U. Hawaii), Sigma Phi Epsilon. Republican. Episcopalian. Office: TransNational Assocs Inc 4100 E Quincy Ave Englewood CO 80110-5051 Fax: 303-221-0359. E-mail: schirmerha@aol.com.

SCHIRO, STEVE, computer software company executive; Bachelors degree in Economics, Claremont McKenna Coll. With Procter & Gamble Co., Intuit Inc., Borland Internat. Inc., Ansa Software; corp. v.p. home & retail divsn. Microsoft Corp., 1995—. Bd. dirs. Software Publishers Assn., 1995—97; retail adv. bd. Gartner Groups. Mem. Seattle Sports & Events Coun. Mem.: Consumer Products Coun. Office: Microsoft Corp Home & Retail Divsn 1 Microsoft Way Redmond WA 98052-6399

SCHLAPBACH, DAVID, lawyer; BA summa cum laude, U. Va.; MA, Stanford U.; JD, Yale U. Atty. Blackwell Sanders Peper Martin LLP, St. Louis; joined First Data, 1996, dep. gen. counsel internat. Paris, 2000—04; gen. counsel, sec. Western Union Co., Englewood, Colo., 2004—06, exec. v.p., sec. gen. counsel, 2006—. Office: Western Union Co PO Box 6992 Greenwood Village CO 80155-6992 Office Phone: 866-405-5012.

SCHLATTER, O. EDWARD, judge; m. Patricia Schlatter; 2 children. BA, So. Ill. U., 1964; JD, U. Denver, 1970. Dist. and chief judge 11th jud. dist. U.S. Dist. Ct. State of Colo., Denver, 1981-92, magistrate judge, 1992—. Mem. Colo. Bar Assn. (exec. coun. criminal law sect 1984-86, bd. govs. 1987-92, sr. v.p. 1991-92), 11th Jud. Dist. Bar Assn. (v.p. 1985-87, pres. 1987-89). Office: US Dist Ct State Colo 1929 Stout St Rm C 162 Denver CO 80294-1929

SCHLEIER-SMITH, JOHANN, Internet company executive; AB in Physics and Math., Harvard U. Co-founder Avivon Inc.; tech. dir. Limespot.com LLC; co-founder, chief tech. officer Jumpstart Technologies, 2000—05, Tagged.com, San Francisco, 2004—. Grantee NSF Grad. Rsch. Fellowship, Hertz Found. Fellowship Rsch. Grant. Office: Tagged Inc 110 Pacific Ave Mall Box #117 San Francisco CA 94111

SCHLESINGER, ADAM, musician; b. Oct. 31, 1967; Grad., Williams Coll. Bassist Ivy, 1994—. Fountains of Wayne, 1995—99, 2001—; prin. Scratchie Records, NYC, 1995—; co-owner Stratosphere Sound, NYC, 1999—. Musician & prodr. (Ivy albums) Lately, 1994, Realistic, 1995, Apartment Life, 1997, Long Distance, 2001, Guestroom, 2002, In the Clear, 2005, (Fountains of Wayne albums) Fountains of Wayne, 1996, I Want an Alien for Christmas, 1997, Utopia Parkway, 1999, Welcome Interstate Managers, 2003, Traffic and Weather, 2007; composer: (songs) Stacy's Mom, 2003 (ASCAP award, BMI Pop award); composer & prodr. (film soundtracks) That Thing You Do!, 1996 (Oscar nomination for Best Original Song, Golden Globe award nominee for Best Original Song, 1997), prodr. There's Something About Mary, 1998, Sweet and Lowdown, 1999, Me, Myself & Irene, 2000, Scary Movie, 2000, Josie & the Pussycats, 2001, Because of Winn-Dixie, 2005, Robots, 2005, composer Music & Lyrics, 2007; composer: (Broadway plays) Cry-Baby, 2008. Office: c/o MOB Agy 6404 Wilshire Blvd #505 Los Angeles CA 90048 also: Stratospheric Sound 239 11th Ave New York NY 10001

SCHLESINGER, DEBORAH LEE, retired librarian; b. Cambridge, Mass., Sept. 13, 1937; d. Edward M. and Edith D. (Schneider) Hershoff; divorced; children: Suzanne, Richard. BA, U. Mass., 1961;

MS, Simmons Coll., 1974; postgrad., U. Pitts., 1983. Reference librarian Bently Coll., Waltham, Mass., 1964-65; dir. Carnegie Library, Swissvale, Pa., 1973-77, South Park Twp. Library, Pa., 1977-81, Monessen (Pa.) Library, 1981-82, Lewis & Clark Library, Helena, Mont., 1983—88, 1989—2004, ret., 2004; state librarian Mont. State Library, Helena, Mont., 1988-89. Vis. scholar Pitts. Regional Library Ctr., 1982-83. Editor Pa. Union List, 1982-83. Mem. exec. bd. Mont. Cultural Advocacy, 1983-2004. Mem. Mont. Libr. Assn. (chmn. legis. com. 1984-92, lobbyist 1992-2001), AAUW (exec. com. 1985-86). Clubs: Montana (Helena). Democrat. Avocations: flying, painting, reading, rafting, travel. Personal E-mail: dbooks@aol.com.

SCHLESSINGER, LAURA, radio talk show host; b. Bklyn., Jan. 16, 1947; d. Monroe and Yolanda Schlessinger; m. Lewis G. Bishop, 1982; 1 child, Deryk. BS in Biological Sciences, SUNY, Stonybrook; MS in Physiology, M Phil in Physiology, Columbia U., PhD in Physiology, 1974. Lic. in marriage and family therapy; cert. marriage, family and child counseling, U. So. Calif. Psychotherapist in private practice, LA, Calif., 1980—90; nat. syndicated radio talk show host The Dr. Laura Schlessinger Program, 1990—; columnist Santa Barbara News Press, 2006—. Past mem. faculty U. So. Calif., Pepperdine U, instr. UCLA, UC Irvine; founder, pres. Dr. Laura Schlessinger Found., 1998- Author: Ten Stupid Things Women Do to Mess Up Their Lives, 1994, How Could You Do That?! The Abdication of Character, Courage and Conscience, 1996, Ten Stupid Things Men Do To Mess Up Their Lives, 1997, The Ten Commandments: The Significance of God's Law in Everyday Life, 1998, Damsels, Dragons, and Regular Guys, 2000, Parenthood by Proxy: Don't Have Them If You Won't Raise Them, 2000, Ten Stupid Things Couples Do To Mess Up Their Relationships, 2002 The Proper Care & Feeding Of Husbands, 2004, Bad Childhood Good Life: How to Blossom and Thrive in Spite of an Unhappy Childhood, 2006, Stop Whining, Start Living, 2008, In Praise of Stay-at-Home Moms, 2009; (children's books) Why Do You Love Me?, 1999, But I Waaannt It!, 2000, Growing Up is Hard, 2001, I Hate My Life!, 2001, Where is God?, 2003; featured on The Oprah Winfrey Show, A&E Biography, Larry King Live, Lifetime's Intimate Portrait, 20/20, The Today Show, PBS, Hannity & Colmes, CBS This Morning, 48 Hours, Meet the Press with Tim Russert, Crier Today, Eye to Eye with Connie Chung, ABC This Week, Dateline; featured in Time, U.S. News and World Report, People, USA Today, The New York Times Magazine, The Los Angeles Times, The Wall Street Journal and others; featured spkr. Nat. Congressional Prayer Breakfast, Mus. Radio and Television, Claremont Inst., PBS, Nat. Religious Broadcasters, Country Radio Seminar. Recipient Marconi Award for Network/Syndicated Personality of the Yr., 1997, Genii Award, American Women in Radio & Television, 1998, Israel 50th Anniversary Tribute award, 1998, Crystal Cathedral Academy award, 1998, Love of a Child award, Childhelp USA, 1998, Chairman's award, Nat. Religious Broadcasters, 2000, Nat. Heritage award, Nat. Council of Young Israel, 2001, Conservative Leadership award, Clare Booth Luce Inst., 2001, Woman of the Yr. award, 2002, Women Extradinaire award, Internat. Women's Conf., 2004, Truth in Media award, Pacific Justice Inst., 2006; named Woman of the Yr., State of Calif. 19th Dist., 2006. Mem.: AFTRA, SAG, Nat. Assn. At-Home Mothers (bd. adv.). Achievements include being broadcasted on approximately 300 stations with 12 million listeners; the second most popular talk show host in the country; show syndicated since June 1994; on air radio career for more than 25 years. Office: Premire Radio Networks 15260 Ventura Blvd Ste 300 Sherman Oaks CA 91403-5337*

SCHLEY, MICHAEL DODSON, lawyer; b. Calif., Jan. 4, 1955; m. Nancy D. Rogers, 2003; children: Nathaniel, Erica, Samuel. BA, Westmont Coll., 1977; JD, U. Calif., San Francisco, 1980. Bar: Calif. 1981, D.C. 1984, U.S. Supreme Ct. 1984. Atty. Fed. Home Loan Bank Bd., Washington, 1980-83; gen. counsel Fed. Home Loan Bank Bd. Credit Union, 1981-82; assoc. Fried, Frank et al, Washington, 1983-85; sr. v.p., gen. counsel Fin. Corp. of Santa Barbara, Calif., 1985-90; pvt. practice, 1990—; ptnr. Schley Look and Guthrie LLP (and predecessor firms), Santa Barbara, Calif., 1993—. Adv. bd. Money and Real Estate. Bd. dirs. Found. for Santa Barbara City Coll., Nonprofit Support Ctr., Transition House, Santa Barbara. Mem. ABA, Santa Barbara (Calif.) Bar Assn. (Richard Abbe Humanitarian award 2001). Republican. Office: Schley Look and Guthrie LLP 311 E Carrillo St Santa Barbara CA 93101

SCHLEYER, WILLIAM T., cable company executive; b. Phila. BS in Mech. Engring., Drexel U.; MBA, Harvard Bus. Sch. Mgr. IBM, Abbott Labs.; from sys. mgr. to pres., COO US West Media Group Continental Cablevision, 1977-97; pres., COO MediaOne, Boston, 1997—2000; prin. Pilot House Ventures, LLC, 2001; pres., CEO, broadband services unit AT&T Corp., 2001—03; chmn., CEO Adelphia Communications Corp., Greenwood Village, Colo., 2003—. Office: Tele Communications Inc 183 Inverness Dr W Englewood CO 80112-5203

SCHLINKERT, WILLIAM JOSEPH, lawyer; b. Bronxville, NY, Feb. 18, 1954; s. William Joseph Schlinkert and Ann Frances (Schilling) S.; m. Meggin Ann Gemmill, Aug. 6, 1978; children: Brian, Kyle, Karly, Evan. BA, U. Dallas, 1975; JD, U. Calif., Berkeley, 1978; LLM in Taxation, Georgetown U., 1981. Bar: Calif. 1978, U.S. Tax Ct. 1981. Atty. Office of Chief Counsel IRS, Washington, 1978-81; assoc. Farella, Braun & Martel, San Francisco, 1981-85, ptnr., 1986—, chmn., 1997—2005. Mem. ABA, Bar Assn. San Francisco, Calif. Bd. Legal Specialization (cert. specialist, taxation law). Avocations: golf, tennis. Office: Farella Braun & Martel 235 Montgomery St Fl 31 San Francisco CA 94104-3159 Business E-Mail: wschlinkert@fbm.com.

SCHLOSS, ERNEST PETER, healthcare facility administrator, planner, professor public health; b. NYC, Mar. 15, 1949; s. Gerd Tobias and Helene (Alberta) S.; m. Janice Gail Callender, Mar. 25, 1972 (div. 1977); 1 child, Jacob Alan; m. Marie Patricia Kearney, Apr. 20, 1985 (div. 1997); m. Marianne Mindell, Feb. 28, 1998. BA in Anthropology, Prscott Coll., Ariz., 1971, MA in counseling Psychology, 2003; MA in Anthropology, U. Ariz., 1973, PhD in Edn. Adminstrn., 1983; MDiv, Interfaith Theol. Sem., Tucson, 2003. Exec. dir. Cochise County Comprehensive Health Planning Coun., Bisbee, Ariz., 1973-74; sr. data analyst Pima Health Systems, Tucson, 1974-76; project coord. Southwestern Ctr. for Behavioral Health Studies, Tucson, 1976; dir. planning Health Systems Agy. Southwestern Ariz., Tucson, 1976-79, exec. dir., 1980-81; exec. dir. community health programs Carondelet Health Svcs., Tucson, 1981-85, dir. planning and rsch., 1985-87; asst. dean of planning Coll. of Medicine U. Ariz., Tucson, 1987—95; v.p. Univ. Med. Ctr., Tucson, 1987—95; outcomes evaluation team leader Health Ptnrs. of So. Ariz., 1996—98; dir. rsch. and edn. Children's Clinics for Rehab. Svcs., Tucson, 1999—2004; spl. asst. for clin. coordination and planning U. Ariz. Coll. Medicine, Univ. Med. Ctr., Univ. Physicians Healthcare, Tucson, 2004—09; admin. clin. coordination & planning, v.p. health affairs U. Ariz., 2009—, asst. prof. cmty. environ. & policy Zuckerman Coll. Pub. Health, 2009—. Clin. lectr. dept. family and cmty. medicine U. Ariz., 1980—, adj. asst. prof. dept. mgmt. and policy, 1985-86, chmn. preventive medicine com. Coll. Medicine, U. Ariz., 1984-86; faculty mem. U. Phoenix, 1983-87; mem. planning com. Healthcare Corp. of Sisters of St. Joseph of Carondelet, St. Louis, 1987; mem. mktg. coun. Univ. Hosp. Consortium, Chgo., 1987-95, chair, 1993-95. Contbr. chpt. to book, articles to profl. jours. Bd. dirs. Pima Coun. on Aging, Tucson, 1980-86, United Way of Greater Tucson, 1986-89, Tucson Tomorrow, 1988-89; assoc. ptnr. Leadership 2000, Scottsdale, 1998-2000. Mem. World Future Soc., The Forge Guild. Democrat. Avocations: reading, hiking, guitar. Home: 6929 E Taos Pl Tucson AZ 85715 Office: U Ariz Coll Medicine Univ Med Ctr Univ Physicians Healthcare PO Box 245017 Tucson AZ 85724-5017 Office Phone: 520-626-1101, 520-626-3591. E-mail: schloss1@email.arizona.edu.

SCHLOSS, KRISTY ANNE, engineering company executive; b. Denver, Jan. 22, 1963; d. Charles Murdock and JoAnn (Bock) S.; m. Mark Edward Kelley, May 7, 1994. BS in Civil Engring., U. Colo., 1986. Project engr. Black & Veatch, Santa Ana, Calif., 1987-89; project mgr., v.p. Schloss Engineered Equipment, Inc., Aurora, Colo., 1989, pres., CEO, 1989—. Mem. small bus. environ. action com. region VIII EPA; mem. engring. adv. bd. U. Colo.; state co-chair Colo. delegation White House Conf. on Small Bus.; appointee Colo. Statehouse Conf. on Small Bus., 1993; appointee roundtable Nat. Women's Bus. Coun.; bd. dirs. Nelson, Coulson and Assocs.; environ. tech. trade adv. com. US Dept. Commerce, chair Export Coun. Rocky Mountain Dist., Fed. Res. Bank Kans. City, Denver br.; spkr. in field. Mem. Class of 1993 Leadership Denver; bd. dirs. Mile High coun. Girl Scouts U.S. Recipient Honor award Colo. Engring. Coun., Award of Heroism, City of Englewood, Nat. Exporter of Yr., Small Bus. Adminstrn., Gov.'s award for Excellence in Exporting, Disting. Engring. Alumni award, U. Colo. Boulder. Fellow: Soc. Women Engrs. (life, nat. co-chair, mem. corp. adv. bd., past pres. RMS, Disting. New Engr. award, Entreprenuer award 2007); mem. ASCE, Am. Water Works Assn., Nat. Assn. Women Bus. Owners (mem. pres.'s roundtable), Water Environment Fedn., Internat. Women's Forum, Women's Forum Colo., U. Colo. Women in Engring. (bd. dirs.), Colo. Women's Leadership Coalition (co-chair bus. com.), Greater Denver C. of C., Colo. Women's C. of C. (bd. dirs.), Chi Epsilon. Office: Schloss Engineered Equipment Inc 10555 E Dartmouth Ave Ste 230 Aurora CO 80014-2633

SCHLOSSER, ANNE GRIFFIN, librarian; b. NYC, Dec. 28, 1939; d. C. Russell and Gertrude (Taylor) Griffin; m. Gary J. Schlosser, Dec. 28, 1965. BA in History, Wheaton Coll., Norton, Mass., 1962; MLS, Simmons Coll., 1964; cert. archives adminstrn., Am. U., 1970. Head UCLA Theater arts Libr., 1964-69; dir. Louis B. Mayer Libr., Am. Film Inst., LA, 1969-88, dir. film/TV documentation workshop, 1977-87; head Cinema-TV Libr. and Archives of the Performing Arts, U. So. Calif., LA, 1988-91; dir. Entertainment Resources Seminar, 1990; dir. rsch. libr. Warner Bros., 1991—2001; part-time libr. Nevada County Libr., 2002—. Project dir. Motion Pictures, Television, Radio: A Union Catalogue of Manuscript and Special Collections in the Wesern U.S., 1977. Recipient numerous grants for script indexing, manuscript cataloging, libr. automation. Mem. Soc. Calif. Archivists (pres. 1982-83), Theater Libr. Assn (exec. bd. 1983-86), Spl. Librs. Assn. Democrat. Episcopalian. Avocations: swimming, reading, dog training.

SCHLUTER, DOLPH A., biologist, educator; b. Montreal, Que., Can., May 22, 1955; s. Antoine Leon and Magdalena (Neiman) S.; m. Andrea Lawson, 1993; 1 child, Magdalen. BSc in Wildlife Biology, U. Guelph, Ont., Can., 1977; PhD in Ecology and Evolution, U. Mich., Ann Arbor, 1983. Rackham predoctoral fellow U. Mich. Rackham Sch. Grad. Studies, 1982; NSERC postdoctoral fellow U. Calif., Davis, 1983—85, U. B.C., Vancouver, Canada, 1983—85, asst. prof. dept. zoology, 1989—91, assoc. prof. dept. zoology, 1991—96, prof. dept. zoology, 1996—, Tier 1 Can. rsch. chair, prof., 2001—, Guggenheim fellow, 2003—04, dir. Biodiversity Rsch. Ctr., Can. rsch., prof. zoology; Guggenheim fellow Stanford U., 2003—04. Dir. Biodiversity Rsch. Ctr., Canada, 2003—; vis. prof. devel. biology Stanford U., 2004. Co-editor: (with R.E. Ricklefs) Species Diversity in Ecological Communities: Historical and Geographical Perspectives, 1993; author: The Ecology of Adaptive Radiation, 2000; contbr. articles to profl. publs. including Science, Nature, Evolution, American Naturalist, etc.; contbr. chpts. to books. E.W.R. Steacie Meml. fellow NSERC, 1993, Izaak Walton Killam Meml. fellow U. BC, 1996; recipient Young Investigators prize Am. Soc. Naturalists, 1984, President's award, 1997, Charles A. McDowell medal U. BC, 1995; named Scholar-in-Residence Peter Wall Inst. Advanced Studies U. BC, 1999, Guggenheim fellowship, 2003, Rosenblatt award, Scripps Inst. Oceanography, 2006. Fellow: Royal Soc. London, Royal Soc. Can.; mem.: Soc. for Study of Evolution (pres. 2005). Achievements include research on natural selection, co-evolution of competing species. Office: U BC Dept Zoology 6270 University Blvd Vancouver BC V6T 1Z4 Canada Business E-Mail: schluter@zoology.ubc.ca.

SCHMALE, NEAL E., utilities company executive; BS in Petroleum Engring., Colo. Sch. Mines; LLD, Loyola U. With UNOCAL, sr. v.p., pres. petroleum products and chem. divsn., CFO; exec. v.p., CFO Sempra Energy, San Diego, 1997—2005, pres., COO, 2006—. Office: Sempra Energy 101 Ash St San Diego CA 92101-3017

SCHMICK, JOE, state legislator; m. Kim Schmick. Grad., Eastern Wash. U., Wash. Agr.and Forestry Edn. Found. Farmer; bus. owner; mem. Dist. 9 Wash. House of Reps., 2007—. Mem. bd. of dirs. Wash. Farm Bur., 1993—; former pres. Whitman County Farm Bur.; mem. Whitman County Wetlands Com. Precinct com. officer Whitman County. Republican. Office: 419 John L O'Brien Bldg PO Box 40600 Olympia WA 98504 Office Phone: 360-786-7844. E-mail: schmick.joe@leg.wa.gov.

SCHMIDLY, DAVID J., academic administrator, biology professor; b. Levelland, Tex., Dec. 20, 1943; m. Janet Elaine Knox, June 2, 1966; children: Katherine Elaine, Brian James. BS in Biology, Tex. Tech U., 1966, MS in Zoology, 1968; PhD in Zoology, U. Ill., 1971. From asst. prof. to prof. dept. wildlife fisheries scis. Tex. A&M U., College Station, 1971-82, prof., 1982-96, head dept. wildlife, 1986-92, CEO, campus dean Galveston, 1992-96; chief curator Tex. Coop. Wildlife Coll., College Station, 1983-86; v.p. Tex. Inst. Oceanography, 1992-96; v.p. rsch. and grad studies, dean grad. sch., tech. transfer Tex. Tech U., Lubbock, 1996—2002, prof. biol. scis., 1996—2002, pres., 2000—02; sys. CEO, pres. Okla. State U., Stillwater, 2002—07; pres. U. N.Mex., 2007—. Cons. Nat. Park Svc., Wildlife Assocs., Walton and Assocs., Continental Shelf Assn., LGL; lectr. in field; press adv. com. Tex. A&M U., 1983-96; charter mem. Tex. A&M U. Faculty Senate, 1983-85, chmn. Scholarship Com., 1978-82. Author: The Mammals of Trans-Pecos Texas including Big Bend National Park and Guadalupe Mountains National Park, 1977, Texas Mammals East of the Balcones Fault Zone, 1983, The Bats of Texas, 1991, The Mammals of Texas, 1994, Texas Natural History: A Century of Change, 2002; contbr. articles to profl. jours. Trustee Tex. Nature Conservancy, 1991—; mem. adv. bd. Ft. Worth Zoo, 2000. Recipient Dist. Prof. award Assn. Grad. Wildlife and Fisheries Scis., 1985, Donald W. Tinkle Rsch. Excellence award Southwestern Assn. Naturalists, 1988, Diploma Recognition La Universidad Autonoma de Guadalajara, 1989, La Universidad Autonoma de Tamaulipas, 1990. Fellow Tex. Soc. Sci. (bd. dirs. 1979-81); mem. AAAS, Am. Soc. Mammalogists (life, editor Jour. Mammalogy 1975-78), Am. Inst. Biol. Scis. (bd. dirs. 1993—, coun. affiliate socs. 1989—), Am. Naturalist, Soc. Marine Mammalogy (charter mem.), Soc. Systematic Zoology, The Wildlife Soc. Soc. Conservation Biology, Nat. Geog. Sci. Soc., S.W. Assn. Naturalists (life mem., bd. govs. 1980-86, 91—, pres. 1981, trustee 1986—), Tex. Mammal Soc. (pres. 1985-86), Assn. Systematic Collections (bd. dirs.), Chihuahuan Desert Rsch. Inst. (v.p. bd. scientists 1982—, bd. dirs. 1991), Mexican Soc. Mammalogists, Sigma Xi (v.p. 1986-87, pres. 1987-88), Disting. Scientist award 1991), Coun. Pub. Univ. Pres. and Chancellors (exec. com. 2000), Golden Key, Beta Beta Beta, Phi Sigma, Phi Kappa Phi. Office: U NMex Office of Pres MSC05 300 Scholes Hall Rm 144 Albuquerque NM 87131 Office Phone: 505-277-2626. Business E-Mail: unmpres@unm.edu.

SCHMID-SCHOENBEIN, GEERT WILFRIED, biomedical engineer, educator; b. Albstadt, Baden-Wurttemberg, Germany, Jan. 1, 1948; came to U.S., 1971; s. Ernst and Ursula Schmid; m. Renate Schmid-Schoenbein, July 3, 1976; children: Philip, Mark, Peter. Vordiplom, Liebig U., Giessen, Germany, 1971; PhD in Bioengring., U. Calif., San Diego, 1976. Staff assoc. dept. physiology Columbia U., NYC, 1976-77, sr. assoc., 1977-79; asst. prof. dept. applied mechs. & engring. scis. U. Calif., San Diego, 1979-84, assoc. prof., 1984-89, prof., 1989-94, prof. dept. bioengring., 1994—. Editor: Frontiers in Biomechanics, 1986, Physiology and Pathophysiology of Leukocyte Adhesion, 1994, Molecular Basis of Microcirculatory Disorders, 2002; author more than 280 rsch. reports. Recipient Melville medal ASME, 1990, Ratschow medal European Soc. Phlebology, 1999. Fellow Am. Inst. for Med. and Biol. Engring., Am. Heart Assn.; mem. NAE, Biomed. Engring. Soc. (pres. 1991-92), Am. Microcirculatory Soc. (pres. 2003-04), N.Am. Soc. Biorheology (pres. 1989-99), European Microciculatory Soc., Am. Physiol. Soc., Am. Mech. Engring. Soc. Achievements include bioengineering research on cardiovascular disease, microcirulation, bioengineering, and lympholgy. Office: U Calif San Diego Dept Bioengineering Gilman Dr 9500 0412 La Jolla CA 92093-0412

SCHMIDT, CHAUNCEY EVERETT, banker, director; b. Oxford, Iowa, June 7, 1931; s. Walter Frederick and Vilda (Saxton) S.; m. Anne Garrett McWilliams, Mar. 3, 1954; children: Carla, Julia, Chauncey Everett. BS, U.S. Naval Acad., 1953; MBA, Harvard U., 1959. With First Nat. Bank, Chgo., 1959-76, v.p., gen. mgr. br. London, Eng., 1965-68, v.p. for Europe, Middle East, Africa, 1968-69, sr. v.p. Chgo., 1969-72, exec. v.p., 1972, vice chmn. bd., 1973, pres., 1974-76; chmn. bd., chief exec. officer, dir. Bank of Calif. N.A., San Francisco, 1976—; chmn. bd., pres., chief exec. officer, dir. BanCal Tri-State Corp., 1976—. Dir. Amfac, Inc., Honolulu; mem. Adv. Council Japan-U.S. Econ. Relations; adv. bd. Pacific Rim Bankers Program. Exec. bd. and pres. San Francisco Bay Area council Boy Scouts Am.; council SRI Internat.; bd. dirs. Bay Area Council; bd. govs. San Francisco Symphony; trustee U.S. Naval War Coll. Fedn., Newport, R.I. Served with USAF, 1953-56. Mem. Assn. Res. City Bankers, Am. Bankers Assn., Internat. Monetary Conf., Calif. Bankers Clearing House Assn. (dir.), Calif. Roundtable (dir.), Japan-Calif. Assn. Clubs: Comml. (Chgo.); Bankers (San Francisco), Bohemian (San Francisco). Home: 40 Why Worry Farm Woodside CA 94062-3654 Office: Ste 140 525 Middlefield Rd Menlo Park CA 94025

SCHMIDT, CYRIL JAMES, librarian; b. Flint, Mich., June 27, 1939; s. Cyril August and Elizabeth Josephine S.; m. Martha Joe Meadows, May 22, 1965; children: Susan, Emily. BA, Cath. U. Am., 1962; MSLS, Columbia U., 1963; PhD, Fla. State U., 1974. Asst. bus. and industry dept. Flint Pub. Library, 1963-65; reference librarian Gen. Motors Inst., Flint, 1965; asso. librarian S.W. Tex. State U., San Marcos, 1965-67; head undergrad. libraries, asst. prof. Ohio State U., 1967-70; dir. libraries SUNY, Albany, 1972-79; also mem. faculty SUNY (Sch. Library and Info. Sci.); univ. librarian Brown U., Providence, 1979-81; exec. v.p. Rsch. Libraries Group, Stanford, Calif., 1981-89; prin. cons. Schmidt & Assocs., Palo Alto, Calif., 1989—; univ. prof. San Jose (Calif.) State U., 1992—. Author papers in field. Libr. Svcs. Act fellow, 1962-63, Higher Edn. Act fellow, 1970-72 Mem. ALA, ACLU, Pi Sigma Alpha, Beta Phi Mu. Home: 244 Forest Ave Palo Alto CA 94301-2510 Office: San Jose State U 1 Washington Sq San Jose CA 95192-0001 Office Phone: 408-924-2465. Business E-Mail: jim_schmidt@sjsu.edu.

SCHMIDT, ELEANORE, library director; Assoc. dir. Long Beach Pub. Libr., Calif., 1989—98, dir. libr. svcs. Calif., 1998—. Bd. dirs. Long Beach Pub. Libr. Found. Office: Long Beach Pub Libr 101 Pacific Ave Long Beach CA 90822 Office Fax: 562-570-6016, 562-570-7408. E-mail: eschmidt@lbpl.org.

SCHMIDT, ERIC EMERSON, information technology executive; b. Washington, Apr. 27, 1955; m. Wendy Schmidt; 2 children. BSEE, Princeton U., 1976; MS in Computer Sci., U. Calif., Berkeley, 1979, PhD in Computer Sci., 1982. With Bell Labs., Zilog; research intern Xerox PARC, Palo Alto, Calif., 1979-80, mem. research staff, 1980-83; software mgr. Sun Microsystems, Mountain View, Calif., 1983-84, software dir., 1984-85, v.p., gen. mgr. software products div., 1985-88, v.p. gen. systems group, 1988-91, chief tech. officer, 1994—97; pres. Sun Tech. Enterprises, Inc., Mountain View, Calif., 1991-94; chmn., CEO Novell, Inc., Provo, Utah, 1997—2001; chmn. exec. com., CEO Google, Inc., Mountain View, Calif., 2001—. Bd. dirs. Google, Inc., 2001—, Apple Inc., 2006—; chmn. New America Found., 2008—. Bd. trustee Princeton U. Named one of Forbes' Richest Americans, 2004—, The World's Richest People, Forbes Mag., 2006—, The 50 Who Matter Now, Business 2.0, 2007, The 50 Most Important People on the Web, PC World, 2007, The 25 Most Powerful People in Bus., Fortune Mag., 2007, The Top 200 Art Collectors, ARTnews, 2007—, The Global Elite, Newsweek mag., 2008, The Top 25 Market Movers, US News & World Report, 2009. Mem. IEEE, Assn. Computing

Machinery, Sigma Xi; fellow Am. Acad. Arts & Scis. Achievements include patents in field. Office: Google Inc 1600 Amphitheatre Pkwy 41 Mountain View CA 94043-1351 Office Phone: 650-623-4000. Office Fax: 650-618-1499.*

SCHMIDT, HARVEY MARTIN, economist, educator, financial analyst, consultant; b. Sept. 15, 1925; s. Joseph David and Dorothy Schmidt; m. Barbara Bebe Bloom, Nov. 25, 1961; children: Ellen Louise, Jay Stephen, Gregg Arthur. Student, U. So. Calif., 1943; BA magna cum laude, Woodbury U., 1947. Assoc. prof. bus. Woodbury U., 1947—48; pvt. practice acctg. LA, 1948—80; cons. mgmt., taxes and fins., 1965—82; econ. forecaster, internat. lectr., investment lectr. on audiotapes, 1989—. Investment lectr. on internat. cruise ships, 1992; fin. cons., Pacific Palisades, 1982—; pres. Harvey Schmidt Mgmt. Inc., 1983—, Med-Plan Operators, 1969—89, Kit Travel, 1987—. Contbr. articles to profl. jours. With USCG, 1943—44. Master: U.S. Contact Bridge League (life); mem.: Internat. Platform Assn., Bruin Athletic Club of UCLA, Exch. Club (pres. local chpt. 1953—56). Personal E-mail: bebe@usinter.net. Business E-Mail: hs@kltrav.com.

SCHMIDT, JAMES CRAIG, retired bank, savings and loan association executive; b. Peoria, Ill., Sept. 27, 1927; s. Walter Henry and Clara (Wolfenbarger) S.; m. Jerrie Louise Bond, Dec. 6, 1958; children: Julie, Sandra, Suzanne. Student, Ill. Wesleyan U., 1945, 48-50, Ph.B. in Bus. Adminstrn, 1952; postgrad., U. Ill. Coll. Law, 1950-52; JD, DePaul U., 1953. Bar: Calif., Calif. Spl. agt. Fidelity & Deposit Co., Chgo., 1956-58; with Home Fed. Savs. & Loan Assn., San Diego, 1958-67; asst. sec. bus. and transp. State of Calif., 1967-69; vice-chmn., pres. Gt. Am. Bank, San Diego, 1969-88. Pres. Conf. Fed. Savs. and Loans of Calif., 1974-75; mem. Calif. Toll Bridge Authority, 1969-74; mem. Calif. State Transp. Bd., 1972-78; past chmn. San Diego Bal. Commn. Task Force. Columnist San Diego Daily Transcript. Pres. San Diego Holiday Bowl Football Game, 1986; bd. dirs. San Diego Internat. Sports Coun., San Diego Hwy. Devel. Assn.; pub. mem. San Diego County Sunset Adv. Bd.; mem. City-County Re-Investment Task Force. Mem. Calif. Bar Assn., Ill. Bar Assn., Calif. League Savs. Instns. (chmn. 1986-87), Calif. C. of C. (bd. dirs. 1987-90), U.S. Savs. Instn. League (exec. com. 1983-86), San Diego East County C. of C. (bd. dirs.), Catfish Club, Sigma Chi, Phi Delta Phi. Office: 8383 Center Dr Ste J La Mesa CA 91942-2913 Home Phone: 619-447-5604.

SCHMIDT, JOSEPH DAVID, urologist; b. Chgo., July 29, 1937; s. Louis and Marian (Fleigel) S.; m. Andrea Maxine Herman, Oct. 28, 1962. BS in Medicine, U. Ill., 1959, MD, 1961. Diplomate Am. Bd. Urology. Rotating intern Presbyn. St. Luke's Hosp., Chgo., 1961-62, resident in surgery, 1962-63; resident in urology The Johns Hopkins Hosp., Balt., 1963-67; faculty U. Iowa Coll. Medicine, Iowa City, 1969-76, U. Calif., San Diego, 1976—, prof., head divsn. urology, 1976—2006; prof., emeritus, 2006; vice-chmn. dept. surgery U. Calif., San Diego, 1985-97. Cons. U.S. Dept. Navy, San Diego, 1976—; attending urologist Vets. Affairs Dept., San Diego, 1976—; assoc. dir. for clin. rsch. U. Calif. San Diego Cancer Ctr., 1997-98. Author, editor: Gynecological and Obstetric Urology, 1978, 82, 93. Capt. USAF, 1967-69. Recipient Francis Senear award U. Ill., 1961. Fellow ACS; mem. AMA, Am. Urol. Assn. Inc., Alpha Omega Alpha. Avocations: collecting antique medical books, manuscripts. Office: U Calif Med Ctr Divsn Urology 200 W Arbor Dr San Diego CA 92103-8897 Home Phone: 858-459-3625; Office Phone: 619-543-5904. Office Fax: 619-543-6573. Business E-Mail: jdschmidt@ucsd.edu.

SCHMIDT, KARL A., lawyer; b. Stockton, Calif., Sept. 18, 1947; BS, U. Calif., Berkeley, 1969, JD, 1974. Bar: Calif. 1974. Mem. Parker, Milliken, Clark, O'Hara & Samuelian, LA. Contbr. Retaliation Matters, to L.A. Daily Jour. Ann. Employment Update, 1997, USC TAx Inst. 2003: Exec. Terminations. Mem. ABA. Home Phone: 310-544-9685; Office Phone: 213-683-6518. Business E-Mail: kschmidt@pmcos.com.

SCHMIDT, MAARTEN, astronomy educator; b. Groningen, Netherlands, Dec. 28, 1929; came to U.S., 1959; s. Wilhelm and Antje (Haringhuizen) S.; m. Cornelia Johanna Tom, Sept. 16, 1955; children: Elizabeth Tjimkje, Maryke Antje, Anne Wilhelmina. BSc, U. Groningen, 1949; PhD, Leiden U., Netherlands, 1956; ScD, Yale U., 1966. Sci. officer Leiden Obs., The Netherlands, 1953-59; postdoctoral fellow Mt. Wilson Obs., Pasadena, Calif., 1956-58; mem. faculty Calif. Inst. Tech., 1959-95, prof. astronomy, 1964-95, exec. officer for astronomy, 1972-75, chmn. div. physics, math. and astronomy, 1975-78, mem. staff Hale Obs., 1959-80, dir. Hale Obs., 1978-80, emeritus prof. astronomy, 1996—. Co-recipient Calif. Scientist of Yr. award, 1964, Kavli prize for Astrophysics, Norwegian Acad. Sci. and Letters in partnership with the Kavli Found. and the Norwegian Ministry Edn. and Rsch., 2008. Fellow Am. Acad. Arts and Scis. (Rumford award 1968); mem. Am. Astron. Soc. (Helen B. Warner prize 1964, Russell lecture award 1978), NAS (fgn. assoc., recip. James Craig Watson Medal, 1991), Internat. Astron. Union, Royal Astron. Soc. (assoc., Gold medal 1980) Office: Calif Inst Tech MC 105 24 1200 E California Blvd Pasadena CA 91125

SCHMIDT, PETER GUSTAV, marine engineer; b. Tumwater, Wash., Dec. 3, 1921; s. Peter G. and Clara Louise (Muench) S.; m. Elva Mary Ingalls, Dec. 3, 1945; children: Mimi Schmidt Fielding, Jill Schmidt Crowson, Janet Schmidt Mano, Hans. BSME, U. Wash., 1948; MS in Naval Architecture and Marine Engring., U. Mich., 1950. Naval architect Nat. Steel Shipbldg. Corp., San Diego, 1950-52, Carl J. Nordstrom/P. Spaulding, Seattle, 1952-53; pres. Marine Constrn. & Design Co., Seattle, 1953—, Astilleros Marco Chilena Ltd., Santiago, Chile, 1960—, Marco Peruana S.A., Lima, Peru, 1965—, Campbell Industries, San Diego, 1979-99, Campbell Ship Design & Engring., Seattle, 2000—; chmn. Marco Global, Inc., 2005—. Author papers on fishing gear and vessels. Served to lt (j.g.) USN, 1942-45, PTO. Recipient Puget Sound's Maritime Man of Yr. award Puget Sound Press Assn., 1975, Naval Arch. and Marine Engring. Merit award U. Mich., 1996. Mem. Soc. Naval Architects and Marine Engrs., Wash. State Boatbuilders Assn. (pres. 1956-58), Alpha Delta Phi. Avocations: sailing, classical music. Office: Marine Constrn & Design 4259 22d Ave W Seattle WA 98199 Office Phone: 206-285-3200.

SCHMIDT, ROBERT MILTON, preventive medicine physician, educator, medical association administrator; b. Milw., May 7, 1944; s. Milton W. and Edith J. (Martinek) S.; children Eric Whitney, Edward Huntington. AB, Northwestern U., 1966; MD, Columbia U., 1970; MPH, Harvard U., 1975; PhD in Law, Medicine and Pub. Policy, Emory U., 1982; MA, San Francisco State U., 1999. Diplomate Am. Bd. Preventive Medicine, Am. Bd. Internal Medicine, Am. Bd. Hematology. Resident in internal medicine Univ. Hosp. U. Calif.-San Diego, 1970-71; resident in preventive medicine Ctr. Disease Control, Atlanta, 1971-74; commd. med. officer USPHS, 1971; advanced through grades to comdr., 1973; dir. hematology div. Nat. Ctr. for Disease Control, Atlanta, 1971-78, spl. asst. to dir., 1978-79, inactive res., 1979—; clin. asst. prof. pediatrics Tufts U. Med. Sch., 1974-86; clin. asst. prof. medicine Emory U. Med. Sch., 1971-81, clin. assoc. prof. community health, 1976-86; clin. assoc. prof. humanities in medicine Morehouse Med. Sch., 1977-79; attending physician dept. medicine Wilcox Meml. Hosp., Lihue, Hawaii, 1979-82, Calif. Pacific Med. Ctr., San Francisco, 1983—; dir. Ctr. Preventive Medicine and Health Rsch., 1983—, dir. Health Watch, 1983—; sr. scientist Inst. Epidemiol. and Behavioral Medicine, Inst. Cancer Rsch., Calif. Pacific Med. Ctr., San Francisco, 1983-88; prof. hematology and gerontology, dir. Ctr. Preventive Medicine and Health Rsch., chair health professions program San Francisco State U., 1983-99, prof. medicine, 1983—, prof. emeritus, Calif. State U. Sys., 1999—; founding dir. Health Watch Internat., 1994—, CEO, pres. Cons. WHO, FDA, Washington, NIH, Bethesda, Md., Govt. of China, Mayo Clinic, Rochester, Minn., Northwestern U., Evanston, Ill., Chgo., U. R.I., Kingston, Pan Am. Health Orgn., Inst. Pub. Health, Italy, Nat. Inst. Aging Rsch. Ctr., Balt., U. Calif., San Diego, U. Ill., Chgo., Columbia U., NYC, Harvard U., Johns Hopkins U., U. Chgo., UCLA, U. Calif. Berkeley, Brown U., Providence, U. Calif., San Francisco, Stanford U., Boston, Emory U., Atlanta, Duke U., NC, U. Tex., Houston, Ariz. State U., U. Hawaii, Honolulu, U. Paris, U. Geneva, U. Munich, Heidelberg U., U. Frankfurt, U. Berlin, Cambridge U., England, U. Singapore, others; vis. rsch. prof. gerontology Ariz. State U., 1989—90; mem. numerous sci. and profl. adv. bd., panels, com. Mem. editorial bd. Am. Jour. Clin. Pathology, 1976-82, The Advisor, 1988—, Generations, 1989—, Contemporary Gerontology, 1994—, Alternative Therapies in Health and Medicine, 1995—, Aging Today, 1997—; book and film reviewer Sci. Books and Films, 1988—, many other jours.; author: 17 books and manuals including Hematology Laboratory Series, 4 vols., 1979-86, CRC Handbook Series in Clinical Laboratory Science, 1976—; assoc. editor: Contemporary Gerontology, 1993—; contbr. more than 400 articles to sci. jours. Alumni regent Columbia U. Coll. Physicians and Surgeons, 1980—. Northwestern U. scholar, 1964-66; NSF fellow, 1964-66; Health Professions scholar, 1966-70; USPHS fellow, 1967-70; Microbiology, Urology, Upjohn Achievement, Borden Rsch. and Virginia Kneeland Frantz scholar awards Columbia U., 1970; recipient Am. Soc. Pharmacol. and Exptl. Therapy award in pharmacology, 1970, Commendation medal USPHS, 1973, Meritorious Performance and Profl. Promise award, 1989, Student Disting. Teaching and Svc. award Pre-Health Professions Student Alliance, 1992, Leadership Recognition awards San Francisco State U., 1984-89, 91-96, Meritorious Svc. award, 1992. Fellow: ACPM, AAAS (med. scis. sect.), ACP (commentator ACP Jour. Club/Annals of Internal Medicine 1993—), Internat. Soc. Hematology, Am. Soc. Clin. Pathology, Am. Coll. Preventive Medicine (sci. com.), Am. Geriat. Soc., Royal Soc. Medicine (London), Gerontol. Soc. Am.; mem.: APHA, AMA, Emory Sch. Pub. Health, Calif. Coun. Gerontology and Geriat., Nat. Assoc. Adv. for Health Professions, Internat. Health Eval. Assn. (v.p. for Ams. 1992—94, bd. dirs. 1992—, pres. 1994—96), Calif. Med. Assn., San Francisco Med. Soc., NY Acad. Sci., Am. Soc. Aging (editl. bd. 1990—, Dychtwald Pub. Speaking award 1991), Am. Soc. Microbiology, Assn. Tchr. Preventive Medicine (edn. com., rsch. com.), Am. Coll. Occupl. and Environ. Medicine, Calif. Coun. Gerontology and Geriat., Am. Assn. Med. Info., Nat. Assn. Advisors for Health Professions (bd. dirs.), Am. Assoc. Blood Banks, Acad. Clin. Lab. Physicians and Scientists, Internat. Soc. Thrombosis and Hemostasis, Am. Soc. Hematology (hon.; emeritus), Internat. Commn. Standardization in Hematology, Am. Assn. Med. Info. (chair prevention and health evaln. informatics WG), Nat. Gallery of Art (Washington), Columbia U. Club No. Calif., Circle Club (Washington), Army and Navy Club, Golden Key (hon. faculty mem.), Harvard Club (NY and San Francisco), Northwestern U. Club. No. Calif., Cosmos Club (mem. art com. 1997—), Knights of Malta, Sigma Xi, Phi Beta Kappa. Home: Whaleship Plaza 25 Hinckley Walk San Francisco CA 94111-2303 Office: Health Watch Med Ctr Calif Pacific Med Ctr San Francisco CA 94120-7999 Home Phone: 415-956-5670; Office Phone: 415-956-5670. Personal E-mail: rmschmidtmd@aol.com.

SCHMIDT, STEPHEN C., real estate developer; Grad., U. Calif., Davis; MS in Bus. Adminstn., Stanford U. Grad. Sch. Various exec. positions, comml., indsl. devel. The Newhall Land & Farming Co., 1976-92, sr. v.p., residential community devel., 1999—. Office: The Newhall Land & Farming Co 23823 Valencia Blvd Valencia CA 91355-2103

SCHMIDT, STEVE (STEPHEN E. SCHMIDT), public relations executive; b. North Plainfield, NJ, 1970; m. Angela Schmidt; children: Madigan, Joseph. Attended, U. Del., Newark, 1988—93. Comm. dir. Matt Fong Senate Campaign, Calif., 1998; sr. staff mem., dep. asst. to Pres. George W. Bush The White House, Washington, spokesman, counselor to Vice Pres. Dick Cheney; media rels. cons. to Amb. Zalmay Khalilzad US Dept. State, Baghdad, Iraq; chief nomination strategist Justice Samuel A. Alito. and Chief Justice John Roberts; comm. dir. Nat. Republican Congl. Com., Washington, 2002; sr. campaign strategist Pres. George W. Bush's Re-Election Campaign, 2004; campaign mgr. Gov. Arnold Swartzenegger's Re-Election Campaign, Calif., 2006; ptnr. Mercury Pub. Affairs, Sacramento; campaign strategist, sr. advisor Senator John McCain's Presdl. Campaign, Arlington, Va., 2007—08. Republican. Office: Mercury Pub Affairs 1801 L St Ste 239 Sacramento CA 95814 Office Phone: 916-444-1380. Office Fax: 916-265-1869. Business E-Mail: sschmidt@mercuryllc.com.*

SCHMIDT, TERRY L., healthcare executive; b. Chgo., Nov. 28, 1943; s. LeRoy C. and Eunice P. Schmidt; children: Christie Anne, Terry L. II. BS, Bowling Green State U., 1965; MBA in Health Care Adminstrn, George Washington U., 1971; Dr Health Adminstrn., Med. U. S.C., 2001. Resident in hosp. adminstrn. U. Pitts. Med. Center, VA Hosp., Pitts., 1968-69; adminstrv. asst. Mt. Sinai Med. Center, NYC, 1969-70; asst. dir. Health Facilities Planning Council of Met. Washington, 1970-71; asst. dir. dept. govtl. relations A.M.A., Washington, 1971-74; contract lobbyist and govtl. rels. Wash. Reps. in Health, Washington, 1974-87; pres. Terry L. Schmidt Inc. Physician Svcs. Group, San Diego, 1987-99, Washington Actions on Health, 1975-79; partner Washington Coun. Medicine and Health, 1979-81; pres. Recreational Enterprises, Inc., Washington, 1977-78; v.p. Crisis Communications Corp. Ltd., 1982-90; pres. Med. Cons. Inc., 1983-84, Ambulance Corp. Am., La Jolla, Calif., 1984-87; exec. dir., chief operating officer Emergency Health Assocs. P.C., Phoenix, 1989-91, Charleston Emergency Physicians, Inc., S.C., 1990-94, Joplin Emergency Physican Assocs., 1991-92, Big Valley Med. Group, 1991-92, Blue Ridge Emergency Physicians, P.C., 1992-94, Berkeley Emergency Physicians, P.C., 1992-94; chmn., pres. Univ. Inst., Inc., 1992—; asst. dir. dept. emergency medicine Med. U.S.C., 1999—2001. Bd. dirs., Univ. Inst., 1997—, lectr., instr. dept. health svcs. adminstrn. George Washington U., 1969-83, preceptor, 1975-84; adj. prof. grad. sch. Pub. Health San Diego State U., 1996—, preceptor, 1989-2002; guest lectr. Bus. Adminstrn. U.S. Internat. U., San Diego, 1994-95; instr. Nat. Naval Sch. Health Care Adminstrn., 1971-73; faculty Civil Svc. Commn. Legis. Insts., 1972-76; fac. Am. Assn. State Colls. and U. Health Tng. Insts., 1975-78; mem. adv. com. ambulatory care standards Joint Commn. Accreditation of Hosps., 1971-72, pres., Recreational Enterprises, Inc., Wash., 1977-78, guest lectr. Med. U.S.C., 1998-99, preceptor, 1999-2001, assoc. prof. Coll. of Health, Med. U.S.C., 1999-2001. Author: Congress and Health: An Introduction to the Legislative Process and the Key Participants, 1976, A Directory of Federal Health Resources and Services for the Disadvantaged, 1976, Health Care Reimbursement: A Glossary, 1983; mem. editl. adv. bd. Nation's Health, 1971-73; contbr. articles to profl. jours. Bd. dirs. Nat. Eye Found., 1976-78. Mem. Med. Group Mgmt. Assn., Health Care Fin. Mgmt. Assn., Assn. Venture Capital Groups (bd. dirs. 1984-89), Amer. Coll. of Health Execs., Amer. Coll. of Med. Prac. Exec., Assn. of Univ. Progs. in Health Admin., San Diego Venture Group (chair 1984-87), Univ. Club (life), Natl. Rep. Club (life), Nat. Dem. Club (life), Capitol Hill Club (life), Alpha Phi Omega (pres. Bowling Green alumni chpt. 1967-70, sec.-treas. alumni assn. 1968-71). Office: University Inst Ste 113 611 7770 Regents Rd San Diego CA 92122-1967

SCHMIDT, VICTOR HUGO, physics professor, researcher; b. Portland, Oreg., July 10, 1930; s. Hugo Andrew Paul and Marie Minna Henrietta (Neils) S.; m. Shirley Ann Schmidt, Sept. 13, 1958; children: Harold Jay, Lawrence Otto, Marie Denise, Gloria Mae. BSME, Wash. State U., 1951; PhD in Physics, U. Wash., 1961. Mech. design engr. Gilfillan Bros., Inc., LA, 1953-54; assoc. rsch. engr. Boeing Airplane Co., Seattle, 1955-57; asst. prof. physics Valparaiso (Ind.) U., 1961-64; assoc. prof. physics Mont. State U., Bozeman, 1964-73, prof. physics, 1973—. Mem. editl. bd. Ferroelectrics, 1997—; author: (with others) Hydrogen Bond, 1976. 1st lt. USAF, 1951—53. Grantee NSF, 1961—, Dept. Energy, 1972—, NASA, 1994—, Dept. Def., 1999— Fellow Am. Phys. Soc.; mem. IEEE (sr.), Am. Assn. Physics Tchrs., Sigma Xi. Achievements include patents for piezoelectric wind generator and pulse modified camera; explained dielectric and conductive behavior in ferroelectric (FE) KH_2PO_4 and discovered its tricritical point; demonstrated that $LiN_2H_5SO_4$ is not FE; found antiferroelectric (AFE) phase at high pressure in tris-sarcosine calcium chloride; discovered coexistence of FE and AFE phases with paraelectric phase in proton glass; invented a piezoelectric polymer actuator. Office: Mont State U Dept Physics 264 Eps Bldg Bozeman MT 59717-0001 Home: 1429 Cherry Dr Bozeman MT 59715-5916

SCHMOLLER, EBERHARD G. H., retired lawyer; b. Menlo Park, CA; BA in engring., Stanford U.; JD, U. Calif. LA. Legal counsel McDonnell Douglas Corp., 1969—74; staff atty. CNF Inc., 1974—76; asst. gen. counsel CF Motor Freight (a subsidiary of CNF Inc.), 1976—83; gen. counsel CF Airfreight, 1983—89; v.p., gen. counsel Menlo Worldwide (formerly Emery Worldwide), 1989—93; sr. v.p., gen. counsel, corp. sec. CNF Inc., 1993—2004; ret. Office: Cnf Inc 2855 Campus Dr Ste 300 San Mateo CA 94403-2512

SCHNABEL, GARY A., health facility administrator, director; Compliance dir. Oreg. Bd. of Pharmacy, 1994-99, acting exec. dir., 1999, exec. dir., 1999—.

SCHNAPP, ROGER HERBERT, lawyer, consultant; b. NYC, Mar. 17, 1946; s. Michael Jay and Beatrice Joan (Becker) S.; m. Candice Jacqueline Larson, Sept. 15, 1979; 1 child, Monica Alexis. BS, Cornell U., 1966; JD, Harvard U., 1969; postgrad. Pub. Utility Mgmt. Program, U. Mich., 1978. Bar: NY 1970, US Ct. Appeals (2d cir.) 1970, US Supreme, 1974, US Dist. Ct. (so. dist.) NY 1975, US Ct. Appeals (4th and 6th cirs.) 1976, US Ct. Appeals (7th cir.) 1977, US Dist. Ct. (so. dist.) NY 1975, US Dist. Ct. (no. dist.) Calif. 1980, US Ct. Appeals (8th cir.) 1980, Calif., 1982, US Dist. Ct. (cen. dist.) Calif. 1982, US Ct. Dist. (ea. dist.) Calif., 1984. Atty. CAB, Washington, 1969-70; labor atty. Western Electric Co., NYC, 1970-71; mgr. employee rels. Am. Airlines, NYC, 1971-74; labor counsel Am. Electric Power Svc. Corp., NYC, 1974-78, sr. labor counsel, 1978-80; indsl. rels. counsel Trans World Airlines, NYC, 1980-81; sr. assoc. Parker, Milliken, Clark & O'Hara, LA, 1981-82; ptnr. Rutan & Tucker, Costa Mesa, Calif., 1983-84, Memel, Jacobs, Pierno, Gersh & Ellsworth, Newport Beach, Calif., 1985-86, Memel, Jacobs & Ellsworth, Newport Beach, 1986-87; pvt. practice Newport Beach, 1987—. Bd. dirs. Dynamic Constrn., Inc., Laguna Hills, Calif., 1986—; commentator labor rels. Fin. News Network; commentator Sta. KOCN Radio, 1990-91; commentator employment law Orange County Register; lectr. Calif. Western Law Sch., Calif. State U.-Fullerton, Calif. State Conf. Small Bus.; lectr. collective bargaining Pace U., NYC; lectr. on labor law Coun. on Edn. in Mgmt.; NE regional coord. Pressler for Pres., 1979-80; adv. bd. manufacturing-zone Web site; dir. Orange County Bur. Jewish Edn., Friends of Fertility Found. Author: Arbitration Issues for the 1980s, 1981, A Look at Three Companies, 1982; editor-in-chief Indsl. and Labor Rels. Forum, 1964-66; columnist Orange County Bus. Jour., 1989-91; contbr. articles to profl. publs. Mem. Bus. Rsch. Adv. Coun. US Dept. Labor; trustee Chapman U., 1991-95; bd. mem., Orange County Bur. Jewish Edn. Mem. Calif. Bar Assn. (chmn.), Labor Law Consulting Group, Calif. Bd. of Legal Specialization, Jewish Cmty. Ctr. Orange County. Republican. Jewish. Office: PO Box 9049 Newport Beach CA 92658-1049 Office Phone: 949-706-7365. Business E-Mail: rhs@schnapp.com.

SCHNEEMAN, BARBARA OLDS, nutritionist, educator; m. Paul Schneeman; 1 child, Eric. BS in Food Sci. and Tech., U. Calif., Davis, 1970; PhD in Nutrition, U. Calif., Berkeley, 1974. NIH postdoctoral fellow gastrointestinal physiology Children's Hosp., Oakland, Calif., 1974-76; faculty mem. nutrition dept. nutrition and food sci. & tech. U. Calif., Davis, 1976—, prof. dept. internal medicine divsn. clin. nutrition, 1986—, assoc. dean Coll. Agrl. and Environ. Scis., 1985-88, chair dept. nutrition, 1988-93, dean Coll. Agrl. and Environ. Scis., 1993-99. Pres., bd. dirs. Dannon Inst., 1996—; vis. scientist Cardiovascular Rsch. Inst., U. Calif., San Francisco, 1991-92; lectr. women in sci. series Coll. St. Catherine, St. Paul, 1987; adv. dir. Blue Cross Calif., 1992-95; mem. dietary guidelines for Ams. adv. com. to Secs. of Agr., Health and Human Svcs., 1989-90, 94-95; mem. expert panel on food safety and nutrition Inst. Food Technologists, 1985-91; mem. external adv. bd. Post Ctr. for Nutrition and Health, 1989-90; councilor Soc. for Exptl. Biology and Medicine, 1988-91. Assoc. editor Jour. Nutrition, 1991-94; contbg. editor Nutrition Revs., 1982-

90; editl. bd. Jour. Nutrition, 1982-87, Procs. for Soc. Exptl. Biology and Medicine, 1985-91, Acad. Press: Food Sci. and Nutrition, 1988-2001. Fellow NDEA, U. Calif., Berkeley; recipient Outstanding Cmty. Svc. award Tierra del Oro coun. Girl Scouts U.S., 1995, Future Leaders award for rsch. Nutrition Found., 1978-80, Samuel Cate Prescott award for rsch. Inst. Food Tech., 1985, Farma Food Internat. Fibre prize, Copenhagen, 1989, Ethel Austin Martin disting. lectr. on Human Nutrition, S.D. State U., 1999. Fellow AAAS; mem. Inst. Food Technologists (sec.-treas. nutrition divsn. 1988-89), Am. Physiol. Soc., Am. Inst. Nutrition (treas. 1989-92), Am. Heart Assn. (fellow arteriosclerosis coun.), Food and Nutrition Bd. IOM, 2001—. Office: U Calif Davis Dept Nutrition Davis CA 95616

SCHNEIDER, BENJAMIN, psychology professor, consultant; b. NYC, Aug. 11, 1938; s. Leo and Rose (Cohen) S.; m. H. Brenda Jacobson, Jan. 29, 1961; children: Lee Andrew, Rhody Yve. BA, Alfred U., 1960; MBA, CUNY, 1962; PhD, U. Md., 1967. Lic. psychologist, Md. Asst. prof. adminstrv. scis. and psychology Yale U., New Haven, 1967-71; prof. psychology-mgmt. U. Md., College Park, 1971-79, prof. psychology and mgmt., 1982—2004, prof. emeritus, 2004—; sr. rsch. fellow Valtera Corp., 2003—; John A. Hannah prof. orgnl. psychology Mich. State U., East Lansing, 1979-82. Vis. prof. Inst. Adminstrn. and Enterprise, U. Aix-Marseille, 1993, 99, 2001, Peking U., 1988, Tuck Sch. Bus. Adminstrn., Dartmouth Coll., 1999. Author: (with D.T. Hall) Organizational Climates and Careers, 1973, Staffing Organizations, 1976, (with N. Schmitt) 2d edit., 1986, (with F.D. Schoorman) Facilitating Work Effectiveness, 1988, Organizational Climate and Culture, 1990, (with D.E. Bowen) Winning the Service Game, 1995, (with S.S. White) Service Quality: Research Perspectives, 2004, (with D.B. Smith) Personality and Organizations, 2004, (with R.E. Ployhart and N. Schmitt) Staffing Organizations, 3d edit., 2006; mem. editl. rev. bd. Jour. Applied Psychology, 1988-98, 02-, Internat. Jour. Svc. Industry Mgmt., 1989—, Jour. Svc. Rsch., 1998—, Orgnl. Behavior and Human Decision Processes, 2002-, Cornell Quar., 2002-. Fulbright grantee, 1973—74. Fellow APA, Am. Psychol. Soc., Soc. for Indsl. and Orgnl. Psychology (pres. 1984-85, Disting. Sci. Contbns. award 2000, Scholarly Contbn. award 2004), Acad. Mgmt. (pres. orgnl. behavior divsn. 1982-83), Am. Mktg. Assn. (svcs. mktg. spl. interest group, Career Contbns. award 2006), San Diego Indsl. and Orgnl. Profls. (pres. 2005-06). Office: 1363 Caminito Floreo Ste G La Jolla CA 92037 Office Phone: 858-488-7594. Business E-Mail: bschneider@valtera.com.

SCHNEIDER, CAROLE M., medical educator, director; PhD, U. Minn., Minneapolis. Prof. Baylor Coll. Medicine, Houston, 1986—88, rschr., 1986—88; prof. U. Kans., Lawrence, 1988—92, rschr., 1988—92; prof. U. No. Colo., Greeley, 1992—, rschr., 1992—. Dir. Rocky Mountain Cancer Rehab. Inst., Greeley, Colo., 1996—. Author: (textbook) Exercise and Cancer Recovery. Office: Univ Northern Colorado BNCC 10th Ave & 19th St Campus Box 6 Greeley CO 80639 Business E-Mail: carole.schneider@unco.edu.

SCHNEIDER, CHARLES IVAN, newspaper executive; b. Chgo., Apr. 6, 1923; s. Samuel Hiram and Eva (Smith) S.; m. Nancy Barrier-Schneider; children: Susan, Charles I. Jr., Kim, Karen, Traci. BS, Northwestern U., 1944. Indsl. engr., sales mgr., v.p. mktg. and sales Curtis-Electro Lighting Corp., Chgo., 1945-54, pres., 1954-62, Jefferson Electronics, Inc., Santa Barbara, Calif., 1962-64; pres. 3 sub., v.p., asst. to pres. Am. Bldg. Maintenance Industries, Los Angeles, 1964-66; group v.p. Times Mirror Co., Los Angeles, 1966-88, ret.; pvt. investor and cons., 1988—. Bd. dirs. Jeppesen Sanderson, Inc., Denver, Graphic Controls Corp., Buffalo, Regional Airports Improvement Corp. Bd. regents Northwestern U., Evanston, Ill.; trustee, past pres. Reiss-Davis Child Study Center, L.A.; bd. govs., past pres. The Music Ctr.; trustee the Menninger Found.; pres. St. John's Hosp. and Health Ctr. Found., Santa Monica, Calif. Served with AUS, 1942-44. Mem. Chief Execs. Orgn. (past pres., bd. dirs.). Clubs: Standard (Chgo.); Beverly Hills Tennis (Calif.); Big. Ten of So. Calif. Avocations: tennis, squash, music, reading. Home: 522 N Beverly Dr Beverly Hills CA 90210-3318

SCHNEIDER, EDWARD LEE, botanist, researcher; b. Portland, Oreg., Sept. 14, 1947; s. Edward John and Elizabeth (Mathews) S.; m. Sandra Lee Alfarone, Aug. 2, 1968; children: Kenneth L., Cassandra L. BA, Ctrl. Wash. U., 1969, MS, 1971; PhD, U. Calif., Santa Barbara, 1974. From asst. to assoc. prof. botany S.W. Tex. State U., San Marcos, 1974-84, prof., 1984-94, chmn. biology dept., 1984-89, dean sci., 1989-92; pres., CEO Santa Barbara (Calif.) Botanic Garden, 1992—. Author: The Botanical World, CEOs and Trustees--Building Working Partnerships; contbr. articles to profl. jours. Bd. dirs. Ctr. for Plant Conservation; bd. dirs. Coun. Sci. Soc. Presidents, 2005-06. Recipient Presdl. Rsch. award S.W. Tex. State U., 1986, Disting. Alumnus award Ctrl. Wash. U., 1996; grantee NSF, 1980, 90. Fellow Tex. Acad. Sci. (pres. 1992-93); mem. Internat. Water Lily Soc. (bd. dirs., sec. 1989-96, inducted into Hall of Fame, Award of Appreciation 1997), Bot. Soc. Am. (bd. dirs., pres.-elect 2004, pres. 2005-06, past pres. 2006-07, Award of Merit 1998, Centennial medallion 2006), Am. Assn. Bot. Gardens and Arboreta (bd. dirs.), Internat. Pollination Congress, Nat. Coun. Deans, Am. Assn. Mus. (assessment program adv. com., nat. program com, Excellence in Peer Rev. Sev. award 2007). Home: 1140 Tunnel Rd Santa Barbara CA 93105-2134 Office: Santa Barbara Botanic Garden 1212 Mission Canyon Rd Santa Barbara CA 93105-2126 Office Phone: 805-682-4726 ext. 123. Business E-Mail: eschneider@sbbg.org.

SCHNEIDER, EDWARD LEWIS, medicine educator, research administrator; b. NYC, June 22, 1940; s. Samuel and Ann S. BS, Rensselaer Poly. Inst., 1961; MD, Boston U., 1966. Intern and resident N.Y. Hosp.-Cornell U., NYC, 1966-68; staff fellow Nat. Inst. Allergy and Infectious Diseases, Bethesda, Md., 1968-70; research fellow U. Calif., San Francisco, 1970-73; chief, sect. on cell aging Nat. Inst. Aging, Balt., 1973-79, assoc. dir., 1980-84, dep. dir., 1984-87; prof. medicine, dir. Davis Inst. on Aging U. Colo., Denver, 1979-80; dean Leonard Davis Sch. Gerontology U. So. Calif., LA, 1986—, exec. dir. Ethel Percy Andrus Gerontology Ctr., 1986—, prof. medicine, 1987—, William and Sylvia Kugel prof. gerontology, 1989—. Sci. dir. Buck Ctr. for Rsch. in Aging, 1989-98; cons. MacArthur Found., Chgo., 1985-93, R.W. Johnson Found., Princeton, N.J., 1982-87, Brookdale Found., N.Y.C., 1985-89. Editor: The Genetics of Aging, 1978, The Aging Reproductive System, 1978, Biological Markers of Aging, 1982, Handbook of the Biology of Aging, 1985, 95, 96, Interrelationship Among Aging Cancer and Differentiation, 1985, Teaching Nursing Home, 1985, Modern Biological Theories of Aging, 1987, The Black American Elderly, 1988, Elder Care and the Work Force, 1990, A Secure Old Age: Financing Long-Term Care, 1998, Ageless: Take Control of Your Age and Stay Youthful for Life, 2003. Med. dir. USPHS, 1968—. Recipient Roche award, 1964. Fellow Gerontology Soc., Am. Soc. Clin. Investigation; mem. Am. Assn. Retired Persons, U.S. Naval Acad. Sailing Squadron (coach 1980-86). Office: U So Calif Andrus Gerontology Ctr Los Angeles CA 90089-0001 E-mail: eschneid@usc.edu.

SCHNEIDER, GERALD L., plastic surgeon; b. Mechanicsburg, Pa., Oct. 25, 1945; s. Gordon Henry and Pauline Emma (Rife) S.; 1 child, Ross Roberts. BS, No. Ariz. U., 1968; MD, U. Ariz., 1973. Intern Naval Regional Med. Ctr., San Diego, 1973-74; resident in gen. surgery U.S. Naval Hosp., San Diego, 1974-78, resident in plastic surgery Portsmouth, Va., 1978-80, staff surgeon divsn. plastic surgery San Diego, 1981-83, chief divsn. plastic surgery, 1983-84; pvt. practice Flagstaff, Ariz., 1984-90; staff surgeon La Jolla (Calif.) Cosmetic Surgery Ctr., 1990-91; surgeon Scripps Clinic & Rsch. Found., La Jolla, 1991—. Capt. USNR Fellow ACS; mem. Am. Soc. Plastic Surgeons. Avocation: golf. Office: Scripps Clinic & Rsch Found 10666 N Torrey Pines Rd La Jolla CA 92037-1092 Office Phone: 858-554-9606. Business E-Mail: schneider.gerald@scrippshealth.org.

SCHNEIDER, HARRY H., JR., lawyer; b. San Antonio, Jan. 12, 1954; AB, U. Calif., Berkeley, 1976; JD, U. Chgo., 1979. Bar: Wash. 1979, US Ct. Appeals (9th Cir.), US Dist. Ct. (We. Dist.) Wash., US Dist. Ct. (Ea. Dist.) Wash. Clk. Contra Costa County Dist. Atty. Office, Martinez, Calif., 1972—76; with Kobin & Meyer, Portland, 1977, Cooley, Godward, Castro, Huddleson & Tatum, San Francisco, 1978; ptnr. Perkins Coie LLP, Seattle, mem. mgmt. com. Office: Perkins Coie LLP 1201 Third Ave Ste 4800 Seattle WA 98101-3029 Office Phone: 206-359-8508. Office Fax: 206-359-9000. Business E-Mail: hschneider@perkinscoie.com.

SCHNEIDER, HILARY A., Internet company executive; BA in Econs., Brown U., 1982; MBA, Harvard Bus. Sch., 1986. Dir. devel. The Balt. Sun Co., 1992—94, v.p. new bus. devel., 1994—95, v.p. sales, 1996—97, v.p. sales and mktg., 1997—98, gen. mgr., 1998—99; v.p. corp. fin. Drexel Burnham Lambert Inc., 1986—90; dir. bus. devel. Times Mirror Corp., 1990—92; pres., CEO Times Mirror Interactive, Balt., 1999—2000, Red Herring Comm., 2000—02; v.p., Knight Ridder Digital Knight Ridder, Inc., 2002—04, pres., CEO, Knight Ridder Digital, 2002—04, sr. v.p., 2005—06; sr. v.p. marketplaces (now called Local Markets and Commerce) Yahoo! Inc., Sunnyvale, Calif., 2006, exec. v.p., local markets and commerce divsn., Yahoo! Pub. Network, 2006—07, exec. v.p., global partner solutions, 2007—. Bd. dirs. CareerBuilder.com, Classified Ventures, Topix.net, ShopLocal; exec. sponsor and leader of significant cross-co. partnership with US publishing companies, including several daily newspapers, 2006—. Mem.: Newspaper Assn. Am. (bd. dirs.). Office: Yahoo Inc 701 1st Ave Sunnyvale CA 94089

SCHNEIDER, MICHAEL (MIKE) A., state legislator; b. McCook, Nebr., Apr. 11, 1950; m to Candice H Hill; children: Andrew. Nevada State Assemblyman, District 42, 93-95; Nevada State Senator, District 8, 1997-2002, Minority Whip, 97, Assistant Minority Floor Leader, 99, Nevada State Senate; Nevada State Senator, Clark Co Senator District 11, 2002-.Real estate develop/sales, currently; board director, Opportunity Village, currently. House of Year, Home Mag, 92; Finalist, Best of America Living, Housing Award; Builder of Show Homes, Nat Association of Homebuilders Conv, 92-93. Gleams Found; Greater Las Vegas & Nevada Asns of Realtors; Southern Nevada Homebuilders Association. Democrat. Mailing: 6381 Sandpiper Way Las Vegas NV 89103-2110 Home Phone: 702-876-5121.

SCHNEIDER, NICHOLAS MCCORD, planetary scientist, educator, textbook author; b. Appleton, Wis., Dec. 17, 1956; s. Ben Ross Jr. and Mackay (McCord) S. BA in Physics and Astronomy, Dartmouth Coll., 1979; PhD in Planetary Sci., U. Ariz., 1988. Assoc. prof. lab. for atmospheric & space physics and dept. of astrophysical & planetary scis. U. Colo., Boulder, 1990—. Recipient Presdl. Young Investigator award NSF, 1991. Mem. Am. Astron. Soc. (divsn. for planetary scis.), Am. Geophys. Union, Internat. Astron. Union, Astron. Soc. of the Pacific. Office: U Colo Lab Atmospheric Space Physics 392 UCB Boulder CO 80309-0392

SCHNEIDER, REBECCA, librarian; b. Parkersburg, W.Va., Dec. 20, 1963; BS in Psychology, Slippery Rock U., 1987. Spl. projects coord./circulation Wilkinsburgh Pub. Libr., 1995—2001; branch mgr. Maricopa County Libr. Dist., 2001—06; overnight libr. supr. Ariz. State U., 2006—. Mem.: NOW, Women's Campaign Forum, League of Conservation Voters, Ctr. Biological Diversity, Democracy for America, Progressive Dem. America, Humane Soc. America, J Street, Emily's List, Sierra Club. Democrat. Office: 1550 E 2nd St Mesa AZ 85203-8931 also: 1970 N Hartford St Unit 1 Chandler AZ 85226 Office Phone: 480-833-5101. Personal E-mail: schneiderforcongress@gmail.com.

SCHNEIDER, ROB, actor; b. Pacifica, Calif., Oct. 31, 1963; s. Marvin and Pilar Schneider; m. London King, 1988 (div. 1990); 1 child, Chole Autumn. Co-owner restaurant Eleven, San Francisco. Actor: (films) Martians Go Home, 1990, Necessary Roughness, 1991, Home Alone 2: Lost in New York, 1992, Surf Ninjas, 1993, Demolition Man, 1993, The Beverly Hillbillies, 1993, Judge Dredd, 1995, Down Periscope, 1996, The Adventures of Pinocchio, 1996, Knock Off, 1998, Susan's Plan, 1998, The Waterboy, 1998, Deuce Bigalow: Male Gigolo, 1999, Big Daddy, 1999, Muppets From Space, 1999, Little Nicky, 2000, The Animal, 2001, The Hot Chick, 2002, Mr. Deeds, 2002, (voice) Eight Crazy Nights, 2002, 50 First Dates, 2004, Around the World in 80 Days, 2004, The Longest Yard, 2005, Deuce Bigalow: European Gigolo, 2005, Grandma's Boy, 2006, The Benchwarmers, 2006, Click, 2006, (voice) Shark Bait, 2006, Little Man, 2006, American Crude, 2007, Juliana and the Medicine Fish, 2007, I Now Pronounce You Chuck & Larry, 2007, Big Stan, 2007, You Don't Mess with the Zohan, 2008, (TV series) Saturday Night Live, 1990-94, Men Behaving Badly, 1996-97, (TV films) The Mummy Parody, 2001, (voice) The Electric Piper, 2003, Back to Norm, 2005.

SCHNEIDER, THOMAS RICHARD, hospital administrator; b. Cin., July 16, 1944; s. Richard Arthur and Janet (Tingley) S.; m. Judith Ann Johnson, June 10, 1967; children: Gregory Thomas, Marcia Kay, Jill Elise. BS in Bus. Adminstrn., Miami U., Oxford, Ohio, 1966; MHA, U. Minn., 1968. Asst. adminstr. Meml. Hosp. of South Bend, Ind., 1971-77, Ft. Hamilton-Hughes Meml. Hosp., Hamilton, Ohio, 1977-82, assoc. adminstr. 5, Ohio, 1982-84, assoc. adminstr., chief oper. officer, 1984-85, v.p. ops. and profl. svcs., 1985-91; adminstr. Shriners Hosp. for Children, Shreveport, La., 1992—2002, Honolulu, 2002—. Chmn. health careers Greater Cin. Hosp. Coun., 1983-90; mem. adv. bd. Xavier U. Ctr. for Health Mgmt. Edn., Cin., 1985-91; trustee Cmty. Blood Ctr., Dayton, Ohio, 1985-91. Trustee, 1st v.p. YMCA of Hamilton-Fairfield, 1990; chmn. city charter comms. com. City of Hamilton, 1990; chmn. pub. svc. div. United Way of Hamilton-Fairfield, 1988-90. Mem. Med. Svc. Corps. USN, 1968-71. Recipient disting. svc. award YMCA, 1982, great American family award of honor, 1990, proclamation Mayor and City Coun. of Hamilton, 1992. Fellow Am. Coll. Healthcare Execs.; mem. Rotary Internat., Masons, Shriner. Republican. Methodist. Avocations: fishing, golf, boating, reading. Home: 10625 Royal Tara Cv Austin TX 78717-4450

SCHNELL, ROGER THOMAS, small business owner, retired state official, military officer; b. Wabasha, Minn., Dec. 11, 1936; s. Donald William and Eva Louise (Barton) Schnell; m. Barbara Ann McDonald, Dec. 18, 1959 (div. Mar. 1968); children: Thomas Allen(dec.), Scott Douglas(dec.). A in Mil. Sci., Command and Gen. Staff Coll., 1975; A in Bus. Administn., Wayland Bapt. U., 1987. Commd. 2d lt. Alaska N.G., 1959, advanced through grades to col., 1975, shop supt. Anchorage, 1965-71, personnel mgr., 1972-74, chief of staff, 1974-87, dir. logistics, 1987; electrician Alaska R.R., Anchorage, 1955-61, elec. foreman, 1962-64; dir. support personnel mgmt. Joint Staff Alaska N.G., 1988-92, ret.; personnel mgr. State of Alaska, 1992, asst. commr. dept. mil. and vets. affairs Ft. Richardson, 1992-95, dep. commr. dept. mil. and vets. affairs, 1995-98, 2002—06, brig. gen., 2007; owner RTS Enterprises, Anchorage, 1999—. Prin., owner RTS Enterprises, 1999—; adv. bd. state joint armed svc. com. State of Alaska, 2001—06; dep. commr. dept. Mil. and Vet. Affairs, 2003—06. Chmn. Alaska Nat. Guard Mus. Trust Fund, 2001—02; appointed to Gov.'s State Seismic Hazard Safety Commn., 2005—06; chmn. pastor parish rels. com. Meth. 1st Ch., 2001—02, mem. fin. com., 2007—08; bd. dirs. Meth. Trust Fund, 2002—04, 2007—. Named Brigadier Gen. (hon.) Alaska NG, Gov. of Alaska, 2007. Mem. Fed. Profl. Labor Relations Execs. (sec. 1974-75), Alaska N.G. Officers Assn. (pres. 1976-78, bd. dirs. 1988—), Assn. U.S. Army (corp.), NG Assn. U.S. (life, retiree rep. from Alaska 1993—), Am. Legion, Amvets, Elks. Republican. Methodist. Avocations: travel, photography. Home and Office: Huntwood Park Estates 6817 Queens View Cir Anchorage AK 99504-5203 Home Phone: 907-333-8001. Personal E-mail: rogertschnell@gci.net, rtschnellenterprises@gci.net.

SCHNELLER, EUGENE STEWART, health administration and policy educator; b. Cornwall, NY, Apr. 9, 1943; s. Michael Nicholas and Anne Ruth (Gruner) Schneller; m. Ellen Stauber, Mar. 24, 1968; children: Andrew Jon, Lee Stauber. AA, SUNY, Buffalo, 1965; BA, LI U., 1967; PhD, NYU, 1973; grad. physician assoc. (hon.), Duke U., 2004. Rsch. asst. dept. sociology NYU, NYC, 1968-70; project dir. Montefiore Hosp. and Med. Ctr., Bronx, NY, 1970-72; asst. prof. Med. Ctr. and sociology Duke U., Durham, NC, 1973-75; assoc. prof., chmn. dept. sociology Union Coll., Schenectady, 1975-79, assoc. prof., dir. Health Studies Ctr., 1979-85; prof., dir. Sch. Health Mgmt. and Policy, Ariz. State U., Tempe, 1985—91, assoc. dean rsch. and adminstrn. Coll. Bus., 1992-94; dir. L. William Seidman Rsch. Ctr., Tempe, 1992-94, counselor to pres. for health profl. edn., 1994-96; clin. prof. cmty. and family medicine U. Ariz., 1995-96, clin. prof. prevention, rsch., 1997—2002; prof., dir. Sch. Health Mgmt. and Policy W.P. Carey Sch. Bus. Ariz. State U., 1996—2002, prof. Sch. Health Mgmt. and Policy, 2002—; dir. Health Sector Supply Chain Initiatives, 2002—; prin. Health Care Sector Advances, 2004—, Dean's Coun. of 100 Disting. Rsch. Scholars, 2007—. Mem. health rsch. coun. N.Y. State Dept. Health, 1977—85; vis. rsch. scholar Columbia U., NYC, 1983—84; fellow Accrediting Commn. Edn. Health Svcs. Adminstrn., 1983—84; chmn. Western Network Edn. Health Adminstrn., Berkeley, Calif., 1987—92; commr. Calif. Commn. Future Med. Edn., 1996—97; mem. Ariz. Medicaid Adv. Bd., 1990—92, Ariz. Data Adv. Bd., 1989—91, Ariz. Health Care Group Adv. Bd., 1989; Dean's Coun. 100 Disting. Rsch. scholar Ariz. State U., 2007—. Author: The Physician's Assistant, 1980; mem. editl. bd. Work and Occupations, 1975—93, Hosps. and Health Svcs. Adminstrn., 1989—92, Health Adminstrn. Press, 1991—94, Health Mgmt. Rev., 1996, Electronic Hallway, 1999; contbr. articles to profl. jours., chapters to books. Trustee Barrow Neurol. Inst., Phoenix, 1989—95; chair nat. adv. com. Investigator Awards Health Svcs. Rsch. Robert Wood Johnson Found., 1993—96. Mem.: APHA, Pharm. and Therapeutics Soc. (trustee 1999—2005, sec. 1999—2005), Assn. Univ. Health Programs Health Adminstrn. (bd. dirs. 1990—96, chmn. bd. dirs. 1994—95), Am. Sociol. Assn. Home: 11843 N 114th Way Scottsdale AZ 85259-2609 Office: Ariz State U Sch Health Mgmt and Policy WP Carey Sch Bus Tempe AZ 85287 Office Phone: 602-320-1512, 480-965-6334. Business E-Mail: gene.schneller@asu.edu.

SCHOCK, ROBERT NORMAN, geophysicist; b. Monticello, NY, May 25, 1939; s. Carl Louis and Norma Elizabeth (Greenfield) S.; m. Susan Esther Benton, Nov. 28, 1959; children: Pamela Ann, Patricia Elizabeth, Christina Benton. BS, Colo. Coll., 1961; MS, Rensselaer Poly. Inst., 1963, PhD, 1966; postgrad., Northwestern U., 1963-64. Cert. Calif. state wine judge. Jr. geophys. trainee Continental Oil Co., Sheridan, Wyo., 1960; jr. geologist Texaco In., Billings, Mont., 1961; teaching asst. Rensselaer Poly. Inst., Troy, NY, 1961-63, research asst., 1964-66; research assoc. U. Chgo., 1966-68; sr. research scientist Lawrence Livermore Nat. Lab., U. Calif., 1968—2006, group leader high pressure physics, 1972-74, sect. leader geoscis. and engring., 1974-76, div. leader earth scis., 1976-81, head dept. earth scis., 1981-87, energy program leader, 1987-92, dep. assoc. dir. for energy, 1992-98, sr. fellow Ctr. Global Security Rsch., 1998—2006. Pres. Pressure Sys. Rsch. Inc.; faculty Chabot Coll., 1969-71; dir. Alameda County Flood Control and Water Conservation Dist., 1984-86, chmn., 1985; adv. panel on geoscis. US Dept. Energy, 1985-87; chmn. adv. com. U. Calif. Energy Inst., 1992-98; rsch. adv. com. Gas Rsch. Inst., Chgo., 1995-2001; dir. studies World Energy Coun., London, 2005—; chmn. Study Group Energy Tech. in 21st Century, 1999-2004, coord. lead author intergovtl. panel on climate change, UN, 2004-07; instrumentation and facilities rev. panel NSF, 2001-04. Mem. editl. bd. Rev. Sci. Instruments, 1975-77; assoc. editor: Jour. Geophys. Rsch., 1978-80; bd. assoc. editors: 11th Lunar and Planetary Sci. Conf., 1980; mem. adv. bd. Physics and Chemistry of Minerals, 1983-97; rsch. and publs. on high pressure physics, solid state physics, physics of earth interior, rock deformation, energy R&D and energy policy. Fulbright sr. fellow U. Bonn, Germany, 1973; vis. research fellow Australian Nat. U. Canberra, 1980-81 Mem. AAAS, Am. Geophys. Union, Sigma Xi, Commonwealth of Calif. Club, Cosmos Club (Washington).

SCHOEN, RICHARD MELVIN, mathematics professor, researcher; b. Celina, Ohio, Oct. 23, 1950; s. Arnold Peter and Rosemary (Heitkamp) S.; m. Doris Helga Fischer-Colbrie, Oct. 29, 1983; children: Alan, Lucy. BS, U. Dayton, 1972; PhD, Stanford U., 1976. Lectr. U. Calif.-Berkeley, 1976-78, prof. math., 1980-85; asst. prof.

Courant Inst. NYU, 1978-80; prof. math. U. Calif.-La Jolla, 1985-87, Stanford U., 1987—. Contbr. articles to profl. jours. Recipient Bocher prize, 1989; fellow NSF, 1972, Alfred P. Sloan Found., 1979, MacArthur Found. prize, 1983, Guggenheim Found., 1996. Mem. Am. Acad. Arts and Scis., Am. Math. Soc., Nat. Acad. Sci. Office: Stanford U Mathematics Dept Stanford CA 94305 Business E-Mail: schoen@math.stanford.edu.

SCHOENER, THOMAS WILLIAM, ecologist, educator; b. Lancaster, Pa., Aug. 9, 1943; BA, Harvard Coll., 1965, PhD, 1969. Asst. prof. Harvard Coll., Cambridge, Mass., 1972-73, assoc. prof., 1973-75, U. Wash., Seattle, 1975-76, prof., 1976-80, U. Calif., Davis, 1980—, chairperson sect. evolution and ecology divsn. biol. scis., 1993-99. Mem. editl. bd. dirs. Oecologia, 1984-93; past mem. editl. bd. Evolution, Am. Naturalist, Sci., Acta Oecologia; contbr. chpts. to books, articles to profl. jours. Recipient MacArthur prize Ecol. Soc. Am., 1987; grantee NSF, 1975—, Nat. Geog. Soc., Australian Rsch. Coun., 2003-; jr. fellow Harvard U., 1969-72; Guggenheim fellow, 1992-93. Mem. NAS, Am. Acad. Arts and Scis., Am. Ornithologists Union (elective), Am. Soc. Naturalists, Ecol. Soc. Am., Am. Soc. Ichthyologists and Herpetologists, Cooper Ornithol. Soc., Am. Arachnological Soc., Soc. Study of Amphibians and Reptiles. Avocations: weightlifting, reading. Office: U Calif Sect Evolution Ecology Davis CA 95616 Office Phone: 530-752-8319. Business E-Mail: twschoener@ucdavis.edu.

SCHOENFELD, ALAN HENRY, mathematics education professor, researcher; b. NYC, July 9, 1947; s. Neil Howard and Natalie (Weinberg) S.; m. Jean Snitzer, June 14, 1970. BS in Math., Queens Coll., 1968; MS in Math., Stanford U., 1969, PhD in Math., 1973. Lectr. U. Calif., Davis, 1973-75; from asst. prof. to assoc. prof. Hamilton Coll., Clinton, NY, 1978-81, U. Rochester, NY, 1981-84; lectr. U. Calif., Berkeley, 1975-78, assoc. prof. edn., math., 1985-86, prof., 1986—, chmn. div. edn. in math., sci. and tech., 1987—98, chmn. Sch. Edn., 1994—98. Chmn. Grad. Group in Sci. and Math. Edn., U. Calif., Berkeley, 1985-87; chief organizer IV Internat. Congress Math. Edn., 1984. Author: Mathematical Problem Solving, 1985, Mathematical Association of America Notes # 1, Problem Solving, 1983; editor: Cognitive Science and Mathematics Education, 1987, A Source Book for College Mathematics Teaching, 1990, Mathematical Thinking and Problem Solving, 1994, Research in Collegiate Mathematics Education, vol. 1, 1994, vol. 2, 1996, vol. 3, 1998, vol. 4, 2000, Assessing Mathematical Proficiency, 2007, A Study of Teaching: Multiple Lenses, Multiple Views, 2008. Mem. State Calif. Math. Framework Com., 1988-90; mem. adv. panel Calif. Assessment Program, 1988—; mem. Supt.'s Math. Task Force, 1995. Grantee NSF, 1979, 85, 87, 90-92, 96-97, 2001-06, Sloan Found., 1984, 87, Spencer Found., 1983, 93. Fellow: AAAS; mem.: Nat. Rsch. Coun. (math. sci. edn. bd. task force on K-12 1986—88, bd. testing/assessment 1993—98), Nat. Bd. for Profl. Tchg. Stds. (math. panel 1990—95), Nat. Coun. Tchrs. Math. (rsch. adv. com. 1990—93, chair 1992—93, leader prins. and stds. 1997—2000), Cognitive Sci. Soc., Am. Math. Soc. (com. on edn. 1992—97), Am. Ednl. Rsch. Assn. (exec. com. Spl. Interest Group Math. Edn. 1984—86, chair publs. com. 1994—, pres. 1998—2000), Math. Assn. Am. (chmn. tchg. undergrad. math. com. 1982—89), Nat. Acad. Edn. (exec. bd. 1995—2006, v.p. 2001—06), Kappa Delta Pi (Laureate 2006). Avocations: food, wine. Home: 830 Colusa Ave Berkeley CA 94707-1839 Office: U Calif Dept Edn Berkeley CA 94720-1670

SCHOENFELD, LAWRENCE JON, real estate developer; b. LA, Nov. 30, 1945; s. Donald and Trudy Schoenfeld; m. Carol Sue Gard, Aug. 24, 1969. AA, LA Valley Coll., Van Nuys, Calif., 1963; BBA, Wichita State U., 1969, MSBA, 1970; grad., Army Med. Acad., 1976, US Army Command/Gen Staff Coll., Ft. Leavenworth, Kans., 1988. Cert. tchr., Calif.; life lic. jr. coll. tchg. credential, Calif.; lic. real estate broker (cert.) developer, Calif.; cert. hotel specialist, Marriott, 2003. Asst. treas. Advance Mortgage, LA, 1970-72; v.p. ops. Unigem Internat., LA, 1972-98; pres. C. & L. Schoenfeld Investments Inc., Manhattan Beach, Calif., 1998—. Bd. dir. The Schoenfeld Constrn. Co., South Star Wours, Uniorr Corp., Execuentre-West, Schoenfeld & Co., Customer Ground Handling Svc. Corp.; co-developer Los-Osos Mini Storage Co., Los Osos, Calif., Bay Osos, 1984, Bay Osos Mini Storage Co., 1984, El Mercadero World Trade Show, Guatemala, 1986, 97, Santiago, 1987, Bahai, 1988, Paraguay, 1989, El Mercado, Costa Rica, 1990, Panama City, 1995, Manaus, 1996, Guayaquil, 1998, Los Osos Mini Storage Co., Quito, 1991, Santa Cruz, 1993, Ecuador, 1998, Uruguay, 1999, Punta del Este, 1999, Fortaleza, Brazil, 2000, San Jose, Costa Rica, 2002, Quilto, 2003, Iquasso Falls, Brazil, 2004, Lima, Peru, 2005, Panama City, 2006, Columbia, 2007, Ecuador, 2008; pres. Accents on Beverly Hills, 1991, Accents at the Biltmore, Santa Barbara, 1995, Accents on Newport Beach, 1996, Accents on San Francisco Travelers Centrury Club, 2001, The Regis, L.A. Mem. Improvement Commn., Hermosa Beach., Calif. 1976-78. Served to maj. Med. Svc. Corps, U.S. Army, 1970-72; lt. col. USAR, 1972—. Recipient Humanitarian award, Richstone Found., 2001. Mem. South Am. Travel Assn., World Trade Assn. (assoc.), Town Hall, Wichita State U. Alumni Assn. (nat. dist. rep., mem. coun. 1992—), Res. Officers Assn., Brit. Am. C. of C., Skal Internat., Travelers Century Club, Navy Golf Club, Palos Verdes Golf Club. Jewish. Office: 8405 Pershing Dr Ste 301 Playa Del Rey CA 90293-7861 Office Fax: 310-318-7106. Personal E-mail: lccorp@earthlink.net, lccorp2@verizon.net.

SCHOENFELD, WALTER EDWIN, manufacturing executive; b. Seattle, Nov. 6, 1930; s. Max and Edna Lucille (Reinhardt) S.; m. Esther Behar, Nov. 27, 1955; children— Lea Anne, Jeffrey, Gary. BBA, U. Wash., 1952. Dir. Reading Railroad, 1964—68; v.p., dir. Sunshine Mining Co., Kellogg, Idaho, 1964-69, First N.W. Industries, Inc. (Seattle Super Sonics), 1968-79; chmn. bd., pres. Schoenfeld Industries, Inc. (diversified holding co.), 1968-93; vice chmn., acting pres., CEO, Vans, Inc., 1993-97, chmn., bd. dirs., 1997—2004; non-exec. chmn. Found. Bank, 2005—06, dir., 2005—, Aritzia, 2007—. Ptnr. Seattle Mariners Baseball Club, 1977-81, Seattle Sounders Soccer Club, 1974-79; bd. dirs. Hazel Bishop Cosmetics. Bd. dirs. Wash. China Rels. Coun., 1980—, Sterling Recreation Orgn., 1985-90; chmn. Access Long Distance of Washington; bd. govs. Weizmann Inst. Sci., Rehovot, Israel, 1980—; trustee Barbara Sinatra Children's Ctr., Eisenhower Hosp., Rancho Mirage, Calif., 1990—. With AUS, 1952-55, Korea. Recipient various service awards. Mem. Chief Execs. Orgn. (v.p., bd. dirs. 1987-93), Rainier Club, Broadmoor Golf Club, Tamarisk Country Club (Rancho Mirage, Calif.), Mission Hills Country Club, Alpha Kappa Psi. Office: 800 5th Ave Ste 4100 Seattle WA 98104

SCHOENKE, MARILYN LEILANI, foundation administrator; b. Wahiawa, Hawaii; m. Donald N. Basham; children: Neil, Steven, Leilani. BB, Corpus Christi State U. Exec. dir. Moanalua Gardens Found., Hawaii, 1994—. Exec. dir. Lawyer's Care; vol. Am. Cancer Soc. Mem. Alzheimer's Assn. (support svcs. coord., vol.), Manu O Ke Kai Canoe Club, Native Hawaiian C. of C., U.S. Tennis Assn., Hawaii Pacific Tennis Assn. Office: Moanalua Gardens Found 1352 Pineapple Pl Honolulu HI 96819-1754

SCHOESLER, MARK GERALD, state legislator; b. Ritzville, Wash., Feb. 16; s. Gerald E. and Dorothy L. (Heinemann) Schoesler; m. Ginger Schoesler; children: Veronica, Cody. AS in Agribus., Spokane CC, Wash. With Schoesler Farms, Inc., 1977—80, Fed. Crop Ins. Corp., 1977—87; self-employed farmer producing wheat, canola and cattle, 1981—; mem. Dist. 9 Wash. House of Reps., Olympia, 1992—2004, Wash. State Senate, Olympia, 2004—, Republican fl. leader, 2007—. Mem. Zion Congl. Ch. Mem.: Adams-Lincoln County Crop Improvement Assn. (past pres., v.p.), Wash. Assn. Wheat Growers (bd. dirs.), Adams County Cattlemen (dir. 1987). Republican. Protestant. Office: 110 Newhouse Bldg PO Box 40409 Olympia WA 98504-0409 Office Phone: 360-786-7620. Office Fax: 360-786-7819.*

SCHOETTLER, GAIL SINTON, former ambassador; b. LA, Oct. 21, 1943; d. James and Norma (McLellan) Sinton; children: Lee, Thomas, James; m. Donald L. Stevens, June 23, 1990. BA in Econs., Stanford U., 1965; MA in History, U. Calif., Santa Barbara, 1969, PhD in History, 1975. Businesswoman, Denver, 1975-83; exec. dir. Colo. Dept. of Personnel, Denver, 1983-86; treas. State of Colo., Denver, 1987—95, lt. gov., 1995—99; chmn. bd. Fischer Imaging Corp. U.S. amb. World Radio Comm. Conf., Istanbul, 1999-2000; bd. dirs. AspenBio, Inc., CancerVax Corp., A4S Security, Inc. Active Douglas County Bd. Edn., Colo., 1979-87, pres., 1983-87; trustee U. No. Colo., Greeley, 1981-87; pres. Denver Children's Mus., 1975-85; bd. dirs. Gunnison Ranchland Conservation Legacy, Colo. Conservation Trust, Progress Now, Ctr. for Women's Health Rsch. Decorated chevalier French Legion of Honor; recipient Disting. Alumna award U. Calif., Santa Barbara, 1987, Trailblazer award AAUW, 1997, Childrens Advocacy award Colo. Soc. Sch. Psychologists, 1997. Mem. Internat. Women's Forum (mem. bd. dirs. 1981-89, pres. 83-85), Women Execs. in State Govt. (bd. dirs. 1981-87, chmn. 1988), Leadership Denver Assn. (bd. dirs. 1987, named Outstanding Alumna 1985), Nat. Congress Lt. Govs., Stanford Alumni Assn. Democrat.

SCHOFIELD, ANTHONY WAYNE, lawyer; b. Farmington, N.Mex., Mar. 5, 1949; s. Aldred Edward and Margueriete (Knudsen) S.; m. Rebecca Ann Rosecrans, May 11, 1971; children: Josie, Matthew Paul, Peter Christian, Addie, Joshua James, M. Thomas, Jacob L., Daniel Z. BA, Brigham Young U., 1973, JD, 1976. Bar: Utah 1976, U.S. Dist. Ct. Utah 1976, U.S. Ct. Appeals (7th and 10th cirs.) 1977. Law clk. to hon. judge A. Sherman Christansen U.S. Dist. Ct. Utah, Salt Lake City, 1976-77; assoc. Ferenz, Bramhall, Williams & Gruskin, Agana, Guam, 1977-79; pvt. practice American Fork, Utah, 1979-80; assoc. Jardine, Linebaugh, Brown & Dunn, Salt Lake City, 1980-81; mem., dir. Ray, Quinney & Nebeker, Provo, Utah, 1981—93; judge 4th Jud. Dist. Ct., Provo, 1993—2007; mem. Kirton & McConkie, Orem, Utah, 2007—. Bishop Mormon Ch., American Fork, 1985-88; commr. American Fork City Planning Commn., 1980-85; trustee American Fork Hosp., 1984-93. Mem. Ctrl. Utah Bar Assn. (pres. 1987, 91). Office: Kirton & McConkie 518 West 800 North 204 Orem UT 84057 Home Phone: 801-756-3074; Office Phone: 801-426-2100. Personal E-mail: aschofield@kmclaw.com.

SCHOHL, JOSEPH, lawyer; b. 1968; children: Annie, Natalie. BA in Fin., U. Ill., 1990; JD, Columbia Law Sch., 1993; MBA, Northwestern U. Kellogg Bus. Sch., 2004. Bar: Calif. 1993, Ill. 1995. Assoc. counsel Milbank, Tweed, Hadley & McCloy, NYC, 1993—95, Sidley Austin Brown & Wood, NYC, 1995—98; corp. counsel Corp. Sec. Group Baxter Healthcare Corp., Chgo., 1998—2001, corp. counsel Transfusion Therapies Bus., 2001—03, corp. counsel Bio-Science Bus. and Transactions Group, 2004; v.p., gen. counsel, corp. sec. DaVita Inc., El Segundo, Calif., 2004—. Office: DaVita Inc 601 Hawaii St El Segundo CA 90245 E-mail: jschohl@davita.com.

SCHOLES, MYRON S., financier, former law and finance educator; b. Timmins, Ont., Can., July 1, 1941; BA, McMaster U., 1959—62, MBA, 1962—64; PhD in finance, U. Chgo., 1964—69; D (hon.), U. Paris-Dauphine, 1989, McMaster U., 1990, U. Leuven, 1998. Rsch. assoc., Ctr. for Math. Studies in Bus. and Econs. U. Chgo., 1966—67, instr. in fin., grad. sch. bus., 1967—68, assoc. prof., 1973—74, prof., 1975—79, dir., Ctr. for Rsch. in Security Prices, 1975—81, Edward Eagle Brown prof. fin., 1979—82; asst. prof. in fin. MIT Mgmt. Sch., Cambridge, 1968—72, assoc. prof., 1972—73; prof. law Stanford U., Calif., 1983—96, Frank E. Buck prof. Grad. Sch. Bus., 1983—96, sr. rsch. fellow, Hoover Instn., 1988—96, Frank E. Buck prof. emeritus fin., 1996—; mng. dir., sr. advisor Salomon Bros., 1990—93; prin. Long-Term Capital Mgmt., Greenwich, Conn., 1994—98; chmn. Oak Hill Platinum Ptnrs., Rye Brook, NY, 1999—2005; mng. ptnr. Oak Hill Capital Mgmt., 1999—2005. Bd. trustees Math. Scis. Rsch. Inst.; bd. dirs. Chgo. Mercantile Exchange, 2000—, chmn. Competitive Markets Adv. Coun., 2004—; bd. dirs. Chgo. Mercantile Exchange Holdings, 2001—, Intelligent Markets, Am Century, FEP/Constellation, UNext Inc., Salomon Swapco Inc. Contbr. articles to profl. jours. Recipient Nobel Prize for econ. scis., 1997. Mem.: Am. Fin. Assn. (v.p. 1989, pres. 1990), Econometrics Soc. Office: Arbor Investors 2775 Sand Hill Rd Ste 220 Menlo Park CA 94025-7019 Address: Oak Hill Platinum Ptnrs Reckson Exec Park 1100 King St Bldg 4 Rye Brook NY 10573 E-mail: mscholes@pacbell.net.

SCHOLTZ, ROBERT ARNO, electrical engineering educator; b. Lebanon, Ohio, Jan. 26, 1936; s. William Paul and Erna Johanna (Weigel) Scholtz; m. Laura Elizabeth McKeon, June 16, 1962; children: Michael William, Paul Andrew. BSEE, U. Cin., 1958; MSEE, U. So. Calif., 1960; PhD, Stanford U., 1964. Co-op student Sheffield Corp., Dayton, Ohio, 1953-58; MS and PHD fellow Hughes Aircraft Co., Culver City, Calif., 1958-63, sr. staff engr., 1963-78; prof. U. So. Calif., LA, 1963—. Vis. prof. U. Hawaii, 1969, 78; cons. LinCom Corp., L.A., 1975-81, Axiomatix Inc., L.A., 1980-86, JPL, Pasadena, 1985, Tech. Group, 1987-89, TRW, 1989, Pulson Comm., 1992-93, Colley-Godward, Palo Alto, 1994-97, Time Domain Corp., 2000-01. Co-author: Spread Spectrum Comm., 3 vols., 1984, Spread Spectrum Communications Handbook, 1994, Basic Concepts in Information Theory and Coding, 1994; contbr. articles to profl. jours. Pres. South Bay Cmty. Concert Orgn., Redondo Beach, Calif., 1975—79. Fellow: IEEE (bd. govs. info. theory group 1981—86, bd. govs. communication soc. 1981—83, chmn. fin. com. NTC 1977, program chmn. ISIT 1981, Leonard G. Abraham award 1983, Donald G. Fink award 1984, Sr. Paper award Signal Processing Soc. 1992, Fred Ellersick Paper award Com. Soc. 1997, Mil. Coms. Conf. award 2001, S.A. Shelkunoff prize Antennas and Propagation Soc. 2003, Eric E. Sumner award 2006); mem.: Nat. Acad. Engring. Office: U So Calif Comm Scis Inst Dept Elec Engring Los Angeles CA 90089-2565 E-mail: scholtz@usc.edu.

SCHOMP, LISA JULIANA, automotive industry executive; b. 1951; d. Ralph and Kay S.; m. Mark Wallace; children: Aaron, Tyler, Logan. From mini-maid to pres. Ralph Schomp Automotive, Littleton, Colo., 1970-88, pres., 1988—. Named 1993 Woman of Yr. Englewood (Colo.) Bus. and Profl. Women. Office: Ralph Schomp Automotive 5700 S Broadway Littleton CO 80121-8007

SCHON, ISABEL, library science specialist, educator; b. Mexico City, Jan. 19; d. Oswaldo and Anita Schon; m. Richard R. Chalquest, Oct. 7, 1977; 1 child, Vera. Student, U. Nat. Autonoma de Mex.; BS cum laude, Minn. State U., Mankato, 1971; MA in Elem. Edn., Mich. State U., 1972; PhD in Edn., U. Colo., 1974. Founding dir. ednl. media ctr. Am. Sch. Found., Mexico City, 1958-72; ednl. evaluator sch. bus. adminstrn. Nat. U. Mex., 1972; evaluator bilingual ednl. materials U. Colo., 1973; asst. prof. dept. ednl. tech./libr. sci. Ariz. State U., Tempe, 1974-79, assoc. prof., 1979-83, prof. reading edn./libr. sci., 1983-89; Barahona Ctr. Study of Books in Spanish for Children & Adolescents Calif. State U., San Marcos, 1989—2008, founding faculty prof. edn., 1989—2008; dir. Isabel Schon Internat. Ctr. Spanish Books for Youth San Diego Pub. Libr., 2009—. Adminstrv. asst. materials dissemination ctr. Kettering Found., Dayton, Ohio, 1966; evaluator Southwestern Coop. Ednl. Lab., Albuquerque, 1967, Nat. Indigenous Inst., Chiapas, Mexico, 1972; vis. prof. Am. Schs., Guayaquil and Quito, Ecuador, 1971, U. Ams., Mexico, 1972; editl. cons. Macmillan Pub. Co., 1985, 87, Holt, Rinehart & Winston Inc., 1994, Harcourt Brace & Co., 1997—, Monterey Bay Aquarium, 1997—; mem. adv. bd. Parents' Choice, 1989—, Santillana Pub. Co., 1991—94; mem. lang. adv. bd. Scholastic Inc., 1992—94. Author: numerous recommended books in Spanish for children and young adults, 1991—2000, The Best of the Latino Heritage: A Guide to the Best Juvenile Books about Latino People and Culture, 1996—2002; reviewer NEH, 1981—, Jour. Nat. Assn. Bilingual Edn., 1982—85, Am. Edn. Rsch. Jour., 1983—85, Libr. Sci. Ann., 1986—, Sch. Libr. Media Quar., 1993—95, contbg. Spanish editor Sch. Libr. Jour., 1984—87, mem. editl. bd. The New Advocate, 1995—, The Reading Tchr., 1998—, columnist Booklist (ALA), 1989—; contbr. articles to profl. jours., chapters to books. Judge ALA's Nat. Libr. Writing Competition, 1977, Arroz con Leche Children's Lit. Contest, 1994—; chair internat. bd. books for young people com. Asahi Reading Promotion Award, 1997—. Recipient Herbert W. Putnam Honor award, ALA, 1979, Grolier Found. award, 1986, Denali Press award, 1992, Nat. Book award, Women's Nat. Book Assn., 1987, Dorothy C. McKenzie award, Children's Lit. Coun. So. Calif., 2005, Dist. Alumni Achievement award, Minn. State U., 2006; named a Role Model in Edn., US Mex. Found., 1992. Avocation: tennis. Office: Isabel Schon Intl Ctr, Spnsh Bks for Yth San Diego Public Library 9005 Aero Dr San Diego CA 92123 Office Phone: 619-238-6638. Office Fax: 619-236-5878.

SCHONFELD, WILLIAM ROST, political science professor; b. NYC, Aug. 28, 1942; s. William A. and Louise R. (Rost) S.; m. Elena Beortegui, Jan. 23, 1964; children: Natalie Beortegui, Elizabeth Lynn Beortegui. Student, Cornell U., Ithaca, NY, 1960-61; BA cum laude with honors, NYU U. Heights Coll., NYC, 1964; MA, Princeton U., NJ, 1968, PhD, 1970. Research asst. Princeton U., 1966-69, research assoc., 1969-70, vis. lectr., 1970; asst. prof. polit. sci. U. Calif.-Irvine, 1970-75, assoc. prof., 1975-81, prof., 1981—, dean Sch. Social Scis., 1982—2002; sr. lectr. Fond. Nat. de Sci. Politique, Paris, 1973-74; researcher Centre de Sociologie des Organisations, Paris, 1976-78; dir. Ctr. for Study of Democracy, 2004—08. Author: Youth and Authority in France, 1971, Obedience and Revolt, 1976, Ethnographie du PS et du RPR, 1985 Recipient Disting. Teaching award U. Calif.-Irvine, 1984, Disting. Faculty Lectureship award for tchg., 1998, Daniel G. Aldrich Disting. Univ. Svc. award, 2000-01; Fulbright fellow Bordeaux, France, 1964-65; Danforth grad. fellow, 1964-69; Fulbright sr. lectr. Paris, 1973-74; NSF-CNRS Exchange of Scientists fellow Paris, 1976-78; Ford Found. grantee France, Spain, 1978-79; finalist Prof. Yr. Council for Advancement and Support of Edn., 1984; Lauds & Laurels Extraordinarious award, U. Calif.-Irvine Alumni Assn., 2002. Mem. Am. Polit. Sci. Assn., Assoc. Francaise de Sci. Pol., Phi Beta Kappa. Office: U Calif Sch Social Scis Irvine CA 92697-0001 Office Phone: 949-824-8801. Personal E-mail: wrschonf@yahoo.com. Business E-Mail: wrschonf@uci.edu.

SCHOOLEY, ROBERT T., medical educator; b. Washington, Nov. 10, 1949; s. Robert Enoch and Lelia Francis (Barnhill) S.; m. Constance Benson; children: Kimberly Dana, Elizabeth Kendall. BS, Washington and Lee U., 1970; MD, Johns Hopkins U., 1974. Diplomate Am. Bd. Internal Medicine. Intern Johns Hopkins Hosp., Balt., 1974—75, resident, 1975—76; clin. assoc. lab. clin. investigation Nat. Inst. Allergy & Infectious Disease, NIH, Bethesda, Md., 1976—77, chief clin. assoc. lab. clin. investigation, 1977—78, med. officer lab. clin. investigation, 1978—79; from instr. to assoc. prof. medicine Harvard Med. Sch., Boston, 1979—90; prof. medicine U. Colo., Denver, 1990—2005, U. Calif., San Diego, 2005—, head Divsn. Infectious Diseases, 2005—. Dir. Colo. Ctr. for AIDS Rsch., 2003—05; head divsn. infectious diseases U. Calif., San Diego, 2005—, vice chair dept. medicine, 2007—. Mem. editl. bd.: Antimicrobial Agts. and Chemotherapy, 1987—2000, Biotherapy, 1987—95, Jour. Acquired Immune Deficiency Syndromes, 1988—, Clin. and Diagnostic Lab. Immunology, 1992, assoc. editor: Clin. Infectious Diseases, 2002—; contbr. articles to profl. jours. Clin. and rsch. fellow Infectious Disease Unit, Mass. Gen. Hosp., Boston, 1979-81; rsch. fellow Medicine Harvard Med. Sch., 1979-81; recipient Bonfils-Stanton award for sci. and medicine. Fellow Infectious Disease Soc. Am.; mem. AAAS, Am. Assn. Immunologists, Am. Soc. Clin. Investigation, Assn. Am. Physicians, Omicron Delta Kappa. Office: U Calif San Diego Mail Stop 0711 9500 Gilman Ave La Jolla CA 92093 Home Phone: 858-350-9610; Office Phone: 858-822-0216. Business E-Mail: rschooley@ucsd.edu.

SCHOONOVER, MARGARET **See LEFRANC, MARGARET**

SCHOPF, JAMES WILLIAM, paleobiologist, researcher, educator; b. Urbana, Ill., Sept. 27, 1941; s. James Morton and Esther Julie (Nissen) S.; m. Julie Morgan, Aug. 7, 1965 (div. 1979); 1 child, James Christopher; m. Jane Shen, Jan. 16, 1980. AB with high honors, Oberlin Coll., 1963; A.M., Harvard U., 1965, PhD (Harvard fellow, NSF fellow), 1968. Research chemist NASA, Ames Research Center, Calif., 1967; mem. lunar sample preliminary exam. team Manned Spacecraft Center, Tex., 1968-71; asst. prof. dept. earth and space scis.

UCLA, 1968-70, assoc. prof., 1970-73, prof., 1973—, mem. Inst. Evolutionary and Environ. Biology, 1970-76, mem. Inst. Geophysics and Planetary Physics, 1973—, dean honors div. Coll. Letters and Sci., 1983-85, dir. Ctr. for Study Evolution and Origin of Life, 1985—, Sigma Xi Disting. lectr., 1976, Rubey lectr., 1976, Golden Yr. Disting. lectr., 1980, Faculty Research lectr., 1984; Sigma Xi Disting. lectr. U. Cin., 1980; Disting. lectr. Buffalo Mus. Sci., 1982; J.A. Bownocker lectr. Ohio State U., 1982, Vis. lectr. Am. Inst. Biol. Scis. Vis. Biologists Program, 1969-72; faculty rsch. learner, UCLA Acad. Senate, 1984, M.W. Haas vis. disting. prof. geology U. Kans., 1979; extraordinary vis. prof. exobiology U. Nijmegen, Netherlands, 1980-81; C. O'Neal lectr. Ohio Wesleyan U., 1982; Sandia disting. lectr. U. N.Mex., 1985; Sigma Xi disting. lectr. U. Oreg., 1985; Du Pont disting. lectr. U. Ill., 1985; R. Stanier disting. lectr. U. Calif.-Berkeley, 1987; H.P. Mangelsdorf disting. lectr. U. N.C., 1987; mem. Bot. Soc. Am. del., People's Republic China, 1978; Academia Sinica vis. research scientist, People's Republic China, 1981, 82; mem. NASA Terrestrial Bodies Sci. Working Group, 1975-76, space program adv. council NASA Life Scis. Com., 1976-78, NASA Working Group on Origins of Life, 1978-79, NASA Space Sci. Adv. Com., 1979-82, mem. NASA Life Scis. Strategic Planning Study Com., 1985—; Alan T. Waterman Award com. NSF, 1978-81; mem. working group on precambrian biostratigraphy Internat. Geol. Correlation Program, UNESCO, 1975—; mem. Working Group on Cambrian-Precambrian Boundary, 1976—; mem. adv. com. USSR and Eastern Europe, Commn. Internat. Relations NRC, 1981-85, mem. bd. earth sci. Commn. Phys. Scis., Math. and Resources, 1982-85, mem. space sci. bd., 1983-86; mem. com. on guidelines for paleontol. collecting, 1984-86, sub.-com. on evolution and diversity Commn. on Life Scis., 1986; mem. Internat. Congress Systematic and Evolutionary Biology, 1990—; mem. com. space research Internat. Council Sci. Unions; chair Gordon Rsch. Conf. Origin of Life, 1999; mem. sci. coun., Geo-bio Ctr., Ludwig-Maximilians U., 2003; lecturer and spkr. in field, 1980—. Mem. editorial bd.: Origins of Life, 1973-87, Precambrian Research, 1973-91, Evolutionary Theory, 1973-85, U. Calif. Press, 1973-82, Paleobiology, 1974-80, Geomicrobiology Jour., 1977—, Evolutionary Monographs, 1977-85, Quarterly Rev. Biology, 1988—, Artificial Life, 1993—, Astrobiology, 2001—, Geokimiya: Internat. Geochemistry, 2005—; contbr. articles to profl. jours. Bd. dirs. Brentwood Glen (Calif.) Assn., 1972-75; trustee UCLA Found., 1983-85; bd. trustees Oberlin Coll., 1992-97. Recipient N.Y. Bot. Garden award Bot. Soc. Am., 1966; Group Achievement award NASA, 1969; Outstanding Paper award Jour. Paleontology, 1971; Charles Schuchert award Paleontol. Soc., 1974; Disting. Teaching award UCLA, 1977; Alan T. Waterman award NSF, 1977; G. Hawk award U. Kans., 1979; spl. recognition diploma NASA, 1979, Group Achievement award, 1997; Outstanding Vol. in Phys. Scis. award Am. Assn. Pubs., 1983; Mary Clark Thompson medal Nat. Acad. Scis., 1986, Profl. and Scholarly Pub. award, Assn. Am. Pubs., 1983, 1992, Disting Sci. award, IGPP Ctr. for Study of Evoluton & The Origin of Life, 2000; Guggenheim fellow, 1973, John Simon Guggenheim Found. fellow, 1988; U.S. Nat. Acad. Scis. exchange scientist USSR, 1975; named one of So. Calif.'s 50 Leading Scientists of 20th Century, 1999. Fellow Geol. Soc. Am. (vice-chmn. Cordilleran sect. 1983-84, chmn. 1984-85); mem. NAS, AAAS, Bot. Soc. Am. (com. on sci. liaison with People's Republic China 1978—), Paleontol. Soc. (mem. Schuchert Award com. 1978-82), Internat. Soc. Study of Origin of Life (treas. 1977-83, nat. meeting adv. com. 1980, 83, 86, councilor, 1983—), Geochem. Soc. (nominating com. 1980-82), Soc. Study of Evolution (edn. com. 1980-83), Am. Philos. Soc., Linnean Soc. London, Internat. Assn. Plant Taxonomy, Internat. Org. Paleobotany, Psychol. Soc. Am., Am. Assn. Univ. Profs., Am. Inst. Biol. Scis., Internat. Psychol. Soc., Am. Soc. Naturalists, Soc. Econ. Paleontologists and Mineralogists, Paleontological Assn., Am. Soc. Mibrobiology, Soc. Molecular Biology and Evolution, Sigma Xi (treas. UCLA chpt. 1972-74, chpt. v.p. 1984-84, pres. 1984-85). Office: UCLA Dept Earth Space Scis Los Angeles CA 90095-0001 Office Phone: 310-825-1170. Business E-Mail: schopf@ess.ucla.edu.

SCHORR, ALAN EDWARD, librarian, publishing executive; b. NYC, Jan. 7, 1945; s. Herbert and Regina S.; m. Debra Genner, June 11, 1967; 1 son, Zebediah. BA, CUNY, 1966; MA, Syracuse U., 1967; postgrad., U. Iowa, 1967-71; MLS, U. Tex., 1973. Tchr., rsch. asst. dept. history U. Iowa, 1967-70; govt. publs. and map libr., asst. prof. Elmer E. Rasmuson Libr., U. Alaska, 1973-78; assoc. prof., dir. libr. U. Alaska, Juneau, 1978-84; prof., dean univ. libr. Calif. State U., Fullerton, 1984-86; pres. The Denali Press, Juneau, 1986—. Freelance indexer and bibliographer; vis. lectr. Birmingham (Eng.) Poly., 1981; mem. Alaska Ednl. Del. to China, 1975. Author: Alaska Place Names, 1974, 4th edit., 1991, Directory of Special Libraries in Alaska, 1975, Government Reference Books, 1974-75, 1976, 1976-77, 1978, Government Documents in the Library Literature 1909-1974, 1976, ALA RSBRC Manual, 1979, Federal Documents Librarianship 1879-1987, 1988, Hispanic Resource Directory, 1988, 3d edit., 1996, Refugee and Immigrant Resource Directory, 1990, 92, 94; editor: The Sourdough, 1974-75, Directory of Services for Refugees and Immigrants, 1987, 3d edit., 1993, Guide to Smithsonian serial publs., 1987; book reviewer, columnist: S.E. Alaska Empire, 1979-82, L.A. Times; contbr. articles to profl. jours. Mem. Auke Bay (Alaska) Vol. Fire Dept., 1978—81, Juneau Borough Libr. Adv. Com., 1981—82, Juneau Borough Cemetery Adv. Com., 1980—81, Am. Book Awards Com., 1980; chmn. program evaluation com., former chmn. facilities com., former chmn. policy com. to v.p. Juneau Bd. of Edn., 2000—; mem. Juneau Bd. Edn., 1991—94, 1995—97, 1997—2000, 2000—03, 2003—04; mem. citizens adv. coun. Juneau Empire Newspaper, 2003—. Mem. ALA (mem. reference and subscription books rev. com. 1975-86, mem. reference and adult svcs. divsn. publs. com. 1975-77, Nat. Assn. Hispanic Publs., Mudge citation commn. 1977-79, 84-86, Dartmouth Coll. Medal Commn., Governing Coun. 1977-84, mem. Dewey medal com. 1984-85, Denali Press award), Alaska Libr. Assn. (mem. exec. bd. 1974-75, mem. nominating com. 1977-79), Pacific N.W. Libr. Assn. (rep. publs. com. 1973-75), Assn. Coll. and Rsch. Libs. (mem. publ. com. 1976-80), Spl. Librs. Assn. (assoc. editor geography and map divsn. bull. 1975-76), Internat. Assn. Ind. Pubs (bd. dirs. 1990-92), True North Fed. Credit Union (bd. dirs. 1997-, treas. 2001-2002, vice chmn., 2002-04, chmn., 2004-), PEN Ctr. USA West, Explorers Club N.Y., Wash. Athletic Club (Seattle). Office: Denali Press PO Box 1535 Juneau AK 99802

SCHORR, S. L., lawyer; b. NYC, Feb. 19, 1930; s. Charles and Clara (Lerech) S.; m. Eleanor Daru, Mar. 23, 1956; children: Lewis, Andrew, Emily, Roberta. Student, L.I. U., 1948-50; LLB, Bklyn. Law Sch., 1953. Bar: N.Y. 1955, Ariz. 1962, U.S. Dist. Ct. Ariz. 1962, U.S. Supreme Ct. 1979. Planning commr. Pima County, Tucson, 1959-62; asst. city mgr. Tucson, 1962-63; ptnr. Lewis and Roca, Tucson, 1988—. Co-chair Continuing Legal Edn. Seminar on Ballot Box Zoning, U. Ariz., 1991, Ariz. State Bar Continuing Legal Edn. Seminar on Land Use Regulation and Litigation, 1977, 86, 89, 95. Bd. dirs. Pima Coll., 1966-67, So. Ariz. Leadership Coun., 1997—; mem. Commn. on Improved Govtl. Mgmt., Tucson, 1974-77, Gov.'s Econ. Planning and Devel. Adv. Bd., Phoenix, 1983-85, Regional Trans. Authority,2003-09; Gov.'s Task Force on Seriously Mentally Ill, Phoenix, 1989-91; Ariz. State Transp. Bd., 2003-2009. Mem. Ariz. Bar Assn., Pima County Bar Assn. Democrat. Office: Lewis Roca 1 S Church Ave Ste 700 Tucson AZ 85701-1611 Office Phone: 520-622-2090.

SCHOTT, STEPHEN C., professional sports team executive; b. Santa Clara, Calif. m. Patricia Schott; children: Lisa, Stephen E., Kristen. Grad., Santa Clara U., 1960. CEO, owner Citation Homes, Award Homes; co-owner, mng. ptnr. Oakland (Calif.) Athletics, 1995—. Advisor athletic dept. Bronco Bench, Santa Clara U. Active Stanford-Amdahl Read to Succeed program; dir. Santa Clara County Role Model program; founding mem. Alexis de Tocqueville Soc.; regent Bellarmine Prep; past chmn. bd. St. Francis H.S. Found.; bd. trustees Santa Clara U.; bd. dirs. Los Altos Tomorrow. Named Disting. Alumnus, Santa Clara U., 1989. Mem. Nat. Assn. Home Builders. Office: Oakland Athletics 7677 Oakport St Ste 200 Oakland CA 94621-1933

SCHOTTENHEIMER, MARTY (MARTIN EDWARD SCOTTENHEIMER), former professional football coach; b. Canonsburg, Pa., Sept. 23, 1943; m. Patricia Schottenheimer; children: Kristen, Brian BA in Eng., U. Pitts., 1964. Profl. football player Buffalo Bills, 1965-68, Boston Patriots, 1969-70, Pitts. Steelers, 1971, Portland Storm, World League Football, 1974; real estate developer Miami and Denver, 1971-74; linebackers coach NY Giants, 1975-77, defensive coord., 1977; linebackers coach Detroit Lions, 1978-79; defensive coord. Cleve. Browns, 1980-84, head coach, 1985-88, Kans. City Chiefs, 1989-99, Wash. Redskins, 2001, San Diego Chargers, 2002—07; tv analyst ESPN, 1999—2000. Motivational spkr. IMG Speakers Bureau. Named Coach of the Year, UPI/AFC, 1995, AP, 2004, Pro Football Weekly, 2004.

SCHOTTLAENDER, BRIAN E.C., university librarian; BA in German Studies, U. Tex., Austin, 1974; MSLS, Ind. U., 1980. Past various libr. positions at Firma Otto Harrassowitz, Wiesbaden, Germany, Ind. U., U. Ariz.; from asst. head cataloging dept. to asst. univ. libr. tech. svc. UCLA, 1984—93, assoc. univ. libr. for collections and tech. svc., 1993—99; univ. libr. U. Calif., San Diego, 1999—. ALA rep. to internat. Joint Steering Com. for Revision Anglo-Am. Cataloguing Rules, 1995—2001; chair Program Coop. Cataloguing Libr. Congress, 1997—98; chair Pacific Rim Digital Alliance, 1999—2001, San Diego Libr. Circuit, 1999—. Editor: Retrospective Conversion: History, Approaches, Considerations, 1992. Sr. fellow Palmer Sch. Libr. Sci., Long Island U., 1995. Mem.: Assn. Rsch. Libr. (bd. dir. 2001—, pres. 2006—07), ALA (bd. dir. Assoc. Libr. Collections and Tech. Svc. 1996—, pres. Assoc. Libr. Collections and Tech. Svc. 2003—, recipient Margaret Mann Citation award 2001), Beta Phi Mu. Office: Adminstrv Office Geisel Libr Univ Calif 9500 Gilman Dr #0175G La Jolla CA 92093-0175 Office Phone: 858-534-3060. E-mail: becs@ucsd.edu.

SCHOVILLE, DENNIS A(RNOLD), lawyer; b. Richland Ctr., Wis., May 31, 1945; BS, U. Wis., 1967; JD with Distinction, Ill. Inst. Tech., 1973; LLM, Northwestern U., 1974. Bar: Wis. 1973, Ill. 1973, U.S. Dist. Ct. (no. dist.) Ill. 1973, Calif. 1974, U.S. Dist. Ct. (so. dist.) Calif. 1974, U.S. Ct. Appeals (9th cir.) 1985, U.S. Ct. Claims. Ptnr. Schoville & Arnell, LLP, San Diego. Capt. U.S. Army, 1968-73. Recipient Broderick award for professionalism, integrity and ethics, 1996; named Consumer Attys. San Diego Trial Lawyer of the Yr., 1995, 99. Mem. ABA, ATLA, Am. Coll. Trial Lawyers, Am. Bd. Trial Advocates (nat. bd. dirs., past pres. San Diego chpt.), Consumer Attys. San Diego (past pres., Trial Advocacy award 2005, Consumer Adv. of Yr. award 2005), Ill. State Bar Assn., State Bar Wis., State Bar Calif., San Diego County Bar Assn. (chair jud. evaluation com. 2006), San Diego Trial Lawyers Assn. (Outstanding Trial Advocacy award-civil 1984, 89, 94), Am. Inns of Ct. (sr. master), DFC Soc. (gen. counsel, nat. dir.). Office: Schoville Arnell Llp 2404 Broadway San Diego CA 92102-2022 Office Phone: 619-232-9901.

SCHRADER, KURT, United States Representative from Oregon, former state senator; b. Bridgeport, Conn., Oct. 19, 1951; m. Martha Schrader; 4 children. BA, Cornell U., Ithaca, NY, 1973; BS, U. Ill., 1975, DVM, 1977. Veterinarian, owner, mgr. Clackamas County Vet. Clinic, Oregon County, Oreg., West Linn, Oreg.; farmer; rsch. analyst to Gov. State of Alaska; mem. Oreg. House of Reps. from Dist. 23, 1997—2003. Oreg. State Senate from Dist. 20, 2003—08, US Congress from 5th Oreg. Dist., 2009—. Mem. emergency bd. Oreg. Senate, co-chair joint ways and means com., 2005. Past chair Canby Planning Commn.; past mem. Mayor's Future Focus Task Force, Canby; past mem. bd. dirs. South Clackamas Rec. Dist.; mem. Clackamas Rec. Task Force; mem. bd. dirs. Blue Heron Rec. Dist. Recipient Disting. Leadership by Cmty. Planner award, Am. Planning Assn. Mem.: Am. Assn. Equine Practitioners, Oreg. Vet. Assn., Am. Vet. Med. Assn., Canby C. of C., Oregon City C. of C., Oreg. Farm Bur., Nat. Fedn. Ind. Bus. Democrat. Office: US Congress 1419 Longworth House Office Bldg Washington DC 20515-3705 also: Dist Office 494 State St Ste 210 Salem OR 97302 Office Phone: 202-225-5711, 503-588-9100. Office Fax: 202-225-5699, 503-588-5517.*

SCHRADER, LAWRENCE EDWIN, plant physiologist, educator; b. Atchison, Kans., Oct. 22, 1941; s. Edwin Carl and Jenna Kathryn (Tobiason) S.; m. Elfriede J. Massier, Mar. 14, 1981 BS, Kans. State U., 1963; PhD, U. Ill., 1967; grad., Inst. Ednl. Mgmt., Harvard U., 1991. Asst. prof. dept. agronomy U. Wis., Madison, 1969-72, assoc. prof., 1972-76, prof., 1976-84; prof., head dept. agronomy U. Ill., Urbana, 1985-89; dean Coll. Agr. and Home Econs. Wash. State U., Pullman, 1989-94, prof. dept. horticulture, 1994—. Chief competitive rsch. grants office Dept. Agr., Washington, 1980-81; trustee, treas. Agrl. Satellite Corp., 1991-94. Contbr. chpts. to books, articles to profl. jours. Active Consortium for Internat. Devel., 1989-94, chair fin. com., vice chair exec. com., 1990-92, trustee 1989-94; mem. exec. com. Coun. Agrl. Heads of Agr., 1992-94. Capt., Rsch. biochemist, US Army, 1967-69. Recipient Soybean Researchers Recognition award 1983, Disting. Service award in Agriculture Kansas State U., 1987; Romnes Faculty fellow U. Wis., 1979 Fellow AAAS (steering group sect. agr. 1991-95, chair-elect sect. on agr., food and renewable resources 1995-96, chmn. 1996-97, past chmn. 1997-98, coun. mem. 1997-98), Am. Soc. Agronomy, Crop Sci. Soc. Am.; mem. Internat. Soc. for Hort. Sci., Am. Soc. for Hort. Sci., Am. Soc. Plant Biologists (sec. 1983-85, pres.-elect 1986, pres. 1987), Am. Chem. Soc., Coun. for Agrl. Sci. and Tech., Blue Key, Sigma Xi, Gamma Sigma Delta (Outstanding Alumnus award, 2005), Phi Kappa Phi, Phi Eta Sigma, Alpha Zeta (named to Centennial Honor Roll 1997). Methodist. Home: 3504 Crestview Rd Wenatchee WA 98801-9668 Office: Wash State U Tree Fruit Rsch & Extension Ctr 1100 N Western Ave Wenatchee WA 98801-1230 Home Phone: 509-662-7301; Office Phone: 509-663-8181 x265. Business E-Mail: schrader@wsu.edu.

SCHRADER, MARTHA, state legislator; m. Kurt Schrader; 5 children. BA in Sci., Cornell U.; M in Entomology, U. Ill.; M in Ed., Portland State U.; PhD coursework in Pub. Admin. & Policy, Portland State U. Hatfield Sch. Govt.; graduated, NY U. Co. Leadership Inst., Portland State U. Exec. Leadership Inst. Farmer; former chief legis. analyst Congressman Kurt Schrader; sr. fellow Am. Leadership Forum; commr. Clackamas Co., 2003—09; mem. Dist. 20 Oreg. State Senate, 2009—. Democrat. Office: 900 Court St NE S-425 Salem OR 97301 Office Phone: 503-986-1720. Business E-Mail: sen.marthaschrader@state.or.us.

SCHRADER, WILLIAM P., organization executive, farmer; b. Phoenix; m. Bondena; children: Alissa Schrader Urshel, William P. Jr., Larry, Travis. Student, Ariz. State U. Bd. dirs. Salt River Project, Phoenix, 1964-90, v.p. bd., 1990-94, pres., 1994—. Pres. Schrader Farms, Inc. Bd. dirs. Greater Phoenix Econ. Coun., Groundwater Users Adv. Coun.; mem. Maricopa C.C.'s Found., East Valley Partnership, Scottsdale (Ariz.) Mcpl. Corp.; former mayor and mem. city coun. City of Scottsdale; 1st chmn. Parada del Sol, Scottsdale Rodeo. Named to Scottsdale Hall of Fame; named Citizen of Yr., City of Scottsdale. Mem. Am. Pub. Power Assn., Am. Mgmt. Assn., Nat. Water Resources Assn., Colorado River Water Users Assn., Scottsdale C. of C., Scottsdale Jr. C. of C. (life, Disting. Svc. award), Scottsdale Charros (life), White Mountain Country Club, Ariz. Club, Mesa Country Club (Ariz.). Methodist. Home: 5611 E Calle Camelia Phoenix AZ 85018-4663 Office: Salt River Project 1521 N Project Dr Tempe AZ 85281

SCHRADY, DAVID ALAN, civilian military employee, educator; b. Akron, Ohio, Nov. 11, 1939; s. Marvin G. and Sheila A. (O'Neill) S.; m. Mary E. Hilt, Sept. 1, 1962; children: Peter, Patrick, Matthew. BS, Case Inst. Tech., 1961, MS, 1963, PhD, 1965. Prof., chmn. Naval Postgrad. Sch., Monterey, Calif., 1974-76, dean acad. planning, 1976-80, provost and acad. dean, 1980-87, prof. ops. rsch., 1988—, Disting. prof., ops. rsch. educator, 1995—. Vis. prof. Cranfield Inst. Tech./Royal Mil. Coll. of Sci., Shrivenham, Eng., fall 1987-spring 88. Contbr. articles to profl. jours. Recipient Goodeve medal Ops. Rsch. Soc., U.K., 1992, Navy Disting. Civilian Svc. medal, 2006, Jancinto Steinhardt Memorial award, 2006. Fellow: Inst. for Ops. Rsch. and the Mgmt. Scis., Mil. Ops. Rsch. Soc., (pres. 1978—79, Wanner medal 1984); mem.: Internat. Fedn. Ops. Rsch. Socs. (hon. treas. 1988—97), Ops. Rsch. Soc. Am. (pres. 1983—84, Kimball medal 1994). Avocations: guitar, motor sports. Office: Naval Postgrad Sch Dept Ops Rsch Monterey CA 93943-5000 Business E-Mail: dschrady@nps.edu.

SCHRAG, PETER, editor, writer; b. Karlsruhe, Germany, July 24, 1931; arrived in U.S., 1941, naturalized, 1953; s. Otto and Judith (Haas) S.; m. Melissa Jane Mowrer, June 9, 1953 (div. 1969); children: Mitzi, Erin Andrew; m. Diane Divoky, May 24, 1969 (div. 1981); children: David Divoky, Benaiah Divoky; m. Patricia Ternahan, Jan. 1, 1988. AB cum laude, Amherst Coll., 1953. Reporter El Paso (Tex.) Herald Post, 1953-55; asst. sec., asst. dir. publs. Amherst Coll., 1955-66, instr. Am. Studies, 1960-64; assoc. edn. editor Sat. Rev., 1966-68, exec. editor, 1968-69; editor Change mag., 1969-70; editor at large Saturday Rev., 1969-72; contbg. editor Saturday Review/Education, 1972-73; editl. adv. bd. The Columbia Forum, 1972-75; editl. bd. Social Policy, 1971—; contbg. editor More, 1974-78, Inquiry, 1977-80, The Am. Prospect, 1995—; editl. page editor Sacramento Bee and McClatchy Newspapers, 1978-96, contbg. editor, 1996—. Vis. lectr. U. Mass. Sch. Edn., 1970-72; fellow in profl. journalism Stanford U., Palo Alto, Calif., 1973-74; lectr. U. Calif., Berkeley, 1974-78, 90—; Pulitzer Prize juror, 1988-89; vis. scholar U. Calif. Inst. Govtl. Studies, Berkeley, 1998—. Author: Voices in the Classroom, 1965, Village School Downtown, 1967, Out of Place in America, 1971, The Decline of the Wasp, 1972, The End of the American Future, 1973, Test of Loyalty, 1974, (with Diane Divoky) The Myth of the Hyperactive Child, 1975, Mind Control, 1978, Paradise Lost: California's Experience, America's Future, 1998, Final Test: The Battle for Adequacy in America's Schools, 2003, California: America's High-Stakes Experiment, 2006; contbr. articles to profl. publs. Adv. com. Student Rights Project, NY Civil Liberties Unon, 1970-72; mem. Com. Study History, 1958-72; trustee Emma Willard Sch., 1967-69; bd. dirs. Park Sch., Oakland, Calif., 1976-77, Ctr. for Investigative Reporting, 1979-81, Ed Source, 1998—; bd. adv. Pub. Policy Inst. Calif. Guggenheim fellow, 1971-72; Nat. Endowment for Arts fellow, 1976-77 Office: 5835 Colton Blvd Oakland CA 94611-2204 Business E-Mail: pschrag@sacbee.com.

SCHRECK, GEORGE CHARLES, lawyer; BS, Babson Coll.; JD, MBA, Boston U. Bar: Tex. 1982, Oreg. 1988. Dir. comml. and legal activities Pacificorp. Mem. ABA. Office: Ste 1700 825 NE Multnomah St Portland OR 97232-2135

SCHRENK, GARY DALE, foundation executive; b. San Jose, Calif., Apr. 29, 1949; s. Robert Shepard and Katherine Mildred (Grant) S.; m. Rhonda Lynn King, Oct. 9, 1981 (div. Jan. 1989); children: Stephen, Kristen, James. BA in Comm., Am. U., 1970; M in Nonprofit Mgmt., Regis U., 2002. TV dir. Sta. WTOP (now WUSA), Washington, 1971-73, Sta. KBTV (now KUSA), Denver, 1973-75; with Denver Area Boy Scouts Am., 1975-80; regional dir. St. Jude Children's Rsch. Hosp., Memphis, 1980-83; dir. devel. Denver Art Mus., 1983-85; asst. dir. devel. The Children's Hosp., Denver, 1985-87; pres. North Colo. Med. Ctr. Found., Greeley, 1987—2007; dir. devel. Nat. Found. Dentistry for the Handicapped, Denver, 2007—. Dir., instr. Fast Start Course, 1985—; pres. Monfort Children's Clinic, Greeley, Colo., 1994—2001. Pres. Vision Together, Weld County, Colo., 1994—95; chmn., founding dir. Weld Citizen Action Network, 1995—98, 2000—02; founding dir. First Steps Weld County, 1993—99; chmn. Weld Cmty. Health Coalition, 1992—98; bd. dirs. North Colo. Health Alliance, 2002—06; chmn. pub. support com. Team Colo. ARC, 1997—2004; regional svc., area 2 public support com. ARC, 2004—06, bd. dirs. Centennial chpt., 2003—08. Recipient Disting. Citizen award Highlanders, Denver, 1974 Mem. Assn. Fundraising Profls. (nat. found. bd. 1998-2003, nat. assembly 1994-98, bd. dirs. Colo. chpt. 1979-2000, 03-, pres. 1984, internat. bd. dirs. 2004-07, Colo. Outstanding Devel. Profl. 2004), Colo. Assn. Nonprofit Orgns. (founding dir. 1987-92), Rotary, Tahosa Alumni Assn. (past pres., past chair). Methodist. Avocation: golf. Office: Nat Found Dentistry Handicapped 1800 15th St Ste 100 Denver CO 80202 Office Phone: 303-534-5360. Business E-Mail: gschrenk@nfdh.org.

SCHRIER, ROBERT WILLIAM, physician, educator; b. Indpls., Feb. 19, 1936; s. Arthur E. and Helen M. Schrier; m. Barbara Lindley, June 14, 1959; children: David, Debbie, Douglas, Derek, Denise. BA, Depauw U., Greencastle, Ind., 1957; DSc (hon.), DePauw U., Greencastle, Ind., 2004; MD, Ind. U., 1962; DSc (hon.), U. Colo., 1996, Silesian Acad. Medicine, Katowice, Poland, 1997. Intern Marion County Hosp., Ind., 1962; resident U. Wash., Seattle, 1963-65; asst. prof. U. Calif. Med. Ctr., San Francisco, 1969—72, assoc. dir. renal divsn., 1971-72, assoc. prof., 1972; prof., head renal disease U. Colo. Sch. Med., Denver, 1972-92, prof., chmn. dept. medicine, 1976—. Editor 45 textbooks in internal medicine, geriat., drug usage, and kidney disease; contbr. over 800 sci. articles to profl. jours. Pres. Western Soc. Clin. Investigation, 1981, Nat. Kidney Found., 1984-86. With US Army, 1966—69. Recipient David Hume award Nat. Kidney Found., 1987, Louis Pasteur medal U. Strasburg, 1987, Mayo Soley award Western Soc. Clin. Investigation, 1989, Robert H. Williams award Assn. Profs. Medicine, 1996, Torchbearer award 1997, Edward N. Gibbs Meml. award NY Acad. Medicine, 2000, Alexander von Humboldt Rsch award 2004, Grand Hamdan Internat. Med. Scis. award 2004. Mem. ACP (master, John Phillips award 1992), Am. Soc. Nephrology (treas. 1979-81, pres. 1983, John Peters award 1997), Internat. Soc. Nephrology (treas. 1981-90, v.p. 1990-95, pres. 1995-97, Jean Hamburger award 2003), Am. Clin. and Climatol. Assn. (v.p. 1986), Assn. Am. Physicians (pres. 1994-95, Francis Blake award 1995), Western Assn. Physicians (pres. 1982), Inst. of Medicine of NAS, Alpha Omega Alpha. Achievements include research contributions centered on the pathogenesis of acute renal failure, genetic renal disorders, mechanisms of cell injury, diabetic nephropathy and renal and hormonal control of body fluid volume; advancement of a unifying hypothesis of sodium and water regulation in health and disease which has stimulated world-wide interest in the medical science community. Office: Univ Colo Health Scis Ctr Renal Divsn C281 Aurora Arvada CO 80004 Business E-Mail: Robert.Schrier@uchsc.edu, robert.schrier@ucdenver.edu.

SCHRIER, STANLEY LEONARD, hematologist, educator; b. NYC, Jan. 2, 1929; s. Harry and Nettie (Schwartz) S.; m. Peggy Helen Pepper, June 6, 1953; children: Rachel, Leslie, David. AB, U. Colo., 1949; MD, Johns Hopkins U., 1954. Diplomate Am. Bd. Internal Medicine (chmn. subsplty. bd. hematology). Intern Osler Med. Service, Johns Hopkins Hosp., 1954-55; resident U. Mich., Ann Arbor, 1955-56, U. Chgo. Hosp., 1958-59; sr. asst. surgeon USPHS, 1956-58; instr. medicine Stanford Sch. Medicine, Calif., 1959-60, asst. prof. medicine, 1960-63, assoc. prof., 1963-72, prof. medicine, 1972-95, chief divsn. hematology, 1968-94, prof. medicine emeritus, hematology, 1996—. Vis. scientist Weizmann Inst., Rehovot, Israel, 1967-68; vis. prof. Oxford U., Eng., 1975-76, Hebrew U., Jerusalem, 1982-83 John and Mary Markle scholar, 1961; recipient Kaiser award Stanford U., 1972, Kaiser award, 1974, 75, David Rytand award, 1982, Eleanor Roosevelt Union Internationale Contre le Cancer award, 1975-76, Albion Walter Hewlett award, 1996, Walter J. Gores award, 2002. Fellow ACP; mem. Am. Soc. Hematology (pres. 2004), Am. Physiol. Soc., Soc. Exptl. Biology and Medicine, Am. Soc. Clin. Investigation, Western Assn. Physicians, Assn. Am. Physicians. Democrat. Jewish. Office: Stanford U Sch Medicine Rm 1155 MC 5156 269 Campus Dr Palo Alto CA 94305-5156 E-mail: sschrier@stanford.edu.*

SCHROCK, THEODORE R., surgeon; b. Berne, Ind., Oct. 21, 1939; s. N.J. and M.A. Schrock; married. AB, U. Calif., San Francisco, 1961, MD, 1964. Diplomate Am. Bd. Surgery. Intern U. Calif. Hosps., San Francisco, 1964-65, resident, 1965-67, 69-71; fellow Mass. Gen. Hosp., Boston, 1967-69; chmn. dept. surgery U. Calif. San Francisco Med. Ctr., 1993-99, J. Englebert Dunphy prof. surgery, 1998—, assoc. dean clin. svcs., chief med. officer, 1999—. Fellow ACS; mem. Am. Gastroenterological Assn., Am. Soc. Colon and Rectal Surgery, Am. Soc. Gastroenterological Endoscopy, Am. Surg. Assn., Soc. Surgery Alimentary Tract. Office: UCSF Campus Box 0296 500 Parnassus Ave San Francisco CA 94143-0296

SCHRODER, DIETER KARL, electrical engineering educator; b. Lübeck, Germany, June 18, 1935; arrived in U.S., 1964; s. Wilhelm and Martha (Werner) S.; m. Beverley Claire (Parchment), Aug. 4, 1961; children: Mark, Derek. BS, McGill U., Montreal, Que., Can., 1962, MS, 1964; PhD, U. Ill., 1968. Sr. engr. rsch. and devel. sect. Westinghouse Electric Corp., Pitts., 1968-73; fellow engr. rsch. and devel. sect. Westinghouse Electric Corp., Pitts., 1973-77, adv. engr., 1977-79, mgr., 1979-81; prof. elec. engring. Ariz. State U., 1981—. Rsch. Inst. Solid State Physics, Freiburg, Fed. Republic Germany, 1978-79. Author: Advanced MOS Devices, 1987, Semiconductor Material and Device Characterization, 2006; patentee in electrical field; contbr. articles to profl. jour. Life Fellow IEEE (life, disting. nat. lectr. 1993-2006); mem. Electrochem. Soc., Sigma Xi, Eta Kappa Nu. Mem. Baha'i Faith. Home: 10572 E Fireweed Dr Scottsdale AZ 85255-1911 Office: Ariz State U Dept Elec Engring Tempe AZ 85287-5706 Office Phone: 480-965-6621. Business E-Mail: schroder@asu.edu.

SCHROEDER, GERALD FRANK, retired state supreme court justice; b. Boise, Idaho, Sept. 13, 1939; s. Frank Frederick and Josephine Ivy (Lucas) S.; children: Karl Casteel, Erich Frank. BA magna cum laude, Coll. of Idaho (now Albertson Coll. of Idaho), 1961; JD, Harvard U., 1964. Bar: Idaho 1965. Assoc. Moffatt, Thomas, Barrett & Blanton, Boise, 1965—66; pvt. practice Boise, 1966—67; asst. U.S. atty. Dept. Justice, Boise, 1967—69; judge Ada County Probate Ct., Boise, 1969—71; magistrate State of Idaho, Boise, 1971—75; dist. judge U.S. Dist. Ct. (4th dist.) Idaho, 1975—95; justice Idaho Supreme Ct., 1995—2007, chief justice, 2004—07. Instr. Boise Bar Rev., 1973—; adj. faculty law Boise State U., 1986—95; former mem. Gov. Coun. on Crime and Delinquency. Author: Idaho Probate Procedure, 1971, (Novel) Triangle of the Sons-Phenomena, 1983; contbr. chpt. to history text. Adminstrv. and dist. judge 4th dist. State of Idaho, 1985—95; Bd. dirs. Boise Philharm. Assn., 1979—81. Fellow Toll fellow, Nat. Coun. State Govt., 1990. Mem.: Idaho Bar Assn., Boise Racquet and Swim Club (pres. bd. dirs. 1991—93). Home Phone: 208-375-6139; Office Phone: 208-334-3324. Business E-Mail: gschroeder@isc.state.io.us.

SCHROEDER, JULIAN IVAN, biology professor; b. Summit, NJ, June 11, 1958; s. Manfred Robert and Anny (Menschik) S.; m. Marion G. Spors, Aug. 9, 1991; children: Julia Sofia K., Nicola A.J. Dr. rer. nat., U. Gottingen, Max Planck Inst., 1987. Postdoctoral rschr. dept. physiology UCLA Sch. Medicine, 1988-90; from asst. to prof. dept. biology U. Calif. San Diego, La Jolla, 1990-2000, Novartis Endowed chair in plant scis., 2000—. Dir. U. Calif. San Diego Plant Sys. Biology Grad. Tng. Program, La Jolla, 2005—, N.Am. arabidopsis steering com, 2007—. Contbr. articles to profl. jours. Recipient Heinz Meier Leibnitz prize, Deutsche Forschungs Gemeinschaft, 1984, Presdl. Young Investigator award NSF, 1991, Blasker award in environ. sci. and engring., San Diego Found., 2001; named Highly Cited Rschr., Inst. for Sci. Info., 2002; vis. scholar guest prof., ETH Zurich, 2005; Alexander von Humboldt fellow, 1988, 1996. Fellow AAAS; mem. Biophys. Soc., Am. Assn. Plant Biologists (Charles Albert Shull award 1997). Achievements include identification of ion channels in higher plant cells, characterization of their functions and regulation in membrane signal transduction and drought stress signaling; cloning and functional roles of mineral nutrient and heavy metal transport and detoxifying enzymes in plants. Office: U Calif San Diego Div Biology Ctr Molec Gene 9500 Gilman Dr La Jolla CA 92093-0116 Home Phone: 858-459-3097; Office Phone: 858-534-7759.

SCHROEDER, KENNETH L., electronics executive; b. 1946; BSEE, U. Wis.; MBA, U. Pa. Gen. mgr. constrn. sys. divsn. Spectra-Physics; ops. mgr. computer group Hewlett-Packard; pres., COO Genus, Inc.; various KLA-Tencor Corp., San Jose, Calif., pres., COO, 1991-99, CEO, 1999—. Bd. dirs. SEMI, GaSonics Internat. Office: KLA Tencor Corp 160 Rio Robles San Jose CA 95134 Fax: 408-875-3030.

SCHROEDER, MARY MURPHY, federal judge; b. Boulder, Colo., Dec. 4, 1940; d. Richard and Theresa (Kahn) Murphy; m. Milton R. Schroeder, Oct. 15, 1965; children: Caroline Theresa, Katherine Emily. BA, Swarthmore Coll., 1962; JD, U. Chgo., 1965; LLD (hon.), Swarthmore Coll., 2006. Bar: Ill. 1966, DC 1966, Ariz. 1970. Trial atty. US Dept. Justice, Washington, 1965—69; law clk. to Hon. Jesse Udall Ariz. Supreme Ct., 1970; mem. Lewis & Roca, Phoenix, 1971—75; judge Ariz. Ct. Appeals, Phoenix, 1975—79, US Ct. Appeals (9th cir.), Phoenix, 1979—, chief judge, 2000—07. Vis. instr. Ariz. State U. Coll. Law, 1976—78. Contbr. articles to profl. jours. Recipient Disting. Achievement award, Ariz. State U. Coll. of Public Programs. Mem.: ABA (Margaret Brent award 2001), Am. Judicature Soc., Am. Law Inst. (coun. mem.), Fed. Bar Assn., Ariz. Bar Assn. (James A. Walsh Outstanding Jurist award 2004), Soroptimists. Office: US Ct Appeals 9th Cir US Courthouse Ste 610 401 W Washington St SPC-54 Phoenix AZ 85003-2156 Fax: 602-322-7320. E-mail: mary_schroeder@ca9.uscourts.gov.

SCHROEDER, MICHAEL JOHN, lawyer; b. Grosse Pointe, Mich., Mar. 29, 1956; s. Paul James and Dessa Marie (Cheyovich) S.; 1 child, Sara. BA, U. So. Calif., LA, 1979, JD, 1982. Bar: Calif. 1982, Hawaii 1987, U.S. Dist. Ct. (cen., ea., no. and so. dists.) Calif. 1987, U.S. Ct. Appeals (9th cir.) 1987, U.S. Dist. Ct. Hawaii 1990, U.S. Supreme Ct. 1990. Assoc. Wyman, Bautzer, Christensen, Kuchel & Silberg, Newport Beach, Calif., 1982-87; ptnr. Case, Schroeder, Knowlson, Mobley & Burnett, Newport Beach, Calif., 1987-90; of counsel Hart, King & Coldren, Santa Ana, Calif., 1991—2005, Carlton, DiSante & Freudenberger, Irvine, Calif., 2002—; pvt. practice Santa Ana, 2006—. Bd. dirs. Legion Lex., U. So. Calif. Law Sch., Los Angeles, 1983—; gen. counsel Calif. Chiropractic Assn., Sacramento, 1983-91. Editor in chief Jour. Major Tax Planning, 1980-82, Jour. Computer/Law, 1980-82. Del. White Ho. Conf. on Productivity, San Diego, 1983; mem. George Deukmejian's Govt. Efficiency Team, Sacramento, 1982; pres. Calif. Rep. Assembly, 1991-93; mem. exec. com. Calif. Rep. Party, treas., 1993-95, vice-chmn., 1995-97, chmn., 1997-99. Mem. Calif. Bar Assn., Hawaii Bar Assn., Orange County Bar Assn. Republican. Roman Catholic. Avocations: travel, photography, whitewater rafting. Office: 1851 E First St Ste 1160 Santa Ana CA 92705 Office Phone: 714-647-6488.

SCHROEDER, STEVEN ALFRED, medical educator; b. NYC, July 26, 1939; s. Arthur Edward and Norma (Scheinberg) Schroeder; m. Sally B. Ross, Oct. 21, 1967; children: David Arthur, Alan Ross. BA, Stanford U., 1960; MD, Harvard U., 1964; LHD (hon.), Rush U., 1994; DSc (hon.), Boston U., 1996, U. Mass. Med. Ctr., 1997, Georgetown U., 2000; DSc, Med. Coll. Wis., 2002; DHL (hon.), U. Medicine Dentistry NJ, 2003. Diplomate Am. Bd. Internal Medicine. Intern and resident in internal medicine Harvard Med. Svc., Boston City Hosp., 1964—66, 1968—70; asst. prof., then assoc. prof. George Washington Med. Ctr., Washington, 1971—76; vis. prof. St. Thomas' Hosp. Med. Sch., London, 1982—83; prof. medicine, chief div. gen. internal medicine, mem. Inst. Health Policy Studies U. Calif., San Francisco, 1976—90; pres., CEO Robert Wood Johnson Found., Princeton, NJ, 1990—2002; clin. prof. medicine U. of Medicine and Dentistry N.J., 1990—2002; disting. prof. health and health care U. Calif., San Francisco, 2003—, dir. smoking cessation leadership ctr., 2003—. Conv. various govtl. and philanthropic health orgns.; chair internat. adv. com. faculty medicine Ben Gurion U., Israel. Sr. editor: Current Med. Diagnosis and Treatment, 1987—93, mem. editl. bd.: New Eng. Jour. Medicine Mag.; contbr. numerous articles to profl. jours. Mem. U.S. Prospective Payment Assessment Commn., 1983—88; bd. overseers Harvard Coll., 2000—06; bd. dirs. Am. Legacy Found., 2000—05, vice chair, 2001—03, chair, 2003—05; dir. James Irvine Found., Charles R. Drew U. Medicine and Sci., 2005—. Named a Nat. Pub. Health Hero, U. Calif. Berkeley, 2004. Master: ACP (James Bruce award 2007); fellow: Am. Acad. Arts & Scis.; mem.: AAAS, APHA, Albany Med. Ctr. (Medicine prize 2000—), Soc. Gen. Internal Medicine (past pres.), Inst. Medicine, Assn. Am. Physicians, Physicians for Social Responsibility, Harvard Med. Alumni Assn. (past pres.), Alpha Omega Alpha, Phi Beta Kappa. Office: U Calif San Francisco 3333 California St Ste 430 San Francisco CA 94143-1211 Home Phone: 415-435-3872; Office Phone: 415-502-1881. Business E-Mail: schroeder@medicine.ucsf.edu.

SCHUB, CRAIG S., health science association administrator; BS in Bus. Adminstrn., Calif. State U.; postgrad., Calif State U. With Johnson & Johnson, Ethicon divsn., 1981-85; acct. supr. health care mktg., ad. agency; dir. corp. planning, devel. PacifiCare Health Systems, 1990-93, pres., Secure Horizons USA, 1993—. Bd. dirs. Orange County Chapt. Am. Red Cross; trustee Alliance Aging Rsch., Washington D.C. Office: PacifiCare Health Systems 3120 W Lake Center Dr Santa Ana CA 92704-6917

SCHUBEL, JERRY ROBERT, marine scientist educator, dean; b. Bad Axe, Mich., Jan. 26, 1936; s. Theodore Howard and Laura Alberta (Gobel) S.; m. Margaret Ann Hostetler, June 14, 1958; children: Susan Elizabeth, Kathryn Ann. BS, Alma Coll., 1957; MA in Tchg., Harvard U., 1959; PhD, Johns Hopkins U., 1968; DSc (hon.), Mass. Maritime Acad., 1997. Rsch. assoc. Chesapeake Bay Inst., Johns Hopkins U., Balt., 1968-69, rsch. scientist, 1969-74, adj. rsch. prof., assoc. dir., 1973-74; dir. Marine Sci. Rsch. Ctr. SUNY, Stony Brook, 1974-83, dean, leading prof., 1983-94, acting dir. Waste Mgmt. Inst., 1985-87, provost, 1986-89, dir. COAST Inst., 1989, disting. svc. prof., 1994-95, prof. emeritus, 1995—; pres. emeritus, CEO New Eng. Aquarium, Boston, 1994—2001; vis. prof. Wash. Coll., Chestertown, Md., 2002—03, dir. Alternative Futures Forum, 2002—03; pres., CEO Aquarium of Pacific, Long Beach, Calif., 2002—. Hon. prof. East China Normal U., Shanghai, 1985—; sec. exec. com. Commn. on Food, Environ. and Renewable Resources, 1993, chair steering com., 1994; mem. governing bd. Regional Marine Rsch. Program, Greater N.Y. Bight, 1993-94; v.p., founding dir. Gulf of Maine Ocean Observing Sys., 1998-02; adv. panel Nat. Whale Conservation Fund Found., 2001-05; mem. Nat. Sea Grant Adv. Panel, 2002-07, chair, 2004-05; bd. dirs. Internat. Resources Group, 2002—, rev. panel Census of Marine Life, U.S. Nat. Com., 2003-07, mem. NSF Edn. and Human Resources Adv. Com., 2003-05, South Bay Salt Pond Restoration, Nat. Sci. Panel, 2003-06; nat. assoc. Nat. Acads. Sci. and Engring.; mem. marine bd. NRC, 1989-94, 2002—; bd. dirs. Inst. for Learning Innovation, 2004—; mem. adv. panel Ocean Rsch. and Resources, 2006—, vice chair, 2007—, chmn., 2007. Author: The Living Chesapeake, 1981, The Life and Death of the Chesapeake Bay, 1 986; (with H.A. Neal) Solid Waste Management and the Environment, 1987, Garbage and Trash: Can We Convert Mountains Into Molehills?, 1992; editor: (with B.C. Marcy Jr.) Power Plant Entrainment, 1978; (with others) The Great South Bay, 1991; sr. editor Coastal Ocean Pollution Assement News, 1981-86; co-editor in chief Estuaries, 1986-88; mem. editl. bd. CRC Revs. in Aquatic Scis.; contbr. articles to profl. jours. Mem. adv. bd. Environ. Sci. Com. Outer Continental Shelf, Minerals Mgmt. Scs., 1984-86, chmn., 1986; bd. dirs. N.E. Area Remote Sensing Sys., 1983-85, L.I. Incubator Corp.; v.p. L.I. Forum for Tech., 1989-92; chair Mass. Outfall Monitoring Task Force, 1995-98; mem. sci. adv. bd. EPA, 1996-98; commr. Nat. Rsch. Coun.'s Commn. on Engring. Tech. Sys., 1996-2000; mem. vis. com. dept. ocean engring MIT, 1995-2002; trustee Natural Heritage Insts., 1995-2001; mem. Boston Artery Bus. Bd. Dirs., 1994-2001; mem. Boston Mcpl. Rsch. Bur. Bd. Dirs., 1994-2001; mem. Annenberg Challenge Adv. Com., 1995-2002; hon. trustee Sci. Mus. L.I., 2000-02. Recipient L.I. Sound Am. Environ. Edn. award, 1987, Stony Brook U. medal, 1989, Matthew Fontaine Maury award, 1990, Ocean Champion award Monmouth U. Uchan Coast Instn., 2007, Ben Gurion U. medal, 1993, sci. achievement award Sci. Mus. L.I., 2000; Alfred P. Sloan fellow, 1959; Wheaton Coll. Disting. fellow, 2000. Mem. NAS (com. on Coastal Ocean 1989-93), Nat. Assn. State Univ. and Land Grant Colls. (bd. dirs. marine divsn., chmn. 1986-88), L.I. Environ. Coun., L.I. Marine Resources Adv. Coun. (chair 1990-94), L.I. Rsch. Inst. (bd. dirs. 1992-94), L.I. Environ.-Econ. Roundtable (co-chair 1991-92), Suffolk County Recycling Commn., (chmn. 1987-88), Estuarine Rsch. Fedn. (v.p. 1982-83, pres. 1985-87), N.Y. Sea Grant Inst. (chmn. governing bd. 1988-90, mem. gov.'s task force on coastal resources 1990-91), Census Marine Life (mem. U.S. nat. com. 2003—), The Nature Conservancy (trustee L.I. chpt. 1991-94), Franklin Electronic Pubs. (bd. dirs. 1991—), Taproot (bd. dirs. 1988-93, vice chair 1990-93), Internat. Resources Group (bd. dirs., 2002—), Sigma Xi, Phi Sigma Pi. Avocation: photography. Office: Aquarium of the Pacific 100 Aquarium Way Long Beach CA 90802 Home Phone: 564-437-5722; Office Phone: 562-951-1608. Business E-Mail: jschubel@lbaop.org.

SCHUCHARD, ROBERT L., lawyer; b. LA, Feb. 14, 1952; BA in Polit. Sci., Stanford U., 1974; JD, Santa Clara U., 1977. Bar: Calif. 1977. Ptnr. Sonnenschein Nath & Rosenthal LLP, LA, 1997—2007, Davis Wright Tremaine LLP, LA, 2007—. Office Phone: 213-633-6800. Office Fax: 213-633-6899. Business E-Mail: robertschuchard@dwt.com.

SCHUDEL, HANSJOERG, international business consultant; b. Wald, Switzerland, Sept. 27, 1937; s. Rene and Alice S. Student, Coll. Bus. Adminstrn., Zurich, Switzerland. With Byk-Gulden, Konstanz, Germany and Sao Paulo, Brazil, 1962-69, Hicksville, N.Y., 1964-69; pres., chief exec. officer, dir. Stinnes Corp., NYC, 1971-83; exec. officer Stinnes A.G., Muelheim, Fed. Republic of Germany, 1978-83; rep. for the Americas First Arab Pacific Corp. Ltd., Chappaqua, NY, 1984—2003; ret., 2003. Mem. German-Am. C. of C. (bd. dirs. 1976-83), Internat. World Travelers Club, Swiss Soc., Confrerie de la Chaine des Rotisseurs, Order des Coteaux de Champagne, Foothills Assn. (bd. dirs., pres.). Office: PMB 307 1275 4th St Santa Rosa CA 95404-4056

SCHUH, ANTONIUS, biotechnology company executive; PhD in Pharm. Chemistry, U. Bonn, Germany. With Fisons Pharms., 1992—93, Helm AG, 1993—96, head Pharma Bus. Devel. Group; mng. dir. German subsidiary Sequenom, Inc., 1996—98, v.p. bus. devel. and mktg. San Diego, 1998—2000, pres., CEO and dir., 2000—.

SCHUHSLER, HELMUT, biotechnology company executive; PhD in social and Econ. Scis., U. Econs., Vienna, Austria. Bd. dirs. Medigene AG, GPC Biotech; with TVM Techno Venture Mgmt., 1990—, mng. ptnr., 1998—; chmn. bd. Sequenom, Inc., San Diego, 1996—.

SCHULER, JAMES K., construction executive; Chmn., pres., CEO Schuler Homes, Inc., Honolulu, 1973—. Office: Schuler Homes Inc 828 Fort Street Mall Ste 400 Honolulu HI 96813-4321

SCHULIAN, JOHN (NIELSEN SCHULIAN), screenwriter, author; b. LA, Jan. 31, 1945; s. John and Estella Katherine (Nielsen) S.; m. Paula Lynn Ellis, Aug. 20, 1977 (div. Oct. 1984). BA, U. Utah, 1967; MS, Northwestern U., 1968. Copy editor Salt Lake City Tribune, 1968; reporter Balt. Evening Sun, 1970-75; sportswriter Washington Post, 1975-77; sports columnist Chgo. Daily News, 1977-78, Chgo. Sun-Times, 1978-84, Phila. Daily News, 1984-86; staff writer Miami Vice, Universal City, Calif., 1986-87, story editor, 1987, The Slap Maxwell Story, North Hollywood, Calif., 1987-88; exec. story editor TV series Wiseguy, Hollywood, 1988-89; co-prodr. TV series Midnight Caller, Burbank, Calif., 1989-90, supervising prodr., 1990-91; co-exec. prodr. TV series Reasonable Doubts, Burbank, 1991-92; creative cons. TV series The Untouchables, LA, 1992-93; co-exec. prodr. TV series Hercules, Universal City, Calif., 1994-96; co-creator Xena: Warrior Princess, Universal City, 1995; assoc. prodr. (documentary) Ben Johnson: Third Cowboy on the Right, 1996; co-exec. prodr. (TV series) Lawless, 1996-97; consulting prodr. (TV series) JAG, 1999-2000; writer producer (TV series) The Outer Limits, Vancouver, Canada, 2000—01; culture columnist MSNBC.com, 2001—02; co-exec prodr. (TV series) Tremors, Universal City, 2002—03. Spl. contbr. Sports Illustrated, 1998—; profl. in residence U. Utah, 2004. Author: Writers' Fighters and Other Sweet Scientists, 1983, Twilight of the Long Ball Gods, 2005; contbg. editor Panorama mag., 1980-81; syndicated columnist UP Syndicate; commentator Nat. Pub. Radio, 1985-86; cons. The Reader's Catalog, 1989, Short Stories (Fiction), thuglit.com Prague Revue; contbr. articles to NY Times, Playboy, Gentlemen's Quar., Oxford Am.Mag., The National,

LA Times; included in The Best Am. Sports Writing, 1994. Mem. Pacific Coast League Hist. Soc. With U.S. Army, 1968-70. Recipient Nat. Headliners Club award, 1980, Column Writing award AP Sports Editors, 1979, 82, Best Sports Stories award, 1983, 84, Nat Fleischer Excellence in Boxing Journalism award Boxing Writers Assn. Am., 1985. Mem. Writers Guild Am., Phi Beta Kappa. Office: Endeavor Talent Agy 9701 Wilshire Blvd 10th Fl Beverly Hills CA 90212 also: Sterling Lord Literistic 35 Bleecker St New York NY 10012 Personal E-mail: jschulian@aol.com.

SCHULMAN, ALAN, lawyer; b. Bklyn., Sept. 7, 1949; BA, NYU, 1971; JD, La. State Univ., 1974. Bar: La. 1974, Tex. 1974, Wash. 1982, Calif. 1986, US Dist. Ct. (so. dist. Calif. 1987, no. & ctrl. dist. Calif. 1989), US Ct. Appeals (5th & 11th cir. 1981, 9th cir. 1982), US Supreme Ct. 1995. Ptnr., Complex Class Action Litigation Bernstein Litowitz Berger & Grossmann, San Diego. Adj. prof. Univ. San Diego Sch. Law, 2000—; co-chmn. so. dist. Calif. Lawyer Reps. Ninth Cir. Judicial Conf., 2000—01, mem. exec. com., 2002—04, Conf. co-chmn., 2005. Editor (assoc.): La. Law Rev. Mem.: ABA (co-chmn. Securities Law com.), Fed. Bar Assn., Wash. State Bar Assn., La. State Bar Assn., State Bar Tex., State Bar Calif., Assn. Bus. Trial Lawyers San Diego (pres. 2001, mem. bd. gov. 1995—2001), Order of the Coif. Office Phone: 858-720-3185. Office Fax: 858-793-0323. Business E-Mail: alans@blbglaw.com.

SCHULMAN, MICHAEL, professional sports team executive, lawyer; m. Sherry Schulman; 4 children. BA in Econs., U. Calif., Berkeley; JD, U. Santa Clara. Ptnr. McDermott, Will & Emery; chmn. bd. Anaheim Arena Mgmt. (AAM); CEO, alt. gov. Anaheim Ducks; mng. dir. H&S Ventures. Prof. law U. So. Calif.; bd. dirs. Comml. Capital Bank Corp, KDOC TV. Mem. U. Calif., Irvine Found. Bd., 1991—; bd. mem. Henry and Susan Samueli Found., Samueli Inst. for Info. Biology, Orange County Jewish Campus. Office: Anaheim Ducks Honda Ctr 2695 E Katella Ave Anaheim CA 92806

SCHULMAN, ROBERT S., lawyer; b. NYC, July 9, 1941; s. Donald Benedict and Edythe (Smythe) Schulman; m. Susan Jan Von Helbig, Sept. 18, 1974; children: Elizabeth Jane, Jennifer Lynn. BA, Rutgers U., New Brunswick, 1963; JD cum laude, Rutgers U., Newark, 1966. Bar: NJ 1967, US Dist. Ct. NJ 1967, US Supreme Ct. 1970, Calif. 1976, US Dist. Cts. (ctrl., no., so. and ea. dists.) Calif. 1976, US Ct. Appeals (9th cir.) 1976. With Pitney, Hardin & Kipp, Newark, 1966-74; dep. atty. gen. Office of NJ Atty. Gen., Trenton, 1974-75; assoc. Cox, Castle & Nicholson, LA, 1976-80; ptnr. Zobrist, Garner & Garrett, LA, 1980-83, Stephens, Berg, Lasater & Schulman, LA, 1984-91, Crosby, Heafey, Roach & May, LA, 1991—2002, Fulbright & Jaworski, LLP, LA, 2002—. Atty. Bd. Adjustment, Fairview, NJ, 1971—73, Bd. Edn., Fairview, 1972. Contbr. articles to profl. jours. Dir. Deafwest Theater, LA, 1991—97. Mem.: State Bar of Calif., Calif. Club. Congregationalist. Home: 13600 Marina Pointe Dr Unit 710 Marina Del Rey CA 90292-9250

SCHULTHEIS, DAVID C., state legislator; b. LA, 1940; m. Sandra; children: two. Attended, Occidental Coll., LA, U. Minn.; BS in Mgmt. Sci., Calif. State U., LA. Pres. RPI Services, Inc.; owner, mgr. residential income properties Colo.; mem. Dist. 22 Colo. House of Reps., Denver, 2000—02, mem. Dist. 14, 2003—06; mem. Dist. 9 Colo. State Senate, 2007—. Bd. dirs. pvt. elem. sch., Pasadena, Calif.; bd. dirs. pvt. HS, Sierra Madre, Calif. Served with US Army Nat. Guard. Mem. Colo. Union Taxpayers, Kappa Sigma, Rocky Mountain Gun Owners, Coun. Nat. Policy, Am. Legislature Exch. Coun. Republican. Presbyterian. Office: Colo State House 200 E Colfax Rm 271 Denver CO 80203 Office Phone: 303-866-4835. Office Fax: 303-866-2012. Business E-Mail: senatorschultheis@gmail.com.*

SCHULTHEIS, PATRICK JOSEPH, lawyer; b. Spokane, Wash., Sept. 3, 1964; s. John Arthur and Catherine Christina (McCann) Schultheis. AB in History, Stanford U., 1986; JD, U. Chgo., 1989. Bar: Calif. 1989, Wash. 1998, US Dist. Ct., No. Dist. Calif., US Ct. Appeals, ninth cir. Assoc. Wilson, Sonsini, Goodrich & Rosati, Palo Alto, Calif., 1989-96, mem., 1997—, Seattle, 1997—. Co-author: The Initial Public Offering: A Guidebook for Executives & Boards of Directors, 2004. Mem.: Federalist Soc., ABA-Bus. Law Sect., Inglewood Golf Club, Bellevue Club, Buck Cardinal Club, Mem. Club Aldarra, Kappa Sigma. Republican. Roman Catholic. Office: Wilson Sonsini Goodrich & Rosati 701 Fifth Ave Ste 5100 Seattle WA 98104-7036 Office Phone: 206-883-2500. Office Fax: 206-883-2699. Business E-Mail: pschultheis@wsgr.com.

SCHULTZ, HOWARD D., beverage service company executive; b. Bklyn., July 19, 1953; m. Sheri Kersch; children: Jordan, Addison. BS, No. Mich. U., 1975. Joined as saleman Xerox Corp.; v.p., gen. mgr. Hammarplast, USA, (divsn. Perstorp); dir. retail ops. & mktg. Starbucks Coffee Co., 1982—85; pres., CEO Il Giornale Coffee Co., 1986—87; founder Starbucks Corp., 1987, chmn., CEO, 1987—2000, chief global strategist, 2000—04, CEO, 2008—; owner, chmn. Seattle Supersonics, 2001—06; co-founder Maveron LLC, 1998—. Bd. govs. Nat. Assn. of Securities Dealers, 1998—2001; bd. dirs. eBay Inc., 1998—2003, Potbelly Sandwich Works, 2001—, DreamWorks Animation SKG, Inc., 2004—. Author (with Dori Jones Young): Pour Your Heart Into It: How Starbucks Built a Company One Cup at a Time, 1996. Recipient Rev. Theodore M. Hesburgh award for Ethics in Bus., Mendoza Coll. Bus. U. Notre Dame, 2007; named Exec. of Yr., Restaurants & Institutions mag., 2000. Office: Starbucks Corp 2401 Utah Ave S Ste 800 Seattle WA 98134

SCHULTZ, LOUIS MICHAEL, advertising agency executive; b. Detroit, Aug. 24, 1944; s. Henry Richard and Genevieve (Jankowski) S.; children: Christian David, Kimberly Ann; m. Diane Lee; stepchildren: Vince, Andrea, Frank. BA, Mich. State U., 1967; MBA, Wayne State U., 1970. Staff Campbell-Ewald, Warren, Mich., 1967-74, v.p. group dir., 1975-77, sr. v.p., assoc. dir., 1977-82, group sr. v.p., 1982-83, exec. v.p., 1984-87, Lintas: USA, 1987-94; chmn. Lintas: WW Media Coun., 1991; mem. devel. council IPG, NYC, 1984—; pres., CEO CE Comm., 1994—; vice chmn. Campbell-Ewald, 1998-99; chmn., CEO Initiative Media N.Am., LA, 2000—; chmn. Initiative Media WW, 2000. Advisor, Detroit Renaissance Com., 1981-84. With USAR, 1967-73. Mem. NATAS, Am. Women in Radio and TV, Am. Mktg. Assn., Detroit Advt. Assn., Promotion Mktg. Assn. (bd. dirs. 1999), Ad Club N.Y. (bd. dirs.), Adcraft Club, Old Club, Hidden Valley Club, Longboat Key Club, Detroit Athletic Club, Am. Advt. Fedn. (bd. dirs.), Forest Lake Country Club, Renaissance Club, Detroit Athletic Club. Episcopalian. Avocations: golf, tennis, travel. Office: Initiative Media 5700 Wilshire Blvd Ste 400 Los Angeles CA 90036-3639 Home: 250 Bird Key Dr Sarasota FL 34236-1614

SCHULTZ, VICTOR M., physician; b. Pitts., Aug. 14, 1932; s. Irvin and Rose (Reiss) S. BS, Kent State U., Ohio, 1955; MD, Ohio State U., Columbus, 1958. Diplomate Am. Bd. Dermatology. Pvt. practice, Santa Monica, Calif., 1965—. Fellow Am. Acad. Dermatology, Pacific Dermatologic Assn.; mem. AMA, Am. Coll. Physicians, Calif. Med. Assn., L.A. County Med. Assn. Avocations: skiing, tennis, golf, music, swimming. Office: 2461 Santa Monica Blvd Santa Monica CA 90404-2049 Home Phone: 310-826-6832; Office Phone: 310-828-7492.

SCHULZ, LAURA JANET, writer, retired executive secretary; b. Alba, Tex., Aug. 12, 1931; d. Joseph Clifton and Laura Oza English; m. Gordon Robert Schulz, Dec. 4, 1953; children: LeAnn Clarinda Barclay, Peggy Gaynell Berry. Grad. h.s., Denison, Tex., 1948. Sec. history dept. Tex. Christian U., Ft. Worth, 1948-49; continuity editor Sta. KDSX, Denison, 1949-51; sec. Perrin AFB, Sherman, Tex., 1951-55; acctg. clk. England AFB, Alexandria, La., 1955; sec. Emile R. Jardine, CPA, Stockton, Calif., 1957-59; tchr. Little Meth. Pre-Sch., Lodi, 1968-69; sec. Heather, Sanguinetti, Caminata & Sakai, CPAs, Stockton, 1983-92; sec., feature writer, photographer Lodi (Calif.) Dist. C. of C., 1993-97. Author: Katy's Children, 1990, Little Rocky's True Adventures, 1991, Depot Days: My Cicada Summer, 2009. Hon. life mem. Wesleyan Svc. Guild Trinity Meth. Ch., Denison, 1955—, Calif. Congress of PTA, 1984—; pres. PTA Needham Sch., Lodi, 1968-70; leader Camp Fire, Lodi, 1974-82; vol. advisor, tchr. Grapevine Newspaper Vinewood Sch., Lodi, 1974-82; tchr. First United Meth. Ch., Lodi, 1961-80, circle chair. Recipient Appreciation awards, Vinewood Sch., Lodi Unified Sch. Dist., 1974—82, Lodi Dist. C. of C., 1993—97, City of Lodi, Lodi Dist. C. of C., 1996. Mem. Nat. League Am. Pen Women, Sierra Club. Democrat. Methodist. Avocations: photography, reading, nature, writing. Home: 1910 W Tokay St Lodi CA 95242-3440

SCHULZ, RENATE ADELE, German studies and second language acquisition educator; b. Lohr am Main, Germany, Feb. 24, 1940; came to U.S., 1958; 1 child, Sigrid Diane. BS, Mankato State Coll., 1962; MA, U. Colo., 1967; PhD, Ohio State U., 1974; D (hon.), U. Leipzig, Germany, 2008. Edn. officer US Peace Corps, Ife Ezinihitte, Nigeria, 1963-65; asst. prof. Otterbein Coll., Westerville, Ohio, 1974-76, State U. Coll. NY, Buffalo, 1976-77; from asst. to assoc. prof. U. Ark., Fayetteville, 1977-81; from assoc. to prof. U. Ariz., Tucson, 1981—, head dept. German, 1984-90, chair PhD program in second lang. acquisition and teaching, 1994-97, acting head, 2008—. Disting. vis. prof. USAF Acad., Colorado Springs, Colo., 1990-91; co-dir. Ctr. Ednl. Resources in Culture, Lang. and Literacy, 2006-07. Recipient Creative Tchg. award, U. Ariz. Found., Tucson, 1984, Stephen A. Freeman award, N.W. Conf. Tchg. Fgn. Langs., 1984, Bundesverdienstkreuz, Fed. Govt. Germany, 1990, Anthony Papalia award for excellence in tchr. edn., Am. Coun. on the Tchg. of Fgn. Langs./N.Y. State Assn. Fgn. Lang. Tchrs., 2002, Henry and Phyllis Koffler prize for outstanding accomplishments in tchg., U. Ariz., 2005, Disting. Svc. to the Profession award, ADFL, 2008. Mem.: Ariz. Lang. Assn. (Outstanding Svc. to Fgn. Edn. award 1989), Nat. Fedn. Modern Lang. Tchrs. Assns. (v.p. 2004—05, pres. 2006—07), Am. Assn. Applied Linguistics, Tchrs. of ESL, Am. Assn. Tchrs. German (v.p. 1988—90, pres. 1990—91), Am. Coun. on the Tchg. of Fgn. Langs. (exec. coun. 1979—81, Florence Steiner award 1993). Office: U Ariz Dept German Studies Tucson AZ 85721-0105 Office Phone: 520-621-1799. Business E-Mail: schulzr@u.arizona.edu.

SCHUMACHER, HENRY JEROLD, museum director, retired military officer; b. Torrance, Calif., June 17, 1934; s. Henry John and Rene S.; m. Barbara Howell, Aug. 24, 1958; children: Sheri Lynn, Henry Jerold II. Student, Stanford U., 1953; BS, U.S. Mil. Acad., 1957; MS, Northeastern U., Boston, 1965; MBA, Auburn U., 1977. Commd. lt. U.S. Army, 1958, advanced through grades to maj. gen., 1982; army attaché Moscow, 1969-71; chief communications ops. Vietnam, 1971-72; exec. officer Office Chief of Staff, 1972-75; comdr. U.S. Army Communications Command, Panama, 1977-79; dir. network integration, Office Asst. Chief of Staff Automation and Communications, Dept. Army, 1979-81; comdr. The White House Communications Agy., Washington, 1981-82; chief U.S. Army Signal Corps, 1981-83; ret., 1983; sr. v.p. Visa Internat., 1983-86; chief oper. officer Fuel Tech., Inc., Stamford, Conn., 1986-87; pres. IMM Systems, Phila., 1987-89; exec. v.p. Cylink Corp., Sunnyvale, Calif., 1990-95; exec. dir. Hiller Mus. of No. Calif. Aviation History, Redwood City, 1995-98; mng. gen. ptnr. Distributed Sys. Ptnrs., 1999—2002, adv. bd. cranite sys., 2003—. Decorated Def. D.S.M., D.S.M., Legion of Merit.

SCHURMAN, DAVID JAY, orthopedic surgeon, educator; b. Chgo., Apr. 25, 1940; s. Shepherd P. and Dorothy (Laskey) S.; m. Martha Ellen Rocker, Mar. 8, 1967; children: Hilary Sue, Theodore Shepherd. BA, Yale U., 1961; MD, Columbia U., 1965. Intern Baylor U., Houston, 1965-67; resident in gen. surgery Mt. Sinai Hosp., NYC, 1966-67; resident in orthop. surgery UCLA, 1969-72; asst. rsch. surgeon UCLA Med. Sch., 1972-73; asst. prof. orthopedic surgery Stanford Med. Sch., 1973-79, assoc. prof., 1979-87, prof., 1987—. Acting chief divsn. orthop. surgery Stanford U. Med. Ctr., 1990-93, fellowship dir. total joint replacement, 1983—, fellowship dir. sports medicine, 1992-95, dir. orthop. rsch. lab., 1973—. Capt. USAF, 1967-69. Fellow NIH, 1972-73; grantee NIH, 1976-96; recipient Top Dr. award, San Francisco Mag., 02, 03, 05. Mem. Am. Orthopaedic Assn. (bd. dirs. 1994-95), Clin. Orthopaedics and Related Rsch. (bd. dirs. 1994-00), Assn. Bone and Joint Surgeons (v.p. 1996-97, pres. 1997-98). Office: Stanford U Sch Medicine R145 Divsn Orthop Surgery 300 Pasteur Dr Palo Alto CA 94304-2203 Office Phone: 650-723-7608. Business E-Mail: djsortho@standford.edu.

SCHUSTER, PHILIP FREDERICK, II, lawyer, writer, educator; b. Denver, Aug. 26, 1945; s. Philip Frederick and Ruth Elizabeth (Robar) S.; m. Barbara Lynn Nordquist, June 7, 1975; children: Philip Christian, Matthew Dale. BA, U. Wash., 1967; JD, Willamette U., 1972. Bar: Oreg. 1972, Wash. 2002, U.S. Dist. Ct. Oreg. 1974, U.S. Ct. Appeals (9th cir.) 1986, U.S. Ct. Appeals (D.C. cir.) 2001, U.S. Supreme Ct. 1986. Dep. dist. atty. Multnomah County, Portland, Oreg., 1972; title examiner Pioneer Nat. Title Co., Portland, 1973-74; assoc. Buss, Leichner et al, Portland, 1975-76; from assoc. to ptnr. Kitson & Bond, Portland, 1976-77; pvt. practice Portland, 1977-95; ptnr. Dierking and Schuster, Portland, 1996—; adj. prof. law Lewis & Clark Coll., 2002. Arbitrator Multnomah County Arbitration Program, 1985—; student mentor Portland Pub. Schs., 1988—, mentor new lawyers divsn. Oreg. State Bar, 2007-. Author: The Indian Water Slide, 1999; contbg. author OSB CLE Publ., Family Law; contbr. articles to profl. jours. Organizer Legal Aid Svcs. Cmty. Clinics, Salem, Oreg. and Seattle, 1969-73; Dem. committeeman, Seattle, 1965-70; judge Oreg. State Bar and Classroom Law Project, HS Mock Trial Competition, 1988—. Mem. ABA, NAACP (exec. bd. Portland, Oreg. chpt. 1979-98), ACLU, Am. Assn. for Justice, Multnomah Bar Assn. (Vol. Lawyers Project), Alpha Phi Alpha. Avocations: river drifting, camping, swimming, walking, writing. Office: 3565 NE Broadway St Portland OR 97232-1820 Office Phone: 503-335-7765. Business E-Mail: schuster@pcez.com.

SCHUSTER, ROBERT PARKS, lawyer; b. St. Louis, Oct. 25, 1945; s. William Thomas Schuster and Carolyn Cornforth (Daugherty) Hathaway; 1 child, Susan Michele. AB, Yale U., 1967; JD with honors, U. Wyo., 1970; LLM, Harvard U., 1971. Bar: Wyo. 1971, US Ct. Appeals (10th cir.) 1979, US Supreme Ct. 1984, Utah 1990. Dep. county atty. County of Natrona, Casper, Wyo., 1971-73; pvt. practice Casper, 1973—76; assoc. Spence & Moriarity, Casper, 1976-78; ptnr. Spence, Moriarity & Schuster, Jackson, Wyo., 1978—2002; pvt. practice Jackson, Wyo., 2002—. Trustee U. Wyo., 1985-89; Wyo. Dem. nominee for US Ho. of Reps., 1994; polit. columnist Casper Star Tribune, 1987-94; pres. United Way Natrona County, 1974; bd. dirs. Dancers Workshop, 1981-83; chair Wyo. selection com. Rhodes Scholarship, 1989-98; mem. bd. visitors Coll. Arts and Scis., U. Wyo., 1991-2000; mem. Dem. Nat. Com., 1992-2000; chair Wyo. Pub. Policy Forum, 1992-98; mem. Wind River Reservation Econ. Adv. Coun., 1998-99; bd. dirs. Internat. Edn. Found., 2005—. Ford Found. Urban Law fellow, 1970-71. Mem. ABA, AJA, Wyo. Trial Lawyers Assn. (named one of Best Lawyers in Am., 2007-, Mountain States Super Lawyer, 2008-), Yale Club (pres. Wyo. chpt., 2004—). Home: PO Box 13160 Jackson WY 83002 Office: Robert P Schuster PC 250 Veronica Ln Ste 204 PO Box 13160 Jackson WY 83002 Office Phone: 307-732-7800.

SCHUSTER, SU'A CARL, political organization administrator, bishop; Mem. Am. Samoa House of Reps., 1996—2000, 2002—04; chmn. Rep. Party of Am. Samoa, 2008—. Bishop Ch. of Jesus Christ of Latter-day Saints, 2000—08. Mem.: Lions Club (pres. 1984—2000). Office: Rep Party American Samoa PO Box 3564 Pago Pago AS 96799*

SCHUTTISH, THOMAS R., oil industry executive; b. Carmel, Calif., 1947; B in Acctg., San Jose State U., Calif.; JD, U. Calif., Davis; M in Tax Law, NYU, NYC. Sr. tax atty. to various positions in the corp. tax dept. Chevron Corp., 1980—94, asst. gen. tax. counsel, 1994—2002, gen. tax. counsel, 2002—. Mem.: Am. Petroleum Inst., State Bar of Calif., Tax Found., Tax Coun. Office: Chevron Corp Hdqs 6001 Bollinger Canyon Rd San Ramon CA 94583

SCHUUR, DIANE JOAN, vocalist; b. Tacoma, Dec. 10, 1953; d. David Schuur. Singer: (albums) Pilot of My Destiny, 1983, Deedles, Schuur Thing, 1986, Timeless (Grammy award for female jazz vocal, 1986), Diane Schuur and the Count Basie Orchestra (Grammy award for female jazz vocal, 1987), Talkin' 'Bout You, 1988, Pure Schuur, 1991 (#1 on Billboard contemporary jazz chart, 1991, nominated for Grammy award, 1991), In Tribute, 1992, Love Songs, 1993 (Grammy nomination, Best Traditional Vocal, Grammy nomination for The Christmas Song), Love Walked In, 1996, Blues For Schuur, 1997, The Best of Diane Schuur, 1997, Music Is My Life, 1999, Friends for Schuur, 2000; singer: (with B.B. King) Heart to Heart, 1994 (No. 1 on Billboard contemporary jazz chart); singer: (with Maynard Ferguson) 'Swingin' for Schuur, 2001, Midnight, 2003; singer: Schuur Fire, 2005, (performances) White House, Monterey Jazz Festival, Hollywood Bowl, Carnegie Hall, Moscow Symphony, (tours) Japan, Far East, Near East, South Am., Europe, South Africa. Recipient 1st Ella Fitzgerald ann. award, Montreal Jazz Festival, 1999, Helen Keller Personal Achievement award, Am. Found. Blind, 2000. Office Phone: 212-362-5684. Business E-Mail: leftside@bway.net.

SCHUYLER, ROBERT LEN, investment company executive; b. Burwell, Nebr., Mar. 4, 1936; s. Norman S. and Ilva M. (Hoppes) S.; m. Mary Carol Huston, June 13, 1958; children: Kylie Anne, Nina Leigh, Melynn Kae, Gwyer Lenn. BS, U. Nebr., 1958; MBA, Harvard U., 1960. Asst. to treas. Potlatch Forests, Inc., Lewiston, Idaho, 1962-64, dir. corp. planning San Francisco, 1964-66; mgr. fin. analysis Weyerhaeuser Co., Tacoma, 1966-68, mgr. investment evaluation dept., 1968-70, v.p. fin. and planning, 1970-72, sr. v.p. fin. and planning, 1972-85, exec. v.p., chief fin. officer, 1985-91; mng. ptnr. Nisqually Ptnrs., Tacoma, 1991-95; bd. dirs. Grande Alberta Paper, Ltd., 1992—. Past mem. nat. adv. bd. Chem. Bank, U. Wash. MBA program, coun. fin. exec. Conf. Bd., Pvt. Sector Coun., exec. com. Am. Paper Inst.; bd. dirs. Paragon Trade Brands Inc., Montrail, Inc. Past chmn. Santa Fe County Bd. Econ. Advs.; chmn. Santa Fe Bus. Incubator; past trustee Santa Fe Chamber Music Festival; commr. N.Mex. Dept. Econ. Devel. Mem. Anglers Club, Sangre de Cristo Flyfishers, Las Campanas Golf & Country Club, Don Quixote Club. Home: PO Box 4225 Tubac AZ 85646-4225 E-mail: skysantafe@msn.com.

SCHWAB, CHARLES ROBERT, JR., (CHUCK SCHWAB), investment company executive; b. Sacramento, July 29, 1937; m. Helen O'Neill; 5 children. BA in Economics, Stanford U., 1959, MBA, 1961. Formerly mut. fund mgr., Marin County, Calif.; founder The Charles Schwab Corp., San Francisco, 1971, chmn., CEO, 1971—2003, 2004—08, exec. chmn., 2008—. Bd. dirs. The Gap, Inc., 1986—2004, The Charles Schwab Corp., 1986—, Seibel Systems, Inc., 1994—2004; dir. U.S. Trust Corp., U.S. Trust Co. of NY; chmn. Charles Schwab Bank, N.A.; trustee Charles Schwab Family of Funds, Schwab Investments, Schwab Capital Trust, Schwab Annuity Portfolios. Author: How to be Your Own Stockbroker, 1984, Guide to Financial Independence, 1998, You're Fifty - Now What?, 2001; co-author (with Carrie Schwab Pomerantz): It Pays To Talk. Chmn. All Kinds of Minds Inst., President's Council on Fin. Literacy, 2008—; co-founder (with Helen Schwab), chmn. Charles and Helen Schwab Found., 2001—; bd. trustees Stanford U. Named one of Forbes' Richest Americans, 1999—, Forbes' Executive Pay, 1999—, World's Richest People, Forbes Mag., 1999—, Top 200 Collectors, ARTnews Mag., 2004—08, 50 Most Generous Philanthropists, BusinessWeek, 2005. Republican. Achievements include pioneer in discount brokerage business since 1974. Avocation: collector of modern & contemporary art. Office: The Charles Schwab Corp 101 Montgomery St San Francisco CA 94104-4175 E-mail: charles.schwab@schwab.com.*

SCHWAB, EVAN LYNN, lawyer; b. Detroit, Apr. 13, 1938; s. Joe Schwab and Vanita Dobbs; m. Heidi Jensen, June 11, 1960 (div. Dec. 1975); children: Mari, Eric, Peter; m. Carole Fuller, Mar. 12, 1976; 1 child, William. BA, U. Wash., 1961, LLB with high honors, 1963. Bar: Wash. 1964, U.S. Dist. Ct. (we. dist.) Wash. 1966, U.S. Supreme Ct. 1967; CPA. Law clk. U.S. Supreme Ct. Justice William O. Douglas, Washington, 1963-64; assoc. Davis, Wright & Jones, Seattle,

1964-69, ptnr., 1969-88, Bogle & Gates, Seattle, 1988—99, co-chair dept. litigation, 1992—99; ptnr. trial group Dorsey & Whitney LLP, Seattle, 1999—; chair Seattle Trial Group, 2005—08. 2nd. lt. USAR, 1962-64. Fellow: Am. Coll. Trial Lawyers (chmn. Wash. state com. 2005—07); mem.: ABA, Seattle-King County Bar Assn., Wash. State Bar Assn., Fed. Bar Assn. Western Dist. Wash. (pres. 1985—86), Seattle Yacht Club (judge adv. 1986, 2005—07). Avocations: sailing, skiing. Office: Dorsey & Whitney LLP Ste 3400 US Bank Ctr 1420 Fifth Ave Seattle WA 98101-4010 Office Phone: 206-903-8858. Office Fax: 206-903-8820. Business E-Mail: schwab.evan@dorsey.com.

SCHWARTZ, ALLEN R., lawyer; b. Greeley, Colo., Oct. 13, 1951; s. David L. and Margaret L. Schwartz; m. Beverly S. Stephens, Mar. 23, 1985; 1 child, Christopher; 1 stepchild, Shawn Jensen. BA in Psychology and Sociology, U. Colo., 1973, JD, 1976. Bar: Colo. 1976, US Dist. Ct. Colo. 1976, US Ct. Appeals (10th cir.) 1983. Law clk. Denver Dist. Ct., 1976-77; assoc. Fischer & Wilmarth, Ft. Collins, Colo., 1977-79; ptnr. Dean, Martin, Mitchell & Schwartz, Ft. Collins, 1979-83; mng. ptnr. Nelson & Schwartz, Ft. Collins, 1983-90; ptnr. Nelson, Reid & Schwartz, Ft. Collins, 1990-96; pvt. practice Ft. Collins, 1996—; county ct. magistrate Larimer County, Colo., 2006—. V.p., legal advisor acad. adv. com. Wingshadow Inc., Frontier HS and Frontier Mid. Sch., Ft. Collins, 1994-2005. Asst. scoutmaster Boy Scouts Am., Ft. Collins, Colo., 1991—94. Mem. Colo. Bar Assn., Larimer County Bar Assn., Overland Sertoma (pres., chmn. bd., Sertoman of the Yr. 1994-95), High Plains Dist. Sertoma (dist. gov. 1996-98, Cmty. Achievement award 1991-92). Home: 1601 Centennial Rd Fort Collins CO 80525-2418 Office: 215 W Oak St Ste 600 Fort Collins CO 80521-2729 Home Phone: 970-223-2978; Office Phone: 970-493-0456. Business E-Mail: allen@allenrschwartz.com.

SCHWARTZ, BERNARD JULIAN, lawyer; b. Edmonton, Alberta, Can., July 29, 1960; came to U.S., 1982; s. Sol and Anne (Motkovich) S. BA, U. Alberta, 1981; JD, McGeorge Sch. Law, 1986. Bar: U.S. Supreme Ct. 1991. Atty. Ropers, Majeski, San Francisco, 1987-88, Riverside County Pub. Defenders, Riverside, Calif., 1988-89; pvt. practice Riverside, 1990—. Coach Riverside County H.S. Mock Trial Team, 1990, 96, 97. Mem. Calif. Attys. Criminal Justice, Calif. Pub. Defenders Assn., Riverside County Bar Assn., Criminal Cts. Bar Assn. (pres.).

SCHWARTZ, GAIL S., state legislator; b. Chgo. m. Alan E. Schwartz; children: Brendan Ash, Aime, Rachel. BS, U. Colo. Real estate & mktg. cons. Sno-Engring., Inc.; Western Slope rep. Colo. Commn. on Higher Edn., 1995—98; vice chair Colo. U. Bd. Regents; mem. Dist. 5 Colo. State Senate, Denver, 2007—. Former dir. devel., acting dir. Pitkin County Housing Authority. Recipient Outstanding Svc. award, Aspen Sch. Dist. Democrat. Office: 200 E Colfax Denver CO 80203 Office Phone: 303-866-4871. Business E-Mail: gail.schwartz.senate@state.co.us.*

SCHWARTZ, IRWIN H., lawyer; b. Bklyn., Mar. 25, 1948; s. Julius and Sylvia (Holzman) S.; m. Barbara T. Granett, July 3, 1971; 1 child, Matthew Lane. BA, Bklyn. Coll., 1968; JD, Stanford U., 1971. Bar: Calif. 1972, Washington 1972, U.S. Ct. Appeals (9th cir.) 1972, U.S. Supreme Ct. 1977, Internat. Criminal Ct., 2005. Asst. U.S. atty. U.S. Dist. Ct. (we. dist.) Wash., Seattle, 1972-74, exec. asst. U.S. atty., 1974-75, fed. pub. defender, 1975-81; pvt. practice Seattle, 1981—. Fellow: Am. Bd. Criminal Lawyers, Am. Coll. Trial Lawyers; mem.: NACDL (pres. 2001—02), ABA (criminal justice sect. coun. 1991—94, 2002—05), Wash. Athletic Club (Seattle). Avocations: photography, woodworking. Office: 710 Cherry St Seattle WA 98104-1925

SCHWARTZ, JEFFREY H., distribution facilities executive; BS with honors, Emory Univ., 1981; MBA, Harvard Univ., 1985. CPA. Acct. Arthur Anderson, Atlanta, 1981—83; with Anderson Properties, Atlanta; co-founder, mng. ptnr. Krauss/Schwartz Co.; mgr. global develop. ProLogis, Denver, 1994—96, vice-chmn. internat. ops. Mexico, 1996, Amsterdam, 1997—2000; CEO Vizional Technologies, 2001; pres., COO Asia ProLogis, Denver, 2002—05, pres. internat. ops., 2003—05, CEO, 2005—07, chmn., CEO, 2007—. Office: ProLogis 4545 Airport Way Denver CO 80239

SCHWARTZ, JONATHAN IAN, information technology executive; b. Oct. 20, 1965; Student, Carnegie Mellon U., Pitts., 1983—84; BS in Econs. and Math., Wesleyan U., Middletown, Conn., 1986. Cons. McKinsey & Co., Inc., 1987—89; co-founder, CEO Lighthouse Design (acquired by Sun Microsystems, Inc.), 1989—96; dir. investment group, devel. tools & Java product mktg. orgn. Sun Microsystems, Inc., Santa Clara, Calif., v.p. venture & strategic investments, 1999—2000, sr. v.p. corp. strategy & planning, 2000—02, exec. v.p. software group, 2002—04, pres., COO, 2004—06, pres., CEO, 2006—. Bd. dirs. Dorado Corp. Office: Sun Microsystems Inc 4150 Network Cir Santa Clara CA 95054 Office Phone: 650-960-1300, 800-555-9786. Office Fax: 408-276-3804. E-mail: jonathan.schwartz@sun.com.

SCHWARTZ, LEON, foreign language educator; b. Boston, Aug. 22, 1922; s. Charles and Celia (Emer) S.; m. Jeanne Gurtat, Mar. 31, 1949; children: Eric Alan, Claire Marie. Student, Providence Coll., 1939-41; BA, UCLA, 1948; certificat de phonetique, U. Paris, 1949; MA, U. So. Cal., 1950, PhD, 1962. Tchr. English, Spanish and Latin Redlands JHS, Calif., 1951—54, tchr. Spanish and French, 1954—59; prof. French Calif. State U., LA, 1959—87, chmn. dept. fgn. langs. and lit., 1970—73, prof. emeritus, 1987—; instr. Osher Learning Inst., 2006. Author: Diderot and the Jews, 1981, Poems That Sing by French Masters, 2008; co-author: Mortier-Tresson, Dictionnaire de Diderot, 1999. Served as 2d lt. USAAF, 1942-45. Decorated Air medal with 5 oak leaf clusters; recipient Outstanding Prof. award Calif. State U. LA, 1976. Mem. Am. Assn. Tchrs. French, Am. Soc. 18th Century Studies, Calif. State U. LA Emeriti Assn. (pres. 1998-2000), Phi Beta Kappa, Phi Kappa Phi, Pi Delta Phi, Sigma Delta Pi, Alpha Mu Gamma. Business E-Mail: lschwar@exchangecalstatela.edu.

SCHWARTZ, PEPPER JUDITH, sociologist, educator; b. Chgo., May 11, 1945; d. Julius J. and Gertrude (Puris) Schwartz; m. John A. Strait, June 19, 1971; m. Arthur M. Skolnick, Jan. 9, 1982 (div. 2001); children: Cooper, Ryder. BA, Washington U., St. Louis, 1968, MA, 1970; M in Philosophy, Yale U., 1972, PhD, 1974. Assoc. prof. sociology, adj. assoc. prof., 1972—88; prof. psychiatry and behavioral sci. U. Wash., Seattle, 1988—. Chmn. rev. com. NIMH; bd. dirs. Women's Rsch. Ctr.; frequent guest and host local and network TV shows; appt. to Pres. Reagan's ad hoc adv. roundtable on the family, 1984; expert appearance in NBC Sacred Sexless, 1987, Some Thoughts on Being Single, 1984, ABC After The Sexual Revolution, 1986; relationship expert LifetimeTV.com, 1998—, PerfectMatch.com, 2003—. Author: Women at Yale, 1976; author: (with Judith Laws et al) Sexual Scripts, 1977; author: (with P. Blumstein) American Couples, 1983; author: (with V. Rutter) The Gender of Sexuality, 1995; author: (with D. Cappello) Ten Talks Parents Must Have with their Children About Sex and Character, 2002; author: Everything You Know About Love & Sex is Wrong, 2002, Lifetime Book of Love & Sex Quizzes, 2003, Finding Your Perfect Match, 2006; contbr. numerous articles to mags. and jours.; profiles in Savvy, Ladies Home Jour., Playboy, Cosmopolitan, NY Times, Newsweek, others, articles on work in Time, Redbook, New West, American Baby Mag., others; co-author, editor: A Student's Guide to Sex on Campus, 1971. Guardian Ad-Litem Program; bd. dirs. Empty Space Theater, Seattle, pres., 1980; past mem. Gov.'s Commn. Venereal Disease; mem. Presdl. Adv. Rountable on Family, 1984; bd. dirs. Nat. Abortion Rights Action League, Anti-Defamation League, ACLU; nat. bd. dirs. YWCA, Jewish Family Svc. Named Oustanding Young Woman of the Future, Time-Life mag., 1978; named one of Most Powerful People of the 1980s, Next mag., 1981. Fellow: Internat. Acad. Sex Rsch.; mem.: Lluminari Women's Expert Health Network, Nat. Conf. Family Relations, Am. Sociol. Assn. (chairperson com. on coms., Outstanding Contbn. Pub. Understanding Sociology 2005), Soc. for Sci. Study of Sexuality (pres. 1998—), Pacific Sociol. Assn. (mem. coun., pres. 2004—), Yale Club (N.Y.C.), The Diet Club. Office: Dept Sociology Dk 40 U Seattle WA 98195-0001 Home Phone: 425-888-6273; Office Phone: 206-543-4036. E-mail: pepperschwartz@hotmail.com.

SCHWARTZ, ROBERT M., lawyer; b. LA, 1959; BS, U. Calif., LA, 1981; JD, U. So. Calif., 1984. Bar: Calif. 1984, US Dist. Ct., Ctrl. Dist. Calif. 1984, US Ct. Appeals, 9th Cir., DC 1987, US Dist. Ct., No. Dist. Calif. 2000, US District Ct., Ea. Dist. Calif. 2001. Litig. ptnr. O'Melveny & Myers LLP, LA, co-chair entertainment and media litig. practice group, mem. class action and appellate practice group. Bd. dir., mem. exec. com. Bet Tzedek- The House of Justice, LA. Named one of 100 Power Lawyers, Hollywood Reporter, 2007. Mem.: Assn. of Bus. Trial Lawyers, ABA (mem. litig. sect.), LA County Bar Assn., Beverly Hills Bar Assn. (co-chair, entertainment law sect. 1998—99, 1999—2000). Office: O'Melveny & Myers LLP 1999 Avenue of the Stars 7th Fl Los Angeles CA 90067-6035 Office Phone: 310-246-6835. Office Fax: 310-246-6779. Business E-Mail: rschwartz@omm.com.

SCHWARTZ, ROBIN, broadcast executive; Asst. ABC; head children's programming NBC; v.p. programming ABC Family; pres. Regency TV, 2004—08, Oprah Winfrey Network, 2008—. Mem. entertainment com. Children's Hosp. LA. Co-chair Girls, Inc. Named one of The 100 Most Powerful Women in Entertainment, Hollywood Reporter, 2005, 2006, 2007. Mem.: Acad. TV Arts and Scis. (gov.), Hollywood Radio and TV Soc. (bd. mem.). Office: Oprah Winfrey Network 9150 Wilshire Blvd Ste 240 West Hollywood CA 90069

SCHWARTZ, STEPHAN ANDREW, entrepreneur, writer; b. Cin., Jan. 10, 1942; s. Abraham Leon and Bertha Culbertson (Watson) S.; m. Katherine Rowland, Jan. 6, 1965 (div. 1979); 1 child, Catherine Rowland; m. Hayden Oliver Gates, July 10, 1982; 1 stepchild, Lea Daniel Meyers. Student, U. Va. Founder, chmn., rsch. dir. The Mobius Soc., LA, 1977—; pres. S. A. Schwartz & Assocs., LA, 1992—. Gen. ptnr. V-Partners, Inc.; chmn. Clearlight TV Prodns., L.A.; former vis. prof. John F. Kennedy U.; adv. bd. PHOENIX: New Directions in the Study of Man; sr. fellow Philos. Rsch. Soc.; cons. to oceanographer USN; spl. asst. rsch. and analysis Chief Naval Ops.; co-inventor ThighMaster; mem. bd, advisors Global Inst. Network N. Inst., Aura Comms. Sys., Inc.; cons. in field. Editor: Seapower Magazine; author: The Secret Vaults of Time, 1978, The Alexandria Project, 1980, 1983, Psychic Detectives, 1987; author: (with others) Stories From Omni, 1984; contbr. over 47 publications to profl. jours.; screenwriter spl. presentations and documentaries. Bd. dirs. World Children's Transplant Found., 1992—. Fellow Royal Geog. Soc.; mem. Internat. Soc. for Subtle Energies and Energy Medicine (bd. dirs., editor Subtle Energies Jour.,), Soc. for the Anthropology of Consciousness (past pres., founding mem.), Soc. for Hist. Archaeology, Calif.-Russia Trade Assn. (bd. dirs.), Explorer's club. N.Y. Avocations: reading, scuba diving, canoeing, sailing, hiking.

SCHWARTZBACH, M. GERALD, lawyer; b. Wilkes-Barre, Pa., Oct. 6, 1944; m. Susan Schwartzbach; 1 child, Micah. BA in Hist., Washington and Jefferson Coll., 1966; JD, George Washington U., 1969. Bar: Mich. 1970, US Dist. Ct. (ea. dist. Mich.) 1970, US District Ct. (no. dist. Calif.) 1974, Calif. 1974, US Ct. Appeals (9th cir.) 1980, US Supreme Ct. 1982, US Dist. Ct. (so. dist. Calif.) 1978. Staff atty. Legal Aid and Defenders Office, Detroit, 1970—71, Mich. State Appellate Defender Office, Detroit, 1971, Bayview Hunter's Point Cmty. Defender, San Francisco, 1974—76; pvt. practice Detroit, 1971—72, San Francisco, 1977—87, 1989—96, Mill Valley, Calif., 1999—; assoc. Law Office of Sheldon Otis, San Francisco, 1976—77, Law Offices of Joseph W. Carcione, Jr., Redwood City, Calif., 1996—99; ptnr. Garry, McTernan, Stender, Walsh & Schwartzbach, San Francisco, 1987—89. Lectr. in field. Vol. Svc. To Am., 1969—70; bd. dirs. La Casa de Las Madres, shelter for battered women, 1981—90. Recipient Outstanding Svc. award, No. Calif. Innocence Project, 2003; named one of Best Lawyers in Am., Woodward/White, Top 10 Trial Lawyers in Am., Nat. Law Jour., 2005. Mem.: Bar Assn. San Francisco (chair criminal justice sect. 1988—91, mem. criminal justice adv. coun. 1988—92), Marin County Bar Assn., Nat. Lawyers Guild, No. Calif. Criminal Trial Lawyers Assn. (bd. govs. 1989—95), Nat. Assn. Criminal Def. Lawyers, Calif. Attys. for Criminal Justice (bd. govs. 1986—93, 2002—07, Skip Glen Outstanding Lawyer award 1986), State Bar Calif. Achievements include the successful defense of actor Robert Blake in the 2004-05 murder trial. Office: 655 Redwood Hwy Ste 277 Mill Valley CA 94941 Office Phone: 415-388-2343. Office Fax: 415-388-2353. Business E-Mail: mgs@mgslawyer.com.

SCHWARTZMAN, JASON FRANCESCO, actor, musician; b. Los Angeles, Calif., June 26, 1980; s. Jack Schwartzman and Talia Shire. Drummer, founder Phantom Planet; band mem. Coconut Records. Actor: (films) Rushmore, 1998 (Best Performance by a Young Actor in a Comedy Film, YoungStar Awards, 1999, Best Actor, Lone Star Film & TV Awards, 1999), CQ, 2001, Odessa or Bust, 2001, Julius and Friends: Hole in One, 2001, Julius and Friends: Yeti, Set, Go, 2002, Slackers, 2002, S1m0ne, 2002, Spun, 2002, Just Like Mona, 2003, I Heart Huckabees, 2004, The Hitchhicker's Guide to the Galaxy, 2005, Bewitched, 2005, Shopgirl, 2005, Marie Antoinette, 2006, (short films) Hotel Chevalier, 2007; actor, writer (films) The Darjeeling Limited, 2007; actor: (TV series) Freaks and Geeks, 2000, Cracking Up, 2004—06. Home: 1875 CENTURY PARK E 700 Los Angeles CA 90057-2508

SCHWARZ, GLENN VERNON, newspaper editor; b. Chgo., Nov. 24, 1947; s. Vernon Edward and LaVerne Louise (Schuster) S.; m. Cynthia Frances Meisenhoelder, June 17, 1984; 1 child, Chloe. BA, San Francisco State U., 1970. Sports writer San Francisco Examiner, 1970—87, sports editor, 1988—2000, San Francisco Chronicle, 2000—. Fundraiser San Francisco Zoological Soc., 1987—. Mem. AP Sports Editors, Baseball Writers Assn. Am. (bd. dirs. 1986-87). Avocation: nature travel. Office: San Francisco Chronicle 901 Mission St San Francisco CA 94103

SCHWARZ, JOHN HENRY, theoretical physicist, educator; b. North Adams, Mass., Nov. 22, 1941; s. George and Madeleine (Haberfeld) S.; m. Patricia Margaret Moyle, July 11, 1986. AB, Harvard U., 1962; PhD, U. Calif., Berkeley, 1966. Instr. physics Princeton (NJ) U., 1966-69, asst. prof., 1969-72; research assoc. Calif. Inst. Tech., Pasadena, 1972-85, Harold Brown prof. theoretical physics, 1985—. Co-author: Superstring Theory, 1987. Trustee Aspen (Colo.) Ctr. for Physics, 1982—. Recipient Dirac medal Internat. Ctr. for Theoretical Physics, 1989; Guggenheim fellow, 1978-79, MacArthur Found. fellow, 1987. Fellow NAS, Am. Acad. Arts & Scis., Am. Phys. Soc., Phi Beta Kappa (vis. scholar 1990-91). Office: Calif Inst Tech # 452 48 Pasadena CA 91125-0001

SCHWARZ, STEVEN EMANUEL, electrical engineering educator, administrator; b. LA, Jan. 29, 1939; s. Carl and Lillian Schwarz; m. Janet Lee Paschal, July 27, 1963. BS, Cal Tech, 1959, MS, 1961, PhD, 1964; AM, Harvard U., 1962. From asst. prof. to prof. elec. engring. U. Calif., Berkeley, 1964-99, assoc. dean Coll. Engring., 1991-96, prof. emeritus, 1999. Author: Electromagnetics for Engineers, 1990; co-author: Electrical Engineering, An Introduction, 1984, 93; contbr. articles to profl. jours. Guggenheim fellow, 1971-72. Fellow IEEE. Office: U Calif Berkeley Electrical Engring Dept 231 Cory Hall Berkeley CA 94720-1713

SCHWARZENEGGER, ARNOLD ALOIS, Governor of California; b. Thal, Styria, Austria, July 30, 1947; arrived in US, 1968, naturalized, 1983; s. Gustav and Aurelia (Jedrny) Schwarzenegger; m. Maria Owings Shriver, Apr. 26, 1986; children: Katherine Eunice, Christina Aurelia, Patrick, Christopher. BA in Bus. and Internat. Econs., U. Wis., Superior; doctorate (hon.), U. Wis. Superior, 1996, Chapman U., 2002. Owner prodn., real estate cos.; gov. State of Calif., Sacramento, 2003—. Speaker Republican Nat. Convention, NYC, 2004. Actor: (films) Stay Hungry, 1976 (Golden Globe award, Best Newcomer in Films, 1976), Pumping Iron, 1977, Conan, The Barbarian, 1982, Conan, The Destroyer, 1983, The Terminator, 1984, Commando, 1985, Red Sonja, 1985, Raw Deal, 1986, Predator, 1987, Running Man, 1987, Red Heat, 1988, Twins, 1988, Total Recall, 1990, Kindergarten Cop, 1990, Terminator 2: Judgement Day, 1991, True Lies, 1994, Junior, 1994, Terminator 2: 3-D, 1996, Jingle All the Way, 1996, Eraser, 1996, Batman & Robin, 1997, End of Days, 1999, Collateral Damage, 2002, Terminator 3: Rise of the Machines, 2003, Around the World in 80 Days, 2004, The Kid and I, 2005; (TV films) The Jayne Mansfield Story, 1980, (TV spl.) Sinatra: 80 Years My Way, 1995; actor, prodr. (films) The Last Action Hero, 1993, The 6th Day, 2000; dir.: (TV series) Tales from the Crypt, 1990; (TV films) Christmas in Connecticut, 1992; author: Arnold: The Education of a Bodybuilder, 1977, Arnold's Bodyshaping for Women, 1979, Arnold's Bodybuilding for Men, 1981, Arnold's Encyclopedia of Modern Bodybuilding, 1985, 2nd. edit., 1998; editor: Muscle & Fitness Mag., Flex Mag. Nat. weight tng. coach Spl. Olympics; vol. prison rehab. programs; chmn. Pres.'s Coun. Phys. Fitness and Sports, 1990—93. Recipient Timmie award, Touchdown Club, 1990, Rave award for politics, WIRED Mag., 2007, Muhammad Ali Humanitarian award, Nat. Leadership award, Simon Wiesenthal Ctr., Father Flanagan Svc. to Youth award, Boys & Girls Town; named Jr. Mr. Europe, 1965, Best Built Man of Europe, 1966, Mr. Europe, 1966, Internat. Powerlifting Champion, 1966, German Powerlifting Champion, 1968, Mr. Internat., Internat. Fedn. Body Builders, 1968, Amateur Mr. Universe, 1969, Nat. Assn. Body Builders, 1967, Profl. Mr. Universe, 1968, 1969; named one of The World's Most Influential People, TIME mag., 2007, 50 Who Matter Now, Bus. 2.0, 2007, America's Best Leaders, US News & World Report, 2007. Republican. Roman Catholic. Office: Office of Governor State Capitol Sacramento CA 95814-4906 Office Phone: 916-445-2841. Office Fax: 916-445-4633.

SCHWARZER, WILLIAM W., federal judge; b. Berlin, Apr. 30, 1925; came to U.S., 1938, naturalized, 1944; s. John F. and Edith M. (Daniel) S.; m. Anne Halbersleben, Feb. 2, 1951; children: Jane Elizabeth, Andrew William. AB cum laude, U. So. Calif., 1948; LLB cum laude, Harvard U., 1951. Bar: Calif. 1953, U.S. Supreme Ct. 1967. Teaching fellow Harvard U. Law Sch., 1951-52; asso. firm McCutchen, Doyle, Brown & Enersen, San Francisco, 1952-60, ptnr., 1960-76; judge U.S. Dist. Ct (no. dist.) Calif., San Francisco, 1976—; dir. Fed. Jud. Ctr., Washington, 1990-95. Sr. counsel Pres.'s Commn. on CIA Activities Within the U.S., 1975; chmn. U.S. Jud. Conf. Com. Fed.-State Jurisdiction, 1987-90; mem. faculty Nat. Inst. Trial Advocacy, Fed. Jud. Ctr., All-ABA, U.S.-Can. Legal Exch., 1987, Anglo-U.S. Jud. Exch., 1994-95, Salzburg Seminar on Am. Studies; ret. disting. prof. Hastings Coll. Law U. Calif., ret. Author: Managing Antitrust and Other Complex Litigation, 1982, Civil Discovery and Mandatory Disclosure, 1994, Federal Civil Procedure Before Trial, 1994; contbr. articles to legal publs., aviation jours. Trustee World Affairs Coun. No. Calif., 1961-88; chmn. bd. trustees Marin Country Day Sch., 1963-66; mem. Marin County Aviation Commn., 1969-76; mem. vis. com. Harvard Law Sch., 1981-86. Served with Intelligence, U.S. Army, 1943-46. Recipient Edward J. Devitt Disting. Svc. to Justice award, 2004. Fellow Am. Coll. Trial Lawyers (S. Gates award 1992), Am. Bar Found.; mem. ABA (Meador Rosenberg award 1995), Am. Law Inst., San Francisco Bar Assn., State Bar Calif., Coun. Fgn. Rels. Office: 450 Golden Gate Ave San Francisco CA 94102-3661 Office Phone: 415-522-4660.

SCHWEBEL, MILTON, psychologist, educator; b. Troy, NY, May 11, 1914; s. Frank and Sarah (Oxenhandler) S.; m. Bernice Lois Davison, Sept. 3, 1939; children: Andrew I., Robert S. AB, Union Coll., 1934; MA, SUNY, Albany, 1936; PhD, Columbia U., NYC, 1949; Cert. in Psychotherapy, Postgrad. Ctr. Mental Health, NYC, 1958. Lic. psychologist, NY, NJ; diplomate Am. Bd. Examiners Profl. Psychology. Asst. prof. psychology Mohawk Champlain Coll., 1946-49; asst. to prof. edn., dept. chmn., assoc. dean NYU, 1949-67; dean, prof. Grad. Sch. Edn., Rutgers U., New Brunswick, NJ, 1967-77; dean emeritus Grad. Sch. Applied and Profl. Psychology, 1977—, prof., 1977-85, prof. emeritus, 1985—. Vis. prof. U. So. Calif., U. Hawaii; postdoctoral fellow Postgrad. Ctr. Mental Health, NYC, 1954-58, lectr. psychology, 1958-90; cons. NIMH, US, state and city depts. edn., UNESCO, ednl. ministries in Europe, Asia, univs. and pub. schs., UNESCO; pvt. cons. psychologist and psychotherapist, 1953—;

disting. cons. & faculty Saybrook Grad. Sch. & Rsch. Ctr., 1999—. Author: A Guide to a Happier Family, 1989, Personal Adjustment and Growth, 1990, Student Teachers Handbook, 3d edit., 1996, Interests of Pharmacists, 1951, Health Counseling, 1953, Who Can Be Educated?, 1968, Remaking America's Three School System: Now Separate and Unequal, 2003; editor: Mental Health Implications of Life in the Nuclear Age, 1986, Facilitating Cognitive Development, 1986, Promoting Cognitive Growth Over the Life Span, 1990, Behavioral Science and Human Survival, 1965, The Impact of Ideology on the I.Q. Controversy, 1975; editor Peace & Conflict: Jour. Peace Psychology, 1993-2000 (vol. 9, no. 4, named Pioneer in Peace Psychology: Milton Schwebel); co-editor Bull. Peace Psychology, 1991-94; mem. editl. bd. Am. Jour. Orthopsychiatry, Readings in Mental Health, Jour. Contemporary Psychotherapy, Jour. Counseling Psychology, Jour. Social Issues, others. Mem. sci. adv. bd. Internat. Ctr. for Enhancement of Learning Potential, 1988—; trustee Edn. Law Ctr., 1973-81, Nat. Com. Employment Youth, Nat. Child Labor Com., 1967-75, Union Exptl. Colls. and Univs., 1976-78; pres. Nat. Orgn. for Migrant Children, 1980-85; pres. Inst. of Arts and Humanities, 1984-95. Served with AUS, 1943-46, ETO. Recipient Disting. Leader in Edn. award, Grad. Sch. Edn. Rutgers U., 2006; Met. Applied Rsch. Coun. fellow, 1970—71. Fellow APA, Am. Psychol. Soc., Am. Orthopsychiatry Assn., Soc. Psychol. Study Social Issues, Jean Piaget Soc. (trustee), Am. Ednl. Rsch. Assn., NY Acad. Scis., Psychologists for Social Responsibility (pres.), Sigma Xi. Home and Office: 431 S Brighton Ln Tucson AZ 85711 Office Phone: 520-745-1725. Business E-Mail: mschwebe@rci.rutgers.edu.

SCHWEIKERT, DAVID, real estate agent, former state legislator; m. Joyce Schweikert. BA in Fin. and Real Estate, Ariz. State U., MBA. Mem. Ariz. State Ho. of Reps.; treas. Maricopa County, Ariz.; real estate agent Fountain Hills, Ariz. Chair State Bd. Equalization. Republican. Roman Catholic. Office: 4110 N Goldwater Blvd #200 Scottsdale AZ 85251 Office Phone: 480-946-1125. E-mail: david@david08.com.

SCHWEITZER, BRIAN, Governor of Montana; b. Havre, Mont., Sept. 4, 1955; s. Adam and Kay Schweitzer; m. Nancy Hupp, 1981; children: Ben, Khai, Katrina. BS in Internat. Agronomy, Colo. State U., 1978; MS in Soil Sci., Mont. State U., 1980. Agronomist Kaercherv Agr., Libya, 1980—81; crop supt. Alfa Laval Engring. Co., Saudi Arabia, 1981—84; farm owner, rancher Flathead, Sanders Rosebud and Judith Basin counties, Mont.; mem. Mont. state farm svc. agency com. USDA, 1993—99; gov. State of Mont., Helena, 2005—. Apptd. Mont. Rural Devel. Partnership Bd., 1996, Nat. Drought Task Force. Recipient Award for outreach efforts to Native Americans, U.S. Sec. Agr., 1995. Democrat. Achievements include development of various immigration systems in Africa, Asia, Europe, and South America; over 28,000 acres of irrigated cropland in Saudi Arabia. Office: Office of the Gov PO Box 200801 Helena MT 59620-0801 Office Phone: 406-444-3111. Office Fax: 406-444-5529. E-mail: governor@mt.gov.

SCHWEIZER, EDWARD SOWERS, insurance agency owner; b. Houston, May 6, 1938; s. John Mel Jr. and Alicia Lucille (Sowers) S.; m. Suzan Lee Peterson, June 20, 1964; children: Edward Jr., Sally, Elizabeth. Degre superieur, U. Paris, 1957; BA, Occidental Coll., 1961; MA, Pepperdine U., 1978. Cert. surface warfare officer USN. Owner ESS Ins. Svcs., Chesapeake City, Md., 1989—. Mem. bd. Laguna Beach Pageant of the Masters; mem. adv. bd. San Diego Found., 1998-2000, Orange County Register Grants Bd., Santa Ana, Calif., 1998-99. Commr. City of Mission Viejo, 1990-92, 97-2000, Parks and Recreation Com., Chesapeake City, 2000—. Capt. USN, 1962-88. Mem.: Surface Navy Assn. (life), Navy League of the U.S. (life), Naval Res. Assn. (life), Res. Officers Assn. (life), Mil. Officers Assn. (life), KC (Grand Knight 1989—90). Republican. Roman Catholic. Avocations: civic affairs, fine art, international traveling, skiing, exercise. Home: 204 Bohemia Ave Chesapeake City MD 21915-0711 Office: ESS Ins Svcs 51 Calle Escalon Camarillo CA 93010-1708 Office Phone: 410-885-3822. Personal E-mail: captained@usa.com.

SCHWEIZER, NIKLAUS R., German educator; b. Zurich, Aug. 24, 1939; arrived in U.S., 1964; s. Rudolf Alexander Schweizer and Hedwig Louise Ulrich. BA, U. Zurich, 1964; PhD, U. Calif., Davis, 1968. Tchr. German Punahou Sch., Honolulu, 1968—70; vis. asst. prof. German Dept. European Lang. and Lit. U. Hawaii, Manoa, 1969—70, asst. prof. German, 1970—74, assoc. prof. German, 1974—83, prof. German, 1983—. Hon. consul of Switzerland, Honolulu, 1972—. Author: (novels) His Hawaiian Excellency, 1987, 1994, 2004, (book) The Ut pictura poesis Controversy in Eighteenth-Century England and Germany, 1972, A Poet Among Explorers: Chamisso in the South Seas, 1973, Hawaii und die deutschsprachigen Völker, 1982, Hawaii and the German Speaking Peoples, 1982, Seine hawaiische Exzellenz, 1990, Turning Tide: The Ebb and Flow of Hawaiian Nationality, 1999, 2002, 2005; editor: By Royal Command: Biographical Notes on Curtis Piehu Iaukea, 1988, Jour. des Malers Ludwig York Choris, 1999; contbr. articles to profl. jours., chpts. to books. Dean Consular Corps of Hawaii, 1986, historian, 1988—; pres. Friends of the Royal Hawaiian Band, 1979—99; steering com. Annexation Observance Hawai'i Loa Ku Like Kakou, 1998; bd. dirs. Friends of Iolani Palace, 1982—, chair spl. events com., 1980—2003; pres., mem. coun. Hui Hanai, aux. Queen Lili 'uokalani Children Trust, 1987, mem. coun., 1981—87; chmn. bd. Friends of the Royal Hawaiian Band, 1999—; bd. dirs. Ahahui Ka'iulani, 1990—, Moanalua Gardens Found., 1994—; del. Friends of Iolani Palace, 1996—. Recipient 1st Ann. Award, German-Hawaiian Friendship Club, 1998. Mem.: PEN Ctr. USA West, Pacific Translators, Royal Order of Kamehameha (hon.), German-Hawaiian Comm. and Friendship Club (hon.). Avocations: amateur radio, tennis, skiing, swimming. Office: Univ of Hawaii at Manoa Lang and Lit of Europe and the Ams 1890 East-West Rd Moore 483 Honolulu HI 96822 Office Phone: 808-956-4184. Business E-Mail: niklaus@hawaii.edu.

SCHWEND, GEORGE THOMAS, sales and marketing executive; b. Newark, Mar. 24, 1947; s. George Eugene and Jean Victory (Camalfa) S.; m. Alice C. Behrens (div.); children: George Thomas Jr., Nicole Marie; m. Jane Claire Poehling; 1 child, Erin O'Donnell. BBA in Mktg., N.E. La. U., 1970. Nat. sales mgr. EG&G Diagnostic Scis., Morris Plains, N.J., 1974-75, v.p. sales and mktg. div., 1975-77; nat. sales mgr. MetPath div. Corning Glass, Teterboro, N.J., 1977-79, gen. mgr., 1979-81; pres. Cen. Med. Lab., Dallas, 1981-84; v.p. sales and mktg. div. Lab Force, Inc., Dallas, 1984-87, v.p. adminstrn., 1987-88; v.p. sales and mktg. div. Western Star, Inc., Portland, Oreg., 1988, also bd. dirs.; general mgr. Corning Med.; pres. Infoscience; sr. v.p., pres., COO Healthcare.com (formerly HIE and Healthcare Comm. Inc.); founder, pres., CEO Health Language, Inc., Aurora, Colo., 2000—, also bd. dir. Cons. Kaplan & Assocs., Dallas, 1985-88. Instr. in hunter safety N.J. Dept. Conservation, 1972-75. Mem. Biomed. Mktg. Assn. Home: 2807 Staffordshire Dr Carrollton TX 75007-4814 Office: Health Language Inc 4600 S Syracuse St Ste 1250 Denver CO 80237-2750 Office Phone: 303-307-4400. Office Fax: 303-375-0656.

SCHWERIN, KARL HENRY, anthropology educator, researcher; b. Bertha, Minn., Feb. 21, 1936; s. Henry William and Audrey Merle (Jahn) S.; m. Judith Drewanne Altermatt, Sept. 1, 1958 (div. May 1975); children: Karl Frederic, Marguerite DelValle; m. Partha Louise, Jan. 25, 1979; stepchildren: Tamara, Brent, Taryn. BA, U. Calif., Berkeley, 1958; PhD, UCLA, 1965. Instr. Los Angeles State Coll., 1963; asst. prof. anthropology U. N.Mex., Albuquerque, 1963-68, assoc. prof., 1968-72, prof., 1972-2001, asst. chmn. dept. anthropology, 1983-85, chmn. dept. anthropology, 1987-93, prof. emeritus, 2001—. Prof. invitado Inst. Venezolano de Investigaciones Cientificas, Caracas, 1979. Author: Oil and Steel Processes of Karinya Culture Change, 1966, Antropologia Social, 1969, Winds Across the Atlantic, 1970; editor: Food Energy in Tropical Ecosystems, 1985; contbr. articles to profl. jours. V.p. Parents without Ptnr., Albuquerque, 1976-77. Grantee Cordell Hull Found., Venezuela, 1961-62, N.Y. Zool. Soc., Honduras, 1981; Fulbright scholar Cañar, Ecuador, 1969-70, Paris, 1986; founded Karl H. Schwerin Fellowship in Ethnology. Fellow Am. Anthropol. Assn.; mem. Am. Ethnol. Soc., Am. Soc. Ethnohistory (pres. 1975), Southwestern Anthropol. Assn. (co-editor Southwestern Jour. Anthropology 1972-75), N.Mex. Cactus and Succulent Soc. (v.p. 1970-71), Internat. Congress of Americanists (35th-40th, 43d, 46th, 48th, 49th, 50th), Netherwood Pk. Neighborhood Assn. (pres. 2005-07), Sigma Xi (chpt. pres. 1980-81) Avocations: photography, gardening, hiking, travel, bicycling. Office: U NMex Dept Anthropology MSC01-1040 Albuquerque NM 87131-0001 Office Phone: 505-277-4614. Business E-Mail: schwerin@unm.edu.

SCHWIETZ, ROGER L., archbishop; b. St. Paul, Minn., July 3, 1930; MA in Philosophy, U. Ottawa; MA in Sacred Theology, Loyola U.; STL in Sacred Theology, Gregorian U., Rome; HHD (hon.), Lewis U., 1998. Ordained priest Oblates of Mary Immaculate, 1967; assoc. pastor St. Thomas Aquinas Parish, International Falls, Minn., 1975—78; dir. Coll. Seminary prog. for Oblates of Mary Immaculate Creighton U., Omaha, 1978—84; pastor Holy Family Parish, Duluth, Minn., 1984—89; ordained bishop, 1990; bishop Diocese of Duluth, 1990—2000; coadjutor archbishop Archdiocese of Anchorage, Alaska, 2000—01, archbishop Alaska, 2001—; apostolic adminstr. Diocese of Juneau, Alaska, 2008—09. Episcopal moderator Teens Encounter Christ (TEC) movement, 1991—; chmn. vocation com. Nat. Conf. Cath. Bishops, 1998; bd. dir. Cath. Relief Services, 1997—2003; mem. adminstrv. bd. Nat. Conf. Cath. Bishops, 1994—97, 1998—2002; regional bd. rep. Am. Coll., Leuven, Belgium. Roman Catholic. Home and Office: Archdiocese of Anchorage 225 Cordova St Anchorage AK 99501-2409*

SCHWIMMER, DAVID, actor; b. Queens, NY, Nov. 12, 1966; BS in Speech/Theater, Northwestern U., 1988. Co-founder The Lookingglass Theater Co., Chgo., 1988. Actor (films) Flight of the Intruder, 1991, Crossing the Bridge, 1992, The Waiter, 1993, Twenty Bucks, 1993, The Party Favor, 1995, The Pallbearer, 1996, Breast Men, 1997, The Thin Pink Line, 1998, Kissing a Fool (also exec. prodr.), 1998, Six Days Seven Nights, 1998, Apt Pupil, 1998, All the Rage, 1999, Picking Up the Pieces, 2000, Hotel, 2001, Duane Hopwood, 2005, (voice) Madagascar, 2005(voice) Madagascar: Escape 2 Africa, 2008, Nothing But the Truth, 2008, (TV films) A Deadly Silence, 1989, Since You've Been Gone, 1998, Uprising, 2001, (TV miniseries) Band of Brothers, 2001, (TV series) The Wonder Years, 1992, Friends, 1994-2004, Monty, 1994, (stage appearances) West, The Odyssey, Of One Blood, In the Eye of the Beholder, The Master and Margarita, Some Girls, 2005; dir. (films) Run Fatboy Run, 2007, (TV series) Little Britain USA, 2008-; (TV appearances) LA Law, NYPD Blue, 1993, L.A. Law, 1992, 93, ER, 1996, The Single Guy, 1997, Curb Your Enthusiasm, 2004; exec. prodr. Humanoid, 2003, Shoot the Moon, 1996

SCHWIMMER, SIGMUND, food enzymologist; b. Cleve., Sept. 20, 1917; s. Solomon and Sarah (Brown) S.; m. Sylvia Klein, Dec. 18, 1941; children: Susan, Elaine. Student Ohio State U., 1935-36; B.S., George Washington U., 1940; M.S., Georgetown U., 1941, Ph.D., 1943. From lab. asst. to research chemist USDA, Washington and Berkeley, Calif., 1936-62; adj. prof. biology Calif. Inst. Tech., Pasadena, 1963-65; chief research biochemist USDA, Berkeley, 1966-72, collaborator emeritus, 1975-; adj. prof. dept. nutritional scis. U. Calif.-Berkeley, 1985-87; sr. expert biochemistry UN Indsl. Devel. Orgn., Haifa, Israel, 1973-74; cons. food enzymology, Berkeley, 1980-; lectr. dept. biotech. food engring. Israel Inst. Tech., Haifa, 1973; vis. scientist Food Industry Rsch. and Devel. Inst., Hsinchu, Taiwan, 1992. Contbr. articles to profl. jours.; editor, Biochem. Sci. Biotech., Cambridge, Eng., 1983—, Trends in Biochemistry, Trends in Biotechnology, 1983—, Jour. Food Biochemistry, 1977-98; author: Source Book of Food Enzymology, 1982 (Jour. Assn. Coll. and Rsch. Librs. award 1983). John S. Guggenheim fellow; NSF fellow; Carlsberg Biol. Inst. fellow, Copenhagen; recipient Superior Service award USDA, 1949, 59, Lifetime Achievement award, 1993, Agrl. and Food Chemistry Divsn. award Am. Chem. Soc., 1996. Fellow Inst. Food Technologists, inductee USDA's ARS Sci. Hall of Fame, 2005; mem. Am. Soc. Biochemistry Molecular Biology, Sigma Xi. Office: Western Regional Ctr USDA 800 Buchanan St Albany CA 94710-1105 also: U Calif Dept Nutritional Sci Berkeley CA 94720-0001 Office Phone: 510-559-5873. Business E-Mail: sig@pw.usda.gov.

SCIFRES, DONALD RAY, finance company executive; m. Carol Scifres. BS, Purdue U., 1968; MS, U. Ill., 1970, PhD, 1972; Doctorate (hon.), Purdue U., 2001. Rsch. and tchg. asst. U. Ill., Urbana, 1968-72; rsch. fellow, area mgr. Xerox Corp., Palo Alto, Calif., 1972-83; founder, pres., CEO SDL, Inc., San Jose, Calif., 1983-2001, dir., 1983-2001, chmn., 1992-2001; co-chmn., chief strategy officer JDS Uniphase Corp., 2001—03; chmn. SDL Capital, LP, 2003—; mng. dir. SDL Ventures, LLC, 2003—. Nat. lectr. IEEE Quantum Electronics Soc., 1979 Bd. editors Jour. Fiber and Integrated Optics, 1978; mem. editorial adv. bd. Photonics Spectra, 1992-2008; contbr. articles to tech. jours.; patentee in field. Recipient Disting. Engring. Alumni award, Purdue U., 1990, Outstanding Elec. Engr. award, 1992, The Gov. Nobert T. Tiemann award, Beta Sigma Pi, 2002, Engring. Alumni award, U. Ill., 1991, Alumni Honor award, 1993, Distinction in Photonics award, Laurin Pub. Co., 1999, Rank prize, Rank Found., U.K., 2001; fellow U. Ill., 1968, Gen. Telephone and Electronics, 1970—72. Fellow IEEE (Jack Morton award 1985, 3d Millenium award 2000, Robert N. Noyce medal 2003, John Tyndall award 2006), IEEE Lasers and Electro-Optics Soc. (pres. 1992, Engring. Achievement award 1994), Optical Soc. Am. (Edward H. Land medal 1996); mem. Am. Phys. Soc. (George E. Pake prize 1997), Lasers and Electro-Optics Mfg. Assn. (bd. dirs. 1992-, sec. 1994, pres. 1996), Nat. Acad. Engring., Tau Beta Pi, Eta Kappa Nu (Eminent Mem. award 2003), Phi Eta Sigma. Office: One First St Ste 14 Los Altos CA 94022

SCILACCI, W. JAMES, JR., utilities executive; BA in Econs., UCLA; MBA, Santa Clara U., Calif. Fin. assoc. Getty Oil Co., Bank of America; treasurer's org. and positions in corp. fin., investor rels. fin. analysis, and cash mgmt. So. Calif. Edison, 1984—93, asst. treas., 1993—95, dir. qualifying facilities resources, 1995—2000, v.p., CFO, 2000—03, gen. rate case team leader, 2003, sr. v.p., CFO, 2003—05, Edison Mission Group, 2005—08; exec. v.p., CFO, and treas. Edison Internat., 2008—. Office: Edison Internat 2244 Walnut Grove Ave Rosemead CA 91770 Office Phone: 626-302-2222.

SCITOVSKY, ANNE AICKELIN, economist, researcher; b. Ludwigshafen, Germany, Apr. 17, 1915; arrived in U.S., 1931, naturalized, 1938; d. Hans W. and Gertrude Margarete Aickelin; 1 child, Catherine Margaret. Student, Smith Coll., 1933—35; BA, Barnard Coll., 1937; postgrad., London Sch. Econs., 1937—39; MA in Econs., Columbia U., 1941. Mem. staff legis. reference svc. Libr. of Congress, 1941—44; mem. staff Social Security Bd., 1944—46; with Palo Alto (Calif.) Med. Found./Rsch. Inst., 1963—, chief health econs. div., 1973—94, sr. staff scientist, 1994—. Lectr. Inst. Health Policy Studies, U. Calif., San Francisco, 1975—94; mem. Inst. Medicine of NAS, Nat. Acad. Social Ins., Pres.'s Commn. for Study of Ethical Problems in Medicine and Biomed. and Behavioral Rsch., 1979—82, U.S. Nat. Com. on Vital and Health Stats., 1975—78, Health Resources and Svcs. Adminstrn., AIDS adv. com., 1990—94; cons. HHS, Inst. Medicine Coun. on Health Care Tech. Assessment, 1986—90. Home: 161 Erica Way Portola Valley CA 94028-7439 Office: Palo Alto Med Found Rsch Inst Ames Bldg 795 El Camino Real Palo Alto CA 94301-2302 Personal E-mail: ascitovsky@aol.com.

SCLATER, JOHN GEORGE, geophysics educator; b. Edinburgh, June 17, 1940; s. John George and Margaret Bennett (Glen) S.; m. Naila Gloria Sclater; children: Iain Andrew, Stuart Michael. B.Sc., Edinburgh U., 1962; PhD, Cambridge U., Eng., 1966. Research geophysicist Scripps Inst. Oceanography, La Jolla, Calif., 1965-72, prof., 1991—; asso. prof. MIT, 1972-77, prof., 1977-83; dir. Joint Program Oceanography Woods Hole Oceanographic Inst., 1981-83; Shell Cos. chair in geophysics U. Tex., Austin, 1983-91; prof. Scripps Instn. Oceanography, U. Calif., San Diego, 1991—, now prof. geophysics La Jolla. Sweeney lectr. Edinburgh U., 1976. Contbr. articles to profl. jours. Guggenheim Found. fellow, 1998-99; recipient Rosenstiel award oceanography, 1979, numerous award for publs. Fellow Geol. Soc. Am., Royal Soc. London, Am. Geophys. Union (Bucher medal 1985); mem. NAS (mem. ocean studies bd., 1985-92, chair 1988-91). Home: 5701 Skylark Pl La Jolla CA 92037-7742 Office: Scripps Instn Oceanography La Jolla CA 92093-0215

SCOGGINS, M. W. (BILL SCOGGINS), academic administrator; Grad., U. Tulsa; M in Petroleum Engring., U. Okla.; PhD in Petroleum Engring., U. Tulsa. With Mobil, 1970—99; mem., exec. com. Mobil Oil; pres. Internat. E & P, Global Exploration; exec. v.p. ExxonMobil Prodn. Co., 1999—2004; pres. Colo. Sch. Mines, 2006—. Mem., exec. com. U. Tulsa Bd. Trustees, 2005, mem., fin., investment, audit com., mem., faculty and curriculum com.; mem., bd. dirs. Questar Corp., Trico Marine Services, Inc., Colo. Renewable Energy Authority. Sec. Bapt. Found. Colo. Named to Coll. Engring. Hall of Fame, 1998. Mem.: Colo. Oil and Gas Assn. Office: Office of Pres Colorado School of Mines 1500 Illinois St Golden CO 80401-1887

SCOLES, EUGENE FRANCIS, lawyer, educator; b. Shelby, Iowa, June 12, 1921; s. Sam and Nola E. (Leslie) S.; m. R. Helen Glawson, Sept. 6, 1942; children— Kathleen Elizabeth, Janene Helen. AB, U. Iowa, Iowa City, 1943, JD, 1945; LLM, Harvard U., Cambridge, Mass., 1949; JSD, Columbia U., NYC, 1955. Bar: Iowa 1945, Ill. 1946. Assoc. Seyfarth-Shaw & Fairweather, Chgo., 1945-46; asst. prof. law Northeastern U., 1946-48, assoc. prof., 1948-49, U. Fla., 1949-51, prof., 1951-56, U. Ill., Champaign, 1956-68, Max Rowe prof. law, 1982-89, prof. emeritus, 1989—; vis. prof. McGeorge Law Sch. U. Pacific, Sacramento, 1989-92; prof. U. Oreg., 1968-82, dean Sch. Law, 1968-74, disting. prof. emeritus, 1982—. Vis. prof. Khartoum U., Sudan, 1964-65; reporter Uniform Probate Code Project, 1966-70; mem. joint editorial bd. Uniform Probate Code, 1972—, Uniform Law Com., 1970-82. Author: (with H.F. Goodrich) Conflict of Laws, 4th edit., 1964, (with R.J. Weintraub) Cases and Materials on Conflict of Laws, 2d edit., 1972, (with E.C. Halbach, Jr., P.G. Roberts, H.D. Begleiter) Problems and Materials on Decedents' Estates and Trusts, 7th edit., 2006, Problems and Materials on Future Interests, 1977, (with P. Hay, P.J. Borchers, S.C. Symeonides) Conflict of Laws, 4th edit., 2004; contbr. articles to profl. jours.; notes and legislation editor Iowa Law Rev., 1945. Mem. ABA, Soc. Pub. Tchrs. Law, Am. Law Inst., Ill. Bar Assn., Assn. Am. Law Schs. (pres. 1978), Order of Coif Office: U Oreg Sch Law 1515 Agate St Eugene OR 97403-1221 Office Phone: 541-346-3862.

SCORGIE, GLEN GIVEN, religious studies educator; b. Mar. 29, 1952; married; 3 children. MA, Wheaton Grad. Sch., 1974; MCS, Regent Coll., 1982; postgrad., Cambridge U., 1983; PhD, U. St. Andrews, 1986. Mktg. asst. IBM Can., Toronto, 1974-76; dir. admissions Can Bible Coll., Regina, 1976-79, asst. prof. theology, 1984-88, assoc. prof. theology, 1988-91; dean, v.p. N.Am. Bapt. Coll., 1991-96; prof. theology Bethel Seminary, San Diego, 1996—. Spkr. in field. Author: A Call for Continuity: The Theological Contribution of James Orr, 1988; contbr. articles to profl. jours. British Govt. Overseas Rsch. scholar, 1981-84. Mem. Am. Acad. Religion, Evang. Theol. Soc., Can. Evang. Theol. Assn., Conf. Faith and History, Delta Epsilon Chi. Office: Bethel Seminary 6116 Arosa St San Diego CA 92115-3999

SCOTCHMER, SUZANNE ANDERSEN, economics professor; b. Seattle, Jan. 23, 1950; d. Toivo Matthias and Margaret A. BA in Econ., U. Wash., 1970; MA in Stats., U. Calif., Berkeley, 1979, PhD in Econ., 1980. Asst., assoc. prof. econ. Harvard U., Cambridge, Mass., 1981—86; prof. econs. and pub. policy U. Calif., Berkeley, 1986—. Vis. prof. U. Toronto, 1993, Tel Aviv U., 1994, U. Paris, Sorbonne, 1992, New Sch. of Econs., Moscow, 1993, U. Auckland, 2002; Stockholm Sch. Econs., 2006, U. Calif., 2007, NYU, 2008, prin. investigator, NSF, 1986-2002; mem. Toulouse Network on Info. Tech., 2005-; mem. sci. tech. econ. policy bd., NAS, 2005-. Author: Innovation and Incentives, 2004; mem. editl. bd. Am. Econ. Rev., 1991-95, Jour. Pub. Econ., 1986-01, Jour. Econ. Perspectives, 1994-

97, Regional Sci. and Urban Econ., 1991—, Jour. Econ. Lit., 1998-01; contbr. articles to profl. jours. Sloan fellow, 1979, Phi Beta Kappa fellow, 1978, Hoover Nat. fellow Stanford U., 1989, Olin fellow Yale Sch. Law, 1993, and Sch. Law U. So. Calif., 2005; France/Berkeley Fund grantee, 1994-95; Kaufmann Found. grantee, 2005. Office: Univ Calif 2607 Hearst Ave Berkeley CA 94720-7320 Business E-Mail: scotch@berkeley.edu.

SCOTT, A. TIMOTHY, lawyer; b. Natchez, Miss., Feb. 16, 1952; s. John William and Patricia (O'Reilly) S.; m. Nancy E. Howard, June 7, 1976; children: Kevin Howard, Brian Howard. BA in Psychology, Stanford U., 1974, JD, 1977. Bar: Calif. 1977, U.S. Tax Ct. 1978. Assoc. then ptnr. Agnew, Miller & Carlson, LA, 1977-83; assoc. Greenberg, Glusker, Fields, Claman & Machtinger, LA, 1983; ptnr. Sachs & Phelps, LA, 1983-91; mem. Heller, Ehrman White & McAuliffe, LA, 1991-96, of counsel, 1996-99; sr. v.p., tax counsel Pub. Storage, Inc., Glendale, Calif., 1996—. Speaker in field. Note editor Stanford Law Rev., 1976-77; contbr. article to profl. publs., chpt. to book. Mem. ABA, L.A. County Bar Assn. (chmn. real estate taxation com. 1988-91, exec. com., taxation sect. 1989-91), Order of Coif. Democrat. Avocations: volleyball, gardening, art, skiing. Office: Pub Storage Inc 701 Western Ave Glendale CA 91201-2349 Business E-Mail: tscott@publicstorage.com.

SCOTT, ALLEN JOHN, public policy and geography educator; b. Liverpool, England, Dec. 23, 1938; came to U.S., 1980; s. William Rule and Nella Maria (Pieri) S.; m. Nga Thuy Nguyen, Jan. 19, 1979. BA, Oxford U., Eng., 1961; PhD, Northwestern U., 1965. Prof. geography UCLA, 1980—, dir. Lewis Ctr. for Regional Policy Studies, 1990-94, assoc. dean Sch. Pub. Policy and Social Rsch., 1994-97. Professeur associé U. Paris, 1974; André Siegfried chair Inst. d'Etudes Plitiques, Paris, 1999; dir. Ctr. Globalization and Policy Rsch., 2000—. Author: Combinatorial Programming, 1971, Urban Land Nexus, 1980, Metropolis, 1988, New Industrial Spaces, 1988, Technopolis, 1993, Regions and the World Economy, 1998, The Cultural Economy of Cities, 2000, On Hollywood, 2005, Geography and Economy, 2006. Fellow Com. on Scholarly Communication with People's Republic China, 1986. Croucher fellow U. Hong Kong, 1984, Vautrin Lud prize, 2003; Guggenheim fellow, 1986-87. Fellow Brit. Acad. (corr.). Office: UCLA Sch Pub Affairs Box 951656 6367 Pub Policy Bldg 1144 Bunche Los Angeles CA 90095 Office Phone: 310-825-7344. Office Fax: 310-206-0337. E-mail: ajscott@geog.ucla.edu.

SCOTT, DAVID J., lawyer, medical products executive; B, St. Lawrence U., Canton, NY; JD, Cornell Law Sch., Ithaca, NY. Pvt. practice lawyer; with RJR Nabisco, Inc., Grand Met. PLC; sr. v.p., gen. counsel Internat. Distillers & Vintners, London, 1996—97; gen. counsel United Distillers & Vintners, London, 1997—99; sr. v.p., gen. counsel Medtronic, Inc., 1999—2004, sec., 2000—04; sr. v.p., gen. counsel, sec., mem. exec. com. Amgen, Inc., Thousand Oaks, Calif., 2004—. Office: Amgen Inc One Amgen Ctr Dr Thousand Oaks CA 91320-1799 Office Phone: 805-447-1000. Office Fax: 805-447-1010.

SCOTT, DEBORAH L., costume designer; Costume designer: (films) E.T. The Extra-Terrestrial, 1982, Twilight Zone-The Movie ("Kick the Can", "Nightmare at 20,000 Feet"), 1983, Back to the Future, 1985, About Last Night..., 1986, Armed and Dangerous, 1986, Who's That Girl?, 1987, Moving, 1988, Coupe de Ville, 1990, Defending Your Life, 1991, Eve of Destruction, 1991, Sliver, 1993, Jack the Bear, 1993, Legends of the Fall, 1994, Indian in the Cupboard, 1995, To Gillian on Her 37th Birthday, 1996, Titanic, 1997 (Acad. award 1998), Wild Wild West, 1999, The Patriot, 2000, Minority Report, 2001. Recipient Academy award, 1998.

SCOTT, DOUGLAS EDWARD, lawyer; b. Evanston, Ill., Jan. 20, 1957; BA in Economics, magna cum laude, U. Ill., 1979, MBA, 1981; JD, UCLA, 1984. Bar: Calif., 1984; U.S. Dist. Ct. (cen. dist.) Calif.; CPA, Ill. Assoc. O'Melveny & Myers, 1984-87; atty. Sci. Applications Internat. Corp., San Diego, 1987—92, corp. v.p., gen. counsel, 1992—97, sr. v.p., gen. counsel, 1997—2003, sr. v.p., sec., gen counsel, 2003—07, exec. v.p., sec., gen. counsel, 2007—. James scholar. Mem. ABA, State Bar of Calif. (sr. v.p., gen. counsel and asst. sec.), Phi Beta Kappa. Office: Sci Applications Internat Corp Mail Stop F 3 10260 Campus Point Dr San Diego CA 92121

SCOTT, EDWARD WILLIAM, JR., computer company executive; b. Panama City, Panama, May 25, 1938; s. Edward William and Janice Gertrude (Grimison) S.; m. Cheryl S. Gilliland, apr. 23, 1988; children: Edward William, Heather Yolanda Deirdre, Reece Donald; 1 stepson, Erik Veit. BA, Mich. State U., 1959, MA, 1963; BA, Oxford U., Eng., 1962. Personnel specialist Panama Canal Co., 1962-64, staff asst. to dir. personnel, 1964-66; personnel officer IRS, Detroit, 1966-68; staff personnel mgmt. specialist U.S. Dept. Justice, Washington, 1968-69, chief personnel systems and evaluation sect., 1970-72, dir. Office Mgmt. Programs, 1972-74, assoc. dep. commr. planning and evaluation U.S. Immigration and Naturalization Svc., 1974-75, dep. asst. atty. gen., 1972-75, asst. sec. for adminstrn. Trans. Dept., 1977-80; pres. Office Power, Inc., Washington, 1980-81; dir. mktg. Computer Consoles, Inc., 1981-84; v.p. mktg. Dest Systems, 1984-85; dir. govt. mktg. Sun Microsystems, Mountain View, Calif., 1985-88; exec. v.p. Pyramid Tech., Mountain View, 1988-95; founder, pres. BEA Sys., Inc., San Jose, Calif., 1995—. Founder, chmn. Ctr. for Global Devel., Washington, (with Bill Gates and George Soros) Data-Debt, AIDS, and Trade-Africa; founder, chmn., Friends of the Global Fight, Wash.; founder, pres. escottVentures, Inc.; owner, chmn., Fla. Bear Com.; owner, Kriz Tennis Club; pres. U.S. Dept. Justice Fed. Credit Union, 1970-73. Bd. mem. Malaria No More, VOXIVA, Holy Trinity Episcopal Acad., Fla. Inst. Tech., King Ctr. Performing Arts. Recipient Presdl. Mgmt. Improvement certificate, 1971; Spl. Commendation award Dept. Justice, 1973; also Spl. Achievement award, 1976; William A. Jump Meml. award, 1974; presdl. sr. exec. service rank of Disting. Exec., 1980; Mich. State U. scholar, 1957-60. Mem.: Phi Kappa Phi, Phi Eta Sigma. Office: Bea Software 5450 Great America Pkwy Santa Clara CA 95054-3644 Business E-Mail: ed@escottventures.com.

SCOTT, EUGENIE CAROL, science foundation director, anthropologist; b. LaCrosse, Wis., Oct. 24, 1945; d. Allen K. and Virginia Meliss (Derr) S.; m. Robert Abner Black, Oct. 18, 1965 (div. 1970); m. Thomas Charles Sager, Dec. 30, 1971; 1 child, Carrie Ellen Sager. BS in Anthropology, U. Wis., Milw., 1967, MS in Anthropology, 1968; PhD in Anthropology, U. Mo., Columbia, 1974; DSc (hon.), McGill U., 2003, Ohio State U., 2005, Mt. Holyoke Coll., 2006, U. Wis., Milw., 2006, Rutgers U., New Brunswick, NJ, 2007, U. New Mex., 2008. Asst. prof. anthropology U. Ky., Lexington, 1974-82; postdoctoral fellow U. Calif., San Francisco, 1983-84; asst. prof., dept. anthropology U. Colo., Boulder, 1984-86; exec. dir., pub. newsletter NCSE Reports, Nat. Ctr. Sci. Edn., Oakland, Calif., 1987—. Vis. prof., U. Kans., 1976; bd. dirs. Biol. Scis. Curriculum Study, Colorado Springs, Colo., 1993-99; pub. Bookwatch Revs., 1988-92. Author, editor: Biology Textbooks, The New Generation, 1990, Evolution and Creationism: An Introduction, 2004, 2nd edit 2009; co-author: Teaching About Evolution and the Nature of Science, 1998; co-editor: Not In Our Classrooms: Why Intelligent Design is Wrong for Our Schools, 2006; prodr.: (videotape series) How Scientists Know About... Mem. nat. adv. bd. Ams. United for Separation of Ch. and State, Washington, 1995—; mem. nat. adv. coun. Am. Civil Liberties Union, 2005-. Recipient Pub. Sci. and Edn. award Com. for Sci. Investigation Claims of Paranormal, 1991, Disting. Alumnus award U. Mo. Arts and Scis., 1993, Isaac Asimov Sci. award Am. Humanist Assn., 1998, James Randi Skeptic of Yr. award Skeptic Soc., 1999, Bruce Alberts award Am. Soc. Cell Biology, 1999, 1st Amendment award Playboy Found., 1999, Outstanding Svc. award, Am. Inst. Biol. Scis, 2002, Pub. Svc. award, Nat. Sci. Bd., 2003, Geol. Soc. Am. Pub. Svc. award, 2001, Margaret Nicholson Dist. Svc. award Calif. Sci. Tchr. Assn., 2002, Ctr. for Inquiry Def. Sci. award, 2003, Anthropology in Media award Anthrop. Assn., 2006, Scientific Freedom and Responsibility award, Am. Assoc Adv. Sci., 2007, Outstanding Educator award, Exploratorium, 2007, UCSF medal, 2008. Fellow Com. Scientific Investigation, Calif. Acad. Scis. (elected 1994), AAAS; mem. Am. Assn. Phys. Anthropology (bd. dirs., exec. com. 1988-93, sec.-treas. 1993-97, pres. 2001-2003), Am. Anthropol. Assn., Nat. Assn. Biology Tchrs. (hon.), Nat. Sci. Tchrs. Assn., Sigma Xi. Office: Nat Ctr Sci Edn PO Box 9477 Berkeley CA 94709-0477 also: Nat Ctr Sci Edn 420 40th St Ste 2 Oakland CA 94609-2509

SCOTT, GREGORY KELLAM, former state supreme court justice, lawyer; b. San Francisco, July 30, 1943; s. Robert and Althea Delores Scott; m. Carolyn Weatherly, Apr. 10, 1971; children: Joshua Weatherly, Elijah Kellam. BS in Environ. Sci., Rutgers U., 1970, EdM in Urban Studies, 1971; JD cum laude, Ind. U., Indpls., 1977. Asst. dean resident instrn. Cook Coll. Rutgers U., 1972-75; trial atty. U.S. SEC, Denver, 1977-79; gen. counsel Blinder, Robinson & Co., Inc., Denver, 1979-80; asst. prof. coll. law U. Denver, 1980-85, assoc. prof., 1985-93, prof. emeritus, 1993—, chair bus. planning program, 1986-89, 92-93; justice Colo. Supreme Ct., Denver, 1993-2000; gen. counselor Kaiser-Hill Co., Golden, Colo., 2000—; judge trial referee Colo. Supreme Ct., Colo., 2000. Of counsel Moore, Smith & Bryant, Indpls., 1987-90; v.p., gen. counsel Comml. Energies, Inc., 1990-91; presenter in field. Author: (with others) Structuring Mergers and Acquisitions in Colorado, 1985, Airport Law and Regulation, 1991, Racism and Underclass in America, 1991; contbr. articles to profl. jours. Mem. ABA, Nat. Bar Assn., Nat. Assn. Securities Dealers, Inc., Nat. Arbitration Panel (arbitrator), Colo. Bar Found., Sam Cary Bar Assn., Am. Inn Ct. (founding mem. Judge Alfred A. Arraj inn). Avocations: golf, reading, travel. Office: Kaiger Hill 11025 Dover St Unit 1000 Westminster CO 80021-5573

SCOTT, GREGORY W., health care company executive; B in Math. Econ., Colgate U.; MS, U. Mich. cert. CLU. Sr. v.p. Prudential Capital Corp.; gen. ptnr. RRY Ptnrs.; v.p. corp. fin. Salomon Brothers, Inc.; exec. v.p., CFO Prudential Securities; pres. no. ctrl. group, healthcare & employee benefits ops. Prudential Ins. Co., v.p., treas., sr. v.p., CFO health care group; COO, CFO Medsite, 1999-01; exec. v.p., CFO PacifiCare Health Sys. Inc., Cypress, Calif., 2001—. Mem. Fin. Exec. Inst. Office: PacifiCare Health Sys 5995 Plaza Dr Cypress CA 90630

SCOTT, J. LENNOX, real estate company executive; s. W. Lennox Scott. BBA, U. Washington. Cert. residential broker. Pres. John L. Scott Real Estate, Bellevue, Wash., 1980—2002, chmn., CEO, 2002—. Author: Next Generation Real Estate, 2002. Active John L. Scott Found.; bd. dirs. Econ. Develop. Coun., Seattle/King County, Wash. Wildlife & Recreation Coalition. Named one of Five Most Admired Individuals' in Real Estate, REAL Trends Inc., 2005, Real Estate's 25 Most Influential Thought Leaders, Realtor Mag., 2006; named to Hall of Leaders, Coun. Real Estate Brokerage Mgrs., 2005. Mem.: Realty Alliance, Young Pres.'s Alumni Orgn., Nat. Assn. Home Builders, Seattle King County Assn. Realtors (former pres., Realtor of Yr. 2002, Pres.'s award 2003), Nat. Assn. Realtors (bd. dirs., Pacesetter award), Rotary Internat. Office: John L Scott 3380 146th Pl SE Ste 450 Bellevue WA 98007 Office Phone: 206-230-7600. Office Fax: 206-230-7650.

SCOTT, JACK ALAN, academic administrator, former state senator; b. Sweetwater, Tex., Aug. 24, 1933; m. Lacreta Isbell Scott; children: Sharon Mitchell, Sheila Head, Amy Schones, Greg, Adam(dec.). BA, Abilene Christian U., 1954; MDiv, Yale U., 1962; MA, Claremont Graduate U., 1967; PhD, Claremont U., 1970; LLD (hon.), Pepperdine U., 1991. Mem. faculty Pepperdine U., 1962-72, provost, 1970-73; dean Orange Coast Coll., 1973-78; pres. Cypress Coll., 1978-87, Pasadena City Coll., 1987-95, pres. emeritus, 1995—; prof. higher edn. Pepperdine U., 1995—; mem. Calif. State Assembly from 44th Dist., 1996—2000, Calif. State Senate from 21st Dist., 2000—08, past chair Accreditation Commn. of Western Assn. of Schs., mem. budget, ins. and transp. coms., chair edn. com. and edn. budget subcommittee; chancellor Calif. CC Sys., 2009—. CEO bd. govs. Co-founder Coalition for a Non-Violent City; past chair Am. Heart Assn. Mem.: Calif. Healthcare Assn., Assn. Calif. C.C. Adminstrs. (past pres.), Pasadena Rotary, Rubio Canon Land and Water Assn. Democrat. Church Of Christ. Office: Calif CC Sys Office 1102 Q St, 4th Fl Sacramento CA 95814 Office Phone: 916-322-4005. E-mail: jscott@cccco.edu.*

SCOTT, JAMES MICHAEL, research biologist; b. San Diego, Sept. 20, 1941; m. 1966; 2 children. BS, San Diego State U., 1966, MA, 1970; PhD in Zoology, Oreg. State U., 1973. Biol. aide U.S. Bur. Comml. Fisheries, 1966-68; asst. curator vertebrates Nat. Hist. Mus., Oreg. State U., 1969-73; rschr. Dept. Fisheries & Wildlife, 1973-74; biologist in charge Mauna Loa Field Sta. U.S. Fish & Wildlife Svc., 1974-84, dir. Condor Field Sta., 1984-86; instr. ornithology Malheur Environ. Field Sta., Pacific U., 1972, 73; leader Fish & Wildlife Rsch. Unit U. Idaho, Moscow, 1986—. Leader Maui Forest Bird Recovery Team, 1975-79, Hawaii Forest Bird Recovery Team, 1975; mem. Palila Recovery Team, 1975; mem. Am. Ornithologists Union Conservation Com., 1974-75, 75-76, sci. adv. bd. Nature Conservancy Hawaii Forest Bird Project, 1981; Richard M. Nixon scholar Whittier Coll. Fellow Am. Ornithologists Union; mem. Nature Conservancy, Ecol. Soc. Am., The Wildlife Soc., Soc. Conservation Biology, Inst. Biol. Sci., Cooper Ornithol. Soc. (pres. 1997—). Office: U Idaho Fish & Wildlife Rsch Unit 1130 Kamiaken St Moscow ID 83843-3855

SCOTT, JILL, poet, musician; b. Phila., 1952; Founder, pres. Blues Babe Found. Singer (with Eric Benet, Will Smith, Roots, Common); musician: (albums) Who is Jill Scott? Words & Sounds, Vol. 1, 2000, Experience: Jill Scott 826+, 2001, Beautifully Human: Words and Sounds, Vol. 2, 2004, The Real Thing, 2007, (songs) God Bless the Child, 2007 (Grammy award for Best Traditional R&B Performance, 2007), Daydreamin', 2007 (Grammy award for Best Urban/Alternative Performance, 2008); co-prodr.(with Dr. Cornel West et. al.): (albums) Never Forget: A Journey of Revelations, 2007; actor: (plays) Rent. Founder Blues Babe Found., Phila. Recipient Grammy Award, 2003. Office: Hidden Beach Recordings 3030 Nebraska Ave Santa Monica CA 90404

SCOTT, JOHN D., pharmacologist; b. Edinburgh, Apr. 13, 1958; married; 2 children. BSc in Biochemistry with honors, Herriot-Watt U., Edinburgh, 1980; PhD in Biochemistry, U. Aberdeen, 1983. NIH postdoctoral fellow dept. pharmacology U. Wash., Seattle, 1983—86, rsch. asst. prof. dept. biochemistry, 1986—88; asst. prof. dept. physiology and biophysics, dept. biol. chemistry U. Calif., Irvine, 1988—89; asst. scientist Ctr. Rsch. Occupl. & Environ. Toxicology Oreg. Health Scis. U., 1989—90, asst. scientist Vollum Inst. Advanced Biomed. Rsch., dept. biochemistry and molecular biology, 1990—92, scientist, 1993—97, sr. scientist, 1997—; investigator Howard Hughes Med. Ctr. (known as Vollum Inst.), 1997—. Spkr. in field. Mem. editl. bd. Jour. Biol. Chemistry; contbr. articles to profl. jours. Recipient John J. Abel award, Am. Soc. Pharmacology and Exptl. Therapeutics, 1996; scholar Med. Endowments Hon., U. Aberdeen, 1980—83. Fellow: Royal Soc.; mem.: Protein Soc., Biochem. Soc., Am. Soc. Biochemistry and Molecular Biology (William C. Rose award 2008). Office: Vollum Inst Oreg Health Scis U 3181 SW Sam Jackson Park Rd Portland OR 97239-3011

SCOTT, KENNETH EUGENE, lawyer, educator; b. Western Springs, Ill., Nov. 21, 1928; s. Kenneth L. and Bernice (Albright) S.; m. Viviane H. May, Sept. 22, 1956 (dec. Feb. 1982); children: Clifton, Jeffrey, Linda; m. Priscilla Gay, July 30, 1989; children: Ashley (dec. Apr. 2002), Shaler. BA in Econs., Coll. William and Mary, 1949; MA in Polit. Sci., Princeton U., 1953; LLB, Stanford U., 1956. Bar: N.Y. 1957, Calif. 1957, D.C. 1967. Assoc. Sullivan & Cromwell, NYC, 1956-59, Musick, Peeler & Garrett, LA, 1959-61; chief dep. savs. and loan commr. State of Calif., LA, 1961-63; gen. counsel Fed. Home Loan Bank Bd., Washington, 1963-67; Parsons prof. law and bus. Stanford (Calif.) Law Sch., 1968-95, emeritus, 1995—; sr. rsch. fellow Hoover Instn., 1978-95, emeritus, 1995—; fellow Am. Acad. Berlin, 2001. Mem. Shadow Fin. Regulatory Com., 1986—, Fin. Economists Roundtable, 1991—. Author: (with others) Retail Banking in the Electronic Age, 1977; co-editor: The Economics of Corporation Law and Securities Regulation, 1980. Mem. Calif. Bar Assn., Phi Beta Kappa, Order of Coif, Pi Kappa Alpha, Omicron Delta Kappa. Home: 610 Gerona Rd Stanford CA 94305-8453 Office: Stanford Law Sch Stanford CA 94305-8610 Home Phone: 650-325-0909; Office Phone: 650-723-3070. E-mail: kenscott@stanford.edu.

SCOTT, MARY CELINE, pharmacologist; b. LA, July 14, 1957; d. Walter Edward and Shirley Jean (Elvin) S. BS in Biol. Sci., U. Calif., Irvine, 1978; MS in Biology, Calif. State U., Long Beach, 1980; PhD in Pharmacology, Purdue U., 1985; MBA in Pharm.-Chem. Studies, Fairleigh Dickinson U., 1995. Tchg. asst. Calif. State U., Long Beach, 1979-80, Purdue U., West Lafayette, Ind., 1980-82, grad. instr., 1982-83, rsch. fellow, 1983-85, 1988-89, Mayo Found., Rochester, Minn., 1985-87; sr. scientist Schering-Plough, Bloomfield, NJ, 1989-92; assoc. prin. scientist Schering-Plough Rsch. Inst., Kenilworth, NJ, 1993-98, prin. scientist, 1998-2000, mgr. U.S. regulatory affairs, 2000—02, mgr. global regulatory affairs, 2002—04; sr. mgr. U.S. regulatory affairs Amgen, Thousand Oaks, Calif., 2004—. Contbr. articles to profl. jours. Mem.: AAAS, Soc. Neurosci., Internat. Soc. for Study Xenobiotics, Am. Soc. Pharm. and Exptl. Therapeutics, Am. Chem. Soc. Democrat. Office: Amgen One Amgen Center Dr Thousand Oaks CA 91320-1799 Office Phone: 805-447-3741. Business E-Mail: mascott@amgen.com.

SCOTT, MATTHEW PETER, biology educator; b. Boston, Jan. 30, 1953; s. Peter Robert and Duscha (Schmid) S.; m. Margaret Tatnall Fuller, May 13, 1990; children: Lincoln Fuller, Julia Fuller. BS, MIT, 1975, PhD, 1980. Postdoctoral tng. Ind. U., Bloomington, 1980-83; from asst. prof. to assoc. prof. U. Colo., Boulder, 1983-90; prof. Stanford (Calif.) U., 1990—, chmn. dept. devel. biology, 1997-98, assoc. chmn. dept. devel. biology, 1999—; assoc. investigator Howard Hughes Med. Inst., 1989-90, investigator, 1993—. Vis. prof. genetics Harvard Med. Sch., 1994-95. Recipient Passano Young Investigator award Passano Found., 1990. Mem. NAS, Inst. Medicine, Am. Acad. Arts and Scis. Achievements include research in developmental genetics, in particular, homeotic genes, signaling systems, and cancer biology. Office: Stanford U Sch Med Dept Devel Biology 279 Campus Dr Beckman B300 Stanford CA 94305-5329*

SCOTT, MCGREGOR W., lawyer, former prosecutor; b. 1962; m. Jennifer Urbanski Scott; 3 children. BA in History, Santa Clara U.; JD, U. Calif. Dep. dist. atty. Contra Costa County, 1989—97; dist. atty. Shasta County, 1997—2003; US atty. (ea. dist.) Calif. US Dept. Justice, Sacramento, 2003—09; ptnr., mem. Litig. Group Orrick, Herrington & Sutcliffe LLP, Sacramento, 2009—. Chair Rural Counties Commn., Calif. Dist. Atty. Assn.; bd. dirs. Calif. Dist. Atty. Assn.; mem. US Atty. Gen. Adv. Com. Lt. col. USNG. Avocations: reading, basketball, golf, exercise, college football, hunting. Office: Orrick, Herrington & Sutcliffe LLP 400 Capitol Mall, Ste 3000 Sacramento CA 95814-4497 Office Phone: 916-329-7982. Office Fax: 916-329-4900. E-mail: mscott@orrick.com.*

SCOTT, MICHAEL DENNIS, lawyer; b. Mpls., Nov. 6, 1945; s. Frank Walton and Donna Julia (Howard) S.; children: Michael Dennis, Cindal Marie, Derek Walton. BS, MIT, 1967; JD, UCLA, 1974. Bar: Calif. 1974, U.S. Dist. Ct. (no., so. and ctrl. dists.) Calif. 1974, U.S. Patent Office 1974, U.S. Ct. Appeals (9th cir.) 1974, U.S. Supreme Ct. 1978, U.S. Ct. Appeals (fed. cir.) 1989. Systems programmer NASA Electronics Rsch. Lab., Cambridge, Mass., 1967-69, Computer Scis. Corp., El Segundo, Calif., 1969-71, Univac, Valencia, Calif., 1971; from assoc. to ptnr. Smaltz & Neelley, LA, 1974-81; exec. dir. Ctr. for Computer/Law, LA, 1977-94; pvt. practice LA, 1981-86, 88-89; pres. Law and Tech. Press, 1981-94; ptnr. Scott & Roxborough, LA, 1986-88, Graham & James, 1989-93; v.p., gen. counsel Sanctuary Woods Multimedia, Inc., San Mateo, Calif., 1993-94; of counsel Steinhart & Falconer, San Francisco, 1995-97; ptnr. Hosie Wes Sacks & Brelsford, Menlo Park, Calif., 1997-98, Perkins Coie LLP, 1998—2003; prof. law Southwestern U., LA, 2003—. Adj. assoc. prof. law, Southwestern U., LA, 1975-80, 01-03, Loyola U., L.A., 1997-99, 02-04, Pepperdine U., LA, 2001-03; chmn. World

Computer Law Congress, LA, 1991, 93; co-chmn. Internat. IT Law Conf., 2005, 2007. Author: (with David S. Yen) Computer Law Bibliography, 1979, Computer Law, 1984, Scott on Computer Law, 1991, Multimedia: Law and Practice, 1993, Scott on Multimedia Law, 1996, (with Warren S. Reid) Year 2000 Computer Crisis: Law Business Technology, 1998, Internet and Technology Law Desk Reference, 1999, Intellectual Property and Licensing Law Desk Reference, 2001, Telecommunications Law Desk Reference, 2003, Scott on Outsourcing Law and Practice, 2006, Scott on Information Technology Law, 2007; editor-in-chief: Computer/Law Jour., 1978-94, Software Protection, 1982-92, Software Law Jour., 1985-94, Internat. Computer Law Adviser, 1986-92, Cyberspace Lawyer, 1996—, E-Commerce Law Report, 1998—. Mem. Computer Law Assn. (bd. dirs. 1994-99), Calif. State Bar Assn.

SCOTT, RACHEL E., lawyer; b. Seattle, Dec. 30, 1976; BA, Univ. Wash., 1998; JD, Univ. Mont. Law Sch., 2001; LLM, Univ. Helsinki Faculty Law, 2002. Bar: Wash. 2001, US Dist. Ct., Western Dist. Wash. 2002. Assoc. atty., personal injury, auto. accidents Scott, Kinney & Fjelstad, Seattle, 2002—. Contbr. articles to numerous profl. jours. Named Wash. Rising Star, SuperLawyer Mag., 2006. Mem.: Wash. State Trial Lawyers Assn., Wash. State Bar Assn., Assn. Trial Lawyers of Am. Office: Scott Kinney & Fjelstad One Union Sq Ste 1928 600 University St Seattle WA 98101-4178

SCOTT, RICHARD G., religious organization administrator; b. Pocatello, Idaho, Nov. 7, 1928; s. Kenneth Leroy and Mary Whittle S.; m. Jeanen Watkins, July 16, 1953; 7 children. Degree in mech. engring., George Washington U.; postgrad. in nuclear engring. Mem. staff naval and land based power plants, 1953-65; head North Mission LDS Ch., Cordoba, Argentina, 1965-69, regional rep. in Uruguay, Paraguay, N.C., S.C., Va., Washington, 1969-77, mem. 1st Quorum of Seventy, 1977-83, mem. presidency of 1st Quorum of Seventy, 1983-88, apostle, 1988—. Avocations: classical music, hiking, bird-watching, painting. Office: LDS Ch 50 E North Temple Salt Lake City UT 84150-0002

SCOTT, RIDLEY, film director; b. South Shields, Tyne and Wear, Eng., Nov. 30, 1937; m. Felicity Heywood, 1964 (div.); 2 children; m. Sandy Watson, 1979 (div. 1989); 1 child. BA, Royal Coll. Art; grad., London Internat. Film Sch. Dir.: (films) The Duellists, 1977, Alien, 1979, Legend, 1985, Black Rain, 1989; prodr.: The Browning Version, 1994, Clay Pigeons, 1998, Where the Money Is, 2000, Six Bullets from Now, 2002, All the Invisible Children, 2005, In Her Shoes, 2005, A Good Year, 2006, The Assassination of Jesse James by the Coward Robert Ford, 2007; exec. prodr.: Monkey Trouble, 1994, The Hire: Hostage, 2002, The Hire: Beat the Devil, 2002, The Hire: Ticker, 2002, Tristan & Isolde, 2006; dir., prodr. (films) Thelma & Louise, 1991, 1492: Conquest of Paradise, 1992, G.I. Jane, 1997, Black Hawk Down, 2001, Matchstick Men, 2003, Kingdom of Heaven, 2005, American Gangster, 2007, Body of Lies, 2008, writer, dir., prodr. Boy on a Bicycle, 1965; dir.(and co-prodr.): Blade Runner, 1982, (and exec. prodr.): Someone to Watch Over Me, 1987, White Squall, 1996, Gladiator, 2000; dir., prodr., exec. music prodr. Hannibal, 2001; dir.: (TV series) Z Cars, 1962, Adam Adamant Lives, 1966, The Informer, 1966; exec. prodr.: The Hunger, 1997, AFP: American Fighter Pilot, 2002, Numb3rs, 2005—; (TV films) RKO 287, 1999, The Last Debate, 2000, The Gathering Storm, 2002 (Emmy award, 2002). Winner Design scholarship, N.Y.; named one of 50 Most Powerful People in Hollywood Premiere mag., 2004, 2005. Address: William Morris Agency One William Morris Pl Beverly Hills CA 90212

SCOTT, ROBERT LANE, chemist, educator; b. Santa Rosa, Calif., Mar. 20, 1922; s. Horace Albert and Maurine (Lane) S.; m. Elizabeth Sewall Hunter, May 27, 1944; children: Joanna Ingersoll (dec.), Jonathan Armat, David St. Clair, Janet Hamilton. S.B., Harvard U., 1942; MA, Princeton U., 1944, PhD, 1945. Sci. staff Los Alamos Lab., 1945-46; Frank B. Jewett fellow U. Calif., Berkeley, 1946-48; faculty UCLA, 1948—, prof. chemistry, 1960-92, prof. emeritus, 1993—, chmn. dept., 1970-75. Author: (with J.H. Hildebrand) Solubility of Nonelectrolytes, 3d edit, 1950, rev., 1964, Regular Solutions, 1962, Regular and Related Solutions, 1970; Contbr. articles to profl. jours. Guggenheim fellow, 1955; NSF sr. fellow, 1961-62; Fulbright lectr., 1968-69 Fellow AAAS, Am. Phys. Soc.; mem. Am. Chem. Soc. (Joel Henry Hildebrand award 1984), Royal Soc. Chemistry (London), Sigma Xi. Home: 11128 Montana Ave Los Angeles CA 90049-3509 Business E-Mail: scott@chem.ucla.edu.

SCOTT, SEANN WILLIAM, actor; b. Cottage Grove, Minn., Oct. 3, 1976; Attended, Glendale Cmty. Coll., Calif. Actor: (films) American Pie, 1999, (voice) Nox, 2000, Final Destination, 2000, Road Trip, 2000, Dude, Where's My Car, 2000, Evolution, 2001, American Pie 2, 2001 (Choice Movie Sleazebag award, Teen Choice awards, 2002, 2004, Best Kiss award, MTV Movie awards, 2002), Jay and Silent Bob Strike Back, 2001, Stark Raving Mad, 2002, Old School, 2003, Bulletproof Monk, 2003, American Wedding, 2003 (Best Dance Sequence award, MTV Movie awards, 2004), The Rundown, 2003, The Dukes of Hazzard, 2005, (voice) Ice Age: The Meltdown, 2006, Ice Age 2: The Meltdown, 2006, Southland Tales, 2006, (voice) Lost Historical Films on the Ice Age Period, 2006, Trainwreck: My Life as an Idiot, 2007, Mr. Woodcock, 2007, The Promotion, 2008, Role Models, 2008; (TV films) Born Into Exile, 1997, Chad's World, 1998; (TV series) Unhappily Ever After, 1996, Something So Right, 1998; host (TV series) Saturday Night Live, 2001. Office: Identity Films Bungalow 4144 100 Universal City Plz Universal City CA 91608

SCOTT, STEPHEN, composer, musician, educator; b. Corvallis, Oreg., 1944; BA, U. Oreg., 1967; MA, Brown U.; fieldwork in African musics, Ghana, Tanzania, Zimbabwe, 1970. Prof. music Colo. Coll., Colorado Springs, 1989—, founder, dir. Bowed Piano Ensemble, 1977—, Nancy Bryson Schlosser and C. William Schlosser prof. arts, 2003—06, assoc. chair, 2007—08, with, 1969—. Composer: (albums) Portraits, Vikings of the Sunrise, New Music for Bowed Piano, 1999, Minerva's Web/The Tears of Niobe, The Deep Spaces, 2006. Recipient Chamber Music prize, New England Conservatory/Rockefeller Found., 1980; grantee Peter S. Reed Found.; Composer's fellowship, Nat. Endowment Arts, 1985—86, US Artists Simon fellow, 2008. Office: Colo Coll Music Dept Packard 111 14 E Cache La Poudre Colorado Springs CO 80903 also: c/o New Albion Records Box 25 Elizaville NY 12523 Office Phone: 719-389-6557. E-mail: sscott@coloradocollege.edu.*

SCOTT, TONY, computer software company executive; BS in Info. Sys. Mgmt., U. San Francisco; JD in Intellectual Property and Internat. Law, Santa Clara U., Calif. Engr. Gt. Am. Pk., Santa Clara, 1976; v.p. of ops. Bristol-Meyers Squibb; chief tech. officer GM, 1999; sr. v.p., chief info. officer The Walt Disney Co., 2005—08; chief info. officer Microsoft Corp., 2008—. Office: Microsoft Corp 1 Microsoft Way Redmond WA 98052-6399

SCOTT, WALTER, JR., telecommunications industry executive; b. May 21, 1931; m. Suzanne Scott. BS, Colo. State U., 1953; LittD, U. Nebr., 1983; LHD, Coll. St. Mary, 1988; D of Commerce, Bellevue U., 1996. With Peter Kiewit Sons, Inc., Omaha, 1953—, engr., project engr., dist. engr., Cleve. dist., 1959—61, asst. dist. mgr., Cleve. dist., 1961—62, dist. mgr. Cleve. dist. Omaha, 1962-64, v.p., 1964, exec. v.p., 1965-79, chmn. bd., 1964, pres., 1979, chmn. bd. dirs., pres., CEO, 1979-97, chmn. emeritus, 1997—; chmn. Level 3 Communications Inc. (former subs. PKS), Broomfield, Colo., 1997—. Bd. trustee Open World Leadership Ctr.; dir. Berkshire Hathaway, Burlington Resources, Commonwealth Telephone Enterprises, MidAmerican Energy Holdings, RCN Corp., Valmont Industries. Served with USAF, 1954-56. Recipient Nebr. Builder award, U. Nebr., 1983, Outstanding Achievement in Construction award, The Moles, 1986, Brotherhood award, Nat. Conf. Christians and Jews, 1986, Horatio Alger award, Horatio Alger Assn., 1997, Spirit Youth award, Uta Halee Girls Village, 1988, Perry W. Branch Disting. Svc. award, U. Nebr. Found., 1989, Golden Beaver for Mgmt., The Beavers, 1990, Order of Tower, U. Nebr., Omaha, 1991, Golden Plate award, Am. Acad. Achievement, 1991, Golden Apple award, Met. Cmty. Coll. Found., 1993, Headliner award, Greater Omaha C. of C., 1996, Nebraskalander award, Nebraskaland Found., 1998, Manresa award, Creighton U., 1998, Cmty. Builder award, Greater Omaha C. of C., 1999, Bus. Vol. of Yr., Nat. Alliance Bus., 1999, Midlander of Yr., Omaha World-Herald, 2000; named Philanthropist of Yr., Nat. Soc. Fund-Raising Execs., 1987, Man of Yr., Mid-Am. Coun. Boy Scouts Am., 1988, King Ak-Sar-Ben XCII, Knights of Ak-Sar-Ben, 1988, Disting. Eagle Scout, Boy Scouts Am., 1991, Citizen of Yr., United Way of the Midlands, 1993, Air Force Assn., 1993, Person of Yr., Pmaha Club, 1996; named one of Forbes Richest Americans, 2006; named to Nebr. Bus. Hall Fame, Nebr. C. of C. and Industry, 1995, Omaha Bus. Hall Fame, Greater Omaha C. of C., 1995. Mem.: Chi Epsilon Soc. (hon.). Office: Peter Kiewit Sons Inc 1000 Kiewit Plz Omaha NE 68131-3302 also: Joslyn Art Mus 2200 Dodge St Omaha NE 68102-1208 Office: Level 3 Communications Inc 1025 Eldorado Blvd Broomfield CO 80021

SCOTT, WALTER, JR., business consultant; b. Balt., July 24, 1925; s. Walter and Margaret Catherine (Pfeiffer) S.; m. Barbara Main, July 6, 1946 (dec. 1964); children: Stephen Walter, Susan Marjorie, Cynthia Margaret, Christopher Main; m. Mary Joan Braun, Aug. 5, 1966 (dec. 1986); m. Helene Lyda Burke, May 1, 1987. AB, Duke U., 1945; MBA with distinction, Harvard U., 1949. Advtg. mgr. The Quaker Oats Co., Chgo., 1950-57; v.p. mktg. J.H. Filbert, Inc., Balt., 1957-67, pres., 1968-77; div. gen. mgr. Cen. Soya Co., Ft. Wayne, Ind., 1972-77; exec. v.p. Fairmont Foods Co., Des Plaines, Ill., 1978-81; pres. McKeon, Scott, Woolf & Assocs., Palo Alto, Calif., 1982-84; chmn. bd. Integral Cons. Group, Mill Valley, Calif., 1986-87, Scott, Woolf & Assocs., Palo Alto, 1984—2001, Mulford Moreland & Assocs., San Jose, Calif., 1986-89. Chmn., speaker pres. courses, Am. Mgmt. Assn., N.Y.C., 1970-90; trustee Calif. Inst. Integral Studies, San Francisco, 1983-89; bd. dirs. West Marine, Inc., Watsonville, Calif., 1995-2001. With USNR, 1943-46, PTO. Mem. Phi Beta Kappa. Home and Office: 1450 Redford Dr Palm Springs CA 92264 Home Phone: 760-416-1451; Office Phone: 760-416-0851.

SCOTT, WAYNE, state legislator; m Marlene Canby; children: three, two grandchildren. Member, Canby Sch Bd, 9 years; Oregon State Representative, District 39, 2003—, Majority Leader, currently, co-chmn, Joint Ways & Means Committee, currently, chairman, State & Federal Affairs Committee, currently, member, Committee on Education, Committee on PERS, formerly, vice chairman, Committee on Revenue, formerly, Oregon House Representative.Owner & operator, business, 30 years. Republican. Mailing: 900 Court St NE H-295 Salem OR 97301 Office Phone: 503-986-1439. E-mail: rep.waynescott@state.or.us.

SCOTTI, JAMES VERNON, astronomer; b. Bandon, Oreg., Aug. 22, 1960; s. Paul Carl and Elizabeth Louise (Garoutte) S.; m. Karriaunna K.-R. Harlan, May 15, 1983; children: Jennifer Anne, Christopher James. BS, U. Ariz., 1983. Planetarium asst. Flandrau Planetarium, Tucson, 1979-82; student rsch. asst. Lunar and Planetary Lab., Tucson, 1982-83, rsch. asst., 1983-93, sr. rsch. specialist, 1993—. Mem. Am. Astron. Soc. (assoc.), Div. for Planetary Scis., Assn. Lunar and Planetary Observers (asst. comets recorder). Achievements include being a leading observer of faint comets, being heavily involved in observing comet P/Shoemaker-Levy 9 before and during its impact on Jupiter in July 1994. Office: U Ariz Lunar And Planetary Lab Tucson AZ 85721-0001

SCOULAR, ROBERT FRANK, lawyer; b. Del Norte, Colo., July 9, 1942; s. Duane William and Marie Josephine (Moloney) Scoular; m. Donna V. Scoular, June 3, 1967; children: Bryan T., Sean D., Bradley R. BS in Aero. Engring., St. Louis U., 1964, JD, 1968. Bar: Mo. 1968, Colo. 1968, ND 1968, US Supreme Ct. 1972, Calif. 1979. Law clk. to chief judge US Ct. Appeals (8th cir.), 1968-69; ptnr. Bryan, Cave, McPheeters & McRoberts, St. Louis, 1969-89, mng. ptnr. LA, 1979—85, exec. com., 1984-85, sect. leader tech., computer and intellectual property law, 1985-89; ptnr. Sonnenschein, Nath, Rosenthal, LA, 1990—, mng. ptnr., 1990—2005. Co-leader intellectual property practice, 1990—98; dir. Mo. Lawyers Credit Union, 1978—79. Contbr. articles to profl. jours. Bd. dirs. St. Louis Bar Found., 1975—76, 1979, bd. dirs., exec. com., pub. counsel, 2004—; bd. dirs., gen. counsel, pres. LA area coun. Boy Scouts Am.; league commr. Am. Youth Soccer Orgn.; mem. alumni coun. St. Louis U., 1979—82, dean's coun. Sch. Law, 2000—; hon. dean Dubourg Soc. Recipient Nat. Disting. Eagle Scout award. Mem.: ABA (nat. dir. young lawyers divsn. 1977—78), Fed. Bar Assn., Mo. Bar Assn. (chmn. young lawyers sect. 1976—77, Disting. Svc. award), Calif. Bar Assn., Assn. Bus. Trial Lawyers (bd. dirs. 2004—), LA County Bar Assn., Bar Assn. Met. St. Louis (chmn. young lawyers sect. 1975—76, v.p. 1978—79, sec. 1979), Calif. Club, Chancery Club. Home: 1505 Lower Paseo La Cresta Palos Verdes Peninsula CA 90274-2066 Office: Sonnenschein Nath Rosenthal 601 S Figueroa St Ste 2500 Los Angeles CA 90017-5709 Home Phone: 310-378-6349; Office Phone: 213-892-5008. Business E-Mail: rscoular@sonnenschein.com.

SCOUTEN, WILLIAM HENRY, chemistry educator, academic administrator; b. Corning, NY, Feb. 12, 1942; s. Henry and M. Anna (Kimble) S.; m. Nancy Jane Coombs, July 16, 1965; children: Lisa, Linda, Michael, William Jr., Thomas, David. BA, Houghton Coll., 1964; PhD, U. Pitts., 1969. NIH postdoctoral fellow SUNY, Stony Brook, 1969-71; asst. prof. Bucknell U., Lewisburg, Pa., 1971-77, assoc. prof., 1977-83, prof., 1983-84; prof., chmn. dept. chemistry Baylor U., Waco, Tex., 1984-93; dir. biotech. ctr. Utah State U., Logan, 1993-2000; dean Coll. Sci. U. Tex., San Antonio, 2000—. Vis. scientist for minority inst. Fedn. Am. Socs. Exptl. Biology, Washington; adj. prof. U. of Utah, 1996, mem. Ctr. for Biopolymers at Interfaces, 1996; chmn. Coun. of Biotech. Ctrs., 1998; mem. govt. rels. coms. Coun. Chem. Rsch., 1996; bd. dirs. emerging cos. sect. Biotechnology Industry Orgn., 1997; mem. Nat. Adv. Bd. Agrl. Rsch. Author: Affinity Chromatography, 1981; editor: Solid Phase Biochem., 1983; editor-in-chief Internat. Jour. Bio-Chromatography, 1994—; mem. editl. bd. Bioconjugate Chemistry, 1994-99, Jour. Molecular Recognition, 1994-99—, Bioseparation, 1995— Fulbright fellow, 1976; Dreyfus Tchr. scholar, Dreyfus Found., 1976; NSF Sci. Devel. NSF, 1978; Lindbach Disting. Tchr. Bucknell U., 1975. Mem. Am. Soc. Biol. Chemists, Am. Chem. Soc., Internat. Soc. for Biorecognition Tech., Coun. for Biotech. Ctrs. (bd. dirs. 1996—), Internat. Soc. for Molecular Recognition (pres. 1990-93), Assn. for Internat. Practical Tng. (bd. dirs. 1991-98), Coun. for Chem. Rsch. (governing bd. 2000—). Republican. Baptist. Office: Utah State U 4700 Old Main Hl Logan UT 84322-4700

SCOZZARI, ALBERT, portfolio manager, inventor; b. Chgo. BA, Northeastern Ill. U., 1973; MPA, Ill. Inst. Tech., 1974; PhD, Columbia Pacific U., 1986; student, Harvard Exec. Devel. Program, 1990. Cons. World Bank Group, 1987—. Adj. prof. bus. studies. Ill. Inst. Tech., 1975, Columbia Pacific U., 1986, Disaster Litigation Protocols, 2008; artist-in-residence Ariz. Coun. Fine Arts, 1999. Author: Mass Communications in Politics, 1978, Managing for Effectiveness, 1986, Management in the 90s, 1990, Vietnam Faces, 1995, Field Cross, 1996, The Mountain, 1997, The Trail, 1997, A Collection of Verses and Poems, 1997, Phobias and Phears, 2005. Pres. Homeowners Assn., Phoenix, 1992-96, Scozzari Meml. Scholarship Fund, 1991—. With USNR, 1961-66, ret. ANG, 1979-87. Mem. Am. Fedn. Musicians (life), Assn. Stage and Film Actors (life), Am. Poets and Writers Guild (life), Am. Mensa Assn. (life), Vietnam Vets. Am. (life), Adventurers Club. (life). Home: PO Box 90263 Phoenix AZ 85066

SCRUGGS, ELAINE M., Mayor, Glendale, Arizona; m. Larry Scruggs; 1 child, Jennifer. Former mgmt. specialist; elected mem. Glendale City Coun., Ariz., 1990-93; mayor City of Glendale, Ariz., 1994—. Past chmn. Maricopa Assn. Govts., past chmn. regional coun.; chmn. Regional Pub. Transp. Authority, Maricopa Assn. Govt. Regional Aviation Systems policy com., Ariz. Mcpl. Tax Code Commn.; chair bd. dirs. Valley Metro Regional Pub. Transportation Authority; bd. dirs., past chmn. Westmarc. Dir. Glendale Leadership Program, 1984-89; mem. Ariz. Coalition for Tomorrow, Ariz. Women in Mcpl. Govt.; active mem. youth adv. commn., Mayor's Alliance Against Drugs and Gangs; adv. bd. YWCA. Recipient Tribute to Women's Pub. Sector Leadership award, YWCA Advisory Board, 2001; named Top 100, Ariz. Woman Mag., 1998, Woman of Yr., 2003. Mem. Glendale C. of C., Ariz. Mcpl. Water Users Assn. (past chair). Office: Office Mayor 5850 W Glendale Ave Glendale AZ 85301-2563*

SCRUGGS, SAMUEL D., lawyer, chemicals executive; b. San Francisco, Sept. 6, 1959; BA, U. Utah, Salt Lake City, 1984; JD, Columbia U., NYC, 1987. Bar: NY 1989. Atty. LeBoef, Lamb, Greene & MacRae, NYC, 1987—89, Skadden, Arps, Slate, Meagher & Flom, NYC, 1989—95; v.p., assoc. gen. counsel, then v.p. corp. tax, then exec. v.p. legal tax & corp. devel. Huntsman Cos., 1995—2002, exec. v.p., corp. gen. counsel, mem. office of chmn., 2002—. Office: Huntsman Corp Legal Dept 500 Huntsman Way Salt Lake City UT 84108 Office Phone: 801-584-5700.

SCUDDER, RICHARD B., newspaper executive; b. Newark, May 13, 1913; s. Edward W. and Katherine (Hollifield) S.; m. Elizabeth A. Shibley, June 24, 944; children: Elizabeth H. (Mrs. Philip Difani), Charles A., Carolyn (Mrs. Peter M. Miller), Jean (Mrs. Joseph Fulmer). AB, Princeton U., 1935; LHD (hon.), Mon Coll. Reporter Newark News, 1935-37, v.p., 1941-51, pub., 1951-72; reporter Boston Herald, 1937-38; chmn. MediaNews Group, Gloucester County Times, Inc., Garden State Newspapers, Inc., Garden State Paper Co., Denver Newspapers, Inc. Trustee Riverview Hosp., N.J. Conservation Found., Monmouth County Conservation Found.; former trustee Rutgers U.; adv. com. Princeton (N.J.) Environ. Inst. Served from pvt. to maj. AUS, 1941-45. Decorated bronze star; recipient TAPPI award, 1971; Nat. Recycling award Nat. Assn. Secondary Materials Industries, 1972; Nat. Resource Recovery Man of Year award, 1978; Papermaker of Yr. award Paper Trade Jour., 1978; named to Paper Industry Hall of Fame, 1995. Mem. N.J. Audubon Soc., Rumson Country Club, Seabright Beach Club, Seabright Lawn Tennis Club, Mill Reef Club, Adirondack League Club. Address: 309 S Broad St Woodbury NJ 08096-2406 Office: Medianews Group 101 W Colfax Ave Denver CO 80202-5315

SCUDDER, THAYER, anthropologist, educator; b. New Haven, Aug. 4, 1930; s. Townsend III and Virginia (Boody) S.; m. Mary Eliza Drinker, Aug. 26, 1950; children: Mary Eliza, Alice Thayer. Grad., Phillips Exeter Acad., 1948; AB, Harvard U., 1952, PhD, 1960; postgrad., Yale U., 1953-54, London Sch. Econs., 1960-61. Rsch. officer Rhodes-Livingstone Inst., No. Rhodesia, 1956-57, sr. rsch. officer, 1962-63; asst. prof. Am. U., Cairo, 1961-62; rsch. fellow Ctr. Middle East Studies, Harvard U., 1963-64; asst. prof. Calif. Inst. Tech., Pasadena, 1964-66, assoc. prof., 1966-69, prof. anthropology, 1969-2000, prof. emeritus, 2000—; dir. Inst. for Devel. Anthropology, Binghamton, NY, 1976—2002; commr. World Commn. on Dams, 1998-2000. Cons. UN Devel. Program, FAO, IBRD, WHO, Ford Found., Navajo Tribal Coun., AID, World Conservation Union, Lesotho Highlands Devel. Authority, South China Electric Power Joint Venture Corp., U.S. Nat. Rsch. Coun., Que.-Hydro, Environ. Def. Fund, Ministry of Energy & Mines, Lao People's Dem. Republic, Nature Conservancy Author: The Ecology of the Gwembe Tonga, 1962, The Future of Large Dams: Dealing with Social, Environmental, Institutional and Political Costs, 2005; co-author: Long-Term Field Research in Social Anthropology, 1979, Secondary Education and the Formation of an Elite: The Impact of Education on Gwembe District, Zambia, 1980, No Place to Go: The Impacts of Forced Relocation on Navajos, 1982, For Prayer and Profit: The Ritual, Economic and Social Importance of Beer in Gwembe District, Zambia, 1950-1982, 1988, The IUCN Review of the So. Okavango Integrated Water Development Project, 1993. Recipient (1st) Lucy Mair medal for applied anthropology, Royal Anthropol. Inst., 1998, John Phillips award, Phillips Exeter Acad, 2005; John Simon Guggenheim Meml. fellow, 1975. Mem. Am. Anthrop. Assn. (1st recipient Solon T. Kimball award for pub. and applied anthropology 1984,

Edward J. Lehman award 1991), Soc. Applied Anthropology (Bronislaw Malinowski award 1999). Office: Calif Inst Tech # 228 77 Pasadena CA 91125-0001 Office Phone: 626-395-4207. Business E-Mail: tzs@hss.caltech.edu.

SCULL, ANDREW T., sociologist, educator; b. Edinburgh, May 2, 1947; arrived in US, 1969; s. Allan Edward and Marjorie Therese Scull; m. Nancy Theresa Principi, Aug. 16, 1970; children: Anna, Andrew, Alexander. BA with first class honours, Oxford U., Eng., 1969; MA, Princeton U., 1971, PhD, 1974. Asst. prof. sociology U. Pa., Phila., 1977—78; vis. assoc. prof. Princeton U., Princeton, NJ, 1978—79; assoc. prof., sociology U. Calif., La Jolla, Calif., 1978—82, prof. sociology, 1982—94, disting. prof. sociology and sci. studies, 1994—. Author: Museums of Madness, 1979, Madhouses, Mad-Doctors, and Madmen, 1981, Decarceration, 1984, Social Order/Mental Disorder, 1989, The Most Solitary of Afflictions: Madness and Society in Britain, 1700-1900, 1993, Masters of Bedlam, 1996, Madhouse: A Tragic Tale of Megalomania and Modern Medicine, 2005, The Race of Insanity, 2006, The Insanity of Place/The Place of Insanity, 2006; co-author (with Steven Lukes): Durkheim and the Law, 1983; co-author: (with Jonathan Andrews) Customers and Patrons of the Mad Trade: The Management of Lunacy in Eighteenth Century London, 2003, Undertaker of the Mind: John Monro and Mad-Doctoring in Eighteenth-Century England, 2001; co-editor (with Stanley Cohen): Social Control and the State, 1983. Office: 401 Social Science Bldg U Calif San Diego 9500 Gilman Dr La Jolla CA 92093-0533 Office Phone: 858-534-0492. Business E-Mail: ascull@ucsd.edu.

SCULLEY, JOHN, investment company executive, former computer company executive; b. NYC, Apr. 6, 1939; s. John and Margaret Blackburn (Smith) S.; m. Carol Lee Adams, Mar. 7, 1978; children: Margaret Ann, John Blackburn, Laura Lee. Student, R.I. Sch. Design, 1960; BArch, Brown U., 1961; MBA, U. Pa., 1963. Asst. account exec. Marschalk Co., NYC, 1963-64, account exec., 1964-65, account supr., 1965-67; dir. mktg. Pepsi-Cola Co., Purchase, NY, 1967-69, v.p. mktg., 1970-71, sr. v.p. mktg., 1971-74, pres., CEO, 1977-83; pres. PepsiCo Foods, Purchase, NY, 1974-77; pres., CEO Apple Computer Inc., Cupertino, Calif., 1983-1993; chmn., CEO Spectrum Info. Technologies, 1993—94; ptnr. Sculley Brothers LLC, 1995—2004; chmn. Live Picture Inc., 1997—98; venture ptnr. Rho Ventures, Palo Alto, 2004—. Co-author (with John A. Byrne): Odyssey: Pepsi to Apple...a Journey of Adventure, Ideas & the Future, 1987. Chmn. Wharton Grad. Exec. Bd., 1980; mem. art adv. com. Brown U., 1980; bd. dirs. Keep Am. Beautiful.; mem. bd. overseers Wharton Sch., U. Pa. Mem. U.S. C. of C. Clubs: Indian Harbor, N.Y. Athletic; Coral Beach (Bermuda); Wharton Bus. Sch. of N.Y. (bd. dirs.); Camden (Maine) Yacht. Republican. Office: Rho Ventures 525 University Ave Ste 1350 Palo Alto CA 94301

SCULLY, VINCENT EDWARD, sports broadcaster; b. Bronx, NY, Nov. 29, 1927; s. Vincent Aloysius and Bridget (Freehill) S.; m. Sandra Hunt, Nov. 11, 1973; children: Michael, Kevin, Todd, Erin, Kelly, Catherine Anne. BA, Fordham U., Bronx, NY, 1949; LLD (hon.), Pepperdine U., Malibu, Calif., 2008. Sports announcer Bklyn. Dodgers, 1950-57, LA Dodgers, 1957—, CBS-TV, 1975-82, NBC-TV, 1982-89. Served with USNR, 1944-45. Recipient TV award Look mag., 1959, Ford C. Frick award, 1982; named Sportscaster of Yr. in Calif., 1959, 60, 63, 69, 71, 73-75; Nat. Sportscaster of Yr., 1966, 78, 82; named to Fordham U. Hall of Fame, 1976, Nat. Baseball Hall of Fame, 1982, Calif. Sports Hall of Fame, 2008; named one of Top 50 Sportscasters Am. Sportscasters Assn., 2009. Mem. AFTRA, Screen Actors Guild, Catholic Actors, TV Acad. Arts and Scis. Clubs: Lambs (N.Y.C.); Bel Air Country, Beach. Roman Catholic. Office: LA Dodgers 1000 Elysian Park Ave Los Angeles CA 90012-1112*

SEABOLT, RICHARD L., lawyer; b. Chgo., Aug. 28, 1949; BGS with distinction, U. Mich., 1971; JD, U. Calif., Hastings, 1975. Bar: Calif. 1975. Ptnr. Duane Morris LLP, San Francisco, 1981—. Mem. Calif. Civil Jury Instr. Adv. Com. Author: Matthew Bender Practice Guides, California Pretrial Civil Procedure and Civil Discovery, 2004. Mem.: Assn. Bus. Trial Lawyers (bd. govs.), State Bar Calif. (chair litig. sect. 2006). Office: Duane Morris LLP One Market Spear Tower San Francisco CA 94111 Office Phone: 415-957-3212. Business E-Mail: rlseabolt@duanemorris.com.

SEABROOK, RAYMOND J., corporate financial executive; b. Toronto, Canada, Mar. 1, 1950; married; 2 children. B in Bus., McMaster U., Hamilton, Ontario, 1975. Cert. arch., Humber Coll., Toronto, 1972. With Coopers and Lybrand, Toronto, Canada, 1976—85; v.p. fin. control Onex Packaging and Am. Can Can., 1985—88; sr. v.p., CFO Ball Packaging Products Canada, 1988—92; v.p., treas. Ball Corp., Broomfield, Colo., 1992—96, v.p. planning & control, 1996—98, sr. v.p. fin., 1998—2000, sr. v.p., CFO, 2000—06, exec. v.p., CFO, 2007—. Bd. dir. Andersen Corp., 2004—. Office: Ball 10 Longs Peak Dr Broomfield CO 80021

SEACREST, RYAN (RYAN JOHN SEACREST), television and radio personality, entrepreneur; b. Atlanta, Dec. 24, 1976; s. Gary and Connie Seacrest. Attended, U. Ga., 1994—95. DJ WSTR/Star 94, Atlanta, 1992—94, 102.7 KIIS-FM morning show, LA. Launched fashion line, R Line, 2005; part owner at Katana, Sushi Roku and Boa. Host (TV series) Gladiators 2000, 1994, Radical Outdoor Challenge, ESPN, 1995, The New Edge, 1996, The Click, 1997, American Juniors, 2003, American Idol, 2002—, host, exec. prodr. On-Air With Ryan Seacrest, 2004, corr. Extra Weekends, 2002, The Tonight Show, 2005—, host (TV) Wild Animal Games, 1995, (radio) Live from the Lounge, Star 98.7, 1995—2001, Ryan Seacrest for the Ride Home, Star 98.7, LA, 1995—2004, American Top 40, 2004—, On-Air With Ryan Seacrest, 102.7 KIIS-FM, 2004—, New Year's Eve: Live From Times Square With Ryan Seacrest, NYC, 2003—; exec. prodr.: New Year's Eve: Live From Times Square With Ryan Seacrest, 2004, New Year's Rockin' Eve 2006, 2005; actor: (TV series) Reality Check, 1995; voice Hey Arnold!, 1999, Robot Chicken, 2005, guest appearances Beverly Hills, 90210, 2000, Mad TV, 2002, 2005, Player$, 2003, guest host Good Day Live, 2003, Larry King Live, 2003, 2004, 2005. Named Marconi Radio award for Personality of Yr. (major market size), Nat. Assn. Broadcasters, 2008; named a Maverick, Details mag., 2007; named one of 50 Most Beautiful People, People Mag., 2003, The 100 Most Powerful Celebrities, Forbes.com, 2007, 2008. Office: William Morris Agy 1 William Morris Pl Beverly Hills CA 90212 Business E-Mail: Ryan@kiisfm.com, ryan@eonline.com. E-mail: Ryan@AT40.com.

SEADER, JUNIOR DEVERE (BOB SEADER), retired chemical engineering professor; b. San Francisco, Aug. 16, 1927; s. George Joseph and Eva (Burbank) S.; m. Joyce Kocher, Aug. 12, 1950 (div. 1960); m. Sylvia Bowen, Aug. 11, 1961; children: Steven Frederick, Clayton Mitchell, Gregory Randolph, Donald Jeffrey, Suzanne Marie, Robert Clark, Kathleen Michelle, Jennifer Anne. BS, U. Calif., Berkeley, 1949, MS, 1950; PhD, U. Wis., 1952. Instr. chem. engring. U. Wis., Madison, 1951-52; group supr. chem. process design Chevron Rsch. Corp., Richmond, Calif., 1952-57, group supr. engring. rsch., 1957-59; prin. scientist heat transfer and fluid dynamics rsch. Rocketdyne div. N.Am. Aviation, Canoga Park, Calif., 1959-65, sr. tech. specialist, summer 1967; prof. chem. engring. U. Idaho, 1965-66, U. Utah, Salt Lake City, 1966—2003, chmn. dept. chem. engring., 1975-78. Tech. cons.; trustee CACHE Corp., Austin, Tex., 1969—2002. Author 15 books; assoc. editor IEC Rsch. jour., 1986-99; contbr. more than 100 articles to tech. publs. With USNR, 1945—46. Recipient Disting. Tchg. award U. Utah, 1975, Donald L. Katz lectureship, 1990, Dean's Tchg. award U. Utah, 1998, CACHE award for excellence in computing in chem. engring. edn. Am. Soc. Engring. Edn., 2004. Fellow: AIChE (Inst. lectr. 1983, bd. dirs. 1983—85, Computing in Chem. Engring. award 1988, Warren K. Lewis award for chem. engring. edn. 2004). Heat transfer research connected with the development of rocket engines associated with the Apollo and Space Shuttle projects, 1960-65; recognition of Seperation Process Principles by Seader and Henley as out of 30 ground breaking chemical engineering book 2008. Home Phone: 801-523-8870. E-mail: j.seader@utah.edu.

SEAGREN, STEPHEN LINNER, oncologist; b. Mpls., Mar. 13, 1941; s. Morley Raymond and Carol Christine (Linner) S.; m. Jill Garrie; 1 child, Sean Garrie. AB, Harvard U., 1963; MD, Northwestern U., 1967. Diplomate Am. Bd. Internal Medicine, Am. Bd. Med. Oncology, Am. Bd. Radiology. From asst. prof. to assoc. prof. radiology and medicine U. Calif., San Diego, 1977-88, prof., 1988—, chief divsn. radiation oncology. Contbr. over 80 articles to profl. jours. Bd. dirs., chmn. profl. adv. com. Wellness Cmty., San Diego, 1988-2003; chmn. radiol. oncology com. Cancer and Acute Leukemia Group, Chgo., 1986-98; assoc. dir. U. Calif. San Diego Cancer Ctr., 1998-2000. Lt. comdr. USNR, 1971-73. Fellow ACP. Avocations: physical fitness, bridge, skiing, golf, tennis. Office: Moores Cancer Ctr 3855 Health Scis Dr #0843 La Jolla CA 92093-0843 Home Phone: 858-272-2053; Office Phone: 858-822-6040. Business E-Mail: sseagren@ucsd.edu.

SEALE, JOHN CLEMENT, director, cinematographer; b. Warwick, Queensland, Australia, Oct. 5, 1942; s. Eric Clement and Marjorie Lyndon (Pool) S.; m. Louise Lee Mutton, Sept. 23, 1967; children: Derin Anthony, Brianna Lee. Grad. high sch., Sydney, Australia; PhD (hon.), Griffith U., 1997. Camera asst. film dept. Australian Broadcasting Com., 1962-68; freelance technician, camera operator various films, series, commls., 1968-76. Dir. feature film, Till There Was You, 1989-90. Dir. photography: Goodbye Paradise (Golden Tripod 1982), Careful, He Might Hear You (Best Cinematography 1983), Witness, 1984 (Golden Tripod 1984, Oscar nomination 1986, Brit. Acad. award nomination 1986), The Hitcher, 1985, Children of a Lesser God, 1985 (Golden Tripod 1985), The Mosquito Coast, 1986, Stakeout, 1987, Gorillas in the Mist (Brit. Acad. award nomination 1989, Premier Mag. Cinematographer of the Yr. 1989), Rainman, 1988 (Acad. award nomination 1988, Artistic Achievement award 1989), Dead Poets Society, 1989, The Doctor, 1991, Lorenzo's Oil, 1992, The Firm, 1993, The Paper, 1993, Beyond Rangoon, 1994, The American President, 1995, The English Patient, 1995-96 (Best Cinematography award L.A. Film Critics Assn., Acad. award Cinematography, 1996, Brit. Acad. award 1996, Best Cinematrography award Am. Soc. Cinematographers 1996, European Best Cinematography award 1997, Chgo. Film Critics award, Fla. Film Critics award), Ghosts of Mississippi, 1996, City of Angels, 1997, At First Sight, 1998, The Talented Mr. Ripley, 1998, The Perfect Storm, 1999, Harry Potter, 2000, Dreamcatcher, 2002, Cold Mountain, 2002. Recipient Film Critics Cir. Australia 1990 Tribute; named European Cinematographer of Yr., 1997. Mem. Australian Cinematographers Soc. (named Cinematographer of Yr. 1982, 84, Inaugural mem. Hall of Fame 1997), Am. Soc. Cinematographers, Order of Australia. Avocations: building boats, sailing.

SEALE, ROBERT MCMILLAN, office services company executive; b. Feb. 1, 1938; s. Robert McMillan and Margaret Sutherland (Miller) S. BA, Emory U., 1959. With N.Y. Life Ins. Co., San Francisco, 1960-67, Dictaphone Office Svcs. divsn. Dictaphone Corp., San Francisco, 1967-69; pres. Am. Profl. Svc., Inc., Dictation West Miss Jones' Word Processing, various locations, 1969-93; pres. Environments West, 1980-86, Los Arcos Properties, 1980—. Founder Seale Orgn., 1993; lectr. in field. Contbr. articles in field to profl. jours. Bd. dirs. The Rose Resnic Ctr. for Blind and Handicapped, Computer Based Patient Record Inst.; med. word processing cons. to hosps., health care insts., office equipment mfrs.; chmn. San Francisco Mayor's Com. for Employment of Handicapped, 1971-73; mem. Calif. Gov.'s Planning and Adv. Com. for Vocat. Rehab. Planning, 1968-69; pres. Calif. League for Handicapped, 1968-70, bd. dirs., 1966-73, 84-89, adv. coun., 1973-77; v.p. Stebbins Found., 1980-89; pres. Stebbins Housing Corp., 1980-89; assoc. St. Francis Hosp. Found., 1990—; sec., founder Palm Springs Coalition of Neighborhoods, mem. Loma LInda U. Med. Ctr., Loma Linda U. Childrens Hosp., 1995. Recipient Spoke and Spark award U.S. Jr. C. of C., 1967, KABL Outstanding Citizen's award, 1965, 71. Mem. Am. Health Info Mgmt. Assn., Adminstrv. Mgmt. Soc., Sales and Mktg. Execs. Assn., Am. Assn. Med. Transcription (Disting. Svc. award 1985), Med. Transcription Industry Alliance, Emory U. Alumni Assn., Emory Lamplighters Soc., U.S. C. of C., Las Palmas Alliance (chmn.), Delta Tau Delta.

SEALEY, RAPHAEL, history professor; b. Middlesbrough, Yorkshire, Eng., Aug. 14, 1927; came to U.S., 1963; s. Bertram Izod and Florence Gladys (Heath) S.; m. Dagmar Schoelermann, Dec. 19, 1972 (div. Oct. 1977); 1 child, Dorte Freyja. BA, Oxford U., Eng., 1947, MA, 1951. Lectr. U. Coll. North Wales, Bangor, 1954—58, U. London, 1958—63; prof. State U. NY, Buffalo, 1963—67, U. Calif., Berkeley, 1967—2000. Author: Essays in Greek Politics, 1967, A History of the Greek City States, 1976, The Athenian Republic, 1987, Women and Law in Classical Greece, 1990, Demosthenes and His Time, 1993, The Justice of the Greeks, 1994. Sgt. British Army, 1947—49. Mem.: Am. Philological Assn. Avocation: literature. Home: 1206 Milvia St Berkeley CA 94709 Office: Univ Calif Dept History Berkeley CA 94720 Business E-Mail: squiley@berkeley.edu.

SEAMAN, ARLENE ANNA, retired musician; b. Pontiac, Mich., Jan. 21, 1918; d. Roy Russell and Mabel Louise (Heffron) S. BS, life cert., Ea. Mich. U., 1939; MMus, Wayne State U., 1951; postgrad., Colo. Coll., 1951-52, Acad. Music, Zermatt Switzerland, 1954-58, U. Mich. Guest conductor Shepherds and Angels, Symphonie Concertante, 1951; asst. conductor Detroit Women's Symphony, 1960-68; adjudicator Mich. State Band and Orch. Festivals, Solo and Ensemble Festivals, 1950-70, Detroit Fiddler's Band Auditions, 1948-52, Mich. Fedn. Music Clubs, 1948-55; tchr. Ea. Mich. U., 1939-42, Hartland Sch. Music, 1939-42, Pontiac (Mich.) Pub. Schs., 1942-45, Detroit Pub. Schs., 1945-73, pvt. studio, 1973-90. Performer cello South Oakland Symphony, 1958-65, Detroit Women's Symphony, 1951-68, Riviera Theatre Orch., 1959, 60, Masonic Auditorium Opera, Ballet Seasons, 1959-65, Toledo Ohio Symphony, 1963-70, others; performer trumpet Detroit Brass Quartet, 1974-78; piano accompanist various auditions, recitals, solo and ensemble festivals; composer: Let There Be Music, 1949, Fantasy for French Horn and Symphonic Band, 1951. Mem. Quota Internat., Delta Omicron. Home: 6231 N Montebella Rd #347 Tucson AZ 85704

SEARFOSS, RICHARD A., aerospace transportation executive, retired astronaut; b. Mt. Clemens, Mich., June 5, 1956; married; 3 children. BS in Aero. Engring. with honors, USAF Acad., 1978; MS in Aeronautics, Calif. Inst. Tech., 1979; grad., USAF Sqaud. Officer Sch., Air Command and Staff Coll., Air War Coll. Enlisted USAF, 1980, advanced through grades to col., 1998, pilot RAF Lakenheath, England, 1981—84, instr. pilot, weapons officer Mountain Home AFB, Idaho, 1984—87; exch. officer US Naval Test Pilot Sch., Patuxent River, Md., 1988; flight instr. USAF Test Pilot Sch., Edwards AFB, Calif.; astronaut, astronaut office rep., flight crew procedures, shuttle computer software devel. NASA, 1991—98; test pilot instr. Nat. Test Pilot Sch., Mojave Spaceport, Calif.; test pilot XCOR Aerospace, Mojave; v.p. Zero Gravity Corp. Pilot, crew performed human and animal physiology experiments in space flight STS-58 Mission (Columbia), 1993; pilot, performed 3rd docking of Am. spacecraft with Russian space station Mir, first ever space walk on combined space shuttle-space station complex STS-76 Mission (Atlantis), 1996; mission comdr., crew performed 26 neuroscience experiments on themselves focusing on the effects of microgravity on the brain and nervous sys. STS-90 Neurolab Mission, 1998; chief judge Ansari X-Prize; motivation spkr. in field. Decorated Commendation medal USAF, Meritorious Svc. medal, Disting. Flying Cross, Def. Meritorious Svc. medal, Def. Superior Svc. medal; recipient 3 Spaceflight medals, NASA, Exceptional Svc. medal, Outstanding Leadership medal, Orbit award, Nat. Space Soc., Calif. Astronaut Hall of Fame award, 2006; named Tactical Air Command Instr. Pilot of Yr., 1985; fellow, NSF, 1979. Mem.: Acad. Model Aeronautics, Air Force Assn., Nat. Eagle Scout Assn., Assn. Space Explorers. Mem. Lds Ch. Avocations: running, soccer, backpacking, classical music. Office: Nat Test Pilot Sch PO Box 658 Mojave CA 93502-0658 Office Phone: 661-824-2977. Office Fax: 661-824-2943. Business E-Mail: rsearfoss@ntps.edu.

SEARS, DAVID O'KEEFE, psychology professor; b. Urbana, Ill., June 24, 1935; s. Robert R. and Pauline (Snedden) S.; married; children: Juliet, Olivia, Meredith. BA in History, Stanford U., 1957; PhD in Psychology, Yale U., 1962. Asst. prof. to disting. prof. psychology and polit. sci. UCLA, 1961—, dean social scis., 1983-92. Dir. Inst. for Social Sci. Rsch., 1993-2008. Author: Public Opinion, 1964, Politics of Violence, 1973, Tax Revolt, 1985, Political Cognition, 1986, Social Psychology, 12th edit., 2005, Racialized Politics, 2000, Oxford Handbook of Political Psychology, 2003, The Diversity Challenge, 2008. Recipient Edward L. Bernays award, Soc. for Psychol. Study of Social Issues, 1979, Warren E. Miller Career award, Am. Polit. Sci. Assn., 2003; fellow, Guggenheim, 1988—89. Fellow Am. Acad. Arts and Scis.; mem. Soc. for Advancement Socio-Econs. (pres. 1991-92), Internat. Soc. Polit. Psychology (pres. 1994-95, Harold D. Lasswell award 1994). Office: UCLA Psychology Dept Los Angeles CA 90095-0001 Office Phone: 310-825-2160. Business E-Mail: sears@psych.ucla.edu.

SEASTRAND, ANDREA H., former congresswoman, state agency administrator; b. Chgo., Aug. 5, 1941; m. Eric Seastrand (dec.); children: Kurt, Heidi. BA in Edn., DePaul U., 1963. Prof. religion U. Santa Barbara; mem. Calif. Assembly, 1990-94, US Congress from Dist. 22 Calif., 1995—97; exec. dir. Calif. Space and Tech. Aliance, Calif. Space Port Authority, 1997—2001, Calif. Space Authority, Santa Maria, Calif., 2001—. Asst. Rep. leader; mem. Rep. caucus; mem. edn. com., agr. com., consumer protection com., new tech. com., govtl. efficiency com., and ways and means com.; mem. rural caucus and select com. on marine resources. Mem. Calif. Fedn. Rep. Women (past pres.). Office: Calif Space Authority Ste 204 3201 Airpark Dr Santa Maria CA 93455 Business E-Mail: andrea.seastrand@californiaspaceauthority.org.

SEATON, PAUL, state legislator; b. Oxnard, Calif., Oct. 1, 1945; m to Tina S; children: Tawny & Rand. AA, Ventura Coll., 1963—65; BS in Biology, U. Alaska, Fairbanks, 1966—68, MA in Tchg. and Biol. Scis., 1968—69; MS in Marine Zoology, San Diego State Coll., 1971—72; studied, U. Calif., Santa Barbara, 1974—76. Alaska State Representative, District 35, 2003-. Teacher; tree clearing business, formerly; owner, fisherman, K-N-S Marine Harvest Priority Committee; N Pacific Fisheries Management Coun; Seward Port & Harbor Comn; panel member West Coast Advisor; Nat Research Coun; Cook Inlet Aquaculture Association; Homer Little League; KELPS of Homer Found (fund advisor); founding board member Alaska Marine Conserv Coun; community coun member Kachemak Bay Research Res. Republican. Avocations: reading, hunting, fishing. Office: State Capitol Rm 102 Juneau AK 99801-1182 also: Dist 35 345 W Sterling Hwy Ste 102-B Homer AK 99603 Office Phone: 907-465-2689, 907-235-2921. Fax: 907-465-3472; Office Fax: 907-235-4008. Business E-Mail: Representative_Paul_Seaton@legis.state.ak.us.*

SEAVEY, WILLIAM ARTHUR, lawyer, vintner; b. LA, Aug. 28, 1930; s. Arthur Jones and Dorothy (Keyes) S.; m. Mary van Beuren, June 25, 1955, (dec. Aug. 29, 2008); children: Dorothy K., Arthur V.B., William G., Frederic A., Charles K. AB, Princeton U., 1952; LLB, Harvard U., 1955; grad. inst. Internat. Studies, U. Geneva, Switzerland, 1956, D in Polit. Sci., 1970. Bar: Calif. 1957, U.S. Dist. Ct. (so. and no. dist.) Calif. 1957, U.S. Ct. Appeals (9th cir.) 1957. Assoc. Luce, Forward, Kunzel & Scripps, San Diego, 1956-57; asst. U.S. atty. U.S. Dist. Ct. (so. dist.) Calif., 1957-59; pvt. practice San Diego, 1959-65; lectr. in internat. law and econ., asst. to pres. Mills Coll., Oakland, Calif., 1968-74; ptnr. Richards & Seavey, San Francisco, 1974-76, Davis, Stafford, Kellman & Fenwick, San Francisco, 1976-78; of counsel Friedman, Olive, McCubbin, Spalding, Bilter, Roosevelt etal, San Francisco, 1987—2004. Founder, proprietor Seavey Vineyard, St. Helena, Napa County, 1981—. Author: Dumping Since the War: The Gatt and National Laws, 1970. Councilman City of Coronado, Calif., 1960-62, mayor 1962-64; trustee French-Am. Internat. Sch., San Francisco, 1968-96; pres. English Speaking Union, San Francisco, 1982-85, Alliance Francaise, San

Francisco, 1979-81; chair Javits Fellowship Bd., Washington, 1989-92; mem. Columbus Fellowship Found. Bd., Washington, 1993-99; dir. San Francisco Com. on Fgn. Rels., 1995-98, 2001—, chmn., 1998-2001. Mem. ABA, Calif. Bar Assn., Am. Soc. Internat. Law, Pacific Union Club, Cercle de l'Union, Met. Club (Washington). Republican. Avocations: hiking, piano. Home and Office: 1310 Conn Valley Rd Saint Helena CA 94574-9624 E-mail: info@seaveyvineyard.com.

SEAWELL, DONALD RAY, lawyer, performing company executive; b. Jonesboro, NC, Aug. 1, 1912; s. A.A.F. and Bertha (Smith) S.; m. Eugenia Rawls, Apr. 5, 1941; children: Brook Ashley, Donald Brockman. AB, U. N.C., 1933, JD, 1936, DLitt, 1980; LHD, U. No. Colo., 1978. Bar: NC 1936, NY 1947. With SEC, 1939-41, 45-47, Dept. Justice, 1942-43; chmn. bd., dir., pub., pres. Denver Post, 1966-81; chmn. bd., dir. Gravure West, LA, 1966-81; dir. Swan Prodns., London; of counsel firm Bernstein, Seawell, Kove & Maltin, NYC, 1979—2006; chmn. bd. Denver Ctr. Performing Arts, 1972—2006, chief exec. officer, 1972—2006; chmn. emeritus, 2007—. Ptnr. Bonfils-Seawell Enterprises, NYC; bd. vis. U. NC Chmn. bd. ANTA, 1965—; theatre panel Nat. Coun. Arts, 1970-74; bd. govs. Royal Shakespeare Theatre, Eng.; trustee Am. Acad. Dramatic Arts, 1967—, Hofstra U., 1968-69, Cen. City Opera Assn., Denver Symphony; bd. dirs., Air Force Acad. Found., Nat. Ints. Outdoor Drama, Walter Hampden Meml. Library, Hammond Mus.; pres. Helen G. Bonfils Found., 1972-97, pres. emeritus, 1997—, Denver Opera Found.; Population Crisis Com., 1982-91; bd. dirs. Family Health Internat., Found. for Internat. Family Health; bd. visitors NC Sch. Arts, 1992-98; pres. Frederick G. Bonfils Found., 1972-92; chmn. Civilian Mil. Inst. Recipient Am. Acad. Achievement award, 1980, Tony award for producing, On Your Toes, 1983, Vocie Rsch. and Awareness award, Voice Found., 1983, Arts and Entertainement Cable Network award, 1987, Third Millennium Leadership award, Am. Diabetes Assn., 1996, Colo. Tourism Hall of Fame award, 1999, Thomas Degaetani award, U.S. Inst. for Theatre Tech., 2000, Benjamin F. Stapleton, Jr. award, 2000, Disting. Svc. award, U. Colo., 2000, Downtown Denver award for Tantalus, 2001, AWARE Honoree award, 2001, Donald Seawell Outstanding Achievement in Theatre award, Colo. Festival World Theatre, 2005, Founders award for Outstanding Contbn. to Am. Theater, Theater Hall Fame, NYC, 2005, Theatre Hall Fame, NYC, 2006; named Officer, Most Excellent Order of the Brit. Empire, 2002. Mem. Bucks Club (London), Dutch Treat Club (NYC), Denver Country Club, Denver Club, Cherry Hills Country Club, Mile High Club (Denver), Garden of Gods Club (Colorado Springs, Colo.). Office: Denver Ctr for Performing Arts 1101 13th St Denver CO 80204 Business E-Mail: dseawell@dcpa.org.

SEBASTIAN, PETER, political scientist, consultant, retired diplomat; b. June 19, 1926; m. Harvel Huddleston, Dec. 11, 1951; 1 child, Christopher. BA, U. Chgo., 1950; postgrad., U. d'Aix-Marseille, Nice, France, 1949, New Sch. for Social Research, NYC, 1950, Nat. War Coll., 1969-70. Dir., owner cons. co., NYC, 1950-57; U.S. Fgn. Service officer Dept. State, Washington, 1957-76, dep. exec. sec., 1976-77, sr. seminar, 1977-78; U.S. consul gen. Casablanca, Morocco, 1978-80; minister, counselor Am. embassy, Rabat, Morocco, 1980-82; dir. for North Africa Dept. State, Washington, 1982-84; ambassador to Tunisia Tunis, 1984-87; ambassador-in-residence Ctr. for Strategic Internat. Studies, Georgetown U., Washington, 1987-88; cons in fgn. affairs to the public and pvt. sector, lectr., 1988—. Mem. V.P. Bush's task force on border control, 1988—89. Contbr. poems to Osmose, 1949; author studies for the pvt. sector U.S. Dept. State and other U.S agys. Bd. dirs. Santa Fe Coun. on Internat. Rels., 2005. Sgt. AUS, 1944-46. Decorated Ouissam Alaouite (Morocco), numerous U.S. mil. decorations; recipient Presdl. Meritorious Service award, 1985. Mem. Am. Group Seminar Assn., Nat. Geog. Soc., Mid. East Inst. Episcopalian. Avocations: painting, drawing, photography. Home Phone: 505-983-6364; Office Phone: 505-992-3402. Personal E-mail: Batuta@aol.com.

SEBRIS, ROBERT, JR., lawyer; b. NYC, May 20, 1950; s. Robert and Ruth Sebris; m. S. Lawson Hollweg, Sept. 8, 1973; children: Jared Matthew, Bryan Taylor. BS in Indsl. Labor Rels., Cornell U., 1972; JD, George Washington U., 1978. Bar: DC 1978, Wash. 1980. Labor rels. specialist Onondaya County Office labor rels., Syracuse, NY, 1973-74, U.S. Dept. Labor, Washington, 1972-75; labor rels. mgr. U.S. Treasury Dept., Washington, 1975-78, employee rels. mgr., 1978-80; assoc. Davis, Wright, Todd, Riese & Jones, Seattle, 1980-84; ptnr. Davis, Wright, Tremain, Bellevue, Wash., 1985-92, Sebris Busto James, Bellevue, 1992—. Expert witness Amendments NLRA US Senate hearing, 1997. Co-author: (book) Employer's Guide to Strike Planning, 1985; contbr. articles to profl. jours. Mem. Bellevue CC Found., 1988—95, pres., 1995—96; chair employment law cert. program U. Wash. Law Sch., 1996—97. Mem.: ABA (health law forum, labo and employment law sect., mem. com. employee rights), Soc. Human Resource Mgmt., Am. Health Lawyers Assn., Pacific Coast Labor Law Conf. (planning com. 1980—93, chmn. 1991—92), Seattle/King County Bar Assn. (chmn. labor law sect. 1991—92), DC Bar Assn., Wash. Bar Assn. Avocations: golf, writing. Home: 16301 Mink Rd NE Woodinville WA 98072-9463 Office: Sebris Busto James Ste 325 14205 SE 36th St Bellevue WA 98006 Office Phone: 425-450-0300. Business E-Mail: rsebris@sebrisbusto.com.

SEDARIS, AMY, writer, actress; b. Endicott, NY, Mar. 19, 1961; d. Lou Sedaris. Performer: (TV series) Exit 57, 1995—96; co-writer (TV series) Exit 57, 1995—96, co-creator, 1995—96; performer: (TV series) Strangers With Candy, 1999—2000; co-writer (TV series) Strangers With Candy, 1999—2000, co-creator, 1999—2000; actor(guest appearances): (TV series) Just Shoot Me, Monk, Sex and the City, Ed, Cracking Up,: (films) Commandments, 1997, Bad Bosses Go to Hell, 1997, Six Days Seven Nights, 1998, Jump Tomorrow, 2001, Maid in Manhattan, 2002, The School of Rock, 2003, Elf, 2003, My Baby's Daddy, 2004, Strangers with Candy, 2005, Stay, 2005, Bewitched, 2005, Romance and Cigarettes, 2005, (voice) Chicken Little, 2005, Full Grown Men, 2006; (TV films) Untitled New York Pilot, 2003; (plays) Jamboree, 1993; co-author (with brother David Sedaris): (plays) Jamboree, 1993; actor: (plays) Stump the Host, 1993; co-author (with brother David Sedaris): (plays) Stump the Host, 1993; actor: (plays) One Woman Shoes, 1995; co-author (with brother David Sedaris): (plays) One Woman Shoes, 1995 (Obie award, 1995); actor: (plays) Froggy, The Country Club, 1998—99 (nominated Drama Desk award, 1999), The Most Fabulous Story Ever Told, 1998—99, The Little Freida Mysteries, 1999; co-author (with brother David Sedaris): (plays) The Little Freida Mysteries, 1997; actor: (plays) The Book of Liz; co-author (with brother David Sedaris): (plays) The Book of Liz, 2001; co-author: (book), 2002; actor: (plays) Drama Department, 2001, Wonder of the World, 2001—02 (Lucille Lortel award for outstanding featured actress League of Off-Broadway Theatres and Prodrs., 2002), (short film) Wheels of Fury, 1998; co-writer (short film) Wheels of Fury, 1998; co-author (with brother David Sedaris): (plays) Stitches, Incident at Cobbler's Knob; co-author: (books) Wigfield: The Can-Do Town That Just May Not, 2003; author: I Like You, 2006. Office: c/o Jonathan Bluman Paradigm 10100 Santa Monica Blvd 25th Fl Los Angeles CA 90067

SEDERBURG, WILLIAM ALBERT, academic administrator, former state senator; b. Chadron, Nebr., Aug. 1, 1947; s. Marion E. and Viola A. (Shalender) S.; m. Joyce I. Witte, July 29, 1972; children: Matthew E., Karl A. BA in Edn. and Polit. Sci., Mankato State Coll., 1969; MA in Polit. Sci., Mich. State U., 1972, PhD in Polit. and Pub. Adminstrn., 1974; LLD (hon.), Kalamazoo Coll. Postdoctoral fellow dept. polit. sci. Mich. State U., East Lansing, 1973-75; dir. rsch. and programs, edn. specialist Mich. Ho. Rep. Caucus, Lansing, 1975—77, exec. dir., 1977—78; pres. Survey Rsch. Co., 1974—91; senator, 24th dist. Mich. Senate, Lansing, 1978—91; v.p. pub. policy, dir. Pub. Opinion Rsch. Inst., 1991—94; pres. Ferris State U., Big Rapids, Mich., 1994—2003, Utah Valley State Coll., Orem, Utah, 2003—. Mem. appropriations com., 1983-95, chmn. higher edn. and tech. com., health policy com., 1987-95, Mich. Capitol com., 1989-95. Contbr. articles to profl. jours. Bd. dirs. Luth. Social Svcs. Mich. Recipient Phil Sirotkin award for Higher Edn. Leadership, Pub. Svc. award, Am. Cancer Soc., Am. Lung Assn., award for Contributions to Ind. Higher Edn., Assn. Ind. Colleges and Universities, William P. Faust award, Am. Cancer award, Dir.'s Conf. award, Mich. Dept. Pub. Health, Pub. Svc. award, Mich. Coll. and U. Placement Coun., Outstanding Alumni award, Mich. State U.; NSF fellow, 1970—73. Mem. Phi Beta Kappa, Kappa Delta Pi, Omicron Delta Kappa, Golden Key Soc., Am. Polit. Sci. Assn. Republican. Office: Utah Valley State Coll 800 W Univ Pkwy Orem UT 84058 Business E-Mail: William.Sederburg@uvsc.edu.

SEDGWICK, KYRA, actress; b. NYC, Aug. 19, 1965; m. Kevin Bacon, Sept. 4, 1988; children: Travis, Sosie. Appeared in off-Broadway prodns. Time Was, 1981, Dakota's Belly Wyoming, 1989; stage appearances in Ah Wilderness!, 1988 (Theatre World award), Maids of Honor, 1990, Oleanna, 1994; Actress (films) War and Love, 1985, Tai-Pan, 1986, Kansas, 1988, Born on the Fourth of July, 1989, Mr. and Mrs. Bridge, 1990, Pyrates, 1991, Singles, 1992, Heart and Souls, 1993, Murder in the First, 1995, Something to Talk About, 1995, Losing Chase, 1996, Phenomenon, 1996, Montana, 1997, Critical Care, 1997, Twelfth Night, 1998, The Red Door, 1999, Labor Pains, 1999, What's Cooking, 2000, Just a Kiss, 2002, Behind the Red Door, 2002, Secondhand Lions, 2003, The Woodsman, 2004, Loverboy, 2005, The Game Plan, 2007; (TV movies) The Man Who Broke 1,000 Chains, 1987, Women & Men II, 1991, Hallmark Hall of Fame, 1992 (Golden Globe award nomination 1993), The Wide Net, 1997, Door to Door, 2002, Cavedweller, 2004, Something the Lord Made, 2004, (TV series) Another World, 1982-83, Talk to Me, 2000, Queens Supreme, 2003-07, The Closer, 2005- (Best Performance by an Actress in a TV Series-Drama, Golden Globe award, Hollywood Fgn. Press Assn., 2007, Favorite TV Drama Diva, People's Choice Awards, 2009); (mini-series) Family Pictures, 1983; (TV appearances) ABC Afternoon Spls., 1985, Am. Playhouse, 1987, 88, Miami Vice, 1985, Amazing Stories, 1986, Ally McBeal, 2002. Named one of Top 25 Entertainers or Yr., Entertainment Weekly, 2007. Office: c/o Handprint Entertainment 9100 Wilshire Blvd Ste 700E Beverly Hills CA 90212-3423

SEDILLO, ORLANDO DELANO, city official; b. Monticello, NY; BA in Sociology and Phys. Edn., U. Albuquerque, 1962. Supr. City of Albuquerque Pks. and Recreation Dept., 1961-66; dir. City of Albuquerque Neighborhood Youth Corps, 1967; manpower devel. specialist U.S. Dept. of Labor, Albuquerque, 1967-70; dir., model cities program City of Albuquerque, 1971; manpower devel. specialist U.S. Dept. Labor, Dallas, 1971-74; dir. Comprehensive Employment and Tng. Program U.S. Dept. Labor/City of Albuquerque, 1974-78; dir. Pks. and Recreation Dept. City of Albuquerque Pks., 1978-86; dir. solid waste collection and disposal dept. City of Albuquerque, 1986-87; dir. state pks. and recreation divsn. State of N.Mex., 1987; dep. county mgr. Bernalillo County, Albuquerque, 1990-91; asst. dir. Human Resource Programs U.S. Forest Svc., USDA, Washington, 1991-96; dir. solid waste mgmt. dept. City of Albuquerque, 1997—. Mem. U.S. Conf. Mayors employment and tng. adv. coun., 1977-78; mem. state manpower svcs. coun. N.Mex., 1974-78; mem. gov.'s recreation priorities adv. com., 1982-86; mem. Bur. Land Mgmt.'s Albuquerque dist. adv. coun., 1986-89; mem. assessment bd., City of El Paso, Tex., for selection of dir. of pks. and recreation dept., 1982, 86; chmn. Albuquerque Bot. Garden adv. bd., 1983-86. Chmn., bd. dirs., N.Mex. Vols. for Outdoors, 1986; bd. dirs. Albuquerque Boys' Clubs, 1983-84. Recipient Outstanding Exec. award Albuquerque Hispano C. of C., 1977, N.Mex. Disting. Pub. Svc. award Gov.'s Disting. Pub. Svc. Award Coun., 1985, Washburn award Ctrl. N.Mex. Autobahn Soc., 1986, cert. of appreciation Nat. Recreation and Pks. Assn., Spl. Olympics Program of N.Mex., Nat. Alliance of Businessmen, LUCAC Nat. Edn. Svc. Ctr., Inc., N.Mex., cert. THANKS U. N.Mex., cert. appreciation dept. health, phys. edn. and recreation; cert. appreciation Albuquerque Internat. Balloon Fiesta, Open Space Task Force, Albuquerque Police Dept., N.Mex. Horse Coun. and Heights Lions Club; recipient Leadership award Keep Am. Beautiful; cert. appreciation for vol. svcs. Gov. of N.Mex.; named Individual of Yr. Albuquerque Conservation Assn., 1986. Mem. Assn. Retarded Citizens (pres. bd. dirs. 1982-83), N.Mex. Recreation and Pks. Assn. (v.p. 1985-86, pres. 1986-87, mem. profl. cert. bd. 1983-86, profl. award 1982). Office: City Albuquerque Dept Solid Waste Mgmt 4600 Edith Blvd NE Albuquerque NM 87107-4043 Fax: 505-761-8167.

SEDIN, HENRIK, professional hockey player; b. Ornskoldsvik, Sweden, Sept. 26, 1980; m. Johanna Sedin; 1 child, Valter. Center MoDo Hockey (Swedish Elite League), 1997—2000, 2004—05, Vancouver Canucks, 2000—. Mem. Swedish Olympic Hockey Team, Torino, Italy, 2006. Named to NHL All-Star Game, 2008. Achievements include being a member of gold medal winning Swedish Hockey Team, Torino Olympics, Italy, 2006. Avocations: boating, golf. Office: Vancouver Canucks 800 Griffiths Way Vancouver BC V6B 6G1 Canada

SEDWICK, JOHN W., federal judge; b. Kittanning, Pa., Mar. 13, 1946; s. Jack D. and Marion (Hilton) S.; m. Deborah Brown, Aug. 22, 1966; children: Jack D. II, Whitney Marie. BA summa cum laude, Dartmouth Coll., 1968; JD cum laude, Harvard U., 1972. Bar: Alaska 1972, U.S. Dist. Ct. Alaska 1972, U.S. Ct. Appeals (9th cir.) 1973. Lawyer Burr, Pease and Kurtz, Anchorage, 1972-81, 1982-92; dir. div. lands State of Alaska, Anchorage, 1981-82; judge US Dist. Ct. Alaska, Anchorage, 1992—, chief judge, 2002—. Mem. Commonwealth North, Anchorage, 1985; bd. dirs. South Addition Alaska R.R. Com., Anchorage, 1984. Sgt. USNG, 1969-72. Mem. ABA, Alaska Bar Assn. (chmn. environ. law sect. 1984, law examiners com. 1986-89, civil rules com. 1990-92, fee arbitration com. 1991-92). Episcopalian. Office: US Dist Ct Box 32 222 W 7th Ave Unit 4 Anchorage AK 99513-7564

SEE, CAROLYN, English language educator, writer, book critic; b. Pasadena, Calif., Jan. 13, 1934; d. George Newton Laws and Kate Louise (Sullivan) Daly; m. Richard Edward See, Feb. 18, 1955 (div. June 1959); 1 child, Lisa Lenine; m. Tom Sturak, June 11, 1959; 1 child, Clara Elizabeth Marya. BA, Calif. State U., LA, 1958; PhD, UCLA, 1963. Prof. English Loyola Marymount Coll., LA, 1970-85, UCLA, 1985—; book critic L.A. Times, 1981-93, Washington Post, 1993—. Author: Rhine Maidens, 1980, Golden Days, 1986, Making History, 1991, Dreaming: Hard Luck and Good Times In America, 1995, The Handyman, 1999, Making a Literary Life, 2002, There Will Never Be Another You, 2006 Bd. dirs. Calif. Arts Coun., L.A., 1987-91, Day Break, for homeless, Santa Monica, Calif., 1989—, Friends of English, UCLA, 1990—; buddy for life AIDS Project L.A., AIDS relief, L.A., 1990—. Recipient award Sidney Hillman Found., 1972, Robert Kirsch award L.A. Times, 1994; PEN Ctr. USA West Lifetime Achievement award 1998; grantee Nat. Endowment for Arts, 1980, Guggenheim fellow, 1990-91. Mem. Writers Guild Am., Libr. Found. Calif., PEN Ctr. USA West (pres. 1990-91), Nat. Book Critics Cir. (bd. dirs. 1986-90). Democrat. Avocations: gardening, sailing, dance, brush clearing. Address: Ms Carolyn See 930 3rd St 203 Santa Monica CA 90403 Office Phone: 310-395-4282. Business E-Mail: csee@ucla.edu.

SEEBACH, LYDIA MARIE, physician; b. Red Wing, Minn., Nov. 9, 1920; d. John Henry and Marie (Gleusen) S.; m. Keith Edward Wentz, Oct. 16, 1959; children: Brooke Marie, Scott. BS, U. Minn., 1942, MB, 1943, MD, 1944, MS in Medicine, 1951. Diplomate Am. Bd. Internal Medicine. Intern Kings County Hosp., Bklyn., 1944; fellow Mayo Found., Rochester, Minn., 1945-51; pvt. practice Oakland, Calif., 1952-60, San Francisco, 1961—. Asst. clin. prof. U. Calif., San Francisco, 1981—; mem., vice chmn. Arthritis Clinic, Presbyn. Hosp., San Francisco, 1961-88, pharmacy com., 1963-78; chief St. Mary's Hosp. Arthritis Clinic, San Francisco, 1968-72; exec. bd. Pacific Med. Ctr., San Francisco, 1974-76. Contbr. articles to med. jours. Fellow ACP; mem. AMA, Am. Med. Womens Assn. (pres. Calif. chpt. 1968-70), Am. Rheumatism Assn., Am. Soc. Internal Medicine, Pan Am. Med. Womens Assn. (treas.), Calif. Acad. Medicine, Calif. Soc. Internal Medicine, Calif. Med. Assn., San Francisco Med. Soc., San Francisco Med. Assn., San Francisco Soc. Internal Medicine, No. Calif. Rheumatism Assn., Internat. Med. Women's Assn., Mayo Alumni (bd. dirs. 1983-89), Iota Sigma Pi. Republican. Lutheran. Avocations: music, cooking, gardening, needlepoint. Office: 490 Post St Ste 939 San Francisco CA 94102-1414 Office Phone: 415-362-6398. Personal E-mail: lseebach@sbcglobal.net.

SEEGAL, JOHN FRANKLIN, lawyer; b. Newton, Mass., May 21, 1946; s. Samuel Melbourne and Martha (Lewenberg) S.; m. Barbara Ellen Wayne, Apr. 2, 1982; children: Sarah Rachel, Laura Rose. BA in econ. summa cum laude, Harvard U., MBA with distinction, 1973, JD magna cum laude, 1973. Bar: Calif. 1973. Assoc. Orrick, Herrington & Sutcliffe, LLP, San Francisco, 1973-78, ptnr., 1979—, practice leader mergers & acquisitions. Co-chmn. Inst. on Securities Regulation, 2001. Author: Bargaining Power, Acquiring or Selling the Privately Held Co., 1999, Private Co. M&A: Deal Structures, Execution & Related Issues, 2001. Mem.: ABA, Practicing Law Inst. (co-chmn. Securities Regulation Inst. 2001), Calif. Bar Assn. Republican. Jewish. Fluent in french. Office: Orrick Herrington & Sutcliffe LLP 405 Howard St San Francisco CA 94105 Office Phone: 415-773-5797. Office Fax: 415-773-5759. Business E-Mail: jseegal@orrick.com.

SEEGER, LAUREEN E., lawyer, health products executive; BBA, U. Wis., Eau Claire, 1983; JD, U. Wis., Madison, 1986. Atty. Jones, Day, Reavis & Pogue, 1986—92; ptnr.-in-charge tech. litigation sect. Morris, Manning & Martin, LLP, 1992—2000; v.p., gen. coun. McKesson Provider Technologies, 2000—06; exec. v.p., gen. counsel, sec. McKesson Corp., San Francisco, 2006—. Office: McKesson Corpn 1 Post St San Francisco CA 94104

SEEGER, LEINAALA ROBINSON, law librarian, educator; b. Wailuku, Hawaii, July 2, 1944; d. John Adam and Anna Hiilani (Leong) Robinson; 1 child, Maile Lea. BA, U. Wash., 1966; JD, U. Puget Sound, 1977; M in Law Librarianship, U. Wash., 1979. Bar: Wash. 1977. Reference librarian U. Puget Sound Sch. Law., Tacoma, 1977-79, assoc. law librarian, 1981-86; asst. librarian McGeorge Sch. Law, U. of Pacific, Sacramento, 1979-81; assoc. librarian pub. svc. Harvard Law Sch., Cambridge, Mass., 1986-89; dir. law library, assoc. prof. law U. Idaho Coll. Law, Moscow, 1989-97, U. Hawaii Sch. of Law, Honolulu, 1997—. Mem. Assn. Am. Law Schs. (librs. and technol. com. 1997-99, chmn. 1998-99), Wash. state Bar Assn., Am. Assn. Law Librs. (chmn. minority com. 1990-91, v.p., pres.-elect Western Pacific chpt. 1985-86, 90-91, pres. 1991-92, vice chmn. edn. com. 1991-92, chmn. 1992-93). Avocations: scuba diving, snorkeling, wine education, flying, aerobics.

SEEGMILLER, F. JAY, state legislator; b. Salt Lake City, Utah, May 29, 1958; m. Michelle Seegmiller; children: Kathryn, Jason, Ashley, Matthew. Attended, U. Utah. Condr. Union Pacific RR, 1976—87, AMTRAK, 1987—; mem. Dist. 49 Utah House of Reps., 2009—. Democrat. Mormon. Office: W030 State Capitol Complex Salt Lake City UT 84114 Mailing: 9152 S Sterling Dr Sandy UT 84093 Office Phone: 801-538-1029. Office Fax: 801-538-1908. Business E-Mail: jseegmiller@utah.gov.

SEEL, CARL E., state legislator; b. Md., July 14, 1969; m. Jamie Seel; children: Matthew, Nathaniel, John. AA, Coll. of the Canyons, Santa Clarita, 1993. Ad sales Directions Pub., 2002; precinct committeeman, 2002—; chmn. Fin. Com. Maricopa County, 2006—; mem.-at-large Ariz. State Exec. Com., 2005—; mem. Dist. 6 Ariz. House of Reps., 2008—. Mem. North Phoenix C. of C., 2003—, Chamber at Antheu, 2005—. Republican. Protestant. Office: Capitol Complex 1700 W Washington Rm 341 Phoenix AZ 85007-2890 Office Phone: 602-926-3018. Office Fax: 602-417-3006. Business E-Mail: cseel@azleg.gov.*

SEELENFREUND, ALAN, retired pharmaceutical company executive; b. NYC, Oct. 22, 1936; s. Max and Gertrude (Roth) S.; m. Ellyn Bolt; 1 child, Eric. BME, Cornell U., 1959, M. in Indsl. Engring., 1960; PhD in Mgmt. Sci., Stanford U., 1967. Asst. prof. bus. adminstrn. Grad. Sch. Bus. Stanford U., Palo Alto, Calif., 1966-71; mgmt. cons. Strong, Wishart and Assocs., San Francisco, 1971-75;

various mgmt. positions McKesson Corp., San Francisco, 1975-84, v.p., chief fin. officer, 1984-86, exec. v.p., chief fin. officer, 1986-89, chmn., CEO, 1989-97, chmn., 1997-99, also bd. dirs., chmn., 1997—2002; ret., 2002. Mem. Nature Conservancy, St. Francis Yacht Club, Villa Taverna Club, Pacific Union Club, Francisco Yacht Club. Avocations: sailing, skiing, hiking. Office: McKesson Corp 1 Post St Ste 2625 San Francisco CA 94104-5296

SEELIG, TINA L., entrepeneurship program director, educator; PhD, Stanford U. Med. Sch., 1985. Entrepreneur, mgmt. cons., author, & scientist; created and taught courses including The History and Philosophy of Brain Function; rsch. assoc. Technology Mus.; tech. and mktg. cons. for several biotechnology companies; mgmt. cons. Booz, Allen and Hamilton; founder BookBrowser, 1991—93; multimedia prodr. Compaq Computer Corp., 1993; exec. dir., Stanford Technology Ventures Program Stanford U., Calif.; Fenwick and West Entrepreneurship educator on creativity & innovation, dept. mgmt. sci. and engring. Stanford U. and Hasso Plattner Inst. for Design, Calif.; dir. Stanford Entrepreneurs Network; co-dir. Mayfield Fellows Program. Written several popular science books, has designed a series of educational games; author: The Epicurean Laboratory: Exploring the Science of Cooking, 1991, Incredible Edible Science (Scientific American Mysteries of Science), 1994 (Internat. Children's Choice award); designer (ednl. card games) Games for Your Brain (12 games) (winner of several awards, including Parents Guide to Children's Media Outstanding Achievement for 1999). Recipient award for Excellence in Undergraduate Tchg., Stanford U., Tau Beta Pi, 2005; co-recipient with Tom Byers, Nat. Olympus Innovation award, Nat. Collegiate Inventors and Innovators Alliance, 2008, with Tom Byers, Bernard M. Gordon prize, NAE, 2009. Office: Stanford U Management Science & Engring Terman Engineering Ctr 3rd Fl Rm 411 380 Panama Way Stanford CA 94305-4026 Office Phone: 650-725-1627. Office Fax: 650-723-1614. Business E-Mail: tseelig@stanford.edu.*

SEEMAN, MELVIN, sociologist, educator; b. Balt., Feb. 5, 1918; s. Morris and Sophie (Kostman) S.; m. Alice Ruth Zerbola, June 30, 1944; children— Teresa E., Paul D. BA, Johns Hopkins U., 1944; PhD, Ohio State U., 1947. Asst. prof. sociology Ohio State U., 1947-52, assoc. prof., 1953-59; prof. UCLA, 1959-88, prof. emeritus, 1988—. Mem. Am. Sociol. Assn. Home: 21532 Paseo Serra St Malibu CA 90265-5112 Office: UCLA Dept Sociology 405 Hilgard Ave Los Angeles CA 90095-9000 E-mail: mseeman@conet.ucla.edu.

SEFF, JAMES M., lawyer; b. NYC, Jan. 27, 1941; AB with honors, U. Mich., 1963; JD, U. Calif., 1966. Bar: Hawaii 1969, Calif. 1970, US Dist. Ct. (no., ctrl. dist Calif., Hawaii), US Supreme Ct. Mem. Pillsbury Winthrop Shaw Pittman LLP, San Francisco, ptnr., chmn. Wine Beer & Spirits practice, co-chair restaurant, food & beverage group. Lectr. Univ. Calif., Davis; co-chmn. CLE Internat. Seminar on Wine Beer & Spirits Law; mem. adv. com. Columbia Univ. Legis. Drafting Rsch. Fund. Author (contributing): Univ. Calif. / Sotheby Book of California Wine; contbr. articles to profl. jours. Dir. Carmel Bach Festival; counsel Soc. Medical Friends of Wine; dir. Lasallian Edn. Fund; past v.p. Jewish Family & Children's Svc., San Francisco. Capt. USNR. Recipient Disting. Cmty. Svc. award, Jewish Family & Children's Svc. of San Francisco. Fellow: Am. Bar Found.; mem.: ABA (past chmn. alcoholic beverage practice com.), Barristers Club San Francisco (past pres.), San Francisco Bar Found. (past pres.), State Bar Calif. (past v.p., gov., vice chmn. conf. del.), Bar Assn. San Francisco (past pres., Award of Merit), Assn. Internationale des Juristes pour le Droit de la Vigne et du Vin, Am. Soc. Enology & Viticulture. Office: Pillsbury Winthrop Shaw Pittman 50 Fremont St San Francisco CA 94105 Office Phone: 415-983-7441. Office Fax: 415-983-1200. Business E-Mail: james.seff@pillsburylaw.com.

SEFF, KARL, zeolite chemist, chemistry educator; b. Chgo., Jan. 23, 1938; s. Joseph and Rose (Hauser) S. BS, U. Calif., Berkeley, 1959; PhD, MIT, 1964. Asst. rsch. chemist UCLA, 1965—67; asst. prof. chemistry U. Hawaii, Honolulu, 1968—73, assoc. prof. chemistry, 1973—75, prof. chemistry, 1975—2006, emeritus prof. chemistry, 2007—. Cons. Filtrol Corp., L.A., 1966-73, Mitsubishi Heavy Industry, Nagasaki, Japan, 1992-94; vis. scholar Princeton (N.J.) U., 1974-75, Oxford (Eng.) U., 1988, 89, Pusan and Kyungpook Nat. Univs., Korea, 1996; assoc. rschr. U. Mex, 1981-82; vis. prof. U. Leuven, Belgium, 1975, Dartmouth U., 1989; lectr. Tokyo Inst. Tech., 1980, 91, Los Alamos Nat. Lab., 1985, U. Bristol, 1988, ETH, Zurich, Switzerland, 1988, Goethe U., Frankfurt, Germany, 1988, Imperial Coll., London, 1989, Cambridge U., 1989, Kyungpook Nat. U., Korea, 1990, Acad. Sci. Leningrad, 1990, Pusan Nat. U., Korea, 1990, Northwestern U., 1994, others; assoc. chair chemistry dept. U. Hawaii, 2000, chair, 2000-03. Contbr. numerous articles to profl. jours. NATO sr. fellow, NSF, 1975, Rsch. Travel award, 1988-90; grantee Army Rsch. Office, 1969-72, NIH, 1972-75, 75-78, NSF, 1973-76, 75, 77, 78-81, Petroleum Rsch. Fund, 1974-76, 95-98, Gordon Conf., 1976, U.S.-Korea Coop. Rsch., NSF, 1982, 84-86, Mitsubishi Industries, 1992-93. Mem. Am. Chem. Soc. (local sect. pres., award 1983, councilor 1992-94, 2005-07), Am. Crystallographic Assn., Vegetarian Soc. Hawaii (exec. com. 1993—), Internat. Zeolite Assn., Sigma Xi. Democrat. Avocations: travel, gardening, cacti. Office: U Hawaii Dept Chemistry 2545 The Mall Honolulu HI 96822-2275 Business E-Mail: seff@hawaii.edu.

SEGAL, HELENE ROSE, periodical editor; b. LA, Jan. 31, 1955; d. Alan and Lila E. Segal. Student, Calif. State U., Fullerton, 1973-75; BA in English, U. Calif., Santa Barbara, 1978. Library asst. ABC-CLIO, Santa Barbara, 1979-80, editorial asst., 1980-81, asst. editor, 1981-83; mng. editor ABC POL SCI, ABC-CLIO, Santa Barbara, 1983-2001; project mgr. ABC-CLIO, Santa Barbara, 2001—. Mem. Am. Polit. Sci. Assn., Current World Leaders (adv. bd. 1989—). Avocations: reading, collecting, swimming. Home: 142 La Vista Grande Santa Barbara CA 93103-2817 Office: ABC CLIO 130 Cremona Dr Ste C Santa Barbara CA 93117-5505 E-mail: hsegal@abc-clio.com.

SEGAL, JACK, mathematics professor; b. Phila., May 9, 1934; s. Morris and Rose (Novin) S.; m. Arlene Stern, Dec. 18, 1955; children: Gregory, Sharon. BS, U. Miami, 1955, MS, 1957; PhD, U. Ga., 1960. Instr. math. U. Wash., Seattle, 1960-61, asst. prof., 1961-65, assoc. prof., 1965-70, prof., 1970-1999, prof. emeritus, 2000—, chmn. dept., 1975-78. Author: Lecture Notes in Mathematics, 1978, Shape Theory, 1982. NSF postdoctoral fellow Inst. Advanced Study, Princeton, N.J., 1963-64; Fulbright fellow U. Zagreb, Croatia, 1969-70, U. Coll. London hon. rsch. fellow, 1988; NAS exch. prof. U. Zagreb, 1979-80. Mem. Am. Math. Soc. Home: 8711 25th Pl NE Seattle WA 98115-3416 Office: U Washington Dept Mathematics Seattle WA 98195-0001 Office Phone: 206-543-1914. Business E-Mail: segal@math.washington.edu.

SEGAL, NANCY LEE, psychology professor, researcher; b. Boston, Mar. 2, 1951; d. Alfred Maurice and Esther (Rubenstein) S. BA in Psychology and English, Boston U., 1973; MA in Social Sci., U. Chgo., 1974, PhD in Human Devel., 1982. Asst. dir., rsch. assoc. Minn. Ctr. for Twin and Adoption Rsch., Mpls., 1985-91; prof. dept. psychology Calif. State U., Fullerton, 1991—. Cons. on twin loss, Mpls., 1984, 87. Author: Entwined Lives: Twins and What They Tell Us About Human Behavior, 1999, Indivisible by Two: Lives of Extraordinary Twins, 2005, Co-editor: Uniting Psychology and Biology: Integrative Perspectives on Human Development, 1997; contbg. editor Twins Mag., 1984—, mem. editorial bd., 1985—; contbr. articles to profl. jours. Recipient Disting. Alumni award Boston U., 1990. Fellow Am. Psychol. Soc., APA (divsn. 7); mem. Twins Found., Internat. Soc. for Twin Studies, Internat. Soc. for Human Ethology (membership chair), N.Y. Road Runners Club, Sigma Delta Epsilon (rsch. award 1989), Sigma Xi. Avocation: running. Office: Calif State U Dept Psychology H-426C 800 N State College Blvd Fullerton CA 92831-3547 Office Fax: 714-278-4843. Business E-Mail: nsegal@fullerton.edu.

SEGEL, KAREN LYNN JOSEPH, lawyer, tax specialist; b. Youngstown, Ohio, Jan. 15, 1947; d. Samuel Dennis and Helen Anita Joseph; m. Alvin Gerald Segel, June 9, 1968 (div. Sept. 1976); 1 child, Adam James. BA in Soviet and East European Studies, Boston U., 1968; JD, Southwestern U., LA, 1975. Bar: Calif., 1996, US Tax Ct., 1996, US Dist. Ct. (ctrl. dist.) Calif., 1996, US Ct. Appeals (9th cir.), 1997. Adminstrv. asst. Olds Brunel & Co., NYC, 1968-69, US Banknote Corp., NYC, 1969-70; tax acct. S.N. Chilkov & Co. CPA's, Beverly Hills, Calif., 1971-74; intern Calif. Corps. Commr., 1975; tax. sr. Oppenheim Appel & Dixon CPA's, LA, 1978, Fox, Westheimer & Co. CPA's, LA, 1978, Zebrak, Levine & Mepos CPA's, LA, 1979; ind. cons. acctg., taxation specialist Beverly Hills, 1980—. Settlement officer LA County Superior Ct., 2000—; law student mentor Southwestern U., 1996—2007; tax moot ct. judge, 1997. High sch. amb. to Europe People-to-People Orgn., 1963. Mem. Calif. State Bar, Women's Inner Circle of Achievement, So. Calif. Bus. Litig. Inns of Ct., LA County Bar Assn, Beverly Hills Tinseltown Rose Soc. Avocations: collecting seashells, art, travel, music. Personal E-mail: kjslaw@earthlink.net.

SEGERBLOM, SHARON B., social services administrator; b. Miami, Okla., Dec. 19, 1948; d. Charles L. and Doris E. (Randall) Butler; m. Richard Segerblom; children: Eva, Carl. Student, Okla. State U.; degree in nursing, U. Tulsa, 1971; BA in Polit. Sci., U. Nev. Past mgr. Neighborhood Response divsn. City of Las Vegas, past intergovtl. cmty. rels. cood., past chief asst. to the mayor, dir. Neighborhood Svcs., 1997—. Rschr. Focus on Nev.'s Children, 1987, Focus on Nev.'s Women, co-editor, video writer, prodr. Issues chairperson Gov.'s Conf. on Women, 1989-90; 1st v.p. Clark County Area Coun. PTA, 1989-90, Girl Scouts USA Frontier Coun., 1991-93; bd. dirs. WE Can, 1989-90, Martin Luther King Jr. Com., Weed and Seed Steering Com.; bd. dirs., past pres. Clark County Atty.'s Wives, 1988-89; past pres. Women's Dem. Club Clark County; mem. Clark County Dem. Ctrl. Com., 1989-90; past bd. dirs. Jr. League of Las Vegas, 1990; mem. adv. bd. REACH-OUT; fundraiser Boy Scouts Am., Boulder Dam Coun. Recipient Cmty. Svcs. award for excellence Gov.'s Conf. on Women, 1990, Heart of Gold award Focus on Nev.'s Women, Jr. League of Las Vegas, 1989-90. Mem. Assn. for Children for Enforcement of Support (bd. dirs. 1989-90). Office: Dept Neighborhood Svcs City Las Vegas City Hall 400 Stewart Ave Las Vegas NV 89101-2927

SEGGER, MARTIN JOSEPH, museum director, educator, art historian; b. Felixtowe, Eng., Nov. 22, 1946; s. Gerald Joseph and Lillian Joan (Barker-Emery) S.; m. Angele Cordonier, Oct. 4, 1968; children: Cara Michelle, Marie-Claire, Margaret Ellen. BA, U. Victoria, 1969, diploma in edn., 1970; MPhil, U. London, 1973. Prof. art history U. Victoria, BC, Canada, 1970—74; museologist Royal B.C. Mus., Victoria, 1974—77; dir. Maltwood Art Mus., prof. art history U. Victoria, 1977—, dir. cmty. rels., 2001—. Cons. Nat. Mus. Corp., Ottawa, 1977, UNESCO, O.E.A., Cairo, 1983; bd. dirs. Canadian Cultural Rsch. Network, Victoria Coll. Art, Can. Rsch. Alliance; bd. advisors Greater Victoria Econ. Devel. Commn.; pres. Pacific northwest chpt. Soc. Archtl. Historians, 2002— Author: exhbn. catalogue House Beautiful, 1975, Arts of the Forgotten Pioneers, 1971, Victoria: An Architectural History, 1979, (commendation Am. Assn. State and Local History 1980), This Old House, 1975, This Old Town, 1979, British Columbia Parliament Buildings, 1979, The Heritage of Canada, 1981, Samuel Maclure: In Search of Appropriate Form, 1986 (Hallmark award 1987, 98), (a guide) St. Andrew's Cathedral, 1990, The Development of Gordon Head Campus, 1988, An Introduction to Museum Studies, 1989, An Introduction to Heritage Conservation, 1990, Botswana Live, 1994, Exploring Victoria's Architecture, 1996; contbr., cons. British Columbia Encyclopedia, 2000, Victoria Modern, 2006. Mem. heritage policy rev. com. Govt. Can., 2001—; Canadian Decorative Arts Soc., 2001—; mem. cultural diversity experts com. Govt. Can., 2002—; v.p. Commonwealth Museums Assn., 2003—; bd. govs. Heritage Can. Found., 1979—83; chmn. City of Victoria Heritage Adv. Com., 1975—79; bd. dirs. Downtown Victoria Cmty. Alliance, Heritage Trust, 1977—86, B.C. Touring Coun., Sta. CFUV Radio, B.C. Govt. Ho. Found., Royal B.C. Mus., 1996—99; co-chair B.C. Arts Festival; mem. B.C. Heritage Adv. Bd., 1973—83; councillor City of Victoria, 1987—93; vice-chair Provincial Capital Commn., 1991—2001; pres. Assn. Vancouver Island Municipalities, 1993—94; chmn. B.C. Festival of the Arts, 1999; bd. dirs. Internat. Coun. Mus.-Can., 1999, Victoria Coll. Art, 2001—, Victoria Harbour Authority, 2002—, dir.; bd. chair Queenswood Soc., 2007—. Decorated knight Equestrian Order of Holy Sepulchre of Jerusalem; recipient award, Heritage Can. Comm., 1976, Heritage Conservation award, Lt. Gov. B.C., 1989, Harley J. McKee award, Assn. Preservation Tech., 1994, Queen's Golden Jubilee medal; named Hon. Citizen, City of Victoria, 2000, Arts Citizen of Yr., 2001. Fellow Royal Soc. Arts, Can. Mus. Assn. (counsellor 1975-77); mem. Internat. Coun. Mus. (chair internat. com. for tng. pers. 1995-98), Internat. Coun. Monuments and Sites (bd. dirs. 1980-82), Soc. Study Architecture Can. (bd. dirs. 1979-81), Can Mus. Dirs. Orgn., Commonwealth Assn. Museums (pres. 2005—), Union Club Victoria. Roman Catholic. Avocations: travel, motor mechanics, water color painting. Home Phone: 250-384-3694; Office Phone: 604-721-8298. Business E-Mail: msegger@uvic.ca.

SEGIL, LARRAINE DIANE, materials company executive; b. Johannesburg, South Africa, July 15, 1948; came to U.S., 1974; d. Jack and Norma Estelle (Cohen) Wolfowitz; m. Clive Melwyn Segil, Mar. 9, 1969; 1 child, James Harris. BA, U. Witwatersrand, South Africa, 1967, BA with honours, 1969; JD, Southwestern U., L.A., 1979; MBA, Pepperdine U., 1985. Bar: Calif. 1979, U.S. Supreme Ct. 1982. Cons. in internat. transactions, L.A., 1976-79; atty. Long & Levit, L.A., 1979-81; chmn., pres. Marina Credit Corp., L.A., 1981-85; pres., chief exec. officer Electronic Space Products Internat., L.A., 1985-87; mng. ptnr. The Lared Group, L.A., 1987—; pres. Lared Presentations Inc.; keynote spkr. and expert on alliances, globalization, and leadership. Author: (novel) Belonging, 1994, Intelligent Business Alliances, 1996. Bd. govs. Cedars Sinai Med. Ctr., L.A., 1984—; bd. dirs. So. Calif. Tech. Execs. Network, 1984-86, DARE. Mem. ABA (chmn. internat. law com. young lawyers div. 1980-84), Internat. Assn. Young Lawyers (exec. coun. 1979-81, coun. internat. law and practice 1983-84), World Tech. Execs. Network (chmn.). Avocations: piano, horseback riding.

SEIBLE, FRIEDER, structural engineer, educator; b. Schwaebisch Gmuend, Germany, 1952; m. Betsy Seible; children: Michael, Daniel, Anika. Dipl. Ing. in civil engring., U. Stuttgart, Germany, 1976; MCE, U. Calgary, Alta., Can., 1978; PhD in civil engring., U. Calif., Berkeley, 1982. Registered profl. engr., 1985. Mem. faculty U. Calif.-San Diego, La Jolla, 1983—, founding chair dept. structural engring., 1995—2001, Eric and Johanna Reissner Prof. Applied Mechanics and Structural Engring., dir. Charles Lee Powell Structural Rsch. Laboratories, prof. Structural Engring., interim dean Irwin & Joan Jacobs Sch. Engring., 2002—03, dean, 2003—. Mem. seismic adv. bd. Calif. Dept. Transp. (Caltrans). Recipient Best paper award Can. Soc. Civil Engring., 1982, K.B. Woods award Transp. Rsch. Bd., 1983, 92, Presdl. Young Investigator award Pres. Reagan, 1986, Japanese Govt. Rsch. award for fgn. rsch. specialists Sci. and Tech. Agy., 1987, Outstanding Paper award N.Am. Masonry Conf. award, 1990, 93, Best Paper award Internat. Conf. on Short and Medium Span Bridges, 1990, Raymond C. Reese Rsch. prize ASCE, 1992, Outstanding Jour. Paper award Masonry Soc., 1993, Shiley Achievement award Chancellor's Assocs., 1994, Outstanding Concrete Project award Am. Concrete Inst., 1994, Orchid award for design of Scripps Crossing pedestrian bridge San Diego Cmty. Awareness Program, 1994, citation for Lighting Design, Internat. Assn. Lighting Designers, 1994, Alan H. Yorkdale award ASTM, 1994, Concrete Bridge award Portland Cement Assn., 1994, Moisseiff award ASCE, 1995, Charles Pankow award for innovation CERF, 1996, Best Paper award ASCE, 1997. Mem.: NAE. Achievements include being one of the world's foremost seismic structural engineers.

SEIDEL, GEORGE ELIAS, JR., zoology educator; b. Reading, Pa., July 13, 1943; s. George E. Sr. and Grace Esther (Heinly) S.; m. Sarah Beth Moore, May 28, 1970; 1 child, Andrew. BS, Pa. State U., 1965; MS, Cornell U., 1968, PhD, 1970; postgrad., Harvard U. Med. Sch., Boston, 1970-71. Asst. prof. physiology Colo. State U., Ft. Collins, 1971-75, assoc. prof., 1975-83, prof., 1983-93, univ. disting. prof., 1993—. Vis. scientist Yale U., 1978-79, MIT, 1986-87; mem. bd. on agr. NRC. Co-editor: New Technologies in Animal Breeding, 1981; contbr. articles to profl. jours. Recipient Alexander Von Humboldt award, N.Y.C., 1983, Animal Breeding Research award Nat. Assn. Animal Breeders, Columbia, Mo., 1983, Clark award Colo. State U., 1982, Upjohn Physiology award, 1986; Gov's. award for Sci. and Tech., Colo., 1986. Mem. AAAS, NAS, Am. Dairy Sci. Assn., Am. Soc. Animal Sci. (Young Animal Scientist award 1983, Physiology, Endocrinology award, 2008), Soc. for Study of Reprodn., Internat. Embryo Transfer Soc. (pres. 1979, disting. svc. award 2001, Pioneer award 2008). Home: 3101 Arrowhead Rd Laporte CO 80535-9374 Office: Colo State U Animal Repro Biotech Lab Fort Collins CO 80523-1683 Office Phone: 970-491-5287. Business E-Mail: gseidel@colostate.edu.

SEILER, FRITZ ARNOLD, physicist; b. Basel, Switzerland, Dec. 20, 1931; came to U.S., 1980; s. Friedrich and Marie (Maibach) S.; m. Mary Catherine Coster, Dec. 22, 1964; children: Monica, Simone, Daniel. BA in Econs., Basel Sch. of Econs., 1951; PhD in Physics, U. Basel, 1962. Rsch. assoc. U. Wis., Madison, 1962-63; scientific assoc. U. Basel, 1963-69, privat dozent, 1969-75, dozent, 1975-80; sr. scientist Lovelace Inhalation Toxicology Inst., Albuquerque, 1980-90; sr. tech. assoc. IT Corp., Albuquerque, 1990-92, disting. tech. assoc., 1992-96; v.p. Inst. Regulatory Sci., Albuquerque, 1996-97; prin. Sigma Five Cons., Los Lunas, N.Mex., 1997—. Cons. Swiss Dept. Def., 1968-74; vis. scientist Lawrence Berkeley Labs., 1974-75. Contbr. numerous articles to profl. jours. With Swiss Army staff, 1964-75. Fellow Am. Phys. Soc., Health Physics Soc., Soc. for Risk Analysis, Fachverband fuer Strahlenschutz, Am. Nat. Stds. Inst. (mgmt. coun. 1987-2002, com. N14 1986-2002), Internat. Hormesis Soc Office: Sigma Five Consulting PO Box 1709 Los Lunas NM 87031-1709 Office Phone: 505-866-5193. Office Fax: 505-866-5197. Business E-Mail: faseiler@nmia.com.

SEILER, STEVEN LAWRENCE, health facility administrator; b. Chgo., Dec. 30, 1941; married. B, U. Ariz., 1963; M, U. Iowa, 1965. Adminstrv. resident Rush-Presbyn.-St. Luke's Med. Ctr., Chgo., 1965, adminstrv. asst., 1965-68; asst. adminstr. Lake Forest (Ill.) Hosp., 1968-71, adminstr., 1971-73, pres., 1973-86; exec. v.p Voluntary Hosps. Am., Park Ridge, Ill., 1987-89, sr. v.p., 1986-92; CEO Good Samaritan Regional Med. Ctr., Phoenix, 1992—. Adj. prof. Contbr. articles to profl. jours. Mem. AHA (svc. com.), Ill. Hosp. Assn. (chair 1980-81). Home: 3930 E Rancho Dr Paradise Valley AZ 85253-5025 Office: Good Samaritan Regional Med Ctr 1111 E Mcdowell Rd Phoenix AZ 85006-2612

SEINFELD, JERRY, comedian, actor, television producer, scriptwriter; b. Bklyn., Apr. 29, 1954; s. Kalman and Betty S.; m. Jessica Sklar, Dec. 25, 1999; children: Sascha, Julian, Shepherd Kellen Grad. with degree in theatre communications, Queens Coll., NY, 1976. Former salesman. Stand-up comedian, 1976—; joke-writer (TV series) Benson, ABC, 1980; actor, co-writer, prod. (TV series) Seinfeld, NBC-TV, 1990-97 (Emmy award Outstanding Comedy Series, 1993, Emmy nomination, Lead Actor - Comedy Series, 1994, Golden Globe winner, 1994, best actor comedy series), (TV movie) The Ratings Game, 1984, I'm Telling You for the Last Time, 1999; (TV specials) The Tommy Chong Roast, 1986, The Seinfeld Chronicles, 1989; (film) exec. prodr. Comedian, 2002, writer, actor A Uniorm Used to Mean Something, 2004, Hindsight is 20/20, 2004, actor The Thing About My Folks, 2005, writer, prodr., actor Bee Movie, (voice), 2007; writer Jerry Seinfeld-Stand-Up Confidential, 1987; author: Sein Language, 1993; guest appearances The Larry Sanders Show, 1992, News Radio, 1995. Recipient Am. Comedy award funniest male comedy stand-up, 1988, funniest actor in a TV series, 1992, 1993; Screen Actors Guild award, Outstanding Performance by an Ensemble in a Comedy Series, 1994, 1996, 1997; People's Choice award, Favorite TV Comedy Series, 1998; named one of The 100 Most Powerful Celebrities, Forbes.com, 2008 Jewish. Avocations: zen, yoga.

SEINFELD, JOHN HERSH, chemical engineering professor; b. Elmira, NY, Aug. 3, 1942; s. Ben B. and Minna (Johnson) S. BS, U. Rochester, 1964; PhD, Princeton U., 1967; DSc honoris causa, U. Patras, Greece, 2002, Carnegie Mellon U., 2002. Asst. prof. chem. engring. Calif. Inst. Tech., Pasadena, 1967-70, assoc. prof., 1970-74, prof., 1974—, Louis E. Nohl prof., 1980—, exec. officer for chem. engring., 1973-90, chmn. engring. and applied sci. div., 1990-2000. Allan P. Colburn meml. lectr. U. Del., 1976; Camille and Henry Dreyfus Found. lectr. MIT, 1979; mem. coun. Gordon Rsch. Confs., 1980-83; Donald L. Katz lectr. U. Mich., 1981; Reilly lectr. U. Notre Dame, 1983; Dean's Disting. lectr. U. Rochester, 1985; Katz lectr. CUNY, 1985; McCabe lectr. N.C. State U., 1986; Lewis lectr. MIT, 1986; Union Carbide lectr. SUNY, Buffalo; Van Winkle lectr. U. Tex., 1988; Bicentennial lectr. La. State U., 1988; Ida Beam lectr. U. Iowa, 1989, David Mason lectr. Stanford U., 1989; Julian Smith lectr. Cornell U., 1990; Merck lectr. Rutgers U., 1991; Henske Disting. lectr. Yale U., 1991; lectr. AIChE, 1980; Centennial lectr. U. Pa., 1993; Miles Disting. lectr. U. Pitts., 1994; Kelly lectr. Purdue U., 1996; Disting. rsch. lectr. Carnegie Mellon U., 1998; Berkeley lectr. U. Calif., Berkeley, 1998; Sigma Xi lectr., 1998—, Merck Sharp & Dohme lectr. U. P.R., 1998; Hess lectr. U. Va., 1998; inaugural disting. lectr. U. Toledo, 1999; Priestley lectr. Commonwealth Sci. and Indsl. Rsch. Orgn., 2000; Amundson lectr. U. Houston, 2002, Hottel lectr. MIT, 2002, Lowrie lectr. Ohio State U., 2004; Fingerson/TSI lectr. U. Minn., 2004; Frontiers lectr. U. Conn., 2005; ICI disting. lectr. U. Alta., 2005; Mah lectr. Northwestern U., 2006; Holtz lectr. Johns Hopkins U., 2006, Quinn lectr. U. Penn., 2008. Author: Numerical Solution of Ordinary Differential Equations, 1971, Mathematical Methods in Chemical Engineering, Vol. III, Process Modeling, Estimation and Identification, 1974, Air Pollution: Physical and Chemical Fundamentals, 1975, Lectures in Atmospheric Chemistry, 1980, Atmospheric Chemistry and Physics of Air Pollution, 1986, Fundamentals of Air Pollution Engineering, 1988, Distributed Parameter Systems--Theory and Applications, 1989, Atmospheric Chemistry and Physics, 1998, 2nd edit., 2006; assoc. editor Environ. Sci., Tech., 1981-97; mem. editorial bd. Computers, Chem. Engring, 1974-96, Jour. Colloid and Interface Sci, 1978-95, Advances in Chem. Engring, 1980-03, Revs. in Chem. Engring, 1980—, Aerosol Sci. and Tech., 1981-93; assoc. editor: Atmospheric Environment, 1976—. Recipient Donald P. Eckman award Am. Automatic Control Coun., 1970, Pub. Svc. medal NASA, 1980, Disting. Alumnus award U. Rochester, 1989, Nev. medal Desert Rsch. Inst., 2001, Haagen-Smit Clean Air award Calif. Air Resources Bd., 2003, Haagen-Smit award, Atmos Environ., 2004; Camille and Henry Dreyfus Found. Tchr. Scholar grantee, 1972. Fellow AIChE (bd. dirs. 1988-91, mem. editl. bd. jours. 1985—, Allan P. Colburn award 1976, William H. Walker award 1986, Warren K. Lewis award 2000), NAE, AAAS, Japan Soc. Promotion Sci., Am. Geophysical Union; mem. Am. Soc. Engring. Edn. (Curtis W. McGraw Rsch. award 1976, George Westinghouse award 1987), Assn. Aerosol Rsch. (bd. dirs. 1983—, v.p. 1988-90, pres. 1990-92), Am. Acad. Arts and Scis., Am. Chem. Soc. (Svc. through Chemistry award 1988, Creative Advances in Environ. Sci. and Tech. award 1993), Internat. Aerosol Rsch. Assembly (Fuchs award 1998), Sigma Xi, Tau Beta Pi. Home: 4409 Beulah Dr La Canada CA 91011 Office: Calif Inst Tech Divsn Chemical and Chemical Engring 210-41 Pasadena CA 91125-0001 E-mail: seinfeld@caltech.edu.

SEITMAN, JOHN MICHAEL, arbitrator, mediator, lawyer; b. Bloomington, Ill., Feb. 9, 1942; BS, U. Ill., 1964, JD, 1966. Bar: Calif., U.S. Dist. Ct. (so., ctrl., no. and ea. dists.) Calif., U.S. Ct. Appeals (9th cir.). Prin. Lindley, Lazar & Scales, San Diego, 1966-97; full-time neutral affiliated with JAMS, 1997—. Lectr. in continuing legal edn. Bd. dirs. San Diego County Bar Found., 1983-89, treas., 1983-84, pres., 1988-89; del. to 9th Cir. Jud. Conf., 1986, 88. Fellow Am. Bar Found.; mem. ABA, State Bar Calif. (pres. 1991-92), San Diego County Bar Assn. (pres. 1986). Office: PO Box 2156 Del Mar CA 92014-1456 Home Phone: 858-793-4426; Office Phone: 858-793-4555. Personal E-mail: jseitman@pacbell.net.

SEJNOWSKI, TERRENCE JOSEPH, science educator; b. Cleve., Aug. 13, 1947; s. Joseph Francis and Theresa (Cudnik) Sejnowski; m. Beatrice Alexandra Golomb, Mar. 24, 1990. BS, Case Western Res. U., 1968; PhD, Princeton U., 1978. Rsch. fellow Harvard Med. Sch., Boston, 1979-82; prof. biophysics Johns Hopkins U., Balt., 1982-90; prof. Salk Inst. U. Calif. San Diego, La Jolla, 1988—, dir. computational neurobiology tng. program, 2001—; Francis Crick prof. Salk Inst., 2005—. Investigator Howard Hughes Med. Inst., 1991—; bd. dirs. San Diego McDonnell-Pew Ctr. for Cognitive Neurosci., 1990-98, Inst. for Neural Computation, U. Calif. San Diego., 1990—. Editor-in-chief Neural Computation, 1989—; co-inventor: (with others) the Boltzmann machine and NET talk; mem. editl. bd. Sci. Mag., 1990—. Pres. Neural Info. Processing System Found. Recipient Presdl. Young Investigator award NSF, 1984, Wright prize Harvey Mudd Coll., 1996; Sherman Fairchild Disting. scholar Calif. Inst. Tech., 1993. Fellow IEEE (Neural Network Pioneer award 2002), AAAS, Soc. Neurosci.; mem. Am. Phys. Soc. (sr. mem.), Internat. Neural Network Soc. (governing bd. 1988-92, Hebb prize 1999), Am. Math. Soc., Assn. Rsch. in Vision and Ophthalmology, Am. Assn. Artificial Intelligence, Biophys. Soc., Optical Soc. Am., Am. Psychol. Soc., Am. Psychol. Assn., N.Y. Acad. Scis., Fedn. Am. Soc. Exptl. Biophysics, Soc. Neuroscience, Internat. Soc. Neuroethology, Soc. Math. Biology, Johns Hopkins U. Soc. Scholars. Achievements include co-invention of the Boltzmann machine, of NETtalk, a neural network for text-to-speech. Office: Salk Inst PO Box 85800 San Diego CA 92186-5800 Home Phone: 858-587-0423. E-mail: sejnowski@salk.edu.

SEKANINA, ZDENEK, astronomer; b. Mlada Boleslav, Czechoslovakia, June 12, 1936; came to U.S., 1969; s. Frantisek Sekanina and Hedvika Sekaninova; m. Jana Soukupova, Apr. 1, 1966; 1 child, Jason. Diploma, Charles U., Prague, Czechoslovakia, 1959, PhD in Astronomy, 1963. Astronomer Stefanik Obs., Prague, 1959-66, Ctr. for Numerical Math., Charles U., Prague, 1967-68; vis. scientist Inst. d'Astrophysique, Univ. de Liege, Cointe-Ougree, Belgium, 1968-69; physicist Smithsonian Astrophys. Obs., Cambridge, Mass., 1969-80; mem. tech. staff Jet Propulsion Lab., Pasadena, Calif., 1980-81, rsch. scientist, 1981-84, sr. rsch. scientist, 1984—. Assoc. Harvard Coll. Obs., Cambridge, 1969-80; mem. NASA Comet Sci. Working Group, 1977-80; cons. Jet Propulsion Lab., 1977-80; prin. U.S. co-investigator Particulate Impact Analyzer Experiment, Dust Impact Detector Sys. Experiment, European Space Agy.'s Giotto Mission to Comet Halley, 1980-89; mem. NASA-European Spacy Agy. Comet Halley Environ. Working Group, 1980-89; discipline specialist Near Nucleus Studies Network, Internat. Halley Watch, 1982-90; mem. imaging sci. subsys. team Comet Rendezvous Asteroid Flyby Mission, 1986-92; mem. sci. definition team ESA/NASA Comet Nucleus Sample Return Mission, 1988—; co-investigator STARDUST Discovery Mission, 1994—. Editor Comet Halley Archive, 1982-91; mem. editorial bd. Kosmicke Rozhledy, 1963-69. Recipient Exceptional Sci. Achievement medal NASA, 1985, 2005; minor planet named Sekanina, 1976. Mem. Internat. Astron. Union (mem. commns. 15, 20, 22, mem. organizing commn. 22 1976-82, organizing commn. 15 1979-85, mem. working group on comets 1988—, assoc. dir. Ctrl. Bur. for Astron. Telegrams 1970-80), COSPAR (working group 3, panel C, exec. mem. 1980-82), Learned Soc of Czech Republic (hon. 1996—), Czech Astron. Soc. (hon. 2001-, Nušl prize 2006). Roman Catholic. Office: Jet Propulsion Lab 4800 Oak Grove Dr Pasadena CA 91109-8001 Business E-Mail: zs@sek.jpl.nasa.gov.

SEKIGUCHI, EUGENE, dentist; BSEE; DDS, U. So. Calif., MS in elec. engring. Pvt. practice dentist, Monterey Park, Calif.; clinical prof., assoc. dean internat. profl. and legis. affairs U. So. Calif. Sch. Dentistry. Pres. ADA, 2003—04, former trustee; past. pres., interim exec. dir. Calif. Dental Assn.; past pres. San Gabriel Valley Dental Soc. Office: 823 S Atlantic Blvd Ste 1 Monterey Park CA 91754 Office Phone: 323-283-3662.

SEKINE, DEBORAH KEIKO, systems analyst, programmer; b. Honolulu, Dec. 1, 1952; d. Yoshiteru and Yaeko (Matsuda) Isa; m. Andrew K. Sekine, May 8, 1993. BA in Math. with distinction, U. Hawaii, 1974, BEd with distinction, 1974, MS in Computer Sci., 1976, MBA, 1987. Data analyst, engr. in-charge Kentron, Honolulu, 1977-81; sys. analyst Am. Savs., Honolulu, 1981-82; analyst, programmer City and County of Honolulu, 1982—. Cons. Am. Savs., Honolulu, 1982. Contbr. articles to profl. jours. Vol. Hawaii Dem. Conv., Honolulu, 1984, Mayoral campaign, 1988, 92; com. co-chair Hui Makaala, Honolulu, 1989—; caregiver Makiki Christian Ch., Honolulu, 1991—. Mem. IEEE, Assn. for Computing Machinery, Am. Fedn. State County Mcpl. Employees, U. Hawaii MBA Alumni Assn., Phi Kappa Phi. Mem. United Ch. of Christ. Avocations: jogging, reading, writing, tennis, music. Home: 3322 George St Honolulu HI 96815-4319

SELANNE, TEEMU, professional hockey player; b. Helsinki, Finland, July 3, 1970; m. Sirpa Vuorinen; children: Eemil, Eetu, Leevi, Veera Johanna. Right wing Winnipeg Jets, 1992—95, Phoenix Coyotes, 1995—97, Anaheim Ducks (formerly Mighty Ducks of Anaheim), 1997—2001, 2005—07, 2008—, San Jose Sharks, 2001—03, Colo. Avalanche, 2004—05. Mem Finnish Nat. Olympic Team, 1992, 98, 2002, Finnish Nat. Team, World Cup of Hockey, 1996, 2004, Finnish Nat. Team, World Championships, 1996, 99. Recipient Calder Meml. Trophy, 1993, Maurice Richard Trophy, 1999, Bill Masterton Trophy, 2006; named World Championships Tournament MVP, 1999; named to All-Rookie Team, 1993, First All-Star Team, NHL, 1993, 1997, NHL All-Star Game, 1993, 1994, 1996—2000, 2002, 2003, 2007. Achievements include being a member of Stanley Cup Champion Anaheim Ducks, 2007. Office: Anaheim Ducks 2695 E Katella Ave Anaheim CA 92806-5904

SELDEN, ANNIE, mathematics professor; b. Torrington, Conn., Feb. 1, 1938; d. Adolf Laurer and Annie (Wopperer) Anderson; m. Herbert Lloyd Alexander Jr., Oct. 7, 1961 (div. July 1970); children: Neil Brooks, Kim Anne; m. John Selden, May 24, 1974. BA, Oberlin Coll., 1959; MA, Yale U., 1962; PhD, Clarkson U., 1974. Instr. SUNY, Potsdam, 1969-71; sr. lectr. Bayero U., Kano, Nigeria, 1978-85; asst. prof. Hampden Sydney Coll., Va., 1973-74, Bosphorus U., Istanbul, Turkey, 1974-78, Tenn. Technol. U., Cookeville, 1985-90, assoc. prof., 1990—95, prof., 1995—2003, emerita, 2003—. Vis. scholar edn. in math., sci. and tech. U. Calif., Berkeley, 1993; sec.-treas. Math. Edn. Resources Co., 1994—; external examiner Fed. Advanced Tchrs. Coll., Katsina, Nigeria, 1979-82, Gumel, Nigeria, 1981-82; reader advanced placement calculus exams., 1990-92; vis. scholar Ctr. for Rsch. in Math. and Sci. Edn., San Diego State U., 1995-96; vis. prof. Ariz. State U., 1999-2000; adj. prof. N.Mex. State U., 2003—. Dept. editor: UME Trends: News and Reports on Undergrad. Math. Edn., 1989—96, MAA Online's Tchg. and Learning Sect., 1996—; mem. editl. bd. Jour. Computers in Math. and Sci. Teaching, 1992—96, Jour. for Rsch. in Math. Edn., 1997-2000; assoc. editor for tchg. and learning MAA Online, 1997—; assoc. editor Media Highlights sect. Coll. Math. Jour., 1994-2006; contbr. articles to profl. jours. Fulbright scholar, 1959—60, Woodrow Wilson fellow, 1960—61, NSF grad. trainee Clarkson U., 1972—73, NSF grantee, 1971, 1994—96. Fellow: AAAS; mem. AAUP (Tenn. Tech. chpt. sec. 1991-92, v.p. 1992-93, pres. 1994—95), Am. Math. Soc., Math. Assn. America (dept. rep. 1986—2000, coord.-elect spl. interest group on rsch. in undergrad. math. edn. 1999-2000, coord. 2000-02, past coord. 2002-03, editl. bd. mem.), Assn. Women in Math. (Louise Hay award for contbns. to math. edn. 2002), Nat. Assn. Math., Am. Math. Assn. Two-Yr. Colls., Benjamin Banneker Assn., Nigerian Math. Soc. (organizer 5th ann. conf. 1984), Internat. Group for Psychology Math. Edn., Am. Ednl. Rsch. Assn., Nat. Coun. Tchrs. Math., Rsch. Coun. for Math. Learning, Tenn. Acad. Sci., Women in Higher Edn. Tenn. (Tenn. Tech. chpt. pres. 1990-92, state 1st v.p. 1991-92, state pres. 1992-93), Women Organizing Women (treas. 1992-93), Am. Coun. Edn. (nat. indentification program for women com. 1992-93), Assn. for Sci. Study of Consciousness, Phi Beta Kappa, Sigma Xi, Pi Mu Epsilon, Kappa Mu Epsilon, Internat. Program Com. 19th Internat. Commn. Math. Instrn. Study Conf. (Taiwan). Office: NMex State U Dept Mathematical Scis PO Box 30001 Las Cruces NM 88003-0001 Business E-Mail: aselden@emmy.nmsu.edu, aselden@math.nmsu.edu.

SELDEN, ROBERT WENTWORTH, physicist, consultant; b. Phoenix, Aug. 11, 1936; s. Edward English and Mary Priscilla (Calder) S.; m. Mary Tania Hudd, June 1958 (div. 1976); 1 child, Ian Scott; m. Marjorie Anne Harmon, Feb. 20, 1977; children: Brock, Thane, Shawna, Kirsten. BA in Physics cum laude, Pomona Coll., 1958; MS in Physics, U. Wis., 1960, PhD in Physics, 1964. Rsch. assoc. Lawrence Livermore Nat. Lab., Calif., 1965—67, staff mem. Calif., 1967—73, group leader Calif., 1973—78, asst. assoc. dir., 1978—80; div. leader applied theoretical physics Los Alamos Nat. Lab., N.Mex., 1980—83, dep. assoc. dir. strategic def. rsch. N.Mex., 1983—84, assoc. dir. theoretical and computational physics, 1984—86, dir. Ctr. for Nat. Securities Studies, 1986—88, assoc. dir for lab. devel., 1991—94; chief scientist USAF, Washington, 1988—91, panel chmn. sci. adv. bd., 1984-88, 91-96, 1991—96, 2002—05, chmn. sci. adv. bd., 1999—2002, mem., 2002—05; cons. Los Alamos, 1994—. Chmn. study group on reactor materials and nuclear explosives U.S. Dept. Energy, 1976-78; mem. ballistic missile def. techs. adv. panel U.S. Congress Office Tech. Assessment, 1984-85, The Pres.'s Defensive Tech. Study Team, Washington, 1983; strat. adv. group U.S. Strat. Command, 1996—, panel chair, 2003-; strat. adv. group jt. adv. com. Sec. Def., Sec. Energy, 1996—. Editor Rsch. Jour. Lawrence Livermore Nat. Lab., 1976-77; contbr. sci. and tech. papers to profl. jours. Pres. Livermore Cultural Arts Coun., 1969-72; chmn. Livermore Sister City Orgn., 1973, Planning Commn. City of Livermore, 1971-76; bd. dirs. Orch. of Santa Fe, 1986-88. Capt. U.S. Army, 1964-67. Grad. fellow Edward John Noble Found., 1958-62; recipient Theodore von Karman award for outstanding contbn. to def. sci., 1989, medal for outstanding pub. svc. U.S. Sec. Def., 1996; decorated for exceptional civilian svc. USAF, 1988, 91, 96, 2005. Mem. AAAS, Am. Phys. Soc., N.Y. Acad. Sci., Air Force Assn. Avocations: tennis, hiking, music. Office: 624 La Bajada Los Alamos NM 87544-3805 E-mail: selden@cybermesa.com.

SELIGMAN, BRAD, lawyer; b. Cin., Aug. 25, 1951; s. Selig J. and Muriel (Bienstock) S.; children: Corina Kasten, Mariana Campos, Sofia Maya Campos. BA, Sonoma State U., Calif., 1975; JD, U. Calif., San Francisco, 1978. Bar: Calif. 1978, US Dist. Ct. (no. dist.) Calif. 1978, US Dist. Ct. (ea. dist.) Calif. 1979. Teaching fellow Law Sch. Stanford U., Calif., 1978-79; sr. law clk. to Hon. Lawrence K. Karlton US Dist. Ct. (ea. dist.) Calif., Sacramento, 1979-80; assoc. Farnsworth, Saperstein & Brand, Oakland, Calif., 1981-85; ptnr. Farnsworth, Saperstein & Seligman, Oakland, 1985-89; mng. dir. Saperstein, Seligman & Mayeda, Oakland, 1989-91; of counsel Saperstein, Mayeda, Larkin & Goldstein, Oakland, Calif., 1991-94; exec. dir. The Impact Fund, Berkeley, Calif., 1992—. Advisor Disability Rights Edn. and Def. Fund, Inc., 1992—; trustee Calif. Rural Legal Assistance, San Francisco, 1982-88; bd. dirs. Equal Rights Advisors, San Francisco, 1989-92. Author: (with others) CEO: Wrongful Employment Termination Practice, 1987, Tax Aspects of Litigation and Settlements, 1989. Named one of 100 Most Influential Lawyers, Nat. Law Jour., 2006. Office: The Impact Fund 125 University Ave Berkeley CA 94710 Business E-Mail: bs@impactfund.org.

SELIGMAN, THOMAS KNOWLES, museum administrator; b. Santa Barbara, Calif., Jan. 1, 1944; s. Joseph L. and Peggy (Van Horne) S.; children: Christopher, Timothy, Dylan. BA, Stanford U., 1965; BFA with honors, San Francisco Acad. Art, 1967; MFA, Sch. Visual Art, NYC, 1968. Tchr., mus. dir. Peace Corps, Liberia, 1968-70; curator dept. Africa, Oceania and Ams. Fine Arts Museums, San Francisco, 1971-88, dep. dir. edn. and exhbns., 1972-88, dep. dir. ops. and planning, 1988-91; dir. Stanford (Calif.) U. Cantor Arts Ctr., 1991—. Mem. cultural property adv. com. USIA, 1988-92, Nat. Endowment for Art Indemnity Panel, 1992-95. Author mus. catalogues, articles in field. Trustee Internat. Coun. Mus./Am. Assn. Mus., 1990-94, Am. Fedn. Arts, 1986-2002, The Christensen Fund, 2002-, v.p., 2004-, Assn. Art Mus. Dirs., 2002-05. Fellow Nat. Endowment Arts, 1974-75, 87. Mem. Assn. Art Mus. Dirs.(trustee 2002—), Am. Assn. Mus., Leaky Found. Address: Cantor Ctr for Visual Arts Stanford U Lomita Dr & Museum Way Stanford CA 94305-5060

SELINGER, PATRICIA GRIFFITHS, computer science professional; b. Cleve., Oct. 15, 1949; d. Fred Robert and Olive Mae (Brewster) Priest; m. James Alan Griffiths, Aug. 29, 1970 (div. 1973); m. Robert David Selinger, July 22, 1978; children: David Robert, Thomas Robert. AB, Harvard U., 1971, MS, 1972, PhD, 1975. Rsch. staff IBM Rsch. Lab, San Jose, Calif., 1975-78, mgr., 1978-83, mgr. computer sci., 1983-86, program dir. Database Technology Inst., 1986, with devel. team, 1997, v.p. Rsch. Area Strategy, Info. and Interaction. Patentee in field; co-author numerous tech. papers. IBM fellow, 1994; recipient YWCA Tribute to Women in Industry award, 1989; named to Hall of Fame, Women in Tech. Internat., 2004. Mem. NAE, Assn. for Computing Machinery (System Software award 1989, former vice-chmn. spl. interest group for mgmt. data). Avocations: cooking, reading.

SELLA, TONY, marketing executive; With Diener Hauser Bates, NYC; v.p. creative svcs. Walt Disney, Touchstone, Hollywood Pictures Walt Disney Co.; sr. v.p. creative advt. Twentieth Century Fox Film Corp, LA, 1991—94, sr. v.p. mktg., creative advt., 1994—2002, co-pres. domestic theatrical mktg., 2002—. Named an Entertainment Marketer of the Yr., Advt. Age Mag., 2007. Office: Twentieth Century Fox Film Corp 10201 W Pico Blvd Los Angeles CA 90035 Office Phone: 310-277-2211. Office Fax: 310-203-1558.

SELLECK, TOM, actor; b. Detroit, Jan. 29, 1945; s. Robert D. and Martha S.; m. Jacquelyn Ray, 1970 (div. 1982); 1 stepson, Kevin; m. Jillie Joan Mack, Aug. 7, 1987; 1 child, Hannah Margaret. Ph.D (hon.), Pepperdine U. Actor: (films) Myra Breckinridge, 1970, The Seven Minutes, 1971, Midway, 1976, Coma, 1982, High Road to China, 1983, Lassiter, 1984, Runaway, 1985, Three Men and a Baby, 1987, Her Alibi, 1989, An Innocent Man, 1989, Quigley Down Under, 1990, Three Men and a Little Lady, 1990, Folks!, 1992, Christopher Columbus: The Discovery, 1992, Mr. Baseball, 1992, In and Out, 1997, The Love Letter, 1999, Angus Magillicutty, 2003, (voice) Meet the Robinsons, 2007; (TV films) The Sacketts, 1979, Divorce Wars, 1982, Louis L'Amour's "The Shadow Riders", 1982, Broken Trust, 1995, Ruby Jean and Joe, 1996, Last Stand at Saher River, 1998, Louis l'Amour's Crossfire Trail, 2000, Monte Walsh, Reversible Errors, Ike: Countdown to D Day, 2004, Stone Cold, 2005, Jesse Stone: Night Passage, 2006; (TV series) The Young and the Restless, 1973-74, Magnum P.I. 1980-88, Las Vegas, 2007-; (TV appearances) Lancer, 1969, Bracken's World, 1969, Sarge, 1971, THe F.B.I., 1973, Marcus Welby, M.D., 1974-75, The Streets of San Francisco, 1975, The Rockford Files, 1978-79, Simon & Simon, 1982, Friends, 1996, 2000, Boston Legal, 2006 Bd. mem. Michael Josephson Inst. Ethics. Mem.: NRA. Office: Creative Artists Agy 2000 Ave of the Stars Los Angeles CA 90067 Office Phone: 323-962-5704.

SELLERS, ROBERT SCOT, real estate developer; b. LA, Jan. 26, 1957; s. Walter DeWitt and Diolenda Teresa (Bernardes) S.; m. Gretchen Alice Geddes, June 6, 1987. BS, Lewis & Clark Coll., 1978; MBA, Stanford U., 1981. Lic. real estate broker, Calif., Colo. Loan officer The Oreg. Bank, Portland, 1978-79; controller CFI Mgmt. Svcs., Portland, 1979; cons. Boston Consulting Group, Palo Alto, Calif., 1980; asst. project mgr. Lincoln Property Co., Denver, 1981-82, v.p., 1982-83, ptnr., Colo., 1983-87, ptnr., So. Calif. San Diego, 1987-91, ptnr. Irvine, Calif., 1991-94; chmn. and CEO Archstone Communities Trust, Englewood, CO, 1994—. Real estate developer apts. and hotels, Denver and San Diego, 1985—. Chmn. bd. Christian Internat. Scholars Found., Seattle, 1988-90; founding mem., bd. advisors High Ground Assocs., San Diego, 1988-91. Mem. Bldg. Industry Assn. (president's coun. 1987—, speakers bur. 1988-91), Apt. Assn. Metro Denver (membership dir. 1987), Constrn. Industry Fedn. Republican. Avocations: tennis, bicycling, golf, cross country skiing, mountain climbing, triathlons.

SELLICK, KATHLEEN A., hospital administrator; b. Phoenix; m. Phil Sellick; 1 child, Grace. BS, Ariz. State U.; MBA, U. Chgo. Grad. Sch. Bus., 1984. With Am. Med. Internat., Beverly Hills, Calif.,

Westgate Med. Ctr., Denton, Tex.; adminstrv. resident Mayo Clinic, Rochester, Minn.; v.p. adminstrn. and dir. outreach devel. Hoag Meml. Hosp. Presbyn., Newport Beach, Calif.; exec. v.p. and COO St. Joseph Hosp., Orange, Calif., 1995—99; assoc. exec. dir. and COO U. Wash. Med. Ctr., Seattle, 1999—2001, acting exec. dir., 2000—01, exec. dir., 2001—. Clin. asst. prof., dept. health services U. Wash. Sch. of Public Health and Community Medicine. Office: U Wash Med Ctr 1959 NE Pacific St Box 356151 Seattle WA 98195-6151 Office Fax: 206-598-6292.

SELWAY, PHILLIP JAMES, musician; b. Huntingdon, England, May 23, 1967; married. Student in English and History, Liverpool Poly, Eng. Drummer touring musicals; sub-editor; tchr. English; drummer Radiohead, 1992—. Musician: (albums) Pablo Honey, 1993, The Bends, 1995, OK Computer, 1997 (Grammy award for Best Alternative Music Performance, 1997), Kid A, 2000 (Grammy award for Best Alternative Music Performance, 2000), Amnesiac, 2001, I Might Be Wrong: Live Reocrdings, 2001, Hail to the Thief, 2003, In Rainbows, 2007 (Grammy award for Best Alternative Music Album, 2009). Office: Capital Records 1750 North Vine St 10th Fl Hollywood CA 90028

SELZ, PETER HOWARD, art historian, educator; b. Munich, Mar. 27, 1919; arrived in US, 1936, naturalized, 1942; s. Eugene and Edith S.; m. Thalia Cheronis, June 10, 1948 (div. 1965); children: Tanya Nicole Eugenia, Diana Gabrielle Hamlin; m. Carole Schemmerling, Dec. 18, 1983 Student, Columbia U., U. Paris; MA, U. Chgo., 1949, PhD, 1954; DFA, Calif. Coll. Arts and Crafts, 1967. Instr. U. Chgo., 1951-56; asst. prof. art history, head art edn. dept. Inst. Design, Ill. Inst. Tech., Chgo., 1949-55; chmn. art dept., dir. art gallery Pomona Coll., 1955-58; chief curator dept. painting and sculpture exhbns. Mus. Modern Art, 1958-65; dir. univ. art mus. U. Calif., Berkeley, 1965-73, prof. history of art, 1965—; Zaks prof. Hebrew U., Jerusalem, 1976. Vis. prof. CUNY, 1987; pres.'s coun. on art and architecture Yale U., 1971-76 Author: German Expressionist Painting, 1957, New Images of Man, 1959, Art Nouveau, 1960, Mark Rothko, 1961, Fifteen Polish Painters, 1961, The Art of Jean Dubuffet, 1962, Emil Nolde, 1963, Max Beckmann, 1964, Alberto Giacometti, 1965, Directions in Kinetic Sculpture, 1966, Funk, 1967, Harold Paris, 1972, Ferdinand Holder, 1972, Sam Francis, 1975, The American Presidency in Political Cartoons, 1976, Art in Our Times, 1981, Art in a Turbulent Era, 1985, Chillida, 1986, Twelve Artists from the GDR, 1989, Max Beckmann: The Self Portraits, 1992, William Congdon, 1992, Beckmann, 1996, Gottfried Helnwein, 1997, Beyond the Mainstream, 1997; co-author: Theories and Documents of Contemporary Art, 1996, Beyond the Mainstream, 1998, Barbara Chase-Riboud, 1999, Nathan Oliviera, 2001, The Art of Engagement, 2006; editor: Art in Am., 1967—, Art Quar., 1969-75, Arts, 1981-92, Cross-Currents in Modern Art, 2000; contbr. articles to profl. jours. Trustee Am. Crafts Coun., 1985—89; mem.adv. coun. archives Am. Art, 1971—; mem. acquisitions com. Fine Arts Mus., San Francisco, 1993; pres. Berkeley Art Project, 1988—93; project dir. Christo's Running Fence, 1973—76; commr. Alameda County Art Commn., 1990—95; bd. dirs. Richmond Art Ctr., 1998—2004; chair Berkeley Arts Festival, 1997—2000; trustee Neue Galerie, New York, 2002—, Kala Inst., Berkley, Calif., 2001—. Decorated Order of Merit Fed. Republic Germany; Fulbright grantee Paris, 1949-50; fellow Belgian-Am. Ednl. Found.; Sr. fellow NEH, 1972; resident Rockefeller Found. Study Ctr., Bellagio, 1994. Mem. Coll. Art Assn. Am. (dir. 1959-64, 67-71, Charles Rufus award 2007), AAUP, Internat. Art Critics Assn. Office: U Calif Dept Art History Berkeley CA 94720-0001 Home Phone: 707-459-6152; Office Phone: 510-524-5402.

SEMANKO, NORMAN M., political organization administrator; BS, U. Idaho; JD, Georgetown U., 1992. Bar: 1993. Legis. asst. to Rep. Larry E. Craig US House of Reps., Washington; legis. asst. and field rep. to Senator Larry E. Craig US Senate, Washington; exec. dir. and gen. counsel Idaho Water Users Assn., Boise; of counsel Barker, Rosholt & Simpson, LLP, Boise; Idaho rep. Western States Water Coun.; mem. city coun. City of Eagle, Idaho, 2008—09; chmn. Idaho Republican Party, Boise, 2008—. Mem.: Idaho State Bar Assn. (past pres. Water Law sect.). Republican. Roman Catholic. Office: Idaho Water Users Assn 1010 W Jefferson Ste 101 Boise ID 83702 also: Idaho Republican Party 802 West Bannock Lower Plz 103 Boise ID 83702 Office Phone: 208-344-6690, 208-343-6405. Office Fax: 208-344-2744, 208-343-6414. E-mail: norm@iwua.org, info@idgop.org.*

SEMEL, GEORGE HERBERT, plastic surgeon; b. NYC, Apr. 20, 1938; s. Louis Bennett and Sara Sonja (Eutis) S. AB, Columbia U., 1959; MD, Boston U., 1963. Diplomate Am. Bd. Plastic Surgery. Intern L.A. County Gen. Hosp., 1963-64; resident gen. surgery Long Beach (Calif.) VA Hosp., 1964-67; residency in plastic surgery Mayo Clinic, Rochester, Minn., 1967-69; chief resident plastic surgery Med. U. S.C., Charleston, 1969-70; pvt. practice LA, 1970—; staff Midway Hosp. Founder L.A. Music Ctr., 1978, Mus. Contemporary Art, 1980. With Calif. NG, 1964-69, USNG, 1969-73. Mem. AMA, Am. Soc. Plastic Surgery, Am. Lipoplasty Soc., L.A. Soc. Plastic Surgeons, Phi Gamma Delta. Office: 450 S Beverly Dr Beverly Hills CA 90212-4402 Office Phone: 310-274-7547. E-mail: drsemel@drsemel.com.

SEMEL, TERRY S., retired Internet company executive; b. NYC, Feb. 24, 1943; s. Ben and Mildred S.; m. Jane Bovingdon, Aug. 24, 1977; children: Eric Scott, Courtenay Jane, Lily Bovingdon Semel, Kate Bovingdon Semel. BS in Acctg., L.I.U., 1964; postgrad. in market research, CCNY, 1966-67; LHD (hon.), Emerson Coll., 2004. Domestic sales mgr. CBS Cinema Center Films, Studio City, Calif., 1970-72; v.p., gen. mgr. Walt Disney's Buena Vista, Burbank, Calif., 1972-75; pres. W.B. Distbn. Corp., Burbank, 1975-78; exec. v.p., COO Warner Bros., Inc., Burbank, 1979-80, pres., COO, 1980-94, chmn., co-CEO, 1994-99, Warner Music Group Inc, 1995-99; chmn. Windsor Media, Inc, 1999—2001; chmn., CEO Yahoo! Inc., 2001—07, non-exec. chmn., 2007—08. Bd. dirs. Polo Ralph Lauren Corp., 1997-, Yahoo! Inc., 2001-08 Vice chmn. Pres.'s Com. for the Arts and Humanities; vice chair San Diego Host Com. for 1996 Rep. Nat. Conv.; bd. trustee Solomon R. Guggenheim Mus., Edn. First, Cedars Sinai Med. Ctr., Environ. Media Assn., Emerson Coll.; bd. dir. Mus. TV and Radio, LA County Mus. Art. Named Pioneer of Yr., 1990, Found. of Motion Pictures Pioneers; named one of the 50 Most Important People on the Web, PC World, 2007; recipient UCLA medal, 2005, Yale Legends in Leadership award, 2005.

SEMENZA, DIRK A., metal fabrication executive; b. Ft. Benton, Mont., Oct. 10, 1962; s. Lenard and Opal E. Semenza. Grad. h.s., Gr. Falls, Mont. Worked in construction; founder, project controller, sec., treas. R Squared Metal Fabrication, Inc., Gt. Falls, Mont., 1990—. FAA approval for R Squared 736 Simulator. Recipient Jay Hollingsworth Speas Airport award AIAA, 1996. Address: Hout PO Box 3293 Great Falls MT 59403-3293

SENCZUK, ANNA MARIA, cell biologist, researcher; b. Czestochowa, Poland, Nov. 3, 1965; arrived in US, 2000, permanent resident, 2006; d. Janusz and Halina Senczuk; m. Miroslaw Josef Studzinski, Dec. 29, 1990; children: Tom Studzinski, Lukas Studzinski. Attended, Academia Medyczna, Wroclaw, Poland, 1990; BS in Cell, Molecular and Microbiology, U. Calgary, Alta., Can., 1996, MS in CMMB, 1999. Assoc. U. Calgary, 1999—2000; assoc. scientist Amgen, Seattle, 2000—. Presenter in field. Contbr. articles to profl. jours. Mentor Sci. Expo., Seattle, 2002—08. Mem.: Sigma Xi. Achievements include patents for HIC dual salt. Office: Amgen 1201 Amgen Ct West AW2D2152 Seattle WA 98119 Personal E-mail: senczukowa@hotmail.com. Business E-Mail: senczuka@amgen.com.

SENDEK, HERB, men's college basketball coach; b. Pitts., Feb. 22, 1963; m. Melanie Scheuer; children: Kristin, Catherine, Kelly. BA in Indsl. Mgmt. summa cum laude, Carnegie-Mellon U., Pitts., 1985. Asst. coach Ctrl. Cath. HS, Pitts., 1984—85; grad. asst. coach Providence Coll. Friars, 1985—86, asst. coach, 1987—89, U. Ky. Wildcats, 1989—93; head basketball coach Miami U. Red Hawks, Ohio, 1994—96, NC State U. Wolfpack, 1996—2006, Ariz. State U. Sun Devils, 2006—. Named Ohio Coach of Yr., 1995, Coach of Yr., Mid-Am. Conf., 1995, Atlantic Coach Conf., 2004, Dist. 5 Coach of Yr., Nat. Assn. Basketball Coaches, 2002, 2004, Dist. IX Coach of Yr., US Basketball Writers, 2008; named to Penn Hills Hall of Fame, Pa., Pa. Hall of Fame, East Boros Chpt., We. Pa. Chpt., Five-Star Basketball Camp Hall of Fame; finalist Naismith Nat. Coach of Yr., 2002. Office: Ariz State Univ Athletics Carson Ctr PO Box 872505 Tempe AZ 85287-2505

SENEKER, CARL JAMES, II, (KIM), lawyer; b. San Jose, Calif., Oct. 12, 1942; s. Carl James and Beth D. (Hearn) S.; m. Julie Marie Pardee, June 17, 1967; children: Mark Gwynn, Todd Christian. AB, Stanford U., 1964; JD, U. Calif., Berkeley, 1967. Bar: Calif. 1969, U.S. Dist. Ct. (no. dist.) Calif. 1973. Law clk. to Hon. William O. Douglas U.S. Supreme Ct., Washington, 1967-68; ptnr. Morrison & Foerster, San Francisco, 1971-84, 96—, LA, 1984—96. Adj. prof. law, lectr. law sch. Stanford U., Palo Alto, Calif., 1982-83. Co-editor: California Real Estate Law and Practice, Vols. 12 & 13, 1983-96; contbr. articles to profl. jours. Bd. dirs. L.A. Hdqs. City Assn., 1988-93. Capt. USAF, 1968-71. Mem. Am. Coll. Real Estate Lawyers (bd. govs. 1989-97, pres.-elect 1996-97, pres. 1997-98), State Bar Calif. (real property law sect., vice-chair exec. com. 1987-90), Am. Coll. Mortgage Attys., Anglo-Am. Real Property Inst., Lambda Alpha Internat. Roman Catholic. Avocations: golf, travel, music. Office: Morrison & Foerster 425 Market St Fl 32 San Francisco CA 94105-2467 Home Phone: 925-377-8420; Office Phone: 415-268-6619. Office Fax: 415-268-7522. Business E-Mail: cseneker@mofo.com.

SENGPIEHL, PAUL MARVIN, lawyer, former state official; b. Stuart, Nebr., Oct. 10, 1937; s. Arthur Paul and Anne Marie (Andersen) S.; BA, Wheaton (Ill.) Coll., 1959; MA in Pub. Adminstrn., Mich. State U., 1961; JD, Ill. Inst. Tech.-Chgo. Kent Coll. Law, 1970. Lic. min., 2007. m. June S. Cline, June 29, 1963; children— Jeffrey D., Chrystal M. Bar: Ill. 1971, U.S. Supreme Ct. 1982. Adminstrv. asst. Chgo. Dept. Urban Renewal, 1962-65; supr. Ill. Municipal Retirement Fund, Chgo., 1966-71; mgmt. officer Ill. Dept. Local Govt. Affairs, Springfield, 1971-72, legal counsel, Chgo., 1972-73; spl. asst. atty. gen. Ill. Dept. Labor, Chgo., 1973-76; asst. atty. gen. Ct. of Claims div. Atty. Gen. of Ill., 1976-83; hearing referee Bd. Rev., Ill. Dept. Labor, 1983-84; local govt. law columnist Chgo. Daily Law Bull., 1975-84; instr. polit. sci. Judson Coll., Elgin, Ill., 1963. Republican candidate for Cook County Recorder of Deeds, 1984; dep. committeeman Oak Park Twp Rep. Orgn.; elected alt. del., served del. Rep. Nat. Conv., 1992; People's Choice candidate pres. Oak Park Village, 1993; Rep. alt. state ctrl. committeeman 7th Congl. Dist., elected commiteeman Oak Park Rep., 1994-98, elected rep. committeeman, 1994-96; elected del. Rep. Nat. Convention, 1996; co-chmn. Cook County Jail Ministry Bd., chmn. 2003-; treas. Cook County Correctional Chaplaincy Coun., 2003-06, chmn., 2006-, lic. min., 2007-. Mem. Ill. Bar Assn. (local govt. law sect. council 1973-79, vice chmn. 1976-77, co-editor local govt. newsletter 1976-77, chmn. 1977-78, editor newsletter 1977-78, state tax sect. council 1979-82, 84-85), Chgo. Bar Assn. (local govt. com., chmn. legis. subcom. 1978-79, sec. 1979-80, vice chmn. 1980-81, chmn. 1981-82, state and mcpl. tax com.), John Ericsson Rep. League Ill. (state sec. 1983-85, 95—, hon. past pres. Cook County 1982-97, pres. 1997—), Oak Park-River Forest C. of C. (small bus. coun. 1991-2000). Baptist (vice chmn. deacons 1973-76, 79-80, moderator 1983-86, supt. Sunday sch. 1986-93). Home and Office: 727 N Ridgeland Ave Oak Park IL 60302-1735 Office Phone: 708-383-8859. Personal E-mail: sengpiehllaw@yahoo.com. Business E-Mail: sengpiehllaw@aol.com.

SENSIPER, SAMUEL, electrical engineer; b. Elmira, NY, Apr. 26, 1919; s. Louis and Molly (Pedolsky) S.; m. Elaine Marie Zwick, Sept. 10, 1950; children: Martin, Sylvia, David. BSEE, MIT, 1939, ScD, 1951; EE, Stanford U., 1941. Asst. project engr. to sr. project engr., cons. Sperry Gyroscope, Garden City, Great Neck, NY, 1941-51; sect. head and sr. staff cons. Hughes Aircraft, Culver City, Malibu, Calif., 1951-60; lab. divsn. mgr. Space Gen. Corp., Glendale, Azuza, L.A., 1960—67; lab. mgr. TRW, Redondo Beach, Calif., 1967—70; cons. elec. engr. LA, 1970—73; dir. engring. Transco Products, Venice, Calif., 1973—75; cons. elec. engr. in pvt. practice LA, 1975—95; cons., 1995—. Faculty U. So. Calif., L.A., 1955-56, 79-80. Contbr. articles to profl. jours.; patentee in field. Recipient Cert. of Commendation U.S. Navy, 1946; indsl. electronics fellow MIT, 1947-48. Fellow IEEE (life), AAAS (life); mem. Calif. Soc. Profl. Engrs., MIT Alumni Assn., Stanford Alumni Assn., U. Calif. Alumni Assn., Electromagnetics Acad., Sigma Xi, Eta Kappa Nu, Nat. Soc. Profl. Engr.(life). Home and Office: 3775 Modoc Rd #117 Santa Barbara CA 93105-4466 Office Phone: 805-879-5560. Personal E-mail: sensiper1@ieee.org.

SENTY, JAMES A., energy executive; BS metallurgical and mining engring., Univ. Wis. Chmn. bd. Western Gas Resources, Inc., 2003—. Chmn. State Wis. Investment Bd.; chmn. bd., pres. Midwest Bottle Gas Co.; chmn. Park Bark, Madison, Wis.

SENTZ, DENNIS, chemical company executive; BBA in Acctg., U. Wisc., 1970. cert. CPA, CMA. Contoller, CFO Instrumentarium Imaging, Inc.; v.p., CFO Foster Wheeler Energy Corp., 1993-97; CFO BE&K-Bechtel Internat., 1997-99; v.p. acctg., controller Eco Soil Sys., Inc., San Diego, 1999-00, CFO, 2000—.

SÉQUIN, CARLO H., computer science educator; b. Winterthur, Switzerland, Oct. 30, 1941; arrived in US, 1970, naturalized, 1994; s. Carl R. and Margrit (Schaeppi) S.; m. Margareta Frey, Oct. 5, 1968; children: Eveline, André. BS, U. Basel, Switzerland, 1965, PhD, 1969. Mem. tech. staff Bell Labs., Murray Hill, NJ, 1970-76; vis. Mackay lectr. U. Calif.-Berkeley, 1976-77, prof. elec. engring. computer scis., 1977—, assoc. chmn. computer sci., 1980-83, assoc. dean capital projects, 2001—. Author: First Book on Charge-Coupled Devices, Charge Transfer Devices, 1975; sculpture designer: Pax Mundi II; H&R Block Headquarters, Kansas City, 2007; contbr. articles to profl. jours. Fellow IEEE (Tech. Achievement award 2003), Assn. Computing Machinery, Swiss Acad. Engring. Scis. Achievements include patents for integrated circuits. Office: U Calif Dept EECS Computer Scis Divsn Soda Hall Berkeley CA 94720-1776 Office Phone: 510-642-5103. Business E-Mail: sequin@cs.berkeley.edu.

SERAFIN, ROBERT JOSEPH, science center administrator, electrical engineer; b. Chgo., Apr. 22, 1936; s. Joseph Albert and Antoinette (Gazda) S.; m. Betsy Furgerson, Mar. 4, 1961; children: Katherine, Jenifer, Robert Joseph Jr., Elizabeth. BSEE, U. Notre Dame, 1958; MSEE, Northwestern U., 1961; PhDEE, Ill. Inst. Tech., 1972. Engr. Hazeltine Rsch. Corp. Ill. Inst. Tech. Rsch. Inst., 1960-62; assoc. engr., rsch. engr., sr. rsch. engr. Nat. Ctr. for Atmospheric Rsch., Boulder, Colo., 1962-73, mgr. field observing facility, 1973-80, dir. atmospheric tech. div. Bouulder, Colo., 1981-89, dir. ctr., 1989-2000. Chair Nat. Weather Svc. Modernization Com. Author: Revised Radar Handbook, 1989; contbr. numerous articles to profl. jours.; editl. bd./com. Acta Meteorologica Sinica; editl. founder Jour. Atmospheric and Oceanic Tech.; patentee in field. Speaker various civic groups in U.S. and internationally. Fellow IEEE, Am. Meteorol. Soc. (pres.); mem. NAE, NAS (human rights com.), Boulder C. of C., Sigma Xi. Avocations: golf, fishing, skiing. Office: Nat Ctr Atmospheric Rsch 1850 Table Mesa Dr PO Box 3000 Boulder CO 80307-3000

SERDAHELY, DOUGLAS J., lawyer, former state judge; b. Rhinelander, Wis., June 1, 1946; AB with highest honors, Northwestern Univ., 1968; JD, Harvard Univ., 1972. Bar: Alaska 1972, US Dist. Ct. (Alaska dist.) 1972, US Ct. Appeals (9th & DC cir.) 1973, US Supreme Ct. 1994. Law clk. Chief Justice Jay A. Rabinowitz, Alaska Supreme Ct., 1972—73; judge Alaska Superior Ct., 1981—89, presiding judge, 1985—89; pro tem panelist Alaska Ct. Appeals, Alaska Supreme Ct., 1981—89; former ptnr. Bogle & Gates, Anchorage; ptnr., Litigation & Dispute resolution, Environ. Health & Safety, Antitrust practices, mem. mgmt. com., office mng. ptnr. Patton Boggs LLP, Anchorage. Instr. Nat. Inst. Trial Advocacy, 1981, Hastings Coll. Trial Advocacy, 1985; adj. prof. Puget Sound Law Sch., 1987. Mem.: ABA, Alaska Bar Assn., Phi Beta Kappa. Office: Patton Boggs LLP Ste 700 601 W Fifth Ave Anchorage AK 99501-2226 Office Phone: 907-263-6310. Office Fax: 907-263-6345. Business E-Mail: dserdahely@pattonboggs.com.

SERKIS, ANDY, actor; b. London, Apr. 20, 1964; m. Lorraine Ashbourne, July 22, 2002; children: Ruby, Sonny, Louis. With Duke's Playhouse, Lancaster, England, 1985, Royal Exchange Theater, Manchester, England, 1989. Actor: (plays) Hush, 1992, Cabaret, 1993, The Queen and I, 1993, Punchbag, 1993, King Lear, 1993, Mojo, 1995, Hurlyburly, 1997, A Lie of the Mind, 2001, Othello, 2002; dir.: The Double Bass, 2003; actor: (films) Prince of Jutland, 1994, The Near Room, 1995, Stella Does Tricks, 1996, Loop, 1997, Career Girls, 1997, Mojo, 1997, Insomnia, 1998, Clueless, 1998, Among Giants, 1998, The Tale of Sweety Barrett, 1998, Five Seconds to Spare, 1999, Topsy-Turvy, 1999, The Jolly Boys' Last Stand, 2000, Pandaemonium, 2000; actor, actor: (films) Shiner, 2000, The Escapist, 2001, The Lord of the Rings: The Fellowship of the Ring, 2001, 24 Hour Party People, 2002, Deathwatch, 2002, The Lord of the Rings: The Two Towers, 2002, The Lord of the Rings: The Return of the King, 2003, Standing Room Only, 2004, 13 Going on 30, 2004, Blessed, 2004, King Kong, 2005, Stories of Lost Souls, 2006, (voice) Stingray, 2006, Stormbreaker, 2006, The Prestige, 2006, (voice) Flushed Away, 2006, Extraordinary Rendition, 2007, The Cottage, 2008, Inkheart, 2008; (TV films) Grushko, 1994, The Pale Horse, 1997, The Jump, 1998, Shooting the Past, 1999, Arabian Nights, 2000, Longford, 2006, Einstein and Eddington, 2008; (TV miniseries) Touching Evil III, 1999, Oliver Twist, 1999, Little Dorrit, 2008. Office: c/o Larry Taube Principal Entertainment 1964 Westwood Blvd Los Angeles CA 90025

SERLET, BERTRAND, information technology executive; PhD in computer sci., U. Orsay, France. Rsch. engr. Xerox PARC, 1985—89; engring./managerial positions NeXT, 1989—97; sr. v.p. software engring. Apple Computer Inc., Cupertino, Calif., 1997—. Achievements include key player in the definition, development and creation of Mac OS X, the world's most advanced operating system. Office: Apple Computer Inc 1 Infinite Loop Cupertino CA 95014 Office Fax: 408-996-1010.

SERLING, JOEL MARTIN, educational psychologist; b. Seneca Falls, NY, Feb. 8, 1936; s. Philip and Cecil Serling; children: Meredith Anne, Rebecca Lynne, Heather Lee. AA, U. Buffalo, 1957; BS in Edn., Ohio Northern U., 1959; MA, Columbia U., 1960. Cert. sch. psychologist NY, NC. Instr. psychology West Liberty State Coll., W.Va., 1961—63; vocat. psychologist Divsn. Child Welfare, Cleve., 1963—64; sch. psychologist Steuben County Bd. Coop. Ednl. Svcs., Bath, NY, 1964—65, Chenango County Bd. Coop. Ednl. Svcs., Norwich, NY, 1965—67, Delaware County Bd. Coop. Ednl. Svcs., Walton, NY, 1967—68, Vestal Ctrl. Sch., NY, 1968—70, Whitesboro Ctrl. Sch., NY, 1970—92. Bd. edn., bd. dirs Hillel Day Sch., Utica-Rome, 1971—75; instr. psychology Am. Inst. Banking, 1971—; bd. profl. advisors Mohawk Valley Learning Disabilities Assn., 1972—76; cons., mentor Empire Coll., SUNY, 1975—; adj. prof. psychology Utica Coll., Syracuse U., 1971—75, 1986—, Mohawk Valley CC, 1971—91, SUNY Coll. Tech., Utica-Rome, NY, 1975—, CC Southern Nev., 1995—; presenter in field. Co-author, co-developer: Early Identification Screening Index, 1971; contbr. articles to profl. publs. Recipient Cert. recognition, Mohawk Valley Learning Disabilities Assn., 1973. Mem.: APA, Phi Delta Kappa, Whitesboro Tchrs. Assn., NY State United Tchrs. Assn., United U. Professions, Ctrl. NY Psychol. Assn., Sch. Psychologists Upper NY, NY Assn. Sch. Psychologists (cert. of recognition 1977), Nat. Assn. Sch. Psychologists (charter), Odd Fellows Club, Zeta Beta Tau. Jewish. E-mail: jssp@cox.net.

SERNA, PATRICIO, state supreme court justice; b. Reserve, N.Mex., Aug. 26, 1939; m. Eloise Serna; children: Elena Patricia, Anna Alicia 1 stepchild, John Herrera. BSBA with honors, U. Albuquerque, 1962; JD, U. Denver, 1970; LLM, Harvard U., 1971; postgrad., Nat. Jud. Coll., 1985, postgrad., 1990, postgrad., 1992, postgrad., 1994; LLD (hon.), U. Denver, 2002. Bar: N.Mex. 1970, Colo. 1971, U.S. Dist. Ct. N.Mex. 1970. Probation and parole officer State of N.Mex., Santa Fe, Las Cruces, 1966—67; spl. asst. to commn. mem. Equal Opportunity Commn., Washington, 1971—75; asst. atty. gen. State of N.Mex., Santa Fe, 1975—79; pvt. practice Santa Fe, 1979—85; dist. judge First Jud. Dist., Santa Fe, 1985—96; justice N.Mex. Supreme Ct., Santa Fe, 1996—, chief justice, 2001—02. Adj. prof. law Georgetown U., Washington, 1973, Cath. U., Washington, 1974—75; faculty advisor Nat. Jud. Coll., Reno, 1987. Bd. dirs. Santa Fe Group Homes Inc. With US Army, 1963—65. Mem.: Santa Fe Bar Assn., No. N.Mex. Am. Inns of Ct., Nat. Hispanic Bar Assn. (Judge of Yr. award 2002, Judge of Yr. 2002), N.Mex. Hispanic Bar Assn., N.Mex. Bar Assn., Elks, Phi Alpha Delta. Avocations: hiking, fishing, Ping Pong, chess, painting. Office: NMex Supreme Ct PO Box 848 Santa Fe NM 87504-0848 Office Phone: 505-827-4886. Business E-Mail: suppms@nmcourts.com.

SESONSKE, ALEXANDER, nuclear and chemical engineer; b. Gloversville, NY, June 20, 1921; s. Abraham and Esther (Kreitzer) S.; m. Marjorie Ann Mach, Apr. 17, 1952 (dec. Jan. 1995); children: Michael Jan, Jana Louise. B.Chem. Engring., Rensselaer Poly. Inst., 1942; MS, U. Rochester, 1947; PhD, U. Del., 1950. Engr. Chem. Constrn. Corp., NYC, 1942; chem. engr. Manhattan Project, 1943-45, Columbia Chem. Corp., 1945-46; staff Los Alamos Sci. Lab., 1950-54, 60-61, cons., 1961-63; faculty Purdue U., Lafayette, Ind., 1954, prof. nuclear and chem. engring., 1959-86, prof. emeritus, 1986—, asst. chmn. dept. nuclear engring., 1966-73. Cons. Oak Ridge Nat. Lab., 1963-67, Electric Power Research Inst., 1974; mem. rev. com. Argonne (Ill.) Nat. Lab., 1965-67, 75-81; ind. cons. 1986—. Author: (with Samuel Glasstone) Nuclear Reactor Engineering, 1963, 4th edit., 1994, Nuclear Power Plant Design Analysis, 1973; mem. editorial bd. Advances in Nuclear Sci. and Tech., 1972—; contbr. numerous articles to profl. jours. Recipient Wall of Fame award U. Del., 1988. Fellow Am. Nuclear Soc. (Arthur H. Compton award 1987); mem. Am. Inst. Chem. Engrs., Am. Soc. Engring. Edn., Sigma Xi, Omega Chi Epsilon. Achievements include research on nuclear fuel mgmt., liquid metal heat transfer and nuclear reactor engring. Home and Office: 700 Black Lake Blvd SW Apt 109 Olympia WA 98502 Office Phone: 360-943-5467.

SESSIONS, DON DAVID, lawyer; BS, Brigham Young U.; JD, Loyola Law Sch., LA, 1976. Bar: Calif. 1976. Sole practice employee rights, Mission Viejo, Calif., 1976—. Adj. prof. Western State U. Coll. Law. Mem. Calif. Bar Assn. (Labor and employment law sect.), Nat. Employment Lawyer's Assn., Calif. Employment Lawyer's Assn., Orange County Bar Assn. (labor and employment law sect.). Office: 23456 Madero Ste 170 Mission Viejo CA 92691-7901

SESSLER, ANDREW MARIENHOFF, physicist; b. Bklyn., Dec. 11, 1928; s. David and Mary (Baron) S.; m. Gladys Lerner, Sept. 23, 1951 (div. Dec. 1994); children: Daniel Ira, Jonathan Lawrence, Ruth. BA in Math. cum laude, Harvard U., 1949; MA in Theoretical Physics, Columbia U., 1951, PhD in Theoretical Physics, 1953. NSF fellow Cornell U., Ithaca, NY, 1953—54; asst. prof. Ohio State U., Columbus, 1954, assoc. prof., 1960; on leave Midwestern Univs. Rsch., 1955—56; vis. physicist Lawrence Radiation Lab., 1959—60; vis. physicist, summer Niels Bohr Inst., Copenhagen, 1961; rschr. theoretical physics Lawrence Berkeley Lab. U. Calif., Berkeley, 1961—73, rschr. energy and environment Lawrence Berkeley Lab., 1971—73, dir. Lawrence Berkeley Lab., 1973—80, sr. scientist plasma physics Lawrence Berkeley Lab., 1980—94, disting. sr. staff scientist Lawrence Berkeley Lab., 1994—2001, disting. vis. scientist Lawrence Berkeley Lab., 2001—02, disting. scientist Lawrence Berkeley Lab., 2002—, dir. emeritus, 2002—. U.S. advisor Panjab U. Physics Inst., Chandigarh, India; mem. U.S.-India Coop. Program for Improvement Sci. Edn. in India, 1966, high energy physics adv. panel to U.S. AEC, 1969-72, adv. com. Lawrence Hall Sci., 1974-78; chmn. Stanford Synchrotron Radiation Project Sci. Policy Bd., 1974-77, EPRI Advanced Fuels Adv. Com., 1978-81, BNL External Adv. Com. on Isabelle, 1980-82; mem. sci. pol. bd. Stanford Synchrotron Radiation Lab., 1991-92; L.J. Haworth dist. scientist Brookhaven Nat. Lab., 1991-92; spokesperson Neutrino Factory and Muon Collider Collaboration, 1999-2002, assoc. spokesperson 2002—. Mem. editl. bd. Nuc. Instruments and Methods, 1969—2000, correspondent Comments on Modern Physics, 1969—71; contbr. articles to profl. jours. Mem. Superconducting Super Collider Sci. Policy Com., 1991—93; mem. radiation effects rsch. bd. Nat. Rsch. Coun., 2001—04, mem. nuclear radiation studies bd., 2005—. Recipient E.O. Lawrence award US Atomic Energy Commn., 1970, US Particle Accelerator Sch. prize, 1988, Nicholson Medal for Humanitarian Svc., 1994, Robert R. Wilson prize 1997; fellow Japan Soc. for Promotion Sci. at KEK, 1985. Fellow AAAS (nominating com. 1984-87), Am. Phys. Soc. (chmn. com. internat. freedom scientist 1982, study of directed energy weapons panel 1985-87, chmn. panel pub. affairs 1988, chmn. divsn. physics of beams 1990, chmn. com. applications of physics 1993, councilor for divsn. physics of beams 1994-97, pres.-elect 1997, pres. 1998, past pres. 1999, vice-chmn. forum on physics and soc. 2001, chmn.-elect 2002, chmn. 2003), N.Y. Acad. Sci.; mem. NAS (bd. on radiation effects rsch. 2002-05, nuclear radiation studies bd., 2005-), IEEE (sr.), Fedn. Am. Scientists Coun. (vice chmn. 1987-88, chmn. 1988-92), Assoc. Univ. Inc. (bd. dirs. 1991-98), Sigma Xi. Avocations: skiing, hiking, jogging, exercise, flute. Office: Lawrence Berkeley Lab Univ Calif MS 71R0259 1 Cyclotron Rd Bldg Berkeley CA 94720-8211 Office Phone: 510-486-4992. Business E-Mail: AMSessler@lbl.gov.

SETTLES, F. STAN, JR., engineering educator, manufacturing executive; b. Denver, Oct. 3, 1938; s. Frank S. and Dorothy Marie (Johnson) S.; m. Evelyn Brown, June 10, 1961; children: Frank S. III, Richard, Charles, Michael. BS in Prodn. Tech., Indsl. Engring., LeTourneau Coll., Longview, Tex., 1962; MS in Indsl. Engring., Ariz. State U., Tempe, 1967, PhD in Indsl. Engring., 1969. Sr. systems analyst AiResearch Mfg. Co., Phoenix, 1968-70, project mgr., 1970-74, mgr. operational planning, 1974-80; mgr. indsl. engrs. Garrett Pneumatic Systems, Phoenix, 1980-83; mgr. indsl. mfg. engring. Garrett Turbine Engring. Co., Phoenix, 1983-85; v.p. mfg. ops. AiResearch Mfg. Co., Torrance, Calif., 1985-87; dir. indusl. mfg. engring. The Garrett Corp., Phoenix, 1987-88; dir. planning Garrett Engine Div., Phoenix, 1988-92; asst. dir. White House Office of Sci. and Tech. Policy, 1992-93; program dir. NSF, 1992-94; prof., chmn. indsl. and systems engring. dept. U. So. Calif., LA, 1994—2003, IBM prof. engring. mgmt., dir. sys. arch. & engring. program, 2003—. Faculty assoc. Ariz. State U., Tempe, 1974-85, 90-92, rsch. prof., 1992-94. Mem. sch. bd. Tempe Elem. Sch. Dist., 1976-80; mem. YMCA Indian Guides, nat. chief, 1978-79. Fellow Inst. Indsl. Engrs. (pres. 1987-88, Ops. Rsch. award 1980), Inst. Ops. Rsch. and Mgmt. Sci., Nat. Acad. Engrs., Soc. Mfg. Engrs. (sr.), IEEE Engring. Mgmt. Soc., Am. Soc. Quality Control, Am. Soc. Engring. Edn. Republican. Presbyterian. Home: 1310 E Ocean Blvd Unit 1602 Long Beach CA 90802-6917 Office: U So Calif Dept Indsl Sys Engring Los Angeles CA 90089-0193 Office Phone: 213-740-0263. Business E-Mail: settles@usc.edu.

SEVERINSEN, DOC (CARL H. SEVERINSEN), retired conductor, musician; b. Arlington, Oreg., July 7, 1927; m. Emily Marshall; children: Nancy, Judy, Cindy, Robin, Allen. Ptnr. Severinsen-Akwright Co.; pops condr. The Phoenix Symphony Orchestra, Ariz.; prin. pops condr. Minn. Orch., Milw. Symphony Orch., Phoenix Symphony Orch.; ret., 2007. Mem. Ted Fio Rito Band, 1945, Charlie Barnet Band, 1947—49, Tommy Dorsey Band, Benny Goodman Band, Vaughn Monroe Band, soloist network band Steve Allen Show NBC-TV, 1954—55, mem. orch. Tonight Show, 1962—67, music dir. Tonight Show, 1967—92, host Midnight Spl., rec. artist Brass Roots album RCA Records, 1971, rec. artist Facets album, 1988, rec. artist The Tonight Show Band, Night Journey album. also: c/o William Morris Agency 151 S El Camino Dr Beverly Hills CA 90212-2704

SEVIGNY, CHLOË, actress; b. Darien, Conn., Nov. 18, 1974; d. Paul Sevigny. Actor: (films) Kids, 1995, Trees Lounge, 1996, Gummo, 1997, Palmetto, 1998, The Last Days of Disco, 1998, Boys Don't Cry, 1999, Julien Donkey-Boy, 1999, A Map of the World, 1999, American Psycho, 2000, Ten Minutes Older: The Trumpet, 2002, Demonlover, 2002, Party Monster, 2003, Death of a Dynasty, 2003, Dogville, 2003, The Brown Bunny, 2003, Shattered Glass, 2003, Melinda and Melinda, 2004, Manderlay, 2005, Broken Flowers, 2005, 3 Needles, 2005, Lying, 2006, Sisters, 2006, Zodiac, 2007; (TV films) Mrs. Harris, 2005, If These Walls Could Talk 2, 2000; (TV series) Big Love, 2006—, (TV appearances) Will & Grace, 2004. Named one of The 50 Most Powerful Women in NYC, NY Post, 2008. Office: Endeavor Talent Agy 9601 Wilshire Blvd 10th Fl Beverly Hills CA 90212

SEVILLA, CARLOS ARTHUR, bishop; b. San Francisco, Aug. 9, 1935; Student, Gonzaga U., Santa Clara U., Jesuiten Kolleg, Innsbruck, Austria, Cath. Inst. Paris. Ordained priest Society of Jesus, 1966, solemn professed, 1974; aux. bishop Archdiocese of San Francisco, 1988—96; ordained bishop, 1989; bishop Diocese of Yakima, Wash., 1996—. Roman Catholic. Office: Diocese of Yakima 5301-A Tieton Dr Yakima WA 98908-3493 Office Phone: 509-965-7117. Office Fax: 509-966-8334.

SEVILLA, STANLEY, lawyer; b. Cin., Apr. 3, 1920; s. Isadore and Dienna (Levy) S.; m. Lois A. Howell, July 25, 1948; children: Stanley, Susan, Donald, Carol, Elizabeth. BA in Econs. with high honors, U. Cin., 1942; JD, Harvard U., 1948. Bar: Calif. 1949. Since practiced in, Los Angeles; assoc. Williamson, Hoge & Curry, 1948-50; mem. firm Axelrod, Sevilla and Ross, 1950-75, Stanley Sevilla (P.C.), 1975—. Gen. counsel La.-Pacific Resources, Inc., 1970-90. Bd. dirs. Caesars World, Inc., 1989-95. With USAAF, 1942-46. Mem. Beverly Hills Bar Assn., Phi Beta Kappa, Tau Kappa Alpha. Home: 16606 Merrivale Ln Pacific Palisades CA 90272-2236 Office: PO Box 308 Pacific Palisades CA 90272-0308 Office Phone: 310-459-8116.

SEWARD, JAMES PICKETT, internist, educator; b. NYC, Oct. 14, 1949; s. George C. and Carroll Frances (McKay) S. AB, Harvard U., 1971; M of Pub. Policy, U. Calif. Berkeley, 1977; MD, U. Calif. San Francisco, 1977; M of Med. Mgmt., Tulane U., 2003. Diplomate Am. Bd. Internal Medicine, Am. Bd. Occupational Medicine, Am. Bd. Med. Mgmt. Resident U. Calif. Hosps., San Francisco, 1977—80; Robert Woods Johnson postdoctoral fellow U. Calif., San Francisco, 1980—82; med. dir. health svcs. Lawrence Livermore Nat. Lab., Calif., 1994—; dir. preventive medicine residency U. Calif., Berkeley, 1991—95, clin. prof. San Francisco, 1983—, clin. prof. Sch. Pub. Health Berkeley, 1986—2005. Fulbright scholar, 1972-73. Fellow Am. Coll. Preventive Medicine (occupl. med. regent 2005-07), Am. Coll. Occupl. an Environ. Medicine, Am. Coll. Physicians Execs., Calif. Acad. Preventive Medicine (past pres.), We. Occupl. and Environ. Med. Assn. (pres.), Calif. Med. Assn. Office: HSD L723 LLNL PO Box 808 Livermore CA 94551-0808

SEWELL, D. BRUCE (BRUCE SEWELL, DURWARD BRUCE SEWELL), lawyer; b. 1958; B, U. Lancaster, UK, 1979; JD, George Washington U., 1986. Bar: Calif. 1986, DC 1987, US Ct. Appeals, Fed. cir. Assoc. Schnader Harrison Segal & Lewis; ptnr. Brown & Bain PC; sr. atty. Intel Corp., Santa Clara, Calif., 1995—2001, v.p. legal & govt. affairs, dep. gen. counsel, 2001—04, v.p., gen. counsel, 2004—05, sr. v.p., gen. counsel, 2005—. Office: Intel Corp 2200 Mission College Blvd Santa Clara CA 95052

SEWELL, ROBERT DALTON, pediatrician; b. Newman, Calif., Apr. 28, 1950; s. James Dalton and Mary Louise (Hartwell) S.; m. Laura Slinkard-Ekberg, May 21, 1998; children: Kevin, David; stepchildren: Nicole, Samantha. BA magna cum laude, Pacific Union Coll., 1972; MD, Loma Linda U., 1975. Diplomate Am. Bd. Pediatrics. Pediat. intern and resident White Meml. Med. Ctr., LA, 1975-77; pediat. resident, chief resident Milton S. Hershey Med. Ctr., Pa. State U., Hershey, 1977-80; pediatrician Children's Med. Ctr. Asheville, N.C., 1980-81, Lincoln City (Oreg.) Med. Ctr. P.C., 1982-95; examining physician C.A.R.E.S. Ctr. Emanuel Hosp. & Health Ctr., Portland, Oreg., 1988-90; asst. prof. Loma Linda (Calif.) U. Sch. Medicine, 1995-97; with Good Shepherd Med. Group, Hemiston, Oreg., 1998-2001; physician examiner Guardian Care Ctr., Pendleton, Oreg., 1999-2001. Chmn. child protection team North Lincoln Hosp., Lincoln City, 1983-89, sec. med. staff, 1990-92, pres. med. staff, 1992-94; mem. Citizens' Rev. Bd. Lincoln County, Newport, Oreg., 1986-92, Early Intervention adv. com., Newport, 1986-90. Mem. North Lincoln Local Sch. Com., Lincoln City, 1983-94, chmn., 1986-90; bd. dirs. Lincoln Shelter and Svcs., Inc., Lincoln City, 1983-89, chmn., 1987-89; mem. North Lincoln divsn. Am. Heart Assn., Lincoln City, 1986-89, v.p., 1987-89; mem. Drug and Alcohol Task Force, Lincoln City, 1988; mem., 2d vice-chmn. Yr. 2000 Plan housing com. Lincoln City Planning Commn., 1987-88; mem. AIDS task force Lincoln County Sch. Dist., 1987-89; mem. Lincoln County Children's Agenda Taskforce, 1988; mem. med. rev. com. Oreg. Med. Assn., 1990-95, mem.-at-large med. staff sect. gov. bd., 1993-95. Named Citizen of Yr. child protection com. Lincoln County, 1984, Man of Yr. Lincoln City C. of C., 1988. Mem. Am. Acad. Pediatrics (sect. on child abuse), Am. Profl. Soc. of Abuse of Children (charter mem.), Nat. Assn. Counsel for Children, Internat. Soc. for Prevention Child Abuse and Neglect, Oreg. Profl. Soc. on Abuse of Children (founding pres. 1992-94), Oreg. Med. Assn. (mem. health care fin. com. 1999-2001). Democrat. Seventh-day Adventist. Avocations: music, sports, boating, auto racing. E-mail: kidsdr@eoni.com.

SEWELL, RUFUS, actor; b. Twickenham, England, Oct. 29, 1967; s. William and Jo Sewell; m. Yasmin Abdallah, Mar. 24, 1999 (div. Mar. 2000); m. Amy Gardner, Feb. 2004; 1 child, William Douglas. Student, Ctrl. Sch. Speech & Drama, London. Actor theatrical debut As You Like It, Shefield's Crucible Theatre, Rock 'n Roll, 2006 (Evening Standard Best Actor award, 2006, Olivier award best actor, 2007); (miniseries) Middlemarch, 1994, Arabian Nights, 1999; (films) Twenty-One, 1991, Dirty Weekend, 1993, Victory, 1995, Carrington, 1995, Hamlet, 1996, The Woodlanders, 1997, Dangerous Beauty, 1998, Dark City, 1998, Martha, Meet Frank, Daniel, and Laurence, 1998, Illuminata, 1998, In Sachem Farm, 1998, In a Savage Land, 1999, Bless the Child, 2000, A Knight's Tale, 2001, Extreme Oops, 2002, Victoria Station, 2003, The Legend of Zorro, 2005, The Illusionist, 2006, Tristan & Isolde, 2006, Paris, I Love You, 2006, Amazing Grace, 2006, The Holiday, 2006; (TV films) Cold Comfort Farm, 1995, King Henry IV, 1995, Arabian Nights, 2000, Mermaid Chronicles Part 1: She Creature, 2001, Helen of Troy, 2003, The Taming of the Shrew, 2005, John Adams, 2008.

SEXTON, RONALD P., academic administrator; b. Greybull, Wyo. Grad., Ea. Mont. Coll.; PhD. Tchr. Mont. State U. (formerly Ea. Mont. Coll.), Billings, 1979, chancellor, 1995—. Chmn. Big Sky Econ. Devel. Authority. Office: Mont State U Office of the Chancellor 1500 University Dr Billings MT 59101-0298 Office Phone: 406-657-2300. E-mail: rsexton@msubillings.edu.

SEYFRIED, AMANDA LOUISE, actress; b. Allentown, Pa., Dec. 3, 1985; Actress (TV series) As the World Turns, 2000—01, All My Children, 2002—03, Veronica Mars, 2004—06, Wildfire, 2006, Big Love, 2006—07, (films) Mean Girls, 2004 (Best On-Screen Team, MTV Awards, 2005), Nine Lives, 2005 (Bronze Leopard award for Best Actress, 2005), America Gun, 2005, Alpha Dog, 2006, Gypsies, Tramps & Thieves, 2006, Solstice, 2008, Mamma Mia!, 2008. Office: c/o Innovative Artists LA 1505 10th St Santa Monica CA 90401

SEYMOUR, JOHN, former senator; b. Chgo., Dec. 3, 1937; M. Judy Thacker, 1972; children: John III, Lisa, Jeffery, Shad, Sarena, Barrett. BS in Fin. and Real Estate, UCLA, 1962. Pres., CEO Seymour Realty and Investment Co., 1964—82; mem. Anaheim City Coun., 1974-78; mayor Anaheim, 1978; state sen. Calif., 1982, 84, 88; sen. U.S. Senate, Washington, 1991—93; dir. Calif. Housing Fin. Agy., 1992—94. Chmn. Calif. Senate Rep. Caucus, 1983-87; mem. Agr., Nutrition and Forestry Com., Energy and Natural Resources Com., Govtl. Affairs Com., Small Bus. Com.; bd. dir. Inco Homes 1995-2001, Indymac Bank, 2000-, Indymac, 2004-, LA Fed. Savings Bank, Irvine Apt. Communities, Countrywide Financial Services; bd. dir., cons. Orange Coast Title Ins., 1995-. Sgt. USMC, 1955-59. Child Care Adv. Am. award, Dayle McIntosh Ctr. for Disabled award, Golden Pineapple award, Leukemia Soc. Am., 1984, 1985, N Anaheim Pony League award; The Founders award, No. & So. Calif. Head Injury Assn., 1988, Legis. Yr., Calif. Sch. Bd. Assn., 1988; Transp. Partnership award, Orange County Transp. Comm., 1988; Senator of Yr., Univ Calif Student Assn., 1989. Mem. Anaheim C. of C. (pres. 1973), Rotary Internat., Nat. Assn. Realtors, Calif. Assn. Realtors (pres., 1980) Republican. Office: Orange Coast Title Co 640 N Tustin Santa Ana CA 92705

SGANGA, JOHN B., retired furniture holding company executive; b. Bronx, NY, Nov. 21, 1931; s. Charles and Marie (Crusco) S.; m. Evelyn Joan Battilana, Jan. 19, 1957; children: Mark, John B. Jr., Matthew. BS in Acctg. cum laude, Bklyn. Coll., 1961; postgrad., Bernard Baruch Coll. Systems analyst DIVCO, Wayne, NY, 1965-67; mgr. mgmt. cons. svcs. Coopers & Lybrand, CPAs, NYC, 1967-74; sr. v.p. fin. and adminstrn. Aurora Products Co. subs. RJR Nabisco, West Hempstead, NY, 1974—78; contr. Gt. Lakes Carbon Corp., NYC, 1979-80, v.p., 1980-81, sr. v.p. fin., CFO, 1981-86; v.p. Cunard Line, Ltd., NYC, 1988; exec. v.p. CFO Consolidated Furniture Corp. (formerly Mohasco Corp.), NYC, 1989—2001, also bd. dirs., mem. Various Othol Furniture Co., 2001—05. Contbr. articles to profl. jours.; editl. adv. to Financial Management mag. Served with USNR, 1950-54. Mem. Inst. Cert. Mgmt. Cons. (a founder), Inst. Mgmt. Accts., Fin. Execs. Internat. (past chmn. com. M.I.S.), Treas.'s Club. Home: 21311 Canea Mission Viejo CA 92692-4992 Personal E-mail: sganga-sr@cox.net.

SHABOT, MYRON MICHAEL, critical care educator; b. Houston, Aug. 5, 1945; s. Sam and Mona Doris (Stalarow) S.; 1 child, Samuel Laib. Student, Tulane U., 1963-64; BA, U. Tex., Austin, 1966; MD, U. Tex., Dallas, 1970. Intern Parkland Meml. Hosp., Dallas, 1970—71; resident Harbor Gen. Hosp., Torrance, Calif., 1973—78; lectr. surgery UCLA Sch. Medicine, 1977-78, asst. prof., 1978-82, clin. assoc. prof. surgery and anesthesiology, 1983-97, prof. surgery, 1997—; dir. surg. ICU, LA County Harbor Med. Ctr.-UCLA Sch. Medicine, 1980-82; med. dir. Enterprise Info. Svcs. Cedars-Sinai Med. Ctr., LA, dir. surg. ICU, 1982—, vice chief of staff, 2000—01, chief of staff, 2002—03, also bd. dirs. Sec. Cedars-Sinai Med. Ctr. Attending Staff, 1999-2000; bd. dirs. eHealth Initiative and Found., 2006—; adj. prof. U. Tex. Health Scis. Ctr., Houston; v.p., chief quality officer Meml. Hermann Healthcare Sys., Houston, 2007, sr. v.p., sys. chief medcial officer, 2007-. Contbr. articles to profl. jours. Served to lt. comdr. USPHS, 1971-73. Fellow ACS (So. Calif. chpt. bd. dirs. 1988—, pres. 1992-93, gov., 1992—), Am. Coll. Critical Care Medicine, Am. Coll. Med. Informatics; mem. Western Surg. Assn., Pacific Coast Surg. Assn., Soc. Critical Care Medicine, Am. Assn. Surgery of Trauma, Soc. Computers in Critical Care and Pulmonary Medicine (bd. dirs. 1988—, treas. 1989—, pres., 1993-94), Soc. Clin. Data Mgmt. Systems (pres. 1985-86), L.A. Surg. Soc. (pres. 1997-98), Phi Eta Sigma. Jewish. Home Phone: 713-647-9894. Business E-Mail: michael.shabot@memorialhermann.org.

SHACHMUT, KENNETH MICHAEL, retail executive; m. Daria Shachmut; children: Spike, Chris. BSEE with honors, Princeton U., NJ, 1970; grad. student in ops. rsch., Columbia U., NYC; MBA, Stanford U., Calif., 1976. Gen. mgmt. cons. Booz Allen Hamilton, San Francisco, McKinsey & Co., San Francisco, London, Amsterdam; exec. officer Safeway, Inc., 1994—99, sr. v.p. strategic initiatives, health initiatives and re-engring., 1999—. Spkr. World Health Care Congress. Lt. (jr. grade) US Navy Civil Engr. Corps, 1971—74. Mem.: Princeton Club No. Calif. Office: Safeway Inc 5918 Stoneridge Mall Rd Pleasanton CA 94588 Office Phone: 925-467-3000. Office Fax: 925-467-3323.

SHACKELFORD, CHARLES DUANE, civil engineering educator, researcher; b. Sewickley, Pa., Sept. 9, 1954; m. Anne Marie Lynch, Apr. 2, 1984; children: Kathryn, David, Daniel. BSCE, U. Mo., Rolla, 1980; MS, U. Tex., 1983, PhD, 1988. Registered profl. engr., Calif., Colo. Civil design engr. Pacific Gas and Electric Co., San Francisco, 1980-81; geotech. engr. Ardaman and Assocs., Inc., Orlando, Fla., 1983-84; rsch. intern Oak Ridge (Tenn.) Nat. Lab., summer 1984; asst. prof. dept. civil engring. Colo. State U., Ft. Collins, 1988-93, assoc. prof. dept. civil engring., 1993-99, prof. dept. civil engring., 1999—. Cons. David E. Daniel, Austin, Tex., 1985-89, Shepard and Miller, Inc., 1990, USAF, 1991, Woodward-Clyde Cons., 1992, Dept. of Energy, 1993, 95; lectr. in field. Editor: Geotechnical News Mag. (environ. geotechnics sect.), 1988—; contbr. articles to Jour. of Contaminant Hydrology, Jour. Geotech. Engring., Jour. Engring. Geology, Nuclear and Chem. Waste Mgmt., Geotech. Testing Jour., others. Vol. sci. fair judge Long's Peak Sci. Fair, U. No. Colo., Greeley, 1988-89. With U.S. Army, 1973-76. U. Tex. Geotech. fellow, 1984-86; grantee NSF Nat., 1992-97; recipient Young Investigator award NSF, 1992. Mem. ASTM, ASCE (mem. environ. geotechnics com. 1988-92, chmn. environ. geotechnics com. 1992—, Walter L. Huber Civil Engring. prize 1995), Assn. Ground Water Scientists and Engrs., Internat. Soc. for Soil Mechanics and Found. Engring. (sec. environ. control com. 1991—), Soil Sci. Soc. of Am. Achievements include research in contaminant transport through saturated and unsaturated porous media, coupled flow processes, diffusion of contaminants in soils, electrokinetics remediation, environmental geotechnics, in situ soil washing, permeability and compatibility of fine-grained soils, permeable reactive walls, physico-chemical properties of soils, soil and waste stabilization, unsaturated flow through clay liners and cover systems. Office: Colo State U Dept Civil Engring Fort Collins CO 80523-0001

SHACKMAN, DANIEL ROBERT, psychiatrist; b. NYC, Nov. 15, 1941; s. Nathan H. and Dorothy K. Shackman. BA, Columbia U., 1962, MD, 1966. Diplomate Am. Bd. Psychiatry and Neurology. Intern Mount Sinai Hosp., NYC, 1966-67, resident, chief resident, fellow, 1967-70; psychiatrist USAF, Spokane, Wash., 1970-72; clin. and adminstrv. staff Brentwood VA Hosp., LA, 1972-79; pvt. practice psychiatry LA, 1975-87, Santa Barbara, Calif., 1984—. Asst. clin. prof. UCLA Sch. Medicine, LA, 1975—87; psychiat. cons. CAlif. Dept. Rehab., LA, 1975—87; cons. psychiatrist Sanctuary Psychiat. Ctrs., Santa Barbara, 1984—2001; chmn. dept. psychiatry Santa Barbara Cottage Hosp., 1990—92. Bd. dirs. Family Counseling Svc., Spokane, 1971-72. Maj. USAF, 1970-72. Mem. Am. Psychiat. Assn., Am. Acad. Child/Adolescent Psychiatry, So. Calif. Psychiat. Soc. (dist. councillor 1989-92), Am. Soc. Clin. Psychopharmacology. Avocations: photography, travel, music, computer science. Office: 924 Anacapa St Santa Barbara CA 93101-2115

SHACTER, DAVID MERVYN, lawyer; b. Toronto, Ont., Can., Jan. 17, 1941; s. Nathan and Tillie Anne (Schwartz) S. BA, U. Toronto, 1963; JD, Southwestern U., 1967. Bar: Calif. 1968, US Ct. Appeals (9th cir.) 1969, US Supreme Ct. 1982. Law clk., staff atty. Legal Aid Found., Long Beach, Calif., 1967-70; asst. city atty. City of Beverly Hills, Calif., 1970; ptnr. Shacter & Berg, Beverly Hills, 1971-83, Selwyn, Capalbo, Lowenthal & Shacter Profl. Law Corp., 1984-99; pvt. practice, 1999—. Del. State Bar Conf. Dels., 1976-2000; lectr. Calif. Continuing Edn. of Bar, 1977, 82-83, 86; judge pro tem LA and Beverly Hills mcpl. cts.; arbitrator LA Superior Ct., 1983—, judge pro tem; disciplinary examiner Calif. State Bar, 1986. Bd. dirs. and pres. Los Angeles Soc. Prevention Cruelty to Animals, 1979-89. Mem.: City of Hope Med. Ctr. Aux., Am. Arbitration Assn. (nat. panel arbitrators, neutral arbitrator, panel chmn.), Beverly Hills Bar Found. (pres. 1995—97, bd. govs. 1998—2001), Beverly Hills Bar Assn. (bd. govs. 1985—90, sec. 1987—88, treas. 1988—89, v.p. 1989—90, pres.-elect 1990—91, pres. 1991—92, editor-in-chief jour.), Nat. Assn. Securities Dealers (arbitrator 1998—), West LA C. of C. Office: 10801 National Blvd Ste 608 Los Angeles CA 90064 Office Phone: 310-474-4115. Business E-Mail: david@shacterlaw.com.

SHADEGG, JOHN BARDEN, United States Representative from Arizona; b. Phoenix, Oct. 22, 1949; s. Stephen and Eugenia Shadegg; m. Shirley Shadegg; children: Courtney, Stephen. BA, U. Ariz., 1972, JD, 1975. Advisor U.S. Sentencing Commn.; spl. asst. atty. gen. State of Ariz., 1983-90; spl. counsel Ariz. State Ho. Rep. Caucus, 1991-92; pvt. practice; mem. U.S. Congress from 4th Ariz. dist., 1995—, asst. whip, mem. commerce com., fin. svcs. com., homeland sec. com. Mem. Victims Bill of Rights Task Force, 1989-90; mem. Fiscal Accountability and Reform Efforts Com., 1991-92; counsel Arizonian's for Wildlife Conservation, 1992; chmn. Proposition 108-Two-Thirds Tax Limitation Initiative, 1992. Rep. Party Ballot Security chmn., 1982; active Corbin for Atty. Gen., 1982-86; Rep. Precinct committeeman; chmn. Ariz. Rep. Caucus, 1985-87; chmn. Ariz. Lawyers for Bush-Quayle, 1988; mem. steering com., surrogate spkr. Jon Kyl for Congress, 1988-92; former pres. Crime Victim Found.; founding dir. Goldwater Inst. Pub. Policy; chmn. Ariz. Juvenile Justice Adv. Coun.; mem. adv. bd. Salvation Army; mem. vestry Christ Ch. of Ascension, 1989-91; mem. class II Valley Leadership; bd. dirs. Ariz. State U. Law Soc. Republican. Episcopalian. Office: US Ho Reps 306 Cannon Ho Office Bldg Washington DC 20515-0001

SHAEVITZ, GEOFF, film company executive; b. Apr. 8, 1974; Student in Hist., Stanford U., Calif.; student, Harvard Bus. Sch. Intern Radar Pictures; v.p. prodn. Warner Premiere. Achievements include acting as a studio executive on the films The Lake House, 2006 and Poseidon, 2006, and the upcoming films Mama's Boy, 2007 and 300, 2007. Avocation: cooking.

SHAFF, BEVERLY GERARD, education administrator; b. Oak Park, Ill., Aug. 16, 1925; d. Carl Tanner and Mary Frances (Gerard) Wilson; m. Maurice A. Shaff, Jr., Dec. 20, 1951 (dec. June 1967); children: Carol Maureen, David Gerrard, Mark Albert MA, U. Ill., 1951; postgrad., Colo. Coll., 1966-73, Lewis and Clark Coll., 1982, Portland State U., 1975-82. Tchr. Haley Sch., Berwyn, Ill., 1948-51; assoc. prof. English, Huntingdon Coll., Montgomery, Ala., 1961-62; tchr. English, William Palmer High Sch., Colorado Springs, Colo., 1964-67, 72-76, dir., 1967-72; tchr. English, Burns (Oreg.) High Sch., 1976-78; tchr. English as 2d lang. Multnomah County Ednl. Svc. Dist., Portland, Oreg., 1979-85; coord. gen. studies Portland Jewish Acad., 1984-90; with Indian Edn. Prog./Student Tng. Edn. Prog. (STEP) Portland Pub. Schs., 1990-92, 95—; tchr. St. Thomas More Sch., Portland, 1992-95; tchr. Indian Edn. Act Program Portland Pub. Schs., 1995—. Del. Colorado Springs Dem. Com., 1968, 72; active Rainbow Coalition, Portland; ct. apptd. spl. adv. CASA; mem. Lake Oswego Libr. Bd., Citizens Rev. Bd. Mem. Nat. Assn. Admnstrs., Nat. Assn. Schs. and Colls., Nat. Coun. Tchrs. Math., Nat. Coun. Tchrs. English. Home: 4625 NE Halsey #211 Portland OR 97213

SHAFFER, BRANDON, state legislator; b. Denver; m. Jessica Shaffer; children: Dylan, Madison Leigh. B in Polit. Sci. with honors, Stanford U., Calif., 1993; JD, U. Colo. Sch. Law, 2001. Bar: Colo. 2001. Pvt. practice atty., Longmont, Colo.; mem. Dist. 17 Colo. State Senate, Denver, 2004—, majority leader. Served with USN, 1993—97. Democrat. Office: Colo State Capitol 200 E Colfax Denver CO 80203 Office Phone: 303-866-5291. Business E-Mail: brandon.shaffer.senate@state.co.us.*

SHAFFER, RAYMOND C., state legislator; b. Wilkes-Barre, Pa., Dec. 12, 1932; m. Sharon Van Allen; children: Thomas, Robin, Diane, James, Cindy. Grad., Youngstown Coll. Profl. code adminstrn. U.S. Marine Corps; mem. Nev. Senate, Dist. 2, 1984—; majority whip Nev. Senate, 1991. Mem. Western States Water Policy Com. Mem. Disabled Am. War Vets Lions, North Las Vegas Luncheon Optimist Club (pres.), Foot Printers, Internat. Conf. Bldg. Ofcls., Marine Corps League, North Las Vegas Twp. Dem. Club, Nat. Conf. State Legislatures. Democrat. Home: 649 10th St Imperial Beach CA 91932-1501

SHAGAN, STEVE, scriptwriter, film producer; b. NYC, Oct. 25, 1927; m. Elizabeth Florance, Nov. 1956. Film technician Consol. Film, Inc., NYC, 1952-56, RCA, Cape Canaveral, Fla., 1956-59; asst. to publicity dir. Paramount Pictures, Hollywood, Calif., 1962-63. Prodr.: (TV series) Tarzan, 1966; prodr., writer movies for TV, Universal and CBS, Hollywood, Calif., 1968-70; writer original screenplay: Save the Tiger, 1972 (Writers Guild award, Acad. award nominee 1973); prodr. film, author screenplay: City of Angels (produced as movie Hustle), 1975, novel, screenplay The Formula, 1979, screenplay Voyage of the Damned, 1976 (Acad. award nominee); writer, prodr. film The Formula, 1980; author: (novels) Save the Tiger, 1972, City of Angels, 1975, The Formula, 1979, The Circle, 1982, The Discovery, 1985, Vendetta, 1986, Pillars of Fire, 1989, A Cast of Thousands, 1993, (screenplays) Primal Fear, 1996, Gotti, 1996 (Emmy nominee Best Screenplay). Served with USCG, 1944-46. Mem. Writers Guild Am. (bd. dirs. West chpt. 1978-82). Office: RBZ Mgmt 11755 Wilshire Blvd 9th Fl Los Angeles CA 90025-1586

SHAH, AJAY, electronics executive; Chmn., pres., CEO Smart Modular Tech., Fremont, Calif. Office: Smart Modular Tech PO Box 1757 Fremont CA 94538-0175

SHAH, HARESH CHANDULAL, civil engineering educator; b. Godhra, Gujarat, India, Aug. 7, 1937; s. Chandulal M. and Rama Shah; m. Mary-Joan Dersjant, Dec. 27, 1965; children: Hemant, Mihir. BEngring., U. Poona, 1959; MSCE, Stanford U., 1960, PhD, 1963. From instr. to assoc. prof. U. Pa., Phila., 1962-68; assoc. prof. civil engring. Stanford (Calif.) U., 1968-73, prof., 1973—, chmn. dept. civil engring., 1985-94, John A. Blume prof. engring., 1988-91, Obayashi prof. engring., 1991-97, dir. Stanford Ctr. for Risk Analysis, 1987-94, Obayashi prof. engring. emeritus, 1998—. Trustee Geohazards Internat.; bd. dir. OYO-RMS, Inc., Japan, ERS, R.M. Software Ltd., India, Risk Mgmt. Solutions, Inc., World Seismic Safety Initiative, Buildfolio, Inc.; cons. in field; pres. World Seismic Safety Initiative, 1994—. Author 1 book; contbr. over 250 articles to profl. jours. Mem. ASCE, Am. Concrete Inst., Earthquake Engring. Rsch. Inst., Seismol. Soc. Am., Sigma Xi, Tau Beta Pi. Avocations: hiking, climbing, travel. Office: Risk Mgmt Solutions Inc 7015 Gateway Bldg Newark CA 94560 E-mail: hshah@stanford.edu, haresh.shah@rms.com.

SHAH, JAMI J., mechanical engineering educator, researcher; s. Maqsood A. and Nasim K. Shah. BSME, NED Engring. Coll., Karachi, 1973; MSMetE, U. Pitts., 1976; PhDME, Ohio State U., 1984. Engr. Pakistan Steel, Karachi, 1973-75; prodn. engr. Pakistan Oxygen, Karachi, 1976-80; assoc. prof. Ariz. State U., Tempe, 1984—2003, prof., 1995—. Cons. rsch. area in application of artificial intelligence techniques to engring. design and mfg. automation; tchr. creativity techniques in engring. & bus. Author: 2 books; contbr. more than 150 rsch. papers to profl. jours.; founding editor: ASME Transactions,: Jour. Computing and Info. Sci. Fellow: ASME. Avocations: hiking, rock climbing. Office: Ariz State U Dept Mech Engring Tempe AZ 85287

SHAH, PREDIMAN K., cardiologist, educator; MBBS, Govt. Med Coll. Srinagar, India, 1969. Diplomate Am. Bd. Internal Medicine. Intern, cardiology Mt. Sinai Hosp., Milw., 1971-72; resident All India Inst. Med. Scis., New Delhi, 1970-71, Montefiore Hosp., NYC, 1973-74, fellow cardiology, 1974-76; hosp. apptd. Cedar Sinai Med. Ctr., LA, dir., divsn. cardiology, dir., Atherosclerosis Rsch. Ctr., Shapell and Webb Family Endowed Chair, Cardiology; prof. medicine UCLA Sch. Medicine. Mem. scientific adv. bd. Larry King Cardiac Found.; nat. chmn. Entertainment Industry Found. Nat. Cardiovascular Rsch. Initiative, 2001—; vis. prof. Cleveland Clinic, Mayo Clinic, Tex. Heart Inst., U. Utah, U. Va., U. Calif., San Diego, U. Calif., San Francisco, U. Tex. Galveston Med. Branch, U. San Antonio & Mass. Gen. Hosp. Harvard Med. Sch.; Fullbright vis. prof. to Japan, Argentina, Chile and Taiwan; spkr. in field. Contbr. scientific papers; mem. editl. bd. Circulation, Am. Jour. Cardiology, Internat. Jour. Heart Failure, Indian Heart Jour., Jour. Preventative Cardiology, Reviews in Cardiovascular Medicine, Current Cardiology Reports, Jour., Jour. Am. Coll. Cardiology, Arteriosclerosis, Thrombosis and Vascular Biology, Cardiovascular Pharmacology &Therapeutics. Named one of Top Cardiovascular Specialist, Am. Health Mag. Fellow Am. Coll. Cardiology (mem. of several committees including Ann. Scientific Program Com., chairperson Clin. Cardiology Spotlight Program (ClinCard), ACP, Coll. Chest Physicians; mem. Am. Heart Assn. (vol., chmn. ednl. task force, LA bd., mem. Western Regional Bd., pres. LA chpt. 2001-2002 (Lifetime Achievement award, 2002, mem. rsch. com., chmn. fall symposium, mem. Young Investigators Award Group, mem. Western Regional Peer-Review Group), European Acad. Scis. Office: Cedars-Sinai Med Ctr 8700 Beverly Blvd Rm 5347 Los Angeles CA 90048-1865 Office Phone: 310-423-3884. Office Fax: 310-423-0144. Business E-Mail: shahp@cshs.org.

SHAHANI, SUDHIN, entrepreneur, Internet company executive; b. India, 1983; BSBA, Babson Coll., Wellesley, Mass. Founder, mng. ptnr. Ready To Go? Animate, Kolkata, India; founder MyMPO. Ptnr. Animaction India. Named one of Best Entrepreneurs Under 25, BusinessWeek mag., 2006. Achievements include creation of the Musicane service, which allows artists to sell audio, video or ringtones online. Office: MyMPO Ste 1003b 201 Ocean Ave Santa Monica CA 90402

SHAHEEN, GEORGE T., former computer software company executive; b. July 11, 1944; BS in Mktg., Bradley U., 1966, MBA, 1968. With Andersen Worldwide Orgn., 1967—89, mng. ptnr.-cons. for N.Am., 1977—89; mng. ptnr., CEO Andersen Cons. (now Accenture), Chgo., 1989-99; chmn., CEO Webvan Group, Inc., Foster City, Calif., 1999—2001; CEO Siebel Systems, Inc., San Mateo, Calif., 2005—06. Bd. dirs. Siebel Systems, Inc., 1996—2006, NetApp, Inc., 2004—. Mem. bd. advisors Northwestern Univ. J.L. Kellogg Grad. Sch. Bus.*

SHAHEEN, ROBERT JOSEPH, bishop; b. Danbury, Conn., June 3, 1937; Attended, Our Lady of Lebanon Maronite Sem, Cath. Univ., Washington. Ordained priest Eparchy of Our Lady of Lebanon of LA (Maronite), 1964; pastor St. Raymond's Maronite Cath. Church, St. Louis; ordained bishop, 2001; bishop Eparchy of Our Lady of Lebanon of LA (Maronite), 2001—. Roman Catholic. Office: Our Lady of Lebanon 333 S Vicente Blvd Los Angeles CA 90048 Mailing: Our Lady of Lebanon PO Box 16397 Beverly Hills CA 90209

SHAKEEL, ARIF, computer company executive; BSME, Memphis State U., 1977; MBA, Pepperdine U., 1982. From product mgr. to v.p. positions in various areas Western Digital Corp., Lake Forest, Calif., 1985—2001, pres., 2002—, COO, 2003—05, CEO, 2005—07, bd. dir., 2004—, spl. adv. to CEO, 2007. Bd. dir. Share Our Selves, Calif. Office: Western Digital Corp 20511 Lake Forest Dr Lake Forest CA 92630-7741

SHAM, LU JEU, physics professor, physicist; b. Hong Kong, Apr. 28, 1938; s. T. S. and Cecilia Maria (Siu) Shen; m. Georgina Bien, Apr. 25, 1965; children: Kevin Shen, Alisa Shen. GCE, Portsmouth Coll., Eng., 1957; BS, Imperial Coll., London U., Eng., 1960; PhD in Physics, Cambridge U., Eng., 1963. Asst. rsch. physicist U. Calif., San Diego, 1963-66, assoc. prof., 1968-75, prof., 1975—, chair dept. physics, 1995-98, dean div. natural scis., 1985-89, Disting. physics prof., 2005—, asst. prof. physics Irvine, 1966-67; rsch. physicist IBM Corp., Yorktown Heights, NY, 1974-75. Reader Queen Mary Coll., U. London, 1967—68. Assoc. editor: Physics Letters A, 1992—; contbr. articles to profl. jours. Recipient Churchill Coll. studentship, Eng., 1960—63, U.S. Scientist award, Humboldt Found., 1978, Faculty Rsch. Letter award, 2000, Lamb medal, 2004, Chancellor Assocs. award for Excellence in Rsch., 1995; fellow, Guggenheim Found., 1984. Fellow: Am. Phys. Soc.; mem.: NAS, AAAS, Optical Soc. Am., Acad. Sinica Republic of China. Democrat. Avocations: tennis, folk dancing. Office: U Calif San Diego Dept Physics 0319 La Jolla CA 92093-0319 Office Phone: 619-534-3269. E-mail: lsham@ucsd.edu.

SHAMOUN, JOHN MILAM, plastic surgeon; b. Greenville, Miss., Apr. 1, 1960; s. Joseph David Shamoun and Phyllis Ann Joseph. BS, U. Miss., 1982, MD, 1986. Bd. cert. Am. Bd. Surgery, Am. Bd. Plastic and Reconstructive Surgery, Am. Bd. Facial Plastic and Reconstructive Surgery, Am. Bd. Forensic Examiners. Gen. surgeon U. South Ala., Mobile, 1986-91; plastic surgeon U. Tex., Dallas, 1991-93, Mt. Sinai Hosp., Miami Beach, Fla., 1993-94, Plastic Surgery Ctr. of the Pacific, Honolulu, 1994-95, Atlanta Plastic Surgery, 1994-95, Newport Inst. Plastic Surgery, Newport Beach, Calif., 1995; solo practice Beverly Hills, Palm Springs, Newport Beach, Calif. Legal cons. Law Firm of Charles G. Shamoun, Dallas, 1995—. Author: (books) Aesthetic Surgery, 1996, Microvascular Atlas, 1997; contbr. articles to profl. jours. Fellow ACS; diplomate Am. Bd. Plastic Surgery; mem. Am. Soc. Plastic and Reconstructive Surgery, Calif. Soc. Plastic Surgery, Anti Aging Soc., Alpha Omega Alpha. Roman Catholic. performed plastic surgery (facelift and forehead lift) on female celebrity, Christopher Templeton, live on the Internet, June 7, 1999; featured in NY Post, Dallas (Tex.) Morning News, London Times, Sunday Mirror (UK), LA bus. Jour., People mag., and Women's Jour. mag. Office: 360 San Miguel Dr Ste 406 Newport Beach CA 92660-7822

SHANAHAN, LAURI M., lawyer, former retail executive; b. 1962; BS in Fin., U. Colo., Boulder; JD, UCLA. Bar: Calif. 1987. Assoc. Thelen, Reid & Priest, San Francisco, 1987—92; dir. legal dept. Gap Inc., San Francisco, 1992—98, sr. v.p., gen. counsel, 1998—2004, corp. sec., 2000—04, chief compliance officer, 2001—04, exec. v.p., chief compliance officer, gen. counsel, corp. sec., 2004—06, chief legal and adminstrv. officer, 2006—08. Co-chmn. Lawyers Com. for Civil Rights.

SHANAHAN, MIKE (MICHAEL EDWARD SHANAHAN), former professional football coach; b. Oak Park, Ill., Aug. 24, 1952; m. Peggy, children: Kyle, Krystal. BS Phys. Edn., Ea. Ill. U., Charleston, 1974, MS Phys. Edn., 1975. Grad. asst. Ea. Ill. U., 1973—74; asst. coach U. Okla., 1975-76; offensive coord. No. Ariz. U., 1976—77, Ea. Ill. U., 1977—78, U. Minn., 1979—80, U. Fla., Gainesville, 1980—84, asst. head coach, 1983—84; receivers coach Denver Broncos, 1984-87; head coach L.A. Raiders, 1988-89; asst. coach Denver Broncos, 1989-91; offensive coord. San Francisco 49ers, 1992-94; head coach Denver Broncos, 1995—2008. Achievements include head coach of the Super Bowl Championship winning Denver Broncos, 1998, 1999. Avocations: golf, travel.*

SHANDLING, GARRY, comedian, scriptwriter, actor; b. Chgo., Nov. 29, 1949; s. Irving and Muriel S. BA in Marketing, U. Ariz. TV screenwriter: Sanford and Son, Welcome Back Kotter, Three's Company; guest host The Tonight Show, 1986-88; host Emmy Awards 1987, 88, Grammy Awards 1990, 91, 92; writer, prodr. (comedy specials) Garry Shandling: Alone in Las Vegas, 1984; exec. prodr., writer (comedy specials) It's Garry Shandling's Show 25th Anniversay Special, 1986, (TV Series) It's Garry Shandling's Show, 1986-90 (CableACE award best comedy series 1989, 90, CableACE award best actor in a comedy series, 1990), Garry Shandling: Stand-Up, 1991; writer, exec. prodr., dir. (TV Series) The Larry Sanders Show, 1992-98 (Emmy award for outstanding writing, 1998, CableACE award writing in a comedy series, 1993, 94, 95, 96, CableACE award best actor in a comedy series, 1995, 96); actor (films) Love Affair, 1994, Mixed Nuts, 1994, Doctor Doolittle (voice), 1998, Hurlyburly, 1998, What Planet Are You From? 2000 (also writer, prodr.), Town & Country, 2001, Run Ronnie Run!, 2002, Comedian, 2002, Over the Hedge (voice), 2006.

SHANK, CHARLES VERNON, science administrator, educator, physicist; b. Mt. Holly, NJ, July 12, 1943; s. Augustus Jacob and Lillian (Peterson) S.; m. Brenda Buckhold, June 16, 1969. BS, U. Calif., Berkeley, 1965, MS, PhD, 1969. Mem. tech. staff AT&T Bell Labs., Holmdel, NJ, 1969-76, head quantum physics and electronics dept., 1976-83, dir. Electronics Rsch. Lab., 1983-89; dir. Lawrence Berkeley Lab., prof. chemistry, physics, elec. engring. and computer scis. U. Calif., Berkeley, 1989—2004. Co-author over 200 sci. pubs. Recipient E. Longstreth medal Franklin Inst., Phila., 1982, Morris E. Leeds award IEEE, 1982, David Sarnoff award IEEE, 1989, Edgerton award Optical Soc. Engring., John Scott award, Edward P. Longstreth award Franklin Soc. Fellow AAAS, IEEE, Am. Phys. Soc. (George E.

Pake prize 1996, Arthur L. Schawlow prize 1997), Optical Soc. Am. (R. W. Wood prize 1981); mem. NAS, NAE, Am. Acad. Arts and Scis. Numerous patents in field. Home: 118 S Kalaheo Ave Kailua HI 96734-2932

SHANK, MAURICE EDWIN, aerospace engineer, consultant; b. NYC, Apr. 22, 1921; s. Edwin A. and Viola (Lewis) S.; m. Virginia Lee King, Sept. 25, 1948; children: Christopher K., Hilary L. Shank-Kuhl, Diana L. Shank. BS in Mech. Engring., Carnegie-Mellon U., 1942; D.Sc., MIT, 1949. Registered profl. engr., Mass. Assoc. prof. mech. engring. MIT, Cambridge, 1949-60; dir. advanced materials R&D Pratt & Whitney, East Hartford, Conn., 1960-70; mgr. materials engring. and rsch., 1971-72; dir. engring. tech., 1972-80; dir. engine design and structures engring. Pratt & Whitney, East Hartford, Conn., 1980-81, dir. engring. tech., 1981-85, dir. engring. tech. assessment, 1985-86; v.p. Pratt Whitney of China, Inc., East Hartford, 1986-87; pvt. exec. cons. to industry and govt., 1987—. Cons. editor McGraw-Hill Book Co., N.Y.C., 1960-80; adv. com. to mechanics div. Nat. Bur. Standards, Washington, 1964-69; vis. com. dept. mech. engring. Carnegie-Mellon U., Pitts., 1968-78; corp. vis. coms. depts. materials sci. and engring., dept. aeros. and astronautics MIT, 1968-74, 79-92; mem. rsch. and tech. adv. coun. com. on aero. propulsion NASA, Washington, 1973-77, mem. aero. adv. com., 1978-86; mem. aero. and space engring. bd. NRC, 1989-92; lectr. in field. Contbr. articles to profl. jours. Served to maj. U.S. Army Corps. of Engrs., Ordnance Corps, 1942-46, Middle East/North Africa. Fellow AIAA, ASME, AIME, Am. Soc. Metals; mem. Nat. Acad. Engring., Conn. Acad. Sci. and Engring. Clubs: Cosmos. Episcopalian. Avocations: boating, fishing.

SHANKS, ERIC, communications executive; b. 1972; Broadcast assoc. CBS Sports, 1993; broadcast assoc., NFL prodn. crew Fox Sports, 1994—95, broadcast assoc., NHL prodn. crew, 1995—96, graphics prodr., 1997—2004; v.p., Enhanced Programming Fox TV Network, 1999—2004; sr. v.p., Adv. Services and Content DirecTV, 2004—. Named one of 40 Executives Under 40, Multichannel News, 2006. Office: DirecTV Group Inc 2230 E Imperial Hwy El Segundo CA 90245

SHANKS, PATRICIA L., lawyer; b. Salt Lake City, Apr. 3, 1940; BA in Microbiology with honors, Stanford U., 1962; JD, U. Colo., 1978. Bar: Calif. 1978. Mng. ptnr. McCutchen, Doyle, Brown & Enersen, LA, 1990-94, ptnr., 1985—. Trustee L.A. County Bar Found., 2001-04. Recipient West Publishing award; Stork scholar. Mem. Order of the Coif, Practice in Environ. Law.

SHANLEY, JOHN PATRICK, playwright, screenwriter; b. NYC, 1950; s. Nicholas and Frances Shanley; m. Jayne Haynes (div.); adopted children: Nick, Frank. Grad., NYU. Disting. artist-in-residence The New Sch. for Drama, NYC, 2006—. Writer (plays) Rockaway, 1982, Welcome to the Moon, 1982, Danny and the Deep Blue Sea, 1984, Savage in Limbo, 1985, the dreamer examines his pillow, 1985, Women of Manhattan, 1986, All for Charity, 1987, Italian-American Reconciliation, 1988, The Big Funk, 1990, Beggars in the House of Plenty, 1991, Four Dogs and a Bone, 1993, Psychopathia Sexualis, 1996, Missing/Kissing, 1997, Cellini, 1998, Where's My Money, 2001, Dirty Story, 2003, Doubt, 2004 (Pulitzer Prize for drama, 2005, Tony Award for best play, 2005), Sailor's Song, 2004, Defiance, 2006, Down and Out, The Red Coat, Let Us Go Out Into the Starry Night, Out West, A Lonely Impulse of Delight, (screen adaptations) Alive, 1993, Congo, 1995, (teleplay) Live From Baghdad, 2002, (screenplays) Moonstruck, 1987 (Acad. Award for best writing- screenplay written directly for the screen, 1988), January Man, 1989, We're Back! A Dinosaur's Story, 1993, writer, assoc. prodr. Five Corners, 1987, writer, dir. Joe Versus the Volcano, 1990, Chain of Command, 2005, Doubt, 2008, Appeared in film Crossing Delancey, 1988. Served USMC. Recipient Ian McLellan Hunter Lifetime Achievement award, Writers Guild America, 2009. Fellow: Am. Acad. Arts & Scis. Office: c/o William Morris Agy 151 S El Camino Dr Beverly Hills CA 90212-2704*

SHANNON, CYNTHIA JEAN, biology professor; b. Phila., Feb. 19, 1961; d. Foster Lloyd and Nancy Ellen (Chapman) Shannon; m. Bryan Carey. AA, Fullerton Coll., Calif., 1981; BA in Psychology, Calif. State U., Fullerton, 1986; BS in Zoology, Calif. Poly. State U., 1985, MS in Biology, 1991; PhD in Biology, U. Calif., Riverside, 2008. Biology instr. Calif. State Poly. U., Pomona, Calif., 1986-91, Mt. San Antonio Coll., Walnut, Calif., 1986—, chair biology dept., 1996-97. Mem. AAAS, Ornithological Soc. N.Am., So. Assn. Naturalists, Golden Key, Phi Kappa Phi. Democrat. Avocations: bird watching, hiking, dogs, food and wine, reading. Office: Mt San Antonio Coll 1100 N Grand Ave Walnut CA 91789-1341 Office Phone: 909-594-5611. E-mail: cshannon@mtsac.edu.

SHANNON, MARYLIN LINFOOT, state legislator; b. LaGrande, Oreg., Sept. 7, 1941; BA in Edn., Ctrl. Wash. U. Mem. Oreg. Legislature, Salem, 1994—, mem. edn. com., mem. gen. govt. com., mem. health and human svcs. com., chair transp. com., mem. water and land use com. Republican. Home: 7955 Portland Rd NE Brooks OR 97305-9401 Office: S 218 State Capitol Salem OR 97310

SHANNON, MOLLY HELEN, actress; b. Shaker Heights, Ohio, Sept. 16, 1964; m. Fritz Chestnut, May 29, 2004; children: Stella Shannon Chestnut, Nolan Shannon Chestnut. BFA in Drama, NYU, 1987. Actor: (films) The Phantom of the Opera, 1989, Return to Two Moon Junction, 1995, Lawnmower Man 2: Beyond Cyberspace, 1996, Dinner and Driving, 1997, The Thin Pink Line, 1998, A Night at the Roxbury, 1998, Happiness, 1998 (Best Acting by Ensemble, Nat. Bd. Review, 1998), Daydream Believer, 1998, Analyze This, 1999, Never Been Kissed, 1999, Superstar, 1999, My 5 Wives, 2000, How the Grinch Stole Christmas, 2000, Wet Hot American Summer, 2001, Osmosis Jones, 2001, Serendipity, 2001, Shallow Hal, 2001, The Santa Clause 2, 2002, American Splendor, 2003, My Boss's Daughter, 2003, Good Boy!, 2003, Shut Up and Sing, 2006, Scary Movie 4, 2006, Marie Antoinette, 2006, Little Man, 2006, Talladega Nights: The Ballad of Ricky Bobby, 2006, Gray Matters, 2006, Year of the Dog, 2007, Evan Almighty, 2007, (voice) Igor, 2008,; (TV films) SNL Fanatic, 2000, Saturday Night Live Primetime Extra 1, 2001, The Music Man, 2003, The Twelve Days of Christmas Eve, 2004, (voice) The Amazing Screw-On Head, 2006, The Mastersons of Manhattan, 2007; (TV series) Saturday Night Live, 1995—2001, Cracking Up, 2004—06, Kath and Kim, 2008. Office: c/o Innovative Artists 1505 10th St Santa Monica CA 90401

SHANNON, THOMAS FREDERIC, German language educator; b. Cambridge, Mass., Mar. 16, 1948; m. Christine D. Höner. BA in German summa cum laude, Boston Coll., 1969; MA in German Lit., SUNY, Albany, 1973; MA in Theoretical Linguistics, Ind. U., 1975, PhD in Germanic Linguistics, 1982. Instr. in German Boston Coll., 1969-70; tchg. fellow in German SUNY, Albany, 1971-73; univ. fellow Ind. U., Bloomington, 1973-74, assoc. instr., 1974-76, 79-80; acting asst. prof. in Germanic linguistics U. Calif., Berkeley, 1980-82, asst. prof., 1982-87, assoc. prof., 1987-94, prof., 1994—, dir. lang. lab., 1989-92, assoc. dir. Berkeley Lang. Ctr., 1994-95, dir. abroad study ctr. Germany, 2000—02. Co-organizer Berkeley Confs. on Dutch Lang. and Lit., 1987, 89, 91, 93, 95, 97, 2005, 10th Interdisciplinary Conf. Netherlandic Studies, 2000; econs. presenter and spkr. in field. Mem. editl. adv. bd. Jour. Germanic Linguistics, 1998—; contbr. articles to profl. jours. With USAR, 1970-76. Grantee Fulbright Found., 1976-78, U. Calif. Berkeley, 1983-84, 94-95, ACLS, 1987, Internat. Assn. Netherlandic Studies, 1988, 91, 94, 97, 06, German Acad. Exch. Svc., summer 1996; NDEA fellow, 1969; Fulbright rsch./lectr. grantee Rijksuniversiteit Groningen, Netherlands, 1992-93; Inst. fuer deutsche Sprache summer rsch. grantee, Mannheim, Germany, 1997. Mem. MLA (exec. com. discussion group in Germanic philology 1989-94, discussion group for Netherlandic Studies 1995-99, divsn. on lang. change 1995-99), Am. Assn. Netherlandic Studies (exec. com. 1988—, editor newsletter 1989-95, series editor publs. 1994-2006), Am. Assn. Tchrs. German, Internat. Assn. Netherlandic Studies, Linguistic Soc. Am., Pacific Ancient and Modern Lang. Assn., European Linguistic Soc., Soc. Germanic Philology (v.p. 1991-92, 95-99), Internat. Cognitive Linguistics Soc., Alpha Sigma Nu. Home: 770 Rose Dr Benicia CA 94510-3709 Office: U Calif Dept German 5319 Dwinelle Hall Berkeley CA 94720-3243 Home Phone: 707-748-1493; Office Phone: 510-642-2004. E-mail: tshannon@berkeley.edu.

SHANSBY, JOHN GARY, investor; b. Seattle, Aug. 25, 1937; s. John Jay and Jule E. (Boyer) S.; m. Joyce Ann Dunsmore, June 21, 1959 (div.); children: Sheri Lee, Kimberly Ann, Jay Thomas; m. Barbara Anderson De Meo, Jan. 1, 1983 (div.); m. Jane Robinson Dettner, May 1, 1990. BA, U. Wash., 1959. Mktg. exec. Colgate-Palmolive Co., NYC, 1959-67; subs. pres. Am. Home Products Corp., NYC, 1968-71; v.p. Clorox Co., Oakland, Calif., 1972-73; ptnr. Booz, Allen & Hamilton, San Francisco, 1974-75; chmn. bd., chief exec. officer, dir. Shaklee Corp., San Francisco, 1975-86; co-founder, chmn. TSG Consumer Ptnrs., San Francisco, 1986—. Former chmn. Calif. State Commn. for Rev. of Master Plan Higher Edn.; founder J. Gary Shansby chair mktg. strategy U. Calif., Berkeley, U. Wash., Seattle; trustee Calif. State U. Mem. San Francisco C. of C. (past pres.), Villa Traverna Club, Pennask Lake Fishing Club (B.C.), Sigma Nu Republican. Office: TSG Consumer Ptnrs 600 Montgomery St Ste 2900 San Francisco CA 94111 Personal E-mail: jgshansby@tsgconsumer.com.

SHANSTROM, JACK D., federal judge; b. Hewitt, Minn., Nov. 30, 1932; s. Harold A. and Willian (Wendorf) S.; m. June 22, 1957; children: Scott S., Susan K. BA in Law, U. Mont., 1956, BS in Bus., 1957, LLB, 1957. Atty. Park County, Livingston, Mont., 1960-65; judge 6th Jud. Dist. Livingston, 1965-82; U.S. magistrate Billings, Mont., 1983-90; U.S. Dist. judge, 1990-96; chief judge U.S. Dist. Ct., Mont., 1996—. Capt. USAF, 1957-60. Office: US Dist Ct PO Box 985 Billings MT 59103-0985

SHAPIRO, LEO J., social researcher; b. NYC, July 8, 1921; m. Virginia L. Johnson, Feb. 9, 1952; children: David, Erik, Owen, Amy. BA, U. Chgo., 1942, PhD, 1952. Survey specialist Fed. Govt. Agy., Washington, 1941-45, Sci. Rsch. Assn., Chgo., 1948-52; prin., founder Leo J. Shapiro and Assocs., Chgo., 1952-91; pres. SAGE LLC Survival & Growth Enterprise, Tucson, 2002—. Bd. dirs. Field of Flowers. Fellow U. Chgo., 1949. Fellow Social Sci. Rsch. Coun.; mem. Am. Sociol. Assn., Phi Beta Kappa.

SHAPIRO, LUCY, molecular biology educator; b. NYC, July 16, 1940; d. Philip and Yetta (Stein) Cohen; m. Roy Shapiro, Jan. 23, 1960 (div. 1977); 1 child, Peter; m. Harley H. McAdams, July 28, 1978; stepchildren: Paul, Heather. BA, Bklyn. Coll., 1962; PhD, Albert Einstein Coll. Medicine, 1966. Asst. prof. Albert Einstein Coll. Medicine, NYC, 1967-72, assoc. prof., 1972-77, Kramer prof., chmn. dept. molecular biology, 1977-86, dir. biol. scis. divsn., 1981-86; Eugene Higgins prof., chmn. dept. microbiology, Coll. Physicians and Surgeons Columbia U., NYC, 1986-89; Joseph D. Grant prof. devel. biology Stanford (Calif.) U. Sch. Medicine, 1989-97, chmn. dept. devel. biology, 1989-97, Virginia and D.K. Ludwig prof. cancer rsch., dept. devel. biology, 1998—; dir. Beckman Ctr. Molecular and Genetic Medicine, Stanford U., 2001—. Mem. bd. sci. counselors NIH, Washington, 1980—84; mem. bd. sci. advisors G.D. Searle Co., Skokie, Ill., 1984—86; trustee Scientists Inst. for Pub. Info., 1990—94; mem. sci. adv. bd. SmithKline Beecham, 1993—2000, Anacor Pharms., Inc., 2001—, PathoGenesis, 1995—2000, Ludwig Found., 2000—, Glaxo Smith Kline, 2001—, Hatteras Ventures, 2008—; mem. adv. bd. Biodesign Inst., Ariz. State U., 2006—, Singapore Inst. Molecular and Cell Biology, 2006—, Lawrence Berkeley Nat. Labs., 2006—; bd. dirs. Anacor Pharms. Inc., 2001—, Gen-Probe Inc., 2008—. Editor: Microbiol. Devel., 1984; mem. editl. bd. Jour. Bacteriology, 1978-86, Trends in Genetics, 1987—, Genes and Development, 1987-91, Cell Regulation, 1990-92, Molecular Biology of the Cell, 1992-98, Molecular Microbiology, 1991-96, Current Opinion on Genetics and Devel., 1991—; contbr. articles to profl. jours. Mem. sci. bd. Helen Hay Witney Found., N.Y.C., 1986-94, Biozentrum, Basel, 1999-2001, Hutchinson Cancer Ctr., Seattle, 1999; mem. grants adv. bd. Beckman Found., 1999—; co-chmn. adv. bd. NSF Biology Directorate, 1988-89; vis. com., bd. overseers Harvard U., Cambridge, Mass., 1987-90; mem. sci. bd. Whitehead Inst., MIT, Boston, 1988-93; mem. sci. rev. bd. Howard Hughes Med. Inst., 1990-94, Cancer Ctr. of Mass. Gen. Hosp., Boston, 1994; mem. Presidio Coun. City of San Francisco, 1991-94; mem. pres. coun. U. Calif., 1991-97. Recipient Hirschl Career Scientist award, 1976, Spirit of Achievement award, 1978, Alumna award of honor Bklyn. Coll., 1983, Excellence in Sci. award Fedn. Am. Soc. Exptl. Biology, 1994, Gairdner Found. Internat. award, 2009; Jane Coffin Child fellow, 1966; resident scholar Rockefeller Found., Bellagio, Italy, 1996. Fellow AAAS, Am. Acad. Arts and Scis., Am. Acad. Microbiology, Calif. Coun. on Sci. and Tech.; mem. NAS (Selman A. Waksman award 2005), Inst. Medicine of NAS, Am. Philos. Soc., Am. Soc. Biochemistry and Molecular Biology (nominating com. 1982, 87, coun. 1990-93), Am. Heart Assn. (sci. adv. bd. 1984-87). Avocation: watercolor painting. Office: Stanford U Sch Medicine Beckman Ctr Dept Devel Biology Stanford CA 94305 Office Phone: 650-725-7678.*

SHAPIRO, MARC ROBERT, retail executive; b. North Hollywood, Calif., Apr. 1, 1959; s. Mel and Sally Shapiro; children: Julie Joseph Jack, Shapiro Shapiro. AA in Bus. Adminstrn., LA Harbor Coll., Wilmington, Calif., 1987; BSBA, U. Phoenix, 2006. Ops. mgr. Name Bears, Inc., Victorville, Calif., 1989—92; exec. v.p. Retail Project Mgrs., LLC, Irvine, Calif., 1992—2007; v.p., mng. dir. Crossmark, 2007. Mem.: Am. Numis. Assn. (life). Jewish. Avocations: travel, languages, home remodeling.

SHAPIRO, MARJORIE D., physics professor; AB in Physics magna cum laude, Harvard U., 1976; PhD in Physics, U. Calif., Berkeley, 1984. Rsch. assoc. Harvard U., 1985—87, asst. prof., 1987—89, Loeb assoc. prof., 1989; asst. prof. U. Calif., Berkeley, 1990—92, assoc. prof., 1992—94, prof., 1994—, chair dept. physics, 2004—. Rschr. Fermilab (CDF), Atlas experiment at CERN, Lawrence Berkeley Labs; spkr. in field. Contbr. articles to numerous profl. jours. Recipient Faculty Assoc. award, U. Calif., 1977, Presdl. Young Investigator award, NSF, 1989. Fellow: Am. Phys. Soc.; mem.: Phi Beta Kappa. Office: U Calif Dept Physics 366 Leconte Hall Berkeley CA 94720-7300 Office Phone: 510-666-3370. Office Fax: 510-643-8497. Business E-Mail: mdshapiro@lbl.gov.

SHAPIRO, MARK HOWARD, physicist, educator, dean; b. Boston, Apr. 18, 1940; s. Louis and Sara Ann (Diamond) S.; m. Anita Rae Lavine, June 8, 1961; children: David Gregory, Diane Elaine, Lisa Michelle. AB with honors, U. Calif., Berkeley, 1962; MS (NSF coop. fellow), U. Pa., 1963, PhD, 1966. Research fellow Kellogg Radiation Lab., Calif. Inst. Tech., Pasadena, 1966-68; vis. assoc. divsn. math., physics and astronomy Calif. Inst. Tech., 1976—; research assoc. Nuclear Structure Research Lab. U. Rochester (N.Y.), 1968-70; mem. faculty Calif. State U., Fullerton, 1970—2002, prof. physics, 1978—2002, acting assoc. dean Sch. Math., Sci. and Engring., 1985-86, acting dir. Office Faculty Research and Devel., 1986-87, chmn. physics dept., 1989-96, 98-01, prof. physics emeritus, 2002—; dir. tchr. enhancement program NSF, Washington, 1987-88. Tour speaker Am. Chem. Soc., 1983—85. Editor, pub.: The Irascible Professor, 1999; webmaster Calif. State U. Fullerton Emeriti Assn.; contbr. over 125 articles to profl. jours, amateur radio. Mem. pub. info. and edn. com. Calif. Task Force on Earthquake Preparedness, 1981—85; dist. team leader Fullerton Cmty. Emergency Response Team, 2007—; pres. Pasadena Young Democrats, 1967—68; bd. dirs. Calif. State U. Fullerton Found., 1982—85. Grantee Research Corp., 1971-74, Calif. Inst. Tech., 1977-78, U.S. Geol. Survey, 1978-85, Digital Equipment Corp., 1982, NSF, 1985-87, 90—; named Vol. of Yr. Cal State Fullerton Emeriti Assn. Fellow Am. Phys. Soc., Materials Rsch. Soc., Coun. on Undergrad. Rsch. (physics/astronomy councillor 1993-2002), Calif. State U. Emeritus and Retired Faculty Assn. (webmaster 2007—, treas. 2008—). Achievements include research in experimental nuclear physics, experimental nuclear astrophysics, geophysics and atomic collisions in solids. Office: Calif State Univ Physics Dept Fullerton CA 92834-6866 Business E-Mail: mshapiro2@roadrunner.com.

SHAPIRO, MARTIN, law educator; b. 1933; BA, UCLA, 1955; PhD, Harvard U., 1961. Instr. polit. sci. Harvard U., Cambridge, Mass., 1960-62, prof., 1971-74; asst. prof. Stanford U., Calif., 1962-65; assoc. prof. U. Calif., Irvine, 1965-70, prof. Berkeley, 1970, prof. law, 1977—, prof. San Diego, 1974-77. Author: Law and Politics in the Supreme Court, 1964, Freedom of Speech, The Supreme Court and Judicial Review, 1966, Supreme Court and Administrative Agencies, 1968, Courts, 1981, Who Guards the Guardians, 1987, Law, Politics and Judicialization, 2002. Mem. Law and Soc. Assn. (trustee 1992-95), Western Polit. Sci. Assn. (pres. 1978), Am. Acad. Arts and Scis., Am. Polit. Sci. Assn. (v.p. 1988). Office: U Calif Law Sch 886 Simon Hl Berkeley CA 94720-0001 Home Phone: 510-482-1206; Office Phone: 510-642-7190.

SHAPIRO, MARVIN SEYMOUR, lawyer; b. NYC, Oct. 26, 1936; s. Benjamin and Sally (Book) S.; m. Natalie Kover, July 12, 1959; children: Donna, Meryl. AB, Columbia U., 1957, LLB, 1959. Bar: D.C. 1959, Calif. 1962. Atty. appellate sect. Civil Div. U.S. Dept. Justice, Washington, 1959-61; ptnr. Irell & Manella, LA, 1962-99, mng. ptnr., 1992-97. Lectr. U. So. Calif. Tax Inst., Calif. Continuing Edn. of the Bar, Practising Law Inst. Articles editor Columbia Law Rev., 1958-59. V.p., bd. dirs. Jewish Fedn. Coun., L.A., 1985-95; treas. Alan Cranston Campaign, 1974, 80, 86; chmn. credentials com. Dem. Nat. Com., 1972-76; bd. dirs. L.A. Opera Co., 1997—. Mem. Beverly Hills Barristers (pres. 1970). Avocations: travel, golf. Home: 432 N Cliffwood Ave Los Angeles CA 90049-2620

SHAPIRO, MEL, playwright, educator, theater director; b. Bklyn., Dec. 16, 1935; s. Benjamin Shapiro and Lillian (Lazarus) Bestul; m. Jeanne Elizabeth Shapiro, Feb. 23, 1963; children: Joshua, Benjamin. BFA, MFA, Carnegie-Mellon U., 1961. Resident dir. Arena Stage, Washington, 1963-65; producing dir. Tyrone Guthrie Theater, Mpls., 1968-70; master tchr. drama NYU, NYC, 1970-80; guest dir. Lincoln Ctr. Repertory, NYC, 1970; dir. N.Y. Shakespeare Festival, NYC, 1971-77; prof. Carnegie Mellon U., Pitts., 1980-90, head. dept., 1980-87. Disting. prof. theater UCLA Sch. Theater, Film and TV, 1990—. Dir. N.Y.C. prodns. The House of Blue Leaves, 1970, Bosoms and Neglect, 1978, Marco Polo Sings a Solo, 1998, Taming of the Shrew, 1999, Big Love (L.A.), 2002; co-adaptor mus. Two Gentlemen of Verona, 1971 (Tony award); author: (plays) The Price of Admissions, 1984 (Drama-Logue mag. award), The Lay of the Land (Joseph Kesselring award 1990), A Life of Crime, 1993; (books) An Actor Performs, 1996, The Director's Companion, 1998. With U.S. Army, 1955-57. Recipient N.Y. Drama Critics award, 1971, 72, Obie award Village Voice, 1972, Drama Desk award, 1973, Drama-logue award, 1993. Mem. Soc. Stage Dirs. and Choreographers (founder, editor The Jour. 1978). Office: UCLA Sch Theatre Film & TV 405 Hilgard Ave Los Angeles CA 90095-9000 Business E-Mail: mshapiro@ucla.edu.

SHAPIRO, ROBERT, lawyer; b. Plainfield, NJ, Sept. 2, 1942; m. Linell Shapiro; children: Brent(dec.), Grant. BS in Fin., UCLA, 1965; JD, Loyola U., LA, 1968. Bar: Calif. 1969, U.S. Ct. Appeals (9th cir.) 1972, U.S. Dist. Ct. (ctrl., no. and so. dists.) Calif. 1982. Dep. dist. atty. Office of Dist. Atty., LA, 1969-72; sole practice LA, 1972—87; of counsel Bushkin, Gaims, Gaines, Jonas, LA, 1987-88, Christensen, Miller, Fink & Jacobs, LA, 1988-95; ptnr. Christensen, Glaser, Fink, Jacobs, Weil & Shapiro, LA, 1995—. Co-founder Legalzoom.com, Inc., 1999—. Author: When The Press Calls: A Lawyer's View, 1991,The Search For Justice: A Defense Attorney's Brief on the O.J. Simpson Case, 1996; co-author: (with Walt W. Becker) Misconception, 2001; frequent guest on network and cable TV shows and is called upon for legal expertise. Bd. dirs. Brent Shapiro Found. for Drug Awareness. Recipient Am. Jurisprudence award Bancroft Whitney, 1969; named Pro-bono Lawyer the Yr., State of Nevada; named one of 100 Super Lawyers, LA Daily Jour. Mem. Nat. Assn. Criminal Def. Lawyers, Calif. Attys. for Criminal Justice, Trial Lawyers for Pub. Justice (founder 1982), Century City Bar Assn. (Best Criminal

Def. Atty. 1993). Avocation: avid sport fan to basketball and boxing. Office: 10250 Constellation Blvd Fl 19 Los Angeles CA 90067 Office Phone: 310-553-3000, 310-556-7886. Office Fax: 310-556-2920. Business E-Mail: rs@chrisglase.com.

SHARER, KEVIN W., medical products executive; b. Clinton, Iowa, Mar. 2, 1948; m. Faye M. Sharer (div.); children: Heather, Keith; m. Carol Sharer. BS in Aero. Engring., US Naval Acad., 1970; MS in Aero. Engring., US Naval Postgraduate Sch., 1971; MBA, U. Pitts., 1982. Commd. lt. to lt. comdr. USN, 1970—78; with AT&T, 1978-82; cons. McKinsey & Co., 1982-84; pres., chief exec. officer GE, Princeton, NJ, 1984-89; exec. v.p., pres. bus. markets divsn. MCI Comm., Washington, 1989—92; pres., COO, bd. dirs. Amgen Inc., Thousand Oaks, Calif., 1992-2000, pres., CEO, 2000—, chmn., 2001—. Bd. dirs. UNOCAL, 3M, Northrup Grumman Corpn., 2003—. US Naval Acad. Found. Chmn. bd. trustees LA County Mus. Natural Hist. Office: Amgen Inc 1 Amgen Ctr Dr Thousand Oaks CA 91320-1799 Office Phone: 805-447-1000. Office Fax: 805-447-1010.

SHARKEY, (JOHN) MICK, biology educator; BS in Biology, Boise State Univ., 1989. Formerly in retail grocery industry; biology tchr. Parma (Idaho) H.S., 1989—. Recipient John 'Mick' Sharkey Day in Idaho, Feb. 27, 2006, Idaho Gov.; named Idaho Tchr. of Yr., 2006; named one of nation's top 5 percent of biology tchrs., Dolan DNA Learning Ctr., 2002; finalist GenzymeInvitrogen Biotech Educator award, 2007; grantee summer fellowship, Cold Spring Harbor Lab., NY. Office: Parma High Sch 908 N 8th Parma ID 83660 Business E-Mail: jsharkey@parmaschools.org.

SHARMA, SANTOSH DEVRAJ, obstetrician, gynecologist, educator; b. Kenya, Feb. 24, 1934; arrived in US, 1972; d. Devraj Chananram and Lakshmi (Devi) S. BS, MB, B.J. Medical Sch., Pune, India, 1960. House surgeon Sasson Hosp., Poona, India, 1960-61; resident in ob-gyn. various hosps., England, 1961-67; house officer Maelor Gen. Hosp., Wrexham, U.K., 1961-62; asst. prof. ob-gyn. Howard U. Med. Sch., Washington, 1972-74; assoc. prof. John A. Burns Sch. Med., Honolulu, 1974-78, prof., 1978—. Fellow Royal Coll. Ob-Gyn., Am. Coll. Ob-Gyn. Avocations: travel, photography, environmental protection. Office: 1319 Punahou St Rm 824 Honolulu HI 96826-1032 Business E-Mail: santosh@hawaii.edu.

SHARMA, SHIV KUMAR, geophysicist; b. India, July 2, 1946; came to U.S., 1977; m. Madhu Malaviya, Aug. 10, 1974; 2 children. BSc, Jiwaji U., India, 1968, MSc, 1973; PhD, Indian Inst. Tech., Delhi, 1980. Rsch. fellow IIT, Delhi, India, 1969-74; rsch. assoc. U. Leicester, 1974-77; with Geophysics Lab., Washington, 1977-80; rschr. Hawaii Inst. Geophysics & Planetology U. Hawaii, Honolulu, 1980—. Contbr. over 160 rsch. papers to profl. jours; patentee in field. Carnegie Postdoctoral fellow; rsch. grantee. Fellow Nat. Acad. Sci. (India); mem. Am. Geophys. Union, Am. Ceramic Soc., Am. Electrochem. Sco., Mineral Soc. Am., Optical Soc. Am., Pacific Congress, Soc. for Applied Spectroscopy. Avocations: reading, writing, travel. Office: U Hawaii Sch Ocean & Earth Sci & Tech Hawaii Inst Geophys & Planet 2525 Correa Rd Honolulu HI 96822-2219

SHARMAN, WILLIAM, professional basketball team executive; b. Abilene, Tex., May 25, 1926; m. Joyce Sharman; children from previous marriage: Jerry, Nancy, Janice, Tom. Student, U. So. Calif. Basketball player Washington Capitols, 1950-51, Boston Celtics, 1951-61; coach LA/Utah Stars, 1968-71, LA Lakers, 1971-76, gen. mgr., 1976-82, pres., 1982-88, spl. cons., 1991—. Author: Sharman on Basketball Shooting, 1965. Named to All Star 1st Team, NBA, 1956-59, 2nd Team, 1953, 55 (game MVP), 60, All League Team, 7 times, named Coach of Yr., 1972, One of Top Players in NBA History, league 50th anniversary, 1997, league leader free-throw percentage, 7 times; named to Basketball Hall of Fame, 1976, Naismith Basketball Hall of Fame (as player), 2004, as coach (3d man ever as both player and coach), 2004; named All-Am., twice; inductee U. So. Calif. Hall of Fame, 1994; Porterville H.S. gymnasium renamed in his honor, 1997; recipient John Wooden All-Time All-Am. award, 2003.

SHARON, TIMOTHY MICHAEL, physicist; s. Lester Clark and Ruth May Sharon; m. Carla Deon Colley, 1977. Student, Santa Ana Coll., 1966—68; BA, U. Calif., Irvine, 1970, MA, 1972, PhD, 1976. Jr. specialist solid state theory U. Calif., Irvine, 1976; rsch. asst. radiation physics Med. Ctr. and Sch. Medicine, 1976—77; cons. to attending staff Rsch. and Edn. Found., 1976—77; mktg. physicist Varian Assoc., Irvine, 1977—78; prin. engr., program mgr. Spectra Rsch. Sys., Newport Beach, Calif., 1977—82; v.p. Brewer-Sharon Corp., Newport Beach, Calif., 1981—86, Micor Instruments, Inc., Irvine, Calif., 1983—86; pres., CEO Medelec Instruments Co., Inc., Newport Beach, Calif., 1986—88; pres. Pacific Crest Enterprises, El Toro, Calif., 1988—91; pres., CEO Novus Group NA, El Toro, Calif., 1991—96; pres. Instafil, Lake Forest, Calif., 1995—2005; CEO Tyronex, Lake Forest, 2006—. Adj. faculty physics and engring. Columbia Pacific U., San Rafael, Calif., 1981—87; dean Sch. Engring., Newport U., Newport Beach, Calif., 1983—87; mem. adv. panel on pub. Am. Inst. Physics, 1974—75. Editor (assoc.): (jour.) Future Oncology, 2000—01; contbr. articles to profl. jours. Fellow: Brit. Interplanetary Soc. (assoc.); mem.: Nat. Hist. Soc., Am. Film Inst., Assn. Advancement Med. Instrumentation, IEEE, Am. Assn. Physicists in Medicine, Am. Phys. Soc., AAAS, Club 33, Smithsonian Instn., Nat. Geographic Soc., Intertel, Mensa, Acad. Magical Arts, Festival of Arts Laguna Beach, Alpha Gamma Sigma, Phi Theta Kappa, Sigma Pi Sigma.

SHARP, ANNE CATHERINE, artist, educator; b. Red Bank, NJ, Nov. 1, 1943; d. Elmer Eugene and Ethel Violet S. BFA, Pratt Inst., Bklyn., 1965; MFA, Bklyn. Coll., CUNY, 1973. Tchr. art Sch. Visual Arts, 1978-89, NYU, 1978, SUNY, Purchase, 1983, Pratt Manhattan Ctr., N.Y.C., 1982-84, Parsons Sch. Design, N.Y.C., 1984-90, Visual Arts Ctr. of Alaska, Anchorage, 1991, Anchorage Mus. Hist. and Art, 1991, 93, 94, 95, U. Alaska, Anchorage, 1994-96, Fashion Inst. Tech., SUNY, 1997-98; lectr. AAAS, The 46th Arctic Divsn. Sci. Conf., U. Alaska, Fairbanks, 1995, Cmty. Ch., Ho-Ho-Ku, N.J., 2005. One-person shows Pace Editions, N.Y.C., Ten/Downtown, N.Y.C., Katonah (N.Y.) Gallery, 1974, Contemporary Gallery, Dallas, 1975, Art in a Public Space, N.Y.C., 1979, Eatontown Hist. Mus., N.J., 1980, N.Y. Pub. Library Epiphany Br., 1988, Books and Co., N.Y., 1989, The Kendall Gallery, N.Y.C., 1990, Alaska Pacific U., Carr-Gottstein Gallery, Anchorage, 1993, Internat. Gallery Contemporary Art, Anchorage, 1993, Art Think Tank Gallery, N.Y.C., 1994, U.S. Geol. Survey, Reston, Va., 1994, Stonington Gallery, Anchorage, 1994, on TV Ltd. Benefit, N.Y.C., 1998-2000; group shows include Arnot Art Mus., Elmira, N.Y., 1975, Bronx Mus., 1975, Mus. Modern Art, N.Y.C., 1975-76, Nat. Arts Club, N.Y.C., 1979, Calif. Mus. Photography, Riverside, 1983-92, Jack Tilton Gallery, N.Y.C., 1983, Lincoln Ctr., N.Y.C., 1983, Cabo Frio Print Biennale, Brazil, 1983, Pratt Graphic Ctr., N.Y.C., 1984, State Mus. N.Y., Albany, 1984, Kenkeleba Gallery, N.Y.C., 1985, Hempstead Harbor Art Assn., Glen Cove, N.Y., 1985, Mus. Mod. Art, Weddel, Fed. Republic of Germany, 1985, Kenkeleba Gallery, N.Y.C., 1985, Paper Art Exhbn. Internat. Mus. Contemporary Art, Bahia, Brazil, 1986, Mus. Salon-de-Provence, France, 1987, Mus. Contemporary Art, Sao Paulo, Brazil, 1985-86, Salon de Provence, France, 1987, Adirondack Lakes Ctr. for Arts, Blue Mountain Lake, N.Y., 1987, Kendall Gallery, N.Y.C., 1988, Exhibition Ctr. Parsons Sch. Design, N.Y.C., 1989, F.M.K. Gallery, Budapest, Hungary, 1989, Galerie des Kulturbundes Schwarzenberg, German Dem. Republic, Q Sen Do Gallery, Kobe, Japan, 1989, Anchorage Mus. History and Art, 1990-91, 94, U. Alaska, Anchorage, 1990, 91, Coos Art Mus., Coos Bay, Oreg., 1990, Spaceship Earth, Mus. Internat. de Neu Art, Vancouver, Can., 1990, Councourse Gallery, Emily Carr Coll. Art and Design, 1990, Nat. Mus. Women in the Arts, Washington, 1991, Visual Arts Ctr. Alaska, 1991, 92, Nomad Mus., Lisbon, Portugal, 1991, Mus. Ostdeutsche Gallery, Regensberg, Germany, 1991, Mcpl. Mus. Cesley Krumlov (So. Bohemia) CSFK, Czechoslovakia, 1991, Böltmiche Dörter Exhbn. Hochstrass 8, Munich, 1992, BBC-TV, Great Britain, U.K., Sta. WXXI-TV, Rochester, N.Y., 1992-93, Site 250 Gallery Contemporary Art., Fairbanks, 1993, Santa Barbara (Calif.) Mus. Art, 1993, The Rochester (N.Y.) Mus. and Sci. Ctr., 1990-94, Space Arc: The Archives of Mankind, Time Capsule in Earth Orbit, Hughes Comm., Divec TV Satellite Launch, 1994, Stonington Gallery, Anchorage, 1994, 95, UAA Art Galley U. Alaska, 1995, Arctic Trading Post, Nome, Alaska, 1995, Allan P. Kikbuarts Ctr. Gallery at the Lawrenceville (N.J.) Sch., 1996, Blue Mountain Gallery, N.Y., 1998, The Book Room, Jersey City, 2000, 01, A.I.R. Gallery, NY, 2002, 03, 04, 05, 06, 07, 08, others; represented in permanent collections Smithsonian Instn., Nat. Air and Space Mus., Washington, Albright Knox Gallery, Buffalo, St. Vincent's Hosp. N.Y.C., N.Y. Pub. Libr., N.Y.C., U.S. Geol. Survey, Reston, Va., White House (Reagan, Bush adminstrns.), Libr. Congress, Washington, Site 250 Gallery Contemporary Art, Fairbanks, Alaska, New Rivers Press, NYC, Anchorage Mus. History and Art, others; Moon Shot series to commemorate moon landing, 1970-76, Cloud Structures of the Universe Painting series, 1980-86, Am. Landscape series, 1987-89, Thoughtlines, fall 1986, Swimming in the Mainstream with Her, U. Va., Charlottesville; author: Artist's Book - Travel Dreams U.S.A., 1989, Artworld-Welt Der Kunst, Synchronicity, 1989—, Art Think Tank: Projects in Art and Ecology, 1990—, The Alaska Series, 1990—, Portraits in the Wilderness, 1990—, Family History Project J. Lindemann, 2004—,; columnist: Anchorage Press, 1995. Sponsor Iditorod Trail Com., Libby Riddles. Tchg. fellow Bklyn. Coll., 1972; Artist-in-residence grantee Va. Ctr. for Creative Arts, 1974, Artpark, Lewiston, N.Y., 1980, Vt. Studio Colony, 1989; recipient Pippin award Our Town, N.Y.C., 1984, certificate of Appreciation Art in Embassy program U.S. Dept. State, 1996. Mem. Mus. Women in Arts, Pratt Inst. Alumni Assn., Internat. Assn.

SHARP, LEWIS INMAN, museum director, curator; b. NYC, Dec. 22, 1941; BA, Lewis & Clark Coll., 1965; MA, U. Del., 1968, PhD. Asst. curator paintings & sculpture Met. Mus. Art, NYC, 1972—75, assoc. curator, 1975—82, curator, adminstr. Am. Wing, 1982—89; dir. Denver Art Mus., 1989—. Office: Denver Art Mus 100 W 14th Ave Pkwy Denver CO 80204-2749 Office Phone: 303-640-2793.

SHARPE, ROLAND LEONARD, structural engineer, consultant; b. Shakopee, Minn., Dec. 18, 1923; s. Alfred Leonard and Ruth Helen Sharpe; m. Jane Esther Steele, Dec. 28, 1946; children: Douglas Rolfe, Deborah Lynn, Sheryl Anne. BSCE, U. Mich., 1947, MSE, 1949. Registered civil engr., structural engr. Designer Cummins & Barnard, Inc., Ann Arbor, Mich., 1947-48; instr. engring. U. Mich., 1948-50; exec. v.p. John A. Blume & Assocs., engrs., San Francisco, 1950-73; chmn., founder Engring. Decision Analysis Co., Inc., Cupertino, Calif., 1974-87; cons. earthquake engr. Sharpe Structural Engrs., Los Altos, Calif., 1987—. Mng. dir. EDAC, GmbH, Frankfurt, Germany, 1974—82; pres. Calif. Devel. & Engring. Co., Inc., Las Vegas, Nev., 1973—81; mem. nat. earthquake hazard reduction program adv. com. overviewing Fed. Emergency Mgmt. Agy., U.S. Geol. Survey, NSF and Nat. Inst. Stds. and Tech., 1990—93. Author (with J. Blume, E. G. Kost): (book) Earthquake Engineering for Nuclear Facilities, 1971; co-author: DOE Seismic Safety Manual, 1996; contbr. articles to profl. jours. Mem. Planning Commn., Palo Alto, 1955—60; mng. dir. Applied Tech. Coun., Palo Alto, 1973—83; dir. Earthquake Engring. Rsch. Inst., 1972—75, mem.; project dir., editor Tentative Provision Devel. Seismic Regulations Bldgs., 1978; tech. mgr., contbr., editor Data Processing Facilities: Guidelines Earthquake Hazard Mitigation, 1987. With USMC, 1942—46. Recipient citation for contbn. to constrn. industry, Engring. News Record, 1978—79, 1986—87, chmn. U.S. Joint Com. Earthquake Engring., 1982—88, citation for devel. of improvements in structural design and constrn. practices, Applied Tech. Coun., Japan Structural Cons. Assn., 1990. Fellow: Assn. Consulting Civil Engrs., India (hon.); mem.: ASCE (hon.; chmn. dynamic effects com. 1978—80, exec. com. structural divsn. 1980—84, chmn. 1983, exec. com. structural divsn. 1989—93, mgmt. group B 1989—93, Earnest E. Howard award 1994), Structural Engrs. World Congress (pres. 1995—2007, chair 1998), Structural Engrs. Assn. Calif. (coll. of fellows dir. 1971—73, chmn. seismology com. 1972—74), Earthquake Engring. Rsch. Inst. (hon.; dir. 1972—75), Am. Concrete Inst. (life), Structural Engrs. No. Calif. (hon.; dir. 1969—71), Japan Structural Cons. Assn. (hon.). Avocations: gardening, hiking, fly fishing. Home: 10320 Rolly Rd Los Altos Hills CA 94024-6568 Office: Sharpe Struct Engrs 10320 Rolly Rd Ste 1 Los Altos Hills CA 94024-6568 Office Phone: 650-948-9095. Personal E-mail: rsharpe3@mindspring.com.

SHARPE, WILLIAM FORSYTH, economics professor; b. Cambridge, Mass., June 16, 1934; s. Russell Thornley Sharpe and Evelyn Forsyth (Jillson) Maloy; m. Roberta Ruth Branton, July 2, 1954 (div. Feb. 1986); children: Deborah Ann, Jonathan Forsyth; m. Kathryn Dorothy Peck, Apr. 5, 1986. AB, UCLA, 1955, MA, 1956, PhD, 1961; DHL (hon.), DePaul U., 1997; D (hon.), U Alicante, Spain, 2003, U. Vienna, Austria, 2004. Economist Rand Corp., 1957—61; asst. prof. econs. U. Wash., 1961—63, assoc. prof., 1963—67, prof., 1967—68, U. Calif., Irvine, 1968—70; Timken prof. fin. Stanford (Calif.) U., 1970—89, Timken prof. emeritus, 1989—92, prof. fin., 1993—95, STANCO 25 prof. fin., 1995—99, prof. emeritus, 1999; prin. William F. Sharpe Assocs., 1986—92; chmn. Fin. Engines, Inc., 1996—2003. Author: The Economics of Computers, 1969, Portfolio Theory and Capital Markets, 1970; co-author: Fundamentals of Investments, 1989, 3d edit., 2000, Investments, 6th edit., 1999. With US Army, 1956—57. Recipient Graham and Dodd award, Fin. Analysts' Fedn., 1972, 1973, 1986—88, Nicholas Molodovsky award, 1989, Nobel prize in econ. scis., 1990, UCLA medal, 1998. Mem.: Am. Econ. Assn., Ea. Fin. Assn. (Disting. Scholar award 1991), Western Fin. Assn. (Enduring Contbn. award 1989), Am. Fin. Assn. (v.p. 1979, pres. 1980), Phi Beta Kappa.

SHARPLESS, JOSEPH BENJAMIN, retired county official; b. Takoma Park, Md., Feb. 4, 1933; s. William Raiford and Julia Maude (Rouse) Sharpless; m. Nancy Kathleen Steffen, July 28, 1962 (dec. Feb. 1988); 1 child, Carole Marie. BA, Earlham Coll., 1955; MS, Pa. State U., 1960. Instr. recreation Montgomery County Recreation Dept., Rockville, Md., 1957—58; from program supr. to dir. Recreation and Parks Dept., Livingston, NJ, 1959—70; chief recreation svc. Md.-Nat. Capital Park and Planning Commn. Prince George's County, Riverdale, Md., 1970—77, parks and recreation div. chief, 1977—95; ret., 1995. Mem. bd. regents, instr. Sch. Sports Mgmt. N.C. State U., 1989—92. Contbr. articles to profl. jours. Dir. volleyball Spl. Olympics Inc., 1994—2007; tech. del. Spl. Olympics World Summer Games, 1995, 1999, 2003, 2007, USA Nat. Spl. Olympics Games, 2006, Spl. Olympics Global Sports Res. Team, 2008; trustee U.S. Volleyball Edn. Found., 1976—2005, sec., 1996—2005; nat. volleyball chmn. AAU, 1966—69, 1972; nat. commr. U.S. Volleyball, 1976—81; mem. volleyball games staff 1996 Olympic Games, Atlanta; staff World Volleyball Congress, Atlanta, 1996; v.p. Montpelier Cmty. Assn., South Laurel, Md., 1983—84, pres., 1985; mem. Md. Sports Adv. Com., 1988—92, Md. State Games Commr., 1986—91; pres. NJAAU, 1968—70, volleyball chmn., 1961—70, Potomac Valley AAU, 1971—73. Recipient Pioneer Volleyball award, AAU, 1998, Breitkeutz Leadership award, 1972; named to, Earlham Coll. Athletic Hall of Fame, 2005. Fellow: Nat. Recreation Pks. Assn. (life Berman Profl. Citation award Mid-Atlantic Regional Coun. 1995, Disting. Svc. award 1995, Disting. Fellow award 1996); mem.: NJ Soccer Ofcls. Assn. (sec., treas. 1966—70), Nat. Capitol Area Bd. Volleyball Ofcls. (sec. 1985—89), Sch. and Coll. Soccer Ofcls. Assn. (sec., treas. 1965—70, del. Mid-Atlantic NRPA regional coun. 1969—79), Md. Recreation and Pk. Assn. (v.p. 1975—77, pres. 1977—78, Mem. of the Yr. 1975, citation 1985), NJ Recreation and Pks. Assn. (sec. 1965, v.p. 1966, pres. 1967, Disting. Fellow 1996), Am. Pk. and Recreation Soc. (bd. dirs. 1977—80, nat. coun., coun. affiliate pres.), Nat. Intercollegiate Soccer Ofcls. Assn. (sec. 1966—68, treas. 1968—70), US Volleyball Assn. (regional commr. 1965—78, nat. ofcl. 1967—96, bd. dirs. 1973—2008, v.p. 1974—90, exec. com. 1976—80, 1985—89, 1992—96, exec. cons. 1989—2004, corp. sec. 1992—96, mng. editor pubs. 1994—98, v.p. 1996—2004, 1996—2004, regional commr., referee, scorekeeper emeritus 2000, numerous awards). Independent. Mem. Soc. Of Friends. Home: 26205 S Cedarcrest Dr Sun Lakes AZ 85248-7206 Personal E-mail: chessycrab@aol.com.

SHARPLESS, K. BARRY, chemist, educator; b. Phila., Apr. 28, 1941; m. Jan Dueser, Apr. 28, 1965; children: Hannah, William, Isaac. BA, Dartmouth Coll., 1963; PhD, Stanford U., 1968; doctorate (hon.), Dartmouth Coll., 1995, Swedish Royal Inst. Tech., 1995, Tech. U. Munich, 1995, Cath. U. Louvain, Belgium, 1996. Postdoctoral assoc. Harvard U., Stanford U., to 1970, faculty dept. chemistry, 1977-80; faculty MIT, Cambridge, 1970-77, 1980-90; W. M. Keck prof. chemistry Scripps Rsch. Inst. and Skaggs Inst. of Chem. Biology, La Jolla, Calif., 1990—. Recipient Pual Janssen prize for Creativity in Organic Synthesis, Chem. Pioneer award, Am. Inst. Chemists, 1988, Prelog medal, Swiss Fed. Inst. Tech., Zurich, 1988, Scheele medal and prize, Swedish Acad. Pharm. Scis., Tetrahedron prize for Creativity in Organic Chemistry, 1993, King Faisal Internat. prize for sci., 1995, Microbial medal, Kitasato Inst., Tokyo, 1997, Harvey medal, Technion-Israel Inst. Tech., 1998, Carothers award, 1999, John Scott Medal, City of Phila, 2001, Benjarmin Franklin medal in chemistry, 2001, Wolf prize in chemistry, Wolf Found., Israel, 2001, Nobel prize in Chemistry, 2001; fellow A. P. Sloan, 1987—88, Guggenheim, 1987—88; scholar Camille and Henry Dreyfus Tchr. Fellow: AAAS, Am. Acad. Arts and Scis., Royal Soc. Chemistry (hon.); mem.: NAS (Award in Chemical Sciences 2000), Am. Chem. Soc. (Creative Work in Synthetic Organic Chemistry award 1983, Harrison Howe award Rochester chpt. 1987, Remsen award Md. sect. 1989, Arthur C. Cope award 1992, Roger Adams award 1997, Richards medal Northeastern sect. 1998, Top 75 Contbrs. to Chem. Enterprise 1998). Office: Scripps Rsch Inst BCC 315 10550 N Torrey Pines Rd La Jolla CA 92037-1000

SHARROW, MARILYN JANE, library administrator; b. Oakland, Calif. d. Charles L. and H. Evelyn Sharrow; m. Larry J. Davis. BS in Design, U. Mich., 1967, MALS, 1969. Libr. Detroit Pub. Libr., 1968-70; head fine arts dept. Syracuse U. Librs., NY, 1970-73; dir. libr. Roseville Pub. Libr., Mich., 1973-75; asst. dir. librs. U. Wash., Seattle, 1975-77, assoc. dir. librs., 1978-79; dir. librs. U. Man., Winnipeg, Canada, 1979-82; chief libr. U. Toronto, Canada, 1982-85; univ. libr. U. Calif., Davis, 1985—. Chair bd. North Regional Libr. Facility, 1999—2001; bd. dirs. Press U. Calif., 2005—08. Named Woman of Yr. in mgmt., Winnipeg YWCA, 1982; named a Woman of Distinction, U. Calif. Faculty Women's Rsch. Grp., 1985. Mem.: ALA, Can. Assn. Rsch. Libr. (pres. 1984—85), Calif. State Network Resources Libr. Com., OCLC-Rsch. Librs. Adv. Com. (vice-chair 1992—93), Assn. Rsch. Librs. (pres.-elect 1989—90, pres. 1990—91, chair sci. tech. work grp. 1994—98, leadership devel. task force 2006—07, rsch. collections com. 1993-95, 2000-2002, preservation com. 1997-99, 2003-05, chair membership com. 2007—). Office: U Calif Shields Libr 100 NW Quad Davis CA 95616-5292 Office Phone: 530-752-2110. E-mail: mjsharrow@ucdavis.edu.

SHARTIN, STACY D., lawyer; b. Mpls., Mar. 10, 1949; AB cum laude, U. Calif., LA, 1970, JD, 1973. Bar: Calif. 1973. Ptnr. Seyfarth, Shaw, Fairweather & Geraldson (now Syefarth Shaw), LA, 1980—. Mem. ABA, Calif. State Bar (exec. com. labor and employment sect.), Los Angeles County Bar Assn. Office: Seyfarth Shaw 2029 Century Park E Ste 3300 Los Angeles CA 90067-3063

SHATZ, CARLA J., biology professor, researcher; b. NYC; BA in Chemistry, Radcliffe Coll., 1969; MPhil, Univ. Coll., London, 1971; PhD, Harvard U., 1976, postdoc., 1976—78. Assoc. prof. neurobiology Sch. Medicine Stanford U., Palo Alto, Calif., 1985—89, prof. neurobiology, 1989—92; investigator Howard Hughes Med. Inst., 1994—2000; Class of 1943 prof. neurobiology U. Calif., Berkeley, 1992—2000; prof., chair dept. neurobiology Harvard Med. Sch., Boston, 2000—07, Nathan Marsh Pusey prof. neurobiology; head Bio-X program, prof. biological scis. and neurobiology Stanford U., 2007—. Mem. commn. on life scis. NRC, 1990—96; nat. adv. NIH, 1996—99; mem. coun. NAS, 1998—2001. Fellow: Inst. Medicine, Am. Philos. Soc., NAS, AAAS. Office: Clark Ctr 318 Campus Dr W 1 1 Rm W157 Stanford CA 94305-5437 Office Phone: 650-723-0534. Business E-Mail: cshatz@stanford.edu.

SHAVER, JAMES PORTER, retired education educator, dean; b. Wadena, Minn., Oct. 19, 1933; BA magna cum laude, U. Wash., Seattle, 1955; MAT, Harvard U., Cambridge, Mass., 1957, EdD, 1961. Instr. Grad. Sch. Edn., Harvard U., 1961-62; asst. prof., dir. Social Studies Curriculum Ctr., Ohio State U., Columbus, 1964-65; assoc. prof. Utah State U. Coll. Edn., Logan, 1962-64, prof., 1965—, chmn. Bur. Rsch. Svcs., 1965-93, assoc. dean rsch., 1978-93, acting dean Sch. Grad. Studies, 1990-91, 92-93, dean, 1993-99, prof. emeritus secondary edn., 1999—. Mem. Commn. Youth Edn. for Citizenship, ABA, 1975-81; mem. edn. task force Am. Hist. Assn.-Am. Polit. Sci. Assn. Project '87, 1981-84; tech. advisor Nat. Ctr. on Effective Secondary Schs., 1988-91; mem. adv. bd. program in civic and moral edn. Inst. for Philosophy and Pub. Policy, U. Md., 1992—; mem. steering com. Nat. Assessment Ednl. Progress Civics Consensus Project, 1995-96. Co-author: Teaching Public Issues in the High School, 1966, 2d edit., 1974, Facing Value Decisions: Rationale-building For Teachers, 1976, 2d edit., 1982; editor: Building Rationales for Citizenship Education, 1977, Handbook of Research on Social Studies Teaching and Learning, 1991; co-editor: Democracy, Pluralism, and the Social Studies, 1968; also others. Recipient Outstanding Svc. and Tchg. award, Utah Coun. for the Social Studies, 1975, 1978, Lifetime Achievement award, 1998. Mem. AAAS, AAUP, Nat. Coun. Social Studies (pres. 1976, Exemplary Rsch. award 1977, Exemplary Rsch. Editor award 1991), Am. Ednl. Rsch. Assn., Phi Beta Kappa, Phi Kappa Phi. Home: 11 Bridger Mountain Rd N Montana City MT 59634-9641 Business E-Mail: jim.shaver@usu.edu.

SHAW, ANTHONY, pediatric surgeon, retired educator; b. Shanghai, Oct. 31, 1929; s. Bruno and Regina (Hyman) S.; m. Iris Violet Azian, Mar. 12, 1955; children: Brian Anthony, Diana Shaw Clark, Daniel Aram. BA cum laude, Harvard Coll., 1950; MD, NYU, 1954. Diplomate Am. Bd. Surgery; cert. spl. competence pediat. surgery. Intern and resident in surgery Columbia-Presbyn. Med. Ctr., NYC, 1954-56, 58-62; resident in pediat. surgery Babies Hosp., NYC, 1962; asst. prof. surgery Columbia U. Coll. Physicians and Surgeons, NYC, 1965-70; chief pediat. surgery St. Vincent's Hosp., NYC, 1963-70, Harlem Hosp. Ctr., NYC, 1965-70; prof. surgery U. Va., Charlottesville, 1970-81, chief pediat. surgery Med. Ctr., 1970-81; prof. surgery UCLA, 1981-2001, emeritus prof. surgery, 2001—; chief pediat. surgery Olive View-UCLA Med. Ctr., Sylmar, 1986-2001, cons. surgeon, 2003—. Expert witness on child abuse L.A. Superior Ct., 1986—; chmn. gov.'s adv. com. child abuse and neglect Commonwealth of Va., 1975-80; vis. prof. pediat. surgery People's Republic of China, 1985. Contbr. more than 220 articles to profl. jours. Mem. Gov.'s Task Force on Child Abuse Va., 1973-74. Capt. U.S. Army, 1956-58. Recipient Commrs. award Va. Dept. Social Svcs., 1980, award Gov.'s Adv. Bd., Cert. of Recognition HEW, 1978. Fellow Am. Pediat. Surg. Assn. (sec. 1982-85), ACS (v.p. 1987-89); mem. AMA, Pacific Coast Surg. Assn. (v.p. 1989-90), Am. Soc. Law, Medicine, and Ethics, Am. Profl. Soc. on Abuse of Children, Alpha Omega Alpha. Avocation: writing humor. Home and Office: One S Orange Grove Blvd # 9 Pasadena CA 91105 Home Phone: 626-796-8588; Office Phone: 626-796-8588. Personal E-mail: shawpas@pacbell.net.

SHAW, ARTHUR E., conductor; Studied with, Sidney Harth; degree, Wichita State U.; postgrad. in Conducting, U. Mich., 1982-85. Asst. condr. Ark. Symphony Orch., 1977-79; music dir., condr. Adrian (Mich.) Symphony Orch., 1979-87, Rogue Valley Symphony, Ashland, Oreg., 1987—. Condr. Rogue Opera, 1987-89; founding dir., guest condr. Youth Symphony So. Oreg.; guest condr. Little Rock Cmty. Theatre, 1979, Summer Music Camp No. Ariz. U., 1988, Ota (Japan) Jr. Symphony, 1990, Jalisco Philharm., Mex., 1992, Ctrl. Oreg. Symphony, 1994, Britt Festivals, 1996. James Robertson Meml. Conducting scholar, 1976-77. Office: Rogue Valley Symphony SOU Music Hall 1250 Siskiyou Blvd Ashland OR 97520-5010

SHAW, ELEANOR JANE, newspaper editor; b. Columbus, Ohio, Mar. 23, 1949; d. Joseph Cannon and Wanda Jane (Campbell) S. BA, U. Del., 1971. With News-Jour. newspapers, Wilmington, Del., 1970-82, editor HEW desk, asst. met. editor, 1977-80, bus. editor, 1980-82; topics editor USA Today, 1982-83; asst. city editor The Miami Herald, 1983-85; projects editor The Sacramento Bee, 1985-87, news editor, 1987-91, exec. bus. editor, 1991-93, editor capitol bur. news, 1993-95, state editor, 1995-99; mgr. employee comm. The McClatchy Co., Sacramento, 1999—2004; associate TMT Worldwide, 2004—08; pres. Shaw Media Consulting, 2008—. Bd. dirs. Del. 4-H Found., 1978—83, Safety Ctr., Inc., Sacramento, 2003—, chair, 2007—08. Mem. Calif. Soc. Newspaper Editors (bd. dirs. 1990-96), No. Calif. Wine Soc. (v.p. 1987-93, pres. 1993-2002). Office Phone: 916-849-6781. Personal E-mail: ellieshaw@sbcglobal.net. Business E-Mail: elliejshaw@gmail.com.

SHAW, JANE ELIZABETH, retired pharmaceutical company executive; b. Droitwich, Eng., Feb. 3, 1939; came to U.S., 1964; m. Peter Fredrick Carpenter, Sept. 25, 1982; 1 son, Jonathan. BS, U. Birmingham, Eng., 1961, PhD in Physiology, 1964. Rsch. scientist Worcester Found., Shrewsbury, Mass., 1964-70; asst. prof. Stanford U., Palo Alto, Calif., 1970-72; prin. scientist ALZA Corp., Palo Alto, 1970-71, project/program dir., 1972-80, v.p. R & D, 1980-84, exec. v.p. rsch., 1984-87, pres., COO, 1987—94; founder Stable Network, 1995—; chmn., CEO Nektar Therapeutics (formerly, Aerogen Inc.), 1998—2005. Bd. dirs. McKesson Corp., 1992—, Intel Corp., 1993—, OfficeMax Inc., 1994—2006, Nektar Therapeutics (formerly, Aerogen Inc.), 1998—2005. Contbr. over 110 sci. papers to profl. publs.; patentee in field. Med. Rsch. Coun. scholar U. Birmingham, 1961-64; hon. rsch. fellow U. Birmingham, 1966. Mem. AAAS, Am. Physiology Soc., Am. Soc. Clin. Pharmacology and Therapeutics, Am. Assn. Pharm. Scientists, N.Y. Acad. Scis., Sigma Xi.*

SHAW, JEFFREY WILLIAM, gas industry executive; b. Salt Lake City, Nov. 9, 1958; s. William R. Jr. and Janet (Engar) S.; m. Cynthia Roberts, July 3, 1984; children: Morgan, Lauren, Catherine, Michael. BA in Acctg., U. Utah, 1983. CPA, Nev. With audit div. Arthur Andersen & Co., Dallas, 1983-85, Las Vegas, Nev., 1985-88; dir. internal audit SW Gas Corp., Las Vegas, Nev., 1988—91, controller, chief acctg. officer, 1991—93, v.p., controller, chief acctg. officer, 1993—94, v.p., treas., 1994—2000, sr. v.p. fin., treas., 2000—02, sr. v.p. gas resources & pricing, 2002—03, pres., 2003—04, CEO, 2004—. Active Boy Scouts Am., Dallas, 1985, Las Vegas, 1987—. Mem. AICPA, Am. Law Assn. (bd. dirs.), Nev. Soc. CPAs, U. Nev. Las Vegas Found. (bd. trustees). Republican. Mem. Lds Ch. Avocations: writing, guitar, composing music, golf, basketball. Office: SW Gas Corp PO Box 98510 Las Vegas NV 89193-8510

SHAW, MICHAEL, biologist, educator; b. Barbados, W.I., Feb. 11, 1924; s. Anthony and Myra (Perkins) S.; m. Jean Norah Berkinshaw, Oct. 16, 1948; children: Christopher A., Rosemary E., Nicholas R., Andrew L. BSc, McGill U., 1946, MSc, 1947, PhD, 1949, DSc (hon.), 1975, U. B.C., 2003, U. Saskatchewan, 2008. NRC Can. postdoctoral fellow Botany Sch., Cambridge U., 1949-50; assoc. prof. biology U. Sask., Canada, 1950-54, prof., 1954-67, prof., head dept. biology, 1961-67; dean faculty agrl. scis. U. B.C., Canada, 1967-75, v.p. acad. devel., 1975-81, acad. v.p., provost, 1981-83, univ. prof., 1983-89, univ. prof. emeritus, 1989—. Mem. Sci. Coun. Can., 1976-82, Natural Scis. and Engring. Rsch. Coun. Can., 1978-80. Contbr. articles to profl. jours. Recipient Queen's Silver Jubilee medal, 1977, Gold medal Biol. Coun. Can., 1983. Fellow Royal Soc. Can. (Flavelle medal 1976), Can. Phytopath. Soc., Am. Phytopath. Soc.; mem. AAAS, Can. Bot. Assn., Can. Soc. Plant Physiologists (Gold medal 1971), Am. Soc. Plant Biologists. Home: 1792 Western Pky Vancouver BC Canada V6T 1V3

SHAW, NINA L., lawyer; b. NYC; BA, Barnard Coll., 1976; JD, Columbia U., 1979. Bar: Calif. 1981. Founding ptnr., entertainment law Del, Shaw, Moonves, Tanaka, Finkelstein & Lezcano, Santa Monica, Calif. Bd. dirs. The Montel Williams MS Found.; mem. Barbara A. Black Professorship Com. Recipient Disting. Alumna/us Award, Columbia Black Law Students Assn., 2002, Women in Film Crystal award, 2005; named one of The 100 Most Powerful Women in Entertainment, Hollywood Reporter, 2003, 2004, 2006, 2007, 100 Power Lawyers, 2007, The 100 Most Influential Blacks in America. Mem.: State Bar Calif., LA County Bar Assn., Kernochan Ctr. Law, Media and Arts (West Coast adv. bd.), Black Women Lawyers Assn. Office: Del, Shaw, Moonves, Tanaka & Finkelstein 2120 Colorado Ave Ste 200 Santa Monica CA 90404 Office Phone: 310-979-7900. Office Fax: 310-979-7999.

SHAW, R. DANIEL, anthropology professor; b. Seattle, Wash., Nov. 19, 1943; s. R. Stanley and Laurel M. Shaw; m. Karen A. Perona, July 30, 1966 (dec. Oct. 23, 2005); m. Georgia R. Grimes, Aug. 19, 2006; children: Richard D., Ryan S., Robert J. BA in Anthropology & Oriental Studies, U. Ariz., Tucson, 1967, MA in Anthropology, 1968; PhD in Anthropology, U. Papua New Guinea, Port Moresby, 1976. Consulting anthropologist US Pub. Health Svc., Tucson, 1966—68; anthrop. linguist, bible translator Summer Inst. Linguistics, Ukarumpa, Papua New Guinea, 1969—81, internat. anthropology cons. Dallas, 1978—; prof. anthropology and transl. Fuller Grad. Sch. Intercultural Studies, Pasadena, Calif., 1982—. Editor: (book) Kinship Studies in Papua New Guinea, 1974; author: Samo Social Structure: A Socio-Linguistic Approach to Understanding Interpersonal Relationships, 1976, Health Concepts and Attitudes of the Papago Indians, 1968, Transculturation: The Cultural Factor in Translation and Other Communication Tasks, 1988 (Top Ten List, 1988), Kandiya: Samo Ceremonialism and Interpersonal Relationships, 1990, From Longhouse to Village: Samo Social Change, 1996; co-author: Understanding Folk Religion: A Christian Response to Religious Belief and Practice, 1999 (Top Ten List, 2000), Communicating God's Word in a Complex World: God's Truth or Hocus-Pocus?, 2003 (Top Ten List, 2004); contbr. articles to profl. jours., papers at soc. meetings, and confs. on anthropology, translation, and mission. Dir. Mission Aviation Fellowship, Redlands, Calif., 1994—2003, Nampa, Idaho, 2005—08; internat. trustee MAF Internat., Ashford, Kent, 2007—08; dir. Providence Mission Homes, Pasadena, Calif., 1997—2008. Recipient Peer Recognition, Directory Am. Scholars, 2002, C. Davis Weyerhaeuser award for Faculty of Yr., Fuller Theol. Sem., 2006, Twenty-five yr. Svc. award, 2007; vis. scholar, U. Stellenbosch, 2004—05. Fellow: Polynesian Soc. (life), Am. Anthrop. Assn. (life); mem.: Summer Inst. Linguistics, Assn. of Evang. Professors of Mission, Am. Soc. Missiologists. Achievements include partnerships with academic institutions in India, Indonesia, Papua New Guinea and Central Africa. Office: Fuller Grad Sch Intercultural Studies 135 N Oakland Ave Pasadena CA 91182 Business E-Mail: danshaw@fuller.edu.

SHAW, RICHARD EUGENE, cardiovascular researcher; b. Springfield, Ohio, Jan. 20, 1950; s. Eugene Russell and Marjorie Caroline Shaw; m. Nov. 26, 1976; 2 children. BA, Duquesne U., 1972; MA, U.S. Internat. U., San Diego, 1977; PhD, U. Calif., San Francisco, 1984. Cert. nuc. med. technologist. Nuclear Medicine Tech. Cert. Bd. Staff nuc. med. technologist Scripps Meml. Hosp., La Jolla, Calif., 1975-79; rsch. asst. U. Calif. San Francisco Sch. Medicine, 1980-85; mgr. rsch. programs San Francisco Heart Inst., Daly City, Calif., 1985-87, dir. rsch., 1988-90, dir. rsch. and ops., 1991—2003; dir. rsch., quality and edn. Sutter Pacific Heart Ctrs., 2003—08, Calif. Pacific Med. Ctr.'s Heart and Vascular Ctr., 2009—. Sr. advisor steering com. for databases Daus. of Charity Nat. Health Sys., St. Louis, 1993-96. Editor-in-chief Jour. Invasive Cardiology, 1989—; contbr. articles to profl. jours; chpts. to books. Coach Am. Youth Soccer Orgn. and Youth Baseball Assn., bd. dirs., Burlingame, Calif., 1990-94; pres. Burlingame H.S. Athletic Boosters, 2000—. Named Impact Player of Yr. award, Mi-Co Corp., 2005. Fellow Am. Coll. Cardiology (nat. cardiac database com., outcomes assessment subcom. 1998—, NCDR task force 2001—, publs. subcom. 2001—), Am. Coll. Angiology; mem. Am. Heart Assn., Soc. for Clin. Trials, N.Y. Acad. Scis., Am. Statis. Assn., Am. Med. Informatics Assn., Soc. Behavioral Medicine. Avocation: music. Office: Sutter Pacific Heart Ctr CPMC 2200 Webster # 303 San Francisco CA 94115 Home Phone: 650-678-2375. Business E-Mail: shawr@sutterhealth.org.

SHAY, ROSHANI CARI, political science professor and healthcare professional; b. Milw., Oct. 5, 1942; d. Walter John and Dorothee May (Dahnke) O'Donnell; 1 child, Mark Sather. Student, Willamette U., 1960—63; BA, U. Oreg., 1968, MA, 1971, PhD, 1974. Adminstrv. asst. Dept. of Youth Svcs., Lubbock, Tex., 1963; tchg. asst., instr. U. Oreg., Eugene, 1969-72; vis. asst. prof. Oreg. State U., Corvallis, 1973-74, Willamette U., Salem, Oreg., 1973-79, Lewis and Clark Coll., Portland, Oreg., 1976, 78; from asst. prof. to prof. Western Oreg. U., Monmouth, 1979—2003, chair history, polit. sci., pub. adminstrn. dept., 1991-94, chair social sci. divsn., 1994-2000; exec. dir. Hawaii Wellness Inst., Honolulu, 2003—. Author: (with others) The People of Rajneeshpuram, 1990, Annual Yearbook in the Sociology of Religion, 1995, (simulation) European Unity Project, 1982; co-prodr., actress: Aging Is Not for Sissies, 2006-. Co-founder, v.p., sec.-treas Ind. Opportunities Unltd., Salem, 1986—; co-founder, sec. Inst. for Justice and Human Rights, San Francisco, 1988-94; bd. dirs. Oreg. UN Assn., Portland, 1982-00, Salem UN Assn., 1982-91; v.p., pres., bd. dirs. Garten Svcs. Inc. for Disabled, Salem, 1989-03; pres. Assn. Oreg. Faculties, 1989-91; adv. bd. Connections Program for Disabled Deaf, Salem, 1989-03; pres., bd. dirs. Model UN of the Far West, San Francisco, 1981-84, 86-88, 95-00, 02-03; Hawaii Alliance Nonprofit Orgns., 2006-. Danforth Found. fellow, 1968-74; named Woman of Achievement YWCA Tribute, Salem, 1990, Mem. of Yr., Oreg. Rehab. Assn., 1995. Mem. AAUW, Am. Fedn. Tchrs. (v.p., legis. officer local 2278 1982-88), Western Polit. Sci. Assn., Communal Studies Assn., Mental Health Assn. Oreg., Oreg. Acad. Sci., Soc. for Utopian Studies, Oreg. Hosp. Found., Oreg. Internat. Coun., Oreg. Mediation Assn., Phi Kappa Phi (pres., sec., treas.), Phi Alpha Delta (Outstanding Faculty Advisor in USA, 2000), Oreg. Women's Polit. Caucus. Democrat. Avocations: volunteer work with multiply disabled deaf, reading, meditation. Office: Hawaii Wellness Inst 3670 Kalihi St Honolulu HI 96819 Home: 106 Independence Way Independence OR 97351 Office Phone: 808-228-9028. Business E-Mail: shayr@wou.edu, hwi@earthlink.net.

SHAYE, ROBERT KENNETH, film company executive; s. Max and Dorothy S.; m. Eva Lindstern, 1970; children: Katja, Juno. BBA, U. Mich., 1960; postgrad., Sorbonne U., 1961; JD, Columbia U., 1964. Bar: N.Y. 1967. Founder, co-chmn., co-CEO New Line Cinema, NYC, 1967—2008. Trustee Am. Film Inst. Recipient 1st prize Rosenthal competition Soc. Cinematologists, 1964, cert. of merit Inst. Copyrights and Patents, U. Stockholm, 1966, award ASCAP/Nathan Burkan Meml. competition, 1964; Fulbright scholar, 1964-66. Mem. Motion Picture Pioneers (bd. dirs.).

SHAYKIN, LEONARD P., investor; b. Chgo., Nov. 17, 1943; s. Lawrence L. and Rose (Yaker) S.; m. Norah Josephine Kan, June 26, 1966 (div.); children: Benjamin, Gabriel, Rebecca. BA, U. Chgo., 1965, MA, 1966, MBA, 1973; postgrad., U. Sussex, Brighton, Eng., 1970. Investment officer First Capital Corp., Chgo., 1970-74; asst. to chmn. Apeco Corp., Chgo., 1975-76; div. pres. Brown Mfg. Co., Woodstock, Ill., 1976-78; v.p. Citicorp Venture Capital, NYC, 1978-79; v.p., dir. Citicorp Capital Investors, NYC, 1979-82; mng. ptnr. Adler & Shaykin, NYC, 1983-94; chmn., dir. NaPro BioTherapeutics, Inc., Boulder, Colo., 1994—, Kimeragen, Inc., Newtown, Pa., 1995—; vice chmn., dir. To Life! LLC, Del Mar, Calif., 1996—. Bd. dirs. Avigen, Inc., The Jerusalem Post; chmn. The Neuroblastoma Found.; governing trustee The Jackson Lab.; trustee U. Chgo. Grad. Sch. Bus. Chmn. Hebrew Arts Sch. and Merkin Concert Hall, N.Y.C., 1983-86. Avocations: sailing, skiing. Office: Napro Biotherapeutics 2945 Wilderness Pl Boulder CO 80301-2255

SHEA, DEBBIE BOWMAN, state legislator; b. Butte, Mont., June 26, 1951; divorced. BS in Elem. Edn., Eastern Mont. Coll., 1974; MA in Edn., U. Mont., 1989. Formerly tchr. 8th grade pub. schs.; mem. Mont. Ho. of Reps., 1994-96, Mont. Senate, Dist. 18, Helena, 1997—; mem. joint appropriations subcom. on corrections/pub. safety Mont. Senate; mem. edn. and cultural resources com. Mont. State Senate, mem. hwys. and transp. com., mem. fin. and claims com. Democrat. Home: 100 Moon Ln Butte MT 59701-3975

SHEA, DION WARREN JOSEPH, academic administrator, fundraiser; b. New London, Conn, June 10, 1937; s. Frank Steven and Violette Marie (Dion) S.; m. Elizabeth M. Siaba, Dec. 31, 1986; children from previous marriage: Dion Warren Joseph, Nancy Wallace. AB, ScB in Physics, Brown U., 1959; MA in Physics, Boston U., 1962; PhD in Physics, U. Colo., 1968. Mem. tech. staff RCA, 1959-62; asst. prof. physics Creighton U., 1967-68; NRC/Environ. Sci. Svc. Adminstrn. fellow, rsch. assoc. Environ. Sci. Svc. Adminstrn., Boulder, Colo., 1968-70; exec. dir. Soc. Physics Students, Am. Inst. Physics, 1970-87, mgr. edn. div., 1972-87; cons. ednl. and computer sytems, 1988—; dir. alumni affairs US Mcht. Marine Acad., Kings Point, NY, 1989-93; asst. dir. devel. CUNY Grad. Sch., 1993-99. Contbr. scientific papers to profl. jours. Fellow AAAS; mem. Am. Phys. Soc., Am. Assn. Physics Tchr., Assn. Coll. Honor Soc. (exec. com. 1984-86), Am. Soc. Assn. Exec., Assn. Fundraising Profl., Coun. Advancement and Support Edn., Sigma Xi, Sigma Pi Sigma, Sigma Chi, Huntington Bicycle Club (treas. 2000-01), Colo. Mountain Club, Port Dive Club (treas. 1980-83). Home: 11821 Lionel Ln Golden CO 80403 Home Phone: 303-642-0699; Office Phone: 303-642-0699. Personal E-mail: dion_shea@yahoo.com.

SHEA, KEVIN MICHAEL, lawyer; b. Indpls., Dec. 23, 1951; s. James Louis and Elizabeth (Walker) S.; children: Brendan Alkire, Maura Kathryn. BS, U. Colo., 1973; JD, U. Detroit, 1976. Bar: Colo. 1976, U.S. Dist. Ct. D.C. 1976, U.S. Ct. Appeals (10th cir. 1980), U.S. Supreme Ct. 1982. Dep. dist. atty., Boulder, Colo., 1976—79; shareholder, dir., assoc. Roath & Brega P.C., Denver, 1980—84; spl. counsel, ptnr. Holme Roberts & Owen, Denver, 1984—94; ptnr. Ballard, Sphar, Andrews & Ingersoll, Denver, 1995—. Named in Best Lawyers in Am., Leading Lawyers Bus. Chambers USA. Fellow Am. Coll. Trial Lawyers; mem. ABA (vice chair environ. crime sect. 1991—), Colo. Bar Assn. (chair criminal law sect. 1990-91), Denver Country Club (bd. dirs.). Democrat. Avocation: fishing. Office: Ballard Sphar Andrews Inger 1225 17th St Ste 2300 Denver CO 80202-5596 Office Phone: 303-299-7337. Business E-Mail: shea@ballardspahr.com.

SHEA, PATRICK A., lawyer; b. Salt Lake City, Feb. 28, 1948; s. Edward J. and Ramona (Kilpack) S.; m. Deborah Fae Kern, Sept. 1, 1980; children: Michael, Paul. BA, Stanford U., 1970; MA in Human Sciences, Oxford U., Eng., 1972; JD, Harvard U., 1975. Bar: Utah 1976, DC 1979. Mem. profl. staff majority leader's office US Senate, 1971; asst. staff dir. US Senate Select Com. on Intelligence Ops., 1975—76; assoc. VanCott, Bagley, Salt Lake City, 1976—79, ptnr., 1980—85; counsel US Senate Fgn. Rels. Com., 1979—80; gen. counsel, corp. sec. Standard Communications, Inc., 1985—91; dir. Bur. Land Mgmt. US Dept. Interior, 1997-98, dep. asst. sec. for land & minerals mgmt., 1998-2000; of counsel Ballard, Spahr, Andrews & Ingersoll LLP, Salt Lake City, 2000—04; founder Patrick A. Shea, P.C., Salt Lake City, 2004—. Cons. Us House Judiciary Com., 1972-73; mem. President's Commn. on Aviation Safety, Security & Air Traffic Control, 1996-97; adj. prof. polit. sci. U. Utah, Salt Lake City, 1981-97,J. Reuben Clark Sch. Law, 1996-97, Kans. State U., 2002—. Chmn. Utah Dem. Party, Salt Lake City, 1983-85; v.p. Tomorrow-Today Found., Salt Lake City, 1982-84. Mem. Am. Rhodes Scholar Assn., Utah Bar Assn., D.C. Bar Assn., Stanford Alumni Assn. (pres.-elect 1983-84), Alta. Club. Roman Catholic. Office: 215 S State St Ste 200 Salt Lake City UT 84111 Office Phone: 801-305-4180. Office Fax: 801-521-9142. E-mail: pas@patrickashea.com.*

SHEAHAN, LARRY L., state legislator, lawyer; b. Spokane, Wash., Dec. 3, 1959; m. Lura Sheahan; 1 child, Ann. BA in Polit. Sci., Wash. State U., 1982; JD, Willamette U., 1985. Ptnr. Sheahan & Sheahan, P.S., Spokane; mem. Wash. Senate, Dist. 9, Olympia, 1999—; mem. higher edn. com.; mem. human svcs. and corrections com.; mem. transp. com. Mem. Rosalia Christian Ch. Mem. Rosalia C. of C. (past pres.), Wash. State Bar Assn., Whitman County Bar Assn., Pullman C. of C., Wash. Assn. Wheat Growers, U.S. Dry Pea and Lentil Assn., Wash. State U. Alumni Assn., Lions (Rosalia), Phi Beta Kappa. Republican. Office: 410A Legislative Bldg Olympia WA 98504-0001

SHEARER, DEREK NOCROSS, political science professor, diplomat, academic administrator; b. LA, Dec. 5, 1946; s. Lloyd and Marva (Peterson) S.; m. Sue Toigo; 1 child, Casey (dec.); stepchildren: Anthony, Julie, Molly. BA, Yale U., 1968; PhD, Union Grad. Sch., Yellow Springs, Ohio, 1977. Lectr. U. Calif., LA, 1979-81; dir. internat. and pub. affairs ctr., prof. of pub. policy Occidental Coll., LA, 1981-94, 98—; dep. undersec. U.S. Dept. Commerce, Washington, 1993; U.S. amb. to Finland U.S. Dept. State, Washington, 1994-97; prof. internat. affairs Occidental Coll., LA, 1997—; internat. advisor Ziff Bros. Investments, 1998—. Fellow Econ. Strategy Inst., Washington, 1993; policy adv. to Presidential Candidate Bill Clinton, 1990-92; adv. on NATO peace keeping USN, 1997—; pub. policy fellow Woodrow Wilson Internat. Scholars Ctr., 1999-2000; dir. global affairs Occidental Coll., 2001—, Chevalier prof. diplomacy and world affairs, 2002—; founder Pacific Coun. Internat. Policy, 1994—; sr. fellow USC Inst. Public Diplomacy. Contbr. articles to profl. publs. Planning commr. City of Santa Monica (Calif.), 1984; bd. mem. Nat. Consumer Bank, Washington, 1991. Fellow Guggenheim Found., 1984, U.S.-Japan Leadership fellow Japan Soc., 1991. Democrat. Avocations: basketball, tennis, travel, mysteries. Office: Global Affairs Occidental Coll Los Angeles CA 90041 Office Phone: 323-259-2681. Business E-Mail: dshearer@oxy.edu.

SHEARER, RONALD ALEXANDER, economics professor; b. Trail, BC, Can., June 15, 1932; s. James Boyd and Mary Ann (Smith) S.; m. Renate Elizabeth Selig, Dec. 20, 1956 (dec.); children: Carl, Bruce. BA, U. B.C., 1954; MA, Ohio State U., 1955, PhD, 1959. Asst. prof. econs. U. Mich., 1958-62; economist Royal Commn. Banking and Fin., Toronto, Canada, 1962-63; mem. faculty U. B.C., Vancouver, 1963—, prof. econs., 1970-98, emeritus prof., 1998—, head dept., 1972-76. Co-author: Money and Banking, 1975, The Economics of the Canadian Financial System, 1994; editor: Trade Liberalization and a Regional Economy, 1971. Mem. Can. Econs. Assn. Office: U BC Dept Econs Vancouver BC Canada Home Phone: 604-266-2852. Business E-Mail: rshearer@interchange.ubc.ca.

SHEARING, MIRIAM, retired state supreme court chief justice; b. Waverly, NY, Feb. 24, 1935; BA, Cornell U., 1956; JD, Boston Coll., 1964. Bar: Calif. 1965, Nev. 1969. Justice of peace Las Vegas Justice Ct., 1977-81; judge Nev. Dist. Ct., 1983-92, chief judge, 1986; justice Nevada Supreme Ct., Carson City, 1993—2005, chief justice, 1997, 2004, sr. justice, 2005—. Mem. ABA, Am. Judicature Soc. (chair 2001-03), Nev. Judges Assn. (sec. 1978), Nev. Dist. Ct. Judges Assn. (sec. 1984-85, pres. 1986-87), State Bar Nev., State Bar Calif., Clark County Bar Assn. Democrat. Personal E-mail: shearing@nvcourts.state.nv.us.

SHEATH, ROBERT GORDON, botanist, educator; b. Toronto, Can., Dec. 26, 1950; arrived in U.S., 1978; s. Harry Gordon and Shirley Irene (Rose) Sheath. BSc, U. Toronto, 1973, PhD, 1977. Nat. Rsch. Coun. Can. postdoctoral fellow U. B.C., 1977-78; asst. prof. aquatic biology U. RI, Kingston, 1978-82, assoc. prof., 1982-86, chmn. dept. botany, 1986-90, prof., 1987-91; head dept. biology Meml. U., St. Johns, Canada, 1991-95; dean coll. biol. sci. U. Guelph, Ont., 1995-2001; provost Calif. State U. San Marcos, 2001—. Mem. evolution and ecology grant selection com. NSERC, 1994—97, chair, 1996—97, selection com. life scis., 1996, chair maj. facilities access life scis. subcom., 2001; mem. Can. Rsch. Chairs Coll. of Reviewers, 2000—01. Editor (with M. M. Harlin): Freshwater and Marine Plants of RI, 1988; editor: (with K. M. Cole) Biology of the Red Algae, 1990; editor: (with J.D. Wehr) Classification and Ecology of Freshwater Algae of North America, 2003; contbr. 131 articles to profl. jours. Recipient G. A. Cox Gold medal, U. Toronto, 1973, Darbaker prize, Bot. Soc. Am., 1997, T. Christensen prize panel, 2000; grantee, NSF, 1980—91, 2001—05, NSERC, 1991—2002. Mem.: Japanese Phycological Soc. (editl. bd. 2000—05), Brit. Phycological Soc. (freshwater flora com. 1993—2002, overseas v.p. 1997—99, assoc. editor 1999—2001), Arctic Inst. N.Am., Phycological Soc. Am. (editl. bd. 1983—86, assoc. editor 1984—89, pres. 1991—92, editl. bd. 1996—2000, publs. com. chair 2001—, bd. trustees 2001—, Bold award 1976), Internat. Phycological Soc. (editl. bd. 1993—95, T. Christensen prize panel 2000, nominating com. 2000—01). Office: Calif State U San Marcos Office of Provost San Marcos CA 92096-0001 Office Phone: 760-750-4050. E-mail: rsheath@csusm.edu.

SHEEHAN, JAMES JOHN, historian, educator; b. San Francisco, May 31, 1937; s. James B. and Sally W. (Walsh) S.; m. 1960; 1 child, Michael L.; m. Margaret L. Anderson, Sept. 2, 1989. BA, Stanford U., 1958; MA, U. Calif., Berkeley, 1959, PhD, 1964. From asst. to assoc. prof. Northwestern U., Evanston, Ill., 1964-79; prof. Stanford (Calif.) U., 1979-86, chmn. dept., 1982-89, Dickason prof. in humanities, 1986—. Author: Lujo Brentano, 1966, German Liberalism, 1978, German History 1770-1866, 1989, Der Ausklang des alten Reiches, 1994, Museums in German Artworld, 2000; editor: The Boundaries of Humanity, 1991; contbr. articles to profl. jours. Decorated officer's cross Order of Merit; fellow Am. Coun. Learned Socs., 1981-82, NEH, 1985-86, Wissenschaftskolleg Berlin; Guggenheim fellow, 2000—. Fellow AAAS (Humboldt Rsch. prize 1995), Am. Acad. Berlin; mem. Royal Hist. Soc. (corr.), Am. Hist. Assn. (nominating com. 1979-81, chmn. conf. group on Ctrl. European history 1985-86, pres. 2005), Am. Philos. Soc. (Orden pour le Mérite). Office: Stanford U Dept History Stanford CA 94305 Home Phone: 510-649-8910. Business E-Mail: sheehan@stanford.edu.

SHEEHAN, LAWRENCE JAMES, lawyer; b. San Francisco, July 23, 1932; AB, Stanford U., 1957, LLB, 1959. Bar: Calif. 1960. Law clk. to chief judge U.S. Ct. Appeals 2d Cir., NYC, 1959-60; assoc. O'Melveny & Myers, LA, 1960-68, ptnr., 1969-94, of counsel, 1995—2004. D. dirs. FPA Mut. Funds, Source Capital, Inc. Mem. ABA, Los Angeles County Bar Assn., Calif. Bar Assn., Order of Coif. Office: O Melveny & Myers 1999 Avenue Of The Stars Los Angeles CA 90067-6035 also: 400 S Hope St Los Angeles CA 90071-2801 Office Phone: 310-246-6895. Business E-Mail: lsheehan@omm.com.

SHEEHAN, MICHAEL JARBOE, archbishop; b. Wichita, Kans., July 9, 1939; s. John Edward and Mildred (Jarboe) Sheehan. MST, Gregorian U., Rome, 1965; D in Canon Law, Lateran U., Rome, 1971. Ordained priest Diocese of Dallas-Ft. Worth, 1964; asst. gen. sec. Nat. Coun. Cath. Bishops, Washington, 1971—76; rector Holy Trinity Sem., Dallas, 1976—82; pastor Immaculate Conception Ch., Grand Prairie, Tex., 1982—83; ordained bishop, 1983; bishop Diocese of Lubbock, Tex., 1983—93; archbishop Archdiocese of Santa Fe, N.Mex., 1993—; apostolic adminstr. Diocese of Phoenix, 2003. Bd. dirs. Tex. Conf. of Chs.; past chmn. Am. Bd. Cath. Missions, 1989—91. Contbr. articles to profl. jours. Trustee St. Mary Hosp., Lubbock, Tex., 1983—89, Cath. Relief Svcs., 1992—. Mem.: Serra Club (chaplain 1983—93, chmn. NCCB com. on Evangelization 1996—99, NCCB adminstrv. com. Washington). Roman Catholic. Avocations: skiing, racquetball. Office: Archdiocese Santa Fe 4000 Saint Josephs Pl NW Albuquerque NM 87120-1714

SHEELER, JIM, journalist, educator; b. Houston, 1969; m. Annick Sheeler; 1 child, James. BA in Journalism, Colo. State U., 1990; MA in Journalism, U. Colo. With Boulder Daily Camera, Colo., 1991—96; sr. staff writer Boulder Planet, 1996—2000; freelance writer Denver Post, 1999—2003; staff writer Rocky Mountain News, Denver, 2004—; scholar-in-residence U. Colo. Sch. Journalism & Mass Comm., Boulder. Author: Obit, 2007, Final Salute, 2008; contbr. Best Newspaper Writing 2006-2007, Life on the Death Beat. Recipient Pulitzer prize for feature writing, 2006. Office: Rocky Mountain News 101 W Colfax Ave # 500 Denver CO 80202-5315 Office Phone: 303-892-2561, 303-868-2386. Office Fax: 303-892-2841. Personal E-mail: jsheeler@mac.com. Business E-Mail: sheelerj@rockymountainnews.com.

SHEEN, MARTIN (RAMON ESTEVEZ), actor; b. Dayton, Ohio, Aug. 3, 1940; s. Francisco and Mary Ann (Phelan) Estevez; m. Janet Sheen, Dec. 23, 1961; children: Emilio, Ramon, Carlos, Renee. Grad. high sch. Made NY stage debut as mem. Living Theatre in The Connection, 1959; Broadway debut in Never Live Over a Pretzel Factory, 1964; other stage appearances include The Subject Was Roses, 1964-66, The Wicked Crooks, 1967, Hamlet, 1967, Romeo and Juliet, 1968, Hello and Goodbye, 1969, The Happiness Cage, 1970, Death of a Salesman, 1975, Julius Caesar, 1988; film appearances include The Incident, 1967, The Subject Was Roses, 1968, Catch-22, 1970, No Drums, No Bugles, 1971, Rage, 1972, Badlands, 1973, The Legend of Earl Durand, 1974, The Cassandra Crossing, 1976, The Little Girl Who Lives Down the Lane, 1977, Apocalypse Now, 1979, The Final Countdown, 1980, Gandhi, 1982, That Championship Season, 1982, The King of Prussia, 1982, No Place to Hide, 1983, The Dead Zone, 1983, Man, Woman, and Child, 1983, Enigma, 1983, Eagle's Wing, 1983, Firestarter, 1984, The Believers, 1987, Wall Street, 1987, Siesta, 1987, Judgement in Berlin, 1988, Walking After Midnight, 1988, Da, 1988 (exec. producer, dir.), Beverly Hills Brats, 1989, Cadence, 1991 (dir.), JFK, 1991 (narrator), Hot Shots, Part Deux!, 1993 (cameo), Hear No Evil, 1993, Gettysburg, 1993, The Break, 1995, The American President, 1995, The War At Home, 1996, Truth or Consequences, 1997, Spawn, 1997, Letter From Death Row, 1998, Stranger in the Kingdom, 1998, Storm, 1998, Monument Avenue, 1998, Free Money, 1998, Catch Me If You Can, 2002, The Departed, 2006, Bobby, 2006; TV series include As the World Turns, The Edge of Night, The West Wing, 1999-2006 (Golden Globe award, 2001, SAG award, 2001, 2002); TV movies and miniseries include Then Came Bronson, 1969, The Subject Was Roses, 1969, Mongo's Back in Town, 1971, Welcome Home, Johnny Bristol, 1972, That Certain Summer, 1972, Catholics, 1973, The Execution of Private Slovik, 1974, The California Kid, 1974, The Story of Pretty Boy Floyd, 1974, The Missiles of October, 1974, Sweet Hostage, 1975, The Last Survivors, 1975, Blind Ambition, 1979, Taxi!!, 1978, The Long Road Home, 1980, Fly Away Home, 1981, Kennedy, 1982, Choices of the Heart, 1983, The Atlanta Child Murders, 1985, Consenting Adult, 1985, Out of Darkness, 1985, Shattered Spirits, 1986, Samaritan, 1986, News at Eleven, 1986, Babies Having Babies (dir.), 1986, Conspiracy: The Trial of the Chicago 8, 1987, No Means No (exec. producer), Night Breaker, 1989, Project Alf, 1996, Marlon Brandon: The Wild One, 1996, D.R.E.A.M. Team, 1999; TV appearances include Mannix, 1967, The Streets of San Francisco, 1972, Murphy Brown, 1988 (Emmy award, Guest Actor - Comedy Series, 1994), The Simpsons (voice), 1989, The Great War, 1996, The Elevator, 1996, Entertaining Angels, 1996, Spin City, 1996, Medusa's Child, 1997, 187 Documented, 1997, Titanic: Anatomy of a Disaster (narrator), 1997, Tudjman (narrator), 1997 Babylon 5: The River of Souls, 1998, Letter From Death Row, 1998, Ambrose Chapel, 1998, Gunfighter, 1998, No Code of Conduct, 1998, Shadrach (voice), 1998, Stranger in the Kingdom, 1998, Talk of the Town, 1998, Voyage of Terror, 1998, Celebrity Poker Showdown, 2003. Recipient Lifetime Achievement award, Imagen Found., 1998, Laetare medal, U. Notre Dame, 2008; named Favorite Actor in a New Series, TV Guide Awards. Roman Catholic.

SHEERAN, MICHAEL JOHN LEO, priest, academic administrator; b. NYC, Jan. 24, 1940; s. Leo John and Glenna Marie (Wright) Sheeran. AB, St. Louis U., 1963, PhL, 1964, AM in Polit. Sci., 1967, AM in Theology, 1971, STL, 1971; PhD, Princeton U., 1977. Joined Soc. of Jesus, 1957, ordained priest Roman Cath. Ch., 1970. Exec. editor Catholic Mind, NYC, 1971-72; assoc. editor Am. Mag., NYC, 1971-72; assoc. chaplain Aquinas Inst., Princeton, NJ, 1972-75; asst. dean Regis U., Denver, 1975-77, dean, 1977-82; v.p. acad. affairs Regis Coll., Denver, 1982-92, acting pres., 1987-88, pres., 1993—. Retreat dir., cons. governance religious cmtys., 1970—. Author: Beyond Majority Rule, 1984; contbr. articles and editls. to publs. Trustee Regis Jesuit HS, 1999—2005; chmn. Mile High United Way, Denver, 1999—2000; nat. bd. dirs. Campus Compact, 2002—06; trustee Rockhurst Coll., Kansas City, Mo., 1982—91, Creighton U., Omaha, 1985—95, U. San Francisco, 1985—94, 2001—, Loyola U., New Orleans, 1994—96, Rocky Mountain Coll. Art and Design, Denver, 1994—99; mem. adv. bd. Cmty. Coll. Aurora, Colo., 2001—; bd. dirs. Colo. Inst. Tech., 2001—06. Ford Found. scholar, 1963. Democrat. Roman Catholic. Home: 3333 Regis Blvd Denver CO 80221-1099 Office: Regis U 3333 Regis Blvd Denver CO 80221-1099 Office Phone: 303-458-4190. Business E-Mail: president@regis.edu.

SHEETS, THOMAS R., lawyer, gas industry executive; BA, Ashland U., 1973; JD, U. Toledo, 1975. Bar: Ohio 1975, Nev. 1982, Tex. 1986. Sr. atty. Tex. Eastern Corp., 1985—87; litig. atty. Southwest Gas Corp., Las Vegas, 1987—89, assoc. gen. counsel, 1989—90, dir. regulatory affairs, 1990—94, asst. gen. counsel, 1994—96, v.p., gen. counsel, 1996—98, sr. v.p., gen. counsel, 1998—. Mem. Nev. Tax Commn., chair; former mem. Nev. Standing Com. Jud. Ethics. Mem.: ABA, Am. Arbitration Assn., Energy Bar Assn., Am. Gas Assn., Clark County Bar Assn. (pres. 1995). Office: Southwest Gas Corp 5241 Spring Mountain Rd Las Vegas NV 89193-8510 Business E-Mail: thom.sheets@swgas.com.

SHEFFIELD, NANCY, city agency administrator; b. Mpls. BA in Sociology and Psychology, U. Minn., 1969; postgrad., U. Wis., 1992. Participant City of Aurora (Colo.) Supervisory Cert. Series Program, 1988-90. Social worker LeSueur County Human Svcs., Le Centre, Minn., 1969-71; quality control reviewer Minn. Dept. Human Svcs., St. Paul, 1971-74, quality control supr., 1974-75; neighborhood planner City of Aurora, 1987, neighborhood support supr., 1987-94, acting mgr. Original Aurora Renewal, 1994-95, acting mgr. neighborhood support divsn., 1995, dir. neighborhood svcs., 1996—. Office: City Aurora Dept Neighborhood Svcs 15151 E Alameda Pkwy Aurora CO 80012 Office Phone: 303-739-7280. Business E-Mail: nsheffie@auroragov.org.

SHEFFIELD, RICHARD LEE, physicist; b. Dayton, Ohio, Sept. 22, 1950; s. Albert H. and Pauline E. (Schutte) S.; m. Antoinette M. Mals, Oct. 28, 1978; children: Nicole, Angela, Michael. BS, Wright State U., 1972; PhD, MIT, 1978. Staff mem. high energy high density physics Los Alamos (N.Mex.) Nat. Lab., 1978-82, staff mem. free electron laser tech., 1982-85, dep. group leader, 1985-89, group leader accelerator theory & free electron laser tech., 1989-93, prin. investigator advanced FEL initiative, 1990—, now project leader advanced accelerator tech. Advisor UV/FEL adv. panel Brookhaven (N.Y.) Nat. Lab., 1991—, Project Leader Advanced Accelevator Tech., 1994—; lectr. U.S. Accelerator Summer Sch., 1989. Editorial bd. Particle Accelerators, 1991—; patentee photoinjector, high brightness electron accelerators. Pres. Los Alamos United Way, 1981-84; vice chmn. Los Alamos County Planning and Zoning Commn., 1983-86, exec. coun. for divsn. of Beams and Particles. Recipient R&D 100 award R&D 100 Mag., 1988, Strategic Def. Tech. Achievements award Strategic Def. Preparedness Assn., 1989. Fellow Am. Phys. Soc. (prize for Achievement in Accelerator Physics and Tech., 1993); mem. Sigma Pi Sigma.

SHEINDLIN, JUDITH (JUDGE JUDY), television personality, judge; b. Bklyn., Oct. 21, 1942; d. Murray and Ethel Blum; m. Ronald Levy, 1964 (div. 1976); children: Jamie, Adam; m. Gerald Sheindlin, 1977 (div. 1990); stepchildren: Greg, Jonathan, Nicole; m. Gerald Sheindlin, 1991. BA, Am. U., Wash., DC, 1963; JD, NY Law Sch., 1965; LLD (hon.), Elizabethtown Coll. Pros. atty. Family Ct., NYC, 1978—82, judge Bronx, 1982—86; supervising judge Manhattan, NYC, 1986—96. Appeared as herself (TV films) ChiPs '99, 1998, (TV series) Judge Judy, 1996— (nominee Daytime Emmy for outstanding special class series, 1999, 2000, 2001, 2002, 2003); author: Don't Pee on My Leg and Tell Me It's Raining: America's Toughest Family Court Judge Speaks Out, 1996, Beauty Fades, Dumb is Forever: The Making of a Happy Woman, 1999, Keep It Simple, Stupid: You're Smarter Than You Look: Uncomplicating Families in Complicated Times, 2000, Judge Judy Sheindlin's Win or Lose by How You Choose, 2000, You're Smarter Than You Look: Uncomplicating Relationships in Complicated Times, 2001, Judge Judy Sheindlin's You Can't Judge a Book By Its Cover: Cool Rules for School, 2001. Named one of The 100 Most Powerful Celebrities, Forbes.com, 2007, 2008.

SHEINER, LEWIS B., pharmacist, educator; b. NYC, May 27, 1940; PhD (hon.), U. Uppsala, Sweden, 1995. Cert. Am. Bd. Internal Medicine. Intern in medicine Columbia Presbyn. Med. Ctr., 1965, resident in medicine, 1966; rsch. assoc. NIMH, NIH, 1968; rsch. physician divsn. computer rsch. and tech. NIH, 1969; resident in medicine Stanford U. Sch. Medicine, 1970; rsch. fellow divsn. clin. pharmacology U. Calif., San Francisco, 1972, instr. depts. lab. medicine and medicine, Sch. Medicine, 1972—73, asst. prof. lab. medicine and medicine and Sch. Pharmacy, dept. biopharm. scis., 1973—78, assoc. prof. lab. medicine and medicine and Sch. Pharmacy, dept. biopharm. scis., 1978—82, prof. lab. medicine and medicine and Sch. Pharmacy, dept. biopharm. scis., 1982—. Mem. anti-virals adv. com. Ctr. for Drug Evaluation and Rsch., FDA, 1991—94; chair Gordon Conf. on Stats. in Chemistry and Chem. Engring., 1989; John G. Wagner lectr. pharmaceutics U. Mich. Coll. Pharmacy, 1994; Leon Goldberg lectr. clin. pharmacology U. Chgo., 1995; Sidney Riegelman lectr. U. Calif., San Francisco, 2000. Mem. editl. bd.: European Jour. Pharm. Scis., Clin. Pharmacology and Therapeutics, 1985—; editor: (pharmacokinetics sect.) Jour. Pharmacokinetics and Biopharmaceutics, 1981—. Recipient MERIT award, NIH, 1996, rsch. grants in field. Fellow: Am. Coll. Clin. Pharmacology (hon.; Therapeutics Frontiers lectr. award 1987); mem.: Am. Soc. for Clin. Investigation (emeritus mem.), Am. Soc. for Clin. Pharmacology and Therapeutics (Rawls-Palmer lectr. on progress in medicine 1989, pres. 1990). Office: U Calif Dept Lab Medicine Box 0626 C255 San Francisco CA 94143-

SHEKHAR, STEPHEN S., obstetrician, gynecologist; b. New Delhi, Jan. 13, 1944; arrived in U.S., 1972; s. S.P. Jain and Shakuntala Mithal; m. Claudette Dorita, Jan. 6, 1978; children: Sasha, Stephen. MBBS, Punjabi U., Patiala, India, 1966. Surgeon Nat. Health Svc. U.K., 1966-72; intern Roosevelt Hosp.-Columbia Coll. Physicians and Surgeons, NYC, 1972-73; resident in ob-gyn. St. Clare's Hosp., N.Y. Med. Coll., NYC, 1973-76, Harlem Hosp.-Columbia U., NYC, 1976-77; pvt. practice Studio City, Calif., 1977—. Mem. staff L.A. County-U. So. Calif. Med. Sch.; clin. prof. ob-gyn. and family medicine U. So. Calif. Sch. Medicine, Oreg. Health Scis. U. Sch. Medicine. Fellow ACS, Am. Coll. Ob-Gyn., L.A. Soc. Ob-Gyn.; mem. AMA, Calif. Med. Assn., L.A. County Med. Assn., Oreg. Med. Assn., Jackson County Med. Assn. Home and Office: PO Box 1742 Medford OR 97501-0136 Office Phone: 541-608-6199. Personal E-mail: drsshekhar@yahoo.com.

SHELBY, CARROLL HALL, automotive designer; b. Leesburg, Tex., Jan. 11, 1923; s. Warren Hall Shelby and Eloise Lawrence; m. Jeanne Fields (separated 1960); children: Sharon Anne, Michael Hall, Patrick Burke. Profl. race car driver Cad-Allard, Aston Martin, and Maserati teams, 1954—60; founder Carroll Shelby Sports Cars, Dallas, 1957, Shelby School of High Performance Driving, 1961, Shelby-Dowd Wheel Co., 1973, Shelby-Am. Automobile Club, 1975, Carroll Shelby Internat., Inc., LA; automobile designer, 1961—, Shelby-Am., 1962—, Ford Motor Co., Chrysler Corp., GM; tech. advisor Ford GT project, 2003. Co-founder Original Tex. Chili Co., 1969, Internat. Chili Soc. Founder Carroll Shelby Children's Found., 1991. 2nd lt. US Army Air Corps. Recipient Kruse Internat. Collector Car Hall of Fame Award, 2002, Robert E. Petersen Lifetime Achievement Award, 2003; named winner, Torrey Pines, 1955, 24 Hours of LeMans, 1959, Continental Divide Raceways, 1960, Sports Car Driver of Yr., Sports Illustrated, 1956, 1957; named to Internat. MotorSports Hall of Fame, 1991, Automotive Hall of Fame, 1992. Achievements include design of original Shelby Cobra Roadster, Ford Motor Co., 1962; Shelby Mustang, 1964; Dodge Viper, 1989; Shelby GT500, 2005. Office: Carroll Shelby Children's Found 19021 S Figueroa St Gardena CA 90248 also: Carroll Shelby Licensing Inc 19021 S Figueroa St Gardena CA 90248-4510

SHELDON, BETTI L., state legislator; b. Aberdeen, Wash. 5 children. Student, Gonzaga U. Mem. Wash. Senate, Dist. 23, Olympia, 1992—; majority flood leader Wash. Senate, Olympia, 1999—; mem. Dem. flood leader Wash. Legislature, Olympia, 1997-98, majority caucus vice chair, 1995, majority whip, 1995-96, majority asst. floor leader, 1993-95, mem. higher edn. com., mem. rules com., mem. ways and means com. Bd. dirs. Small Bus. Improvement Coun., Commn. on Student Learning's K-123 Accountability Task Force., Nat. Assn. Adminstrv. Rules Rev., YMCA Youth and Govt., Gov.'s Regulatory Reform Task Force, Big Bros. and Big Sisters Kitsap County, Kitsap County Econ. Devel. Coun., Puget Sound Naval Bases Assn., West Sound Arts Coun., Bremerton Olympic Peninsula Coun. Navy League; mem. Wash. Devel. Fin. Authority; mem. adv. bd. for corp. rels. Martha & Mary Luth. Svcs.; mem. delivery plan adv. group Dept. Health Am. Indian Health Care; trustee Keyport Naval Undersea Mus. Found. Recipient Woman of Yr. Bremerton Kitsap YWCA, 1993, Strong Kids, Strong Families, Strong Cmtys. award YMCA, 1999, Dem. Woman of Yr. Wash. State Fedn. Women's Clubs, 1997. Mem. Bremerton Area C. of C. (past exec. dir.), Wash. C. of C. Execs. (v.p.). Democrat. Office: 410A Legislative Bldg Olympia WA 38504-0482

SHELDON, GARY, conductor, music director; b. Bay Shore, NY, Jan. 21, 1953; Student, Wash. U., St. Louis, 1972; BMus, Juilliard Sch. Music, 1974; diploma, Inst. Hautes Etudes Musicales, Montreux, Switzerland, 1975. Prin. condr. Opera Theater, Syracuse, 1976-77; asst. condr. Syracuse Symphony Orch., 1976-77, New Orleans Symphony Orch., 1977-80; assoc. condr. Columbus (Ohio) Symphony Orch., 1982-89; music dir. Lancaster (Ohio) Festival, 1988—, Marin Symphony Orch., San Rafael, Calif., 1990—. Composer: Variations on a Theme of Handel, 1984, Mississippi River (for documentary film Miss. River Mus.), Memphis; rec. performances include Beauty and the Beast (with Frank DiGiacomo), 1977, Ballet Class with Karen Hebert, 1982. Recipient New Orleans Music and Drama Found. award, 1982, 3d prize Rupert BBC Symphony Found., London, 1982, 4th prize Leopold Stokowski Conducting Competition, 1986. Mem. Am. Symphony Orch. League (youth orch. div. bd. dirs. 1980—). Office: Marin Symphony Orch 4340 Redwood Hwy San Rafael CA 94903-2121

SHELDON, JEANNE, computer software company executive; m. Marvin Sheldon; 1 child. BA in History & Physical Sci., San Jose State U. Section mgr., software quality assurance divsn. Software Publ. Corp.; with Microsoft Corp., 1989—, software test mgr., 1989, gen. mgr. Microsoft Office sustaining engring. services, corp. v.p. Microsoft Office authoring applications. Avocations: photography, hiking. Office: Microsoft Corp Bus Divsn 1 Microsoft Way Redmond WA 98052-6399

SHELDON, TIMOTHY M., state legislator; b. Shelton, Wash., Mar. 9, 1947; son of T R Sheldon & Lillian Carlson S; married 1981 to Linda Honan S; children: Alexandra. Chairman, Port of Hoodsport, 87-; Washington State Representative, District 35, 91-98; Washington State Senator, District 35, 1997-, vice chairman, Agriculture & Rural Econ Develop, Natural Resources, Parks & Recreation Committees, member, Commerce, Trade, Housing & Financial Inst & Transportation Committees, currently. Washington State Senate: member, Joint Task Force on Rural Land Use & Econ Develop, currently; member, Community Econ Revitilization Bd, currently; chairman Senator Econ Develop Committee, currently.Manager, Sheldon Properties, 80-; business manager, Squaxin Island Indian Tribe, 84-86; exec director, Econ Develop Coun of Mason Co, 86-; manager, Potlatch Mutual Water Co, 87-; member, Washington State WWII Member Fund Raising Committee, Pacific NW Econ Region Deleg Coun, Community Econ Revitilization Bd & Olympic Col Shelton Bldg Fund, currently; economic development, NW Indian Tribes, formerly. Toastmasters; Shelton High Sch Voc Education Advisor Committee (chairman, 87-); Washington Farm Forestry Association; Washington Forest Protection Association; Mason Co Hist Soc; Boys & Girls Club North Mason Co (board gov, currently). Democrat. Protestant. Fax: 360-786-1999. E-mail: sheldon_ti@leg.wa.gov.

SHELL, ART (ARTHUR SHELL JR.), former professional football coach; b. Charleston, SC, Nov. 26, 1946; m. Janice Shell; children: Arthur III, Christopher. BS in Industrial Arts, Md. State Coll., 1968. Offensive lineman Oakland Raiders, 1968—81, L.A. Raiders, 1982, asst. coach, 1983-89, head coach, 1989-94; offensive line coach Kans. City Chiefs, 1995-96, Atlanta Falcons, 1997—2000; appeals officer NFL, 2001—04, sr. v.p. football ops. & devel., 2004—06; head coach Oakland Raiders, 2006. Inducted into Pro Football Hall of Fame, 1989; recipient, Jackie Robinson Award for Athletics (Ebony mag.), 1990; named All-Pro, 1973, 1974, 1976, 1977; named to Pro Bowl, 1972-78, 1980; named NFL Coach of Yr., 1991 member of two Super Bowl Champion teams with Oakland Raiders, 1977, 1981; the first African-American to become an NFL head coach, 1989.

SHELLAN, RONALD A., lawyer; b. Everett, Wash., Oct. 17, 1949; s. Henry and Sondra Ilsa (Hess) S.; m. Rebecca Rae, March 24, 1972; children: Elisabeth S., David W. BA magna cum laude, U. Wash., 1972; LLM, Willamette U., 1975. Bar: Oreg. 1975, U.S. Dist. Ct. Oreg. 1979, U.S. Tax Ct. 1982; CPA, Oreg. 1978. Law clk. Oreg. Tax Ct., Salem, 1976; tax sr. Coopers & Lybrand, Portland, 1977-79; atty. Sussman, Shank, Wapnick, Caplan & Stiles, Portland, 1979-91, Weiss, Jensen, Ellis & Botteri, Portland, 1991; ptnr. Miller, Nash, Wiener, Hager & Carlsen (name now Miller Nash LLP), Portland, 1991—. Author: G Reorganization Tax Free Acquisition of Financially Distressed Corporations; assoc. editor Willamette Law Jour., 1974-75. V.p. Nat. Multiple Sclerosis Soc. Oreg. Chapter, 1989-96, Robison Jewish Home, Portland, 1990-96. Mem. Oreg. State Bar (chair tax section), Oreg. Soc. CPA's (dir. 1978), Portland Tax Forum (pres.). Avocations: racquetball, skiing. Office: Miller Nash LLP 111 SW 5th Ave Ste 3500 Portland OR 97204-3638

SHELLER, JOHN WILLARD, lawyer; b. LA, Oct. 29, 1950; s. Willard and Barbara S.; m. Mary Elizabeth Hodor, Aug. 9, 1975; children: Matthew John, James Henry. BA, Stanford U., 1972; JD, Loyola U., LA, 1975. Bar: Calif. 1975. Ptnr. in charge Hinshaw & Culbertston, LA. Mem. Am. Bd. Trial Advs. Contbr. articles to profl. jours. Mem. Calif. State Bar Assn., LA County Bar Assn., LA Country Club. Avocation: golf. Office: Hinshaw & Culbertson 11601 Wilshire Blvd Ste 800 Los Angeles CA 90025 Home: 16 Park Ave Venice CA 90291-3222 Office Phone: 310-909-8000. Business E-Mail: jsheller@hinshawlaw.com.

SHELLEY, KEVIN FRANCIS, former state official; b. Washington, Nov. 16, 1955; s. John Francis and Thelma (Smith) Shelley; m. Dominique Shelley; 1 child, Jack. BA in Polit. Sci., U. Calif., Davis, 1978; JD, Hastings Coll. Law, 1983. Asst. to U.S. Congressman Phil Burton US Ho. Reps., 1978—87; mem. bd. suprs., pres. bd. San Francisco Bd. Suprs., 1990—96; mem., majority leader Calif. State Assembly, 1996—2002; sec. state State of Calif., 2003—05; atty. Calif., 2005—. Mem.: Calif. State Bar.

SHELLEY, MARKE R., career officer; BArch, U. Idaho, 1971; MA in Nat. Security, Coll. of Naval Warfare, 1987. Lic. profl. architect, Wash., NSW/Australia. Commd. 2d lt. USN, 1971, advanced through ranks to rear adm.; various assignments to comdr. Maritime Def. Zone Pacific, 1988-89; comdr. Joint Task Force Mid. East in Bahrain, 1989-90; team chief for European Command's Mil. Liaison Team Bucharest, 1994; comdr. Mil. Sealift & Command Pacific and Far East; ind. architect, comml. real estate developer Seattle, Wash. Adj. prof. Naval War Coll., Seattle, 1990-94. Decorated Def. Meritorious Svc. medal, Meritorious Svc. medal, Navy and Marine Corps Commendation medal, Navy Achievement medal. Mem. Naval Res. Assn. (pres. 13th dist.), Res. Officers Assn., The Naval Inst., Navy League, Surface Navy Assn., Fleet Res. Assn., Am. Legion. Office: 11424 NE 94th St Kirkland WA 98033-5706

SHELTON, ROBERT NEAL, academic administrator, physics professor, researcher; b. Phoenix, Oct. 5, 1948; s. Clark B. and Grace M. (McLaughlin) S.; m. Adrian Ann Millar, Aug. 30, 1969; children: Christian, Cameron, Stephanie. BS, Stanford U., 1970; MS, U. Calif., San Diego, 1973, PhD, 1975. Postdoctoral researcher U. Calif.-San Diego, La Jolla, 1975-76, asst. rsch. physicist, 1976-78; asst. prof. Iowa State U., Ames, 1978-81, assoc. prof., 1981-84, prof. physics, 1984-87; prof. physics, chmn. dept. U. Calif.-Davis, 1987-90, vice chancellor for rsch., 1990-96, vice provost for rsch., 1996-2001; exec. vice chancellor, provost U. N.C., Chapel Hill, 2001—06; pres. U. Ariz., Tucson, 2006—. Contbr. over 200 articles to profl. jours. Fellow Am. Phys. Soc., Calif. Coun. on Sci. and Tech.; mem. AAAS, Materials Rsch. Soc., Sigma Xi, Phi Beta Kappa. Office: Univ Ariz Adminstrn Bldg Rm 712 PO Box 210066 Tucson AZ 85721-0066

SHEMIN, RICHARD JAY, cardiothoracic surgeon, educator; b. Little Rock, Sept. 25, 1950; s. Saul and Beverly (Newfield) S.; m. Susan Helaine Packer, Aug. 25, 1971; children: Stephanie Leigh, Michael Andrew, Michelle Elizabeth. BA magna cum laude, Boston U., 1970, MD magna cum laude, 1974. Cert. Am. Bd. Thoracic Surgery. Intern, gen. surgery Peter Bent Brigham Hosp./Harvard Med. Sch., Boston, 1974—75, resident, cardiothoracic vascular surgery, 1975—76, 1978—80; asst. prof., cardiothoracic surgery Harvard Med. Sch., Boston, 1982—87; fellow in cardiothoracic surgery NYU Sch. Medicine, NYC, 1980-82; clin. assoc., cardiothoracic surgery NHLBI/NIH, The Clinical Ctr., Bethesda, Md., 1976-78; sr. resident in surgery Brigham and Women's Hosp./Harvard Med. Sch., Boston, 1978-80, assoc. surgery, cardiac surgeon, prof., 1982-87; med. dir., cardiac surgery, ICU Brigham and Women's Hosp., Boston, 1984—87; assoc. cardiothoracic surgery Children's Hosp. Med. Ctr., Boston, 1984; prof., chmn. Boston U. Sch. Medicine, 1987—2007, chief, cardiothoracic surgery, 1995—2007, vice chair dept. cardiothoracic surgery, 1997—2007; chair dept. cardiothoracic surgery Boston Med. Ctr., 1987—2007, co-dir., Cardiovascular Ctr., 2000—07; prof., surgery David Geffen UCLA Sch. Medicine, 2007—; vice-chmn., dept. surgery UCLA Med. Ctr., 2007—, chief cardiothoracic surgery, chmn. cardiothoracic surgery, 2007—, co-dir., Cardiovascular Ctr., 2007—. Cons. Dana Farber Canc Inst, Boston, MA, 1983, Baxter Healthcare, Orange County, Calif., 1990-; pres., Boston U. Cardiothoracic Surgery Found., Inc.; presenter in the field Contbr. several articles to profl. jours; assoc. editor Circulation, Jour. Cardiac Surgery; reviewer for several jours. including Annal of Thoracic Surgery, Jour. Thoracic and Cardiac Vascular Surgery. Lt. comdr. USPHS, 1996-98. Recipient Roche award Boston U. Med. Sch., 1974, Boston U. Sch. Medicine Alumni award, 1987, Outstanding Leadership, Thoracic Surgery Found. for Rsch. and Edn. Fellow ACS (coun. Mass. Chpt.), Am. Surg. Assn., Am. Coll. Cardiology (coun. Mass. Chpt.), Am. Heart Assn. (pres. greater Boston divsn.), Am. Coll. Chest Physicians; mem. Soc. Thoracic Surgeons (chair workforce com. 1998-), Am. Assn. Thoracic Surgery, Thoracic Surgery Tng. Dirs. Assn. (exec. com., editor Adult Cardiac Surgery), Algonquin Club Boston (exec. com., bd. dirs.), Northeast Cardiac Surgery Soc. (immediate past pres.), Phi Beta Kappa, Alpha Omega Alpha. Avocations: sailing, hunting, golf, reading history and biographies. Office: UCLA Divsn Cardiothoracic Surgery 10833 LeConte Los Angeles CA 90095 Office Phone: 310-206-8232. Office Fax: 310-825-7473.

SHENK, GEORGE H., lawyer; b. NYC, Sept. 10, 1943; BA, Princeton U., 1965; M in Internat. Affairs, Columbia U., 1967; JD, Yale U., 1970. Bar: N.Y. 1971, Calif. 1985. Assoc. Coudert Bros., Paris, 1970, NYC, 1970-73, Hong Kong, 1973-75, Tokyo, 1975-78, ptnr. NYC, 1978-91, San Francisco, 1991-94, Heller Ehrman LLP, 1994—. Exec. dir. San Francisco Com. on Fgn. Rels. Contbr. articles to publs. Mem. Bar Assn. City of N.Y., Calif. State Bar Assn., Coun. Fgn. Rels., Pacific Coun. on Internat. Policy. Office: Heller Ehrman LLP 333 Bush St San Francisco CA 94104-2806

SHEPARD, SAM (SAMUEL SHEPARD ROGERS), playwright, actor; b. Ft. Sheridan, Ill., Nov. 5, 1943; s. Samuel Shepard and Jane Elaine (Schook) Rogers; m. O-Lan Johnson Dark, Nov. 9, 1969 (div. 1984); 1 child, Jesse Mojo; life ptnr. Jessica Lange; children: Hannah Jane, Samuel Walker. Student, Mt. San Antonio Jr. Coll., Walnut, Calif., 1961-62. Playwright-in-residence Magic Theatre, San Francisco. Author: (plays) 4-H Club, Up to Thursday, Dog, Rocking Chair, 1965, Cowboys, The Rock Garden, 1964, Chicago, 1965 (Obie award, 1966), Icarus's Mother, 1965 (Obie award, 1966), Fourteen Hundred Thousand, 1966, Red Cross, 1966 (Obie award, 1966), Melodrama Play, 1966 (Obie award, 1968), La Turista, 1967 (Obie award, 1967), Cowboys #2, 1967, Forensic and the Navigators, 1967 (Obie award, 1968), The Holy Ghostly, The Unseen Hand, 1969, Operation Sidewinder, Shaved Splits, 1970, Mad Dog Blues, Terminal, (with Patti Smith) Cowboy Mouth, Black Bog Beast Bait, 1971, The Tooth of Crime, 1972 (Obie award, 1973), Blue Bitch, (with Megan Terry and Jean-Claude van Itallie) Nightwalk, 1973, Geography of a Horse Dreamer, Little Ocean, Killer's Head, 1974, Action, 1974 (Obie award, 1975), Starving Class, 1977, Buried Child, 1978 (Obie award, 1977, Pulitzer Prize in drama, 1979, Obie award, 1979), Tongues, Savage/Love, Seduced, 1979, True West, 1981, Fool for Love, 1983 (Obie award, 1984), Superstitions, The Sad Lament of Pecos Bill on the Eve of Killing his Wife, 1983, A Lie of the Mind, 1985 (New York Drama Critics' Circle award, 1986), States of Shock, 1991, Simpatico, 1993, The Late Henry Moss, 2000, The God of Hell, 2004, Kicking a Dead Horse, 2008, (collections of plays) Five Plays by Sam Shepard, 1967, The Unseen Hand and Other Plays, 1971, 1986, Mad Dog Blues and Other Plays, 1972, The Tooth of Crime and Geography of a Horse Dreamer, 1974, Angel City, Curse of the Starving Class and Other Plays, 1976, Buried Child, Seduced, Suicide in B-Flat, 1979, (collection of plays) Four Two-Act Plays by Sam Shepard, 1980, Chicago and Other Plays, Seven Plays, 1981, Fool for Love and The Sad Lament of Pecos Bill on the Eve of Killing His Wife, 1983, Fool For Love and Other Plays, 1984, 1986, contbr. to Oh! Calcutta, 1976, (with Bob Dylan) Renaldo and Clara, 1978, (collection of plays) Paris, Texas, 1984, (other writings) Rolling Thunder Logbook, 1977, Hawk Moon: A Book of Short Stories, Poems and Monologues, 1981, Motel Chronicles, 1982; dir.(writer): (plays) Fool for Love, 1983, A Lie of the Mind, 1985; (screenplays) Far North, 1988, Silent Tongue, 1993; actor: (plays) A Number, 2004—05; (films) Renaldo and Clara, Days of Heaven, 1978, Resurrection, 1980, Raggedy Man, 1981, Frances, 1982, The Right Stuff, 1983 (Academy award nomination best supporting actor, 1984), Country, 1984, Fool for Love, 1985, Crimes of the Heart, 1986, Baby Boom, 1987, Steel Magnolias, 1989, Hot Spot, 1990, Bright Angel, Defenseless, 1991, Thunderheart, 1992, The Pelican Brief, 1993, Safe Passage, 1994, The Good Old Boys, 1995, Curtain Call, The Only Thrill, 1997, All the Pretty Horses, 2000, The Pledge, 2001, Swordfish, 2001, Black Hawk Down, 2001, Leo, 2002, Blind Horizon, 2003, The Notebook, 2004, Don't Come Knocking, 2005, Stealth, 2005, Bandidas, 2006, Walker Payne, 2006, The Return, 2006, Charlotte's Web, 2006, The Assassination of Jesse James by the Coward Robert Ford, 2007, The Accidental Husband, 2008; (TV films) Streets of Laredo, 1995, Lily Dale, 1996, Purgatory, Dash & Lilly, 2000 (nominated for Golden Globe, Best Actor), After the Harvest, 2001, Shot in the Heart, 2001, Ruffian, 2007. Recipient Nat. Inst. and Am. Acad. Arts and Letters award for lit., 1974, Creative Arts award Brandeis U., 1975; named to Theater Hall of Fame, 1994; grantee Rockefeller Found., 1967, Guggenheim Found., 1968, 1971; Fellow, U. Minn., 1966, Yale U., 1967. Mem.: Am. Acad. and Inst. of Arts and Letters.

SHEPARD, THOMAS HILL, physician, educator; b. Milw., May 22, 1923; s. Francis Parker and Elizabeth Rhodes (Buchner) S.; m. Alice B. Kelly, June 24, 1946; children: Donna, Elizabeth, Ann. AB, Amherst Coll., 1945; MD, U. Rochester, 1948. Intern Strong Meml. Hosp., Rochester, NY, 1948-49, resident, 1950-52, Albany (N.Y.) Med. Ctr., 1949-50; pediatric endocrine fellow Johns Hopkins Hosp., 1954-55; pediatrician U. Wash., Seattle, 1955-61, teratologist, 1961—, prof. pediat., head ctrl. lab. for human embryology, 1961-93, prof. emeritus, 1993—; embryologist dept. anatomy U. Fla., 1961-62; rsch. assoc. dept. embryology Carnegie Inst., 1962, U. Copenhagen, 1963. Cons. NIH, FDA, EPA, 1971-; vis. prof. pediat. U. Geneva, 1972, 73-74. Author: A Catalog of Teratogenic Agents, 1973, 11th edit., 2004; contbr. articles to profl. jours. With US Army, 1946—48, with USAF, 1952—54. Mem.: Am. Pediatric Soc., Western Soc. Pediatric Rsch. (pres. 1970), Orgn. for Teratogen Answering Svcs. (hon. Thomas Shepard Ann. lectr.), Japanese Teratology Soc. (hon.), Teratology Soc. (hon.; pres. 1968). Home: 3015 98th Ave NE Bellevue WA 98004-1818 Office: U Wash Sch Medicine Dept Pediatrics Seattle WA 98195-0001

SHEPHERD, BRUCE P., lawyer; BA, Harvard U., 1979; MBA, JD, U. Calif., Berkeley, 1983. Bar: Calif. 1984. Mng. ptnr. Latham & Watkins LLP, San Diego, and mem. fin. and real estate dept. Bd. dir. San Diego County Big Brothers and Big Sisters, Coronado Schools Found.; elected sch. bd. mem. (pres. 2001-02) Coronado Sch. Dist., 1998—2002. Mem.: ABA. Office: Latham & Watkins LLP Ste 1800 600 W Broadway San Diego CA 92101-3375 also: Latham And Watkins Llp 12636 High Bluff Dr Ste 400 San Diego CA 92130-2071

SHEPHERD, CYBILL LYNNE, actress, singer; b. Memphis, Feb. 18, 1950; d. William Jennings and Patty Shobe (Micci) S.; m. David Ford, Nov. 19, 1978 (div., 1982); 1 child, Clementine; m. Bruce Oppenheim, March 1, 1987 (div., 1990); children: Molly Ariel and Cyrus Zachariah (twins) Student, Hunter Coll., 1969, Coll. of New Rochelle, 1970, Washington Sq. Coll., NYU, 1971, U. So. Calif., 1972, NYU, 1973. Actor: (films) Last Picture Show, 1971, The Heartbreak Kid, 1973, Daisy Miller, 1974, At Long Last Love, 1975, Taxi Driver, 1976, Special Delivery, 1976, Silver Bears, 1977, The Lady Vanishes, 1978, Earthright, 1980, The Return, 1986, Chances Are, 1988, Texasville, 1990, Alice, 1990, Married to It, 1991, Once Upon a Crime, 1992, The Last Word, 1995, The Muse, 1999, Marine Life, 2000, Open Window, 2006, (TV series) The Yellow Rose, 1983-84, Moonlighting, 1985-89, Cybill, 1994-98 (also prodr.), The L Word, 2007-, (TV films) A Guide for the Married Woman, 1978, Secrets of a Married Man, 1984, Seduced, 1985, The Long Hot Summer, 1985, Which Way Home, 1991, Memphis, 1992 (also co-writer, co-exec. prodr.), Stormy Weathers, 1992, Telling Secrets, 1993, There Was a Little Boy, 1993, Journey of the Heart, 1997, Due East, 2002, Martha, Inc.: The Story of Martha Stewart, 2003, Martha Behind Bars, 2005; record albums include Cybill Does It To Cole Porter, 1974, Cybill and Stan Getz, 1977, Vanilla with Phineas Newborn, Jr, 1978; appeared in stage plays A Shot in the Dark, 1977, Picnic, 1980, Vanities, 1981, The Muse, 1999, Marine Life, 2000; co-author Cybill Disobedience, 2000.

SHEPHERD, JOHN FREDERIC, lawyer; b. Oak Park, Ill., May 22, 1954; s. James Frederic Shepherd and Margaret Joanne (Crotchett) Woollen; m. Jane Lowell Montgomery; children: Eliza Marion, Justine Catherine, Austin Frederic, Jack Lowell. AB magna cum laude, Dartmouth Coll., Hanover, NH, 1976; JD, U. Denver, 1979. Bar: Colo. 1979, US Dist. Ct. Colo. 1979, DC 1981, Okla. 2005, US Dist. Ct. DC 1981, US Ct. Appeals (10th cir.) 1981, US Ct. Appeals (DC cir.) 1982, US Supreme Ct. 1984, US Ct. Appeals (9th cir.) 1990. Assoc. Holland & Hart, Denver, 1979-81, Washington, 1981-85, ptnr., 1985-87, Denver, 1987—; natural resources disting. practitioner in residence U. Denver Coll. Law, 1998. Reporter Mineral Law Newsletter, 1985-92. Mem. 50 for Colo., Denver, 1989. Mem. ABA (chmn. pub. lands and land use com. 1991-93, mem. coun. sect. of natural resources energy and environ. law 1993-96), Rocky Mountain Mineral Law Found. (mem. long-range planning com. 1988—, trustee 1993-95), Inst. Energy Law (exec. com. 2006-), Dartmouth Alumni Club (pres. Washington chpt. 1985-86, trustee Rocky Mt. chpt., 1998-2001), Denver Athletic Club. Avocations: fly fishing, basketball, bicycling. Home: 320 Clermont St Pky Denver CO 80220-5642 Office: Holland & Hart 555 17th St Ste 3200 Denver CO 80202-3950 Office Phone: 303-295-8309. Business E-Mail: jshepherd@hollandhart.com.

SHEPHERD, JOHN MICHAEL, lawyer; b. St. Louis, Aug. 1, 1955; s. John Calvin and Bernice Florence (Hines) S.; m. Deborah Tremaine Fenton, Oct. 10, 1981; children: Elizabeth White, Katherine Tremaine. BA, Stanford U., 1977; JD, U. Mich., 1980. Bar: Calif. 1981, D.C. 1991, U.S. Dist. Ct. (no. dist.) Calif. 1981. Assoc. McCutchen, Doyle, Brown & Enersen, San Francisco, 1980-82; spl. asst. to asst. atty. gen. U.S. Dept. Justice, Washington, 1982-84, dep. asst. atty gen., 1984-86; assoc. counsel to The President The White House, Washington, 1986-87; sr. dep. comptroller of the currency Dept. Treasury, Washington, 1987-91; spl. counsel Sullivan & Cromwell, NYC, 1991-93, Washington, 1993; exec. v.p., gen. counsel Shawmut Nat. Corp., Boston, 1993-95; ptnr. Brobeck, Phleger & Harrison LLP, San Francisco, 1995-2000; exec. v.p., gen. counsel, sec. Bank of New York

Co., Inc., NYC, 2001—04; exec. v.p., gen. counsel, chief risk officer, sec. Bank of the West, San Francisco, 2004—, pres., COO, 2006—07, pres., CEO, 2008—. Bd. dirs. Promontory Interfin. Corp., Pacific Mutual Holding Co., Pacific LifeCorp. Contbr. articles to profl. jours. Asst. dir. policy Reagan-Bush Presdl. Transition Team, Washington, 1980-81; bd. dirs. Reagan Dep. Asst. Secs., Washington, 1985-90, Episc. Charities N.Y., 2001-2004, Episc. Charities Calif., 2005-, Common Good, Presidio Trust, 2008-; trustee New Eng. Aquarium, 1994-96. Named one of Outstanding Young Men Am., U.S. Jaycees, 1984; Wardack Research fellow Washington U., 1976. Mem. ABA (chmn. fin. markets and ins. com., antitrust law sect. 1992-95, banking law com. 1983—, vice chair 1998-2002, chmn. bank holding co. acquisitions subcom. 1995-98, bus. law sect., standing com. on law and nat. security 1984-96), DC Bar Assn., Am. Judicature Soc., Coun. Fgn. Rels., Chevy Chase Club, Met. Club, Olympic Club, Fin. Svcs. Roundtable. Office: Bank of the West 180 Montgomery St San Francisco CA 94104 Business E-Mail: michaelshepherd@bankofthewest.com.

SHEPHERD, KAREN, former congresswoman; b. Silver City, N.Mex., July 5, 1940; m. Vincent P. Shepherd. BA, U. Utah, 1962; MA, Brigham Young U., 1963. Former instr. Brigham Young U., Am. U., Cairo; former pres. Webster Pub. Co.; former adminstr. David Eccles Sch. Bus., U. Utah; former dir. Salt Lake County Social Svcs., Utah; former dir. continuing edn. Westminster Coll.; former mem. Utah Senate; mem. 103d Congress from 2d Utah dist., Washington, 1993—94; exec. dir., U.S. rep. European Bank for Reconstruction Devel., London, 1996—2002; mem. exec. com., chair East West Trade and Investment Forum Am. C. of C., England, 1998—2002; dir. EMILY's List, 2002. Mem. nat. governing bd. Common Cause, Washington, 1995—96, Internat. Del. to Monitor Elections in West Bank and Gaza, Israel, Nat. Planned Parenthood Action Fund, 2004—; founder Karen Shepherd Fund; founding mem. Utah Women's Polit. Caucus, Project 2000; mem. trustee KeyBank Victory Funds; bd. dirs. UBS Bank, USA, O.C. Tanner; fellow Inst. Politics, Harvard U., 1995. Former mem. United Way, Pvt. Industry Coun.; former mem. adv. bd. U.S. West Grad. Sch. Social Work; trustee Westminster Coll.; bd. dirs. Utah Red Cross, 2003-06; chair Grad. Sch. Social Work, U. Utah, 1986-88, David Essler Sch. Bus., 1996—. Recipient Women in Bus. award, US Small Bus. Assn., Woman of Achievement award, Pathfinder award, Leadership award, YWCA, 1st pl. award, Nat. Assn. Journalists, Disting. Alumni award, U. Utah Coll. Humanities, Eleanor Roosevelt award, Utah Dem. Party, 2002, Merit of Honor award, U. Utah, 2004. Fellow Inst. Politics Kennedy Sch. Govt., Internat. Women's Forum, Salt Lake Area C. of C. (pub. rels. com.)., Coun. on Fgn. Rels. Home: PO Box 1049 Salt Lake City UT 84110-1049

SHEPHERD, MARY LOU, state legislator; m. James Shepherd. Ret. bus. owner; mem. Dist. 4 Idaho House of Reps., Boise, mem. Dist. 2, 2003—. Democrat. Office: Dist Office 273 Crescent Dr Wallace ID 83873 also: Legis Services Office PO Box 83720 Boise ID 83720 Office Phone: 208-682-4771. Office Fax: 208-682-2319.*

SHEPHERD, PAUL H., school system administrator; b. Salt Lake City, Sept. 6, 1955; s. Richard Lawrence and Janis (Hoskings) S.; m. Marlene Wade, Aug. 31, 1978; children: Janice, Faith, Matthew, Andrew, Luke, Christian. BS in Elem. Edn., U. Utah, 1981, MEd, 1985. Cert. elem. tchr. Utah, adminstrv. certification Utah. Printer Transamerica Film Svc., Salt Lake City, 1978-81; tchr. Granite Sch. Dist., Salt Lake City, 1981—. Pres. Granite Fedn. Tchrs., 1985-87, treas., 1990-92. Chmn. rels. com. Boy Scouts Am., 1972-98. Recipient Outstanding Tchr. award Excel Found., 1985, Elem. Tchr. of Yr. award Utah Fedn. Tchrs., 1991. Mem. ASCD, Utah Assn Gifted Children. Democrat. Avocations: fishing, guitar. Home: PO Box 65671 Salt Lake City UT 84165-0671 Office Phone: 801-646-4123. E-mail: shepfam@concentric.net, paul.shepherd@granite.k12.ut.us, paul.shepherd@comcast.net.

SHEPPARD, JACK W., retired career officer; b. Parkersburg, W.Va., Aug. 8, 1931; s. James Lee and Audrey Irene (Heiney) S.; m. Norma Ann Stutler, Sept. 4, 1953; children: Bradley, Gregory. BAC, U. Akron, Ohio, 1955; MA in Pub. Adminstrn., George Washington U., 1965. Advanced through grades to maj. gen. USAF; vice comdr. 60 Mil. Airlift Wing, USAF, Travis AFB, Calif., 1977-79; comdr. 1606 Air Base Wing, USAF, Kirtland AFB, N.Mex., 1979-81; dir. internat. staff Inter Am. Def. Bd., USAF, Washington, 1981-82; dep. chief of staff for pers. USAF Mil. Airlift Command, Scott AFB, Ill., 1982-83, chief of staff, 1983-85; comdr. Twenty First Air Force, McGuire AFB, NJ, 1985-87; asst. dep. chief staff programs and resources Hdqrs. USAF, Washington, 1987-88, ret., 1988. Mem. Albuquerque Armed Forces Adv. Assn., Order of Daedalians, Air Force Assn., Airlift Assn., USAF Order of the Sword, USAF Order of the Bayonet, Theta Chi. Presbyterian. Home: PO Box 908 21 Beaver Ln Cedar Crest NM 87008-0908 E-mail: jackgenusaf@cs.com.

SHER, BYRON D., state legislator, law educator; b. 1928; BSBA, Washington U., St. Louis, 1949; JD, Harvard U., 1952. Bar: Mass. 1952. Sole practice, Boston, 1952-54; teaching fellow Harvard U., Cambridge, Mass., 1954-55; asst. prof. law So. Methodist U., Dallas, 1955-57; asst. prof. Stanford (Calif.) U. Law Sch., 1957-59, assoc. prof., 1959-62, prof., 1962—; senator Calif. State Legislature, Sacramento, 1996—. Cons. Fulbright research scholar Victoria U., Wellington, N.Z., 1964; mem. Calif. State Assembly, 1980-96. Author: (with others) Law and Society, 1960, mem., Calif. Senate, 1996. Mem. Nat. Conf. Commrs. Uniform State Laws. Address: 260 Main St Ste 201 Redwood City CA 94063-1733 also: State Capitol Rm 2082 Sacramento CA 95814

SHER, PAUL PHILLIP, pathologist; b. Bklyn., Oct. 25, 1939; s. Louis and Lottie (Kloner) S.; m. Joan E. Zeffren, June 9, 1964; children: Matthew, Andrew, Lawrence. BS cum laude, Hobart Coll., 1961; MD, Washington U., 1965. Diplomate Am. Bd. Pathology. Intern Columbia-Presbyn. Hosp., NYC, 1965-66, resident in pathology, 1966-69; instr. pathology Columbia Presbyn. Hosp., NYC, 1968-70; resident in pathology Englewood (N.J.) Hosp., 1969-70; dir. clin. chemistry Frances Delafeld Hosp., NYC, 1970-71; dir. blood bank Bethesda Naval Hosp., Rockville, Md., 1971-72, dir. hematology, 1973; dir. clin. chemistry NYU Med. Ctr., Tisch Hosp., 1973, dir. clin. labs., 1980-93. Editor Lab. Med.; contbr. articles to profl. jours. Lt. comdr. USN, 1971-73. Fellow Coll. Am. Pathologists, Am. Soc. Clin. Pathologists, Explorer's Club.

SHER, STACEY M., film and television producer; b. Oct. 8, 1961; MFA, U. Southern Calif., 1985. Dir. devel. Hill/Obst Prodns., 1985, v.p. prodn.; sr. v.p. Lynda Obst Prodns., 1991; joined Jersey Films, 1992, ptnr. Assoc. prodr. (films) Heartbreak Hotel, 1988, The Fisher King, 1991; exec. prodr.: (films) Reality Bites, 1994, Pulp Fiction, 1994, Drowning Mona, 2000, Garden State, 2004; prodr.: (films) Get Shorty, 1995, Matilda, 1996, Feeling Minnesota, 1996, Gattaca, 1997, Out of Sight, 1998, Living Out Loud, 1998, Man on the Moon, 1999, Erin Brockovich, 2000, The Caveman's Valentine, 2001, How High, 2001, Camp, 2003, Be Cool, 2005, The Skeleton Key, 2005, World Trade Center, 2006, Freedom Writers, 2007, Reno 911!: Miami, 2007; exec. prodr.: (TV series) Kate Brasher, 2001, The American Embassy, 2002, Karen Sisco, 2003, The Funkhousers, 2002, Other People's Business, 2003. Named one of The 100 Most Powerful Women in Entertainment, The Hollywood Reporter, 2005—07. Mem.: Prodrs. Guild America (mem. bd. dirs.). Office: Jersey Films PO Box 491246 Los Angeles CA 90049

SHERFY, BRADLEY LLOYD, professional golfer; b. Jan. 9, 1956; m. Jeannette Meier; children: Kelli, Corinne, James. BS in Econs., UCLA, 1978. Profl. golfer, 1978—; head golf profl. Harbor Golf Practice Ctr., Wilmington, Calif., 1995—. Head profl. PGA Mulligan Golf Ctr., Torrance, Calif. Named So. Calif. PGA Player of Yr., 1993, 94, 95, SCPGA Match & Stroke Play Champion; record holder Desert Falls Country Club, Palm Valley Country Club, Hillcrest Country Club, Spanish Hills Country Club, De Bell Golf Course, Buenaventura Golf Coiurse. Office: UCLA 325 Westwood Plz Los Angeles CA 90095-8356

SHERIDAN, CHRISTOPHER FREDERICK, human resources executive; b. Syracuse, NY, June 7, 1953; s. Frederick John and Patricia Ann S.; m. Diane Marie Harman, Dec. 31, 1977; children: Ryan, Kelly. BS in Indsl. Relations, LeMoyne Coll., 1975. Employee rels. trainee Anaconda Co., Buffalo, 1975-76, employee rels. rep. LA, 1976-78; pers. mgr. HITCO, Gardena, Calif., 1978-80; labor rels. rep. Miller Brewing Co., Fulton, NY, 1980-82, labor rels. mgr. LA, 1982-90; employee rels. mgr. Ryder Distbn. Resources, Anaheim, Calif., 1990-91; dir. human resources Alta-Dena Cert. Dairy Inc., City of Industry, Calif., 1991-99; regional human resources dir. west/southwest Dean Foods Co., 1999—2004; regional human resources dir. Mission Foods, 2004—05; fin. cons. Am. Nat. Fin. Svcs. Corp., Upland, Calif., 2006—08; mgr. regional human rels. Bimbo Bakeries USA, 2008—. Mem. Soc. Human Resources Mgmt. Roman Catholic. Avocations: golf, basketball, reading, music. Office: 366 S Acacia Ave Fullerton CA 92831

SHERIDAN, MICHAEL JOHN, bishop; b. St. Louis, Mar. 4, 1945; Grad., Cardinal Glennon Coll., Kenrick Seminary. Ordained priest Archdiocese of St. Louis, Mo., 1971; prof. theology Kenrick Seminary, St. Louis, 1977-87; assoc. pastor St. Stephen Protomartyr Parish, 1987-88; pastor King Parish, St. Louis, 1988-93, Immacolata Parish, St. Louis, 1993-97; aux. bishop Roman Cath. Ch., St. Louis, 1997—2001; ordained bishop, 1997; coadjutor bishop Diocese of Colorado Springs, 2001—03, bishop, 2003—. Roman Catholic. Office: Diocese of Colorado Springs 228 N Cascade Ave Colorado Springs CO 80903 Office Phone: 719-636-2345. Office Fax: 719-636-1216.

SHERIDAN, NICOLLETTE, actress; b. Worthing, Sussex, Eng., Nov. 21, 1963; d. Sally Sheridan; m. Harry Hamlin, Sept. 7, 1991 (div. 1993). Actor: (films) The Sure Thing, 1985, Noises Off, 1992, Spy Hard, 1996, Beverly Hills Ninja, 1997, I Woke Up Early the Date I Died, 1998, Raw Nerve, 1999, .com for Murder, 2002, Lost Treasure, 2003, Code Name: The Cleaner, 2007, (voice) Fly Me to the Moon, 2008,; (TV series) Knots Landing, 1986—93 (Soap Opera Digest award, 1990, 1991), Paper Dolls, 1984, Desperate Housewives, 2004— (co-recipient, Outstanding Performance by an Ensemble in a Comedy Series, Screen Actors Guild award, 2005, 2006); (TV films) Dead Man's Folly, 1986, Deceptions, 1990, Somebody's Daughter, 1992, A Time to Heal, 1994, Indictment: The McMartin Trial, 1995, Silver Strand, 1995, The People Next Door, 1996, Murder in My Mind, 1997, Dead Husbands, 1998, The Spiral Staircase, 2000, Haven't We Met Before?, 2002, Deadly Betrayal, 2003, Deadly Visions, 2004; (TV miniseries) Lucky/Chances, 1990, Knots Landing: Back to the Cul-de-Sac, 1997; TV appearances include Paradise, 1991, Will & Grace, 2003, Becker, 2003. Office: Desperate Housewives Touchtone Television 100 Universal City Plaza Bldg 212B Ste G Universal City CA 91608

SHERK, KENNETH JOHN, lawyer; b. Ida Grove, Iowa, Feb. 27, 1933; s. John and Dorothy (Myers) Sherk; children: Karin Fulton, Katrina, Keith, Kyle. BSc, U. Iowa, 1955; JD, George Washington U., 1961. Bar: Ariz. 1962, U.S. Dist. Ct. Ariz. 1962, U.S. Ct. Appeals (9th cir.) 1966, U.S. Supreme Ct. 1974. Assoc. Moore & Romley, Phoenix, 1962-67, ptnr., 1967-79, Romley & Sherk, Phoenix, 1979-85; dir. Fennemore Craig, Phoenix, 1985—. 1st lt. U.S. Army, 1955-58, Korea. Recipient Profl. Achievement Svcs. award George Washington Law Assn., 1986, Ariz. Judges Assn., 1989, Disting. Svc. award Phoenix Assn. Def. Counsel, 1990; named Mem. of Yr. State Bar of Ariz., 1994. Fellow Am. Coll. Trial Lawyers, Am. Acad. Appellate Lawyers, Am. Bar Found., Ariz. Bar Found. (Walter E. Craig award 1999); mem. ABA (ho. of dels. 1990-93), Ariz. Bar Assn. (pres. 1985-86), Maricopa County Bar Assn. (pres. 1978-79). Republican. Congregationalist. Avocations: fishing, hiking, bicycling. Home: 1554 W Las Palmaritas Dr Phoenix AZ 85021-5429 Office: Fennemore Craig 3003 N Central Ave Ste 2600 Phoenix AZ 85012-2913 Office Phone: 602-916-5383. Business E-Mail: ksherk@fclaw.com. E-mail: ksherk@cox.net.

SHERMAN, BRADLEY JAMES, United States Representative from California; b. LA, Oct. 24, 1954; s. Maurice H. and Lane (Moss) Sherman. BA summa cum laude, UCLA, 1974; JD magna cum laude, Harvard U., 1979. CPA Calif.; bar: Calif. 1979. Pvt. practice, LA, 1980-91; mem. Calif. Franchise Tax Bd., 1991-95, US Congress from 27th Calif. dist., 1996—, internat. rels. com., judiciary com., fgn. affairs com., fin. svcs. com. Instr. Harvard Law Sch. Internat. Tax Prog.; mem. Calif. State Bd. Equalization, Sacramento, 1990—97, chmn., 1991—95; mem. Dem. Homeland Security Task Force, New Dem. Coalition. Contbr. articles to profl. jours.; lectr. in field (tax law and policy). Bd. dirs., rep. tax issues Calif. Common Cause, 1985—89. Mem.: Calif. Bar Assn. Democrat. Jewish. Office: US Ho Reps 1030 Longworth HOB Washington DC 20515-0527 Office Phone: 202-225-5911. E-mail: brad.sherman@mail.house.gov.

SHERMAN, CRAIG, Internet company executive; AB magna cum laude, Princeton U. Joined Cendant Corp., 1991, v.p. internat. divsn., 1994—96; CEO Cendant Japan, 1998—99; regional v.p. Am. Internat. Group (AIG), 1999—2000; exec. v.p., gen. mgr. ThirdAge Media; COO MyFamily.com, 2000—05; entrepreneur in residence Benchmark Capital, 2005—06; CEO Gaia Interactive, 2006—. Spkr. in field. Office: Gaia Interactive, Inc Ste 125 50 Airport Parkway San Jose CA 95110 Office Phone: 408-573-8800. Office Fax: 408-573-9800.

SHERMAN, IRWIN WILLIAM, biological sciences educator, academic administrator; b. NYC, Feb. 12, 1933; s. Morris and Anna (Ezaak) S.; m. Vilia Gay Turner, Aug. 25, 1966; children: Jonathan Turner, Alexa Joy. BS, CCNY, 1954; MS, Northwestern U., Evanston, Ill., 1959, PhD, 1960. Asst. prof. U. Calif., Riverside, 1962-67, assoc. prof., 1967-70, prof. biology, 1970—2005, chmn. biology dept., 1974-79, dean Coll. Natural and Agrl. Scis., dir. agrl. expt. sta., 1981-88, exec. vice chancellor, 1993-94, emeritus prof., 2006—; vis. scientist Scripps Rsch. Inst., 2006—. Instr. marine biol. lab., Woods Hole, Mass., 1963-68; mem. study sect. tropical medicine NIH, 1970-73; cons. Agy. Internat. Devel., 1978-90; mem. ad hoc study group U.S. Army, 1975-78. Author: The Invertebrates: Function and Form, 1976, Biology: A Human Approach, 1989, Malaria: Parasite Biology, Pathogenesis, Protection, 1998, Molecular Approaches to Malaria, 2005, The Power of Plagues, 2006, Twelve Diseases That Changed Our World, 2007, Reflections on a Century of Malaria Biochemistry, 2009. Steering com. World Health Orgn., 1978-87. With U.S. Army, 1954-56. USPHS fellow Rockefeller Inst., 1960-62, Guggenheim fellow, 1967, NIH/Nat. Inst. Med. Rsch. fellow 1973-74, Walter and Eliza Hall Inst. for Med. Rsch. fellow, 1986; Wellcome Trust lectr. Brit. Soc. Parasitology, 1987, Scripps Rsch. Inst. fellow 1991, 2003-07. Fellow AAAS, Am. Acad. Microbiology; mem. Am. Soc. Tropical Medicine and Hygiene, Soc. Protozoology, Soc. Parasitology, Sigma Xi. Democrat. Jewish. Avocations: painting, reading. Office: Scripps Research Inst Dept Cell Biology ICND 202 10550 N Torrey Pines La Jolla CA 92037 Office Phone: 858-784-2302. E-mail: isherman@scripps.edu.

SHERMAN, RANDOLPH, plastic and reconstructive surgeon, educator; b. St. Louis, May 27, 1951; s. Leon and Pearl (Lichtenfeld) S.; 1 child, Max Lassen. BA, U. Rochester, 1973; MD, U. Mo., 1977. Diplomate Am. Bd. Surgery, Am. Bd. Plastic Surgery (cert. added qualification in hand surgery). Intern in gen. medicine U. Wis., Madison, 1978; intern in surgery U. Calif., San Francisco, 1978-79, resident in surgery, 1979-81, SUNY, Syracuse, 1981-83; fellow in plastic and reconstructive surgery U. So. Calif., 1983-85, asst. prof. surger and orthopedics LA, 1985-91, assoc. prof. clin. surgery and orthopaedics, 1991-92, assoc. prof. clin. surgery, orthopaedics and neurol. surgery, 1992-96, chmn. divsn. plastic and reconstructive surgery, 1994—, prof. clin. surgery, orthopaedics and neurol. surgery, 1996—. Mem. cons. staff City of Hope Nat. Med. Ctr., Duarte, Calif., 1985-91, 94—, St. John's Hosp., Santa Monica, 1989—, USC Univ. Hosp., 1997—; mem. staff, med. dir. Microsurg. Ctr. Hosp. Good Samaritan, L.A., 1985-93; mem. plastic and reconstructive surgery staff Kenneth Norris Jr. Cancer Hosp., L.A., 1985—, L.A. County/U. So. Calif. Med. Ctr., L.A., 1985—; mem. staff St. Vincent Med. Ctr., L.A., 1986-92, Orthop. Hosp., L.A., 1986—; Shriner's Hosp. for Crippled Children, L.A., 1987-92, Children's Hosp. L.A., 1987—, Cedars Sinai Med. Ctr., L.A., 1987—, Estelle Doheny Eye Hosp., L.A., 1994—, numerous others; chief plastic and reconstructive surgery divsn. U. So. Calif. U. Hosp., L.A., 1991—, mem. active staff; dir. Am. Bd. Plastic Surgery 2000—, Am. Bd. Surgery, 2004—; vice-chair dept. surgery Keck Sch. Medicine, 2004-; assoc. med. dir. surg. svcs. L.A. County/U. So. Calif. Med. Ctr., 2005; mem plastic reconstructive surgery staff U. So. Calif. Hosp., 1991—; vice chair dept. surgery Keck Sch. Medicine, U. So. Calif. lectr., 2005; rschr. in field. Editor: Orthopedic Clinics, 1993; assoc. editor Surg. Rounds, 1989—, Jour. Hand Surgery, 1992-96, Am. Jour. Reconstructive Microsurgery, 1995—; sect. editor PRS 2005—; contbr. articles to profl. jours., chpts. to books. Founder L.A. chpt. Operation Smile Internat., 1993—. Recipient L.A. Humanitarian award Calif. Hosp., 1994; Microsurg. Devel. grantee Hosp. Good Samaritan, 1987-92, U. So. Calif. U. Hosp., 1992—; grantee Searle R&D, 1995-97, Cohesion Corp., 1997. Fellow ACS, Am. Assn. Plastic Surgeons, Am. Assn. Hand Surgeons (bd. dirs. 1991-95), Am. Soc. Hand Surgery, Am. Soc. Reconstructive Microsurgery (past pres.), Calif. Soc. Plastic Surgery; mem. Am. Soc. Plastic and Reconstructive Surgery, Am. Soc. Peripheral Nerve, Internat. Soc. Reconstructive Microsurgery, Calif. Med. Assn., Calif. Soc. Plastic Surgery, Assn. Acad. Chmn. Plastic Surgery, Plastic Surgery Rsch. Coun., Musculoskeletal Infection Soc., Undersea Med. Soc., Flying Physicians Assn., Wound Healing Soc. Avocations: flying, mountain climbing, scuba diving, jazz piano, gardening. Office: 1450 San Pablo St Ste 2000 Los Angeles CA 90089-0106 Office Phone: 323-442-6470. Business E-Mail: rsherman@surgery.usc.edu.

SHERMAN, ROBERT B(ERNARD), composer, lyricist, screenwriter; b. Dec. 19, 1925; s. Al and Rosa (Dancis) S.; m. Joyce Ruth Sasner, Sept. 27, 1953; children: Laurie Shane, Jeffrey Craig, Andrea Tracy, Robert Jason. Student, UCLA, 1943; BA, Bard Coll., 1949; MusD (hon.), Lincoln U., 1990. Songwriter Walt Disney Prodns., Beverly Hills, Calif.; composer, lyricist United Artist, Beverly Hills; v.p. Musi-Classics, Inc.; founder, CEO, exec. prodr. Music World Corp., Beverly Hills, 1958—. Songs include Tall Paul, Pineapple Princess, You're Sixteen (Gold Record), It's a Small World, Winnie the Pooh, Let's Get Together; songwriter films including The Parent Trap, 1961, Summer Magic, 1963, Mary Poppins, 1964 (Acad. awards for best score, best song, 1964, Grammy award, 1965), That Darn Cat, 1965, Winnie The Pooh, 1965, Jungle Book, 1967, Chitty Chitty Bang Bang, 1969, Bedknobs and Broomsticks, 1971; songs Snoopy, Come Home!, 1972; song scores Charlotte's Web, 1972, Cabbage Patch Kids, 1974, Little Nemo, 1992, The Mighty Kong, 1996, The Tigger Movie, 2000; co-producer NBC-TV spl. Goldilocks, 1970; co-producer, composer, lyricist stage musical Victory Canteen, 1971; composer-lyricist Broadway show Over Here!, 1975, Busker Alley, 1995, stage prodn. Chitty Chitty Bang Bang, London, 2002 (Musical Theater award, Variety Club of Great Britain, 2003), Broadway, 2005, Mary Poppins, London, 2004, Broadway, 2006), screenplay and song score Tom Sawyer, 1972, Huckleberry Finn, 1974, The Slipper and the Rose, 1977, The Magic of Lassie, 1978. Served with inf. AUS, 1943-45 ETO. Decorated Purple Heart. Recipient Mousecar award Disney Studios, Disney Legend award, 1990, Winsor McCay award for lifetime achievement and contbn. to animation, Intenat. Animated Film Soc., 2003, Nat. Medal Arts, 2008; named to Hollywood Walk of Fame, 1976, Songwriters Hall of Fame, 2005. Mem. Acad. Motion Picture Arts and Scis. (exec. bd. music br. 12 yrs.), Broadcast Music, Inc. (Pioneer award, 1977, Lifetime Achievement award, 1991), AFTRA, Nat. Acad. Rec. Arts and Scis., Composers and Lyricists Guild (exec. bd.), Dramatists Guild, Authors League. Office: Music World Corp PO Box 16425 Beverly Hills CA 90209-2425 Office Phone: 310-576-8100. E-mail: info@musicworldcorp.com.

SHERMAN, ZACHARY, civil engineer, aerospace engineer, consultant; b. NYC, Oct. 26, 1922; s. Harry and Minnie (Schulsinger) Sherman; m. Bertha Leikin, Mar. 23, 1947; children: Gene Victor, Carol Beth. BCE, CCNY, 1943; MCE, Polytech. U. N.Y., Bklyn., 1953, PhD in Civil Engring. & Mechanics, 1969; MME, Stevens Inst. Tech., 1968. Registered profl. engr., N.Y., N.J. Stress analyst Gen. Dynamics, San Diego, 1943-45; sr. stress analyst Republic Aviation, Farmingdale, NY, 1945-47, 59-62; prof. civil engring. U. Miss., Oxford, 1954-59; lectr. Stevens Inst. Tech., Hoboken, NJ, 1962-67, CUNY, 1967-69; assoc. prof. aerospace engring. Pa. State U., State College, 1969-73; prin. Dr. Zachary Sherman Cons. Engrs., Santa Monica, Calif., 1973—; aerospace engr. FAA, NYC, 1980-86. Designated cons. engr. rep. FAA, 1986—. Contr.: articles to profl. jours. including Jour. of Aircraft AIAA. NSF grantee, 1972. Fellow: ASCE; mem.: AIAA (v.p. Western Conn. chpt. 1977—78), N.Y. Acad. Scis., Sigma Xi. Achievements include development of beam/beam-column deck suspension bridge; solutions to pothole problems; prestressed aircraft wing. Home and Office: 2021 California Ave Apt 7 Santa Monica CA 90403-4531 Office Phone: 310-264-5990. Fax: 310-264-5990. Personal E-mail: aerozach@earthlink.net.

SHERR, ELLIOTT HAROLD, neurologist, researcher; s. Walter R. and Karen Sherr; m. Linda M. Rubinstein, July 2, 1989; children: Rachel J., David A., Jessica C. BAS in Biology and Philosophy, Stanford U., Calif., 1984; MD, PhD, Columbia U., NYC, 1995. Diplomate Am. Bd. of Psychiatry and Neurology. Vis. scientist La Catolica U., Santiago, Chile, 1995—96; resident in pediats. U. Calif., San Francisco, 1996—2000, instr. neurology and pediats., 2000—02, asst. prof., 2002—, assoc. prof., 2008—. Mem. exec. com. Nat. Orgn. Dosirders of Corpus Callosum, Calif., 2003—06. Recipient Sci. Award, Child Neurology Found., 2004—06, Philip Dodge Young Investigator award, Child Neurology Soc., 2006. Mem.: Am. Acad. Neurology. Independent. Avocations: travel, cooking, cycling. Office: U Calif San Francisco Dept Neurology 350 Parnassus Ave San Francisco CA 94143-0137

SHERRARD, WILLIAM ROBERT, retired operations management educator; b. Langford, SD, July 16, 1932; s. Earl George and Isabel Ann (Williams) S.; m. Miriam Elaine Murren, June 11, 1960. BBA, U. Wash., 1957, MBA, 1958, PhD, 1965. Indsl. engr. Boeing Airplane Co., Seattle, 1957-59; prof. Idaho State U., Pocatello, 1959-60, U. NC, Chapel Hill, 1965-68, San Diego State U., 1968—2006; ret., 2006. Cons. various orgns., San Diego, 1968—. Author: (textbook) Production Management, 1990; contbr. articles to profl. jours. Mem. Decision Scis. Inst. (program chmn. 1972-79), Acad. Mgmt., Am. Inst. Mgmt. Scis., Am. Prodn. Inventory Control Soc., Ops. Rsch. Soc. Am., Beta Gamma Sigma, Sigma Iota Epsilon. Avocations: golf, hiking, jogging. Office Phone: 858-481-3159. Business E-Mail: sherrard@mail.sdsu.edu.

SHERRELL, JOHN BRADFORD, lawyer; b. Indpls., Jan. 27, 1951; s. Carl and Mary Jean (Bell) S.; m. Sherry Naomi Calhoun, Apr. 28, 1974; children: David Alan, Corinne Elizabeth. BA, Yale U., 1973; JD, U. Mich., 1977. Bar: Calif. 1977. Ptnr. Latham & Watkins, Los Angeles, 1977—. Dep. gen. counsel to Ind. Commn. on L.A. Police Dept. Named an Am.'s Top Black Lawyers, Black Enterprise Mag., 2003. Mem. ABA, Calif. Bar Assn. (co-chair real estate fin. subsect. of real property sec. 1990-92), L.A. County Bar Assn. (barrister's exec. com. 1978-80, bd. trustees 1991-93). Office: Latham Watkins 355 S Grand Ave Los Angeles CA 90071-1560 Home: 11576 Chiquita St Studio City CA 91604-2914 Office Phone: 213-891-8174. E-mail: john.sherrell@lw.com.

SHERRER, CHARLES DAVID, dean, clergyman; b. Marion, Ohio, Sept. 21, 1935; s. Harold D. and Catherine E. (Fye) S. AB, U. Notre Dame, 1958, MA, 1965; S.T.L., Gregorian U., 1962; PhD, U. N.C., 1969; HHD, King's Coll., 1997. Ordained priest Roman Cath. Ch., 1961. Instr. English U. Portland, Oreg., 1963-64, asst. prof. Oreg., 1969-74, prof. Oreg., 1990—2005, prof. emeritus Oreg., 2005—, chmn. dept. Oreg., 1970-74, dean Grad. Sch. Oreg., 1982-87, mem. Bd. Regents Oreg., 1986-87, acad. v.p. Oreg., 1987-96; pres. King's Coll., Wilkes Barre, Pa., 1974-81. Bd. trustees Stonehill Coll., 1992-98; dir. studies Holy Cross Fathers, Ind. Province, 1979-88. Office Phone: 503-943-7596. Business E-Mail: sherrer@up.edu.

SHERRIFFS, RONALD EVERETT, communication and film educator; b. Salem, Oreg., Apr. 10, 1934; s. Robert William and Margaret Kathleen (Tutt) S.; m. Mary Lona West, July 9, 1960; children: Ellen, Matthew. BA, San Jose State U., 1955, MA, 1957; PhD, U. So. Calif., 1964. Instr. theater Mich. State U., East Lansing, 1960-61; asst. prof. broadcasting Tex. Tech U., Lubbock, 1964-65; asst. prof. speech U. Oreg., Eugene, 1965-70, assoc. prof., 1970-79, prof. telecomm. and film, 1979-92, chmn. dept. speech, 1978-84, 88-90, prof. journalism and comm., 1993-2000, prof. emeritus, 2000. Author: (with others) Speech Communication via Radio and TV, 1971, TV Lighting Handbook, 1977, Small Format TV Production, 1985, 3d edit., Video Field Production and Editing, 1994, 4th edit., 1996; prodr., dir. TV programs, 1965—. Mem. Oreg. Pub. Broadcasting Policy Adv. Bd., 1980-88. Served to lt. comdr. USNR, 1957-68, PTO. Faculty enrichment program grantee Can., 1984, 91. Mem. Nat. Communication Assn., AAUP, We. States Communication Assn. Clubs: Oreg. Track; McKenzie Flyfishers (Eugene). Office: U Oreg Journalism Sch Eugene OR 97403 E-mail: sherriff@oregon.uoregon.edu.

SHERWOOD, ARTHUR LAWRENCE, lawyer; b. LA, Jan. 25, 1943; s. Allen Joseph and Edith S. Sherwood; m. Frances Merele, May 1, 1970; children: David, Chet. BA magna cum laude, U. Calif., Berkeley, 1964; MS, U. Chgo., 1965; JD cum laude, Harvard U., 1968. Bar: Calif. 1969, U.S. Dist. Ct. (cen. dist.) Calif. 1968, U.S. Dist. Ct. (no. dist.) Calif. 1971, Calif. 1971, U.S. Dist. Ct. (so. and ea. dists.) Calif. 1973, U.S. Ct. Appeals (9th cir.) 1973, U.S. Ct. Appeals (D.C. cir.) 1991, U.S. Supreme Ct. 1980. Instr. UCLA Law Sch., 1968—69; assoc. Gibson, Dunn & Crutcher, LA, 1968—75, ptnr., 1975—98, of counsel, 1998—. Judge pro tem L.A. Mcpl. and Superior Ct., 1980—98; instr. law UCLA, 1968—69; arbitrator N.Y. Stock Exch., Nat. Futures Assn. Co-author: Civil Procedure During Trial, 1995, Civil Procedure Before Trial, 1990; contbr. articles to profl. jours. Chmn. East Asian Art Coun., L.A. County Mus. Art, 1992—97, 2005—06. NASA fellow, U. Chgo., 1964—65. Master: Am. Contract Bridge League; mem.: Calif. Bar Assn., Phi Beta Kappa. Republican. Avocations: art, history. Office: 10430 Wilshire Blvd. Unit 502 Los Angeles CA 90024

SHERWOOD, ROD(ERICK), III, computer company executive; BA with hons. in Econs., Stanford U.; MBA, Harvard U. With Chrysler Corp., 1981—95; from corp. v.p., treas. to pres. Spaceway Broadband Svcs. Hughes Electronics, 1995—98, pres. Spaceway Broadband Svcs., 1998—99; sr. v.p., CFO BroadStream Corp., 1999—2000, Loudcloud Inc., 2000—02, Gateway Inc., Poway, Calif., 2002—03, exec. v.p., CFO, 2003—. Office: Gateway Inc 7565 Irvine Ctr Dr Irvine CA 92618-2930

SHIBA, WENDY C., lawyer; BA, Mich. State U., 1973; JD cum laude, Temple U. Sch. of Law, 1979. Atty. corp. and securities law O'Melveny & Myers, Los Angeles & NYC; corp. chair Phila. Law Dept., Phila.; v.p., sec., asst. gen. counsel Bowater, Inc., Greenville, SC, 1993—2000; gen. counsel PolyOne Corp., Avon Lake, Ohio, 2000—01, v.p., chief legal officer, sec., 2001—07; exec. v.p., gen. counsel, corp. sec. KB Home, LA, 2007—. Former bd. mem. Legal Services Agency of Western Carolina, S.C. Bd. of Accountancy, Greenville Little Theater, Palmetto Soc. of United Way of Greenville County; former mem. United Way of Greenville County Campaign Cabinet, Palmetto Soc. Women's Leadership Council, Greenville Professional Women's Forum. Office: KB Home 10990 Wilshire Blvd Los Angeles CA 90024

SHIDELER, ROSS PATRICK, literature and language educator, writer, translator, poet; b. Denver, Apr. 12, 1936; BA, San Francisco State U., 1958; MA, U. Stockholm, 1963; PhD, U. Calif., Berkeley, 1968. Instr. in comparative lit. U. Calif., Berkeley, 1967-68; asst. prof. English Hunter Coll., NYC, 1968-69; asst. prof. Scandinavian lang. and comparative lit. UCLA, 1969-73, assoc. prof., 1973-79, prof., 1979—, chmn. program in comparative lit., 1979-86, 92-96, assoc. dean Grad. Divsn., 2003—. Author: (monograph) Voices Under the Ground: Themes and Images in the Poetry of Gunnar Ekelof, 1973, Per Olov Enquist-A Critical Study, 1984, Questioning the Father: From Darwin to Zola, Ibsen, Strindberg and Hardy, 1999; translator: (plays) The Night of the Tribades (Per Olov Enquist), 1977, The Hour of the Lynx (Per Olov Enquist), 1990; co-editor (with Kathleen L. Komar): Lyrical Symbols and Narrative Transformations, Essays in Honor of Ralph Freedman, 1998; U.S. assoc. editor Swedish Book Rev., 1984—. Fellow, Nat. Defense Fgn. Language, 1964—65; Fulbright-Hays fellow, 1966—67. Mem. MLA (exec. com. divsn. Scandinavian Langs. and Lits. 1993-97), Soc. Advancement Scandinavian Study (exec. coun. 1985-89, v.p. 1997-99, pres. 1999-2001), Internat. Comparative Lit. Assn. (treas. 2004-). Office: UCLA Dept Comparative Lit Los Angeles CA 90095

SHIELDS, BROOKE CHRISTA CAMILLE, actress, model; m. Andre Agassi, Apr. 19, 1997 (annulled 1999); m. Chris Henchy, Apr. 4, 2001; children: Rowan Francis Henchy, Grier Hammond Henchy. BA, Princeton U., 1987. Model for Ivory Soap commls. starting in 1966, later for Calvin Klein jeans and Colgate toothpaste commls.; Actor (films) Alice, Sweet Alice, 1975, Pretty Baby, 1977, King of the Gypsies, 1978, Wanda Nevada, 1978, Just You and Me Kid, 1978, Blue Lagoon, 1979, Endless Love, 1980, Sahara, 1983, Backstreet Strays, 1989, Brenda Starr, 1992, Seventh Floor, 1993, Running Wild, 1993, Freaked, 1993, Freeway, 1996, The Misadventures of Margaret, 1998, The Weekend, 1999, The Bachelor, 1999, Black & White, 1999, After Sex, 2000, Rent-A-Husband, 2004, Bob the Butler, 2005, Bag Boy, 2007, The Midnight Meat Train, 2008; (TV movies) The Prince of Central Park, 1977, After the Fall, Wet Gold, I Can Make You Love Me: The Stalking of Laura Black, 1993, Nothing Lasts Forever, 1995, What Makes a Family, 2001, Miss Spider's Sunny Patch Kids, 2003; (TV mini-series) Widows, 2002; (TV series) Suddenly Susan, 1996-99 (People's Choice award Favorite Female in New Series 1997), Lipstick Jungle, 2008-; TV appearances include: The Tonight Show, Bob Hope spls., The Diamond Trap, 1988, Friends, 1996, Just Shoot Me, 1997, I'm With Her, 2004, That 70's Show, 2004, Niptuck 2006; appeared on Broadway in Grease, 1994-95 (Theatre World award 1995), Wonderful Town, 2004, Chicago, 2005; Author: Down Came the Rain: My Journey Through Postpartum Depression, 2005 (NY Times Bestseller list, 2005). Recipient People's Choice award Favorite Young Picture Performer, 1981—84; named Time Mag. Face of the '80s.

SHIELDS, FRANK W., state legislator; b. New Castle, Pa., Mar. 26, 1945; m. Suzanne Shields; 2 children. BA in Secondary Edn., Slippery Rock State Coll., 1967; MDiv, Eastern Bapt. Sem., 1972; DMin, Drew U., 1981. Pastor Trinity United Meth. Ch., 1973-75, Chihoquin United Meth. Ch., 1975-78, Sunnyside United Meth. Ch., 1978-98; mem. Oreg. Legislature, Salem, 1998—, mem. gen. govt. com., vice chair health and human svcs. com., mem. subcom. on human resources. Democrat. Methodist.

SHIERSHKE, NANCY FAY, artist, educator, property manager; b. St. Helens, Oreg., May 10, 1935; d. David Cline and Matilda Ruth (Pearce) Morrison; m. H. McNeal Kavanagh, Sept. 4. 1955 (dec. Dec. 1978); children: Marjorie L. Wood, David M. Kavanagh, Katherine F. Fiske; m. Richard M. Shiershke, Nov. 29, 1980. AA, Pasadena City Coll., Calif., 1956; BA, UCLA, 1965. Substitute elem. sch. tchr., Buena Park, Calif., 1967-69; property mgr. Pky. Cts., Arcadia, Calif., 1977—; libr. Reading Rm., Arcadia, 1979-87; freelance artist Nancy-Shiershke Art St., Arcadia, Calif., 1985—; art gallery hostess Descanso Gardens, La Canada, Flintridge, Calif., 1990—; display and sales person Village Fine Arts Gallery, Arcadia, 1991-92; art instr. Tri Cmty. Adult Edn., Covina, Calif., 1994—. Art instr. Claremont (Calif.) Adult Edn. Group shows include Pasadena Presbyn. Ch., 1985—, Hillcrest Ch., 1992—, Descanso Gardens, 1994—, San Gabriel Fine Arts, 1994—. Named Artist of the Yr. Mid Valley art League, 1990; Recipient Best of Show San Gabriel Fine Arts, 1991, Hulsebus award Pasadena Prebyn. Ch., 1996, Best of Show Eagle Rock Rennaisance Plein Air, 2002. Mem. Nat. Watercolor Soc., San Gabriel Fine Arts, Mid Valley Arts League (Artist of Yr. 1998), East Valley Art Assn., Valley Watercolor Soc., Foothill Creative Arts Group, Water Color West, Calif. Art Club, So. Calif. Plein Air Painters Assn.

SHIFFMAN, MICHAEL A., lawyer; b. Newark, July 23, 1941; LLB magna cum laude, Lincoln U., 1973. Bar: Calif. 1973, U.S. Dist. Ct. (no. dist.) Calif. 1973; lic. real estate broker. Atty. Lanahan & Reilley, San Francisco, EVP and GC-New City N. Am. Editor: Lincoln U. Law Rev., 1972-73. Mem. ABA, Internat. Bar Assn., State Bar Calif. Office: New City N Am 575 Market No 3050 San Francisco CA 94105 Business E-Mail: shifflaw@aol.com.

SHIFLETT, CHRIS, musician; Band mem. Lost Kittenz; guitarist Me First & the Gimme Gimmes, 1995—; lead guitarist No Use For A Name, 1995—99; guitarist Foo Fighters, 1999—; band mem. Viva Death, 2002—, Jackson United, 2005—. With Me First & the Gimme Gimmes (albums) Have a Ball, 1997, Are a Drag, 1999, Blow in the Wind, 2001, Take a Break, 2002, Ruin Jonny's Bar Mitzvah, 2004, with No Use For A Name Leche Con Carne, 1995, Making Friends, 1997, More Betterness!, 1999, with Foo Fighters One by One, 2002 (Grammy Award, Best Rock Album, 2004), In Your Honor, 2005, Echoes, Silence, Patience & Grace, 2007 (Grammy Award, Best Rock Album, 2008), with Viva Death Viva Death, 2002, with Jackson United Jackson United, 2005, with Foo Fighters (songs) All My Life, 2002 (Grammy Award, Best Hard Rock Performance, 2003), The Pretender, 2007 (Grammy Award, Best Hard Rock Performance, 2008). Office Phone: 212-930-4000.

SHIFRIN, DONALD LEE, pediatrician; b. Portland, Oreg., Jan. 10, 1949; m. Barbara Sue Chamberlin, Nov. 3, 2002; children: Max Burton, Alexis Chamberlin. MD, Georgetown U., Washington, 1970. Cert. Am. Bd. Pediatics, 1981. Physician Pediatric Assocs., Bellevue, Wash., 1978—. Clin. prof. pediat. U. Wash. Sch. Medicine, Seattle; nat. adv. bd. Civitas. Chair Maimonides Soc. Jewish Fedn. Greater Seattle, 2000—. Fellow: Am. Acad. Pediat. Office: Pedatric Associates 2700 Northup Way Bellevue WA 98004 Office Fax: 425-828-2256; Home Fax: 206-275-3244. Business E-Mail: dshifrin@peds-associates.com.

SHIMODA, JERRY YASUTAKA, retired national historic park manager; b. Haleiwa, Hawaii, Mar. 21, 1930; s. Tamotsu and Sasai Shimoda; m. Clara H. Segawa, Aug. 7, 1954; children: Karen Marie K., Randall T., Shaun T., Teri Ellen H., Jacqueline Y., David Y. BA in Govt., U. Hawaii, 1952, MA in Far Ea. Area Studies, 1957; postgrad., St. Louis U., 1957-59; PhD in Pub. Adminstrn., Kennedy-Western U., 2004. Historian Jefferson Nat. Expansion Meml. Nat. Hist. Site, St. Louis, 1957-60; chief historian, in charge hist. rsch. and visitor svcs. Saratoga Nat. Hist. Park, Stillwater, NY, 1960-66; chief historian Home of Franklin D. Roosevelt Nat. Hist. Site and, Frederick Vanderbilt Nat. Hist. Site, Hyde Park, NY, 1966-69; instr. Nat. Park Svc. Stephen T. Mather Tng. Ctr., Harpers Ferry, W.Va., 1969-72; supt. Pu'uhonua o Honaunau (Hawaii) Nat. Hist. Park, 1972-96, Puukohola Heiau Nat. Hist. Site, Kawaihae, 1972-96, Asian Descent, First Nat. Park; ret., 1996. Lectr. environ. edn. Pa. State U., U. W.Va., Shepard Coll., 1969—72; acting supr. Kaloko-Honokohau Nat. Hist. Pk., 1988—90; instr. environ. edn., interpretive and basic instructing techniques U. Hawaii, Hilo, Kapiolani C.C.; instr. Japanese culture U. Hawaii, Hilo, 1994; U.S. del. and translator U.S.-Japan Panel on Nat. Parks and Equivalent Res., 1968—97, 2nd. World Conf. Nat. Parks, Yellowstone, Okla., 1972, World Conf. on Marine Parks, Tokyo, 1975; mem. internat. bd. dirs. Heritage Interpretation Internat., 1989—98; trainer Japan Pk. Interpreters, 1997—2006; cons., presenter in field. Contbr. articles to profl. jours., popular mags., local newspapers. Bd. dirs. Volcano Art Ctr.; adv. com. Wailoa State Ctr.; active Hawaii Gov.'s Task Force on Ocean and Recreation; chmn. restoration com. St. Benedict's Ch., Honaunau, 1982-95; chmn. bd. dirs. Kahua Na'au 'Ao, 1996-97; vol. training cons. Nat. Pk. Svc., 1996-2005. Recipient Spl. Achievement award Nat. Park Svc., 1964, 68, 70, resolution W.Va. Senate, 1971, Hawaii Ho. of Reps., 1982, sec.'s cert. Dept. Interior, 1971, Exec. of Yr. award West Hawaii chpt. Profl. Secs. Internat., 1981, cert. Govt. of Japan, 1981, staff plaque Pu'uhonua o Honaunau Nat. Hist. Park, Puukohola Heiau Nat. Hist. Site and Kaloko-Honokohau Nat. Hist. Park, 1988, cert. Japan Nat. Parks Assn., 1989, cert. of appreciation South Kona Aloha Lions Club, 1990, Meritorious Svc. award Sec. Interior, 1996, others. Mem.: Hawaii Mus. Assn. (bd. dirs. 1988—92), Kona Hist. Soc. (bd. dirs. 1988—92), Big Island Ocean Recreation and Tourism Assn. (exec. com.), Hawaii Natural History Assn. (bd. dirs. 2007—), Polynesian Voyaging Soc. (life; hon.), Kona Judo Club (pres. 1977—96), Rotary (pres. Kona Mauka 1978—79, co-founder Volcano chpt. 2001, Disting. Svc. award 1992, Paul Harris fellow 1991). Avocations: writing, reading, travel, teaching.

SHIMPFKY, RICHARD LESTER, bishop; b. Albuquerque, Oct. 18, 1940; m. Jamel Shimpfky, 1966; children: Trevor, Allison, Joshua. Grad., U. Colo., 1963, Va. Theol. Seminary, 1970. Ordained to diaconate Episc. Ch., 1970. With William L. Philips Found., Richmond, Va., 1963-67; curate St. Peter's Ch., Arlington, 1970-72; vicar All Saints' Sharon Chapel, Alexandria, Va., 1972-73, rector, 1973-77, Christ Ch., Ridgewood, N.J., 1977-90; bishop Diocese El Camino Real, Monterey, Calif., 1990—. Avocations: reading, travel. Office: Diocese El Camino Real PO Box 1903 Monterey CA 93942-1903

SHIN, PAULL HOBOM, state legislator, investment company executive; b. Kumchon, Korea, Sept. 27, 1935; came to U.S., 1955; adopted s. Ray and Eloise (Siddoway) Paull; m. Donna June Skaggs, June 12, 1963; children: Paull Y., Alisa M. BA, Brigham Young U., 1962; MPIA, U. Pitts., 1964; MA, U. Wash., 1972, PhD, 1978. Asst. prof. Brigham Young U., Laie, Hawaii, 1964-67; prof. Shoreline Coll., Seattle, 1969-72; pres. A.P.S. Investment Co., Seattle, 1982—; chmn. T.T.I. Telecom. Inc., Bellevue, Wash., 1992—; mem. Wash. Ho. of Reps., Olympia, 1992-94, Wash. Senate, Dist. 21, Olympia, 1998—. Commr., chmn. Office of Pres. Korea, Seoul, 1985-88. Mission pres. LDS Ch., Seoul, 1988-91; bd. dirs. Asian-Ams. for Political Action, Seattle, 1982-84, United Way, Snohomish County, 1992—; advisor internat. trade Office Gov., Wash. State, 1983-88, Boy Scouts Am., 1986-88. With U.S. Army, 1958-60. Recipient Outstanding Svc. award Pres. Korea, 1985. Mem. Wash. State Korean Assn. (pres. 1983-84, Community Svc. award 1983), Rotary Club. Avocations: reading, travel, fishing. Office: 405 John Obrien Bldg Olympia WA 98504-0001 Address: Legis Bldg Rm 412B Olympia WA 98504-0001 E-mail: shin_pa@leg.wa.gov.

SHINDELL, SIDNEY, preventive medicine physician, educator, department chairman; b. New Haven, May 31, 1923; s. Benjamin Abraham and Freda (Mann) S.; m. Gloria Emhoff, June 17, 1945; children: Barbara, Roger, Lawrence, Judith. BS, Yale U., 1944; MD, L.I. Coll. Medicine, 1946; postgrad., Emory U., 1948-49; LLB, George Washington U., 1951. Diplomate Am. Bd. Preventive Medicine in Occupl. Medicine, Am. Bd. General Preventive Medicine. With USPHS, 1947-52; med. dir. Conn. Commn. on Chronically Ill and Aged, 1952-57, Am. Joint Distbn. Com., 1957-59; asst. prof. preventive medicine U. Pitts., 1960-65; dir. Hosp. Utilization Project Western Pa., 1965-66; prof. dept. preventive medicine Med. Coll. Wis., Milw., 1966-93, chmn. dept., 1966-89, dir. Office Internat. Affairs, 1989-93, prof. emeritus, 1993—; exec. dir. Health Svc. Data of Wis., 1967-73. Mem. bd. sci. advisors Am. Coun. Sci. and Health, 1978—87, 1992—, chmn., 1988—92; mem. Nat. Adv. Com. on Occupl. Safety and Health U.S. Dept. Labor, 1982—84; cons. Caribbean Epidemiology Ctr. Pan Am. Health Orgn./WHO, 1988; field edpiemiology tng. program Ctr. Disease Control, Thailand, 1989; field epidemiology tng. program Nat. Office Occupl. and Environ. Medicine Royal Thai Ministry of Pub Health, 1990; mem. gov.'s white paper com. on health care reform, Wis., 93; acad. cons. Facilities of Medicine Padjadjaran U., Airlangga U., Indonesia, 1993, 94; cons. Project C.U.R.E., 2002—. Author: Statistics, Science and Sense, 1964, A Method of Hospital Utilization Review, 1966, The Law in Medical Practice, 1966, A Coursebook on Health Care

Delivery, 1976; contbr. 120 articles to profl. jours. Trustee Med. Coll. Wis., 1996-2002; mem. sch. bd. Fox Point-Bayside (Wis.), Sch. Dist., 1970-71; vice chmn. Citizens' Adv. Com. Met. Problems, 1971-72; bd. dirs. Med. Care Evaluation S.E. Wis., 1973-76; trustee Interfaith Caregivers Aliance, 2001-2002. With AUS, 1943-46. Recipient Frank L. Babbott Meml. award SUNY Health Sci. Ctr., Bklyn., 1996. Fellow Am. Coll. Preventive Medicine (mem. bd. regents 1982-85), APHA, Am. Coll. Occupl. and Environ. Medicine (Pres.'s award 1999), Am. Coll. Legal Medicine; mem. Am. Assn. Health Data Sys. (sec. 1972-73), Assn. Tchrs. Preventive Medicine (dir. 1973-74, pres. 1976-77, spl. recognition award 1992, Duncan Clark award 2002), Assn. Occupl. Health Profls. (pres. 1980-90), Wis. Med. Soc. (mem. coun. on health care financing and delivery, mem. coun. on govt. affairs, mem. ho. of dels., 50 Yr. recognition award 1996, svc. award 2000), Am. Coll. Physician Execs., Internat. Commn. on Occupl. Health, Aircraft Owners and Pilots Assn., Masons, CAP. Home and Office: One Polo Creek Unit 201 2400 Cherry Creek South Drive Denver CO 80209-3251 Office Phone: 303-778-0141.

SHINDLER, MERRILL KARSH, writer, radio personality; b. NYC, July 2, 1948; s. Joseph and Miriam (Karsh) S. BA, CCNY, 1970; MFA, NYU, 1971. Entertainment editor San Francisco Bay Guardian, 1972-75; music editor Rolling Stone mag., San Francisco, 1976-79; film critic Los Angeles mag., 1979-89; restaurant critic L.A. Examiner, 1979-88; editor Zagat Los Angeles Restaurant Survey, 1986—; restaurant critic L.A. Reader, 1990-96, Daily Breeze, 1990—, Daily News, 1989-94, San Gabriel Valley Newspapers, 1994—. Author: Best Restaurants of L.A., 1989, Zagat, L.A. Restaurant Survey, 1986—, American Dish, 1996, El Cholo: A History, 1998; writer (radio shows) Am. Top 40, 1979-89, 98—, Casey's Top 40, 1989—, Casey's Biggest Hits, 1990—, USA Top 20, 1990—, (TV shows) Am. Top 10, 1980-93, Cinemattractions, 1990—, USA Music Today, 1990—; host radio show Feed Your Face with Merrill Shindler, KLSX-FM, 1988—; contr. to Gault-Millau Best of Los Angeles, 1988, Gault-Millau Best of Hong Kong, 1989; contbr. articles to jours. Avocations: cooking, jogging, travel.

SHINEFIELD, HENRY ROBERT, pediatrician; b. Paterson, NJ, Oct. 11, 1925; s. Louis and Sarah (Kaplan) Shinefield; m. Jacqueline Marilyn Walker; children: Jill, Michael, Kimberley Putzer, Melissa Strome. BA, Columbia U., 1945, MD, 1948. Diplomate Diplomate: Am. Bd. Pediat. (examiner, 1975—, bd. dirs., 1979-84, v.p., 1981-84). 1949Rotating intern Mt. Sinai Hosp., NYC, 1948; pediatric intern Duke Hosp., Durham, NC, 1949-50; asst. resident pediatrician N.Y. Hosp. (Cornell), 1950-51, pediatrician to outpatients, 1953-59, instr. in pediatrics, 1959-60, asst. prof., 1960-64, asso. prof., 1964-65, asst. attending pediatrician, 1959-63, asso. attending pediatrician, 1963-65; pediatrician to outpatients Children's Hosp., Oakland, Calif., 1951-53; chief of pediatrics Kaiser-Permanente Med. Center, San Francisco, 1965-89, chief emeritus, 1989—; co-dir. Kaiser-Permanente Vaccine Study Ctr., San Francisco, 1984—2005; assoc. clin. prof. pediatrics Sch. Medicine U. Calif., 1966-68, clin. prof. pediatrics, 1968—, clin. prof. dermatology, 1970—; asso. attending pediatrician Paterson (N.J.) Gen. Hosp., 1955-59; chief of pediatrics Kaiser Found. Hosp., San Francisco, 1965-86; attending Moffitt Hosp., San Francisco, 1967-88; practice medicine specializing in pediatrics Paterson, 1953-59. Cons. San Francisco Gen. Hosp., 1967—88, Children's Hosp., San Francisco, 1970—88, Mt. Zion Hosp., San Francisco, 1970—88; mem. rsch. grants rev. br. NIH, HEW, 1970—74; med. dir. USPHSR, 1969—; bd. dirs. San Francisco Peer Rev. Orgn., 1975—81, sec., exec. com., 1976—81; chmn. Calif. State Child Health Disability Bd., 1973—82; mem. Inst. Medicine NAS, 1980—; cons. Bur. Drugs FDA, 1970, NIH, HEW, 1974—85. Editl. bd. We. Jour. Medicine, 1968—80, Am. Jour. Diseases of Children, 1970—82; contbr. articles to profl. publs. Chmn. San Francisco Med. Adv. Com. Nat. Found. March of Dimes, 1969—80. Served USPHS, 1951—53. Fellow: Am. Acad. Pediat. (com. fetus and newborn 1969—76, com. on drugs 1978—82); mem.: AMA, Am. Pediatric Soc., We. Soc. Clin. Rsch., We. Pediatric Soc., Infectious Diseases Soc. Am., Soc. Pediatric Rsch., Phi Beta Kappa. Home: 2240 Hyde St 2 San Francisco CA 94109-1509 Office Phone: 415-519-8613. Personal E-mail: henryshinefield@aol.com.

SHINOZUKA, MASANOBU, civil engineer, educator; b. Tokyo, Dec. 23, 1930; came to U.S., 1957, naturalized, 1971; s. Akira and Kiyo S.; m. Fujiko Sakamoto, Oct. 25, 1954; children: Rei, Naomi, Megumi. BS, Kyoto U., Japan, 1953, MS, 1955; PhD, Columbia U., 1960. Rsch. asst. civil engring. Columbia U., NYC, 1958-61, asst. prof., 1961-65, assoc. prof., 1965-69, prof., 1969-88, Renwick prof., 1977-88; prof. Princeton U., 1988-94, Sollenberger prof. civil engring., 1989-94, on leave, 1990—; dir. Nat. Ctr. for Earthquake Engring. Rsch. SUNY, Buffalo, 1990-94; prof. civil engring. U. So. Calif., LA, 1994—. Vis. Capen prof. structural engring., dept. civil engring., 1990—; vis. scholar N.C. State U., Raleigh, 1967-68; pres. Modern Analysis Inc., Princeton, N.J., 1972—; co-chmn. 2d Internat. Conf. on Structural Safety and Reliability, 1978, 3d, 1981, 4th, 1985, 5th, 1989, also co-editor Proc. of 2d, 3d and 4th confs.; mem. steering com. U.S. Panel on Structural Control Rsch., 1990—; cons. in field. Editor: Probabilistic Engineering Mechanics, 1987—, Reliability Approach in Structural Engineering, 1975; co-editor Proc. ASCE Symposium on Probabilistic Methods in Structural Engring., 1981. Recipient Wessex Inst. Tech. medal, 1991; NSF grantee, 1968—. Mem. NAE, ASCE (Walter L. Huber prize 1972, State of the Art of Civil Engring. award 1973, Alfred M. Freudenthal medal 1978, Nathan M. Newmark medal 1985, Moisseiff award 1988, C. Martin Duke award 1991, Theodore Von Karman medal 1994), ASME, AIAA, Japan Soc. Civil Engrs., Sigma Xi. Office: U So Calif Dept Civil Engring 3620 S Vermont Ave Los Angeles CA 90089-0082 Home: 7 Murasaki St Irvine CA 92617-4087

SHIPMAN, JEAN PUGH, medical librarian; b. Chambersburg, Pa., Aug. 6, 1957; d. Andrew Richard and Sara Elizabeth (Bert) Pugh; m. Mark James Shipman, Oct. 8, 1988. BA, Gettysburg Coll., 1979; MSLS, Case Western Res. U., 1980. Reference libr. Johns Hopkins Sch. Medicine, Balt., 1980-81, sr. reference libr., 1981-82, access libr., 1982-84, psychiatry-neuroscis. librarian, 1984-88; mgr. libr. and audiovisual svcs. Greater Balt. Med. Ctr., 1988-90, NN/LM southeastern/atlantic regional coord., 1990—93; outreach info. svcs. libr. Health Scis. Libr., U. Wash., 1993—95, acting head access svcs., 1993—95, assoc. dir. info. resources mgmt., 1995—2000; dir. Tompkins-McCaw Libr. for Health Scis., assoc. Univ. Libr. Va. Commonwealth Univ. Librs., Richmond, Va., 2000—08; dir. Spencer S. Eccles Health Scis. Libr., U. Uttah, Salt Lake, 2008—. Contbr. articles to profl. jours. Mem. Med. Libr. Assn. (bd. dirs. 1999-2002, sec. 2000-02, pres.-elect 2005-06, pres. 2006-2007, immediate past pres., 2007-08), Beta Phi Mu, Beta Beta Beta. Democrat. Lutheran. Avocations: tennis, reading, cooking. Office: Spencer S Eccles Health Scis Libr Univ Utah 10 N 1900 E Bldg 589 Salt Lake City UT 84112-5890 Home: 7909 S Desert Ridge Core Cottonwood UT 84121-5682

SHIPPEY, SANDRA LEE, lawyer; b. Casper, Wyo., June 24, 1957; d. Virgil Carr and Doris Louise (Conklin) McClintock; m. Ojars Herberts Ozols, Sept. 2, 1978 (div.); children: Michael Ojars, Sara Ann, Brian Christopher; m. James Robert Shippey, Jan. 13, 1991; 1 child, Matthew James. BA with distinction, U. Colo., 1978; JD magna cum laude, Boston U., 1982. Bar: Colo. 1982, U.S. Dist. Ct. Colo. 1985. Assoc. Cohen, Brame & Smith, Denver, 1983-84, Parcel, Meyer, Schwartz, Ruttum & Mauro, Denver, 1984-85, Mayer, Brown & Platt, Denver, 1985-87; counsel western ops. GE Capital Corp., San Diego, 1987-94; assoc. Page, Polin, Busch & Boatwright, San Diego, 1994-95; v.p., gen. counsel First Comml. Corp., San Diego, 1995-96; legal counsel NextWave Telecom Inc., San Diego, 1996-98; ptnr. Procopio, Cory, Hargreaves and Savitch, LLP, 1998—, mgmt. com. Spkr. in field. Contbr. articles to profl. jours. Active Pop Warner football and cheerleading; bd. dirs. Southwestern Christian Schs., Inc., 2002—, San Diego Christian Found., 2001—. Mem. Calif. State Bar (co-chair uniform comml. code com., 2004-05), Phi Beta Kappa, Phi Delta Phi. Republican. Mem. Ch. of Christ. Avocations: tennis, golf, photography. Home: 15839 Big Springs Way San Diego CA 92127-2034 Office: Procopio Cory Et Al 530 B St Ste 2100 San Diego CA 92101-4496 Home Phone: 858-722-6072; Office Phone: 619-515-3226. Business E-Mail: sls@procopio.com.

SHIRLEY, DAVID ARTHUR, chemistry professor, science administrator; b. North Conway, NH, Mar. 30, 1934; m. Virginia Schultz, June 23, 1956 (dec. Mar. 1995); children: David N., Diane, Michael, Eric, Gail; m. Barbara Cerny, Dec. 26, 1995. BS, U. Maine, 1955, ScD (hon.), 1978; PhD in Chemistry, U. Calif.-Berkeley, 1858; D honoris causa, Free U. Berlin, 1987. With Lawrence Radiation Lab. (now Lawrence Berkeley Lab.), U. Calif., Berkeley, 1958-92, assoc. dir., head materials and molecular research div., 1975-80, dir., 1980-89, lectr. chemistry, 1959-60, asst. prof., 1960-64, assoc. prof., 1964-67, prof., 1967-92, vice chmn. dept. chemistry, 1968-71, chmn. dept. chemistry, 1971-75; sr. v.p. rsch., dean grad. sch. Pa. State U., University Park, 1992-96; dir. emeritus Lawrence Berkeley Nat. Lab., 1997—. Chair bd. overseers Fermilab. Contbr. over 400 rsch. articles. NSF fellow, 1955-58, 66-67, 70; recipient Ernest O. Lawrence award AEC, 1972, Humboldt award (sr. U.S. scientist); listed by Sci. Citation Index as one of the world's 300 most cited scientists for work published during 1965-78. Fellow Am. Phys. Soc.; mem. Nat. Acad. Scis., Am. Chem. Soc., AAAS, Am. Acad. Arts and Scis., Bohemian Club, Explorers Club, Sigma Xi, Tau Beta Pi, Sigma Pi Sigma, Phi Kappa Phi.

SHIRLEY, JON ANTHONY, former computer software company executive; b. San Diego, Apr. 12, 1938; s. Joseph Roy and Mercedes (Miller) Shirley; m. Gail Grieg (div. June 1964); 1 child, Erickson; m. E. Mary L. Johanson, July 7, 1964; children: Peter, Mary. Attended, MIT, 1956-57. With Radio Shack divsn. Tandy Corp., Ft. Worth, 1963-72, v.p. computer merchandising, 1972-83; pres., COO Microsoft Corp., Redmond, Wash., 1983—90, bd. dir., 1983—. Bd. dir. Manzanita Capital, Seattle. Chmn. bd. trustees Seattle Art Mus.; trustee Mus. Flight, Seattle, Hill Sch., Pottstown, Pa.; mem. chmn. council Mus. Modern Art, NYC. Named one of Top 200 Collectors, ARTnews Mag., 2004—08. Mem.: Assn. Data Processing Service Orgn. (bd. dirs. 1986—), Seattle Yacht. Democrat. Avocations: Collector of Modern & Contemporary Art, Collecting, restoring, showing and racing of Vintage Ferrari Motor Cars. Office: Microsoft Corp One Microsoft Way Redmond WA 98052

SHIRTCLIFF, JOHN DELZELL, business owner, oil jobber; b. Roseburg, Oreg., Mar. 2, 1948; s. Henry Marion and Sheila Nell (Delzell) S.; m. Connie Lee Cantrell, June 13, 1975; children: Darcie, Danielle, Andrew. BS, Oregon State U., 1970. Pres. Shirtcliff Oil Co., Myrtle Creek, Oreg., 1971—. Engr. Myrtle Creek (Oreg.) Vol. Fire Dept., 1971—, emergency technician, 1981—; mem. Rep. Cen. Com., Roseburg, Oreg., 1982-88; chmn. Umpqua Community Coll. Budget Com., Roseburg, 1983-96; bd. dirs. Mercy Hospice, Roseburg, 1988-96; dir. Myrtle Creek Bldg. Authority, 2001-. 2nd lt. U.S. Army, 1970-71. Named Citizen of Year, Myrtle Creek City, 1986, Vol. of Year, Douglas County C. of C., 1987. Mem. Petroleum Marketers Assn. Am. (dir. Oreg. 1988), Oreg. Petroleum Marketers Assn. (v.p. legis. chmn. 1986, pres. 1987, PMAA dir. 1988), Pacific Oil Conf. (bd. dirs., v.p. 1995, gen. chmn. 1997), Lions, Elks, Masons, Shriners. Republican. Avocations: landscaping, jogging, golf. Office: Shirtcliff Oil Co 283 SW Western Ave PO Box 6003 Myrtle Creek OR 97457-0051 Office Phone: 541-863-5268.

SHIRVANI, SIR HAMID, architect, educator, philosopher, writer, university president; b. Tehran, Iran, Oct. 20, 1950; arrived in US, 1974, naturalized, 1986; s. Majid and Taji (Granpisheh) Shirvani; m. Fatemeh Shokrollahi, Oct. 4, 2002. Diploma in architecture, Poly. of Cen. London, 1974; MArch, Pratt Inst., 1975; MS, Rensselaer Poly. Inst., 1977; MLA, Harvard U., 1978; MA, Princeton U., 1979, PhD, 1980; LHD (hon.), Soka U., Japan, 2003. Project designer London Borough of Barnet, 1973-74; asst. prof. architecture Pa. State U., 1979-82; prof., dir. grad. studies SUNY, Syracuse, 1982-85; prof., dir. Sch. Urban Planning and Devel., U. Louisville, 1985-86; prof. architecture and urban design U. Colo., Denver, 1986-92, dean Sch. of Architecture and Planning, 1986-91; prof. philosophy, dean Coll. Arts and Scis. U. Mass., Lowell, 1992-95; v.p. grad. studies and rsch., prof. urban studies CUNY Queens Coll., Flushing, 1995-2000; provost, exec. v.p., Martha Masters prof. art/architecture Chapman U., Orange, Calif., 2000—05; pres., prof. art and architecture Calif. State U., Stanislaus, 2005—. Vis. faculty So. Calif. Inst. Architecutre, U. So. Calif.; lectr. in field. Author: Urban Design: A Comprehensive Reference, 1981, Urban Design Review, 1981, Urban Design Process, 1985, Beyond Public Architecture, 1990; editor Urban Design Rev., 1982-85, Urban Design and Preservation Quar., 1985-88; mem. editorial bd. Jour. Archtl. Edn., 1988-94, Avant Garde, 1988-93, Jour. Planning Edn. and Rsch., 1987-93, Art and Architecture, 1974-78, Jour. Am. Planning Assn., 1982-88. Recipient Gold medal in Architecture and Urbanism, 1988, Faculty Honor award, 1990, Acad. Leadership award, Faculty Rsch. award, Commendation award AIA, 2003, Justice award SGI, 2003, 09, Pres. of Yr. award Calif. State U. Student Assn., 2007, 09; Knight of Holy Sepulchre, 2004. Fellow World Acad. Arts and Scis., Am. Soc. Landscape Archs. (recognition award), Royal Geog. Soc., Royal Soc. Arts, World Acad. Arts and Scis.; mem. NCAA (pres. coun.), Am. Inst. Cert. Planners, Am. Planning Assn. (chmn. urban design divsn. 1987-89, Disting. award 1984, Urban Design award 1985), Sigma Xi, Omicron Delta Epsilon, Tau Sigma Delta (Silver medal in archtl. edn. 1988), Tau Beta Pi, Sigma Lambda Alpha, Phi Kappa Phi. Office: Calif State U One University Cir Turlock CA 95382 Office Phone: 209-667-3201. Office Fax: 209-667-3206. Business E-Mail: president@csustan.edu.

SHMAVONIAN, GERALD S., political organization administrator; b. LA, June 26, 1945; s. Sergius Neshan and Berje-Lucia (der Hareutunyan) Shmavonian. Student, U. Calif., Berkeley, 1964-70. Leader archaeol. excavation team, Guatemala, Turkey, 1970-75; pub. City Mags., 1975-80; spl. advisor Bicentennial Commission, Washington, DC, 1975; chmn. Am. Nationalities Coun., Stanford U., 1983-86; pres. Am. Talent, 1986—2000; ptnr. Assembly Plant Ptnrs., 2001—. Founder Tommorw Party, 2000—; pres. emeritus C.A.U.S.E., 2007—. Recipient Intercollegiate Boxing Championship, 1965. Fellow Am. Documentary Film Acad.; mem. Calif. Scholarship Fedn. (life, pres. 1963), Nat. Forensic League (pres. 1963, degree of honor). Avocation: art. Home: 6219 N Prospect Ave Fresno CA 93711-1658

SHMUGER, MARC, film company executive; Grad., Wesleyan U. Sr. v.p. creative advt. Columbia Pictures, Sony Pictures Entertainment, 1991—92, v.p., creative dir., 1992—94, exec. v.p. worldwide mktg. Columbia TriStar, 1994—2000; pres. mktg. Universal Pictures, Universal City, Calif., 1998—2000, vice chmn., 2000—06, chmn., 2006—. Founder Art of War Prodn. Co., 1996. Prodr., writer (films) Dead of Winter, 1987. Named Entertainment Marketer of Yr., Advt. Age, 1999, 2000; named one of 50 Most Powerful People in Mktg., 1999, 2000, 50 Most Powerful People in Hollywood, Premiere mag., 2006. Mem.: Phi Beta Kappa. Office: Universal Pictures 100 Universal City Plz Universal City CA 91608

SHNEOUR, ELIE ALEXIS, biophysicist, researcher, historian; b. Neuilly-sur-Seine, France, Dec. 11, 1925; came to U.S., 1941, naturalized, 1944; s. Zalman and Salomea (Landau) S.; children, Mark Zalman, Alan Brewster. BA, Columbia U., 1947; DSc (hon.), Bard Coll., 1969; MA, U. Calif., Berkeley, 1955; PhD, UCLA, 1958. Tchr. and rsch. fellow U. Calif., Berkeley, 1953-55, Am. Heart Assn. rsch. fellow, 1958-62, tchg. and rsch. fellow LA, 1958; rsch. fellow Nat. Cancer Inst., 1956-57; Am. Heart Assn. rsch. fellow NYU, 1958-59; rsch. assoc. genetics Stanford U., 1962-65; assoc. prof. biology and neuroscis. U. Utah, 1965-69; rsch. neurochemist City of Hope Nat. Med. Ctr., Duarte, Calif., 1969-71. Dir. rsch. Calbiochem., 1971-75; pres. Biosystems Insts., Inc., 1975—; dir. Biosystems Rsch. Inst., 1979; steering com. Nat. Acad. Sci. Study Group on Biology and the Exploration of Mars, 1964; chmn. Western Regional coun. Rsch. in Basic Bioscis. for Manned Orbiting Missions, Am. Inst. Biol. Scis., NASA, 1966-69; fellow Com. Skeptical Inquiry, 1996—; mem. editl. bd. Skeptic Mag., 1992-2008. Author: Extraterrestrial Life, 1965, (with Eric A. Ottesen) National Academy of Sciences, National Rsch. Coun., 1966, (with S. Moffat) Life Beyond the Earth, 1966, The Malnourished Mind, 1974; contbr. articles to profl. jours. Chmn. citizens adv. coun. San Diego Pub. Schs., 1971-72; adv. coun. Cousteau Soc., 1977-98; bd. dir. Lunar Power System Coalition, 1993-2002; internat. v.p. Transinnova S.A. France, 1990—; chmn. sci. adv. bd. County of San Diego, 1995-2002, 2006-08. With U.S. Army, 1944-45. Recipient William Lockwood prize, Bard Coll. of Columbia U., 1947. Mem. IEEE, AAAS (chmn. So. Calif. Skeptics soc. Pacific divsn. 1988-90), Am. Chem. Soc., N.Y. Acad. Scis., Am. Inst. Biol. Scis., Am. Soc. for Biochemistry and Molecular Biology (chmn. sci. advisors program 1973-75, mem. com. on pub. policy 1974-76, congl. liaison 1992—), Am. Soc. Neurochemistry (mem. coun. 1971-73), Soc. Neurosci., Internat. Soc. Neurochemistry, U.S. C. of C. (bd. dirs. 1993-98), La Jolla Chamber Music Soc. (bd. dirs. 1994-97), Internat. Coun. for Global Health Progress (N.Am. adv. bd. 1996—), Sigma Xi, Phi Sigma. Office: Biosystems Rsch Inst 700 Front St m/s CDM 608 San Diego CA 92101-6085

SHOCKLEY-ZALABAK, PAMELA SUE, academic administrator; b. May 25, 1944; d. James William and Leatha Pearl (Cartwright) Shockley; m. Charles Zalabak, Dec. 30, 1975. BA in Comm., Okla. State U., 1965, MA in Comm., 1972; PhD in Orgnl. Comm., U. Colo., 1980. Instr. comm. Coll. Letters, Arts and Scis. U. Colo., 1976, from asst. to full prof., 1992, prof. comm. Colorado Springs, 1992—, dir., net and media ctr., 1992, spl. asst. to chancellor, 1994, vice chancellor for student success Colorado Springs, 1998—2001, interim chancellor, 2001—02, chancellor, 2002—. Cons. in field. Author six books; prodr.: (six video documentaries); contbr. articles to profl. jours. Recipient Disting. Svc. award, Colo. Speech Comm. Assn., Telly award; Lew Wentz Tri Delt scholar, 1961—65. Mem.: Internat. Comm. Assn., Speech Comm. Assn., Phi Kappa Phi. Democrat. Avocations: skiing, hiking, fly fishing. Office: Univ Colorado Chancellor's Office 1420 Austin Bluffs Pkwy Colorado Springs CO 80918

SHOCKRO, MICHAEL J., lawyer; b. Laconia, NH, Nov. 21, 1942; BA with distinction, Stanford U., 1964; LLB magna cum laude, Columbia U., 1967. Bar: Calif. 1967. Ptnr. Corp. Dept., founder & chair Tech. Transactions Practice Group Latham & Watkins LLP, LA. Mem. exec. com. CalTech/MIT Enterprise Forum. Editor: Columbia Law Review 1966-67. Mem. bd. dirs., legal advisor Pasadena Symphony Assn. Mem. ABA, L.A. County Bar Assn. Office: Latham Watkins 355 S Grand Ave Los Angeles CA 90071-1560 Office Fax: 213-891-8763.

SHOEMAKER, CAROLYN SPELLMAN, planetary astronomer; b. Gallup, N.Mex., June 24, 1929; d. Leonard Robert and Hazel Adele (Arthur) Spellmann; m. Eugene Merle Shoemaker, Aug. 18, 1951 (dec. July 1997); children: Christine Shoemaker Abanto, Patrick Gene, Linda Shoemaker Salazar. BA cum laude, Chico State Coll., 1949, MA, 1950; ScD, No. Ariz. U., 1990, St. Mary's U., NS, Can., 2003. Vis. scientist Br. astrogeology U.S. Geol. Survey, Flagstaff, Ariz., 1980—; rsch. asst. Calif. Inst. Tech., Pasadena, 1981-85; rsch. prof. astronomy No. Ariz. U., Flagstaff, 1989—; mem. staff Lowell Obs., Flagstaff, 1993—. Guest observer Palomar Obs., Palomar Mountain, Calif., 1982-94; Ruth Northcott Meml. lectr. R.A.S.C., 1995; co-McGovern lectr. Cosmos Club Found., 1995. Co-recipient Rittenhouse medal Rittenhouse Astron. Soc., 1988, Scientist of Yr. award ARCS Found., 1995, James C. Watson medal NAS, 1998; recipient Woman of Distinction award Soroptimists, 1994, 20th Anniversary Internat. Women's Yr. award Zonta and 99s, 1995, NASA Exceptional Scientific Achievement medal, 1996, Woman of Distinction award Nat. Assn. Women in Edn., 1996, Shoemaker award Am. Inst. Profl. Geologists, 1997, plaque Internat. Forest Friendship, Atchison, Kans., 1997, Robert Burnham Jr. award Western Regional Astron. League, 2000, Ariz. Woman of Distinction award Alpha Delta Kappa, 2004; named Disting. Alumna of the Calif. State U., Chico, 1996. Fellow AAAS, Am. Acad. Arts and Scis., Am. Geophys. Union; mem. Meteoritical Soc., Sigma Xi. Achievements include discovery of 32 comets including Periodic Comet Shoemaker-Levy 9 which impacted Jupiter in July 1994, more than 500 asteroids including 44

Earth approachers and approximately 68 Mars crossers, meteorites at Veevers Crater, Australia and impactites at Wolfe Creek Crater, Australia. Home: 5231 Hidden Hollow Rd Flagstaff AZ 86001-3821 Office: Lowell Obs 1400 W Mars Hill Rd Flagstaff AZ 86001-4499 Business E-Mail: cshoemaker@usgs.gov.

SHOEN, EDWARD JOSEPH, transportation and insurance companies executive; s. Leonard and Anna (Carty) S. BA, Coll. Holy Cross, 1971; MBA, Harvard U., 1973; JD, Ariz. State Univ., 1981. With Amerco Corp, 1971—; pres. U-Haul Internat., Inc., 1990—; pres., chmn. Amerco Corp., Reno, 1986—. Office: Amerco 1325 Airmotive Way Reno NV 89502

SHOHET, STEPHEN BYRON, medical educator; b. Boston, Nov. 29, 1934; s. Harmon Abraham and Grace (Cohen) S.; m. Geraldine Poplack, July 22, 1956; children: Ralph, Grace, Jason, Juliet. BA, Harvard U., 1956, MD, 1960. Diplomate: Am. Bd. Internal Medicine. Intern, resident in medicine Beth Israel Hosp., Boston, 1960—62; clin. assoc. NIH, 1962—64, sr. staff assoc., 1965; fellow in hematology, instr. medicine Peter Bent Brigham Hosp., 1965—69; asst. prof. Harvard U., 1969—71; assoc. prof. U. Calif., San Francisco, 1971—76, prof. medicine and lab. medicine, 1976—2003, prof. emeritus, 2003—, chief hematology, 1974—84, dir. Cancer Rsch. Inst., 1974—80, dir. MacMillan-Cargill Hematology Rsch. Lab., 1980—2003. Contbr. articles to med. jours., also chpts. on hematology and biology of blood cell membranes to books. Recipient various research and tng. grants NIH. Mem. Am. Soc. Clin. Investigation, Am. Soc. Hematology, Biophys. Soc., Am. Assn. Physicians, Red Cell Club, Western Assn. Physicians. Office Phone: 415-922-3070. E-mail: sbshohet@aol.com.

SHONK, ALBERT DAVENPORT, JR., advertising executive; b. LA, May 23, 1932; s. Albert Davenport and Jean Spence (Stannard) S. BS in Bus. Adminstrn., U. So. Calif., 1954. Field rep. mktg. divsn. LA Examiner, 1954-55, asst. mgr. mktg. and field supr. mktg. divsn., 1955-56, mgr. mktg. divsn., 1956-57; account exec. Hearst Advt. Svc., LA, 1957-59; account exec., mgr. Keith H. Evans & Assocs., San Francisco and Los Angeles, 1959-65; owner, pres. Albert D. Shonk Co., LA, 1965-97; gen. ptnr. Shonk Land Co. Ltd., Charleston, W.Va., 1989-00; dir. Shonk, LLC, Del., 2001—. Pres. Signet Cir. Corp., Inc., 1977-81, dir., 1962-81, hon. life dir., 1981—, treas., 1989-2002, pres., 2002—. Founding chmn. Crittenton Assocs.; bd. dirs. Balboa Island Improvement Assn., 2000—07, pres., 2005—07, immediate past pres., 2008—; bd. dirs. Balboa Island Mus. & Hist. Soc., 1999—2008, pres., 2008—; co-chair Centennial com. Florence Crittenton Ctr., 1992, bd. dirs., sec., 1978, 1st v.p., 1978—79, exec. v.p., 1979—81, pres., 1981—83, chmn. bd., 1983—85, hon. life dir., 1986, treas., 1997, pres., 1997—2001, chmn. bd. dirs., 2002—03, pres., 2004—05, pres. emeritus, 2006. Recipient Medallion of Merit Phi Sigma Kappa, 1976, Founders award, 1961, NIC Interfraternal award, 1989. Mem.: Jr. Advt. Club LA (hon. life, dir., treas., 1st v.p.), Nat. Assn. Pubs. Reps. (past v.p. West Coast 1981—83), Pubs. Rep. Assn. of So. Calif., Advt. Club LA, Town Hall, U. So. Calif. Alumni Assn. (bd. govs. 2000—03, 2007—08, Pres.s' award 2008), U. So. Calif. Marshall Sch. Bus. Alumni Assn. (nat. bd. 1991—99, treas. 1995—99), World Affairs Coun., U. So. Calif. Assocs., Marshall Assocs. (bd. dirs. 1999—), U. So. Calif. Half Century Trojans (co-chair 50 yr. reunion 2004, bd. dirs. 2004—, pres.-elect 2006—07, pres. 2007—, officer 2008), Rotary (bd. dirs., sec. LA Rotary Found. 2006—, Paul Harris fellow), Trojan Club, Skull and Dagger (Arnold Eddy Vol. Svc. award 2009), U. So. Calif. Cardinal and Gold, Alpha Kappa Psi, Phi Sigma Kappa (dir. grand coun. 1962—70, 1977—79, grand pres. 1979—83, v.p. meml. found. 1979—84, chancellor 1983—87, pres. meml. found. 1984, found. trustee pres. 1984—95, chancellor 1990—91, recorder 1995—, found. trustee emeritus 1995—), Inter-Greek Soc. (v.p. 1976—79, pres. 1984—86, co-founder, hon. life, dir.). Home and Office: 225 Sapphire Ave Newport Beach CA 92662-1148 E-mail: adshonk@msn.com.

SHONTERE, JAMES G., construction executive; CFO, sec. JF Shea, Walnut, Calif. Office: JF Shea 655 Brea Canyon Rd Walnut CA 91789

SHOOK, JON, chef; b. Miami, 1981; Grad., Inst. Ft. Lauderdale. Chef The Strand restaurant, South Beach, Mark's, Café Maxx, The River House, Wildflower Restaurant, Vail, Chadwick Restaurant, LA; co-owner, exec. chef Animal Restaurant, LA, 2008—. Co-owner, chef catering bus. Chef (TV series) Two Dudes Catering, The Food Network; co-author: Two Dudes One Pan, 2008 (Top 10 Cookbooks of 2008, Nat. Pub. Radio). Named one of America's Best New Chefs, Food & Wine Mag., 2009. Office: Animal Restaurant 435 N Fairfax Ave Los Angeles CA 90036 Office Phone: 323-782-9225.*

SHOOTER, ERIC MANVERS, retired neurobiology professor, consultant; b. Mansfield, Eng., Apr. 18, 1924; arrived in U.S., 1964; s. Fred and Pattie (Johnson) Shooter; m. Elaine Staley Arnold, May 28, 1949; 1 child, Annette Elizabeth. BA, Cambridge U., Eng., 1945, MA, 1949, PhD, 1950, ScD, 1986; DSc, U. London, 1964. Sr. scientist biochemistry Brewing Industry Rsch. Found., 1950—53; biochemistry lectr. Univ. Coll., London, 1953—63; assoc. prof. genetics Stanford U., 1963—68, prof. genetics and biochemistry, 1968—75, prof., chmn. neurobiology dept., 1975—87, prof. neurobiology, 1987—2004, prof. neurobiology emeritus, 2004—, chmn. Neurosci. PhD Program, 1972—82. Assoc. Neurosci. Rsch. Program, NYC, 1979—89; mem. tchg. staff Internat. Sch. Neurosci., Praglia, Italy, 1987—93; sr. cons. Markey Charitable Trust, Miami, Fla., 1985—97; bd. dirs. Regeneron Pharm., Inc., Tarrytown, NY. Assoc. editor (book series) Ann. Rev. Neuroscis., 1984—2001; contbr. articles to profl. jours. Recipient Wakeman award, Duke U., 1988, Award for Disting. Achievement in Neurosci. Rsch., Bristol-Myers-Squibb, 1997; scholar, Josiah Macy Jr. Found., N.Y.C., 1974—75. Fellow: AAAS, Am. Acad. Arts and Scis., Royal Soc. (London); mem.: NAS, Am. Philos. Soc., Internat. Brain Rsch. Orgn., Internat. Soc. Neurochemistry, Am. Soc. Neurochemistry, Am. Assn. Biol. Chemists, Soc. for Neurosci. (Ralph W. Gerard prize 1995), Inst. Medicine of NAS, Alpha Omega Alpha (hon.). Avocation: travel. Home: 370 Golden Oak Dr Portola Valley CA 94028-7757 Office: Stanford U Sch Medicine Dept Neurobiology 299 Campus Dr Stanford CA 94305-5125 Office Phone: 650-723-7559. Business E-Mail: eshooter@stanford.edu.

SHORE, HOWARD LESLIE, composer; b. Toronto, Ontario, Canada, Oct. 18, 1946; s. Mac and Bernice (Ash) S.; m. Elizabeth Ann Cotnoir, Aug. 3, 1990; 1 child, Mae. Student, Berklee Sch. Music, 1965-67, Forest Hill Collegiate, Toronto, Ont., Can., 1961-64. Composer The Gorfaine/Schwartz Agy., Sherman Oaks, Calif. Composer film scores including I Miss You, Hugs and Kisses, 1978, The Brood, 1979, Scanners, 1981, Videodrome, 1983, Nothing Lasts Forever, 1984, After Hours, 1985, Belizaire the Cajun, 1987, Fire with Fire, 1986, The Fly, 1986, Nadine, 1987, The Local Stigmatic, 1987, Heaven, 1987, Moving, 1988, Dead Ringers, 1988 (Genie award), Big, 1988 (ASCAP award), She-Devil, 1989, An Innocent Man, 1989, Signs of Life, 1989, The Silence of the Lambs, 1991 (ASCAP award), A Kiss Before Dying, 1989, Naked Lunch, 1990, Prelude to a Kiss, 1992, Single White Female, 1992, (TV score) Scales of Justice, 1990, Guilty as Sin, 1993, Sliver, 1993, M. Butterfly, 1993, Mrs. Doubtfire, 1993 (ASCAP award), Philadelphia, 1993 (ASCAP award), The Client, 1994 (ASCAP award), Ed Wood, 1994, Nobody's Fool, 1994, Moonlight and Valentino, 1995, White Man's Burden, 1995, Se7en, 1995 (ASCAP award), Before and After, 1996, The Truth About Cats and Dogs, 1996, Looking for Richard, 1996, Crash, 1996, Looking For Richard, 1996, That Thing You Do, 1996, The Game, 1997, Cop Land, 1997, Last Night, 1998, Silver, 1998, Analyze This, 1999 (ASCAP award), Dogma, 1999, High Fidelity, 2000, The Yards, 2000, The Cell, 2000, The Score, 2001, Jay and Silent Bob Strike Back, 2001, The Lord of the Rings: The Fellowship of the Ring, 2001 (ASCAP award, Acad. award for Best Original Score, 2002, Broadcast Film Critics Assn. award for Best Composer, 2002, Grammy award for Best Score Soundtrack Album, 2003), Panic Room, 2002 (ASCAP award), Spider, 2002, The Lord of the Rings: The Two Towers, 2002 (ASCAP award, Grammy award for Best Score Soundtrack Album, 2004), Gangs of New York, 2002, The Lord of the Rings: the Return of the King, 2003 (ASCAP award, Acad. awards for Best Original Score & Best Original Song, 2004, Golden Globe awards for Best Original Score & Best Original Song, 2004, Grammy award for Best Score Soundtrack Album & Best Song, 2005, Broadcast Film Critics Assn. award for Best Composer, 2005), The Aviator, 2004 (Broadcast Film Critics Assn. award for Best Composer, 2005, Golden Globe award for Best Original Score 2005), A History of Violence, 2005, The Departed, 2006 (ASCAP award), The Last Mimzy, 2007, Eastern Promises, 2007; composer (orchestral works) The Lord of the Rings Symphony, (operas) The Fly, 2008, others; music supr. Places in the Heart, 1984, Postcards From the Edge, 1990; music dir. The Hart & Lorne Terrific Hour, 1970, Saturday Night Live, 1975-80, 1985-86. Recipient Most Performed Theme(s) award, ASCAP, 2000—05, Henry Mancini award, 2004, Hollywood Film award for Outstanding Achievement in Music in Film, Hollywood Film Festival, 2003, Career Achievement award for Film Music Composition, Nat. Bd. Review, 2005. Mem. ASCAP, Lighthouse (founding mem.). Home: Wee Wah Lodge Tuxedo Park NY 10987 Office: The Gorfaine Schwartz Agency Inc 4111 W Alameda Ave Ste 509 Burbank CA 91505-4171

SHORE, JAMES H(ENRY), psychiatrist; b. Winston-Salem, NC, Apr. 6, 1940; s. James Henry and Ellen Elizabeth (Hayes) S.; m. Christine Lowenbach, Aug. 24, 1963; children— Ellen Ottilie, James Henry. MD, Duke U., 1965. Diplomate Am. Bd. Psychiatry and Neurology. Intern U. Utah Med. Ctr., 1965-66; resident in psychiatry U. Wash., 1966-69; chief mental health office Portland Area Indian Health Svc., Oreg., 1969-73; assoc. prof. psychiatry, dir. cmty. psychiatry tng. program U. Oreg. Health Sci. Ctr., 1973-75, prof., chmn. dept. psychiatry, 1975-85; from chmn. dept. psychiatry Health Sci. Ctr. to chancellor U. Colo., Aurora, 1985—2004, chancellor Health Scis. Ctr., 2004—05, chancellor emeritus Health Scis. Ctr., 2006—. Mem. exptl. and spl. edn. com. NIMH-Internal Rev. Group, 1976-80; dir. Colo. Psychiatry Hosp., 1985-99; interim dir. U. Colo. Hosp., Denver, 1987-88, interim exec. vice chancellor, 1995-97, chancellor, 1998-2005; cons. in field. Contbr. numerous articles to profl. publs. Mem. Various community bds. Served with USPHS, 1969-73. Decorated USPHS Commendation medal; various grants. Fellow Am. Psychiat. Assn., Am. Coll. Psychiatry (pres. 2003-04); mem. Am. Assn. Chmn. Depts. Psychiatry (pres. 1989), Am. Bd. Psychiatry and Neurology (dir. 1987—, pres. 1994), Residency Rev. Com. for Psychiatry (chmn. 1991-92). Office: U Colo Health Scis Ctr Mail Stop F800 PO Box 6508 Aurora CO 80045

SHORENSTEIN, DOUGLAS W., corporate executive; BA, U. Calif., Berkeley; JD, Hastings Coll. Atty. Real Estate Group Shearman & Sterling LLP, NY, 1980—83; joined Shorenstein Properties LLC, San Francisco, 1983, chmn., CEO, 1995—. Chair United Way of the Bay Area, 1998—. Office: Shorenstein 555 California St Ste 4900 San Francisco CA 94104

SHORENSTEIN, ROSALIND GREENBERG, internist; b. NYC, Jan. 14, 1947; d. Albert Samuel and Natalie Miriam (Sherman) Greenberg; m. Michael Lewis Shorenstein, June 18, 1967; children: Anna Irene, Claire Beth. BA in Chemistry, Wellesley Coll., 1968; MA in Biochemistry and Molecular Biology, Harvard U., 1970, PhD in Biochemistry and Molecular Biology, 1973; MD, Stanford U., 1976. Diplomate Am. Bd. Internal Medicine. Resident in internal medicine UCLA Med. Ctr., 1976-79; pvt. practice internal medicine Santa Cruz, Calif., 1979—. Mem. dept. internal medicine Dominican Hosp., Santa Cruz, 1979—; co-dir. med. svcs. Health Enhancement & Lifestyle Planning Systems, Santa Cruz, 1983—. Contbr. articles to profl. journals. Dir. Santa Cruz Chamber Players, 1993-94, pres., bd. dirs., 1994—. Recipient Charlie Parkhurst award Santa Cruz Women's Commn., 1989; NSF fellow, 1968-72, Sarah Perry Wood Med. fellow Wellesley Coll., 1972-76. Mem. Am. Soc. Internal Medicine (del. 1994, 95), Calif. Soc. Internal Medicine (trustee 1994—, sec.-treas. 1996-2000), Am. Med. Women's Assn. (Outstanding Svc. award 1987, br. #59 pres. 1986—), Calif. Med. Assn. (com. on women 1987-93), Santa Cruz County Med. Soc. (mem. bd. govs. 1993—, sec. 1997-99, pres. 2000-01, sec. 2002-), Phi Beta Kappa, Sigma Xi. Jewish. Office: 700 Frederick St Ste 103 Santa Cruz CA 95062-2239 Office Phone: 831-458-1002.

SHORENSTEIN, WALTER HERBERT, commercial real estate development company executive; b. Glen Cove, NY, Feb. 23, 1915; m. Phyllis J. Finley, Aug. 8, 1945 (dec.); children: Joan (Dec.), Carole, Douglas. Student, Pa. State U., 1933-34, U. Pa., 1934-36; D in Econs. (hon.), HanYang U., Seoul, Republic of Korea, 1988. With property sales mgmt. depts. Milton Meyer & Co., San Francisco, 1946-51, ptnr., 1951-60, owner, chmn. bd. dirs., 1960—, Shorenstein Group, San Francisco, Shorenstein Co., San Francisco, 1960—. Appt. by Pres. Johnson adv. del. UN Econ. Commn. for Asia and Far East, 1967, Pub. Advisory Com. U.S. Trade Policy; apptd. Pres. Carter Com. for Preservation fo White House; appt. by Pres. Clinton bd. dirs. Corp. Nat. Svc., 1994-96, adv.com. U.S. Commerce Dept. Industry, 1995-96. Past chmn. bd. trustees Hastings Law Ctr., U. Calif., San Francisco; founding mem. exec. adv. com. Hubert H. Humphrey Inst. Pub. Affairs, U. Minn.; bd. visitors; past pres., hon. life bd. dirs. San Francisco Park and Recreation Commn.; chmn. Vietnam Orphans Airlift; bd. dirs. San Francisco Performing Arts Ctr.; trustee Asia Found.; fin. chmn. Dem. Nat. Conv., 1984; founder Joan Shorenstein Ctr. on Press, Politics and Public Policy, Harvard U., 1986; apptd. by Pres. Clinton to Nat. Svc. Commn., 1994, Bd. of Americorp, founding mem. WWII Nat. Monument com., Nat. Endowment Arts, White House Endowment Fund; apptd. by Pres. Carter chair White House Preservation Fund; apptd. by Mayor Frank Jordon chair Save the San Francisco Giants com.; personal advisor Pres. Johnson, Carter, Clinton; chmn. Pacific Rim Econ. Coun., San Francisco; bd. visitors Internat. Studies Bd. Stanford U.; co-founder Orpheum, Curran and Golden Gate Theatres, San Francsico; founder Johnson Presdl. Libr., Carter Ctr.; chmn. San Francisco U. N50 nat. com., 1995, also numerous polit. activities. Maj. USAF, 1940-45. Named Leader of Tomorrow, Time mag., 1953, Calif. Dem. of Yr., 1985; recipient Nat. Brotherhood award NCCJ, 1982, Disting. Svc. award Dem. Nat. Com., 1983, Golden Plate award Am. Acad. Achievement, 1991, Svc. to Youth award Cath. Youth Orgn., 1994, Lifetime Achievement award Dem. Party, 1997; inducted Real Estate Legends Hall of Fame, 1997, Bay Area Coun. Bay Area Bus. Hall of Fame, 1998; Shorenstein award named in his honor Dem. Nat. Com., 1999. Mem. Calif. C. of C. (past bd. dirs.), San Francisco C. of C. (past chmn. bd. dirs., life bd. dirs.). Office: Shorenstein Co 555 California St Ste 4900 San Francisco CA 94104-1714

SHORENSTEIN HAYS, CAROLE, theater producer; b. San Francisco, Sept. 15, 1948; d. Walter and Phyllis Shorenstein; m. Jeffrey Hays; children: Wally, Gracie. Co-owner Curran Theatre, Golden Gate Theatre, Orpheum Theatre, San Francisco. Prodr.: (Broadway plays) Can-Can, 1981, Woman of the Year, 1981—83 (Tony nom. best musical, 1981), Oliver!, 1984, Fences, 1987 (Tony award best play, 1987), A Midsummer Night's Dream, 1996 (Tony nom. best revival of a play, 1996), The Old Neighborhood, 1997—98, The Chairs, 1998 (Tony nom. best revival of a play, 1996), Not About Nightingales, 1999 (Tony nom. best play, 1999), Closer, 1999 (Tony nom. best play, 1999), The Tale of the Allergist's Wife, 2000—02 (Tony nom. best play, 2001), Proof, 2000—03 (Tony award best play, 2001), The Goat, or Who Is Sylvia?, 2002 (Tony award best play, 2002), Topdog / Underdog, 2002 (Tony nom. best play, 2002), Take Me Out, 2003—04 (Tony award best play, 2003), Caroline, or Change, 2004 (Tony nom. best musical, 2004), Gem of the Ocean, 2004—05 (Tony nom. best play, 2005), Doubt, 2005—06 (Tony award best play, 2005, Drama Desk award outstanding new play, 2005), Julius Caesar, 2005; (plays) Well, 2006; (Broadway plays) Rock 'n' Roll, 2007—08. Office: Curran Theatre 445 Geary St San Francisco CA 94102 also: Golden Gate Theatre P O Box 7110 San Francisco CA 94102

SHORS, CLAYTON MARION, retired cardiologist; b. Beemer, Nebr., June 10, 1925; s. Joseph Albert and Morva Edith (Clayton) S.; m. Arlene Towle, June 6, 1948; children: Susan Debra, Clayton Robert, Scott Towle BS, U. Nebr., 1950, MD, 1952. Diplomate Am. Bd. Internal Medicine (subspecialty cardiovascular disease). Intern Detroit Receiving Hosp., 1952-53, resident, 1953-56; practice medicine specializing in cardiology Detroit; chief cardiology St. John Hosp., Detroit; ret., 2005. Bd. dirs. Sedona Acad.; mem. Sedona 30. Served with U.S. Army, 1943-46 Fellow Am. Coll. Cardiology, Internat. Coll. Angiology, Am. Heart Assn. Council on Clin. Cardiology; mem. Alpha Omega Alpha Home and Office: 6562 E Crested Saguaro Ln Scottsdale AZ 85266-7373

SHORT, JAY MILTON, biotechnology company executive; b. Lebanon, Ind., Mar. 5, 1958; s. Roy Milton and Patricia Ann (Brewer) S.; m. Heidi Patrice Messinger, July 26, 1980; children: Ryan Milton, Cole Evan. BA in Chemistry with honors, Taylor U., Upland, Ind., 1980; PhD in Biochemistry, Case Western Res. U., 1985. Tchg. asst. Taylor U., 1978-80, Kent (Ohio) State U., 1981, Case Western Res. U., Cleve., 1981-85; staff scientist R & D, Stratagene Cloning Systems, La Jolla, Calif., 1985-88, sr. staff scientist, 1988-89, v.p. long term rsch. and biol. ops., 1989-92, v.p. long term rsch. and ops., 1992-94; pres. Stratcyte, Inc., La Jolla, 1992-94, Diversa Corp., San Diego, 1994—, CEO, 1994—, chief tech. officer, 1994—, bd. dir. Bd. dirs. Stressgen, Inc., Invitrogen, Synomyx, Chem. Engring. News, BioCom, Innovase, Zymetrics; reviewer human genome project and patenting DNA sequences U.S. Congl. Office Tech. Assessment; chmn., ofcl. Instnl. Animal Care and Use Com.; mem. peer rev. com. Nat. Inst. Environ. Health Scis., Molecular Biology, Microbiology, NAS, Genetic Analysis Techniques, Analytical Biochemistry, Nucleic Acids Rsch.; cons. on transgenic toxicology testing EEC, 1991-94; lectr. in field; mem. adj. faculty U. Calif., San Diego, 1991; lectr. Ctr. for Drug Evaluation and Rsch., FDA, 1992, others. Editor Mutation Rsch.; contbr. numerous articles and abstracts to sci. jours Recipient 1st place award for innovation and entrepreneurship in biotech. U. Calif., 1990, 91; named Entrepreneur of Yr., Ernst and Young, 2001; numerous grants including Nat. Inst. Environ. Health Scis., 1989-94, NIH, 1990-94, Nat. Cancer Inst., 1992-95. Mem. AAAS, Am. Soc. Biochemistry and Molecular Biology, Am. Soc. Microbiology, Environ. Mutagenesis Soc., Soc. Toxicology (chmn. conf. discussion group 1993), Japanese Environ. Mutagen Soc., N.Y. Acad. Scis. Achievements include patents in field. Avocations: flying, photography, collecting fossils, scuba diving. Office: Recombinant BioCatalysis Inc 10665 Sorrento Valley Rd San Diego CA 92121-1609

SHORT, MARTIN, actor, comedian, film critic; b. Hamilton, Ont, Canada, Mar. 26, 1950; s. Charles Patrick and Olive Short; m. Nancy Dolman, 1980; children: Katherine, Oliver, Henry. Degree in social work, McMaster U., 1972. Actor: (films) Three Amigos, 1986, Innerspace, 1987, Cross My Heart, 1987, Three Fugitives, 1989, The Big Picture, 1989, Pure Luck, 1991, Father of the Bride, 1991, Captain Ron, 1992, (voice) We're Back! A Dinosaur's Story, 1993, Clifford, 1994, (voice) The Pebble and the Penguin, 1995, Father of the Bride 2, 1995, Mars Attacks!, 1996, Jungle 2 Jungle, 1997, The Fairy Godmother, 1997, A Simple Wish, 1997, Mumford, 1998, Akbar's Adventure Tours, 1998, (voice) Prince of Egypt, 1998, Get Over It, 2001, (voice) Jimmy Neutron: Boy Genius, 2001, (voice) Treasure Planet, 2001, Cinemagique, 2002, (voice) Treasure Planet, 2002, The Santa Clause 3: The Escape Clause, 2006, The Spiderwick Chronicles, 2008; (TV series) The Associates, 1979, I'm a Big Girl Now, 1980-81, SCTV Network 90, 1982-84 (Emmy award for Outstanding Writing 1983), Saturday Night Live, 1985-86, (voice) The Completely Mental Misadventures of Ed Grimley, 1988-89, The Martin Short Show, 1994, (miniseries) Merlin, 1998; (TV films) The Family Man, 1979, Sunset Limousine, 1983, Alice in Wonderland, 1999, Prince Charming, 2001; writer (TV films) Martin Short's Concert for the North Americas, 1985, I, Martin Short Goes Hollywood, 1989, (TV series) Second City TV, 1981, SCTV Network 90, 1981-82, SCTV Channel, 1983, Saturday Night Live, 1984-85; exec. prodr. (TV series) The Martin Short Show, 1994, 99, Primetime Glick, 2001-03; writer, prodr. (TV films) Martin Short Shorts, 2003; dir. (TV films) Friends of Gilda, 1993; actor, writer, prodr. (films) Jiminy Glick in La La Wood, 2004; also numerous revues and cabaret appearances with Second City comedy troupe; 1977-78, Broadway appearances include The Goodbye Girl, 1993, Little Me, 1999 (Tony award for Best Actor in a Musical); stage appearances Martin Short: Fame Becomes Me, 2006. Office: William Morris Agency care Ames Cushing 1 William Morris Pl Beverly Hills CA 90212-2775

SHORTELL, STEPHEN MICHAEL, dean, health services researcher; b. New London, Wis., Nov. 9, 1944; BBA, U. Notre Dame, 1966; MPH, UCLA, 1968; MBA, U. Chgo., 1970, PhD in Behavioral Sci., 1972. Rsch. asst. Nat. Opinion Rsch. Ctr., 1969; instr., rsch. assoc. Ctr. Health Adminstrv. Studies, 1970—72; acting dir. grad. program hosp. adminstrn. U. Chgo., 1973—74, from asst. prof. to assoc. prof., 1974—79; prof. dept. health svc. Sch. Pub. Health and Cmty. Medicine, U. Wash., 1979—82; A.C. Buehler Disting. prof. health svc. mgmt. Northwestern U., Evanston, Ill., 1982—98; Blue Cross disting. prof. health policy and mgmt. Sch. Pub. Health, U. Calif., Berkeley, 1998—; dean Sch. Pub. Health, U. Calif, Berkeley, 2002—. Cons. VA, Robert Wood Found., Henry Kaiser Found.; asst. prof. Health Svcs. Orgn. U. Chgo., 1972—74; adj. asst. prof. dept. sociology U. Wash., 1975—76, dir. doctoral program dept. health svcs. Sch. Pub. Health and Cmty. Medicine, 1976—78; prof. sociology dept. sociology Northwestern U., 1982, prof. preventive medicine Sch. Medicine. Contbr. numerous articles to profl. jours. Recipient Baxter prize, Baxter-Allegiance Found., 1995, Honorary AHA Lifetime Mem. award, Gold Medal award, Amer. Coll. of Healthcare Exec., 1998, Dist. Investigator award, Assoc. for Health Services Research, 1998, Best Paper award, Acad. of Mgmnt., 1996, George R. Terry Book of the Year award, 1990. Fellow: Am. Coll. Healthcare Execs. (Gold medal 1998); mem.: Inst. Med.-NAS. Office: Univ Calif Berkeley Sch Pub Health 407 Warren Hl Berkeley CA 94720-0001

SHORTLIFFE, LINDA MARIE DAIRIKI, urology educator, researcher; b. Boston, Feb. 28, 1949; d. Setsuo and Norma Masako (Yoshida) Dairiki; children: Lindsay Ann, Lauren Leigh. AB in Hist. and Sci., Harvard U., 1971; MD, Stanford U. Sch. Medicine, Calif., 1975. Diplomate Am. Bd. Urology. Resident gen. surgery Tufts-New Eng. Med. Ctr., Boston, 1976-77; intern Stanford U. Med. Ctr., 1975-76, resident urology, 1977-81, chief pediat. urology, 1991—, chair dept. urology, 1995—; asst. prof. surgery urology Stanford U. Sch. Medicine, 1981-88, assoc. prof., 1988-93, prof., 1993—. Com. mem. spl. grants Nat. Inst. Diabetes, Digestive and Kidney Diseases, Bethesda, Md., 1990—94; pres. elect, trustee Am. Bd. Urology, 2001—07; pres. Soc. Univ. Urologists, 2004—05; bd. dirs. VIVUS, Inc., 1999—; dir. Am. Found. Urol. Disease, Balt., 2004—. Contbr. articles to profl. jours. Named one of Best Dr.'s in America, Woodward and White, Inc., America's Top Dr.'s, Castle Connolly Med. LTD; named to Nat. Libr. Med. Fellow: ACS, Am. Acad. Pediat. (chair-elect urology sect. 2007—08); mem.: Soc. Pediat. Urology, Am. Urol. Assn. Office: Stanford U Med Ctr Dept Urology 300 Pasteur Dr S287 Stanford CA 94305-5118 Office Phone: 650-498-5042. Business E-Mail: lindas@stanford.edu.

SHORTZ, RICHARD ALAN, lawyer; b. Chgo., Mar. 11, 1945; s. Lyle A. and Wilma Warner (Wildes) S.; m. Jennifer A. Harrell; children: Eric, Heidi. BS, Ind. U., 1967; JD, Harvard U., 1970. Bar: Calif. 1971, U.S. Supreme Ct. 1980. Assoc. Gibson, Dunn & Crutcher, LA, 1970-73; sr. v.p., gen. counsel, sec. Tosco Corp., LA, 1973-83; ptnr. Jones, Day, Reavis & Pogue, LA, 1983-95, Rogers & Wells, LA, 1995-97, Morgan Lewis & Bockius, LA, 1997—. Mem. L.A. World Affairs Inst., 1983—, Town Hall L.A., 1983—. 2nd lt. US Army, 1970—71. Mem.: Calif. Bar Assn., L.A. Bar. Assn., ABA, Merion Golf Club (Ardmore, Pa.), Loch Lomond Golf Club (Scotland), L.A. Country Club (Bd. Dir.), Beach Club (Santa Monica, Calif.), Calif. Club. Republican. Episcopalian. Home: 1343 Pavia Pl Pacific Palisades CA 90272-4047 Office: Morgan Lewis & Bockius 300 S Grand Ave Ste 2200 Los Angeles CA 90071-3132 Office Phone: 213-612-2526. Office Fax: 213-612-2501. Business E-Mail: rshortz@morganlewis.com.

SHOSTAK, LINDA E., lawyer; b. May 9, 1948; BA, Vassar Coll., 1970; JD, Harvard U., 1973. Bar: NY 1974, Calif. 1975. Lawyer Morrison & Foerster, San Francisco, 1974, ptnr., 1979—. Lectr. CEB, Rutter Grp.; taught (advanced pro. of trial advocacy) Nat. Inst. of Trial Advocacy; spkr. in field. Mem. Phi Beta Kappa. Office: Morrison & Foerster 425 Market St San Francisco CA 94105 Office Phone: 415-268-7202. Office Fax: 415-268-7522. Business E-Mail: lshostak@mofo.com.

SHOTTS, WAYNE J., nuclear scientist, federal agency administrator; b. Des Plaines, Ill., Mar. 20, 1945; s. Norman Russell Shotts and Winnifred Mae (Averill) Shotts Goeppinger; m. Melinda Maureen Antilla, June 24, 1967 (dec. Feb. 1975); children: Kenneth Wayne Shotts, Jeffrey Alan Shotts; m. Jacquelyn Francyle Willis, Aug. 11, 1979. BA in Physics, U. Calif., Santa Barbara, 1967; PhD, Cornell U., 1973. Rsch. physicist E.I. duPont deNemours & Co., Wilmington, Del., 1973-74; physicist U. Calif., Livermore, Calif., 1974—, Lawrence Livermore Nat. Lab., Livermore, 1974-79, group leader, thermonuclear design divsn., 1979-85, divsn leader, nuc. chemistry, 1985-86, divsn. leader, prompt diagnostics, 1986-88, prin. dep. assoc. dir., military applications, 1988-92, prin. dep. assoc. dir. def. and nuc. techs., 1992-95, assoc. dir. nonproliferation arms control/internat. security, 1995—2004, dep. dir. ops., 2004—06; ret., 2006. Sci. advisor Dept. Energy Office of Def. Programs; tech. advisor Nuclear Weapons Council Standing and Safety Com.; mem. Navy Steering Task Group. Recipient Ernest Orlando Lawrence Meml. award U.S. Dept. Energy, Washington, 1990. Mem. Am. Phys. Soc., Am. Assn. Advancement Sci. Office: Lawrence Livermore Nat Lab PO Box 808 Livermore CA 94551-0808

SHOUP, ANDREW JAMES, JR., retired oil industry executive; b. Monroe, La., Mar. 26, 1935; s. Andrew James Sr. and Ruth (Landis) S.; m. Sue Cowles, Sept. 12, 1959 (dec. May 1998); children: Catherine Shoup Collins, Andrew James III; m. Julia Conger Galloway, May 6, 2000. BS in Petroleum Engring., La. State U., 1957; M in Indsl. Adminstrn., Yale U., 1959. Registered engr., Tex. Prodn. engr. Continental Oil Co., Houston, 1959-65; v.p. DeGolyer and MacNaughton, Dallas, 1965-74; chmn., CEO Sabine Corp., Dallas, 1974-89; pres. Pacific Enterprises Oil Co. U.S.A, Dallas, 1989-90; pres., CEO The Wiser Oil Co., Dallas, 1991-2000; ret., 2000. 2nd lt. U.S. Army, 1959-60. Mem. Soc. Petroleum Engrs. of AIME, Dallas Petroleum Club, Dallas Country Club. Avocations: skiing, golf.

SHOUP, TERRY EMERSON, dean, engineering educator; b. Troy, Ohio, July 20, 1944; s. Dale Emerson and Betty Jean (Spoon) S.; m. Betsy Dinsomore, Dec. 18, 1966; children: Jennifer Jean, Matthew David. BME, Ohio State U., 1966, MS, 1967, PhD, 1969. Asst. prof. to assoc. prof. Rutgers U., New Brunswick, N.J., 1969-75; assoc. prof. to prof. U. Houston, 1975-80; asst. dean, prof. Tex. A&M U., College Sta., 1980-83; dean, prof. Fla. Atlantic U., Boca Raton, 1983-89; dean, Sobrato prof. Santa Clara (Calif.) U., 1989—. Cons., software specialist Numerical Methods in Engring. Author: (books) A Practical Guide to Computer Methods for Engineers, 1979, Resheniye Ingenyernikh Zadach NA EVM Prakticheskoye rukovodstvo, 1982, Narichnik Po Izchislitelni Methodi Za Ingeneri, 1983, Numerical Methods for the Personal Computer, 1983, Applied Numerical Methods for the Microcomputer, 1984, (with L.S. Fletcher) Introduction to Engineering with FORTRAN Programming, 1978, Solutions Manual for Introduction to Engineering Including FORTRAN Programming, 1978, Introduccion a la ingenieria Incluyendo programacion FORTRAN, 1980, (with L.S. Fletcher and E.V. Mochel) Introduction to Design with Graphics and Design Projects, 1981, (with S.P. Goldstein and J. Waddell) Information Sources, 1984, (with Carl Hanser Verlag) Numerische Verfahren fur Arbeitsplatzrechner, 1985, (with F. Mistree) Optimization Methods with Applications for Personal Computers, 1987; (software) Numerical Methods for the Personal Computer-Software User's Guide, Version 2, 1983, Optimization Software for the Personal Computer, 1986; editor in chief Mechanism and Machine Theory, 1977—; contbr. more than 100 articles to profl. jours. Fellow ASME (chmn. Design Engring. div. 1987-88, Mech. Engring. div. 1980-81, Centennial medal 1980, Gustus Larson award 1981); mem. Am. Soc. for Engring. Edn. (Dow Outstanding Faculty award 1974, Western Electric award 1984), Fla. Engring. Soc. Home: 440 Galleria Dr Apt 12 San Jose CA 95134-2467 Office: Santa Clara U Coll Engring Office of Dean 500 El Camino Real Santa Clara CA 95053-0001

SHOWALTER, MARILYN GRACE, trade association administrator, director; AB, Harvard U., 1972, JD, 1975. Bar: Wash. 1975. Dep. pros. atty. King County, Wash., 1975—81, counsel to gov., 1981—83; pvt. practice, 1985—89; counsel house appropriations com. Wash. State House of Reps., 1989—92, dep. chief clk., house counsel, 1992—93, chief clk., 1994—95; advisor to Gov. Gary Locke, 1997—99; chair Utilities and Transp. Com., Portland, Oreg., 1999—2005, exec. dir., 2005—. Home Phone: 360-754-7238. Business E-Mail: mshowalter@ppcpdx.org.

SHREEVE, JEAN'NE MARIE, chemist, educator; b. Deer Lodge, Mont., July 2, 1933; d. Charles William and Maryfrances (Briggeman) Shreeve. BA in Chemistry, U. Mont., 1953, DSc (hon.), 1982; MS in Analytical Chemistry, U. Minn., 1956; PhD in Inorganic Chemistry, U. Wash., 1961. From asst. prof. to assoc. prof. chemistry U. Idaho, Moscow, 1961—67, prof., 1967-73, 2000—, acting chmn. dept. chemistry, 1969-70, 1973, head dept. and prof., 1973-87, v.p. rsch. and grad. studies, prof. chemistry, 1987-99, Jean'ne M. Shreeve chemistry prof., 2004—. Mem. nat. com. Stds. Higher Edn., 1965—67, 1969—73; Lucy W. Pickett lectr. Mt. Holyoke Coll., 1976; George H. Cady lectr. U. Wash., 1993; chmn. com. nat. medal sci. Pres. U.S., 2003—07. Mem. editl. bd. Jour. Fluorine Chemistry, 1970—2003, Jour. Heteroatom Chemistry, 1988—95, Accounts Chem. Rsch., 1973—75, Inorganic Synthesis, 1976—; contbr. articles to sci. jours. Mem. bd. govs. Argonne (Ill.) Nat. Lab., 1992—98. Recipient Disting. Alumni award, U. Mont., 1970, Outstanding Achievement award, U. Minn., 1975, Sr. U.S. Scientist award, Alexander Von Humboldt Found., 1978, Excellence in Tchg. award, Chem. Mfrs. Assn., 1980; named Hon. Alumnus, U. Idaho, 1972; named to Idaho Hall of Fame, 2001; NSF Postdoctoral fellow, U. Cambridge, Eng., 1967—68, U.S. Hon. Ramsay fellow, 1967—68, Alfred P. Sloan fellow, 1970—72. Mem.: AAUW (officer Moscow chpt. 1962—69), AAAS (bd. dirs. 1991—95), Idaho Acad. Sci. (Disting. Scientist 2001), Am. Chem. Soc. (bd. dirs. 1985—93, chmn. fluorine divsn. 1979—81, mem. adv. bd. Petroleum Rsch. Fund 1975—77, mem. women chemists com. 1972—77, Harry and Carol Mosher award Santa Clara Valley sect. 1992, Shirley B. Radding award Santa Clara Valley sect. 2003, Garvan medal 1972, award for creative work in fluorine chemistry 1978), Göttingen (Germany) Acad. Scis. (corr.), Phi Beta Kappa. Avocations: fishing, gardening. Office: U Idaho Dept Chemistry Box 442343 Moscow ID 83844-2343 Office Phone: 208-885-6215. Business E-Mail: jshreeve@uidaho.edu.

SHRIRAM, K. RAM, investment company executive; married; 2 children. BS, U. Madras, India. Mem. exec. team Netscape; pres. Junglee; v.p. bus. devel. Amazon.com, 1998—99; mng. ptnr. Sherpalo Ventures, 2000—. Bd. mem. Google, Inc., 1998—, 247customer.com, Plaxo, Zazzle.com, PodShow, Bus. Signatures. Named one of 400 Richest Americans, Forbes, 2006.

SHRIVER, MARIA OWINGS, former news correspondent; b. Chgo., Nov. 6, 1955; d. Robert Sargent and Eunice Mary (Kennedy) S.; m. Arnold Schwarzenegger, Apr. 26, 1986; children: Katherine Eunice, Christina Maria Aurelia, Patrick Arnold, Christopher Sargent BA, Georgetown U. Coll. Am. Studies, Washington, 1977. News producer Sta. KYW-TV, 1977-78; producer Sta. WJZ-TV, 1978-80; nat. reporter PM Mag., 1981-83; news reporter CBS News, Los Angeles, 1983-85; news correspondent, co-anchor CBS Morning News, NYC, 1985-86; co-host Sunday Today, NBC, 1987-90; anchor Main Street, NBC, 1987; co-anchor Yesterday, Today, and Tomorrow, NBC, 1989; anchor NBC Nightly News Weekend Edition, 1989-90, Cutting Edge with Maria Shriver, NBC, 1990, First Person with Maria Shriver, NBC, 1990—2004; First Lady of Calif., 2003—. Co-anchor Summer Olympics, Seoul, Korea, 1988; substitute anchor NBC News at Sunrise, Today, NBC Nightly News with Tom Brokaw; contbg. anchor Dateline, NBC, 1995-2004. Author: What's Heaven, 1999, Ten Things I Wish I'd Known Before I Went Into the Real World, 2000, What's Wrong With Timmy, 2001, What's Happening to Grandpa?, 2003, And One More Thing Before You Go..., 2005, Just Who Will You Be?: Big Question, Little Book, Answer Within, 2008; exec. prodr: (documentary) The Alzheimer's Project, 2009 Recipient Christopher award for "Fatal Addictions", 1990, Exceptional Merit Media award Nat. Women's Political Caucus, first-place Commendation award Am. Women in Radio and TV, 1991, Emmy nomination, George Peabody Award, 1998. Democrat. Roman Catholic. Office: First Lady Maria Shriver State Capitol Bldg Sacramento CA 95814-4906*

SHROPSHIRE, DONALD GRAY, hospital executive; b. Winston-Salem, NC, Aug. 6, 1927; s. John Lee and Bess L. (Shouse) S.; m. Mary Ruth Bodenheimer, Aug. 19, 1950; children: Melanie Shropshire David, John Devin. BS, U. NC, 1950; postgrad Erickson fellow, U. Chgo., 1958-59; LLD (hon.), U. Ariz., 1992; PhD (hon.), Tucson U., 1994. Personnel asst. Nat. Biscuit Co., Atlanta, 1950-52, asst. personnel mgr. Chgo., 1952-54; adminstr. Eastern State Hosp., Lexington, Ky., 1954-62; assoc. dir. U. Md. Hosp., Balt., 1962-67; adminstr. Tucson Med. Ctr., 1967-82, pres., 1982-92, pres. emeritus, 1992—; pres. Tucson Hosps. Med. Edn. Program, 1970-71, sec., 1971-86; pres. So. Ariz. Hosp. Council, 1968-69; bd. dirs. Ariz. Blue Cross, 1967-76, chmn. provider standards com., 1972-76; chmn. bd. Healthways, Inc., 1985-92. Mem. bd. La Posada at Park Centre, Inc., Green Valley, Ariz., 1996-2000, chmn., bd. emeritus, 2000—. Bd. dirs. Health Planning Coun. Tucson, mem. exec. com., 1969-74; chmn. profl. divsn. United Way, Tucson, 1969-70, vice chmn. campaign, 1988, Ariz. Health Facilities Authority, bd. dirs., 1992-2005; chmn. dietary svcs. com., vice chmn., 1988, Md. Hosp. Coun., 1966-67; bd. dirs. Ky. Hosp. Assn., 1961-62, chmn. coun. profl. practice, 1960-61; past pres. Blue Grass Hosp. Coun.; trustee Assn. Western Hosps., 1974-81, pres., 1979-80; mem. accreditation Coun. for Continuing Med. Edn., 1982-87, chair, 1986; bd. govs. Pima C.C., 1970-76, sec., 1973-74, chmn., 1975-76, bd. dirs. Found., 1978-82, Ariz. Bd. Regents, 1982-90, sec., 1983-86, pres., 1987-88; mem. Tucson Airport Authority, 1987—, bd. dirs., 1990-95, pres., 1995; v.p. Tucson Econ. Devel. Corp., 1977-82; founder, dir., bd. dirs. Vol. Hosps. Am., 1977-88, treas., 1979-82; mem. Ariz. Adv. Health Coun. Dirs., 1976-78; bd. dirs. Tucson Tomorrow, 1983-87, Tucson Downtown Devel. Corp., 1988-95, Rincon Inst., 1992-97, Sonoran Inst., 1992-97, Pima County Med. Res. Corps, 2006—; dir. Mus. No. Ariz., 1988-2002, dir. emeritus, 2002—; nat. bd. advisors Eller Coll. Mgmt. U. Ariz., 1990-2007, mem. Dean's Bd. Coll. Fine Arts, 1992—, chmn., 1992-96, pres. Ariz. Coun. Econ. Edn., 1993-95; vis. panel Sch. Health Adminstrn. and Policy Ariz. State U., 1990-92; bd. dirs. Cmty. Found. So. Ariz., 1996-2001; mem. adv. bd. Steele Meml. Rsch. Ctr., U. Ariz. Coll. Medicine, 1996-2004; mem. student health adv. com. U. Ariz., 1990-07, Med. Reserve Corps Southern Ariz., 2006-, Ariz. Skill Stds. Commn., 2007. Named to Hon. Order Ky. Cols.; named Tucson Man of Yr. 1987, Tucson Father of Yr. 1997, Hon. Alumnus, Coll. Nursing, U. Ariz., 1998; recipient Disting. Svc. award Anti-Defamation League B'nai B'rith, 1989, Sticking-Your-Neck-Out award Pima Coun. on Aging, 1991, Il Magnifico award U. Ariz. Coll. Fine Arts, 1996, Humanitarian award Arthritis Found. S.Am., 2001, Crystal Apple Lifetime Achievement award Tucson Metro Edn. Commn., 2004, Pima Med. Found. award, 2005, Humanitarian Achievement award, Ednl. Enrichment Found., 2005; co-recipient Paloma Family Svcs. Commitment to Children award, 2005; Pima CC Dinner honoree, 1986, 92. Mem. Am. Hosp. Assn. (nominating com. 1983-86, trustee 1975-78, ho. dels. 1972-78, chmn. coun. profl. svc. 1973-74, regional adv. bd. 1969-78, chmn. joint com. with NASW 1963-64, Disting. Svc. award 1989), Ariz. Hosp. Assn. (Salisbury award 1982, bd. dirs. 1967-72, pres. 1970-71), Ariz. C. of C. (bd. dirs. 1988-93), Assn. Am. Med. Colls. (mem. assembly 1974-77), Health Care Study Soc., Tucson C. of C. (bd. dirs. 1968-69, 1974), Nat. League for Nursing, Ariz. Town Hall (bd. dirs. 1982-92, chmn. 1990-92, treas. 1985, Circle of Disting. Svc. award 2002), Pima County Acad. Decathlon Assn. (dir. 1983-85), Rotary Club (Tucson) (pres. 1993-94, McPherson award, 2008), U. Ariz. Alumni Assn. Coll. Nursing (hon. alumnus 1998), Pi Alpha Alpha (hon.). Baptist/Presbyterian (ch. moderator, chmn. finance com., deacon, ch. sch. supt., trustee, bd. dirs. ch. found.) Office: Tucson Med Ctr 5301 E Grant Rd Tucson AZ 85712-2805

SHU, FRANK HSIA-SAN, astronomy educator, researcher, writer; b. Kunming, China, June 2, 1943; came to U.S., 1949; s. Shien-Siu and Irene I-Jen (Hsia) S.; m. Helen Chien-Ping Pu, June 22, 1968 BS in Physics, MIT, 1963; PhD in Astronomy, Harvard U., 1968. Asst. prof. SUNY-Stony Brook, 1968-71, assoc. prof., 1971-73, U. Calif.-Berkeley, 1973-76, prof. astronomy, 1976—, chmn. dept. astronomy, 1984-96, chancellor's prof. astronomy, 1996—, univ. prof., 1998—. Research assoc. MIT, Cambridge, 1968, sr. research assoc., 1971; vis. scientist Kapteyn Astron. Lab., Groningen, The Netherlands, 1973; mem. Inst. Advanced Study, Princeton, N.J., 1982; Oort Professorship, Leiden U., The Netherlands, 1996, Thomas Gold lectureship, Cornell U., 2002; served US Nat. Rsch. Coun. Blue-Ribbon com. 2001; pres. Nat. Tsing Hua Univ., Taiwan, 2002-03, former prof.; mem. bd. adjudicators, The Shaw Prize (Hong Kong), 2005-, chmn. selection com. in astronomy, 2005-. Author: The Physical Universe, 1982; also numerous sci. and popular articles Pamphlet writer McGovern Campaign, Suffolk County, N.Y., 1972 Recipient Bok prize Harvard U., 1972, Warner prize, 1977, Dirk Brouwer award for Dynamical Astronomy, 1996, Heinemann prize, 2000; Sloan research fellow, 1972-74; named Oort Prof., Leiden U., 1996. Mem. AAAS, NAS, Academia Sinica, Am. Acad. Arts and Sciences, Internat. Astron. Union, Am. Astron. Soc. (councilor 1982-85, pres., 1994-96, Warner prize 1977, Dannie Heineman prize for Astrophysics, 2006), Astron. Soc. of Pacific (bd. dirs. 1985-86), Am. Philos. Soc., Academia Sinica (Taiwan), Sigma Xi Democrat. Avocations: chess; poker; bridge; sports; wine and food. Office: U Calif Berkeley Dept Astronomy 601 Campbell Hall Berkeley CA 94720-3411

SHUBB, WILLIAM BARNET, judge; b. Oakland, Calif., May 28, 1938; s. Ben and Nellie Bernice (Fruechtenicht) Shubb; m. Sandra Ann Talarico, July 29, 1962; children: Alisa Marie, Carissa Ann, Victoria Ann. AB, U. Calif., Berkeley, 1960, JD, 1963. Bar: Calif. 1964, US Ct. Internat. Trade 1981, US Customs Ct. 1980, US Ct. Appeals (9th cir.) 1964, US Supreme Ct. 1972. Law clk. US Dist. Ct., Sacramento, 1963—65; asst. US atty. US Dist. Ct. Ea. Dist. Calif., 1965—71, chief asst. US atty., 1971—74, chmn. com. drafting of local criminal rules, 1974, mem. speedy trial planning com., 1974—80, US atty., 1980—81, judge, 1990—, chief judge, 1996—2003; assoc. Diepenbrock, Wulff, Plant & Hannegan, Sacramento, 1974—77, ptnr., 1977—80, 1981—90. Instr. McGeorge Sch. Law U. Pacific, 1964—66; lawyer rep. 9th cir. US Jud. Conf., 1975—78; mem. faculty Fed. Practice Inst., 1978—80. Mem.: ABA, Sacramento County Bar. Coun., Am. Bd. Trial Advs., Assn. Def. Counsel, Calif. Bar Assn., Sacramento Rotary Club.

SHUER, LAWRENCE MENDEL, neurosurgery educator; b. Toledo, Apr. 12, 1954; s. Bernard Benjamin and Estelle Rose (Drukker) S.; m. Paula Ann Elliott, Sept. 4, 1976; children: Jenna, Tammy, Nichole. BA with high distinction, U. Mich., 1975, MD cum laude, 1978. Diplomate Am. Bd. Neurol. Surgery, Nat. Bd. Med. Examiners. Fellow in neurology Inst. Neurology, London, 1979; intern in surgery Stanford (Calif.) U. Sch. Medicine, 1978-79, resident in neuropathology, 1980, resident in neurosurgery, 1980-84, clin. asst. prof. surgery and neurosurgery, 1984-90, assoc. prof., 1990—2002, acting chmn. dept. neurosurgery, 1992-95, 96—, assoc. dean, 1996—, chief of staff Stanford Health Sys., 1996—; chief of staff Stanford U. Hosp. and Clinics, 1996—2008, prof., 2002—. Numerous presentations in field. Contbr. articles and abstracts to med. jours., chpts. to books. Recipient Kaiser tchr. award Stanford U., 1993; James B. Angell scholar. Mem. AMA, Am. Assn. Neurol. Surgeons, Congress Neurol. Surgeons, Western Neurosurg. Soc., Calif. Assn. Neurol. Surgeons (bd. dirs., treas. 1995—98, 2nd v.p. 1998-99, 1st v.p. 1999-2000, pres.-elect 2000-01, pres. 2002-03), Calif. Med. Assn., Am. Heart Assn. (fellow stroke coun.), Santa Clara County Med. Assn., San Francisco Neurol. Soc., Alpha Omega Alpha. Conservative. Jewish. Avocations: skiing, swimming, travel. Office: Stanford U Med Ctr 300 Pasteur Dr R229 Palo Alto CA 94304-5327 Home Phone: 650-222-5433; Office Phone: 650-723-6093. Business E-Mail: lshuer@stanford.edu.

SHUGART, HOWARD ALAN, physicist, researcher; b. Orange, Calif., Sept. 21, 1931; s. Howard Ancil and Bertha Elizabeth (Henderson) S.; m. Elizabeth L. Hanson, Feb. 6, 1971. BS, Calif. Inst. Tech., 1953; MA, U. Calif., Berkeley, 1955, PhD, 1957. Tchg. asst. physics U. Calif., Berkeley, 1953-56, assoc., 1957, lectr., 1957-58, acting asst. prof., 1958-59, asst. prof., 1959-63, assoc. prof., 1963-67, prof., 1967-93, prof. emeritus, 1993—, vice chmn., 1968—70, 1979—87, 1989—2001, acting chmn., 1979—81, 1983—84, 1987. Cons. Convair divsn. Gen. Dynamics Corp., 1960-61; mem. com. nuc. constants NRC, 1960-63; atomic beam group leader Lawrence Berkeley (Calif.) Nat. Lab., 1965-79, guest rschr., 1999—. Fellow Am. Phys. Soc. (acting sec. Pacific Coast 1961-64, exec. com. divsn. electron and atomic physics 1972-74), Nat. Speleological Soc. (gov. 1954-56); mem. Sigma Xi. Office: U Calif Dept Physics Berkeley CA 94720-7300

SHULER, DENNIS W., entertainment company executive; b. NY; married; 2 children. BS in Bus Adminstrn., magna cum laude, SUNY, Oswego; MA in Human Resources Mgmt., summa cum laude, U. Ala. Lectr. Highline CC, Seattle; assoc. Kaiser Aluminum and Chem. Corp.; various position including human resources mgr. and dir. human resources UK/Ireland Procter and Gamble Co., 1984—2002, v.p. human resources, beauty and health & well being, 2002—08; exec. v.p., chief human resources officer Walt Disney Co., 2008—. Vis. prof., bus. adminstrn. Northumbria U., Newcastle, England; vis. prof. Durham U. Mem. Am. C. of C., London; vol. Jr. Achievement; active Greater Cin. Fine Arts Fund; fin. contbr. Cin. Children's Hosp.; bd. governors Woking Coll.; former bd. mem. Coll. Mt. St. Joseph, Cin.; bd. visitors U. Ala., Tuscaloosa; adv. bd. mem. Durham U.; bd. mem. Xavier U. Williams Coll. Bus., Cin. Fellow: Royal Soc. Arts London; mem.: Phi Beta Kappa (Beta Gamma Sigma Chpt. Disting. Alumni award 2007). Office: Walt Disney Co 500 S Buena Vista St Burbank CA 91521

SHULER, KURT EGON, chemist, educator; b. Nuremberg, Germany, July 10, 1922; came to U.S., 1937, naturalized, 1944; s. Louis and Donie (Wald) Schulherr; m. Beatrice Gwyn London, Nov. 11, 1944. BS, Ga. Inst. Tech., 1942; PhD, Cath. U. Am., 1949. Fellow Johns Hopkins U., 1949-51; sr. staff mem., asst. group supr., chem. physics group Applied Physics Lab., Johns Hopkins, 1951-55; supervisory phys. chemist Nat. Bur. Standards, 1955-58, cons. to dir., 1958-61, asst. dir., sr. research fellow, 1963-68; rsch. staff, sci. adviser to v.p. rsch. Gen. Motors Corp., 1958; spl. asst. to dir. rsch. Inst. Def. Analyses, 1961-63; vis. prof. chemistry U. Calif., San Diego, 1966-67, prof. chemistry, 1968-91, prof. emeritus, 1991—, chmn. dept., 1968-70, 84-87. Cons. in field; mem. Solvay Conf., 1962, 78; mem. adv. panel, chemistry div. NSF, 1973-75. Author, editor tech. books; assoc. editor: Jour. Math. Physics, 1963-66; bd. editors: Jour. Statis. Physics, 1968-80; mem. adv. bd.: Chem. Engring. News, 1967-70; contbr. articles to profl. jours. Served with U.S. Army, 1944-46. Recipient Distinguished Service award Nat. Bur. Standards, 1959, Gold medal award Dept. Commerce, 1968; Solvay Found. fellow, 1975 Fellow Am. Inst. Chemists, AAAS, Am. Phys. Soc., Washington Acad. Sci.; mem. Am. Chem. Soc., Washington Philos. Soc. Clubs: Rancho Santa Fe Golf. Achievements include the department of chemistry and biochemistry at the University of California San Diego establishing an endowed chair in his name in 2006. Home: PO Box 1504 Rancho Santa Fe CA 92067-1504 Office: Univ Calif San Diego Dept Chemistry La Jolla CA 92093 Business E-Mail: kshuler@ucsd.edu.

SHULMAN, LEE S., former educational association administrator; b. Chgo., Sept. 28, 1938; BA, MA, U. Chgo., 1959, PhD, 1963; doctorate (hon.), U. Judaism, 1989, Hebrew Union Coll., 1995, Mich. State U., 1996, Drury Coll., 1999, U. Aveiro Portugal, 1999, So. Ill. U., 2001. Prof. ednl. psychology and med. edn. Mich. State U., 1963—82; prof. edn. and psychology Stanford U., Calif., 1982-98, Charles E. Ducommun prof. edn. emeritus, 1998—; pres. Carnegie Found. for the Advancement of Tchg., Stanford, Calif., 1997—2008, pres. emeritus, 2008—. Co-author: Educating Lawyers: Preparation for the Profession of Law, 2007; author: The Wisdom of Practice: Essays on Teaching, Learning, and Learning to Teach, 2004, Teaching as Community Property: Essays on Higher Education, 2004. Recipient Grawemeyer Prize in Edn., 2006; fellow Ctr. Advanced Study in Behavioral Scis.; vis. scholar Guggenheim Fellow. Fellow: AAAS, Am. Acad. Arts and Scis.; mem.: Am. Psychol. Assn. (E.L. Thorndike Award for Disting. Psychol. Contributions to Edn. 1995), Nat. Acad. Edn., Am. Ednl. Rsch. Assn. (past pres.). Office: Carnegie Found for Advancement of Tchg 51 Vista Lane Stanford CA 94305 Office Phone: 650-566-5110. Office Fax: 650-326-0278. E-mail: shulman@carnegiefoundation.org.

SHULTZ, GEORGE PRATT, economics professor, former United States Secretary of State; b. NYC, Dec. 13, 1920; s. Birl E. and Margaret Lennox (Pratt) S.; children: Margaret Ann Shultz Tilsworth, Kathleen Pratt Shultz Jorgensen, Peter Milton, Barbara Lennox Shultz White, Alexander George; m. Charlotte Mailliard, Aug. 15, 1997. BA in econs., Princeton U., 1942; PhD in indsl. econs., MIT, 1949; Hon. degree, Yeshiva U., U. Tel Aviv, Technion-Israel Inst. Tech., Keio U., Tokyo, Brandeis U., U. Notre Dame, Princeton U., Loyola U., U. Pa., U. Rochester, Carnegie-Mellon U., Baruch Coll., Northwestern U., Tblisi State U.; Hon. degree (hon.), Columbia U. Mem. faculty MIT, 1949-57, assoc. prof. indsl. relations, 1955-57; prof. indsl. relations Grad. Sch. Bus., U. Chgo., 1957-68; dean sch. Grad. Sch. Bus. U. Chgo., 1962-68, fellow Ctr. for Advanced Study in Behavioral Scis., 1968-69; sec. US Dept. Labor, 1969-70; dir. Office Mgmt. & Budget Exec. Office of the Pres., 1970-72; sec. US Dept. Treasury, 1972-74; asst. to the Pres. The White House, 1972—74; chmn. Council on Econ. Policy, East-West Trade Policy com.; exec. v.p. Bechtel Corp., San Francisco, 1974-75, pres., 1975-81, vice chmn., 1977-81; also dir.; pres. Bechtel Group, Inc., 1981-82; prof. mgmt. and pub. policy Stanford U., 1974-82, prof. internat. econs., 1989-91, prof. emeritus, 1991—; chmn. Pres. Reagan's Econ. Policy Adv. Bd., 1981-82; sec. US Dept. State, 1982-89; Thomas W. and Susan B. Ford disting. fellow Hoover Instn., Stanford, 1989—. Bd. dirs. Accretive Health, Fremont Group; mem. adv. coun. Bechtel Inc.; chmn. J.P. Morgan Chase Internat. Coun.; chmn. adv. coun. Inst. Internat. Studies, 2002—07; mem. Calif. Gov.'s Econ. Policy Adv. Bd., 1995—98, 2003—; chmn. Govs. Coun. Econ. Advisors, 2004—. Author: Pressures on Wage Decisions, 1950, (with Charles A. Myers) The Dynamics of a Labor Market, 1951, (with John R. Coleman) Labor Problems: Cases and Readings, 1953, (with T.L. Whisler) Management Organization and the Computer, 1960, (with Arnold R. Weber) Strategies for the Displaced Worker, 1966, (with Robert Z. Aliber) Guidelines, Informal Controls and the Marketplace, 1966, (with Albert Rees) Workers and Wages in the Urban Labor Market, 1970, Leaders and Followers in an Age of Ambiguity, 1975, (with Kenneth W. Dam) Economic Policy Beyond the Headlines, 1977, 2d edition, 1998, Turmoil and Triumph: My Years as Secretary of State, 1993, (with John B. Shoven)A Putting Our House in Order: Citizens Guide to Social Security and Health Care Reform, 2008; also articles, chpts. in books, reports, and essays. Served to maj. USMCR, 1942—45. Recipient Medal of Freedom, 1989, Seoul Peace prize, 1992, Eisenhower medal for Leadership and Svc., 2001, Reagan Disting. Am. award, 2002, Ralph Bunche award for diplomatic excellence, 2002, Am. Spirit award, Nat. WWII Mus., 2006. Fellow Am. Econ. Assn. (disting.); mem. Indsl. Rels. Rsch. Assn. (pres. 1968), Nat. Acad. Arbitrators. Republican. Office: Stanford U Hoover Instn Stanford CA 94305-6010 Business E-Mail: shultz@hoover.stanford.edu.

SHULTZ, JOHN DAVID, lawyer; b. LA, Oct. 9, 1939; Student, Harvard Coll., Cambridge, Mass., 1960—61; BA, U. Ariz., Tucson, 1964; JD, U. Calif., Berkeley, 1967. Bar: N.Y. 1968, Calif. 1978. Assoc. Cadwalader, Wickersham & Taft, NYC, 1968—77; ptnr. Lawler, Felix & Hall, LA, 1977—83, mem. exec. com., chmn. planning com., co-chmn. recruiting and hiring com.; ptnr. Morgan, Lewis & Bockius, LA, 1983—, chmn. mgmt. com., mem. lateral entry com., chmn. profl. evaluation com., chmn. practice devel. com., chmn. recruiting com. Mem. adv. bd. Internat. and Comparative Law Ctr., Southwestern Legal Found., 1981—; active Practicing Law Inst. Adv. Bd., Corp. and Securities Law, 1992—; Trustee St. Thomas Ch., NYC, 1969—72, Shore Acres Point Corp., Mamaroneck, NY, 1975—77. Mem.: N.Y. State Bar Assn., State Bar Calif., Assn. Bar City of N.Y., ABA. Office: Morgan Lewis & Bockius LLP 300 S Grand Ave Ste 22 Los Angeles CA 90071-3109

SHULTZ, LEILA MCREYNOLDS, botanist, educator; b. Bartlesville, Okla., Apr. 20, 1946; 1 child, Kirsten. BS, U. Tulsa, 1969; MA, U. Colo., 1975; PhD, Claremont Grad. Sch., 1983. Curator Intermountain Herbarium Utah State U., 1973-92, rsch. prof., 1994—; rschr. Harvard U., Cambridge, Mass., 1994—. Vis. prof., acting curator dept. botany U. Okla., 1992-93; bibliographer Gray Herbarium Index, Harvard U., Cambridge, 1994-95. Author: Atlas of the Vascular Plants of Utah, 1988; taxon editor, author: Flora of North America (7 vols.), 1993—. Office: Utah State U Logan UT 84322-5230

SHUMAN, THOMAS ALAN, protective services official, consultant; b. Fairmont, W.Va., Dec. 31, 1946; BA, N.Mex State U., 1969-73; postgrad., U. N.Mex, 1988. Mgr. Drum Appliance, Inc., Las Cruces, N.Mex., 1971-75; classification supr. N.Mex. Corrections Dept., Santa Fe, 1976-80, mgmt. analyst supr., 1981-83, dir. classification, 1983-84, dep. sec., 1984-87; pres. Correctional Data Sys., Santa Fe, 1987—; owner Desktop Publ. Co., Santa Fe, 1988—; dir. N.Mex. Corrections Tng. Acad., 1991-95, probation, parole dir., 1995—; pres. Silicon Wizard Corp., 1989—. Cons. Nat. Inst. Corrections, Wash., 1988, Am. Correctional Assn., Md., 1987—. Mem. Smithsonian Inst., US Naval Inst. Served to lt. U.S. Army, 1969-71, Vietnam. Decorated Bronze Star, Presdl. Commendation. Mem. NRA, N.Mex. State U. Alumni Assn. Republican. Presbyterian. Avocations: fishing, painting, photography, writing. E-mail: alans76@comcast.net.

SHUMWAY, ERIC BRANDON, academic administrator; s. James Carroll and Merie Kartchner Shumway; m. Carolyn Merrill, June 1963; 7 children. BA, Brigham Young U., 1964, MA, 1966; PhD in English Lit., U. Va., 1973. Tchr., English Ch. Coll. of Hawaii, 1966—70; academic v.p. Brigham Young U.-Hawaii, 1980—86, 1990—94, prof. English and modern languages, 1966—, pres., 1994—; acting pres. Polynesian Cultural Ctr., 1991. Trainer, Tongan language US Peace Corps, 1967—68. Missionary, Tonga, 1959—62; pres. Tonga Nuku'alofa Mission, 1986—89; Area Authority Seventy Hawaii, Calif.; bishop Hauula 2nd Ward, 1968—70. Office: Brigham Young U-Hawaii 55-220 Kulanui St Laie HI 96762 Business E-Mail: shumwaye@byuh.edu.

SHURTLEFF, MARK L., state attorney general; b. Utah, Aug. 9, 1957; m. M'Liss Shurtleff; 5 children. BA in Polit. Sci., Brigham Young U., 1981; JD, U. Utah, 1985. Officer, atty. JAG USN, 1985—90; pvt. practice in law Calif., 1990—93; asst. atty. gen. State of Utah, 1993—97; dep. county atty. Salt Lake County, 1997—98; commr. Salt Lake County Commn., 1999—2000, chmn., 2000; atty. gen. State of Utah, 2001—. Leader Boy Scout troops, 1980—; anti-drug lectr., at-risk youth mentor. Republican. Office: Office of Atty Gen State Capitol Rm 236 Salt Lake City UT 84114-0810 Office Phone: 801-538-9600.*

SHURTLIFF, MARVIN KARL, lawyer; b. Idaho Falls, Nov. 6, 1939; s. Noah Leon and Melba Dorothy (Hunting) S.; m. Peggy J. Griffin, Nov. 23, 1963; 1 dau., Jennifer Karyl. BA, Idaho State Coll., 1962; JD, U. Idaho, 1968. Bar: Idaho 1968. Tchr. pub. schs., Jefferson County, Idaho, 1964-65; atty. U.S. Dept. Justice, Washington, 1968-74; commr. Idaho Pub. Utilities Commn., 1974-75, pres., 1975-76; spl. asst., legal counsel Gov. of Idaho, Boise, 1977; U.S. atty. for Dist. of Idaho, Boise, 1977-81; practice law Boise, 1981—. Mem. Idaho Ho. of Reps., 1962-64 Mem. Idaho State Bd. Edn., 1990—95, Idaho Commn. on Redistricting, 2001. Mem. Idaho Bar Assn. Democrat. Home: 62 Horizon Dr Boise ID 83702-4419 Office: PO Box 1652 Boise ID 83701-1652

SHUSTER, ALVIN, journalist, reporter; b. Washington, Jan. 25, 1930; s. Fred and Dora (Levy) S.; m. Miriam Schwartz, June 22, 1952; children: Fred, Jessica, Beth. AB, George Washington U., 1951. Reporter Washington Bur. N.Y. Times, 1952-61, asst. news editor, 1961-66, reporter London Bur., 1967-70; bur. chief Saigon, Vietnam, 1970-71, London, 1971-75, Rome, 1975-77; dep. editor editorial pages L.A. Times, 1977-83, fgn. editor, 1983-95, sr. consulting editor, 1995—. Pres. Fgn. Corrs. Assn., London, 1973-74; trustee Monterey (Calif.) Inst. Internat. Studies, 1983-99; chmn. Pulitzer Prize Jury Internat. Reporting, 1999. Editor: The Witnesses, 1964, Washington: The New York Times Guide to the Nations' Capital, 1967, International Press Institute Report, 1995-99; assc. editor Global Journalist, 1999-2004; contbg. author: The Kennedy Years, 1964; contbg. editor Columbia Journalism Rev., 1999-2004. Nieman fellow Harvard U., 1966-67. Mem. Reform Club (London). Office: Los Angeles Times 202 W 1st St Los Angeles CA 90012

SHUSTERMAN, NEAL DOUGLAS, writer, scriptwriter; b. NYC, Nov. 12, 1962; s. Milton and Charlotte Ruth (Altman) S.; m. Elaine Gale Jones, Jan. 31, 1987; children: Brendan, Jarrod, Joelle, Erin. BA in Psychology and Drama, U. Calif., Irvine, 1985. Author, screenwriter, 1987—. Author: Guy Talk, 1987, The Shadow Club, 1988 (Children's CHoice award Internat. Reading Assn. 1989), Dissidents, 1989, Speeding Bullet, 1991 (Best Book for Teens award N.Y. Pub. Libr., nominated Calif. Young Reader Medal 1995-96), Kid Heroes, 1991, What Daddy Did, 1991 (Best Book for Young Adults award ALA, Outstanding Work of Fiction award So. Calif. Coun. Lit. for Children and Young People, Children's Choice award and Young Adult Choice award Internat. Reading Assn., Pick of the List award ABA, Best Book for Teens award N.Y. Pub. Libr., Okla. Sequoyah award 1994), The Eyes of Kid Midas, 1992 (ALA Best Book for Reluctant Readers), Darkness Creeping, 1993, Piggyback Ninja, 1994, Scorpion Shards, 1995 (N.Y. Pub. Libr. Best Book for the Teenaged), Darkness Creeping II, 1995, Mindquakes, 1996 (ALA YALSA Quick Pick), Mindstorms, 1996, Mindtwisters, 1997, The Dark Side of Nowhere, 1997 (ALA Best Book, ALA Quick Pick--Top 10 Book), Thief of Souls, 1999, Downsiders, 1999 (ALA Best Book, ALA Quick Pick), MindBenders, 2000, The Shadow Club Rising, 2002, Shattered Sky, 2002, Full Tilt, 2003 (Tex. Lonestar award), The Schwa Was Here, 2004 (Boston Globe Horn Book award, ALA Best Book, ALA Notable, Calif. Young Reader medal 2008), Dread Locks, 2005 (ALA Quick Pick, IRA Young Adult Choice), Red Rider's Hood, 2005 (ALA Quick Pick), Duckling Ugly, 2006 (IRA Young Adult Choice), Everlost, 2006, Unwind, 2007 (ALA Best Book, ALA Top Ten Quick Pick), Antsy Does Time, 2008; screenwriter: Double Dragon, 1992, Evolver, 1993; dir. Heart on a Chain, 1991 (Golden Eagle award CINE), What About the Sisters, 1993 (Golden Eagle award CINE), Games: How to Host a Teen Mystery, Hot Times at Hollywood High, 1994, Barbecue with the Vampire, 1997, Roswell that Ends Well, 1999, How to Host a Murder: Roman Ruins, 1996, The Good, the Bad and the Guilty, 1997, The Tragical Mystery Tour, 1998, The Maiming of the Shrew, 2000, Saturday Night Cleaver, 2000, An Affair to Dismember, 2003, (TV) Goosebumps: The Werewolf of Fever Swamp, 1996, Goosebumps: Night of the Living Dummy III, 1997, Animorphs (staff writer), 1998, Pixel Perfect, 2004. Mem. PEN, Writers Guild Am. West, Soc. Children's Book Writers and Illustrators. Avocations: swimming, tennis, storytelling. Home: P O Box 80093 Rancho Santa Margarita CA 92688 E-mail: NStoryman@aol.com.

SHUTLER, MARY ELIZABETH, retired academic administrator; b. Oakland, Calif., Nov. 14, 1929; d. Hal Wilfred and Elizabeth Frances (Gimbel) Hall; m. Richard Shutler Jr., Sept. 8, 1951 (div. 1975); children: Kathryn Allice (dec.), John Hall, Richard Burnett. BA, U. Calif., Berkeley, 1951; MA, U. Ariz., 1958, PhD, 1967. Asst., assoc., full prof. anthropology, chmn. dept. San Diego State U., 1967-75; prof. anthropology, dept. chmn. Wash. State U., Pullman, 1975-80; dean Coll. Arts and Scis., prof. anthropology U. Alaska, Fairbanks, 1980-84; vice chancellor, dean of faculty, prof. anthropology U. Wis. Parkside, Kenosha, 1984-88; provost, v.p. for acad. affairs, prof. anthropology Calif. State U., LA, 1988-94; prof. emeritus, 1994—2007; provost West Coast U., LA, 1994-97; dean Sch. of Arts and Scis. Nat. U., La Jolla, Calif., 1997—2004, dean emeritus, 2004—07; ret., 2007. Mem. core staff Lahav Rsch. Project, Miss. State U., 1975-92. Co-author: Oceanic Prehistory, 1975, Deer Creek Cave, 1964, Archaeological Survey of Southern Nevada, 1963, Stuart Rockshelter, 1962; contbr. articles to jours. in field. Mem. coun. Gamble House; mem. bd. trustees San Diego Archeol. Ctr. 2005-. Fellow Am. Anthropol. Assn.; mem. Soc. for Am. Archaeology, Am. Schs. for Oriental Rsch., Am. Coun. Edn., Am. Assn. for Higher Edn., Am. Assn. State Colls. and Univs., Delta Zeta. Republican. Roman Catholic. Avocations: travel, gardening. Home Phone: 858-673-5200.

SHWARTS, ROBERT S., lawyer; b. NYC, 1965; BA, Rutgers U., 1987; JD, George Washington U., 1990. Bar: N.J. 1990, N.Y. 1991, Calif. 1998. Adminstr. ptnr. Orrick, Herrington & Sutcliffe LLP, San Francisco. Mem.: N.Y. State Bar Assn., Calif. State Bar Assn., ABA (litig. sect., employment sect.). Office: Orrick Herrington & Sutcliffe LLP The Orrick Building 405 Howard St San Francisco CA 94105 Office Phone: 415-773-5760. Office Fax: 415-773-5759. Business E-Mail: rshwarts@orrick.com.

SHYAMALAN, M. NIGHT (MANOJ NELLIYATTU SHYAMALAN), film director; b. Pondicherry, Tamil-Nadu, India, Aug. 6, 1970; s. Jayalakshmi Shyamalan and Nelliate C; m. Bhavna Vaswani, 1993; 2 children. Grad., NYU, 1992. Actor, dir., prodr., writer: (films) Praying with Anger, 1992, Unbreakable, 2000, Signs, 2002, The Village, 2004, Lady in the Water, 2006, The Happening, 2008; actor, dir., writer: The Sixth Sense, 1999 (Bram Stoker Award for Best Screenplay, 1999, Golden Satellite Award for Best Original Screenplay, 1999, Visionary Award, Palm Springs Internat. Film Festival, 2000, Nebula Award for Best Script, Sci. Fiction and Fantasy Writers Am., 1999, nominated for Best Dir. and Best Original Screenplay, Acad. Awards 2000, Nominated for Best Screenplay, Golden Globes, 2000); dir., writer: Praying Wide Awake, 1998; writer screenplay Stuart Little, 1999; actor (TV appearances) Entourage, 2007 Recipient Samman award, Pravasi Bharatiya Divas, 2005, Padma Shri, India, 2008; named one of 50 Most Powerful People in Hollywood, Premiere mag., 2003—05. Office: Creative Artists Agency 2000 Avenue Of The Stars Los Angeles CA 90067-4700

SIA, CALVIN CHIA JUNG, pediatrician; b. Beijing, June 3, 1927; arrived in U.S., 1939; s. Richard Ho Ping and Mary Ling Sang Sia; m. Katherine Wai Kwan Li, June 3, 1951; children: Richard, Jeffrey, Michael. BA, Dartmouth Coll., 1950; MD, Western Res. U., 1955; PhD in Humanities (hon.), U. Hawaii, 1992. Intern William Beaumont Army Hosp., El Paso, Tex., 1955—56; pediat. resident Children's Hosp., Honolulu, 1956—58; pvt. practice pediat., 1958—96; clin. prof. dept. pediat. U. Hawaii Sch. Medicine, 1966—99, prof. pediat. dept. pediat., 1999—. Rschr. in field. Staff sgt. US Army, 1945—47, 1st lt. US Army, 1955—56. Recipient Pvt. Citizen award, Nat. Govs. Assn., 1997. Fellow: Am. Acad. Pediat. (chmn. Hawaii chpt. 1968—76, Clifford G. Grulee award 2001, Job Lewis Smith award 2001), Am. Bd. Pediat. (cert.); mem.: AMA (chmn. sect. coun. on pediat. 1983—, Abraham Jacob award 1992, Benjamin Rush award 1998), Hawaii Med. Assn. (pres. 1976—77). Avocations: tennis, travel. Office: U Hawaii Dept Pediat 1319 Punahou St Honolulu HI 96826

SIA, JEFFREY H.K., lawyer; b. Honolulu, June 10, 1956; BA magna cum laude, Brown U., 1978; JD, Villanova U., 1981. Bar: Hawaii 1981. Ptnr. Ayabe Chong Nishimoto Sia & Nakamura LLP, Honolulu. Mem.: Hawaii State Bar Assn. (sec. 2001, treas. 2002, pres.-elect 2006—07). Office: Ayabe Chong Nishimoto Sia & Nakamura LLP Pauahi Tower Ste 2500 1001 Bishop St Honolulu HI 96813 Office Phone: 808-537-6119. Office Fax: 808-526-3491.

SIAS, JOHN B., former multi-media company executive, newspaper publisher, publishing executive; b. 1927; AB, Stanford U., 1949. Group v.p. Metromedia Inc., 1962—71; with Capital Cities Comm., 1971—93; pres. Fairchild Pubs. Inc., 1971—75, exec. v.p., pres. pub. divsn., 1975—85; pres. ABC-TV Network Group, NYC, 1986—93; also former exec. v.p. Capital Cities/ABC Inc. (parent), NYC; former pres., chmn Chronicle Pub. Co., San Francisco. With US Army, 1945—46. Office: Chronicle Pub Co 901 Mission St San Francisco CA 94103-2905 also: Capital Cities ABC Inc 24 E 51st St New York NY 10022-6801

SIBLEY, WILLIAM AUSTIN, neurologist, educator; b. Miami, Okla., Jan. 25, 1925; s. William Austin and Erna Johanna (Quickert) S.; m. Joanne Shaw, Sept. 4, 1954; children: John, Mary Jane, Peter, Andrew. BS, Yale U., 1945, MD, 1948. Intern Univ. Hosp., Cleve., 1948-50; asst. resident neurologist Neurol. Inst. Presbyn. Hosp., NYC, 1953-55, chief resident neurologist, 1955-56; asst. prof. neurology Western Res. U., Cleve., 1956-63, assoc. prof., 1963-67; prof. U. Ariz. Coll. Medicine, Tucson, 1967—, head dept. neurology, 1967-82. Chmn. therapy com. Internat. Fedn. Multiple Sclerosis Socs., 1986-92, 96-98. Served to capt. M.C. USAF, 1951-53. Recipient LaFayette B. Mendel prize in physiol. chemistry, Yale U., 1945, John Dystel award, Am. Acad. Neurolgy and Nat. Multiple Scerosis Soc., 2006. Mem. Am. Neurol. Assn. (v.p. 1979-80), Am. Acad. Neurology (v.p. 1985-87), Central Soc. for Neurol. Research (pres. 1968) Achievements include helping establish effectiveness of beta-interferon therapy in multiple sclerosis. Home: 2150 E Hampton St Tucson AZ 85719-3810 Office: 1501 N Campbell Ave Tucson AZ 85724-0001

SICILIAN, JAMES MICHAEL, retired research engineer; b. Bronx, NY, May 25, 1947; s. Leonard James and Veronica Patricia (Reinwald) S. BS, MIT, 1969; MS, Stanford U., 1970, PhD, 1973. Tech. editor C.S. Draper Lab., Cambridge, Mass., 1968-69; research analyst Savannah River Lab., Aiken, S.C., 1973-76; staff Los Alamos Sci. Lab, 1976-79, asst. group leader, 1979-80; sr. scientist Flow Science, Inc., Los Alamos, 1980-96, sec. of corp., 1980-96, v.p., 1990-96; treas. LFD Techs., Inc., 1998—2002; mem. staff Los Alamos Nat. Lab., 2001—07, Telluride project leader, 2002—04, dep. group leader, 2005—07; ret., 2007. Cons., Los Alamos, N.Mex., 1996—2002. Mem. Cultural Ctr. adv. com., Los Alamos, 1987-89; vice chmn. Park and Recreation Bd., Los Alamos, 1989-90; treas. N.Mex. Theater Assn., 1983-85; pres. Los Alamos Little Theater, 1978-79, v.p., 1997-98, sec., 2000-02; sec. Los Alamos Light Opera, 1990-91. Los Alamos Living Treasure, 2001—, treas., 2005—. Recipient AEC spl. fellowship, U.S. AEC, 1969-72. Mem.: Sigma Xi. Avocations: theatrical productions, skiing. Home Phone: 505-662-9352; Office Phone: 505-665-6827. Personal E-mail: sicilian@alum.mit.edu. Business E-Mail: sicilian@lanl.gov.

SIDBURY, ROBERT, pediatrician; b. Durham, NC, Sept. 23, 1963; s. James Buren Jr. and Alice Rayle Sidbury; 1 child, Claire Winnie. BS in Psychology, Duke U., 1985, MD, 1993; MPH, Harvard Sch. Pub. Health, 2008. Diplomate Am. Bd. Dermatology, Am. Bd. Pediat. Dermatology. Intern U. Calif., San Francisco, 1993—94, rsch. fellow, 1994—95; resident in dermatology Oreg. Health & Sci. U., Portland, Oreg., 1995—98; fellow pediat. dermatology Childrens Meml. Hosp., Chgo., 1998—2000; asst. prof. pediat. Childrens Hosp., Seattle, 2000—; rsch. fellow Harvad Pediat. Health Svc., 2007—08; asst. prof., dept. dermatology Harvard Med. Sch., Boston Children's Hosp., 2006—09; chief, div. dermatology assoc. prof., dept. pediat. Seattle Children's Hosp., U. Wash. Sch. Medicine, 2009—. Faculty U. Wash. Sch. Medicine, 2004—05; instr. dermatology Bastyr U.; presenter, lectr. in field. Mem. editl. bd.: On The Surface; contbr. articles to profl. jours., chapters to books. Recipient Dermatology Investigator award, Dermatology Found., 1998; named Tchr. of Yr., Providence Family Practice, 2003, Top Doctor, Seattle Mag., 2004. Fellow: Am. Acad. Pediatrics, Am. Acad. Dermatology (edn. slide series task force 2004); mem.: Soc. for Pediat. Dermatology. Democrat. Office: Childrens Hosp Univ Wash Sch Med 4800 Sand Point Way NE Seattle WA 98105 Office Phone: 206-987-2158. Office Fax: 206-987-2217. Business E-Mail: robert.sidbury@seattlechildrens.org.

SIDNER, ROBERT BROWN, museum director; BA in English, St. Meinrad Coll., Ind.; STB, Gregorian U., Rome; MA in Liturgy, Notre Dame U., Ind. Assoc. pastor, Ohio, 1969—77; asst. prof., dir. formation St. Meinrad Coll., 1977—81; pastor St. John's Ch., Delphos, Ohio, 1981—85, St. Charles Ch., Lima, Ohio, 1985—91; owner, dir. Cable Gallery, San Diego, 1991—92; membership coord. Mingei Internat. Mus., 1993—94, dir., pub. rels., 1994—96, asst. dir., 1996—2005, acting dir., 2005—06, dir., 2006—. Spkr. in field. Bd. dirs. Akaloa Resource Found., 2007—. Mem.: San Diego/Tijuana Japan Soc., Nat. Fedn. Spiritual Dirs. (pres. 1977—81). Office: Mingei Internat Mus 1439 El Prado San Diego CA 92101 Office Phone: 619-239-0003.

SIDRAN, MARK HARRIS, lawyer; b. Seattle, July 7, 1951; married. BA in Govt. magna cum laude, Harvard U., 1973; JD, U. Wash., 1976. Bar: Wash. With King County Prosecuting Atty.'s Office, 1975-80, asst. chief criminal dep. juvenile sect., 1980-85; ptnr. McKay & Gaitan, 1986-89; city atty. City of Seattle, 1989—. Apptd. spl. counsel to Gov. Booth Gardner State of Wash., 1987—. Mem. Am. Jewish Com. Bd.; past bd. dirs. United Way King County.

SIEBEL, KENNETH, investment advisor; BBA in Fin., MBA, U. Wisconsin. With Smith, Barney & Co., NYC, San Francisco; co-founder, ptnr. Robertson, Colman & Siebel (now Bank of Am. Securities and Bank of Boston Robertson Stephens), 1969—77; chmn., CEO Wood Island Associates, 1977—98; chief investment officer US Trust Co., 1998—; chmn. Private Wealth Partners, LLC, Larkspur, Calif. Mem. fin. and investment comm., corp. partnerships comm., and resources commitment comm. Conservation Internat. Trustee San Francisco Museum of Modern Art, Gordon & Betty Moore Found. Office: Us Trust 555 California St Fl 7 San Francisco CA 94104-1510

SIEBEL, THOMAS M., software company executive; BA, U. Ill., Urbana-Champaign, MS in Computer Sci., MBA. Various positions including group v.p., gen. mgr. Oracle Corp.; CEO Gain Tech., until 1992, Siebel Systems, San Mateo, Calif., 1993—2004, chmn., 1993—. Author: Virtual Selling, Cyber Rules, Taking Care of eBusiness. Bd. advisors U. Ill., Coll. Engring., Stanford U. Grad. Sch. Bus., Stanford U. Law Sch. Recipient David Packard Award, Bus. Executives for Nat. Security, 2002, CEO of the Year, Industry Week mag., 2002; named one of top 25 managers in the world, Business Week mag., 2000, 2001, 400 Richest Americans, Forbes, 2006.

SIEBERT, DAVE, City Councilman, Phoenix, Arizona; m to Kim. Member, Deer Valley Village Planning Committee, formerly; city councilman, District 1, Phoenix, Arizona, 95-, vmayor, 98-, chairman, Environ & Natural Resources Subcomt; chairman, Ethics & Public Safety Subcomt; member Natural Resources, Transport & Techno subcomt; member Governor Efficiency subcomt.Vice Chairman, Phoenix Parks & Recreation Bd, formerly; hearing officer, Justice Court, currently. Mailing: 200 W Washington St 11th Fl Phoenix AZ 85003-1611 Fax: 602-495-2036. E-mail: dhoward@ci.phoenix.az.us.

SIEFER, STUART B., architect; b. Detroit, Nov. 28, 1942; s. Louis and Esther (Ressler) S.; m. Nancy Ann Feldman, Apr. 23, 1967; children: Eric S., Jeremy M., Ted B. BA, Wayne State U., 1965; postgrad., U. Detroit, 1965-68; BArch, Ariz. State U., 1971. Registered architect, Ariz. Designer, draftsman various firms, Detroit, 1966-68; rschr. Detroit Bd. Edn., 1967; archtl. designer Peace Corps, Tegucigalpa, Honduras, 1968-70; designer, job capt. various firms, Phoenix, 1970-73; prin. Siefer Assocs., Tempe, Ariz., 1973—. Bd. dirs. Downtown Tempe Community, Inc., 1993—; vol. bd. mem. Tempe Ctr. for Habilitation, 1993—; mem. Ariz. Town Hall, Phoenix, 1993—. Recipient 16 design awards Tempe Beautification Com., 1975—, merit & Crescordia award Valley Forward Assn. AIA Ariz., 1988, 93, Beautification award City of Mesa, Ariz., AIA Ariz. Archs. medal, 1996. Mem. AIA (pres. Rio Salado chpt.), Rio Salado Architecture Found. (exec. mem.), Tempe C. of C. (pres. 1992-93) Found. (founding bd. mem. 1995). Avocations: jogging, skiing, hiking, tennis.

SIEGEL, BARRY, journalist, writer, literature educator; b. St. Louis, Sept. 7, 1949; m. Marti Devore; 1 child, Alexandra Nicole. BA magna cum laude, Pomona Coll., 1971; MS in Journalism, Columbia U., 1972. Stringer LA bur. Newsweek, 1973; news editor West Coast Women's Wear Daily, 1973—76; writer View sect. LA Times, 1976—78, writer spl. assignment, 1979, corr. Nat., 1980—83, corr./sr. writer, 1983—2003, spl. corr., 2003—; prof. English & comparative lit. U. Calif., Irvine, 2003—, dir. lit. journalism program, 2003—. Vis. lectr. U. So. Calif., 1988. Author: A Death in White Bear Lake, 1990, Shades of Gray, 1992, The Perfect Witness, 1998, Actual Innocence, 1999, Lines of Defense, 2002, Claim of Privilege:A Mysterious Plane Crash, a Landmark Supreme Court Case, and the Rise of State Secrets, 2008; contbr. articles to profl. jours. Recipient USA West Journalism award, PEN Ctr., 1987, USA West Lit. award in Journalism, 2000, Golden Medallion Media award, State Bar Calif., 1984, Silver Gavel award, ABA, 1985, Paul Tobenkin Meml. award, 1997, Pulitzer Prize for Feature Writing, 2002. Office: U Calif Mail Code: 2650 408 Humanities Instructional Bldg Irvine CA 92697 Office Phone: 949-824-3023. Office Fax: 949-824-2916. Personal E-mail: barry@barrysiegel.com. Business E-Mail: bsiegel@uci.edu.

SIEGEL, CLARK BYRON, lawyer; b. Tehran, Iran, Feb. 7, 1958; BA with highest honors, Stanford U., 1980; JD with highest honors, U. Chgo., 1984. Bar: Calif. 1984. Ptnr. Irell & Manella, LLP, LA, co-chair internat. property group. Spkr. in field. Contbr. articles to profl. jours. Mem.: State Bar Calif., Order of Coif, Phi Beta Kappa. Office: Irell & Manella LLP 1800 Ave of the Stars Century City Ste 900 Los Angeles CA 90067-4276 Office Phone: 310-203-7051. Office Fax: 310-203-7199. E-mail: csiegel@irell.com.

SIEGEL, DAVID M., construction executive; CFO, sr. v.p., treas. William Lyons Homes, Newport Beach, Calif., 1991—. Office: William Lyons Homes The Presley Companies 4490 Von Karman Ave Newport Beach CA 92660-2008

SIEGEL, JAY STEVEN, chemistry educator; b. Inglewood, Calif., Aug. 16, 1959; s. Erwin and Jeanne (Strzesak) S. BS, Calif. State U., Northridge, 1980; MA, Princeton U., 1982, PhD, 1985. Researcher Princeton (N.J.) U., 1981-83, 84-85, Eidgenossische Technishche Hochschule, Zürich, Switzerland, 1983-84, U. Louis Pasteur, Strasbourg, France, 1985-86; asst. prof. U. Calif., San Diego, 1986—. Observer, mem. com. on stereochemistry Internat. Union of Pure and Applied Chemists, 1985—. Contbr. articles to sci. jours. Calif. State scholar, 1977-70; Swiss U. grantee, 1983-84, NSF-CNRS Sci. Exchange grantee, 1985-86; named Presdl. Young Investigator NSF, 1988—. Mem. Am. Chem. Soc., N.Y. Acad. Scis., Sigma Xi. Office: U Calif San Diego Dept Chemistry B-014 La Jolla CA 92093

SIEGEL, LOUIS PENDLETON, retired forest products executive; b. Richmond, Va., Nov. 6, 1942; s. John Boschen Jr. and Francis Beale (Tyler) S.; m. Nancy Dicks Blanton, Apr. 10, 1974 (dec. July 1976); m. Nancy Northon, June 26, 1982; children: Kathryn Tyler. AB in Econs., Dartmouth Coll., 1967. Asst. cashier, security researcher First Nat. Citibank, NYC, 1967-71; v.p. security rsch. Drexel Burnham Lambert, NYC, 1971-79; with Potlatch Corp., San Francisco and Spokane, Wash., 1979—, sr. v.p. fin. and adminstrn. San Francisco, 1989, group v.p. wood products and corp. planning, 1989-92, group v.p. pulp and paperboard and corp. planning, 1992-93, exec. v.p. pulp-based ops. and corp. planning, 1993-94, pres., COO San Francisco and Spokane, Wash., 1994-99, also bd. dirs. Spokane, CEO, 1999—2006, chmn., 1999; ret., 1999. Bd. dirs. San Francisco Fed. Corp., 1985-96. Pres., bd. dirs. Bay Area Sci. Fair, San Francisco, 1989-90; trustee Am. Forest Found., 1999-, chmn. trustees, 2000-; bd. dirs. Nat. Coun. for Air and Stream Improvement, 1999-, chmn. bd., 2003-06; pres. Area One, Boy Scouts Am., 2003-05. With USCG, 1964-65. Mem.: Am. Forest & Paper Assn. (bd. dirs. 1999—). Republican. Episcopalian. Avocations: golf, fishing. Office: Potlatch Corp 601 W First Ave Ste 1600 Spokane WA 99201 Office Phone: 509-835-1565.

SIEGEL, MICHAEL ELLIOT, nuclear medicine physician, educator; b. NYC, May 13, 1942; s. Benjamin and Rose (Gilbert) S.; m. Marsha Rose Snower, Mar. 20, 1966; children: Herrick Jove, Meridith Ann. AB, Cornell U., 1964; MD, Chgo. Med. Sch., 1968. Diplomate Nat. Bd. Med. Examiners. Intern Cedars-Sinai Med. Ctr., LA, 1968-69, resident in radiology, 1969-70; NIH fellow in radiology Temple U. Med. Ctr., Phila., 1970-71; NIH fellow in nuclear medicine Johns Hopkins U. Sch. Medicine, Balt., 1971-73, asst. prof. radiology, 1972-76; assoc. prof. radiology and medicine U. So. Calif., LA, 1976—, prof. radiology, 1989—, dir. divsn. nuclear medicine, 1982-99. Dir. Sch. Nuclear Medicine, Los Angeles County-U. So. Calif. Med. Ctr., 1976-99; dir. divsn. nuclear medicine Kenneth Norris Cancer Hosp. and Rsch. Ctr., L.A., 1983-99; dir. dept. nuclear medicine Orthopaedic Hosp., L.A., 1981-2006, Intercmty. Hosp., Covina, Calif., 1981-2006, U. So. Calif. Univ. Hosp., L.A., 1993—; clin. prof. radiology U. Calif., San Diego, 2000—. Author: Textbook of Nuclear Medicine, 1978, Vascular Surgery, 1983, 88, numerous other textbooks; editor: Nuclear Cardiology, 1981, Vascular Disease: Nuclear Medicine, 1983. Mem. Maple Ctr., Beverly Hills. Served as maj. USAF, 1974-76. Recipient Outstanding Alumnus award Chgo. Med. Sch., 1991. Fellow Am. Coll. Nuclear Medicine (sci. investigator 1974, 76, nominations com. 1980, program com. 1983, trustee 1993, disting. fellow, 1993, bd. reps. 1993—, bd. dirs. 1994—, treas. 1996—, chmn. ann. sci. program 1996—, pres.'s award 1997, v.p. 1997-98, pres. 1999—, CEO 2005—); mem. Soc. Nuclear Medicine (sic. exhbn. com. 1978-79, program com. 1979-80, Silver medal 1975), Calif. Med. Assn. (sci. adv. bd. 1987—), Radiol. Soc. N.Am., Soc. Nuclear Magnetic Resonance Imaging, Friars So. Calif., Alpha Omega Alpha. Achievements include research on development of nuclear medicine techniques to treat recurrent joint effusions, evaluate cardiovascular disease and diagnose and treat cancer; clinical utilization of video digital displays in nuclear medicine development; invention of pneumatic radiologic pressure system. Office: U So Calif Med Ctr Rm 5250 1200 N State St Los Angeles CA 90033-1029 Business E-Mail: mesiegel@usc.edu.

SIEGEL, ROBERT (BOB) A., lawyer; AB with great distinction, U. Calif., Berkeley, 1971; JD magna cum laude, U. Mich. Bar: Calif. Ptnr. O'Melveny & Myers LLP, LA, vice-chair LA firm, chair adversarial law dept., mem. office of chair. Tchr., lectr. ALI-ABA, Am. Arbitration Assn., Practisng Law Inst. Sr. editor The Railway Labor Act (BNA). Mem.: ABA (labor and employment law sect., equal opportunity com., railway and airline labor law com. (past co-chmn.)), Order of the Coif, Phi Beta Kappa. Office: O'Melveny & Myers LLP 400 S Hope St Los Angeles CA 90071 Office Phone: 213-430-6005. Office Fax: 213-430-6407. Business E-Mail: rsiegel@omm.com.

SIEGEL, SHELDON C., pediatrician, immunologist, allergist; b. Mpls., Jan. 30, 1922; s. Carl S.; m. Priscilla Rikess, Mar. 3, 1946; children— Linda, Nancy. AA, Va. Jr. Coll., 1940; BA, BS, U. Minn., 1942, MD, 1945. Intern U. Minn. Hosp., 1946, resident in pediatrics, 1947-48; fellow in pediatric allergy Rochester, NY, 1949-50; practice medicine specializing in pediatric allergy and pediatrics St. Paul, 1950-52, San Antonio, 1952-54, Los Angeles, 1954—; clin. instr. pediatrics U. Rochester, 1949-50, U. Minn., 1950-51; asst. prof. pediatrics U. Tex., 1952-54; asst. clin. prof. U. Calif. at Los Angeles Med. Sch., 1955, clin. asso. prof., 1957-62, clin. prof., 1963—, co-chief pediatric allergy clinic, 1957—. Editorial bd.: Jour. Allergy, 1973-75; contbr. articles to med. jours. Fellow Am. Acad. Allergy (pres. 1974), Am. Coll. Allergists, Am. Acad. Pediatrics; mem. AMA, Allergy Found. Am. (pres. 1976), Calif. Med. Assn., LA County Med. Assn., LA Pediatric Soc., Calif. Soc. Allergy, LA Soc. Allergy, Western Pediatric Rsch. Soc., Am. Bd. Med. Specialists, Sigma Xi.

SIEGELE, PAUL K., oil industry executive; b. Tokyo, 1959; BSc in Geology, Calif. Luth. U., Thousand Oaks, 1980; MSc in Geology, Calif. State U., Northridge, 1990. Petroleum geologist, LA divsn. to numerous tech. and managerial positions and exploration assignments in North and South America Texaco, 1980—95, upstream coord., corp. planning and econs. group Harrison, NY, 1995—97, regional mgr., internat. exploration divsn., regional mgr., exploration and new ventures divsn. Bellaire, Tex.; exploration mgr. Chevron North America Exploration and Prodn. Co., New Orleans, 2001—05, v.p. deepwater exploration and projects Gulf of Mex., 2005—08; v.p. strategic planning Chevron Corp., 2008. Mem.: Am. Assn. Petroleum Geologists, Geol. Soc. America. Office: Chevron Corp Hdqs 6001 Bollinger Canyon Rd San Ramon CA 94583

SIEGMAN, ANTHONY EDWARD, electrical engineer, educator; b. Detroit, Nov. 23, 1931; s. Orra Leslie and Helen Salome (Winnie) S.; married. AB summa cum laude, Harvard U., 1952; MS, UCLA, 1954; PhD, Stanford U., 1957. Faculty Stanford (Calif.) U., 1957—, assoc. prof. elec. engring., 1960-64, prof., 1964-98, prof. engring. emeritus, 1998—. Dir. Edward L. Ginzton Lab., 1978-83; cons. Lawrence Livermore Labs., Coherent Inc., GTE; mem. Air Force Sci. Adv. Bd.; vis. prof. Harvard U., 1965 Author: Microwave Solid State Masers, 1964, An Introduction to Lasers and Masers, 1970, Lasers, 1986; contbr. over 200 articles to profl. jours. Recipient Schawlow award Laser Inst. Am., 1991; Guggenheim fellow IBM Rsch. Lab., Zurich, 1969-70; Alexander von Humboldt Found. sr. scientist Max Planck Inst. Quantum Optics, Garching, Fed. Republic Germany, 1984-85. Fellow AAAS, IEEE (W.R.G. Baker award 1971, J.J. Ebers award 1977), Am. Phys. Soc., Laser Inst. Am., Optical Soc. Am. (R.W. Wood prize 1980), IEEE Laser Electro-Optics Soc. (Quantum Electronics award 1989), Am. Acad. Arts and Scis.; mem. NAS, NAE, AAUP, Phi Beta Kappa, Sigma Xi. Achievements include patents for microwave and optical devices and lasers, including the unstable optical resonator. Office: Stanford U 550 Junipero Serra Blvd Stanford CA 94305-8442

SIERACKI, ERIC P., diversified financial services company executive; BS in Econs., U. Pa. Mgr. Grant Thornton; sr. v.p. Countrywide Asset Mgmt. Corp., 1988—89; exec. v.p. corp. fin. Countrywide Fin. Corp., Calabasas, Calif., 1989—94, mng. dir., 1994—2002, sr. mng. dir. corp. fin., treas., & corp. develop., investor rels., 2002—05, exec. mng. dir., CFO, 2005—. Recipient Best Fin. Exec., Am. Bus. Awards, 2007. Office: Countrywide Fin Corp 4500 Park Granada Calabasas CA 91302-1613

SILAK, CATHY R., lawyer, former state supreme court justice; b. Astoria, NY, May 25, 1950; d. Michael John and Rose Marie (Janor) S.; m. Nicholas G. Miller, Aug. 9, 1980; 3 children. BA, NYU, 1971; M in City Planning, Harvard U., 1973; JD, U. Calif., 1976. Bar: Calif. 1977, U.S. Dist. Ct. (no. dist.) Calif. 1977, D.C. 1979, U.S. Ct. Appeals (D.C. cir.) 1979, U.S. Dist. Ct. (so. dist.) N.Y. 1980, Idaho 1983, U.S. Dist. Ct. Idaho 1983, U.S. Ct. Appeals (2nd cir.) 1983, U.S. Ct. Appeals (9th cir.) 1985. Law clk. to Hon. William W. Schwarzer US Dist. Ct. (no dist.), Calif., 1976-77; pvt. practice San Francisco, 1977-79, Washington, 1979-80, Boise, Idaho, 1984-90; asst. US atty. US Dist. Ct. (so. dist.) NY, 1980-83; spl. asst. US atty. Dist. of Idaho, 1983-84; judge Idaho Ct. Appeals, 1990-93; justice Idaho Supreme Ct., Boise, 1993—2000; ptnr. Hawley, Troxell, Ennis, and Hawley, 2001—. Assoc. gen. counsel Morrison Knudsen Corp., 1989-90; mem. fairness com. Idaho Supreme Ct. and Gov.'s Task Force on Alternative Dispute Resolution; instr. and lectr. in field. Assoc. note and comment editor Calif. Law Rev., 1975-76. Land use planner Mass. Dept. Natural Resources, 1973; founder Idaho Coalition for Adult Literacy; bd. dirs. Literacy Lab., Inc.; mem. adv. bd. Boise State U. Legal Asst. Program. Recipient Jouce Stein award Boise YWCA, 1992, Women Helping Women award Soroptimist, Boise, 1993. Fellow Idaho Law Found (ann., lectr.); mem. ABA (nat. conf. state trial judges jud. adminstrn. divsn.), Nat. Assn. Women Judges, Idaho State Bar (corp./securities sect., instr.), Am. Law Inst., Fellows of the Am. Bar Found, Am. Judicature Soc. (bd. dirs.). Office: Hawley Troxell Ennis & Hawley PO Box 1617 Boise ID 83702-1617

SILBERGELD, ARTHUR F., lawyer; b. St. Louis, June 1, 1942; s. David and Sabina (Silbergeld) S.; m. Carol Ann Schwartz, May 1, 1970; children: Diana Lauren, Julia Kay. BA, U. Mich., 1968; M in City Planning, U. Pa., 1971; JD, Temple U., 1975. Bar: N.Y. 1976, Calif. 1978, D.C. 1983, U.S. Ct. Appeals (2nd cir.), U.S. Ct. Appeals (9th cir.), U.S. Ct. Appeals (D.C. cir.), U.S. Supreme Ct. 1999. Assoc. Vladeck, Elias, Vladeck & Lewis, NYC, 1975-77; field atty. NLRB, LA, 1977-78; ptnr., head employment law practice group McKenna, Conner & Cuneo, LA, 1978-89; ptnr. Graham & James, LA, 1990-96; labor ptnr. Sonnenschein Nath & Rosenthal, LA, 1996-99; ptnr. Proskauer Rose LLP, LA, 1999—. Instr. extension divsn. UCLA, 1981-89. Author: Doing Business in California: An Employment Law Handbook, 2nd edit., 1997, Advising California Employers, 1990-95 supplements; contbr. articles to profl. jours. Founding mem. L.A. Mus. Contemporary Art; bd. dirs. Bay Cities unit Am. Cancer Soc., Calif., 1981-85, Jewish Family Svc., L.A., 1981-85, So. Calif. Employers Roundtable, Leadership coun., So. Poverty Law Ctr., Leadership Task Force, Drs. Without Borders; pres. Mo. Valley Fedn. of Temple Youth, 1959-60, Exec. Com., Calif. Com. South Human Rights Watch, 2005-; treas. L.A. Child Devel. Ctr., 2001-. Mem. ABA (labor and employment law sect.), L.A. County Bar Assn. (mem. exec. com. 1984-, chmn. labor and employment law sect. 1999-2000, trustee 2000-01), Mus. Modern Art (N.Y.C.), Coll. of Labor and Employment Lawyers. Office: Proskauer Rose LLP 2049 Century Park E Fl 32 Los Angeles CA 90067-3101 Office Phone: 310-557-2900.

SILJAK, DRAGOSLAV D., engineering educator, researcher; b. Belgrade, Serbia, Sept. 10, 1933; came to U.S. 1964, naturalized; s. Dobrilo T. and Ljubica Z. (Zivanovic) S.; m. Dragana T. Todorovic, Sept. 28, 1967; children— Ana, Matija. BSEE, U. Belgrade, 1958, MSEE, 1961, ScD, 1963. Docent prof. U. Belgrade, 1963-64; assoc. prof. U. Santa Clara, Calif., 1964-70, prof. engring., 1970-84, B. and M. Swig Univ. chair, 1984—. Author: Nonlinear Systems, 1969, Large Scale Systems, 1978, Decentralized Control of Complex Systems, 1991; mem. editl. bd. Jour. Difference Equations, Nonlinear World, Comm. in Applied Analysis, Internat. Jour. Computer Rsch., Nonlinear Analysis: Theory, Methods and Applications, Dynamics of Cont., Disc. and Impulsive Systems, Math. Problems in Engring., Stability and Control: Theory and Applications. Disting. prof. Fulbright Found., 1984. Life fellow IEEE; mem. Serbian Acad. Scis. and Arts (hon.) Mem. Christian Orthodox Ch. E-mail: dsiljak@scu.edu.

SILL, MELANIE, editor-in-chief; m. Bennett Groshong. BA in Journalism, U. NC, Chapel Hill, 1981. With News & Observer, Raleigh, NC, 1982—2007, mng. editor, 1998—2002, exec. editor, sr. v.p., 2002—07; editor, sr. v.p. Sacramento Bee, 2007—. Recipient Pulitzer prize for Public Svc. Reporting, 1996; Nieman fellow, Harvard U., 1993—94. Mem.: Investigative Reporters & Editors, Am. Soc. Newspaper Editors. Office: Sacramento Bee PO Box 15779 Sacramento CA 95852 Office Phone: 916-321-1002. E-mail: msill@sacbee.com.

SILLARS, MALCOLM O., communications educator; b. Union City, NJ, Feb. 12, 1928; s. Malcolm Osgood and Dorothy Edna (Browning) S.; m. Charlotte Jane Grimm, June 1, 1948; children: Paul Louis, Bruce Malcolm, Alan Leslie. BA, U. Redlands, 1948, MA, 1949; PhD, U. Iowa, 1955. Asst. prof. comm. Iowa State U., Ames, 1949-53; asst. prof. Calif. State U., LA, 1954-56, prof., 1956—71, dean, 1970-71; pres. Calif. State U. Northridge, 1969-70; prof. U. Mass., Amherst, 1971-74; prof. communication U. Utah, Salt Lake City, 1974-97, dean humanities, 1974-81, ret., 1998. Author: Speech: Content and Communications, 6th edit., 1991, Argumentation and Critical Decision Making, 7th edit., 2009, Communication Criticism, 2d edit., 2001; contbr. articles to profl. jours. Recipient Silver Beaver award Boy Scouts Am. Mem. ACLU, Nat. Comm. Assn. (pres.), We. States Comm. Assn. (pres.). Democrat. Home: 3508 Eastoaks Dr Salt Lake City UT 84124-3811 E-mail: m.sillars@utah.edu.

SILLERMAN, ROBERT F. X., communications executive, banker; b. NYC, Apr. 12, 1948; s. Michael McKinley and Estelle (Levande) Sillerman; m. Jane Waxenberg, July 13, 1969 (div. Dec. 1970); m. Laura Baudo, Feb. 25, 1974. BS magna cum laude, Brandeis U., 1969. CEO, chmn. bd. Youth Markets Cons., Inc., Boston, 1966-74, Nat. Discount Mktg., Great Neck, NY, 1974-78, Sillerman-Morrow Broadcasting Group, Middletown, NY, 1978-85; co-chmn. bd. Legacy Broadcasting, LA, 1985-89; CEO, chmn. bd. Sillerman-Magee Comm. Mgmt. Corp. (now Sillerman Comm. Mgmt. Corp.), NYC, 1985, TV Programs of Am., Hollywood, Calif., 1985; founder, CEO, chmn. SFX Broadcasting, Inc.(acquired by Hicks, Muse, Tate & Furst), 1992—95, exec. chmn., 1995—98; founder, exec. chmn., mem. of the office of the chmn., dir. SFX Entertainment, Inc. (acquired by Clear Channel Communications), 1997—2000; chmn. FXM, Inc., 2000—05; founder, mng. mem. FXM Asset Mgmt. LLC, 2003—; mng. mem. MJX Asset Mgmt., 2003—; CEO, pres., chmn. bd. CKX, Inc., Las Vegas, Nev., 2005—. Co-chmn. Legacy Broadcasting, Inc., 1986—; chmn. Met. Broadcasting, Inc., 1988-89. Recipient Bearer of the Torch award Anti-Defamation League, N.Y.C., 1982. Mem. Nat. Assn. Broadcasters, Nat. Radio Broadcasters Assn. Office: CKX Inc 6730 S Las Vegas Blvd Las Vegas NV 89119 also: Southampton College Liu 121 Speonk Riverhead Rd Riverhead NY 11901-3444 Office Phone: 702-798-7777, 631-283-4000. Office Fax: 702-798-6847, 631-283-4081.

SILLMAN, ARNOLD JOEL, physiologist, educator; b. NYC, Oct. 10, 1940; s. Philip and Anne L. (Pearlman) S.; m. Jean Fletcher Van Keuren, Sept. 26, 1969; children: Andrea Jose Callaway, Diana Van Keuren Taylor. AB, UCLA, 1963, MA, 1965, PhD, 1968. Asst. prof. UCLA, 1969-73, U. Calif., Davis, 1975-78, assoc. prof., 1978-85, prof., 1985—2007, prof. emeritus, 2007—; asst. prof. U. Pitts., 1973-75, interim dir. aquaculture and fisheries program, 1994—95, vice chair sect. neurobiology, physiology and behavior, 1998—, acting chair, 2001. Contbr. articles to profl. jours. USPHS trainee, UCLA, 1966-67; fellow NSF, 1967-68, Fight for Sight, Inc., 1968-69. Recipient Acad. Senate Disting. Tchg. award, 1996. Jewish. Avocations: backpacking, gardening, woodworking. Home: 1140 Los Robles St Davis CA 95618-4927 Office: U Calif Dept Neurobiology Physiology & Behavior Coll Biol Scis Davis CA 95616 Office Phone: 530-752-3207. Business E-Mail: ajsillman@ucdavis.edu.

SILVA, CLARENCE RICHARD, bishop; b. Honolulu, Aug. 6, 1949; Student, St. Joseph Sem., Mountain View, Calif., St. Patrick Sem., Menlo Pk. Ordained priest Diocese of Oakland, Calif., 1975; parochial vicar St. Bernard Parish, Oakland, St. Bede Parish, Hayward, Calif.; pastor St. Peter Martyr Parish, Pittsburgh, Pa., St. Anthony Parish, Oakland, Calif., St. John the Baptist Parish, El Cerrito, Calif., St. Andrew-St. Joseph Parish, Oakland, Calif., St. Leonard-St. Paul Parish, Fremont, Calif.; vicar gen. & moderator of curia Diocese of Oakland, 2004—05; ordained bishop, 2005; bishop Diocese of Honolulu, Hawaii, 2005—. Roman Catholic. Office: Diocese of Honolulu 1184 Bishop St Honolulu HI 96813-2858 Office Phone: 801-533-1791. Office Fax: 801-521-8428.

SILVA, CLARICE F. (CLARICE F. CHAVIRA-SLIVA), lawyer; b. LA, Sept. 14, 1973; BA cum laude, Calif. State Univ., Northridge, 1998; JD, Loyola Univ., 2001. Bar: Calif. 2001. Assoc., real estate practice Shumaker Steckbauer Weinhart LLP, LA. Named a Rising Star, So. Calif. Super Lawyers, 2006. Mem.: ABA, State Bar Calif., Women Lawyers Assn. LA, LA County Bar Assn. Office: Shumaker Steckbauer Weinhart 36th Fl 333 S Hope St Los Angeles CA 90071 Office Phone: 213-229-2868. Office Fax: 213-229-2870. Business E-Mail: csilva@sswesq.com.

SILVA, ERNEST R., visual arts educator, artist; b. Providence, Dec. 11, 1948; BFA, U. R.I., 1971; MFA, Tyler Sch. Art, 1974. Instr. U. R.I., Kingston, 1977-79; lectr. dept. visual arts U. Calif. San Diego, La Jolla, 1979-87, prof. dept. visual arts, 1987—; represented by Jan Baum Gallery, LA, Lenore Gray Gallery, Providence, R.I. Bd. dirs. Installation Gallery, San Diego, mem. arts adv. bd., 1992—, exec. com., 1993—; lectr. Phila. Coll. Art, 1973, U. R.I., 1974, 84, 91, RISD, 1977, Tyler Sch. Art, Elkins Park, Pa., 1979, U. Calif. Irvine, 1981, Southwestern Coll., Chula Vista, 1982, San Diego State U., 1985, Nat. Soc. Arts and Letters, Washington, 1986, Friends of Jung, San Diego, 1991. One-person exhbns. include Inst. Contemporary Art, Boston, 1972, Artists Space, N.Y.C., 1975, Anyart Contemporary Art Ctr., Providence, R.I., 1976, Lenore Gray Gallery, Providence, 1978, 79, 92, Roy Boyd Gallery, L.A., 1982, 84, 87, Quint Gallery, San Diego, 1982, 83, 86, Jan Baum Gallery, L.A., 1989, 91, Tuttle Gallery, McDonogh, Md., 1990, Porter Randall Gallery, La Jolla, 1994, Mus. Contemporary Art, Roskilde, Denmark, 1995, many others; group exhbns. include Mus. Phila. Civic Ctr., 1973, Cheltenham (Pa.) Art Ctr., 1973, Pratt Graphic Ctr., N.Y.C., 1975, Corcoran Art Gallery, Washington, 1975, Ft. Worth Art Mus., 1976, Baker Gallery, La Jolla, 1980, Ind. Contemporary Exhbns., L.A., 1982, Navy Pier, Chgo., 1983, 84, 85, Roy Boyd Gallery, Chgo., 1983, 85, 86, Heckscher Mus. Art, Huntington, N.Y., 1984, Indpls. Mus. Art, 1984, Forum Internat. Kunstmesse, Zurich, Switzerland, 1984, Nat. History Mus., San Diego, 1985, Visual Arts Ctr. Alaska, Anchorage, 1985, San Francisco Airport Mus., 1985, Sonrisa Gallery, L.A., 1985, Alaska State Mus., Juneau, 1986, Foire Internat. De L'Art Contemporain, Nice, France, 1986, Lyceum Theatre, San Diego, 1987, Installation Gallery, San Diego, 1986, 87, 88, Chgo. Internat. Art Exposition, 1987,L.A. Convention Ctr., 1987, Cmty. Arts, San Francisco, 1989, 90, Annex Gallery, La Jolla, 1990, Bill Bace Gallery, N.Y.C., 1991, David Lewinson Gallery, Del Mar, Calif., 1991, Southwestern Coll. Art, Chula Vista, Calif., 1992, Boehm Gallery Palomar Coll, San Marcos, Calif., 1993, Porter Randall Gallery, La Jolla, 1992, numerous others; represented in permanent collections Fogg Art Mus. Harvard U., Cambridge, Mass., Grand Rapids (Mich.) Art Mus., La Jolla Mus. Contemporary Art, Laguna Mus. Art, De Saisset Mus. U. Santa Clara, Newport Harbor Art Mus., Newport Beach, Calif., Mus. Contemporary Art, San Diego, La Jolla, San Jose Mus. Art, San Diego Mus. Art; subject reviews, articles, 1974—. Office: U Calif San Diego Visual Arts 0084 9500 Gilman Dr La Jolla CA 92093-5004

SILVA, JIM, state legislator; m to Connie; children: Chad & Donna (Mrs Ethan Waitte). BA in Bus., San Jose State U.; MA in Edn., Chapman U. California State Assemblyman, District 67, 2006-; vice chairman, Jobs, Econ Develop & Economy Committee, currently. Republican. Office: Dist 67 17011 Beach Blvd Ste 570 Huntington Beach CA 92647-5995 Office Phone: 714-843-4966. Office Fax: 714-843-6375. Business E-Mail: Assemblymember.Silva@assembly.ca.gov.

SILVA, JOSEPH, JR., dean, medical educator; BA in biol. scis., Rutgers U., 1962; MD, Northwestern U., 1966. Diplomate Am. Bd. Internal Medicine, 1972. Intern Johns Hopkins Hosp., Balt., 1962—66, asst. resident in medicine, 1967—68, sr. resident in medicine, 1968—69; fellow in infectious diseases U. Mich. Med. Ctr., Ann Arbor, 1969—70; asst. prof. internal medicine divsn. infectious diseases U. Mich., prof., 1980—82; prof. and chair. of internal med. U. Calif. Davis, 1982—97; dean U. Calif. Davis Sch. Medicine, 1997—2005, sr. adv. to chancellor health sciences, 2005—, dean emeritus; CEO U. Calif. Davis Health Sys.1, 1997—. Served 2 yrs. in USAF. Fellow: Royal Soc. Medicine, London, Infectious Diseases Soc. Am., ACP (regent); mem.: Sociedad Medica de Santiago, Chile (assoc. mem.), Internat. Immunocompromised Host Soc., Sacramento/Sierra Med. Soc., Western Assn. Physicians, Western Assn. Clin. Investigation, Soc. Intestinal Microecology and Disease, Soc. Hosp. Epidemiologists of Am., Sacramento/El Dorado Med. Soc. (affiliate), Reticuloendothelial Soc., Mich. Soc. Med. Rsch., Mich. Soc. Infection Control, Ctrl. Soc. Clin. Rsch., Calif. Acad. Medicine, Am. Soc. Tropical Medicine and Hygiene, Am. Soc. Internal Medicine, Am. Fedn. Clin. Rsch., Calif. Med. Assn., AMA, AAAS, Alpha Omega Alpha. Office: U Calif Sch Medicine 2315 Stockton Blvd Rm 1501 Sacramento CA 95817 Office Phone: 530-752-0321. E-mail: josilva@ucdavis.edu.

SILVA, ROBERT OWEN, retired protective service official; b. La Junta, Colo., Sept. 5, 1935; s. Owen Delbert and Gertrude H. (Kerr) S.; m. Meredith Ann Ginn, Dec. 18, 1953; children— Edward, Andrew, Colleen. Student Pueblo Jr. Coll., 1953, FBI Nat. Acad., 1975, Police Found. Exec. Program, 1979-80. Cert. peace officer, Colo. Police officer Pueblo Police Dept., Colo., 1958-66, sgt., 1966-72, capt., 1972-77, chief of police, 1977-92, ret. dir. Colo. Police Officers Standards and Tng. Bd. dirs. Salvation Army, Pueblo, Easter Seals Soc., Pueblo, Community Corrections Bd., Pueblo, Served with U.S. Army, 1955-57; apptd. by gov. Colo. Crim. Justice Comsn., 1990. Mem. Pueblo Community Coll. Criminal Justice Adv. Bd., Leadership Pueblo Steering Com., Pikes Peak Community Coll. Criminal Justice Program (chmn. adv. bd. 1981), Organized Crime Strike Force (bd. dirs. 1977-84, chmn. 1982, 83, 84); Colo. Assn. Chiefs of Police (pres. 1984-85), Rocky Mountain Info. Network (chmn. bd. dirs. 1986—), Presbyterian (elder). Lodges: Kiwanis (bd. dirs. 1982-84), Elks.

SILVER, MARY WILCOX, oceanography educator; b. San Francisco, July 13, 1941; d. Philip E. and Mary C. (Kartes) Wilcox; children: Monica, Joel. BA in Zoology, U. Calif., Berkeley, 1963; PhD in Oceanography, U. Calif., La Jolla, 1971. Asst. prof. biology San Francisco State U., 1971-72; prof. marine sci. U. Calif., Santa Cruz, 1972—, chmn. dept., 1992-95. Contbr. numerous articles on biol. oceanography to profl. jours. Recipient Bigelow medal, 1992, Mary Sears Woman Pioneer award, 2002; NSF grantee, 1979—. Mem. Am. Soc. Limnology and Oceanography, Am. Phycological Soc. Office: U Calif Dept Ocean Sci Santa Cruz CA 95064 Office Phone: 831-459-2908. E-mail: msilver@ucsc.edu.

SILVER, MICHAEL, education educator; b. Landsberg, Germany, Jan. 30, 1948; came to U.S., 1949; s. Norman and Esther Silver; m. Beverley Ann Moss, May 16, 1971; children: Sabina, Joseph. AB, Washington U., 1970, MEd, 1973, PhD, 1982. Cert. supt. Mo., Wash. Tchr. Normandy Sch. Dist., St. Louis, 1970-72, Parkway Sch. Dist., St. Louis, 1972-75, asst. prin., 1976-79, adminstrv. asst., 1979-83, asst. to supt., 1983-84, asst. supt., 1984-86; supt. Tukwila Sch. Dist., Seattle, 1986—2003; asst. prof. ednl. adminstrn. Seattle U. Bd. dirs. Cities in Schs., Seattle; mem. adv. bd. Sta. KCTS, Seattle, 1990-2003; vis. exec. Seattle U. Sch. Edn., 1995. Author: Values Education, 1976, Facing Issues of Life and Death, 1976. Pres. SeaTac Task Force, Seattle, 1989; bd. dirs. Anti-Defamation League, Seattle, 1987—; mem. City of Tukwila (Wash.) 2000 Com., 1988-90. Recipient A Plus award Wash. Coun. Econ. Edn., 1992, Excellence in Ednl. Leadership award Univ. Coun. for Ednl. Adminstrn., 1998, Art Tribute award, Wash. Art Edn. Assn., 2001; named Exec. Educator, 100 Exec. Educator Mag., 1985, 1996 Assoc. for Inst. for Ednl. Inquiry Leadership Program; named to Homework Ctrl.; 100 Most Influential People in U.S. Pub. Edn.; I/D/E/A fellow Charles F. Kettering Found., 1978, 88, Title VI fellow Washington U., 1971-73, Svc. Learning Faculty fellow Seattle U., 2005-06; New Prin. grantee Wash. Mutual, 2005; named Supt. of Yr. Wash. Libr. Media Assn., 2000. Mem. ASCD, Am. Assn. Sch. Adminstrs., Wash. Assn. Sch. Adminstrs. (met. chpt., pres. 1989-90), King County Supts. (chmn. adv. com. 1989-90, 95-96), Southcenter Rotary Club (Paul Harris fellow 1994), Southwest King County C. of C., Phi Delta Kappa. Home: 14127 SE 50th St Bellevue WA 98006-3409 Office: Seattle U Sch Edn PO Box 222000 901 12th Ave Seattle WA 98122 Office Phone: 206-296-5798. Personal E-mail: 4silver@gmail.com. Business E-Mail: silverm@seattleu.edu.

SILVER, ROSLYN OLSON, federal judge; b. Phoenix, Feb. 28, 1946; BA, U. Calif. Santa Barbara, 1968; JD cum laude, Ariz. State U., 1971. Bar: Ariz. 1971, U.S. Ct. Appeals (9th cir.) 1980, U.S. Supreme Ct. 1984. Law clk. Hon. Lorna E. Lockwood Ariz. Supreme Ct., Phoenix, 1971-72; advisor, litigator Navajo Nation Native Am. Rights Fund, Phoenix, 1974-76; legal labor counsel Dial Corp., Phoenix, 1976-78; ptnr. Logan and Aguirre, Phoenix, 1978-79; legal counsel EEOC, Phoenix, 1979-80; asst. U.S. Atty. Dist. Ariz., Phoenix, 1980-84; asst. atty. gen. Ariz. Atty. Gen.'s Office, Phoenix, 1984-86; acting 1st asst., chief criminal divsn. dist. Ariz. U.S. Atty. Office, Phoenix, 1986-94; judge Dist. Ariz. U.S. Dist. Ct., Phoenix, 1994—. Chair local rules com. Ariz. Dist. Ct.; mem. regional sect. panel Harry S Truman Scholarship Found. Contbg. editor: Rutter Group Practice Guide; contbr. articles to profl. jours. Mem. bd. visitors U. Ariz. Law Sch.; mem. adv. panel Lodestar Mediation Clinic, Ariz. State U. Law Sch. Named one of 100 Significant Women and Minorities in Ariz.'s Legal History, 2000. Mem. ABA, Fed. Bar Assn., Nat. Assn. Women Judges, Ariz. Bar Assn. (Pub. Lawyer of Yr. 1990), Ariz. Women Lawyers Assn. (outstanding legal practitioner award 1999), Ariz. State U. Alumni Assn. (outstanding alumnus award 1996). Office: US Dist Ct 401 W Washington SPC 59 Phoenix AZ 85003 Office Phone: 602-322-7520.

SILVERBERG, LEWIS HENRY, lawyer, consultant; b. LA, Nov. 1, 1934; s. Milton Henry and Marjorie Vella (Coates) S.; children: Stephen, Richard, Donna; m. Alice Ellen Deakins, Mar. 9, 1979. BA, Pomona Coll., 1955; JD, UCLA, 1958. Bar: Calif. 1959, U.S. Supreme Ct. 1966. Pvt. practice, San Diego, 1959-89; bus. cons., 1993—. Active various pub., charitable and ednl. orgns. Office: 1515 Merritt Dr El Cajon CA 92020-7847 Home Phone: 619-447-9173; Office Phone: 619-588-8083. Personal E-mail: lew@the-silverbergs.net.

SILVERMAN, ALAN HENRY, lawyer; b. NYC, Feb. 18, 1954; s. Melvin H. and Florence (Green) S.; m. Gretchen E. Freeman, May 25, 1986; children: Willa C.F., Gordon H.F. BA summa cum laude, Hamilton Coll., 1976; MBA, JD, U. Pa., 1980. Bar: N.Y. 1981, U.S. Dist. Ct. (so. and ea. dists.) N.Y. 1981, U.S. Ct. Internat. Trade 1981, D.C. 1986, U.S. Supreme Ct. 1990. Assoc. Hughes, Hubbard & Reed, NYC, 1980-84; asst. counsel Newsweek, Inc., NYC, 1984-86; v.p., gen. counsel, sec., dir. adminstrn. Cable One, Inc., Phoenix, 1986—. Contbr. articles to profl. jours. Mem. prevention adv. com. Gov. Pa. Justice Commn., 1975-79; bd. dirs. Lawyers' Alliance for N.Y., 1982-85, N.Y. Lawyers Pub. Interest, 1983-85, Nat. Assn. JD-MBA Profls., 1983-85, Bus. Vols. for Arts, Inc., Phoenix, 1989-93, Ariz. Vol. Lawyers for the Arts, Inc., 1994-97, First Amendment Coalition Ariz., Inc., 1991—, Phoenix Falcons Fencing Club, Inc., 2003-05; mem. Maricopa County Citizens Jud. Adv. Coun., 1990-93; mem. citizens' bond com. City of Phoenix, 2000. Mem. ABA, Assn. of Bar of City of N.Y., D.C. Bar Assn., Phi Beta Kappa. Home: 5833 N 30th St Phoenix AZ 85016-2401 Office: Cable One Inc 1314 N 3d St Phoenix AZ 85004 Office Phone: 602-364-6190.

SILVERMAN, BARRY G., federal judge; b. NYC, Oct. 11, 1951; 1 child, Bagel Ann. BA summa cum laude, Ariz. State U., 1973, JD, 1976. Bar: Ariz. 1976, US Dist. Ct. Ariz. 1976, US Ct. Appeals (9th cir.) 1976, US Supreme Ct. 1980. Asst. city prosecutor, Phoenix, 1976—77; dep. atty. Maricopa County, 1977—79; ct. commr., 1979—84; judge Superior Ct. Ariz. Maricopa County, 1984—95; apptd. magistrate judge US Dist. Ct. Ariz., 1995—98; judge US Ct. Appeals (9th cir.), 1998—. Instr. constnl. law Coll. Law, Ariz. State U., 1983, adj. prof. advanced criminal procedure, 89; lectr. cmty. property BAR/BRI Ariz., Idaho and Nev. Bar Rev. Courses, 1989—94. Recipient Exel award, Soc. Nat. Assn. Publs., 1992. Mem.: ABA, Maricopa County Bar Assn. (Henry Stevens award 1991), State Bar Ariz. Avocations: magic, beagles, baseball, wine tasting. Office: US Ct of Appeals 401 W Washington St SPC 78 Phoenix AZ 85003

SILVERMAN, BEN, broadcast executive, television producer; b. Pittsfield, Mass., Aug. 15, 1970; BA in Hist., magna cum laude, Tufts U. V.p. New World/Marvel Entertainment; head of internat. packaging divsn. & NY cons. br. William Morris Agy.; founder, CEO, exec. prodr. Reveille Prodns., 2002—07; co-chmn. NBC Entertainment & NBC Universal TV Studio (name changed to Universal Media Studios), 2007—. Writer (TV series) The Restaurant, 2003—04, co-creator & exec. prodr. Nashville Star, 2003—, The Biggest Loser, 2004—; exec. prodr.: (TV series) Coupling, 2003, $25 Million Dollar Hoax, 2004, Blow Out, 2004—, The Club, 2004—05, 30 Days, 2005, The Office, 2006—, Ugly Betty, 2006—07, Are You Smarter Than a 5th Grader?, 2007—; (TV miniseries) The Tudors, 2007; prodr.: (TV films) 9/11, 2002. Active in Seeds of Peace. Named a Maverick, Details mag., 2007, 2008; named one of 40 Under 40, Advt. Age, 2007. Office: Universal Media Studios 100 Universal City Plz Universal City CA 91608

SILVERMAN, BRUCE GARY, advertising executive, consultant; b. NYC, Feb. 16, 1945; s. Edward E. and Lillian (Brill) S.; children: Jennifer, Matthew; m. Nancy Cole, 1996; children: Christen Cole, Larry Cole. BA, Adelphi U., 1965; JD, Albany Law Sch., 1967. Sr. v.p., exec. creative dir. Ogilvy & Mather Inc., NYC, 1967-80; exec. v.p., exec. creative dir. Bozell & Jacobs Inc., Dallas, 1981-83, Batten, Barton, Durstine & Osborn Inc., LA, 1984-85; exec. v.p., creative dir. Asher/Gould Advt. Inc., LA, 1986-89, pres., chief creative officer, 1989-95, pres., COO, 1996-97; pres. Western Internat. Advocacy Group, LA, 1997-98; exec. v.p., mng. dir. Initiative Media, LA, 1998—; pres., CEO Initiative Ptnrs., USA, 1999—2002; pres. WONGDOODY Advt., LA, 2003—05; chmn., CEO Pocket Billboards, Inc., Studio City, Calif., 2005—; prin. Silverman Consulting, LA, 2005—. V.p., bd. dirs. L.A. Children's Mus., 1984-88; chmn. Resource Devel. com. Starbright Pavillion Found., 1993. Mem. Acad. TV Arts and Scis., Am. Assn. Advt. Agys. (bd. dirs., vice chmn. western region 2002), UCLA Ext. (dean adv. bd.). Home: 3168 Dona Mema Pl Studio City CA 91604-4264 Office: Pocket Billboards Inc 4400 Coldwater Cyn Ave Ste 355 Studio City CA 91604 Personal E-mail: bgsla@roadrunner.com.

SILVERMAN, DEBORA LEAH, history professor; BA, Princeton U., 1975, PhD, 1983. With hist. dept. UCLA, 1981—, prof. history and art history, presdl. chair modern European history, art and culture. Author: Selling Culture: Bloomingdale's, Diana Vreeland, and the New Aristocracy of Taste in Reagan's America, 1986, Art Nouveau in Fin-de-Siecle France: Politics, Psychology and Style, 1989 (Berkshire History prize, 1990), Van Gogh and Gauguin: The Search for Sacred Art, 2000 (PEN Am. Ctr./Archtl. Digest Nat. prize for Arts Writing, 2001, Ralph Waldo Emerson prize, Phi Beta Kappa Soc., 2001, J. Russell Major prize, Am. Hist. Assn., 2001). Fellow John S. Guggenheim Meml. Found., 1992, NEH, 2005—06; Getty scholar, 1998. Fellow: Am. Acad. Arts and Sciences. Office: UCLA Dept History 6265 Bunche Hall Box 951473 Los Angeles CA 90095-1473 Office Phone: 310-825-4601. Office Fax: 310-206-9630. E-mail: silverma@history.ucla.edu.

SILVERMAN, JOSH, communications executive; Grad. magna cum laude, Brown U.; MBA, Stanford Grad. Sch. Bus. Staff mem. to US Senator Bill Bradley; mgmt. positions ADAC Labs; sr. cons. Booz Allen & Hamilton; co-founder, CEO Evite, 1998—2001; gen. mgr. Marktplaats.nl; CEO Shopping.com Ltd. (eBay, Inc. Co.), 2003—08; pres., CEO Skype, Ltd., 2008—. Office: Skype (eBay Inc Co) 2145 Hamilton Ave San Jose CA 95125 Address: Skype Technologies SA 22/24 Boulevard Royal 6e etage L-2449 Luxembourg Germany

SILVERMAN, LEONARD M., dean, electrical engineering educator; BS, Columbia U., 1962, MS, 1963, PhD, 1966. Prof. elec. engring. U. So. Calif., Los Angeles, 1966—, dean sch. engring., 1966—. Mem. Nat. Acad. Engring. Office: U So Calif Sch Engring University Park Los Angeles CA 90089-0001

SILVERMAN, TREVA, scriptwriter, television producer, consultant; b. NYC; d. Nathan and Janno (Harra) S. Student, U. Chgo., 1956; BA, Bennington Coll., 1958. Staff writer: (TV) The Entertainers, 1964, The Monkees, 1966, 67, 68, Captain Nice, 1968, Room 222, 1969, The Mary Tyler Moore Show, 1970-75 (Emmy award Best Comedy Writer 1974, Writer of Yr. 1974); episode writer He and She, 1968, Get Smart, 1968; writer: (TV pilots) Dates from Hell, 1991, Boy, Girl, Boy, 1991, Home Again, 1992, Ladies Night, 1992, The Rev, 1995, San Diego Presents, 1996; (features) A Nice Girl, 1980, Going All the Way, 1986, Act One, 1987; writer, prodr. children's musicals Theatre East, N.Y.C., 1960-63, Scandal, 1985, Hearts' Desire: Out of Town, 1992; contbg. writer: Julius Monk's Upstairs at the Downstairs, 1962-64; cons. Columbia pictures TV comedy devel., 1985-86, MTM Prodns., 1986, Just in Time, ABC-TV, 1987. Named one of TV Women of Yr., Ladies Home Jour., 1975. Mem. Writers Guild Am. (Best Writer of a Spl. award 1969), Dramatists Guild, Acad. TV Arts and Scis. Democrat. Home Phone: 818-752-1968. Business E-Mail: trevas@ix.netcom.com.

SILVERSTEIN, RICHARD, advertising agency executive; b. 1949; m. Carla Emil Silverstein; children: Aaron, Simone. Grad., Parsons Sch. Design, NYC. Various graphic design positions in San Francisco including art dir. Rolling Stone mag., McCann Erickson, Bozell & Jacobs, Foote, Cone & Belding, Ogilvy & Mather; co-chmn., co-creative dir. Goodby, Silverstein & Ptnrs. (formerly Goodby, Berlin, & Silverstein), San Francisco, 1983—. Active Corp. Design Found., Cambridge, Mass.; bd. dirs. USA Cycling Fedn., Golden Gate Nat. Parks Assn. Named Creative Dir. of Yr., Adweek mag., 1990, 1992, Agy. Exec. of Yr., 1994; named to Hall of Fame, Art Dirs. Club NY, 2002, Creative Hall of Fame, The One Club for Art & Copy, 2004. Office: Goodby Silverstein & Ptnrs 720 California St San Francisco CA 94108-2404 Office Phone: 415-392-0669.*

SILVERSTEIN, ROBERT P., lawyer; BA magna cum laude, UCLA, 1990; JD, Univ. Calif., Hastings, 1996. Bar: Calif. Judicial extern Assoc. Justice Marvin Baxter Calif. Supreme Ct., 1995; assoc. Demetriou, Del Guerico, Springer & Moyer LLP, LA, 1996—99; assoc. to ptnr., bus. & real estate litigation Hill, Farrer & Burrill LLP, LA, 1999—2005; founder, principal, real estate & bus. litigation Silverstein Law Firm, LA, 2005—. Editor (articles): Hastings Internat. & Comparative Law Rev. (Am. Jurisprudence award in legal writing & rsch.). Named a Rising Star, So. Calif. Super Lawyers, 2006. Mem.: Calif. State Bar, LA County Bar Assn., Phi Beta Kappa. Office: Silverstein Law Firm 3d Fl 215 N Marengo Ave Pasadena CA 91101-1504 Office Phone: 626-449-4200. Office Fax: 626-449-4205. Business E-Mail: robert@robertsilversteinlaw.com.

SILVERSTONE, LEON MARTIN, neuroscientist, cardiologist, educator, research scientist; b. London, May 21, 1939; came to US, 1976; s. Jack Stanley and Sadie (Osen) S.; children from previous marriage: Samantha, Frances, Mark; m. Deborah Advani, Sept. 13, 1998. Student, U. London, 1958-59; L.D.S., U. Leeds, UK, 1963, B.Ch.D., 1964, D.D.Sc., 1971; L.D.S., Royal Coll. Surgeons, Eng., 1964; PhD, U. Bristol, Eng., 1967; postgrad., U. London, 1969-76. House surgeon Leeds Dental Hosp., England, 1963-64; rsch. fellow med. rsch. coun. unit Bristol Med. and Dental Sch., 1964-67; lectr. dental surgery U. Bristol, 1967-68; sr. lectr. child dental health Med. Coll., Royal London Hosp., 1969-75, reader in preventive and pediat. dentistry, 1975-76; cons. Royal London Hosp., 1973-76; vis. Lasby prof. Dental Sch. U. Minn., Mpls., 1974-75; prof., head divsn. cardiology Dows Inst. Dental Rsch., Coll. Dentistry, U. Iowa, Iowa City, 1976-82; assoc. dean rsch. U. Colo. Health Scis. Ctr., Denver, 1982-89, dir. Oral Scis. Rsch. Inst., 1986-89; biomed. cons., 1990; v.p. R & D Synaptic Corp., La Jolla, Calif., 1990-95; dir. R & D BioSciences Sys. LLC, La Jolla, Calif., 1995—2002; pres., chmn. NeuroMed Devices Inc., 2003—. Vis. Nicholaysen prof. U. Oslo, 1972; cons. Pan Am. Health Orgn., WHO, 1973-85, dental rsch. Va, 1978-85; mem. study sect. and program adv. com. NIH-Nat. Inst. Dental Rsch., 1976-84, chmn. subcom. on dental caries, 1982-83, chmn. program adv. com., 1983-84; pres. Neura Corp., La Jolla, Calif., 1997-98. Mem. editorial bd. Caries Research, 1976-86; contbr. chpts. to books, articles in field to profl. publs. Recipient Nobel-Pharma A.B. Bofors prize, Copenhagen, 1971, ORCA-ROLEX rsch. prize, Zurich, 1973, Disting. award child dental health, 1981; NIH/Nat. Inst. Rsch. grantee, 1976-89. Mem. European Orgn. Caries Rsch.(mem. bd., sci. councillor 1971-83, pres. 1977-79), Internat. Assn. Dental Research (pres. cariology group 1982-83, Disting. Scientist award 1984), Am. Assn. Dental Rsch. (pres. cariology group chpt. 1982-83, chmn. publs. com. 1985-86), Brit. Dental Assn., Internat. Assn. Pedodontics (exec. com. 1972-79, jour. editor 1971-79), AAAS, Soc. Exptl. Biology and Medicine, Space Medicine Com., AAUP, Am. Acad. Pedodontics, Omega Kappa Upsilon, Sigma Xi. Office: Neuro Med Devices PO Box 100 Oakley UT 84055 Home Phone: 435-655-1081; Office Phone: 435-783-6696. Personal E-mail: neuromed@allwest.net.

SILVERTON, NANCY, chef; b. June 20, 1954; m. Mark Peel (div.); 3 children. Student, Calif. State U., Cordon Bleu, London, Ecole Le Notre, France. Asst. pastry chef Michael's Restaurant, Santa Monica, Calif.; 1st exec. pastry chef Spago, West Hollywood, Calif., 1982—85, 1987—89; v.p. product devel., exec. v.p., baker, owner LaBrea Bakery, LA, 1989—2001, Las Vegas, 1998—2001; pastry chef, co-owner Campanile restaurant; chef, co-owner Pizzeria Mozzo, LA, 2006—, Osteria Mozza, LA, 2006—. Author: Desserts, 1991, Nancy Silverton's Breads from the La Brea Bakery, 1996, Nancy Silverton's Pastries from the La Brea Bakery, 2000, Nancy Silverton's Sandwich Book, 2002, Twist of the Wrist, 2007; co-author: Mark Peel and Nancy Silverton At Home: Two Chefs Cook for Family and Friends, 1994, The Food of Campanile, 1997. Involved in Garden Sch. Project, LA, Meals-on-Wheels, Chgo., NYC, LA. Recipient Fine Dining award, Nation's Restaurant News, 1996, RCA Pioneer award, 2003, Internat. Star Diamond award for Outstanding Hospitality, 2004, WCR Golden Bowl award, 2005; named Best Pastry Chef of Yr., James Beard Found., 1990, LA Culinary Master of Yr., 1994, Restaurateur of Yr. and Restaurant of Yr., Southern Calif. Restaurant Writers, 1995, Pastry Chef of Yr., Chocolatier Mag., 1995; named a Who's Who in Am. Cooking, James Beard Found., 1990, Food Artisan, Bon Appetite Best of Food & Entertaining, 1999; named one of America's Best New Chefs, Food & Wine mag., 1990, 50 New Taste Makers, Nation's Restaurant News, 1999; named to The West 100: The most influential people in Southern Calif., LA Times, 2006. Office: Osteria Mozza 6602 Melrose Ave Los Angeles CA 90038 Office Phone: 323-297-0100.

SILVESTRI, ALAN ANTHONY, film composer; b. NYC, Mar. 26, 1950; s. Louis and Elizabeth (Clarke) S.; m. Sandra Dee Shue; children: Alexandra, Joseph, James. PhD in Music (hon.), Berklee Coll. Music, Boston, 1995. Film scores include The Doberman Gang, 1972, The Amazing Dobermans, Las Vegas Lady, 1976, Romancing the Stone, 1984, Par ou t'es rentre? On t'as vu sortir, 1984, Fandango, 1984, Cat's Eye, 1984, Back to the Future, 1985 (Grammy award nominations best instrumental composition and best album of original score for a motion picture, 1985), Summer Rental, 1985, Clan of the Cave Bear, 1986, The Delta Force, 1986, American Anthem, 1986, Flight of the Navigator, 1986, No Mercy, 1986, Critical Condition, 1987, Outrageous Fortune, 1987, Predator, 1987, Overboard, 1987, Who Framed Roger Rabbit?, 1988 (Grammy award nominations best instrumental composition and best album of original score for a motion picture, 1988), My Stepmother Is an Alien, 1988, Mac and Me, 1988, She's Out of Control, 1989, Downtown, 1989, The Abyss, 1989, Back to the Future II, 1989, Back to the Future III, 1990, Young Guns II, 1990, Predator II, 1990, Soapdish, 1991, Dutch, 1991, Ricohet, 1991, Shattered, 1991, Father of the Bride, 1991, Ferngully: The Last Rainforest, 1992, Death Becomes Her, 1992, Stop! Or My Mom Will Shoot, 1992, The Bodyguard, 1992, Cop and a Half, 1993, Sidekicks, 1993, Super Mario Bros., 1993, Judgment Night, 1993, Grumpy Old Men, 1993, Clean Slate, 1994, Blown Away, 1994, Forrest Gump, 1994 (Academy award nomination best original score, Grammy award nomination best instrumental performance for "Feather Theme from Forrest Gump," Golden Globe award nomination best original score), Richie Rich, 1994, The Quick and the Dead, 1994, The Perez Family, 1995, Judge Dredd, 1995, Father of the Bride II, 1995, Sgt. Bilko, 1995, Grumpier Old Men, 1995, Eraser, 1996, Long Kiss Goodnight, 1996, Fools Rush In, 1996, Volcano, 1997, Contact, 1997, Mousehunt, 1997, Odd Couple II, 1998, Parent Trap, 1998, Holyman, 1998, Practical Magic, 1998, Siegfried & Roy, The Magic Box, 1999, Stuart Little, 1999, Reindeer Games, 2000, What Lies Beneath, 2000, What Women Want, 2000, Castaway, 2000 (Grammy award winner for best instrumental composition for "Theme from Castaway"), The Mexican, 2001, What Women Want, 2000,The Mummy Returns, 2001, Serendipity, 2001, Showtime, 2002, Lilo & Stitch, 2002, Stuart Little 2, 2002, Maid in Manhattan, 2002, Identity, 2003, Lara Croft Tomb Raider: The Cradle of Life, 2003, Two Soldiers, 2003, Van Helsing, 2004, The Polar Express, 2004, The Wild, 2006, Night at the Museum, 2006 (ASCAP award); TV themes include CHiPs, 1978-83, Manimal, 1983. Recipient ACE award Nat. Acad. Cable Programming for Tales from the Crypt - All Through the House, 1990, Saturn award Acad. Arts and Sci. for fantasy and horror film, 1987, Grammy award for Best Song Written for Motion Picture for The Polar Express, 2006; Grammy nominations for Back to the Future, 1985, Who Framed Rger Rabbit?, 1988, Forrest Gump, 1994, Castaway, 2001, Henry Mancini award, ASCAP, 2002; nominated for Golden Globe, Forrest Gump, 1994.

SIMERVILLE, JAMES JASPER, pediatrician; b. Bend, Oreg., Sept. 15, 1939; s. George Melvin and Clara Louise (Jasper) S.; m. Carol Marie Smith, Dec. 26, 1961; children: Pamela Marie, Steven James, Jeffrey Alan. BS, Oreg. State U., 1961; MD, U. Oreg., 1965. Diplomate Am. Bd. Pediatrics; diplomate in occupational medicine Am. Bd. Preventive Medicine. Commd. 2d lt. USAF, 1964, advanced through grades to col., 1979; intern USAF Hosp. Travis, Travis AFB, Calif., 1965-66; resident USAF Hosp. Wilford Hall, Lackland AFB, Tex., 1966-68; chief pediatric svc. USAF, Westover AFB, Mass., Lakenheath, Eng., and Scott AFB, Ill., Eng., 1968-75; dir. med. edn. USAF Hosp. Scott, Scott AFB, 1975-84; cons. in pediatrics, then dep. comdr. U.S. Air Force Acad. Hosp., Colorado Springs, Colo., 1976-84; retired USAF, 1984; dir. Colorado Springs Sports Medicine Clinic, 1984-87, Colo. Ctr. Occupational Medicine, Colorado Springs, 1985-92; med. dir. Colorado Springs Health Ptnrs., 1992-96, Pacific Care, 1996—. Med. cons. sports medicine program, Chapman Coll., Colorado Springs, 1983-88. Fellow Am. Acad. Pediatrics; mem. Colo. Med. Soc., El Paso County Med. Soc. Roman Catholic. Avocations: walking, hiking, camping, golf, skiing. Office: Pacificare 5755 Mark Dabling Blvd Ste 104 Colorado Springs CO 80919-2228

SIMINI, JOSEPH PETER, accountant, financial consultant, writer, former educator; b. Buffalo, Feb. 15, 1921; s. Paul and Ida (Moro) S.; m. Marcelline McDermott, Oct. 4, 1968. BS, St. Bonaventure U., 1940, BBA, 1949; MBA, U. Calif.-Berkeley, 1957; DBA, Western Colo. U., 1981. CPA, Calif. Insp. naval material Bur. Ordnance, Buffalo and Rochester, N.Y., 1941-44; mgr. Paul Simini Bakery, Buffalo, 1946-48; internal auditor DiGiorgio (Fruit) Corp., San Francisco, 1950-51; tax acct. Price Waterhouse & Co., San Francisco, 1953; sr. acct. Richard L. Hanlin C.P.A., San Francisco, 1953-54; prof. acctg. U. San Francisco, 1954-79, emeritus prof., 1983—. Mem. rev. bd. Calif. Bd. Accountancy, 1964-68; host The Bus. Doctor Stas. WALE and KCCF, 1998. Author: Accounting Made Simple, 1967, rev. edit., 1987, Cost Accounting Concepts for Nonfinancial Executives, 1976, Become Wealthy! Using Tax Savings and Real Estate Investments, 1982, Balance Sheet Basics for the Nonfinancial Managers, 1989, Petals of the Rose, 1990, How to Become Financially Independent, 1996, 10 Steps to Financial Independence Guaranteed, 2000, Entwined Lives, 2003; tech. editor Accounting Essentials, 1972; patentee Dial-A-Trig and Verbum Est card game. Mem. coun. com. Boy Scouts Am., Buffalo, San Francisco, 1942-65, Souters Key, San Francisco coun.; bd. dir. Nat. Italian Am. Found., Washington, 1979-85. Lt. j.g. USNR, 1944-46. Recipient Bacon-McLaughlin medal St. Bonaventure U., 1940, Laurel Key, 1940; Outstanding Tchr. award Coll. Bus. Adminstrn., U. San Francisco, 1973, Disting. Tchr. award U. San Francisco, 1975, Joseph Per Simini award, 1977, Crown Zellerbach Found. fellow, 1968-69, Gold Medal Associazione Piemontese nel Mondo, Turin, Italy, 1984; decorated Knight Order of Merit, Republic of Italy, 1982. Mem. AICPA's, MENSA, Calif. Soc. CPAs (past chmn. ednl. stds., student rels. com. San Francisco chpt.), Inst. of Mgmt. Accts. (past pres. San Francisco chpt.), Am. Acctg. Assn., Am. Mgmt. Assn. (lectr. 1968-78), Serra (past pres. Golden Gate chpt.), Il Cenacolo (past pres.), Toastmasters (past pres. Magic Word, treas. Dist. 4, 1996-97), K.C., Rotary (past pres. Daly City), Delta Sigma Pi (past pres. San Francisco alumni club), Beta Gamma Sigma. Roman Catholic. Office: PO Box 31420 San Francisco CA 94131-0420 Home: 5235 Diamond Heights Blvd #209 San Francisco CA 94131

SIMMON, VINCENT FOWLER, biotechnology executive; b. LA, Aug. 9, 1943; s. Vincent Joseph and Gertrude (Fowler) S.; m. Carol Ann Lamboy, Dec. 28, 1963 (div. 1973); 1 child, Stacy Anne; m. Berniece Irene Yocum, Jan. 2, 1983 (dec. 1988); children: Vincent F. Jr., Geoffrey Hamilton; m. Susan Lynn Sweeten, Nov. 3, 1990; children: Marcus Wesley, Katlyn Shea. BA, Amherst Coll., 1964; MS, U. Toledo, 1966; PhD, Brown U., 1971. Postdoctoral fellow Stanford U., Palo Alto, Calif., 1971-73; rschr. SRI Internat., Menlo Park, Calif., 1973-75, mgr., 1975-77, asst. dir., 1977-79; dept. dir. Genex Corp., Rockville, Md., 1979-80, v.p., 1980-83, sr. v.p., 1984-85; v.p. rsch. divsn. W.R. Grace & Co., Columbia, Md., 1985-90; pres., CEO Alpha 1 Biomeds., Inc., Washington, 1990-94, Viral Techs. Inc., Washington, 1990-94, Prototek, Inc., Potomac, Md., 1994—; also chmn. bd. dirs. Prototech, Inc., Potomac, Md. Councilor Enviorn. Mutagen Soc., 1977-79; bd. dirs. chem. Industry Ins. for Toxicology, Research Triangle Park, N.C., 1986-90, Viral Tecs, Inc., Alpha I Biomedics, Inc. Mem. AAAS, Am. Chem. Soc. Address: Prototek Inc 11902 Coldstream Dr Potomac MD 20854-3615 Office: Cortex Pharmaceuticals Inc 15241 Barranca Pkwy Irvine CA 92618

SIMMONS, GENE (CHAIM WITZ, GENE KLEIN), musician; b. Haifa, Israel, Aug. 25, 1949; came to U.S., 1958, naturalized, 1963; s. Flora Witz; (children with Shannon Tweed). Nicholas, Sophie BE, SUNY, 1970; BA in Edn., Richmond Coll., CUNY, 1972. Tchr., Spanish Harlem, NY; asst. to editor Glamour and Vogue; asst. to dir. Puerto Rican InterAgeny Coun.; member in bands called Bullfrog Beer, Coffee, Long Island Sounds, Cathedral, and Wicked Lester; co-founder Kiss, 1973—; founder $immons Records; ptnr. Simmons Abramson Mktg., 2006—; chmn. NGTV (No Good TV), 2006—. Singer: (albums with Kiss): Kiss, 1974, Hotter Than Hell, 1974, Dressed to Kill, 1975, Alive, 1975, Destroyer, 1976, Rock & Roll Over, 1976, Love Gun, 1977, Alive II, 1977, Double Platinum, 1978, Dynasty, 1979, Unmasked, 1980, Music From the Elder, 1981, Killers, 1982, Creatures of the Night, 1982, Lick It Up, 1983, Animalize, 1984, Asylum, 1985, Crazy Nights, 1987, Hot In The Shade, 1989, Smashes, Thrashes and Hits, 1989, Revenge, 1992, Alive III, 1993, Kiss My Ass, 1995, MTV: Kiss Unplugged, 1996, Carnival of Souls, 1997, You Wanted the Best You Got the Best!, 1997, Greatest Kiss, 1997, Psycho Circus, 1998, Kiss: The Box Set, 2001, The Very Best of Kiss, 2002, Kiss Symphony Alive VI, 20th Century Masters: Millenium Collection Vol. 1 and 2, Kiss Gold, Kiss Rock the Nation; (solo albums) Gene Simmons, 1978, ***Hole, 2004; actor (films) Runaway, 1984, Never Too Young To Die, 1986, Trick or Treat, 1986, Wanted: Dead or Alive, 1987, The Decline of Western Civilization Part II: The Metal Years, 1988, The Return of Bruno, 1988, Red Surf, 1990, Detroit Rock City, 1999, Wish You Were Dead, 2000, The New Guy, 2002; (TV series) My Dad the Rock Star, 2003 Gene Simmons' Rock School, 2005, Gene Simmons Family Jewels, 2005-; (TV appearances) The Paul Lynde Halloween Special, 1976, KISS Meets the Phantom of the Park, 1978, Miami Vice, 1985, Hitchhiker, 1986, Millennium, 1996, Talk to Me, 2000, (voice only) Family Guy, 2001, 2002, 2005, King of the Hill, 2003 Who Wants to Be a Millionaire, 2001, At Any Cost, 2002, (voice only) King of the Hill, 2003, Gene Simmons TV Special '24/7', 2004, Third Watch, 2004; creater (TV) Baby 101, Mr. Romance, The Apprentice 3, 2005; guest judge American Idol: The Search for a Superstar, 2005; composer (films) Reform School Girls, 1986, Less Than Zero, 1987, (TV) Kiss: The Last Kiss, 2000, Kiss: Beyond the Makeup, 2001, (video game) Underground, 2003; prodr. (TV series) Detroit Rock City, 1999, Smash, 2001; writer (video) KISS: eXposed, 1987; author: Kiss and Makeup, 2001, Sex Money Kiss (both NY Times Best Selling Books), 2005; founder Simmons Publishing; published(magazine) Gene Simmons Tongue, 2001-(Sterling/Macfadden), Gene Simmons Game mag.; released (audio visual, CD) Speaking in Tongues; launched fashion label, Gene Simmons-Dragonfly, 2002; perfomer, writer (song) I Am Indy, 2006; TV commericals, shows and advertising associated with KISS include Cannon Camera (Japan), NASCAR, Nat. Hot Rod Assn. (NHRA), Pepsi Cola, Coca Cola, Holiday Inn, VISA cards, KISS/Platinum online comics, KISS Girls; sponsor Worldwide Mktg. and Branding of Indy Racing League, 2006-. Winner 27 Gold Record Albums, 9 Platinum Record Albums, 7 Multi-Platimun Record Albums. Mem. Am. Fedn. Musicians, AFTRA, ASCAP. Discovered Van Halen in 1977 and produced 15 song demo album; inventor of Axe bass guitar in 1980; speaks several languages English, Hungarian, Hebrew, German, learning Japanese and Mandarin Chinese; Kiss has been America's Number One Gold Record award winning group of all time according to RIAA; in honor of Gene Simmons US Postage Stamp; self-titled debut from the group BAG to mark first release from Gene Simmons' Simmons Records in over a decade in 2005. Office: $immons Records PO Box 15097 Beverly Hills CA 90210

SIMMONS, GEOFFREY STUART, physician, educator, writer; b. Camp Gordon, Ga., July 28, 1943; s. Ted R. and Jane A. (Lavander) Simmons; m. Sherry Simmons, Sept. 7, 1985; children: Bradley, Anais. BS, U. Ill., 1965, MD, 1969. Diplomate Am. Bd. Internal Medicine; cert. instr., ham operator, trainer Cmty. Emergency Response Team. Intern U. So. Calif., LA, 1969-70, resident, 1971-74; pvt. practice Astoria, Oreg., 1974-77, Eugene, Oreg., 1977—; chmn. internal medicine dept. Peace Health Med. Group, 1996-98, 2000—. Med. corres. KUGN Radio, 1993—95; chair Med. Res. Corps Coun., 2002—; trainer Cmty. Emergency Response Team; bd. govs. Am. Acad. Disaster Medicine, 2006—; bd. dirs. Physicians and Surgeons Sci. Integrity, 2006—. Author: (book) The Z Papers, 1977, The Adam Experiment, 1978, Pandemic, 1980, Murdock, 1982, The Glue Factory, 1995, To Glue or Not to Glue, 1997, What Darwin Didn't Know, 2004, Billions of Missing Links, 2007; med. commentator KABC Radio, 1970. Fellow: Discovery Inst. (sr.); mem.: Eugene Citizen Corps., Lane County Med. Soc. (chmn. task force for disaster preparedness 2001—02, trainer cmty. emergency response team 2004—, vol. mgr. cert. program 2004—, lead cert. trainer cmty. emergency response teams). Avocations: writing, teaching disaster preparedness.

SIMMONS, GEORGE FINLAY, retired mathematics professor; b. Austin, Tex., Mar. 3, 1925; s. George Finlay and Armede Victoria (Hatcher) S.; m. Hope Bridgeford, Sept. 11, 1954; 1 child, Nancy Bingham. BS, Caltech, 1946; MS, U. Chgo., 1948; PhD, Yale U., 1957. Instr. U. Chgo., 1947-50, U. Maine, Orono, 1950-52, Yale U., New Haven, 1952-56; asst. prof. U. R.I., Kingston, 1956-58, Williams College, Williamstown, Mass., 1958-62; assoc. prof. math. Colo. Coll., Colorado Springs, 1962-65, prof., 1965-90, prof. emeritus, 1990—. Author: Introduction Topology and Modern Analysis, 1962, Differential Equations, 1972, 3d edit., 2006, Precalculus Mathematics in a Nutshell, 1981, Calculus with Analytic Geometry, 1985, 2nd edit., 1995, Calculus Gems: Brief Lives and Memorable Mathematics, 1992, repub., 2007. Mem. Math. Assn. Am. Avocations: travel, cooking, fishing, billiards. Home: 1401 Wood Ave Colorado Springs CO 80907-7348 Office: Colorado College Dept Math Colorado Springs CO 80903

SIMMONS, HARRIS H., bank executive; b. Salt Lake City, June 25, 1954; s. Roy William and Elizabeth (Ellison) S. BA in Econs., U. Utah, 1977; MBA, Harvard U., 1980. Comml. loan officer Allied Bancshares, Houston, 1980-81; asst. v.p. Zions Bancorp, Salt Lake City, 1981, fin. v.p., 1981-82; sr. v.p. fin. Zions Utah Bancorp, Salt Lake City, 1982-83, exec. v.p., sec., treas., 1984-86, pres., 1986—90; pres., CEO Zions 1st Nat. Bank, Salt Lake City, 1990—98, chmn., 1990—; pres., CEO Zions Bancorporation, Salt Lake City, 1990—, chmn., 2002—. Bd. dirs. Questar, Inc., Salt Lake City, Entrada Industries, Inc., Salt Lake City, Keystone Comm., Salt Lake City, Simmons Family, Inc., Salt Lake City, Zions 1st Nat. Bank, Salt Lake City, Nat. Bank Ariz., Tucson, Nev. State Bank, Las Vegas. Bd. dirs. United Way, Salt Lake City, 1983-89; bd. dirs. Utah Symphony, 1986—, vice chmn., 1990-95, chmn., 1995—; trustee Salt Lake City C.C., 1993—; v.p. fin. Great Salt Lake coun. Boy Scouts Am., 1991-95; co-chair Greater Salt Lake Shelter-the-Homeless Com., 1986-89, v.p., 1989—. Pres., dir., past vice-chmn. ABA; mem. Utah Bankers Assn. (bd.dirs. 1987-92, chmn. 1990-91), Salt Lake Area C. of C. (bd. dirs. 1991-94), Phi Beta Kappa. Mem. Lds Ch. Office: Zions Bancorporation 1 S Main St Salt Lake City UT 84111

SIMMONS, RICHARD J., lawyer; b. Brockton, Mass., Nov. 26, 1951; BA summa cum laude, U. Mass., 1973; JD, U. Calif., Berkeley, 1976. Bar: Calif. 1976. Ptnr. Sheppard, Mullin, Richter & Hampton LLP, LA, 1995—. Lectr. State of Calif., 1977-88; instr. UCLA, 1980-87; appointed to bd. Calif. Minimum Wage Bds. 1982, 84, 87; adv. bd. U. Calif. Boalt Hall Law Sch. Indsl. Relations Law Journal, 1985—. Reviews editor, editor in chief: Indsl. Relations Law Jour. 1975-76; Author: Wrongful Discharge and Employment Practices Manual, 1989, 2001, Employee Handbook and Personnel Policies Manual, 1983, 87, 92, 2004, Wage and Hour Manual for California Employers, 1982, 86, 88, 89, 91, 2001, 04, 05, Employment Discrimination and EEO Practice Manual for California Employers, 1982, 85, 91, 2000, 05, Employer's Guide to the American with Disabilities Act, 1990, 91, 92, The Employer's Guide to the California Family Rights Act of 1991, 92, 2000, Employer Obligations Under the Federal Plant Closing Law, 1989, 90, The New Federal Polygraph Law, 1989, The New Federal Immigration Law: The Immigration Reform and Control Act of 1986, 1987, COBRA: The Federal Health Insurance Rules for the 1990's, 1987,90, 2001; contbr. articles to profl mags. and jours. Commonwealth scholar. Mem. ABA (labor, employment law, tax sect.), L.A. County Bar Assn. (tax, labor sect.), The State Bar Calif., Calif. Soc. Health Care Attys., Am. Soc. Health Care Attys., Phi Kappa Phi. Office: Sheppard Mullin Richter & Hampton 333 S Hope St Ste 4700 Los Angeles CA 90071-1448 Office Phone: 213-617-5518. Business E-Mail: rsimmons@smrh.com.

SIMMONS, SABRINA L., apparel executive; BS in Fin., U. Calif., Berkeley; MBA, UCLA. CPA Calif. Accountant KPMG, Hewlett Packard Co.; asst. treas. Americas Levi Strauss & Co.; dir. fin. planning & analysis PIC Internat. Group PLC, Sygen Internat. PLC, 1999—2000, group fin. dir., bd. dirs., 2000—01; v.p., treas. to sr. v.p. corp. fin. Gap Inc., San Francisco, 2001—07, exec. v.p. fin., acting CFO, 2007—08, mem. exec. leadership team, 2007—, exec. v.p. corp. fin., CFO, 2008—. Bus. adv. coun. mem. U. San Francisco, Sch. Bus. and Mgmt., 2003—. Office: Gap Inc Two Folsom St San Francisco CA 94105 Office Phone: 650-952-4400. Office Fax: 415-427-2553.

SIMMONS, SARAH R., lawyer; b. Ducktown, Tenn., Jan. 23, 1948; BA magna cum laude, U. Ariz., 1970, postgrad.; JD magna cum laude, U. Denver, 1973. Bar: Colo. 1974, Ariz. 1975. Mem. Molloy, Jones & Donahue, Tucson, Brown & Bain, P.A., Lewis & Roca LLP, 2002—05; judge Ariz. Superior Ct. Pima County, 2006—. Mem. Davis Monthan 50, 1991—, pres., 1998-2000; trustee Tohono Club Park, 1995-2004, sec., 1997-99, v.p. 1999-2001, pres., 2001-03; trustee Tucson Airport Authority, 1996-2006, bd. dir., 2005-06; mem. Law Coll. Assn. Bd., 1996—, sec. 1998-99, pres. 2000-01; 4th R bd. Tucson Unified Sch., 1996-2003; bd. dir. United Way Tucson, 1995-2000, Family Advocacy Resource and Wellness Ctrs., Resources Women, 1995-2000; bd. dir. Ariz. Town Hall, 1998-2003; mem. adv. bd. Ariz. Drug Free Workplace, 1991-2002, So. Ariz. Sports Devel. Corp., U. Ariz. Social and Behavioral Scis., 1994-96; sec. So. Ariz. Minutemen, 1996-98; mem. bd. visitors Coll. Law, chair, 2002-06; v.p. Met. Tucson Conv. and Visitors Bur., 2003-05, pres. 2005-07. Recipient Outstanding Alumni award U. Ariz. Coll. of Law, 1993, Tucson Woman of Yr. C. of C., 1994, Women on the Move award YWCA, 1995, Alice Truman Leadership award, 2003; named one of 100 Women and Minorities in the Law, 2000, Women Who Lead, U. Ariz. Women's Studies Adv. Coun., 2003. Fellow ABA, Ariz. Bar Assn.; mem. Nat. Assn. Bond Lawyers, State Bar Ariz. (bd. govs. 1987-95, sec.-treas. 1989-90, 2d v.p. 1990-91, 1st v.p. 1991-92, pres.-elect 1992-93, pres. 1993-94, employment law sect., profl. conduct com., fee arbitration com., co- mem. of yr. 2004), Ariz. Women Lawyers Assn. (charter), Colo. Bar Assn., Pima County Bar Assn. (bd. dirs. 1985-94), Am. Judicature Soc., So. Ariz. Legal Aid (bd. dir. 1990-93), Lawyers Against Hunger, Order St. Ives, Phi Beta Kappa, Phi Kappa Phi, Phi Alpha Theta, Kappa Beta Pi. Office: Ariz Supreme Ct in Pima County 110 W Congress Tucson AZ 85701 Office Phone: 520-740-8441. E-mail: ssimmons@sc.pima.gov.

SIMMONS, WILLIAM, retired aerospace engineer, research and development company executive; b. Chgo., Apr. 24, 1932; s. Walter Garfield and Edna Dean (Winch) S.; m. Barbara Millet Haury, Oct. 4, 1954; children: Sheryl Lee, Cynthia Jane, Shelly Jean. BA in Physics, Carleton Coll., 1953; MS in Physics, U. Ill., 1955, PhD in Physics, 1960. Mem. tech. staff Space Tech. Labs., Redondo Beach, Calif., 1960-62; sr. rsch. scientist Gen. Tech., Torrance, Calif., 1962, TRW, Redondo Beach, 1962-71, dir. rsch., 1984-89, chief engr. spl. projects assigned to Lawrence Livermore (Calif.) Labs., 1989-92; engring. mgr. Lawrence Livermore Labs., 1972-84, rsch. reviewer, 1985-89; prof. engring. UCLA, 1968-72. Tech. panel mem. U. Calif., Berkeley, 1985; tech. reviewer Dept. Energy, Washington, 1986—, mem. rev. com., 1987—; cons. in field, 1992-2006. Editor, reviewer 2 books, 1982, 83; contbr. numerous articles to profl. jours. Named Disting. Engring. Prof. of Yr. UCLA, 1972, one of Top 100 Innovators in U.S.A, Sci. Digest, 1986; George F. Baker Found. scholar Carleton Coll., 1949-53; Disting. Alum. Engring Svcs. award, engring U. Ill., 2009. Mem. IEEE (sr., life, gen. chmn. symposia 1988, 89, Simon Ramo Major medal 1987), Laser Engring. and Optical Soc., Am. Phys. Soc., Soc. of Photographic and Instrumentation Engrs., U.S. Chess Club, Phi Beta Kappa, Sigma Xi. Republican. Achievements include 11 patents for electro-optics devices. Avocations: chess, ping pong/table tennis, bridge. Office: Sys Solutions 1621 W 25th St Ste 231 San Pedro CA 90732-4300 Office Phone: 310-541-4140. Business E-Mail: wwsimmons@cox.net.

SIMON, GREGORY E., psychiatrist, researcher; MD, U. N.C., 1982; MPH, U. Wash., 1990. Diplomate Am. Bd. Internal Medicine 1985, Am. Bd. Adult Psychiatry 1990. Scientific investigator Ctr. for Health Studies, Group Health Coop., Seattle, 1990—2000, staff psychiatrist, 1990—, sr. scientific investigator Seattle, 2000—; rsch. prof. psychiatry and behavioral sciences U. Wash., Seattle, 2005—. Named one of Best Doctors, Seattle Met. mag., 2006, Puget Sound Consumers' Checkbook, 2007. Mem.: Am. Psychiatric Assn. (Eli Lilly "Welcome Back" award 2002, sr. scholar health services rsch. award 2002), Depression and Bipolar Support Alliance (sci. adv. bd., Gerald R. Klerman sr. investigator award 2005). Office: Group Health Coop 1730 Minor Ave #1600 Seattle WA 98112 Business E-Mail: simon.g@ghc.org.

SIMON, HORST D., computer scientist; b. Aug. 8, 1953; married; 2 children. Diploma in Math., Technische U. Berlin, 1978; PhD, U. Calif., 1982. Asst. prof. SUNY, Stony Brook, NY, 1982—83; with Boeing Computer Svcs., 1983—89, coord. engring. and tech. applications divsn., 1983—86, mgr. computational math. group, 1986—87; mgr. rsch. dept. computer sci. corp. NASA Ames Rsch. Ctr., Moffett Field, Calif., 1989—94; rsch. market devel. mgr. advanced sys. divsn. Silicon Graphics, 1994—96; dir. Nat. Energy Rsch. Sci. Computing Ctr. Lawrence Berkeley Nat. Lab., 1996—, dir. Computational Rsch. Divsn., 2002—, assoc. lab. dir. computing scis., 2004—. Spkr. in field; mem. indsl. adv. bd. dept. computer sci. U. Calif., Davis; mem. internat. adv. panel Inst. HPC, Singapore. Editor: (books) Scientific Applications of the Connection Machine, 1989, Parallel Computational Fluid Dynamics, 1992, Parallel Processing for Scientific Computing, 1995, Solving Irregularly Structured Problems in Parallel, 1998; contbr. articles to profl. jours., chapters to books; mng. editor: Internat. Jour. High Speed Computing, 1989—97, mem. editl. bd.: SIAM Jour. Sci. and Statistical Computing, 1989—95, Jour. Sci. Programming, NHSE Review, Advances in Engineering Software (formerly Computing Systems Engineering), others. Recipient (with NAS Parallel Benchmarks Team) H. Julian Allen award, 1995, (with group from Cray and Boeing) Gordon Bell Prize, 1988. Office: NERSC Divn Dir Berkeley Lab MS 50B-4230 One Cyclotron Rd Berkeley CA 94720-8150 Office Phone: 510-486-7377. Office Fax: 510-486-4300. E-mail: hdsimon@lbl.gov.

SIMON, JAMES LOWELL, lawyer; b. Nov. 8, 1944; s. K. Lowell and Elizabeth Ann (Unholz) S.; m. RuthAnn Beck, July 4, 1997; children: Heather Lyn Small, Brandon James; stepchildren: Gary G. Mower, Richard M. Nazareth II, Juliet A. Nazareth. Student, U. Ill., 1962-63, JD with honors, 1975; BSEE magna cum laude, Bradley U., 1967. Bar: Fla. 1975, Utah 1999, Calif. 2002, U.S. Dist. Ct. (mid. dist.) Fla. 1976, U.S. Dist. Ct. Utah 1999, U.S. Dist. Ct. (no. dist.) Calif. 2002, U.S. Ct. Appeals (11th cir.) 1981, U.S. Patent Office 1983. Engr. Pan Am. World Airways, Cape Kennedy, Fla., 1967-68; assoc. Akerman, Senterfitt & Eidson, Orlando, Fla., 1975-80; ptnr. Bogin, Munns, Munns & Simon, Orlando, 1980-87, Holland & Knight, LLP, 1987-99; corp. counsel Agilent Technologies Inc., Palo Alto, Calif., 2000—. With Seminole County Sch. Adv. Coun., Fla., 1981-88, chmn., 1982-83; with Forest City Local Sch. Adv. Com., Altamonte Springs, Fla., 1981-84, Code Enforcement Bd., Altamonte Springs, 1983-84, Cen. Bus. Dist. Study com., Altamonte Springs, 1983-85, Rep. Coun. of '76, Seminole County, 1982-87; mem. Seminole County Libr. Adv. Bd., 1989-92, sec., 1990, pres., 1991, Seminole County Citizens for Quality Edn., 1990-92; mem. Seminole County Sch. Dist. Strategic Planning Com., 1991-99, Leadership Orlando Alumni, 1992-99; bd. dirs. Found. for Seminole County Pub. Schs., Inc., 1992-95, chmn., 1993-94; bd. dirs. Greater Seminole C. of C., 1993; active Lake Brantley HS Band Boosters, 1995-2000, Lake Brantley HS PTSA, 1995-2000, Chorus Boosters, 1997, Leadership Club-Heart of Fla. United Way, 1997; sponsor concerts Orlando Philharm. Orch. for Boys and Girls Clubs. Cen. Fla., 1996-97; regional dir. region 5 Holocaust Remembrance Project, 1997-99. Capt. USAF, 1968-72. Mem. ABA, Am. Corp. Counsel Assn., Am. Intellectual Property Law Assn., Intellectual Property Owners Assn. (chmn. copyright law com. 2003-05), U. Ill. Alumni Club, Phi Kappa Phi, Tau Beta Pi, Sigma Tau, Eta Kappa Nu Republican. Home: 1675 Tupolo Dr San Jose CA 95124-4754 Office: M/S 1A-PB 5301 Stevens Creek Blvd Santa Clara CA 95051 Office Phone: 408-553-2772. Personal E-mail: JimandRuthann@comcast.net. Business E-Mail: jim_simon@agilent.com.

SIMON, JOHN R., utilities executive; B, Colo. Coll., Colo. Springs; law degree, Georgetown U., Washington. Ptnr. Hallenbeck, Lascell, LLP, Rochester, NY; exec. v.p. global human capital TeleTech Holdings, Inc., Denver; sr. v.p. human resources PG&E Corp., San Francisco, sr. v.p. human resources Pacific Gas & Electric Co. subs. Office: PG&E Corp One Market Spear Tower Ste 2400 San Francisco CA 94105-1126 Office Phone: 415-267-7070. Office Fax: 415-267-7268.

SIMON, MELVIN I., molecular biologist, educator; b. NYC, Feb. 8, 1937; s. Hyman and Sarah (Liebman) S.; m. Linda, Jan. 7, 1959; children— Joshua, David, Rachel BS, CCNY, 1959; PhD, Brandeis U., 1963. Postdoctoral fellow Princeton U., N.J., 1963-65; prof. biology U. Calif.-San Diego, La Jolla, 1965-82, Calif. Inst. Tech., Pasadena, 1982—, chmn., 1995-2000, prof., 2000—. Pres., dir. Agouron Inst., La Jolla, 1980— Contbr. articles to profl. jours. Mem. Nat. Acad. Scis. (Selman A. Waksman microbiology award 1991), Am. Soc. Microbiology

SIMON, NANCY LYNN, performing arts educator, director; b. Chgo., June 20, 1942; d. Otis Benjamin Simon and Virginia Ruth Gilliland. BA, Whitman Coll., Walla Walla, Wash., 1959—63; MA, Tufts U., Somerville, Mass., 1963—65; PhD, U. Wash., Seattle, 1965—75. Paul Garrett prof. dramatic arts Whitman Coll., 1967—, dir. Harper Joy Theatre, 1967—. Freelance theatre/opera dir. Tacoma Opera, 1983—, Seattle Opera Cmty. Outreach, 1983—, Bellevue Civic Theatre, 1983—, Walla Walla Opera, 1983—, Juneau Lyric Opera, Alaska, 1983—, Shepherd Sch. Music Rice U., Houston, 1983—. Recipient George Ball Advising Excellence award, Whitman Coll., 1997, Thomas D. Howells award for disting. tchg. in humanities and arts, 2005, Paul Garrett Endowed Professorship award, 2006, Faculty award, Whitman Alumni Assn., 2007. Mem.: Artists Trust, Theatre Comm. Group, US Inst. Theater Tech., Actors' Equity Assn. Office: Whitman Coll 345 Boyer Ave Walla Walla WA 99362

SIMON, RALPH E., electronics executive; b. Passaic, NJ, Oct. 20, 1930; s. Paul and Sophie (Epstein) S.; m. Elena Schiffman, June 22, 1952; children: Richard L., David P., Michael A. BA, Princeton U., 1952; PhD, Cornell U., 1959. Mem. tech. staff RCA Labs., Princeton, N.J., 1958-67, dir., 1967-69; mgr. RCA Electronic Components, Lancaster, Pa., 1969-75; v.p. RCA Solid State Div., Lancaster, Pa., 1975-80; v.p. optoelectronics div. Gen. Instrument Corp., Palo Alto, Calif., 1980-84; pres. Lytel Inc., Somerville, N.J., 1984-87; pres., CEO QT Optoelectronics, Sunnyvale, Calif., 1989—. Dir. Xsirius Scientific, Inc., Marina Del Rey, Calif., 1988-91, Applied Electron Corp., Santa Clara, Calif., 1987—. Pres., mem. Lawrence Twp. Bd. Edn., Lawrenceville, N.J., 1964-69, Community Action Orgn., 1967-69. Recipient UK Zworykin prize IEEE, 1973. Office: QT Optoelectronics 3001 Orchard Pkwy San Jose CA 95134-2017

SIMON, RONALD ISAAC, financial executive; b. Cairo, Nov. 4, 1938; came to U.S., 1942; s. David and Helene (Zilkha) S.; m. Anne Faith Hartman, June 19, 1960; children: Cheryl, Eric, Daniel. BA, Harvard U., 1960; MA, Columbia U., 1962, PhD, 1968. V.p. Harpers Internat., NYC, 1959-62; fin. analyst Amerace Corp., NYC, 1965-66; v.p. Am. Foresight Inc., Phila., 1966-67; asst. to pres. Avco Corp., Greenwich, Conn., 1967-70; exec. v.p. Avco Community Developers Inc., La Jolla, Calif., 1970-73; pres. Ronald I. Simon Inc., La Jolla, 1973—99; pres., CEO Delta Data Systems Corp., Phila., 1980-81; exec. v.p. Towner Petroleum Corp., Houston, 1983-85; mng. dir., chief fin. officer The Henley Group Inc., La Jolla, 1986-90; pvt. practice fin. cons. La Jolla, 1990—2000. Vice-chmn. bd. dirs. Softnet Corp., San Francisco, 1998—2002, acting chmn. and CEO, 2001; CFO WingCast LLC, San Diego, 2001—02; bd. dirs. Collateral Therapeutics, Inc., San Diego, 1999—2002; exec. v.p., CFO/bd. dirs. Western Water Co., San Diego, 1997—2000; bd. dirs. Am. Independence Corp., NY, 2002—, WFS Fin., Inc., Irvine, Calif., 2003—06, BDI Investments, San Diego, 2003—05, Cardium Therapeutics, 2006—, Ellington Fin. LLC, 2007—. Bd. dirs. San Diego Opera Co., 1988-90, Univ. Art Gallery U. Calif., San Diego, 1991-95; bd. dirs., treas. Lyric Opera, San Diego, 2003-2005; audit com. San Diego Zool. Soc. Ford Found. fellow, 1963-65.

SIMON, SHELDON WEISS, political science professor; b. St. Paul, Jan. 31, 1937; s. Blair S. and Jennie M. (Dim) S.; m. Charlann Lilwin Scheid, Apr. 27, 1962; 1 child, Alex Russell BA summa cum laude, U. Minn., 1958, PhD, 1964; MPA, Princeton U., 1960; postgrad., U. Geneva, 1962—63. Asst. prof., then prof. U. Ky., 1966-75; prof. polit. sci. Ariz. State U., 1975—, chmn. dept., 1975-79, dir. Ctr. Asian Studies, 1980-88. Vis. prof. George Washington U., 1965, U. B.C., Can., 1972-73, 79-80, Carleton U., 1976, Monterey Inst. Internat. Studies, 1991, 96, Am. Grad. Sch. Internat. Mgmt., 1991-92; cons. USIA Rsch. Analysis Corp., Am. Enterprise Inst. Pub. Policy Rsch., Hoover Instn., Orkand Corp.; cons., dir. S.E. Asian Projects, Nat. Bur. Asian Rsch., 1998—; Smithsonian Instn. lectr. internat. politics Crystal and Regent Cruise Lines, 2000—; vis. Asia-Pacific mentor prof. US Naval War Coll., 2008-09. Author: Asian Neutralism and U.S. Policy, 1975, The ASEAN States and Regional Security, 1982, The Future of Asian-Pacific Security Collaboration, 1988; editor: The Military and Security in the Third World, 1978, East Asian Security in the Post-Cold War Era, 1993, Southeast Asian Security in the New Millenium, 1996, The Many Faces of Asian Security, 2001, Disrupting Violence: Religion and Conflict in South and Southeast Asia, 2007, China, the United States and Southeast Asia, Contending Perspectives on Politics, Economics and Security, 2008, others; contbr. articles to profl. jours., chpts. to books. Mem. Com. Fgn. Relations, Phoenix, 1976—; bd. dirs. Phoenix Little Theater, 1976-79 Grantee Am. Enterprise Inst., 1974, Earhart Found., 1979, 81, 92, 84, 88, U.S. Inst. Peace, 1994-96, 2000-01, Nat. Bur. Asian Rsch., 1998, W. Alton Jones Found., 2000, U.S. Pacific Command, 2002-03; Hoover Instn. fellow, 1980, 85; named Outstanding Alumni Notable Achievement, U. Minn., 2007. Mem. Am. Polit. Sci. Assn., Assn. Asian Studies, Internat. Studies Assn. (profl. ethics com. 1987-91, v.p. 1991-93), Asia Soc. (contemporary affairs com. 1987-92), U.S. Coun. for Asia-Pacific Security (exec. bd. 1998-2003), Phi Beta Kappa. Democrat. Jewish. Avocations: acting, singing, tennis. Home: 5630 S Rocky Point Rd Tempe AZ 85283-2134 Office: Ariz State U Polit Sci Dept Tempe AZ 85287-3902 Office Phone: 480-965-1317. Business E-Mail: shells@asu.edu.

SIMONDS, JOHN EDWARD, retired newspaper editor; b. Boston, July 4, 1935; s. Alvin E. and Ruth Angeline (Rankin) S.; m. Rose B. Muller, Nov. 16, 1968; children— Maximillian P., Malia G.; children by previous marriage— Rachel F. Cobb, John B. BA, Bowdoin Coll., 1957. Reporter Daily Tribune, Seymour, Ind., 1957-58, UPI, Columbus, Ohio, 1958-60; reporter, asst. city editor Providence Jour. Bull., 1960-65, Washington Evening Star, 1965-66; corr. Gannett News Svc., Washington, 1966-75; mng. editor Honolulu Star Bull., 1975-80, exec. editor, 1980-87, sr. editor, editl. page editor, 1987-93; exec. Hawaii Newspaper Agy., Honolulu, 1993-99; reader rep. The Honolulu Advertiser, Honolulu, 1999—2002; ret., 2002. Served with U.S. Army, 1958. Mem. Am. Soc. Newspaper Editors, AP Mng. Editors, Soc. Profl. Journalists, Nat. Conf. Editl. Writers, Orgn. News Ombudsmen, Hawaii Lit. Arts Coun. Home: 5316 Nehu Pl Honolulu HI 96821-1941 Office: The Honolulu Advertiser 605 Kapiolani Blvd Honolulu HI 96813-5195 Home Phone: 808-373-3609; Office Phone: 808-383-7984. Personal E-mail: simondsj001@hawaii.rr.com.

SIMONE, ROBERT M., broadcast executive; b. Springfield, Mass., Dec. 11, 1949; V.p., gen. mgr. Sta. KDVR-TV, Denver, 1997—. Office: Sta KDVR TV 100 E Speer Blvd Denver CO 80203-3437

SIMONI, ROBERT D., biology educator; married; 3 children. BA in Biology, San Jose State Coll., 1962; PhD in Biochemistry, U. Calif., Davis, 1966. Postdoct. fellow biology dept. Johns Hopkins U., Balt., 1966-68, rsch. assoc., 1968-71; asst. prof. dept. biol. scis. Stanford (Calif.) U., 1971-77, assoc. prof. dept. biol. scis., 1977-82, prof. dept. biol. scis., 1982—, chmn. dept. biol. scis., 1985-86, 89-94. Vis. scholar Max-Planck Inst. Biology, Tubingen, Germany, 1977-78; ad hoc mm. cell biology study sect. NIH, 1973, biochemistry study sect., 1975, mem. biochemistry study sect., 1976-80, mem. chmn.'s adv. com. to dir. on peer review, 1979, chmn. phys. biochemistry study sect., 1979-80, mem. cellular and molecular basis of disease rev. pcoml. Gen. Med. Scis., 1987-91; spkr., lectr. in field. Editor: Jour. Biochemistry, 1996, Jour. Biochemistry, Molecular Biology and Biophysics, 1996; assoc. editor, mem. editl. bd. Jour. Biol. Chemistry, 1987—; mem. editl. bd. Jour. Supramolecular Structure, 1978-86; developer Jour. biol. Chemistry On Line, 1994. contbr. numerous articles to profl. jours. Fellow NSF, 1966-68, Fulbright fellow, 1977-78; recipient William C. Rose award Am. Soc. Biochemistyr and Molecular Biology, 1998. Mem. Am. Cancer Soc. (biochemistry-carcinogenesis rev. panel 1979-80, chmn. 1986-87). Home: 563 Jefferson Dr Palo Alto CA 94303-2834 Office: Stanford U Biol Scis Dept Gilbert Bldg 326 B Stanford CA 94305-5020

SIMONS, LYNN OSBORN, educator; b. Havre, Mont., June 1, 1934; d. Robert Blair and Dorothy (Briggs) Osborn; m. John Powell Simons, Jan. 19, 1957; children: Clayton Osborn, William Blair. BA, U. Colo., 1956. Tchr. Midvale (Utah) Jr. H.S., 1956-57, Sweetwater county Sch. Dist. 1, Rock Springs, Wyo., 1957-58, U. Wyo., 1959-61, Natrona County Sch. Dist. 1, Casper, Wyo., 1963-64; credit mgr. Gallery 323, Casper, 1972-77; Wyo. state supt. pub. instrn. Cheyenne, 1979-91; sec.'s regional rep. region VIII U.S. Dept. Edn., Denver, 1993—2001; mem. Denver Fed. Exec. Bd., 1995-2001; mem. exec. bd. combined Fed. campaign, 1994—2001; ednl. cons., 2001—03; state planning coord. Capitol Bldg., Cheyenne, Wyo., 2003; adj. instr. Laramie County CC, 2008—. Mem. State Bds. Charities and Reform, Land Commrs., Farm Loan, 1979-91; mem. State Commns. Capitol Bldg., Liquor, 1979-91; Ex-officio mem. bd. trustees U. Wyo., 1979-91; ex-officio mem. Wyo. Community Coll. Commn., 1979-91; adjunct English instr. Laramine County Cmty. Coll., Cheymne, Wyo; mem. steering com. Edn. Commn. of the States, 1988-90; mem. State Bd. Edn., 1971-77, chmn., 1976-77; advisor Nat. Trust for Hist. Preservation, 1980-86; bd. visitors coll. arts and scis. U. Wyo., 1998—. Bd. dirs. Cheyenne Bot. Gardens Found., 2004—. Mem. LWV (pres. 1970-71). Democrat. Episcopalian.

SIMONS, STEPHEN, mathematics professor, researcher; b. London, Aug. 11, 1938; came to U.S., 1965; s. Jack Isidore Simons and Ethel Esther (Littman) Harris; m. Jacqueline Mania Berchadsky, Aug. 13, 1963; 1 son, Mark. BA, Cambridge U., Eng., 1959, PhD, 1962. Instr. U. B.C., Vancouver, Can., 1962-63; asst. prof. U. BC., Vancouver, Can., 1964-65, U. Calif., Santa Barbara, 1965-67, assoc. prof., 1967-73, prof., 1973—2002, prof. emeritus, 2002—, chmn. dept., 1975-77, 88-89. Trustee Math. Scis. Rsch. Inst., Berkeley, Calif., 1988-94. Peterhouse rsch. fellow, Cambridge U., 1963-64. Mem. Am. Math. Soc. Office: Univ Calif Dept Math Santa Barbara CA 93106

SIMONSON, SUSAN KAY, social worker; b. La Porte, Ind., Dec. 5, 1946; d. George Randolph and Myrtle Lucille (Opfel) Menkes; m. Richard Bruce Simonson, Aug. 25, 1973. BA with honors, Ind. U., 1969; MA, Washington U., St. Louis, 1972. Perinatal social worker Yakima Valley Meml. Hosp., Yakima, Wash., 1979-81, dir. patient support program, 1981—98, dir. social svc., 1982-98; instr. Spanish, ethnic studies, sociology Yakima Valley Coll., Yakima, Wash., 1981—2009. Pres. Yakima Child Abuse Council, 1983-85; developer nat. patient support program, 1981. Contbr. articles to profl. jours. Mem. adv. council Robert Wood Johnson Found. Rural Infant Health Care Project, Yakima, 1980, Pregnancy Loss and Compassionate Friends Support Groups, Yakima, 1982—, Teen Outreach Program, Yakima, 1984—. Recipient NSF award, 1967, discharge planning program of yr. regional award Nat. Glasrock Home Health Care Discharge Planning Program, 1987; research grantee Ind. U., 1968, Fulbright grantee U.S. Dept. State, 1969-70; Nat. Def. Edn. Act fellowship, 1970-73, Lillian World award, 2007. Mem. NASW, Soc. Hosp. Social Work Dirs. Am. Hosp. Assn. (regional award 1989), Nat. Assn. Childrens Hosp. (bd. trustee, 2008-), Phi Beta Kappa.

SIMONYI, CHARLES, software engineer; b. Budapest, Hungary, Sept. 10, 1948; m. Lisa Persdotter. BS in Engring. Math., U. Calif., Berkeley, 1972; PhD in Computer Sci., Stanford U., 1976; PhD (hon.), U. Pecs, Hungary, 2001. Developer Xerox Palo Alto Rsch. Ctr. (PARC), Calif., 1972-80; dir. application develop., chief architect, and disting. engr. Microsoft Rsch. Corp., Redmond, Wash., 1981—2002; co-founder, pres., CEO Intentional Software Corp., Bellevue, Wash., 2002—. Trustee Inst. for Advanced Study, Princeton, NJ, 1997—, pres. of the corp., 2003—, elected chmn. bd. trustees, 2008—. Recipient Wharton Infosys Bus. Transformaton award, 2004; named one of 400 Richest Americans, Forbes mag., 2006. Mem. NAE, Hungarian Acad. Sci. (corres. mem.); fellow Am. Acad. Arts & Scis. Achievements include development of new approaches in programming technology; program representation where new abstraction mechanisms can be introduced without invalidating legacy code; created the first WYSIWYG (what you see is what you get) text editor called Bravo; endowed a chair for the Public Understanding of Science at Oxford University (1995) and a Charles Simonyi Professorship for Theoretical Physics at the Institute for Advanced Study, Princeton, NJ (1997), among many other educational and charitable contributions through the Charles Simonyi Fund for Arts and Sciences; fulfilled a lifelong dream and became the fifth space tourist for $25 million to take a trip to the International Space Station with Russian cosmonauts on the Russian Soyuz TMA-10 mission in April, 2007. The trip lasted a total of 13 days. Returned to Earth on April 21, 2007; paid $35 million for second trip on the Russian Soyuz TMA-14 mission to the International Space Station in March, 2009. The trip will last 13 days. This trip that makes him the first two-time space tourist. Office: Charles Simonyi Fund For Arts And Scienc PO Box 85900 Seattle WA 98145-1900 Office Phone: 425-467-6600. Office Fax: 425-467-6601. E-mail: charles@intentsoft.com.

SIMPLOT, SCOTT R., diversified food products company executive; b. Boise, Idaho, Oct. 11, 1946; s. John Richard and Ruby Simplot; m. Maggie Simplot. BA, U. Idaho, 1968; MBA, U. Pa., 1973; D Adminstrv. Sci (hon.), U. Idaho, 2004. Chmn. The J.R. Simplot Co., Boise, 1994—. Named one of Forbes' Richest Americans, 2006. Office: The J R Simplot Co PO Box 27 Boise ID 83707-0027

SIMPLOT, TOM, Councilman; Bar: Ariz.; lic. realtor. Former sr. adv. Gov. Fife Symington; former adv. Maricopa County Supr. Betsey Bayless; councilman, Dist. 4 Phoenix City Coun., 2003—; vice mayor City of Phoenix. Former pres. Maricopa County Bd. Health, Maricopa County Indsl. Devel. Authority; mem. Fed. Comm. Commn. Intergovernmental Adv. Com., Housing & Neighborhoods, Seniors, Families & Youth, Transp. & Infrastructure Coms. Chmn. METRO Bd. Dirs.; vice chmn. Phoenix Encanto Village Planning Com.; former chmn. Phoenix Hist. Preservation Commn.; bd. mem. Valle del Sol; mem. Phoenix Housing Commn. Mem.: Arizona Multi-housing Assn. (pres.). Office: 200 W Washington St 11th Fl Phoenix AZ 85003 Office Phone: 602-262-7447. Office Fax: 602-534-5438. Business E-Mail: council.district.4@phoenix.gov.*

SIMPSON, ALAN KOOI, lawyer, former senator; b. Cody, Wyo., Sept. 2, 1931; s. Milward Lee and Lorna (Kooi) S.; m. Ann Schroll, June 21, 1954; children: William Lloyd, Colin Mackenzie, Susan Lorna Simpson Gallagher. BS, U. Wyo., 1954, JD, 1958; LLD (hon.), Calif. Western Sch. of Law, San Diego, 1983, Colo. Coll., Colo. Springs, 1986, Notre Dame U., South Bend, Ind., 1987, Am. U., DC, 1989, Rocky Mountain Coll., Billings, Mont., 1996, U. Wyo., Laramie, 1999. Bar: Wyo. 1958, U.S. Supreme Ct. 1964. Asst. atty. gen. State of Wyo., 1959; city atty. City of Cody, 1959-69; ptnr. Simpson, Kepler, and Simpson, Cody, Wyo., 1959-78; mem. Wyo. Ho. of Reps., 1964-77, majority whip, 1973-75, majority floor leader, 1975-77, speaker pro tem, 1977; US Senator from Wyo., 1979—97; asst. majority leader, 1985—87; asst. mimority leader, 1987—95; chmn. vets. affairs com., 1980—84; chmn. fin. subcom. on Social Security and Family Policy; chmn. subcom. on Immigration and Refugee Policy; mem. Spec. Com. on Aging; dir. Inst. Politics Kennedy Sch. Govt. Harvard U., 1999—2000; ptnr. & shareholder Burg Simpson Eldredge Hersh Jardine and Simpson Kepler & Edwards PC, Cody, Wyo. Guest lectr. London exchange program Regent's Coll., London, 1987; vis. lectr. Lombard chair Shorenstein Ctr. for Press, Politics and Pub. Policy, Kennedy Sch. Govt., Harvard U., 1997-2000; mem. Presdl. Debate Commn.; former commr., Am. Battle Monuments Commn., co-chair Continuity in Govt. Commn., 2002-; mem. Iraq Study Group, 2006; mem. external adv. bd. BP Am.; bd. visitors Kennedy Sch. Govt.; co-chmn. Americans for Campaign Reform, adv. com. The Common Good. Author: Right in the Old Gazoo: A Lifetime of Scrapping with the Press, 1997. Chmn. bd. trustees Buffalo Bill Hist. Ctr., Cody; trustee emeritus, Grand Teton Music Festival; former regent Smithsonian Inst., Washington; past adv. bd. Folger Shakespeare Libr., Washington, past bd. mem. Kennedy Ctr. for Performing Arts, Washington. Recipient Nat. Assn. Land Grant Colls. Centennial Alumni award U. Wyo., 1987, Disting. Alumnus award, 1985, Lifetime Svc. award Vietnam Vets. Am., 1993, Thomas Jefferson award in Law U. Va., 1998. Mem. Wyo. Bar Assn., Park County Bar Assn., U. Wyo Alumni Assn. (pres. 1962, 63, Disting. Alumnus award 1985), VFW (life), Am. Legion, Amvets (Silver Helmet award). Lodges: Eagles, Elks, Masons (33 deg., Order of Grand Cross), Shriners, Rotary. Republican. Office: Burg Simpson Eldredge Hersh & Jardine 1135 14th St PO Box 490 Cody WY 82414 also: 1220 Sunshine Ave Ste B Cody WY 82414

SIMPSON, ALLYSON BILICH, lawyer; b. Pasadena, Calif., Feb. 5, 1951; d. John Joseph and Barbaran Rita (Bessolo) Bilich; m. Roland Gilbert Simpson, Aug. 11, 1979; children: Megan Elise, Erin Marie, Brian Patrick. BS, U. So. Calif., LA, 1973, JD, 1976. Bar: Calif. 1976. Staff atty. Gen. Telephone Co., Thousand Oaks, Calif., 1978-79; group staff atty., dir. legis. compliance Pacific Mut. Life Ins. Co., Newport Beach, Calif., 1980-86; corp. counsel and sec. Amicare Ins. Co., Beverly Hills, Calif., 1986; assoc. Leboeuf, Lamb, Leiby & MacRae, LA, 1986-87; from assoc. to ptnr. Musick, Peeler & Garrett, LA, 1988-94; ptnr. Sonnenschein Nath & Rosenthal, LA, 1994-95; sr. v.p., sec., gen. counsel Fremont Compensation Ins. Group, Glendale, Calif., 1995—. Vis. pro. bus. law U. So. Calif., L.A., 1981. Trustee St. Anne's Maternity Home Found., L.A., 1991-97; bd. dirs. St. Anne's Maternity Home, L.A., 1993-97. Mem. Western Pension and Benefits Conf., Conf. Ins. Counsel, Am. Corp. Counsel Assn. Republican. Roman Catholic. Avocations: music, reading. Office: Fremont Compensation Ins Group 500 N Brand Blvd Ste 1100 Glendale CA 91203-3392

SIMPSON, COLIN M., state legislator; b. Cheyenne, Wyo., Mar. 5, 1959; m. Debbie Simpson; children: Mac, Nic. BA, Colo. Coll., 1982; JD, U. Wyo., 1985. Atty. Simpson, Kepler & Edwards LLC, 1986—; precinct committeeman, 1988—94; state ctrl. committeeman, 1992—96; mem. Park Co. Planning & Zoning, 1994—98, chmn., 1997—98; mem. Dist. 24 Wyo. House of Reps., 1999—, Spkr. Pro-Tem., 2005—06, Majority Fl. Leader, 2007—08, Spkr. of the House, 2009—. Wyo. & Park Co. Bar Assns.; Cody Co. C of C. Mem. Episc. Ch. Vestry, 1992—95, chmn., 1997—98. Republican. Episcopalian. Mailing: PO Box 490 Cody WY 82414 Office: 213 State Capitol Bldg Cheyenne WY 82002 Office Phone: 307-777-7881, 307-527-7891. Office Fax: 307-777-5466, 307-527-7897. Business E-Mail: csimpson@cody.wtp.net, csimpson@skelaw.com.*

SIMPSON, DAVID WILLIAM, artist, educator; b. Pasadena, Calif., Jan. 20, 1928; s. Frederick and Mary Adeline (White) S.; m. Dolores D. Debus, July 30, 1954; 1 stepchild, Gregory C. Vose; 1 child, Lisa C. B.F.A., Calif. Sch. Fine Arts, 1956; MA, San Francisco State Coll., 1958. Instr. art Am. River Jr. Coll., Sacramento, 1958-60, Contra Costa Jr. Coll., San Pablo, Calif., 1960-65; prof. art U. Calif., Berkeley, 1967-91, prof. emeritus, 1991—. One-man shows include Robert Elkon Gallery, NYC, 1961, 63-64, San Francisco Mus. Art, 1967, Henri Gallery, Washington, 1968, Oakland Mus., 1978, Modernism, San Francisco, 1980-81, 84, 86, 2001, 09, Sheldon Meml. Art Gallery, Lincoln, Nebr., 1990, Mincher/Wilcox Gallery, San Francisco, 1991-93, Angles Gallery, Santa Monica, Calif., 1991-92, 94, 99, Bemis Found., Omaha, 1991, Anthony Ralph Gallery, NYC, 1992, John Berggruen Gallery, San Francisco, 1994, Charlotte Jackson Fine Art, Santa Fe, 1995, 2005, 2007-, Laguna Art Mus., Laguna Beach, Calif., 1995 Haines Gallery, San Francisco, 1997, 99, 2004, 07, Studio La Citta, Verona, Italy, 1998, 2002, 08, Renate Schröder Gallery, Cologne, Germany, 2000-02, Artothek, Cologne, 2002, James Kelly Contemporary, Santa Fe, 2003, Studio G-7, Bologna, Italy, Sonja Roesch Gallery, Houston, 2005, 07, 09; exhibited in group shows at Mus. Modern Art, NYC, 1963, Carnegie Internat., Pitts., 1961-62, 66-67, LA Mus. Art, 1964, U. Ill., 1969, Expo '70, Osaka, Japan, 1970, Josly Art Mus., Omaha, 1970, John Berggruen Gallery, San Francisco, 1979, 93, Angles Gallery, Santa Monica, 1988, 90, John Good Gallery, NY, 1992, Cheryl Haines Gallery, San Francisco, 1996, Mus. di Arte Moderna e Contemporanea, Trento, Italy, 1996, Studio La Citta, Verona, Italy, 1996-2005, Llonja, Palma De Majorca, Spain, 1997, Mus. Cantonale d'Arte, Lugano, Switzerland, 1997, Haines Gallery, San Francisco, 1997, 2008, Palazzo Ducale, Gubbio, Italy, 1999, Palazzo Ducale, Panza Della Gran Guardia, Verona, 2002, Albright-Knox Gallery, Buffalo, NY, 2005, 2007-, Fondazione Marenostrum Porto Venere, Italy, Kunstverein Lingen Kuntshauz, Germany, 2005, Lausberg Gallery, Toronto, Can., 2007, Dusseldorf, Germany, 2007, Dorsky Gallery, Long Island City, NY, 2009, others; represented in permanent collections including Phila. Mus. Art, Nat. Collection Fine Arts, Wash., Seattle Art Mus., La Jolla (Calif.) Mus. Art, Mus. Modern Art, NYC, San Francisco Mus. Art, Oakland (Calif.) Mus., Panza Collection, Italy, Laguna Art Mus., Laguna Beach, Calif., U. Art Mus., Berkeley, Calif., Mus. Cantonale d'Arte Lugano, Switzerland, Mus. Di Arte Moderna e Contemporanea Di Trento e Roverato, Sassuolo, Panza Collection, Italy, Albright Knox Gallery, Buffalo, San Jose Mus., Calif. Home: 565 Vistamont Ave Berkeley CA 94708-1244 Office: U Calif Dept Art Berkeley CA 94720

SIMPSON, ERIK, state legislator; m. Fawn Simpson; children: Brooke, Colter 1 stepchild, Clancy. BS, U. Idaho, 1988. Journalist, Blackfoot, Idaho; tech. writer Idaho Nat. Lab., 1990; mem. Dist. 32 Idaho House of Reps., 2008—. Bd. dirs. Greater Idaho Falls C. of C., Partnership for Sci. & Technol., Eastern Idaho Cmty. Action Partnership. Republican. Office: Capitol Annex PO Box 83720 Boise ID 83720-0054 also: 6117 N 5th W Idaho Falls ID 83401 Office Phone: 208-334-2475, 208-360-0426. Office Fax: 208-334-2125, 208-542-5447.*

SIMPSON, MICHAEL K., United States Representative from Idaho; b. Burley, Idaho, Sept. 8, 1950; m. Kathy Johnson, 1971. Student, Utah State U.; DDS, Washington U., St. Louis, 1978. Dentist, Blackfoot, Idaho, 1978—; councilmember Blackfoot City Coun., 1980—84; mem. Idaho Ho. Reps., 1985—99, asst. majority leader, 1989, speaker, 1991—99; mem. US Congress from 2nd Idaho dist., Washington, 1999—, ho. appropriations com., agr., resources, transp. & infrastructure com., vet. affairs com. Former spkr. majority caucus chmn. and asst. majority leader Idaho Ho. Reps. Recipient Boyd A. Martin award, Assn. Idaho Cities, Friend of Edn. award, 1994, Citizen of Yr. award, Idaho Family Forum, 1996; named to Idaho's Rep. Party Hall of Fame. Mem.: Am. Legis. Exch. Coun. (state chmn., nat. bd. dirs., Jefferson award 1994), Idaho State Dental Assn. (Pres.'s award 1998). Republican. Avocations: golf, chess, painting. Office: US Ho Reps 1339 Longworth Ho Office Bldg Washington DC 20515-1202 Office Phone: 202-225-5531. Office Fax: 202-225-8216.

SIMPSON, MURRAY L., lawyer; b. Chgo., 1937; BA, U. Ill., 1959; JD, DePaul U., 1961. Staff atty. Securities and Exchange Commn., 1961—64; atty. priv. practice, 1964—91; CEO, mng. dir. Franklin Templeton Investments-Asia, Hong Kong, 1994—2000; exec. v.p., gen. counsel Franklin Resources, Inc., San Mateo, Calif., 2000—06, exec. v.p., 2006—. Mem. unit trust com. Securities and Futures Commn., 1998—2000; chmn. Hong Kong Investment Funds Assn., 2000; mem. financial services advisory com. Hong Kong Trade Devel. Council; former bd mem. Franklin Resources, Inc. Office: Franklin Resources Inc One Franklin Pkwy San Mateo CA 94403 Business E-Mail: mlsimpson@frk.com.

SIMPSON, ROBERT GLENN, lawyer; b. Seattle, June 27, 1932; s. Harold Vernon and Anna Rondeau (McCabe) S.; m. Josephine Anne Heald, June 7, 1959; children: Jenifer Jane, Thomas Glenn, Mary Elizabeth. BS, U. Oreg., 1954; LLB, Willamette U., 1959. Bar: Oreg. 1959. Assoc. William B. Adams Law Office, Portland, Oreg., 1959-67; ptnr. Adams McLaughlin & Simpson, Portland, 1967-70, Schwabe Williamson & Wyatt, P.C., Portland, 1970—. Trustee, sec. Legacy Good Samaritan Hosp. and Med. Ctr., Portland, 1983-89, mem. cmty. bd., 1989-98; trustee, chancellor Episcopal Diocese of Oreg., Portland, 1988-2007. Mem. Oreg. State Bar (exec. com. health law sect. 1987-90), Am. Health Lawyers Assn. (program com. 1987-88), Oreg. Health Lawyers Assn.(pres. 1977-78, legis. com. 1989). Home: 13345 SW Iron Mountain Blvd Portland OR 97219-9306 Office: Schwabe Williamson & Wyatt, PC 1211 SW 5th Ave Ste 1800 Portland OR 97204-3795

SIMS, DOUGLAS D., bank executive; b. 1946; Grad., U. Ill., Urbana, 1968. With St. Louis Bank for Cooperatives, St. Louis, 1969-74; v.p. Ctrl. Bank for Coops., 1974-78; pres. St. Louis Bank for Coops., 1978-84; exec. v.p. Farm Credit Banks of St. Louis, 1984-86, pres., 1986-88, Nat. Bank for Cooperatives, Englewood, Colo., 1988-93; CEO CoBank, Englewood, 1994—. Office: CoBank 5500 S Quebec St Greenwood Village CO 80111-1914

SIMSON, CLAUDINE, computer company executive; married; 2 children. BEE, INSA, Toulouse, France, PhD in Semiconductor Physics, 1978; three hon. degrees. Device physicist Bell-Northern Rsch., France; R&D and sr. exec. positions, including gen. mgr. global microelectronics & microwave components bus. Nortel Networks, v.p., global tech rsch. & intellectual property, 1997; v.p., chief tech. officer, semiconductor products sector (now Freescale Semiconductor) Motorola, Inc., 2003—07; exec. v.p., chief tech. officer LSI Logic Corp., Milpitas, Calif., 2007—. Established the Nat. Chair for Women in Engring., 1988; involved with Adv. Coun. for Sci. & Tech. to the Prime Minister Can., NRC; Can. rep. US President's Adv. Com. on Internat. Cooperation Policy; hon. chair US Nat. Task Force on Intellectual Property and Knowledge Mgmt.; chmn. bd. directors Micronet R&D, Inc.; spkr. in field. Recipient Chevalier de l'Ordre Nat. du Merite, Pres. France, 1998; named to Hall of Fame of Women in Tech. Internat., 1999; Disting. Fellow, Field Inst., 2004. Fellow: Royal Soc. Can. Achievements include being the youngest PhD in France. Office: LSI Logic Corp 1621 Barber Ln Milpitas CA 95035

SINAY, JOSEPH, retail executive; b. Chgo., Dec. 5, 1920; s. Hyman and Ella S.; m. Ruth Milman, Mar. 7, 1961; 1 dau., Elise Sinay Spilker. Student, Herzl Jr. Coll., 1939. Gen. mgr. Fanchon & Marco Theatres, LA, 1943-54; v.p., founder Interstate United, Chgo., 1953-56; ptnr. Josam Investment Co., LA, 1956-97, Sinay Co. L.L.C., LA, 1997—; pres., CEO R B Industries Inc., LA, 1956-89, also chmn. bd. dirs., cons.; chmn. bd. dirs. Gorian Sinay Land Co., Inc., LA, 1997—. Bd. dirs. Am. Acad. Dramatic Arts; pres. Variety Clubs Internat., 1985-87; gen. chmn. United Jewish Welfare L.A., 1976; pres. We. region Am. Friends Hebrew U., 1980; Calif. fin. chmn. Muskie for Pres., 1972; trustee Idyllwild Arts Found., 1968-73; bd. dirs. Constl. Rights Found., 1973-78. Mem. Nat. Home Furnishing Assn. Jewish. Office: Sinay Co LLC 1801 Century Park E Los Angeles CA 90067-2302 Home Phone: 310-553-2340. Business E-Mail: joe@sinaycompany.com.

SINCLAIR, ALASTAIR JAMES, geology educator; b. Hamilton, Ont., Can., Aug. 1, 1935; s. Burton Leslie and Grace (Isherwood) S.; m. Elizabeth Mary Sylvia Hill, June 13, 1964; children: Alison Trevena, Fiona Tamsin. BS, U. Toronto, Can., 1957, MS, 1958; PhD, U. B.C., Can., 1964. Asst. prof. U. Wash., Seattle, 1962-64, U. B.C., Vancouver, 1964-68, assoc. prof., 1968-74, prof., 1974-98, prof. emeritus, 1999—, head dept. geol. scis., 1985-90, dir. Geol. Engring., 1979-80, 81-82, 92-98. Pres. Sinclair Cons. Ltd., Vancouver, 1980—, Internat. Croesus Venture Corp. (now Zinco Mining Corp.), 2004—07; dir. Deal Capital, 2006—07, Eureka Resources, 2006—, Zinco Mining, 2007—, Waverly Biotech Inc., 2008—. Author: Applied Mineral Inventory Estimation, 2002, Applied Ore Microscopy and Minerology, 2003, Quality Control of Assay Data, 2004, Empirical Methods of Resource/Reserve Estimation, 2006; contbr. articles to profl. jours. Recipient Spl. Tribute Information of Mineral Deposit Research Unit, U. BC, 2008, Selwyn G Blaylock medal, Canadian Inst. Mining Metallurgy & Petroleum, 2009, Frank Woodside Disting Svc. award, Assn. Mineral Exploration British Columbia, 2008; Killam Sr. fellow, 1990—91. Fellow Geol. Assn. Can. (treas. mineral deposits divsn. 1978-89, Disting. Svc. award 2001), Soc. Econ. Geologists; mem. Assn. Profl. Engrs. B.C., Assn. Exploration Geochemists (councillor 1992-96), Can. Inst. Mining, Metallurgy and Petroleum (life, disting. lectr. 1999-2000, Robert Elver award 1991), Geol. Soc. Brazil (hon. mem. sci.-tech. commn. geochemistry 1982), Brazilian Geochem. Soc. (hon.), Assn. Mineral Exploration BC (life Frank Woodside award 2008). Avocations: classical music, skiing, golf. Home: 2972 W 44th Ave Vancouver BC Canada V6N 3K4 Office: U BC Dept Earth and Ocean Scis Vancouver BC Canada V6T 1Z4 Home Phone: 604-261-8477; Office Phone: 604-822-3086. E-mail: asinclai@eos.ubc.ca, ajsincon@shaw.ca.

SINCLAIR, JAMES WALTER, lawyer; b. Twin Falls, Idaho, June 17, 1953; s. James A. and Orriette (Coiner) S.; m. Jeanne L. Williams, Mar. 18, 1983. BA, Stanford U., 1975; JD, U. Idaho, 1978. Bar: Idaho 1978, U.S. Dist. Ct. Idaho 1978. Assoc. Benoit & Alexander, Twin Falls, 1978-81; ptnr. Benoit, Alexander & Sinclair, Twin Falls, 1981-85, Benoit, Alexander, Sinclair, Harwood & High, Twin Falls, 1985—. Pres. Magic Valley Regional Med. Ctr. Found., Inc., Twin Falls, 1987-89; chair ind. affiliates Am. Heart Assn., 1992-93, chair-elect Rocky Mountain com., 1993-94; chmn. profl. com. United Way, 1980, bd. dirs., 1981-83, assoc. campaign chmn., 1982, v.p., campaign chmn., 1983, loaned exec., 1989-90; mem. guidance adv. bd. Twin Falls Sch. Dist., 1989-91, incorporator and legal counsel, 1991, sec., bd. dirs. Ednl. Found., Inc., 1991—; bd. dirs. Magic Valley Regional Med. Ctr. Found., Inc., 1987-90, pres., 1989; mem. profl. adv. com. Coll. So. Idaho Estate Planning Coun., 1991—. Mem. ABA (young lawyers divsn. 1978-83, chmn. membership Idaho young lawyer divsn. 1978-80, arson project com. 1982-83, law & media com. 1982-83), Am. Heart Assn. (bd. dirs. Idaho 1987—, chmn. 1992-93, divsn. pres. 1993—, co-chair divsn. heart ball 1993—, chair North West Rocky Mountain Region heart com. 1994, chair Idaho long range/ strategic planning com. 1994—, bd. dirs. 1996—, nominating issues task force 1996, co-chair structure task force 1996, Meritorious Achievement award 1996), Internat. Assn. Def. Coun., Def. Rsch. Inst., Idaho Bar Assn. (profl. conduct review com. 1982-84, civil rules adv. bd. 1984-88, fee arbitration com. 1996, sec./treas. Ffith Jud. Dist. 1980-81, v.p. Fifth Dist. 1981), Idaho Def. Counsel Assn., Young Family Christian Assn. (bd. dirs. 1981-83, membership com. 1982-83, first v.p. 1983), Stanford Club Idaho (co-pres. 1982-83). Avocations: skiing, golf, tennis, jogging. Office: Benoit Alexander Sinclair Harwood & High PO Box 366 126 2d Ave N Twin Falls ID 83303-0366

SINCLITICO, DENNIS J., lawyer; b. St. Louis, Jan. 9, 1947; BA, U. San Diego, 1968; JD cum laude, U. Wis., 1971. Bar: Wis. 1971, Calif. 1972, U.S. Dist. Ct. (cen. and so. dists.) Calif. 1972. Prof. Calif. Coll. Law, 1972; ptnr. Sinclitico & Burns PLC, Long Beach, Calif. Arbitrator spl. arbitration plan Los Angeles County Superior Ct., 1975—. Mem. Am. Bd. Trial Advocates (nat. exec. com. 1978—, pres. L.A. chpt., editor newsletter), Long Beach Bar Assn., State Bar Wis., State Bar Calif., Assn. So. Calif. Def. Counsel (program chmn. 1980-81, bd. dirs. 1980—), Cal-Abota (chair 1994), Ball-Hunt Ins of Ct. (barrister), Phi Alpha Delta. Office: Sinclitico & Burns PLC 330 Golden Shore # 410 Long Beach CA 90802 Office Phone: 562-628-1919. Business E-Mail: dsinclitico@sin-burns.com.

SINCOFF, STEVEN LAWRENCE, chemistry educator; b. NYC, Apr. 17, 1948; s. Murray B. and Lillian (Goldberg) S.; m. Marcella Seay, June 12, 1993; children by previous marriage: Kristina Lynne, Carolyn Suzanne. BSChemE, N.J. Inst. Tech., 1969, MSChemE, 1972; PhD in Analytical Chemistry, Ohio State U., 1980. Commd. 2d lt. USAF, 1969, advanced through grades to lt. col., 1987, retired, 1991, fuels mgmt. officer Albuquerque and Galena, Alaska, 1970-74; chem. engr. Aero. Systems Div., Wright-Patterson AFB, Ohio, 1974-77; assoc. prof. chemistry USAF Acad., Colorado Springs, Colo., 1980-84, dir. continuing edn. dept. chemistry, 1982-84; chief gas analysis lab. McClellan (AFB) Cen. Lab., Calif., 1984-88; exec. officer to comdr. Tech. Ops. Div. McClellan AFB, Calif., 1988-89, chief info. officer Calif., 1989-91; gen. mgr. ChemWest Analytical Lab., Sacramento, 1991-92; dir. ops. Barringer Labs., Inc., Golden, Colo., 1992-94; instr. chemistry C.C. Aurora, Colo., 1995-98, Butte Coll., Oroville, Calif., 1998—, Met. State Coll. of Denver, 1995—98. Reviewer chemistry textbooks Saunders Pub., Phila., 1983-84, Prentice-Hall Pub., 2003-. Mem. Am. Chem. Soc., Air Force Assn. Jewish. Avocation: hiking. Home and Office: 14574 Carnegie Rd Magalia CA 95954-9647 Office: Butte Coll Dept Chemistry Oroville CA 95965 Office Phone: 530-895-2595. E-mail: sincoffst@butte.edu.

SINEGAL, JAMES D., wholesale distribution executive; b. 1936; BA, San Diego State U., 1959. With Fed-Mart Corp., 1954-77, exec. v.p.; v.p. Builders Emporium, 1977-78; exec. v.p. Price Co., 1978-79; with Sinegal/Chamberlin & Assocs., 1979-83; COO Costco Wholesale Corp., Issaquah, Wash., 1983—93, pres., 1993—, CEO, 1988—, bd. dir. Named one of 100 Most Influential People, Time mag., 2006. Address: Costco Wholesale PO Box 34331 999 Lake Dr Ste 200 Issaquah WA 98027-8982*

SINEMA, KYRSTEN, state legislator; b. Tucson, July 12, 1976; MS in Social Work, Ariz. State U., 1999, JD, 2004. Social worker Washington Elem. Sch. Dist., Phoenix, 1995—2002; pvt. practice atty., 2005—; mem. Dist. 15 Ariz. House of Reps., 2005—, asst. minority leader. Adj. prof. Ariz. State U. Sch. Social Work, 2003—; mem. Commn. Prevent Violence Against Women, 2006—. Bd. dirs. Ariz. Death Penalty Forum, 2003—, Girls for a Change, 2005—, Ariz. Ctr. Progressive Leadership, 2006—; pres. bd. dirs. Cmty. Outreach & Advocacy for Refugees (COAR), 2005—. Recipient Stonewall Dem.'s Legislator of Yr. award, 2005, CHOICE award, Planned Parenthood, 2006; named Legislator of Yr., Ariz. Pub. Health Assn., 2006; named a Legis. Hero, Ariz. League Conservation Voters, 2006. Mem.: NOW, Progressive Dem.'s of America (nat. bd. dirs. 2005—), Nat. Assn. Social Workers (Legislator of Yr. 2006), League of Women Voters, Ariz. Edn. Assn., Ariz. Atty.'s for Criminal Justice, Ariz. Advocacy Network, Sierra Club (Most Valuable Player 2005, 2006). Democrat. Office: Ariz House Reps Capitol Complex 1700 W Washington Rm 321 Phoenix AZ 85007 Office Fax: 602-926-5058, 602-417-3015. Business E-Mail: ksinema@azleg.gov.*

SINGER, ALLEN MORRIS, lawyer; b. Mpls., Dec. 30, 1923; s. William and Ida (Simenstein) S. JD, U. Chgo., 1948; LLM, Harvard U., Cambridge, Mass., 1958. Bar: Ill. 1948, Calif. 1949. Pvt. practice, 1950-55, 59—; v.p., sec., gen. counsel ABM Industries, San Francisco, 1969-85. Assoc. prof. law U. Oreg., 1955-59; lectr. law Stanford (Calif.) U., 1960-62; of counsel Cooper, White & Cooper, San Francisco, 1970-97. Contbr. articles to profl. jours. Mem. U. Chgo. Nat. Alumni Cabinet, 1978-80. 2nd lt., USAAF, 1943-45. Mem. ABA, San Francisco Bar Assn., Calif. Bar Assn. Office: 1070 Green St Ste 703 San Francisco CA 94133-5414 Home Phone: 415-447-5495; Office Phone: 415-673-9149.

SINGER, FREDERICK RAPHAEL, medical researcher; b. St. Louis, June 27, 1939; s. Meyer and Lee (Minkle) S.; m. Sandra Joy Barnes, Aug. 16, 1964; children: Stefanie, Jeffrey. Student, UCLA, 1956—59; BS, U. Calif., Berkeley, 1960; MD, U. Calif., San Francisco, 1963. Diplomate Am. Bd. Internal Medicine, Am. Bd. Endocrinology and Metabolism. Intern UCLA Affiliated Hosp., 1963-64; resident VA Hosp., LA, 1964-65, 68-69; instr. in medicine Harvard U., Boston, 1971-72; asst. prof. medicine UCLA, 1972-73, U. So. Calif., LA, 1973-74, assoc. prof., 1974-78, prof., 1978-89, prof. orthop. surgery, 1980-89; dir. Bone Ctr. Cedars-Sinai Med. Ctr., LA, 1989-92, clin. prof. medicine, 1993—. Dir. Osteoporosis/Metabolic Bone Disease program St. Johns Hosp. and Health Ctr., Santa Monica, Calif., 1992—; dir. Skeletal Biology Lab, John Wayne Cancer Inst., Santa Monica, 1992—; mem. endocrine and metabolic drug adv. com. FDA, USPHS, Bethesda, Md., 1983-87. Author: Paget's Disease of Bone, 1977; contbr. numerous articles, revs. to profl. jours. Vice chmn. cmty. adv. com. Univ. H.S., L.A., 1984. Capt. USAF, 1965-67. Calif. State scholar, 1956-60; clin. investigator VA, 1971-73. Mem. Endocrine Soc., Am. Soc. Clin. Investigation, Am. Soc. Bone and Mineral Rsch. (chmn. pub. affairs 1981-86, coun. 1987, pres.-elect 1989, pres. 1990), Paget's Disease Found. (chmn. bd. dirs. 1990—2006), Fibrosis Dysplasia Found. (bd. dirs. 2006—). Office: John Wayne Cancer Inst 2200 Santa Monica Blvd Santa Monica CA 90404-2302 Personal E-mail: singerf@yahoo.com.

SINGER, GARY JAMES, lawyer; b. LA, Oct. 8, 1952; s. Stanley Merle and Ernestine Alice (Brandstatter) S.; m. Melanie Carol Rabin, Mar. 19, 1978; children: Brian, Kimberly, Andrew. BA magna cum laude, U. Calif., Irvine, 1974; JD cum laude, Loyola U., 1977. Bar: Calif. 1977, U.S. Dist. Ct. (fed. dist.) 1978. Assoc. O'Melveny & Myers LLP, LA, 1977-84, Newport Beach, Calif., ptnr., head Irvine, Calif., 1985—, ptnr., head bus. practice group Newport Beach, Calif. Bd. dirs. Irvine Barclay Theatre, 1990-98, chmn. 1993-96; chair bd. dir. Com. on Product Liability and Tort Reform, 1999-; lectr. Continuing Legal Edn., Merger and Acquisition Practice (1997, 1999), Calif. Continuing Edn. of the Bar, Calif. State Bar Assn., Euromoney Conf. Editor-in-chief Loyola of LA Law Review, 1976—77. Bd. dir. Calif. C. of C., Orange County Bus. Com. Arts, 1999—, U. Calif. Irvine Found., 1998—, Human Options, 1982—86, Big Canyon Country Club, 1990—93; past pres. U. Calif. Irvine Chancellor's Club. Recipient Lauds and Laurels, 1998; named Disting. Alumni Recipient. Mem.: ABA, Orange County Bar Assn. (past chmn., corp. and bus. law sect.), St. Thomas More Law Honor Soc., Phi Beta Kappa, Alpha Sigma Nu. Avocations: golf, skiing, reading. Office: O'Melveny & Myers LLP 610 Newport Center Dr 17th Fl Newport Beach CA 92660

SINGER, ROBERT, plastic surgeon; b. Buffalo, Oct. 22, 1942; s. Murray and Fay Singer; m. Judith Harris. Student, SUNY, Buffalo, 1960-63; MD, SUNY, 1967. Lic. physician, Calif.; diplomate Am. Bd. Plastic and Reconstructive Surgery. Resident in gen. surgery Stanford Med. Ctr., Palo Alto, Calif., 1967-69, Santa Barbara Cottage and Gen. Hosp., 1972-74; resident in plastic surgery Vanderbilt U., 1974-76; pvt. practice specializing in emergency and trauma San Diego, 1971-72; pvt. practice plastic, reconstructive and aesthetic surgery La Jolla, Calif., 1976—. Clin. prof. plastic surgery U. Calif., San Diego; sr. staff, chief plastic surgery Scripps Meml. Hosp., La Jolla, 1980-86, vice chmn. dept. surgery, 1989-91; co-chmn. editl. adv. bd. New-Beauty Mag. Contbr. articles to profl. jours. Active San Diego Opera, San Diego Mus. of Man, La Jolla Playhouse, Voices for Children, San Diego Zoo, Mus. Photog. Arts, KPBS, others. Served, Vietnam, ret. lt. comdr. USNR, served in emergency dept., Balboa Naval Hosp., San Diego. Named one of Best Cosmetic Surgeons in Country, Town & Country Mag.; named to Best Doctors in America. Fellow ACS; mem. AMA, Calif. Med. Assn., San Diego County Med. Soc. (named to Best Plastic Surgeons in San Diego), San Diego Internat. Soc. Plastic Surgery (pres. 1988-89), Calif. Soc. Plastic Surgeons (pres. 1995-96), Am. Soc. Aesthetic Plastic Surgeons (pres. 1994-95, traveling vis. prof., Plastic Surgery Leadership award), Internat. Soc. Clin. Plastic Surgeons, Am. Soc. Plastic and Reconstructive Surgeons (trustee 1996—, chmn. bd. trustees 1998-99), J.B. Lynch Soc., Royal Soc. Medicine, Am. Assn. for Accreditation of Ambulatory Surgery Facilities (pres. 1991-2000), San Diego Plastic Surgery Soc. (pres. 1989-90), Aesthetic Surgery Edn. and Rsch. Found. (pres., 2000—) Avocations: tennis, travel, pre-columbian art. Office: 9834 Genesee Ave Ste 100 La Jolla CA 92037-1214 Office Phone: 866-660-0206, 858-455-0240.

SINGH, LOREN CHAN, writer, educator; b. Palo Alto, Calif., Sept. 10, 1943; s. Shau Wing and Anna Mae Chan; m. Frances Anastasia Chow, Apr. 19, 1975 (div. Jan. 1988); children: Karen Monique Chan, Pierre Benedict Chan, Marc Henri Chan; m. Sandra Marie Miner, Mar. 14, 2000. AB, Stanford U., Calif., 1965, AM, 1966; MS, Golden Gate U., San Francisco, 1988; PhD, UCLA, 1971. Tchg. asst. UCLA, 1968—69, tchg. assoc., 1969—70; lectr. in history Calif. State U., Northridge, 1970—71, San Jose State U., Calif., 1971—72, asst. prof. history, 1972—76, assoc. prof. history, 1976—80; lectr. history Calif. State U., East Bay, 1980—81; prodn. test technician Nicolet Paratronics Corp., Fremont, Calif., 1982; computer svc. technician Bell-No. Rsch., Mountain View, Calif., 1982—83, rsch. analyst, 1984—85, tech. writer, 1985—87; sr. tech. writer StrataCom, Inc., Campbell, Calif., 1987—88; tech. writer Sun Microsystems, Palo Alto, 1988—90, sr. tech. writer, 1990—2000; tech. editor Brocade Comms. Sys., Inc., San Jose, 2000—02; instr. adult edn. Santa Clara Unified Sch. Dist., Calif., 2002—03; bus driver Serendipity Land Yachts, Ltd., Santa Clara, 2002—05; adminstrv. asst. Microcontroller Pros Corp., Morgan Hill, Calif., 2005—08, editl. consultant, 2008—. Author: Sagebrush Statesman, 1973, Collected Technical Support Notes, 1988, SPARCstation 1 Installation Guide, 1989, Desktop Storage Pack Installation Guide, 1989—90, SPARCstation 2 Installation Guide, 1990, SPARCstation 10 Installation Guide, 1992, SPARCstation 10 Networking and Communication Guide, 1993, SPARCstation 10SX VSIMMs Installation, 1993, SPARCstation 20 HyperSPARC Module Upgrade, 1995, SPARCstation 20 SuperSPARC-II Module Upgrade, 1995, Sun Ultra 1 Reference Material, 1995—96, Sun Ultra 2 Reference Manual, 1996, Sun Ultra 30 Installation Guide, 1997, SPARCstorage FlexiPack Removable Storage Tray Installation Guide, 1997, Sun StorEdge Long Wave Gigabit Interface Converter Service Manual, 1999, Sun StorEdge PCI Dual Fibre Channel Host Adapter Installation, 2000; editor: Chinese-American History Reader, 1976; contbr. articles to profl. jours. Radio sta. trustee ARC, Menlo Park, Calif., 1975—80. Recipient Presdl. Sports award, Pres.'s Coun. Phys. Fitness and Sports, 1973. Mem.: Am. Radio Relay League, South Valley YMCA. Democrat. Sikh. Avocations: swimming, amateur radio, stamp collecting/philately. Home: 195 Blossom Hill Rd # 123 San Jose CA 95123-2348 Personal E-mail: ad6yu@yahoo.com.

SINGLETARY, MIKE, professional football coach, retired professional football player; b. Houston, Oct. 9, 1958; m. Kim Singletary; children: Kristen, Matthew, Jill, Jackie, Brooke, Becky, John. BA in Mgmt., Baylor U., 1981. Middle linebacker Chgo. Bears, 1981-93; linebackers coach Balt. Ravens, 2003—04; asst. head coach, linebackers coach San Francisco 49ers, 2005—08, head coach, 2008—. Motivational spkr. Wash. Speakers Bur. Author: Calling the Shots, 1986; co-author (with Jerry B. Jenkins): Singletary on Singletary, 1991; co-author: (with Russ Pate) Daddy's Home at Last: What it Takes for Dads to Put Families First, 1999; co-author: (with Jay Carty) Mike Singletary One-on-One: The Determination That Inspired Him to Give God His Very Best, 2005. Named NFL Defensive Player of Yr., AP, 1985, 88, Walter Payton Man of Yr., 1990; named to Sporting News Coll. All-Am. team, 1980, NFL Pro Bowl team, 1983-92, Sporting News All-Pro team, 1984-89, 91, College Football Hall of Fame, 1995, Pro Football Hall of Fame, 1998. Achievements include being a member of Super Bowl XX Championship winning Chicago Bears, 1985. Office: San Francisco 49ers 4949 Centennial Blvd Santa Clara CA 95054*

SINGLETON, JOAN VIETOR, publishing executive, writer, film producer; b. LA, Nov. 8, 1951; d. Carl William and Elizabeth Anne (Caulfield) Vietor; m. W. Alexander Sheafe, Apr. 23, 1977 (div. 1981); m. Ralph Stuart Singleton, Dec. 21, 1984. Premiere degre, Universite de Paris, 1971; BA, Hollins Coll., 1972. Asst. to pres. Calif. Fed. Savs., Los Angeles, 1972-73, dir. promotion, publicity, 1973-74; publicist Dave Mirisch Enterprises, Beverly Hills, Calif., 1974-75; owner, pres. Joan Vietor Enterprises, Los Angeles, 1975-79; bus. affairs staff Warner Bros., Inc., Burbank, Calif., 1979-80; pres. Lone Eagle Pub. Co., Los Angeles, 1981—. Assoc. prodr. Stephen King's Graveyard Shift, 1990; prodr., writer Because of Winn-Dixie, 2005. Bd. dirs. The Curtis Sch., 1993—, Crestwood Hills Sch., 1993-95. Mem. Pubs. Mktg. Assn. (bd. dirs. 1984-87). Democrat. Presbyterian. Avocations: skiing, needlepoint, tennis, scuba diving, reading. Office: Lone Eagle Pub Co 2337 Roscomare Rd Los Angeles CA 90077-1851

SINGLETON, MARVIN AYERS, state legislator, otolaryngologist; b. Baytown, Tex., Oct. 7, 1939; s. Henry Marvin and Mary Ruth Singleton. BA, U. of the South, 1962; MD, U. Tenn., 1966. Diplomate Am. Bd. Otolaryngology. Intern City of Memphis Hosps., 1966-67; resident in surgery Highland Alameda City Hosp., Oakland, Calif., 1967-68; resident in otolaryngology U. Tenn. Hosp., Memphis, 1968-71; fellow in otolaryngic pathology Armed Forces Inst. Pathology, Washington, 1971; fellow in otologic surgery U. Colo. at Gallup (N.Mex.) Indian Med. Ctr., 1972; practice medicine specializing in otolaryngology/allergies Joplin, Mo., 1972—. Founder, operator Home and Farm Investments, Joplin, 1975—, staff mem. Freeman Hosp., Dameron Hosp. Stockton, St. John's Hosp., Joplin; cons. in otolaryngology Mo. Crippled Children's Service; pres. Ozark Mfg. Co., Inc., Joplin; mem. St. Joaquin Commn. on Aging, 2005—; dir. St. Mary's Interfaith Svcs., Stockton, 2007—; med. dir. Health Choice NW Mo. Mem. Internat. Arabian Racing Bd., 1983-88; mem. Mo. State Senate, 1990-2003; del. Rep. Nat. Conv., 1988, 92. Served with USNG, 1966-72. Fellow Am. Coll. Surgeons, Am. Acad. Otolaryngologic Allergy (past pres.), Am. Assn. Acad. Asthma, Allergy and Immunology; mem. AMA (Mo. del.), Mo. State Med. Assn., So. Med. Assn., Mo. State Allergy Assn., Ear Nose & Throat Soc. Mo. (past. pres.), Calif. Med. Assn. (trustee 2005—), San Joaquin Med. Soc. (pres. 2006-07), Masons (32d degree), Sigma Alpha Epsilon, Phi Theta Kappa, Phi Chi. Republican. Episcopalian. Home: 1637 W Swain Rd Stockton CA 95207-4172 Office: 7373 W Ln Stockton CA 95210 Home Phone: 209-951-7273; Office Phone: 209-476-5623. Personal E-mail: senatorsingleton@hotmail.com.

SINGLETON, WILLIAM DEAN, publishing executive; b. Graham, Tex., Aug. 1, 1951; s. William Hyde and Florence E. (Myrick) S.; m. Adrienne Casale, Dec. 31, 1983; children: William Dean II, Paige, Adam Nicholas. Student, Tyler Jr. Coll., Tex., El Centro Coll., Dallas; BS, U. Tex., Arlington. Vice chmn., CEO MediaNews Group Inc., Denver, 1983—. Chmn. and pub. Denver Post; chmn. bd. Denver Newspaper Agency; pub. Salt Lake City Tribune; bd. dir. Associated Press, chmn. bd. dir., 2006—; former chmn. Newspaper Assn. Am. Mem. Salvation Army, Am. Heart Assn. of Ft. Bend County. Mem.

Newspaper Assn. Am. (bd. govs.), So. Newspapers Assn., New Eng. Newspaper Assn., NJ Press Assn., Tex. Daily Newspaper Assn., Greater Houston Partnership Assn. Baptist. Office: Denver Post 101 W Colfax Ave Denver CO 80202

SINHA, SUNIL KUMAR, physicist; b. Calcutta, India, Sept. 13, 1939; came to U.S., 1965; s. Sushil Kumar and Romola Sinha; m. Lonny Linde Olsen, Jan. 27, 1962; children: Arjun, Ranjan. BA in Natural Scis., Cambridge U., Britain, 1960, PhD in Physics, 1964. Vis. scientist Bhabha Atomic Rsch. Ctr., Trombay, India, 1965; asst. prof. physics dept. Iowa State U., Ames, 1966-69, assoc. prof., 1969-71, prof. physics, 1972-75; sr. physicist Argonne (Ill.) Nat. Lab., 1975-82; sr. rsch. assoc. Corp. Rsch., Exxon Rsch., Annandale, NJ, 1982-95; sr. scientist and assoc. dir., exptl. facilities div. Argonne (Ill.) Nat. Lab., 1995-2001; prof. physics U. Calif., San Diego, 2001—. Chmn. Div. Condensed Matter Physics Fellowship Com. of Am. Phys. Soc., 1990-91, Conf. X-Ray Physics, 1999; mem. adv. com. US Dept. Energy, 1997-02; co-chair Basic Energy Scis. Advisry Com. subcom. Dept. Energy facilities, 2003. Editor: Ordering in Two Dimensions, 1980, Spin Waves and Magnetic Excitations, 1990; contbr. articles to profl. jours. Recipient Dept. Energy Rsch. Achievement award, 1981, Ernest Orlando Lawrence Meml. award, 1996, Arthur H. Compton award Advanced Photon Source, 2000; Guggenheim fellow, 1982; MRS medal, 2004. Fellow AAAS, Am. Phys. Soc.; mem. Materials Rsch. Soc., Am. Crystallographic Assn. Achievements include research in antiferromagnetism in High Tc materials by neutron diffraction; theory of diffuse X-ray scattering from surfaces.

SINISCALCO, GARY RICHARD, lawyer; b. NYC, Aug. 14, 1943; BA in Econs., Le Moyne Coll., 1965; JD, Georgetown U., 1969. Bar: Calif. Regional counsel, sr. trial atty. EEOC, San Francisco, 1969-78; ptnr. Orrick, Herrington & Sutcliffe, San Francisco, 1978—, past co-chair employment law dept. Mem. adv. bd. Nat. Employment Law Inst.; fellow, Coll. of Labor and Employment Lawyers; lectr. in field. Co-author: Manager's Guide to Lawful Terminations, 1991; author: (with others) Employment Discrimination Law, 1979, 3rd edit., 1996; contbr. articles to profl. jours. Mem. ABA (mem. com. on internat. labor rels. and equal employment opportunity, mgmt. co-chair equal employment opportunity com. 1996-98, co-chair internat. labor law com. 2006—), State Bar Calif., Am. Employment Law Coun. (founder and mem. of the bd.). Office: Orrick Herrington 405 Howard St San Francisco CA 94105 Office Phone: 415-773-5833. E-mail: grsiniscalo@orrick.com.

SINOFSKY, STEVEN J., computer software company executive; BA with hon., Cornell U., 1987; MS in Computer Sci., U. Mass., 1989. With Microsoft Corp., Redmond, Wash., 1989—, software design engr., project lead, develop. tools group, 1989—94, dir., program mgmt., Microsoft Office, 1994—98, v.p., Microsoft Office, 1998—99, sr. v.p. Microsoft Office, 1999—2006, sr. v.p. Windows and Windows Live Engring. group, 2006—. Vis. scholar Harvard U. Bus. Sch., Cambridge, Mass., 1998. Office: One Microsoft Way Redmond WA 98052-6399

SINSHEIMER, ROBERT LOUIS, retired academic administrator, educator; b. Washington, Feb. 5, 1920; s. Allen S. and Rose (Davidson) S.; m. Flora Joan Hirsch, Aug. 8, 1943 (div. 1972); children: Lois June (Mrs. Wickstrom), Kathy Jean (Mrs. Vandagriff), Roger Allen; m. Kathleen Mae Reynolds, Sept. 10, 1972 (div. 1980); m. Karen Current, Aug. 1, 1981. S.B., MIT, 1941, MS, 1942, PhD, 1948. Staff mem. radiation lab. MIT, Cambridge, 1942-46; assoc. prof. biophysics, physics dept. Iowa State Coll., Ames, 1949-55, prof., 1955-57; prof. biophysics Calif. Inst. Tech., Pasadena, 1957-77, chmn. div. biology, 1968-77; chancellor U. Calif., Santa Cruz, 1977-87, chancellor emeritus, 1987—, prof. Santa Barbara, 1988-90, prof. emeritus, 1990—. Editor: Jour. Molecular Biology, 1959-67, Ann. Rev. Biochemistry, 1966-72. Named Calif. Scientist of Year, 1968; recipient N.W. Beijerinck-Virologie medal Netherlands Acad. Sci., 1969 Fellow Am. Acad. Arts and Scis.; mem. Am. Soc. Biol. Chemists, Biophys. soc. (pres. 1970), AAAS, Nat. Acad. Scis. (mem. council 1970-73, chmn. bd. editors Proc. 1972-80), Inst. Medicine. Achievements include discovery of single-stranded DNA, circular DNA; research in first in vitro replication of infective DNA. Avocations: photography, travel. Office: U Calif MCD Biology Santa Barbara CA 93106 Home Phone: 805-683-2247; Office Phone: 805-893-8038. Business E-Mail: sinsheim@lifesci.ucsb.edu.

SION, MAURICE, mathematics professor; b. Skopje, Yugoslavia, Oct. 17, 1928; came to Can., 1960; s. Max and Sarah (Alalouf) S.; m. Emilie Grace Chisholm, Sept. 15, 1957; children: Crispin, Sarah, Dirk. BA, NYU, 1947, MA, 1948; PhD, U. Calif., Berkeley, 1951. Mathematician Nat. Bur. Stds., Washington, 1951-52; instr. U. Calif., 1952-53; asst. prof. U. Calif., 1957-60; mem. Inst. for Advanced Study, Princeton, NJ, 1955-57, 62; asst. prof. U. B.C., Vancouver, Canada, 1960, assoc. prof., 1961, prof., 1964-89, prof. emeritus, 1989—, head math. dept., 1984-86, dir. Quadra Inst. Math., 1970-89. Author: Introduction to Methods of Real Analysis, 1969, Theory Semi Group Valued Measures, 1973; contbr. articles to profl. jours. With U.S. Army, 1953-55. Mem. Am. Math. Soc., Can. Math. Soc. (v.p. 1972-74). Office: U BC Dept Math Vancouver BC Canada V6T 1Z2

SIPCHEN, BOB, reporter; b. Chgo., June 13, 1953; m. Pamela Jean Sipchen; children: Ashley Rose-Anna, Emily Sage, Robert John III. BA in English, U. Calif. Santa Barbara, 1976. Freelance writer, 1980—87; staff writer Orange County Edit. LA Times, 1987—88, staff writer, 1988—98, sr. editor Mag., 1998—2001, assoc. editor Editl. Pages, 2001—. Author: Baby Insane and the Buddha, 1993. Recipient Pulitzer prize, 2002. Mem.: PEN, Nat. Writers Union, Soc. Profl. Journalists, Sigma Delta Chi. Office: LA Times 202 W 1st St Los Angeles CA 90012

SIRIGNANO, WILLIAM ALFONSO, aerospace and mechanical engineer, educator; b. Bronx, NY, Apr. 14, 1938; s. Anthony P. and Lucy (Caruso) S.; m. Lynn Haisfield, Nov. 26, 1977; children: Monica Ann, Jacqueline Hope, Justin Anthony. B.Aero.Engring., Rensselaer Poly. Inst., 1959; PhD, Princeton U., 1964. Mem. research staff Guggenheim Labs., aerospace, mech. scis. dept. Princeton U., 1964-67, asst. prof. aerospace and mech. scis., 1967-69, assoc. prof., 1969-73, prof., 1973-79, dept. dir. grad. studies, 1974-78; George Tallman Ladd prof., head dept. mech. engring. Carnegie-Mellon U., 1979-85; dean Sch. Engring., U. Calif.-Irvine, 1985-94, prof., 1994—. Cons. industry and govt., 1966—; lectr., cons. NATO adv. group on aero. rsch. and devel., 1967, 75, 80; chmn. nat. and internat. tech. congs.; chmn. acad. adv. coun. Indsl. Rsch. Inst., 1985-88; mem. space sci. applications adv. com. NASA, 1985-90, chmn. combustion sci. microgravity disciplinary working group, 1987-90; chmn. com. on microgravity rsch. space studies bd. NRC, 1991-94, Henry Samueli endowed chair in engring., 2004-. Spl. issues editor: Combustion Sci. and Tech., 1969-70, 2000-06; assoc. tech. editor Jour. Heat Transfer, 1986-92; contbr. articles to profl. jours. Recipient Disting. Alumni Rsch. award U. Calif. Irvine, 1992, Recognition award Am. Electronics Assn., 1994, Excellence award Orange County Engring. Coun., 1994; United Aircraft rsch. fellow, 1973-74. Fellow: AAAS, ASME (Freeman scholar 1992), AIAA (Pendray Aerospace Lit. award 1991, Propellants and Combustion award 1992, Energy Systems award 2004, Sustained Svc. award 2006), Am. Phys. Soc.; mem.: NAE, Soc. Indsl. and Applied Math., Combustion Inst. (treas. internat. orgn., chmn. ea. sect., Alfred C. Egerton Gold medal 1996), Inst. Dynamics Explosives and Reactive Sys. (v.p. 1991—95, pres. 1995—99, Oppenheim award 1993). Office: U Calif Irvine Sch Engring S3202 Engring Gtwy Irvine CA 92697-3975 Office Phone: 949-824-3700.

SISK, DANIEL ARTHUR, lawyer; b. Albuquerque, July 12, 1927; s. Arthur Henry and Myrl (Hope) S.; m. Katharine Banning, Nov. 27, 1954; children: John, Sarah, Thomas. BA, Stanford U., 1950, JD, 1954. Bar: N.Mex. 1955, Calif. 1954. Ptnr. firm Modrall, Sperling, Roehl, Harris & Sisk, Albuquerque, 1954-70, 71—; justice N.Mex. Supreme Ct., Santa Fe, 1970. Chmn. bd. Sunwest Fin. Svcs., Inc., Albuquerque, 1975-90. Pres. Legal Aid Soc., Albuquerque, 1960-61; trustee Sandia Sch., 1968-72, Albuquerque Acad., 1971-73, A.T. & S.F. Meml. Hosps., Topeka, 1966-82; bd. dirs. N.Mex. Sch. Banking Found., 1981-85. Served with USNR, 1945-46, PTO; to capt. USMCR, 1951-52, Korea. Mem. N.Mex. Bar Assn., Albuquerque Bar Assn. (dir. 1962-63), ABA, State Bar Calif. Presbyn. (elder). Office: 500 4th St NW Albuquerque NM 87102-5324

SISLEY, BECKY LYNN, physical education educator; b. Seattle, May 10, 1939; d. Leslie James and Blanche (Howe) S.; m. Jerry Newcomb, 1994. BA, U. Wash., 1961; MSPE, U. N.C., Greensboro, 1964, EdD, 1973. Tchr. Lake Washington H.S., Kirkland, Wash., 1961-62; instr. U. Wis., Madison, 1963-65, U. Oreg., Eugene, 1965-68, prof. phys. edn., 1968—2004, women's athletic dir., 1973-79, head undergrad. studies in phys. edn., 1985-92. Co-author: Softball for Girls, 1971; contbr. over 70 articles to profl. jours. Mem. athletic adv. bd. Women's Sports Found., 1993-96. Recipient Honor award, N.W. Dist. AAHPERD, 1988, Nat. Assn. for Girls and Women in Sports, 1995, Disting. Alumni award, Sch. Health and Human Performance, U. N.C., Greensboro, 1996; named to Hall of Fame, U. Oreg. Athletics, 1998, Hall Fame, N.W. Women's Sports Found., Seattle, 1981, Nat. Masters Track and Field Hall of Fame, 2001. Mem. AAHPERD, Oreg. Alliance Health, Phys. Edn., Recreation and Dance (hon. life mem.), Western Soc. for Phys. Edn. of Coll. Women (hon. mem., exec. bd. 1982-85), Oreg. High Sch. Coaches Assn., N.W. Coll. Women's Sports Assn. (pres. 1977-78), Oreg. Women's Sports Leadership Network (dir. 1987-97), Phi Epsilon Kappa, others. Office: U Oreg Phys Activity & Recreation Svcs Eugene OR 97403

SITOMER, ALAN LAWRENCE, literature and language educator; m. Tracy Sitomer; 1 child, Sienna. Lang. arts tchr. Lynwood (Calif.) H.S.; and instr., grad. sch. edn. Loyola Marymount Univ. Co-author (with Michael Cirelli): Hip-Hop Poetry and the Classics, 2004; author: The Hoopster, 2005, Hip-Hop High School, 2006, Homeboyz, 2007. Recipient Classroom Excellence award, So. Calif. Tchrs. of English, 2006; named Tchr. of Yr., Calif. Literacy, 2003, Calif. Tchr. of Yr., 2007. Office: Lynwood High Sch 4050 E Imperial Hwy Lynwood CA 90262 Address: Milk Mug Pub– Ste #253 9190 W Olympic Blvd Beverly Hills CA 90212 E-mail: alanlawrencesitomer@yahoo.com.

SITRICK, MICHAEL STEVEN, public relations executive; b. Davenport, Iowa, June 8, 1947; s. J. Herman and Marcia B. (Bofman) S.; m. Nancy Elaine Eiseman, July 1, 1969; children: Julie, Sheri, Alison. BS in Bus. Adminstrn. and Journalism, U. Md., 1969. Coord. press services Western Elec., Chgo., 1969-70; asst. dir. program services City of Chgo., 1970-72; asst. v.p. Selz, Seabolt & Assocs., Chgo., 1972-74; dir. comm. and pub. affairs Nat. Can Corp., Chgo., 1974-81; dir. comm. Wickes Cos., Inc., San Diego, 1981-82, v.p. comm. Santa Monica, Calif., 1982-84, sr. v.p. comm., 1984-89; chmn., CEO Sitrick & Co., LA and NYC, 1989—. Bd. dirs. Turnaround Mgmt. Assn., Jewish Television Network; mem. adv. bd. The 1939 Club. Author: Spin--How to Turn the Power of the Press to Your Advantage, 1998. Office: Sitrick and Co 1840 Century Pk E Ste 800 Los Angeles CA 90067

SIVORI, JOHN P., health and medical products executive; BBA, Calif. State U., Chico. CPA. Audit mgr. KPMG Peat Marwick; various fin. positions Sutter Health, Sacramento; various sr. mgmt. positions Found. Health Corp., 1994—98; sr. v.p., CFO Health Net Pharm. Svcs. (formerly Integrated Pharm. Svcs.), 1998—2001, pres., 2001; sr. v.p. Health Net, Inc. Office: Health Net Inc 21650 Oxnard St Woodland Hills CA 91367 Office Phone: 818-676-6000.

SIZEMORE, HERMAN MASON, JR., newspaper executive; b. Halifax, Va., Apr. 15, 1941; s. Herman Mason and Hazel (Johnson) S.; m. Connie Catterton, June 22, 1963; children: Jill, Jennifer. AB in History, Coll. William and Mary, 1963; postgrad., U. Mo., 1965; MBA, U. Wash., 1985. Reporter Norfolk (Va.) Ledger-Star, summers 1961, 62, 63; copy editor Seattle Times, 1965-70, copy-desk chief, 1970-75, asst. mng. editor, 1975-77, mng. editor, 1977-81, prodn. dir., 1981-83, asst. gen. mgr., 1984, v.p., gen. mgr., 1985, pres., chief operating officer, 1985—. Vis. instr. Sch. Comms. U. Wash., 1972-78; bd. dirs. Times Comms. Co., Walla Walla Union-Bull, Inc., Yakima Herald-Republic, Blethen Maine Newspapers, Northwestern Mut. Life Ins. Co., 1993—, mem. policyowner examining com., 1985, chmn., 1986. Bd. dirs. Ctrl. Puget Sound Campfire Coun., 1985-91, pres., 1989-90; bd. dirs. Ptnrs. in Pub. Edn., 1987-88, Downtown Seattle Assn.; chmn. bd. dirs. United Way; adv. coun. Puget Sound Blood Ctr. and Program; adv. bd. USO-Puget Sound Area, U. Wash. Sch. Bus. Named Seattle Newsmaker of Tomorrow, 1978; recipient Alumni medallion Coll. William and Mary, 1998. Mem. AP Mng. Editors, Soc. Profl. Journalists, Pacific N.W. Newspaper Assn. (bd. dirs.), Newspaper Assn of Am. (vice-chair newsprint com.), Allied Daily Newspapers Washington, Coll. William and Mary Alumni Assn., Greater Seatt C. of C. (bd. dirs.), U. Wash. Exec. MBA Alumni Assn. (pres. 1988), Wash. Athletic Club (chmn. bd. dirs.), Rainier Club, Rotary. Methodist. Office: Seattle Times PO Box 70 Seattle WA 98111-0070

SKAFF, ANDREW JOSEPH, lawyer, transportation and utilities executive; b. Sioux Falls, SD, Aug. 30, 1945; s. Andrew Joseph and Alice Maxine (Skaff) Skaff; m. Lois Carol Phillips, Oct. 4, 1971; 2 children. BS in Bus. Adminstrn, Miami U., Oxford, Ohio, 1967; JD, U. Toledo, 1970. Bar: Calif. 1971, U.S. Supreme Ct. 1974. Prin., sr. counsel Calif. Pub. Utilities Commn., 1977; gen. counsel Delta Calif. Industries, Oakland, Calif., 1977-82, sec., 1978-82; mem. Silver Rosen, Fischer & Stecher, San Francisco, 1982-84; sr. ptnr. Skaff and Anderson, San Francisco, 1984-90; pvt. practice Law Office of Andrew J. Skaff, 1990-95; ptnr. Knox Ricksen LLP, Oakland, Calif., 1995-97, Crosby, Heafey Roach & May, Oakland, Calif., 1997-99, Energy Law Group LLP, Oakland, Calif., 2000—02. Officer Delta Calif. Industries and subs. Contbr. articles to legal jours.; contbg. mem. law rev. U. Toledo, 1970. Mem. ABA, Calif. Bar Assn., Conf. Calif. Pub. Utilities Counsel, Calif. Cogeneration Coun., Alameda County Bar Assn. Home: 220 The Knoll Orinda CA 94563-2703 E-mail: andy@skafflaw.com.

SKAGGS, BEBE REBECCA PATTEN, college dean, clergywoman; b. Berkeley, Calif., Jan. 30, 1950; d. Carl Thomas and Bebe (Harrison) P. BS in Bible, Patten Coll., 1969; BA in Philosophy, Holy Names Coll., 1970; MA in Bibl. Studies New Testament, Wheaton Coll., 1972; PhD in Bibl. Studies New Testament, Drew U., 1976; MA in Philosophy, Dominican Sch. Philosophy & Theology, 1990; postgrad., U. Calif., Berkeley, 1991-92. Ordained to ministry Christian Evang. Ch., 1963. Co-pastor Christian Cathedral, Christian Evang. Chs. Am., Inc., 1964—; assoc. prof. Patten Coll., Oakland, Calif., 1975-82, dean, 1977—, prof. N.T., 1982—. Presenter in field. Author: Before the Times, 1980, The World of the Early Church, 1990; contbg. author: Internat. Standard Bibl. Ency., rev. edit., 1983, Women's Study Bible, Pneuma Faculty Dialogue. Active Wheaton Coll. Symphony, 1971-72, Drew U. Ensemble, 1971-75, Young Artists Symphony, N.J., 1972-75, Somerset Hill Symphony, N.J., 1973-74, Peninsula Symphony, 1977, 80-81, Madison Chamber Trio, N.J., 1973-75. Named one of Outstanding Young Women of Am., 1976, 77, 80-81, 82; St. Olaf's Coll. fellow, 1990. Mem. AAUP, Am. Acad. Religion, Soc. Bibl. Lit., Internat. Biographical Assn., Christian Evang. Chs. of Am., Inc. (bd. dirs. 1964—), Inst. for Bibl. Rsch., Soc. for Pentecostal Studies (pres. 1998-99), Phi Delta Kappa.

SKAGGS, DAVID EVANS, state official, former congressman; b. Cin., Feb. 22, 1943; s. Charles and Juanita Skaggs; m. Laura Locher, Jan. 3, 1987; 1 child, Matthew; stepchildren: Clare, Will. BA in Philosophy, Wesleyan U., 1964; student law, U. Va., 1964-65; LLB, Yale U., 1967. Bar: NY 1968, Colo. 1971. Assoc. Patterson, Belknap & Webb, NYC, 1967-68, Newcomer & Douglass, Boulder, Colo., 1971-74, 77-78; chief of staff to Rep. Tim Wirth US Congress, Washington, 1974-77; ptnr. Skaggs, Stone & Sheehy, Boulder, 1978-86; mem. Colo. Ho. of Reps., 1980—86, minority leader, 1982—85; mem. US Congress from 2nd Colo. dist., Washington, 1987-99, appropriations com., 1991-98, select. com. on intelligence, 1993—94, 1996—98; exec. dir. Democracy and Citizenship program The Aspen Inst., Washington, 1999—2001; of counsel Hogan & Hartson LLP, 1999—2007; exec. dir. Center for Dem. & Citizenship Council for Excellence in Govt., Washington, 2001—07; exec. dir. Colo. Dept. Higher Edn., 2007—. Alt. delegate, Dem. Nat. Convention, 1984, '88, '92, '96; mem. Tasl Force on Nonproliferation Programs in Russia, 1999-2000, Overseas Presence Advisory Panel, 1999; adj. prof. U. Colo., 1999-2002; vice chair US Pub. Interest Declassification Bd.; mem. advisory coun., Nat. Ctr. Atmospheric Rsch.; steering com., East West Parliamentary Project Former bd. dirs. Rocky Mountain Planned Parenthood, Mental Health Assn. Colo., Boulder County United Way, Boulder Civic Opera; bd. trustees Wesleyan U., 1991-94 Capt. USMC, 1968—71, South Vietnam, major USMC Res., 1971—77. Decorated Navy Commendation medal, Navy Achievement medal with Combat V. Mem. Colo. Bar Assn., Boulder County Bar Assn., Boulder C. of C., US Capitol Historical Soc., US Assn. Former Members of Congress Democrat. Congregationalist. Office: Colo Dept Higher Edn 1560 Broadway Ste 1600 Denver CO 80202

SKAGGS, SANFORD MERLE, lawyer; b. Berkeley, Calif., Oct. 24, 1939; s. Sherman G. and Barbara Jewell (Stinson) Skaggs; m. Sharon Ann Barnes, Sept. 3, 1976; children: Stephen, Paula Ferry, Barbara Gallagher, Darren Peterson. BA, U. Calif., Berkeley, 1961; JD, U. Calif., 1964. Bar: Calif. 1965. Atty. Pacific Gas and Electric Co., San Francisco, 1964-73; gen. counsel Pacific Gas Transmission Co., San Francisco, 1973-75; ptnr. Van Voorhis & Skaggs, Walnut Creek, Calif., 1975-85, McCutchen, Doyle, Brown & Enersen, San Francisco and Walnut Creek, 1985—2002, Bingham McCutchen LLP, 2002—; dir. John Muir Mt. Diablo Health Sys., 1997—2005. Mem. Calif. Law Revision Commn., 1990—2001, chmn., 1993. Councilman City of Walnut Creek, 1972-78, mayor 1974-75, 76-77; bd. dirs. East Bay Mcpl. Utility Dist., 1978-90, pres., 1982-90; dir. Episcopal Homes Found., 2005-. Mem.: Contra Costa County Bar Assn., Calif. State Bar Assn., Phi Delta Phi, Alpha Delta Phi, Lambda Alpha. Episcopalian. Office: Bingham McCutchen LLP Three Embarcadero Ctr San Francisco CA 94111-4067 Office Phone: 415-393-2528. Office Fax: 415-262-9233. Business E-Mail: s.skaggs@bingham.com.

SKANDERA TROMBLEY, LAURA ELISE, academic administrator, literature educator; b. LA, Nov. 1, 1960; d. John and Mary Ruth (Chaney) S.; m. Nelson Edmund Trombley, July 13, 1991. BA, Pepperdine U., 1981, MA summa cum laude, 1993; PhD in English Lit., U. So. Calif., 1989. Asst. prof. Dept. English SUNY, Potsdam, 1990—92, assoc. prof., 1993—97, spl. asst. to pres., 1994—97, dir. Tchg., Tenure and Promotion Assistance Program, 1994—97, asst. provost, 1995—97; v.p. academic affairs, dean faculty Coe Coll., Cedar Rapids, Iowa, 1997—2002; pres. Pitzer Coll., Claremont, Calif., 2002—. Asst. lectr. writing program U. So. Calif., 1983—85, 1987; vis. prof. Am. studies U. Eichstaett, Bavaria, Germany, 1985—86, Bavaria, 1987—88; vis. asst. prof. Dept. English Pepperdine U., 1988—90. Author: Epistemology: Turning Points in the History of Poetic Knowledge, 1986, Mark Twain's Literary Marriage, 1992, Mark Twain in the Company of Women, 1994; editor: Critical Essays on Maxine Hong Kingston, 1998; co-editor: Constructing Mark Twain: New Directions in Scholarship, 2001; contbr. articles to profl. jours. Named Quarry Farm fellow Ctr. for Mark Twain Studies, 1988, Finklestein fellow U. Soc. Calif., 1988. Mem.: Internat. Assn. Univ. Prof. English, Internat. Assn. Univ. Pres., Am. Assn. Univ. Women, Mark Twain Circle of Am. Office: Office of Pres Pitzer Coll 1050 N Mills Ave Claremont CA 91711 Office Phone: 909-621-8198. E-mail: president@pitzer.edu.

SKEFF, KELLEY MICHAEL, health facility administrator; b. Center, Colo., 1944; MD, U. Chgo., 1970. Diplomate Am. Bd. Internal Medicine. Intern Harbor Gen. Hosp., Torrance, Calif., 1970-71; resident in internal medicine U. Colo. Med. Ctr., Denver, 1974-75, Stanford (Calif.) U. Hosps., 1975-76, fellow in internal medicine, 1976; resident in internal medicine Stanford U., 1989—, assoc. prof. medicine. Recipient Alpha Omega Alpha award Assocs. Am. Med. Coll., 1994. Office: Stanford U Dept Med 300 Pasteur Dr Palo Alto CA 94304-2203

SKIENS, WILLIAM EUGENE, electrical interconnect systems scientist, polymer engineer; b. Burns, Oreg., Feb. 21, 1928; s. William Poleman and Eugenia Glenn (Hibbard) S.; m. Vesta Lorraine Franz, Nov. 4, 1955; children: Rebecca, Beverly, Michael. Student, N.W. Nazarene U., 1946-48; BS in Chemistry, Oreg. State U., 1951; PhD in Phys. Chemistry, U. Wash., 1957. Chemist Dow Chem. Co., Pittsburg, Calif., 1951-53, rsch. chemist Midland, Mich. and Walnut Creek, Calif., 1957-58, 1958-73, E.I DuPont de Nemours, Wilmington, Del., 1955; sr. rsch. chemist Battelle Meml. Inst., Richland, Wash., 1973-84, also cons., 1984—; mgr. media system devel. Optical Data, Inc., Beaverton, Oreg., 1984-89; chief scientist Precision Interconnect, Portland, Oreg., 1989—. Cons. WHO, Geneva, 1978-85, PI Med., Portland, 1991—. Contbr. chpts. to books, articles to profl. jours.; patentee in field. Com. chmn. Concord, Calif. council Boy Scouts Am., 1969-72; sec. Tri-Cities Nuclear Council, Richland, Wash., 1984. Named Alumni of Yr. N.W. Nazarene U., 1982. Mem. Am. Chem. Soc. (chmn. Richland sect. 1982), Soc. Plastic Engrs., Sigma Xi. Republican. Mem. Ch. Nazarene. Avocations: skiing, photography, backpacking, golf. Office: Precision Interconnect 10025 SW Freeman Dr Wilsonville OR 97070-9289 Home: 2200 Primrose Dr Nampa ID 83686-7982 E-mail: gene.skiens@precisionint.com.

SKINNER, ANDREW CHARLES, history professor, writer; b. Durango, Colo., Apr. 25, 1951; s. Charles La Verne and Julia Magdalena (Schunk) S.; m. Janet Corbridge, Mar. 22, 1974; children: Cheryl Lyn, Charles Lon, Kelli Ann, Mark Andrew, Holly, Suzanne. BA with distinction, U. Colo., 1975; MA with distinction, Iliff Sch. Theology, Denver, 1978; ThM, Harvard U., 1980; PhD, U. Denver, 1986. Group mgr. May Co. Dept. Store, Denver, 1980-83; assoc. studio dir. Talking Books Pub. Co., Denver, 1984-88; instr. history Metro. State Coll., Denver, 1984-88; prof. history Ricks Coll., Rexburg, Utah, 1988-92; prof. ancient scripture Brigham Young U., Provo, Utah, 1992—, chmn. ancient scripture, 1997—2000, dean Coll. of Religious Edn., 2000—06, dir. Religious Studies Ctr., 2000—; exec. dir. Neal A. Maxwell Inst. Religious Scholarship, 2005—; chmn. Coun. Religious Endeavors, 2005—. Vis. instr. ancient scripture Brigham Young U., 1987; vis. prof. Jerusalem Ctr. for Nr. Eastern Studies, Israel; cons. Univ. Without Walls, Loretto Heights Coll., Denver, 1985-88; mem. editl. staff Dead Sea Scrolls, publ. bd. Israel Antiquities Authority; gen. editor New Testament Commentary, Brigham Young U. Author chpts. numerous books including Gethsemane, 2002, Parables of the Latter Days, Golgotha, 2004, Garden Tomb, 2005; Temple Norsitip, 2007; co-author: Jerusalem-The Eternal City, 1996, New Testament Apostles Testify of Christ, 1998, C.S. Lewis: The Man and His Message, 1999, Parables of the Latter Days, 2001, Discoveries in the Judaean Desert XXXIII-Qumran Cave 4; What Da Vinci Didn't Know, 2006; contbr. articles to profl. jours. Bishop Mormon Ch., Denver, 1986-88, Utah, 1996—; varsity scout leader Teton Parks coun. Boy Scouts Am., Rexburg, 1988-89; host Internat. Scholars Conf. on Holocaust and the Chs., 1995; dir. Orson Hyde Found., 2008-; bd. dirs. Children of Israel Found., 2001—, Inst. for Study and Preservation of Ancient Religious Texts, 2001—. Mil. history fellow U.S. Mil. Acad., 1989. Mem. Am. Hist. Assn., Soc. Bibl. Lit., Mormon History Assn., Phi Theta Kappa, Phi Alpha Theta. Mem. Lds Ch. Office: Brigham Young U Coll Religious Edn JSB 375-A Provo UT 84602 Office Phone: 801-422-9229. E-mail: Andrew_Skinner@byu.edu.

SKINNER, G(EORGE) WILLIAM, anthropologist, educator; b. Oakland, Calif., Feb. 14, 1925; s. John James and Eunice (Engle) S.; m. Carol Bagger, Mar. 25, 1951 (div. Jan. 1970); children: Geoffrey Crane, James Lauriston, Mark Williamson, Jeremy Burr; m. Susan Mann, Apr. 26, 1980; 1 dau., Alison Jane. Student, Deep Springs Coll., Calif., 1942-43; BA with distinction in Far Eastern Studies, Cornell U., Ithaca, NY, 1947, PhD in Cultural Anthropology, 1954; LLD (hon.), U. Hong Kong, 2001. Field dir. Cornell U. S.E. Asia program, also Cornell Research Center, Bangkok, 1951-55; rsch. assoc. in Indonesia, 1956-58; assoc. prof., then prof. anthropology Cornell U., Ithaca, NY, 1960-65; asst. prof. sociology Columbia, 1958-60; sr. specialist in residence East-West Ctr. Honolulu, 1965-66; prof. anthropology Stanford, 1966-89; Barbara Kimball Browning prof. humanities and scis., 1987-89; prof. anthropology U. Calif., Davis, 1990—. Vis. prof. U. Pa., 1977, Duke U., 1978, Keio U., Tokyo, 1985, 1988, U. Calif., San Diego, 1986, Hong Kong U., 2002; field rsch. China, 1949-50, 77, S.E. Asia, 1950-51, Thailand, 1951-53, 54-55, Java and Borneo, 1956-58, Japan, 1985, 88, 95; joint com. on contemporary China Social Sci. Research Coun.-Am. Acad. Learned Socs., 1961-65, 80-81, internat. com. on Chinese studies, 1963-64, mem. joint com. on Chinese studies, 1981-83; mem. subcom. rsch. Chinese Soc. Social Sci. Rsch. Coun., 1961-70, chmn., 1963-70; dir. program on East Asian Local Systems, 1969-71; dir. Chinese Soc. Bibliography Project, 1964-73; assoc. dir. Cornell China Program, 1961-63; dir. London-Cornell Project Social Rsch., 1962-65; mem. com. on scholarly communication with People's Republic of China, Nat. Acad. Scis., 1966-70, social scis. and humanities panel, 1982-83; adv. com. Ctr. for Chinese Rsch. Materials, Assn. Rsch. Libraries, 1967-70; bd. dirs. Nat. Ctr. for Geog. Info. and Analysis, 1989-92; policy and planning com. China in Time and Space, 1993-96; mem. mgmt. com. China Hist. GIS, 2000—. Author: Chinese Society in Thailand, 1957, Leadership and Power in the Chinese Community of Thailand, 1958; also articles; Editor: The Social Sciences and Thailand, 1956, Local, Ethnic and National Loyalties in Village Indonesia, 1959, Modern Chinese Society: An Analytical Bibliography, 3 vols, 1973, (with Mark Elvin) The Chinese City Between Two Worlds, 1974, (with A. Thomas Kirsch) Change and Persistence in Thai Society, 1975, The City in Late Imperial China, 1977, The Study of Chinese Society, 1979. Served to ensign USNR, 1943-46. Fellow Center for Advanced Study in Behavioral Scis., 1969-70, Guggenheim fellow, 1969, NIMH spl. fellow, 1970 Mem. NAS, AAAS, Am. Anthrop. Assn., Am. Sociol. Assn., Assn. Asian Studies (bd. dirs. 1962-65, chmn. nominating com. 1967-68, pres. 1983-84), Soc. for Cultural Anthropology, Internat. Union for Sci. Study of Population, Social Sci. History Assn., Am. Ethnol. Soc., Population Assn. Am., Siam Soc., Soc. Qing Studies, Soc. Econ. Anthropology, Phi Beta Kappa, Sigma Xi. Office: U Calif Dept Anthropology 1 Shields Ave Davis CA 95616-5270 Business E-Mail: gwskinner@ucdavis.edu.

SKINNER, NANCY, state legislator; m. Lance Skinner; 1 child, Sirona. BS, MEd., U. Calif., Berkeley. Mem. Berkeley City Coun., 1984—92; field mgr. Barbara Lee for US Congress, 2002; coord. Lori Hancock for State Assembly, 2002; mem. Dist. 14 Calif. State Assembly, 2008—. Democrat. Office: PO Box 942849 Rm 4126 Sacramento CA 94249-0014 also: Elihu Harris State Bldg 1515 Clay St Ste 2201 Oakland CA 94612 Office Phone: 916-319-2014, 510-286-1400. Office Fax: 916-319-2114, 510-286-1406.*

SKLANSKY, JACK, electrical and computer engineering educator, researcher; b. NYC, Nov. 15, 1928; s. Abraham and Clara S.; m. Gloria Joy Weiss, Dec. 24, 1957; children: David Alan, Mark Steven, Jeffrey Paul. BEE, CCNY, 1950; MSEE, Purdue U., 1952; D in Engring. Sci., Columbia U., 1955. Research engr. RCA Labs., Princeton, NJ, 1955-65; mgr. Nat. Cash Register Co., Dayton, Ohio, 1965-66; prof. elec. and computer engring. U. Calif., Irvine, 1966—94; pres. Scanicon Corp., Irvine, 1980-89; prof. radiology Charles R. Drew U. of Medicine and Sci., LA, 1995—2004. Author: (with others) Pattern Classifiers and Trainable Machines, 1981; editor: Pattern Recognition, 1973, (with others) Biomedical Images and Computers, 1982; editor-in-chief: Machine Vision and Applications, 1987. Recipient best paper award Jour. Pattern Recognition, 1977, 2000; rsch. grantee NIH, 1971-84, Army Rsch. Office, 1984-91, NSF, 1992-96, Office of Naval Rsch., 1995-97, Naval Air Warfare Ctr., 1997-98, Calif. Breast Cancer Rsch. Program, 1997-99, US Army Med. Rsch. and Materiel Command, 1999-2004, Calif. Telehealth and Telemedicine Ctr., 2000-02. Fellow IEEE, Internat. Assn. for Pattern Recognition; mem. ACM. Office: U Calif Dept Elec Engring & Computer Sci MSTB 211 Irvine CA 92697 E-mail: sklansky@uci.edu.

SKLAR, MARTY (MARTIN A. SKLAR), entertainment company executive; b. New Brunswick, NJ; m. Leah Sklar. Grad., UCLA. Asst. news editor Media Agy. Clients Publs.; with Walt Disney Co., Burbank, Calif., 1956—; v.p. concepts/planning Walt Disney Imagineering, Walt Disney Co., Burbank, Calif., 1974—79, v.p. creative devel., 1979—87, pres., 1987—96, vice chmn., prin. creative exec., 1996—2006, internat. amb., 2006—. One of founders Ryman Program for Young Artists. Contbr. articles to Showman of the World films. Mem. bd. edn. Anaheim City Sch. Dist., 1969, 1973; pres. Orange County, Calif. Sch. Bds. Assn.; commr. Anaheim City; founding chmn. Michael L. Roston Creative Writing Awards. Recipient Cmty. Svc. award for Anaheim, Cypress Coll., 1977, Lifetime Achievement award, Themed Entertainment Assn., 1995; inducted into, Hall of Fame, Internat. Assn. Amusement Pks. and Attractions, 2002. Office: Walt Disney Co 500 S Buena Vista St Burbank CA 91521-9722

SKOGEN, HAVEN SHERMAN, investment company executive; b. Rochester, Minn., May 8, 1927; s. Joseph Harold and Elpha (Hemphill) S.; m. Beverly R. Baker, Feb. 19, 1949; 1 child, Scott H. BS, Iowa State U., 1950; MS, Rutgers U., 1954, PhD, 1955; MBA, U. Chgo., 1970. Registered profl. engr., Wis. Devel. engr. E.I. duPont, Wilmington, Del., 1955—57; prof. Elmhurst (Ill.) Coll., 1957—58; chief engr. Stackpole, St. Marys, Pa., 1958—62; plant mgr. Magnatronics, Elizabethtown, Ky., 1962—65; mgr. Allen-Bradley, Milw., 1965—70; v.p. Dill-Clithrow, Chgo., 1970—74; oil co. exec. Occidental Oil Co., Grand Junction, Colo., 1974—92; ptnr. H&B Investment Co., 1992—. Author: Synthetic Fuel Combustion, 1984; inventor radioactive retort doping, locus retorting zone. Naval Rsch. fellow, 1951-55. Fellow Am. Inst. Chemists; mem. Internat. Platform Assn., Masons, Elks, Sigma Xi, Phi Beta Kappa, Phi Lambda Upsilon. Republican. Avocations: fly fishing, travel, reading, teaching. Home: 3152 Primrose Ct Grand Junction CO 81506-4147

SKOLL, JEFFREY S., philanthropist, former internet company executive; b. Montreal, Jan. 16, 1965; BSEE, U. Toronto, 1987; MBA, Stanford U., 1995; LLD (hon.), U. Toronto, 2003. Founder Skoll Engring., 1987, Micros on the Move Ltd., 1990; mgr. distbn. channels online news info. Knight-Ridder Info.; co-founder, pres., v.p. strategic analysis and planning eBay Inc., San Jose, Calif., 1995—99; founder, CEO Participant Productions, LA, 2004—. Exec. prodr.: (films) Good Night, and Good Luck, North Country, Syriana, American Gun, An Inconvenient Truth, The World According to Sesame Street, Fast Food Nation. Bd. dirs. e-Bay Found., 1998—; founder, chmn. Skoll Found., 1999—; bd. dirs. Cmty. Found. Silicon Valley; mem. advisory bd. Stanford Grad. Sch. Bus. Recipient Leafy award, 1999, Visionary award, Software Development Forum, 2001, Outstanding Philanthropist award, Silicon Valley chapter Assn. Fundraising Professionals, 2002, Internat. Assn. Fundraising Professionals, 2003, Nat. Leadership Award, Commonwealth Club Silicon Valley, 2004, Visionary award, Prodrs. Guild America, 2009; named a WIRED Renegade, WIRED Rave Awards, 2006; named one of the most innovative philanthropists of the past decade, BusinessWeek, 2002, 2003, 50 Most Generous Philanthropists, Fortune Mag., 2005, World's Richest People, Forbes, 1999—, 100 Most Influential People, Time Mag., 2006, 50 Smartest People in Hollywood, Entertainment Weekly, 2007. Office: Skoll Foundation 250 University Ave Ste 200 Palo Alto CA 94301 Office Phone: 650-331-1031. Office Fax: 650-331-1033.*

SKOOG, WILLIAM ARTHUR, retired oncologist; b. Culver City, Calif., Apr. 10, 1925; s. John Lundeen and Allis Rose (Gatz) Skoog; m. Ann Douglas, Sept. 17, 1949; children: Karen, William Arthur, James Douglas, Allison. AA, UCLA, 1944; BA with great distinction, Stanford U., 1946, MD, 1949. Intern in medicine Stanford Hosp., San Francisco, 1948-49, asst. resident in medicine, 1949-50, N.Y. Hosp., NYC, 1950-51; sr. resident in medicine Wadsworth VA Hosp., LA, 1951, attending specialist in internal medicine, 1962-68; pvt. practice internal medicine Los Altos, Calif., 1959-61; pvt. practice hematology and oncology, Santa Monica, Calif., 1971-72; pvt. practice med. oncology, San Bernardino, Calif., 1972-94; ret. Assoc. staff Palo Alto-Stanford Med. Ctr., 1959-61, U. Calif. Med. Ctr., San francisco, 1959-61; assoc. attending physician UCLA Hosp. and Clinics, 1961-78; vis. physician in internal medicine Harbor Gen. Hosp., Torrance, Calif., 1962-65, attending physician, 1965-71; cons. in chemistry Clin. Lab., UCLA Hosp., 1963-68; affiliate cons. staff St. John's Hosp., Santa Monica, 1967-71, courtesy staff, 1971-72; courtesy attending med. staff Santa Monica Hosp., 1967-72; staff physician St. Bernardine (Calif.) Hosp., 1972-94, hon. staff, 1994—; staff physician San Bernardino Cmty. Hosp., 1972-90, courtesy staff, 1990-94; chief sect. oncology San Bernardino County Hosp., 1972-76; cons. staff Redlands(Calf.) Cmty. Hosp., 1972-83, courtesy staff, 1983-94, hon. staff, 1994—; asst. in medicine Cornell U. Med. Coll., N.Y.C., 1950-51; jr. rsch. physician UCLA Atomic Energy Project, 1954-55; instr. medicine, asst. rsch. physician dept. medicine UCLA Med. Ctr., 1955-56, asst. prof. medicine, asst. rsch. physician, 1956-59; clin. assoc. in hematology VA Ctr., L.A., 1956-59; co-dir. metabolic rsch. unit UCLA Ctr. for Health Scis., 1955-59, 61-65; co-dir. Health Scis. Clin. Rsch. Ctr., 1965-68, dir., 1968-72; clin. instr. medicine Stanford U., 1959-61; asst. clin. prof. medicine, assoc. rsch. physician U. Calif. Med. Ctr., San Francisco, 1959-61; lectr. medicine UCLA Sch. Medicine, 1961-62, assoc. prof., 1962-72, assoc. clin. prof., 1973—. Contbr. articles to med. jours. Active duty USNR, 1943—46, lt. M.C. USNR, 1951—53. Fellow: ACP, Am Soc. Internal Medicine; mem.: AMA, San Bernardino County Med. Soc., Am. Soc Clin. Oncology, L.A. Acad. Medicine, Am. Fedn. Clin. Rsch., Western Soc. Clin. Rsch., So. Calif. Acad. Clin. Oncology, Calif. Med. Assn., Redlands Country Club, Alpha Omega Alpha, Sigma Xi, Phi Beta Kappa, Alpha Kappa Kappa. Episcopalian (vestryman 1965-70). Home: 1119 Kimberly Pl Redlands CA 92373-6786 Home Fax: 909-798-5016. Personal E-mail: wasredarrow@aol.com.

SKOPIL, OTTO RICHARD, JR., federal judge; b. Portland, Oreg., June 3, 1919; s. Otto Richard and Freda Martha (Boetticher) Skopil; m. Janet Rae Lundy, July 27, 1956; children: Otto Richard III, Casey Robert, Shannon Ida, Molly Jo. BA in Econs., Willamette U., 1941, LLB, 1946, LLD (hon.), 1983. Bar: Oreg. 1946, US Dist. Ct. Oreg., US Ct. Appeals (9th cir.), US Supreme Ct. 1946. Assoc. Skopil & Skopil, 1946—51; ptnr. Williams, Skopil, Miller & Beck (and predecessors), Salem, Oreg., 1951—72; judge US Dist. Ct., Portland, 1972—79, chief judge, 1976—79; judge US Ct. Appeals (9th cir.), Portland, 1979—85, sr. judge, 1986—. Chmn. com. adminstrn. of fed. magistrate sys. US Jud. Conf., 1980—86; co-founder Oreg. chpt. Am. Leadership Forum; chmn. 9th cir. Jud. Coun. Magistrates Adv. Com., 1988—91; chmn. US Jud. Conf. Long Range Planning Com., 1990—95. Hi-Y adviser Salem YMCA, 1951—52; appeal agt. SSS Marion County (Oreg.) Draft Bd., 1953—66; master of ceremonies 1st Gov.'s Prayer Breakfast for State Oreg., 1959; citizens adv. com. City of Salem, 1970—71; Gov.'s Com. on Staffing Mental Instns., 1969—70; pres., bd. dirs. Marion County Tb and Health Assn., 1958—61; bd. dirs. Willamette U., 1969—71; elder Mt. Park Ch., 1979—81; bd. dirs. Willamette Valley Camp Fire Girls, 1946—56, Internat. Christian Leadership, 1959, Fed. Jud. Ctr., 1979. Lt. USNR, 1942—46. Recipient Oreg. Legal Citizen of Yr. award, 1986, Disting. Alumni award, Willamette U. Sch. Law, 1988. Mem.: ABA, Internat. Soc. Barristers, Assn. Ins. Attys. U.S. and Can. (Oreg. rep. 1970), Def. Rsch. Inst., Oreg. Assn. Def. Counsel (bd. dirs.), Am. Judicature Soc., Marion County Bar Assn., Oreg. Bar Assn. (bd. dirs.), Prayer Breakfast Movement (fellowship coun.), Illahe Hills Country Club (pres., bd. dirs. 1964—67), Exchange Club (pres. 1947), Salem Club. Office: Sr Circuit Judge 827 US Courthouse 1000 SW 3rd Ave Portland OR 97204-2930

SKOTHEIM, ROBERT ALLEN, academic administrator, educator; b. Seattle, Jan. 31, 1933; s. Sivert O. and Marjorie F. (Allen) S.; m. Nadine Vail, June 14, 1953; children: Marjorie, Kris, Julia. BA, U. Wash., 1955, MA, 1958, PhD, 1962; LLD (hon.), Hobart and William Smith Colls., Geneva, NY, 1975; LittD (hon.), Whitman Coll., 1988; LHD (hon.), Coll. Idaho, 1988, Occidental Coll., 1989, Ill. Wesleyan U., 1990; DFA (hon.), Willamette U., 1989; DFA (hon.), Whittier Coll., 2000, Gustavus Adolphus Coll., 2000. Prof. history U. Wash., 1962-63, Wayne State U., Detroit, 1963-66; prof. UCLA, 1966-67, U. Colo., Boulder, 1967-72; provost, dean faculty Hobart and William Smith Colls., 1972-75; pres. Whitman Coll., Walla Walla, Wash., 1975-88, Huntington Libr., Art Collections & Bot. Gardens, San Marino, Calif., 1988-2001, Occidental Coll., Los Angeles, Calif., 2008—. Author: American Intellectual Histories and Historians, 1966, Totalitarianism and American Social Thought, 1971; Editor: The Historian and the Climate of Opinion, 1969; co-editor: American Social Thought: Sources and Interpretations, 2 vols, 1972. Guggenheim fellow, 1967-68 Mem. Phi Beta Kappa (hon.) Office: Occidental Coll Office of Pres 1600 Campus Rd Los Angeles CA 90041 Home: 1852 Campus Rd Los Angeles CA 90041 Office Phone: 323-259-2691. Office Fax: 323-259-2907.

SKURZYNSKI, GLORIA JOAN, writer; b. Duquesne, Pa., July 6, 1930; d. Aylmer Kearney and Serena Elizabeth (Decker) Flister; m. Edward Joseph Skurzynski, Dec. 1, 1951; children: Serena Nolan, Janine Skurzynski-Mahoney, Joan Alm, Alane Ferguson, Lauren Thliveris. Student, Carlow Coll., 1948-50. Author: The Magic Pumpkin, 1971, The Remarkable Journey of Gustavus Bell, 1973, The Poltergeist of Jason Morey, 1975, In a Bottle with a Cork on Top, 1976, Two Fools and a Faker, 1977, Bionic Parts for People, 1978 (Golden Kite Honor Bk. award Soc. Children's Bk. Writers), Martin by Himself, 1979, What Happened in Hamelin, 1979 (telecast on Storybreak, CBS, 1987, Christopher award, Reviewer's Choice award, Horn Bk. Honor List, ALA Booklist), Honest Andrew, 1981, Safeguarding the Land, 1981, Three Folktales, 1981, Manwolf, 1981 (Best Bks. for Young Adults award ALA, Reviewer's Choice award ALA Booklist, Bks. of Yr. award Child Study Assn., Notable Children's Trade Bk. in Field of Social Studies), Lost in the Devil's Desert, 1982 (Utah Children's Bk. award), The Tempering, 1983 (Golden Kite award Soc. Children's Bk. Writers, Best Bks. for Young Adults award ALA, Best Bks. of Yr. award Sch. Libr. Jour., Children's Bks. of Yr. award Libr. Congress, Bks. of Yr. award Child Study Assn.), Trapped in the Slickrock Canyon, 1984 (Golden Spur award Western Writers Am., Am. Booksellers Pick of the List, Jr. Lit. Guild Selection), Caught in the Moving Mountains, 1984, Swept in the Wave of Terror, 1985, The Minstrel in the Tower, 1988, Dangerous Ground, 1989, Robots, 1990 (100 Children's Bks. award N.Y. Pub. Libr. 1990, Outstanding Science Trade Bk. for Children award NSTA/CBC 1991), Almost the Real Thing, 1991 (Children's Sci. Bk. award Am. Inst. Physics 1992), Here Comes the Mail, 1992, Good-Bye, Billy Radish, 1992 (Best Bks. of Yr. award Sch. Libr. Jour., Jefferson Cup Hon. award Va. Libr. Assn., Judy Lopez Meml. Hon. Bk., Women's Nat. Bk. Assn.), Get the Message, 1993 (Outstanding Sci. Trade Bks. for Children award NSTA/CBC 1994, Bks. for the Teen Age award N.Y. Pub. Libr. 1994), Know the Score, 1994 (Bks. for the Teen Age award N.Y. Pub. Libr. 1995), Zero Gravity, 1994 (Outstanding Sci. Trade Bks. for Children award NSTA/CBC 1995, Children's Bk. of Yr., Bank Street Coll. Child Study Com.), Cyberstorm, 1995, Caitlin's Big Idea, 1995, Waves, the Electromagnetic Universe, 1996, Virtual War, 1997, (with Alane Ferguson) The Mystery of the Spooky Shadow, 1996, The Mystery of the Vanishing Creatures, 1996, Wolf Stalker, 1997, Rage of Fire, 1998, Discover Mars, 1998, Cliff-Hanger, 1999, Spider's Voice, 1999, Deadly Waters, 1999, On Time, 2000, Ghost Horses, 2000, The Hunted, 2000, Over the Edge, 2001 (Ind. Children's Choice award), Valley of Death, 2001, Rockbuster, 2001 (Western Writers Am. award), Escape From Fear, 2002, Out of the Deep, 2002, Running Scared, 2002, Buried Alive, 2003, Are We Alone: Scientists Search for Life in Space, 2004, The Virtual War Chronologs, Book One, Virtual War, 2004, Book Two, The Clones, 2004. Mem. Soc. of Children's Book Writers and Illustrators, Utah Women's Forum, Internat. Women's Forum. Home and Office: 5898 W Riverbend Ln Boise ID 83703-6249 E-mail: gloriabooks@qwest.net.

SKYLSTAD, WILLIAM STEPHEN, bishop; b. Omak, Wash., Mar. 2, 1934; s. Stephen Martin and Reneldes Elizzbeth (Danzl) Skylstad. Student, Pontifical Coll.Josephinium, Worthington, Ohio, 1948—60; student Wash. State U., 1960—61; MA in Edn., Gonzaga U., 1966. Ordained priest Diocese of Spokane, Wash., 1960; asst. pastor Pullman, Wash., 1960-62; tchr. Mater Cleri Sem., 1961-68, rector,

1968-74; pastor Assumption Parish, Spokane, 1974-76; chancellor Diocese of Spokane, 1976-77; ordained bishop, 1977; bishop Diocese of Yakima, Wash., 1977-90, Diocese of Spokane, Wash., 1990—. V.p. US Conf. of Catholic Bishops, 2001—04, pres., 2004—. Roman Catholic. Office: Diocese of Spokane PO Box 1453 1023 W Riverside Ave Spokane WA 99210-1453 E-mail: bishop@dioceseofspokane.org.

SLACK, DONALD CARL, agricultural engineer, educator; b. Cody, Wyo., June 25, 1942; s. Clarence Ralbon and Clara May (Beightol) S.; m. Marion Arline Kimball, Dec. 19, 1964; children: Jonel Marie, Jennifer Michelle. BS in Agrl. Engring., U. Wyo., 1965; MS in Agrl. Engring., U. Ky., 1968, PhD in Agrl. Engring., 1975. Registered profl. engr., Ky., Ariz. Asst. civil engr. City of LA, 1965; research specialist U. Ky., Lexington, 1966—70, agrl. engring. advisor Tha Phra, Thailand, 1970—73, rsch. asst. Lexington, 1973—75; from asst. prof. to assoc. prof. agrl. engring. U. Minn., St. Paul, 1975—84; prof. U. Ariz., Tucson, 1984—, head dept. agrl. and biosystems engring., 1991—, prof. watershed mgmt., Cecil H. Miller endowed chair, 2006—; co-dir. AMD Lands Sustainable Bioenergy Inst., 2008—. Mem. Mid. East and Mediterranean Desert Devel. Program, 1997—; vis. prof. dept. atmospheric sci. Fed. U. Paraiba, Campina Grande, Brazil, 1997; vis. prof. dept. irrigation Chapingo Autonomous U., Mexico, 2000; tech. adv. Ariz. Dept. Water Resources, Phoenix, 1985—, Tucson active mgmt. area, 1996—; cons. Winrock Internat., Morrilton, Ark., 1984, Water Mgmt. Synthesis II, Logan, Utah, 1985, Desert Agrl. Tech. Sys., Tucson, 1985—, Portek Hermosillo, Mexico, 1989—, World Bank, Washington, 1992—, Malawi Environ. Monitoring Project, 1996, Mex. Inst. for Water Tech., 1997, Nat. Agrl. Rsch. Inst., La Serema, Chile, 1997; cons. F.J. Hansen Inst. for World Peace San Diego State U., 1997—; cons. Internat. Ctr. for Agrl. Rsch. in Dry Areas, 2005; dep. program support mgr. Rsch. Irrigation Support Project for Asia and the Near East, Arlington, Va., 1987—94; mem. adv. team Cearan Found. for Meteorology and Hydrology, Fortaleza, Brazil, 1995—; mem. internat. adv. panel Matrou Resources Mgmt. Project, World Bank, Egypt, 1996—2000; bd. dirs. Sonoita Vineyards, Ltd., Watershed Mgmt. Group, Inc. Contbr. articles to profl. jours. Named Adminstr. of Yr., Coll. Agrl. & Life Scis., 2004—05. Fellow ASCE (Outstanding Jour. Paper award 1988), Am. Soc. Agrl. Engrs. (Ariz. sect. Engr. of Yr. 1993); mem. US Com. on Irrigation and Drainage (life), Am. Soc. Engring. Edn. (program evaluator accreditation bd. for enring. and tech., 2001—), SAR, Brotherhood of Knights of the Vine (master knight), Rocky Mountain Elk Found. (life), Wyo. Wildlife Fedn. (life); Sigma Xi, Tau Beta Pi, Alpha Epsilon, Gamma Sigma Delta. Democrat. Lutheran. Achievements include patents pending in field; development of infrared based irrigation scheduling device. Avocations: hunting, camping, hiking, model railroading, fishing. Home: 9230 E Visco Pl Tucson AZ 85710-3167 Office: U Ariz Agrl Biosystems Engring Tucson AZ 85721-0038 Home Phone: 520-722-2162; Office Phone: 520-621-7230. Business E-Mail: slackd@email.arizona.edu.

SLADE, BERNARD, playwright; b. St. Catharines, Ont., Can., May 2, 1930; s. Frederick and Bessie (Walbourne) Newbound; m. Jill Florence Hancock, July 25, 1953; children: Laurel, Christopher. Actor: Garden Ctr. Theatre, Vineland, Ont., Crest Theatre, Toronto, CBC-TV, Citadel Theatre, Edmonton, Alta.; screenwriter of over 20 hour TV plays for CBC, CBS, ABC, NBC, 1957—; writer/creator (TV series) Love on a Rooftop, The Partridge Family, The Flying Nun, The Girl with Something Extra, Bridget Loves Bernie; story editor, writer 15 episodes of TV series Bewitched; writer/creator (plays) A Very Close Family, 1962, Same Time Next Year (Drama Desk award 1975, Tony award nomination 1975), Tribute, 1978, Romantic Comedy, 1979, Special Occasions, 1981, Fatal Attraction, 1984, Return Engagements, 1986, Sweet William, 1987, An Act of the Imagination, 1987, I Remember You, 1991, You Say Tomatoes, 1993, Everytime I See You, 1994, Same Time, Another Year, Fling!, 2000, Les Grande Occasions, Paris, 2007; feature films: Same Time, Next Year, 1977, Tribute, 1978, Romantic Comedy, 1979, Shared Laughter-a memoir, 2000, Moving Day, 2005, (film biography) Comedic Genius of Bernard Slade, 2003. Recipient Acad. award nomination Motion Picture Arts and Scis., 1978. Mem. Dramatists Guild Am., Writers Guild Am. (award nomination), Acad. Motion Picture Arts and Scis. (Acad. award nomination 1978), Soc. Authors and Artists (France). Avocation: tennis. Home: 261 S Reeves Dr # 102 Beverly Hills CA 90212-4004 Office Phone: 310-360-6532. Personal E-mail: bernslade@aol.com.

SLADE, COLIN L., electronics manufacturing executive; m. Marianne; 2 children. BS in Acctg., U. Oreg. CPA. Internat. svc. Price Waterhouse, London; audit mgr.; corp. controller, CFO Graphic Software; fin. mgr. info. display group Tektronix, Inc., Beaverton, Oreg., 1987; v.p. fin.; corp. controller; controller color printing and imaging divsn.; CFO, 2000—. Office: Tektronix Inc 14200 SW Karl Braun Dr Beaverton OR 97077

SLADE, LYNN, lawyer; b. Santa Fe, Jan. 29, 1948; m. Susan Zimmerman, 1 child, Benjamin, 1 child from a previous marriage, Jessica. BA in Econs., U. N.Mex., 1973, JD, 1976. Bar: N.Mex. 1976, US Dist. Ct. N.Mex. 1976, US Ct. Appeals (10th cir.) 1978, US Ct. Appeals (DC cir.) 1984, US Supreme Ct. 1984, US Ct. Appeals (9th cir.) 2007. Ptnr. Modrall, Sperling, Roehl, Harris & Sisk, PA, Albuquerque, 1976—. Adj. prof. U. N.Mex. Sch. Law, Albuquerque, 1990. Editor N.Mex. Law Rev., 1975-76; contbr. articles to profl. jours. Bd. dirs. N.Mex. First, 1999—, chair, 2005—06; trustee-at-large Rocky Mountain Min. L. Found., 1995—97, 2005—; mem. bd. adv. Utton Ctr. for Transboundary Resources, 2005—. Mem. ABA (sect. environ., energy and resources, membership officer 1998-00, chair com. on Native Am. natural resources 1991-94, 2002-, coun. mem. 1995-98, mem. sects. litig., dispute resolution, pub. utilities and comm., and transp. law), N.Mex. State Bar (chair, bd. dirs. sect. natural resources 1983-87, bd. dirs. Indian law sect. 2002-04). Home: 143 Olguin Rd Corrales NM 87048-6930 Office: Modrall Sperling Roehl Harris & Sisk PA 500 4th St NW Ste 1000 Albuquerque NM 87102-2186 Office Phone: 505-848-1828. Business E-Mail: lynn.slade@modrall.com.

SLAGER, DONALD W., waste management executive; Various mgmt. positions Gen. Waste Svcs., 1985—90, gen. mgr., 1990—92; dist. mgr. Chgo. metro dist. Allied Waste Industries, Scottsdale, Ariz., 1992—96, regional v.p. west region, 1996—97, asst. v.p. ops., 1997—98, v.p. ops., 1998—2001, sr. v.p. ops., 2001—03, exec. v.p., COO, 2003—04, pres., COO, 2005—. Office: Allied Waste Industries 18500 N Allied Way Phoenix AZ 85054

SLAGHT, KENNETH D., career officer; b. Chgo. Grad., U.S. Naval Acad., 1970; student, Def. Sys. Mgmt. Coll.; M in Computer Sys. Mgmt., Naval Postgrad. Sch. Commd. ensign USN, advanced through grades to rear adm.; divsn. dir. for automation Navy Recruiting Command; divsn. dir. automated plans and programs Jt. Chiefs of Staff; dep. dir. material profl. policy Naval Mil. Personnel Command; dep. dir. info. transfer sys. dir. Space and Naval Warfare Sys. Command; project officer Comm. Support Sys.; program mgr. Jt. Maritime Comm. Sys.; chief engr. Space and Naval Warfare Sys. Command, 1997—, vice comdr., 1999—. Decorated Legion of Merit, Def. Meritorious Svc. medal, Navy Meritorious Svc. medal with Gold star, Nat. Der. Svc. medal with Bronze star.

SLATE, JOHN BUTLER, biomedical engineer; b. Schenectady, NY, Sept. 27, 1953; s. Herbert Butler and Violet (Perugi) S. BSEE, U. Wis., 1975, MEE, 1977, PhDEE, 1980. Spl. fellow of cardiovascular surgery U. Ala., Birmingham, 1980-81, dept. biomed. research engr., 1981-82; microbiology fellow, 1981-82; sr. research engr. IMED Corp., San Diego, 1982-83, sr. research scientist, 1983-86; sci. dir. Pacesetter Infusion Ltd. (dba MiniMed Technologies), Sylmar, Calif., 1986-87; v.p. tech. MiniMed Technologies, Sylmar, Calif., 1987-91; v.p. R & D Siemens Infusion Systems, Sylmar, Calif., 1991-93; v.p. tech. devel. Via Med., San Diego, 1993-94; pres. Slate Engring., San Diego, 1997—2003, Avant Drug Delivery Sys., Inc., San Diego, 1997—2002; v.p. ops. Avant Med. Corp., San Diego, 2002—, pres., 2002—. Mem. IEEE (IEE Ayrton award), Sigma Xi. Office: Avant Med Corp 10225 Barnes Canyon Rd Ste A113 San Diego CA 92121 Home Phone: 858-273-3674; Office Phone: 858-202-1560 Ext. 1. E-mail: jslate@avantmedical.com.

SLATER, JAMES MUNRO, radiation oncologist; b. Salt Lake City, Jan. 7, 1929; s. Donald Munro and Leone Forestine (Fehr) S.; m. JoAnn Strout, Dec. 28, 1948; children: James, Julie, Jan, Jerry, Jon. BS in Physics, U. Utah, Utah State U., 1954; MD, Loma Linda U., 1963; PhD (hon.), Andrews U., Berrien Springs, Mich., 1996. Diplomate Am. Bd. Radiology. Intern Latter Day Saints Hosp., Salt Lake City, 1963-64, resident in radiology, 1964-65; resident in radiotherapy Loma Linda U. Med. Ctr., White Meml. Med. Center, LA, fellow in radiotherapy, 1967-68, U. Tex.-M.D. Anderson Hosp. and Tumor Inst., Houston, 1968-69; dir. radiation oncology sect. Loma Linda U. Med. Ctr., Calif., 1970—79, dir. radiation sect. Calif., 1975—79, chmn. dept. radiation scis. Calif., 1978—90, chmn. dept. radiation medicine Calif., 1990—2001, dir. Cancer Inst., 1993—97, treas. Calif., 1995-96, exec. v.p. Calif., 1994—95; founder, dir. Loma Linda U./NASA Radiation Biology Lab., Calif., 1997—; vice chair radiation medicine Loma Linda U. Med. Ctr., 2003—. Co-dir. cmty. radiology oncology program L.A. County-U. So. Calif. Comprehensive Cancer Ctr., 1978-83; mem. cancer adv. coun. State of Calif., 1980-85; clin. prof. U. So. Calif., 1982—; founding mem. Proton Therapy Coop. Group, 1985—, chmn. 1987-91; cons. charged particle therapy program Lawrence Berkeley Lab., 1986-94; cons. R&D monoclonal antibodies Hybritech Inc., 1985-94, bd. dirs., 1985-94; cons. Berkeley lab., 1986-94; mem. panel cons. Internat. Atomic Energy Agy. UN, 1994-98; cons. Sci. Applications Internat. Corp., 1979, 89-91. Bd. dirs. Am. Cancer Soc., San Bernardino/Riverside, 1976-84, exec. com., 1976—; pres. Inland Empire chpt., 1981-83. NIH fellow, 1968-69; recipient exhbn. awards Radiol. Soc. N.Am., 1973, exhbn. awards European Assn. Radiology, 1975, exhbn. awards Am. Soc. Therapeutic Radiologists, 1978, Alumnus of Yr. award, 1993-94. Fellow Am. Coll. Radiology; mem. AAAS, AMA, ACS (liaison mem. to commn. on cancer 1976-84), Am. Radium Soc., Am. Soc. Clin. Oncology, Am. Soc. Therapeutics Radiologists, Assn. Univ. Radiologists, Soc. for Clinical Trials, N.Y. Acad. Scis., Calif. Med. Assn., Calif. Radiol. Soc., Gilbert H. Fletcher Soc. (pres. 1981-82), Loma Linda U. Med. Sch. Alumni Assn., Radiol. Soc. N.Am., Bernardino County Med Soc., Soc. Chairmen Of Acad. Radiation Oncology Programs, Alpha Omega Alpha. Achievements include development of proton accelerator system for treating patients with cancer and some benign diseases in a hospital environment; development of computer assisted radiation treatment planning system utilizing patient's digitized anatomic images with overlying radiation distribution images, Loma Linda U. Proton Facility renamed James M. Slater Proton Treatmant and Rsch. Ctr., 2007. Office: Loma Linda Univ Med Ctr 25590 Prospect Ave Apt 27c Loma Linda CA 92354-3150 Business E-Mail: jmslater@dominion.llumc.edu.

SLATER, MARY JO, former broadcasting executive, casting director; b. Trenton, NJ, Apr. 19, 1946; d. Leonard Joseph and Anna Mae (Sweeny) Lawton; m. Michael Hawkins, 1966 (div. 1976); 1 child, Christian; m. William Henry Taron, Sept. 9, 1990; children: Josh, Emily, Ryan. Diploma, Am. Acad. Dramatic Arts, 1967. Dir. casting ABC TV, NYC, 1976-86; v.p. casting Metro Goldwyn Mayer/United Artists TV, Culver City, Calif., 1986-90; prin. Slater & Assoc., Santa Monica, Calif., 1990—. Mem.: Casting Soc. America (Artios award for Best Casting for TV Daytime 1986, Artios award for Best Casting for TV Miniseries 2004). Office: Slater & Assoc 2425 Colorado Ave Ste 204 Santa Monica CA 90404-3584 Home: 10945 Bluffside Dr Apt 301 Studio City CA 91604-4488

SLAVKIN, HAROLD CHARLES, dean, biologist; b. Chgo., Mar. 20, 1938; m. Lois S. Slavkin; children: Mark D., Todd P. BA in English lit., U. So. Calif., 1961, DDS, 1965; Doctorate (hon.), Georgetown U., 1990, U. Paris, 1996, U. Md., 1997. Mem. faculty U. So. Calif. Sch. Dentistry, LA, 1968—, mem. faculty gerontology inst., 1969, chmn. dept. biochemistry and nutrition, 1969—75, prof., 1974—, chmn. grad. program in craniofacial molecular biology, 1975-85, founding dir. Ctr. for Craniofacial Molecular Biology, 1989-95, George & Mary Lou Boone prof. craniofacial molecular biology, 1989-95, dean, 2000—, G. Donald and Marian James Montgomery Dean's Chair in Dentistry, 2000—; dir. Nat. Inst. Dental and Craniofacial Rsch., NIH, Bethesda, Md., 1995—2000. Vis. prof. Israel Inst. Tech., Haifa, 1987-88; cons. U.S. News and World Report, 1985-95, L.A. Edn. Partnership, 1983-95, Torstar Books, Inc., 1985-95. Contbr. articles to profl. jours. Mem. sci. adv. bd. Calif. Mus. Sci. and Tech., 1985-95. Rsch. scholar U. Coll. London, 1980. Mem. AAAS, Am. Assn. Anatomists, Am. Inst. Biol. Scis., Am. Soc. for Cell Biology, Am. Assn. for Dental Rsch. (pres. 1993-94), N.Y. Acad. Scis., Inst. Medicine of NAS, Internat. Coll. Dentistry, Am. Coll. Dentistry, Los Angeles County Art Mus. Assocs. Office: 925 W 34th St Los Angeles CA 90089 Office Phone: 213-740-2811. Office Fax: 213-740-1509. E-mail: slavkin@usc.edu.

SLEEP, NORMAN H., geophysics educator; BS in Math., Mich. State U., 1967; MS in Geophysics, MIT, 1969, PhD in Geophysics, 1973. Postdoc. rsch. assoc. Mass. Inst. Tech., Cambridge, 1973; asst. prof. Geophysics Northwestern U., Evanston, Ill., 1973-79; from assoc. prof. to prof. Geophysics Stanford U., Palo Alto, Calif., 1979—. Contbr. articles to profl. jours. including Earth Planetary Sci., J. Geophysical Rsch., Nature. Recipient James B. Macelwane award, 1980, George P. Woollard award, 1991. Fellow Am. Geophysical Union (Walter H. Bucher medal 1998), Geological Soc. Am., AAAS. Office: Stanford U Dept Geophysics Mitchell Bldg Rm 373A Palo Alto CA 94305-2215

SLEICHER, CHARLES ALBERT, chemical engineer; b. Albany, NY, Aug. 15, 1924; s. Charles Albert and Beatrice Eugena (Cole) S.; m. Janis Jorgensen, Sept. 5, 1953; children— Jeffrey Mark, Gretchen Gail. BS, Brown U., 1946; MS, M.I.T., 1949; PhD, U. Mich., 1955. Asst. dir. M.I.T. Sch. Chem. Engring.; Practice Bangor, Maine, 1949-51; research engr. Shell Devel. Co., Emeryville, Calif., 1955-59; assoc. prof. chem. engring. U. Wash., Seattle, 1960-66, prof., 1966-92, prof. emeritus, 1993—, dept. chmn., 1977-89. Cons. Westinghouse-Hanford Co.; profl. photographer, 1994—. Contbr. articles on extraction, heat transfer, fluid mechanics, pesticide transport to profl. jours.; contbr. photos to mags., books & calendars. Served with USN, 1943-47. NSF postdoctoral fellow, 1959-60; SEED grantee, 1973-74; research grantee NSF; research grantee Chevron Research Corp.; research grantee Am. Chem. Soc. Fellow AIChE (program and awards coms.), AAAS; mem. Am. Chem. Soc., N.Am. Nature Photography Assn., Photographic Soc. Am., Sigma Xi. Achievements include chem. reactor design patents, nat. photography awards, co-founder Columbia Winery. Office: U Wash Dept Chem Engring PO Box 351750 Seattle WA 98195-1750 Home: 116 Fairview Ave N Unit 310 Seattle WA 98109-5328

SLETTEN, JOHN ROBERT, construction company executive; b. Gt. Falls, Mont., Sept. 19, 1932; s. John and Hedvig Marie (Finstad) S.; m. Patricia Gail Thomas, Dec. 16, 1962; children: Leighanne, Kristen Gail, Erik John. BS in Archtl. Engring., Mont. State U., 1956, PhD (hon.), 1993. Estimator Sletten Constrn. Co., Gt. Falls, 1956-63, v.p., area mgr. Las Vegas, Nev., 1963-65, pres., chief exec. officer Gt. Falls, 1969—2001, chmn. bd., 1991—. Bd. dirs. 1st Banks, Gt. Falls, Blue Cross-Blue Shield, Helena, Mont. Chmn. Gt. Falls Mil. Affairs Com., 1985; pres. President's Cir., Mont. State U., Bozeman, 1986; trustee Mont. Hist. Soc., Helena, 1987. with USMC, 1950-52. Mem. Mont. Contractors Assn. (bd. dirs. 1969-75, pres. 1974), Mont. C. of C. (chmn. 1984), Pachyderm Club, Rotary (bd. dirs. Gt. Falls), Elks. Republican. Lutheran. Avocations: skiing, fishing, hunting. Office: Sletten Inc 1000 25th St N PO Box 2467 Great Falls MT 59403-2467

SLEZKINE, YURI, history professor; b. Moscow, Feb. 7, 1956; came to US, 1983; s. Lev Y. and Karma M. (Goldstein) S.; m. Lisa C. Little, Nov. 21, 1984; 1 child, Peter A. BA, MA, Moscow State U., 1978; PhD, U. Tex., 1989. Transl., Port Beira, Mozambique, 1978-79; editor Progress Pub., Moscow, 1980-82; instr. Linguacoop Lang. Inst., Lisbon, Portugal, 1982-83; instr. Slavic Studies U. Tex., 1983-86; asst. prof. history Wake Forest U., Winston-Salem, NC, 1989—92, Univ. Calif., Berkeley, 1992—94, assoc. prof. history, 1994—98, prof. of history, 1998—, dir. Inst. Slavic, East European & Eurasian studies. Bd. trustees Nat. Coun. Soviet and East European Rsch., 1995—2001; disting. vis. prof. Vassar Coll., Poughkeepsie, NY, 2002; spl. prof. U. Nottingham, England, 2006—09. Author: Arctic Mirrors: Russia and the Small Peoples of the North, 1994 (Book of Yr. award, Am. Hist. Assn., 1995), The Jewish Century, 2004 (Best Scholarly Book in Religion, Assn. Am. Publishers, 2004, Wayne S. Vucinich book prize, Am. Assn. Advancement Slavic Studies, 2005, Nat. Jewish Book award, 2005, Ronald S. Lauder award, 2005); co-author: Speak Russian, 1990; asst. editor Slavic Rev., 1985-87; co-editor: In the Shadow of Revolution: Life Stories of Russian Women from 1917 to the Second World War, 2000, Between Heaven and Hell: The Myth of Siberia in Russian Culture, 1993. Pew grantee Wake Forest U., 1990; Postdoctoral fellow Social Sci. Rsch. Coun., 1990, Fgn. Lang. and Area Studies fellow U. Tex., 1988-89, Univ. fellow U. Tex., 1987-88. Fellow Am. Acad. Arts and Sciences; mem. Am. Hist. Assn. (prog. com., 1995), Am. Assn. Advancement Slavic Studies (bd. dirs.). Office: UC Berkeley History Dept 2220 Dwindle Hall Berkeley CA 94720 also: UC Berkeley ISEES 260 Stephens Hall 2304 Berkeley CA 94720-2304 Office Phone: 510-642-3230, 510-642-2224. Office Fax: 510-643-5045. E-mail: isees@berkeley.edu, slezkine@berkeley.edu.

SLIPSAGER, HENRIK C., building services company executive; CFO ISS Internat. Svc. Sys., Inc., 1984-85, exec. v.p., COO, 1985-88, pres., CEO, 1988-94; exec. v.p. janitorial svcs. ABM Industries Inc., San Francisco, 1994-99, sr. v.p., 1997-99, pres. Am. Bldg. Maintenance Co., 1999-2000, CEO, pres., 2000—. Office: Abm Industries Inc 420 Taylor St # 200 San Francisco CA 94102-1702

SLOAN, ANNE ELIZABETH, food scientist, writer; d. Thomas and Anne Sloan; m. James Murtland, June 14, 2003. BS, Rutgers U., 1973; PhD, U. Minn., 1976. Mgr. nutrition comm. Gen. Mills, Mpls., 1976—78; dir. Good Housekeeping Inst., NYC, 1978—85; editor-in-chief McCall's Mag., NYC, 1985—92; pres. Sloan Trends and Solution, Stuart, Fla., 1993—2003, Sloan Trends, Escondido, Calif., 2004—. Author: Food For Thoughts, 1977, Contemporary Nutrition Controversies, 1979; contbr. articles to numerous profl. jours. and mag. Recipient Pub. Rels. award, John W. Hill Found.; George Cook scholar, Rutgers U., 1973.

SLOAN, HARRY EVANS, film company executive; BA, UCLA, 1971; JD, Loyola Law Sch., 1976. Founder, entertainment lawyer Sloan, Kuppin and Ament, LA, 1976—83; co-chmn. New World Entertainment Ltd., Los Angeles, 1983—89; chmn. SBS Broadcasting S.A., Luxembourg, 1990—2002, CEO, 1993—2001, exec. chmn., 2002—05; chmn., CEO Metro-Goldwyn-Mayer Inc., 2005—. Dir. ZeniMax Media Inc. Office: Metro Goldwyn Mayer Inc 10250 Constellation Blvd Los Angeles CA 90067

SLOAN, JERRY (GERALD EUGENE SLOAN), professional basketball coach; b. McLeansboro, Ill., Mar. 28, 1942; m. Bobbye (dec. 2004); 3 children: Kathy, Brian, Holly. Student, Evansville Coll., Ind., 1965. Player Balt. Bullets, 1965—66, Chgo. Bulls, 1966—76, scout, 1976—77, asst. coach, 1977—79, head coach, 1979—82; scout Utah Jazz, Salt Lake City, 1983—84, asst. coach, 1984—88, head coach, 1988—. Named NBA Coach of Yr., The Sporting News, 2004; named to NBA All-Star Team, 1967, 1969, NBA All-Def. First Team, 1969, 1972, 1974, 1975, Naismith Meml. Basketball Hall of Fame, 2009. Office: Utah Jazz EnergySolutions Arena 301 W South Temple Salt Lake City UT 84101*

SLOAN, L. LAWRENCE, publishing executive; b. NYC, 1947; Grad., UCLA. Chmn. Price Stern Sloan, Inc., West Hollywood, Calif. Pres. Sloan Co. Office: 11150 W Olympic Blvd Los Angeles CA 90064-1817

SLOAN, SHELDON HAROLD, lawyer; b. Mpls., Dec. 25, 1935; s. Leonard Norman Sloan and Mary (Wasserman); m. Loraine Bayer, Nov. 28, 1964; children: Stephen Howard, Jennifer Blair; m. Shelby Jean Sloan. BSBA, UCLA, 1958; JD, U. So. Calif., 1961. Bar: Calif. 1962, US Dist. Ct. (so. and cen. dists.) Calif. 1962, US Claims Ct. 1962, US Supreme Ct. 1962. Atty. US Dept. Justice, Washington, 1962-63; assoc. Brown & Brown, LA, 1963-73, ptnr., 1976-79; judge LA Mcpl. Ct., 1973-76; sole practice, 1980—; of counsel Lewis, Brisbois Bisgaard & Smith LLP. Bd. dirs. ACA JOE, San Francisco, Pioneer Magnetics Inc., Santa Monica, Calif. Trustee, treas. Westlake Sch. for Girls, Los Angeles, 1980; pres., chmn. Coro Found., LA, 1980-81, Frater Friends Music Ctr., LA, 1981-85; chmn. Senator Pete Wilson's Jud. Selection Com., 1982-84, 85—; pres. Guardians Jewish Homes for the Aged, LA, 1986, LA Meml. Coliseum Commn., 1999-2000. Mem.: State Bar Calif. (pres. 2006—07), LA County Bar Assn. (chmn. Jud. Appointments Com. 1984, pres. 1996—97). Republican. Avocation: golf. Office: Lewis, Brisbois Bisgaard & Smith LLP Ste 1200 221 N Figueroa St Los Angeles CA 90012-2601 also: 11111 Santa Monica Blvd Ste 230 Los Angeles CA 90025-3347 Office Phone: 310-268-0622. Personal E-mail: ssloanlaw@aol.com. E-mail: Sloan@lbbslaw.com.

SLOANE, THOMAS O., speech educator; b. West Frankfort, Ill., July 12, 1929; s. Thomas Orville and Blanche (Morris) S.; m. Barbara Lee Lewis, Nov. 1, 1952; children— Elizabeth Alison, David Lewis, Emily. BA, So. Ill. U., 1951, MA, 1952; PhD, Northwestern U., 1960. Instr. English, Washington and Lee U., 1958-60; asst. prof. speech U. Ill., 1960-65, assoc. prof., 1965-70, assoc. head dept., 1967-68, asst. dean liberal arts and scis., 1966-67; prof. rhetoric, chmn. rhetoric dept. U. Calif., Berkeley, 1970-92, pres.'s chair, 1987-90, prof. emeritus, 1993—. Dir. Nat. Endowment Humanities Summer Seminar for Coll. Tchrs., 1979 Editor: The Oral Study of Literature, 1966, The Passions of the Minde in Generall (Thomas Wright), 1971, (with Raymond B. Waddington) The Rhetoric of Renaissance Poetry, 1974, (with Joanna H. Maclay) Interpretation, 1972; Donne, Milton and the End of Humanist Rhetoric, 1985, On the Contrary, 1997, (with Peter Oesterreich) Rhetorica Movet, 1999; editor in chief: Encyclopedia of Rhetoric, 2001; contbr. articles to profl. jours. Served to lt. USNR, 1952-55. Faculty research fellow, 1964; U. Ill. instructional devel. awardee, 1965; Henry H. Huntington Library research awardee, 1967; U. Calif. humanities research fellow, 1974; Guggenheim fellow, 1981-82 Office: U Calif Berkeley CA 94720-0001 E-mail: tos@berkeley.edu.

SLONECKER, CHARLES EDWARD, anatomist, medical educator, writer; b. Gig Harbor, Wash., Nov. 30, 1938; s. William Mead and Helen Spencer (Henderson) S.; m. Jan Hunter, June 24, 1961; children— David Charles, Derron Scott, John Patrick. Student, Olympic Coll., 1957-58; student in Sci., U. Wash., 1958-60, DDS, 1965, PhD in Biol. Structure, 1967. Sci. asst. in pathology U. Bern, Switzerland, 1967-68; asst. prof. U. B.C., Vancouver, Canada, 1968-71, assoc. prof., 1971-76, prof., 1976, head of anatomy, 1981-92, dir. ceremonies and univ. rels., 1989—2003, acting v.p. external affairs, 1998-99, 00-01, prof. emeritus, 2003—. Advisor Community Unit YMCA, Vancouver, 1981-92; group com. chmn. Boy Scouts, Can., 1976-82; mem. cabinet United Way Lower Mainland, 1997-99. With USAR, 1955-63. Recipient Award of Merit Am. Acad. Dental Medicine, 1965; recipient Award of Merit Wash. State Dental Assn., 1965, Dennis P. Duskin Meml. award U. Wash., 1965, Master Tchr. award, Cert. of Merit U. B.C., 1975-76, U. B.C. Pres.'s award for excellence, 2001, Individual Exceptional Svc. award United Way, Vancouver, 2005. Fellow Am. Coll. Dentists; mem. Am. Assn. Anatomists (Centennial Gold medal 1987, program sec. 1982-90, v.p. 1991-93, pres. 1994, A. Ladman award for svc. 2003), Can. Assn. U. Tchrs. (U. B.C. Killam Tchg. prize 1995), U. B.C. Prof. Emeriti Assn. (pres. 2006—), Sigma Xi (pres. U. B.C. 1981-82, 88-89), Omicron Kappa Upsilon (chpt. sec.). Anglican. Home: 6007 Dunbar St Vancouver BC Canada V6N 1W8 E-mail: csloneck@interchange.ubc.ca.

SLUDIKOFF, STANLEY ROBERT, publisher, writer; b. Bronx, NY, July 17, 1935; s. Harry and Lillie (Elberger) S.; m. Ann Paula Blumberg, June 30, 1972; children: Lisa Beth, Jaime Dawn, Bonnie Joy. B.Arch., Pratt Inst., 1957; grad. student, U. So. Calif., 1960-62. Cert. planner Am. Inst. Cert. Planners. Project planner Robert E. Alexander, F.A.I.A. & Assos., Los Angeles, 1965-66, Daniel, Mann, Johnson & Mendenhall (City and Regional Planning Cons.), Los Angeles, 1967-70; pres., editor, pub. Gambling Times Inc., also Two Worlds Mgmt., Inc., Los Angeles, 1971—2003; v.p. Prima Quality Farms, Inc., PR; chmn. Creative Games, Inc., 1992—. Pres. Las Vegas TV Weekly, also Postal West, Las Vegas, 1975-79; founder Stanley Roberts Sch. Winning Blackjack, 1976; instr. city and regional planning program U. So. Calif., 1960-63; founding mem. Mfrs. Direct, 1996. Author: (under pen name Stanley Roberts) Winning Blackjack, 1971, How to Win at Weekend Blackjack, 1973, Gambling Times Guide to Blackjack, 1983; author: The Beginner's Guide to Winning Blackjack, 1983, Begin to Win at Blackjack, 1997, Begin to Win at Video Poker, 1997, Begin to Win at Craps, 1997; also monthly column, 1977—; creator & tournament dir. The World Casino Games; editor/pub. Poker Player Newspaper, 1982-88, 2003—; inventor Daily Digit lottery game, Straight Out casino game; founder www.gamblingtimes.com, www.pokerplayernewspaper.com; patentee in field. Mem. Destination 90 Forum, Citizens Planning Group, San Fernando Valley, Calif., 1966-67, Rebuild L.A. land use com., 1992-94; pres. Sludikoff Gaming Tournaments, chmn., 2007-. Served to lt. col. US Army, served to lt. col. Aus., ret. Recipient commendation from mayor Los Angeles for work on model cities funding, 1968 Mem. AIA, Am. Planning Assn., Am. Inst. Cert. Planners, Internat. Casino Assn. (sec. 1980-85), Res. Officers Assn. (life), Mensa (life) Achievements include invention of Straight Out gambling game. Avocation: poker. Office: 3883 W Century Blvd Inglewood CA 90303-1003 Office Phone: 310-674-3365. Business E-Mail: srs@gamblingtimes.com.

SMALES, FRED BENSON, materials product company executive; b. Keokuk, Iowa, Oct. 7, 1914; s. Fred B. and Mary Alice (Warwick) S.; m. Constance Brennan, Dec. 11, 1965; children: Fred Benson III, Catherine (Mrs. Jonathan Christensen); children by previous marriage: Nancy (Mrs. Bruce Clark). Student public schs., Los Angeles. With U.S. Plywood Corp., 1933-68, successively San Francisco mgr., 1938-44, Los Angeles, Western div. mgr., 1944-55, v.p. Western sales div., 1955-65, v.p., regional dir., 1965-68, pres. Lewers & Cooke, Inc. div. Honolulu, 1966-68; chmn. Securities of Am., Inc., 1968-70; chmn., pres., dir. Hawaiian Cement Co., 1970-84; pres. Transpacific Cons., 1984-94; owner Plywood Hawaii, 1995—. Trustee Hawaii-Pacific U., Hawaii Maritime Ctr. Recipient Disting. Citizen award Nat. Govs. Assn., 1986. Mem. C. of C. Hawaii (past chmn.), So. Calif. Yachting Assn. (sr. staff commodore), Balboa Yacht Club (Corona del Mar, Calif, sr. staff commodore), Transpacific Yacht, Waikiki Yacht (staff commodore), Pacific Club (past pres.), Sequoia Yacht Club (Redwood City, Calif., sr. staff commodore). Home: 46-422 Hulupala Pl Kaneohe HI 96744-4243 Office: 1062 Kikowaena Pl Honolulu HI 96819-4413

SMALL, ELISABETH CHAN, psychiatrist, educator; b. Beijing, July 11, 1934; came to U.S., 1937; d. Stanley Hong and Lily Luella (Lum) Chan; m. Donald M. Small, July 8, 1957 (div. 1980); children Geoffrey Brooks, Philip Willard Stanley; m. H. Sidney Robinson, Jan. 12, 1991 (div. 2001). Student, Immaculate Heart Coll., LA, 1951-52; BA in Polit. Sci., UCLA, 1955, MD, 1960. Intern Newton-Wellesley Hosp., Mass., 1960-61; asst. dir. for venereal diseases Mass. Dept. Pub. Health, 1961-63; resident in psychiatry Boston State Hosp., Mattapan, Mass., 1965-66, Tufts New Eng. Med. Ctr. Hosps., 1966-69, psychiat. cons. dept. gynecology, 1973-75; asst. clin. prof. psychiatry Sch. Medicine Tufts U., 1973-75, assoc. clin. prof., 1975-82, asst. clin. prof. ob-gyn, 1977-80, assoc. clin. prof. ob-gyn, 1980-82; from assoc. prof. to prof. psychiatry U. Nev. Sch. Med., Reno, 1982-95; practice psychiatry specializing in psychological effects of bodily changes on women, 1969—; emeritus prof. psychiatry and behavioral scis. U. Nev. Sch. Medicine, Reno, 1995—, from assoc. prof. to clin. assoc. prof. ob-gyn, 1982-88; mem. staff Tufts New Eng. Med. Ctr. Hosps., 1977-82, St. Margaret's Hosps., Boston, 1977-82, Washoe Med. Ctr., Reno, 1983—2006, St. Mary's Regional Med. Ctr., Reno, Truckee Meadows Hosp., Reno, St. Mary's Hosp., Reno; chief psychiatry svc. Reno VA Med. Ctr., 1989-94. Lectr., cons. in field; mem. psychiatry adv. panel Hosp. Satellite Network; mem. office external peer rev. NIMH, HEW; psychiat. cons. to Boston Redevelopment Authority on Relocation of Chinese Families of South Cove Area, 1968-70; mem. New Eng. Med. Ctr. Hosps. Cancer Ctr. Com., 1979-80, Pain Control Com., 1981-82; reproductive sys. curriculum com. Tufts Univ. Sch. Medicine, 1975-82. Mem. editorial bd. Psychiat. Update Am. (Psychiat. Assn. ann. rev.), 1983-85; reviewer Psychosomatics and Hosp. Community Psychiatry, New Eng. Jour. of Medicine, Am. Jour. of Psychiatry Psychosomatic Medicine; contbr. articles to profl. jours. Fellow, Radcliffe Inst., 1967—70; Immaculate Heart Coll. scholar, 1951—52, Mira Hershey scholar, UCLA, 1955. Fellow Am. Coll. Psychiatrists (sci. program com. 1989-98); mem. AMA, Am. Psychiat. Assn. (life, rep. to sect. com. AAAS, chmn. ad hoc com. Asian-Am. Psychiatrists 1975, task force 1975-77, task force cost effectiveness in consultation 1984—, caucus chmn. 1981-82, sci. program com. 1982-88, courses subcom. chmn. sci. program com. 1986-88), Nev. Psychiat. Assn., Assn. for Acad. Psychiatry (fellowship com. 1982), Washoe County Med. Assn., Nev. Med. Soc. Avocations: skiing, cooking. Home and Office: 825 Caughlin Crossing Reno NV 89519-0647

SMALL, STACY H., luxury travel company executive, former magazine editor; b. Rochester, NY, 1969; BS in Mag. Journalism, Syracuse U. Samuel Irving Newhouse Sch. Pub. Comm., NY, 1991. With Caribbean Travel & Life mag., Washington; sr. editor Travel Agent Mag., NYC, LA, 1994—2000; founder, pres., chief content provider TheWriteCrowd, LLC, Marina del Rey, Calif., 2000—01; editl. dir. Elite Traveler Mag., 2001—03; contbg. editor Ocean Home Mag., NY Family Mag., Agent@Home Mag., 2004—; founder, pres. Elite Travel International, Brentwood, Calif., 2005—. Contbr. Breast Cancer Rsch. Found. Named Nat. Woman of Yr., Leukemia & Lymphoma Soc., 2006. Mem.: Beverly Hills C. of C., Ladies Who Launch, Travel Tourism & Hospitality Grp., Luxury & Lifestyle Profls., Travel Industry Profls. Worldwide, Travel Industry Exec. Womens Network, World Luxury Travelers Soc., St. Barts Network, Luxury Industry Profls., Women in Tech. Internat. Office: Elite Travel Internat 1011 S Barrington Ave Los Angeles CA 90049 Office Phone: 310-979-9036. Business E-Mail: stacy@elitetravelinternational.com.

SMART, JEAN, actress; b. Seattle, Sept. 13, 1951; m. Richard Gilliland, June 7, 1987; 1 child, Connor Douglas. Actor: (films) Gangsters, 1979, Flashpoint, 1984, Protocol, 1984, Fire with Fire, 1986, Project X, 1987, Baby Talk, 1992, Mistress, 1992, Homeward Bound: The Incredible Journey, 1993, The Brady Bunch Movie, 1995, The Odd Couple II, 1998, Guinevere, 1999, Forever Fabulous, 1999, Snow Day, 2000, The Kid, 2000, Sweet Home Alabama, 2002, Bringing Down the House, 2003, Garden State, 2004, I Heart Huckabees, 2004, Lucky You, 2007, Hero Wanted, 2008; (TV films) Before and After, 1979, Piaf, 1984, Single Bars, Single Women, 1984, A Fight for Jenny, 1986, Place at the Table, 1987, A Seduction in Travis County, 1991, Locked Up: A Mother's Rage, 1991, Overkill: The Aileen Wuornos Story, 1992, Just My Imagination, 1992, The Yarn Princess, 1994, The Yearling, 1994, A Stranger in Town, 1995, Undue Influence, 1996, A Change of Heart, 1998, The Man Who Came to Dinner, 2000, Audrey's Rain, 2003, Killer Instinct: From the Files of Agent Candice DeLong, 2003, Kim Possible: A Sitch in Time, 2003, A Very Married Christmas, 2004, Kim Possible: So the Drama, 2005; (TV series) Maximum Security, 1984, Designing Women, 1986—91, High Society, 1995—96, Style and Substance, 1998, Frasier, 2000—01 (Primetime Emmy Outstanding Guest Actress in a Comedy Series, Acad. TV Arts and Scis., 2000, 2001), The District, 2000—04, The Oblongs, 2001, In-Laws, 2002—03, Kim Possible, 2002—07, Center of the Universe, 2004—05, 24, 2006—07, Samantha Who?, 2007— (Primetime Emmy for Outstanding Supporting Actress in a Comedy Series, Acad. TV Arts and Scis., 2008). Office: CBS Studio Ctr Bungalow 15 4024 Radford Ave Studio City CA 91604 also: c/o Untitled Entertainment 1801 Century Park E, Ste 700 Los Angeles CA 90067

SMARTT, RICHARD A., museum director; married. BS, MS, U. Tex., El Paso; PhD in Zoology and Botany, U. N.Mex. Prof. U. Tex., El Paso; dir., chmn. sci. divsn., curator zoology and collections N.Mex. Mus. Natural History, Albuquerque; now exec. dir. The Wildlife Experience, Parker, Colo. Contbr. articles to profl. jours. Office: The Wildlife Experience 10035 S Peoria Parker CO 80134 Office Phone: 720-488-3301. Office Fax: 720-488-3399.

SMATHERS, JAMES BURTON, medical physicist, educator; b. Prairie du Chien, Wis., Aug. 26, 1935; s. James Levi and Irma Marie (Stindt) S.; m. Sylvia Lee Rath, Apr. 20, 1957; children: Kristine Kay, Kathryn Ann, James Scott, Ernest Kent. B.Nuclear Enging., N.C. State Coll., 1957, MS, 1959; PhD, U. Md., 1967. Diplomate Am. Bd. Radiology, Am. Bd. Health Physics, Am. Bd. Medical Physics; cert. in radiation oncology physics; registered profl. engr., D.C., Tex., Calif. Research engr. Atomics Internat., Canoga Park, Calif., 1959, Walter Reed Army Inst. Research, Washington, 1961-67; prof. nuclear enging. Tex. A. and M. U., College Station, 1967-80, prof., head bioengring., 1976-80; prof., head med. physics, dept. radiation oncology UCLA, 1980-2001, prof. emeritus, 2001—. Cons. U.S. Army, Dept. Energy, also pvt.; industry. Served with U.S. Army, 1959-61. Recipient Excellence in Teaching award Gen. Dynamics, 1971; Excellence in Research award Tex. A. and M. U. Former Students Assn., 1976 Mem. Health Physics Soc., Am. Assn. Physcists in Medicine, Am. Coll. Med. Physics, Am. Soc. Therapeutic Radiation Oncology, Am. Coll. Radiology. Home: 18229 Minnehaha St Northridge CA 91326-3427 E-mail: smathers@ucla.edu.

SMEGAL, THOMAS FRANK, JR., lawyer; b. Eveleth, Minn., June 15, 1935; s. Thomas Frank and Genevieve (Andreachi) S.; m. Susan Jane Stanton, May 28, 1966; children: Thomas Frank, Elizabeth Jane. BS in Chem. Enging., Mich. Technol. U., 1957; JD, George Washington U., 1961. Bar: Va. 1961, D.C. 1961, Calif. 1964, U.S. Supreme Ct. 1976. Patent examiner U.S. Patent Office, Washington, 1957-61; staff patent atty. Shell Devel. Co., San Francisco, 1962-65; patent atty. Townsend and Townsend, San Francisco, 1965-91, mng. ptnr., 1974-89; sr. ptnr. Graham and James, San Francisco, 1992-97; ptnr. Knobbe, Martens, Olson & Bear, San Francisco, 1997—2005, Law Offices Thomas F. Smegal, Jr., 2006—. Mem. U.S. del. to Paris Conv. for Protection of Indsl. Property; mem. adv. com. Ct. of Appeals for Fed. Cir., 1992-96. Contbr. articles to profl. jours. Pres. bd. dirs. Legal Aid Soc. San Francisco, 1982-84, Youth Law Ctr., 1973-84; bd. dirs. Nat. Ctr. for Youth Law, 1978-84, San Francisco Lawyers Com. for Urban Affairs, 1972—, Legal Svcs. for Children, 1980-88; bd. dirs., presdl. nominee Legal Svcs. Corp., 1984-90, 1993-2003. Capt. Chem. Corps, U.S. Army, 1961-62. Recipient St. Thomas More award, 1982. Mem. ABA (chmn. PTC sect. 1990-91, ho. of dels. 1988-2000,2006, mem. standing com. Legal Aid and Indigent Defendants 1991-94, 2004—07, chair sect. officer conf. 1992-94, bd. govs. 1994-97, standing com. on Pro Bono and Pub. Svc. 1997-2001, standing com. on Gavel awards 2001-04), Intellectual Property Law Assn. (chmn. nat. coun. 1989), Nat. Inventors Hall of Fame (pres. 1988), Calif. Bar Assn. (v.p. bd. dirs. 1986-87), Am. Patent Law Assn. (pres. 1986), Internat. Assn. Intellectual Property Lawyers (pres. 1995-2001), Bar Assn. San Francisco (pres. 1979), Patent Law Assn. San Francisco (pres. 1974), Olympic Club, Golden Gate Breakfast Club, Claremont Country Club (Oakland). Republican. Roman Catholic. Office: One Sansome Ste 3500 San Francisco CA 94104 Home: 107 King Ave Piedmont CA 94610 Home Phone: 510-547-5309; Office Phone: 415-217-8383. Business E-Mail: tomsmegal@smegallaw.com.

SMELSER, NEIL JOSEPH, sociologist; b. Kahoka, Mo., July 22, 1930; s. Joseph Nelson and Susie Marie (Hess) S.; m. Helen Thelma Margolis, June 10, 1954 (div. 1965); children: Eric Jonathan, Tina Rachel; m. Sharin Fateley, Dec. 20, 1967; children: Joseph Neil, Sarah Joanne. BA, Harvard U., 1952, PhD, 1958; BA, Oxford U., Eng., 1954, MA, 1959; grad., San Francisco Psychoanalytic Inst., 1971. Mem. faculty U. Calif., Berkeley, 1958-94, prof. sociology, 1962—, asst. chancellor ednl. devel., 1966-68; assoc. dir. Inst. of Internat. Studies, Berkeley, 1969-73, 80-89; prof. sociology U. Calif., Berkeley, 1972-94; prof. emeritus, 1994—; dir. edn. abroad program for U. Calif., Berkeley, 1977-79, spl. advisor Office of Pres., 1993-94, dir. Ctr. for Advanced Study in Behavioral Scis., 1994-2001. Bd. dirs. Social Sci. Rsch. Coun., chmn., 1971-73, com. econ. growth, 1961-65; trustee Ctr. for Advanced Study in Behavioral Scis., 1980-93, 1994-2007, chmn., 1984-86; trustee Russell Sage Found., 1990-2000; subcom. humanism Am. Bd. Internal Medicine, 1981-85, 89-90, adv. com., 1992-99, chmn. adv. com., 1995-99; chmn. sociology panel Behavioral and Social Scis. survey NAS and Social Sci. Rsch. Coun., 1967-69; com. on basic rsch. in behavioral and social scis. NRC, 1980-89, chmn., 1984-86, co-chmn., 1986-89; chmn. com. of selection Guggenheim Found., 1996-; chmn. Commn. for Behavioral and Social Scis. and Edn. (NAS/NRC), 1996-2003, German-Am. Acad. Coun., 1999-2000. Author: (with T. Parsons) Economy and Society, 1956, Social Change in the Industrial Revolution, 1959, Theory of Collective Behavior, 1962, The Sociology of Economic Life, 1963, 2d edit., 1975, Essays in Sociological Explanation, 1968, Sociological Theory: A Contemporary View, 1971, Comparative Methods in the Social Sciences, 1976, (with Robin Content) The Changing Academic Market, 1980, Sociology, 1981, 2d edit., 1984, 3d edit., 1987, 4th edit., 1991, 5th edit., 1995, Social Paralysis and Social Change, 1991, Effective Committee Service, 1993, Sociology, 1994, Problematics of Sociology, 1997, The Social Edges of Psychoanalysis, 1999, The Faces of Terrorism, 2007; editor: (with W.T. Smelser) Personality and Social Systems, 1963, 2d edit., 1971, (with S.M. Lipset) Social Structure and Mobility in Economic Development, 1966, Sociology, 1967, 2d edit., 1973, (with James Davis) Sociology: A Survey Report, 1969, Karl Marx on Society and Social Change, 1973, (with Gabriel Almond) Public Higher Education in California, 1974, (with Erik Erikson) Themes of Work and Love in Adulthood, 1980, (with Jeffrey Alexander et al) The Micro-Macro Link, 1987, Handbook of Sociology, 1988, (with Hans Haferkamp) Social Change and Modernity, 1992; (with Richard Munch) Theory of Culture, 1992; (with Richard Swedberg) The Handbook of Economic Sociology, 1994, 2d. edit. 2005; (with Jeffrey Alexander) Diversity and Its Discontents, 1999; (with William Julius Wilson and Faith Mitchell) American Becoming: Racial Trends and their Consequences, 2001, (with Paul B. Baltes) International Encyclopedia of the Social and Behavioral Sciences, 2001; editor Am. Sociol. Rev., 1962-65; adv. editor Am. Jour. Sociology, 1960-62. Rhodes scholar, 1952-54; Jr. fellow Soc. Fellows, Harvard U., 1955-58, fellow Russell Sage Found., 1989-90. Mem. Am. Sociol. Assn. (coun. 1962-65, 67-70, exec. com. 1963-65, pres. elect 1995-96, pres. 1996-97), Pacific Sociol. Assn., Internat. Sociol. Assn. (exec. com. 1986-94, v.p. 1990-94), Am. Acad. Arts and Scis. (hon.), Fedn. State Med. Bds. (bd. dirs. 2006-), (Am. Philos. Soc. (hon.), Nat. Acad. of Scis. (hon.). Business E-Mail: nsmelser@berkeley.edu.

SMERDON, ERNEST THOMAS, engineering educator; b. Ritchey, Mo., Jan. 19, 1930; s. John Erle and Ada (Davidson) Smerdon; m. Joanne Duck, June 9, 1951; children: Thomas, Katherine, Gary. BS in Enging., U. Mo., 1951, MS in Enging., 1956, PhD in Enging., 1959, DSc (hon.), 2003. Registered profl. engr., Ariz. Chmn. dept. agrl. enging. U. Fla., Gainesville, 1968-74, asst. dean for rsch., 1974-76; vice chancellor for acad. affairs U. Tex. System, Austin, 1976-82; dir. Ctr. for Rsch. in Water Resources U. Tex., 1982-88; dean Coll. Enging. and Mines U. Ariz., Tucson, 1988-92, vice provost, dean Enging, 1992-97; sr. edn. assoc. NSF, Arlington, Va., 1997-00; prof. civil enging. and hydrology U. Ariz., Tucson, 1988—2001, dean emeritus, 2001—. Mem. bd. sci. and tech. internat. devel. NRC, 1990—94, mem. com. planning and remediation irrigation-induced water quality problems, 1990—96, chair com. Yucca Mountian peer rev., 1995, mem. com. study rsch.-doctorate programs U.S., 1991—95, mem. com. Mo. River Ecosys. Sci., 1999—2001; chair com. Water Resources Mgmt. Instream Flow and Salmon Survival in Columbia River, 2002—04, Sci. Bases Colorado River Water Mgmt., 2005—07, others. Editor: Managing Water Related Conflicts: The Engineer's Role, 1989. Mem. Ariz. Gov.'s Sci. and Tech. Coun., Tucson, 1989—96; bd. dirs. Greater Tucson Econ. Coun., 1990—95.

Recipient Disting. Svc. in Engring. award, U. Mo., 1982, Lifetime Achievement award, Environ. and Water Resources Inst., 2002. Fellow: NAE (acad. adv. bd. 1989—95, tech. policy options com. 1990—91, chair com. career-long edn. engrs. 1997—2000, acad. adv. bd. 1998—99, peer com. 2002—05, chmn. sect. 12 2003—04, com. capacity U.S. Engr. Rsch. Enterprise 2004, peer com. 1986—90, 2002—, steering com. engr. 2020, policy com. Engr. 2020), ASCE (hon. Outstanding Svc. award irrigation and drainage divsn. 1988, Royce Tipton award 1989, Robert C. Park Outstanding Civil Engr. award 2005); mem.: Ariz. Soc. Profl. Engrs. (Engr. of Yr. award 1990), Univ. Coun. Water Resources, Am. Geophys. Union, Am. Soc. Engring. Edn. (chmn., bd. dirs. engring. dean's coun. 1995—97, pres. 1998—99, Outstanding Projects and Leaders award 2008, Benjamin Garver Lamme award 2008), Am. Water Resources Assn. (Icko Iben award 1989), Am. Soc. Agrl. Engrs., Pi Mu Epsilon, Tau Beta Pi, Phi Kappa Phi, Sigma Xi. Avocations: hiking, golf, scuba diving, painting. Office: U Ariz AME Bldg Rm N521 Tucson AZ 85721-0001

SMILEY, RICHARD WAYNE, researcher; b. Paso Robles, Calif., Aug. 17, 1943; s. Cecil Wallace and Elenore Louise (Hamm) S.; m. Marilyn Lois Wenning, June 24, 1967; 1 child, Shawn Elizabeth. BSc in Soil Sci., Calif. State Poly. U., San Luis Obispo, 1965; MSc in Soils, Wash. State U., 1969, PhD in Plant Pathology, 1972. Asst. soil scientist Agrl. Rsch. Svc., USDA, Pullman, Wash., 1966-69; rsch. asst. dept. plant pathology Wash. State U., Pullman, 1969-72; soil microbiologist Commonwealth Sci. and Indsl. Rsch. Orgn., Adelaide, Australia, 1972-73; rsch. assoc. dept. plant pathology Cornell U., Ithaca, NY, 1973-74, asst. prof., 1975-80, assoc. prof., 1980-85; supt. Columbia Basin Agr. Rsch. Ctr., 1985-2000; prof. Oreg. State U., 1985—. Vis. scientist Plant Rsch. Inst., Victoria Dept. Agr., Melbourne, Australia, 1982-83. Author: Compendium of Turfgrass Diseases, 1983, 3d edit., 2005; contbr. more than 200 articles to profl. jours. Postdoctoral fellow NATO, 1972. Fellow Am. Phytopath. Soc. (sr. editor APS Press 1984-87, editor-in-chief 1987-91); mem. Coun. Agrl. Sci. and Tech., Rotary (pres. Pendleton chpt. 1991-92, Paul Harris fellow 1993). Achievements include discovery of the etiology of a serious disease of turfgrasses, which led to a redefinition of studies and disease processes in turfgrasses. Office: Oreg State U Columbia Basin Agr Rsch Ctr PO Box 370 Pendleton OR 97801-0370 Business E-Mail: richard.smiley@oregonstate.edu.

SMILEY, ROBERT HERSCHEL, dean; b. Scottsbluff, Nebr., Mar. 17, 1943; s. Eldridge Herschel and Lucile Agnes (Kolterman) S., m. Sandra P. Mason (div. 1975); children: Peter, Michael, Robin; m. JoAnn Charlene Cannon, June 3, 1978; 1 child, Matthew. BS, UCLA, 1966, MS, 1969; PhD, Stanford U., 1973. Sr. aerospace engr. Martin Marietta Co., Littleton, Colo., 1966-67; mem. tech. staff, engr. Hughes Aircraft Co., Culver City, Calif., 1967-69; prof. econs. and policy, assoc. dean Grad. Sch. Mgmt. Cornell U., Ithaca, N.Y., 1973-89; dean, prof. mgmt. Grad. Sch. Mgmt. U. Calif., Davis, 1989—. Econ. cons. IBM, GM, Amex, SBA, Air Transport Assn., others; mem. rsch. adv. bd. NFIB, 1988—, policy adv. com. Ctr. for Coops., Davis, 1989—, adv. bd. Tech. Devel. Ctr., Davis, 1990—. Editor Sinergie, 1984—, Small Bus. Econs., 1988—; mem. editorial bd. Comstock's Mag., 1989—; contbr. articles to econs. and mgmt. jours. Bd. dirs. Sacramento Valley Forum, 1990—, Japan-Am. Conf., Sacramento, 1991—; chair sponsors com. Access '91, Sacramento, 1991; bd. govs. Capitol Club. SBA grantee, DOE grantee. Mem. Am. Econs. Assn., European Assn. for Rsch., Western Econs. Assn., Beta Gamma Sigma, Capitol Club. Avocations: skiing, tennis, swimming, bicycling. Office: U Calif AOB4 Dept Grad Sch Mgmt Davis CA 95616-8609

SMILEY, ROBERT WILLIAM, JR., investment banker; b. Lansing, Mich., Nov. 17, 1943; s. Robert William Sr. and Rebecca Lee (Flint) S. AB in Econs., Stanford U., 1970; postgrad., San Fernando Valley Coll. Law, 1973—75; MBA in Corp. Fin., City U. L.A., 1979; LLB, LaSalle U., 1982. Bar: Calif. 1984. Sr. v.p. mktg. Actuarial Systems Inc., San Jose, Calif., 1972-73; founder, chmn. Benefit Systems Inc., L.A. and S.E. Nev., 1973-84, Brentwood Sq. Savs. and Loan, LA, 1982-84; chmn., CEO The Benefit Capital Cos. Inc., L.A. and S.E. Nev., 1984—. Lectr. U. Calif. Ext., L.A. and Berkeley, 1977—; instr. Am. Coll. Life Underwriters. Editor, contbg. author: Employee Stock Ownership Plans: ESOP Planning, Implementation, Law and Taxation, 1989, 3d edit. 2006; contbg. author: The Handbook of Employee Benefits, 1984, 7th edit., 2005; contbr. articles to profl. jours. Mem. nat. adv. coun., trustee Reason Found., L.A., 1983-91; bd. dirs. Nat. Ctr. for Employee Ownership, Oakland, Calif.; former trustee The Employee Ownership Found., Washington, 2000-04. With USN, 1961-64, Vietnam. Recipient Spl. Achievement award Pres.' Commn. on Pension Policy, 1984. Fellow Life Mgmt. Inst.; mem. Employee Stock Ownership Plan Assn. (founder, pres., bd. dirs., lifetime dir.), Assn. for Corp. Growth, Western and SW Pension Confs., Nat. Assn. Bus. Economists, ABA, Calif. Bar Assn. Office: The Benefit Capital Cos Inc PO Box 542 Logandale NV 89021-0542 Office Phone: 702-398-3222.

SMILEY, TAVIS, television talk show host, writer; b. Biloxi, Miss., Sept. 13, 1964; s. Emory G. and Joyce M. Smiley. Grad., Ind. U., 1986, D (hon.). Asst. to Mayor Tomilea Allison, LA, 1984—85; coun. aide, 1987; spl. asst. to exec. dir., 1978—88; adminstrv. aide to Mayor Tom Bradley, 1988—90; commentator The Smiley Report, 1990—2001; contbr. CNN, 2001—, HuffingtonPost.com; spl. correspondent ABC-TV, 2001—; commentator Tom Joyner Morning Show; pres., CEO Smiley Group, Inc. Host (TV series) BET Tonight with Tavis Smiley, 1998—2001, supervisory prodr. Tavis Smiley, 2004— (Outstanding TV News, Talk or Information (Series or Spl.), NAACP Image award, 2006), TV appearances include For Your Love, 1999, The Parkers, 2000, Any Day Now, 2001, American Dreams, 2004; author: Hard Left: Straight Talk about the Wrongs of the Right, 1996, Doing What's Right: How to Fight for What You Believe and Make a Difference, 2000, How to Make Black America Better: Leading African Americans Speak Out, 2002, Keeping the Faith: Stories of Love, Courage, Healing and Hope from Black America, 2002; co-author (with David Ritz): What I Know for Sure: My Story of Growing up in America, 2006; editor: The Covenant with Black America, 2006; host TavisTalks.com. Founder Tavis Smiley Found.; bd. dirs. Challengers Boys and Girls Club, Black Coll. Tour, LA; mem. adv. bd. Martin Luther King Jr. Ctr. Non-Violent Social Change, 1992—93, Inner City Found. Excellence in Edn., 1989—91, After Class Scouting, Scouting USA, 1991; chmn. ops. com. Young Black Profls., LA, 1988—90; mem. steering com. United Way Greater L.A., 1989—90. Recipient Outstanding Bus. Profl. award, Dollars & Sense Mag., 1992, Image award, NAACP, 2000, Mickey Leland Humanitarian award, Nat. Assn. Minorities in Communications, NAACP Image award for News, Talk or Information, Series or Spl. for Katrina-One Year Later, 2007, NAACP Image award for Outstanding Talk-Crisis in Darfur, 2008, NAACP Image award for Outstanding Literary Work-Instructional, The Covenant in Action, 2008; named one of 50 Most Promising Young Leaders, Time Mag., 100 Most Influential Black Americans, Ebony mag., 2006, The World's Most Influential People, TIME mag., 2009; named to Hall of Fame, Vanity Fair, 1996, Power 150, Ebony mag., 2008. Office: 3870 Crenshaw Blvd Ste 391 Los Angeles CA 90008*

SMITH, ADAM, United States Representative from Washington; b. Washington, June 15, 1965; s. Ben Smith; m. Sara Bickle-Eldridge, Aug. 1993; 2 children. BA, Fordham U., NY, 1987; JD, U. Wash., 1990. Driver United Parcel Svc., 1985-87; mem. Wash. State Senate, 1990-96; atty. Cromwell, Mendoza and Belur, 1991—92; asst. pros. atty. Seattle, 1993—95; pro tem judge, 1996; mem. US Congress from 9th Wash. dist., 1997—, mem. armed svcs. com., mem. internat. rels. com. Mem. Kent Drinking Driver Task Force, Highline Citizens for Schs., Kent Meridian HS Site-Based Coun.; bd. mem. Judson Pk. Retirement Home. Mem.: Kiwanis Internat. Democrat. Office: US House of Reps 2402 Rayburn House Office Bldg Washington DC 20515 Office Phone: 202-225-8901. Office Fax: 202-225-5893.

SMITH, A.J., professional sports team executive; b. Feb. 28, 1949; m. Susan Smith; children: Andrea, Kyle. Grad. in Health and Phys. Edn., Ky. Wesleyan Coll., Owensboro, 1971. Tchr. health and phys. edn. Providence Jr. HS Sys., 1971—85; asst. coach Cranston West HS, RI, 1971—76, U. RI, 1978; wide receiver Ea. Football League Attleboro Kings, Mass., 1972—74; head coach Ea. Football League RI Kings, 1976; vol. part-time scout NFL NY Giants, 1977; part-time scout NFL New Eng. Patriots, 1978—80, NFL Houston Oilers, 1981; scouting position US Football League Chgo. Blitz., 1982—83, US Football League Pitts. Maulers, 1984; dir. pro pers. NFL San Diego Chargers, 1985—86, asst. gen. mgr., dir. pro pers., 2001—03, exec. v.p., gen. mgr., 2003—; area scout NFL Buffalo Bills, 1987—89, asst. dir. coll. scouting, 1989—93, dir. pro pers., 1993—2000. Named NFL Exec. of Yr., Pro Football Weekly, 2004, Profl. Football Writers of Am., 2004, FoxSports.com, 2004, CBSSportsline.com, 2004; named to Am. Football Assn. Minor/Semi-Pro Football Hall of Fame, 1990. Office: San Diego Chargers PO Box 609609 San Diego CA 92160-9609*

SMITH, ALAN JAY, computer science educator, consultant; b. NYC, Apr. 10, 1949; s. Harry and Elsie Smith. SB, MIT, 1971; MS, Stanford U., Calif., 1973, PhD in Computer Sci., 1974. From asst. prof. to full prof. U. Calif., Berkeley, 1974—; assoc. editor ACM Trans. on Computers Systems, 1982-93. Vice-chmn. elec. engring. and computer sci. dept. U. Calif., Berkeley, 1982-84; nat. lectr. ACM, 1985-86; mem. editl. bd. Jour. Microprocessors and Microsystems, 1988—2005, Microprocessor Report, 2005-07; subject area editor Jour. Parallel and Distbn. Computing, 1989—; mem. IFIP working group 7.3; program chmn. Sigmetrics 89, Performance 1989, Hot Chips Symposium, 1990, 94, 97, 2005. Recipient AA Michaelson award, Comp. Measurement Group, 2003, Harry Goode award, IEEE computer Soc., 2006. Fellow: AAAS, IEEE (disting. visitor 1986—87, Reynold Johnson Info. Storage Sys. award 2008), Assn. for Computing Machinery (chmn. spl. interest group on ops. sys. 1983—87, nat. lectr. 1985—86, bd. dirs. spl. interest group on performance evaluation 1989—89, chmn. spl. interest group on computer architecture 1991—93, bd. dirs. spl. interest group on computer architecture 1993—2003); mem.: Computer Measurement Group. Office: U Calif Dept Computer Sci Berkeley CA 94720-1776

SMITH, ALEX (ALEXANDER DOUG SMITH), professional football player; b. Seattle, Wash., May 7, 1984; s. Douglas D. and Pam Smith. BS in Econ., Utah U., 2003. Quarterback San Francisco 49ers, 2005—. Founder Alex Smith Found., 2005—. Named Nat. Player Yr., The Sporting News, 2004, Mountain West Conf. Player of Yr., 2004. Achievements include being the first overall selection in the 2005 NFL Draft. Office: San Francisco 49ers Marie P DeBartolo Sports Ctr 4949 Centennial Blvd Santa Clara CA 95054

SMITH, ANN DELORISE, municipal official; b. Union, SC, June 26, 1941; 1 child. BS in Social Svc., Ea. Mich. U., 1962, postgrad., 1992-93. Planner III demonstration agy. City of L.A., 1970-75, sr. grants mgmt. specialist cmty. devel. dept., 1975-83, sr. mgmt. analyst I dept. aging, 1983-94, gen. mgr. dept. aging, 1994—. Del. White House Conf. on Aging, 1995; tchr. h.s. social studies, Flint and Ecors, Mich., 1962-63, grant cons., 1964-69, L.A./Detroit. Mem. adv. bd. Roybal Inst., Drew/RAND Ctr. on Health and Aging, KCET; mem. L.A. Urban League; mem. bd. dirs. Delta Sigma Theta HeadStart/State Presch.; involved in fed. grant programs including War on Poverty, 1960's. Mem. Am. Soc. on Aging, Nat. Ctr. and Caucus on Black Aging, Nat. Assn. of Area Agencies on Aging, Calif. Assn. of Area Agencies on Aging, Nat. Coun. on Aging, Gerontol. Soc. Am., Delta Sigma Theta. Home: 3580 Wilshire Blvd #300 Los Angeles CA 90010-2501 also: 610 Cover Ln Accokeek MD 20607-3415

SMITH, ANNA DEAVERE, actress, playwright, educator; b. Balt., Sept. 18, 1950; d. Deavere Young and Anna (Young) S. BA, Beaver Coll., Pa., 1971, doctorate (hon.), 1973; MFA, Am. Conservatory Theatre, 1977; doctorate (hon.), U. NC, 1995; degree (hon.), Wheelock Coll., 1995, Colgate U., 1997, Sch. Visual Arts, 1997, Wesleyan U., 1997, Northwestern U., 1997, Coll. Holy Cross, 1997. Ann O'Day Maples prof. arts and drama Stanford U. Artist-in-residence Ford Found., 1997. Playwright, performer one-woman shows On the Road: A Search for American Character, 1983, Aye, Aye, Aye, I'm Integrated, 1984, Piano, 1991 (Drama-Logue award), Fires in the Mirror, 1989 (Obie award 1992, Drama Desk award 1992, N.Y. Drama Critics spl. citation 1993-94), Twilight: Los Angeles 1992 (Obie award, 2 Tony award nominations, Drama Critics Cir. spl. citation, Outer Critics Cir. award, Drama Desk award, Audelco award, Beverly Hills, Hollywood NAACP theatre awards), House Arrest, 1997; writer libretto for Judith Jamison, performer Hymn, 1993; appeared in (films) Dave, 1993, Philadelphia, 1993, The American President, 1995, Twilight: Los Angeles, 2000. Founding dir. The Inst. on Arts and Civic Dialogue Harvard U., 1998; trustee, Mus. Modern Art, N.Y.C. Named One of Women of Yr., Glamour mag., 1993; fellow Bunting Inst., Radcliffe Coll.; genius fellow The MacArthur Found., 1996. also: Stanford U Dept Drama Memorial Hall Stanford CA 94305

SMITH, ANNICK, writer; b. Paris, May 11, 1936; came to U.S., 1937; d. Stephen and Helene Deutch; m. David James Smith (dec. 1974); children: Eric, Stephen, Alex, Andrew. Student, Cornell Univ., 1954-55, U. Chgo., 1955-57; BA, U. Wash., 1961. Editor U. Wash. Press, Seattle, 1961-64, Montana Bus. Quarterly, U. Montana, Missoula, 1971-72; founding bd. mem. Sundance Film Inst., Sundance, Utah, 1981-85; founding mem. Ind. Film Project, NYC, 1981-84; acting dir. Montana Com. for the Humanities, Missoula, 1983-84; devel. dir. Hellgate Writers, Inc., Missoula, 1986-96; creative dir. Yellow Bay Writers Workshop, U. Montana Continuing Edn. Dept, Missoula, 1987-98. Freelance filmmaker, producer, arts administrator, writer, Mont., 1974—; past H.S. tchr., cmty. organizer, environ. worker. Exec. prodr. Heartland, 1981; co-prodr. A River Runs Through It, 1992; co-editor: (with William Kittredge) The Last Best Place, (Susan O'Connor) The Wide Open; author: Homestead, 1994, Big BlueStem A Journey into the Tall Grass, 1996, In This We Are Native, 2001; contbr. to anthologies including Best Am. Short Stories, 1992. Recipient Western Heritage award Cowboy Hall of Fame, 1981; Mont. Humanites award Mont. Com. for Humanities, 1988, Okla. Book award, 1997, Bancroft Prize Denver Pub. Libr., 1998. Mem. Trout Unlimited, Blackfoot Challenge. Democrat. Office: 898 Bear Creek Rd Bonner MT 59823

SMITH, BRADFORD LEE, computer software company executive, lawyer; b. Milw., Jan. 17, 1959; m. Kathy Surace-Smith; 2 children. AB, summa cum laude, Princeton U., 1981; JD, Columbia U., 1985; student, U. Geneva Grad. Inst. Internat. Studies, Geneva, Switzerland, 1984. Ptnr. Covington & Burling LLP, Washington; mgr., European Law & Corp. Affairs group, Microsoft Corp., Paris, 1993—96, dep. gen. counsel for worldwide sales Redmond, Wash., 1996—2001, sr. v.p., gen. counsel for law & corp. affairs, 2001—. Lectr. Hague Acad. Internat. Law. Contbr. articles. Office: Microsoft One Microsoft Way Redmond WA 98052-6399

SMITH, BRIAN D., lawyer; AB, Brown U., 1972; JD, U. Va. Law Sch., 1977; PhD, Cambridge U., 1986. Bar: Calif., NY, Am. Bar Assn. Atty., real estate, shareholder Heller, Ehrman, White, & McAuliffe LLP, San Francisco, 1991—. Mem.: Lambda Alpha Internat. Office: Heller Ehrman 333 Bush St San Francisco CA 94104 Office Phone: 415-772-6534. Fax: 415-772-6268. E-mail: bsmith@hewm.com.

SMITH, BURTON JORDAN, computer designer; b. Durham, NC, Mar. 21, 1941; s. Sherman Everett and Rebecca Frances (Jordan) S.; m. Dorothy Nan Duncan, Dec. 28, 1966; children: Katherine Page, Julia Jordan. BSEE, U. N.Mex., Albuquerque, 1967; SM, MIT, Cambridge, 1968, Elec. Engring. Diploma, 1969, ScD, 1972. Asst. prof. U. Colo., Denver, 1972-78, assoc. prof., 1978-79; v.p. R&D Denelcor, Inc., Denver, 1979-85; fellow Supercomputing Rsch. Ctr., Lanham, Md., 1985-88; co-founder, chief scientist Tera Computer Co. (purchased Cray Rsch. from Silicon Graphics, Inc. in 2000, renamed Cray, Inc.), Seattle, 1988—2005; chmn. Cray, Inc., Seattle, 1988—99, also bd. dir., 1988—2005; tech. fellow Microsoft Corp., Redmond, Wash., 2005—. Adv. com. on computer rsch. NSF, Washington, 1984-87; fellow, Supercomputing Rsch. Ctr. (now Ctr. for Computing Sciences), divsn. Inst. for Def. Analysis, 1985-88; sci. coun. Universities Space Rsch. Assn., Washington, 1987-91; blue ribbon panel on high performance computing NSF, Washington, 1993, presdl. faculty fellows final selection panel, Washington, 1992-93, Computer Sci. Telecom. Bd. Nat. Rsch. Coun., Washington, 1999-2004. Editor: (book) Multithreaded Computer Architecture, 1994. Precinct committeeman Dem. Party, Denver, 1980-84. With USN, 1960-64. Recipient Eckert-Marchly award, 1990, awarded jointly by IEEE Computer Soc. and Assn. for Computer Machinery, Seymour Cray award IEEE Computer Soc., 2003. Fellow IEEE, Assn. for Computing Machinery; mem. NAE, Eta Kappa Nu, Sigma Xi. Democrat. Avocation: choral singing. Office: Microsoft Corp 1 Microsoft Way Redmond WA 98052-6399

SMITH, CALVIN BRUCE, museum director; b. Odessa, Tex., Oct. 22, 1940; s. Calvin Carroll and Elga Sam (McCallum) S.; m. Shirley Gail East, June 4, 1965 (div. 1972); m. Sylvia Sydney Boutwell, July 2, 1973; 1 child, Selena Michelle BS in Anthropology, Eastern N.Mex. U., 1970, BS in Zoology, 1970, MS in Biology, 1973. Dir. edn. Tex. Meml. Mus., Austin, 1974-75; dir. mus. services Lamar U., Beaumont, Tex., 1975-79; dir. Ark. Mus. Services, Little Rock, 1979-82, Strecker Mus., Baylor U., Waco, Tex., 1983—2003; chmn., tenured assoc. prof. dept. mus. studies Baylor U., Waco, 1993—2003, assoc. prof. emeritus, dept. mus. studies, 2003; pres., CEO Legacy Mus. Consulting, Pueblo, Colo., 2003—07; mus. and cultural resource mgmt. cons., 2003—; exec. dir. Western Heritage Mus. & Lea County Cowboy Hall of Fame, N.Mex Jr. Coll., Hobbs, 2007—. Dir. Waco Mammoth Site, 1984—2002; cons. Tex. Forestry Mus., Lufkin, 1982, Dr. Pepper Mus., Waco, 1982, Nat. Broadcast Mus., Dallas, 1983, Mus. of Gulf Coast, 1989, Helen Marie Taylor Mus., 1989; dir. Central Tex. Regional Sci. Fair, Waco, 1985; dir. Heart of Tex. History Fair, Waco, 1983. Author: (monograph) Mescalero Sands Natural Studies Plan, 1971, The Peopling of North America, The Paleo-Indians of the Great Plains; contbr. articles to profl. jours. Dir. Gov. Bill and Vara Daniel Hist. Village, 1986—. Recipient Organizer's award Boy Scouts Am., Buckeye, N.Mex., 1962, Nat. Med. Honor DAR, 1987, The State of Tex. Ho. of Reps. Cert. of Citation, Tex. State Cultural and Hist. Resources Com., 1990, Disting. Svc. award Women's Caucus of the Tex. Assn. of Mus., 1991, City of Waco Hospitality award, 1991, Cmty. Builder award, Masonic Grand Lodge Tex., Gov. Bill Daniel Statesmanship award, State Bar Tex.; named Outstanding Archaeologist of Yr., Archaeol. Soc. N.Mex., 1972, Disting. Former Odessan, Heritage Found. Odessa. Mem. Am. Assn. Mus., Am. Assn. State and Local History, Internat. Coun. Mus., Can. Mus. Assn., Mountain-Plains Museums Assn., Tex. Assn. Mus. (v.p. 1979, 85, Outstanding Profl. award Dallas, 1980, President's award), Ctrl. Tex. Mus. Assn., Mus. Assn. Waco, Beta Beta Beta. Democrat. Mem. Christian Ch. Lodge: Rotary Avocations: photography; camping; hunting; fishing. Home: 3108 Pioneer Cir Waco TX 76712-9643 Office: Western Heritage Mus Complex 5317 Lovington Hwy Hobbs NM 88240 Office Phone: 575-492-2676. Business E-Mail: c.smith@nmjc.edu.

SMITH, CARY, state legislator; b. Salt Lake City, Ut., Dec. 8, 1950; m. Susan Smith; children: Brandon, Melissa, Natalie, Jessica, Nathan, Ashley. BS in Psychology, U. Ut., 1972. Mgmt. Sears Roebuck & Co., 1973—2005; mem. Dist. 55 Mont. House of Reps., 2008—. Republican. Mormon. Office: Montana House of Representatives PO Box 200400 Helena MT 59620-0400 Mailing: 5522 Billy Casper Dr Billings MT 59106-1029 Home Phone: 406-652-1828; Office Phone: 406-444-4800. Office Fax: 406-444-4825. Business E-Mail: cary@bresnan.net.

SMITH, CHARLES CONARD, refractory company executive; b. Mexico, Mo., Feb. 10, 1936; s. Charles Adelbert and Waldine (Barnes) S.; m. Constance Nagel, Oct. 6, 1962; children: Stewart Ashley, Graham Prior. BS in Ceramic Engring., Iowa State U., 1958; MBA, Stanford U., 1962. Process engr. Kaiser Refractory divsn. Kaiser Aluminum, Moss Landing, Calif., 1962-65, materials mgr. Mexico, Mo., 1965-67, divsn. planning Oakland, Calif., 1967-69; v.p., gen. mgr. Kaiser Refractories Argentina, Buenos Aires, 1969-74; with divsn. planning Kaiser Refractories divsn. Kaiser Aluminum, Oakland, 1974-77, mktg. mgr., 1977-80, gen. mgr. mfg., 1980-82, v.p., gen. mgr. refractories divsn., 1982-85; chmn., pres., CEO Nat. Refractories and Mineral Corp., Livermore, Calif., 1985—. Patentee in refractory field. Lt. USNR, 1958-60. Mem. Refractories Inst. (past chmn., exec. com.). Republican. Avocations: fishing, bicycling, kite flying, photography, music.

SMITH, CHARLES Z., retired state supreme court justice; b. Lakeland, Fla., Feb. 23, 1927; s. John R. and Eva (Love) S.; m. Eleanor Jane Martinez, Aug. 20, 1955; children: Carlos M., Michael O., Stephen P., Felica L. BS, Temple U., 1952; JD, U. Wash., 1955. Bar: Wash. 1955. Law clk. Wash. Supreme Ct., Olympia, 1955-56; dep. pros. atty., asst. chief criminal div. King County, Seattle, 1956-60; ptnr. Bianchi, Smith & Tobin, Seattle, 1960-61; spl. asst. to atty. gen. criminal div. U.S. Dept. Justice, Washington, 1961-64; judge criminal dept. Seattle Mcpl. Ct., 1965-66; judge Superior Ct. King County, 1966-73; former assoc. dean, prof. law U. Wash., 1973—83; justice Wash. Supreme Ct., Olympia, until 2002. Mem. adv. bd. NAACP, Seattle Urban League, Wash. State Literacy Coun., Boys Club, Wash. Citizens for Migrant Affairs, Medina Children's Svc., Children's Home Soc. Wash., Seattle Better Bus. Bur., Seattle Foundation, Seattle Symphony Orch., Seattle Opera Assn., Community Svc. Ctr. for Deaf and Hard of Hearing, Seattle U., Seattle Sexual Assault Ctr., Seattle Psychoanalytic Inst., The Little Sch., Linfield Coll., Japanese Am. Citizens League, Kawabe Meml. Hous, Puget Counseling Ctr, Am. Cancer Soc., Hutchinson Cancer Rsch. Ctr., Robert Chinn Found.; pres. Am. Bapt. Chs. U.S.A., 1976-77, U.S. Commn. on Internat. Religious Freedom, 1999-2000. lt. col. ret. USMCR Mem. ABA, Am. Judicature Soc., Washington Bar Assn., Seattle-King County Bar Assn., Order of Coif., Phi Alpha Delta, Alpha Phi Alpha. Mailing: PO Box 146 Olympia WA 98507-0146 Home Phone: 206-324-0776; Office Phone: 360-273-0964. Business E-Mail: czsmith@usa.net.

SMITH, DANIEL WALTER, engineering educator; BS in Civil Engring., Calif. State U., 1967; MS in Sanitary Engring., San Jose State U., 1968; PhD in Environ. Health Engring., U. Kans., 1970. Registered profl. engr. Alta., Can., Calif., Alaska, N.W. Territories, Inst. Water and Environ. Mgmt. Eng. Tchg. asst. dept. civil engring. U. Kans., Lawrence, 1969-70; asst. prof. environ. health engring. U. Alaska, Fairbanks, 1971, asst. prof. water resources Inst. Water Resources, 1972-75, asst. prof. environ. quality engring., 1972-75; head No. Tech. Ctr. Environ. Protection Svc. Dept. of the Environment, Edmonton, Alta., Can., 1975-77; sr. environ. engr. R&M Cons., Inc., Anchorage, 1977-78; assoc. prof. civil engring. U. Alta., Edmonton, 1978-80, prof. civil engr., 1980—2006, chair dept. civil engring., 1990-94, dir. environ. engring. program, 1996—2005, prof. emeritus, 2006—; environ. engring. specialist UMA Engring. Ltd., Edmonton, Alta., 2006—. Pres. Daniel W. Smith & Assocs. Ltd., Edmonton, Alta., 1979—; sr. v.p., tech. dir. TekTran Internat., Info. and Edn., Inc., Alta. and Ont., 1979—86; cons. Edmonton Bd. Health, 1989—95, Stanley Cons. Group Ltd., Stanley Environ., Health Can. Med. Svcs. Br., Alta., 1998—, organizer internat. symposia on cold regions environ. engring.; lead instr. faculty extension U. Alta., Canada, 1985; mem. grant selection com. NSERC, 1995—96, re-allocations steering com., 1997; organizer, co-instr., instr. numerous workshops; adj. prof. U. Calgary, Ont., 2007—. Co-author: Cold Climate Utilities Delivery Design Manual, 1979; editor, co-editor numerous books including Design of Water and Wastewater Services for Cold Climate Communities, 1981, Scale-Up of Water and Wastewater Treatment Processes, 1983, Cold Climate Utilities Manual, 1986; tech. editor: Cold Regions Utilities Monograph, 1996; mem. editl. com. Cold Region Engring. Jour., 1992-94, mem. editl. bd., 1995-97; editor NRC Can. Jour. Environ. Engring. and Sci., 2000—; assoc. editor Ozone Sci. and Engring.; contbr. numerous articles to profl. jours., chpts. to books. Recipient Award of Merit Soc. Tech. Comm., 1987, Profl. Award of Merit Assn. Profl. Engrs., Geologists and Geophysicists of N.W. Territories, 1993, Edmonton Amb. award Edmonton Conv. Bur. Econ. Devel. Edmonton, 1997, Gold medal Polish Assn. San. Engrs. and Tech., Harvey M. Rosen Meml. award Ozone Sci. and Engring. Fellow ASCE (mem. tech. affairs com. cold regions engring. splty. confs. 1978, 81, 84, 86, 89, 91, 94, chair 1984, co-chair 1994, 2004, mem. exec. com. tech. coun. on cold regions engring. 1980-85, 96—, chmn. 1983-84, 99-2000, chmn. CSCE/ASCE Environ. Engring. Conf., 1997, design and constrn. com. 1988—, edn. com. 1989—, mem. profl. affairs com. environ. engring. divsn. 1996—, Elbert F. Rice Meml. Lectr. award 1989, Can-Am Amity Civil Engring. award 1989, Rudolph Hering medal 2002, Harold R. Payton award 2004), Engring. Inst. Can., Canadian Soc. Civil Engring. (chmn. environ. engring. divsn. 1979-84, chair tech. activities com. 1984-86, sr. v.p. 1986-87, pres. 1987-88, invited spkr. cold regions environ. engring. Nat. Lecture Tour 1997, T.C. Keefer medal (with G.R. Finch) 1987, (with H. Mao) 1998, Albert E. Berry medal 1988), Canadian Acad. Engring., Royal Soc. Can.; mem. Am. Water Works Assn. (life, student mem. award 1966-67), Am. Acad. Environ. Engrs. (BCEE), Canadian Pulp and Paper Assn., Internat. Assn. Water Quality, Internat. Ozone Assn., Engring. Inst. Can. (fellow), Assn. Environ. Engrs., Instn. Water and Environ. Mgmt. (Eng., mem. profl. review com. 1995-96), Western Can. Water and Wastewater Assn. (elected to Select Soc. Sanitary Sludge Shovelers 1995), Assn. Profl. Engrs. and Geologists B.C. (mem. CCPE environ. engring. syllabus com. 1997), Chi Epsilon. Achievements include patents for automated oxygen uptake rate measurement device; contbn. to application of laser Doppler rsch. tools for studying treatment processes fundamentals; rsch. in ozone water, wastewater treatment, distbn. sys. corrosion studies, advanced wastewater treatment studies, solid waste mgmt., freeze separtion wastewater treatment, river quality; indicator organism modelling, pulp mill wastewater treatment. Office: U Alta Dept Civil & Environ 3-095 Nat Resources Engring Facility Edmonton AB Canada T6G 2W2 Home Phone: 780-435-3269; Office Phone: 780-492-4138. Fax: (780) 492-8189. E-mail: dwsmith@ualberta.ca.

SMITH, DAVID ELVIN, physician; b. Bakersfield, Calif., Feb. 7, 1939; s. Elvin W. and Dorothy (McGinnis) S.; m. Millicent Buxton; children: Julia, Suzanne, Christopher Buxton-Smith, Sabree Hill-Smith. BS, U. Calif., Berkeley; MS in Pharmacology, U. Calif., San Francisco, 1964, MD, 1967. Intern San Francisco Gen. Hosp., 1965; fellow pharmacology and toxicology U. Calif., San Francisco, 1965-67; clin. prof. U. Calif., San Francisco Med. Ctr., 1967—, dir. psychopharmacology study group, dir. Inst. of Health, 1966-70, assoc. clin. prof., rsch. physician Med. Sch.; clin. prof. U. Calif., San Francisco; practice specializing in toxicology/addiction medicine San Francisco, 1965—. Physician Presbyn. Alcoholic Clinic, 1965—67, Contra Cost Alcoholic Clinic, 1965—67; dir. alcohol and drug abuse screening unit San Francisco Gen. Hosp., 1967—68; co-dir. Calif. drug abuse info. project U. Calif. Med. Ctr., 1967—72; founder, pres., stct med. dir. Haight-Ashbury Free Med. Clinic, San Francisco, 1967—2006; rsch. dir. Merritt Peralta Chem. Dependency Hosp., Oakland, Calif., 1984—2003; med. dir. Drug Abuse Scis., 1999—2003, Calif. Alcohol and Drug Programs, U. Calif. San Francisco Substance Abuse Policy Ctr., 1999; exec. med. dir. Prometa Ctr., Santa Monica and San Francisco, Calif.; assoc. med. dir., med. rev. officer Betty Ford Ctr. Profl. Recovery Program; chmn. Nat. Drug Abuse Conf., 1996—2006, Calif. Gov.'s Commn. on Narcotics and Drug Abuse, 1977—; nat. health adviser to former U.S. Pres. Jimmy Carter; mem. Pres. Clinton's Health Care Task Force on Addiction and Nat. Health Reform, 1993; with Office Drug Abuse Policy, White House Task Force Physicians for Drug Abuse Prevention; dir. Benzodiazepine Rsch. and Tng. Project, Substance Abuse and Sexual Concerns Project, PCP Rsch. and Tng. Project; med. editor Alcohol-MD.com, OpiateMD.org, Alcohol MD (CD-ROM); vis. assoc. prof. U. Nev. Med. Sch., 1975—; clin. prof. U. Calif. San Francisco Med. Ctr.; v.p. corp. med affairs Hythiam; cons. in field; chief Addiction Medicine Svcs. Bayside Marin, San Rafael, 2006—; med. dir. Centerpoint, 1996—. Author: Love Needs Care, 1970, The New Social Drug: Cultural, Medical and Legal Perspectives on Marijuana, 1971, The Free Clnic: Community Approaches to Health Care and Drug Abuse, 1971, Treating the Cocaine Abuser, 1985, The Benzodiazepines: Current Standard Medical Practice, 1986, Physicians' Guide to Drug Abuse, 1987; co-author: It's So Good, Don't Even Try it Once: Heroin in Perspective, 1972, Uppers and Downers, 1973, Drugs in the Classroom, 1973, Barbiturate Use and Abuse, 1977, A Multicultural View of Drug Abuse, 1978, Amphetamine Use, Misuse and Abuse, 1979, PCP: Problems and Prevention, 1981, Sexological Aspects of Substance Use and Abuse, Treatment of the Cocaine Abuser, 1985, The Haight Ashbury Free Medical Clinic: Still Free After All These Years, Drug Free: Alternatives to Drug Abuse, 1987, Treatment of Opiate Dependence, Designer Drugs, 1988, Treatment of Cocaine Dependence, 1988, Treatment of Opiate Dependence, 1988, The New Drugs, 1989, Crack and Ice in the Era of Smokeable Drugs, 1992, Clinical Guide to Substance Abuse, 2001, others; also drug edn. films; founder, editor Jour. Psychedelic Drugs (now Jour. Psychoactive Drugs), 1967—; co-author: Clinical Guide to Substance Abuse; contbr. over 300 articles to profl. jours. Mem. Physicians for Prevention White House Office Drug Abuse Policy, 1995; pres. Youth Projects, Inc.; founder, chmn. bd., pres. Nat. Free Clin. Coun., 1968-72; med. dir. Calif. Alcohol and Drug Programs, 1998, U. Calif. Drug Policy Ctr., San Francisco, 1998—99. Recipient Rsch. award, Borden Found., 1964, AMA Rsch. award, 1977, Cmty. Svc. award U. Calif., San Francisco, 1974, Calif. State Drug Abuse Treatment award, 1984, Vernelle Fox Drug Abuse Treatment award, 1985, UCLA Sidney Cohen Addiction Medicine award, 1989, U. Calif. San Francisco medal of honor, 1995, Lifetime Achievement award for sr. workers, Gov. of Calif., 2003; named one of Best Drs. in US, 1995, 1996, 1997, 2002. Mem. AMA (alt. del.), Calif. Med. Assn. (alt. del.), Am. Soc. on Addiction Medicine (bd. dirs., pres. 1995), San Francisco Med. Soc., APHA, Calif. Soc. on Addiction Medicine (pres., bd. dirs.), Am. Soc. Addiction Medicine, Cosmos Club, 2006-, Sigma Xi, Phi Beta Kappa. Methodist. Home and Office: David E Smith MD and Assocs 856 Stanyan St San Francisco CA 94117 Office Phone: 415-933-8759, 415-933-8759. Business E-Mail: drsmith@drdave.org.

SMITH, DAVID MICHAEL, financial planner; b. Fresno, Calif., Dec. 29, 1944; s. Ralph S. and Verla Fern Smith; m. Barbara J. Bryson, June 27, 1964; children: Brandon, Eric. AA, Fresno City Coll., 1964; AB, Calif. State U., Fresno, 1966. Tchr. English Fresno Unified Sch. Dist., 1967-79; registered rep. TMI Equities, Inc., Fresno, 1979-82, regional mgr. Camarillo, Calif., 1982-85; fin. planner Associated Planners Securities Corp., Camarillo, 1985-89, David M. Smith & Assocs., Camarillo, 1989—2002, Lifetime Planning, Inc., 2003—. Coun. mem. City of Camarillo, 1988—96, mayor, 1991, 1996; pres. Fresno Dem. Coalition, 1979. Mem.: Fin. Planners Assn. Ventura County (pres. 2004), Fin. Planning Assn., Camarillo Noontime Optimists Club. Office: Lifetime Planning Inc 1200 Paseo Camarillo Ste 190 Camarillo CA 93010-6085 Home Phone: 805-987-5919; Office Phone: 805-987-8938. Personal E-mail: dms.planners@verizon.net.

SMITH, DAVID WAYNE, retired psychologist, educator; b. Ind., Apr. 16, 1927; s. Lowell Wayne and Ruth Elizabeth (Westphal) S.; m. Marcene B. Leever, Oct. 20, 1948; children: David Wayne, Laurreen Lea. BS, Purdue U., 1949; MS, Ind. U., 1953, PhD, 1955. Diplomate Am. Bd. Psychol. Specialities. Prof. rehab., dir. Rehab. Ctr.; assoc. dean, later asst. v.p. acad. affairs Ariz. Health Scis. Ctr., U. Ariz., Tucson, 1955-80; rsch. prof. rehab., adj. prof. medicine, cons. in rsch. S.W. Arthritis Ctr., Coll. Medicine, 1980-87; prof. rehab. and rheumatology, dept. medicine U. Ariz., 1987—, also dir. disability assessment program, Ariz. Arthritis Ctr., Tucson; dir. Disability Assessment Rsch. Clinic, 1987—. Pres. allied health professions sect. Nat. Arthritis Found.; bd. dirs. Nat. Arthritis Found. (S.W. chpt.); nat. vice chmn. bd. dirs.; mem. NIH Nat. Arthritis Adv. Bd., 1977-84; also chmn. subcom. community programs and rehab.; mem. staff Ariz. Legislature Health Welfare, 1972-73; Mem. Gov.'s Council Dept. Econ. Security, 1978-85; pres., bd. dirs. Tucson Assn. for Blind, 1974-86; chmn. Gov.'s Council on Blind and Visually Impaired, 1987—; active Gov.'s Coun. on Arthritis and Musculoskeletal Disease, 1987—, Gov.'s State wide Coun. on Rehab., 1998—, Am. Bd. Forensic Examiners, 1997—. Author: Worksamples; contbr. chpts. to books and articles to profl. jours. Mem. Gov.'s State Rehab. Coun., 1998—, commr. Commn. on Civil Rights, Az., 2002. Recipient Gov.'s awards for leadership in rehab., 1966, 69, 72, 73; awards for sci. and vol. services Nat. Arthritis Found., 1973, 75; 1st nat. Addie Thomas award Nat. Arthritis Found., 1983, Benson award, 1989, Govt. Affairs award, 1989; Arthritis Found. fellow, 1983. Fellow Am. Coll. Forensics; mem. Am. Psychol. Assn. (div. 17 counseling psychology), Assn. Schs. Allied Health Professions, Nat. Rehab. Assn., Ariz. Psychol. Assn. Home: 5765 N Camino Real Tucson AZ 85718-4213 Personal E-mail: davesfolly@earthlink.net.

SMITH, DEREK E., lawyer; b. Salt Lake City, Feb. 25, 1964; BS in computer sci., Brigham Young U., 1988; JD, Cornell U., 1991. Bar: Calif. 1991. Ptnr. Paul, Hastings, Janofsky & Walker LLP, LA, co-vice chmn. real estate dept. Fluent in spanish. Office: Paul Hastings Janofsky & Walker LLP 515 S Flower St Twenty-fifth Floor Los Angeles CA 90071-2228 Office Phone: 213-683-6178. Office Fax: 213-996-3178. Business E-Mail: dereksmith@paulhastings.com.

SMITH, DERRIN RAY, information systems company executive; b. Columbus, Ohio, Feb. 19, 1955; s. Ray Stanley Smith and Clara (Diddle) Craver; m. Catherine Marie Massey, Aug. 18, 1979; children: Shannon Cathleen, Allison Collette, Micayla Colleen, Nicole Catherine. BS, Regis U., 1981; MBA, U. Phoenix, 1984; PhD, U. Denver, 1991. Test lab. mgr. Ball Aerospace Systems, Ball Corp., Boulder, 1975-84; sr. systems engr. Martin Marietta Info. Systems, Denver, 1984-87; tech. cons. MITRE Fed. R & D Ctr., Colorado Springs, 1988-92; pres. DRS Scis., Inc., Denver, 1992—; nat. program mgr. cable/telephone/full svc. network The Nat. Program Dir. Time Warner, 1994—; chmn., CEO GETGO, Inc., 2000—. Tech. cons. U.S. Space Command-RAPIER, Colorado Springs, 1989-91, Unisys Corp., Greenwood Village, Colo., 1992; adj. prof. CIS dept. Univ. Coll., U. Denver, 1992; secretariat Corp. Planner's Roundtable, St. Louis, 1982-84; spkr. in field. Author: Evolving the Mountain; Defense Acquisition Management of Strategic Command and Control System Procurements, 1991; contbr. articles to profl. jours. Res. police officer Federal Heights (Colo.) Police Dept., 1979-82. With USMC, 1978-84. Recipient Outstanding Achievement award Rocky Mountain News, 1981, Reservist of Yr. award Navy League U.S., 1981. Mem. Assn. Former Intelligence Officers (pres. Rocky Mountain chpt.). Roman Catholic. Avocations: martial arts, skiing, sailing, creative writing, mountain climbing. Home: 1050 17th St Ste 1700 Denver CO 80265-2077 also: 4062 El Shaddiai Sq Plant City FL 33565-5106

SMITH, DWIGHT MORRELL, chemistry professor, academic administrator; b. Hudson, NY, Oct. 10, 1931; s. Elliott Monroe and Edith Helen (Hall) S.; m. Alice Beverly Bond, Aug. 27, 1955 (dec. 1990); children— Karen Elizabeth, Susan Allison, Jonathan Aaron; m. Elfi Nelson, Dec. 28, 1991. BA, Ctrl. Coll., Pella, Iowa, 1953; PhD, Pa. State U., 1957; ScD (hon.), Ctrl. Coll., 1986; LittD (hon.), U. Denver, 1990. Postdoctoral fellow, instr. Calif. Inst. Tech., 1957—59; sr. chemist Texaco Rsch. Ctr., Beacon, NY, 1959—61; asst. prof. chemistry Wesleyan U., Middletown, Conn., 1961—66; assoc. prof. Hope Coll., Holland, Mich., 1966—69, prof., 1969—72; prof. chemistry U. Denver, 1972—, chmn. dept., 1972—83, 1999—2001, vice chancellor for acad. affairs, 1983—84, chancellor, 1984—89; pres., bd. trustees Hawaii Loa Coll., Kaneohe, 1990—92. Mem. Registry for Interim Coll. and Univ. Pres.; mem. adv. bd. Solar Energy Rsch. Inst., 1989—91; mem. vis. com. Zettlemoyer Ctr. for Surface Studies Lehigh U., 1990—96; dept. chemistry and geochemistry Colo. Sch. Mines; mem. sci. adv. bd. Denver Rsch. Inst.; sr. advisor Rocky Mountain Ctr. Homeland Def. Editor Revs. on Petroleum Chemistry, 1975-78; editl. adv. bd. Recent Rsch. Devels. in Applied Spectroscopy, 1998—; contbr. articles to profl. jours. Chmn. Chs. United for Social Action, Holland, 1968-69; mem. adv. com. Holland Sch. Bd., 1969-70; bd. commrs. Colo. Adv. Tech. Inst., 1984-88, Univ. Senate, United Meth. Ch., Nashville, 1987-88, 91-93; mem. adv. bd. United Way, Inst. Internat. Edn., Japan Am. Soc. Colo., Denver Winter Games Olympics Com.; mem. ch. bds. or consistories Ref. Ch. Am., N.Y., Conn., Mich., United Meth. Ch., Colo. DuPont fellow, 1956-57, NSF fellow Scripps Inst., 1971-72; recipient grants Rsch. Corp., Petroleum Rsch. Fund, NSF, Solar Energy Rsch. Inst., Camille & Henry Dreyfus Found., Inc. Mem. AAAS, Am. Assn. Aerosol Rsch., Am. Chem. Soc. (chmn. Colo. 1976, sec. we. Mich. 1970-71, joint coun. and bd. com. on sci. 1997-98, award Colo. sect. 1986), Soc. Applied Spectroscopy, Mile High Club, Sigma Xi. Achievements include patents for selective hydrogenation and fuel, lubricant additives. Home: 1931 W Sanibel Ct Littleton CO 80120-8133 Office: U Denver Dept Chem & Biochem Denver CO 80208-0001 Office Phone: 303-871-2938. Personal E-mail: elfidwight@comcast.net. Business E-Mail: dwismith@du.edu.

SMITH, EDWARD JOHN, geophysicist, physicist; b. Dravosburg, Pa., Sept. 21, 1927; married, 1953; 4 children. BA, UCLA, 1951, MS, 1952, PhD in Physics, 1960. Rsch. geophysicist Inst. Geophysics UCLA, 1955-59; mem. tech. staff Space Tech. Labs., 1959-61, Jet Propulsion Lab, 1961—. Recipient medal Exceptional Sci. Achievement NASA, Arctowski medal, 2005. Mem. AAAS, Internat. Sci. Radio Union, Am. Geophys. Union, Am. Astron. Soc., Sigma Xi. Achievements include research in planetary magnetism, space physics, interplanetary physics, wave-particle interactions in plasmas, propagation of electromagnetic waves, solar-terrestrial relations. Office: Calif Inst Tech Jet Propulsion Lab 4800 Oak Grove Dr M/S 169-506 Pasadena CA 91109-8001 E-mail: edward.j.smith@jpl.nasa.gov.

SMITH, EDWIN P., security studies center director, career officer; b. Allentown, Pa., Aug. 8, 1945; Grad., U.S. Mil. Acad., 1967; MA, U. Ky., 1976; MBA, L.I. U., 1979; grad., Command and Gen. Staff Coll., Can. Nat. Def. Coll. Commd. 2d lt. U.S. Army, 1967, advanced through grades to lt. gen., 1998, various assignments U.S. and overseas; dir. Asia-Pacific Ctr. Security Studies, 2006—. Decorated Purple Heart; recipient Def. Disting. Svc. medal.

SMITH, ELAINE E., school system administrator; b. Gooding, Idaho; m. Rich L. Smith, June 8, 1968; children: Camille, Kirk, Brenda. BA in Secondary Edn., Idaho State U. Cert. secondary tchr. Coord. vol. svcs.-bus. and edn. partnerships Sch. Dist. # 25, Pocatello, Idaho, 1985—. Coord. Expanding Your Horizons Conf., S.E. Idaho, 1986—. Past pres. Community Svcs. Coun., Pocatello; active Bannock County Youth at Risk, Pocatello, 1988—; mem. Pocatello Area Foster Grandparents Adv., Pocatello, 1989—; bd. dirs. YWCA of Ea. Idaho, 1990—; mem. Idaho West Point Parents Club, 1990-95; active United Way of S.E. Idaho; mem., coord. Portneuf Cropwalk. Recipient Friend of Edn. award Pocatello Edn. Assn., 1990, Disting. Young Woman of Yr. Jaycees, 1980. Mem. AAUW (past state pres.), Nat. Assn. Ptnrs. Edn., Nat. Coalition for Sex Equity Edn., Assn. Vol. Adminstrs., Greater Pocatello C. of C. (K-12 edn. com 1985—, state issues com. 1985—), Soroptimists (Women Helping award 1993 Pocatello chpt.), Alpha Omicron Pi, Delta Kappa Gamma. Office: Sch Dist # 25 3115 Poleline Rd Pocatello ID 83201-6119

SMITH, ELDEN LEROY, recreational vehicle and manufactured housing company executive; b. Berwyn, Ill., June 1, 1940; s. Frederick M. and Margaret I. (Larson) Smith; m. Barbara G. Whaley, Apr. 4, 1963; children: Jill Marie, David Elden. BA in Bus. Adminstrn., Whittier Coll., Calif., 1962. Mkt. analyst autonetics divsn. N.Am. Aviation, Anaheim, Calif., 1963—66; sales mgr. Pendleton Tool Industries, LA, 1966—68; plant gen. mgr. Fleetwood Enterprises, Inc., Hancock, Md., 1969—71, v.p. recreational vehicle group Riverside, Calif., 1972—88, sr. v.p., 1988—97, pres., dir., CEO, 2005—. Trustee Whittier Coll., 1991—99. Served with USNR, 1962—63. Mem.: Recreation Vehicle Industry Assn. (chmn. 1980—82, dir. 1975—97). Office: Fleetwood Enterprises 3125 Myers St Riverside CA 92503

SMITH, ELDON, cardiologist, physiologist, educator; MD, Dalhousie U., Halifax, NS, Can., 1967. From asst. prof. to assoc. prof. medicine and physiology Dalhousie U., 1973—80; prof. medicine and physiology and biophysics U. Calgary, Canada, 1980—2004, prof. emeritus, 2004—, chief divsn. cardiology, 1980—86, chair dept. medicine, 1985—90, assoc. dean clin. affairs, 1990—92, dean faculty of medicine, 1992—97. Corp. dir. Can. Natural Resources, Ltd., 1997—, Vasogen, Inc., 1998—, Sernova Corp., 2000—09, Aston Hill Fin., Inc., 2005—. Editor-in-chief: Can. Jour. Cardiology, 1997—2009. Bd. dirs., pres. Peter Lougheed Med. Rsch. Found., 1999—2007, Premier's adv. coun. health, 2000—02, health professions adv. bd., 2002—07; trustee Alta. Heritage Found. for Med. Rsch., Canada, 2000—07. Recipient officer Order of Can. Fellow: Can. Acad. Health Scis., Am. Heart Assn., Internat. Acad. Cardiovasc. Scis., Am. Coll. Cardiology, Royal Coll. Physicians and Surgeons Can. Office: U Calgary Faculty Medicine 3330 Hosp Dr Calgary AB Canada T2N 4N1 Home Phone: 403-286-6800; Office Phone: 403-220-5500. Business E-Mail: esmith@ucalgary.ca.

SMITH, ELDRED GEE, church leader; b. Lehi, Utah, Jan. 9, 1907; s. Hyrum Gibbs and Martha E. (Gee) S.; m. Jeanne A. Ness, Aug. 17, 1932 (dec. June 1977); children: Miriam Smith Skeen, Eldred Gary, Audrey Gay Smith Vance, Gordon Raynor, Sylvia Dawn Smith Isom; m. Hortense H. Child, May 18, 1978; stepchildren: Carol Jane Child Burdette (dec.), Thomas Robert Child. Employed with sales div. Bennett Glass & Paint Co., Salt Lake City, 6 years; mech. design engr. Remington Arms Co., 2 years; design engr., prodn. equipment design Tenn. Eastman Corp., Oak Ridge, Tenn., 3 years; now presiding patriarch Ch. Jesus Christ of Latter-day Saints. Mem. Lds Ch. Home: 2942 Devonshire Cir Salt Lake City UT 84108-2526 Office: 47 E South Temple Salt Lake City UT 84150-9701

SMITH, EMIL L., biochemist, educator; b. NYC, July 5, 1911; s. Abraham and Esther (Lubart) S.; m. Esther Press, Mar. 29, 1934; children: Joseph Donald, Jeffrey Bernard BS, Columbia U., 1931, PhD, 1936. Instr. biophysics Columbia U., NYC, 1936-38; John Simon Guggenheim fellow Cambridge U., Eng., 1938-39, Yale U., New Haven, 1939-40; fellow Rockefeller Inst., NYC, 1940-42; biophysicist, biochemist E. R. Squibb & Sons, New Brunswick, N.J., 1942-46; assoc. prof. to prof. biochemistry U. Utah, Salt Lake City, 1946-63; prof. biol. chemistry Sch. Medicine UCLA, 1963-79, prof. emeritus, 1979—. Cons. NIH, Am. Cancer Soc., Office Naval Research Author: (with others) Principles of Biochemistry, 7th edit., 1983; also numerous articles Recipient Stein-Moore award Protein Soc., 1987. Mem. NAS, Am. Acad. Arts and Scis., Am. Philos. Soc., Am. Soc. Biochemistry and Molecular Biology, Am. Chem. Soc., Acad. Scis. Russia (fgn.). Office: UCLA Sch Medicine Los Angeles CA 90095-1737

SMITH, EPHRAIM PHILIP, academic administrator; b. Fall River, Mass., Sept. 19, 1942; s. Jacob Max and Bertha (Horvitz) S.; m. Linda Sue Katz, Sept. 3, 1967; children: Benjamin, Rachel, Leah. BS, Providence Coll., 1964; MS, U. Mass., 1965; PhD, U. Ill., 1968. Chmn. dept. acctg. U. R.I., Kingston, 1972-73; dean Sch. Bus. Shippensburg State Coll., Pa., 1973-75; dean Coll. Bus. Adminstrn. Cleve. State U., 1975-90; dean Sch. Bus. Adminstrn. and Econ. Calif. State U., Fullerton, 1990-98, v.p. acad. affairs, 1998—. Co-author: Principles of Supervision: First and Second Level Management, 1984, Federal Taxation-Advanced Topics, 1995, Federal Taxation-Basic Principles, 2008, Federal Taxation Comprehensive Topics, 2008; contbr. articles to profl. jours. Mem. Am. Acctg. Assn., Am. Taxation Assn., Am. Inst. Decision Scis., Fin. Execs. Inst., Beta Gamma Sigma, Beta Alpha Psi. Office: Calif State Univ - Fullerton VPAA Office MH-133 800 N State College Blvd Fullerton CA 92831-3599 Business E-Mail: esmith@fullerton.edu.

SMITH, ERNEST KETCHAM, electrical engineer; b. Peking, China, May 31, 1922; (parents Am. citizens); s. Ernest Ketcham and Grace (Goodrich) S.; m. Mary Louise Standish, June 23, 1950; children: Priscilla Varland, Nancy Smith Johnson, Cynthia Jackson. BA in Physics, Swarthmore Coll., 1944; MSEE, Cornell U., 1951, PhD, 1956. With Mut. Broadcasting Sys., 1946-49, chief plans and allocations engr., 1949; with radio propagation lab. Nat. Bur. Stds., Boulder, Colo., 1951-65, chief ionosphere rsch. sect., 1957-60, divsn. chief, 1960-65; dir. aeronomy lab. Environ. Sci. Svcs. Adminstrn., Boulder, 1965-67; dir. Inst. Telecom. Scis., 1968, dir. univ. rels., 1968-70; assoc. dir. Inst. Telecom. Scis. Office of Telecom., Boulder, 1970-72, cons., 1972-76; tech. staff Jet Propulsion Lab. Calif. Inst. Tech., Pasadena, 1976-87; adj. prof. dept. elec. and computer engring. U. Colo., Boulder, 1987—. Vis. fellow Coop. Inst. Rsch. on Environ. Scis., 1968; assoc. Harvard Coll. Obs., 1965-75; adj. prof. U. Colo., 1969-76; internat. vice-chmn. study group 6, Internat. Radio Consultative Com., 1958-70, chmn. U.S. study group, 1970-76; mem.-at-large U.S. nat. com. Internat. Sci. Radio Union, 1985-88; convenor Boulder Gatekeepers to the Future, 1990—. Author: Worldwide Occurrence of Sporadic E, 1957; (with S. Matsushita) Ionospheric Sporadic E, 1962. Contbr. numerous articles to profl. jours. Editor: Electromagnetic Probing of the Upper Atmosphere, 1969; assoc. editor for propagation IEEE Antennas and Propagation Mag., 1989—. Mem. 1st Congl. Ch., moderator, 1995-97. Recipient Diplôme d'Honneur, Internat. Radio Consultative Com., Internat. Telecom. Union, 1978; named to Gallery of Disting. Scientists, Engrs. and Adminstrs., Nat. Bur. Stds., Nat. Inst. Stds. and Tech., Gaithersburg, Md., 2003, USNC - URSI Special Recognition award, 2008. Fellow: IEEE (com. mem. 1993-1995, AAAS, Electromagnetics Acad.; mem. Am. Geophys. Union, Athenaeum (Pasadena), UN Assn. of US (convenor Boulder chpt., treas. 1994-2005), Sigma Xi (pres. U. Colo. chpt. 1994-95, v.p. 95-98). Home: 4900 Thunderbird Dr Apt 605 Boulder CO 80303-3802 Home Phone: 720-562-8175. Business E-Mail: ernest.smith@colorado.edu, ernestksmith@comcast.net.

SMITH, F. D. (RICKY SMITH), rail transporation executive; Pres. Stevedoring Svcs. Am., Seattle, 1979-81, CEO, chmn., 1981—. Office: 1131 SW Klickitat Way Seattle WA 98134-1108

SMITH, FRED WESLEY, retired communications company executive; b. Arkoma, Okla., Jan. 1, 1934; s. Erma (Howard) Wells; m. Mary Blanche Moore, May 1961; children: Fred W. Jr., Jonathan Paul, Deborah Lee. Student, Ark. Poly. Tech. Coll. Classified advt. salesman S.W. Times Record, Ft. Smith, Ark., 1951-53; classified advt. mgr. Southwest Times Record, Ft. Smith, Ark., 1953-55, nat. advt. mgr., 1956-59, advt. mgr., 1959-60, asst. gen. mgr., 1960-61; gen. mgr. Las Vegas Rev. Jour., 1961-66; v.p. western newspaper div. Donrey Media Group, Las Vegas, 1966-73, exec. v.p., 1973-87, pres., 1987—90, CEO, 1990—93. Bd. dirs. First Interstate Bank of Nev., Reno, Nev. Develop. Authority, ALLTell Corp., 2001-, Safefoods Corp., 2003-. Former bd. dirs. United Fund, Clark County Boys Club, Las Vegas; mem. exec. bd. Boy Scouts Am., Las Vegas; former mem., chmn. adv. bd. Salvation Army, Las Vegas; bd. trustees U. Nev. Las Vegas Found., U. of the Ozarks; nat. adv. bd. First Comml. nank, Little Rock, chmn., Donald W. Reynolds Found, 1996-. Mem. Sigma Delta Chi. Avocations: boating, golf, skiing. Office: DW Reynolds Found 1701 Village Ctr Circle Las Vegas NV 89134

SMITH, FREDRICA EMRICH, rheumatologist, internist; b. Princeton, NJ, Apr. 28, 1945; d. Raymond Jay and Carolyn Sarah (Schleicher) Emrich; m. Paul David Smith, June 10, 1967. AB, Bryn Mawr Coll., Pa., 1967; MD, Duke U., Durham, NC, 1971. Intern, resident U. N.Mex. Affiliated Hosps., 1971-73; fellow U. Va. Hosp., Charlottesville, 1974-75; pvt. practice, Los Alamos, N.Mex., 1975—. Chmn. credentials com. Los Alamos Med. Ctr., 1983—, chief staff, 1990, 2003; bd. dirs. N.Mex. Physicians Mut. Liability Ins. Co., Albuquerque, 1988-97; regional adv. bd. Am. Physicians Assurance, 1997-; cons. PPAC, 2008-. Contbr. articles to med. jours. Mem. bass sect. Los Alamos Symphony, 1975—; active Los Alamos County Parks and Recreation Bd., 1984-88, 92-96, 2007-, Los Alamos County Med. Indigent Health Care Task Force, 1989—2003; ops. subcom. Aquatic Ctr., Los Alamos County, 1988—,Los Alamos Country Pk. Recreation Bd., 2009-. Fellow ACP, Am. Coll. Rheumatology; mem. N.Mex. Soc. Internal Medicine (pres. 1993-96), Friends of Bandelier. Democrat. Avocations: swimming, music, reading, hiking. Office: Los Alamos Med Ctr 3917 West Rd Los Alamos NM 87544-2275 Office Phone: 505-662-9400.

SMITH, GLENN A., lawyer; b. Oakland, Calif., July 11, 1946; BA, Pomona Coll., 1968; JD, U. Calif., Berkeley, 1971; LLM in Taxation, NYU, 1973. Bar: Calif. 1972, D.C. 1975. Law clerk to Hon. William M. Drennen U.S. Tax Ct., 1973-75; ptnr. Heller, Ehrman, White & McAuliffe, Palo Alto, San Francisco, Calif., 1981—2001; KPMG Mountain View, san Fransisco, 2001—04; pvt. practice Palo Alto, Calif., 1985—. Office: Ste 205 459 Hamilton Ave Palo Alto CA 94301 Office Phone: 650-473-1000. Office Fax: 650-473-9550.

SMITH, GORDON E., publishing executive; Bureau chief Copley News Svc., LA, 1998—. Office: Copley News Svc 500 W Temple St Rm 479 E Los Angeles CA 90012

SMITH, GORDON PAUL, management consultant; b. Salem, Mass., Dec. 25, 1916; s. Gordon and May (Vaughan) S.; m. Daphne Miller, Nov. 23, 1943 (div. 1968); m. Ramona Chamberlain, Sept. 27, 1969; children: Randall B., Roderick F. BS in Mgmt., U. Mass., 1947; MS in Govt. Mgmt, U. Denver, 1948; postgrad. in polit. sci, NYU, 1948-50; DHL (hon.), Monterey Inst. Internat. Studies, Middlebury Coll., 1994. With Econ. Rsch. Tax Found., Inc., NYC, 1948—51, Booz, Allen & Hamilton, 1951-70, partner San Francisco, 1959-62, v.p., 1962-67, mng. pntr. Western U.S., 1968-70; ptnr. Harrod, Williams and Smith, San Francisco, 1962—69; dir. fin. State of Calif., Calif., 1967—68; mem. Calif. State Bds. and Commrs.; pres. Gordon Paul Smith & Co., Mgmt. Cons., 1968—; pres., CEO Golconda Corp., 1972—74, chmn. bd., 1974-85. Pres. Cermetek Corp., 1978-80; adviser task force def. procurement and contracting Hoover Commn., 1954-55; spl. asst. to pres. Republic Aviation Corp., 1954-55; cons., Hawaii, 1960-61, Alaska, 1963; cons. Wash. Hwy. Adminstrn., 1964, Am. Baseball League and Calif. Angels, 1960-62, others; bd. dirs. Monterey Coll. Law; chmn. Ft. Ord Econ. Devel. Adv. Group, 1991; chmn. Coalition on Rsch. and Edn., 1993—97; spkr. in field. Contbr. articles to profl. jours. Mem. Calif. Select Com. on Master Plan for Edn., 1971—73; mem. alumni coun. U. Mass., 1950—54, bd. dirs. alumni ass., 1964—70; chmn. West Coast Cancer Found., 1976—87, Coalition Rsch. and Edn., 1993—, Jim Tunney Youth Found., 1994—; trustee, chmn. Monterey Inst. Internat. Studies, 1978—92, trustee emeritus, 1995—; trustee Northfield Mt. Hermon Sch., 1983—93, Robert Louis Stevenson Sch., 1993—; mem. devel. coun. Cmty. Hosp. of Monterey Peninsula, 1983—84; sr. advisor Pres. Calif. State U., Monterey, Calif., 1998—; mem. 15 bds. and commns. State of Calif., 1967—72; bd. dirs. Alumni Assn. Mt. Hermon Prep. Sch., 1963; bd. dirs. Stanford Med. Ctr., 1960—62, pres., chmn., 1962—66; bd. dirs. Friends of the Performing Arts, 1985—, Monterey County Symphony Orch., 1991—96, Monterey Bay Futures Project, 1992—, Ctr. for Nonproliferation of Weapons of Mass Destruction, 1998—, Calif. Inst. for Local Self Govt., 2000—. Recipient spl. commendation Hoover Commn., 1955, Alumni of Yr. award U. Mass., 1963, Trustee of Yr. award Monterey-Peninsula, 1991, Monterey-Peninsula Outstanding Citizen of Yr. award, 1992, Laura Bride Powers Heritage award, 1991, U.S. Congl. award, 1992, Calif. Senate and Assembly Outstanding Citizen award, 1992, Wisdom award of honor Wisdom Soc., 1992; named Global Citizen of Yr., Internat. Sch. Monterey, Calif, 2005; permanent Gordon Paul Smith Disting. Chair for Internat. Studies established at Monterey Inst. Internat. Studies; named Gordon Paul Smith Scholarship Fund in his honor Northfield Mt. Hermon Sch.and Robert Louis Stevenson Sch.; named to Honorable Order of Ky. Cols. Mem. Monterey History and Art Assn. (bd. dirs. 1987-92, pres. 1985-87, chmn. 1987-92, hon. lifetime dir. 1992—), The Stanton Heritage Ctr. (chmn. 1987-92, chmn. emeritus 1992—), Salvation Army (bd. dirs., chmn. hon. cabinet), Monterey Peninsula Mus. Art, Carmel Valley (Calif.) Country Club, Monterey Peninsula Country Club, Old Capitol Club, San Francisco Stock Exch. Club. Home: 253 Del Mesa Carmel CA 93923 Home Phone: 831-624-8119. Personal E-mail: gp1225@aol.com.

SMITH, GORDON RAY, utilities executive; b. San Francisco, Feb. 26, 1948; s. Margaret C. Orlando; m. Elizabeth Anne Rulfo, Sept. 26, 1981; children: Adam R., Alexandra R. BS in Fin., U. Calif., Berkeley, 1970; MBA in Fin., U. San Francisco, 1974. Fin. analyst Pacific Gas & Electric Co., San Francisco, 1970-76, sr. fin. analyst, 1976-78, dir., project financing, 1978-80, asst. treas., 1980-82, treas., 1982-83, v.p. fin., treas., 1983-87, v.p. fin. and rates, 1987—91, CFO, 1991—97, pres., CEO, 1997—. Mem. Mayor's Fiscal Adv. Com., San Francisco, 1986, Investment Rev. Com., San Francisco Found., 1986; dir. Calif.Chamber of Commerce, Bay Area Council, trustee, Monterey Bay Aquarium. Mem. Fin. Officers No. Calif., Pacific Coast Electric Assn., Pacific Coast Gas Assn., Bankers Club San Francisco, Moraga Country Club.

SMITH, GREG V., state legislator; b. Portland, Oreg., Nov. 7, 1968; m. Sherri Smith; 5 children. BS in Liberal Studies, Eastern Oreg. U., 1992. Former aide, use Majority Leader Greg Walden; advisor mem., Morrow Co Sch; chmn. Morrow Co Republican Cent Com.; former cmty. advisor mem. US Senator Gordon Smith; mem. Dist. 57 Oreg. House of Reps., 2000-; former bus devel. prof., Port of Morrow; former bd. dir., Greater Eastern Oreg. Devel & Morrow Cold Storage; former advisor mem. Blue Mountain Cmty. Coll. Small Bus Develop Ctr. Republican. Mormon. Office: 900 Court St NE H-482 Salem OR 97301 Office Phone: 503-986-1457. Business E-Mail: rep.gregsmith@state.or.us.

SMITH, GREGORY C., lawyer; b. Salt Lake City, 1963; BA with distinction, Stanford U., 1985; JD Harlan Fiske Stone Scholar, Columbia Law School, 1988. Bar: Calif. 1988. Ptnr. Skadden, Arps, Slate, Meagher & Flom LLP. Contbg. author, gen. editor Start-up and Emerging Companies, 2004. Dir. Friends of Music, Stanford U. Named one of The World's Leading Lawyers Bus., Chambers Global, 2002—04, 2004—05, Am.'s Leading Bus. Lawyers, Chambers USA, 2004—05. Mem.: Phi Beta Kappa. Office: Skadden 525 University Avenue Suite 1100 Palo Alto CA 94301 Office Phone: 650-470-4590.

SMITH, GREGORY R., lawyer; b. Chgo., Jan. 9, 1944; BA summa cum laude, Claremont Men's Coll., 1965; JD magna cum laude, Harvard U., 1968; MS, London Sch. Econs., 1969. Bar: Calif. 1969. Ptnr. Irell & Manella, LA. Vis. prof. U. Kansas Sch. Law, 1975. Mem. bd. editors Harvard Law Review, 1966-68. Mem. State Bar Calif., Phi Alpha Delta. Office: Irell & Manella Ste 900 1800 Avenue Of The Stars Los Angeles CA 90067-4276

SMITH, GREIG LOUIS, councilman; b. South Pasadena, Calif., Nov. 26, 1948; s. John Harold and Gloria Mae (Pitre) S.; m. Christine Marie Crippen, Apr. 14, 1973; children: Krista Lynn, Matthew John. AA, Pierce Coll., 1978; cert. advt., UCLA, 1988. Area dir. Rep. Ctrl. Com., 1969-70; youth dir. Re-elect Senator Murphy, LA, 1970-71; mktg. dir. V.I.V.A., LA, 1971-72; exec. dir. Ams. for Agnew, Washington, 1972-73; owner Greig's Formal Wear, Northridge, Calif., 1973-81; chief dep. for Councilman Bernson LA City Coun., 1979; reserve police officer, Valley's Devonshire divsn. LA Police Dept., 1992, reserve police officer, detective hdqs. robbery homicide divsn.; councilman, Dist. 12 LA City Coun., 2003—. Govt. rels. officer L.A. Olympic Organizing Com., 1984. Vice chmn. San Fernando Valley Breakfast Forum, 1975-78, C.I.V.I.C.C., San Fernando Valley, 1976-78; pres. North Hills Jaycees, Granada Hills, Calif., 1976-77; chmn. bd. North Valley YMCA, Mission Hills, Calif., 1979-80, 92—; founding mem. North Valley Rep. Assembly, 1992., founding mem. SOLID Foundation, bd. mem. U. Southern Calif. Sch. Pub. Policy Planning and Devel. Named Citizen of Yr. Granada Hills C. of C., 1977, Vol. of Yr. North Valley YMCA, 1988, Citizen of Yr. Internat. Order of Foresters, 1990, Reserve Officer of Yr., LA Police Dept., 1996. Mem. Jr. Chamber Internat. (senator, life). Alpha Sigma Gamma. Office: City Hall 200 North Spring St Rm 405 Los Angeles CA 90012 Office Phone: 213-473-7012. Office Fax: 213-473-6925. Business E-Mail: councilmember.smith@lacity.org.*

SMITH, HARVEY ALVIN, mathematics professor, consultant; b. Easton, Pa., Jan. 30, 1932; s. William Augustus and Ruth Carolyn (Krauth) S.; m. Ruth Wismer Kolb, Aug. 27, 1955; children: Deirdre Lynn, Kirsten Nadine, Brinton Averil. BS, Lehigh U., 1952; MS, U. Pa., 1955, AM, 1958, PhD, 1964. Asst. prof. math Drexel U., 1960-65; mem. tech. staff Inst. Def. Analyses, Arlington, Va., 1965-66; assoc. prof. math Oakland U., 1966-68; ops. rsch. scientist Exec. Office of Pres., Washington, 1968-70; prof. math. Oakland U., 1970-77; prof. Ariz. State U., Tempe, 1977—2003, prof. emeritus, 2003—. Cons. U.S. Army Security Agy., 1967—68, Inst. Def. Analyses, 1967—69, Exec. Office Pres., 1967—73, U.S. Arms Control and Disarmament Agy., 1973—79, Los Alamos Nat. Lab., 1980—93. Author: Mathematical Foundations of Systems Analysis, 1969. NSF fellow, 1964-65; recipient Meritorious Service award Exec. Office of Pres., 1970 Mem. Soc. Indsl. and Applied Math., Am. Math. Soc., AAAS, Sigma Xi Home: 18 E Concorda Dr Tempe AZ 85282-3517 Office: Ariz State U Dept Math Tempe AZ 85287-1804 Office Phone: 480-968-6813. Business E-Mail: hsmith@math.asu.edu.

SMITH, H(OWARD) DUANE, zoology educator; b. Fillmore, Utah, June 25, 1941; s. Howard Martell and Mary Ellen (Mitchell) S.; m. Dahnelle Bower, Dec. 18, 1961; children: Cory, Neichol. BS, Brigham Young U., 1963, MS, 1966; PhD, U. Ill., 1969. From asst. prof. to prof. Brigham Young U., Provo, Utah, 1969—; pvt. practice Orem, Utah, 1973—; dir. Monte L. Bean Life Sci. Mus., Provo, Utah. Dir. Life Sci. Mus. Co-author: Special Publications-Mammalogy, 1994; contbr. articles to profl. jours. State chair Mule Deer Found. Mem. Am. Soc. Mammalogists (sec. 1987-1992), Wildlife Soc., Rocky Mountain Elk Found., Mule Deer Found. (state chair), Safari Club Internat., Sigma Xi (pres. 1996-97). Republican. Mem. Lds Ch. Avocations: hunting, fishing. Office: Brigham Young Univ 290 MLBM Provo UT 84602-1049 E-mail: Duane@Museum.BYU.EDU.

SMITH, HOWARD RUSSELL, manufacturing executive, director; b. Clark County, Ohio, Aug. 15, 1914; s. Lewis Hoskins and Eula (Elder) S.; m. Jeanne Rogers, June 27, 1942; children: Stewart Russell, Douglas Howard, Jeanne Ellen Smith James. AB, Pomona Coll., 1936. Security analyst Kidder, Peabody & Co., NYC, 1936-37; economist ILO, Geneva, 1937-40; asst. to pres. Blue Diamond Corp., Los Angeles, 1940—; v.p., gen. mgr., dir. Avery Dennison Corp., Pasadena, Calif., 1946-56, pres., 1956-75, chmn. bd., 1975-84, chmn. exec. com., 1984-95; dir. emeritus, 1995—; chmn. bd. Kinsmith Fin. Corp., San Marino, Calif., 1979—. Bd. dirs., past pres., chmn. Los Angeles Philharm. Assn.; chmn. emeritus, bd. trustees Pomona Coll., Claremont, Calif.; past chmn. bd. Children's Hosp. Los Angeles, Community TV of So. Calif. (Sta. KCET), Los Angeles. Lt. USNR, 1943-46. Home: 1458 Hillcrest Ave Pasadena CA 91106-4503 Office: Avery Dennison Corp 150 N Orange Grove Blvd Pasadena CA 91103-3534 Office Phone: 626-304-2153.

SMITH, HYRUM WAYNE, management executive; b. Salt Lake City, Oct. 16, 1943; s. Joseph F. and Ruth (Pingree) S.; m. A. Gail Cooper, Dec. 21, 1966; Glenna, Stacie, Sharwan, Joseph, Rebecca, Jacob. BS in Bus., Brigham Young U., Provo, Utah, 1971. Ins. salesman Conn. Mut. Life, Honolulu, 1971-72; div. mgr. Nat. Inventory Control Systems, Portland, Oreg., 1972-73; v.p. sales western div. Automated Data Processing, Portland, 1973-78; mission pres. Later-Day Saints Ch., Ventura, Calif., 1978-81; owner Golden Eagle Motivation, Ventura, 1981-82; cons. Charles Hobbs, Salt Lake City, 1982-83; co-owner Hyrum Smith & Assocs., Salt Lake City, 1983-84; owner, chmn. bd. Franklin Internat. Inst., Inc., Salt Lake City, 1984—. Author: Where Eagles Rest, 1982; co-author: Excellence Through Time Management, 1985; author: Advanced Day Planner Users Guide, 1987. Bd. mem. Great Salt Lake Coun., Boy Scouts Am., 1982—, Explorers, 1982—. 1st lt. U.S. Army, 1967-69. Recipient Pub. Svc. award Assn. Fed. Investigators, Washington, 1988. Mem. Am. Soc. Tng. and Devel. Republican. Mem. Lds Ch. Avocations: boating, reading. Office: Franklin Covey Co 2200 W Pkwy Blvd Salt Lake City UT 84119-2099 Home: PO Box 40 Gunlock UT 84733-0040

SMITH, IRBY JAY, film producer; b. San Antonio, Apr. 17, 1938; s. Irby Jay and Virginia Lee (Algee) S.; m. Elaine Nicholson, June 8, 1956; children: Kimberly, Carrie, Jay. Student, Occidental Coll., 1955-56; BA summa cum laude, U. Calif., Berkeley, 1960. Pub. info. spcialist, tv interview host, writer U.S. Dept. Health, Edn. and Welfare, LA, 1960-66; writer, dir. CRM/McGraw-Hill Films, LA, 1969-70; pvt. practice asst. dir., prodn. mgr., prodr., dir., 1966—. Prodr. City Slickers, Prefontaine, Wild America, Rookie of the Year,

Angels in the Outfield, Enemies a Love Story, Major League, Young Guns I and II. Recipient ALA award for writing and directing edn1. films, 1970, 2 Cine Golden Eagle awards for writing and directing ednl. films, 1970. Mem. Dirs. Guild Am., Phi Beta Kappa. Democrat.

SMITH, JAMES LAWRENCE, research physicist; b. Detroit, Sept. 3, 1943; s. William Leo and Marjorie Marie (Underwood) S.; m. Carol Ann Adam, Mar. 27, 1965; children: David Adam, William Leo. BS, Wayne State U., 1965; PhD, Brown U., 1974. Mem. staff Los Alamos Nat. Lab., N.Mex., 1973—82, fellow, 1982—86, 1987—, dir. Ctr. Materials Sci., 1986—87; chief scientist Superconductivity Tech. Ctr., 1988—99. Sci. editor: Los Alamos Rsch. Quar., 2002-03; N.Am. editor: Philos. mag., 1990-95, 03-06; editor: Philos. mag. B, 1995-02, Philos. Mag., 2003-06; contbr. articles to profl. jours. Recipient E.O. Lawrence award, 1986, Disting. Alumni award Wayne State U., 1993. Fellow Am. Phys. Soc. (internat. prize for new materials 1990); mem. AAAS, Materials Rsch. Soc., Minerals Metals Materials Soc., Am. Crystallographic Assn., Brown Alumni Assn. (bd. govs. 1998-2000), Phi Beta Kappa. Achievements include patents for design of magnetic field and high-strength conductors. Office: Los Alamos Nat Lab Mail Stop G770 Los Alamos NM 87545-0001 Office Phone: 505-667-4476. Business E-Mail: jlsmith@lanl.gov.

SMITH, JAMES PATRICK, economist; b. Aug. 3, 1943; s. James P. and Winefred (Harrison) S.; m. Sandra Berry, Oct. 25, 1983; children: Gillian Clare, Lauren Theresa. BS, Fordham U., 1965; PhD, U. Chgo., 1972. Rsch. assoc. Nat. Bur. Econ. Rsch., NYC, 1972-74; sr. economist Rand Corp., Santa Monica, Calif., 1974—, dir. of rsch. labor and population, 1977-93. Bd. dirs. Occupl. Safety and Health Standards State Calif. Editor: Female Labor Supply, 1980, The New Americans, 1997, The Immigration Debate, 1998, Wealth, Work, and Health, 1999, Disease Disadvantage in United States and England; bd. editors: Am. Econ. Rev., 1980-83; contbr. articles to profl. jours. Recipient Merit award NIH, 1995-2005 Mem. NIA (monitoring com., health and retirement survey, chair NAS panel on immigration, chair adv. com. Korean HRS KLOSA, Chinese HRS CHARLES and Indian HRS LASI), Am. Econ. Assn., Phi Beta Kappa. Office: RAND PO Box 2138 Santa Monica CA 90407-2138 Business E-Mail: smith@rand.org.

SMITH, JANET HUGIE, lawyer; b. Logan, Utah, Aug. 1, 1945; BA magna cum laude, Utah State U., 1967; MA cum laude, Stanford U., 1969; JD, U. Utah, 1976. Bar: Utah 1976, US Supreme Ct. 1992, U.S. Ct. Appeals (10th cir.) 1977, (9th cir.) 2003, US Dist. Ct. Colo. 2004. Shareholder, exec. com. Ray, Quinney & Nebeker, Salt Lake City, 1983—. Mem. ABA (labor and employment law sect.), Utah State Bar (labor and employment law sect.), CUE (labor lawyers adv. coun.), Am. Law Coun., Am. Coll. Trial Lawyers, Aldon J. Anderson Am. Inns of Ct. Office: Ray Quinney & Nebeker 36 S State St Ste 1400 Salt Lake City UT 84111-1431 Business E-Mail: jhsmith@rqn.com.

SMITH, JEFFERSON, state legislator; Attended, U. Oreg.; graduated, Harvard Law Sch. Former cowhand Hermiston farm; former atty. NYC; founder Oreg. Bus Project; mem. Dist. 47 Oreg. House of Reps., 2008—. Democrat. Office: 900 Court St NE H-486 Salem OR 97301 Office Phone: 503-986-1447. Business E-Mail: rep.jeffersonsmith@state.or.us.

SMITH, JIMMIE DEE, lawyer; BBA, No. Ariz. U.; JD, Ariz. State U., 1970. Solo law practice, Yuma, Ariz., 1970—. Mem.: State Bar Ariz. Bd. Govs. (sec.-treas., 2nd v.p., 1st v.p., pres.-elect 2005—06, pres. 2006—07), Yuma County Bar Assn. (former pres.). Office: Atty at Law 221 S 2nd Ave Yuma AZ 85364-2265 Office Phone: 928-783-7809. Office Fax: 928-783-7800. E-mail: jimmiedeesmith@azbar.org.

SMITH, JOSEF RILEY, retired internist; b. Council Bluffs, Iowa, Oct. 1, 1926; s. George William Smith and Margaret (Wood) Hill; divorced; children: Sarah L. Kratz, David L., Mary E. Loeb, John R., Ruthann P. Sherrier, Mark A.; m. Susan Frances Irwin, Feb. 9, 1973; 1 child, Christopher I. Student, Tulane U., 1944-46; BM, Northwestern U., 1950, MD, 1951; MSEE, Marquette U., 1964. Diplomate Am. Bd. Internal Medicine. Instr. internal medicine U. Miss. Med. Sch., Jackson, 1956-59; asst. prof. Marquette U. Med. Sch., Milw., 1959-63; from assoc. prof. to full prof. U. Mich. Med. Sch., Ann Arbor, 1963-72; physician Youngstown (Ohio) Hosp., 1972-79, Group Health Med. Assn., Tucson, 1979-84, Assocs. in Internal Medicine, Tucson, 1985-87; pvt. practice Tucson, 1987—2006; ret., 2006. Co-author: Clinical Cardiopulmonary Physiology, 1960, Textbook of Pulmonary Disease, 1965, 2d rev. edit., 1974; contbr. articles to profl. jours. Controller Mahoning County TB Clinic, Youngstown, 1973-79. Served to lt. USNR, 1952-54. Fellow ACP, Sigma Xi; mem. Ariz. Med. Assn., Pima County Med. Assn., Am. Thoracic Soc., Ariz. Thoracic Soc., Bioengring. Med. Soc. (founder). Avocations: photography, computers. Personal E-mail: jrsmith2@qwest.net.

SMITH, JULIE ANN, pharmaceutical executive; BS, Cornell Univ. Mktg. div. Bristol-Myers Squibb; comml. team Novazyme Pharmaceutical Corp.; v.p. product strategy and devel. Genzyme Corp., v.p. global mktg.; v.p., mktg. Jazz Pharmaceuticals, 2006—. Clinical rschr. neuroendocrinology Mass. Gen. Hosp. Named one of 40 Under 40, Boston Bus. Jour., 2005. Office: Jazz Pahrmaceuticals 3180 Porter Dr Palo Alto CA 94304

SMITH, KEITH E., hotel and gaming company executive; b. 1960; Corp. controller Boyd Gaming Corp., 1990, sr. v.p., controller, exec. v.p., ops., 1998—2001, COO, 2001—05, pres., COO, 2005—07, pres., CEO, 2008—. Dir., bd. of dirs. Boyd Gaming Corp.; vice-chmn., bd. of dirs. NV Resort Assn., Las Vegas Convention and Visitors Authority. Office: Boyd Gaming Corp 3883 Howard Hughes Pkwy Ninth Fl Las Vegas NV 89118 Office Phone: 702-792-7200. Office Fax: 702-792-7263.

SMITH, KERRY CLARK, lawyer; b. Phoenix, July 12, 1935; s. Clark and Fay S.; m. Michael Waterman, 1958; children: Kevin, Ian. AB, Stanford U., 1957, JD, 1962. Bar: Calif. 1963, U.S. Supreme Ct. 1980. Assoc. Chickering & Gregory, San Francisco, 1962-70, ptnr., 1970-81, Pettit & Martin, San Francisco, 1981-95, Hovis, Smith, San Francisco, 1995-99; pvt. practice San Francisco, 1999—. Mem. editl. bd. Stanford Law Rev., 1961-62. Lt. USN, 1957-60. Mem. Calif. Bar Assn., Orinda County Club, La Quinta Citrus Golf Club.

SMITH, KIRK ROBERT, environmental health sciences educator, researcher; b. Calif., Jan. 19, 1947; MPH, U. Calif., Berkeley, PhD in Biomed. & Environ. Health Scis., 1977. Founder, leader energy program East-West Ctr., Honolulu, 1978-85, sr. fellow, program area coord. environ. risk, 1985—; prof. environ. health scis. U. Calif., Berkeley, 1995—; dep. dir. Inst. Global Health, 2000—, Brian and Jennifer Maxwell chair in pub. health, 2003—. Author: 8 books; contbr. numerous articles to profl. jours. Named One of Am.'s 100 Brightest Young Scientists, Sci. Digest, 1984, Alumnus of Yr., U. Calif. Sch. Pub. Health, 1982. Mem. NAS. Achievements include research on pollution in developing countries. Office: U Calif Sch Pub Health Environ Health Scis Warren Hall Berkeley CA 94720-7360 E-mail: KRKSmith@uclink.berkeley.edu.

SMITH, LESLIE C., federal judge; BA, Vanderbilt U., 1962; JD with high distinction, U. Ky.; LLM, U. Western Australia, Perth. Dist. judge 7th Jud. Dist. N.Mex., 1989-95; magistrate judge U.S. Dist. Ct. N.Mex., Las Cruces, 1995—. Office: US Courthouse 200 E Griggs Ave Las Cruces NM 88001-3523

SMITH, LESLIE ROPER, hospital and health facility administrator; b. Stockton, Calif., June 20, 1928; s. Austin J. and Helen (Roper) S.; m. Edith Sue Fischer, June 22, 1952; children: Melinda Sue, Leslie Erin, Timothy Brian. AB, U. Pacific, 1951; MS in Pub. Adminstrn, U. So. Calif., 1956. Adminstrv. asst. Ranchos Los Amigos Hosp., Downey, Calif., 1953-57; asst. adminstr. Harbor Gen. Hosp., Torrance, Calif., 1957-65; adminstr. Harbor UCLA Med. Ctr., 1966-71; acting regional dir. Los Angeles County Coastal Health Services Region, 1973; pres. San Pedro Peninsula Hosp., San Pedro, Calif., 1974-86; exec. dir. Los Angeles County/U. So. Calif. Med. Center, 1971-73; adminstr. Long Beach (Calif.) Hosp., 1965-66; asso. clin. prof. community medicine and pub. health, also emergency medicine U. So. Calif., 1968-78; instr. U. So. Calif. (Sch. Pub. Adminstrn.), 1968; preceptor hosp. adminstrn. UCLA Sch. Pub. Health, 1964—; chief exec. officer French Hosp. Med. Ctr. and Health Plan, 1986-87; dir. health care services McCormack & Farrow, 1987—. Lectr. in field, 1963—; cons. emergency health services HEW, 1970-73; chmn. com. disaster preparedness Hosp. Council So. Calif., 1966-72, sec., 1971—, pres., 1973; mem. Calif. Assembly Com. on Emergency Med. Services, 1970, Calif. Emergency Med. Adv. Com., 1972-75, Los Angeles County Commn. on Emergency Med. Services, 1975-83, Los Angeles Health Planning and Devel. Agy. Commn., 1980-83; bd. dirs. Blue Cross of So. Calif.; mem. hosp. relations com. Blue Cross of Calif.; mem. adv. com. on emergency health services Calif. Dept. Health, 1974-75; bd. dirs., mem. exec. com. Truck Ins. Exchange of Farmers Ins. Group, 1977-82; bd. dirs. Hosp. Council of So. Calif., 1966-76, 81-86, Health Resources Inst., 1985-86; chmn. Preferred Health Network, 1983-86 Mem. goals com., Torrance, 1968—; pres. Silver Spur Little League, Palos Verdes, 1969-70. With US Army, 1946—48. Recipient Silver Knight and Gold Knight award Nat. Mgmt. Assn., 1970, 85, Walker Fellowship award, Calif. Hosp. Assn, 1976 Fellow Am. Coll. Health Care Execs. (life); mem. Am., Nat. mgmt. assns., Am. Hosp. Assn. (chmn. com. on community emergency health services 1973), Calif. Hosp. Assn. (chmn. com. emergency services 1965-70, trustee 1973-76, bd. dirs. Calif. Ins. Service Group 1980-82), County Suprs. Assn. Calif. (chmn. joint subcom. on emergency care 1970) Presbyn. (elder, trustee). Methodist.

SMITH, LLOYD HOLLINGSWORTH, physician; b. Easley, SC, Mar. 27, 1924; s. Lloyd H. and Phyllis (Page) S.; m. Margaret Constance Avery, Feb. 27, 1954; children— Virginia Constance, Christopher Avery, Rebecca Anne, Charlotte Page, Elizabeth Hollingsworth, Jeffrey Hollingsworth. AB, Washington and Lee U., 1944, D.Sc., 1969; MD, Harvard, 1948. Intern, then resident Mass. Gen. Hosp., Boston, 1948-50, chief resident physician, 1955-56; mem. Harvard Soc. Fellows, 1952-54; asst. prof. Harvard Soc. Fellows (Med. Sch.), 1956-63; vis. investigator Karolinska Inst., Stockholm, 1954-55, Oxford (Eng.) U., 1963-64; prof. medicine, chmn. dept. U. Calif. Med. Sch., San Francisco, 1964-85, assoc dean, 1985-2000. Mem. Pres.'s Sci. Adv. Com., 1970-73 Bd. overseers Harvard, 1974-80. Served to capt., M.C. AUS, 1950-52. Mem. Am. Acad. Arts and Scis., Am. Soc. Clin. Investigation (pres. 1969-70), Western Soc. Clin. Rsch. (pres. 1969-70), Assn. Am. Physicians (pres. 1974-75), Am. Fedn. Clin. Rsch. Achievements include special research genetic and metabolic diseases. Home: 309 Evergreen Dr Kentfield CA 94904-2709 Office: U Calif San Francisco Med Ctr San Francisco CA 94143-0001 E-mail: lloydhsmith@aol.com.

SMITH, LONNIE MAX, diversified industries executive; b. Twin Falls, Idaho, July 28, 1944; s. Lonnie E. and Christie (Stuart) S.; m. Cheryl Diane Smith, June 10, 1968; children: Kristen, Maryam, Rebecca, Michael, Catherine. BSEE, Utah State U., 1967; MBA, Harvard U., 1974. Engr., mgr. field services, mgr. tech. services to asst. to v.p. plans and control IBM Corp., San Francisco, Palo Alto, Calif., and White Plains, NY, 1967-74; mgr., corp. strategy, then cons. Boston Cons. Group, 1974-76; exec. v.p. Am. Tourister, Inc., Warren, R.I., 1978-81; sr. v.p. corp. planning Hillenbrand Industries, Inc., Batesville, Ind., 1977-78, sr. exec. vp., 1982-97, also bd. dirs., 1997; pres., CEO Intuitive Surgs., Mountain View, Calif., 1997—. Pres. Biosite Diagnostics, Lozion Corp. Served to 1st lt. U.S. Army, 1969-72. Mem. Lds Ch. Avocations: tennis, skiing. Office: Intuitive Surg 950 Kifer Rd Sunnyvale CA 94086-5206

SMITH, MARIE B., college president; BA, San Francisco State U.; MA in Biology, Sonoma State U.; DEdn, U. San Francisco. Biology instr. to acting pres. Indian Valley Coll., Novato, Calif., 1974; dean Coll. at Life Chiropractic Coll.-West San Lorenzo, 1985; staff to dean instrn. Coll. of Alameda, 1990, pres., 1991-94, Am. River Coll., 1995—. Chair planning team McClennan AFB Privatization and Reuse adv. com.; co-chair strategic planning teams Los Rio C.C. Dist. Mem. Grant Joint Union H.S. Dist. Vol. Integration Cmty. adv. coun.; mem. Golden Gate U. Women's Leadership Inst., Calif. Ctr. for Health Improvement, Life College West, San Lorenzo, Calif.; pres. ARC. Mem. Biol. Field Svc. Assn. Office: Am River Coll 4700 College Oak Dr Sacramento CA 95841-4217

SMITH, MARSHA H., state agency administrator, lawyer; b. Boise, Idaho, Mar. 24, 1950; d. Eugene F. and Joyce (Ross) Hatch; 2 children. BS in Biology/Edn., Idaho State U., 1973; MLS, Brigham Young U., 1975; JD, U. Wash., 1980. Bar: Idaho, U.S. Dist. Ct. Idaho, U.S. Ct. Appeals (9th cir.), U.S. Ct. Appeals (D.C. cir.). Dep. atty. gen. Bus./Consumer Protection Divsn., Boise, 1980-81, Idaho Pub. Utilities Commn., Boise, 1981-89, dir. policy and external rels., 1989-91, commr., 1991—, pres., 1991-95. Mem. Harvard Electricity Policy Group, Nat. Coun. on Electricity Policy; com. for regional electric power coop. Western Interstate Energy Bd., 1999-2005; dir. Western Electricity Coordinating Coun., 2002—; mem. adv. coun. Electric Power Rsch. Inst. Legis. dist. chair Ada County Democrats, Idaho, 1986-89. Mem. Nat. Assn. Regulatory Utility Commrs. (bd. dirs. 1999—, chair electricity com. 2000-03, 2nd v.p. 2005). Office: Idaho Pub Utilities Commn PO Box 83720 Boise ID 83720-0074 Office Phone: 208-334-3912.

SMITH, MARSHALL SAVIDGE, foundation executive; b. East Orange, NJ, Sept. 16, 1937; s. Marshall Parsons and Ann Eileen (Zulauf) S.; m. Carol Goodspeed, June 25, 1960 (div. Aug. 1962); m. Louise Nixon Claiborn, Aug. 1964; children: Adam, Jennifer, Matthew, Megan. AB, Harvard U., 1960, EdM, 1963, EdD, 1970. Systems analyst and computer programmer Raytheon Corp., Andover, Mass., 1959-62; instr., assoc. prof. Harvard U., Cambridge, Mass., 1966-76; asst., assoc. dir. Nat. Inst. Edn., Washington, 1973-76; asst. commr. edn. HEW, Washington, 1976-79, chief of staff to U.S. Dept. Edn. sec., 1980; prof. U. Wis., Madison, 1980-86, Stanford (Calif.) U., 1986—2003, dean Sch. Edn., 1986—94; under-sec. edn. U.S. Dept. Edn., 1993-2000, acting dep. sec. edn., 1996-2000; program dir. Hewlett Found., 2001—. Task force, chmn. Clinton Presdl. Transition Team, 1992-93; chmn. PEW Forum on Ednl. Reform; chmn. bd. internat. com. studies in edn. NAS, 1992-93. Author: The General Inquirer, 1967, Inequality, 1972; contbr. articles to profl. jours, chpts. to books. Pres. Madison West Hockey Assn., 1982-84. Mem. Am. Ednl. Rsch. Assn. (chmn. orgn. instl. affiliates 1985-86), Nat. Acad. Edn. Democrat. Avocations: environmental issues, philanthropy. Home: 1256 Forest Ave Palo Alto CA 94301 Office: Wm & Flora Hewlett Found Menlo Park CA Business E-Mail: msmith@hewlett.org.

SMITH, MARTIN BERNHARD, retired journalist; b. San Francisco, Apr. 20, 1930; s. John Edgar and Anna Sophie (Thorsen) S.; m. Joan Lovat Muller, Apr. 25, 1953; children: Catherine Joan, Karen Anne. AB, U. Calif., Berkeley, 1952, M Journalism, 1968. Reporter, city editor Modesto (Calif.) Bee, 1957-64; reporter, mng. editor Sacramento Bee, 1964-75; polit. editor, columnist McClatchy Newspapers, Sacramento, 1975-92; ret., 1992. Episcopalian. Personal E-mail: Joan_and_Marty@msn.com.

SMITH, MEREDITH WOOD, political organization administrator; b. Attleboro, Mass. m. Joe Smith; 4 children. BA in Edn., U. Ky. Small bus. owner, pres. of a local bus. assn., sales rep. for a mid-sized nat. corp.; dir. Clackamas County Juvenile Svc. Commn.; western states vice chair rep. Assn. State Dem. Chairs Exec. Com.; vice chair Dem. Party of Oreg., chairwoman, 2008—. Active John F. Kennedy Presdl. Campaign, Ky., 1961. Democrat. Office: Dem Party of Oreg 232 NE 9th Ave Portland OR 97232-2915 Office Phone: 503-224-8200. E-mail: chair@dpo.org.

SMITH, MICHAEL PETER, social sciences educator, researcher; b. Dunkirk, NY, Aug. 2, 1942; s. Peter Joseph and Rosalie Barbara (Lipka) S.; m. Patricia Anne Lendway, Aug. 21, 1965. BA magna cum laude, St. Michael's Coll., 1964; MA in Polit. Sci., U. Mass., 1966, PhD in Polit. Sci., 1971. Instr., asst. prof. dept. govt. Dartmouth Coll., Hanover, NH, 1968—71; asst. prof. dept. polit. sci. Boston U., 1971—74; assoc. prof., prof. dept. polit. sci. Tulane U., New Orleans, 1974—86; prof. cmty. studies U. Calif., Davis, 1986—, chmn. dept. applied behavioral scis., 1986—91, chmn. cmty. studies and devel. program, 2001—. Vis. prof. pub. policy U. Calif., Berkeley, 1981, city planning U. N.C., Chapel Hill, 1982, city planning U. Calif., Berkeley, 1985; vis. scholar in govt. U. Essex, Eng., 1979; vis. scholar polit. and social sci. U. Cambridge, Eng., 1982; vis. scholar Inst. Urban and Regional Devel., U. Calif., Berkeley, 1990, 94 Internat. Ctr. for Advanced Studies, NYU, 1998, Ctr. Migration, Policy and Soc., Oxford U., 2005 Author: The City & Social Theory, 1979, City, State and Market, 1988, Transnational Urbanism, 2001; co-author: Restructuring the City, 1983, California's Changing Faces, 1993, Citizenship Across Borders, 2008; editor: Cities in Transformation, 1984, Breaking Chains, 1991, After Modernism, 1992, Marginal Spaces, 1995, Comparative Urban & Community Research, 1986—; co-editor: The Capitalist City, 1987—, The Bubbling Cauldron, 1995, Transnationalism from Below, 1998, City and Nation: Rethinking Place and Identity, 2001, The Human Face of Global Mobility, 2006, Transnational Ties, 2008; mem. editl. bd. Global Networks., 1999—. Office: Dept Human & Cmty Devel Univ Calif Davis CA 95616 Office Phone: 530-752-2243. Business E-Mail: mpsmith@ucdavis.edu.

SMITH, MICHAEL S., interior designer, furniture designer; b. Newport Beach, Calif. Grad., Otis Coll. Art and Design, LA. With Gep Durenberger, John Saladino, NYC; opened home furnishings store, Calif.; owner, designer Michael S. Smith Inc., Santa Monica, 1990—; designer fabric and leather collection Cowtan and Tout, 1997; designer lines for Kallista brand and Anna Sacks Tile Kohler, 1999; design partnerships with Visual Comfort Lighting, Mansour Modern Rugs, Patterson, Flynn and Martin Carpeting, Samuel and Sons Passementrie, Agaria Home Fragrances. Mem. bd. trustees Otis Coll. Art and Design; co-chair Am. Friends of Olympia Internat. Fine Art and Antique Fair; family quarters decorator The White House, 2009. Author: (books) Elements of Style, 2007, Houses, 2008; featured in Elle Decor Mag., Archtl. Digest, House Beautiful, Town and Country, Domino mag., Metro. Home, Interior Design, W. Named Designer of Yr., Elle Decor, 2003; named one of The AD 100, Archtl. Digest, 2002, 2004, Stars of Design, LA Pacific Design Ctr., 2004. Achievements include winning the commission to redecorate The White House, 2009. Office: Michael S Smith Inc 1646 19th St Santa Monica CA 90404 Office Phone: 310-315-3018. Office Fax: 310-315-3059. Business E-Mail: info@michaelsmithinc.com.*

SMITH, MILTON RAY, computer company executive, lawyer; b. Idaho, 1935; AA, Long Beach City Coll., Calif., 1958; BS, Portland State U., 1962; MS, Oreg. State U., 1969; JD, Lewis and Clark Coll., 1970. Bar: Oreg. 1970, U.S. Dist. Ct. Oreg. 1970, U.S. Ct. Appeals (9th cir.) 1971, U.S. Supreme Ct. 1973. Tech. writer Northrop Corp., Hawthorne, Calif., 1957-58; engring. writer Tektronix Inc., Beaverton, Oreg., 1958-60, design engr., 1960-63, project engr., 1963-65, program mgr., 1966-70; asst. engring. mgr. Eldorado Electronics, Concord, Calif., 1965-66; ptnr. Acker, Underwood & Smith, Portland, Oreg., 1970-86; chmn., chief exec. officer Floating Point Systems Inc., Beaverton, 1986-88, pres., chief exec. officer, 1991-92, also vice chmn. bd. dirs.; pres., chief exec. officer Thrustmaster Inc., Tigard, Oreg., 1992-94; pres., CEO Zeelan Tech., Inc., Beaverton, Oreg., 1994-95; mgmt. cons., 1995—. CEO, Test Sys. Strategies, Inc., Beaverton, 1992-93; bd. dirs. ThrustMaster, Inc., Beaverton, Integrated Measurement Sys., Beaverton. Bd. dirs. Oreg. Bus. Council, Portland, 1986-88; mem. bd. visitors Northwestern Sch. Law, Portland, 1986—. With USN, 1953-56. Mem. Am. Electronics Assn. (exec. com. Oreg. coun. 1987-93, vice chmn. 1994-95, chmn. 1995-96), Oreg. State Bar, Founders Club Portland. Republican.

SMITH, NORMA, state legislator; b. Pensacola, Fla. d. Chapman and Alice Creighton; m. Stephen Smith (dec. Sept. 2005); 4 children. Special asst. for veterans, military and local govtl. affairs Office Congressman Jack Metcalf; dir. sen. cmty. programs CRISTA; writer Lindsay Comm., 2005; mem. Dist. 10 Wash. House of Reps., 2009—.

Writer Lindsay Comm. Republican. Office: District 22 Front St NW Ste C Coupeville WA 98239 also: 417 John L O'Brien Bldg PO Box 40600 Olympia WA 98504 Office Phone: 360-678-3604, 360-786-7884. E-mail: smith.norma@leg.wa.gov.

SMITH, NORMAN RANDY, federal judge; b. Logan, Utah, Aug. 11, 1949; s. Norman Busby and Patricia (Mendenhall) S.; m. La Dean Egbert, Jan. 3, 1984. BS magna cum laude, Brigham Young U., 1974, JD, 1977. Bar: Idaho 1977, U.S. Dist. Ct. Idaho 1977, U.S. Ct. Claims 1979, U.S. Tax Ct. 1978, U.S. Ct. Appeals (9th cir.) 1979, U.S. Supreme Ct. 1981. Asst. gen. counsel J.R. Simplot Co., Boise, Idaho, 1977-82; assoc. Merrill & Merrill, Pocatello, Idaho, 1982—84, ptnr., 1984—95; dist. judge Idaho 6th Judicial Dist., 1995—2007, adminstrv. dist. judge, 2004—07; judge US Ct. Appeals (9th cir.), 2007—. Adj. prof., Boise St. U., 1979-81, Idaho State U., 1984- Party chmn. Idaho Rep. Party, 1993-96; county chmn. Bannock County Rep. Party, Pocatello, 1991-93; pres. Idaho State Civic Symphony, Pocatello, 1992-95, 98-99. Recipient George G. Granada award, Outstanding judge in Idaho, 2004; named Idaho Statesman of Yr., 2005; named a Tchr. of Yr., Coll. Bus., 2005. Mem. Idaho Dist. Judges Assn. (pres. 1998-2000), Idaho Def. Counsel (pres. 1992-93), Def. Rsch. Inst. (del. Idaho state 1992-94, Exceptional Performance Citation 1993), 6th Dist. Bar Assn. (pres. 1994-95), Rotary (Gate City pres. 1993-94). Avocations: golf, gardening, work. Office: US Courthouse 801 E Sherman Pocatello ID 83201 Office Phone: 208-478-4140.

SMITH, ORIN C., retired beverage service company executive; b. 1942; BA, U. Wash., 1965; MBA, Harvard U., 1967. With Touche Ross & Co., 1969—77, 1980—85; chief policy & fin. officer Office Mgmt. & Budget State of Wash., 1977—80, 1985—87; exec. v.p., CFO, chief adminstrv. officer Danzas Corp., 1987—90; v.p., CFO Starbucks Corp., Seattle, 1990—94, pres., COO, 1994—2000, pres., CEO, 2000—05. Bd. dirs. Starbucks Corp., 1996—2005, Nike, Inc., 2004—, Washington Mutual Inc., 2005—08, Walt Disney Co., 2006—. Bd. dirs. Conservation Internat.; advisory bd. U. Wash. Sch. Bus.; bd. dirs. U. Wash. Medicine. Avocations: golf, skiing, reading.*

SMITH, ORVILLE AUVERNE, physiology educator; b. Nogales, Ariz., June 16, 1927; s. Orville Auverne and Bess (Gill) S.; m. Clara Jean Smith; children— Nanette, Marcella. BA in Psychology, U. Ariz., 1949; MA, Mich. State U., 1950, PhD, 1953. Instr. psychology Mich. State U., East Lansing, 1953-54; fellow U. Pa., Phila., 1954-56; trainee dept. physiology and biophysics U. Wash., Seattle, 1956-58, instr. physiology and biophysics, 1958-59, asst. prof., 1959-61, 62-63; asst. dir. Regional Primate Research Ctr., 1962-69, assoc. prof., 1963-67, prof., 1967-97; assoc. dir. Regional Primate Research Center, 1969-71, dir., 1971-88, prof. emeritus, 1997—. Contbr. articles to profl. jours. Mem. Am. Physiol. Soc., Am. Soc. Primatologists (pres. 1977-79), Internat. Congress Physiol. Scis., Am. Assn. Anatomists, AAAS, Pavlovian Soc. N.Am. (pres. 1977-78), Internat. Primatological Soc., AAUP, Neurosci. Soc. Home: 30311 201st Ct SE Kent WA 98042-5920 Office: U Wash Nat Primate Rsch Ctr PO Box 357330 Seattle WA 98195-7330

SMITH, OTTO J. M., electrical engineering educator; b. Urbana, Ill., Aug. 6, 1917; s. Otto Mitchell and Mary Catherine (Carr) S.; m. Phyllis P. Sterling, Sept. 3, 1941; children: Candace B., Otto J.A., Sterling M., Stanford D. BS in Chemistry, Okla. State U., 1938; BSEE, U. Okla., 1938; PhDEE, Stanford U., 1941. Registered profl. engr., Calif. Instr. elec. engring. Tufts U., Medford, Mass., 1941-43; asst. prof. elec. engring. Denver U., 1943-44; rsch. engr. Westinghouse Rsch. Labs., Forest Hills, Pa., 1944-46; sr. rsch. fellow econs. and engring. Monash U., Melbourne, Australia, 1966-67; prof. elec. engr. U. Calif., Berkeley, 1947—. Chief engr. Smith and Sun, Berkeley, 1976—; mem. coop. sci. program NSF, Romania, 1973; chief energy efficiency EPA, Poland, 1992. Author: Feedback Control Systems, 1958; contbr. articles to profl. jours.; patentee in field. Dist. commr. Boy Scouts Am., Berkeley, 1949-53; trustee South Campus Community Ministry, Berkeley, 1968-70, Wesley Found., Berkeley, 1969-72; vol. Natural Resources Conservation Svc., U.S. Dept. Agr., 1996—. Guggenheim fellow, 1960. Fellow AAAS, IEEE; mem. Am. Solar Energy Soc., Internat. Solar Energy Soc., Am. Wind Energy Assn., Calif. Writer's Club. Clubs: Berkeley City Commons (pres. 1963). Democrat. Methodist. Avocations: photography, travel, guitar, violin, chorus. Home: 612 Euclid Ave Berkeley CA 94708-1332 Office: U Calif Dept Elec Engring & Computer Scis Berkeley CA 94720-0001 Office Phone: 510-525-9126. Business E-Mail: otto.enabler@olympus.net.

SMITH, PATRICK (PATRICK SANTOSUOSSO), columnist, pilot; b. 1966; Airline pilot; air travel columnist salon.com, 2001—. Author: Ask the Pilot: Everything You Need To Know About Air Travel, 2004. Office: c/o Salon Media Group Inc 101 Spear St Ste 203 San Francisco CA 94105 Office Phone: 415-645-9200. Office Fax: 415-645-9204. Personal E-mail: aviateur@askthepilot.com. Business E-Mail: PatrickSmith@salon.com.

SMITH, PATTI, state legislator; m to Leroy. Oregon State Representative, District 52, currently.Tax preparer, realtor, support enforcement office, Baker Co District Atty, payroll staff, Woodland Prk Hosp, staff member, Multnomah Co Charter Review Committee, formerly; owner, Ranch, Farm & Logging Bus, currently. Citizen Involvement Award, Northeast Mutnomah Co Community Association. Farm Bureau; Columbia & Keating Granges; 4-H; Crown Point Hist Soc; East Multnomah Co Pioneer's Association; Northeast Multnomah Co Community Association (president, currently). Republican. Office: 900 Court St NE H-276 Salem OR 97301 Office Phone: 503-986-1452.

SMITH, PETER HOPKINSON, political scientist, consultant, writer; b. Bklyn., Jan. 17, 1940; s. Joseph Hopkinson and Mary Edna (Sullivan) S.; children: Jonathan Yeardley, Peter Hopkinson Jr, Joanna Alexandra. BA, Harvard U., 1961; MA, PhD, Columbia U., 1966. Asst. prof. Dartmouth Coll., Hanover, N.H., 1966-68; from asst. prof. to prof. U. Wis., Madison, 1968-80; prof. MIT, Cambridge, 1980-86; Simón Bolívar prof. L.Am. studies U. Calif., San Diego, 1987—, dir. Ctr. for Iberian and L.Am. studies, 1989—. Cons. Ford Found., N.Y.C., 1984—; vis. mem. Inst. for Advanced Study, Princeton, N.J., 1972-73. Author: Politics and Beef in Argentina: Patterns of Conflict and Change, 1969, Argentina and the Failure of Democracy: Conflict among Political Elites, 1904-55, 1974, Labyrinths of Power: Political Recruitment in Twentieth-Century Mexico, 1979, Mexico: The Quest for a U.S. Policy, 1980, Mexico: Neighbor in Transition, 1984; co-author: Modern Latin America, 1984, 89, 92, editor: Statistics, Epistemology, and History, 1984, Drug Policy in the Americas, 1992, The Challenge of Integration: Europe and the Americas, 1993, Talons of the Eagle, 1995; co-editor: New Approaches to Latin Am. History, 1974, The Family in Latin America, 1978; series editor: Latin America in Global Perspective, 1995—; contbr. articles to profl. jours. Guggenheim fellow, 1975-76; disting. Fulbright lectr. Mexico, 1984. Mem. Latin Am. Studies Assn. (pres. 1981), Am. Polit. Sci. Assn., Am. Hist. Assn., Coun. for Internat. Exch. Scholars, Coun. on Fgn. Rels. Office: U Calif Ctr Iberian & LAm Studies 9500 Gilman Dr La Jolla CA 92093-0528

SMITH, PHILIP MEEK, science administrator, consultant; b. Springfield, Ohio, May 18, 1932; s. Clarence Mitchell S. and Lois Ellen (Meek) Dudley. BS, Ohio State U., 1954, MA, 1955; DSc (hon.), NC State U., 1986. Mem. staff U.S. Nat. Com. for Internat. Geophys. Yr., NAS, 1957-58; program dir. NSF, 1958-63, dir. ops. U.S. Antarctic Rsch. program, 1964-69, dep. head divsn. polar programs, 1970-73, exec. asst. to dir. and sci. advisor to pres., 1974-76; chief gen. sci. br. Office Mgmt. and Budget Exec. Office of Pres., 1973-74; assoc. dir. Office Sci. and Tech. Policy, Exec. Office of Pres., 1976-81; exec. officer NRC-NAS, Washington, 1981-94; ptnr. McGeary and Smith, Washington, 1995—2004; chmn. external adv. com. Nat. Computational Sci. Alliance, 1997—2001, mem., 2002—03; prin. Smith Sci. Policy and Mgmt., Santa Fe, 2004—. Bd. dirs. Aurora Flight Scis. Corp.; adv. cons. bd. U. Ala. Geophys. Inst., 1994—98; adv. bd. Sci.'s Next Wave, 1998—2002; advisor Com. for Econ. Devel., 1997; com. on sci., tech. and health aspects fgn. policy agenda US NRC, 1998—2000, com. on sci. and tech. counter terrorism, 2001—02, mem. com. sci. bases Colo. River Basin water mgmt., 2005—07, mem. com. sci. basis decision making internat. sustainable devel. orgns., 2002—05; chair com. orgn. & strategy Sci. Com. Antarctic Rsch., 1999—2000; co-chair adv. bd. Calif. Inst. Telecom. & Info. Tech., 2000—; mem. US Nat. Com. Internat. Polar Yr., 2003—05; history of geophysics com. Am. Geophys. Union, 2004—; bd. dirs. found. Los Alamos Nat. Lab., 2006—07; advisor Lapides Found., 2007—; chair Review Group Sci. Com. Antarctic Rsch., 2008—09. Author: (with others) The Frozen Future, a Prophetic Report from Antarctica, 1973; contbr. articles to profl. jours. Bd. dirs. Washington Project for Arts, 1983-84, Washington Sculptors Group, 1983-84; mem. N.Mex. First., 2008-. 1st lt. U.S. Army, 1955-57. Fellow AAAS, Antarctican Soc.; mem. Cosmos Club (Washington), Am. Alpine Club (Golden, Colo.), Sigma Xi. Office: Smith Sci Policy & Mgmt 767 Acequia Madre 2 Santa Fe NM 87505-2868 Personal E-mail: smithphilip67@gmail.com.

SMITH, PHILLIP J., food products executive; V.p., controller various divsn. Cullum Cos. Inc., Dallas, 1975-84; v.p., CFO Market Basket Food Stores, Tex., 1984-87; controller Stater Bros., Colton, Calif., 1987, v.p., controller, sr. v.p., CFO, 2000—. Office: Stater Bros Markets PO Box 150 San Bernardino CA 92402-0150

SMITH, PHYLLIS, actress; b. Lemay, Mo., July 10, 1951; Studied ballet and tap with Majorie Mendolia; B in Elementary Edn., U. Mo., St. Louis. Former St. Louis Cardinals Cheerleader; ballet dancer St. Louis Civic Ballet, The St. Louis Dance Theater; profl. jazz dancer under Raoul Appel; toured the country as a dancer with Able's Baggy Pants Burlesque; toured the country as a dancer and comic skit performer with Mercer Brother's show, Giggles Galore; pre-school tchr. Casting asst. (TV films) A Taste for Killing, 1992, casting assoc. (TV series) Dr. Quinn, Medicine Women, 1993, Spin City, 1996; actor: (TV series) The Office, 2005— (Outstanding Performance by an Ensemble in a Comedy Series, SAG, 2007, 2008); (films) I Want Someone to Eat Cheese With, 2006; guest appearances Arrested Development, 2005, Curb Your Enthusiasm, 2005. Mem.: SAG.

SMITH, RALPH EARL, virologist; b. Yuma, Colo., May 10, 1940; s. Robert C. and Esther C. (Schwarz) S.; m. Sheila L. Kondy, Aug. 29, 1961 (div. 1986); 1 child, Andrea Denise; m. Janet M. Keller, 1988. BS, Colo. State U., 1961; PhD, U. Colo., 1968. Registered microbiologist Am. Soc. Clin. Pathologists. Mem. faculty Duke U. Med. Ctr., Durham, NC, 1968—80, prof. virology, 1980-82; prof., head dept. microbiology Colo. State U., Ft. Collins, 1983-88, prof. microbiology, assoc. v.p. rsch., 1989-99, interim v.p. rsch., 1990-91, prof. microbiology, assoc. v.p. rsch., 1991-99, interim head dept. microbiology, 1999—2002, prof. microbiology, immunology and pathology, 2002—; dir. Rocky Mt. Regional Biocontainment Lab., 2004—07; assoc. dir. Rocky Mt. Regional Ctr. Excellence, 2005—08; interim dir. Infectious Disease Rsch. Ctr., 2007—, Infectious Disease Super Cluster, 2008—. Cons. Bellco Glass Co., Vineland, N.J., 1976-80, Procter & Gamble Co., Cin., 1985-86, Schering Plough Corp., Bloomfield, N.J., 1987-89, Rose Biomed., 2002-06. Contbr. articles to profl. jours.; patentee in field. Bd. dirs. Colo. Ctr. for Environ. Mgmt., v.p. for rsch.; mem. pollution prevention adv. bd. Colo. Dept. Pub. Health and Environment; mem. Rocky Mountain U. Consortium on Environ. Restoration, Environ. Inst. Rocky Flats; asst. scoutmaster Boy Scouts Am., Durham, 1972-82, com. mem., Ft. Collins, 1986-91; mem. adminstrv. bd. 1st United Meth. Ch., Ft. Collins. Eleanor Roosevelt fellow Internat. Union Against Cancer 1978-79. Mem. AAAS, Am. Soc. Microbiology, N.Y. Acad. Scis., Am. Soc. Virology, Gamma Sigma Delta. Democrat. Methodist. Avocations: photography, hiking. Home: 2406 Creekwood Dr Fort Collins CO 80525-2034 Office: Colo State U Infectious Disease Rsch Ctr Fort Collins CO 80523-2025 Office Phone: 970-491-6119. Business E-Mail: ralph.smith@colostate.edu.

SMITH, RICHARD ALAN, neurologist, medical association administrator; Student, Brandeis U., 1958-61; grad., U. Miami, 1965. Intern in medicine Jackson Meml. Hosp., Miami, Fla., 1965-66; resident in neurology Stanford U. Hosp., Palo Alto, Calif., 1966-69; head neurology br. Navy Neuropsychiatric Rsch. Unit, San Diego, 1969-71; mem. assoc. staff microbiology Scripps Clinic and Rsch. Found., La Jolla, Calif., 1972-79, mem. assoc. staff neurology, 1972-82; dir. Ctr. Neurologic Study, San Diego, 1979—; mem. sr. staff Scripps Meml. Hosp., La Jolla, 1982—. Mem. med. adv. bd. Multiple Sclerosis Soc., San Diego; founder neurosci. network Ams. Drs., Gurnee, Ill., 1995—; pres. Coordinated Clin. Rsch. Corp., San Diego, 1996—; vis. scholar neurosci. dept. U. Calif., San Diego, 2000—. Editor: Interferon Treatment for Neurologic Disorders, 1988, Handbook of Amyotrophic Lateral Sclerosis, 1992; contbr. articles to profl. jours. Recipient Henry Newman award San Francisco Neurologic Soc., 1968; NIH STTR grantee, 1996-97; Skaggs Clin. scholar Scripps Rsch. Inst., 1998—. Mem. AAAS, Am. Acad. Neurology (assoc.). Achievements include 6 U.S. patents; work on methodology for enhancing the systemic delivery of Dextromethorphan for the treatment of neurological and medical disorders, including emotional lability, pain, cough. and drug addiction. Office: 9850 Genesee Ave Ste 320 La Jolla CA 92037-1208 E-mail: cns@cts.com.

SMITH, RICHARD HOWARD, banker; b. Tulare, Calif., Aug. 27, 1927; s. Howard Charles and Sue Elizabeth (Cheyne) S.; B.A., Principia Coll, 1958; LL.B., LaSalle U., 1975; postgrad. Sch. Banking U. Wash., 1970-72; m. Patricia Ann Howery, Mar. 12, 1950 (dec. Sept. 2001); children: Jeffrey Howard, Holly Lee, Gregory Scott, Deborah Elaine; m. Charlene Burruel, Mar. 27, 2004. Prin., Aurora Elementary Sch., Tulare, 1951-53; prin. Desert Sun Sch., Idyllwild, Calif., 1953-55; trust adminstr. trainee Bank of Am., San Diego, 1955-58, asst. trust officer, Ventura, Redlands, Riverside and L.A., 1958-65; asst. trust officer Security Pacific Bank, Fresno, Calif., 1965-68; trust officer, 1968-72, v.p., mgr., 1972-88, Pasadena, 1988-94; v.p. Bank of Am., L.A., 1994-95; ret., 1995; pres. Fiduciary Svcs., Fresno, 1995—; instr. San Bernardino Valley Coll., 1962-, Fresno City Coll., 1977-. With USN, 1945-46. Home: 3222 W Dovewood Ln Fresno CA 93711-2125 Office: Smith Fiduciary Svc 163 7081 N Marks Ave #104 Fresno CA 93711-0232 Office Phone: 559-432-6573.

SMITH, ROBERT LONDON, SR., commissioner, retired air force officer, political scientist, educator; b. Alexandria, La., Oct. 13, 1919; s. Daniel Charleston and Lillie (Roberts) S.; m. Jewel Busch, Feb. 5, 1949; children: Jewel Diane, Robert London, Karl Busch. BA, Coll. St. Joseph, 1954; MA, U. Okla., 1955; PhD, Am. U., 1964. Commd. 2d lt. USAAF, 1941; advanced through grades to lt. col. USAF, 1961, various assignments in aircraft engring., command and logistics, 1941-60; rsch. logistics Hdqs. Office Aerospace Rsch., 1960-63; project sci., adminstr. postdoctoral rsch. program, asst. dir. NAS, Hdqs. Office Sci. Rsch., 1963-65; ret., 1965; assoc. prof. polit. sci., head dept. evening classes and corr. study U. Alaska Coll., 1966-68, dean Coll. Bus., Econs. and Govt., 1968-70, prof., head dept. polit. sci., 1966-84, prof. emeritus, 1984—; commr. Alaska Dept. Health and Social Svcs., 1983—, mem. govt. panels and planning groups. Dir. Arctic 1st Fed. Savs. & Loan Assn.; corporator Mt. McKinley Mut. Savs. Bank. Author: (with others) Squadron Adminstration, 1951; also publs. on nat. security and nat. def.; contbr.: (with others) The United Nations Peace University, 1965. Committeeman Western region Boy Scouts Am., 1968-73; mem. exec. bd. Midnight Sun coun., 1973-74, committeeman-at-large nat. coun., 1968-; mem. Alaska Gov.'s Employment Commn.; pres. USO Coun., Fairbanks, Alaska; mem. active corps execs. SBA. Recipient Silver Beaver award Boy Scouts Am. Mem. Nat. Acad. Econs. and Polit. Sci., AAAS, Air Force Hist. Found., Nat. Inst. Social and Behavioral Scis., Nat. Inst. U.S. in World Affairs, Am. Polit. Sci. Assn., Assn. U.S. Army (bd. dirs. Polar Bear chpt.), Alaska C. of C. (edn. com.), Rotary, Pi Gamma Mu, Pi Sigma Alpha. Roman Catholic. Home: Smithhaven 1100 9th Ave Fairbanks AK 99701-4105 Home Phone: 907-458-7228. Personal E-mail: lundy@alaska.com.

SMITH, SAMUEL HOWARD, academic administrator, plant pathologist; b. Salinas, Calif., Feb. 4, 1940; s. Adrian Reed and Elsa (Jacop) Smith; m. Patricia Ann Walter, July 8, 1960; children: Samuel, Linda Kjelgaard. BS in Plant Pathology, U. Calif., Berkeley, 1961, PhD in Plant Pathology, 1964; D (hon.), Nihon U., Tokyo, 1989, Far Eastern State U., Vladivostok, Russia, 1997. NATO fellow Glasshouse Crops Research Inst., Sussex, England, 1964-65; asst. prof. plant pathology U. Calif., Berkeley, 1965-69; assoc. prof. Pa. State U., University Park, 1969—74, prof., 1974—85, head dept. plant pathology, 1976—81, dean Coll. Agr., dir. Pa. Agrl. Expt. Sta. and Coop. Extension Service, 1981—85; pres. Wash. State U., Pullman, 1985—2000, pres. emeritus, 2000—. Bd. dirs. Blethen Corp., 1994—, Met. Mortgage & Securities, 2000—04, Nat. Assn. State Univs. & Land-Grant Colls., 1994—, chair, bd. dirs., 1999—2000, exec. dir., W.K. Kellogg Found., Food & Soc. Project, 2000—04, mem. Audit & Fin. Com., 1999—2000, chair, Coun. Pres.', 1998—99, exec. dir., Com. Food & Soc., 2000—04, mem. Ad-Hoc Com. Fed. Support Agrl. Sci., Ext., & Edn., 1998—2000, mem. Commn. Info. Tech., 1994—2000, chair, Commn. Info. Tech., 1994—96, mem. Pres.' Policy Bd. Info. Tech., 1997—2000, mem. Kellogg Commn. Twenty-First Century State & Land-Grant Univs., 1995—2000; chair, exec. com. NCAA, 1997—99, Div. I bd. dirs., 1997—99, mem. Pres.' Commn., 1994—97, chair, Pres.' Commn., 1996—97, div. I chair, Pres.' Commn., 1995; bd. dirs. The Tech. Alliance, 1996—2000, Assn. Western Univs., 1993—2000; mem. adv. com. Wash. Sch. Employees Credit Union, 1993—95, Battelle Pacific N.W. Lab., 1993—2000; mem. Wash. Coun. Internat. Trade; chair of pres.' and chancellors Pacific-10 Conf. CEOs, 1993—94; bd. dirs. Norman Borlaug U., 2000—02, Seattle Times, 1998—; pres., bd. dirs. Talaris Rsch. Inst., 2000—; bd. trustees Western Gov.'s U., 1997—, spl. adv. to pres., 2000—05, chair, pres. adv. coun., 1996—2005, exec. com., 1997—, chair, acad. policy com., 1997—, mem., nominating com., 1997—. Founding bd. mem. Coll. Success Found., Washington, 1997—; bd. trustees Pilchuck Glass Sch., 2000—04, Wash. State Hist. Soc., 2000—04, highly edn. coordinating bd., 2007—, exec. com., 2007—, chair, edn. com. Mem.: Am. Phytopath Soc., Pi Kappa Alpha (hon.). Business E-Mail: smithsh@wsuwest.edu.

SMITH, SARAH JANE (SALLY SMITH), mayor; b. Pekin, Ill., Jan. 23, 1945; d. Claude P. and Jane (Prettyman) Smith. BS in Music Edn., U. Ill.; postgrad., U. Alaska. Jr. HS tchr. LA City Schs., 1968—69; adminstrv. asst. Office of Gov. of Alaska, 1971—74; project field rep. Alaska Dept. Cmty. and Regional Affairs, 1974—76; expeditor H.W. Blackstock, Inc., 1979—82; exec. dir. Fairbanks Pvt. Industry Coun., 1983—84; dir. divsn. pub. svcs. Alaska Dept. Revenue, 1984—; mayor City and Borough of Juneau, 2000—. Mem. Alaska House of Reps. from 20th Dist., 1977—83, majority whip, 1977—79, mem. fin. com., 1979—81, chmn. rules com., 1981. Historian Fairbanks Drama Assn., 1974—76; adv. bd. Assn. Children with Learning Disabilities, 1978—80; commr. Fairbanks Historic Preservation Commn., 1982—84; dir. choir Juneau Meth. and Presbyn. chs., 1972—74, 1986—, Fairbanks Presbyn. Ch., 1974—75; bd. dirs. Friends of U. Alaska Mus., 1983—84. Named Outstanding Freshman Legislator, 1976. Mem.: Fairbanks Assn. Arts, PEO. Democrat.

SMITH, SCOTT, Mayor, Mesa, Arizona, business, financial and legal consultant; m. Kim Smith. BS in Acctg., Brigham Young U., Utah, 1980; MBA, Ariz. State U., Tempe, 1985; JD, Ariz. State U. Coll. Law, 1996. Mgr. NWL&O, 1985; fin. and bus. cons. ExecuShare, Ltd., 1986—; acctg. and fin. instr. U. Phoenix, 1988—93; pres. Great Western Homes, 1994—2003; regional pres. K. Hovnanian Homes, 2003—07; mayor City of Mesa, Ariz., 2008—. Chmn. Phoenix-Mesa Gateway Airport Authority, 2008—. Mem. Superstition Vistas Steering Com., Mesa Bldg. Bd. Appeals; pres. Mesa Cmty. Found.; bd. dirs., campaign chmn. Mesa United Way; bd. dirs. East Valley Partnership, Esperanza, Inc., Southwest Shakespeare Co. Address: Office of the Mayor City of Mesa PO Box 1466 Mesa AZ 85211 Office Phone: 480-644-2388. Business E-Mail: mayor.smith@cityofmesa.org.*

SMITH, SCOTT A., lawyer; b. Grand Forks, ND, July 17, 1957; married. BA, Stanford U., 1978; JD, U. Calif., Berkeley, 1981. Bar: Wash. 1981, U.S. Ct. Appeals (9th cir) 1982, U.S. Dist. Ct. (Ea. and We. dists.) Wash. Law clk. to Hon. Jerome Farris 9th Cir. U.S. Ct. of Appeals, 1981—82; assoc. Preston, Gates & Ellis, Seattle, 1982—88; ptnr. Short, Cressman & Burgess, Seattle, 1988—2004; prin. Riddell Williams, Seattle, 2004—. Chair Wash. State Access to Justice Bd., Seattle, 2002—04. Recipient Pro Bono award, Wash. State Bar Assn., Allies for Justice award, LEGALS of Wash. Fellow: Am. Bar Found.; mem.: King County Bar Assn. (pres. 1996—97, trustee 1991—97, Helen Geisness award Exemplary Svc.). Office: Riddell Williams Ste 4500 1001 Fourth Ave Seattle WA 98154 Business E-Mail: SSmith@riddellwilliams.com.

SMITH, SELMA MOIDEL, lawyer, composer; b. Warren, Ohio, Apr. 3, 1919; d. Louis and Mary (Oyer) Moidel; 1 child, Mark Lee. Student, UCLA, 1936-39, U. So. Calif. Law School, 1939-41; JD, Pacific Coast U., 1942. Bar: Calif. 1943, U.S. Dist. Ct. 1943, U.S. Supreme Ct. 1958. Gen. practice law; mem. firm Moidel, Moidel, Moidel & Smith, 1943—. Field dir. civilian adv. com. WAC, 1943—45; charter mem. nat. bd. Med. Coll. Pa. (formerly Woman's Med. Coll. Pa.), 1953—, mem. exec. bd., 1976—80, pres., 1980—82, chmn, past pres. com., 1990—92, spkr., honoree 50th anniversary gala, 2003. Author: A Century of Achievement: The National Association of Women Lawyers, 1998, The First Women Members of the ABA, 1999; composer: Espressivo-Four Piano Pieces (orchestral premiere, 1987, performance Nat. Mus. Women in the Arts, 1989), numerous works. Decorated La Orden del Merito Juan Pablo Duarte (Dominican Republic), 1956. Fellow Am. Bar Found. (life); mem. ASCAP, ABA (jr. bar. conf., 1946-52, activities com., 1948-49), Sr. Lawyers divsn. ABA (vice-chair editl. bd. Experience mag. 1997-99,2008-, chair arts com. 1998-99, chair editl. bd. Experience Mag. 1999-2001, exec. coun. 1999-2003, Experience mag. adv. bd. 2001-08, nominating com. 2003-04, co-chair newsletter 2003-04, chair newsletter 2004-05, asst. sec., 2005-07, Dist. Svc. award 2003, 07), Calif. Supreme Ct. Hist. Soc. (bd. dirs. 2001-, programs and pubs. com., 2004-, State Bar program coord., 2006, founding chair writing competition, 2007-, chair. publs., 2008-, editor in chief Calif. Legal Hist. 2009), Assn. Learning in Retirement Orgns. in West (pres. 1993-94, exec. com. 1994-95, Disting. Svc. award 1995), Plato Soc. UCLA (discussion leader Constitution Bicentennial Project 1985-87, moderator extension lecture series 1990, Toga editor 1990-93, sec. 1991-92, chmn. colloquium com. 1992-93, Exceptional Leadership award 1994), Euterpe Opera Club (chair auditions 1972, chair awards 1973-75, v.p. 1974-75), Docents L.A. Philharm. (press and pub. rels. 1972-75, cons. coord. 1973-75, v.p. 1973-83, chair Latin Am. Cmty. Rels., Recognition and Honor award, 1978), Calif. Fedn. Music Clubs (chair Am. music 1971-75, conv. chair 1972), Nat. Fedn. Music Clubs (vice-chair Western region 1973-78), Nat. Assn. Composers USA (dir. 1974-79, luncheon chair 1975), Calif. Pres. Coun. (1st v.p.), L.A. Bus. Women's Coun. (pres. 1952), Calif. Bus. Women's Coun. (dir. 1951), Coun. Bar Assns. L.A. County (charter sec. 1950), Inter-Am. Bar Assn., League of Ams. (dir.), Nat. Assn. Women Lawyers (regional dir. western states, Hawaii 1949-51, jud. adminstrn. com. 1960, nat. chair world peace through law com. 1966-67, liaison to ABA Sr. Lawyers Divsn. 1996, chair bd. elections 1997-98, centennial com. 1997-99, chair com. unauthorized practice of law, social commn. UN, Lifetime Svc. award 1999, honoree annual Selma Moidel Smith law student writing competition 2005), L.A. Lawyers Club (pub. defenders com. 1951), L.A. Bar Assn. (servicemen's legal aid com. 1944-45, psychopathic ct. com. 1948-53, Outstanding Svc. award 1993), State Bar Calif. (conf. com. on unauthorized practice of medicine 1964, Disting. Svc. award 1993), Women Lawyers Assn. LA (formerly So. Calif. Women Lawyers Assn.)(hon life; pres., 1947, 48, chair law day com. 1966, subject of oral hist. project 1986, 2001), Iota Tau Tau Legal Scholastic Soc. (1st prize 1942, dean L.A. 1947, supreme treas. 1959-62). Home: 5272 Lindley Ave Encino CA 91316-3518

SMITH, SHERWOOD PAUL, plastic surgeon; b. Sault St. Marie, Ont., Can., May 25, 1941; came to U.S., 1972; s. Irwin and Sophie Edith (Freeman) S.; m. Judith Ann Gebhard, Jan. 24, 1966; 1 child, Stephen Barclay. MD, U. Toronto, 1965; MSc, McGill U., 1969. Diplomate Am. Bd. Plastic Surgery. Plastic surgeon Olympia (Wash.) Plastic Surgeons Inc. PS, 1972—. Vol. plastic surgeon Gen. Hosp. Columbo, Sri Lanka, 1985—. Fellow ACS, Royal Coll. Physicians and Surgeons of Can.; mem. Olympia Yacht Club, South Sound Sailing Soc. Avocations: sailing, bicycling, hiking, mountain climbing.

SMITH, STACY J., computer company executive; BBA, Univ. Tex., Austin, MBA, 1988. IT mgr. Matt David Corp.; mgmt. positions Intel Corp., Santa Clara, Calif., 1988—96, group contr. assembly test mfg. group, 1996—99, group contr. worldwide sales & mktg., 1999—2001, gen. mgr. Europe, Asia & Middle East, 2001—04, v.p. sales & mktg., 2002—04, v.p., CIO, 2004—06, v.p., asst. CFO, 2006—07, v.p., CFO, 2007—. Mem. advisory bd. McCombs Sch. Bus., Univ. Tex., Austin. Office: Intel Corp 2200 Mission Coll Blvd Santa Clara CA 95054-1549

SMITH, STEVEN RAY, law educator; b. Spirit Lake, Iowa, July 8, 1946; s. Bymard L. and Dorothy V. (Fischbeck) S.; m. Lera Baker, June 15, 1975. BA, Buena Vista Coll., 1968; JD, U. Iowa, 1971, MA, 1971. Bar: Iowa 1971, Ky. 1987, Ohio 1992. From asst. to assoc. dean Sch. Law U. Louisville, 1974-81, acting dean, 1974-75, 76, prof. law, 1971-88, assoc. in medicine Med. Sch., 1983-88; dep. dir/ Assn. Am. Law Schs., 1987-88; dean, prof. law Cleve. State U., 1988-96; pres., dean and prof. Calif. Western Sch. of Law, 1996—. Author: Law, Behavior and Mental Health: Policy and Practice, 1987; contbr. chpts. to books, articles to profl. jours. Trustee U. Louisville, 1980-82, SCRIBES, 1993—; pres. Ky. Congress of Senate Faculty Leaders, 1982-84; bd. trustees Am. Bd. Profl. Psychology, 1994-2001; bd. dirs. Nat. Register of Health Svc. Providers in Psychology, 2002—, San Diego Vol. Lawyers Program, 1998—, Nat. Conflict Resolution Ctr., 2003—; sec., bd. dirs. Assn. for Accreditation of Human Rsch. Protection Programs, 2001—. Recipient Grawemeyer award Innovative Teaching. Metroversity Consortium, 1983. Fellow Ohio State Bar Found. ABA (stds. rev. com. 1991-95, govt. rels. com. 1993-95, joint commn. ABA/Assn. Am. Law Schs. financing of legal edn. 1993-94, 97-98, coun. sect. legal edn. and admission to the bar 1997—, chmn.-elect sect. on legal edn. and admission to the bar 2004-05, chmn. sect. of legal edn. and admissions to the bar 2005-06, bd. govs. San Diego Found. 2006—); mem. APA (pub. mem. ethics com.), Am. Econs. Assn., Assn. Am. Law Schs. (chmn. librs. com., dep. dir. 1987-88, mem. accreditation com. 1993-96, chair accreditation com. 1994-96), Ohio State Bar Assn. (coun. of dels. 1992-96), Order of Coif, City Club of Cleve. (pres. 1994-95). Office: Calif Western Sch Law Office of Dean 225 Cedar St San Diego CA 92101-3046

SMITH, THOMAS WINSTON, cotton marketing executive; b. Crosbyton, Tex., Mar. 16, 1935; s. Lance L. and Willie Mae (Little) Smith; m. Patricia Mae Zachary Smith, Dec. 13, 1958; children: Janna Olean, Thomas Mark. BS Tex. A&M U., 1957; PMD, Harvard U., 1964. Various positions Calcot Ltd., Bakersfield, Calif., 1957—77, exec. v.p., pres, 1977—; v.p. Amcot, Inc., Calif., 1977—2002, Amcot Internat., Inc., Bakersfield, Calif., 1977—2002; ret., 2002. Chmn. Amcot Inc., Bakersfield, Calif., 2003—; bd. mgrs. NY Cotton Exchange, NYC, v.p., Memphis; bd. dir. Greater Bakersfield Meml. Hosp.; mem. pres. adv. commn. Calif. State Coll., Bakersfield, Calif. Mem.: Rotary, Nat. Cotton Coun. (v.p.). Business E-Mail: twsmith@calcot.com.

SMITH, TOM, state legislator, military officer; b. St. Paul, Mar. 16, 1927; m. Sarah Jane Smith; 7 children. BA, Roosevelt U., 1968; MA, Ariz. State U., 1973. Ret. lt. col. USMC, 1945-68; ret. educator, 1970-84; mem. Ariz. Ho. of Reps., 1991-98, Ariz. Senate, Dist. 26, Phoenix, 1998—; mem. appropriations com., mem. edn. com. Ariz. State Senate, vice-chmn. judiciary com., chmn. rules com. Active Scottdale Cultural Ctr., Phoenix Symphony; mem. Scottsdale Sch. Dist. Governing Bd., 1983-86. Mem. VFW (life), 1st Marine Divsn. Assn. (life), Ret. Officers Assn., Ret. Tchrs. Assn., Navy Mutual Aid Assn., Mustang Assn., China Marine Assn. Republican. Roman Catholic. E-mail: tsmith@azleg.state.az.us.

SMITH, V. KERRY, economics professor; b. Jersey City, Mar. 11, 1945; s. Vincent C. and Dorothy E. S.; m. Pauline Anne Taylor, May 10, 1969; children: Timothy, Shelley. AB, Rutgers U., 1966, PhD, 1970. Asst. prof., then assoc. prof. Bowling Green State U., Ohio, 1969-72; rsch. assoc. Resources for Future, Washington, 1971-73; assoc. prof. SUNY, Binghamton, 1973-75, prof., 1975-78; sr. fellow Resources for Future, Washington, 1976-79; prof. U. NC, Chapel Hill, 1979-83; Centennial prof. Vanderbilt U., Nashville, 1983-87; univ. disting. prof. NC State U., 1987-94, univ. disting. prof., dir. Ctr. Environ. and Resource Econ. Policy, 1999—; Arts and Scis. prof. environ. econs. Duke U., 1994-99; W.P. Carey prof. econs. Ariz. State U., Tempe, 2006—; rsch. assoc. Nat. Bureau Econ. Rsch., 2007—. Adviser energy div. Oak Ridge Nat. Lab., 1978-80, U. NC Inst. Environ. Studies, 1980-83; mem. panel NSF, 1981-83, sci. adv. bd. EPA. Author: Monte Carlo Methods, 1973, Technical Change, Relative Prices and Environmental Resource Evaluation, 1974, The Costs of Congestion: An Econometric Analysis of Wilderness Recreation, 1976, Structure and Properties of a Wilderness Travel Simulator: An Application to the Spanish Peaks Area, 1976, The Economic Consequences of Air Pollution, 1976, Scarcity and Growth Reconsidered, 1979, (with others) Explorations in Natural Resource Economics, 1982, (with others) Environmental Policy Under Reagan's Executive Order, 1984, (with W.H. Desvousges) Measuring Water Quality Benefits, 1986, (with others) Environmental Resources and Applied Welfare Economics, 1988, (with R.J. Kopp) Valuing Natural Assets: The Economics of Natural Resource Damage Assessment, Resources for the Future, 1993, Estimating Economic Values for Nature, 1996, (with others) The Smoking Puzzle: Information, Perception and Choices, 2003; editor Advances in Applied Micro Econs. series; contbr. numerous articles to profl. jours. Guggenheim fellow, 1976; grantee Resources for Future, 1970, 73, 74, 86, Fed. Energy Adminstrn. 1975, NY Sea Grant Inst., 1975, Ford Found., 1976, NSF, 1977, 79, 83, Electric Power Rsch. Inst., 1978, Nat. Oceanic and Atmospheric Adminstrn., 1980, Sloan Found., 1981, 86, EPA, 1983-88, NC Sea Grant Program, 1987-93. Russell Sage Found., 1989-91; recipient Frederick V. Waugh medal Am. Agrl. Econ. Assn., 1992. Fellow Am. Agrl. and Econ. Assn., Assn. Environ. and Resource Economists (bd. dirs. 1975-79, v.p. 1979-80, chmn. com. 1982-83, pres. 1985-86, Disting. Svc. award 1989); mem. NAS, Am. Econ. Assn., Econometric Soc., So. Econ. Assn. (exec. com. 1981-83, 1st v.p. 1987, pres.-elect 1988, pres. 1989). Office: Ariz State U PO Box 873806 Tempe AZ 85287-3806 Home: PO Box 7437 Cave Creek AZ 85327

SMITH, VALENE LUCY, anthropologist, educator; b. Spokane, Wash., Feb. 14, 1926; d. Ernest Frank and Lucy (Blachly) S.; m. Edwin Chesteen Golay, June 7, 1970 (dec. June 1980); m. Stanley George McIntyre, Nov. 26, 1983 (dec. Oct. 2000); m. George Addison Posey, Oct. 5, 2005. BA in Geography, U. Calif., 1946, MA in Geography, 1950; PhD in Anthropology, U. Utah, Salt Lake City, 1966. Cert. travel counselor. Prof. earth sci. LA City Coll., 1947-67; prof. anthropology Calif. State U., Chico, 1967—. Cons. World Tourism Orgn., Madrid, 1987. Editor: Hosts and Guests: The Anthrop, 1989, Tourism Alternatives: Potentials and Problems in the Development of Tourism, 1992, Hosts and Guests Revisited, 2001. Mem. Soroptimist Internat., Chico, 1968—; founding pres. Chico Mus. Assn., 1978. Recipient Athena award, US C. of C., 1988; named Fulbright prof., Peshawar, Pakistan, 1953—54. Mem. Internat. Acad. for Study Tourism, Cert. Travel Counselors, Am. Anthrop. Assn., AAUW, Soroptimists. Republican. Avocations: travel, aviation, photography. Office: U Calif Dept Anthropology Chico CA 95929-0004 Office Phone: 530-891-1155. Business E-Mail: vsmith@csuchico.edu.

SMITH, VERNON LOMAX, economist, educator; b. Wichita, Kans., Jan. 1, 1927; s. Vernon Chessman and Lula Belle (Lomax) S.; m. Candace C. Smith, Mar. 13, 2002. BSEE, Calif. Inst. Tech., 1949; MA in Econs., U. Kans., 1952; PhD in Econs., Harvard U., 1955; D of Mgmt. (hon.), Purdue U., 1990. Asst. prof. econs. Purdue U., West Lafayette, Ind., 1955-58, assoc. prof., 1958-61, prof., 1961-65, Krannert prof., 1965-67; prof. Brown U., Providence, 1967-68, U. Mass., Amherst, 1968-75, U. Ariz., Tucson, 1975—2001, Regents' prof., 1988—2001; prof. econs. & law George Mason U., 2001—07, Chapman U. Sch. Law, Orange, Calif., 2008—. Contbr. articles to profl. jours. Fellow Ctr. for Advanced Study in Behavioral Scis., Stanford, Calif., 1972-73; Sherman Fairchild Disting. Scholar Calif. Inst. Tech., Pasadena, 1973-74; adj. scholar CATO Inst., Washington, 1983—; recipient Nobel prize in econs., 2002. Fellow AAAS, Am. Acad. Arts and Scis., Econometric Soc., Am. Econ. Assn. (Disting. fellow); mem. NAS, Pvt. Enterprise Edn. Assn. (Adam Smith award). Office: Chapman U Sch Law One University Dr Orange CA 92866

SMITH, WILL (WILLARD CHRISTOPHER SMITH JR.), actor, film producer; b. Phila., Sept. 25, 1968; s. Willard and Caroline Smith; m. Sheree Smith, May 9, 1992 (div. 1995); 1 child, Willard III; m. Jada Pinkett Smith, Dec. 31, 1997; children: Jaden Christopher Syre, Willow Camille Reign. Ptnr. Overbrook Entertainment. Albums (as The Fresh Prince with DJ Jazzy Jeff): And in this Corner..., 1989, Homebase, 1991, Rock the House, 1987, He's the DJ, I'm the Rapper, 1988, Code Red, 1993, Big Willie Style, 1997, Willennium, 1999, Maximum Will Smith, 2000, Born to Reign, 2002, Greatest Hits, 2002, Lost and Found, 2005; (singles) Just One of Those Days, 1987, Girls Ain't Nothing But Trouble, 1988, Brank New Funk, 1988, A Nightmare on My Street, 1988, Jazzy's Groove, 1989, I Think I Can Beat Mike Tyson, 1989, Parents Just Don't Understand, (Grammy award for Best Rap Performance, 1989), The Things That U Do, 1991, Summertime, 1991 (Grammy award), Ring My Bell, 1991, I'm Looking for the One (To Be With Me), 1993, Boom! Shake the Room, 1993; Actor: (TV series) The Fresh Prince of Bel-Air, 1990-96, (also exec. prodr. 1994-96), Happily Ever After: Fairy Tales for Every Child (voice), 1995, All of Us, 2003 (also writer, exec. prodr.); (TV appearances) Blossom, 1991, All of Us, 2003; (films) Where the Day Takes You, 1992, Made in America, 1993, Six Degrees of Separation, 1993, Bad Boys, 1995, Independence Day, 1996 (Blockbuster Entertainment award Favorite Actor Sci-Fi), Men In Black, 1997 (MTV Movie awards Best Fight, Best Movie Song, ASCAP award Most Performed Songs for Motion Picture, Blockbuster Entertainment award Favorite Actor Sci-Fi), Welcome to Hollywood, 1998, Enemy of the State, 1998, Wild Wild West, 1999, The Legend of Bagger Vance, 2000, Ali, 2001, Men in Black II, 2002, Bad Boys II, 2003, I, Robot, 2004 (also exec. prodr.), Shark Tale (voice), 2004, Hitch, 2005 (also prodr.), The Pursuit of Happyness, 2006 (also prodr.)(Choice Movie Actor: Drama, Teen Choice Awards, 2007), I Am Legend, 2007 (Best Male Performance, MTV Movie Awards, 2008, Choice Movie Actor: Horror/Thriller, Teen Choice Awards, 2008), Hancock, 2008, Seven Pounds, 2008 (Outstanding Actor in a Motion Picture, NAACP Image award, 2009); exec. prodr., Showtime, 2002, The Seat Filler, 2004; prodr. Saving Face, 2004, ATL, 2006. Recipient ShoWest Conv. awards Actor of Yr., 1999, Spl. Internat. Box Office Achievement award 1997, BET award for Best Actor, 2002, Am. Music Award, Favorite Male Artist, 2005; named one of 50 Most Powerful People in Hollywood, 2004-06, The 100 Most Influential People, Time Mag., 2006, The 100 Most Powerful Celebrities, Forbes.com, 2007, 2008, The Top 25 Entertainers of Yr., Entertainment Weekly, 2007, The 50 Smartest People in Hollywood, 2007, The Ten Most Fascinating People of 2008, Barbara Walters, Favorite Male Movie Star People's Choice Awards, 2009, Favorite Male Action Star, 2009; named to Power 150, Ebony mag., 2008. Office: Overbook Entertainment 450 N Roxbury Dr Fl 4 Beverly Hills CA 90210-4232

SMITH, ZANNIE O., retired career officer; b. Columbia, SC, Mar. 27, 1943; BA in History, U. Tampa; M in Bus. Mgmt., Webster U., St. Louis. Enlisted 82d airborne divsn. U.S. Army, 1962, commd. 2d lt., advanced through grades to maj. gen.; chief of staff U.S. Army Res. Command, Atlanta, 1995; asst. divsn. comdr. ops. 10th Mountain Divsn. and Ft. Drum, 1997; dep. comdg. gen., chief of staff I Corps and Ft. Lewis, 1998—2003; ret., 2003. Decorated Def. Superior Meritorious Svc. award, Legion of Merit with 5 oak leaf clusters, Def. Meritorious Svc. medal, Meritorious Svc. medal with 4 oak leaf clusters, Army Commendation medal with 2 oak leaf clusters, Armed Forces Expeditionary medal, four Vietnam Svc. medals, Good Conduct medal, Bronze Star medal with V and 2 oak leaf clusters, Air medal with oak leaf cluster; recipient Combat Infantryman's badge, Ranger Tab, Air Assault badge.

SMOLENSKY, EUGENE, economics professor; b. Bklyn., Mar. 4, 1932; s. Abraham and Jennie (Miller) S.; m. Natalie Joan Rabinowitz, Aug. 16, 1952; children: Paul, Beth. BA, Bklyn. Coll., 1952; MA, Am. U., 1956; PhD, U. Pa., 1961. Prof. econs. U. Wis., Madison, 1968-88, chmn. dept., 1978-80, 86-88; dir. Inst. for Research on Poverty, U. Wis., 1980-83; dean Grad. Sch. Pub. Policy, U. Calif., Berkeley, 1988-97, prof. pub. policy, 1997—. Author: Public Expenditures, Taxation and the Distribution of Income: The U.S., 1950, 61, 70, 77. Mem. Nat. Acad. Pub. Adminstrn., 1994; mem. com. on child devel. rsch. and pub. policy NAS, Washington, 1982-87, mem. com. on status of women in labor market, 1985-87. With USN, 1952-56. Mem. Am. Econs. Assn. Democrat. Jewish. Avocation: master etching and lithograph collecting. Home: 669 Woodmont Ave Berkeley CA 94708-1233 Office: U Calif Dept Pub Policy 2607 Hearst Ave Berkeley CA 94720-7305 Office Phone: 510-643-3979. Business E-Mail: geno@berkeley.edu.

SMOOT, GEORGE FITZGERALD, III, astrophysicist; b. Yukon, Fla., Feb. 20, 1945; BS in Math and Physics, MIT, 1966, PhD in Physics, 1970. Rsch. physicist MIT, 1970; rsch. physicist, space sciences lab. Univ. Calif., Berkeley, Calif., 1971—, prof. physics, 1994—; rsch. physicist Lawrence Berkeley Lab., 1974—. Team leader, differential microwave radiometer experiment, COBE (Cosmic Background Explorer) satellite; mem. steering group on cosmic background explorer satellite, prin. investigator on isotrophy experiment (NASA), 1975; 80 mem. Mgmt. and Ops. Working Group for Shuttle Astronomy, 1976-80; mem. adv. com. White Mountain Rsch. Station, 1982; mem. superconducting magnet facility for the space station study team, 1985; mem. Ctr. for Particle Astrophysics, U. Calif. Berkeley, 1988; mem. adv. com. Radio Astronomy Lab., 1990. Author: (with Keay Davidson) Wrinkles in Time, 1993; contbr. articles to profl. jours. Recipient Space/Missiles Laurels award Aviation Week & Space Technology, 1992, Popular Sci. award, 1992, Disting. Scientist, ARCS Found., Inc., 1993, Kirby award, 1993, Golden Plate award, 1994, Ernesto Orlando Lawrence award US Dept Energy, 1994, Einstein medal, 2003, Grober prize with John Mather, 2006, Daniel Chalonge medak, 2006; co-recipient Nobel Prize in Physics, Nobel Found., 2006. Mem. Internat. Astron. Union, Am. Phys. Soc. (mem. com. on the safety comml. nuclear reactors, 1974-75), Am. Astron. Soc., Sigma Xi., AAAS. Office: Lawrence Berkeley Nat Lab 1 Cyclotron Rd 5OR5008 Berkeley CA 94720

SMOOT, LEON DOUGLAS, chemical engineer, educator, retired dean; b. Provo, Utah, July 26, 1934; s. Douglas Parley and Jennie (Hallam) S.; m. Marian Bird, Sept. 7, 1953; children: Analee, LaCinda, Michelle, Melinda Lee. BS, Brigham Young U., Provo, Utah, 1956; B in Engring. Sci., Brigham Young U., 1957; MS, U. Wash., Seattle, 1958; PhD, U. Wash., 1960. Registered profl. engr., Utah. Engr. Boeing Corp., Seattle, 1956; teaching and research asst. Brigham Young U., 1954-57; engr. Phillips Petroleum Corp., Arco, Idaho, 1957; engr., cons. Hercules Powder Co., Bacchus, Utah, 1961-63; asst. prof. Brigham Young U., 1960-63; engr. Lockheed Propulsion, Redlands, Calif., 1963-67; vis. asst. prof. Calif. Inst. Tech., 1966-67; assoc. prof. to prof. Brigham Young U., 1967—2003, prof. emeritus, 2003—, chmn. dept. chem. engring., 1970-77, dean Coll. Engring. and Tech., 1977-94, dean emeritus, 1994—; prin. Combustion Resources, Inc., 1994—. Expert witness on combustion and explosions; founding dir. Advanced Combustion Engring. Research Ctr. (NSF), 1986-97; cons. Hercules, Thiokol, Lockheed, Teledyne, Atlantic Research Corp., Raytheon, Redd and Redd, Billings Energy, Ford, Bacon & Davis, Jaycor, Intel Com Radiation Tech., Phys. Dynamics, Nat. Soc. Propellants and Explosives, France, DFVLR, West Germany, Martin Marietta, Honeywell, Phillips Petroleum Co., Exxon, Nat. Bur. Standards, Eyring Research Inst., Systems, Sci. and Software., Los Alamos Nat. Lab., others. Author 5 books on coal combustion; contbr. over 200 articles and tech. jours.

Recipient Nichols award, Am. Soc. Mech. Engring., 2002, Homer H. Lowry Gold Medal, U.S. Dept. Energy, 2002. Mem. AIChE, Nat. Fire Protection Assn., Combustion Inst., Rsch. Soc. Am., Sigma Xi, Tau Beta Pi. Republican. Mem. Lds Ch. Office: Brigham Young U Chem Engring Dept 435 T CTB Provo UT 84602

SMOTHERS, TOM, actor, singer; b. NYC, Feb. 2, 1937; s. Thomas B. and Ruth Smothers; children: Tom, Bo, Riley Rose; m. Marcy Carriker, Sept. 9, 1990. Student, San Jose State Coll. Owner winery, Kenwood, Calif. Nightclub appearances in Reno, Lake Tahoe, Las Vegas, Nev., and various venues in the U.S.; co-star TV situation comedy Smothers Brothers Show, 1965-66, Smothers Brothers Comedy Hour, CBS-TV, 1967-69, 70, weekly variety show The Smothers Brothers Show, NBC-TV, 1975; starred in films The Silver Bears, Get To Know Your Rabbit, A Pleasure Doing Business, Serial, There Goes the Bride, Pandemonium, Speed Zone; starred on Broadway in I Love My Wife, 1978-79; appeared in TV movie Terror at Alcatraz, 1982; starred in Smothers Brothers Spl. and Series, 1988-89. Office: Knave Prodns Ste 107B 6442 Coldwater Canyon Ave North Hollywood CA 91606-1137 Office Phone: 818-754-0351. E-mail: smobro1@aol.com.

SMYSER, MELINDA, state legislator; m. Charles Smyser. MEd, Idaho Coll. Mem. Dist. 11 Idaho State Senate, 2009—. Republican. Office: Capitol Annex PO Box 83720 Boise ID 83720-0054 also: 26298 Lee Ln Parma ID 83660 Office Phone: 208-334-2475, 208-722-6658. Office Fax: 208-334-2125, 208-332-1422.*

SMYTH, CORNELIUS EDMONSTON, retired hotel executive; b. NYC, Aug. 20, 1926; s. Cornelius Joseph and Roberta Ernestine (Anderson) S.; m. Jeanne Laura Dillingham, Nov. 25, 1950 (dec. Oct. 1996); m. Jeanette M. Hubbard, Apr. 18, 1998; children: Cornelius E. Jr., Loretta M., William D., James B., Laura I., Robert B. BS in Econs., U. Pa., Phila., 1946. Cert. hospitality account exec. Contr. Caesars Palace Hotel and Casino, Las Vegas, Nev., 1970-73, fin. v.p., 1974, adminstrv. v.p., 1975-77, exec. v.p., 1977-81; pres. Sands Hotel and Casino, Las Vegas, 1981-83; exec. v.p. Latin Am. ops. Caesars World Internat., LA, 1983-89, pres. Mexican ops., 1989-90; bd. dirs. Venture Catalyst, Inc., San Diego, 1994—2006. Co-author: A Uniform System of Accounts for Hotels, 7th rev. edit., 1977. Comdr. USNR, 1944-70. Named to U.S. Table Tennis Hall of Fame, 1996. Mem. Pi Gamma Mu, Sigma Chi. Republican. Roman Cath. Avocation: ping pong/table tennis.

SMYTH, GLEN MILLER, management consultant; b. Abingdon, Va., July 26, 1929; s. Glen Miller and Kathleen (Dunn) S.; m. Cynthia Olson, Aug. 25, 1954 (div. 1967); children: Catherine Ellen, Glen Miller, III, Cynthia Allison; m. Lilian Castel Edgar, Oct. 31, 1968; children: Stephanie Castel, Kimberley Forsyth, Lindsay Dunn. BA, Yale U., 1951; MS in Psychology, Rutgers U., 1958. Mktg. rep. Wheeling Stamping Co., NYC, 1953-56; personnel dir. Celanese Internat., NYC, 1958-71; mgr. orgn. and Manpower Internat. and Can. group Gen. Electric Co., NYC, 1971-73; sr. v.p. human resources Northwest Bancorp., Mpls., 1973-82; sr. v.p. Calif. Fed. Savs., LA, 1983-85; v.p. Career Transition Group, LA, 1985-87; pres. Fuchs, Cuthrell & Co., Inc., LA, 1987-93, Fuchs & Co., LA, 1993-94; pres., CEO Smyth, Fuchs & Co., Inc., LA, 1995-99; v.p. Spherion, 1998—. Leader seminars. Co-author: International Career Pathing, 1971; Contbr. articles to profl. jours. Served with AUS, 1951-53. Mem. Am. Psychol. Assn., Nat. Fgn. Trade Coun. (founder, past chmn. human resources, orgn. com. 1966—), Human Resources Planning Soc., Employment Mgmt. Assn., Jonathan Club, Yale Club of N.Y., North Ranch Country Club, Phi Gamma Delta. Home: 1115 Westcreek Ln Westlake Village CA 91362-5467

SNAPP, MARY E., computer software company executive, lawyer; b. Manhattan, Kans., Sept. 7, 1953; BS, U. Kans., 1974; MBA, Wayne State U., 1981; JD, U. Mich., 1984. Bar: Wash. 1984. Assoc. Preston, Thorgrimson, Ellis & Hollman, Seattle, 1984—88; corp. atty. Microsoft Corp., Redmond, Wash., 1988, assoc. gen. counsel, dep. gen. counsel, dep. gen. counsel & corp. v.p., 2002—. Bd. dirs. Greater Seattle C. of C., King County-Snohomish County YWCA, Artist Trust, ArtsFund; active in Food Lifeline, Ryther Child Ctr., Cath. Cmty. Services. Mem.: ABA, ABA Forum on Comm. Law (mem. governing com.), Wash. State Bar Assn., Seattle-King County Bar Assn., Phi Beta Kappa. Office: Microsoft Corp Law & Corp Affairs Dept 1 Microsoft Way Redmond WA 98052-6399 Office Phone: 425-882-8080. Office Fax: 425-936-7329.

SNEDDON, THOMAS WILLIAM, JR., prosecutor; b. LA, 1941; m. Pam Sneddon. BA, U. Notre Dame, 1963; JD, UCLA, 1966; grad., Nat. Dist. Atty. Sch., U. Houston, 1972, Nat. Homicide Acad., 1977. Dep. dist atty. Santa Barbara County, 1969—77, supr. criminal ops., 1977—82, dist. atty., 1983—. Mem. faculty Santa Barbara Coll. Law, 1989—; chair Com. for Child Support Enforcement, 1991—; advisor Am. Prosecutor's Rsch. Ctr.; pres. Calif. Dist. Atty. Assn., 1989—90; co-chair Nat. Dist. Atty. Child Support Com., Nat. Dist. Atty. Assn. Nat. Com., 1997, v.p., 2000—. Served in US Army, 1967—69. Recipient Leadership award, Calif. Dept. Social Services, 1993, Director's award, Calif. Family Support Coun., 1995, Disting. Faculty award, Nat. Dist. Atty. Coll., 2000. Office: Thomas W Sneddon Jr 1112 Santa Barbara St Santa Barbara CA 93101-2008

SNEED, JOSEPH DONALD, philosophy educator, writer; b. Durant, Okla., Sept. 23, 1938; s. Dabney Whitfield and Sallybelle (Atkinson) S. BS, Rice U., 1960; MS, U Ill., 1962; PhD, Stanford U., 1964. Prof. Stanford U., Palo Alto, Calif., 1966-73; policy analyst SRI Internat., Menlo Park, Calif., 1973-74; prof. U. Munich, 1974-75, U. Eindhoven, Holland, 1976-77, SUNY, Albany, 1977-79; prof. philosophy Colo. Sch. Mines, Golden, 1980—. Author: The Logical Structure of Mathematical Physics, 1971, (with W. Balzer and C. Moulines) An Architectonic for Science, 1987; editor: (with S. Waldhorn) Restructuring the Federal System, 1974. Mem. Am. Philos. Assn. Office: Colo Sch Mines Golden CO 80401 E-mail: jsneed@mines.edu.

SNELL, MARK A., utilities executive; B in acctg., San Diego State Univ. CPA. Sr. mgr. KPMG Peat Marwick; exec. v.p., CFO World Oil Corp.; CFO, CAO Latham & Watkins; exec. v.p., CFO Dames & Moore, Earth Tech, Long Beach, Calif.; v.p. planning & develop. Sempra Energy, San Diego, 2001; CFO Sempra Global, San Diego, 2001—04, group pres., 2004—06; exec. v.p., CFO Sempra Energy, San Diego, 2006—. Bd. dir. Venoco Inc. Office: Sempra Energy 101 Ash St San Diego CA 92101

SNELL, PATRICIA POLDERVAART, retired librarian, consultant; b. Santa Fe, Apr. 11, 1943; d. Arie and Edna Beryl (Kerchmar) Poldervaart; m. Charles Eliot Snell, June 7, 1966. BA in Edn., U. N.M., 1965; MSLS, U. So. Calif., 1966. Asst. edn. libr. U. So. Calif., LA, 1966—68; med. libr. Bedford (Mass.) VA Hosp., 1968—69; asst. law libr. U. Miami, Coral Gables, Fla., 1970—71; acquistions libr. U. N.Mex. Law Sch. Libr., Albuquerque, 1971—72; order libr. Los Angeles County Law Libr., 1972—76, cataloguer, 1976—90; libr. Parks Coll., Albuquerque, 1990—92; records technician Technadyne Engring. Cons. to Sandia Nat. Labs., 1992—93; libr. Tireman Learning Materials Ctr. U. N.Mex., Albuquerque, 1993—96, instr. libr. sci. program Coll. Edn., 1991—2003; legal rsch. technician City of Albuquerque, 1996—2006, Bernalillo County, 2006—09, ret., 2009. Ch. libr. Beverly Hills Presbyn. Ch., 1974-90, ch. choir libr., 1976-90. Southwestern Library Assn. scholar, 1965. Mem.: ALA, N.Mex. Libr. Assn., Pi Lambda Theta. Avocations: travel, reading. Business E-Mail: psnell@bernco.gov.

SNIDER, DARRYL, lawyer; BA, U. Mich., 1971, JD magna cum laude, 1974, PhD in Econ. with highest distinction, 1975. Bar: Calif., U.S. Supreme Ct., Am. Bar Assoc. Adjunct prof. Law Golden Gate Univ., 1977—78, Univ. San Francisco, 1979; atty., shareholder Heller, Ehrman, White, & McAuliffe LLP, Los Angeles, Calif., 1998—. Panel mem. Inst. Con. on Securities Litigation, 1996—97. Mem.: Phi Beta Kappa. Office: Heller Ehrman LLP 333 S Hope St Los Angeles CA 90071-1406 Office Phone: 213-689-7577. Office Fax: 213-614-1868. E-mail: dsnider@hewm.com.

SNIDER, STACEY, film company executive; b. Phila., Apr. 29, 1961; m. Gary Jones; children: Katie, Natalie. BA, U. Penn., 1982; JD, U. Calif. LA, 1985. Dir. of devel. Guber-Peters Entertainment Co., 1986—90, exec. v.p., 1990—92; pres. prodn. TriStar Pictures, 1992-96; co-pres. prodn. Universal Pictures, Universal City, Calif., 1996—98, pres. prodn., 1998—99, chmn., CEO, 1999—2006; co-chmn., CEO DreamWorks SKG, Glendale, Calif., 2006—. Bd. dirs. Am. Film Inst. Bd. dirs. Spl. Olympics of So. Calif.; bd. trustees Art Ctr. Coll. of Design, Pasadena, Calif. Recipient Dorothy and Sherrill C. Corwin Human Rels. Award, Am. Jewish Com., 2003; named one of The 100 Most Powerful Women in Entertainment, Hollywood Reporter, 2005, 2006, 2007, The Most Powerful Women, Forbes mag., 2005, The 50 Most Powerful People in Hollywood, Premiere mag., 2004—05, The 100 Most Powerful Women in Bus., Fortune mag., 2005—07, America 's Top Women in Bus.-Game Changers, Pink mag. & Forté Found., 2007, The 50 Smartest People in Hollywood, Entertainment Weekly, 2007. Office: DreamWorks SKG 1000 Flower St Glendale CA 91201

SNIDER, TIMOTHY R., retired mining executive; BS in Chemistry and Geology, No. Ariz. U., 1979; grad. advanced mgmt. program, U. Pa., 1996. Joined Phelps Dodge Corp., 1970; pres. Phelps Dodge Morenci Inc., Morenci, Ariz.; pres., COO Phelps Dodge Mining Co., Phoenix, 1998—; sr. v.p. Phelps Dodge Corp., Phoenix, 1998, pres., COO, 2003—07, Freeport-McMoRan Copper & Gold Inc., Phoenix, 2007—08.

SNOOP DOGG, (CALVIN BROADUS), vocalist, actor; b. Long Beach, Calif., Oct. 20, 1972; s. Beverly Tate; m. Shante Taylor, June 1997; 1 child, Corde Calvin Broadus;children from previous marriage: Cordell Broadus, Cori Broadus. Founder, owner Doggy Style Records, Inc. (formerly DoggHouse Records), 1999—. Musician: (albums) Doggystyle, 1993, Tha Doggfather, 1996, Da Game Is To Be Sold Not To Be Told, 1998, No Limit Top Dogg, 1999, Tha Last Meal, 2000, Doggy Style Allstars: Welcome to Tha House, 2002, Paid Tha Cost to Be da Bo$$, 2002, Soundtrack Raw N Uncut, Vol. 1, 2002, Welcome to Church: Mix Tape, Vol. 1, 2003, R&G - Rhythm and Gangster: The Masterpiece, 2004, Dogg Pound Mix, 2005, Me & My Homies, 2005, Tha Blue Carpet Treatment, 2006, The Chronicalz, Vol. 1: The Mixed Up Album, 2006, Ego Trippin', 2008; actor: (films) Half Baked, 1998, I Got the Hook Up, 1998, Ride, 1998, Caught Up, 1998, Urban Menace, 1999, The Wrecking Crew, 1999, Hot Boyz, 1999, Tha Eastsidaz, 2000, Baby Boy, 2001, Training Day, 2001, Bones, 2001, The Wash, 2001, Crime Partners, 2001, Malibu's Most Wanted, 2003, Old School, 2003, Starsky & Hutch, 2004, Soul Plane, 2004, (voice only) Racing Stripes, 2005,: (TV appearances) Just Shoot Me, 2001; co-author (with David Seay): The Doggfather: The Times, Trials, and Hardcore Truths of Snoop Dogg, 1999. Founder Snoop Youth Football League, Calif., 2005. Office: Doggy Style Records 1142 S Diamond Bar Blvd #504 Diamond Bar CA 91765

SNOW, MARLON O., trucking executive, state agency administrator; m. Ann; children. Gen. mgr. spl. commodities Milne Truck Lines, Phoenix, LA, 1970-81; gen. mgr. spl. commodities, sales Motor Cargo, Salt Lake City, 1981-82; owner MST Trucking, Inc., Salt Lake City, 1982—. V.p. Utah Motor Carriers for State of Utah, 1997-98; mem. adv. bd. Zions Bank. Mem. State Bd. Edn., 1994-97, chair, 1995-97; trustee Utah Valley State Coll., 1998; mem. Ho. of Reps., Utah, 1999-2001; bd. regents Bd. Higher Edn. State of Utah, 2001—; bd. dirs. Children's Justice Ctr., State of Utah, 2002-, Riverside Country Club; mem. bd. I.H.C. Hosp. Utah County. Mem. Utah Valley State Coll. Found. (bd. dirs. 1991—), Alpine Sch. Dist. Found. (bd. dirs. 1990-94). Office: 1247 E 430 N Orem UT 84097-5400

SNOW, THEODORE PECK, astrophysics educator; b. Seattle, Jan. 30, 1947; s. Theodore P. and Louise (Wertz) S.; m. Constance M. Snow, Aug. 23, 1969; children: McGregor A., Tyler M., Reilly A. BA, Yale U., 1969; MS, U. Wash., 1970, PhD, 1973. Mem. rsch. staff Princeton (N.J.) U., 1973-77; prof. U. Colo., Boulder, 1977—, dir. Ctr. for Astrophysics and Space Astronomy, 1986-96, dir. Fiske Planetarium, 2000—. Mem. instrument devel. teams for far Ultraviolet Spectroscopic Explorer, 1999—, Cosmic Origins Spectrograph to be installed in Hubble Space Telescope. Author: (textbook) The Dynamic Universe, 1983, 4th edit., 1991, Essentials of the Dynamic Universe 4th edit., 1993 (textbook excellence award Text and Academic Authors Assn. 1994), Physics, 1986, Universe: Origins and Evolution, 1997; contbr. over 200 articles to profl. jours. Fellow Royal Astron. Soc.; mem. Am. Astron. Soc., Astron. Soc. Pacific, Sigma Xi. Achievements include discovery, through observations in ultraviolet visible, and infrared wavelengths, and through laboratory measurement of chemical reactions, of several important processes involving interstellar gas and dust, and their roles in star formation and late stages of stellar evolution. Office: U Colo Ctr Astrophysics Space Astronomy 389 UCB Boulder CO 80309-0389 Business E-Mail: tsnow@casa.colorado.edu.

SNOW, TOWER CHARLES, JR., lawyer; b. Boston, Oct. 28, 1947; s. Tower Charles and Margaret (Harper) S. BA in English, Dartmouth Coll., 1969; JD, U. Calif., Berkeley, 1973. Bar: Calif. 1973, US Dist. Ct. (no. dist.) Calif. 1973, US Ct. Appeals (9th cir.) 1973, US Supreme Ct. 1976, US Dist. Ct. (ea. dist.) Calif. 1979, US Ct. Appeals (fed. cir.) 1980, US Ct. Claims 1980, US Ct. Appeals (2d cir.) 1987, NY 1988, US Dist. Ct. (ea. and so. dists.) NY 1988, US Dist. Ct. (ctrl. dist.) Calif. 1989, US Dist. Ct. (no. dist.) Tex. 1995, US Dist. Ct. (so. dist.) Calif. 1996, US Dist. Ct. Ariz. 1996. Ptnr., chmn. litigation dept. Orrick, Herrington & Sutcliffe, San Francisco, 1973-89; ptnr. Shearman & Sterling, San Francisco, 1989-94; ptnr., chmn. securities litigation group, mem. policy com. Brobeck, Phleger & Harrison, LLP, San Francisco, 1995-97; chmn., CEO Brobeck, Phleger & Harrison, San Francisco, 1998—2001; ptnr., mem. Americas Mgmt. Group, Clifford Chance, LLP, 2002—04, cons., 2005—06; ind. cons., 2007—09; ptnr. Howard Rice Nemerovski Canady Falk & Rabkin, San Francisco, 2009—. Arbitrator Nat. Assn. Securities Dealers, Am. Stock Exch., N.Y. Stock Exch., Pacific Coast Stock Exch., Superior Ct. City and County San Francisco, Am. Arbitration Assn.; lectr. in field. Author numerous law handbooks and articles to prof. jours. Mem. San Francisco Mus. Soc., San Francisco Symphony, San Francisco Ballet, San Francisco Opera, Am. Conservatory Theatre. Named Best Lawyer in the U.S. in his Field, Corp. Bd. Member Mag., 2001; named one of The 100 Most Influential Lawyers in America, Nat. Law Jour., 2000, The 100 Most Influential Lawyers in Calif., Calif. Law and Bus., 2000, 2002, Lawyer Mag. (U.K.), 2002, America's Leading Lawyers for Bus., Chambers USA, 2003, 2004, 2005; Rufus Choate scholar, Dartmouth Coll., 1969. Mem. ABA (chmn. subcom. pub. offering litig. 1984-88, co-chair task force on securities arbitration 1988-89, vice chair securities litig. com. 1986-88), Continuing Edn. Bar (bus. law inst. planning com. 1986), Securities Industry Assn., Nat. Inst. Trial Advocacy, San Francisco Bar Assn. (pres. securities litig. sect. 1995). Democrat. Avocations: travel, skiing, running, scuba diving, films. Office: Howard Rice Nemerovski Canady Falk & Rabkin Three Embarcadero Ctr Seventh Fl San Francisco CA 94111 Office Phone: 415-987-5877, 415-677-3475. Personal E-mail: tower.snow@gmail.com. E-mail: tsnow@howardrice.com.*

SNOWDEN, DAVID L., protective services official; BA, Calif. State U., Fullerton. Chief of police, Beverly Hills, Calif. Recipient Am.'s Star award U.S. Marshal's Office, Sherman Block Law Enforcement Profl. of Yr. award Calif. Peace Officers Assn., 2003. Mem. Calif. Police Chiefs Assn. (past pres.), Orange County Chiefs and Sheriffs Assn. (past pres.), L.A. County Chiefs Assn. (past pres.). Office: 464 N Rexford Dr Beverly Hills CA 90210 E-mail: dsnowden@beverlyhills.org.

SNYDER, ALAN CARHART, finance company executive; b. NYC, May 25, 1946; s. John I. and Elfrida (Bendix) S.; m. Mary Burgoyne, Feb. 9, 1974. BS, BA, Georgetown U., 1968; MBA, Harvard U., 1973. Cons. Reynolds Securities, NYC, 1972-73; exec. v.p. Dean Witter Reynolds, NYC, 1975-85; sole proprietor Shinnecock Ptnrs., NYC, 1985-89, mng. ptnr., 1989—; pres., chief oper. officer, bd. dirs. First Exec. Corp., LA, 1990-91; COO, Exec. Life Ins. Co., LA, 1991-93; CEO, Aurora Nat. Life Assurance Co., LA, 1993-94, cons., 1994-95; mng. ptnr. Shinnecock Group L.L.C., LA, 1994—; chmn., CEO, pres. Answer Fin. Inc., LA, 1997—2006. Baker scholar Harvard Bus. Sch., 1973.

SNYDER, ALLEGRA FULLER, dancer, film director, educator; b. Chgo., Aug. 28, 1927; d. R. Buckminster and Anne (Hewlett) Fuller; m. Robert Snyder, June 30, 1951 (div. Apr. 1975, remarried Sept. 1980); children: Alexandra, Jaime. BA in Dance, Bennington Coll., 1951; MA in Dance, UCLA, 1967. Asst. to curator, dance archives Mus. Modern Art, NYC, 1945-47; dancer Ballet Soc. of N.Y.C. Ballet Co., 1945-47; mem. office and prodn. staff Internat. Film Found., NYC, 1950-52; editor, dance films Film News mag., NYC, 1966-72; lectr. dance and film adv., dept. dance UCLA, 1967-73, chmn. dept. dance, 1974-80, 90-91, acting chair, spring 1985, chair of faculty Sch. of the Arts, 1989-91, prof. dance and dance ethnology, 1973-91, prof. emeritus, 1991—; pres. Buckminster Fuller Inst., Santa Barbara, Calif., chairwoman bd. dirs., 1984—. Vis. lectr. Calif. Inst. Arts, Valencia, 1972; co-dir. dance and TV workshop Am. Dance Festival, Conn. Coll., New London, 1973; dir. NEH summer seminar for coll. tchrs. Asian Performing Arts, 1978, 81; coord. Ethnic Arts Intercoll. Interdisciplinary Program, 1974-73, acting chmn., 1986; vis. prof. performance studies NYU, 1982-83; hon. vis. prof. U. Surrey, Guildford, Eng., 1983-84; cons. Thyodia Found., Salt Lake City, 1973-74; mem. dance adv. panel Nat. Endowment Arts, 1968-72, Calif. Arts Commn., 1974-91; mem. adv. screening com. Coun. Internat. Exch. of Scholars, 1979-82; mem. various panels NEH, 1979-85; core cons. for Dancing, Sta. WNET-TV, 1988—. Dir. film Baroque Dance 1625-1725, in 1977; co-dir. film Gods of Bali, 1952; dir. and wrote film Bayanihan, 1962 (named Best Folkloric Documentary at Bilboa Film Festival, winner Golden Eagle award); asst. dir. and asst. editor film The Bennington Story, 1952; created films Gestures of Sand, 1968, Reflections on Choreography, 1973, When the Fire Dances Between Two Poles, 1982; created film, video loop and text Celebration: A World of Art and Ritual, 1982-83; supr. post-prodn. film Erick Hawkins, 1964, in 1973. Also contbr. articles to profl. jours. and mags. Adv. com. Pacific Asia Mus., 1980-84, Festival of the Mask, Craft and Folk Art Mus., 1979-84; adv. panel Los Angeles Dance Currents II, Mus. Ctr. Dance Assn., 1974-75; bd. dirs. Council Grove Sch. III, Compton, Calif., 1976-81; apptd. mem. Adv. Dance Com., Pasadena (Calif.) Art Mus., 1970-71, Los Angeles Festival of Performing Arts com., Studio Watts, 1970; mem. Technology and Cultural Transformation com., UNESCO, 1977. Fulbright research fellow, 1983-84; grantee Nat. Endowment Arts, 1981, Nat. Endowment Humanities, 1977, 79, 81, UCLA, 1968, 77, 80, 82, 85; recipient Amer. Dance Guild Award for Outstanding Achievement in Dance, 1992. Mem. Am. Dance Therapy Assn., Congress on Rsch. in Dance (bd. dirs. 1970-76, chmn. 1975-77, nat. conf. chmn. 1972), Coun. Dance Adminstrs., Am. Dance Guild (chmn. com. awards 1972), Soc. for Ethnomusicology, Am. Anthrop. Assn., Am. Folklore Soc., Soc. Anthropology of Visual Comm., Soc. Humanistic Anthropology, Calif. Dance Educators Assn. (conf. chmn. 1972), L.A. Area Dance Alliance (adv. bd. 1978-84, selection com. Dance Kaleidoscope project 1979-81), Fulbright Alumni Assn. Home: 15313 Whitfield Ave Pacific Palisades CA 90272-2548 Office: Buckminster Fuller Institute 181 N 11th St Apt 402 Brooklyn NY 11211-1175

SNYDER, DANIEL JAMES, military career officer; b. Clarkson, NY, Dec. 31, 1954; s. James Orman and Marilyn Malita (Ophardt) S.; m. Carrie Sue Grimes, May 11, 1985; children: Robert James, Ryan Benjamin. BS Health Svcs. Adminstrn., So. Ill. U., 1977; MA Nat. Resources Strategy, Webster U., 1978. Enlisted USN, 1975, commd. ensign, 1979, advanced through grades to comdr., hosp. corpsman Naval Hosp. Great Lakes, Ill., 1976-79, comptroller Naval Hosp. Okinawa, Japan, 1979-81, dir. adminstrn. Naval Hosp. Annapolis, Md., 1981-85, head med. planning, chief naval ops. Washington, 1985-88, dir. adminstrn. Naval Hosp. Rota, Spain, 1988-91, head med. planning., chief naval ops. Washington, 1991—. Decorated Meritorious Svc. medal, Navy Commendation medal, numerous Navy Achievement medals. Fellow Am. Coll. Healthcare Execs. (mem. bd. govs. dist. 8, Regent 1993-96). Republican. Lutheran. Avocations: sailing, running.

SNYDER, DARIN W., lawyer; b. Kansas City, Mo., 1963; BA cum laude, Georgetown U., 1985; JD cum laude, U. Chgo., 1988. Bar: Calif. 1988, US Dist. Ct., (Ctrl, No., Ea., and So. Dists. of Calif.), US Ct. of Appeals (Ninth and Fed. Circuits), US Ct. Veterans Appeals. Head O'Melveny & Myers LLP, San Francisco, co-chair patent and tech. litig. practice group, head intellectual property and tech. dept. No. Calif. Divsn. LA. Dir. Bar Assn. San Francisco, Legal Aid Soc. Employment Law Ctr. Bradley Law & Government Fellow, 1987—88. Mem.: Am. Intellectual Property Law Assn., Santa Clara County Bar Assn., ABA (former co-chair intellectual property com., co-chair trade secrets subcommittee litig. sect. 1997—98). Office: O'Melveny & Myers LLP Embarcadero Ctr West 2 Embarcadero Ctr Ste 2800 San Francisco CA 94111-3903 Office Phone: 415-984-8846. Office Fax: 415-984-8701. Business E-Mail: dsnyder@omm.com.

SNYDER, DAVID L., film production designer; b. Buffalo, Sept. 22, 1944; s. Albert R. and Louise M. (Passero) S.; m. Terry Finn, Aug. 1, 1990; children: David Michael, Amy Lynne, Finn Henry. Grad. high sch., Niagara Falls, NY. Ind. film prodn. designer, Hollywood, Calif.; pres. Snyder Bros. Prodns., Inc., Hollywood. Guest speaker Tokyo Internat. Film Festival, 1985. Art dir. (films) In God We Trust, 1980, The Idolmaker, 1980, Blade Runner, 1982 (Academy award nomination best art direction 1982), Brainstorm, 1983; prodn. designer (films) Strange Brew, 1983, Racing With the Moon, 1984, The Woman In Red, 1984, My Science Project, 1985, Armed and Dangerous, 1986, Back to School, 1986, Summer School, 1987, Moving, 1988, She's Out of Control, 1989, Bill & Ted's Bogus Journey, 1991, Class Act, 1992, Super Mario Brothers, 1993, Demolition Man, 1993, Terminal Velocity, 1994, Rainbow, 1995, Vegas Vacation, 1997, Burn, Hollywood, Burn, 1997, Soldier, 1998, The Whole Nine Yards, 1999; assoc. prodr.: (film) Cold Dog Soup, 1990; exec. prodr. (film) Rainbow, 1995. Mem. NATAS, Motion Picture Art Dirs. Guild, Acad. Motion Picture Arts and Scis., Dirs. Guild Am. Democrat. Avocations: history, filmmaking, films.

SNYDER, DAVID RICHARD, lawyer; b. Kalamazoo, Oct. 9, 1949; s. Richard E. and Margaret L. (Vanderplough) S.; m. Phyllis Alford, Aug. 14, 1971; children: Jason Richard, Carrie Lynn. BA with high honors, Mich. State U., East Lansing, 1971; JD with distinction, Cornell U., Ithaca, NY, 1974. Bar: Calif. 1974. Assoc. Jenkins & Perry, San Diego, 1974-77, ptnr., 1978-83, Aylward, Kintz & Stiska, San Diego, 1983-86, Luce, Forward, Hamilton & Scripps, San Diego, 1986-93, Pillsbury Madison & Sutro LLP, San Diego, 1993—2005; mng. bd. Pillsbury Winthrop LLP, San Diego, 1999—2005, vice chmn., 2004—05; chair bus. dept., ptnr., corp. & securities practice, mem. mng. bd. Pillsbury Winthrop Shaw Pittman LLP, San Diego, 2005—. V.p., dir. San Diego Venture Group, 1989-91; adj. prof. Calif. Western Sch. Law, San Diego, 1982-84; lectr. Calif. Continuing Edn. of Bar, 1983—. Co-author: Drafting Legal Instruments, 1982; editor Cornell Law Rev., 1973-74. Bd. dirs. Boys Club Chula Vista, Calif., 1979-83, San Diego Symphony Orch. Assn., 2006-; pres. Corpus Christi Parish Coun., Bonita, Calif., 1988-90; trustee Children's Hosp. Found., San Diego, 1988-2004, chmn., 1990-92. Mem.: ABA (fed. securities law com. 1987—, chmn. subcom. on ann. rev. fed. securities regulation, dir. corp. dirs. forum), Corp. Dirs. Forum (bd. dirs. 2001—), San Diego County Bar Assn., State Bar Calif., Am. Electronics Assn. (bd. dirs., mem. exec. com. San Diego chpt. 1991—93), Order of Coif, Phi Beta Kappa. Republican. Roman Catholic. Office: Pillsbury Winthrop Shaw Pittman LLP 501 W Broadway Ste 1100 San Diego CA 92101-8298 Office Phone: 619-544-3369. Office Fax: 619-236-1995. Business E-Mail: dave.snyder@pillsburylaw.com.

SNYDER, EVAN, stem cell biologist, neuroscientist, physician, educator; MD and PhD in Neuroscience, U. Pa., 1980. Resident and fellow in pediatrics, neurology, and newborn intensive care Children's Hosp.-Boston and Harvard Medical School; postdoctoral rsch. Harvard Med. Sch., instr. neurology, 1992—96, asst. prof. neurology, 1996—2003; prof., dir. stem cell and regeneration prog. Burnham Inst., La Jolla, Calif., 2003—. Contbr. articles in high profl. jours. Office: Burnham Inst Mail Stop 7261 10901 N Torrey Pines Rd La Jolla CA 92037 Office Phone: 858-646-3158. Fax: 858-646-3199; Office Fax: 858-713-6273. Business E-Mail: esnyder@burnham.org.

SNYDER, H(ELEN) DIANE, state legislator; New Mexico State Senator, District 15, 2000-, Bernalillo Co, member Corps & Transportation Committee, Indian & Cultural Affairs Committee, interim member, Legislature Committee on Compacts, Corrections Oversight & Justice Committee, Judicial Sys Study Committee, New Mexico Finance Authority Oversight Committee, Redistricting Committee, Water & Natural Resources Committee, New Mexico State Senate. Republican. Mailing: 7006 Elna Ct NE Albuquerque NM 87110 E-mail: senate@state.nm.us.

SNYDER, HENRY LEONARD, historian, educator, writer; b. Hayward, Calif., Nov. 3, 1929; s. Henry Runyon and Mary (Rosenberg) Snyder; m. Janette Marie Hannus, July 21, 1961; children: Michael Jesse, Christopher Henry, David Lyle. BA, U. Calif., Berkeley, 1951, MA, 1960, PhD, 1963. Sr. buyer Dohrmann Comml. Co., San Francisco, 1951—59; instr. to prof. U. Kans., Lawrence, 1963—78, assoc. dean to dean rsch. adminstrn., 1967—78; dir. English Short Title Catalogue for N.Am., 1978—; prof. history, dean arts and scis. La. State U., Baton Rouge, 1979—86; prof. history U. Calif., Riverside, 1986—; dir. Ctr. for Bibliog. Studies, 1989—. Sigmund, Martin, Heller traveling fellow U. Calif., Berkeley, 1962—63; vis. lectr. Bedford Coll., U. London, 1965—66; sr. fellow Am. Council Learned Soc., 1969—70; Fulbright lectr., rsch. scholar U. Hamburg, Germany, 1974; dean humanities and social scis. U. Calif., Riverside, 1986. Co-editor: (book) The Marlborough Godolphin Correspondence, 1975, The Scottish World: History and Culture of Scotland, 1981; co-author: The English Heritage, 1988. United Way, 1977; pres. Baton Rouge Opera, 1981—83, Riverside Opera, 1987—90; bd. dirs. Arts and Humanities Com., Baton Rouge, 1981—85. Served with Nat. US Army. Recipient Nat. Humanities medal for digitizing the past, NEH, 2007. Fellow: Gt. Brit. Bibliog. Soc., Royal Hist. Soc.; mem.: Internat. Fed. Librs. (chair rarebooks sect. 1995—99), Am. Hist. Assn., Conf. Brit. Studies (exec. com. 1978—83), Am. Soc. 18th Century Studies (pres. 1980—81). Republican. Congregationalist. Home: 220 Trinity Ave Kensington CA 94708-1139 Office: U Calif Ctr For Bibliog Studies Riverside CA 92521-0154 Office Phone: 951-827-5841. Personal E-mail: hlsnyder@earthlink.net.

SNYDER, HOWARD ARTHUR, aerospace engineering educator, consultant; b. Palmerton, Pa., Mar. 7, 1930; s. Howard Franklin and Mary Rachel (Landis) S.; m. Nancy Jane Simon, Sept. 14, 1961 (div. Feb. 1975); m. Kaye Elizabeth Bache, Mar. 21, 1975. BS in Physics, Rensselaer Poly. Inst., 1952; MS in Physics, U. Chgo., 1957, PhD in Physics, 1961. From asst. prof. to assoc. prof. Brown U., Providence, 1961-68; from assoc. prof. to prof. aerospace engring. U. Colo., Boulder, 1968—. Cons. Storage Tech. Corp., Louisville, Colo., 1980-84, 89-91, Ball Aerospace Systems, Boulder, 1984-2002, Superconducting Super Collider, 1992-93. Contbr. articles to profl. jours. Served to lt. (j.g.) USN, 1948-55. Mem. Am. Phys. Soc., Colo. Mountain Club (Denver). Home: 251 Gay St Longmont CO 80501-5336 Office: U Colo PO Box 429 Boulder CO 80309-0429 Office Phone: 303-492-7635. Business E-Mail: howard.sndyder@colorado.edu.

SNYDER, LESTER M., sports association executive; b. Red Lion, Pa. m. Audrene Snyder; children: Kim, Ky. Degree, Millersville State U.; doctorate, U. Mich. Past v.p., treas., presdl. appointee to exec. com., Pacific region v.p., sect. del., pres. southwest sect., chmn. and mem. various coms. U.S. Tennis Assn., Tempe, Ariz., pres., chmn. bd. dirs., 1995-97, past pres., 1997—. Prof. counseling psychology Ariz. State U., Tempe, 1967—; founding dir. Rio Salado Bank; pres. The Heuristic Syss., Inc.; past mem. com. mgmt. Internat. Tennis Fedn., Davis Cup and budget coms., del.; bd. dirs., exec. com. Internat. Tennis Hall of Fame; past Grand Slam com. rep. to Women's Tennis Fedn. Office: 1324 E Whalers Way Tempe AZ 85283-2148

SNYDER, RICK (RICHARD D. SNYDER), computer company executive; BGS with high distinction, Univ. Mich., 1977, MBA with high distinction, 1979, JD, 1982. CPA; bar: Mich. Acct. Coopers & Lybrand, 1982—88, ptnr., 1988—91; exec. v.p. Gateway, Inc., Irvine, Calif., 1991—97, pres. & COO, 1996—97, dir., 1991—97, chmn., 2005—, interim CEO, 2006; pres. Avalon Investments, 1997—2000; founder, CEO, chmn. Ardesta LLC, Ann Arbor, Mich., 2000—. Adj. prof. acctg. U. Mich., 1982—84; dir. Launch Media Inc. Trustee The Henry Ford; bd. mem. U. Mich. Coll. Engring. Nat. Adv. Com.; mem. tech. transfer nat. adv. com. U. Mich.; mem. Gov. e-Mich. Adv. Council; mem. adv. bd. Samuel Zell & Robert H. Lurie Inst. for Entrepreneurial Studies, NanoBus. Alliance; mem. vis. com. Purdue Univ. Sch. Engring.; chmn. Ann Arbor SPARK; mem. The Nature Conservancy, Mich. Chpt. Mem.: Mich. Bar Assn. Office: Gateway Inc 7565 Irvine Center Dr Irvine CA 92618

SNYDER, ZACK, film director; b. Green Bay, Mar. 1, 1966; m. Denise Snyder (div.); m. Deborah Snyder, Sept. 25, 2004; 6 children. Grad., Art Ctr. Coll. Design, Pasadena, Calif.; student, Heatherlies Sch. Fine Art, London. Dir.: various sports and car commercials; (films) Dawn of the Dead, 2004, The Lost Tape: Andy's Terrifying Last Days Revealed, 2004, Watchmen, 2009; dir., writer (films) 300, 2006 (Hollywood Movie of Yr., Hollywood Film Festival, 2007, Saturn award for best direction, 2008). Recipient 2 Clio awards, Gold Lion award, Cannes Festival; named a Maverick, Details mag., 2008; named one of 50 Smartest People in Hollywood, Entertainment Weekly, 2007. Office: c/o Creative Artists Agy 2000 Ave of the Stars Los Angeles CA 90067

SOBEL, NOAM, science educator; BA, MA Psychobiology, Tel Aviv U., 1995; PhD Neurosci., Stanford U., 1999. Asst. prof. Wills Neurosci. Inst. U. Calif., Berkeley, assoc. prof., Wills Neuroscience Inst., asst. prof. Psychology, assoc. prof., Psychology. Contbr. articles to profl. jours. Recipient Moskowitz Jacobs Inc. award, Assn. for Chemoreception Sciences, 2003; fellow, Helen Hay Whitney Found., 2000; Searle Scholar, 2001. Office: U Calif Berkeley Dept Psychology 3210 Tolman Hall Rm G95 Berkeley CA 94720 Office Phone: 510-643-0131, 510-643-0132. Business E-Mail: nsobel@socrates.berkeley.edu.

SOBELLE, RICHARD E., lawyer; b. Cleve., Mar. 18, 1935; BA, Stanford U., 1956, JD, 1960; LLM, U. So. Calif., 1967. Bar: Calif. 1961, U.S. Supreme Ct. 1969. Exec. Tracinda Corp. Mem. ABA (corp., banking and bus. law sect. 1969-95), State Bar Calif. (del. to conf. state bar dels. 1965-77, exec. com. bus. law sect. 1977-78), L.A. County Bar Assn. (exec. coun., jr. barristers 1965-68, exec. com. bus. and corps. sect. 1973-75). Office: Tracinda Corp 150 S Rodeo Dr Ste 250 Beverly Hills CA 90212-2417

SOBEY, EDWIN J. C., museum director, oceanographer, consultant; b. Phila., Apr. 7, 1948; s. Edwin J. and Helen (Chapin) S.; m. Barbara Lee, May 9, 1970; children: Ted Wooddall, Andrew Chapin. BS, U. Richmond, 1969; MS, Oreg. State U., 1974, PhD, 1977. Rsch. scientist Sci. Applications, Inc., Boulder, Colo., 1977-79, divsn. mgr., 1979-81; exec. dir. Sci. Mus., West Palm Beach, Fla., 1981-88, Mus. Sci. and History, Jacksonville, Fla., 1988, Nat. Invention Ctr., Akron, Ohio, 1989-92, Fresno Met. Mus., Calif., 1993-95; ednl. cons., 1995—. Exec. dir. A.C. Gilbert's Discovery Village, Salem, Oreg., 1997-99; pres. Northwest Invention Ctr., 1999—; founder Nat. Toy Hall of Fame, 1998; instr. mus. mgmt. U. Wash., 1998-2001. Author: Complete Circuit Training Guide, 1980, Strength Training Book, 1981, The Whole Backpacker's Catalog, 1988, Increasing Your Audience, 1989, Inventing Stuff, 1995, Wrapper Rockets and Trombone Straws-Science at Every Meal, 1996, Car Smarts, 1997, Just Plane Smart, 1998, Young Inventors at Work, 1999, How to Enter and Win an Invention Contest, 1999, Fantastic Flying Fun with Science, 2000, Wacky Water Fun with Science, 2000, Inventing Toys: Kids Having Fun Learning Science, 2001, How to Build Your Own Prize-Winning Robot, 2002, Loco-Motion, 2005, Rocket-Powered Science, 2005, A Field Guild to Roadside Technology, 2006, A Field Guide to Office Technology, 2007, Wax Toys Work, 2008; co-author: Aerobic Weight Training Book, 1982; mem. editl. adv. bd. Invent Mag., 1989—92; exec. prodr.: (TV show) Idea Factory, Sta. KFSN-30, 1995—97; co-host (ednl. TV show) Blow the Roof Off, 1992. Alumni v.p. Leadership Palm Beach County; expdn. leader Expdn. Tng. Inst., S.E. Alaska, 1980; mem. U.S. Antarctic Rsch. Program, 1974; founder, bd. dirs. Visually Impaired Sports Program, Boulder, 1978-81; fitness instr. YMCA Boulder, 1977-81; convener 1st Nat. Conf. Sports for the Blind, 1979; bd. dirs. Leadership Palm Beach; vice chmn. County Com. on Artificial Reefs; treas. Leadership Akron Alumni Assn., 1990-91, class pres. Leadership Akron; v.p. Ohio Mus. Assn., 1991-92, pres., 1992-93; bd. dirs. Fla. Mus. Assn., 1988-89; mem. adv. bd. Marine Sci. Inst., 1990—. Lt. USN, 1970-73. Recipient Disting. award, Akron Coun. Engring. and Scientific Socs., 1992, award, Ohio Ednl. Broadcasting Network Commn., 1994, Congl. award for inventing equitable futures, 2005; named to Nonfiction Honor List, Voice of Youth Activities, 2003. Fellow Explorers Club (chair Pacific Midwest chpt. 2002-07); mem. Marine Tech. Soc. (sect. chmn. 1982-84), Coral Reef Soc. (chpt. pres. 1982-87), Nat. Inventive Thinking Assn. (bd. dirs. 1989—). Home: 2420 178th Ave NE Redmond WA 98052-5820 Office Phone: 425-861-8685. Personal E-mail: sobey@gte.net.

SOBIESKI, LEELEE (LILIANE RUDABET GLORIA ESLVETA SOBIESKI), actress; b. NYC, June 10, 1983; d. Jean Sobieski and Elizabeth Soloman. Attended, Brown U. Actress (TV films) Reunion, 1994, A Horse for Danny, 1995, Joan of Arc, 1999 (Best Performance by a Young Actress in a Mini-Series/Made for TV Film, YoungStar award, 1999), Uprising, 2001, Hercules, 2005, (TV series) Charlie Grace, 1995, (films) Jungle 2 Jungle, 1997, Deep Impact, 1998, A Soldier's Daughter Never Cries, 1998, Never Been Kissed, 1999, Eyes Wide Shut, 1999, Here on Earth, 2000, My First Mister, 2001, Joy Ride, 2001, Glass House, 2001, The Idol, 2002, Max, 2002, Lying, 2006, Heavens Fall, 2006, In a Dark Place, 2006, The Wicker Man, 2006, The Elder Son, 2006, In the Name of the King: A Dungeon Siege Tale, 2007, 88 Minutes, 2007, Walk All Over Me, 2007, Acts of Violence, 2008, (TV miniseries) Dangerous Liaisons, 2003, voice (films) Coven, 2006. Named Superstar of Tomorrow - Female, Young Hollywood Awards, 2000. Avocations: painting, ceramics, poetry, martial arts, horseback riding. Office: c/o Pinnacle PR 8265 Sunset Blvd Ste 201 Los Angeles CA 90046

SOBOLEWSKI, JOHN STEPHEN, computer scientist, director, consultant; b. Krakow, Poland, July 14, 1939; came to U.S., 1966; s. Jan Zygmund and Stefania (Zwolinska) S.; m. Helen Skipper, Dec. 17, 1965 (div. July 1969); m. Carole Straith, Apr. 6, 1974; children: Anne-Marie, Elisa, Martin. BE, U. Adelaide, Adelaide, South Australia, 1962, ME, 1966; PhD in Computer Sci., Wash. State U., 1971. Sci. officer Weapons Research Establishment, Salisbury, South Australia, 1964-66; asst. prof. computer sci. Wash. State U., Pullman, 1966-73; dir. research, assoc. prof. U. Wash., Seattle, 1973-80, dir. computer svcs., 1980-88; assoc. v.p. computing U. N.Mex., Albuquerque, 1988—. Cons. govt. and industry, Seattle, 1973—; mem. bd. trustees Fisher Found., Seattle, 1984—. Author: Computers for the Dental Office, 1986; contbr. articles to profl. jours. Served as engr. with Royal Australian Army, 1957-60. Australian govt. scholar, 1954-60, Elec. Res. Bd. scholar CSIRO, Melbourne, Australia, 1961-64. Mem. IEEE, Computer Soc. Roman Catholic. Avocation: mineral collecting. Home: 18422 57th Ave NE Kenmore WA 98028 Personal E-mail: nwminerals@hotmail.com.

SOBRATO, JOHN A., construction executive; married; 3 children. Real estate agt., Palo Alto, 1957; founder, prin. Sobrato Devel. Cos., Cupertino, Calif. Trustee U. Santa Clara; vice chmn. Nat. Hispanic U. Named Philanthropist of Yr., NSFRE, 1998; named one of Forbes' Richest Americans, 2006. Office: Sobrato Devel Cos Ste 200 10600 N De Anza Blvd Cupertino CA 95014-2075

SOCHYNSKY, YAROSLAV, lawyer, arbitrator, mediator; b. Feb. 5, 1946; BA in English, Colgate U., 1967; JD, Georgetown U., 1970. Bar: Calif., N.Y. Assoc. White & Case, NYC, 1970-71; law clerk to Hon. William T. Sweigert U.S. Dist. Ct. (no. dist.) Calif., 1971-73; assoc. Landels, Ripley & Diamond LLP, San Francisco, 1973-76; sr. ptnr. Landels, Ripley & Diamond, San Francisco, 1976-2000; mediator Am. Arbitration Assn., San Francisco, 2000—. Lectr. Calif. Continuing Edn. Bar, 1985, Equity Asset Mgr.'s Assn., 1987, Calif. Dept. Real Estate, 1986-89). Originator, co-author California ADR Practice Guide, 1992; co-author Real Property Practice and Litigation, 1990; case and notes editor, mem. editorial bd. Georgetown Law Jour.; contbr. articles and monographs to profl. jours. Fellow, Coll. Comml. Arbitrators. Fellow Chartered Inst. Arbitrators (London); mem. ABA (mem. exec. coun. sect. on real property, probate and trust, lectr. 1988, 89, 91), Am. Arbitration Assn. (cert. mediator, mem. pres.' panel of mediators, large and complex case panel, internat. panel, real property valuation panel, No. Calif. adv. coun., lectr. 1990, speaker various panels, No. Calif. Outstanding Mediator award 1991), San Francisco Bar Assn.

SODEN, JOHN P., publishing executive; b. Yakima, Wash., Aug. 25, 1942; BA, U. Wash., 1964. Paperback buyer Univ. Bookstore, Seattle, 1964-66; libr. svcs. coord. Am. News Co., 1966-68; trade sales rep. Little Brown & Co., LA, 1968-70; sales mgr. U. Wash. Press, Seattle, 1971-76, mktg. mgr., 1977-90, assoc. dir., gen. mgr., 1991-96, dir., 1996—. Bd. dirs. Wash. Ctr. for the Book. Recipient Nancy Pryor Blakenship award Wash. State Gov.'s Writers Awards, 1995. Mem. Pacific N.W. Booksellers Assn. (v.p. 1975-78, bd. dirs.). Office: U Wash Press PO Box 50096 Seattle WA 98145-5096

SODHANI, ARVIND, computer company executive; Bachelor's, Master's, U. London; MBA, U. Mich., 1978. Asst. treas. Intel Europe Intel Corp., 1981—84, asst. treas., 1984—88, treas., 1988—90, v.p. and treas., 1990—2005, sr. v.p., pres. Intel Capital, 2005—07, exec. v.p., pres. Intel Capital, 2007—. Office: 2200 Mission College Blvd Santa Clara CA 95052

SOELDNER, JOHN STUART, physician, educator; b. Boston, Sept. 22, 1932; s. Frank and Mary Amelia (Stuart) S.; m. Elsie Irene Harnish, Aug. 25, 1962; children: Judith Marie, Elizabeth Anne, Stephen J.D. BS magna cum laude, Tufts U., 1954; MD, Dalhousie U., Halifax, NS, 1959; LLD (hon.), Dalhousie U., 1996. Diplomate Am. Bd. Med. Examiners; lic. Med. Coun. Can. Intern then resident Victoria Gen. Hosp., Halifax, 1958-61; from instr. medicine to assoc. prof. medicine Harvard U., Boston, 1964-87; prof. medicine U. Calif. Davis Med. Ctr., Sacramento, 1987—97; ret., 1997. Contbr. 300 articles to sci. publs.; patentee in field. Founding mem. med. bd. Juvenile Diabetes Found., N.Y.C. Recipient Sci. award Juvenile Diabetes Found., 1973, U.S. Sr. Scientist award Von Humboldt Found., 1975; fellow Dalhousie U., 1959-60, Harvard Med. Sch., 1961-63, Pfizer traveling fellow, 1973. Mem. Am. Physol. Soc., Am. Soc. Clin. Investigation, Am. Diabetes Assn. (profl. edn. com. 1975-81, 83-85, bd. dirs. 1982-85, Calif. affiliate bd. dirs. 1989—), Columbian Assn. Internal Medicine (corr.), New Eng. Diabetes Assn., Am. Fedn. Clin. Rsch., European Assn. Study of Diabetes, Endocrine Soc., Soc. Exptl. Biology and Medicine, Assn. Advancement Med. Instrumentation, Am. Soc. Artificial Internal Organs, Internat. Soc. Artificial Organs, We. Assn. of Physicians, Dalhousie Med. Alumni Assn. (bd. dirs. Can. 1977). Democrat. Roman Catholic.

SOFAER, ABRAHAM DAVID, lawyer, former federal judge, educator, consultant; b. Bombay, May 6, 1938; arrived in U.S., 1948, naturalized, 1959; m. Marian Bea Scheuer, Oct. 23, 1977; children: Daniel E., Michael J., Helen R., Joseph S., Aaron R., Raphael J. BA in History magna cum laude, Yeshiva Coll., 1962; LLB cum laude, NYU, 1965. Bar: N.Y. 1965, D.C. 1988. Law clk. to Hon. J. Skelly Wright U.S. Ct. Appeals (DC cir.), Washington, 1965-66; law clk. to

Hon. William J. Brennan Jr. US Supreme Ct., Washington, 1966-67; asst. U.S. atty. (so. dist.) NY US Dept. Justice, NYC, 1967-69; prof. law Columbia U., NYC, 1969-79; judge US Dist. Ct. (so. dist.) NY, 1979-85; legal adv. US Dept. State, Washington, 1985-90; ptnr. Hughes Hubbard & Reed, Washington, 1991-94; George P. Shultz disting. scholar, sr. fellow Hoover Instn., Stanford U., 1994—. Hearing officer N.Y. Dept. Environ. Conservation, 1975-76. Author: War, Foreign Affairs and Constitutional Power: The Origins, 1976; contbr. articles to legal, polit., fgn. jours.; editor-in-chief: NYU Law Rev, 1964-65. Served with USAF, 1956-59. Root-Tilden scholar NYU, 1965. Mem. ABA, Fed. Bar Assn., N.Y.C. Bar Assn., N.Y. Bar Assn., Am. Law Inst. Jewish. Office: Stanford Univ The Hoover Instn Stanford CA 94305-6010 Office Phone: 650-725-3763. Office Fax: 650-723-2103. Business E-Mail: sofaer@hoover.stanford.edu.

SOH, CHUNGHEE SARAH, anthropology educator; b. Taegu, Korea, May 1, 1947; came to U.S., 1970; d. Sang Yung and Ock Yun (Choi) S.; m. Jerry Dee Boucher. BA in English summa cum laude, Sogang U., 1971; postgrad., U. Calif., Berkeley, 1971; MA in Anthropology, U. Hawaii, 1983, PhD in Anthropology, 1987. Staff instr. English Korean Air Lines, Edn. & Tng. Ctr., Seoul, 1978-79; instr. anthropology Ewha Womans U., Seoul, 1985; post-doctoral assoc. Inst. of Culture and Comm., East-West Ctr., Honolulu, 1987; asst. prof. U. Hawaii, 1990; asst. prof. anthropology Southwest Tex. State U., San Marcos, 1991-94, San Francisco State U., 1994-96, assoc. prof. anthropology, 1996—2006, prof., 2006—. Guest lectr. Chaminade U. Honolulu, 1988; vis. asst. prof. anthropology U. Ariz., 1990-91; adj. prof. Intercultural Inst. Calif., 1996-98; cons. in field. Author: The Chosen Women in Korean Politics: An Anthropological Study, 1991, Women in Korean Politics, 1993; contbr. articles to profl. jour. Bd. dirs. Women Devel. Inst. Internat., 2000—. Grantee East-West Ctr., 1981-87, NSF, 1985-86; fellow Korea Found., 1993, Japan Found., 1997-98, Inst. Social Sci., U. Tokyo, 1997-98, Leiden U. Internat. Inst. for Asian Studies, The Netherlands, 1998, Inst. for Corean-Am. Studies, 1998—; Hoover Inst. scholar, 1996-97, Stanford U. Inst. for Rsch. on Women and Gender scholar, 2000-01; Rsch. and Writing grantee John D. and Catherine T. MacArthur Found., 2000-01, Fulbright Scholor grant, 2008. Fellow Am. Anthrop. Assn. (treas. East Asia sect. 2001-03), Inst. for Corean-Am. Studies; mem. Am. Ethnological Soc., Soc. Psychol. Anthropology, Assn. Asian Studies (exec. bd. Com. Women Asian Studies 1995-97), Korean Assn. Womens Studies, Royal Asiatic Soc. Korean Br. Office: San Francisco State U Dept Anthropology 1600 Holloway Ave San Francisco CA 94132-1722 Business E-Mail: soh@sfsu.edu.

SOHN, HONG YONG, chemical and metallurgical engineer, educator; b. Kaesung, Kyunggi-Do, Republic of Korea, Aug. 21, 1941; arrived in U.S., 1966; s. Chong Ku and Soon Deuk (Woo) Sohn; m. Victoria Bee Tuan Ngo, Jan. 8, 1971; children: Berkeley Jihoon, Edward Jihyun. BSChemE, Seoul Nat. U., Republic of Korea), 1962; MSChemE, U. NB, Can., 1966; PhD, U. Calif., Berkeley, 1970. Engr. Cheil Sugar Co., Busan, Republic of Korea, 1962-64; rsch. assoc. SUNY, Buffalo, 1971-73; rsch. engr. DuPont Co., Wilmington, Del., 1973-74; prof. metall. engring., adj. prof. chem. engring. U. Utah, Salt Lake City, 1974—. Cons. Lawrence Livermore Nat. Lab., 1976—, Cabot Corp., 1984—, DuPont Co., 1987—, Utah Power and Light Co., 1987—, H. C. Starck, 1997—. Co-author: (book) Gas-Solid Reactions, 1976; co-editor: Rate Processes of Extractive Metallurgy, 1979, Extractive Metallurgy of Refractory Metals, 1980, Advances in Sulfide Smelting, 2 vols., 1983, Recycle and Secondary Recovery of Metals, 1985, Gas-Solid Reactions in Pyrometallurgy, 1986, Flash Reaction Processes, 1988, Metallurgical Processes for the Year 2000 and Beyond, 1988, Metallurgical Processes for the Early Twenty-First Century, 2 vols., 1994, Proceeding of the Julian Szekely Memorial Symposium on Materials Processing, 1997, Value-Addition Metallurgy, 1998, Sulfide Smelting, 2002, Metallurgical and Materials Processing: Principles and Technologies, 3 vols., 2003; contbr. articles to profl. jours. Recipient Fulbright Disting. lectureship, 1983; Camille and Henry Dreyfus Found. Tchr. scholar, 1977, Japan Soc. Promotion Sci. fellow, 1990. Mem.: AIChE, AIME (James Douglas Gold medal 2001), Korean Inst. Chem. Engrs., Korean Acad. Sci. and Tech. (Fellow award 1998), Minerals, Metals and Materials Soc. (past dir., Extractive Metallurgy Lectr. award 1990, Extraction and Processing Sci. award 1990, champion H. Mathewson Gold medal award 1993, Extraction and Processing Sci. award 1994, 1999, 2007, symposium named in his honor). Achievements include patents for process for treating sulfide-bearing ores, continuous solvent extraction with bottom gas injection. Office: U Utah 135 S 1460 E Rm 412 Salt Lake City UT 84112-0114 Office Phone: 801-581-5491. Business E-Mail: h.y.sohn@utah.edu.

SOHN, SUNG WON, former bank executive; b. 1945; Grad., U. Pitts., Harvard U. Sr. economist Coun. Econ. Advisors, Exec. Office of the Pres.; exec. v.p., chief econ. officer Wells Fargo Banks; pres., CEO Hanmi Fin. Corp., 2005—08. Prof. Pa. State U. Sys. Bd. dirs. LA World Affairs Coun., Children's Bur., Claremont Grad Sch. Named most accurate forcaster for We. U.S., Blue Chip Publications, 2002, most accurate economist in U.S., Wall Street Jour., 2006; named one of five most accurate forcasters in U.S., 2001, 100 most influential Minnesotans of 20th century, The Star Tribune; named to Board of Economists, Time mag., 2001.

SOIFER, AVIAM, dean, law educator; b. Worcester, Mass., Mar. 18, 1948; married; 2 children. BA cum laude, Yale U., 1969, MA in Urban Studies, 1972, JD, 1972. Bar: Conn. 1974, U.S. Dist. Ct. Conn. 1974, U.S. Supreme Ct. 1994. Law clk. to Judge Jon O. Newman U.S. Dist. Ct. Conn., 1972-73; asst. prof. U. Conn. Sch. Law, 1976-77, assoc. prof., 1977-78, prof., 1978-80, Boston U. Sch. Law, 1980—93, 1998—2003; dean Boston Coll. Law Sch., 1993-98, U. Hawaii, Sch. Law, Honolulu, 2003—. Vis. prof. Boston U. Sch. Law, 1979-80; vis. colleague William S. Richardson Sch. Law, 1999-2000. Author: Law the the Company We Keep, 1995 (Alpha Sigma Nu Nat. Jesuit Book Prize, 1998); contbr. articles to profl. jours. Vice chair Supreme Jud. Ct. Mass. Task Force on Jud. Edn., 1996-2001; mem. steering com. 1st Cir. Task Force on Gender, Race and Ethnicity, 1995-99; trustee New Eng. Med. Ctr., 1997-2002, Cambridge Health Alliance, 2002-03. Recipient Disting. Sr. Rsch. award Boston Coll., 2001-02; named Disting. Scholar Legal Studies Inst., U. Wis., 2001-; Harvard Program in Law and Humanities fellow, 1976-77; Kellog Nat. fellow, 1981-84. Mem. ABA (commn. on coll. and univ. legal studies 1996-2000. Office: William S Richardson Sch Law U Hawaii 2515 Dole St Honolulu HI 96822 Office Phone: 808-956-6343. E-mail: soifer@hawaii.edu.

SOIFER, SCOTT JAY, pediatrician; b. 1952; MD, SUNY Upstate Med. Ctr., Syracuse, 1977. Cert. in pediat. 1981, in pediatric cardiology 1981, in pediatric critical care medicine 2002. Residency in pediat. Yale U., New Haven; fellowship in pediatric cardiology U. Calif. Med. Ctr., San Francisco, program and clin. med. dir., pediatric intensive care unit, vice chair clin. affairs, dept. pediat. Contbr. articles to profl. jours. Office: Univ Calif Med Ctr Pediatric Critical Care Medicine 505 Parnassus Ave Box 0106 San Francisco CA 94143 Office Phone: 415-476-5153. Office Fax: 415-476-6083. Business E-Mail: SoiferS@peds.ucsf.edu.

SOKOL, JAN D., lawyer; b. NYC, May 27, 1952; BS magna cum laude, Rutgers U., 1974; JD Northwestern Sch. of Law, Lewis and Clark Coll., 1977. Bar: Oreg. 1978, U.S. Dist. Ct. (dist. Oreg.), U.S. Ct. Appeals (9th cir.) 1981, U.S. Claims Ct. 1982, U.S. Supreme Ct. 1982. Law clerk to Hon. George A. Juba U.S. Dist. Ct. (dist. Oreg.), 1978-79, law clerk to Hon. Gus J. Solomon, 1979-80, law clerk to Hon. James A. Redden, 1980; mng. mem. Stewart, Sokol & Gray, 1994. Case note and comment editor Environmental Law, 1976-77. Mem. ABA (mem. forum com. on the construction industry, fidelity and surety, forest resources com.), Multnomah County.

SOKOL, RONALD JAY, pediatric gastroenterologist, researcher; b. Chgo., July 18, 1950; s. Max Charles and Edith Sokol; m. Lori Lubman, Aug. 20, 1989; children: Skylar Paul, Jared Todd. BS, U. Ill., 1972; MD, U. Chgo., 1976. Diplomate Am. Bd. Pediat., Am. Bd. Pediatric Gastroenterology. Asst. prof. pediat. U. Colo., Denver, 1983—88; assoc. prof. pediat. U. Colo. Sch. Medicine, Denver, 1989—95, prof. pediat., 1995—, vice chair pediat., 1999—. Program dir. Pediatric Gen. Clin. Rsch. Ctr., Denver, 1998—2008, head sect. pediat. gastroenterology, hepatology and nutrition, 2006—; dir. and prin. investigator Colo. Clin. and Translational Scis. Inst., 2008—. Editor: (med. textbook) Liver Disease in Children. Chair children's liver coun. Am. Liver Found., NYC, 1997—2003. Rsch. grantee, NIH, 1985—. Fellow: Am. Acad. Pediat. (nutrition rsch. award 2003); mem.: Am. Pediat. Soc., N. Am. Soc. for Pediat. Gastroenterology, Hepatology and Nutrition (pres. 1996—98), Am. Assn. for Study of Liver Disease, Soc. Pediat. Rsch., Am. Gastroent. Assn. Achievements include patents for antioxidant solution for treatment of cholestatic liver disease and for treatment of non-alcoholic steatohepatitis. Business E-Mail: sokol.ronald@tchden.org.

SOKOLSKY, ROBERT LAWRENCE, journalist; b. Boston, May 18, 1928; s. Henry and Lillian (Gorodetzky) S.; m. Sally-Ann Moss, Aug. 11, 1955; 1 son, Andrew E. AB, Syracuse U., NY, 1950. Reporter Springfield (Mass.) Union, 1950; asst. dir. pub. info. ARC, Syracuse, 1952-54; entertainment editor Syracuse Herald-Jour., 1954-61, Buffalo Courier Express, 1961-72, Phila. Bull., 1972-82; entertainment writer Riverside (Calif.) Press-Enterprise, 1983-2000; syndicated TV columnist Ottaway News Svc., 1988-96, Scripps Howard, 1996-2000; freelance writer, radio commentator pub. radio, 2000—; columnist San Bernardino Sun, 2001—08; entertainment editor Inland Empire News Radio, 2001—; feature writer instantriverside.com, 2005—. Radio show host; freelance writer; guest lectr. Contbr. columns in newspapers, 2001, articles to profl. jours. Bd. dirs. Brush Hollow Civic Assn., Evesham Twp., N.J. Served with U.S. Army, 1950-52. Recipient Sigma Delta Chi award for feature writing, 1950, award for entertainment coverage Twin Counties Press Club, 1984, 87, Lifetime Achievement award Inland Theatre League, 2001. Mem. Am. Newspaper Guild (Page One award for opinion writing), Syracuse Press Club, Greater Buffalo Press Assn., TV Critics Assn., Soc. Profl. Journalists (Excellence in Journalism award 1989, 93), Pen and Pencil Club of Phila., Variety Club. Republican. Jewish. Home and Office: 3080 Saratoga St Riverside CA 92503-5435 Office Phone: 951-785-0798. E-mail: rsokolsky@charter.net.

SOLA, JURE, electronics executive; BSEE, San Jose State U., 1972. Various mgmt. positions Lika Corp., Stockton, Calif., 1972-80; co-founder, held various mgmt. positions Sanmina Corp. and predecessor, 1980—, pres. & chmn., 1991—2001; co-chmn. Sanmina-SCI, 1999—2002, CEO, 2001—, chmn., 2002—. Recipient Ernst & Young Master Entrepreneur of Yr. award, 2004. Office: Sanmina SCI Corp 2700 N 1st St San Jose CA 95134-2015

SOLANO, JUDITH ANNE, state legislator; m. Manuel Solano; 2 children; 2 stepchildren. BS in Edn., Kans. State Tchrs. Coll., 1971; MEd, U. Colo., Denver, 1992. Pub. sch. tchr. Bailey, Erie Pub. Schs.; former co-owner Artes Solano; mem. Dist. 31 Colo. House of Reps., Denver, 2004—. Vol. Meals on Wheels; mem. Adams County Democratic Party; bd. mem. After Sch. Network. Recipient Achievement award, Erie Police Dept., Commitment to Children award, Colo. Assn. the Edn. Young Children, 2006, Working Families Legislator of Yr. award, AFL-CIO, 2006, Legislator of Yr. award, United Veterans Com., 2006, Colo. Humane Voters League, 2006, Rocky Mountain Farmers Union, 2007, The Colorado Recyclers, 2008, Friend of Gifted award, Colo. Assn. Gifted and Talented, 2007, Honorary award, Colo. Solar Energies Industries Assn., 2008. Mem.: NEA, Colo. Edn. Assn., Colorado Environ. Coalition, Sierra Club Rocky Mt. Chpt. Democrat. Mailing: Colo State Capitol 200 E Colfax Denver CO 80203 Office Phone: 303-866-2918. E-mail: judy.solano.house@state.co.us.*

SOLIMON, RONALD JAMES (RON SOLIMAN), museum administrator; m. Elaine Solimon; children: Kristin, Justin. BBA, N.Mex State U., 1973; JD, U. N.Mex Law Sch., 1976. Pres., CEO Indian Pueblo Cultural Ctr., Albuquerque, Indian Pueblos Mktg., Inc., Albuquerque. Bd. mem. Nat. Ctr. Am. Indian Enterprise Devel., Walking Shield, N.Mex Workforce Devel. Bd., N.Mex Comm. on Community Volunteerism, Laguna Devel. Corp., Pueblo Tesuque Devel. Corp. Bd. mem. Albuquerque Conv. & Visitors Bur. Mem.: Tourism Assn. N.Mex (bd. mem.). Office: Indian Pueblo Cultural Ctr Inc 2401 12th St NW Albuquerque NM 87104

SOLIS, CARLOS, lawyer; b. Managua, Nicaragua, May 15, 1945; came to US, 1952; s. Carlos and Luisa (Serrano) S. BA, U. San Francisco, 1967, JD, 1969. Bar: Calif. 1970, US Dist. Ct. (cen. and no. dists.) Calif. 1970, US Ct. Appeals (9th cir.) 1970, US Dist. Ct. (ea. dist.) Calif. 1972, US Dist. Ct. (so. dist.) Calif. 1973, US Supreme Ct. 1973. Assoc. Kindel & Anderson, LA, 1969—76, ptnr., 1976—96, Heller Ehrman LLP, 1996—2005; pvt. practice, 2005—. Exec. legal counsel, bd. dirs. internat. student ctr. UCLA, 1976-86, exec. v.p., 1981-86; instr. atty. asst. program UCLA, 1977-79; bd. advisors LA Internat. Trade Devel. Corp., 1981-87; bd. dirs. Pub. Counsel of LA, 2003-05. Assoc. editor U. San Francisco Law Rev., 1968-69; contbr. articles to profl. jours. Bd. dirs. ARC, LA, 1978-93, 95-05, chmn. audit com., 1985-88, bd. advisors, 1993-05; bd. dirs. March of Dimes, LA, 1982-87, LA Pub. Theater Found., 1978-81, Young Musicians Found., 1979-80, Boys and Girls Club East LA, 1986-89; bd. dirs. Am. Diabetes Assn., LA, 1986-93, chmn., 1989-91, bd. dirs. Calif., 1988-93, chmn., 1992-93, mem. nat. minority initiative task force, 1986-92, bd. dirs. Nat., 1993-95; vice chmn. bd. LA United Way, 1982-83, bd. dirs., 1980-03, corp. bd. dirs., 1982-96, treas., 1989-93; pres. LA Open Golf Found., 1979-80. Recipient Alumni Award U. San Francisco, 1969, Province award Phi Delta Phi, 1969. Mem. LA Jr. Chamber (pres., chmn. bd. dirs. 1980-81, Most Improved com. award 1975, Dir. of Yr. award 1977, Outstanding Bus. Leader award 1980), Assocs. LA C. of C., LA Area C. of C. (bd. dirs. 1979-80), U. San Francisco Alumni Assn. (pres. San Gabriel Valley chpt. 1976-80), Latin Am. Ctr. Assocs. (pres. 1980-82, bd. advisors 1980-88), Alpha Sigmu Nu, Phi Delta Phi. Avocation: travel. Home: 201 La Vereda Rd Pasadena CA 91105-1227 Personal E-mail: carlossolis1000@yahoo.com.

SOLIS, OSCAR AZARCON, bishop; b. San Jose City, Philippines, Oct. 13, 1953; arrived in US, 1984; s. Anselmo dela Fuente Solis and Antonio Ortega Azarcon. BST cum laude, U. Santo Tomas, Manila, 1978. Ordained priest Diocese of Cabanatuan, Philippines, 1979; assoc. pastor St. Rocco Ch., Union City, NJ, 1984—98, St. Joseph Co-Cathedral, Thibodaux, La., 1988—92, pastor, 1999—2003, Our Lady of Prompt Succor Ch., Golden Meadow, La., 1993—99, St. Luke Ch., Thibodaux, La., 1999—2003; ordained bishop, 2004; aux. bishop Archdiocese of LA, 2004—, coord. ethnic ministries. Roman Catholic. Achievements include becoming first Filipino-American bishop ordained in the US. Office: Archdiocese of LA 3424 Wilshire Blvd Los Angeles CA 90010-2202 Office Phone: 213-637-7000. E-mail: info@la-archdiocese.org.

SOLLENDER, JOEL DAVID, management consultant, financial executive, accountant; b. NYC, Nov. 11, 1924; s. Samuel and Flora (Blumenthal) S.; m. Dorothy Leaf, Aug. 6, 1958; children: Jeffrey D., Jonathan L. BS, N.Y. U., 1946. CPA N.Y., 1947. Staff auditor Ernst & Young, NYC, 1946-50; with United Mchts. & Mfrs., Inc., NYC, 1950-86, chief acctg. officer, 1976—, corp. contr., 1977—, sr. v.p., 1980—, mem. exec. mgmt. com. also bd. dirs. subsidiary cos.; assoc. dir. N.Y. Hist. Soc., NYC, 1986—89; mem. adv. coun. to Office of Charities Registration Dept. State, N.Y. State, 1988-89; v.p. fin. Piedmont Industries, NYC, 1989-90; exec. v.p., CFO Earthworm Inc., 1990—92; fin. mgmt. cons.; sr. cons. Internat. Exec. Svc. Corps Agy. for Aid for Internat. Devel., Kazakstan, 1996—. Adv. coun. San Diego State U., 1997—; audit com. San Diego Mus. Art, 1997-2002; fin. com. Globe Theater, 2003-04, audit com., 2004—. With US Army, 1943—45, WW II. Decorated Combat Infantry Badge, Purple Heart with oak leaf cluster, Prisoner of War medal, Bronze Star. Mem. AICPA, N.Y. State Soc. CPAs (chief fin. officer com.), Am. Inst. Corp. Contrs., Rancho Bernardo (Calif.) Men's Club, Bailiwick Club (Greenwich, Conn.), Greenhaven Yacht Club (Rye).

SOLLMAN, GEORGE HENRY, venture capitalist; b. Michigan City, Ind., Nov. 2, 1941; s. Henry Charles and Margaret Elisabeth (Gockel) S.; m. Maureen Tosh, July 12, 1968; children: Jennifer, Erich. Spl. student, MIT, 1965—66; BSEE, Northwestern U., 1964; MSEE, Northeastern U., 1967. Engring. dir. Honeywell Info. Systems, Waltham, Mass., 1964—73; product line mgr. Control Data, Hawthorne, Calif., 1973—76; v.p., gen. mgr. Shugart/Xerox, Sunnyvale, 1976—84; spl. ptnr. Sand Hill Venture Group, Menlo Park, 1984; pres., CEO Centigram Corp., San Jose, 1985—97, AtMotion Inc. (now OpenWave Corp.), Redwood City, Calif., 1997—2000, Arabesque Investments LLC, Atherton, Calif., 2000—; chmn. First Virtual Corp., Redwood Shores, Calif., 2004—, Corticon Techs., San Mateo, Calif., 2000—. Bd. dirs. T-Ventures, Venture Capital arm of Deutsche Telecom, Bonn, Germany, 2001-; chmn. nat. bd. dirs. Am. Elec. Assn.; presdl. nomination Semicondr. Tech. Coun.; co-chmn. Alexis d'Toqueville Soc.; mem. adv. coun. Joint Venture Silicon Valley; chmn. adv. bd. Leavey Sch. Bus., Santa Clara U., 2000-. Patentee in field. Co-chmn. United Way of Santa Clara County; mem. steering com. George Lucas Ednl. Found., Marin County. Home: 242 Polhemus Ave Atherton CA 94027-5439 Office: Arabesque Investments LLC 242 Polhemus Ave Atherton CA 94027-5439 Home Phone: 650-364-9164; Office Phone: 650-365-8186. Personal E-mail: george_sollman@hotmail.com.

SOLMER, RICHARD, surgeon; b. South Bend, Ind., Feb. 11, 1947; MD, U. Mich., 1972. Diplomate Am. Bd. Plastic Surgery. Surgical intern Hosp. of the U. Pa., Phila., 1972-73; gen. surgical resident Calif. Hosp. Med. Ctr., LA, 1976-80; plastic surgery resident Allentown (Pa.) Affiliated Hosp., 1980-82; pvt. practice Huntington Beach, and Newport Beach, Calif., 1982—. Fellow Am. Coll. Surgeons; mem. Am. Soc. Plastic Surgeons. Office: 307 Placentia Ave Ste 208 Newport Beach CA 92663-3308 Office Phone: 949-548-0227.

SOLOFF, LAURA J., academic administrator; BA in English, UCLA. Human resources position Broadway Dept. Stores; dir. career planning & placement Fashion Inst. Design & Merchandising, Calif., campus dir. Calif., regional dir. Calif., dir. student financial svcs. Calif.; dir. human resources & adminstrn. Sony Pictures Entertainment, Culver City, Calif.; mem. Edn. Mgmt. Corp., 1998—; pres. Art Inst. Calif.-Orange County, 2000—03, Art Inst. Calif.-LA, 2003—; regional v.p. Edn. Mgmt. Corp., 2004—. Office: Office Pres Art Institute California LA 2900 31st St Santa Monica CA 90405-3035

SOLOMON, DARLENE J.S., electronics executive; BS, Stanford Univ.; PhD, MIT; grad. exec. develop. program, Stanford Univ. Rsch. & mgmt. positions Hewlett-Packard Laboratories, 1984—99; dir. Life Sciences Technologies Lab. & sr. dir. rsch. & develop. tech. life sciences & chem. analysis Agilent Technologies, Palo Alto, Calif., 1999—2003, v.p. Agilent Labs & chief tech. officer, 2003—. Chair. R&D Calif. Blue Ribbon Task Force on Nanotechnology; mem. adv. bd. NSF Nanobiotechnology Ctr., A-STAR Singapore Econ. Develop., Univ. Calif. Davis, Viterbi Sch. Engring. Univ. So. Calif., Joint Venture Tech. Convergence Consortium, Bay Area Sci. & Innovation Consortium. Recipient Tribute to Women and Industry award, YWCA, 2004; named one of Women Worth Watching, Diversity Jour., 2007; named to Women in Tech. Internat. Hall of Fame, 2001. Achievements include patents in field. Office: Agilent Technologies Inc 5301 Stevens Creek Blvd Santa Clara CA 95051-7201

SOLOMON, DAVID HARRIS, geriatrician, educator; b. Cambridge, Mass., Mar. 7, 1923; s. Frank and Rose (Roud) Solomon; m. Ronda L. Markson, June 23, 1946; children: Patti Jean Sinaiko, Nancy Ellen. AB, Brown U., 1944; MD, Harvard U., 1946. Intern Peter Bent Brigham Hosp., Boston, 1946—47, resident, 1947—48, 1950—51; fellow endocrinology New Eng. Center Hosp., Boston, 1951—52; faculty UCLA Sch. Medicine, 1952—, prof. medicine, 1966—93, vice chmn. dept. medicine, 1968—71, chmn. dept., 1971—81, assoc. dir. geriatrics, 1982—89; dir. UCLA Ctr. on Aging, 1991—96; prof. emeritus UCLA, 1993—. Chief med. svc. Harbor Gen. Hosp., Torrance, Calif., 1966—71; cons. Wadsworth VA Hosp., LA, 1952—93, Sepulveda VA Hosp., 1971—93; cons. metabolism tng.

com. USPHS, 1960—64, endocrinology study sect., 1970—73; cons. RAND Corp., 1997—. Editor: Jour. Am. Geriatric Soc., 1988—93; contbr. numerous articles to profl. jours. Recipient Ollie Randall award, Nat. Coun. on the Aging, 2004. Master: ACP (John Phillips Meml. award 2002); mem.: AAAS, Gerontol. Soc. Am. (Freeman award 1997), Am. Geriatrics Soc. (bd. dir. 1985—93, Milo Leavitt award 1992, Disting. Svc. award 1993, Edward Henderson award 1999, David H. Solomon Disting. Svc. award named in his honor), Am. Fedn. Aging Rsch. (Irving S. Wright award 1990), Western Assn. Physicians (councillor 1972—75, pres. 1983—84), Inst. Medicine Nat. Acad. Sci., Am. Thyroid Assn. (pres. 1973—74, Disting. Svc. award 1986), Endocrine Soc. (Robert H. Williams award 1989), We. Soc. Clin. Rsch. (councillor 1963—65, Mayo Soley award 1986), Am. Soc. Clin. Investigation, Assn. Am. Physicians, UCLA Med. Alumni Assn. (Extraordinary Merit award 2002), Assn. Profs. of Medicine (pres. 1980—81), Alpha Omega Alpha, Sigma Xi, Phi Beta Kappa. Achievements include The Parlow-Solomon Chair on Aging named in his honor at UCLA School of Medicine. Home: 3640 Dragonfly Dr Apt 202 Thousand Oaks CA 91360-8445 Home Phone: 310-471-5256; Office Phone: 310-471-5256. Personal E-mail: dsolomon1@earthlink.net.

SOLOMON, EDWARD IRA, chemistry professor, researcher; b. NYC, Oct. 20, 1946; s. Mordecai L. and Sally S. Solomon; m. Darlene Joy Spira, Sept. 15, 1984; children: Mitchell Landau, Paige Elana. BS, Rensselaer Poly. Inst., 1968; PhD, Princeton U., 1972. Rsch. assoc. Princeton U., NJ, 1972-73; postdoctoral fellow H.C. Ørsted Inst., Copenhagen, 1973-74, Calif. Inst. Tech., Pasadena, 1974-75; asst. prof. MIT, Cambridge, Mass., 1975-79, assoc. prof., 1979-81, prof., 1981-82, Stanford U., Calif., 1982-91, Monroe E. Spaght prof. humanities and sci., 1991—, SSRL prof., 2005—. Cons. prof., World Bank lectr. Xiamen U., People's Republic of China, 1984; O.K. Rice lectr. U. NC, 1984, Reilly lectr. U. Notre Dame, 1985; invited prof. U. Paris, 1987; 1st Glen Seaborg lectr. U. Calif., 1990; Frontiers in Chem. Rsch. lectr. Tex. A&M U., 1990; ACS lectr., Argentina, 1992; invited prof. Tokyo Inst. Tech., 1992; Xerox lectr. U. Alta., 1993; lectr. NSC Republic of China, 1993; Leermakers lectr. Wesleyan U., 1994; Amoco lectr. Ind. U., 1995; Kahn lectr. U. N.Mex., 1996, Golden Jubilee invited prof. Tata Inst., India, 1996; Karcher lectr. U. Okla., 1997; Colloquium 3eme Cucle, Switzerland, 1998; FMC lectr. Princeton U., 1998; A.D. Little lectr. MIT, 1998, Nobel Found. lectr. Stockholm U., 2000; invited prof. Tata Inst. Bombay, India, 2000; Crawford lectr. in spectroscopy U. Minn., 2004; McElvain lectr. U. Wis.; Walton lectr. Purdue U., Hill Meml. lectr., Cady lectr., U. Wash.; Kieler Woche lectr., Kiel U., Dawson lectr., U. Ky.; Andreas Albrecht Lectureship, Cornell U., 2009; Proctor & Gamble lecturer, U. Ariz., 2008; Thomas Chemistry Scholar, U. Mo.- Columbia, 2007; Frontiers Lecturer, Tex. A & M U., 2007, Highly Cited rschr.; Inst. Sci. Info., 2005. Assoc. editor Inorganic Chemistry, 1985—; bd. editors Jour. Inorganic Biochemistry, 1991-; mem. editl. bd. Chem. Revs., 1990—, Chemtracts Inorganic Chemistry, 1992-, Chemistry Biology, 1993-94, Jour. Biol. Inorganic Chemistry, 1995-03, Coord. Chem. Revs., 1996-, Indian Jour. Chemistry, 2001-, Ctrl. European Jour. Chemistry, 2003-, Inorganica Chemica Acta, 2005-, Metal Based Drugs, 2006-, Chemistry Ctrl. Jour., 2007-; contbr. articles to profl. jours. including Jour.; numerous other lectureships; Am. Chem. Soc., Inorganic Chemistry, Procs. of NAS, Phys. Rev. Sci. Mem. panels NIH, NSF, Washington; mem. vis. coms. Exxon, U. Calif., Santa Cruz. Recipient Dean award for disting. tchg., 1990, Remsen award Md. ACS and Johns Hopkins U., 1994, NIH Merit award, 1995, G.W. Wheland medal, U. Chgo., 2001, Aldrich Sponsored lectureship, Northwestern, 2001, Frontiers Biol. Chem. award, Max Planck Inst., NIH Merit award, 2002, Centenary medal and lectureship Royal Soc. UK, 2003, Chakravorty award & lectr., Chemical Rsch. Soc. India, 2008, Bailar medal, U. Ill., 2007, Solomon award, Symposium Nat. ACS Meeting, San Diego, 2001, Atlanta, 2006, ACS award, Disting. Svc. Advancement Inorganic Chemistry, 2006, Endicott/Rorabacker Frontiers lecturership, Wayne State U., 2006. Fellow AAAS, NAS, Japan Soc. for Promotion of Sci., Am. Acad. Arts and Scis.; mem. Am. Chem. Soc. (chmn. bioinorganic divsn.), Am. Phys. Soc., Internat. EPR Soc., Soc. Biol. Inorganic Chemistry, Sigma Xi, Open Inorganic Chemistry Jour. (editl. bd. mem. 2007-), Biochemistry (editl. adv. bd. 2008-), Rsch. Letters Inorganic Chemistry (editl. bd. mem. 2008-) Achievements include research in physical-inorganic and bioinorganic chemistry emphasizing application of a wide variety of spectroscopic and computational methods to determine the electronic structure of transition; metal complexes to define in detail electronic structure high symmetry small molecule complexes to define in detail electronic structure contributions to chemical and physical properties, and metal ion; active sites in catalysis to understand their unusual spectral features in terms of electronic and geometric structure and to evaluate these structural contributions to reactivity; fundamental problems in bionorganic chemistry. Office: Stanford U Dept Chemistry Roth Way Stanford CA 94305 Office Phone: 650-723-9104. Business E-Mail: edward.solomon@stanford.edu.

SOLOMON, JACK AVRUM, JR., lawyer, automotive executive, art dealer; b. Omaha, Oct. 25, 1928; s. John A. and Matilda (Bienstok) S.; m. Josephine J. Kleiman, June 1948 (div. Mar. 1971); children: Debra, Alisa, Michael, Rena; m. Carolyn Summers, Dec. 1973. BS, U. Nebr., 1950, LLB cum laude, 1952; LLM (Cook fellow), U. Mich., 1953. Bar: Nebr. 1950, Ill. 1951. Practice law, Chgo., 1950—; with firm Stiefel, Greenberg, Burns, Baldridge & Solomon, 1953-66, ptnr., 1958-66, Solomon, Rosenfeld, Elliot & Stiefel, and predecessor, 1966—, sr. ptnr., 1966—. Bd. dirs. Amco Industries, Inc., Chgo., chmn. bd., 1968-69, sec., gen. counsel, 1969-72; sec. Mogen David Wine Corp., Chgo., 1964-71; chmn. bd. Arts and Leisure Corp., 1969-76; pres., chmn. bd. Circle Fine Art Corp., 1968-94; chmn. bd. dirs. S2 Art Group, Ltd., 1996—, Re Soc., 1997—, Art of the Movies.com, 1999—; pres. Las Vegas Art Dist., 2002-05; mng. dir. C&J Properties LLC, 2005-, Carjack Properties LLC, 2005—; chmn., CEO Jack Gallary, Inc., 2005— Commr. City of Las Vegas Arts Commn., 2005—; pres. temple, 1959—61; bd. dirs. Boulder Plz. Sculpture Park Found. Mem. Ill., Nebr. Bar Assns., Fine Art Pubs. Assn. (pres. 1982—, Lifetime Achievement award, Art Expo and Art Bus. News)), Order of Coif.; Club: Nat. Arts (NYC). Jewish. Home: 2870 Augusta Las Vegas NV 89109 Office: 1 E Charleston Las Vegas NV 89104 Office Phone: 702-868-7880. Personal E-mail: jsolomon@s2art.com.

SOLOMON, JOHN DAVIS, aviation executive; b. Kingfisher, Okla., Oct. 22, 1936; s. Edward Dempsey and Mary Blanche (Smith) S.; m. Mildred Oraline Brammer, July 16, 1968 (div. Mar. 1984); children: Jennifer Leigh, Jason Lewis; m. Sheila Mary McLeod, Nov. 23, 1985. BA, Okla. State U., 1958. Asst. mgr. airport City of Oklahoma City Dept. Aviation, 1963-66, City of Tulsa Airport Authority, 1966-70; dir. aviation City of Oklahoma City., 1970-77, Clark County Dept. Aviation, Las Vegas, Nev., 1977-86; dir. environ. planning Landrum & Brown. Aviation Planners, Cin., 1986-88; dep. dir. aviation City of Houston Airport System, 1988-90; dir. aviation City of Kansas City, Mo., 1990-96; asst. dir. aviation City of Phoenix, 1997—. Editor Airport Mgmt. Jour., 1975; contbr. articles to aviation jours. Mem. Am. Assn. Airport Execs. (bd. dirs., ex-officio, accredited 1965, pres. 1979, Pres.'s award 1975, Disting. Svc. award 1991), Airports Coun. Internat. (bd. dirs. 1985-86), Kappa Sigma. Avocations: art, music, collecting miniatures.

SOLOMON, MARK A., lawyer; b. Cedar Rapids, Iowa, Aug. 30, 1950; BA summa cum laude, Calif. State U., San Jose, 1972; JD magna cum laude, U. Santa Clara, 1975. Bar: Calif. 1975, Nev. 1976. Mem. Lionel Sawyer & Collins, Las Vegas, Nev., 1976—. Mem. ABA, State Bar Calif., State Bar Nev., Clark County Bar Assn. Office: Lionel Sawyer & Collins 1700 Bank Am Plz 300 S 4th St Ste 1700 Las Vegas NV 89101-6053

SOLOMON, RUTH, state legislator, educational association administrator; b. Phila., Apr. 16, 1941; d. David and Bella (Azeff) Epstein; m. Arthur Solomon; 1 child, Barry. BA, U. Ariz., 1971. Tchr. Tucson (Ariz.) Unified Sch. Dist., 1971—; mem. Ariz. Ho. of Reps., Phoenix, 1988-94, Ariz. Senate, Dist. 14, Phoenix, 1994—. Pres. Tucson Edn. Assn., 1983-85; dir. Ariz. Edn. Assn., Phoenix, 1986—. Bd. dirs. Pima County Community Action Agy., Tucson, 1986—, Mayor's Coun. Youth Initiatives, Tucson, 1987—. Mem. Bus. and Profl. Women's Coun., Alpha Delta Kappa, Phi Kappa Phi. Avocation: swimming. Office: Ariz Senate 1700 W Washington St Rm 313 Phoenix AZ 85007-2812

SOLOMON, SUSAN, atmospheric chemist; d. Leonard Marvin and Alice Solomon. BS in Chemistry, Ill. Inst. Tech., 1977; MS in Chemistry, U. Calif., Berkeley, 1979, PhD in Chemistry, 1981; D (hon.), Tulane U., Williams Coll., SUNY at Stony Brook, Ill. Inst. Tech., U. Colo. Sr. scientist aeronomy lab. NOAA, Boulder, Colo., 1981—, program leader middle atmosphere group aeronomy lab., 1988—. Adj. faculty U. Colo., 1982—; head project sci. Nat. Ozone Expdn., McMurdo Station, Antarctica, 1986, McMurdo Station, Antarctica, 87; co-chair Intergovernmental Panel on Climate Change. Co-author: Aeronomy of the Middle Atmosphere, 1984; contbr. articles to sci. jours. Recipient Gold medal, US Dept. Commerce, 1989, Nat. Medal of Sci., 2000, Victor Moritz Goldschmidt Medal, Geochemical Soc., 2006, Arthur S. Flemming award, Common Wealth Trust award, Ozone award, UN Environ. Programme; named Scientist of Yr., 1992, Solomon Glacier and Solomon Saddle in honor of leadership in Antarctic rsch., 1994, CIRES Fellow; named one of The 100 Most Influential People in the World, TIME mag., 2008; named to Women in Tech. Inst. Hall of Fame, 2004, Colo. Women's Hall of Fame, 2006. Fellow: Am. Geophys. Union (J.B. McElwane award 1985), Am. Meteorol. Soc. (Henry G. Houghton award, Carl-Gustaf Rossby award 2000), Royal Meteorol. Soc.; mem.: NAS, European Acad. Scis. (foreign assoc.), French Acad. Scis. (foreign assoc.), US Nat. Acad. Scis., Am. Acad. Arts and Scis. Avocations: creative writing, crafts, scuba diving. Office Phone: 303-497-3483. Business E-Mail: ssolomon@al.noaa.gov.

SOLORIO, JOSE, state legislator; m to Linn; children: two. BA, U. Calid., Irvine; MPA in Pub. Policy, Harvard U. California State Assemblyman, District 69, 2006-; chair, Committee on Public Safety, currently. Democrat. Office: Dist 69 2400 E Katella Ave Anaheim CA 92806 Office Phone: 714-939-8469. Office Fax: 714-939-8986. Business E-Mail: Assemblymember.Solorio@assembly.ca.gov.

SOLTYS, JOHN JOSEPH, lawyer; b. Portsmouth, Va., Feb. 4, 1942; children: John J. III, Amy Elaine. BS, USCG Acad., 1963; JD, Willamette U., 1970. Bar: Wash. 1970, U.S. Dist. Ct. (we. and ea. dists.) Wash. 1970. From assoc. to sr. ptnr. Karr, Tuttle, Seattle, 1970-89; shareholder Cozen, O'Connor, Seattle, 1999—. Writer, spkr. in field of product liability, med. malpractice and toxic torts; editor Wash. State Bar Assn. Motor Vehicle Accident Litig. Deskbook, 2000-01; elected super lawyer Wash. State Lt. (j.g.) USCG, 1963-67. Mem. Wash. Def. Trial Lawyers (pres. 1986-87), Fedn. Def. and Corp. Counsel. Avocations: fishing, hunting, gardening. Office: Cozen O'Connor 1201 3rd Ave Ste 5200 Seattle WA 98101-3071 Home Phone: 425-883-2322; Office Phone: 206-340-1000. Business E-Mail: jsoltys@cozen.com.

SOMASEGAR, SIVARAMA KICHENANE, computer software company executive; b. 1965; m. Akila Somasegar; children: Sahana, Archana. BSEE, Anna U., India; MS in Computer Engring., La. State U.; PhD (hon.), Anna U., India, 2006. From software design engr. to v.p. Microsoft Corp., Redmond, Wash., 1989—2000, v.p. Windows engring. solutions & svc. group, 2000—04, corp. v.p. developer divsn., 2004—08, sr. v.p. developer divsn., 2008—; dir. Microsoft India Devel. Ctr., Hyderabad, 1998—, Microsoft Can. Devel. Ctr., Vancouver. Recipient Asian Am. Engr. of Yr. award, Chinese Inst. Engrs., USA, 2008. Office: One Microsoft Way Redmond WA 98052-6399

SOMERMAN, MARTHA J., dean, dental educator; m. Norm Schiff. DDS, NYU, 1975; PhD, U. Rochester, 1980. Diplomate Am. Acad. Periodontology. Asst. prof., periodontics and pharmacology Balt. Coll. Dental Surgery, 1984—87, assoc. prof., pharmacology, 1987—91; William K. and Mary Anne Najjar prof., dept. periodontics, prevention and periodontics U. Mich. Sch. Dentistry, 1991—2002, chair dept. periodontics, prevention and geriatrics, 1991—2001, assoc. dean rsch., 2001—02; assoc. prof., pharmacology U. Mich. Med. Sch., 1991—95, prof., pharmacology, 1995—2002; dean U. Wash. Sch. Dentistry, 2002—. Adv. coun. mem. Nat. Inst. of Dental and Craniofacial Rsch. Contbr. articles to profl. jours. Recipient Rsch in Oral Biology Award, Internat. Assn. Dental Rsch., 2005. Fellow: AAAS; mem.: Am. Assn. Dental Rsch. (past pres.). Office: RM D-322 Box 356365 Seattle WA 98195 Office Phone: 206-543-5982. Office Fax: 206-616-2612. Business E-Mail: somerman@u.washington.edu.

SOMERO, GEORGE NICHOLLS, biology educator; b. Duluth, Minn., July 30, 1940; s. George Theodore and Mary Elizabeth (Nicholls) S.; m. Amyelia Anderson, July 2, 1988. BS, Carleton Coll., Northfield, Minn., 1962; PhD, Stanford U., 1967. Postdoctoral fellow U. B.C., Vancouver, 1967-70; asst. prof. Scripps Inst. Oceanography, La Jolla, Calif., 1970-76, assoc. prof., 1976-80, prof., 1980-91; prof. dept. zoology Oreg. State U., 1991-95; David and Lucile Packard chair of Marine Sci. Hopkins Marine Sta., Stanford U., Pacific Grove, Calif., 1995—. Co-author: Biochemical Adaptation, 1974, 84. Endowed chair named in his honor U. Calif., San Diego, 1984, Wayne and Gladys Valley chair of Marine Biology, Oreg. State U. Fellow AAAS; mem. NAS. Home: 25010 Outlook Dr Carmel CA 93923-8960 Office: Hopkins Marine Sta Pacific Grove CA 93950

SOMERVILLE, CHRISTOPHER ROLAND, biochemist, educator; b. Oct. 11, 1947; naturalized, US, 1995; BSc in Math., U. Alta., Can., 1974, MSc in Genetics, 1976, PhD in Genetics, 1978; DSc (hon.), Queen's U., 1993, U. Alta., 1997, Wageningen U., 1998. Rsch. assoc. dept. agronomy U. Ill., 1978—81; asst. prof. dept. genetics U. Alta., 1981; assoc. prof. dept. botany and plant pathology Mich. State U., 1982-86, prof., 1986—93; prof. dept. biol. scis. Stanford U., Calif., 1994—2008; dir. dept. plant biology Carnegie Instn. Washington, Stanford, Calif., 1994—2008; dir. Energy Bioscis. Inst., Uc Berkeley, Calif., 2007—, prof., 2007—. Panel mem. fed. support for soybean rsch. USDA-ARS, 1981; mem. adv. bd. molecular genetics Mass. Gen. Hosp., 1989—92; mem. plant adv. group Cold Spring Harbor Lab., 1990; mem. adv. bd. The Inst. Genomic Rsch., 1992—, Noble Found., 1993—97, Danforth Ctr., 1999—2001; mem. bd. agr. NRC, 1994—96; mem. vis. com. Swedish Found. for Strategic Rsch., 1995, Cornell U. Plant Biology, 1998; mem. President's Adv. Panel on Plant Biodiversity, 1997—98, Alta. Heritage Found., 2000—04; vis. prof. U. Glasgow, 1998—2006; mem. sci. adv. bd. Wellcome Trust, 1999—2001; mem. adv. com. life scis. Cornell U., 2001—04; mem. adv. com. U. Wis. Structural Biology Ctr., 2001—04; CEO Mendel Biotech., 2002—07. Contbr. articles to sci. jours.; mem. editl. com.: Photosynthesis Rsch., 1984—87, Plant Physiology, 1985—91, Development, 1986—93, Archives Biochemistry and Biophysics, 1986—2003, Devel. Genetics, 1989—91; editor: The Plant Jour., 1990—94; co-editor: Biochemistry and Molecular Biology of Membrane and Storage Lipids of Plants, 1993, Arabidopsis, 1994, The Arabidopsis Book, 2002; assoc. editor: Ann. Rev. Plant Physiology and Plant Molecular Biology, 1993—97, The Plant Cell, 1995—2000, mem. editl. bd.: Current Biology, 1996—97, Procs. NAS, 1997—2000, mem. bd. reviewing editors: Science, 1996—2007, mem. sr. editl. com.:, 2001—; editor: Current Opinion in Plant Sci., 1997—2000. Recipient Young Presdl. Investigator award, NSF, 1984, Humboldt Sr. Rsch. award, 1992, Kuhmo award, 2001, Mendel medal, Genetics Soc., 2004, Balzan award, 2006. Fellow: AAAS, Royal Soc. London, Royal Soc. Can.; mem.: Internat. Soc. Plant Molecular Biology, Academia Europaea, NAS (bd. mem. 1993—97), Am. Soc. Plant Physiologists (mem. publ. com. 1989—91, Gibbs medal 1993, Schull award 1987). Business E-Mail: crs@berkeley.edu.

SOMERVILLE, MASON HAROLD, mechanical engineering educator, university dean; b. Worcester, Mass., Dec. 21, 1941; s. Harold Mervin and Eleanor Ruth (Archibald) S.; children: Mark, Matthew, Meredith, Michael, Michelle. BSM.E., Worcester Polytech. Inst., 1964; MSM.E., Northeastern U., 1966; PhD in Mech. Engring., Pa. State U., 1971. Profl. engr., N.D., Ark., Tex. Grad. teaching asst Northeastern U., Boston, 1964-66; engr. Norton Co., Worcester, Mass., 1965; instr. mech. engring. dept. Pa. State U., State College, 1966-71; sr. engr. Bettis Atomic Power Lab., West Mifflin, Pa., 1971-73; prof., dir. Engring. Expt. Sta., U. N.D., Grand Forks, 1973-80; prof., head mech. engring dept. U. Ark., Fayettesville, 1980-84; prof., dean engring. Tex. Tech U., Lubbock, TX, 1984-94; dean engring. No. Ariz. U., Flagstaff, 1994—, interim provost, 1999—. Cons. Natural Gas Pipeline, Chgo., 1974-79, Archtl. Alliance, Mpls., 1978-80; bd. dirs. Mid-Am. Solar Energy Corp., Mpls., 1978-80, Ctr. for Advanced Engring and Rsch., TTU/HSC Rsch. Found.; chmn. bd. dirs. N.D. Energy Assn., 1979-80; energy advisor State of N.D., 1978-80; mem. ABET/EAC Commn., 1987-92; speaker to pub. service groups Author: Coal Gasification Environmental Impact, Analysis of U.S. Weather, 1980; numerous tech. papers. Mem. Lubbock Bd. City Devel., 1985-87 Recipient Ralph R. Teetor award Soc. Automotive Engrs., 1974, Haliburton award; rsch. grantee. Mem. ASME, ASHRAE, Am. Soc. Engring. Edn., Sigma Xi, Pi Tau Sigma. Republican. Episcopalian. Home: # 300-285 2700 Woodlands Village Blvd Flagstaff AZ 86001-7127 Office: Northern Arizona U Coll Engring & Tech PO Box 15600 Flagstaff AZ 86011-0001

SOMERVILLE, RICHARD CHAPIN JAMES, atmospheric scientist, educator; b. Washington, May 30, 1941; s. James William and Mollie (Dorf) S.; m. Sylvia Francisca Bal, Sept. 17, 1965; children: Anatol Leon, Alexander Chapin. BS in Meteorology, Pa. State U., 1961; PhD in Meteorology, NYU, 1966. Postdoctoral fellow Nat. Ctr. Atmospheric Rsch., Boulder, Colo., 1966-67; rsch. assoc. geophysical fluid dynamics lab. NOAA, Princeton, NJ, 1967-69; rsch. scientist Courant Inst. Math. Scis., NYC, 1969-71; meteorologist Goddard inst. space studies NASA, NYC, 1971-74; adj. prof. Columbia U., NYU, 1971-74; head numerical weather prediction sect. Nat. Ctr. Atmospheric Rsch., Boulder, 1974-79; prof. meteorology Scripps Inst. Oceanography, U. Calif.-San Diego, La Jolla, 1979—. Author: The Forgiving Air: Understanding Environmental Change, 1996. Fellow: AAAS, Am. Meteorol. Soc.; mem.: Am. Geophys. Union. Office: U Calif San Diego Scripps Inst Oceanography 9500 Gilman Dr Dept 0224 La Jolla CA 92093-0224

SOMMERS, STEPHEN, film director, producer, scriptwriter; b. Indpls. Motion picture dir., writer, prodr. Writer, dir. Catch Me If You Can, 1989, The Adventures of Huck and Finn, 1993, The Jungle Book, 1994, Deep Rising, 1998, The Mummy, 1999; The Mummy Returns, 2001; writer, prodr. Tom and Huck, 1995, The Scorpion King, 2002; writer, prodr., dir., Van Helsing, 2004; prodr. T.V. movie Oliver Twist, 1997; dir. Terror Eyes, 1989; writer Gunmen, 1994. Office: c/o Jim Wiatt William Morris Agy 151 El Camino Dr Beverly Hills CA 90212

SOMORJAI, GABOR ARPAD, chemist, educator; b. Budapest, Hungary, May 4, 1935; came to US, 1957, naturalized, 1962. s. Charles and Livia (Ormos) S.; m. Judith Kaldor, Sept. 2, 1957; children: Nicole, John. BS, U. Tech. Scis., Budapest, 1956; PhD, U. Calif., Berkeley, 1960; Dr. Honoris Causa (hon.), Tech. U., Budapest, 1989, U. Pierre et Marie Curie, Paris, 1990, U. Libre Brussels, 1992, U. degli de Ferrara, Italy, 1998, Jozsef Attila U., Szeged, Hungary, 1999, Royal Inst. Tech., Stockholm, 2000; D (hon.), U. Manchester, Eng., 2001. Mem. rsch. staff IBM, Yorktown Heights, NY, 1960-64; dir. Surface Sci. and Catalysis Prog. Lawrence Berkeley Lab., Calif., 1964—; mem. faculty dept. chemistry U. Calif., Berkeley, 1964—, assoc. prof., 1967-72, prof., 1972—, Miller prof., 1978, univ. prof., 2002. Unilever prof. dept. chemistry U. Bristol, Eng., 1972; vis. fellow Emmanuel Coll., Cambridge, Eng., 1989; Baker lectr. Cornell U., Ithaca, NY, 1977; edit. bd. mem. Catalysis Reviews J. Am. Chem. Soc., 2004—; hon. fellow Cardiff U., 2006. Author: Principles of Surface Chemistry, 1972, Chemistry in Two Dimensions, 1981, Introduction to Surface Chemistry and Catalysis, 1994; editor-in-chief Catalysis Letters, 1988—; contbr. articles to profl. jours. Recipient Emmett award Am. Catalysis Soc., 1977, Kokes award Johns Hopkins U., 1976, Albert award Precious Metal Inst., 1986, Sr. Disting. Scientist award Alexander von Humboldt Found., 1989, E.W. Mueller award U. Wis., Chem. Pioneer award Am. Inst. Chemists, 1995, Von Hippel award Materials Rsch. Soc., 1997, Wolf prize in chemistry, Wolf Found., Israel, 1998; Guggenheim fellow, 1969; hon. fellow

Cardiff U., 2006Priestlex medal, 2008. Fellow: AAAS, Am. Phys. Soc. (Langmuir award 2007); mem.: NAS (Irving Langmuir prize in Chem. Physics 2007), Catalysis Soc. N.Am., Am. Chem. Soc. (chmn. colloid and surface chemistry 1981, Surface and Colloid Chemistry award 1981, Peter Debye award 1989, Arthur W. Adamson award 1994, Award for creative rsch. in homogeneous and heterogeneous catalysis 2000, Cotton medal 2002, Remsen award 2006, Priestley medal 2008), Hungarian Acad. Scis. (hon. Pauling medal 2000, Nat. Medal of Sci. 2001), Am. Acad. Arts and Scis. Home: 665 San Luis Rd Berkeley CA 94707-1725 Office: U Calif Dept Chemistry D 58 Hildebrand Hl Berkeley CA 94720-0001 E-mail: somorjai@socrates.berkeley.edu.

SONE, HIRO, chef, restaurant owner, writer; b. Ichihasama, Japan; m. Lissa Doumani. Grad., Ecole Technique Hoteliere Tsuji, Osaka, Japan. From dishwasher to sous chef Italian restaurant, Tokyo; from mem. staff to head chef Spago, LA, former sous chef Tokyo; co-owner, chef Terra, St. Helena, Calif., 1988—. Author (with Lissa Doumani): Terra, Cooking from the Heart of the Napa Valley, 2001. Recipient Best Chef Calif. award, James Beard Found., 2003, Outstanding Svc. award (with Lissa Doumani), 2008; nominee Am. Express Best Chef, Calif., 2001. Office: Terra 1345 Railroad Ave Saint Helena CA 94574

SONKIN, DANIEL JAY, marriage and family therapist, writer; Pvt. practice marriage, child, and family counseling, Sausalito, Calif. Lectr. dept. counseling Calif. State U., Sonoma. Author: The Counselor's Guide to Learning to Live Without Violence, Learning to Live Without Violence: A Handbook for Men. Mem.: Calif. Assn. Marriage & Family Therapists (mem. state ethics com.). Office: 1505 Bridgeway Ste 105 Sausalito CA 94965

SONNEBORN, WILLIAM CHARLES, diversified financial services company executive; b. 1970; BA with honors, Georgetown U., Washington. Cons. KPMG Peat Marwick, Washington; various corp. fin. positions Goldman, Sachs & Co., NY, Hong Kong, 1992—98; mng. dir., CFO TCW Group Inc., 1998—2001, COO, 2001—08, pres., 2005—08; CEO The TCW Funds, Inc., 2005—08; CEO, bd. dirs., head asset mgmt. divsn. KKR Fin. Holdings LLC (Kohlberg Kravis Roberts & Co.), San Francisco, 2008—. Bd. dirs. Sompo Japan Asset Mgmt., Tokyo; mem. internat. exec. com. Société Générale Asset Mgmt., S.A., Paris. Trustee St. John's Health Ctr. Found., Santa Monica, Calif.; bd. dirs., mem. exec. com. LA Coun. Boy Scouts of America. Served in Naval ROTC, Washington. Office: KKR Asset Mgmt 555 California St 50th Fl San Francisco CA 94104 Office Phone: 415-315-3620.*

SONNENBERG, JERRY, state legislator; m. Vonnie Constance; children: Ashley, Afton, Joshua, Ryan. Grad. Colo. agr. & rural leadership program, Colorado State U., Ft. Collins. Owner & operator trucking bus.; farm owner; substitute tchr. Sterling Sch. Dist.; part-time tchr. Northeastern Jr. Coll.; precinct chmn. Logan County Rep. Party; mem. Dist. 65 Colo. House of Reps., Denver, 2007—. Umpire & coach of youth, HS and coll. sports. Bd. dirs. Colo. Farm Bur., Colo. Farm Bur. Mutual Ins. Co., Rep. River Water Conservation Dist.; pres. Coloradan's for Water Conservation & Devel., Logan County Farm Bur.; mem. Colo. Water Congress Policy Com., Sterling Sch. Bldg. Accountability Com., Logan County Planning Commn.; chmn. Logan County Right to Farm Com.; music ministry dir. First Christian Ch.; choir dir. Berean Ch. Named Logan County Rep. of Yr., 2005. Mem. NRA, 4H, Colo. Young Farmers, Future Farmers America, Sterling Baseball Orgn. (bd. mem.), Elks Club. Republican. Office: Colo State Capitol 200 E Colfax Denver CO 80203 Office Phone: 303-866-3706. Business E-Mail: jerry.sonnenberg.house@state.co.us.*

SONNENFELD, BARRY, director, cinematographer; b. NYC, Apr. 1, 1953; m. Susan Ringo, 1989; 1 child. Grad., NY U., 1978. Cinematographer (films) In Our Water, 1982, Blood Simple, 1984, Compromising Positions, 1985, Three O'Clock High, 1987, Raising Arizona, 1987, Throw Momma from the Train, 1987, Big, 1988, When Harry Met Sally..., 1989, Miller's Crossing, 1990, Misery, 1990, (TV movies) How to Be a Perfect Person In Just Three Days, 1983, Out of Step, 1984 (Emmy award best cinematography 1984), Double Take, 1985, Welcome Home, Bobby, 1986, Classified Love, 1986; dir. (films) The Addams Family (uncredited cameo appearance), 1991, Addams Family Values (also actor), 1993, Get Shorty, 1995 (also exec. prodr., actor), Men In Black, 1997, Maximum Bob (TV series, also exec. prodr.), 1998, Wild Wild West, 1999 (also prodr.), Chippendales, 2000, Men In Black II, 2002 (also actor), R.V., 2006; dir., co-prodr.: For Love or Money, 1993; exec. prodr.: (films) Out of Sight, 1998, Lemony Snicket's A Series of Unfortunate Events, 2004, (TV Series) Fantasy Island, 1998, Pushing Daisies (also dir.)(Outstanding Directorial Achievement in Comedy Series for 2007, Directors Guild Am., 2008, Primetime Emmy for Outstanding Directing for a Comedy Series, Acad. TV Arts and Scis., 2008), (TV) Partners, 1999; prodr. (TV Series) Secret Agent Man, 2000 (also creator), The Tick, 2001 (also dir.), Karen Sisco, 2003, (film) The Crew, 2000, Big Trouble, 2002 (also dir.), Ladykillers, 2004. also: United Talent Agency 9560 Wilshire Blvd Fl 5 Beverly Hills CA 90212-2401

SONNENSCHEIN, RALPH ROBERT, physiologist; b. Chgo., Aug. 14, 1923; s. Robert and Flora (Kieferstein) S.; m. Patricia W. Niddrie, June 21, 1952; children— David, Lisa, Ann. Student, Swarthmore Coll., 1940—42, U. Chgo., 1942—43; BS, Northwestern U., 1943, BM, MS, Northwestern U., 1946, MD, 1947; PhD, U. Ill., 1950. Research asst. in physiology Northwestern U. Med. Sch., 1944-46; intern Michael Reese Hosp., Chgo., 1946-47; successively research fellow clin. sci., research asst. psychiatry, research asso. psychiatry U. Ill. Med. Sch., Chgo., 1947-51; mem. faculty U. Calif. Med. Sch., Los Angeles, 1951-88, prof. physiology, 1962-88, prof. emeritus, 1988—; liaison scientist Office Naval Research, London, 1971-72. Author papers on pain, innervation of skin, peripheral circulation. Served with AUS, 1943-46. Spl. research fellow USPHS, 1957-58; fellow Swedish Med. Research Council, 1964-65; grantee USAF; grantee Office Naval Research; grantee NIH; grantee NSF. Mem. Am. Physiol. Soc., Microcirculatory Soc., Soc. Exptl. Biology and Medicine, AAAS, Hungarian Physiol. Soc. (hon.). Home: 18212 Kingsport Dr Malibu CA 90265-5636 Office: U Calif Sch Medicine Dept Physiology Los Angeles CA 90095-1751

SONNIER, PATRICIA BENNETT, business management educator; b. Park River, ND, Mar. 25, 1935; d. Benjamin Beekman Bennett and Alice Catherine (Peerboom) Bennett Brenckinridge; m. William McGregor Castellini (dec.); m. Cecil Sherwood Sonnier (dec.); m. Joseph N. Pagano; children: Bruce Bennett Wells (Nabil Subhani), Barbara Lea Ragland. AA, Allan Handcock Coll., Santa Maria, Calif., 1964; BS magna cum laude, U. Great Falls, 1966; MS, U. N.D., 1967, PhD, 1971. Fiscal acct. USIA, Washington, 1954-56; pub. acct. Bremerton, Wash., 1956; statistician USN, Bremerton, Wash., 1957-59; med. svcs. accounts officer USAF, Vandenberg AFB, Calif., 1962-64; instr. bus. adminstrn. Western New Eng. U., 1967—69; vis. prof. econs. Chapman Coll., 1970; vis. prof. U. So. Calif. Sys., Griffith AFB, NY, 1971-72; assoc. prof., dir. adminstrv. mgmt. program Va. State U., 1973-74; assoc. prof. bus. adminstrn. Oreg. State U., Corvallis, 1974-81, prof. mgmt., 1982-90, emeritus prof. mgmt., 1990—, univ. curriculum coord., 1984-86, dir. adminstrv. mgmt. program, 1974-81, pres. Faculty Senate, 1981. Mem. Interinstl. Faculty Senate, 1986-90, pres., 1989-90; exec. dir. Bus. Enterprise Ctr., 1990-92, Enterprise Ctr. LA, Inc., 1992-95; commr. Lafayette Econ. Devel. Authority, 1994-2000, treas., 1995-96, vice chmn., 1996-97, chmn., 1997-98, past chmn., 1998-99, sec., chmn. bldg. com., 1999-2000; cons. process tech. devel. Digital Equipment Corp., 1981. Pres., chmn. bd. dirs. Adminstrv. Orgnl. Svcs., Inc., Corvallis, 1976—83, Dynamic Achivement, Inc., 1983—92; cons. Oregonians in Action, 1990—91, sec., 1999, 2000; cert. adminstrv. mng. pres. TYEE Mobile Home Park, Inc., 1987—92; mem. Leadership LA, 1986; del various convs.; mem. parish coun. St. Patrick's Cath. Ch., 1998—2000, Risen Savior Ch., 2005—06. Fellow: Assn. Bus. Comm. (internat. bd. 1980—86, v.p. Northwest 1981, 2d v.p. 1982—83, 1st v.p. 1983—84, pres. 1984—85); mem.: AAUP (chpt. sec. 1973, chpt. bd. dirs. 1982, pres. Oreg. conf. 1983—85, chpt. bd. dirs. 1984—89, pres. chpt. 1985—86), Corvallis Area C. of C. (v.p. chamber devel. 1987—88, pres. 1988—89, chair bd. 1989—90, Pres.'s award 1986), La. Bus. Incubation Assn. (sec.-treas. 1993—95), Nat. Assn. Tchr. Edn. for Bus. Office Edn. (pres. 1976—77, chair pub. rels. com. 1978—81), Better Bus. Bur. (sec. 1994, treas. 1995, vice-chair 1996, chair 1997, past chair 1998, sec. 1999, chair nominating com. 1999, chair pub. rels., Lafayette Blue Ribbon 1999—2000), Nat. Bus. Edn. Assn., Associated Oreg. Faculties, Am. Vocat. Assn. (nominating com. 1976), Adminstrv. Mgmt. Soc., Assn. Info. Sys. Profls. (chpt. v.p. 1977, chpt. pres. 1978—81), Am. Bus. Women's Assn. (chpt. v.p. 1979, pres. 1980, Top Businesswoman in Nation 1980, Bus. Assoc. of Yr. 1986), Albuquerque Federated Rep. Women (hospitality chair 2003—04, 1st v.p. 2004—), Acadiana Rep. Women (gen. chmn. La. Fedn. Rep. Women's Clubs State Conv. 1997, 1st v.p. 1997—98, pres. 1998—2000, asst. state CAP chmn. 1999—2000, Ahrens for Gov. Com. 2002), Rotary (co-chmn. fundraiser com. 2002), Boys and Girls Club of Corvallis (pres. 1991—92), Lafayette Rotary (cmty. svc. dir. 1993—94, bd. dirs. 1993—2000, treas. 1995—96, sec. 1996—97, v.p. 1997—98, pres. 1998—99, Dist. 6200 Found. award 2000), Rotary of Albuquerque del Norte (silent auction chair 2001—02, dep. dir. internat. svc. com. 2002, dist. 5520 dep. dir. permanent fund, asst. gov. 2003—04, dist. 5520 found. chair 2003—06, dist. 5520 internat. chmn. 2004—06, chmn. Shrimp Fiesta 2005, Dist. 5520 Found. award 2003, 2004, Dist. 5520 Svc. Above Self award 2004—05, Dist. 5520 Found. award 2005, Dist. 5520 Svc. Above Self award 2005—06, Rotarian of Yr. 2006—07, 25 Yr. Perfect Attendance award), Sigma Kappa. Home and Office: Landing at Newport 890 SE Bay Blvd #213 Newport OR 97365

SONNTAG, BERNARD H., agronomist, researcher, public information officer; b. Goodsoil, Sask., Can., June 27, 1940; s. Henry R. and Annie (Heesing) S.; m. Mary L. Ortman, Aug. 10, 1963; children: Calvin, Galen, Courtney Anne. BSA, Sask. U., Saskatoon, 1962, MSc, 1965; PhD, Purdue U., 1971. Economist Agriculture Can., Saskatoon, 1962-66; cons. D.W. Carr & Assoc., Ottawa, Ont., Canada, 1966-68; economist Agriculture Can., Lethbridge, Alta., 1968-79, Saskatoon, 1979-80, dir. rsch. sta. Brandon, Man., 1980-86, Swiftcurrent, Sask., 1986-89, Lethbridge, 1989-95; dir. gen. Prairie Farm Rehab. Adminstrn., Regina, Sask., Canada, 1996-01; pres. Sonntag Agrl. Svcs., Saskatoon, Sask., Canada, 2001—. Pres. Man. Inst. Agrologists, Brandon, 1984. Recipient Leadership award Bell Can., 1993; named Disting. Agrologist, Alta. Inst. Agrologists, 1995. Fellow Agrl. Inst. Can.; mem. Rotary. Roman Catholic.

SONSINI, LARRY W., lawyer; b. Rome, NY, Feb. 5, 1941; AB, U. Calif., Berkeley, 1963, LLB, 1966; PhD (hon.), Pacific Grad. Sch.of Psychology. Bar: Calif. 1966. Assoc. McCloskey Wilson & Mosher, Palo Alto, 1966—73, ptnr., 1973—78; mng. ptnr., chmn. CEO Wilson, Sonsini, Goodrich & Rosati, Palo Alto, 1978—; prof. securities regulation Boalt Hall Sch. law U. Calif., Berkeley, 1985—. Bd. dirs. NY Stock Exchange (NYSE), 2001—03, Silicon Valley Bancshares, 2003—, Brocade Communications Systems, Inc., Echelon Corp., LSI Logic Corp., Lattice Semiconductor Corp., Pixar, Inc., Tesla Motors, Inc., 2008—; chmn. Regulation, Enforcement and Listing Standards Com., Legal Adv. Com., 2003—. Trustee Santa Clara U. Recipient Spl. Achievement Award in Commerce and Law, Nat. Italian Am. Found. (NIAF), 2003, Cmty. Svc. Award exemplary leadership, Nat. Conf. Cmty. & Justice, 1993, Visionary Award, Software Devel. Forum, 2000, Dir.'s Award, San Francisco Exploratorium, Boalt Hall Sch. of Law Citation Award, U. Calif., Berkeley, Bus. Hall of Fame Award, Bay Area Coun.; named Bus. Leader of the Yr., Harvard Bus. Sch. Assn. of No. Calif., 2005; named one of Top Ten Lawyers in Bay Area, San Francisco Chronicle, 2003, 100 Most Influential Lawyers, Nat. Law Jour., 2006. Mem.: ABA (com. on fed. regulation securities, subcom. on registration statements), Am. Acad. Arts and Scis., Am. Law Inst. Office: Wilson Sonsini Goodrich & Rosati 650 Page Mill Rd Palo Alto CA 94304-1050 Office Phone: 650-493-9300. Office Fax: 650-493-6811. E-mail: lsonsini@wsgr.com.

SONTAG, FREDERICK EARL, philosophy educator; b. Long Beach, Calif., Oct. 2, 1924; s. M. Burnett and Cornelia (Nicholson) S.; m. Carol Furth, June 10, 1950; children: Grant Furth, Anne Burnett Karch. BA with great distinction, Stanford U., Calif., 1949; MA, Yale U., New Haven, Conn., 1951, PhD, 1952; LLD (hon.), Coll. Idaho, 1971. Instr. Yale U., 1951-52; asst. prof. philosophy Pomona Coll., Claremont, Calif., 1952-55, assoc. prof., 1955-60, prof., 1970—, Robert C. Denison prof. philosophy, 1972—, chmn. dept. philosophy, 1960-67, 76-77, 1980-84; chmn. coord. com. in philosophy Claremont Grad. Sch. and Univ. Ctr., 1962-65. Vis. prof. Union Theol. Sem., NYC, 1959-60, Collegio de Sant' Anselmo, Rome, 1966-67, U. Copenhagen, 1972; theologian-in-residence Am. Ch. in Paris, 1973; fulbright regional vis. prof., India, East Asia, Pacific areas, 1977-78; nat. adv. coun. Kent Fellowship Program of Danforth Found., 1963-66. Author Divine Perfection, 1962, The Future of Theology, 1966, The Existentialist Prolegomena, 1969, The Crisis of Faith, 1969, The God of Evil, 1970, God, Why Did You Do That, 1970, Problems Metaphysics, 1970, How Philosophy Shapes Theology, 1971, and other numerous books, the most recent being; Love Beyond Pain: Mysticism Within Christianity, 1977, Sun Myung Moon and the Unification Church, 1977, also German, Japanese and Korean transl.; (with John K. Roth) God and America's Future, 1977, What Can God Do?, 1979, A Kierkegaard Handbook, 1979, The Elements of Philosophy, 1984, (with John K. Roth) The Questions of Philosophy, 1988, Emotion, 1989, The Return of the Gods, 1989, Willgenstein and the Mystical, 1995, Uncertain Truth, 1995, The Descent of Women, 1997, The Acts of the Trinity, 1997, Truth and Imagination, 1998, 2001; A Spiritual Odyssey, 2001, The Mysterious Presence, 2002, A Kierkegaard Handbook, 2003, American Life, 2006. Pres. bd. dirs. Claremont Family Svc., 1960-64; trustee The Coro Found., LA and San Francisco, 1967-71; bd. dirs., chmn. ways and means com. Pilgrim Place, Claremont, 1970-77. With AUS, 1943-46. Vis. scholar Ctr. for Study Japanese Religions, Kyoto, Japan, spring 1974; vis. fellow East-West Ctr., Honolulu, summer 1974; Wig Disting. prof. award, 1970, 76. Mem.: Am. Philos. Assn., Metaphys. Soc. Am., Soc. on Religion in Higher Edn. (Kent fellow 1950—52), Am. Acad. Religion, Phi Beta Kappa. United Ch. Of Christ. Office: Pomona Coll 551 N College Ave Claremont CA 91711-4410 Business E-Mail: f.sontag@pomona.edu.

SOODIK, LYNN, lawyer; b. Pitts., Aug. 6, 1956; BS with distinction, Pa. State U., 1978; student, Durham U., Eng.; JD, U. Calif. Hastings Coll. Law, San Francisco, 1982. Bar: Calif. 1982, cert.: State Bar Calif. Bd. Legal Specialization (family law) 1988. Prin. Law Offices of Lynn Soodik, P.C., Santa Monica, Calif. Instr., mentor Harriet Buhai Ctr. Family Law, 1990—93. Assoc. articles editor: COMM/ENT, A Jour. of Comm. and Entertainment Law, 1980—82; contbr. articles to profl. jours. Mem.: Beverly Hills Bar Assn., LA County Bar Assn. (sec. 1995—96, vice chair 1996—97, chair-elect 1997—98, chair family law sect. 1998—99, mem. exec. com. 1986—99). Office: Law Offices of Lynn Soodik 233 Wilshire Blvd Ste 525 Santa Monica CA 90401-1205 Office Phone: 310-393-8000. Office Fax: 310-394-8182. E-mail: info@lynnsoodik.com.

SOPP, MARK W., corporate financial executive; B in acctg., New Mex. State Univ., 1987. CPA. CPA Arthur Andersen & Co., 1987—90; sr. acct. through dir. & internat. controller Taylor Made Gold Co., 1990—98; dir. fin. & bus. ops. Titan Systems Corp., 1998—99, v.p. fin. & bus. ops., 1999—2001; sr. v.p., CFO, treas. Titan Corp., 2001—05; exec. v.p., CFO Sci. Applications Internat. Corp., San Diego, 2005—. Office: SAIC 10260 Campus Point Dr San Diego CA 92121

SORBY, DONALD LLOYD, retired dean; b. Fremont, Nebr., Aug. 12, 1933; s. Lloyd A. and Orpha M. (Simmons) S.; m. Jacquelyn J. Burchard, Nov. 7, 1959; children: Thomas, Sharon. BS in Pharmacy, U. Nebr., 1955; MS, U. Wash., 1958, PhD, 1960. Dir. pharm. services U. Calif., San Francisco, 1970-72; chmn. dept. pharmacy practice Sch. Pharmacy, U. Wash., Seattle, 1972-74; dean Sch. of Pharmacy, U. Mo., Kansas City, 1974-84, Sch. of Pharmacy, U. Pacific, Stockton, Calif., 1984-95, dean emeritus, 1995—. Contbr. articles to profl. jours. Named Disting. Alumnus, U. Nebr. Coll. Pharmacy, 2000. Am. Assn. Colls. of Pharmacy (pres. 1980-81), Calif. Pharm. Assn., Calif. Soc. Health-Sys. Pharmacists, Sigma Xi, Phi Kappa Phi, Rho Chi. Home: 4362 Yacht Harbor Dr Stockton CA 95204-1126 Business E-Mail: donsorby@sbcglobal.net.

SORDELLO, STEVE, communications executive; b. 1970; BA in Fin. and Mgmt., Santa Clara U., MBA. Cert. Mgmt. Acct. Various positions in finance and acctg. Syntex Corp., Palo Alto, Calif.; sr. dir., fin. planning Adobe Systems, Inc.; joined Ask Jeeves, Inc., Oakland, Calif., 1999, dir., fin. planning and analysis, 1999—2000, v.p. fin. planning and analysis, 2000, acting CFO, 2000—01, exec. v.p., CFO, 2001—05; CFO TiVo Inc., 2006—. Office: TiVo Inc PO Box 2160 Alviso CA 95002-2160 Office Phone: 510-985-7400. Office Fax: 510-985-7412.

SOREGAROLI, A(RTHUR) E(ARL), mining executive, geologist; b. Jan. 4, 1933; arrived in Can., 1962; s. Arthur Samuel and Margaret Alice S.; m. Rosalie Ann Lawrick, Dec. 22, 1962; children: Carla Jean, Brian Arthur. BSc in Geology, Iowa State U., 1959; MSc in Geology, U. Idaho, 1961; PhD in Geology, U. B.C., Vancouver, Can., 1968. Geologist Idaho Bur. Mines and Geology, Moscow, 1961-62, Noranda Exploration Co. Ltd., Vancouver, 1963-68, chief geologist western dist., 1968-72; asst. prof. geology U. B.C., Vancouver, 1972-74; rsch. scientist Geol. Survey Can., Ottawa, Ont., 1974-76; v.p. exploration Westmin Resources Ltd., Vancouver, 1976-90; chief geoscientist Teck Corp., Vancouver, 1990-98; pres. AES Enterprises, Ltd., Vancouver, 1998—. Dir. Mineral. Record, 1995—, pres., 1999—2001. Contbr. scientific papers to profl. jours. Pres. Britannia Beach Hist. Soc. which operates BC Mus. Mining, 1995-03; dir. Pacific Mineral Mus. Soc., 1998-04. With US Army, 1952-54. Fellow Geol. Assn. Can. (Duncan R. Derry Gold medal 1997), Soc. Econ. Geologists (pres. 1985), Geol. Soc. Am.; mem. Prospector and Developers Assn. Can. (life), Assn. Exploration Geochemists (pres. 1989-90), Can. Inst. Mining and Metallurgy (chmn. geology divsn. 1978, Dist. Proficiency Gold medal 1986, Julian Boldly Meml. award 1989, hon. fellow 1990, v.p. Dist. 6 1982-84, Disting. Svc. medal 1991, A.O. Dufresne award 2000, life 2005-), Mineral Assn. Can., Friends of Mineralogy (dir. 1997-00, 03—), Assn. for Mineral Exploration BC (life, Frank Woodside Disting. Svc. award 2004). Avocations: sports, mineral collecting.

SOREN, DAVID, archaeologist, educator, writer, filmmaker; b. Phila., Oct. 7, 1946; s. Harry Friedman and Erma Elizabeth (Salamon) Soren; m. Noelle Louise Schattyn, Dec. 22, 1967. BA, Dartmouth Coll., 1968; MA, Harvard U., 1972, PhD, 1973. Cert. Rome Classics Ctr. Curator of coins Fogg Art Mus., Cambridge, Mass., 1972; asst. prof. U. Mo., Columbia, 1972-76, assoc. prof., dept. head, 1976-81; prof. U. Ariz., Tucson, 1982-97, Regents prof., 1997—, dept. head, 1984-89. Guest curator Am. Mus. Natural History, NYC, 1983—90, lectr, 1993—; creator, dir. Kourion Excavations, Cyprus, 1982—89, Portugal, 1983—84, Am. Excavations, Lugnano, Italy, 1988—93; pot cons., field dir. Tunisa Excavations, Chgo. Oriental Inst./Smithsonian Instn., 1973—78; dir. excavations Chianciano, Terme, Italy, 1995—; dir. Orvieto (Italy) Inst. Classical Studies, 2002—; resident in classical archaeology Am. Acad., Rome, 2002. Author: (book) Unreal Reality, 1978, Rise and Fall of Fantasy Film, 1980, Carthage, 1990, Carthage, French edit., 1994, Vera-Ellen: The Magic and the Mystery, 1999, 2d edit., 2003, Lugnano! Excavation of a Roman Villa, 1999, Kourion: Search for a Lost Roman City, 1988, Corpus des Mosaiques de Tunisie, 1972, Corpus des Mosaiques de Tunisie, 3d rev. edit., 1986, Carthage: A Mosaic of Ancient Tunisia, 1987; editor: Excavations at Kourion I, 1987; contbg. editor: Archaeology Mag.; prodr.: (films) Carthage: A Mirage of Antiquity, 1987; creator, guest curator (internt traveling exhbn.) Carthage: A Mosaic of Ancient Tunisia, 1987—92; editor, founder: Roscius, 1993—95; creative cons. (TV miniseries) Lost Civilizations, 1994; contbr. articles to profl. jours.; prodr.: (documentaries) BBC-TV documentary Malaria and the Fall of Rome, 2002; author: Vera-Ellen: The Magic and the Mystery; 2d edit., 2003; cons.: The History Channel, 2004; cons., on-screen contbr. The Colosseum, History Channel, 2005, Where Did it Come From? 3rd

Episodes for History Channel As On Screen Personality and Creative Consultaut, 2006; editor: (reports) Archaeological Excavations, 2007; prodr.: (TV reality show) Forgotten Lives, 2008. Recipient Cine Golden Eagle, 1980, Angenieux Film award, Indsl. Photography Mag., 1980, Oustanding Am. Under 40 award, C. Johns Hopkins-Britain's Royal Inst. Internat. Affairs, 1985; named Outstanding Am. Under 40, Esquire Mag., 1985, hon. Italian citizen, Lugnano, Italy, 1989; grantee, NEH, 1979, 1987, Fulbright, Lisbon, 1983. Fellow: Brit. Royal Inst. Internat. Affairs; mem.: Am. Acad. Rome (mem. internat. com. 2003—, bd. dirs. 2003—), Luso-Am. Commn. (citation 1983—84), Archaeol. Inst. Tucson (pres. 1983—86), Am. Sch. Oriental Rsch. (dept. rep. 1981—85), Nat. Geog. Soc. (project dir. 1983—84). Office: Univ Ariz Dept Classics PO Box 210105 206 Learning Svcs Bldg Tucson AZ 85721-0001 Office Phone: 520-621-1689. Business E-Mail: soren@u.arizona.edu.

SORENSEN, LINDA, lawyer; b. Eureka, Calif., Mar. 3, 1945; BS, U. Wis., 1967; JD, U. Calif., 1976. Bar: Calif. 1976, U.S. Dist. Ct. (no. dist.) Calif. 1976, U.S. Ct. Appeals (9th cir.) 1976, U.S. Dist. Ct. (ea. dist.) Calif. 1977. Assoc., ptnr. Rothschild, Phelan & Mortali, San Francisco, 1976-88; dir. Howard, Rice, Nemerovski, Canady, Falk & Rabkin, San Francisco, 1988-95; shareholder Feldman, Waldman & Kline, P.C., San Francisco, 1997-99; pvt. practice Berkeley, Calif., 1999—; of counsel Stromsheim & Assoc., 2001—. Mem. ABA (mem. subcom. on avoiding powers, bus. bankruptcy com. 1983-95), Bar Assn. of San Francisco (chmn. comml. law and bankruptcy sect. 1984, editor fed. cts. com., no. dist. Calif. digest 1979-82). Office: PO Box 325 Bodega Bay CA 94923 Office Fax: 707-875-9287. Personal E-mail: lindasorensen@earthlink.net.

SORENSEN, SHEILA, state legislator; b. Chgo., Sept. 20, 1947; d. Martin Thomas Moloney and Elizabeth (Koehr) Paulus; m. Wayne B. Slaughter, May, 1969 (div. 1976); 1 child, Wayne Benjamin III; m. Dean E. Sorensen, Feb. 14, 1977; (stepchildren) Michael, Debbie, Kevin, Dean C. BS, Loretto Heights Coll., Denver, 1965; postgrad. pediatric nurse practicioner, U. Colo., Denver, 1969-70. Pediatric nurse practicioner Pub. Health Dept., Denver, 1970-71, Boise, Idaho, 1971-72, Boise (Idaho) Pediatric Group, 1972-74, Pediatric Assocs., Boise, 1974-77; mem. Idaho Ho. Reps., 1987-92, Idaho Senate, Dist. 13, Boise, 1992—; chair senate health and welfare com. Idaho Senate, 1992-94, chair senate majority caucus, 1994-96, vice chair state affairs com., 1996-98, chair state affairs, 1998—. State chair Am. Legis. Exchange Coun. Precinct committeeman Ada County Rep. Ctrl. Com., Boise, 1982-86, dist. vice chair, 1985-88; polit. chair Idaho Med. Assn. Aux., 1984-87, Ada County Med. Assocs., 1986-87; bd. dirs. Family Practice Residency Program, 1992-94, Univ./Cmty. Health Sci. Assn., Bishop Kelly Found., 1993—99; chair Senate Majority Caucus, 1995-96, chair state affairs com., 1999—; mem. adv. com. on health care edn. and workforce devel. State Bd. Edn., mem. adv. bd. Drug Free Idaho., Boise State U. Master of Health Sci. Recipient AMA Nathan Davis award for Outstanding State Legislator, 1994. Mem. Nat. Conf. State Legislators, Nat. Orgn. Women Legislators (state chair), Am. Legis. Exch. Coun. (Legis of Yr. award 1999). Roman Catholic. Office Phone: 208-870-8081. Personal E-mail: sheilasorensen@hawaii.rr.com.

SORENSON, STEPHEN JAY, lawyer; b. Salt Lake City, Aug. 9, 1949; s. Peter Jay and Jeannette (Hanks) S.; m. Corinne Clyde, Jan. 24, 1974; children: Jeannette, Peter, Richard, Michael, Rebecca. Student, Yale U., 1967-69; BA, U. Utah, 1973, JD, 1977. Bar: Utah 1977, U.S. Dist. Ct. Utah 1977, U.S. Ct. Appeals (10th cir.) 1982. Asst. atty. gen. State of Utah, Salt Lake City, 1977-90, chief litig. divsn., 1986-90; asst. US atty. Dist. Utah US Dept. Justice, Salt Lake City, 1990—, chief civil divsn., 1995-98, 2006—09, first asst. US atty., 1998—2006, acting US atty., 2006. Mem. Utah Bar Assn. Office: US Atty's Office 185 S State St Ste 300 Salt Lake City UT 84111-1552 Office Phone: 801-325-3218.

SORGE, JOSEPH ANTHONY, molecular biologist; b. Newark, Mar. 23, 1954; s. Joseph S. and Margaret (Ticken) S.; m. Maryanne Kinchla, July 2, 1984. BS in Biology, MIT, 1975, BS in Chemistry, 1975; MD cum laude, Harvard U., Boston, 1979. Intern Brown U., Providence, 1979-80; post-doctoral fellow Cold Spring Harbor (N.Y.) Lab., 1980-82; asst. mem. Scripps Clinic and Research Inst., La Jolla, Calif., 1983—, staff physician, 1985—. Sci. dir. Stratagene, San Diego, 1984-86, chief exec. officer, 1985—. Contbr. articles on molecular biology to profl. jours. Recipient Research Service award NIH, 1981-83, Research Investigator award NIH, 1983-91, Jr. Faculty award Am. Cancer Soc., 1985-86, Pew Scholars award, Pew Meml. Trust, 1985-89. Mem. AAAS, Am. Soc. Microbiology. Avocations: skiing, surfing. Office: Stratagene Holding Corporation 11011 N Torrey Pines Rd La Jolla CA 92037

SORVINO, PAUL, actor; b. NYC, 1939; Attended, Am. Musical and Dramatic Acad. Artistic dir. Am. Stage Co., Teaneck, NJ 1986-90. N.Y.C. stage debut in Bajour, 1964; actor in (plays) including The Baker's Wife, Mating Dance, Skyscraper, That Championship Season, King Lear, An American Millionaire, For My Last Number, We'll Get By, Philemon, (films) The Gambler, 1970, Where's Poppa, 1970, Panic in Needle Park, 1971, Cry Uncle, Made for Each Other, 1971, The Day of the Dolphin, 1973, A Touch of Class, 1973, I Will, I Will... For Now, 1976, Oh God!, 1977, The Brink's Job, 1978, Shoot It, Black, Shoot It, Blue, Slow Dancing in the Big City, 1978, The Bloodbrothers, 1979, Lost and Found, 1979, Cruising, 1980, Reds, 1981, That Championship Season, 1982, I, The Jury, 1982, Off the Wall, Turk 1982, A Fine Mess, 1985, The Stuff, 1986, Vasectomy, 1986, Dick Tracy, 1990, Goodfellas, 1990, The Rocketeer, 1991, The Firm, 1993, Nixon, 1995, Romeo and Juliet, 1996, Love Is All There Is, 1996, Escape Clause, 1996, Dog Watch, 1996, Love is All There Is, 1996, Romeo and Juliet, 1996, Men with Guns, 1997, Money Talks, 1997, American Perfekt, 1997, Most Wanted, 1997, Bulworth, 1998, Knock Off, 1998, Ringside, 1999, That Championship Season, 1999, Prince of Central Park, 1999, Harlem Aria, 1999, Goodnight Joseph Parker, 1999, Dead Broke, 1999, Amati Girls, 2000, Family Man, 2000, Longshot, 2000, Perfume, 2001, See Spot Run, 2001, Plan B, 2001, Witches to the North, 2001, Rhode Island Blue, 2001, Irishman: The Legend of Danny Greene, 2001, Ciao America, 2002, Hey Arnold! (voice), 2002, The Cooler, 2003, Mambo Italiano, 2002, Goodnight, Joseph Parker, 2004, Mr. 3000, 2004, The Wild Stallion, 2006, Mr. Fix It, 2006, Greetings from the Shore, 2007, Last Hour, 2008, Camera: The Walking Mountain, 2008, Repo! The Genetic Opera, 2008; (TV miniseries) Seventh Avenue, 1977, (TV movies) Tell Me Where it Hurts, 1974, It Couldn't Happen to a Nicer Guy, 1974, Dummy, 1979, A Question of Honor, 1982, Chiefs, 1983, My Mother's Secret Life, 1984, With Intent to Kill, 1984, Surviving, 1985, Betrayed by Innocence, 1986, Don't Touch My Daughter, 1991, Perry Mason: The Case of the Wicked Wives, 1993, Parallel Lives, 1994, The Art of the Cigar (host), 1996, Joe Torre: Curveballs Along the Way, 1997, That Championship Season, 1999, The Thin Blue Lie, 2000, Mafia Doctor, 2003; (TV series) We'll Get By, 1975, Bert D'Angelo/Superstar, 1976, The Oldest Rookie, 1987, Law and Order, 1991-92, Star Trek: The Next Generation (guest appearance), 1994, That's Life, 2000-02. Office: Gersh Agy c/o Larry Taube 232 N Canon Dr Beverly Hills CA 90210-5302

SOSNICK, STEPHEN HOWARD, economics educator; b. Portland, Oreg., Feb. 24, 1930; s. Benjamin and Natalie (Schmulowitz) S.; m. Galya Chernow, July 14, 1951; children: Beryl, Elika, Randall, Tobin. AB, U. Calif. Berkeley, 1950, PhD, 1954. Inst., Princeton U., NJ, 1954-57; mem. faculty U. Calif., Davis, from 1957, now prof. emeritus, agrl. econs. Author: Hired Hands, 1978; Budget's New Clothes, 1971; also articles.

SOTELO, EDUARDO (EL PIOLÍN), radio personality; b. Ocotlán, Jalisco, Mexico, 1971; arrived in US, 1986, permanent resident, 1996; Broadcaster local radio stations, Calif., 1991—2003, KSCA FM101.9, LA, 2003—; with Univision Radio, LA, 2003—. Host (radio shows) Piolín por la Mañana, 2003—. Recipient Marconi Radio award for Spanish Format Personality of Yr., Nat. Assn. Broadcasters, 2006, 2008. Achievements include support and organization of demonstrations for immigrants' rights through radio broadcasts. Office: La Nueva #2500 655 N Central Ave Glendale CA 91203 Office Phone: 818-500-4500. Office Fax: 818-500-4550. E-mail: elshowdepiolin@univision.com.

SOTO, JAIME, bishop; b. Inglewood, Calif., Dec. 31, 1955; BA in Philosophy, St. John's Sem. Coll., Camarillo, Calif., 1978, MDiv, 1982; MSW, Columbia U. Sch. Social Work, 1986. Ordained priest Diocese of Orange, Calif., 1982; assoc. pastor St. Joseph Ch., Santa Ana, 1982—84; assoc. dir. Cath. Charities of Orange, 1986, dir. immigration & citizenship services, 1986—89; episcopal vicar for Hispanic cmty. Diocese of Orange, 1989—2000, vicar for charities, 1999—2000; ordained bishop, 2000; aux. bishop Diocese of Orange, 2000—07; coadjutor bishop Diocese of Sacramento, 2007—08, bishop Calif., 2008—. Roman Catholic. Office: Pastoral Ctr 2110 Broadway Sacramento CA 95818 Office Phone: 916-733-0100.

SOURAY, SHELDON, professional hockey player; b. Elk Point, Alta., Can., July 13, 1976; m. Angelica Bridges (div.); children: Valentina Raine, Scarlett Skye. Defenseman NJ Devils, 1997—2000, Montreal Canadiens, 2000—07, Edmonton Oilers, 2007—. Co-owner La Pizzeria etc., Montreal. Named to NHL All-Star Game, 2004, 2007, 2009. Achievements include setting NHL record for most powerplay goals scored by a defenseman in a single season, 2007. Office: Edmonton Oilers Hockey Club 11230 - 110 St Edmonton AB Canada*

SOUTHERN, NANCY C., utilities executive; m. Jonathan Asselin; children: Kelly Asselin, Kyle Asselin, Benjamin Asselin. Pres., CEO ATCO Ltd. and Can. Utilities, Calgary, Alba., Canada. Exec. v.p. Spruce Meadows; bd. dirs. Akita Drilling Ltd., Sentgraf Enterprises Ltd. Mem. Calgary Econ. Devel. Authority. Named Bus. Woman of Yr., Consumer's Choice Awards, 2005. Office: ATCO Ltd 1600 909 11th Ave SW Calgary AB Canada T2R 1N6

SOUTHWICK, CHARLES HENRY, zoologist, educator; b. Wooster, Ohio, Aug. 28, 1928; s. Arthur F. and Faye (Motz) S.; m. Heather Milne Beck, July 12, 1952; children: Steven, Karen. BA, Coll. Wooster, 1949; MS, U. Wis., 1951, PhD, 1953. NIH fellow, 1951-53; asst. prof. biology Hamilton Coll., 1953-54; NSF fellow Oxford U., England, 1954-55; faculty Ohio U., 1955-61; assoc. prof. pathobiology Johns Hopkins Sch. Hygiene and Pub. Health, Balt., 1961-68, prof., 1968-79; assoc. dir. Johns Hopkins Internat. Ctr. for Med. Rsch. and Tng., Calcutta, India, 1964-65; chmn. dept. environ., population and organismic biology U. Colo., Boulder, 1979-82, prof. biology, 1979—, prof. emeritus, 1993—. Rschr. and author publs. on animal social behavior and population dynamics, influences animal social behavior on demographic characteristic mammal populations, primate ecology and behavior, estuarine ecology and environ. quality; mem. primate adv. com. Nat. Acad. Sci.-NRC, 1963-75, com. primate conservation, 1974-75; mem. Gov.'s Sci. Adv. Com. State of Md., 1975-78; mem. com. on rsch. and exploration Nat. Geog. Soc., 1979-2000; mem. adv. bd. Caribbean Primate Rsch. Ctr., 1987-99, Wis. Primate Rsch. Ctr., 1990-98; mem. Integrated Conservation Rsch., 1989-2002; mem. or leader of more than 85 rsch. expdns. on five continents. Editor, author: Primate Social Behavior, 1963, Animal Aggression, 1970, Nonhuman Primates in Biomedical Research, 1975, Ecology and the Quality of Our Environment, 1976, Global Ecology, 1985; Ecology and Behavior of Food-Enhanced Primate Groups, 1988; author: Global Ecology in Human Perspective, 1996. Recipient Fulbright Rsch. award, India, 1959—60, Tchg. Excellence award, U. Colo., 1993. Fellow AAAS, Acad. Zoology, Animal Behavior Soc.; mem. Am. Soc. Zoologists, Ecol. Soc. Am., Am. Soc. Mammalogists, Am. Soc. Primatology (Disting. Primatologist award 1994), Internat. Primatology Soc., Am. Inst. Biol. Scis. Home: 6507 Baseline Rd Boulder CO 80303-3065 Office Phone: 303-492-5468.

SOWDER, ROBERT ROBERTSON, architect; b. Kans. City, Dec. 29, 1928; s. James Robert and Agnes (Robertson) S.; m. Joan Goddard, July 26, 1954; 1 dau., Lisa Robertson Lee. BA, U. Wash., 1953; B.Arch., U. Va., 1958; grad. diploma in Architecture, Ecole Des Beaux Arts, Fontainebleau, France, 1952. Designer Architects Collaborative, Boston, 1958-59, Peirce & Pierce (architects), Boston, 1959-63; asso. Fred. Bassetti & Co. (architects), Seattle, 1963-67; partner Naramore, Bain, Brady & Johanson (architects), Seattle, 1967-81; pres. NBBJ Internat., 1976-81; architect TRA, Seattle, 1981-83; v.p. Daniel, Mann, Johnson & Mendenhall, San Francisco, 1983-93; prin. RRS Consulting, 1993—. Archtl. design critic Boston Archtl. Ctr., 1961-62. Important works include Ridgeway III Dormitories, Bellingham, Wash. (Dept. Housing and Urban Devel. Honor award), Seattle Rapid Transit (HUD Excellence award), Safeco Ins. Co. Home Office Complex, Seattle, King County Stadium, Balt. Conv. Ctr., Oreg. Conv. Ctr., San Francisco (Moscone) Conv. Ctr. Expansion, Honolulu Conv. Ctr., Wilmington (Del.) Conv. Ctr. Mem. Redmond (Wash.) Design Rev. Bd., 1996-2000. Served with CIC U.S. Army, 1954-56, Thomas Jefferson Soc., U. Va. Recipient Premier Prix D'Architecture Ecole Des Beaux Arts, Fontainebleau, 1951, 52, Prix D'Remondet Fontainebleau, 1952 Mem. AIA (emeritus), Internat. Assn. Assembly Mgrs., Seattle Tennis Club, Seattle Rainier Club, Scarab, Sigma Chi. Episcopalian. Home and Office: 17032 NE 135th Ct Redmond WA 98052-1715

SOWELL, THOMAS, economist, syndicated columnist; b. Gastonia, NC, June 30, 1930; AB, Harvard U., 1958; A.M., Columbia U., 1959; PhD, U. Chgo., 1968. Economist Dept. Labor, 1961-62; instr. econs. Douglass Coll., Rutgers U., 1962-63; lectr. econs. Howard U., 1963-64; econ. analyst AT&T, 1964-65; asst. prof. Cornell U., 1965-69; assoc. prof. Brandeis U., 1969-70; assoc. prof. econs. UCLA, 1970-74, prof., 1974-80; project dir. Urban Inst., Washington, 1972-74; fellow Center Advanced Study Behavioral Scis., Stanford, Calif., 1976-77; sr. fellow Hoover Instn., 1977, 1980—. Vis. prof. Amherst Coll., 1977 Author: Economics: Analysis and Issues, 1971, Black Education: Myths and Tragedies, 1972, Say's Law: An Historical Analysis, 1972, Classical Economics Reconsidered, 1974, Race and Economics, 1975, Knowledge and Decisions, 1980, Markets and Minorities, 1981, Ethnic America: A History, 1981, The Economics and Politics of Race: An International Perspective, 1983, Civil Rights: Rhetoric or Reality, 1984, Marxism: Philosophy and Economics, 1985, A Conflict of Visions: Ideological Origins of Political Struggles, 1987, revised ed., 2007, Choosing a College: A Guide for Parents and Students, 1989, Preferential Policies: An International Perspective, 1990, Inside American Education: The Decline, the Deception, the Dogmas, 1993, 1993, Race and Culture: World View, 1994, The Vision of the Anointed: Self-Congratulation as a Basis for Social Policy, 1995, Migrations and Cultures: A World View, 1996, Late-Talking Children, 1997, Conquests and Cultures: An International History, 1998, The Quest for Cosmic Justice, 1999, A Personal Odyssey, 2000, Basic Economics: A Citizen's Guide to the Economy, 2000, 2nd. ed., 2004, 3rd ed., 2007, The Einstein Syndrome: Bright Children Who Talk Late, 2001, Applied Economics: Thinking Beyond Stage One, 2003, Affirmative Action Around the World: An Empirical Study, 2004, Black Rednecks and White Liberals, 2005, On Classical Economics, 2006 A Man of Letters, 2007 Economic Facts and Fallacies, 2008; contbr. articles to profl. publs, syndicated columnist. Served with USMC, 1951-53. Fellow, Hoover Instn., 1977; sr. fellow, 1980—. Mem. Am. Econ. Assn., Nat. Acad. Edn. Office: Stanford Univ Hoover Instn Stanford CA 94305 also: Creators Syndicate 5777 W Century Blvd Los Angeles CA 90045 Business E-Mail: sowell@stanford.edu.

SPAFFORD, MICHAEL CHARLES, artist; b. Palm Springs, Calif., Nov. 6, 1935; BA, Pomona Coll., 1959; MA, Harvard U., 1960. Artist-in-residence Dartmouth Coll., 2005. One man shows include Seattle Art Mus., 1982, 86, Reed Coll., 1984, Whitcom county Mus., 1987, U. Puget Sound, Tacoma, Wash., 1973, Tacoma Art Mus., 1975, 86, Utah Mus. Fine Arts, Salt Lake City, 1975, Francine Seders Gallery, Seattle, 1965—, Bellevue Art Mus., 1991, Cheney-Cowles Mus., Spokane, Wash., 1994, Hallie Ford Mus. Art, Willamette U., Salem, Oreg., 1999; exhibited in group shows at Wilcox Gallery, Swarthmore Coll., Pa., 1977, Seattle Art Mus., 1977, 80, 84, Am. Acad. and Inst. Arts and Letters, N.Y.C., 1980, 83, 89, 95, Kobe, Japan, 1981, Eastern Wash. U., 1982, Henry Art Gallery, 1982, 86, Bellevue Art Mus., 1987, 95, Cheney Cowles Mus., 1988, Holter Mus. of Art, Helena, Mont. Recipient Rome Prize Am. Acad. in Rome, 1967-69, award Am. Acad. and Inst. Arts and Letters, 1983, Lifetime Achievement in Arts award Corp. Coun. Arts, Seattle, 1999. Flintridge Found. award for visual artists, 2006; Louis Comfort Tiffany Found. grantee, 1965-66; Neddy fellow, 1996. Address: c/o Francine Seders Gallery 6701 Greenwood Ave N Seattle WA 98103-5225

SPANGLER, DAVID ROBERT, academic administrator, engineer, educator; b. Flint, Mich., Aug. 17, 1940; s. John Solomon and Margaret Inger (McKinley) S.; m. Sally Jeanne Henry, Aug. 28, 1965; children: Timothy David, Megan Marie. BS, U.S. Mil. Acad., 1962; MS in Engring., U. Ill., 1966, PhD in Structural Dynamics, 1977. Registered profl. engr. Commd. 2d lt. U.S. Army, 1962, advanced through grades to lt. col., 1979, prof. math. U.S. Mil. Acad. West Point, N.Y., 1968-71, engr. Korea Support Command, 1972-73, dep. dist. engr. C.E. Walla Walla, Wash., 1973-74, research coordinator Def. Nuclear Agy. Washington, 1976-79, bn. comdr. Hawaii, 1979-81, inspector C.E. San Francisco, 1981-82, ret., 1982; prof. engring. St. Martin's Coll., Lacey, Wash., 1982-84, pres., 1984—. Mem. Nat. Com. for Tunnelling Tech., Washington, 1977-79; cons. Thurston County, Olympia, Wash., 1982-84. Contbr. articles to profl. jours. Bd. dirs. Econ. Devel. Coun., Thurston County, 1985-88, Wash. State Capitol Mus., 1988-91. Decorated Bronze Star with 2 oak leaf clusters, Meritorious Service medal, Def. Nuclear Agy. Joint Service medal. Mem. Soc. Mil. Engrs. (v.p. 1980-81, pres. 1973-74), Nat. Assn. Ind. Colls. and Univs. (bd. dirs. 1992-95, treas. 1994), Ind. Colls. Wash. (bd. dirs.), Assn. Benedictine Colls. and Univs. (pres. 1994-95), Rotary (mem. gov.'s oversight com. on tech. 1996—). Roman Catholic. Avocation: running. Office: St Martins Coll Office of Pres Lacey WA 98503

SPANOS, ALEXANDER GUS, construction and professional sports team executive; b. Stockton, Calif., Sept. 28, 1923; m. Faye Spanos; children: Dean, Dea Spanos Berberian, Alexis Spanos Ruhl, Michael. LLD (hon.), U. Pacific, 1984, Eureka Coll., 1984; DHL (hon.), Wayne State Coll., 2003, Calif. Polytechnic State U., 2004, Anatolia Coll., Thessaloniki, Greece, 2004; HHD (hon.), Hellenic Coll., 2004, Holy Cross Greek Orthodox Sch. Theology, 2004. Chmn. bd. dirs. A.G. Spanos Constrn. Inc., Stockton, Calif., 1960—; chmn. bd. dirs. A.G. Spanos Mgmt. Inc., Stockton, Calif., 1967—, A.G. Spanos Enterprises Inc., Stockton, Calif., 1971—, A.G. Spanos Devel. Inc., Stockton, Calif., 1973—, A.G. Spanos Realty Inc., Stockton, Calif., 1978—, A.G.S. Fin. Corp., Stockton, Calif., 1980—, A.G. Spanos Securities Corp., Stockton, Calif., 1981—, San Diego Chargers, 1984—. Chmn. bd. dirs. AGS Internat. Corp., Stockton, Calif., The Spanos Corp., Stockton, A.G. Spanos Ventures, Stockton, AGS Comms., LLC, Stockton. Former trustee Children's Hosp., San Francisco, San Francisco Fine Arts Mus.; trustee Eisenhower Med. Ctr., Rancho Mirage, Calif., John F. Kennedy Ctr. Performing Arts; hon. regent U. Pacific, Stockton, 1972-82; gov. USO, Washington, 1982—; former gov. Ronald Reagan Presdl. Found.; chmn. U.S. chpt. U.S. Greece bus. coun. Served with USAF, 1942-46. Recipient Albert Gallatin award Zurich-Am. Ins. Co., 1973, Horatio Alger award Horatio Alger Found., 1982, medal of Honor Statue of Liberty-Ellis Islan Found., 1982; named one of Forbes' Richest Americans, 2006. Mem. Am. Hellenic Ednl. Progressive Assn., Calif. C. of C. (bd. dirs. 1980-85). Republican. Greek Orthodox. Avocation: golf. Office: San Diego Chargers Qualcomm Stadium PO Box 609609 San Diego CA 92160-9609 also: A G Spanos Cos 10100 Trinity Pkwy 5th Fl Stockton CA 95219 Business E-Mail: agspr@agspanos.com.

SPARKS, DALE BOYD, allergist, health facility administrator; b. Springfield, Mo., July 14, 1929; s. Roscoe R. and Ruby V. (Boyd) S.; children: Susan L., Laura A., Lisa M., Jennifer G.; m. Leeanna M. Molccyk Priboy, Apr. 21, 2001. AB, BS, Southwest Mo. State U., 1951; BS in Medicine, U. Mo., 1953; MD, St. Louis U., 1955.

Diplomate Am. Bd. Allergy and Immunology. Intern Kansas City (Mo.) Gen. Hosp. U. Med. Ctr., 1955-56; resident U. Mo. Hosp., 1958-60; fellow in allergy and immunology Northwestern U., 1960-61; mem. cons. staff Parkview Cmty. Hosp., 1961—; mem. med. staff Riverside County Regional Med. Ctr., 1961-2000, dir. respiratory therapy, 1968-85, dir. respiratory therapy and diagnostic svcs., 1965—, chmn. dept. medicine, 1978-98, chief med. staff, 1990-98; acting dir., health officer Riverside Pub. Health Dept., 1991-93; ret., 1993. Clin. prof. medicine Loma Linda U. Mem. editl. bd. Immunology and Allergy in Practice, 1980—. Lt. USNR. Fellow ACP (coun. subsplty. socs. 1988—), Am. Coll. Allergy and Immunology (disting., bd. regents 1989-93, pres. 1990-91, chmn. fin. com., treas. 1990-93, recert. com.), Coll. Allergy, Asthma and Immunology; mem. AMA, Am. Lung Assn. (bd. dirs. 1990-95), Am. Heart Assn. (bd. dirs. 1964-70, pres. 1966), Joint Coun. Am. Allergy and Immunology (bd. dirs. 1985-90), Calif. Med. Assn., Calif. Soc. Allergy, Inland Soc. Internal Medicine, Riverside County Med. Assn. (bd. councilors 1980-99, del. CMA 1988-99), Riverside County Found. Med. Care (sec., past pres.). Home and Office: 29368 Big Range Rd Canyon Lake CA 92587 Personal E-mail: dsparksmd@aol.com.

SPARKS, JOHN EDWARD, lawyer; b. Rochester, Ind., July 3, 1930; s. Russell Leo and Pauline Anna (Whittenberger) S.; m. Margaret Joan Snyder, Sept. 4, 1954; children: Thomas Edward, William Russell, Kathryn Chapman McCarthy. AB, Ind. U., 1952; LL.B., U. Calif., Berkeley, 1957; postgrad., London Sch. Econs., 1957-58. Bar: Calif. 1958, U.S. Supreme Ct., 1968. Assoc. Brobeck, Phleger & Harrison, San Francisco, 1958-66, ptnr., 1967-95, of counsel, 1996—2003; pvt. practice, 2003—. Adj. prof. law U. San Francisco, 1967-69; pres. Legal Aid Soc. San Francisco, 1978-79, dir., 1971-81. Editor U. Calif. Law Rev., 1956-57. Served to 1st lt. Q.M.C. U.S. Army, 1952-54, Korea. Recipient Wheeler Oak Meritorious award U. Calif., Berkeley, 1986. Fellow Am. Bar Found., Am. Coll. Trial Lawyers; mem. ABA, State Bar Calif., Bar Assn. San Francisco (bd. dirs. 1974-75), Boalt Hall Alumni Assn. (pres. 1983-84). Democrat. Home Phone: 510-524-6106; Office Phone: 510-524-5404. E-mail: jsparks458@aol.com.

SPARKS, MILDRED THOMAS, state agency administrator, educator; b. Montgomery, Ala., Oct. 2, 1942; d. Leon and Annie Lee (Johnson) Thomas; m. John H. Sparks, Aug. 29, 1964; children: Melanie J. Thomas Bosak, Jennifer L. Gerhartz, Regina F. BS, Ala. State U., 1964; MS, Pepperdine U., 1978; postgrad., Claremont Coll., Calif. State U., Boston Coll. Cert. reading specialist, contract mgmt., U. Phoenix, U. Wyo. Tchr. Dayton (Ohio) Schs., 1964-66, Oxon Hill (Md.) Schs., 1966-70; technician Reading Lab. Grambling (La.) State U., 1972; reading lab. aide Calif. City (Calif.) Schs., 1975; reading instr. Cerro Coso So. Outreach, Edwards AFB, Calif., 1976-78; substitute tchr. San Bernardino City Schs., 1979, Aquinas H.S., San Bernardino, 1978-79; reading lab. tchr. San Bernardino H.S., 1979; instr. reading lab. San Bernardino Valley Coll., 1980-81, assoc. prof. reading, dept. head, 1981-86; contract adminstr. Hercules Missile Ordinance and Space Group, Magna, Utah, 1986, Alliant Techsys. (formerly Hercules Missile Ordinance and Space Group), 1987-97; dir. Office of Black Affairs State of Utah, 1997—2000; assoc. prof. Salt Lake CC, Salt Lake City, 2003—. Mem. Pres.'s Diversity Coun. Tchg. Cir. - Courage Teach Salt Lake City (Utah) C.C., 2003—, mem. gen. edn. com. Mem. Black Adv. Coun., Office of Black Affairs, AARP (mem. Utah bd., safety program instr.); presenter workshops, cmty. events; troop vol. Girl Scouts U.S.; vol. The March of Dimes, Am. Heart Assn., Visitation of the Elderly Homebound, Am. Cancer Soc. and Marriage and Family Workshop for Teens, Cath. Cmty. Svcs.; civil rights movement participant Ala. Bus Boycott; mem. minority health adv. bd. Utah Health Dept.; mem. Cath. Women League, Black Caths. Utah, Salt Lake City, African Am. Task Force, Gov.'s Initiative on Family Today, Anti-Discrimination Com.; planning com. United Way Greater Salt Lake, vol.; past pres. Salt Lake Diocesan Pastoral Coun., vol.; mem. Americorp Legacy program, Salt Lake County, Utah State Bd. Aging and Adult Svcs. Mem. Calif Tchrs. Assn., Nat. Coun. Tchrs. English, Assn. Supervision and Curriculum Devel., Western Coll. Reading Assn., Bus. and Profl. Women's Club, Link's, Jack and Jill of Am. Inc., Delta Kappa Gamma, Alpha Kappa Alpha. Roman Catholic (Norton lav lector). Avocations: reading, writing, gardening, cross country skiing. Home: 3790 Becky Cir Salt Lake City UT 84109-3302 Office: Salt Lake CC Coll Devel Edn 4600 S Redwood Rd Salt Lake City UT 84123

SPARKS, ROBERT DEAN, medical administrator, gastroenterologist; b. Newton, Iowa, May 6, 1932; s. Albert John and Josephine Emma (Kleinendorst) S.; children: Steven Robert, Ann Louise, John James. BA, U. Iowa, 1955, MD, 1957; D of Humanitarian Svc. (hon.), Creighton U., 1978. Diplomate Am. Bd. Internal Medicine. Intern Charity Hosp. of La., New Orleans, 1957-58, resident in internal medicine, 1958-59, asst. in medicine, 1958-59; fellow in gen. medicine and gastroenterology Tulane U. Sch. Medicine, 1959-62, instr. medicine, 1959-63, asst. prof., 1963-64, assoc. prof., 1964-68, prof., 1968-72, asst. dean, 1964-67, assoc. dean, acting dean, 1967-68, vice dean, 1968-69, dean, 1969-72, chief sect. gastroenterology, 1968-72; chancellor Med. Ctr. U. Nebr., 1972-76, prof. medicine, 1972-76; v.p. U. Nebr. System, 1972-76; health program dir. W.K. Kellogg Found., Battle Creek, Mich., 1976-81, v.p. programming, 1981-82, sr. v.p., 1982, pres., chief programming officer, 1982—88, trustee, 1988, pres. emeritus, cons., 1988-92; pres., CEO, Calif. Med. Assn. Found., Sacramento, 1995-98, sr. assoc., 1998—. Cons. U. Tenn. Health Sci. Ctr., 1988-90, Boston U. Health Policy Inst., 1989-90; mem. sci., compensation and trust rev. coms. Syntex Corp., Palo Alto, Calif., 1987-91, v.p. product safety and compliance, 1991-93; mem. overseers com. to visit Harvard U. Med. and Dental Schs., 1984-90; mem. vis. com. U. Miami Sch. Medicine, 1982-86; assoc. med. dir. for addiction treatment svcs., dir. for edn. and rsch., Battle Creek Adventist Hosp., 1990-91; v.p. Howe-Lewis Internat Inc., Menlo Park, N.Y., 1993-94, cons., 1994-95; mem. adv. coun. to dean Tulane U. Sch. Medicine, 2004—. Mem. editl. bd. Alcoholism Treatment Quar., 1985--; contbr. articles to profl. jours. Bd. dirs. Nat. Coun. on Alcoholism and Drug Dependence, NYC, 1982-93, treas., 1986-88, chmn., 1989-90, past chmn., 1991-92; bd. dirs. Battle Creek Symphony Orch., 1981-88, Lakeview Sch. Dist., Battle Creek, 1979-83, 88-91, Omni Med, 2001-; trustee Monsour Med. Found., Jeannette, Pa., 1976-90, interim pres. 1989, chmn. bd., pres., 1989-90; mem. President's Adv. Bd. on Pvt. Sector Initiatives, Washington, 1986-89; chmn. bd. dirs. Bard Coll. Health Policy and Practice Inst., 1988-96, Consumer Health Info. Rsch. Inst., 1990-95, Chelsea-Arbor Treatment Ctr., 1990-91; bd. dirs. Calhoun County Bd. Health, 1988-91, chmn., 1989-91; mem., bd. dirs. Mental Health and Addictions Found. Mich., Battle Creek, 1991-93; mem. adv. coun. CMA Found., 2004-07; mem. cmty. adv. com., Taser Found., Scottsdale, Ariz., 2005—, bd. dirs. 2006—, chair, 2006—. Recipient Harvard Dental award Harvard U. Sch. Dental Medicine, 1992, Disting. Alumni award for achievement U. Iowa Coll. Medicine, 1998, U. Iowa Alumni Assn, 2009, Disting. Alumni Achievement award, annual Robert D. Sparks Cmty. Health Leadership Achievement award CMA Found., 1997— Fellow ACP; mem. AMA, Nat. Acad. Scis. Inst. Medicine (com. study of treatment and rehab. svcs. for alcoholism and alcohol abuse, bd. mental health and behavioral medicine), Coun. Mich. Founds. (trustee 1986-88), Assn. Am. Med. Colls. (disting. svc. mem. 1975—), Phi Eta Sigma, Alpha Omega Alpha, Ph Kappa Psi. Republican. Methodist. Avocations: tennis, bridge, reading, travel. Home and Office: 5004 Gresham Dr El Dorado Hills CA 95762-7703 Office Phone: 916-230-0719. Personal E-mail: rdsparksmd1@earthlink.net.

SPARKS, THOMAS E., JR., lawyer; b. Little Rock, Jan. 11, 1942; children: Thomas Gunnar, Erik Richard, Andrew Pal. BS, Washington and Lee U., 1963; JD, U. Ark., 1968; LLM, Harvard U., 1970. Bar: Ark. 1968, Calif. 1970. Assoc. Pillsbury Madison & Sutro, San Francisco, 1970-76; ptnr. Pillsbury, Madison & Sutro, San Francisco, 1977-84, Baker & McKenzie, San Francisco, 1984-87, Pillsbury Madison & Sutro, San Francisco, 1987-2000, Pillsbury Winthrop, San Francisco, 2001—. Trustee Grace Cathedral, San Francisco. 1st lt. U.S. Army, 1965. Mem. ABA, Calif. Bar Assn., Calif. Tennis Club (pres. 2000). Office: Pillsbury Winthrop LLP 50 Fremont St San Francisco CA 94105-2230

SPARLING, MARY LEE, biology professor; b. Ft. Wayne, Ind., May 20, 1934; d. George Hewson and Velmah Evelyn (McClain) S.; m. Albert Alcide Barber, Sept. 1, 1956 (div. Jan. 1975); children: Bonnie Lee Barber, Bradley Paul Barber. BS, U. Miami, Coral Gables, Fla., 1955; MA, Duke U., 1958; PhD, UCLA, 1962. Lectr. UCLA, 1962-63; asst. prof. Calif. State U., Northridge, 1966-72, assoc. prof., 1972-76, prof., 1976—2006, prof. emeritus, 2006—. Statewide acad. senator Calif. State U., 1996-98. Contbr. articles to profl. jours. NSF grantee Calif. State U., Northridge, 1971-72, 81-83, 89, NIH grantee Calif. State U., Northridge, 1987-89. Mem. AAUP (pres. 1981-82), Am. Soc. Cell Biology, Soc. for Devel. Biology, Am. Soc. Zoologists, Sigma Xi (bd. dirs. Research Triangle, N.C. 1974-91). Avocations: tennis, gardening, travel. Office Phone: 818-677-2754. Office Fax: 818-677-2034. E-mail: marylee.sparling@csun.edu.

SPEAR, ROBERT CLINTON, environmental health educator, consultant; b. Los Banos, Calif., June 26, 1939; s. Clinton Wentworth Spear and Maytie Izetta (Patten) Gill; m. Patricia Warner, Dec. 15, 1962; children: Andrew Warner, Jennifer Ellen. BS, U. Calif., Berkeley, 1961, MS, 1962; PhD, Cambridge U., 1968. Registered profl. engr., Calif. Sys. engr. U.S. Naval Weapons Ctr., China Lake, Calif., 1962-65, 68-69; from asst. prof. to assoc. prof. environ. health U. Calif. Sch. Pub. Health, Berkeley, 1970-81, prof., 1981—, dir. No. Calif. Occupational Health Ctr., 1980-89, assoc. dean, 1988-91, dir. environ. engring. and health scis. lab., 1991-96; assoc. dean U. Calif. Coll. Engring., Berkeley, 1994-96; dir. Ctr. for Occupl. and Environ. Health U. Calif., Berkeley, 1992-2000. Vice-chair Berkeley divsn. Acad. Senate, 1998-99, chair, 1999-2000; hon. prof. Sichuan Inst. Parasitic Disease. Contbr. articles on engring. aspects of environ. health to profl. jours. Mem. Nat. Adv. Com. on Occupational Safety and Health, U.S. Dept. Labor, 1986-88. NSF grad. fellow Cambridge U., 1965-68, sr. internat. fellow Fogarty Ctr., NIH, Australian Nat. U., 1977-78, research grantee Nat. Inst. Occupational Safety and Health NIH, State of Calif., 1971—. Mem. ASME, AAAS, Am. Indsl. Hygiene Assn., Nat. Inst. Occupl. Safety and Health (bd. scientific counselors), Assn. Univ. Programs in Occupational Health and Safety (pres. 1984-85) Democrat. Avocation: sailing. Home: 1963 Yosemite Rd Berkeley CA 94707-1631 Office: U Calif Sch Pub Health Berkeley CA 94720-0001 E-mail: spear@uclink4.berkeley.edu.

SPECK, EUGENE LEWIS, internist; b. Boston, Dec. 17, 1936; s. Robert A. and Anne (Rosenberg) S.; m. Rachel Shoshana; children: Michael Robert, Keren Sara. AB, Brandeis U., Waltham, Mass., 1958; MS, U. Mass., 1961; PhD, George Washington U., 1966, MD, 1969. Diplomate Am. Bd. Internal Medicine with subspecialty in infectious diseases. Intern N.Y. Hosp.-Cornell, 1969-70; rsch. assoc. NIH, Bethesda, Md., 1970-72; resident Barnes Hosp.-Washington U., 1972-73; instr. medicine Washington U., St. Louis, 1972-73; fellow Strong Meml. Hosp.-U. Rochester, 1973-75; instr. medicine U. Rochester, N.Y., 1973-75, asst. prof. medicine N.Y., 1975-80, U. Nev., Las Vegas, 1980-85, assoc. prof., 1985-95, prof. medicine, 1995—; dir./co-dir. infectious disease unit U. Med. Ctr. of So. Nev., Las Vegas, 1980—; ptnr. Infectious Diseases Consultants, 1983—. Cons. Clark County Health Dept., Las Vegas, 1980—, U. Med. Ctr. So. Nev., Las Vegas, 1980—, Sunrise Hosp., Las Vegas, 1980—, Valley Hosp., Las Vegas, 1980—; Am. coll. physicians gov., State Nev. Contbr. articles to profl. jours., chpts. to books. Recipient Disting. Physician award, State of Nev., 2002. Fellow ACP (elected gov. Nev.), Infectious Disease Soc. Am.; mem. Am. Soc. Microbiology, Alpha Omega Alpha. Avocations: tennis, skiing, racquetball. Home: 2228 Chatsworth Ct Henderson NV 89074-5309 Office: Infectious Diseases Cons 3006 S Maryland Pkwy Ste 780 Las Vegas NV 89109-2292 Home Phone: 702-433-1850; Office Phone: 702-737-0740. Personal E-mail: disdoc@aol.com.

SPEER, SUSAN H., bank executive; b. 1941; Sr. v.p., pvt. banking mgr. Zions First Nat. Bank, Salt Lake City, 1997—. Creator pvt. med. svcs. initiative Zions First Nat. Bank. Mem. deferred giving bd. U. Utah, Salt Lake City; mem. adv. coun. Westminster Coll., Salt Lake City. Named one of 25 Women to Watch, US Banker mag., 2006. Mem.: Utah Bankers Assn. (mem. convention com.). Office: Zions First Nat Bank 1 S Main St Salt Lake City UT 84111

SPEIDEL, JOHN JOSEPH, public health professional, educator; b. Iowa City, Iowa, Sept. 17, 1937; s. Thomas Dennis and Edna (Warweg) Speidel; m. Melissa Jane Webster, Oct. 7, 2001; 1 child from previous marriage, Sabrina Brett. AB cum laude, Harvard U., 1959, MD, 1963, MPH, 1965. Diplomate Nat. Bd. Med. Examiners, Am. Bd. Preventive Medicine. Intern St. Luke's Hosp., NYC, 1963-64; resident N.Y.C. Dept. Health, 1965-67, dep. dir. maternal and infant care project, 1966-67; chief rsch. divsn. Office Population, AID, Dept. of State, Washington, 1969-76, assoc. dir., 1977, dep. dir., acting dir. office, 1978-83; v.p. Population Action Internat. (formerly Population Crisis Com.), 1983-87, pres., 1987-95; program dir. population Hewlett Found., 1995—2003; prof. Bixby Ctr. Global Reproductive Health U. Calif., San Francisco, 2003—. Lectr. population and family planning Georgetown U., 1973—75. Editor (with others): (book) Female Sterilization, 1971, Hysteroscopic Sterilization, 1974, Intrauterine Devices, 1974, Control of Male Fertility, 1975, Advances in Female Sterilization Technology, 1976, Risks, Benefits and Controversies in Fertility Control, 1978, Reversal of Sterilization, 1978, Pregnancy Termination, 1979, Vaginal Contraception, 1979; contbr. articles to profl. jours. Served to maj. US Army, 1967—69. Recipient Meritorious Unit citiation, Office of Population, 1969—71, Arthur S. Flemming award, Washington Downtown Jaycees, 1972, Family Planning Visionary award, Nat. Family Planning & Reproductive Health Assn., 2008, Allan Rosen Guild award, Internat. Family Planning Soc. Family Planning, 2009. Mem.: Population Assn. Am., Am. Pub. Health Assn. (Carl S. Shultz award 1982). Office: U Calif San Francisco BCGRH Dept Ob Gyn 3333 California St Ste 335 Box 0744 San Francisco CA 94118 Office Phone: 415-502-3928. Business E-Mail: speidelj@obgyn.ucsf.edu.

SPEIER, JACKIE (KAREN LORRAINE JACQUELINE SPEIER), United States Representative from California, former state senator; b. San Francisco, May 14, 1950; m. Steven K. Sierra, 1987 (dec. 1994); children: Jackson Kent, Stephanie Katelin; m. Barry Dennis, 2001. BA, U. Calif., Davis, 1972; JD, U. Calif. Hastings Coll. Law, 1976. Legal coun., legis. asst. to Rep. Leo J. Ryan US Congress, 1973-78; mem. San Mateo County Bd. Suprs., Calif., 1980—84, chair Calif., 1985—86; mem. Calif. State Assembly from Dist. 19, 1987—96, majority whip, 1988—92, chair consumer protection com., 1991-95; v.p. govtl. & cmty. affairs Electronic Arts Inc., 1996—98; dir. govtl. & corp. affairs Poplar ReCare, 1996—98; mem. Calif. State Senate from Dist. 8, 1999—2006; of counsel Hanson, Bridgett, Marcus, Viahos, & Rudy LLP, San Francisco, 2007—08; mem. US Congress from 12th Calif. Dist., 2008—, US House Financial Services Com., 2009—, US House Oversight & Govt. Reform Com., 2009—, US House Spl. Com. on Energy Independence & Global Warming, 2009—. Author: This Is Not the Life I Ordered: 50 Ways to Keep Your Head Above Water When Life Keeps Dragging You Down, 2007. Named Legis. of Yr., Met. Transp. Commn., 2004. Democrat. Roman Catholic. Office: US Congress 2413 Rayburn Ho Office Bldg Washington DC 20515 also: 400 S El Camino Real Ste 410 San Mateo CA 94402

SPEIGHT, JOHN BLAIN, lawyer; b. Cheyenne, May 29, 1949; s. Jack B. and Kathryn Elizabeth (Schmidt) S.; m. Sally Karolee Sullivan, Aug. 20, 1960; children— Sheryl, Tricia, Jackie; m. Carol Ann McBee, Sept. 16, 1979. BA, U. Wyo., 1962, JD, 1965. Bar: Wyo. 1966, U.S. Dist. Ct. Wyo. 1967, U.S. Dist. Ct. Colo. 1967, U.S. Ct. Appeals (10th cir.) 1967, U.S. Supreme Ct. 1970; diplomate Am. Bd. Trial Attys. Atty., Standard Oil Co. of Calif., 1965-67; asst. atty. gen. State of Wyo., 1967-69; adminstrv., legal asst. to Gov. Wyo., 1969-71; atty. for Reorgn. Commn., State of Wyo., 1969-71; asst. U.S. atty. Litigation divsn., 1971-72; cons. sec. interior, 1975; ptnr. Speight McCue & Assocs, Cheyenne, 1972—; bd. dirs. First Wyo. Bank, East Cheyenne, Laramie County Legal Svc. Inc. Bd. dirs. Laramie County United Fund. Mem. Wyo. Bar Assn., ABA, Wyo. Trial Lawyers Assn., Am. Trial Lawyers Assn., Laramie County United Fund. Mem. Wyo. Bar Assn., ABA, Wyo. Trial Lawyers Assn. (bd. dirs. 1982—), Am. Trial Lawyers Assn., Laramie County Bar Assn. (pres. 1982-83), Commrs. for Uniform State Laws from the State of Wyo., Jud. Supervisory Commn., Cheyenne Kiwanis Club (bd. dirs.) Young Men's Literary Club. Republican. Roman Catholic. Home: 4021 Snyder Ave Cheyenne WY 82001-1170 Office: PO Box 1709 Cheyenne WY 82003-1709 Office Phone: 307-634-2994. Business E-Mail: jspeight@speightmccue.com.

SPELLMAN, JOHN DENNIS, lawyer, former governor of Washington, Former Governor, Washington; b. Seattle, Dec. 29, 1926; s. Sterling B. and Lela (Cushman) S.; m. Lois Elizabeth Murphy, Feb. 20, 1954; children: Margo, Bart, David, Jeffrey, Teresa, Katherine. BS, Seattle U., 1949, LLD (hon.), 1981; JD, Georgetown U., 1953; LLD (hon.), Gonzaga Law Sch., Walla Walla Coll. Bar: Wash. 1953. Practiced in, Seattle, 1954-67; commr. King County, Wash., 1967-69; exec., 1969-81; gov. State of Wash., Olympia, 1981-85; of counsel Carney Stephenson Badley Smith & Spellman, Seattle, 1985—. Vice chair US Coastal Zone Mgmt. Adv. Commn., 1974—76; mem. US Export/Import Bank Adv. Coun., 1984—85; prof. adminstrv. law Seattle U., 1992—2004. Chmn. Evergreen Safety Coun., mem. bd. Gerald P. Murphy Cancer Inst., TVW, Camp Brotherhood, Sierra Club Seattle. Served with USNR, World War II. Mem. ABA, Wash. State Bar Assn. Republican. Roman Catholic. Office: Carney Badley Spellman PS Ste 3600 701 5th Ave Seattle WA 98104-7010 Office Phone: 206-622-8020. Office Fax: 206-622-8983. E-mail: spellman@carneylaw.com.

SPELTS, RICHARD JOHN, lawyer; b. Yuma, Colo., July 29, 1939; s. Richard Clark and Barbara Eve (Pletcher) S.; children: Melinda, Meghan, Richard John Jr.; m. Gayle Merves, Nov. 14, 1992. BS cum laude, U. Colo., 1961, JD, 1964. Bar: Colo. 1964, U.S. Dist. Ct. Colo. 1964, U.S. Supreme Ct. 1968, U.S. Ct. Appeals (10th cir.) 1970, U.S. Dist. Ct. (ea. dist.) Mich. 1986. With Ford Motor Internat., Cologne, Germany, 1964-65; legis. counsel to U.S. Senator, 89th and 90th Congresses, 1967-68; minority counsel U.S. Senate Subcom., 90th and 91st Congresses, 1968-70; asst. U.S. atty., 1st asst. U.S. atty. Fed. Dist. of Colo., 1970-77; pvt. practice Denver, 1977-89; risk mgr. sheriff's dept. Jefferson County, Golden, Colo., 1990-91. Selected for Leadership Denver, 1977; recipient cert. for outstanding contbns. in drug law enforcement U.S. Drug Enforcement Adminstrn., 1977, spl. commendation for criminal prosecution U.S. Dept. Justice, 1973, spl. commendation for civil prosecution U.S. Dept. Justice, 1976. Mem. Fed. Bar Assn. (chmn. govt. torts seminar 1980), Colo. Bar Assn. (bd. govs. 1976-78), Denver Bar Assn., Colo. Trial Lawyers Assn., Denver Law Club, Order of Coif. Republican. Methodist. Home and Office: 9715 Sunset Hill Cir Lone Tree CO 80124-6716

SPENCE, ANDREW MICHAEL, former dean, finance educator; b. Montclair, NJ, 1943; m. Ann Bennett (div.); children: Graham, Catherine, Marya; m. Monica Spence. BA in Philosophy summa cum laude, Princeton U., 1966; BA, MA in Maths., Oxford U., 1968; PhD in Econs. with honors, Harvard U., 1972. Asst. prof. polit. econ. Kennedy Sch. Govt. Harvard U., Cambridge, Mass., 1971-75, hon. rsch. fellow, 1975—76, vis. prof. econs. dept., 1976-77, prof. econs., 1977-83, prof. bus. adminstrn., 1979-83, George Gund prof. econs. and bus. adminstrn., 1983-86, chmn. bus. econs. PhD program, 1981-83, chmn. econs. dept., 1983-84, dean Faculty Arts and Scis., 1984-90; assoc. prof. dept. econs. Stanford U., Calif., 1973-75, Philip H. Knight Prof., dean Grad. Sch. Bus. Calif., 1990-99, Philip H. Knight Prof. Emeritus, prof. mgmt. Calif., 1999—; ptnr. Oak Hill Venture Ptnrs. and Oak Hill Capital Ptnrs., Menlo Park, Calif., 1999—. Bd. dirs. Gen. Mills, Inc., Nike, Inc., Exult Inc., Siebel Syss. Inc., Blue Martini Software, Torstar Corp., ITI Edn.; mem. econs. adv. panel NSF, 1977-79; chmn. Nat. Rsch. Coun. Bd. on Sci., Tech. and Econ., Policy, 1990-97. Author: Market Signaling: Informational Transfer in Hiring and Related Processes, 1974; Co-author: Industrial Organization in an Open Economy, 1980, Competitive Structure in Investment Banking, 1983; past mem. editl. bd. Am. Econs. Rev., Bell. Jour. Econs., Jour. Econ. Theory and Pub. Policy; contbr. over 50 articles to profl. jours. Mem. econs. adv. com. Sloan Found., 1979—. Recipient J.K. Galbraith prize for excellence in tchg., 1978, Nobel prize in econ. scis., 2001, Golden Plate award, Acad. Achievement, 2006; Danforth fellow, 1966, Rhodes scholar, 1966. Fellow Am. Acad. Arts & Scis., 1983-, Econometric Soc.; mem. Am. Econ. Assn. (John Bates Clark medal 1981). Office: Stanford U Grad Sch Bus Bldg 350 Memorial Way Stanford CA 94305-5015 also: Oak Hill Venture Partnership 2775 Sand Hill Rd Ste 220 Menlo Park CA 94025-7085

SPENCE, GERRY (GERALD LEONARD SPENCE), lawyer, writer; b. Laramie, Wyo., Jan. 8, 1929; s. Gerald M. and Esther Sophie (Pfleeger) S.; m. Anna Wilson, June 20, 1947; children: Kip, Kerry, Kent, Katy; m. LaNelle Hampton Peterson, Nov. 18, 1969. BSL, U. Wyo., 1949, LLB, 1952, LLD (hon.), 1990. Bar: Wyo. 1952, U.S. Ct. Claims 1952, U.S. Supreme Ct. 1982. Sole practice, Riverton, Wyo., 1952-54; county and pros. atty. Fremont County, Wyo., 1954-62; ptnr. various law firms, Riverton and Casper, Wyo., 1962-78; sr. ptnr. Spence, Moriarity & Schuster, Jackson, Wyo., 1978—2002, Spence, Moriarity & Shockey, 2002—03, Spence Law Firm, 2004—. Founder Trial Lawyers Coll.; lectr. legal orgns. and law schs. Author: (with others) Gunning for Justice, 1982, Of Murder and Madness, 1983, Trial by Fire, 1986, With Justice for None, 1989, From Freedom to Slavery, 1993, How To Argue and Win Every Time, 1995, The Making of a Country Lawyer, 1996, O.J.: The Last Word, 1997, Give Me Liberty, 1998, A Boy's Summer, 2000, Gerry Spence's Wyoming: The Landscapes, 2000, Half Moon and Empty Stars, 2001, Seven Simple Steps to Personal Freedom, 2001, The Smoking Gun, 2003, Win Your Case, 2005, Bloodthirsty Bitches and Pious Pimps of Power: The Rise and Risk of the New Conservative Hate Culture, 2006. Mem. ABA, Wyo. Bar Assn., Wyo. Trial Lawyers Assn., Assn. Trial Lawyers Am., Nat. Assn. Criminal Def. Lawyers Office: The Spence Law Firm LLC PO Box 548 Jackson WY 83001-0548 Office Phone: 307-733-7290. Office Fax: 307-733-5248. Business E-Mail: infointake@spencelawyers.com.

SPENCE, NANCY, state legislator; b. Denver, Dec. 12, 1936; m. Peter Spence; 4 children. Attended, Colo. State U., Ft. Collins. Mem. Dist. 39 Colo. House of Reps., Denver, 1999—2004; mem. Dist. 27 Colo. State Senate, Denver, 2004—, minority whip. Republican. Roman Catholic. Office: Colo State Capitol 200 E Colfax Rm 200 Denver CO 80203 Office Phone: 303-866-4883. Business E-Mail: nancyspence@qwest.net.*

SPENCER, CAROLE A., medical association administrator, educator; BSc in Applied Biochemistry, Bath U. Tech., Bath, Somerset, Eng., 1969; PhD, Glasgow U., Scotland, 1972. Lic. clin. chemist med. technologist Calif., 1985. Lectr. in biochemistry Glasgow U., Scotland, 1972—73; asst. prof. rsch. medicine U. So. Calif., LA, 1980—88, assoc. prof. rsch. medicine, 1988—94, prof. rsch. medicine, 1995—, dir. Endocrine Svcs. Lab., 1980—, GCRC Core Lab. dir. Clin. Rsch. Ctr., 1977—, GCRC Core Low Level Ligand Detection lab. dir., 1993—. Biochemist dept. pathol. biochemistry Glasgow Royal Infirmary, 1973—77; lectr. in field; cons. in field. Editl. bd. Jour. Clin. endocrinology and Metabolism, 1984—88, Am. Assn. Clin. Chemistry Jours., 1996—, Hormone and Metabolic Rsch., 1996—, reviewer Annals of Internal Medicine, —, Clin. Chemistry, —, Gerontology, —, Hormone and Metabolic Rsch., —, Jour. of Clin. Endocrinology and Metabolism, —, Jour. of Clin. Investigation, —, Jour. of Endocrinol. Investigation, —; contbr. articles to profl. jours. Mem.: European Thyroid Assn., Assn. Clin. Biochemists U.K., Endocrine Soc., Clin. Ligand Assay Soc. (Disting. Scientist award 1998), Am. Thyroid Assn. (pub. health com. 1991—, pres., exec. coun. 1995—), Am. Fedn. Clin. Rsch., Am. Assn. Clin. endocrinologists, Am. Assn. Clin. Chemists (Outstanding Spkr. award 1992, 1997), Cross-Town Endocrine Club. Achievements include research in includes thyroid physiology and pathology; thyroglobulin and thyroid cancer; thyroid hormone metabolism; immunoassay techniques. Office: U Southern Calif EDM111 9560 Los Angeles CA 90089

SPENCER, JOHN ANDREW, real estate development corporation executive; b. Ft. Pierce, Fla., Sept. 26, 1948; s. Andrew Jackson and Kathryn Samantha (Gray) S.; m. Maria Ester Cascante, Sept. 29, 1979; 1 child, Sarah. BS, Fla. State U., 1970; MS, Ariz. State U., 1976. CPA, Ariz. Sr. auditor Peat, Marwick, Mitchell & Co., Phoenix, 1976-79; asst. controller, controller Sahara Hotel and Casino, Las Vegas, 1979-80; asst. treas. Del Webb Hotels, Las Vegas, 1980-82; asst. controller, controller Del E. Webb Corp., Phoenix, 1982-85, v.p., controller, 1985-98, exec. v.p., CFO, 1998—. Mem. profl. adv. bd. Ariz. State U. Acctg. Dept., Tempe, 1985—. Served with USAR, 1970-76. Mem. Am. Inst. CPA's, Ariz. State Soc. CPA's. Republican. Methodist. Office: Del Webb Corp 15333 N Pima Rd Ste 300 Scottsdale AZ 85260-2782

SPENCER, MARGARET GILLIAM, lawyer; b. Spokane, Aug. 30, 1951; d. Jackson Earl and Margaret Kathleen (Hindley) Gilliam; m. John Bernard Spencer, Feb. 21, 1993. BA in Sociology, U. Mont., 1974, MA in Sociology, 1978, JD, 1982. Bar: Mont. 1982, Colo. 1982. Assoc. Holland & Hart, Denver, 1982-84, Roath & Brega, P.C., Denver, 1984-88, shareholder, dir., 1988-89; spl. counsel Brega & Winters, P.C., Denver, 1989; corp. counsel CH2M Hill, Inc., Denver, 1989—. Democrat. Episcopalian. Avocations: skiing, scuba diving. Office: CH2M Hill Inc 9191 S Jamaica St Englewood CO 80112 Business E-Mail: pspencer@ch2m.com.

SPENCER, PETER SIMNER, neurotoxicologist; b. London, Nov. 30, 1946; U.S. citizen; married; 2 children. BSc, U. London, 1968, PhD in Pathology, 1971. Rsch. asst. Nat. Hosp. Nervous Disorders U. London, 1968-70, rsch. fellow Royal Free Hosp. Sch. Medicine, 1970-71; fellow pathology Albert Einstein Coll. Medicine, 1971-73, asst. prof., 1973-81, assoc. prof. neurosci., 1977-83, prof. neurosci., 1983-88, assoc. prof. pathology, dir. Inst. Neurotoxicology, 1979-88; dir., cr. scientist Ctr. Rsch. of Occupl. Environ./Toxicol. Oreg. Health Sci. U., 1988—, prof. neurology and mem. neurosci. faculty, 1988—. Cons. Nat. Inst. Occupational Safety & Health, 1976-77, EPA, 1977—; chmn. adv. bd. Jour. Neurotoxicology, 1978—; mem. adv. bd. Rutgers U. Toxicology Program, 1984, Howe & Assocs., 1985, Peripheral Nerve Repair & Regeneration, 1985; mem. bd. toxicol. and environ. health hazards NAS, 1984, Safe Drinking Water Com., 1985; sec. Third World Med. Rsch. Found., 1985—; adj. prof. Coll. Vet. Medicine Oreg. State U. Assoc. editor Jour. Neurocytology, 1977—; author: Experimental and Clin. Neurotoxicology. Fellow Joseph P. Kennedy Jr. Found., 1974-76; recipient Silvio O. Conte Nat. prize for Neuroscience contbns. relevant to environ. health, 1993, Sr. Travel award Alzheimer Assn. Mem. AAAS, Am. Assn. Neuropathologists (Weil award 1976, Moore award), Am. Soc. Cell Biologists, Am. Neurological Assn., Anatomic Soc. Gt. Britain & Ireland, Brit. Neuropathology Soc., World Fedn. Neurology, Royal Coll. Pathologists, Pan-Am. Neuroepidiology Found. (hon.). Achievements include research in cellular relationships in the nervous system and the effects of neurotoxic chemicals. Office: Oregon Health Scis U # L606 3181 SW Sam Jackson Park Rd Portland OR 97201-3079

SPENCER, ROBERT C., retired political science educator; b. Chgo., Mar. 28, 1920; m. Edith Maxham McCarthy, Sept. 13, 1941; children: Margaret, Catherine, Anne, Thomas More, David. AB, U. Chgo., 1943, MA, 1952, PhD in Polit. Sci. (Univ. fellow 1952-53), 1955. Instr. polit. sci. and sociology St. Michaels Coll., 1949-51, asst., then assoc. prof. polit. sci., 1953-60, prof. govt., 1960-63, dir. summer sessions, 1960-61, asst. to pres., 1963-65; prof. polit. sci., chmn. dept., dean summer sessions U. R.I., 1965-67; grad. dean U. R.I. (Grad. Sch.), 1967-69; founding pres. Sangamon State U., Springfield, Ill., 1969-78, prof. govt. and public affairs, 1978-88; prof. emeritus U. Ill. Springfield, 1988-93, retired, 1993—. Research assoc. Indsl. Relations Center, U. Chgo., 1952-58; extension lectr. N.Y. State Sch. Indsl. and Labor Relations, Cornell U., 1956-57; vice chmn. West Central Ill. Ednl. Telecommunications Consortium, 1975-77, chmn., 1977-78; chmn. task force personnel Vt. Little Hoover Commn., 1957-58; mem. Ill. adv. com. U.S. Commn. on Civil Rights, 1979-87; bd. mgrs. Franklin Life Variable Annuity Funds, 1974—; vis. prof. polit. sci., sr. rsch. assoc. local govt. ctr. Mont. State U., Bozeman, 1985, 89, 90—. Author: (with Robert J. Huckshorn) The Politics of Defeat, 1971. Bd. dirs. City Day Sch., Springfield, 1979-83, Gt. Am. People Show Repertory Co., 1980-90; vice chmn. Petersburg Libr. Bd., 1982-88; chmn. Petersburg Zoning Bd. Appeals, 1984-90; mem. Vt. Senate, 1959-63; faculty fellow Ford Found.'s Nat. Ctr. for Edn. in Politics, rsch. dir. Dem. Nat. Com., 1962-63; mem. adv. bd. Landmark Preservation Coun. Ill., 1986-89; mem., treas. Gallatin County Coun. on Aging, 1993—. Roman Catholic. Home: 2303 S 3rd Ave Bozeman MT 59715-6009

SPENCER, TED M., museum director; Exec. dir. Alaska Aviation Heritage Mus., Anchorage, 1977-2000; curator Alaska Hist. Aviation Inst., Anchorage, San Diego, 2000—. Home and Office: 6561 Green Gables Ave San Diego CA 92119-2927

SPENCER, TERRY R., state legislator, lawyer; b. Logan, Utah, Mar. 19, 1960; m. Sharon Perschon; 2 children. BS in Polit. Sci., Utah State U., MS in Econs., PhD in Econs., Utah State U.; JD, Brigham Young U. Bar: Utah, Idaho, Calif. Atty. TR Spencer & Assocs.; mem. Utah Senate, Dist. 22, Salt Lake City, 1998—; chair judiciary com.; mem. state/local affairs com., higher edn. appropriations. Active Boy Scouts Am. Republican. Home: 2161 W 2300 S Syracuse UT 84075-9362 E-mail: vimcla@sprynet.com.

SPERBER, BURTON S., construction executive; b. 1929; Chmn., pres. Valley Crest Landscape, Inc., Calabasas, Calif., 1949—. Office: Environ Industries Inc 24121 Ventura Blvd Calabasas CA 91302-1449

SPERLING, GEORGE, psychologist, educator; s. Otto and Melitta Sperling BS in Math., U. Mich., 1955; MA in Psychology, Columbia U., 1956; PhD in Psychology, Harvard U., 1959. Rsch. asst. in biophysics Brookhaven Nat. Labs., Upton, NY, summer 1955; rsch. asst. in psychology Harvard U., Cambridge, Mass., 1957-59; mem. tech. rsch. staff Acoustical and Behavioral Rsch. Ctr., AT&T Bell Labs., Murray Hill, NJ, 1958-86; prof. psychology and neural sci. NYU, NYC, 1970-92; disting. prof. cognitive scis., neurobiology and behavior U. Calif., Irvine, 1992—. Instr. psychology Washington Sq. Coll., NYU, 1962-63; vis. assoc. prof. psychology Duke U., spring 1964; adj. assoc. prof. psychology Columbia U., 1964-65; acting assoc. prof. psychology UCLA, 1967-68; hon. rsch. assoc. Univ. Coll., U. London, 1969-70; vis. prof. psychology U. Western Australia, Perth, 1972, U. Wash., Seattle, 1977; vis. scholar Stanford (Calif.) U., 1984; mem. sci. adv. bd. USAE, 1988-92. Recipient Meritorious Civilian Svc. medal USAF, 1993; Gomberg scholar U. Mich., 1953-54; Guggenheim fellow, 1969-70, APS fellow. Fellow: APA (Disting. Sci. Contbn. award 1988), AAAS, Am. Psychol. Soc. (William James fellow), Optical Soc. Am. (Tillyer award 2002), Am. Acad. Arts and Sci.; mem.: NAS, Internat. Neural Network Soc. (founding mem., mem. governing bd. 1987—91, Helmholtz award 2004), Soc. Math. Psychology (exec. bd. 1979—85, chmn. 1983—84), Soc. Exptl. Psychologists (Warren medal 1996), Psychonomic Soc., Soc. Computers in Psychology (steering com. 1974—78), Eastern Psychol. Assn. (bd. dirs. 1982—85), Am. Interdisciplinary Conf. (organizer 1975—, founder), Assn. Rsch. in Vision and Ophthalmology, Sigma Xi, Phi Beta Kappa. Office: U Calif SS Plz A Dept Cognitive Scis Irvine CA 92697-5100 E-mail: sperling@uci.edu.

SPERLING, JOHN GLEN, education company executive, educator; b. Willow Springs, Mo., Jan. 9, 1921; s. Leon Birchfield and Lena (McNama) S.; m. Virginia Vandergrift, June 1951 (div. 1965); 1 child, Peter Vandegrift. BA, Reed Coll., 1948; MA, U. Calif., 1952; PhD, U. Cambridge, Eng., 1955. Mem. faculty Northern Ill. U.; instr. U. Md., Europe, 1955-57; asst. professor Ohio State U., Columbus, 1957—61; prof. Humanities San Jose (Calif.) State U., 1961—73, dir., Right to Read Project, dir., NSF Cooperative Coll.-Sch. Sci. Prog in Econ.; pres. Inst. Profl. Devel., San Jose, 1972-76; founder, pres. U. Phoenix, 1976-80; founder, dir. Apollo Group Inc., Phoenix, 1973—, pres., 1973—98, CEO, 1973—2001, chmn. bd. dir., 1973—2004, acting exec. chmn., 2006—. Author: The South Sea Company, 1964, Great Depressions: 1837, 1893, and 1929, 1966, Against All Odds, 1989; co-author: (with Peter Dixon) War Finance 1698-1714, (with Suzanne Helburn) Economic Concepts and Institutions, 1974, Industry Performance, 1974, National Economic Policies, 1974, Social and Economic Priorities, 1974, Communist Economics, 1974, Third World Economics, 1974, (with Robert Tucker) For Profit Higher Education: Developing a World Class Workforce, 1997; contbr. articles to profl. jours. including Hist. Jour., Econ. History Rev., Bull. NASSP, Rule Mag., among others. Cons. Combating Juvenile Delinquency, Sunnyvale, Calif., 1972-75. Recipient Ehrman Studentship, Kings Coll., Cambridge U., 1953-55, Acad. Freedom award Calif. Fedn. Tchrs., L.A., 1988; named of Forbes Richest Americans, 2006. Mem. Arizona Club. Democrat. Founder the U. Phoenix, which has established itself as a leading provider of higher education programs for working adults by focusing on servicing the needs of the working adult; Primary investor in Genetic Savings and Clone, Inc., "Missyplicity Project" (cloned dog) and "Operation CC" (cloned cat that was created was called CopyCat), made first sale: a cloned male kitten, for $50,000 in December, 2004; latest quest: to research, develop, and sell the new science of longevity; opponent of drug prohibition and is actively financing initiatives to legalize medical marijuana in the US. Office: Apollo Group Inc 4615 E Elwood St Phoenix AZ 85040-1958 Office Phone: 480-921-5394.

SPEYER, JASON LEE, aeronautical engineer, educator; b. Boston, Apr. 30, 1938; s. Joseph Louis and Ruth Sylvia (Steinmetz) S.; m. Barbara Joan Sachs, Sept. 11, 1966; children— Gil, Gavriel, Rakhel, Joseph BS, MIT, 1960; MS, Harvard U., 1964, PhD, 1968. Registered profl. engr., Tex. Engr. Boeing Co., Seattle, 1960-61; sr. engr. Raytheon Co., Bedford, Mass., 1961-68; sr. analyst Analytical Mechanics Assocs., Inc., Cambridge, Mass., 1968-70; mem. research staff Charles Stark Draper Lab., Cambridge, Mass., 1970-76; Harry H. Power prof. engring. U. Tex., Austin, 1976-90; prof. engring. UCLA, 1990—. Lectr. MIT, 1971-76; vis. scientist Weizmann Inst. Sci., 1972-73; Lady Davis prof. Technion, Haifa, Israel, 1983; Hunsaker vis. prof. aeros. and astronautics MIT, 1989-90. Recipient Hocott Disting. Engring. Rsch. award Coll. Engring., U. Tex., 1985, Exceptional Civil Svc. award USAF, 1991; Raytheon fellow, 1963-67; Hugh L. Dryden lectureship Am. Inst. of Aeronautics and Astronautics, 1995 Fellow IEEE (bd. govs. Control Sys. Soc. 1982—, assoc. editor Transaction on Automatic Control), AIAA (Mechanics and Control of Flight award 1985, Dryden lectureship in rsch. 1995, assoc. editor Jour. Spacecraft and Rockets, Jour. Guidance and Control), NAE. Home: 11358 Chalon Rd Los Angeles CA 90049-1721 Office: UCLA Dept Mech Aerospace Engring 420 Westwood Plz # 951597 Los Angeles CA 90095-8357

SPIEGELBERG, HANS LEONHARD, medical educator; b. Basel, Switzerland, Jan. 8, 1933; came to U.S., 1961; s. Hans G. S.; m. Elizabeth von der Crone, May 19, 1962; children: Franzi, Daniel, Markus. MD, U. Basel, Basel, 1958. Med. diplomate, Switzerland. Intern and resident in pediatric allergy and immunology Dept. of Medicine, U. of Basel, Switzerland; intern and resident in allergy and immunology NYU, NYC, 1961-63; with Scripps Rsch. Inst., La Jolla, Calif., 1963-90; prof. U. Calif., San Diego, 1990—, now prof. emeritus. Cons. VA Med. Ctr., L.A., 1966-90. Editor (jour.) Seminars in Immunopathology, 1988—. Home: 2234 Paseo Dorado La Jolla CA 92037-3208

SPIEGELMAN, ART, writer, cartoonist; b. Stockholm, Feb. 15, 1948; s. Wladek and Andzia (Zylberberg) S.; m. Francoise Mouly, July 12, 1977; children: Nadja, Dashiell. Student, Harpur Coll. (now SUNY), Binghamton, NY. Creative cons., artist, designer, editor, writer Topps Chewing Gum, Inc., Bklyn., 1966-88; editor Douglas Comix, 1972; contbg. editor Arcade, the Comics Revue, 1975-76; founding editor Raw, 1980—; artist, contbg. editor New Yorker, 1992—2003. Instr. San Francisco Acad. Art, 1974-75, NY Sch. Visual Arts, 1979-87. Author, illustrator: The Complete Mr. Infinity, 1970, The Viper Vicar of Vice, Villainy, and Vickedness, 1972, Ace Hole, Midge Detective, 1974, The Language of Comics, 1974, Breakdowns: From Maus to Now: An Anthology of Strips, 1977, Work and Turn, 1979, Every Day Has Its Dog, 1979, Two-Fisted Painters Action Adventure, 1980, Maus: A Survivor's Tale, 1986 (Joel M. Cavior award for Jewish Writing 1986, Nat. Book Critics Cir. nomination 1986, Pulitzer prize 1992), Maus, Part Two, 1992 (Nat. Book Critics Cir. nomination 1992, Pulitzer prize 1992, Eisner award, 1992, Harvey award, 1992), Open Me...I'm a Dog!, 1997; (with J.M. March) The Wild Party, 1994, Kisses from New York; (with F. Mouly) Read Yourself Raw, 1987, In the Shadow of No Towers, 2004 (named one of the 100 Notable Books of 2004, NY Times Book Review), Breakdowns: Portrait of the Artist as a Young %@&*!, 2008; contbr. The Apex Treasury of Underground Comics, 1974; compiling editor (with B. Schneider) Whole Grains: A Book of Quotations, 1972; creator (with composer Phillip Johnston) Drawn to Death: A Three Panel Opera, Am. Repertory Theatre Co., Cambridge, Mass.; editor (comic series) Little Lit, 2000-03; exhbns. include NY Cultural Ctr., Inst. Contemporary Art, London, Seibu Gallery, Tokyo, Mus. Modern Art, NYC, 1991, Galerie St. Etienne, NYC, 1992, Ft. Lauderdale Mus. Art, 1993, LA Mus. Contemporary Art, 2005; creator Wacky Packages, Garbage Pail Kids and other novelties; contbr. to numerous underground comics. Named one of Time Mag. 100 Most Influential People, 2005; named to Will Eisner Award Hall of Fame, 1999, Art Dir.'s Club Hall of Fame, 2006; recipient Playboy Editorial award for best comic strip, 1982, Yellow Kid award for best comic strip author, 1982, Regional Design award, Print mag., 1983, 1984, 1985, Inkpot award, San Diego Comics Conv., 1987, Stripschappening award for best fgn. comics album, 1987, Alpha Art award, Angoulerne, France, 1993, Chevalier de l'Ordre des Arts et des Lettres, France, 2005. Fellow: Am. Acad. Arts and Sciences. Office: c/o The Steven Barclay Agency 321 Pleasant St Petaluma CA 94952-2648 Office Phone: 888-965-7323.

SPIELBERG, STEVEN ALLAN, film director, producer; b. Cin., Dec. 18, 1946; m. Amy Irving, Nov. 27, 1985 (div. Feb. 2, 1989); 1 child: Max Samuel; m. Kate Capshaw Oct. 12, 1991; children: Theo (adopted), Sasha, Sawyer, Mikaela (adopted), Destry, Jessica (stepchild). BA, Calif. State U., Long Beach; D of creative arts (hon.), Brandeis U., 1986; DHL (hon.), Yale U., 2002. Founder Amblin Entertainment, 1984—; co-founder (with Jeffrey Katzenberg & David Geffen), ptnr. DreamWorks SKG, Universal City, 1994—. Co-founder DreamWorks SKG, 1995—2005; co-creator of concept, story and design of new game franchises EA Games, LA, 2005—; artistic adv. 2008 Olympic Games, Beijing, 2007—08. Dir.: (films) The Last Gun, 1959, Jaws, 1975, 1941, 1979, Raiders of the Lost Ark, 1981 (Acad. Award nomination for best dir., 1982), Indiana Jones and the Temple of Doom, 1984, Indiana Jones and the Last Crusade, 1989, Hook, 1991, Jurassic Park, 1993, The Lost World: Jurassic Park, 1997, Minority Report, 2002, War of the Worlds, 2005, Indiana Jones and the Kingdom of the Crystal Skull, 2008; dir., prodr. (films) E.T. the Extra-Terrestrial, 1982 (Acad. Award nomination for best dir., 1983, Acad. Award nomination for best picture, 1983), Twilight Zone: The Movie, 1983; dir.: (TV films) Columbo: Murder by the Book, 1971, Duel, 1971, Something Evil, 1972, Savage, 1973, (episodes for TV series) The Name of the Game, 1968, Marcus Welby, M.D., 1969, Night Gallery, 1970, The Psychiatrist, 1971, Owen Marshall: Counselor at Law, 1971; exec. prodr.: (films) I Wanna Hold Your Hand, 1978, Used Cars, 1980, Continental Divide, 1981, Gremlins, 1984, Back to the Future, 1985, Young Sherlock Holmes, 1985, The Money Pit, 1986, An American Tail, 1986, Innerspace, 1987, *batteries not included, 1987, Who Framed Roger Rabbit, 1988, The Land Before Time, 1988, Tummy Trouble, 1989, Dad, 1989, Back to the Future Part II, 1989, Joe Versus the Volcano, 1990, Yume, 1990, Back to the Future Part III, 1990, Roller Coaster Rabbit, 1990, Gremlins 2: The New Batch, 1990, Arachnophobia, 1990, Trail Mix-Up, 1993, We're Back! A Dinosaur's Story, 1993, I'm Mad, 1994, The Flintstones, 1994, Casper, 1995, Balto, 1995, Twister, 1996, The Lost Children of Berlin, 1997, Men in Black, 1997, Deep Impact, 1998, The Mask of Zorro, 1998, The Last Days, 1998, The Haunting, 1999, Eyes of the Holocaust, 2000, Jurassic Park III, 2001, Price for Peace, 2002, Men in Black II, 2002, The Legend of Zorro, 2005, Monster House, 2006, Disturbia, 2007, Transformers, 2007; (TV films) Class of '61, 1993, Survivors of the Holocaust, 1996, Shooting War, 2000, Semper Fi,

2001, We Stand Alone Together, 2001, Burma Bridge Busters, 2003, Dan Finnerty & the Dan Band: I Am Women, 2005; (TV miniseries) Band of Brothers, 2001 (Emmy for outstanding miniseries, 2002), Broken Silence, 2002, Taken, 2002 (Emmy for outstanding miniseries, 2003), Into the West, 2005; (TV series) The Plucky Duck Show, 1992, Family Dog, 1992, SeaQuest DSV, 1993—96, ER, 1994, Pinky and the Brain, 1995—98, Freakazoid!, 1995—97, Toonsylvania, 1998—2000, Pinky, Elmyra & the Brain, 1998, On the Lot, 2007; prodr.: (films) An American Tail: Fievel Goes West, 1991; writer (films) Ace Eli and Rodger of the Skies, 1973, dir., prodr. The Color Purple, 1985 (Acad. Award nomination for best picture, 1986), Empire of the Sun, 1987, Always, 1989, Schindler's List, 1993 (Acad. Award for best dir., 1994, Acad. Award for best picture, 1994, Golden Globe for best dir., 1994), Amistad, 1997, Saving Private Ryan, 1998 (Acad. Award for best dir., 1999, Acad. Award nomination for best picture, 1999, Golden Globe for best dir., 1999, Disting. Pub. Svc. Award USN, 1999), Catch Me If You Can, 2002, The Terminal, 2004, Munich, 2005, dir., writer Fighter Squad, 1961, Escape to Nowhere, 1961, Firelight, 1964, Slipstream, 1967, Amblin', 1968, The Sugarland Express, 1974, Close Encounters of the Third Kind, 1977 (Acad. Award nomination for best dir., 1978); prodr.: (films) Memoirs of a Geisha, 2005, Flags of Our Fathers, 2006, Letters from Iwo Jima, 2006; prodr., writer (films) Poltergeist, 1982, exec. prodr., writer The Goonies, 1985, (TV series) Amazing Stories, 1985—87, Tiny Toon Adventures, 1990—92, Animaniacs, 1993—98, consulting prodr. The Unites States of Tara, 2009—, dir., prodr., writer (films) Artificial Intelligence: AI, 2001, asst. dir. action scenes Star Wars III: Revenge of the Sith, 2005. Mem. adv. bd. Sci. Fiction Mus. and Hall of Fame. Recipient Man of Yr. award Hasty Pudding Theater, Harvard U., 1983, Outstanding Directorial Achievement award for feature films Dirs. Guild Am., 1985, Film award Brit. Acad. Film and TV Arts, 1986, Irving Thalberg Mem. award Acad. Motion Picture Arts and Scis., 1987, Golden Lion award for career achievement Venice Film Festival, 1993, Life Achievement award Am. Film Inst., 1995, John Huston award Artists Rights Found., 1995, Kennedy Ctr. Honor, John F. Kennedy Center for Performing Arts, 2006, The French Legion of Honor, 2008, Cecil B. DeMille award, Hollywood Fgn. Press Assn., 2009; named Entertainment Weekly's Most Powerful Person in Entertainment, 1997, Lifetime Achievement award, Dir. Guild Am., 2000; named one of 50 Most Powerful People in Hollywood Premiere mag., 2004-06, Forbes' Richest Americans, 1999—, World's Richest People, Forbes mag. 2001—, 100 Top Celebrities, Forbes mag., 2001—, The 100 Most Powerful Celebrities, 2007, 2008, Forbes.com, 50 Smartest People in Hollywood, Entertainment Weekly, 2007, America's Best Leaders, US News & World Report, 2008; named a Knight Comdr. of the British Empire (KBE), Her Majesty Queen Elizabeth II, 2001. Fellow Brit. Acad. Film and TV Arts. Achievements include winning film contest with 40-minute war movie, Escape to Nowhere, at age 13; made film Firelight at age 16, and made 5 films while in coll.; became TV dir. at Universal Pictures at age 20. Office: c/o Dreamworks SKG 100 Universal City Plz Bldg 477 Universal City CA 91608-1002

SPIERKEL, GREGORY M., information technology executive; b. 1957; BA, Carleton U., Ottawa, Can.; MBA, Georgetown U.; attended, Advanced Manufacturing Program at INSEAD, Fontainbleau, France. Mng. dir. Mitel Telecom, United Kingdom, 1986—89; gen. mgr. Mitel Far East Ltd., Hong Kong, 1989—90; pres., CEO, N. Am. Mitel Inc., Reston, Va., 1992—96, v.p., global sales and marketing Canada, 1996—97; sr. v.p., pres. Ingram Micro Inc., Santa Ana, Calif., 1997—99; pres. Ingram Micro Asia-Pacific, 1997—99; exec. v.p. Ingram Micro Inc., 1999—2004, officer, 1997—; pres. Ingram Micro Europe, 1999—2004, Ingram Micro Inc., 2004—05, CEO, 2005—. Bd. dir. PACCAR Corp., 2008—. Bd. mem. Sch. Bus., U. Calif., Irvine. Office: Ingram Micro Inc 1600 E St Andrew Pl Santa Ana CA 92705-4931 Office Phone: 714-566-1000. Office Fax: 714-566-7900.

SPILKER, LINDA JOYCE, aerospace scientist; b. Mpls., Apr. 26, 1955; d. Arthur Elzear and Bonnie Joy (Jansen) Bies; m. John Leonard Horn, Jr., July 31, 1976 (div.); children: Jennifer, Jessica; m. Thomas Richard Spilker, 1997. BA in Physics, Calif. State U., Fullerton, 1977; MS in Physics, Calif. State U., LA, 1983; PhD in Geophysics and Space Physics, UCLA, 1992. Rep. Voyager Infrared Radiometer and Spectrometer expt. Jet Propulsion Lab., Pasadena, Calif., 1977-90, sci. assoc. Voyager Photopolarimeter, 1984-90, sc. assoc. Voyager Infrared Radiometer and Spectrometer, 1988-90, study scientist Cassini asst., 1988-90, co-investigator Cassini Composite Infrared Spectrometer, 1990—, dep. project scientist Cassini mission, 1990—, prin. investigator planetary geology and geophysics, 1993—. Mem. planetary sci. data steering group NASA, Washington, 1991-95, adv. coun. for planetary data sys. ring node, Moffett Field, Calif., 1990—. Contbr. chpt. Van Nostrand Encyclopedia of Planetary Science, 1994; contbr. jour. articles Icarus. Pres. North San Gabriel Valley Dem. Club, Monrovia, Calif., 1992-94. Recipient Exceptional Svc. medal, NASA, 1990, Sci. Achievement award, 1992, Disting. Alumna award, Calif. State U., L.A., 1996, Calif. State U., Fullerton, 2005; named one of Hottest 25 in Orange County, Orange County Metro mag., 2004; named to Hall of Fame, Placentia-Yorba Linda Unified Sch. Dist., 1998—99. Mem. AAAS, AAUW, Divsn. of Planetary Sci. Democrat. Presbyterian. Avocations: hiking, astronomical observing, piano, jogging. Home: 457 Granite Ave Monrovia CA 91016-2324 Office: Jet Propulsion Lab MS 230-205 4800 Oak Grove Dr Pasadena CA 91109-8001 Business E-Mail: Linda.J.Spilker@jpl.nasa.gov.

SPILLER, EBERHARD ADOLF, physicist, researcher; b. Halbendorf, Ger., Apr. 16, 1933; came to U.S., 1968; s. Walter Richard and Ruth Elfriede Spiller; children: Michael, Bettina. Diploma, U. Frankfurt, Ger., 1960, PhD, 1964. With U. Frankfurt, 1960-68; physicist IBM Research Center, Yorktown Heights, NY, 1968-93; emeritus physicist IBM, 1993-97; owner Spiller X-Ray Optics, 1996—. Guest prof. Tech. U. Denmark, 1994—95, U. Ctrl. Fla., 1996; vis. scientist European Synchrotron Radiation Facility Nat. Inst. Stds. and Tech., 1996—97; vis. scientist Lawrence Livermore Lab., Calif., 1997—. Author: Soft X-Ray Optics, 1994. Fellow AAAS, Am. Optical Soc., Photo-Optic Instrumentation Soc.; mem. German Phys. Soc. Achievements include research in solid state physics, laser and coherence optics, nonlinear optics, thin films, soft x-rays, x-ray microscopy, lithography; inventor multilayer x-ray optics, x-ray astronomy, x-ray lithography. Office: Lawrence Livermore Nat Lab MS-L210 Livermore CA 94551 Office Phone: 925-423-4938. E-mail: spiller@llnl.gov.

SPINDEL, ROBERT CHARLES, electrical engineering educator; b. NYC, Sept. 5, 1944; s. Morris Tayson and Isabel (Glazer) S.; m. Barbara June Sullivan, June 12, 1966; children: Jennifer Susan, Miranda Ellen BSEE, Cooper Union, 1965; MS, Yale U., 1966, MPhil, 1968, PhD, 1971. Postdoctoral fellow Woods Hole Oceanographic Instn., Mass., 1971-72, asst. scientist Mass., 1972-76, assoc. scientist Mass., 1976-82, sr. scientist Mass., 1982-87, chmn. dept. ocean engring. Mass., 1982-87; dir. applied physics lab. U. Wash., Seattle, 1987—. Mem. naval studies bd. NRC, 1987-99; mem. Naval Rsch. Adv. Com., 1998—. Contbr. articles to profl. jours.; patentee on underwater nav. Recipient A.B. Wood medal Brit. Inst. Acoustics, 1981, Gano Dunn medal The Cooper Union, 1989, Ocean Engr. Soc. Tech. Achievement award, 1990. Fellow IEEE (assoc. editor jour. 1982—), Acoustical Soc. Am., Marine Tech. Soc. (pres. elect 1991-93, pres. 1993-95), Oceanography Soc. (Munk award 2001). Independent. Jewish. Avocations: auto restoration, hiking. Home: 14859 SE 51st St Bellevue WA 98006-3515 Office: U Wash Applied Physics Lab 1013 NE 40th St Seattle WA 98105-6606 E-mail: spindel@APL.Washington.edu.

SPINDLER, GEORGE DEARBORN, anthropologist, educator, writer; b. Stevens Point, Wis., Feb. 28, 1920; s. Frank Nicholas and Winifred (Hatch) S.; m. Louise Schaubel, May 29, 1942 (dec. Feb. 1997); 1 dau., Sue Carol Spindler Coleman. BS, Central State Tchrs. Coll., Wis., 1940; MA, U. Wis., 1947; PhD, U. Calif. at Los Angeles, 1952. Tchr. sch. in, Wis., 1940-42; rsch. assoc. Stanford U., 1950-51, prof. anthropology and edn., 1954—2006, exec. head dept., 1963—67. Cons. editor Holt, Rinehart & Winston, 1965-91, Harcourt, 1991-99, Wadsworth-Thomson, 2002-; vis. prof. U. Wis., 1979-85, U. Calif., Santa Barbara, 1986-91, Harvard U., 1999. Author: Menomini Acculturation, 1955, (with A. Beals and L. Spindler) Culture in Process, 1967, rev. edit., 1973, Transmission of American Culture, 1959, (with L. Spindler) Dreamers Without Power, 1971, rev. edit., 1984, Burgbach: Urbanization and Identity in a German Village, 1973, (with Louise Spindler) The American Cultural Dialogue and its Transmission, 1990, (with Lorie Hammond) Innovations in Educational Ethnography, 2006; editor: Education and Anthropology, 1955, (with Louise Spindler) Case Studies in Cultural Anthropology, 1960—, Am. Anthropologist, 1962-66, Methods in Cultural Anthropology, 1965-71, Case Studies in Education and Culture, 1966-72, Basic Units in Anthropology, 1970, (with Janice Stockard) Globalization and Urbanization in Fifteen Cultures-Born in One World, Living in Another, 2006; editor, contbr.: Education and Culture, 1963, Being An Anthropologist, 1970, Education and Cultural Process, 1974, rev. edit., 1987, 97, The Making of Psychological Anthropology, 1978, 2nd edit., 1994, Doing the Ethnography of Schooling, 1982, Interpretive Ethnography of Schooling at Home and Abroad, 1987, Pathways to Cultural Awareness: Cultural Therapy with Students and Teachers, 1994, Fifty Years of Anthropology and Education: A Spindler Anthology, 2000. Pres. Peninsula Sch. Bd., Menlo Park, Calif., 1954-56. Served with AUS, 1942-45. Recipient Lloyd W. Dinkelspeil award Stanford U., 1978, Disting. Svc. award Soc. Internat. Diplomacy and Third World Anthropologists, 1984, Disting. Career Contbn. award Com. on Role and Status of Minorities, Am. Edn. Rsch. Assn., Nat. Acad. Edn., 1994, Father of Ednl. Ethnography award Nat. Ednl. Ethnography Conf., 2000, George and Louise Spindler Excellence award Stanford U., 2001; fellow Ctr. Advanced Study of Behavioral Scis., 1956-57; subject of Vol. 17 Psychoanalytic Study of Soc. essays, 1992. Fellow Am. Anthrop. Assn.; mem. Southwestern Anthrop. Assn. (pres. 1962-63), Coun. for Anthropology and Edn. (pres. 1982, George and Louise Spindler award for outstanding contbns. to ednl. anthropology 1987, disting. Scholar award 1998), Nat. Acad. Edn. Office: Ethnographics 1247 Alice St Davis CA 95616-2174 Personal E-mail: geospinner@aol.com.

SPINDLER, PAUL, communications executive, consultant; b. Chgo., May 2, 1931; s. Isaac Edward and Sophie (Stein) Spindler; m. Gail Klynn; children from previous marriage: Kevin, Makayla, Sydney, Jeffrey. BA in Journalism, Temple U., 1952. Reporter Akron Beacon Jour., Akron, Ohio, 1955-58, San Francisco Examiner, 1958-59; editor Santa Clara (Calif.) Daily Jour., 1959-63; dir. pub. affairs Litton Industries, Inc., Beverly Hills, Calif., 1963-68; dir. pub. relations Internat. Industries, Beverly Hills, 1968-70; pres. Paul Spindler & Co., LA, 1970-75; exec. v.p. Manning Selvage & Lee, Inc., NYC, 1975-85; pres. The Spindler Co., LA, 1985-87; pres. Western div. GCI Group, LA, 1987-91; pres. GCI Spindler, LA, 1991-96; chmn. Bristol Retail Solutions, Inc., Newport Beach, Calif., 1996-98; pres. Paul Spindler Co., LA, 1998—. Bd. dirs. Phoenix House Calif.; bd. visitors, Temple U. Sch. Comm. and Theatre; co-pres., dir., The Partnership Scholars, 2004—. Bd. dirs. Bright Future Adoption Found. Cpl. US Army, 1952—54. Mem. Mountain Gate Country Club (L.A.). Democrat. Jewish. Office: Paul Spindler Co 1901 Ave of the Stars 2nd Flr Los Angeles CA 90067 Office Phone: 310-286-0102. Business E-Mail: paul@spindlercompany.com.

SPINELLA, JUDY LYNN, health facility administrator; b. Ft. Worth, Apr. 8, 1948; d. Gettis Breon and Velrea Inez (Webb) Prothro; children: Scott Slater, Jennifer. BS, U. Tex., 1971; MS, Tex. Woman's U., 1973; MBA, Vanderbilt U., 1993. RN, Tex., Calif., Tenn. Asst. prof. U. Tex., Arlington, 1976-81; dir. emergency svcs. San Francisco Gen. Hosp., 1981-84, assoc. adminstr. for clin. svcs., 1984-88; exec. dir. for nursing svcs. Vanderbilt U. Med. Ctr., Nashville, 1988-93, dir. patient care svcs., 1993-94; dir., COO Vanderbilt U. Hosp., Nashville, 1994-96; healthcare cons. APM, Inc., NYC, 1996—98; health care cons. The Meth. Hosp., Houston, 1998—2001, v.p. ops., 2001—04; pres., CEO Gunnison Valley Hosp., Colo., 2004—05; chief nursing officer U. N. Mex. Hosp., 2005—. Wharton fellow Johnson & Johnson, 1987. Mem. Am. Orgn. Nurse Execs., Am. Coll. Healthcare Execs., Emergency Nurses Assn. (bd. dirs., treas. 1979-86), Tenn. Orgn. Nurse Execs. (bd. dirs. 1989-91), Sigma Theta Tau. Avocations: hiking, skiing, travel. Office: U N Mex Hosp Chief Nursing Office 2211 Lomas Blvd NE Albuquerque NM 87106 Office Phone: 970-641-1456. Business E-Mail: jspinella@gvh-colorado.org. E-mail: jlspinella@aol.com.

SPINRAD, HYRON, astronomer; b. NYC, Feb. 17, 1934; s. Emanuel B. and Ida (Silverman) S.; m. Bette L. Abrams, Aug. 17, 1958; children— Michael, Robert, Tracy. AB, U. Calif., Berkeley, 1955; MA, U. Calif., 1959, PhD (Lick Obs. fellow), 1961. Studied galaxies U. Calif. at Berkeley, 1960-61; planetary atmospheres work Jet Propulsion Lab., Pasadena, Calif., 1961-63; investigation atmospheres of coolest stars U. Calif. at Berkeley, 1964-70. Mem. Am. Astron. Soc., Astron. Soc. Pacific. Achievements include spl. research water vapor on Mars, molecular hydrogen on Jupiter, Saturn, Uranus and Neptune, temperature measurements on Venus atmosphere, spectra of galaxies and near-infrared observations, 71-72, location of faint radio galaxies, redshifts of galaxies, galaxy evolution and cosmology, 1973, spectroscopic observations of volatile gases in comets. Office: U Calif Dept Astronomy Berkeley CA 94720-0001 Home: 613 Red Wing Ct Walnut Creek CA 94595-3927

SPIRO, MELFORD ELLIOT, anthropology educator; b. Cleve., Apr. 26, 1920; s. Wilbert I. and Sophie (Goodman) Spiro; m. Audrey Goldman, May 27, 1950; children: Michael, Jonathan. BA, U. Minn., 1941; PhD, Northwestern U., 1950. Mem. faculty Washington U., St. Louis, 1948—52, U. Conn., 1952—57, U. Wash., 1957—64; prof. anthropology U. Chgo., 1964—68; prof., chmn. dept. anthropology U. Calif., San Diego, 1968—99, prof. emeritus, 1999—. Author (with E.G. Burrows): An Atoll Culture, 1953; author: Kibbutz: Venture in Utopia, 1955, Children of Kibbutz, 1958, Burmese Supernaturalism, 1967, Buddhism and Society: A Great Tradition and Its Burmese Vicissitudes, 1971, Kinship and Marriage in Burma, 1977, Gender and Culture: Kibbutz Women Revisited, 1979, Culture and Human Nature, 1993, Oedipus in the Trobriands, 1982, Anthropological Other or Burmese Brother: Studies in Cultural Analysis, 1992, Gender Ideology and Psychological Reality, 1997; editor: Context and Meaning in Culture Anthropology, 1965. Bd. dirs. Social Sci. Rsch. Coun., 1960—62. Fellow: NAS, Am. Acad. Arts and Scis.; mem.: AAAS, Soc. for Psychol. Anthropology (pres. 1979—80), Am. Ethnol. Soc. (pres. 1967—68), Am. Anthrop. Assn. Home: 2500 Torrey Pines Rd La Jolla CA 92037-3400 Office: U Calif-San Diego 9500 Gilman Dr La Jolla CA 92093-0532 Business E-Mail: mspiro@ucsd.edu.

SPISAK, JOHN FRANCIS, corporation executive; b. Cleve., Mar. 27, 1950; s. Ernest Lawrence and Adele Marie (Chipko) S.; m. Barbara Ann Heisman, June 10, 1972; children: John Stefan, Theresa Rose. BS in Chemistry, Purdue U., 1972, BS in Biology with honors, 1972. Rsch. engr. Anaconda Minerals, Tucson, 1972-79; chief metallurgist Fed. Am. Uranium, Riverton, Wyo., 1979-80; v.p. ops. Anschutz Mining Corp., Denver, 1980-87; chmn. bd. dirs. Warrenton Refining (subs. of Anschutz Corp.), Denver, 1987-89; dir., owner BE&K/Terranext, Inc., Denver, 1989—; pres. Continental Supply, Woodland, Calif., 2003—; pres., CEO Precision Assessment Tech. Corp., Lone Tree, 2006—. Mem. Western States-U.S. Senate Coalition for Superfund Reform; CEO, Am. Purification Corp., Newport Beach, Calif., 1998-02, pres. Prosonic Corp., Marietta, Ohio, 2002-03; CEO, Exegesis, 2005-, mgmt. cons., exec. coach, 2003-06. Contbr. articles to profl. publs.; patentee sequential flotation of sulfide ores. Named One of Fifty Colo. Top Bus. Leaders, Colo. Assn. Commerce and Industry. Mem. AIME, Soc. Mining, Metallurgy and Exploration, Nat. Assn. Environ. Mgrs. (co-founder, bd. dirs. Washington chpt., co-chmn. govt. liaison and advocacy com.). Denver Petroleum Club, Elks. Republican. Roman Catholic. Avocations: classical piano, bicycling, model railroads. Home: 9384 Oakbrush Way Lone Tree CO 80124-3070 Office: Precision Assessment Tech Corp 9980 Park Meadows Dr Ste 112F Lone Tree CO 80124 Office Phone: 720-279-2392, 303-339-9638. Personal E-mail: tnxtceo@aol.com. Business E-Mail: john.spisak@patc-usa.com.

SPITZER, HUGH D., lawyer; b. Seattle, Feb. 14, 1949; s. George Frederick and Dorothy Lea (Davidson) S.; m. Ann Scales, Oct. 14, 1983; children: Johanna Spitzer, Claudia Spitzer, Jenny Spitzer. BA, Yale U., 1970; JD, U. Wash., 1974; LLM, U. Calif., 1982. Bar: Wash. 1974, U.S. Dist/ Ct. (ea. and we. dists.) Wash. 1975, U.S. Ct. Appeals (9th and D.C. cirs.) 1975, U.S. Supreme Ct. 1980. Program analyst N.Y.C. Health and Hosp. Corp., 1970-71; labor lawyer Hafer, Cassidy & Price, Seattle, 1974-76; legis. asst. Seattle City Coun., 1976-77; legal counsel to mayor City of Seattle, 1977-81; mcpl. bond lawyer Foster Pepper & Shefelman, PLLC, Seattle, 1982—. Affiliate prof. sch. law U. Wash. Contbr. articles to profl. jours. Chair Seattle Law Income Housing Levy Oversight com., 1988-96, Wash. State Affordable Housing Adv. Bd., 2000—; vice chair Puget Sound Water Quality Authority Wash. State, 1989-96, State Tax Structure Com., 2001-02. Mem. Nat. Assn. Bond Lawyers, Am. Judicature Soc. (mem. exec. com. Coun. on Pub. Legal Edn.). Democrat. Avocations: piano, hiking, skiing. Office: Foster Pepper & Shefelman PLLC 1111 3rd Ave Bldg Ste 3400 Seattle WA 98101-3292 Office Phone: 206-447-8965. E-mail: spith@foster.com.

SPITZER, MATTHEW LAURENCE, law educator; b. LA, June 23, 1952; s. William George and Jeanette Dorothy S.; m. Jean Fuksman, July 8, 1973; 1 child, Amanda Elizabeth. BA in Math., UCLA, 1973; JD, U. So. Calif., 1977; PhD in Social Scis., Calif. Inst. Tech., 1979. Assoc. Nossaman, Guthner, Knox & Elliott, LA, 1977—79; asst. prof. Northwestern U., Chgo., 1979—81; William T. Dalessi prof. law U. So. Calif., LA, 1987—2000, assoc. prof., 1981—84, prof., 1984—, dir. law and rational choice programs, 1990—2000, co-dir. Ctr. Comms. Law and Policy, 1998—, dean, Carl Mason Franklin prof. law, 2000—06, Robert C. Packard Trustee Prof. Law, 2006—; prof. law and social scis. Calif. Inst. Tech., Pasadena, 1992—2000, 2006—. Vis. prof. law U. Chgo., 1996, Stanford U., Calif., 1997, NYU, 2007; mem. organizing com. Telecoms. Policy Rsch. Conf., Washington, 1991-94. Author: Seven Dirty Words and Six Other Stories, 1986; co-author: (with T. Hazlett) Public Policy Toward Cable Television, 1997. Recipient (shared with Elizabeth Hoffman) Ronald H. Coase prize U. Chgo., 1986. Mem.: Am. Law and Econs. Assn. (bd. dirs. 1997—2000). Avocations: paperweight collecting, audiophile. Office: U So Calif Gould Law School Los Angeles CA 90089-0071 Home Phone: 323-550-8609; Office Phone: 213-740-6473.

SPITZER, ROBERT J., academic administrator; BBA, Gonzaga U.; MPhil, St. Louis U.; STB, Gregorian U., Rome; ThM, Weston Sch. Theology, Cambridge, Mass.; PhD in Philosophy, Cath. U. of Am. Tchr. Georgetown U., 1984-90, Seattle U., 1978-80, 90-98; pres. Gonzaga U., 1998—. Co-founder U. Faculty for Life; founder, adv. Life Principles. Office: Gonzaga U 502 E Boone Ave Spokane WA 99258-0001

SPIVEY, BRUCE E., ophthalmologist, educator, health facility administrator; b. Cedar Rapids, Iowa, Aug. 29, 1934; s. William Loranzy and Grace Loretta (Barber) S.; children: Lisa, Eric; m. Patti Amanda Birge, Dec. 20, 1987. BA, Coe Coll., 1956; MD, U. Iowa, 1959, MS, 1964; MEd, U. Ill., 1969; DSc (hon.), Coe Coll., 1978. Diplomate Am. Bd. Ophthalmology (fellow, bd. dirs. 1975-83, chmn. oral exam 1976-81). Asst. prof. U. Iowa Coll. Medicine, Iowa City, 1966, assoc. prof., 1968—71; dean Sch. Med. Scis. U. Pacific, San Francisco, 1971—76; prof., chmn. dept. ophthalmology Pacific Med. Ctr. (now Calif. Pacific Med. Ctr.), San Francisco, 1971—87; pres., CEO, dir. Calif. Pacific Med. Ctr., San Francisco, 1976—91; exec. v.p., CEO Am. Acad. Ophthalmology, San Francisco, 1977—93; pres., CEO Calif. Healthcare Sys., Bay area, 1986—92; CEO Northwestern Healthcare Network, Chgo., 1992—97, Columbia Cornell Care, NYC, 1997—2000, Columbia Cornell Network Physicians, NYC, 1998—2000. Bd. dirs. Reliance Group Holdings Inc., NYC; trustee, bd. dirs., sec. bd. MedEx, Balt., 1999—; v.p. Am. Bd. Med. Spltys., 1978—80, pres., 1980—82, Coun. Med. Splty. Socs., 2000—02, 1975—2008, dep. exec. v.p., 2002—08; chmn. bd. dirs. Vol. Hosps. of

Am.-No. Calif., 1985—87, nat. bd. dirs., 1991—96; nat. adv. coun. NEI/NIH, 1987—92; spl. med. adv. group Dept. Vets Affairs, 1987—93; trustee, bd. dirs., sec. bd. Ophthal. Mut. Ins. Co., 1988—2007; trustee, sec. bd. PrimeSight, San Francisco, 1996—99. Contbr. over 120 articles to profl. jours.; inventor instruments for eye surgery. Bd. dirs. Pacific Vision Found., San Francisco, 1978—, U.S.-China Ednl. Inst., 1979—; trustee Coe Coll., 1985—, Found. AAO, 1981—, Internat. Coun. Ophthalmology, 1985—, Helen Keller Internat., 1999—; trustee Medbiquitous, 2000-07, chmn, 2001—07. Served to capt. U.S. Army, 1964-66, 85th Duke Hosp., Vietnam, 1965-66. Decorated Bronze Star; recipient Emile Javal Gold medal Internat. Contact Lens Council, San Francisco, 1982, Gradle medal Pan-Am. Assn. Ophthalmol., Disting. Alumni award U. Iowa, 2003, others. Fellow ACS, Am. Acad. Ophthalmology (Disting. Svc. award 1972, Sr. Honor award 1986, Guest of Honor 1996, Lifetime Achievement award, 2002, Internat. Blindness Prevention award, 2007); mem. AMA, Am. Ophthal. Soc. (Howe medal 1993, bd. dirs. 1986-91, pres. 1994-95), Academia Ophthal. Internat. (Bernardo Streiff Gold medal 2002), Soc. Med. Adminstrs. (pres. 1999-2001), Internat. Congress Ophthalmology (sec.-gen. 1978-82), Internat. Coun. Ophthalmology (sec.-gen. 1994—2006, trustee 1985—, pres. 2006—, Jules Francois Gold medal 2006, Sir John Wilson award 2007), Pacific-Union Club, Chevy Chase Club, Knickerbocker Club, Cosmos Club. Presbyterian. Office: 945 Green St San Francisco CA 94133 Business E-Mail: bruce@spivey.org.

SPLINTER, MICHAEL R., manufacturing executive; BEE, U. Wis., Madison, 1972, MEE, 1974. Gen. mgr., exec. v.p. Intel Corp., Santa Clara, Calif., 1984—96; v.p. and asst. Gen. mgr. Tech. and Mfg. Group, Intel Corp., Santa Clara, Calif., 1996—98, v.p. and Gen. mgr., 1998—99, sr. v.p. and Gen. mgr., 1999—2001, exec. v.p. and Gen. mgr., 2001, exec. v.p. and dir., Sales and Mktg. group, 2001—03; pres. and CEO Applied Materials, Inc., Santa Clara, Calif., 2003—09, chmn., pres., CEO, 2009—. Mem. Computer Sys. Policy Project; bd. dir. Semiconductor Equipment and Materials Intern., Silicon Valley Leadership Group. Recipient Intern. Partnership Award, Calif.-Israel C. of C., Disting. Alumni Award, U. Wis.; named to, Jr. Achievement Hall of Fame. Mem.: Governors' Coun. of World Econ. Forum, Applied Materials (bd. dir. 2003). Office: Applied Materials Inc 3050 Bowers Ave Santa Clara CA 95054*

SPOFFORD, ROBERT HOUSTON, advertising agency executive; b. NYC, Apr. 3, 1941; s. Robert Knowlton and Linda Prieber (Houston) S.; m. Susan Proctor Allerton; children: Margaret, Robert Christopher. B.E.E., Cornell U., 1964. Account exec. Batten, Barton, Durstine & Osborn, Inc., NYC, 1964-71, v.p., 1971-84, sr. v.p., 1984-88, exec. v.p., dir. strategic planning, 1988-96; exec. v.p. BBDO Univ., Barcelona, Spain, 1997—. Contbr. articles to advt. and data processing jours. Mem. Westchester County Democratic Com. N.Y. 1974-78; ch. organist First recipient Founder's medal Batten, Barton, Durstine & Osborn, Inc., 1985 Congregationalist. Home: 61 Dunfries Ter San Rafael CA 94901-2415 Office: BBDO LA 10960 Wilshire Blvd Los Angeles CA 90024-3702 E-mail: spoffo@bbdowest.com.

SPOHN, NOR RAE, computer company executive; married; 2 children. BS in Computer Sci., Iowa State U., Calif., 1980; MEE, Stanford U. R&D engr. Hewlett-Packard Co., 1980, R&D mgr. LaserJet Divsn., 1998—2002, v.p., gen. mgr. Personal LaserJet Solutions, 2002—07, sr. v.p. LaserJet Printing Bus., 2007—. Mem. Gov.'s Sci. & Tech. Adv. Coun., Idaho, 2006—. Chair Idaho Sci., Math. and Tech. Coalition; bd. mem. Treasure Vallet Math. & Sci. Ctr.; bd. adv. Sch. Engring. Boise State U. Named to Women in Tech. Internat. Hall of Fame, 2006. Office: Hewlett Packard Co Personal LaserJet Solutions Divsn 3000 Hanover St Palo Alto CA 94304-1185

SPOOR, RHYS, dentist; Grad., U. Wash., 1983. With Aesthetic & Restorative Dentistry, Seattle. Fellow: Pierre Fauchard Acad., Acad. Gen. Dentistry; mem.: Am. Acad. Cosmetic Dentistry. Office: Aesthetic & Restorative Dentistry 701 5th Ave Ste 4660 Seattle WA 98104 Office Phone: 206-682-8200. E-mail: info@rhysspoor.com.

SPRAGUE, ANN LOUISE, aerospace scientist; b. Bellfonte, Pa., Feb. 25, 1946; d. David Carpenter and Opal (Wheat) S.; m. Donald M. Hunten, 1995. BA Geology, Syracuse U., 1969; MA, Boston U., 1980; PhD, U. Ariz., 1990. Tchr. sci. Selinsgrove Mid. Sch., 1970—79; space scientist Lunar and Planetary Lab. U. Ariz., Tucson, 1990—. Mem. Lunar and Planetary Exploration com. NRC, 2000— Contbg. author: Caloris Basin: An Enhanced Source for Potassium in Mercury's Atmosphere, 1990, Sulfur at Mercury, Elemental at the Poles and Sulfides in the Regolith, 1995, Water Brought In to Jupiter's Atmosphere by Fragments R and W of Comet SL-9, 1996, Distribution and Abundance of Sodium in Mercury's Atmosphere, 1985-1988, 1997, Exploring Mercury: The Iron Planet, 2003; editl. bd. ICARUS Mem. AAAS, Internat. Astron. Union, Am. Astron. Soc. (com. divsn. planetary scis.), Am. Geophys. Union Office: U Ariz Lunar & Planetary Lab Tucson AZ 85721-0001 Business E-Mail: sprague@lpl.arizona.edu.

SPRATT, RANDALL N., healthcare services and information technology executive; BS in Biology, U. Utah. Various exec. positions to COO Advanced Lab. Systems; joined McKesson Corp., 1986, sr. v.p. imaging, tech. and bus. process improvement, 2000—03, chief process officer MPT (McKesson Provider Technologies) Alpharetta, Ga., 2003—05, exec. v.p. chief info. officer San Francisco, 2005—, chief tech. officer, 2009—. Office: McKesson Corpn 1 Post St San Francisco CA 94104 Office Phone: 415-983-8300. Business E-Mail: randall.spratt@mckesson.com.*

SPRINGER, CHARLES EDWARD, retired judge; b. Reno, Feb. 20, 1928; s. Edwin and Rose Mary Cecelia (Kelly) S.; m. Jacqueline Sirkegian, Mar. 17, 1951; 1 dau., Kelli Ann. BA, U. Nev., Reno, 1950; LLB, Georgetown U., 1953; LLM, U. Va., 1984; student Grad. Program for Am. Judges, Oriel Coll., Oxford U., Eng., 1984. Bar: Nev. 1953, U.S. Dist. Ct. Nev. 1953, D.C. 1954, U.S. Supreme Ct. 1962. Pvt. practice law, Reno, 1953-80; atty. gen. State of Nev., 1962, legis. legal adv. to gov., 1958-62; legis. bill drafter Nev. Legislature, 1955-57; mem. faculty Nat. Coll. Juvenile Justice, Reno, 1978—; juvenile master 2d Jud. Dist. Nev., 1973-80; justice Nev. Suprem Ct., Carson City, 1981—99; vice-chief justice Nev. Supreme Ct., Carson City, 1987, chief justice, 1998-99, ret., 1999. Mem. Jud. Selection Commn., 1981, 98, Nev. Supreme Ct. Gender Bias Task Force, 1981—; trustee Nat. Coun. Juvenile and Family Ct. Judges, 1983—; mem. faculty McGeorge Sch. Law, U. Nev., Reno, 1982—; mem. Nev. Commn. for Women, 1991-95. With AUS, 1945-47. Recipient Outstanding Contbn. to Juvenile Justice award Nat. Coun. Juvenile and Family Ct. Judges, 1989, Midby-Byron Disting. Leadership award U. Nev., 1988. Mem. ABA, Am. Judicature Soc., Am. Trial Lawyers Assn., Phi Kappa Phi. Home: 1001 Dartmouth Dr Reno NV 89509 Office: Nev Supreme Ct Capitol Complex 201 S Carson St Carson City NV 89701-4702

SPRINGER, GEORGE STEPHEN, mechanical engineering educator; b. Budapest, Hungary, Dec. 12, 1933; came to U.S., 1959; s. Joseph and Susan (Grausz) S.; m. Susan Martha Flory, Sept. 15, 1963; children: Elizabeth Anne, Mary Katherine. B in Engring., U. Sydney, Australia, 1959; M in Engring., Yale U., 1960, MSc in Engring., 1961, PhD, 1962; D (hon.), Tech. U. Budapest, 2000, U. Sydney, 2007. Registered profl. engr., Mass. Asst. prof. mech. engring. MIT, Cambridge, 1962-67; prof. mech. engring. U. Mich., Ann Arbor, 1967-83; Paul Pigott prof. Stanford (Calif.) U., 1983—, chmn. dept. aeronautics and astronautics, 1990—2001. Author: Erosion by Liquid Impact, 1975; co-author, co-editor 14 books; contbr. over 200 articles to scholarly and profl. jours. Recipient Pub. Svc. Group Achievement award, NASA, 1988, Medal of Excellence in Composite Materials U. Del., 1999. Fellow AIAA (Engr. of Yr. 1995, Structures Structural Dynamics and Materials award 2000), ASME (Worcester Reed Warner medal 1994), Soc. Advancement Materials and Process Engring. (Delmonte award 1991); mem. Am. Phys. Soc., Soc. Automotive Engrs. (Ralph Teetor award 1978), NAE, Hungarian Nat. Acad. Sci. (fgn. mem.), Am. Soc. Composites (Outstanding Rschr. award 1997). Achievements include patents in field. Office: Stanford U Dept Aeronautics & Astronautics Stanford CA 94305 Office Phone: 650-723-4135. Business E-Mail: gspringer@stanford.edu.

SPRINGER, PAUL DAVID, lawyer, film company executive; b. NYC, Apr. 27, 1942; s. William W. and Alma (Markowitz) S.; m. Mariann Frankfurt, Aug. 16, 1964; children: Rob, Will. BA, U. Bridgeport, 1963; JD, Bklyn. Law Sch., 1967. Bar: N.Y. 1968, U.S. Dist. Ct. (so. and ea. dists.) N.Y. 1968, U.S. Ct. Appeals (2d cir.) 1970, U.S. Supreme Ct. 1973, Calif. 1989. Assoc. Johnson & Tannenbaum, NYC, 1968—70; assoc. counsel Columbia Pictures, NYC, 1970, Paramount Pictures, NYC, 1970—79, v.p., theatrical distbn. counsel, 1979—85, sr. v.p., chief resident counsel East Coast, 1985—87, sr. v.p., asst. gen. counsel LA, 1987—. Bar: N.Y. 1968, U.S. Dist. Ct. (so. and ea. dists.) N.Y. 1968, U.S. Ct. Appeals (2d cir.) 1970, U.S. Supreme Ct. 1973, Calif. 1989. Trustee West Cunningham Park Civic Assn., Fresh Meadows, N.Y., 1978—. Mem. ABA, Assn. of Bar of City of N.Y., L.A. Copyright Soc., Acad. Motion Picture Arts and Scis., Motion Picture Pioneers. Office Phone: 323-956-8408. Business E-Mail: paul_springer@paramount.com.

SPRINGER, WAYNE RICHARD, healthcare system official, research biochemist; b. Milw., Nov. 16, 1946; s. Richard Andrew and Irma Edna (Richter) S.; m. Jane Bradley, Aug. 19, 1972; children: Matthew Bradley, Katherine Jane. BA, Northwestern U., 1968; PhD, U. Calif., Berkeley, 1977. Vol. Peace Corps, Somalia, Antigua, 1969-72; postdoctoral fellow U. Calif., San Diego, 1977-79, rsch. biochemist, 1979-92, assoc. project biochemist, 1992-99; rsch. biochemist VA Healthcare Sys., San Diego, 1979-99; chem. hygiene officer VA Med. Ctr., San Diego, 1992-94, biosafety officer, 1992—, chief environ. health and safety, 1994—. Mem. Am. Biol. Safety Assn. Avocations: travel, gardening. Office: VA San Diego Healthcare Sys (138S) 3350 La Jolla Village Dr San Diego CA 92161-0002 Home Phone: 858-452-8832. Business E-Mail: Wayne.Springer@va.gov.

SPRITZER, RALPH SIMON, lawyer, educator; b. NYC, Apr. 27, 1917; s. Harry and Stella (Theuman) S.; m. Lorraine Nelson, Dec. 23, 1950; children: Ronald, Pamela. BS, Columbia U., 1937, LL.B., 1940. Bar: N.Y. bar 1941, U.S. Supreme Ct. bar 1950. Atty. Office Alien Property, Dept. Justice, 1946-51; anti-trust div. Dept. Justice, 1951-54, Office Solicitor Gen., 1954-61; gen. counsel FPC, 1961-62; 1st asst. to solicitor gen. U.S., 1962-68; prof. law U. Pa., Phila., 1968-86, Ariz. State U., Tempe, 1986—; gen. counsel AAUP, 1983-84. Adj. prof. law George Wasington U., 1967; cons. Adminstrv. Conf. U.S., Ford Found., Pa. Gov.'s Justice Commn. Served with AUS, 1941-46. Recipient Superior Service award Dept. Justice, 1960; Tom C. Clark award Fed. Bar. Assn., 1968 Mem. Am. Law Inst. Office: Ariz State Univ Coll Law Tempe AZ 85287 Home: 7017 S Priest Dr Apt 2017 Tempe AZ 85283-6013 Office Phone: 480-965-7419.

SPROLES, KEVIN, entrepreneur, Internet company executive; b. 1983; Founder & CEO Volusion, Inc., Simi Valley, Calif., 1999—. Named one of Best Entrepreneurs Under 25, BusinessWeek, 2006. Office: Volusion Inc 1736 Erringer Rd Simi Valley CA 93065 Office Phone: 800-646-3517. Office Fax: 805-435-7476.

SPROUL, JOHN ALLAN, retired utilities executive; b. Oakland, Calif., Mar. 28, 1924; s. Robert Gordon and Ida Amelia (Wittschen) S.; m. Marjorie Ann Hauck, June 20, 1945; children: John Allan, Malcolm J., Richard O., Catherine E. AB, U. Calif., Berkeley, 1947, LL.B., 1949. Bar: Calif. 1950. Atty. Pacific Gas & Electric Co., San Francisco, 1949-52, 56-62, sr. atty., 1962-70, asst. gen. counsel, 1970-71, v.p. gas supply, 1971-76, sr. v.p., 1976-77, exec. v.p., 1977-89; ret.; gen. counsel Pacific Gas Transmission Co., 1970-73, v.p., 1973-79, chmn. bd., 1979-89, also bd. dirs. Atty. Johnson & Stanton, San Francisco, 1952-56. Bd. dirs. emeritus Hastings Coll. Law. Served to 1st lt. USAAF, 1943-46. Mem. Calif. Bar Assn. (inactive), Pacific Coast Gas Assn., Pacific-Union Club, Orinda Country Club. Home: 8413 Buckingham Dr El Cerrito CA 94530-2531 Office: Pacific Gas & Electric Co Mail Code B26 PO Box 770000 San Francisco CA 94177-0001 also: Pacific Gas & Electric Co 77 Beale St Rm 2680 San Francisco CA 94105-1814 Office Phone: 415-973-2693. Office Fax: 415-973-8808. Personal E-mail: johnsproul@comcast.net.

SPROULE, JAMES MICHAEL, communications educator, writer; b. Dayton, Ohio, Feb. 8, 1949; s. John Harper and Katherine Veronica Sproule; m. Betty Ann Mathis, Mar. 3, 1973; children: John Harold, Kevin William. BA, MA, Ohio State U., Columbus, 1971, PhD, 1973. Asst. prof. U. of Tex. of Permian Basin, Odessa, 1973—77; assoc. prof. Ind. U. S.E., New Albany, 1977—86; vis. lectr. U. of Calif., Berkeley, 1986—87; prof., dir. Bowling Green (Ohio) State U., 2001—04; prof. St. Louis U., 2004—08, dean, 2004—06; prof. San Jose (Calif.) State U., 1987—2001, prof. emeritus, 2001—. Author: (book) The Rhetoric of Western Thought, Propaganda and Democracy, Channels of Propaganda, Speechmaking, Communication Today, Argument: Language and Its Influence. Recipient Golden Anniversary Monograph award, Nat. Comm. Assn., 1988; fellow, NEH, 1983. Mem.: Western States Comm. Assn., Internat. Soc. for the History of Rhetoric, Author's Guild, Nat. Comm. Assn. (pres. 2007). Home: 110 7th St Pacific Grove CA 93950-2907

SPUDICH, JAMES A., biology professor; b. Collinsville, Ill., Jan. 7, 1942; married, 1964; 2 children. BS, U. Ill., 1963; PhD in Biochemistry, Stanford U., 1968. Asst. prof. biochemistry U. Calif., San Francisco, 1971-74, assoc. prof., 1974-76; prof. structural biology, biochemistry and devel. biology Stanford U. Sch. Medicine, 1977—92. Editor: Annual Rev. Cell Biology, 1987-1998. Recipient Lewis S. Rosentiel award for disting. work in basic med. rsch., 1996, Repligen Corp. award, 1997. Mem. Am. Soc. Cell Biologists (pres. 1989), Nat. Acad. of Sci., 1991, Am. Acad. of Arts and Scis., 1997. Achievements include research in molecular basis of cytokinesis amoeboid movement and other forms of cell motility. Office: Stanford U Sch Medicine Dept Biochemistry Stanford Med Ctr Beckman Ctr B400 Stanford CA 94305-5307

SPUDIS, PAUL D., geologist; b. Bowling Green, Ky., Aug. 29, 1952; s. Frank Paul and M. Erlene (Wren) S.; m. Anne M. Seaborne, Oct. 21, 1982; children: Janelle Kathryn, Diane Michelle. BS in Geology, Ariz. State U., 1976; Sc.M. in Geology, Brown U., 1977; PhD in Geology, Ariz. State U., 1982. Geologist NASA Ames Research Ctr., Mountain View, Calif., 1976-78; geologist, Br. Astrogeology U.S. Geol. Survey, Flagstaff, Ariz., 1980—82, 1982—90; faculty rsch. assoc. Ariz. State U., 1982—85; vis. scientist Lunar and Planetary Inst., Houston, 1978, staff scientist, 1990—2002, dep. dir., 1999—2002, dir., regional planetary image facility, Ctr. for Info. and Rsch. Services, 1999—2002, sr. staff scientist, 2008—; sr. prof. staff Johns Hopkins U. Applied Physics Lab., 2002—08. Vis. scientist U. Hawaii, Honolulu, 1980; mem. exploration sci. planning, synthesis group, Washington, DC, 1990-91; prin. investigator on NASA grant, The Geology of Lunar Multi-ring Basins, 1980-82, NASA Planetary Geology Program, 1982-85, NASA Planetary Geology Program, 1982-1990, NASA Planetary Geology and Geophysics Program, 1990-2002, 2002-2008, mini-SAR experiment on Indian Chandrayaan mission to the Moon, 2007, 2008; vis. scientist, Ctr. for Earth and Planetary Studies, Nat. Air and Space Mus., Smithsonian Institution, Washington, DC, 1991; cons. Lawrence Livermore Nat. Lab., Calif., 1992-94; adj. prof., dept. geology and geophysics, Rice U., Houston, Tex., 1993-2003; dep. leader sci. team, Dept. Def. Clementine mission to the Moon, 1994; team mem. mini-RF technology demonstration experiment, Lunar Reconnaissance Orbiter mission to the Moon, 2008; com. mem. numerous NASA sci. adv. panels, 1983-; mem. White House panel that analyzed a return to the Moon to establish a base and the first human mission to Mars, 1990-91; Commr. Predsl. Commn. on the Implementation of the US Space Exploration Policy, 2004; security, Top Secret, Applied Physics Lab., 2004-,prin. profl. staff, 2005; US Dept. Energy "Q" Clearance, 1992-94. Contbr. numerous articles to profl. jours.; co-author books; editor for books and reports. NASA grantee, 1980-; U. Fellowship, Brown U., 1976-77, hon. rsch. fellow, dept. geol. scis., U. Coll. London, 2000-; aviation week and space tech. laurels award, 1994, NASA Pub. Svc. medal, 2004; named in honor of Asteroid 7560 Spudis, 1999; Frank Howard Disting. Lecture, George Washington U., 2006. Mem. Am. Geophys. Union., AIAA (von Karman lectureship, 2006), Geol. Soc. America, Phi Kappa Phi, Sigma Xi. Avocations: reading, tropical fish, boomeranging. Office: Lunar and Planetary Inst 3600 Bay Area Blvd Houston TX 77058 Business E-Mail: spudis@lpi.usra.edu.

SPURLOCK, MORGAN, television producer, film producer; b. Parkersburg, W.Va., Nov. 7, 1970; m. Alexandra Jamieson, May 3, 2006; 1 child, Laken James. BFA, NYU, 1993. Prodr.: (TV series) I Bet You Will, 2002; exec. prodr.: 30 Days, 2005—; (films) Class Act, 2006, Chalk, 2006, The Third Wave, 2007; prodr.: What Would Jesus Buy?, 2007; prodr., dir., writer: Super Size Me, 2004; Where in the World is Osama Bin Laden?, 2008; actor: Drive-Thru, 2006; author: Don't Eat This Book: Fast Food and the Supersizing of America, 2006. Mem.: ACLU.

SQUIRES, WILLIAM RANDOLPH, III, lawyer; b. Providence, Sept. 6, 1947; s. William Randolph and Mary Louise (Gress) S.; children: Shannon, William R. IV, Mayre Elisabeth, James Robert. BA in Econs., Stanford U., 1969; JD, U. Tex., 1972. Bar: Wash. 1973, U.S. Dist. Ct. (we. dist.) Wash. 1973, U.S. Dist. Ct. (ea. dist.) Wash. 1976, U.S. Ct. Appeals (9th cir.) 1976, U.S. Supreme Ct. 1976, U.S. Ct. Fed. Claims 1982. Assoc. Oles, Morrison, Rinker, Stanislaw & Ashbaugh, Seattle, 1973-78; ptnr., chmn. litig. group Davis Wright Tremaine, Seattle, 1978-97; mem. Summit Law Group, Seattle, 1997—2007, chmn., 2005—07; of counsel Corr Cronin Michelson Baumgardner & Preece, Seattle, 2007—. Fellow Am. Coll. Trial Lawyers; mem. ABA, Internat. Bar Assn., Wash. State Bar Assn., King County Bar Assn., Wash. Athletic Club, Rainier Club (Seattle). Episcopalian. Office: Corr Cronin Michelson Baumgardner and Preece 1001 Fourth Ave Ste 3900 Seattle WA 98154 Home: 1622 35th Ave Seattle WA 98122-3411 Office Phone: 206-652-8658. Business E-Mail: rsquires@corrcronin.com.

SREENIVASAN, SREENIVASA RANGA, physicist, researcher; b. Mysore, Karnataka, India, Oct. 20, 1933; came to U.S., 1959; s. Sreenivasachari and Alamelammal (Rangaswami) S.; m. Claire de Reineck, Nov. 16, 1963; children: Gopal, Govind, Gauri, Gayatri, Aravind. BS, U. Mysore, 1950, BS, 1952; PhD, Gujarat U., India, 1958. Lectr. St. Philomena's Coll., Mysore, 1952-54; rsch. fellow Harvard U., Cambridge, Mass., 1959-61; rsch. assoc. NASA Inst. for Space Studies, NYC, 1961-64; vis. scientist Max Planck Inst. Physics and Astrophysics, Munich, 1964-66; prof. physics U. Calgary, Alta., Canada, 1967—. Vis. prof. Royal Inst. Tech., Stockholm, 1974-75. Contbr. articles to profl. jours. Chmn. Coun. South Asians, Calgary, 1981-84; pres. Calgary Interfaith Cmty. Action Assn., 1986; pri. Sch. East Indian Langs. and Performing Arts, Calgary, 1986. Govt. of India Sr. Rsch. scholar, Ahmedabad, 1955-58. Achievements include research in force-free fields, electrostatic instabilities in plasmas, evolution of massive stars, size of convective cores in rotating stellar models. Home: 2110 30 Ave SW Calgary AB Canada T2T 1R4 Office: U Calgary 2500 University Dr NW Calgary AB Canada T2N 1N4 E-mail: srs@ucalgary.edu.

SRIKANTIAH, JAYASHRI, law educator; BSEE, U. Calif., Berkeley, 1991; JC magna cum laude, NYU, 1996. Bar: Calif., US Ct. Appeals (fed., 5th, 9th. cir.), US Dist. Ct. (no., ea., so. dists.) Calif., US Supreme Ct. Graduate rotation engr. Intel Corp., Santa Clara, Calif., 1991—92, tech. mktg. engr., 1992—93; law clk., Hon. David R. Thompson US Ct. Appeals (9th cir.), 1996—97; assoc., litig. Howard, Rice, Nemerovski, Canady, Falk & Rabkin, San Francisco, 1997—98; staff atty. ACLU Immigrants' Rights Project, 1998—2001, ACLU No. Calif., 2001—03, assoc. legal dir., 2003—04; assoc. prof. law Stanford Univ. Law Sch., 2004—, and dir. Immigrants' Rights Clin., 2004—. Sr. note & comment editor NYU Law Rev. Named one of 40 Indian-Am. Faces of the Future, India Today, 2000, Best Lawyers Under 40, Nat. Asian Pacific Am. Bar Assn., 2004. Mem.:

Clin. Legal Edn. Assn., Nat. Lawyers Guild, Am. Immigration Lawyers Assn., Assn. Am. Law Schs., S. Asian Bar Assn. and Minority Bar Coalition (Outstanding Svc. to Legal Cmty. award 2000), Asian Law Alliance (Cmty. Impact award 2002), Asian Am. Bar Assn. (bd. dir. 2002—, co-chair civil rights com. 2001), Order of Coif. Office: Crown Quadrangle Stanford Law Sch 559 Nathan Abbot Way Stanford CA 94305-8610 Office Phone: 650-724-2442. Business E-Mail: jsrikantiah@law.stanford.edu.

SRINIVASAN, VENKATARAMAN, marketing and management educator; b. Pudukkottai, Tamil Nadu, India, June 5, 1944; came to U.S., 1968; s. Annaswamy and Jambagalakshmi Venkataraman; m. Sitalakshmi Subrahmanyam, June 30, 1972; children: Ramesh, Mahesh. B Tech., Indian Inst. Tech., Madras, India, 1966; MS, Carnegie-Mellon U., 1970, PhD, 1971. Asst. engr. Larsen & Toubro, Bombay, 1966-68; asst. prof. mgmt. and mktg. U. Rochester, NY, 1971-73, assoc. prof. NY, 1973-74, Stanford (Calif.) U., 1974-76, prof., 1976-82, dir. PhD program in bus., 1982-85, Ernest C. Arbuckle prof. mktg. and mgmt. sci., 1982—2003, Adams disting. prof. mgmt., 2003—; mktg. area coord. Stanford U., 1976—78, 1988—93, 2000—03. Mem. bd. acad. trustees Mktg. Sci. Inst., 2004—; cons. in field. Mem. editl. bd. Jour. Mktg. Rsch., 1988—, Mktg. Sci., 1980—, Mgmt. Sci., 1974-91; contbr. articles to profl. jours. Mem. Am. Mktg. Assn., Inst. Ops. Rsch./Mgmt. Scis. Hindu. Avocation: classical music.

SRIVASTAVA, AMITABH, computer software company executive; BSEE, Indean Inst. Tech., Kanpur, 1979; MS in Computer Sci., Penn. State U., 1984. Rschr. Tex. Instruments Inc., Dallas, 1984—91; with Digital Equipment Corp. Western Rsch. Labs, Palo Alto, Calif., 1991; chief tech. officer, v.p. enging. Tracepoint Tech. Inc.; with Microsoft Rsch., 1997—2003, sr. rschr., 1997, disting. engr., 2001; founder, dir. Programmer Productivity Rsch. Ctr., 1999—2003, Ctr. Software Excellence, 2003—; corp. v.p. Windows core operating sys. devel. Microsoft Corp., 2003—07, corp. v.p. Cloud infrastructure services, 2007—. Recipient Disting. Alumnus award, Indian Inst. Tech., Kanpur, 2004, Outstanding Engring. Alumnus award, Penn. State U., 2004; named Disting. Engr., Microsoft Corp., 2001. Achievements include development of OM, ATOM and SCOOPS software systems; Vulcan binary transformation system.

STABBERT, FREDERICK JOSEPH, paper company executive; b. Seattle, Nov. 17, 1943; s. Wallace Roger and Eleanor Clarice (Joringdal) S.; m. Faith Edna Jordan, Nov. 22, 1963; children—Monica, Michael BA in Bus. Adminstrn., U. Puget Sound, 1968. Trainee div. Zellerback Paper Co., South San Francisco, Calif., 1960-70, sales rep., 1970-71, mng., adminstr. Los Angeles, 1971-75, mgr. div. Sacramento, 1975-76, mgr. indsl. bus. unit San Francisco, 1976-79, v.p., regional mgr., 1979-80, exec. v.p., 1980-83; sr. v.p. Crown Zellerbach Corp., San Francisco, 1983—; pres. Zellerbach Paper Co., San Francisco, 1983—. Mem. Nat. Paper Trade Assn. (treas. 1984—, bd. dirs. 1983—) Republican. Avocations: golf, skiing, tennis. Home: 3550 Tripp Rd Redwood City CA 94062-3636 Office: Zellerback Paper Co 3130 Crow Canyon Pl San Ramon CA 94583-1346

STABILE, BRUCE EDWARD, surgeon; b. Monterey Park, California, Apr. 14, 1944; s. Edward Emilio and Angela (Tramantozzi) S.; m. Caroline Graston, Sept. 18, 1967; children: Jessica, Drew. BA, UCLA, 1966; MD, U. Calif., San Francisco, 1970. Diplomate Am. Bd. Surgery. From assoc. prof. to prof. vice chmn. dept. surgery Sch. Medicine U. Calif., San Diego, 1985—93; from asst. prof. to assoc. prof. Sch. Medicine UCLA, 1977—85, vice chmn. dept. surgery Sch. Medicine, 1993—. Chmn. dept. surgery Harbor UCLA Med. Ctr., Torrance, 1993—, acting med. dir., 1997-98; interim assoc. dean UCLA Sch. Medicine, 1997-98; med. expert Med. Bd. Calif., 1980—; bd. dirs. Am. Bd. Surgery, 1998-2004. Mem. editl. bd.: Jour. Surg. Rsch., 1993—97, Archives of Surgery, 1991—2004. Fellow, ACS (gov. 2001-07, pres. So. Calif. chpt. 2005-06), Am. Surg. Assn.; mem. Soc. Univ. Surgeons, Assn. Acad. Surgery, Am. Gastroenterol. Assn., San Diego Soc. Gen. Surgeons (pres. 1992-93), L.A. Surg. Soc. (pres. 2000-01), Pacific Coast Surg. Assn. (pres. 2007-08). Office: Harbor U Calif at L A Med Ctr 1000 W Carson St Torrance CA 90502-2004 Office Phone: 310-222-2701. Business E-Mail: bstabile@ucla.edu.

STACK, GEOFFREY LAWRENCE, real estate developer; b. Trinidad, Brit. West Indies, Sept. 16, 1943; s. Gerald Francis and V. Louise (Bell) S.; m. Victoria Hammack, 1970 (div. 1986); 1 child, Kathryn; m. Nancy J. Haarer, Apr. 19, 1987; children: Alexandra, Natalie. BA, Georgetown U., 1965; MBA, U. Pa., 1972. Dir. acquisitions J.H. Snyder Co., LA, 1972-75; from project mgr. to exec. v.p. Richards West, Newport Beach, Calif., 1975-77; pres. Regis Homes Corp., Newport Beach, 1977-93; mng. dir. Sares-Regis Group, Irvine, Calif., 1993—. Bd. dirs. Arral & Ptnrs., Hong Kong, Calif. Housing Coun., Sacramento, Tejon Ranch Co. Chmn. bd. dirs. Nat. Multihousing Coun., 1987—; bd. regents Georgetown U., 2005; trustee Cystinosis Rsch. Found., 2006, Urban Land Inst. Capt. USMC, 1967—70. Decorated 2 Bronze Stars, 21 Air medals, Navy Commendation medal, Purple Heart. Mem. Young Pres. Orgn., Big Canyon Country Club, Pacific Club, Olympic Club, Calif. Club. Democrat. Roman Catholic. Office: SARES REGIS Group 18802 Bardeen Ave Irvine CA 92612-1521 Office Phone: 949-756-5959. Business E-Mail: jstack@sares-regis.com.

STACK, KEVIN J., lawyer; b. NYC, Aug. 12, 1951; BA cum laude, UCLA, 1973; JD cum laude, Loyola U., LA, 1976. Bar: Calif. 1976, U.S. Dist. Ct. (ctrl. dist.) Calif. 1977. Ptnr. Knapp, Petersen & Clarke, Glendale, Calif., 1984—. Office: Knapp Petersen & Clarke 500 N Brand Blvd Fl 20 Glendale CA 91203-1923

STACY, ANGELICA M., chemistry educator; Prof. dept. chemistry U. Calif., Berkeley. Recipient Francis P. Garvan-John M. Olin medal Am. Chem. Soc., 1995. Office: U Calif Dept Chemistry 419 Latimer Hall Berkeley CA 94720-1460

STACY, RICHARD A., judge; b. Eldorado, Ark., Mar. 7, 1942; s. Jack Leonard S. and Estelle (Mabry) Carrier; m. Karen Kay King, Aug. 20, 1961; children: Mark L., Andrea L. BA, U. Wyo., 1965, JD, 1967. Bar: Wyo. 1967, Colo. 1967, U.S. Supreme Ct. 1972. Revisor Wyo. Statute Revision Com., Cheyenne, 1967-69; asst. atty. gen. State of Wyo., 1969-72; asst. U.S. atty. Dept. Justice, Cheyenne, 1972-75; U.S. atty. Dis. Wyo., Cheyenne, 1981-94; adminstrv. law judge Office of Hearing & Appeals, San Jose, Calif., 1994-99, Denver, 1999—; mem. atty. gen.'s adv. com. of U.S. attys. Dept. Justice, 1981-84. Mem. Gov.'s Statewide Drug Alcohol Adv. Bd., 1988-94. Mem. ABA, Wyo. Bar Assn., Colo. State Bar, Santa Clara County Bar Assn. (hon., com. on bench, bar, media, police relationships 1995—). Clubs: Kiwanis (charter pres. Wheatland 1977). Republican. Episcopalian. Office: Hearings & Appeals 1244 Speer Blvd Ste 752 Denver CO 80204-3584

STAEHELIN, LUCAS ANDREW, cell biology professor emeritus; b. Sydney, Feb. 10, 1939; came to U.S., 1969; s. Lucas Eduard and Isobel (Malloch) S.; m. Margrit Weibel, Sept. 17, 1965; children: Daniel Thomas, Philip Roland, Marcel Felix. Dipl. Natw., Swiss Fed. Inst. Tech., Zurich, 1963, PhD in Biology, 1966. Research scientist N.Z. Dept. Sci. and Indsl. Research, 1966-69; research fellow in cell biology Harvard U., Cambridge, Mass., 1969-70; asst. prof. cell biology U. Colo., Boulder, 1970-73, assoc. prof., 1973-79, prof., 1979—2007, prof. emeritus, 2007—. Vis. prof. U. Freiburg, 1978, Swiss Fed. Inst. Tech., 1984, 92, U. Melbourne, Australia, 1998; mem. cellular biology and physiology study sect. NIH, Bethesda, Md., 1980-84; mem. DOE panel on rsch. directions for the energy bioscis., 1988, 92; mem. NSF adv. panel for cellular orgn., 1994-96; mem. plant biology panel NASA; mem. adv. bd. BioEnergy Sci. Ctr., Oak Ridge, Teen., 2008-. Editl. bd. Jour. Cell Biology, 1977-81, European Jour. Cell Biology, 1981-90, Plant Physiology, 1986-92, Plant Jour., 1991-97, Biology of the Cell, 1996-99, Planta, 2003—, Current Opion in Plant Biology, 2003-2007; editor: (with C.J. Antzen) Encyclopedia of Plant Physiology, Vol. 19, Photosynthesis III, 1986; contbr. numerous articles to sci. jours. Recipient Humboldt award Humboldt Found., 1978, Sci. Tchr. award U. Colo., 1984, Outstanding Faculty award U. Colo.-Boulder Parents Assn., 2001, Highly Cited Rschr. ISI, 2004, Haselkorn Scholar award, U. Chgo., 2006; grantee NIH, 1971-, USDA, 1994-, NASA, 1997-; hon. sr. fellow U. Melbourne, Australia, 1998, Am. Assn. Adv. Sci., 2005. Mem. AAAS, Am. Soc. Cell Biology, Am. Soc. Plant Physiology, German Acad. Natural Scis. Leopoldina, Bio Energy Sci.(Sci. Adv bd., 2007-); fellow Am Soc. Plant Physiologist. Home: 2855 Dover Dr Boulder CO 80305-5305 Office: Dept Molecular Cell U Colo 347 UCB Boulder CO 80309-0347 Office Phone: 303-492-8843. E-mail: staeheli@colorado.edu.

STAEHLE, ROBERT L., foundation executive; b. Rochester, NY, Apr. 22, 1955; s. Henry Carl and Isabel Montgomery S. BS in Aero. and Astronautic Engring., Purdue U., 1977. Prin. investigator Skylab Expt. ED-31 (bacteria aboard Skylab), NASA/Marshall Space Flight Center, Huntsville, Ala., 1972-74, student trainee engring., 1974-77; sci. observation analyst Caltech/Jet Propulsion Lab., Pasadena, Calif., 1977-78, engr. advanced projects group, 1978-83, mem. tech. staff system integration sect. of Space Sta., 1983-87, mem. tech. staff and space sta., user ops. team leader, 1987-88; from tech. mgr. to dep. mgr. various positions Jet Propulsion Lab., Pasadena, Calif., 1988—2007; asst. mgr. Advanced Concepts Instruments and Data Sys. Divsn., 2007—. Prin. founder, pres. World Space Found., South Pasadena, Calif., 1979—; founding dir. So. Calif. Space Bus. Roundtable, 1987-95; bd. dirs. Altadena Foothills Conservancy, 2000—. Co-author: Project Solar Sail, New Am. Libr., 1990; contbr. articles to profl. jours. Mem. Cmty. Leaders Adv. Bd. for Irvine Scholars, Occidental Coll., L.A., 1996-97; bd. dirs. Caltech Y, 1987-93. Nat. Space Club Goddard scholar, 1977; Charles A. Lindbergh Fund grantee, 1986. Fellow Brit. Interplanetary Soc.; mem. Tau Beta Pi, Sigma Gamma Tau. Avocations: photography, hiking, mountain biking. Office: Jet Propulsion Lab Pasadena CA 91109 Business E-Mail: robert.l.staehle@jpl.nasa.gov.

STAFFELDT, DARLENE MARIA PREBLE, library director; b. Great Falls, Mont. d. Ardith and Lowell Preble; m. Bill Staffeldt; children: Carla, Dora. MLS, U. Wash. With State Libr. Mont., Helena, 1976—, reference libr., libr. devel. cons., dir. info. resources, dir. statewide libr. resources, state libr., 2004—. Recipient Gov.'s award for Excellence, 1993, Sheila Cates Libr. of Yr. award, Mont. Libr. Assn., 1999. Office: Montana State Libr PO Box 201800 Helena MT 59620-1800 Office Phone: 406-444-3115. Office Fax: 406-444-0266. E-mail: dstaffeldt@mt.gov.

STAFFORD, DEBBIE, state legislator; b. Rapid City, SD, Apr. 5, 1953; d Paul & Pat Dressen; State repr, 40th District, Colorado, 2000-, member, Appropriations and Health and Human Servs, currently, Colorado House Representative; precinct leader, Colorado House Representative, currently; chairman, Key Community Response Team, Aurora, Colorado; White House appointment to Federal Home Loan Bd, 2003-2006.Counselor, Domestic Violence, formerly; owner, small business, currently; ordained minister, currently; voice overs, formerly; board member, Project Heritage, currently, member, Aid to Agencies Blue Ribbon Panel, Govs Child Support Comn & Mayor Webb's Citizen Against Hate Comn, formerly. Shattered Dreams, A Biblical Outlook on Domestic Violence. Citizenship Award, Daughters of America Revolution, Aurora Fire Department. Aurora Chamber of Commerce; Nat Association Women Bus Owners; America Legislature Exchange Coun; Nat Conf State Legislature. Republican. Address: Aurora CO Mailing: State Capitol 200 E Colfax Rm 271 Denver CO 80203 Office Phone: 303-866-2944. Fax: 303-866-2218. E-mail: debbie.stafford.house@state.co.us.

STAGER, DONALD K., retired construction company executive; Chmn., pres., CEO Dillingham Constrn. Holdings Inc., Pleasanton, Calif., 1982-99; with Guy F. Atkinson Co., 1952—82; ret., 1999. Recipient, Roebling award Am. Soc. of Civil Engineers, 1995, Golden Beaver award for Mgmt Beavers, Inc., 1998. Office: 957 Wapato Way Manson WA 98831-9595

STAGGS, THOMAS O., entertainment company executive; Mgr. strategic planning Walt Disney Co., Burbank, Calif., 1990—94, v.p. planning & development, 1995—97, exec. v.p., CFO, 1998—99, sr. exec. v.p., CFO, 2000—. Office: Walt Disney Co 500 S Buena Vista St Burbank CA 91521-0006 Office Phone: 818-560-1000.

STAGLIN, GAREN KENT, computer company executive, venture capitalist; b. Lincoln, Nebr., Dec. 22, 1944; s. Ramon and Darlene (Guilliams) S.; m. Sharalyn King, June 8, 1968; children: Brandon Kent, Shannon King. BS in Engring. with honors, UCLA, 1966; MBA, Stanford U., 1968. Assoc. Carr Mgmt. Co., NYC, 1971-75; v.p. Crocker Nat. Bank, San Francisco, 1975-76; dir. fin. Itel Corp., San Francisco, 1976-77, pres. ins. services divsn., 1977-79; corp. v.p., gen. mgr. ADP Automotive Svcs. Group, San Ramon, Calif., 1978-91; chmn., CEO Safelite Glass Corp., Columbus, Ohio, 1991-97, chmn., 1998-2000; owner Staglin Family Vineyard, Rutherford, Calif., 1985—; pres., CEO eOne Global L.L.C., Napa, Calif., 2000—05; sr. advisor FT Capital, San Francisco, 2005—, Irving Place Pvt. Equity, NYC. Bd. dir. Certive Corp., Specialized Bicycle Corp., Global Document Solutions, Inc., ExL Svcs., Inc., Free Run Techs., Bottom-line techs. Bd. dir. Peralta Hosp. Cancer Inst., 1977-78, Berkeley Reportory Theatre, 1979-85, Nat. Alliance for Rsch. Schizophrenia & Depression, 2000-2008; trustee Justin Sienna HS, Napa, Calif., 1995-20; chmn. major gifts program East Bay region Stanford U., Calif., 1989-92; mem. adv. bd. Stanford Bus. Sch., 1995-2000; judge Cambridge Bus. Sch., 2004-; chmn. 75th anniversary campaign Stanford Grad. Sch. Bus., 1998-00; capital campaign UCLA Coll. Letters Sci., 2004-07; pres. bd. trustees Am. Ctr. Wine, Food and Arts, Napa, Calif., 1998-03;founder Music Festival Mental Health, 1994-. Lt. USN, 1968—71. Recipient Gold Spike award, Stanford U., 2000, Honors Fellow award, UCLA, 2006. Mem. Stanford Assocs. (bd. govs. 1985-92), World Pres. Orgn., Internat. Inst. Soc. (bd. govs. 1985-92), Nappa Valley Vintners Assn. Democrat. Lutheran. Home: PO Box 680 1570 Bella Oaks Ln Rutherford CA 94573 Office Phone: 707-280-5374. Business E-Mail: garen.stagline@staglinfamily.com.

STAHELI, KORY D., law librarian; BA, Brigham Young U., 1984, JD, 1987, MLIS, 1991. Atty. Snow, Nuffer, Engstrom & Drake, St. George, Utah, 1987—90; reference libr. Brigham Young U. Law Library, Provo, Utah, 1990—91, head of reference svcs., 1991—95, assoc. dir. pub. svc. Howard W. Hunter Law Libr., 1995—98, assoc. dir. collection devel. and faculty outreach, 2004—05, dir., 2005—; assoc. dir., head pub. svcs. Wiener-Rogers Law Libr., U. Nev., Las Vegas, 1998—2004, interim dir., 2002. Spkr. in field. Contbr. articles to profl. jours. Mem.: Am. Assn. Law Libs. Office: Howard W Hunter Law Lib 256 JRCB PO Box 28000 Provo UT 84602-8000 Office Phone: 801-422-9223. E-mail: stahelik@lawgate.byu.edu.

STAHL, DAVID A., microbiologist, educator; BS magna cum laude, U. Wash., Seattle, 1971; MS, U. Ill., 1975, PhD, 1978. Pre-doctoral fellowship U. of Ill., 1971—73; tchg. asst. U. of Ill., Sch. of Life Sciences, 1973—74; grad. studies U. of Ill., 1974—77; NIH post doctoral fellowship Nat. Jewish Hosp. and Rsch. Ctr., Denver, 1978—80, sr. rsch. assoc.; asst. prof., dept. of vet. pathobiology U. of Ill., 1984—91, assoc. prof., dept. of vet. pathobiology, 1991—94; assoc. prof., dept. of civil enging. Northwestern U., 1994—96; scientist in residence DuPont CR&D, Wilmington, Del., 1998—99; prof. Northwestern U., 1996—2001; adj. prof. U. of Wash., Sch. of Medicine, 2001—. Vis. prof. U. of Minn., 1987—89, 1992; panel mem. NASA, Mars Curation and Receiving Oversight Panel, 1997—98; mem. J. Roger Porter award com., 1998—99. Recipient Bergey award, 1999, Orton K. Stark disting. lectr., Miami U., 1998, award for rsch. excellence, SmithKline Beecham, 1992, Beckman rsch. award, U. of Ill., 1992, Norman and Helen Levine award for rsch. excellence, U. of Ill., Dept. of Vet. Pathobiology, 1991. Fellow: Am. Acad. of Microbiology. Achievements include research in microbial ecology, evolution and phylogeny of microorganisms, ribosomal RNA processing, molecular phylogeny of microorganisms, molecular approaches to microbial ecology, nucleic acid structure; ribosomal RNA processing, structure and evolution of the 23S ribosomal RNA. Office: University of Washington Office: More 302 Seattle WA 98195

STAHL, FRANKLIN WILLIAM, biology educator; b. Boston, Oct. 8, 1929; AB in Biology, Harvard U., 1951; PhD in Biology, U. Rochester, 1956; DSc (hon.), Oakland U., 1966, U. Rochester, 1982. Grad. tchg. asst., rsch. asst. U. Rochester, 1951-54, predoctoral fellow NSF, 1954-55; postdoctoral fellow NSF, NRC, divsn. med. sci. Calif. Inst. Tech., 1955-57, rsch. fellow, 1957-58; assoc. prof. biology, rsch. assoc. Inst. Molecular Biology, U. Oreg., Eugene, 1959-63, prof. biology, mem., 1963—, acting dir., 1973-74. Vol. scientist divsn. molecular genetics Med. Rsch. Coun., Cambridge, Eng., 1964-65; mem. virology study sect. NIH, 1968-71; sabbatical leave MRC Unit of Molecular Genetics, U. Edinburgh, Scotland, 1969-70, Internat. Genetics and Biophysics Lab., Napoli, Italy, 1969-70; Lady Davis vis. prof. genetics dept. Hebrew U., Jerusalem, 1975-76; mem. microbial genetics study sect. NSF, 1987—. Mem. editl. bd. Virology, 1959-62, Molecular and Gen. Genetics, 1967-78, 80-82, Genetics, 1971-76, Jour. Genetics, 1986—; contbr. articles to profl. jours. Recipient Thomas Hunt Morgan medal for lifetime achievement in genetics Genetics Soc. Am., 1996; named Am. Cancer Soc. rsch. prof. molecular genetics, 1985—; Guggenheim fellow, 1975, 85, MacArthur fellow, 1985-90. Mem. NAS, European Molecular Biology Orgn., Am. Acad. Arts and Scis. Office: U Oregon Inst Molecular Biology Eugene OR 97403-1229

STAHL, JACK LELAND, real estate company executive; b. Lincoln, Ill., June 28, 1934; s. Edwin R. and Edna M. (Burns) S.; m. Carol Anne Townsend, June 23, 1956; children: Cheryl, Nancy, Kellea BS in Edn., U. N.Mex., 1957. Tchr. Albuquerque Pub. Schs., 1956-59; pres. House Finders, Inc., Albuquerque, 1959-65; v.p. N.Mex. Savs. & Loan Assn., Albuquerque, 1965-67; chmn. bd. Hooten-Stahl, Inc., Albuquerque, 1967-77; mem. N.Mex. Ho. of Reps., 1969-70; pres. The Jack Stahl Co., Albuquerque, 1977—; mem. N.Mex. Senate, 1981-86; lt. gov. State of N.Mex., 1987-90. Mem. exec. bd. Gr. S.W. Coun. Boy Scouts Am, 1982-89; bd. dirs. BBB N. Mex., 1968-82, pres. 1975-76; trustee Univ Heights. Hosp.,1980-85; vice chmn. N. Mex. Bd. Fin., 1987-90, N. Mex. Cmty. Devel. Coun., 1987-90; bd. dirs. Ctr. for Entrepreneurship and Econ. Devel., 1994-96; mem. Gov.'s Bus. Adv. Coun., 1995-97. Named Realtor of Yr., Albuquerque Bd. Realtors, 1972. Mem. Nat. Assn. Realtors, Nat. Homebuilders Assn., N.Mex. Amigos, 20-30 Club (pres. 1963-64), Rotary. Republican. Methodist. Office: 1911 Wyoming Blvd NE Albuquerque NM 87112-2865 Office Phone: 505-292-6635.

STAHL, JAMES F., engineer; Grad. in Civil Engring., Loyola Marymount U., 1965. Chief engr., gen. mgr. County Sanitation Dists. LA County, Whittier, Calif., 2000—07; ret., 2007. Mem.: NAE. Office: County Sanitation Dists LA County 1955 Workman Mill Rd Whittier CA 90601 Office Phone: 562-908-4288 ext. 2301. Office Fax: 562-695-6139.

STAHL, LOUIS A., lawyer; b. Oct. 31, 1940; s. Louis A. and Dorothy (Cox) S.; m. Mary Kathleen Quinn, Apr. 4, 1960; children: Lisa, Suzanne, Gretchen, Nicole. BA magna cum laude, Wheeling Jesuit U., 1962; postgrad., Duquesne U., 1965-66; JD summa cum laude, Notre Dame U., 1971. Bar: Ariz. 1971, U.S. Dist. Ct. Ariz. 1971, U.S. Ct. Appeals (9th cir.) 1974, U.S. Supreme Ct. 1975. Ptnr. Streich Lang P.A., Phoenix, 1971—. Mem. Maricopa County Superior Ct. Rule 26.1 Study Com., 1992—; Frances Lewis lawyer in residence Washington & Lee Univ. Law Sch., 1986; seminar panelist Ariz. Bankers Assn., 1987, Profl. Ednl. Systems, Inc., 1989; mediator, arbitrator U.S. Arbitration and Mediation of Ariz., Nev. and N. Mex., 1993—. Contbg. author: Arizona Attorneys' Fees Manual, 1987, Arizona Professionalism Manual, 1992; contbr. papers to law revs. and jours. Active Phoenix and Maricopa County Young Reps., Ariz. Rep. Party's Lawyers' Ballot Security Com., 1980, Vols. for Reagan-Bush, 1980, Re-elect Rep. Ernest Baird Fin. Com., 1992, Ariz. Rep. Caucus.; founding mem., v.p., dir., legal counsel Performing Arts

Combined Talent; pres., bd. dirs. Make a Wish Found. Ctrl. & So. Ariz., 1995—. Mem. ABA (vice-chmn. health ins. com., sect. ins., negligence and compensation law 1973-79, contbg. editor The Forum 1976-79), State Bar Ariz. (mem. profl. liability com. 1979-86, chmn. 1983-86, mem. com. on rules of profl. conduct ethics com. 1981-93, com. on professionalism 1989-91, discipline task force 1991-92, co-chmn. peer rev. com. 1991—), Def. Rsch. Inst., Ariz. Assn. of Def. Counsel, Ariz. Bar Found., Phoenix C. of C. (military affairs com.), Am. Numismatic Assn., Phoenix Coin Club. Office: Streich Lang PA Renaissance One 2 N Central Ave Fl 2 Phoenix AZ 85004-2345

STAHL, NICK, actor; b. Harlingen, Tex., Dec. 5, 1979; Actor: (TV miniseries) Seasons of Love, 1999; (TV series) Carnivàle, 2003—05; (TV films) Stranger at My Door, 1991, Woman with a Past, 1992, Incident in a Small Town, 1994, Blue River, 1995, My Son Is Innocent, 1996, Wasted, 2002; (films) The Man Without a Face, 1993, Safe Passage, 1994, Tall Tale, 1995, Eye of God, 1997, Disturbing Behavior, 1998, Soundman, 1998, The Thin Red Line, 1998, All Forgotten, 2000, Sunset Strip, 2000, In the Bedroom, 2001, The Sleepy Time Gal, 2001, Bully, 2001, Taboo, 2002, Bookies, 2003, Terminator 3: Rise of the Machines, 2003, Twist, 2003, Sin City, 2005, The Night of the White Pants, 2006, How to Rob a Bank, 2007, Quid Pro Quo, 2008, Sleepwalking, 2008. Office: c/o 1 Management 9000 Sunset Blvd Ste 1550 Los Angeles CA 90069

STAHL, RICHARD G. C., journalist, editor; b. Chgo., Feb. 22, 1934; m. Gladys C. Weisbecker; 1 child, Laura Ann. Student, Northwestern U., U. Ill., Chgo. Editor Railway Purchases and Stores Mag., Chgo., 1960-63; editor pub. rels. dept. Sears Roebuck & Co., Chgo., 1963-68; dir pub. rels. dept. St. Joseph's Hosp. Med. Ctr., Phoenix, 1968-72; v.p. pub. rels. Consultation Svcs., Inc., Phoenix, 1972-73; creative dir. Don Jackson and Assoc., Phoenix, 1973; editor, pub. rels. mgr. Maricopa County Med. Soc., Phoenix, 1974-76; sr. editor Ariz. Hwys. mag., Phoenix, 1977-99; ret., 1999. Regional editor: (travel guides) Budget Travel, 1985, USA, 1986, Arizona, 1986; free-lance writer and editor. Mem. Soc. Profl. Journalists. Avocation: woodworking. Office: Ariz Hwys Mag 2039 W Lewis Ave Phoenix AZ 85009-2819

STAHMANN, ROBERT F., education educator; b. Peoria, Ill., Nov. 26, 1939; s. Fred Soeffner and Mary Emma (Thompson) S.; m. Kathleen Cook, Dec. 21, 1965; children: Benjamin C., John C., Paul C., Mark C., Anne. BA, Macalester Coll., 1963; MS, U. Utah, 1965, PhD, 1967. Research fellow U. Utah, 1966-67; sr. counselor U. Iowa, Iowa City, 1967-71, coordinator counseling service, 1971-72, dir. counseling service, 1972-75, asst. prof. edn., 1967-71, asso. prof., 1971-75; prof. family scis. Brigham Young U., Provo, Utah, 1975—, chmn. dept. family scis., 1983-89, dir. Marriage and Family Counseling Clinic, 1976-83, coordinator program in marriage and family therapy, 1977-83; program dir. marriage and family therapy, 2001—. Vis. prof. sex and marital therapy clinic Coll. Medicine, U. Utah, 1980-81; mem. Utah State Marriage and Family Therapy Licensing Bd., 1982-92; mem. Commn. Accreditation for Marriage and Family Therapy Edn., 1989-94, chair, 1990-94. Co-author: Premarital Counseling, 1980, 2d edit., 1987, Dynamic Assessment in Couples Therapy, 1993, Premarital and Remarital Counseling, 1997, Becoming One: Intimacy in Marriage, 2004; co-editor: Ethical and Professional Issues for Marital and Family Therapists, 1980; co-editor, contbr.; Counseling in Marital and Sexual Problems: A Clinician's Handbook, 1977, 3d edit., 1984; assoc. editor: Jour. Coll. Student Pers., 1971-77; editor: Jour. Assoc. Mormon Counselors and Psychotherapists, 1977-78; contbr. chpts. to books., articles to profl. jours. Scoutmaster Boy Scouts Am., 1969-72, 83-87, cubmaster, 1976-79; mem. Orem City Beautification Commn., 1976-77; mem. adv. bd. Ret. Sr. Vol. Program for Utah County, 1987-89. Fellow Am. Assn. Marriage and Family Therapy (bd. dirs. 1977-79); mem. Internat. Family Therapy Assn., Am. Assn. Sex Educators, Counselors and Therapists (cert.), Utah Assn. Marriage and Family Counselors (pres. 1978-80), Nat. Coun. on Family Rels., Utah Coun. on Family Rels. (pres. 1987-88), Sigma Xi, Phi Kappa Phi. Mem. Lds Ch. Office: Brigham Young Univ 240 TLRB Provo UT 84602 E-mail: robert_stahmann@byu.edu.

STAKY, RICHARD, real estate development company executive; Degree, Albion Coll.; grad. degree, U. Detroit. Chief fin. officer, exec. v.p. no. Calif., divsn. pres. Pulte Homes, Tucson, Denver, regional pres. Rocky Mtn. divsn. Denver, WL Homes LLC, Greenwood Village, Colo. Office: John Laing Homes 19520 Jamboree Rd Ste 500 Irvine CA 92612-2457

STALLINGS, CHARLES HENRY, retired physicist; b. Durham, NC, Dec. 28, 1941; s. Henry Harroll and Dorothy (Powers) S.; m. Elizabeth Bright, Sept. 4, 1965; children: Deborah, Sharon. BS, N.C. State U., 1963, MS, 1964; PhD, U. Wis., 1970. Sr. physicist Physics Internat. Co. (now Maxwell Physics Internat.), San Leandro, Calif., 1970-73, dep. dept. mgr., 1974-76, dept. mgr., 1976-79, dir. satellite x-ray test facility office, 1979-81, dir. bus. devel., 1981-83, v.p., dir. rsch. devel., v.p., gen. mgr., 1983—2001; ret., 2001. Contbr. articles to tech. jours. Mem. Gen. Plan Rev. Com., Pleasanton, Calif., 1983. Mem. Am. Phys. Soc., IEEE (mem. pulsed power sci. and tech. com. 1996—, chmn. 12th internat. pulsed power conf. 1999), Def. Sci. Bd. Task Force, 2003-05. Home: 3608 Fieldview Ct Pleasanton CA 94588

STALLINGS, VALERIE AILEEN, retired councilwoman, consultant; b. Chgo., Dec. 23, 1939; d. Jay Sims and Mary Elizabeth (Batson) Spire; adoptive dau. Willian Mundo Spire; m. John R. Stallings, July 14, 1961 (div. 1970); children: Dana Elizabeth, Marshall Brigg. AA, Palomar (Calif.) Coll., 1978; BA, U. Calif., San Diego, 1980. Rschr., lab. mgr. Salk Inst., La Jolla, Calif., 1970-91; mem. coun. City of San Diego, 1991-2001, ret., 2001. Sabbatical rschr. Netherlands Cancer Inst., 1981; city rep. Jack Murphy Stadium Authority, San Diego, 1991-2000; chmn. pub. facilities and recreation City of San Diego, 1992-95; chmn. fiscal policy San Diego Wastewater, 1993-94; dir. San Diego Area Wastewater Mgmt. Dist., 1993—. Contbr. articles to sci. jours. Pres. Pacific Beach Dem. Club, San Diego; mem. Pacific Beach Planning Commn., San Diego. Named Legislator of Yr., SEIU Svc. Coun., 1992. Mem. Nat. Women's Polit. Caucus, Calif. Elected Women's Assn. for Edn. and Rsch., U. Calif. Alumni Assn. (bd. dirs.). Democrat. Avocations: triathlons, jogging, safaris, photography.

STALLONE, SYLVESTER GARDENZIO, actor, film director, scriptwriter, producer; b. NYC, July 6, 1946; s. Frank and Jacquline (Labofish) Stallone; m. Sasha Czack, Dec. 28, 1974 (div. Feb. 14, 1985); children: Sage, Seth; m. Brigitte Nielsen, Dec. 15, 1985 (div. July 13, 1987); m. Jennifer Flavin, May 17, 1997; children: Sophia, Sistine, Scarlet. Student, Am. Coll. of Switzerland, 1965-67, U. Miami, 1967-69. Actor: (films) The Party at Kitty and Stud's, 1970, No Place to Hide, 1970, The Prisoner of Second Avenue, 1975, Capone, 1975, Death Race 2000, 1975, Farewell, My Lovely, 1975, Cannonball!, 1976, Nighthawks, 1981, Victory, 1981, Lock Up, 1989, Tango & Cash, 1989, Oscar, 1991, Stop! Or My Mom Will Shoot, 1992, Demolition Man, 1993, The Specialist, 1994, Judge Dredd, 1995, Assassins, 1995, Daylight, 1996, The Good Life, 1997, Cop Land, 1997, An Alan Smithee Film: Burn Hollywood Burn, 1998, (voice) Antz, 1998, Get Carter, 2000, D-Tox, 2002, Avenging Angelo, 2002, Shade, 2003, Spy Kids 3-D: Game Over, 2003; writer, actor (films) The Lord's of Flatbush, 1974, Rocky, 1976, F.I.S.T, 1978, First Blood, 1982, Rhinestone, 1984, Rambo: First Blood Part II, 1985, Cobra, 1986, Over the Top, 1987, Rambo III, 1988, Rocky V, 1980, Cliffhanger, 1993, dir., writer, actor Paradise Alley, 1978, Rocky II, 1979, Rocky III, 1982, Rocky IV, 1985, Rocky Balboa, 2006, prodr., dir., writer, actor Staying Alive, 1983, Rambo, 2008; prodr.: (films) Heart of a Champion: The Ray Mancini Story, 1985; prodr., writer, actor (films) Driven, 2001, exec. prodr., writer Father Lefty, 2002; actor(guest appearances): (TV series) Police Story, 1975, Kojak, 1975, Liberty's Kids: Est. 1776, 2002, Las Vegas, 2005; prodr.: The Contender, 2005, The Contender Rematch: Mora vs. Manfredo, 2005; author: Sly Moves: My Proven Program to Lose Weight, Build Strength, Gain Will Power, and Live Your Dream, 2005. Recipient Star of Yr. award, 1977, Artistic Achievement award, Nat. Italian Am. Found., 1991, Order of Arts and Letters, French Ministry, 1992, Caesar award for Career Achievement, 1992; named Show West Actor of Yr., 1979. Mem.: SAG, Dirs. Guild, Writers Guild, Stuntmans Assn. (hon.). Achievements include being nominated for two Oscars (acting and writing) in same year (1976); occurred for only 3d time in history.

STAMBAUGH, LARRY G., strategic business consultant; b. Topeka, Feb. 1, 1947; s. Merle L and Eileen M. (Denslow) S.; m. Sallie M. Underwood, Jan. 18, 1969 (div. Oct. 1981); children: Matt, Julie; m. Suzanne Van Slyke, May 14, 1982 (div. Oct. 2006); children: Todd, Scott, Andy; m. Pamela Truax, Oct. 27, 2007. BBA, Washburn U., 1969. CPA, Kans. Mgr. KPMG Peat, Marwick, Mitchell Co., Kansas City, Mo., 1969-76; co-owner Automotive Investment & Devel. Co., Olathe, Kans., 1976-82; EVP, CFO CNB Fin. Corp., Kansas City, Kans., 1983—90; CFO ABC Labs., Columbia, Mo., 1990, pres., CEO, 1990-92; chmn., pres., CEO Maxim Pharms., San Diego, 1993—2006; prin. Apercu Cons., 2006—, pres., 2007—08; CEO Calando Pharmaceuticals, 2007; chmn., pres., CEO CryoPort, Inc., 2009—; chmn to bd. dir. Ridge Diagnostics Inc., 2007; bd. dir. Elixir Industries, 2007—08, Ecodog, 2008—, Assure Controls, 2008—09. Bd. dirs. BioCom, Eco Dog Inc., 2008-; mem. adv. bd. U. Calif. San Diego Rady Sch. Bus. Chmn. bd. dirs. Forum for Corp. Dirs., 1996-99. Recipient Dir. of Yr. award, Forum for Corp. Dirs., 2002, 2006—07, Jim Mcgraw Disting. award, 2008. Mem. Am. Mgmt. Assn., Nat. Assn. Corp. Dirs. (Jim McGraw award 2008). Avocations: photography, golf. Home: 645 Front St 314 San Diego CA 92101 Office Phone: 858-531-9201. Personal E-mail: lgstambaugh@gmail.com.

STAMBAUGH, RONALD DENNIS, physicist, researcher; b. Milw., May 15, 1947; s. Wilbert Foster and Joyce Elaine (Miller) S.; m. Mildred Alice Considine, June 22, 1968; children: James, Emily, Claire, Margaret. BS, U. Wis., 1969; MPhil, Yale U., 1971, PhD, 1974. Computer programmer U. Wis., Madison, 1967-69; rsch. asst. Yale U., New Haven, Conn., 1970-74; sr. scientist Gen. Atomics, San Diego, 1975-77, br. mgr., 1978-79, plasma control coord., 1979-84, mgr. physics dept., 1984-91, divsn. dir., 1991—. Chmn. divertor expert group ITER, 1994—; BPX dep. physics head Princeton (N.J.) Plasma Lab., 1990-91; exec. com. APS-DPP, 1987-89, 91-92. Mem. editl. bd. Nuclear Fusion, 1991—. Recipient award for Excellence in Plasma Physics Research Am. Physical Society, 1994 Fellow Am. Phys. Soc. (Excellence in Plasma Physics 1994). Achievements include experimental verification of plasma stability theory for Tokamaks. Office: Gen Atomics PO Box 85608 San Diego CA 92186-5608

STAMEY, THOMAS ALEXANDER, urologist, educator; b. Rutherfordton, NC, Apr. 26, 1928; s. Owen and Virginia (Link) S.; m. Kathryn Simmons Dec. 1, 1973; children: Fred M., Charline, Thomas A. III, Allison, Theron. BA, Vanderbilt U., 1948; MD, Johns Hopkins U., 1952. Diplomate Am. Bd. Urology. Intern, then resident Johns Hopkins Hosp., 1952-56; asst. prof. urology Johns Hopkins U. Sch. Medicine, Balt., 1958-60, assoc. prof., 1960-61; assoc. prof., chmn. divsn. urology Stanford U., Calif., 1961-64, assoc. prof., 1964-90, prof., 0191—, chmn. dept., 1964-95. Author: Renovascular Hypertension, 1967, Pathogenesis and Treatment of Urinary Tract Infections, 1980, Urinalysis and Urinary Sediment: A Practical Guide for the Health Science Professional, 1985; editor: Campbell's Urology, edits. 4-6, 1978-92, Monographs in Urology, 1980-99. Capt. M.C., USAF, 1956-58. Recipient Sheen award ACS, 1990, Ferdinand C. Valentine award N.Y. Acad. Medicine, 1991. Mem. Am. Urol. Assn. (Ramon Guiteras award 1995, John K. Lattimer award 2000, Eugene Fuller Triennial Prostate award 2001), Am. Surg. Assn. (sr.), Inst. Medicine of NAS. Avocations: fishing, astronomy. Office: Stanford U Med Ctr Dept Urology S 287 300 Pasteur Dr Stanford CA 94305-5118 Home Phone: 650-851-3100. Business E-Mail: tstamey@stanford.edu.

STAMM, ALAN, lawyer; b. Galesburg, Ill., Nov. 22, 1931; s. Gustave Frederick and Miriam (Simon) S.; m. Shelley Lynn Ramage, Mar. 19, 1978; 1 child, Lucinda Anne. Student, Universidad Nacional de Mex., summer 1950; AB, Yale U., 1952; JD, Harvard U., 1957. Bar: Calif. 1957, U.S. Supreme Ct. 1963. Assoc. Thelen Reid, Brown Raysman & Steiner LLP, San Francisco, 1957—60; staff atty. Litton Industries Inc., Beverly Hills, Calif., 1960-66, asst. sec., 1963-66; sec., gen. counsel Internat. Rectifier Corp., LA, 1966-69, v.p., 1968-69; v.p., gen. counsel Republic Corp., LA, 1969-71, bd. dirs., 1970-71; v.p., gen. counsel Sat. Rev. Industries, NYC, 1971-72, Mattel Inc., Hawthorne, Calif., 1972-74, staff cons., 1974-75; of counsel Long & Levit, LA, 1975-82, O'Donnell & Gordon, LA, 1983-87, Hedges, Powe & Caldwell, LA, 1988-90; pvt. practice LA, 1990—. Judge pro tem Mcpl. Ct. LA Jud. Dist., 1977—, LA Superior Ct. 1989—; arbitrator Fin. Industry Regulatory Authority, Nat. Assn. Securities Dealers, 1981—, NYSE, 1994-2007. Founding trustee Ctr. for Law in Pub. Interest; former trustee Marlborough Sch., LA; former mem. bd. govs. Century City Hosp., LA; counsel bus. and profl. com. LA Philharm.; mem. bd. dirs. Yale Alumni Fund. Lt. j.g. USNR, 1952—54, ret. lt. comdr. USNR. Mem. ABA, State Bar of Calif., LA Bar Assn., Harvard Law Sch. Assn., LA County Art Mus., Am. Arbitration Assn. (nat. panel arbitrators 1968—), Sierra Club (life), Nat. Assn. Yale Alumni (former bd. govs.), Yale Club of So. Calif. (mem. dir.), Harvard Club of So. Calif., Phi Beta Kappa. Home: 422 Denslow Ave Los Angeles CA 90049-3507 Office: 1950 Pelham Ave Unit 1 Los Angeles CA 90025-5835

STAMM, CAROL ANN, obstetrician, gynecologist; b. Denver, Aug. 8, 1959; d. Robert L. and Mary Ellen Stamm. BA in Biology cum laude, U. Colo., 1981; MD with honors, U. Colo., Denver, 1991. Diplomate Am. Bd. Ob-Gyn; cert. in elem. tchg. U. Colo., 1986. Bilingual elem. tchr. Denver Pub. Schs., 1986—87; intern in ob-gyn U. Colo. Sch. Medicine, Denver, 1991—92, resident in ob-gyn, 1992—95, asst. prof., 1997—2003; staff ob-gyn, asst. prof. Denver Health Med. Ctr., 1995—2003; dir. women's health rotation Colo. Health Found. (formerly High St. Primary Care Clinic), Denver, 2003—, asst. prof. clin. medicine, 2003—, dir. women's svcs., 2004—. Mem. Patient and Family Edn. Work Group, 1996—97; mem. ob-gyn edn. com. U. Colo. Health Scis. Ctr., 1997—2003; dir. ob-gyn Grand Rounds, 1997—2001; provider design team Lifetime Clin. Record Project, 1998—2001; alt. mem. Colo. Multiple Instl. Rev. Bd., 1998—2003; presenter in field. Co-author: (book) Management of High-Risk Pregnancy, 4th edit., 1999, Medical Care of the Pregnant Patient, 2000, The Female Athlete, 2002, Contemporary Therapy in Obstetrics and Gynecology, 2002; contbr. articles to profl. jours.; peer reviewer Jour. Obstetrics and Gynecology, 1999—, Am. Jour. Obstetrics and Gynecology, 1999—. Recipient Richard Whitehead award, Phi Rho Sigma, 1989; grantee, March of Dimes, 2000—01; Trust fellow, Am. Cancer Soc. Brooks, 1988, Acad. Enrichment grantee, U. Colo. Health Scis. Ctr., 1993—95, NIH subcontract grantee, U. Pitts., 2000—03, NIH grantee, IBBEX, 2002. Fellow: ACOG (History fellow 2006); mem.: N.Am. Menopause Soc, Golden Key, Phi Beta Kappa (mem. mortar bd.). Avocations: reading, running, pilates, symphony, opera. Home: 155 S Jackson St Unit C Denver CO 80209 Office: Colorado Health Found 1801 High St Denver CO 80218 Office Phone: 303-869-2158. Business E-Mail: cstamm@coloradohealth.org.

STAMPER, NORMAN HARVEY, former police chief; b. San Diego, 1944; BS, MS in Criminal Justice Adminstrn., San Diego State U.; PhD in Leadership & Human Behavior, US Internat. U. With San Diego Police Dept., 1966—94, patrolman, 1966—71, lt., 1971—75; chief of police Seattle Police Dept., 1994—2000. Exec. dir. Mayor Pete Wilson's Crime Control Commn.; apptd. (by U.S. Atty. Gen. and Sec. Health and Human Svcs.) Adv. Coun. Violence Against Women; mem. adv. panel on Excessive Force by Police, Police Exec. Rsch. Forum, Major Cities Chiefs; mem. steering com. Seattle Equal Justice Coalition; co-chair Ptnr's. in Pub. Edn's. Urban Scholar's Program; mem. bd. dirs. Leadership Tomorrow; trustee Ctr. for Ethical Leadership; mem. advisory bd., Law Enforcement Against Prohibition (LEAP). Author: Removing Managerial Barriers to Effective Police Leadership, 1992, Breaking Rank: A Top Cop's Exposé of the Dark Side of American Policing, 2005; technical adv. Municipal Police Admminstrn., 1992. Named to Alumni Hall of Fame Boys and Girls Club of Am.; recipient Katharine M. Bullitt award for Leadership Ptnrs. in Pub. Edn. Mem. Internat. Assn. Chiefs of Police. E-mail: norm@rockisland.com.*

STAMPER, ROBERT LEWIS, ophthalmologist, educator; b. NYC, July 27, 1939; m. Naomi T. Belson, June 23, 1963; children: Juliet, Marjorie, Alison. BA, Cornell U., 1961; MD, SUNY-Downstate, 1965. Diplomate Am. Bd. Ophthalmology (assoc. examiner 1976-92, bd. dirs. 1992-99). Intern Mt. Sinai Hosp., NYC, 1965-66; resident in ophthalmology Washington U.-Barnes Hosp., St. Louis, 1968-71; Nat. Eye Inst.-NIH fellow dept. ophthalmology Washington U., St. Louis, 1971-72, from instr. ophthalmology to asst. prof. dept. ophthalmology, 1971-72; asst. prof. dept. ophthalmology Pacific Presbyn. Med. Ctr., San Francisco, 1972-76, assoc. prof. ophthalmology, 1976-87; chmn. dept. ophthalmology Calif. Pacific Med. Ctr. (formerly Pacific Presbyn. Med. Ctr.), San Francisco, 1987-96; vice-chmn. dept. ophthalmology U. Calif., San Francisco, 1999—2003, prof. clin. ophthalmology, dir. glaucoma, 1999—. Asst. opthalmologist Barnes Hosp., St. Louis, 1971-72, Harkness Hosp., San Francisco, 1973-74; dir. ophthalmic photography and fluorescin angiography, dept. ophthalmology Washington U., St. Louis, 1969-72; dir. resident tng. Pacific Presbyn. Med. Ctr., 1972-89, dir. glaucoma svc., vice-chmn. dept. ophthalmology, 1974-87; chief ophthalmology svc. Highland Hosp., Oakland, Calif., 1974-76; clin. instr. dept. ophthalmology U. Calif., San Francisco, 1974-77, prof. clin. ophthalmology, 1998—; clin. asst. prof. ophthalmology U. Calif., Berkeley, 1974-78, asst. clin. prof. ophthalmology, 1978-85; sr. rsch. assoc. Smith-Kettlewell Inst. Visual Scis., San Francisco, 1972-89; project co-dir. ophthalmic curriculum for med. students Nat. Libr. Medicine, 1973-75; commr. Joint Commn. on Allied Health Pers. in Ophthalmology, 1975-87, bd. dirs., 1978-88, sec., 1980, v.p., 1982-83, pres., 1984-85; provisional asst. chief dept. ophthalmology Mt. Zion Hosp., San Francisco, 1976-87, assoc. chief dept. ophthalmology, 1982-86; ophthalmic cons. Ft. Ord, Calif., 1976-1984, Oakland Naval Hosp., 1978-83; instr. Stanford U., Calif., 1977—1992; glaucoma cons. U. Calif., Davis, 1978-84; vis. lectr. dept. ophthalmology Hadassah Hebrew U. Med. Ctr., Jerusalem, 1978, Oxford U. Eye Hosp., Eng., 1986; ind. med. examiner State of Calif., 1979—; mem. appeals hearing panel Accreditation Coun. for Grad. Med. Edn., 1986-93, mem. residency rev. com. for ophthalmology, 1993-98; mem. provisional courtesy staff Peralta Hosp., Oakland, 1988-92; mem. ophthalmic devices adv. panel USFDA, 1989-92; presenter, lectr. in field. Co-author: Update in Glaucoma, 2004, 2d edit., 2006; editor Ophthalmology Clinics of North Am., 1988-2004, 06; mem. editl. adv. com. Ophthalmology, 1982-89, mem. editl. bd., 1983-94; co-author: Becker and Shaffer's Diagnosis and Management of the Glaucomas, 7th edit., 1999, 8th edit., 2009; co-editor Essentials in Ophthalmology: Glaucoma, 2007, 2009; contbr. articles to profl. jours. Chmn. bd. Agy. Jewish Edn., Oakland, 1986-89; bd. dirs. Jewish Fedn. Greater East Bay, Oakland, 1992-94; bd. dirs. Found. Glaucoma Rsch.; mem. glaucoma adv. com. Nat. Soc. to Prevent Blindness, 1981-2004; mem. Am. Diabetes Assn. Surgeon USPHS, 1966-68. Recipient Self-Instrnl. Material in Ophthalmology award Nat. Soc. for Performance and Instrn., 1975, Honor award Am. Acad. Ophthalmology, 1982, Sr. Honor award, 1992, lifetime Achievement award, 2008, Am. Acad. Ophthalmology, 2008, Statesmanship award Joint Commn. on Allied Health Pers. in Ophthalmology, 1989, Disting. Alumnus award Wash. U. Sch. Medicine, 2004; named Troutman Master Tchr. in Ophthalmology, 2000; Regents scholar NY State, 1961, scholar NY State, 1965; Blalock fellow UCLA Sch. Medicine, 1961, Fight for Sight fellow Dept. Ophthalmology NY Hosp. and Cornell Med. Ctr., 1962, 63, 64. Fellow Am. Acad. Ophthalmology and Otolaryngology (rep. to joint commn. on allied health pers., faculty home study course sect. X, chmn. sect. VIII 1983-85, bd. councilors, editl. adv. com. Opthalmology jour. 1982-89, editl. bd. Ophthalmology jour. 1983-94, and many others), ACS; mem. AMA (Physician's Recognition award 1989), Am. Ophthalmologic Soc., Assn. for Rsch. in Vision and Ophthalmology, Calif. Med. Assn. (asst. sec. sect. ophthalmology, chmn., sci. bd. rep. adv. panel on ophthalmology 1985-91), Nat. Soc. Prevent Blindness (mem. glaucoma adv. com. 1981-2004), No. Calif. Soc. Prevent Blindness (bd. dirs. 1986—, pres.-elect 2006—, pres. 2008-), Calif. Assn. Ophthalmology, Pan Am. Ophthal. (bd. dirs. 1992—), Soc., NY Acad. Scis., Las Vegas Ophthal. Soc. (hon.), Am. Glaucoma Soc. (v.p. 1997-99, pres. 1999-2000), Glaucoma Rsch. Found. (bd. dirs.). Office: Dept Opht UCSF Med Ctr 8 Koret Way San Francisco CA 94143-0730 Business E-Mail: stamperr@vision.ucsf.edu.

STAMPS, JUDY A., retired biology professor; m. Vaidyanadhan Venkaka Krishnan, 2005. MA in Zoology, U. Calif., Berkeley, 1971, PhD in Zoology, 1974. Prof. U. Calif., Davis, 1973—2007, prof. emerita, 2007—. Fellow: AAAS, Animal Behavior Soc. (Exemplar award, Disting. Animal Behaviorist award). Achievements include research in theoretical and empirical studies of territoriality, habitat selection, and personality traits in animals.

STANBRIDGE, ERIC JOHN, biology professor; b. London, May 28, 1942; came to U.S., 1965; BS, Brunel U., 1964; PhD, Stanford U., 1971. Rsch. asst. Wistar Inst., Phila., 1965—67; mem. sci. staff Nat. Inst. Med. Research, London, 1968-69; research assoc. med. microbiology Stanford (Calif.) U., 1972-73, instr. med. microbiology, 1973-75; asst. prof., dept. microbiology U. Calif., Irvine, 1975-78, assoc. prof., dept. microbiology, 1978-82, prof., dept. microbiology and molecular genetics, 1982—, disting. prof., dept. microbiology and molecular genetics, 2002—. Chmn. Gordon Conf. Cancer Biology, 1985; advisor Office of Tech. Assessment, 1986; co-organizer UCLA-Triton Bioscis. Symposium, 1986; mem. external adv. bd., U. Calif. San Francisco Comprehensive Cancer Ctr., 2000-; bd. sci. advisors, Norwegian Inst. Gene Ecology, 2002-; coll. reviewers, Can. Rsch. Chairs Program, 2003-;lectr. in the field. Editorial bd. mem. Microbiol. Revs., 1985-, In Vitro, 1987-, J. Cellular Biochemistry, 1990-, Oncology Rsch., 1992-, Geno Methods, 1993-, Cancer Rsch. Ency., 1999-, Cancer Letters, 1998-; assoc. editor Cancer Research, 1985-, J. Cellular Physiology, 1989-, Molecular and Cellular Differentation, 1992-, Cancer Sci. (Japan), 2004-; contbr. articles to profl. jours. and chpts. to books; 4 US patents in the field. Fellow Leukemia Soc., 1976-1978, Internat. Union Against Cancer, 1979, Eleanor Roosevelt Internat., 1983-84, Am. Acad. Microbiology, 1986, AAAS, 1993; recipient Research Career Devel. award, NIH, 1978-83, NIH Merit award, 1987-96, Phi Kappa Phi Biology Colloquium award, Oregon State U., 1988; named one of Outstanding Young Men of Am., Jaycees, 1979. Mem. AAAS, NY Acad. Scis., Internat. Orgn. Mycoplasmologists, Am. Soc. Microbiology, Sigma Xi, Tissue Culture Assn., Internat. Orgn. Mycolplasmologist, Am. Assn. for Cancer Rsch., Internat. Soc. for Differentiation, UICC Acad. Fellows Office: U Calif Irvine B235/B210 Med Sciences Mail Code 4025 Irvine CA 92697-4025 Office Phone: 949-824-7042, 949-824-5259. Office Fax: 949-824-8598. Business E-Mail: ejstanbr@uci.edu.

STANCILL, JAMES MCNEILL, retired finance educator; b. Orange, NJ, July 30, 1932; s. James Sr. and Anne Jeanne (Sauter) S.; m. Catherine Jackson, Sept. 25, 1954; children: Martha A., Mary C., Christine E. AB, George Wash. U., Washington, DC, 1954, MBA, 1957; PhD in Fin. and Econs., U. Pa., Phila., 1965. Buyer Melpar Inc., Falls Church, Va., 1954-59; instr., adminstrv. officer U. Pa., Phila., 1959-64; prof. fin. U. So. Calif., LA, 1964—2007; prof. emeritus, 2007—. Prin. Stancill & Assocs., Pasadena, Calif., 1964—, The McNeill Bush Co. Ltd.; chmn. S.W. Products Co., 1991—97. Author: Management of Working Capital, 1970, Entrepreneurial Finance: for New and Emerging Businesses, 2004; contbr. numerous articles to Harvard Bus. Rev., 1977—. Avocations: genealogy, sailing, travel. Business E-Mail: stancill@marshall.usc.edu.

STANEK, ALAN EDWARD, retired music educator, performing arts association administrator; b. Longmont, Colo., July 3, 1939; s. Edward Thomas and Mary Rose Stanek; m. Janette Elizabeth Swanson, Aug. 23, 1963; children: Michael Alan, Karen Leigh. MusB Edn., U. Colo., 1961; MusM, Eastman Sch. Music, 1965; DMusArts, U. Mich., 1974. Dir. instrumental music Ainsworth Pub. Sch., Nebr., 1961-64, Cozad Pub. Sch., Nebr., 1965-67; asst. prof. music Hastings Coll., Nebr., 1967-76; prof., chmn. music dept. Idaho State U., Pocatello, 1976-2001, ret., 2001. Contbr., editor, reviewer profl. jours. including The Clarinet, Idaho Music Notes, Nebr. Music Educator. Mem. Music Educators Nat. Conf., Idaho Music Educators Assn. (chmn. higher edn. 1978-86, 97-98, pres. 1988-90, chair state solo contest 1990-92), Internat. Clarinet Assn. (sec. 1978-84, v.p. 1986-88, pres. 1996-98, historian 2002—), Coll. Music Soc., Nat. Assn. Coll. Wind and Percussion Instrs. (chmn. Idaho 1978-88), Nat. Assn. Schs. Music (sec. N.W. region 1979-82, vis. evaluator 1990—2002, chair N.W. region 1991-94), Rotary (pres. Gate City chpt. 1994-95). Business E-Mail: stanalan@isu.edu.

STANFILL, DENNIS CAROTHERS, corporate financial executive; b. Centerville, Tenn., Apr. 1, 1927; s. Sam Broome and Hattie (Carothers) S.; m. Therese Olivieri, June 29, 1951; children: Francesca, Dennis Carothers. BS, U.S. Naval Acad., 1949; MA (Rhodes scholar), Oxford U., 1953; LHD (hon.), U. S.C. Corporate finance specialist Lehman Bros., NYC, 1959-65; v.p. finance Times Mirror Co., Los Angeles, 1965-69; exec. v.p. 20th Century-Fox Film Corp., 1969-71, pres., 1971, chmn. bd., chief exec. officer, 1971-81; pres. Stanfill, Bowen & Co., 1981-90; chmn. bd. dirs., chief exec. officer AME, Inc., 1990-91; co-chmn., co-CEO Metro-Goldwyn-Mayer, Inc., 1992-93; sr. advisor Credit Lyonnais, 1993-95; pres. Dennis Stanfill Co., 1995—. Trustee Calif. Inst. Tech. Served to lt. USN, 1949-59; politico-mil. policy div. Office Chief Naval Ops., 1956-59.

STANFORD, JANET LEE, physician, epidemiologist; RN, Grady Meml Hosp., Atlanta, 1974; BS, Ga. State U., 1980; MPH, Emory U., 1982; PhD, John Hopkins U., 1985. Various to asst. prof. dept. epidemiology Sch. of Pub. Health and Cmty. Medicine/U. Wash., Seattle, 1986-92; assoc. prof. Sch. Pub. Health and Cmty. Medicine U. Wash., Seattle, 1992-98, prof. epidemiology Sch. Pub. Health and Cmty. Medicine, 1999—; assoc. mem. program in epidemiology Divsn. Pub. Health Scis. Fred Hutchinson Cancer Rsch. Ctr., Seattle, 1991-96, co-investigator Cancer Surveillance System, 1993-96, coprin. investigator Tracking Resource Ctr., 1995-96; dir. Utah State Cancer Registry/U. Utah, Salt Lake City, 1996-97; prof. Divn. Pub. Health Scis./Huntsman Cancer Inst. U. Utah, Salt Lake City, 1996-97; mem. program in epidemiology/Divsn. Pub. Health Scis. Fred Hutchinson Cancer Rsch. Ctr., Seattle, 1996—, head program in prostate cancer rsch., 1997—, affil. mem. cancer prevention rsch. program, 1999—. Rschr. and investigator in field of hormonal and environ. exposures that may alter cancer risk, and how such risks may be modified by genetic predisposition. Editor: Am. Jour. Epidemiology, 1999—, assoc. editor 1991-96; editl. bd.: Human Genome Epidemiology Network, 1999—; editl. positions: Am. Jour. Pub. Health, Annals of Epidemiology, Cancer, Cancer Causes and Control, Cancer Epidemiology, Biomarkers and Prevention, Human Molecular Genetics, others; contbr. numerous articles to profl. jours. and publs. Granteee HHS, 1982-83, NIH, 1983-85; fellowships Nat. Cancer Inst., NIH, HHS, 1985-86; recipient Preventive Oncology Acad. awards Nat. Cancer Inst., NIH, HHS, 1988-93. Mem. AHA, Soc. Epidemiologic Rsch., APHA, Assn. of Wash. State Epidemiologists, Sigma Theta Tau, others. Office: Fred Hutchinson Cancer Rsch Ctr PO Box 19024 1100 Fairview Ave N MW 814 Seattle WA 98109-1024

STANFORD, JOSEPH BARNEY, medical educator, physician; b. July 9, 1961; s. Kathleen Barnett; children: Matthew Joseph, Jesse Barnett, Hyrum Porter, Caleb Dean, Thomas Barnett. BA magna cum laude, Mankato State U., 1984; MD, U. Minn., 1988. Diplomate Am. Bd. Family Practice. Resident family and cmty. medicine U. Mo.-Columbia, 1988-91, chief resident family and cmty. medicine, 1990-91, academic fellow, clinical instr. dept. family and cmty. medicine, 1991-93; asst. prof. dept. family and preventive medicine U. Utah, Salt Lake City, 1993—. Part time staff physician Cherchez La Femme Birth Svcs. Ltd., Columbia, Mo., 1991-93; med. cons. U. Utah BirthCare HealthCare, 1994—; physician N.E. Family Health Ctr., Salt Lake Regional Med. Ctr., U. Utah Hosp., Primary Children's Med. Ctr., 1993; invited observer Pontifical Acad. Scis. Working Group on Natural Fertility Regulation, Vatican, Italy, 1994. Contbr to prof. jours. Mem. Soc. Tchrs. of Family Medicine (mem. group family centered perinatal care 1990—), Am. Acad. Family Physicians, Am. Acad. Natural Family Planning (chairperson sci. and rsch. com. 1993—), Am. Holistic Med. Assn., Am. Soc. Clinical Hypnosis, Collegium Aesculapium, North Am. Primary Care Rsch. Group, Alpha Omega Alpha, Phi Kappa Phi. Avocations: hiking, camping, reading, writing, skiing. Office: U Utah Dept Family Preventive Med 50 N Medical Dr Salt Lake City UT 84132-0001

STANG, PETER JOHN, organic chemist; b. Nürnberg, Germany, Nov. 17, 1941; came to U.S., 1956; s. John Stang and Margaret Stang Pollman; m. Christine Schirmer, 1969; children: Antonia, Alexandra. BS, DePaul U., Chgo., 1963; PhD, U. Calif., Berkeley, 1966; degree (hon.), Moscow State Lomonossov U., 1992, Russian Acad. Scis., 1992. Instr. Princeton (N.J.) U., 1967-68; from asst. to assoc. prof. U. Utah, Salt Lake City, 1969-79, prof., 1979-92, Disting. prof. chemistry, 1992—. Co-author: Organic Spectroscopy, 1971; author: (with others) Vinyl Cations, 1979; editor: (with F. Diederich) Modern Acetylene Chemistry, 1995, Metal Catalyzed Cross Coupling Reactions, 1998, (with Z. Rappaport) Dicoordinated Carbocations, 1997; editor-in-chief Jour. Organic Chemsitry, 2000-01; contbr. numerous articles to sci. publs. Recipient Humboldt-Forschungspreis, 1977, Linus Pauling medal, 2006; JSPS fellow, 1985; Fulbright-Hays sr. scholar, 1988. Fellow AAAS; mem. NAS, Am. Acad. Arts and Scis., Am. Chem. Soc. (assoc. editor jour. 1982-99, editor 2002-, George A. Olah award in hydrocarbon chemistry 2003, award for creative rsch. and applications iodine chemistry, 2007), Chinese Acad. Scis. (fgn. mem.), Hungarian Academy of Sciences(fgn. mem.). Office: U Utah Dept Chemistry 315 South 1400 East Salt Lake City UT 84112-0850 Office Phone: 801-581-8329. E-mail: stang@chemistry.utah.edu.

STANISLAO, JOSEPH, engineering educator, consultant; b. Manchester, Conn., Nov. 21, 1928; s. Eduardo and Rose (Zaccaro) S.; m. Bettie Chloe Carter, Sept. 6, 1960. BS, Tex. Tech. U., Lubbock, 1957; MS, Pa. State U., Univ. Park, 1959; DSc in Industrial Engring, Columbia U., NYC, 1970. Registered profl. engr., Mass., Mont. Asst. engr. Naval Ordnance Research, University Park, Pa., 1958-59; asst. prof. NC State U., Raleigh, 1959-61; dir. rsch. Darlington Fabrics Corp., Pawtucket, RI, 1961-62; from asst. prof. to prof. U. RI, Kingston, 1962-71; prof., chmn. dept. Cleve. State U., 1971-75; prof., dean ND State U., Fargo, 1975-94, acting v.p. agrl. affairs, 1983-85; asst. to pres. N.D. State U., Fargo, 1983—, dir. Engring. Computer Ctr., 1984—, prof. emeritus indsl. engring. and mgmt. Fargo, 1994—; pres. XOX Corp., 1984-90; chmn. bd., CEO ATSCO, 1989-94, chief engr., 1993—; prof. emeritus ND State U., 1994. Adj. prof. Mont. State U., 1994—, dir. indsl. and mgmt. engring. program, 1996—, mfg. rsch., sponsored by Nat. Sci. Found. 1997—; pres., CEO J&B Inc., 1996—2006; v.p., co-owner, bd. dirs. D.T.&J., Inc., Fargo, ND, 1999-2006, London, 1999—; v.p. engring. Roll-A-Ramp, Rolla-A-Latter, and Rolla-A-conveyor, 2000-05; cons. to healthcare sys., 1999-2005. Contbr. chpts. to books, articles to profl. jours. Served to sgt. USMC, 1948-51. Recipient Sigma Xi award, 1968; Order of the Iron Ring award N.D. State U., 1972, Econ. Devel. award, 1991; named Best Tchr., Alpha Pi Mu, 2005; USAF recognition award, 1979, ROTC appreciation award, 1982. Mem. Am. Inst. Indsl. Engrs. (sr.; v.p. 1964-65), ASME, Order of the Engr., Am. Soc. Engring. Edn. (campus coord. 1979-81), Acad. Indsl. Engrs. Tex. Tech U., Lions, Elks, Am. Legion, Phi Kappa Phi, Tau Beta Pi (advisor 1978-79). Roman Catholic. Achievements include patents for pump apparatus, pump fluid housing, roll-conveyer, and handicap loading dock; roll-a-ramp; invention of Telescopic Sliding Ramp, Thermal-Brick. Avocations: pool, billiards. Home: 8 Park Plaza Dr Bozeman MT 59715-9343 Office: Mont State U M&IE Dept 304 Roberts Hall Bozeman MT 59717-3800 Office Phone: 406-994-5943. Personal E-mail: bstanislao2314@msn.com. Business E-Mail: jstanslo@ie.montana.edu.

STANLEY, HEIDI B., bank executive; b. 1956; m. Ron Stanley. Grad., Wash. State U., 1979. With IBM, San Francisco, Tucson; joined Sterling Savings Bank, Spokane, Wash., 1985, exec. v.p. Corp. Adminstrn., vice chair, COO, 2003—07, pres., CEO, 2007—. Vice chmn. Am.'s Cmty. Banker's Membership Com.; mem. Govt. Affairs Steering Com.; bd. govs. WSU Found., chmn. planning com. Named one of 25 Most Powerful Women in Banking, US Banker, 2006, 2007. Mem.: Wash. State U. Alumni Assn., Spokane C. of C. (bd. mem.). Avocation: golf. Office: Sterling Savings Bank 111 N Wall St Spokane WA 99201

STANLEY, PETER WILLIAM, former academic administrator; b. Bronxville, NY, Feb. 17, 1940; s. Arnold and Mildred Jeanette (Pattison) Stanley; m. Mary-Jane Cullen Cosgrove, Sept. 2, 1978; 1 child, Laura. BA magna cum laude, Harvard U., 1962, MA, 1964, PhD, 1970; LHD (hon.), Occidental Coll., 1994, Rhodes Coll., 2001. Asst. prof. history U. Ill., Chgo., 1970—72, Harvard U., 1972—78, lectr. history, 1978—79; dean of coll. Carleton Coll., Northfield, Minn., 1979—84; program officer in charge edn. and culture program Ford Found., 1984—87, dir. edn. and culture program, 1987—91; pres. Pomona Coll., Claremont, Calif., 1991—2003, pres. emeritus, 2003—; v.p. Isaacson, Miller, Boston, 2004—. Lectr. Fgn. Service Inst., Arlington, Va., 1977—89. Author: A Nation in the Making: The Philippines and the United States, 1974; co-author: Sentimental Imperialists: The American Experience in East Asia, 1981; editor: Reappraising an Empire: New Perspectives on Philippine-American History, 1984; contbr. articles to profl. jours. Trustee The Coll. Bd., 1991—99, vice-chmn., 1993—94, chmn., 1994—96, Barnard Coll., 2000—06; humanities and scis. coun. Stanford U., 1986—2002; nat. adv. coun. Nat. Fgn. Lang. Ctr., 1991—2002; bd. dirs. The James Irvine Found., 1997—2006, chmn., 2003—06; bd. dirs. The Pacific Basin Inst., 1998—, chmn., 1998—2003; bd. dirs. The Hitachi Found., 1993—2000, Assn. Am. Colls. and Univs., 1995—2001, vice-chmn., 1998—99, chmn., 1999—2000; bd. fellows Claremont Grad. U. and Claremont U. Consortium, 1991—2003; bd. overseers Nat. Bd. Ednl. Testing and Pub. Policy, 2000—. Fellow Frank Knox Meml. fellow, Harvard U., 1962—63, Charles Warren Ctr. for Studies in Am. History fellow, 1975—76. Mem.: Coun. on Fgn. Rels., Assn. Asian Studies, Am. Hist. Assn., Phi Beta Kappa. Home: 65 Knollwood Dr Old Saybrook CT 06475 Office: Pomona Coll Pres Office Claremont CA 91711-6301

STANLEY, STEVEN MITCHELL, paleontologist, educator; b. Detroit, Nov. 2, 1941; s. William Thomas and Mildred Elizabeth (Baker) S.; m. E. Ellen Reynolds, Dec. 28, 2005. AB with highest honors, Princeton U., 1963; PhD, Yale U., 1968. Asst. prof. U. Rochester, 1967-69; asst. prof. paleobiology Johns Hopkins U., 1969-71, assoc. prof., 1971-74, prof., 1974—2005, chmn. dept. Earth and planetary Scis., 1987-88, chmn. MS program in environ. scis. and policy, 1993—2005; rsch. prof. U. Hawaii, 2005. Assoc. in rsch. Smithsonian Instn., 1972—; mem. bd. earth scis. NRC, 1985—, vice chmn., 1988, mem. bd. earth scis. resources, 1988-88, com. on solid earth scis., exec. and steering com., 1988, 2004—, com. on geoscis., environ. and resources, 1990-96. Author: Relation of Shell Form to Life Habits in the Bivalvia, 1970, (with D.M. Raup) Principles of Paleontology, 1971, Macroevolution: Pattern and Process, 1979, The New Evolutionary Timetable: Fossils, Genes, and the Origin of species, 1981, Earth and Life Through Time, 1986, Extinction, 1987, Exploring Earth and Life Through Time, 1992, Children of the Ice Age: How a Global Catastrophe Allowed Humans to Evolve, 1996, Earth System History, 1999; mem. editl. bd. Am. Jour. Sci., 1975—, Paleobiology, 1975-82, 88—, Evolutionary Theory, 1973—. Recipient Outstanding Paper award Jour. Paleontology, 1968, Allan C. Davis medal Md. Acad. Scis., 1973, Outstanding Tech. Paper award Washington Geol. Soc., 1986, Bownocker medal Ohio State U., 1997; Guggenheim fellow, 1981 Fellow NAS (Mary Clark Thompson Medal, 2006), Am. Acad. Arts and Scis., Geol. Soc. Am. (chmn. Penrose com. 1978, councilor 2002—); mem. Paleontol. Soc. (councilor 1976-77, sr. councilor 1991-93, pres. 1993-94, Charles Schuchert award 1977, medal 2007), Soc. for Study Evolution (councilor 1982-84), Am. Geophys. Union (pub. affairs com.), Paleontol. Rsch. Inst., Am. Geol. Inst. (mem. exec. com. 1996-99, pres. 2001—), Nat. Assn. Geosci. Tchrs. (James H. Shea award, 2004), Soc. Sedimentary Geology (Twenhofel medal 2008). Business E-Mail: stevenst@hawaii.edu.

STANLEY, TIM, information technology executive; BS in Engring., U. Wash.; degree in Internat. Bus. and Tech. Mgmt., Thunderbird U., Ariz. State U. With Intel Corp., Optima/KPMG, Innova Tech, Kimberly-Clark Corp.; v.p. info. sys. Nat. Airlines, chief info. officer; ptnr. USWeb (now marchFIRST); v.p., info. tech. devel. Harrah's Entertainment, Las Vegas, 2001—03, sr. v.p., chief info. officer, 2003—. With USAF. Named one of the Top 25 Unsung Heroes of the Internet, Interactive Week Mag., Top 25 Chief Tech. Officers, InfoWorld mag., 2006. Office: Harrahs Entertainment Inc One Harrahs Ct Las Vegas NV 89119

STANSKY, PETER DAVID LYMAN, historian, writer, retired professor; b. NYC, Jan. 18, 1932; s. Lyman and Ruth (Macow) Stansky. BA, Yale U., 1953, King's Coll., Cambridge U., Eng., 1955, MA, 1959; PhD, Harvard U., 1961; DL (hon.), Wittenberg U., 1984. Tchg. fellow history and lit. Harvard U., 1957-61, from instr. to asst. prof. history, 1961-68; assoc. prof. Stanford (Calif.) U., 1968-73, prof., 1973-74, Frances and Charles Field prof., 1974—2004, Frances and Charles Field prof. emeritus, 2004—, chmn. dept. history, 1975-78, 79-82, 89-90, assoc. dean humanities and scis., 1985-88. Chmn. publs. com. Conf. Brit. Studies, 1970—78; vis. fellow Wesleyan Ctr. Humanities, Middletown, 1972; pres. Pacific Coast Conf. Brit. Studies, 1974—76, N.Am. Conf. Brit. Studies, 1983—85; vis. fellow All Soul's Coll. Oxford (Eng.) U., 1979, vis. fellow St. Catherine's Coll., 83. Author: Ambitions and Strategies, 1964, England Since 1867, 1973, Gladstone, 1979, William Morris, 1983, Redesigning the World, 1985, On or About December 1910, 1996, Another Book that Never Was, 1998, From William Morris to Sergeant Pepper, 1999, Sassoon: The Worlds of Philip and Sybil, 2003, The First Day of the Blitz, 2007; co-author: Journey to the Frontier, 1966, The Unknown Orwell, 1972, Orwell: The Transformation, 1979, London's Burning, 1994. Guggenheim fellow, 1966—67, 1973—74, Am. Coun. Learned Socs. fellow, 1978—79, NEH fellow, 1983, 1998—99, Royal Hist. Soc. fellow, Ctr. Advanced Study Behavioral Scis., 1988—89. Fellow: Am. Acad. Arts and Scis. (coun. 1994—98, 2002—05); mem.: AAUP, Century Assn., William Morris Soc., Victorian Soc., Conf. Brit. Studies, Am. Hist. Assn. Home: 375 Pinehill Rd Hillsborough CA 94010-6612 Office: Stanford U Dept History Stanford CA 94305-2024 Office Phone: 650-723-2663. Business E-Mail: stansky@stanford.edu.

STANTON, JOHN W., communications executive; b. Seattle; BA in Polit. Sci., Whitman Coll.; MBA, Harvard U. Chmn., CEO Western Wireless (now Alltel Corp.), Bellevue, Wash., 1992—2005; chmn. Telocator, 1986—95; chmn., CEO VoiceStream Wireless, 1992—2002; cons. cellular and long-distance bus.; v.p. McCaw Comms., 1983; exec. v.p., COO McCaw Cellular, 1985—88, vice-chmn., 1988—91; dir. McCaw and LIN Broadcasting, 1991—94; co-founder Stanton Comms., 1988; founder, chmn., CEO (now Western Wireless) Pacific N.W. Cellular, 1992; dir. Columbia Sportswear Co., 1997—. Bd. dirs. Advanced Digital Info. Corp., Columbia Sportswear, Pacific Sci. Ctr.; trustee Whitman Coll. Mem.: Cellular Telecomms. Industry Assn. (chmn. emeritus). Office: c/o Columbia Sportswear 14375 NW Science Park Drive Portland OR 97229

STANTON, JULIA A., lawyer; b. Torrance, Calif., Feb. 14, 1968; BA, Pomona Coll., 1990; JD, Loyola law Sch., 1993. Bar: Calif. 1993, US Dist. Ct. Ctrl. Calif. Ptnr., family law practice Brandmeyer & Stanton, Long Beach, Calif. Named a Rising Star, So. Calif. Super Lawyers, 2006. Mem.: State Bar Calif., LA County Bar Assn., Women Lawyers Assn. LA, South Bay Bar Assn. Office: Brandmeyer & Stanton Ste 1940 1 World Trade Ctr Long Beach CA 90802 Office Phone: 562-499-2131. Office Fax: 562-499-2132.

STANTON, LEWIS HARRIS, Internet learning company executive; b. London, Apr. 2, 1954; came to U.S., 1980; s. Gerald and Carole (Harris) S.;divorced; children: Graham, Joshua. BS, U. Birmingham, Eng., 1976. CPA, Calif.; chartered acct., Eng. Sr. mgr. Arthur Andersen & Co., L.A., London, 1976-88; chief fin. officer Data

Analysis Inc., LA, 1988-96; CEO WorldSite Networks Inc., Beverly Hills, Calif., 1996-97; exec. v.p., COO, CFO MAI Sys. Corp., Irvine, Calif., 1997-99; exec. v.p., CFO Univ. Access, Inc., LA, 1999—2000; CEO Personic, Inc., San Francisco, 2000—02, E Team, Inc., Canoga Park, Calif., 2002—. Chmn. L.A. Youth non-profit orgn., 1997. Fellow Inst. Chartered Accts.; mem. AICPA, Calif. Soc. CPAs (chmn. mems. in industry com. 1990-94), Assn. Western Securities Mgmt. (pres. 1989). Avocations: tennis, visual arts. Office: E Team Inc 21700 Oxnard St Woodland Hills CA 91367-3642

STANTON, MICHAEL JOHN, newspaper editor; b. New Britain, Conn., Mar. 30, 1944; s. John Martin and Helen (McNally) S.; m. Barbara Ann Mucha, Aug. 27, 1966; 1 child, Sean AB in English, Holy Cross Coll., 1966. Reporter, editor Providence (R.I.) Jour., 1968-72; press sec. Gov. R.I., Providence, 1972-77; asst. news editor St. Louis Globe-Dem., 1977-81; news copy desk chief Detroit Free Press, 1981-83, exec. news editor, 1983-85, asst. to exec. editor, 1985-86; exec. news editor Seattle Times, 1986—. Office: The Seattle Times PO Box 70 Fairview Ave N & John St Seattle WA 98111

STANTON, ROBERT JAMES, JR., geologist, educator; b. LA, June 17, 1931; s. Robert James and Audrey (Franke) S.; m. Patricia Ann Burns, Sept. 13, 1953; children: John, Carol. BS, Calif. Inst. Tech., 1953, PhD, 1960; MA, Harvard U., 1956. Research geologist Shell Devel. Co., Houston, 1959-67; mem. faculty Tex. A&M U., 1967—, prof. geology, 1972-86, Ray C. Fish prof. geology, 1986-98, head dept., 1979-83, prof. geology emeritus, 1998—. Vis. prof. U. Nuremburg-Erlangen, Germany, 1984; rsch. assoc. invertebrate paleontology Natural History Mus. L.A. County, 2000-. Co-author: Paleoecology: Principles and Applications, 1981, 2d edit., 1990. Served with AUS, 1953-55. Fellow Geol. Soc. Am.; mem. Internat. Paleontol. Union, Paleontol. Soc., Paleontol. Research Inst., Soc. Econ. Paleontologists and Mineralogists (Outstanding Paper award 1970), Sigma Xi, Tau Beta Pi. Home: 2297 Valleyfield Ave Thousand Oaks CA 91360 Office: Nat Hist Mus LA County Dept Invertebrate Paleontol 900 Exposition Blvd Los Angeles CA 90007 Home Phone: 805-493-1517. Personal E-mail: starton.robertj@gmail.com.

STANTON, RUSS W., editor-in-chief; b. 1958; married; 3 children. BS, Calif. State U., 1981. Bus. reporter Visalia Times-Delta; with San Bernardino County Sun, Riverside Press-Enterprise, Orange County Register; Orange county bus. reporter LA Times, 1997—98, Orange county bus. editor, 1998—2000, asst. bus. editor, 2000—01, sr. tech. editor, 2001—02, dep. bus. editor, 2002—05, bus. editor, 2005—07, innovation editor, 2007—08, editor, 2008—. Fellow Herbert J. Davenport Econ. Prog., U. Mo. Office: LA Times 202 W 1st St Los Angeles CA 90012 E-mail: russ.stanton@latimes.com.

STANTON, WILLIAM JOHN, JR., marketing educator, author; b. Chgo., Dec. 15, 1919; s. William John and Winifred (McGann) S.; m. Imma Mair, Sept. 14, 1978; children by previous marriage: Kathleen Louise, William John III. BS, Ill. Inst. Tech., 1940; MBA, Northwestern U., 1941, PhD, 1948; D (hon.), Cath. U. Santo Domingo, Dominican Republic, 2003. Mgmt. trainee Sears Roebuck & Co., 1940-41; instr. U. Ala., 1941-44; auditor Olan Mills Portrait Studios, Chattanooga, 1944-46; asst. prof., asso. prof. U. Wash., 1948-55; prof. U. Colo., Boulder, 1955-90; prof. emeritus, 1990—; head mktg. dept. U. Colo., 1955-71, acting dean, 1963-64; assoc. dean U. Colo. (Sch. Bus.), 1964-67; ret. Author: Economic Aspects of Recreation in Alaska, 1953; author: (with others) Challenge of Business, 1975; author: (with M. Etzel and B. Walker) Marketing, 14th edit., 2007, Marketing, Spanish, Chinese, Portuguese, Indonesian and Korean transl., 2003; author: (with R. Varaldo) Italian edit., 2d edit., 1989; author: (with others) South African edit., 1992; author: (with M.S. Sommers and J.G. Barnes) Canadian edit., Fundamentals of Marketing, 11th edit., 2004; author: (with K. Miller and R. Layton) Australian edit., 4th edit., 2000; author: (with Rosann Spiro and G.A. Rich) Management of a Sales Force, 12th edit., Spanish, Portuguese, Chinese, and Russian transl., 2007; contbr. articles to profl. jour. Mem. Am. Mktg. Assn., Mktg. Educators Assn., Beta Gamma Sigma. Roman Catholic. Home: 1445 Sierra Dr Boulder CO 80302-7846

STANUTZ, DONALD J., chemicals executive; Various sr. positions Texaco Chem. Co.; with Huntsman Corp., 1994—, exec. v.p. polyurethanes, PO and performance chems., 1999—2000, exec. v.p. global sales and mktg., 2000—01, exec. v.p., COO Huntsman LLC, 2001—04, divsn. pres. performance products, 2004—. Office: Huntsman Corp 500 Huntsman Way Salt Lake City UT 84108 Office Phone: 801-584-5700.

STAPLES, MAVIS, singer; b. Chgo., 1940; d. Roebuck "Pops" and Oceloa S. Singer Staple Singers, 1951—; represented by United, 1954, Vee Jay Label, 1956, CBS/Epic, 1964, Stax, 1968, Curtom, 1975. Opened for Prince's overseas tour, 1990; provided back-up vocals for Ray Charles, Kenny Loggins, Marty Stuart and others. Albums include Mavis Staples, 1969, Only for the Lonely, 1970, A Piece of the Action, 1977, Mavis Staples, 1984, Time Waits for No One, 1989, The Voice, 1993, Spirituals & Gospel: Dedicated to Mahalia Jackson, 1996, Have a Little Faith, 2004, We'll Never Turn Back, 2007, Live: Hope at the Hideout, 2008. Single "Uncloudy Day" reached number one on gospel charts; single "I'll Take you There" reached number one on gospel and rythym and blues charts, 1993. Office: c/o 525 Worldwide Music PO Box 957 Salem MA 01970 also: c/o The Rosebud Agy PO Box 170429 San Francisco CA 94117

STAPLETON, COREY, financial planner; b. Seattle, Sept. 17, 1967; BS, U.S. Naval Acad., 1992; MA, Temple U., 1995. Commd. officer USN, 1986, advanced through grades, 1997; fin. planner Prudential Ind. Fin. Svcs., 1997—; mem. Dist. 10 Mont. State Senate, 2001—05, mem. Dist. 27, 2005—08. Mem. Midland Empire Pachyderm Club, 1998—; campaign aide Bob Dole for Pres. Campaign, 1996; campaign mgr. Norm Mills, Mont. State House Dist. 19, 1998; chair Yellowstone County Young Reps., 1999-2000. Mem. Am. Legion, Billings C. of C., Rotary. Office: 2015 Eastridge Dr Billings MT 59102-7904 E-mail: stapletonct@aol.com.

STAPLETON, F. BRUDER, pediatric nephrologist, academic administrator; b. Lawrence, Kans., Dec. 19, 1946; s. Harold Jack and Hazel Maria Stapleton; m. Barbara R. Stapleton, Sept. 16, 1969; children: Hillary J., F. Reed. BA, U. Kans., 1968, MD, 1972. Cert. Am. Bd. Pediat., in pediatric nephrology. Residency U. Kans. Med. Ctr., Kansas City, fellowship; residency U. Wash. Sch. Medicine, Seattle, Ford/Morgan Prof. and Chair, dept. pediat., 1996—; prof. pediat. U. Tenn. Coll. Medicine, Memphis, 1979—89; pediatrician Children's Hosp. Buffalo, 1989—96; chair dept. pediat. SUNY, 1989—96; pediatrician-in-chief Children's Hosp. and Med. Ctr., Seattle, 1996—, sr. v.p., chief academic officer, dir., dept. medicine. Contbr. articles to profl. jours.; founding editor-in-chief: Jour. Watch Pediat. and Adolescent Medicine, 2002—. Bd. dirs. Seattle Cancer Care Alliance, Ronald McDonald Children's Home, Buffalo, 1993—95, Seattle, 2000—. Lt. comdr. USN, 1977—79. Fellow pediatric nephrology, U. Kans., Kansas City, 1974—77. Mem.: Am. Bd. Pediat. (bd. dirs. 1998—2004, chair subspecialties com.), Am. Soc. Pediatric Nephrology (pres. 1995—96), Assn. Med. Sch. Dept. Chairs (pres. 2005—07), Internat. Pediatric Nephrology Assn. (treas. 2001—04). Home: 4693 NE 89th St Seattle WA 98115 Office: Childrens Hosp Dept Pediatrics CH-65 4800 Sand Point Way NE T-0211 Seattle WA 98105 E-mail: bstaplet@u.washington.edu.

STAPLETON, SHERYL WILLIAMS, state legislator; b. July 30, 1957; m. Edreade Stapleton; children: David, Veronica. BEd, N.Mex. State U., 1978; MA, U. N.Mex., 1987, edn. specialist, edn. adminstr., 1990. Asst. prin. & educator sch.-to-careers coord. Albuquerque Pub. Schs.; state rep. dist. 19 N.Mex. House of Reps., Santa Fe, 1995—, chair, labor and human resources com., mem. N.Mex. fin. authority oversight interim com., mem. legis. edn. study interim com., edn. com., and legis. health and human svcs. interim com., mem. Dist. 19, 1994—. Vice chair, state chair N.Mex. Dem. Party. Democrat. Office: State Capitol Room 312A Santa Fe NM 87503 E-mail: sheryl.stapleton@nmlegis.gov.*

STAPRANS, ARMAND, electronics executive; b. Riga, Latvia, Feb. 28, 1931; s. Theodore and Elvira (Ulmanis) S.; m. Vija Spalvins, Sept. 25, 1955; children: Silvija, Armin, Erik. Student, Willamette U., 1949-52; BSEE, U. Calif., Berkeley, 1954, MSEE, 1955, PhDEE, 1959. Rsch. asst. dept. elec. engring. U. Calif., 1955-57; engr. microwave tube div. Varian Assocs., Palo Alto, Calif., 1957-60, engring. mgr., 1960-68, ops. mgr., 1978-78, 86-89, chief engr., 1978-86, gen. mgr. coupled cavity tube divsn., 1989-92, v.p., 1990-95; gen. mgr. microwave power tube products, 1992-95; pres. microwave power tube products divsn. Comms. and Power Inds., Palo Alto, Calif., 1995-98; mgmt. cons., 1999—. Contbr. articles to profl. jours., chpt. to book; patentee microwave tubes field. Fellow IEEE (electron device adminstrv. com. 1983-88). Home: 445 Knoll Dr Los Altos CA 94024-4732 Office: Comm & Power Inds M S B 100 Microwave Power Tube Prod Divsn PO Box 50750 Palo Alto CA 94303-0665 Home Phone: 650-948-9521.

STARING, GRAYDON SHAW, lawyer; b. Deansboro, NY, Apr. 9, 1923; s. William Luther and Eleanor Mary (Shaw) S.; m. Joyce Lydia Allum-Poon, Sept. 1, 1949; children: Diana Hilary Agnes, Christopher Paul Norman. AB, Hamilton Coll., 1947; JD, U. Calif., Berkeley, 1951. Bar: Calif. 1952, U.S. Supreme Ct. 1958. Atty. Office Gen. Counsel, Navy Dept., San Francisco, 1952-53; atty. admiralty and shipping sect. U.S. Dept. Justice, San Francisco, 1953-60; assoc. Lillick & Charles (now Nixon Peabody), San Francisco, 1960-64, ptnr., 1965—88, of counsel, 1989—. Titulary mem. Internat. Maritime Com.; bd. dirs. Marine Exch. at San Francisco, 1984-88, pres. 1986-88; instr. pub. speaking Hamilton Coll., 1947-48; adj. prof. Hastings Coll. Law, 1996-97, Boalt Hall, U. Calif., 1999. Author: Law of Reinsurance, 1993; assoc. editor Am. Maritime Cases, 1966-92, editor, 1992-2008; contbr. articles to legal jours. Mem. San Francisco Lawyers Com. for Urban Affairs, 1972-90; bd. dirs. Legal Aid Soc., San Francisco, 1974-90, v.p., 1975-80, pres., 1980-82. With USN, 1943-46, comdr. USNR. Fellow Am. Bar Found., Am. Coll. Trial Lawyers; mem. ABA (chmn. maritime ins. com. 1975-76, mem. standing com. admiralty law 1976-82, 86-90, chmn. 1990, ho. dels. 1986-90), Fed. Bar Assn. (pres. San Francisco chpt. 1968), Bar Assn. San Francisco (sec. 1972, treas. 1973), Calif. Acad. Appellate Lawyers, Maritime Law Assn. U.S. (exec. com. 1977-88, v.p. 1980-84, pres. 1984-86), Brit.-Am. C. of C. (bd. dirs. 1987-2001), Tulane Admiralty Inst. (permanent adv. bd.), Assocs. Maritime Mus. Libr. (dir. 1990-2001, pres. 1992-94). Office: Nixon Peabody LLP 1 Embarcadero Ctr Fl 18 San Francisco CA 94111-3900 Home Phone: 510-540-7722; Office Phone: 415-984-8310. Personal E-mail: Starlaw@att.net. Business E-Mail: gstaring@nixonpeabody.com.

STARK, FORTNEY HILLMAN (PETE STARK), United States Representative from California; b. Milw., Nov. 11, 1931; s. Fortney Hillman and Dorothy M. (Mueller) Stark; m. Deborah Roderick; children: Hannah Marie, Andrew Peter; children: Jeffrey Peter, Beatrice Ann, Thekla Brumder, Sarah Gallun, Fortney Hillman III. BS in Engring., MIT, 1953; MBA, U. Calif. Berkeley, 1960. Teaching asst. MIT, Cambridge, 1953-54; prin. Skaife & Co., Berkeley, Calif., 1957-61; founder Beacon Savs. & Loan Assn., Antioch, Calif., 1961; pres., founder Security Nat. Bank, Walnut Creek, Calif., 1963-72; mem. US Congress from 13th (formerly 9th) Calif. dist., 1973—, mem. ways and means com., formerly chmn., now ranking minority mem. health subcom., mem. joint com. taxation. Del. Dem. State Ctr. Com.; bd. trustees Calif. Dem. Coun.; mem. Progressive Caucus. Bd. dirs., former chmn. Starr King Sch. Ministry; past bd. dirs. Common Cause; past bd. mem. Housing Devel. Corp., Coun. Civic Unity. Capt. USAF, 1955—57. Mem.: Delta Kappa Epsilon. Democrat. Unitarian Universalist. Office: US Ho Reps 239 Cannon Ho Office Bldg Washington DC 20515-0513 Office Phone: 202-225-5065.

STARK, MARTIN J., international management consultant; b. NYC, May 29, 1941; s. Nathan and Lola (Belmont) S.; m. Shigemi Matsumoto, Apr. 27, 1967. AA, Glendale Coll., 1960; BA, Calif. State U., 1966; postgrad., San Fernando Valley Coll. Law, 1967—70. Prodn. control supr. Indsl. Electronic Engrs., Van Nuys, Calif., 1967—69, sys. analyst, 1969—71, internat. sales mgr., 1971—73; sales rep. Columbia Artists Mgmt., Inc., NYC, 1973—78, sales mgr., 1978—79, v.p. bus. affairs, and mgr. data processing, 1979—82; dir. corp. affairs Kolmar-Luth Entertainment, Inc., NYC, 1982—84; pres. Oryx & Corp., NYC, 1984—85; exec. v.p. Asco Aerospace Products, Inc., El Segundo, Calif., 1985—87, Internat. Engine Parts, Inc., Chatsworth, Calif., 1987—92; pres. Stark & Assocs., Northridge, Calif., 1985—91; owner Mail Boxes Etc., 1992—2008. Lectr. Calif. State U., Long Beach, U. So. Calif., Chapman U.; cons. City of N.Y., Memory Data Software, IEPO, Inc.; advisor Thornton Protégé Program Thornton Sch. Music U. So. Calif.; bd. dirs. Holy Cross Hosp.; mentor Thornton Sch. Music, U. So. Calif. Mem.: Calabas C. of C., Classical Singer's Assn., Delta Upsilon. Avocations: sports cars, antiques, travel. Office: 18342 Chatham Ln Northridge CA 91326-3603 Personal E-mail: mbe1047@aol.com, starkconsultancy@aol.com.

STARK, NELLIE MAY, forester, ecologist, educator; b. Norwich, Conn., Nov. 20, 1933; d. Theodore Benjamin and Dorothy Josephine (Pendleton) Beetham; m. Oscar Elder Stark, Oct. 1962 (dec.). BA, Conn. Coll., 1956; AM, Duke U., 1958, PhD, 1962. Botanist Exptl. Sta., U.S. Forest Svc., Old Strawberry, Calif., 1958-66; botanist, ecologist Desert Rsch. Inst., Reno, 1966-72; prof. forest ecology Sch. Forestry, U. Mont., Missoula, 1972-92; pvt. cons. Philomath, Oreg. Pres. Camas Analytical Lab., Inc., Missoula, 1987—92. Author: Will Your Family Survive the 21st Century, 1997, Memories of Wren, Oregon, 1998, So You Want to Build a Little Log Cabin in the Woods, 2002, Thirteen Days of Christmas, 2005, Midshipman Randel, 2009; contbr. articles to profl. jours. Named Disting. Dau. Norwich, Conn., 1985; recipient Conn. award Conn. Coll., 1986, 54 grants. Mem. Ecol. Soc. Am. (chair ethics com. 1974, 76), Soc. Am. Foresters (taskforce 1987-88).

STARKS, JOHN LEVELL, professional basketball player; b. Tulsa, Aug. 10, 1965; m. Jacqueline Starks; children: John Jr., chelsea. Student, Okla. State U., 1988. Guard Golden State Warriors, 1988-89, Continental Basketball Assn./Cedar Rapids Silver Bullets, 1989-90, World Bakestball League/Memphis Rockers, 1990, New York Knicks, 1990-98. Active boys Brotherhood Republic, N.Y.C.; founder John Starks Found., Tulsa. Honoree in downtown parade on John Starks Day, tulsa, 1994; winner NBA Sixth Man award, 1996-97; named 1993 NBA All Defensive Second Team; participant in 1994 NBA All-Star Game. Avocations: tennis, jazz. Office: Golden State Warriors 1221 Broadway Fl 20 Oakland CA 94612-1837

STARR, BRUCE, state legislator; b. Portland, Oreg. m 1992 to Rebecca; children: Brooke. Legislature intern to Senator Bob Kintigh, 87 & 89; delegate, Oreg Republican State Conv, 88, 92 & 96; Republican precinct committeeman, 1988-2002; chairman, Portland State Univ Col Republican, formerly; alt delegate from Washington County, Oregon State Cent Committee, 92-94, delegate, 94-97; legislation asst to Representative Charles Starr, 93-98; member, Budget Committee, Washington County Consol Communications Agency (911 Emergency Serv), 1995-2002; city councilman, Hillsboro, 95-98; member, Hillsboro Street & Budget Committees, 95-98, Budget Committee, Oregon Republican Party, 97; Oregon State Representative, District 3, 1999-2002, vice chairman, Rules, Elections & Public Affairs Committee, 1999-2002, member, General Govt, Joint Stream Restoration & Species Recovery Committee & Ways & Means Subcomt on Transportation & Econ Develop, 1999-2002, Oregon House Representative; Oregon State Senator, District 15, 2003-.Bd trustees, Western Washington Co Interfaith Shelter Network, currently; small business owner, roofing & residential construction, 91-. Hillsboro Optimist Club. Republican. Office: 900 Court St NE S-411 Salem OR 97301 Mailing: 5651 NE Farmcrest St Hillsboro OR 97124-6154 Office Phone: 503-986-1715. E-mail: sen.brucestarr@state.or.us.

STARR, CHARLES, state legislator, farmer, contractor; b. Eastland, Tex., Oct. 1932; m. Kathy Starr. BS in Agrl. Edn., U. Idaho; MS in Agrl. Bus. Mgmt., U. Calif., Davis. Mem. Oreg. Legislature, Salem, 1998—, mem. bus. and consumer affairs com., mem. pub. affairs com., mem. rev. com., chair rules and election com. Mem. Groner Elem. Sch. Bd., Hillsboro Union H.S. Bd. Republican. Home: 8330 SW River Rd Hillsboro OR 97123-9131 Office: S 312 State Capitol Salem OR 97310

STARR, KENNETH WINSTON, dean, lawyer; b. Vernon, Tex., July 21, 1946; s. W. D. and Vannie Maude (Trimble) Starr; m. Alice Jean Mendell, Aug. 23, 1970; children: Randall Postley, Carolyn Marie, Cynthia Anne. BA, George Washington U., 1968; MA, Brown U., 1969; JD, Duke U., 1973; LLD (hon.), Hampden Sydney Coll., 1992, Shenandoah U., 1993, John Marshall Coll. Law, 1993, Pepperdine U., 1996. Bar: Calif. 1973, D.C. 1979, Va. 1979. Law clk. to Judge David Dyer U.S. Ct. Appeals (5th cir.), Miami, Fla., 1973—74; assoc. Gibson, Dunn & Crutcher, Los Angeles, 1974—75; law clk. to Chief Justice Warren E. Burger U.S. Supreme Ct., Washington, 1975—77; assoc., ptnr. Gibson, Dunn & Crutcher, Washington, 1977—81; counselor to atty gen. of U.S. Dept. Justice, Washington, 1981—83; judge U.S. Ct. Appeals (D.C. circuit), Washington, 1983—89; solicitor gen. US Dept. Justice, Washington, 1989—93; ptnr. Kirkland & Ellis LLP, Washington, 1993—2005, of counsel LA, 2005—; ind. counsel for Whitewater, 1994—99; Duane and Kelly Roberts Dean and Dean, prof. law Pepperdine U. Sch. of Law, Malibu, Calif., 2004—. Author: First Among Equals: The Supreme Court in American Life, 2002; contbr. articles to legal jours. Legal advisor CAB transition team office of pres.-elect, 1980—81, SEC transition team, 1980—81; bd. adv. Duke Law Jour. Recipient Disting. Alumni awards, George Washington U., Duke U., Atty. Gen.'s award for disting. svc., 1993, Am. Values award, U.S. Indsl. Coun. Ednl. Found., 1993; named one of 75 Best Lawyers In Washington, Washingtonian survey mag., 2002. Fellow: Am. Bar Found. (jud. fellows com., jud. conf. com. on bicentennial of U.S. constn.); mem.: ABA, Am. Inns of Court, Va. Bar Assn., D.C. Bar Assn., Calif. Bar Assn., Supreme Ct. Hist. Soc., Inst. Jud. Adminstrn. (pres.), Am. Judicature Soc., Am. Law Inst., Phi Delta Phi (Hughes chpt. Man of Yr. 1973), Order of Coif. Republican. Office: Pepperdine U Sch of Law 24255 Pacific Coast Hwy Malibu CA 90263 Fax: 310-506-4266. Business E-Mail: ken.starr@pepperdine.edu.*

STARR, KEVIN, librarian, educator; b. San Francisco, Sept. 3, 1940; m. Sheila Gordon, June 10, 1963; children: Marian, Jessica. BA, U. San Francisco, 1962; MA, Harvard U., 1965, PhD, 1969; MLS, U. Calif., Berkeley, 1974; postgrad., Ch. Div. Sch. Pacific, Berkeley, 1983-84. From asst. to assoc. prof. Am. lit. Harvard U., Cambridge, Mass., 1969-74; city libr. San Francisco, 1973-76; prin. Kevin Starr Assocs., San Francisco, 1983-85; prof. comm. arts U. San Francisco, 1981-89; prof. Sch. Planning and Devel. U. So. Calif., 1989—98, univ. prof., 1998—; state libr. Calif., 1994—2004; state libr. emeritus, 2004—. Allston Burr sr. tutor Eliot House Harvard U., Cambridge, 1970-73; cons. Beyl and Boyd, Inc., San Francisco, 1979-83; sr. cons. Hill and Knowlton USA, San Francisco, 1983-84; vis. assoc. prof. English U. Calif., Berkely, 1974, vis. lectr. polit. sci., 1976, lectr. librarianship, 1978; adj. prof. humanities San Francisco State U., 1975-76; Regent's lectr. polit. sci. U. Calif., Riverside, 1977; adj. prof. English Santa Clara (Calif.) U., 1977-78; vis. prof. history U. Calif., Davis, 1985-86; vis. scholar, media fellow Hoover Inst., 1986-88; vis. fellow Ctr. Humanistic Studies, Claremont McKenna Coll., 1987; faculty master Embassy Residential Coll., 1990-94. Sr. editor New West Mag., 1977; vatican corr. Hearst Newspapers, Rome, 1978; columnist Examiner, San Francisco, 1977-83; contbng. editor L.A. Times, 1994—; contbr. articles to profl. jours., chpts. to books; auth. Americans and the California Dream, 1850-1915, 1973, Inventing the Dream: California Through the Progressive Era, 1985, Material Dreams: Southern California Through the 1920s, 1990, Endangered Dreams: The Great Depression in California, 1996, The Dream Endures: California Enters the 1940s, 1997, Embattled Dreams: California in War and Peace, 1940-1950, 2002, Coast of Dreams: California on the Edge, 1990-2003, 2004, California: A History, 2005. Exec. aide to mayor San Francisco, 1973; bd. trustees Am. Issues

Forum, 1975-76, Calif. Hist. Soc., 1992—; co-chmn. sister city com., San Francisco and Sydney, Australia, 1981-86; advisor Jr. League San Francisco, 1982-84; canidate San Francisco Bd. Suprs., 1984; councilor Am. Antiquarian Soc., 1996—; mem. Calif. Coun. Humanities, 1996—; regent Cathedral St. Mary Assumption, San Francisco, 1996—. Lt. German Army, 1962-64. Recipient Nat. Humanities Medal, NEH, 2006. Mem.: Calif. Historical Soc., Calif. Coun. Humanities, Am. Antiquarian Soc. Office: Univ So Calif SOS 175 Los Angeles CA 90089

STARR, ROSS MARC, economist, educator; b. Oak Ridge, Nov. 14, 1945; s. Chauncey and Doris E. S.; m. Susan S. Strauss, July 2, 1967; children: Daniel, Diana. BS, Stanford U., 1966, PhD, 1972. Cons. Rand Corp., summers 1966, 67, Western Mgmt. Sci. Inst., Grad. Sch. Mgmt., UCLA, summers 1967, 71; Cowles Found. staff rsch. economist Yale U., New Haven, 1970, faculty, 1970-74, assoc. prof. econs., 1974, U. Calif., Davis, 1975-76, prof. econs., 1976-80, San Diego, 1980—, chmn. dept., 1987-90. Vis. lectr. London Sch. Econs., 1973-74, Peoples U. China, Beijing, 1987; vis. scholar U. Calif., Berkeley, 1978-80, vis. prof., 1997; vis. prof. European U. Inst. Florence, Italy, 2007. Author: General Equilibrium Theory: An Introduction, 1997; co-editor: Essays in Honor of Kenneth J. Arrow, 1986: v.1, Social Choice and Public Decision Making, v.2, Equilibrium Analysis, v.3, Uncertainty, Information and Communication; editor: Gen. Equilibrium Models of Monetary Economies, 1989; contbr. articles to profl. jours. NDEA fellow, 1966-69, Yale jr. faculty fellow, 1973-74, Guggenheim fellow, 1978-79; NSF grant, 1979-81, 83-85. Office: U Calif San Diego Dept Econs 0508 9500 Gilman Dr La Jolla CA 92093-0508 Home Phone: 858-455-1630; Office Phone: 858-534-3879. Business E-Mail: rstarr@ucsd.edu.

STARRETT, LUCINDA, lawyer; b. Washington, June 21, 1957; BA magna cum laude, Princeton U., 1979; student, U. Nigeria, Nsukka, 1980-84; JD cum laude, U. Pa., 1984. Bar: Calif. 1986. Law clerk to Hon. Dorothy W. Nelson U.S. Ct. Appeals (9th cir), 1984-85; ptnr. Latham & Watkins, LA, 1991—. Chief comment editor Jour. Capital Markets and Securities Regulation, 1983. Mem. bd. alternative dispute resolution Western Justice Ctr. Fulbright scholar, Nigeria, 1980—81. Mem. ABA, L.A. County Bar Assn. Office: Latham Watkins 355 S Grand Ave Los Angeles CA 90071-1560 E-mail: cindy.starrett@lw.com.

STARRFIELD, SUMNER GROSBY, astrophysics educator, researcher; b. LA, Dec. 29, 1940; s. Harold Ernest and Eve (Grosby) S.; m. Susan Lee Hutt, Aug. 7, 1966; children: Barry, Brian, Sara. BA, U. Calif., Berkeley, 1962; MA, UCLA, 1965, PhD, 1969. From lectr. to asst. prof. Yale U., New Haven, 1967-71; rsch. scientist IBM, Yorktown Heights, N.Y., 1971-72; asst. prof. Ariz. State U., Tempe, 1972-75, assoc. prof., 1975-80, prof., 1980—2001, Regents' prof., 2002—. Vis. assoc. prof. Steward Observatory, Tucson, 1978-79; vis. staff mem. Los Alamos (N.Mex.) Nat. Lab., 1974-94. Author numerous scientific papers. Grantee Ariz. State U., 1973, NSF, 1974—, NASA, 1981—; Los Alamos summer fellow, 1974, 86; Joint Inst. Lab. Astrophysics fellow, 1985-86. Fellow Royal Astron. Soc., Am. Phys. Soc. (astrophysics divsn.); mem. Internat. Astron. Union, Am. Astron. Soc. (high energy astrophyics div., mem. publs. bd. 1978-81, chmn. publs. bd. 2002-05). Achievements include discovery of thermonuclear runaway theory of nova outburst; co-discovery of hottest known class of pulsating variable stars and the cause of their pulsations, ultraviolet studies of nova cygni, 1992; HST and CHANDRA X-ray studies of novae in outburst; theoretical studies of Supernova 1a progenitors. Office: Ariz State U Sch Earth Space PO Box 871404 Tempe AZ 85287-1504 Home Phone: 480-705-8977. Business E-Mail: starrfield@asu.edu.

STARSHAK, JAMES L., lawyer; b. Chgo., Feb. 3, 1945; s. Norbert Phillip and Enda (Reiter) S.; m. Susanne M. Smith, Oct. 25, 1969; children: Lesle M., Phillip E. BBA, U. Notre Dame, 1966, JD, 1969. Bar: Ill. 1969, Hawaii 1972, U.S. Dist. Ct. (no. dist.) Ill., U.S. Tax Ct., U.S. Supreme Ct. Atty. estate tax IRS, Chgo., 1969-71, Honolulu, 1971-77; ptnr. Steiner & Starshak, Honolulu, 1971-79; assoc. Conahan & Conahan, Honolulu, 1979-86; ptnr. Carlsmith, Ball et al, Honolulu, 1986—. Office: Carlsmith Ball Pacific Tower 22d Fl 1001 Bishop St Honolulu HI 96813-3429

STASHOWER, ARTHUR L., lawyer; b. Cleve., Apr. 12, 1930; s. Joseph G. and Tillie (Merlin) S.; m. Joy Schary, Sept. 1, 1957 (div. 1982); children: Keren, Saul, David; m. Barbara Hayden, Jan. 17, 1985. AB, U. Mich., 1951, JD with distinction, 1953. Bar: Ohio 1953, Mich. 1953, Calif. 1957, U.S. Dist. Ct. (mid. dist.) Calif. 1957, U.S. Ct. Appeals (9th cir.) 1962. Assoc. Kaplan Livingston Goodwin & Berkowitz, Beverly Hills, Calif., 1957-64; exec. United Artists Corp., LA, 1964-65, Artists Agy. Corp., LA, 1965-67; assoc. Greenberg & Glusker, Beverly Hills, 1967-68; ptnr. Swerdlow Glikbarg & Shimer, Beverly Hills, 1968-71, Sklar Coben & Stashower, LA, 1971-84; of counsel Shea & Gould, LA, 1985-88; ptnr. Chrystie & Berle, LA, 1988-92, of counsel, 1993-97, Kenoff & Machtinger, LA, 1997—. Arbitrator Hughes Aircraft, E.A.S.T. Mem. Anti-Defamation League, 1961-79, exec. com. 1967-73; mem. Assn. Alternative Pub. Schs., L.A., 1973-79. Lt. USCGR, 1953-57. Mem. ABA, Am. Arbitration Assn., L.A. Bar Assn., State Bar Assn. Calif., Beverly Hills Bar Assn., L.A. Copyright Soc. (trustee 1986-90), Fed. Mediation and Conciliation Svc. Democrat. Jewish. Office: 1901 Avenue Of The Stars Ste 1775 Los Angeles CA 90067-4609 Home: 502 San Vicente Blvd Unit 304 Santa Monica CA 90402-1834 Home Phone: 310-394-7565. Personal E-mail: abstash1@sbcglobal.net.

STATLER, IRVING CARL, aerospace engineer; b. Buffalo, Nov. 23, 1923; s. Samuel William and Sarah (Strauss) S.; m. Renee Roll, Aug. 23, 1953; children: William Scott, Thomas Stuart BS in Aero. Engring., U. Mich., 1945, BS in Engring. Math., 1945; PhD, Calif. Inst. Tech., 1956. Research engr. flight research dept. Cornell Aero. Lab., Inc., Buffalo, 1946-53, prin. engr. flight research dept., 1956-57, asst. head aero-mechanics dept., 1957-63, head applied mechanics dept., 1963-70, sr. staff scientist aeroscis. div., 1970-71; research scientist U.S. Army Air Mobility Research and Devel. Lab., Moffett Field, Calif., 1971-73, dir. Aeromechanics Lab., 1973-85, dir. AGARD, 1985-88; sr. staff scientist NASA Ames Rsch. Ctr., 1988-92, chief Human Factors Rsch. Divsn., 1992—2008, assoc. emeritus, 2008—. Research scientist research analysis group Jet Propulsion Lab., Pasadena, Calif., 1953-55; chmn. flight mechanics panel adv. group aerospace research and devel. NATO, 1974-76; lectr. U. Buffalo, Millard-Fillmore Coll., Buffalo, 1957-58 Served with US-AAF, 1945-46 Fellow AIAA (Internat. Cooperation in Space Sci. medal 1992), AAAS, German Aerospace Soc., Royal Aero Soc.; mem. Am. Helicoptor Soc., Sigma Xi. Home: 1362 Cuernavaca Circulo Mountain View CA 94040-3571 Office: NASA Ames Rsch Ctr MS 262-4 Moffett Field CA 94035 Home Phone: 650-966-1364. E-mail: irving.c.statler@nasa.gov.

STAUBUS, GEORGE JOSEPH, finance educator; b. Brunswick, Mo., Apr. 26, 1926; s. George Washington and Florence Lidwina (Pittman) S.; m. Sarah Mayer, Apr. 11, 1949; children: Lindsay, Martin, Paul, Janette. BS, U. Mo., 1947; MBA, U. Chgo., 1949, PhD, 1954. C.P.A., Ill. Instr. U. Buffalo, 1947-49, U. Chgo., 1950-52; asst. prof. then prof. acctg. U. Calif.-Berkeley, from 1952, now Michael N. Chetkovich prof. emeritus. Vis. prof. NYU, 1965, London Bus. Sch., 1966-67, U. Kans., 1969-70; Erskine lectr. U. Canterbury, New Zealand, 1972, 91. Author: A Theory of Accounting to Investors, 1961, Activity Costing and Input-Output Accounting, 1971, Making Accounting Decisions, 1977, An Accounting Concept of Revenue, 1980, Activity Costing for Decisions, 1988, Economic Influences on the Development of Accounting in Firms, 1996, The Decision-Usefulness Theory of Accounting: A Limited History, 2000. Served with USN, 1944-46. Recipient Disting. prof. Calif. Soc. C.P.A.s, 1981 Mem. Am. Acctg. Assn. (disting. internat. lectr. 1982), AICPA, Fin. Execs. Inst. Office: UC Berkeley Haas Sch Bus Berkeley CA 94720-0001 Business E-Mail: staubus@haas.berkeley.edu.

STAUFFER, THOMAS MICHAEL, university president; b. Harrisburg, Pa., Dec. 5, 1941; s. John Nisley and Louise Lee Stauffer; children: Amity Juliet, Courtney Amanda, Winston Thomas; m. Susie Heller; stepchildren: Lauren Heller, Adam Heller, Elizabeth Stinson. BA cum laude, Wittenberg U., Ohio, 1963; Cert. in E. European Politics, Freie U. Berlin, 1964; MA, PhD, Josef Korbel Sch. Internat. Studies, U. Denver, 1973; Doctorate (hon.), Jackson State U., 2002. Dir. office leadership devel., v.p., external rels. Am. Coun. on Edn., 1972—82; pres., prof. pub. policy U. Houston-Clear Lake, 1982—91; spl. asst. to adminstr. NASA, 1991—92; pres., prof. pub. policy and internat. rels. Golden Gate U., 1992—99; mng. ptnr. Global Consultation and Family Bus. Internat., 1985—; CEO Young Pres. Orgn. Internat., 1999—2001; exec. dir. Lincoln Ctr. for Internat. Mgmt. Ethics; prof. global bus. Thunderbird Sch. Global Mgmt., 2003—05; pres., CEO, prof. mgmt. Am. U. Afghanistan, Kabul, 2006—. Exec. sec. Fedn. Assn. of Acad. Health Care Profls.; chmn. task force Am. Coun. Edn.; exec. dir. Bus. Higher Edn. Forum, Nat. Com. Higher Edn. Issues, 1975—82; bd. dirs. Am. U. Afghanistan Found. Contbr. chpts. to books and articles to profl. jours. and newspapers. Chair, nat. bd. Challenger Ctr. for Space Sci. Edn.; chair Ctr. for Advanced Space Studies; com. advanced tech. Tex. Econ. Devel.; chmn. Houston Com. on Econ. Diversification Planning, Houston World Trade Ctr. Task Force; chmn. com. advanced tech. Clear Lake Area Econ. Devel. Found.; co-chair Tex. Sci. and Tech. Coun.; pres. St. John Hosp.; co-chair San Francisco World Trade Assn.; chair San Francisco Consortium on Higher Edn., San Francisco Mayor's Blue Ribbon Com. on Econ. Devel.; mem. steering com. Silicon Valley Mfrs. Group; bd. dirs. San Francisco C. of C., San Francisco YMCA, Acad. of Art U.; lectr. George Washington U., Regis U. Oceania Cruise Line. Recipient Disting. Alumni award Joseph Korbel Sch. Internat. Studies U. Denver, 1989, Tex. Senate Resolution of Commendation, 1991, Challenger Ctr. Nat. award, 1990, ACE Fellow Anniversary award, 1990, 05, Leadership HS Do the Right Thing award, 1998; Am. Coun. on Edn. fellow in acad. adminstrn., 1971-72, Ford Found. and Social Sci. Found. fellow, 1963-68, sr. fellow Am. Leadership Forum. Mem.: Cosmos Club, Washington, DC. Home: 3080 Coombsville Rd Napa CA 94558 Office Phone: 415-516-8767. Office Fax: 707-255-4999. Business E-Mail: globalcosultation@gmail.com.

STAUSBOLL, ANNE, pension fund administrator; b. 1956; BA in English, Oberlin Coll., Ohio; JD, U. Calif. Davis Sch. Law. With legal office Calif. Pub. Employees' Retirement Sys. (CalPERS), Sacramento, 1993—97, dep. gen. counsel, 1997—99, asst. exec. officer investment ops., 2004—08, interim chief investment officer, 2008—09, CEO, 2009—; gen. counsel Calif. State Treas. Phil Angelides, Sacramento, 1999—2000, chief dep. treas., 2000—04. Mem. Ceres Bd.; governing bd. UN Principles for Responsible Investment; adv. bd. Toigo Found. Named one of Top 20 Nonbank Women in Fin., US Banker, 2007. Mem.: Order of the Coif. Office: Calif Pub Employees' Retirement Sys - CalPERS Lincoln Plz N 400 Q St Sacramento CA 95811 Office Phone: 916-795-3829.*

STAVIG, MARK LUTHER, language educator; b. Northfield, Minn., Jan. 20, 1935; s. Lawrence Melvin and Cora (Hjertaas) S.; m. Donna Mae Ring, July 3, 1957; children— Anne Ragnhild, Thomas Edward, Rolf Lawrence BA, Augustana Coll., 1956, Oxford U., 1958, MA, 1962; PhD, Princeton U., 1961. Instr. to asst. prof. English U. Wis., Madison, 1961-68; from assoc. prof. to prof. English Colo. Coll., Colorado Springs, 1968—2001; ret., 2001—. Author: John Ford and the Traditional Moral Order, 1968, The Forms of Things Unknown: Renaissance Metaphor in Romeo and Juliet and A Midsummer Night's Dream, 1995; editor: Ford, 'Tis Pity She's a Whore, 1966. Fellow Danforth Found., 1956-61, Woodrow Wilson Found., 1956-57; Fulbright scholar Oxford U., 1956-58 Mem.: Shakespeare Assn. Am. Democrat. Home: 1409 Wood Ave Colorado Springs CO 80907-7348

STEADMAN, JOHN MARCELLUS, III, retired language educator; b. Spartanburg, SC, Nov. 25, 1918; s. John Marcellus and Medora Rice (Rembert) S. AB, Emory U., 1940, MA, 1941, DHL (hon.), 1976; MA (T.W. Hunt scholar), Princeton U., 1948, PhD, 1949; DHL (hon.), St. Bonaventure U., 1998. Instr. English Ga. Inst. Tech., 1941-42; asst. prof. U. N.C., 1949-51; ind. study and rsch. in English lit., 1953-61; from rsch. assoc.to sr. rsch. assoc. Henry E. Huntington Libr., San Marino, Calif., 1962—2002; mem. faculty U. Calif., Riverside, 1966—2002, prof. English, 1967—2002, faculty rsch. lectr., 1977, prof. emeritus, 1989—. Vis. disting. prof. CUNY, fall, 1974 Author numerous books including Milton and the Renaisannce Hero, 1967, Milton's Epic Characters, 1968, The Myth of Asia, 1970, Disembodied Laughter: Troilus and the Apotheosis Tradition, 1972, The Lamb and The Elephant: Ideal Imitation and the Context of Renaissance Allegory, 1974, Epic and Tragic Structure in Paradise Lost, 1976, Nature into Myth: Medieval and Renaissance Moral Symbols, 1979, Milton's Biblical and Classical Imagery, 1984, The Hill and the Labyrinth: Discourse and Certitude in Milton and His Near-Contemporaries, 1984, The Wall of Paradise: Essays on Milton's Poetics, 1985, Milton and the Paradoxes of Renaissance Heroism, 1987, Redefining a Period Style: "Renaissance," "Mannerist," and "Baroque" in Literature, 1990, Ryoanji Temple and Other Poems, 1993, Moral Fiction in Milton and Spenser, 1995, Reconnaissances: Poems, 1995, Winter Harvest, A Retrospective, 1996, In Earnest or Game: A Seriocomic Medley. Verses Early or Late, 1998, Siege of Contraries: Rumors of Wars Real or Metaphorical, Stories and Sketches, 1998; co-editor latest being A Milton Ency., vols. I-IX, 1978-83; editor: latest being Huntington Libr. Quar., 1962-81; mem. numerous editl. and advisory bds.; contbr. articles to profl. jours. Served to capt. USAAF, 1942-46; capt. AUS, 1951-52. Grantee Huntington Libr., 1961-62; Procter fellow Princeton U., 1949, Guggenheim fellow, 1979. Mem. Milton Soc. Am. (pres. 1973, honored scholar 1976), So. Calif. Renaissance Conf., Phi Beta Kappa, Chi Phi, Fine Arts Club. Democrat. Home: 4720 Morrison Dr Apt 111 Mobile AL 36609-3341 Home Phone: 251-380-0053.

STEARNS, ROBERT LELAND, curator; b. LA, Aug. 28, 1947; s. Edward Van Buren and Harriett Ann (Hauck) S.; m. Sheri Roseanne Lucas, Oct. 2, 1982 (div. 1994); children: Marissa Hauck, Caroline Lucas. Student, U. Calif., San Diego, 1965-68, BFA, 1970; student, Calif. Poly. State U., San Luis Obispo, 1968. Asst. dir. Paula Cooper Gallery, NYC, 1970-72; prodn. asst. Avalanche Mag., NYC, 1972; dir. Kitchen Ctr. for Video/Music, NYC, 1972-77, Contemporary Arts Ctr., Cin., 1977-82; dir. performing arts Walker Art Ctr., Mpls., 1982-88; dir. Wexner Ctr. for Arts, Columbus, Ohio, 1988-92; mem. Wexner Ctr. Found., Columbus, 1990-92; dir. Stearns & Assocs./Contemporary Exhbn. Svcs., Columbus, Ohio, 1992—2000; sr. prgm. dir. Arts Midwest, Mpls., 1998—2005; cons. curator Franklin Park Conservatory, Columbus, Ohio, 2005—, Bellevue Arts Mus., Wash., 2008—. Adj. prof. dept. art, assoc. dean Coll. Art, Ohio State U., Columbus, 1988-92; lectr. Sch. of the Art Inst. Chgo., 2002; cons. McKnight Found., St. Paul, 1978, Jerome Found., 1978-79; chmn. Artists TV Workshop, N.Y.C., 1976-77; bd. dirs., chmn. Minn. Dance Alliance, Mpls., 1983-88; bd. dirs. Haleakala, Inc., N.Y.C.; mem. various panels Nat. Endowment for Arts, Washington, 1977-91; mem. pub. arts policy Greater Columbus Arts Coun., 1988-90; adv. coun. Bklyn. Acad. Music, 1982-84, Houston Grand Opera, 1991-93; fundraising cons. Art for Life Columbus AIDS Task Force, 2000-2006; mem. Advocacy Com. Ballet Met, Columbus, 2003-2006; mem. db. dirs. Architecture and Design Coun. Palm Springs Atr Mus., 2008-, Laquinta Arts Found., 2008-, Coachella Valley Art Alliance, 2008-; chair leadership coun. Calif. Desert Arts Incubator, 2008-. Author, editor: Robert Wilson: Theater of Images, 1980, Photography and Beyond in Japan, 1995; author: Mexico Now: Point of Departure, 1997, Robert Wilson: Scenografie e Installazioni, 1997, Illusions of Eden: Visions of the American Heartland, 2000, Aspirations: Toward a Future in the Middle East, 2001, The View from Here: Recent Pictures from Central Europe and the American Midwest, 2002, Russel Wright: Living with Good Design, 2006, Bending Nature, 2008; editor: Dimensions of Black, 1970; exec. editor: Breakthroughs: Avant Garde Art in Europe and America 1950-1990, 1991; author and editor numerous catalogues. Mem. gov.'s residence com. State of Ohio, 2004—. Decorated chevalier Order of Arts and Letters (France); Travel grantee Jerome Found., 1986, Japan Found., 1991, Can. Cultural Ministry, 2004. Office: 2218 N Sunshine cir Palm Springs CA 92264 Office Phone: 760-832-7882. E-mail: arts2020@aol.com.

STEARNS, SHEILA MACDONALD, academic administrator; b. Ft. Snelling, Minn., Aug. 30, 1946; d. Alexander Colin and Marie Kristine (Peterson) MacD.; m. Hal Stearns, June 22, 1968; children: Scott, Malin. BA, Univ. Mont., Missoula, 1968, MA, 1969, EdD, 1983. English and history tchr. Wiesbaden (Germany) Jr. High Sch., 1969-72; libr. media specialist Missoula Pub. Schs., 1975-77; dir. alumni rels. Univ. Mont., Missoula, 1983-87, v.p. univ. rels., 1987-93; chancellor Univ. Mont. Western, Dillon, 1993—99; pres. Wayne State Coll., Mich., 1999—2003; commr. higher ed. State of Mont., Helena, 2003—. Contbr. articles to profl. publs. Chair gov. bd. dirs. St. Patrick Hosp., Missoula, 1991-93; mem. Mayor's Adv. Bd., Missoula; nat. chair NAIA Coun. of Pres., 1996-97; chair NAIA Gender Equity com. Mem. Missoula C. of C. (v.p. exec. com.), Rotary (bd. dirs.) Alpha Phi (Chi chpt.), Phi Delta Kappa. Roman Catholic. Avocations: golf, reading, writing. Office: Commissioner Of Higher Education 46 N Last Chance Gulch St Helena MT 59601-4122 Office Phone: 406-444-0311.

STEARNS, SUSAN TRACEY, lighting design company executive, lawyer; b. Seattle, Oct. 28, 1957; d. Arthur Thomas and Roberta Jane (Arrowood) S.; m. Ross Alan De Alessi, Aug. 11, 1990; 1 child, Chase Arthur. AA, Stephens Coll., 1977, BA, 1979; JD, U. Wash., Seattle, 1990. Bar: Calif. 1990, U.S. Ct. Appeals (9th cir.) 1990, U.S. Dist. Ct. (no. dist.) Calif 1990, U.S. Dist. Ct. (we. dist.) Wash. 1991, Wash. 1991. TV news prodr. KOMO, Seattle, 1980-86; atty. Brobeck, Phleger & Harrison, San Francisco, 1990-92; pres. Ross De Alessi Lighting Design, Seattle, 1993—. Author periodicals in field. Alumnae Assn. Coun. Stephens Coll., Columbia, Mo., 1995—. Named Nat. Order of Barristers, U. Washington, Seattle, 1990. Mem. ABA (mem. state labor and employment law subcom.), Wash. State Bar Assn. (mem. bench-bar-press com.), State Bar Calif., King County Bar Assn., Bar Assn.San Francisco, Wash. Athletic Club. Avocations: travel, dance. Office: Ross De Alessi Lighting Des 2330 Magnolia Blvd W Seattle WA 98199-3813

STEBBINS, ROBERT ALAN, sociology educator; b. Rhinelander, Wis., June 22, 1938; s. William Nelson and Dorothy May (Guy) S.; m. Karin Yvonne Olson, Jan. 11, 1964; children: Paul, Lisa, Christi. BA, Macalester Coll., 1961; MA, U. Minn., 1962, PhD, 1964. Assoc. prof. Presbyterian Coll., Clinton, SC, 1964-65; assoc. prof.to prof. Meml. U. Nfld., St. John's, Canada, 1965-73; prof. U. Tex.-Arlington, 1973-76; prof. sociology U. Calgary, Alta., Canada, 1976-99, faculty prof. social scis. Alta., 2000—, dept. head Alta., 1976-82; head dept. sociology and anthropology Meml. U. Nfld., 1968-71. Author: Commitment to Deviance, 1971, The Disorderly Classroom: Its Physical and Temporal Conditions, 1974, Teachers and Meaning, 1975, Amateurs, 1979, The Magician, 1984, Sociology: The Study of Society, 2d edit., 1990, Canadian Football: The View from the Helmet, 1987, Deviance: Tolerable Differences, 1988, The Laugh-Makers: Stand-Up Comedy as Art, Business, and Life-Style, 1990, Amateurs, Professionals and Serious Leisure, 1992; co-editor: Fieldwork Experience, 1980, The Sociology of Deviance, 1982, Experiencing Fieldwork, 1991, Career, Culture, and Social Psychology in a Variety Art, 1993, Predicaments: Moral Difficulty in Everyday Life, 1993, The Franco-Calgarians: French Language, Leisure and Linguistic Lifestyle in an Anglophone City, 1994, The Connoisseur's New Orleans, 1995, The Barbershop Singer: Inside the Social World of a Musical Hobby, 1996, Tolerable Differences: Living with Deviance, 2d edit., 1996; After Work: The Search for an Optimal Leisure Lifestyle, 1998, The Urban Francophone Volunteer: Searching for Personal Meaning and Community Growth in a Linguistic Minority, 1998, The French Enigma: Survival and Development of Canada's Francophone Societies, 2000, Exploratory Research in the Social Sciences, 2001, New Directions in the Theory and Research of Serions Leisure, 2001, The Organizational Basis of Leisure Participation: A Motivational Exploration, 2002, Francophonie et langue dans un monde diverse en évolution: contacts interlinguistiques socioculturels, 2003, Volunteering as Leisure/Leisure as Volunteering: An International Assessment, 2004, Between Work and Leisure: A Study of the Common Ground of Two Separate Worlds, 2004, Challenging Mountain Nature: Risk, Motive, and Lifestyle in Three Hobbyist Sports, 2005, Serious Leisure: A Perspective for our Own Time, 2007, A Dictionary of Nonprofit Terms and Concepts, 2006, The Pivotal Role of Leisure Education: Finding Personal Fulfillment in This Century, 2007, Personal Decisions in the Public Square: Beyond Problem Solving into a Positive Sociology, 2008. Pres. St. John's Orch., 1967-68; mem. Dallas Civic Symphony, 1973-76, Orch. Soc. of Calgary, 1978-97. Can. Coun. Sabbatical Leave fellow, 1972-72, Calgary Inst. for Humanities fellow, 1987-88, Killam resident fellow, 1990; NEH summer stipend, 1976; Acad. Leisure Scis. fellow, 1996—, Royal Soc. Can. fellow, 1999—. Mem. Leisure Studies Assn., Can. Sociology and Anthropology Assn. (pres. 1988-89), Internat. Sociol. Assn., Assn. for Can. Studies, World Leisure and Recreation Assn. (bd. dirs. 1997-2002), Social Sci. Fedn. Can. (pres. 1991-92), Can. Assn. for Leisure Studies (v.p. 1993-96). Home: 144 Edgemont Estates Dr NW Calgary AB Canada T3A 2M3 Office: U Calgary Dept Sociology 2500 University Dr NW Calgary AB Canada T2N 1N4 Office Phone: 403-220-5827. E-mail: stebbins@ucalgary.ca.

STECKEL, RICHARD J., retired radiologist, educator, academic administrator; b. Scranton, Pa., Apr. 17, 1936; s. Morris Leo and Lucille (Yellin) Steckel; m. Julie Raskin, June 16, 1960; children: Jan Marie, David Matthew. BS magna cum laude, Harvard U., 1957, MD cum laude, 1961. Diplomate Am. Bd. Radiology. Intern UCLA Hosp., 1961-62; resident in radiology Mass. Gen. Hosp., Boston, 1962-65; clin., rsch. assoc. Nat. Cancer Inst., 1965-67; faculty UCLA Med. Sch., 1967—, prof. radiol. scis. and radiation oncology, 1974—2000; chmn. dept. radiol. scis. UCLA Med. Ctr., 1994-2000, prof. emeritus, 2000—; pres. Assn. Am. Cancer Insts., 1981. Dir. Jonsson Comprehensive Cancer Ctr., 1974—94; mem. staff UCLA Med. Ctr., Cottage Hosp., Santa Barbara, Calif. Author, editor 3 books; contbr. more than 130 articles to profl. jours. Fellow: Am. Coll. Radiology; mem.: Assn. Univ. Radiologists, Am. Roentgen Ray Soc., Radiol. Soc. N.Am.

STECKLER, CRAIG THEODORE, protective services official; b. Scottsfield, Ill., Feb. 3, 1944; s. Albert George and Mary Lorene (Johnston) S.; m. Karen Capellutto, Mar. 11, 1978; children: Theresa, Rachael, Suzanne, Mark. AA, Saddleback Coll., 1973; BA, Calif. State U., LA, 1975; postgrad., U. Va., 1982, Peace Officer Standards & Tng., Pomona, Calif., 1986. Dist. mgr. Orange County Register, Santa Ana, Calif., 1962-68; police officer, sgt., then lt. City of San Clemente, Calif., 1968-80; police chief City of Piedmont, Calif., 1980-86; dep. police chief City of Fremont, Calif., 1986-92, chief of police Calif., 1992—. Instr., Cypress (Calif.) Coll., 1975-77, Los Mondos Coll., Pittsberg, calif., 1982-83. Mem. Am. Mgmt. Assn., Calif. Peace Officers Assn., Calif. Police Chiefs Assn. (bd. dirs.), Command Coll. Grads. (bd. dirs.), Rotary. Republican. Roman Catholic. Avocation: golf. Office: Fremont Police Dept 2000 Stevenson Blvd Fremont CA 94538-2336

STECKLER, LARRY, publishing executive, writer; b. Bklyn., Nov. 3, 1933; s. Morris and Ida (Beekman) S.; m. Catherine Coccozza, June 6, 1959 (div. June 1999); children: Gail Denise, Glenn Eric, Kerri Lynn, Adria Lauren; m. Lorraine Mary Rubsamen, Oct. 16, 1999. Student, CCNY, 1951; degree in Grad. Realtor's Inst., Parkstate Inst., 2007. Lic. realtor Ariz., 2005, cert. E-Pro Nat. Assn. Realtors. Assoc. editor Radio-Electronics mag., NYC, 1957-62, editor, 1967-85; pub., editor-in-chief Radio Electronics mag., NYC, 1985-92; electronics editor Popular Mechanics mag., NYC, 1962-65; assoc. editor Electronic Products mag., Garden City, NY, 1965-67, Electro-Tech., 1967; editl. dir. Merchandising 2-Way Radio mag., NYC, 1975-77; v.p., dir. Gernsback Publs., NYC, 1975-84, pres., dir., 1984—2003; pub., editl. dir. Spl. Projects mag., 1980-84, Radio-Electronics Ann., 1982-84; pub., editor-in-chief Hands-On Electronics, 1984-88, Computer Digest, 1985-90, Experimenters Handbook, 1986-96, Modem Short Stories, 1987-90, Video/Stereo Digest, 1989-91, Popular Electronics Mag., 1988-99, GIZMO, 1988-99, Hobbyists Handbook, 1989-96, Sci. Probe! mag., 1989-93, StoryMasters, 1989—2001, Electronics Shopper, 1990-99, Electronics Market Ctr., 1991-99, Electronics Now Mag., 1992-99, Radio Craft, 1993-96, Poptronix Handbook, 1996—2003; pres. Claggk, Inc., 1986—2003, Silicon Chip, 1993-94, Sci. Probe Inc., 1989-93, Poptronix Inc., 1997—2005, Ariz., 2005—; realtor Long Realty Co., Tucson, 2005—. Mem. electronics adv. bd. Bd. Coop. Ednl. Svcs., Nassau County, NY, 1975—77; pres. Electronics Industry Hall of Fame, 1985—2001; bd. dirs. Pub. Hall of Fame, 1987—89. Pub., editor-in-chief Poptronics, 2000-03, Poptronics Shopper, 2000-03, PC Tech, 2000-03; co-editor The Shofar, 1998-2002; contbr. articles to profl. jours., popular mags.; author Hugo Gernsback, A Man Well Ahead of His Time, 2007. Bd. dirs. Nassau County coun. Camp Fire Girls, 1971-72; 1st v.p. bd. dirs. Temple Beth Am, Las Vegas, 1998-2002 pres. 2001-02; apptd. bd. adjusters, Marana, Ariz., 2005—; apptd. sec.-treas. Dove Mt. Civic Assn., Marana, 2005—; appt. adv. bd. Citizens Park, Marana, 2007—, chair, 2007—; mem. adv. commn. Dove Mountain Preserve, 2008-. With US Army, 1953—56. Recipient Coop. award Nat. Alliance TV and Electronic Svcs. Assns., 1974, 75; inducted into Electronics Industry Hall of Fame, 1985; ISCET Gov's. award, 1998, FESA Pres. award, 1998. Mem.: IEEE, Marana C. of C. (chair adv. com., parks and recreation 2007—), LA Press, Soc. Profl. Journalists, Internat. Performing Magicians (exec. dir.), Internat. Underwater Explorers Soc., Am. Mgmt. Assn., Nat. Electronics Sales and Svc. Dealers Assn. (rec. sec. NY State 1976—78, treas. 1991—94, Man of Yr. award 1975, 1985, M.L. Finneyberg Excellence award 1994), Internat. Soc. Cert. electronic Technicians (chmn. 1974—76, 1979—81, dir.-at-large 1991—93, rep. to NESDA bd. 1991—93, chmn. 1993—95, Region 9 dir. 1995—97, chmn. 1999—2001, Chmn.'s award 1985), Am. Soc. Bus. Press Editors (sr.), Radio Club Am. Home: 12317 N Fallen Shadows Dr Marana AZ 85658 Office: Long Realty Co 12080 N Dove Mountain Blvd Ste 100 Marana AZ 85653 Home Phone: 520-572-8144; Office Phone: 520-918-5761. Personal E-mail: lartronics@aol.com, larrysteckler@aol.com.

STECKLER, PHYLLIS BETTY, business owner; b. NYC; d. Irwin H. and Bertha (Fellner) Schwartzbard; m. Stuart J. Steckler; children: Randall, Sharon Steckler-Slotky. BA, Hunter Coll.; MA, NYU. Editl. dir. R.R. Bowker Co., NYC, Crowell Collier Macmillan Info. Pub. Co., NYC, Holt Rinehart & Winston Info. Systems, NYC; pres., CEO Oryx Press, Scottsdale, Ariz., 1973-76, Phoenix, 1976—2000, Zephyr Info., Phoenix, 2001—; publ. cons., 2001—. Adj. prof. mktg. scholarly publs. Grad. History dept., Ariz. State U., Tempe; mem. dean's coun. Coll. of Extended Edn., Ariz. State U., Phoenix; mem. adv. coun. Republic Bank Ariz., NA. Past chmn. Info. Industry Assn.; past chair Ariz. Ctr. for the Book; past pres. Contemporary Forum of Phoenix Art Mus.; founding mem. Nat. Edn. Network, U.S. Dept. Edn.; past pres. Friends of the Libr., U.S.A.; mem. Ariz. Women's Forum; bd. dirs. Ariz. region Com. for the Weizmann Inst. Sci.; mem. order coun. Republic Bank, Ariz.; mem. Young Arts Ariz. Bd. Recipient Women Who Make a Difference award The Internat. Women's Forum, 1995, Excellence in Pub. award Ariz. Book Pub. Assn., 1997, The Pub. History Program Ariz. State U. Founding Friend award, 2000; elected to Hunter Coll. Hall of Fame. Mem.: ALA, Ariz. Libr. Assn., Univ. Club of Phoenix. Home and Office: 6446 N 28th St Phoenix AZ 85016-8946 Home Phone: 602-955-4288. E-mail: pbs.zephyr@cox.net.

STEDMAN, DONALD HUGH, chemist, educator; BA, Cambridge U., 1964; MSc, U. East Anglia, 1965, PhD, 1967. Postdoctoral fellow Kans. State U., Manhattan, 1967-69; sr. rsch. scientist Ford Motor Co., Dearborn, Mich., 1969-71; from vis. lectr. to prof. U. Mich., Ann Arbor, 1971-83; Brainerd F. Phillipson prof. chemistry U. Denver, 1983—. Mem. AAAS, Am. Chem. Soc. (award for creative advances in environ. technology 1996), Air Waste Mgmt. Soc. (Frank A Chambers award 1996). Home: 2620 S Fillmore St Denver CO 80210-6213 Office: U Denver Dept Chemistry University Park Denver CO 80208-0001

STEDMAN, JOHN ADDIS, management consultant; b. LA, June 30, 1960; s. Saul Addis Fonseca and Marie Edith S.; m. Kelly Jean Francis (div.); 1 child, Abrielle Francis. AS, SUNY, Albany, 1981, BS, 1991. Mem. LUTCF. Dir. of sales U.S. Mktg., San Diego, Calif., 1989-91; fin. planner Prin. Fin. Group, San Diego, 1991-95; market mgr. PepsiCo, Inc., Chula Vista, Calif., 1995-96; account exec. Pitney Bowes Corp., Henderson, Nev., 1997; account mgr. Xerox Corp., Las Vegas, 1998-99, govt. and edn. mgr. Santa Barbara, Calif., 1999—. Cons. Meadows Cons., Las Vegas, 1999, Jr. Achievement, San Diego and Las Vegas, 1996-99. Chmn. Kiwanis, San Diego, 1992; mem. USCG aux., Santa Barbara, Calif., 1999, U.S. Naval Inst., San Diego, 1985—; instr. U.S. Naval Sea Cadets, San Diego, 1986. Recipient Spl. Achievement award U.S. Navy League, Honolulu, 1981, Navy Cup, San Diego, 1986; cons. grantee Jr. Achievement of So. Nev., Las Vegas, 1997. Republican. Roman Catholic. Avocations: yachting, competitive running, golf, squash.

STEED, ALLAN J., physical science research administrator; Dir. Space Dynamics Lab. Utah State U., Logan, Utah. Office: Utah State U Space Dynamics Lab Logan UT 84341-1942

STEEFEL, DAVID SIMON, lawyer; b. Mpls., June 27, 1951; s. Lawrence D. Jr. and Marion (Charlson) S.; m. Mary Ann Moody, May 24, 1981; children: Emily, Daniel, Katherine. BA, Carleton Coll., 1973; JD, U. Colo., 1978. Bar: Colo. 1978, U.S. Dist. Ct. Colo. 1978, U.S. Ct. Appeals (10th cir.) 1978. Assoc. Gorsuch, Kirgis, Denver, 1978-80, Holme Roberts & Owen, Denver, 1980-84, ptnr., 1984—, litig. practice group leader, 1999—2006. Instr. U. Colo. Law Sch., Boulder, 1978, 91. Home: 1300 Green Oaks Dr Littleton CO 80121-1331 Office: Holme Roberts & Owen 1700 Lincoln St Ste 4100 Denver CO 80203-4541 Home Phone: 303-347-2913; Office Phone: 303-866-0348. Business E-Mail: david.steefel@hro.com.

STEEL, JOHN MURRAY, lawyer; b. Dec. 14, 1945; s. John Murray and Jo Ellen (Collins) Steel; m. Rebecca Maria Hunt, June 10, 1989; children: Britta J., Cerise O., Jacob C., Sara B. BA in Polit. Sci., Stanford U., 1967; JD, U. Wash., 1970. Bar: Wash. 1970, U.S. Dist. Ct. (we. dist.) Wash. 1970, U.S. Tax Ct. 1974, U.S. Ct. Appeals (9th Cir.) 1970. Assoc. Garvey, Schubert, Adams & Barer, Seattle, 1970—73, ptnr., 1974—88, Riddell Williams, Bullitt & Walkinshaw, Seattle, 1988—2000, Gray Cary Ware & Freidenrich, Seattle, 2000—04; ptnr., co-chmn. retail and consumer practice group DLA Piper Rudnick Gray Cary, Seattle, 2005—. Bd. editors Wash. Law Rev., 1969—70. Bd. mem., chmn. strategic planning com. Wash. Spl. Olympics, 1993—98. Mem.: ABA, Wash. State Bar Assn. (exec. com. 1988—2001, corp. act com. 1990—, mem. securities com., chair 1991—92, co-chair 1993—2001, bus. law sect.), Seattle-King County Bar Assn., Wash. Biotechnology and Biomedical Assn. (bd. dirs. 2003—), Tower Club (Seattle), Wash. Athletic Club (Seattle), Order of Coif. Office: DLA Piper Rudnick Gray Cary 701 Fifth Ave Ste 7000 Seattle WA 98104 Office Phone: 206-839-4833. Office Fax: 206-839-4801. Business E-Mail: john.steel@dlapiper.com.

STEEL, MICHAEL J., lawyer; b. Marysville, Calif., May 9, 1955; BA, Univ. Calif., Davis, 1977; JD, Univ. Calif., Hastings, 1982. Bar: Calif. 1982. Ptnr., co-leader Environ. Litigation practice Pillsbury Winthrop Shaw Pittman, San Francisco. Office: Pillsbury Winthrop Shaw Pittman 50 Fremont St San Francisco CA 94105 Office Phone: 415-983-7320. Office Fax: 415-983-1200. Business E-Mail: michael.steel@pillsburylaw.com.

STEEL, RONALD LEWIS, writer, historian, educator; b. Morris, Ill., Mar. 25, 1931; BA magna cum laude, Northwestern U., 1953; MA, Harvard U., 1955. Vice consul US Fgn. Svc., 1957-58; editor Scholastic mag., NYC, 1959-62; sr. assoc. Carnegie Endowment for Internat. Peace, 1982-83; fellow Woodrow Wilson Internat. Ctr. Scholars, 1984-85; prof. internat. relations U. So. Calif., Los Angeles, Calif., 1986—; fellow Wissenschaftskolleg zu Berlin, Germany, 1988; French-Am. found. prof. U. Paris, France, 2001—02; Shephardson sr. fellow coun. on Fgn. Rels., 2002—03. Vis. fellow Yale U., 1971-73; vis. prof. U. Tex., 1977, 79, 80, 85, Wellesley Coll., 1978, Rutgers U., 1980, UCLA, 1981, Dartmouth Coll., 1983, Princeton U., 1984; Shapiro prof. internat. rels. George Washington U., 1995-97; fellow Am. Acad., Berlin, 2005. Author books including: The End of Alliance: America and the Future of Europe, 1964, (with G. Kimble) Tropical Africa Today, 1966, Pax Americana, 1967, Imperialists and Other Heroes, 1971, Walter Lippmann and the American Century, 1980, Temptations of a Superpower, 1995, In Love With Night: The American Romance with Robert Kennedy, 2000; editor various publs. for H.W. Wilson Co., 1961-67; contbr. to N.Y. Rev. Books; contbg. editor New Republic. Served with U.S. Army, 1954-56. Recipient Sidney Hillman award, 1968, Washington Monthly book award, 1980, L.A. Times book award for non-fiction, 1980, Nat. Book Critics Circle award, 1981, Bancroft prize Columbia U., 1981, Am. Book award for biography, 1982; Guggenheim fellow, 1973-74; French-Am. Found. fellow Ecole des Hautes Etudes, Paris, 2001-02. Mem. Council on Fgn. Relations Office: U So Calif Sch Internat Rels Los Angeles CA 90089-0043

STEEL, VIRGINIA (GINNY STEEL), university librarian; BA, U. Rochester; MLS, U. Chgo. Libr. Asst. Ariz. State U. Librs., Tempe; head Social Scis. and Humanities Libr., head Access Svcs. Dept., acting asst. univ. libr. pub. svcs. U. Calif., San Diego, 1988—97; assoc. dir. pub. svcs. MIT, Cambridge, 1997—2001; dir. librs. Wash. State U., Pullman, 2001—05; univ. libr. U. Calif., Santa Cruz, 2005—. Office: U Calif Santa Cruz Univ Libr 320 McHenry Libr 1156 High St Santa Cruz CA 95064 Office Phone: 831-459-2076. E-mail: vsteel@ucsc.edu.

STEELE, (MARGARET) ANITA MARTIN, law librarian, educator; b. Haines City, Fla., Dec. 30, 1927; d. Emmett Edward and Esther Majulia (Phifer) Martin; m. Thomas Dinsmore Steele, June 10, 1947 (div. 1969); children: Linda Frances, Roger Dinsmore, Thomas Garrick, Carolyn Ann; m. James E. Beaver, Mar. 1980 (dec. Feb. 1996). BA, Radcliffe Coll., 1948; JD, U. Va., 1971; M in Law Librarianship, U. Wash., 1972. Asst. prof. law U. Puget Sound, Tacoma, 1972—74, assoc. prof. law, 1974—79, prof. law, 1979—94, dir. law libr., 1972—94; prof. law, dir. law libr. Seattle U., Tacoma, 1994—98, prof. law emeritus, 1998—. Author: (book) Martin and Carmichael Descendants in Ga., 1811-1994, 1994; contbr. articles to profl. jours.; mem. editorial adv. bds.: various law book pubs. Treas. Congl. Campaign Orgn., Tacoma, 1978, 1980; mem. adv. bd. Clover Pk. Vocat.-Tech. Sch., Tacoma, 1980—82. Mem.: DAR, Colonial Dames XVII Century. Republican. Home: 4434 Pheasant Ridge Rd Condo # 303 Roanoke VA 24014-5280 E-mail: ams145@cox.net.

STEELE, BRUCE CARL, magazine editor; b. York, Pa., Sept. 9, 1959; s. William Melvin and Kaye Marilyn (Meyer) S.; m. Christopher Cornell Oakley, Feb. 14, 1987. BA, U. Ala., 1981; MFA, Columbia U., 1987. Staff editor Alexandria (La.) Daily Town Talk, 1982-85; sr. editor Cahners Pub., NYC, 1987-92; mng. editor Out Mag., NYC, 1992-95, exec. editor, 1995-97, entertainment editor, 1997-99; exec. editor The Advocate, LA, 1999—. Office: The Advocate 6922 Hollywood Blvd Fl 10 Los Angeles CA 90028-6117 Home: PO Box 2625 Fairview NC 28730-2600

STEELE, CHARLES GLEN, retired accountant; b. Faulkton, SD, July 24, 1925; s. Clifford D. and Emily O. (Hanson) S.; m. Shirley June Ferguson, Nov. 9, 1947; children: Richard Alan (dec.), Deborah Ann Steele Most (dec.). BBA, Golden Gate U., San Francisco, 1951, MBA, 1962. With Deloitte Haskins & Sells, 1951-86, partner, 1963-86, partner charge Chgo. office, 1973-76, partner charge personnel and adminstrn. NYC, 1976-78, chmn., chief exec. officer, 1978-86. Instr. evening program Golden Gate U., 1952-58. Served with USNR, 1943-48, aircraft carrier fighter pilot, 1946-48. Recipient Elijah Watts Sells Gold medal for highest grade in U.S. for C.P.A. exam., 1951 Mem. AICPA. Home: 7831 Rush Rose Dr Unit 124 Carlsbad CA 92009-6843

STEELE, CHARLES RICHARD, biomedical and mechanical engineering educator; b. Royal, Iowa, Aug. 15, 1933; married, 1969; 4 children. BS, Tex. A&M U., 1956; PhD in Applied Mechanics, Stanford U., 1960; PhD (hon.), Zaporozhye State U., Ukraine, 1997. Engrng. specialist aircraft structure Chance-Vought Aircraft, Dallas, 1959-60; rsch. scientist shell theory Lockheed Rsch. Lab., Palo Alto, 1960-66; assoc. prof. Stanford (Calif.) U., 1966-71, prof. applied mechanics, 1971—. Lectr. U. Calif., Berkeley, 1964-65; vis. prof. Swiss Fed. Inst. Technology, Zurich, 1971-72, U. Luleá, Sweden, 1982, Chung Kung U., Taiwan, 1985, U. Cape Town, South Africa, spring 1993, U. Trento, Italy, fall 1999; tech. dir. Shelltech Assoc. Editor-in-chief: Internat. Jour. Solids Structures, 1985—2005, Jour. Mechanics of Materials and Structures, 2005-. Recipient NIH Claude Pepper award, 1988, Humboldt award, 1994; named Eminent Academician Ukrainian Acad., 1998. Fellow ASME (chmn. exec. com. applied mechanics divsn. 1983-84, Warner T. Koiter medal 1999), Am. Acad. Mechanics (pres. 1989-90); mem. AIAA, NAE, Acoustical Soc. Am. Achievements include research in asymptotic analysis in mechanics; thin shell theory; mechanics of the inner ear; noninvasive determination of bone stiffness; and morphology of plants. Office: Stanford Univ Divsn Mechanics and Computation Durand Bldg 355A Stanford CA 94305-4040

STEELE, CLAUDE MASON, psychology professor; b. Chgo., Jan. 1, 1946; s. Shelby and Ruth (Hootman) Steele; married, Aug. 27, 1967; children: Jory, Claude Benjamin. BA in Psychology, Hiram Coll., 1967; MA in Social Psychology, Ohio State U., 1969, PhD in Social Psychology, minor in Statistical Psychology, 1971; PhD (hon.), Yale U., 2002, Princeton U., 2003. Asst. prof. U. Utah, Salt Lake City, 1971-73; from asst. to prof. U. Washington, Seattle, 1978-87, prof. psychology, 1985—87; prof. U. Mich., Ann Arbor, 1987-91, rsch. scientist Inst. Social Rsch., 1989—91; prof. psychology Stanford U., Calif., 1991—, fellow Ctr. Advanced Study in Behavioral Sciences, 1994—95, chmn. Dept. Psychology, 1997—2000, Lucie Stern prof. social sciences, 1997—, co-dir. Ctr. Comparative Studies in Race and Ethnicity, 1999—2002, dir. Ctr. Comparative Studies in Race and Ethnicity, 2002—, dir. Ctr. for Advanced Study in the Behavioral Scis. Mem. psychosocial rsch. study sect. Nat. Inst. Alcohol Abuse and Alcoholism, 1984—88; mem. rev. panel and mental health rsch. edn. rev. panel Nat. Inst. Mental Health, 1979—83. Assoc. editor Personality and Social Psychology Bull., 1984—87, consulting editor Jour. of Social Issues, 1983—90, Jour. Personality and Social Psychology, 1990—, Attitudes and Social Cognition, 1990—, Psychol. Rev., 1990—, Motivation and Emotion, 1990—, Basic and Applied Social Psychology, 1990—, Jour. Exptl. Social Psychology, 1990—. Mem. King County Alcoholism and Drug Abuse Adminstrv. Bd., 1980—85. Recipient numerous rsch. grants. Fellow: Am. Psychol. Assn. (Cattell Fellowship), Am. Psychol. Soc. (bd. dirs. 1991—96, William James Fellow award 2000, Gordon Allport Prize); mem.: NAS, Nat. Acad. Edn., Am. Acad. Arts and Scis., Soc. Personality and Social Psychology (pres. 2002—03, Donald Campbell award 2001), Soc. Exptl. Social Psychology (sec.-treas. 1987—88, chmn. 1988—89). Home: 562 Junipero Serra Blvd Stanford CA 94305-8442 Office: Stanford U Dept Psychology Jordan Hall Bldg 420 Stanford CA 94305 Office Phone: 650-725-9849. Office Fax: 650-725-5699.*

STEELE, DALE F., women's healthcare company executive; Co-founder, CFO, M.W. Steele Group, 1983-89, corp. sec., treas., 1994-96; owner, mgr. Dale Fitzmorris, 1989-94; co-founder, co-CEO, As We Change, LLC, 1995-98; v.p. catalog ops. Women First HealthCare, Inc., San Diego, 1998—.

STEELE, DAVID H., state legislator; m. Sharon Nauta; 7 children. BS in Math., Utah State U., 1971, MEd, 1978, postgrad., 1986, Calif. Poly, 1984. Cert. tchr. and adminstr., Utah. Dir. instructional tech., dir. adult and continuing edn. Davis Sch. Dist.; mem. Utah Senate, Dist. 21, Salt Lake City, 1986—; mem. transp. and pub. safety com., mem. edn. com.; co-chair exec. and natural resources appropriations. Mem. steering com. Edn. Commn. of the states; chair Edn. and Job Tng. Com.; co-chair Info. Tech. Commn. Utah. Republican. Office: 320 S 500 E Kaysville UT 84037-3307

STEELE, ELISA ANNE, Internet company executive, marketing professional; b. 1966; BS, U. NH Whittemore Sch. Bus. & Econs., 1988; MBA, San Francisco State U. Sch. Bus., 1990. Gen. mgr. bus. svcs. AT&T Inc., 1991—99; mktg. exec., v.p. Sun Microsystems, Inc., 1999—2004; sr. v.p. corp. mktg. NetApp Inc., 2005—09; chief mktg. officer Yahoo! Inc., 2009—. Office: Yahoo Inc 701 First Ave Sunnyvale CA 94089 Office Phone: 408-349-3300. Office Fax: 408-349-3301.*

STEELE, KAREN DORN, journalist; b. Portland, Oreg., Oct. 27, 1943; d. Ronald and Margaret Elizabeth (Cates) Moxness; m. Charles Stuart Dorn, Oct. 30, 1965 (div. Oct. 1982); children: Trilby Constance Elizabeth Dorn, Blythe Estella Dorn; m. Richard Donald Steele, July 4, 1983. BA, Stanford U., 1965; MA, U. Calif., Berkeley, 1967. Prodr. Sta. KSPS-TV, Spokane, Wash., 1970—72, dir. news and pub. affairs, 1972—82; reporter Spokesman-Rev., Spokane, 1982—87, environ./spl. projects reporter, 1987—2005, investigative reporter, 2005—. Contbr. articles to sci. publs. (Olive Br. award NYU Ctr. War, Peace & The Media, 1989). Bd. dirs. Women Helping Women, Spokane, 1994; trustee St. George's Sch., Spokane, 1988-92. Mid-career fellow Stanford Knight Fellowship Program, 1986-87, Arms Control fellow Ctr. for Internat. Security and Arms Control, Stanford U., 1986-87; Japan Travel grant Japan Press Found., Tokyo, 1987, Rsch. grantee John D. and Catherine T. MacArthur Found., 1992; recipient Gerald Loeb award Anderson Sch. Mgmt. UCLA, 1995, George Polk award L.I. U., 1995, William Stokes award U. Mo., 1988, Nat. Headliner award, Excellence in Legal Journalism award Wash. State Bar Assn., 2000, Payne award U. Oreg., 2006; named to State Hall of Journalistic Achievement, Wash. State U., Pullman, 1995. Unitarian Universalist. Office: Spokesman Review 999 W Riverside Ave Spokane WA 99210-2160 Office Phone: 509-459-5462. Business E-Mail: karend@spokesman.com.

STEELE, SHELBY, writer, educator; b. Chgo., 1946; s. Shelby Sr. and Ruth S. Grad., Coe Coll., 1968; M in Sociology, So. Ill. U., 1971; PhD in English, U. Utah, 1974. Prof. dept English Calif. State U., San Jose; Robert J. and Marion E. Oster sr. fellow Hoover Instn., Stanford, Calif., 1994—. Author: The Content of Our Character: A New Vision of Race in America, 1991 (Nat. Book Critics Circle award 1991), A Dream Deferred: The Second Betrayal of Black Freedom in America, 1998, White Guilt: How Blacks and Whites Together Destroyed the Promise of the Civil Rights Era, 2006, A Bound Man: Why We Are Excited About Obama and Why He Can't Win, 2007 (TV documentary) Seven Days in Bensonhurst (Emmy award, San Francisco Film Festival award); contbr. essays to profl. jours. Recipient Nat. Humanities Medal, 2004, Bradley prize, 2006. Mem.: Ctr. for New Am. Cmty. at Manhattan Inst. (nat. bd.), Univ. Accreditation Assn., Am. Acad. Liberal Edn. (nat. bd.), Nat. Assn. Scholars. Office: Hoover Inst Pub Affairs Stanford Univ Stanford CA 94305-6010

STEEN, PAUL JOSEPH, retired broadcasting executive; b. Williston, ND, July 4, 1932; s. Ernest B. and Inez (Ingebrigtson) S.; m. Judith Smith; children— Michael M., Melanie. BA, Pacific Luth. U., 1954; MS, Syracuse U., 1957. Producer, dir. Sta. KNTV, San Jose, Calif., 1957-58, Sta. KVIE, Sacramento, 1958-60; asst. prof. telecommunications Pacific Luth. U., Tacoma, 1960-67; dir. ops. Sta. KPBS San Diego State U., 1967-74; gen. mgr., 1974-93; prof. telecommunications and film, 1974-93; dir. univ. telecommunications. Co-chmn. Office of New Tech. Initiatives. Dir. (tel. program) Troubled Waters (winner Nat. Ednl. TV award of excellence 1970). With AUS. Named Danforth Assoc. Mem. Pacific Mountain Network (bd. dirs., chmn., bd. of govs. award 1993), NATAS, Assn. Calif. Pub. TV Stas. (pres.), San Diego County Sr. Golf Assn. (past pres.), Pi Kappa Delta. Home: 6068 Caminito De La Taza San Diego CA 92120-5323 Business E-Mail: psteen@mail.sdsu.edu.

STEER, REGINALD DAVID, lawyer; b. NYC, July 16, 1945; s. Joseph D. and Rozica (Yusim) S.; m. Marianne Spizzy, July 22, 1983; children: Derek B., Trevor A. BA, U. Minn., 1966, JD, 1969. Bar: Minn. 1969, Calif. 1973, U.S. Dist. Ct. (no., ea. so. and ctrl. dists.) Calif., U.S. Ct. Mil. Appeals 1969, U.S. Ct. Appeals (9th cir.), U.S. Ct. Appeals (11th cir.), U.S. Supreme Ct. 1981, U.S. Ct. Internat. Trade, 1994. Ptnr. Akin Gump Strauss Hauer & Feld, LLP, San Francisco. Capt. US Army, 1969—73. Fellow Am. Coll. Trial Lawyers; mem. ABA (antitrust and litigation sects.), San Francisco (Calif.) Bar Assn. Office: Akin Gump Strauss Hauer & Feld LLP 580 California St Ste 1500 San Francisco CA 94104 Home Phone: 415-665-9037; Office Phone: 415-765-9520. E-mail: rsteer@akingump.com.

STEERS, GEORGE W., lawyer; b. NYC, Jan. 29, 1941; BA, Yale U., 1963; LLB cum laude, Columbia U., 1966. Bar: Wash. 1970. Law clk. U.S. Ct. Appeals (2d cir.), 1966-67; prin. Stoel Rives, LLP, Seattle, Wash., 1974—. Mem. ABA, Wash. State Bar Assn., Seattle-King County Bar Assn. Office: Stoel Rives LLP One Union Sq 600 University St Ste 3600 Seattle WA 98101-4109

STEFANI, GWEN RENEE, singer; b. Anaheim, Calif., Oct. 3, 1969; d. Dennis and Patti Stefani; m. Gavin McGregor Rossdale, Sept. 14, 2002; children: Kingston James McGregor, Zuma Nesta Rock. Student, Calif. State U., Fullerton. Singer No Doubt, 1986—. Designer, creator fashion line L.A.M.B. (Love. Angel. Music. Baby.), 2004—; launched toy doll line (8 dolls) Love. Angel. Music. Baby. Fashion Dolls, 2006. Singer: (albums with No Doubt) No Doubt, 1992, Tragic Kingdom, 1995, Beacon Street Collection, 1995, Collector's Orange Crate, 1997, Return of Saturn, 2000, Rock Steady, 2001 (Grammy awards: Best Pop Performance By A Duo Or Group With Vocal for song "Hey Baby", 2002, Best Pop Performance By A Duo Or Group With Vocal for song "Underneath it All", 2003), The Singles 1992-2003, 2003, Everything In Time, 2005, (solo albums) Love, Angel, Music, Baby, 2004, The Sweet Escape, 2006, (songs) Just A Girl, Spiderwebs, Don't Speak, 1995, Simple Kind of Life, 2000, Hella Good, Hey Baby, Underneath It All, 2001, It's My Life, 2003 (MTV Video Music award Best Group Video, 2004, MTV Video Music award Best Pop Video, 2004), Hollaback Girl, 2005 (Billboard awards, Digital Song of Yr., 2005), (with Moby) South Side, 1999, (with eve) Let Me Blow Your Mind, 2001 (Grammy award, Best Rap/Song Collaboration, 2001); actor: (films) Zoolander, 2001, The Aviator, 2004, (voice only): (TV appearances) King of the Hill, 2001, (TV guest appearances) Saturday Night Live, 1996, 2001, Mad TV, 2000, Dawson's Creek, 2002. Recipient Best Choreography In a Video for Hollaback Girl, MTV Video Music Awards, 2005, Best Art Direction In a Video for What You Waiting For?, Favorite Female Artist, Am. Music Awards, 2005, New Artist of Yr., Billboard Music Awards, 2005, Best-Selling New Female Artist, World Music Awards, 2005; named Favorite Female Singer, People's Choice Awards, 2008; named one of The 100 Most Powerful Celebrities, Forbes.com, 2008. Office: c/o David Schiff Schiff Co 9465 Wilshire Blvd #480 Beverly Hills CA 90212

STEFFAN, WALLACE ALLAN, entomologist, educator, museum director; b. St. Paul, Aug. 10, 1934; m. Sylvia Behler, July 16, 1966; 1 child, Sharon. BS, U. Calif., Berkeley, 1961, PhD, 1965. Entomologist dept. entomology Bishop Mus., Honolulu, 1964-85, head diptera sect., 1966-85, asst. chmn., 1979-85; dir. Idaho Mus. Natural History, Idaho State U., Pocatello, 1985-89, U. Alaska Mus., 1989-92; prof. biology, dir. U. Alaska, Fairbanks, 1989—92; exec. dir. Gt. Valley Mus. Natural History, 1992-94, Sun Cities Mus. Art, 1995-97, Burpee Mus. Natural History, Rockford, Ill., 1997-00, West Valley Art Mus., 2000—. Mem. grad. affiliate faculty dept. entomology, U. Hawaii, 1969-85; reviewer NSF, 1976-94; mem. affiliate faculty biology, Idaho State U., 1986-89. Acting editor Jour. Med. Entomology, 1966; assoc. editor Pacific Insects, 1980-85. Bd. dirs. Idaho State U. Fed. Credit Union, 1986-89; mem. adv. coun. Modesto Conv. and Visitors Bur., 1992-95; mem. Ft. Hall Replica Commn., 1986-89; judge Hawaii State Sci. and Engring. Fair, 1966-85, chief judge sr. display divsn., 1982, 83, 84; advisor to bd. Fairbanks Conv. and Visitors Bur., 1989-91; mem. vestry St. Christopher's Episcopal Ch., 1974-76, St. Matthew's Episcopal Ch., Fairbanks, 1990-91; pres. Alaska Visitors Assn., Fairbanks, 1991; advisor Fairbanks Conv. and Visitors Bur. Bd., 1989-91; bd. dirs. Kamehameha Fed. Credit Union, 1975-77, chmn., mem. supervisory com., 1980-84. With USAF, 1954-57. Grantee NIH, 1962, 63, 67-74, 76-81, 83-85, U.S. Army Med. Rsch. and Devel. Command, 1964-67, 73-74, NSF, 1968-76, 83-89, City and County of Honolulu, 1977, U.S. Dept. Interior, 1980, 81. Mem. Entomol. Soc. Am. (standing com. on systematics resources 1983-87), Pacific Coast Entomol. Soc., Soc. Systematic Zoology, Hawaiian Entomol. Soc. (pres. 1974, chmn. coms. 1966-85, editor procs. 1966), Hawaiian Acad. (councillor 1976-78), Sigma Xi (pres. San Joaquin chpt. 1994-95), Northwest Passage Immigrants and Ingenuity (pres. exec. com. 1998-00, v.p.), Ill. Assn. Museums (bd. dirs. 1998-00), Assn. Midwest Mus. (chair local arrangements com.), N.W. Valley C. of C. (bd. dirs. 2001—). Office: West Valley Art Mus 17420 N Ave of Arts Surprise AZ 85374

STEFFEN, THOMAS LEE, retired judge, lawyer; b. Tremonton, Utah, July 9, 1930; s. Conrad Richard and Jewel (McGuire) S.; m. LaVona Ericksen, Mar. 20, 1953; children— Elizabeth, Catherine, Conrad, John, Jennifer Student, U. So. Calif., 1955-56; BS, U. Utah, 1957; JD with honors, George Washington U., 1964; LLM, U. Va., 1988. Bar: Nev. 1965, U.S. Dist. Ct. Nev. 1965, U.S. Tax Ct. 1966, U.S. Ct. Appeals 1967, U.S. Supreme Ct. 1977. Contracts negotiator U.S. Bur. Naval Weapons, Washington, 1961-64; private practice Las Vegas, 1965-82; justice Supreme Ct. Nev., Carson City, 1982-94, chief justice, 1995-97, ret., 1997, chmn. code of jud. conduct study com., 1991; of counsel Hutchison & Steffen, Las Vegas, also Provo, Utah, 1997—. Vice chmn. Nev. State Jud. Edn. Coun., 1983-84; chmn. Nev. State-Fed. Jud. Coun., 1986-91, mem., 1986-93. Mem. editorial staff George Washington U. Law Rev., 1963-64; contbr. articles to legal jours. Bd. dirs. So. Nev. chpt. NCCJ, 1974-75; mem. exec. bd. Boulder Dam Area coun. Boy Scouts Am., 1979-83; bd. visitors Brigham Young U., 1985-89. Recipient merit citation Utah State U., 1983 Mem. Nev. Bar Assn. (former chmn. So. Nev. med.-legal screening panel), Nev. Trial Lawyers Assn. (former dir.) Republican. Mem. Lds Ch. Avocations: reading, sports. Office: Lakes Business Park 8831 W Sahara Ave Las Vegas NV 89117-5865 also: 481 E Normandy Dr Provo UT 84604-5963 E-mail: Tlsrcjnsct@aol.com.

STEFFEY, EUGENE PAUL, veterinary medicine educator; b. Reading, Pa., Oct. 27, 1942; s. Paul E. and Mary M. (Balthaser) S.; children: Michele A., Bret E., Michael R., Brian T. Student, Muhlenberg Coll., 1960-63; D in Vet. Medicine, U. Pa., 1967; PhD, U. Calif., Davis, 1973; D (hon.), U. Bern, Switzerland, 2002. Diplomate Am. Coll. Vet. Anesthesiologists (pres. 1980), European Coll. Vet. Anaesthesia. NIH spl. research fellow U. Calif., San Francisco, 1973, asst. prof. Davis, 1974-77, assoc. prof., 1977-80, prof. vet. medicine, 1980—, also chmn. dept. vet. surgery, 1980-93. Mem. scientific reviewers Am. Jour. Vet. Research, Schaumburg, Ill., 1984-87. Contbr. more than 150 articles to profl. jours. Recipient Alumni Achievement award, U. Calif. Sch. Vet. Medicine, 2005. Mem. AVMA, Am. Coll. Vet. Anesthesiologists, Am. Physiol. Soc., Am. Soc. Pharmacology Exptl. Therapeutics, Am. Soc. Anesthesiologists, Assn. Vet. Anaesthetists, Calif. Soc. Anesthesiologists, European Coll. Vet. Anesthesia, Internat. Anesthesia Rsch. Soc., Pa. Vet. Med. Assn., Royal Coll. Vet. Surgeons (hon. assoc.), Sigma Xi, Phi Zeta. Office: U Calif Dept Surg Radiol Scis School of Vet Medicine Davis CA 95616

STEGMAYER, JOSEPH HENRY, housing industry executive; b. Teaneck, NJ, Jan. 4, 1951; s. Arthur Harry and Alicia (Ward) S.; m. Delene Russell. BS in Fin., U. Louisville, 1973. Spl. projects Worthington Industries Inc., Columbus, Ohio, 1973-75, dir. investor rels., 1975-77, dir. corp. rels., 1977-80, v.p. corp. devel., 1980-82, v.p., CFO, treas., 1982-93, also bd. dirs.; pres., vice chmn. Clayton Homes, Inc., Knoxville, Tenn., 1985—98, also bd. dirs.; pres. retail & CFO Champion Enterprises, Inc., Auburn Hills, Mich., 1998-2000; chmn., CEO Centex Mfg. Housing Group, Dallas, 2000—03; chmn., pres., CEO Cavco Industries, 2003—. Editor: We've Only Scratched the Surface, 1981. Chmn. YMCA, Columbus, 1981-83; pres. and chmn. Columbus Zoo, 1987-93; bd. dirs. Muskingum Coll., 1984-93, Knoxville Zoo, Found. of Diocese of Columbus, United Way Knoxville; chmn. Ronald McDonald House, Columbus; mem. chancellor's assocs. bd. U. Tenn.; dir. Desert Voices Oral Learning Ctr.; mem. provost's bd. Ariz. State U. Named Citizen of Yr., Columbus Jaycees, 1984; recipient Outstanding Achievement in Fin. award Phi Beta Kappa, 1984. Roman Catholic. Avocations: scuba diving, travel, investing. Office: CAVCO 1001 N Central Ave Phoenix AZ 85004 Office Phone: 602-256-6263.

STEGNER, JOE, state legislator; m. Deborah Stegner; 4 children. BA, U. Idaho. Owner Stegner Grain & Seed Co., 1972—95; mem. Dist. 7 Idaho State Senate, 1998—, asst. majority leader. Republican. Office: State Capitol Bldg PO Box 83720 Boise ID 83720-0081 Office Phone: 208-334-2475. Office Fax: 208-334-2125. Business E-Mail: jstegner@senate.idaho.gov.*

STEIDEL, CHARLES C., astronomy educator; b. Ithaca, NY, Oct. 14, 1962; married. AB in Astrophysy. Scis., Princeton U., NJ, 1984; PhD in Astronomy, Calif. Inst. Tech., Pasadena, 1990. Parisot fellow U. Calif., Berkeley, 1989—90, Hubble fellow, 1990—93; asst. prof. physics MIT, Cambridge, Mass., 1993—95; asst. prof. astronomy Calif. Inst. Tech., 1995—97, assoc. prof., 1997—98, prof., 1998—. Mem. telescope allocation com. Cerro Tololo Inter-Am. Obs., 1994—97; mem. sci. steering com. Keck Obs., 1996—2003, co-chair sci. steering com., 1997—2003; mem. Hubble space telescope second decade com., 1998—99; mem. external sci. rev. panel Next Generation Space Telescope, 1998—99; mem. space scis. origins sub-com. NASA, 1998—2000; chair sci. working grp. Calif. Extremely Large Telescope, 1999—2002, co-chair steering com., 2000—02; mem. Hubble fellowship selection com., 2000; chair sci. adv. com. Thirty Meter Telescope (formerly Calif. Extremely Large Telescope), 2003—. Contbr. articles to sci. jours. Recipient Young Investigator award, NSF, 1994—99, Helen B. Warner prize, Am. Astron. Soc., 1997; fellow Alfred P. Sloan Found., 1994—96, David and Lucile Packard Found., 1997—2002, MacArthur Found., 2002. Mem.: NAS (US/Japan Frontiers in Sci. organizing com. 1997—98). Office: Calif Inst Tech Dept Astronomy 1201 E Calif Blvd Pasadena CA 91125-0001 Home: 230 S Arroyo Blvd Pasadena CA 91105

STEIN, BEN (BENJAMIN JEREMY STEIN), television personality, writer, lawyer, economist; b. Washington, Nov. 25, 1944; s. Herbert and Mildred (Fishman) S.; m. Alexandra Denman, June 22, 1968 (div. 1974); m. Alexandra Denman, 1977; 1 child, Thomas. BA, Columbia U., 1966; LLB, Yale U., 1970. Bar: Conn. Trial lawyer FTC, Washington, 1970-72; speechwriter The White House, Washington, 1973-74; columnist Wall St. Jour., NYC, 1974-76; writer, commentator, columnist LA Herald-Examiner, 1978-87; TV personality Win Ben Stein's Money, Comedy Ctrl., 1997—2003; host Turn Ben Stein On, Comedy Ctrl., 1999—2001. Fin. cons. LAACO, Inc., LA; contbg. editor Am. Spectator, 1980—; law and econs. tchr. Pepperdine, Malibu, 1992—; adj. prof. Am. U., Washington, U. Calif. Santa Cruz; spokesperson Clear Eyes eye drops. Author: On The Brink, 1977, The View from Sunset Boulevard, 1978, DREEMZ, 1978, Moneypower, 1980, 'Ludes, 1981, Financial Passages, 1986, A License to Steal, 1992, Tommy and Me, 1999, How To Ruin Your Life, 2002, How to Ruin Your Love Life, 2003, How to Ruin Your Financial Life, 2004, How Succesful People Win: Using Bunkhouse Logic to Get What You Want in Live, 2006; co-author (with Phil DeMuth) Mechanical and Electrical Equipment for Buildings, 1999, Yes, You Can Time the Market!, 2003, Can America Survive? The Rage of the Left, the Truth, and What to Do about It, 2004, Yes, You Can Be a Successful Income Investor: Reaching for Yield in Today's Market, 2005, Yes, You Can Still Retire Comfortably: The Baby-Boom Retirement Crisis and How to Beat It, 2005, Yes, You Can Get a Financial Life!: Your Lifetime Guide to Financial Planning, 2007, The Real Stars: In Today's America, Who Are the True Heroes?, 2007, How to Ruin the United States of America, 2008; author numerous articles on leveraged buy-outs and other fin. frauds for Barrons, 1984—; syndicated columnist King Features Syndicate; regular columnist LA Mag., NY Mag., E! Online, NY Times (Everybody's Money) SundayBusiness; contbr. Wash. Post, Wall St. Jour., CBS TV News; guest speaker on fin. Fox News Channel; co-creater: (TV series) Fernwood Tonight; actor: (films) The Wild Life, 1984, Ferris Bueller's Day Off, 1986, Planes, Trains, and Automobiles, 1987, Ghostbusters II, 1989, Soapdish, 1991, Honeymoon in Vegas, 1992, Dennis the Menace, 1993, My Girl 2, 1994, North, 1994, The Mask, 1994, Richie Rich, 1994, Miami Rhapsody, 1995, Casper, 1995; (TV series) The Wonder Years, 1988-91, (voice only) Animaniacs, 1993, Freakazoid, 1995, Earthworm Jim, 1995, The Mask, 1995, Bruno the Kid, 1996, The Secret Files of the SpyDogs, 1998; (TV films) Mastergate, 1992, The Day My Parents Ran Away, 1993, (voice only) Santa vs. the Snowman, 1997, Breakfast with Einstein, 1998; exec. prodr. Turn Ben Stein On, 1999; host: (TV series) Win Ben Stein's Money, 1997-2002 (Daytime Emmy award Outstanding Game Show Host, 1999); (TV appearances) Charles in Charge, 1987, 88, 90, MacGyver, 1991, Melrose Place, 1993, Full House, 1993, Hearts Afire, 1993, 94, Tales from the Crypt, 1995, Lois & Clark: The New Adventures of Superman, 1995, Married...With Children, 1995, The Marshal, 1995, (voice only) Duckman, 1996, 97, Seinfeld, 1997, Murphy Brown, 1997, Muppets Tonight!, 1998, (voice only) Rugrats, 1998, The Drew Carey Show, 2001, (voice only) The Adventures of Jimmy Neutron: Boy Genius, 2002, Family Guy, 2003, The Fairly Odd Parents, 2004; writer: (documentaries) Expelled: No Intelligence Allowed, 2008 Mem. Writers Guild Am., Screen Actors' Guild, Am. Fedn. TV and Radio Actors, Yale Club NYC, Friars, LA Athletic Club, Calif. Yacht Club, Morningside Country Club. Republican. Jewish. Office: 8787 Shoreham Dr West Hollywood CA 90069-2231 Office Phone: 310-652-9406. Personal E-mail: benstein@aol.com.

STEIN, CHRIS, musician; b. Bklyn., Jan. 5, 1950; m. Barbara Sicuranza, 1999; 1 child, Akira. Co-founder, guitarist Blondie, 1974—82, 1997—. Musician: (albums) Blondie, 1976, Plastic Letters, 1977, Parallel Lines, 1978, Eat to the Beat, 1979, Autoamerican, 1980, The Hunter, 1982, No Exit, 1999, Livid, 2000, The Curse of Blondie, 2004, Live, 2004, Best Live, 2005. Named to Rock and Roll Hall of Fame, 2006. Office: c/o 10th St Entertainment Ste G410 700 San Vicente Blvd West Hollywood CA 90069

STEIN, KARL N., plastic and reconstructive surgeon; b. Phila., July 1, 1940; BA in Chemistry, Temple U., 1962, MD, 1966. Diplomate Am. Bd. Plastic Surgery. Intern U. Pa. Grad. Hosp., 1966-67; resident in surgery Abington Meml. Hosp., 1967-68, SUNY Up-State Med. Ctr., 1970-71, instr. in surgery, 1970—; resident in plastic surgery Hosp. Albert Einstein Coll. Medicine, Bronx Mcpl. Hosp. Ctr., 1971-74, asst. instr. plastic surgery and hand surgery, 1974; pvt. practice in plastic surgery, 1974—. Surgeon Sherman Oaks (Calif.) Burn Ctr., 1975—; cons. L.A. Dept. Water and Power; med. legal expert for burns and plastic surgery; med. legal cons. Author (patent) Treatment of Tar Burns, 1980. Capt. USAF, 1969-71. Fellow Am. Coll. Surgeons; mem. AMA, Am. Soc. Plastic and Reconstructive Surgeons, Am. Burn Assn., Am. Soc. Aesthetic Plastic Surgery, Calif. Soc. Plastic Surgeons, Calif. Med. Assn., L.A. County Med. Assn. Office: PO Box 220340 Newhall CA 91322-0340 Office Phone: 661-255-5451.

STEIN, LAURA, lawyer, consumer products company executive; b. 1961; children: Amanda, Christopher. BA, Dartmouth Coll., 1983; JD, Harvard Law Sch., 1987; MA, Dartmouth Coll. Bar: Calif., 1987. Tracsactional corp. lawyer Morrison & Foerster, San Francisco; asst. gen. counsel, regulatory affairs The Clorox Co., Oakland, Calif., 1992—99; sr. v.p., gen. counsel H.J. Heinz Co., Pittsburgh, Pa., 2000—05, The Clorox Co., Oakland, Calif., 2005—. Dir. Franklin Resources, Inc. Mem.: Am. Soc. Corp. Sect., ABA (chmn. Commn. on Domestic Violence), Assn. Corp. Counsel (treas., mem. exec. com.), Calif. State Bar. Office: Clorox Co 1221 Broadway Oakland CA 94612-1888

STEIN, LAURENCE JAY, lawyer; b. West Hartford, Conn., Mar. 20, 1961; s. Milton and Selma (Roth) S.; m. Miriam Beth Siegel, Aug. 17, 1986. AB magna cum laude, Harvard Coll., 1982; JD, Stanford U.,

1985. Bar: Ill. 1986, Calif. 1999. Clk. to Chief Judge Walter J. Cummings U.S. Ct. Appeals (7th cir.), Chgo., 1985-86; assoc. Latham & Watkins, Chgo., 1986-92, partner, 1993-97, LA, 1997—, global chmn. Tax Dept., 2000—. Recipient Urban A. Sontheimer award Stanford U., 1985, John Harvard Scholarships, Harvard Coll., 1979-82. Mem. ABA, Calif. Bar Assn., Order of the Coif, Phi Beta Kappa. Avocation: golf. Office: Latham Watkins 355 S Grand Ave Los Angeles CA 90071-1560

STEIN, MICHAEL A., pharmaceutical executive; BSBA, Univ. Md. Ptnr. Arthur Andersen LLP, Washington; with Marriott Internat., Inc., Washington, 1989—98, CFO, 1993—98; exec. v.p., CFO Nordstrom Inc., 1998—2000; v.p., CFO ICOS Corp., Bothell, Wash., 2001—05, sr. v.p., CFO, 2005—. Trustee Fred Hutchinson Cancer rsch. Ctr.; bd. dir. Apartment Investment & Mgmt. Co., Getty Images Inc. Office: ICOS Corp 22021 20th Ave SE Bothell WA 98021

STEIN, SHERYL E., lawyer; b. Bklyn., Apr. 20, 1952; BA cum laude, Univ. Miami, 1974; JD, Southwestern Univ., 1978. Bar: Calif. 1979. Ptnr., office mng. ptnr., leader office Corp. & Securities practice sect. Pillsbury Winthrop Shaw Pittman, LA. Mem.: LA County Bar Found. (bd. mem.), LA County Bar Assn., Org. Women Exec. Office: Pillsbury Winthrop Shaw Pittman Suite 2800 725 S Figueroa St Los Angeles CA 90017 Office Phone: 213-488-7194. Office Fax: 213-629-1033. Business E-Mail: sheryl.stein@pillsburylaw.com.

STEINBERG, CHARLES ALLAN, electronics manufacturing company executive; b. Bklyn., June 7, 1934; s. Joseph and Rose (Graff) S.; m. Helen Greene, June 16, 1956; children— Ruth, Steven, Bruce. BSE.E., CCNY, 1955; MSE.E., M.I.T., 1958. Mem. tech. staff Bell Telephone Labs., Whippany, N.J., 1955; research and teaching asst. MIT, 1955-58; engring. sect. mgr. Airborne Instruments Lab. div. Eaton Corp., Deer Park, N.Y., 1958-63; exec. v.p. Ampex Corp., Redwood City, Calif., 1963-86, pres., chief exec. officer, 1986-88; pres. broadcast and profl. co. Sony Corp. Am., Montvale, N.J., 1988-99, sr. advisor San Jose, Calif., 1999—. Exec.-in-res. UC Davis, 2002. Contbr. numerous articles on med. electronics and diagnosis, info. systems to profl. jours.; patentee computer techniques in medicine. Bd. dirs. Santa Clara County (Calif.) United Fund, 1969-71. Mem. IEEE, CCNY Alumni Assn., M.I.T. Alumni Assn., Sigma Xi, Tau Beta Pi, Eta Kappa Nu. Office: Sony Electronics 1730 N 1st St San Jose CA 95112-4508

STEINBERG, DANIEL, preventive medicine physician, educator; b. Windsor, Ont., Can., July 21, 1922; came to US, 1922. s. Maxwell Robert and Bess (Krupp) S.; m. Sara Murdock, Nov. 30, 1946 (dec. July 1986); children: Jonathan Henry, Ann Ballard, David Ethan; m. Mary Ellen Stratthaus, Aug. 11, 1991; 1 stepchild: Katrin Seifert. BS with highest distinction, Wayne State U., Detroit, 1941, MD with highest distinction, 1944; PhD with distinction, Harvard U., Boston, 1951; MD (hon.), U. Gothenburg, Sweden, 1991. Intern Boston City Hosp., 1944-45; physician Detroit Receiving Hosp., 1945-46; instr. physiology Boston U. Sch. Medicine, 1947-48; joined USPHS, 1951, med. dir., 1959; research staff lab. cellular physiology and metabolism Nat. Heart Inst., 1951-53, chief sect. metabolism, 1956-61, chief of lab. metabolism, 1962-68; lectr. grad. program NIH, 1955, mem. sci. adv. com. ednl. activities, 1955-61, com. chmn., 1955-60; mem. metabolism study sect. USPHS, 1959-61; chmn. heart and lung research rev. com. B Nat. Heart, Lung and Blood Inst., 1977-79; vis. scientist Carlsberg Labs., Copenhagen, 1952-53, Nat. Inst. Med. Research, London, 1960-61, Rockefeller U., 1981; pres. Lipid Research Inc., 1961-64, adv. bd., 1964-73; prof. medicine Sch. Medicine, U. Calif., San Diego, 1968—2000, prof. emeritus, 2000—. Former editor Jour. Lipid Research; mem. editorial bd. Jour Clin. Investigation, 1969-74, Jour. Biol. Chemistry, 1980-84, Arteriosclerosis, 1980—; exec. editor Analytical Biochemistry, 1978-80; contbr. articles to profl. jours. Bd. dirs. Found. Advanced Edn. in Scis., 1959-68, pres., 1956-62, 65-67. Served to capt. M.C. AUS, World War II. Fellow, Am. Cancer Soc., 1950—51. Mem. Nat. Acad. Scis., AAAS, Am. Acad. Arts and Scis., Am. Heart Assn. (mem. exec. com. coun. on arteriosclerosis 1960-63, 65-73, chmn. coun. arteriosclerosis 1967-69), Fedn. Am. Scientists (exec. com. 1957-58), Am. Soc. Biol. Chemists, Am. Soc. Clin. Investigation, Assn. Am. Physicians, Am. Fedn. Clin. Rsch., Inst. Medicine, European Atherosclerosis Discussion Group, Alpha Omega Alpha. Home: 7742 Whitefield Pl La Jolla CA 92037-3810 Office: U Calif San Diego Dept Medicine 9500 Gilman Dr La Jolla CA 92093-0682 Home Phone: 858-454-0597; Office Phone: 858-534-0569. Personal E-mail: dsteinb1@san.rr.com. Business E-Mail: dsteinberg@ucsd.edu.

STEINBERG, DARRELL S., state legislator; b. San Francisco, Oct. 15, 1959; m to Julie; children: Jordana & Ari. BA, U. Calif., LA, 1981; JD, U. Calif., Davis, 1984. City coun, Sacramento, 6 years; California State Assemblyman, District 9, formerly, member, Labor & Employ, Appropriations, Health & Judiciary Committees, formerly, Select Committees on Jobs-Housing Balance & Mental Health, formerly, California State Assembly; California State Senator, District 6, 2006-, pres. pro tem., currently; Founder, Students Today Achieving Results for Tomorrow, 95; vice chairman, Army Depot Reuse Comn, formerly; board member, Sacramento Employ & Training Agency, Sacramento Air Quality Management District & Sacramento Transportation Authority, formerly; employees rights attorney, California State Employees Association, 10 years; atty. Hanson, Brigett, Marcus, Vlahos, and Rudy LLP, 2004-. Regional Transit (president, formerly, board director, currently); co-found Tahoe Park Neighborhood Association. Democrat. Office: State Capitol Rm 205 Sacramento CA 95814 also: Hanson Bridget LLP 980 9th St Ste 1500 Sacramento CA 95814 also: Dist 6 1020 N St Ste 578 Sacramento CA 95814 Office Phone: 916-651-4006, 916-324-4937. Office Fax: 916-327-8754; Home Fax: 916-323-2263. Business E-Mail: Senator.Steinberg@senate.ca.gov.

STEINBERG, LEIGH WILLIAM, sports agent; b. LA, 1949; 3 children. BA in Polit. Sci., UCLA, 1970; JD, U. Calif., Berkeley, 1973. Founder, ptnr. Steinberg, Moorad & Dunn, 1975—99; CEO Assante Sports Mgmt. Group, 1999—2003; founder, ptnr. Steinberg, Tollner & Moon, Newport Beach, Calif., 2003—. Co-author (with Michael D'Orso): Winning with Integrity: Getting What You Want Without Selling Your Soul, 1998. Office: 660 Newport Ctr Dr Ste 1000 Newport Beach CA 92660

STEINBOCK, JOHN THOMAS, bishop; b. LA, July 16, 1937; Student, LA Diocesan sems. Ordained priest Archdiocese of LA, Calif., 1963; ordained bishop, 1984; aux. bishop Diocese of Orange, 1984—87; bishop Diocese of Santa Rosa, 1987—91, Diocese of Fresno, 1991—. Roman Catholic. Office: Diocese of Fresno 1550 N Fresno St Fresno CA 93703-3788 Office Phone: 559-488-7400. Fax: 559-488-7464. E-mail: malanis@dioceseoffresno.org.

STEINEM, GLORIA, writer, editor, advocate; b. Toledo, Mar. 25, 1934; d. Leo and Ruth (Nuneviller) S.; granddaughter of suffragette Pauline Steinem; m. David Bale, Sept. 3, 2000 (dec. Dec. 30, 2003); step-son Christian Bale. BA in Govt., magna cum laude (hon.), Smith Coll., 1956; postgrad. (Chester Bowles Asian fellow), India, 1957-58; D. Human Justice, Simmons Coll., 1973, PhD (hon.). Co-dir., dir. ednl. found. Ind. Rsch. Svc., Cambridge, Mass. and NYC, 1959-60; contbg. editor Glamour Mag., NYC, 1962-69; co-founder, contbg. editor New York Mag., 1968-72; feminist lectr., 1969—; co-founder, editor Ms. Mag., 1971-87, columnist, 1980-87, cons. editor, 1987—. Active various civil rights and peace campaigns including United Farmworkers, Vietnam War Tax Protest, Com. for the Legal Def. of Angela Davis (treas., 1971-72); active polit. campaigns of Adlai Stevenson, Robert Kennedy, Eugene McCarthy, Shirley Chisholm, George McGovern; Co-founder, bd. dirs. Women's Action Alliance, 1970-2001, (now Feminist Majority Found.); co-founder, convenor, mem. nat. adv. com. Nat. Women's Polit. Caucus, 1971; co-founder, pres. bd. dirs. Ms. Found. for Women, 1972-1990; founding mem. Coalition of Labor Union Women, 1974, Pres. Voters for Choice, 1979; mem. Internat. Women's Year Commn., 1977, pres. Choice USA, co-founder, chmn. Liberty Media for Women, 1998 (current owner and operator Ms. mag); editorial cons., Conde Nast Publications, 1962-69, Curtis Publishing, 1964-65, Random House Publishing, 1988-, McCall Publishing. Author: The Thousand Indias, 1957, The Beach Book, 1963, Wonder Woman, 1972, Outrageous Acts and Everyday Rebellions, 1982, Marilyn: Norma Jeane, 1986, Revolution from Within: A Book of Self-Esteem, 1992; contbg. corr. NBC Today Show, 1987—88; author: Moving Beyond Words: Age, Rage, Sex, Power, Money, Muscles - Breaking the Boundaries of Gender, 1994; contbr. to various anthologies. Recipient Penney-Missouri Journalism award, 1970, Award for Journalism, Gov. Ohio, 1972, Bill of Rights award, ACLU of So. Calif., 1975, Mo. Honor Medal for Disting. Svc. in Journalism, U. Mo. Sch. Journalism, 2005; named Woman of Yr., McCall's mag., 1972; named to Nat. Women's Hall of Fame, 1993; Woodrow Wilson Internat. Ctr. for Scholars Fellow, 1977. Mem.: Author's Guild, Soc. Mag. Writers, Nat. Press Club, AFTRA, NOW, Phi Beta Kappa. Coined phrase "reproductive freedom" during 1972 nat. abortion debate. Office: MS Magazine 433 S Beverly Dr Beverly Hills CA 90212-4401 also: Choice USA 712 Hershey Ave Monterey Park CA 91755-1473

STEINER, FRANCES JOSEPHINE, conductor, musician, educator; b. Portland, Oreg., Feb. 25, 1937; d. Ferenz Joseph and Elizabeth (Levy) Steiner; m. Mervin Israel Tarlow, June 8, 1965; 1 child, Sarah Leah Tarlow. EdB with hon., Temple U., 1956; MusB, Curtis Inst. Music, 1956; student with Nadia Boulanger, France, 1957; MA, Radcliffe Coll., 1958; Mus D arts, U. So. Calif., 1969; student with Hans Beer, 1972—82. Tchr., orch. dir. Roosevelt Jr. HS, Phila., 1956, Brown Jr. HS, Malden, Mass., 1957—58; mem. faculty Newton Jr., Sr. HS, 1958—62; instr. Bklyn. Coll., 1962—65; mem. faculty Fullerton Jr. Coll., Calif., 1966—67; soloist Glendale Symphony, 1970—71; asst. prin. cellist Pasadena Symphony, 1970—71, L.A. Chamber Orch., 1970—73; prin. cellist Calif. Chamber Symphony, 1970—76; condr., music dir. Baroque Consortium Chamber Orch. (now named Chamber Orch. of the So. Bay), 1974—; mem. faculty Calif. State U., Dominguez Hills, 1967—2005, prof., 1975—2005, prof. emeritus, 2005—, chmn. Dept. Music, 1978—84; condr., music dir. Carson-Dominguez Hills Symphony Orch., 1977—; prin. cellist Glendale Symphony Orch., 1975—85, asst. condr. Calif., 1984—85. Guest condr. MIT Orch., Cambridge, Mass., 1980, Maracaibo Symphony, Venezuela, 1984, Nat. Symphony Orch. of Dominican Republic, Brevard (County) Symphony Orch., 1986, Bay Area Women's Philharm., 1986, Billings (Mont.) Symphony, 1987, Wis. Chamber Orch., Calif. All-State Honor Orch., 2005, Wis. Chamber Orch., 1994, Sofia Chamber Orch., Nizhny Nougorod, Russia, 2003. Co-editor: Introduction to Music, 1964; co-author (with Max Kaplan): Musicianship for the Classroom, 1966; arranger: menuets Six Minuets in Two Celli (Haydn), 1967. Recipient citation Nat. Fedn. Music Clubs, 1975—76, Elizabeth Mathias award, CSUDH Status of Women award, 1991, Mu Phi Epsilon award of merit; fellow Thomas Dana fellow, 1956—57; scholar, Temple U., 1952—56; Curtis Inst. Music scholar, 1945—56, Russell Kingman scholar, 1957. Mem.: Am. Symphony Orch. League, Condrs. Guild. Democrat. Jewish. Avocations: gourmet, wines. Home and Office: 21 La Vista Verde Dr Rancho Palos Verdes CA 90275 Business E-Mail: fsteiner@csudh.edu.

STEINER, GREG, Internet company executive; BS in Fin., U. Ill., Urbana-Champaign, 1990. With Interstate Consolidation Services; v.p. ops. Pacer Internat., 1990—99, NetFreight.com, 1999—2000; COO eHarmony.com, 2000—. Office: eHarmony PO Box 60157 Pasadena CA 91116 Office Phone: 626-795-4814.

STEINER, HENRY-YORK, English language and literature educator; b. Chgo., Mar. 12, 1932; s. Richard Morrow and Deborah (Lantz) S.; m. Margaret Gray, June 3, 1957 (div.); children: Anne Elizabeth, Edward Yagi, Riley Jane; m. Leonor Coleman Flores, Jan. 13, 1990. BA, Grinnell Coll., 1956; MA, Yale U., 1957; PhD, U. Oreg., 1963. Instr. Grinnell (Iowa) Coll., 1957-59, assoc. prof., assoc. dean faculty, 1964-68; instr. U. Oreg., Eugene, 1959-62; assoc. prof. Yankton (S.D.) Coll., 1959-62; dean undergrad. studies Ea. Wash. U., Cheney, 1968-77, prof. English, 1977—. Chmn. Wash. State Folklife Coun., Olympia, 1988-92. Editor: (autobiography) St. Peter & I, 1967, (anthology) 12 Poets, 1967; contbr. articles to profl. jours., including Internat. Edn. Chmn. Spokane (Wash.) Cmty. Action, 1971-76; bd. dirs. Expo '74, Spokane World's Fair, 1972-75; dir. 49 Degrees N. Ski Patrol, Chewelah, Wash., 1982-86, 97-2001; sect. chief Inland Empire Region Nat. Ski Patrol, Spokane, 1994-97, 01, dir. 2001--. Named Patroller of Yr., Inland Empire region Nat. Ski Patrol, 1998, Patrol Dir. of Yr., Pacific N.W. divsn., 1998; Fellow Yale U. and Ford Found., 1957. Mem. AAUP (sec. Wash. State coun. 1993-98), Nat. Ski Patrol (founding mem., Patroller Com., 2005—). Avocations: skiing, sailing, gardening. Home: 2627 W Gardner Ave Spokane WA 99201 Office: Ea Wash U Dept English Cheney WA 99004 Business E-Mail: hsteiner@mail.ewu.edu.

STEINER, HERBERT MAX, physics professor; b. Goeppingen, Germany, Dec. 8, 1927; came to U.S., 1939, naturalized, 1944; s. Albert and Martha (Epstein) S. BS, U. Calif., Berkeley, 1951, PhD, 1956. Physicist Lawrence Berkeley Lab., Berkeley, Calif., 1956—; mem. faculty U. Calif., Berkeley, 1958—, prof. physics, 1966-2000, prof. emeritus, 2000—, William H. McAdams prof. physics, chmn. dept., 1992-95; vis. scientist European Center Nuclear Research, 1960-61, 64, 68-69, 82-83, Max Planck Inst. Physics and Astrophysics, Munich, 1976-77; vis. prof. Japanese Soc. Promotion Sci., 1978. Vis. prof. physics U. Paris, 1989-90; vis. scientist Deutsches Electron Synchrotron Lab., 1995-96. Author articles in field. Served with AUS, 1946-47. Recipient Sr. Am. Scientist award Alexander von Humboldt Found., 1976-77; Guggenheim fellow, 1960-61 Fellow Am. Phys. Soc. Office: U Calif Berkeley Dept Physics 7300 Berkeley CA 94720-0001 Home Phone: 510-527-8692; Office Phone: 510-486-6805. Business E-Mail: steiner@lbl.gov.

STEINER, KENNETH DONALD, bishop; b. David City, Nebr., Nov. 25, 1936; s. Lawrence Nicholas and Florine Marie (Pieters) Steiner. BA, Mt. Angel Sem., 1958; MDiv, St. Thomas Sem., 1962. Ordained priest Archdiocese of Portland, Oreg., 1962, aux. bishop, 1978—, vicar clergy, 1978—80, clergy personnel dir., 1978—80, vicar worship & ministry, 1979—81, vicar sr. & infirm priests, 2002—, interim adminstr., 1995—96, 1997; assoc. pastor St. Monica Parish, Coos Bay, Oreg., 1962—67, St. Mary's Cathedral, Portland, 1967—70, St. Stephen Parish, Portland, 1970—72; pastor Holy Name Parish, Coquille, 1972-76, St. Francis Ch., Roy, 1976—78, St. Mary's Ch., Corvallis, 1987—2000, St. John the Baptist Parish, Milwaukie, 2000—02, St. Edward Parish, North Plains, 2002—; adminstr. St. Mary Parish, Vernonia, 1976—78, St. Mary's Ch., Corvallis, 1986—87; ordained bishop, 1978. Bd. dirs. Oreg. Cath. Conf., Portland. Mem. bd. Martha & Mary Home, Poulsbo, Wash. Democrat. Roman Catholic. Office: Archdiocesan Pastoral Ctr 2838 E Burnside St Portland OR 97214

STEINER, SAMUEL J., judge; BA, U. Wash., 1949, JD, 1951. Bar: Wash. Pvt. practice, Seattle, 1954-78; bankruptcy judge for western Wash., 1978—. With U.S. Army, 1951-54; mem. USAR, 1954-78. Home: 700 Stewart St Seattle WA 98101-1271

STEINMAN, LISA MALINOWSKI, English literature educator, writer; b. Willimantic, Conn., Apr. 8, 1950; d. Zenon Stanislaus and Shirley Belle Malinowski; m. James A. Steinman, Apr. 1968 (div. 1980); m. James L. Shugrue, July 23, 1984. BA, Cornell U., 1971, MFA, 1973, PhD, 1976. Asst. prof. English Reed Coll., Portland, Oreg., 1976-82, assoc. prof., 1982-90, prof., 1990—, Kenan prof. English lit. and humanities, 1993—. Cons. NEH, Washington, 1984—85. Author: Lost Poems, 1976, Made in America, 1987, All That Comes to Light, 1989, A Book of Other Days, 1992, Ordinary Songs, 1996, Masters of Repetition, 1998, Carslaw's Sequences, 2003, Invitation to Poetry, 2008; editor: Hubbub Mag., 1983—; mem. editl. bd. PMLA, 2006—09, Williams Rev., 1991—, Stevens Jour., 1994—; contbr. articles to profl. jours. Fellow Danforth Found., 1971-75, NEH, 1983, 96, 2006, Oreg. Arts Commn., 1983, Nat. Endowment for Arts, 1984; Rockefeller Found. scholar, 1987-88; recipient Pablo Neruda award, 1987, Oreg. Inst. Lit. Arts award, 1993. Mem. MLA, Poets and Writers, PEN (N.W. chpt., co-founder, officer 1989-93). Home: 5344 SE 38th Ave Portland OR 97202-4208 Office: Reed Coll Dept English 3203 SE Woodstock Blvd Portland OR 97202-8138 Business E-Mail: lisa.steinman@reed.edu.

STEINMANN, JOHN COLBURN, architect; b. Monroe, Wis., Oct. 24, 1941; s. John Wilbur and Irene Marie (Steil) S.; m. Susan Koslosky, Aug. 12, 1978 (div. July 1989); m. Genevieve Sim, Aug. 29, 1998. BArch, U. Ill., 1964; postgrad., Ill. Inst. Tech., 1970-71. Registered architect, Wash., Oreg., Calif., N.Mex., Ariz., Utah, Alaska, Wis., Ill., Hawaii. Project designer C.F. Murphy Assocs., Chgo., 1968-71, Steinmann Architects, Monticello, Wis., 1971-73; design chief, chief project architect State of Alaska, Juneau, 1973-78; project designer Mithun Assos., architects, Bellevue, Wash., 1978-80; owner, prin. John C. Steinmann Assos., Architect, Kirkland, Wash., 1980-94; supr. head facilities sect. divsn. fin. Dept. Edn. State of Alaska, Juneau, 1994-96; docs. mgr. Loschky Marquardt and Nesholm, Architects, Seattle, 1996-98; project mgr. Dept. Gen. Adminstrn. Divsn. Engring. and Archtl. Svsc., State of Wash., Olympia, 1998-99; project mgr. URS Architects, Seattle, 2000—04, RIM Architects, Honolulu, 2005—07, Architects Hawaii, Honolulu, 2007—. Bd. dirs. Storytell Internat.; lectr. Ill. Inst. Tech., 1971-72. Prin. works include Grant Park Music Bowl, Chgo., 1971, Menomonee Falls (Wis.) Med. Clinic, 1972, Hidden Valley Office Bldg., Bellevue, 1978, Kezner Office Bldg., Bellevue, 1979, The Pines at Sunriver, Oreg., 1980, also Phase II, 1984, Phase III, 1986, The Pines at Sunriver Lodge Bldg., 1986, 2d and Lenora highrise, Seattle, 1981, Bob Hope Cardiovascular Rsch. Inst. lab animal facility, Seattle, 1982, Wash. Ct., Bellevue, 1982, Anchorage Bus. Pk., 1982, Garden Townhouses, Anchorage, 1983, Vacation Internationale, Ltd. Corp. Hdqs., Bellevue, 1983, Vallarta Torres III, Puerto Vallarta, Mex., 1987, Torres Mazatlan (Mex.) II, 1988, Canterwood Townhouses, Gig Harbor Wash., 1988, Inn at Ceres (Calif.), 1989, Woodard Creek Inn, Olympia, Wash., 1989, Northgate Corp. Ctr., Seattle, 1990, Icicle Creek Hotel and Restaurant, Leavenworth, Wash., 1990, Bellingham (Wash.), Market Pl., 1990, Boeing Hot Gas Test Facility, Renton, Wash., 1991, Boeing Longacres Customer Svc. Tng. Ctr. Support Facilities, Renton, 1992, Boeing Comml. Airplane Group Hdqs., Renton, 1996, U. Wash./Cascade C.C., Bothell, 1999, Wash. State U., Pullman, Wash., Sea-Tac Airport Comm. Control Ctr., Seattle, 2000, McCarty, Internet Cafe and Residence Hall Renovation, U. Wash., Seattle, 2001, K'ima Med. Ctr. Dental Clinic, Hoopa, Calif., 2001, Sea-Tac Airport Flight Info. Mgmt. Sys., 2002; 600 Bed student housing, classroom, parking mixed use project, U. Idaho, Moscow, The Vegetable Bin, Seattle, 2004, Kona Coffee and Tea Plantation Visitors Ctr., Hawaii, 2006, Misawa Family Housing, Misawa, Japan, 2007, 1723 Kalakaua Mixed Use Condominium High Rise, Honolulu, 2008, 1830 Kapiolani Mixed Use Condominium High Rise, Honolulu, Laie Resort Hotel, Hawaii, 2009; also pvt. residences. Served to 1st lt. C.E., USAR, 1964-66, Vietnam. Decorated Bronze Star. Mem. AIA, Am. Mgmt. Assn., Nat. Coun. Archtl. Registration Bds., U. Wash. Yacht Club, Columbia Athletic Club, Alpha Rho Chi. Republican. Roman Catholic. Mailing: PO Box 2041 Honolulu HI 96805

STEINMETZ, SEYMOUR, pediatrician; b. Czechoslovakia, Oct. 6, 1934; arrived in U.S., 1947; s. Nathan and Gisela S. Steinmetz. BA, Yeshiva U., NYC, 1956; MD, Albert Einstein Coll. Medicine, Bronx, NY, 1960. Diplomate Am. Bd. Pediat. Intern UCLA Hosp., 1960-61, resident in pediat., 1961-62; chief resident in pediat. Montefiore Hosp., Bronx, 1964-65; fellow in child psychiatry Jacobi Hosp., Bronx, 1965-66; pvt. practice Great Neck, NY, 1966-74, Fremont (Calif.) Pediatric Med. Group, 1974—, pres., 1984—. With M.C. USAF, 1962—64. Fellow: Am. Acad. Pediat. Office: Fremont Pediatric Med Group 43971 Boscell Rd Fremont CA 94538 Office Phone: 510-979-0603.

STELCK, CHARLES RICHARD, geology educator; b. Edmonton, Alta., Can., May 20, 1917; s. Robert Ferdinand and Florella Maud (Stanbury) S.; m. Frances Gertrude McDowell, Apr. 24, 1945;

children: David, Brian, Leland, John (dec.). BSc, U. Alta., 1937, MSc, 1941, DSc (hon.), 2003; PhD, Stanford U., 1951. Registered profl. geologist Alta. Field geologist B.C. Dept. Mines, Victoria, Canada, 1939-41, Canol Project, Norman Wells, N.W.T., Canada, 1941-43, Imperial Oil Co., Calgary, Alta., 1943-49; from lectr. to prof. emeritus geology U. Alta., Edmonton, 1946—. Contbr. numerous articles principally on biostratigraphy of Cretaceous to sci. publs. Decorated officer Order of Can.; recipient Disting. Educator award Am. Assn. Petroleum Geologists, 2001, Queen's Golden Jubilee medal, 2002, Alberta Centenial medal, 2005; named to Can. Petroleum Hall Fame, 2005. Fellow Royal Soc. Can.; mem. Assn. Profl. Engrs., Geologists and Geophysicists Alta. (Centennial award 1979), Geol. Assn. Can. (Logan medal 1982), Geol. Soc. Am., Can. Soc. Petroleum Geologists (Douglas medal 1994, Stanley Slipper gold medal 2002), Order of Can. (officer 1997). Conservative. Office: U Alta Dept Earth & Atmospheric Scis Edmonton AB Canada T6G 2E3

STELL, JOE M., JR., state legislator; b. Wilson, Tex., June 15, 1928; s. Joe M. Sr. and Mary Louise (Stiles) S.; m. Verna Jeanne Renfro, Aug. 30, 1948; children: James William, Cathy Jeanne Stell Kinzer, Jo Beth Stell Hawk, Linda Lee. BS, U. N.Mex., 1950; MS, Western N.Mex. U., 1956; postgrad., N.Mex. State U., Ea. N.Mex. U., 1960-80. Tchr., coach Deming (N.Mex.) Pub. Schs., 1950-53, Carlsbad (N.Mex.) Mcpl. Schs., 1953-86; rancher, farmer Eddy County, Carlsbad, 1955—; mem. dist. 54 N.Mex. Ho. Reps., Carlsbad and Artesia, 1986—. Bd. dirs. Eddy County Soil and Water Conservation, Carlsbad, 1986; active Mountain States Legal Found., Denver, 1980, Eddy County Sheriff's Posse, Carlsbad, 1986. Named Outstanding Legislator, N.Mex. Farm and Livestock Bur., 1992. Mem. NEA, N.Mex. Cattle Growers, S.E. N.Mex. Grazing Assn., Elks, Carlsbad Sportsman Club. Democrat. Methodist. Avocations: trout fishing, horseback packing. Office: Hat Bar Ranch 22 Colwell Ranch Rd Carlsbad NM 88220-2503

STELLWAGEN, ROBERT HARWOOD, biochemistry professor; s. Harwood John and Alma Dorothy S.; m. Joanne Kovacs, June 15, 1963; children: Robert Harwood, Alise Anne. AB, Harvard U., 1963; PhD, U. Calif., Berkeley, 1968. Staff fellow NIH, Bethesda, Md., 1968-69; postdoctoral scholar U. Calif., San Francisco, 1969-70; asst. prof. biochemistry, molecular biology U. So. Calif., LA, 1970-74, assoc. prof., 1974-80, prof., 1980—2008, chmn. dept., 1981-86, vice chmn. dept., 1993—2006, emeritus prof., 2008—. Vis. scientist Nat. Inst. for Med. Rsch., Mill Hill, Eng., 1979. Contbr. articles to profl. jours. Recipient Henderson prize Harvard U., 1963; NSF fellow, 1963-67; NIH grantee, 1971-84. Mem. Sierra Club, Phi Beta Kappa. Democrat. Office: U So Calif Keck Sch Medicine 1333 San Pablo St Los Angeles CA 90089-9151 Home Phone: 805-532-9986; Office Phone: 323-442-1149. Business E-Mail: stellwag@usc.edu.

STELMAR, WAYNE J., building company executive; m. Lisa Stelmar; children: Danielle, Katy, Brian. BA in Bus. Adminstrn., Calif. State U., Northridge. CPA, lic. corp. broker, Ca. Sr. mgr. EY Kenneth Leventhal Real Estate Group, LA; mgr. Grant Thorton, LA; contr. Watt Industries, Inc., Santa Monica, 1988-90, CFO, 1990-94, 1994-98, WL Homes, Inc., 1998—. Mem. Am. Inst. CPA, Ca. Soc. CPA.

STENCHEVER, MORTON ALBERT, obstetrician, gynecologist; b. Paterson, NJ, Jan. 25, 1931; s. Harold and Lena (Suresky) Stenchever; m. Diane Bilsky, June 19, 1955 (dec. 1999); children: Michael A., Marc R., Douglas A.; m. Luba Kane, Sept. 8, 2001. AB, NYU, 1951; MD, U. Buffalo, 1956. Diplomate Am. Bd. Ob-gyn., 1965, recertified 1986. Intern Mt. Sinai Hosp., 1956-57; resident obstetrics and gynecology Columbia-Presbyn. Med. Center, NYC, 1957-60; asst. prof., Oglebey research fellow Case-Western Res. U., Cleve., 1962-66, asso. prof. dept. reproductive biology, 1967-70, dir. Tissue Culture Lab., 1965-70, coordinator Phase II Med. Sch. program, 1969-70; prof., chmn. dept. obstetrics-gynecology U. Utah Med. Sch., Salt Lake City, 1970-77; prof. ob-gyn. U. Wash. Sch. Medicine, Seattle, 1977-98; prof. emeritus, 1998—; chmn. dept. U. Wash. Sch. Medicine, Seattle, 1977-96. Chmn. test com. for ob-gyn. Nat. Bd. Med. Examiners, 1979-82; cons. in urogynecology Fedn. Internat. for Gynecology & Obstetrics, 1998—. Author: Labor: Workbook in Obstetrics, 1968, Labor: Workbook in Obstetrics, 2d edit., 1993, Human Sexual Behavior: A Workbook in Reproductive Biology, 1970, Human Cytogenics: A Workbook in Reproductive Biology, 1973, Introductory Gynecology: A Workbook in Reproductive Biology, 1974; co-author: Comprehensive Gynecology, 1987, Comprehensive Gynecology, 4th edit., 2001, Caring for the Older Woman, 1991, Health Care for the Older Woman, 1996, Office Gynecology, 1992, Office Gynecology, 2d edit., 1996, Good Health, Great Sex After 40: A Woman's Guide, 1997; sr. editor: Atlas of Gynecology, 5 vols., 1997—99, assoc. editor: Ob-Gyn., 1986—2001, Ob-Gyn. Survey; editor: Clinical Updates in Women's Health Care, 2001—, ACOG Clin. Review, 2001—; mem. editl. bd.: Western Jour. Medicine; contbr. articles to profl. jours. Served to capt. USAF, 1960-62. Fellow Am. Coll. Obstetricians and Gynecologists (com. on residency edn. 1974-80, learning resource commn. 1980-86, vice chmn. 1982-83, chmn. prolog self-assessment program 1982-86, vice chair com. health care for the underserved women 1995-97), Am. Assn. Obstetricians and Gynecologists, Am. Gynecol. Soc., Am. Gyencol. and Obstetrical Soc., Pacific Coast Ob-Gyn. Soc.; mem. AAAS, AMA, Am. Bd. Ob-Gyn. (bd. dir. 1988-2004, v.p. 1990-92, treas. 1992-96, chmn. 1996-98, mem. resident rev. com. 1993-97, chmn. divsn. female pelvic medicine/reconstructive surgery), Assn. Profs. Gynecology and Obstetrics (chmn. steering com. teaching methods in ob-gyn. 1970-79, v.p. 1975-76, pres. 1983-84, v.p. Found. 1986-87, pres. Found. 1987-91), Pacific N.W. Ob-Gyn. Soc., Wash. State Med. Assn., Seattle Gynec. Soc. (v.p. 1981, pres.-elect 1982, pres. 1982-83), Am. Soc. Human Genetics, Ctrl. Assn. Ob-Gyn., Soc. Gynecologic Investigation, Wash. State Obstet. Soc., Tissue Culture Assn., N.Y. Acad. Sci., Utah Ob-Gyn. Soc., Utah Med. Assn., Teratology Soc., Am. Fertility Soc., Internat. Pelvic Floor Dysfunction Soc. Home: 8301 SE 83rd St Mercer Island WA 98040-5644 Office: Ob-Gyn 130 Knickerson St Ste 211 Seattle WA 98109 Office Phone: 206-286-1775. Business E-Mail: mstenchever@acog.org.

STENGEL, JOSEPH P., former state legislator; b. Denver, Apr. 8, 1954; m. Bettye Stengel; children: Jeffrey, Tyler. BS in Econs., We. State Coll., 1976; postgrad., Denver U. Cert. pvt. pilot. State rep. dist. 38 Colo. Ho. of Reps., Denver, 1998—2007, chair fin. com., mem. appropriations and judiciary coms. Mem.: AOPA, NRA, Civil Air Patrol, Interfaith Task Force, Littleton Rotary, Fraternal Order of Old Goats. Republican. Presbyterian. Avocations: gardening, hunting, flying.

STENMARK, KURT R., medical educator, researcher; b. Denver, Sept. 2, 1951; s. Carle E. and Margaret Stenmark; m. Sandra Hoyt Hoyt; children: Matthew Hoyt, Spencer Morgan. BS, U. Colo., Boulder, 1973. Cert. U. Colo., 1977. Prof. pediat. U. Colo., Denver, 1994—, prof. medicine, 1994—. Dir. critical care and cardiovasc. pulmonary rsch. U. Colo., 1987—2008. Contbr. scientific papers to profl. jour. Scor, NIH, 1993—2008. Mem.: Am. Thoracic Soc. (bd. dirs.). Achievements include research in lung development. Office: Univ Colo Denver Health Sci Ctr 4200 e 9th Ave Denver CO 80262 Office Fax: 303-315-8353. Business E-Mail: kurt.stenmark@uchsc.edu.

STENNETT, WILLIAM CLINTON (CLINT), state legislator, entrepreneur; b. Winona, Minn., Oct. 1, 1956; s. William Jessie and Carole Lee Stennett; m. Michelle Stennett. BA in Journalism, Idaho State U., 1979. Gen. mgr. Wood River Jour., Hailey, Idaho, 1979-85, pres., pub., 1985-87; pres. Sta. KSVT-TV, Ketchum, Idaho, Sta. KSKI-FM, Sun Valley, Idaho; mem. Idaho House of Reps., Boise, 1990-94; mem. Dist. 25 Idaho State Senate, Boise, 1996—, minority leader, 1996—. Recipient Gen. Excellence award, Idaho Newspaper Assn., 1985, 1986—87; named Legislator of Yr., Idaho Soil Conservation Dists., 1994, Idaho Wildlife Found., 1996, Idaho Assn. Recyclers, 2002, Idaho Profl. Firefighters Assn., 2002. Mem.: Idaho Broadcasters (bd. dirs.), Ketchum Sun Valley C. of C. (bd. dirs. 1990—95), Rotary. Democrat. Office: Dist 25 PO Box 475 Ketchum ID 83340 Office Phone: 208-726-8106. Business E-Mail: stennett@senate.idaho.gov.*

STENSTROM, MICHAEL KNUDSON, civil engineering educator; b. Anderson, SC, Nov. 28, 1948; s. Edward Farnum and Virginia Frances (Garrett) S.; m. Linda Ann Moxley, Aug. 15, 1974 (div. Nov. 1976); m. Margaret Merle Allen, Jan. 13, 1977 (div. Apr. 1994). BSEE, Clemson U., 1971, MS in Environ. Engring., 1972, PhD in Environ. Engring., 1976. Registered profl. engr., Calif. Project mgr. Amoco Oil Co., Naperville, Ill., 1975—77; asst. prof. civil engring. UCLA, 1977—81, assoc. prof., 1981—84, prof., 1984—, dir. Engring. Computer Ctr., 1985—89, asst. dean, 1989—92, chair dept. civil engring., 1991—98, assoc. dean, 2001—03. Cons. in field. Contbr. articles to profl. jours. Chmn. sci. adv. bd. Heal-the-Bay, L.A., 1987-88. With USAF, 1969-70. Recipient numerous grants. Mem. ASCE (Walter L. Huber award 1989), Am. Acad. Environ. Engrs., Assn. Environ. Engring. Profs., Water Environ. Fedn. (Harrison Prescott Eddy medal 1992, Calif. EPA Water Quality Protection award, 2002, 05), Internat. Assn. on Water Quality, Am. Chem. Soc., Blue Key, Sigma Xi, Tau Beta Pi. Democrat. Avocations: photography, amateur radio. Home: 3032 Motor Ave Los Angeles CA 90064 Office: UCLA 5714 Boelter Hall Los Angeles CA 90095-1593 Office Phone: 310-825-1408. Business E-Mail: stenstro@seas.ucla.edu.

STEP, EUGENE LEE, retired pharmaceutical executive; b. Sioux City, Iowa, Feb. 19, 1929; s. Harry and Ann (Keiser) S.; m. Hannah Scheuermann, Dec. 27, 1953; children: Steven Harry, Michael David, Jonathan Allen. BA in Econs., U. Nebr., 1951; MS in Acctg. and Fin., U. Ill., 1952. With Eli Lilly Internat. Corp., London and Paris, 1964-69, dir. Elanco Internat. Indpls., 1969-70, v.p. marketing, 1970-72, v.p. Europe, 1972; v.p. mktg. Eli Lilly and Co., Indpls., 1972-73, pres. pharm. div., 1973-86, exec. v.p., 1986—. Bd. dirs. Cell-Genesys. 1st lt. U.S. Army, 1953-56. Mem. Pharm. Mfrs. Assn. (bd. dirs. 1980-92, chmn. 1989-90), Internat. Pharm. Mfrs. Assn. (pres. 1991-92). Home: PO Box 8997 Rancho Santa Fe CA 92067-8997 Office Phone: 858-759-8958.

STEPHENS, ALBERT LEE, JR., federal judge; b. LA, Feb. 14, 1913; m. Barbara, Sept. 29, 1939; 2 children. AB, U. So. Calif., 1936, LLB, 1938. Bar: Calif. 1939, U.S. Dist. Ct. Nev. 1939. Pvt. practice, LA, 1939-43, 46-59; judge Superior Ct., LA, 1959-61; now sr. judge U.S. Dist. Ct. (ctrl. dist.) Calif. Mem. legal profession panel U. So. Calif. Law Sch., 1961-65; lectr. UCLA Law Sch., 1954-55; sponsor, chair Dist. Judges Seminar (9th cir.), 1964-66. Lt. USNR, 1943-46, WWII. Nominated for appt. in 1961 by Pres. Kennedy. Mem. ABA, Calif. Bar Assn., L.A. County Bar Assn., Am. Jud. Soc., Jud. Conf. U.s. (trial practice and technique com.), U.S. Dist. Judges Assn. 9th Cir., Maritime Law Assn., U.s. Lawyers Club L.A., Chancery Club (pres. 1959). Office: US Dist Ct 232 S June St Los Angeles CA 90004-1046

STEPHENS, AMY, state legislator; m. Ron Stephens; 1 child, Nicholas. BA, Calif. State U., Fullerton. Pub. policy & youth cultural specialist Focus on the Family, 1991—2001; founder, dir. Fresh Ideas Comm. & Cons.; mem. Dist. 20 Colo. House of Reps., 2007—, minority caucus chmn. Mem. Human Rels. Commn. Contbr. opinion editorials to newspapers including USA Today, The NY Times, LA Times, Washington Times, Washington Post, Denver Post, The Rocky Mountain News, others, articles to magazines including In Touch, Focus on the Family, others. Appointee Gov. Task Force on the Welfare of Children; Colo. del. Rep. Nat. Convention, 1996, 2004. Republican. Office: Colo State Capitol 200 E Colfax Rm 271 Denver CO 80203 Office Phone: 303-866-2924. Business E-Mail: amy.stephens.house@state.co.us.*

STEPHENS, BOB, electronics executive; Pres., CEO Adaptec, Inc., Milpitas, Calif. Office: Adaptec Inc 691 S Milpitas Blvd Milpitas CA 95035-5484

STEPHENS, DONALD R(ICHARDS), investor; b. San Francisco, June 28, 1938; s. Donald Lewis and Anona Marie (O'Leary) S.; m. Christina Brinkman, Sept. 11, 1971 (div. 1996); m. Patricia Hamilton, Oct. 21, 2000; children: Lane B., Justin H., Nicholas W., Adam H. BS, U. So. Calif., 1961; JD, Hastings Coll., 1969. Pres. Campodonico & Stephens, San Francisco, 1963-65; pres., owner Union Investment Co., San Francisco, 1966-69; assoc. Law Offices of Louis O. Kelso, 1969-72; pres. D.R. Stephens & Co., San Francisco, 1972—; mng. ptnr. Stephens & Stephens, San Francisco, 1999—. Chmn., bd. dirs., CEO Bank of San Francisco Co., 1978-91; chmn., bd. dirs. N.Am. Trust REIT; bd. dirs. Am. Inst. for Fgn. Study, Charles Schwab Family of Funds Inc. Bd. dirs. Bay Area Coun.; trustee St. Francis Meml. Hosp., San Francisco, 1976-82; mem. policy adv. bd. U. Calif., 1985—. Mem. Urban Land Inst., World Bus. Coun., Bohemian Club, Reserve Palm Desert, Napa Valley Reserve. Republican. Presbyterian. Avocations: tennis, bridge. Business E-Mail: info@drstephens.com, drstephens@drstephens.com.

STEPHENS, ELISA, college president; d. Richard A. Stephens; married; 1 child. BA, Vassar Coll.; JD, U. San Francisco, 1985. Law clk. San Francisco Superior Ct., Calif., 1985—86; in-house counsel Cellular Holdings, Inc., 1987—88, Acad. of Art Coll., San Francisco, 1989—92, pres., 1992—. Contbg. editor Barclays Law Publishers, 1986—88. Bd. dirs. Am. Red Cross Bay Area Chpt., San Francisco Lyric Opera. Mem.: Royal Soc. Arts, Assn. Rewards for Coll. Scientists, Nob Hill Assn. (pres. 2003—05), San Francisco Jr. League, San Francisco Rotary Club, Univ. Club, Met. Club, San Francisco City Club, Young Pres. Orgn., Calif. Bar Assn. Office: 79 New Montgomery St 6th Fl San Francisco CA 94105-3410

STEPHENS, MARTIN R., state official; b. Ogden, Utah, Mar. 26, 1954; m. Carole Stephens. BSin Bus. Administrn., Webder State U. Mayor Farr West City, Utah, 1986-88; mem. hos. reps. State of Utah, 1988—, house speaker, 1999—. Coun. mem. Farr West City, 1984-85, vice chair Weber Area Coun. of Govts., 1986-87, chair, 1988, elected Utah rep. White House Conf. Small Bus., Washington, 1986, majority leader, 1993-94, chair legis. mgmt. com., judiciary standing com., govt. ops. standing com., retirement com., exec. appropriations com. (chair 1993-94), commerce and revenue appropriations com., 1999—. Recipient Roy B. Gibson Freedom of Information award Soc. Profl. Journalists, 1991. Office: Utah Legis 318 State Capitol Salt Lake City UT 84114 also: 3159 N Higley Rd Farr West UT 84404-9380

STEPHENS, MICHAEL DEAN, hospital administrator; b. Salt Lake City, May 1, 1942; married. B, Columbia U., 1966, MHA, 1970. Adminstrv. resident Mt. Sinai Med. Ctr., NYC, 1969-70; asst. adminstr. Greenville (S.C.) Gen. Hosp., 1970-71, assoc. adminstr., 1971-72, adminstr., 1972-75; pres., ceo. Hoag Meml. Hosp.-Presbyn., Newport Beach, Calif., 1975—. Trustee Am. Hosp. Assn. Recipient Citizen of the Yr., Newport Chamber of Comm., 1995, Excellence in Leadership award, Leadership Tomorrow, 1996. Mem. Am. Coll. Healthcare Execs. Home: 900 Alder Pl Newport Beach CA 92660-4121 Office: Hoag Meml Hosp Presbyn 1 Hoag Blvd PO Box 6100 Newport Beach CA 92658-6100

STEPHENS, ROBERT, horticulturist; m. Julie Packard. Grad. in Computer Sci., UCSC. Former pres. Santa Cruz Natural History Museum; owner, gen. mgr. Elkhorn Native Plant Nursery. Former chmn. Audubon Calif. Bd. dirs. David and Lucile Packard Found.; adv. bd. mem. O'Neill Sea Odyssey, Elkhorn Slough Found.; trustee Future of Children, Los Altos. Named Man of the Yr., Santa Cruz Chamber of Commerce, 1999. Office: Elkhorn Native Plant Nursery 1957B Highway 1 Moss Landing CA 95039-9629

STEPHENS, SHAND SCOTT, lawyer; b. Pasadena, Calif., Mar. 25, 1949; s. Elmer Shand and Gladys Joy (Baker) S.; m. Marcia Pizzo, July 25, 1982 (div. Dec. 1985); m. Kieran Candy, Feb. 6, 1999; children: Sofia, Shannon, Shand BA, Yale U., 1971; JD, U. Calif., San Francisco, 1975. Bar: Calif. 1975, U.S. Dist. Ct. (no., so., ea. and cen. dists.) Calif. 1975, U.S. Ct. Appeals (8th, 9th, 11th cir.) 1975. Assoc. Bronson, Bronson & McKinnon, San Francisco, 1978-82, ptnr., 1982—93; counsel Aon Corp., Nat. Litigation, 1993—2004; ptnr. DLA Piper Rudnick Gray Cary US, LLP, 2004—. Gen. counsel San Francisco State U. Found., 1987-93; gen. counsel Westamerica Bank, San Rafael, Calif., 1987-93; bd. dirs. Russian Art Found., Kydsncars. Recipient Calif. Lawyer of Yr. award, 1998; named No. Calif. Super Lawyer, 2005, So. Bay Area Best Lawyer, 2005. Mem. ABA, Calif. Bar Assn., Order of Coif. Avocations: american civil war history and archaeology, skiing, tennis. Home Phone: 415-435-2606; Office Phone: 415-615-6028. Business E-Mail: shand.stephens@dlapiper.com.

STEPHENSON, ARTHUR EMMET, JR., investment company executive; b. Bastrop, La., Aug. 29, 1945; s. Arthur Emmet and Edith Louise Stephenson; m. Toni Lyn Edwards, June 17, 1967; 1 child, Tessa. BS in Fin. magna cum laude, La. State U., 1967; MBA (Ralph Thomas Sayles fellow), Harvard U., 1969. Chartered fin. analyst. Adminstrv. aide to U.S. Sen. Russell Long of La., Washington, 1966; security analyst Fidelity Funds, Boston, 1968; sr. ptnr. Stephenson Ventures; founder, chmn. Gen. Comm., Inc., Denver; founder, chmn. bd. dirs. StarTek, Inc., 1987—2006. Bd. dirs. Danaher Corp., 1986—2008; founder Charter Bank and Trust, chmn., 1980—91; mem. adv. bd. First Berkshire Fund, 1984—2002, Capital Resources Ptnrs., L.P., 1987—2004; former pub. Law Enforcement Product News, Colo. Book, Pub. Safety Product News, 1990—98, Denver mag., Denver Bus. mag.; founder Stephenson Disaster Mgmt. Inst., La. State U.; bd. dean's adv. Bus. Sch. Harvard U., 2006—. Del. White House conf., 1980; past. nat. trustee Nat. Symphony Orch., John F. Kennedy Ctr. Performing Arts, 1995—98; past mem. nat. steering com. Norman Rockwell Mus., Stockbridge, Mass.; past mem. Colo. Small bus. Coun.; past mem. assocs. coun. Templeton Coll., Oxford (Eng.) U. Recipient Hall of Fame award, Inc. mag., 1994, Albert Einstein Tech. medal, 1999; named to Hall of Distinction, Coll. Bus. Adminstrn., La. State U., 1999, La. State U., 2006. Mem.: Young Pres. Orgn. (chpt. chmn. 1992—93), Colo. Investment Advisors Assn. (treas., bd. dirs. 1975—76), World Pres.'s Orgn., Chief Execs. Orgn., Harvard U. Bus. Sch. Assn. (internat. pres. 1987—88), So. Calif. Harvard Bus. Sch. Club, Jonathan Club (L.A.), Thunderbird Country Club (Rancho Mirage, Calif.), Colo. Harvard Bus. Sch. Club (pres. 1980—81, chmn. 1981—82), Delta Sigma Pi, Kappa Sigma, Beta Gamma Sigma, Phi Kappa Phi, Omicron Delta Kappa. Office: 400 Nevada Way Boulder City NV 89005

STEPHENSON, HERMAN HOWARD, retired banker; b. Wichita, Kans., July 15, 1929; s. Herman Horace and Edith May (Wayland) S.; m. Virginia Anne Ross, Dec. 24, 1950, (dec. March 2004); children: Ross Wayland, Neal Bevan, Jann Edith. BA, U. Mich., 1950; JD with distinction, U. Mo., Kansas City, 1958, LLD (hon.), 1993. Bar: Kans. 1958. With City Nat. Bank, Kansas City, Mo., 1952-54, City Bond & Mortgage Co., Kansas City, 1954-59, Bank of Hawaii, Honolulu, 1959-94, CEO, 1989-94, ret. chmn., 1994—. Bd. dirs. Friends of Cancer Rsch. Ctr. Hawaii. With US Army, 1950—52. Mem.: Pacific Forum/CSIS (bd. govs.), Navy League U.S., Waialae Country Club, Oahu Country Club, Eagle Bend Country Club, Rotary, Pi Eta Sigma, Kappa Sigma.

STEPHENSON, LARRY KIRK, geography educator, financial planner; b. Seattle, Sept. 22, 1944; s. Norman Eugene and Virginia Dare (Frost) S.; m. Margery Alsever, Aug. 15, 1992 (dec. Sept. 2006); children: Matthew Alan, Leah Anela. BS, Ariz. State U., 1966, MA, 1971; PhD, U. Cin., 1973. Manpower rsch. analyst Employment Security Commn. of Ariz., 1969-70; asst. prof. geography U. Hawaii, Hilo, 1973-76, assoc. prof., 1976-78, chmn. dept. geography, 1975-77; planner Ariz. Dept. Health Svcs., Phoenix, 1978-84; strategic planner City of Glendale, Ariz., 1984-92; pub. health analyst Gila River Indian Cmmty., Ariz., 1992-98, econ. devel. planner, 1998—2005; exec. dir. Eastern Ariz. Counties Orgn., 2006—. Vis. lectr. dept. geography Ariz. State U., 1978, adj. assoc. prof., 1979—; vis. assoc. prof. dept. geography, area devel. and urban planning U. Ariz., 1978; faculty U. Phoenix, 1979—; adj. prof. Golden Gate U., 1981—, Coll. St. Francis,

1982—; ptnr. Urban Rsch. Assocs., Phoenix, 1981—; faculty Troy State U., 1990-. Author: Statistics for Health Managers, 1981; co-author: Student Study Guide and Instructor's Manual to accompany Geography: A Modern Synthesis, 4 edits., 1975-83; editor: Kohala keia: Collected Expressions of a Community, 1977; contbr. articles to profl. jours., chpts. to textbooks. Active. Hawaii Island Health Planning Coun., 1974-78, Glendale Cmty. Colls. Pres.'s Coun., 1986-92. With US Army, 1966-68. NDEA fellow 1971-72. Mem. Am. Inst. Cert. Planners, Am Planning Assn., Assn. Am. Geographers, Ariz. Planning Assn. (pres. 1987—), SW Profl. Geog. Assn., Lambda Alpha, Gila County CC Dist. (Ariz.) (mem. governing bd. 2004-). Unitarian Universalist. Home: HC 4 Box 28K Payson AZ 85541 Office: PO Box 2010 Payson AZ 85547 Office Phone: 928-972-5378. Personal E-mail: lstephe739@aol.com.

STEPNER, MICHAEL JAY, architect; b. Chgo., Aug. 7, 1940; s. Lester Harry and Florence (Addison) S.; m. Rosemary Reiser, Apr. 2, 1965; children: Rachel, Jessica, Adam, Joshua, Rebekah. Student, U. Minn., 1961-62; BArch, U. Ill., 1964; postgrad., U. Calif., Berkeley, 1971, U.S. Navy Engring. Schs., 1965-66. Registered architect, Calif. Urban designer, planner Crosstown Assocs., Chgo., 1968-71; urban designer, planner planning dept. City of San Diego, 1971-81, asst. planning dir., 1981-88, acting planning dir., 1987-88, city architect, 1988-92, asst. to city mgr., spl. projects coord., 1992-94, city urban design coord., 1984—97; pvt. practice The Stepner Design Group, San Diego; dean New Sch. Arch. and Design, 1997—2001. Vis. critic in urban design U. Ill, Chgo., 1970-71, San Diego State U. Grad. Sch. Planning and Pub. Adminstrn., Urban Design & Site Planning Inst., 1974-85; lectr. Urban Conservation Grad. Sch. History, U. San Diego, 1978, 81, 82, 84; asst. prof., lectr., design critic New Sch. Arch. and Design, San Diego City U., 1988—, prof. arch. and urban design; faculty assoc. for transp. and land use planning Lincoln Inst. Land Policy, Cambridge, Mass., 1993—; former mem. hist. bldg. code bd. State of Calif.; peer profl. Federal Govt. Design Excellence Program, 2002-04; mem., dir. Community Planning and Design Ctr., San Diego, 1971-74; mem. faculty New Sch. Arch. and Design.; mem. post licensure competency task force Calif. Archtl. Registration Bd. Bd. dirs. Citizens Coordinate for Century III, 1991—; mem. Regional Urban Design Assistance Team, Seattle, Washington, and Liverpool, Eng.; past bd. dirs. Californians for Preservation Action; mem. Congress for the New Urbanism; mem. Calif. State Bd. Arch. Exams, 1999; peer profl. Fed. Ct. Fed. Design Excellence Program, 2002-04. Recipient Leadership in Planning award New Sch. Architecture, 1992, Gaslamp Pioneer award San Diego Gaslamp Quarter Found., 1993, Ellen and Roger Revelle award Citizens Coordinate for Century III, 1993. Fellow AIA (co-chair housing assistance team City of Washincton, 1990, bd. dirs. San Diego chpt. 1976-78, 94-95, 97—, pres-elect 2001, mem. nat. urban design com., past mem. Calif. coun., hist. preservation-urban conservation com., urban design commr. San Diego chpt. 1975-76, Spl. award for Excellence in Govt. 1983), Am. Inst. Cert. Planners, Inst. for Urban Design; mem. Am. Planning Assn. (Disting. Leadership award Calif. chpt. 1991), San Diego Fed. Courthouse Design Team (selection panel), Urban Land Inst., Lambda Alpha. Home: 4260 Hortensia St San Diego CA 92103-1105 Office: 3620 30th St Ste B San Diego CA 92104 Office Phone: 619-234-2112. Business E-Mail: stepner1@pacbell.net.

STERBA, JEFFRY E., energy executive; BA in Econ. summa cum laude, Washington Univ., St. Louis; post-grad study in Econ., Washington Univ., Univ. N.Mex. Various positions PNM (subs. PNM Resources), Albuquerque, 1977—98; exec. v.p. USEC, Md., 1998—2000; pres. PNM (subs. PNM Resources), Albuquerque, 2000; chmn., pres., CEO PNM Resources, Albuquerque, 2000—08, chmn., CEO, 2008—. Chmn. Edison Elec. Inst., 2007—, Elec. Power Rsch. Inst. Former campaign chmn. United Way Ctrl. N. Mex.; mem. Gov. Bus. Adv. Coun.; bd. dir. US C. of C.; co-chmn. Albuquerque Econ. Forum. Mem.: Mortar Board, Omicron Delta Kappa. Office: PNM Resources Alvarado Sq Albuquerque NM 87158-0001 Office Phone: 505-241-4568. Office Fax: 505-241-2368. Business E-Mail: jeff.sterba@pnmresources.com.*

STERLING, DONALD T., real estate mogul, professional sports team owner; b. Chgo., 1934; m. Shelly Stein, 1957; 3 children. BA, Calif. State U., LA; JD, Southwestern U. Sch. Law, LA. Owner NBA LA (formerly San Diego) Clippers, 1981—, chmn. bd. Bd. govs. NBA. Founder Donald T. Sterling Charitable Foundation. Office: LA Clippers Staples Ctr 1111 S Figueroa St Ste 1100 Los Angeles CA 90015

STERMER, DUGALD ROBERT, designer, writer, illustrator, consultant; b. LA, Dec. 17, 1936; s. Robert Newton and Mary (Blue) S.; children: Dugald, Megan, Chris, Colin, Crystal. BA, UCLA, 1960. Art dir., v.p. Ramparts mag., 1965-70; freelance designer, illustrator, writer, cons. San Francisco, 1970—; founder Pub. Interest Communications, San Francisco, 1974; chmn. illustration dept. Calif. Coll. Arts and Crafts, 1994—, disting. prof., 1994—. Bd. dirs. Am. Inst. Graphic Arts, Illustration Partnership Am.; mem. San Francisco Art Commn., 1997—. Cons. editor: Communication Arts mag., 1974-90; designer: Oceans mag., 1976-82; editor: The Environment, 1972, Vanishing Creatures, 1980; author: The Art of Revolution, 1970, Vanishing Creatures, 1980, Vanishing Flora, 1994, Birds and Bees, 1994; illustration exhbn. Calif. Acad. Scis., 1986; one-man show Jernigan Wicker Gallery, San Francisco, 1996 Mem. Grand Jury City and County San Francisco, 1989; bd. dirs. Delancey St. Found., 1990—. Recipient various medals, awards for design and illustration nat. and internat. competitions. Achievements include design of 1984 Olympic medals. Office: 600 The Embarcadero # 204 San Francisco CA 94107-2121 Office Phone: 415-777-0110. Business E-Mail: ds@dugaldstermer.com.

STERN, DAVID R., retail executive; V.p. fin. planning and analysis Safeway, Inc., 1994—2002, sr. v.p. planning and bus. devel., 2002—. Office: Safeway Inc 5918 Stoneridge Mall Rd Pleasanton CA 94588 Office Phone: 925-467-3000. Office Fax: 925-467-3323.

STERN, EDWARD ABRAHAM, physics professor; b. Detroit, Sept. 19, 1930; s. Jacob Munich and Rose (Kravitz) S.; m. Sylvia Rita Sidell, Oct. 30, 1955; children: Hilary, Shari, Miri. BS, Calif. Tech., 1951, PhD, 1955. Post-doctoral fellow Calif. Tech., Pasadena, 1955-57; asst. prof. U. Md., College Park, 1957-61, assoc. prof., 1961-64, prof., 1964-65, U. Wash., Seattle, 1965—2000, emeritus, 2000—. Contbr. over 200 articles to profl. jours.; editor; three books. Recipient B. Warren award Am. Crystallography Assn., 1979, Outstanding Achievement award Internat. XAFS Soc., 2000; named Guggenheim fellow, Cambridge, Eng., 1963-64, NSF Sr. Post-doctoral fellow, Haifa, Israel, 1970-71, Fulbright fellow, Jerusalem, Israel, 1985-86. Fellow AAAS, Am. Physical Soc.; mem. Materials Rsch. Soc. Achievements include patent for x-ray focusing device; development of x-ray absorption fine structure technique; research on surface plasmons, nonlinear reflection from surfaces, electronic properties of alloys, structural phase transition; named Father of EXAFS. Office: U Wash Dept Physics PO Box 351560 Seattle WA 98195-1560 Home Phone: 206-525-2771; Office Phone: 206-543-2023. Business E-Mail: stern@phys.washington.edu.

STERN, JAMES D., film and theater producer; Former hedge fund mgr.; founder, CEO Endgame Entertainment, West Hollywood, Calif. Co-owner Chgo. Bulls. Assoc. prodr.: (films) Jeffrey, 1985; dir., prodr. All the Rage, 1999; Michael Jordan to the Max, 2000; Year of the Yao, 2004; prodr.: 35 Miles from Normal, 1997, Pulse: A Stomp Odyssey, 2002, The Alibi, 2005; co-exec. prodr.: Let the Devil Wear Black, 1999; exec. prodr.: Stage Beauty, 2004, Harold & Kumar Go to White Castle, 2004, Five Children and It, 2004, Rag Tale, 2005, Lord of War, 2005; prodr.: (Broadway plays) The Producers (Tony award), Hairspray (Tony award, 2003), Little Shop of Horrors, Diary of Anne Frank, Sound of Music, (off-Broadway play) Stomp. Named one of 50 Most Powerful People in Hollywood, Premiere mag., 2005.

STERN, JUDITH SCHNEIDER, nutritionist, researcher, educator; b. Bklyn. d. Sidney and Lillian (Rosen) Schneider; m. Richard C. Stern; 1 child, Daniel Arthur. BS, Cornell U., 1964; MS, Harvard U. Sch. Pub. Health, 1966, ScD, 1970. Rsch. asst., dept. food sci. and nutrition MIT, Cambridge, 1964—65; rsch. assoc. dept. human behavior and metabolism The Rockefeller U., NYC, 1968—72, asst. prof. dept. human behavior and metabolism, 1972—74; contbg. editor Vogue Mag., Conde Nast Publs., NYC, 1974; asst. prof. nutrition U. Calif., Davis, 1975—77, assoc. prof. dept. nutrition, 1977—82, dir. food intake lab. group, 1980—2001, prof. dept. nutrition, 1982—, prof. divsn. endocrinology, clin. nutrition and vascular biology, 1988—, disting. prof., 2003—. Mem. editl. bd. Internat. Jour. Obesity, 1976-85, Appetite, 1990, Obesity Rsch., 1993—2002, Nutrition Today, 1999—. Bd. sci. advisors Am. Coun. Sci. and Health, 1980—; mem. U.S. Dept. Agr. Dietary Guidelines Adv. Com., 1983—85; mem. obesity task force NIDDK, 1996—2002, AAAS; mem. expert com. U.S. Pharmacopeia Bioavailability and Nutrient Absorption, 2000—03; mem. adv. bd. USDA Nat. Agrl. Rsch. Ext., Edn. and Econs., 2000—03. Recipient Sec.'s Honor award USDA, 2004; NIH tng. grantee, 1979-2006. Fellow Am. Heart Assn.; mem. Am. Soc. Clin. Nutirition (pres. 1995-96), Am. Dietetic Assn., Am. Diabetes Assn., Am. Obesity Assn. (co-founder, v.p. 1995-2006), N.Am. Assn. for Study of Obesity (pres. 1992-93), Inst. Medicine of NAS, Inst. Food Technologists, Am. Soc. Nutrition Sci. (chair pub. info. com. 1992-94), Sigma Xi, Delta Omega. Office: U Calif Dept Nutrition 1 Shields Ave Davis CA 95616-5271 Home Phone: 530-753-4216; Office Phone: 530-752-6575. Business E-Mail: jsstern@ucdavis.edu.

STERN, LEONARD BERNARD, television and motion picture production company executive; b. NYC, Dec. 23, 1923; s. Max and Esther (Marton) S.; m. Gloria Jane Stroock, Aug. 12, 1956; children: Michael Stroock, Kate Jennifer. Student, NYU, 1944. Dir. TV, LA, 1946-53; writer, dir., producer Jackie Gleason Show/Honeymooners, Sergeant Bilko, Steve Allen Show NYC, 1953-60; founder Price-Stern-Sloan, LA, 1959-64, v.p., 1964-69, dir., 1969-80; pres. Heyday Prodns., LA, 1962-69, 75-97; v.p. Talent Assocs./Norton Simon, L.A. and NYC, 1965-75; pres. Tallfellow Prodns., LA, 1997—. Author: (with Roger Price) Mad Libs, 1958, What Not to Name the Baby, 1960, Dear Attila the Hun, 1985; (with Roger Price and Larry Sloan) The Baby Boomer Book of Names, 1985, (with Diane L. Robison) A Martian Wouldn't Say That, 1994; writer, dir.: (motion pictures) Just You and Me, Kid, 1979, Target, 1985, Missing Pieces, 1990; creator, writer, dir. 21 TV series, including Get Smart, McMillan and Wife and He and She, 1953-89; media editor Dialogue newsletter. Mem. adv. coun. Sch. of Arts, NYU; bd. dirs. Nat. Coun. for Families and TV, Inst. for Mental Health Initiatives. Recipient Peabody award U. Ga., Writers Guild award 1956, 66, Nat. Assn. TV Arts and Scis. award 1956, 66-67, Emmy award 1956, 1966. Mem. Writers Guild Am., Dirs. Guild Am., Caucus for Producers, Writers and Dirs. (co-chmn., Mem. of Yr award 1987, Disting. Svc. award 1987), Producers Guild Am. (pres.), Bd. Motion Picure and TV Fund Found. Office: Tallfellow Productions 9454 Wilshire Blvd Ste 550 Beverly Hills CA 90212-2905

STERN, MORT(IMER) P(HILLIP), communications educator, editor, reporter, consultant; b. New Haven, Feb. 20, 1926; s. Bernard and Louise Eleanor (Spiro) S.; m. Patricia Ruth Freeman, Jan. 10, 1946; children: Susan C., Margaret L. AB, U. Ark., 1947; MS, Columbia U., NYC, 1949; postgrad., Harvard U., Cambridge, Mass., 1954—55; PhD, U. Denver, 1969. Reporter S.W.-Am., Ft. Smith, Ark., 1946-47; night bur. mgr. UPI, Little Rock, 1947-48; reporter, polit. writer, state editor Ark. Gazette, Little Rock, 1949-51; reporter, rewrite man Denver Post, 1951-53, night city editor, 1953-54, asst. editor Rocky Mountain Empire sect., 1955-56, mng. editor, 1956-58, assoc. editor, 1958, editl. page editor, 1958-65, asst. to pub., 1965-70, editl. page editor, 1971-73; dean Sch. Pub. Comm. U. Ala., 1973-74; dean Sch. Journalism U. Colo., Boulder, 1974-77; lectr. journalism U. Denver, 1953-54, adj. prof., 1970, exec. dir. pub. affairs, 1977-78, exec. asst. to chancellor, 1978-84; prof., chmn. dept. journalism and mass communication U. No. Colo., Greeley, 1985-90. Atwood prof. journalism U. Alaska, Anchorage, 1981-82. With USAAF, 1944-45. Mem. Georgetown Bd. of Selectmen, 1997-99; mem. Georgetown Bd. Adjustment, 2001-07. Nieman fellow Harvard U., 1954-55; named Disting. Alumnus dept. journalism U. Ark., 1999; inducted to Fulbright Coll. Alumni Acad. U. Ark., 1999. Mem.: Georgetown Libr. Assn. (v.p. 1999, pres. 2001—04, bd. dirs.), Phi Beta Kappa, Sigma Delta Chi, Omicron Delta Kappa. Baptist. Home: PO Box 549 Georgetown CO 80444-0549

STERN, RICHARD DAVID, investment company executive; b. New Rochelle, NY, Nov. 5, 1936; s. Leo and Grace Marjorie S.; m. Phyllis Marlene Edelstein, Nov. 20, 1966; children: Marjorie Anne, Andrew Howard. AB, Princeton U., 1958; MBA, Harvard U., 1962. CFA. 1st v.p. Newburger, Loeb & Co., NYC, 1962-74, also bd. dirs., 1969-74; sr. investment officer Ctrl. Trust Co. (now known as PNC Bank), Cin., 1974—76, owner bus. valuation cons. co., 1976—78; v.p. Gt. Western Bank & Trust Co. (now Wells Fargo Bank), Phoenix, 1978-84; pres. Stern, Ludke & Co. (now Stellar Capital Mgmt. LLC.), Phoenix, 1984—, mng. mem., 2000—. Co-author: Air Cushion Vehicles, 1962. Trustee endowment trust Phoenix Chamber Music Soc., 1982-91; v.p., 1986-90, bd. dirs., 1982-91, 93-94; pres. Cen. Ariz. chpt. Arthritis Found., 1982-84, chmn. planned giving com., 1986-91, mem. nat. planned giving com., 1987-89; chmn. endowments and trusts com. Temple Beth Israel, Phoenix, 1980-83; dir., investment com. Endowment Found., Temple Solel, Paradise Valley, 1990-92; pres. Am. Jewish Com., Phoenix, 1983-84, bd. dirs., 1980-84, adv. bd., 1985-2005; prof. adv. com. Jewish Cmty. Found., 2007-; bd. dirs. Asian Arts Coun., Phoenix Art Mus., 1987-93, v.p., 1989-90, pres., 1990-92; trustee Ariz. Theatre Co., 1990-97, mem. regional nominating com., 1995-97, chmn., 1995-96, asst. treas., 1996-97; grants award panelist Phoenix Office of Arts and Culture, 2002, 05. Mem. CFA Inst., Phoenix CFA Soc. (chmn. profl. conduct com. 1980-83, membership com. 1990-91, bd. dirs.), Anti-Defamation League (dir. Ctrl. Ariz. chpt. 1986—, exec. bd. 1989—, chair nominating com. 1990-94, 2001—, chair bd. devel. 1993-94, treas. 1994-2004, assoc. nat. commr. 1998—), Princeton Alumni Assn. No. Ariz. (alumni schs. com. 1992—, v.p. 2005—), Univ. Club Phoenix (bd. dirs. 1990-92, fin. com. 1990-91), Harvard Bus. Sch. Club Ariz. (bd. dirs. 1991—, pres. 1993-95), Clearwater Hills Improvement Assn. (dir. 2002-08, sec. 2006-08). Republican. Home: 7547 N Lakeside Ln Paradise Valley AZ 85253-2857 Office: 2200 E Camelback Rd Ste 130 Phoenix AZ 85016-3455 Business E-Mail: rstern@stellarmgt.com.

STERN, ROBIN LAURI, medical physicist; b. Urbana, Ill., Mar. 12, 1959; d. Morris Stern and Myrna (Tanzer) Stern Longenecker; m. Donald Neil Bittner, May 20, 1989. BA in Physics and German Studies, Rice U., 1981; MS in Physics, U. Mich., 1983, PhD in Physics, 1987. Rsch. assoc. Duke U., Durham, N.C., 1987-89; postdoctoral rsch. fellow U. Mich., Ann Arbor, 1989-91; asst. prof. U. Calif.-Davis, San Francisco, 1992-98; assoc. prof. U. Calif., Davis, 1998—2004, prof., 2004—. Cons. Scanditronix, Inc., Livonia, Mich., 1991. Contbr. articles to jours. Rev. of Sci. Instruments, Magnetic Resonance Imaging, Med. Physics. Argonne Nat. Lab. grantee, 1985-86; Nat. Merit scholar, 1977-81. Fellow Am. Assn. Physicists in Medicine; mem. Am. Soc. Therapeutic Radiology and Oncology, Sigma Pi Sigma, Phi Beta Kappa. E-mail: robin.stern@ucdc.udavis.edu.

STERN, SANDRA, film company executive; Grad., City U. NY-Bklyn. Coll.; JD, UCLA. Bar: Calif. Exec. v.p. bus. legal affairs Lionsgate TV, 2003; exec. v.p., COO Lionsgate Films, 2005—. Named one of The 100 Most Powerful Women in Entertainment, Hollywood Reporter, 2007. Office: Lionsgate Entertainment 2700 Colorado Ave #200 Santa Monica CA 90404 Office Phone: 310-255-3724. Office Fax: 310-255-3970. Business E-Mail: sandrastern@sbcglobal.net.

STERN, STANLEY, psychiatrist; b. NYC, Apr. 5, 1933; s. Frank and Gussie S.; children: Marcus F., David S. BA cum laude, NYU, 1953; MD, SUNY, 1957. Intern Ohio State U. Hosp., Columbus, 1957-58; resident in psychiatry Inst. Living, Hartford, Conn., 1958-60, Austen Riggs Ctr., Stockbridge, Mass., 1960-61; psychoanalytic tng. We. New Eng. Inst. for Psychoanalysis, New Haven, 1965-73; asst. clin. prof. psychiatry Yale U., New Haven, 1975-81; assoc. clin. prof. psychiatry U. Calif., San Diego, 1982-84; pvt. practice New Haven, 1965-82, La Jolla, Calif., 1982-84, Phoenix, 1984—. Mem. faculty San Diego Psychoanalytic Inst., 1980-84; pres. Ariz. Psychoanalytic Study Group, Phoenix, 1986-88, Phoenix Psychoanalytic Study Group, 1986-88; tng. and supervising analyst So. Calif. Psychoanalytic Inst., 1989; chmn. edn. com. Ariz. Psychoanalytic New Tng. Facility, 1990-91; lectr., presenter, participant seminars and confs. in field. Contbr. article to profl. jours. Trustee, Gesell Inst., New Haven, 1986-88, Ctr. for the Exceptional Patient, New Haven; bd. dirs. ACLU. Capt. USAF, 1961-63. Mem. Am. Coll. Psychoanalysts, Am. Psychoanalytic Assn. (cert.), Am. Psychiat. Assn., Am. Acad. Psychoanalysts, Irene Josselyn Group Advancement of Psychoanalysis, So. Calif. Psychoanalytic Inst. and Soc. (faculty), San Diego Psychoanalytic Inst., Council for the Advancement of Psychoanalysis (treas. 1972-73, pres.-elect 1973-74, pres. 1974-75, councillor 1975-80), Phi Beta Kappa, Beta Lambda Sigma, Psi Chi. Home and Office: 3104 E Camelback Rd # 601 Phoenix AZ 85016 Address: 4438 E Arlington Rd Phoenix AZ 85018-1262 Office Phone: 602-840-5614.

STERN, WALTER EUGENE, neurosurgeon, educator; b. Portland, Oreg., Jan. 1, 1920; s. Walter Eugene and Ida May (McCoy) S.; m. Elizabeth Naffziger, May 24, 1946; children: Geoffrey Alexander, Howard Christian, Eugenia Louise, Walter Eugene III. AB cum laude, U. Calif., MD, 1943. Diplomate Am. Bd. Neurol. Surgery (vice chmn. 1975-80). Surg. intern, asst. resident surgery and neurol. surgery U. Calif. Hosp., 1943-46, asst. resident neurol. surgery and neuropathology, 1948; clin. clk. Nat. Hosp. Paralyzed and Epileptic, London, 1948-49; Nat. Rsch. fellow med. sci. Johns Hopkins, Balt., 1949-50; asst. resident, resident U. Calif. Svc., 1951; clin. instr. U. Calif., 1951; asst. prof. neurosurgery UCLA, 1952-56, assoc. prof., 1956-59, prof., 1959—87, prof. emeritus, 1987—, chief divsn. neurosurgery, 1952-85, chmn. dept. surgery, 1981-87; NIH spl. fellow univ. lab. physiology Oxford (Eng.) U., 1961-62. Cons. neurosurgery Wadsworth VA Hosp. Former mem., chmn. editl. bd. Jour. Neurosurgery; contbr. articles to sci. jours., chpts. to books. Lt. to capt. M.C. AUS, 1946-48. Fellow ACS (sec.); mem. AMA, Am. Surg. Assn., Pacific Coast Surg. Assn., L.A. Surg. Soc. (pres. 1978), Am. Assn. Neurol. Surgeons (pres. 1979-80, Cushing medalist, 1992), James IV Assn. Surgeons, Western Neurosurg. Soc. (past pres.), Soc. Neurol. Surgeons (past pres., Disting. Svc. award 1999), Neurosurg. Soc. Am., Am. Neurol. Assn., Soc. Univ. Surgeons, Soc. Brit. Neurol. Surgeons (hon.), Calif. Assn. Neurol. Surgery (Disting. Svc. award 2004), Phi Beta Kappa, Sigma Xi, Alpha Omega Alpha. Episcopalian. Home: 435 Georgina Ave Santa Monica CA 90402-1909

STERRETT, JAMES KELLEY, II, lawyer; b. St. Louis, Nov. 26, 1946; s. James Kelley and Anastasia Mary (Holzer) S.; 1 child, Brittany. AB, San Diego State U., 1968; JD, U. Calif., Berkeley, 1971; LLM, U. Pa., 1973. Bar: Calif. 1972, U.S. Dist. Ct. (so. dist.) Calif. 1972. From assoc. to ptnr. Gray, Cary, Ames & Frye, San Diego, 1972-83; ptnr. Lillick, McHose & Charles, San Diego, 1983-90, Pillsbury, Madison & Sutro, San Diego, 1991-96, Dostart Clapp Sterrett & Coveney, LLP, 1996-99; sole practice, 1999—. Contbr. articles to profl. jours. Bd. dirs. Holiday Bowl, San Diego, 1980—, Mus. Photog. Arts, San Diego, 1985-88, San Diego Internat. Sports Coun., 1980—, pres., 1990, chmn., 1992. Capt. USAFR, 1972. Fellow U. Pa. Ctr. Study Fin. Instns., 1971-72. Mem. ABA, Calif. Bar Assn., San Diego County Bar Assn. Clubs: Fairbanks Ranch Country (Rancho Santa Fe) (bd. dirs. 1985-87). Republican. Episcopalian. Avocations: golf, hiking, football.

STESKAL, CHRISTOPHER JAMES, lawyer, former prosecutor; b. 1966; JD, Harvard Law Sch., 1992. Law clk. to Hon. Harry L. Hupp US Dist. Ct.; law clk. to Hon. James R. Browning US Ct. Appeals (9th Cir.); assoc. Cravath, Swaine & Moore, Howard, Rice, Nemerovski, Canady, Falk; asst. U.S. atty. (no. dist.) Calif. US Dept. Justice,

2001—07; ptnr., chair white collar practice Fenwick & West LLP, San Francisco, 2007—. Office: Fenwick & West LLP 555 California St 12th Fl San Francisco CA 94104 Office Phone: 415-875-2300. Office Fax: 415-281-1350.

STETLER, RUSSELL DEARNLEY, JR., investigator; b. Phila., Jan. 15, 1945; s. Russell Dearnley and Martha Eleanor (Schultz) S. BA with honors in Philosophy, Haverford Coll., Pa., 1966; postgrad., New Sch. Social Rsch., 1966-67. Research asst. to Bertrand Russell, 1967; lectr. Hendon Coll., London, 1968-69; pres. Archetype, Inc., Berkeley, Calif., 1971-78; pub. Westworks, Berkeley, 1977-80; pvt. investigator, 1980-90; chief investigator Calif. Appellate Project, 1990-95; dir. of investigation and mitigation N.Y. State Capital Defender Office, NYC, 1995—2005; nat. mitigation coord. Office of the Fed. Pub. Defender, Oakland, Calif., 2005—. Cons., dir. Ramparts Press, Palo Alto, 1971-80; editorial cons. Internews, Berkeley, 1973-78; faculty Caribbean Sch., Ponce, P.R., 1978-80 Author: The Battle of Bogside, 1970; co-editor: The Assassinations: Dallas and Beyond, 1976. Research grantee Atlantic Peace Found., 1969-70 Mem. Calif. Assn. Lic. Investigators, Nat. Assn. Legal Investigators, Calif. Soccer Referees Assn.-North (treas. Marin County chpt. 1982-90), Amigos de las Americas (pres. Marin chpt. 1985-88). Clubs: Mill Valley Soccer (dir. 1981), Albany-Berkeley Soccer (pres. 1977-78). Office: Office of the Fed Pub Defender 555 12th St Ste 650 Oakland CA 94607 E-mail: russell_stetler@fd.org.

STEUERT, DOUGLAS MICHAEL, engineering and construction management company executive; b. Oklahoma City, May 21, 1948; s. Douglas Anselm and Geraldine (Sparks) S.; m. Nancy Elizabeth Ridd, Aug. 22, 1970. BS in Physics, Carnegie-Mellon U., Pitts., 1971, MS in Indsl. Mgmt. Staff asst. TRW, Inc., Cleve., 1971-73, mgr. fin. rsch. and analysis, 1973-75, dir. fin. US, 1975-76, dir. fin. Europe Frankfurt, Germany, 1976-79, asst. treas. internat. Cleve., 1979-81, sr. fin. dir. automotive worldwide sector, 1981-84, contr. valve divsn., 1984-86; v.p., treas. GenCorp Inc., Ohio, 1986-87, v.p. fin. and planning Ohio, 1987-90, v.p, CFO, treas. Ohio, 1990-94, sr. v.p., CFO Ohio, 1994—99, Litton Industries, Inc., 1999—2001, Fluor Corp., Calif., 2001—. Dir. Weyerhaeuser Co., 2004—. Dir. Mental Health Assn. Summit County, 1993; mem. coun. on fin. Grad. Sch. Indsl. Adminstrn., Carnegie-Mellon U., 1994—. Mem. Fin. Execs. Inst. (nat. chpt., NE Ohio chpt.), Mfrs. Alliance for Productivity and Innovation, Conf. Bd. Coun. of CFOs, Leadership Akron, Alumni Assn. Carnegie-Mellon U. Office: Fluor Enterprises 3 Polaris Way Aliso Viejo CA 92698 Office Phone: 949-349-2000. Office Fax: 949-349-2585.

STEVENS, BEN, former state legislator; b. Washington, 1959; m. Elizabeth Stevens; children: Susan, Ben Jr., Augustus, Theodore. BA in Econs., Ariz. State U.; postgrad., George Washington U. Mem. Alaska State Senate, 2002—07, majority leader, 2002—03, pres., 2005—06. Bd. dirs. Aleut Enterprise Corp. Pres. bd. dirs. DARE Alaska; bd. dirs. Spl. Olympics Alaska. Mem.: Anchorage C. of C., Rotary. Republican.

STEVENS, BERTON LOUIS, JR., data processing executive; b. Chgo., Apr. 4, 1951; s. Berton Louis Sr. and Mary Cover (Kochavaris) S.; m. Janet Alene Madenberg, May 20, 1990. Student, Ill. Inst. Tech., Chgo., 1969-73. Systems and applications programmer Judge & Dolph, Ltd., Elk Grove Village, Ill., 1978-91, mgr. data processing, 1991-99; bus. sys. coord. Meml. Med. Ctr., Inc., 2000-2001, lead sys. analyst, 2001—02; svc. ctr. mgr. Siemens Health Sys., 2002—04; mgr. applications Province Healthcare, Las Cruces, N.Mex., 2004—06; dir. MIS LifePoint Hosps., Las Cruces, N.Mex., 2006—. Instr. Adler Planetarium and Astron. Mus., Chgo., 1980-86; dir. Desert Moon Observatory #448. Editor and author newsletter Bert's Bull., 1987-90; editor newsletter No. Lights, 1990-98; columnist Starry Dome, 2004- Recipient Regional award North Ctrl. Region Astron. League, 1989. Mem. Nat. Assn. Sys. Programmers, Internat. Occulation Timing Assn. (sec. 1975-78), Chgo. Computer Soc., Chgo. Astron. Soc. (pres. 1977, 80, 84), Racine Astron. Soc. (pres. 1979), Astron. League (exec. sec. 1993-95, webmaster 1995-02), Desert Moon Observatory (dir.), Astron. Soc. Las Cruces (pres, 2001, 2007). Personal E-mail: bstevens@zianet.com. Business E-Mail: Berton.Stevens@lpnt.net.

STEVENS, CHARLES J., lawyer, former prosecutor; BA in English, Colgate U., 1979; JD, U. Calif., Berkeley, 1982. Assoc. Gibson, Dunn & Crutcher, LA, 1982-84, ptnr. in charge Sacramento, 1987-93; asst. U.S. atty. Office U.S. Atty., LA, 1984-87; U.S. atty. ea. dist. Calif. U.S. Dept. Justice, Sacramento, 1993-97; ptnr. Steven & O'Connell LLP, Sacramento, 1997—. Mem. com. for ea. dist. Civil Justice Reform Act com. for ea. dist., 1991—, lawyer rep. to 9th cir., 1999—; panel spkr. and lectr. in field. Contbr. articles to profl. jours. Master Anthony M. Kennedy Am. Inn. of Ct.; mem. FBA (chair program com. Sacramento chpt. 1992-93), State Bar Calif. (bd. editors Criminal Law News 1991-93) Office: 400 Capitol Mall Ste 1400 Sacramento CA 95814-4498

STEVENS, GARY, state legislator; b. McMinnville, Oreg., Aug. 21, 1941; m to Rita; children: Anna, Matthew, Natalie. BA, Linfield Coll., McMinnville, Oreg., 1959—63; MFA, U. Oreg., 1963—65, PhD, 1982—84. Mayor, City of Lodiak, formerly; Alaska State Representative, District 6, 2001; Alaska State Representative, District 36, 2003; Alaska State Senator, District R, 2003-, majority leader, 2005-08, Alaska State Senate, currently Senate Pres. Prof, Univ Alaska, formerly; gen. mgr. Northern Processors; dir. Kodiak Oral History Project; pres. Alaska Hist. Soc.; mem. bd. dirs. Alaska Humanities Forum. 1st Lt. US Army. Decorated Army Commendation medal, Nat. Def. medal. Rotary Int, Alaska, Yukon Territory & Siberia. Republican. Office: State Capitol Rm 103 Juneau AK 99801-1182 also: Dist R 345 W Sterling Hwy Ste 102 Homer AK 99603 Office Phone: 907-465-4925, 907-235-0690. Office Fax: 907-465-3517, 907-235-4008. Business E-Mail: Senator_Gary_Stevens@legis.state.ak.us.*

STEVENS, GEORGE RICHARD, business consultant, public information officer; b. Chgo., Sept. 6, 1932; s. George and Irene (Kaczmarek) S.; m. Jeanne E. Sowden, Aug. 2, 1957; children: Stacey, Samantha, Pamela. BS with honors, Northwestern U., 1954. CPA, Ill. With Arthur Andersen & Co., 1954-78, mng. ptnr. Brussels, 1957—71, ptnr. Chgo., 1971-78; pres. Daubert Industries, Oak Brook, Ill., 1978-80, G.R. Stevens Group, 1981—; founder, pres. Stevens Ctr. for Pub. Policy Studies, 1981—. Commr. Ill. Ednl. Facilities Authority, 1989-04. Commr. Ill. State Scholarship Commn., 1981-87; vice chmn. Ill. Ind. Higher Edn. Loan Authority, 1982-88. Home and Office: 22615 N Las Lomas Ln Sun City West AZ 85375-2022

STEVENS, GLENN H., lawyer; Grad., Johns Hopkins U.; JD, NYU. Positions in legal dept. US West Inc., 1979—92; atty. pvt. practice, 1992—94; v.p., gen. counsel, sec. Maxtor Corp., Milpitas, Calif., 1994—2001, sr. v.p., gen. counsel, sec., 2001; spl. counsel Stevens, Littman, Biddison, Tharp & Weinberg, LLC, Boulder, Colo., 2005—. Mem.: Nebr. State Bar Assn., Colo. Bar Assn. Office: Stevens, Littman, Biddison, Tharp & Weinberg, LLC 250 Arapahoe, Ste 301 Boulder CO 80302 Office Phone: 303-443-6690. Office Fax: 303-449-9349. E-mail: glenn@slb-llc.com.

STEVENS, PAUL IRVING, manufacturing executive; b. Lawrence, Kans., Mar. 22, 1915; s. Ira F. and Ida M. S.; m. Artie Faye Womack, Nov. 10, 1935; children: Richard Irving, Constance Irene. Student bus. adminstrn., Pasadena Coll., Calif., 1933-35. Indsl. engr. Consol. Aircraft Co., San Diego, 1940-49; founder, prin. stockholder, pres. United Machine Co., Ft. Worth, 1950-61; exec. v.p. Clary Corp., San Gabriel, Calif., 1962-65; pres., owner Stevens Corp., Ft. Worth, 1965-69; pres., chief exec. officer Waltham Industries, NYC, 1969-71, Stevens Industries, La Jolla, Calif., 1972—, Campbell Industries, San Diego., 1976-79; chmn., pres. Stevens Air Systems, El Cajon, Calif., 1974-81; pres. Womack Motors, Inc., El Centro, Calif., 1982-90. Chmn. bd. dirs., CEO Stevens Graphics Corp., Ft. Worth, 1986-95; bd. dirs. Rancho Santa Fe Nat. Bank, Calif., 1982-85, chmn. 1985-95; chmn., CEO Stevens Internat., Inc., 1995—; bd. dirs. Rancho Santa Fe. Mem. Nat. Mgmt. Assn. (exec. com.), Presidents Assn., Civic Round Table, La Jolla Country Club, Colonial Country Club, Canyon Country Club, University Club, Ft. Worth Club, Shady Oaks Country Club. Republican. Methodist.

STEVENS, SHARON COX, lawyer; b. 1948; m. Michael Callahan. BA, Washington State Univ.; JD, McGeorge Sch. Law. Bar: Oreg. 1977. Ptnr. Callahan & Stevens, Keizer, Oreg. Mem.: ABA (bd. gov. 2004—). Office: Callahan & Stevens 5845 Shoreview Lane N PO Box 20937 Keizer OR 97307-0937 also: Callahan & Stevens 156 Chemawa Rd N Salem OR 97303-5356 Office Phone: 503-240-4133.

STEVENS, STANLEY DAVID, historian, researcher, retired librarian, archivist; b. San Francisco, Nov. 10, 1933; s. David Franklin and Ellen Myrtle (Wixson) S.; m. Carli Ann Lewis, Sept. 3, 1960; adopted children: Alexander Lewis, Nikolas Harriman, Brooke Cayton Stevens. BA, San Jose State U., Calif., 1959. Conf. officer polit. and security com. 14th Gen. Assembly, UN, NYC, 1959; map libr. U. Calif., Santa Cruz, 1965-93, ret., 1993, coord. Hihn-Younger Archive, Univ. Libr., 1994—. Mem. Cartographic Users Adv. Coun., 1976-86, chmn., 1982-86; presenter in field; adj. prof. libr. sci. San Jose State U., 1989, 91. Author: Index to Guinn's Biographical Record of Santa Cruz, San Benito, Monterey and San Luis Obispo Counties, Catalog of aerial photos by Fairchild Aerial Surveys, Inc. now in the collections of the Dept. Geography, UCLA, 1982, Correspondence of Charles B. Younger Sr. and Charles B. Younger Jr., Santa Cruz, California Attorneys and Counsellors at Law, vols. 1-13, 1996—, indexed edit. Santa Cruz County, Calif., 1997, Index to Personal Names, Portraits & Illustrations Appearing in California City, County & Regional Histories 1867-1910, 2005; editor: Santa Cruz County History Jour., 1994-96, 98, Index to Sidewalk Companion to Santa Cruz Architecture, 3d edit., 2005; co-author: A Legal History of Santa Cruz County: an account of the local bench and bar through the end of the Twentieth Century, 2006, Index to Morton Marcus, Striking Through The Marks, 2008, The Rowland Website & The Content of the Leon Rowland Collection, 2006, Index to Lime Kiln Legacies: The History of the Lime Industry in Santa Cruz County, 2007, Index to Santa Cruz County History Jour., 2009, others; prodn. editor: Index to Boulder Creek Mountain Echo, 1896-1916, 1999; contbr. articles to profl. jours. and Map Collections Mem. adv. com. archaeol. program Cabrillo Coll., Aptos, Calif., 1985—; bd. dirs. Santa Cruz County Hist. Soc., 1985-94, chmn. publs. com., 1985-96, mem. programs adv. coun., 1994-95; mem. Santa Cruz Orgn. for Progress and Euthenics, 1987—; bd. dirs. Friends of U. Calif.-Santa Cruz Libr., 1994-97; founding mem. Rschr. Anonymous, Santa Cruz, 1993—; mem. U. Calif.-Santa Cruz Emeriti Group, sec.-treas. 1996—; mem. collections adv. com. Santa Cruz City Mus. Natural History, 1995—; mem. hist. publs. com. Mus. Art and History, 2000—, chmn., 2006—; vol. Spl. Collections, Univ. Libr., U. Calif., Santa Cruz, 1994—. With U.S. Army, 1954-56. Recipient honors award geography and map divsn. for outstanding achievement in map librarianship Spl. Librs. Assn., 1981, cert. of commendation Santa Cruz Hist. Soc., 1986, appreciation cert. for svcs. Assn. Info. and Image Mgmt., 1989, Proclamation of Honor, Santa Cruz County Bd. Suprs., 1998, Historian of Yr. award History Forum of Santa Cruz Mus. of Art and History, 2001; grantee Librs. Assn. U. Calif., 1981-82, Rsch. grantee Office of Pres., U. Calif., 1985-86. Mem. ALA (publs. com. Map and Geography Round Table 1985-86, editl. bd. Meridian 1989-2000, honors award Map and Geography Round Table 1992), ACLU (chmn. bd. dirs. Santa Cruz County chpt. 1962-68, bd. dirs. No. Calif. br. 1973-76), Western Assn. Map Librs. (hon. life, founding pres. 1967-68, treas. 1968-89, editor Info. Bull. 1969-84, Exec. Com. award 1984, Stanley D. Stevens Hon. Map presented at 30th anniversary meeting 1997, Calif. Hist. Soc., Calif. Map Soc., Pajaro Valley Hist. Assn., Santa Cruz County Geneal. Soc., Capitola Hist. Soc., El Paso de Robles Hist. Soc. (life). Democrat. Avocations: researching local history, listening to jazz and classical music. Home: 231 13th Ave Santa Cruz CA 95062-4831 Office: U Calif Dean E McHenry Libr Santa Cruz CA 95064 Business E-Mail: sstevens@library.ucsc.edu.

STEVENS, TED (THEODORE FULTON STEVENS), former United States Senator from Alaska; b. Indpls., Nov. 18, 1923; s. George A. and Gertrude (Chancellor) S.; m. Ann Mary Cherrington, Mar. 29, 1952 (dec. 1978); children: Susan B., Elizabeth H., Walter C., Theodore Fulton, Ben A.; m. Catherine Chandler, 1980; 1 child, Lily Irene. BA, U. Calif. at Los Angeles, 1947; LL.B., Harvard U., 1950. Bar: Calif., Alaska, D.C., U.S. Supreme Ct. bars. Atty. Northcutt Ely, Washington, 1950—52, Collins & Clasby, Fairbanks, Alaska, 1953; U.S. atty. Dist. Alaska US Dept. Justice, Fairbanks, 1953-56; legis. counsel US Dept. Interior, Washington, 1956—57, asst to sec., 1958—59, solicitor, 1960; ptnr. Stevens & Roderick, Anchorage, 1961—63, Stevens & Stringer, Anchorage, 1964, Stevens, Savage, Holland, Erwin & Edwards, Anchorage, 1964—65, Stevens & Holland, Anchorage, 1966—68; mem. Alaska Ho. of Reps., 1965-68, majority leader, speaker pro tem, 1967-68; US Senator from Alaska, 1968—2009; minority whip, 1977—81; majority whip, 1981—85; pres. pro tempore, 2003—07; chmn. appropriations com., 1997—2001, 2003—05, commerce, sci., & transp. com., 2005—07, vice chmn., 2007—09. Served in USAF, 1943—46. Decorated Disting. Flying Cross, Air medal with Cluster, Yuan Hai Medal Chinese Nationalist Govt., China-Burma-India Ribbion; recipient Alaska 49'er, Alaska Press Club, 1963, Disting. Svc. Award, UCLA, 1971, Man of Yr. Award, Nat. Fisheries Inst., 1975; named Alaskan of Yr., 1974. Mem. ABA, Alaska Bar Assn., Calif. Bar Assn., D.C. Bar Assn., Am. Legion, VFW. Lodges: Rotary, Pioneers of Alaska, Igloo #4. Republican. Episcopalian.*

STEVENS, VAL, state legislator; m to Keith Stevens; children: two sons, four grandchildren. Washington State director, Concerned Women for America, 87-91; elected member, Nat Bd Director, 91; Washington State Representative, District 39, 92-96, Assistant Majority Floor Leader, formerly, Washington House Representative; Washington State Senator, District 39, 96-, chairwoman, Children & Family Servs & Corrections, vchairwoman, Govt Opers & Elections, Technology & Communications, currently, Washington State Senate.Interior Decorator, currently. Private Enterprise Gold Medal, Int Bus Association; Sentinel Award, Washington State Law Enforcement Association, 96; Cornerstone Award, Association Washington Bus; Outstanding Support, Washington Retail Association, 96; Guardian Small Bus, Nat Fedn Ind Bus; Public Safety Award, Snohomish Co Law Enforcement, 93. Grange; Snohomish Co Property Rights Alliance; America Legislature Exchange Coun; Christian Armed Servs Association (ad hoc board member, currently); Better Govt Bureau. Republican. Lutheran. Mailing: State Senate 105 Irving R Newhouse Bldg PO Box 40439 Olympia WA 98504-0482 Fax: 360-786-1999. E-mail: stevens_va@leg.wa.gov.

STEVENS, YVETTE MARIE See KHAN, CHAKA

STEVENSON, DAVID JOHN, planetary scientist, educator; b. Wellington, New Zealand, Sept. 2, 1948; arrived in US, 1971, permanent resident; s. Ian McIvor and Gwenyth (Carroll) S. BS in Physics, Victoria U., New Zealand, 1971, MS in Physics, 1972; PhD in Theoretical Physics, Cornell U., 1976. Rsch. fellow Australian Nat. U., Canberra, Australia, 1976-78; asst. prof. UCLA, LA, 1978-80; assoc. prof. Calif. Inst. Tech., Pasadena, 1980-84, prof., 1984—, George van Osdol prof., 1995—. Chmn. divsn. geol. & planetary scis. Calif. Inst. Tech., 1989-94; mem. NASA solar system exploration subcom., 2000—. Assoc. editor ICARUS, 1990—; Contbr. 100 articles to profl. jours. Named Fulbright scholar, USA, 1971-76; in 1996, at suggestion of discoverers asteroid, (5211) Stevenson, named in his honor. Fellow Am. Geophysical Union (Whipple award 1994, Harry H. Hess medal 1998; pres. planetary scis. sect. 2000-02), Royal Soc. London, 1993, AAAS; Am. Astron. Soc. (Urey prize 1984), NAS (fgn. assoc.). Office: Calif Inst Tech 1200 E California Blvd Pasadena CA 91125-0001 Office Phone: 626-395-6534. Office Fax: 626-585-1917. E-mail: djs@gps.caltech.edu.

STEVENSON, ROBERT MURRELL, music educator; b. Melrose, N.Mex., July 3, 1916; s. Robert Emory and Ada (Ross) S. AB, U. Tex., El Paso, 1936; grad., Juilliard Grad. Sch. Music, 1938; MusM, Yale, 1939; PhD, U. Rochester, 1942; STB cum laude, Harvard U., 1943; BLitt, Oxford U., Eng.; Th.M., Princeton Theol. Sem.; DMus honoris causa, Cath. U. Am., 1991; LHD honoris causa, Ill. Wesleyan U., 1992; LittD honoris causa, Universidade Nova de Lisboa, 1993. Instr. music U. Tex., 1941-43, 46; faculty Westminster Choir Coll., Princeton, NJ, 1946-49; faculty rsch. lectr. UCLA, 1981, mem. faculty to prof. music, 1949—. Vis. asst. prof. Columbia, 1955-56; vis. prof. Ind. U., Bloomington, 1959-60, U. Chile, 1965-66, Northwestern U., Chgo., 1976, U. Granada, 1992; adj. prof. Cath. U. Am., 1991—; cons. UNESCO, 1977; Louis Charles Elson lectr. Libr. of Congress, Washington, 1969; inaugural prof. musicology Nat. U. Mex., 1996; spkr. Dumbarton Oaks Pre-Columbian Music Workshop, 1998, Internat. Colonial Music Congress, Lima, Peru, 2000; lectr. Tureck Bach Rsch. Found., Oxford U., 2000; hon. prof. Conservatorio Nacional, Peru, 2000, Real Conservatorio Superior, Madrid, 1991-2003; hon. lectr. Royal Conservatory, Madrid, 2004; keynote spkr. Morales Colloquium, Oxford U., 2004. Author: Music in Mexico, 1952, Patterns of Protestant Church Music, 1953, La musica en la catedral de Sevilla, 1954, 85, Music Before the Classic Era, 1955, Shakespeare's Religious Frontier, 1958, The Music of Peru, 1959, Juan Bermudo, 1960, Spanish Music in the Age of Columbus, 1960, Spanish Cathedral Music in the Golden Age, 1961, La musica colonial en Colombia, 1964, Protestant Church Music in America, 1966, Music in Aztec and Inca Territory, 1968, Renaissance and Baroque Musical Sources in the Americas, 1970, Music in El Paso, 1970, Philosophies of American Music History, 1970, Written Sources for Indian Music Until 1882, 1972, Christmas Music From Baroque Mexico, 1974, Foundations of New World Opera, 1973, Seventeenth Century Villancicos, 1974, Latin American Colonial Music Anthology, 1975, Vilancicos Portugueses, 1976, Josquin in the Music of Spain and Portugal, 1977, American Musical Scholarship, Parker to Thayer, 1978, Liszt at Madrid and Lisbon, 1980, Wagner's Latin American Outreach, 1983, Spanish Musical Impact Beyond the Pyrenees, 1250-1500, 1985, La Música en las catedrales españolas del Siglo de Oro, 1993; contbg. editor: Handbook Latin Am. Studies, 1976—; editor Inter-Am. Music Rev., 1978—; contbr. to New Grove Dictionary of Music and Musicians, 17 other internat. encys. Decorated Army Commendation ribbon, 1946; fellow Folger Shakespeare Library, 1950, Ford Found., 1953-54, Gulbenkian Found., 1966, 81, Guggenheim Found., 1962, NEH, 1974, Comité Conjunto Hispano-Norteamericano (Madrid), 1989; recipient Fulbright rsch. awards, 1958-59, 64, 70-71, 88-89, Carnegie Found. tchg. award, 1955-56, Gabriela Mistral award OAS, 1985, Heitor Villa Lobos Jury award OAS, 1988, OAS medal, 1986, Cert. Merit Mexican Consulate San Bernardino, Calif., 1987, Silver medal Spanish Ministry Culture, 1989, Gold medal Real Conservatorio Superior, 1994, 97, 1st Lifetime Achievement award Sonneck Soc., 1999, All-Calif. Constantine Penunzio award, 2004. Mem. Real Academia de Bellas Artes (hon.), Hispanic Soc. Am., Am. Liszt Soc. (cons. editor), Heterofonia (cons. editor), Brazilian Musicol. Soc. (hon.), Portuguese Musicol. Soc. (hon.), Argentinian Musicol. Soc. (hon.), Venezuelan Musicol. Soc. (hon.), Am. Musicol. Soc. (hon.), Orden Andrés Bello, Primera Clase, Venezuela, 1992. Avocation: playing piano. Office: UCLA Dept Music 405 Hilgard Ave Los Angeles CA 90095-9000 Business E-Mail: info@ericdilauro.com.

STEVENSON, THOMAS RAY, plastic surgeon; b. Kansas City, Mo., Jan. 22, 1946; s. John Adolph and Helen Ray (Clarke) S.; m. Judith Ann Hunter, Aug. 17, 1968; children: Anne Hunter, Andrew Thomas. BA, U. Kans., 1968, MD. Diplomate Am. Bd. Plastic and Reconstructive Surgery, Am. Bd. Surgery. Resident in gen. surgery U. Va., Charlottesville, 1972-78; resident in plastic surgery Emory U., Atlanta, 1980-82; asst. prof. surgery U. Mich., 1982-88, assoc. prof. surgery, 1988-89. Chief plastic surgery Ann Arbor VA Hosp., 1982—, U. Calif., Davis, 1989—. Served to maj. USAR, 1978-80. Fellow ACS; mem. Am. Soc. Plastic and Reconstructive Surgery, Am. Bd. Plastic Surgery, chair-elect 2006- Office: UC Davis Divsn Plastic Surg 2221 Stockton Blvd 2d Fl Sacramento CA 95817-2214

STEWART, DEBORAH CLAIRE, dean; b. Freeport, Ill., Sept. 14, 1951; Student, Monterey Peninsula Coll., 1969-71; BS in Zoology, U. Calif., Davis, 1973; MD, U. Calif., San Francisco, 1977. Diplomate Am. Bd. Peds. Intern Children's Hosp. L.A., 1977-78, resident in peds., 1978-79, fellow in adolescent medicine, 1979-81, attending physician emergency med. svcs., 1980-81; med. dir. comprehensive adolescent program dept. ob-gyn. Charles R. Drew Postgrad. Med. Sch., LA, 1981-83; asst. prof. dept. ob-gyn. UCLA/Charles R. Drew Postgrad. Med. Sch., 1982-83; mem. ped. staff Children's Hosp. of Orange County, Orange, Calif., 1983-86, U. Calif. Irvine Med. Ctr., Orange, 1983-99; assoc. prof. ob-gyn., assoc. prof. medicine U. Calif., Irvine, 1983-99, dir. child sexual abuse program, 1983-99, assoc. prof. clin. peds., chief divsn. gen. peds., dir. adol, 1988-95, assoc. dean for med. student and resident affairs, 1992-99; med. dir. child protection ctr. Meml. Miller Children's Hosp., Long Beach, Calif., 1995-99; assoc. dean med. edn. program U. Calif.-San Francisco, Fresno, 1999—. Project dir. South Ctrl. L.A. Sexual Trauma Program, 1983; med. cons. L.A. Commn. on Assaults Against Women, 1982-84, Calif. Children's Svcs., 1980-85, Sexual Assault Protocol Office of Criminal Justice Planning, 1984-86, Sexual Assault Protocol L.A. County, 1984-86; med. dir. Child Abuse Svcs. Team County of Orange, 1987—; physician mem. Calif. State Atty. Gen.'s Investigative Pilot Projects Rsch. and Evaluation Adv. Panel; cons. County of Orange Coroner's Office, 1994-99. Contbr. articles to profl. jours.; presenter in field; reviewer: Ped. and Adolescent Gyn., 1988—, Jour. Adolescent Health Care, 1986—, Peds., 1988—, Am. Jour. Obs. and Gyn., 1991— Mem. med. adv. bd. Planned Parenthood, 1983-94. Fellow Am. Acad. Pediatrics (pres. Dist. IX Chpt. 4, 1995-97, sec. chpt. IV, chair chpt. IV com. on child abuse 1983—); mem. N.Am. Soc. Pediatric And Adolescent Gynecology (co-chair collaborative rsch. com. 1988—), Orange County Ped. Assn. Office: U Calif San Francisco-Fresno Med Edn Program 2615 E Clinton Ave Fresno CA 93703-2223 E-mail: deborah.stewart@ucsfresno.edu.

STEWART, FRANK MAURICE, JR., federal agency administrator; b. Okalona, Miss., Apr. 1, 1939; s. Frank Maurice Stewart and Henryne Annette (Walker) Goode; m. Regina Diane Mosley, Dec. 26, 1964; children: Lisa Ann, Dana Joy. BA, Wesleyan U., 1961, MA in Teaching, 1963, diploma further study, 1963; postgrad., Am. U., 1982-84. Dir. urban edn. corps N.J. State Dept. Edn., Trenton, 1969-70; dir. urban teaching intern program Sch. Edn. Rutgers U., New Brunswick, N.J., 1970-71; staff asst. White House Conf. on Aging, Washington, 1971-73; chief program devel. U.S. Office of Equal Edn. Opportunity, Washington, 1973-74; chief policy analysis U.S. Adminstrn. on Aging, Washington, 1974-75; asst. exec. sec. U.S. HEW, Washington, 1975-77; dir. govt. programs U.S. Dept. Energy, Washington, 1977-80, dir. instnl. conservation programs, 1980-84, dir. state and local assistance programs, 1984-90, dep. asst. sec. for tech. and fin. assistance, 1990-93; acting asst. sec. for energy efficiency and renewable energy, 1993-94; mgr. Golden (Colo.) Field Office, U.S. Dept. Energy, 1994—. Bd. dirs. Renewable Energy for African Devel., 1992-94; mem. U.S. Presdl. Del. on Sustainable Energy Devel. to South Africa, 1995, U.S. Del. to African-African-Am. Summit, Dakar, Senegal, 1995; bd. advisors Internat. Sustainable Tech. Bus. Ctr. Bd. dirs. Urban League of Met. Denver. Recipient Svc. Recognition award Assn. Phys. Plant Adminstrs., Washington, 1982, Svc. Appreciation award Nat. Assn. State Energy Officials, Washington, 1987, Midwest Rsch. Inst., 1996; named Energy Exec. of Yr. Assn. Energy Engrs., Atlanta, 1988. Mem. Sr. Execs. Assn., Nat. Assn. of Black Environmentalists (bd. dirs.), Am. Assn. of Blacks in Energy (bd. dirs. Denver chpt.), Denver Fed. Exec. Bd. Episcopalian. Office: US Dept Energy Field Office 1617 Cole Blvd Golden CO 80401-3305 Home: 13880 NW 20th St Pembroke Pines FL 33028-2614 E-mail: frank_stewart@nrel.gov.

STEWART, ISAAC DANIEL, JR., retired state supreme court justice; b. Salt Lake City, Nov. 21, 1932; s. Isaac Daniel and Orabelle (Iverson) S.; m. Elizabeth Bryan, Sept. 10, 1959; children: Elizabeth Ann, Shannon. BA with high honors, U. Utah, 1959, JD with high honors, 1962. Bar: Utah 1962, U.S. Dist. Ct. Utah 1962, U.S. Ct. Appeals (10th cir.) 1962, U.S. Ct. Appeals (4th cir.) 1963, U.S. Ct. Appeals (9th cir.) 1964, U.S. Ct. Appeals (8th cir.) 1965, U.S. Supreme Ct. 1965. Atty. antitrust divsn. Dept. Justice, Washington, 1962-65; asst. prof., then assoc. prof. U. Utah Coll. Law, 1965-70; ptnr. Jones, Waldo, Holbrook & McDonough, Salt Lake City, 1970-79; assoc. justice Utah Supreme Ct., 1979-2000, assoc. chief justice, 1986-88, 94-98, assoc. justice, 1999-2000; ret., 2000. Lectr. in field; mem. Utah Bd. Oil, Gas and Mining, 1976-78, chmn., 1977-78; Utah rep. Interstate Oil Compact Commn., 1977-78, exec. com. 1978-79; mem. adv. com. rules of procedure Utah Supreme Ct., 1983-87; chmn. com. on bar-press guidelines Utah Bar; mem. U. Utah search com., 1968-70; legal advisor, 1966-68. Editor-in-chief Utah Law Rev.; contbr. articles to legal jours. Chmn. subcom. on legal rights and responsibilities of youth Utah Gov's Com. on Youth, 1972; pres. Salt Lake chpt. Coun. Fgn. Rels., 1982; mem. Salt Lake City C. of C., 1974-79, mem. govtl. modernization com., 1976-78; missionary for Mormon Ch. in Fed. Republic Germany, 1953-56; bd. dirs. U. Utah Alumni Assn., 1986-89 Recipient Alumnus of Yr. award U. Utah Coll. Law, 1989. Mem. ABA, Utah Bar Assn. (com. on law and poverty 1967-69, com. on specialization 1977-78, pub. rels. com. 1968-69, chmn. com. on antitrust law 1977-78, com. on civil procedure reform 1968, mem. exec. com. bd. of appellate judges 1990—, liaison to supreme and adv. coms. evidence & profl. conduct 1986—, Appellate Judge of Yr. 1986), Salt Lake County Bar Assn., Am. Judicature Soc., Order of Coif, Phi Beta Kappa, Phi Kappa Phi, Sigma Chi (Significant Sig award 1987).

STEWART, JOHN TODD, economist, consultant; AB, Stanford U., 1961; MA, Tufts U., 1962, MALD, 1970. With Am. Fgn. Svc., 1962-98; U.S. amb. to Republic of Moldova, 1995-98; dep. head U.S. diplomatic missions to Can., Costa Rica and Jamaica; dir. office maritime and land transport Dept. of State, Washington; dir. GATT affairs Pres.'s Spl. Rep. for Trade Negotiations; dep. dir. Inst. Internat. Econs., Washington, 1998—2002; diplomat-in-residence Am. U., 2003—04. Vis. fellow Inst. Internat. Econs., 2002—. Home and Office: PO Box 3200 Sun Valley ID 83353 Office Phone: 208-622-7343. E-mail: todd.stewart@stanfordalumni.org.

STEWART, JOHN WRAY BLACK, college dean; b. Coleraine, Northern Ireland, Jan. 16, 1936; s. John Wray and Margaret Reid (Black) S.; m. Felicity Ann Patricia Poole, Aug. 7, 1965; children: J.W. Matthew, Hannah Louise. BSc with honors, Queen's U., Belfast, Northern Ireland, 1958, BSA with honors, 1959, PhD, 1963, DSc, 1988. Registered profl. agrologist. Sci. officer chem. rsch. divsn. Ministry of Agr., Belfast, 1959-64; asst. prof. soil sci. dept. U. Sask., Saskatoon, Canada, 1966-71, assoc. prof., 1971-76, prof., 1976-81, dir. Sask. Inst. Pedology, 1981-89, dean Coll. Agr., 1989-99, prof. emeritus, 1999—, dean emeritus, 1999—, interim dir. Inter-Am. Inst. for Global Change Rsch., 2002, 2005. Tech. expert, cons. FAO/IAEA, U.N.D.P., Vienna, 1971, Vienna, 1974—75; mem. program com. Can. Global Change, 1985—98; sec.-gen. Sci. Com. on Problems of Environ., Paris, 1988—92, pres., 1992—95, editor-in-chief, 1999—2006; cons. UNESCO, Paris, 1990; trustee Internat. Inst. Tropical Agr., Nigeria, 1991—97; chair sci. adv. com. Inter-Am. Inst. for Global Change Rsch., 1994—2001. Contbr. articles to profl. publs., chapters to books. Fellow: Can. Soc. Soil Sci., Berlin Inst. Advanced Study, Soil Sci. Soc. Am., Am. Soc. Agronomy, Agrl. Inst. Can.; mem.: Internat. Assn. Agrl. Sci. and Tech. Devel. (bureau mem. 2005—08), Internat. Soc. Soil Sci., Brit. Soc. Soil Sci. Avocations: golf, tennis. Personal E-mail: stew9250@telus.net.

STEWART, KIRK T., public relations executive; b. 1951; BA in Polit. Sci., U. So. Calif., 1973, MA in Pub. Rels. and Journalism, 1976. Account exec. Burson-Marsteller, 1976—79; pub. affairs dir. Info. Svcs. Dir. TRW, 1979—81; group supr. Manning Selvage & Lee, 1981—82, v.p., 1982—83, exec. v.p., 1983—84; exec. v.p., mng. dir. Manning Selvage & Lee/L.A., Calif., 1984—89; pres. Manning, Selvage & Lee Inc., NYC, 1989—91, pres., CEO, 1992; chmn., CEO Manning, Selvage & Lee, Inc., NYC, 1993—97; v.p. corp. comms. Nike Inc., Beaverton, Oreg., 1997—.

STEWART, LINDSAY D., lawyer, apparel executive; b. Portland, Oreg. married. BA in Econs., Willamette U., Salem, Oreg., 1969, JD, 1973. Bar: Oreg. 1973. Pvt. practice atty.; corp. counsel Ga.-Pacific Corp.; asst. corp. counsel Nike, Inc., Beaverton, Oreg., 1981—83, gen. counsel, 1983—91, v.p., gen. counsel, 1991—96, v.p. law and corp. affairs, 1996—2001, v.p., chief of staff, 2001—. Mem. Oreg. State Internat. Trade Commn. Avocations: tennis, golf, running. Office: Nike Inc 1 Bowerman Dr Beaverton OR 97005-0979 Office Phone: 503-671-6453.

STEWART, MILTON ROY, lawyer; b. Clovis, N.Mex., Dec. 16, 1945; s. Virgil Maurice and E. Marie (Collins) S. BA, Ind. U., 1968, JD summa cum laude, 1971. Bar: Oreg. 1971, U.S. Ct. Appeals (9th cir.) 1971, U.S. Dist. Ct. (no. dist.) Oreg. 1971. Assoc. Davies, Biggs et al, Portland, Oreg., 1971-75; v.p., gen. counsel U.S. Datacorp, Portland, 1975-77; pvt. practice Portland, 1977-86; bus. devel. ptnr. Davis, Wright, Tremaine, Portland, 1987—2006; spl. counsel AIG Corp., NY, 2007—. Bd. dir. Lex Mundi assn. internat. law firms. Past chmn., mem emeritus Oreg. chpt. Nat. Multisclerosis Soc., 1994—, immediate past mem.; bd. dirs. Nat. Multiple Sclerosis Soc.; emeritus bd. visitors Ind. U. Law Sch.; active Bd. Ind. U. Found. Capt. U.S. Army, 1968-78 State Farm Found. fellow, 1970, John H. Edwards fellow Ind. U. Found., 1971. Mem. Oreg. State Bar Assn., Wash. State Bar Assn., Multnomah Athletic Club, Astoria Golf and Country Club. Office: Davis Wright Tremaine 1300 SW 5th Ave Ste 2200 Portland OR 97201-5667 Business E-Mail: miltstewart@dwt.com.

STEWART, MIRIAM KAY (MIMI STEWART), state legislator; b. Sarasota, Fla., Jan. 27, 1947; d. Wilbur H. Stewart and Alice Miriam Beck; m. David Margolin; children: Boris Nathan Margolin, Hannah Beck Margolin. BA cum laude, Boston U., 1971; MS, Wheelock Coll., 1977. Spl. educator, 1977—2004; ward chair N.Mex. Democratic Party, 1992—; mem. Dist. 21 N.Mex. House of Reps., Albuquerque, 1994—. Democrat. Address: 313 Moon St NE Albuquerque NM 87123-1151 Office: State Capitol Rm 312B Santa Fe NM 87501 Office Phone: 505-880-8249 ext. 113, 505-986-4840. E-mail: mstewart@osogrande.com, mstewart@osogrande.com.*

STEWART, PATRICK, actor; b. Mirfield, Eng., July 13, 1940; s. Alfred and Gladys (Barraclough) S.; m. Sheila Falconer, Mar. 3, 1966 (div. 1990); 2 children; m. Wendy Neuss, Aug. 25, 2000 (div. 2003). Trained, Bristol Old Vic Theatre Sch. Actor: (theatre) Treasure Island (UK, debut), 1959, (US) A Midsummer Night's Dream (Broadway debut), 1970, A Christmas Carol, 1991, 92, 94, Macbeth, West End, 2007, Broadway, 2008, Hamlet, Royal Shakespeare Co., 2008 (Laurence Olivier award for best supporting actor, 2009); (TV series) Star Trek: The Next Generation, 1987-94, Eleventh Hour, 2006, (narrator) High Spirits with the Ghostman, 2005, (mini series) Fall of Eagles, 1974, I, Claudius, 1977, Tinker, Sailor, Soldier, Spy, 1979, Maybury, 1981, Smiley's People, 1982, Playing Shakespeare, 1983, When the Lion Roars, 1992, (voice) 500 Nations, 1995, Mysterious Island, 2005, (TV movies) The Gathering Storm, 1974, Anthony and Cleopatra, 1974 (Olivier award best supporting actor), North and South, 1975, The Madness, 1976, Hamlet, Prince of Denmark, 1980, Little Lord Fauntleroy, 1980, John Paul II, 1984, The Devil's Disciple, 1987, Death Train, 1993, In Search of Dr. Seuss, 1994, (also co-prodr.) The Canterville Ghost, 1996, Moby Dick, 1997, Safe House, 1998, (voice) Animal Farm, 1999, (also exec. prodr.) A Christmas Carol, 1999, (also exec. prodr.) King of Texas, 2002, The Lion in Winter, 2003; host on Saturday Night Live, 1994, (films) Hennessy, 1975, Hedda, 1975, Excalibur, 1981, The Plague Dogs (voice) 1982, Dune, 1984, Uindii, 1984, Lifeforce, 1985, Code Name: Emerald, 1985, Wild Geese II, 1985, The Doctor and the Devils, 1985, Lady Jane, 1986, L.A. Story, 1991, Robin Hood: Men in Tights, 1993, Gunmen, 1994, Star Trek: Generations, 1994, The Pagemaster, 1994 (voice), Jeffrey, 1995, Let It Me Be (aka Love Dance), 1995, Star Trek: First Contact, 1996, Conspiracy Theory, 1997, Safe House, 1997, Dad Savage, 1997, Master Minds, 1997, (voice) Prince of Egypt, 1998, X-Men, 2000, (voice) Jimmy Neutron: Boy Genius, 2001, Star Trek: Nemesis, 2002, X-Men 2, 2003, (voice) Back to Gaya, 2004, Steamboy, 2004, The Game of Their Lives, 2005, (voice) Chicken Little, 2005, X-Men: The Last Stand, 2006, TMNT, 2007, (voice) Earth, 2007; assoc. prodr. Star Trek IX: Insurrection, 1998; assoc. artist with Royal Shakespeare Co., 1967—; recording: Prokofiev: Peter and the Wolf (Grammy award best spoken word album for children 1996). Recipient Sir John Gielgud award, Nat. Arts Club, 2008. Office: William Morris Agy 151 El Camino Dr Beverly Hills CA 90212

STEWART, RICHARD A., former mayor; m. Susan B. Stewart. Postgrad, Air War Coll.; BA, Calif. State U., 1965; MA, No. Mich. U., 1972; JD, Calif. So. Law Sch., 1982. Mayor City of Moreno Valley, Calif., 1996—2000; ptnr. Gellar Stewart and Foley, Riverside, Calif., 1995—; mem. Moreno Valley City Coun., 1990—. Active Res. Deputy Riverside County Sheriff's Dept., 1992—.: 3430 Bundy Ave Ste 107 March Air Force Base CA 92518 E-mail: richards@moval.org.

STEWART, RICHARD ALFRED, business executive; b. Hartford, Conn., Nov. 2, 1945; s. Charles Alfred and Theresa (Procopio) S. BS, Valley Coll., 1967. Account exec. Bank Printing Inc., Los Angeles, 1967-70; pres. Carpet Closet Inc., Los Angeles, 1970-73; western sales mgr. Josten's, Los Angeles, 1973-84; pres. Western Internat. Premiums, Los Angeles, 1984-87; dir. corp. sales Tiffany and Co., Beverly Hills, Calif., 1987-90, dir. major program sales, 1990-92, dir. regional sales NYC, 1992-93, dir. major programs, 1992-93; v.p. sales mktg. and recognition divsn. Jostens, Memphis, 1993—; prin. The Stewart Group Sales & Mktg. Cons., 1994—. V.p. sales & mktg. Am. Gem Corp.; recognition cons. L.A. Olympic Com., 1983-84. Contbr. articles to profl. mags.; developer medals for 1984 summer Olympics. Chmn. bd. dirs. Athletes and Entertainers for Kids. Avocations: tennis, basketball, photography.

STEWART, ROBERT LEE, retired career officer, astronaut; b. Washington, Aug. 13, 1942; s. Lee Olin and Mildred Kathleen (Wann) S.; m. Mary Jane Murphy; children: Ragon Annette, Jennifer Lee. BS in Math., U. So. Miss., 1964; MS in Aerospace Engring., U. Tex., 1972; grad., U.S. Army Air Def. Sch., 1964, grad. advanced course, guided missile systems officers course, 1970. Commd. 2d lt. U.S. Army, 1964, advanced through grades to brig. gen., 1986, fire team leader armed helicopter platoon 101st Aviation Bn., instr. pilot Primary Helicopter Sch., 1967-69, bn. ops. officer, bn. exec. officer 309th Aviation Bn., Seoul, Korea, 1972-73, exptl. test pilot Aviation Engring. Flight Activity Edwards AFB, Calif., 1974-78; astronaut candidate NASA, 1978, mission specialist Space Shuttle Mission 41-B, 1984; mission specialist STS-51J, 1985; dep. comdr. U.S. Army Strategic Def. Command, Huntsville, Ala., 1987-89; dir. of plans U.S. Space Command, 1989-92. Decorated D.S.M., (2) Legion of Merit, (4) DFC, (2) Purple Hearts, Bronze star, Def. Superior Svc. medal, others; recipient NASA Space Flight medal, 1984, 85, Fineburg Meml. award Am. Helicopter Soc., 1984, Herman Oberth award AIAA, 1990; named Army Aviator of Yr., 1984. Mem. Soc. Exptl. Test Pilots, Assn. U.S. Army, Army Aviation Assn. Am., Assn. Space Explorers. Avocations: photography, woodworking, skiing. Home and Office: 815 Sun Valley Dr Woodland Park CO 80863-7729

STEWART, TERRY, lawyer; b. San Francisco; life ptnr. Carole Scagnetti; 1 adopted child. Diploma, Cornell U., 1981; JD, Boalt Hall Sch. Law, 1981. Law clk. 11th cir. Ct. Appeals, Savannah, Ga., 1981—82; ptnr. Howard, Rice, Nemerovski, Canady, Robertson, & Falk; chief dep. city attorney San Francisco, 2002—. Pro bono counsel Internat. Dog Racing Assn.; vol. asst. Iditarod. Mem.: Bar Assn. San Francisco (founder Sch.-to-Coll. program 1999—, pres. 1999). Known for representing same-sex marriage rights in San Francisco. Office: City Hall Rm 234 1 Dr Carlton B Goodlet Pl San Francisco CA 94102-4682

STEWART, THOMAS J., wholesale distribution executive; b. Mar. 28, 1945; CEO Svc. Group Am., 1985—.

STEYER, THOMAS FAHR, investment company executive; b. 1957; s. Roy H. and Marnie (Fahr) Steyer; m. Kathryn Taylor, Aug. 16, 1986; 4 children. BA in Economics and Polit. Sci., summa cum laude, Yale U., 1979; MBA, Stanford U., 1983. Assoc. risk arbitrage dept. Goldman, Sachs & Co.; with mergers and acquisitions dept. Morgan Stanley & Co.; founder, sr. mng. mem. Farallon Capital Mgmt. LLC, 1986—; mng. dir. Hellman & Friedman LLC, 1986—. Bd. dirs CapitalSource, Chevy Chase, Md. Fellow: Am. Acad. Arts and Sciences; mem.: Phi Beta Kappa. Office: Hellman & Friedman LLC One Maritime Plz 12th Fl San Francisco CA 94111 also: Farallon Capital Mgmt Ste 2100 One Maritime Plaza San Francisco CA 94111*

STICKEL, FREDERICK A., publishing executive; b. Weehawken, NJ, Nov. 18, 1921; s. Fred and Eva (Madigan) S.; m. Margaret A. Dunne, Dec. 4, 1943; children: Fred A., Patrick F., Daisy E., Geoffrey M., James E., Bridget A. Student, Georgetown U., 1939-42; BS, St. Peter's Coll., 1943. Advt. salesperson Jersey Observer daily, Hoboken, NJ, 1945-51; retail advt. salesperson Jersey Jour., Jersey City, 1951-55, advt. dir., 1955-66, pub., 1966-67; gen. mgr. Oregonian Pub. Co., Portland, Oreg., 1967-72, pres., 1972-86, pub., 1975—. Bd. regents U. Portland; adv. bd. Portland State U., St. Vincent's Hosp.; bd. dirs. Portland Rose Festival Assn., United Way Oreg.; chmn. Portland Citizens Crime Commn. Capt. USMC, 1942-45. Mem. Assn. for Portland Progress (dir.), Portland C. of C. (dir.), Oreg. Newspaper Pubs. Assn. (past pres.), Pacific N.W. Newspaper Assn. (past pres.), Newspaper Assn. Am., University Club, Multnomah Athletic Waverley Country Club, Arlington Club, Rotary. Office: Oregonian Pub Co 1320 SW Broadway Portland OR 97201-3499 Office Phone: 503-221-8140. Office Fax: 503-294-4175.

STICKLES, BONNIE JEAN, retired nurse; b. Waukesha, Wis., Nov. 24, 1944; d. Donald William and Betty Jane S. BSN, U. Wis., 1967; MSN in Midwifery, Columbia U., 1974. Mem. nursing staff Grace Hosp., Detroit, 1970-73; mem. faculty and staff U. Minn. Sch. Nursing and Nurse-Midwifery Svc., Mpls., 1974-76; chief nurse-midwife, clin. instr. St. Paul-Ramsey Med. Ctr., 1976-84; midwifery supr. IHS/PHS Chinle Hosp., 1984-85; program mgr. maternal health sect. N.Mex. Dept. Health and Environ., 1985-90, Lovelance Med. Ctr., 1990-91, St. Vincent's Hosp., 1991-94, NMC Dialysis Divsn., 1994-95; blackjack dealer, 1995-97; nurse CMS Penitentiary, N.Mex., 1997—2002; ret. Author articles in field; patentee tchg. model. Mem. FDA Anesthetics, Life Support Adv. com.; adv. bd. Childbirth Edn. Assn., 1980-85. Served with USNR, 1965-70. Mem. Am. Coll. Nurse-Midwives (chmn. profl. affairs com. 1975-80), Nurses Assn. Am. Coll. Obstetricians and Gynecologists (charter), Aircraft Owners and Pilot Assn., Gt. Plains Perinatal Orgn., Alpha Tau Delta.

STICKNEY, ROBERT ROY, fisheries educator; b. Mpls., July 2, 1941; s. Roy E. and Helen Doris (Nelson) S.; m. LuVerne C. (Whiteley), Dec. 29, 1961; children: Robert Roy, Marolan Margaret. BS, U. Nebr., 1967; MA, U. Mo., 1968; PhD, Fla. State U., 1971. cert. fisheries scientist. Rsch. assoc. Skidaway Inst. Oceanography, Savannah, Ga., 1971—73, asst. prof., 1973—75, Tex. A and M U., Coll. Sta., 1975—78, assoc. prof., 1978—83, prof., 1983—84; prof. zoology, dir. Fisheries Rsch. Lab., So. Ill. U., Carbondale, 1984—85; dir. Sch. of Fisheries U. Wash., Seattle, 1985—91, prof., 1985—96; dir. Sea Grant Coll. program Tex. A&M U., Coll. Sta., 1996—. Author: Principles of Warmwater Aquaculture, 1979, Estuarine Ecology of the Southeastern U.S. and Gulf of Mex., 1984; editor: Culture of Non Salmonid Freshwater Fishes, 1986, 1992, Flagship: A History of Fisheries at the U. of Washington, 1989; co-editor: Fisheries: Harvesting Life from Water, 1989, Culture of Salmonid Fishes, 1992, Fisheries: Harvesting Life from Water, 1995, Principles of Aquaculture, 1994, Fish Culture in the United States: A Hist. Survey, 1996, Responsible Marine Aquaculture, 2002, Aquaculture: An Introductory Text, 2005; editor: revs. in Fisheries Sci., Ency. of Aqua-culture, World Aquaculture mag.; contbr. articles to profl. jour. Served in USAF, 1959-63. Mem.: Sea Grant Assn. (pres. 2003—04). Home Phone: 979-279-3094; Office Phone: 979-845-3854. Personal E-mail: rrstickney@aol.com. E-mail: stickney@tamu.edu.

STIEBER, TAMAR, journalist; b. Bklyn., Sept. 15, 1955; d. Alfred and Florence (Spector) Stieber. Student, Rockland C.C., 1972—75, West Chester CC, NY, 1973—74; BA in Film cum laude, U. Calif., Berkeley, 1985, postgrad. in comparative lit., 1985—86; grad. Police Res. Acad. cum laude, Napa Valley Coll., 1988. Office mgr., confidential sec. AP, San Francisco, 1981—83; stringer Daily Californian, Berkeley, Calif., 1983—84; film rsch. tchg. asst. U. Calif., Berkeley, 1984—86; libr. and rsch. asst. Pacific Film Archive, Berkeley, 1984—86; intern San Francisco Examiner, 1984; reporter Sonoma (Calif.) Index-Tribune, 1987—88, Vallejo (Calif.) Times-Herald, 1988—89, Albuquerque Jour., 1989—94, freelancer, 1994—. Recipient Pulitzer Prize for specialized reporting, 1990, 1st pl. pub. svc. divsn., N.Mex. Press Assn., 1990, Pub. Svc. award, Albuquerque Press Club, 1990, 1st pl. newswriting, N.Mex. Press Assn., 1991, Hon. Mention, AP Mng. Editors, 1994. Mem.: AAUW, Phi Beta Kappa. Home: PO Box 9835 Santa Fe NM 87504-9835 E-mail: tstieber@isp.com.

STIEHM, E. RICHARD, pediatrician, educator; b. Milw., Jan. 22, 1933; s. Reuben Harold and Marie Dueno S.; m. Judith Hicks, July 12, 1958; children: Jamie Elizabeth, Carrie Eleanor, Meredith Ellen. BS, U. Wis., 1954, MD, 1957. Diplomate Am. Bd. Pediat., Am. Bd. Allergy and Clin. Immunology (bd. dirs. 1977-83), Am. Bd. Diagnostic Lab. Immunology. Intern Phila. Gen. Hosp., 1957-58; fellow in physiol. chemistry U. Wis., 1959-61, asst. prof. pediat., 1965—68, assoc. prof., 1968—69; med. officer USNR, Johnsville, Pa., 1961-63; resident in pediat. Babies Hosp., NYC, 1963-65; rsch. fellow in pediat. immunology U. Calif., San Francisco, 1965-68; assoc. prof. UCLA, 1969—72, chief divsn. immunology, allergy and rheumatology, 1969—2003, prof., 1972—, assoc. dir. Ctr. for Interdisciplinary Rsch. in Immunologic Diseases, 1981-82, co-dir. Cystic Fibrosis Ctr., 1988—95, vice chair acad. affairs dept. pediat., 1989—99; vis. scientist metabolism br. Nat. Cancer Inst., Bethesda, Md., 1982-88. Vis. prof. Yale U., Mayo Clinic, U. Cin., Great Ormond St. Hosp., U.K., U. Wis.; bd. sci. dirs. Immune Deficiency Found., 1981—, Eczema Found., 1988—, Pediat. AIDS Found., 1989-99; task force on pediatric allergy NIH, 1977; mem. gen. clin. rsch. ctr. study sect. NIH, 1978-82, 84-88; adv. com. Hartford Fellowship, 1984-88; co-dir. LA Pediatric AIDS Consortium, 1988—. Editor: Immunologic Disorders in Infants and Children, 1972, 80, 89, 96, 2004; Am. editor: Pediatric Rsch., 1984-89; assoc. editor: Pediat. Update, 2003-; mem. editl. bd. Pediat., 1972-78, Pediat. in Rev., 1978-81, Jour. Allergy and Clin. Immunology, 1976-80, Jour. Clin. Immunology, 1985-89, Jour. Asthma Pediatric Allergy and Immunology, 1987-91, Am. Jour. Diseases of Children, 1987-97, Contemporary Pediat., 1991-96, Am. Jour. Clin. Nutrition, 1992-97; contbr. articles to profl. jours. Commr. HHS Commn. on Childhood Vaccines, 1988-90; mem. clin. rsch. adv. com. Nat. Found. March of Dimes, 1992-97, 2004-09. Recipient Career Devel. award Nat. Inst. Allergy and Infectious Diseases, 1967-69, E. Mead Johnson award for Pediat. Rsch., 1974, Alumni Citation award U. Wis. Med. Sch., 1988, Lifetime Achievement award Immune Deficiency Found., 1995, Med. Sci. award UCLA Med. Alumni, 1999, Disting. Alumni award Babies and Children's Hosp. Alumni Assn., N.Y., 1999, Abbott Labs. award, Clin. and Diagnostic Immunology Am. Soc. Microbiology, 2007; Markle scholar, 1967-72. Fellow AAAS; mem. Am. Assn. Immunologists, Western Soc. Pediat. Rsch. (coun. 1977-80, pres. 1983, Ross Rsch. award 1971), Soc. Pediat. Rsch., Am. Pediat. Soc., Am. Acad. Allergy, Asthma and Clin. Immunology, Am. Acad. Pediat. (infectious diseases com. 1971-77), Am. Soc. Clin. Investigation, Clin. Immunology Soc., Phi Beta Kappa, Alpha Omega Alpha. Office: UCLA Dept Peds Divsn Immunology 10833 Le Conte Ave Los Angeles CA 90095-3075 Office Phone: 310-825-6481. Business E-Mail: estiehm@mednet.ucla.edu.

STIEHM, JUDITH HICKS, political scientist; b. Madison, Wis., Oct. 9, 1935; d. Stratton Elson and Eleanor Spencer (Kilbourn) Hicks; m. E. Richard Stiehm, July 12, 1958; children: Jamie Elizabeth, Carrie Eleanor, Meredith Ellen. Student, Oberlin Coll., 1953; BA in E. Asian Studies, U. Wis., 1957; MA in Am. History, Temple U., 1961; PhD in Polit. Theory, Columbia U., 1969. Dir. resident hons. program U. So. Calif., LA, 1970-73, asst. prof., 1970-74, assoc. prof., 1974-83, dir. program for study of women and men in soc., 1975-81, prof. polit. sci., 1983, vice provost, 1984-87; provost Fla. Internat. U., Miami, 1987-91, prof. polit. sci., 1987—. Vis. prof. U. Wis., 1994, U.S. Army Peacekeeping Inst., U.S. Army War Coll., 1995-96, U.S. Army Strategic Studies Inst., U.S. Army War Coll., 1996, U. So. Calif., 2002-; lectr. U. Wis., Madison, 1966-69, UCLA, 1969-70; vis. lectr. San Francisco State U., 1965-66; affiliate NAS Project, 1981-82; cons. UN Div. for the Advancement of Women, Calif. Elected Women, Dept. HEW, AAUW, LWV L.A., UN Lessons Learned Unit, Dept. Peacekeeping Ops. Author: Nonviolent Power: Active and Passive Resistance in America, 1972, Bring Me Men and Women..., 1981, Arms and the Enlisted Woman, 1989, The U.S. Army War College: Military Education in a Democracy, 2002, Champions for Peace: Women Winners of the Nobel Peace Prize, 2006; editor: The Frontiers of Knowledge, 1976, Women and Men's Wars, 1983, Women's Views of the Political World of Men, 1984, It's Our Military, Too!, 1996; mem. editorial bd. Western Polit. Quar., 1972-75, Signs, 1981-84, Women and Politics, 1986-88, 2000-. Mem. Calif. Postsecondary Edn. Commn., 1978, Calif. Adv. Coun. on Vocat. Edn., 1978-82, Def. Adv. Com. on Women in Svcs., 1979-82; bd. dirs. So. Calif. and Miami chpts. ACLU. Named Woman of Yr., Santa Monica YWCA, 1981; recipient Outstanding Civilian Svc. medal U.S. Army, 1996, U. Wis. Disting Alumni award, 2006. Mem. Am. Polit. Sci. Assn. (exec. coun. 1989, sec. 2000, Frank Goodnow award, 2008), Western Polit. Sci. Assn. (pres. 1986), Women's Caucus Polit. Sci. (pres. 1996-97), Nat. Council for Research on Women (exec. council 1982), Council on Fgn. Relations, Phi Beta Kappa, Phi Kappa Phi (Victoria Schuck Book award 1990). Avocations: tennis, skiing, stained glass. Home: 434 24th St Santa Monica CA 90402-3102 Personal E-mail: stiehmj@fiu.edu.

STINEHART, WILLIAM, JR., retired lawyer; b. LA, Dec. 15, 1943; s. William Sr. and Martha T. S.; m. Patricia Kidney, June 22, 1968; children: Jacqueline Elaine, William III. BA with distinction, Stanford U., 1966; LLB, UCLA, 1969. Bar: Calif. 1970, US Dist. Ct. (cen. dist.) Calif. 1970. Assoc. Gibson, Dunn & Crutcher LLP, LA, 1969-76, ptnr. tax dept., 1977—; ret., 2005. Bd. dir. Tribune Co. Trustee Harvard Westlake Sch., N. Hollywood, 1983-89, SW Mus., 1986-89. Mem. LA County Bar Assn., Order of Coif, LA Country Club, Beach Club of Santa Monica, Calif., LA Tennis Club. Republican. Episcopalian. Office: Gibson Dunn & Crutcher LLP 1043 Roscomare Rd Los Angeles CA 90077-2227 Office Phone: 310-552-8557. Office Fax: 310-552-7027. Business E-Mail: wstinehart@gbsondunn.com.

STINI, WILLIAM ARTHUR, anthropologist, educator; b. Oshkosh, Wis., Oct. 9, 1930; s. Louis Alois and Clara (Larsen) S.; m. Mary Ruth Kalous, Feb. 11, 1950; children: Patricia Laraine, Paulette Ann, Suzanne Kay. BBA, U. Wis., 1960, MS, 1967, PhD, 1969. Planner cost acct. Kimberly-Clark Corp., Niagara Falls, NY, 1960-62; from asst. prof. to assoc. prof. Cornell U., Ithaca, NY, 1968-73; assoc. prof. U. Kans., Lawrence, 1973-76; prof. anthropology U. Ariz., Tucson, 1976—, prof. family and cmty. medicine, 1978—; panelist anthropology program NSF, 1976-78; cons. NIH, 1974—. Mem. Ariz. Cancer Ctr., 1995—; adj. prof. Nutritional Scis., 1997—; head dept. anthropology U. Ariz., 1980-89, prof. pub. health, 1998—; panelist NRC/NSF Grad. Fellowship Program, 1991-95. Author: Ecology and Human Adaptation, 1975, Nature, Culture and Human History - A Biocultural Introduction to Anthropology (with Davydd J. Greenwood), 1977, Physiological and Morphological Adaptation and Evolution, 1979 (with Frank E. Poirier and Kathy B. Wreden) In Search of Ourselves: An Introduction to Physical Anthropology, 1990, 5th edit., 1994; field editor phys. anthropology The Am. Anthropologist, 1980-83; editor-in-chief Am. Jour. Phys. Anthropology, 1983-89; assoc. editor Nutrition and Cancer, 1981-95; cons. editor Collegium Antropologicum, 1985—. Mem. Gov.'s Adv. Coun. on Aging, State of Ariz., 1980—83. Nat. Inst. Dental Rsch. tng. grantee, 1964-68; Clark Found. grantee Cornell U., 1973; Nat. Dairy Coun. grantee, 1985-88; Wenner-Gren Found. grantee, 1991—; fellow Linacre Coll., Oxford, 1985; vis. fellow U. London, 1991. Fellow AAAS (steering group sect. H 1987-91), Am. Anthrop. Assn., N.Y. Acad. Scis.; mem. Am. Assn. Phys. Anthropologists (exec. com. 1978-81, pres. 1989-91), Human Biology Assn. (exec. com. 1978-81), Soc. for Study Social Biology, Am. Soc. Nutritional Scis., Am. Soc. on Aging, Sigma Xi. Home: 6240 N Camino Miraval Tucson AZ 85718-3025 Home Phone: 520-299-3703. Business E-Mail: stini@u.arizona.edu.

STISKA, JOHN CHARLES, lawyer; b. Chgo., Feb. 14, 1942; s. Rudolph and Elsie Sophie (Nelson) S.; m. Janet Hazel Osuch, Aug. 8, 1964; children: Julie, Thomas, Michael, Matthew. BBA, U. Wis., 1965, JD, 1970. Bar: Wis. 1970, Calif. 1971. Assoc., ptnr. Luce, Forward, Hamilton & Scripps, San Diego, 1970-81; ptnr. Aylward, Kintz & Stiska, San Diego, 1981-86; pres., CEO Triton Group Ltd., La Jolla, Calif., 1986-87; ptnr. Brobeck, Phleger & Harrison, San Diego, 1987-90; pres., COO Intermark, Inc., La Jolla, Calif., 1990-92; pres., CEO Triton Group Ltd., 1993-94; chmn., CEO, 1994-96; sr. v.p. Qualcomm, Inc., San Diego, 1996-98; pres., ceo DC Acquisition Corp., San Diego, 1998; chair Comml. Bridge Capital LLC, La Jolla, Calif., 1998—. Of counsel Latham & Watkins, San Diego, 1998—. 1st lt. U.S. Army, 1965-67. Mem. ABA. San Diego County Bar Assn., Calif State Bar Assn. Lutheran.

STITLEY, JAMES WALTER, JR., food manufacturing executive; b. York, Pa., May 23, 1944; s. James Walter and Geraldine Salome (Horn) S.; m. Tresa Rose Adkins, 1996. BS in Chemistry, Millersville U., 1970. Med. technician York Hosp., 1962-66; rsch. biochemist Carter-Wallace, Inc., Cranbury, N.J., 1970-75; mgr. Ward Labs. divsn. Ward Foods, East Orange, N.J., 1975-77; mgr. tech. svcs. Pepperidge Farm, Inc., Norwalk, Conn., 1977-86; dir. tech. devel. Am. Inst. Baking, Manhattan, Kans., 1986-88; dir. baking and cereal sci. rsch. and biscuit product devel. internat. Campbell Soup Co., Camden, N.J., 1988-90; nat. dir. rsch. and tech. Domino's Pizza, Inc., 1990-91, divsn. v.p. consumer and product rsch., 1992—; pres., CEO Techno-Vation Network, Inc., 1992—; dir. new product innovation Weider Nutrition Internat., Salt Lake City, 1999—. Cons. biochemistry and toxicology. Contbr. articles to profl.jours. Asst. scoutmaster Boy Scouts Am. Mem. AAAS, Am. Chem. Soc., Am. Mgmt. Assn., Am. Assn. Cereal Chemists, Am. Inst. Baking (ednl. adv. com. 1978—), Instrument Soc. Am. (assoc. dir.-food industry liaison), Am. Astron. Rsch. Group, York Astron. Soc. (v.p. 1960). Achievements include patents in field; publs. in field. Office: Schiff Nutrition Internat 2002 S 5070 W Salt Lake City UT 84104 Home: 5519 Philadelphian Ct West Jordan UT 84088-6232 E-mail: sitf2000@yahoo.com.

STITZINGER, JAMES FRANKLIN, religious studies educator, library director; b. Abington, Pa., July 27, 1950; s. James Franklin and Elizabeth (Kocher) S.; m. Deborah Lynn Benner, July 22, 1972; children: Rachael, James, David, Jonathan. BA, Northwestern Coll., Roseville, Minn., 1975; MDiv, Central Sem., 1975; ThM, Grace Theol. Sem., 1977; MLS, Drexel U., 1978; postgrad., Westminster Theol. Sem., 1991—. Acquisition libr. Grace Theol. Sem., Winona Lake, Ind., 1975-77; libr., prof. ch. history Calvary Bapt. Sem., Lansdale, Pa., 1977-87; dir. libr. svcs., assoc. prof. hist. theology The Master's Coll. and Sem., Sun Valley, Calif., 1987—; chief exec. officer Books for Libraries, Inc., North Hollywood, Calif., 1989—. Mem. Am. Theol. Libr. Assn., Am. Soc. Ch. History, Evang. Theol. Soc. Republican. Baptist. Office: The Masters Sem 13248 Roscoe Blvd Sun Valley CA 91352-3739

STOCK, DAVID EARL, mechanical engineering educator; b. Balt., Feb. 2, 1939; s. Walter E. and Minnie H. (Bauer) S.; m. Mary R. Wilford, Aug. 4, 1962; children: Joseph W., Katherine W. BS, Pa. State U., 1961; MS, U. Conn., 1965; PhD, Oreg. State U., 1972. Test engr. Pratt & Whitney Aircraft, East Hartford, Conn., 1961-65; vol. Peace Corps, Ghana, 1965-68; prof. Wash. State U., Pullman, 1972—. Contbr. articles to profl. jours. Fellow ASME (chair multiphase flow com. 1988-90, Freeman scholar 1994, chair exec. com. fluid engring. divsn., 2000-01). Office: Wash State U Sch Mech Materials Engr PO Box 642920 Pullman WA 99164-2920 Office Phone: 509-335-3223. Business E-Mail: stock@wsu.edu.

STOCKARD, R. L., state legislator; b. Bloomfield; Student, U. Albuquerque. State police capt.; mem. N.Mex. Legislature, Santa Fe, 1996—, mem. jud. com., mem. pub. affairs com. Republican. Office: PO Box 1364 Bloomfield NM 87413-1364

STOCKDALE, STEWART A., data processing company executive; b. 1961; BBA in Mktg., U. Denver. Brand mgmt. Procter & Gamble, American Express, Citibank; sr. v.p. global mktg. and product mgmt. MasterCard Internat.; exec. v.p., chief mktg. officer Conseco, Inc.; chief mktg. officer Simon Property Group, Inc. (SPG), 2002—08; pres. Simon Brand Ventures (SBV), 2002—08; exec. v.p., pres. US & Can. Western Union Co., Englewood, Colo., 2008—. Named #2 Mktg. Exec. of Yr., Fin. Svc. Mktg., 2000; nominee Marketer of Yr., Direct Marketing Assn., 2002. Office: Western Union Co 12500 E Belford Ave Englewood CO 80112

STOCKHOLM, CHARLES M., diversified financial services company executive; BA, Stanford Univ.; grad. degree, Am. Grad. Sch. Internat. Mgmt. Sr. officer Citibank; chmn. Citibank Internat.; sr. exec. vice-pres. Crocker Nat. Bank; mng. dir. Trust Co. West; chmn. bd. dir. Matson Navigation Co., Inc., Alexander & Baldwin, Inc. Trustee Am. Graduate Sch. Internat. Mgmt., Asian Art Mus. San Francisco.

STOCKWELL, ROBERT PAUL, linguist, educator; b. Oklahoma City, June 12, 1925; s. Benjamin P. and Anna (Cunningham) S.; m. Lucy Louisa Floyd, Aug. 29, 1946; 1 child, Paul Witten; m. Donka Minkova, Jan. 13, 2005. BA, U. Va., 1946, MA, 1949, PhD, 1952. Instr. English, Oklahoma City U., 1946-48; mem. linguistics staff Sch. Langs., Fgn. Service Inst., State Dept., 1952-56; mem. faculty UCLA, 1956-94, prof. English, 1962-66, prof. linguistics, 1966—94, chmn. dept., 1966-73, 80-84, prof. emeritus, 1994—. Mem. com. lang. programs Am. Coun. Learned Socs., 1965-69 Author: (with J.D. Bowen) Patterns of Spanish Pronunciation, 1960, Sounds of English and Spanish, 1965, (with J. D. Bowen, J.W. Martin) The Grammatical Structures of English and Spanish, 1965, The Major Syntactic Structures of English, 1973, (with P.M. Schachter, B.H. Partee) Foundations of Syntactic Theory, 1977, Workbook in Syntactic Theory and Analysis, 1977, (with Donka Minkova) English Words: History and Structure, 2001; also numerous articles.; editor: (with R.S.K. Macaulay) Linguistic Change and Generative Theory, 1972, (with Donka Minkova) Studies in the History of the English Language: A Millennial Perspective, 2003; assoc. editor: Lang., 1973-79, Festschrift: Rhetorica, Phonologica, Syntactica: A Festchrift for Robert P. Stockwell, 1988. Served with USNR, 1943-45. Am. Coun. Learned Socs. fellow, 1963-64. Mem. Linguistic Soc. Am. (exec. com. 1965-68), Philol. Assn. Great Britain. Home: 1929 Manning Ave #301 Los Angeles CA 90025 Office: UCLA Linguistics Dept Los Angeles CA 90095 Business E-Mail: stockwel@ucla.edu.

STOESSINGER, JOHN GEORGE, political science professor; b. Vienna, Oct. 14, 1927; arrived in US, 1947; s. Oscar and Irene Stoessinger; m. Carolyn Stoessinger, 1966 (div. 1985); children: Richard Victor (dec.), Anna. BA, Grinnell Coll., 1950, LLB (hon.), 1970; MA, Harvard U., 1952, PhD, 1954; LLB (hon.), Am. Coll. in Switzerland, Leysin, 1981; LHD (hon.), Drury U., 2007. Prof. polit. scis. CUNY, NYC, 1957-83; dir. polit. affairs divsn. UN, NYC, 1967-74; disting. prof. internat. affairs Trinity U., San Antonio, 1983-2000; disting. prof. global diplomacy U. San Diego, 2000—. Teaching fellow Harvard U., Cambridge, Mass., 1952-54; asst. prof. polit. sci. Wellesley Coll., Mass., 1954-56; vis. prof. internat. affairs Columbia U., NYC, 1963-67, Princeton U., NJ, 1978. Author: The Might of Nations, 1962, 10th edit., 2000 (Bancroft prize 1963), Nations at Dawn, 1979, 6th edit., 1996, Henry Kissinger, 1979, Why Nations Go To War, 1983, 10th edit., 2007. Active UNA-USA, NY, 1960—. Mem. Coun. on Fgn. Rels. (book rev. editor Fgn. Affairs 1968-78). Jewish. Avocation: classical music. Office: U San Diego 5998 Alcala Park San Diego CA 92110 Home: 1337 Neptune Ave Encinitas CA 92024 Office Phone: 760-632-8682. Personal E-mail: johngstoessinger@cox.net.

STOFFLE, CARLA JOY, university library dean; b. Pueblo, Colo., June 19, 1943; d. Samuel Bernard and Virginia Irene (Berry) Hayden; m. Richard William Stoffle, June 12, 1964; children: Brent William, Kami Ann. AA, So. Colo. State Coll., Pueblo, 1963; BA, U. Colo., 1965; MLS, U. Ky., 1969; postgrad., U. Wis., 1980. Head govt. publ. dept. John G. Crabbe Library, Eastern Ky. U., Richmond, 1969-72; from head pub. svcs. to asst. chancellor edn. svcs. U. Wis. Parkside Libr., Kenosha, 1972—85; dep. dir. U. Mich. Libr., Ann Arbor, 1986—91; prof. libr. sci. U. Ariz., Tucson, 1991—, dean librs. and Ctr. for Creative Photography, 1991—, acting dir. Sch. Info. Resources and Libr. Sci., 1999—2001. Adv. bd. Bowker Librs., NY, 1985—90; bd. dirs. Trejo Foster Found., 2000—; state adv. com. Ariz. State Dept. of Libr. Archives and Pub. Records, 2000—; adv. com. U. Mich. Sch. Libr. Sci., 1986—92, OCLC Rsch. Librs., 1995—2000. Co-author: Administration of Government Documents Collection, 1974, Materials and Method for History Research, 1979, Materials and Methods for Political Science Research, 1979; mem. editl. bd. The Collection Bldg., 1978—95, The Bottom Line, 1989—95, Internet and Higher Edn., 1998—99, The Univ. Ariz. Press, 1992—. Vol. Peace Corps, Barbados, West Indies, 1965—67; mem. bd. Pima County Pub. Libr., 2004—; mem. bd. libr. examiners Ariz. State Libr. Recipient Pres.'s award, Ariz. Ednl. Media Assn., 1993, YWCA Tucson Outstanding Woman of 1992: A Woman on the Move award, 1992, Ariz. Libr. of Yr. award, 2000, Dir.'s award for Outstanding Svc., Sch. Info. Resources Libr. Sci., 2006; named Outstanding Alumnus, Coll. Libr. and Info. Sci., U. Ky., 1989. Mem.: ALA (councilor 1983—93, exec. bd. dirs. 1985—93, treas. 1988—93, endowment trustee 1988—93, endowment campaign com. 1989—93, pres. adv. com. 1993—96, legis. com. 1994—96, nominations com. 1997, Lippincott award com. 1997, spectrum scholarship com. 1998—2002, endowment trustee 2001—, chair com. accreditation 2002—04, libr. and outreach svcs. adv. com. 1997-99, chair 1997-98, Miriam Dudley Bibliographic Instrn. Libr. of Yr. award 1991, Acad. Rsch. Libr. of Yr. 1992, Elizabeth Futas Catalyst for Change award 2002, Equality award 2003, Loleta Fyan award Jury 2003—04), Greater Western Libr. Alliance (incoming chair 2006—), Ctr. Rsch. Librs. (budget and fin. com. 1994—2001, exec. com., bd. dirs. 1998—, treas. 1999—2000, vice chair, bd. dirs. 2001—03, chair, bd. dirs. 2003), Ariz. State Libr. Assn., Assn. Coll. Rsch. Librs. (bd. dirs. 1978—84, mem. exec. com. 1981—84, pres. 1982—83, planning com. 1993—95, chair nat. conf. planning com. 1995—97), Assn. Rsch. Librs. (com. stats. and measurement 1994—2003, bd. dirs. 1997—2001, mem. steering com. Scholarly Pub. and Acad. Resource Coalition 1998—2001, mem. govt. documents digitization project work group 2004—, bd. dirs. info. policies com. 2004—). Office: U Arizona Main Libr 1510 E University Blvd Tucson AZ 85721-0055 Office Phone: 520-621-2101. E-mail: stofflec@u.library.arizona.edu.

STOKKE, DIANE REES, lawyer; b. Kansas City, Mo., Jan. 29, 1951; d. William James and Marybeth (Smith) Rees; m. Larry Ernst Stokke, June 9, 1973; children: Michelle, Megan, Carly. AB magna cum laude, Gonzaga U., 1972; JD with high honors, U. Wash., 1976. Bar: Wash. 1976, U.S. Dist. Ct. (ea. dist.) Wash. 1976, U.S. Dist. Ct. (we. dist.) Wash. 1976, U.S. Ct. Appeals (9th cir.) 1980. Assoc. Preston, Thorgrimson, Ellis & Holman, Seattle, 1976-83; ptnr. Kirkpatrick & Lockhart Preston Gates Ellis LLP (formerly known as Preston, Gates & Ellis LLP), Seattle, 1983—. Atty. Seattle Ctr. Found., 1977-83. Trustee Seattle Infant Devel. Ctr., 1984—86, Fremont Pub. Assn., 1994—2001, 2003—05. Gonzaga U. scholar, 1968. Mem. ABA, Wash. State Bar Assn. (spl. dist. counsel 1985-88), Seattle-King County Bar Assn., Wash. Women Lawyers, Order of Coif, Wash. Women Real Estate Lawyers, Am. Coll. of Mortgage Attys., Comml. Real Estate Women. Roman Catholic. Office: Kirkpatrick Lockhart Preston Gates Ellis LLP 925 Fourth Ave Ste 2900 Seattle WA 98104-1158 Office Phone: 206-623-7580. Business E-Mail: diane.stokke@klgates.com.

STOLL, CRAIG, chef; m. Anne Spencer, May 2000; 1 child, Lucy Rose. Grad., Culinary Inst. America, Hyde Park, NY; B in Hospitality Mgmt., Fla. Internat. U., Miami. Cook Campton Place, Postrio, Splendido; intern Italian Culinary Inst. for Foreigners, Turin; exec. chef Tutto Bene, Timo's, Palio d'Asti, Frog and Peach, Mill Valley, Calif., 1997—98; co-owner, exec. chef Delfina Restaurant, San Francisco, 1998—. Named Best Chef: Pacific, James Beard Found., 2008. Office: Delfina Restaurant 3621 18th St San Francisco CA 94110

STOLLER, CLAUDE, architect; b. NYC, Dec. 2, 1921; s. Max and Esther (Zisblatt) S.; m. Anna Maria Oldenburg, June 5, 1946 (div. Oct. 1972); children: Jacob, Dorothea, Elizabeth; m. Rosemary Raymond Lax, Sept. 22, 1978. Student, Black Mountain Coll., NC, 1942; M.Arch., Harvard U., 1949. Architect Architects Collaborative, Cambridge, Mass., after 1949, Shepley, Bulfinch, Richardson & Abbot, Boston, 1951; co-founder, partner firm Marquis & Stoller, San Francisco, 1956; pvt. practice architecture NYC and San Francisco, 1974-78; founder, partner Stoller/Partners, Berkeley, Calif., 1978, Stoller, Knoerr Archs., 1988-95. Mem. faculty Washington U., St. Louis, 1955-56; mem. faculty U. Calif., Berkeley, 1957-91, prof. architecture, 1968-92, acting chmn. dept., 1965-66, chair grad. studies, 1984-91, prof. emeritus, 1991—; mem. Berkeley Campus Design Rev. Bd., 1985-91, chmn., 1992-93; commr. Calif. Bd. Archtl. Examiners, 1980-90, mem. exam. com., 1985-88; mem. diocesan commn. arch. Episcopal Diocese Calif., 1961-98; vis. arch. Nat. Design Inst., Ahmedabad, India, 1963; planning commr. City of Mill Valley, 1961-66, Marin County Planning Commn., 1966-67; mem. pub. adv. panel archtl. svcs. GSA, 1969-71; citizens urban design adv. com. City of Oakland, Calif., 1968; vis. com. nat. archtl. accrediting bd. U. Minn. and U. Wis., Milw., 1971; coun. Harvard Grad. Sch. Design Assn., 1976-77; mem. design rev. com. The Sea Ranch, Calif., 1990-2002. Prin. works include St. Francis Sq. Coop. Apts., San Francisco, 1961, Pub. Housing for Elderly, San Francisco, 1974, Learning Resources Bldg, U. Calif., Santa Barbara, 1975, Menorah Park Housing for Elderly, San Francisco, 1979, San Jose State U. Student Housing Project, 1984, Delta Airlines Terminal, San Francisco Internat. Airport, 1988. Served with AUS, 1943-46. Recipient numerous awards including AIA Honor awards, 1963, 64, AIA Bay Region Honor award, 1974, Concrete Reinforced Steel Inst. award, 1976, AIA award, 1976, CADA Site I Solar Housing award Sacramento, Calif., 1980, State of Calif. Affordable Housing award, 1981, PG&E Suntherm award, 1981, San Francisco Housing Authority award, 1983, Orchid award City of Oakland, 1989, Citation for achievement and svc. U. Calif., Berkeley, 1991, Design award Berkeley Design Advocates. Fellow AIA. Home: 2816 Derby St Berkeley CA 94705-1325 Home Phone: 510-843-7214. Business E-Mail: stoller@berkeley.edu.

STOLOV, WALTER CHARLES, medicine physiatrist, educator; b. NYC, Jan. 6, 1928; s. Arthur and Rose F. (Gordon) S.; m. Anita Carvel Noodelman, Aug. 9, 1953; children: Nancy, Amy, Lynne. BS in Physics, CCNY, 1948; MA in Physics, U. Minn., 1951, MD, 1956. Diplomate Am. Bd. Phys. Med. and Rehab., Am. Bd. Electrodiagnostic Medicine. Physicist U.S. Naval Gun Factory, Nat. Bur. Stds., Washington, 1948-49; teaching and rsch. asst. U. Minn., Mpls., 1950-54; from instr. to assoc. prof. U. Wash., Seattle, 1960-70, prof., 1970-99, prof. emeritus, 1999—, also chmn., 1987-99, prof. emeritus, 1999—. Editl. bd. Archives Phys. Medicine and Rehab., 1967-78, Muscle and Nerve, 1983-89, 92-95; cons. Social Security Adminstrn., Seattle, 1975—; sec. Am. Bd. Electrodiagnostic Medicine, 1995—. Co-editor: Handbook of Severe Disability, 1981; contbr. articles to profl. jours. Surgeon USPHS, 1956-57. Recipient Townsend Harris medal CCNY, 1990. Fellow: AAAS, Am. Heart Assn.; mem.: Am. Spinal Cord Injry Assn., Am. Assn. Electrodiagnostic Medicine (pres. 1987—88, Lifetime Achievement award 2001), Assn. Acad. Physiatrists, Am. Congress Rehab. Medicine (Essay award 1959), Am. Acad. Phys. Medicine and Rehab. (Disting. Clinician award 1987). Avocations: dance, singing. Office: U Wash Box 356490 1959 NE Pacific St Seattle WA 98195-0001 Office Phone: 206-543-7065.

STOLPER, EDWARD MANIN, secondary school educator; b. Boston, Dec. 16, 1952; s. Saul James and Frances A. (Liberman) S.; m. Lauren Beth Adoff, June 3, 1973; children: Jennifer Ann, Daniel Aaron. AB, Harvard U., 1974, PhD, 1979; MPhil, U. Edinburgh, Scotland, 1976. Asst. prof. geology Calif. Inst. Tech., Pasadena, 1979-82, assoc. prof. geology, 1982-83, prof. geology, 1983-90, William E. Leonhard prof. geology, 1990—, chmn. divsn. geol. and planetary sci., 1994—2004, acting provost, 2004. Marshall scholar Marshall Aid Commemoration Commn., 1974-76; recipient Newcomb Cleve. prize AAAS, 1984, F.W. Clarke medal Geochem. Soc., 1985, Arthur Holmes medal European Union Geosci., 1997; Geochemistry fellow Geochem. Soc. and The European Assn. for Geochemistry, 1997. Fellow Meteoritical Soc. (Nininger Meteorite award 1976), Am. Geophys. Union (James B. Macelwane award 1986), Mineral Soc. Am., Am. Acad. Arts and Scis., Geol. Soc. Am. (Arthur L. Day medal 2004); mem. NAS, Sigma Xi. Office: Calif Inst Tech Div Geol Planetary Sci Pasadena CA 91125-0001

STOLTZE, BILL, state legislator; b. Anchorage, Alaska, July 30, 1961; BA in Polit. Sci., U. Alaska, Anchorage/Fairbanks, 1984. Alaska State Representative, District 16, 2003-; Legislature aide, Alaska Legislature, formerly; Staff to Senate President and Speaker of House, formerly; Bd director, Alaska Outdoor Coun Polit Action Committee-.Director, sec, board director, Chugiak Sr Housing, Inc. Lions; Elks; NRA; Alaska Outdoor Coun; Special Olympics World Winter Games. Republican. Avocations: fishing, baseball, gardening. Office: State Capitol Rm 501 Juneau AK 99801-1182 Office Phone: 907-465-4958. Office Fax: 907-465-4928. Business E-Mail: representative_bill_stoltze@legis.state.ak.us.*

STONE, ALAN JAY, retired academic administrator; b. Ft. Dodge, Iowa, Oct. 15, 1942; s. Hubert H. and Bernice A. (Tilton) S.; m. Jonieta J. Smith; 1 child, Kirsten K. Stone Morlock. BA, Morningside Coll., Sioux City, Iowa, 1964, HD, 2001; MA, U. Iowa, Iowa City, 1966; MTh, U. Chgo., 1968, DMin, 1970; PhD (hon.), Kyonggi U., Korea, 1985; LLD, Stillman Coll., Tuscaloosa, Ala., 1991, Sogong U., Korea, 1992, Alma Coll., Mich., 2001. Admissions counselor Morningside Coll., Sioux City, Iowa, 1964-66; dir. admissions, asso. prof. history George Williams Coll., Downers Grove, Ill., 1969-73; v.p. coll. relations Hood Coll., Frederick, Md., 1973-75; v.p. devel. and fin. affairs W.Va. Wesleyan Coll., Buckhannon, 1975-77; dir. devel. U. Maine, 1977-78; pres. Aurora U., Ill., 1978-88, Alma Coll., 1988-2000; pres., CEO Alzheimer's Assn., Chgo., 2001—02; ret., 2002; lectr. for cruises. Home: 28897 N 94th Pl Scottsdale AZ 85262 Personal E-mail: thestones3@cox.net.

STONE, CAROL, library director; City libr. Anaheim Pub. Libr., Calif. Office: Anaheim Pub Libr Ctrl Libr 500 W Broadway Anaheim CA 92805-3699 Office Phone: 714-765-1710. Office Fax: 714-765-1730. E-mail: cstone@anaheim.net.

STONE, EDWARD C., physicist, researcher; b. Knoxville, Iowa, Jan. 23, 1936; s. Edward Carroll and Ferne Elizabeth (Baber) Stone; m. Alice Trabue Wickliffe, Aug. 4, 1962; children: Susan, Janet. AA, Burlington Jr. Coll., 1956; MS, U. Chgo., 1959, PhD, 1964, DSc (hon.), 1992, Washington U., St. Louis, 1992, Harvard U., 1992, U. So. Calif., 1998. From rsch. fellow in physics to prof. Calif. Inst. Tech., Pasadena, Calif., 1964—94, Voyager project scientist, 1972—, chmn. divsn. physics, math. and astron., 1983—88, v.p., 1988—2001, dir. jet propulsion lab., 1991—2001, David Morrisroe prof. physics, 1994—, mem. Draper Lab., 2001, vice provost for spl. projects, 2004—. Cons. Office of Space Sci., NASA, 1969—85, adv. com. outer planets, 1972—73; high energy astrophysics mgmt. oper. working group NASA, 1976—84, cosmic ray program working group, 1980—82, outer planets working group, 1981—82, solar sys. exploration com., 1981—82, U. rels. study group, 1983; exec. com. Com. on Space Rsch. Interdisciplinary Sci. Commn., 1982—86; com. on space astronomy and astrophysics Space Sci. Bd., 1979—82, steering group study on maj. directions for space sci., 1984—85; mem. Space Sci. Bd., NRC, 1982—85; commn. on phys. sci., math. and resources NRC, 1986—89; adv. com. vis. sr. scientist program NASA/Jet Propulsion Labs., 1986—90; com. on space policy NAS/NAE, 1988—89; chmn., chief sci. advisor The Astronomers, KCET, 1989—91; chmn. adv. panel NAS/WQED TV program "Sail on, Voyager!", 1989—90; v.p. COSPAR Bur., 2001—. Mem. editl. bd. Space Sci. Instrumentation, 1975—81, Space Sci. Rev., 1982—85, Astrophysics and Space Sci., 1982—, Sci. mag. Bd. dir. W.M. Keck Found., 1994—. Recipient medal for exceptional sci. achievement, NASA, 1980, Am. Edn. award, 1981, DSM, 1981, 1998, 2001, Dryden award, 1983, Disting. Pub. Svc. medal, 1985, Outstanding Leadership medal, 1986, 1995, Achievement award, Soc. for Tech. Comm., 1984, Space Achievement award, AIAA, 1986, Oppenheimer Mem. Lecture Aviation Week and Space Tech. Aerospace Laureate, 1989, Sci. Man of Yr. award, ARCS Found., 1991, Nat. Medal of Sci., 1991, Golden Plate award, Am. Acad. Achievement, 1992, COSPAR award, 1992, LeRoy Randle Grumman medal, 1992, Disting. Pub. Svc. award, Aviation/Space Writers Assn., 1993, Internat. von Karman Wings award, 1996, Space Flight Award, Am. Astron. Soc., 1997, Alumni award, S.E. C.C., Burlington, Iowa, 1997, CEO of Yr. award, ARC, 1998, Allan D. Emil Meml. award, Internat. Astronautical Fedn., 1999, Carl Sagan award, Am. Astronautical Soc. and Planetary Soc., 1999, Prof. Achievement award, Alumni, U. Chgo., 2002, Nat. Award for Op., Assn. for Unmanned Sys., Nat. Medal of Sci., Pres. Bush; named an asteroid Edward C. Stone in his honor, 1996; named to Hall of Fame, Aviation Week and Space Tech., 1997, Hall of Honor, Burlington Comm., 1999; fellow Sloan Found., 1971—73. Fellow: AAAS (award 1993), AIAA (assoc.; Calif. coun. sci. and tech. 1996—2001, Space Sci. award 1984, von Karman lectureship in astronautics 1999), Internat. Astron. Union, Am. Geophys. Union, Am. Phys. Soc. (exec. com. 1974—76, chmn. cosmic physics divsn. 1979—80); mem.: NAS, Sci. Edit. Bd., Comm. of Phys. Sci., Math., and Applications, NRC, Am. Philos. Soc., Calif. Assn. Rsch. in Astronomy (bd. dirs., vice-chmn. 1986—88, vice-chmn. 1986—2003, bd. dirs., vice-chmn. 1991—94, chmn. bd. dirs. 1994—97, bd. dirs., vice-chmn. 1997—2000, chmn. bd. dirs. 2000—03), Royal Aero. Soc., Nat. Space Club (bd. govs., Sci. award 1990), Astron. Soc. Pacific, Am. Philos. Soc. (Magellanic award 1992), Am. Astron. Soc. (divsn. planetary sci. com. 1981—84, Space Flight award 1997), Internat. Acad. Astronautics (trustee 1989—2001, v.p. 2001—). Office: Calif Inst Tech Space Radiation Lab M/C 220-47 Pasadena CA 91125 Office Phone: 626-395-8321. Business E-Mail: ecs@srl.caltech.edu.

STONE, GARY LEON, retired lawyer; b. Fruitridge, Calif., Oct. 29, 1941; s. Xerxes and Martha (Houts) S.; m. Lori Knoll, Aug. 17, 1985; children by a previous marriage: Diane Stone Bossert, Richard. BA in English, U. Calif., Berkeley, 1968; JD, Harvard U., 1972. Bar: Calif. 1972, U.S. Dist. Ct. (no. dist.) Calif., U.S. Ct. Appeals (9th cir.). Assoc. Petty, Andrews, Tufts & Jackson, San Francisco, 1972-75; counsel TRW Inc., Redondo Beach, Calif., 1975-80; sr. counsel Ralph M. Parsons Co., Pasadena, 1980-82, asst. gen. counsel, 1982-84; v.p. to sr. v.p., gen. counsel, sec. Parsons Corp., Pasadena, 1984—2008. Pres. Am. Cancer Soc., Northeast Los Angeles County. Mem. ABA, Los Angeles County Assn.

STONE, GEORGE, artist, educator; BA, Calif. State U., Long Beach, 1972; MFA, R.I. Sch. Design, 1974. Instr. R.I. Sch. Design, Providence, 1972-74; instr. sculpture Portsmouth (R.I.) Abbey Sch., 1973-74, Wayne State U., Detroit, 1974-75; vis. lectr., sculpture dept. Ohio U., Athens, 1976-77; instr., found. dept. Otis/Parsons Sch. Design, LA, 1982-83; vis. lectr., sculpture dept. UCLA, 1986; assoc. prof. fine arts Art Inst. So. Calif., Laguna Beach, 1989-93; assoc. prof. visual art U. La Verne, Calif., 1994-2000. Vis. artist Calif. State U. Long Beach, 1986, Crossroads H.S. for Arts and Sci., Santa Monica, 1987, Claremont (Calif.) Grad. Sch., 1987, 88, U. Calif. Santa Barbara, 1989, Art Ctr. Coll. Design, Pasadena, Calif., 1991, Yale U., New Haven, 1992, Chatham Coll., Pitts., 1992, Calif. State U. San Francisco, 1993; commd. artist City of West Hollywood, 1986, City of L.A. Cmty. Redevel. Agy., 1987, Metro Art L.A. County Met. Transp. Auth., 1990-97, City of L.A. Cultural Affairs Dept., 1995-97. Solo exhbns. include Forsythe Bldg., Detroit, 1975, Cline Bldg., Athens, Ohio, 1976, Lake Hope, Athens, 1977, Otis/Parsons Gallery, 1981, East Gallery Claremont Grad. Sch., 1985, Calif. State U. Long Beach Art Mus., 1986, Meyers/Bloom Gallery, Santa Monica, Calif., 1988, 91, Laguna Art Mus., Costa Mesa, Calif., 1990, Capp St. Project, 1991, New Langton Arts, San Francisco, 1991, Ruth Bloom Gallery, Santa Monica, 1993, Pitts. Ctr. Arts, 1994; 2-person exhbns. L.A. Contemporary Exhbns., 1985, Claremont Grad. Sch. Gallery, 1988; group exhbns. include Lehigh U. Art Gallery, Bethlemen, Pa., 1975, Wayne State U., 1975, U. Calif. Santa Cruz, 1978, Vanguard Gallery, L.A., 1979, L.A. Inst. Contemporary Art, 1979, NYU Art Gallery, N.Y.C., 1980, Charles Kobler and Assoc. Architects, L.A., 1983, Design Ctr. L.A., 1984, Univ. Art Mus. Calif. State U. Long Beach, 1985, IDM Corp. and Pub. Corp. Arts, Long Beach, 1985, CRA, L.A., 1987, Newport Harbor Art Mus., Newport Beach, Calif., 1988, Meyers/Bloom Gallery, 1989, Galerie Antoine Candeau, Paris, 1990, Sezon Mus. Art, Tokyo and Osaka, Japan, 1991, Muckenthaler Cultural Ctr., Fullerton, Calif., 1991, Contemporary Arts Ctr., New Orleans, 1993, Next Thread Waxing Space, N.Y.C., 1993, Contemporary Arts Forum, Santa Barbara, 1996, Armand Hammer Mus. Art and Cultural Ctr., UCLA, 1997, others; subject numerous catalogs, publs., and revs., 1984—. Home: 1815 Laurel Canyon Blvd Los Angeles CA 90046-2028 Fax: 323-654-3012.

STONE, GREGORY PAUL, lawyer; b. Ventura, Calif., July 21, 1952; BS in Chem. Engring., MS in Chem. Engring., Calif. Inst. Tech., 1974; JD, Yale U., 1977. Bar: Calif. 1977. Law clk. to Hon. William Matthew Byrne, Jr. US Dist. Ct. (ctrl. dist. Calif.), 1977—78; ptnr. Munger, Tolles & Olson LLP, LA, 1978—. Bd. dirs. Constl. Rights Found., Pasadena Playhouse, Huntington-USC Inst. on Calif. and the West. Recipient Jack E. Froelich Meml. award, Donald S. Clark award, John F. Casky Prize for trial advocacy; named one of Top 10 Trial Lawyers in Am., Nat. Law Jour., 2006. Mem.: ABA, State Bar Calif., LA County Bar Assn. Office: Munger Tolles & Olson LLP 355 S Grand Ave 35th Fl Los Angeles CA 90071-1560 Office Phone: 213-683-9255. Office Fax: 213-683-5155. E-mail: Gregory.Stone@mto.com.

STONE, HERBERT ALLEN, management consultant; b. Washington, Sept. 14, 1934; s. Joseph and Marion (Solomon) S.; m. Marjorie Nelke Sterling, June 14, 1964; children: Joanna, Lisa. BSc, U. Mass., 1955, MSc, 1958; PhD, U. Calif., Davis, 1963. Specialist Exptl. Sta. U. Calif., Davis, 1961-62; food scientist SRI, Menlo Park, Calif., 1962-67, dir. food and plant sci., 1967-74; pres. Tragon Corp., Redwood City, Calif., 1974—; adj. prof. Fuzhou U., 2004—. Mem. adv. bd. U. Mass. Food Sci., 1992—, Calif. Poly. U. Food Sci. and Nutrition, 1996—2001; chair leadership bd., food sci. dept. U. Calif., Davis, 2005—; vis. prof. So. Yangtze U., 2004—, Fuzhou U., 2004—. Author: Sensory Evaluation Practices, 2004; assoc. editor: Jour. Food Sci., 1977—80, 2000—, chair editl. bd.: World of Food Sci.; contbr. sci. and tech. articles to profl. jours. Fellow Inst. Food Sci. and Tech., Inst. Food Exec. Com. (pres. S.E. divsn. 1977-78, exec. com., pres. mktg. and mgmt. divsn.); mem. AAAS, Inst. Food Technologists (nat. exec. com. 1994-97, pres. 2004-05), Am. Soc. Enology, European Chemoreception Orgn., Ladera Oaks Club (Menlo Park, Calif.). Achievements include patents in field. Home: 990 San Mateo Dr Menlo Park CA 94025-5640 Office: Tragon Corporation 350 Bridge Pkwy Redwood City CA 94065-1061 Business E-Mail: hstone@tragon.com.

STONE, ISSAC (BIZ STONE), application developer, consultant; m. Livia Stone. Student, Northeastern U., U. Mass. Designer Little, Brown and Co., 1994—97; creative dir. Xanga, Inc., 1999—2001; sr. specialist Google, Inc., 2003—05; dir. cmty. Odeo, Inc., 2005—06; co-founder Obvious Corp. (spun off Twitter, Inc.), 2006, Twitter, Inc., Calif., 2007, creative dir. Calif., 2007—. Advisor to start-ups such as Fluther.com, Trazzler.com (also co-founder), Plinky.com, Justgive.org. Author: Blogging: Genius Strategies for Instant Web Content, 2002, Who Let the Blogs Out?, 2004. Named one of The World's Most Influential People, TIME mag., 2009. Office: Twitter Inc 539 Bryant St Ste 402 San Francisco CA 94107*

STONE, JEFFREY KYLE, mycologist, educator; b. East Liverpool, Ohio, Mar. 13, 1954; s. Harry C. and Mary L. (Coleman) S.; m. Daphne Fisher Smith, Aug. 29, 1981; children: Laurel Rebecca, Eliot Kyle. BA in Biology, Antioch Coll., 1976; PhD in Biology (Mycology), U. Oreg., 1986. Grad. rsch. assoc. dept. biology U. Oreg., Eugene, 1979-82, 84, grad. tchg. fellow dept. biology, 1982-85, postdoct. rsch. assoc. dept. biology, 1986, vis. asst. prof. dept. biology, 1987; rsch. assoc. dept. botany and plant pathology Oreg. State U., Corvallis, 1987-90, 90-93, asst. prof. dept. botany and plant pathology, 1993—. Invited participant, spkr. foliar fungi in old-growth forests; participant 5th Internat. Mycological Congress, 1994; invited spkr., instr. Workshop on Fungi and Sustainable Forestry, Xiacui, Oaxaca, Mex., 1997; bd. dirs. N.W. Mycological Cons., 1997—; mem. panel Nat. Biol. Survey Nat. Mus. Natural History Biodiversity Inventory, 1995. Assoc. editor: Mycologia, 1995—; reviewer manuscripts: Canadian Jour. Botany, Canadian Jour. Microbiology, Canadian Jour. Forest Pathology, Sydowia, APS Press, Mycologia, numerous others; contbr. numerous articles to profl. jours. Grantee USDA Forest Svc., 1993-94, 94-95, 95-96, 97-98, 98—, USDA ARS Nursery Crops Rsch., 1995-96, OSU Swiss Needle Cast Coop., 1997-98, 98—, Oregon Filbert Commn., 1998—. Mem. AAAS, Am. Phytopathological Soc. (mem. phylloplane microbiology com. 1995, Lee Hutchins award 1998), Brit. Mycological Soc., Internat. Symbiosis Soc., Lat. Am. Mycological Assn. Mycological Soc. Am. (chair local arrangements annual meeting 1992, chmn. 1995-98, mem. endowment com. 1995-98, councillor ecology/pathology 1996-98, treas. 1998—), N.W. Scientific Assn., Sigma Xi. Achievements include research in ecology, distribution, biodiversity of fungi causing asymptomatic infections of plants (endophytes); pathology, ecology and taxonomy of foliar and stem fungi of woody hosts, particularly those on conifers; taxonomy of conidial fungi, ecology, distribution, and diversity of microfungi; systematics and evolutionary biology of inoperculate discomycetes, particularly those parasitic on plants; research in alternatives to chemical fumigaion for control of Fusarium diseases in conifer nurseries, fungal and parasitic infections of Douglas fir and European hazelnut. Home: 30567 Le Bleu Rd Eugene OR 97405-9216 Office: Oreg State U Bot & Plant Pathology Dept Cordley 2082 Corvallis OR 97331-2902 Fax: 541-737-3573. E-mail: stonej@bcc.orst.edu.

STONE, LAWRENCE MAURICE, lawyer, educator; b. Malden, Mass., Mar. 25, 1931; s. Abraham Jacob and Pauline (Bernstein) S.; m. Anna Jane Clark, June 15, 1963; children: Abraham Dean, Ethan Goldthwaite, Katharine Elisheva. AB magna cum laude, Harvard U., 1953, JD magna cum laude, 1956. Bar: Mass. 1956, Calif. 1958. Rsch. asst. Am. Law Inst., Cambridge, Mass., 1956-57; assoc. Irell and Manella, LA, 1957-61, ptnr., 1963, 79-96, of counsel, 1997—; internat. tax coordinator U.S. Treasury Dept., Washington, 1961-62, tax. legis. counsel, 1964-66; prof. law U. Calif., Berkeley, 1966-78. Vis. prof. law Yale U., New Haven, 1969, Hebrew U. Jerusalem, 1973-74, U. So. Calif., L.A., 1984; mem. adv. group to commr. IRS, Washington, 1973-74; mem. President's Adv. Commn. on Tax Ct. Appointments, Washington, 1976-80; tax advisory bd. Little Brown Co., 1994-96. Author: (with Doernberg) Federal Income Taxation of Corporations and Partnerships, (with Klein, Bankman and Bittker) Federal Income Taxation; bd. editors Harvard Law Rev., 1955-56. Fellow Am. Coll. Tax Counsel; mem. ABA, Am. Law Inst., Internat. Fiscal Inst., Am. Arbitration Assn., L.A. County Bar Assn. (recipient Dana Latham award 1995), Phi Beta Kappa. Office: Irell & Manella 1800 Avenue Of The Stars Los Angeles CA 90067-4276

STONE, NORMAN CLEMENT, psychologist, foundation administrator; b. Evanston, Ill., Apr. 28, 1939; s. W. Clement and Jessie Verna (Tarson) Stone; m. Norah Grace Sharpe, June 1, 1986; children: Bryan C., Norman Clifford, Mark C., Amy M. ABA, Nichols Jr. Coll., 1959; BA, Stanford U., 1962; PhD, Wright Inst., 1985. Pvt. investigator, 1964—70; gen. ptnr., founder San Francisco Venture Capital, 1970—76; trustee, co-founder Nueva Day Sch. and Learning Ctr., Hillsborogh, Calif., 1976; psychotherapist Bay View Hunter's Point Found. for Cmty. Improvement, San Francisco, 1980—. Trustee San

Francisco Mus. Modern Art; nat. com. Whitney Mus. Am. Art, NYC; mem. Tate Internat. Coun., London. Pres. W. Clement and Jessie V. Stone Found., San Francisco Friends of the Homeless. Named one of Top 200 Art Collectors, ARTnews Mag., 2008. Mem.: Napa Valley Vintners. Democrat. Avocations: winemaking, contemporary art collection. Home and Office: 2790 Broadway St San Francisco CA 94115-1105

STONE, OLIVER, film director, producer, scriptwriter; b. NYC, Sept. 15, 1946; s. Louis and Jacqueline (Goddet) S.; m. Najwa Sarkis May 22, 1971 (div. 1977); m. Elizabeth Stone June 6, 1981 (div. 1993); 2 children. Student, Yale U., 1965; BFA, NYU Film Sch., 1971. Tchr., Cholon, Vietnam, 1965-66; wiper U.S. Mcht. Marine, 1966; taxi driver NYC, 1971. Screenwriter: Midnight Express, 1978 (Acad. award for screenplay, Writers Guild Am. for screenplay), Evita, 1996; screenwriter, dir.: Seizure, 1974 The Hand, 1981, (with John Milius) Conan, the Barbarian, 1982 (writer), Scarface, 1983, (writer with Michael Cimino) Year of the Dragon, 1985, (writer with David Lee Henry) 8 Million Ways to Die, 1986; dir., writer (with Richard Boyle) Salvador, 1986, Platoon, 1986 (Acad. award for best dir., Dirs. Guild award, British Acad. award),(documenatary) Looking for Fidel, 2004; co-writer, dir.: Wall Street, 1987, Talk Radio, 1988, The Doors, 1991, Any Given Sunday, 1999; screenwriter, prodr., dir.: Born on the Fourth of July, 1989 (Acad. award for best dir. 1990), Heaven & Earth, 1993, Comandante, 2003, Looking for Fidel, 2004, Alexander, 2004, World Trade Center (Hollywood Dir. of the Yr. Hollywood Awards, 2006), 2006; co-writer, prodr., dir.: JFK, 1991, Natural Born Killers, 1994, Nixon, 1995 (Acad. award nominee for best screenplay with Stephen J. Rivele and Christopher Wilkinson 1996); prodr.: Love, Death, 1972, Sugar Cookies, 1973, Reversal of Fortune, 1991, South Central, 1992, Zebrahead, 1992, The Joy Luck Club, 1993, The New Age, 1994, The People vs. Larry Flynt, 1996, Savior, 1998, The Corruptor, 1999, (TV mini-series) Wild Palms, 1993; exec. prodr. The Iron Mze, 1991, Freeway, 1996, Killer: A Journal of Murder, 1996, Indictment: The McMartin Trial, 1995 (Emmy award), Cold Around the Heart, 1997, The Last Days of Kennedy and King, 1998, The Day Reagan was Shot, 2003; dir. only (short film) Last Year in Viet Nam, 1971, Mad Man of Martinique, 1979, U-Turn, 1992, Persona Non Grata, 2003, (films) W., 2008; film appearances include The Battle of Lover's Return, 1971, The Hand, 1981, Platoon, 1986, Wall Street, 1987, Born on the Fourth of July, 1989, The Doors, 1991, Nixon (voice only), 1995, Any Given Sunday, 1999. Served with U.S. Army, 1967-68. Decorated Purple Heart with oak leaf cluster, Bronze Star; Lifetime Achievement award, Stockholm Internat. Film Festival, 2004. Mem. Writers Guild Am., Dirs. Guild Am., Acad. Motion Picture Arts and Scis.

STONE, PATRICK F., insurance company executive; Grad., Oreg. State U. Various positions in title ins. industry; pres. Fidelity Nat. Title Co., Portland, Oreg., 1989, exec. v.p. Fidelity Nat. Fin. Inc. Irvine, Calif., 1995—, pres., COO Fidelity Nat. Fin. Inc., 1995—. Trustee Portland Art Mus. Mem. Bldg. Materials Dealers Assn. Portland (bd. dirs.), Oreg. Land Title Assn., Am. Land Title Assn. Office: Fidelity Nat Fin Inc 4050 Calle Real Ste 200 Santa Barbara CA 93110

STONE, RICHARD JAMES, lawyer; b. Apr. 30, 1945; s. Milton M. and Ruth Jean (Manaster) S.; m. Lee Lawrence, Sept. 1, 1979; children: Robert Allyn, Katherine Jenney, Grant Lawrence. BA in Econs., U. Chgo., 1967; JD, UCLA, 1970. Bar: Calif. 1971, Oreg. 1994, D.C., 2000, Wash. State, 2004. Assoc. O'Melveny & Myers, LA, 1971-77; dep. asst. gen. counsel US Dept. Def., Washington, 1978-79; asst. to sec. US Dept. Energy, Washington, 1979-80; counsel Sidley & Austin, LA, 1981, ptnr., 1982-88; ptnr., head litig. dept. Milbank, Tweed, Hadley & McCloy, LA, 1988-94; mng. ptnr. Zelle & Larson, LLP, LA, 1994-97; counsel Ball Janik LLP, Portland, Oreg., 1998—2006, ptnr., 2007—. Adj. prof. law Lewis and Clark Northwestern Sch. Law, 1998—99; lawyer rep. 9th Cir. Jud. Conf., 1998—99; mem. legal ethics com. Oreg. State Bar, 2002—03, com. on spl. rules, 2002—03. Editor (editor-in-chief): (profl. jourl.) UCLA Law Rev., 1970; contbr. articles to profl. jours. Dir. Legal Aid Found., L.A., 1991—99, officer, 1994—98, pres., 1997—98; dir. Portland City United Soccer Club, 1999—2000, classic coach, 2002—04; gen. counsel and staff dir. Study of L.A. Civil Disturbance for Bd. Police Commrs., 1992; mem. vestry St. Aidan's Episcopal Ch., 1990—93, 1997—98, sr. warden, 1998; mem. pub. sector task force State Senate Select Com. on Long Range Policy Planning, Calif., 1985—86; mem. Oreg. Pub. Health Adv. Bd., 2008—; mem. adv. panel Coun. Energy Resource Tribes, 1981-85;, 1981—85; U.S. del. Micronesian Polit. Status Negotiations, 1978-79, 1978—79. With U.S. Mil. Acad. at West Point Oreg. Field Force, 2003—. Recipient Amos Alonzo Stagg medal and Howell Murray Alumni medal U. Chgo., 1967; honoree Nat. Conf. Black Mayors, 1980; recipient spl. citation for outstanding performance Sec. Dept. Energy, 1981. Fellow Am. Bar Found.; mem. ABA, Fed. Bar Assn., Calif. Bar Assn., Oreg. Bar Assn., Wash. Bar Assn., L.A. County Bar Assn. (trustee 1986-88), D.C. Bar Assn., Assn. Bus. Trial Lawyers, Multnomah County Bar Assn., Phi Gamma Delta. Home: 3675 NW Gordon St Portland OR 97210-1285 Office: Ball Janik LLP 101 SW Main St 11th Fl Portland OR 97204-3228 Office Phone: 503-228-2525. Business E-Mail: rstone@bjllp.com.

STONE, SHARON, actress; b. Meadville, Pa., Mar. 10, 1958; d. Joe and Dorothy S; m. George Englund Jr. (div.); m. Michael Greenburg, Aug. 18, 1984 (div. Jan. 20, 1987); m. Phil Bronstein, Feb. 14, 1998 (div. Jan. 29, 2004); 3 adopted sons, Roan Joseph, Laird Vonne, Quinn Kelly. Diploma in Creative Writing and Fine Arts, Edinboro State U. Model Eileen Ford Modeling Agy.; owner Chaos prodn. co. Actress (films) Stardust Memories, 1980, Deadly Blessing, 1981, Irreconcilable Differences, 1984, King Solomon's Mines, 1985, Allan Quatermain and the Lost City of Gold, 1986, Cold Steel, 1987, Police Academy 4: Citizens on Patrol, 1987, Action Jackson, 1988, Above the Law, 1988, Beyond the Stars, 1989 (Personal Choice award), Total Recall, 1990, Year of the Gun, 1991, Diary of a Hitman, 1991, He Said/She Said, 1991, Scissors, 1991, Basic Instinct, 1991, Where Sleeping Dogs Lie, 1992, Last Action Hero, 1993, Sliver, 1993, Intersection, 1994, The Specialist, 1994, (also co-prodr.) The Quick and the Dead, 1995 (also co-prodr.), Casino, 1995 (Golden Globe award for best actress in film 1996, Acad. award nominee for best actress 1996), Diabolique, 1996, Last Dance, 1996, Sphere, 1998, The Mighty, 1998 (Golden Global nominee), Antz, 1998 (voice), Gloria, 1999, The Muse, 1999, Simpatico, 1999, Beautiful Joe, 2000, Picking Up the Pieces, 2000, Cold Creek Manor, 2003, Cold Creek Manor, 2003, Catwoman, 2004, Jiminy Glick in La La Wood, 2004, A Different Loyalty, 2004, Broken Flowers, 2005, Alpha Dog, 2006, Basic Instinct 2, 2006, Bobby, 2006; TV appearances include Not Just Another Affair, 1982, Bay City Blues, 1983, Calendar Girl Murders, 1984, The Vegas Strip Wars, 1984, War and Remembrance, 1988, Tears in the Rain, 1988, (guest) The Larry Sanders Show, 1994, Big Guns Talk: The Story of the Western (tv spl.), 1997; narrator: Harlow: The Blond Bombshell, 1993, If These Walls Could Talk 2, 2000, Harold and the Purple Crayon, 2001, Cold Creek Manor, 2003. Chmn. Campaign for AIDS Rsch. amfAR, The Found. for AIDS Rsch., 2005—, global fundraising chmn., 2007—.

STONE, THOMAS EDWARD, defense contractor, retired career officer; b. Selfridge, Mich., Oct. 21, 1939; m. Lucy Lee, June 9, 1962. BS, U.S. Naval Acad., 1962; MS in Elec. Engring., Naval Postgrad. Sch., 1968; postgrad., Destroyer Dept. Head Sch., 1969. Advanced through grades to rear adm. USN, 1990, ops. officer USS Sampson, 1970; aide, flag sec. to commdr. Attack Carrier striking Force /CTF 77, 7th Fleet Vietnam, 1971-72; communications/ops. officer to comdr. in chief U.S. Naval Forces, Europe, 1972-75; exec. officer USS Mitscher, 1976-78; asst. chief of staff for communications, comdr. Naval Surface Force Atlantic, 1978-80; comdg. officer USS Preble, 1980-82; surface ops. officer, staff of comdr. Cruiser Destroyer Group 12, 1982-83; dir. Space, Command and Control Devel. Div. USN, 1984-85; comdr. U.S. Naval Communications Master Sta., Western Pacific, Guam, Marianas Island, 1985-87; comdr. Naval Telecommunications Command, 1988-90; dir. Naval Commns. info systems of Naval opers. staff, 1990-91; dir. communication programs Space & Naval Warfare Systems Command, 1991-93; v.p. Def. Contractor. Decorated Legion of Merit with three gold stars. Roman Catholic. Office: American Systems 2878 Camino Del Rio S San Diego CA 92108-3872 E-mail: thomas.stone@2asc.com.

STONE, WILLIAM EDWARD, academic administrator, consultant; b. Peoria, Ill., Aug. 13, 1945; s. Dean Proctor and Katherine (Jamison) S.; m. Deborah Ann Duncan; children: Jennifer, Allison, Molly. AB, Stanford U., 1967, MBA, 1969. Asst. dean Stanford U., 1969—71, asst. to pres., 1971—77; exec. dir. Stanford Alumni Assn., 1977—90, pres., CEO, 1990—98; pres., dir. Stanford Alumni Assn. divsn. Stanford U., 1998—2001, Stanford Sierra Programs LLC, South Lake Tahoe, Calif., 1998—2001, Alpine Chalet, Inc., Alpine Meadows, Calif., 1987—2001; pres.-emeritus Stanford Alumni Assn. Stanford U., 2001—, cons. in ednl. advancement, 2001—; prin. eAdvancement Consortium, 2001—. Dir. Coun. Alumni Assn. Execs., 1989-93, v.p., 1990-91, pres., 1991-92; trustee Coun. for Advancement and Support of Edn., 1988-91; bd. dirs. Univ. ProNet, Inc., chmn., 1990-92, sec. 1996-00. Bd. dirs. North County YMCA, 1975-76; bd. dirs., chmn. nominating com. faculty club Stanford U., 1979-81; trustee Watkins Discretionary Fund, 1979-82; mem. cmty. adv. bd. Resource Ctr. Women; dir. Stanford Hist. Soc., 2002—, v.p., 2003-06, pres., 2006-2008, past pres., 2008- Recipient K.M. Cuthbertson award Stanford U., 1987, Tribute award Coun. for Advancement and Support of Edn., 1991, Steuben Apple award, 2002, Stanford Assocs. award of merit, 2005. Mem.: Stanford Assocs., Stanford Faculty Club. Home: 1061 Cathcart Way Stanford CA 94305-1048 Office Phone: 650-494-6959. Business E-Mail: stone@eadvancement.org.

STONESIFER, PATTY (PATRICIA Q. STONESIFER), former foundation administrator; b. Indpls., 1956; m. Michael Kinsley; 2 children from previous marriage. BA in Gen. Studies, Ind. U., 1982. Editor-in-chief Que Corp., Indpls.; sr. mgr. Microsoft Press, 1988-89; gen. mgr. Microsoft Can., 1989-90; gen. mgr., then v.p. product support svcs. consumer divsn. Microsoft Corp., Redmond, Wash., 1990-93, sr. v.p. consumer divsn., 1993—96; chairwoman, pres. Gates Learning Found., 1997—99; pres., co-chair The Bill & Melinda Gates Found., Seattle, 1997—2006, CEO, 2000—08, sr. advisor to trustees, 2008—; bd. regents Smithsonian Inst., Washington, 2001—, chairwoman, 2009—. Mem. US delegation to UN Gen. Assembly Spl. Session on AIDS; bd. dirs. Amazon.com, 1997—, Viacom Inc., 2000—07, The Seattle Found. Mem. bd. regents Smithsonian Inst. Named one of The 25 Most Influential People in America, TIME mag., 1996. Fellow: Am. Acad. Arts & Sci. (founding bd. mem.). Democrat. Office: Office of the Regents Smithsonian Inst MRC 050 PO Box 37012 Washington DC 20013-7012*

STONINGTON, EMILY S., state legislator; b. Oak Park, Ill., Jan. 12, 1947; m. Tim Swanson; 2 children. BA, Bennington Coll.; MA, U. Calif., Berkeley. Mem. Mont. Ho. of Reps., Mont. Senate, Dist. 15, Helena, 1996—.

STOOPS, MIKE, college football coach; b. Youngstown, Ohio, Dec. 31, 1961; m. Nicole Stoops; children: Payton, Colton. Grad., U. Iowa, Iowa City, 1986. Defensive back Chgo. Bears, Pitts. Gladiators, Arena Football League; grad. asst. coach U. Iowa Hawkeyes, 1986—87, vol. coach, 1988—91; defensive ends coach Kansas State U. Wildcats, 1992—95, co-defensive coord., 1996—97, asst. head coach, 1998; assoc. head coach U. Okla. Sooners, 1999—2003; head coach U. Ariz. Wildcats, 2004—. Named First Team All-Am., UPI, 1984, First Team All-Conf., Big 10 Conf., 1983, 1984; finalist Asst. Coach of Yr., Am. Football Coaches Assn., 2001. Office: Univ Ariz Athletics McKale Ctr 1 National Championship Dr PO Box 210096 Tucson AZ 85721

STOPPELMAN, JEREMY, Internet company executive, entrepreneur; b. Arlington, Va., 1978; BS in computer engring., U. Ill., 1999; student, Harvard Bus. Sch., 2003—04. With @Home Networks, X.com, Confinity; v.p. engring. PayPal, 2002—03; co-founder & CEO Yelp Inc., San Francisco, 2004—. Office: Yelp Inc 706 Mission St Fl 7 San Francisco CA 94103-3167 E-mail: info@yelp.com.

STORER, MARYRUTH, law librarian; b. Portland, Oreg., 1953; d. Joseph and Carol Storer; m. David Bailey, 1981; children: Sarah, Allison. BA in History, Portland State U., 1974; JD, U. Oreg., 1977; M in Law Librarianship, U. Wash., 1978. Bar: Oreg. 1978. Assoc. law libr. U. Tenn., Knoxville, 1978-79; law libr. O'Melveny & Myers, LA, 1979-88; dir. Orange County Pub. Law Libr., Santa Ana, Calif., 1988—. Mem. Am. Assn. Law Librs. (exec. bd. 1999-2002), So. Calif. Assn. Law Librs. (pres. 1986-87), Coun. Calif. County Law Librs. (sec./treas. 1990-94, pres. 1994-96), Arroyo Sero Libr. Network (chair 2000-03). Democrat. Episcopalian. Office: Orange County Public Law Library 515 N Flower St Santa Ana CA 92703-2304 Office Phone: 714-834-3002.

STOREY, NORMAN C., lawyer; b. Miami, Fla., Oct. 11, 1943; BA cum laude, Loyola-Marymount U., LA, 1965; JD, U. Ariz., 1968. Bar: Ariz. 1968. Law clk. to Hon. James A. Walsh U.S. Dist. Ct. Ariz.; ptnr. Squire, Sanders & Dempsey, L.L.P., Phoenix. Fin. Coun. Diocese Phoenix Cath. Ch.; mem. Mens Art Coun. Phoenix Art Mus. Mem.: State Bar Ariz. Office: 40 N Central Ave Ste 2700 Phoenix AZ 85004-4498 Business E-Mail: nstorey@ssd.com.

STOREY, RICHARD D., academic administrator, biology professor; m. Martha Storey; children: Beth, Justin. BS, Univ. N.Mex.; MS, PhD, Univ. Okla. Asst. prof., assoc. prof. Colo. Coll., Colo. Springs., 1978—92, prof., biology dept. Colo. Springs, 1992—99, dean of faculty, 1999—2004, acting pres., 2000; chancellor Univ. Mont. Western, Dillon, 2004—. Office: Univ of Montana Western Office of the Chancellor 710 S Atlantic Dillon MT 59725

STORMS, WILLIAM WALLACE, physician; b. Racine, Wis., May 18, 1942; m. Bette Bear. BA, Northwestern U., 1964; MD, U. Wis., 1968. Diplomate Am. Bd. Internal Medicine, Am. Bd. Allergy and Immunology. Intern San Francisco Gen. Hosp., 1968-69; resident in internal med. U. Wis. Hosps., Madison, 1969-70, 73-73, fellow in allergy/immunology, 1973-75; prof. medicine Health Scis. Ctr. U. Colo., Denver, 1981—; practice medicine specializing in immunology William Storms Allergy Clinic, Colorado Springs, Colo., 1975—. Mem. bd. regents Am. Coll. Allergy and Immunology, 1990-93. Contbr. articles to profl. jours. Vestryman Chapel Our Saviour Episcopal Ch., Colorado Springs, 1978-81. Served with U.S. Army, 1970-72. Fellow ACP, Am. Acad. Allergy, Am. Coll. Allergists, Coll. Chest Physicians; mem. Am. Thoracic Soc., Western Soc. Allergy and Immunology (exec. coun. 1983-88, pres. 1987-88), Colo. Allergy Soc. (pres. 1988-90). Republican. Avocations: skiing, tennis, golf, fly fishing. Office: William Storms Allergy Clinic 1625 Medical Center Point Ste 190 Colorado Springs CO 80907 Home Phone: 719-632-2702; Office Phone: 719-955-6000. Business E-Mail: sneezedoc@stormsallergy.com.

STORY, JOAN H., lawyer; b. Parsons, Kans., Feb. 7, 1944; AB, Occidental Coll., 1965; MA, UCLA, 1968; JD, U. Calif., Davis, 1977. Bar: Calif. 1977. Ptnr., mem. exec. com. Sheppard, Mullin, Richter & Hampton LLP, San Francisco. Co-chair Calif. adv. bd. Trust for Pub. Land. Volume editor U. Calif. at Davis Law Rev., 1976-77. Mem. alumni bd. govs. Occidental Coll., 1982-85. Mem.: Practicing Law Inst. (real estate law adv. com.), Am. Coll. Real Estate Lawyers, Bar Assn. San Francisco, State Bar Calif. (mem. real property law sect.), U. Calif. Davis Law Sch. Alumni Assn. (bd. dirs.), Lambda Alpha. Office: Sheppard, Mullin, Richter & Hampton LLP 17 Fl Four Embarcadero Ctr San Francisco CA 94111 Office Phone: 415-774-3211. Office Fax: 415-434-3947. E-mail: jstory@sheppardmullin.com.

STOTLAR, DOUGLAS W., transportation executive; b. Newbury, Ohio; BS, Ohio State Univ. Freight ops. supr. through regional mgr. Con-Way Transp. Svcs., Ann Arbor, Mich., 1985—96, v.p., gen mgr. Con-Way NOW, 1996—99, exec. v.p. ops., 1999—2002, exec. v.p., COO, 2002—04, pres., CEO, 2004—05, Con-Way Inc. (formerly CNF Inc.), San Mateo, Calif., 2005—. V.p., mem. exec. com. Am. Trucking Assn.; bd. dir. Am. Transp. Rsch. Inst. Office: Con-Way Inc 2855 Campus Dr Ste 300 San Mateo CA 94403-2512

STOTLER, ALICEMARIE HUBER, federal judge; b. Alhambra, Calif., May 29, 1942; d. James R. and Loretta M. Huber; m. James Allen Stotler, Sept. 11, 1971. BA, U. So. Calif., 1964, JD, 1967. Bar: Calif. 1967, U.S. Dist. Ct. (no. dist.) Calif. 1967, U.S. Dist. Ct. (ctrl. dist.) Calif. 1973, U.S. Supreme Ct. 1976; cert. criminal law specialist. Dep. Orange County Dist. Attys. Office, 1967-73; mem. Stotler & Stotler, Santa Ana, Calif., 1973-76, 83-84; judge Orange County Mcpl. Ct., 1976-78, Orange County Superior Ct., 1978-83, U.S. Dist. Ct. (ctrl. dist.) Calif., LA, 1984—. Assoc. dean Calif. Trial Judges Coll., 1982; lectr., panelist, numerous orgns.; standing com. on rules of practice and procedure U.S. Jud. Conf., 1991-98, chair, 1993-98; chair 9th cir. Pub. Info. and Cmty. Outreach, 2000-04; mem. exec. com. 9th Cir. Jud. Conf., 1989-93, Fed. State Jud. Coun., 1989-98, jury com., 1990-92, planning com. for Nat. Conf. on Fed.-State Jud. Relationships, Orlando, 1991-92, planning com. for We. Regional Conf. on State-Fed. Jud. Relationships, Stevens, Wash., 1992-93; chair dist. ct. symposium and jury utilization Ctrl. Dist. Calif., 1985, chair atty. liaison, 1989-90, chair U.S. Constn. Bicentennial com., 1986-91, chair magistrate judge com., 1992-93; mem. State Adv. Group on Juvenile Justice and Delinquency Prevention, 1983-84, Bd. Legal Specializations Criminal Law Adv. Commn., 1983-84, victim/witness adv. com. Office Criminal Justice Planning, 1980-83, U. So. Calif. Bd. Councilors, 1993-2001; active team in tng. Leukemia Soc. Am., 1993, 95, 97, 2000; legion lex bd. dirs. U. So. Calif. Sch. Law Support Group, 1981-83. Winner Hale Moot Ct. Competition, State of Calif., 1967; named Judge of Yr., Orange County Trial Lawyers Assn., 1978, Most Outstanding Judge Orange County Bus. Litig. Sect., 1990. Mem. ABA (jud. adminstrn. divsn. and litig. sect. 1984—, nat. conf. fed. trial judges com. on legis. affairs 1990-91), Am. Law Inst., Am. Judicature Soc., Fed. Judges Assn. (bd. dirs. 1989-92), Nat. Assn. Women Judges, U.S. Supreme Ct. Hist. Soc., Ninth Cir. Dist. Judges Assn., Calif. Supreme Ct. Hist. Soc., Orange County Bar Assn. (mem. numerous coms., Franklin G. West award 1984), Calif. Judges Assn. (mem. com. on jud. coll. 1978-80, com. on civil law and procedure 1980-82, Dean's coll. curriculum commn. 1981), Calif. Judges Found. Office: Ronald Reagan Fed Bldg & Courthouse 411 W 4th St Santa Ana CA 92701-4500

STOTT, BRIAN, software company executive, consultant; b. Eccles, Eng., Aug. 5, 1941; came to U.S., 1983; s. Harold and Mary (Stephens) S.; m. Patricia Ann Farrar, Dec. 3, 1983. BSc, Manchester U., 1962, MSc, 1963, PhD, 1971. Asst. prof. Mid. East Tech. U., Ankara, Turkey, 1965—68; lectr. Inst. Sci. and Tech., U. Manchester, England, 1968—74; assoc. prof. U. Waterloo, Ont., Canada, 1974—76; cons. Electric Energy Rsch. Ctr. Brazil, Rio de Janeiro, 1976—83; prof. Ariz. State U., Tempe, 1983—84; chmn. Power Computer Applications Corp., Mesa, Ariz., 1984—2000; pres. Stott Inc. Cons. in field. Contbr. numerous articles to rsch. publs. Fellow IEEE (Millennium medal); mem. NAE. Home and Office: 10222E Southwind Lane #1004 Scottsdale AZ 85262 Business E-Mail: brianstott@ieee.org.

STOTT, PETER WALTER, investment company executive; b. Spokane, Wash., May 26, 1944; s. Walter Joseph and Rellalee (Gray) S.; m. Julie L. Neupert, Oct. 12, 1996; 1 child, Preston. Student, Portland State U., 1962-63, 65-68, U. Americas, Mexico City, 1964-65. Founder, bd. chmn. emeritus Market Transport Ltd., Portland, Oreg., 1969—2006; pres. Columbia Investments, Ltd., Portland, 2005—; vice chmn., CEO, prin. ScanlanKemperBard Cos., Portland, 2005—. Pres., CEO, prin. Crown Pacific, 1988-2004; bd. dir. Con-Way Inc. Mem. cabinet Bldg. Our Future Campaign; trustee Portland Art Mus.; founding bd. dir. Crater Lake Nat. Park Trust; bd. dir. Portland State U. Found. With USAR, 1966-72. Mem. Nat. Football Found. and Hall of Fame, Oreg. Sports Hall of Fame (lifetime), Stop Oreg. Litter and Vandalism (founders' circle), Arlington Club, Mazamas Club, Multnomah Athletic Club, Univ. Club, Waverley Country Club, Valley Club. Republican. Roman Catholic. Office: Columbia Investments Ltd Ste 2600 1211 SW Fifth Ave Portland OR 97204 Business E-Mail: pstott@skbcos.com.

STOTTER, LAWRENCE HENRY, lawyer; b. Cleve., Sept. 24, 1929; s. Oscar and Bertha (Lieb) S.; m. Ruth Rapoport, June 30, 1957; children: Daniel, Jennifer, Steven. BBA, Ohio State U., 1956, LLB, 1958, JD, 1967. Bar: Calif. 1960, U.S. Supreme Ct. 1973, U.S. Tax Ct. 1976. Pvt. practice, San Francisco, 1963—; ptnr. Stotter and Coats, San Francisco, 1981-97; sole practitioner, 1997—; mem. faculty Nat. Judicial Coll.; mem. Calif. Family Law Adv. Commn., 1979-80. Editor in chief: Am. Bar Family Advocate mag, 1977-82; TV appearances on Phil Donahue Show, Good Morning America. Pres. Tamalpais Conservation Club, Marin County, Calif.; U.S. State Dept. del. Hague Conf. Pvt. Internat. Law, 1979-80; legal adv. White House Conf. on Families, 1980—. Served with AUS, 1950-53. Mem. ABA (past chmn. family law sect.), Am. Acad. Matrimonial Lawyers (past nat. v.p.), Calif. State Bar (past chmn. family law sect.), San Francisco Bar Assn. (past chmn. family law sect.), Calif. Trial Lawyers Assn. (past chmn. family law sect.) Home and Office: 2244 Vistazo St E Belvedere Tiburon CA 94920-1970 Office Phone: 415-435-3568. Personal E-mail: lhstotter@aol.com.

STOTTLEMYRE, MEL (MELVIN LEON STOTTLEMYRE SR.), professional baseball coach, former professional baseball player; b. Hazelton, Mo., Nov. 13, 1941; m. Jeannie Stottlemyre; children: Mel Jr., Todd, Jason (dec.). Attended, Yakima Valley CC. Pitcher NY Yankees, Bronx, 1964—74; roving instr. Seattle Mariners, 1977-81; pitching coach NY Mets, 1984-93, Houston Astros, 1994-95, NY Yankees, 1996—2005, Seattle Mariners, 2008—. Owner Stottlemyre's Athletic Stores, Yakima and Sunnyside, Wash. Mem. sports com. Leukemia Soc. Am.; active Multiple Myeloma Rsch. Found. Co-recipient (with Jeannie Stottlemyre) Nat. Recognition award Leukemia Soc. Am., 1992; named to Am. League All-Star Team, 1965, 66, 68, 69, 70. Office: c/o Seattle Mariners Safeco Field PO Box 4100 Seattle WA 98104 Office Phone: 206-346-4000.

STOUDEMIRE, AMARE CARSARES, professional basketball player; b. Lake Wales, Fla., Nov. 16, 1982; Player Phoenix Suns, 2002—. Mem. US Olympic Basketball Team, Athens, Greece, 2004. Named McDonald's All-Am., 2002, NBA Rookie of Yr., 2003, MVP, Rookie Challenge, 2004; named to NBA All-Rookie First Team, 2003, All-NBA First Team, 2007, Western Conf. All-Star Team, NBA, 2005, 2007—09. Office: c/o Phoenix Suns 201 E Jefferson St Phoenix AZ 85004*

STOUGHTON, W. VICKERY, healthcare executive; b. Peoria, Ill., Mar. 1, 1946; s. Warner Vickery and Mary Olive (McNamara) S.; m. Anne Stoughton; children: Zachary Benjamin, Samantha. BS, St. Louis U., 1968; MBA, U. Chgo., 1973. Asst. dir. Boston Hosp. for Women, 1973-74, Peter Bent Brigham Hosp., Boston, 1975-77, dir., 1978-80; pres. The Toronto Hosp., Ont., Can.; asst. prof. U. Toronto, 1982-90, assoc. prof., 1991; vice chancellor health affairs, chief exec. officer Duke U. Hosp., Durham, N.C., 1991-92; pres. Smithkline Beecham Clin. Labs., Collegeville, Pa., 1992-95, Smithkline Beecham Diagnostic Systems, King of Prussia, Pa., 1996; chmn., CEO Careside, Culver City, Calif., 1996—; dir. Biomira, 1988—. Bd. dirs. Sun Life Assurance Co. Bd. dirs. Toronto Symphony, 1983-86, Toronto United Way, 1988-91. Served to capt. AUS, 1969-72. Fellow Am. Coll. Hosp. Adminstrs. Home: 8820 Lookout Mountain Ave Los Angeles CA 90046-1820

STOUT, DENNIS LEE, prosecutor; b. 1948; BA, U. Calif., Riverside, 1970; JD, U. LaVerne, Calif., 1977. Adminstrv. aide City of Fontana, Calif., 1972-73; planning technician City of Pomona, Calif., 1973; dep. dist. atty. San Bernardino County, Calif., 1977-94, dist. atty. Calif., 1995—. Mayor City of Rancho Cucamonga, Calif., 1986-94. Named Vet. of the Yr., San Bernardino County, 1989. Office: 316 N Mountain View Ave San Bernardino CA 92415-1016

STOUT, LYNN ANDREA, law educator; b. Albany, NY, Sept. 14, 1957; d. Warren White and Sally (Cowan) Stout. BA, Princeton U., 1979, MPA, 1982; JD, Yale U., 1982. Law clk. to the Hon. Gerhard A. Gesell US Dist. Ct. D.C., Washington, 1982-83; assoc. Williams & Connolly, Washington, 1983-86; prof. George Washington U., Washington, 1986-90; prof. Law Ctr. Georgetown U., Washington, 1990—2001, dir. Georgetown-Sloan Project on Bus. Insts.; prof. law UCLA, 2001—, Paul Hastings prof. corp. & securities law, 2006—; prin. investigator UCLA-Sloan Found. Rsch. Program on Bus. Orgns.; prof. (corp. and Securities Law) UCLA, Wash. Vis. prof. Harvard Law Sch., NYU Law Sch., George Washington U. Nat. Law Ctr.; guest scholar Brookings Inst., Washington. Contbr. articles to law jours. Bd. trustee Eaton Vance family of mutual funds. Vis. scholar Nat. Merit scholar, 1975. Mem.: Am. Assn. of Law Sch. (past chair Sect. on Law and Econ. and Sect. Bus. Assns.), Am. Law and Econs. Assn. (bd. dirs.), Phi Beta Kappa. Office: UCLA Sch Law Box 951476 Los Angeles CA 90095-1476 Office Phone: 310-206-8402, 310-825-4841. Office Fax: 310-825-6023. E-mail: stout@law.ucla.edu.

STOVAL, LINDA, political coach, consultant; b. Kans. m. Toby Stoval. Chairperson Wyo. Dem. Party, 2001—03; polit. leadership coach, 2005—. Mgr. Trauner for Congress, 2006; mem. campaign staff to local presdl. activist; ograniizer; campaign cons.; owner Gravilas Coaching & Consulting. Former chair Make-A-Wish, Wyo.; former vice chair Habitat for Humanity, Wyo.; former chair Serve Wyo. (Americorps).

STOVER, MILES RONALD, management consultant; b. Glendale, Calif., Dec. 23, 1948; s. Robert Miles and Alberta Mae (Walker) S.; m. Cynthia McNeil, Jan. 25, 1975; children: Christopher, Matthew. BS, U. So. Calif., 1974; MBA, Pepperdine U., 1979; PhD, Kennedy Western U., 2005. Cert. fraud examiner; cert. turnaround profl.; cert. profl. cons.; cert. mgmt. cons.; cert. confidentiality officer; cert. insolvency advisor. V.p., gen. mgr., CFO Johnson Controls Inc., LA, 1974-82; gen. mgr. MG Products Inc., San Diego, 1982-84; exec. v.p., gen. mgr. ICU Med. Inc., Mission Viejo, 1984-86; v.p., COO B.P. John Inc., Santa Ana, Calif., 1986-88; gen. mgr. MG Products Inc., San Diego, 1988-90; pres. Lucks Co., Kent, Wash., 1991-96, also bd. dirs.; prin. Crossroads LLC, 1998—2002; pres. Turnaround, Inc., 1996—98, 2002—. Cons. Turnaround Mgmt. Assn., Tacoma, 1990. With USN, 1967-71. Decorated Gallantry Cross USN; recipient award for Productivity US Senate, 1978, Congl. medal of Distinction Nat. Rep. Congl. Com.; named Businessman of Yr. Wash., 2006, Campaign medal NAM Mem. Inst. Mgmt. Cons., Turnaround Mgmt. Assn., Am. Bankruptcy Inst., Nat. Assn. Corp. Dirs., Assn. Cert. Fraud Examiners, Assn. Insolvency and Restructuring Advisors, Inst. Mgmt. Accts., Mensa. Republican. Methodist. Home: 3415 A St NW Gig Harbor WA 98335-7843 Home Phone: 253-851-7687; Office Phone: 253-857-6730, 253-857-6730, 253-857-6730. Business E-Mail: mstover@turnaround-inc.com.

STOVER, WILBUR G., JR., manufacturing executive; BSBA, Wash. State U., 1975. Audit mgr. Cooper & Lybrand; with Micron, 1989, dir. subs. sales; v.p. fin., CFO, Micron Semiconductor, 1992; v.p. fin., CFO Micron Tech., Inc., Boise, Idaho, 1994—2007.

STOWELL, CHRISTOPHER R., performing company executive, choreographer, retired dancer; b. NYC, June 8, 1966; s. Kent and Francia (Russell) S. Student, Pacific N.W. Ballet Sch., 1979-84, Sch. Am. Ballet, 1984-85. Entered corps de ballet San Francisco Ballet, 1986, promoted to soloist, 1987, prin., 1990—2001; freelance choreographer for ballet and opera cos., 2001—; ballet master Balanchine Trust, 2001—; artistic dir. Oreg. Ballet Theater. Guest artist Ballet Met, Ohio, Pacific N.W. Ballet, Seattle, and with Jean Charles Gil, Marseilles, France, Asami Maki Ballet, Tokyo. Created leading roles in Handel-A Celebration, Con Brio, The Sleeping Beauty, New Sleep, Connotations, Pulcinella, Meistens Mozart; other roles include Calcium Light Night, Rubies, The Sons of Horus, The Four Temperaments, Hearts, Tarantella, Flower Festival, La Fille Mal Garde, Haffner Symphony, Forgotten Land, The End, Agon, In the Middle Somewhat Elevated, Le Quattro Stagioni, Swan Lake, Job, Company B, Tchaikousky Pas de Deux, Maelstrom, Mercutio in Romeo and Juliet, The Dance House, Stars and Stripes, Ballo Della Regina, Drink to me Only With Thine Eyes, Pacific; performed in Reykjavik Arts Festival, Iceland, 1990, San Francisco Ballet at the Paris Opera Garnier, 1994, Bolshoi Theatre, Moscow, 1998; artistic dir. Oreg. Ballet Theatre, Portland, 2003—. Avocations: cooking, reading, camping. Office: Oreg Ballet Theatre 818 SE 6th Ave Portland OR 97214

STOWELL, ETHAN, chef; s. Kent Stowell and Francia Russell; life ptnr. Michelle Rasnic. Co-owner, exec. chef Union, Seattle, 2003—, Tavolàta, Seattle; co-owner How To Cook A Wolf, Seattle, 2007—. Guest appearances on (TV series) The Today Show, 2008. Named one of America's Best New Chefs, Food & Wine Mag., 2008; nominee Best Chef: Northwest, James Beard Found., 2008. Office: Union Restaurant 1400 First Ave Seattle WA 98101

STOWELL, KENT, retired ballet director; b. Rexburg, Idaho, Aug. 8, 1939; s. Harold Bowman and Maxine (Hudson) S.; m. Francia Marie Russell, Nov. 19, 1965; children: Christopher, Darren, Ethan. Student, San Francisco Ballet Sch., Sch. Am. Ballet; LHD (hon.), Seattle U., 2003, PhD (hon.), 2004. Lead dancer San Francisco Ballet, 1957—62, NYC Ballet, 1962—68; ballet dir., ballet master Frankfurt (Fed. Republic Germany) Opera Ballet, 1973—77; artistic dir. Pacific NW Ballet, Seattle, 1977—2005. Prof. dance Ind. U., Bloomington, 1969-70; bd. dirs. Sch. of Am. Ballet, Dance/USA, Washington, 1986—; bd. dirs. Sch. of Am. Ballet, NYC, 1981—; mem. Goodwill Games Arts Com., Seattle, 1987—; chmn. dance panel NEA, 1981-85. Grantee NEA, 1980, 85; fellow NEA, 1979. Choreographer: Silver Lining, Cinderella, Carmina Burana, Coppelia, Time & Ebb, Fauré Requiem, Hail to the Conquering Hero, Firebird, Over the Waves, Nutcracker, The Tragedy of Romeo and Juliet, Delicate Balance, Swan Lake, Time and Ebb, Through Interior Worlds, Quaternary, Orpheus. Recipient Arts Service award King County Arts Commn., 1985, Outstanding Contbn. to Pacific NW Ballet State of Was., 1987, Best Dance Co. award The Weekly Newspaper, Seattle, 1987, Gov. Arts award, 1988, Dance Mag. award, 1996, Lifetime Achievement award U. Utah, 2004, Lifetime Achievement in Arts award ArtsFund, 2004, award Seattle (Wash.) Ctr., 2004, Entrepreneur of Yr. award Ernst and Young, 2004, Mayor's Art award, 2004. Office: Pacific NW Ballet 301 Mercer St Seattle WA 98109-4600

STOWELL, ROBERT EUGENE, pathologist, retired educator; b. Cashmere, Wash., Dec. 25, 1914; s. Eugene Francis and Mary (Wilson) S.; m. Eva Mae (Chambers), Dec. 1, 1945; children: Susan Jane, Robert Eugene Jr. Attended, Whitman Coll., 1932-33; BA, Stanford Univ., 1936, MD, 1941; PhD, Washington Univ., 1944. Fellow in cytology Wash. U. Sch. Medicine, St. Louis, 1940-42; rsch. fellow Barnard Free Skin and Cancer Hosp., St. Louis, 1940-42, rsch. assoc., 1942-48; asst. resident in pathology Barnes, McMillan, St. Louis Children's Hosps., St. Louis, 1942-43, resident in pathology, 1943-44, asst. pathologist, 1944-48; instr. in pathology Washington U. Sch. Medicine, St. Louis, 1943-45, asst. prof., assoc. prof., 1948; advanced med. fellow Inst. for Cell Rsch., Stockholm, 1946-47; chmn. dept. oncology U. Kans. Med. Ctr., Kans. City, Kans., 1948-51, prof. pathology and oncology, dir. cancer rsch., 1948-59, chmn., 1951-59; sci. dir. Armed Forces Inst. Pathology, Washington, 1959-67; chmn. dept. pathology Sch. of Medicine U. Calif., Davis, 1967-69, asst. dean Sch. Medicine, 1967-72, prof. pathology Sch. Medicine, 1967-82, prof. emeritus, 1982—; dir. div. pathology Sacramento Med. Ctr., 1967-69. Vis. prof. U. Md. Sch. Medicine, Balt., 1960-67; acting dir. Nat. Ctr. for Primate Biology, U. Calif., Davis, 1968-69, dir., 1969-71; cons. U.S. Atomic Energy commn., Los Alamos, N.Mex., 1949-54; NIH, 1949-74; Cancer Control Div. USPHS, 1949-59, others; mem. adv. med. bd. Leonard Wood Meml. found., Washington, 1965-67, numerous univs.; prin. investigator, chmn. Expert Panel on Authentication Review of Selected Materials Submitted to the FDA Relative to Application of Searle Lab. to Market Aspartame, 1977-78; Assessment of the Practical Risk to Human Health from Nitrilotriacetic Acid in Household Laundry Products, 1984-85. Contbr. 121 articles, 34 abstracts to jour. in field; editor 35 biomed. books, monographs and conf. reports, 1941-88; mem. editorial bd. Cancer Rsch., 1949-59, Lab. Investigation, 1952-71, editor, 1967-71. Recipient Meritorious Svc. Award, Dept. Army, 1963; Exceptional Civilian Svc. Award, Dept. Army, 1965; Disting. Svc. Award U. Calif., 1988, Robert E. Stowell ann. Med. Student Award Outstanding Excellence in Pathology, 1981—; Robert E. Stowell ann. lectureship established U. Calif. Sch. Medicine, 1991 and Am. Registry of Pathology, Washington, 1991; endowed Robert E. Stowell professorship, 2002-. Mem. AMA; Am. Registry of Pathology (bd. dir. 1976-83, exec. com. 1976-82, v.p. 1976-78, pres. 1978-79, Disting. Svc. Award 1995), Am. Assn. Cancer Rsch., Am. Assn. Pathologists (Gold-headed Cane Award 1990), Am. Assn. Pathologists and Bacteriologists (councilor 1965-72, v.p. 1969-70, pres. 1970-71); Am. Soc. Clin. Pathologists; Am. Soc. Expd. Pathology (councilor 1962-66, v.p. 1963-64, pres. 1964-65); Calif. Med. Soc.; Calif. Soc. Pathologists; Binford-Dammin Soc. Infectious Disease Pathologists; Coll. Am. Pathologists; Histochem. Soc.; Internat. Acad. Pathology (councilor 1954-61, pres.-elect 1958-59, pres. 1995-60); Disting. Svc. Award 1970; Diamond Jubilee Award 1981; Stowell-Orbison Award established 1982—); Soc. Cryobiology (bd. gov. 1968-71); Soc. Exptl. Biology and Medicine; U.S. and Can. Acad. Pathelog:, Yolo County Med. Soc.; Assn. Mil. Surgeons U.S. (sustaining membership award 1965), Univ. Associated for Rsch. and Edn. in Path. (bd. dir. 1975-90, sec.-treas. 1978-82, hon. dir. 1990-2002); Sigma Xi; Alpha Omega Alpha. Home: 44752 N El Macero Dr El Macero CA 95618-1090

STRAATSMA, BRADLEY RALPH, ophthalmologist, educator; b. Grand Rapids, Mich., Dec. 29, 1927; s. Clarence Ralph and Lucretia Marie (Nicholson) S.; m. Ruth Campbell, June 16, 1951; children: Cary Ewing, Derek, Greer. Student, U. Mich., 1947; MD cum laude, Yale U., New Haven, Conn., 1951; DSc (hon.), Columbia U., NYC, 1984; JD cum laude, U. West LA, 2002. Diplomate Am. Bd. Ophthalmology (vice chmn. 1979, chmn. 1980). Intern New Haven Hosp., Yale U., 1951-52; resident in ophthalmology Columbia U., NYC, 1955-58; spl. clin. trainee Nat. Inst. Neurol. Diseases and Blindness, Bethesda, Md., 1958-59; assoc. prof. surgery/ophthalmology UCLA Sch. Medicine, 1959-63, chief div. ophthalmology, dept. surgery, 1959-68, prof. surgery/ophthalmology, 1963-68, prof. ophthalmology, 1968—2001, dir. Jules Stein Eye Inst., 1964-94, chmn. dept. ophthalmology, 1968-94, prof. emeritus, 2001—; ophthalmologist-in-chief UCLA Med. Ctr., 1968-94. Lectr. numerous univs. and profl. socs. 1971—; cons. to surgeon gen. USPHS, mem. Vision Research Tng. Com., Nat. Inst. Neurol. Diseases and Blindness, NIH, 1959-63, mem. neurol. and sensory disease program project com., 1964-68; chmn. Vision Rsch. Program Planning Com., Nat. Adv. Eye Coun., Nat. Eye Inst., NIH, 1973-75, 75-77, 85-89; mem. med. adv. bd. Internat. Eye Found., 1970-79; mem. adv. com. on basic clin. rsch. Nat. Soc. to Prevent Blindness, 1971-87; mem. med. adv. com. Fight for Sight, 1960-83; bd. dirs. So. Calif. Soc. to Prevent Blindness, 1967-77, Ophthalmic Pub. Co., 1975-93, v.p. 1990-93, Pan-Am. Ophthalmol. Found., 1985-95; chmn. sci. adv. bd. Ctr. for Partially Sighted, 1984-87; mem. nat. adv. panel Found. for Eye Rsch., Inc., 1984-94; mem. cons. com. Palestra Oftalmologica Panamericana, 1976-81; coord. com. Nat. Eye Health Edn. Program, 1989; mem. sci. adv. bd. Rsch. to Prevent Blindness, Inc., 1993—2003. Editor-in-chief Am. Jour. Ophthalmology, 1993-2002; mem. editorial bd. UCLA Forum in Med. Scis., 1974-82, Am. Jour. Ophthalmology, 1974-91, Am. Intra-Ocular Implant Soc. Jour., 1978-79, EYE-SAT Satellite-Relayed Profl. Edn. in Ophthalmology, 1982-86; mng. editor von Graefe's Archive for Clin. and Exptl. Ophthalmology, 1976-88; contbr. over 500 articles to med. jours. Trustee John Thomas Dye Sch., LA, 1967-72. Lt. USNR, 1952-54. Recipient William Warren Hoppin award NY Acad. Medicine, 1956, Univ. Service award UCLA Alumni Assn., 1982, Miguel Aleman Found. medal, 1992, Benjamin Boyd Humanitarian award Pan Am. Assn. Ophthalmology, 1991, Lucian Howe medal, Am. Ophthalmological Soc., 1992, Internat. Gold Medal award 3rd Singapore Nat. Eye Ctr. Internat. Meeting and 11th Internat. Meeting on Cataract, Implant, Microsurgery and Refractive Keratoplasty, 1998, award of merit in retinal rsch. Retina Rsch. Found., 2002, Jose Rizal gold medal Asia-Pacific Acad. Ophthalmology, 2003, Gold medal Barraquer Inst., 2005. Fellow Royal Australian and New Zealand Coll. Ophthalmologists (hon.); mem. Academia Ophthalmologica Internationales (pres. 1998-2002), Am. Acad. Ophthalmology (bd. councillors 1981, Life Achievement award 1999), Found. of Am. Acad. Ophthalmology (trustee 1989, chmn. bd. trustees 1989-92), Am. Acad. Ophthalmology and Otolaryngology (pres. 1977), Am. Soc. Cataract and Refractive Surgery, AMA (asst. sec. ophthalmology sect. 1962-63, sec. 1963-66, chmn. 1966-67, coun. 1970-74), Am. Ophthalmol. Soc. (coun. 1985-90, v.p. 1992, pres. 1993), Assn. Rsch. in Vision and Ophthalmology (Mildred Weisenfeld award 1991), Assn. U. Profs. of Ophthalmology (trustee 1969-75, pres.-elect 1973-74, pres. 1974-75), Assn. VA Ophthalmologists, Calif. Med. Assn. (mem. ophthalmology adv. panel 1972-94, chmn. 1974-79, sci. bd. 1973-79, ho. of dels. 1974, 77, 79), Chilean Soc. Ophthalmology (hon.), Columbian Soc. Ophthalmology (hon.), Glaucoma Soc. Internat. Congress of Ophthalmology (hon.), Heed Ophthalmic Found. (chmn., bd. dirs. 1990-98), Hellenic Ophthalmol. Soc. (hon.), Internat. Coun. Ophthalmology (bd. dirs. 1993-, Jules Francois medal 2002, Internat. Duke-Elder medal 2006), LA County Med. Assn., LA Soc. Ophthalmology, Pan-Am. Assn. Ophthalmology (coun. 1972—, pres. elect 1985-87, pres. 1987-89, Harry S. Gradle Tchg. award 2007), Peruvian Soc. Ophthalmology (hon.), Retina Soc., Barraquer Inst. Ophthalmology (pres. 1996-05), Academia Ophthalmol. Internat. (pres. 1998-02), Internat. Coun. Ophthalmology Found.(pres. 2002-08, dir. 2009-; Philip M. Corboy award 2005, Internat. Duke-Elder medal 2006, Middle East African Coun. Opthamology, Prince Abdul Aziz Ahmed Al-Saud Prevention of Blindness award, 2007), Internat. Coun. Opthamology (hon. life trustee, 2008-),The Jules Gonin Club. Republican. Presbyterian. Avocations: music, scuba diving. Home: 3031 Elvido Dr Los Angeles CA 90049-1107 Office: UCLA 100 Stein Plz Los Angeles CA 90095-7065 Office Phone: 310-825-5051. Business E-Mail: straatsma@jsei.ucla.edu.

STRAHAN, JULIA CELESTINE, electronics company executive; b. Indpls., Feb. 10, 1938; d. Edgar Paul Pauley and Pauline Barbara (Myers) Shawver; m. Norman Strahan, Oct. 2, 1962 (div. 1982); children: Daniel Keven, Natalie Kay. With Bechtel Nev./Lockheed Martin Nev. Techs., Las Vegas, 1967—; sect. head EG&G Co., 1979-83, mgr. electronics dept., 1984—. Recipient award Am. Legion, 1952, Excellence award, 1986. Mem. NAFE, Am. Nuclear Soc. (models and mentors), Internat. Platform Assn. Home: 5222 Stacey Ave Las Vegas NV 89108-3078 Office: Bechtel Nevada/Lockheed Martin Tech PO Box 98521 Las Vegas NV 89193 Office Phone: 702-295-2859. Personal E-mail: jeweljcs@aol.com.

STRAIGHT, RICHARD COLEMAN, photobiologist, natural philosopher; b. Rivesville, W.Va., Sept. 8, 1937; BA, U. Utah, 1961, PhD in Molecular Biology, 1967. Asst. dir. radiation biology summer inst. U. Utah, 1961-63; supervisory chemist med. svc. VA Hosp., 1965—; dir. VA Venom Rsch. Lab., 1975—; adminstrv. officer rsch. svc. VA Ctr., 1980—; dir. Dixon laser inst. U. Utah, Salt Lake City, 1985-90; pres. Western Inst. for Biomed. Rsch., Salt Lake City, 1990—2003. Dir. Utah Ctr. for Photo Medicine, Salt Lake City, 1993-; assoc. chief of staff for rsch. VA Salt Lake City Health Care Sys., 1997-2003; chmn. bd. dirs. VAMCU FEd. Credit Union, 1980-; cons. to NIH, NSF, Dept. Def., 1985-. Assoc. editor Lasers in Surgery and Medicine, 1990-95, Jour. Biomed. Optics, 1998—. Mem. AAAS, Am. Chem. Soc., Am. Soc. Photobiology, Biophysics Soc., Am. Soc. for Laser Medicine and Surgery, Utah Life Sci. Industries Assn. (charter). Achievements include research in photodynamic action on biomonomers and biopolymers, tumor immunology, effect of antigens on mammary adenocarcinoma of C3H mice, biochemical changes in aging, venom toxicology, mechanism of action of photoactive drugs, optical imaging and spectroscopy. Office: Protherics-Utah Univ Utah PO Box 58603 Salt Lake City UT 84158 Office Phone: 801-913-4799. E-mail: rcsrcsrcs3@aol.com.

STRAIT, EDWARD J., research physicist; Prin. scientist Stability Physics Group Gen. Atomics, San Diego. Recipient Excellence in Plasma Physics Rsch. award Am. Phys. Soc., 1994. Office: General Atomics PO Box 85608 San Diego CA 92186-5608

STRAKA, LASZLO RICHARD, retired publishing consultant; b. Budapest, Hungary, June 22, 1934; came to U.S., 1950, naturalized, 1956; s. Richard J. and Elisabeth (Roeck) S.; m. Eva K. von Viczian, Jan. 20, 1962 (div. May 1981); children: Eva M., Monika E., Viktoria K. BA cum laude, NYU, 1959. Acct. Greatrex Ltd., NYC, 1952-53; pres. Maxwell Macmillan Internat. Pub. Group, NYC, 1991-92; with Pergamon Press, Inc., Elmsford, NY, 1954-90, v.p., 1964-68, exec. v.p., treas., 1968-74, pres., 1974-75, 80-88, chmn. bd., 1975-77, 88-90, vice chmn. bd., 1977-80, 88-89, also dir.; vice chmn. bd. Pergamon Books Ltd., Oxford, England, 1986-88; group v.p. Macmillan Inc., NYC, 1989-91; pub. cons. Alta Loma, Calif., 1992—2005; ret., 2005. Treas. Brit. Book Centre, Inc., N.Y.C., 1956-67; pres. Pergamon Holding Corp., 1981-86; chmn. bd. Microforms Internat., Inc., 1971-87. D. dirs., sec. Szechenyi Istvan Soc., N.Y.C., 1967-80, 89-93. Mem. Phi Beta Kappa. Home: 6405 Caledon Pl Alta Loma CA 91737 Home Phone: 909-912-4140. Personal E-mail: nagyapul@yahoo.com.

STRALING, PHILLIP FRANCIS, bishop emeritus; b. San Bernardino, Calif., Apr. 25, 1933; s. Sylvester J. and Florence E. (Robinson) Straling. BA, U. San Diego, 1963; MS in Child and Family Counseling, San Diego State U., 1971. Ordained priest Diocese of San Diego, 1959; mem. faculty St. John Acad., El Cajon, Calif., 1959—60, St. Therese Acad., San Diego, 1960—63; chaplain Newman Club, San Diego State U., 1960—72; mem. faculty St. Francis Sem., San Diego, 1972—76; pastor Holy Rosary Parish, San Bernardino, 1976—78; ordained bishop, 1978; bishop Diocese of San Bernardino, 1978—95; pub. Inland Cath. newspaper, 1979—95; bishop Diocese of Reno, 1995—2005, bishop emeritus Nev., 2005—. Bd. dirs. Calif. Assn. Cath. Campus Mins., 1960; exec. sec. Diocesan Synod II, 1972—76; Episcopal vicar San Bernardino Deanery, 1976—78. Mem.: Nat. Cath. Campus Ministries Assn. (bishop rep. 1992—98). Roman Catholic.

STRAND, CURT ROBERT, hotel executive; b. Vienna, Nov. 13, 1920; naturalized Am. citizen, 1943; m. Fleur Lillian Emanuel, June 14, 1946. BS, Cornell U., 1943. Supt. service Plaza, NYC, 1947-49; asst. to v.p. Hilton Hotels Corp., 1949-53; v.p. Hilton Internat. Co., NYC, 1953-64, exec. v.p., 1964-67, pres., chief exec. officer, 1967-86, chmn., 1986-87. Sr. v.p., dir. Trans World Air Lines, Inc.; lectr. Cornell U. Sch. Hotel Adminstrn., Ecole Superieure de Scis. Econs., Paris, NYU, Houston U.; sr. cons. Am. Express; mem. adv. panel com. Am. Hotel and Motel Assn.; dir. Sherry Netherland Corp.; mem. exec. com. Bd. Exec. Svc. Corps, Aspen. Mem. coun. Cornell U.; adv. bd. Aspen Found.; bd. govs. Snowmass Resort Assn., also pres.; fellow Aspen Inst. With Mil. Intelligence US Army, 1943—46. Mem. Cornell Soc. Hotelmen (Hotelier of Yr. 1986), Aspen Exec. Svc. Corps (mem. bd., v.p.), Snowmass Club. Home: PO Box 6359 Snowmass Village CO 81615

STRAND, ROGER GORDON, federal judge; b. Peekskill, NY, Apr. 28, 1934; s. Ernest Gordon Strand and Lisabeth Laurine (Phin) Steinmetz; m. Joan Williams, Nov. 25, 1961. AB, Hamilton Coll., 1955; LLB, Cornell U., 1961; grad., Nat. Coll. State Trial Judges, 1968. Bar: Ariz. 1961, U.S. Dist. Ct. Ariz. 1961, U.S. Supreme Ct. 1980. Assoc. Fennemore, Craig, Allen & McClennen, Phoenix, 1961-67; judge Ariz. Superior Ct., Phoenix, 1967-85, U.S. Dist. Ct. Ariz., Phoenix, 1985—2001, now sr. judge. Assoc. presiding judge Ariz. Superior Ct., 1971-85; lectr. Nat. Jud. Coll., Reno, 1978-87; mem. jud. conf. U.S. com. on info. tech., 1996-2002; mem. 9th Cir. Jud. Coun., 2004-2007 Past pres. cen. Ariz. chpt. Arthritis Found. Lt. USN, 1955-61. Mem. ABA, Ariz. Bar Assn., Maricopa County Bar Assn., Nat. Conf. Fed. Trial Judges, Phi Delta Phi, Lodges: Rotary. Avocations: computer applications, golf, fishing. Home: 5825 N 3rd Ave Phoenix AZ 85013-1537 Office: Sandra Day O'Connor US Courthouse SPC 57 401 W Washington Phoenix AZ 85003-2156 Office Phone: 602-322-7550. Business E-Mail: roger_strand@azd.uscourts.gov.

STRASBURGER, VICTOR C., pediatrician; b. Balt., Oct. 7, 1949; s. Arthur Charles and Marjorie (Cohen) S.; m. Alison Reeve, Aug. 18, 1984; children: Max, Katya. BA summa cum laude, Yale U., 1971; MD, Harvard U., 1975. Intern Children's Hosp.- U. Wash., Seattle, 1975-76, residency, 1976-77, Boston Children's Hosp., 1977-78; dir. adolescent medicine Bridgeport (Conn.) Hosp., 1979-86; vis. lectr. St. Mary's Hosp. Med. Sch., London, 1986-87; chief div. adolescent medicine sch. medicine U. N.Mex., Albuquerque, 1987—, prof. pediats., 1997—. Cons. Nat. PTA, Washington and Chgo., 1978-86. Author: Rounding Third and Heading Home, 1974, Adolescent Medicine: A Practical Guide, 1991, 2d edit., 1998, Getting Your Kids to Say No in the '90's When You Said Yes in the '60's, 1993, (with B. Wilson) Children, Adolescents, and the Media, 2002, (with R. Brown, P. Braverman, C. Holland, P. Rogers and S. Coupey) Care of the Adolescent: A Handbook for Primary Care, 2006; editor: Basic Adolescent Gynecology, 1990; editor-in-chief Adolescent Medicine: State of the Art Revs., 1989—. Recipient Adele Hofmann award, 2000. Fellow Am. Acad. Pediatrics (Holyroyd-Sherry award 2000), Soc. for Adolescent Medicine; mem. Phi Beta Kappa. Office: U NM Sch Medicine Dept Pediatrics MSC10 5590 1 Univ New Mexico Albuquerque NM 87131-0001 Home Phone: 505-856-7943; Office Phone: 505-272-0338. E-mail: vstrasburger@salud.unm.edu.

STRATTON, GREGORY ALEXANDER, application developer, director, mayor; b. Glendale, Calif., July 31, 1946; s. William Jaspar and Rita Phyllis (Smith) S.; m. Yolanda Margot Soler, 1967 (div. 1974); 1 child, Tiffany Schwarzer; m. Edith Carter, Sept. 27, 1975; stepchildren: Paul Henkell, D'Lorah Henkell Wismar. Student, Harvey Mudd Coll., 1964-65; BS in Physics, UCLA, 1968; MBA, Calif. Luth. U., 1977. Elec. engr. Naval Ship Weapon System Engring. Sta., Port Hueneme, Calif., 1968-73; sr. staff mem. Univac, Valencia, Calif., 1973-74; v.p. Digital Applications, Camarillo, Calif., 1974-75; cons. Grumman Aerospace, Point Mugu, Calif., 1975-76; F-14 software mgr. Pacific Missle Test Ctr., Pt. Mugu, 1976-84; software mgr. Teledyne Systems, Northridge, Calif., 1984-92, dir. engring. software dept., 1992-93; dep. dir. software engring. Teledyne Electronic Systems, Northridge, Calif., 1993-94; software mgr. Litton Guidance and Controls, Woodland Hills, Calif., 1995-2001, Northrop/Grumman Nav. Sys., Woodland Hills, Calif., 2001—. Mem. strategic planning Simi Valley Hosp. Mem. City Coun., City of Simi Valley, Calif., 1979-86, mayor, 1986-98; mem. Rep. County Cen. Com., Ventura County, 2000-04; mem. Rep. State Cen. Com., Calif., 1990—; bd. dirs. Simi Valley Hosp., 1987-2001; pres. Simi Valley Cultural Arts Found., 1999-2005; trustee Simi Valley Unified Sch. Dist, 2002—. Mem. Rotary (Paul Harris award Simi Sunrise chpt. 1989), Jaycees (pres. Simi Valley chpt. 1974-75, nat. bd. dirs. 1975-76, v.p. Calif. state 1976-77). Republican. Lutheran. Office: Northrop Grumman Navigation Sys 5500 Canoga Ave Woodland Hills CA 91367-6698 Office Phone: 818-715-2371. Personal E-mail: gastratton@sbcglobal.net. Business E-Mail: greg.stratton@ngc.com.

STRATTON, RICHARD JAMES, lawyer; b. Sandwich, Ill., May 17, 1946; s. James L. and Dorothy (Olson) S.; m. Michele Disario, June 13, 1970; children: Matthew A., Laura D. AB, Harvard U., 1968, JD, 1972; MS, London Sch. of Econs., 1969. Bar: Calif. 1972, U.S. Dist. Ct. (no. dist.) Calif. 1972, U.S. Ct. Appeals (9th cir.) 1972, U.S. Dist. Ct. (cen. dist.) Calif. 1978, U.S. Dist. Ct. (so. and ea. dists.) Calif. 1979, U.S. Supreme Ct. 1979. Assoc. Bronson, Bronson & McKinnon LLP, San Francisco, 1972-79, ptnr., 1980—99, Hanson Bridgett, 1999—. Early neutral evaluator, mediator U.S. Dist. Ct. Co-author: Real Property Litigation, 1994. Trustee San Francisco Day Sch., 1987-94; bd. dirs. Legal Aid Soc. of San Francisco, 1989—2002. Fellow Am. Bar Found., Am. Coll. Trial Lawyers, ABOTA; mem. ABA, Bar Assn. of San Francisco (bd. dirs. 1988-90), Calif. Bar Assn., No. Calif. Assn. Bus. Trial Lawyers, San Francisco Barristers Club (pres. 1980), City Club (bd. givs., 2002-), Harvard Club (San Francisco). Office Phone: 415-995-5002. Business E-Mail: rstratton@hansonbridgett.com.

STRAUS, DAVID A., architectural firm executive; b. Medford, Oreg., 1943; m. Sherry Straus; 2 children. BArch, U. Oreg., 1967. Registered architect, Oreg. Founding ptnr. Skelton, Straus & Seibert, Medford, 1989—. Mem Oreg Transp Comn, Rogne Valley Area Comn Transp. Past pres Medford Arts Comn, Arts Coun Southern Oreg; coach Rogue Valley Soccer Asn; leader Boy Scouts Am; bd dirs, past pres Schneider Mus Art SOSC; bd dirs Medford YMCA, Rogue Valley Art Asn. Lt USNR, Vietnam. Mem.: AIA (pres. so. Oreg. chpt.), Archit Found Oreg (past bd. dirs.), Medford/Jackson County CofC (past bd. dirs., Mem of the Yr 2000), Univ Oreg Alumni Asn, Oreg Club Southern Oreg (past pres.), Univ Club Medford (past pres.), Rotary. Office: Skelton Straus & Seibert Arch 26 Hawthorne St Medford OR 97504-7114 Office Phone: 541-779-4363. Business E-Mail: dstraus@sssarchitects.com.

STRAUSS, HERBERT LEOPOLD, chemistry professor; b. Aachen, Germany, Mar. 26, 1936; came to U.S., 1940, naturalized, 1946; s. Charles and Joan (Goldschmidt) S.; m. Carolyn North Cooper, Apr. 24, 1960; children: Michael Abram, Rebecca Anne, Ethan Edward. AB, Columbia U., 1957, MA, 1958, PhD, 1960; postgrad, Oxford U., 1960-61. Mem. faculty U. Calif., Berkeley, 1961—, prof. chemistry, 1973—2003, prof. grad. divsn., 2003—, vice chmn. dept. chemistry, 1975-81, 92-95, asst. dean. Coll. Chemistry, 1986-92, assoc. dean, 1995—2008. Vis. prof. Indian Inst. Tech., Kanpur, 1968-69, Fudan U., Shanghai, 1982, U. Tokyo, 1982, U. Paris du Nord, 1987; mem. IUPAC Commn. I.1, 1990-2005. Author: Quantum Mechanics, 1968; assoc. editor Ann. Rev. Phys. Chemistry, 1976-85, editor, 1985-2000. Recipient Bomen-Michaelson award Coblentz Soc., 1994, Ellis Lippincott award Optical Soc. Am., 1994, The Berkeley Citation, 2003, Faculty Svc. award, 2008; Alfred P. Sloan fellow, 1966-70. Fellow Am. Phys. Soc., AAAS; mem. Am. Chem. Soc., Sigma Xi, Phi Beta Kappa, Phi Lambda Upsilon. Achievements include research in elucidation of vibrational spectra associated with large amplitude molecular motion in gases, liquids and solids. Home: 2447 Prince St Berkeley CA 94705-2021 Office: U Calif Dept Chemistry Berkeley CA 94720-1420 Home Phone: 510-848-3522; Office Phone: 510-642-7114. Business E-Mail: hls@berkeley.edu.

STRAUSS, JON CALVERT, retired academic administrator; b. Chgo., Jan. 17, 1940; s. Charles E. and Alice C. (Woods) S.; m. Joan Helen Bailey, Sept. 19, 1959 (div. 1985); children: Susan, Stephanie; m. Jean Anne Sacconaghi, June 14, 1985; children: Kristoffer, Jonathon. BSEE, U. Wis., 1959; MS in Physics, U. Pitts., 1962; PhD in E.E., Carnegie Inst. Tech., 1965; LLD (hon.), U. Mass., 1996. Assoc. prof. computer sci., elec. engring. Carnegie Mellon U., Pitts., 1966-70; dir. computer ctr., prof. computer sci. Tech. U. Norway, Trondheim, Norway, 1970; vis. assoc. prof. elec. engring. U. Mich., Ann Arbor, 1971; assoc. prof. computer sci. Washington U., St. Louis, 1971-74, dir. computing facilities, 1971-73; dir. computing activities U. Pa., Phila., 1974-76, faculty master Stouffer Coll. House, 1978-80, prof. computer, info. scis., prof. decision sci. Wharton Sch., 1974-81, exec. dir. Univ. Budget, 1975-78, v.p. for budget, fin., 1978-81; prof. elec. engring. U. So. Calif., Los Angeles, 1981-85, sr. v.p. adminstrn., 1981-85; pres. Worcester Poly. Inst., Mass., 1985-94, pres. emeritus; v.p., chief fin. officer Howard Hughes Med. Inst., Chevy Chase, Md., 1994-97; pres. Harvey Mudd Coll., Claremont, Calif., 1997—2006, pres. emeritus, 2006—. Cons. Electronics Assocs., Inc., 1965, IBM Corp., 1960-64, Westinghouse Elec. Corp., 1959-60; bd. dirs. Transamerica Income Fund, Variable Ins. Fund, United Educators Ins., mem. NSF Nat. Sci. Bd., 2004-. Contbr. articles on computer systems and university mgmt. to profl. jours.; co-holder patent. Bd. dirs. Presbyn.-U. Pa. Med. Ctr., Phila., 1980-81, U. So. Calif. Kenneth Norris Jr. Cancer Hosp., L.A., 1981-85, Med. Ctr. of Ctrl. Mass., 1986-94, Worcester Acad., 1986-91, Mass. Biotech. Rsch. Inst., 1985-94. Mem. New. Eng. Assn. Schs. and Colls., Inc., Commn. on Instns. of Higher Edn., Nat. Collegiate Athletic Assn. (pres.'s commn. 1990-94). Avocations: hiking, running, swimming. Office: Harvey Mudd Coll Kingston Hall Rm 201 301 E 12th St Claremont CA 91711-5980 Office Fax: 909-321-8360. Business E-Mail: jon_strauss@hmc.edu.

STRAUSS, RICKY, film company executive, producer; BA in English and Theater, cum laude, U. Vt. Advt. exec. Columbia Pictures Industries, Inc., 1988—97; mktg. cons., sr. v.p. prodn. Sony Pictures Entertainment, Inc.; mktg. cons. Revolution Studios; founder, pres. Ricochet Entertainment; pres. Participant Prodns., LLC, 2005—. Prodr.: (films) Grownups, 2001, Double Vision, 2002; exec. prodr.: The Sweetest Thing, 2002, Fast Food Nation, 2006, An Inconvenient Truth, 2006, The Visitor, 2007, Chicago 10, 2007. Past bd. dirs. Project Angel Food, LA; vice-chmn. The Trevor Project; mentor Project: Involved; hon. bd. mem. Teamworks charity. Named a Maverick, Details mag., 2008. Office: Participant Prodns LLC 335 N Maple Dr Ste 354 Beverly Hills CA 90210

STREEP, MERYL (MARY LOUISE STREEP), actress; b. Summit, NJ, June 22, 1949; d. Harry, Jr. and Mary W. Streep; m. Donald J. Grummer, Sept. 15, 1978; children: Henry, Mary Willa, Grace, Louisa. BA in Drama, Vassar Coll., 1971; MFA, Yale U., 1975, DFA (hon.), 1983, Dartmouth Coll., 1981. Co-founder Mothers & Others for a Livable Planet. Appeared with: Green Mountain Guild; actress: (Broadway plays) Trelawny of the Wells, 1975; (plays) 27 Wagons Full of Cotton (Theatre World award); A Memory of Two Mondays; Henry V; Secret Service; The Taming of the Shrew; Measure for Measure; The Cherry Orchard; Happy End; Wonderland; Taken in Marriage; Alice in Concert (Obie award, 1981); Mother Courage, 2006; (films) Julia, 1977; The Deer Hunter, 1978 (Best Supporting Actress award nat. Soc. film Critics, Acad. award nomination, 1978); Manhattan, 1979; The Seduction of Joe Tynan, 1979; Kramer vs. Kramer, 1979 (N.Y. Film Critics' award, Los Angeles Film Critics' award, both for best actress, Golden Globe award, Acad. award for best supporting actress, 1980); The French Lieutenant's Woman, 1981 (Los Angeles Film Critics award for best actress, Brit. Acad. award, Golden Globe award for best actress, Acad. award nomination, 1982); Sophie's Choice, 1982 (Acad. award for best actress, Los Angeles Film Critics award for best actress, Golden Globe award for best actress, 1983); Still of the Night, 1982; Silkwood, 1983 (Acad. award nomination); Falling in Love, 1984; Plenty, 1985; Out of Africa, 1985 (Los Angeles Film Critics award for best actress, Golden Globe award, 1985); Heartburn, 1986; Ironweed, 1987 (Acad. award nomination); A Cry in the Dark, 1988 (named Best Actress N.Y. Film Critics' Circle, Best Actress Cannes Film Festival, 1989, Acad. award nomination); She-Devil, 1989; Postcards From the Edge, 1990; Defending Your Life, 1991; Death Becomes Her, 1992; The House of Spirits, 1993; The River Wild, 1994; The Bridges of Madison County, 1995 (Acad. award nominee for best actress, 1996); Before and After, 1996; Marvin's Room, 1996; Dancing at Lugnasa, 1998; One True Thing, 1998; Music of the Heart, 1999 (Acad. award nominee for best actress); The Hours, 2002; Adaptation, 2002 (Southeastern Film Critics Assn. award for best supporting actress, 2002, Chgo. Film Critics Assn. award for best supporting actress, 2003, Golden Globe for best supporting actress, 2003); The Manchurian Candidate, 2004; Lemony Snicket's A Series of Unfortunate Events, 2004; Prime, 2005; A Prairie Home Companion, 2006 (Best Supporting Actress, Nat. Soc. Film Critics, 2007); The Devil Wears Prada, 2006 (Best Supporting Actress, Nat. Soc. Film Critics, 2007, Best Performance by an Actress in a Motion Picture-Musical or Comedy, Golden Globe awards, Hollywood Fgn. Press Assn., 2007); Dark Matter, 2007; Evening, 2007; Rendition, 2007; Lions for Lambs, 2007; Mamma Mia!, 2008; Doubt, 2008 (Best Actress Washington DC Area Film Critics Assn., 2008, 2008 Best Actress, Critics' Choice award, Broadcast Film Critics Assn., 2009, Outstanding Performance by a Female Actor in a Leading Role, SAG, 2009); (voice only) Rabbit Ears: The Tale of Peter Rabbit, 1987; Rabbit Ears: The Tale of Jeremy Fisher, 1987; The Tailor of Gloucester, 1988; Rabbit Ears: The Fisherman and His Wife, 1989; Chrysanthemum, 1999; Artificial Intelligence: AI, 2001; The Ant Bully, 2006; actress: (TV films) Secret Service, 1977; The Deadliest Season, 1977; Uncommon Women and Others, 1979; Alice at the Palace, 1982; actress, exec. prodr. First Do No Harm, 1997; narrator The Velveteen Rabbit, 1984 (Emmy award Best Children's Rec.); A Vanishing Wilderness, 1990; actress: (TV miniseries) Holocaust, 1978 (Emmy award for Outstanding Lead Actress in a Miniseries, 1978); Angels in America, 2003 (Screen Actors Guild Award for best actress, Golden Globe for best actress, Emmy award Outstanding Lead Actress in a Mini-series or a movie, 2004). Recipient Mademoiselle award, 1976, Woman of Yr. award, B'nai Brith, 1979, Hasty Pudding Soc., Harvard U., 1980, Best Supporting Actress award, Nat. Bd. of Rev., 1979, Best Actress award, 1982, Star of Yr. award, Nat. Assn. Theater Owners, 1983, People's Choice award, 1983, 85, 86, 87, 1990, Women in Film Crystal award, 1998, Gotham award for Lifetime Achievement, 1999, Bette Davis Lifetime Achievement award, 1999, Lifetime Achievement award, Am. Film Inst., 2004, Dana Reeve HOPE award, Christopher and Dana Reeve Found., 2007, Marcos Aurelius Lifetime Achievement award, Rome Film Festival, 2009, most nominated actor ever for an Academy Award; named Officer, French Ordre des Arts et des Lettres, 2000; named one of The 100 Most Influential People in the World, TIME mag., 2006, 50 Smartest People in Hollywood, Entertainment Weekly, 2007; named to NJ Hall of Fame, 2007. Office: c/o 42 West 11400 W Olympic Blvd Los Angeles CA 90064

STREET, HUSTON LOWELL, professional baseball player; b. Austin, Tex., Aug. 2, 1983; s. James, Janie. Attended, U. Tex., Austin, 2002—03. Relief pitcher Oakland Athletics, 2004—08, Colo. Rockies, 2008—. Named First-Team All-Conf., Big 12 Conf., 2002—03, First-Team All-Am., NCAA, 2003, Ctrl. Tex. Coll. Pitcher of Yr., 2003, USA Baseball Athlete of Yr., 2003, Am. League Rookie of Yr., Maj. League Baseball, 2005. Office: Colo Rockies 2001 Blake St Denver CO 80205

STREET, PAUL SHIPLEY, lawyer; b. Klamath Falls, Oreg., Mar. 4, 1948; s. Leon Rex and Mary Rebecca (Shipley) S.; children: Adam, Blake. BA, Coll. Idaho, 1970; JD, U. Wash., 1973. Bar: Idaho 1973, U.S. Dist. Ct. Idaho 1973, Idaho Supreme Ct. 1973. Law clerk Idaho Supreme Ct., Boise, 1973-74; pres., mng. ptnr. Moffatt, Thomas, Barrett, Rock & Fields, Boise, 1974—99; sr. v.p., gen. counsel, corp. sec. Bldg. Materials Holding Co., San Francisco, 1999—, chief adminstrv. officer, 2001—. Sec. BMC West Corp., Boise. Co-author: Idaho Law Review, 1991, Digest of Environmental Law of Real Property, 1991. Pres. Coll. Idaho Alumni Assn., Caldwell, 1986, Am. Diabetes Assn., 1984—; formerly bd. dirs. First United Meth. Ch., Boise; chairperson United Way of Ada County, Boise, 1982-83. Mem. ABA (sec. mem. patent, trademark and copyright law; litigation, econs. law practice), Am. Soc. Med. Assn. Counsel, Am. Soc. Law and Medicine, Am. Arbitration Assn., Idaho State Bar (chmn. corp. and securities law sect. 1992-93), Boise Bar Assn., Boise Ins. Adjusters Assn., Real Estate Lawyers Assn., Boise Area C. of C. (vice chmn. 1991—). Avocation: bird hunting. Office: Bldg Materials Holding Corp Four Embarcadero Ctr Ste 3200 San Francisco CA 94111 Office Phone: 415-627-9100. Office Fax: 415-627-9119.

STREET, ROBERT A., research physicist; Sr. rsch. fellow Xerox Corp., Palo Alto, Calif. Recipient David Adler Lectureship award Am. Phys. Soc., 1992. Office: Palo Alto Rsch Ctr Xerox Corp 3333 Coyote Hill Rd Palo Alto CA 94304-1314 E-mail: street@parc.xerox.com.

STREET, ROBERT LYNNWOOD, civil, mechanical and environmental engineer; b. Honolulu, Dec. 18, 1934; s. Evelyn Mansel and Dorothy Heather (Brook) S.; m. Norma Jeanette Ensminger, Feb. 6, 1959; children: Brian Clark (dec.), Deborah Lynne, Kimberley Anne. Student, USN ROTC Program, 1952-57; MS, Stanford U., 1957, PhD (NSF grad. fellow 1960-62), 1963. Mem. faculty Sch. Engring. Stanford U., 1962—2005, prof. civil engring., assoc. chmn. dept. Sch. Engring., 1970-72, chmn. dept. Sch. Engring., 1972-80, 94-95, prof. fluid mechanics and applied math. Sch. Engring., 1972—2004, founding dir. environ. fluid mechanics lab. Sch. Engring., 1985-91, assoc. dean rsch. Sch. Engring., 1971-83, vice provost acad. computing and info. sys., 1983-85, vice provost, dean rsch. and acad. info. sys., 1985-87, v.p. for info. resources, 1987-90, acting provost, 1987, v.p. librs. and info. resources, 1990-92, vice provost, dean of librs. and info. resources, 1992—94, William Alden and Martha Campbell prof. Sch. Engring., 1997—2004, prof. emeritus fluid mechanics, applied math, 2005. Vis. prof. U. Liverpool, Eng., 1970-71, Ctr. for Water

Rsch., U. Western Australia, 1985; vis. prof. mech. engring. James Cook U., Australia, 1995; trustee Univ. Corp. Atmospheric Rsch., 1983-94, chmn. sci. programs evaluation com., 1981, treas. corp., 1985, vice chmn. bd., 1986, chmn. bd., 1987-91; bd. dirs., sec.-treas. UCAR Found., 1987-91, mem. rep., 2005-; bd. govs. Rsch. Libr. Group, 1990-91; chmn. Com. Preservation Rsch. Libr. Materials, Assn. Rsch. Librs., 1993; mem. higher edn. adv. bds. computer corps., 1983-94; mem. basic energy sci. adv. com. U.S. Dept. Energy, 1993-96; bd. dirs. Stanford U. Bookstore, Inc., 1993-98; cons. Design of Libr., Sch. Engring., Stanford U., 2007; bd. dir. Stanford Campus Residential Leaseholder, 2008-, chair, capital planning com., 2009-. With C.E.C., USN, 1957-60. Sr. postdoc. fellow Nat. Ctr. Atmospheric Rsch., 1978-79, faculty fellow, 2007; sr. Queen's fellow in marine sci., Australia, 1985; fellow N.E. Asia-U.S. Forum on Internat. Policy at Stanford U., 1985-89; named to Beverly Hills H.S. Hall of Fame, 2005. Fellow: AAAS; mem.: NAE (sect. 4 peer com. mem. 2006—08), ASME (R.T. Knapp award 1986), ASCE (chmn. publs. com. hydraulics divsn. 1978—80, Walter Huber prize 1972, Hilgard Hydraulic Engring. prize 2002, Rouse Hydraulic Engring. award 2005), Am. Meteorol. Soc., Oceanographic Soc., Am. Geophys. Union, Sigma Xi, Phi Beta Kappa, Tau Beta Pi. Office: Dept Civil and Environ Engring Stanford Univ Yang Yamasaki Environ & Energy Bldg MC 4020 473 Via Ortega Stanford CA 94305 Office Phone: 650-723-4969. Business E-Mail: street@stanford.edu.

STREISAND, BARBRA JOAN, singer, actress, film director; b. Bklyn., Apr. 24, 1942; d. Emanuel and Diana (Rosen) S.; m. Elliott Gould, Mar. 21, 1963 (div. July 9, 1971); 1 son, Jason Emanuel; m. James Brolin, July 1, 1998. Grad. high sch., Bklyn.; student, Yeshiva of Bklyn.; Doctorate of Arts and Humanities (hon.), Brandeis U., 1995. NY theatre debut Another Evening with Harry Stoones, 1961; appeared in Broadway musicals I Can Get It for You Wholesale, 1962, Funny Girl, 1964-65; motion pictures include Funny Girl, 1968, Hello Dolly, 1969, On a Clear Day You Can See Forever, 1970, The Owl and the Pussy Cat, 1970, What's Up Doc?, 1972, Up the Sandbox, 1972, The Way We Were, 1973, For Pete's Sake, 1974, Funny Lady, 1975, The Main Event, 1979, All Night Long, 1981, Nuts, 1987, Meet the Fockers, 2004; actor, prodr. (films): A Star is Born, 1976; prodr., dir., actor (films) Yentl, 1983, The Prince of Tides, 1991, The Mirror Has Two Faces, 1996 (ASCAP Award for score, 1996; exec. prodr.: (TV movies) Serving in Silence: The Margarethe Cammermeyer Story, 1995; (TV spls.) My Name is Barbra, 1965 (5 Emmy awards), Color Me Barbra, 1966, Barbra Streisand: The Concert, 1995 (Cable ACE award for best performance and for best direction, Two Emmy awards), Barbra Streisand: Timeless, 2001 (Emmy award); rec. artist on Columbia Records; (albums) People, 1965, My Name is Barbra, 1965, Color Me Barbra, 1966, Barbra Streisand: A Happening in Central Park, 1968, Barbra Streisand: One Voice, Stoney End, 1971, Barbra Joan Streisand, 1972, The Way We Were, 1974, A Star is Born, 1976, Superman, 1977, The Stars Salute Israel at 30, 1978, Wet, 1979, (with Barry Gibb) Guilty, 1980, Emotion, 1984, The Broadway Album, 1986, Til I Loved You, 1989; other albums include: A Collection: Greatest Hits, 1989, Just for the Record, 1991, Back to Broadway, 1993, Concert at the Forum, 1993, The Concert Recorded Live at Madison Square Garden, 1994, The Concert Highlights, 1995, Higher Ground, 1997, A Love Like Ours, 1999, Christmas Memories, 2001, The Essential Barbara Streisand, 2002, The Movie Album, 2003, Guilty Pleasures, 2005, Guilty Too, 2005, Nur das Beste, 2006, Live in Concert 2006, 2007. Recipient: Emmy award, CBS-TV spl. (My Name Is Barbra), 1964, Acad. award as best actress (Funny Girl), 1968, Golden Globe award (Funny Girl), 1969, co-recipient Acad. award for best song (Evergreen), 1976, Georgie award AGVA 1977, Grammy awards for best female pop vocalist, 1963, 64, 65, 77, 86, for best song writer (with Paul Williams), 1977, 2 Grammy nominations for Back to Broadway, 1994; Nat. Acad. of Recording Arts & Sciences Lifetime Achievement Award, 1994, Cecil B. Demille Lifetime Achievement Award, 2000, Life Achievement award, Am. Film Inst., 2001, Liberty & Justice Award, Rainbow/PUSH Coalition, 2001, Humanitarian award, Human Rights Campaign, 2004, Kennedy Ctr. Honors, John F. Kennedy Ctr. for the Performing Arts, 2008; Inducted into French Legion Of Honor, 2007 Office: Barbra Streisand c/o Martin Erlichman Assoc Inc 5670 Wilshire Blvd Ste 2400 Los Angeles CA 90036 also: Nigro Karlin Segal 10100 Santa Monica Blvd Ste 1300 Los Angeles CA 90067

STREITWIESER, ANDREW, JR., retired chemistry professor; b. Buffalo, June 23, 1927; s. Andrew and Sophie Streitwieser; m. Mary Ann Good, Aug. 19, 1950 (dec. May 1965); children: David Roy, Susan Ann; m. Suzanne Cope Beier, July 29, 1967 (dec. Apr. 2006); m. Joyce Hessel, May 2007. AB, Columbia U., 1949, MA, 1950, PhD, 1952; postgrad. (AEC fellow), MIT, 1951-52. Faculty U. Calif., Berkeley, 1952-92, prof. chemistry, 1963-92, prof. emeritus, 1993—. Cons. to industry, 1957—. Author: Molecular Orbital Theory for Organic Chemists, 1961, Solvolytic Displacement Reactions, 1962, (with J.I. Brauman) Supplemental Tables of Molecular Orbital Calculations, 1965, (with C.A. Coulson) Dictionary of Pi Electron Calculations, 1965, (with P.H. Owens) Orbital and Electron Density Diagrams, 1973, (with C.H. Heathcock and E.M. Kosower) Introduction to Organic Chemistry, 4th edit., 1992, A Lifetime of Synergy with Theory and Experiment, 1996; also numerous articles; co-editor: Progress in Physical Organic Chemistry, 11 vols., 1963-74. Recipient Humboldt Found. Sr. Scientist award, 1976, Humboldt medal, 1979, Berkeley citation, 1993. Fellow AAAS; mem. NAS, Am. Chem. Soc. (Calif. sect. award 1964, award in Petroleum Chemistry 1967, Norris award in phys. organic chemistry 1982, Cope scholar award 1989), Am. Acad. Arts and Scis., Bavarian Acad. Scis. (corr.), Phi Beta Kappa, Sigma Xi. Achievements include research in organic reaction mechanisms; application molecular orbital theory to organic chemistry; chemical structures on carbon acidities; f-element organometallic chemistry. Office: U Calif Dept Chemistry Berkeley CA 94720-1460 Home Phone: 510-841-6877; Office Phone: 510-642-2204. Business E-Mail: astreit@berkeley.edu.

STREVER, KEVIN KIRK, lawyer; b. Denver, July 4, 1960; s. Merle A. and Donna Jo (Ritchie) S.; m. Lauri Jean Rask, Apr. 1, 1989. BS in Polit. Sci. cum laude, So. Oreg. State Coll., 1982; JD, U. Oreg., 1985. Bar: Oreg. 1985, U.S. Dist. Ct. Oreg. 1986, U.S. Ct. Appeals (9th cir.) 1986. Musician, 1977-84; legal clk. E.F. Hutton & Co., NYC, 1984; atty. Barton & Strever P.C., Newport, Oreg., 1985—. Contbr. chapters to books. Bd. mem. Oregon Law Found., 2000—. Mem. Oreg. State Bar (pres. 1997-98, bd. govs. 1995-98), Oreg. Criminal Def. Lawyers Assn., Assn. Trial Lawyers Am., Oreg. Trial Lawyers Assn. (Pres.'s club 1989—), Lincoln County Bar Assn. (pres. 1989). Avocations: guitar, scuba diving, vacuum tube amplification, electronics. Home: 421 NW 13th St Newport OR 97365-2402 Office: Barton & Strever PC 214 SW Coast Hwy Newport OR 97365-4927 Office Phone: 503-265-5377. Business E-Mail: attorneys@bartonstrever.com.

STRICK, JEREMY, curator, museum director; BA in History of Art with highest honors, U. Calif., Santa Cruz, 1977; postgrad., Harvard U. Asst. curator 20th Century art Nat. Gallery Art, Washington, 1986-89, assoc. curator 20th Century art, 1989-93, acting dept. dept. 20th Century art, 1992-93, curator Nat. Sculpture Garden project, 1989-93; curator modern art St. Louis Art Mus., 1993-96; Frances and Thomas Dittmer curator 20th Century painting and sculpture Art Inst. Chgo., 1996-99; dir. Mus. Contemporary Art, LA, 1999—. Curator N.Y. Interpreted: Joseph Stella and Alfred Stieglitz, Nat. Gallery Art, 1987, Milton Avery, 1990, Mark Rothko: The Spirit Myth, 1990-95, asst. curator A Century of Modern Sculpture: The Patsy and Raymond Nasher Collection, 1987, co-curator Twentieth-Century Art: Selections for the Tenth Anniversary of the East Building, 1987; curator Brice Marden: A Painting, Drawings, Prints, St. Louis Art Mus., 1993, Currents 58: Susan Crile—The Fires of War, 1994, Louise Bourgeois: The Personages 1946-1954, 1995, Currents 60: Jerald Ieans, 1994, Masterworks from Stuttgar: The Romantic Age in German Art, 1995, Currents 66: Michael Byron, 1996, Currents 67: Leonardo Drew, 1996; curator The Sublime Is Now: The Early Work of Barnett Newman, Walker Art Ctr., Mpls., Pace Gallery, N.Y.C., 1994; curator In the Light of Italy: Corot and Early Open-Air Painting, Nat. Gallery Art, Bklyn. Mus., St. Louis Art Mus., 1996; lectr., symposia participant and organizer, 1980—; juror Showhegan awards, 1995. Contbg. author: Works by Antoine-Louis Barye in the Collection of the Fogg Art Museum, Vol. IV, 1982; contbr. articles to exhbn. catalogs, newspapers, mags., ency. Instnl. fellow Samuel H. Kress Found., Paris, 1983-85, fellow Mrs. Giles Whiting Found., 1985-86. Office: Mus Contemporary Art Dept 20th Century Painting 250 S Grand Ave Los Angeles CA 90012-3021 Home: 261 N Bundy Dr Los Angeles CA 90049-2825 E-mail: jstrick@moca.org.

STRICKLAND, AUDRA, state legislator; m Tony Strickland. BA in Polit. Sci., U. Calif., Irvine. California State Assemblywoman, District 37, 2005-; vchairwoman, Arts, Entertain, Sports, Tourism & Internet Media, member, Environ Safety & Toxic Materials, Health comts, currently.Temple Christian School Jr High, teacher, formerly. Republican. Office: Dist 37 2659 Townsgate Rd Ste 236 Westlake Village CA 91361 Office Phone: 805-230-9167. Office Fax: 805-230-9183. Business E-Mail: assemblymember.strickland@assembly.ca.gov.

STRICKLAND, JULIA B., lawyer; b. San Francisco, Aug. 21, 1954; Student, Dartmouth Coll.; BA with honors, Univ. Calif., San Diego, 1975; JD, UCLA, 1978. Bar: Calif. 1978. Summer intern Stroock & Stroock & Lavan LLP, LA, 1977, ptnr., chair, fin. svcs. litig. practice, mem., operating exec. com, 1996—. Chair, consumer fin. svcs. litig. program Practising Law Inst., 1997—. Bd. of editors Banking Law Jour., editorial bd. Wall St. Lawyer, frequent lectr., writer in field. Named a Super Lawyer, LA Mag.; named one of Top 50 Women Litigators, LA Daily Jour., 2004. Mem.: Mortgage Bankers Assn., Assn. Bus. Trial Lawyers (bd. dir.). Office: Stroock & Stroock & Lavan LLP 2029 Century Pk E Los Angeles CA 90067-3086 Office Phone: 310-556-5806. Office Fax: 310-556-5959. Business E-Mail: jstrickland@strook.com.

STRICKLER, JEFFREY HAROLD, pediatrician; b. Mpls., Oct. 14, 1943; s. Jacob Harold and Helen Cecelia (Mitchell) S.; m. Karen Anne Stewart, June 18, 1966; children: Hans Stewart, Liesl Ann. BA, Carleton Coll., 1965; MD, U. Minn., 1969. Diplomate Am. Bd. Pediatrics. Resident in pediatrics Stanford U., Calif., 1969-73; pvt. practice Helena, Mont., 1975—2005; chief staff Shodair Children's Hosp., Helena, 1984-86; consulting ptnr. Strickler Enterprises, 2006—. Dir. maternal-child health Lewis and Clark County, Helena, 1978-88; chief of staff St. Peters Hosp., Helena, 1994-96; bd.chmn. Helena Health Alliance, 1996-99; founding mem., bd. dirs. Caring Found. Mont., 1992-2005; bd. mem. Intermountain Opera Assn., 2007-. Author: Big Sky Names, An Amble Through Western History and Ecology on the Roads, Streams, and Developments of Big Sky Montana, 2008. Mem. Mont. Gov.'s Task Force on Child Abuse, 1978-79; mem. steering com. Region VIII Child Abuse Prevention, Denver, 1979-82; bd. dirs. Helena Dist. 1 Sch. Bd., 1982-88, vice chmn., 1985-87. Maj. MC USAF, 1973—75. Fellow: Am. Acad. Pediatrics (vice chmn. Mont. chpt. 1981—84, chmn. 1984—87, mem. nat. nominating com. 1987—90, chmn. 1989—90, coun. on govt. affairs 1990—96, future of pediatric edn. II 1996—2000, Wyeth award 1987); mem.: Am. Bd. Pediatrics (PMCP-G practice performance com. 2001—), Rotary (youth exch. chmn. dist. 539 1984—88, pres. Helena 1988—89, polio plus chair dist. 5390 1996—, asst. gov. dist. 5390 2002—04, dist. gov. elect 2005—06, gov. 2006—07). Avocations: skiing, hiking. Home: PO Box 161815 2125 Yellowtail Rd Big Sky MT 59716-1815 Office Phone: 406-431-4331. Personal E-mail: j.strickler@3rivers.net.

STRINGFELLOW, GERALD B., engineering educator; b. Salt Lake City, Apr. 26, 1942; s. Paul Bennion and Jean (Barton) S.; m. Barbara Farr, June 9, 1962; children: Anne, Heather, Michael. BS, U. Utah, 1964; PhD, Stanford U., 1968. Staff scientist Hewlett Packard Labs., Palo Alto, Calif., 1967-70, group mgr., 1970-80; disting. prof. elec. engring., materials sci. U. Utah, Salt Lake City, 1980—, chmn., 1994-98, adj. prof. physics, 1988—, dean Coll. Engring., 1998—2003. Cons. Tex. Instruments, Dallas, 1995-97, AT&T-Bell Labs., Holmdel, N.J., 1986-90, Brit. Telecom., London, 1989-92; editor-in-chief Phase Diagrams for Ceramics, Vol. IX. Author: Organometallic Vapor Phase Epitaxy, 1989, 2d edit., 1999; editor: Metal Organic Vapor Phase Epitaxy, 1986, 2004, American Crystal Growth, 1987, Alloy Semiconductor Physics and Electronics, 1989, Phase Equilibria Diagrams-Semiconductors and Chalcogenides, 1991, High Brightness LEDs, 1997; prin. editor Jour. Crystal Growth, 1998-2003; letters editor Jour. Electronic Materials, 1992-99; contbr. over 360 articles to profl. jours. Recipient U.S. Sr. Scientist award Alexander von Humboldt Soc., Bonn, Germany, 1979, Gov.'s Sci. Tech. medal State of Utah, 1997, John Bardeen award TMS, 2003; guest fellow Royal Soc., London, 1990. Fellow IEEE, Japan Soc. Promotion of Sci.; mem. Am. Phys. Soc., Electronic Materials Com. (pres. 1985-87), Nat. Acad. Engring. Achievements include pioneering development of organometallic vapor phase epitaxy, development of theories of thermodynamic properties of alloy semiconductors; discovery of phenomenon of compositional latching in alloy semiconductor layers grown by epitaxial techniques. Office: U Utah Dept ECE 3280 MEB Salt Lake City UT 84112-1109 Business E-Mail: stringfellow@coe.utah.edu.

STRINGHAM, RENÉE, physician; b. Mpls., July 16, 1940; d. Clifford Leonard and Helen Pearl (Marcineak) Heinrich; children: Lars Eric, Leif Erik, Lance Devon. BS, St. Lawrence U., 1962; MD, U. Ky., 1972. Diplomate Am. Bd. Family Practice. Intern U. Fla., Gainesville, 1972-73; physician Lee County Coop. Clinic, Marianna, Ark., 1973-74; pvt. practice Coastal Health Practitioners, Lincoln City, Oreg., 1975-84; county med. officer Lincoln County Health Dept., Newport, Oreg., 1986-90; pvt. practice, 1984-90; student health Miami U., Oxford, Ohio, 1991-93; pvt. practice Macadam Clin., Portland, 1994; cons. student health Willamette U., 1994-95; contract physician West Salem Clinic, 1995-97; med. dir. Capital Manor, 1997-99; locum tenens, 1999—; physician Oreg. State Hosp., 2001—03. Trustee Coast Home Nursing, Lincoln County, 1984-86; expert witness EPA, 1980. Facilitator Exceptional Living, 1984-86. Fellow Am. Acad. Family Practice; mem. Lincoln County Med. Soc. (pres. 1984), Oreg. Med. Assn. Avocations: spontaneous music, folk dancing, sailing.

STRITTMATTER, PETER ALBERT, astronomer, educator; b. London, Eng., Sept. 12, 1939; came to U.S., 1970. s. Albert and Rosa S.; m. Janet Hubbard Parkhurst, Mar. 18, 1967; children— Catherine D., Robert P. BA, Cambridge U., Eng., 1961, MA, 1963, PhD, 1967. Staff scientist Inst. for Astronomy, Cambridge, Eng., 1967-70; staff scientist dept. physics U. Calif.-San Diego, La Jolla, 1970-71; assoc. prof. dept. astronomy U. Ariz., Tucson, 1971-74, prof. dept. astronomy, 1974—, Regent's prof., 1994—. Dir. Steward Observatory, Tucson, 1975—; mem. staff Max Planck Inst. Radio-astronomy, Bonn, W. Germany, 1981—. Contbr. articles to profl. jours. Recipient Sr. award Humboldt Found., 1979-80, Karl Schwarzschild medal, 1998. Fellow Royal Astron. Soc.; mem. Am. Astron. Soc., Astronomische Gesellschaft. Office: U Ariz Steward Obs Tucson AZ 85721-0001

STROBER, MYRA HOFFENBERG, education educator, consultant; b. NYC, Mar. 28, 1941; d. Julius William Hoffenberg and Regina Scharer; m. Samuel Strober, June 23, 1963 (div. Dec. 1983); children: Jason M., Elizabeth A.; m. Jay M. Jackman, Oct. 21, 1990. BS in Indsl. Rels., Cornell U., 1962; MA in Econs., Tufts U., 1965; PhD in Econs., MIT, 1969. Lectr., asst. prof. dept. econs. U. Md., College Park, 1967-70; lectr. U. Calif., Berkeley, 1970-72; asst. prof. grad. sch. bus. Stanford (Calif.) U., 1972-86, assoc. prof. sch. edn., 1979-90, prof. edn., 1990—, assoc. dean acad. affairs, 1993-95, interim dean, 1994; program officer in higher edn. Atlantic Philanthropic Svcs., Ithaca, N.Y., 1998-2000. Organizer Stanford Bus. Conf. Women Mgmt., 1974; founding dir. ctr. rsch. women Stanford U., 1974-76, 79-84, dir. edn. policy inst., 1984-86, dean alumni coll., 1992, mem. policy and planning bd., 1992-93, chair program edn. adminstrn. and policy analysis, 1991-93, chair provost's com. recruitment and retention women faculty, 1992-93, chair faculty senate com. on coms., 1992-93; mem. adv. bd. State of Calif. Office Econ. Policy Planning and Rsch., 1978-80; mem. Coll. Bd. Com. Develop Advanced Placement Exam. Econs., 1987-88; faculty advisor Rutgers Women's Leadership Program, 1991-93. Author: (with others) Industrial Relations, 1972, 1990, Sex, Discrimination and the Division of Labor, 1975, Changing Roles of Men and Women, 1976, Women in the Labor Market, 1979, Educational Policy and Management: Sex Differentials, 1981, Women in the Workplace, 1982, Sex Segregation in the Workplace: Trends, Explanations, Remedies, 1984, The New Palgrave: A Dictionary of Economic Theory and Doctrine, 1987, Computer Chips and Paper Clips: Technology and Women's Employment, Vol. II, 1987, Gender in the Workplace, 1987, Challenge to Human Capital Theory: Implications for the HR Manager, American Economic Review, 1995, Rethinking Economics Through a Feminist Lens, Feminist Economics, 1995, Making and Correcting Errors in Economic Analyses: An Examination of Videotapes, (with Agnes M.K. Chan) the Road Winds Uphill All the Way: Gender, Work, and Family in the U.S. and Japan, 1999, (with Jay M. Jackman) Fear of Feedback, 2003, Children As a Public Good, 2004, Can Harvard Ever Play a Positive Role for Women in Higher Education?, 2005; editor (with Francine E. Gordon) Bringing Women Into Management, 1975, (with others) Women and Poverty, 1986, Industrial Relations, 1990, Challenges to Human Capitol Theory: Implications for HR Managers, 1995, (with Sanford M. Dornbusch) Feminism, Children and the New Families, 1988, Rethinking Economics Through a Feminist Lens, 1995, (with Agnes M.K. Chan) The Road Winds Uphill All The Way: Gender, Work and Family in the U.S. and Japan, 1999, (with Jay M. Jackman) Fear of Feedback, 2003, Application of Mainstream Economics Constructs to Education: A Feminist Analysis, 2003, Children as a Public Good, 2004, Feminist Economics: Implications for Education, 2005, Can Harvard Ever Play a Positive Role for Women in Higher Education, 2005; Habits of the Mind: Challenges for Multidisciplinarity, 2006; Faculty Salaries and Maximization of Prestige, 2007, (with Tatiana Melguizo); mem. bd. editors Signs: Jour. Women Culture and Soc., 1975-89, assoc. editor, 1980-85; mem. bd. editors Sage Ann. Rev. Women and Work, 1984—; mem. editorial adv. bd. U.S.-Japan Women's Jour., 1991—; assoc. editor Jour. Econ. Edn., 1991—; contbr. chpt. to book, articles to profl. jours. Mem. rsch. adv. task force YWCA, 1989—; chair exec. bd. Stanford Hillel, 1990-92; bd. dirs. Resource Ctr. Women, Palo Alto, Calif., 1983-84; pres. bd. dirs. Kaider Found., Mountain View, Calif., 1990-96; bd. trustees Mills Coll., 2004—. Fellow Stanford U., 1975-77, Schiff House Resident fellow, 85-87. Mem.: NOW (bd. dirs. legal def. and edn. fund 1993—98), Ctr. Gender Equality (bd. dirs. 2000—), Internat. Assn. Feminist Econs. (assoc. editor Feminist Econs. 1994—, pres. 1997), Indsl. Rels. Rsch. Assn., Am. Ednl. Rsch. Assn., Am. Econ. Assn. (mem. com. status of women in profession 1972—75). Office: Stanford U School Edn Stanford CA 94305 Office Phone: 650-723-0387. Business E-Mail: myra.strober@stanford.edu.

STROBER, SAMUEL, immunologist, educator; b. NYC, May 8, 1940; s. Julius and Lee (Lander) S.; m. Linda Carol Higgins, July 6, 1991; children: William, Jesse; children from a previous marriage: Jason, Elizabeth. AB in Liberal Arts, Columbia U., 1961; MD magna cum laude, Harvard U., 1966. Intern Mass. Gen. Hosp., Boston, 1966-67; resident in internal medicine Stanford U. Hosp., Calif., 1970-71; rsch. fellow Peter Bent Brigham Hosp., Boston, 1962-63, 65-66, Oxford U., England, 1963-64; rsch. assoc. Lab. Cell Biology Nat. Cancer Inst. NIH, Bethesda, Md., 1967-70; instr. medicine Stanford U., 1971-72, asst. prof., 1972-78, assoc. prof. medicine, 1978-82, prof. medicine, 1982—, Diane Goldstone Meml. lectr., 1978-97, John Putnam Merrill Meml. lectr., chief div. immunology & rheumatology, 1978-97. Investigator Howard Hughes Med. Inst., Miami, Fla., 1976-81; chmn., bd. dirs. La Jolla Inst. for Allergy and Immunology; founder Dendreon, Inc. Assoc. editor: Jour. Immunology, 1981-84, Transplantation, 1981-85, 99—, Internat. Jour. Immunotherapy, 1985—, Transplant Immunology, 1992—, Biol. Bone Marrow Transplantation, 1999—; contbr. articles to profl. jours. Served with USPHS, 1967-70. Recipient Leon Reznick Meml. Rsch. prize, Harvard U., 1966. Mem. Am. Assn. Immunology, Am. Soc. Clin. Investigation, Am. Coll. Rheumatology, Transplantation Soc. (councilor 1986-89), Am. Soc. Tranplantation Physicians, Western Soc. Medicine, Am. Assn. Physicians, Clin. Immunology Soc. (pres. 1996), Alpha Omega. Office: Stanford U Sch Medicine 300 Pasteur Dr Palo Alto CA 94304-2203

STROCK, DAVID RANDOLPH, brokerage house executive; b. Salt Lake City, Jan. 31, 1944; s. Clarence Randolph and Francis (Hornibrook) S.; m. Phyllis A. Tingley, Dec. 13, 1945 (div. June 15, 1982); children: Sarah, Heidi. AA, San Mateo Coll., 1967; BS, San Jose State U., 1970. Investment exec. Paine Webber, San Jose, Calif., 1970-78, corp. trainer NYC, 1978-79, rsch. coord., 1979-82, br. mgr. Northbrook, Ill., 1982-84, Palos Verdes, Calif., 1984-89, Napa, Calif., 1989-90, investment exec., 1990—. Contbr. articles to profl. jours. Mem. San Jose Jr. C. of C. (chmn. 1977, v.p. 1978), North Napa Rotary (past pres.), Moose. Republican. Avocations: reading, indy car racing, formula one racing, biking, whitewater rafting. Home: 3324 Homestead Ct Napa CA 94558-4275 Office: Paine Webber 703 Trancas St Napa CA 94558-3014 Office Phone: 707-254-1504. Business E-Mail: dave_strock@hotmail.com.

STROCK, JAMES MARTIN, communications executive, writer, entrepreneur; b. Austin, Tex., Aug. 19, 1956; s. James Martin Strock Sr. and Augusta (Tenney) Cumby. AB, Harvard U., 1977, JD, 1981; postgrad, New Coll. Oxford U., 1981—82. Bar: Colo. 1983. Tchg. asst. Harvard U., 1980—81; spl. cons. to majority leader U.S. Senate, Washington, 1982—83; spl. asst. to adminstr. EPA, Washington, 1983—85, asst. adminstr. for enforcement, 1989—91; spl. counsel U.S. Senate Com. on Environment and Pub. Works, Washington, 1985—86; assoc. Davis, Graham & Stubbs, Denver, 1986—88; acting dir., gen. counsel U.S. Office Pers. Mgmt., Washington, 1988—89; sec. for environ. protection State of Calif., Sacramento, 1991—97; prin. James Strock & Co., Scottsdale, Ariz., 1997—. Adj. prof. U. So. Calif., 1996-97; mem. Intergovtl. Policy Adv. Com., rep. U.S. Trade, 1991-97; mem. Calif. State Pers. Bd., 1998; guest prof. U. Konstanz, 1998; mem. Calif. State Personnel Bd., 1997-99; spkr. in field Author: Reagan on Leadership, 1998, Theodore Roosevelt on Leadership, 2001; contbr. articles to profl. jours. Capt. JAGC USAR, 1987—96. Recipient Ross Essay award ABA, 1985, Environ. Leadership award Calif. Environ. Bus. Coun., 1994, Fed. Republic Germany Friendship award, 1996; Environ. Soc. India fellow, 1997, commendation Calif. Dist. Attys. Assn., 1997 Mem. Coun. Fgn. Rels., Authors' Guild, Phi Beta Kappa. Republican. Office: Ste B-111-601 15029 N Thompson Peak Pky Scottsdale AZ 85260 Business E-Mail: jms@jamesstrock.com.

STROHMEYER, JOHN, writer, retired editor; b. Cascade, Wis., June 26, 1924; s. Louis A. and Anna Rose (Saladunas) S.; m. Nancy Jordan, Aug. 20, 1949 (dec. 2000); children: Mark, John, Sarah; m. Sylvia Ciernick Broady, Oct. 25, 2003. Student, Moravian Coll., 1941—43; AB, Muhlenberg Coll., 1947; MA in Journalism, Columbia U., 1948; LHD (hon.), Lehigh U., 1983. With Nazareth Item, Pa., 1940—41; night reporter Bethlehem Globe-Times, Pa., 1941—43, 1945—47; investigative reporter Providence Jour.-Bull., 1949—56; editor Bethlehem Globe-Times, 1956—64, v.p., 1961—84, dir., 1963—84. African-Am. journalism tchr. in Nairobi, Freetown, 1964; Atwood prof. journalism U. Alaska, Anchorage, 1987-88, writer-in-residence, 1989—; Clendinen Prof., U. S. Fla., 2001. Author: Crisis in Bethlehem: Big Steel's Struggle to Survive, 1986, Extreme Conditions: Big Oil and The Transformation of Alaska, 1993, Historic Anchorage, 2001. Lt. (j.g.) USNR, 1943-45. Pulitzer Traveling fellow, 1948; Nieman fellow, 1952-53; recipient Comenius award Moravian Coll., 1971; Pulitzer prize for editl. writing, 1972; Alicia Patterson Found. fellow, 1984, 85. Mem. Am. Soc. Newspaper Editors, Pa. Soc. Newspaper Editors (pres. 1964-66), Anchorage Racquet Club. Home (Summer): 6633 Lunar Dr Anchorage AK 99504-4550 E-mail: jstroh@gci.net.

STROMBERG, ROSS ERNEST, lawyer; b. Arcata, Calif., May 5, 1940; s. Noah Anders and Anne Laura (Noyes) S.; m. Toni Nicholas, Dec. 16, 1961; m. Margaret Telonicher, Oct. 3, 1965; children: Kristin, Matthew, Gretchen, Erik. BS, Humboldt State U., 1962; JD, U. Calif., Berkeley, 1965. Bar: Calif. 1966, U.S. Dist. Ct. (no. dist.) Calif. 1966, U.S. Ct. Appeals (9th cir.) 1966. Assoc. Hanson Bridgett, San Francisco, 1965-70, ptnr., 1970-85, Epstein Becker Stromberg & Green, San Francisco, 1985-90, Jones Day, San Francisco, 1990—. Past chmn. Jones Day's Healthcare Specialized Industry Practice; pres. Stromberg Vineyards, Healdsburg, Calif., 2002—. Author: Economic Joint Venturing, 1985, Acquisition and Enhancement of Physician Practices, 1988. Pres. Am. Acad. Hosp. Attys. of Am. Host. Assn., Chgo., 1978; bd. dirs. Sutter Med. Ctr., Santa Rosa, 2001—, chair, 2003—; pres. East Bay AHEC, Oakland, Calif., 1984—87; bd. dirs. Am. Cancer Soc., Oakland, 1984—95, Wildflowers Inst., San Francisco, 1984—2008; chair Pediat. Dental Initiative of the North Coast, Healdsburg, Calif., 2004. Mem.: Am. Health Lawyers Assn. Democrat. Office: Jones Day 26th Fl 555 Calif St San Francisco CA 94104 Office Phone: 415-875-5724. Business E-Mail: restromberg@jonesday.com.

STRONG, ANNSLEY CHAPMAN, interior designer, volunteer; b. Paterson, NJ, July 18, 1947; d. Donald John and Margaret Brawley Chapman; m. George Gordon Strong, Jr., Nov. 30, 1974; children: George Gordon III, Courtney Chapman Strong Thomas, Meredith Annsley, Alexis Palmer. BA, Wheaton Coll., Norton, Mass., 1969. Cert. N.Y. Sch. Design, 1969, Interior Designers Guild, 1975. Pres. Strong Studio Designs, La Canada, Calif., 1984—. Treas., commr. AYSO Region 13, Pasadena, Calif., 1993—97; mem. Bishop Stevens Found. Bd., Pasadena, Calif., 1994—; co-founder La Canada Sports Coalition, 1996; chmn. bd. Hathaway Sycamores, Pasadena, Calif., 2007—; past chair Verdugo Hills Hosp. Found., 2008—; bd. chair Verdugo Hills Hosp., Glendale, 2008—. Recipient 20th Century award, Pasadena YMCA, 1990, Bill Carroll Lifetime Achievement award, Am. Youth Soccer Orgn., 2000. Republican. Avocations: painting, piano, Bridge, skiing, golf. Office Phone: 818-957-0086.

STRONG, JOHN OLIVER, plastic surgeon, educator; b. Montclair, NJ, Feb. 1, 1930; s. George Joseph and Olivia (LeBrun) S.; m. Helen Louise Vrooman, July 19, 1958 (dec. Mar. 1973); m. Deborah Sperberg, May 20, 1978; children: John Jr., Jean LeB., Andrew D. BS, Yale U., 1952; MD, U. Pa., 1957. Cert. vol. paleontologist Calif. Practice medicine specializing in plastic and reconstructive surgery, Santa Ana, Calif., 1964-97; asst. clin. prof. plastic and reconstructive surgery U. Calif., Irvine, 1970—. Chief of staff Western Med. Ctr., Santa Ana, 1996-97, interim chmn. bd., 1996-97, bd. dirs.; bd. dirs. United Western Med. Ctrs., Healthcare Found. Orange County, chmn.; vol. Anza Borrego Desert State Pk., steering com., 1998-2003. Vol. Anza -Borrego Desert State Pk. Fellow ACS; mem. Calif. Med. Assn. (chmn. sci. adv. panel 1983-89), Calif. Soc. Plastic Surgeons (pres. 1991-92). Republican. Office: PO Box 94 Borrego Springs CA 92004-0094 Address: 511 Seaward Rd Corona Del Mar CA 92625-2600 Personal E-mail: jostrong1@sbcglobal.net.

STRONG, JOHN WILLIAM, lawyer, educator; b. Iowa City, Aug. 18, 1935; s. Frank Ransom and Gertrude Elizabeth (Way) S.; m. Margaret Waite Cleary, June 16, 1962; children— Frank Ransom, Benjamin Waite. BA, Yale U., 1957; JD, U. Ill., 1962; postgrad, U. N.C., 1966-67. Bar: Ill. 1963, Oreg. 1976. Assoc. firm LeForgee, Samuels, Miller, Schroeder & Jackson, Decatur, Ill., 1963-64; asst. prof. law U. Kans., 1964-66; assoc. prof. Duke U., 1966-69; prof. U. Oreg., 1969-75; legal counsel Oreg. Task Force on Med. Malpractice, 1976; prof. U. Nebr., 1977-84, dean, 1977-82, vice chancellor for acad. affairs, 1981-84; Rosenstiel Disting. prof. law U. Ariz., 1984-98, prof. emeritus, 1998—. Nat. sec.-treas. Order of the Coif, 1992-98; cons. Nat. Judicial Coll. Author: (with others) Handbook on Evidence, 5th edit., 1999. Served with U.S. Army, 1957-59. Mem. Ill. Bar Assn., Oreg. Bar Assn., ABA, Am. Law Inst., Phi Delta Phi. Independent. Congregationalist. Office: U Ariz Coll Law Tucson AZ 85721-0001 Home: PO Box 8063 Black Butte Ranch OR 97759 Business E-Mail: strong@law.arizona.edu.

STRONG, PAMELA KAY, material and process engineer; b. Mesa, Ariz., Oct. 17, 1950; d. Wayland Thorton and Adele (Gaumer) S. BS in Organic Chemistry, Phila. Coll. Pharmacy and Sci., 1972; MS in Organic Chemistry, Bryn Mawr Coll., 1974. Cons. formulation, rsch. chemist Western Indsl. Enterprises, Phoenix, 1974-75; analytical chemist Henkel Corp., Hawthorne, Calif., 1975-80; mem. tech. staff, process engr. Radar div. Hughes Aircraft, El Segundo, Calif., 1980-83; sr. process engr. Irvine Sensors Corp., Costa Mesa, Calif., 1983; sr. advanced composite and composite quality engr. Aircraft Engine Bus. Group, GE, Albuquerque, 1983-85; Mantech engring. specialist sr., sr. quality assurance engr. Advanced Systems div. Northrop Corp., Pico Rivera, Calif., 1985-87; material and process engring. tech. specialist, lead engr. McDonnell Douglas Missile and Space Systems Co., Huntington Beach, Calif., 1987—97; assoc. tech. fellow, prin. engr., scientist Boeing Co. (merged with McDonnell Douglas), 1997—2007; sr. engring. specialist for systems engring. divsn. Aerospace Corp., LA, 2007—. Recipient GE Mfg. Tech. Excellence award, 1984, Boeing Performance award, 2002, Boeing Chief Tech Officer Profl. Excellence award, 2004, J. Cordell Breed Women's Leadership award, Soc. Automotive Engrs., 2005; Bryn Mawr Coll. scholar; NSF rsch. fellow, 1971. Fellow Am. Inst. Chemists, Royal Australian Tech. Inst., Soc. Advancement Materials and Process Engrs. (treas. 1984-85), Soc. Women Engrs. (life, Achievement award 2007); mem. AAAS, Am. Chem. Soc. (Petroleum Rsch. fellow 1971, Scholastic award 1972), Soc. Applied Spectroscopy (chairperson 1977-79, sec. 1979-81), Soc. Women Chemists, NAFE, Iota Sigma Pi. Office: Aerospace Corp PO Box 92957 Los Angeles CA 90009-2957

STROOCK, THOMAS FRANK, oil and gas company executive; b. NYC, Oct. 10, 1925; s. Samuel and Dorothy (Frank) S.; m. Marta Freyre de Andrade, June 19, 1949; children: Margaret, Sandra, Elizabeth, Anne. BA in Econs., Yale U., 1948; LLB (hon.), U. Wyo., 1995; PhD (hon.), Universidad del Valle, Guatemala, 2001. Landman Stanolind Oil & Gas Co., Tulsa, 1948-52; pres. Stroock Leasing Corp., Casper, Wyo., 1952-89, Alpha Exploration, Inc., 1980-89; ptnr. Stroock, Rogers & Dymond, Casper, 1960-82; dir. First Wyo. Bank, Casper, 1967-89; mem. Wyo. Senate, 1969-89, chmn. appropriations com., 1983-89, co-chmn. joint appropriations com., 1983-89, mem. mgmt. and audit com., pres., 1988-89; mem. steering com. Edn. Commn. of States; amb. to Guatemala Govt. of U.S., 1989-93; pres. Alpha Devel. Corp., 1992—; prof. pub. diplomacy U. Wyo., Laramie, 1993—2002, chmn. internat. adv. bd., 2001—. Dir. Wyo. Med. Ctr., 1996-2004. Rep. precinct committeeman, 1960-68; pres. Natrona County Sch. Bd., 1966, 69; pres. Wyo. State Sch. Bds. Assn., 1965-66; chmn. Casper Cmty. Recreation, 1955-60; chmn. Natrona County United Fund, 1963-64, Wyo. State Rep. Com., 1975-78, exec. com. 1954-60; del. Rep. Nat. Conv., 1956-76, 92; regional coord. campaign George Bush for pres., 1979-80, 87-88; chmn. Western States Rep. Chmn. Assn., 1977-78; chmn. Wyo. Higher Edn. Commn., 1969-71, Wyo. Health Access Task Force, 2003-04; mem. Nat. Petroleum Coun., 1972-77; chmn. trustees Sierra Madre Found. for Geol. Rsch., New Haven; chmn. Wyo. Nat. Gas Pipline Authority, 1987-88; bd. dirs. Ucross Found., Denver; mem. Nat. Pub. Lands Adv. Coun., 1981-85; trustee Nature Conservancy, 1993-2005; chmn. Wyo. Health Reform Commn., 1993-95, Universidad del Valle Found., Guatemala City, 1995-2000, trustee, 2000-2005. Sgt. USMC, 1943-46. Mem. Rocky Mountain Oil and Gas Assn., Petroleum Assn. Wyo., Kiwanis, Casper Country Club, Casper Petroleum Club, Yale Club N.Y. Republican. Unitarian Universalist. Home and Office: PO Box 2875 Casper WY 82602-2875 Office Phone: 307-234-8925.

STROPE, MICHAEL LEE, protective services official; BS cum laude, Drury Coll., 1975; MS, Cen. Mo. State U., 1978. From police officer to police lt. Mo. Police Dept., Springfield, 1970-84; chief of police City of Stillwater, Okla., 1984-87, City of College Station, Tex., 1987-92, Peoria (Ariz.) Police Dept., 1992—. Instr. Ariz. State U., Phoenix, 1996—, Wayland U., Luke AFB, Ariz., 1993—; security-mgmt. cons. SSRS Properties, Inc., College Station, 1992; dept. chmn. criminal justice Blinn Coll., Brenham, Tex., 1992; project assessor Commn. on Accreditation for Law Enforcement Agencies, Inc., 1990; lectr. Okla. Mcpl. League, 1986; adj. faculty Columbia (Mo.) Coll., 1982-84, Drury Coll., Springfield, 1976-82; project dir. Mo. Police Dept., Springfield, 1979-81; adv. bd. chmn. Tex. A&M Engring. Ext. Svc. Police Acad., 1990-92. Contbr. articles to profl. jours. Criminal justice adv. com. Brazos Valley Cmty. Devel. Coun., 1987-92; exec. bd. dirs. Brazos Valley Coun. on Alcohol and Substance Abuse, 1987-91; dep. chmn. Brazos County Emergency Mgmt. Coun., 1987-92. Recipient Mayors award C. of C., 1996, Best of the West award Cmty. Svc., 1994, Cmty. Svc. award SAR, Tex., 1992, Spl. Recognition award Spl. Olympics, Okla., 1986, Outstanding Cmty. Svc. award Delta Tau Delta, 1985; named one of Outstanding Young Men of Am., 1982. Mem. Internat. Assn. Chiefs Police (tng. and edn. com. 1984-92, juvenile justice com. 1995—), FBI Nat. Acad. Assoc., Ariz. Police Chiefs Assn. Office: Peoria Police Dept 8343 W Monroe St Peoria AZ 85345-6559 Fax: 623-773-9015.

STROTE, JOEL RICHARD, lawyer; b. NYC, Apr. 19, 1939; s. Jack and Fortuna (Benezra) S.; children: Jared, Noah, Sebastian; m. Elisa Ballestas, Dec. 14, 1991. BA, U. Mich., 1960; JD, Northwestern U., 1963. Bar: N.Y. 1964, D.C. 1965, Calif. 1967, U.S. Dist. Ct. (cen. dist.) Calif. 1967, U.S. Supreme Ct. 1971, Nev., 2003. Assoc. Damman, Blank, Hirsh & Heming, NYC, 1964-65, ICC, Washington, 1965-66, Capitol Records, Hollywood, Calif., 1966-67; ptnr. Strote & Whitehouse, Beverly Hills, Calif., 1967-89; of counsel Selvin, Weiner & Ruben, Beverly Hills, Calif., 1989-94; ptnr. with Cohen, Strote & Young, 1992-94; sole practice law, 1994—. Judge pro tem L.A. County Mcpl. Ct., 1973—; probation monitor Calif. State Bar Ct., L.A., 1985-2005; pres., Wheda Found., Las Vegas, Nev., 1987-2005; bd. chmn. Tuesday's Child, L.A., 1989-91. Mem. Thousand Oaks Arts Commn., 1997-99. Cpl. USMC, 1963-64. Mem. Calif. State Bar Assn., L.A. County Bar Assn., L.A. Copyright Soc., Beverly Hills Bar Assn., Assn. Internat. Entertainment Lawyers, Internat. Fedn. of Festival Orgns. Democrat. Jewish. Avocations: swimming, bicycling, hiking, opera, travel. Office: 200 N Westlake Blvd Ste 204 Westlake Village CA 91392 Home Phone: 818-259-2939; Office Phone: 818-707-1923. Personal E-mail: joelstrote@verizon.net.

STROTHER, ALLEN, biochemical pharmacologist, researcher; b. Nolan County, Tex., Feb. 20, 1928; s. Henry Allen and Minnie Etta (Taylor) S.; m. Julia Ann Gutch, Feb. 7, 1957; children: Wesley Allen, Lori Ann. BS, Tex. Tech U., 1955; MS, U. Calif., 1957; PhD, Tex. A&M U., 1963. Rsch. asst. Tex. A&M, Coll. Sta., 1959-63; rsch. biochemist FDA, Washington, 1963-65; asst. prof. pharmacology Loma Linda (Calif.) U., 1965-70, assoc. prof., 1970-75, prof., 1975-95, retired, vol. faculty, 1995—, prof. emeritus Physiology and Pharmacology, 1997—. Cons. WHO, Geneva, 1982-86. Contbr. numerous articles to profl. jours.; chpt. to WHO Bull. Pilot CAP/USAF Search and Rescue San Bernardino, Calif., 1967-95; pilot examiner CAP Air Force Aux., Norton AFB, 1970-86. Named Investigator of Yr. Walter E. McPherson Soc., Loma Linda U., 1984, Basic Sci. Fellow of Yr., 1986, Outstanding Faculty Rschr. of Yr. award, 1997. Mem. Am. Soc. Pharmacology and Exptl. Therapeutics, Am. Chem. Soc., Xzenobiotic Soc. Avocations: flying, golf. Home: 74448 Nevada Cir E Palm Desert CA 92260-2269 Office: Loma Linda U Sch Medicine Dept Physiology and Pharmacology Loma Linda CA 92354

STROTHER, JAMES M., lawyer; b. 1951; BA, JD, Univ. Minn. Pvt. practice, Mpls.; asst. gen. counsel Norwest Corp. (now Wells Fargo Home Mortgage), 1986—98; gen. counsel Wells Fargo Home Mortgage, 1998—2001; dep. gen. counsel Wells Fargo & Co., San Francisco, 2001—03, exec. v.p., gen. counsel, 2004—. Office: Wells Fargo Retechs 333 Market St Fl 3 San Francisco CA 94105-2104

STROUP, ELIZABETH FAYE, librarian; b. Tulsa, Okla., Mar. 25, 1939; d. Milton Earl and Lois (Buhl) S. BA in Philosophy, U. Wash., 1962, MLS, 1964. Intern Libr. of Congress, Washington, 1964-65; asst. dir. North Cen. Regional Libr., Wenatchee, Wash., 1966-69; reference specialist Congl. Reference div. Libr. of Congress, Washington, 1970-71, head nat. collections Div. for the Blind and Physically Handicapped, 1971-73, chief Congl. Reference div., 1973-78, dir. gen. reference, 1978-88; city libr., chief exec. officer Seattle Pub. Libr., 1988-96; exec. dir. Wash. Literacy, Seattle, 1996-99; reference coord. Timberland Regional Libr., Olympia, Wash., 1999—. Cons. U.S. Info. Svc., Indonesia, Feb. 1987. Mem. adv. bd. KCTS 9 Pub. TV, Seattle, 1988—; bd. visitors Sch. Librarianship, U. Wash., 1988—; bd. dirs. Wash. Literacy, 1988—. Mem. ALA (pres. reference and adult svcs. div. 1986-87, div. bd. 1985-88), Wash. Libr. Assn., D.C. Libr. Assn. (bd. dirs. 1975-76), City Club, Ranier Club. Avocations: gardening, mountain climbing, reading. Office: Wash Literacy 220 Nickerson St Seattle WA 98109-1622

STROVINK, MARK WILLIAM, physics professor; b. Santa Monica, Calif., July 22, 1944; s. William George and Barbara (Marsh) S.; m. Joyce Catharine Hodgson, Dec. 22, 1965 (div. June 1988); children: Kurt Gregory, Karl William; m. Linda Margaret Cooper, July 5, 1991. BS, MIT, 1965; PhD, Princeton U., 1970. Instr. Princeton U., NJ, 1970-71, asst. prof., 1970-73, U. Calif., Berkeley, 1973-76, assoc. prof., 1976-81, prof., 1981—. Vis. asst. prof. Cornell U., Ithaca, N.Y., 1971-72; chmn. physics adv. com. Stanford Linear Accelerator Ctr., Stanford, Calif., 1985-86, Fermilab, Batavia, Ill., 1988-90; mem. high energy physics adv. panel U.S. Dept. Energy, Washington, 1988-92. Contbr. articles to profl. jours. Fellow Am. Phys. Soc. Office: U Calif Dept Physics Berkeley CA 94720-7300 Office Phone: 510-486-7087, 510-642-9685. E-mail: strovink@lbl.gov.

STRUHL, STANLEY FREDERICK, real estate developer; b. Bklyn., Oct. 10, 1939; s. Isidore and Yvette (Miller) Struhl; m. Patricia Joyce Wald, Feb. 26, 1966; children: Marc Howard, Lisa Lynn. BS in Engring. with honors, UCLA, 1961, MBA in Data Processing, 1963. Lic. real estate broker Calif., 1977. Tech. staff Hughes Aircraft Co., Fullerton, Calif., 1963—65; sr. assoc. Planning Rsch. Corp., LA, 1965—70; mgr. corp. info. sys. Logicon, Inc., Torrance, Calif., 1970—73; mgr. ops. analysis Sys. Devel. Corp., Santa Monica, Calif., 1973—77; gen. ptnr. TST Developers, Canyon Country, Calif., 1977—81; pres. Struhl Enterprises, Inc., Northridge, Calif., 1977—85; owner Struhl Properties, West Hills, 1977—2003; ret., 2003. Planning sub. com. 12th Coun. Dist., LA, 1986—98. Mem.: Trail Dusters, Tau Beta Pi, Beta Gamma Sigma, Alpha Phi Omega.

STRUTZEL, JOD CHRISTOPHER, escrow company executive; b. LA, Sept. 20, 1947; s. James Rudolph and Charlotte Elizabeth (Weiss) S.; m. Christine Melba Kemp, Dec. 28, 1969; children: Jason James, Jess Warren. BS in Bus. Mgmt., Calif. State U., Long Beach, 1970. Bellman Edgewater Hyatt House Hotel, Long Beach, 1970, night auditor, 1970-71; asst. mgr. Sands Resort Hotel, Palm Springs, Calif., 1971-72, gen. mgr., 1972-73; sales coordinator Bendix Home Systems, Santa Fe Springs, Calif., 1973-74; loan rep. J.E. Wells Fin. Co., LA, 1974-75; v.p. Express Escrow Co., Huntington Beach, Calif., 1976-78, pres., chmn. bd., bd. dirs., 1978—. Pres., chmn. bd., bd. dirs Elsinore (Calif.) Escrow, Inc., 1977-79; bd. dirs. Sorrell Devel., Redondo Beach, Calif.; expert witness on escrow, litigation and cons., 1982—; chmn. liability reduction com. Escrow Agts. Fidelity Corp., 1983-84, legis. chmn., 1985-86, 87-90, 95-97, vice-chmn. bd., 1989-90, 94-95, treas., 1992-93; bd. dirs., sec. Discovery Escrow Co., 1989-94; drafted sections of Calif. Fin. Code, Health and Safety Code, Calif. Adminstrv. Code. Contbr. articles to profl. jours. Bd. dirs. publicity chmn. Fountain Valley (Calif.) Youth Baseball, 1986-87; AD HOC com. on Escrow Regulations Dept. Housing and Cmty. Devel., 1980; escrow adv. com. Dept. Corps., 1990-93. Recipient J.E. Wells Meml. award, 1988. Mem. Escrow Agts. Fidelity Corp. (bd. dirs. 1983-97), Escrow Inst. Calif. (bd. dirs. 1991), Calif. Manufactured Housing Assn. (treas., bd. dirs. 1984-86), Calif. Manufactured Housing Inst. (bd. dirs. 1986—, treas. 1986-87, legis. chmn. 1993—, Polit. Action Com. Man of Yr. award 1988, Orange County chpt. Man of Yr. award 1988, Chmn.'s award 1997, Pres. award 1999), Western Mobilehome Assn. (renaissance com. 2001—). Avocations: golf, war games, athletic coaching. Office: Express Escrow Co 7812 Edinger Ave Ste 300 Huntington Beach CA 92647-3727

STRYER, LUBERT, biochemist, educator; b. Tientsin, China, Mar. 2, 1938; BS with honors, U. Chgo., 1957; MD magna cum laude, Harvard U., 1961; DS (hon.), U. Chgo., 1992. Helen Hay Whitney fellow Harvard U., also Med. Research Council Lab., 1961-63; from asst. prof. to assoc. prof. biochemistry Stanford U., 1963-69; prof. molecular biophysics and biochemistry Yale U., 1969-76; Winzer prof. neurobiology Stanford U. Sch. Medicine, 1976—2004, chmn.

dept. structural biology, 1976-79, prof. emeritus, 2004—; chmn. sci. adv. bd. Affymetrix, Inc., 1993—; founder, chmn., chief sci. officer Senomyx, Inc., La Jolla, Calif., 1999-2001, chmn. sci. adv. bd., 2001—. Cons. NIH, NRC; pres., sci. dir. Affymax Rsch. Inst., Palo Alto, Calif., 1989-90; mem. sci. adv. bd. Jane Coffin Childs Fund, 1982-90, Rsch. to Prevent Blindness, 1984-93, Pew Scholars Profs. in Biomed. Scis.; chmn. sci. adv. bd. Perlegen Sciences, Inc. Mem. editorial bd.: Jour. Molecular Biology, 1968-72, Jour. Cell Biology, 1981-84; assoc. editor: Annual Revs. Biophysics and Bioengineering, 1970-76. Trustee Helen Hay Whitney Found., 1997—2001, McKnight Endowment for the Neuroscis., 1999—2007. Named 2006 Nat. Medal Sci. Laureate, NSF, 2007; recipient Alcon award in vision Alcon Rsch. Inst., 1992, Disting. Inventors award, Intellectual Property Owners' Assn., 1994, Molecular Bioanalytics award German Soc. Biochemistry and Molecular Biology, 2002, Frank Westheimer prize Harvard U., 2006, Carl Branden award Protein Soc., 2007. Fellow AAAS (Newcomb Cleveland prize 1992), Am. Acad. Arts and Scis.; mem. NAS, Am. Chem. Soc.(award in biol. chemistry Eli Lilly & Co., 1970), Am. Soc. Biol. Chemists, Biophys. Soc., Am. Philos. Soc., Phi Beta Kappa. Office: Stanford Sch Medicine Fairchild Ctr D221 Stanford CA 94305-5125

STRZEMP, JOHN, hotel and gaming company executive; b. Nov. 3, 1951; Pres. Treasure Island Corp., Las Vegas, Nev., 1997—98; exec. v.p., CFO Bellagio, LLC, Las Vegas, 1998—2000; exec. v.p. Wynn Resorts, Las Vegas, 2002—, CFO, 2002—08, treas., 2003—06, chief adminstrv. officer, 2008—. Office: Wynn Resorts 3131 Las Vegas Blvd S Las Vegas NV 89109 Office Phone: 702-770-7000.

STUART, ANDREW MARK, mechanical engineering educator; PhD, Oxford U., 1987. Assoc. prof. mech. engring. Stanford (Calif.) U. Office: Stanford U Dept Mech Engring Durand Bldg Rm 257 Stanford CA 94305

STUART, DAVID R., academic administrator; Asst. exec. dir. Faculty Assn. Calif. C.C.s, Sacramento, 1997—. Office: FACCC Faculty Association 1823 11th St Sacramento CA 95814-6514

STUART, GARY LESTER, lawyer; b. Gallup, N.Mex., Oct. 8, 1939; s. Arthur Lester and DeAva (Cato) S.; m. Kathleen Ann Stuart, Aug. 31, 1962; children: Gregory Lester, Kara Stuart Lewis, Tosh Forrest. Student, St. Michael's Coll., Santa Fe, N.Mex., 1961-62; BS, U. Ariz., 1965, JD, 1967. Bar: Ariz. 1967, U.S. Dist. Ct. Ariz. 1967, U.S. Ct. Appeals (9th cir.) 1968, U.S. Supreme Ct. 1973, U.S. Tax Ct. 1976. Assoc. Jennings, Strouss & Salmon, Phoenix, 1967-71, ptnr., 1971—. Chmn. ethics com. Ariz. Bar, Phoenix, 1976-86; mem. faculty Ariz. Coll. Trial Advocacy, 1987—; chmn. Ariz. Adv. Commn. on Litigation, Phoenix, 1989—. Fellow Ariz. Bar Found.; mem. Am. Bd. Trial Advocates (faculty mem. 1976—, pres. 1986), Ariz. Inn. of Ct. Roman Catholic. Avocations: horses, woodworking. Home: 2039 E Glenn Dr Phoenix AZ 85020-5647 Office: Jennings Strouss & Salmon 2 N Central Ave Fl 14 Phoenix AZ 85004-4471

STUART, KENNETH D., plant research administrator, microbiologist; b. Boston, 1940; married; 3 children. BA, Northeastern U., 1963; MA, Wesleyan U., 1965; PhD in Zoology, U. Iowa, 1969. Rsch. biochemist Nat. Inst. Med. Rsch., London, 1969-71, SUNY, Stony Brook, 1971-72; rsch. biologist U. San Francisco, 1972-76; dir. Seattle Biomed. Rsch. Inst., 1982—; affiliate prof. microbiology U. Wash., Seattle, 1984—. Fellow AAAS; mem. Am. Soc. Microbiology, Am. Soc. Parasitology, Am. Soc. Cell Biology, Am. Soc. Advancement Sci. Office: 307 Westlake Ave N #500 Seattle WA 98109-5219

STUBBERUD, ALLEN ROGER, electrical engineering educator; b. Glendive, Mont., Aug. 14, 1934; s. Oscar Adolph and Alice Marie (LeBlanc) S.; m. May B. Tragus, Nov. 19, 1961; children: Peter A., Stephen C. BS in Elec. Engring, U. Idaho, 1956; MS in Engring, UCLA, 1958, PhD, 1962. From asst. prof. to assoc. prof. engring. UCLA, 1962-69; prof., then prof. emeritus, elec. engring. U. Calif., Irvine, 1969—, assoc. dean engring., 1972-78, dean engring., 1978-83, chair elec. and computer engring., 1993-98, interim dean engring., 1994-96; chief scientist U.S. Air Force, 1983-85. Dir. Elec. Communications and Systems Engring. divsn. NSF, 1987-88. Author: Analysis and Synthesis of Linear Time Variable Systems, 1964, (with others) Feedback and Control Systems, 2d edit., 1990, (with others) Digital Control System Design, 2d edit., 1994; contbr. articles to profl. jours. Recipient Exceptional Civilian Svc. medal USAF, 1985, 90, Meritorious Civilian Svc. medal, 1996. Fellow IEEE (Centennial medal 1984, Millennium medal 2000), AIAA, AAAS, NYAS; mem. INFORMS, Sigma Xi, Sigma Tau, Tau Beta Pi, Eta Kappa Nu. Office: Univ Calif Elec Engring Dept zotcode 2625 Irvine CA 92697-2625 E-mail: arstubbe@uci.edu.

STUBER, SCOTT, film company executive; Past mktg. dept. Universal Pictures; exec. Donner/Schuler-Donner Prodns.; v.p. prodn. Universal Pictures, Universal City, Calif., 1997—2000, exec. v.p. prodn., 2000—01, co-pres. prodn., 2001—03, vice chmn., worldwide prodn., 2003—05, prodr., 2006—. Actor: (films) Free Willy 2: The Advanture Home, 1995, Assassins, 1995; assoc. prodr.: Volcano, 1997; prodr.: The Break-Up, 2006, You, Me and Dupree, 2006; exec. prodr.: (films) Accepted, 2006, Dead Silence, 2007. Office: Universal Pictures 100 Universal City Plaza Universal City CA 91608

STUDLEY, JAMIENNE SHAYNE, lawyer, educator; b. NYC, Apr. 30, 1951; d. Jack Hill and Joy (Cosor) Studley; m. Gary J. Smith, July 14, 1984. BA magna cum laude, Barnard Coll., 1972; JD, Harvard U., 1975. Bar: DC 1975, U.S. Dist. Ct. DC 1978. Assoc. Bergson, Borkland, Margolis & Adler, Washington, 1976—80; spl. asst., sec. U.S. HHS, 1980—81; assoc. Weil, Gotshal & Manges, Washington, 1981—83; assoc. dean law sch. Yale U., New Haven, 1983—87, lectr. law, 1984—87; exec. dir. Nat. Assn. for Law Placement, Washington, 1987—90; syndicated columnist Am. Lawyer Media, 1990—91; exec. dir. Calif. Abortion Rights Action League, 1992—93; dep. gen. counsel U.S. Dept. Edn., 1993—99, acting gen. counsel, 1997—99; pres. Skidmore Coll., Saratoga Springs, NY, 1999—2003; scholar-in-residence Carnegie Found. for the Advancement of Tchg., Palo Alto, Calif., 2003—04; pres. Pub. Advocates, Inc., 2004—. Vis. scholar adj. faculty U. Calif., Berkeley Law Sch., 1992; bd. dirs. Assn. Am. Colls. & U., 2001—, treas., 2006—; bd. dirs. Adirondack Trust Co., 1999—2003; vis. com. Harvard Law Sch., 1999—2005; vice chair for program The Annapolis Group, 2001—03; chair legis. com. Commn. on Ind. Colls. and Univs. N.Y. State, 2002—03. Pres. Conn. Women's Ednl. and Legal Fund, Hartford, 1986—87; co-founder Washington Area Women's Found., 1997; founding bd. dirs. Wood Art Collectors; mem. Jacob Javits fellowship bd. U.S. Dept. Edn., 2000—03; mem. policy com. Campus Compact, 2002—; co-chmn. Calif. Coalition for Civil Rights, 2005—; bd. dirs. The Urban Sch., San Francisco, 2004—, v.p., 2005—; bd. dirs. San Francisco Mus. Craft and Design, 2004—, Am. Craft Coun., 2005—. Mem.: ABA (commn. on women in the profession 1991—94, chair editl. bd. Perspectives 1991—99, chair coord. coun. legal edn. 1996—97, com. on loan repayment and forgiveness 2001—03), Nat. Adv. Coun., First Book, Nat. Assn. for Ind. Colls. and Univs. (accountability com. 1999—2002), DC Bar Assn., Barnard in Washington (pres. 1977—78), Assn. Alumnae Barnard Coll. (bd. dirs. 1978—81), Phi Beta Kappa. Office: 131 Steuart St 300 San Francisco CA 94105-1241 Office Phone: 415-431-7430.

STUEBER, NANCY, museum director; m. Dan Stueber. BS in Environ. Biology and Terrestrial Ecology, U. Pitts. Mgr. cmty. events and temporary exhibits Ore. Mus. Sci. and Industry, Portland, 1981, v.p. exhibits, COO, interim pres., pres. Bd. mem. Portland Streetcar, Inc., Ore. Natural Step Network. Mem.: AAM, Ore. Women's Forum, Assn. Sci.-Tech. Centers (bd. v.p.), Portland Ore. Visitors Assn. (bd. chair 2006—07). Office: Ore Mus Sci and Industry 1945 SE Water Ave Portland OR 97214-3354 Office Phone: 503-797-4514. Office Fax: 503-797-4500.

STUMP, DAVID JAMES, philosopher, educator; b. Santa Monica, Calif., Mar. 21, 1955; s. John and Sarah Stump. BA, U. Calif., Berkeley, 1977; MA, Northwestern U., Ill., 1984, PhD, 1988. Prof., philosophy U. San Francisco, 1992—. Editor: Disunity of Science. Postdoctoral fellowship, NSF, 1989-1990. Mem.: The Internat. Soc. History of Philosophy of Sci. (steering com. 2003—06). Office: U San Francisco 2130 Fulton St San Francisco CA 94118

STUMPF, JOHN GERARD, bank executive; b. Pierz, Minn., 1953; BS in Acctg., St. Cloud State U., 1976; MBA in Fin., U. Minn. V.p. loan adminstrn. Norwest Nat. Bank, 1982—83, sr. v.p., chief credit officer, 1982—89; chmn., CEO Norwest Bank Ariz., 1989—91; regional pres. Greater Colo./Ariz Norwest Bank, Colo., 1991—94, head Tex., 1994—98; head southwestern banking group Wells Fargo & Co., San Francisco, 1998—2000, exec. v.p. we. banking group, 2000—02, group exec. v.p. cmty. banking, 2002—05, pres., COO, 2005—07, pres., CEO, 2007—. Bd. dirs. Visa U.S.A. Inc., 2005—, Wells Fargo & Co., 2006—. Bd. dir. San Francisco Zool. Soc., Bay Area chpt. Jr. Achievement, San Francisco Com. on Jobs; trustee San Francisco Mus. Modern Art. Mem.: Fin. Services Roundtable, Calif Bus. Roundtable. Office: Wells Fargo & Co 420 Montgomery St San Francisco CA 94163

STURGES, MOLLY, performing company executive, composer; MA in composition, Wesleyan U. Dir. edn. Ctr. Contemporary Arts, Santa Fe; co-founder, artistic dir. Littleglobe Inc., Santa Fe, 2005—; co-founder, mem. BING pop musical ensemble, 2001—; founder, primary vocalist mJane ensemble, N.Mex., 2003—. Guest artistic dir. The Creative Ctr.: Arts for People with Cancer, NYC; creator, dir. Moment intergenerational project, Cork, Ireland, 2005; artist in residence Santa Fe Opera; creator, dir. Memorylines: Voces de Nuestras Jornadas, Santa Fe. Composer, performer: live music for silent films, 2001—, sub)merge, 2001, In Situ, 2005, La Reina Roja, 2004, Night, 2005; singer: (albums) (with mJane) Prayers from the Underbelly; dir.: (Operas) Cuentos del Valle, 2006. Fellow US Artists, 2008. Office: Littleglobe Inc 223 N Guadalupe #427 Santa Fe NM 87501 Office Phone: 505-989-1437. E-mail: molly@littleglobe.org.*

STURGULEWSKI, ARLISS, state legislator; b. Blaine, Wash., Sept. 27, 1927; BA, U. Wash., Seattle, 1949; LLD (hon.), U. Alaska, Anchorage, 1993. Mem. Assembly Municipality of Anchorage; interim exec. dir. Alaska Sci. and Tech. Found., 1995. Vice chmn. New Capital Site Planning Commn., mem. Capital Site Selection Com.; chmn. Greater Anchorage Area Planning and Zoning Commn.; mem. Alaska State Senate, 1978-93; Rep. nominee Office Gov. Alaska, 1986, 90. Home: 2957 Sheldon Jackson St Anchorage AK 99508-4469 Office: 3201 C St Ste 405 Anchorage AK 99503-3967 Office Phone: 907-561-5286. Business E-Mail: a.sturgulewski@swallingcpas.com.

STURROCK, PETER ANDREW, space science and astrophysics educator; b. South Stifford, Essex, Eng., Mar. 20, 1924; came to U.S., 1955; s. Albert Edward and Mabel Minnie Sturrock; m. Marilyn Fern Stenson, June 29, 1963; children: Deirdre, Colin; 1 child from previous marriage, Myra. BA, Cambridge U., Eng., 1945, MA, 1948, PhD, 1951. Scientist Telecomms. Rsch. Establishment, Malvern, England, 1943-46, Nat. Bur. Standards, Washington, 1949-50, Ecole Normale Superieure, Paris, 1950-51, Atomic Energy Rsch. Establishment, Harwell, 1951-53; fellow St. John's Coll., Cambridge U., 1952-55; rsch. assoc. Stanford (Calif.) U., 1955-61, prof. applied physics, 1961-98, dir. Inst. for Plasma Rsch., 1964—74, 1980—83; dep. dir. Ctr. for Space Sci. and Astrophysics, 1983-92, dir., 1992-98. Author: Static and Dynamic Electron Optics, 1955, Plasma Physics, 1993, The UFO Enigma, 1999; editor: Plasma Astrophysics, 1967, Solar Flares, 1980, Physics of the Sun, vols. I, II, III, 1986. Recipient Gravity prize Gravity Found., 1967, Hale prize Am. Astron. Soc., 1986, Henryk Arctowski medal NAS, 1990, Space Sci. award AIAA, 1992; European Ctr. for Nuclear Rsch. fellow, 1957-58. Fellow AAAS, Royal Astron. Soc., Am. Phys. Soc.; mem. Internat. Astron. Union, Internat. Acad. Astronautics, Soc. Sci. Exploration (pres. 1982-2001, Dinsdale prize 2006). Office: Stanford U Dept Physics Varian Bldg Rm 302 Stanford CA 94305

STYNE, DENNIS MICHAEL, physician, educator; b. Chgo., July 31, 1947; s. Irving and Bernice S.; m. Donna Petre, Sept. 5, 1971; children: Rachel, Jonathan, Juliana, Aaron. BS, Northwestern U., 1969, MD, 1971. Diplomate Am. Bd. Pediat. Intern in pediatrics U. Calif., San Diego, 1971-72, resident in pediatrics, 1972-73, Yale U., New Haven, 1973-74; fellow in pediatric endocrinology U. Calif., San Francisco, 1974-77, asst. prof. pediatrics, 1977-83, assoc. prof. Davis, 1983-90, prof., 1990—, chair pediatrics, 1989-97; prof., sect. chief and Rumsey chair of pediatric endocrinology U. Calif. Davis Med. Ctr., Sacramento, 1997—. Author numerous book chpts., contbr. articles to profl. jours. Mem. Endocrine Soc., Soc. Pediat. Rsch., Am. Pediat. Soc., Am. Acad. Pediat., Lawson Wilkins Soc. for Pediat. Endocrinology, Western Assn. of Physicians. Avocations: sailing, music. Office: UC Davis Med Ctr Dept Pediat 2516 Stockton Blvd Fl 3 Sacramento CA 95817-2208

SU, JUDY YA HWA LIN, pharmacologist; b. Hsinchu, Taiwan, Nov. 20, 1938; came to U.S., 1962; d. Ferng Nian and Chiu-Chin (Cheng) Lin; m. Michael W. Su; 1 child, Mawin. BS, Nat. Taiwan U., 1961; MS, U. Kans., 1964; PhD, U. Wash., 1968. Asst. prof. dept. biology U. Ala., Huntsville, 1972-73; rsch. assoc. dept. anesthesiology U. Wash., Seattle, 1976-77, acting asst. prof. dept. anesthesia, 1977-78, rsch. asst. prof., 1978-81, rsch. assoc. prof., 1981-89, rsch. prof., 1989—. Mem. surg. anesthesiology & trauma study sect. NIH, 1987-91; vis. scientist Max-Planck Inst. Med. Rsch., Heidelberg, West Germany, 1982-83; vis. prof. dept. anesthesiology Mayo Clinic, Rochester, Minn., Med. Coll. Wis., 1988; editorial bd. cons. Jour. Molecular & Cellular Cardiology, London, 1987—, European Jour. Physiology, Berlin, Germany, Muscle & Nerve, Kyoto, Japan, 1989—, Anesthesiology, Phila., 1987—, Molecular Pharmacology, 1988—, Jour. Biol. Chemistry, 1989—, Am. Jour. Physiology, 1990—; mem. rsch. study com. Am. Heart Assn., 1992-95. Contbr. articles to profl. jours. Grantee Wash. Heart Assn., 1976-77, 1985-87, Pharm. Mfrs. Assn. Found., Inc., 1977, Lilly Rsch. Labs, 1986-88, Anaquest, 1987—, NIH, 1978—; recipient Rsch. Career Devel. award NIH, 1982-87; rsch. fellowship San Diego Heart Assn., 1970-72, Max-Planck Inst., 1982-83. Mem. AAAS, Biophys. Soc., Am. Soc. for Pharmacology and Exptl. Therapeutics, Am. Physiol. Soc., Am. Soc. Anesthesiologists. Office: U Wash Dept Anesthesiology PO Box 356540 Seattle WA 98195-6540 Home: 23818 NE 124th Ter Redmond WA 98053-5691

SUAZO, PETE, state legislator; b. Salt Lake City, June 5, 1951; m. Alicia Suazo; 4 children. BA in Criminology and Corrections, U. Utah, MS in Econs. Bus. cons.; mem. Utah Ho. of Reps., 1992-96, Utah Senate, Dist. 2, Salt Lake City, 1996—; mem. judiciary com., edn. com.; mem. exec. office, criminal justice and legis. appropriations. Active Girl Scouts U.S., Boy Scouts Am. Mem. NAACP (life), Footprinters Internat., Utah Falconers and Raptors Assn., Utah Hispanic C. of C., Utah Amateur Boxing Fedn. Democrat. Recipient Youth Svc. award Salt Lake Area Gang Project, 1992, Caesar Chavez Peace and Justice award, Dr. Martin Luther King Freedom award, 1994; named to Outstanding Young Men of Am., 1983. Home: 1307 Garnette St Salt Lake City UT 84116-1626

SUBBIONDO, JOSEPH L., academic administrator; V.p. academic affairs U. Pacific, Stockton, Calif.; dean Santa Clara U. Coll. Arts & Sciences, St. Mary's Coll. Calif. Sch. Liberal Arts, Moraga; pres. Calif. Inst. Integral Studies, San Francisco, 1999—. Author: Borrowed Time, 1972; co-author: Fifty Years of Innovations in Undergraduate Education: Change & Stasis in the Pursuit of Quality, 1999; editor: John Wilkins & 17th-Century British Linguistics, 1992; contbr. articles. Office: Calif Inst Integral Studies Office of the Pres 1453 Mission St San Francisco CA 94103 Office Phone: 415-575-6105. Office Fax: 415-575-1268. E-mail: jsubbiondo@ciis.edu.

SUBER, ROBIN HALL, former medical and surgical nurse; b. Bethlehem, Pa., Mar. 14, 1952; d. Arthur Albert and Sarah Virginia (Smith) Hall; m. David A. Suber, July 28, 1979; 1 child, Benjamin A. BSN, Ohio State U., 1974. RN, Ariz., Ohio. Formerly staff nurse Desert Samaritan Hosp., Mesa, Ariz. Lt. USN, 1974-80. Mem. ANA, Sigma Theta Tau.

SUDARSKY, JERRY M., industrialist; b. Russia, June 12, 1918; s. Selig and Sara (Ars) S.; m. Mildred Axelrod, Aug. 31, 1947; children: Deborah, Donna (dec.). Student, U. Iowa, 1936—39; BS in Chem. Engring., Poly. U. Bklyn., 1942; DSc (hon.), Poly. U. NY, 1976; PhD Hebrew U. Jerusalem (hon.), 2002. Founder, CEO Bioferm Corp., Wasco, Calif., 1946-66; cons. to Govt. of Israel, 1966—72; founder, chmn. Israel Chems., Ltd., Tel Aviv, 1967-72; chmn. I.C. Internat. Cons., Tel Aviv, 1971-73; vice chmn., bd. dirs. Daylin, Inc., LA, 1972-76; pres., chmn. J.M.S. Assocs., LA, 1976—; vice chmn. bd. dirs. Jacobs Engring. Group Inc., Pasadena, Calif., 1982-94; chmn., CEO Health Sci. Prop. Holding Corp., 1994-97; chmn. Alexandria Real Estate Equities, Pasadena, 1997—2007, chmn. emeritus, 2007—. Patentee in field of indsl. microbiology. Bd. govs. Hebrew U., Jerusalem; trustee Polytechnic U. NY, 1976—; bd. dirs. Mgmt. Edn. Assn., UCLA, 1990-99. Served with USNR, 1943-46. Recipient Richard J. Bolt award for supporting industries, Chem. Heritage Found., 2008. Mem. AAAS, Am. Chem. Soc., Brentwood Country Club, Sigma Xi.

SUDWEEKS, JAY DEAN, lawyer; b. Ft. Peck, Mont., June 10, 1940; s. Harold D. and Rachel N. Sudweeks; m. Isabell Murray, Feb. 25, 1966. AA, Ricks Coll., 1960; BS, Brigham Young U., 1966; JD, U. Utah, 1969. Bar: Idaho 1969, U.S. Supreme Ct. 1973. Ptnr. May, Sudweeks & Browning, Twin Falls, Idaho, 1969—. Bd. dirs. United Way, Twin Falls. Mem.: Idaho Trial Lawyers Assn. (pres. 5th jud. dist. 1975—76), Idaho Bar Assn. (bd. dirs. bankruptcy sect. 1984—90). Office: 516 Hansen St E PO Box 1846 Twin Falls ID 83303-1846 Office Phone: 208-733-7180.

SUE, MICHAEL ALVIN, allergist; b. LA, Apr. 15, 1956; MD, U. Chgo., 1980. Diplomate Am. Bd. Internal Medicine, Am. Bd. Allergy and Immunology. Intern, resident and fellow West Los Angeles VA Med. Ctr., LA, 1980-86; allergist Kaiser Permanent, Panorama City, Calif., 1986—. Fellow Am. Coll. Allergy, Asthma, and Immunology; mem. Am. Acad. Allergy, Asthma, and Immunology. Office: Kaiser Permanente 13652 Cantara St Panorama City CA 91402-5497 Office Phone: 818-375-1720.

SUEDFELD, PETER, psychologist, educator; b. Budapest, Hungary, Aug. 30, 1935; emigrated to US, 1948, naturalized, 1952; s. Leslie John and Jolan (Eichenbaum) Field; m. Gabrielle Debra Guterman, June 11, 1961 (div. 1980); children: Michael Thomas, Joanne Ruth, David Lee; m. Phyllis Jean Johnson, Oct. 19, 1991. Student, U. Philippines, 1956-57; BA, Queens Coll., 1960; MA, Princeton U., 1962, PhD, 1963. Rsch. assoc. Princeton U.; lectr. Trenton State Coll., 1963-64; vis. asst. prof. psychology U. Ill., 1964-65; asst. prof. psychology Univ. Coll. Rutgers U., 1965-67, assoc. prof., 1967-71, prof., 1971-72, chmn. dept., 1967-72; prof. psychology U. B.C., Vancouver, 1972-2001, head dept., 1972-84, dean faculty grad. studies, 1984-90, disting. scholar-in-residence, P. Wall Inst. Adv. Studies, 2000, dean and prof. emeritus, 2001—. Chmn. Can. Antarctic Rsch. Program, 1994—98; Disting. vis. scholar Ohio State U., 2000—03; affiliated prof. U. Haifa, 2005—; cons., lectr. in field. Author: Restricted Environmental Stimulation: Research and Clinical Applications, 1980; editor: Attitude Change: The Competing Views, 1971, Personality Theory and Information Processing, 1971, The Behavioral Basis of Design, 1976, Psychology and Torture, 1990, Restricted Environmental Stimulation: Theoretical and Empirical Developments in Flotation REST, 1990, Psychology and Social Policy, 1991, Light from the Ashes, 2001, Understanding the Bush Doctrine, 2007; editor Jour. Applied Social Psychology, 1975-82; assoc. editor Environment and Behavior, 1992—; contbr. articles to profl. jours. Served with US Army, 1955-58. Recipient Antarctica svc. medal, NSF, US Navy, 1994, Zachor award, Parliament of Can., 2000; grantee, NIMH, 1970—72, Can. Coun., 1973—2006, Nat. Rsch. Coun. Can., 1973—90, NIH, 1980—84, Can. Space Agy., 2003—, Def. Rsch. and Dev. Can., 2007—. Fellow Royal Soc. Can., Can.

Psychol. Assn. (pres. 1998-99, Donald O. Hebb award 2001), APA, Am. Psychol. Soc., Acad. Behavioral Medicine Resch., Soc. Behavioral Medicine, NY Acad. Sci., Royal Can. Geog. Soc.(hon.); mem. Internat. Soc. Polit. Psychol. (v.p. 1999-2001, Harold D. Lasswell award 2001, Roberta Sigel award 2005), Internat. Acad. Astronautics (corr.), Soc. Exptl. Social Psychology, Phi Beta Kappa, Sigma Xi. Office: U BC Dept Psychology Vancouver BC Canada V6T 1Z4 Home Phone: 604-687-8886; Office Phone: 604-822-5713. Business E-Mail: psuedfeld@psych.ubc.ca.

SUGAR, RONALD D., aerospace transportation company executive; b. Toronto, July 1948; m. Valerie Sugar; 2 children. BSEE summa cum laude, UCLA, 1968, MS, 1969, PhD, 1971. Dir. advanced R & D programs TRW Inc., Cleve., 1981-83, chief engr., dep. program mgr. Milstar Satellite payload program, 1983-87, v.p., gen. mgr. space comms. divsn., 1987-92, v.p. strategic bus. devel. space and def. sector, 1992-94, exec. v.p., CFO, 1994-96, exec. v.p., gen. mgr. automotive electronics group, 1996-98, exec. v.p. spl. projects, 1998-99, pres., COO space and info. sys. sector, 1999-2000; pres., COO Litton Industries, Inc., Woodland Hills, Calif., 2000—01, Northrop Grumman Corp., LA, 2001—03, pres., CEO, chmn., 2003—06, chmn., CEO, 2006—. Mem. adv. com. Nat. Security Telecom. Adv. Com.; bd. dirs. Chevron Corp., 2005—. Nat. trustee Boys & Girls Clubs of Am.; mem. bd. vis. UCLA Anderson Sch. Mgmt., 2008—; dir. LA Philharmonic Assn.; trustee U. So. Calif.; nat. fundraising chmn. Pearl Harbor Meml. Fund. Recipient Engring. Alumnus of the Yr., UCLA, 1996, Daniel Epstein Engring. Mgmt. award, U. So. Calif., 2003, Semper Fidelis award, USMC Found., 2003, John R. Alison Leadership to Nat. Def. award, Air Force Assn., 2003, Eisenhower Disting. Citizen award, Army Distaff Found. Fellow: Royal Aeronautical Soc., Am. Inst. of Aeronautics and Astronautics; mem.: NAE, Aerospace Industries Assn. (vice chmn., former chmn.), Assn. US Army. Office: Northrop Grumman Corp 1840 Century Park E Los Angeles CA 90067-2199

SUGARMAN, MICHAEL, physician, rheumatologist; b. Galveston, Tex., May 26, 1945; s. Harold and Amelia Sugarman; m. Hilda Roberta Krug, Aug. 26, 1967; children: Jason, Steven. BS, U. Calif., Berkeley, 1966; MD, U. Calif., San Francisco, 1970. Diplomate Am. Coll. Physicians, Am. Coll. Rheumatology. Rheumatologist Fullerton (Calif.) Internal Medicine Ctr., Fullerton, Calif., 1976-94. Pres. St. Jude Heritage Med. Group, 1996—. Bd. trustees St. Jude Hosp. Fellow Am. Coll. Rheumatology, Orange County Rheumatism Soc.; mem. AMA, Orange County Med. Assn. Office: St Jude Heritage Med Group 433 W Bastanchury Rd Fullerton CA 92835-3404 Home Phone: 714-525-4422.

SUGARMAN, MYRON GEORGE, lawyer; b. San Francisco, Nov. 7, 1942; s. Irving Carden and Jane Hortense (Weingarten) S.; m. Cheryl Ann Struble, June 8, 1968 (div. 1993); children: Andrew, Amy, Adam; m. Cynthia Wilson Woods, Apr. 16, 1994. BS, U. Calif., Berkeley, 1964, JD, 1967. Bar: Calif. 1967, US Tax Ct. 1994. Assoc. Cooley Godward Kronish LLP, San Francisco, 1972-77, ptnr., 1977—. Served to capt. US Army, 1968-71. Fellow Am. Coll. Trust and Estate Counsel, Am. Coll. Tax Counsel, Am. Bar Found.; mem. U. Calif. Alumni Assn. (bd. dirs. 1985-88), U. Calf. Berkeley Found. (bd. trustees), San Francisco Tax Club (pres. 1990), San Francisco Grid Club, Order of Coif, Phi Beta Kappa, Beta Gamma Sigma. Avocations: skiing, tennis. Office: Cooley Godward Kronish LLP 101 California St 5th Fl San Francisco CA 94111-5800 Office Phone: 415-693-2040. Office Fax: 415-693-2222. Business E-Mail: msugarman@cooley.com.

SUGARMAN, PAUL WILLIAM, lawyer; b. Cambridge, Mass., July 31, 1947; s. Louis Edward and Natalie (Waldman) S.; m. Susan Lee Richard, July 16, 1978; children: Sarah, Emily, Hannah. BA magna cum laude (hon.), Harvard U., 1969; JD, Yale U., 1975. Bar: Calif. 1976, US Dist. Ct. (no. dist.) Calif. 1976, US Ct. Appeals (9th cir.) 1976. Law clk. to judge U.S. Dist. Ct. (no. dist.) Calif., San Francisco, 1975-76; assoc. Heller, Ehrman, White & McAuliffe, San Francisco, 1976-81, ptnr., 1982; shareholder Heller, Ehrman LLP, San Francisco. Spkr. in field. Contbr. articles to profl. jour. Vol. U.S. Peace Corps, Ethiopia, 1969-72. Mem. ABA (litig., tort & ins. practice sect.), Calif. Bar Assn., San Francisco Bar Assn., Phi Beta Kappa. Home: 1200 Sunnyhills Rd Oakland CA 94610-1818 Office: Heller Ehrman LLP 333 Bush St San Francisco CA 94104-2806 Office Phone: 415-772-6000, 415-772-6217. Office Fax: 415-772-6268. Business E-Mail: paul.sugarman@hellerehrman.com.

SUH, DAE-SOOK, political science professor; b. Hoeryong, Korea, Nov. 22, 1931; came to U.S., 1952; s. Chang-Hee and Chong-Hee (Paek) S.; m. Yun-Ok Park, Oct. 29, 1960; children: Maurice, Kevin. BA, Tex. Christian U., 1956; MA, Ind. U., 1958; PhD, Columbia U., 1964. Asst. prof. U. Houston, 1965-67, assoc. prof., 1968-71; prof. polit. sci., dir. Ctr. for Korean Studies, U. Hawaii, Honolulu, 1972-95, Korea Found. prof. policy studies, 1994-99; George L. Paik prof. Yonsei U., 1999; prof. polit. sci. U. Hawaii, Manoa, Hawaii, 1972—. Vis. prof. polit. sci. UCLA, 2005. Author: The Korean Communist Movement, 1967, Documents of Korean Communism, 1970, Korean Communism, 1980, Kim Il Sung, 1988, Kim Il Sung and Kim Jong Il, 1996. Mem. Conv. Ctr. Authority, Honolulu, 1989-94. Grantee Social Sci. Rsch. Coun.-Am. Coun. Learned Socs., 1963, East-/West Ctr., Columbia U., 1971, The Woodraw Wilson Internat. Ctr. for Scholars, 1985, Fulbright, 1988. Mem. Am. Polit. Sci. Assn. (life), Assn. for Asian Studies. Avocations: tennis, golf. Office: U Hawaii Manoa Dept Political Sci 2424 Maile Way Honolulu HI 96822-2223 Home: 5150 Via EL Molino Thousand Oaks CA 91320-6996 Personal E-mail: daesook@roadrunner.com.

SUINN, RICHARD MICHAEL, psychologist; b. Honolulu, May 8, 1933; s. Maurice and Edith (Wong) S.; m. Grace D. Toy, July 26, 1958; children: Susan, Randall, Staci, Bradley. Student, U. Hawaii, 1951-53; BA summa cum laude, Ohio State U., 1955; MA in Clin. Psychology, Stanford U., 1957, PhD in Clin. Psychology, 1959; Doctorate (hon.), Calif. Sch. Profl. Psychology, 1999. Lic. psychologist, Colo.; diplomate Am. Bd. Profl. Psychology. Counselor Stanford U., Calif., 1958-59, rsch. assoc. Med. Sch., 1964-66; asst. prof. psychology Whitman Coll., Walla Walla, Wash., 1959-64; assoc. prof. U. Hawaii, Honolulu, 1966-68; prof. Colo. State U., Ft. Collins, 1968-99, head dept. psychology, 1972-93, emeritus prof., 2000—. Cons. in field; psychologist US Ski Teams, 1976, Olympic Games, US Women's Track and Field, 1980 Olympic Games, US Ski Jumping Team, 1988, US Shooting Team, 1994; mem. sports psychology adv. com. US Olympic Com., 1983-89; reviewer NIMH, 1977-80, 94-98. Author: The Predictive Validity of Projective Measures, 1969, Fundamentals of Behavior Pathology, 1970, The Innovative Psychological Therapies, 1975, The Innovative Medical-Psychiatric Therapies, 1976, Psychology in Sport: Methods and Applications, 1980, Fundamentals of Abnormal Psychology, 1984, 88, Seven Steps to Peak Performance, 1986, Anxiety Management Training, 1990; editorial bd.: Jour. Cons. and Clin. Psychology, 1973-86, Jour. Counseling Psychology, 1974-91, Behavior Therapy, 1977-80, Behavior Modification, 1977-78, Jour. Behavioral Medicine, 1978-83, Behavior Counseling Quar., 1979-83, Jour. Sports Psychology, 1980-91, Clin. Psychology: Science and Practice, 1994-97, Professional Psychology, 1994-97; author: tests Math. Anxiety Rating Scale, Suinn Test Anxiety Behavior Scale, Suinn-Lew Asian Self-identity Acculturation Scale. Mem. City Coun., Ft. Collins, 1975-79, mayor, 1978-79; mem. Gov.'s Mental Health Adv. Coun., 1983, Colo. Bd. Psychologist Examiners, 1983-86. Recipient cert. merit US Ski Team, 1976, APA Career Contbn. to Edn. award, 1995, Lifetime Contbn. to Ethnic Minority Issues award, 2004, Raymond D. Fowler award, 2005; NIMH grantee, 1963-64; Office Edn. grantee, 1970-71. Fellow APA (chmn. bd. ethnic minority affairs 1982-83, chmn. edn. and tng. bd. 1986-87, policy and planning bd. 1987-89, publs. bd. 1993-97, bd. dirs. 1990-93, pres.-elect 1998, pres. 1999, chmn. membership com. 2005, chmn. presdl. task force on enhancing diversity, 2005), Behavior Therapy and Rsch. Soc. (charter); mem. Am. Psychol. Found. (trustee 2000-04), Assn. for Advancement Psychology (trustee 1983-86), Assn. for Advancement Behavior Therapy (sec.-treas. 1986-89, pres. 1992-93), Asian Am. Psychol. Assn. (bd. dirs. 1983-88), Am. Bd. Behavior Therapy (bd. dirs. 1987-2000), Phi Beta Kappa, Sigma Xi. Home: 808 Cheyenne Dr Fort Collins CO 80525-1560 Office: Colo State U Dept Psychology Fort Collins CO 80523-0001 Office Phone: 970-491-1351. Business E-Mail: suinn@lamar.colostate.edu.

SUJANSKY, EVA BORSKA, pediatrician, geneticist, educator; b. Bratislava, Slovak Republic, Feb. 14, 1936; d. Stefan and Terezia (Kaiserova) Borsky; m. Eduard Sujansky, Apr. 2, 1960 (dec. Sept. 1979); children: Paul, Walter. MD, Comenius U., Bratislava, Czechoslovakia, 1959. Diplomate Am. Bd. Pediats., Am. Bd. Med. Genetics. Resident in pediats. U. Iowa, Iowa City, 1969-71; fellow in human genetics Mt. Sinai Sch. Medicine, NYC, 1971-73; clin. geneticist Beth Israel Hosp., NYC, 1973-74; dir. clin. genetics Sch. Medicine, U. Colo., Denver, 1974-90, assoc. prof. pediats., 1981—, assoc. prof. biochemistry, biophysics and genetics, 1981—98; co-dir. divsn. genetic svcs. The Children's Hosp., U. Colo., Denver, 1990—2000. Contbr. articles to profl. jours. Fellow Am. Acad. Pediats., Am. Soc. Human Genetics, Am. Coll. Med. Genetics (founding fellow). Avocations: fine arts, reading, travel. Office: U Colo Med Ctr/TCH 1056 E 19th Ave Denver CO 80218-1007 Office Phone: 303-861-6395. Business E-Mail: sujansky.eva@tchden.org.

SUKO, LONNY RAY, judge; b. Spokane, Wash., Oct. 12, 1943; s. Ray R. and Leila B. (Snyder) Suko; m. Marcia A. Michaelson, Aug. 26, 1967; children: Jolynn R., David M. BA, Wash. State U., 1965; JD, U. Idaho, 1968. Bar: Wash. 1968, U.S. Dist. Ct. (ea. dist.), Wash. 1969, U.S. Dist. Ct. (we. dist.), Wash. 1978, U.S. Ct. Appeals (9th cir.) 1978. Law clk. U.S. Dist. Ct. Ea. Dist., Wash., 1968—69; assoc. Lyon, Beaulaurier & Aaron, Yakima, Wash., 1969—72; ptnr. Lyon, Beaulaurier, Weigand, Suko & Gustafson, Yakima, Wash., 1972—91; ptnr., shareholder Lyon, Weigand, Suko & Gustafson, Yakima, Wash., 1991—95; U.S. magistrate judge Yakima, Wash., 1971—91, 1995—2003; judge U.S. Dist. Ct., 2003—. Mem.: Phi Kappa Phi, Phi Beta Kappa. Office: PO Box 2726 Yakima WA 98907-2726

SULENTIC, ROBERT E., real estate company executive; Various positions Trammell Crow Co., Dallas, 1984—94, pres. Trammell Crow NE, Inc., 1995—98, exec. v.p., nat. dir. devel. and investment, 1997—98, exec. v.p., CFO, 1998—2000, pres., CEO, 2000—06, chmn., 2002—06; group pres. EMEA, Asia Pacific, develop. & investment CB Richard Ellis, LA, 2006—09, CFO, 2009—. Office: CB Richard Ellis 11150 Santa Monica Blvd Los Angeles CA 90025 Business E-Mail: bsulentic@cbre.com.

SULL, WONHEE, telecommunications industry executive; BS, Seoul Nat. U.; MS in Computer Sci. and Engring., U. Mich.; PhD in Elec. and Computer Engring., Purdue U. Sr. mem. tech. staff Microelectronics and Computer Tech. Corp.; sr. engr. GE Med. Sys.; asst. rsch. prof. U. Miami, Fla.; dir. Platform R&D Ctr., SK Telecom, Republic of Korea, v.p.; pres., COO HELIO LLC (formerly SK-EarthLink), Westwood, Calif., 2005—08, bd. dirs., CEO, 2008—. Office: HELIO LLC 10960 Wilshire Blvd Ste 600 Westwood CA 90024

SULLENBERGER (SULLY), CHESLEY BURNETT, III, pilot, airline safety consulting company executive; b. Jan. 1951; m. Lorrie Sullenberger (Sully); 2 children. BS in Psychology, USAF Acad., Colo., 1973; MS in Indsl. Psychology, Purdue U., West Lafayette, Ind., 1973; MPA, U. No. Colo., Greenley, 1979. Cert. Flight Instr. (Airplane Single and Multi-Engine, Glider, Instrument Airplane), Flight Engr. (Turbojet Powered), Ground Instr. (Advanced and Instrument). Fighter F-4 pilot, capt. USAF, 1973—80; pilot, capt. on Airbus A319/320/321 US Airways, 1980—; founder, pres., CEO Safety Reliability Methods, Inc. (SRM), 2007—. Panel mem. High Reliability Orgn. Internat. Conf., Deauville, France, 2007; participated in several USAF and Nat. Transportation Safety Bd. accident investigations; safety and reliability cons. and spkr. Recipient Outstanding Cadet in Airmanship award, 1973; co-recipient (with crew of 1549) Key to NYC, 2009; named one of The World's Most Influential People, TIME mag., 2009; vis. scholar, Ctr. for Catastrophic Risk Mgmt., U. Calif. Berkeley. Mem.: Air Line Pilots Assn. (served as local air safety chmn., mem. noise abatement com., rep. during negotiations leading to adoptions of adv. circular 91-53). Key achievements and contributions with US Airways: served as Check Airman, supervising and instructing other airline pilots upgrading from First Officer to Captain and to different aircraft. Recognized as one of best Check Airman/Line Instructors; Spearheaded efforts to improve maintenance efforts of MD-80 fleet, focusing on reliability of air conditioning systems. Helped identify and reduce number of faulty air conditioning systems from 24 to zero on fleet. Received formal commendation from MD-80 Fleet Manager for work on this project; Instrumental in delivering better, more competitive passenger service by presenting and receiving approval for suggestion to apply for and receive lower-than-standard takeoff minima in Canada; Realized operational safety and efficiency improvements by providing numerous suggestions that improved company gate charts that pilots use taxiing to/from airport gates; Enhancing situational awareness and safety by incorporating entry/exit taxiways on airport charts used by pilots to transition from gate areas to runways, working closely with airline vendor that provides pilot charts; Improving efficiency and reliability of air service in National Airspace System. Identified hundreds of FAA Instrument Landing System procedures used by all operators to land at airports that utilized incorrect visibility minima and collaborated with chart vendor to correct them; Selected as airline pilot representative to work with vendor that provides Flight Management System (FMS) for several of airline's aircraft to improve software and hardware that positively impacted operational safety and efficiency of airline operations. FMS improvements led to savings in both time and money (1% savings in fuel costs); Driving force behind development of airline's first CRM course and presenting course to hundreds of USAirways pilots. Significantly reduced number of operational incidents and realized reduction in number of altitude deviations. Course focuses on multi-disciplinary approach involving leadership, communication, decision-making and error management-airline went from 5 major accidents to zero; Served as NASA Aviation Safety Research Consultant evaluating cockpit systems for reducing runway incursions. Co-authored published technical paper on crew decision-making errors in aviation working with NASA Ames researchers which provided blueprint for safer pilot training, procedures and standardization; Instrumental in guiding all aviation groups to adopt safer, more uniform standard with respect to departure procedures that ultimately was incorporated into new FAA standard for all operators; Teamed with SFO to adopt new airport taxiway signage that met latest FAA standards while improving safety and operational efficiency; Played integral role working with ATA, FAA, NATCA and NTSB to improve operations and investigate several major airline accidents. As member of ALPA National Noise Abatement Committee, directly involved in development of FAA Advisory Circular 91-53 which set new standard for aircraft noise abatement departure procedures industry-wide and improved safety and standardization; Key contributor/member of National Transportation Safety Board Survival Factors Group during investigation of major airline accident at LAX, leading to improved airline procedures and training for emergency evacuations of aircraft; Participated in joint FAA/ALPA All-Weather Flying Committee simulator study of Head-Up-Display (HUD) symbology effectiveness during low visibility landings; Widely recognized as pilot advocate and champion of high professional standards that consistently result in safer, smoother and more efficient flights. Employ leadership-by-example approach in the facilitation of CRM courses, teaching captains to be more effective leaders and make better decisions; Pilot from US Airways Flight 1549 that safely landed in the Hudson River in NYC on January 15th, 2009 saving all 155 passengers. Office Phone: 925-997-9332. Office Fax: 925-648-1166. E-mail: sully@safetyreliability.com.*

SULLIVAN, DENNIS C., lawyer; b. San Francisco, 1946; AB, U. Calif., Berkeley, 1968, JD, 1972. Bar: Calif. 1972. Counsel Pacific Gas & Elec., 1972—76; assoc. Wilson Sonsini Goodrich & Rosati, 1976—78; founding ptnr. Mosher Pooley & Sullivan, 1978—88; ptnr. Graham & James, Palo Alto, Calif., 1988—93, Gray Cary Ware & Freidenrich, 1993—2004; ptnr., co-chmn. Capital Markets practice group DLA Piper Rudnick Gray Cary, Ea. Palo Alto, Calif., 2005—. Office: DLA Piper Rudnick Gray Cary 2000 University Ave Palo Alto CA 94303 Office Phone: 650-833-2243. Office Fax: 650-833-2001. Business E-Mail: dennis.sullivan@dlapiper.com.

SULLIVAN, DONAL D., federal judge; b. 1931; Attended, Loyola U., Chgo., 1949-50, Ill. Inst. Tech., 1952-54; LLB, De Paul U., 1957. Bar: Oreg. 1957, Ill. 1958. 1st asst. U.S. atty. for Oreg., Portland, 1962-65; clk. U.S. Dist. Ct. Oreg., Portland, 1966-69, bankruptcy judge, 1969—98; ret., 1998; recalled, 1998—. Office: US Bankruptcy Ct 1001 SW 5th Ave 7th Fl Portland OR 97204-1147

SULLIVAN, EDWARD JOSEPH, lawyer; b. Bklyn., Apr. 24, 1945; s. Edward Joseph and Bridget (Duffy) S.; m. Patte Hancock, Aug. 7, 1982; children: Amy Brase, Molly Elsasser, Mary Christine. BA, St. John's U., 1966; JD, Willamette U., 1969; MA, cert. Urban Studies, Portland State U., 1973; LLM, Univ. Coll., London, 1978; diploma in law, Univ. Coll., Oxford, 1984; MA, U. Durham, 1999. Bar: Oreg. 1969, D.C. 1978, Wash. 2001, U.S. Dist. Ct. Oreg. 1970, U.S. Ct. Appeals (9th cir.) 1970, U.S. Supreme Ct. 1972. Counsel Washington County, Hillsboro, Oreg., 1969-75; legal counsel Gov. of Oreg., Salem, 1975-77; ptnr. O'Donnell, Sullivan & Ramis, Portland, Oreg., 1978-84, Sullivan, Josselson, Roberts, Johnson & Kloos, Portland, Salem and Eugene, Oreg., 1984-86, Mitchell, Lang & Smith, Portland, 1986-90, Preston Gates & Ellis, Portland, 1990—2003; owner Garvey Schubert Barer, Portland, Oreg., 2003—. Bd. dirs., pres. Oreg. Law Inst. Contbr. numerous articles to profl. jours. Chmn. Capitol Planning Commn., Salem, 1975-77, 78-81. Mem. ABA (local govt. sect., com. on planning and zoning, adminstrv. law sect.) Oreg. State Bar Assn., D.C. Bar Assn., Wash. State Bar Assn., Am. Judicature Soc., Am. Polit. Sci. Assn. Democrat. Roman Catholic. Office: Garvey Schubert Barer 121 SW Morrison Ste 1100 Portland OR 97204-3141 Office Phone: 503-228-3939. Business E-Mail: esullivan@gsblaw.com.

SULLIVAN, G. CRAIG, household products executive; b. 1940; BS, Boston Coll., 1964. With Procter & Gamble Co., 1964-69, Am. Express Co., 1969-70; regional sales mgr. Clorox Co., Oakland, Calif., 1971-76, v.p. mktg., 1976-78, mgr. food svc. sales devel., mgr. bus. devel., 1978-79, gen. mgr. food svc. products divsn., 1979-81, v.p. food svc. products divsn., 1981, v.p. household products, 1981-89, group v.p. household products, 1989-92, chmn. bd., pres., CEO, 1992-99, chmn. bd., CEO, 1999—2003; ret., 2003.

SULLIVAN, GEORGE MURRAY, transportation executive, consultant, retired mayor; b. Portland, Oreg., Mar. 31, 1922; s. Harvey Patrick and Viola (Murray) S.; m. Margaret Eagan, Dec. 30, 1947; children: Timothy M., Harvey P. (dec. July 1996), Daniel A., Kevin Shane, Colleen Marie, George Murray, Michael J., Shannon Margaret, Casey Eagan. D.P.A. (hon.), U. Alaska, 1981. Line driver Alaska Freight Lines, Inc., Valdez-Fairbanks, 1942-44; US dep. marshal Alaska Dist., Nenana, 1946-52; mgr. Alaska Freight Lines, 1952-56; Alaska gen. mgr. Consol. Freightways Corp. of Del., Anchorage, 1956-67; mayor of Anchorage, 1967-82; exec. mgr. Alaska Bus. Council, 1968; sr. cons. to pres. Western Air Lines Inc., 1982-87; former legis. liaison for Gov. of Alaska; now cons. Past mem. Nat. Adv. Com. on Oceans and Atmosphere, Joint Fed.-State Land Use Planning Commn.; past chmn. 4-state region 10 adv. com. OEO; mem. Fairbanks City Council, 1955-59, Anchorage City Council, 1965-67, Greater Anchorage Borough Assembly, 1965-67, Alaska Ho. of Reps., 1964-65. Trustee U. Alaska Found.; chmn. Anchorage Conv. and Visitors Bur.; bd. dirs. Western council Boy Scouts Am., 1958-59. Served with U.S. Army, 1944-46. Mem. Nat. Def. Transp. Assn. (life mem., pres. 1962-63), Nat. League Cities (dir.), Pioneers of Alaska, Alaska Mcpl. League (past pres.), Anchorage C. of C. (exec. com. 1963-65, treas. 1965-66, dir.), Alaska Carriers Assn. (exec. com.), Alaska Transp. Conf. (chmn.), U.S. Conf. Mayors (exec. com.), VFW (comdr. Alaska 1952) Clubs: Elks. Home and Office: George M Sullivan Co 1345 W 12th Ave Anchorage AK 99501-4252 Office Phone: 907-272-2918.

SULLIVAN, JACQUELYN F., engineering education program administrator; Co-founder, Integrated Tchg. and Learning (ITL) Prog. U. Colo., Boulder, 1992—, co-dir., Integrated Tchg. and Learning (ITL) Prog., dir., K-12 engring. edn., ITL Prog. Co-recipient Bernard M. Gordon prize, NAS, 2008. Office: ITL Lab Drescher Undergraduate Engring Coll Engring and Applied Sci U Colo 522 UCB 1045 Regent Dr Boulder CO 80309-0522 Office Phone: 303-492-8303. Business E-Mail: jacquelyn.sullivan@colorado.edu.

SULLIVAN, JAMES KIRK (KIRK SULLIVAN), management consultant, former political organization administrator; b. Greenwood, SC, Aug. 25, 1935; s. Daniel Jones and Addie (Brown) S.; m. Elizabeth Miller, June 18, 1960; children: Hal N., Kim J. BS in Chemistry, Clemson U., 1957, MS, 1964, PhD, 1966; postgrad. program for sr. execs., MIT, 1975; DSc (hon.), U. Idaho, 1990. Prodn. supr. FMC Corp., South Charleston, W.Va., 1957-62, tech. supt. Pocatello, Idaho, 1966-69, mktg. mgr. NYC, 1969-70; v.p. govtl. and environ. affairs Boise (Idaho) Cascade Corp., 1970-98; exec. com., chmn. trust and investment com., dist. bd. dirs. Key Bank of Idaho, 1983—2006; sr. ptnr. Veritas Advisors, LLP, 1999—2006; chmn. Idaho Rep. Party, 2004—08. Bd. dirs., chmn. audit com. Key Trust Co. of the West, 1980—83; mem. Accreditation Bd. Engring. and Tech., Inc., 1994—99; bd. dirs. Pub. Employees Retirement Sys. of Idaho. Contbr. articles to profl. jours.; patentee in field. Mem. Coll. of Forest and Recreation Resources com. Clemson U., mem. Golden Tiger Soc.; mem. Idaho Found. Pvt. Enterprise and Econ. Edn., Idaho Rsch. Found., Inc., Idaho Task Force on Higher Edn., Len B. Jordan Pub. Affairs Symposium; trustee Idaho Children's Emergency Fund, 1984—90, Bishop Kelly HS, 1987—89; chmn. adv. bd. U. Idaho Coll. Engring., 1966—70, 1980—87, centennial campaign, 1987—89, rsch. found., 1980—82; chmn. adv. bd. Am. Forest and Paper Assn., Govtl. Affairs Com., Environ. Com., Options Adv. Group, Idaho State Rep. Com.; pres Ore-Ida coun. Boy Scouts Am., St. Al's Found.; trustee St. Al's Med. Ctr.; bd. dirs. Idaho Found. for Excellence in Higher Edn., Exptl. Program to Stimulate Competitive Rsch. NSF, NW Nazarene Coll., 1988—90, Boise Philharm., 1996—99, Boise Master Chorale, 1995—98. Recipient Presdl. Citation U. Idaho, 1990, Disting. Eagle award Boy Scouts Am., 2005, Good Shepard award Presbyn. Ch., 2005, Named Outstanding Citizen award Saint Alphowsus Regional Medical Ctr., 2007, Outstanding Hospital Trustee of The Year, Idaho Hosp. Assoc. Mem. AIChE, Am. Chem. Soc., Bus. Week Found. (chmn. Bus. Week 1980), Am. Forest and Paper Assn. (environ. and health coun., product and tech. com., solid waste task force), Bus. Roundtable (environ. com.), Idaho Assn. Commerce and Industry (past chmn. bd. dirs.), C. of C. of U.S. (pub. affairs com.). Republican. Home: 5206 Sorrento Cir Boise ID 83704-2347 Personal E-mail: j.kirksullivan@att.net.*

SULLIVAN, KATHLEEN MARIE, lawyer, law educator; b. Sault Sainte Marie, Mich., Aug. 20, 1955; BA, Cornell U., 1976, Oxford U., Eng., 1978; JD, Harvard U., 1981. Bar: NY 1982, US Supreme Ct. 1985, Mass. 1988, Calif. 2006. Law clk. to Hon. James L. Oakes US Ct. Appeals (2nd cir.), 1981-82; pvt. law practice, 1982-84; asst. prof. law Harvard U., Cambridge, Mass., 1984-89, prof., 1989-93, Stanford U. Law Sch., Calif., 1993—, Robert E. Paradise fellow, 1995-96, Stanley Morrison prof., 1996—, dean, Richard E. Lang prof. law, 1999—2004; of counsel Quinn Emanuel Urquhart Oliver & Hedges LLP, Redwood Shores, Calif., 2005—. Vis. prov. U. So. Calif. Law Ctr., 1991, Stanford U., 1992; lectr., commentator on constnl. law. Co-editor: (with Gerald Gunther) Constitutional Law, 15th edit., 2004. Named one of 100 Most Influential Lawyers in America Nat. Law Jour., 2000, 2006, 50 Most Influential Women Lawyers in America, 2007, 100 Most Influential Lawyers in Calif., Daily Jour.; recipient Albert M. Sacks-Paul A. Freund award for Tchg. Excellence, Harvard U., 1992, John Bingham Hurlbut award for Excellence in Tchg. Stanford U., 1996. Fellow Am. Acad. Arts and Scis, Am. Philosophical Soc.; bd. trustees, The Century Found. Office: Quinn Emanuel Urquhart Oliver & Hedges LLP 555 Twin Dolphin Dr Ste 560 Redwood City CA 94065 also: Stanford U Law Sch Crown Quadrangle 559 Nathan Abbott Way Stanford CA 94305-8610 Office Phone: 650-801-5000. Business E-Mail: sullivan@law.stanford.edu.

SULLIVAN, MICHAEL JOHN, lawyer, former ambassador; b. Omaha, Sept. 22, 1939; s. Joseph Byrne and Margaret (Hamilton) S.; m. Jane Metzler, Sept. 2, 1961; children: Michelle, Patrick, Theresa. BS in Petroleum Engring., U. Wyo., 1961, JD, 1964. Bar: Wyo. 1964, U.S. Ct. Appeals (10th cir.) 1968, U.S. Supreme Ct. 1980. Assoc. Brown, Drew, Apostolos, Barton & Massey, Casper, Wyo., 1964-67; ptnr. Brown, Drew, Apostolos, Massey & Sullivan, Casper, 1967-86, 95-98; gov. State of Wyo., Cheyenne, 1987-95; amb. to Ireland Dublin, 1998-2001; spl. counsel Rothgerber, Johnson & Lyons, LLP, Casper, Wyo., 2001—. Trustee St. Joseph's Children's Home, Torrington, Wyo., 1986-87; bd. dirs. Natrona County Meml. Hosp., Casper, 1976-86. Mem. ABA, ATLA, Wyo. Bar Assn., Wyo. Trial Lawyers Assn., Rotary (pres. Casper club). Democrat. Roman Catholic. Avocations: fly fishing, golf, tennis, jogging. Office: Casper Bus Ctr 123 W 1st St Ste 200 Casper WY 82601 Home: 1124 S Durbin St Casper WY 82601-4328 E-mail: msullivan@rothgerber.com.

SULLIVAN, PETER MEREDITH, lawyer; b. Santa Monica, Calif., Nov. 9, 1952; s. Charles H. and Mary Jane (Menzel) S.; m. Mary T. Krueger, May 25, 1978. AB, Columbia Coll., 1974; JD, Fordham U., 1977. Assoc. atty. Kaye, Scholer, NYC, 1977-81, Gibson Dunn & Crutcher, LA, 1981-86, litigation, antitrust ptnr., 1986—. Contbr. articles to profl. jours. Mem. ABA, N.Y. State Bar Assn., Calif. State Bar Assn. Episcopalian. Office: Gibson Dunn & Crutcher 333 S Grand Ave Ste 50 Los Angeles CA 90071-1504 also: 200 Park Ave New York NY 10166-0005

SULLIVAN, ROBERT EDWARD, lawyer; b. San Francisco, May 18, 1936; s. Edward C. S. and Mary Jane (Sullivan); m. Maureen Lois Miles, June 14, 1958 (dec. 1972); children: Teresa Ann, Andrew Edward, Edward Braddock; m. Lynn Bryant, Aug. 28, 2002. BS, U. San Francisco, 1958; LLB, U. Calif-Berkeley, 1961. Bar: Calif. 1962. Assoc. Pillsbury, Madison & Sutro, San Francisco, 1963-70, ptnr., 1971—2000, Pillsbury Winthrop LLP, San Francisco, 2001—05, Pillsbury Winthrop Shaw Pittman LLP, San Francisco, 2005—. Lectr. bus. law Calif. Continuing Edn. Bar and Practicing Law Inst.; v.p., treas., dir. MPC Ins., Ltd., 1986-93. Contbr. articles to profl. jours. Bd. dirs., exec. com. mem., sec. San Francisco Opera Assn., 1993-2007. 1st lt. U.S. Army, 1961-63. Mem. ABA, State Bar Calif. (com. corps. 1979-82, chmn. 1981-82, mem. exec. com. bus. law sect. 1982-85, vice chmn. 1983-84, chmn. 1984-85, advisor 1985-86, mem. partnership com. 1990-92, chmn. ltd. liability co. drafting com. 1992-93), San Francisco Bar Assn., Bankers Club San Francisco (bd. dirs., sec.). Democrat. Roman Catholic. Office: Pillsbury Winthrop Shaw Pittman LLP 50 Fremont St San Francisco CA 94105-2228

SULLIVAN, ROBERT S., college dean; BA in Math., Boston Coll., 1966; PhD in Ops. Mgmt., Pa. State U., 1968; MBA in Prodn. Mgmt., Cornell U., 2003. Various U. Tex., Austin, 1968—91; dean graduate sch. Indsl. Adminstrn. Carnegie Mellon U., Pitts., 1991-95; dir. IC2 inst. U. Tex., Austin, 1995-97; dean Kenan-Flagler U. N.C., Chapel Hill, 1998—2003; dean Rady Sch. Mgmt. U. Calif., San Diego, 2003—. Peace Corps. vol. Addis Ababa U., 1968-70. Office: U Calif Rady Sch Mgmt 9500 Gilman Dr La Jolla CA 92093-0093 Office Phone: 858-822-0830. Business E-Mail: rss@ucsd.edu.

SULLIVAN, WILLIAM FRANCIS, lawyer; b. San Francisco, May 6, 1952; s. Francis Michael and Jane Frances (Walsh) S.; children: Matthew, Meghan, Kathleen; m. Kait Sullivan. AB, U. Calif., Berkeley, 1974; JD, UCLA, 1977. Bar: Calif. 1977, U.S. Dist. Ct. (no. dist.) Calif. 1977, U.S. Ct. Appeals (9th cir.) 1977, U.S. Dist. Ct. (ea. dist.) Calif. 1978, U.S. Ct. Appeals (D.C. cir.) 1979, U.S. Ct. Appeals (fed. cir.) 1985, U.S. Dist. Ct. (so. dist.) Calif. 1986, U.S. Dist. Ct. (cen. dist.) Calif. 1990, U.S. Supreme Ct. 1986. Assoc. Chickering & Gregory, San Francisco and Washington, 1977-81, Brobeck, Phleger & Harrison, San Diego and San Francisco, 1981-84, ptnr., 1984—2002, mng. ptnr. San Diego, 1992-96, 2001—03, securities litig. group leader, 2002—03, firmwide mng. ptnr., 1996-98; ptnr. Paul Hastings Janofsky & Walker LLP, San Diego and LA, 2003—, chair nat. securities litig. practice group, mem. litig. steering com., 2003—. Named Calif. Lawyer of Yr. in Securities, Chambers USA, 2006; named an Best Lawyers in Am. Mem. ABA, Assn. Bus. Trial Lawyers (bd. govs. San Diego chpt. 1993-95), Calif. Bar Assn. (litig. sect.), LA County Bar Assn., San Diego Bar Assn., Barristers Club San Francisco (bd. dirs. 1984-86, pres. 1985), Calif. Young Lawyers Assn. (bd. dirs. 1986-89, sec. 1987-99, 1st v.p. 1988-89), Am. Arbitration Assn. Democrat. Roman Catholic. Home: 1089 Prospect Blvd Pasadena CA 91103 Home Phone: 626-584-1909; Office Phone: 213-683-6000. Business E-Mail: williamsullivan@paulhastings.com.

SULLIVAN, WILLIAM P., electronics executive; b. Yakima, Wash., 1949; BS, U. Calif.-Davis. With Hewlett-Packard Co., 1976—99, various positions, 1976—95, gen. mgr. Optical Comm. Divsn., 1995—97, gen. mgr. Comm. Semiconductor Solutions Divsn., 1997—98, gen. mgr., v.p. Components Group (now Semiconductor Products Group), 1998—99; senior v.p., gen. mgr. SPG Agilent Technologies Inc. (spin-off from HP Co.), 1999—2002; exec. v.p., COO Agilent Technologies Inc., 2002—05, pres., CEO, 2005—. Bd. dir. Children's Discovery Mus., San Jose, Calif., Lumileds, URS Corp., 2006—, Avnet Inc. Office: Agilent Technologies Inc 5301 Stevens Creek Blvd Santa Clara CA 95051-7201

SULLIVAN, WOODRUFF TURNER, III, astronomy educator, research scientist; b. Colorado Springs, Colo., June 17, 1944; s. Woodruff Turner Jr. and Virginia Lucille (Ward) S.; m. Barbara Jean Phillips, June 8, 1968; children: Rachel, Sarah. SB in Physics, MIT, 1966; PhD in Astronomy, U. Md., 1971. Astronomer Naval Research Lab., Washington, 1969-71; postdoctoral fellow U. Groningen, The Netherlands, 1971-73; mem. faculty U. Wash., Seattle, 1973—, prof. astronomy, 1986—. Mem. NASA Search of Extraterrestrial Intelligence Group, Ames Rsch. Ctr., Calif., 1980-94. Editor: Classics in Radio Astronomy, 1982, The Early Years of Radio Astronomy, 1984, Preserving the Astronomical Sky, 2001; contbr. articles to profl. jours. Grantee NSF, NASA. Mem. Internat. Astron. Union, Am. Astron. Soc., History of Sci. Soc., Eukaryotes of Seattle, Astron. Unit Club (Seattle). Avocations: hiking, softball, pardating, Scrabble.

SULLOWAY, FRANK JONES, social sciences educator, historian; b. Concord, NH, Feb. 2, 1947; s. Alvah Woodbury and Alison (Green) Sulloway; 1 child, Ryan. AB summa cum laude, Harvard U., Cambridge, Mass., 1969, AM in History Sci., 1971, PhD in History Sci., 1978. Jr. fellow Harvard U. Soc. Fellows, 1974-77; mem. Sch. Social Sci. Inst. Advanced Study, Princeton, NJ, 1977-78; rsch. fellow Miller Inst. Basic Rsch. Sci. U. Calif., Berkeley, 1978-80, vis. Miller rsch. prof., 1999—2000, vis. prof., 2000—; rsch. fellow MIT, Cambridge, 1980-81, vis. scholar, 1989-98; postdoctoral fellow Harvard U., Cambridge, 1981-82, vis. scholar, 1984-89; rsch. fellow U. Coll., London, 1982-84; Vernon prof. biography Dartmouth Coll., Hanover, NH, 1986. Author: (book) Freud, Biologist of the Mind, 1979 (Pfizer award History Sci. Soc., 1980), Born to Rebel, 1996; contbr. articles to profl. jours. Recipient Randi award, Skeptics Soc., 1997, Golden Plate award, Am. Acad. Achievement, 1997; fellow, NEH, 1980—81, NSF, 1981—82, John Simon Guggenheim Meml. Found., 1982—83, MacArthur Found., 1984—89, Dibner Inst., MIT, 1993—94, Ctr. Advanced Study Behavioral Scis., Stanford, Calif., 1998—99. Fellow: AAAS (mem. electorate nominating com. sect. L 1988—91, 1994—97), Assn. Psychol. Sci., Linnean Soc. London; mem.: History Sci. Soc. (mem. fin. com. 1987—92, mem. com. devel. 1988—92), Human Behavior and Evolution Soc., Am. Psychol. Soc. Home: 1709 Shattuck Ave Apt 205 Berkeley CA 94709-1753 Office: U Calif Dept Psychology IPSR 4125 Tolman Hall Berkeley CA 94720-1603 Home Phone: 510-540-9336; Office Phone: 510-642-7139. Business E-Mail: sulloway@berkeley.edu.

SUMMER, DONNA (LA DONNA ADRIAN GAINES), singer, songwriter, actress; b. Boston, Dec. 31, 1948; d. Andrew and Mary Gaines; m. Helmut Sommer (div.); 1 child, Mimi; m. Bruce Sudano; children: Brooklyn, Amanda. Has sold over 20 million records. Singer, 1967—; actress: (German stage prodn.) Hair, 1967-75, (Vienna Folk Opera prodns.) Porgy and Bess, (German prodns.) The Me Nobody Knows, (cable TV spl.) Donna Summer Special, 1980; recorded albums including The Wanderer, Star Collection, Love To Love You Baby, Love Trilogy, Four Seasons of Love, I Remember Yesterday, The Deep, Shut Out, Once Upon A Time, Bad Girls, On The Radio, Walk Away, She Works Hard For The Money, Cats Without Claws, All Systems Go, 1988, Another Place and Time, 1989, Mistaken Identity, 1991, Endless Summer, 1994, Christmas Spirit, 1994, I'm a Rainbow, 1996, Live & More Encore, 1999, Crayons, 2008; subject My Life VH1 Concert, 1999; recorded theme song for Hunchback of Notre Dame, Disney; forerunner of disco style. Named Best Rhythm and Blues Female Vocalist, Nat. Acad. Rec. Arts and Scis., 1978, Best Female Rock Vocalist, 1979, Favorite Female Pop Vocalist, Am. Music Awards, 1979, Favorite Female Vocalist of Soul Music, 1979, Soul Artist of Yr., Rolling Stone mag., 1979; recipient Best Favorite Pop Single award, 1979, Best-selling Black Music Album for Female Artist award Nat. Assn. Record Merchandizers, 1979, Ampex Golden Reel award for album On the Radio, 1979, Best-selling Album for Female Artist, 1980, Ampex Golden Reel award for single On the Radio, 1980, Ampex Golden Reel award for album Bad Girls, Best of Las Vegas Jimmy award for best rock performance, 1980, Grammy award for best inspirational performance, 1984. Office: 2401 Main St Santa Monica CA 90405-3515

SUMMERS, CAROL, artist; b. Kingston, NY, Dec. 26, 1925; s. Ivan Franklin and Theresa (Jones) S.; m. Elaine Smithers, Oct. 2, 1954 (div. Aug. 1967); 1 child, Kyle; m. Joan Ward Toth, May 6, 1974 (dec. 1998); 1 child, Ethan. BA, Bard Coll., 1951, DFA (hon.), 1974. Tchr. Hunter Coll., Sch. Visual Arts, Haystack Mountain Sch. Crafts, Bklyn. Mus. Art Sch., Pratt Graphic Art Ctr., Chelterham Twp. Art Ctr., Valley Stream Community Art Ctr., U. Pa., Columbia Coll., U. Calif., Santa Cruz, San Francisco Art Inst., U. Utah, Logan, Art Study Abroad, Paris, Casa de Espiritus Alegres Marfil, Mex., USIS workshop tour, India, 1974, 79; folk art and textiles tour leader to Rajasthan, India, 1995-2007. Represented in permanent collections at, Mus. Modern Art, Bklyn. Mus., N.Y. Pub. Libr., Libr. of Congress, Nat. Gallery, Victoria and Albert Mus., London, Bibliotheque Nationale, Paris, Kunstmuseum, Basil, Lugano (Switzerland) Art Mus. Grenchen (Switzerland) Art Mus., Malmo (Sweden) Mus., Los Angeles County Mus., Phila. Mus., Balt. Mus., Seattle Mus., Boston Mus., Art Inst. Chgo., Am. embassies in Russia, Can., India, Thailand, Fed. Republic Germany and Eng.; traveling exhibit, Mus. Modern Art, 1964-66; retrospective exhbn. Brooklyn Mus., 1977, Nassau County Mus. Art, 1990, Belles Artes, San Miquel de Allende, Mex., 1992, Miami U. Art Mus., Oxford, Ohio, 1995, Egon Schiele Centrum Česky Krumlov, Czech Republic, 1997-98; 50-yr. retrospective at Mus. Art and History, Santa Cruz, 1999, Woodstock (N.Y.) Artists Assn., 1999, Museo del Peublo de Guarajuato, Mex., 2007; author: A Treasury of Indian Folk Textiles, 2002, Another Treasury of Indian Folk Textiles, 2006. Served with USMCR, 1944-48, PTO. Recipient Outstanding Printmaker award, Mid Am. Print Coun., 2004; named Artist of Yr., Santa Cruz County Arts Commn., 2001; fellow, Louis Comfort Tiffany Found., 1955, 1960, John Simon Guggenheim Found., 1959, Fulbright, Italy, 1961; study grantee, Italian govt., 1954—55, rsch. grantee, Coun. Internat. Exch. Scholars, India, 1993—94. Mem. NAD (academician, 1994-), Calif. Soc. Printmakers. Office Phone: 831-423-0181. Personal E-mail: carol@casaspirit.com.

SUMMERS, CATHLEEN, film producer; b. Chgo. d. Paul and Elizabeth Summers; m. Patrick Crowley. BA, U. So. Calif., 1973. Film editor, comml. producer, dir.'s asst. Roman Polanski, Rome, 1972; story editor Albert S. Ruddy Prodns. Paramount Pictures, LA, 1973-74; exec. asst. Columbia Pictures, Burbank, Calif., 1974, story editor, 1974-76; devel. exec., v.p., producer Martin Ransohoff Prodns. Columbia Pictures, 1976; sr. v.p. Tri-Star Pictures, Century City, Calif., 1984-87; motion picture producer Cathleen Summers Prodns., LA, 1989—; ptnr. ESN, Film Prodn. Resource Co.; cons., ptnr. Estudio Network. Motion picture producer, ptnr. Summers-Kouf Prodns., Burbank, 1986-87; motion picture producer Cathleen Summers Prodns., L.A., 1987, Summers-Quaid Prodns., Century City, Culver City, Calif., 1988—. Producer: (motion picture) Stakeout, 1987, DOA, 1991, Vital Signs, 1990, Mystery Date, 1991, Dogfight, 1991, The Sandlot, 1993, Stakeout II, 1993; exec. prodr. Derivations, Who New/The Real Deal, 2003. Co-founder Diane Thomas Scholarship, UCLA, 1988—; bd. dirs. L.A. chpt. Nat. Parkinsons Found.; founding bd. dirs. U.S. Comedy Arts Festival, Aspen, Colo. Mem. Am. Film Inst. (pres. 3d Decade Coun. 1995, 96, 97). Personal E-mail: july4bu@charter.net.

SUMMERS, KEN, state legislator; m. Debbie Summers. Mem. Dist. 22 Colo. House of Reps., Denver, 2007—. Republican. Office: Colo State Capitol 200 E Colfax Denver CO 80203 Office Phone: 303-866-2927. Business E-Mail: ken.summers.house@state.co.us.*

SUMNER, DANIEL ALAN, economist, educator; b. Fairfield, Calif., Dec. 5, 1950; BS in Agrl. Mgmt., Calif. State Poly. U., 1971; MA in Econs., Mich. State U., 1973, U. Chgo., 1977, PhD, 1978. Postdoctoral fellow, labor and population group, econ. dept., Rand Corp., Santa Monica, Calif., 1977-78; asst. prof. N.C. State U., Raleigh, 1978-83, assoc. prof., 1983-87, prof., 1987-92; resident fellow Resources for the Future, Washington, 1986-87; sr. economist Pres.'s Council of Econ. Advisers, 1987-88; dep. asst. sec. for econs. USDA, 1990-91, asst. sec. for econs., 1992-93; Frank H. Buck Jr. prof. dept. agrl. econs. U. Calif., Davis, 1993—. Dir. U. Calif. Agrl. Issues Ctr., 1997—; chair Internat. Agrl. Trade Rsch. Consortium, 1997-99; mem. USDA Agrl. Policy Adv. Com. for Trade, 2001-03. Author and editor books and monographs; contbr. chpts. to books, articles in profl. jours. Named Alumnus of Yr., Calif. State Poly. U., 1991; recipient Quality of Rsch. Contbn. award Am. Agrl. Econ. Assn., 1996, Policy Contbn., 1995, fellow, 1999; Fulbright Sr. Spl. Scholar Australia, 2002. Mem. Am. Agrl. Econs. Assn., Internat. Assn. Agrl. Economists. Office: U Calif Davis Dept Agrl Econ Davis CA 95616 Office Phone: 530-752-1668. Business E-Mail: dasumner@ucdavis.edu.

SUMNER, GORDON, JR., retired military officer; b. Albuquerque, July 23, 1924; s. Gordon and Esstella (Berry) S.; m. Frances Fernandes, May, 1991; children: Ward T., Holly Rose. AS, N.Mex. Mil. Inst., Roswell, 1943; BA, La. State U., 1955; MA, U. Md., 1963. Commd. 2d. lt. US Army, 1944, advanced through grades to lt. gen., 1975, ret., 1978; founder, chmn. Cypress Internat., 1978-96; chmn. La Mancha Co., Inc., 1981-89, Sumner Assoc. Cons. US Depts. State and Def; amabassador at large for Latin Am.; spl. advisor US Dept. State; nat. security advisor Pres.' Bi-Partisan Commn. Ctrl. Am.; cons. Los Alamos Nat. Lab. Contbr. articles to profl. jours. Decorated D.S.M., Silver Star, Legion of Merit with three oak leaf clusters, D.F.C., Air medal with 13 oak leaf clusters, Bronze Star, Army Commendation medal with oak leaf cluster, Purple Heart. Mem. Phi Kappa Phi, Pi Sigma Alpha. Office: La Mancha Co 100 Cienega St Ste D Santa Fe NM 87501-2003 Office Phone: 505-984-8041.

SUN, YILIN, language educator; arrived in US, 1994, permanent resident; d. Jieqing and Jing Mei; m. Jian Zou; children: Lydia Zou, David Zou. BA, Ctrl. China Normal U., Wuhan, China, 1982; MEd, U. Toronto, Can., 1989, PhD (hon.), 1992. Tchr. faculty edn. York U., Toronto, Canada, 1992—94; prof. Seattle Ctrl. C.C., 1994—, dir. faculty devel., 2000—02. Curriculum writer, rschr. Ont. Province English Lang. Instrn. for Newcomers Curriculum Guidelines Employment and Immigration Can./TESL Ont., 1993; adj. prof. Seattle Pacific U., 2004—06, Seattle U., 2006—; program lead Seattle Ctrl. C.C., 2006—. Illustrator: The Illustrated Otolaryngological Operation, 1977; contbr. chapters to books. Mem. adv. com. the yr. China City Seattle, Seattle Art Mus, Asian Art Mus., 2000—01; mem. title II grant adv. com. US Dept. Edn., Washington, 1999—99. Recipient Exceptional Faculty award, Seattle C.C. Dist., 2002, Innovation of Yr. award, League Innovation in C.C., 2002, Svc. citation, Wash. State Faculty and Staff of Color in Higher Edn. Ann. Conf. Planning Com., 2005, 2006; named Outstanding Student Orgn. Advisor, Seattle Ctrl. C.C., 1997; grantee, Office of Adult Literacy, State Bd. Cmty. and Tech. Colls., 1995, 2005, 2006; scholar, Fulbright Hayes Found., 1998, 2005. Mem.: TESOL (chmn. affiliate leadership coun. 2005—07, chmn. conf. 2006—07, bd. dirs. 2008—), Wash. Assn.

Edn. Spkrs. Other Langs. (pres. 2002—03), Am. Assn. Applied Linguistics (corr.; mem. 1990—95), Am. Fedn. Tchrs. (assoc.; chmn. profl. issues Wash. chpt. 2004—07, mem. exec. bd. 2005—07, Svc. citation 2002, 2004), Global Edn. Design Team (co-chmn. 2004—06). Office: Seattle Central CC 1701 Broadway Seattle WA 98122 Office Fax: 206-344-4384. Business E-Mail: yilsun@sccd.ctc.edu.

SUNDBORG, STEPHEN V., academic administrator; s. George and Mary Sundborg. PhD, Pontifical Gregorian Univ., Rome, 1982. Ordained Jesuit, 1974. Tchr. religion and Latin Gonzaga Prep. Sch., Spokane, Wash., Jesuit High, Portland, Oreg.; tchr. theology Seattle U.; rector Seattle U. Jewish Cmty., 1986-90; provincial Oreg. Province, 1990-97; pres. Seattle U., 1997—. Office: Admin Bldg 109 900 Broadway Seattle WA 98122-4340

SUNDEL, HARVEY H., marketing research analyst, consultant; b. Bronx, NY, July 24, 1944; s. Louis and Pauline (Brotman) S. BBA, St. Mary's U., San Antonio, 1969, MBA, 1970; PhD, St. Louis U., 1974. Asst. dir. research Lone Star Brewery, San Antonio, 1970-71; cons. Tri-Mark, Inc., San Antonio, 1972-73; asst. prof. mktg. Lewis and Clark Coll., Godfrey, Ill., 1973-74, Met. State Coll., Denver, 1974-77, chmn., prof. mktg., 1977-86; pres. Sundel Rsch., Inc., Denver, 1976—. Cons. Frederick Ross Co., Denver, 1979-84, U.S. West Direct, Denver, 1986—, Monsanto Chems. Co., St. Louis, 1985-97, Mountain Bell, Denver, 1979-88, U.S. West Comm., Denver, 1988—, AT&T, 1986-91, Melco Industries, 1987-90, Norwest Banks, 1990-94, PACE Membership Warehouse, 1992-93, U.S. Meat Export Fedn., 1992—, G.D. Searle, 1996-98, Nextel Comms., 1996-2000, Solutia, 1997—, Ethyl Corp., 2000—, Watlow Electric Mfg. Co., 2000—; expert witness in legal cases. Contbr. papers and proceedings to profl. jours. Com. mem. Mile High United Way, Denver, 1975-80, Allied Jewish Fedn. Cmty. Rels. Action Com., 1995—, Hewlett Packard, 1998—, Agilent Techs., 1999—, Encore Media, 2000—, Xcel Energy, 2003-. Jewish. Avocation: handball. Home: 1616 Glen Bar Dr Lakewood CO 80215-3014 E-mail: sundel@rm.incc.net.

SUNDGREN, DONALD E., construction executive; BS, La. State U. V.p. exec. dir. Dillingham Constrn. Holdings, Inc., Pleasanton, Calif., 1996-97; pres., CEO Dillingham Construction Corp., Pleasanton, Calif., 1997—. Office: Dillingham Construction Holdings PO Box 1268 Placerville CA 95667-1268

SUNG, KUO-LI PAUL, bioengineering educator; MA in Biology, Coll. William and Mary, 1975; MS in Physiology, Columbia U., 1977; PhD in Physiology, Rutgers U., 1982; PhD in Bioengring. (hon.), Chongqing U., China, 1993. Rsch. asst. dept. biology Coll. Willam and Mary, 1972-74; lectr. divsn. of circulatory physiology and biophysics dept. of physiology and cellular biophysics, Coll. Physicians and Surgeons Columbia U., 1986, 87; lectr. Inst. Biomedical Sci. Academia Sinica, 1987; assoc. rsch sci. dept. physiology and cellular biophysics Coll. Physicians and Surgeons, Columbia U., 1982-88; organizer and instr. Cell Biophysics Workshop Academia Sinica and Nat. Sci. Coun., Taiwan, China, 1987; assoc. rsch. bioengineer III, lectr. dept. applied mechanics and engring. scis.-bioengineering U Calif.-San Diego, La Jolla, 1988-92, assoc. prof. of orthopaedic dept., Sch. Medicine, 1992-95, assoc. prof. orthopaedics and bioengring. depts., 1992-96; prof. U. Calif.-San Diego, La Jolla, 1996—; lectr. bioengineering ctr. Chongqing U., China, 1993. Full mem. cancer ctr. U. Calif., San Diego, 1991, Inst. for Biomedical Engring., 1991—; organizer Cellular Adhesion: Signaling and Molecular Regulation Am. Physiol. Soc., 1994, main speaker Cell Biophysics Workshop Academia Sinica and Nat. Sci. Coun., China, 1987, Cellular Adhesion Workshop, West China of Med. Scis., China, 1993; hon. prof. Chongqing U., China, 1992, West China U. Med. Sci., 1992, Sch. Medicine Shanghai Med. U. China, 1996. Author various publs. Recipient New Investigator Rsch. award NIH, 1984-87, Best Jour. Paper award ASME, 1989, Chancellor award U. Calif., San Diego, 1988-89, The Whitaker Found. award, 1990, Melville medal ASME, 1990, Lamport award Biomedical Engring. Soc., 1992; Dr. Yat-Sen Sun Fellow Taiwan, China, 1967; Walter Russell Scholar, 1980-82. Mem. AAAS, Am. Physiol. Soc., N.Am. Soc. of Biorheology, Internat. Soc. of Biorheology, Biomedical Engring. Soc., Microcirculatory Soc., Sigma Xi. Achievements include research in influence of tumor suppressor genes on tumor cell metastasis, biophysical properties and molecular organization of cell membranes, healing mechanism of human ligament cells, adhesion between osteoblast and biomaterials, biophysical properties of blood cells and endothelial cells in inflammatory reponse, energy balance and molecular mechanisms of cell-cell interactions in immune response, intracellular ions, intracellular transmition and cell activation. Office: U Calif San Diego Bioengring Orthop 0412 9500 Gilman Dr La Jolla CA 92093 Fax: 619-534-6896. E-mail: klpsung@bioeng.ucsd.edu.

SUNIA, AITOFELE TOESE F., Lieutenant Governor of American Samoa; b. Mar. 26, 1943; JD, U. San Francisco. Various gov. positions including asst. atty. gen., temp. dist. ct. judge Ter. of Am. Samoa, territorial treas., 1997—2003, lt. gov., 2003—. Democrat. Office: Office Lt Governor Territory American Samoa Pago Pago AS 96799 Office Phone: 684-633-4116. Office Fax: 684-633-2269.

SUNSHINE, PHILIP, pediatrician; b. 1930; MD, U. Colo., 1955. Bd. cert. neonatal-perinatal medicine Am. Bd. Pediat. Resident Stanford Hosp. and Clinics, 1957, 1961, fellow, 1963; co-dir. MCCPOP Stanford U. Sch. Medicine, Palo Alto, Calif.; staff mem. Lucile Packard Childrens Hosp. Recipient Virgina Apgar award, Am. Acad. Pediat., 2001. Avocations: tennis, bicycling. Office: Stanford Univ Sch Medicine MC 5731 750 Welch Rd #315 Palo Alto CA 94304-1510 Home Phone: 650-854-1120; Office Phone: 650-723-5711. E-mail: psunshine@stanford.edu.

SUNSHINE, STEVEN H., lawyer; AB, UCLA, 1973, JD, 1976. Bar: Calif. 1976. Ptnr., mem. exec. com. Bryan Cave LLP, Irvine, Calif. Office: Bryan Cave Llp 3161 Michelson Dr Ste 1500 Irvine CA 92612-4414 Office Phone: 949-223-7200. E-mail: shsunshine@bryancave.com.

SUPPES, PATRICK, statistician, philosopher, psychologist, educator; b. Tulsa, Mar. 17, 1922; s. George Biddle and Ann (Costello) Suppes; m. Joan Farmer, Apr. 16, 1946 (div. 1970); children: Patricia, Deborah, John Biddle; m. Joan Sieber, Mar. 29, 1970 (div. 1973); m. Christine Johnson, May 26, 1979; children: Alexandra Christine, Michael Patrick. BS, U. Chgo., 1943; PhD (Wendell T. Bush fellow), Columbia U., 1950; LLD, U. Nijmegen, Netherlands, 1979; Dr. honoris causa (hon.), U. Rene Descartes, Paris, 1982, U. Regensburg, Germany, 1999, U. Bologna, Italy, 1999. Instr., Stanford U., 1950—52, asst. prof., 1952—55, assoc. prof., 1955—59, prof. philosophy, statistics, psychology and edn., 1959—92, prof. emeritus. Founder, CEO Computer Curriculum Corp., 1967—90. Author: Introduction to Logic, 1957, Axiomatic Set Theory, 1960, Sets and Numbers, books 1-6, 1966, Studies in the Methodology and Foundations of Science, 1969, A Probabilistic Theory of Causality, 1970, Logique du Probable, 1981, Probabilistic Metaphysics, 1984, Estudios de Filosofia y Metodologí de la Ciencia, 1988, Language for Humans and Robots, 1991, Models and Methods in the Philosophy of Science, 1993, Representation and Invariance of Scientific Structures, 2002; author: (with Davidson and Siegel) Decision Making, 1957; author: (with Richard C. Atkinson) Markov Learning Models for Multiperson Interactions, 1960; author: (with Shirley Hill) First Course in Mathematical Logic, 1964; author: (with Edward J. Crothers) Experiments on Second-Language Learning, 1967; author: (with Max Jerman and Dow Brian) Computer-assisted Instruction, 1965—66, Stanford Arithmetic Program, 1968; author: (with D. Krantz, R.D. Luce and A. Tversky) Foundations of Measurement, Vol. 1, 1971, Vol. 2, 1989, Vol. 3, 1990; author: (with M. Morningstar) Computer-Assisted Instruction at Stanford, 1966-68, 1972; author: (with B. Searle and J. Friend) The Radio Mathematics Project: Nicaragua, 1974-75, 1976; author: (with Colleen Crangle) Language and Learning for Robots, 1994; author: (with Mario Zanotti) Foundations of Probability with Applications, 1996. Served to capt. USAAF, 1942-46. Recipient Nicholas Murray Butler Silver medal, Columbia U., 1965, Disting. Sci. Contbr. award, APA, 1972, Tchrs. Coll. medal for disting. svc., 1978, Nat. medal Sci., NSF, 1990, Henry Chauncey award for disting. svc., Ednl. Testing Svc., 2003, Lakatos Book Award prize, London Sch. Econs., 2003, Lauener Prize in Philosophy, Lauener Found., 2004; fellow, Ctr. for Advanced Study Behavioral Scis., 1955—56, NSF, 1957—58. Fellow: APA, AAAS, Assn. Computing Machinery, Am. Acad. Arts and Scis.; mem.: NAS, Chilean Acad. Scis., European Acad. Scis. and Arts, Norwegian Acad. Sci. and Letters (fgn.), Russian Acad. Edn. (fgn.), Am. Ednl. Rsch. Assn. (pres. 1973—74), Internat. Union History and Philosophy of Sci. (pres. divsn. logic, methodology and philosophy of sci. 1975—79), Finnish Acad. Sci. and Letters, Internat. Inst. Philosophy, Croatian Acad. Scis. (corr.), Brazilian Acad. Philosophy (corr.), Nat. Acad. Edn. (pres. 1973—77), Acad. Internat. de Philosophie des Scis. (titular), Am. Math. Soc., Assn. Symbolic Logic, Am. Philos. Soc., Am. Philos. Assn., Math. Assn. Am., Sigma Xi. Home Phone: 650-321-6594; Office Phone: 650-725-6030. E-mail: psuppes@stanford.edu.

SURI, JASJIT S., research scientist; BS in Computer Engring., Regional Engring. Coll., Bhopal, India, 1988; MS, U. Ill., Chgo., 1991; PhD in Elec. Engring., U. Wash., 1997. Lectr. dept. electronic and computer engring. Regional Engring. Coll., Bhopal, 1988-89; rsch. asst. biomed. visualization dept. U. Ill., Chgo., 1989-90; rsch. programmer image sci. group IBM Palo Alto (Calif.) Sci. Ctr., summer 1990-91; rsch. assoc. U. Wash., Seattle, 1992-97; rsch. software engr. radiation treatment planning group Siemens Med. Sys., Calif., 1991-92; rsch. scientist Gammex Inc., Middleton, Wis., 1997, Sch. Medicine, U. Wis., Madison, 1997; rsch. scientist software devel. TSI, N.Y., 1997; rsch. staff scientist image guided surgery dept. Image Processing and Computer Graphics Picker Internat., Cleve., 1999—. With Bharat Heavy Elec. Ltd., Bhopal, 1986, Larson & Tubro Ltd., Bombay, India, 1987, Nat. Info. Tech. Ltd., Bhopal, 1987; presenter in field; mem. Mayo Clinic Procs., Rochester, Minn.; rev. com. Internat. Conf. in Pattern Analysis and Applications, Plymouth, Eng., 1998. Author: (with others) Model Based Segmentation, 2d. rev. edit., 2000; mem. editl. bd. Radiology, Jour. Computer Assisted Tomography, Internat. Jour. Pattern Analysis and Applications, Internat. Conf. Pattern Analysis and Applications; contbr. over 150 articles. to profl. jours.; patentee in field. Scholar Regional Engring. Coll., 1985-88 Mem. IEEE, Assn. Computing Machinery, Artificial Intelligence, Optical Engring. Soc. Am., Engring. in Medicine and Biology Soc. (mem. editl. bd.), Am. Assn. Artificial Int., USENIX-Tcl/Tk. Office: Eigen LLC 13366 Grass Valley Ave Grass Valley CA 95945 Office Phone: 916-580-8341. Personal E-mail: suri0256@msn.com.

SUSCHITZKY, PETER, cinematographer; Cinematographer The Skouras Agy., 1987—. Cinematographer: (films) It Happened Here, 1962, Privilege, 1967, A Midsummer Night's Dream, 1968, Charlie Bubbles, 1968, Leo the Last, 1970, Melody/Swalk, 1971, The Pied Piper, 1972, Henry VIII and His Six Wives, 1972, That'll Be the Day, 1974, All Creatures Great and Small, 1975, Lisztomania, 1975, The Rocky Horror Picture Show, 1976, Valentino, 1977, The Empire Strikes Back, 1980, Krull, 1983, Falling in Love, 1984, Dead Ringers, 1988, Where the Heart Is, 1990, Naked Lunch, 1992, The Public Eye, 1992, The Vanishing, 1993, M. Butterfly, 1993, Immortal Beloved, 1994, Crash, 1996, Mars Attacks!, 1996, eXistenZ, 1998, The Man in the Iron Mask, 1998, The Empire Strikes Back - Spl. Edition, 1999, Star Wars Trilogy- Spl. Edition, 1999, The Red Planet, 1999, Spider, 2005, A History of Violence, 2005, Shopgirl, 2005, le concile de pierre, 2005. Office: The Skouras Agency 1149 3rd St #3 Santa Monica CA 90403

SUSSKIND, LEONARD, physicist, educator; BS, CCNY, 1962; PhD, Cornell U., 1965. NSF postdoc. fellow Cornell U., Ithaca, NY, 1965-66; asst. prof. physics Belfer Grad. Sch. Sci. Yeshiva U., NYC, 1966—68, assoc. prof., 1968—70, prof., 1970—79; prof. physics Stanford U., Stanford, Calif., 1979—, Felix Bloch prof. physics, 2000—. Visiting prof. Physics U. Tel Aviv 1971-72. Co-author (with James Lindesay): An Introduction To Black Holes, Information And The String Theory Revolution: The Holographic Universe, 2004; author: The Cosmic Landscape: String Theory and the Illusion of Intelligent Design, 2005, The Black Hole War: My Battle with Stephen Hawking to Make the World Safe for Quantum Mechanics, 2008. Recipient Pregel award 1975, J.J. Sakurai prize 1997; Loeb lectr. Harvard U. 1976. Mem. AAAS, Nat. Acad. Sci. Achievements include being credited as the father of String Theory; co-inventor, Holographic Principle. Office: Stanford Univ Dept Physics Varian Bldg 382 Via Pueblo Mall Rm 332 Stanford CA 94305-4060 Business E-Mail: susskind@stanford.edu.

SUSSKIND, TERESA GABRIEL, publishing executive; came to U.S., 1945; d. Aaron and Betty (Fox) Gabriel; m. Charles Susskind, May 1, 1945; children: Pamela Pettler, Peter Gabriel, Amanda. Student, U. London, 1938-40. Profl. libr. Calif. Inst. Tech., Pasadena, 1946-48, Yale U., New Haven, 1948-51, Stanford (Calif.) U., 1951-52, SRI Internat., Menlo Park, Calif., 1953; founder, pres. San Francisco Press, Inc., 1959—. Active in cultural affairs; bd. govs. San Francisco Symphony, 1986-89. With Women's Royal Naval Svc., 1943—45. Mem. Town and Gown Club (Berkeley, Calif.; pres. 1984-85). Office: 660 Spruce St Berkeley CA 94707-1730

SUSSMAN, MICHAEL DAVID, orthopedic surgeon; b. Balt., Feb. 20, 1943; s. Sidney and Leonora H. (Applebaum) S.; m. Nancy Evans Whiteley, Aug. 13, 1971; children: Evans, Tovah. AB, Washington and Lee U., 1963; MD, U. Md., Balt., 1967. Diplomate Am. Bd. Orthopaedic Surgery. Intern, jr. resident surgery Med. Coll. Va., Richmond, 1967-69; rsch. assoc. NIH, Bethesda, Md., 1969-71; resident orthopaedic surgery Johns Hopkins Hosp., Balt., 1971-75; fellow pediatric orthopaedic surgery Childrens Hosp. Med. Ctr., Boston, 1975-76; from asst. prof. to prof. dept. orthopaedic surgery and dept. pediat. U. Va., Charlottesville, 1976—92, head div. pediatric orthopaedics, 1985—92; chief med. staff Shriners Hosps. for Children, Portland, Oreg., staff surgeon. Mem. rsch. adv. bd. Shrine Hosp., 1984—; mem. grant rev. bd. Orthopaedic Rsch. Edn. Found., 1985—. Mem. editl. bd.: Jour. Pediatric Orthopedics, Jour. Pediatric Orthopedics B; contbr. articles to profl. jours., chapters to books. Bd. dirs. Bloomfield Inc., Ivy, Va., 1979-83, Dyslexia Ctr., Charlottesville, 1987-92. Served to lt. commdr. USPHS, 1969-71. Frank Ober fellow, 1976, Gianestras-Schmerge Traveling fellow, 1978. Fellow Am. Acad. Orthopaedic Surgery (mem. com. on pediatric orthopaedics 1986—), Am. Acad. Cerebral Palsy and Devel. Medicine (sci. program com. 1986—, membership com. 1986—), Am. Acad. Pediat., Scoliosis Rsch. Soc.; mem. Pediatric Orthopaedic Soc. (Arthur H. Huene award). Democrat. Jewish. Office: Shriners Hospitals Children 3101 SW Sam Jackson Park Rd Portland OR 97239-5090 Office Phone: 503-241-5090. Office Fax: 503-221-3701.

SUTHERLAND, DONALD, actor; b. St. John, NB, Can., July 17, 1935; m. Lois Hardwick, 1959 (div. 1966); m. Shirley Douglas, 1966. (div. 1970); children: Kiefer, Rachel; m. Francine Racette, 1972; children: Roeg, Rossif, Angus. Grad., U. Toronto, 1958. Actor: London Acad. Music and Dramatic Art, Perth Repertory Theatre, Scotland, also Nottingham, Chesterfield, Bronley, Sheffield, (plays) The Spoon River Anthology, The Male Animal, The Tempest, August for People (London debut), On a Clear Day You Can See Canterbury, The Shewing Up a Blanco Posnet, Enigma Variations, 2000, Ten Unknowns, 2001 (films) The World Ten Times Over, 1963, The Castle of the Living Dead, 1964, Dr. Terror's House of Horrors, 1965, Fanatic, 1965, The Bedford Incident, 1965, Promise Her Anything, 1966, The Dirty Dozen, 1967, Billion Dollar Brain, 1967, Oedipus the King, 1967, Sebastian, 1968, Interlude, 1968, Joanna, 1968, The Split, 1968, Start the Revolution Without Me, 1970, The Act of the Heart, 1970, M*A*S*H, 1970, Kelly's Heroes, 1970, Alex in Wonderland, 1970, Little Murders, 1971, Klute, 1971, Johnny Got His Gun, 1971, Lady Ice, 1973, Steelyard Blues, 1973, Don't Look Now, 1973, Alien Thunder, 1974, S*P*Y*S, 1974, The Day of the Locust, 1975, End of the Game, 1975, Fellini's Casanova, 1976, 1900, 1976, The Eagle Has Landed, 1976, The Kentucky Fried Chicken Movie, 1977, The Disappearance, 1977, Blood Relatives, 1978, Animal House, 1978, Invasion of the Body Snatchers, 1978, The Great Train Robbery, 1979, Murder by Decree, 1979, Bear Island, 1979, A Man, A Woman and a Bank, 1979, North China Commune (voice), 1980, Nothing Personal, 1980, Ordinary People, 1980, Eye of the Needle, 1981, Gas, 1981, The Disappearance, Blood Relative, Threshold, 1981, Max Dugan Returns, 1983, Crackers, 1984, Heaven Help Us, 1985, Revolution, 1985, The Wolf at the Door, 1986, The Trouble with Spies, 1987, The Rosary Murders, 1987, Apprentice to Murder, 1988, Lock Up, 1989, Lost Angels, 1989, A Dry White Season, 1989, Bethune: The Making of a Hero, 1990, Buster's Bedroom, 1991, Backdraft, 1991, JFK, 1991, Eminent Domain, 1991, Cerro Torre: Schrei aus Stein, 1991, Buffy the Vampire Slayer, 1992, The Setting Sun, 1992, Shadow of the Wolf, 1992, The Railway Station Man, 1992, Younger and Younger, 1993, Six Degrees of Separation, 1993, The Shadow Catcher (voice), 1993, Red Hot, 1993, Benefit of the Doubt, 1993, Punch, 1994, The Puppet Masters, 1994, Disclosure, 1994, Outbreak, 1995, Bethune: The Making of a Hero, 1990, FTA, A Time to Kill, 1996, Hollow Point, 1996, The Shadow Conspiracy, 1997, The Assignment, 1997, Fallen, 1997, Without Limits, 1998, Free Money, 1998, Toscano, 1999, CSS Hunley, 1999, Virus, 1999, Instinct, 1999, Panic, 2000, Space Cowboys, 2000, The Art of War, 2000, Threads of Hope (voice), 2000, Final Fantasy: The Spirit Within(voice), 2001, Da wan, 2001, Five Moons Plaza, 2003, The Italian Job, 2003, Baltic Storm, 2003, Cold Mountain, 2003, Aurora Borealis, 2005, Fierce People, 2005, Pride & Prejudice, 2005, Lord of War, 2005, An American Haunting, 2005, Land of the Blind, 2006, Ask the Dust, 2006, Beerfest, 2006, Sleepwalkers, 2007, Reign Over Me, 2007, Fool's Gold, 2008; (TV films) Terry-Thomas, 1963, Marching to the Sea, Hamlet at Elsinore, 1964, The Death of Bessie Smith, 1965, The American Civil War, 1965, The Sunshine Patriot, 1968, Bethune, 1977, The Saint, The Avengers, Gideon's Way, The Champions, The Winter of Our Discontent, 1984, Ordeal By Innocence, 1984, Quicksand: No Escape, 1992, The Lifeforce Experiment, 1994, Oldest Living Confederate Widow Tells All, 1994, Citizen X, 1995 (Emmy award), Natural Enemy, 1997, Behind the Mask, 1999, The Hunley, 1999, The Big Heist, 2001, Uprising, 2001, Path to War, 2002, Salem's Lot, 2004, Frankenstein, 2004; (TV mini series) A Farewell to Arms, 1966; (TV series) Commander in Chief, 2005-06; guest appearance Suspense, 1963, Gideon's Way, 1965, The Saint, 1965, 1966, Man in a Suitcase, 1967, 1968, The Name of the Game, 1969, (voice) The Simpsons, 1996 and others; narrator The Poky Little Puppy's First Christmas, 1992; exec. prodr. Steelyard Blues, 1973. Decorated officier dans l'Ordre des Artes et des Lettres (France); officer Order of Can.

SUTHERLAND, DONALD WOOD, retired cardiologist; b. Kansas City, Mo., July 29, 1932; s. Donald Redeker and Mary Frances (Wood) S.; m. Margaret Sutherland, Sept. 11, 1954 (div. 1994); children: Kathleen Sutherland, Ellen Baltus, Richard, Ann, Julia McMurchie; m. Roslyn Ruggiero Elms, Mar. 31, 1995. BA, Amherst Coll., 1953; MD, Harvard U., 1957. Intern, resident Mass. Gen. Hosp., Boston, 1957-60; fellow in cardiology U. Oreg., Portland, 1961-63; pvt. practice Portland, 1963—2006; ret. Assoc. clin. prof. medicine Oreg. Health Sci. U., Portland, 1967—; chief of staff St. Vincent Hosp. and Med. Ctr., Portland, 1971-72. Contbr. articles to profl. jours. Fellow Am. Heart Assn., Am. Coll. Cardiology (pres. Oreg. chpt. 1972); mem. Multnomah Athletic Club, North Pacific Soc. Internal Medicine (pres. 1985), Pacific Interurban Clin. Club (pres. 2000). Avocations: flying, scuba diving. Home: 4405 SW Council Crest Dr Portland OR 97239 Personal E-mail: dwscardio@comcast.net.

SUTHERLAND, DOUGLASS B., former mayor, tent and awning company executive; b. Helena, Mont., May 2, 1937; s. Chris and Marie Sutherland; m. Grace Sutherland, Sept. 5, 1986; children: Karen, Scott. BA, Central Wash. U., 1959. Program specialist Boeing Co., Tacoma, 1960-71; owner, pres. Tacoma Tent & Awning, Inc., 1971-86; sec., pres., 1986-98; county exec. Pierce County, Wash., 2001—09. Bd. dirs. Tacoma-Pierce County Bd. Health, Tacoma-Pierce County Employment and Tng. Consortium; mayor City of Tacoma, 1982-89; pres. Puget Sound Regional Coun.; chair Urban

County Caucus, Wash. Assn. of Counties. Mem. Assn. Wash. Cities, Tacoma-Pierce County C. of C. Lodges: Rotary. Republican. Avocation: sailing. Mailing: PO Box 2375 Olympia WA 98507

SUTHERLAND, IVAN E., computer scientist; b. Hastings, Nebr., May 16, 1938; children: Juliet, Dean. BSEE, Carnegie Inst. Tech., 1959; MSEE, Calif. Inst. Tech., 1960; PhD in Elec. Engring., MIT, 1963; MA (hon.), Harvard U., 1966. Elec. engr., 1st lt. Nat. Security Agy., 1963; dir. office info. processing techniques Advance Rsch. Projects Agy., 1964-66; prof. elec. engring. Harvard U., 1966-68, U. Utah, Salt Lake City, 1968—73; co-founder Evans & Sutherland, 1968; rschr. Rand Corp., 1975; chmn. dept. computer sci. Calif. Inst. Tech., 1976—80; established, v.p., Tech. dir. Sutherland, Sproull, and Assocs., 1980; fellow, v.p. Sun Microsystems Lab., Menlo Park, Calif., 1990—. Honored guest spkr., elec. engring. computer sci. dept. U. Calif. Berkeley, 2006; spkr. in field. Contbr. articles to profl. publs. Recipient Smithsonian Price Waterhouse Info. Tech. Leadership award for Lifetime Achievement, Fellow award, Computer History Mus., 2005; co-recipient, R&D 100 award, 2004. Fellow Assn. Computing Machinery (A.M. Turing award 1988); mem. NAE (First Zworkin award 1972), NAS, IEEE (John von Neumann medal 1998). Achievements include pioneer in computer graphics; inventor of computer program, known as Sketchpad, and head-mounted three-dimensional display, an integral part of many virtual reality systems; several patents in field. Office: Sun Microsystems Lab 16 Network Cir umpk16-161 Menlo Park CA 94025

SUTHERS, JOHN WILLIAM, state attorney general; b. Denver, Oct. 18, 1951; s. William Dupont and Marguerite A. (Ryan) S.; m. Janet Gill, May 21, 1976; children: Alison, Catherine. BA in Govt. magna cum laude, U. Notre Dame, 1974; JD, U. Colo., 1977. Bar: Colo. 1977, U.S. Dist. Ct. Colo. 1977, U.S. Ct. Appeals (10th cir.) 1979, U.S. Supreme Ct. 2003. Dep. dist. atty. 4th jud. dist. State of Colo., Colorado Springs, 1977-79, chief dep. dist. atty. 4th jud. dist., 1979-81, dist. atty. 4th jud. dist., 1989—97; assoc. Sparks, Dix, Enoch, Colorado Springs, 1981-82; ptnr. Sparks, Dix, Enoch, Suthers & Winslow, Colorado Springs, 1982-89; sr. counsel Sparks, Dix, Colorado Springs, 1997—99; exec. dir. Colo. Dept. Corrections, 1999—2001; US atty. dist. Colo. US Dept. Justice, 2001—05; atty. gen State of Colo., Denver, 2005—. Mem. adv. bd. Sec. of State, Denver, 1983—89; Colo. commr. Uniform State Laws, 1993—97. Author: Fraud and Deceit, 1982, No Higher Calling, 2008. Pres., chmn. bd. dirs. Cmty. Corrections of Pikes Peak Region, Inc., 1984—87; bd. dirs. Crimestoppers, Inc., Colorado Springs, 1985—88; mem. exec. com. Colo. Dist. Atty.'s Coun., 1992—97, pres., 1994—95, treas., 1993; El Paso County Rep. Ctrl. com. Colorado Springs, 1985—2001; Colo. State Rep. Ctrl. com., 1989—2001. Zimmerman Found. scholar, 1970-74. Mem. Colo. Bar Assn. (com. chmn.), El Paso County Bar Assn. (pres. 1990-91), Notre Dame Colorado Springs (pres. 1983-84). Republican. Roman Catholic. Avocations: baseball cards, golf. Office: Colo Dept Law 1525 Sherman St 5th Fl Denver CO 80203 Office Phone: 303-866-3557. Business E-Mail: john.suthers@state.co.us.*

SUTPHIN, BRIAN, information technology executive; Grad. in Econs., U. Wis., Madison; law degree, Stanford U., Calif. Pvt. practice atty.; various sr. mgmt. positions in mktg., bus. devel. and engring. Sun Microsystems, Inc., Santa Clara, Calif., v.p. bus. devel., exec. v.p. corp. devel. & alliances, mem. exec. mgmt. group. Office: Sun Microsystems Inc 4150 Network Cir Santa Clara CA 95054 Office Phone: 650-960-1300.

SUTTER, DARRYL JOHN, professional sports team executive, former professional hockey coach; b. Viking, Alta., Can., Aug. 19, 1958; m. Wanda Sutter; children: Brett, Christopher, Jessie. Player Chgo. Blackhawks, 1980-86, asst. coach, 1987-88, assoc. coach, 1991-92, head coach, 1992-95, cons., 1995-97; head coach San Jose Sharks, 1997—2002, Calgary Flames, 2002—06, gen. mgr., 2003—. Recipient Dudley Red Garrett Meml. Trophy, 1980, Commrs. Trophy, 1990; named to Alberta Sports Hall of Fame, 2000. Office: Calgary Flames PO Box 1540 Stn M Calgary AB Canada T2P 3B9

SUTTER, JOSEPH F., aeronautical engineer, consultant, retired air transportation executive; b. Seattle, Mar. 21, 1921; m. Nancy Ann French, June 14, 1943. BA, U. Wash., 1943; Doctorate, Nova Gorcia Poly. Inst., 2004. Various engring. positions Boeing Comml. Airplane Co., Seattle, 1946—65, dir. engring. for Boeing 747, 1965—71, v.p., gen. mgr. 747 div., 1971—74, v.p. program ops., 1974—76, v.p. ops. and product devel., 1976—81, exec. v.p., 1981—86, cons., 1986—87, 1987—. Chmn. aerospace safety adv. panel NASA, 1986; mem. Challenger Accident Commn., 1986. Served to lt. j.g. USN, 1943—45. Recipient Master Design award, Product Engring. mag., 1965, Franklin W. Kolk Air Transp. Progress award, Soc. Aero. Aerospace Coun., 1980, Elmer A. Sperry award, 1980, Nuts & Bolts award, Transport Assn., 1983, Nat. Medal Tech., U.S. Pres. Reagan, 1985, Sir Kingsford Smith award, Royal Aero. Soc. in Sydney, 1980, Wright Bros. Meml. Trophy, 1986, Alumnus Summa Laude Dignatus award, U. Wash., 2001; named Joseph F. Sutter professorship established in his honor, U. Wash., Boeing Co., 1992; named to, Interant. Air Cargo Assn. Hall of Fame, Gallery of Legends, Pacific Asian Travel Assn., 2005. Fellow: AIAA (Daniel Guggenheim award 1990), Royal Aero Soc. (hon.); mem.: Internat. Fedn. Airworthiness (pres. 1989), Slovenian Acad. Engring. (hon.). Office: Boeing Co PO Box 3707 Seattle WA 98124-2207

SUTTON, DANA FERRIN, classics educator; b. White Plains, NY, Oct. 10, 1942; s. Joseph Guy Jr. and Eleanor Sutton; m. Kathryn A. Sinkovich, Aug. 16, 1975. BA, The New Sch. for Social Rsch., NYC, 1965; MA, U. Wis., 1966, PhD, 1970. Lectr. Herbert Lehman Coll., CUNY, 1969-72; postdoctoral rsch. Darwin Coll., Cambridge, Eng., 1972-74, U. Auckland, New Zealand, 1974-75; asst. prof. U. Ill., Urbana, 1975-79; prof. U. Calif., Irvine, 1979—2005, prof. emeritus, 2005—, dept. chair., 1986-94. Author: The Greek Satyr Play, 1975, numerous other books and monographs; editor: William Gager: The Complete Works, 1994, The Complete Works of Thomas Watson (1556-1592), 1995, The Complete Latin Poetry of Walter Savage Landor, 1999; contbr. articles to profl. jours. John Guggenheim fellow, 1975—76, hon. fellow, The Shakespeare Inst., Stratford-upon-Avon, 2004. Office: U Calif Dept Classics 120 HOB II Irvine CA 92697-2000 E-mail: danasutton@mac.com.

SUTTON, JOHN PAUL, lawyer; b. Youngstown, Ohio, July 24, 1934; m. Jane Williamson, Aug. 20, 1958; children: Julia, Susan, Elizabeth. BA, U. Va., 1956; JD, George Washington U., 1963. Bar: Calif. 1965. Patent examiner U.S. Patent Office, Washington, 1956, 59-62; law clk. U.S. Ct. Customs and Patent Appeals, Washington, 1962-64; assoc. Flehr, Hohbach, Test, Albritton & Herbert, San Francisco, 1964-68; ptnr. Limbach, Limbach & Sutton, San Francisco, 1969-91; spl. counsel Heller, Ehrman, White & McAuliffe, San Francisco, 1992-95; of counsel Medlin & Carroll, San Francisco, 1995, Bryan, Hinshaw & Barnet, San Francisco, 1996-99; sole practice San Francisco, 2000—. Adj. instr. Practicing Law Inst., 1968-69; continuing edn. program Calif. State Bar, 1972, 75, U. Calif. Law Sch., Berkeley, 1975, 84. Contbr. articles to legal jours. Served with USNR, 1956-59. Mem.: Am. Chem. Soc., Fedn. Internat. des Conseils en Propriete Indsl. (pres. U.S. sect. 2003—06), State Bar Calif. (exec. com. patent sect. 1975—77), San Francisco Patent Law Assn. (pres. 1976), Calif. Patent Law Assn. (pres. 1975). Democrat. Episcopalian. Home and Office: 123 Race St Grass Valley CA 95945 Office Phone: 530-477-8535. Personal E-mail: JohnPSutton@earthlink.net.

SUTTON, PHILIP D(IETRICH), psychologist, educator; b. June 20, 1952; s. Clifton C. and Ida-Lois (Dietrich) S.; m. Kathleen E. Duffy, June 17, 1973; children: Heather, Shivonne. BA, So. Ill. U., 1974; MA, U. Chgo., 1975; PhD, U. Utah, 1979. Lic. psychologist, Colo. Psychologist VA Hosp., Salt Lake City, 1975-76; psychology intern Salt Lake Cmty. Mental Health Ctr., 1976-78; counselor, instr. Counseling Ctr. U. Utah, 1976-78; counselor, acting dir. spl. svcs. program Met. State Coll., Denver, 1978-80; staff psychologist Kaiser-Permanente Health Plan, 1980—83; pvt. practice Boulder, 1983—. Adj. prof. U. Colo., 1979-83; cons. spl. program for disacvantaged students in higher edn. HEW, 1980. Mem. APA, Biofeedback Soc., Am. Soc. Behavioral Medicine. Office: Box 1781 Nederland CO 80466 Office Phone: 720-406-0400. Personal E-mail: pdsphd@aol.com.

SUTTON, RAYMOND L., JR., lawyer; b. Detroit, Oct. 4, 1951; BA, U. Mich., 1973; JD, U. Colo., 1976; LLM, U. Denver, 1979. Bar: Mich. 1976, Colo. 1978, US Tax Ct., 1980. Mng. ptnr., mem. policy com. Baker & Hostetler, Denver. Adj. prof. law U. Denver, 1980-81, vis. asst. prof. law, 1981-82. Editor: Colo. Lawyer, 1984-86; contbr. articles to profl. jours. Fellow Am. Coll. Trust and Estate Coun.; mem. ABA, Colo. Bar Assn., State Bar Mich. Office: Baker & Hostetler 303 E 17th Ave Ste 1100 Denver CO 80203-1264 Office Phone: 303-764-4103. Office Fax: 303-861-7805. Business E-Mail: rsutton@bakerlaw.com.

SUTTON, THOMAS C., retired insurance company executive; b. Atlanta, June 2, 1942; m. Marilyn Sutton; children: Stephen, Paul, Matthew, Meagan. BS in Math. and Physics, U. Toronto, 1965; postgrad., Harvard U., 1982. With Pacific Mut. Life Ins. Co., Newport Beach, Calif., 1963—, actuarial asst., 1966-69, successively asst. actuary, assoc. actuary, asst. v.p., 2d v.p., v.p. individual ins., 1969-80, successively v.p. individual fin., sr. v.p. corp. devel., exec. v.p. individual ins., 1980-87, pres., 1987—90; CEO Pacific Life Ins. Co., Newport Beach, Calif., 1990—2007, chmn., 1990—2008. Bd. dirs. Pacific Life Ins. Co., 1997-, Irvine Co., Edison Internat.; dir & past chmn. Am. Council Life Insurers, Assn. Calif. Life & Health Ins. Cos., Health Ins. Assn. Am. Trustee South Coast Repertory 1984-94, pres. 1992-94; bd. dir. Orange County Perf. Arts Ctr. 1995-98, Calif. C. of C.; chmn. Pub. Policy Inst. Calif. Fellow Soc. of Actuaries (mem. numerous coms.); mem. Am. Acad. Actuaries (com. on dividend prins. and practices, 1978), Pacific States Actuarial Club, L.A. Actuarial Club (sec. 1974-75, pres. 1978-79).

SUVARI, MENA, actress; b. Newport, RI, Feb. 9, 1979; d. Ando and Candance Suvari; m. Robert Brinkmann, Mar. 4, 2000 (div. 2006). Actor: (films) Nowhere, 1997, Snide and Prejudice, 1997, Kiss the Girls, 1997, Slums of Beverly Hills, 1998, The Rage: Carrie 2, 1999, American Pie, 1999, American Beauty, 1999, American Virgin, 2000, Loser, 2000, Sugar & Spice, 2001, American Pie 2, 2001, The Musketeer, 2001, Sonny, 2002, Spun, 2002, Trauma, 2004, Beauty Shop, 2005, Standing Still, 2005, Edmond, 2005, Domino, 2005, Rumor Has It..., 2005, Caffeine, 2006, The Dog Problem, 2006, Factory Girl, 2006, Brooklyn Rules, 2007, Stuck, 2007, The Garden of Eden, 2008, The Mysteries of Pittsburgh, 2008, Day of the Dead, 2008; (TV films) Atomic Train, 1999, Orpheus, 2006; (TV series) Six Feet Under, 2004—, (TV appearances) Boy Meets World, 1995, 1996, ER, 1996, Minor Adjustments, 1996, High Incident, 1996, 1997, Chicago Hope, 1997, 413 Hope St, 1997. Office: c/o Gersh Agy 232 N Canon Dr Beverly Hills CA 90210

SUZUKI, BOB H., retired academic administrator; b. Jan. 1936; BS in Aeronautics, PhD in Aeronautics, Calif. Inst. Tech., Pasadena; MS in Mech. Engring., U. Calif., Berkeley. Formerly v.p. acad. affairs Calif. State Univ., Northridge; pres. Calif. State Poly. Univ., Pomona, 1991—2003; ret., 2003. Recipient Human Rights award Leadership Asian and Pacific Island Affairs, NEA, 1976, Order of Rising Sun, Japanese Govt., 2003. Home: 3012 W Ross Ave Alhambra CA 91803 Personal E-mail: bsuzuki1@charter.net.

SUZUKI, ICHIRO, professional baseball player; b. Kasugai, Japan, Oct. 22, 1973; m. Yumiko Suzuki. Player Orix Blue Waves, Japan, 1992—2001; right fielder Seattle Mariners, 2001—. Mem. Japanese nat. team World Baseball Classic, 2006, 09. Recipient 8 Gold Glove awards, Nippon Profl. Baseball League, Matsutaro Shoriki prize, 1994—95, Silver Slugger award, 2001, 2007, Gold Glove award, 2001—08; named Pacific League MVP, 1994—96, Am. League Rookie of Yr., 2001, Am. League MVP, 2001, Maj. League All-Star Game MVP, 2007; named to Am. League All-Star Team, 2001—08, All-Tourney Team, World Baseball Classic, 2006. Achievements include becoming the second player in Major League Baseball history named Rookie of the Year and MVP in the same season, 2001; leading the American League in: at bats, 2001, 2004-08; hits, 2001, 2004, 2006-08; singles, 2001-08; batting average, 2001, 2004; stolen bases, 2001; setting MLB records for hits (262) and singles (225) in a season, 2004; member of the World Baseball Classic winning Japanese national team, 2006, 2009; recording his 3,000 career hit (Japanese League and MLB), 2008; tying the MLB record for consecutive 200 hit seasons (8), 2001-08; becoming the Japanese all-time hits leader, 2009. Office: Seattle Mariners PO Box 4100 Seattle WA 98104*

SVAHN, JOHN ALFRED, federal agency administrator; b. New London, Conn., May 13, 1943; s. Albert Russell and Esther Marilu (Caffero) S.; m. Jill Weber, July 12, 1977; children: Kirsten Marie, John Alfred III. BA in Polit. Sci, U. Wash., 1966; postgrad., U. Pacific, 1970-73, Georgetown U., 1973-74. Spl. asst. to dir. Calif. Dept. Public Works, 1968-70; chief dep. dir. Calif. Dept. Social Welfare, 1971-73, dir., 1973; acting commr. Community Services Adminstrn., HEW, Washington, 1973-74; commr. Assistance Payments Adminstrn., 1973-76; dep. adminstr. Social and Rehab. Service, 1974-75; adminstr. Social and Rehab. Svcs., 1975-76; mgr. Haskins and Sells, 1976-79; pres. John A. Svahn, Inc., Annapolis, Md., 1979-81; U.S. commr. social security Balt., 1981-83; undersec. HHS, Washington, 1983-84; assst. to Pres. for policy devel. Washington, 1984-86; chmn. Maximus Inc., Washington, 1988-94; U.S. commr. Commn. for Study of Alternatives for Panama Canal, 1987-92; exec. v.p. The Wexler Group, Washington, 1995—; chmn. Captial Assocs., Inc., 1994—; bd. dirs. Logisticare, Inc., 2000—, EpicEdge, Inc., 2001—. Mem. Nat. Devel. Disability Adv. Council, 1975-76, Pres.'s Transition Team, 1980-81, Calif. Health Care Commn., 1972, pub. affairs com. United Way Am., 1987—; chmn. Govs. Commn. on Corrections Health Care, Md., 1990—; assoc. mem. Calif. Republican State Cen. Com., 1970-72; bd. dirs. Nat. Aquarium, Balt.; bd. dirs. Health Care Svcs. NAS Inst. Medicine, 1987-92; bd. dirs. Logisticare, Inc., 2001-; bd. dirs. Epic Edge, Inc., 2001-04; mem. Gov.'s Privatization Coun., 1992—. Served to lt. USAF, 1966-68. Named Outstanding Young Man in HEW, 1974; recipient Sec.'s citation, 1975, Adminstr.'s spl. citation, 1975 Mem. Annapolis Yacht Club, Sailing Club of the Chesapeake, Kent Island Yacht Club, Phi Delta Phi, Zeta Psi. Republican. Office: 4790 Caughlin Pkwy 317 Reno NV 89509 Personal E-mail: jacksvahn@aol.com.

SVEE, GARY DUANE, newspaper editor, writer, journalist; b. Billings, Mont., Nov. 11, 1943; s. Sigvart Oluf and Beatrice Evelyn (Lund) S.; m. C. Diane Schmidt, June 26, 1966; children— Darren Kirk, Nathan Jared BA, U. Mont., 1967. Unit mgr. Midland Bank, Billings, Mont., 1967-69; reporter Billings Gazette, 1969-76, opinion editor, 1982—; pub. Bridger (Mont.) Bonanza, 1976-77; feature editor Missoulian, Missoula, Mont., 1977-81. Author: Spirit Wolf, 1987, Incident at Pishkin Creek, 1989, Sanctuary, 1990 (Best Western novel Western Writers Am. 1990), Single Tree. Vestryman St. Luke's Meml. Bd., Billings, 1989, Salvation Army, Missoula, 1980-82; vestryman Holy Spirit Parish, Missoula, 1980-82. Served to lt. USAR, 1966-72 Recipient Business Writing award U. Mo., 1974, Minority Affairs Reporting award N.W. region Sigma Delta Chi, 1980 Mem. Kiwanis (bd. dirs. Billings club 1988-89, 2d v.p. 1989, pres. 1990, 91-92), Theta Chi. Episcopalian. Avocations: fishing, golf, writing, sculpting, reading. Office: Billings Gazette PO Box 36300 Billings MT 59107-6300 Home: 1821 Gleneagles Blvd Billings MT 59105-3572

SVET, DON J., federal judge; Bar: N.Mex. Magistrate judge for N.Mex., U.S. Magistrate Ct., Albuquerque, 1994—. Address: US Magistrate 333 Lomas Blvd NW # 670 Albuquerque NM 87102-2276

SVOBODNY, RICHARD A., state attorney general; b. 1948; BA, Calif. State U., Sacramento, 1970; JD, Northwestern Sch. Law, 1973. Sr. asst. dist. atty. State of Alaska, dep. atty. gen. criminal divsn., 2005—09, acting atty. gen., 2009—. Former acting chair Coun. on Domestic Violence & Sexual Assault, State of Alaska. Office: Office of Atty Gen PO Box 110300 Juneau AK 99811-0300 Office Phone: 907-465-2133. Office Fax: 907-465-2075. E-mail: attorney.general@alaska.gov.*

SWAFFORD, LESLIE EUGENE, physician assistant, consultant; b. Long Beach, Calif., Aug. 31, 1950; s. Leslie Eugene Swafford, Sr. and Kathryn Shirley (Gros) Jarvis; children: Jayson Patrick, Jonathan Allyn, Jude Christopher, Joshua Douglas; m. Cheryl Kaleen Killman, Apr. 10, 1993; 1 child, Lesli Tayte. BS in Allied Health, physician asst. degree of completion, George Washington U., 1978; postgrad. in Occupl. Medicine, U. Cin., 1994-95; M. in Physician Asst. Studies, U. Nebr., 2001. Cert. physician's asst. NCCPA, ACLS, PALS, ATLS, CDC AIDS Counselor, EBT (Alco-Sensor IV), EBT (EC/IR) QAP, TTT, lic. JBORPA. Chief EEG technologist Group Health Assn., Washington, 1974-76; physician asst. Pediat. Assocs., Frederick, Md., 1978-81, Heart Inst. for Care, Amarillo, Tex., 1981-84, Maricopa County Medicine Assocs., Avondale-Goodyear, Ariz., 1984-89; mgr. Samarital Occupl. Health Svcs. Samaritan Health System, Phoenix, 1989-98; dir. employee health/occupl. medicine, worker's comp program Maryvale Hosp. Med. Ctr., Phoenix, 1998, MRO asst., dir. adminstr. respiratory protection program, 1998-2001; with Emergency Assocs. Ariz. St. Joseph's Emergency Rm. and Trauma Ctr., Phoenix, 2001—05. Med. edn. and policy cons. Occupl. Health and Med. Edn. Consultants; adminstr. drug test program Samaritan Health Svcs., Phoenix, 1991—95; mem. com. Ariz. Rural Health Conf., 1992—96; adj. asst. prof. physician asst. tng. program Kirksville Coll. of Osteo. Medicine, Phoenix, 1995—; instr. Calif. Tech. Contbr. articles to profl. jours. Chmn. sex edn. com. North Ctrl. Accreditation-Aqua Fria H.S., Avondale, Ariz., 1991; physician asst. Camp Geronimo (Boy Scouts of Am.), Phoenix, 1989-94; team mem. Young People's Beginning Experience Grief Recovery Program for Children, Phoenix, 1989-93; mem. com. Ariz. Dept. Health Svcs.-Robert Wood Johnson Application, Phoenix, 1992-93. With USN, 1969-74. Recipient scholarship NIH, 1976, Squibb Pharm. Rural Physician Asst. of Yr. award honorable mention Am. Acad. Physician Assts., 1987, Dr. Paul L. Singer award for disting. cmty. svc. Samaritan Found., 1991. Fellow Ariz. State Assn. Physician Assts. (pres.-elect 1990-91, pres. 1991-92, chmn. Ariz. physician asst. tng. program task force 1990-94). Republican. Christian. Avocations: fishing, hiking, softball, basketball, golf. Home: 17723 Cactus Flower Dr Goodyear AZ 85338-5232 Office: Banner Estrella Med Ctr ER 9201 Ww Thomas Rd Phoenix AZ 85037 Office Phone: 623-910-1204.

SWAIM, MICHAEL E., lawyer, former mayor; BA, UCLA, 1967, MA, 1968, JD, 1971. Lawyer Simon, McKinsey & Miller, 1971-78; pvt. practice, 1978—; mayor City of Salem, Oreg., 1997—2003. Office: Law Office 270 Cottage St NE Salem OR 97301 E-mail: mswaim@open.org.

SWALIN, RICHARD ARTHUR, scientist, company executive; b. Mpls., Mar. 18, 1929; s. Arthur and Mae (Hurley) S.; m. Helen Marguerite Van Wagenen, June 28, 1952; children: Karen, Kent, Kristin. BS with distinction, U. Minn., 1951, PhD, 1954. Rsch. assoc. GE, 1954-56; mem. faculty U. Minn., Mpls., 1956-77, prof., head Sch. Mineral and Metall Engring., 1962-68, assoc. dean Inst. Tech., 1968-71, dean Inst. Tech., 1971-77; acting dir. Space Sci. Center, 1965; v.p. tech. Eltra Corp., NYC, 1977-80; v.p. R & D Allied-Signal Corp., Morristown, NJ, 1980-84; dean Coll. Engring. and Mines U. Ariz., Tucson, 1984-87, prof., 1984-94; pres. Ariz. Tech. Devel. Corp., Tucson, 1987; prof. emeritus U. Ariz., Tucson, 1995—. Guest scientist Max Planck Inst. für Phys. Chemie, Göttingen, Fed. Republic Germany, 1963, Lawrence Radiation Lab., Livermore, Calif., 1967; cons. to govt. and industry; bd. dirs. emeritus Medtronic Corp., BMC Industries; corp. adv. bd. AMP Inc., 1990-93. Author: Thermodynamics of Solids, 2d edit, 1972; Contbr. articles to profl. jours. Dir. div. indsl. coop. U. Ariz. Found., 1985-86; trustee Midwest Research Inst., 1975-78, Sci. Mus. Minn., 1973-77, Nat. Tech. U., 1983-90. Recipient Disting. Teaching award Inst. Tech., U. Minn., 1967, Leadership award U. Minn. Alumni, 1993; NATO sr. fellow in sci., 1971. Mem.

Sigma Xi, Tau Beta Pi, Phi Delta Theta, Gamma Alpha. Home: Splendido 518 13500 Rancho Vistoso Blvd Oro Valley AZ 85755 Personal E-mail: rswalin@gmail.com.

SWAN, ROBERT H., Internet company executive; BS in Mgmt., SUNY, Buffalo; MBA, SUNY, Binghamton. Fin. positions Gen. Electric, 1985—99; CFO GE Transportation Systems, 1994—97; v.p. fin. GE Med. Systems, 1997—98; v.p. fin., CFO GE Lighting, 1998—99, Webvan Group, 1999—2001, COO, 2000—01, CEO, 2001; CFO, exec. v.p. TRW Inc., 2001—02; exec. v.p., CFO EDS, Plano, Tex., 2003—06; sr. v.p. fin., CFO eBay Inc., San Jose, Calif., 2006—. Office: eBay Inc 2145 Hamilton Ave San Jose CA 95125 Office Phone: 972-604-6000. Office Fax: 972-605-6033.

SWANSON, DONALD ALAN, geologist; b. Tacoma, July 25, 1938; s. Leonard Walter and Edith Christine (Bowers) S.; m. Barbara Joan White, May 25, 1974. BS in Geology, Wash. State U., 1960; PhD in Geology, Johns Hopkins U., 1964. Geologist U.S. Geol. Survey, Menlo Park, Calif., 1965—68, 1971—80, Hawaii National Park, 1968—71, sr. geologist Cascades Volcano Obs. Vancouver, Wash., 1980—90, rsch. scientist-in-charge, 1986—89, sr. geologist Seattle, 1990—96; assoc. dir. Volcano Systems Ctr. U. Wash., 1993—96; scientist-in-charge Hawaiian Volcano Obs., 1997—2004. Affiliate prof. U. Wash., 1992—; adj. prof. U. Hawaii, 2002--; cons. U.S. Dept. Energy, Richland, Wash., 1979-83; volcanologist New Zealand Geol. Survey, Taupo, 1984; advisor Colombian Volcano Obs., Manizales, 1986. Assoc. editor Jour. Volcanology and Geothermal Rsch., 1976—, Jour. Geophys. Rsch., 1992-94; editor Bull. of Volcanology, 1985-90, exec. editor, 1995-99; contbr. numerous articles to profl. jours. Recipient Superior Svc. award U.S. Geol. Survey, 1980, Meritorious Svc. award U.S. Dept. Interior, 1985, Disting. Svc. award, U.S. Dept. Interior, 2005; postdoctoral fellow NATO, 1964-65. Fellow Geol. Soc. Am., Am. Geophys. Union, AAAS; mem. Sigma Xi. Avocation: hiking. Home: 417 Linaka St Hilo HI 96720-5927 Office: US Geol Survey Hawaiian Volcano Obs PO Box 51 Hawaii National Park HI 96718-0051 Office Phone: 808-967-8863. Business E-Mail: donswan@usgs.gov.

SWANSON, ERIK CHRISTIAN, museum director; b. Breckenridge, Colo., June 17, 1940; s. Glen Leonard and Eveitte Leona (Snell) S.; m. Elizabeth Jane Thompson, Aug. 22, 1976; children: Johannah Elizabeth, Nils Christian. Student, Royal U., Lund, Sweden, 1960-64; BA in History, German Lang., tchg. cert., U. No. Colo. Curator South Pk. City Mus., Fairplay, Colo., 1974-89; dir. Alma (Colo.) Fire House Mus., 1976-82; exec. dir. Cripple Creek (Colo.) Dist. Mus., 1988—. Chief of police Alma, Colo., 1977-80. With U.S. Army, 1966-68. Mem. Odd Fellows (past grand South Park Lodge # 10, Fairplay, Colo.), Swedish Order of VASA (Lodge #178), Masons (sr. warden Cripple Creek chpt. 1995), Elks. Republican. Home: PO Box 27 Alma CO 80420-0027 Home Phone: 719-836-2627; Office Phone: 719-689-9540.

SWANSON, KENNETH J., museum administrator; Adminstr. Idaho State Hist. Mus., Boise. Office: Idaho State Hist Mus 610 Julia Davis Dr Boise ID 83702-7677

SWANSON, MARY CATHERINE, educational association administrator; b. Kingsburg, Calif., Sept. 3, 1944; d. Edwin Elmore and Corrine (Miller) Jacobs; m. Thomas Edward Swanson, Aug. 27, 1966; 1 child, Thomas Jacobs. BA in English and Journalism, Calif. State U., San Francisco, 1966; standard teaching credential in secondary edn., U. Calif., 1966; MA in Edn., U. Redlands, 1977; DHL (hon.), U. San Diego, 2002, U. LaVerne, 2003. Svc. adminstrv. credential, Calif.; specialist learning handicapped, Calif.; gifted cert., Calif. Tchr. English and journalism Woodland (Calif.) High Sch., 1966-67, Armijo High Sch., Fairfield, Calif., 1967-69, Moreno Valley High Sch., Sunnymead, Calif., 1969-70, Clairemont High Sch., San Diego, 1970-86; coord. San Diego County Office Edn., 1986-90, dir. AVID project, 1990-92; founder, exec. dir. AVID Ctr., 1992—. Newspaper and yearbook advisor Moreno Valley High Sch., Moreno Valley Sch. Dist., 1969-70; reading program coord. Clairemont High Sch., 1974-80, project English coord. and site plan coord., 1975-80, English dept. chairperson, 1978-86, coord. Advancement Via Individual Determination and WASC accreditation, 1980-86, in-sch. resource tchr., 1982-86; mem. numerous positions and coms. San Diego City Schs., 1974-91; mem. com. univ. and coll. opportunities comm. Calif. State Dept. Edn., 1981-82; mem. adv. com. tchr. edn. program Pt. Loma Coll., 1982-83, tchr. English methods course for tchrs. secondary edn., 1986-87; mem. accreditation vis. com. WASC, 1983, integration monitoring team Crawford High Sch., 1984, adv. com. San Diego Area Writing Project, 1987—; developer numerous curricular programs, 1967—. Community leader Olivenhain Valley 4-H Club, 1981-90; founder Olivenhain Valley Soccer Club, 1982; coord. Clairemont High Sch./Sea World Adopt-A-Sch., 1982-84. Recipient EXCEL award for excellence in tchg., 1985, Exemplary Program award, Nat. Coun. States on Insvc. Edn., 1990, Pioneering Achievement in Edn. award, Charles A. Dana Found., 1991, Lifetime Achievement award, Calif. Assn. Tchrs., 2006; named Headliner of Yr.-Edn./Creative Tchg., San Diego Press Club, 1991, Headline of Yr.-Cmty. Activist, 2002, Woman of Vision, LWV-San Diego, 1992, Nat. Educator of Yr., McGraw Hill, 2001, America's Best Tchr., Time Mag. and CNN, 2001; named to Pres.'s Forum on Tchg. as a Profession, Am. Assn. Higher Edn., 1991; grantee, BankAmerica Found., 1980, UCSD Acad. Support Svcs., 1980, San Diego Gas and Elec. Found., 1984. Mem. Nat. Coun. Tchrs. English (Nat. Ctr. Excellence award 1985-87), Calif. Coun. Tchrs. English, Calif. Assn. Gifted Edn., Golden Key Nat. Honor Soc. (hon. mem.), Phi Kappa Phi. Office: Avid Center 9246 Lightwave Ave # 200 San Diego CA 92123-6404 Business E-Mail: mcswanson@avidcenter.org.

SWANSON, PAUL RUBERT, minister; b. Bakersfield, Calif., May 13, 1943; s. Roland Hilding and Myrtle Isabelle (Magnuson) S.; m. Mary Elizabeth Greene, June 18, 1967; children: Kristen Ann, Karlynn Marie, Jonathan Paul. BA, Pacific Luth. U., 1966; MDiv, Luth. Sch. Theology, 1970. Ordained minister, Luth. Ch. Pastor 1st Luth. Ch., Anaconda, Mont., 1970-76, King of Kings Luth. Ch., Milwaukie, Oreg., 1976-84; asst. to bishop Pacific N.W. Synod-Luth. Ch. in Am., Portland, Oreg., 1984-87; bishop Oreg. Synod-Evang. Luth. Ch. Am., Portland, 1987—. Bd. dirs. Legacy Health System, Portland. Regent Pacific Luth. U., Tacoma, 1987—; bd. dirs. Emanuel Hosp., Portland, 1987; chmn. bd. dirs. Hearthstone, Inc., Anaconda, 1973-76; bd. dirs. Ecumenical Ministries Oreg., Portland, 1984—. Recipient Disting. Svc. award Pacific Luth. U., 1993. Avocation: golf.

SWANSON, PHILLIP DEAN, neurologist; b. Seattle, Oct. 1, 1932; s. William Dean and Kathryn C. (Peterson) S.; m. Sheila N. Joardar, Apr. 20, 1957; children: Stephen, Jennifer, Kathryn, Rebecca, Sara. BS, Yale U., 1954; student, U. Heidelberg, 1952-53; MD, Johns Hopkins U., 1958; PhD in Biochemistry, U. London, 1964. Intern Harvard med. svc. Boston City Hosp., 1958-59; resident in neurology Johns Hopkins Hosp., Balt. City Hosp., 1959-62; asst. prof. U. Wash. Sch. Medicine, Seattle, 1964-68, assoc. prof., 1968-73, prof., 1973—, head divsn. neurology, 1967-95, dir. neurology residency program, 1967—. Mem. med. adv. bd. Puget Sound chpt. Nat. Multiple Sclerosis Soc., 1967-97, chmn., 1970-74; mem. com. to combat Huntington's Disease Nat. Sci. Council, 1975-84. Author: (with others) Introduction to Clinical Neurology, 1976; editor: Signs and Symptoms in Neurology, 1984; contbr. articles to profl. jours. NIH spl. fellow, 1962-64; NIH grantee. Fellow Am. Acad. Neurology; mem. Am. Neurol. Assn., Assn. Univ. Profs. Neurology (pres. 1975-76), Am. Heart Assn., Am. Soc. Neurochemistry, Internat. Soc. Neurochemistry, Biochem. Soc. (London), Am. Soc. Clin. Investigation (emeritus) Home: 6537 29th Ave NE Seattle WA 98115-7234 Office: U Wash Sch Medicine Dept Neurology PO Box 356465 Seattle WA 98195-6465 E-mail: swansonp@u.washington.edu.

SWANSON, RICHARD WILLIAM, retired statistician; b. July 26, 1934; s. Richard and Erma Marie (Herman) Swanson; m. Laura Yoko Arai, Dec. 30, 1970. BS, Iowa State U., Ames, 1958, MS, 1964. Ops. analyst Stanford Rsch. Inst., Monterey, Calif., 1958—62; statistician ARINC Rsch. Corp., Washington, 1964—65; sr. scientist Booz-Allen Applied Rsch., Vietnam, 1965—67, LA, 1967—68; sr. ops. analyst Control Data Corp., Honolulu, 1968—70; mgmt. cons. Honolulu, 1970—73; exec. v.p. SEQUEL Corp., Honolulu, 1973—75; bus. cons. Hawaii Dept. Planning and Econ. Devel., Honlulu, 1975—77; tax rsch. and planning officer Dept. Taxation, 1977—82; ops. rsch. analyst U.S. Govt., 1982—89, shipyard statistician, 1989—97; ret., 1997. Mem.: Hawaiian Acad. Sci., Sigma Xi. Home: 583 Kamoku St Apt 3505 Honolulu HI 96826-5241 Home Phone: 808-949-4868. Personal E-mail: hnlrichardswanson@msn.com.

SWANSON, ROBERT H., JR., electronics executive; BS in Indsl. Engring., Northeastern U. V.p., gen. mgr. Nat. Semiconductor, 1968—81; founder, pres., CEO, dir. Linear Tech. Corp., Milpitas, Calif., 1981, chmn. bd. dirs., CEO, 1999—. Office: Linear Tech Corp 1630 Mccarthy Blvd Milpitas CA 95035-7417

SWANSON, VICTORIA CLARE HELDMAN, lawyer; b. Aug. 28, 1949; d. Paul F. and Anne F. (Thomas) Schmitz; m. Louis M. Heldman, Sept. 21, 1971 (div. 1973); m. John Askins, Feb. 28, 1975 (div. 1977); m. Thomas C. Swanson, Feb. 13, 1988 (div. 2004); m. Spellman T. Richard, Oct. 11, 2008. BA in journalism with distinction, Ohio State U., 1972; JD, U. Detroit, 1975. Bar: Mich. 1975, Colo. 1984, U.S. Dist. Ct. (ea. and we. dists.) Mich. 1975, U.S. Ct. Appeals (6th cir.) 1977, U.S. Ct. Appeals (3d cir.) 1980, U.S. Supreme Ct. 1983, U.S. Ct. Appeals (10th cir.) 1984, U.S. Ct. Appeals (5th cir.) 1989, cert.: NBTA (civil trial advocate) 1994. Assoc. Lopatin, Miller, Bindes & Freedman, Detroit, 1973—76; ptnr. Schaden, Swanson & Lampert, Detroit, 1977—90, Sears, Anderson & Swanson, P.C., Colorado Springs, Colo., 1991—96, Sears & Swanson, Colorado Springs, 1997—. Adj. prof. U. Detroit Sch. Law, 1982. Author (chpt.): (non-fiction) Anatomy of a Personal Injury Lawsuit, 1992; author, editor: handbook Colorado Auto Litigators Handbook, 1995, Colorado Courtroom Handbook, 1998, author, editor: 2nd edit., 2006, Colorado Evidence Handbook, 2005; co-author (with Richard F. Schaden): (non-fiction) Product Design Liability, 1982; co-author: (with others) Women Trial Lawyers: How They Succeed in Practice and in the Courtroom, 1986. Mem.: Mich. Trial Lawyers Assn., Colo. Trial Lawyers Assn. (past pres., Kripke Lifetime Achievement award 2005), Am. Assn. Justice, Colo. Bar Assn., Mich. Bar Assn. Home Phone: 719-481-4210; Office Phone: 719-471-1984. Business E-Mail: victoria@searsandswanson.com.

SWARTOUT, WILLIAM R., mathematician, educator, director; s. Charles W. and June Swartout; m. Janet P. Swartout, 2008 (dec.); children: Robin, David. BS in Math. Scis. with distinction, Stanford U., Palo Alto, Calif., 1974; MS in Elec. Engring. & Computer Sci., MIT, Cambridge, Mass., 1977, PhD in Computer Sci., 1981. Dir., intelligent sys. divsn. U. So. Calif. Info. Scis. Inst., Marina del Rey, 1989—99; dir. of tech. U. So. Calif. Inst. for Creative Technologies, Marina del Rey, 1999—. Rsch. assoc. prof. computer sci. U. So. Calif., 1985—2006, rsch. prof. computer sci., 2006—. Mem. Air Force Sci. Adv. Bd., Washington, 2003—07, Bd. Army Sci. and Tech., Washington, 2004—, Joint Forces Command Transformation Adv. Group, 2004. Fellow: Am. Assn. Artificial Intelligence (mem. bd. councilors 1989—92); mem.: Assn. Computing Machinery (chair Spl. Interest Group on Artificial Intelligence 1985—87). Presbyterian. Achievements include pioneering research in automatic program explanation, and development of virtual humans. Avocations: photography, bicycling. Office: Univ So Calif Inst Creative Technologies 13274 Fiji Way Marina Del Rey CA 90292

SWARTZ, JACK, retired chamber of commerce executive; b. Nov. 24, 1932; s. John Ralph and Fern (Cave) S.; m. Nadine Ann Langlois, Aug. 4, 1956; children: Dana, Shawn, Tim, Jay. AA, Dodge City C.C., 1953; student, St. Mary of Plains Coll., 1953-55, 58; BBA, Washburn U., 1973, BA in Econs., 1974. V.p. D.C. Terminal Elevator Co., Dodge City, Kans., 1957-65; exec. v.p. Kans. Jaycees, Hutchinson, 1965-68, Kans. C. of C. and Industry, Topeka, 1968-82; pres. Nebr. C. of C. and Industry, Lincoln, 1982—2000, ret., 2000. Past chmn., bd. regents U.S. C. of C. Inst. U. Colo. With U.S. Army, 1955-57, USAR, 1961. Named Outstanding Local Pres. in State, Kans. Jaycees, 1961, Outstanding Young Man of Yr., Dodge City Jaycees, 1961, Outstanding State V.P., U.S. Jaycees, 1962, Outstanding Nat. Dir., 1963; named to Nebr. Bus. Hall of Fame, 2000, Sublette H.S. Wall of Honor, 2002. Mem. Am. Soc. Assn. Execs. (cert.), Am. C. of C. Execs. (bd. dirs., cert.), Nebr. C.of C. Execs. (sec.-treas.), Nebr. Soc. Assn. Execs. (past pres.), Nebr. Fedn. Bus. Assns. (pres. 1986-88), Nebr. Thoroughbred Breeders Assn. (past bd. dirs.), Washburn U. Alum. (past bd. dirs.), Am. Legion, Rotary. Republican. Roman Catholic. Home: 625 W Gibraltar Ln Phoenix AZ 85023-5243

SWARTZ, JAMES R., chemical engineer, educator; B in Chem. Engring., S.D. Sch. Mines and Tech.; DSci, MIT, 1978. Rsch. scientist Eli Lilly & Co., Indpls., Genentech, Inc., San Francisco, 1981—2003, dir. dept. fermentation rsch. and process devel.; prof. chem. engring. Stanford U., Palo Alto, Calif., 2003—. Mem. NAE, Am. Chem. Soc. Office: Dept Chem Engring Stanford U Keck 185 381 North South Mall Stanford CA 94305-5025 E-mail: swartz@chemeng.stanford.edu.

SWATT, STEPHEN BENTON, communications executive, consultant; b. LA, June 26, 1944; s. Maurice I. and Lucille E. (Sternberger) S.; m. Susan Ruth Edelstein, Sept. 7, 1968; 1 child, Jeffrey Michael. BSBA, U. Calif., 1966, M in Journalism, 1967. Writer San Francisco Examiner, 1967; reporter United Press Internat., LA, 1968-69; producer news Sta. KCRA-TV, Sacramento, 1969-70, reporter news, 1970-79, chief polit. and capitol corres., 1979-92; mng. ptnr. NCG Porter Novelli, Sacramento, 1992—2003, sr. counselor, 2003—. Adj. prof., guest lectr. Calif. State U., Sacramento. Contbr. articles to profl. jours. With USCG, 1966. Recipient No. Calif. Emmy NATAS, 1976-77, Pub. Svc. award Calif. State Bar, 1977, Exceptional Achievement Coun. advancement and Support of Edn., 1976, Nat. Health Journalism award Am. Chiropractic Assn., 1978. Mem. Soc. Profl. Journalists (8 awards), Capitol Corres. Assn., U. Calif. Alumni Assn., Sacramento Press Club. Avocations: hiking, jogging, fishing. Office: Porter Novelli 1215 K St # 2100 Sacramento CA 95814 Office Phone: 916-443-3354. Business E-Mail: steve.swatt@porternovelli.com.

SWEARENGIN, ASHLEY, Mayor, Fresno, California; b. Tex. m. Paul Swearengin; children: Sydney, Samuel. BS in bus. adminstrn., MS in bus. adminstrn., Calif. State U., Fresno. Dir. cmty. and econ. devel. Calif. State U., Fresno, 2000—08; co-founder, COO Regional Jobs Initiative, Fresno, 2002—05; lead exec. Calif. Partnership for the San Joaquin Valley, 2005—08; mayor City of Fresno, Calif., 2009—. Mem. Fresno Utility Commn., Calif. Commn. Econ. Devel., 2007. Named Alumnus of the Yr., Leadership Fresno, 2007; named one of Fresno's Top Bus. and Profl. Women of the Yr., Marjaree Mason Ctr., 2006. Office: Office of the Mayor 2600 Fresno St Fresno CA 93721 Office Phone: 559-621-8000. Office Fax: 559-621-7990. E-mail: mayor@fresno.gov.*

SWECKER, DAN, state legislator; b. Bozeman, Mont., Feb. 28, 1947; m to Debby; children: Jenny, Joel, Devin & Amy. Washington State Senator, District 20, 95-, member, Agriculture & Rural Econ Develop, Education Environ Quality & Water Resources & Transportation Committees, currently, chairman, Republican Caucus Policy Committee, currently, Assistant Majority Whip, 97-98, Washington State Senate; member, Family Policy Coun & Joint Task Force on Land Use & Econ Develop, currently.Owner & operation, Swecker Salmon Farm, Inc, 20 years; fireman & fire commissioner, District 1, Thurston, formerly; board member & chairman, Centralia Christian Sch, formerly; member, Water Rights Fee Task Force, 93 & Washington Water Policy Alliance, 94. 100 Percent Voting Record, Washington State Farm Bureau; Guardian Small Bus Award, Nat Fedn Independent Bus. Washington Fish Growers Association (exec director, currently); Nature Conserv Washington (board trustees, currently). Republican. Mailing: State Senate 103 Irving R Newhouse Bldg, PO Box 40420 Olympia WA 98504-0482 Office Phone: 360-786-7638; 800-562-6000. Fax: 360-786-1999. E-mail: swecker_da@leg.wa.gov.

SWEENEY, ANNE M., cable television company executive; b. Nov. 4, 1957; m. Philip Miller; children: Rosemary, Christopher. BA, Coll. of New Rochelle, NYC, 1979; EdM, Harvard U., 1980. With Nickelodeon/Nick at Nite, 1981-93, sr. v.p. program enterprises; chmn., CEO Fx Networks, NYC, 1993-96; exec. v.p. Disney/ABC Cable Networks, pres. Disney Channel Walt Disney Co., 1996—98, pres. Disney/ABC Cable Networks, Disney Channel, 1998—2000, pres. ABC Cable Networks Group, Disney Channel Worldwide, 2000—04, co-chair Media Networks divsn., pres. Disney/ ABC TV, 2004—. Bd. dirs. Hulu, 2009—, Mus. Radio & TV; hon. chair Cable Positive. Bd. trustees Coll. of New Rochelle, Harvard U. Ptnrs. Coun.; hon. chair Cable Positive; bd. dirs. Walter Kaitz Found, Spl. Olympics Internat. Recipient Lucy award, Women in Film, 2002, Chair Award, Caucus for TV Prodrs., Writers, and Dirs., 2003, President's award, Cable TV Pub. Affairs Assn., 2004; named one of 100 Most Powerful Women in Entertainment, Hollywood Reporter, 2004—07, 50 Women to Watch, Wall St. Jour., 2005, 2006, 100 Most Powerful Women, Forbes mag., 2005—08, Next 20 Female CEOs, Pink Mag. & Forté Found., 2006, 50 Most Powerful Women in Bus., Fortune mag., 2006, 2007, 2008; named to Hall of Achievement, Am. Advt. Fedn., 1996. Mem. Nat. Acad. Cable Programming (bd. dirs.), Women in Cable NY (founding mem.), Women in Cable (Exec. of Yr. 1994, Woman of Yr. 1997, Advocate Leader award So. Calif. Chpt. 1998). Office: The Walt Disney Co 500 S Buena Vista St Burbank CA 91521

SWEENEY, DAVID BRIAN, lawyer; b. Seattle, June 23, 1941; s. Hubert Lee and Ann Louise (Harmon) S.; m. Janice Kay Goins, June 18, 1983; children: Stuart, Jennifer, Ann, Katharine. BA Magna cum laude, Yale U., 1963; LLB, Harvard U., 1967. Bar: Wash. 1968, U.S. Dist. Ct. (we. dist.) Wash. 1968, U.S. Ct. Appeals (9th cir.) 1968. Assoc. Roberts, Shefelman, Lawrence, Gay and Moch, Seattle, 1968-75; ptnr. Roberts, Shefelman, Lawrence, Gay & Moch (then Robert & Shefelman, then Foster, Pepper & Shefelman), 1976—2002; of counsel Smith & Zuccarini, P.S., Bellevue, Wash., 2002—. Mem. Seattle-King County Bar Assn., Wash. State Bar Assn., ABA, Estate Planning Coun. Seattle, College Club, Harbor Club. Home: 17506 SE 46th St Bellevue WA 98006-6527 Office: Smith & Zuccarini PS 2155 112th Ave NE Bellevue WA 98004 Home Phone: 425-641-8323; Office Phone: 425-990-1586. Business E-Mail: d.sweeney@smithzuccarini.com.

SWEENEY, JAMES LEE, engineering educator; b. Waterbury, Conn., Mar. 22, 1944; s. James Wallace and Aletha B. S.; m. Susan L. Van Every, Aug. 21, 1971; children: Erin, Ryan, Regan, Wesley. BSEE, MIT, 1966; PhD in Engring.-Econ. Sys., Stanford U., 1971. With Stanford U., 1967—, prof. engring.-econ. sys., 1971—, chmn. dept. engring.-econ. sys., 1991—, prof. and chmn. dept. ops. rsch., engring.-econ. sys., 1996—99, prof. mgmt. sci. and engring., 2000—; sr. fellow Hoover Inst., 2001—; dir. office energy sys., modeling and forecasting U.S. Fed. Energy Adminstrn., Washington, 1974-76. Dir. Energy Modeling Forum, 1978-85, chmn. Inst. Energy Studies, 1981-84, cons. faculty Sch. of Law, 1980-82, mem. steering com. Ctr. Econ. policy Rsch., 1982—, dir., 1984-86; sr. fellow Ctr. for Econ. Policy Rsch., 1997—; dir. Precourt Inst. Energy Efficiency; cons. Cornerstone Rsch., NRC, Exxon Mobil. Author: The California Electricity Crisis, 2001; co-author: Macroeconomics Impacts of Energy Shocks, 1987, Fuels to Drive Our Future, 1990; editor: Handbook of Natural Resources and Energy Economics, 1985, 93; contbr. numerous publs., in field to profl. jours. Bd. pres. Stanford Campus Residential Leaseholders, 1998—. Recipient Disting. Svc. award Fed. Energy Adminstrn., 1975, Adelman-Frankel award US Assoc. Energy Econs., 2007. Mem. Am. Econ. Assn., Internat. Assn. Energy Econs. (Past v.p. for publs.), Rotary (past pres.), Menlo Circus Club, Eta Kappa Nu, Tau Beta Pi. Home: 445 El Escarpado Stanford CA 94305-8430 Office: Stanford University 473 Via Ortega Stanford CA 94305-4121 Office Phone: 650-723-2847. Business E-Mail: jim.sweeney@stanford.edu.

SWEENEY, JOSEPH J., lawyer, manufacturing executive; AB, Harvard Coll., 1970; JD, Boston U., 1973. Sr. atty. Data Gen. Corp.; v.p., gen. counsel MIPS Computer Systems, Inc.; v.p. adminstrn. MIPS Technologies, Inc.; with Applied Materials Inc., Santa Clara, Calif., 1993—, group v.p. legal affairs & intellectual property, corp. sec., 2002—05, sr. v.p., gen. counsel, corp. sec., 2005—. Office: Applied Materials 3050 Bowers Ave PO Box 58039 Santa Clara CA 95054-3299

SWEENEY, PAUL W., JR., lawyer; BA cum laude, U. So. Calif., 1972; JD, Columbia U., 1975. Bar: D.C. 1975, Calif. 1984. White House Fellow Chief of Staff Asst. to Pres. for Intergovernmental Affairs, Washington, 1979—81; adminstrv. ptnr. & mem. mgmt. com Kirkpatrick & Lockhart Nicholson Graham LLP, LA. Contbr. articles to profl. jours. Bd. dir. Prevent Child Abuse Am., Hollywood Wilshire YMCA, Public Counsel. Mem.: Am. Law Inst. Office: Kirkpatrick & Lockhart Nicholson Graham LLP 7th Fl 10100 Santa Monica Blvd Los Angeles CA 90067-4003 Office Phone: 310-552-5055. Office Fax: 310-552-5001. Business E-Mail: psweeney@klng.com.

SWEITZER, MICHAEL COOK, healthcare product executive; b. Cin., July 29, 1961; s. Charles Samuel and Louise (Cook) S. BS in Biomedical Engring., Rensselaer Poly. Inst., 1983, M in Engring., 1985. Product specialist Siemens Med. Sys., Iselin, N.J., 1985-89, tech. mgr, 1989-90, nat. sales mgr., 1993-94, product mgr., 1994-96, cons., 1996-98, product specialist San Francisco, 1990-92; product mgr. Toshiba Am. Med. Sys., S. San Francisco, 1992-93, Varian Med. Sys., Palo Alto, Calif., 1998—2001, bus. unit mgr., 2001—03, mgr. emerging techs., 2003—06, dir., rsch. collaborations, 2006—. Contbr. chpt. to MRI Guide for Technologists, 1994. Mem. Am. Healthcare Radiology Adminstrs., Inst. for Indsl. Engrs. Office: Varian Med Sys Inc MS E 263 3100 Hansen Way Palo Alto CA 94304-1129

SWENSON, RICHARD ALLEN, business owner, animal trainer; b. Willmar, Minn., Dec. 1, 1950; s. LeRoy Oswald Boe and Delores G. (Malghist) S.; children: Kristen, Richard Andrew, Kevin. Author: Secrets of Long Distance Sled Dog Racing. Treas. Pride, Alaska, 1993—. Recipient 1st pl. Iditarod, 1977, 79, 80, 81, 91 among others. Office: Denali Sled Dog Tours PO Box 86 Denali National Park AK 99755-0086

SWERDLOFF, RONALD S., physician, educator, researcher; b. Pomona, Calif., Feb. 18, 1938; s. Julius Lewis and Eva (Kelman) S.; m. Christina Wang; children: Jonathan Nicolai, Peter Loren, Paul Im, Michael Im. BS, U. Calif., 1959, MD, 1962. Diplomate Am. Bd. Internal Medicine, Am. Bd. Endocrinology. Intern U. Wash., Seattle, 1962-63, resident, 1963-64; rsch. assoc. NIH, Bethesda, Md., 1964-66; resident UCLA Sch. Medicine, 1966-67; rsch. fellow Harbor-UCLA Med. Ctr., Torrance, Calif., 1967-69, asst. prof., 1969-72, assoc. prof. divsn. Endocrinology, 1972-78, chief divsn. Endocrinology, 1973—, prof., 1978—, assoc. chair dept. medicine, 1997—; dir. UCLA Population Rsch. Ctr., Torrance, 1986-92, Mellon Found. Ctr. in Reproductive Medicine, 1997—. Dir. WHO Collaborating Ctr. Reproduction, Torrance, NIH Contraceptive Clin. Trials Ctr., 2005—, Torrance; cons. WHO Geneva, 1982-90, NIH, Bethesda, 1982—, UN Fertility Planning Assn., Geneva, 1983—, Am. Bd. Internal Medicine, Phila., 1989—; inaugural lectr. Australian Soc. Reproductive Biology, Perth, 1990; mem. tech. adv. com. Contraceptive R & D Agy. (CONRAD, AID), 1992—. Editor: 3 books; contbr. chapters to books 100, articles 250 to profl. jours. Bd. dirs., vice chair Harbor-UCLA Rsch. and Edn. Inst; bd. dirs. Scaplanes Corp. Recipient Sherman Mellinkoff award, UCLA, 1998. Fellow: ACP; mem.: We. Soc. Clin. Rsch. (pres. 1983—84, Sherman Mellinkoff award UCLA, Mayo Soley award 2000), Endocrinology Soc., Pacific Coast Fertility (pres. 1984, Outstanding Rsch. award 1976, 1984, Wyeth award 1984, Squibb award), Am. Soc. Clin. Rsch. (pres. we. sect. 1972—73), Am. Assn. Physicians, Am. Soc. Andrology (pres. 1992—93, Serono award 1986, Disting. Andrologist award 2004). Office: Harbor UCLA Med Ctr Divsn Endocrinology 1000 W Carson St Torrance CA 90502-2004 Office Phone: 310-222-1867. Business E-Mail: swerdloff@labiomed.org.

SWETTE, BRIAN T., online company executive; 5 children. BA in Econ. (summa cum laude), Az. State U., 1976. Brand mgr. Procter & Gamble; joined Pepsi-Cola Internat., 1981; various positions including exec. v.p. mktg., sr. v.p., gen. mgr., new beverage ventures, dir. ops., and v.p. nat. mktg. Pepsi-Cola N.Am.; exec. v.p.,chief mktg. officer Pepsi-Cola; exec. v.p. mktg. eBay, Inc., 1998—2001, COO, 1999—2002. Bd. dir. Texas Pacific Group holdings, CBL Partners, TheLadders.com, 2005; non-exec. chmn. Burger King Corp., Miami, Fla., 2006—08; invited spkr. Trustee Pine Crest Prep Sch., Cmty. Found. Broward County.

SWIFT, GREGORY, physicist; b. Omaha, July 7, 1952; BS in physics and math., U. Nebr., 1974; PhD in physics, U. Calif., Berkeley, 1980. Dir. postdoctoral fellow condensed matter and thermal physics group Los Alamos Nat. Lab., J. Robert Oppenheimer fellow condensed matter and thermal physics group, tech. staff mem. condensed matter and thermal physics group, lab. fellow condensed matter and thermal physics group. Author: Thermoacoustics: A Unifying Perspective for Some Engines and Refrigerators. Recipient Los Alamos Disting. Performance award, "Thermoacoustic natural-gas liquefier", 1996, R&D-100 award, "Acoustic Stirling Heat Engine", R&D mag., 1999, World Oil's New Horizons Idea award, "Thermoacoustics for gas liquefaction", 2003, Ernest and Orlando Laurence award, US Dept Energy, 2004, Los Alamos Disting. Patent award, 2004, Los Alamos Disting. Licensing award, 2004. Fellow: Am. Physical Soc., Los Alamos Nat. Lab., Acoustical Soc. Am. (Silver Medal in Physical Acoustics 2000). Achievements include 24 patents. Office: Los Alamos Nat Lab PO Mail Stop K764 Los Alamos NM 87545

SWIG, KENT M., real estate company executive; b. San Francisco, Jan. 20, 1961; m. Elizabeth Swig; children: Simon, Oliver. BA in Chinese History, Brown U.; JD, U. Calif., Berkeley. V.p. The Swig Co. (formerly Swig, Weiler & Dinner Devel. Co.), San Francisco, prin., bd. dirs.; exec. v.p. The Macklowe Orgn., pres. Manhattan Pacific Mgmt. Co., Inc.; co-founder, pres. Swig Equities, LLC (formerly Swig Burris Equities), 2001—, co-chair Brown Harris Stevens; owner, co-chair Terra Holdings, LLC; owner, pres. Helmsley Spear, LLC; owner Falcon Pacific Construction, LLC. Chmn. real estate and construction industries State of Israel Bonds, nat. bd. dirs., 2004. Bd. mem. Downtown Alliance, Wall Street Rising, Assn. Builders and Owners of NY, Bus. Execs. for Nat. Security; v.p. Realty Found. of NY; pres. Am. Friends of the Jaffa Inst. Recipient Man of Yr. Award, Big Brothers/Big Sisters of NY, 2000; named Man of Yr., Realty Found. of NY, 2005. Office: Swig Equities, LLC 770 Lexington Ave New York NY 10065 also: 450 Sansome St San Francisco CA 94111 Office Phone: 212-508-7373. Office Fax: 212-508-7488.

SWIG, ROSELYNE CHROMAN, community consultant; b. Chgo., June 8, 1930; m. Richard Swig, Feb. 5, 1950 (dec.); children—Richard, Jr., Susan, Marjorie, Carol. Student, U. Calif.-Berkeley, UCLA; MFA (hon.), DHL (hon.), San Francisco Art Inst., 1988. Founder, pres. Roselyne C. Swig Artsource, San Francisco, 1977-94; apptd. by Pres. Clinton as dir. Art in Embassies Program U.S. Dept. of State, 1994-97; founder, pres. Comcon Internat., 1998—. Founder Ptnrs. Ending Domestic Abuse, San Francisco. Trustee San Francisco Mus. Modern Art, U. Art Mus., Berkeley, Calif.; ex officio bd. mem. Jewish Mus. San Francisco; bd. dirs., former treas. Am. Jewish Joint Distbn. Com.; vice chair fine art adv. panel Fed. Res., Washington; past trustee Mills Coll., Oakland, Calif.; past past pres., bd. dirs. Jewish Cmty. Fedn. San Francisco, the Peninsula, Marin and Sonoma Counties; past commr. San Francisco Pub. Libr.; past bd. dirs. San Francisco Opera, Am. Coun. for Arts, KQED Broadcasting Sys.; past. pres. Calif. State Summer Sch. Arts, past chair bd. trustees San Francisco Art Inst.; past pres. San Francisco Arts Commn.; past nat. v.p. Am./Israel Pub. Affairs Com.; past trustee United Jewish Appeal; past chair bd. trustees Univ. Art Mus. Mem. Women's Forum West (bd. dirs.), Internat. Women's Forum. Avocations: skiing, boating, tennis, fishing.

SWIHART, H. GREGG, real estate company executive; b. San Francisco, Sept. 25, 1938; s. Lawson Benjamin and Violet Mary (Watters) S.; m. Ilse Paula Rambacher, Dec. 24, 1958; children: Tatjana Etta, Brett Marc, Natascha Theda. BA, U. Ariz., 1958; postgrad., Heidelberg U., Germany, 1958—59, Harvard U., 1959-60; MA, Boston U., 1961; postgrad., Freiburg U., Germany, 1961-65. Cert. property mgr. Stockbroker Walston & Co., Tucson, 1966-71; with Solot Co., Tucson, 1971-74; pres. Cienega Properties, Inc., property mgmt. and investment, Tucson, 1975-77, GT Realty Assocs., Ltd., Tucson, 1977—2004; ret., 2004. Mem Tucson Com. Fgn. Rels., 1973—; pres. Forum for Greater Outdoors, 1977-79; bd. dirs. Tucson Mus. Art, 1968-74, pres., 1969-70; pres. and trustee, Canelo Hills Sch., 1977-79. Mem. Tucson Bd. Realtors, Inst. Real Estate Mgmt. (pres. Tucson-So. Ariz. chpt. 1982, mem. nat. governing coun. 1985-87), Inst. Real Estate Mgmt. (governing coun. 1985-87, Property Mgr. of Yr. award So. Ariz. chpt. 1988), Realtors Nat. Mktg. Inst., Harvard Club (pres. 1973-74), Active 20-30 Club (pres. 1969-70), Downtown Tucson Club. Home: 5390E Placita del Mesquite Tucson AZ 85712

SWIHART, JAMES W., JR., diplomat; b. Washington, July 25, 1946; s. James Wilbur and Ruth (Inge) S.; m. Ellen Jane Cendo Mar. 30, 1968; children: Jennifer Anne, Christopher John; m. Kimberly Ann Mack, May 12, 2001. BA, Columbia Coll., 1968. Vice consul Am. Embassy, Belize, Brit. Honduras, 1970-72, 2nd sec., polit. officer Belgrade, Yugoslavia, 1972-74; ops. officer ops. ctr. Dept. State, Washington, 1974-75, country officer for Italy and the Vatican, 1975-78, polit./mil. officer for U.S. Mission Berlin, 1978-82, officer C.S.C.E. Bur. European Affairs Washington, 1982-83, officer for Fed. Republic of Germany, 1983-84; consul gen., prin. officer U.S. Consulate Gen., Zagreb, Yugoslavia, 1984-1988; mem. sr. seminar Dept. State, Washington, 1988-89, dir. Bur. for Ea. European and Yugoslavia Affairs, 1989-1991; min. counselor, deputy chief of mission Am. Embassy, Vienna, Austria, 1991-94, Chargé d'Affaires ad interim, 1993, amb. to Lithuania Vilnius, 1994-97; sr. fellow Inst. for Strategic Studies/Nat. Def. U., Washington, 1997-99; polit. advisor U.S. Space Command, Colorado Springs, Colo., 1999—. Avocations: piano, harpsichord, jogging, classical music.

SWINBURN, PETER, brewery company executive; married; 2 children. BSc in Econs. with honors, U. Wales. Joined Coors Brewing Co., 1974; sales dir. Bass Brewers, 1994—2002; dir. Grolsch UK; COO Coors Brewers Ltd., 2002—03, pres., CEO, 2005—07; pres. Coors Brewing Worldwide, 2003—05; pres., CEO Coors Brewing Co., 2007—08, Molson Coors Brewing Co., 2008—. Chmn. Tradeteam; bd. dirs. Molson Coors Brewing Co., 2008—. Office: Molson Coors Brewing Co 1225 17th St Ste 1875 Denver CO 80202 E-mail: peter.swinburn@molsoncoors.com.

SWING, WILLIAM EDWIN, bishop; b. Huntington, W.Va., Aug. 26, 1936; s. William Lee and Elsie Bell (Holliday) S.; M. Mary Willis Taylor, Oct. 7, 1961; children— Alice Marshall, William Edwin BA, Kenyon Coll., Ohio, 1954-58; D.Div. (hon.), Kenyon Coll., 1980; MA, Va. Theol. Sem., 1958-61, D.Div., 1980. Ordained priest Episcopal Ch. Asst. St. Matthews Ch., Wheeling, W.Va., 1961-63, vicar Chester, W.Va., 1963-69, St. Thomas Ch., Weirton, W.Va., 1963-69; rector St. Columba's Episcopal Ch., Washington, 1969-79; bishop Episcopal Ch. Calif., San Francisco, 1980—. Chmn. bd. Ch. Div. Sch. of the Pacific, 1983-84; founder, chmn. Episcopal Found. for Drama, 1976—. Republican. Home: 105 Pepper Ave Burlingame CA 94010-5234

SWINTON, STEPHEN P., lawyer; b. Charles City, Iowa, Sept. 25, 1951; BS, Iowa State Univ., 1973; JD with honors, Drake Univ., 1982. Bar: Calif. 1982, US Dist. Ct. (so., no., ctrl. dist. Calif.), US Ct. Appeals (9th, Fed. cir.), US Patent & Trademark Office, US Supreme Ct. Process & mfg. engr. Proctor & Gamble; extern Judge Roy L. Stephenson, US Ct. Appeals, 8th cir.; ptnr., bus. litigation Cooley Godward LLP, San Diego, 1994—, chmn. Intellectual Property Litigation practice. Faculty mem. Nat. Inst. Trial Advocacy. Served surface line officer USN. Mem.: ABA, State Bar Calif., San Diego Bar Assn., Order of the Coif. Office: Cooley Godward LLP 4401 Eastgate Mall San Diego CA 92121-1909 Office Phone: 858-550-6028. Office Fax: 858-550-6420. Business E-Mail: swintonsp@cooley.com.

SWISSTACK, THOMAS E., state legislator; b. Passaic, NJ, Nov. 26; m Kathy Swisstack; children: James Martinez. Mayor, Rio Rancho, NM, formerly; member, Juvenile Justice Committee, currently, Nat Juvenile Detention Affiliate, currently; director, Bernalillo Co Juvenile Detention Center, currently; New Mexico State Representative, District 60, 2003-. Democrat. Roman Catholic. Office: Capitol Add NM State Capitol Rm 203CCN Santa Fe NM 87503 Mailing: 300 Encantado Ridge Ct NE Albuquerque NM 87124-2571 E-mail: tswisstake@msn.com.

SWOFFORD, BETH, agent; Motion picture agent Creative Artists Agency (CAA), Beverly Hills. Trustee Mus. of Contemporary Art, LA; media com. mem. Gold Mus. Modern Art, 2007—09. Named one of Top 200 Collectors, ARTnews Mag., 2004—08, The 100 Most Powerful Women in Entertainment, Hollywood Reporter, 2004, 2005, 2006, 2007, The 50 Smartest People in Hollywood, Entertainment Weekly, 2007. Avocation: Collector of Contemporary Art. Office: Creative Artists Agy 2000 Ave of the Stars Los Angeles CA 90067 also: PO Box 240002 Los Angeles CA 90024

SWOFFORD, ROBERT LEE, editor, journalist; b. Berryville, Ark., Aug. 22, 1949; s. Andrew Madison and Verna Mae (England) S.; m. Karan King, Jan. 24, 1969 (div. 1977); children: Teri, Toby; m. Sandra Dunn, 1978 (div. 1979); m. B. Joanna Rongren, Feb. 14, 1981 (div. 2001); 1 child, Tyler. AA, Coll. of the Sequoias, 1969; student, Calif. State U., 1969-71. Photographer, reporter, news editor The Advance-Register, Tulare, Calif., 1965-78; city editor The Record Searchlight, Redding, Calif., 1978-81; suburban editor, Neighbors editor The Sacramento Bee, 1981-86; assoc. metro. editor, cmty. editor The Orange County Register, Santa Ana, Calif., 1986-89; exec. news editor The Press Democrat, Santa Rosa, Calif., 1989-90, mng. editor, 1990—. Mem. Am. Soc. Newspaper Editors, Calif. Soc. Newspaper Editors (bd. mem., past pres.). Office: The Press Democrat 427 Mendocino Ave Santa Rosa CA 95401-6385 Business E-Mail: bob.swofford@pressdemocrat.com.

SYDANSK, ROBERT DUNN, chemist, petroleum engineer; b. 1943; BS in Chemistry, U. Colo., 1967. With Petroleum Tech. Rsch. Ctr. Marathon Oil Co., Littleton, Colo., 1967—, now sr. tech. cons. Cons. and lectr. in field. Tech. editor publs. Soc. Petroleum Engrs.; contbr. some 30 articles to profl. jours.; 56 patents in chem. improved oil recovery processes. Mem. Am. Chem. Soc. (award in indsl. chemistry 1997), Soc. Petroleum Engrs. (Henry Mattson Tech. Achievement award 1993, Disting. Lectr. 1997).

SYKES, WANDA, comedienne, actress; b. Portsmouth, Va., Mar. 7, 1964; m. Alex Sykes, Oct. 25, 2008; children: Olivia Lou, Lucas Claude. BS, Hampton U. Actor: (TV series) Best of Chris Rock, 1999, Larry David: Curb Your Enthusiasm, 1999, Crank Yankers, 2003—, Wanda Does It, 2004, The New Adventures of Old Christine, 2006—09, Back at the Barnyard, 2007—08; (films) Tomorrow Night, 1998, Nutty Professor II: The Klumps, 2000, Down to Earth, 2001, Pootie Tang, 2001, Monster-in-Law, 2005 (Outstanding Supporting Actress in a Theatrical Film, BET Comedy award, 2005), Clerks II, 2006, My Super Ex-Girlfriend, 2006, (voice) Over the Hedge, 2006, Barnyard: The Original Party Animals, 2006, CondomNation, 2006, Evan Almighty, 2007, License to Wed, 2007; actor, writer (TV series) The Chris Rock Show, 1997—2000 (Emmy award for outstanding writing, 1999), The Downer Channel, 2001, writer, creator, actor, prodr. Wanda at Large, 2003, writer The Keenen Ivory Wayans Show, 1997, guest appearances include The Drew Carey Show, Chappelle's Show, appears on Inside the NFL, 2002—; author: Yeah I Said It, 2004. Recipient Am. Comedy award for Funniest Female Stand-Up Comic, 2001. Office: c/o William Morris Agy One William Morris Pl Beverly Hills CA 90212*

SYLVESTER, ROBERT, dean, musician; b. NYC; Dir. cultural affairs Western Wash. U., dean Sch. Fine & Performing Arts; pres. Portland State U., 1997—. Cofounder Chamber Music at Guggenheim Festival, NYC, Cape & Island Festival, Cape Cod, Mass., Bellingham Festival Music. Avocation: cello. Office: Office of the Dean Sch Fine & Performing Arts Portland State U 349 Lincoln Hall Portland OR 97207-0751 Office Phone: 503-725-3105. E-mail: sylvesterr@pdx.edu.

SYMES, LAWRENCE RICHARD, computer science educator, university dean; s. Oliver Lawrence and Maybell Melita Blanche Symes; m. Evelyn Jean Hewett, Apr. 3, 1964; children: Calvin Richard, Michelle Louise, Erin Kathleen. BA, U. Sask., Saskatoon, Can., 1963, postgrad. in math., 1964; MS, Purdue U., 1966, Phd, 1969. Asst. prof. Purdue U., West Lafayette, Ind., 1969-70; assoc. prof. computer sci. U. Regina, Sask., Canada, 1970-74, prof. Sask., 1974—, dir. computer ctr. Sask., 1970-75, head dept. computer sci. Sask., 1972-81, dean of sci. Sask., 1982-92, dean grad. studies, assoc. rsch. v.p. Sask., 1997-99, dir. info. svcs. Sask., 1999—. Dir. tng. Software Tech. Ctr., 1993-94; exec. dir. postsecondary svcs. br. Saskatchewan Edn. Tng. and Employment Govt. of Saskatchewan, 1994-95, exec. dir. multimedia learning, 1995-96; invited lectr. Xian Jiaotong U., 1983; invited lectr., Shandong Acad. Sci., China, 1987, guest prof.; vis. prof. Ednl. Inst. Jilin Province, Shandong U., Jinan, China; co-chair IT cluster Regina Regional Econ. Authority, 2002—. Contbr. articles to profl. jours. Bd. dirs. Hosp. Sys. Study Group, Saskatoon, 1978-94, chmn. bd., 1980-83; dir. SSTA Computer Svcs., Regina, 1972-89; mem. adv. coun. Can./Sask. Advanced Tech. Agreement, 1985-87; mem. Sask. Agrl. Rsch. Found. Bd., 1987-88; mem. steering com. IBM/Sask. Agreement, 1990-92; mem. adv. bd. Plant Biotech. Inst., NRC. Can. Fed. Govt. grantee, 1977-84. Mem. Assn. Computing Machinery, Can. Info. Processing (pres. 1979-80, accreditation com. 1988-94), IEEE Computer Soc., Sask. ADA Assn. (bd. dirs. 1990-93), Software Tech. Ctr. (bd. dirs. 1993-98), Regina Regional Econ. Authority (IT cluster co-chair). Office: U Regina Info Svcs 3737 Wascana Pkwy Regina SK Canada S4S 0A2

SYMINGTON, J. FIFE, III, former governor, political consultant; b. NYC, Aug. 12, 1945; s. John Fife Jr. and Martha (Frick) S.; m. Leslie Marion Barker, June 1, 1968 (div. Jan. 1973); childen: Fife IV, Scott; m. Ann Pritzlaff, Feb. 7, 1976; children: Whitney, Richard, Tom. Student, Harvard U., 1968. Ptnr. Lincoln Property Co., Phoenix, 1972-76; chmn. of the bd. The Symington Co., Phoenix, 1976-89; gov. State of Ariz., 1991-97; founder Ariz. Culinary Inst., 2001; ptnr. Symington Private Equity Group. Precinct committeeman Ariz.'s Legis. Dist. 24, Paradise Valley; fin. chmn. State Republican Party, Phoenix, 1982-84; campaign advisor Rep. John Rhodes, Sen. John McCain, Ariz.; chmn. Phoenix Citizens Police Protection Bond Com., 1988; v.p. bd. trustees Heard Mus.; mem. Men's Art Coun., Environ. Quality Commn., 1971-73, Ariz. Children's Found.; dep. sheriff Maricopa County Air Posse; exec. bd. Phoenix Community Alliance. Capt. USAF, 1968-71. Mem. Western Govs.' Assn. (chmn. 1992—). Episcopalian.

SYMONE, RAVEN (RAVEN-SYMONÉ CHRISTINA PEARMAN), actress, singer; b. Atlanta, Dec. 10, 1985; d. Christopher B. Pearman and Lydia Gaulden. Actor: (TV series) The Cosby Show, 1989—92, A Different World, 1989, The Fresh Prince of Bel-Air, 1992, Hangin' with Mr. Cooper, 1994—97, Happily Ever After: Fairy Tales for Every Child, 1998, My Wife and Kids, 2001, (voice) Kim Possible, 2002—07, That's So Raven, 2003—07 (Blimp Award for Favorite TV Actress, Kids' Choice Awards, 2004, 2005, Outstanding Performance, Children's Program, NAACP Image award, 2005, 2006, 2007, 2008), Fillmore!, 2004, Higglytown Heroes, 2005; (films) The Little Rascals, 1994, Doctor Dolittle, 1998, Dr. Dolittle 2, 2001, The Princess Diaries 2: Royal Engagement, 2004, (voice) Fat Albert, 2004, Everyone's Hero, 2006, College Road Trip, 2008, (voice): (video)

Kim Possible: The Secret Files, 2003, That's So Raven: Supernaturally Stylish, 2004, That's So Raven: Raven's Makeover Madness, 2006, Raven Symone: Raven's Postcards from Spain, 2006; (TV films) The Cheetah Girls, 2003, (voice) Kim Possible: A Sitch in Time, 2003, Kim Possible: So the Drama, 2005, Zenon: Z3, 2004, For One Night, 2006; prodr.: (TV series) That's So Raven, 2006; actor, co-prodr.: (TV films) The Cheetah Girls 2, 2006; singer: (soundtrack) Ella Enchanted, 2004, That's So Raven, 2004, The Princess Diaries 2: Royal Engagement, 2004. Former amb. Children First program; spkr. for Nat. Safe Kids Campaign. Home: c/o Internat Creative Mgmt 8942 Wilshire Blvd Beverly Hills CA 90211-1934

SYMONS, JAMES MARTIN, theater and dance educator; b. Jacksonville, Ill., May 7, 1937; s. James and Pauline (Barton) S.; m. Judith White, Nov. 14, 1959; children: Tracy, Kelly, Carrie. BA, Ill. Coll., 1959; MA, So. Ill. U., 1964; PhD, Cornell U., 1970. Asst. prof. Yankton (S.D.) Coll., 1964-67; assoc. prof. Coll. St. Catherine, St. Paul, 1970-74, SUNY, Albany, 1974-77; prof., chair Trinity U., San Antonio, 1977-84; prof., chair theatre and dance dept. U. Colo., Boulder, 1984-99, prof., 1999—, Pres.'s Tchg. scholar, 2000—. Actor Off-Broadway, N.Y.C., 1959, Mo. Repertory Theatre, Kansas City, 1984; dir., actor Colo. Shakespeare Festival, Boulder, 1985—, producing artistic dir., 1994-95; leader People-to-People Del. of Theater Educators, USSR and Czechoslovakia, 1991. Author: Meyerhold's Theatre of the Grotesque, 1971 (Freedley Meml. award Theatre Libr. Assn. 1971); contbr. articles to scholarly jours. Lt. (j.g.) USN, 1960-63. Recipient Outstanding Tchr. award, ATHE, 2004. Mem. Assn. for Theatre in Higher Edn. (pres. 1989-91), Assn. for Communication Adminstrn. (pres. 1990), Coll. Fellows Am. Theatre. Democrat. Methodist. Office: U Colo Dept Theatre & Dance Cb 261 Boulder CO 80309-0001 Office Phone: 303-492-3388. E-mail: james.symons@colorado.edu.

SZABLYA, HELEN MARY, writer, language educator; b. Budapest, Hungary, Sept. 6, 1934; came to U.S., 1963; d. Louis and Helen (Bartha) Kovacs; m. John Francis Szablya, June 12, 1951; children: Helen, Janos, Louis, Stephen, Alexandra, Rita, Dominique-Mary. Diploma in Sales, Mktg., U.B.C., 1962; BA in Fgn. Lang., Lit., Wash. State U., 1976. Freelance writer, translator, 1967—; columnist Cath. News, Trinidad, West Indies, 1980-91; adult educator TELOS Bellevue (Wash.) C.C., 1987-89; adult educator Pullman-Spokane (Wash.) C.C., 1976-80; faculty Christian Writers' Conf., Seattle, 1983-88, Pacific N.W. Writers' Conf., Seattle and Tacoma, 1987—92; hon. consul for Wash., Oreg., Idaho Republic of Hungary, 1993—; pres. Consular Assn. WA, 2009—. Lectr. Washington Commn. for Humanities, 1987-89. Author (with others): Hungary Remembered, 1986 (Guardian of Liberty award, 1986, George Washington Honor medal, Freedoms Found. award, 1988); author: 56-os Cserkèszcsapat, 1986; author: (with others) The Fall of the Red Star, 1996, Hungarian transl., 1999 (1st prize Wash. Press Assn., 1st prize Nat. Fedn. Press Women); pub., editor Hungary Internat. newsletter, 1990—93, columnist Hungarian Bus. Weekly, 1994—95; translator: Emlèkezünk, 1986, Mind Twisters, 1987, A vörös csillag lehull, 1999. Recipient Nat. 1st place editl. Nat. Fedn. Press Women, 1987, Senator Tom Martin Meml. award Pacific N.W. Writers Conf., 1979, Pro Auxilio Civium Hungarorum, Min. Fgn. Affairs, Republic of Hungary, 2003, Order of Merit, Republic of Hungary, 2005, Pro Communitate, City of Pecs, Hungary, 2006; grantee Hungarian Am. Assn. Wash., 1986, Wash. Com. for Humanities, 1986; named Cmty. Woman of Yr. Am. Bus. Women Assn., 1990. Mem. AAUW, Wash. Press Assn. (pres. 1987-88, 1st and 2nd place awards, several editl. and profile awards 1983, 87, 89, 90, 91, 92, 96, Communicator of Achievement award 1987), Nat. Fedn. Press Women (Affiliate Pres.' award 1988, bd. dirs. edn. fund N.W. quadrant, mem. 21st century planning com.), Authors Guild, Am. Translators Assn., Arpad Acad. (Gold medal 1987), Nat. Writers Club, Internat. PEN Club, Sigma Delta Chi (editl. award 1989), Hungarian-Am. Coalition (bd mem. 1992—, chair bd. 2007), Am.-Hungarian Fedn. Avocations: children, reading, dance, swimming, travel. Home and Office: PO Box 578 Kirkland WA 98083-0578 Office Phone: 425-739-0631. Personal E-mail: szablyahj@aol.com.

SZABO, PETER JOHN, investment company executive, mining engineer, financial planner, lawyer; b. Bklyn., Nov. 22, 1946; s. Paul Simon and Marita Ellen (Coughlin) S.; m. Dorothy Anne Steward, Nov. 14, 1970; children: Peter, David, John Paul Steward. BS in Mining Engring., Columbia U., 1968; LLB, LaSalle Law Sch., 1975; MS in Fin. Planning, Coll. Fin. PLanning, 1994. registered profl. engr., CFP. Mining engr. Halecrest Co., Mt. Hope, NJ, 1973-74; mgr. solid fuels & minerals Ford, Bacon & Davis, NYC, 1974-75; asst. v.p. Mfrs. Hanover Trust Co., NYC, 1975-77, Irving Trust Co., NYC, 1977; v.p. Republic Nat. Bank of Dallas, 1977-80; mgr. bus. devel. AMOCO Minerals, Denver, 1980-84; investment broker B.J. Leonard, Denver, 1984-85; investment exec. Wedbush Nobel Cook, Denver, 1985; regional sr. v.p. Alliance Fund Distbrs., NYC, 1985-92, sr. v.p., 1992—. Mining engr. U.S. Bur. Mines, Dallas, 1971-72, IRS, Washington, 1972-73. Treas. Columbia Sch. Engring., 1968—. Lt. USMC, 1969-71, Vietnam, capt. Res. Mem. VFW (post sr. vice comdr. 1993-94, post comdr. 1994-95, all state team post comdrs. 1995, 16th dist. jr. vice comdr. 1995—, 16th dist. sr. vice comdr. 1996—, nat. aide-de-camp 1995-96), Mil. Order of the Cootie (sr. vice comdr. 1994-95). Republican. Roman Catholic. Avocations: sailing, golf, tennis, jogging. Home and Office: Alliance Fund Distbrs 810 Oxford Way Benicia CA 94510-3646

SZEFLER, STANLEY JAMES, pediatrics and pharmacology educator; b. Buffalo, Aug. 24, 1948; s. Stanley and Bernice Laura (Platt) Szefler; m. Christine M. Drezek, Dec. 26, 1970; children: David, Paul. BS, SUNY, Buffalo, 1971, MD, 1975. Resident pediat. Children's Hosp. Buffalo, 1975—77; postdoctoral fellow in clin. pharmacology and allergy immunology SUNY, Buffalo, 1977—79, asst. prof. pediat. and pharmacology, 1979—82; assoc. prof. pediat. and pharmacology U. Colo., Denver, 1982—90, prof. pediat., pharmacology, 1990—. Dir. clin. pharmacology Children's Hosp., Buffalo, 1979—82, Nat. Jewish Ctr. for Immunology and Respiratory Medicine, Denver, 1982—. Contbr. articles to profl. jours. Mem. steering com., Asthma Camp for Children Am. Lung Assn., Denver, 1987—96. Maj. USAR, 1979—88. Grantee NIH, 1980—84, 1990—, FDA, Denver, 1988—91. Fellow: Am. Acad. Pediat. (liaison mem. com. drugs), Am. Acad. Allergy, Asthma and Immunology (chmn. asthma, rhinitis and respiratory disease interest sect. 1995—97). Avocations: literature, history, reading. Office: Nat Jewish Med & Rsch Ctr Dept Pediat 1400 Jackson St Denver CO 80206-2761 Business E-Mail: szeflers@njc.org.

SZEGO, CLARA MARIAN, cell biologist, educator; b. Budapest, Hungary, Mar. 23, 1916; arrived in U.S., 1921, naturalized, 1927; d. Paul S. and Helen (Elek) S.; m. Sidney Roberts, Sept. 14, 1943. AB, Hunter Coll., 1937; MS, U. Minn., 1939, PhD, 1942; DSc (hon.), CUNY, 2007. Instr. physiology U. Minn., 1942-43; Minn. Cancer Rsch. Found. fellow, 1943—44; rsch. assoc. OSRD, Nat. Bur. Stds., 1944-45, Worcester Found. Exptl. Biology, 1945-47; rsch. instr. physiol. chemistry Yale U. Sch. Medicine, 1947-48; mem. faculty UCLA, 1948—, prof. biology, 1960—. Contbr. articles to profl. jours., book chapters and revs. Garvan fellow U. Minn., 1939; Guggenheim fellow, 1956; named Woman of Year in Sci. Los Angeles Times, 1957-58; named to Hunter Coll. Hall of Fame, 1987. Fellow AAAS; mem. Am. Physiol. Soc., Am. Soc. Cell Biology, Endocrine Soc. (CIBA award 1953), Soc. for Endocrinology (Gt. Britain), Biochem. Soc. (Gt. Britain), Internat. Soc. Rsch. Reproduction, Phi Beta Kappa (pres. UCLA chpt. 1973-74), Sigma Xi (pres. UCLA chpt. 1976-77). Home: 1371 Marinette Rd Pacific Palisades CA 90272-2627 Office: U Calif Dept Molecular Cell & Devel Biology Los Angeles CA 90095-1606 Business E-Mail: cmszego@ucla.edu.

SZKUTAK, TOM, corporate financial executive; married; 2 children. BS in Fin. magna cum laude, Boston U. Fin. mgmt. positions through exec. v.p. fin. GE Investments, CFO GE Lighting GE, 1982—2002; sr. v.p., CFO Amazon.com, Seattle, 2002—. Office: Amazon.com 1200 12th Ave S Seattle WA 98144

TABACHNICK, NORMAN DONALD, psychiatrist, educator; b. Toronto, Ont., Can., Feb. 21, 1927; BS, U. Ill., 1947, MD, 1949; PhD in Psychoanalysis, So. Calif. Psychoanalytic Inst., 1977. Diplomate Am. Bd. Med. Examiners, Am. Bd. Psychiatry and Neurology. Intern Michael Reese Hosp., 1949-50; resident in psychiatry U.S. VA Hosp., Bedford, Mass., 1950-51, U.S. AFB, Biloxi, Miss., 1951-52, L.A. County Gen. Hosp., 1953-54; staff psychiatrist Sepulveda VA Hosp., 1976-78; pvt. practice LA; mem. staff Resthaven Sanitarium, U. So. Calif. Med. Ctr., L.A. County, Westwood Hosp., Edgemont Hosp., Cedars-Sinai Med. Ctr.; mem. staff Neuropsychiatric Inst. UCLA; clin. prof. psychiatry U. So. Calif., LA, 1970-75, UCLA, 1975—2008, disting. clin. prof. psychiatry, 2008—. Hon. mem. med. staf. Resthaven Cmty. Med. Health Ctr., 1973; guest lectr. Cedars-Sinai Med. Ctr., 1985; mem. adv. bd. divsn. psychoanalysis Nassau County Med. Ctr.; mem. faculty Calif. Sch. Profl. Psychology, L.A. Ctr. Group Psychotherapy, Grad. Ctr. Child Devel. and Psychotherapy; cons. L.A. County Coroner's Office, 1963-70, Bur. Vocat. Rehab., Jewish Family Svc., profl. adv. bd. Resthaven Sanitarium, Marianne Frostig Sch. Ednl. Therapy, W. Valley Ctr. Edl. Therapy. Author: Accident or Suicide?, 1973; mem. edtl. bd. Jour. Acad. Psychoanalysis, book rev. editor, 1978; mem. edtl. bd. Internat. Jour. Psycho-analytic Psychotherapy, 1979-83; reviewer Am. Jour. Psychiatry, 1983—, Jour. Neuropsychiatry and Clin. Neuro Scis., 1988-90; contbr. articles to profl. jours.; cons. (film) Suicide Prevention: The Physician's Role, 1967, Highlights of the 1964 American Psychiatric Association; cons., participant The Thin Edge--Guilt., 1975; author book revs. Assoc. chief psychiatrist L.A. Suicide Prevention Ctr., 1968-76, prin. investigator; adv. com. Walter Briehl Human Rights Found., 1984; v.p., bd. dirs. Suicide Prevention Ctr., Inc.; bd. dirs. Inst. Suicide Prevention, L.A., 1996, chmn. funding a crisis line com., 1997; bd. dirs. We. divsn. Am. Found. Suicide Prevention, 1998, chair program com., 1999-2002. Recipient award for disting. creativity and leadership, Am. Found. for Suicide Prevention, 2003; rsch. grantee, Founds. Fund Rsch. Psychiatry, 1963, NIMH, 1970. Fellow Am. Psychiatric Assn. (life), Am. Acad. Psychoanalysis (pres. 1974, chmn. nominating com. 1975, trustee, chmn. com. on rsch., mem. editl. bd. The Acad., presdl. citation 1975); mem. Internat. Psychoanalytic Assn., Internat. Assn. Suicide Prevention, Am. Psychoanalytic Assn. (cert., mem. com. liason with AAAS 1977-80), Am. Assn. Suicidology, (founder, mem. editl. bd. Life-Threatening Behavior, cert. recognition 1996) Inst. Contemporary Psychoanalysis (founding mem., trustee 1990-93), So. Calif. Psychoanalytic Inst. (pres., tng. and supervising analyst, selection rsch. clin. assocs. com., dir. rsch. divsn. 1970-81, chief investigator 1976-88, chmn. com. rsch. award stds. 1979, pres.-elect 1980, 86, pres. 1981, 87-90, mem. tng. and supr. analyst, new ctr. for psychoanalysis), Am. Coll. Psychiatrists, Med. Rsch. Assn. So. Calif., So. Calif. Psychiat. Soc. (consultation and violence panel), L.A. County Med. Assn. Office: 505 N Bonhill Rd Los Angeles CA 90049-2325 Office Phone: 310-472-5044. Personal E-mail: ndtmd@aol.com.

TABAZADEH, AZADEH, environmental scientist, researcher; b. Tehran, Iran, Feb. 17, 1965; came to U.S., 1982; d. Modjtaba and Fatema (Beigi) T.; m. Mark Z. Jacobson, Aug. 30, 1993; children: Dionna Shelly Jacobson, Daniel Forest Jacobson. BS in Chemistry, UCLA, 1988, MS in Chemistry, 1990, PhD, 1994. Rsch., tchg. asst. UCLA, 1989-94; postdoctoral NASA, Moffett Field, Calif., 1994-97, rsch. sci., 1997—. Lectr. in field. Contbr. articles to profl. jours. including Jour. Geophys. Rsch., Geophys. Rsch. Letters, Sci. NASA fellow, 1991-94, 94-97; recipient Presdl. Early Career award for Scientist and Engrs., 1998; named to Brilliant 10, Popular Science Mag., 2002. Mem. Am. Chem. Soc., Am. Geophysical Union (James B. Macelwane medal, 2001), Am. Assn. Aerosol Rsch., Air and Waste Mgmt. Assn., UCLA Chemist Assn. Achievements include discovery of narrow rings of cold air over the Earth's poles that help to form clouds which contribute to the destruction of the ozone layer. Fax: 650-604-3625. Business E-Mail: azadeh.tabazadeh-1@nasa.gov.

TACHDJIAN, RAFFI, pediatrician; b. July 8, 1969; BS, UCLA, 1992; MPH, Univ. Ala., Birmingham, 1994; MD, Morehouse Sch. Med., Atlanta, 2001. Cert. Am. Bd. Pediatrics, 2007. Epidemiologist in diphtheria surveillance Centers for Disease Control & Prevention, 1995—97; intern & resident in pediatrics Harvard Med. Sch., Mass. Gen. Hosp., 2001—04; fellow in pediatric immunology & rheumatology Mattel Children;s Hosp., UCLA, 2004—07. Vis. prof. Berklee Coll., Boston, 2004—; Chrysalis Mentor Am. Acad. of Allergy, Asthhma & Immunology, 2006. Contbr. articles to profl. jours. Mem.: Am. Acad. of Allergy, Asthma & Immunology, Am. Coll. of Allergy, Asthma & Immunology, Am. Acad. Pediatrics. Office: Mattel Children's Hosp MDCC 22-464 10833 LeConte Ave Los Angeles CA 90095-1752 Office Phone: 310-825-0731. Business E-Mail: rtachdjian@mednet.ucla.edu.

TACHNER, LEONARD, lawyer; b. Bklyn., Jan. 18, 1944; BEE, CCNY, 1965; MSEE, Calif. State U., Long Beach, 1969; JD, Western State U., Fullerton, Calif., 1973. Bar: Calif. 1973, US Patent Office 1972. Supr. electronic counter measures sect. Ford Aerospace Corp., Newport Beach, Calif., 1969—73; patent atty. Reed C. Lawlor, LA, 1973—76, Rockwell Internat. Corp., Anaheim, Calif., 1976—78; ptnr. Fischer, Tachner & Strauss, Newport Beach, 1978—84; pvt. practice Irvine, Calif., 1984—. Instr. intellectual property Calif. State U., Long Beach, 1979—82; com. maintenance profl. competence Calif. State Bar, 1978—81. Mem. editl. bd. Western State U. Law Rev., 1972—73, columnist Interface Age mag., 1979—82, Bus.-to-Bus. mag., 1983—85. Mem.: Orange County Patent Law Assn., Calif. Bar Assn., Greater Irvine Indsl. League, Phi Kappa Phi. Office: 17961 Sky Park Cir Ste 38-E Irvine CA 92614 Home Phone: 949-786-7767; Office Phone: 949-752-8525. Personal E-mail: ltachner@aol.com.

TAEKMAN, MICHAEL SEYMOUR, neurological surgeon; b. Chgo., June 30, 1937; s. Harry Joseph and Rose Anne (Sturner) T.; m. Ilene Roberta Erlich, Dec. 18, 1960; children: Jeffrey Marc, Jennifer Lynn, Jessica Beth. MD, U. Ill., Chgo., 1962. Diplomate Am. Bd. Neurol. Surgery. Intern U. Ill., Chgo., 1962—63, resident in gen. surgery, 1963—64, 1971; resident in neurosurgery U. Ill. Neuropsychiat. Hosp., Chgo., 1964—67; fellow U. Edinburgh, Scotland, 1967; attending neurosurgeon Chgo. Mcpl. Contagious Disease Hosp., 1967; pres. East Bay Med. Group, Berkeley, Calif., 1969—99. Asst. clin. prof. U. Calif., San Francisco, 1990-99, assoc. clin. prof., 1999—; instr. U. Ill., Chgo., 1963-67; lectr. U. Calif., Berkeley, 1975—1992; chmn. dept. surgery Childrens Hosp. Med. Ctr., Oakland, Calif., 1980-90; assoc. clin. prof., Stanford U., 1999—; assoc. prof. pediatric neurosurgery Leland Packard Childrens Hosp. Contbr. articles to profl. jours. Adv. mem. San Rafael Sch. Bd., 1976-77; med. examiner State Calif., Berkeley, 1976—, docent, chmn. acad. sci. Served to capt. USAF, 1964-71. Scholar Internat. Coll. Surgeons, 1967, Med. Rsch. Coun. Great Britain, 1967. Fellow ACS, Am. Assn. Neurol. Surgeons, Am. Assn. Pediatric Neurol. Surgeons; mem. Calif. Acad. Medicine, Alameda Contra Costa Med. Assn., Rafael Racket Club, Phi Eta Sigma. Republican. Jewish. Office: 4350 Clement St San Francisco CA 94121 Office Phone: 415-459-3616. Personal E-mail: michaeltaekman@sbcglobal.net.

TAFOYA, ARTHUR NICHOLAS, bishop; b. Alameda, N.Mex., Mar. 2, 1933; s. Nicholas and Rosita Tafoya. Student, St. Thomas Sem., Denver, Conception Sem., Mo. Ordained priest Archdiocese of Santa Fe, 1962; asst. pastor Holy Rosary Parish, Albuquerque, 1962-65; pastor Northern N.Mex., from 1965, San Jose Parish, Albuquerque; rector Immaculate Heart of Mary Sem., Santa Fe; ordained bishop, 1980; bishop Diocese of Pueblo, Colo., 1980—. Roman Catholic. Office: Diocese of Pueblo 1001 N Grand Ave Pueblo CO 81003-2915

TAFT, DAVID DAKIN, chemicals executive; b. Cleve., Mar. 27, 1938; s. Kingsley A. and Louise D. T.; m. Sararose Leonard, July 8, 1961; children: Amy Rose, Kingsley Leonard, Elisabeth. AB, Kenyon Coll., 1960; PhD in Chemistry, Mich. State U., 1963. Sr. rsch. chemist Archer-Daniels Midland, 1964-67; mgr. polymer rsch. Ashland Chem., 1967-72; dir. comml. devel. Gen. Mills Chems., 1972-74; v.p., dir. R&D, Henkel Corp., 1973-78, group v.p. consumer and splty. products, 1978-81, exec. v.p. chem. products div., dir., 1981-82; gen. mgr. materials div. Raychem Corp., Menlo Park, Calif., 1983-84; gen. mgr. Telecom group, 1983-86; v.p. Raychem Corp., 1984-93, v.p. manufacuturing, 1986-93; COO Landec Corp., Menlo Park, Calif., 1993—2001, 2005—; pres., COO Dock Resins Corp., 2001—02; COO Apio, Inc., 2002—05. Author: Fundamentals of Powder Coatings; bd. editors: Rsch. Mgmt. Jour.; patentee in field. Trustee Mpls. Soc. Fine Arts, 1981-83, Kenyon Coll., 1990—2002; vice chmn. Mem. Comml. Devel. Assn., Indsl. Research Inst., Am. Chem. Soc., Kenyon Alumni Assn. (pres. 1978), Circus Club. Republican. Office: Landec Corp 3603 Haven Ave Menlo Park CA 94025-1010 Office Phone: 650-261-3695. E-mail: dtaft@landec.com.

TAGGART, JENNIFER T., lawyer; b. Hammond, Ind., Oct. 8, 1968; d. William E. and Mary Beth (Silvian) T. BS, Calif. Polytechnic State Univ., 1990; JD cum laude, Southwestern Univ., 1995. Cert. engr., Ca. Environ. engr., Rocketdyne div. Rockwell Internat.; ptnr., environ. law practice Demetriou, Del Guercio, Springer & Francis LLP, LA. Contbr. articles to profl. jours. Commr. LA City Environ. Affairs Commn., 1996—2000, 2004—05, v.p., 2003—04, pres., 2000—02. Recipient GM Spirit award/Pres.'s award Calif. Poly., 1990, Rocketdyne Leadership award, 1991, Am. Jurisprudence Book award Constitutional Law I, 1992, Acad. Excellence Juvenile Law, 1993, Acad. Excellence in Environ. Law, 1994; named Outstanding Contbr. to Goals & Pub. Image of Sch. Engring., 1990; Paul Wildman scholar Southwestern U., 1991. Mem. ABA, ASME, Air & Waste Mgmt. Assn., Tau Beta Pi (pres. 1989-90). Home: Demetriou Del Guercio Springer & Francis 10th Fl 801 S Grand Ave Los Angeles CA 90017-4613 Office Phone: 213-624-8407. Office Fax: 213-624-0174. Business E-Mail: jtaggart@ddsffirm.com.

TAGGART, RICHARD J., retired paper company executive; BS, U. Wyo., 1967, MS in Agrl. Econs., 1970; grad. exec. mgmt. program, U. Wash. CPA. With ops. rsch. and systems devel. depts. Ford Motor Co., 1970—74; with Weyerhaeuser Co., Federal Way, Wash., 1974—, dir. investor rels., 1994—96, v.p. investor rels., 1996—98, v.p., treas., 1998—2001, v.p. fin., 2001—03, exec. v.p., CFO, 2003—07.

TAGOMORI, HOWARD H., protective services official; Chief of police, Maui, Hawaii; U.S. marshall Honolulu, 1999—. Office: US Marshall 300 Ala Moana Blvd Rm C101 Honolulu HI 96850-0101

TAJIK, A(BDUL) J(AMIL), cardiologist, educator; b. Pakistan, Apr. 8, 1943; MBBS, King Edward Med. Coll., Lahore, Pakistan, 1965. Cert. Internal Medicine, 1973, Cardiovascular Disease, 1973. Intern cardiology Hamilton Civic Hosp., 1966—67, resident, 1967—68; resident internal medicine Mayo Grad. Sch. Medicine, Mayo Clinic, Rochester, Minn., 1968—70, fellowship cardiovascular diseases, 1970—72; appointment Mayo Clinic, Rochester, Minn., St. Mary's Hosp., Rochester, Minn., Rochester Meth. Hosp.; cardiology Divsn. Cardiovascular Medicine Mayo Clinic, Scottsdale, Ariz. Thomas J. Watson, Jr., prof. medicine and pediatrics Mayo Med. Sch., Rochester, Minn. Contbr. articles to med. jours. Office: Mayo Clinic 13400 East Shea Blvd Scottsdale AZ 85259 Office Phone: 480-301-8000. Office Fax: 480-301-7006.

TAKAHASHI, MASATO, pediatric cardiologist, educator; b. Tokyo, Feb. 10, 1933; came to U.S., 1952; s. Noboru and Fujiko (Tarumoto) T.; m. Marcia Parnell, Jan. 16, 1966; children: Rumi Anne, Yuki Lynn. AB, Wabash U., 1956; MD, Ind. U., 1960. Attending physician Children's Hosp., LA, 1968—; prof. pediatrics,, Keck Sch. Medicine U. So. Calif., LA, 1986—2005, prof. pediat. emeritus, 2005—. Chmn. 4th Internat. Kawasaki Disease Symposium, 1991. Vol. Habitat for Humanity, San Fernando Valley, Calif., 1993-94, Am. Heart Assn. L.A., 1982-85, com. mem. 1991-93 (Disting. Achievement award 1983). Mem. Am. Acad. Pediatrics, Am. Coll. Cardiology, Meth. Avocations: long distance running, wood working. Office: Divsn Cardiology Children's Hosp LA MS#34 4650 Sunset Blvd Los Angeles CA 90027 Office Phone: 323-669-4634. Business E-Mail: mtakahashi@chla.usc.edu.

TAKASUGI, PATRICK A., state agency administrator; m. Suzanne Takasugi; children: Taylor, Cole, Paige. BA in Polit. Sci., Albertson Coll. of Idaho, 1971. Dir./sec. Idaho State Dept. Agr., 1996—. Served to capt. U.S. Army. Recipient Outstanding Young Farmer and Rancher award Idaho Farm Bur., 1979, Young Farmer of Idaho award Idaho Jaycees, 1981, Outstanding Svc. award Idaho Crop Improvement Assn., 1991, Disting. Alumni Svc. award Albertson Coll. Idaho, 1996; named to Idaho Co-op Hall of Fame, 2000. Mem. Idaho Farm Bur. Fedn. (v.p.), Idaho Farm Bur. (bd. dirs.), Canyon County Farm Bur. (pres.), Western Assn. State Dirs. Agr. (v.p., pres., sec.-treas.), Nat. Assn. State Dirs. Agr. (bd. dirs.), Idaho Crop Improvement Assn. (pres.), N.W. Alfalfa Seed Growers Assn. (pres.), Idaho Alfalfa Seed Growers Assn. (pres.). Office: Idaho Dept Agr PO Box 790 Boise ID 83701-0790

TAKASUGI, ROBERT MITSUHIRO, federal judge; b. Tacoma, Sept. 12, 1930; s. Hidesaburo and Kayo (Otsuki) T.; m. Dorothy O. Takasugi; children: Jon Robert, Lesli Mari. BS, UCLA, 1953; LLB, JD, U. So. Calif., 1959. Bar: Calif. bar 1960. Practiced law, Los Angeles, 1960-73; judge East Los Angeles Municipal Ct., 1973-75, adminstrv. judge, 1974, presiding judge, 1975; judge Superior Ct., County of Los Angeles, 1975-76; U.S. dist. judge U.S. Dist. Ct. (cen. dist.) Calif., 1976—. Nat. legal counsel Japanese Am. Citizens League; guest lectr. law seminars Harvard U. Law Sch. Careers Symposium; commencement spkr.; mem. Legion Lex U. So. Calif. Law Ctr.; mem. Civil Justice Reform Act and Alt. Dispute Resolution Com., mem. Adv. Com. on Codes of Conduct of the Jud. Conf. of the U.S., 1987-92, Code of Conduct of Judges. Mem. editorial bd. U. So. Calif. Law Rev., 1959; contbr. articles to profl. jours. Calif. adv. com. Western Regional Office, U.S. Commn. on Civil Rights, 1983-85; chmn. blue ribbon com. for selection of chancellor L.A. C.C. With U.S. Army, 1953-55. Harry J. Bauer scholar, 1959; recipient U.S. Mil. Man of Yr. award for Far East Theater U.S. Army, 1954, Jud. Excellence award Criminal Cts. Bar Assn., Disting. Svc. award Asian Pacific Ctr. and Pacific Clinics, 1994, Freedom award Sertoma, 1995, Pub. Svc. award Asian Pacific Am. Legal Ctr. So. Calif., 1995, cert. of merit Japanese-Am. Bar Assn., Lifetime Achievement award, 2000, Trailblazer award So. Calif. region NAPABA, 1995, Spl. award Mex.-Am. Bar Assn., 1996, Spirit of Excellence award ABA, 1998, Pub. Svc. award Japanese Am. Citizens League, 1999, lifetime achievement award Japanese-Am. Bar Assn., 2000, PACE-Setter award Pacific Asian Consort. in Employment, 2003, Individual Diversity award State Bar Calif., 2004; named Judge of Yr. Century City Bar Assn., 1995. Mem. U. So. Calif. Law Alumni Assn. (dir.), Criminal Cts. Bar Assn. (Jud. Excellence award 2002, Jud. Courage award 2003). Office: US Dist Ct 312 N Spring St Los Angeles CA 90012-4701

TAKENAKA, TOSHIKO, lawyer, educator; b. Tokyo, July 10, 1958; LLB, Seikei Univ., Tokyo, 1981; LLM, Univ. Wash., 1990, PhD, 1992. Bar: N.Y. 1993. Patent preparation analyst Texas Instruments Japan, 1981—86; assoc. Yamasaki Law & Patent Office, Tokyo, 1987—89; vis. rsch. assoc. U. Tokyo, 1999; adj. prof. George Washington U., 1998; vis. scholar US Ct. Appeals Fed cir., 1998; assoc. prof. U. Washington Sch. Law, 1993—2003, W. Hunter Simpson prof., 2003—, dir. Ctr. Advanced Study & Rsch. Intellectual Property; vis. scholar Max Planck Inst., Munich; vis. prof. Wasenda U., Tokyo, 2003—. Contbr. articles to prof. jour. Mem.: Internat. Assn. for Advancement of Tchg. & Rsch. in Intellectual Property, Am. Intellectual Property Law Assn. (mem. exec. com., Intellectual Property sect.), N.Y. State Bar Assn., Assn. Am. Law Sch. Office: University of Washington Law School 1100 NE Campus Pky Seattle WA 98118

TAKESH, FAHI, lawyer; b. Teheran, Iran, Sept. 12, 1969; BA magna cum laude, UCLA, 1992; JD, Loyola Law Sch., 1996. Bar: Calif. 1996. Ptnr., family law practice Harris Ginsberg LLP, LA. Bd. dir., v.p., pres.-elect Harriet Buhai Ctr. for Family Law. Contbg. editor: Calif. Evidence for the Family Law Lawyer, LA County Bar Assn., 1998. Named a Rising Star, So. Calif. Super Lawyers, 2006. Mem.: ABA, State Bar Calif., LA County Bar Assn., Santa Monica Bar Assn., Phi Beta Kappa. Office: Harris Ginsberg LLP Ste 1870 6500 Wilshire Blvd Los Angeles CA 90048 Office Phone: 310-444-6333. Office Fax: 310-444-6330. Business E-Mail: ftakesh@harris-ginsberg.com.

TAKIS, STEPHANIE, state legislator; b. Salt Lake City, Oct. 16, 1944; Member, Aurora Elec Comn, formerly; member, Citizens Advisor Budget Committee, formerly; congress liaison asst, United States Department Commerce, formerly; staff asst, United States Senate Banking, Housing & Urban Affairs Committee, formerly; mem-at-lg, Aurora City Coun, 89-93; Colorado State Representative, District 36, 96-01, member, Bus Affairs & Labor & Finance Committees, Govt Mil Transportation Committee & Audit Committee, formerly, Colorado House Representative; Colorado State Senator, District 25, 01-, chairwoman, Transportation Committee, member, Bus, Labor & Technology, Legislature Audit and Joint Computer Committees, currently, Colorado State Senate.Financial Specialist, Federal Emergency Management Agency, formerly; management analyst, Fitzsimons Army Med Center, formerly; exec secretary, Association for Experiential Education, formerly; director, Humana Hosp/Aurora Regional Med Center, formerly; member, Spirit of Aurora Bd, Fitzsimons Redevelop Advisor Committee, Aurora Rehabilitation Authority. Democrat. Mailing: State Capitol 200 E Colfax Denver CO 80203 E-mail: stakis@sni.net; stephanie.takis.senate@state.co.us.

TAKUMI, ROY MITSUO, state legislator; b. Honolulu, Oct. 13, 1952; m. Wanda A. Kutaka; children: Aisha, Jaron. BA, Friends World Coll., 1991; MPA, U. Hawaii, 1993. Laborer Pearl Harbor Naval Shipyard; cmty. organizer Osaka, Japan, 1977-83; tchr. ESL; program dir. Am. Friends Svc. Com., Honolulu, 1984-90; polit. dir. Hawaii State AFL-CIO, Honolulu, 1990-92, comms. dir., 1992—; mem. Dist. 36 Hawaii House of Reps., Honolulu, 1992—. Precinct pres. Dem. Party; del. Dem. Party State Conv. Democrat. Office: Hawaii State Capitol 415 South Beretania St Rm 444 Honolulu HI 96813 Office Phone: 808-586-6170. Business E-Mail: reptakumi@capitol.hawaii.gov.

TALBOT, STEPHEN HENDERSON, television producer, documentary filmmaker, writer; b. Hollywood, Calif., Feb. 28, 1949; s. Lyle and Margaret (Epple) T.; m. Pippa Gordon; children: Dashiell, Caitlin. BA, Wesleyan U., 1970. Asst. to pres., lectr. Am. studies SUNY, Old Westbury, 1970-73; reporter Internews, Berkeley, Calif., 1973-79; producer, reporter KQED-TV, San Francisco, 1980-89; producer, writer Frontline (PBS), San Francisco, 1992—2008; series editor Frontline World, 2002—08; lectr. U. Calif. Berkeley, Grad. Sch. Journalism, 2004—08; pres. Talbot Players, 2008—. Appeared in Leave It To Beaver as Gilbert, 1958-63, also Twilight Zone, Perry Mason, Lassie, others; correspondent Frontline Diet Wars, 2004; prodr., co-writer for Frontline: The Best Campaign Money Can Buy (Columbia U. Dupont award), 1992, Rush Limbaugh's America, 1995, The Long March of Newt Gingrich, 1996, Justice for Sale, 1999 (Gold medal Houston Internat. Film Festival 2000); writer, co-prodr.: (PBS-TV) Beryl Markham, 1986, Ken Kesey, 1987, Carlos Fuentes, 1989, Maxine Hong Kingston, 1990, John Dos Passos, 1994, Frontline: Spying on Saddam, 1999; sr. prodr. Iraq: Saddam's Road to Hell (Emmy award 2007), Libya: Out of the Shadow (Emmy award 2007); prodr., writer: The Case of Dashiell Hammett, 1982 (Peabody award, Edgar Allan Poe award), 1968: The Year That Shaped a Generation, 1998, Frontline: The Battle Over School Choice, 2000 (First prize Edn. Writers Assn.); co-prodr., reporter: Broken Arrow, 1980 (George Peabody & George Polk award); co-prodr., co-writer The Sixties, 2005, others; contbr. articles to mags. including Salon, Washington Post Mag., San Francisco Chronicle and Frontline World Web Site. Recipient Thomas Storke Internat. Journalism award World Affairs Coun. No. Calif., San Francisco, 1983, 86, Golden Gate award San Francisco Film Festival, 1986, 89, Emmy award NATAS, 1980-83, 87-88, 90-91, 2007, Online Journalism award Columbia U, Edward R. Murrow award, Overseas Press Club, NYC for Frontline World series, Webby award, 2008. Mem. Writer's Guild Am. West, Am. Fedn. TV and Radio Artists. Office: Talbot Players 916 Kearny St 501 San Francisco CA 94133 Office Phone: 415-788-9602. Business E-Mail: steve@talbotplayers.com.

TALLMAN, RICHARD C., federal judge, lawyer; b. Oakland, Calif., 1953; s. Kenneth A. and Jean M. Tallman; m. Cynthia Ostolaza, Nov. 14, 1981. BSc, U. Santa Clara, 1975; JD, Northwestern U., 1978. Bar: Calif. 1978, Wash. 1979, US Dist. Ct. (no. dist.) Calif. 1979, US Dist. Ct. (we. dist.) Wash. 1979, US Dist. Ct. Hawaii 1986, US Ct. Fed. Cl. 1999, US Ct. Appeals (9th cir.) 1979, US Dist. Ct. (ea. dist.) Wash. 1998, US Supreme Ct. 1997. Law clk. to Hon. Morrell E. Sharp US Dist. Ct. (we. dist.) Wash., Seattle, 1978—79; trial atty. US Dept. Justice, Washington, 1979—80; asst. US atty. (we. dist.) Wash., Seattle, 1980—83; assoc., then ptnr. Schweppe, Krug & Tausend, PS, Seattle, 1983—89; mem. Bogle & Gates, PLLC, Seattle, 1990—99; ptnr. Tallman & Severin, LLP, Seattle, 1999—2000; apptd. US cir. judge US Ct. Appeals (9th cir.), 2000—. Chmn. western dist. Wash. Lawyer Reps. to Ninth Cir. Jud. Conf., 1996—97. Instr. Nat. Pk. Svc. Seasonal Ranger Acad., Everett, Mt. Vernon, Wash., 1983—93; chmn. Edmonds C.C. Found., Lynnwood, Wash., 1990—92; gen. counsel Seattle-King County Crime Stoppers, 1987—99; mem. exec. bd. Chief Seattle coun. Boy Scouts Am., 1997—; chmn. US Jud. Conf. Adv. Com. Criminal Rules, 2007—. Mem.: Fed. Judges Assn. (bd. dirs. 2002—06), King County Bar Assn., Fed. Bar Assn. (we. dist. trustee 1992—93, v.p. 1994, pres. 1995), Wash. Athletic Club, Rainier Club. Office: Park Place Bldg 1200 Sixth Avenue 21st FL Seattle WA 98101-3123

TALMADGE, PHILIP ALBERT, retired judge, state senator; b. Seattle, Apr. 23, 1952; s. Judson H., Jr. and Jeanne C. Talmadge; m. Darlene L. Nelson, Sept. 6, 1970; children: Adam, Matthew, Jessica, Jonathan, Annemarie. BA magna cum laude, Yale U., 1973; JD, U. Wash., 1976. Bar: Wash. 1976. Atty. Karr Tuttle Campbell, 1976—89; pres. Talmadge & Cutler, P.S., 1989—95; senator State of Wash., 1979—94; justice Supreme Ct. Wash., 1995—2001; ptnr. Talmadge Law Group PLLC, 2001—. Author: The Nixon Doctrine and the Reaction of Three Asian Nations, 1973; editor: Law Rev., 1975—76; contbr. articles to profl. jours. Chair Senate Judiciary Com., 1981, 1983—87, Senate Health and Human Svcs. Com., 1992—95, Wash. Senate, 1978—94, ways and means com. Fellow: Am. Assn. Appellate Lawyers; mem.: Wash. Appellate Lawyers Assn., King County Bar Assn., Wash. State Bar Assn. Office: Talmadge Law Group PLLC 18010 Southcenter Pkwy Tukwila WA 98188

TALMAGE, DAVID WILSON, retired microbiologist, educator, dean; b. Kwangju, Korea, Sept. 15, 1919; s. John Van Talmage and Eliza (Emerson) Talmage; m. LaVeryn Marie Hunicke, June 23, 1944; children: Janet, Marilyn, David, Mark, Carol. Student, Maryville Coll., Tenn., 1937—38; BS, Davidson Coll., NC, 1941; MD, Washington U., St. Louis, 1944. Intern Ga. Baptist Hosp., 1944—45; resident medicine Barnes Hosp., St. Louis, 1948—50, fellow medicine, 1950—51; asst. prof. pathology U. Pitts., 1951—52; asst. prof., then assoc. prof. medicine U. Chgo., 1952—59; prof. medicine U. Colo., 1959—, prof. microbiology, 1960—86, disting. prof., 1986—, chmn. dept., 1963—65, assoc. dean, 1966—68, dean, 1969—71; dir. Webb-Waring Lung Inst., 1973—83, assoc. dean for rsch., 1983—86. Mem. nat. council Nat. Inst. Allergy and Infectious Diseases, NIH, 1963—66, 1973—77. Author (with John Cann): Chemistry of Immunity in Health and Disease; editor: Jour. Allergy, 1963—67; editor: (with M. Samter) Immunological Diseases. With M.C. AUS, 1945—48. Scholar Markle, 1955—60. Mem.: Am. Assn. Immunologists, Am. Acad. Allergy, Inst. Medicine, NAS, Alpha Omega Alpha, Phi Beta Kappa. Home Phone: 303-388-1898. Home Fax: 303-388-6955.

TALWALKAR, ABHI Y. (ABHIJIT Y. TALWALKAR), computer company executive; b. Pune, India, 1965; BEE, Oreg. State Univ., 1985. Sr. engring., mktg. mgmt. Sequent Computer Sys. (now part of IBM), Bipolar Integrated Tech. Inc., Lattice Semiconductor Inc.; with Intel Corp., Santa Clara, Calif., 1993—2005, various positions including v.p., gen. mgr., enterprise platform group, v.p., co-gen. mgr., digital enterprise group; pres., CEO, dir. LSI Logic Corp., Milpitas, Calif., 2005—. Office: LSI Logic Corp 1621 Barber Ln Milpitas CA 95035 Office Phone: 408-433-8000.

TAM, ROD, state legislator; b. Honolulu, Oct. 3, 1953; s. Robert H.C. and Patsy Y.T. (Young) T.; m. Lynnette Tam, two children. BBA, U. Hawaii, 1977. Mem. Hawaii Ho. of Reps., Honolulu, 1982-94, Hawaii Senate, Dist. 13, Honolulu, 1994—; bus. agent Hawaii State Org. Police Ofcrs.; research analyst Hawaii Transportation Assoc.; admin. specialist Research Corp. U. Hawaii; budget analyst State Senate Ways & Means Com. Chmn. Neighborhood Bd., Honolulu, 1979-82; v.p. Chinese Physical Culture Assoc.; Kalihi-Liliha-Nuuanu-Palama Community Network. Named to Three Outstanding Young Persons o1 1983, Hawaii Jaycees, 1983; recipient Freedom award Sertoma Club, 1984, Librs. award for Leadership and Support, Librs. Assn. Hawaii, 1987. Democrat. Roman Catholic. Office: Hawaii State Capitol 415 S Beretania St Rm 220 Honolulu HI 96813-2407

TAMADDON, SINA, information technology executive; b. Aug. 27, 1957; V.p. Advanced Tech. Software Alliance Inc.; v.p. profl. svcs. NeXT, 1994—96, v.p. Europe, 1996—97; sr. v.p. worldwide svc. and support Apple Computer Inc., v.p. and gen. mgr. Newton Group, sr. v.p. applications Cupertino, Calif., 1997—. Office: Apple Computer Inc 1 Infinite Loop Cupertino CA 95014 Office Phone: 408-996-1010.

TAMBLYN, AMBER ROSE, actress; b. Santa Monica, Calif., May 14, 1983; d. Russ and Bonnie Tamblyn. Actor: (TV series) General Hospital, 1995—2001, Joan of Arcadia, 2003—05; (films) Live Nude Girls, 1995, Rebellious, 1995, Johnny Mysto: Boy Wizard, 1996, The Ring, 2002, The Sisterhood of the Traveling Pants, 2005, Stephanie Daley, 2006, The Grudge 2, 2006, Blackout, 2007, Spiral, 2007, Normal Adolescent Behavior, 2007, The Sisterhood of the Traveling Pants 2, 2008; (TV films) Prep, 2002, Babylon Fields, 2007, The Russell Girl, 2008, (guest appearances): Buffy the Vampire Slayer, 2001, Boston Public, 2002, Twilight Zone, 2002, CSI: Miami, 2002, Without a Trace, 2003, Punk'd, 2003. Office: c/o Hyler Mgmt 20 Ocean Park Blvd Ste 25 Santa Monica CA 90405

TAMBOR, JEFFREY, actor, theater director, educator; b. San Francisco, July 8, 1944; m. Kasia Ostlun, Oct. 6, 2001; children: Gabriel Kasper, Eve Julia. BA, San Francisco State; MFA, Wayne State U. Acting tchr. Milton Katselas' Acting Workshops, Beverly Hills, Calif. Actor (theatre) Sly Fox, 1976 (Broadway and L.A.), Measure for Measure, The Hands of the Enemy, Flea in Her Ear, American Mosaic; (films) ...And Justice For All, 1979, Saturday the 14th, 1981, Dreamchasers, 1982, The Man Who Wasn't There, 1983, Mr. Mom, 1983, No Small Affair, 1984, Desert Hearts, 1985, Three O'Clock High, 1987, Brenda Starr, 1989, Lisa, 1990, City Slickers, 1991, Life Stinks, 1991, Pastime, 1991, Article 99, 1992, Crossing the Bridge, 1992, The Webbers, 1993, A House in the Hills, 1993, Radioland Murders, 1994, Heavyweights, 1995, My Teacher's Wife, 1995, Big Bully, 1996, Dr. Dolittle, 1998, There's Something About Mary, 1998, Meet Joe Black, 1998, Muppets From Space, 1999, Teaching Mrs. Tingle, 1999, Girl Interrupted, 1999, Pollock, 2000, How the Grinch Stole Christmas, 2000, Never Again, 2001, Get Well Soon, 2001, Scorched, 2002, The Freshman, 2002, Malibu's Most Wanted, 2003, My Boss's Daughter, 2003, Nobody's Perfect, 2004, Hellboy, 2004, Funky Monkey, 2004, (voice) The SpongeBob SquarePants Movie, 2004, The King of Central Park, 2006, Slipstream, 2007, The Chubbchubbs Save Xmas, 2007, Superhero Movie, 2008, Hellboy II: The Golden Army, 2008, (voice) Monsters vs. Aliens, 2009; (TV series) The Ropers, 1979-80, Hill Street Blues, 1981-87, 9 to 5, 1982, Mr. Sunshine, 1986, (voice) Jonny Quest, 1986, Max Headroom, 1987-88, Studio 5-B, 1989, American Dreamer, 1990, The Larry Sanders Show, 1992-98 (Emmy award nominee 1993), Me & George, 1998, (voice) The Lionhearts, 1998, Everything's Relative, 1999, The Lot, 1999, (voice) Sammy, 2000, That Was Then, 2002, 3-South, 2002, Hollywood Squares (announcer), 2002-03, Arrested Development, 2003-06, Welcome to the Captain, 2008; (TV episodes) M*A*S*H, Barney Miller, L.A. Law, The Golden Girls, Empty Nest, Who's The Boss, Doogie Houser, M.D., Equal Justice, Murder She Wrote, Tales From The Crypt (Dead Right) (TV movies) Eddie and Herbert, 1977, Alcatraz: The Whole Shocking Story, 1980, A Gun in the House, 1981, The Star Maker, 1981, Pals, 1981, The Awakening of Candra, 1981, Take Your Best Shot, 1982, The Zertigo Diamond Caper, 1982, Cocaine: One Man's Seduction, 1983, Sadat, 1983, The Three Wishes of Billy Grier, 1984, Wildfire, 1986, A Quiet Little Neighborhood, a Perfect Little Murder, 1990, The Burden of Proof, 1992, 1775, 1992, (voice) Jonny's Golden Quest, 1993, Another Midnight Run, 1994, (voice) Jonny Quest vs. the Cyber Insects, 1995, The Man Who Captured Eichmann, 1996, Weapons of Mass Distraction, 1997, Eloise at the Plaza, 2003, Eloise at the Plaza, 2003, Eloise at Christmastime, 2003, The Muppets' Wonderful Wizard of Oz, 2005; (TV spls.) Living and Working in Space: The Countdown Has Begun; (TV miniseries) Robert Kennedy and His Times, 1985; dir. for numerous theatre companies including Seattle Repertory Theatre, Actors Theatre of Louisville, Milw. Repertory Theatre, Acad. Festival Theatre, Chgo., San Diego Shakespeare Festival, South Coast Repertory Theatre, Loeb Drama Ctr., Cambridge, Mass., Sky Light Theatre, L.A. Office: Care The Gersh Agency c/o Leslie Siebert 232 N Canon Dr Beverly Hills CA 90210-5302

TAMBS, LEWIS ARTHUR, diplomat, historian, educator; b. San Diego, July 7, 1927; s. Fred B. and Marguerite Johanna (Tambs) Jones; m. Phyllis Ann Greer, 1982. BS, U. Calif., Berkeley, 1953; MA, U. Calif., Santa Barbara, 1962, PhD, 1967. Plant engr. Std. Brands, San Francisco, 1953—54; pipeline engr. Creole Petroleum Co., Caracas, Maracaibo, Venezuela, 1954—57; gen. mgr. Cacyp, Maracaibo, 1957—59; instr. Creighton U., 1965—67, asst. prof., 1967—69; prof. history Ariz. State U., Tempe, 1969—82, 1987—2002, dir. Ctr. L.Am. Studies, 1972—76; cons. NSC, 1982—83; U.S. amb. to Colombia, 1983—85; U.S. amb. to Costa Rica, 1985—87; ret., 2002. Author: East European and Soviet Economic Affairs, 1975, Historiography, Method and History Teaching, 1975, Hitler's Spanish Legion, 1979; editor: United States Policy Toward Latin America, 1976, Inter-American Policy for the 80's; co-editor: Santa Fe IV, 2000, English translation of Karl Haushofer's Geopolitics of the Pacific, 2002; co-author periodical guides; contbr. articles to profl. jours. Bd. dirs. Ariz.-Mex. Commn., 1974-82, Coun. Inter-Am. Security, 1979-90. With U.S. Army, 1945-47, 50-51. Faculty grantee, Ariz. State U., 1970, 1971, 1974, 1978, 1979. Roman Catholic. E-mail: lewtambs@aol.com.

TAMKIN, CURTIS SLOANE, real estate development company executive; b. Boston, Sept. 21, 1936; s. Hayward and Etta (Goldfarb) T.; m. Priscilla Martin, Oct. 18, 1975; 1 child, Curtis Sloane. BA in Econs., Stanford U., Calif., 1958. V.p., treas., dir. Hayward Tamkin & Co., Inc., mortgage bankers, LA, 1963-70; mng. ptnr. Property Devel. Co., LA, 1970-82; pres. The Tamkin Co., 1982—2000; chmn. Tamkin Capital Group L.L.C., 1999—. Mem. bd. govs. Music Ctr. LA, 1974—98; pres. LA Master Chorale Assn., 1974—78; mem. vis. com. Stanford U. Librs., 1982—86; vice-chmn. bd. dirs., mem. exec. com. LA Philharm. Assn., 1985—2006, vice chmn. bd., 2004—06, chmn. bd. overseers, 2001—07. Lt. (j.g.) USNR, 1960—63. Mem.: Nat. Coun. World Wildlife Fund, Pacific Council Internat. Policy, L.A. Jr. C. of C. (dir. 1968—69), Founders League L.A. Music Ctr. (pres. 1988—98, chmn. emeritus 1998—, chevaliers 2008—), Hillcrest Country Club, Burlingame Country Club. Home: 1230 Stone Canyon Rd Los Angeles CA 90077-2920 Office: 9460 Wilshire Blvd Beverly Hills CA 90212-2732

TAMKIN, S. JEROME, manufacturing executive, consultant; b. LA, Apr. 19, 1926; s. William W. and Thelma (Brandel) T.; m. Judith Deborah, Mar. 23, 1963; children: Steven Marc, Windy Lynn, Gary William, Sherry Dawn. BS, U. So. Calif., 1950; MA, Fremont Coll., 1951, PhD, 1952; LLD., St. Andrews U., London, 1954. Rsch. staff chemistry dept. U. Calif., LA, 1943; rsch. chemist, analyst supr. synthetic rubber div. U.S. Rubber Co., 1943-44; rsch. engr. Coll. Engring., U. So. Calif., 1946-48; gen. mgr. Pan Pacific Oil Co., Long Beach, Calif., 1948-55; plant mgr. indsl. sales and mfg., 1953-55; v.p., sales mgr. Wilco Co., LA, 1948-55, v.p. charge indsl. sales and mfg.,

1953-55; v.p., sales mgr. Unit Chem. Corp., LA, 1955-56; pres. Phillips Mfg. Co. (merger Instl. Food Equipment Corp.), LA, 1957-62, Waste King Corp. (subs. Instl. Food Equipment Corp.), 1962-67; also dir.; v.p., dir. Dyna Mfg. Co., LA, 1962-68; pres., dir. Profl. Rsch. Inc., LA, 1965-73; exec. v.p. Am. Med. Internat., Inc., Beverly Hills, Calif., 1966-71, dir., 1966-89; sec., dir. Rodger Young, Inc., LA, 1971-77; pres., chmn. bd. TGT Petroleum Corp., Wichita, 1972—; pres., dir. Tamkin Cons. Corp., 1978—; owner, operator Tamkin Securities Co., 1979-86; vice chair bd., dir. Integrated Voice Solutions Inc., Chattanooga, 1991-96; bd. dirs. CAPP Care Inc., Newport Beach, Calif., 1991-99. Tech. cons. Daylin Inc., Beverly Hills, 1973-75; bd. dirs. Healthcare Decisions, Inc., Newport Beach, Calif., 1996-99. Contbr. articles to profl. jours.; patentee electronic gas detector, circuits for automatic control hazardous vapors. Cmty. warden W. Adams-Baldwin Hills Cmty. CD, 1950—52; bd. govs. West LA County coun. Boy Scouts Am., 1977—; bd. govs. Technion-Israel Inst. of Tech., 2001—; dep. sheriff L.A. County, 1949; city commr. L.A. Bd. Environ. Quality, 1972—73; bd. dirs. Sunair Home Asthmatic Children, Recovery Found., Fund for Higher Edn., U. of Judaism, 1999—, UCLA Brain Mapping Found., 1999—, UCLA Ctr. on Aging, LA, 2005—; bd. visitors UCLA Sch. Medicine, 1990—; exec. com. adv. coun. crime prevention LA Police, 1985—; trustee, bd. visitors U. Calif.-Irvine Coll. Medicine, 1989—; trustee Morehouse Sch. Medicine, 1995—2005, Scripps Found. for Medicine and Sci., 1996—. Officer USNR, 1944—46. Mem. AIM, Am. Mgmt. Assn., Inst. Aero. Scis., Am. Soc. Naval Engrs., Soc. Am. Mil. Engrs., Am. Chem. Soc., IEEE, Soc. Motion Picture and TV Engrs., Am. Inst. Chem. Engrs., Soc. Advancement Mgmt., U.S. Naval Inst., Calif. Scholarship Fedn. (life), Nat. Eagle Scout Assn., Sunrise Country Club, The Springs Country Club, Malibu Riding and Tennis Club, Alpha Eta Rho. Office: 2100 Sawtelle Blvd Ste 201 Los Angeles CA 90025-6264 Office Phone: 310-479-2555.

TAN, ENG MENG, immunologist, biomedical researcher; b. Seremban, Malaysia, Aug. 26, 1926; arrived in US, 1950; s. Ming Kee and Chooi Eng (Ang) T.; m. Liselotte Filippi, June 30, 1962; children: Philip, Peter. BA, Johns Hopkins U., 1952, MD, 1956. Intern Duke U., Durham, NC, 1956-57; resident, fellow Case-We. Res. U., Cleve., 1957-62; rsch. assoc. Rockefeller U., NYC, 1962—65; asst. prof. Washington U. Sch. Medicine, St. Louis, 1965—67; assoc. mem. and mem. Scipps Rsch. Inst., LaJolla, Calif., 1967—77; prof. Scripps Rsch. Inst., LaJolla, Calif., 1982—2006, prof. emeritus, 2006—; prof. U. Colo. Sch. Medicine, Denver, 1977-82. Chmn. allergy & immunology rsch. com. NIH, Bethesda, Md., 1982-84; mem. nat. arthritis adv. bd. HHS, Washington, 1981-85; hon. prof. Shanghai Jiao Dong U., Zhengzhou U., China. Contbr. chapters to books, articles to profl. jours. Recipient US Sr. Scientist award, Humboldt Found., Germany, 1986, Ciba-Giegy-Internat. League against Rheumatism award, 1989, Carol Nachman award, Wiesbaden, Germany, 1989, Lee Howley Sr. award, Arthritis Found., 1989, Paul Klemperer award and medal, NY Acad. Medicine, 1993, City Medicine award, Durham, NC, 1996, Disting. Med. Alumnus award, Duke U., 2000, Mayo Soley award, Western Soc. Clin. Investigation, 2002, Japan Rheumatism Found. Internat. prize, 2003, Meritorious Svc. award, European League Against Rheumatism, 2005, Lifetime Achievement award, 8th Internat. Lupus Congress, China, 2007; named to Nat. Lupus Hall Fame, 1984. Fellow AAAS; mem. Am. Coll. Rheumatology (pres. 1984-85, chmn. Blue Ribbon com. Future Acad. Rheumatology 1997-98, Disting. Investigator award 1991, Gold medal award 1998), Assn. Am. Physicians, Am. Soc. Clin. Investigation, Western Assn. Physicians (v.p. 1980-81), Am. Assn. Immunologists, Brazilian Soc. Rheumatology (hon.), Australian Rheumatism Assn. (hon.), Brit. Soc. Rheumatology (hon.), Mex. Nat. Acad. Medicine (hon.). Achievements include research on antibodies and antigens in cancer and in autoimmune diseases, systemic lupus erythematosus, scleroderma, Sjogren's syndrome, myositis and mixed connective tissue disease; relationship of autoantibodies to pathogenesis. Home: 8303 Sugarman Dr La Jolla CA 92037-2224 Office: Scripps Rsch Inst 10550 N Torrey Pines Rd La Jolla CA 92037-1000 Office Phone: 858-784-8686. Business E-Mail: emtan@scripps.edu.

TANABE, CHARLES Y., lawyer; b. Denver, Nov. 27, 1951; BA cum laude, U. Colo., 1973; JD, U. Calif., Berkeley, 1976. Bar: Colo. 1976. Atty. Sherman & Howard LLC, Denver; gen. counsel Liberty Media Corp., Englewood, Colo., 1999—2001, sr. v.p., sec., gen. counsel, 2001—07, exec. v.p., sec., gen. counsel, 2007—. Bd. dir. FUN Technologies Inc. Mem. ABA, Phi Beta Kappa. Office: Liberty Media Corp 12300 Liberty Blvd Englewood CO 80112

TANAKA, JOE SUEO, state legislator; b. Lahaina Maui, Hawaii, Sept. 15, 1941; m. Barbara Tanaka; children: Joanne, Aimee. AA, Golden West Coll.; BA in Econs. and Bus. Adminstrn., U. Hawaii, Hilo. Mem. Hawaii Senate, 1992—, asst. majority leader, 1992-93, mem. various coms., 1992-96, chair tourism and recreation com., 1993-96, vice chair transp. com., 1994, vice chair transp. & govt. affairs com., 1995-96; mem. Maui County Council, 1986-92. Mem. County Bd. Water Supply, Hawaii Criminal Justice Commn., Mayor's Com. for Betterment of Youth; mem. PTSA and band boosters Lihikai Sch.; mem. adv. bd. Family Cmty. Leadership; bd. dirs. Maui Econ. Opportunity, Inc., Maui Visitors Bur., Maui Econ. Bus. Devel.; chmn. econ. devel. and water devel. County Coun., 1986-88, chmn. econ. devel. and agr., 1988-90, chmn. human svcs., pks. and housing com., 1990-92. With U.S. Army, Vietnam. Democrat. Office: Hawaii State Capitol 415 S Beretania St Rm 223 Honolulu HI 96813-2407

TANAKA, KOUICHI ROBERT, hematologist, educator; b. Fresno, Calif., Dec. 15, 1926; s. Kenjiro and Teru (Arai) T.; m. Grace Mutsuko Sakaguchi, Oct. 23, 1965; children: Anne M., Nancy K., David K. BS, Wayne State U., 1949, MD, 1952. Cert. in internal medicine Am. Bd. Internal Medicine, 1961, recertified in internal medicine Am. Bd. Internal Medicine, 1974, cert. in hematology Am. Bd. Internal Medicine, 1972. Intern Los Angeles County Gen. Hosp., 1952—53; resident, fellow Detroit Receiving Hosp., 1953—57; instr. Sch. Medicine UCLA, 1957—59, asst. prof. medicine, 1959—61, assoc. prof. medicine, 1961—68, prof. Sch. Medicine, 1968—97, prof. emeritus, 1998—. Chief hematology divsn. Harbor-UCLA, Torrance, Calif., 1961—97, chief hematology, 1998—2000. Author 137 rsch. publs. Served US Army, 1946—48. Recipient Disting. Alumni Svc. award, Wayne St. U. Sch. Med. Alumni Assn., Med. Alumni Assn. Disting. Svc. award, UCLA. Master ACP (gov. So. Calif. region I 1993-97); mem. Am. Fedn. Med. Rsch., We. Soc. Clin. Investigation, Am. Soc. Hematology, Internat. Soc. Hematology, We. Assn. Physicians, Am. Soc. Clin. Investigation, Assn. Am. Physicians, Sigma Xi, Alpha Omega Alpha. Achievements include research on red cell metabolism. Home: 4 Cayuse Ln Rancho Palos Verdes CA 90275-5172 Office: Dept Med Box 400 Harbor-UCLA Med Ctr Torrance CA 90509 Home Phone: 310-377-7687; Office Phone: 310-222-3695.

TANAKA, RICHARD KOICHI, JR., architect, planner; b. San Jose, Calif., Oct. 16, 1931; s. Richard Inoru and Mae Yoshiko (Koga) T.; m. Barbara Hisako Kumagai, Oct. 7, 1961; children: Craig, Todd, Sandra, Trent. BArch, U. Mich., Ann Arbor, 1954; M in Urban Planning, Calif. State U., San Jose, 1978. Arch., planner Steinberg Group, San Jose, L.A., 1954. Chair, bd. dirs. Happi House Restaurants, Inc., 1972—. Author: American on Trial, 1988. Dir. Human Rels. Com., San Jose, 1969-73; past pres., trustee East Side HS Dist., San Jose, 1971-92, Japanese Am. Citizens League, San Jose; dir., pres. Bicentennial Com., San Jose, 1974-77; past pres. Tapestry and Talent, 1976-80; mem. bd. govs. NCCJ, San Jose, 1976—, Boy Scouts Am., San Jose, 1978—; bd. dirs. Santa Clara County Sch. Bd. Assn., 1980—, Calif. CC Trustees, 1993-2002, pres., 1997-98; pres. Internment of Local Japanese Ams., San Jose, 1984—; trustee San Jose/Evergreen CC, 1992—, pres., 1993-94, 97-98, 2001-02, 07-08. Mem. AIA, Am. Planning Inst., Constrn. Specification Inst., Rotary. Avocations: golf, painting. Home: 14811 Whipple Ct San Jose CA 95127-2570 Office: 60 Pierce Ave San Jose CA 95110-2819 Personal E-mail: rktanaka@sbcglobal.net.

TANANBAUM, JAMES, medical engineering company executive; b. NYC, May 5, 1963; s. David J. and Elizebeth Zelda (Belfer) T. BS cum laude, Yale U., 1985; postgrad. health scis., tech. program, Harvard U., Cambridge, 1985-89; postgrad., Harvard Bus. Sch., Boston, 1989—. Rsch. asst. MIT, Cambridge, 1986—; chmn. Med. Engring. Devices, Inc., Boston, 1987—. Computer cons. Nat. Retirement Programs, Inc., N.Y.C., 1981—, Software Engring., Inc., N.Y.C., 1985, Clin. Computing Ctr., Inc., Boston, 1985—; student pres. Health, Scis., and Tech. Program, Harvard U. and MIT, 1986—. Mem. Sigma Xi. Office: Advanced Medical Inc 901Gateway Blvd South San Francisco CA 94080

TANCREDO, TOM (THOMAS GERARD TANCREDO), retired United States Representative from Colorado; b. North Denver, Dec. 20, 1945; s. Gerald and Adeline (Lombardi) Tancredo; m. Jackie Tancredo; 2 children. BA in Polit. Sci., U. North Colo., 1968. Tchr. Drake Jr. H.S.; mem. Colo. State Ho. Reps., 1977-81; regional rep. US Dept. Edn., 1981-93; mem. US Congress from 6th Colo. Dist., 1999—2009; mem. edn. and workforce, budget, internat. rels., and resources committees. Author: In Mortal Danger: The Battle for America's Border and Security, 2006. Republican. Evangelical Presbyterian Church.*

TANENBAUM, BASIL SAMUEL, engineering educator; b. Providence, Dec. 1, 1934; s. Harry Milton and Rena Ada (Herr) Tanenbaum; m. Carol Binder, Aug. 26, 1956; children: Laurie, Stephen, David. BS summa cum laude, Brown U., 1956; MS, Yale U., 1957, PhD in Physics, 1960. Staff physicist Raytheon Co., Waltham, Mass., 1960—63; prof. engring. Case We. Res. U., Cleve., 1963—75; prof. Harvey Mudd Coll., Claremont, Calif., 1975—2003, dean faculty, 1975—93, Norman F. Sprague, Jr. prof. life scis., 1996—2003, prof. emeritus, 2003—; interim assoc. dean joint sci. dept. The Claremont Colls., 2003—05, adj. prof., 2005—. Vis. scientist Arecibo (P.R.) Obs. Cornell U., 1968—69; vis. assoc. prof. Northwestern U., Evanston, Ill., 1970; mem. sci. adv. com. Nat. Astronomy and Ionosphere Ctr., 1972—77; dir. Minority Engrs. Indsl. Opportunity Program, 1973—75; mem. sci. adv. com. Calif. Poly. Inst., Pomona, 1976—87; mem. engring. and sci. adv. com. Calif. State U., Fullerton, 1976—87; dir. summer sci. program Thacher Sch., Ojai, Calif., 1977—82; vis. scholar Beckman Laser Inst. U. Calif., Irvine, Calif., 1993—94, 1998, 2006—, mem. biomed. engring. adv. com., 2000—05; mem. nat. adv. com. Rowan Coll., Glassboro, NJ, 1993—2000; mem. Eisenhower adv. com. Calif. Postsecondary Edn. Com., 1993—97; pres.'s adv. coun. Olin Coll. Engring., Needham, Mass., 2001—08, vice chmn., 2001, chmn., 2002—06; cons. in field. Author: Plasma Physics, 1967. Trustee Western U. Health Scis., Pomona, 1997—2004. Recipient Wittke Tchg. award, Case We. Res. U., 1973; Woods Hole Oceanog. Inst. fellow, 1959, NSF fellow, Yale U., 1956—60, Sr. Sterling fellow, 1959. Mem.: AAUP, IEEE, AAAS, Am. Soc. Engring. Edn., Am. Phys. Soc., Sigma Xi (Rsch. award 1969). Home: 611 W Delaware Dr Claremont CA 91711-3458 Office: Harvey Mudd Coll 301 E Platt Dr Claremont CA 91711-5901 Office Phone: 909-607-0716. Business E-Mail: sam_tanenbaum@hmc.edu.

TANG, MAN-CHUNG, civil engineer, company executive; b. Xiao Qing, China, Feb. 22, 1938; came to U.S., 1968; s. Yu-Fung and Jing Tse Tang; m. Yee-Yun Fung, Aug. 26, 1966; children: Chin-Chung, Chin-Ning. BSc, Chu-Hai Coll., Hong Kong, 1959; DLitt (hon.), Chu-Hai U., Hong Kong, 1997; MS, Tech. U. Darmstadt, Germany, 1964, PhD, 1965; D of Engring. (hon.), Kassel U., Germany, 2001. Registered profl. engr., N.Y., Mass., Fla., Ill., Wash., others. Bridge engr. GHH, Germany, 1965-68; sr. engr. Severud & Assocs., NYC, 1968-70; v.p., chief engr. Dyckerhoff & Widmann, NYC, 1970-78; pres. DRC Cons. Inc., NYC, 1978—; chmn. bd. T.Y. Lin Internat., San Francisco, 1995—. Contbr. more than 100 articles to profl. jours. Recipient Leadership award Am. Segmental Bridge Inst., 1991, Roebling Life Achievement award Internat. Bridge Conf., 1998. Mem. ASCE (hon.), named N.Y. Civil Engr. of Yr. 1989, Roebling award 1999, Nat. Acad. Engring. (life), Chinese Acad. Engring. (life mem.). Achievements include pioneer work in design and construction of cable-stayed and segmental bridges. Office: TY Lin Internat Two Harrison St Ste 500 San Francisco CA 94105 Office Phone: 415-291-3707. E-mail: mtang@tylin.com.

TANGHERLINI, TIMOTHY R., literature educator; b. Durham, NC, Oct. 2, 1963; AB magna cum laude, Harvard U., 1985; MA in Scandinavian Studies, U. Calif., Berkeley, 1986, PhD, 1992. Cert. in Modern Icelandic, Korean lang. Video producer/editor Harvard-Danforth Ctr. for Teaching and Learning/Harvard U., Cambridge, Mass., 1981-85; rsch. asst. U. Calif., Berkeley, 1987, teaching asst. in Danish, 1986-91; vis. asst. prof. Scandinavian sect. Program in Folklore/Myth UCLA, 1991—. Contbr. articles to profl. jours. John Harvard scholar, 1984, Luce scholar, 1987-88, Bernard Osher Found. fellow, Am. Scandinavian Found. fellow, 1990, Regents fellow U. Calif., Berkeley, 1985, 91; recipient other grants and awards. Mem. MLA, Am. Anthrop. Assn., Am. Folklore Soc., Assn. Asian Studies, Foreningen Danmarks Folkeminder, Internat. Soc. for Folk Narrative Rsch., Nordic Inst. Folklore, Soc. for Advancement of Scandinavian Study. Office: UCLA Scandinavian Sect 332 Royce Hall Los Angeles CA 90024

TANI, LLOYD YASUO, pediatrician, educator; b. LA, Aug. 6, 1956; s. Lorraine Hiroko Tani; m. Yvette Friede Tani, May 30, 1990; children: Ryan Yasuo, Jaclyn Christine. BA in Biology, UCLA, 1978; MD, U. Calif., LA, 1982. Diplomate Nat. Bd. Med. Examiners, 1986, Am. Bd. Pediatrics, 1987, pediatric cardiology Am. Bd. Pediatrics, 1991, lic. Utah, 1989. Internship and residency pediat. Baylor Coll. Medicine, 1982—86, fellowship pediat. cardiology, 1986—89; pediat. cardiologist Sch. Medicine U. Utah, 1989—, prof. pediat. Sch. Medicine, 1989—, assoc. dir. divsn. pediat. cardiology, 2002—07, dir. divsn. pediat. cardiology, 2007—. Mem.: Utah Med. Assn., Am. Acad. Pediatrics, Am. Soc. Echocardiography, Am. Heart Assn. Office: University of Utah School of Medicine 100 N Medical Drive Salt Lake City UT 84113 Office Fax: 801-662-5404.

TANNER, GLORIA TRAVIS, state legislator; b. Atlanta, July 16, 1935; d. Marcellus and Blanche Arnold Travis; m. Theodore Ralph Tanner, 1955 (dec.); children: Terrance Ralph, Tanvis Renee, Tracey Lynne. BA, Met. State Coll., 1974; MUA, U. Colo., 1976. Office mgr. Great Western Mfg. Co., Denver, 1965-67; writer Rage mag., 1969-70; reporter, feature writer Denver Weekly News, 1970-75; dir. East Denver Cmty. Office, 1974—; also real estate agt.; mem. Colo. Ho. of Reps., 1985-94; mem. from dist. 33 Colo. Senate, 1994—. Minority caucus chairwoman; mem. appropriations, bus. affairs, labor coms. Dist. capt. Denver Dem. Com., Colo., 1973-75; chairwoman Senatorial Dist. 3 Dem. Com., 1974-82; adminstrv. aide Colo. State Senator Regis Groff, Denver, 1974-82; alt. del. Dem. Nat. Conv., 1976, del., 1980; commr. Colo. Status of Women, 1977—; chairwoman Colo. Black Women for Polit. Action, 1977—; exec. asst. to Lt. Gov., 1978-79; mem. adv. bd. United Negro Coll. Fund, Colo. State Treas. Served USAF, 1952-55. Recipient Outstanding Cmty. Leadership award Scott's Meth. Ch., 1974, Tribute to Black Women award, 1980; named Woman of Yr., Colo. Black Women Caucus, 1974. Mem. Colo. Black Media Assn. (pub. dir. 1972—), Reginas' Civic Club (founder, first pres. 1959—, Outstanding Woman of Yr. 1975), Nat. Assn. Real Estate Brokers. Roman Catholic. Democrat. Office: State Senate 200 E Colfax Ave Ste 274 Denver CO 80203-1716

TANNER, R. MARSHALL, lawyer; b. Santa Monica, Calif., Dec. 4, 1946; s. Stanley Robert and Kathryn (Lau) Tanner; m. Colleen Bonner, Sept. 3, 1969; children: David, Brent, Julie, Glenn, Scott, Holly. BA, Brigham Young U., 1970; JD, UCLA, 1977. Ptnr. Lawler, Felix & Hall, LA, 1977-86, Pettit & Martin, Newport Beach, Calif., 1986-95, Sheppard, Mullin, Richter & Hampton, 1995—. Lt. USNR, 1970-74. Mem. Calif. State Bar Assn., Orange County Bar Assn. Mem. Lds Ch. Office: Sheppard Mullin Richter & Hampton 650 Town Center Dr Fl 4 Costa Mesa CA 92626-1993 Business E-Mail: mtanner@smrh.com.

TANNO, JOHN W., university librarian; b. Bklyn., Sept. 28, 1939; s. John C. and Hildegarde (Whitaker) T.; children: Maria Elena, Luisa. AA, Phoenix Jr. Coll., 1959; MusB, Ariz. State U., 1963; MusM, U. So. Calif., 1965, MLS, 1970. Music librarian SUNY, Binghamton, 1965-68; order librarian Claremont Colls., Calif., 1970; music librarian U. Calif., Riverside, 1970-72, head monographs sect., 1972-78, asst. univ. librarian, 1978-83, assoc. univ. librarian, 1983—2002, assoc. univ. libr. Davis, 2002—. Mem. ops. com. So. Regional Library Facility, 1984—, task group Intercampus Transp., 1984, negotiating team CLSI, 1981-84, bldg. com. So. Regional Compact Shelving Facility, 1979-82, steering com. Univ. Bibliographic Access System, 1978-82; chair Systemwide Ops. and Planning Adv. Group, 2001-04. Editor Soundboard, 1976-80; contbr. articles to profl. jours. Mem. ALA, The Music Library Assn., Coll. Music Soc., Assn. Recorded Sound Collections, Guitar Found. Am. (exec. com. 1976-80), Beta Phi Mu. Home: 130 Eastbrook Cir Sacramento CA 95835 Office: Gen Libr U Calif Davis 100 NorthWest Quad Davis CA 95616-5292 Office Phone: 530-752-2110. Business E-Mail: jwtanno@ucdavis.edu.

TANOUE, DONNA A., bank executive, former federal agency administrator; BA, U. Hawaii, 1977; JD, Georgetown U., 1981. Spl. dep. atty. gen. Dept. Commerce and Consumer Affairs, Hawaii, 1981-83; commr. financial inst. State of Hawaii, 1983-87; ptnr. Goodsill Anderson Quinn & Stifel, Hawaii, 1987-98; chmn. FDIC, Washington, 1998—2002; vice chmn. Bank of Hawaii, 2002—. Office: PO Box 2900 Honolulu HI 96846-6000

TANS, PIETER P., research scientist; PhD in Exptl. Physics, Rijksuniversitet Groningen, The Netherlands, 1978. Postdoctoral Scripps Inst. Oceanography, La Jolla, Calif., 1978—79; staff scientist, astrophysics group Lawrence Berkeley Lab., Berkeley, Calif., 1979—85; rsch. assoc. Cooperative Inst. for Rsch. in Environ. Sciences (CIRES), U. Colo., Boulder, Colo., 1985—90, fellow, 1997—; supervisory physicist, climate monitoring and diagnostics lab. Nat. Oceanic and Atmospheric Adminstrn. (NOAA), Boulder, Colo., 1990—96, chief scientist, climate monitoring and diagnostics lab., 1996—. Mem. dept. chemistry & biochemistry U. Colo. at Boulder, 1992—2000; mem. com. on oceanic carbon, ocean studies bd. NRC, 1992—93, mem. Dec-Cen panel, bd. on atmospheric sciences and climate, 1995—97; mem. working group drafting a multi-agy. US Carbon Cycle Sci. Plan, 1998. Assoc. editor Journal of Climate, 1996—, mem. editl. adv. bd. Tellus B, 1997—; contbr. articles to profl. jours. Recipient Gold medal, Dept. Commerce, 2000—; named ISI Highly Cited, 2002—. Fellow: Am. Geophysical Union; mem.: Royal Dutch Acad. Sciences (corr. mem. 1995—). Office: Environ Rsch Lab Climate Monitoring and Diagnostics Lab Nat Oceanic and Atmospheric Adminstrn 325 Broadway Mail Code R/GMD1 Boulder CO 80303-3328 Office Phone: 303-497-6811, 303-497-6678. Office Fax: 303-497-5590. Business E-Mail: Pieter.Tans@noaa.gov.

TAO, TERENCE CHI-SHEN, mathematics professor; b. Adelaide, South Australia, Australia, July 17, 1975; arrived in US, 1992; s. Billy and Grace Tao; married. BSc with honors in Math., Flinders U., 1991, MSc in Math., 1992; PhD in Math., Princeton U., 1996. Asst. rschr. Flinders Med. Ctr., 1992—94, Princeton U., 1993—94; Hedrick asst. prof. UCLA, 1996—98, acting asst. prof., 1999, asst. prof., 2000, prof., 2000—. Mem. Math. Scis. Rsch. Inst., 1997; vis. fellow U. NSW, Sydney, 1999—2000, vis. prof., 2000; long-term prize fellow Clay Math. Inst., Boston, 2001—03; hon. prof. Australian Nat. U., 2001—03; mem. sci. adv. bd. Australian Math. Scis. Inst., 2002—; mem. adv. bd. Internat. Math. Rsch. Surveys (IRMS), 2003—. Reviewer Zentralblatt Math., 1998—2005, assoc. editor J. Am. Math. Soc., 2002—04, full editor, 2004—06, assoc. editor Am. Jour. Math., 2002—, Dynamics of Partial Differential Equations, 2003—; author: Solving Mathematical Problems: A Personal Perspective, 1992, 2006, Analysis Vol. I, Analysis Vol. II, 2006. Recipient Bronze medal, Internat. Math. Olympiad, 1986, Silver medal, 1987, Gold medal, 1988, medal, Flinders U., 1992, Fulbright postgraduate award, Fulbright Assn., 1992—95, Salem prize, Salem Prize Com., 2000, medal, Australian Math. Soc., 2005, Bocher Meml. prize, Am. Math. Soc., 2000, Fields medal, Internat. Math. Union, 2006, SASTRA Ramanujan prize, 2006, Alan T. Waterman award, NSF, 2008; co-recipient Levi L. Conant prize, Am. Math. Soc., 2005; named one of Brilliant 10, Popular Sci. mag., 2006; Packard Found. fellow, David & Lucille

Packard Found., 1999—, Rsch. fellow, Sloan Found., 1999—2001, MacArthur Fellow, John D. and Catherine T. MacArthur Found., 2006. Fellow: Royal Soc. UK; mem.: NAS, Australian Acad. Sci. (corr.). Achievements include research in partial differential equations, combinatorics, number theory and harmonic analysis which is an advanced form of calculus that uses equations from physics. Office: UCLA Dept Math Math Sciences 5622 MS 6364 405 Hilgard Ave Los Angeles CA 90095-1555 Office Phone: 310-206-4844. Business E-Mail: tao@math.ucla.edu.

TAPIA, ABEL J., state legislator; b. Las Vegas, Nev., July 23, 1949; AS, U. So. Colo., Pueblo, 1970; BS, Colo. State U., Ft. Collins, 1973. Mem. Dist. 46 Colo. House of Reps., Denver, 1999—2002; mem. Dist. 3 Colo. State Senate, 2003—. Democrat. Roman Catholic. Office: 200 E 14th Ave 3rd Fl Denver CO 80203 also: Colo State Capitol 200 E Colfax Denver CO 80203 Office Phone: 303-866-2581. Business E-Mail: abel.tapia.senate@state.co.us.*

TAPPER, JOAN JUDITH, magazine editor; b. Chgo., June 12, 1947; d. Samuel Jack and Anna (Swoiskin) T.; m. Steven Richard Siegel, Oct. 15, 1971. BA, U. Chgo., 1968; MA, Harvard U., 1969. Editor manuscripts Chelsea House, NYC, 1969-71, Scribners, NYC, 1971; editor books Nat. Acad. Scis., Washington, 1972-73; assoc. editor Praeger Pubs., Washington, 1973-74; editor New Rep. Books, Washington, 1974-79; mng. editor spl. pubs. Nat. Geog. Soc., Washington, 1979-83; editor Nat. Geog. Traveler, Washington, 1984-88; editor-in-chief Islands, internat. mag., Santa Barbara, Calif., 1989—; editl. dir. Islands Pub. Co., Santa Barbara, 1996—. Recipient Pacific Asia Travel Assn. Journalist of the Yr. award, 1995. Mem. Am. Soc. Mag. Editors, Soc. Am. Travel Writers (editors' coun.), Channel City Club. Democrat. Jewish. Avocations: travel, reading, tennis. Home: 603 Island View Dr Santa Barbara CA 93109-1508

TARANIK, JAMES VLADIMIR, geologist, educator; b. LA, Apr. 23, 1940; s. Vladimir James and Jeanette Downing (Smith) T.; m. Colleen Sue Glessner, Dec. 4, 1971; children: Debra Lynn, Danny Lee. BSc in Geology, Stanford U., 1964; PhD, Colo. Sch. Mines, 1974. Chief remote sensing Iowa Geol. Survey, Iowa City, 1971-74; prin. remote sensing scientist Earth Resources Observation Systems Data Ctr., U.S. Geol. Survey, Sioux Falls, SD, 1975-79; chief non-renewable resources br., resource observation div. Office of Space and Terrestrial Applications, NASA Hdqrs., Washington, 1979-82; dean mines Mackay Sch. Mines U. Nev., Reno, 1982-87, prof. geology and geophysics, 1982—98, Arthur Brant chair of geophysics, 1998—; pres. Desert Rsch. Inst., Univ. and C.C. Sys. Nev., 1987-98, Regents's prof. and pres. emeritus, 1998—; adj. prof. geology U. Iowa, 1971-79; vis. prof. civil engring. Iowa State U., 1972-74; adj. prof. earth sci. U. S.D., 1976-79; HQ program scientist space shuttle OSTA-1 Payload on STS-2 NASA, 1981—82, large format camera expt. for heat capacity mapping mission and for magnetic field satellite mission; liaison, 1981—82; dir. NOAA Coop. Inst. Aerospace Sci. & Terrestrial Applications, 1986-94; program dir. NASA Space Grant consortium Univ. and C.C. Sys. Nev., Reno, 1991—2005, dir. NASA EPSCOR program, 1998—2005; bd. dirs. NASA Challenger Learning Ctr., Reno, 2006—; dir. Great Basin Ctr. Geothermal Energy, 2000—03; acting dean Mackay Sch. Mines, 2003; dir. Mackay Sch. Earth Sci. and Engring., U. Nev, 2004—. Team mem. Shuttle Imaging Radar-B Sci. Team NASA, 1983-88, NASA space applications adv. com., 1986-88; chmn. remote sensing subcom. SAAC, 1986-88; chmn. working group on civil space commercialization Dept. Commerce, 1982-84, mem. civil operational remote sensing satellite com., 1983-84; bd. dir. Newmont Mining Corp., 1986-; adv. com. NASA Space Sci. and Applications Com., 1988-90, Nat. Def. Exec. Res., 1986-94, AF studies bd., com. on strategic relocatable targets, 1989-91; pre-launch rev. bd., NASA, Space Radar Lab., 1993-94; fed. lab. rev. task force, NASA, 1994-96; prin. investigator Japanese Earth Resources Satellite, 1991-94; environ. task force MEDEA, Mitre Corp., McLean, Va., 1993-98; mapping scis. com. Nat. Rsch. Coun., 2001-04; cons. Jet Propulsion Lab., Calif., Hughes Aircraft Corp., Lockheed-Marietta Corp., Mitre Corp., TRW; developer remote sensing program and remote sensing lab. State of Iowa, ednl. program in remote sensing Iowa univs. and U. Nev., Reno; program scientist 2d space shuttle flight Office Space and Terrestrial Applications Program; mem. terrestrial geol. applications program NASA, 1981-82; co-investigator Can. Radarsat Program, 1995-97; mem. geol. scis. bd., NAS; dept. of energy prin. investigator nuclear non-proliferation sci. program, 2004-. Contbr. articles to profl. jours. Bd. dirs. Mountain States Legal Found., 2000—, sec., 2006-, Northwest Mining Assn., 2006-08. Served with C.E. U.S. Army, 1965-67; mil. intellegence officer Res. Decorated Bronze Star medal; recipient Spl. Achievement award U.S. Geol. Survey, 1978, Exceptional Sci. Achievement medal NASA, 1982, NASA Group Achievement award Shuttle imaging radar, 1990, NASA Johnson Space Ctr. Group Achievement award for large format camera, 1985; NASA prin. investigator, 1973, 83-88, prin. investigator French Spot-1 Program to Evaluate Spot 1986-88; NDEA fellow, 1968-71. Fellow: AAAS, AIAA (assoc.), Am. Soc. Photogrammetry Remote Sensing, Explorers Club, Geol. Soc. Am.; mem.: IEEE (sr.), N.W. Mining Assn. (trustee 2005—), Mining and Metall. Soc. Am., St. Mary's Hosp. Found., Soc. Econ. Geologists, Am. Geol. Inst. Found. (trustee 1999—), Am. Astron. Soc. (sr.), Am. Inst. Metall. Engrs., Soc. Mining Engrs. Am. (gen. chmn. ednl. sustainability task force 2005—), Am. Assn. Petroleum Geologists (chmn. rsch. com. 2000—), Am. Geophys. Union, Soc. Exploration Geophysicists, Internat. Acad. Astronautics. Home: PO Box 7175 Reno NV 89510-7175 Office Phone: 775-682-8735, 775-784-6987. Business E-Mail: jtaranik@mines.unr.edu.

TARANTINO, QUENTIN JEROME, film director, scriptwriter; b. Knoxville, Tenn., Mar. 27, 1963; s. Tony and Connie Tarantino. Co-founder (with Lawrence Baker) A Band Apart Records. Actor: (films) My Best Friend's Birthday, 1987, Eddie Presley, 1993, (voice) The Coriolis Effect, 1994, Sleep With Me, 1994, Somebody to Love, 1994, Destiny Turns on the Radio, 1995, The Anatomy of Horror, 1995, Desperado, 1995, Girl 6, 1996, Steven Spielberg's Director's Chair, 1996, Full Tilt Boogie, 1997, Little Nicky, 2000, Planet of the Pits, 2004, Epreuves d'artistes, 2004, (voice) Diary of the Dead, 2008; actor, writer & prodr.: From Dusk Till Dawn, 1996, writer (story): Natural Born Killers, 1994, writer & dir.: CSI: Crime Scene Investigation, Episode 5.23, 2003, writer, dir. & prodr.: Kill Bill: Vol. 1, 2003, Kill Bill: Vol. 2, 2004, actor, writer & dir.: Reservoir Dogs, 1992, Pulp Fiction, 1994, actor (voice), writer & dir.: Jackie Brown, 1997, writer & prodr.: Curdled, 1996, actor, writer, prodr. & dir.: (with Alexandre Rockwell, Robert Rodriguez & Allision Anders) Four Rooms, 1995, Grindhouse, 2007; exec. prodr.: God Said, 'Ha!", 1998, From Dusk Till Dawn 2: Tex. Blood Money, 1999, From Dusk Till Dawn 3: The Hangman's Daughter, 2000; exec. prodr.: Hostel, 2005, Daltry Calhoun, 2005, Freedom's Fury, 2006; prodr.: Siunin Wong Fei-hung tsi titmalau (aka Iron Monkey), 1993, released 2001; TV appearances Golden Girls, 1998, 1990, All-American Girl, The Muppets' Wonderful Wizard of Oz, 2005; dir.: (TV series) ER, episode 'Motherhood', 1994, Jimmy Kimmel Live, episode 5/18/2004. Recipient Building Bridges award, Asian Excellence Awards, 2006; named one of Time Mag. 100 Most Influential People, 2005. Home: 8439 W Sunset Blvd West Hollywood CA 90069-1921

TARAVELLA, ROSIE, actress; b. Mt. Morris, NY, July 8, 1962; d. Charles James and Carrie (Sardinia) T.; m. Michael Anthony Valerio, May 27, 1994. BA in Dramatic Arts, San Diego State U., 1985. Entertainment dir., staff trainer Johnny Rockets, Inc., LA, 1986-98; staff writer, voice talent The Rick Dees Weekly Top 40, LA, 1990-93; freelance writer, voice talent The Premiere Comedy Radio Network, LA, 1992-98; actress LA, 1992—; writer L.A. Times Calendar Live! Website, 1999—. Theatrical prodr., cons. The Tamarind Theater, L.A., 1993-94. Author (plays) Rose's Bowl-O-Rama, 1992, The Wives, 1994, Pa's Funeral, 1995; (with Diane Kelber) Blue Grass, 1999; screenwriter: Carlo's Wake, 1997; actress (comml s.) AT&T, Dial, Radio Shack and others, 1992—, (TV) Who's the Boss, Ellen, Full House, Married with Children, The Client, Almost Perfect, Brooklyn South, Sinatra, Norma Jean and Marilyn, George and Leo, Roswell; actress, co-writer (film) Carlo's Wake, 1999. Pres. Boards and Boards Prodns., North Hollywood, Calif., 1994-98. Recipient Am.'s Best Sitcom Writing Competition award, 1999. Mem. Mus. TV and Radio, KCRW-Nat. Pub. Radio, Am. Soc. Prevention Cruelty Animals, Nat. Geog. Soc. Democrat. Roman Catholic. Avocations: cooking, genealogy, internet, film and tv history. Office: Broads and Boards 12828 Victory Blvd Ste 334 North Hollywood CA 91606-3013 Home: 5334 Lindley Ave Unit 106 Encino CA 91316-2907

TARBI, WILLIAM RHEINLANDER, secondary education curriculum consultant, researcher; b. San Bernardino, Calif., Feb. 23, 1949; s. William Metro and Sue (Rheinlander) T.; m. Jenny Workman, Apr. 10, 1980 (div. 1985); m. Michele Hastings, July 4, 1990; children: Amy, Melissa. AA, Santa Barbara City Coll., 1969; BA in History, U. Calif., Santa Barbara, 1976; MA, U. Redlands, 1992. Cert. secondary edn. social studies tchr., Calif. Reporter AP, Santa Barbara, Calif., 1976-80, UPI, Seattle, 1980-85, Golden West Radio Network, Seattle, 1980-85; tchr. Redlands (Calif.) Unified Sch. Dist., 1986—. Cons. IMCOM, Redlands, 1985—. Mem. E Clampus Vitus, Phi Delta Kappa. Avocations: painting, photography, writing, gardening, fencing.

TARDIO, THOMAS A., public relations executive; V.p. strategic planning and other positions Columbia Pictures Industries, 1979-88; CFO, v.p. adminstrn. Rogers & Cowan, Inc., LA, 1988-89, exec. v.p. entertainment sect., 1989-91, pres., 1991-95; CEO Rogers & Cowan, LA, 1995—. Mem. Pub. Rels. Soc. Am., Nat. Acad. Recording Arts and Scis., Pub. Communicators L.A., Contry Music Assn. Office: Rogers & Cowan 8687 Melrose Ave 7th Fl Los Angeles CA 90069

TARIN, DAVID, oncologist, researcher; b. UK, Aug. 28, 1939; BSc Honors Class I, Leeds U., Eng., 1961; BM, BChir, Oxford U., Eng., 1963, DM, MA, 1969. House surgeon/physician Radcliffe Infirmary, Oxford, 1964-65; MC Smith lectr. pathology Brimingham (Eng.) U., 1965-67; lectr. anatomy Leeds (Eng.) U., 1967-73; sr. registrar neuropathology Gen. Infirmary, Leeds, 1973-74; sr. lectr. histopathology, hon. cons. pathologist Royal Postgrad. Med. Sch., London, 1975-79; clin. reader pathology John Radcliffe Hosp., Oxford, 1979-80, Nuffield reader pathology, 1980-97; dir. cancer ctr., prof. pathology U. Calif. San Diego, La Jolla, 1997—. Professorial fellow Green Coll. Oxford, 1984—. Author: Tissue Interactions in Carcinogenesis, 1972; contbr. articles on cancer diagnosis and tumor invasion and metastasis to sci. and med. jours. Mem. Royal Coll. Pathologists, Path. Soc., Internat. Soc. Differentiation (bd. dirs., mem. exec. com., pres. 1987-90), Brit. Assn. Cancer Rsch., Am. Assn. Cancer Rsch. Avocations: literature, poetry, music, art, cinema. Office: Rebecca and John Moores UCSD Cancer Center 0658 9500 Gilman Drive La Jolla CA 92093-0658

TARN, NATHANIEL, poet, educator, translator; b. Paris, June 30, 1928; s. Marcel and Yvonne (Suchar) T.; children: Andrea, Marc. BA with honors, Cambridge U., Eng., 1948, MA, 1952; postgrad., U. Sorbonne, U. Paris, 1949-51; MA, U. Chgo., 1952, PhD, 1957; postgrad., London Sch. Econs., 1953-58. Anthropologist, Guatemala, Burma, Alaska, and other locations, 1952—; prof. comparative lit. Rutgers U., 1970-85, prof. emeritus modern poetry, comparative lit, anthropology, 1985. Vis. prof. SUNY, Buffalo and Princeton, 1969-70. Author: Old Savage/Young City, 1964, Where Babylon Ends, 1968, The Beautiful Contradictions, 1969, October, 1969, A Nowhere for Vallejo, 1971, Lyrics for the Bride of God: Section: The Artemision, 1972, The Persephones, 1974, Lyrics for the Bride of God, 1975, The House of Leaves, 1976, Birdscapes, with Seaside, 1978, The Desert Mothers, 1985, At the Western Gates, 1985, Palenque, 1986, Seeing America First, 1989, Flying the Body, 1993, Multitude of One, 1995, Views from the Weaving Mountain: Selected Essays in Poetics and Anthropology, 1991, Scandals in the House of Birds: Shamans & Priests on Lake Atitlan, 1997, The Architextures, 2000, Three Letters From The City: The St. Petersburg Poems 1968-1998, 2000, Selected Poems 1950-2000, 2002, Dying Trees, 2003, Recollections of Being, 2004, The Embattled Lyric, 2007; co-author: (with Janet Rodney) The Forest, 1978, Atitlan/Alashka, 1979, The Ground of Our Great Admiration of Nature, 1978; contbg. author: Penguin Modern Poets No. Seven: Richard Murphy, Jon Silkin, Nathaniel Tarn, 1965, A.P.E.N. Anthology of Contemporary Poetry, 1966, The Penguin Book of Modern Verse Translation, 1966, Poems Addressed to Hugh MacDiarmid, 1967, Music and Sweet Poetry: A Verse Anthology, 1968, Frontier of Going: Anthology of Space Poetry, 1969, Shaking the Pumpkin, 1972, America: A Prophecy, 1973, Open Poetry, 1973, Active Anthology, 1974, Symposium of the Whole, 1983, Random House Book of Twentieth Century French Poetry, 1983, Beneath a Single Moon: Buddhism in American Poetry, 1991, American Poetry since 1950: Innovators and Outsiders, 1993; translator: The Heights of Macchu Picchu (Pablo Neruda), 1966, Stelae (Victor Segalen), 1969, Zapotec Struggles, 1993; editor, co-translator: Con Cuba: An Anthology of Cuban Poetry of the Last Sixty Years, 1969, Selected Poems (Pablo Neruda), 1970; editor Cape Edits. and founder-dir. Cape Goliard Press, J. Cape Ltd., 1967-69. Recipient Guinness prize for poetry, 1963.

TARNOFF, PETER, federal agency administrator, consultant; b. NYC, Apr. 19, 1937; s. Norman Tarnoff and Henrietta (Goldfarb) Laing; m. Daniele Oudinot, Jan. 13, 1962 (div. Oct. 1981); children: Nicholas, Alexander; m. Mathea Falco, Dec. 24, 1981; 1 child, Benjamin. Student, U. Paris, 1956-57, postgrad., 60-61; BA, Colgate U., 1958; postgrad., U. Chgo., 1958-60. Joined Fgn. Svc., Dept. State, 1961; spl. asst. to amb. Am. Embassy, Bonn, Fed. Republic Germany, 1969; trainee Nat. Sch. Adminstrn., Paris, 1970; prin. officer Am. Consulate Gen., Lyon, France, 1971-73; dep. chief of mission Am. Embassy, Luxembourg, 1973-75; dir. Office Rsch. and Analysis for Western Europe Dept. State, Washington, 1975-76, exec. sec. Dept. State, 1977-81, fgn. affairs fellow San Francisco, 1981-82; exec. dir. World Affairs Coun. No. Calif., San Francisco, 1983-86; pres., dir. Coun. on Fgn. Rels., NYC, 1986-93; under sec. state for polit. affairs Dept. State, Washington, 1993-97; pres. Internat. Adv. Corp., San Francisco, 1997—. Office: Internat Adv Corp 2028 Green St San Francisco CA 94123-4813 Home Phone: 415-567-4241; Office Phone: 415-235-2547. Personal E-mail: iacmail@aol.com.

TARR, GREGORY L., health and medical products company executive; With Alpha Beta Co., McKesson Corp., 1986-99, v.p., mgr. distbn. ctr. Sacramento, v.p. sales and ops. Everett, until 1997, sr. v.p. customer ops. group western region, 1997—; pres., CEO, URM Stores, Inc., Spokane, Wash., 1999—. Office: URM Stores Inc 7511 N Freya St Spokane WA 99217-8043

TARR, RALPH WILLIAM, lawyer, former federal government official; b. Bakersfield, Calif., Sept. 29, 1948; BA, Dartmouth Coll., 1970; MPA, Calif. State U., Sacramento, 1973; JD, U. Calif., Hastings, 1976. Staff asst. Calif. Gov. Ronald Reagan, 1971—73; extern to assoc. justice Calif. Supreme Ct., 1976; rsch. atty. to presiding justice Ct. Appeal (5th dist.) Calif., 1976-77; assoc. Baker, Manock & Jensen, Fresno, Calif., 1977-81, dir., mem. exec. com., 1981-82; mem. adminstrv. com. Fed. Register, Washington, 1982-85; dep. asst. atty. gen. US Dept. Justice, Washington, 1982-84, acting asst. atty. gen., 1984-85; solicitor US Dept. Interior, Washington, 1985-89, counselor, 1989-90; pvt. practice LA, 1990—. Home: 24011 Alder Pl Calabasas CA 91302-2394 Office: Andrews Kurth LLP Ste 3700 601 S Figueroa St Los Angeles CA 90017-5742 Office Phone: 213-896-3136. Business E-Mail: rtarr@andrewskurth.com.

TARRANT, ALISON, broadcast company executive; b. 1970; Assoc. to v.p., grp. dir. nat. broadcast divsn. Universal McCann, 1993—2000; dir. promotions Kids' WB! to v.p. integrated sales and mktg. Warner Bros. TV Network, 2000—06; v.p. integrated sales and mktg. CW TV Network, 2006—. Mem. media coun. Paley Ctr. for Media. Named a Woman to Watch, Advt. Age, 2008. Office: CW TV Network 4000 Warner Blvd Burbank CA 91522 Office Phone: 818-977-2500. Office Fax: 818-954-7667.

TARTER, CURTIS BRUCE, physicist, science administrator; b. Louisville, Sept. 26, 1939; s. Curtis B. and Marian Turner (Cundiff) T.; divorced; 1 child, Shana Lee; m. Gabriela Odell, 2003. BS, MIT, 1961; PhD, Cornell U., 1967. Tchg. asst. Cornell U., Ithaca, NY, 1961—63, rsch. asst., 1964—67; physicist, summers Lawrence Radiation Lab., Livermore, Calif., 1962—63; staff mem. theoretical physics divsn. U. Calif., Lawrence Livermore Nat. Lab., 1967—69, group leader macroscopic properties of matter, 1969—71, assoc. divsn. leader, 1971—74, group leader opacities, 1972—78, divsn. leader, 1974—84; dep. assoc. dir. for physics Lawrence Livermore Nat. Lab., 1984—88, assoc. dir. for physics, 1988—94, dep. dir., 1994, dir., 1994—2002, assoc. dir. at large, 2002—04, dir. emeritus, 2004—. Sr. scientist Applied Rsch. Labs. Aeronutronic divsn. Philco-Ford Corp.; cons. Hertz Found., field com. study on astronomy in the 80's, NRC, 1980; mem. Army Sci. Bd., Washington, 1989-96; adj. prof. dept. applied sci., U. Calif., Davis, 1999-2002; mem. Calif. Coun. on Sci. and Tech., 1996-2002, Pacific Coun. on Internat. Policy, 1998—, lab. opers. bd. DOE, 1998-2002, Nuc. Energy Rsch. Adv. Bd., 1999-2002, Coun. Fgn. Rels., 1999—; bd. dirs. Draper Lab; chair nuc. weapons assessment com. AAAS. Contbr. numerous articles to profl. jours. Recipient Roosevelts Gold Medal award for sci., NNSA Gold medal for disting. svc., U.S. Dept. Energy Exceptional Pub. Svc. award, Sec. of Energy's Gold award. Fellow AAAS (chair nuc. weapons complex assessment com. 2006—), Calif. Coun. Sci. and Tech., Am. Phys. Soc. (phys. policy com. 2002-05); mem. Am. Astron. Soc., Internat. Astron. Union. Avocations: golf, running, music. Office: Lawrence Livermore Nat Lab PO Box 808 Livermore CA 94551-0808 Office Phone: 925-422-4169. Business E-Mail: tarter1@llnl.gov. E-mail: cbtarter@yahoo.com.

TARTER, MICHAEL ERNEST, biostatistician, educator; b. Bronx, NY, Dec. 20, 1938; s. William Tarter and Frieda Browdy; m. Orna Benzenburg, Aug. 30, 1975; children: Douglas, Robin. BA in Math., UCLA, 1959, MA in Math., 1961, PhD in Biostats., 1963. Asst. prof. U. Mich., Ann Arbor, 1964-66, assoc. prof., 1967, U. Calif., Irvine, 1968-70, Berkeley, 1970-76, prof., 1977—. Author books and articles; editor: Jour. Am. Statis. Assn. (screening editor for applications 1971-80). Fellow Am. Statis. Assn. (chmn. com. resources biometrics sect. 1981—, editorial bds. computational stats. and data analysis 1983-86, biometrics 1976-84, stats. 1977-97). Office: U Calif Sch Pub Health Dept Biomed Environ Health Scis 140 Warren Hall Berkeley CA 94720-7360 Business E-Mail: tarter@uclink.berkeley.edu.

TASH, BILL, state legislator; b. Dillon, Mont., Aug. 21, 1932; m to Marlene; children: four. Montana State Representative, District 73, 1993-94, District 34, 1995-01; Montana State Senator, District 17, 2001-05, District 36, 2005-, Montana State Senate.Rancher, currently; board member, Barrett Hosp, currently. Montana & America Hosp Association (trustee, currently). Republican. Home: 240 Vista Dr Dillon MT 59725 Mailing: State Capitol Helena MT 59620-1701 Office Phone: 406-633-2746.

TASH, GRAHAM ANDREW, JR., automobile retail company executive; b. Seattle, Dec. 18, 1956; s. Graham Andrew and Charlotte Eleanor (Hawes) Tash; m. Julie Thompson Titus, Aug. 8, 1981; children: Jacqueline E., Katherine J., Graham A. III. BA, U. Puget Sound, 1979. Dist. mgr. Kenworth Truck Co., Atlanta, 1984-86; ops. mgr. Titus-Will Ford/Toyota, Tacoma, Wash., 1987-90, gen. mgr., 1991-94, pres., 1994—, bd. dirs. Bd. dirs. Titus-Will Ent. Bd. dirs. Christian Brotherhood Acad., Tacoma, 1996—; mem. activities coun. Tacoma Art Mus., 1993, 94, 95. Recipient Chairman's award Ford Motor Co., 1986, 87, 92, Pres.'s award Toyota Motor Sales USA, 1991, 92, 94, 95, 96. Mem. Tacoma C. of C. (bd. dirs. 1996—), Tacoma Country and Golf Club, Wash. Athletic Club, Tacoma Lawn Tennis Club. Republican. Episcopalian. Avocations: skiing, boating, hunting, golf. Office: Titus-Will Ford Toyota Sales Inc 3606 S Sprague Ave Tacoma WA 98409-7444

TASH, MARTIN ELIAS, publishing company executive; b. NYC, Jan. 24, 1941; s. David and Esther (Milch) T.; m. Arlene Sue Klein, June 23, 1962; children: Nathan, Faye, Jill. BBA, Baruch Sch. City Coll. N.Y., 1962. C.P.A. Staff accountant S.D. Leidesdorf & Co. (C.P.A.'s), NYC, 1962-66; v.p. fin., dir. LMC Data Inc., NYC,

1966-71; with Plenum Pub. Corp., NYC, 1971-98, chmn. bd., pres., 1977-98; chmn. bd., pres., CEO Gradco Systems, Inc., 1990—. Office: Gradco Systems Inc 3753 Howard Hughes Pkwy Ste 200 Las Vegas NV 89109-0952

TASHIMA, ATSUSHI WALLACE, federal judge; b. Santa Maria, Calif., June 24, 1934; s. Yasutaro and Aya (Sasaki) Tashima; m. Nora Kiyo Inadomi, Jan. 27, 1957; children: Catherine Y., Christopher I., Jonathan I. AB in Polit. Sci., UCLA, 1958; LLB, Harvard U., 1961. Bar: Calif. 1962. Dep. atty. gen. State of Calif., 1961—67; atty. Spreckels Sugar divsn. Amstar Corp., 1968—72, v.p., gen. atty. Spreckels Sugar divsn., 1972—77; ptnr. Morrison & Foerster, LA, 1977—80; judge US Dist. Ct. (ctrl. dist.), LA, 1980—96, US Ct. Appeals (9th cir.), Pasadena, Calif., 1996—2003, sr. judge, 2003—. Mem. Calif. Com. Bar Examiners, 1978—80. With USMC, 1953—56. Mem.: ABA, LA County Bar Assn. Democrat. Office: Richard A Chambers US Ct Appeals PO Box 91510 125 S Grand Ave Pasadena CA 91109-1510

TASOOJI, MICHAEL B., retail executive; m. Linda Tasooji; 3 children. BS in Internat. Trade and Quantitative Bus. Analysis, U. So. Calif., MBA in Internat. Fin. and Bus. Econs. With Getty Oil Co., Columbia Pictures Studio; v.p. application systems Bergen Brunswig Corp.; v.p. info. svcs. Disneyland, 1995—2000; sr. v.p., chief info. officer Walt Disney Attractions, 2000, Walt Disney Co., 2000—03; exec. v.p., chief info. officer Gap, Inc., 2003—. Office: Gap Inc 2 Folsom St San Francisco CA 94105 Office Phone: 650-952-4400.

TATA, GIOVANNI, publishing executive; b. Taranto, Italy, Apr. 26, 1954; came to U.S., 1974, naturalized, 1982; s. Vito and Angela (Colucci) T.; m. Brenda Susan Smith, Feb. 14, 1978; children: Elizabeth Ariana, Katherine Allison, Margaret Anne, Michael Anthony, Hanna Amelia. BS cum laude, Brigham Young U., 1977, MA, 1980; grad. cert. area studies, U. Utah, 1980, PhD, 1986; postgrad., U. Turin, Italy, 1980-81. Archaeologist Utah State Hist. Soc., Salt Lake City, 1979; instr. dept. langs. U. Utah, Salt Lake City, 1983-85; Mediterranean specialist Soc. Early Hist. Archaeology, Provo, Utah, 1978-91; rsch. fellow Direzione Gen. Cooperazione Sci. Culturale e Technica, Rome, 1980-81; mus. curator Pioneer Trail State Park, Salt Lake City, 1982-83; instr. dept. art Brigham Young U., Provo, 1982-84, dir. creative works, 1996—; rsch. curator Utah Mus. Fine Arts, Salt Lake City, 1985-87; pres. Mus. Info. Sys., 1987-93, Transoft Internat., Inc., 1988—. Chmn. 35th Ann. Symposium on the Archaeology of the Scriptures, 1986, Taras Devel. Corp., 1994—97, Muse-Media, Inc., 1995—2000. Patentee method and system for computerized learning, response, and evaluation. Brigham Young U. scholar. Mem.: Intellectual Property Owners Assn., Assn. Univ. Tech. Mgrs., Nat. Coun. Museums, Am. Assn. Museums. Republican. Mem. Ch. Jesus Christ of Latter-day Saints. Home Phone: 801-224-4973; Office Phone: 801-422-3724. Business E-Mail: giovanni_tata@byu.edu. E-mail: tata@lexinet.com.

TATÁR, ANNA, retired library director; d. Joseph and Elizabeth Tatár; m. Julio Martinez (div.); 1 child, Julius. Grad., DePauw U., Greencastle, Ind.; MLS, U. Mich., Ann Arbor. Dir. San Diego Pub. Libr., 1997—2008; ret., 2008. Bd. dirs. STAR/PAL (Sports, Tng., Academics and Recreational/Police Athletic League), San Diego. Named one of 50 People to Watch in 2003, San Diego Mag. Mem.: ALA.

TATARINOV, KIRILL, computer software industry expert; b. Moscow, Sept. 17, 1964; came to US, 1994; s. Lev Gorinshteyn and Inna Tatarinova; m. Oksana Grekina Tatarinov, Jan. 18m 1986; children: Katherine, Konstantin. MS in Elec. Engring., Moscow U. Railroad Engring., 1986; MBA, Houston Bapt. U., 1997. Tech. lead Fibronics Ltd., Haifa, Israel, 1990-91; dir. R&D Patrol Software Pty. Ltd., Sydney, 1991-94; v.p. R&D BMC Software, Inc., Houston, 1994-98, v.p. strategic planning, 1998-2000, sr. v.p., chief tech. officer, 2000—02; corp. v.p. mgmt. & solutions divsn. Microsoft Corp., 2002—. Inventor: System for monitoring and managing computer resources, 1997, 99. Office: Microsoft Corp Microsoft Bus Solutions 1 Microsoft Way Redmond WA 98052-6399 Office Phone: 425-707-8978. E-mail: kirill@tatarinov.com.

TATARSKII, VALERIAN IL'ICH, physics researcher; b. Kharkov, USSR, Oct. 13, 1929; s. Il'ya A. and Elizabeth A. (Lapis) T.; m. Maia S. Granovskaia, Dec. 22, 1955; 1 child, Viatcheslav V. MS, Moscow State U., 1952; PhD, Acoustical Inst. Acad. Scis., 1957; DSc, Gorky State U., 1962. Scientific rschr. Geophys. Inst. Acad. Sci. USSR, Moscow, 1953-56, Inst. Atmospheric Physics, Acad. Sci. USSR, Moscow, 1956-59, sr. scientific rschr., 1959-78, head lab., 1978-90; head dept. Lebedev. Phys. Inst. Acad. Sci., Moscow, 1990-91; sr. rsch. assoc. U. Colo. Coop. Inst. for Rsch. in Environ. Sci., Boulder, 1991—2001; sr. rsch. scientist Zel Techs. and NOAA/Phys. Sci. Dept., Boulder, 2001—06, Radio Hydro Physics LLC, Boulder, 2006—. Author: Wave Propagation in a Turbulent Medium, 1961, 67, The Effect of the Turbulent Atmosphere on Wave Propagation, 1971, Principles of Statistical Radiophysics, 1989; contbr. articles to profl. jours. Recipient USSR State prize, 1990. Fellow Optical Soc. Am. (Max Born award 1994), Inst. Physics; mem. Russian Acad. Sci., USA Nat. Acad. Engring., NY Acad. Sci., MIT Electromagnetic Soc. Avocations: classical music, fine art, photography. Office: Radio Hydro Physics NOAA Phys Sci Dept Mail Stop ZelTech 325 Broadway St Boulder CO 80305-3328 Personal E-mail: vtatarskii@hotmail.com.

TATE, JOHN WILLIAM, consumer products company executive, former food products executive; BA in Econs., U. Tex., 1972. Various fin. and gen. mgmt. positions Dole Food Co. Inc., Westlake Village, Calif.; CFO fresh vegetables divsn. Dole Food Co., 1993-96, CFO Dole Europe Paris, CFO Westlake Village, Calif., 1998—2000, Krispy Kreme Doughnuts, Inc., Winston-Salem, NC, 2000—02; COO Krispy Kreme Doughnuts Inc., Winston-Salem, NC, 2002—04; exec. v.p., COO Restoration Hardware, Inc., Corte Madera, Calif., 2004—. With USAF, 1973-79. Office: Restoration Hardware Inc 15 Koch Rd Ste J Corte Madera CA 94925

TATE, PENFIELD, state senator; b. Phila., May 19; m. Valencia Tate. BA, Colo. State U., 1978; JD, Antioch U., 1981. Atty. FTC, 1981-84, 1984—; Dem. rep. dist. 8 Colo. Ho. of Reps., 1996-2000; Dem. senator dist. 33 Colo. State Senate, 2000—. Mem. bus. affairs and labor and fin. coms. Colo. Ho. of Reps.; mem. joint budget com. Colo. State Senate, vice chmn. appropriations com. Mem. bd. dirs. Metro State Coll. Found., Colo. Housing and Fin. Authority; adminstr. asst. to Mayor of Denver, 1990-91; exec. dir. Colo. Dept. Adminstrn., 1993-94; 2d vice chair Colo. Dem. Party, 1995-97. Mem. Denver Metro C. of C. (bd. dirs.). Office: Colo State Senate 200 E Colfax Rm 263 Denver CO 80203 also: 2520 Ash St Denver CO 80207-3118 E-mail: ptate@csn.net, ptate@sni.net.

TATMAN, DAVID C., state agency administrator; Grad., U. Oreg. Sch. Law, 1981. Bar: Oreg. 1981. With Oreg. Divsn. Fin. & Corp. Securities, 1988—, chief enforcement securities sect., dep. adminstr., 2004—05, acting adminstr., 2005—06, adminstr., 2006—; spl. asst. atty. gen. Oreg. Dept. Justice. Office: Dept Consumer & Bus Svcs Divsn Fin and Corp Securities PO Box 14480 Salem OR 97309-0405 Office Phone: 503-378-4140. Office Fax: 503-947-7862. E-mail: david.c.tatman@state.or.us.

TATUM, CHANNING, actor; b. Cullman, Ala., Apr. 26, 1980; Actor: (films) Coach Carter, 2005, Supercross, 2005, Havoc, 2005, She's the Man, 2006 (Choice Breakout Make, Teen Choice Awards, 2006), Step Up, 2006, A Guide to Recognizing Your Saints, 2006 (co-recipient Best Actor, Gijón Internat. Film Festival, Special Jury Prize, Sundance Film Festival, 2006), Battle in Seattle, 2007, The Trap, 2007, Step Up 2: The Streets, 2008, Stop-Loss, 2008 (Choice Movie Actor: Drama, Teen Choice Awards, 2008), Fighting, 2009, (guest appearance): (TV series) CSI: Miami, 2004. Avocation: Kung Fu. Office: c/o Management 360 9111 Wilshire Blvd Beverly Hills CA 90210

TATUM, JACKIE, former parks and recreation manager, municipal official; b. Kansas City, Mo., June 11, 1932; 2 children. BS in Phys. Edn., U. So. Calif. Tchr., Calif. With Ctrl. Recreation Ctr. Parks and Recreation Ctr. City of L.A., 1955; recreation dir. various recreation ctrs.; prin. recreation supr.; asst. gen. mgr. Valley Region, 1989-92; gen. mgr., 1992-98; cons. City of L.A., Dept. Recreation and Parks, 1998—. Chair nat. exec. com., creator, developer Wonderful Outdoor World (WOW); presenter in field. Contbr. articles to profl. jours.; appearances in tv, radio shows. Recipient Ticket to Life award Inner City Games; named Woman of the Yr. World Ops. Internat., 1976, City Employee of Yr. All City Employees Benefits Svc. Assn., 1992., One of Ten Most Powerful Black Women in L.A. Mem. Nat. Recreation and Parks Assn. (Disting. Svc. award 1997, tchr. Pacific Mktg. and Revenue Sources Mgmt. Sch.), Chi Kappa Rho (v.p., pres., past pres. Helen I. Pontius Nat. award of merit).

TAU, LEONARD, communications company executive; Chmn. bd. dirs. Century Comms. Corp., 1989-90, CEO, chmn., 1990-91, CFO, 1991-97; dir., chmn. bd. dirs. Electric Lightwave, Vancouver, Wash., 1994—. Office: Electric Lightwave Inc 1201 NE Lloyd Blvd Ste 500 Portland OR 97232-1259

TAUER, ED, Mayor, Aurora, Colorado; m. Betsy Tauer; 1 child. MBA, U. Colo; BME, Colo. State U. Mem. Aurora City Coun., 1997—; mayor City of Aurora, Colo., 2003—. Bd. dirs. Aurora Econ. Develop. Coun. Mem. Denver Regional Coun. Govts., Regional Air Quality Coun., Linkages for Older Adults, Fitzsimons Redevelopment Authority; chmn. Commn. & Youth Programs. Mem.: Nat. League of Cities, US Conf. Mayors, Village East Neighborhood Assn., Aurora C. of C. Republican. Avocations: Sports, family activities, making wood furniture. Office: Office of Mayor 15151 E Alameda Pkwy 5th Floor Aurora CO 80012 Office Phone: 303-739-7015. E-mail: etauer@auroragov.org.*

TAUER, PAUL E., mayor, educator; b. 1935; m. Katherine Eldredge, Sept. 1, 1956; children: Paul E. Jr., Edward, Roch, Eugene, Kathryn, Tammie, Andrew, Timothy. BA in Historyand Edn., Regis Coll., 1961; MA in Edn. Adminstrn., U. No. Colo., 1964. Tchr. Denver Pub. Schs., 1961-92; ret., 1992. Mayor City of Aurora, Colo., 1987-2003, mem. Aurora City Coun., 1979-1987; mem. Adams County Coordinating Com., Gov.'s Met. Transp. Roundtable; active Aurora airport coms. Mem. N.O.I.S.E. E-mail: ptauer@ci.aurora.co.us.

TAURASI, DIANA LURENA, professional basketball player; b. Glendale, Calif., June 11, 1982; d. Mario Taurasi and Lili. Grad. in Sociology, U. Conn., 2004. Player Phoenix Mercury, Ariz., 2004—. Mem. USA Basketball Women's Sr. Nat. Team, Athens, Greece, 2004, Beijing, 08. Recipient Honda award for Women's Basketball Finalist, 2001—02, Honda Trophy Award, 2003, Wade Trophy, 2003, ESPY award, Best Female Coll. Athlete, ESPN, 2003, 2004, ESPY award, Best Female Athlete, 2004, Gold medal, women's basketball, Athens Olympic Games, 2004, Beijing Olympic Games, 2008; named Big East Preseason Rookie of Yr., 2000—01, Most Outstanding Player of NCAA East Region, 2000—01, Big East Championship Most Outstanding Player, 2000—01, Kodak All-Am. and AP Second Team All Am., 2001—02, Naismith Player of Yr., 2001—02, 2003, Big East First Team Performer, 2002—03, NCAA Final Four and East Regional Most Outstanding Player, 2003, Nat. Player of Yr., US Basketball Writers Assn., 2003, Preseason All-Am., 2003, WNBA Rookie of Yr., 2004, WNBA Peak Performer, 2006, Female Athlete of Yr., USA Basketball, 2006; named to All Big East All-Rookie Team, 2000—01, NCAA Mideast Region All-Tournament Team, 2001—02, All Big-East First Team, 2002, Big East All-Tournament Team, 2002, 2003, All-WNBA First Team, 2004, 2006, WNBA Western Conf. All-Star Team, 2005—07. Achievements include winning a WNBA Championship as a member of the Mercury, 2007. Office: Phoenix Mercury 201 E Jefferson St Phoenix AZ 85004

TAUSCHER, ELLEN O'KANE, United States Representative from California; b. Newark, Nov. 15, 1951; 1 child, Katherine. BS in Early Childhood Edn., Seton Hall U., 1974. With Bache Securities, NYC, 1974—79; officer NY Stock Exch., 1980—83; with Bear Stearns Cos. Inc., 1983—85, Drexel Burnham Lambert, NYC, 1985—89; founder, CEO Child Care Registry Inc., 1991—96; mem. US Congress from 10th Calif. dist., 1997—, regional whip, 2008—, mem. armed svcs. com., transp. & infrastructure com., environment com. Co-chair US Senate Campaign Dianne Feinstein, 1992, 1994; mem. Blue Dog Coalition; co-chair Troop Capitol Hill: Hon. Girl Scout Caucus, Intelligent Transp. Sys. Caucus, Dept. Energy Facilities Caucus, Iraqi Women's Caucus, 2004—; chair New Dem. Coalition, 2005—, co-chair Entitlement Reform Task Force; com. mem. N. Am. Treaty Orgn. Parliamentary Assembly; nat. vice chair Dem. Leadership Coun. Author: The ChildCare Sourcebook, 1996. Bd. vis. US Mil. Acad.; bd. mem. Alumnae Resources, Battered Women's Alternative, Breast Cancer Fund, Bus. Execs. for Nat. Security, Calif. Symphony; bd. regents Seton Hall U. Democrat. Roman Catholic. Office: US Congress 1034 Longworth Ho Office Bldg Washington DC 20510-0510 Home: 2121 N California Ste 555 Walnut Creek CA 94596 Office Phone: 202-225-1880.

TAUSSIG, LYNN MAX, healthcare administrator, pulmonologist, pediatrician, educator; b. Milw., July 19, 1942; m. Lisa Peter; children: Heather, Jennifer. AB cum laude, Harvard U., 1964; MD, Washington U., St. Louis, 1968. Diplomate Am. Bd. Pediat., Nat. Bd. Med. Examiners, Am. Bd. Pediat. Pulmonary. Rsch. asst. dept. neuroanatomy Marquette U., Milw., 1965; intern in pediat. St. Louis Children's Hosp., 1968-69; resident in pediat. U. Colo. Med. Ctr., Denver, 1969-70; clin. assoc. pediat. metabolism br. Nat. Inst. Arthritis, Metabolism, and Digestive Diseases, NIH, Bethesda, Md., 1970-72; pulmonary fellow Montreal (Que., Can.) Children's Hosp., 1972-74; asst. prof. pediat. Ariz. Health Scis. Ctr., Tucson, 1974-77, cystic fibrosis ctr. dir., 1974-85, assoc. chief pulmonary function labs., 1974-85, dir. pulmonary sect., 1974-85, asst. dir. divsn. respiratory scis., 1976-92, assoc. prof. pediat., 1977-81, assoc. head dept. pediat., 1979-84, prof., 1981-93, head dept. pediat., 1985-93, dir. Steele Meml. Children's Rsch. Ctr., 1986-93; prof. pediats. U. Colo. Health Scis. Ctr., Denver, 1993—; pres., CEO Nat. Jewish Med. and Rsch. Ctr., Denver, 1993—. Frank Stevenson vis. prof. U. Con., 1977, 82; Robert Chinnock Meml. lectr. Loma Linda U., Calif., 1983; Jour. Pediats. vis. prof. U. Chgo., 1984; Brennenman lectr. L.A. Pediat. Soc., 1988, 94; Danis Meml. lectr. St. Louis U., 1989; Talamo Meml. lectr. Johns Hopkins U., Balt., 1989; Anna Zager vis. lectr. in pediats. Technion U., Haifa, Israel, 1990; Sir Clavering Fison vis. prof. Inst. Child Health, U. London, 1992; Benjamin Meaker vis. prof. U. Bristol, Eng., 1992; Ben Kagan vis. lectr. Cedars-Sinai Hosp., L.A., 1993. Mem. editl. bd. Chest, 1983-88, Am. Rev. Respiratory Diseases, 1983-89; contbr. articles to profl. jours. Trustee Congregation Anshei Israel, 1978-80; bd. dirs. Jerwish Cmty. Ctr., 1982-90, sec., 1984-86, v.p., 1987-89; mem. allocations com. Jewish Fedn. So. Ariz., 1985, 88, Allied Jewish Fedn. Denver, 1996—; bd. dirs. Colo. Biomed. Venture Ctr., 1994—, Congregation Rodef Shalom, 1996—; active Martin Luther King Jr. Minority Scholarship Program, 1994—, Colo. Concern, 1995—. Cystic Fibrosis Found. Clin. fellow, 1972-74, Sr. Internat. fellow Fogarty Internat. Ctr., 1980-81; Young Investigator Pulmonary Rsch. grantee Nat. Heart and Lung Inst., 1974-76, and numerous other med. grants; Pfizer Labs. Med. scholar, 1966; recipient Lange Med. Book award, 1966 Mem. Am. Acad. Pediat. (mem. exec. com. sect. on diseases of chest 1978-80, mem. ad hoc com. for pediat. pulmonary bds., sect. on diseases of chest 1978-85), Am. Pediat. Soc., Am. Thoracic Soc. (mem. com. to advise pres. 1975-76, sec. sci. assembly for pediats. 1975-77, mem. respiratory care com. 1976-78, mem. nominating com. 1977, 84-85, chmn. prograom com. 1979-81, mem. ann. meeting com. 1979-81, mem. rsch. rev. com. 1981-82, chmn. publs. policy com. 1988-89, 90-92, mem. exec. com. 1989-90, sec.-treas. 1989-90, active many other coms.), Am. Coll. Chest Physicians (mem. steering group for com. on cardiopulmonary diseases in children 1977-79), Ariz. Pediat. Soc., Ariz. Lung Assn., Pima County Pediat. Soc., Soc. Pediat. Rsch. (founder Lung Club 1985), Western Soc. Pediat. Rsch. (mem. nominating com. 1979-80, elected to coun. 1994—), Rotary, Harvard Club of So. Ariz. (schs. com. 1982-93, sec.-treas. 1989-93), Harvard Club of Colo., Alpha Omega Alpha. Office: Nat Jewish Med & Rsch Ctr 1400 Jackson St Denver CO 80206-2761

TAVERNA, RODNEY ELWARD, financial services company executive; b. Springfield, Ill., Aug. 8, 1947; s. Jerome Thomas and Virginia (Holcomb) T.; m. Cheryl Ann Walters, Sept. 4, 1968 (div. 1983); children: Lara Lyn, Melinda Marie, Ryan Thomas; m. Caroline Whiffen, Apr. 1985. BA, U. Mo., 1969; MBA in Fin., Nat. U., 1988. Commd. 2d lt., supply officer USMC, 1969, advanced through grades to maj., 1979; supply officer Central Svcs. Agy., Danang, Vietnam, 1970-71, Marine Air Control Squadron, Futenma, Okinawa, 1977-78; logistics officer Hdqrs. Marine Corps Recruit Depot, Paris Island, S.C., 1972-75; support officer Marine Barracks, Treasure Island, San Francisco, 1975-77; regimental supply officer 1st Marine Divsn., Camp Pendleton, Calif., 1978-79, asst divsn. supply officer, 1985-88; brigade supply officer 1st Marine Brigade, Kaneohe Bay, Hawaii, 1980-82; exec. officer 1st Maintenance Bn., Camp Pendleton, 1982-85; asst div. supply officer 1st Marine Div., 1985-88; pres. Freedom Fin. Group, 1991—2000; br. mgr. WMA Securities, Inc., 1994-97; sr. field dir. Premier Fin. Am., 1997-2000; CEO Freedom Fin. Solutions, Inc., 2000—; pres. Best Discount Benefits, 2003—; founder Smart Consumer Group, 2003—. Owner, mgr. Opportunities Unltd., Oceanside, Calif., 1985-91; cons. Incentive Leasing Corp., San Diego, 1985-86, The Profit Ctr., Santa Ana, Calif., 1991; founding mgr. Meditrend Internat., San Diego, 1987-88; founding dir. Am. 3-D Corp., Henderson, Nev., 1990-91. Mem.: Fed. C. of C. (bd. advisors 2002—03). Republican. Avocations: computers, skiing, racquetball, scuba diving. Office: PO Box 4022 Oceanside CA 92052 Home Phone: 760-631-4300; Office Phone: 760-631-4300. Business E-Mail: ceo@freedomfinancialsolutionsinc.com.

TAYLOR, ALLAN ROSS, linguist, educator; b. Palisade, Colo., Dec. 24, 1931; s. Athel Ross and Marjorie Verle (Walters) T.; m. Mary Callas, Sept. 8, 1958; children: Artemisia, Anthony, Peter, Anna, Yoana. AB, U. Colo., Boulder, 1953; PhD (Woodrow Wilson fellow, Fulbright fellow, NDEA fellow), U. Calif., Berkeley, 1969; MA, U. Colo., Boulder, 2004. Teaching asst., lectr. U. Calif., Berkeley, 1958-63; instr. U. Colo., 1964-65, asst. prof., 1965-70, assoc. prof., 1970-77, prof., 1977-93, prof. emeritus, 1998—, also past chmn. dept. linguistics, dept. French and Italian. Cons. bilingual edn. for Native Ams. Active Dem. Party and in environ. issues. With U.S. Army, 1954-57. NEH grantee, 1972-76, 80-82, 87-90, 89-93. Home: 787 17th St Boulder CO 80302-7601 Office: U Colo Dept Linguistics PO Box 295 Boulder CO 80309-0295 E-mail: allan.taylor@colorado.edu.

TAYLOR, BARRY E., lawyer; b. Mineola, NY, Mar. 14, 1948; BA magna cum laude, U. Va., 1970, JD, 1975. Bar: Calif. 1975. With Wilson, Sonsini, Goodrich & Rosati P.C., Palo Alto, Calif. Mem. ABA, State Bar Calif., Order Coif, Phi Beta Kappa. Office: Wilson Sonsini Goodrich & Rosati PC 650 Page Mill Rd Palo Alto CA 94304-1050

TAYLOR, BARRY LLEWELLYN, microbiologist, educator; b. Sydney, May 7, 1937; arrived in US, 1967; s. Fredrick Llewelyn and Vera Lavina (Clarke) T.; m. Desmyrna Ruth Tolhurst, Jan. 4, 1961; children: Lyndon, Nerida, Darrin. BA, Avondale Coll., Cooranbong, New South Wales, 1959; BSc with honors, U. New South Wales, Sydney, 1966; PhD, Case Western Res. U., 1973; postgrad., U. Calif., Berkeley, 1973-75. Vis. postdoctoral fellow Australian Nat. U., Canberra, 1975-76; asst. prof. biochemistry Loma Linda (Calif.) U., 1976-78, assoc. prof. biochemistry, 1978-83, prof. biochemistry, 1983—, prof., chmn. dept. microbiology and molecular genetics, 1988-2000, interim dir. Ctr. for Molecular Biology, 1989-94, 96-98, v.p. for rsch. affairs, 2000—06, prof. microbiology and molecular genetics, 2006—. Contbr. articles to profl. publs. Rsch. grantee Am. Heart Assn., 1978-85, NIH, 1981—. Mem. Am. Soc. Microbiology,

Am. Soc. Biochemistry and Molecular Biology. Office: Divsn Microbiology and Molecular Genetics Loma Linda U Loma Linda CA 92350-0001 Office Phone: 909-558-4881. Business E-Mail: bltaylor@llu.edu.

TAYLOR, CARSON WILLIAM, retired electrical engineer; b. Superior, Wis., May 24, 1942; s. William Stanley and Elizabeth Marie (Christophersen) T.; m. Gudrun Renate Leistner, Dec. 28, 1966; 1 child, Natasha Marie. BSEE, U. Wis., 1965; M in Engring., Rensselaer Poly. Inst., 1969. Elec. engr. U.S. Bur. Reclamation, Billings, Mont., 1967-68, Bonneville Power Adminstrn., Portland, Oreg., 1969-89, prin. engr., 1989—2006; ret. Prin. Carson Taylor Seminars, Portland, 1986—. Author: Power System Voltage Stability, 1994; contbr. papers to profl. publs.; patentee in field. Lt. U.S. Army, 1965-67. Lt. U.S. Army, 1965-67. Fellow IEEE (chmn. subcom. 1982—); mem. NAE, Conférence Internationale des Grands Réseaux Électriques a Haute Tension (CIGRE, disting. mem.), Eta Kappa Nu. Lutheran. Avocations: fishing, hunting, woodworking, reading, computers.

TAYLOR, CHARLES A. (CHUCK TAYLOR), oil industry executive; b. Ind., 1957; BS in Engring., Purdue U., Ind., 1980; MBA, Tulane U., New Orleans, 1992. Drilling engr. to domestic and internat. engring. and mgmt. positions in upstream operations in the US, Indonesia, the UK and Nigeria Chevron Corp.; mgr. asset devel., area ops. mgr., Bekasap Strategic Bus. Unit Caltex Pacific, Duri, Sumatra, Indonesia, 1996—99; gen. mgr. Chevron UK, Aberdeen, Scotland, 1999—2003; gen. mgr., joint venture Chevron Nigeria Ltd. and Nigerian Nat. Petroleum Co., Nigeria, 2003—07; v.p. health, environment and safety Chevron Corp., 2007—. Chevron rep., bd. dirs. Offshore Prodrs. Trade Sect., UK Offshore Operators Assn.; Chevron rep., oil and gas sector Step Change Initiative. Recipient Allen R. Vorholt award, Tulane U., 1992. Mem.: Beta Gamma Sigma. Office: Chevron Corp Hdqs 6001 Bollinger Canyon Rd San Ramon CA 94583

TAYLOR, CHARLES ELLETT, biologist, educator; b. Chgo., Sept. 9, 1945; s. Stewart Ferguson and Barbara (Ellett) Taylor; m. Minna Glushien, June 22, 1969. AB, U. Calif., 1968; PhD, SUNY, Stony Brook, 1973. Prof. U. Calif., Riverside, 1974-80, UCLA, 1980—. Cons. artificial life and population genetics; dir. UCLA Cognitive Sci. Rsch. Program, 1990—99; mem. adv. bd. Computer Mus. Fishtank. Co-author: Artifical Life II, 1992, Artifical Life VI, 1998; editor: Artificial Life, 1997—2001; assoc. editor: IEEE Transactions on Evolutionary Computing, 1997—99; assoc. editor Artifical Life and Robotics, 1999—, Artificial Life, 2002—; mem. editl. bd.: Internat. Jour. Distributed Sensor Networks, 2004—; contbr. articles to profl. publs. Office: Dept Ecology and Evolutionary Biology UCLA Box 951606 Los Angeles CA 90095-1606 E-mail: ctaylor@ucla.edu.

TAYLOR, CHRISTINE, actress; b. Allentown, Pa., July 30, 1971; d. Skip and Joan Taylor; m. Ben Stiller, May 13, 2000; children: Ella Olivia, Quinlin Dempsey. Actor: (films) Calendar Girl, 1993, Showdown, 1993, The Brady Bunch Movie, 1995, Breaking Free, 1995, The Craft, 1996, A Very Brady Sequel, 1996, Cat Swallows Parakeet and Speaks, 1996, Campfire Tales, 1997, The Wedding Singer, 1998, Overnight Delivery, 1998, Denial, 1998, Kiss Toledo Goodbye, 1999, Desperate But Not Serious, 1999, Zoolander, 2001, Dodgeball: A True Underdog Story, 2004, The First Year's A Bitch, 2004, Room 6, 2006, Kabluey, 2007, Dedication, 2007, License to Wed, 2007; (TV films) Here Come the Munsters, 1995, To the Ends of Time, 1996, Heat Vision and Jack, 1999. Office: United Talent Agy 9560 Wilshire Blvd Ste 500 Beverly Hills CA 90212

TAYLOR, DAVID, state legislator; m. Molly Taylor; children: Tiffany, Brock. BA in Geography, Central Wash. U. Owner Taylor Angus Ranch, Taylor Consulting Group; planning dir. Kittitas County Planning Dept.; dir. Kittitas County Cmty. Devel. Svcs. Dept.; mem. Dist. 15 Wash. House of Reps., 2009—. Mem.: Land Use Com., Wash. State Farm Bur. (state chmn., Excellence in Agr.), Wash. Agr. and Forestry Edn. Found., Land Use Com., Wash. Cattleman's Assn. Republican. Office: 438 John L O'Brien Bldg PO Box 40600 Olympia WA 98504 Office Phone: 360-786-7874. E-mail: taylor.david@leg.wa.gov.

TAYLOR, FINLEY L., lawyer; b. Florence, Ala., Aug. 31, 1945; BA, U. Calif., Santa Barbara, 1967; JD, Vanderbilt U., 1970. Bar: Calif. 1971. Ptnr. Bus. Trial Practice Group Sheppard, Mullin, Richter & Hampton LLP, Costa Mesa, Calif. Articles editor Vanderbilt Law Review, 1969-70. Mem.: ABA (mem. Litig. Sec.), Orange County Bar Assn. (bd. dirs. 2000—02), State Bar Calif., Order of Coif. Office: Sheppard, Mullin, Richter & Hampton LLP 4th Fl 650 Town Ctr Dr Costa Mesa CA 92626 Office Phone: 714-513-5100. Office Fax: 714-513-5130. E-mail: ftaylor@sheppardmullin.com.

TAYLOR, FRANCIS MICHAEL, auditor, municipal official; b. Munich, 1960; came to the U.S., 1961; BS, Va. Tech., 1982. CPA Va., cert. internal auditor. Pub. acct., Roanoke, Va., 1982-84; controller ARC Roanoke, Inc., Roanoke, 1984-87; audit supr. City of Roanoke, 1987-94; city auditor City of Stockton (Calif.), 1994—. Nat. coord. com. Key Nat. Indicators Initiative. Mem. AICPA, Nat. Assn. Local Govt. Auditors (past pres.), Calif. Soc. CPAs, Inst. Internal Auditors, Govt. Fin. Officers Assn., Info. Sys. Audit and Control Assn., Bay Area Local Govt. Auditors. Office: 22 E Weber Ave Ste 325 Stockton CA 95202-1951

TAYLOR, GEORGE FREDERICK, newspaper publisher, editor; b. Portland, Oreg., Feb. 28, 1928; s. George Noble and Ida Louise (Dixon) T.; m. Georga Bray, Oct. 6, 1951; children— Amelia Ruth, Ross Noble. BS, U. Oreg., 1950. Reporter Astoria (Oreg.) Budget, 1950-52, Portland Oregonian, 1952-54; copy reader Wall St. Jour., 1955-57, reporter, 1957-59, Detroit Bur. chief, 1959-64, Washington corr., 1964-68, asst. mng. editor San Francisco, 1968-69, mng. editor NYC, 1970-77, exec. editor, 1977-86; pub. North Bend (Oreg.) News, 1981-86, Prime Time, 1987—, Coquille Valley Sentinel, 1989-2000. Lt. USAF, 1955-57. Mem. Oregon Newspaper Publishers Assn. (bd. dirs. 1997-2000). E-mail: Ftaylor@harborside.com.

TAYLOR, HOWARD S., chemistry and physics educator, researcher; b. NYC, Sept. 17, 1935; m. 1959; 3 children. BA, Columbia U., 1956; PhD in Chem. Physics, U. Calif., Berkeley, 1959. NSF post-doctoral fellow in chemistry Free U. Brussels, 1959-61; from asst. prof. to prof. chemistry U. So. Calif., LA, 1961—, Humboldt prof., 1974, prof. physics, 1975—. Cons. Jet Propulsion Lab. Calif. Inst. Tech., 1960—, Lawrence Livermore Nat. Lab., Los Alamos Sci. Lab.; guest prof. U. Amsterdam, U. Paris-Sud, Freiberg U. Recipient Max-Planck-Forschungs-prize Physics, Maths., Astronomy, 1992. Fellow Am. Phys. Soc.; mem. Am. Chem. Soc. Achievements includes research in atomic and molecular physics, lasers, dynamics, spectroscopy, chaotic phenomena, signal processing in chemistry and physics. Office: USC Dept Chemistry University Park Los Angeles CA 90007 E-mail: taylor@chem4.usc.edu.

TAYLOR, HUGH PETTINGILL, JR., geologist, educator; b. Holbrook, Ariz., Dec. 27, 1932; s. Hugh Pettingill and Genevieve (Fillerup) T.; m. Candis E. Hoffman, 1982. BS, Calif. Inst. Tech., 1954; A.M., Harvard U., 1955; PhD, Calif. Inst. Tech., 1959. Asst. prof. geochemistry Pa. State U., 1960-62; mem. faculty div. geol. and planetary scis. Calif. Inst. Tech., 1962—, now prof. geology, Robert P. Sharp prof., 1981. Crosby vis. prof. M.I.T., 1978; vis. prof. Stanford U., 1981; William Smith lectr. Geol. Soc. London, 1976; Hofmann lectr. Harvard U., 1980; Cloos lectr. Johns Hopkins U., 1986; with U.S. Geol. Survey, Saudi Arabia, 1980-81 Author: The Oxygen Isotope Geochemistry of Igneous Rocks, 1968, Stable Isotopes in High Temperature Geological Processes, 1986, Stable Isotope Geochemistry, 1991; assoc. editor Bull. Geol. Soc. Am, 1969-71, Geochimica Cosmochimica Acta, 1971-76; editor Chem. Geology, 1985-91. Recipient Day medal Geol. Soc. Am., Urey medal European Assn. Geochem., 1995. Fellow NAS, Soc. Econ. Geol., Geol. Soc. Am., Am. Geophys. Union, Mineral. Soc. Am. (councillor), Am. Acad. Arts and Scis.; mem. Geochem. Soc. (councillor). Republican.

TAYLOR, JACK, state legislator; b. Chgo., Nov. 22, 1935; m to Geneva; children: Vicki, two grandchildren. Member, W Steamboat Water & Sanitation District Bd, formerly, Steamboat Springs Home Rule Charter Comn, formerly, Steamboat Springs Chamber/Resort Association Bd, formerly, Irrigation Water Co, currently; chairman, Routt Co Republican, Colorado, 89-92; member, Senator Hank Brown's Mil Acad Selection Committee, currently; Colorado State Representative, District 56, 92-01, chairman, Bus Affairs & Labor & Agriculture, Livestock & Natural Resources Committees, 93-01, vice chairman, Legislature Audit Committee, formerly, Colorado House Representative; Colorado State Senator, District 8, 2001-, member, Agriculture, Natural Resources & Energy, Finance and Legislature Audit, currently, Colorado State Senate.Boeing Aerospace Apollo Moon Landing Proj, 62-67; management team, Peat Marwick Mitchell, Kuwait, Arabia, 67-68; self-employed businessman, currently. Legislator of Year, Colorado Ski Country USA, 94; 100% Rating, Nat Federal Independent Bus; Bus Legislator of Year, Colorado Association Commerce & Indust, 96 & 98; Guardian Small Bus Award, Nat Fedn Independent Bus, 96 & 98; Colorado Legislator of Year, Colo/Wyo Petroleum Marketers Association, 98. United States Chamber of Commerce; Nat Fedn of Independent Businessmen; Steamboat Springs Kiwanis Club (president, formerly). Republican. Protestant. Mailing: PO Box 5656 Steamboat Springs CO 80477

TAYLOR, JANET R., Mayor, Salem, Oregon; b. 1942; m. Duane Taylor; 5 children. Student, Chemeketa C.C. Lic. pvt. pilot 1981. Co-founder, exec. Taylor Metal Products, Salem, Oreg.; mayor City of Salem, Oreg., 2003—. Past chairwoman Salem Econ. Devel. Corp., S.E. Mill Creek Neighborhood Assn.; mem. Willamette River Bridge Task Force; sponsor A.C. Gilbert Discovery Village. Mem.: Salem Area C. of C. (v.p.), Salem Futures, Salem City Club, Salem Downtown Rotary. Office: 555 Liberty St SE Rm 220 Salem OR 97301 Office Phone: 503-588-6159. Business E-Mail: jtaylor@cityofsalem.net.*

TAYLOR, JOHN BRIAN, economist, educator; b. Yonkers, NY, Dec. 8, 1946; s. John Joseph and Lorraine (Crowley) T.; m. Raye Allyn Price, Dec. 30, 1972; children: Jennifer Lynn, John Andrew. AB in Econs. summa cum laude, Princeton U., 1968; PhD, Stanford U., 1973. Asst. prof. econs. Columbia U., NYC, 1973-77, assoc. prof., 1977-79, prof., 1979-80; prof. econs. and pub. affairs Princeton U., 1980-84; prof. economics Stanford U., 1984—93, Mary & Robert Raymond prof. economics, 1993—, dir. Ctr. for Econ. Policy Rsch., 1994-97, dir. Introductory Econs. Ctr., 1997-2001; under sec. for internat. affairs US Dept. Treasury, Washington, 2001—05. Vis. prof. econs. Yale U., 1980; sr. staff economist Pres.'s Coun. Econ. Advisers, 1976—77, mem., 1989—91; econometric cons. Townsend-Greenspan and Co., NY, 1978—81; rsch. advisor Fed. Res. Bank, Phila., 1981—84; rsch. assoc. Nat. Bur. Econ. Rsch., 1980—; rsch. economist Bank of Japan, Tokyo, 1987, hon. adviser, 1994—2001; panel of econ. advisers Congl. Budget Office, 1995—2001; sr. fellow Hoover Instn., 1996—. Author: (non-fiction) Macroeconomics, 1986, Macroeconomic Policy in the World Economy, 1993, Economics, 1995, Unemployment, Inflation, and Monetary Policy, 1998, Monetary Policy Rules, 1999, Handbook of Macroeconomics, 2000, Global Financial Warriors: The Untold Story of International Finance in the Post 9/11 World, 2007, Getting Off Track: How Government Actions and Interventions Caused, Prolonged and Worsened the Financial Crisis, 2009; co-editor: Am. Econ. Rev., 1985—89; assoc. editor: Econometrica, 1981—85, Jour. Econ. Dynamics and Control, 1978—85, Jour. Monetary Econs., 1978—83, Jour. Econ. Perspectives, 1997—2001, mng. editor: Internat. Jour. Ctrl. Banking, 2005—; contbr. articles to profl. jours. NSF grantee, 1979-81, 81-83, 83-86, 86-89, 92-95; Guggenheim Found. fellow, 1983-84. Fellow Econometric Soc., Am. Acad. of Arts and Sci.; mem. Am. Econ. Assn. (exec. com. 1991-94, v.p. 2000-01). Office: Stanford University 579 Serra Mall Stanford CA 94305 Office Phone: 650-723-9677. Business E-Mail: johnbtaylor@stanford.edu.*

TAYLOR, JOHN JOSEPH, nuclear engineer, researcher; b. Hackensack, NJ, Feb. 27, 1922; s. John J.D. and Johanna F. (Thibideau) T.; m. Lorraine Crowley, Feb. 5, 1943; children: John B., Nancy M., Susan M. BA, St. John's U., Jamaica, NY, 1942, DSc (hon.), 1975; MS, U. Notre Dame, Ind., 1947. Mathematician Bendix Aviation Corp., Teterboro, NJ, 1946-47; engr. Kellex Corp., NYC, 1947-50; v.p. water reactor divsn. Westinghouse Electric Corp., Pitts., 1950-81; v.p. nuc. power Electric Power Rsch. Inst., Palo Alto, Calif., 1981-95; energy cons., 1995—. Adv. com. Oak Ridge Nat. Lab., Tenn., 1973-83, Brookhaven Nat. Lab., Upton, NY, 1986-92, Inst. for Nuc. Power Ops., 1988-95; adv. com. Argonne Nat. Lab., Ill., 1980-86, bd. dirs.; cons. Office Tech. Assessment, Washington, 1975-93; internat. adv. group IAEA, Vienna, Austria, 1992-95; nuc. rsch. rev. com. NRC, 1995-97; mem. US-Russian Commn. on Weapons Plutonium Disposition, 1996-2001, Nat. Acad. Bd. Radioactive Waste Mgmt., 1998-2001, DOE Nuc. Energy Rsch. Adv. Bd., 1998-2002; co-chair Atoms for Peace Study, Livermore Lab., 2003-04; com. on rev. of Dept. Energy Nuc. Energy R&D, Nat. Acad., 2006-07. Co-author: Reactor Shielding Manual, 1953, Naval Reactor Physics Manual, 1956, Nuclear Power, Policy and Prospects, 1987, Management and Disposition of Excess Weapons Plutonium, 1995; contbr. articles to profl. jours. Bd. regents emeritus St. Mary's Coll., Moraga, Calif., Bd of Regents, St. Patrick's U. Calif. Lt. (j.g.) USN, 1942—45. Recipient Order of Merit Westinghouse Electric Corp., 1957, George Westinghouse Gold medal ASME, 1990. Fellow AAAS, Am. Phys. Soc., Am. Nuc. Soc. (bd. dirs., Walter Zinn award 1993, Nuclear Builders award, 2007); mem. NAE (chair), Elec. Power/Energy Sys. Engrs. Republican. Roman Catholic. Office: Electric Power Rsch Inst PO Box 10412 3412 Hillview Ave Palo Alto CA 94304-1344 Home: 620 Sand Hill Rd Apt 303b Palo Alto CA 94304-2069

TAYLOR, LESLIE GEORGE, mining and finance company executive; b. London, Oct. 8, 1922; arrived in U.S., 1925; s. Charles Henry and Florence Louisa (Renouf) Taylor; m. Monique S. Schuster, May 1964 (div. 1974); children: Leslie G. Anthony II, Sandra J. Mira, Linda S. Marshall(dec.); m. Wendy Ann Ward, July 4, 1979. BBA, U. Buffalo, 1952. Asst. to pres. Kelsey Hayes Co., 1952—60; pres. Aluminum Industries and Glen Alden Co., Cin., NYC, 1960—63; pres., chmn. bd. dirs. DC Internat. (and European subs.), Denver, 1963—68; prin. Taylor Energy Enterprises, Denver, 1968—, Taylor Mining Enterprises, Denver, 1968—, Leslie G. Taylor and Co., Denver, 1968—; gen. ptnr., sr. v.p. Am. Universal Mgmt. Corp., Miami Beach, Fla., exec. v.p. Grants Pass, Oreg., 2007—; sr. advisor 1st US Capital Corp., NY, Miami. Del. Internat. Astronautical Soc., Stockholm, 1968, London, 69, Speditur Conv., 1976, Spring Hill Capital LLC, Miami Beach, Fla. Mem. USCG Aux. Mem.: Soc. Automotive Engrs., Scottish Rite, Masons, Shriners. Republican. Episcopalian. Office Phone: 541-956-9600. Business E-Mail: lgtaylor@terragon.com.

TAYLOR, MIKE A., state legislator; b. Lewistown, Mont., June 12, 1941; m. Janna Taylor. Grad., Wilmington (Ohio) H.S. In bus. and agr.; mem. Mont. Senate, Dist. 37, Helena, 1996—; vice chair fish and game com.; vice chair jt. appropriations subcom. gen. govt. and transp.; mem. fin./claims com., natural resources com., rules com. Mem. Elks, Rotary. Republican. Home: PO Box 210 Dayton MT 59914-0210

TAYLOR, MINNA, lawyer; b. Washington, Jan. 25, 1947; d. Morris P. and Anne (Williams) Glushien; m. Charles Ellett Taylor, June 22, 1969; 1 child, Amy Caroline. BA, SUNY, Stony Brook, 1969; MA, SUNY, 1973; JD, U. So. Calif., 1977. Bar: Calif. 1977, U.S. Dist. Ct. (cen. dist.) Calif. 1978. Extern to presiding justice Calif. Supreme Ct., 1977; field atty. NLRB, LA, 1977-82; dir. employee rels., legal svcs. Paramount Pictures Corp., LA, 1982-85, v.p. employee rels. legal svcs., 1985-89; dir. bus. and legal affairs Wilshire Ct. Prodns., LA, 1989-91; sr. counsel Fox Broadcasting Co., LA, 1991-92, v.p. legal affairs, 1992-97, sr. v.p. legal affairs, 1997—. Webmaster www.if-come.com, 2001—. Editor notes and articles: U. So. Calif. Law Rev., 1976-77. Mentor MOSTE, L.A., 1986-87, 88-89; pres. Beverly Hills chpt. ACLU, LA, 1985; mem. Jr. League LA, 2003-, sec. 2006-07. Fellow ABA, Calif. State Bar (mem. copyright subcom. 1994-95), L.A. County Bar Assn.; mem. Beverly Hills Bar Assn., L.A. Bead Soc. (membership sec. 1992-94, mem. bd. dirs. 1994-95), Order of Coif. Office: Fox Broadcasting Co 10201 W Pico Blvd Los Angeles CA 90064-2606

TAYLOR, REESE HALE, JR., lawyer, former government administrator; b. LA, May 6, 1928; s. Reese Hale and Kathryn (Emery) T.; m. Lucille Langdon, Dec. 29, 1948 (div. 1959); children: Reese Hale (dec.), Stuart Langdon, Anne Kathryn, Lucille Emery; m. Jolene Yerby, June 30, 1972. BA with distinction, Stanford U., 1949; LL.B., Cornell U., 1952. Bar: Calif. 1954, Nev. 1966. Assoc. Gibson, Dunn & Crutcher, Los Angeles, 1952-58; pvt. practice Los Angeles, 1958-65; assoc. Wiener, Goldwater & Galatz, Las Vegas, Nev., 1966-67; chmn. Nev. Pub. Service Commn., Carson City, 1967-71; ptnr. Laxalt, Berry & Allison, Carson City, 1971-78, Allison, Brunetti, MacKenzie & Taylor, Carson City, 1978-81; chmn. ICC, Washington, 1981-85; ptnr. Heron, Burchette, Ruckert & Rothwell, Washington, 1986-90, Taylor & Morell, Washington and Long Beach, Calif., 1990-91, Taylor, Morell & Gitomer, Washington and Long Beach, 1992-94; of counsel Keesal, Young & Logan, Long Beach, 1994—. Vice chmn. Nev. Tax Commn., Carson City, 1967-69; mem. Nev. Gov.'s Cabinet, Carson City, 1967-70, Carson City Bd. Equalization, 1979-81, chmn., 1979-80; bd. dirs. U.S. Rail Assn., Washington, 1981-85 Del. Republican Nat. Conv., Kansas City, Mo., 1976, mem. platform com., 1976, alt. del., Detroit, 1980; mem. Rep. Nat. Com., 1980-81. Mem. ABA, Am. Judicature Soc., Order of Coif, Phi Gamma Delta, Phi Delta Phi. Episcopalian. Office: Keesal Young & Logan Union Bank Bldg PO Box 1730 Long Beach CA 90801-1730

TAYLOR, RICHARD EDWARD, physicist, researcher; b. Medicine Hat, Alta., Can., 1929; arrived in U.S., 1952; s. Clarence Richard and Delia Alena Taylor; m. Rita Jean Bonneau, 1951; 1 child, Norman Edward. BS, U. Alta., 1950, MS, 1952; PhD, Stanford U., 1962; DHC (hon.), U. Paris-Sud, 1980; DSc, U. Alta., 1991; LLD (hon.), U. Calgary, Alta., 1993; DSc (hon.), U. Lethbridge, Alta., 1993, U. Victoria, B.C., Can., 1995; DHC (hon.), U. Blaise Pascal, 1997; DSc (hon.), Carleton U., Ottawa, Ont., 1999, U. Liverpool, UK, 1999, Queen's U., Kingston, Ont., 2000. Boursier Lab. de l'Accelerateur Lineaire, Orsay, France, 1958—61; physicist Lawrence Berkeley Lab., Berkeley, Calif., 1961—62; staff mem. Stanford Linear Accelerator Ctr., 1962—68, assoc. prof., 1968—70, prof., 1970—2003, assoc. dir., 1982—86, Lewis M. Terman Prof., 1993—99, emeritus prof., 2003—. Recipient Nobel prize in Physics, 1990; named Companion, Order of Can., 2005; fellow Guggenheim Found., 1971—72, von Humboldt Found., 1982. Fellow: AAAS, Royal Soc. London, Royal Soc. Can., Am. Acad. Arts and Scis.; mem.: NAS (fgn. assoc.), Can. Assn. Physicists, Am. Phys. Soc. (W.K.H. Panofsky prize divsn. particles and fields 1989). Achievements include first to conduct investigations concerning deep inelastic scattering of electrons on protons and bound neutrons, which have been of essential importance for the development of quark model in particle physics. Office: Stanford Linear Accelerator Ctr M/S 43 2575 Sand Hill Rd Menlo Park CA 94025-7015 E-mail: retaylor@slac.stanford.edu.

TAYLOR, ROBERT BROWN, physician, educator, writer; b. Elmira, NY, May 31, 1936; s. Olaf C. Taylor and Elizabeth (Place) Brown; m. Anita Dopico; children: Diana Taylor Root, Sharon Taylor Oliverio. Student, Bucknell U., 1954-57; MD, Temple U., 1961. Diplomate Am. Bd. Family Medicine. Gen. practice medicine, New Paltz, NY, 1964-78; faculty physician Sch. Medicine Wake Forest U., Winston-Salem, NC, 1978-84; prof. dept. family medicine Oreg. Health Scis. U. Sch. Medicine, Portland, 1984—, chmn., 1984-98, prof. emeritus family medicine, 1998—. Mem. comprehensive part II com. Nat. Bd. Med. Examiners, Phila., 1986-91. Author: Common Problems in Office Practice, 1972, A Primer of Clinical Symptoms, 1973, The Practical Art of Medicine, 1974; editor: Family Medicine: Principles and Practice, 1978, 6th edit., 2003, Health Promotion: Principles and Clinical Applications, 1982, Difficult Diagnosis, 1985,

Difficult Medical Management, 1991, Difficult Diagnosis II, 1992, Fundamentals of Family Medicine, 1996, 3rd edit. 2003, Manual of Family Practice, 1997, 2d edit., 2002, Taylor's Review of Family Medicine, 1998, Manual of Ten-Minute Diagnosis, 2000, The Clinician's Guide to Medical Writing, 2004, Taylor's Diagnostic and Therapeutic Challenges, 2005, Taylor's Cardiovascular Diseases, 2006, Academic Medicine: A Guide for Clinicians, 2006, Taylor's Musculoskeletal Problems and Injuries, 2006, White Coat Tales: Medicine's Heroes, Heritage and Misadventures, 2008; contbg. editor Physicians Mgmt. Mag., 1972-99; editl. bd. Family Practice Rsch. Jour., 1980-90, Female Patient, 1984-2006, Am. Family Physician, 1990-98, Jour. Family Practice, 1990-93, Med. Tribune, 1993-99. Served as surgeon USPHS, 1961-64. Recipient J. David Bristow MD award, Oreg. Health Scis. U., 1993, F. Marian Bishop Leadership award, Soc. Tchrs. Family Medicine Found., 2007. Fellow Am. Acad. Family Physicians (sci. program com., Thomas W. Johnson award 1998, bd. curators found. archives, John G. Walsh Lifetime Achievement award 2003, Outstanding Sci. Paper award 1982); mem. Soc. Tchrs. Family Medicine (bd. dirs., Excellence cert. 1989), Assn. Am. Med. Colls., Am. Assn. for Study Headache, World Orgn. Family Doctors (chmn. sci. program com.), Portland City Club, Multnomah Athletic Club, Phi Beta Kappa (award 1957), Alpha Omega Alpha (award 1961). Home: 1414 SW 3rd Ave Apt 2904 Portland OR 97201-6629 Office: Oreg Health Sci U Sch Medicine Mail Code FM 3181 SW Sam Jackson Park Rd Portland OR 97239-3098 Home Phone: 503-241-1826; Office Phone: 503-494-6611.

TAYLOR, ROBERT P., lawyer; b. Douglas, Ariz., May 6, 1939; s. Paul Burton and Mary Ruth (Hart) T.; m. Sybil Ann Cappelletti, May 30, 1963 (div. Apr. 1974); children: David Scott, Nicole; m. Anne Dale Kaiser, Sept. 21, 1991. BSEE, U. Ariz., 1961; JD, Georgetown U., 1969. Bar: U.S. Ct. Appeals (9th circ.) 1969, U.S. Ct. Appeals (1st, 2d, 3d, 6th, and Fed. circs.), U.S. Supreme Ct., 1975. Elec. engr. Motorola Corp., Phoenix, 1961, Bell & Howell, Pasadena, Calif., 1964-65; examiner U.S. Patent Office, Washington, 1966-69; atty. Pillsbury Madison & Sutro, San Francisco, 1969-96, Howrey, Simon, Arnold & White, LLP, Menlo Park, Calif., 1996—. Mem. adv. commn. Patent Law Reform, Washington, 1990-92; mem. adv. bd. Litigation Risk Analysis, Palo Alto, Calif., 1985—. Contbr. articles to profl. jours. Dir. Ind. Colls. of No. Calif., San Francisco, 1982-96, officer, 1988-96. Fellow Am. Coll. Trial Lawyers; mem. ABA (chair sect. antitrust 1991-92), Am. Law Inst. Avocations: bicycling, cooking, hiking.

TAYLOR, ROBIN L., state legislator, lawyer; b. Sedro Woolley, Wash., Feb. 5, 1943; m. Kaye Marie Taylor; children: Robin, Tracy Lynn. BA, U. Wash., 1965; MA, Oreg. Coll. Edn., 1966; JD, Willamette U., 1969. Mem. Alaska Senate, Dist. A, Juneau, 1992—; chair adminstrv. regulation rev. com. Alaska Senate, chair judiciary com., vice-chair resources com. Pres. Alaska Judges Conf., 1981-82. Mem. Borough Assembly/City Coun., Ketchikan, 1973-76; vice mayor City of Ketchikan, 1974-75; dist. ct. judge, Alaska, 1977-82; pres. Pacific Conf., 1995-96; chmn. Western Legis. Forestry Task Force, 1996. Mem. NRA, Am. Judicature Soc. (nat. bd. dirs. 1980-83), Alaska Bar Assn., Pioneers of Alaska, Ketchikan Masons Lodge, Wrangell Elks Lodge, Petersburg Moose Lodge. Republican. Avocations: fishing, hunting, golf, gardening. Address: PO Box 1441 Wrangell AK 99929-1441 also: 50 Front St Ste 203 Ketchikan AK 99901-6439 Fax: 907-465-3922/907-874-3470/907-225-0713. E-mail: senatorrobintaylor@legis.state.ak.us.

TAYLOR, RUTH ANNE, lawyer; b. Honolulu, Feb. 18, 1961; d. Gerald Lou and Charlotte Anne (Nelson) Allison; m. Thomas Scott Taylor, Dec. 28, 1985; children: Kyle Thomas, Kelly Gerald, Kory Scott. BA in Journalism, U. So. Calif., 1984; JD, N.Y. Law Sch., 1987. Bar: Calif. 1987, U.S. Dist. Ct. (so. dist.) Calif., U.S. Ct. Appeals (9th cir.). Assoc. Carlsmith, Wichman, Case Mukai & Ichiki, L.A., LA, 1987-89, Christensen, White, Miller, Fink & Jacobs, LA, 1989-93; assoc. gen. counsel Warner Bros. Records, Inc., 1993-98, v.p. legal and bus. affairs, 1998—. Mem. Los Angeles County Bar Assn., Beverly Hills Bar Assn. Republican. Avocations: scuba diving, skiing, photography, cooking.

TAYLOR, S. BROOKE, lawyer; b. Port Angeles, Wash. BA in Polit. Sci., Stanford U., 1965; JD, U. Va., 1968. Bar: Wash. 1968. Dep. prosecuting atty. Clallam County, 1969—70, prosecuting atty., 1970—75; co-owner, ptnr. Taylor & Taylor P.S., Port Angeles, 1975—90, Platt Irwin Taylor, Port Angeles, 1991—. Spkr. in field. Dir., pres. Clallam County Family YMCA; dir. G.M. Lauridsen Found.; dir., pres. Clallam County Cmty. Mental Health Ctr.; mem., dir. Port Angeles C. of C.; mem. Penninsula Coll. Found. Named Citizen of Yr., Clallam County, 1999. Mem.: ABA, Assn. Trial Lawyers Am., Wash. State Trial Lawyers Assn., Clallam County Bar Assn. (pres. 1981), Wash. State Bar Assn. (mem. bd. govs. 2000—02, treas. 2001—02, chmn. facilities com. 2001—, liaison dist. and mcpl. ct. judges assn. 2003—04, pres.-elect 2004, pres. 2005), Kiwanis Club (dir.). Achievements include contributions to the Washington State Bar Association's "Diversity Amendment" (later called the "Taylor Draft") which expanded the Association's definition of diversity and led to the creation of three governor-at-large positions. Office: Platt Irwin Taylor 403 S Peabody Port Angeles WA 98362 Office Phone: 360-457-3327. Office Fax: 360-452-5010.

TAYLOR, SHELLEY E., psychology researcher, educator; b. Mt. Kisco, NY, Sept. 10, 1946; d. Charles Fox and Pearl May (Harvey) T.; m. Mervyn Francis Fernandes, May 1, 1972; children: Sara F., Charles F. AB magna cum laude in Psychology, Conn. Coll., 1968; PhD in Social Psychology, Yale U., 1972. Asst. prof. psychology and social rels. Harvard U., Cambridge, Mass., 1972-77, assoc. prof., 1977-79; assoc. prof. psychology UCLA, 1979-81, prof., 1981—. Mem. vis. faculty dept. adminstrv. scis. Yale U., New Haven, 1971-72, vis. Sloane fellow, 1978; mem. basic sociocultural rsch. rev. com. NIH, 1979-83; Katz-Newcomb lectr. U. Mich., 1982; cons. to pub. houses and TV producers. Author: Social Cognition, 1986, 2d edit., 1991, Health Psychology, 1986, 3d edit., 1995, 5th edit., 2002. Positive Illusions: Creative Self-Deception and the Healthy Mind, 1989, The Tending Instinct: How Nurturing is Essential to Who We Are and How We Live, 2002; contbr. numerous articles to sci. publs. Active numerous charitable and fund-raising orgns. including Curtis Sch. PTA and U. So. Calif./Norris Cancer Ctr. Recipient Rsch. Scientist Devel. award NIMH, 1981-86, 86-91, MERIT award, 1987, Donald Campbell award for disting. sci. contbn. to sociology, 1995; numerous rsch. grants in field; Winthrop scholar, 1967; Woodrow Wilson fellow, 1968, NIMH fellow, 1968-72. Fellow APA (Sci. Weekend lectr. 1988, Disting. Sci. award 1980, Outstanding Sci.Contbn. award Divsn. 38, 1994), Brit. Psychol. Soc. (flying fellow), Acad. Behavioral Medicine Rsch., Soc. Psychol. Study Social Issues, Soc. Behavioral Medicine; mem. AAAS, Soc. Exptl. Social Psychology, Western Psychol. Assn. (pres. 1993-94), Inst. Medicine. Office: UCLA Dept Psychology Franz 4611 Box 951563 Los Angeles CA 90095-1563

TAYLOR, STEVEN BRUCE, agriculture company executive; b. Salinas, Calif., Dec. 29, 1954; s. Edward Horton and Joanne (Church) T.; m. Kathryn Hagler, Dec. 17, 1978; children: Meghan Jean, Kyle Hagler, Christian Steven. BA, U. Calif., Berkeley, 1978; MBA, Harvard U., 1985. Pres. Fresh Concepts, San Marino, Calif., 1985-87; mktg. staff Bruce Church, Inc., Salinas, Calif., 1987-91; pres. Fresh Express Retail Mktg., Salinas, 1991-93, Fresh Internat., Salinas, 1991-93; CEO, chmn. Fresh Express Fresh Foods (formerly Fresh Internat.), Salinas, 1993—. V.p. Salinas Valley Lettuce Co-op, Salinas, 1990—; bd. dirs. Produce for Better Health, Del., 1991—. Bd. Elders First Presbyn. Ch., Salinas, 1989-92, personnel com. 1989-94, bldg. com. 1990—; founding mem. Lincoln Club of Monterey County, Salinas, 1990. Avocations: basketball, skiing, soccer, bible study, board games. Home: 515 Santa Paula Dr Salinas CA 93901-1517 Office: Fresh Express 950 E Blanco Rd Salinas CA 93901-4419

TAYLOR, TERESA, telecommunications industry executive; BS, U. Wis., LaCrosse. With US West (now Qwest), 1988—2000; exec. v.p. products and pricing group Qwest Comm. Internat., Inc., Denver, 2000—03, exec. v.p. wholesale markets group, 2003—04, exec. v.p., chief human resources officer, 2004—07, exec. v.p., chief adminstrv. officer, 2007—08, exec. v.p. Bus. Markets Group (BMG), 2008—. Bd. dirs. Colo. Inst. Tech., Colo. Children's Campaign, Colo. Symphony Orch. Office: Qwest Comm Internat Inc 1801 California St Denver CO 80202 Office Phone: 303-992-1400. Office Fax: 303-896-8515.

TAYLOR, TONY S., research scientist; Dir. exptl. sci. divsn. Gen. Atomics, San Diego. Recipient Excellence in Plasma Physics Rsch. award Am. Phys. Soc., 1994. Office: General Atomics PO Box 85608 San Diego CA 92186-5608

TAYLOR, WILLIAM AL, state supreme court justice; b. Lusk, Wyo., Nov. 2, 1928; m. Jane Y.; 3 children. BA, U. Wyo., 1951, LLD, 1959. Bar: Wyo. 1959. Teacher, Lusk, 1950-51,54-55; pvt. practice, 1959-78; city atty. Town of Lusk, 1962-74; atty. Niobrara County, Wyo., 1964-77; judge Wyo. Dist. Ct. (8th dist.), Cheyenne, 1980-93; justice Wyoming Supreme Ct., 1993—, chief justice, 1996-98. Exec. dir. Wyo. State Bar, 1977-80. Staff sgt. U.S. Army, 1951-53. Mem. Wyo. State Bar (Civil Rules com.), Wyo. Judicial Conf. (chmn. 1984-85),Tenth Cir. Bar Assn., Nat. Trial Judges, Am. Legion, Sigma Alpha Epsilon. Office: State Wyo Supreme Ct Supreme Ct Bldg Cheyenne WY 82002-0001

TAYLOR, WILLIAM JAMES (ZAK), lawyer; b. Milw., Jan. 26, 1948; s. William Elmer and Elizabeth Emily (Lupinski) T.; m. Marlou Belyea, Sept. 20, 1975; children: Danielle Belyea, James Zachary Belyea. BA in Econs., Yale U., 1970; JD, Harvard U., 1976. Bar: Calif. 1976, US Dist. Ct. (cen. dist.) Calif. 1976, US Dist. Ct. (no. dist.) Calif. 1977, US Ct. Appeals (9th cir.) 1977, US Dist. Ct. (ea. dist.) Calif. 1980, US Supreme Ct. 1980, US Tax Ct. 1988. Law clk. to hon. Shirley M. Hufstedler U.S. Ct. Appeals (9th cir.), LA, 1976-77; assoc. Broebeck, Phleger & Harrison, San Francisco, 1977-83; ptnr. Broebeck, Phleger and Harrison, San Francisco, 1983-95; shareholder Taylor & Jenkins, P.C., Oakland, Calif., 1995-96, Chilvers & Taylor, P.C., Oakland, 1996-99; of counsel Brobeck, Phleger & Harrison, LLP, San Francisco, 2000—03, Morgan Lewis & Bockius, LLP, San Francisco, 2003—04, ptnr., 2004—. Bd. dirs. Berkeley (Calif.) Law Found., 1988-91, Legal Svcs. for Children (recipient Jean Waldman Child Advocacy award, San Francisco 1988), 1983-89; co-chmn. Attys. Task Force for Children, San Francisco, 1983-89. Editor-in-chief Harvard Civil Rights, Civil Liberties Law Rev., 1976; bd. editors No. Dist. Calif. Digest, 1978-83; co-author: California Antitrust Law, 1991; contbg. editor: Calif. Bus. Law Reporter, 1995—, Antitrust Law Developments, 1997, 4th edit., 2002. With US Army, 1970—73. Mem. ABA, Bar Assn. San Francisco (bd. dirs. 1986-87, chair antitrust sect. 1987, chair fed. cts. sect. 1995-97; award of merit 1987), Am. Bus. Trial Lawyers Assn., Am. Health Lawyers Assn., Calif. Soc. Healthcare Attys., Barristers of San Francisco (bd. dirs. 1980-82, v.p. 1982-83). Democrat. Office: Morgan Lewis & Bockius LLP 1 Market Spear Tower San Francisco CA 94105-1420 Office Phone: 415-442-1315. Business E-Mail: wtaylor@morganlewis.com.

TCHAIKOVSKY, LESLIE J., federal judge; b. 1943; BA, Calif. State Univ., Hayward, 1967; JD, Univ. of Calif., Berkeley, 1976. Law clk. to Hon. John Mowbray Nev. Supreme Ct., 1976-77; with Dinkelspiel, Steefel, Leavitt & Weiss, 1977-80, Gordon, Peitzman & Lopes, 1981, Dinkelspiel, Donovan & Reder, 1981-88; bankruptcy judge U.S. Bankruptcy Ct. (Calif. no. dist.), 9th circuit, Oakland, 1988—. Office: US Courthouse 1300 Clay St Oakland CA 94612-1425

TEAGLE, RACHEL, museum director; PhD in Art History, Stanford U. Cur. San Francisco Mus. Modern Art; cur., co-dept. head Mus. Contemporary Art San Diego; exec. dir. Children's Mus. San Diego, 2007—. Office: Childrens Museum San Diego 200 W Island Ave San Diego CA 92101-6850 Office Phone: 619-233-8792.

TEAGUE, HARRY, United States Representative from New Mexico; b. Gracemont, Okla., June 29, 1949; m. Nancy Teague; 2 children. Founder, owner, pres. Teaco Energy Services, N.Mex.; mem. Lea County Bd. Commissioners, N.Mex., 1999—2006, chmn. N.Mex., 2003—06; mem. US Congress from 2nd N.Mex. Dist., 2009—. Bd. mem. Black Gold Race Track and Casino, LES Enrichment Facility; mem. N.Mex. State Transportation Com. Bd. mem. Lea County Big Brothers Big Sisters, Lea County Fair, Boys and Girls Club of Hobbs. Mem.: N.Mex. Oil and Gas Assn., Assn. Commerce and Industry. Democrat. Office: US Congress 1007 Longworth House Office Bldg Washington DC 20515-3102 also: Dist Office 200 E Broadway Ste 200 Hobbs NM 88240 Office Phone: 202-225-2365, 575-393-0510. Office Fax: 202-225-9599.*

TEAGUE, LAVETTE COX, JR., systems educator, consultant; b. Birmingham, Ala., Oct. 8, 1934; s. Lavette Cox and Caroline Green (Stokes) T. Student, Auburn U., 1951-54; BArch, MIT, 1957, MSCE, 1965, PhD, 1968; MDiv with distinction, Ch. Div. Sch. Pacific, 1979. Cert. computer profl. Inst. Cert. Computer Profls. Archtl. designer Carroll C. Harmon, Birmingham, 1957, Fred Renneker, Jr., Birmingham, 1958-59; architect Rust Engring. Co., Birmingham, 1959-62, Synergetics, Inc., Raleigh, NC, 1962-64, Rust Engring. Co., Birmingham, 1964-68; rsch. asst., instr., rsch. assoc. MIT, Cambridge, 1964-68; dir. computer svcs. Skidmore Owings & Merrill, San Francisco, Chgo., 1968-74; postdoctoral fellow UCLA, 1972; adj. assoc. prof. arch. and civil engring. Carnegie-Mellon U., Pitts., 1973-74; archtl. systems cons. Chgo., 1974-75, Berkeley, Calif., 1975-80, Pasadena, 1980-82, Altadena, Calif., 1982—. Lectr. info. systems Calif. State Poly. U., Pomona, 1980-81, prof., 1981-98, prof. emeritus, 1998—, asst. chair, 1990-91, chair, 1991-93, 96-98; Fulbright lectr., Uruguay, 1985; lectr. Peking U., 2004. Author: Event-Based Analysis and Design: An Introduction to Structured Methods, 2000; co-author: Structured Analysis Methods for Computer Information Systems, 1985, Object-Oriented Systems Analysis and Design with UML, 2005, Chinese edit., 2005. Mem. adv. bd. Ch. Div. Sch. of the Pacific. Recipient Tucker-Voss award MIT, 1967. Mem. AIA (Arnold W. Brunner scholar 1966), Assn. Computing Machinery, Sigma Xi, Phi Eta Sigma, Scarab, Scabbard and Blade, Tau Beta Pi, Chi Epsilon, Beta Gamma Sigma. Episcopalian. Home: 1696 N Altadena Dr Altadena CA 91001-3623 Office: 3801 W Temple Ave Pomona CA 91768-2557 Business E-Mail: lcteague@csupomona.edu.

TEAGUE, ROBERT COLE, physician; b. Waxahachie, Tex., June 13, 1930; s. Isaac Lawson and Frances (Cole) Teague; m. Virginia M. Teague, Nov. 11, 1960 (dec. May 1, 2005); children: Patrick, Michael. BA in Chemistry, Baylor U., Waco, Tex., 1951; MD, U. Tex., Galveston, 1955. Lic. physician Ariz. Intern McLaren Hosp., Flint, Mich., 1955—56; med. officer, active duty USNR, 1956—58; physician family practice LaJolla, Calif., 1958—63, Phoenix, 1963—. Med. dir., pres. Vis. Nurse Svc., Phoenix; chmn. Family Practice Humana Hosp., 1984—86, past chmn.; chmn. Family Practice Good Samaritan Hosp., 1990—91. Fellow Am. Acad. Family Physicians (charter); mem. Ariz. Acad. Family Physicians (pres. 1988). Republican. Episcopalian. Avocation: travel. Office: 7200 W Bell Rd G-103 Glendale AZ 85308

TEBEDO, MARYANNE, state legislator; b. Denver, Oct. 30, 1936; m. Don Tebedo; children: Kevin, Ronald, Linda, Thomas, Christine. Profl. registered parliamentarian. Mem. Colo. Ho. of Reps., Denver, 1982-88, Colo. Senate, Denver, 1988—2001; owner, pres. Colo. Mediation and Parliamentary Profls., Colorado Springs. Mediator 4th Jud. Dist. Colo. Mem.: Nat. Assn. Parliamentarians, Colo. Assn. Parliamentarians (pres.). Republican. Office Phone: 719-471-2561. E-mail: matebedo@isp.com.

TECK, RONALD JAY, state legislator; b. Pueblo, Colo., Sept. 22, 1947; s. John Alan Teck and Chloie Beatrice (Barnett) Morris; m. Beverly Merline Smith Kanda, Sept. 9, 1978 (div. 1987); m. Patricia Kay Artz, Nov. 6, 1989; children: Michael Alan, John Franklin. BA in Chemistry, U. Colo., 1970. Chemist Nat. Ctr. Atmosphere Rsch., Boulder, Colo., 1970-74; cons. Dames & Moore, Park Ridge, Ill., 1974-75, Ambient Analysis Inc., Boulder, 1975; sales rep. Sargent-Welch Scientific, Denver, 1975-77; program analyst Bendix Field Engring., Grand Junction, Colo., 1977-83; realtor Gale & Co., others, Grand Junction, 1983-92; assessor Mesa County Govt., Grand Junction, 1992-98; mem. Colo. Senate, Dist. 7, Denver, 1998—. Contbr. articles to profl. jours. Mem. legis. com. Grand Junction Bd. of Realtos, 1988-92, pres. 1986-87. Named Realtor of Yr. Grand Junction Bd. of Realtors, 1988-92. Mem. Colo. Assessors Assn., Grand Junction C. of C. (govtl. affairs). Republican. Avocations: camping, cooking. Address: State Capitol 200 E Colfax Ave Ste 346 Denver CO 80203-1716

TEDFORD, CHARLES FRANKLIN, biophysicist; b. Lawton, Okla., June 26, 1928; s. Charles E. and Loula B. (Waters) T.; m. Julie Reme Sauret, Sept. 15, 1951; children: Gary Franklin, Mark Charles, Philip John. BS with distinction in Chemistry, S.W. Tex. State U., 1950, MS, 1954; postgrad. in radiobiology Reed Coll., 1957, in biophysics U. Calif., Berkeley, 1961-63. Enlisted USN, 1945-47, commd. ensign, 1950, advanced through grades to capt., 1968; biochemist U.S. Naval Hosp., San Diego, 1953-54, U.S. Naval Biol. Lab., Oakland, Calif., 1954-56; sr. instr., radiation safety officer Nuclear, Biol. and Chem. Warfare Def. Sch., Treasure Island, Calif., 1956-61; asst. chief nuclear medicine div. Navy Med. Sch., Bethesda, Md., 1963-66; adminstrv. program mgr. radiation safety br. Bur. Medicine and Surgery, Washington, 1966-72; dir. radiation safety and health physics program Navy Regional Med. Center, San Diego, 1972-74; mgr. Navy Regional Med. Clinic, Seattle, 1974-78, ret., 1978; dir. radiation health unit Ga. Dept. Human Resources, Atlanta, 1978-79; dir. Ariz. Radiation Regulatory Agy., Tempe, 1979-91; chief, Radiological Health Prog., Juneau, Alaska, 1991-93, ret. 1993; cons. 1993—. elected chmn. Conf. Radiation Program Dirs., 1987; named Ariz. Southwestern Low Level Radioactive Waste Compact Commr., 1990. Recipient Ariz. Adminstr. of Yr. award Ariz. Adminstrs. Assn., 1988; decorated Legion of Merit, Meritorious Service medal. Mem. Health Physics Soc., Am. Nuclear Soc. Contbr. articles on radiation safety to profl. publs. Home Phone: 480-860-0608.

TEDFORD, JEFF, college football coach; b. Lynwood, Calif., Nov. 2, 1961; BS in physical edn., Fresno State U., 1983. Profl. football player Hamilton, Calgary, Saskatchewan, and Winnipeg (CFL), 1983—87; volunteer asst. coach Fresno State U., 1987—88; coached Calgary Stampede (CFL), 1989—91; quarterback coach Fresno State U., 1992—97; offensive coord. U. Oregon, 1998—2001; head coach U. Calif. Golden Bears, 2002—. Named Pac-10 coach of the year, 2002. Achievements include winning the Insight Bowl (2003), Las Vegas Bowl (2005); creating a team that earned the school's highest national ranking (No. 4) since 1952 and registered its best regular-season record (10-1) in 54 years. Office: UC Berkeley Intercollegiate Athletics 209 Memorial Stadium Berkeley CA 94720 Office Phone: 510-642-3857.

TEEGUARDEN, DENNIS EARL, forest economist, educator; b. Gary, Ind., Aug. 21, 1931; s. Gary Leon and Mary Dessa (Purciful) T.; m. Sally Annette Gleason, Dec. 23, 1954; children: Jason Earl, Julie Annette, Justin Gary. BS in Forestry with honors, Mich. Tech. U., Houghton, 1953; M.Forestry, U. Calif., Berkeley, 1958, PhD in Agrl. Econs. (Bidwell research fellow 1962-63), 1964. Rsch. aid U.S. Forest Service, 1957; asst. rsch. specialist U. Calif., Berkeley, 1958-63, mem. faculty, 1963-91, prof. forestry econs. Sch. Forestry, 1963-91, S.J. Hall prof. forest econs., 1989-91, prof. emeritus, 1991—, chmn. dept. forestry and resource mgmt., 1978-86, acting dir. forest products lab., 1987-88, assoc. dean for acad. affairs, 1990-92, assoc. dean rsch. and extension, 1992-93. Mem. Calif. Commn. on Agr. and Higher Edn., 1993-95, com. scientists Dept. Agr., 1977-80; cons. in field; mem. adv. bd. U. Calif. Forest Products Lab., 1994-98; mem. adv. coun. Alberta Heritage Found. for Sci. and Engring. Rsch., 2001-03. Co-author: Forest Resource Management: Decision-Making Principles and Cases, 1979; contbr. articles to profl. jours. Trustee Mich. Tech. Fund, Mich. Tech. U., Houghton, 1994-2004, life trustee, 2004—. Lt. USNR, 1953-57, Korea. Recipient Outstanding Alumnus award Mich. Tech. U., 1993, Berkeley citation U. Calif., Berkeley, 1994, Outstanding Svc. award Mich. Tech. Alumni Assn., 2007; grantee U.S. Forest Svc., Bur. Land Mgmt.; named to Honor Acad. Sch. Forestry and Wood Products, Mich. Tech. U., 1995. Fellow Soc. Am. Foresters; mem. Western Forest Economists, Calif. Water Fowl Assn. Home: 4732 Westwood Ct Richmond CA 94803-2441 Office: U Calif Coll Natural Resources Berkeley CA 94720-0001

TEEL, JOYCE RALEY, retail executive; b. 1930; m. James Teel. Dir. Raley's, West Sacramento, 1950—; co-chmn. bd. dirs. Raley's, Bel Air Markets, Food Source, Nob Hill Foods, No. Calif., Nev., NMex., 1991—. Dir. non-profit Food for Families. Named one of Forbes' Richest Americans, 2006. Office: Raleys & Belaire 500 W Capitol Ave West Sacramento CA 95605-2696

TEELE, CYNTHIA LOMBARD, lawyer; b. Boston, Oct. 11, 1961; d. John Hughes and Patricia Jeanne (Linder) T. AB in Urban Studies magna cum laude, Brown U., 1983; JD, U. Va., 1986. Bar: Calif. 1986. Assoc. Lillick McHose & Charles, LA, 1986-87, Wyman Bautzer Kuchel & Silbert, LA, 1987-91; sr. atty. Paramount Pictures Corp.-TV Divsn., Hollywood, Calif., 1991-92, dir., legal, 1992-94, v.p., legal, 1994—. Home: 3644 Berryman Ave Los Angeles CA 90066-3306

TEEMANT, MELANIE J., middle school educator; BS in Elem Edn., Univ. Nev., Las Vegas; MS student in Ednl. Leadership, Nova Southeastern Univ. Tchr. Clark County Sch. Dist., 1997—, Wengert Elem. Sch., Las Vegas, 1997—2001; reading tchr. Bob Miller Mid. Sch., Henderson, Nev., 2001—. Named Nev. Tchr. of Yr., 2007. Office: Bob Miller Middle Sch 2400 Cozy Hills Dr Henderson NV 89052 E-mail: mteemantx6@msn.com.

TEES, RICHARD CHISHOLM, psychology professor emeritus; b. Montreal, Que., Can., Oct. 31, 1940; s. Ralph Charles and Helen Winnifred (Chisholm) T.; m. Kathleen F. Coleman, Sept. 1, 1962; children: Susan M., Carolyn V. BA, McGill U., 1961; PhD, U. Chgo., 1965. Asst. prof. U. B.C., Vancouver, Canada, 1965-67, assoc. prof., 1969-75, prof. psychology, 1975—, head dept. psychology, 1984—94, 1999—2004, U. B.C. Okanogen transition mgmt. exec., 2004—07, acting dep. vice chancellor, acad. v.p., 2006. Rsch. prof. U. Sussex, Brighton, Eng., 1972-73, 77-78; chmn. grant selection panel Nat. Scis. and Engring. Rsch. Coun. Can., Ottawa, 1993-96, B.C. Health Care Rsch. Found., Vancouver, 1984-87; chmn. studentship com. Med. Rsch. Coun., Ottawa, 1985-92; chmn. Can. Coun. Dept. Psychology, 1987-93; mem. B.C. Degree Quality Assessment Bd., 2006—; chair bd. dirs. Cetacea Networks Corp., 2005—. Author: (with Kolb) Cerebral Cortex of the Rat, 1990; mem. editl. bd. Can. Jour. Exptl. Psychology, 1975-84, 87—; contbr. articles to profl. jours., chpts. to books. Rsch. fellow Killam Found., 1972-73, 77-78; Rsch. fellow Can. Coun., 1972-73. Fellow APA, Am. Psychol. Soc., Can. Psychol. Assn.; mem. Soc. for Neurosci., Psychonomic Soc., Can. Soc. Brain, Behaviour, and Cognitive Sci. (pres. 1997-98, Richard C. Tees Leadership award, 2004), U. B.C. Senate, Nat. Ctr. Excellence Can. Stroke Network. Office: U BC Dept Psychology Vancouver BC Canada V6T 1Z4 Home: 4506 W 14th Ave Vancouver BC V6R 2Y4 Canada Home Phone: 604-224-6030. Business E-Mail: rtees@psych.ubc.ca.

TEITELBAUM, STEVEN, plastic surgeon; b. LA, Aug. 22, 1962; AB, U. Calif. Berkeley; MD, UCLA, 1988. Lic. Mass., 1989, Calif., 1993, DEA, 1993, cert. Am. Bd. Plastic Surgery, 1997, Am. Bd. Plastic Surgery, 2006, Am. Bd. Surgery, 1995. Intern Harvard/Beth Israel Hosp., Boston, 1988—89, gen. surgery resident, chief resident, 1989—93; plastic & reconstructive surgery resident U. Southern Calif., 1993—95; at Santa Monica/ULCA Med. Ctr., 1995—2006, St. John's Hosp., Santa Monica, Calif., 1995—, UCLA Ctr. Health Sciences, 2006—; asst. clin. prof. plastic surgery UCLA David Geffen Sch. Medicine, 2006—; pvt. practice Santa Monica, Calif. Guest editor Aesthetic Surgery Jour., 2002—, Plastic & Reconstructive Surgery, 2006—. Chair new leadership div. Israel Bonds; state pres. Am. Jewish Congress; bd. mem. Maestro Found. U. Calif. Presdl. rsch. grant, 1982, Heart Assn. rsch. grant, 1985. Mem.: Internat. Soc. Aesthetic Plastic Surgeons, Internat. Ultrasonic Soc., Am. Coll. Surgeons, Calif. Soc. Plastic Surgeons, Bay Surg. Soc., LA Soc. Plastic Surgery (bd. dirs. 2005—, sec. 2005—), Calif. Soc. Plastic Surgery (ethics com. 2000—, co-chair exhibits com. 2001—04, co-chair legis. com. 2003—, exec. coun. 2006—), Calif. Med. Assn. (alt. del. 2004), Am. Soc. Plastic Surgeons (legis. com. 2002—04, exhibits com. 2004—06, performance metrics task force 2007—), Am. Soc. Aesthetic Plastic Surgery (govt. rels. com. 2001—03, electronic comms. com. 2003—, breast implant task force exhibits com. 2004, practice rels. com. 2004—, emerging trends task force & innovative procedures com. 2005—). Avocations: sailing, triathlon, photography, piano, scuba diving. Office: 1301 20th St Ste 350 Santa Monica CA 90404 Office Phone: 310-315-1121. Office Fax: 310-315-9921. Business E-Mail: steve@drteitelbaum.com.

TELLEM, NANCY REISS, broadcast executive; b. Danville, Calif., Dec. 13, 1953; m. Arn Tellem; children: Michael, Matthew, Eric. BA in Polit. Sci., U. Calif., Berkeley, 1975; JD, Hastings Coll. Law, 1979. Intern to Congressman Ron Dullums, Washington, 1974; with legal affairs dept. Lorimar TV; joined Warner Bros. TV, 1987, exec. v.p. bus. and fin. affairs; exec. v.p. bus. affairs CBS Entertainment, exec. v.p. CBS Prodns. CBS, 1997—98, pres. CBS Entertainment, 1998—2004; pres. CBS Paramount Network TV Entertainment Group, 2004—. Bd. dirs. ThirdAge Media. Named one of The 100 Most Powerful Women in Entertainment, Hollywood Reporter, 2005—07, The 100 Most Powerful Women, Forbes mag., 2007, 2008. Avocations: tennis, yoga, hiking, photography. Office: CBS Entertainment 7800 Beverly Blvd Los Angeles CA 90036

TELLEM, SUSAN MARY, public relations executive; b. NYC, May 23, 1945; d. John F. and Rita C. (Lietz) Cain; m. Marshall R.B. Thompson; children: Tori, John, Daniel. BS, Mt. St. Mary's Coll., LA, 1967. Cert. pub. health nurse; RN. Pres. Tellem Pub. Rels. Agy., Marina del Rey, Calif., 1977-80, Rowland Grody Tellem, LA, 1980-90; chmn. The Rowland Co., LA, 1990—; pres., CEO Tellem, Inc., LA, 1992-93. Instr. UCLA Extension, 1983-97; adj. prof. Pepperdine U., 1999—; speaker numerous seminars and confs. on pub. rels. Editor: Sports Medicine for the '80's, Sports Medicine Digest, 1982-84. Bd. dirs. Marymount High Sch., 1984-87, pres., 1984-86; bd. dirs. L.A. Police Dept. Booster Assn., 1984-87; mem. Cath. Press Coun.; mem. pres.'s coun. Mus. Sci. and Industry. Mem. Am. Soc. Hosp. Mktg. and Pub. Rels., Healthcare Mktg. and Pub. Rels. Assn., Pub. Rels. Soc. Am. (bd. dirs. 1994—), L.A. Counselors, PETA, Am. Lung Assn. (chair comm. com. L.A. chpt.) Soc. for Prevention of Cruelty to Animals (chair PetSet), Sports Club (L.A.). Roman Catholic. Avocations: reading, tennis, aerobics. Office: 23852 Pacific Coast Hwy # 928 Malibu CA 90265-4879 Office Phone: 310-479-6111. Fax: 310-589-6101. Business E-Mail: stellem@tellem.com.

TELLES, CYNTHIA ANN, psychologist; b. El Paso, Tex., Aug. 10, 1952; d. Raymond Lawrence and Delfina Telles; m. David Jimenez (div. Aug. 1991); 1 child, Raymond Jimenez. BA, Smith Coll., Northampton, Mass., 1974; PhD in Clin. Psychology, Boston U., 1982. Cert. psychologist, Calif. Psychologist U. Hosp. Boston U. Med. Ctr., 1977-78; rsch. fellow psychology dept. Spanish Speaking Mental Health Rsch. Ctr. UCLA, 1978-79, co-investigator, rsch. diagnostician, ucla dept. psychiatry, 1982-84, investigator and mgr. Spanish instrument tng. Epidemiologic Catchment Area Program Dept. Psychiatry, 1981-87; clin. project dir., co-investigator NIMH Grant, 1984-86; investigator NIMH, 1986-90; project dir., co-prin. investigator Calif. State Dept. Mental Health Grant, 1986—; psychologist adult outpatient dept. UCLA Neuropsychiat. Inst., 1979-80; dir. UCLA Spanish Speaking Psychosocial Clinic, 1980—. Media psychologist for TV and radio; cons. Boston City Police, 1975, Boulder County Community Mental Health Ctr., 1978, Spl. Svc. for Groups, LA, 1982, Ministry of Health, Lima, Peru, 1982, NIMH, 1984—, LA County Dept. Mental Health, 1985—, Calif. Sch. Profl. Psychology, 1986—; presenter in field; teaching fellow Boston U. Sch. Medicine, 1975-78; lectr. dept. psychiatry UCLA, 1980-85, asst. clin. prof., 1986-96, assoc. clin. prof., 1996-, mem. faculty adv. com. Chicano Studies Rsch. Ctr., 1988—; bd. dirs. United Calif. Bank, 1994-2002, Kaiser Health Plan and Hosps., 2004-, Calif. Cmty. Found., 2005-. Author: (with others) Psychiatric Epidemiology and Prevention: The Possibilities, 1985, Violence and Homicide in Hispanic Communities, 1988; contbr. articles to profl. jours.; mem. editorial bd. Hispanic Jour. Behavioral Scis., 1978-79; ad hoc reviewer Psychology of Women Quar., 1986-87. Bd. dirs. Coalition Pro-Salud Hispana, Boston, 1977-78, Nat. Hispanic Psychol. Assn., 1984-86, Ctr. for Study of Youth in Groups/Teen Line, Dept. of Psychiatry, Cedars-Sinai Med. Ctr., 1986-88, NCCJ, Southern Calif., 1990—, El Centro Human Svcs. Corp., 1988-90, Calif. Commerce Found., Calif. Endowment, 2001-, bd. chair, 2004-; mem. Nat. Adv. Com. on Hispanic Women and AIDS, Ctrs. for Disease Control and Hispanic Designers Inc., 1989—; pres., founder Hispanic Health Found., 1988-98. Boston U. Grad. scholar, 1975-79, APA Minority fellow, 1975-79; recipient Humanitarian award East LA Coll., 1988, Civic and Cmty. Leadership award Nat. Network of Hispanic Women, 1989, First Annual Achievement award for mental health pub. svc. APA Minority Fellowship Program, 1989, Crystal Eagle award CORO Found., 2006, Pioneer for Justice award Mex. Am. Found., LA, 2006, others. Mem. Nat. Hispanic Psychol. Assn. (charter), APA. Roman Catholic. Office: UCLA Dept Psychiatry 300 Ucla Medical Plz Los Angeles CA 90095-8346 Office Phone: 310-825-4568.

TELLIER, RICHARD DAVIS, management educator; b. Darby, Pa., Feb. 18, 1942; s. Joseph Campbell and Jane Grace (Davis) T.; m. Susan Gammon, June 10, 1974; children: John-Jo and Tiekka (twins). BSEE, Drexel U., 1967; MBA, Fla. State U., 1971, DBA, 1973. Elec. engr. Philco-Ford Corp., Phila., 1960-67; aerospace sys. engr. GE, Cape Canaveral, Fla., 1967-70; lectr. Fla. State U., Tallahassee, 1970-73; prof. mgmt. Calif. State U., Fresno, 1973-2000, chmn. dept. mgmt. and mktg., 1979-84, assoc. dean Sch. Bus., 1984-85, asst. dean, 1990-92, assoc. provost acad. resources, 1995-99, prof. emeritus, 2000—. Cons. ops. mgmt., market rsch. orgnl. behavior. Author: Operations Management: Fundamental Concepts and Methods, 1978, Production and Operations Management Test Bank, 1990; contbr. articles to profl. jours. Grantee 1975; recipient Meritorious Performance award, 1987, 88, 90. Mem. Ops. Research Soc. Am., Phi Kappa Phi. Home: 8294 N Academy Ave Clovis CA 93619-9454 Office: Calif State U Shaw and Maple Ave Fresno CA 93740-0001 Business E-Mail: rickt@csufresno.edu.

TEMBREULL, MICHAEL A., automotive executive; Grad., Stanford U., Calif., 1985. Gen. mgr. PACCAR, Inc., 1985—90, sr. v.p., 1990-92, exec. v.p., 1992-95, bd dirs., 1994—, vice chmn., 1995—; prin. fin. officer, vice chmn. PACCAR Fin. Corp. Office: PACCAR PO Box 1518 Bellevue WA 98009 Office Phone: 425-468-7400. Office Fax: 425-468-8216.

TEMES, GABOR CHARLES, electrical engineering educator; s. Erno and Rozsa (Angyal) Wohl-Temes; m. Ibi Kutasi-Temes, Feb. 6, 1954; children: Roy Thomas, Carla Andrea. Dipl.Ing., Tech. U. Budapest, 1952, DSc (hon.), 1991; Dipl. Phys., Eotvos U., Budapest, 1954; PhD, U. Ottawa, Ont., Can., 1961. Asst. prof. Tech. U. Budapest, 1952-56; project engr. Measurement Engring. Ltd., 1956-59; dept. head No. Electric Co. Ltd., 1959-64; group leader Stanford Linear Accelerator Center, 1964-66; corp. cons. Ampex Corp., 1966-69; prof. elec. engring. UCLA, 1969-90, chmn. dept., 1975-80; dept. head Oreg. State U., Corvallis, 1990—. Cons. Xerox Corp., ANT GmbH Author: (with others) Introduction to Circuit Synthesis and Design, 1977, Analog MOS Integrated Circuits for Signal Processing, 1986; assoc. editor: (with others) Jour. Franklin Inst, 1971-82; co-editor, contbg. author: (with others) Modern Filter Theory and Design, 1973, Oversampling Delta-Sigma Data Converters, 1991. Recipient Western Electric Fund award Am. Soc. Engring. Edn., 1982, Humboldt Sr. Rsch. award, 1991; NSF grantee, 1970— Fellow IEEE (life, editor Transactions on Circuit Theory 1969-71 Best Paper award 1969, 81, 85, Centennial medal 1984, Edn. award 1987, Tech. Achievement award 1989, Grad. Tchg. award 1998, Millenium medal 2000, CAS Golden Jubilee medal 2000, Gustav Robert Kirchhoff award 2006, Mac Valkenburg award, 2009). Home: 7100 NW Grandview Dr Corvallis OR 97330-2708 Office: Oreg State U Dept Elec Engring Corvallis OR 97331 Personal E-mail: temes@ieee.org. Business E-Mail: temes@ece.orst.edu.

TEMPELIS, CONSTANTINE HARRY, immunologist, educator; b. Superior, Wis., Aug. 27, 1927; s. Harry and Thelma Marie (Hoff) T.; m. Nancy Louise Foster, Aug. 27, 1955; children: William H., Daniel S. BS, U. Wis.-Superior, 1950; MS, U. Wis.-Madison, 1953, PhD, 1955. Project assoc. immunology U. Wis., Madison, 1955-57; instr. immunology U. W.Va., Morgantown, 1957-58; asst. rsch. immunologist U. Calif., Berkeley, 1958-66, assoc. prof. immunology, 1966-72, prof., 1972-95, prof. emeritus, 1995—, prof. grad. sch., 1996—. Vis. scientist Wellcome Rsch. Labs., Beckenham, Kent, Eng., 1977-78, U. Innsbruck, Austria, 1985, 90, 91; cons. in field. Contbr. articles to profl. jours. Served with USNR, 1945-46. Recipient Rsch. Career Devel. award, 1965-70; Fogarty sr. internat. fellow NIH, 1977-78 Mem. AAAS, Am. Assn. Immunologists, Fedn. Am. Soc. Exptl. Biology, Sigma Xi. Office: U Calif Sch Pub Health Berkeley CA 94720-0001 Home Phone: 510-524-7742; Office Phone: 510-642-3744. Business E-Mail: chtemp@berkeley.edu, champ@berkeley.edu.

TEMPEST, RICHARD BLACKETT, state senator, general contractor; b. Salt Lake City, Oct. 4, 1935; s. John Henry and Kathryn (Blackett) T.; m. Ruth Ottosen, Sept. 8, 1958; childrn: Robert, Lynne Anne, Michael, Mathew, David. BS, U. Utah, 1959. Sec.-treas. The Tempest Co., Murray, Utah, 1960—; senator Utah State Senate, Salt Lake City, 1987—. Bd. dirs. Sta. KUED, Salt Lake City. With U.S. Army, 1958-59. Mem. Associated Gen. Contractors (past sec.-treas.). Republican. Mem. Lds Ch. Avocations: shooting, hunting, gun collecting. Home: 4671 S 300 W Murray UT 84107-3737 Office: The Tempest Co 4681 S 300 W Salt Lake City UT 84107-3737

TEMPLE, THOMAS C., oil company executive; V.p. supply and distbn. U.S. Oil & Refining Co., LA, 1981-86, pres., CEO Tacoma, 1984—; exec. v.p. MacMillan Ring-Free Oil Co. Inc., NYC, 1986—. Office: US Oil & Refining Co 3001 E Marshall Ave Tacoma WA 98421-3116

TENNEN, LESLIE IRWIN, lawyer, consultant; b. Toronto, Aug. 26, 1952; came to U.S., 1961; s. Edward and Elsie (Liberbaum) T.; m. Patricia MargaretSterns. BA with distinction, U. Ariz., Tucson, 1973, JD, 1976; Mount Scopus, Hebrew U., Jerusalem, 1975. Bar: Ariz. 1977, US Dist. Ct. Ariz. 1979, US Ct. Appeals (9th cir.) 2007. Sole practice, Tucson, 1977—79; ptnr. Sterns and Tennen, Phoenix, 1979—. Cons. internat. law and aerospace activities; lectr. univs., colls. and law schs., UN(Vienna); mem. Ariz. Space Commn., 1994-2000, inventor, profl. aviation and aerospace congresses and seminars in N.Am., Europe, Asia, S.Am., Australia; judge Jessup Internat. Moot Court Competition, 1982, 83, 85, 92; dir., treas. Assn. US Mems. Internat. Inst. Space Law; com. mem. U. Belarusian Culture Internat. Orgn. Mem. editl bd. Space Regulations Libr.; contbr. Ariz. Law Rev., 1975-76; contbr. articles to profl. jours. Precinct committeeman State Dem. Conv., 1972-73. Received highest score Ariz. Bar Exam., Feb. 1977. Mem. AIAA (sr.), Ariz. Bar Found., Internat. Eurasian Acad. Scis., Internat. Inst. Space Law (Appreciation award 1998, Disting. Svc. award 2006), Internat. Acad. Astronautics, Am. Soc. Internat. Law, Soc. Aerospace Communicators Inc., Internat. Law Assn., Planetary Soc., Fedn. Aerospace Socs. in Tucson (exec. bd.). Office: 2915 N 16th Ave Phoenix AZ 85015 Office Phone: 602-254-5197. Business E-Mail: LTennen@astrolaw.com.

TENNENBAUM, MICHAEL ERNEST, investor; b. St. Petersburg, Fla., Sept. 17, 1935; s. Reubin and Frieda (Miller) T.; m. Suzanne Stockfisch; children by previous marriage: Mark Stephen, Andrew Richard. BS, Ga. Inst. Tech., 1958; MBA with honors, Harvard U., 1962. Assoc. Burnham & Co., NYC, 1962-64, Bear, Stearns & Co., NYC, 1964-69, sr. mng. dir., 1969-96, vice chmn. investment banking divsn., 1988-93; chmn. bd. dirs. Tech. Park, Atlanta, 1978-81; sr. mng. ptnr. Tennenbaum Capital Ptnrs., LLC, LA, 1996—. Bd. dirs. Pemco Aviation Group, chmn.; bd. dirs. Anacomp, Inc.; chmn. LA World Affairs Coun., WinCnp; founder Tennenbaum Inst. Enterprise Transformation, Ga. Tech. Sch. Indsl. and Systems Engring., Tennenbaum Interdisciplinary Ctr. Neuropsychiatric Inst. UCLA. Bd. govs., vice chmn. Boys and Girls Clubs Am.; mem. nat. adv. bd. Ga. Inst. Tech., 1971-77; mem. vis. com. Harvard U. Sch. Bus., Cambridge, Mass., 1986-92, bd. assocs., 1992—; trustee emeritus Ga. Tech. Found., Inc., Atlanta, 1988-96; bd. dirs. Joffrey Ballet, 1990-92, chmn. exec. com., 1991-92; bd. dirs. Music Ctr. LA County Unified Fund Cabinet, 1990-91; bd. vistiors UCLA Sch. Medicine, 2000-; chmn. LA Mayor's Spl. Adv. Com. on Fiscal Adminstrn., 1993-94, Calif. High Speed Rail Authority, 1998-2001; commr. Calif. Intercity HighSpeed Ground Transp. Commn. Home: 118 Malibu Colony Rd Malibu CA 90265-4642 Office: Tennenbaum Capital Partners Llc 2951 28th St Ste 1000 Santa Monica CA 90405-2993 Office Phone: 310-899-4950, 310-566-1001.

TENNYSON, PETER JOSEPH, lawyer; b. Winona, Minn., Mar. 18, 1946; s. Richard Harvey and Sylvia Josephine (Jadrich) T.; m. Mary Eileen Fay, Jan. 3, 1970; children: Mark Christian, Rachel Christine, Matthew Patrick, Erica Ruth. BA, Purdue U., 1968; JD, U. Va., 1975. Bar: Calif. Assoc. atty. O'Melveny & Myers, LA, 1975-82; v.p., gen. counsel Cannon Mills Co., Kannapolis, NC, 1982-84; ptnr. Stradling, Yocca, Newport Beach, Calif., 1984-89, Jones, Day, Reavis & Pogue, Irvine, Calif., 1990-95, Paul, Hastings, Janofsky & Walker, Costa Mesa, Calif., 1995—. Mem. Calif. Commn. on Future of Legal Profession and State Bar, 1994; lectr. in field. Mem. adv. bd. St. Joseph Hosp., Orange, Calif., 1987-; bd. dirs. Lincoln Club Orange County, 1991-93, South Coast Symphony, 1989-92; mem. found. bd. Orange County H.S. Arts. Capt. US Army, 1968—72. Recipient Attys. of Yr. award, Calif. Lawyer, 2003; named one of Best Lawyers in Am., 2006—07. Mem.: Orange County Bar Assn., South Coast Repertory Silver Circle, Performing Arts Bus. Alliance. Roman Catholic. Avocations: downhill skiing, swimming. Home: 19 Monaco Newport Beach CA 92660 Office: Paul Hastings Janofsky & Walker LLP 695 Town Center Dr Fl 17 Costa Mesa CA 92626-1924 Office Phone: 714-668-6237. Business E-Mail: petertennyson@paulhastings.com.

TEPER, JEFFREY ALLEN, computer software company executive; b. 1964; s. Gary Teper; m. Sandy Rynczak, Sept. 14, 1991; 2 children. BS in Info. Systems and Finance, NYU; MBA, Harvard U. Sr. v.p. Colonial Consulting Corp., NYC; with Windows Corp., 1992—, dir. orgn. mktg. & info, gen. mgr. SharePoint Portal Server bus. group, 2001—07, corp. v.p. Office SharePoint Server group, 2007—. Office: Microsoft Corp SharePoint Server Group 1 Microsoft Way Redmond WA 98052-6399

TEPSTEIN, DANIEL C., lawyer; b. Encino, Calif., May 28, 1971; BA, Loyola Marymount Univ., 1993; JD cum laude, Southwestern Univ., 1997. Bar: Calif. 1997, D.C. 1999, US Dist. Ct. Ctrl. & No. Calif., US Ct. Appeals Ninth Cir., US Supreme Ct. Judicial extern Judge Arthur Alarcon, US Ct. Appeals Ninth Cir., 1997; assoc. Haight, Brown & Bonesteel LLP, Santa Monica, Calif., 1997—99, O'Donnell & Mortimer LLP, LA, 1999—2004, ptnr., 2004—06; ptnr., intellectual property & antitrust litigation Hunton & Williams LLP, LA, 2006—. Adj. assoc. prof. Southwestern Univ. Sch. Law, 2002—04. Editor (in-chief): Southwestern Univ. Law Rev., 1997. Named a Rising Star, So. Calif. Super Lawyers, 2005—06. Mem.: State Bar Calif. Office: Hunton & Williams LLP Ste 2000 550 S Hope St Los Angeles CA 90071-2627 Office Phone: 213-532-2109. Office Fax: 213-532-2020.

TERADA, ALICE MASAE, retired elementary school educator; b. Hilo, Hawaii, Nov. 13, 1928; d. David Matsuo and Mitsuko (Sekido) Marutani; m. Harry T. Terada, Aug. 25, 1951; children: Suzanne T. Henderson, Keith Y., Lance S. Diploma, Queen's Hosp. Sch. Nursing, 1950; BS, We. Res. U., 1953; MEd, U. Hawaii, 1971. Cert. tchr., Hawaii. Registered nurse County Meml. Hosp., Hilo, Hawaii, 1950-51, U. Hosps., Cleve., 1952-53; lang. arts tchr. Dept. Edn., Honolulu,

1967-68; reading tchr. Reading Ctr., Honolulu, Hawaii, 1968-82; ret. Author: Under the Starfruit Tree, 1989, The Magic Crocodile, 1994. Mem. AAUW, Internat. Reading Assn., Zonta Club Internat., Zonta Club Honolulu (bd. dirs. 1996-97). Avocations: art, art history, porcelain antiques, yoga, swimming.

TERESI, JOSEPH, publishing executive; b. Mpls., Mar. 13, 1941; s. Cliff I.A. and Helen Ione (Leslie) (dec.); 1 child, Nicholas (dec.). CEO Jammer Cycle Products Inc., Burbank, Calif., 1968—80, Paisano Pubs. LLC, Agoura Hills, Calif., 1970—; chmn. bd., CEO V-Twin Expo, Agoura Hills, Calif., 1998—. Promoter motorcycle events; prodr. Easyriders Video mag.; owner Teresi Dyno Drags. Pub. (mags.) Easyriders, 1971—, In the Wind, 1974—, Biker, 1986—, Tattoo, 1986—, Am. Rodder, 1987-2001, Womens Enterprise, 1987-89, V-Twin News, 1989—, V-Twin, 1989, Tattoo Flash, 1993—, Tattoo Savage, 1993—, VQ, 1994—, Early-Riders, 1994-96, Quick Throttle, 1995-99, Roadware, 1995—, Tailgate, 2000, Tattoo Industry, 2000, Highbeams, 2003, Street Customs, 2004, Am. Choppers, 2004, Rebel Rodz, 2007; cable TV prodr.: V-Twin TV, 2004. Achievements include holding the world speed record for motorcycles set at 322 miles per hour, 1990-2006. Office: Paisano Pubs LLC PO Box 3000 Agoura Hills CA 91376-3000

TERR, LENORE CAGEN, psychiatrist, writer; b. NYC, Mar. 27, 1936; d. Samuel Lawrence and Esther (Hirsch) Cagen; m. Abba I. Terr; children: David, Julia. AB magna cum laude, Case Western Res. U., 1957; MD with honors, U. Mich., 1961. Diplomate Am. Bd. Psychiatry and Neurology (subspecialty bd. child and adolescent psychiatry). Intern U. Mich. Med. Ctr., Ann Arbor, 1961-62; resident Neuropsychiat. Inst. U. Mich., Ann Arbor, 1962-64, fellow Children's Psychiat. Hosp., 1964-66; from instr. to asst. prof. Case Western Res. U. Med. Sch., Cleve., 1966-71; pvt. practice Terr Med. Corp., San Francisco, 1971—; from asst. clin. prof. to clin. prof. psychiatry Sch. Medicine U. Calif., San Francisco, 1971—. Lectr. law, psychiatry U. Calif., Berkeley, 1971—90, Davis, 1974—88; dir. Am. Bd. Psychiatry and Neurology, 1988—96, chair psychiatry coun., 1996. Author: Too Scared to Cry, 1990, Unchained Memories, 1994, Beyond Love and Work, 1999, Magical Moments of Change, 2008; contbr. articles to profl. jours.; exhibited works in art show at Canessa Gallery, San Francisco, 2002. Recipient Career Tchr. award, NIMH, 1967—69, Child Advocacy award, APA, 1994; named to Cleveland Heights H.S. Disting Alumni Hall of Fame, 2003; grantee project, Rosenberg Found., 1977, William T. Grant Found., 1986—87, Leon Lowenstein Found., 2002; scholar-in-residence, Rockefeller Found., Italy, 1981, 1988. Fellow: Am. Acad. Child and Adolescent Psychiatry (coun. 1984—87), Am. Coll. Psychiatrists (program chair 1991—92, Bowis award 1993), Am. Psychiat. Assn. (Child Psychiatry Rsch. award 1984, Clin. Rsch. award 1987, Marmor Sci. award 2002); mem.: Phi Bet Kappa, Alpha Omega Alpha. Avocations: piano, walking, travel, gardening, needlepoint. Office: Terr Med Corp 450 Sutter St Rm 1336 San Francisco CA 94108-4204 Office Phone: 415-433-7800. Office Fax: 415-433-2130. E-mail: lenoreterrmd@sbcglobal.net.

TERRAS, AUDREY ANNE, mathematics professor; b. Washington, Sept. 10, 1942; d. Stephen Decatur and Maude Mae Bowdoin. BS with high honors in Math., U. Md., 1964; MA, Yale U., 1966, PhD, 1970. Instr. U. Ill., Urbana, 1968-70; asst. prof. U. P.R., Mayaguez, 1970-71, Bklyn. Coll., CUNY, 1971-72; asst. prof. math. U. Calif.-San Diego, La Jolla, 1972-76, assoc. prof., 1976-83, prof., 1983—. Prin. investigator NSF, 1974-88; vis. positions MIT, fall 1977, 83, U. Bonn West Germany, spring 1977, Inst. Mittag-Leffler, Stockholm, winter, 1978, Inst. Advanced Study, spring 1984, Math. Scis. Rsch. Inst., Berkeley, Calif., winter 1992, spring 1995, U. Aachen, Germany, 1998, Tsuda Coll., Tokyo, 1999, CRM, U. Montreal, 1999, U. Colo., Boulder, 2006, Newton Inst., Cambridge, Eng., 2007; dir. West Coast Number Theory Conf., U. Calif.-San Diego, 1976, AMS joint summer rsch. conf., 1984; Co-organizer, UCLA IPAM Workshops on Expanders, 2004, 2008; lectr. in field. Author: Harmonic Analysis on Symmetric Spaces and Applications, Vol. 1, 1985, Vol. II, 1988, Fourier Analysis on Finite Groups and Applications, 1999; editor: The Selberg Trace Formula and Related Topics, 1986; contbr. chapters to books, articles to profl. jours. Woodrow Wilson fellow, 1964, NSF fellow, 1964-68; NSF grantee Summer Inst. in Number Theory, Ann Arbor, Mich., 1973. Fellow: AAAS (nominating com. math. sect. project 2061); mem.: Assn. for Women in Sci., Assn. for Women in Math. (travel grants com. 1996, noether lectr. 2008), Soc. Indsl. and Applied Math., Math. Assn. Am. (program com. for nat. meeting 1988—90, chair joint program com. Am. Math. Soc. and Math. Assn. Am. 1991), Am. Math. Soc. (com. employment and ednl. policy com. on coms., coun., trans. editor, com. for the yr. 2000, western sect. program com., assoc. editor book revs. Bull., assoc. editor Notices). Achievements include research in harmonic analysis on symmetric spaces; number theory; graph theory. Office: U Calif San Diego Dept Math La Jolla CA 92093-0112

TERRELL, (NELSON) JAMES, physicist; b. Houston, Aug. 15, 1923; s. Nelson James Sr. and Gladys Delphine (Stevens) T.; m. Elizabeth Anne Pearson, June 9, 1945; children— Anne (dec.), Barbara, Jean BA, Rice U., 1944, MA, 1947, PhD, 1950. Rsch. asst. Rice U., Houston, 1950; asst. prof. physics We. Res. U., Cleve., 1950—51; mem. staff Los Alamos Nat. Lab., U. Calif., 1951—89, assoc., 1989—94; affiliate, 1994—2005; ret., 2005. Producer (computer generated movie) The X-Ray Sky, 1969-76; contbr. articles to profl. jours. and encys. Served to 1st lt. AUS, 1944-46 Graham Baker scholar Rice U., 1943-44; fellow Rice U., 1946-48, AEC, 1948-50 Fellow Am. Phys. Soc., AAAS; mem. Am. Astron. Soc., Internat. Astron. Union, Phi Beta Kappa, Sigma Xi Achievements include research in relativity, quasars, x-ray and gamma ray astronomy, nuclear physics, lasers. Home: 85 Obsidian Loop Los Alamos NM 87544-2528 Office Phone: 505-662-7582.

TERRITO, MARY C., health facility administrator, hematologist, educator; BS in Biology, Wayne State U., 1965, MD, 1968. Intern/resident in internal medicine Parkland Hosp., Dallas, 1971-73; fellow in hematology/oncology Harbor-U. Calif., LA, 1973-74, UCLA, 1974-75; rsch. assoc. Wadsworth VA Hosp., LA, 1975-81; asst. prof. dept. medicine UCLA, 1975-81, assoc. prof., 1981-96, prof., 1996—2007, dir. bone marrow transplant program Ctr. Health Scis., 1981—. Contbr. articles to profl. jours. Office: UCLA Bone Marrow Transplantation Program Ctr 42-121 CHS 10833 Le Conte Ave Los Angeles CA 90095-3075

TERRY, ROBERT DAVIS, neuropathologist, educator; b. Hartford, Conn., Jan. 13, 1924; m. Patricia Ann Blech, June 27, 1952; 1 son, Nicolas Saul. AB, Williams Coll., 1946, DSc (hon.), 1991; MD, Albany Med. Coll., NY, 1950. Diplomate: Am. Bd. Pathology, Am. Bd. Neuropathology. Postdoctoral tng. St. Francis Hosp., Hartford, 1950, Bellevue Hosp., NYC, 1951, Montefiore Hosp., N.Y.C., 1952-53, 54-55, Inst. Recherches sur le Cancer, Paris, 1953-54, sr. postdoctoral fellow, 1965-66; asst. pathologist Montefiore Hosp., 1955-59; assoc. prof. dept. pathology Einstein Coll. Medicine, Bronx, NY, 1959-64, prof., 1964-84, acting chmn. dept. pathology, 1969-70, chmn., 1970-84; prof. depts. neuroscis. and pathology U. Calif.-San Diego, 1984-94, prof. emeritus, 1994—. Mem. study sect. pathology NIH, 1964-68; study sects. Nat. Multiple Sclerosis Soc., 1964-72, 74-78; mem. bd. sci. counselors Nat. Inst. Neurol. and Communicative Disorders and Stroke, NIH, 1976-80, chmn., 1977-80; mem. nat. sci. coun. Huntington's Disease Assn., 1978-81; mem. med. and sci. adv. bd. Alzheimer Assn., 1978-88; mem. sci. adv. bd. Max Planck Inst., Martinsried, 1990-96. Mem. editorial adv. bd. Jour. Neuropathology and Exptl. Neurology, 1963-83, 85-88, Lab. Investigation, 1967-77, Revue Neurologique, 1977-87, Annals of Neurology, 1978-82, Ultrastructural Pathology, 1978-86, Am. Jour. Pathology, 1985-89. Served with U.S. Army, 1943-46, ETO. Recipient Potamkin prize for Alzheimer Rsch., 1988, Met. Life Found. award, 1991, Irving Wright award Am. Fedn. Aging Rsch., 2006. Fellow AAAS, Am. Acad. Arts and Sci.; mem. Am. Assn. Neuropathologists (pres. 1969-70, Meritorious Contbn. award 1989), N.Y. Path. Soc. (v.p. 1969-70, pres. 1971-73), Am. Assn. Pathologists, Am. Neurol. Assn., Am. Acad. Neurology. Achievements include research and publications on Alzheimer disease and Tay Sachs disease.

TERTELING-PAYNE, CAROLYN ANN, city official; b. Buhl, Idaho, Dec. 20, 1936; d. Carl Treva and Ann Christine (Witt) Edwards; m. Joseph Loyd Terteling, June 20, 1959 (div. Sept. 1991); children: Joseph Nixon, Steven Loyd, Thomas Edward, Andrew James; m. Frank Adrian Payne, May 13, 1995. BA with highest honors, U. Idaho, Moscow, 1959. Grad. tchg. asst. Ariz. State U., Phoenix, 1959-60; mem. Boise City Coun., 1993—, pres., 1996—2003; mayor City of Boise, Idaho, 2003—. Sustainer Boise Jr. League; mem. Collector's Forum, Boise Art Mus.; trustee, mem. exec. com., mem. bldg. and planning com. St. Lukes Regional Med. Ctr.; pres. Boise Pub. Libr. Found.; dir., past pres. U. Idaho Found.; dir. Fundsy Charitable Found., Boise River Festival; mem. adv. bd. Lit. Lab, Warm Springs Counseling Ctr.; hon. bd. Idaho Zool. Soc.; emeritus dir. Boise Philharmonic; past dir. Boise Mus. Art, Boise Bicentennial Commn., Boise Sch. Vols., Idaho Hist. Preservation Coun., Morriso Ctr. for Ars, Endowment Dr., Women's Life at St. Lukes, Idaho Law Found.; mem. adv. bd. Children at Risk Evaluative Svcs.; past dir. area coun. 11 Western states, Assn. Jr. Leagues Am.; past pres. St. Lukes Hosp. Aux., U. Idaho Found., Boise Jr. League; past chair symposium Albertson Coll. Idaho, Grand Opening of Morrison Ctr. for Arts, Sun valley, Arts and Humanities Benefit, Alternate Mobility Adventure Seekers, Boise State U. Named Idaho Statesman Disting. Citizen, 1979, Woman of Yr., C. of C., 1986; recipient Woman of Today and Tomorrow award Girl Scouts, 1992, Disting. Svc. award Idaho State Bar, 1992, Cultural Heritage award Coll. Letters and Sci. U. Idaho, 1994. Mem. U. Idaho Alumni Assn., Hillcrest Country Club (past dir.), PEO, Phi Beta Kappa, Gamma Phi Beta. Avocations: golf, tennis, gardening, reading. Home: 2050 Table Rock Rd Boise ID 83712-6663 Office: City Hall 150 N Capitol Blvd Boise ID 83702-5920

TERWILLIGER, MOLLY, lawyer; b. Wausau, Wisc., Sept. 27, 1972; BA, Northwestern Univ., Chgo., 1994; JD, Univ. Wis., Madison, 1998. Bar: Wis. 1998, Wash. 1998. Assoc. atty., antitrust, trade regulation Heller Ehrman LLP, Seattle. Contbr. articles to numerous profl. jours. Named Wash. Rising Star, SuperLawyer Mag., 2006. Mem.: ABA, Wash. Bar Assn. Office: Heller Ehrman LLP Ste 6100 701 Fifth Ave Seattle WA 98104-7098 E-mail: molly.terwilliger@hellerehrman.com.

TESH, JOHN, television talk show host, musician; b. Garden City, NY, 1953; s. John and Mildred Tesh; m. Connie Sellecca, Apr. 4, 1992; children: Gib, Prima. Co-host Entertainment Tonight, 1986-96; host One-On-One with John Tesh, 1991; co-host John and Leeza from Hollywood, 1993. Television appearances include: The U.S. Open Tennis Championship, 1985, Macy's Thanksgiving Day Parade, 1987, Wimbledon, 1991, TV film Hollyrock-a-Bye Baby, 1993, The Olympic Games, Barcelona, 1992, Atlanta, 1996, Star Trek, 1987; film appearances include Shocker, 1989, Soapdish, 1991, Love Affair, 1996; albums include Tour de France, 1988, The Early Years, 1990, Ironman, 1992, The Games, 1992, Monterey Nights, 1993, A Romantic Christmas, 1993, Wintersong, Sax by the Fire, Sax on the Beach, John Tesh Live at Red Rocks, Discovery, Avalon, A Family Christmas, 1995, Music in the Key of Love, 1995, Choirs of Christmas, 1996, Holiday Collection, 1996, Victory: The Sports Collection, 1997, Sax All Night, 1997, Grand Passion, 1998, One World, 1999; composers theme music Bobby's World, 1990, The Knife and Gun Club, 1990, One on One, 1991, NFL Live, NCA in NBC Theme, 1993. Recipient 4 Emmy awards for composing, 2 Emmy awards for reporting. Office: Garden City Music Teshmedia Group 13245 Riverside Dr # 305 Sherman Oaks CA 91423

TESTER, JON(ATHAN), United States Senator from Montana, former state legislator, farmer; b. Havre, Mont., Aug. 21, 1956; m. Sharla Tester; children: Christine, Shon. BS in Music, U. Great Falls, 1978. Tchr. Big Sandy School District, 1978—80; farmer organic wheat, barley, lentils, peas, millet, buckwheat, alfalfa and hay; mem. Mont. Senate from Dist. 45, Helena, 1998—2005, 2005—06, minority whip, 2001—03, minority leader, 2003—05, pres., 2005—06; US Senator from Mont., 2007—. Mem. Big Sandy Sch. Bd., 1983—91, chmn., 1986—91. Named an Outstanding Agrl. Leader, Coll. Agrl., Mont. State U., 2005. Democrat. Office: US Senate B-40E Dirksen Senate Office Bldg Washington DC 20510 Office Phone: 202-224-3121. E-mail: jontester@yahoo.com.*

TETZ, KAREN BONNIE, nurse, educator; b. Winnipeg, Manitoba, Can., Aug. 15, 1955; d. Ernest Alfred and Evelyn Anette Kay; m. Gerald Lee Tetz, June 13, 1977; children: Scott Jeffrey, Ashley Kay. PhD, Oreg. Health & Scis. U., Portland, 2003. Registered Wash. State Bd. Nursing, 1977. Prof. Walla Walla U., Portland, Oreg., 1986—. Predoctoral scholar John A. Hartford Found., 2001—03. Contbr. articles to profl. jours. Mem.: Gerontol. Soc. America. Office: Walla Walla Univ 10345 SE Market Portland OR 97216

TEVANIAN, AVADIS, JR., information technology executive; BA in Math., U. Rochester; MS in Computer Sci., PhD in Computer Sci., Carnegie Mellon U. Principal designer and engr. Mach operating system Carnegie Mellon U.; engr. to mgr. NEXTSTEP, NeXT, 1988—95; v.p. engring. NeXT, 1995—97; sr. v.p. software engring. Apple Computer Inc., 1997—2003, chief software tech. officer, 2003—06. Bd. dir. Tellme Networks, 2006—.

TEVRIZIAN, DICKRAN M., JR., judge; b. LA, Aug. 4, 1940; s. Dickran and Rose Tevrizian; m. Geraldine Tevrizian, Aug. 22, 1964; children: Allyson Tracy, Leslie Sara. BS, U. So. Calif., 1962, JD, 1965. Tax acct. Arthur Andersen and Co., LA, 1965-66; atty., ptnr. Kirtland and Packard, LA, 1966-72; judge LA Mcpl. Ct., 1972-78, State of Calif. Superior Ct., LA, 1978-82; ptnr. Manatt, Phelps, Rothenberg & Tunney, LA, 1982-85, Lewis, D'Amato, Brisbois & Bisgaard, LA, 1985-86; judge U.S. Dist. Ct., LA, 1986—. Adv. dir. UCLA Sch. Pub. Policy. Recipient Peter the Great Gold Medal of Honor Russian Acad. Natural Scis., 1998, Ellis Island Medal of Honor award, 1999, Disting. Pub. Svc. award Orange County Fed. Bar Assn., 2003. Mem. Calif. Trial Lawyers Assn. (Trial Judge of Yr. 1987), LA County Bar Assn. (Trial Judge of Yr. 1994-95), Malibu Bar Assn. (fed. ct. trial judge of yr. 1998, Maynard Toll award 2002, Jud. Svcs. award DSR Emil Gumpert ADR, 2005, Justice Armand Arabian Leaders in Pub. Svc. award 2005).

TEWKSBURY, TED (THEODORE L. TEWKSBURY III), communications executive; b. 1956; BSEE, MSEE, MIT, Cambridge, PhD in Elec. Engring. Sr. design engr. Analog Devices, Inc.; dir. SiGe RF/Analog Product Devel. IBM Microelectronics; gen. mgr., mng. dir. Maxim Integrated Products, Inc., Sunnyvale, Calif., 2000—06; pres., CEO AMI Semiconductor, Inc., Pocatello, Idaho, 2006—08, Integrated Device Tech., Inc., San Jose, Calif., 2008—. Bd. dirs. Integrated Device Tech., Inc., 2008—. Contbr. articles to profl. jours. Achievements include patents in field. Office: Integrated Device Tech Inc 6024 Silver Creek Valley Rd San Jose CA 95138 Office Phone: 408-284-8200. Office Fax: 408-284-2775.

TEXTOR, ROBERT BAYARD, cultural anthropology educator, writer, consultant; b. Cloquet, Minn., Mar. 13, 1923; s. Clinton Kenney and Lillian (Nickles) T.; divorced; children: Alexander Robertson, Marisa Elizabeth. Student, Lafayette Coll., 1940—41, Antioch Coll., 1941—43; BA in Asian Studies, U. Mich., 1945; PhD in Cultural Anthropology, Cornell U., 1960. Civil info. and edn. officer Mil. Govt., Kyoto-Wakayama, Japan, 1946-48; rsch. fellow anthropology and S.E. Asia studies Yale U., 1959-60, assoc., 1960-61; rsch. fellow in stats. Harvard U., 1962-64; assoc. prof. edn. and anthropology Stanford U., 1964-68, prof. edn. and anthropology, 1968-86, prof. anthropology, 1986-90, prof. anthropology emeritus, 1990—; co founder EFR Source Inc., Spoken, Wash., 2008. Vis. prof. U. Saar, Saarbrücken, Germany, 1984-85; cons. Motorola, Inc., 1991-2001, Ministry of Planning, Kuwait, 1999; mem. S.E. Asia Coun., 1974-77; cons. cultural anthropology to govt. agys., 1957-58, 61-62. Author: (with Arthur S. Banks) A Cross-Policy Survey, 1963, A Cross-Cultural Summary, 1967, Roster of the Gods: An Ethnography of The Supernatural in a Thai Village, 6 vols., 1973, Austria 2005: Projected Sociocultural Effects of the Microelectronic Revolution, 1983,(with Sippanondha Ketudat) The Middle Path for the Future of Thailand, 1990; (with others) Uncompromising Integrity: Motorola's Global Challenge, 1998; editor, commentator: Margaret Mead and the World Ahead: An Anthropologist Anticipates the Future, 2005; editor, commentator; (with Ernst Eugen Veselsky and others) The Future of Austria: Opportunities and Dangers in the Age of Nanotechnology, 2006; assoc. editor Jour. Conflict Resolution, 1965-70; mem. editl. bd. Human Orgn., 1966-71, Jour. Cultural Futures, 1979-87; adv. editor Behavior Sci. Rsch., 1974-86. Bd. dirs. Vols. in Asia, Stanford, Calif., 1968-73; mem. Metro Portland Future Vision Commn., 1993-95; Served with U.S. Army, 1943-46. Fellow Rockefeller Found., 1951-52, fgn. area tng. fellow Ford Found., Thailand 1955-58, Carnegie fellow, 1958-59, Fulbright West Europe rsch. fellow, 1984-85, East-West Ctr. fellow, 1988-90; NSF grantee, Thailand, U.S., 1969-73, Volkswagen Found. grantee, Thailand and Germany, 1984. Fellow Am. Anthrop. Assn. (life, chair resource devel. com. 2003-04), Soc. Applied Anthropology; mem. Siam Soc. (life), Assn. Asian Studies (life), Council on Anthropology and Edn. (pres. 1974-75), AAUP (pres. Stanford chpt. 1975-76), Phi Kappa Phi.

THACHER, CARTER POMEROY, diversified manufacturing company executive; b. 1926; With Wilbur-Ellis Co., San Francisco, 1960—, v.p., 1963-67, pres., from 1967, vice chmn., 1989—, also bd. dirs. Office: Wilbur-Ellis Co 345 California St Fl 27 San Francisco CA 94104-2644

THARP, FRED C., JR., federal judge, lawyer; BS, Hardin-Simmons U., 1958; JD, U.N.Mex., 1967. Bar: N.Mex. 1967. Ins. claims adjuster, claims mgr. Gen. Adjustment Bur., Clovis, 1958-64; law clk. to Hon. Joe Wood N.Mex. Ct. Appeals, 1967-68; pvt. practice Clovis, N.Mex., 1968—; part-time magistrate judge for N.Mex. U.S. Magistrate Ct., Clovis. Mem. staff U. N.Mex. Natural Resources Jour., 1966-67. Office: 716 Mitchell St Clovis NM 88101-6568

THAYER, MICHAEL J., secondary school educator; Tchr. Las Cruces (N.Mex.) Mid. Sch., 1972-94, Las Cruces H.S., 1994—. Named N.Mex. Tchr. of Yr., 1992. Office: Las Cruces HS 1755 El Paseo St Las Cruces NM 88001-6011

THEOLOGIDES, STERGIOS, lawyer, real estate company executive; BA, Princeton U.; JD, Columbia U. Assoc. corp. dept. O'Melveny & Myers, LLP, 1992—96; corp. counsel Wynn's International, Inc., 1996—98; v.p., gen. counsel New Century Fin. Corp., Irvine, Calif., 1999—, corp. sec., 1999—2005, exec. v.p. corp. affairs, 2003—. Exec. v.p. corp. affairs, sr. legal counsel, sec. New Century Mortgage; exec. v.p., dir. NC Capital; corp. sec. Home123, 2004—. Harlan Fiske Stone Scholar, Charles Evans Hughes Fellow. Office: New Century Fin Corp 18400 Von Karman Ste 1000 Irvine CA 92612

THERIOT, JULIE, microbiologist, medical educator; BS, MIT, 1988; PhD in Cell Biology, U. Calif. San Francisco, 1993; predoctoral fellow, Howard Hughes Med. Inst., 1988—93; fellow, Whitehead Inst.for Biomedical Rsch., 1993—97. Asst. prof., biochemistry, microbiology and immunology Stanford U. Sch. Medicine, Calif., 1997—. Author: of numerous articles pub. in such acad. jour. as Nature, Proceedings of the Natl. Acad. of Sci. USA, and Jour. of Cell Biology. Named a MacArthur Fellow, 2004. Office: Theriot Lab Beckman Ctr Dept Biochemistry Stanford Univ Med Sch Stanford CA 94305

THEROUX, DAVID JON, economist, educator, research and development company executive; b. Lansing, Mich., May 25, 1949; s. Paul Richard and Marjorie Erma (Withrow) Theroux; m. Elaine Laconia Shipp, 1976 (div. 1991); children: Paul Jacques, Drake Emeri; m. Mary Lyn Garvey, 1991. AB in Applied Math., U. Calif., Berkeley, 1973, BSME, 1973, MSME, 1974; MBA, U. Chgo., 1977. Rsch. asst. Richmond Field Sta., U. Calif., Berkeley, 1974, U. Chgo., 1976; project engr. Exxon Co. U.S.A., 1975—76; dir. vis. lectr. program in econ. sci. U. Chgo., 1977; v.p., dir. acad. affairs, dir. pub. policy studies Cato Inst., San Francisco, 1977—79; pres., dir. Pacific Rsch. Inst. Pub. Policy, San Francisco, 1979—86, Ind. Inst., Oakland, Calif., 1986—90; pres., gen. ptnr. LTN Ptnrs., 1986—90; pub., editor LibertyTree Network, 1986—; pub. Independent Review: A Journal of Political Economy. Adv. bd. No. Calif. Econ. Seminars, 1981—; bd. dirs. Grocery Express, Ltd., 1986—; mem. Coun. for Monetary Reform. Sr. editor Policy Report, 1978—79; editor: Cato Papers, 1978—79, The Energy Crisis: Government Policy and the Economy, 1978; editor: (with P. Truluck) Private Rights and Public Lands, 1983; editor: Politics and Tyranny: Lessons in Pursuit of Freedom, 1985. Trustee William Koch Found., 1978—79; mem. Mencken award book com. Free Press Assn., 1990—; exec. com. Templeton Honor Roll for Higher Edn. in a Free Soc. With USAF, 1967—72. Recipient George Washington Honor medal for excellence, Freedoms Found., 1983, Mencken award for Best Book, Free Press Assn., 1988. Mem.: Pub. Choice Soc., Nat. Assn. Bus. Economists, So. Econ. Assn., Western Econ. Assn., Royal Econ. Soc., Am. Econ. Assn., John Randolph Club, Omicron Delta Epsilon, Pi Tau Sigma. Home: 11990 Skyline Blvd Oakland CA 94619-2421 Office: 100 Swan Way Oakland CA 94621-1428

THERRIAULT, GENE, state legislator; b. Fairbanks, Alaska, Jan. 31, 1960; m to Jo; children: Justin & Jordyn. BBA, U. Alaska, Fairbanks, 1978—83. Assoc Students, Univ Alaska, Senate, 82; Legislature asst to Representative Mike Miller, 84-92; Alaska State Representative, District 33, 93-01, co-chmn, House Finance Committee, formerly, member, House Committee on Committees, Legislature Budget & Adult Committees, formerly, Alaska House Representative; Alaska State Senator, District Q, 2001-02; Alaska State Senator, District F, 2003-, currently minority leader; board director, North Pole Paper, Printing & Off Products, 87-91; partner, Hectors Welding, Inc, THE Company, currently. Jr Achievement Fairbanks (volunteer teacher, 89-91, board director, 90-); Mothers Against Drunk Driving; Alaska Outdoor Coun; Nat Fedn Independent Businesses. Republican. Mailing: 119 N Cushman Fairbanks AK 99701 Office: Dist F 3340 Badger Rd Ste 290 North Pole AK 99705 also: State Capitol Rm 427 Juneau AK 99801 Office Phone: 907-465-4797, 907-488-0857. Office Fax: 907-465-3884, 907-488-4271. Business E-Mail: Senator_Gene_Therriault@legis.state.ak.us.*

THIEBAUT, WILLIAM, state legislator, lawyer; b. Santa Fe, Dec. 11, 1947; m. Mary Ann Thiebaut. BA, U. N.Mex.; JD, Oklahoma City U. Bar: Colo. Mem. Colo. Ho. of Reps., Denver, 1986-93, Colo. Senate, Dist. 3, Denver, 1993—; asst. minority leader. Mem. appropriations com., edn. com., judiciary com., transp. com., joint legis. coun. Mem. Colo. Gov.'s Task Force on Govtl. Immunity, on Deinstitutionalization Mentally Ill, on Worker's Compensatoin Premium Rate Increases, Criminal Justice Comm.; mem. adv. com. Colo. 4-H Youth; chmn. labor-mgmt. com. Pueblo (Colo.) Depot Activity Assistance Program. Mem. Colo. Bar Assn., Pueblo County Bar Assn., Eagles. Democrat. Office: Colo State Senate State Capitol 200 E Colfax Ave Ste 274 Denver CO 80203-1716 also: PO Box 262 Pueblo CO 81002-0262 Fax: 719-544-8899.

THIEL, PETER ANDREAS, hedge fund manager; b. 1967; BA in Philosophy, Stanford U., JD. Securities law atty. Sullivan & Cromwell; derivatives trader CS Fin. Products; founder, head Thiel Capital Mgmt. LLC; chmn., CEO Confinity, Inc; co-founder PayPal, Inc., 1998, chmn., CEO, 1998—2002; founder, pres., chmn. Investment Com. Clarium Capital Mgmt., LLC, 2003—. Rsch. fellow, bd. dirs. Independent Inst.; bd. dirs. Pacific Rsch. Inst., Facebook, Inc., 2004—. Co-author: The Diversity Myth, 1998. Bd. visitors Stanford Law Sch.; bd. dir. The Hoover Inst. Avocation: chess. Office: Clarium Capital Management LLC 1 Letterman Dr Ste 400 San Francisco CA 94129-1495 Office Phone: 415-248-5140. Office Fax: 415-248-5141.*

THIEL, PHILIP, retired design educator; b. Bklyn., Dec. 20, 1920; s. Philip and Alma Theone (Meyer) T.; m. Midori Kono, 1955; children: Philip Kenji, Nancy Tamiko, Susan Akiko, Peter Akira (dec.) BSc, Webb Inst. Naval Architecture, 1943; MSc, U. Mich., 1948; BArch, MIT, Cambridge, 1952. Registered arch., Wash. Instr. naval architecture MIT, Cambridge, 1949—50; instr. architecture U. Calif., Berkeley, 1954—56, asst. prof., 1956—60; assoc. prof. U. Wash., Seattle, 1961—66, prof. visual design and experiential notation, 1966—91; guest prof. Tokyo Inst. Tech., 1976—78; vis. prof. Sapporo Sch. Arts, Japan, 1992—98. Lectr., US, Can., Japan, Norway, Denmark, Sweden, Eng., Austria, Switzerland, Peru, Bolivia, Korea; cons. FAO, Rome, 1952; co-founder Environment and Behavior, 1969; founder Ctr. for Exptl. Notation, Seattle, 1981 Author: Freehand Drawing, 1965, Visual Awareness and Design, 1981, People, Paths and Purposes, 1997; patentee in field Soc. Naval Architects and Marine Engrs. scholar, 1947; Rehmann scholar AIA, 1960; grantee NIMH, 1967, Nat. Endowment for Arts, 1969, Graham Found., 1995 Mem. Soc. Naval Archs. and Marine Engrs. (assoc.), Phi Beta Kappa, Sigma Xi

THIEMENS, MARK H., chemistry professor; b. St. Louis, Jan. 6, 1950; m. Nasrin Thiemens; 2 children. BS, U. Miami, 1972; MS, Old Dominion U., 1974; postgrad., Fla. Inst. Technology, 1974-75; PhD, Fla. State U., 1977. Grad. rsch. asst. dept. oceanography Old Dominion U., Norfolk, Va., 1972-74; grad. rsch. asst. dept. physics Fla. Inst. Technology, Melbourne, 1974-75; participant trace element aerosol rsch. program Fla. State U., Tallahassee, 1975-76; researcher dept. atmospheric chemistry Brookhaven Nat. Labs., Upton, N.Y., 1976-77; postdoctoral fellow Enrico Fermi Inst. U. Chgo., 1977-80; vis. prof. dept. chemistry U. Calif., San Diego, La Jolla, 1980-81, asst. prof. step II dept. chemistry, 1981-83, asst. prof. step IV dept. chemistry, 1983-85, assoc. prof. step I dept. chemistry, 1985-87, assoc. prof. dept. chemistry step II, 1987-88, assoc. prof. step III dept. chemistry, 1988-89, prof. step I dept. chemistry, 1989-91, prof. step II dept. chemistry, 1991-93, prof. step III dept. chemistry, 1993-95, prof. step VII dept. chemistry, 1996-2000, prof. step IX dept. chemistry, 2000—, chair dept. chemistry, 1996-99, dean divsn. phys. sci., 1999—. Dir. Cr. Environ Rsch. and Tng. U. Calif., San Diego, 1996—, mem. Ctr. Astrophysicis and Space Sci., 1980—, Scripps Inst. Oceanography, 1996—; mem. workshop panel Origins of Solar Sys. NASA, 1989, mem. panel cosmochemistry divsn. group b isotope geochemistry, 1996—, cosmochemistry rev. panel Johnson Space Ctr., 1997; organizer, convenor 1997 Informal Symposium on Kinetic and Photochemical Processes in the Atmosphere, 1997. Contbr. numerous articles to profl. jours. Alexander von Humboldt fellow Inst. Phys. Chemistry U. Göttingen (Germany), 1990-91, 93; Camille and Henry Dreyfus tchg. scholar, 1984-89; recipient Ernest Orlando Lawrence Meml. award US Dept. of Energy, 1999, Disting. Scientist of Yr. award Am. Chem. Soc., 2002. Fellow Meteoritical Soc.; mem. Am. Acad. Arts Scis., NAS. Achievements include development of analytical capability to measure stable isotope variations at ultra-high precision in sulfur, oxygen, carbon and nitrogen to use in development of experimental programs in varying research fields including atmospheric chemistry, physical chemistry of gas phase photochemical eractions, electrical plasmas, early solar system history, and gas-solid conversion mechanisms; development of the ability to measure sulfur isotopic in meteoritic and lunr material to a precision greater than an order-of-magnitude over previous laboratory determination to determine the nature of pre-solar sulfur chemistry, cosmic-ray-spallation, and nucleosynthetic inputs; development of rocket borne atmospheric sampling and analysis.

THIGPEN, STEPHEN P., horticulture products company executive; b. 1956; BS in Plant and Soil summa cum laude, U. Mass.; PhD in Plant Physiology, U. Calif., Davis. Joined Weyerhauser Co., 1981, gen. mgr. Vacaville nursery, 1985; pres., CEO Hines Horticulture, Inc., Irvine, Calif., 1995—, chmn. bd., 2000—. Bd. dirs. Coun. for a Green Environment. Office: Hines Horticulture Inc 12621 Jeffrey Rd Irvine CA 92620 Office Fax: 949-786-0968.

THIRLBY, OLIVIA, actress; b. NYC, Oct. 6, 1986; Attended, Royal Acad. Dramatic Art, London. Tng. Shakespearian acting Am. Globe Theatre, NYC. Actress (films) United 93, 2006, Unlocked, 2006, Snow Angels, 2007, Juno, 2007, Love Comes Lately, 2007, The Secret, 2007, The Wackness, 2008. Office: c/o Mgmt 360 9111 Wilshire Blvd Beverly Hills CA 90210

THIRLBY, RICHARD COLLER, surgeon; b. Traverse City, Mich., Aug. 30, 1952; s. Richard Leeson Thirlby; m. Patricia Rosso, July 17, 1976; children: Marjorie Rose, David Ryan. BA, Dartmouth U., Hanover, NH, 1974; MD, U. Mich., Ann Arbor, 1978. Contbr. articles to profl. jours. Mem.: ACS (pres. Wash. State chpt. 2003—04), Am. Bd. Surgery (bd. dirs. 2006—), Western Surg. Assn. (pres. 2005—06). Office: Virginia Mason Med Ctr 1100 9th Ave Mailstop C6-GSUR Seattle WA 98111

THIRY, KENT J., health products executive; BA in Polit. Sci., Stanford U., 1978; MBA with honors, Harvard U., 1983. Sr. cons. Andersen Consulting, 1978-81; ptnr., v.p. Bain & Co., 1983—91; pres., COO Vivra, Inc., San Francisco, 1991-92, pres., CEO, 1992-97; chmn., CEO Vivra Holdings Inc., 1997—99, Da Vita Inc., El Segundo, Calif., 1999—. Dir. Oxford Health Plans, 1998—2004, chmn., 2002—04. Bd. dirs. Val. Ctr. San Mateo County. Mem. Phi Beta Kappa. Office: 601 Hawaii St El Segundo CA 90245-4814

THISTLETHWAITE, DAVID RICHARD, architect; b. Burlington, Iowa, Aug. 24, 1947; s. Robert and Nona (Binder) T.; m. Carol Anne Armstrong, Aug. 22, 1970. BArch, Iowa State U., 1971. Registered arch., Calif., 1979, Minn., 1975; registered Nat. Coun. Archtl. Registration Bds., 1978; cert. Health Care arch., Am. Coll. Healthcare Archs., 2000. Designer Morrison Architects, St. Paul, 1971-73, Times Architects, Mpls., 1973-74; project architect Bentz/Thompson Assocs., Mpls., 1974-77; project mgr. Setter Leach Lindstrom, Mpls., 1977-78; project architect Wurster Bernardi Emmons, San Francisco, 1978-79, Strotz & Assocs., Tiburon, Calif., 1979-81, Hood Miller Assoc., San Francisco, 1981-84; prin., ptnr. R S T Architects, San Francisco, 1984-88; prin. Thistlethwaite Archtl. Group, San Francisco, 1988—2007; v.p., prin. HGA Archs. & Engrs., Inc., 2007—. Contbr. articles to profl. jours. Mem. AIA (nat. profl. devel. com. 1983-86, treas. San Francisco chpt. 1985-86, chmn. Calif. coun. health facilities com. 1994-96, chmn. design com. Acad. Architecture for Health, 1994-96, Calif. coun. ins. bd. trustees 1988-2002, Calif. coun. legis. com. 1996-98) Am. Coll. Healthcare Archs. (mem. pub. rels. com. 2004-05), Am. Soc. Healthcare Engring., Design Profls. Safety Assn. (bd. dirs.). Office Phone: 415-814-6910.

THOM, RICHARD DAVID, retired electronics executive; b. St. Louis, Oct. 4, 1944; s. Reginald James and Vlasta (Koukl) T.; m. Linda Marie Hunt, Sept. 9, 1967; children: Elizabeth Marie, Robert James. BS in Physics, U. Mo., Rolla, 1967; MSEE, UCLA, 1971. Co-op engr. McDonnell Aircraft Corp., St. Louis, 1962-67; head advanced tech. group IR systems dept., aerospace group Hughes Aircraft Co., Culver City, Calif., 1967-72; mem. tech. staff Santa Barbara Rsch. Ctr., Hughes Aircraft Co., Goleta, Calif., 1972-76, asst. mgr. R&D Lab., 1976-80, mgr. advanced applications, 1980-83, chief engr., 1984-86, chief scientist, 1986-90, dir. tech., 1990-95; tech. program exec. Hughes Aircraft Co., Goleta, Calif., 1995-98; asst. mgr. Raytheon Santa Barbara Rsch. Ctr., Goleta, Calif., 1998-99; ret. Contbr. articles to profl. jours.; patentee in field. Recipient Hughes Group Patent award for pioneering contbns. in infrared detector tech., 1990. Mem. IEEE, Tau Beta Pi, Sigma Pi Sigma, Delta Sigma Phi. Republican. Avocations: freelance travel writing and photography, specializing in railway travel around the world. Home: 38 Fawn Run Pl PO Box 326 Coupeville WA 98239-0326 Home Phone: 360-678-1444. Personal E-mail: richthommail@aol.com.

THOMAS, ANDREW P., prosecutor; b. Long Beach, Calif., 1966; BA Political Science, Univ. of Missouri, 1988; JD, Harvard Univ., 1991. Bar: Arizona 1991. Lawyer private practice, 1991—94; asst. atty. gen. State of Arizona; chief atty. Arizona Dept. of Corrections; deputy county atty. Maricopa County, Ariz., 2003—04, dist. atty. Ariz., 2005—. Office: District Attorney 301 W Jefferson St Ste 800 Phoenix AZ 85003

THOMAS, BRIAN CHESTER, retired state legislator, engineer; b. Tacoma, May 19, 1939; s. Ralph R. and Katheryne Thomas; m. Judith Lynn Adams, Feb. 20, 1965; children: Jeffrey, Kyle, Cheryl. BS in Engring., Oreg. State U., 1961; student in Law, U. Wash., 1968—70; MBA, Pacific Luth. U., 1979. Civil engr. U.S. Coast Guard, Seattle, 1962-63, ops. officer Astoria, Oreg., 1964-65; sr. sales engr. Puget Sound Power & Light Co., Bellevue, Wash., 1965-70, mgr. market rsch., 1971-80, rsch. adminstr., 1981-89, prin. engr., rsch. dir., 1989-97; mem. Wash. Ho. of Reps., Olympia, 1993-2001, mem. forecast coun., 1996-2001, mem. joint select com. on edn. restructuring, 1995-2001, chmn. fin. com., 1995-2001, chmn. Sch. Constrn. Task Force, 1998-99, energy, utilities com., 1999-2001, mem. Edn. Com., 1999-2001. Chair EEI Rsch. Mgmt. Com., Washington, 1988-89, EPRI Renewable Com., Palo Alto, Calif., 1989-90; adv. bd. Nat. Renewable Energy Lab., Golden, Colo., 1990-93; mem. adv. bd. sch. elec. engring. Oreg. State U., Corvallis, 1991-97; dep. dir. region 10 U.S. Dept. Transp. Emergency Orgn., Seattle, 1989-93. Bd. dirs. Issaquah (Wash.), Sch. Dist., 1989-93, pres. 1992; trustee Mcpl. League of King County, 2000-03; pres. Friendship Force of Seattle, 2002. Capt. USCGR, 1961-84, ret Master: Knights St. Andrew; mem.: Issaquah Rotary (pres. 1982—83), Preston Aboretum (dir., pres. 1999—2002), Navy League, Scottish Rite and York Rite, past master: Myrtle Lodge 108 F&AM, Wash., Royal Order of Scotland, Phi Sigma Kappa. Republican/Libertarian. Home: 14715 182nd Pl SE Renton WA 98059-8028 Home Phone: 425-226-0463.

THOMAS, CHARLES ALLEN, JR., molecular biologist, educator; b. Dayton, Ohio, July 7, 1927; s. Charles Allen and Margaret Stoddard (Talbott) T.; m. Margaret M. Gay, July 7, 1951; children: Linda Carrick, Stephen Gay. AB, Princeton U., NJ, 1950; PhD, Harvard U., 1954. Rsch. scientist Eli Lilly Co., Indpls., 1954-55; NCR fellow U. Mich., Ann Arbor, 1955-57; prof. biophysics Johns Hopkins U., Balt., 1957-67; prof. biol. chemistry Med. Sch. Harvard U., Boston, 1967-78; chmn. dept. cellular biology Scripps Clinic & Rsch. Found., La Jolla, Calif., 1978-81; pres., dir. Helicon Found., San Diego, 1981—; founder, CEO The Syntro Corp., San Diego, 1981-82; founder, CEO, now dir. of R & D Pantox Corp., San Diego, 1989—. Mem. genetics study sect. NIH, 1968-72; mem. rsch. grants com. Am. Cancer Soc., 1972-76, 79-85. Mem. editl. bd. Virology, 1967-73, Jour. Molecular Biology, 1968-72, BioPhysics Jour., 1965-68, Chromosoma, 1969-79, Analytic Biochemistry, 1970-79, Biochim Biophys. ACTA, 1973-79, Plasmid, 1977—. With USNR, 1945-46. NRC fellow, 1965-66. Mem. AAAS, Am. Acad. Arts and Scis., Am. Fedn. Biol. Chemists, Genetics Soc. Am., Am. Chem. Soc. Achievements include research in genetic and structural organization of chromosomes and development of a practical assessment of the antioxidant defense system by analytical biochemistry. Home: 1640 El Paso Real La Jolla CA 92037-6304 E-mail: cathomas@pantox.com.

THOMAS, CLAUDEWELL SIDNEY, psychiatrist, educator; b. NYC, Oct. 5, 1932; s. Humphrey Sidney and Frances Elizabeth (Collins) T.; m. Carolyn Pauline Rozansky, Sept. 6, 1958; children: Jeffrey Evan, Julie-Anne Elizabeth, Jessica Edith. BA, Columbia U., 1952; MD, SUNY, Downstate Med. Ctr., 1956; MPH, Yale U., 1964. Diplomate Nat. Bd. Med. Examiners, Am. Bd. Psychiatry. From instr. to assoc. prof. Yale U., New Haven, 1963-68, dir. Yale tng. program in social community psychiatry, 1967-70; dir. div. mental health service programs NIMH, Washington, 1970-73; chmn. dept. psychiatry UMDNJ, Newark, 1973-83; prof., chmn. dept. psychiatry Drew Med. Sch., 1983—93, chmn. dept. psychiatry, 1983-93; prof. dept. psychiatry UCLA, 1983-94, vice chmn. dept. psychiatry, 1983-93, prof. emeritus dept. psychiatry, 1994—; med. dir. Tokanui Hosp., TeAwamutu, N.Z., 1996. Cons. A.K. Rice Inst., Washington, 1978—80, SAMSA/PHS Cons., 1991—99, L.A. County Homeless Outreach Program, 2001—04; mem. LA County Superior Ct. Psychol. Panel, 1991—97; cons. psychiatrist L.A. County AB2034 Homeless Outreach Program (Skid Row Dual Diagnoses), 2001—04. Author: (with B. Bergen) Issues and Problems in Social Psychiatry, 1966; editor (with R. Bryce LaPorte) Alienation in Contemporary Society, 1976, (with J. Lindenthal) Psychiatry and Mental Health Science Handbook; mem. editl. bd. Adminstrn. Mental Health. Bd. dirs. Bay Area Found., 1987—. Served to capt. USAF, 1959-61. Fellow APHA, Am. Psychoanalytic Assn. (hon.), Am. Psychiat. Assn. (disting. life), NY Acad. Sci., NY Acad. Medicine; mem. Am. Sociol. Assn., Am. Coll. Mental Health Adminstrs., Am. Coll. Psychiatrists (emeritus), Sigma Xi. Avocations: tennis, racquetball, violin, piano. Office: 30676 Palos Verdes Dr E Palos Verdes Peninsula CA 90275-6354 Personal E-mail: cysid32@ucla.edu, cst240@columbia.edu.

THOMAS, DANIEL FOLEY, retired diversified financial services company executive; b. Washington, Aug. 24, 1950; s. Richard Kenneth and Margaret (Foley) T.; m. Barbara Jane Clark, June 30, 1973; 1 child, Alison Clark. BS in Acctg., Mt. St. Mary's Coll., 1972. CPA, Va. Auditor Deloitte & Touche, Washington, 1972-74; various fin. positions Comm. Satellite Corp., Washington, 1974-78, asst. treas., 1984-85, treas., 1986-87, contr., 1987-89, Comsat Telesystems, Washington, 1978-79; mgr. acctg. and taxes Satellite Bus. Systems, McLean, Va., 1979-81, treas., 1981-84; v.p. fin. Comsat Tech. Products, Inc., Washington, 1985-86, Comsat Video Enterprises, Inc., Washington, 1989-90; exec. v.p. Leasetec Corp., Boulder, Colo., 1990—2002; ret., 2002. Instr. acctg. Colo. State U., 2003—, U. Colo., 2003—. Active cmty. svc. activities. Mem. AICPA, Va. Jaycees (life), Great Falls Jaycees (pres. 1978). Roman Catholic. Avocations: running, golf. Home: 36495 Peak to Peak Hwy Nederland CO 80466 Office Phone: 303-808-1181. E-mail: dfthomas@aol.com.

THOMAS, DAVID ALBERT, law educator, director; b. LA, Feb. 4, 1944; s. Albert Rees and Betty Lou (Adams) T.; m. Paula Rasmussen, Aug. 7, 1967; children: Rebecca, David R., John H., Matthew A., Susannah, Amanda, Christina, Erin. BA, Brigham Young U., 1967; JD, Duke U., 1972; MLS, Brigham Young U., 1977. Jud. clk. U.S. Dist. Ct. Utah, Salt Lake City, 1972-73; pvt. practice, 1973-74; asst. prof. Law Sch. Brigham Young U., Provo, 1974-76, dir. law libr. Law Sch., 1974-90, assoc. prof. Law Sch., 1976-79, prof. Law Sch., 1979—, Rex E. Lee endowed chair, prof. law, 2005—. Accreditation site insp. ABA, Chgo., 1978—. Author: Utah Civil Procedure, 1980, (with others) A Practical Guide to Disputes Between Adjoining Landowners, 1989, Utah Civil Practice, 1992, 6th edit., 2007, (with others) Thomas and Backman on Utah Real Property Law, 1999, 2d edit., 2005; prin. author, editor-in-chief: Thompson on Real Property, Thomas Edition, 15 vols., 1994; contbr. articles to profl. jours. With U.S. Army, 1969-71, Vietnam. Mem. ABA (mem. sect. coun., chmn. real property trust and estate sect.) Office: Brigham Young U Law Sch Provo UT 84602 Business E-Mail: david_thomas@byu.edu.

THOMAS, DAVID G., advertising executive; b. Ogden, Utah, Oct. 15, 1950; s. Glenn and Norma (Beard) T.; m. Kathleen Lynn Alford, Aug. 27, 1969; children: Troy, Matthew, Brett. BS, Weber State Coll., 1977; MS, Brigham Young U., 1980. Musician, Utah, 1968-77; tchr., counselor Sandridge Jr. High Sch., Roy, Utah, 1977-81; writer, producer Salt Lake City, 1981-82; chmn. Thomas/Phillips/Clawson Advt., Salt Lake City, 1982-86; exec. v.p., mng. dir. Cole & Weber Advt., Inc., Salt Lake City, 1986—; pres. Publicis, Salt Lake City. Councilman, asst. mayor, Plain City, Utah, 1972-78; scout master Boy Scouts Am., Farmington, Utah, 1977-85. Recipient Clio finalist award, 198-86, IBA awards (7) Hollywood Broadcasters, N.Y. Film and Video Gold awards N.Y. Film Soc., 1987. Mem. Utah Advt. Fedn. (43 Gold awards 1981-87), AAAA. Democrat. Mem. Lds Ch. Avocations: skiing, water-skiing, camping. Home: 2073 Kingston Rd Farmington UT 84025-4107 Office: Publicis 110 Social Mall Ave Salt Lake City UT 84111

THOMAS, DAVID SNOW, plastic surgeon; b. Chgo., Feb. 7, 1951; s. Allan Perry and Verna Bea (Snow) T.; m. Becky Williams Thomas, Aug. 25, 1973; children: Nathan David, Abigail, Elizabeth. BA, U. Utah, 1974, MD, 1978. Diplomate Am. Bd. Plastic Surgery, Am. Bd. Surgery. Resident surgery UCLA, 1978-83, resident plastic surgery, 1983-85, fellow craniofacial surgery, 1985; pvt. practice Salt Lake City, 1986—; chief plastic surgery Primary Childrens Med. Ctr., Salt

Lake City, 1988-90, LDS Hosp., 1993-99. Clin. asst. prof. U. Utah Plastic Surgeons, Salt Lake City, 1986-89, assoc. prof. surgery, 1990-93, clin. assoc. prof., 1993—. Bd. Dirs. AMICUS, Salt Lake City, Utah, 1990-92. Fellow ACS; mem. Am. Soc. Plastic and Reconstructive Surgery, Am. Soc. Maxillofacial Surgery, Am. Cleft Palate Craniofacial Assn., Am. Soc. Aesthetic Plastic Surgery, Interplast (pres. Salt Lake City, 1992—, bd. dirs. Palo Alto, Calif., 1992—), The Country Club (Salt Lake City), Alta Club (sec.). Office: 370 9th Ave Ste 200 Salt Lake City UT 84103-3185 Home Phone: 801-355-0104; Office Phone: 801-355-0731. Business E-Mail: dst@davidsthomasmd.com.

THOMAS, DENE KAY, academic administrator, educator; 3 children. B Lit., S.W. State U., cert. in secondary edn., 1978; PhD English, U. Minn., 1984; course, Bryn Mawr's Women in Higher Edn. Adminstrn. program, 1990. Vice provost acad. affairs to tchr., dept. chmn., dean U. Idaho; pres. Lewis-Clark State Coll., 2001—. Office: Lewis-Clark State Coll 500 8th Ave Lewiston ID 83501

THOMAS, EDWARD DONNALL, internist, hematologist, retired medical educator; b. Mart, Tex., Mar. 15, 1920; m. Dorothy Thomas; 3 children. BA, U. Tex., 1941, MA, 1943; MD, Harvard U., 1946; MD (hon.), U. Cagliari, Sardinia, 1981, U. Verona, Italy, 1991, U. Parma, 1992, U. Barcelona, Spain, 1994, U. Warsaw, Poland, 1996, U. Jagiellonski, Cracow, Poland, 1996. Lic. physician Mass., N.Y., Wash., diplomate Am. Bd. Internal Medicine. Intern in medicine Peter Bent Brigham Hosp., Boston, 1946—47, rsch. fellow hematology, 1947—48; NRC postdoctoral fellow in medicine dept. biology MIT, Cambridge, 1950—51; chief med. resident, sr. asst. resident Peter Bent Brigham Hosp., 1951—53, hematologist, 1953—55; instr. medicine Harvard Med. Sch., Boston, 1953—55; rsch. assoc. Cancer Rsch. Found. Children's Med. Ctr., Boston, 1953—55; physician-in-chief Mary Imogene Bassett Hosp., Cooperstown, NY, 1955—63; assoc. clin. prof. medicine Coll. Physicians and Surgeons Columbia U., NYC, 1955—63; attending physician U. Wash. Hosp., Seattle, 1963—90; prof. medicine Sch. Medicine U. Wash., Seattle, 1963—90, head divsn. oncology Sch. Medicine, 1963—85, prof. emeritus medicine Sch. Medicine, 1990—; dir. med. oncology Fred Hutchinson Cancer Rsch. Ctr., Seattle, 1974—89, assoc. dir. clin. rsch. programs, 1982—89, mem., 1974—. Mem. hematology study sect. NIH, 1965—69; mem. bd. trustees and med. sci. adv. com. Leukemia Soc. Am., Inc., 1969—73; mem. clin. cancer investigation rev. com. NCI, 1970—74; 1st ann. Eugene C. Eppinger lectr. Peter Bent Brigham Hosp. and Harvard Med. Sch., 1974; Lilly lectr. RCP, London, 1977; Stratton lectr. Internat. Soc. Hematology, 1982; Paul Aggeler lectr. U. Calif., San Francisco, 1982; 65th Mellon lectr. U. Pitts. Sch. Medicine, 1984; Stanley Wright Meml. lectr. Western Soc. Pediat. Rsch., 1985; Adolfo Ferrata lectr. Italian Soc. Hematology, Verona, Italy, 1991. Mem. editl. bd. Blood, 1962—75, 1977—82, Transplantation, 1970—76, Proc. of Soc. for Exptl. Biology and Medicine, 1974—81, Leukemia Rsch., 1977—87, Hematological Oncology, 1982—87, Jour. Clin. Immunology, 1982—87, Am. Jour. Hematology, 1985—, Bone Marrow Transplantation, 1986—. With US Army, 1948—50. Recipient A. Ross McIntyre award, U. Nebr. Med. Ctr., 1975, Philip Levine award, Am. Soc. Clin. Pathologists, 1979, Disting. Svc. in Basic Rsch. award, Am. Cancer Soc., 1980, Kettering prize, GM Cancer Rsch. Found., 1981, Spl. Keynote Address award, Am. Soc. Therapeutic Radiologists, 1981, Robert Roesler de Villiers award, Leukemia Soc. Am., 1983, Karl Landsteiner Meml. award, Am. Assn. Blood Banks, 1987, Terry Fox award, Can., 1990, Internat. award, Gairdner Found., 1990, Hong Kong prize, N.Am. Med. Assn., 1990, Nobel Prize in Medicine, 1990, Presdl. medal of sci., NSF, 1990, Lifetime Achievement award, Am. Soc. Blood and Marrow Transplantation, 2004. Mem.: NAS, Soc. Exptl. Biology and Medicine, Western Assn. Physicians, Swiss Soc. Hematology, Internat. Soc. Hematology, Internat. Soc. Exptl. Hematology, Am. Soc. Hematology (pres. 1987—88, Henry M. Stratton lectr. 1975), Am. Soc. Clin. Investigation, Am. Soc. Clin. Oncology (David A. Karnoksky Meml. lectr. 1983), Am. Fedn. Clin. Rsch., Assn. Am. Physicians (Kober medal 1992), Am. Assn. Cancer Rsch., Academie Royale de Medicine de Belgique (corr.), Nat. Acad. Medicine Mex. (hon.), Royal Coll. Physicians and Surgeons Can. (hon.), Swedish Soc. Hematology (hon.). Office: Fred Hutchinson Cancer Ctr 1100 Fairview Ave N D5-100 PO Box 19024 Seattle WA 98109-1024 Office Phone: 206-667-4319. Business E-Mail: ethomas@fhcrc.org.

THOMAS, FRANK EDWARD, professional baseball player; b. Columbus, Ga., May 27, 1968; Student, Auburn U. Outfielder Chgo. White Sox, 1990—2006; designated hitter Oakland Athletics, 2006, 2008, Toronto Blue Jays, 2006—08. Recipient Silver Slugger award, 1991, 1993, 1994, Most Valuable Player award, Am. League, 1994; named Maj. League Player of Yr., Sporting News, 1993, AL Comeback Player Yr., Players Choice Awards, 2006; named to All-Star Coll. All Am. team, Sporting News, 1989, All-Star Team, 1991, 1993—94, Am. League, 1993—95. Achievements include becoming the 21st player in major league history to hit 500 home runs, June 28, 2007. Office: Oakland Athletics 7000 Coliseum Way Oakland CA 94621

THOMAS, FRED, state legislator; b. Stevensville, Mont., June 27, 1958; m. Suzzie Thomas. BS, Mont. State U., 1981. Cert. ins. counselor. Ins. agt.; mem. Mont. Ho. of Reps., 1985-92, Mont. Senate, Dist. 31, Helena, 1996—2002; vice chair labor and employment rels. com.; vice chair pub. health, welfare and safety com.; mem. bus. and industry com., conf. com., rules com.; mem. select com. on Constl. amendments. Bd. dirs. Stevensville Cmty. Found. Mem. Profl. Inst. Agts. Mont. (past pres., Agt. of Yr.), Mont. C. of C., Bitterroot C. of C. (bd. dirs. 1994—), Civic Club Stevensville (pres. 1982-83). Republican. Home: 1004 S Burnt Fork Rd Stevensville MT 59870-6658 E-mail: fthomas@bitterroot.net.

THOMAS, GARETH, metallurgy educator; b. Maesteg, UK, Aug. 9, 1932; came to U.S., 1960, naturalized, 1977; s. David Bassett and Edith May (Gregory) T.; 1 child, Julian Guy David. B.Sc., U. Wales, 1952; PhD, Cambridge U., 1955, Sc.D., 1969; DCs (hon.), Lehigh U., 1996. I.C.I. fellow Cambridge U., 1956-59; asst. prof. U. Calif., Berkeley, 1960-63, asso. prof., 1963-67, prof. metallurgy, 1967—, assoc. dean grad. div., 1968-69, asst. chancellor, acting vice chancellor for acad. affairs, 1969-72; founder, sci. dir. Nat. Ctr. Electron Microscopy, 1982-93. Cons. to industry. Author: Transmission Electron Microscopy of Metals, 1962, Electron Microscopy and Strength of Crystals, 1963, (with O. Johari) Stereographic Projection and Applications, 1969, Transmission Electron Microscopy of Materials, 1980; manual dir. Acta Met. Inc., 1998—; contbr. articles to profl. jours.; patentee in field. Recipient Curtis McGraw Rsch. award Am. Soc. Engring. Edn., 1966, E.O. Lawrence award Dept. Energy, 1978, I-R 100 award R & D mag., 1987, Henry Clifton Sorby award Internat. Metallographic Soc., 1987, Albert Sauveur Achievement award, 1991; Guggenheim fellow, 1972. Fellow Am. Soc. Metals (Bradley Stoughton Young Tchrs. award 1965, Grossman Publ. award 1966), Am. Inst. Mining, Metall. and Petroleum Engrs.; mem. Electron Microscopy Soc. Am. (prize 1965, pres. 1976), Am. Phys. Soc., Nat. Acad. Scis., Nat. Acad. Engring., Brit. Inst. Metals (Rosenheim medal 1977), Internat. Fedn. Electron Microscopy Socs. (pres. 1986-90), Brit. Iron and Steel Inst. Clubs: Marylebone Cricket (Eng.). Office: U Calif Dept Materials Sci & Engring 481 Hearst Mining Bldg Berkeley CA 94720-1760

THOMAS, GARY EDWARD, science educator, researcher; b. Lookout, W.Va., Oct. 25, 1934; s. Garland Eugene Thomas and Dorothy Mae (Fish) Johnson; m. Susan Jude Cherup, Jan. 20, 1963; 1 child, Jennifer Ann. BS, N.Mex. State U., 1957; PhD, U. Pitts., 1963. Rsch. assoc. Svc. d'Aeronomie du CNRS, Paris, 1962-63; staff scientist Aerospace Corp., El Segundo, Calif., 1965-67; prof., now prof. emeritus U. Colo., Boulder, 1967—. Sec. Internat. Comm. on Meteorology of the Upper Atmosphere, 1988-95; disting. vis. prof. U. Adelaide, Australia, 1995. Contbr. more than 100 articles to profl. jours. 1st lt. Signal Corps U.S. Army, 1963-65. Recipient Award Rsch. Excellence U. Colo., 1994; fellowship U. Colo., 1974-75. Mem. Am. Geophysical Union (assoc. editor 1992-95). Office: U Colo Cb 392 Boulder CO 80309-0001

THOMAS, GEOFFREY L., lawyer; b. Lindsay, Calif., May 12, 1944; AB cum laude, Harvard U., 1967; JD, Stanford, 1971. Bar: Calif. 1972. Ptnr. Paul, Hastings, Janofsky & Walker LLP, LA, gen. counsel, chmn. profl. responsibility com. Mem. bd. editors Stanford Law Rev., 1970—71. Contbr. (chapter) Examining Witnesses to Civil Procedure During Trial. Office: Paul Hastings Janofsky & Walker LLP 515 S Flower St Los Angeles CA 90071-2228 Office Phone: 213-683-6149. Office Fax: 213-627-0705. Business E-Mail: geoffreythomas@paulhastings.com.

THOMAS, GEORGE LEO, bishop; b. Anaconda, Mont., May 19, 1950; s. Mary (Cronin) and George Thomas. BA, Carroll Coll., 1972; MDiv, St. Thomas Sem., Bothell, Wash.; MS in Counseling & Cmty. Mental Health, U. Wash., 1983, PhD, 1986. Ordained priest Archdiocese of Seattle, 1976, chancellor, vicar gen., 1987—99, aux. bishop, 2000—04; assoc. pastor Holy Family Parish, Kirkland, Wash., St. James Cathedral, Seattle; parish adminstr. Sacred Heart Parish, Bellevue, Wash.; with Holy Innocents Mission, Duvall, Wash.; ordained bishop, 2000; bishop Diocese of Helena, Mont., 2004—. Chancellor, bd. trustees Carroll Coll., Helena, Mont., 2004—; bd. dirs. Found. Cath. Diocese of Helena, Cath. Soc. Svcs. for Mont., Cath. Relief Svcs. Recipient Gordon C. Lee award, U. Wash., 1986. Mem.: US Conf. Cath. Bishops (comm. com., comm. subcommittee policy & practices, ad hoc com. for Native Am. Catholics), Mont. Assn. Churches (bd. dirs.), Mont. Cath. Conf. (bd. dirs.). Roman Catholic. Office: Diocese of Helena PO Box 1729 Helena MT 59624-1729 Office Phone: 406-442-5820.

THOMAS, JACK E., state legislator; Mem. Dist. 60 N. Mex. House of Reps., 2009—. Democrat. Home: 200 Lisbon Ave Rio Rancho NM 87124 Office: House of Representatives State Capitol North Rm 203ACN Santa Fe NM 87501 Home Phone: 505-892-1320; Office Phone: 505-934-0254. E-mail: jpkthomas@prodigy.net.

THOMAS, JACK WARD, retired wildlife biologist, educator; b. Ft. Worth, Sept. 7, 1934; s. Scranton Boulware and Lillian Louise (List) T.; m. Farrar Margaret Schindler, June 29, 1957 (dec. Feb. 1994); children: Britt Ward, Scranton Gregory; m. Kathleen Connelly, Feb. 11, 1997. BS, Tex. A&M U., 1957; MS, W.Va. U., 1969; PhD, U. Mass., 1972; PhD (hon.), Lewis & Clark Coll., 1994, Lakehead U., 2001. Biologist Tex. Game & Fish Commn., Sonora, 1957-60; rsch. biologist Tex. Parks & Wildlife Dept., Plano, 1962—67; wildlife rsch. biologist, forestry sci. lab., Northeastern Forest Exptl. Sta. U.S. Forest Svc., Morgantown, W.Va., 1967-71; project dir. environ. forestry rsch. Pinchot Inst. Environ. Forestry, 1971-73; project leader range & wildlife habitat rsch. Pacific Northwest Forest Exptl. Sta. U.S. Forest Svc., LaGrande, Oreg., 1973-93; chief U.S. Dept. Agr.- Forest Svc., Washington, 1993-96; Boone & Crockett prof. wildlife conservation U. Mont., Missoula, 1996—2005, prof. emeritus, 2006—. Author, editor: Wildlife Habitats in Managed Forests, 1979 (award The Wildlife Soc. 1980), Elk of North America, 1984 (award The Wildlife Soc. 1985), North American Elk: Ecology and Management, 2002; contbr. over 500 articles to profl. jours. Served to lt. USAF, 1957, USNR, 1952-57. Recipient Conservation award Gulf Oil Corp., 1983, Earle A. Childs award Childs Found., 1984, Disting. Svc. award USDA, Disting. Citizen's award, E. Oreg. State Coll., Nat Wildlife Fedn. award for Sci., 1990, Disting. Achievement award Soc. for Cons. Biology, 1990, Giraffe award The Giraffe Project, 1990, Scientist of Yr. award Oreg. Acad. Sci., 1990, Disting. Svc. award Soc. Conservation Biology, 1991, Sci. Conservation award Nat. Wildlife Fedn., 1991, Disting. Achievement award Soc. Conservative Biology, 1991, Chuck Yeager award Nat. Fish and Wildlife Found., 1992, Conservationist of Yr. award Oreg. Rivers Coun., 1992, Chief's Tech. Transfer award USDA, 1992, Tech. Transfer award Fed. Lab. Consortium, 1993, named Outstanding Scientist N.W. Sci. Assn., 1995, Disting. Alumni award Coll. Agr., Tex. A&M U., 1995, Disting. Svc. award Oreg. State U., 1996, Fed. Statesman award Found. N.Am. Wild Sheep, 1997, Claus J. Murie award Rocky Mountain Elk Found., 1999, Sustained Achievement award Renewable Natural Resources Found., 1999. Fellow Soc. Am. Foresters; mem. NAS (bd. agr. and natural resources 2001-2003), The Wildlife Soc. (cert., hon., pres. 1977-78, Oreg. Chpt. award 1980, Arthur Einarsen award 1981, spl. svcs. award 1984, Aldo Leopold Meml. medal 1991, group achievement award 1990), Am. Ornithologists Union, Am. Soc. Mammalogists, W.Va. U. Alumni Assn. (Disting. Alumni award 1996), U. Mass.-Amherst Alumni Assn. (Disting. Alumni award 1995), Rocky Mountain Elk Found. (bd. dirs. 1997-2003, chmn. 2003—), Bear Trust Internat., Forest Trust (adv. bd. gen. acctg. office 1999-2003), Lions, Elks. Avocations: hunting, fishing, white-water rafting, shooting, carpentry. Office: U Mont Sch Forestry Missoula MT 59812-0001

THOMAS, JOHN, professional sports team executive; Grad. in Bus., U. Minn. With KSTP-TV, Mpls./St. Paul, KFAN Sports Radio, Maj. League Baseball Seattle Mariners, NHL Minn. North Stars, NBA Minn. Timberwolves, NBA Rockets, WNBA Comets and Arena Football League Thunderbears, Houston, 1994—99; pres. Maloof Sports & Entertainment (NBA Kings, WNBA Monarchs and ARCO Arena), Sacramento, 1999—. Bd. dirs. Sacramento Conv. and Visitors Bur., Sacramento Metro Chamber, Valley Vision's Leadership Coun. Office: Sacramento Kings ARCO Arena 1 Sports Pky Sacramento CA 95834-2301

THOMAS, JOHN D., JR., career officer; b. Plymouth, Pa. BA in History, Wilkes Coll.; MA in Internat. Rels., U. So. Calif.; grad., disting. grad. in Field Artillery, Officer's Candidate Sch., Ft. Sill, Okla. Enlisted U.S. Army, commd. 2d lt., advanced through grades to maj. gen., early assignments include command and staff positions, co. comdr. Augsburg, Germany, exec. officer 1st Army Security Aviation Co., svc. in intelligence and electronic warfare staff positions Korea, comdr. 3d Mil. Intelligence bn. Ft. Humphreys, Korea; dep. chief for Intelligence, Spl. Tech. Ops. Divsn. The Jt. Staff, Washington; comdr 111th Mil. Intelligence brigade U.S. Army, Ft. Huachuca, Ariz.; dep. comdg. gen., asst. comdr. U.S. Army Intelligence Ctr., Ft. Huachuca; assoc. dep. dir. ops., Mil. Support Nat. Security Agy.; dep. chief Ctrl. Security Svc.; comdr. U.S. Army Intelligence Security Command, U.S. Mil. Intelligence Corps, Ft. Huachuca, 1998—. Decorated Legion of Merit with oak leaf cluster, Meritorious Svc. Medal with oak leaf cluster, Jt. Svc. Commendation medal, Def. Disting. Svc. medal, Def. Superior Svc. medal, others. Achievements include being a master army aviator. E-mail: John.thomas@hua.army.mil.

THOMAS, JOHN VAL, architect; b. San Diego, Feb. 26, 1943; Grad arch., Rice Univ., Houston; MArch, MCP, U. Pa. Prin. Val Thomas, Inc., Seattle, 1985—; devel. mgr. Pike Pl. Market Preservation and Devel. Authority, Seattle, 1974. Cons. ptnr. Cardwell/Thomas & Assoc., Seattle. Conversion, W. Queen Anne Sch. (Award for Excellence, Nat. Endowment for the Arts). Fellow: Am. Inst. Arch.; mem.: Housing Comm. of the Greater Seattle Chamber of Commerce, Univ. of Wash. Profl. Coun. for the Sch. of Urban Planning, Seattle Planning Commission (chrmn.). Democrat. Episcopalian. Achievements include development of Thomas Incorporated; headed the development team for the new headquarters building of the Fremont Public Association on North 45th Street. Avocations: skiing, aerobics, painting, gardening. Office: STE 420 2025 1ST Ave Seattle WA 98121-2176 Office Phone: 206-621-1221.

THOMAS, JOSEPH FLESHMAN, retired architect; b. Oak Hill, W.Va., Mar. 23, 1915; s. Robert Russel and Effie (Fleshman) T.; m. Margaret Ruth Lively, Feb. 28, 1939 (dec.); children: Anita Carol, Joseph Stephen; m. Dorothy Francene Root, Apr. 29, 1967 (div.); m. Bonnie Abbott Buckley, June 15, 1991 (dec.). Student, Duke U., 1931—32; BArch, Carnegie-Mellon U., 1938. Practice architecture various firms, W.Va., Va., Tenn., Calif., 1938-49; staff arch. Calif. Divsn. Architecture, LA, 1949-52; prin. Joseph F. Thomas, Arch., Pasadena, Calif., 1952-53; pres. Neptune & Thomas (archs.-engrs.), Pasadena and San Diego, 1953-78. Mem. Pasadena Planning Commn., 1956-64, chmn., 1963-64; pres. Citizens Coun. for Planning, Pasadena, 1966-67; steering com. Pasadena NOW, 1970-74; mem. Pasadena Design Com., 1979-86; adv. bd. Calif. Office Architecture and Constrn., 1970-72; archtl. adv. com. Calif. State U. Sys., 1981-84; adv. coun. Sch. Environ. Design Calif. Poly. Inst., 1983-2002; outreach for architecture com. Carnegie Mellon U., 1989-95, pres.'s devel. com., 1991-95. Prin. works include Meth. Hosp., Arcadia, Calif., Foothill Presbyn. Hosp., Glendora, Calif., master plans and bldgs., Citrus Coll., Azusa, Calif., Riverside (Calif.) Coll., Westmont Coll., Monticeto, Calif., Northrop Inst. Tech., Inglewood, Calif, Indian Valley Coll., Marin County, Calif., Pepperdine U., Malibu, Calif., UCLA, U. Calif., San Diego, Long Beach (Calif.) State U., Calif. Inst. Tech., Pasadena, Pacific Tel. Co., Pasadena, LA County Superior Ct. Bldg., U.S. Naval Hosp., San Diego, others Trustee Almansor Edn. Ctr., 1986-92; bd. dirs., co-founder Syncor Internat., 1973-83; founding dir. Bank of Pasadena, 1962-65. Lt. (j.g.) USNR, 1943-46. Recipient Svc. award, City of Pasadena, 1964, Disting. Svc. award, Calif. Dept. Gen. Svcs., 1972, Gold Crown award, Pasadena Arts Coun., 1981. Fellow AIA (dir. Calif. coun. 1966-68, exec. com. 1974-77, pres. Pasadena chpt. 1967, chmn. Calif. sch. facilities com. 1970-72, mem. nat. jud. bd. 1973-74, nat. dir. 1974-77, treas. 1977-79, exec. com., planning com., chmn. finance com., 4 awards honor, 13 awards merit 1957-78, Lifetime Achievement award 2007); mem. Breakfast Forum (chmn. 1983), Annandale Golf Club, Pi Kappa Alpha. Republican. Methodist. Home: 330 San Miguel Rd Pasadena CA 91105-1446

THOMAS, JOSEPH JAMES, JR., state legislator; b. Fairbanks, Alaska, Oct. 17, 1948; s. Joseph James Sr. and Myrtle Rose (Harris) T.; children: Damian, Natalie, Ryan. BS in Psychology, W.Va. U., 1974. Constrn. worker Laborers Local 942, Fairbanks, bus. agt., bus. mgr.; mem. Alaska State Senate from Dist. D, 2006—. Trustee Alaska Laborers Trust, 1978—; v.p. Alaska State AFL-CIO, 1984-96; mem. Alaska Worker's Compensation Bd., Resource Devel. Coun. Exec. Bd., 1980-86, Main Street Fairbanks, 1985-88, Fairbanks Indsl. Devel. Authority, 1988-90, Fairbanks Devel. Authority, 1988-92, bd. regents U. Alaska, 1995-2003. Vol. various polit. campaigns. Democrat. Roman Catholic. Avocations: skiing, soccer, golf, boating, fishing, reading. Home: 879 Vide Way Fairbanks AK 99712-1132 Office: Dist D 1292 Sadler Way Ste 313 Fairbanks AK 99701 also: State Capitol Rm 510 Juneau AK 99801-1182 Office Phone: 907-456-8161, 907-465-2327. Office Fax: 907-456-8763, 907-465-5241. Business E-Mail: Senator_Joe_Thomas@legis.state.ak.us.

THOMAS, KAREN P., composer, conductor; b. Seattle, Sept. 17, 1957; BA in Composition, Cornish Inst., 1979; MusM in Composition and Conducting, U. Wash., 1985. Condr. The Contemporary Group, 1981-85; condr., music dir. Wash. Composers Forum, 1984-86; artistic dir., condr. Seattle Pro Musica, 1987—. Conducting debut Seattle, 1987; composer: Four Delineations of Curtmantle for Trombone or Cello, 1982, Metamorphoses on a Machaut Kyrie for Strong Orch. or Quartet, 1983, Cowboy Songs for Voice and Piano, 1985, There Must Be a Lone Range for Soprano and Chamber Ensemble, 1987, Brass Quintet, 1987, Four Lewis Carroll Songs for Choir, 1989, (music/dance/theater) Boxiana, 1990, Elementi for Clarinet and Percussion, 1991, (one-act children's opera) Coyote's Tail, 1991, Clarion Dances for Brass Ensemble, 1993, Roundup for Sax Quartet, 1993, Three Medieval Lyrics for Choir, 1992, Sopravvento for Wind Quartet and Percussion, 1994, When Night Came for Clarinet and Chamber Orch. or Clarinet and Piano, 1994, Over the City for Choir, 1995, also numerous others. Recipient Composers Forum award N.W. Chamber Orch., 1984, King County Arts Commn., 1987, 90, Artist Trust, 1988, 93, 96, Seattle Arts Commn., 1988, 91, 93, New Langton Arts, 1988, Delius Festival, 1993, Melodious Accord award 1993; fellow Wash. State Arts Commn., 1991; Charles E. Ives scholar AAAL. Mem. Am. Choral Dirs. Assn., Broadcast Music, Am. Music Ctr., Internat. Alliance for Women in Music, Soc. Composers, Chorus Am., Conductors Guild. Home: 4435 1st Ave Nw Seattle WA 98107-4307 E-mail: kpthomas1@aol.com.

THOMAS, LOWELL, JR., writer, retired military officer, state senator; b. London, Oct. 6, 1923; s. Lowell Jackson and Frances (Ryan) T.; m. Mary Taylor Pryor, May 20, 1950; children: Anne

Frazier, David Lowell. Student, Taft Sch., 1942; BA, Dartmouth Coll., 1948; postgrad., Princeton Sch. Pub. and Internat. Affairs, 1952. Asst. cameraman Fox Movietone News, S.Am., 1939, Bradford Washburn Alaskan mountaineering expdn., 1940; illustrated lecturer, 1946—; asst. economist, photographer with Max Weston Thornburg, Turkey, 1947, Iran, 1948; film prodn. Iran, 1949; Tibet expdn. with Lowell Thomas, Sr., 1949; field work Cinerama, S.Am., Africa, Asia, 1951-52; travels by small airplane with wife, writing and filming Europe, Africa, Middle East, 1954-55; mem. Rockwell Polar Flight, first flight around the world over both poles, Nov., 1965; mem. Alaska State Senate, 1967-74; lt. gov. State of Alaska, 1974-79; owner Talkeetna Air Taxi, Inc., air contract carrier, Anchorage, Alaska, 1980-94. Producer series of films Flight to Adventure, NBC-TV, 1956; producer, writer TV series High Adventure, 1957-59; producer documentary film Adaq, King of Alaskan Seas, 1960; producer two films on Alaska, 1962, 63, film on U. Alaska, 1964, South Pacific travel documentary, 1965, film on Arctic oil exploration, Atlantic-Richfield Co., 1969. Author: Out of this World, A Journey to Tibet, 1950, (with Mrs. Lowell Thomas, Jr.) Our Flight to Adventure, 1956, The Silent War in Tibet, 1959, The Dalai Lama, 1961, The Trail of Ninety-Eight, 1962, (with Lowell Thomas Sr.) More Great True Adventures, 1963, Famous First Flights that Changed History, 1968. Past pres. Western Alaska coun. Boy Scouts Am.; bd. dirs. Anchorage unit Salvation Army, Alaska Conservation Found. 1st lt. USAAF, 1943-45. Mem. Nat. Parks and Conservation Assn. (bd. dirs.), Alaska C. of C., Aircraft Owners and Pilots Assn. Clubs: Explorers, Marco Polo, Dutch Treat (N.Y.C.); Rotary, (Anchorage), Press (Anchorage); Dartmouth Outing; American Alpine. Address: 10800 Hideaway Lake Dr Anchorage AK 99507-6139

THOMAS, SIDNEY R., federal judge; b. Bozeman, Mont., Aug. 14, 1953; m. Martha Sheehy. BA in Speech-Comm., Mont. State U., 1975, JD cum laude, 1978; D (hon.), Rocky Mountain Coll., 1998. Bar: Mont. 1978, US Dist. Ct. Mont. 1978, US Ct. Appeals (9th cir.) 1980, US Dist. Ct. (9th cir.) 1980, US Ct. Fed. Claims 1986, US Supreme Ct. 1994. Shareholder Moulton, Bellimgham, Longo and Mather, P.C., Billings, Mont., 1978—96; judge US Ct. Appeals (9th cir.), Billings, 1996—. Adj. instr. Rocky Mountain Coll., Billings, 1982—95. Contbr. articles to profl. jours. Recipient Gov.'s award for Pub. Svc., 1978, Outstanding Faculty award, Rocky Mountain Coll., 1988. Mem.: ABA, Yellowstone County Bar Assn., State Bar Mont. Office: US Ct Appeals Ninth Circuit PO Box 31478 Billings MT 59107-1478

THOMAS, THOMAS DARRAH, chemistry educator; b. Glen Ridge, NJ, Apr. 8, 1932; s. Woodlief and Jean (Darrah) T.; m. Barbara Joan Rassweiler, Sept. 8, 1956; children: David, Steven, Kathleen, Susan. BS, Haverford Coll., 1954; PhD, U. Calif., Berkeley, 1957. Instr. chemistry U. Calif., Berkeley, 1957-58, asst. prof., 1958-59; rsch. assoc. Brookhaven Nat. Lab., Upton, N.Y., 1959-61; asst. prof. Princeton (N.J.) U., 1961-66, assoc. prof., 1966-71; prof. Oreg. State U., Corvallis, 1971-89, disting. prof., 1989-97, chmn. dept. chemistry, 1981-84, dir. Ctr. Advanced Materials Rsch., 1986-91, Disting. prof. emeritus, 1997—. Cons. Los Alamos (N.Mex.) Sci. Lab., 1965. Contbr. articles to profl. jours. Fellow Alfred P. Sloan Found., 1966-68, Guggenheim Found., 1969, U. Liverpool, Eng., 1984-85. Fellow AAAS, Am. Phys. Soc.; mem. Am. Chem. Soc., Sigma Xi, Phi Beta Kappa. Home: 1470 NW Greenwood Pl Corvallis OR 97330-1827 Office: Oreg State U Dept Chemistry 153 Gilbert Hall Corvallis OR 97331-8546 E-mail: thomast@chem.orst.edu.

THOMAS, TIMOTHY R., lawyer; b. Olney, Ill. B in Fin., U. Ill., JD. With Judge Advocate Gen.'s Corps USN, San Diego; atty. corp. law dept. Unocal, El Segundo, Calif., 1974-76, assoc. counsel, 1976-90, dep. counsel, 1990-93, gen. counsel 76 Products Co., 1993—. Mem. Calif. Bar Assn., L.A. County Bar Assn. Office: 2141 Rosecrans Ave Ste 4000 El Segundo CA 90245

THOMAS, WILLIAM SCOTT, lawyer; b. Joliet, Ill., Aug. 16, 1949; AB, Stanford U., Calif., 1971; JD, U. Calif., Hastings, 1974; LLM in Taxation, Golden Gate U., 1981. Bar: Calif. 1975, US Dist. Ct. (no. dist. Calif.) 1975, US Tax Ct. 1982. Tax editor Internat. Bur. Fiscal Documentation, Amsterdam, 1974-75; tax atty. Chevron Corp., San Francisco, 1975-77; assoc. to ptnr. Brobeck, Phleger & Harrison, San Francisco, 1978—2003; ptnr. Morgan Lewis & Bockius, San Francisco, 2003—07, Dickenson, Peatman & Fogarty, Napa, Calif., 2007—. Named one of Top 100 Attys., Worth mag., 2005—07. Mem. ABA (taxation sect.), Calif. Bar Assn. (exec. com. taxation sect. 1984-89, chmn. 1987-88). Office: Dickenson Peatman & Fogarty 809 Coombs Napa CA 94559 Office Phone: 707-252-7122. Office Fax: 707-255-6876. Business E-Mail: sthomas@dpf-law.com.

THOMASCH, ROGER PAUL, lawyer; b. NYC, Nov. 7, 1942; s. Gordon J. and Margaret (Molloy) T.; children: Laura Leigh, Paul Butler. BA, Coll. William and Mary, 1964; LLB, Duke U., 1967. Bar: Conn. 1967, Colo. 1974. Assoc. atty. Cummings & Lockwood, Stamford, Conn., 1967-70; trial atty. U.S. Dept. Justice, Washington, 1970-73; ptnr. Roath & Brega, Denver, 1975-87; mng. ptnr. Denver office of Ballard, Spahr, Andrews & Ingersoll LLP, 1987—, chmn. litigation practice, 2005—. Vis. assoc. prof. of law Drake U. Sch. Law, Des Moines, 1973-74; frequent lectr. in field, U.S. and Can.; adj. faculty mem. U. Denver Coll. Law, 1976-80. Recipient Leland Forrest Outstanding Prof. award, Drake U. Sch. Law, 1973. Fellow Am. Coll. of Trial Lawyers, Am. Bar Found., Colo. Bar Found.; mem. ABA, Colo. Bar Assn., Denver Country Club, Univ. Club. Office: Ballard Spahr Andrews & Ingersoll LLP 1225 17th St Ste 2300 Denver CO 80202-5535 Home Phone: 303-744-8434; Office Phone: 303-299-7301. E-mail: Thomasch@BallardSpahr.com.

THOMAS-GRAHAM, PAMELA, apparel executive; b. Detroit, 1963; d. Albert and Marian Thomas; m. Lawrence Otis Graham; 3 children. Grad., AB, Harvard Coll.; MBA, Harvard Bus. Sch.; JD, Harvard Law Sch. With McKinsey & Co., 1989—99, ptnr., 1995—99; pres., CEO CNBC.com, 1999—2001, CNBC, Ft. Lee, NJ, 2001—05, chmn., 2005; group pres. Liz Claiborne, Inc., NYC, 2005—. Editor: Harvard Law Rev.; author: Ivy League Mystery Series, (novels) A Darker Shade of Crimson, 1998, Blue Blood, 1999, Orange Crushed, 2004. Bd. dirs. Clorox, Idenix Pharms., NYC Opera. Recipient Matrix award, N.Y. Women Comm., 2001; named Woman of Yr., Finl. Women's Assn.; named one of Forty Under Forty Rising Young Bus. Leaders, Crain's N.Y. Bus., Top 20 Women in Fin., Global Fin. Mag., Top 10 Cons. in Am., Cons. Mag. Mem.: Phi Beta Kappa.

THOMPSON, ANNE KATHLEEN, entertainment journalist; b. NYC, Aug. 10, 1954; d. Charles Torrington Thompson and Eleanor Josephine (Callahan) Dekins; m. David Christopher Chute, Oct. 23, 1983; 1 child, Nora Thompson Chute. BA in Cinema Studies, NYU, 1976. Asst. mgr. Bleecker St. Cinema, NYC, 1975—76; publicist United Artists, NYC, 1976—79; account exec. P/M/K Pub. Rels., NYC, 1979—81; assoc. editor Film Comment Mag., NYC, 1981-82, west coast editor, 1982-96; publicity dir. Twentieth Century Fox Pictures, 1983-85; wrote column Risky Bus. LA Weekly, LA Times Syndicate, 1985-93; columnist Inside Film, 1988-90; U.S. editor Empire Mag., London, 1989-91; sr. writer Entertainment Weekly, 1993-96; west coast editor Premier Mag., 1996—2002; contbr. Premiere, Filmmaker, Wired, NY Times, Washington Post, NY mag., London Observer; dep. film editor The Hollywood Reporter, LA, 2005—. Mem. Nat. Writer's Union, Women in Film. Office: The Hollywood Reporter 5055 Wilshire Blvd Los Angeles CA 90036-4396

THOMPSON, ANTHONY WAYNE, metallurgist, educator, consultant; b. Burbank, Calif., Mar. 6, 1940; s. William Lyman and Mary Adelaide (Nisbet) T.; m. Mary Ruth Cummings, Aug. 24, 1963; children: Campbell Lyman, Michael Anthony. BS, Stanford U., 1962; MS, U. Wash., 1965; PhD, MIT, 1970. Research engr. Jet Propulsion Lab., Pasadena, Calif., 1962-63; mem. tech. staff Sandia Labs., Livermore, Calif., 1970-73, Rockwell Sci. Ctr., Thousand Oaks, Calif., 1973-77; assoc. prof. Carnegie Mellon U., Pitts., 1977-79, prof., 1980-94, dept. head, 1987-90; staff scientist Lawrence Berkeley Lab., Berkeley, Calif., 1994-99; rsch. engr. U. Calif., Berkeley, Calif., 1995—. Vis. scientist U. Cambridge, Eng., 1983, Risø, Denmark, 1987, U. Calif., 1991; cons. Sandia Labs., 1977—1998, GE, 1988-2000. Editor: Work Hardening, 1976, Metall. Transactions, 1983-88, Signature Press Book Pubs., 1993-; co-editor: Hydrogen in Metals, 1974, Hydrogen Conf. Proc., 1976, 81, 89, 94, 2002; mem. editl. bd. Internat. Metals Revs., 1980-88; contbr. articles to profl. jours. Overseas fellow Churchill Coll. Cambridge U., 1982 Fellow Am. Soc. Metals; mem. Clubs: Sierra, Nat. Model R.R. Assn. Democrat. Home: 2906 Forest Ave Berkeley CA 94705

THOMPSON, BUZZ (BARTON H. JR.), law educator; b. 1951; AB in Economics, Stanford U., 1972, MBA, JD, Stanford U., 1976. Law clk. to Judge Joseph T. Sneed US Ct. Appeals 9th Cir., San Francisco, 1976—77; law clk. to Justice William H. Rehnquist US Supreme Ct., 1977—78; assoc. O'Melveny & Myers, LA, 1978—83, ptnr., 1984—86; mem. faculty Stanford Law Sch., 1986—, Robert E. Paradise fellow, 1993—95, Robert E. Paradise prof. natural resources law, 1996—, vice dean, 2000—04; co-dir. Stanford Inst. for the Environment, 2004—. Instr. water resources UCLA, 1980—83; vis. fellow Hoover Instn. for War, Revolution, and Peace Stanford U., 1999. Bd. dirs. Nat. Heritage Inst. Office: Stanford Law Sch Crown Quadrangle 559 Nathan Abbott Way Stanford CA 94305-8610 Office Phone: 650-723-2518. Office Fax: 650-725-8509. Business E-Mail: buzzt@stanford.edu.

THOMPSON, CAROLINE WARNER, film director, screenwriter; b. Washington, Apr. 23, 1956; d. Thomas Carlton Jr. and Bettie Marshall (Warner) T.; m. Alfred Henry Bromell, Aug. 28, 1982 (div. 1985). BA summa cum laude, Amherst Coll., 1978. Film dir., screenwriter William Morris Agy., Inc., Beverly Hills, Calif. Author: First Born, 1983; screenwriter: (films) Edward Scissorhands, 1990, The Addams Family, 1991, Homeward Bound: The Incredible Journey, 1993, The Secret Garden, 1993, Tim Burton's The Nightmare Before Christmas, 1993; screenwriter, dir.: Black Beauty, 1994, Buddy, 1997. Mem. Phi Beta Kappa. Avocation: horseback riding. Office: William Morris Agency Inc 151 S El Camino Dr Beverly Hills CA 90212-2775

THOMPSON, CHARLOTTE ELLIS, pediatrician, educator, writer; d. Robert and Ann Ellis; divorced; children: Jennifer Ann, Geoffrey Graeme. BA, Stanford U., 1950, MD, 1954. Diplomate Am. Bd. Pediat. Intern Children's Hosp., San Francisco, 1953-54; resident UCLA, 1960-61, L.A. Children's Hosp., 1962-63; pvt. practice La Jolla, Calif., 1963-75; dir. Muscle Disease Clinic Univ. Hosp.-U. Calif. Sch. Medicine, San Diego, 1969-80, asst. clin. prof. pediat., 1969—; founder, dir. Ctr. for Handicapped Children and Teenagers, San Francisco, 1981—2004. Cons. U.S. Naval Hosp., San Diego, 1970-91; dep. dir. Santa Clara County Child Health and Disability, Santa Clara, Calif., 1974-75; dir. Ctr. for Multiple Handicaps, Oakland, Calif., 1976-81; co-dir. Muscle Clinic Children's Hosp., San Diego, 1963-69; dir. muscle program U. Rochester, 1957-60. Author: Raising a Handicapped Child: A Helpful Guide for Parents of the Physically Disabled, 1986, 4th edit., 1991, rev., expanded edit., 2000, Allein leben: Ein umfassendes Handbuch für Frauen, 1993, Making Wise Choices: A Guide for Women, 1993, Raising a Child with a Neuromuscular Disorder, 1999, Raising A Handicapped Child, 1999, 101 Ways To The Best Medical Care, 2006, Grandparenting a child with special needs Jersica Kingsley, 2009; contbr. articles to med. jours., including Clin. Pediat., New Eng. Jour. Medicine, Neurology, Jour. Family Practice, Mothering, Jour. Pediatric Orthopedics, Pediatrician, Am. Baby, Pediatric News, also chpts. to books. Mem. Calif. Children's Svc. Com., 1977—. Fellow: Am. Acad. Pediat. Avocations: tennis, ice skating, opera. Office: 8070 La Jolla Shores Dr # 514 La Jolla CA 92037-3296 Office Phone: 858-456-2105. Personal E-mail: cetmd@earthlink.net.

THOMPSON, CRAIG SNOVER, corporate communications executive; b. Bklyn., May 24, 1932; s. Craig F. and Edith (Williams) T.; m. Masae Sugizaki, Feb. 21, 1957; children: Lee Anne, Jane Laura. Grad., Valley Forge Mil. Acad., 1951; BA, Johns Hopkins U., 1954. Newspaper and radio reporter Easton (Pa.) Express, 1954-55, 57-59, Wall St. Jour., 1959-60; account exec. Moore, Meldrum & Assocs., 1960; mgr. pub. relations Cen. Nat. Bank of Cleve., 1961-62; account exec. Edward Howard & Co., Cleve., 1962-67, v.p., 1967-69, sr. v.p., 1969-71; dir. pub. relations White Motor Corp., Cleve., 1971-76; v.p. pub. relations No. Telecom Inc., Nashville, 1976-77, White Motor Corp., Farmington Hills, Mich., 1977-80, v.p. corp. communications, 1980-81; dir. exec. communications Rockwell Internat. Corp., Pitts., 1981-86, El Segundo, Calif., 1986-91, Seal Beach, Calif., 1992-97, sr. communications exec., 1997; pres. Craig S. Thompson. Inc., 1997—. Bd. dirs. Shaker Lakes Regional Nature Center, 1970-73. Served to 1st lt., inf. U.S. Army, 1955-57. Mem. Pub. Rels. Soc. Am. (accredited), Alumni Assn. Valley Forge Mil. Acad. (bd. dirs. 1988-94).

THOMPSON, DAVID ALFRED, industrial engineer; b. Chgo., Sept. 9, 1929; s. Clifford James and Christobel Eliza (Sawin) T.; children: Nancy, Brooke, Lynda, Diane, Kristy. B.M.E., U. Va., 1951; BS in Indsl. Engring, U. Fla., 1955, MS in Engring, 1956; PhD, Stanford U., 1961. Registered profl. engr., Calif; cert. profl. ergonomist; bd. cert. diplomate in forensic engring. Research asst. U. Fla. Engring. and Industries Exptl. Sta., Gainesville, 1955-56; instr. indsl. engring. Stanford U., 1956-58, acting asst. prof., 1958-61, asst. prof., 1961-64, asso. prof., 1964-72, prof., 1972-83, prof., asso. chmn. dept. indsl. engring., 1972-73, prof. emeritus, 1983—; clin. faculty occupational medicine U. Calif. Med. Sch., San Francisco, 1985—; pres., chief scientist Portola Assocs., Palo Alto, Calif., 1962—97, Incline Village, Nev., 1997—; prin. investigator NASA Ames Rsch. Ctr., Moffatt Field, Calif., 1974-77. Cons. Dept. State, Fed. EEO Commn., maj. U.S. and fgn. cos.; cons. emergency commn. ctr. design Santa Clara County Criminal Justice Bd., 1974, Bay Area Rapid Transit Control Ctr., 1977, Govt. of Mex., 1978, Amadahl Corp., 1978-79, Kerr-McGee Corp., 1979, Chase Manhattan Bank, 1980, St. Regis Paper Co., 1980-82, Pacific Gas & Electric, 1983-85, Pacific Bell, 1984-86, 89-93, IBM, 1988-91, Hewlett-Packard, 1990-91, 98-99, Reuter's News Svc., 1990-92, Safeway Corp., 1992-94, New United Motors Mfg., 1993-95, Sun Microsys., 1993-94, Microsoft, 1995-00; mem. com. for office computers Calif. OSHA. Dir., editor: documentary film Rapid Answers for Rapid Transit, Dept. Transp., 1974; mem. editorial adv. bd. Computers and Graphics, 1970-85; reviewer Indsl. Engring. and IEEE Transactions, 1972-86; contbr. articles to profl. jours. Served to lt. USNR, 1951-58. HEW grantee, 1967-70 Fellow Nat. Assn. Forensic Engrs.; mem. IEEE, Am. Inst. Indsl. Engrs., Human Factors and Ergonomics Soc., Am. Soc. Safety Engrs., Soc. Forensic Engrs. and Scientists, Am. Assn. Forensic Scientists. Home: PO Box 6685 Incline Village NV 89450-6685 Address: PO Box 6088 Incline Village NV 89450-6088 Office Phone: 775-833-3304. Personal E-mail: davidthompson@pyramid.net. Business E-Mail: davidthompson@humanfactors.org.

THOMPSON, DAVID C., electronics manufacturing company executive; b. 1930; Pres., CEO Stephens Engring. Assocs., Inc., SEA Inc.; prin. fin. and acctg. officer Datamarine Internat., Inc., 1995-97, sec., treas., 1996—, pres., CEO Mountlake Terrace, Wash., 1997—. Office: 7030 220th St SW Mountlake Terrace WA 98043-2125

THOMPSON, DAVID M., computer software company executive; b. NJ; married; 2 children. Bachelors in Engring., Masters in Engring., Cornell U. With Digital Equipment Corp.; dir. software devel. Concord Comm.; with Microsoft Corp., 1990—, corp. v.p. Windows Server Product group, 2000—04, corp. v.p. Microsoft Exchange group, 2004—07, corp. v.p. Microsoft Online, 2007—. Avocations: skiing, snowboarding, bicycling, hiking.

THOMPSON, DAVID RENWICK, federal judge; b. 1930; BS in Bus., U. So. Calif., 1952, LLB, 1955. Pvt. practice Thompson & Thompson (and predecessor firms), 1957—85; judge US Ct. Appeals (9th cir.), 1985—98, sr. judge, 1998—. With USN, 1955—57. Mem.: ABA, Am. Bd. Trial Lawyers (sec. San Diego chpt. 1983, v.p. 1984, Pres. 1985), San Diego County Bar Assn. Office: US Ct Appeals 940 Front St Rm 2193 San Diego CA 92101-8919

THOMPSON, DAVID W.J., atmospheric scientist, educator; BS in Aerospace Engring., U. Colo., Boulder, 1994; MS in Atmospheric Scis., U. Wash., Seattle, 1998, PhD in Atmospheric Scis., 2000. Asst. prof. Colo. State U., Ft. Collins, 2001—06, assoc. prof., 2006—. Contbr. articles to sci. jours.; assoc. editor: Jour. Climate, 2004—. Recipient CAREER award, NSF, 2001; named one of Brilliant 10, Popular Sci. mag., 2006. Fellow: Am. Geophys. Union (Macelwane medal 2004). Achievements include one of the first to identify the Arctic Oscillation. Office: Colo State U Dept Atmospheric Sci Fort Collins CO 80523 Office Phone: 970-491-3338. Office Fax: 970-491-8449. E-mail: davet@atmos.colostate.edu.

THOMPSON, DENNIS PETERS, plastic surgeon; b. Chgo., Mar. 18, 1937; s. David John and Ruth Dorothy (Peters) T.; m. Virginia Louise Williams, June 17, 1961; children: Laura Faye, Victoria Ruth, Elizabeth Jan. BS, U. Ill., 1957, BS in Medicine, 1959, MS in Physiology, 1961, MD, 1961. Diplomate Am. Bd. Surgery, Am. Bd. Plastic Surgery. Intern Presbyn.-St. Lukes Hosp., Chgo., 1961—62; resident in gen. surgery Mayo Clinic, Rochester, Minn., 1964—66, fellow in gen. surgery, 1964—66; resident in gen. surgery Harbor Gen. Hosp., LA, 1968—70; resident in plastic surgery UCLA, 1971—73, clin. instr. plastic surgery, 1975—82, asst. clin. prof. surgery, 1982—97, assoc. clin. prof. plastic surgery, 1998—; clin. prof. Plastic Surgery. Practice medicine specializing in plastic and reconstructive surgery, LA, 1974-78, Santa Monica, Calif., 1978—2008; chmn. plastic surgery sect. St. John's Hosp., 1986-91; staff Olive View Hosp., 1982—2008, St. John's Hosp., 1982-; chmn. dept. surgery Beverly Glen Hosp., 1978-79; pres. Coop. of Am. Physicians Credit Union, 1978-80; bd. dirs. Coop. Am. Physicians, 1980-97, chmn. membership devel. com., 1983-97, treas., 1985-97. Contbr. articles to med. jours. Moderator Congl. Ch. of Northridge (Calif.), 1975-76, chmn. bd. trustees, 1973-74, 80-82; bd. dirs. L.A. Bus. Coun., 1987-90. Am. Tobacco Inst. rsch. grantee, 1959-60. Fellow ACS; mem. AMA (Physicians Recognition award 1971, 74, 77, 81, 84, 87, 90, 93, 96, 99, 2002, 05), Calif. Med. Assn., L.A. County Med. Assn. (chmn. bylaws com. 1979-80, chmn. ethics com. 1980-81, 2000-01, sec.-treas. dist. 5 1982-83, program chmn. 1983-84, pres. 1985-86, councilor 1988-96, 2001-03, councilor-at-large 2004—, v.p. 1999-2000), Pan-Pacific Surg. Assn., Am. Soc. Plastic Surgeons, Calif. Soc. Plastic Surgeons (chmn. bylaws com. 1982-83, chmn. liability com. 1983-85, councilor 1988-91, sec. 1993-95, v.p. 1995-96, pres.-elect 1996-97, pres. 1997-98), L.A. Soc. Plastic Surgeons (sec. 1980-82, pres. 1982-97), Lipoplasty Soc. N.Am., UCLA Plastic Surgery Soc. (treas. 1983-84, v.p. 1996-98, pres. 1998-2003, 2005), Am. Soc. Aesthetic Plastic Surgery, Internat. Soc. Clin. Plastic Surgeons (bd. dirs. 1999-2006, pres. 2004-06), Am. Assn. Accreditation of Ambulatory Surg. Facilities (bd. dirs. 1995-97, 2002-, ofcl. observer to AMA ho. of dels. 1999—), Western L.A. Regional C. of C. (bd. dirs. 1981-84, 86-89, chmn. legis. action com. 1978-80), Phi Beta Kappa, Alpha Omega Alpha, Nu Sigma Nu, Phi Kappa Phi, Delta Sigma Delta, Omega Beta Pi, Phi Eta Sigma. Republican. Home Phone: 818-347-8369; Office Phone: 310-829-6876. Business E-Mail: dthompson@dslextreme.com.

THOMPSON, GEORGE ALBERT, geophysicist, educator; b. Swissvale, Pa., June 5, 1919; s. George Albert Sr. and Maude Alice (Harkness) T.; m. Anita Kimmell, July 20, 1944; children: Albert J., Dan A., David C. BS, Pa. State U., 1941; MS, MIT, 1942; PhD, Stanford U., 1949. Registered profl. geophysicist Calif., 1970, profl. geologist Calif., 1970. Geologist, geophysicist U.S. Geol. Survey, Menlo Park, Calif., 1942-49; asst. prof. Stanford (Calif.) U., 1949-55, assoc. prof., 1955-60, prof. geophysics, 1960—, chmn. geophysics dept., 1967-86, chmn. geology dept., 1979-82, Otto N. Miller prof. earth scis., 1980-89, dean sch. earth scis., 1987-89. Part-time geologist US Geol. Survey, Menlo Park, 1949-76; cons. adv. com. on reactor safeguards Nuclear Regulation Commn., Washington, 1974-94; mem. bd. earth sci. NRC, 1986-88, vice chmn. Yucca Mountain Hydrology-tectonics panel NRC, 1990-92; mem. sr. external events rev. com. Lawrence Livermore Nat. Lab., 1989-93; mem. exec. com. Inc. Rsch. Inst. for Seismology, Washington, 1990-92; mem. Coun. on Continental Sci. Drilling, 1990-94; cons. Los Alamos Nat. Lab. on volcano-tectonic processes, 1993-96, S.W. Rsch. Inst., 1993; chair com. to review sci. issues NRC, Ward Valley, Calif., 1994-95; mem. panel on probabalistic volcanic hazard analysis Geomatrix Cons., Inc., 1995-96, 2005— Author over 100 research papers. With USN, 1944—46. Recipient John Wesley Powell award US Geol. Survey, 1999; NSF postdoctoral fellow, 1956-57, Guggenheim Found. fellow, 1963-64 Fellow AAAS, Geol. Soc. Am. (coun. mem. 1983-86, George P. Woollard award 1983, v.p. 1995, pres. 1996, Penrose Medal, 2008), Am. Geophys. Union; mem. NAS (chair geology sect. 2000-03), Seismol. Soc. Am., Soc. Exploration Geophysicists. Avocation: forestry. Home: 421 Adobe Pl Palo Alto CA 94306-4501 Office: Stanford U Geophysics Dept Stanford CA 94305-2215 Home Phone: 650-493-3230; Office Phone: 650-723-3714. Business E-Mail: gathomps@stanford.edu.

THOMPSON, GORDON, JR., federal judge; b. San Diego, Dec. 28, 1929; s. Gordon and Garnet (Meese) T.; m. Jean Peters, Mar. 17, 1951; children— John M., Peter Renwick, Gordon III. Grad., U. So. Calif., 1951, Southwestern U. Sch. Law, Los Angeles, 1956. Bar: Calif. 1956. With Dist. Atty.'s Office, County of San Diego, 1957-60; partner firm Thompson & Thompson, San Diego, 1960-70; U.S. dist. judge So. Dist. Calif., San Diego, 1970—, chief judge, 1984-91, sr. judge, 1994—. Mem. ABA, Am. Bd. Trial Advocates, San Diego County Bar Assn. (v.p. 1970), San Diego Yacht Club, Delta Chi. Office: US Dist Ct 940 Front St San Diego CA 92101-8994

THOMPSON, JACK EDWARD, mining company executive; b. Central City, Nebr., Nov. 17, 1924; s. Ray Elbert and Bessie Fay (Davis) T.; m. Maria del Carmen Larrea, May 8, 1948; children: Jack Edward, Ray Anthony, Robert Davis. Student, Northwestern U., 1942-43, Colo. Sch. Mines, 1943-45, D of Engring. (hon.), 1993. V.p. Cía. Química Comercial de Cuba S.A., 1946-60, Cía. de Fomento Químico S.A., 1946-60; with Newmont Mining Corp., NYC, 1960-86, asst. to pres., 1964-67, v.p., 1967-71, dir., 1969-86, exec. v.p., 1971-74, pres., 1974-85, vice chmn., 1985-86, cons., 1986-90. Chmn. bd. trustees Minerals Industry Ednl. Found. Recipient Distinguished Achievement medal Colo. Sch. Mines, 1974 Mem. AIME, Mining and Metall. Soc. Am., Mining Found. of S.W. (past pres., bd. govs.), Tucson Country Club. E-mail: rayonera@aol.com.

THOMPSON, JEFF, state legislator; b. Harlingen, Tex., Sept. 16, 1963; m. Chanin Thompson. BS in Bus. & Fin., Liberty U., 1986; MA in Human Resource Training & Devel., Idaho State U., 2006. Former regional mgr. ARAMARK; former cons. Idaho Nat. Lab.; mem. Psychol. Dept. Idaho Falls Sch. Dist.; mem. Dist. 33 Idaho House of Reps., 2008—. Republican. Baptist. Office: Capitol Annex PO Box 83720 Boise ID 83720-0054 also: 1739 Peggys Ln Idaho Falls ID 83402 Office Phone: 208-334-2475, 208-681-4310. Office Fax: 208-334-2125, 208-524-7367.*

THOMPSON, JEFFREY L., automotive parts manfacturing executive; V.p./gen. mgr., COO Edelbrock Corp., Torrance, Calif., 1988—, dir., 1994—. Office: Edelbrock Corp 2700 California St Torrance CA 90503

THOMPSON, JILL LYNETTE LONG, former congressman; b. Warsaw, Ind., July 15, 1952; m. Don Thompson, 1995. BBA, Valparaiso U., 1974; MBA, Ind. U., 1978, PhD, 1984. Asst. instr., lectr. Ind. U., Bloomington, 1977—80; asst. prof. Valparaiso U., 1981—88; mgmt. cons. Campbell and Pryor, 1985-86; mem. US Congress from 4th Ind. Dist., 1989-95, mem. agrl. com., vets. affairs com.; under sec. for rural devel. USDA, Washington, 1995—2001; CEO Nat. Ctr. for Food & Agrl. Policy, Washington, 2003—08. Adj. prof. Indiana U.-Purdue U. Ft. Wayne, 1987-89; Manchester Coll., 2002-03 asst. prof. Valparaiso U. Councilwoman City of Valparaiso, Ind., 1984-86; chair Congrl. Rural Congress. Fellow: Inst. of Politics. Democrat. Methodist.

THOMPSON, JOE D., physicist; BS in Physics, 1969, PhD in Physics, 1975. Postdoctoral Cryogenics Group Los Alamos Nat. Lab., N.Mex., 1975—77, tech. staff mem. Condensed Matter and Thermal Physics Group, 1977—2001, dep. group leader, 1989—92, group leader, 1992—2001, Lab. fellow, 2001—. Fellow: AAAS, Am. Phys. Soc. Office: Los Alamos Nat Lab MSK-764 PO Box 1663 Los Alamos NM 87545

THOMPSON, JOHN WENDELL, information technology executive; b. Ft. Dix, NJ, Apr. 24, 1949; s. John H. and Eunice Thompson; m. Sandi Thompson; children: John E., Ayanna. BBA, Fla. A&M U., 1971; MBA in Mgmt. Sci., MIT's Sloan School Mgmt., 1982. Sales rep. IBM Corp., 1971—75, branch office mgr., 1975—79, regional adminstrv. asst., regional mktg. dir., 1980—84, asst. to CEO, 1984, dir. Midwest ops., 1990—93, head mktg. US ops., 1993, gen. mgr. personal software products, 1994—98, gen. mgr. IBM Americas, 1997—99; chmn., CEO Symantec Corp., Cupertino, Calif., 1999—2009, chmn., 2009—. Bd. dirs. Symantec Corp., 1999—, United Parcel Svc., Inc. (UPS), 2000—, Seagate Tech., 2004—; mem. Nat. Infrastructure Adv. Com., Washington, 2002—; chair Silicon Valley Blue Ribbon Task Force on Aviation Security & Tech. Chmn. Fla. A&M U. Cluster; Ill. Gov's human resource adv. coun. Named one of 50 Who Matter Now, CNNMoney.com Bus. 2.0, 2006; named to Power 150, Ebony mag., 2008. Office: Symantec Corp 20330 Stevens Creek Blvd Cupertino CA 95014*

THOMPSON, JOSEPH STANTON, career officer; m. Sandra Kay Kirby; children: Sarah, Joshua, Annah. BSc, U. Mo., 1970, B in Journalism, 1974. Enlisted USN, 1970, advanced through grades to rear adm.; stationed on USS Kilauea, 1970-72; recalled to active duty Operations Desert Shield/Desert Storm, 1990; exec. dir. Lafayette County Mo. Office Farm Svc. Agy. U.S. Dept. Agrl., 1972—; various assignments Inshore Undersea Warfare Group One, San Diego; comdr. Inshore Undersea Warfare Group Two, 1992-95; dep. comdr. Hdqs. Staff Naval Reserve Readiness Command Region Ten, New Orleans, 1995-96, U.S. Coast Guard Maritime Defense Command Seven, Miami, Fla., 1996—. Decorated Legion of Merit, Meritorious Svc. medal with two gold stars.

THOMPSON, JUDITH KASTRUP, nursing researcher; b. Marstal, Denmark, Oct. 1, 1933; arrived in US, 1951; d. Edward Kastrup and Anna Hansa (Knudsen) Pedersen; m. Richard Frederick Thompson, May 22, 1960; children: Kathryn Marr, Elizabeth Kastrup, Virginia St. Claire. BS, RN, U. Oreg., Corvallis, 1958; MSN, U. Oreg., 1963. RN Calif., Oreg. Staff nurse U. Oreg. Med. Sch., Eugene, 1957-58, Portland, 1958-61, head staff nurse, 1960-61; instr. psychiat. nursing U. Oreg. Sch. Nursing, Portland, 1963-64; rsch. asst. U. Oreg. Med. Sch., Portland, 1964-65, U. Calif., Irvine, 1971-72; rsch. assoc. Stanford (Calif.) U., 1982-87; rsch. asst. Harvard U., Cambridge, Mass., 1973-74; rsch. assoc. U. So. Calif., LA, 1987—. Contbg. author: Behavioral Control and Role of Sensory Biofeedback, 1976; contbr. articles to profl. jours. Treas. LWV, Newport Beach, Calif., 1970-74; scout leader Girl Scouts Am., Newport Beach, 1970-78. Named Citizen of Yr. State of Oreg., 1966. Mem. Soc. for Neurosci., Am. Psychol. Soc. (charter), ANA, Oreg. Nurses Assn. Republican. Lutheran. Avocations: art collecting, travel, tennis. Office: U So Calif University Park Los Angeles CA 90089-0001 Home: 952 Jacqueline Pl Nipomo CA 93444-6605 Office Phone: 213-740-7350, 213-740-7339. Business E-Mail: judith@usc.edu.

THOMPSON, KENNETH, software engineer; b. New Orleans, 1943; BSEE, U. Calif., Berkeley, 1965, MSEE, 1966. With Computer Scis. Rsch. Ctr. Bell Labs/Lucent Technologies, Murray Hill, NJ, 1966—2000; disting. mem. tech. staff Bell Labs/Lucent Techs, Murray Hill, NJ; fellow Entrisphere, Inc. Vis. prof. U. Calif., Berkeley, 1975—76, U. Sydney, Australia, 1988. Recipient Fellow award, Computer History Mus., 1997, Emmanuel R. Piore award, IEEE, Richard Hamming medal, Harold Pender Award, Sch. Engring. and Applied Sci., U. Pa., 2003; co-recipient U.S. Nat. Medal of Tech., 1999, C&C prize, NEC, 1989; named Bell Labs Fellow, 1983. Mem.: Assn. Computing Machinery (Turing award and software sys. award 1983), NAE, NAS, IEEE Computer Soc. (Tsutomu Kanai award 1999). Achievements include patents for computer technology; research in operating systems, programming languages, software for voice and data communications, security, computer games and digital music distribution; co-developer of UNIX operating system in 1969; with J.H. Condon was involved with the development of Belle, a chess computer, which won the US and World Computing Chess Championships in 1980.

THOMPSON, LEONARD RUSSELL, pediatrician; b. Columbus, Ohio, Sept. 29, 1934; s. Oliver Bernard and Christina (Nichols) T.; m. Candice Elizabeth Brisken, Dec. 6, 1980; children: Ryan, Deron, Hillary, Jon, Christina, Lisa. BA, Ohio State U., 1956, MD, 1960. Diplomat Am. Bd. Pediatrics. Intern Fitzsimmons Gen. Hosp., Denver, 1960-61, resident, 1961-63; chief pediatrics Ireland Army Hosp., Ft. Knox, Ky., 1965-66; chmn. dept. pediatrics Fresno (Calif.) Med. Group, 1966-80; pediatrician pvt. practice, Fresno, 1990—; clinical prof. pediatrics UCSF, Fresno, 1990—. Pres. med. staff Valley Children's Hosp., Fresno, 1992. Maj. U.S. Army, 1960-66. Fellow Am. Acad. Pediatrics. Office: 1187 E Herndon Ave # 104 Fresno CA 93720-3114 E-mail: lrthompson1@att.net.

THOMPSON, LOHREN MATTHEW, oil company executive; b. Sutherland, Nebr., Jan. 21, 1926; s. John M. and Anna (Ecklund) T.; children: Terence M., Sheila M., Clark M. Ed., U. Denver. Spl. rep. Standard Oil Co., Omaha, 1948-56; sales mgr. Frontier REF. Co., 1956-67, v.p. mktg., 1967-68; mgr. mktg. U.S. region Husky Oil Co., Denver, 1968-72; v.p. Westar Stas., Inc., Denver, 1967-70; chmn. bd. Colo. Petroleum, Denver, 1971—. Served with USAAF, 1944-46 Mem. Colo. Petroleum Council, Am. Petroleum Inst., Am. Legion Clubs: Denver Petroleum, Denver Oilman's. Lodges: Lions. Lutheran. Home: 2410 Spruce Ave Estes Park CO 80517-7146 Office: Colo Petroleum 4080 Globeville Rd Denver CO 80216-4906

THOMPSON, MARK LEE, art educator, sculptor; b. Ft. Sill, Okla., 1950; s. James B. and Beverly J. T. Student, Va. Polytech Inst., 1968-70; BA in Art, U. Calif., Berkeley, 1972, MA in Sculpture, 1973. Lectr. conceptual design San Francisco State U., 1988-89, lectr. sculpture, 1991-93; adj. prof. sculpture Calif. Coll. Arts and Crafts, 1993—. Vis. lectr. U. Coll. London, 1990; grad. workshop San Francisco State U., 1992, U. Colo., Boulder, 1994, Chgo. Sch. Art Inst. Chgo., 1995, Stanford U., 1995, So. Ill. U., Carbondale, 1995; presenter in field. Exhibits include Va. Polytech. Inst., Blacksburg, 1969, U. Calif., Berkeley, 1973, San Francisco Civic Ctr. Plz., 1975, San Francisco Art Commn. Gallery, 1986, Headlands Ctr. for Arts, Fort Barry, Calif., 1987, Headlands Ctr. Arts, 1987, Steirischer Herbst '87, 1987, Intersection for Arts, 1989, Artpark, 1989, Kunstlerhaus Bethanien, Ressource Kunst, 1989, New Langton Arts, 1989, Palo Alto (Calif.) Cultural Ctr., 1990, Whitechapel Art Gallery, London, 1990, M.H. de Young Meml. Mus., Ctr. Arts, Yerba Buena Gardens, Exploratorium, Haus am Waldsee, 1990, Edge 90, 1990, Hartnell Coll., Salinas, Calif., 1993, M.H. de Young Meml. Mus., San Francisco, 1995, Oliver Art Ctr. Calif. Coll. Arts and Crafts, 1995, Boulder Mus. Contemporary Art, 1996, Pro Arts Gallery, 1997, Gallery Paule Anglim, 2001, Yerba Buena Ctr. Arts, 1999, mus. Contemporary Art, 1998-99, others; contbr. articles to profl. jours. Recipient Visual Artists award Flintridge Found., 1997-1998, Wattis Artists-in-Residence award Yuerba Buena Ctr. Arts, 1999; project grantee fund U.S. Artists Internat. Festivals Rockefeller Found. U.S. Info. Agy. Nat. Endowment Arts, 1989, project grantee, Inc., Art Matters, N.Y., 1989, Visual Arts fellowship grantee Nat. Endowment Arts, 1989, AVA 11 Artist fellowship grantee Awards in Visual Arts, 1991-92, New Genre Artists fellowship grantee Calif. Arts Coun., 1992; U.S.-Japan Creative Artist Exch. fellow Nat. Endowment Arts/Japan-U.S. Friendship Commn., 1990, Creative Artist sculpture fellow Cultural Arts, City of Oakland, Calif., 1994, Civitella Ranieri Ctr. fellow, Umbertide, Italy, 2001—. Office: Calif Coll Arts & Crafts 5212 Broadway Oakland CA 94618-1426

THOMPSON, MIKE (C. MICHAEL THOMPSON), United States Representative from California; b. Jan. 24, 1951; s. Charles Thompson and Beverly (Forni) Powell; m. Janet Thompson, Mar. 8, 1982; children: Christopher, Jon. BA in Political Sci., Calif. State U., Chico, 1982, MA in Pub. Adminstrn., 1996. Owner, maintenance supr. Beringer Winery; mem. Calif. State Senate, 1991—98, U.S. Congress from 1st Calif. dist., 1999—; mem. armed svcs. com., agr. com. Former chair select com. Calif. Wine Industry; former chair budget com. Calif. Senate, former vice chair natural resources com.; instr. Army Airborne Sch.; instr. pub. adminstrn. and state govt. San Francisco State U., Calif. State U., Chico. Co-founder, co-chair Congl. Wine Caucus; co-vice chair Congl. Sportsmen's Caucus; mem. New Dem. Coalition, Blue Dog Coalition. Staff sgt. US Army, Vietnam. Decorated Purple Heart, US Army; recipient Disting. Svc. award, Calif. State Assn. Counties, Calif. Assn. Hosps., Legis. Leadership award, Calif. Assn. Health Svcs., 1994, Disting. Svc. award, Aids Project LA, 1995, Outstanding Senator award, Planned Parenthood Affiliates Calif., 1996; named Legislator of Yr., Calif. Abortion Rights Action League, Calif. Assn. Persons with Handicaps, Police Officers Rsch. Assn. Calif., Disabled in State Svc., 1994, Senator of Yr., Calif. Assn. Homes & Svcs. for Aging, 1995, Outstanding Senator of Yr., Calif. Sch. Bds. Assn., 1996, Calif. Profl. Firefighters, 1996. Mem.: Calif. Faculty Assn., Bus. & Profl. Women's Assn., Vietnam Vets. of America, Am. Legion, Native Sons of Golden West, Sons of Italy. Democrat. Roman Catholic. Office: US Ho Reps 231 Cannon Ho Office Bldg Washington DC 20515-0501 Office Phone: 202-225-3111. Office Fax: 202-225-4335.

THOMPSON, PATRICK S., lawyer; b. Muskegon, Mich., July 24, 1967; BA with high honors, U. Mich., 1989; JD, Harvard Law Sch., 1992. Bar: Calif. 1992. Ptnr., antitrust, telecom., complex litig. Pillsbury Winthrop LLP, San Francisco; ptnr. Goodwin Procter LLP, 2006—. Editor: Antitrust Law Jour., 1996—2002. Vice chair, conservatory com. Am. Conservatory Theater; sec., bd. trustees Grace Cathedral; chmn. bd. dirs. Calif. Pacific Med. Ctr., 2003—04, dir., 1996—2004; sec., bd. trustees Am. Conservatory Theater; bd. dirs. Francis of Assisi Cmty. Named one of Am. Top Black Attys., Black Enterprise, 2003, Top 20 Lawyers Under Age 40, Daily Jour., Calif., 2004, N. Calif. Super Lawyers, 2004—05. Mem.: ABA (mem. antitrust section, mem. editl. bd. Antitrust Source, liaison to commn. racial and ethnic diversity in legal profession), State Bar Calif. (vice chair, exec. com. antitrust and unfair competition section 2005). Office: Goodwin Procter LLP 101 Calif St San Francisco CA 94111 Office Phone: 415-733-6068. Office Fax: 415-677-9041. Business E-Mail: pthompson@goodwinprocter.com.

THOMPSON, PAUL HAROLD, university president; b. Ogden, Utah, Nov. 28, 1938; s. Harold Merwin and Elda (Skeen) T.; m. Carolyn Lee Nelson, Mar. 9, 1961; children: Loralyn, Kristyn, Shannyn, Robbyn, Daylyn, Nathan. BS, U. Utah, 1964; MBA, Harvard U., 1966, D Bus. Adminstrn., 1969. Rsch. assoc. Harvard U., Cambridge, Mass., 1966-69, asst. prof., 1969-73; assoc. prof. bus. Brigham Young U., Provo, Utah, 1973-78, prof., 1978-84, asst. dean, 1978-81, dean, 1984-89, v.p., 1989-90; pres. Weber State U., Ogden, Utah, 1990—. Cons. Goodyear, Hughes Aircraft, Portland GE, Esso Resources Ltd., GE. Co-author: Organization and People: Readings, Cases, and Exercises in Organizational Behavior, 1976, Novations: Strategies for Career Management, 1986; also articles. Named Outstanding Prof. of Yr., Brigham Young U., 1981; Baker scholar Harvard U., 1966. Mem. Am. Assn. State Colls. and Univs. (com. 1991—), Ogden C. of C. (exec. com. 1990—), Rotary (prograam com. Ogden 1991—, Harris fellow 1992—), Phi Beta Kappa. Office: Weber State U Presidents Office 3750 Harrison Blvd Ogden UT 84408-0001

THOMPSON, PAUL MATTHEW, neuroscientist; b. York, Eng., June 13, 1971; s. Derek and Cynthia (Jenkinson) T.; m. Lynn Lee Hodges, Sept. 9, 1995. BA in Classical Langs., Oxford U., Eng., 1991, MA in Math., 1993; PhD in Neurosci., UCLA, 1998. Rsch. scholar Oxford U., 1989-93; Fulbright scholar Brain Mapping divsn. UCLA, 1993-98; fellow Howard Hughes Med. Inst., Bethesda, Md., 1993-98; prof. neurology UCLA Brain Rsch. Inst., 1998—. Cons. Nathan Kline Inst., N.Y.C., 1998—; sci. investigator NIH Neuro-Imaging Resource, L.A., 1998—, NSF, Bethesda, 1998—. Contbr. over 70 articles to profl. jours. Recipient SPIE Medical Imaging award, 1997, Outstanding Grad. Student of the Yr., UCLA Chancello's Svc. award, 1998, Eiduson award for Neuroscience Rsch., 1998, Di Chiro Outstanding Scientific Paper award, 1998; Rsch. grantee Nat. Ctr. for Rsch. Resources, 1998—, NIH, 1998—, NINDS, 1998—, NSF, 1998—. Mem. U. Calif. Alumni Assn. Achievements include design of new algorithms for brain image analysis and pathology detection; developed new strategies for analyzing brain image data bases and for brain mapping in large human populations; creation of systems to detect and map alterations in brain structure and function; developed system to map growth patterns in brain development. Office: Lab of Neuro Imaging UCLA Sch Med 635 Charles E Young Dr S Ste 225E Los Angeles CA 90095 E-mail: thompson@loni.ucla.edu.

THOMPSON, PETER LAYARD HAILEY, SR., landscape and golf course architect, architectural firm executive; b. Modesto, Calif., Apr. 26, 1939; BS in East Asian Studies, U. Oreg., 1962, B in Landscape Architecture, 1971, M in Urban Planning, 1971; postgrad., U. Calif., Berkeley, 1975, Nat. U. Registered landscape arch., Calif., Oreg., Wash., Nev. With Oreg. Planning Commn., Lane County, 1965-70, commr. Eugene, 1981-83; sr. assoc. Ruff, Cameron, Lacoss, Eugene, 1971-75; prin. Peter L. H. Thompson & Assocs., Eugene, 1975-83, John H. Midby & Assocs., Las Vegas, Nev., 1983-86, Thompson-Wihlborg, Ltd., Corte Madera, Calif., 1982-89, Thompson Planning Group (now Thompson Golf Planning), Ltd., Novato, Calif., 1989—. With Oreg. Planning Commn., commr., 1981-83, Novato, Calif. Planning Commn., commr. 1989-93, pres. 1989-93; spkr. Oreg. Home Builders Conf., 1980, Pacific Coast Builders Conf., 1984, Tacoma Country Club Pro-Pres. Tournament, 1991, Madrona Links Men's Golf Club, 1991, Twin Lakes Country Club Pro-Pres. Tournament, 1992, Golf Expo, Palm Springs, Calif., 1993, 95, Golf Expo, Nashville, 1993, Golf Expo, Monterey, Calif., 1994, others. Contbr. articles to mags. Mem. citizen's adv. bd. City of Eugene, Oreg., City of Las Vegas. Mem. USGA, Am. Soc. Landscape Archs., Am. Assn. Planners, Nat. Golf Found., Urban Land Inst., Rotary Internat. Office: Thompson Golf Planning Ltd 1510 Grant Ave Ste 305 Novato CA 94945-3146 Office Phone: 415-878-2020.

THOMPSON, RAYMOND HARRIS, retired anthropologist, educator; b. Portland, Maine, May 10, 1924; s. Raymond and Eloise (MacIntyre) T.; m. Molly Kendall, Sept. 9, 1948; children: Margaret Kelsey Luchetta, Mary Frances. BS, Tufts U., 1947; A.M., Harvard U., 1950, PhD, 1955. Fellow div. hist. research Carnegie Instn., Washington, 1950-52; asst. prof. anthropology, curator Mus. Anthropology, U. Ky., 1952-56; faculty U. Ariz., 1956-97, prof. anthropology, 1964—, Riecker Disting. prof., 1980-97, head dept., 1964-80; emeritus, 1997; dir. Ariz. State Mus., 1964-97; emeritus, 1997. Mem. adv. panel program in anthropology NSF, 1963-64, mem. mus. collections program, 1983-85; mem. NSF grad. fellowship panel Nat. Acad. Scis.-NRC, 1964-66; mem. research in nursing in patient care rev. com. USPHS, 1967-69; com. on social sci. commn. edn. in agr. and natural resources Nat. Acad. Scis., 1968-69; mem. anthropology com. examiners Grad. Record Exam., 1967-70, chmn., 1969-70; mem. com. recovery archaeol. remains, 1972-77, chmn., 1973-77; collaborator Nat. Park Service, 1972-76; mem. Ariz. Hist. Adv. Commn., 1966-97, chmn., 1971-74, chmn. hist. sites rev. com., 1971-83; mem. editl. bd. Science, 1972-77; chmn. Ariz. Humanities Council, 1973-77, mem., 1979-85; adv. bd. Ariz. Hist. Recors, 1976-84; mem. research review panel for archaeology NEH, 1976-77, mem. rev. panel mus., 1978, Ariz. Archaeology Adv. Commn., 1985-97; cons. task force on archaeology Adv. Council on Historic Preservation, 1978; editl. advisor, Jour. of the Southwest. Author: Modern Yucatecan Maya Pottery Making, 1958; editor: Migrations in New World Culture History, 1958, When is a Kiva, 1990. Trustee Mus. No. Ariz., 1969-84, 86-90; bd. dirs. Tucson Art Mus., 1974-77; cons. Nat. Mus. Act Coun., 1984-86. Served with USNR, 1944-45, PTO. Recipient Pub. Svc. award, Dept. Interior, 1990; named Raymond H. Thompson award in his name, Dept. Anthrop., U. Ariz., 2006. Fellow AAAS (chmn. sect. H 1977-78), Tree-Ring Soc., Am. Anthrop. Assn. (Disting. Svc. award 1980); mem. Soc. Am. Archaeology (editor 1958-62, exec. com. 1963-64, pres. 1976-77, disting. svc. award 1998), Am. Soc. Conservation Archaeology (Conservation award 1980), Seminario de Cultura Maya, Am. Assn. Museums (accreditation vis. com. 1972, 82-90, cons. mus. assessment program 1983-89, repatriation task force 1987, steering com. mus. data collection program 1988-93), Internat. Coun. Museums (assoc.), Coun. Mus. Anthropology (dir. 1978-79, pres. 1980-83), Assn. Sci. Mus. Dirs. (sec.-treas. 1978-80), Ariz. Acad. Sci., Ariz. Archaeol. and Hist. Soc. (Byron Cummings award 1993), Mus. Assn. Ariz. (pres. 1983, 84), Phi Beta Kappa, Sigma Xi. Office: Univ Ariz Ariz State Museum Tucson AZ 85721-0026

THOMPSON, RICHARD, financial executive; B, Western Wash. U., 1965; JD, U. Wash., 1968. Pvt. law practice, Snohomish, Wash., 1968-76; atty., then adminstr. city govt. Wash., 1976-80; city mgr. city govt. Puyalla, Wash., 1981-84; chief of staff Gov. Booth Gardner Wash., 1987-88; sec. Dept. Social and Health Svcs., Wash., 1989-92; chair Western Wash. Growth Mgmt. Bd., 1992-93; pres. United Way King County, Seattle, 1993-96; dir. Office of Fin. Mgmt., Olympia, Wash., 1997-99; dir. govt. rels. U. Wash. Office Govt. Rels., Seattle, 1999—. Recipient Citizenship award Comty. of Color of State of Wash., 1991. Mem. Nat. Assn. State Budgeters, Wash. Bar Assn. Office: U Wash Office Govt Rels PO Box 531278 Seattle WA 98195-0001

THOMPSON, RICHARD DICKSON, lawyer; b. Lexington, Ky., Aug. 14, 1955; s. Lawrence Sidney and Algernon Smith (Dickson) T.; m. Bobbi Dale Magidoff, Aug. 3, 1980; children: Anne Katherine, Harrison Asher, Tracey Ruth. AB, Harvard U., 1977; JD, Stanford U., 1980. Bar: Calif. 1980, U.S. Dist. Ct. (so. dist.) Calif. 1980. Assoc. Rosenfeld Meyer & Susman, Beverly Hills, Calif., 1980-83, Silverberg Rosen Leon & Behr, LA, 1983-86, assoc. ptnr., 1986-89; ptnr. Silverberg Katz Thompson & Braun, LA, 1989-95, Bloom, Hergott, Diemer, & Cook, Beverly Hills, Calif., 1995—2000; sr. v.p., corp. devel. then COO The Brodia Group, San Francisco, 2000—02; of counsel Bloom, Hergott Diemer Rosenthal & LaViolette, LLP, Beverly Hills, Calif., 2002—. Former bd. trustees L.A. Copyright Soc. (former pres.). Mem. Order of the Coif, Phi beta Kappa. Office: Bloom Hergott et al 150 S Rodeo Dr Beverly Hills CA 90212 Office Phone: 310-859-6839. E-mail: rdt@bhdrl.com.

THOMPSON, RICHARD FREDERICK, psychologist, neuroscientist, educator; b. Portland, Oreg., 1930; s. Frederick Albert and Margaret St. Clair (Marr) T.; m. Judith K. Pedersen, May 22, 1960; children: Kathryn M., Elizabeth K., Virginia St. C. BA, Reed Coll., 1952; MS, U. Wis., 1953, PhD, 1956. Asst. prof. med. psychology Med. Sch. U. Oreg., Portland, 1959-63, assoc. prof., 1963-65, prof., 1965-67; prof. psychobiology U. Calif., Irvine, 1967-73, 75-80; prof. psychology Harvard U., Cambridge, Mass., 1973-74, Lashley chair prof., 1973; prof. psychology, Bing prof. human biology Stanford U., Palo Alto, Calif., 1980-87; Keck prof. psychology and biol. scis. U. So. Calif., LA, 1987—, dir. neuroscience program, 1989—2001. Mem. Nat. Sci. Bd., 2006—. Author: Foundations of Physiological Psychology, 1967, (with others) Psychology, 1971, Introduction to Physiological Psychology, 1975; Psychology editor (with others), W.H. Freeman & Co. publs., chief editor, Behavioral Neurosci., 1983—; editor: Jour. Comparative and Physiol. Psychology, 1981-83; regional editor: (with others) Physiology and Behavior; contbr. (with others) articles to profl. jours. Recipient Rsch. Scientist Award, Nat. Institutes of Mental Health, D.G. Marquis Behavioral Neurosci. Award, 1999. Fellow AAAS (John P. McGovern Award, 1999), APA (Disting. Sci. Contbn. award 1974, governing coun. 1974—), Soc. Neurosci. (councilor 1972-76); mem. NAS, Am. Acad. Arts and Scis., Internat. Brain Rsch. Orgn., Am. Philos. Soc., Psychonomic Soc. (gov. 1972-77, chmn. 1976), Am. Psychol. Soc. (pres. 1994-96), Western Psychol. Assn. (pres. 1994-95), Soc. Expl. Psychology (Warren medal). Office: Univ of So Calif Neuroscis Program HNB 122 Univ Park Los Angeles CA 90007 Office Phone: 213-740-7350. Business E-Mail: thompson@usc.edu.

THOMPSON, RICK, computer software company executive; married; 2 children. BA, Bates Coll., 1981. Product mgr. for Microsoft Mouse Microsoft Corp., 1987—91, gen. mgr. Microsoft Hardware, 1991—96, v.p. Microsoft Hardware, 1996—99, with Xbox team, 1999—2000, corp. v.p. Windows Client extended platform divsn., 2002—06, corp. v.p. Windows live advt. & monetization platforms, 2006—; CFO, v.p. product devel. Go2Net Inc., 2000—02. Owner Seattle Chocolates; co-owner Ferrari of Seattle. Office: Microsoft Corp 1 Microsoft Way Redmond WA 98052-6399

THOMPSON, ROBERT CHARLES, lawyer; b. Council, Idaho, Apr. 20, 1942; s. Ernest Lavelle and Evangeline Montgomery (Carlson) T.; m. Marilyn Anne Wilcox, Jan. 17, 1960 (dec. Mar. 1962); m. Patricia Joan Price, June 1, 1963 (div. 1969); m. Jan Nesbitt, June 29, 1973 (dec. May 1998); m. Shari Lewis, Feb. 7, 1999; children: Christopher, Eric, Tanya, Carrie AB, Harvard U., Cambridge, Mass., 1963, LLB, 1967. Bar: Mass. 1967, Calif. 1983, US Dist. Ct. (ea. dist.) Mass. 1975, US Ct. Appeals (1st cir.) 1976, US Ct. Appeals (9th cir.) 1984, US Dist. Ct. (no. dist.) Calif. 1983, US Dist. Ct. (ea. dist.) Calif., 1996. Assoc. Choate, Hall & Stewart, Boston, 1967-73; asst. regional counsel EPA, Boston, 1973-75, regional counsel, 1975-82, assoc. gen. counsel, 1979-82, regional counsel San Francisco, 1982-84; ptnr. Graham & James, San Francisco, 1984-91, LeBoeuf, Lamb, Greene & MacRae LLP, San Francisco, 1992—99, of counsel, 2000—. Co-author: Crime and Conflict, 2006; contbr. articles to profl. jours. Bd. dirs. Peninsula Indsl. and Bus. Assn., Palo Alto, Calif., 1986-98, chmn. Cambridge Conservation Commn., Mass., 1972-74; co-chmn. The Clift Confs. on Environ. Law, 1983-98; assoc. mem. Bay Conservation and Devel. Commn., 1998-2000. John Russell Shaw traveling fellow Harvard Coll., 1963-64; recipient Regional Adminstrs. Bronze medal EPA, 1976, 84. Mem. ABA (chmn. natural resources sect., chmn. com. native Am. natural resources law, spl. com. mktg.), HumanRights Watch, Internat. Pub. What You Pay Campaign, Human RightsFirst, OxFan Am., Phi Beta Kappa. Democrat. Episcopalian. Avocations: yoga, antiques, cooking, gardening, opera. Office: LeBoeuf Lamb Greene & MacRae One Embarcadero Ctr San Francisco CA 94111 E-mail: thomps925@aol.com.

THOMPSON, RONALD EDWARD, lawyer; b. Bremerton, Wash., May 24, 1931; s. Melville Herbert and Clara Mildred (Griggs) T.; m. Marilyn Christine Woods, Dec. 15, 1956; children: Donald Jeffery, Karen, Susan, Nancy, Sally, Claire BA, U. Wash., 1953, JD, 1958. Bar: Wash. 1959. Asst. city atty. City of Tacoma, 1960—61; pres. firm Thompson, Krilich, LaPorte, West & Lockner, P.S., Tacoma, 1961—99. Judge pro tem Mcpl. Ct., City of Tacoma, Pierce County Dist., 1972—, Pierce County Superior Ct., 1972—. Chmn. housing and social welfare com. City of Tacoma, 1965-69; mem. Tacoma Bd. Adjustment, 1967-71, chmn., 1968; mem. Tacoma Com. Future Devel., 1961-64, Tacoma Planning Commn., 1971-72; bd. dirs., pres. Mcpl. League Tacoma; bd. dirs. Pres. Tacoma Rescue Mission, Tacoma Pierce County Cancer Soc., Tacoma-Pierce County Heart Assn., Tacoma Grand Cinema, Tacoma-Pierce County Coun. for Arts, Econ. Devel. Coun. Puget Sound, Tacoma Youth Symphony, Kleiner Group Home, Tacoma C.C. Found., Pierce County Econ. Devel. Corp., Wash. Transp. Policy Inst.; Coalition to Keep Wash. Moving, precinct committeeman Rep. party, 1969-73. With AUS, 1953-55; col. Res. Recipient Internat. Cmty. Svc. award Optimist Club, 1970, Patriotism award Am. Fedn. Police, 1974, citation for cmty. svc. HUD, 1974, Disting. Citizen award Mcpl. League Tacoma-Pierce County, 1985; named Lawyer of the Yr. Pierce County Legal Secs. Assn., 1992. Mem. ATLA, Am. Arbitration Assn. (panel of arbitrators), ABA, Wash. State Bar Assn. (Local Hero award 2002), Tacoma-Pierce County Bar Assn. (sec. 1964, pres. 1979, mem. cts. and judiciary com. 1981-82), Wash. State Trial Lawyers Assn., Tacoma-Pierce County C. of C. (bd. dirs., exec. com., v.p., chmn.), Downtown Tacoma Assn. (com. chmn., bd. dirs. exec. com., chmn.), Variety Club (Seattle), Lawn Tennis Club, Tacoma Club, Optimist (Tacoma, internat. pres. 1973-74), Phi Delta Phi, Sigma Nu. Roman Catholic. Home: 3101 E Bay Dr NW Gig Harbor WA 98335-7610 Office: PO Box 2091 4411 Point Fosdick Dr Ste 207 Gig Harbor WA 98333-4091 Office Phone: 253-853-7449. Personal E-mail: retpllc@att.net.

THOMPSON, RUFUS E., lawyer; b. Lubbock, Tex., Aug. 15, 1943; s. Glenn Wesley and Naomi Elvina T.; m. Sandra Jean Lemons, Aug. 8, 1965; children— Michael Glenn, Mark Gregory, Matthew Wesley. BBA, U. Tex., Austin, 1965, JD, 1968. Bar: Tex. bar 1968, N.Mex. bar 1969. Assoc. firm Atwood & Malone, Roswell, N.Mex., 1968-71; ptnr. firm Atwood, Malone, Mann & Cooter, Roswell, 1971-78; U.S. Atty. Dist. N.Mex., Albuquerque, 1978-81; now ptnr. firm Modrall, Sperling, Roehl, Harris & Sisk, Albuquerque, 1981—. Mem. Nat. Conf. Commrs. on Uniform State Laws, 1975-79; chmn. N.Mex. Supreme Ct. Com. on Rules of Evidence, 1972-94; U.S. Atty. for N.Mex. Com., 1978-82; mem. U.S. Atty. Gen.'s Adv. Com., 1980—, chmn., 1981. Mem. N.Mex. Democratic Party Central Com., 1972-78; mem. N.Mex. State Senate, 1973-78; mem. Gov.'s. Commn. on Prevention of Organized Crime, 1985-89. Mem. Am. Bar Assn. (exec. council young lawyers sect. 1972), N.Mex. Bar Assn. (chmn. young lawyers sect. 1970) Baptist. Office: PO Box 2168 Albuquerque NM 87103-2168 also: Modrall Sperling Roehl Harris & Sisk 500 4th St NW Albuquerque NM 87102-5324

THOMPSON, SCOTT, Internet company executive; BS in Acctg. & Computer Sci., Stonehill Coll. With Coopers & Lybrand; chief info. officer Barclays Gobal Investors; chief info. officer, exec. v.p. tech. & support systems VISA USA, 1997—2000; exec. v.p. tech. solutions, global chief info. officer Inovant LLC, 2001—05; sr. v.p., chief tech. officer PayPal, Inc., 2005—08, pres., 2008—. Bd. dirs. F5 Networks, Inc., 2008—. Office: PayPal Inc 2211 N First St San Jose CA

THOMPSON, TERENCE WILLIAM, lawyer; b. Moberly, Mo., July 3, 1952; s. Donald Gene and Carolyn (Stringer) T.; m. Caryn Elizabeth Hildebrand, Aug. 30, 1975; children: Cory Elizabeth, Christopher William, Tyler Madison. BA in Govt. with honors and high distinction, U. Ariz., 1974; JD, Harvard U., 1977. Bar: Ariz. 1977, U.S. Dist. Ct. Ariz. 1977, U.S. Tax Ct. 1979. Assoc. Brown & Bain P.A., Phoenix, 1977-83, ptnr., 1983-92, Gallagher and Kennedy, P.A., Phoenix, 1992—. Legis. aide Rep. Richard Burgess, Ariz. Ho. of Reps., 1974; mem. bus. adv. bd. Citibank Ariz. (formerly Great Western Bank & Trust, Phoenix), 1985-86. Mem. staff Harvard Law Record, 1974-75; rsch. editor Harvard Internat. Law Jour.,1976; lead author, editor-in-chief: Arizona Corporate Practice, 1996—; contbr. articles to profl. jours. Mem. Phoenix Mayor's Youth Adv. Bd. 1968-70, Phoenix Internat.; active 20-30 Club, 1978-81, sec. 1978-80, Valley Leadership, Phoenix, 1983-84, citizens task force future financing needs City of Phoenix, 1985-86; exec. coun. Boys and Girls Clubs of Met. Phoenix, 1990-2000, sr. coun. 2000—; bd. dirs. Phoenix Bach Choir, 1992-94; deacon Shepherd of Hills Congl. Ch., Phoenix, 1984-85; pres. Maricopa County Young Dems., 1982-83, Ariz. Young Dems., 1983-84, sec. 1981-82, v.p. 1982-83; exec. dir. Young Dems. Am., 1985, exec. com. 1983-85; others. Recipient Best of Ariz. State Bar, Ariz. Bus. Jour., 2004. Fellow Ariz. Bar Found.; mem. State Bar Ariz. (vice chmn. internt. law sect. 1978, sec. securities law sect. 1990-91, vice chmn. sect. 1991-92, chmn.-elect 1992-93, chmn. 1993-94, exec. coun. 1988-96, sec. bus. law sect. 1992-93, vice chmn. 1993-94, chmn. 1994-95, exec. coun. 1996-98, 07-), Nat. Assn. Bond Lawyers, Nat. Health Lawyers, Selden Soc., Greater Phoenix Black C. of C. (bd. dirs. 1999-2001), Blue Key, Phi Beta Kappa, Phi Kappa Phi, Phi Eta Sigma. Home: 202 W Lawrence Rd Phoenix AZ 85013-1226 Office: Gallagher & Kennedy PA 2575 E Camelback Rd Phoenix AZ 85016-9225 Home Phone: 602-248-8237; Office Phone: 602-530-8515. Business E-Mail: twt@gknet.com.

THOMSEN, CARL, electronics company executive; b. 1945; BSBA, Valparaiso U.; MBA, U. Mich. CPA. Former controller Audio-Video Systems Divsn. Ampex; former sr. v.p., chief fin. officer Measurex Corp.; chief fin. officer, sr. v.p., sec. DMC Stratex Networks, Inc., San Jose, Calif., 1995—. Mem. Fin. Exec. Inst., Calif. Soc. CPAs. E-mail: www.dmcwave.com.

THOMSON, JAMES ALAN, think-tank executive; b. Boston, Jan. 21, 1945; s. James Alan and Mary Elizabeth (Pluff) T.; m. Darlene Thomson; children: Kristen Ann, David Alan. BS, U. NH, 1967, DSC (hon.), 2007; MS, Purdue U., 1970, PhD, 1972, DSc (hon.), 1992; LLD (hon.), Pepperdine U., 1996. Research fellow U. Wis., Madison, 1972-74; systems analyst Office Sec. Def. US Dept. Def., Washington, 1974-77; staff mem. Nat. Security Council, The White House, Washington, 1977-81; v.p. The RAND Corp., Santa Monica, Calif., 1981-89, pres., CEO, 1989—. Bd. dirs. L.A. World Affairs Coun., AK Steel Holding Corp., Encysive Pharms., Object Reservoir. Contbr. articles to profl. jours. and chpts. to books. Mem. Internat. Inst. for Strategic Studies (coun. 1985-99), Coun. Fgn. Rels. Office: The RAND Corp 1776 Main St Santa Monica CA 90401-3297 Office Phone: 310-451-6936. Business E-Mail: thomson@rand.org.*

THOR, LINDA M., college president; BA, Pepperdine U., 1971, EdD, 1986; MPA, Calif. State U., LA, 1980. Dir. pub. info. Pepperdine U., Los Angeles, 1971-73; pub. info. officer L.A. C.C. Dist., 1974-75, dir. comm., 1975-81, dir. edn. svcs., 1981-82, dir. high tech., 1982-83, sr. dir. occupl. and tech. edn., 1983-86; pres. West Los Angeles Coll., Culver City, Calif., 1986-90, Rio Salado Coll., Phoenix, 1990—. Contbr. articles to profl. jours. Active Continuous Quality Improvement Network for Cmty. Colls., 1991—; mem. Ariz. Gov.'s Adv. Coun. on Quality, 1992—97; pres. Ariz. Cmty. Coll. Pres.'s Coun., 1995—96; bd. dirs. Coun. for Adult and Experiential Learning, 1990—2005, C.C. Baccalaureate Assn., 2000—, Ariz. Town Hall, 2005—, Nana's Children Mental Health Found., 2003—, Friends of Pub. Radio Ariz., Ariz. Quality Alliance, 2008—. Recipient Delores award, Pepperdine U., 1986, Alumni Medal of Honor, 1987, Outstanding Achievement award Women's Bus. Network, 1989, Shirley B. Gordon award of distinction, Phi Theta Kappa Internat. Honor Soc., 2000, Paul A. Elsner Excellence in Leadership award, Chair Acad., 2003, Pioneer award, CC Baccalaureate Assn., 2007, Disting. Alumni award, Calif. State U., LA Coll. Natural Soc. Scis., 2007; named Woman of the Yr., Culver City Bus. and Profl. Women, 1988, Pacesetter of Yr., Nat. Coun. Mktg. and Pub. Rels., 1998. Office: 2323 W 14th St Tempe AZ 85281-6950 Business E-Mail: linda.thor@riomail.maricopa.edu.

THOREN-PEDEN, DEBORAH SUZANNE, lawyer; d. Robert Roy and Marguerite Natalie (Geoghegan) Thoren; m. Steven E. Peden, Aug. 10, 1985. BA in Philosophy, Polit. Sci./Psychology, U. Mich., 1978; JD, U. So. Calif., 1982. Bar: Calif. 1982. Assoc. Bushkin, Gaines & Gaims, LA, 1982-84, Rutan & Tucker, Costa Mesa, Calif., 1984-86; sr. counsel First Interstate Bancorp, LA, 1986-96; ptnr. Pillsbury Winthrop LLP, LA, 1996—; asst. gen. counsel CarsDirect-.com; gen. counsel CD1 Financial.com; gen. counsel, sr. v.p., chief privacy officer PayMyBills.Com, 2000; ptnr. Pillsbury Winthrop LLP, 2000—; (Pillsbury Winthrop LLP merged with Shaw Pittman LLP, 2005); ptnr., corp. & securities dept., co-chair, consumer and retail industry team Pillsbury Winthrop Shaw Pittman LLP, Los Angeles, 2005—. Lectr. on e-commerce, privacy Bank Secrecy Act and Ethics, Office of Fgn. Assets Control. Supervising editor U. So. Calif. Entertainment Law Jour., 1982-83, Entertainment Publishing and the Arts Handbook, 1983-84; contbr. articles to profl. jours. Mem. ABA (past vice-chmn. compliance exec. com., money laundering task force, privacy task force, co chmn. BSA staff commentary com.), Calif. Bankers Assn. (regulatory compliance com., co-chmn. regulatory compliance conf., past ex-officio mem. state govt. rels. com., co-vice chmn., vice-chmn., Regulatory Compliance Profl. award 1997, Frandzel award for outside counsel 2001, award 2001), Calif. State Bar Assn. (chmn., consumer fin. com.). Avocations: horseback riding, travel, reading, skiing. Office: Pillsbury Winthrop Shaw Pittman LLP Ste 2800 725 S Figueroa St Los Angeles CA 90017-5443 Office Phone: 213-488-7320. Office Fax: 213-629-1033. Business E-Mail: deborah.thoren-peden@pillsburylaw.com.

THORNBURG, GARRETT, JR., finance company executive; BA, Williams Coll.; MBA, Harvard Univ. CFO NY State Urban Develop. Corp.; limited ptnr., founding mem. pub. fin. dept. Bear Stearns & Co., NYC; sole dir. Thornburg Investment Mgmt. Inc., 1982—, Thornburg Securities Corp.; founder, chmn., CEO Thornburg Mortgage Inc., Santa Fe, 1993—2007, founder, chmn., 2007—. Bd. gov. Investment Co. Inst., Nat. Assn. REIT Inc. Bd. mem. Nat. Dance Inst. N. Mex.; trustee Coll. Santa Fe. Office: Thornburg Mortgage Inc Ste 302 150 Washington Ave Santa Fe NM 87501

THORNE, DAVID W., lawyer; b. Walla Walla, Wash., Aug. 9, 1945; BA, Wash. State U., 1967; MBA, U. Wash., 1969, JD, 1974. Bar: Wash. 1974. Mem. Davis Wright Tremaine LLP, Seattle. Mem. ABA, Am. Coll. Real Estate Lawyers, Am. Coll. Mortgage Attys., Am. Land Title Assn. Lender Counsel Group, Wash. State Bar Assn. (past mem. exec. com. real property, probate and trust sect., past chmn. 1991-92), Pacific Real Estate Inst. (past pres. 1994, founding trustee 1989-96), Phi Delta Phi. Office: Davis Wright Tremaine 1201 3rd Ave Ste 2200 Seattle WA 98101-3047

THORNE, KIP STEPHEN, physicist, researcher; b. Logan, Utah, June 1, 1940; s. David Wynne and Alison (Comish) T.; m. Linda Jeanne Peterson, Sept. 12, 1960 (div. 1977); children: Kares Anne, Bret Carter; m. Carolee Joyce Winstein, July 7, 1984. BS in Physics, Calif. Inst. Tech., 1962; A.M. in Physics (Woodrow Wilson fellow, Danforth Found. fellow), Princeton U., 1963, PhD in Physics (Danforth Found. fellow, NSF fellow), 1965, postgrad. (NSF postdoctoral fellow), 1965-66; D.Sc. (hon.), Ill. Coll., 1979; Dr.h.c., Moscow U., 1981; D.Sc. (hon.), Utah State U., 2000, U. Glasgow, 2001; D.H.L. (hon.), Claremont Grad. U., 2002. Research fellow Calif. Inst. Tech., 1966-67, assoc. prof. theoretical physics, 1967-70, prof., 1970—, William R. Kenan, Jr. prof., 1981-91, Feynman prof. theoretical physics, 1991—. Fulbright lectr., France, 1966; vis. assoc. prof. U. Chgo., 1968; vis. prof. Moscow U., 1969, 75, 78, 82, 83, 86, 88, 90, 98; vis. sr. rsch. assoc. Cornell U., 1977, A.D. White prof.-at-large, 1988-92; adj. prof. U. Utah, 1971-98; mem. Internat. Com. on Gen. Relativity and Gravitation, 1971-80, 92-01, Com. on U.S.-USSR Coop. in Physics, 1978-79, Space Sci. Bd., NASA, 1980-83; co-founder, chair steering com. LIGO, 1984-87. Co-author: Gravitation Theory and Gravitational Collapse, 1965, Gravitation, 1973, Black Holes: The Membrane Paradigm, 1986, Black Holes and Time Warps: Einstein's Outrageous Legacy, 1994. Alfred P. Sloan Found. Rsch. fellow, 1966-68; John Simon Guggenheim fellow, 1967; recipient Sci. Writing award in physics and astronomy Am. Inst. Physics, 1969, 94, P.A.M. Dirac Meml. lectureship Cambridge U., 1995, Karl Schwarzschild medal Astron. Soc. Germany, 1996, J. Robert Oppenheimer Meml. lectureship U. Calif., 1999, Charles Darwin Meml. Lectureship Royal Astron. Soc., 2000, Arthur Holly Compton Meml. lectureship Washington U., 2001, Herzberg Meml. Lectureship Can. Assn. Physicists, 2001; recipient Common Wealth award, Sci. Invention, 2005; Robinson Prize in Cosmology, U. Newcastle, 2002; named Calif. Scientist of Yr., 2004. Fellow Am. Phys. Soc. (Julius Edgar Lilienfeld prize 1996, chair topical group in gravity 1997-98); mem. Am. Philosophical Soc., Nat. Acad. Scis., Am. Acad. Arts and Scis., Am. Astron. Soc., Internat. Astron. Union, AAAS, Russian Acad. Scis., Ligo Sci. Collaboration, Lisa Internat. Sci. Team, Sigma Xi, Tau Beta Pi. Office: California Inst Tech 130-33 Theoretical Astrophysics 1200 E California Blvd Pasadena CA 91125

THORNE, RICHARD MANSERGH, physicist; b. Birmingham, Eng., July 25, 1942; s. Robert George and Dorothy Lena (Goodchild) T.; children: Peter Baring, Michael Thomas, Thomas Mansergh. BSc, Birmingham U., 1963; PhD, MIT, 1968. Grad. asst. M.I.T., 1963-68; asst. prof. dept. atmospheric scis. UCLA, 1968-71, asso. prof., 1971-75, prof., 1975—, chmn. dept., 1976-79. Vis. fellow St. Edmund's Coll., Cambridge (Eng.) U., 1986-87, 92; cons. NATO Adv. Group for Aerospace R&D, 1973, Jet Propulsion Lab., Aerospace Corp. Contbr. articles to profl. jours. Recipient numerous grants NSF, NASA, NATO, Jet Propulsion Lab.; Fulbright scholar, 1963-70; fellow Royal Norwegian Coun. for Sci. and Indsl. Rsch., 1973, sr. vis. fellow U. Sussex, 1979-80, rsch. fellow Royal Soc. London, 1986-87.

Fellow Am. Geophys. Union; mem. Internat. Union Radio Scis. Home: 10390 Caribou Ln Los Angeles CA 90077 Office: UCLA Dept Atmospheric and Oceanic Scis Los Angeles CA 90095-1565 Business E-Mail: rmt@atmos.ucla.edu.

THORNLEY, ANTHONY S., telecommunications company executive; BS in Chemistry, U. Manchester, Eng. With Coopers and Lybrand; corp. contr. Nortel Ltd., various mgmt. positions; v.p. fin., CFO Qualcomm Inc., San Diego, Calif., 1994-96, sr. v.p., 1996-97, exec. v.p., CFO, 1997—. Fellow Inst. of Chartered Accts. in Eng. and Wales. Office: Qual Comm Inc 5775 Morehouse Dr San Diego CA 92121

THORNTON, CHARLES VICTOR, lawyer; b. Takoma Park, Md., July 18, 1942; s. Charles Victor and Margaret Louise (Wiggins) T.; m. Suzanne Thorne, May 16, 1970; children: Christopher, Matthew, Joshua, Jeremy. AB, Cornell U., 1964; JD, U. Mich., 1967. Bar: Calif. 1969, US Dist. Ct. (ctrl. dist.) Calif. 1969. Instr. U. Pa. Law Sch., Phila., 1967-68; assoc. Paul, Hastings, Janofsky & Walker, LA, 1968-74, ptnr., 1975—, mng. ptnr. L.A. office, 1992-96, mng. ptnr. San Francisco office, 1997-2000. Contbr. articles to publs. Pres. Info. and Referral Fedn. LA County, 1988-95; mem. exec. com. LA County United Way, 1988-92; chmn. bd. dir. San Francisco YMCA, 2006-. Named Bd. Vol. of Yr. United Way, 1986, Bd. Vol. of Yr. YMCA, 2004. Mem. Calif. Club, LA Country Club, San Francisco YMCA (bd. dirs., 1998—, chmn. bd., 2006-). Avocations: running, golf. Office: Paul Hastings Janofsky & Walker 24th Flr 55 Second San Francisco CA 94105 Office Phone: 415-856-7001. Business E-Mail: charlesthornton@paulhastings.com.

THORNTON, FELICIA D., food service company executive; BSc Econs., Santa Clara U.; MBA Corp. Fin., Mktg., U. So. Calif. V.p., corp. planning and acctg. Ralphs Grocery Co., v.p., admin., 1998, group v.p., fin. and adminstrn., 1999—2001; group v.p. retail ops. Kroger Co., 2000—01; exec. v.p., CFO Albertson's, Inc., 2001—.

THORNTON, J. DUKE, lawyer; b. Murray, Ky., July 11, 1944; s. Arthur Lee and Ruth Maxine (Billings) T.; m. Carol Caceres, Dec. 26, 1966 (dec.); children: Jennifer, Carey. BBA, U. N.Mex., Albuquerque, 1966, JD, 1969. Bar: N.Mex. 1969, U.S. Ct. Appeals (10th cir.) 1969, N.Y. 1985, U.S. Supreme Ct. 1992. With Butt, Thornton & Baehr, P.C., Albuquerque, 1971—, now chmn. bd. Legal counsel N.Mex. Jaycees, 1972; clk. N.Mex. Supreme Ct., Santa Fe, 1969; mem. com. N.Mex. Uniform Jury Instructions, 1987-88. Author: Trial Handbook for New Mexico Lawyers, 1992. Bd. dirs. N.Mex. Bd. of Dentistry, Santa Fe, 1987-88; commr. N.Mex. Racing Commn., Albuquerque, 1988-95. Mem. ABA, Am. Bd. Trial Advs., Albuquerque Bar Assn. (bd. dirs. 1978-79), Nat. Collegiate Athletic Assn. (agt.). Avocation: pilot. Office: Butt Thornton & Baehr PC PO Box 3170 Albuquerque NM 87190-3170

THORNTON, JOE, professional hockey player; b. London, Ont., Can., July 2, 1979; Center Boston Bruins, 1997—2005, HC Davos, Switzerland, 2004—05, San Jose Sharks, 2005—. Mem. Team Can., World Championships, 2001, 05, Team Can., World Cup of Hockey, 2004, Team Can. Olympic Games, Torino, Italy, 2006. Recipient Art Ross Trophy, 2006, Hart Meml. Trophy, 2006; named to Second All-Star Team, NHL, 2003, 2008, First All-Start Team, 2006, NHL All-Star Game, 2002—04, 2007, 2008, 2009. Achievements include being a member of World Cup Champion Team Canada, 2004. Office: c/o San Jose Sharks 525 W Santa Clara St San Jose CA 95113*

THORNTON, JOHN S., IV, retired bishop; Bishop Diocese of Idaho, Boise, 1990-98; ret. Address: 6715 N Mockingbird Ln Scottsdale AZ 85253-4344

THORNTON, ROLAND, telecommunications industry executive; married; 3 children. BSBA, Ind. U.; grad. student in Info. Systems, U. Ill. Co-founder Acquired Knowledge, Ltd.; v.p. customer ops. Ameritech; v.p. interconnection svcs. SBC; sr. v.p. customer svc. ops. Wholesale Markets Qwest Comm. Internat., Inc., exec. v.p. wholesale markets, 2004—. Bd. dirs. Rotary Internat., 2007—, Food Bank of the Rockies, Colo. Black C. of C., chmn. Mem.: Rotary Club Denver (mem. world coun. com.). Office: Qwest Comm Internat Inc 1801 California St Denver CO 80202 Office Phone: 303-992-1400. Office Fax: 303-896-8515.

THORPE, GEOGORY B., lawyer; b. LA, 1953; BA cum laude, U. Calif., Santa Barbara, 1977; JD cum laude, Loyola Marymount U., 1982. Bar: Calif. 1982. Ptnr., real estate and natural resources practice O'Melveny & Myers LLP, Santa Barbara, Calif., 1982—, chair, project development and fin. practice group. Staff mem. and chief article editor Loyola LA Law Review, 1980—82. Mem.: LA County Bar Assn. (mem. general real property subsection), ABA (mem. real property sect.), St. Thomas More Law Soc. Office: O'Melveny & Myers LLP 400 S Hope St Los Angeles CA 90071-2899 Office Phone: 213-430-6593. Office Fax: 213-430-6407. Business E-Mail: gthorpe@omm.com.

THORPE, JASON M., non-profit organization director; b. 1982; Dir., cmty. edn. and outreach Open-Inn Inc. Bd. co-chair Western States Youth Services Network; mem. Ariz. Statewide Devel. Taskforce, Wingspan award com.; co-chair, bd. of incorporators Porch Light Found. Nat. Safe Place adv. bd. mem. YMCA; official organizer Tucson V-Day. Named one of 40 Under 40, Tucson Bus. Edge, 2006. Office: Open Inn Inc PO Box 5766 Tucson AZ 85703-0766 Office Phone: 520-670-9040.

THORSEN, NANCY DAIN, retired real estate broker; b. Edwardsville, Ill., 1944; d. Clifford Earl and Suzanne Eleanor (Kribs) Dain; m. David Massie, 1968 (div. 1975); 1 child, Suzanne Dain Massie; m. James Hugh Thorsen, May 30, 1980. BSc in Mktg., So. Ill. U., 1968, MSc in Bus. Edn., 1975; grad., Realtor Inst., Idaho, 1983. Cert. residential and investment specialist, fin. instr., luxury home mktg. specialist, 2004; designated real estate instr. State of Idaho; accredited buyer rep. Personnel officer J.H. Little & Co. Ltd., London, 1969-72; instr. in bus. edn. Spl. Sch. Dist. St. Louis, 1974-77; mgr. mktg./ops. Isis Foods, Inc., St. Louis, 1978-80; asst. mgr. store Stix, Baer & Fuller, St. Louis, 1980; assoc. broker Century 21 Sayer Realty, Inc., Idaho Falls, Idaho, 1981-88, RE/MAX Homestead Realty, 1989—2009. Spkr. in field; real estate fin. instr. State of Idaho Real Estate Commn., 1994; founder Nancy Thorsen Seminars, 1995; pres. S.E. Idaho Women's Coun. of Realtors, 2006 Bd. dirs. Idaho Vol., Boise, 1981-84, Idaho Falls Symphony, 1982; pres. Friends of Idaho Falls Libr., 1981-83; chmn. Idaho Falls Mayor's Com. for Vol. Coordination, 1981-84; power leader Power Program, 1995; mem. Mtn. River Valley Red Cross, chair capital campaign, cmty. gifts chair ARC. Recipient Idaho Gov.'s award, 1982, cert. appreciation City of Idaho Falls/Mayor Campbell, 1982, 87, Bus. Women of the Yr. award C. of C., 1998, Gifar Anne Alexander award Greater Idaho Falls Assoc. of Realtors, 2007; named to Two Million Dollar Club, 1987, 88, Four Million Dollar Club, 1989, 90, Top Investment Sales Person for Eastern Idaho, 1985, Realtor of Yr. Idaho Falls Bd. Realtors, 1990, Outstanding Realtors Active in Politics, Women of Yr. Am. Biog. Inst., 1991, Profiles of Top Prodrs. award Real Estate Edn. Assn., Above the Crowd award 1997; named Western Region Power Leader, Darryl Davis Seminars, Lifetime Achievement award Idaho Falls Assn. Relators, 2008 Mem. Nat. Spkrs. Assn., Idaho Falls Bd. Realtors (chmn. Orientation 1982-83, chmn. edn. 1983, chmn. legis. com. 1989, 95—, chmn. program com. 1990, 91), Idaho Assn. Realtors (pres. Million Dollar Club 1988-2001, edn. com. 1990-93, Mem. of Yr. 1991), Idaho Women's Coun. Realtors (Mem. of Yr. 2006, 2007), Am. Bus. Women's Assn., So. Ill. U. Alumni Assn., Idaho Falls C. of C. (Bus. Woman of the Yr.-Professions, 1997), newcomers Club, Civitan (pres. Idaho Falls chpt. 1988-89, Civitan of Yr. 1986, 97, Outstanding Pres. award 1990, Hall of Fame 1998), Real Estate Educators Assn. Office: RE/MAX Homestead Inc 1301 E 17th St Ste 1 Idaho Falls ID 83404-6273 E-mail: thorsen@srv.net.

THORSON, LEE A., lawyer; b. Seattle, Nov. 10, 1949; s. Theodore Arthur and Irene Mary (Dakers) T.; m. Elizabeth Clayton Hay, June 7, 1975; children: Kirk Hunter, Alex Peter. BA, U. Wash., 1971; JD, U. Pacific, Sacramento, 1975; LLM Taxation, Boston U., 1976. Atty. Dahlgren & Dauenhauer P.S., Seattle, 1976-79, Lane Powell Spears Lubersky, Seattle, 1980-93; shareholder Birmingham Thorson & Barnett, P.C., 1993—; affiliate prof. U. Wash. Grad. Program in Taxation, 1995—. Mem. ABA (health law forum), Employee Benefits and Health Law coms., Wash. State Bar Assn. Avocations: bicycling, skiing. Office: Birmingham Thorson Barnett 601 Union St Ste 3315 Seattle WA 98101-4018 E-mail: lthorson@btbpc.com.

THOULESS, DAVID JAMES, retired physicist, educator; b. Bearsden, Scotland, Sept. 21, 1934; arrived in U.S., 1979, naturalized, 1994; s. Robert Henry and Priscilla (Gorton) T.; m. Margaret Elizabeth Scrase, July 26, 1958; children: Michael, Christopher, Helen. BA, U. Cambridge, Eng., 1955, ScD, 1986; PhD, Cornell U., 1958. Physicist Lawrence Berkeley Lab., Calif., 1958-59; rsch. fellow U. Birmingham, England, 1959—61, prof. math. physics, 1965—78; lectr., fellow Churchill Coll. U. Cambridge, England, 1961—65; prof. physics Queen's U., Kingston, Ont., Canada, 1978; prof. applied sci. Yale U., New Haven, 1979-80; prof. physics U. Wash., Seattle, 1980—2003; ret. Author: Quantum Mechanics of Many Body Systems, 2d edit., 1972, Topological Quantum Numbers in Nonrelativistic Physics, 1998. Recipient Maxwell medal Inst. Physics, 1973, Holweck prize Soc. Francaise de Physique-Inst. Physics, 1980, Fritz London award for Low temperature physics, Fritz London Meml. Fund, 1984, Wolf prize in physics, Wolf Found., Israel, 1990, Paul Dirac medal Inst. Physics, 1993, Lars Onsager prize Am. Phys. Soc., 2000; Edwin Uehling disting. scholar U. Wash., 1988-98. Fellow: Royal Soc.; mem.: NAS. Office: U Wash PO Box 351560 Seattle WA 98195-1560 Business E-Mail: Thouless@u.washington.edu.

THRASHER, JACK DWAYNE, toxicologist, researcher, consultant; b. Nashville, Kans., Aug. 13, 1936; s. Harold A. and Margaret E. (Bolin) T.; m. Diane L. Walton, June 29, 1963; children: Traci L., Kristen I. BS, Long Beach State U., 1959; PhD, UCLA, 1964. Asst. prof. U. Colo. Sch. Medicine, Denver, 1964-66, UCLA Sch. of Medicine, 1966-72; application specialist Millipore Corp., Bedford, Mass., 1973-75; cons. Thrasher and Assocs., LA, 1975-92, Alto, N.Mex., 1992-96; mem. faculty E. N. Mex. U., Ruidoso, 1992-97; mentor Columbia Pacific U., San Rafael, Calif., 1992-96. Bd. dirs., chmn. Internat. Inst. Rsch. for Chem. Hypersensitivity, Alto, N. Mex., 1991-94; advisor Chem. Impact Project Mill Valley, Calif., 1993—. Author: (books) Cellular and Molecular Renewal in the Mammalian Body, 1971, The Poisoning of our Homes and Work Places, 1990; editor-in-chief Informed Consent, 1993-94. Grantee: USPHS, NIH, 1966-69. Avocations: golf, fishing, wood working.

THRASHER, JOHN, music educator; b. McAlester, Okla., Aug. 2, 1942; m. Jackie Thrasher; children: Jason, Jessica. BA, No. Ariz. U., 1965, MA in Music Edn., 1970. Band dir. Prescott HS, Ariz., 1965—67, Cortez HS, Phoenix, 1967—70, Maricopa Coll., Glendale Coll., 1970—99, Deer Valley Union Sch. Dist., 1999—2008. Mem.: Deer Valley Edn. Assn., Ariz. Music Educators Assn., Coll. Band Dir.'s Nat. Assn. (Western divsn.). Democrat. Lutheran. Office: 16845 N 29th Ave, Ste 1-301 Phoenix AZ 85053 Office Phone: 602-978-6767.

THREEDY, DEBORA LYNN, law educator; b. Chgo., June 10, 1951; d. Edward Clarence and Irene Frances (Palenik) T. BA, Beloit Coll., 1973; JD, Loyola U., 1980. Bar: Ill. Law clk. to Hon. Getzendanner U.S. Dist. Ct. (no. dist.) Ill., Chgo., 1980-82; assoc. Mayer Brown & Platt, Chgo., 1982-86; assoc. prof. law U. Utah, Salt Lake City, 1986—, prof. law, assoc. dean academic affairs, acting dean, 2004—. Contbr. articles to profl. jours. Bd. dirs. ACLU, Salt Lake City, 1990; trustee Theater Works West, Salt Lake City, 1990. McCormick Scholar Loyola U., 1980, Owens Scholar, 1980. Mem. Phi Beta Kappa. Office: U Utah Coll Law 332 South 1400 East Salt Lake City UT 84112-1107

THROCKMORTON, REX DENTON, lawyer; b. Lima, Ohio, June 4, 1941; s. Francis and Jane (Corwin) T.; m. Barbara Catherine Poore, July 21, 1962; children: Scott, John. BS, Denison U., 1963; JD, Ohio State U., 1965. Bar: Ohio 1966, N. Mex. 1971, U.S. Dist. Ct. N. Mex. 1971, U.S. Ct. Appeals (10th cir.) 1973. Assoc. Squire, Sanders & Dempsey, Cleve., 1965-66; shareholder, bd. dirs. Rodey, Dickason, Sloan, Akin & Robb, P.A., Albuquerque, 1971—, ptnr., pres., mng. dir., 1999—2004. Editor Ohio State Law Jour., 1965. Pres. Albuquerque Civic Light Opera Assn., 1985; sec. Accion, N.Mex. Capt. JAGC, USAF, 1966-71. Named one of best lawyers in Am., 2003—04. Mem. ABA, N.Mex. Bar Assn. (bd. of bar commrs. 1990-98, sec.-treas. 1994, v.p. 1995, pres.-elect 1996, pres. 1997), Albuquerque Bar Assn. (pres. 1982). Republican. Avocations: golf, running. Office: Rodey Dickason Sloan Akin & Robb PO Box 1888 Albuquerque NM 87103-1888 Office Phone: 505-765-5900. Office Fax: 505-768-7395. Business E-Mail: rthrockmorton@rodey.com.

THRONER, GUY CHARLES, JR., aerospace engineering executive, scientist, inventor, consultant; b. Mpls., Sept. 14, 1919; s. Guy Charles and Marie (Zechar) T.; m. Jean Holt, Dec. 5, 1943; children—Richard, Carol Anne, Steven. BA, Oberlin Coll., 1943; postgrad., UCLA, 1960-61. Registered profl. engr., Calif. Br. head Naval Weapon Ctr., China Lake, Calif., 1946-53; mgr. ordnance div., mgr. weapon systems div. Aerojet Gen. Corp., Azusa, Calif., 1953-64; v.p., div. mgr. FMC Corp., San Jose, Calif., 1964-74; research dir. Vacu Blast Corp., Belmont, Calif., 1976-78; v.p., devel. mfg. Dahlman, Inc., Braham, Minn., 1978-79; mgr. ordnance systems & tech. Battelle Meml. Inst., Columbus, Ohio, 1979-85; pres. Guy C. Throner & Assocs., tech. and mgmt. cons., 1985—. Dir. Omron Corp. Am., Chgo., 1976-77 Inventor, patentee indls., med. and mil. systems design. Served as officer USNR, World War II Recipient Am. Order St. Barbara medal U.S. Army Arty, 1983, IR-100 award Indsl. Rsch. Mag., Chgo., 1971, Congl. Commendation, 1985, Commendation, State of Ohio Ho. of Reps., 1995, also various commendations. Mem. AIAA, Am. Def. Preparedness Assn. (Bronze medal 1974, Simon Silver medal 1985), Lake Wildwood Country Club, Sigma Xi. Republican. Avocations: astronomy, photography, golf. Home and Office: 3939 Walnut Ave #152 Carmichael CA 95608 Personal E-mail: jeannguy@comcast.net.

THRUN, SEBASTIAN BURKHARD, computer science educator, researcher; b. Solingen, Germany, May 14, 1967; s. Winfried and Kristin (Grüner) T.; m. Petra Dierkes, July 1, 1995. BSc in Computer Sci., Econs. and Medicine, U. Hildesheim, Germany, 1988; MSc in Computer Sci. and Stats., U. Bonn, Germany, 1993, PhD summa cum laude in Computer Sci. and Stats., 1995. Rsch. asst. German Nat. Rsch. Ctr. for Info. Tech., Sankt Augustin, Germany, 1989-91; project scientist Carnegie Mellon U., Pitts., 1991-92, rsch. computer scientist, 1995-98, asst. prof. computer sci., 1998-2001, assoc. prof., 2001—03; rsch. assoc. U. Bonn, 1993-95; assoc. prof. computer sci. Stanford U., Calif., 2003—, assoc. prof. elec. engring., 2006—; dir. Stanford Artificial Intelligence Lab., 2004—. Cons. Daimler Benz Rsch., Berlin, 1995, Real World Interface, Inc., Jaffrey, NH, 1996; v.p. devel. Neural Info. Processing Systems Found., 2003-. Author: Explanation-Based Neural Network Learning: A Lifelong Learning Approach, 1996; editor: Recent Advances in Robot Learning, 1996, Learning to Learn, 1997; co-author: Principles of Robotic Motion: Theory, Algorithms, and Implementation, 2004, Probabilistic Robotics, 2005; contbr. articles to profl. jours., chpts. to books. Recipient CAREER award, NSF, 1999—2003, Olympus award, German Soc. Pattern Recognition, 2001; named one of Brilliant 10, Popular Sci., 2005. Fellow: European Coordinating Com. Artificial Intelligence, Am. Assn. Artificial Intelligence (2nd place in autonomous mobile robot competition 1994, 1st place in autonomous mobile robot competition 1996), World Tech. Network (World Tech. award-IT Software 2006); mem.: NAE. Achievements include leading the development of the robotic vehicle Stanley, which won the Def. Advanced Rsch. Projects Agy. Grand Challenge in 2005. Avocations: singing, connoisseur. Office: Stanford Artificial Intelligence Lab Gates Bldg 154 353 Serra Mall Stanford CA 94305-9010 Office Phone: 650-723-2797. Office Fax: 650-725-1449. E-mail: thrun@stanford.edu.

THUESON, DAVID OREL, pharmaceutical executive, researcher, writer, educator; b. Twin Falls, Idaho, May 9, 1947; s. Orel Grover and Shirley Jean (Archer) T.; m. Sherrie Linn Lowe, June 14, 1969; children: Sean, Kirsten, Eric, Ryan, Todd. BS, Brigham Young U., 1971; PhD, U. Utah, 1976. Postdoctoral fellow U. Tex. Med. Br., Galveston, 1976-77, asst. prof., 1977-82; sr. rsch. assoc. Parke-Davis Pharms., Ann Arbor, Mich., 1982-88; dir. pharmacology Immunetech Pharms., San Diego, 1988-90; dir. immunopharmacology Tanabe Rsch. Labs., San Diego, 1990-92; v.p. discovery Cosmederm Techs., San Diego, 1992-97. Contbr. articles to profl. jours.; patentee in field. Scout leader Boy Scouts Am., Mich., Tex. and Calif., 1979—. NIH grantee, 1978-81. Mem. Am. Acad. Allergy and Clin. Immunology, Am. Assn. Immunologists, Am. Thoracic Soc. Republican. Mem. Lds Ch. Avocations: water-skiing, tennis, scuba diving. Home: 1356 Winchester Ave Mckinleyville CA 95519-8801 Office: 2330 Central Ave Ste 3 Mckinleyville CA 95519-3696 Home Phone: 707-839-4935; Office Phone: 707-840-0623. Business E-Mail: thueson@reninet.com.

THURAI, MERHALA, research scientist; b. Jaffna, Sri Lanka, Jan. 6, 1960; d. Jeevaratnam Victor and Sornagandhimalar Thurai-Rajasingam. BSc (hon.), Imperial Coll., U. London, Eng., 1980; PhD, King's Coll., U. London, 1985. Cert. Chartered Engr., Inst. Elec. Engring., 1997. Sr. rsch. fellow Nat. Inst. Info. and Comm. Tech., Tokyo; sr. sci. officer Rutherford Appleton Lab., Chilton, Didcot, Oxon, England, 1986—2001; sr. rschr. Colo. State U., Fort Collins, 2004—. Cons. Gematronik - Selex, Neuss, Germany, 2004—. Contbr. articles to profl. jours. Del. ITU-R propagation study group, 2004—08. Recipient Best Radiowave Propagation paper, 1997. Mem.: IEEE. Achievements include research in experimentally derived drop shapes in rain; the effect of rain microstructure on radiowave propagation; using rain microstructure information to improve rain estimations from weather radars. Avocation: travel. Office: Colorado State Univ Dept Elec Engring Fort Collins CO 80523 Personal E-mail: thurai@theiet.orgn. Business E-Mail: merhala@engr.colostate.edu.

THURSTON, MORRIS ASHCROFT, lawyer; b. Logan, Utah, May 25, 1943; s. Morris Alma and Barbara (Ashcroft) T.; m. Dawna Lyn Parrett, Sept. 10, 1966; children: Morris III, David, Ashley, Tyson. BA, Brigham Young U., 1967; JD, Harvard U., 1970. Bar: Calif. 1971, U.S. Dist. Ct. (cen. dist.) Calif. 1971, U.S. Supreme Ct. 1978. Assoc. Latham & Watkins, LA, 1970-77, ptnr. Costa Mesa, Calif., 1978—. Jud. arbitrator Orange County Superior Ct., Calif., 1980—. Mem. Calif. Bar Assn., Orange County Bar Assn., Assn. Bus. Trial Lawyers. Republican. Mem. Lds Ch. Avocations: genealogy, writing, basketball. Home: 9752 Crestview Cir Orange CA 92861-1313 Office: Latham & Watkins 650 Town Center Dr Ste 2000 Costa Mesa CA 92626-7135

THURSTON, WILLIAM RICHARDSON, oil and gas industry executive, geologist; b. New Haven, Sept. 20, 1920; s. Edward S. and Florence (Holbrooke) T.; m. Ruth A. Nelson, Apr. 30, 1944 (div. 1966); children: Karin R., Amy R., Ruth A.; m. Beatrice Furnas, Sept. 11, 1971; children: Mark P., Stephen P., Douglas P., Jennifer P. AB in Geol. Sci. with honors, Harvard U., 1942. Field geologist Sun Oil Co., Corpus Christi, Tex., 1946-47, asst. to div. geologist Dallas, 1947-50; chief geologist The Kimbark Co., Denver, 1952-59; head exploration dept. Kimbark Exploration Co., Denver, 1959-66; co-owner Kimbark Exploration Ltd., Denver, 1966-67, Kimbark Assocs., Denver, 1967-76, Hardscrabble Assocs., Denver, 1976-80; pres. Weaselskin Corp., Durango, Colo., 1980—. Bd. dirs. Denver Bot. Gardens, 1972-99, Crow Canyon Ctr. for Archaeology, Cortez, Colo., 1980-92. Comdr. USNR, World War II, Korea. Decorated D.F.C. with 2 gold stars, air medal with 10 gold stars. Mem. Am. Assn. Petroleum Geologists, Rocky Mountain Assn. Petroleum Geologists, Four Corners Geol. Soc. Republican. Avocations: photography, gardening, reading. Office: Weaselskin Corp 12995 US Hwy 550 Durango CO 81303-6674

TIANO, ANTHONY STEVEN, television producer, publishing executive; b. Santa Fe, Mar. 27, 1941; s. Joseph A. and Marian (Adlesperger) T.; m. Kathleen O'Brien, Dec. 29, 1972; children: Mark A., A. Steven. BA, U. N.Mex., 1969, MA, 1971; LittD (hon.), Calif. Sch. Profl. Psychology, 1985. Dir. programming Sta. KNME-TV U. N.Mex., Albuquerque, 1968-72; sta. mgr. Sta. WHA-TV U. Wis., Madison, 1972-76; exec. dir. Sta. KETC-TV, St. Louis, 1976-78; pres., CEO KQED, Inc., San Francisco, 1978-93; chmn., CEO Santa Fe Ventures, Inc., San Francisco, 1993—2003; CEO Santa Fe Prodns., Inc., Albuquerque, 2003—. Vice-chair bd. dirs. Calif. Sch. Profl. Psychology, San Francisco, 1985-90. Mem. Nat. Assn. Pub. TV Stas. (vice chair bd. dirs. 1986).

TIANO, LINDA V., lawyer, insurance company executive; b. 1957; BA summa cum laude, U. Cin.; JD cum laude, Boston U. Assoc. Epstein Becker and Green, P.C., 1981—90, ptnr., stockholder, 1990—92; v.p. for legal and govt. affairs, gen counsel MVP Health Plan, 1992—95; sr. v.p., gen. counsel Empire BlueCross BlueShield, 1995—2002, WellChoice, Inc., NYC, 2002—05; v.p., dep. gen. counsel for Ea. region & nat. accounts WellPoint, Inc., Indpls., 2005—07; sr. v.p., gen. counsel, sec. Health Net, Inc., Woodland Hills, Calif., 2007—. Office: Health Net Inc 21650 Oxnard St Woodland Hills CA 91367

TIBSHRAENY, JAY, state legislator; b. Chandler, Ariz., 1955; m. Karen M. Tibshraeny; 1 child, Lauren Noel Rose. BS in Acctg., Ariz. State U. Planning/zoning commr. Chandler City Coun., 1980—86, mem., 1986—90, vice mayor, 1990—94, mayor, 1994—2002; mem. Dist. 21 Ariz. State Senate, 2003—, vice chair commerce & econ. devel. com., mem. pub. safety & human svcs. com. Chair Regional Pub. Transp. Authority, 1994—2002, Ariz. Municipal Water Users Assn., 1994—2002; mem. Williams Air Force Base Redevel. Partnership, 1994—2002; sec., treas. Maricopa Assn. Govt.'s, 1997—2002; mem. exec. com. Ariz. League Cities & Towns, 2000—02, Greater Phoenix Econ. Coun., 2002. Mem.: Chandler C. of C., Chandler Hist. Soc. Republican. Office: Ariz State Senate Capitol Complex 1700 W Washington Rm 306 Phoenix AZ 85007 Office Phone: 602-926-4481. Office Fax: 602-417-3252. Business E-Mail: jtibshraeny@azleg.gov.*

TICKNOR, CAROLYN M., computer company executive; BA in Psychology, U. Redlands, Calif.; MA in Indsl. Psychology, San Francisco State U.; MBA, Stanford U. From programming, ops. mgr. to pres., CEO Hewlett-Packard Co., Palo Alto, Calif., 1977-94, pres., CEO laser jet imaging sys., 1994—. Office: Hewlett Packard Co 300 Hanover St Palo Alto CA 94304

TIDWELL, JERRY, retail executive; With Pepsi Cola Co., 1974—98, Safeway, Inc., 1998—2000, dir. grocery bus. unit, 2000—01, v.p. milk and beverage mfg., 2001—03, sr. v.p. supply ops., 2003—. Office: Safeway Inc 5918 Stoneridge Mall Rd Pleasanton CA 94588 Office Phone: 925-467-3000. Office Fax: 925-467-3323.

TIEMESSEN, JOHN J., lawyer; b. Fairbanks, Alaska, Jan. 21, 1966; BS magna cum laude, Ariz. State U., 1987; JD, Willamette U., 1991. Bar: Alaska 1991. Ptnr. Clapp, Peterson, Van Flein, Tiemessen & Thorsness LLC, Fairbanks, Alaska. Mem. Def. Rsch. Inst. Mem.: ABA, Alaska Bar Assn. (pres. 2006—07), Tanana Valley Bar Assn., Order of Barristers. Office: Clapp Peterson Van Flein Tiemessen & Thorsness LLC Ste 300 411 4th Ave Fairbanks AK 99701 Office Phone: 907-479-7707. Office Fax: 907-479-7966. E-mail: jjt@cplawak.com.

TIERNAN, BOB (ROBERT TIERNAN), political organization administrator, former state legislator; m. Susan Tiernan; 3 children. BA, Oreg. State U., 1977; JD, Seattle U. Sch. Law, 1980; LLM, Georgetown U., 1983. Mem. Oreg. House of Reps. from 24th Dist., 1993—97, chair Gen. Govt. and Crime and Corrections Com., mem. Judiciary and Labor Com.; pres. Tiernan and Assocs.; chmn. Oreg. Republican Party, 2009—. Founder PayLess Drug. Comdr. USNR. Office: Oreg Rep Party PO Box 25406 Portland OR 97298-0406 Office Phone: 503-595-8881. Office Fax: 503-595-8882.*

TIERNEY, MAURA, actress; b. Boston, Feb. 3, 1965; m. Billy Morrissette, 1994. Student, NYU. Cir. in the Sq. Theatre Sch. Actor: (TV series) 704 Hauser St., —, News Radio, 1995—2000, ER, 2000—; (TV films) Flying Blind, 1990—, Out of Darkness, —, Student Exchange, —, Crossing the Mob, —, (guest appearance): (TV series) Growing Pains; (TV films) Family Ties; (TV series) Law & Order, The Van Dyke Show,; (films) Dead Women in Lingerie, 1991, The Linguini Incident, 1991, White Sands, 1992, Fly By Night, 1993, The Temp, 1993, Primal Fear, 1996, Primary Colors, 1997, Liar, Liar, 1997, Primary Colors, 1998, Forces of Nature, 1999, Instinct, 1999, Welcome to Mooseport, 2004, Danny Roane: First Time Director, 2006, Semi-Pro, 2008, Baby Mama, 2008; (plays) Some Girl(s), 2006. Office: c/o Creative Artists Agy 9830 Wilshire Blvd Beverly Hills CA 90212

TIFFANY, JOSEPH RAYMOND, II, lawyer; b. Dayton, Ohio, Feb. 5, 1949; s. Forrest Fraser and Margaret Watson (Clark) T.; m. Terri Robbins, Dec. 1, 1984. AB magna cum laude, Harvard U., Cambridge, Mass., 1971; MS in Internat. Relations, London Sch. Econs., 1972; JD, U. Calif., Berkeley, 1975. Bar: US Dist. Ct. (no. dist.) 1975, US Dist. Ct. (ea. dist.) 1977, US Ct. Appeals (9th cir.) 1982, US Ct. Appeals (fed. cir.) 2004. Assoc. Pillsbury, Madison & Sutro, San Francisco, 1975-82, ptnr., 1983-2001, Pillsbury Winthrop LLP, Palo Alto, Calif., 2001—05, Pillsbury Winthrop Shaw Pittman LLP, 2005—. Mem. ABA (antitrust sect.), Calif. Bar Assn. (antitrust and unfair competition sect.). Office: Pillsbury Winthrop Shaw Pittman LLP 2475 Hanover St Palo Alto CA 94304-1115 Office Phone: 650-233-4644. Business E-Mail: joseph.tiffany@pillsburylaw.com.

TIFFANY, SANDRA L., state legislator; b. Spokane, Wash., June 30, 1949; m. Ross M. Tonkens; 1 child, Courtney. Student, U. Calif. Mem. Nev. Assembly, 1993—. Mem. Nev. Rep. State Ctrl. com., Clark County Rep. Ctrl. com.; mem. adv. bd. Boys and Girls Club of Henderson; bd. dirs. Desert Rsch. Inst. Mem. Nat. Assn. Women Bus. Owners, Nat. Conf. State Legislatures, Nat. Orgn. Women Legislators, Am. Legis. Exchange coun., Nat. Rep. Leadership Assn., Exec. Devel. Assn., Henderson C. of C. (mktg. and tourism com., issues com.), Nev. Rep. Women's Club, Green Valley Cmty. Assn., Variety Club. Home: 2144 Eaglepath Cir Henderson NV 89074-0684

TIFFT, WILLIAM GRANT, retired physics professor, scientist; b. Derby, Conn., Apr. 5, 1932; s. William Charles and Marguerite Howe (Hubbell) T.; m. Carol Ruth Nordquist, June 1, 1957 (div. July 1964); children: Jennifer, William John; m. Janet Ann Lindner Homewood, June 2, 1965; 1 child, Amy, stepchildren: Patricia, Susan, Hollis. AB, Harvard Coll., 1954; PhD, Calif. Inst. Tech., 1958. Postdoctoral fellow Australian Nat. U., Canberra, 1958-60; rsch. assoc. Vanderbilt U., Nashville, 1960-61; astronomer Lowell Obs., Flagstaff, Ariz., 1961-64; assoc. prof. U. Ariz., Tucson, 1964-73, prof., 1973—2002, prof. emeritus, 2002—; prin. scientist Sci. Assn. Study of Time in Physics and Cosmology, 2000—. Joint author: Revised New General Catalog, 1973; joint editor: Modern Mathematical Models of Time and Their Applications to Physics and Cosmology, 1997; contbr. over 100 articles to profl. jours. NSF Predoctoral fellow, 1954-58, NSF Postdoctoral fellow, 1958-60; grantee NASA, NSF, ONR, Rsch. Corp. Fellow Am. Astron. Soc.; mem. Internat. Astron. Union, Sci. Assn. Study of Time in Physics and Cosmology (prin. scientist 2000-). Achievements include discovery of redshift quantization and correlations relating to it, including possible variability; first to detect voids in mapping of large scale supercluster structure; investigations of three-dimensional time in cosmology and particle physics. Office: U Arizona Dept Astronomy Tucson AZ 85721-0001

TIGHT, DEXTER CORWIN, lawyer; b. San Francisco, Sept. 14, 1924; s. Dexter Junkins and Marie (Corwin) T.; m. Elizabeth Callander, Apr. 20, 1951; children: Dexter C. Jr., Kathyryn Marie Loken, Steven M., David C. AB, Denison U., 1948; JD, Yale U., 1951. Bar: Calif. 1951. Assoc. Pillsbury, Madison & Sutro, San Francisco, 1953-60; gen. atty. W.P. Fuller & Co., San Francisco, 1960-61; gen. counsel Schlage Lock Co., San Francisco, 1961-77; dir. govt. affairs Crown Zellerbach Corp., San Francisco, 1977-78; sr. v.p., internat. and gen. counsel The Gap Inc., San Bruno, Calif., 1978-90; gen. coun. The Nature Co., 1990—95. Bd. dirs. Shaw-Clayton Plastics, San Rafael, Calif., Granite Rock Co., Watsonville, Calif., Boys and Girls Club of the Peninsula; mem. World Affairs Coun., Internat. Diplomacy Coun.; chmn. That Man May See, San Francisco, 1997, 98. Trustee Denison U., 1978-99, chmn. capital fund dr., 1988-94; Trustee, Global Council, URI 2003-, trustee Calvary Presbyn. Ch., 1968, 73, elder, 1969-90; elder Valley Presbyn. Ch., 1992—; vol. Internat. Exec. Svc. Corps., participant People to People Internat. 2002. 2d lt. USAR, 1943—45, 1st Lt. USAR, 1951—52. Mem. ABA, Calif. Bar Assn., San Francisco Bar Assn. (chmn. various coms.), Commonwealth Club Calif. (past bd. dirs., exec. com.), Menlo Country Club, Bohemian Club (San Francisco), Guardsman Club (1st v.p. 1961), Phi Beta Kappa. Republican. Presbyterian. Avocations: horseback riding, fishing, tennis, golf, photography. Home: 501 Portola Rd Apt 8002 Portola Valley CA 94028-7666

TILLINGHAST, CHARLES CARPENTER, III, retired marketing company executive; b. NYC, Nov. 16, 1936; s. Charles Carpenter, Jr. and Lisette (Micoleau) T.; m. Cynthia Branch, Sept. 28, 1974; children by previous marriage: Avery D., Charles W., David C. BS in Mech. Engring., Lehigh U., 1958; MBA, Harvard U., 1963. Asst. to dir. devel. Lehigh U., Bethlehem, Pa., 1958-61; adminstrv. asst. Boise Cascade Corp., Portland, Oreg., 1963; asst. to v.p. Boise (Idaho) Cascade Corp., 1964-65, gen. mgr. office supply divsn., 1965-67, gen. mgr. paper distbn. divsn., 1966, v.p. bus. products, 1967-69, sr. v.p. housing group, 1969-71, sr. v.p., 1971-73; pres. CRM divsn. Ziff-Davis Pub. Co., Inc., Del Mar, Calif., 1971-75; pres., treas. Value Communications, Inc., La Jolla, Calif., 1975-76; pres. Oak Tree Publs., Inc., San Diego, 1976-81; co-founder, pres. Advanced Mktg. Svcs. Inc., San Diego, 1982-94, chmn., 1994—2004, pres., CEO, 2004; ret., 2004. Served to 2d lt. AUS, 1959.

TILTON, DAVID LLOYD, savings and loan association executive; b. Santa Barbara, Calif., Sept. 21, 1926; s. Lloyd Irvine and Grace (Hart) T.; m. Mary Caroline Knudtson, June 6, 1953; children: Peter, Jennifer, Michael, Catharine. AB, Stanford U., 1949, MBA, 1951. With Santa Barbara Savs. & Loan Assn., 1951-90, pres., 1965-84; now pres. Fin. Corp., Santa Barbara. Trustee, chmn. Calif. Real Estate Investment Trust, 1988. Served with USNR, World War II. Mem. Calif. Savs. and Loan League (dir. 1980), Delta Chi. Home: 630 Oak Grove Dr Santa Barbara CA 93108-1402 Office: Fin Corp Santa Barbara 311 E Carillo St Santa Barbara CA 93101-2761 E-mail: dtilton@earthlink.net.

TILTON, JOHN ELVIN, mineral economics educator; b. Brownsville, Pa., Sept. 16, 1939; s. John Elvin Sr. and Margaret Julia (Renn) T.; m. Elizabeth Martha Meier, June 18, 1966; children: Margaret Ann, John Christian. AB, Princeton U., 1961; PhD in Econs., Yale U., 1965. Staff analyst Office of Sec. of Def., Washington, 1965-67; rsch. assoc. Brookings Inst., Washington, 1967-70; asst. prof. econs. U. Md., College Park, 1970-72; assoc. prof. mineral econs. Pa. State U., University Park, 1972-75, prof., 1975-85; Coulter prof. Colo. Sch. Mines, Golden, 1985—, dir. Divsn. Econs. and Bus., 1987-98. Officer econ. affairs commodities divsn. UN Conf. on Trade and Devel., Geneva, 1977; leader rsch. Internat. Inst. Applied Systems Analysis, Laxenburg, Austria, 1982-84; vice chmn. bd. mineral and energy resources NRC, Washington, 1980-83, mem. nat. materials adv. bd., 1987-89; vis. prof. Pontifica Cath. U., Santiago, Chile, 1998-99. Author: International Diffusion of Technology, 1971, The Future of Nonfuel Minerals, 1977, On Borrowed Time? Assessing the Threat of Mineral Depletion, 2002; editor: Material Substitution, 1983, World Metal Demand, 1990, Mineral Wealth and Economic Development, 1992, View from the Helm, 1995; co-editor: Economics of Mineral Exploration, 1987, Competitiveness in Metals, 1992. Capt. US Army, 1965—67. Fulbright scholar Ecole Nat. Supérieure des Mines de Paris, 1992. Mem. Am. Econ. Assn., Am. Inst. Mining Metall. and Petroleum Engrs. (Mineral Econs. award 1985), Mineral Econs. and Mgmt. Soc. (pres. 1993-94), Mining and Metall. Soc. Am. Avocations: skiing, hiking. Office: Colo Sch Mines Divsn Econs & Bus Golden CO 80401 E-mail: jtilton@mines.edu.

TIMLIN, ROBERT J., judge; b. 1932; BA cum laude, Georgetown U., 1954, JD, 1959, LLM, 1964. Atty. Douglas, Obear and Campbell, 1960-61, Law Offices of A.L. Wheeler, 1961; with criminal divsn. U.S. Dept. Justice, 1961-64; atty. U.S. Atty. Office (ctrl. dist.) Calif., 1964-66, Hennigan, Ryneal and Butterwick, 1965-67; city atty. City of Corona, Calif., 1967-70; prin. Law Office of Robert J. Timlin, 1970-71, 75-76; ptnr. Hunt, Palladino and Timlin, 1971-74, Timlin and Coffin, 1974-75; judge Mcpl. Ct., Riverside, Calif., 1976-80, Calif. Superior Ct., Riverside, 1980-90; assoc. justice Calif. Ct. Appeals, 1990-94; judge U.S. Dist. Ct. (ctrl. dist.) Calif., LA, 1994—. Part-time U.S. Magistrate judge Ctrl. Dist. Calif., 1970-74. Served U.S. Army, 1955-57. Mem. Calif. Judges Assn. Office: US Dist Ct Central Distric Calif Western Divsn 312 N Spring St Los Angeles CA 90012 Home Phone: 805-566-0756; Office Phone: 213-894-5272.

TIMMER, BARBARA, state agency administrator; b. Holland, Mich., Dec. 13, 1946; d. John Norman and Barbara Dee (Folensbee) T. BA, Hope Coll., Holland, Mich., 1969; JD, U. Mich., 1975. Bar: Mich. 1975, U.S. Supreme Ct. 1995. Assoc. McCrosky, Libner, VanLeuven, Muskegon, Mich., 1975-78; apptd. to Mich. Women Commn. by Gov., 1976-79; staff counsel subcom. commerce, consumer & monetary affairs Ho. Govt. Ops. Com., U.S. Ho. of Reps., 1979-82, 85-86; exec. v.p. NOW, 1982-84; legis. asst. to Rep. Geraldine Ferraro, 1984; atty. Office Gen. Counsel Fed. Home Loan Bank Bd., 1986-89; gen. counsel Com. on Banking, Fin. and Urban affairs U.S. Ho. of Reps., Washington, 1989-92; asst. gen. counsel, dir. govt. affairs ITT Corp., Washington, 1992-96; sr. v.p., dir. govt. rels. Home Savs. of Am., Irwindale, Calif., 1996-99; ptnr. Manatt, Phelps & Phillips, Washington, 1999—; gen. counsel MyPrimeTime, Inc., San Francisco, 2000-01; asst. sec. U.S. Senate, 2001—02, asst. sgt. at arms, 2003; chief info. officer Calif. Dept. Transp., Sacramento, 2003—. Mem. info. tech. coun. Women's Transp. Seminar, Calif., 2004—. Editor: Compliance With Lobbying Laws and Gift Rule Guide, 1996. Mem. Calif. State CIO Coun., 2004—05; bd. dirs. Women's High Tech Coalition. Recipient Affordable Housing award, Nat. Assn. Real Estate Brokers, 1990, Disting. Alumni award, Hope Coll., 2003; named to Acad. of Women Achievers, YWCA, 1993. Mem.: FBA (chair exec. coun. banking law com.), ABA (bus. law sect., electronic fin. svcs. subcom.), Bar of D.C., Mich. Bar Assn., Supreme Ct. Hist. Soc., Supreme Ct. Bar Assn., Women in Housing and Fin. (bd. dirs. 1992—94, gen. counsel 1994—98), Exchequer Club. Episcopalian. Office: 2629 Main St PMB 115 Santa Monica CA 90405 E-mail: btimmerdc@earthlink.net.

TIMMERHAUS, KLAUS DIETER, chemical engineering professor; b. Mpls., Sept. 10, 1924; s. Paul P. and Elsa L. (Bever) T.; m. Jean L. Mevis, Aug. 3, 1952; 1 dau., Carol Jane. BS in Chem. Engring, U. Ill., 1948, MS, 1949, PhD, 1951. Registered profl. engr., Colo. Process design engr. Calif. Rsch. Corp., Richmond, 1952-53; extension lectr. U. Calif., Berkeley, 1952; mem. faculty U. Colo., Boulder, 1953-95, prof. chem. engring., 1963—86, assoc. dean engring., 1963—86, dir. engring. rsch. ctr. coll. engring., 1963—86, chmn. aerospace dept., 1983—86, chmn. chem. engring. dept., 1986-89, Patten Chair Disting. prof., 1986-89, presdl. tchg. scholar, 1989—95; ret., 1995. Chem. engr. cryogenics lab. Nat. Bur. Standards, Boulder, summers 1955,57,59,61; lectr. U. Calif. at L.A., 1961-62; sect. head engring. div. NSF, 1972-73; cons. in field. Bd. dirs. Colo. Engring. Expt. Sta., Inc., Engring. Measurements Co. Editor: Advances in Cryogenic Engineering, vols. 1-25, 1954-80; co-editor: Internat. Cryogenic Monograph Series, 1965-. Served with USNR, 1944-46. Recipient Disting. Svc. award Dept. Commerce, 1957, Samuel C. Collins award for outstanding contbns. to cyrogenic tech., 1967, Meritorious Svc. award Cryogenic Engring. Conf., 1987, Disting. Pub. Svc. award NSF, 1984, Exemplary Contbr. award Cryogenic Engring. Conf., 2005; named CASE Colo. Prof. of Yr., 1993, Disting. Lectr., L-T Fan, 2001. Fellow AAAS (v.p. 1985, pres. 1986, Southwestern and Rocky Mountain divsn. Pres.'s award 1989), AIChE (v.p. 1975, pres. 1976, Alpha Chi Sigma award for chem. engring. rsch., 1968, Founders award 1978, Eminent Chem. Engring. award 1983, 2008, W.K. Lewis award 1987, F.J. Van Antwerpen award 1991, Inst. Lecture award 1995), Am. Soc. for Engring. Edn. (bd. dirs. 1986-88, George Westinghouse award 1968, 3M Chem. Engring. divsn. award 1980, Engring. Rsch. Coun. award 1990, Delos Svc. award 1991, Lifetime Achievement award 2008), Cryogenic Soc. Am.; mem. Internat. Inst. Refrigeration (v.p. 1979-87, pres. 1987-95, US nat. commn. 1983-2006, W.T. Pentzer award 1989, hon. co-chair, IIR World Congress, 2003); mem. NAE, Am. Astron. Soc., Austrian Acad. Sci., Cryogenic Engring. Conf. (chmn. 1956-67, bd. dirs. 1967-), Internat. Cryocooler Conf. (bd. dirs. 1980-2006, Outstanding Svc. award, 2006), Soc. Automotive Engrs. (Ralph Teetor award 1991), Sigma Xi (v.p. 1986-87, pres. 1987-88, bd. dirs. 1981-89), Verein Deutscher Ingenieure, Sigma Tau, Tau Beta Pi, Phi Lambda Upsilon. Home: 905 Brooklawn Dr Boulder CO 80303-2708 Business E-Mail: klaus.timmerhaus@colorado.edu.

TIMMINS, TIMOTHY A., telecommunications industry executive; BSBA, Portland State U., Oreg.; MBA, U. So. Calif. CPA. Formerly with investment banking divsn., former sr. v.p. Kemper Securities, Inc., 1985—93; exec. v.p., CFO Metro One Telecomm., Inc., Beaverton, Oreg., 1993—95, pres., CEO, 1995—. Office: Metro One Telecomm Inc 11200 Murray Scholls Pl Beaverton OR 97007

TIMMS, EUGENE DALE, wholesale business owner, state senator; b. Burns, Oreg., May 15, 1932; s. Morgan Oscar and Dorothy Vera (Payne) T.; m. Edna May Evans, Aug. 24, 1953; children: Tobi Eugene, Trina Maria. BA, Willamette U., 1954; grad. studies, U. Wash. Mem. Oreg. Senate, Salem, 1982—; st. republican leader, 1992-94. Sen. State of Oreg., 1982, 84, 88, 92; pres. Harney City C. of C.; bd. trustees Assoc. Oreg. Industries; chmn. Parks & Recreation Dist. Bd.; mem. Harney City Hosp. Bd. Mem. SBA, Jaycees (state v.p.), Elk Lodge, Masonic Lodge, Al Kader Harney City Shrine Club. Presbyterian. Avocations: fishing, hunting, reading, movies, sports. Home: 1049 N Court Ave Burns OR 97720-1016 Address: Oreg Senate S-219 State Capitol Salem OR 97310-0001

TIMMS, MICHELE, retired professional basketball player; b. Australia, June 28, 1965; Guard Australia's Women's Nat. Basketball League - Bulleen Boomers, 1984-85, Nunawading Spectres, 1985, Lotus Munchen, Germany, 1989-90, Perth Breakers, Australia, 1991-92, Basket Firenze, Italy, 1993-94, Sydney Flames, Australia, 1995, WTV Wuppertal, Germany, 1995-96, Phoenix Mercury, 1997—2001. Named WNBL Player of Yr., 1995, 96; named to Women's Basketball Hall of Fame, 2007. Avocations: tennis, golf.

TINDALL, ROBERT EMMETT, lawyer, educator; b. NYC, Jan. 2, 1934; s. Robert E. and Alice (McGonigle) T.; children: Robert Emmett IV, Elizabeth. BS in Marine Engring., SUNY, 1955; postgrad., Georgetown U. Law Sch., 1960—61; LLB, U. Ariz., 1963; LLM, NYU, 1967; PhD, City U., London, 1975. Bar: Ariz. 1963. Mgmt. trainee GE, Schenectady, NY, Lynn, Mass., Glens Falls, NY, 1955-56, 58-60; law clk. Haight, Gardner, Poor and Havens, NYC, 1961; prin., mem. Robert Emmett Tindall & Assocs., Tucson, 1963—; prof. mgmt. U. Ariz., Tucson, 1969—2003; prof. emeritus, 2003. Vis. prof. Grad. Sch. of Law, Soochow U., China, 1972, Grad. Bus. Ctr., London, 1974, NYU, 1991-96, UCSD, 2005-07; dir. MBA program U. Ariz., Tucson, 1975-81, dir. entrepreneurship program, 1984-86; investment cons. Saudi Arabia, 1981—; lectr. USIA, Eng., India, Mid. East, 1974; lectr. bus. orgn. and regulatory laws Southwestern Legal Found., Acad. Am. and Internat. Law, 1976-80. Actor cmty. theatres, Schenectady, 1955-56, Harrisburg, Pa., 1957-58, Tucson, 1961-71; appeared in films Rage, 1971, Showdown at OK Corral, 1971, Lost Horizon, 1972; appeared in TV programs Gunsmoke, 1972, Petrocelli,

1974; author: Multinational Enterprises, 1975; contbr. articles on domestic and internat. bus. to profl. jours. Served to lt. USN, 1956-58. Fellow Ford Found., 1965-67; grantee Asia Found., 1972-73. Mem. Strategic Mgmt. Soc., State Bar Ariz., Acad. Internat. Bus., SAG, Honourable Soc. of Mid. Temple (London), Phi Delta Phi, Beta Gamma Sigma, Assn. Corp. Growth, Royal Overseas League (London). Home: PO Box 42196 Tucson AZ 85733-2196

TING, ALBERT CHIA, biomedical engineer, researcher; b. Hong Kong, Sept. 7, 1950; came to U.S., 1957; s. William Su and Katherine Sung T.; m. Shirley Roung Wang, July 30, 1988, (dec. Aug. 2003). BA, UCLA, 1973; MS, Calif. State U., LA, 1975, Calif. Inst. Tech., 1977; PhD, U. Calif., San Diego, 1983. Rsch. asst. Calif. Inst. Tech., Pasadena, 1975-77, U. Calif., San Diego, 1982-83; sr. staff engr. R&D Am. Med. Optics, Irvine, Calif., 1983-86; project engr., rsch. Allergan Med. Optics, Irvine, Calif., 1987-89, sr. project engr., rsch., 1989-92, sr. project engr., engring., 1993-94; bioengr. cons. Pharmacia Iovision, Inc., Irvine, Calif., 1995-97; sr. engr. D & E, 1997, sr. engr., project mgr., 1998-99; rsch. and devel. mgr., surg. Bausch & Lomb, Irvine, 1999—2001; R & D mgr. Visiogen, Inc., Irvine, 2001—02, sr. R & D mgr., 2002—. Contbr. articles to profl. jours. Mem. AAAS, Biomed. Engring. Soc., Assn. for Rsch. in Vision and Ophthalmology, Biomed. Optics Soc. Achievements include invention of med. and optical devices. Office: Visiogen Inc 2 Goodyear Ste B Irvine CA 92618 Office Phone: 949-900-3352. Business E-Mail: ating@visiogen.com.

TINGLE, JAMES O'MALLEY, retired lawyer; b. NYC, June 12, 1928; s. Thomas Jefferson and Mercedes (O'Malley) T. BS, U. Mont., 1950, BA, LL.B., U. Mont., 1952; LL.M., U. Mich., 1953, S.JD, 1958. Bar: Calif. 1959, Mont. 1952, N.Y. 1961. Asst. prof. law U. Mont., Missoula, 1955-56; atty. Shell Oil Co., NYC, 1957-62; assoc. Pillsbury, Madison & Sutro, San Francisco, 1962-68, ptnr., 1969-2000. Author: The Stockholder's Remedy of Corporate Dissolution, 1959; editor: State Antitrust Laws, 1974. Served to 1st lt. USAF, 1953—55. William W. Cook fellow U. Mich. Mem. Mont. Bar Assn., Calif. Bar Assn., ABA Democrat.

TINSLEY, JEFFREY, Internet company executive; married, June 2003. CEO Intelligent Bus. Concepts, GreatDomains.com; CEO, chmn. Reunion.com, Inc., 2002—. Chmn. RealtyTracker. Office: Reunion.com Inc 12100 Wilshire Blvd Ste 150 Los Angeles CA 90025 Office Phone: 310-571-3144. Office Fax: 310-571-3145.

TIONG, TAMRA A., elementary school educator; BA in English, Santa Clara (Calif.) Univ., 1998; Spl. edn. alt. lic., No. N.Mex. Cmty. Coll., 2003. AmeriCorps Co-tchr./Sch. Garden Coord. New Brighton Mid. Sch., 1998—99; tchr. Hidden Villa Environ. Edn. Program, 1999—2002; spl. edn. tchr. Dulce (N.Mex) Elem. Sch., Jicarilla Apache Indian Reservation, 2002—; after sch. tutor Advantage Tutoring Svc., 2004—05. Named N.Mex. Tchr. of Yr., 2007, Dulce ISD Tchr. of Yr., 2007; finalist Nat. Tchr. of Yr., 2007. Mem.: Phi Sigma Tau, Alpha Sigma Nu, Sigma Tau Delta. Office: Dulce Elem Sch PO Box 590 Dulce NM 87528 Personal E-mail: tammy_tiong@hotmail.com. Business E-Mail: ttiong@dulceschools.com.

TIPTON, HARRY BASIL, JR., state legislator, physician; b. Salida, Colo., Mar. 14, 1927; s. Harry Basil Sr. and Nina Belle (Hailey) T.; m. Dorothy Joan Alexander, Sept. 16, 1950; children: Leslie Louise, Harry Basil III, Robert Alexander. BA, U. Colo., 1950, MD, 1953. Diplomate Am. Bd. Family Practice. Postgrad. med. tng. Good Samaritan Hosp., Phoenix., Ariz., Maricopa County Hosp., Phoenix; ptnr., dir. Lander (Wyo.) Med. Clinic, 1954—; mem. Wyo. Ho. Reps., Cheyenne, 1981—, chmn. judiciary com., 1986-98, speaker pro tem, 1999-2001, mem. appropriations com., 2001—. Cons. Indian Health Svc., Ft. Washakie, Wyo., 1968—; dir NOWCAP Family Planning, Worland, Wyo., 1975-90. Mem., pres. Fremont County Sch. Dist. # 1, Lander, 1958-78. With USMC, 1945-46, capt. USNR Med. Corps, 1950-87. Recipient Dr. Nathon Davis award, AMA, 1999, Silver and Gold award, U. Colo., 2003; named Capt. Med. Corps. USNR, 1974. Fellow Am. Coll. Ob.-Gyn., Am. Assn. Family Practice (charter); mem. Wyo. Med. Soc. (Physician of Yr. 1989), Rotary (pres. 1960-61), Elks. Republican. Avocations: fishing, skiing, hunting, history.

TIPTON, SCOTT, state legislator; m. Jean Tipton; children: Liesl, Elizabeth. BA in Polit. Sci., Fort Lewis Coll. Pres. Tipton Ltd., Tipton Properties; owner Mesa Verde Pottery, Mesa Indian Trading Co.; mem. Dist. 58 Colo. House of Reps., 2008—. Chmn. McInnis for Congress, 1992, 2002, 3rd Congl. dist., 1997—2008, Montezuma County Rep. Party. Bd. trustees Crow Canyon Archeol. Ctr.; bd. mem. Mesa Verde Found.; bd. trustees Mesa Verde Nat. Park; mem. Pueblo Cmty. Coll. Adv. Bd. Mem.: Montezuma County 100 Club. Republican. Office: State House 200 E Colfax Denver CO 80203 Office Phone: 303-866-2955. Business E-Mail: COHD58@yahoo.com.*

TIRADOR, GABRIEL, insurance company executive; Asst. contr. Mercury Ins. Group, LA, 1994—96; v.p., contr. Automobile Club Calif., 1997—98; v.p., CFO Mercury Gen. Corp., LA, 1998—2001, pres., COO, 2001—06, pres., CEO, 2007—. Office: Mercury Gen Corp 4484 Wilshire Blvd Los Angeles CA 90010

TIRRELL, DAVID A., research scientist, educator; b. Jan. 10, 1953; BS in Chemistry, MIT, 1974; MS in Polymer Sci. and Engring., U. Mass., 1976, PhD in Polymer Sci. and Engring., 1978; D honoris causa (hon.), Tech. Univ. Eindhoven, 2001. Rsch. assoc. Kyoto U., 1978; asst. prof. chemistry Carnegie-Mellon U., 1978-82, assoc. prof. chemistry, 1982-84; assoc. prof. polymer sci. and engring. U. Mass., 1984-87, prof. polymer sci. and engring., 1987-92, Barrett prof. polymer and sci. and engring., 1992-98; Ross McCollum-William H. Corcoran prof. Calif. Inst. Tech., 1998—, chair chemistry divsn. & chem. engring., 1999—. Mem. molecular and cellular biology faculty, 1990—; adj. prof. chemistry U. Mass., 1991; dir. NSF materials rsch. lab., 1991, NSF materials rsch. sci. and engring. ctr., 1994—; vis. prof. chemistry Queensland U., Australia, 1987, Inst. Charles Sadron, Strausbourg, Austria; mem. materials rsch. adv. com. NSF, 1988—91; chmn. com. on synthetic hierarchical structures Nat. Rsch. Coun., 1990—94, mem. panel on biomolecular materials, 1991—; mem. polymers in biosystems com. Naval Rsch. Lab., Oxnard, 1994; co-chmn. grad. polymer rsch. conf., State Coll., Pa., 1994; co-chmn. program com. IUPAC Macromolecular Symposium, 1994; chmn. Gordon Rsch. Conf. on Chemistry of Supramolecules and Assemblies, 1995; Fellow American Association for the Advancement of Science, 2003, 2003. Editor: (profl. jours.) Jour. of Polymer Sci., 1988—99; assoc. editor: New Polymeric Materials, 1986—87, editl. bd.: Indsl. and Engring. Chemistry, Product Rsch. and Devel., 1983—86, Jour. Bioactive and Compatible Polymers, 1986—, Biomaterials, 1986—, New Polymeric Materials, 1987, Jour. of Macromolecular Sci-Chemistry, 1990—, Progress in Polymer Sci., 1992—, Macromolecular Reports, 1992, Materials Sci. and Engring., 1993—, Chem. and Engring. News, 1995—; contbr. articles to profl. jours. Recipient Presdl. Young Investigator award, 1984—89, Fulbright Sr. scholar award, 1987, Chancellor's medal, Univ. Mass., 1997; fellow Univ., 1974—77, Alfred P. Sloan Rsch., 1982—84, Rothschild, Curie Inst., 1995—97. Fellow: Am. Inst. Med. & Biol. Engring., AAAS; mem.: NAS, Phi Lambda Upsilon, Materials Rsch. Soc., NY Acad. Scis., Am. Chem. Soc. (Carl S. Marvel Polymer Chem. award 1991, Harrison Howe award 1996, Polymer Chem. award 2001, Arthur C. Cope Scholar award 2007), Sigma Xi. Office: Calif Inst Tech Divsn Chemistry Mail Code 164-30 Pasadena CA 91125

TIRRELL, JOHN ALBERT, organization executive, consultant; b. Boston, Feb. 11, 1934; s. George Howard and Helen Sarah (Hitchings) T.; m. Helga Ruth Eisenhauer, Jan. 29, 1966; children: Steffanie Ruth, Sabina Lisette, Monica Susanne. BA in Psychology, King's Coll., Briarcliff Manor, NY, 1961; MEd, U. Ariz., Tucson, 1975. Various positions for several orgns., 1962-68; analyst instrnl.-ednl. systems GE, Daytona Beach, Fla., 1969-72; dir. curriculum and program devel. Brookdale CC, Lincroft, NJ, 1972; dir. learning and faculty resources Pima CC, Tucson, 1972-76; dir. human resources planning and devel. Miami divsn. Cyprus Copper Co., Claypool, Ariz., 1976-79; exec. dir. Calvary Missionary Fellowship, Tucson, 1983-85; interim pastor Sagauro Evang. Ch., Tucson, 1985-86; pastor Midvale Evangelical Ch., Tucson, 1986-87; founder, pres. The Jethro Consultancy, Birmingham, Mich., 1979—88, Tucson, 1979—; v.p. mgmt. svc. AA Gage, Ferndale, Mich., 1987; pastor Desert Hills Bapt. Ch., Tucson, 1993-95. Mem. adv. bd. UIM Internat., Greeley, Colo., 1983-92, mem. fin. com., 1983-94, sec. support svcs. field bd., 1993-01, sec. bus. and devel. field bd., 2002-, sec., chmn. pers. com., 1997-2008, sec., 1998-2008, bd. dirs., 1993-2008, mem. policy revision com., 2004-08, v.p. internat. bd., 2005-08, mem. search com., 2005-, vice pres., sec. 2005-08, mem. bus. and devel. bd., chmn. nominating com., 2005-08, interim exec. dir., 2008-; assoc. faculty mem. Gila Pueblo Campus Ea. Ariz. Coll., Globe, 1978; adj. prof. Montclair State Coll., NJ, 1972; chmn. mgmt. and pers. com. Wildwood Ranch, Inc., Howell, Mich., 1989-92; interim pres., v.p. programs, v.p. devel. Detroit Rescue Mission Ministries, 1990-92; v.p. corp. planning, tng., productivity George Instrument Co., Royal Oak, 1988-89; faculty mem. mgmt., comm., sociology, psychology So. Ariz. and Phoenix campuses U. Phoenix, Tuscon and Phoenix, 1997—, area chair for social scis., 2001-04; adj. faculty mem. psychology Pima County CC, 1999-2002. Contbr. articles to profl. jours. Mem. Ariz. Coun. for Econ. Conversion, 1992-94; mem. facilities task force Grace Evang. Free Ch., Birmingham, 1989-90, chmn. bylaws revision com., 1989-90, chmn. property devel. com., 1990-92; interim pastor Desert Hills Bapt. Ch., Tucson, 1992-93; elder 1st Evang. Free Ch., Tucson, 1979-81, 86-87, 97, supt. Sunday sch., 1981-84, supr. adult Sunday sch., 1992-93, chmn. gen. bd., elder bd., 1979-82, short-term missions coord., missions bd., 1992-93; bd. dirs. S.W. Border dist. Evang. Free Ch. Am., 1996-00, mem. comm. com., 1996-01, chmn. comm. com., 1998-99; bd. dirs. Clearing House of Operational Resources for Christian Orgns., Royal Oak, Mich., 1991; bd. dirs. Shadow Roc Homeowners Assn., 1996-98, treas., 1997; v.p. parent-tchr. fellowship Palo Verde Christian Sch., Tucson, 1980-81. Staff sgt. USAF, 1952-56. Mem. ASTD (treas., Old Pueblo chpt. 1982, bd. dirs.-at-large 1983, Human Resources Devel. award Valley of the Sun chpt. 1977), Birmingham-Bloomfield C. of C. (mem. profl. devel. edn. com. 1987-91, mem. pub. rels. mktg. com. 1989), King's Coll. Alumni Assn. (class gov. 1988-95, 2000-03). Independent. Avocation: Bible teaching. Home and Office: 1205 E Deer Canyon Rd Tucson AZ 85718-1069 Office Phone: 520-544-9750. Personal E-mail: jack.tirrell@comcast.net.

TIRRELL, MATTHEW V., engineering educator; b. Phillipsburg, NJ, Sept. 5, 1950; s. Matthew Vincent Tirrell Jr. and Loraine (Wier) Gonsky; m. Pamela LaVigne, Aug. 1993. BS in chem. engring., Northwestern U., 1973; PhD in polymer sci. and engring., U. Mass., 1977. Mem. coop. edn. program Cin. Milacron Chem. Inc., 1970-72; tchg. and rsch. asst. U. Mass., Amherst, 1973-77; asst. prof. U. Minn., Mpls., 1977-81, assoc. prof., 1981-85, prof. chem. engring. and materials sci., 1985—99, Shell disting. chair. chem. engring., 1986-91, Earl E. Bakken Prof. Biomed. Engring., 1993—97, head chem. engring. and materials sci., 1995-99; dir. Biomed. Engring. Inst., 1995-98; dean Coll Engring. U. Calif., Santa Barbara, 1999—, Richard A. Auhll Prof., 1999—, also prof. materials engring.; venture ptnr. NGEN Partners, LLC. Mem. adv. panel Grad. Sch. Integrative Sciences and Engring. Nat. U. Singapore, 2003—05, vis. com. chem. and environ. engring., 2003—05; cons. Institut Francais du Petrole, 1982—, Kimberly-Clark Corp., 2000—, Edwards Lifesciences, 2000—, Santa Barbara Tech. Group, 2000—, bd. mem.; editl. adv. bd. Jour. Polymer Sci., Polymer Physics Edit., 1986—2000, Macromolecules, 1987—90, McGraw-Hill Chem. Engring. Series, 1987—98, Jour. Rheology, 1990—, Progress in Polymer Sci., 1992—97, Polymerica Acta, 1992—, Jour. Adhesion Sci. and Tech., 1993—96, Langmuir, 1995—, Current Opinion in Colloid and Interface Sci., 1996—, Oxford Univ. Press, Chem. Engring. Series, 1998—2000, Chemistry of Materials, 1998—, Gordon and Breach, 2000—; editl. bd. Jour. Chem. Physics, 1991—93; US editor Chem. Engring. Sci., 1988—91; assoc. editor Reviews in Macromolecular Sci., 1992—2000, editor, 2000—; Sci. and Tech. Panel U. Calif. Pres.'s Coun. for Nat. Lab. Adminstrn., 2000—; bd. dirs. Cottage Health Sys., Santa Barbara, 2000—; US Chair German-Am. Frontiers of Engring., 1999—. Author: Modeling of Polymerization Processes, 1995. Advisor Camille and Henry Dreyfus Found., 1998—. Recipient Camille and Henry Dreyfus Tchr.-Scholar Award, 1980, George Taylor/IT Alumni Soc. Disting. Rsch. Award, U. Minn. Inst. Tech., 1981, Gordon Starr Outstanding Contribution Award, U. Minn., 1981, Presdl. Young Investigator Award, NSF, 1984, Chancellor's Medal, U. Mass. Amherst, 1987, Alumni Merit Award, Northwestern U., 1997; named Outstanding Young Chem. Engr. of Minn., 1981; Alfred P. Sloan Found. Fellowship, 1982, John Simon Guggenheim Meml. Found. Fellowship, 1986. Fellow AAAS, Am. Inst. Med. and Bio. Engineers, Am. Phys. Soc. (John H. Dillon Medal 1987); mem. NAE, AIChE (editor jour. 1991—2001, inst. lectr. 2001, Allan P. Colburn award 1985, Profl. Progress award 1994, Charles M.A. Stine Award 1996), Am. Chem. Soc., Materials Rsch. Soc., Biomed. Engring. Soc., Controlled Release Soc., Soc. Biomaterials, Soc. Polymer Sci. Japan, Soc. Rheology Avocations: gourmet cooking, movies, distance running. Office: U Calif Dean's Office Coll Engring Santa Barbara CA 93106-5080*

TITLE, ALAN M., astrophysicist; BA in Math., UCLA, 1960; PhD in Physics, Calif. Inst. Tech., 1996. Rsch. assoc. Harvard U., 1967—71; scientist, sr. fellow Lockheed Martin Corp., 1971—; prin. investigator TRACE solar telescope project Lockheed Martin Space Systems Advanced Tech. Ctr., Palo Alto, prin. investigator Atmospheric Imaging Assembly, Solar Dynamics Observatory. Prof. physics Stanford U. Recipient Public Svc. award, NASA, Hale prize, Am. Astronomical Soc.; Nat. Acad. Scis. Rsch. fellow, Smithsonian Astrophysical Observatory. Mem.: Internat. Acad. Astronauts, Nat. Acad. Engring., NAS. Achievements include research in techniques and development of optical systems for observing the sun from orbiting spacecraft. Office: Lockheed Palo Alto Rsch Lab Dept 91-30 Bldg 252 3251 Hanover St Palo Alto CA 94304-1191

TITLE, GAIL MIGDAL, lawyer; b. Waldenberg, Germany; AB, Wellesley Coll.; JD, U. Calif., Berkeley. Bar: Calif. Mng. ptnr. Katten Muchin Rosenman, LLP, LA. Adj. prof. law Loyola U.; head Nat. Entertainment Litigation Practice; former trustee Ctr. for Law in the Pub. Interest, 1976-96; exec. com., bd. Pub. Counsel Law Ctr. & Constl. Rights Found; co-chair USDC Magistrate Selection Com., ctrl. Calif. Named a Woman of Distinction, Women's Lawyer's Assn. LA; named one of 100 Power Lawyers, Hollywood Reporter, 2007. Mem. ABA (litigation sect., forum com. entertainment), Assn. Bus. Trial Lawyers, State Bar Calif. (standing com. pub. interest law 1976—), Beverly Hills Bar Assn., LA Copyright Soc. (trustee). Office: Katten Muchin Rosenman LLP 2029 Century Park E Los Angeles CA 90067 Office Phone: 310-788-4727. Office Fax: 310-712-8427. Business E-Mail: gail.title@kattenlaw.com.

TITLEY, SPENCER ROWE, geology educator; b. Denver, Sept. 27, 1928; m. Clara Helen Ruxton, May 1951; children: Ronald, Jane, Jennifer. Geol. Engr., Colo. Sch. Mines, 1951; PhD in Geology, U. Ariz., 1958. Ops. geologist N.J. Zinc Co., Gilman, Colo., 1951, 53-55; instr. U. Ariz., Tucson, 1955-58; regional geologist S.W. N.J. Zinc Co., 1958-60; from asst. to full prof. geology U. Ariz., 1960—. Panel mem. NSF, Divsn. Biol., Math. and Geophysical Scis. and Engring., 1978-81; sec. Soc. Econ. Geologists Found., 1972-83; mem. Apollo Field Geology Investigation Team, U.S. Geol. Survey, 1969-72; pres. Ariz. Geol. Soc., 1973-74. Mem. editl. bd. Econ. Geology, 1970-75, Ore Geology Reviews, 1984-2003; editor 5 books; contbr. over 85 articles to profl. jours. Pres. Mining Found. SW, 2007. With U.S. Army Corps Engrs., 1951-53, Korea. Decorated Bronze Star; recipient Disting. Achievement medal Colo. Sch. Mines, 1975, Excellence in Tchg. award Burlington No. Found., 1985, Creative Tchg. award U. Ariz. Found., 1986, D.C. Jackling award Soc. Mining, Mettalurgy and Exploration of AIME, 1997, Merit medal Am. Mining Hall of Fame, 1997; Fulbright Sr. lectr. Fed. U. Para'Brazil, 1986, Phoebe Apperson Hearst Disting. lectr. U. Calif., Berkeley, 1988. Fellow Geol. Soc. Am., Soc. Econ. Geologists (councilor 1980-83, Thayer Lindsley lectr. 1985, Disting. lectr. 1995, Penrose medal 1996), Mineral. Soc. Am., Australasian Inst. Mining and Metallurgy; mem. Nat. Acad. Engring., Soc. Applied Geology Home: 6920 E Taos Pl Tucson AZ 85715-3343 Office: Univ Ariz Dept Geosciences Simpson Bldg Tucson AZ 85721-0001 Office Phone: 520-621-6018. Business E-Mail: stitley@email.arizona.edu.

TITUS, ALICE COSTANDINA (DINA TITUS), United States Representative from Nevada, former state legislator; b. Thomasville, Ga., May 23, 1950; m. Thomas Clayton Wright. AB, Coll. William and Mary, 1970; MA, U. Ga., 1973; PhD, Fla. State U., 1976. Lectr. North Tex. State U., Denton; prof. polit. sci. U. Nev., Las Vegas, 1977—2009; mem. Nev. State Senate from Dist. 7, 1989—2009, minority leader, 1993—2008, mem. legis. commn.; mem. US Congress from 3d Nev. Dist., 2009—. Chmn. Nev. Humanities Com., 1984-86; mem. Eldorado Basin adv. group to Colo. River Commn.; active Gov. Commn. Bicentennial of U.S. Constn.; former mem. Gov. Commn. on Aging. Author: Bombs in the Backyard: Atomic Testing and American Politics, 1986, Battle Born: Federal-State Relations in Nevada during the 20th Century, 1989. Mem. Western Polit. Sci. Assn., Clark County Women's Dem. Club, Amer. Pen Women, Aquavision, PEO. Democrat. Greek Orthodox. Office: US Congress 319 Cannon House Office Bldg Washington DC 20515-2803 also: Dist Office 8215 S Eastern Ave Ste 205 Las Vegas NV 89123 Office Phone: 202-225-3252, 702-387-4941. Office Fax: 202-225-2185, 702-837-0728.*

TJIAN, ROBERT TSE NAN, biochemistry educator, biology and virology researcher; b. Hong Kong, Sept. 22, 1949; naturalized Brit. citizen. m. 1976. BA in Biochemistry, U. Calif., Berkeley, 1972; PhD in Biochemistry and Molecular Biology, Harvard U., 1976. Staff investigator molecular virology Cold Spring Harbor Lab., 1976-79, Robertson fellow, 1978; asst. prof. biochemistry U. Calif., Berkeley, 1979—82, prof. biochemistry, 1982—, prof. molecular and cell biology; co-founder Tularik, Inc., 1991. Howard Hughes investigator Howard Hughes Inst., 1987—; adj. prof. biochemistry and biophysics U. Calif., San Francisco. Contbr. several articles to profl. jours. Named Passano Found. laureate, 1994, Calif. Scientist of the Yr., 1994; recipient Lewis S. Rosentiel award for disting. work in basic med. rsch. Brandeis U., 1995, Monsanto award, Louisa Gross Horwitz prize, Columbia U., MERIT award, Nat. Cancer Inst., 2004; co-recipient Alfred P. Sloan Jr. prize, General Motors Cancer Rsch. Found., 1999. Mem. NAS (Molecular Biology award 1991). Achievements include research in oncogenic viruses and their interactions with the host cell; control of gene expression; simian virus 40; a small DNA containing oncogenic virus, tumor antigen, its structure and function. Office: U Calif Molecular and Cell Biology Dept 16 Barker Hall # 3204 Berkeley CA 94720-3204 Home and Office: U Calif Molecular and Cell Biology 161A Koshland Hall Berkeley CA 94720 Office Phone: 510-642-8258 2-4442. Office Fax: 510-642-0884. Business E-Mail: jmlim@berkeley.edu.

TOBEY, BRIAN, computer software company executive; married; 2 children. BSChemE, U. Calif., Berkeley; Masters in Mfg. Mgmt., Northwestern U., MBA. Prin. A.T. Kearney; v.p. N.Am. Bath & Spa mfg. & supply chain ops. Jacuzzi Brands; gen. mgr. supply chain & info. tech. services Microsoft Corp., 2004, corp. v.p. mfg. & ops., Entertainment & Devices divsn., 2008—. Office: Microsoft Corp Entertainment & Devices Divsn 1 Microsoft Way Redmond WA 98052-6399

TOBIN, ALLAN JOSHUA, biologist; b. Manchester, NH, Aug. 22, 1942; s. Maurice and Eve (Alter) T.; m. Elaine Munsey, Apr. 7, 1968 (div.); children: David, Adam; m. Janet Ruth Hadda, Mar. 22, 1981. BS, MIT, 1963; PhD, Harvard U., 1969. Asst. prof. biology Harvard U., Cambridge, Mass., 1971-75, UCLA, 1975-81, assoc. prof. biology, 1981-86, prof. biology, 1986—, chair interdepartmental program for neurosci., 1989-95, dir. Brain Rsch. Inst., 1995—. Eleanor Leslie Chair in neuroscience, 1996—. Sci. dir. Hereditary Disease Found., Santa Monica, Calif., 1979—, mem. sci. adv. bd., 1979—; vis. scientist Laboratoire de Neurobiologie Moleculaire, Inst. Pasteur, Paris, 1982; cons. Curriculum Resources Group, Inst. for Svs. to Edn.,

Ednl. Devel. Ct., Newton, Mass.; centennial speaker Nat. Student Rsch. Forum, U. Tex. Med. Br., 1991. Named Research fellow Dept. Biology MIT, 1970-71, Vis. Research fellow Dept. Biophysics Weizmann Inst. Science, 1969-70, Mary Jennifer Selznick fellow Herediltary Disease Found., 1978, fellow Com. to Combat Huntington's Disease, 1973-75, Postdoctoral fellow U.S. Pub. Health Service; recipient Javits Neuroscience Investigator award Nat. Inst. Neurological Disorders, 1993, Nat. Med. Rsch. award Nat. Health Coun., 1993, David Gillespie Meml. Lectureship Med. Coll. Pa. and Hahnemann U., Phila., 1996, Excellence award Text and Acad. Authors Assn., 1999, 2000; named to Manchester (N.H.) Ctrl. H.S. Hall of Fame, 1998-00. Mem. AAAS, Soc. for Neurosci., NIH (mem. Neurology C. study sect. 1985-89), NINDS (chair stategic planning group neurodegenerative disease 1998—), Molecular Biology Inst., Soc. for Devel. Biology, Am. Soc. Neurochemistry. Office: UCLA Brain Rsch Inst 2506 Gonda Neurosci Genetics Ctr PO Box 951761 Los Angeles CA 90095-1761 E-mail: atobin@mednet.ucla.edu.

TOBIN, ANDREW MICHAEL, state legislator; b. NYC, June 27, 1958; m. Jennifer Tobin; children: Andrew Michael Jr., Chris, Meagan, Kelly, Laura. Lic. Ariz. Dept. Ins. Mgr. pvt. bus. TLC Employee Benefits, 1995—; mem. Dist. 1 Ariz. House of Reps., 2006—, majority whip, 2008—, mem. rules com., banking & ins. com. Nat. pres. US Jr. C. of C., 1988—89. Bd. dirs. Sharlot Hall Mus., Prescott, Ariz., Young Men's Christian Assn. Named Freshman Legislator of Yr., Ariz. Sch. Bd. Assn., 2007, Legislator of Yr., Ariz. Sch. Superintendents, 2008, Ariz. Small Bus. Assn., 2008. Republican. Roman Catholic. Office: Ariz House Reps Capitol Complex 1700 W Washington Rm 217 Phoenix AZ 85007 Home Phone: 602-978-3267; Office Phone: 602-926-5172. Office Fax: 602-417-3085. Business E-Mail: atobin@azleg.gov.*

TOBIN, JAMES MICHAEL, lawyer; b. Santa Monica, Calif., Sept. 27, 1948; s. James Joseph and Glada Marie (Meisner); m. Kathleen Marie Espy, Sept. 14, 1985; children: Kristina Claire, Victoria Elizabeth Joy. BA with honors, U. Calif., Riverside, 1970; JD, Georgetown U., DC, 1974. Bar: Calif. 1974, Mich. 1987. From atty. to gen. atty. So. Pacific Co., San Francisco, 1975-82; v.p. regulatory affairs So. Pacific Comm. Co., Washington, 1982-83; v.p., gen. counsel Lexitel Corp., Washington, 1983-85; v.p., gen. counsel, sec. ALC Comm. Corp., Birmingham, Mich., 1985-87, sr. v.p., gen. counsel, sec., 1987-88; of counsel Morrison & Foerster, San Francisco, 1988-90, ptnr., 1990—2005, Tobin Law Group, P. C., 2006—. Mem. ABA, Calif. Bar Assn., Fed. Comm. Bar Assn. Democrat. Episcopalian. Avocations: carpentry, travel. Home: 17 Reed Ranch Rd Tiburon CA 94920 Office: 1628 Tiburon Blvd Tiburon CA 94920 Office Phone: 415-732-1700. Business E-Mail: jim@tobinlaw.us.

TOBIN, VINCENT MICHAEL, professional football coach, former sports team executive; b. Burlington Junction, Mo., Sept. 29, 1943; BE, U. Mo., 1965, M in Guidance and Counseling, 1966. Def. ends coach Missouri, 1967-70, def. coord., 1971-76, Brit. Columbia Lions CFL, 1977-82, Phila./Balt. Stars USFL, 1983-85, Chgo. Bears NFL, 1986-92, Indpls. Colts NFL, 1994-95; head coach Ariz. Cardinals, 1996—2000.

TOBIN, WILLIAM JOSEPH, newspaper editor; b. Joplin, Mo., July 28, 1927; s. John J. and Lucy T. (Shoppach) Tobin; m. Marjorie Stuhldreher, Apr. 26, 1952; children: Michael Gerard, David Joseph, James Patrick. BS, Butler U., 1948; LLD (hon.), Gonzaga U., 2006. Staff writer AP, Indpls., 1947-52, news feature writer NYC, 1952-54, regional membership exec. Louisville, 1954-56, corr. Juneau, Alaska, 1956-60, asst. chief bur. Balt., 1960-61, chief bur. Helena, Mont., 1961-63; mng. editor Anchorage Times, 1963-73, assoc. editor, 1973-85, gen. mgr., 1974-85, v.p., editor-in-chief, 1985-89, editor editl. page, 1990, asst. pub., 1991; sr. editor Voice of the Times, 1991—. Mem. devel. com. Anchorage Winter Olympics, 1984-91, bd. dirs. Anchorage organizing com., 1985-91; bd. dirs. Alaska Coun. Econ. Edn., 1978-84, Boys Clubs Alaska, 1979-83, Anchorage Symphony Orch., 1986-87, Blue Cross Wash. and Alaska, 1987—, chmn., 1990-91; chmn. Premera Corp., 1994-99; mem. adv. bd. Providence Hosp., Anchorage, 1974-91, chmn., 1980-85. Sgt. U.S. Army, 1950-52. Mem. Alaska AP Mems. Assn. (pres. 1964), Anchorage C. of C. (bd. dirs. 1969-74, pres. 1972-73), Alaska World Affairs Coun. (pres. 1967-68), Alaska Press Club (pres. 1968-69), Commonwealth North Club (Anchorage). Home: 2130 Lord Baranof Dr Anchorage AK 99517-1257 Office: Anchorage Times PO Box 100040 Anchorage AK 99510-0040 Office Phone: 907-565-2263. Personal E-mail: wjt@alaskalife.net.

TOBIS, JEROME SANFORD, physician; b. Syracuse, NY, July 23, 1915; s. David George and Anna (Feinberg) T.; m. Hazel Weisbard, Sept. 18, 1938; children: David, Heather, Jonathan. BS, CCNY, 1936; MD, Chgo. Med. Sch., 1943. Diplomate Am. Bd. Phys. Medicine and Rehab. Intern Knickerbocker Hosp., 1943-44; resident Bronx VA Hosp., 1946-48; med. dir. state fever therapy unit USPHS, Brookhaven, Miss., 1944-46; practice medicine NYC, 1948-70; prof. dir. dept. phys. medicine and rehab. N.Y. Med. Coll., Flower and Fifth Av. Hosps., 1948-61; prof. rehab. medicine Albert Einstein Coll. of Medicine, 1963-70; chief div. rehab. medicine Montefiore Hosp., 1961-70; dir. vis. physician Met., Bird S. Coler hosps., 1952-61; prof., chmn. dept. phys. medicine and rehab. Calif. Coll. Medicine, U. Calif. at Irvine, 1970-82, prof., dir. program in geriatric medicine and gerontology, 1980-86; mem. adv. com. Acad. Geriatric Resource program, 1984-86, 95—. Expert med. com. Am. Rehab. Found., 1961-70; cons. Dept. Health, NYC, Long Beach VA Hosp., 1970—, Fairview State Devel. Ctr., 1976—; adv. coun. phys. medicine and rehab. for appeals com. Calif. Med. Assn., 1971-74, adv. com. U. Calif. Acad. Geriatric Resource Program, 1995—; NIH Internat. Fogarty fellow, hon. lectr., dept. geriat. medicine U. Birmingham, 1979-80; rev. panel musculoskeletal diseases NIH, 1996; rsch. prof. dept. phys. medicine & rehab. U. Calif., Irvine, 1986—, chair med. ethics com., 1986—; mem. Ctr. Health Policy Rsch. U. Calif., Davis, 1996—. Author: (book) Fundamentals of the Stem Cell Debate: The Sci., Religious, Ethical, and Polit. Issues Monroe, K. R., Miller, R. B. and Tobis, J., U. Calif. Press, 2008; mem. editorial bd.: Heart and Lung, 1973-76, Geriatrics, 1975-80, Archives of Phys. Medicine and Rehab, 1958-73. Named Physician of the Year, 1957; recipient Distinguished Alumnus award Chgo. Med. Sch., 1972, Acad. award Nat. Inst. on Aging, 1981-86; named hon. faculty mem. Calif. Zeta chpt. Alpha Omega Alpha, 1981; Leavitt Meml. lectureship Baylor Coll. Medicine, 1983, Griffith Meml. lectureship Am. Geriatric Soc., 1984; Australian Coll. Rehabilitation Medicine, 1984; Jerome S. Tobis Ann. Conf. on Geriatric Medicine established in his name, U. Calif. at Irvine, 1986. Fellow ACP, Am. Coll. Cardiology, Am. Congress Rehab. Medicine (hon.); mem. AMA (mem. residency rev. com. Coun. Med. Edn. 1973), AAAS, Am. Acad. Cerebral Palsy, Am. Acad. Phys. Medicine and Rehab. (Disting. Clinician award 1993), Am. Congress Rehab. Medicine (pres. 1962), Calif. Coun. Gerontology and Geriatrics (bd. dirs. 1980-86, pres. 1985), N.Y. Acad. Medicine, N.Y. Acad. Sci., Orange County Med. Soc., Assn. U. Calif. Irvine (chair emeritae/i 1996-97). Home: 1115 Goldenrod Ave Corona Del Mar CA 92625-1508 Office Phone: 714-456-5626. Personal E-mail: jstobis@uci.edu.

TOBISMAN, STUART PAUL, lawyer; b. Detroit, June 5, 1942; s. Nathan and Beverly (Porvin) T.; m. Karen Sue Tobisman, Aug. 8, 1965; children: Cynthia Elaine, Neal Jay. BA, UCLA, 1966; JD, U. Calif., Berkeley, 1969. Bar: Calif. 1969. Assoc. O'Melveny & Myers, LA, 1969-77, ptnr., 1977—2006, Loeb & Loeb LLP, LA, 2006—. Contbr. articles to profl. jours. Trustee L.A. County Bar Assn., 1983-84. With USN, 1961-63. Fellow Am. Coll. Trust and Estate Counsel; mem. Phi Beta Kappa, Order of Coif. Office: Loeb & Loeb LLP 10100 Santa Monica Blvd Los Angeles CA 90067-4120

TOCHTROP, LOIS ANNE, state legislator; b. St. Louis, Jan. 31, 1942; d. Walter and Elizabeth Werner; m. Paul Tochtrop. Grad., St. Louis Hosp. Sch. Nursing, 1963; BS, Met. State Coll., Denver, 1988. V.p. Tri-County Health Dept.; dir. nursing services Park Forest Care Ctr., 1999—; mem. Dist. 34 Colo. House of Reps., Denver, 1999—2004; mem. Dist. 24 Colo. State Senate, Denver, 2004—, asst. majority leader. Mem. Eagles, Abate Colo. Democrat. Office: Colo State Capitol 200 E Colfax Denver CO 80203 Office Phone: 303-866-4863. Business E-Mail: lois.tochtrop.senate@state.co.us.*

TODARO, GEORGE JOSEPH, pathologist, researcher; b. NYC, July 1, 1937; s. George J. and Antoinette (Piccinni) Todaro; m. Jane Lehv, Aug. 12, 1962; children: Wendy C., Thomas M., Anthony A. BS, Swarthmore Coll., 1958; MD, NYU, 1963. Intern NYU Sch. Medicine, NYC, 1963—64, fellow in pathology, 1964—65, asst. prof. pathology, 1965—67; staff assoc. Viral Carcinogenesis br. Nat. Cancer Inst., Bethesda, Md., 1967—70, head molecular biology sect., 1969—70; chief Viral Carcinogenesis br. Nat. Cancer Inst. (Lab. Viral Carcinogenesis), 1970—83; sci. dir., pres. Oncogen, Seattle, 1987—90; sr. v.p. exploratory biomed. rsch. Bristol-Myers Squibb Pharm. Rsch. Inst., 1990; pres., CEO Cytokine Networks, Inc., Seattle, 1998—; now prof. pathobiology U. Wash., Seattle. Adj. prof. pathology U. Wash., Seattle, 1983—, past chmn. dept. pathobiology; sr. v.p., sci. dir. Pathogenesis Corp., Seattle, 1992—95; mem. Fred Hutchinson Cancer Rsch. Ctr., Seattle, 1991—93. Editor: Cancer Rsch., 1973—86, Archives of Virology, 1976—, Jour. Biol. Chemistry, 1979; contbr. articles to profl. jours. Med. officer USPHS, 1967—69. Recipient Borden Undergrad. Rsch. award, 1963, Career Devel. award, USPHS, 1967, HEW Superior Svc. award, 1971, Gustav Stern award for virology, 1972, Parke-Davis award in exptl. pathology, 1975; named Walter Hubert lectr., Brit. Cancer Soc., 1977. Mem.: Am. Soc. Clin. Investigation, Am. Soc. hemists, Soc. Exptl. Biology and Medicine, Am. Assn. Cancer Rsch., Am. Soc. Microbiology, NAS. Home: 1940 15th Ave E Seattle WA 98112-2829 Office Phone: 206-336-5572. E-mail: gtodaro@targetedgrowth.com.

TODD, BEVERLY, actress; b. Chgo., July 11, 1946; d. Virena T.; 1 child, Malik Smith. Ind. film, TV actress, 1971—. Actress: (films) They Call Me Mr. Tibbs, 1970, The Lost Man, 1970, Brother John, 1971, Moving, 1988, Clara's Heart, 1988, Lean On Me, 1989, Exquisite Tenderness, 1995, Crash, 2004, Ascension Day, 2007, The Bucket List, 2007; (TV film) Don't Look Back...The Story of Leroy Satchel Paige, 1982, A Different Affair, 1987, Class of '61, 1993, Ali: An American Hero, 2000; TV series regular Falcon Crest, Benson, Hill St. Blues, The Redd Foxx Show; other TV appearances include (episodes) Magnum P.I., Wiseguy, Equal Justice, (miniseries) Roots, 1977; co-producer (2-hour TV comedy spl.) A Laugh, A Tear. Office: Triad Artists Inc 1173 N Ardmore Ave Apt 2 Los Angeles CA 90029-1443

TODD, HAROLD WADE, retired medical association administrator, military officer; b. Chgo., Jan. 17, 1938; s. Harold Wade and Jeanne (Fayal) T.; m. Wendy Yvonne Kendrick, July 12, 1981; children by previous marriage: Hellen J. Wilson, Kenneth J., Stephen D., Joseph M., Michelle M. Adams, Mark A.; stepchildren: Jamie Y. White, James K. Mills, Timothy S. Emerson. BS, U.S. Air Force Acad., 1959; grad., Nat. War Coll., 1975. Commd. 2d lt. U.S. Air Force, 1959, advanced through grades to maj. gen., 1982; aide to comdr. (2d Air Force (SAC)), Barksdale AFB, La., 1970-71; exec. aide to comdr.-in-chief U.S. Air Forces Europe, Germany, 1971-74; spl. asst. chief of staff USAF, 1975-76; chief Concept Devel. Divsn., 1976-77; chief Readiness and NATO Staff Group, Hdqrs. USAF, 1977-78; exec. asst. to chmn. Joint Chiefs Staff Washington, 1978-80; comdr. 25th region N. Am. Aerospace Def. Command McChord AFB, Wash., 1980-82; chief staff 4th Allied Tactical Air Force Heidelberg, 1982-85; commandant Air War Coll., 1985-89; vice comdr. Air U., 1985-89, ret., 1989; ind. cons. Colorado Springs, Colo., 1989-95; pres., CEO, Nat. Stroke Assn., Englewood, Colo., 1995-00. Founder, pres. Bossier City (La.) chpt. Nat. Assn. for Children with Learning Disabilities, 1970-71. Decorated Def. DSM, Air Force DSM (2), Legion of Merit (2), DFC, Air medal (8), Air Force Commendation medal. Mem. Air Force Assn., USAF Acad. Assn. Grads., Nat. War Coll. Alumni Assn. Home: 1250 Big Valley Dr Colorado Springs CO 80919-1015

TODD, HARRY WILLIAMS, aircraft propulsion system company executive; b. Oak Park, Ill., 1922; BSME, U. So. Calif., 1947, BSIE, 1948, MBA, 1950. With Rockwell Internat., Pitts., 1947-76, former v.p. ops.; pres., chmn., chief exec. officer, bd. dirs. The L.E. Myers Co., Pitts., 1976-80; with Rohr Industries, Inc., Chula Vista, Calif., 1980-90, chief operating officer, 1980-82, pres., chief exec. officer, chmn., 1982-90, retired, 1990; mng. ptnr. Carlise Enterprises, 1990-97, mng. dir., 1990, limited ptnr., 2005—. Bd. dirs. Rohr Industries, Pacific Scientific, Helmerich & Payne, Garrett Aviation Svcs. Trustee Scripps Clinic and Rsch. Found. With U.S. Army, 1944-46. Office: Carlisle Enterprises Llc 4330 La Jolla Village Dr Ste 270 San Diego CA 92122-6229

TODD, KATHLEEN GAIL, physician; b. Portland, Oreg., Aug. 31, 1951; d. Horace Edward and Lois Marie (Messing) T.; m. Andrew Richard Embick, March 31, 1980; children: Elizabeth Todd Embick, Margaret Todd Embick. BA, Pomona Coll., 1972; MD, Washington U., St. Louis, 1976. Diplomate Am. Bd. Family Practice. Resident U. Wash. Affiliated Hosps., Seattle, 1976-79; pvt. practice Valdez (Alaska) Med. Clinic, 1980—; chief of staff Valdez Community Hosp., 1986—95. Mem. AMA, AAFP, Am. Acad. Family Practice, Alaska State Med. Assn. (counselor-at-large 1986-87). Democrat. Episcopalian. Avocations: skiing, kayaking, camping, music. Office: Valdez Med Clinic PO Box 1829 Valdez AK 99686-1829

TODD, NANCY JANANN, state legislator; b. Lawrence, Kans., Oct. 28, 1948; m. Terry Todd; 2 children. BEd, U. Kans., 1970; M in Reading, U. No. Colo., 1990. Tchr. Cherry Creek Sch. Dist. #5, 1970—73, 1983—2004; mem. Dist. 41 Colo. House of Reps., Denver, 2004—. Literacy chmn. Nat. Bd. Am. Mothers, Inc.; mem. Greenwood Cmty. Ch.; bd. mem. Colo. HS Activities Assn., Ridge View Acad., Fitzsimmons Veterans Home, Mile High Lung Assn. Mem.: PEO, Am. Assn. Univ. Women, Aurora C. of C., Aurora Rotary Club. Democrat. Office: Colo State Capitol 200 E Colfax Denver CO 80203 Office Phone: 303-866-2919. Business E-Mail: nancy.todd.house@state.co.us.*

TOKUDA, JILL N., state legislator; BA in Internat. Affairs, George Wash. U. Exec. aide Office of Lt. Gov. Mazie Hirono, Honolulu, 1996—2002; pres., founder Charitable Ventures, Inc., Honolulu, 2002; dir. cmty. rels. and govtl. affairs Reynolds Recycling, Wahiawa, Hawaii, 2002—06; mem. Dist. 24 Hawaii State Senate, Honolulu, 2006—. Devel. dir. Nat. Kidney Found. Hawaii; interim dir. Dem. Party Hawaii, Honolulu; founder Charitable Ventures, Inc., Honolulu. Democrat. Office: Hawaii State Senate 415 S Beretania St Rm 218 Honolulu HI 96813 Office Phone: 808-587-7215. Office Fax: 808-587-7220.

TOLBERT, MARGARET A., geochemistry educator; AB in Chemistry, with honors, Grinnell Coll., 1979; MS in Chemistry, U. Calif., Berkeley, 1985; PhD in Chemistry, Calif. Inst. Tech., 1986. Postdoctoral fellow Stanford Rsch. Inst., 1986—87; rsch. asst. U. Calif., Berkeley, 1979—83, Calif. Inst. Tech., 1983—86; staff scientist, Chemistry Lab. SRI Internat., 1986—91, leader Atmospheric Chemistry Group, 1990—91; assoc. prof. Dept. Chemistry and Biochemistry U. Colo., 1991—98, prof., 1998—. Author: Stratispheric Ozone Depletion, 2000. Recipient James B. Macelwane Young Investigator medal Am. Geophys. Union, 1993. Fellow: Am. Geophysical Union (James B. Macelwane Young Investigator medal 1993); mem.: NAS. Office: U Colo CIRES 166 Campus Box 216 Boulder CO 80309-0216 Office Phone: 303-492-3179. Fax: 303-492-1149. Business E-Mail: tolbert@colorado.edu.

TOLIVER, LEE, mechanical engineer; b. Wildhorse, Okla., Oct. 3, 1921; s. Clinton Leslie and Mary (O'Neall) T.; m. Barbara Anne O'Reilly, Jan. 24, 1942 (dec. Jan. 1999); children: Margaret Anne, Michael Edward. BSME, U. Okla., 1942. Engr. Douglas Aircraft Co., Santa Monica, Calif., 1942, Oklahoma City, 1942-44, Los Alamos Sci. Lab., N.Mex., 1946; instr. mech. engring. Ohio State U., Columbus, 1946-47; engr. Sandia Nat. Labs., Albuquerque, 1947-82; instr. computer sci. and math. U. N.Mex., Valencia County, 1982-84; number theory researcher Belen, N.Mex., 1982—. Author: Relations Between Prime and Relatively Prime Integers, 1998, Prime Number Problems: Solved, 2006. With Manhattan Project (Atomic Bomb) U.S. Army, 1944-46. Home: 206 Howell St Belen NM 87002-6225

TOLLE, ECKHART, writer; b. Germany, Feb. 6, 1948; BA, U. London. Rschr. Cambridge U.; counselor, spiritual tchr., London. Author: (books) The Power of Now: A Guide to Spiritual Enlightenment, 1999, Practicing the Power of Now: Essential Teachings, Meditations, and Exercises from The Power of Now, 2001, Stillness Speaks: Whispers of Now, 2003, A New Earth: Awakening to Your Life's Purpose, 2005 (Publishers Weekly bestseller). Achievements include having books translated into 32 languages. Mailing: Eckhart Tolle PO Box 93664 Nelson Park RPO Vancouver BC V6E 4L7 Canada Personal E-mail: DearEckhart@eckharttolle.com.

TOLLENAERE, LAWRENCE ROBERT, retired industrial products company executive; b. Berwyn, Ill., Nov. 19, 1922; s. Cyrille and Modesta (Van Damme) T.; m. Mary Elizabeth Hansen, Aug. 14, 1948; children: Elizabeth, Homer, Stephanie, Caswell, Mary Jennifer. BS in Engring., Iowa State U., 1944, MS in Engring., 1949; MBA, U. So. Calif., 1969; LLD (hon.), Claremont Grad. Sch., 1977. Specification engr. Aluminum Co. Am., Vernon, Calif., 1946-47; asst. prof. indsl. engring. Iowa State U., Ames, 1947-50; sales rep. Am. Pipe and Constrn. Co. (now AMERON), South Gate, Calif., 1950-53, spl. rep. S.Am., 1952-54, 2nd v.p., mgr. Columbian divsn. Bogota, S.Am., 1955-57, divsn. v.p., mgr. Calif., 1957-63, v.p. concrete pipe ops. Monterey Park, Calif., 1963-65, pres. corp. hdqrs., 1965-67; pres., CEO Ameron Inc., Monterey Park, Calif., 1967-89, CEO, pres. Pasadena, 1989-93, chmn. bd. dirs., 1989-94, ret., 1994. Trustee The Huntington Library, Art Gallery and Bot. Gardens; emeritus mem. bd. fellows Claremont U. Ctr.; bd. gov.'s Iowa State U. Found. Mem. Calif. C. of C. (bd. dirs. 1977-92), Calif. Club (past pres.), Jonathan Club, Bohemian Club, San Francisco Club, Beavers Club (past pres., hon. dir.), Alpha Tau Omega. Republican. Avocations: fishing, hunting, horseback riding, stamp collecting/philately. Home: 9493 Sandpiper Ln West Palm Beach FL 33411-6315

TOLMAN, BRETT L., prosecutor; b. Provo, UT; BA, Brigham Young U., 1994, JD, 1998. Asst. US atty. Dist. Utah US Dept. Justice, Salt Lake City, 2000—03, US atty., 2006—; chief counsel crime and terrorism Senate Judiciary Com., Salt Lake City, 2003—05. Office: US Attys Office 185 S State St Ste 300 Salt Lake City UT 84111 Office Phone: 801-524-5682. Office Fax: 801-524-6924.

TOLO, VERNON THORPE, orthopedist, educator; b. Onawa, Iowa; MD, Johns Hopkins U., 1968. Diplomate Am. Bd. Orthopaedic Surgery. Intern Johns Hopkins Hosp., Balt., 1969—70, resident orthop. surgery, 1972—75; fellow pediat. orthop. Hosp. Sick Children, Toronto, Canada, 1975—76; asst. prof. Johns Hopkins U. Sch. Medicine, Balt., 1976—82, assoc. prof., 1982—87; prof. orthop. surgery U. So. Calif., LA, 1987—; and head, divsn. orthop surgery Children's Hosp., LA. Attending physician Johns Hopkins Hosp., Balt., 1976—87, Children's Hosp., LA, 1987—. Mem.: Calif. Orthop. Assn., Scoliosis Rsch. Soc. (past pres.), Pediat. Orthopedics Soc. N. Am. (past pres., bd. dir. 1989—97), Am. Acad. Pediatricians, Am. Orthop. Assn., Am. Acad. Orthop. Surgeons (1st v.p. 2001—02, pres. 2002—03). Office: Children's Hosp MS 69 4650 W Sunset Blvd Los Angeles CA 90027-6062 Office Phone: 323-442-5860. Business E-Mail: vtolo@chla.usc.edu.

TOLSTEDT, CARRIE L., bank executive; BS in Bus. Adminstrn., U. Nebr.; degree in Banking, U. Wash. From credit tng. program to corp. banking officer United Bank Denver, corp. banking officer; from v.p. corp. banking to sr. v.p. downtown Omaha (Nebr.) retail banking Norwest Bank Nebr., Omaha, 1986—95; sr. v.p. corp. retail FirstMerit Corp., Akron, Ohio, 1995—96, pres., CEO Citizens Nat. Bank and Peoples Nat. Bank, 1996—98, exec. v.p., 1996—98; with Norwest Corp., 1998; regional pres. Ctrl. Calif. Wells Fargo & Co., San Francisco, 1998—2001, exec. v.p. regional banking, 2001—. Bd. dirs. The Cmty. Coll. Found. Named one of 25 Most Powerful Women in

Banking, US Banker, 2006, 2007. Mem.: Consumer Bankers Assn. (bd. dirs.), U. Nebr. Alumni Assn. (bd. dirs.), Calif. C. of C. (bd. dirs.). Office: Wells Fargo & Co 420 Montgomery St San Francisco CA 94163

TOM, LAWRENCE, technology executive; b. LA, Jan. 21, 1950; BS, Harvey Mudd Coll., 1972; JD, Western State U., San Diego, 1978; spl. diploma, U. Calif., San Diego, 1991. Design engr. Rockwell Internat., LA, 1972-73, Goodrich Corp. (formerly Rohr, Inc.), Chula Vista, Calif., 1973-76, sr. design engr., 1980, computer graphics engring. specialist, 1980-83, chief engring. svcs., 1989-91, chief engring. quality, 1991-93, project mgr., 1993-98, info. tech. specialist, 1998—2002. Sr. engr. Rohr Marine, Inc., Chula Vista, 1977-79; chief exec. officer Computer Aided Tech. Svcs., San Diego, 1983-87; software cons. Small Systems Software, San Diego, 1984-85; computer graphics engring. specialist TOM & ROMAN, San Diego, 1986-88; dir. Computervision Users Group, 1986-88, vice chmn. 1988-91, pres., 1991-93, exec. chmn., 1992-94; bd. dirs. Exec. Program for Scientists and Engrs.-Alumni Assn. U. Calif., San Diego, 1991—; CFO Global Peregrine Users Group, 2001-03; pres. Art to Art, San Diego, 1994-99; pres. SGL Computer Profls., San Diego, 1999—; ptnr. San Diego Tech. Movers, 2007—; cons. in field. George H. Mayr Found. scholar, 1971, Bates Found. Aero. Edn. scholar, 1970-72. Mem. Nat. Mgmt. Assn. (chpt. v.p.), Aircraft Owners and Pilots Assn., Infiniti Club. Office: 7770 Regents Rd Ste 113-190 San Diego CA 92122-1967 Home Phone: 858-546-9090; Office Phone: 619-985-9850. Business E-Mail: larry.tom@sglpro.com.

TOMAN, MARY ANN, federal official; b. Pasadena, Calif., Mar. 31, 1954; d. John James and Mary Ann Zajec T.; m. Milton Allen Miller, Sept. 10, 1988; 1 child, Mary Ann III. BA with honors, Stanford U., Calif., 1976; MBA, Harvard U., Cambridge, Mass., 1981. Mgmt. cons. Bain and Co., Boston, 1976—77; mgr. brand Procter & Gamble Co., Cin., 1977—79; summer assoc. E.F. Hutton, NYC, 1980; head corp. planning Burton Group, PLC, London, 1981—84; pres., founder Glenclair Ltd., London, 1984—86; pres. London Cons. Group, London, Beverly Hills, Calif., 1987—88; mem. U.S. Presdl. Transition Team, Bus. and Fin., 1988—89; dep. asst. sec. commerce, automotive affairs, consumer goods U.S. Dept. Commerce, Washington, 1989—93; commr., chmn. L.A. Indsl. Devel. Authority, 1993—95; dep. treas. State of Calif., Sacramento, 1995—99. Bd. dirs. US Coun. of Devel. Fin. Agencies, 1994-97. Founder, chair Stanford U. Fundraising, London, 1983-88; chair Reps. Abroad Absentee Voter Registration, London, 1983-88; bd. dirs. Harvard Bus. Sch. Assn., London, 1984-87; vol. Bush-Quayle Campaign, 1988; trustee Bath U., Eng., 1988—; apptd. by Gov. Wilson to State of Calif. Econ. Devel. Adv. Coun., 1994-97, Jobs Tng. Coordinating Coun., 1998-2000; first vice chmn. Rep. Party L.A. County, 1996-99, chmn., 1999—; mem. exec. bd. Coun. Calif. County Chairmen, 1999—; mem. US Presdl. Transition Team, 2000-2001; Rep. candidate for Calif. State Treas., 2002. Named Calif. Mother of Yr., 1997. Mem. Stanford Club U.K. (pres. 1983-88), Harvard Club NY, Harvard Club Washington, Harvard Club Boston, Nat. Assn. of Urban Rep. County Chmn. Roman Catholic. Home: 604 N Elm Dr Beverly Hills CA 90210-3421 Office: PO Box 71483 Los Angeles CA 90071-0483 Home Phone: 310-550-5799; Office Phone: 310-274-4822. Business E-Mail: tomanmail@aol.com.

TOMASH, ERWIN, retired computer company executive; b. St. Paul, Nov. 17, 1921; s. Noah and Milka (Ehrlich) T.; m. Adelle Ruben, July 31, 1943; children: Judith Sarada Tomash Diffenbaugh, Barbara Ann Tomash Bussa. BS, U. Minn., Minneapolis, 1943; MS, U. Md., College Park, 1950. Instr. elec. engring. U. Minn., 1946; assoc. dir. computer devel. Univac div. Remington Rand Corp., St. Paul, 1947-51; dir. West Coast ops. Univac div. Sperry Rand Corp., LA, 1953-55; pres. Telemeter Magnetics, Inc., LA, 1956-60; v.p. Ampex Corp., LA, 1961; founder, pres. Dataproducts Corp., LA, 1962-71, chmn. bd., 1971-80, chmn. exec. com., 1980-89; chmn. bd., dir. Newport Corp., Irvine, Calif., 1982-94. Founder, trustee, dir. Charles Babbage Found., U. Minn.; dir. and nat. gov. Coro Found., L.A. Served to capt. Signal Corps AUS, 1943-46. Decorated Bronze Star; recipient Outstanding Grad. award U. Minn., 1983. Mem. IEEE (sr., computer entrepreneur award 1988), Am. Soc. for Technion, History of Sci. Soc., Soc. for History of Tech., Assn. Internationale du Bibliophile. Home: 3918 Mainsail Pl Soquel CA 95073

TOMASI, DONALD CHARLES, architect; b. Sacramento, Oct. 24, 1956; s. Thomas M. and Anita (Migliavacca) T.; m. Loretta Elaine Goveia, Feb. 1, 1986; children: Jeffrey, Genna, Michael. AB in Architecture with honors, U. Calif., Berkeley, 1979; MArch, U. Wash., 1982. Registered architect, Calif. Project mgr. Robert Wells and Assocs., Seattle, 1982-84, Milbrandt Architects, Seattle, 1984, T.M. Tomasi Architects, Santa Rosa, Calif., 1984-86; prin. Tomasi Architects, Santa Rosa, 1986-93, sr. prin.; prin. TLCD Architecture, Santa Rosa, 1993—. Grad. Leadership Santa Rosa, 1992; mem. design rev. com. Sonoma County, 1988-90; chmn. Santa Rosa Design Rev. Bd., 1990-97. Recipient Honor award Coalition for Adequate Sch. Housing, 1991, 93, 96, 99, 2000, 02, 04, Merit award, 1991. Mem. AIA (chpt. bd. dirs. 1990-91, 98, v.p. 1999, pres. 2000, Calif. Coun. bd. dirs. 2002-03, Merit award 1986). Avocations: skiing, wine, travel. Office Phone: 707-525-5600. E-mail: don.tomasi@tlcd.com.

TOMASSON, HELGI, dancer, choreographer, company executive; b. Reykjavik, Iceland, 1942; m. Marlene Rizzo; children: Kristinn, Erik. Student, Sigridur Arman, Erik Bidsted, Vera Volkova, Sch. Am. Ballet, Tivoli Pantomime Theatre, Copenhagen. With Joffrey Ballet, 1961-64; prin. dancer Harkness Ballet, 1964-70, NYC Ballet, 1970-85; artistic dir. San Francisco Ballet, 1985—, also dir. Dancer debut Tivoli Pantomime Theatre, 1958, A Season of Hell, 1967, Stages and Reflections, 1968, La Favorita, 1969, The Goldberg Variations, 1971, Symphony in Three Movements, 1972, Coppelia, 1974, Dybbuk Variations, 1974, Chansons Madecasses, 1975, Introduction and Allegro, 1975, Allegro, 1975, Union Jack, 1976, Vienna Waltzes, 1977, choreographer Theme and Variations, Polonaise, Op. 65, 1982, Ballet d'Isoline, 1983, Menuetto, N.Y.C. Ballet, 1984, Beads of Memory, 1985, Swan Lake, 1988, Handel-a Celebration, 1989, Sleeping Beauty, 1990, Romeo and Juliet, 1994, Prism, 2000, Bartok Divertimento, 2002, Chi-Lin, 2002, Concerto Grosso, 2003, 7 for Eight, 2003. Decorated Knight Order of Falcon Iceland, Comdr. Order of Falcon; recipient Silver medal, Internat. Moscow Ballet Competition, 1969, Golden Plate award, Am. Acad. Achievement, 1992, Dance Mag. award, 1992, Disting. Citizen, Commonwealth Club Calif., 1991. Office: San Francisco Ballet 455 Franklin St San Francisco CA 94102-4438

TOMBRELLO, THOMAS ANTHONY, JR., physics professor; b. Austin, Tex., Sept. 20, 1936; s. Thomas Anthony and Jeanette Lilian (Marcuse) T.; m. Esther Ann Hall, May 30, 1957 (div. Jan. 1976); children: Christopher Thomas, Susan Elaine, Karen Elizabeth; m. Stephanie Carhart Merton, Jan. 15, 1977; 1 stepchild, Kerstin Arusha (dec.). BA in Physics, Rice U., Houston, 1958, MA, 1960; PhD, Rice U., 1961; PhD (hon.), Uppsala U., Sweden, 1997. Rsch. fellow in physics Calif. Inst. Tech., Pasadena, 1961-62, 64-65, asst. prof. physics, 1965-67, assoc. prof., 1967-71, prof., 1971—, William R. Kenan Jr. prof., 1997—, tech. assessment officer, 1996—, chair divsn. physics, math. and astronomy, 1998—2008; asst. prof. Yale U., New Haven, 1963. Cons. in field; disting. vis. prof. U. Calif.-Davis, 1984; v.p., dir. rsch. Schlumberger-Doll Rsch., Ridgefield, Conn., 1987-89; mem. US V.P.'s Space Policy Adv. Bd., 1992; mem. sci. adv. bd. Ctr. of Nanoscale Sci. and Tech., Rice U., 1995-2004; bd. dirs. Schlumberger Tech. Corp., Schlumberger Found., 1987-89, Thirty Meter Telescope, 2004-08, Combined Array Rsch. Millimeter Astronomy, 2003-08, Cornell-Caltech-Atacama Telescope, 2007-08, Am. Friends Uppsala U., 2008-. Assoc. editor Nuc. Physics, 1971-91, Applications Nuc. Physics, 1980-89, Radiation Effects, 1985-88, Nuc. Instruments and Methods B, 1993-96; mem. editl. bd. Blue Origin, 2003-07, Applied Minds, 2004—, Arrowhead Rsch., 2005—, Form Factor, 2005—, Trilience Rsch., 2005— Recipient Alexander von Humboldt award von Humboldt Stiftung, U. Frankfurt, Germany, 1984-85; named Disting. Alumnus, Rice U., 1998; NSF fellow Calif. Inst. Tech., 1961-62, A.P. Sloan fellow, 1971-73. Fellow Am. Phys. Soc.; Phi Beta Kappa, Sigma Xi, Delta Phi Alpha. Democrat. Avocations: reading, jogging. Office: Calif Inst Tech Dept Physics Mail Code 200 36 Pasadena CA 91125-0001 Office Phone: 626-395-4581. Business E-Mail: tat@caltech.edu.

TOMEI, CAROLYN, state legislator; m to Gary; children: seventeen children, stepchildren & foster children, three grandchildren. Oregon State Representative, District 25, formerly, member, Streams Restoration & Species Recovery, Govt Efficiency & Health & Public Advocacy Committees, currently; mayor, Milwaukee, Wisconsin, 1999-2001, member, City Coun, 96-99, Planning Coun, formerly; Oregon State Representative, District 41, 2003-.Child development specialist, Portland Public Schs, formerly, consultant, Multnomah Co Mental Health & Children's Serv Div, formerly; teacher, Portland Community Col, formerly. Democrat. Office: 900 Court St NE H-279 Salem OR 97301 Address: 11907 SE 19th Ave Portland OR 97222 Home Phone: 503-653-5180; Office Phone: 503-986-1441. E-mail: Tomei.rep@state.or.us.

TOMEI, MARISA, actress; b. Bklyn., Dec. 4, 1964; d. Gary and Patricia Tomei. Attended, Boston U. TV appearances include (series) As the World Turns, 1983-88, A Different World, 1987, Only Love, 1998, My Own Country, 1998, Since You've Been Gone, 1998, (films) The Flamingo Kid, 1984, Playing for Keeps, 1986, Parker Kane, 1990, Oscar, 1991, Zandalee, 1991, My Cousin Vinny, 1992 (Acad. award best supporting actress 1993), Chaplin, 1992, Untamed Heart, 1993, Equinox, 1993, The Paper, 1994, Only You, 1994, The Perez Family, 1994, Four Rooms, 1995, Unhook the Stars, 1996, What Women Want, 2000, Dirk and Betty, 2000, Driven, 2000, King of the Jungle, 2000, In the Bedroom, 2001 (ShoWest award best supporting actress, 2002), Someone Like You, 2001, The Guru, 2002, The Wild Thornberrys Movie (voice), 2002, Anger Management, 2003, Loverboy, 2004, Alfie, 2004, Marilyn Hotchkiss Ballroom Dancing and Charm School, 2005, Factotum, 2005, Danika, 2006, Wild Hogs, 2007, Before the Devil Knows You're Dead, 2007, Grace Is Gone, 2007, War, Inc., 2008, The Wrestler, 2008; theatre appearances include Slavs! Thinking About the Longstanding Problems of Virtue and Happiness, 1994, Welcome to Sarajevo, 1997, This Is How It Goes, 2005; Broadway plays include Wait Until Dark, 1998, Salome, 2003, Top Girls, 2008. Office: c/o Bella Vita Prodns 8033 W Sunset Blvd Ste 891 West Hollywood CA 90046

TOMICH, LILLIAN, lawyer; b. LA; d. Peter S. and Yovanka P. (Ivanovic) T. AA, Pasadena City Coll., 1954; BA in Polit. Sci., UCLA, 1956, cert. secondary tchg., 1957, MA, 1958; JD, U. So. Calif., 1961. Bar: Calif., US Ct. Appeals (9th Cir.) 1978, 2002, US Ct. Appeals (4th Appellate Dist.), 2007. Sole practice, 1961-66; house counsel Mfrs. Bank, LA, 1966; assoc. Hurley, Shaw & Tomich, San Marino, Calif., 1968-76, Driscoll & Tomich, San Marino, Calif., 1976—2005, Conway & Tomich, San Marino, Calif., 2005—. Dir. Continental Culture Specialists Inc., Glendale, Calif. Trustee St. Sava Serbian Orthodox Ch., San Gabriel, Calif. Recipient Episcopal Gramata award Serbian Orthodox Met. of Midwestern Am., 1993, Episcopal Gramata award Serbian Orthodox Bishop of Western Am., 1996, 2002; Charles Fletcher Scott fellow, 1957; U. So. Calif. Law Sch. scholar, 1958. Mem.: ABA, ATLA, Women Lawyers Assn., Los Angeles County Bar Assn., Calif. Bar Assn., Order Mast and Dagger, San Marino C. of C., UCLA Alumni Assn., Town Hall and World Affairs Coun., Pi Kappa Delta, Alpha Gamma Sigma, Iota Tau Tau. Office: 2460 Huntington Dr San Marino CA 91108-2643 Office Phone: 626-287-1248. E-mail: lilliantomich@yahoo.com.

TOMJACK, THOMAS J., lumber company executive; b. Aug. 25, 1942; BBA, U. Notre Dame, 1964. With Peat Marwick Mitchell & Co., 1964-71, Potlatch Corp., 1971-85; exec. v.p. sales North Pacific Lumber Co., Portland, Oreg., 1971-85, exec. v.p., COO, 1987, pres., 1988—, chmn., CEO, 1989—. Bd. dir. Capital Pacific Bank. Mem. bd. regents Univ. Portland.

TOMLIN, LILY, actress; b. Detroit, Sept. 1, 1939; Student, Wayne State U.; studied mime with Paul Curtis, studied acting with Peggy Feury. Co-founder Lily Tomlin Jane Wagner Cultural Arts Ctr., LA. Appearances in concerts and colls. throughout U.S.; TV appearances include The Music Scene, 1969-70, Laugh In, 1970-73, Lily Tomlin, CBS Spls., 1973, 81, 82; 2 ABC Spls., 1974, 75, Edith Ann Animated Specials, ABC, 1994, The Magic School Bus, 1994 (voice), Murphy Brown, 1996-98, The West Wing, 2002-06, 12 Miles of Bad Road, 2008, Desperate Housewives, 2008-09; motion picture debut in Nashville, 1975 (N.Y. Film Critics award); also appeared in The Late Show, 1977, Moment by Moment, 1978, The Incredible Shrinking Woman, 1981, Nine to Five, 1980, All of Me, 1984, Big Business, 1987, Shadows and Fog, 1992, The Player, 1992, Short Cuts, 1993, The Beverly Hillbillies, 1993, And the Band Played On, HBO, 1993 (Best Supporting Actress Emmy nominee - Special, 1994, Emmy nominations guest appearance Homicide, 1996), Getting Away with Murder, 1995, The Celluloid Closet, 1995, Blue in the Face, 1995, Flirting With Disaster, 1996, Reno Finds Her Mom, 1997, Get Bruce, 1999, Krippendorf's Tribe, 1998, Tea with Mussolini, 1999, Picking Up the Pieces, 2000, The Kid, 2000, Orange County, 2002, I Heart Huckabees, 2004, A Prairie Home Companion, 2006, (voice) The Ant Bully, 2006, The Walker, 2007, The Pink Panther 2, 2009; exec. prodr. TV series Citizen Reno, 2001; one-woman Broadway show Appearing Nitely, 1977 (Spl. Tony award), The Search for Signs of Intelligent Life in the Universe, 1985 (Drama Desk award, Outer Critics Circle award, Tony award 1986, Cable Ace award); recs. include This is a Recording, And That's The Truth, Modern Scream, On Stage. Recipient Grammy award 1971, 5 Emmy awards for CBS Spl. 1973, 81, Emmy award for ABC Spl. 1975, Emmy award Magic Sch. Bus, 1995, Peabody award Celluloid Closet, 1997, Peabody Edith Ann's Christmas, 1997, Mark Twain Prize for Am. Humor, Kennedy Center, 2003. Office: Lily Tomlin Jane Wagner Cultural Arts Ctr Village at Ed Gould Plz 1125 N McCadden Pl Los Angeles CA 90038-1212

TOMLINSON, LADAINIAN, professional football player; b. Rosebud, Tex., June 23, 1979; s. Oliver Tomlinson and Loreane Chappell; m. LaTorsha Tomlinson. BA in Gen. Studies, Tex. Christian U., Ft. Worth, 2001. Running back San Diego Chargers, 2001—. Founder Tomlinson Touching Lives Found., 2005—. Recipient NFL MVP award, AP, 2006, ESPY award, Male Athlete of Yr., ESPN, 2007, ESPY award, Best NFL Player, 2007, ESPY award, Record-breaking Performance, 2007, ESPY award, Like Nothing Else award, 2007, Bart Starr award, 2008; co-recipient Walter Payton Man of Yr. award, 2006; named First Team All-Pro, NFL, 2004, 2006—07, Player of Yr., NBC, 2006, NFL Offensive Player of Yr., AP, 2006, Sportsman of Yr., The Sporting News, 2006; named one of Most Influential People in the World of Sports, Bus. Week, 2007; named to Am. Football Conf. Pro Bowl Team, 2002, 2004—07. Achievements include leading the NFL in: rushing yards, 2003, rushing touchdowns, 2004, 2006, 2007, rushing yards per game, 2006, total touchows, 2006, points scored, 2006; becoming the first and only player in NFL history to rush for 1000 yards and receive 100 passes in a single season, 2003; reaching 100 career touchdowns faster than any other player in NFL history, 2006; setting the NFL single-season record for: most rushing touchdowns (28), 2006, total touchdowns (31), 2006, points scored (186), 2006; setting the NFL record for consecutive games with a rushing touchdown (18), consecutive multi-touchdown games (8). Office: c/o San Diego Chargers 4020 Murphy Canyon Rd San Diego CA 92123

TOMLINSON, WILLIAM M., lawyer; b. Paris, Sept. 2, 1948; BA, Princeton U., 1970; JD, U. Oreg., 1974. Bar: Oreg. 1974, Wash. 1986. Atty. Lindsay, Hart, Neil & Weigler, Portland, Oreg. Mem. ABA (mem. torts and ins. practice sect.), Oreg. State Bar, Oreg. Assn. Def. Counsel, Wash. State Bar Assn., Multnomah County Bar Assn. Office: Lindsay Hart Neil & Weigler 1300 SW 5th Ave Ste 3400 Portland OR 97201-5640

TOMLINSON-KEASEY, CAROL ANN, academic administrator; b. Washington, Oct. 15, 1942; d. Robert Bruce and Geraldine (Howe) Tomlinson; m. Charles Blake Keasey, June 13, 1964; children: Kai Linson, Amber Lynn. BS, Pa. State U., University Park, 1964; MS, Iowa State U., Ames, 1966; PhD, U. Calif., Berkeley, 1970. Lic. psychologist, Calif. Asst. prof. psychology Trenton (NJ) State Coll., 1969-70, Rutgers U., New Brunswick, NJ, 1970-72; prof. U. Nebr., Lincoln, 1972-77, U. Calif., Riverside, 1977-92, acting dean Coll. Humanities and Social Scis., 1986-88, chmn. dept. psychology, 1989-92, vice provost for acad. planning and pers. Davis, 1992-97, vice provost for acad. initiatives, 1997-99, chancellor, 1996—2006. Author: Child's Eye View, 1980, Child Development, 1985, numerous chpts. to books; contbr. articles to profl. jours. Recipient Disting. Tchr. award U. Calif., 1986. Mem. APA, Soc. Rsch. in Child Devel., Riverside Aquatics Assn. (pres.). Office: PO Box 2039 Merced CA 95344 Home Phone: 404-321-7433. Personal E-mail: caroltk@yahoo.com.

TOMPKINS, EMIL, chiropractor; b. 1975; Degree in Chiropractic, Iowa State U.; grad., Palmer Coll. of Chiropractic. Owner, pres. Tompkin Family Chiropractic. Organized Hoops for Hope basketball camp; foster and adoptive parent Christian Family Care Agy. Mem. Marana Chamber of Commerce, Tucson Black Chamber of Commerce, Palmer Student Alumni Found.; organizer Marana Sch. Dist. Thanksgiving food drive, Marana Sch. Dist. Christmas toy drive, Picture Rocks Intermediate Sch. donation drive; mem. Marana Wellness Coun.; mem., sponsor Marana Healthy You Initiative. Recipient Humanitarian Svc. award, Palmer Coll. of Chiropractic; named one of 40 Under 40, Tucson Bus. Edge, 2006. Mem.: Am. Black Chiropractic Assn., Am. Chiropractic Assn., Internat. Chiropractic Assn., Vogt Leadership Soc. Office: Tompkins Family Chiropractic 7620 N Hartman Ste 124-2 Tucson AZ 85743 Office Phone: 520-572-2596.

TOMPKINS, RONALD K., retired surgeon, educator; b. Malta, Ohio, Oct. 14, 1934; s. Kenneth Steidley and Mildred Lillian (Loomis) T.; m. Suzanne Colbert, June 9, 1956; children: Gregory Alan, Teresa Susan, Geoffrey Stuart. BA, Ohio U., 1956; MD, Johns Hopkins U., 1960; MS, Ohio State U., 1968; DSc (hon.), U. Bordeaux, 1995. Diplomate Am. Bd. Surgery. Intern in surgery Ohio State U., 1960-61, resident in surgery, 1964-68, adminstrv. chief resident in surgery, 1968-69, NIH trainee in acad. surgery, instr. physiol. chemistry, 1966-69; asst. prof. surgery UCLA, 1969-73, assoc. prof., 1973-79, prof., 1979-2001, prof. emeritus, 2001—, chmn. basic surg. tng. program, 1970-79, asst. dean student affairs, 1979-82, chief divsn. gen. surgery, 1982-88, chief gastrointestinal surgery, 1986-97, assoc. dean, 1988-91, dir. surg. edn., 1996—2004; ret., 2004. Cons. VA Hosps. Editor-in-chief World Jour. Surgery, 1993-2004. With M.C. USAF, 1961-64. Recipient Disting Alumni award, Ohio U. Arts & Scis., 2001; grantee, NIH, 1968—70, John A. Hartford Found., 1970—79; fellow, Royal Soc. Medicine Eng., 1976—77. Fellow ACS (So. Calif. chpt. pres. 1987); mem. Am. Surg. Assn., Am. Gastroenterol. Assn., Am. Fedn. Clin. Rsch. Am. Inst. Nutrition, AMA, Assn. Acad. Surgery, Pacific Coast Surg. Assn. (recorder 1986-91, pres. 1995), Japan Surgical Soc. (hon.), Soc. Clin. Surgery, Soc. Surgery Alimentary Tract (sec. 1982-85, pres.-elect 1985, pres. 1986, chmn. bd. trustees 1987), Soc. Univ. Surgeons, Societe Internationale de Chirurgie (U.S. chpt. sec. 1990-94, pres. 1996-98), Internat. Biliary Assn. (pres. 1979-81), Internat. HepatoPancreato-Biliary Assn. (hon.), Bay Surg. Soc., LA Surg. Soc. (pres. 1981), Robert M. Zollinger/Ohio State U. Surg. Soc. (pres. 1988-90), Longmire Surg. Soc. (pres. 1997-99), Phi Beta Kappa, Sigma Xi, Alpha Omega Alpha, Delta Tau Delta, Soc. Surg. Alimonary Tract (Founders medal, 2008). Achievements include numerous research publications in gastrointestinal surgery and gastrointestinal metabolism and biochemistry. Home: 309 20th St Santa Monica CA 90402

TOMS, JUSTINE WILLIS, educational organization executive; b. Evanston, Ill., Oct. 16, 1942; d. Robert Jacques and Ruth (Herzfeld) W.; m. Donald Carroll Welch, Nov. 1962 (div. 1969); 1 child, Robert Gregory Welch; m. Michael Anthony Toms, Dec. 16, 1972. BS, Auburn U., 1967. Elem. sch. tchr. Sylacauga (Ala.) Sch. System, 1966-69; exec. dir. New Dimensions Radio, Ukiah, Calif., 1973—.

Seminar leader in field. Co-author: True Work: Doing What You Love and Loving What You Do, 1998; editor (quar. jour.) New Dimensions Jour., 1987—. Democrat. Buddhist. Avocations: horseback riding, drums.

TONELLO-STUART, ENRICA MARIA, political scientist, economist; b. Monza, Italy; d. Alessandro P. and Maddalena M. (Marangoni) Tonello; m. Albert E. Smith; m. Charles L. Stuart. BA in Internat. Affairs, Econs., U. Colo., 1961; MA, Claremont Grad. Sch., 1966, PhD, 1971. Sales mgr. Met. Life Ins. Co., 1974-79; pres., CEO, ETS R&D, Inc., Palos Verdes Peninsula, Calif., 1977—2004; ret. Pub., editor Tomorrow Outline Jour., 1963—, The Monitor, 1988; pub. World Regionalism-An Ecological Analysis, 1971, A Proposal for the Reorganization of the United Nations, 1966, The Persuasion Technocracy, Its Forms, Techniques and Potentials, 1966, The Role of the Multinationals in the Emerging Globalism, 1978; developed the theory of social ecology and econsociometry. Organizer 1st family assistance program Langley FB Tractical Air Command, 1956-58. Recipient vol. svc. award VA, 1956-58, ARC svc. award, 1950-58. Mem. Corp. Planners Assn. (treas. 1974-79), Investigative Reporters and Editors, World Future Soc. (pres. 1974-75), Soc. Environ. Journalists, Chinese Am. Assn. (life), Palos Verdes C. of C., L.A. Press Club (bd. dirs.), Zonta (chmn. internat. com. South Bay), Pi Sigma Alpha. Avocations: writing, collecting old books and maps, community service, travel, pediatric activist. Office Phone: 310-377-7608. Personal E-mail: stuarteeix@netcom.com, stuarte@cox.net.

TONEY, ANITA KAREN, printmaker; b. NYC; d. Anthony and Edna Greenfield Toney. BFA, Syracuse Univ.; MA, San Francisco State Univ. Instr. printmaking City Coll. San Francisco, 1979—. Exhibited in group shows at Nancy Dodds Gallery, Carmel, Calif., Le Celle Gallery, San Anselmo, Calif., Andrea Schwartz Gallery, San Francisco, Images Gallery, Briarcliff, NY, exhibitions include with father, Anthony Toney, Coll. of Marin, 2003. Mem.: Calif. Soc. Printmakers, NAD (academician 1995—). Office: Printmaking City Coll San Francisco 50 Phelan Ave San Francisco CA 94112 Office Phone: 415-239-3000.

TONG, SIU WING, computer programmer; b. Hong Kong, May 20, 1950; came to U.S., 1968; BA, U. Calif., Berkeley, 1972; PhD, Harvard U., 1979; MS, U. Lowell, 1984. Rsch. assoc. Brookhaven Nat. Lab., Upton, N.Y., 1979-83; software engr. Honeywell Info. Systems, Billerica, Mass., 1984-85; sr. programmer, analyst Hui Computer Cons., Berkeley, Calif., 1985-88; sr. v.p. devel., chief fin. officer Surgicenter Info. Systems, Inc., Orinda, Calif., 1989-94; sr. sys. specialist Info. Sys. Divsn. Contra Costa County Health Svcs., Martinez, Calif., 1995-97, info. tech. supr. Info. Sys. Divsn., 1997—. Vol. tchr. Boston Chinatown Saturday Adult Edn. Program of Tufts Med. Sch., 1977-79. Muscular Dystrophy Assn. fellow, 1980-82. Mem. AAAS, IEEE, Assn. Computing Machinery, N.Y. Acad. Scis. Home: 17 Beaconsfield Ct Orinda CA 94563-4203 Office: Contra Costa County Health Svcs 595 Center Ave Ste 210 Martinez CA 94553-4634 E-mail: swtong@hsd.cccounty.us.

TONN, ELVERNE MERYL, pediatric dentist, dental benefits consultant, forensic odontologist; b. Stockton, Calif., Dec. 10, 1929; s. Emanuel M. and Lorna Darlene (Bryant) T.; m. Ann G. Richardson, Oct. 28, 1951; children: James Edward, Susan Elaine (dec.). AA, La Sierra U., Riverside, Calif., 1949; DDS, U. So. Calif., 1955; BS, Excelsior Coll., 1984; grad., Citizens Police Acad., Manteca, 2003, San Joaquin County Citizens Sheriff's Acad. Cert. lifetime cmty. coll. instr., tchg. credential Calif., 1982; lic. dentist Calif., 1955, diplomate Am. Bd. Quality Assurance and Utilization Rev. Physicians, Am. Bd. Forensic Dentistry, Am. Bd. Spl. Care Dentistry, Am. Bd. for Cert. in Homeland Security, cert. dental cons., forensic cons. Am. Coll. Forensic Examiners, 2004, med. investigator Am. Coll. Forensic Examiners, 2004. Pediat. dentistry intern Childrens Hosp. LA, 1957—59; pediatric dentist, assoc. Walker Dental Group, Long Beach, Calif., 1957-59, Children's Dental Clinic, Sunnyvale, Calif., 1959-61; pediatric dentist in pvt. practice Mountain View, Calif., 1961-72; pediatric dentist, ptnr. Pediatric Dentistry Assocs., Los Altos, Calif., 1972-83; pediatric dentist, ptnr. Valley Oak Dental Group, Manteca, Calif., 1987—2003; from clin. instr. to assoc. prof. Sch. Dentistry, U. Pacific, San Francisco, 1964-84; assoc. prof. Sch. Dentistry, U. Calif., San Francisco, 1984-86. Pediat. dental cons. Delta Dental Plan, San Francisco, 1985—2002; chief dental staff El Camino Hosp., Mountain View, Calif., 1964—65, 1984—85; dental cons. Interplast program Stanford U. Sch. Medicine, 1973; cert. physician adv. Physicians' Review Network, Phoenix, 2004—; forensic dental cons. San Joaquin County Sheriff/Coroner, 2007—; appt. Weekly columnist Manteca Bull., 1987-92; producer 2 teaching videos, 1986; contbr. articles to profl. jours. Extern, dentist for disabled Long Island Jewish Med. Ctr., 1970. Capt. US Army, 1955—63. Recipient Dr. Willard Fleming Meritorious Svcs. award, Am. Coll. Dentists, 2006. Fellow Am. Coll. Dentists, Internat. Coll. Dentists, Am. Acad. Pediatric Dentistry, Royal Soc. Health, Acad. of Dentistry for Handicapped, Pierre Fauchard Acad., Acad. Dental Materials, Am. Soc. Dentistry for Children (mastership award 2001), Am. Acad. Forensic Scis., Am. Coll. Forensic Examiners; mem. ADA, Internat. Assn. Pediatric Dentistry, Internat. Assn. Dental Rsch., Am. Soc. Forensic Odontology, Fedn. Dentaire Internationale, Am. Assn. Dental Cons., Calif. Dental Assn., Calif. Soc. Dentistry for Children (pres. 1968), Calif. Soc. Pediatric Dentistry, NY Acad. Scis., Calif. Acad. Sci., Rotary Internat. (Paul Harris fellow 1990), Manteca Police Dept. (Badge 2003), Nat. Disaster Med. Svc., Disaster Mortuary Org. Response Team (DMORT region 9), Am. Coll. Med. Quality, Manteca Cert. Emergency Response Team, Calif. State Dental Identification Team, AMA (assoc.). Republican. Avocations: photography, travel, medieval history, anthropology. Home and Office: Tonn Forensic Cons Svcs 2420 Bellchase Dr Manteca CA 95336-5108 Personal E-mail: emtonn@comcast.net.

TONSETH, RALPH G., airport executive; Dir. aviation San Jose (Calif.) Airport, 1990—. Office: San Jose Airport 1732 N 1st St Ste 600 San Jose CA 95112-4544

TOOLE, KENNETH R., JR., Public Svc Commissioner, Montana; b. Missoula, Mont., June 18, 1955; m. Nancy Toole; 3 children. BA, U. Mont., 1981. Program dir. Rural Employment Opportunities; investigator Mont. Human Rights Commn.; personnel dir. Mont. Office Pub. Interest; co-dir. Mont. Human Rights Network, 1996-2000; Dem. senator dist. 27 Mont. State Senate, 2000—06; public service commr. State of Mont., 2007—. Mem. Mont. Adv. Com. to U.S. Commn. on Civil Rights. Caucus chair N.W. Energy Coalition; bd. dirs. No. Plains Resource Coun., Plan Helena, Renewable N.W.; chair Local Ctrl. Com. Dems.; west chair rep. Mont. State Dem. Bd. Office: PO Box 202601 Helena MT 59620-2601 E-mail: samt@mcn.net.

TOOLSON, KAY, transportation executive; Exec. positions with two major motor coach co., 1973—86; pres. Monaco Coach Corp., 1986—95, 1997—2000, CEO, 1986—, chmn., 1993—. Office: Monaco Coach 91320 Coburg Industrial Way Eugene OR 97408 Office Phone: 541-686-8011. Office Fax: 541-681-8899.

TOPIK, STEVEN CURTIS, historian, educator; b. Montebello, Calif., Aug. 6, 1949; s. Kurt and Trudy Topik; m. Martha Jane Marcy, Feb. 3, 1979; children: Julia, Natalia. BA, U. Calif., San Diego, 1971; MA, U. Tex., 1973, PhD, 1978. Asst. prof. U. Fed. Fluminense, Rio de Janeiro, 1978-81, Colgate U., Hamilton, NY, 1981-84; prof. U. Calif., Irvine, 1984-96, chair history dept., 1996-2000. Vis. prof. Universidade Fed. Fluminense, Rio de Janeiro, 1984—, U. Ibero Americana, Mexico City, 1982, Ecoles des Hautes Etudes en Sci. Social, Paris, 1990, London Sch. Econs., 2002; cons. in field. Author: (book) The Political Economy of the Brazilian State, 1987, Trade and Gunboats, The United States and Brazil in the Age of Empire, 1996; author: (with Allen Wells) The Second Conquest of Latin America, 1998; author: (with Kenneth Pomeranz) The World Trade Created, 1999; editor (with Dorothy Solinger and David Smith): States and Sovereignty in the Global Economy, 1999; editor: (with William Clarence-Smith) The Global Coffee Economy in Africa, Asia and Latin America 1500-1989, 2003; contbr. revs. to profl. publs.; mem. editl. com. U. Calif. Press, Berkeley, 1987—89. Mem. Mayor's Adv. Bd. Sister Cities, Irvine, 1989—90; mem. adv. bd. Orange County (Calif.) Com. L.Am., 1989—90. Fellow, Rockerfeller Found., 1977, Fulbright-Hayes Found., 1978—79, 1984, Social Sci. Rsch. Coun. Mexico City, 1982—83, NEH, 1987, 1989—90, U. Calif., 1988—89. Mem.: Pacific Coast Coun. L.Am. Studies (bd. govs. 1987—90), Conf. L.Am. History (mem. com. hist. statis., mem. com. projects and publs., chair Brazilian studies com. 1988—90), Am. Hist. Assn., L.Am. Studies Assn. Home Phone: 949-856-3045; Office Phone: 949-824-8053. E-mail: sctopik@uci.edu.

TORGERSON, JOHN, state senator; b. Iowa City, Oct. 21, 1947; m. Marjorie Torgerson; children: Leila, Jolene, Marissa. Gen. edn. diploma, 1966. Mem. Kenai Peninsula Borough Assembly; Rep. senator dist. D Alaska State Senate, 1994—2002. Former pres. Alaska Mcpl. League, Kenai Peninsula Caucus. Founding bd. dirs., past pres. Peninsula Winter Games; mem., past pres. Kenai Eagles; mem. Kasilof Eagles, Pioneers of Alaska. With U.S. Army. Mem. Nat. Assn. Devel. Orgns., VFW (life), Seward Am. Legion, Soldotna Elks, Soldotna C. of C. (past pres.), Ala. C. of C. (former bd. dirs.). Avocations: hiking, goldpanning.

TORGERSON, LINDA BELLE, music educator; b. Sioux City, Iowa, Dec. 16, 1951; d. Fredric William and Clara Jeanette Wilson; m. Peter Kinsey Torgerson; children: Christopher, Patricia. Diploma, Ctrl. H.S., 1971; MusB Edn., Morningside Coll., 1976; MEd, City U., 1999. Cert. Iowa tchr., tchr. Mont., Washington. Choral dir. First United Meth. Ch., Sioux City, Iowa, 1974—76, First Presbyn. Ch., Kalispell, Mont., 1976—80; pvt. music instr. Self-employed, Kalispell, Mont., 1976—80; music tchr. St. Matthews Sch., Kalispell, Mont., 1976—77; music dir., coord. Flathead County Rural Schools, Kalispell, Mont., 1979—85; music dir. Clarkston Sch. Dist., Wash., 1985—. Treas. Clarkston Edn. Assn., 1988—90, v.p., 1990—92, 2001—03, pres., 1991—92, bldg. rep., 1993—94, 2000—01; sec. Wash. uniserv polit. action com. Wash. Edn. Assn., Olympia, 1992—93; jazz band dir. Lincoln Mid. Sch., Clarkston, 1996—2003; co-director for asotin county teens against smoking Asotin County Devel. Services, Clarkston, 2001—02. Singer (composer): (commercial) Flathead County Milk Music Ad for the Radio, 1978; contbr. articles to profl. jours. Mem. U-Pac bd. for SE Wash. Edn. Assn., Kennewick, Wash., 1992—93. Grantee Dist., Clarkston Sch. Dist., 1994, 1995. Mem.: NEA, SE Wash. Music Educators Assn. (pres. 2002—04), Wash. Music Educators Assn., Music Educators Nat. Conf. Home: 1505 8th St Clarkston WA 99403 Office: Lincoln Mid Sch 1945 4th Ave Clarkston WA 99403 Office Phone: 509-758-5506 x5245. Personal E-mail: torgersons@cableone.net. Business E-Mail: torgersonl@csdk12.org.

TORLAKSON, TOM, state legislator; b. San Francisco, Aug. 19, 1949; son of Allen Daniel Torlakson & Catherine Leary T; married 1970 to Diana Bravos; children: Tiffany & Tamara. BA in History, U. Calif. Berkeley, 1971, MA in Edn., 1977. Member, Antioch City Coun, 78, councilman formerly; mayor pro tem, Antioch, California, formerly; member, Contra Costa Co Bd Supervisors, 80-96; California State Assemblyman, District 11, 96-2001, 2008-; chairman, Delta Protection Comn, currently; California State Senator, District 7, 2001-08. Teacher & Educator, 73. Founder, chair Calif. Task Force on Youth and Workplace Wellness. Served in Merchant Marine, Vietnam. Association Bay Area Govt (president, 94-95). Democrat. Roman Catholic. Avocations: running, bicycling. Office: Dist 11 815 Estudillo St Martinez CA 94553 also: State Capitol PO Box 942849 Sacramento CA 94249-0011 Office Phone: 925-372-7990, 916-319-2011. Office Fax: 925-372-0934, 916-319-2111. Business E-Mail: Assemblymember.Torlakson@assembly.ca.gov.*

TORME, MARGARET ANNE, public relations executive, management consultant; b. Indpls., Apr. 5, 1943; d. Ira G. and Margaret Joy (Wright) Barker; children: Karen Anne, Leah Vanessa. Student, Coll. San Mateo, 1961—65. Pub. rels. mgr. Hoefer, Dieterich & Brown (now Chiat-Day), San Francisco, 1964-73; v.p., co-founder, creative dir. Lowry & Ptnrs., San Francisco, 1975-83; pres., founder Torme and Lauricella Comm., San Francisco, 1983—. Cons. in comm. Mem. Coun. Pub. Rels. Firms, Jr. League (adv. bd.), Pub. Rels. Orgn. Internat. Office: 847 Sansome St San Francisco CA 94111-2908 Office Phone: 415-956-1791. Business E-Mail: margaret@torme.com.

TORN, RIP (ELMORE RUAL TORN JR.), actor, theater director; b. Temple, Tex., Feb. 6, 1931; s. Elmore and Thelma (Spacek) T.; m. Ann Wedgeworth, Jan. 15, 1955 (div. 1961); 1 child, Danae; m. Geraldine Page, 1963 (div. June 13, 1987); children: Angelica, Anthony, Jonathan; m. Amy Wright. Grad., Tex. A & M U., 1952. Performances include: (stage) Cat on a Hot Tin Roof, 1955, Orpheus Descending, 1958, Chaparral, 1958 (Theatre World award 1959), Sweet Bird of Youth, 1959, on tour, 1960, Daughter of Silence, 1961, Macbeth, 1962, Desire Under the Elms, 1963, Strange Interlude, 1963, Blues for Mr. Charlie, 1964, The Kitchen, 1966, The Country Girl, 1966, The Deer Park, 1967 (Obie award), The Cuban Thing, 1968, The Honest-to-God Schnozzola, 1969, Dream of a Blacklisted Actor, 1969, The Dance of Death, 1970-71, The Marriage Proposal, 1971, Marriage and Money, 1971, Barbary Shore, The Little Foxes, 1974, The Father, 1975, The Glass Menagerie, 1975, Fever for Life, 1975, Creditors, 1977, Night Shift, 1977, Seduced, 1979, Anna Christie, 1992; (motion pictures) Baby Doll, 1956, A Face in the Crowd, 1957, Time Limit, 1957, Pork Chop Hill, 1959, King of Kings, 1961, Hero's Island, 1962, Sweet Bird of Youth, 1962, Critic's Choice, 1963, The Cincinnati Kid, 1965, One Spy Too Many, 1966, Beach Red, 1967, You're a Big Boy Now, 1967, Beyond the Law, 1968, Sol Madrid, 1968, Coming Apart, 1969, Tropic of Cancer, 1970, Slaughter, 1972, Payday, 1973, Crazy Joe, 1974, Birch Interval, 1976, Maidstone, The Man Who Fell to Earth, 1976, Nasty Habits, 1977, Coma, 1978, The Seduction of Joe Tynan, 1979, First Family, 1980, Heartland, 1980, One Trick Pony, 1980, Jinxed, 1982, Airplane II: The Sequel, 1982, The Beastmaster, 1982, A Stranger is Watching, 1982, Cross Creek, 1983, City Heat, 1984, Misunderstood, 1984, Night Shadows, 1984, Song Writer, 1984, Flashpoint, 1984, Summer Rental, 1985, Beer, 1985, Extreme Prejudice, 1987, Defending Your Life, 1991, Beautiful Dreamers, 1992, Hard Promises, 1992, Robocop 3, 1993, Where the Rivers Flow North, 1994, How to Make an American Quilt, 1995, Down Periscope, 1996, Trial and Error, 1997, Men in Black, 1997, Hercules, 1997, The Mouse, 1997, Senseless, 1998, Wonder Boys, 2000, Men in Black Alien Attack, 2000, Men in Black II, 2002, Rolling Kansas, 2003, Welcome to Mooseport, 2004, Dodgeball: A True Underdog Story, 2004, Eulogy, 2004, Forty Shades of Blue, 2005, Yours, Mine and Ours, 2005, Marie Antoinette, 2006, Zoom, 2006, Bee Movie (voice), 2007, August, 2008; (TV films and miniseries) Two Plays, 1971, The President's Plane Is Missing, 1973, The FBI Versus the Ku Klux Klan, 1975, Song of Myself, 1976, Betrayal, 1976, The Gift of Love, 1978, Blind Ambition, 1979, A Shining Season, 1979, Sophia Loren: Her Own Story, 1980, Rape and Marriage: The Rideout Case, 1980, The Blue and the Gray, 1982, When She Says No, 1984, Dream West, 1986, April Morning, 1988, Sweet Bird of Youth, 1989, By Dawn's Early Light, 1990, Another Pair of Aces: Three of a Kind, 1991, My Son Johnny, 1991, Death Hits the Jackpot, 1991, T-Bone and Weasel, 1992, Dead Ahead: The Exxon Valdez Disaster, 1992, A Mother's Right: The Elizabeth Morgan Story, 1993, The Almost Perfect Bank Robbery, 1996, Seasons of Love, 1998, Passing Glory, 1999, Balloon Farm, 1999, A Vision of Murder: The Story of Donielle, 2000, Maniac Magee, 2003, The Lyon's Denn, 2003; (TV series) The Larry Sanders Show, HBO, 1992-98 (Emmy nominee for best supporting actor 1993, 94, Cable Ace award for best supporting actor 1994), Ghost Stories, 1997 (narrator); dir. plays: The Beard, 1968 (Obie award), Look Away, 1973. Mem. AFTRA, SAG, Actors Equity Assn., Actors' Studio (bd. dirs., prodn. bd., 1st chmn. founding com.), Dirs. Guild Am. Office: 118 S Beverly Dr 504 Beverly Hills CA 90212

TORNESE, JUDITH M., financial institution executive; b. Pitts., Aug. 26, 1942; d. Ilario and Rose Mary Tornese; m. Jerry E. Winters. Student, U. Pitts., Golden Gate U. CPCU. Various positions Transam Corp., San Francisco, 1971-81; dir. risk mgmt. TransAm. Corp., San Francisco, 1981-87; dir. X.L. Ins. Co., 1987-92; v.p. risk mgmt. TransAm. Corp., San Francisco, 1987—; dir., chair devel. com. St. Vincent de Paul Soc., 1994—. Dir. San Francisco Suicide Prevention, 1984-90; mem. Earthquake Ins. and Recovery Fin. Com. of Seismic Safety Commn., 1988-91. Named Risk Mgr. of Yr. Bus. Ins. Mag., 1992. Mem. Risk and Ins. Mgmt. Soc. (soc. dir. 1981—, chair nominating com. 1987-92, strategic planning com., 1996—), Mfr.'s Alliance Productivity and Innovation (risk mgmt. coun. 1981-85).

TORRE, JOE (JOSEPH PAUL TORRE), professional baseball team manager; b. Bklyn., July 18, 1940; s. Joseph Sr. & Margaret Torre; m. Ali Torre, Aug. 23, 1987; one child, Andrea Rea; children from previous marriages: Michael, Lauren, Tina. HHD (hon.), Rider U., 2006. Profl. baseball player Milw. Braves, 1960-69, St. Louis Cardinals, 1969-74, NY Mets, 1974-77, player-mgr., 1977-82; mgr. Atlanta Braves, 1982-84, St. Louis Cardinals, 1990-94, NY Yankees, 1995—2007, LA Dodgers, 2008—. TV broadcaster Calif. Angels, 1984—90; co-founder (with Ali Torre) Joe Torre Safe at Home Found., 2002—. Author: (novels) Chasing the Dream: My Lifelong Journey to the World Series, 1997, Joe Torre's Ground Rules for Winners: 12 Keys to Managing Team Players, Tough Bosses, Setbacks, and Success, 1999; co-author (with Tom Verducci): The Yankee Years, 2009 (#1 Publishers Weekly bestseller); actor: (films) Taking Care of Business, 1990, Analyze That, 2002, (voice) Everyone's Hero, 2006. Named Nat. League MVP, 1971, Player of Yr. Sporting News, 1971, Mgr. of Yr. AP, 1982, Am. League Mgr. of Yr., 1996, 1998; named to All-Star Team, 1963-67, 70-73, coach 1997, 1999-2002, 2004; recipient Gold Glove award, 1965, MLB.com's Mgr of Yr. award, 2007; hit for cycle, 1973; winner World Series NY Yankees, 1996, 1998, 1999, 2000. over 1,000 career wins, 2006; four world championships. Office: c/o LA Dodgers Dodgers Stadium 1000 Elysian Park Ave Los Angeles CA 90012*

TORRES, ART, former political organization administrator, former state legislator; b. LA; children: Joaquin, Danielle. AA, East L.A. C.C.; BA, U. Calif., Santa Cruz; JD, U. Calif. John F. Kennedy tchg. fellow Harvard U., Cambridge, Mass.; mem. Calif. State Assembly, Sacramento, 1973—81, Calif. State Senate, Sacramento, 1982—93; chmn. Calif. Dem. Party, 1996—2009. Chmn. Senate Com. Ins., Claims and Corps., Assembly Health Com., Senate Toxics and Pub. Safety Mgmt. Com., Select Com. Pacific Rim, Senate Spl. Rask Force on New L.A.; founder Calif. EPA; sr. mem. Senate Edn. Com.; author 1992 Immigrant Workforce Preparation Act; mem. Nat. Conf. State Legislatures Coalition on Immigration, Senate Appropriations Com., Senate Energy and Pub. Utilities Com., Senate Govtl. Orgn. Com., Senate Judiciary Com., Senate Natural Resources Com., Senate Transp. Com. Mem. Coun. Fgn. Rels., NY, Nat. Commn. Internat. Migration and Econ. Devel.; participant IVth Nobel Prizewinners Meeting Nova Spes Internat. Found., Vatican, Rome, 1989. Recipient Legislator of Yr. award Calif. Orgn. Policy and Sheriffs, 1990, Outstanding Legislator of Yr. award Calif. Sch. Bd. Assn., 1990, Outstanding Alumnus award U. Calif. Santa Cruz, Dreamer award Boys and Girls Club Am., 1990, Achievement award Latin Am. Law Enforcement Assn., 1992. Democrat. Office: 911 20th St Sacramento CA 95814-3115 Office Phone: 916-442-5707. Office Fax: 916-442-5714.*

TORRES, ESTEBAN EDWARD, former congressman, trade association administrator; b. Miami, Ariz., Jan. 27, 1930; s. Esteban Torres and Rena Baron (Gomez) T.; m. Arcy Sanchez, Jan. 22, 1955; children: Carmen D'Arcy, Rena Denise, Camille Bianca, Selina Andre, Esteban Adrian. Student, East Los Angeles Coll., 1960, Calif. State U., Los Angeles, 1963, U. Md., 1965, Am. U., 1966; PhD (hon.), Nat. U., 1987; DHL (hon.), Whittier Coll., 2001. Chief steward United Auto Workers, local 230, 1954-63, dir. polit. com., 1963; organizer, internat. rep. United Auto Workers (local 230), Washington, 1964;

asst. dir. Internat. Affairs Dept., 1975-77; dir. Inter-Am. Bureau for Latin Am., Caribbean, 1965-67; exec. dir. E. Los Angeles Community Union (TELACU), 1967-74; U.S. ambassador to UNESCO, Paris, 1977-79; chmn. Geneva Grp., 1977-78; chmn. U.S. del. Gen. Conf., 1978; spl. asst. to pres. U.S., dir. White House Office Hispanic Affairs, 1979-81; mem. 98th-103rd Congresses from 34th Dist. Calif., 1983-98; mem. appropriations com., subcom. fgn. ops., subcom. transp.; chmn. ho. subcom. coinage; mem. ho. banking com., 1983; mem. ho. small bus. com., 1983. Campaign coord. Jerry Brown for Gov., 1974; Hispanic coord. LA County campaign Jimmy Carter for Pres., 1976; mem. Sec. of State Adv. Group, 1979-81; v.p. Nat. Congress Cmty. Econ. Devel., 1973-74; pres. Congress Mex.-Am. Unity, 1970-71; dir. Nat. Com. on Citizens Broadcasting, 1977; cons. U.S. Congress office of tech. assessment, 1976-77; del to IMF gen. conf., Geneva, 1975, del to U.S. Congress European Parliament meetings, 1984; ofcl. congl. observer Geneva Arms Control Talks; chmn. Congl. Hispanic Caucus, 1987; speaker Wrights Del. to USSR, 1987; Dem. dep. Whip, 1990; chmn. bd. Nat. Latino Media Coun., 1999—. Contbr. numerous articles to profl. jours. Co-chmn. Nat. Hispanic Dems., 1988—; chmn. Japan-Hispanic Inst. Inc.; bd. visitors Sch. Architecture UCLA, 1971-73; bd. dirs. LA County Econ. Devel. Com., 1972-75, Internat. Devel. Conf., 1976-78; chmn. Congrl. Hispanic Caucus, 1985-86; pres. Plaza de la Raza Cultural Ctr., 1972-73, chmn. bd. la Plaza de Cultural Art, 2007—; trustee Am. Coll. Paris, 1977-79; active Calif. Transp. Commn., Sacramento. With AUS, 1949-53, ETO. Recipient Congrl. award Nat. Leadership award 1997; sr. fellow UCLA Sch. Pub. Policy, 2000-05. Mem. Americans for Dem. Action (exec. bd. 1975-77), VFW Post 6315, Pico Rivera, Calif., Am. Legion, Smithsonian Inst. (regent emeritus 1999—), Willy C. Velasqez Inst., Calif. Transp. Commn. Democrat. Home: 1104 Montezuma Way West Covina CA 91791 Personal E-mail: etorres_nlmc@hotmail.com.

TORRES, NORMA, state legislator; b. Guatemala; m. Louis Torres; children: Robert, Christopher, Matthew. Former 911 dispatcher City of Los Angeles Police Dept.; councilwoman City of Pomona from Dist. 6, 2000—06; mayor City of Pomona, 2006—08; mem. Dist. 61 Calif. State Assembly, 2008—. Treas. Exec. Com. Nat. Conf. Dem. Mayors. Founder Neighbors for Pomona Com.; bd. mem. Pomonoa Valley Transp. Authority, Tri-City Mental Health, Fairplex Blue Ribbon Com.; vol. Suicide Prevention Ctr., Big Sisters Program, Am. Youth Soccer Org., Boy Scouts Am. Mem.: AFSCME Local 3090. Democrat. Office: Dist 61 PO Box 660 Pomona CA 91769 also: 505 South Garey Ave 2nd Fl Pomona CA 91766 Office Phone: 909-620-2051. Office Fax: 909-620-3707. Business E-Mail: Assemblymember.Torres@assembly.ca.gov.*

TORRES-GIL, FERNANDO M., academic administrator; b. Salinas, Calif., June 24, 1948; BA in Polit. Sci., San Jose State U., 1970; MSW, Brandeis U., 1972, PhD in Social Policy, Planning and Rsch., 1976. Spl. asst. to sec. Dept. Health, Edn. and Welfare, Washington, 1978-79, Dept. Health and Human Svcs., Washington, 1979-80; prof. gerontology and pub. adminstrn. U. So. Calif., 1981-91, assoc. dir. Nat. Resource Ctr. on Minority Aging Populations, 1988-92, prof. social welfare, 1991-93; assoc. dean Sch. Pub. Policy and Soc. Rsch. UCLA, 1993—, dir., Ctr. for Policy Rsch. on Aging. Staff dir. Select Com. on Aging, U.S. Ho. of Reps., Washington, 1985-87. Contbr. articles to profl. jours. Bd. dirs. Nat. Steinbeck Ctr., Families USA Found., AARP Andrus Found., Calif. Endowment, 2003—. White House fellow, 1978-79. Mem. Am. Soc. Aging (pres. 1989-92), Nat. Acad. Social Insurance; fellow Gerontological Soc. of Am., 1985, Nat. Acad. Public Administration, 1995. Office: UCLA Sch Pub Plicy & Social Rsch Box 951656 3250 Public Policy Blvd Los Angeles CA 90095-1656

TORREY, JAMES D., mayor, communications executive, consultant; b. Drayton, ND, July 16, 1940; s. Howard J. Torrey and Gertrude (Carpenter) Steenson; m. Katherine Joann Kowal, Sept. 2, 1958; children: Tamara, Timonthy (dec.), Teresa, Todd. Student, U. Oreg., 1959-61. Mgr. Waldport (Oreg.) Food Market, 1959-67; dist. mgr. Obie Outdoor Advt., Aberdeen, Wash., 1967-68; dir. sales Obie Media Corp., Eugene, Oreg., 1968-71, exec. v.p., 1971-78, pres., CEO, 1980-88, Total Comm., Inc., Eugene, Oreg., 1989-91; N.W. area market mgr. 3M Nat. Advt., Eugene, Oreg., 1978-80; dir. mktg. State Accident Ins. Fund, Salem, Oreg., 1988-89. Mem. exec. com. affiliate bd. Mut. Broadcasting, 1981-87. Pres. Waldport City Coun., 1962-67; coach Eugene Kidsports, 1968-92, Am. Softball Assn. Girls Softball Team, 1988; mem. adv. com. 4 J Sch. Dist., 1988-90; bd. dirs. Lane County United Way, 1983-86, dir., 1992, Lane County Goodwill Industries, 1989-90; mem. Eugene City Budget Com., 1992-94, Eugene City Coun., 1994-97; mayor City of Eugene, Oreg., 1997—. Named JCI senator, Oreg. State Jaycees, 1966, Citizen of Yr., City of Waldport, 1967, Outstanding Vol., City of Eugene, 1991, First Citizen, Eugene, Oreg., 2001—. Mem. Oreg. Outdoor Advt. Assn. (pres. 1971-80), Oreg. Assn. Broadcasters (dir. 1984-87), Eugene C. of C. (bd. dirs., pres. 1991-92), Eugene Rotary (dir., pres. 1984, Paul Harris fellow 1985). Republican. Roman Catholic. Office: Mayor's Office 777 Pearl St Ste 105 Eugene OR 97401-2720

TORRICO, ALBERTO, state legislator; b. Fremont, Calif. m to Raquel; children: Mateo & Amy-Elizabeth. BS in Polit. Sci., Santa Clara U.; JD, Hastings Coll. of Law, San Francisco. Councilman & vice mayor, Newark, California, 2001-2004; California State Assemblyman, District 20, 2004-, majority floor leader, currently, asst. majority whip, 2005-2006, dir. majority affairs. Assoc. atty., Weinberg, Roger & Rosenfeld, 1996-99; asst gen counsel, Santa Clara Valley Transportation Agency, 2000; owner, Law Offices of Alberto Torrico, 2001-; adj. instr., San Jose City Coll. Democrat. Office: State Capitol Rm 319 PO Box 942849 Sacramento CA 94249-0020 also: Dist 20 39510 Paseo Padre Pkwy Ste 280 Fremont CA 94538 Office Phone: 916-319-2020, 510-440-9030. Office Fax: 916-319-2120, 510-440-9035. Business E-Mail: Assemblymember.torrico@assembly.ca.gov.

TORVALDS, LINUS BENEDICT, application developer; b. Helsinki, Finland, Dec. 28, 1969; s. Nils and Anna Torvalds; m. Tove Torvalds; children: Patricia Miranda, Daniela Yolanda, Celeste Amanda. MS in Computer Sci., Helsinki U., 1996. Developer Transmeta Corp., Santa Clara, Calif., 1997—2003; fellow Open Source Develop. Labs (OSDL), Beaverton, Oreg., 2003—. Co-author (with David Diamond): (autobiography) Just for Fun: The Story of an Accidental Revolutionary, 2001. Recipient Nokia Found. Award, 1997, Lifetime Achievement Award, Uniforum, 1997, Takeda award, 2001; named One of the Most Influential People in the World, TIME mag., 2004. Achievements include invention of Linux operating system. Office: Osdl 210 Fell St # 16 San Francisco CA 94102-5145

TOSTI, DONALD THOMAS, psychologist, consultant; b. Kansas City, Mo., Dec. 6, 1935; s. Joseph T. Tosti and Elizabeth M. (Parsons) Tosti Addison; m. Carol J. Curless, Jan. 31, 1957 (dec. 1980); children: Rene, Alicia, Roxanna, Brett, Tabitha, Todd Marcus; m. Annette Brewer, Dec. 29, 1989. BSEE, U. N.Mex., 1957, MS in Psychology, 1962, PhD in Psychology, 1967. Chief editor Tchg. Machines, Inc., Albuquerque, 1960-64; divsn. mgr. Westinghouse Learning Corp., Albuquerque, 1964-70; founder, sr. v.p. Ind. Learning Sys., San Raphael, Calif., 1970-74, pres., 1974-76; chmn. bd. Omega Performance, San Francisco, 1976-77; pres. Operants, Inc., San Rafael, 1978-81; v.p. Forum Corp., San Rafael, 1981-83; mng. ptnr. Vanguard Cons. Group, San Francisco, 1983—. Author: Basic Electricity, Advanced Algebra, Fundamentals of Calculus, TMI Programmed Mathematics Series, 1960-63, Behavior Technology, 1970, A Guide to Child Development, Tactics of Communication, 1973; co-author: Learning Is Getting Easier, 1973, Indtroductory Psychology, 1981, Usibility Factors in Hardware and Software Design, 1982, Comparative Usibility, 1983, Performance Based Management, Positive Leadership, 1986, Strategic Alliances, 1990, The Professional Manager, 1995, Power and Governance, 1996, Global Fluency, 1999, Organizational Alignment, 2000, Internal Branding, 2000, Principles of Performance Consulting, 2001. Mem. AAAS, APA, Internat. Soc. for Performance Improvement (v.p. rsch. 1983-85, treas. 1997-99, pres., 2003-, Outstanding Mem. award 1984, Life Membership award 1984, Outstanding product award 1974), Sigma Xi. Home: 41 Marinita Ave San Rafael CA 94901-3443 Office Phone: 415-259-0160. Personal E-mail: change111@aol.com.

TOTTON, CARL ALLEN, II, psychologist; b. LA, May 10, 1948; s. Carl Allen and Elva T. Student, Calif. State U., 1976, BS in Rehab. Counseling, 1978, MS in Counseling, 1980; PsyD in Clin. Psychology, Pepperdine U., Malibu, Calif., 1998. Cert. sch. psychologist, counselor, Calif.; lic. psychologist, Calif., Diagnostic Ctr. South, 2008; ordained Taoist abbot, 1983. Sch. psychologist Alhambra (Calif.) Sch. Dist., LA, 1990—2006; dir. Taoist Inst., North Hollywood, Calif., 1981—. Faculty mem. Calif. State U., Northridge, 1993-96, SAMRA U. Oriental Medicine, 1996-98; dir., counselor Rehab. Counseling Assocs., North Hollywood, 1981-83; stress mgmt. cons., hypnotherapist; adj. and core faculty Phillips Grad. Inst. Clin. Psychology, 2005—, adj. faculty sch. psychology, 2006—; bd. advisors Rancho San Antonio Home for Boys, Chatsworth, Calif., 1996—. Author: Comprehensive Guide to Chinese Medicine and Structural Tui Na, Martial Arts Chi Kung, 1997, Pediatric Tui Na, 1998; editor: Tui Na: Chinese Healing and Acupressure Massage, 1984; author, pub., prodr., The Core System for Martial Arts, Health, and Chi Kung, 2005; contbr. articles to mags. Recipient Presdl. Sports award, 1993, 95, 97; elected to US Martial Arts Hall Fame as Grandmaster, 2002. Mem. APA, Calif. Rehab. Counseling Assn. (pres. 1983-84), Assn. Transpersonal Psychology, Nat. Assn. Sch. Psychologists, Calif. Assn. Sch. Psychologists (bd. dirs., 2001-2003, named Outstanding Sch. Psychologist 2000), Calif. Assn. Lic. Ednl. Psychologists (named Lic. Ednl. Psychologist of Yr. 1999), Calif. Assn. Marriage and Family Therapists. Democrat. Office: Taoist Inst 10630 Burbank Blvd North Hollywood CA 91601-2511 Office Phone: 818-760-4219.

TOUFF, MICHAEL, lawyer; b. 1945; AB, Harvard U.; JD, U. Michigan. Officer, law firm Holmes & Starr, Ireland, Stapleton, Pryor & Pascoe, P.C., 1992-94; v.p., gen. counsel MDC Holdings, Inc (Richmond Am. Homes), 1994—99, sr. v.p., gen. counsel, 1999—. Mem.: ABA. Office: MDC Holdings Inc 4350 S Monaco St Denver CO 80237

TOULMIN, STEPHEN EDELSTON, humanities educator; b. London, Mar. 25, 1922; BA in Math. and Physics, King's Coll., Cambridge, Eng., 1942; PhD, King's Coll., 1948; D Tech. (hon.), Royal Inst. Tech., Stockholm, 1991. Lectr. in philosophy of sci. Oxford U., Eng., 1949-55; prof., chmn. dept. of philosophy U. Leeds, Yorkshire, Eng., 1955-59; dir. unit for history of ideas Nuffield Found., London, 1960-65; prof. history of ideas and philosophy Brandeis U., Waltham, Mass., 1965-69; prof. philosophy Mich. State U., East Lansing, 1969-72; prof. humanities U. Calif., Santa Cruz, 1972-73; prof. com. social thought U. Chgo., 1973-86; Avalon prof. humanities Northwestern U., Evanston, Ill., 1986-92, Avalon prof. emeritus, 1992—; prof. U. So. Calif., LA, 1993-2001, 2001—. Vis. prof. U. Melbourne, Australia, 1954-55, Stanford U., 1959, Columbia U., N.Y.C., 1960, Hebrew U., Jerusalem, 1964, U. South Fla., 1972, Dartmouth Coll., 1979, SUNY, Plattsburgh, 1980, Colo. Coll., 1980, 82, MacMaster U., 1983, Harvard Project Physics Grad. Sch. Edn., Harvard U., 1965; counselor Smithsonian Inst., Washington, 1967-77; cons., staff mem. Nat. Commn. Protection Human Subjects Biomed. Behavioral Rsch., 1975-78; sr. vis. scholar, fellow Inst. Soc. Ethics and Life Scis., Hastings-on-Hudson, N.Y., 1981-2001; regent's lectr. U. Calif. Med. Sch., Davis, 1985; Mary Flexner lectr. Bryn Mawr Coll., 1977; Reyerson lectr. U. Chgo., 1979, John Nuveen lectr., 1980; Tate-Wilson lectr. So. Meth. U., 1980; Or Emet lectr. Osgoode Hall Law Sch., 1981; McDermott lectr. U. Dallas, 1985; lectr. Sigma Xi, 1965-66, Phi Beta Kappa, 1978-79, Phi Beta Kappa-AAAS, 1984, Thomas Jefferson lectr. NEH, Washington, 1997; Tanner lectr. Clare Hall, Cambridge U., 1998; guest prof. social and human scis. Wolfgang Goethe Universitat, Frankfurt, Germany, 1987; vis. fellow Internationales Forschungszentrum Kulturwissenschaften (IFK), Vienna, 1995. Author: The Place of Reason in Ethics, 1949, The Philosophy of Science: an Introduction, 1953, The Uses of Argument, 1958, Foresight and Understanding, 1961, Human Understanding, vol. 1, 1972, Knowing and Acting, 1976, The Return to Cosmology, 1982, Cosmopolis, 1989; (with J. Goodfield) The Fabric of the Heavens, 1961, The Architecture of Matter, 1963, The Discovery of Time, 1965; (with A. Janik) Wittgenstein's Vienna, 1973; (with R. Rieke and A. Janik) An Introduction to Reasoning, 1978; (with A. Jonsen) The Abuse of Casuistry, 1987; (with B. Gustavsen) Beyond Theory, 1996, Return to Reason, 2001; contbr. numerous sci. articles to profl. jours. Recipient Honor Cross 1st class (Austria), 1991; Getty Ctr. for History of Art and Humanities scholar, 1985-86, First Book of the Year prize Am. Soc. Social Philosophy, 1992; Ctr. for Psychosocial Studies fellow, 1974-76. Fellow Am. Acad. Arts and Scis.

TOURTELLOTTE, WALLACE WILLIAM, neurologist, educator; b. Great Falls, Mont., Sept. 13, 1924; B in Philosophy, Hutchin's Coll., U. Chgo., 1945; BS in Anatomy, U. Chgo., 1945, PhD in Neurochemical Pharmacology, 1948, MD, 1951. Instr. biochem Neuro pharmacology U. Chgo., 1948—50; intern Strong Meml. Hosp. Straight Medicine U. Rochester Sch. Medicine and Dentistry, NY, 1951—52; resident in neurology U. Mich. Med. Ctr., Ann Arbor, 1954-57, asst. prof. neurology, 1957-59, assoc. prof., 1959-66, prof., 1966-71; prof. dept. neurology UCLA, 1971—, vice chmn. dept. neurology, 1971-98, disting. prof., 1992—, emeritus vice chmn. dept. neurology, 1998; chief neurology svcs. VA Wadsworth, West LA, Calif., 1971-99, emeritus dir. neurology tng. program, 1999—, staff neurologist, neuroscientist, 1999—; neuroscientist Inst. Sci. Info., 1981—99. Vis. assoc. prof. pharmacology Washington U., St. Louis, 1963-64; hon. mem. med. adv. bd. Nat. Multiple Sclerosis Soc., 1968—, So. Calif. Multiple Sclerosis Socs., 1972—; dir. Multiple Sclerosis Rsch. and Treatment Ctr., 1971-, Human Brain and Spinal Fluid Resource Ctr., 1961—; reviewer profl. jours. in field, Inst. Sci. Info., 1967-2002. Co-editor (with Cedric Raines, Henry McFarland): Multiple Sclerosis, Clinical and Pathogenetic Basis, 1997; dedicated The Wallace W. Tourtellotte Clin. and Neurosci. Libr., Va. Wadsworth, LA, 1999; author Post Lambda Headache WWT, 1967, Quantitative Examination Of human Neurologic Function, 1985. Lt. (j.g.) M.C., USNR, 1952-54. Recipient Disting. Alumni Service award U. Chgo., 1982. Fellow Am. Acad. Neurology (S. Weir Mitchell Neurology Reseach award 1959); mem. Am. Neurol. Assn. (counselor 1982—, v.p. 1992), World Fedn. Neurology (founding mem. 1969), Am. Assn. Neuropathologists, Internat. Soc. Neurochemsitry (founding mem. 1969), Am. Soc. Pharmacology and Exptl. Therapeutics, Am. Soc. Neurochemistry (founding mem.), Soc. Neurosci., Confrerie de la Chaine des Rotisseur, Argentier du Baillage de Los Angeles (vice chanceller, comdr. 1971), Pasadena Wine and Food Soc., Physician Wine and Food Soc., Culinary Club French Cuisine LA. Office Phone: 310-268-4635. Fax: 310-454-7650. Business E-Mail: wtourtel@ucla.edu.

TOVAR, ANNA, state legislator; m. Carlos Tovar; 2 children. BA in Elem. Edn., Ariz. State U. Councilwoman Tolleson City Coun., 2001—09, vice mayor, 2007—09; mem. Dist. 13 Ariz. House of Reps., 2009—. Former tchr. Tolleson Elem. Sch. Dist. Bd. mem. JAG-Jobs for Ariz. Grads., Southwest Valley C. of C., Found. for Surviving Depression & Anxiety; v.p. PTA Tolleson Elem., 2000—02, Tolleson Tchr. Edn. Assn., 2000—01; mentor Tolleson Teen Coun.; mem. Eloisa Diaz Scholarship Found. Com. Mem.: Maricopa Assn. Govts., League Ariz. Cities & Towns, Nat. Assn. Latino Elected Officials, Women in Mcpl. Govt., Hispanic Elected Local Officials, Nat. League Cities. Democrat. Office: Capitol Complex 1700 W Washington Rm 325 Phoenix AZ 85007-2890 Office Phone: 602-926-3392. Office Fax: 602-417-3013. Business E-Mail: atovar@azleg.gov.*

TOWE, A. RUTH, retired museum director; b. Circle, Mont., Mar. 4, 1938; d. David and Anna Marie (Pedersen) James; m. Thomas E. Towe, Aug. 21, 1960; children: James Thomas, Kristofer Edward. BA, U. Mont., 1960, MA, 1970; postgrad., Am. U., 1964. Cert. master gardener 2005. Bookkeeper, copywriter Sta. KGVO, Missoula, Mont., 1960-61; grad. asst. Sch. of Journalism U. Mont., Missoula, 1961-62; editl. asst. Phi Gamma Delta mag., Washington, 1964; reporter The Chelsea (Mich.) Standard, 1965-66; dir. Mont. Nat. Bank, Plentywood, 1966-73; bookkeeper, legal sec. Thomas E. Towe, Atty. of Law, Billings, Mont., 1967-68; dir. Mont. Nat. Bank, Browning, 1972-73; mus. exec. dir. The Moss Mansion Mus., Billings, 1988—2003; ret., 2003. Bd. dirs. Billings Depot, Inc., sec., 1999-2003. Mem. Mont. Coun. of Family Rels. & Devel., 1970, Mont. Com. Humanities, 2005—; pres. Mont. Assn. of Symphony Orchs., 1987-88; sheriff Yellowstone Corral of Westerners, Billings, 1993; pres. Yellowstone Hist. Soc., 1998-2000; vice-chmn. Yellowstone Dem. Ctrl. Com., Billings, 1983-84; mem. Billings Friends Mtg., 1986—. Mem. AAUW, PEO, Mus. Assn. Mont. (pres. 1990-92, bd. dirs. 1989-96), Jr. League, Theta Sigma Phi (hon.). Avocation: gardening. E-mail: r.towe@bresnan.net.

TOWE, THOMAS EDWARD, lawyer; b. Cherokee, Iowa, June 25, 1937; s. Edward and Florence (Tow) T.; m. Ruth James, Aug. 21, 1960; children: James Thomas, Kristofer Edward. Student, U. Paris, 1956; BA, Earlham Coll., 1959; LLB, U. Mont., 1962; LLM, Georgetown U., 1965; student, U. Mich., Ann Arbor, 1965—67. Ptnr. Towe, Ball, Enright, Mackey & Sommerfeld, Billings, Mont., 1967—; legislator Mont. House of Rep., Billings, 1971-75, Mont. State Senate, Billings, 1975-87, 91-94. Com. mem. Mont. Senate, 1975—87, 1991—94. Contbr. articles to law revs. Mem. Alternatives, Inc., Halfway House, Billing, 1977-99, pres., 1985-86; mem. adv. com. Mont. Crime Control Bd., 1973-78, Youth Justice Coun., 1981-83; mem. State Dem. Exec. Com., 1969-73; Dem. candidate for Congress, 1976; bd. dirs. Mont. Consumer Affairs Coun., Regl. Cmty. Svcs. for the Devel. Disabled, 1975-77, Rimrock Guidance Found., 1975-80, Vols. of Am., Billings, 1984-89, Youth Dynamics Inc., 1989-96, Zoo Mont., 1985-2001, Inst. for Peace Studies, 1993—, Mont. State Parks Assn., 1993—. Capt. JAGC US Army, 1962—65. Named as one of 100 Most Influential Montanans in 20th Century, Missoulian newspaper, 1999, one of 12 state officials in US as "Stars of the States," Washington Monthly mag., one of 10 best state and local officials in US, Mother Jones mag, Jeanette Rankin Civil Liberties award, ACLU, 2008. Mem. Mont. Bar Assn., Yellowstone County Bar Assn., Billings C. of C. Mem. Soc. Of Friends. Avocation: outdoor recreation. Home: 2739 S Gregory Dr Billings MT 59102-0509 Office: Towe Ball Enright Mackey & Sommerfeld 2525 6th Ave N Billings MT 59101 Office Phone: 406-248-7337. Personal E-mail: t.towe@bresnan.net. Business E-Mail: towe@tbems.com.

TOWERY, JAMES E., lawyer; b. Los Alamos, N.Mex., July 12, 1948; s. Lawson E. and Irma (Van Apeldorn) T.; 1 child, Mark J. BA, Princeton U., 1973; JD, Emory U., 1976. Assoc. Morgan Beauzay Hammer, San Jose, Calif., 1977-79; ptnr. Morgan & Towery, San Jose, Calif., 1979-89; assoc. Hoge Fenton Jones & Appel, San Jose, Calif., 1989-90, ptnr., 1990—. Chmn. bd. trustees Alexian Bros. Hosp., San Jose, Calif., 1995-98. Mem. ABA (ho. of dels. 1989-98, standing com. client protection 1996—2000, chair 1998-00), State Bar Calif. (v.p. and chair discipline com. 1994-95, pres. 1995-96, bd. govs. 1992-96, pres. 1995-96, presiding arbitrator, fee arbitration program 1990-92), Santa Clara County Bar Assn. (counsel 1984-85, treas. 1987, pres. 1989). Office: Hoge Fenton Jones 60 S Market St San Jose CA 95113-2351 Home Phone: 408-279-8687; Office Phone: 408-947-2432. Business E-Mail: jet@hogefenton.com.

TOWNE, DAVID L., zoological park administrator; b. Winslow, Wash., Dec. 1, 1931; BA, U. Wash., 1958. Supt. Dept. Parks and Recreation, Seattle, 1972-77; v.p. Earl Combs, Inc., Bellevue, Wash., 1982-84; dir. Woodland Park Zool. Gardens, Seattle, 1984-2000. Fellow Am. Zoos and Aquariums; mem. N. Am. Giant Panda Plan (pres.), Am. Assn. Zoos and Aquariums (past pres.), Woodland Park Zool. Soc. (pres., CEO). Office: Woodland Park Zoological Gardens 5500 Phinney Ave N Seattle WA 98103-5865 E-mail: clave.towne@zoo.org.

TOWNES, CHARLES HARD, physics professor; b. Greenville, SC, July 28, 1915; s. Henry Keith and Ellen Sumter (Hard) Townes; m. Frances H. Brown, May 4, 1941; children: Linda Lewis, Ellen

Screven, Carla Keith, Holly Robinson. BA, BS, Furman U., 1935; MA, Duke U., 1937; PhD, Calif. Inst. Tech., 1939. Mem. tech. staff Bell Telephone Lab., 1939—47; assoc. prof. physics Columbia U., 1948—50, prof. physics, 1950—61; exec. dir. Columbia Radiation Lab., 1950—52, chmn. physics dept., 1952—55; provost and prof. physics MIT, 1961—66, inst. prof., 1966—67; v.p., dir. rsch. Inst. Def. Analyses, Washington, 1959—61; univ. prof. physics U. Calif., Berkeley, 1967—86, prof. physics emeritus, 1986—94, prof. grad. sch., 1994—. Guggenheim fellow, 1955—56; Fulbright lectr. U. Paris, 1955—56, U. Tokyo, 1956; dir. Enrico Fermi Internat. Sch. Physics, 1963; Richtmeyer lectr. Am. Phys. Soc., 1959; Scott lectr. U. Cambridge, 1963; Centennial lectr. U. Toronto, 1967; Lincoln lectr., 1972—73; Halley lectr., 1976; Krishnan lectr., 92; Nishina lectr., 92; Weinberg lectr. Oak Ridge (Tenn.) Nat. Lab., 1997; Rajiv Gandhi lectr., 97; Henry Norris Russell lectr. Am. Astron. Soc., 1998; dir. Gen. Motors Corp., 1973—86, Perkin-Elmer Corp., 1966—69; mem. Pres.'s Sci. Adv. Com., 1966—69, vice chmn., 1967—69; chmn. sci. and tech. adv. com. for manned space flight NASA, 1964—70; mem. Pres.'s Com. on Sci. and Tech., 1976; rschr. on nuc. and molecular structure, quantum electronics, interstellar molecules, radio and infrared astrophysics; Greenstein lectr., 2009. Author (with A.L. Schawlow): Microwave Spectroscopy; author: Making Waves, 1996, How the Laser Happened. Adventures of a Scientist, 1999; author, co-editor Quantum Electronics, 1960, Quantum Electronics and Coherent Light, 1964, mem. editl. bd. Rev. Sci. Instruments, 1950—52, Phys. Rev., 1951—53, Jour. Molecular Spectroscopy, 1957—60, Procs. NAS, 1978—84, Can. Jour. Physics, 1995—, contbr. articles to sci. publs. Mem. corp. Woods Hole Oceanographic Instn.; bd. mem. Calif. Inst. Tech., Carnegie Instn. Washington, Ctr. for Theology and Natural Scis., Mount Wilson Inst. Decorated officier Légion d'Honneur (France); recipient Stuart Ballantine medal, Franklin Inst., 1962, Thomas Young medal and prize, Inst. Physics and Phys. Soc., Eng., 1963, Nobel prize for Physics, 1964, Disting. Pub. Svc. medal, NASA, 1969, Wilhelm Exner award, Austria, 1970, Niels Bohr Internat. Gold medal, 1979, Nat. medal of Sci., 1982, Berkeley citation, U. Calif., 1986, CommonWealth award, 1993, ADION medal, Obs. Nice, 1995, Mendel award, Villanova U., 1999, Frank Annunzio award, Christopher Columbus Fellowship Found., 1999, Rabindranath Tagore Birth Centenary plaque, Asiatic Soc., 1999, Karl Schwarzschild medal, Astronomische Gesellschaft, 2002, Drake award, SETI Inst., 2003, Templeton prize, 2005, Vannevar Bush medal, 2006; named to Nat. Inventors Hall of Fame, 1976, Engring. and Sci. Hall of Fame, 1983. Fellow: IEEE (life medal of honor 1967), Calif. Acad. Scis., Indian Nat. Sci. Acad., Optical Soc. Am. (Mees medal 1968), Am. Phys. Soc. (pres. 1967, Plyler prize 1977, Frederick Ives medal 1996); mem.: NAE (founders award 2000), NAS (coun. 1968—72, 1978—81, chmn. space sci. bd. 1970—73, Comstock award 1959, Carty medal 1962), N.Y. Acad. Scis., Max-Planck Inst. Physics and Astrophysics (fgn. mem.), Pontifical Acad. Scis., Russian Acad. Scis. (Lomonosov medal 2000, fgn. mem.), Royal Soc. (fgn. mem.), Am. Acad. Arts and Scis., Am. Astron. Soc., Am. Philos. Soc. Achievements include patents for masers and lasers. Office: U Calif Dept Physics 366 Leconte # 7200 Berkeley CA 94720-0001 Office Phone: 510-642-1128. Business E-Mail: cht@ssl.berkeley.edu.

TOWNSEND, JAMES DOUGLAS, chief financial officer, accountant; b. Kokomo, Ind., May 20, 1959; s. Lemon Dale and Diamond Sue (Turner) T.; m. Ariane Antonia Atkins, May 7, 1983 (div. July 1992); 1 child, Bradley Alan; m. Mildred Ann Kurtz, Oct. 18, 1992 (div. Aug. 2004); children: Heather Marie, Tyler Neil; m. Rand Jayne Latham, Oct. 17, 2007. Student, Ind. U., 1977, Ind. State U., 1977—78; BS Acctg. summa cum laude, Ball State U., 1980. CPA, Ind., Colo.; cert. mgmt. acct. Acctg. intern Chevrolet Motor Divsn. GM, Muncie, Ind., 1979; from staff acct. to sr. mgr. Price Waterhouse, Indpls., 1980—89; from contr. to v.p. fin. Raffensperger, Hughes & Co., Inc., Indpls., 1989—95; sr. v.p., chief adminstrv. officer Nat. City Investments, Inc., Indpls., 1995—99; pres. Fin. Mgmt., Inc., Indpls., 1994—2005; sr. v.p. Madison Ave. Capital Group LLC, 1999—2000; CFO Colo.'s Ocean Journey, 2000—01, exec. v.p., COO, 2001, CEO, 2001—05; v.p., contr. Curian Capital LLC, 2004—07, Jackson Nat. Life Distbr., Inc., 2004—07; sr. v.p., chief fin. officer, 2008—. Coord. Seek Program Ind. U., Indpls., 1985-86; cons. project bus. Jr. Achievement, Indpls., 1986; treas., asst. sec. Sagamore Funds Trust, 1991-94; treas. Raffensberger Hughes Capitol Corp., 1991-94, RHGP, Inc., 1993-95. Baseball coach Pike Twp. (Ind.) Youth League, 1986-87; cubmaster Pike Twp. Coun. Boy Scouts Am., 1987-88; mem. Pike Twp. Sch. Bd., 1988-92, v.p., 1989-90, pres., 1990-92; bd. dirs. Project I-Star, 1992-94, Crooked Creek Villages Homeowners Assn., 1998-99; fin. com. Highlands Ranch Cmty. Assn., 2000—02. Fellow Life Mgmt. Inst.; mem. AICPA, Inst. Mgmt. Accts., Ind. CPA Soc. (vice chmn. edn. com. 1988-89, chmn. 1989-90, chmn. govt. rels. com. 1999), Colo. Soc. CPAs, Indpls. C. of C. (SKLA exec. coun. 1992-94). Republican. Avocations: boating, guitar, chess, scuba diving, skiing. Address: 10586 Parkington Ln B Highlands Ranch CO 80126

TRACY, ROBERT (EDWARD), literature and language professor, translator; b. Woburn, Mass., Nov. 23, 1928; s. Hubert William and Vera Mary (Hurley) T.; m. Rebecca Garrison, Aug. 26, 1956; children: Jessica Janes, Hugh Garrison, Dominick O'Donovan. AB in Greek with honors, Boston Coll., 1950; MA, Harvard U., 1954, PhD, 1960. Teaching fellow Harvard U., Cambridge, Mass., 1954-58; instr. Carleton Coll., Northfield, Minn., 1958-60; from asst. prof. English, to assoc. prof., then prof. U. Calif., Berkeley, 1960-89, prof. English and Celtic Studies, 1989—, assoc. dir. Dickens Project, 1994-95. Vis. prof., Bruern fellow in Am. studies U. Leeds, Eng., 1965-66; vis. prof., Leverhulme fellow Trinity Coll., Dublin, 1971-72; vis. Kathryn W. Davis prof. slavic studies Wellesley (Mass.) Coll., 1979; Charles Mills Gayley lectr. U. Calif., Berkeley, 1989-90; vis. prof. Anglo-Irish lit. Trinity Coll., 1995-96. Author: Trollope's Later Novels, 1978, The Unappeasable Host: Studies in Irish Identities, 1998; translator (poems by Osip Mandelstam): Stone, 1981, 2d edit., 1991; editor J.M Synge's The Aran Islands, 1962, The Way We Live Now (Anthony Trollope), 1974, The Macdermots of Ballycloran (Anthony Trollope), 1989, Nina Balatka and Linda Tressel (Anthony Trollope), 1991, In A Glass Darkly (Sheridan Le Fanu) 1993, Rhapsody in Stephen's Green (Flann O'Brien), 1994; adv. editor The Recorder, 1985—, LIT (Lit., Interpretation, Theory), 1989—, Dickens Studies Annual, 2001--; contbr. articles and revs. to numerous jours. including Shakespeare Quarterly, So. Rev., Nineteenth-Century Fiction, Irish Univ. Rev., Eire-Ireland, Irish Literary Supplement, others; poetry translations in New Orleans Rev., Poetry, N.Y. Rev. of Books, Ploughshares, others. Appointed mem. cultural panel San Francisco-Cork Sister City Com. Fulbright travel grantee, 1965-66; recipient humanities research fellowships U. Calif., Berkeley, 1962, 69, 78, 81, 86, 92; Guggenheim fellow, 1981-82. Mem. MLA, Philol. Assn. Pacific Coast, Am. Conf. for Irish Studies, Internat. Assn. for Study of Irish Lit. Avocation: exploring western Ireland and northern California. Office: U Calif Dept English Berkeley CA 94720-1030 E-mail: rtracy@uclink4.berkeley.edu.

TRAFTON, STEPHEN J., bank executive; b. Mt. Vernon, Wash., Sept. 17, 1946; m. Diane Trafton; children: John, Roland. BS in Zoology, Wash. State U., 1968. V.p., mgr. dept. money market Seattle-First Nat. Bank, 1968-79; v.p., mgr. bank consulting group Donaldson Lufkin Jennrette, NYC, 1980; exec. v.p., treas. Gibraltar Savings Bank, LA, 1980-84; banking cons., 1984-86; v.p., treas. Hibernia Bank, San Francisco, 1986-88; sr. v.p., treas. Goldome Bank, Buffalo, N.Y., 1988-90; sr. exec. v.p., CFO Glenfed Inc., 1990-91, vice chmn., CFO, 1991—, pres., 1992—; sr. exec. v.p., CFO Glendale Fed. Bank, 1990-91, vice chmn., CFO, 1991, pres., COO, 1991-92, chmn. bd., pres., CEO, 1992-99, COO, also bd. dirs.; exec. v.p. Golden State Bancorp, 1999—. Mem. Phi Eta Sigma.

TRAIL, THOMAS F., state legislator; b. Moscow, Idaho, July 29, 1935; m. Jo Ann Trail; children: Ruth, Mark, Steven. BS in Animal Sci., U. Idaho, 1958; MA, U. Md., 1960; EdD in Exptl. Psychology, Mont. State U., 1966. Dir., mem. Keifer Project Peace Corps, Ecuador, 1963—65; assoc. prof. U. Nebr., 1966—69; head social sci. program Ministry of Agr., Colombia, 1969—71; prof. Washington State U., 1971—94; mem. Dist. 6A Idaho House of Reps., Boise, 1996—, mem. agrl. affairs, commerce and human resources, and edn. coms. Served Med. Co. USAR, 1953—61. Mem.: LWV, Latah County Fairboard, Northwest Adult Educators Assn., Assn. Internat. Agrl. Educators, Moscow Rotary Club (Outstanding U. Tchr. award 1993). Republican. Office: State Capitol PO Box 83720 Boise ID 83720-0038 Address: Dist 6A 1375 Mountain View Rd Moscow ID 83843 Office Phone: 208-332-1000, 800-626-0471. Fax: 208-882-0896. Business E-Mail: ttrail@house.idaho.gov.*

TRAN, KHANH T., insurance company executive; BA in Econ. and Polit. Sci., Whittier Coll.; MBA in Fin. and Mktg., UCLA. With United Calif. Bank, Flying Tiger Line, Inc.; asst. treas. Vons Cos., Inc.; treas. Pacific Life Ins. Co., Newport Beach, Calif., 1990—91, v.p., treas., 1991—95, v.p. corp. develop., treas., 1995—96, sr. v.p., CFO, 1996—2001, exec. v.p., CFO, 2001—. Mem.: ACLI (CFO Conf.). Office: Pacific Life Ins Co PO Box 9000 Newport Beach CA 92658-9030

TRAN, VAN, state legislator; b. Saigon, Vietnam; m. Cyndi Tran; 1 child, Alexander. BA in Polit. Sci., U. Calif. Irvine, 1990; JD, Hamline U., St. Paul, Minn.; MA in Pub. Adminstrn., Hamline U. California State Assemblyman, District 68, 2005-; vice chairman, Environ Safety & Toxic Materials; member, Bank & Finance, Bus & Professions comts, currently; member, Select Committee on Critical Issues & Asian Pacific Islander Joint Caucus. Republican. Office: Dist 68 1503 S Coast Dr Ste 205 Costa Mesa CA 92626 Office Phone: 714-668-2100. Office Fax: 714-668-2104. Business E-Mail: assemblymember.tran@assembly.ca.gov.*

TRAPA, PETER ENGEL, mathematics professor; BA, Northwestern Univ., 1993; PhD in Math., MIT, 1998. Mem. sch. math. inst. for adv. study Princeton Univ., 1998—2000; NSF postdoctoral fellow Harvard Univ., 2000—03; asst prof., math. Univ. Utah, 2001—05, assoc. prof., 2005—. Achievements include being one of 18 top mathematicians and computer scientists (Atlas of Lie Groups Project) from the US to successfully map E8, one of the largest and most complicated structures in mathematics. Office: Dept Math LCB 118 Univ Utah Salt Lake City UT 84112 Office Phone: 801-585-7671. Office Fax: 801-581-4148. Business E-Mail: ptrapa@math.utah.edu.

TRAPP, LANSFORD E., air force officer; m. Nancy Trapp; 1 child, Bethany. BSEE, S.D. State U., 1969; posgrad., Squadron Officer Sch., Maxwell AFB, Ala., 1974; MPA, Pepperdine U., 1976; postgrad., Armed Forces Staff Coll., Norfolk, Va., 1981, Nat. War Coll., Washington, 1988, MIT, 1993, Syracuse U., 1997, Johns Hopkins U., 1997. Commd. 2d lt. USAF, 1969, advanced through grades to lt. gen., 1997, OV-10A forward air contr., 22nd Tactical Air Control Bien Hoa AB, Vietnam, 1970-71, OV-10A instr. pilot 549th Tactical Air Control Tng. Squadron Hurlburt Field, Fla., 1971-74, A-7D fighter pilot, 74th Tactical Fighter Squadron England AFB, La., 1974-77, fighter assignment officer, dep. chief fighter Randolph AFB, Tex., 1977-80, F-4E and F-16A fighter pilot, ops. officer 10th Tactical Hahn AB, West Germany, 1981-83, chief std. and evaluation divsn. 50th Tactical Command, 1983, ops. officer, comdr. 313th Tactical Fighter Squadron, 1983-85, tactical force programmer, directorate programs Hdqrs. Washington, 1985-86, exec. officer, dep. chief of staff programs and resources, 1986-87, comdr. 832nd Combat Support Group Luke AFB, Ariz., 1988, comdr. 24th Composite Wing Howard AFB, Panama, 1989-90, chief Gen. Officer Group Hdqrs. Washington, 1990-91, mil. asst. sec. Air Force, Hdqs., 1991-93, comdr. 355th Wing Davis-Monthan AFB, Ariz., 1993—94, comdr. 366th Wing Mountain Home AFB, Ohio, 1994—95, dep. dir. to leg. liaison office of sec. Washington, 1995—97, comdr. 12th Air Force and U.S. Southern Command Air Forces Davis-Monthan AFB, Ariz., 1997—99; vice comdr. hdqrs. Pacific Air Forces, Hickam AFB, Hawaii, 1999—; vice comdr. FAF. Decorated Legion of Merit with two oak leaf clusters, Disting. Flying Cross with oak leaf cluster, Purple Heart, Disting. Svc. medal, Meritorious Svc. medal with two oak leaf clusters, air medal with eight oak leaf clusters, Air Force commendation medal with oak leaf cluster, Presdl. unit citation with oak leaf cluster, Rep. of Vietnam Campaign medal with four svc. stars, Rep. of Vietnam Gallantry Cross with Palm. Office: 25 E St Ste G214 Hickam AFB HI 96853-5400

TRASK, ROBERT RILEY CHAUNCEY, writer, educator, foundation administrator; b. Albuquerque, Jan. 2, 1939; s. Edward Almon Trask and Florence Jane (White) Jones; m. Katie Lucille Bitters (div. 1981); m. Mary Jo Chiarottino, Dec. 1, 1984; 1 child, Chauncey Anne. Student pub. schs., San Diego. Lic. master sea capt. Entertainer, singer, comedian, 1964--; founder, pres. Nat. Health & Safety Svcs., San Francisco, 1968-71, ARAS Found., Issaquah, Wash., 1978—; capt., dive master San Diego Dive Charters, 1972-75; sr. capt., dive master Pacific Sport Diving Corp., Long Beach, Calif., 1975-77; lectr., bus. cons., 1978—. Cons., tng. developer Nissan, Gen. Dynamics, AT&T, religious orgns., also other corps., 1978--. Author: (manual) Tulip, 1971, Living Free, 1982, God's Phone Number, 1987, (video program for adolescents) Breaking Free, Realtor, 2006-, also seminar manuals. Mem. SAG. Avocations: fishing, boating, diving, exploring, gardening. Office: ARAS Found 3020 Issaquah Pine Lake Rd SE #93 Sammamish WA 98075 Office Phone: 425-868-8448. Business E-Mail: bob@arasfoundation.org. E-mail: arasfdn@earthlink.net.

TRAUGOTT, ELIZABETH CLOSS, linguist, educator, researcher; b. Bristol, Eng., Apr. 9, 1939; d. August and Hannah M. M. (Priebsch) Closs; m. John L. Traugott, Sept. 26, 1967; 1 child, Isabel. BA in English, Oxford U., Eng., 1960; PhD in English Lang., U. Calif., Berkeley, 1964. Asst. prof. English U. Calif., Berkeley, 1964-70; lectr. U. East Africa, Tanzania, 1965-66, U. York, Eng., 1966-67; lectr., then assoc. prof. linguistics and English Stanford (Calif.) U., 1970-77, prof., 1977—2003, chmn. linguistics dept., 1980-85, vice provost, dean grad. studies, 1985-91, mem. grad. record examinations bd., 1989-93, mem. test of English as a fgn. lang. bd., 1990—92, chmn. test of English as a fgn. lang. bd., 1991—92. Mem. higher edn. funding coun. Eng. Assessment Panel, 1996, 2001, 08. Author: (book) A History of English Syntax, 1972; author: (with Mary Pratt) Linguistics for Students of Literature, 1980; author: (with Paul Hopper) Grammaticalization, 1993, rev. edit., 2003; author: (with Richard Dasher) Regularity in Semantic Change, 2002; author: (with Laurel J. Brinton) Lexicalization and Language Change, 2005; editor (with ter Meulen, Reilly, Ferguson): (book) On Conditionals, 1986; editor: (with Heine) Approaches to Grammaticalization, 2 vols., 1991; series co-editor: Topics in English Linguistics; contbr. articles to profl. jours. Am. Coun. Learned Socs. fellow, 1975—76, Guggenheim fellow, 1983—84, Ctr. Advanced Study Behavioral Scis. fellow, 1983—84. Fellow: AAAS; mem.: AAUW, AAUP, MLA, Internat. Soc. Linguistics English (pres. 2007—), Internat. Pragmatics Assn. (bd. dirs. 2000—), Internat. Soc. Hist. Linguistics (pres. 1979—81), Linguistic Soc. Am. (pres. 1987, sec.-treas. 1994—98). Office: Stanford Univ Dept Linguistics Bldg 460 Stanford CA 94305-2150 Business E-Mail: traugott@stanford.edu.

TRAUGOTT, PETER S., television producer, broadcast executive; b. 1964; V.p. Brillstein-Grey TV, 1996—2005, pres., 2005—. Actor: (TV series) Party of Five; (films) Silent Men, 2005; exec. prodr.: (TV series) Numb3rs, Way Downtown, 2002, My Big Greek Fat Life, 2003, The Showbiz Show With David Spade, 2005, Jake in Progress, 2005, Girls on the Bus, 2006, 52 Fights, 2006, Mr. Nice Guy, 2006, Cracking Up, 2006, Sam I Am, 2007, Frangela, 2007, See Jayne Run, 2007. Named a Maverick, Details mag., 2007. Office: Brillstein Grey Entertainment 9150 Wilshire Blvd Ste 350 Beverly Hills CA 90212 Office Phone: 310-275-6135. Office Fax: 310-275-6180.

TRAUNER, GARY, entrepreneur; m. Terry Trauner; children: Benjamin, Aaron. Grad., Colgate U., Hamilton, NY; MBA, NYU Stern Sch. Bus., NYC. V.p. fin. Teton Trust Co., Wyo.; co-founder, CFO OneWest.net, Wyo., Cell Response Formulation, LLC, Wyo. At-large candidate US House of Reps., 2006; past chmn. Teton County Sch. Dist. #1 Bd. Trustees; chmn. Aspens Water & Sewer Dist.; former vice-chmn. Teton County Pathways Task Force; mem. open range com. Jackson Hole Land Trust. Democrat. Office: Cell Response Formulation LLC PO Box 7396 4115 S Pub Pl Jackson WY 83002 Office Phone: 307-734-7839. Office Fax: 307-734-4667.

TRAUTMAN, WILLIAM ELLSWORTH, lawyer; b. San Francisco, Nov. 27, 1940; s. Gerald H. and Doris Joy (Tucker) T.; m. Dorothy (Williamson), June 17, 1962; children: Darcey, Torey. BA, U. Calif., Berkeley, 1962, LLB, 1965. Bar: Calif. 1966, US Supreme Ct., Calif. Dist. Ct., US Ct. Appeals (9th and Fed. Cir.). Assoc. Chickering and Gregory, San Francisco, 1965-71, ptnr., 1972-81, Brobeck, Phleger, and Harrison, San Francisco, 1981—2003, litig. dept. chair, 1984-91, San Francisco mng. ptnr., 1992-96; ptnr. Morgan, Lewis, and Bockius, San Francisco, 2003—05; pvt. practice San Francisco, 2005—. Pres. Oakland, Calif. Mus. Assn., 1981-83; mem. profl. ethics com. State Bar Calif., 1974-77. Fellow: Am. Coll. Trial Lawyers; mem.: Barrister's Club of San Francisco (v.p. 1973), Calif. Barristers (bd. dirs., v.p.), Bar Assn. San Francisco (bd. dirs. 1972—73), Legal Aid Soc. (bd. dirs. 1982—93, pres. 1985—88), U. Calif.-Berkeley Found. (trustee 1998—2000), Boalt Hall Alumni Assn. (bd. dirs. 1993—99, pres. 1997—98). Office: 5283 Broadway Terr Oakland CA 94618 Home Phone: 707-255-5570; Office Phone: 510-547-1555. Business E-Mail: trautman17@sbcglobal.net.

TRAVERS, JUDITH LYNNETTE, human resources executive; b. Buffalo, Feb. 25, 1950; d. Harold Elwin and Dorothy (Helsel) Howes; m. David Jon Travers, Oct. 21, 1972; 1 child, Heather Lynne. BA in Psychology, Barrington Coll., 1972; cert. in paralegal course, St. Mary's Coll., Moraga, Calif., 1983; postgrad., Southland U., 1982-84. Exec. sec. Sherman C. Weeks, P.A., Derry, N.H., 1973-75; legal asst. Mason-McDuffie Co., Berkeley, Calif., 1975-82; paralegal asst. Blum, Kay, Merkle & Kauftheil, Oakland, Calif., 1982-83; CEO, bd. dirs. Dela Pers. Svcs. Inc., Concord, Calif., 1983—; pres. All Ages Sitters Agy., Concord, 1986-95; CEO, bd. dirs. Guardian Security Agy., Concord, Calif., 1992—. Sec., bd. dirs. Per Diem Staffing Systems, Inc., Securicorp. Vocalist record album The Loved Ones, 1978. Vol. local Congl. campaign, 1980, Circle of Friends, Children's Hosp. No. Calif., Oakland, 1987—; mem. Alameda County Sheriff's Mounted Posse, 1989, Contra Costa Child Abuse Prevention Coun., 1989; employer adv. coun. Ctrl. Contra Costa County, 1993—; mem. Carondelet/De La Salle H.S. Adult Choir, 1998— Recipient Outstanding Achievement in Amateur Photography award, Internat. Soc. Photographers, 2004. Mem. NAFE, Am. Assn. Respiratory Therapy, Soc. for Human Resource Mgmt., Am. Mgmt. Assn., Gospel Music Assn., Palomino Horse Breeders Am., DAR, Barrington Oratorio Soc., Commonwealth Club Calif., Nat. Trust Hist. Preservation, Alpha Theta Sigma. Republican. Baptist. Avocations: boating, horses. Home: 3900 Brown Rd Oakley CA 94561-2664 Office: Delta Pers Svcs Inc 1820 Galindo St Ste 3 Concord CA 94520-2447 Home Phone: 925-625-0240; Office Phone: 925-356-3050. Personal E-mail: jltravers@aol.com.

TRAVIS, VANCE KENNETH, petroleum business executive; b. Coriander, Sask., Can., Jan. 30, 1926; s. Roy Hazen and Etta Orilla (Anderson) T.; m. Louise Mary, Nov. 30, 1948 (div. 1979); children: Stuart, Shirley, Gordon, Donald, Marian; m. Mildred Elaine, June 29, 1979; stepchildren: Susan, Nancy, Gordon, Sandra, Karen. Chmn. bd. Turbo Resources Ltd., 1970-83, Challenger Internat., 1977-83, Bankeno Mines Ltd., 1977-83, Queenston Gold Mines Ltd., Toronto, Ont., Canada, 1977-84, Health Risk Mgmt. Inc., Mpls., 1984-86, Triad Internat. Inc., 1985—96; dir. Health Resource Mgmt. Ltd., Edmonton, Alta., Canada, 1990-97. Bd. dirs. Vencap Equities Alta. Ltd., Edmonton, 1981-86, L.K. Resources Ltd., Calgary, 1973-84. Mem. Young. Pres.'s Orgn., Calgary, 1964-76, World Pres. Orgn. Recipient Presdl. pin Jr. Achievement, 1963, Best Pitcher award Petroleum Fastball League, 1955. Mem.: Calgary Petroleum Club. E-mail: kentravis@telus.net.

TRAVOUS, KENNETH E., state agency administrator; Exec. dir. Ariz. State Parks Bd., Phoenix. Office: Ariz State Parks Bd 1300 W Washington St Phoenix AZ 85007-2929

TRAYNOR, J. MICHAEL, retired lawyer; b. Oakland, Calif., Oct. 25, 1934; s. Roger J. and Madeleine (Lackmann) Traynor; m. Shirley Williams, Feb. 11, 1956; children: Kathleen Traynor DeRose, Elizabeth Traynor Fowler, Thomas. BA, U. Calif., Berkeley, 1955; JD, Harvard U., 1960; LLD (hon.), U. SC, Columbia, 2007. Bar: Calif. 1961, U.S. Supreme Ct. 1966. Dep. atty. gen. State of Calif., San Francisco, 1961—63; spl. counsel Calif. Senate Com. on Local Govt., Sacramento, 1963; assoc. firm Cooley Godward Kronish, LLP, San Francisco, 1963—69, ptnr., 1969—2004, sr. counsel, 2005—08. Adviser 3d Restatement of Unfair Competition, 1988—95, 3d Restatement of Torts, Products Liability, 1992—98, Apportionment, 1994—99, 2d Restatement of Conflict of Laws revs., 1988, 3d Restatement of Restitution and Unjust Enrichment, 1997—; lectr. Boalt Hall Sch. Law U. Calif., 1982—89, 1996—98; chmn. Earthjustice Legal Def. Fund (formerly Sierra Club Legal Def. Fund), 1991—92; trustee EarthJustice Legal Def. Fund (formerly Sierra Club Legal Def. Fund), 1974—96; prin. World Trade Law, 2008. Mem. bd. overseers Inst. for Civil Justice RAND, 1991—97; bd. dirs. Environ. Law Inst., 1991—97, 1999—2005, Ecojustice Can. (formerly Sierra Legal Def. Fund), Canada, 1990—96. 1st lt. USMC, 1955—57, USMCR, 1957—63. Recipient John P. Frank award, 2004. Fellow: Am. Acad. Appellate Lawyers, Am. Acad. Arts & Scis., Calif. Acad. Appellate Lawyers, Am. Bar Found. (life); mem.: Bar Assn. San Francisco (pres. 1973), Am. Law Inst. (coun. 1985—, pres. 2000—08, chair coun. 2008—). Home: 3131 Eton Ave Berkeley CA 94705-2713 Office Phone: 510-658-8839. Office Fax: 510-658-5162. Personal E-mail: mtraynor@traynorgroup.com.

TREADWELL, DAVID, computer software company executive; b. 1967; s. David R. Treadwell and Carol A. Ritter, Elizabeth S. Treadwell (Stepmother) and Donald E. Williams (Stepfather); m. Lynn Treadwell; children: David, Aiden. BEE, Princeton U., 1989. With Microsoft Corp., 1989—, v.p. .NET Devel. Platform divsn., corp. v.p. Live Platform services, 2007—. Avocations: marathons, triathlons, photography. Office: Microsoft Corp 1 Microsoft Way Redmond WA 98052-6399

TREAS, JUDITH KAY, sociology educator; b. Phoenix, Jan. 2, 1947; d. John Joseph and Hope Catherine (Thomas) Jennings; m. Benjamin C. Treas II, May 14, 1969; children: Stella, Evan. BA, Pitzer Coll., Claremont, Calif., 1969; MA, UCLA, 1972, PhD, 1976. Instr. U. So. Calif., LA, 1974-75, asst. prof., 1975-81, assoc. prof., 1981-87, dept. chair, 1984-89, prof., 1987-89, U. Calif., Irvine, 1989, dept. chair, 1989-94. Bd. overseers Gen. Social Survey, 1986-88; cons. social sci. and population study sect. NIH, 1989-92. Contbr. articles to profl. jours. Trustee Pitzer Coll., 1977-79. Recipient Rsch. award NSF, 1978-81, 84-91, NIH, 1979-81; Univ. scholar U. So. Calif., 1982-83. Fellow Gerontological Assn. Am.; mem. Golden Key (hon.), Am. Sociol. Assn., Population Assn. Am. Office: U Calif Dept Sociology Irvine CA 92697-0001

TREBON, THOMAS, academic administrator; m. Scottie Trebon. B magna cum laude, Seattle U.; M, PhD, U. Denver. Tchr., adminstr. Seattle U.; acad. dean Coll. Arts and Scis. Rockhurst Coll., Kansas City; provost, v.p. acad. affairs Sacred Heart U., Trumbull, Conn., St. Norbert Coll., 1995—2001, v.p. acad. affairs, dean; pres. Carroll Coll., Helena, Mont., 2001—. Office Phone: 406-447-4401.

TREFNY, JOHN ULRIC, retired college president; b. Jan. 28, 1942; s. Ulric John and Mary Elizabeth (Leech) T.; m. Sharon Livingston, 1992; 1 child from previous marriage, Benjamin Robin. BS, Fordham U., 1963; PhD, Rutgers U., 1968; doctorate (hon.), Colo. Sch. of Mines, 2006. Rsch. assoc. Cornell U., Ithaca, NY, 1967-69; asst. prof. physics Wesleyan U., Middletown, Conn., 1969-77, Colo. Sch. Mines, Golden, 1977-79, assoc. prof., 1979-85, prof., 1985—, assoc. dean rsch., 1988—90, head physics dept., 1990—95, v.p. for acad. affairs, dean faculty, 1995—2000, pres., 2000—06. Dir. Amorphous Materials Ctr. Colo. Sch. Mines, 1986-90; cons. Solar Energy Rsch. Inst., Golden, Energy Conversion Devices, Troy, Mich., others. Contbr. articles to profl. jours. Mem. Golden Civic Found., Red Rocks CC Found.; bd. mem. Denver region Inst. Internat. Edn. Recipient Tchg. award AMOCO Found., 1984, Friend of Sci. Edn. award, 1990. Avocations: golf, travel. Home: 14268 W 1st Ave Golden CO 80401 Personal E-mail: jtrefny@mines.edu.

TREGEMBA, ROBERT D., telecommunications industry executive; married; 2 children. BS in Civil Engring., U. Kans., Lawrence, 1971. With ops. group Southwestern Bell; several exec. positions including v.p. engring. and planning and v.p. mktg. for local exch. divsn. Sprint Corp.; COO Long Distance US West (now Qwest), 1996; exec. v.p. engring. and ops. Qwest Comm. Internat., Inc., v.p. network svcs., 2004—07, exec. v.p. network ops., 2007—. Office: Qwest Comm Internat Inc 1801 California St Denver CO 80202 Office Phone: 303-992-1400. Office Fax: 303-896-8515.

TREIGER, IRWIN LOUIS, lawyer; b. Seattle, Sept. 10, 1934; s. Sam S. and Rose (Steinberg) T.; m. Betty Lou Friedlander, Aug. 18, 1957; children: Louis H., Karen I., Kenneth B. BA, U. Wash., 1955, JD, 1957; LLM in Taxation, NYU, 1958. Bar: Wash. 1958, D.C. 1982, U.S. Dist. Ct. (we. dist.) Wash., U.S. Ct. Appeals (9th cir.), U.S. Supreme Ct. Assoc. Bogle & Gates, Seattle, 1958—63, ptnr., 1964—99, chmn., 1986—94; ptnr. Dorsey & Whitney LLP, Seattle, 1999—. Trustee Am. Tax Policy Inst., 2004—06. Pres. Jewish Fedn. Greater Seattle, 1993-95; chmn. Mayor's Symphony Panel, 1986, Corp. Coun. for the Arts, 1987-88; pres. Seattle Symphony Found., 1986—; trustee, co-chmn. Cornish Coll. of the Arts, 1990-96, chair elect 2003—; trustee The Seattle Found., 1992—, vice chair, 1999-2003, chair, 2003-05; trustee, sec. Samis Found., 1989—; chmn. King County Baseball Pk. Commn., 1995; chmn. task force tax reform Prosperity Partnership Puget Sound Regional Coun., 2006—. Fellow Am. Coll. Tax Counsel; mem. ABA (chmn. taxation sect. 1988-89, sect. del. 1990-96, bd. govs. 2000-03), Wash. State Bar Assn. (chmn. taxation sect. 1975, co-chmn. nat. conf. lawyers and accts. 1997-2000, 09, ABA Sec.Dist. Svc. award), Greater Seattle C. of C. (chmn. 1993-94), Seattle Rotary (trustee 1998-2000), Seattle Rotary Svc. Found. (v.p. 1995-96, pres. 1996-97). Jewish. Office: Irwin L Treiger 600 University St Ste 3600 Seattle WA 98101-4109 Home Phone: 206-328-8404; Office Phone: 206-386-7215, 206-386-7511. Business E-Mail: iltreiger@stoel.com.

TREISTER, GEORGE MARVIN, lawyer; b. Oxnard, Calif., Sept. 5, 1923; s. Isadore Harry and Augusta Lee (Bloom) T.; m. Jane Goldberg, Jan. 24, 1946; children: Laura, Neil, Adam, Dana. BS, UCLA, 1943; LL.B., Yale U., 1949. Bar: Calif. 1950. Law clk. to chief justice Calif. Supreme Ct., 1949-50; law clk. to Assoc. Justice Hugo L. Black U. S. Supreme Ct., 1950-51; asst. U.S. atty. So. Dist. Calif., 1951-53; dep. atty. gen. Calif., 1953; practiced in Los Angeles, 1953—; mem. Stutman, Treister and Glatt, 1953—; instr. U. So. Calif. Law Sch., 1954-98, Stanford U. Law Sch., 1977-81. Mem., former vice chmn. Nat. Bankruptcy Conf., emeritus,2007-; former mem. adv. com. on bankruptcy rules Jud. Conf. U.S. Contbr. articles to profl. jours. Served with USNR, 1943-46. Mem. Am. Law Inst. Home: 1201 Neil Creek Rd Ashland OR 97520-9778 Office: 1901 Ave of the Stars 12th fl Los Angeles CA 90067 Home Phone: 541-488-3100; Office Phone: 800-201-3030.

TREMBLAY, MARC, information technology executive; B in Physics Engring., Laval U., Can.; M in Computer Sci., D in Computer Sci., UCLA. Co-arch. UltraSPARC I Sun Microsystems, Inc., chief arch. UltraSPARC II, chief arch. MAJC program, arch. picoJava processor core, sr. v.p., chief tech. officer Microelectronics, Sun fellow. Mem.: IEEE, Assn. Computing Machinery. Achievements include patents in field. Office: Sun Microsystems Inc 4150 Network Cir Santa Clara CA 95054 Office Phone: 650-960-1300.

TRENBERTH, KEVIN EDWARD, atmospheric scientist; b. Christchurch, New Zealand, Nov. 8, 1944; came to US, 1977; s. Edward Maurice and Ngaira Ivy (Eyre) T.; m. Gail Neville Thompson, Mar. 21, 1970; children: Annika Gail, Angela Dawn. BSc with honors, U. Canterbury, Christchurch, 1966; ScD, MIT, Cambridge, 1972. Meteorologist New Zealand Meteorol. Service, Wellington, 1966-76, supt. dynamic meteorology, 1976-77; assoc. prof. meteorology U. Ill., Urbana, 1977-82, prof., 1982-84; scientist Nat. Ctr. Atmospheric Research, Boulder, Colo., 1984-86, sr. scientist, 1986—, leader empirical studies group, 1987, head sect. climate analysis, 1987—; dep. dir. climate and global dynamics divsn. Nat. Ctr. Atmospheric Rsch., Boulder, Colo., 1991-95. Joint sci. com. for world climate rsch. programme, com. climate changes and the ocean Tropical Oceans Global Atmosphere Program Sci. Steering Group, 1990-94; mem. Climate Variability and Predictability Sci. Steering Group, 1995—2004, co-chair, 1996-99; joint sci. com. World Climate Rsch. Program, 1999-2006, officer 2002-2006, chair observations and assimilation panel, 2004—, mem. global energy and water cycle experiment, 2007—. Editor: Climate System Modeling, 1992, Earth Interactions, 1996-98; contbr. Intergovernmental Panel on Climate Change, 1990, 92, lead author, 1995, 2001, 07; shared Nobel Peace Prize For IPCC, 2007; contbr. articles to profl. jours. Recipient Disting. Achievement award Nat. Ctr. Atmospheric Rsch., 2003; grantee NSF, NOAA, NASA. Fellow Am. Meteorol. Soc. (editor sci. jour. 1981-86, com. chmn. 1985-87, Editor's award 1989, Jule G. Charney award 2000), AAAS (coun. del. sect. atmosphere and hydrosphere sci. 1993-97), Royal Soc. New Zealand (hon.), Am. Geophys. Union (editor's award 2007); mem. NAS (earth scis. com. 1982-85, tropical oceans global atmosphere adv. panel 1984-87, polar rsch. bd. 1986-90, climate rsch. com. 1987-90, global oceans atmosphere land sys. panel 1994-98, panel on reconciling temperature observations, 1999-2000, com. on global change rsch. 1999-02), Meterol. Soc. New Zealand. Home: 5697 Pennsylvania Pl Boulder CO 80303 Office: Nat Ctr Atmospheric Rsch PO Box 3000 Boulder CO 80307-3000 Home Phone: 303-443-1446; Office Phone: 303-497-1318. Business E-Mail: trenbert@ucar.edu.

TRENTO, ALFREDO A., thoracic surgeon, educator; b. Padua, Italy, July 3, 1950; MD, U. Padova, 1975. Cert. Am. Bd. Surgery, Am. Bd. Thoracic Surgery. Intern, internal medicine Cittadella Gen. Hosp., Padua, Italy; intern, gen. surgery U. Mass., Worcester, Mass., 1977, fellow, 1982; resident, thoracic surgery U. Mass. Med. Ctr., Worcester, Mass., 1977—82; resident, surgery U. Pitts. Sch. Medicine, Pa., 1983—85, faculty mem.; dir., ECMO Program Children's Hosp. Pitts.; dir., divsn. cardiothoracic surgery Cedars-Sinai Med. Ctr., LA, Estelle, Abe and Marjorie Sanders Endowed Chair, cardiac surgery; prof., surgery, David Geffen Sch. Medicine UCLA Sch. Medicine, Calif. Presenter in field. Contbr. articles to profl. jours., chapters to books. Fellow: ACS; mem.: Western Assn. Transplant Surgeons, Am. Assn. for Thoracic Surgery, Soc. Thoracic Surgeons, Internat. Soc. for Heart Transplantation. Office: Cedars Sinai Med Ctr 8700 Beverly Blvd Ste 6215 Los Angeles CA 90048 Office Phone: 310-423-3851. Office Fax: 310-423-0127. Business E-Mail: alfredo.trento@cshs.org.

TRESHIE, R. DAVID, former newspaper publishing executive; Publ. The Orange County Register, Santa Ana, Calif., ret., 1999. Office: The Orange County Register 625 N Grand Ave Santa Ana CA 92701-4347

TREVINO, MARIO H., protective services official; b. Bellingham, Wash., July 27, 1952; AAS, Shoreline C.C.; BA in Pub. Adminstrn. summa cum laude, Seattle U., 1986. Firefighter Seattle Fire Dept., 1973-96, bat. chief, capt. fire investigations, chief emergency med. svcs., dep. chief support svcs.; fire chief Las Vegas Fire Dept., 1996—. Mem. Met. Fire Chiefs, Internat. Assn. Fire Chiefs, Western Fire Chiefs, Nev. Fire Chiefs, So. Nev. Fire Chiefs. Office: Las Vegas Fire Svcs Dept 500 N Casino Center Blvd Las Vegas NV 89101-2944

TRILLING, GEORGE HENRY, physicist, researcher; b. Bialystok, Poland, Sept. 18, 1930; came to U.S., 1941; s. Max and Eugenie (Walfisz) T.; m. Madeleine Alice Monic, June 26, 1955; children: Stephen, Yvonne, David. BS, Calif. Inst. Tech., Pasadena, 1951, PhD, 1955. Rsch. fellow Calif. Inst. Tech., Pasadena, 1955-56; Fulbright post-doctoral fellow Ecole Polytechnique, Paris, 1956-57; asst. to assoc. prof. U. Mich., Ann Arbor, 1957-60; assoc. to prof. dept. physics U. Calif., Berkeley, 1960-94, prof. emeritus, 1994—. Fellow Am. Phys. Soc., Am. Acad. Arts and Scis.; mem. NAS. Achievements include research in high energy physics. Office: Lawrence Berkeley Nat Lab Berkeley CA 94720-0001 Office Phone: 510-486-6801. Business E-Mail: ght@lbl.gov.

TRIMBLE, PHILLIP RICHARD, law educator; b. Springfield, Ohio, Nov. 12, 1937; s. Melvin R. and Dorothy T.; m. Stephanie Gardner, July 20, 1963 (div. 1977); children: John, William; m. Valeria Vasilevski, Dec. 21, 2000. BA, Ohio U., 1958; MA, Fletcher U., 1959; JD, Harvard U., 1963. Bar: NY 1964. Legal writing instr. U. Calif., Berkeley, 1963-64; assoc. Cravath, Swaine & Moore, NYC, 1964-70; staff mem. fgn. rels. com. U.S. Senate, Washington, 1971-72; asst. legal adviser Dept. State, Washington, 1973-78; counsel to the mayor NYC, 1978; dep. mayor, 1979; U.S. ambassador Nepal, 1980-81; prof. law UCLA, 1981—2001, vice provost internat. studies, 1999—2000; founding mem. Dalai Lama Found., 2001—. Mem. exec. com. Asia Soc. So. Calif. Ctr., L.A., 1981-94; vis. prof. law Stanford U., 1988-89, U. Mich., 1995-96; U.S. panelist under U.S.-Can. Free Trade Agreement, NAFTA; cons. ACDA, 1989-92. Mem. bd. editors Am. Jour. Internat. Law, 1993-98. Bd. dirs. Milarepa Tibetan Buddhist Ctr., 2001—06, Am. Alpine Club, 1978—80, 1982—85. Fellow Explorers Club. Democrat.

TRIMBLE, STANLEY WAYNE, hydrologist; b. Columbia, Tenn., Dec. 8, 1940; s. Stanley Drake and Clara Faye (Smith) T.; m. Alice Erle Gunn, Aug. 16, 1964; children: Alicia Anne, Jennifer Lusanne. BS, U. North Ala., 1964; MA, U. Ga., 1970, PhD, 1973. Asst. prof. hydrology and geography U. Wis., Milw., 1972-75; from asst. prof. to prof. UCLA, 1975—. Vis. asst. prof. U. Chgo., 1978, vis. assoc. prof., 81, vis. prof. environ. geography, 1990—; vis. prof. U. Durham, England, 1998; vis. lectr. U. London, 1985; hydrologist US Geol. Survey, 1974—84; vis. prof. U. Vienna, 1994, 99; Frost lectr. Brit. Geomorphol. Rsch. Group, Durham, 1994; vis. rsch. lectr. Oxford U., 1995; Fulbright scholar in UK, 95; vis. fellow Keble Coll., Oxford U., 1995, Hatfield Coll., U. Durham, 1998. Author: Culturally Accelerated Sedimentation on the Middle Georgia Piedmont, 1971, Man-Induced Erosion on the Southern Piedmont, 1700-1970, 1974, Soil Conservation and the Reduction, 1982, Sediment Characteristics of Tennessee Streams, 1984, (with A Ward) Environmental Hydrology, 2004 (ASAE Blue Ribbon award); joint editor-in-chief: Catena, 1995-2006; editor: Dekker Encyclopedia of Water Science, 2003-; contbr. articles to profl. jours; editor, Enclopedic Water Sci., 2003-07. 1st lt. 101 Airborne Divsn. US Army, 1963—65. Grantee U.S. Geol. Survey, Washington, 1974-79, Wis. Dept. Natural Resources, Madison, 1978, 82, 93, 94, 95, NSF, Washington, 1976, Agrl. Rsch. Svc. of USDA, Washington, 1972, Nat. Geographic Soc., 1993. Mem.: NAS-NRC (Com. on Watershed Mgmt. 1996—98, Com. on Miss. River and Clean Water Act 2005—07), Brit. Geomorphol. Rsch. Group, Soil Conservation Soc. Am., Am. Geophys. Union, Assn. Am. Geographers (Disting. Career award 2006), Sigma Xi. Republican. Avocations: historic houses, documentation and restoration, landscape gardens. Office: UCLA Dept Geography 1255 Bunche Hall Los Angeles CA 90095-1524 Home Phone: 931-363-0457; Office Phone: 310-825-1071. Business E-Mail: trimble@geog.ucla.edu.

TRIPP, ALAN H., educational association administrator, consultant; AB in Econ. and Internat. Rels., Stanford U., 1985, MBA, 1989. Editor, reporter Wall St. Jour., European edit., Brussels, 1985—86; cons. Boston Consulting Group, San Francisco, 1989—91; founder, CEO, Score! Ednl. Crs., San Francisco, 1992—99, InsideTrack Learning, Inc., San Francisco, 1999—. Bd. chair GreatSchools.net, San Francisco, 2001—. Mem.: Phi Beta Kappa. Office: InsideTrack Learning Inc 703 Market St 20th Fl San Francisco CA 94114

TRITTEN, JAMES JOHN, retired federal agency administrator; s. James Hanley and Jennie (Szucs) Tritten; m. Kathleen Brattesani (div. 1983); children: Kimberly, James John Jr.; m. Jasmine Clark, Dec. 29, 1990. BA in Internat. Studies, Am. U., 1971; MA in Internat. Affairs, Fla. State U., 1978; AM in Internat. Rels., U. So. Calif., 1982, PhD in Internat. Rels., 1984. Commd. officer USN, 1967, advanced through grades to commdr., 1981; joint strategic plans officer Office Chief Naval Ops., Washington, 1984—85; asst. dir. net assessment Office Sec. Def., Washington, 1985—86; chmn. dept. nat. security affairs Naval Postgrad. Sch., Monterey, Calif., 1986—89; ret. USN, 1989; assoc. prof. nat. security affairs Naval Postgrad. Sch., Monterey, 1989—93; spl. asst. comdr. Naval Doctrine Command, Norfolk, Va., 1993—96; chief policy and plan divsn. US Joint Forces Command, Suffolk, Va., 1996—2001, mem. joint doctrine divsn., 2001—02; chief Def. Threat Reduction U./Def. Threat Reduction Agy., Albuquerque, 2002—09; asst. chief staff Def. Threat Reduction Agy., 2002—09. Cons. Rand Corp., Santa Monica, Calif., 1982—84; with Nat. Security Rsch., Fairfax, Va., 1992, Amerind, Alexandria, Va., 1996. Author: (book) Soviet Naval Forces and Nuclear Warfare, 1986, Our New National Security Strategy, 1992 (George Washington Honor medal, 1991), A Doctrine Reader, 1996; contbr. chapters to books, articles to profl. jours. Mem. Adv. Bd. on Alcohol Related Problems, Monterey, 1987—90; bd. dirs., officer Leadership Monterey Peninsula, 1989—92, Carmel Valley (Calif.) Property Owners Assn., 1989—91; commr. Airport Land Use Commn., Monterey County, 1990—93; officer Kiwans Club of Corrales, 2006, Concerned Citizens of Conales, 2008. Decorated Def. Superior Svc. medal Sec. Def., Washington, DC, Meritorious Svc. medal Sec. Navy, Navy Civilian Supr. Svc. medal; recipient Joint Meritorious Civilian Svc. award, Chmn. Joint Chiefs Staff, 1998, Alfred Thayer Mahan award literary achievement, Navy League US, 1986. Mem.: Mil. Ops. Rsch. Soc. (v.p. 1990—91), U.S. Naval Inst. (Silver and Bronze medals), Naval Order U.S., Pi Gamma Mu, Pi Sigma Alpha. Republican. Presbyterian. Avocation: writing. Personal E-mail: jtritten121@comcast.net.

TRIVELPIECE, ALVIN WILLIAM, physicist, educator, consultant; b. Stockton, Calif., Mar. 15, 1931; s. Alvin Stevens and Mae (Hughes) Trivelpiece; m. Shirley Ann Ross, Mar. 23, 1953; children: Craig Evan, Steve Edward, Keith Eric. BEE, Calif. Poly. Coll., 1953; MEE, Calif. Inst. Tech., Pasadena, 1955, PhD in Elec. Engring. and Physics, 1958. Fulbright scholar Delft U., Netherlands, 1958—59; asst. prof., then assoc. prof. U. Calif. at Berkeley, 1959—66; prof. physics U. Md., 1966—76; on leave as asst. dir. for rsch. divsn. controlled thermonuclear rsch. AEC, Washington, 1973—75; v.p. Maxwell Labs. Inc., San Diego, 1976—78; corp. v.p. Sci. Applications, Inc., La Jolla, Calif., 1978—81; dir. Office of Energy Rsch., US Dept. Energy, Washington, 1981—87; exec. officer AAAS, Washington, 1987—88; dir. Oak Ridge Nat. Lab., Tenn., 1989—2000; v.p. Martin Marietta Energy Systems, 1989—95, Lockheed Martin Energy Systems, 1995; pres. Lockheed Martin Energy Rsch. Corp., 1996—2000; cons. Sandia Nat. Labs., Albuquerque, 2000—. Head del. joint NAS and Soviet Acad. Scis. mtg. and conf. on energy and global ecol. problems USSR, 1989; chmn. math. scis. ednl. bd. NAS, 1990—93; chmn. coordinating coun. for edn. NRC, 1991—93, chmn. com. small innovative firms in Russian nuclear cities, 2001, chmn. com. on Sci. and Tech. in Kazakhstan, 2006—07; mem. Commn. on Phys. Scis., Math. and Applications, 1993—96, com. on tech. issues related to the comprehensive test ban treaty NAS, 2000—02, Tenn. Sci. and Tech. Adv. Commn., 1993—96, chmn., 1996—99, adv. com. Fedn. Networking Coun., 1992—96; chmn. and pres. Tenn. Tech. Devel. Corp., 1998—2000; workshop chmn. NAS and Russian Acad. Scis., Yekaterinburg, Russia, 2004; founding bd. mem., sec., treas. Am. Coun. on Global Nuc. Competitiveness, 2006—; bd. dirs. Environ. Literacy Coun. Author: Slow Wave Propagation in Plasma Wave Guides, 1966, Principles of Plasma Physics, 1973; contbr. articles to profl. jours. Recipient Gold medal for Disting. Svc., US Sec. Energy, 1986, Disting. Assoc. award, 2000, Tenn. Outstanding Svc. commendation, Senate Joint Resolution #530, 2000; named Disting. Alumnus, Calif. Poly. State U., 1978, Calif. Inst. Tech., Pasadena, 1987; fellow Guggenheim, 1966. Fellow: IEEE (Outstanding Engr. award region 3 1995), AAAS, Am. Phys. Soc.; mem.: NAE, AAUP, Am. Assn. Physics Tchrs., Am. Nuc. Soc., Nat. Press Club, Capital Hill Club, Tau Beta Pi, Sigma Xi. Achievements include patents in field. Home and Office: 14 Wade Hampton Trail Henderson NV 89052-6635 Office Phone: 702-492-1602. Personal E-mail: awt511@cox.net.

TROIDL, RICHARD JOHN, banker; b. Buffalo, July 2, 1944; s. Henry Albert and Lola Julian (Davern) T.; m. Diane Budney, Nov. 20, 1982; children: Nicholas, Holly. AAS, SUNY, Buffalo, 1973. Sr. v.p. Empire Am. Fed. Savs. Bank, Buffalo, 1969-93; pres. Express Svcs. of Am., Inc., Las Vegas, Nev., 1993—. With U.S. Army, 1965-71. Office: Express Svcs Am Inc 6120 W Tropicana Ave Ste A16 Las Vegas NV 89103-4697

TRONCOSO, JOSE GERARDO, protective services official; b. Juarez-Chin, Mex., Dec. 26, 1952; MA in Pub. Adminstrn., LaSalle U., 1991. Cert. Peace Officer Standards-Tng., Nev. Police officer N. Las Vegas Police Dept., 1974-97; U.S. marshall U.S. Marshall Svc., 1997—. Tchr. Clark Co. traffic sch., City Las. Vegas traffic sch./DUI instr. Mem. Nat. Safety Council., Hispanics in Politics. Mem. N. Las Vegas Police Officers Assn. (chmn. bd. dirs.), Nev. Conf. Police and Sheriffs, Lation Peace Officers Assn., Latin C. of C., Internat. Union Police Assocs., Internat. Assn. Chiefs of Police.

TROST, BARRY MARTIN, chemist, educator; b. Phila., June 13, 1941; s. Joseph and Esther T.; m. Susan Paula Shapiro, Nov. 25, 1967; children: Aaron David, Carey Daniel. BA cum laude, U. Pa., Phila., 1962; PhD, MIT, Cambridge, 1965; D (hon.), U. Claude Bernard, Lyons, France, 1994, Technion, Israel, 1997. Mem. faculty U. Wis., Madison, 1965—, prof., chemistry, 1969—, Evan P. and Marion Helfaer prof. chemistry, from 1976, Vilas rsch. prof. chemistry; prof. chemistry Stanford U., 1987—, Tamaki prof. humanities and scis., 1990, chmn. dept., 1996—2002; Lord Todd vis. prof. Cambridge U., England, 2002—. Cons. Merck, Sharp & Dohme, E.I. duPont de Nemours.; hon. prof. Shanghai Inst. Organic Chemistry, 2006. Author: Problems in Spectroscopy, 1967, Sulfur Ylides, 1975; editor-in-chief Comprehensive Organic Synthesis, 1991—, ChemTracts/Organic Chemistry, 1993—; editor: Structure and Reactivity Concepts in Organic Chemistry series, 1972—; assoc. editor Jour. Am. Chem. Soc., 1974-80; mem. editl. bd. Organic Reactions Series, 1971—, Chemistry A European Jour., 1995—, Sci. of Synthesis, Houben-Weyl Methods of Molecular Transformations, 1995—; contbr. numerous articles to profl. jours. Recipient Dreyfus Found. Tech.-Scholar award, 1970, 1977, Creative Work in Synthetic Organic Chemistry award, 1981, Baekland medal, 1981, Alexander von Humboldt award, 1984, Guenther award, 1990, Janssen prize, 1990, Roger Adams award, Am. Chem. Soc., 1995, Presdl. Green Univ. Challenge award, 1998, Nicholas medal, 2000, Yamada prize, 2001, ACS Nobel Laureate Signature award, Graduate Ed. Chemistry, 2002, John Scott award, City of Phila., 2004, Nagoya medal, 2008; named Chem. Pioneer, Am. Inst. Chemists, 1983; fellow, NSF, 1963—65, Sloan Found., 1967—69, Am. Swiss Found., 1975—, Zeneca, 1997; scholar Cope scholar, 1989. Mem.: NAS, AAAS, Chem. Soc. London, Am. Acad. Arts and Scis., Am. Chem. Soc. (award in pure chemistry 1977, Roger Adams award 1995, Herbert C. Brown award for creative rsch. in synthetic methods 1999, Nobel Laureate Signature award for grad. edn. in chemistry 2002, Arthur C. Cope award 2004, centenary lectr. 1982). Office: Stanford U Dept Chemistry Stanford CA 94305

TROST, GLENN W., lawyer; b. Boston, Mar. 27, 1956; BS, MIT; JD cum laude, Southwestern Univ., 1984. Bar: Calif. 1984, US Dist. Ct. (no. & ctrl. dist. Calif.), US Ct. Appeals (9th & Fed. cir.), Supreme Ct. Calif., Supreme Ct. Colo., US Supreme Ct. 2000. Ptnr. mng. partner LA office Coudert Bros. LLP, LA. Adj. prof. Southwestern Univ. Sch. Law, 1986—91. Office Phone: 213-229-2900. Office Fax: 213-229-2999. Business E-Mail: gtrost@coudert.com.

TROTT, MENA, application developer; b. 1977; m. Ben Trott. Webblogger dollarshort.org, 2001; co-founder, pres. Six Apart, Inc., 2004—. Spkr. in field. Named one of People of the Year, PC Mag., 2004, Top 100 Young Innovators, MIT Tech. Review, 2004, Fast 50 for 2004, Fast Company, Most Influential Women in Technology, 2009. Achievements include creator of TypePad and Moveable Type, software tools for publishing weblogs. Office: Six Apart 548 4th St San Francisco CA 94107-1621*

TROTT, STEPHEN SPANGLER, federal judge; b. Glen Ridge, NJ, Dec. 12, 1939; s. David Herman and Virginia (Spangler) Trott; m. Carol C. Trott; children: Christina, Shelley. BA, Wesleyan U., 1962; LLB, Harvard U., 1965; LLD (hon.), Santa Clara U., 1992; LLD (hon.), U. Idaho, 2001. Bar: Calif. 1966, US Dist. Ct. (ctrl. dist.) Calif. 1966, US Ct. Appeals (9th cir.) 1983, US Supreme Ct. 1984. Guitarist, mem. The Highwaymen, 1958—; dep. dist. atty. LA County Dist. Atty.'s Office, LA, 1966—75, chief dep. dist. atty., 1975—79; US dist. atty. Ctrl. Dist. Calif., LA, 1981—83; asst. atty. gen. criminal divsn. US Dept. Justice, Washington, 1983—86; faculty Nat. Coll. Dist. Attys., Houston, 1973—80; chmn. central dist. Calif. Law Enforcement Coord. Com., Houston, 1981—83; coord. LA-Nev. Drug Enforcement Task Force, 1982—83; assoc. atty. gen. US Dept. Justice, Washington, 1986—88; chmn. US Interpol, 1986—88; judge US Ct. Appeals (9th cir.), Boise, Idaho, 1988—2004, sr. judge, 2004—. Trustee Wesleyan U., 1984—87; adv. council Big Brothers, Big Sisters S.W. Idaho, 2001—03; ofcl. photographer World Cup Wrestling Championship, 2003—; bd. dirs., pres. Children's Home Soc., Idaho, 1990—2004. Recipient Gold record as singer-guitarist for Michael Row the Boat Ashore, 1961, Disting. Faculty award, Nat. Coll. Dist. Attys., 1977. Mem.: Am. Coll. Trial Lawyers, Boise (Idaho) Philharm. Assn. (bd. dirs. 1995—, v.p. 1997—99, pre-concert lectr. 1997—, pres. 1999—2003), Idaho Classic Guitar Soc. (founder, pres. 1989—2004), Internat. Brotherhood Magicians, Idaho Racing Pigeon Assn., Magic Castle, Brentwood Racing Pigeon Club (pres. 1977—82), Wilderness Fly Fishers Club (pres. 1975—77). Republican. Office: US Ct Appeals 9th Cir 666 US Courthouse 550 W Fort St Boise ID 83724-0040

TROTTER, F(REDERICK) THOMAS, retired academic administrator; b. LA, Apr. 17, 1926; s. Fred B. and Hazel (Thomas) T.; m. Gania Demaree, June 27, 1953; children: Ruth Elizabeth, Paula Anne (dec.), Tania, Mary. AB, Occidental Coll., 1950, DD, 1968; STB, Boston U., 1953, PhD, 1958; LHD, Ill. Wesleyan U., 1974, Cornell Coll., 1985, Westmar Coll., 1987; LLD, U. Pacific, 1978, Wesleyan Coll., 1981; EdD, Columbia Coll., 1984; LittD, Alaska Pacific U., 1987; DD, Emory U., 1989. Exec. sec. Boston U. Student Christian Assn., 1951-54; ordained elder Calif.-Pacific, Methodist Ch., 1953; pastor Montclair (Calif.) Meth. Ch., 1956-59; lectr. Sch. Theology at Claremont, 1959—73; gen. sec. Bd. Higher Edn. and Ministry United Meth. Ch., 1973—87; pres. Alaska Pacific U., Anchorage, 1988-95; ret., 1995. Author: Jesus and the Historian, 1968, Loving God with One's Mind, 1987, God Is with Us, 1997, Politics, Morality, and Higher Education, 1997, weekly column local newspapers; editor-at-large: Christian Century, 1969-84. Trustee Dillard U. Served with USAAF, 1944-46. Kent fellow Soc. for Values in Higher Edn., 1954; Dempster fellow Meth. Ch., 1954 Mem. Rotary Internat. (Anchorage Downtown), Commonwealth North. Home: 900 E Harrison Ave Pomona CA 91767-2075

TROUNSTINE, PHILIP JOHN, communications consultant; b. Cin., July 30, 1949; s. Henry P. and Amy May (Joseph) Trounstine; children: Jessica, David; m. Deborah Williams, May 1, 1993; children: Amy, Ryan, Patrick Wilkes. Student, U. Vt., 1967-68, Stanford U., 1968-70; BA in Journalism, San Jose State U., 1975. Graphic artist Eric Printing, San Jose, Calif., 1972-75; reporter Indpls. Star, Ind., 1975-78, San Jose Mercury News, Calif., 1978-83, editl. writer Calif., 1983-86, polit. editor Calif., 1986-99; ednl. cons. Teen Recovery Strategies, 1995-99; comms. dir. Gov. Gray Davis, Calif., 1999-2001, comm. cons. Calif., 2001—; dir. Survey and Policy Rsch. Inst. at San Jose State U., 2001—08. Co-author: Movers & Shakers: The Study of Community Power, 1981. Creator, writer SPJ Gridiron Show, San Jose, 1981-91. Pulliam fellow, 1975, Duke U., 1991, J.S. Knight fellow Stanford U., 1993-94. Mem. Soc. Profl. Journalists (nat. ethics com. 1993-96), Am. Assn. Pub. Opinion Rsch., Seascape Golf Club. Jewish. Avocations: golf, fishing. Home: 620 Middlefield Dr Aptos CA 95003-3560 Office Phone: 408-924-6993.

TROUSDALE, STEPHEN RICHARD, newspaper editor; b. LA, May 29, 1963; s. Richard Gardner Trousdale and Geraldine Barbara Wisdom. AB, Stanford U., 1985. News editor LA Daily Commerce, 1986—87, edit. page editor, 1987—89, mng. editor, 1989—96; bus. editor Copley LA Newspapers, 1996—97; dep. bus. editor Contra Costa Times, 1997—2000, bus. editor, 2000—07; dep. bus. editor San Jose Mercury News, Calif., 2006—07, bus. editor, 2007—. Mem. Soc. Profl. Journalists (past pres. L.A. chpt.), AP Mng. Editors, Calif. Soc. Newspaper Editors, Soc. Am. Bus. Editors and Writers. Avocation: motorcycling. Home: 2335 Valley St Berkeley CA 94702-2133 Office: San Jose Mercury News 750 Ridder Park Dr San Jose CA 95190 Office Phone: 408-920-5800. Business E-Mail: strousdale@mercurynews.com.

TROUT, LINDA COPPLE, former state supreme court justice; b. Tokyo, Sept. 1, 1951; BA, U. Idaho, 1973, JD, 1977; LLD (hon.), Albertson Coll. Idaho, 1999. Bar: Idaho 1977. Atty. Blake, Feeney & Clark, 1978—83; judge magistrate divsn. Idaho Dist. Ct. (2d jud. divsn.), 1983—90, dist. judge Lewiston, 1991-92, acting trial ct. adminstr., 1987-91; justice Idaho Supreme Ct., 1992—2007, chief justice, 1997—2004. Instr. coll. law U. Idaho, 1983, 88; chair Idaho State Supreme Ct. Judicial Education Com. Mem. bd. directors Lewiston City Library, Northwest Children's Home, Lewiston YWCA. Mem. Idaho State Bar Assn., Clearwater Bar Assn. (pres. 1980-81).

TROWBRIDGE, THOMAS, JR., mortgage company executive; b. Troy, NY, June 28, 1938; s. of Thomas and Elberta (Wood) T.; m. Delinda Bryan, July 3, 1965; children: Elisabeth Tacy, Wendy Bryan. BA, Yale U., 1960; MBA, Harvard U., 1965. V.p. James W. Rouse & Co., Balt., 1965-66, Washington, 1966-68, San Francisco, 1968-73, 76-78; pres. Rouse Investing Co., Columbia, Md., 1973-76, Trowbridge, Kieselhorst & Co., San Francisco, 1978-97, CEO, chmn., 1997-2000; ret., 2000. Bd. dirs. Columbia Assn., 1975-76; trustee, treas. The Head-Royce Sch., Oakland, Calif., 1980-84; trustee, pres. Gen. Alumni Assn. Phillips Exeter Acad., 1984-90. Lt. USNR, 1960-63. Mem. SAR, Urban Land Inst., Calif. Mortgage Bankers Assn. (bd. dirs. 1991-98, pres. 1996-97), Mortgage Bankers Assn. Am. (bd. govs. 1993-2000), Naval War Coll. Found., 2000-, Olympic Club, Pacific Union Club, Orinda Country Club (bd. dirs. 2005-09, pres. 2008). LOPC Found. (trustee 2005-09, pres 2009). Republican. Presbyterian. Avocation: golf. Home: 4 Ridge Ln Orinda CA 94563-1318

TROXEL, DAVID B., pathologist; b. Elgin, Ill., 1936; MD, Northwestern U., 1962. Intern Chgo. Wesley Meml. Hosp., 1962—63; residency Mayo Clinic Found., Rochester, 1963—64, Presbyn. Hosp., Denver, 1966—68; clinical prof. Divsn. of Health & Med. Sci., U. Calif., Berkeley. Cons., govr. Doctors Ins. Com. Contbr. articles to jours. Mem.: Calif. Soc. of Pathologists (former pres.), Am. Bd. of Pathology (former pres.). Office: U Calif Berkeley 570 Univ Hall Berkeley CA 94720

TROY, FREDERIC ARTHUR, II, medical biochemistry professor; b. Evanston, Ill., Feb. 16, 1937; s. Charles McGregor and Virginia Lane (Minto) T.; m. Linda Ann Price, Mar. 23, 1959; children: Karen M., Janet R. BS, Washington U., St. Louis, 1961; PhD, Purdue U., 1966; postdoctoral, Johns Hopkins U., Balt., 1968. Asst. prof. U. Calif. Sch. Medicine, Davis, 1968-74, assoc. prof., 1974-80, prof., 1980—2006, emeritus prof., 2006—, chmn., 1991-94, 2006—; cofounder SialoGen Therapeutics, Inc., Davis, Calif., 2003—, pres., 2003—, CEO, 2003—. Cons. NIH, Bethesda, Md., 1974—, NSF, Washington, 1975—, Damon Runyon Cancer Found., NYC, 1980-81, VA, Washington, 1984-88, US Army Breast Cancer Study Sect., 1999—; vis. prof. Karolinska Inst. Med. Sch., Stockholm, Sweden, 1976-77. Mem. editl. bd. Jour. Biol. Chem., 1988—, Glycobiol., 1990—; contbr. articles to profl. jours. Recipient Research Cancer Devel. award Nat. Cancer Inst., 1975-80; Eleanor Roosevelt Internat. Cancer fellow Am. Cancer Soc., 1976-77. Mem. AAAS, Am. Soc. Biol. Chemistry and Molecular Biology, Am. Assn. Cancer Rsch., Am. Chem. Soc., Am. Soc. Enologists, Biochemistry Soc., Biophysics Soc., Am. Fedn. for Clin. Rsch., NY Acad. Scis., Soc. for Glycobiol. (pres. 1991-92), Am. Med. and Grad. Sch. Dept. Biochem. (pres.-elect 1995—), Sigma Xi. Office: Sch Medicine Dept Biochem and Molecular Medicine U Calif Davis CA 95616 Business E-Mail: fatroy@ucdavis.edu.

TROY, NANCY J., art history educator; BA in Art magna cum laude with honors, Wesleyan U., 1974; MA, Yale U., 1976, PhD, 1979. Gallery asst. Waddington Galleries, London, 1973; rsch. asst. Soc. Anonyme Collection, Yale U., New Haven, 1975, tchg. asst. history of art dept., 1975-76; asst. prof. dept. history of art Johns Hopkins U., Balt., 1979-83; asst. prof. dept. art history Northwestern U., Evanston, Ill., 1983-85, assoc. prof., 1985-92, prof., 1992-93, chmn. dept., 1990-92; vis. prof. UCLA, 1994; vis. prof. art history U. So. Calif., LA, 1994-95, prof., 1995—, chmn. dept., 1997—. Scholar-in-residence Getty Rsch. Inst. for History Art and Humanities, L.A., 1993-96, organizer Work in Progress lecture series, 1993-98; series co-editor Histories, Cultures, Contexts, Reaktion Book, London; curatorial coord., spl. cons. to Ilya Bolotowsky Retrospective, Solomon R. Guggenheim Mus., N.Y.C., summers 1972-74; asst. to curator French paintings Nat. Gallery Art, Washington, summer 1975, bd. advisors Ctr. for Advanced Study in Visual Arts, 1999-2002; guest curator Yale U. Art Gallery, 1979; mem. fine arts accessions com. and com. on collections Balt. Mus. Art, 1979-82; cons. De Stijl: 1917-1931, Visions of Utopia exhbn. Walker Art Ctr., Mpls., Washington, The Netherlands, 1982; cons. amplifying art program Art Inst. Chgo., 1984-85; mem. vis. com. Harvard U. Art Mus., Cambridge, Mass., 1992-98; lectr., chmn., moderator numerous symposia, 1980—; numerous invited lectures, 1975—, including U. Brighton, Eng., U. London, Middlexex U., London, Royal Coll. Art, London, U. Toronto, Mt. Holyoke Coll., Barnard Coll., Columbia U., Newcomb Coll., Tulane U., Los Angeles County Mus. Art, Art Inst. Chgo., Terra Mus. Am. Art, Chgo., N.C. Mus. Art, Raleigh, McGill U., Montreal, Vassar Coll; mus. projects peer rev. panelist NEH, 1991; peer reviewer Woodrow Wilson Ctr., Washington, 1994, 96; external reviewer dept. art history U. Mich., 1987; bd. dirs. Nat. Com. for History Art, 1998—; peer reviewer for promotion and tenure Boston U., Lake Forest Coll., Middlesex U., Occidental Coll., U. Mo., Columbia, U. Va., 1996-98. Author: The De Stijl Environment, 1983, Modernism and the Decorative Arts in France: Art Nouveau to Le Corbusier, 1991, (exhbn. catalog) Mondrian and Neo-Plasticism in America, 1979; editor-in-chief The Art Bull., 1994-97; editor: (with Eve Blau) Architecture and Cubism, 1997; series co-editor Histories, Cultures, Contexts; mem. editl. bd. Art Bull., 1993—, Grey Room, 1998—; contbr. articles and book revs. to profl. jours., including Decorative Arts Soc. Jour., Design Issues, Art Bull., October, Archithese, Arts mag., Portfolio, Design Book Rev., chpts. to books. Mem. Md. Coun. on Arts, 1981-82; trustee Wesleyan U., 1994-97. Recipient Disting. Alumna award Wesleyan U., 1991, postdoctoral tchg. award Lilly Endowment, 1985, Andrew W. Mellon professorship for advanced study in the visual arts Nat. Gallery Art (declined), 2000-02; Fulbright-Hays grantee, The Netherlands, 1977-78, travel grantee Kress Found., summer 1976, spring 1977, grantee Am. Coun. Learned Soc., summers 1981, 91, 98-99; grantee Graham Found. for Advanced Studies in Fine Arts, 1982, publ. grantee, 1989; grantee NEH, 1982-83, Am. Philos. Soc., 1986, Inst. for Advanced Study Sch. Hist. Studies, 1987, Getty Rsch. Inst. for History Art and Humanities, 1989-90, Zumberge Faculty Rsch. and Innovation Fund, U. So. Calif., 1998-99, Guggenheim Found., 1998-99; AT&T rsch. fellow Northwestern U., 1992-93. Mem. Coll. Art Assn. Am. (nominating com. 1990, bd. dirs. 1992-97, ann. meeting local host com. L.A. 1998-99), Soc. Archtl. Historian (sec. Chgo. chpt. 1984-85, peer reviewer Jour. 1996), Nat. Com. for the History of Art (bd. dirs.), Sterling and Francine Clark Art Inst. (mem. fellowship com.). Office: U So Calif Dept Art History University Park 104 Watt MC 0293 Los Angeles CA 90089-0001

TROYER, VERNE, actor; b. Sturgis, Mich., Jan. 1, 1969; m. Genevieve Gallen, Jan. 22, 2004 (div.). Actor: (films) Pinocchio's Revenge, 1996, Men in Black, 1997, Wishmaster, 1997, My Giant, 1998, Fear and Loathing in Las Vegas, 1998, The Wacky Adventures of Ronald McDonald: Scared Silly, 1998, Mighty Joe Young, 1998, Here Lies Lonely, 1999, Instinct, 1999, Austin Powers: The Spy Who Shagged Me, 1999 (Best On-Screen Duo (with Mike Myers) MTV Movie Awards, 2000), Bit Players, 2000, How the Grinch Stole Christmas, 2000, Bubble Boy, 2001, Harry Potter and the Sorcerer's Stone, 2001, Run for the Money, 2002, Austin Powers in Goldmember, 2002, The Love Guru, 2008; (TV series) Jack of All Trades, 2000—01; (TV films) Karroll's Christmas, 2004. Office: c/o Elena Bertagnolli Fonolli Mgmt Inc 11218 Osborne St Lake View Terrace CA 91342

TRUCE, WILLIAM EVERETT, chemist, educator; b. Chgo., Sept. 30, 1917; s. Stanley C. and Frances (Novak) T.; m. Eloise Joyce McBroom, June 16, 1940; children: Nancy Jane, Roger William. BS, U. Ill., 1939; PhD, Northwestern U., 1943. Mem. faculty Purdue U., 1946-88, prof. chemistry, 1956-88, prof. chemistry emeritus, 1988—, asst. dean Grad. Sch., 1963-66. Com. mem. numerous univ.; chmn. profl. meetings; exec. officer Nat. Organic Symposium, 1961; chmn. Gordon Rsch. Conf. on Organic Reactions and Processes; cons. in field. Co-author book; contbr. articles to profl. jours., chpts. to books. Guggenheim fellow Oxford U., 1957 Mem. Am. Chem. Soc., Phi Beta Kappa (sec. Purdue chpt.), Sigma Xi (pres. Purdue chpt.). Achievements include research in new methods of synthesis, devel. new kinds of compounds and reactions. Home: 350 Ponca Pl Boulder CO 80303-3802

TRUEBLOOD, HARRY ALBERT, JR., oil industry executive; b. Wichita Falls, Tex., Aug. 28, 1925; s. Harry A. and Marguerite (Barnhart) T.; m. Lucile Bernard, Jan. 22, 1953; children: Katherine T. Astin, John B. Student, Tex. A&M Coll., 1942; BS in Petroleum Engring., U. Tex., 1948. Petroleum engr. Cal. Co., 1948-51; chief engr. McDermott & Barnhart Co., Colo., Tex., 1951-52; cons. petroleum and geol. engr. Denver, 1952-55; pres. Colo. Western Exploration Inc., Denver, 1955-58, Consol. Oil & Gas., Inc., 1958-88, chmn. bd., CEO, 1969-88, Princeville Devel. Corp., 1979-87, pres., 1984-86; chmn. bd., CEO Columbus Energy Corp., 1983-2000; pres., mng. mem. HAT Resources LLC, 2001—. Chmn. bd., CEO, Princeville Airways, Inc., 1979-87; chmn. bd. dirs., pres. CEC Resources, Ltd., 1984-99; bd. dirs. NYTIS Exploration Co. With USNR, 1944-46, ensign, 1949-55. Named to Rocky Mountain Oil and Gas Hall of Fame, 2004. Mem. Soc. Petroleum Engrs. (legion of honor), Am. Petroleum Inst. (25 Yr. Club), World Pres. Orgn., Chief Execs. Orgn. (bd. dirs.), Ind. Petroleum Assn. Am. (exec. com.); Ind. Pet Assn. Mountain States (recipient Wildcatter 2006 award for Lifetime Achievement), 2007 Disting. Grad. Sch. Engring. award, U. Tex., Austin, Disting. Eagle Scout. award, Boy Scouts Am., Natural Gas Supply Assn. (exec. com.), Cherry Hills Country Club, One Hundred Club. Roman Catholic. Office: 1720 S Bellaire St Ste 912 Denver CO 80222-4334 Home: 9039 Ranch River Cir Highlands Ranch CO 80126 Office Phone: 303-300-6792. E-mail: hajtrueblood@yahoo.com.

TRUJILLO, MARC, painter; b. Albuquerque, N.Mex., 1966; BA, U. Tex., Austin, 1991; MFA, Yale. U., 1994. Cartoonist Daily Texan, 1989; instr. drawing and painting Dougherty Arts Ctr., Austin, 1995, Santa Monica Coll., Calif., 2007; instr. printmaking and 2-D design Caldwell Coll., NJ, 1997—98; painting instr. Art Ctr. Coll. Design, Pasadena, Calif., 1999, 2003; drawing instr. Pierce Coll., Woodland Hills, Calif., 2000. Vis. artist U. Calif., Riverside, 2003. One-man shows include Tim Gleason Gallery, NYC, 1994, Contemporary Realist Gallery, San Francisco, 1994, 1995, Hackett-Freedman Gallery, San Francisco, 1997, 1998, 2007, Ruth Bachofner Gallery, Santa Monica, 2000, The Plainness of Plain Things, 2003, Minor Works, Santa Monica Coll., 2007, exhibited in group shows at Mexicarte, Austin, 1989, Flood Gallery, U. Tex., Austin, 1990, 10th Anniversary Exhbn., Hackett-Freedman Gallery, San Francisco, 1997, Speculative Terrain, Carnegie Art Mus., Oxnard, Calif., 2004, A View from Here, Judson Gallery Contemporary and Traditional Art, LA, 2008, Invitational Exhbn. Visual Art, AAAL, 2008; composer, music performer:

(films) El Mariachi, 1992. Recipient Rosenthal Family Found. award for Painting, AAAL, 2008; fellow Guggenheim Found., 2008. Mailing: 4424 Murietta Ave #11 Sherman Oaks CA 91423 Office: c/o Hackett-Freeman Gallery Ste 400 250 Sutter St San Francisco CA 94108 E-mail: marc_trujillo@aya.yale.edu.

TRULY, RICHARD H., academic and federal agency administrator, retired pilot; b. Fayette, Miss., Nov. 12, 1937; s. James B. Truly; m. Coleen Hanner; children: Richard Michael, Daniel Bennett, Lee Margaret. B in Aero. Engring., Ga. Inst. Tech., 1959; D in Sci. (hon.), Millsaps Coll., Duquesne U.; D in Engring. (hon.), Colo. Sch. Mines, Stevens Inst. Tech. Commd. ensign USN, 1959; advanced through grades to vice adm.; assigned Fighter Squadron 33; served in U.S.S. Intrepid; served in U.S.S. Enterprise; astronaut Manned Orbiting Lab. Program USAF, 1965—69, NASA, 1969—, comdr. Columbia Flight 2, 1981, Challenger Flight 3, 1983; dir. Space Shuttle program, 1986—89; adminstr. NASA, 1989—92; v.p., dir. Georgia Tech Rsch. Inst., Atlanta, 1992—97; dir. Nat. Renewable Energy Lab., Golden, Colo., 1997—2004; ret., 2004. Recipient Robert H. Goddard Astronautics award, AIAA, 1990, Presdl. Citizen's Medal, 1989. Mem.: NAE. Office: Nat Renewable Energy Lab 1617 Cole Blvd Golden CO 80401-3305

TRUSSELL, R(OBERT) RHODES, environmental engineer; b. National City, Calif. s. Robert L. and Margaret (Kessing) T.; m. Elizabeth Shane, Nov. 26, 1969; children: Robert Shane, Charles Bryan. BSCE, U. Calif., Berkeley, 1966, MS, 1967, PhD, 1972. With Montgomery Watson Inc. (formerly Mongomery Cons. Engrs.), Pasadena, Calif., 1972—, v.p., 1977, sr. v.p., 1986, dir. applied tech., 1988-92, sr. v.p., dir. corp. devel., 1992—. Mem. com. on water treatment chems. Nat. Acad. Sci., 1980-82, mem. com. 3d part cert., 1982-83, com. on irrigation-induced water quality problems, 1986-88, indirect potable reuse, 1996-98, chmn. com. on drinking water contaminants, 1998—, Am. Water Work Commn. on mixing of water treatment chems., 1988-90; mem. U.S./German rsch. com. on corrosion of water sys., 1984-85, U.S./Dutch rsch. com. on organics in water, 1982-83, U.S./USSR rsch. com. on water treatment, 1985-88, U.S./E.C. Com. Corrosion in Water, 1992-94; mem. Water Sci. and Tech. Bd., 1998—. Mem. jt. editl. bd. Standards Methods for Examination of Water and Wastewater, 1980-89; mem. editl. adv. bd. Environ. and Sci. and Tech., 1977-83; mng. editl. bd. Environ. Sci. and Tech., 2001—; contbr. articles to profl. publs. Mem. AIChE, AEEP, Acad. Environ. Engring. (Kappe lectr. 1999), Nat. Acad. Engrs., Water Works Assn. (editl. adv. bd. jour. 1987-94, EPA SAB com. on drinking water 1988-91, 94—, cons. radon disinfectant by-products, 1993, cons. on disinfection and disinfection by-products 1994, ad hoc sci. adv. com. on arsenic 1995-96), Bd. Sci. Couns. Com. on AS, 1997, Internat. Water Supply Assn. (U.S. rep. to standing com. on water quality and treatment 1990-94, chmn. com. disinfection and mem. sci. and tech. coun. 1994—), Water Environ. Fedn., Internat. Water Quality Assn., Am. Chem. Soc., Nat. Assn. Corrosion Engrs., Sigma Xi. Office: Montgomery Watson 618 Michillinda Ave Ste 200 Arcadia CA 91007-1625

TRYGSTAD, LAWRENCE BENSON, lawyer; b. Holton, Mich., Mar. 22, 1937; BA, U. Mich., 1959; JD, U. So. Calif., 1967. Bar: Calif. 1968, U.S. Supreme Ct. 1974. Legal counsel Calif. Tchrs. Assn., United Tchrs. L.A., LA, 1968-71; ptnr. Trygstad & Odell, LA, 1971-80; pres. Trygstad Law Corp., LA, 1980—2004; ptnr. Trygstad, Schwab & Trygstad, LA, 2004—. Instr., tchr. negotiation U. Calif.-Northridge; panelist TV shows Law and the Teacher. Bd. dirs. George Washington Carver Found., L.A. Mem. ABA, Calif. Bar Assn., Consumer Attys. Calif., L.A. County Bar Assn., Nat. Orgn. Lawyers for Edn. Assns., Am. Assoc. Justice, Consumer Attys. L.A., Phi Alpha Delta. Home: 4209 Aleman Dr Tarzana CA 91356-5405 Office: 1880 Century Park E Ste 1104 Los Angeles CA 90067-1609 Office Phone: 310-552-0500. Business E-Mail: ltrygstad@trygstadlawoffice.com.

TRZYNA, THADDEUS CHARLES, academic institution administrator; b. Chgo., Oct. 26, 1939; s. Thaddeus Stephen and Irene Mary (Giese) T.; divorced; 1 child, Jennifer. BA in Internat. Rels., U. So. Calif., 1961; PhD in Govt., Claremont Grad. U., 1975. Vice consul US Govt., Elisabethville, Katanga, Congo, 1962-63, consul Leopoldville, 1963-64, sec. Nat. Mil. Info. Disclosure Policy Com. Washington, 1964-67; pres. Calif. Inst. Pub. Affairs, Claremont, 1969-89, Sacramento, 1989—; sr. assoc. Sch. Politics and Econs., Claremont Grad. U., 1989—; dir. Internat. Ctr. Environment and Pub. Policy, 1990—; rsch. assoc. U. Calif., Santa Cruz, 2009—. Mem. coun. Internat. Union for Conservation of Nature and Natural Resources, 1990-96, chmn. commn. on environ. strategy and planning, 1990-96, world commn. protected areas, 1990—; sr. adv. cities and conservation, 2005—; chmn. Calif. Forum on Hazardous Materials, 1985-88, Calif. Farmlands Project Task Force, 1981-84; cons. U.S. and Calif. State Agys. on Environ. Policy; cons. on devel. of natural resources Univ. for Peace, Costa Rica; lectr. internat. rels. Pomona Coll. Author: The California Handbook, rev. 8th edit. 1999, The Power of Convening, 1990, A Sustainable World, 1995, The Urban Imperative, 2005. Mem. World Acad. Art and Sci., Sierra Club (v.p. 1975-77, chmn. internat. com. 1977-79). Democrat. Office: Calif Inst Pub Affairs PO Box 189040 Sacramento CA 95818-9040 Office Phone: 916-442-2472.

TSCHERNISCH, SERGEI P., academic administrator; BA, San Francisco State U.; MFA in Theatre, Stanford U.; student, San Francisco Actors' Workshop, Stanford Repertory Theatre. Founding mem. Calif. Inst. of Arts, 1969, mem. faculty, assoc. dean Sch. Theatre, dir., 1969-80; prof. dept. theatre U. Md., College Park, 1980-82; dir. divsn. performing and visual arts Northeastern U., Boston, 1982-92; dean Coll. of Comm. and Fine Arts Loyola Marymount U., LA, 1992-94; pres. Cornish Coll. of Arts, Seattle, 1994—. Advisor NEA; mem. com. USIA; cons. to many festivals. Office: Cornish College of the Arts 1000 Lenora St Seattle WA 98121-2718 Office Phone: 206-726-5001. E-mail: stschernisch@cornish.edu.

TSCHIRHART, JOHN THOMAS, economist, educator; b. NYC, Oct. 23, 1946; s. John A. and Mary Ellen (McManus) T.; children: Deborah, Daniel. BS, Johns Hopkins U., 1970; MS, Purdue U., 1972, PhD, 1975. Instr. Purdue U., West Lafayette, Ind., 1973-75; asst. prof. SUNY, Buffalo, 1975-78; assoc. prof. U. Wyo., Laramie, 1978-81, prof., 1982—. Author: Regulation of Natural Monopolies, 1988; contbr. articles to profl. jours. Midshipman USN, 1964-66. Mem. Am. Econs. Assn. Home: 5887 Obenchain Rd Laporte CO 80535-9729 Office: U Wyo Dept Econs 1000 E University Ave Laramie WY 82071-3985 Office Phone: 307-766-2356.

TSENG, GREG, Internet company executive; AB in Chemistry, Physics & Math., Harvard U. Founder Avivon Inc.; COO Limespot-.com LLC; co-founder, CEO Jumpstart Technologies, 2000—05, Tagged.com, San Francisco, 2004—. Co-author: Harvard Entrepreneurs Club Guide to Starting Your Own Business, 1999. Mem.: Harvard Entrepreneurs Club (HEC) (dir. 1998—2000). Office: Tagged Inc 110 Pacific Ave Mall Box #117 San Francisco CA 94111

TSENG, ROSE, academic administrator; BS, Kansas State U.; MS, U. Calif., Berkeley, PhD Nutrition. Registered dietician. Prof., chair, dir., assoc. dean San Jose State U., 1970—86, dean Coll. Applied Scis. and Arts, 1986—93; chancellor, CEO West Valley-Mission C.C., Calif., 1993—98; chancellor U. Hawaii-Hilo, 1998—. Office: U Hawaii-Hilo 200 W Kawili Hilo HI 96720-4091

TSIEN, RICHARD WINYU, biology professor; b. Tating, Kweichow, People's Republic China, Mar. 3, 1945; s. Hsue-Chu and Yi-Ying (Li) T.; m. Julia Shiang Aug. 29, 1971; children: Sara Shiang-Ming, Gregory Shiang-An, Alexa Tsien-Shiang. BS, MIT, 1965, MS, 1966; DPhil, Oxford U., Eng., 1970. Rsch. student Eaton Peabody Lab. Auditory, Physiology, Mass. Eye and Ear Infirmary, 1966; asst. prof. dept. physiology, Yale U. Sch. Medicine, New Haven, 1970-74, assoc. prof., 1974-79, prof., 1979-88; George D. Smith prof. molecular and cellular physiology Stanford (Calif.) U., 1988—, chmn. dept., 1988-94. Established investigator Am. Heart Assn., 1974-79. Author: Electric Current Flow in Excitable Cells, 1975. Recipient Otsuka award Internat. Soc. Heart Rsch., 1985; Rhodes Scholar, 1966; Weir Rsch. fellow, 1966-70 Univ. Coll., Oxford, 1966-70, lecturing fellow Balliol Coll., Oxford, 1969-70 Mem. Soc. Gen. Physiologists (pres. 1988), Biophys. Soc. (Kenneth S. Cole award 1985), Soc. for Neurosci. Democrat. Home: 866 Tolman Dr Palo Alto CA 94305-1026 Office: Stanford U Dept Molecular & Cellular Physiology 300 Pasteur Dr Palo Alto CA 94304-2203

TSIEN, ROGER YONCHIEN, chemist, cell biologist; b. NYC, Feb. 1, 1952; s. Hsue Chu and Yi Ying (Li) T.; m. Wendy M. Globe, July 30, 1982. AB in Chemistry and Physics summa cum laude, Harvard Coll., 1972; PhD in Physiology, U. Cambridge, 1977; PhD (hon.), Cath. U., Leuven, Belgium, 1995. Rsch. asst. U. Cambridge, Eng., 1975-78; asst. prof. Dept. Physiology-Anatomy U. Calif., Berkeley, 1981-85, assoc. prof., 1985-87, prof., 1987-89, prof. pharmacology, chemistry and biochemistry San Diego, 1989—; biological investigator Howard Hughes Med. Inst. Rsch. Lab, Calif., 1989—; co-found. Aurora Bioscis. Corp., 1994, Senomyx, Inc., 1998. T.Y. Shen vis. prof. Medicinal Chem., MIT, 1991, Todd vis. prof. Chem., U. Cambridge, 2003. Contbr. chpts. to books, articles to profl. jours. Recipient: Lamport prize NY Acad. Scis., 1986, Javits Neurosci. Investigator award Nat. Inst. Neurol. Disorders and Stroke, 1989, Young Scientist award Passano Found., 1991, W. Alden Spencer Neurobiology award Columbia U., 1991, Bowditch lectureship Am. Physiol. Soc., 1992, Gairdner Found. Internat. award, 1995, Artois-Baillet-Latour Health prize (Belgium), 1995, Basic Rsch. prize Am. Heart Assn., 1995, Faculty Rsch. lectureship U. Calif., San Diego, 1997, Faculty Rsch. Lectureship, Univ. Calif., San Diego, Acad. Senate, 1997, EG&G Wallac award for Innovation in High Throughput Screening Soc. for Biomolecular Screening, 1998, Herbert Sober Lectureship, Am. Soc. Biochemistry and Molecular Biology, 2000, Pearse Prize, Royal Microscopical Soc., 2000, Am. Chem. Soc. award for Creative Invention, 2002, Anfinsen award, Protein Soc., 2002, Dr. H.P. Heineken Prize for Biochemistry and Biophysics, 2002,Max Delbrück medal, Max Delbrück Centrum für Molekulare Medizin, Berlin, 2002, Wolf prize in Medicine, Israel, 2004, Keio Med. Sci. prize, Keio U., 2004, Assn. Biomolecular Resource Facilities award, 2006, Nobel Prize in Chemistry, 2008; Comyns Berkeley Rsch. fellow Gonville & Caius Coll., 1977-81; Marshall scholar British Govt., 1972-75, Searle scholar, 1983-86; Hugh Davson Disting. Lecturer, Am. Physiological Soc., 2003, Konrad Bloch Lectureship, Harvard U., 2003, Keith Porter Lectureship, Am. Soc. Cell Biology, 2003. Mem. Amer. Acad. Arts & Sciences, NAS, IOM, Phi Beta Kappa. Achievements: development and extensive biological application of molecules to measure and/or manipulate intracellular calcium, sodium, and hydrogen ions, cyclic adenosine-3', 5'-monophosphate, nitric oxide, inositol phosphates, membrane potential, protein trafficking, protein-protein interaction, and gene expression; developed biochemistry and redesign of green fluorescent protein; elucidation fo signal transduction mechanisms in calcium oscillations and synaptic plasticity; inventor new methods for microscopic imaging and pharmaceutical high-throughput screening. Office: Tsien Lab HHMI - UCSD CMM West 310 9500 Gilman Dr La Jolla CA 92093-0647 Office Phone: 858-534-4891. Fax: 858-534-5270. E-mail: rtsien@ucsd.edu.

TSOSIE, LEONARD, state legislator, lawyer; b. 1958; BS, JD, U. N.Mex. Pvt. practice, Crown Point; mem. N.Mex. Senate, Dist. 22, Santa Fe, 1992—; mem. fin. com. N.Mex. Senate, mem. jud. com. Democrat. Office: PO Box 1003 Crownpoint NM 87313

TSOULFANIDIS, NICHOLAS, engineering educator, dean; b. Ioannina, Greece, May 6, 1938; arrived in US, 1963; s. Stephen and Aristea (Ganiou) T.; m. Zizeta Koutsombidou, June 21, 1964; children: Stephen, Lena. BS in Physics, U. Athens, Greece, 1960; MS in Nuclear Engring., U. Ill., 1965, PhD in Nuclear Engring., 1968. Registered profl. engr., Mo. Prof. nuclear engring. U. Mo., Rolla, 1968—2002, vice chancellor acad. affairs, 1985-86, assoc. dean for rsch. Sch. Mines and Metallurgy, 1989; prof. chem. and metall. engring. U. Nevada, Reno. Sr. engr. Gen. Atomic Co., San Diego, 1974-75; researcher Cadarache France, 1986-87. Author: Measurement and Detection of Radiation, 1984, 2d edit. 1995; co-author: The Nuclear Fuel Cycle: Analysis and Management, 1990; editor: Nuclear Technology, 1997-. Recipient Glenn Murphy award, outstanding contributions in profession and tchg. of nuclear engring., Am. Soc. for Engring. Edn., 1995. Mem. Am. Nuclear Soc. (chmn. radiation protection shielding div. 1987-88), Health Physics Soc., Nat. Soc. Profl. Engring., Rotary. Office: Chemical & Metallurgical Engring Univ Nevada Mail Stop 388 Reno NV 89557 Office Phone: 775-784-8287. Office Fax: 775-327-5059. E-mail: nikost@unr.edu.

TUCCI, STANLEY, actor; b. Peekskill, NY, Nov. 11, 1960; s. Stanley and Joan (Tropiano) Tucci; m. Kate Tucci, 1995 (dec. 2009); children: Camilla, Nicolo Robert, Isabel Concetta. BFA, SUNY, Purchase, 1982. Actor (films) Fear Anxiety and Depression, 1990, Billy Bathgate, 1991, Men of Respect, 1991, In The Soup, 1992, Beethoven, 1992, Prelude to A Kiss, 1992, Undercover Blues, 1993, The Pelican Brief, 1993, Somebody to Love, 1994, It Could Happen to You, 1994, Mrs. Parker and the Vicious Circle, 1994, Jury Duty, 1995, Kiss of Death, 1995, A Modern Affair, 1995, Captive, 1995, The Daytrippers, 1996, Montana, 1997, Life During Wartime, 1997, The Eighteenth Angel, 1997, Deconstructing Harry, 1997, A Life Less Ordinary, 1997, The Imposters, 1998, A Midsummer Night's Dream, 1999, Joe Gould's Secret, 1999, In Too Deep, 1999, The Whole Shebang, 2000, Bull, 2000, Sidewalks of New York, 2001, America's Sweethearts, 2001, Big Trouble, 2002, Road to Perdition, 2002, Maid in Manhattan, 2002, The Core, 2003, The Life and Death of Peter Sellers, 2004, The Terminal, 2004, Shall We Dance?, 2004, (voice) Robots, 2005, Lucky Number Slevin, 2006, Four Las Songs, 2006, The Devil Wears Prada, 2006, The Hoax, 2006, Kit Kittredge: An American Girl, 2008, (voice) Space Chimps, 2008, Swing Vote, 2008, What Just Happened, 2008, (voice) THe Tale of Despereaux, 2008; actor, co-dir., co-prodr. (films) Big Night, 1996 (Ind. Spirit award for best 1st screenplay 1996); actor (TV series) Murder One, 1995, 3 Lbs., 2006-, (TV movies) Winchell, 1998 (Emmy award 1998), Conspiracy, 2001 (Golden Globe award 2001) Recipient Creative Arts Primetime Emmy for Outstanding Guest Actor in Comedy Series, Acad. TV Arts and Scis., 2007. Office: William Morris Agy c/o David Yocum 151 S El Camino Dr Beverly Hills CA 90212-2775

TUCK, CHRIS S., state legislator; b. Taft, Calif., July 8, 1966; 1 child, Devon. Lic. electrician Alaska Joint Elec. Training Sch., 1998. Electrician Alcan Electric, 1996—98, Hotwire Electric, 1998—2001; instr. Alaska Joint Electrical Apprenticeship Sch., 1999—, U. Tenn. Nat. Training Inst., 2003—; bus. rep. Internat. Brotherhood of Electrical Workers Local 1547, 2001—; mem. Alaska House of Reps from Dist. 29, 2008—. Bd. mem. AJEAT Electrical Appreticeship Sch., 2002—, Mcpl. Edn. Commn., 2004—; mem. NECA/IBEW Joint Safety Com. Mem.: Brotherhood of Elec. Workers (mem Joint Safety Com.). Democrat. Office: State Capitol Terry Miller Bldg Ste 111 Rm 426 Juneau AK 99801-1182 Office Phone: 907-465-4648, 907-465-2095. Office Fax: 907-465-2864. Business E-Mail: Representative_Chris_Tuck@legis.state.ak.us.

TUCKER, ROY W., lawyer; b. Buffalo, Aug. 31, 1952; BA in Polit. Sci. & English, with dist. in Polit. Sci., magna cum laude, Kenyon Coll., 1974; JD, SUNY Buffalo, 1979. Bar: NY 1980, Oreg. 1985. Law clk. to Hon. Reid S. Moule Appellate Divsn., NY State Supreme Ct., 1979—80; with Davis Polk & Wardwell, NY, 1980—84; ptnr., mem. exec. com. Perkins Coie LLP, Portland, Oreg. Assoc. editor Buffalo Law Rev., 1977—78, sr. editor, 1978—79. Mem.: Phi Beta Kappa. Office: Perkins Coie LLP 1120 NW Couch St Floor 10 Portland OR 97209-4128 Office Phone: 503-727-2044. Office Fax: 503-727-2222. Business E-Mail: rtucker@perkinscoie.com.

TUCKER, SHIRLEY LOIS COTTER, botanist, educator; b. St. Paul, Apr. 4, 1927; d. Ralph U. and Myra C. (Knutson) Cotter; m. Kenneth W. Tucker, Aug. 22, 1953. BA, U. Minn., 1949, MS, 1951; PhD, U. Calif., Davis, 1956. Asst. prof. botany La. State U., Baton Rouge, 1967-71, assoc. prof., 1971-76, prof., 1976-82, Boyd prof., 1982-95, prof. emerita, 1995—. Adj. prof. dept. biology U. Calif., Santa Barbara, 1995—. Co-editor: Aspects of Floral Development, 1988, Advances in Legume Systematics, Vol. 6, 1994; contbr. numerous articles on plant devel. to profl. jours. Recipient, Outstanding Alumni Achievement award U. Minn., 1999; fellow Linnean Soc., London, 1975—, Fulbright fellow Eng., 1952-53; named to Hall of Distinction La. State U., Baton Rouge, 2006. Mem. Bot. Soc. Am. (v.p. 1979, program chmn. 1975-78, pres.-elect 1986-87, pres. 1987-88, Merit award 1989, Centennial award 2006), Am. Bryological and Lichenological Soc., Brit. Lichenological Soc., Am. Inst. Biol. Scis., Am. Soc. Plant Taxonomists (pres.-elect 1994-95, pres. 1995-96), Phi Beta Kappa, Sigma Xi. Home: 3987 Primavera Rd Santa Barbara CA 93110-1467 Office: U Calif Dept Biology EEMB Santa Barbara CA 93106 Home Phone: 805-898-0908. Business E-Mail: tucker@lifesci.ucsb.edu.

TUELL, JACK MARVIN, retired bishop; b. Tacoma, Nov. 14, 1923; s. Frank Harry and Anne Helen (Bertelson) T.; m. Marjorie Ida Beadles, June 17, 1946; children: Jacqueline, Cynthia, James. BS, U. Wash., 1947, JD, 1948; MDiv, Boston U., 1955; MA, U. Puget Sound, 1961, DHS, 1990; D.D., Pacific Sch. Religion, 1966; LLD, Alaska Pacific U., 1980. Bar: Wash. 1948; ordained to ministry Meth. Ch., 1955. Practice law with firm Holte & Tuell, Edmonds, Wash., 1948-50; pastor Grace Meth. Ch., Everett, Wash., 1950-52, South Tewksbury Meth. Ch., Tewksbury, Mass., 1952-55, Lakewood Meth. Ch., Tacoma, 1955-61; dist. supt. Puget Sound dist. Meth. Ch., Everett, 1961-67; pastor 1st United Meth. Ch., Vancouver, Wash., 1967-72; bishop United Meth. Ch., Portland, Oreg., 1972-80, Calif.-Pacific Conf., United Meth. Ch., LA, 1980-92, ret., 1992; interim sr. pastor First United Meth. Ch., Boise, Idaho, 1995; interim supt. Seattle Tacoma Dist., 2004—05. Mem. gen. conf. United Meth. Ch., 1964, 66, 68, 70, 72; pres. coun. of Bishops United Meth. Ch., 1989-90. Author: The Organization of the United Methodist Church, 1970, 11th edit. 2008, (autobiography) From Law to Grace, 2004. Pres. Tacoma U.S.O., 1959-61, Vancouver YMCA, 1968; v.p. Ft. Vancouver Seamens Cnt., 1969-72; vice chmn. Vancouver Human Rels. Commn., 1970-72; pres. Oreg. Coun. Alcohol Problems, 1972-76; trustee U. Puget Sound, 1961-73, Vancouver Meml. Hosp., 1967-72, Alaska Meth. U., Anchorage, 1972-80, Willamette U., Salem, Oreg., 1972-80, Willamette View Manor, Portland, 1972-80, Rogue Valley Manor, Medford, Oreg., 1972-76, Sch. Theology at Claremont, Calif., 1980-92, Methodist Hosp., Arcadia, Calif., 1983-92; pres. nat. div. bd. global ministries United Meth. Ch., 1972-76, pres. ecumenical and interreligious concerns div., 1976-80, Commn. on Christian Unity and intereligious concerns, 1980-84, Gen. Bd. of Pensions,1984-92, Calif. Coun. Alcohol Problems, 1985-88. Jacob Sleeper fellow, 1955. Methodist. Home and Office: 816 S 216th St 637 Des Moines WA 98198-6331

TUGGLE, FRANCIS DOUGLAS, entrepreneur, consultant, management educator, scientist; b. Portsmouth, Va., Jan. 19, 1943; s. Francis Joyner and Florence Eleanor (Dahlgren) T.; m. Mary Ann Tredway, June 3, 1967; children: Wendy Elizabeth, Laura Michelle. SB, MIT, 1964; MS, Carnegie-Mellon U., 1967, PhD, 1971. Prof. bus. adminstrn. and computer sci. U. Kans., Lawrence, 1968-78; Jesse H. Jones prof. mgmt. Rice U., Houston, 1978-90; dean Kogod Coll. Bus. Adminstrn., Am. U., Washington, 1990-96, prof. info. systems and strategic planning, 1996—2002; Robert J. & Carolyn A. Waltos Jr. dean Argyros Sch. Bus. Econs. Chapman U., Orange, Calif., 2002—06, prof., 2006—; founder Family Health Info. Svcs., Inc., Yorba-Linda, Calif., 2006—, Anderson & Tuggle Inc., 2002—; ptnr. Insight Cons., 2006—. Bd. dirs. Equus Total Return Inc., Houston; dir.-at-large Inst. for Ops. Rsch. and Mgmt. Scis., 1995; cons. in field; bd. trustees, Internat U. Creative Leadership Entrepreneurship, Breda, Holland, 2007- Author: How to Program a Computer, 1975, Organizational Processes, 1978. Com. chmn. United Way Tex. Gulf Coast, Houston, 1985-88. Fellow, Ford Found., 1966. Mem. Inst. for Ops. Rsch. and Mgmt. Scis. (bd. dirs. 1995, v.p. 1992-94), Am. Assn. Artificial Intelligence, Assn. for Computing Machinery, Acad. of

Mgmt., Sigma Xi, Beta Gamma Sigma, Alpha Kappa Psi. Episcopalian. Avocations: golf, bicycling, jogging, painting, drawing. Home: 20465 Via Torralba Yorba Linda CA 92887 Office: Argyros Sch Bus Econs Chapman U 1 University Dr Orange CA 92866 Office Phone: 714-997-6537. Business E-Mail: tuggle@chapman.edu.

TULAFONO, TOGIOLA T.A., Governor of American Samoa; b. Aunu'u Island, American Samoa, Feb. 28, 1947; s. Aitu and Silika (Vaatu'itu'i) T.; m. Maryann Taufaasau Mauga, Sept. 17, 1984; children: Puataunofo, Olita, Cherianne, Emema, Timoteo, Rosie. Grad., Honolulu Police Acad., 1967; BA, Chadron State Coll., 1970; JD, Washburn U., 1975. Bar: Kans., Am. Samoa. Police instr. Am. Samoa Police Dept., Pago Pago, 1967; adminstrv. asst. Sec. of Samoan Affairs, Pago Pago, 1970-71; legal asst. Atty. Gen., Pago Pago, 1971-72; assoc. Law Offices of George A. Wray, Pago Pago, 1975-77; v.p. South Pacific Island Airways, Pago Pago, 1977-79; judge Dist. Ct. of Am. Samoa, Pago Pago, 1979-80; chmn. bd. dirs. Am. Samoa Power Authority, Pago Pago, 1978-80; mem. Am. Samoa Senate, Pago Pago, 1981-85, 89—; pres. Nayram Samoa, Ltd., Pago Pago, 1985-88; lt. gov. Am. Samoa Pago Pago, 1997—2003; gov. Am. Samoa, 2003—. Chmn. Senate Investigation Com., 1993—. Chmn. Bd. Higher Edn., Am. Samoa, 1993—; bd. dirs. Am. Samoa Jr. Golfers' Assn.; deacon Sailele Congrl. Ch. Mem. ATLA, Am. Samoa Bar Assn., Kans. Bar Assn., Samoa Profl. Golfer's Assn. (pres. 1985-87), Am. Samoa Golf Assn. (pres.). Democrat. Congregationalist. Office: Office of the Gov Ter of American Samoa Pago Pago AS 96799 Office Phone: 684-633-4116. Office Fax: 684-633-2269.

TULLY, HERBERT BULLARD, chemical manufacturing executive; b. Glen Ridge, NJ, Sept. 3, 1943; s. Richard Golfe and Marie Foster (Towne) T.; m. Nancy Dee Zook, Dec. 22, 1967; children: Kimberly, Christine, Gregory. BS, U. Calif., Berkeley, 1967. Mem. fin. mgmt. staff Gen. Electric Co., San Jose, Calif., 1967-70, mem. corp. audit staff Schenectady, N.J., 1970-73, mgr. acct. dept. San Leandro, Calif., 1973-75; mgr. audit dept. Am. Express Co., Fireman's Fund, San Francisco, 1975-77; asst. controller Fireman's Fund Ins. Co., San Francisco, 1977-81; controller Wilbur-Ellis Co., San Francisco, 1981-86, asst. treas., 1986-89, vp treas., 1989—2000, CEO, pres., 2000—. Bd. dirs. Overseas Cos., San Francisco. Office: Wilbur Ellis 345 California Street Flr 27 San Francisco CA 94104

TULLY, MAC, publishing executive; m. Cindy Tully. BA, U. Kans. Pres. & pub. Bradenton Herald, Fla.; v.p. advt., pub. Arlington Star-Telegram, Tex.; corp. v.p. ops. Knight Ridder, 2004; pub. Kansas City Star, Mo., 2005—08; v.p. Bay Area News Group MediaNews Group, 2008—; pres., pub. San Jose Mercury News, 2008—. Recipient John S. Knight Gold medal, Knight Ridder. Office: San Jose Mercury News 750 Ridder Park Dr San Jose CA 95190 Office Phone: 816-234-4490. E-mail: mtully@kcstar.com.

TULOWITZKI, TROY TREVOR, professional baseball player; b. Santa Clara, Calif., Oct. 10, 1984; s. Ken and Susan Tulowitzki. Grad. in Kinesiology, Calif. State U., Long Beach, 2005. Shortstop Colo. Rockies, 2006—. Shortstop Grand Canyon Rafters (Ariz. Fall League), 2006. Recipient Fielding Bible award, 2007; named Spring Tng. MVP, Colo. Rockies, 2007; named to Topps Maj. League Rookie All-Star Team, 2007. Achievements include reaching the Major Leagues in the shortest time span between draft day and debut in Rockies franchise history (one year, 83 days); turning the 13th unassisted triple play in Major League history, April 29, 2007; setting a new record for the most home runs in a single season by a National League rookie with 20, 2007; leading all Major League shortstops in fielding percentage (.987) and double plays turned (114) during the 2007 season; being a member of the 2004 National League Champion Colorado Rockies; signing the largest contract ever for a player with less than two year experience, 2008. Office: c/o Colo Rockies Coors Field 2001 Blake St Denver CO 80205

TULSKY, FREDRIC NEAL, journalist; b. Chgo., Sept. 30, 1950; s. George and Helen (Mailick) T.; m. Kim Rennard, June 20, 1971; children: Eric George, Elizabeth Rose. B.J., U. Mo., 1972; JD cum laude, Temple U., Phila., 1984. Bar: Pa. 1984. Reporter Saginaw News, Mich., 1973-74, Port Huron Times Herald, Mich., 1974-75, Jackson Clarion-Ledger, Miss., 1975-78, Los Angeles Herald Examiner, 1978-79, Phila. Inquirer, 1979-93; mng. editor Ctr. for Investigative Reporting, San Francisco, 1993-94, exec. dir., 1994; reporter L.A. Times, 1995—. Adj. prof. urban studies U. Pa., 1990-93. Recipient nat. awards including Robert F. Kennedy Found. award, 1979, Heywood Broun award Newspaper Guild, 1978, Disting. Svc. medal Sigma Delta Chi, 1978, 97, Pub. Svc. award AP Mng. Editors, 1978, Silver Gavel award ABA, 1979, 87, Pulitzer prize for investigative reporting, 1987, Pub. Svc. award Nat. Headliners Club, 1987, Investigative Reporters and editors medal, 1997; Nieman fellow Harvard U., 1989, Alicia Patterson fellow, 1998. Mem. Investigative Reporters and Editors (pres. 1988-91, chair 1991-93), Kappa Tau Alpha. Office: LA Times Times Mirror Sq Los Angeles CA 90053 E-mail: rick.tulsky@latimes.com.

TUNE, BRUCE MALCOLM, pediatrics educator, renal toxicologist; b. NYC, Aug. 26, 1939; s. Buford M. and Sylvia Tune; m. Nancy Carter Doolittle, Sept. 13, 1969; children: Sara E., Steven M. AB, Stanford U., 1963, MD, 1965. Diplomate Am. Bd. Pediat., Am. Bd. Pediatric Nephrology, Nat. Bd. Med. Examiners. Intern in medicine and pediatrics Strong Meml. Hosp., Rochester, NY, 1965—66; rsch. assoc. Lab. Kidney and Electrolyte Metabolism, Nat. Heart Inst., NIH, Bethesda, Md., 1967—69, clin. assoc., 1968—69; resident in pediat. Stanford (Calif.) U. Sch. Medicine, 1966—67, chief resident, 1969—70, fellow in pediatric renal and metabolic disease, 1970—71, asst. prof. pediat., 1971—77, assoc. prof., 1977—83, prof., 1983—, acting chmn. dept., 1991—93, dir. pediatric nephrology, 1971—97, prof. pediat. divsn. pediatric nephrology, 1998—, now emeritus prof. pediat. divsn. pediatric nephrology. Attending physician, chief pediatric renal svcs. Stanford U. Hosp., Palo Alto, Calif., 1971—76, Children's Hosp. at Stanford, Palo Alto, 1971—91; cons. physician Santa Clara Valley Med. Ctr., San Jose, Calif., 1973—; attending physician, chief pediatric renal svcs. Lucile Salter Packard Children's Hosp. at Stanford, 1991—98, acting chief pediatric medicine, 1991—93, attending physician, 1997; mem. rev. panel internat. study kidney diseases in children N.Y.C. NIH, 1973—74; polycystic kidney disease study group, Albuquerque, 1984; mem. spl. study sect. on genetics and kidney maturation, Bethesda, Md., 92; cons. Lilly Rsch. Labs., Indpls., 1980, Merck Sharp and Dohme Labs., Rahway, NJ, 1980, Bristol Labs., Syracuse, NY, 1982, ICI Pharms., Cheshire, England, 1992, Gilead Scis., Foster City, Calif., 1993, Zeneca Pharms., Mereside, England, 1994—; organizing mem., chmn. session on antibiotics NIH and EPA Conf. on Nephrotoxicity of Drugs and Environ. Toxicants, Pinehurst, NC, 1981; co-dir. Coop. Study Therapy of Steroid-Resistant Focal Glomerulosclerosis in Children, 1988—; mem. rsch. grant rev. panel Ont. (Can.) Ministry Health, 1992—, Wellcome Trust, London, 1994—; reviewer bd. environ. studies and toxicology NRC, 1994. Edit. bd. Am. Jour. Kidney Diseases, 1981—94, guest editor Contemporary Issues in Nephrology, 1984, Jour. Am. Soc. Nephrology, 1991; contbr. articles to med. jours. Grantee NIH, 1974—77, 1979—83, 1985—89, 1990—95. Mem.: Am. Soc. Pharmacology and Exptl. Therapeutics, Am. Heart Assn. (coun. on kidney diseases, grantee 1985—88, 1989—92), Western Soc. for Pediatric Rsch., Internat. Pediatric Nephrology Assn., Am. Soc. Pediatric Nephrology (coun. 1978—82, rsch. subcom. 1993—), Internat. Soc. Nephrology, Am. Soc. Nephrology, Alpha Omega Alpha, Phi Beta Kappa. Office: Stanford U Sch Medicine Dept Pediatrics 300 Pasteur Dr Rm G306 Palo Alto CA 94304-2203

TUNE, JAMES FULCHER, lawyer; b. Danville, Va., May 13, 1942; s. William Orrin and Susan Agnes (Fulcher) T.; m. Katherine Del Mickey, Aug. 2, 1969; children: Katherine Winslow, Jeffrey Bricker. BA, U. Va., 1964; MA, Stanford U., 1970, JD, 1974. Bar: Wash. 1974, U.S. Dist. Ct. (we. dist.) Wash. 1974. Assoc. Bogle & Gates, Seattle, 1974-79, ptnr., 1980-99, head comml./banking dept., 1985-93, mng. ptnr., 1986-93, chmn., 1994-99; ptnr. Dorsey & Whitney LLP, Seattle, 1999—2000, Stoel Rives LLP, Seattle, 2001—05, Seattle mng. ptnr., 2001—05; pres., CEO ArtsFund, Seattle, 2006—. Bd. dirs. Keynetics Inc., Boise, Idaho, Click Sales Inc., Boise, Kount Inc., Boise, Pay-Track Inc., Boise, Puget Sound Bank, Bellevue, Wash.; chmn. Seattle-King City Econ. Devel. Coun., 1992. Chmn. Seattle Repertory Theatre, 1995, Corp. Coun. for the Arts, 2001—02, United Way King County, 2004. Lt. USN, 1964—69, Vietnam. Woodrow Wilson fellow, 1964, Danforth Found. fellow, 1964. Mem. ABA, Wash. State Bar Assn. (lectr. CLE 1976, 78, 84, 99, 02), Seattle C. of C. (vice chmn. City Budget Task Force 1980-82), Greater Seattle C. of C. (trustee 2006—), Ranier Club (trustee 2006—), Seattle Tennis Club, Phi Beta Kappa. Presbyterian. Office: ArtsFund PO Box 19780 10 Harrison St Ste 200 Seattle WA 98109 Home Phone: 206-329-0372; Office Phone: 206-281-9050. Business E-Mail: jimtune@artsfund.org.

TUNG, PRABHAS, plastic surgeon; b. Ubol, Thailand, Apr. 3, 1944; s. Sathee and Seng (Ngium) T.; m. Patarin C. Sinjin; children: Tony, Tommy. MD, Mahidol U., Bangkok, 1968. Diplomate Am. Bd. Plastic Surgery. Plastic surgeon pvt. practice, Flint, Mich., 1980-82, Sacramento, Calif., 1982—. Office: 2801 K St Ste 200 Sacramento CA 95816-5118

TUNNEY, JOHN VARICK, lawyer, former United States Senator from California; b. NYC, June 26, 1934; s. Gene and Mary (Lauder) T.; m. Kathinka Osborne, April 1977; children: Edward Eugene, Mark Andrew, Arianne Sprengers, Tara Theodora. BA in Anthropology, Yale, 1956; JD, U. Va., 1959; student, Acad. Internat. Law, The Hague, Netherlands, 1957. Bar: N.Y. 1959, Calif. 1963, Va. 1963. With firm Cahill, Gordon, Reindel & Ohl, NYC, 1959-60; tchr. bus. law U. Calif., Riverside, 1961-62; practice law Riverside, 1963—; mem. 89th-91st Congresses from Calif. 38th Dist., U.S. Senate from Calif., 1971-77; mem. firm Manatt, Phelps, Rothenberg & Tunney, Los Angeles, 1977-86; chmn. bd. Cloverleaf Group, Inc., Los Angeles, 1986—; gen. ptnr. Sun Valley Ventures, 1994—; pres. JVT Consulting, Inc., 1997—. Chmn. bd. Enterprise Plan, Inc., chmn. bd. Trusted Brands Inc.; bd. dirs. Prospect Group Inc., Garnet Resources Corp., Ill. Central Railroad, The Forschner Group, Inc., Foamex Internat.; bd. dir. Prescpect Group Inc. Polit. commentator Station KABC-TV. Trustee Westminster Sch., St. Matthews Sch.; bd. visitors Loyola Law Sch.; vice chmn. Limited Incomes Housing Corp.; mem. Lawyers Adv. Council. Constl. Rights Found., Citizens Rsch. Found., Commn. on Soviet Jewry. Served to capt. USAF, 1960-63. Chubb fellow Yale U., 1967 Mem. Am. Bar Assn. Democrat. Episcopalian. Office: 1819 Ocean Ave Santa Monica CA 90401-3223

TUPA, RON, state legislator; b. Harbor Beach, Mich., Aug. 25, 1966; Colorado State Representative, District 14, 1995-2001, Minority Whip, 1997-2001, member, Education, State & Vet & Mil Affairs Committees, formerly, Colorado House Representative; Colorado State Senator, District 18, 2003-, majority caucus chairman, currently, chairman, State, Veterans & Military Affairs, member, Education, Finance, Legislature Coun Committees, currently, Colorado State Senate.Teacher, currently. Democrat. Mailing: Colo State Senate 200 E Colfax Denver CO 80203 Office Phone: 303-866-4872. E-mail: ron.tupa.senate@state.co.us.

TURBIN, RICHARD, lawyer; b. NYC, Dec. 25, 1944; s. William and Ruth (Fiedler) T.; m. Rai Saint Chu-Turbin, June 12, 1976; children: Laurel Mei, Derek Andrew. BA magna cum laude, Cornell U., 1966; JD, Harvard U., 1969. Bar: Hawaii 1971, U.S. Dist. Ct. Hawaii 1971. Asst. atty. gen., Western Samoa, Apia, 1969-70; dep. pub. defender Pub. Defender's Office, Honolulu, 1970-74; dir. Legal Aid Soc. Hawaii, Kaneohe, 1974-75; sr. atty., pres. Law Offices Richard Turbin, Honolulu, 1975—. Legal counsel Hawaii Crime Commn., 1980-81. Co-author: Pacific; author: Medical Malpractice, Handling Emergency Medical Cases, 1991; editor Harvard Civil Rights-Civil Liberties Law Rev., 1969. Legal counsel Dem. Party, Honolulu County, 1981-82; elected Neighborhood Bd., 1985, elected chair, 1990-97; bd. dirs. Hawaii chpt. ACLU, 1974-78, East-West Ctr. grantee, 1971, 72; commn. State of Hawaii Civil Rights com., 2002-05. Recipient Traphagen Disting. Alumnus award, Harvard Law Sch. Mem. ATLA, ABA (chair internat. torts and ins. practice section 1999-2000., governing coun., chair tort and ins. practice sect. 1999-2000), Hawaii Bar Assn. (pres. 2005), Hawaii Trial Lawyers Assn. (pres. 2002), Hawaii Jaycees (legal counsel 1981-82), Chinese Jaycees Honolulu (legal counsel 1980-81), Honolulu Tennis League (undefeated player 1983), Hawaii Harlequin Rugby Club (sec., legal counsel 1978-82), Pacific Club, Outrigger Canoe Club.' Jewish. Home: 4817 Kahala Ave Honolulu HI 96816-5231 Office Phone: 808-528-4000. Personal E-mail: richturbin@aol.com.

TURCOTTE, DONALD LAWSON, geophysical sciences educator; b. Bellingham, Wash., Apr. 22, 1932; s. Lawson Phillip and Eva (Pearson) Turcotte; m. Joan Meredith Luecke, May 17, 1957; children: Phillip Lawson, Stephen Bradford. BS, Calif. Inst. Tech., 1954, PhD, 1958; M in Aero. Engring., Cornell U., 1955; PhD (hon.), U. Paris, 2005. Asst. prof. aero. engring. U.S. Naval Postgrad. Sch., Monterey, Calif., 1958-59; asst. prof. aero. engring. Cornell U., Ithaca, NY, 1959-63, assoc. prof., 1963-67, prof., 1967-73, prof. geol. scis., 1973-85, Maxwell Upson prof., 1985—2000, chmn., 1981-90; disting. prof. geology U. Calif. Davis, 2003—. Author (with others): Statistical Thermodynamics, 1963, Space Propulsion, 1965, Geodynamics, 1982, Fractals and Chaos in Geology and Geophysics, 1992, Mantle Convection, 2001. Trustee U. Space Rsch. Assn., 1975—79. Recipient Wegener medal, European Union Geosci., 1991, Disting. Alumni award, Calif. Inst. Tech., 1999; sr. postdoctoral rsch. fellow, NSF, 1965—66, Guggenheim fellow, 1972—73. Mem.: NAS, Am. Acad. Arts and Scis., Seismol. Soc. Am., Geol. Soc. Am. (Day medal 1982), Am. Geophys. Union (Charles A. Whitten medal 1995, William Bowie Medal 2003), El Macero Country Club. Home: 27104 Middle Golf Dr El Macero CA 95618 Office: Univ Calif Dept Geology Davis CA 95616 Office Phone: 530-572-6808. Business E-Mail: turcotte@geology.ucdavis.edu.

TURK, AUSTIN THEODORE, social studies educator; b. Gainesville, Ga., May 28, 1934; s. Hollis Theodore and Ruth (Vandiver) T.; m. Janet Stuart Irving, Oct. 4, 1957 (div. 1977); children: Catherine, Jennifer; m. Ruth-Ellen Marie Grimes, July 27, 1985. BA cum laude, U. Ga., 1956; MA, U. Ky., 1959; PhD, U. Wis., 1962. Acting instr. sociology U. Wis., Madison, 1961-62; from instr. to prof. sociology Ind. U., Bloomington, 1962-74; prof. U. Toronto, Can., 1974-88, U. Calif., Riverside, 1988—, chmn. dept. sociology, 1989-94; interim dir. Robert B. Presley Ctr. for Crime and Justice Studies, 1994-95. Author: Criminality and Legal Order, 1969, Political Criminality, 1982; gen. editor crime and justice series SUNY Press, Albany, 1990—; contbr. articles to jours. in field. Mem. Calif. Mus. Photography, 1988—, Citizens Univ. Com., 1990—. Recipient Paul Tappan award Western Soc. Criminology, 1989. Fellow Am. Soc. Criminology (pres. 1984-85); mem. Am. Sociol. Assn. (chair criminology sect. 1975-76), Law and Soc. Assn. (trustee 1982-85), Acad. Criminal Justice Scis. Democrat. Avocations: gardening, reading, swimming, tennis. Office: Dept Sociology U Calif Riverside Riverside CA 92521-0001 E-mail: austin.turk@ucr.edu.

TURNAGE, JEAN ALLEN, retired state supreme court chief justice; b. St. Ignatius, Mont., Mar. 10, 1926; JD, Mont. State U., 1951; D of Laws and Letters (hon.), U. Mont., 1995. Bar: Mont. 1951, US Supreme Ct. 1963. Former ptnr. Turnage, McNeil & Mercer, Polson, Mont.; former Mont. State senator from 13th Dist.; pres. Mont. State Senate, 1981—85; chief justice Supreme Ct. Mont., 1985-2001. Mem. Mont. State Bar Assn., Nat. Conf. Chief Justices (past pres.), Nat. Ctr. State Courts (past chair). Office: Turnage & Mercer PO Box 460 Polson MT 59860 Office Phone: 406-883-5367. Personal E-mail: jeanturnage@centurytel.net.

TURNBAUGH, ROY CARROLL, archivist; b. Peoria, Ill., Oct. 16, 1945; s. Roy Carroll and Zora (Alexander) T.; m. Donna Marie Chase, Mar. 28, 1970; children: Andrew, Peter. BA, Aurora Coll., 1969; AM, U. Ill., 1973, PhD, 1977. Asst. prof. U. Ill., Urbana, 1977-78; archivist Ill. State Archives, Springfield, 1978-85; dir. Oreg. State Archives, Salem, 1985—. Mem. Nat. Hist. Publs. and Records Commn., 2000—. Mem. Nat. Assn. Govt. Archives Records Adminstrs. (pres. 1998-2000), Soc. Am. Archivists (C.F.W. Coker prize 1984, Fellows Posner prize 1999). Office: Oreg State Archives 800 Summer St NE Salem OR 97310-1347 E-mail: roy.c.turnbaugh@state.or.us.

TURNER, ANDREW L., healthcare management company executive; BA, Ohio State Univ. Adminstr skilled nursing facility, Springfield, Ohio, 1970-75; mgr. regional nursing home chain; sr. v.p. ops. Hillhaven Corp.; co-founder Horizon Healthcare Corp., 1986-89; founder, chmn.,CEO Sun Healthcare Group, Albuquerque, 1989—2000; chmn. Ballantrae Healthcare, 2000—; founder, chmn. Endura Care, 2000—, Code Blue Staffing Solutions, 2001—; mem. bd. of directors Sports Clubs/L.A., Watson Pharmaceuticals.

TURNER, BONESE COLLINS, artist, educator; b. Abilene, Kans. d. Paul Edwin and Ruby (Seybold) Collins; m. Glenn E. Turner; 1 child, Craig Collins. BS in Edn., MEd, U. Idaho, Moscow; MA, Calif. State U., Northridge, 1974. Adj. prof. L.A. Pierce Coll., Woodland Hills, Calif., 1964—. Prof. art Calif. State U., Northridge, 1986-89; adj. prof. L.A. Valley Coll., Van Nuys, 1987-89, Moorpark Coll., Calif., 1988-98, Arrowmont Coll. Arts and Crafts, Gatlinburg, Tenn., 1995-96; advisor Coll. Art and Arch. U. Idaho, 1988—; juror for art exhbns. including Nat. Watercolor Soc., 1980, 91, San Diego Art Inst., Brand Nat. Watermedia Exhbn., 1980, 96-97, prin. gallery Orlando Gallery, Tarzana, Calif.; juror South Bay Watercolor Soc., 2008, Montrose Verdugo Juried Art Exhibit, 2005; tchr. watercolor seminar Dale Chihuly Found., W.Hills, Calif., 2005. Represented in permanent collections Smithsonian Inst., U. Idaho Hartung Performing Arts Ctr., Moscow Idaho Installation, 1994, Olympic Arts Festival, L.A.; one-woman shows include Angel's Gate Gallery, San Pedro, Calif., 1989, Art Store Gallery, Studio City, Calif., 1988, L.A. Pierce Coll. Gallery, 1988, Brand Art Gallery, Glendale, Calif., 1988, 93, 2000, 05, Coos (Oreg.) Art Mus., 1988, U. Nev., 1987, Orlando Gallery, Sherman Oaks, Calif., 1993, 98, 2002, 05, Burbank (Calif.) Creative Arts Ctr., 2000, 07, Village Sq. Gallery, Montrose, Calif., 2002, 05, Pierce Art Gallery, 2005, Calif. Inst. Tech., 2007, La Galeria Gitana San Fernando, Calif, 2003-2009, Of Dreams & Memories, 2009, The Sacred in Art, Birger Sandzen Gallery, Lindsborg, Kans., 2007, La Galiriagitana, San Fernando, Calif., 2009, Torrance Art Mus., 2008, Springfield Art Mus., Mo., 2008; prin. works in pub. collections include The Smithsonian Inst., Hartung Performing Arts Ctr., Moscow, Idaho, Robert V. Fulton Mus. Art, Calif. State U., San Bernardino, Calif., Springfield (Mo.) Art Mus, Home Savs. and Loan, San Bernardino Sun Telegram Newspapers, Oreg. Coun. for the Arts, Newport, Oreg. Pub. Librs., Brand Libr., Glendale, Calif., Lincoln (Nebr.) Pub. Lib., Indsl. Tile Corp., Lincoln. Recipient Springfield (Mo.) Art Mus. award, 1989, 2002, 1st prize Brand XXVIII, 1998, Glendale, Calif., Butler Art Inst. award, 1989, 1st award in graphics Diamond Jubilee Exhibit/Pasadena Soc. Artists, 2002, Nat. award Acrylic Painters Assn. Eng. and U.S.A., 1996, Ruth Kain award, LA Brewery, 2003. Mem. Nat. Acrylic Painters Assn. of Eng. (award 1996), Nat. Mortar Bd. Soc., Nat. Watercolor Soc. (life, past pres., Purchase prize 1979), Watercolor U.S.A. Honor Soc. (awards), Watercolor West. Avocations: bicycling, music, singing. Personal E-mail: boneseturner@yahoo.com.

TURNER, HAROLD EDWARD, retired education educator; b. Hamilton, Ill., Nov. 22, 1921; s. Edward Jesse and Beulah May (White) T.; m. Catherine Skeeters, Apr. 5, 1946; children: Michele Turner Nimerick, Thomas, Barbara Turner McMahon, Krista Turner Landgraf. AB, Carthage Coll., 1950; MS, U. Ill. - Urbana, 1951, Ed.D. (George Peabody fellow), 1956. Tchr. Taylorville (Ill.) Jr. H.S., 1951-52, Moline (Ill.) Jr. H.S., 1952-54; dir. elem. edn. Jefferson County, Colo., 1955-57; prin. Jefferson County H.S., 1957-60; asst. prof. edn. North Tex. State U., Denton, 1960-63; asst. supt. curriculum Sacramento City Schs., 1963-66; assoc. prof., chmn. dept. curriculum and instrn. U. Mo., St. Louis, 1966-69, prof., 1971-85, prof. emeritus, 1985—, chmn. dept. adminstrn., founds., secondary edn., 1977-78, dept. chmn., 1983-85. Vis. prof. Adams State Coll., Alamosa, Colo., 1959, U. Ga., Athens, 1981-82; adj. prof. NYU, 1965, U. Ill., 1980; cons. various sch. dists., Tex., Mo.; spl. cons. Mo. State Dept. Edn.,

1973. Author: (with Adolph Unruh) Supervision for Change and Innovation, 1970; contbr. articles to profl. jours. Served with USNR, 1942-46. Presbyterian. Home: 685 S La Posada Cir # AL 52 Green Valley AZ 85614 E-mail: gazvk@aol.com.

TURNER, HENRY BROWN, finance company executive, director; b. NYC, Sept. 3, 1936; s. Henry Brown III and Gertrude (Adams) T.; m. Sarah Jean Thomas, June 7, 1958 (div.); children: Laura Eleanor, Steven Bristow, Nancy Carolyn. AB, Duke U., 1958; MBA, Harvard U., 1962. Controller Fin. Corp. of Ariz., Phoenix, 1962-64; treas., dir. corporate planning Star-Kist Foods, Terminal Island, Calif., 1964-67; dir., 1st v.p. Mitchum, Jones & Templeton, Los Angeles, 1967-73; asst. sec. Dept. Commerce, Washington, 1973-74; v.p. fin. N-Ren Corp., Cin., 1975-76; v.p. Oppenheimer & Co., NYC, 1976-78; exec. v.p., mng. dir. corporate fin. Shearson Hayden Stone Inc., NYC, 1978-79; sr. mng. dir. Ardshiel Inc., 1980-81, pres., 1981-93, chmn. emeritus, 1994—. Vis. lectr. U. Va. Sch. of Bus.; bd. dirs. MacDonald & Co., Pembrook Mgmt., Inc., Golden State Vitners, Inc., Cellu-Tissue Corp., Rio Verde, Ariz; quarter horse trainer; prof. piano player. Sponsor Jr. Achievement, 1964-67. Served to lt. USNR, 1958-60. Coll. Men's Club scholar Westfield, N.J., 1954-55 Mem. Fed. Govt. Accountants Assn. (hon.), Duke Washington Club, Omicron Delta Kappa.

TURNER, JANA L., real estate company executive; b. 1955; BSBA in Mktg., No. Ariz. U., 1977. Cert. property mgr. Inst. Real Estate Mgmt. Leasing receptionist R&B Comml. Mgmt., LA; pres. Pacific S.W. Region Koll Real Estate Svcs., Newport Beach, Calif., 1990—97; exec. v.p., mgr. western divsn. CB Comml., 1997—98; pres. asset svcs. CB Richard Ellis, 1998—. Bd. dirs. SiteStuff, Inc. Office: CB Richard Ellis 3501 Jamboree Rd Ste 100 Newport Beach CA 92660 Office Phone: 949-809-4057. E-mail: jana.turner@cbre.com.

TURNER, KEVIN (B. KEVIN TURNER), computer software company executive; m. Shelly Turner; 3 children. BS, E. Ctrl. U., 1987. Cashier Wal-Mart Stores, Inc., Ada, Okla., 1985—88, with internal audit dept., 1988—89, bus. analyst info. sys. div., strategy mgr. info. sys. div., dir. info. sys. div., v.p. and asst. chief info. officer info. sys. div., chief info. officer info. sys. div., 2000—03, exec. v.p., 2000, pres. and CEO Sam's Club div., 2002—05; COO Microsoft Corp., Redmond, Wash., 2005—. Recipient inaugural Sam M. Walton Entrepreneur of the Yr. award, 1997, Disting. Alumnus award, E. Ctrl. U., 2003; named one of Top 25 Most Innovative Execs., CRN Mag., 2007; named to CIO Hall of Fame, CIO Mag., 2007. Office: Microsoft Corp 1 Microsoft Way Redmond WA 98052-6399

TURNER, MARCELLUS, library director; MS in Libr. Sci., U. Tenn., Knoxville, 1988. Departmental supr. Tacoma Pub. Libr., Wash., Atlantic City Free Pub. Libr., NJ; asst. exec. dir. Rockford Pub. Libr., Ill.; joined Jefferson County Pub. Libr., Lakewood, Colo., 2002, dir. pub. svcs., dep. county libr., 2005—08, exec. dir., 2008—. Mem.: ALA (mem. Black Caucus, sec. Joint Conf. Librs. of Color), Libr. Adminstrn. & Mgmt. Assn., Colo. Assn. Librs., Pub. Libr. Assn. Office: Jefferson County Pub Libr 10200 W 20th Ave Denver CO 80215 Office Phone: 303-235-5275.

TURNER, NORV(AL) (EUGENE), professional football coach; b. LeJeune, NC, May 17, 1952; m. Nancy Turner; children: Scott, Stephanie, Drew. Asst. coach U. So. Calif. Trojans, 1976—84; receivers coach LA Rams, 1985—90; offensive coord. Dallas Cowboys, 1991—93, San Diego Chargers, 2001, Miami Dolphins, 2002—03, San Francisco 49ers, 2006—07; head coach Washington Redskins, 1994—2000, Oakland Raiders, 2004—06, San Diego Chargers, 2007—. Achievements include being a member of Super Bowl Championship winning Dallas Cowboys, 1993, 1994. Office: c/o San Diego Chargers PO Box 609609 San Diego CA 92160

TURNER, RALPH HERBERT, sociologist, educator; b. Effingham, Ill., Dec. 15, 1919; s. Herbert Turner and Hilda Pearl (Bohn) T.; m. Christine Elizabeth Hanks, Nov. 2, 1943; children: Lowell Ralph, Cheryl Christine. BA, U So. Calif., 1941, MA, 1942; postgrad., U. Wis., 1942-43; PhD, U. Chgo., 1948. Rsch. assoc. Am. Coun. Race Relations, 1947-48; faculty UCLA, 1948—, prof. sociology and anthropology, 1959-90, prof. emeritus, 1990—, chmn. dept. sociology, 1963-68; chmn. Acad. Senate U. Calif. System, 1983-84. Vis. summer prof. U. Wash., 1960, U. Hawaii, 1962; vis. scholar Australian Nat. U., 1972; vis. prof. U. Ga., 1975, Ben Gurion U., Israel, 1983; vis. fellow Nuffield Coll. Oxford U., 1980; disting. vis. prof. Am. U., Cairo, Egypt, 1983; adj. prof. China Acad. Social Scis., Beijing, People's Republic China, 1986. Author: (with L. Killian) Collective Behavior, 1957, 2d edit., 1972, 3d edit., 1987, The Social Context of Ambition, 1964, Robert Park on Social Control and Collective Behavior, 1967, Family Interaction, 1970, Earthquake Prediction and Public Policy, 1975, (with J. Nigg, D. Paz, B. Young) Community Response to Earthquake Threat in So. Calif., 1980, (with J. Nigg and D. Paz) Waiting for Disaster, 1986; editl. cons., 1959-62; editor: Sociometry, 1962-64; acting editor: Ann. Rev. of Sociology, 1977-78; assoc. editor, 1978-79, editor, 1980-86; adv. editor: Am. Jour. Sociology, 1954-56, Sociology and Social Rsch., 1961-74; editl. staff: Am. Sociol. Rev., 1955-56; assoc. editor: Social Problems, 1959-62, 67-69; cons. editor: Sociol. Inquiry, 1968-73, Western Sociol. Rev., 1975-79; mem. editl. bd. Mass Emergencies, 1975-79, Internat. Jour. Crit. Sociology, 1974-76, Symbolic Interaction, 1977-90, 95—, Mobilization, 1996—. Mem. behavioral scis. study sect. NIH, 1961-66, chmn., 1963-64; dir.-at-large Social Sci. Rsch. Coun., 1965-66; chmn. panel on pub. policy implications of earthquake predictions Nat. Acad. Scis., 1974-75, also mem. earthquake study del. to Peoples Republic of China, 1976; mem. policy adv. bd. So. Calif. Earthquake Preparedness program, 1987-92, mem. com. social edn. and action L.A. Presbytery, 1954-56. Served to lt. (j.g.) USNR, 1943-46. Recipient Faculty prize Coll. Letters and Scis. UCLA, 1985; Faculty Rsch. fellow Social Sci. Rsch. Coun., 1953-56; Sr. Fulbright scholar U.K., 1956-57; Guggenheim fellow, U.K., 1964-65; Faculty Rsch. lectr. UCLA, 1987, UCLA Emeritus of Yr., 1997. Mem. AAAS (exch. del. to China 1988), AAUP, Am. Sociol. Assn. (coun. 1959-64, chmn. social psychology sect. 1960-61, pres. 1968-69, chmn. sect. theoretical sociology 1973-74, chmn. collective behavior and social movements sect. 1983-84, Cooley-Mead award 1987), Pacific Sociol. Assn. (pres. 1957), Internat. Sociol. Assn. (coun. 1974-82, v.p. 1978-82), Soc. Study Social Problems (exec. com. 1962-63), Soc. for Study Symbolic Interaction (pres. 1982-83, Charles Horton Cooley award 1978, George Herbert Mead award 1990), Sociol. Rsch. Assn. (pres. 1989-90), Am. Coun. of Learned Soc. (exec. com. of coun. 1990-93), UCLA Emeriti Assn. (coun., pres. 1992-93), U. of Calif. Emeriti Assns. (chair-elect 1996-97, chair 1997-98, Panunzio award 2002, Lifetime Svc. award 2007). Home: 1126 Chautauqua Blvd Pacific Palisades CA 90272-3808 Office: UCLA 405 Hilgard Ave Los Angeles CA 90095-9000

TURNER, ROBERT ELWOOD, physicist; b. Covington, Ky., Dec. 8, 1937; s. Elwood Fletcher and Margaret Belle (Gunn) T. BS in Physics, U. Cin., 1959, MS in Physics, 1960; MA in Physics, Columbia U., 1963; PhD in Physics, Washington U., St. Louis, 1970. Research physicist U. Mich., Ann Arbor, 1970-73, Environ. Research Inst. Mich., Ann Arbor, 1973-77; sr. scientist Sci. Applications Internat. Corp., Monterey, Calif., 1977—. Rsch. assoc. Inst. for Space Studies, NASA, N.Y.C., 1962, Washington U., 1964-69; astronomer McDonnell Planetarium, St. Louis, 1965-68; lectr. U. Mich., 1971-77; Gordon Conf. lectr., 1980. Contbr. articles to profl. jours. and books. Rep. precinct leader, Ann Arbor, 1972. Laws fellow, 1959; recipient Group Achievement award NASA, 1976. Mem. AAAS, Am. Assn. Physics Tchrs., Monterey Inst. Rsch. in Astronomy, Toastmasters (ednl. v.p. Dayton 1986, pres. 1987, sec. 1989, treas. 1991), Sigma Xi (programs co-chair Air Force chpt. 1988-89). Clubs: Toastmasters (ednl. v.p. Dayton 1986, pres. 1987, sec. 1989). Methodist. Avocations: swimming, tennis, ice skating, hiking. Home: 930 Casanova Ave Apt 40 Monterey CA 93940-6821 Office: Science Applications International Corp 550 Camino El Estero Ste 103 Monterey CA 93940-3231

TURNER, WALLACE L., reporter; b. Titusville, Fla., Mar. 15, 1921; s. Clyde H. and Ina B. (Wallace) T.; m. Pearl Burk, June 12, 1943; chldren: Kathleen Turner, Elizabeth Turner Everett. B.J., U. Mo., 1943; postgrad. (Nieman fellow), Harvard U., 1958-59. Reporter Springfield (Mo.) Daily News, 1943, Portland Oregonian, 1943-59; news dir. Sta. KPTV, Portland, 1959-61; asst. sec. HEW, Washington, 1961-62; reporter N.Y. Times, San Francisco, 1962—, bur. chief, 1970-85, Seattle bur. chief, 1985-88. Author: Gamblers Money, 1965, The Morman Establishment, 1967. Recipient Heywood Broun award for reporting, 1952, 56; Pulitzer Prize for reporting, 1957 Office: Box 99269 Magnolia Sta Seattle WA 98199-4260

TURNER, WILLIAM WEYAND, writer; b. Buffalo, Apr. 14, 1927; s. William Peter and Magdalen (Weyand) T.; m. Margaret Peiffer, Sept. 12, 1964; children: Mark Peter, Lori Ann. BS, Canisius Coll., 1949. Spl. agt. in various field offices FBI, 1951-61; free-lance writer Calif., 1963—; sr. editor Ramparts Mag., San Francisco, 1967—. Investigator and cons. Nat. Wiretap Commn., 1975; U.S. del. J.F.K. Internat. Seminar, Rio de Janeiro, 1995. Author: The Police Establishment, 1968, Invisible Witness: The Use and Abuse of the New Technology of Crime Investigation, 1968, Hoover's F.B.I.: The Men and the Myth, 1970, Power on the Right, 1971, (with Warren Hinckle and Eliot Asinof) The Ten Second Jailbreak, 1973, (with John Christian) The Assassination of Robert F. Kennedy, 1978, (with Warren Hinckle) The Fish is Red: The Story of the Secret War Against Castro, 1981, updated, expanded, retitled as Deadly Secrets: The CIA-Mafia War Against Castro and the Assassination of JFK, 1992, Rearview Mirror: Looking Back at the FBI, the CIA and Other Tails, 2001, Mission Not Accomplished: How George Bush Lost the War on Terrorism, 2004; contbg. author: Investigating the FBI, 1973; contbr. articles to popular mags.; book reviewer L.A. Times. Dem. candidate for U.S. Congress, 1968. Served with USN, 1945-46. Mem. Authors Guild, Internat. Platform Assn., Press Club of San Francisco. Roman Catholic. Avocation: tennis. Home and Office: 163 Mark Twain Ave San Rafael CA 94903-2820 Office Phone: 415-479-7945. Business E-Mail: fanofjfk@aol.com.

TURNER THORNE, CHARLI, women's college basketball coach; d. Jim Turner; m. Will Thorne, May 14, 1994; children: Conor, Liam, Quinn. BA in Psychology, Stanford U., Calif., 1988; MEd, U. Wash., Seattle, 1990. Grad. asst. U. Wash. Huskies, 1988-90; asst. coach, recruiting coord. Santa Clara U. Broncos, Calif., 1990-93; head coach No. Ariz. U. Lumberjacks, Flagstaff, 1993—96, Ariz. State U. Sun Devils, Tempe, 1996—. Bd. dirs. Women's Basketball Coaches Assn. Named Dist. VIII Coach of Yr., Women's Basketball Coaches Assn., 2006. Office: Ariz State U Womens Basketball Carson Ctr PO Box 872505 Tempe AZ 85287-2505 Office Phone: 480-965-6086. E-mail: ASUHoop@asu.edu.

TURNLUND, JUDITH RAE, nutritionist; b. St. Paul, Sept. 28, 1936; d. Victor Emanuel and Vida Mae (Priddy) Hanson; m. Richard Wayne Turnlund, Nov. 9, 1957; children: Michael Wayne, Mark Richard, Todd Hanson. BS in Chemistry and Psychology, Gustavus Adolphus Coll., 1958; PhD in Nutrition, U. Calif., Berkeley, 1978. Registered dietitian. Postdoctoral fellow U. Calif., Berkeley, 1978-80, lectr., 1984-92, adj. assoc. prof., 1989-97; rsch. nutrition scientist Western Regional Rsch. Ctr./Western Human Nutrition Ctr., USDA, San Francisco, Albany, and Davis, Calif., 1980—; rsch. leader Western Human Nutrition Ctr. USDA, San Francisco, 1993-96; adj. prof. nutrition U. Calif., Davis, 2000—. Vis. asst. prof. Am. U. Beirut, Lebanon, 1979, 80. Editor: Stable Isotopes in Nutrition, 1984; contbr. articles to profl. jours. Recipient Cert. of Merit, USDA/ARS, 1984, 93, 98, Disting. Alumni citation Gustavus Adolphus Coll., 1988, Am. Inst. Nutrition's Lederle award in Human Nutrition, 1996; USDA grantee, Nat. Dairy Coun. grantee. Fellow Am. Soc. Nutritional Scis.; mem. Am. Soc. Clin. Nutrition, Am. Dietetic Assn. Home: 2276 Great Hwy San Francisco CA 94116-1555 Office: U Calif USDA/ARS Western Human Nutrition Rsch One Shields Ave Davis CA 95616 E-mail: jturnlun@whnrc.usda.gov.

TURNOVSKY, STEPHEN JOHN, economics professor; b. Wellington, New Zealand, Apr. 5, 1941; came to U.S., 1981; s. Frederick and Liselotte Felicitas (Wodak) T.; m. Michelle Henriette Louise Roos, Jan. 21, 1967; children: Geoffrey George, Jacqueline Liselotte. BA, Victoria U., Wellington, 1962, MA with honors, 1963; PhD, Harvard U., 1968. Asst. prof. econs. U. Pa., Phila., 1968-71; assoc. prof. U. Toronto, Ont., Canada, 1971-72; prof. Australian Nat. U., Canberra, 1972-82; IBE disting. prof. econs. U. Ill., Champaign, 1982-87; prof. econs. U. Wash., Seattle, 1987—, chmn. dept., 1990-95; Castor prof., 1993—. Rsch. assoc. Nat. Bur. Econ. Rsch., Cambridge, Mass., 1983-93. Author: Macroeconomic Analysis and Stabilization Policy, 1977, International Macroeconomic Stabilization Policy, 1990, Methods of Macroeconomic Dynamics, 1995, 2d edit., 2000, International Macroeconomic Dynamics, 1997; mem. editl. bd. several jours.; contbr. articles to profl. jours. Fellow Econometric Soc., Acad. Social Scis. in Australia; mem. Soc. Econ. Dynamics and Control (pres. 1982-84, editor Jour. Econ. Dynamics and Control 1981-87, 95-2001), Soc. Computational Econs. (pres. 2004-05). Avocations: skiing, hiking, music. Home: 6053 NE Kelden Pl Seattle WA 98105-2045 Office: Dept Econs U Wash Box 353330 Seattle WA 98195-3330 Office Phone: 206-685-8028. E-mail: sturn@u.washington.edu.

TURPIN, DAVID HOWARD, biologist, educator, academic administrator; b. Duncan, BC, Can., July 14, 1956; s. George Howard and Marilyn Elizabeth (Jones) T.; children: Chantal, Joshua. BSc in Biology, U. BC, 1977, PhD in Botany and Oceanography, 1980. Postdoctoral rsch. fellow Natural Scis. Engring. Rsch. Coun., 1980—81; rsch. assoc. Simon Fraser U., 1980; v.p. Sigma Resource Cons., Vancouver, BC, 1980—81; from asst. prof. to assoc. prof. Queen's U., Kingston, Ont., Canada, 1981—90, prof. biology, 1990—91, dean arts and sci., 1993—95, vice prin. acad., 1995—2000; prof., head botany U. BC, 1991—93; pres., vice-chancellor U. Victoria, BC, 2000—. Invited spkr. profl. meetings univs. worldwide. Co-editor: Plant Physiology, Biochemistry and Molecular Biology, 1990, 2d edit., 1996; mem. editl. bd. Jour. Phycology, 1992-96, Plant Physiology, 1988-92, Plant Cell and Environ., 1994-96, Jour. Exptl. Botany, 1995-98; contbr. chpts. in books; author numerous articles, conf. procs. V.p. Great Lakes Tomorrow, 1986-90; mem. program com. Great Lakes Course-Ont. Sci. Ctr., 1988; Kingston City rep. Cataraqui Regional Conservation Authority, 1984-86; hon. adv. mem. Soong Ching Ling Found. Ltd., 2001-. Recipient Excellence in Tchg. Alumni award Queen's U., 1989, Outstanding Alumni award U. B.C., 1990, Darbaker prize in phycology Am. Bot. Assn., 1991; Natural Scis. and Engring. Rsch. Coun. E.W.R. Stacie Meml. fellow, 1989-90, Royal Soc. Can. fellow, 1998-; Capt. T.S. Byrne Meml. scholar U. B.C., 1980; postgrad. scholar Natural Scis. and Engring. Rsch. Coun., 1979-81, Edith Ashton Meml. scholar U. B.C., 1979, NRC scholar, 1978-79; Natural Scis. and Engring. Rsch. Coun. grantee, 1982—. Mem. Phycological Soc. Am., Am. Soc. Limnology and Oceanography, Can. Soc. Plant Physiologists (C.D. Nelson award 1989), Am. Soc. Plant Physiologists (cert. recognition 1992), Minister Nat. Defence Edn. Adv. Bd., Discovery Found. Bd., Assn. Univs. and Colls. Can. (mem. bd. dirs. 2002-). Office: Office of the Pres U Victoria Bus and Econ Bldg Rm 454 Victoria BC Canada V8W 2Y2 Business E-Mail: pres@uvic.ca.

TURRENTINE, HOWARD BOYD, federal judge; b. Escondido, Calif., Jan. 22, 1914; s. Howard and Veda Lillian (Maxfield) T.; children: Howard Robert, Terry Beverly; m. Marlene Lipsey, Nov. 1, 1991. AB, San Diego State Coll., 1936; LLB, U. So. Calif., 1939. Bar: Calif. 1939. Practiced in, San Diego, 1939-68; judge Superior Ct. County of San Diego, 1968-70. U.S. Dist. Ct. (so. dist.) Calif., Calif., sr. judge San Diego, 1970—. Served with USNR, 1941-45. Mem. ABA, Fed. Bar Assn., Am. Judicature Soc. Office: US Dist Ct 940 Front St San Diego CA 92101-8994 Office Phone: 619-557-6630.

TUTHILL, WALTER WARREN, accountant, management consultant; b. Madison, NJ, Nov. 28, 1941; s. Walter Warren and Elizabeth Emma (Kniskern) T.; m. Barbara Ann Stephens, Apr. 22, 1967. BSBA, U. NC, Chapel Hill, 1964. CPA NY, NJ, NC; cert. info. systems auditor. Sr. mgr. Price Waterhouse, NYC, 1964-77; dir. internal audit Carter Hawley Hale Stores Inc., LA, 1977-82, gen. auditor, 1982-85, v.p., 1985-93; sr. v.p. retail control Broadway Stores, Inc., LA, 1993-96; v.p. retail control Federated Dept. Stores, Inc., LA, 1996-97; COO Gelfand, Rennert & Feldman divsn. PricewaterhouseCoopers LLP, LA, 1997-2001; dir. comprehensive bus. svcs. WongHolland LLP, CPAs, Woodland Hills, Calif., 2001—. Lectr. in field. Contbr. articles to profl. jours. Mem. AICPA, NY Soc. CPAs, Am. Acctg. Assn., Nat. Retail Fedn. (chmn. bd. internal audit group 1982-84, bd. dirs.), Info. Sys. Audit and Control Assn. Avocations: international travel, computers, classical music, photography, philanthropy. Office: WongHolland LLP CPAs and Cons 4919 Topanga Canyon Blvd Woodland Hills CA 91364-3113 Home Phone: 818-609-8099; Office Phone: 818-999-5273. Office Fax: 818-999-5274. Personal E-mail: wwtuthill@earthlink.net. Business E-Mail: wtuthill@wongholland.com.

TUTOR, RONALD N., construction executive; b. Oct. 13, 1940; BS in Fin., U. So. Calif., LA, 1963. Pres., CEO Tutor-Saliba Corp., Calif.; bd. dirs. Perini Corp., 1997—, COO, 1997—2000, vice chmn., 1998—99, chmn., 1999—, CEO, 2000—. Bd. dirs. Southdown Corp.; mem. adv. com. U. So. Calif. Sch. Engring. Recipient LA Conservancy Preservation award, 1994, Greater LA African-Am. C. of C. Contractor of Yr. award, 1994, US Army C.E. LA Dist. Contractor of Yr. award, 1994, NCCJ Real Estate and Constrn. Industry Humanitarian award, 1992. Mem. Am. Concrete Inst. Office: Tutor-Saliba 15901 Olden St Sylmar CA 91342-1093 also: Perini Corp 73 Mt Wayte Ave Framingham MA 01701

TUTTLE, RICK, city controller; b. New Haven, Jan. 5, 1940; s. Frederick Burton and Mary Emily; m. Muff Singer; 1 child, Sarah Emily Tuttle Singer. BA with honors and distinction, Wesleyan U., 1962; MA, UCLA, 1964, PhD, 1975. From asst. dean of students to student affairs officer UCLA, 1971-85; contr. City of L.A., 1985—. Civil rights worker, Ga. and Miss., 1963; co-chmn. Calif. Young Citizens Robert F. Kennedy, 1968; pres. Calif. Fedn. Young Dems., 1969-71; trustee L.A. Community Coll., 1977-85, pres. 1982-83; bd. dirs. univ. rel. conf. UCLA. Recipient Svc. award, UCLA Alumni Internship Assn., 1988, Equal Justice in Govt. award, NAACP Legal Def. and Edn. Fund, L.A., 1986, Disting. Pub. Svc. award Anti Defamation League, L.A., 1991, Pub. Svc. award UCLA Alumni Assn., 1994, Disting. Leadership award Local Govt. Assn. Govt. Accts., 1996. Mem. Govt. Fin. Officers Assn., L.A. Bus. Coun. (life). Democrat. Office: City of Los Angeles Office Contr Rm 1200 200 N Main St Ofc Contr Los Angeles CA 90012-4110

TUTVEDT, BRUCE, state legislator; b. Kalispell, Mont., Nov. 2, 1955; m. Linda Tutvedt; children: Valerie, Emily, Andora. BS in Agrl. Bus., Mont. State U., 1978. Owner/operator Bruce Tutvedt Farm, 1984—2008; mem. Mont. Farm Svcs. Agy., 2001—07, chmn., 2007—08; mem. Dist. 3 Mont. State Senate, 2008—. Republican. Presbyterian. Office: Montana Senate PO Box 200500 Helena MT 59620-0500 Mailing: 2335 W Valley Dr Kalispell MT 59901-6958 Home Phone: 406-257-9732; Office Phone: 406-444-4800. Office Fax: 406-444-4875. Business E-Mail: tutvedt@montanasky.us.

TWIGG, NANCY L., nursing association administrator; Exec. dir. State of N.Mex. Bd. Nursing, Albuquerque.

TWIGGS, JERRY T., state legislator; b. Blackfoot, Idaho, Mar. 25, 1933; m. Sandra Twiggs; children: Jerry D., Quinn D., Cindy, Ted, Thane. Farmer; in agribus.; ret.; elected senator, dist. 31 Idaho Senate, Boise, 1984—. Senate pres. pro tempore; mem. state affairs com. Republican. Office: State Capitol PO Box 83720 Boise ID 83720-3720

TWIGG-SMITH, THURSTON, newspaper publisher; b. Honolulu, Aug. 17, 1921; s. William and Margaret Carter (Thurston) Twigg-S.; m. Bessie Bell, June 9, 1942 (div. Feb. 1983); children: Elizabeth, Thurston, William, Margaret, Evelyn; m. Laila Roster, Feb. 22, 1983 (div. Dec. 1994); m. Sharon Smith, Feb. 28, 1996. B.Engring., Yale U., 1942. With Honolulu Advertiser, 1946-2000, mng. editor, 1954-60, asst. bus. mgr., 1960-61, pub., 1961-86; pres., dir., chief exec. officer Honolulu Advertiser, Inc., 1962-93, chmn., 1993-2000. Chmn., dir., CEO Persis Corp., 1962-2002, chmn. Twigg-Smith Group LLC, 2002—. Trustee Honolulu Acad. Arts, The Contemporary Mus., Hawaii, Yale Art Gallery, New Haven. Maj. AUS, 1942-46. Mem. Waialae Country Club, Pacific Club, Oahu Country Club, Outrigger Canoe Club. Office Phone: 808-735-3883. Personal E-mail: ttwiggsmith@aol.com.

TWINING, CHARLES HAILE, ambassador; b. Balt., Nov. 1, 1940; s. Charles Haile and Martha R. (Caples) T.; m. Irene Verann Metz, May 30, 1972; children: Daniel, Steven. BA, U. Va., 1962; MA, Johns Hopkins U., 1964; postgrad., Cornell U., 1977-78. Joined Fgn. Svc., Dept. State, Washington, 1964; with Am. Embassy, Tananarive, 1964-66, Cords Dalat, Vietnam, 1966-68; desk officer Ivory Coast, Upper Volta, Nigeria; with Dept. of State, Washington, 1970-72, Am. Embassy, Abidjan, 1972-74, Bangkok, 1975-77; dep. office dir. for Australia and New Zealand Dept. of State, Washington, 1978-80, with East Asian pers., 1980-82; former charge d'affaires Am. Embassy, Cotonou, 1982-83; former prin. officer Am. Con Gen, Douala, 1983-85; former dep. chief of mission Am. Embassy, Ouagadougou, Burkina Faso, 1985-88; former dir. Office of Vietnam, Laos and Cambodia Dept. State, Washington, 1988-91; spl. rep., amb. to Cambodia Phnom Penh, 1991-95; amb. to Cameroon and Equatorial Guinea Dept. State, Yaounde, 1996-98; fgn. policy advisor USCINCPAC. Contbr.: Cambodia: 1975-78, 1990. Office: Fgn Policy Advisor HQ USCINCPAC PO Box 64028 Camp H M Smith HI 96861-4028

TWISS, ROBERT MANNING, prosecutor; b. Worcester, Mass., Aug. 2, 1948; s. Robert Sullivan Jr. and Marion (Manning) T.; m. Joan Marie Callahan, Aug. 4, 1979. BA, U. Mass., 1970; JD, U. San Francisco, 1975; MA in Criminal Justice, Wichita State U., 1979; LLM, Georgetown U., 1981. Bar: Mass. 1976, Calif., 1988, U.S. Ct. Appeals Armed Forces 1976, U.S. Dist. Ct. Mass. 1976, U.S. Ct. Appeals (1st cir.) 1976, U.S. Ct. Appeals (5th cir.) 1986, U.S. Ct. Appeals (9th cir.) 1988, U.S. Dist. Ct. (ea. and cen. dist.) Calif. 1989. Atty. office chief counsel IRS, Washington, 1980-86; trial atty. criminal div. U.S. Dept. Justice, Washington, 1986-87, asst. U.S. atty. Sacramento, 1987-93, 94—, chief organized crime and narcotics, 1991-92, 1st asst. U.S. atty., 1992-93, U.S. atty., 1993, exec. assst. U.S. atty., 1994, sr. litigation counsel, 2002—03, chief narcotics and violent crime, 2003—. Vis. prof. U. Calif. Law Sch., 2001—02; prof. The JAG Sch., 1998—2006; mil. judge USAR, 2006—. Contbr. articles to profl. jours. Capt. JAGC US Army, 1976—80, mil. judge USAR, 1980—85, maj. JAGC USAR, 1998—2004, lt. col. JAGC USAR, 2004—. Named to McAuliffe Honor Soc. U. San Francisco, 1975; recipient Markham award Office Chief Counsel IRS, Washington, 1985. Avocation: sports. Office: Office US Atty 501 I St 10th Fl Sacramento CA 95814-7306

TYKESON, DONALD ERWIN, broadcast executive; b. Portland, Oreg., Apr. 11, 1927; s. O. Ansel and Hillie Martha (Haveman) T.; m. Rikla Margaret Steigleder, July 1, 1950; children: Ellen, Amy, Eric. BS, U. Oreg., 1951. V.p., dir. Liberty Comm., Inc., Eugene, Oreg., 1963-67, pres., CEO, dir., 1967-83; mng. ptnr. Tykeson/Assocs. Enterprises, 1983—; chmn. bd. Bend Cable Comm., LLC, 1983—2002, vice chmn., 2002—; chmn. bd. Ctrl. Oreg. Cable Advt., LLC, 1992—. Mem. coun. pub. reps. NIH, 2002-05, NIH Pub. Access Working Group Bd of Regents Nat. Libr. Medicine, 2005-; trustee. Tykeson Family Charitable Trust, 1995—; mem. Hoover Instn. bd. overseers Stanford U., 2002-. Vice-chmn. we. area Nat. Multiple Sclerosis Soc., 1983—2002, bd. dirs., 1987—2003, life bd. dirs., 2004—; bd. dirs. Nat. Coalition Rsch. in Neurol. and Communicative Disorders, 1984—89, Sacred Heart Med. Ctr. Found., 1995—2004; chmn. pub. and gov. info. com. Nat. Coaltion in Rsch., C-SPAN, 1980—89; trustee U. Oreg. Found., 1996—2006, Eugene Art Found., 1980—85, Oreg. Health Scis. U. Found., 1988—91; trustee emeritus Sacred Heart Med. Ctr. Found., 2004—; mem. bus. adv. coun. U. Oreg. Coll. Bus. Adminstrn., 1973—, mem. steering com., 1997—2001, dean search com., 1998; mem. Oreg. Investment Coun. State of Oreg., vice chmn., 1988—92. Recipient 1st Citizen honoree, Eugene C. of C., 2006. Mem. Nat. Assn. Broadcasters, Nat. Cable TV Assn. (dir. 1976-83), Chief Execs. Orgn., Vintage Club (bd. dirs. 1996-99, chmn. fin. com., treas. 1996-99, pres. Custom Lot Assn. 1992-97), Country Club Eugene (dir. 1975-77, sec. 1976, v.p. 1977), Multnomah Athletic Club, Arlington Club, Rotary, Alexis de Tocqueville Soc., Confrérie Chevaliers du Tastevin Sous Commanderie de Coachella Valley. Home: 447 Spyglass Dr Eugene OR 97401-2091 Office: Tykeson Assocs Enterprises PO Box 70006 Eugene OR 97401-0101 Office Phone: 541-683-4511.

TYLE, CRAIG S., lawyer, investment company executive; b. Syracuse, NY, 1960; BA with high honors, Swarthmore Coll., 1982; JD magna cum laude, Harvard Univ., 1985. Bar: NY 1988, DC 2004. Assoc. Sullivan & Cromwell, NYC, 1982—88; atty. Investment Company Inst., Washington, 1988—97, gen. counsel, 1997—2004; ptnr., asset mgmt. group Shearman & Sterling LLP, Washington, 2004—05; exec. v.p. & gen. counsel Franklin Resources Inc. (Franklin Templeton Investments), San Mateo, Calif., 2005—. Mem. NASDAQ Quality of Markets com., 1997—2003, co-chmn., 2003. Contbr. articles to profl. jours. Mem.: ABA, Assn. Bar City of NY. Office: Franklin Resources Inc 1 Franklin Pkwy San Mateo CA 94403-1906 Office Phone: 202-508-8016. Office Fax: 202-508-8100. Business E-Mail: craig.tyle@shearman.com.

TYLER, GAIL MADELEINE, nurse; b. Dhahran, Saudi Arabia, Nov. 21, 1953; (parents Am. citizens); d. Louis Rogers and Nona Jean (Henderson) T.; m. Alan J. Moore, Sept. 29, 1990; 1 child, Sean James. AS, Front Range C.C., Westminster, Colo., 1979; BSN, U. Wyo., 1989. RN, Colo. Ward sec. Valley View Hosp., Thornton, Colo., 1975-79; nurse Scott and White Hosp., Temple, Tex., 1979-83, Meml. Hosp. Laramie County, Cheyenne, Who., 1983-89; dir. DePaul Home Health, 1989-91; field staff nurse Poudre Valley Hosp. Home Care/Poudre Care Connection, 1991-98, Rehab. and Vis. Nurses Assn., Fort Collins, Colo., 1999—2003; resource pool nurse Poudre Valley Hosp., Fort Collins, Colo., 2003—. Parish nurse Rocky Mountain Parish Health Ministry Orgn., pres., 2004—05, past. pres., 2005—06. Avocations: doll collecting, sewing, reading, travel. Office: Poudre Valley Hosp 1024 S Lemay Ave Fort Collins CO 80524

TYLER, GEORGE LEONARD, electrical engineering educator; b. Bartow, Fla., Oct. 18, 1940; s. George Leonard and Mable Leona (Bethea) T.; m. Joanne Lynne Phelps, Nov. 17, 1977; children: Virginia L., Matthew L. BEE, Ga. Inst. Tech., 1963; MS, Stanford U., 1964, PhD in Elec. Engring., 1967. Engr. Lockheed Aircraft Corp., Marietta, Ga., 1963; rsch. assoc. Ctr. for Radar Astronomy, Stanford (Calif.) U., 1967-69, rsch. engr., 1969-72, sr. rsch. assoc., 1972-74, rsch. prof. elec. engring., 1974-90, prof., 1990—, dir. Space, Telecom. and Radiosci. Lab., 1993-98. Cons. SRI-Internat., NASA, Jet Propulsion Lab., also other orgns., 1972—; mem. com. on planetary exploration of space sci. bd. NAS, 1983-87, mem. naval studies bd. panel on advanced radar tech., 1990-91. Contbr. over 200 articles to sci. jours., chpts. to books. Recipient Medal for Exceptional Sci. Achievement, NASA, 1977, 81, 86, Pub. Svc. medal, 1992; fellow NSF, 1964-66. Fellow IEEE; mem. Am. Geophys. Union, Am. Astron. Soc., Internat. Astron. Union, Internat. Radio Sci. Union, Electromagnetics Acad., Phi Kappa Phi, Tau Beta Pi. Achievements include co-discovery of Crab Nebula pulsar, first high-resolution measurement of the directional spectrum of the sea, development and application of occultation technique for outer planets, measurement of Titan's atmosphere. Office: Stanford U Ctr Radar Astronomy Dept Elec Engring Stanford CA 94305-9515

TYLER, MICHAEL ROBERT, lawyer; b. Hollywood, Calif., May 20, 1956; m. Christine D. von Wrangel. BA in history, UCLA, 1979, MA in history, 1980; JD, Loyola Law Sch., LA, 1983; LLM in comparative law, Fitzwilliam Coll., Cambridge U., 1986. Bar: Calif. 1984. Law clk. to the Hon. Arthur Alcaron US Ct. Appeals (9th Cir.), San Francisco, 1987—88; assoc. Heller Ehrman White & McAuliffe, LA, 1991—95; sr. corp. counsel internat. Northrop Grumman Corp., LA, 1995—2000; v.p., group counsel for Europe, Middle East, and Africa ops. Gateway Inc., London, 2000—02, v.p. law for procurement activities Irvine, Calif., 2002—03, v.p., asst. gen. counsel, 2003—04, sr. v.p., gen. counsel, sec., 2004—05, sr. v.p., chief legal & adminstrv. officer, 2005—07; exec. v.p., gen. counsel Sanmina-SCI Corp., San Jose, Calif., 2007—. Mem.: State Bar Calif. (chair internat. law sect. 1999), ABA (editor-in-chief European Law Bulletin 1989—91, chair European law com. of internat. law and practice sect. 1998). Office: Sanmina-SCI Corp 2700 N 1st St San Jose CA 95134

TYLER, RICHARD, fashion designer; b. Sunshine, Australia, Sept. 22, 1950; m. Doris Taylor (div.); 1 child, Sheridan; m. Lisa Trafficante, 1989; 1 child, Edward Charles. Prin. Zippity-doo-dah, Melbourne, Australia, 1968-80, Tyler-Trafficante, LA, 1988—; design dir. Anne Klein Collection, NYC, 1993-94, 99; fashion dir. owner Tyler Trafficante, Inc., 1999—. Designer Richard Tyler Couture introduced for Women, 1989, Richard Tyler Collection debut for Men, April 1997, Richard Tyler Shoes for Women, 1996, Richard Tyler Collection for Women, 1997, Richard Tyler Shoes for Men, 1997. Recipient New Fashion Talent Perry Ellis award Coun. Fashion Designers Am., 1993, Womenswear Designer of Yr. award, 1994, Perry Ellis award for new fashion talent in menswear, 1995.

TYMKOVICH, TIMOTHY MICHAEL, federal judge; b. Denver, Nov. 2, 1956; married; 2 children. BA, Co. Coll., 1979; JD, U. Colo. Sch. Law, 1982. Clk. Co. Supreme Ct., 1982—83; assoc. Davis, Graham, & Stubbs, 1983—89; of counsel Bradley Campbel Carney & Madsen, 1990—91; solicitor gen. Office of Co. Atty. Gen., 1991—96; ptnr. Hale Hackstaff Tymkovich & ErkenBrack, 1996—2003; judge US Ct. of Appeals (10th cir), 2003—. Mem.: ABA, Internat. Soc. Barristers, Colo. Bar Found., Am. Law Inst. Office: Byron White US Courthouse 1823 Stout St Denver CO 80257

TYNDALL, GAYE LYNN, secondary school educator; b. Reno, Apr. 21, 1953; d. Chris H. and Ellen (Hutchinson) Gansberg; m. Dave Tyndall, Mar. 17, 1973; children: Jody, Dave. BS, U. Nev., Reno, 1987, postgrad. Cert. secondary tchr. Tchr. math, sci. Douglas High Sch., Minden, Nev., 1987—. Treas. Nev. Sci. Project, Reno, 1990—; presenter Reading and Writing in the Math Classroom Internat. Reading Assn., Nat. Sci. Tchrs. Assn., 1990-92. Recipient Nev. State Tchr. of Yr. award Nev. Bd. Edn., 1993. Mem. Nat. Coun. Tchrs. Math., Calif. Math Coun. Avocation: rodeo. Office: Douglas High Sch PO Box 1888 Minden NV 89423-1888

TYNER, NEAL EDWARD, retired insurance company executive; b. Grand Island, Nebr., Jan. 30, 1930; s. Edward Raymond and Lydia Dorothea (Kruse) T.; children: Karen Tyner Redrow, Morgan. BBA, U. Nebr., 1956. Jr. analyst Bankers Life Nebr., Lincoln, 1956-62, asst. v.p. securities, 1962-67, v.p. securities, treas., 1967-69, fin. v.p., treas., 1970-72, sr. v.p. fin., treas., 1972-83, pres., chief exec. officer, 1983-87, chmn., pres., chief exec. officer, 1987-88; chmn., CEO Ameritas Life Ins., Lincoln, 1988—95; pres. Net Cons., Paradise Valley, Ariz., 1995—. Bd. dirs. Union Bank & Trust Co. Trustee U. Nebr. Found., Lincoln Found. Capt. USMC, 1950-54, Korea. Fellow: CFAs. Lutheran. Avocations: tennis, computers. Office: 8225 N Golf Dr Paradise Valley AZ 85253-2716

TYSON, JOSEPH JUDE, bishop; b. Moses Lake, Wash., Oct. 16, 1957; BA, U. Wash., 1980, MA, 1984; MDiv, Cath. U. Am., Washington, 1989. Ordained priest Archdiocese of Seattle, 1989; pastor St. Edward, St. George & St. Paul parishes, Seattle; ordained bishop, 2005; aux. bishop Archdiocese of Seattle, 2005—. Roman Catholic. Office: Archdiocese of Seattle 710 9th Ave Seattle WA 98104 Office Phone: 206-382-4560.

TYSON, LAURA D'ANDREA, economics professor, former dean; b. Bayonne, NJ, June 28, 1947; m. Erik Tarloff; 1 child. BA, Smith Coll., 1969; PhD, MIT, 1974. Asst. prof. econ. Princeton U., 1974—77; prof. econ. U. Calif., Berkeley, 1977—2001; prof. econ. & bus. adminstrn. Haas Sch. Bus., U. Calif., Berkeley, 1990—2001, 2007—, dean, 1998—2001; chmn. Coun. Econ. Advisors Exec. Office of the Pres., Washington, 1993-95; dir. Nat. Econ. Coun., Washington, 1995-96; dean London Bus. Sch., 2002—06; dir. LECG, LLC, Emeryville, Calif., 2007—. Bd. dirs. Eastman Kodak Co., 1997—, Morgan Stanley, 1997—, 24/7 Customer, 2007; bd. economists L.A. Times, 1989—92; bd. dirs. Coun. Fgn. Rels., 1997; bd. trustees Brookings Instn., 2003—; econ. viewpoint columnist Business Week mag., 1997—2006; mem. President's Econ. Recovery Advisory Bd., 2009—. Editor: (with John Zysman) American Industry in International Competition, 1983, (with Ellen Comisso) Power, Purpose and Collective Choice: Economic Strategy in Socialist States, 1986, (with William Dickens and John Zysman) The Dynamics of Trade and Employment, 1988, (with Chalmers Johnson and John Zysman) Politics and Productivity: The Real Story of How Japan Works, 1989, Who's Bashing Whom? Trade Conflict in High Technology Industries, 1992 Mem. Nat. Bipartisan Commn. Future Medicare, 1997—99. Democrat. Office: Haas Sch Bus U Calif Berkeley 545 Student Services Bldg #1900 Berkeley CA 94720 also: LECG LLC 2000 Powell St Ste 600 Emeryville CA 94608 Business E-Mail: tyson@haas.berkeley.edu.

TYUS, HAROLD MAURICE, ichthyologist; b. Lake City, Fla., Mar. 8, 1942; s. Howard Kelly and Minnie (Louise) T.; m. Ruby J. Slone, Nov. 25, 1974 (div. 1979); 1 child, Christopher Scott. BS, Fla. So. Coll., 1964; MS, N.C. State U., 1969, PhD, 1971. Instr. Fla. So. Coll., 1965-66; field biologist State of Fla., Tampa, 1966; fishery biologist U.S. Army C.E., Wilmington, N.C., 1971-74; fishery biologist U.S. Fish and Wildlife Service, Miami, Fla., 1974, Raleigh, N.C., 1975-76, environ. specialist, Denver, 1976-79, project leader Colorado River Fish Project, Vernal, Utah, 1979—; cons. Coastal Zone Resources Corp., Wilmington, 1973. Author sci. articles, govt. reportsl mem. Colo. River Fishes Recovery Team. Recipient Spl. Achievement award, U.S. Fish and Wildlife Service, Denver, 1982, appreciation award, U.S. Dept. Interior, 1978; NSF grad. trainee, 1965-69; Nat. Wildlife Fedn. grad. scholar, 1970-71. Mem. Am. Inst. Fishery Research Biologists, Am. Fisheries Soc. (cert. fisheries scientist), Am. Soc. Ichthyologists and Herpetologists, Desert Fishes Council, Sigma Xi, Lambda Chi Alpha. Democrat. Methodist. Home: 78 Pine Rd Golden CO 80401-9337 Office: US Fish and Wildlife Service 1680 W Hyw 40 # 1210 Vernal UT 84078

UDALL, MARK, United States Senator from Colorado; b. Tucson, July 18, 1950; m. Maggie Fox; children: Jed, Tess. B in Am. Civilization, Williams Coll., Mass., 1972. Course dir., educator Colo. Outward Bound Sch., 1975-85, exec. dir., 1985-95; mem. dist. 13 Colo. Ho. of Reps., 1997—98; mem. US Congress from 2d Colo. dist., Washington, 1999—2008, dep. regional whip; mem. armed svcs. com., resources com., sci. & tech. com., small bus. com., agrl. com.; US Senator from Colo., 2009—. Mem. Dem. Homeland Security Task Force, North Atlantic Treaty Orgn. Parliamentary Assembly, Congl. Fitness Caucus; v.p. Dem. Freshman Class; co-chair Renewable Energy & Energy Efficiency Caucus. Mem. Parkinson's Action Network; bd. dirs. Berger Found. Mem.: Am. Alpine Club. Democrat. Avocation: mountain climbing. Office: Ste 206 8601 Turnpike Dr Westminster CO 80031-7044 also: B40E Dirksen Senate Office Bldg Washington DC 20510 Office Phone: 202-244-5941. E-mail: Senator_Mark_Udall@markudall.senate.gov.*

UDALL, THOMAS S. (TOM), United States Senator from New Mexico; b. Tucson, May 18, 1948; s. Stewart and Lee Udall; m. Jill Z. Cooper; 1 child, Amanda. BA in Govt./Polit. Sci., Prescott Coll., Ariz., 1970; LLB in Internat. Law, Cambridge U., Eng., 1975; JD, U. N.Mex. Sch. Law, 1977. Bar: N.Mex. 1978. Legis. asst. Staff of US Senator Joseph R. Biden of Del., 1973; law clk. to Chief Justice Oliver Seth US 10th Cir. Ct. Appeals, Santa Fe, 1977-78; asst. US atty. criminal divsn. US Atty.'s Office, 1978-81; atty. pvt. practice, Santa Fe, 1981-83; chief counsel N.Mex. Health and Environ. Dept., 1983-84; atty. to ptnr. Miller, Stratvert, Togerson and Schlenker, P.A., Albuquerque, 1985-90; atty. gen., 1991—99; mem. US Congress from 3rd N.Mex. dist., 1999—2009, mem. appropriations com., co-vice chair Native Am. caucus, mem. Bipartisan Rural Caucus; US Senator from NMex., 2009—. Pres. Rio Chama Preservation Trust; mem. N.Mex. Environ. Improvement Bd., 1986—87; bd. dirs. La Compania de Teatro de Albuquerque, Santa Fe Chamber Music Festival, Law Fund, 1991—98. Recipient Leadership award, Nat. Commn. Against Drunk Driving, Legal Impact award, N.Mex. Bar Prosecution Sect., Pub. Svc. award, Nat. Highway Traffic Safety Adminstrn. Mem.: Nat. Assn. Atty. Gens. (pres. 1996). Democrat. Office: US Senate B40D Dirksen Senate Office Bldg Washington DC 20510 Mailing: Ste A & B 3311 Candelaria Ave Albuquerque NM 87107 Office Phone: 202-225-6190. Office Fax: 202-226-1331.*

UDLAND, DUANE S., protective services official; b. Minot, ND, Apr. 15, 1950; m. Judi Udland; 1 child, Eric. Grad., Spokane Police Acad., 1973; BA in Sociology, Ea. Washington State Coll., 1973; grad., FBI Nat. Acad., 1987. From law enforcement officer to detective Spokane (Wash.) County Sheriffs Office, 1972-78; from patrol officer to sgt. Soldotna (Alaska) Police Dept., 1978-82, chief, 1982-88; dep. chief Anchorage (Alaska) Police Dept., 1988-97, chief, 1997—. Bd. dirs. Alaska Native Justice Ctr.; past chmn. Cen. Peninsula 911 Bd.; mem. Govs. Juvenile Justice Conf. on Youth and Justice; criminal justice adv. bd. State of Alaska; we. states working group FBIs Criminal Justice Info. Sys.; dept. rep. Police Minority Rels. Task Force. Mem. FBI Nat. Acad. Assn., Internat. Assn. Chiefs of Police, Alaska Assn. Chiefs of Police, Alaska Peace Officers Assn., Anchorage C. of C. (crime com.). Office: Anchorage Police Dept 4501 S Bragaw St Anchorage AK 99507-1500 Home: 1140 E Fort Pierce Dr N Unit 102 Saint George UT 84790-8881

UDVAR-HAZY, STEVEN F., leasing company financial executive; b. Budapest, Hungary, Feb. 23, 1946; came to U.S., 1958. m. Christine L. Henneman, June 7, 1980; 4 children. BA, UCLA, 1968; HHD (hon.), U. Utah, 1990; D (hon.), Emory Riddle Aero. U., 2000. Cert. airline transp. jet pilot. Chmn., CEO Internat. Lease Fin. Corp., Beverly Hills, Calif., 1973—. Bd. dirs. Sky West Inc., St. George, Utah; chmn. bd. dirs. Ocean Equities, Inc. Active Smothsonian's Udvar-Hazy Nat. Air & Spave Mus. Named one of Forbes' Richest Americans, 2000—, World's Richest People, Forbes mag., 2001—. Mem. Wings Club (Achievement to Aviation award 1989). Office: Internat Lease Fin Corp 10250 Constellation Blvd 35th Fl Los Angeles CA 90067 Office Phone: 310-788-1999.

UDWADIA, FIRDAUS ERACH, engineering educator, consultant; b. Bombay, Aug. 28, 1947; arrived in US, 1968; s. Erach Rustam and Perin P. (Lentin) Udwadia; m. Farida Gagrat, Jan. 6, 1977; children: Shanaira, Zubin. BS, Indian Inst. Tech., Bombay, 1968; MS, Calif. Inst. Tech., 1969, PhD, 1972; MBA, U. So. Calif., 1985. Mem. faculty Calif. Inst. Tech., Pasadena, 1972-74; asst. prof. engring. U. So. Calif., LA, 1974-77, assoc. prof. mech., civil, and aerospace engring. and bus. adminstrn., 1977-83, prof., 1983-86, bd. dirs. Structural Identification Computing Facility, prof. engring. bus. adminstrn., maths., 1986—2005, prof. civil engring., aerospace mech. engring., math., info. ops., mgmt., and sys. architecture engring., 2005—. Cons. Jet Propulsion Lab., Pasadena, 1978—, Argonne Nat. Lab., 1982—83, Air Force Rocket Lab., Edwards AFB, Calif., 1984—, Air Force Rsch. Lab., 1990—; vis. prof. applied mechanics and mech. engring. Calif. Inst. Tech., Pasadena, 1993. Author: Analytical Dynamics, A New Approach, 1996; hon. editor: Jour. Math. Ctrl. Sci. and Applications, assoc. editor: Applied Math. and Computation, Applied Mechanics Reviews, Discrete Dynamics Nature and Soc., Jour. Optimization Theory and Applications, Jour. Franklin Inst., Jour. Differential Equations and Dynamical Sys., Nonlinear Studies, Jour. Math. Analysis and Applications, Jour. Math. Problems in Engring.; editor: Jour. Aerospace Engring., Advances in Dynamics and Control, 2000; co-editor: Dynamics and Control, 1999; chief editor Dynamical Systems and Control, 2004; hon. editor: Jour. Math. Control and its Applications; mem. adv. bd. Jour. Tech. Forecasting and Social Change; contbr. articles to profl. jours. Bd. dirs. Crisis Mgmt. Ctr. U. So. Calif., LA. Recipient Golden Poet award, 1990; NSF grantee, 1976—. Fellow: ASME, AIAA; mem.: ASCE (Outstanding Tech. Contributions award 2006), Seismol. Soc. Am., Soc. Indsl. and Applied Math., Am. Acad. Mechanics, Sigma Xi (mem. Earthquake Engring. Rsch. Inst. 1971, 1974, 1984). Achievements include patents in field; patents for control of nonlinear systems, 2002. Avocations: poetry, piano, chess. Home: 2100 S Santa Anita Ave Arcadia CA 91006-4611 Office: U So Calif 430K Olin Hall University Park Los Angeles CA 90007 Office Phone: 213-740-0495.

UEBERROTH, JOHN A., air transportation executive; b. Phila., 1944; Student, U. Calif., Berkeley, U. So. Calif. Formerly pres. Ask Mr. Foster Travel, Encino, Calif.; formerly v.p. TCU Travel Corp.; formerly pres., COO 1st Travel Corp., Van Nuys, Calif.; with Carlson Travel Group, Mpls., 1983-89, Contrarian Group Inc., Newport Beach, Calif., 1989—; chmn. bd., CEO Hawaiian Airlines, Inc., 1990—, also bd. dirs. Office: Ambassadors International Inc Dwight D Eisenhower Bldg 110 S Ferrall St Spokane WA 99202 also: First Travel Corp 7833 Haskell Ave Van Nuys CA 91406-1908 also: Carlson Cos Inc 12755 Highway 55 Minneapolis MN 55441-3837

UEBERROTH, PETER VICTOR, sports association executive; b. Evanston, Ill., Sept. 2, 1937; s. Victor and Laura (Larson) U.; m. Virginia Nicolaus, Sept. 1959; children: Vicky, Heidi, Keri, Joe BS in Bus., San Jose State Coll., 1959. Ops. mgr. then v.p. Trans Internat., 1959-62; founder, chmn. Transp. Cons. Internat., 1963-79; pres., mng. dir. LA Olympic Organizing Com., 1979-84; commr. Maj. League Baseball, NYC, 1984-89; mng. dir. Contrarian Group, 1990—; co-chmn. Doubletree Hotels Corp., Phoenix, 1993—; co-owner, co-chmn. Pebble Beach Co., 1999—; dir. McLeodUSA, 2001—; chmn. US Olympic Com., 2004—. Former chmn. Ask Mr. Foster Travel Service; chmn. Colony Hotels, Intercontinental Tours, Inc., First Travel Corp; mem. bd. dirs. California Angels. Ambassadors Internat., Coca-Cola Co., Hilton Hotels Corp. Author: Made in America, 1985 Named Man of Yr., Time Mag. and Sporting News, 1984; recipient Scopus award Am. Friends of Hebrew U., Jerusalem, 1985; named one of Most Influential People in the World of Sports, Bus. Week, 2008. Fellow: Am. Acad. Arts and Scis. Office: Ambassadors Intl Inc 110 S Ferrall St Spokane WA 99202

UFIMTSEV, PYOTR YAKOVLEVICH, physicist, electrical engineer, educator; b. Ust'-Charyshskaya Pristan', Altai Region, Russia, July 8, 1931; s. Yakov Fedorovich and Vasilisa Vasil'evna (Toropchina) U.; m. Tatiana Vladimirovna Sinelschikova; children: Galina, Ivan, Vladimir. Grad., Odessa State U., Ukraine, 1954; PhD, Ctrl. Rsch. Inst. Radio Industry, 1959; DSc, St. Petersburg State U., Russia, 1970. Engr., sr. engr., sr. scientist Ctrl. Rsch. Inst. of Radio Industry, Moscow, 1954-73; sr. scientist, head scientist Inst. Radio Engring. & Electronics Acad. Scis., Moscow, 1973-90; prin. engr. Northrop Grumman Corp., 1995—2000; prof. U. Calif., Irvine, 2003—04. Vis. prof., adj. prof. UCLA, 1990—2003; mem. sci. bd. radio waves Acad. Scis., Moscow, 1960—90. Author: Method of Edge Waves in the Physical Theory of Diffraction, 1962, Theory of Edge Diffraction in Electromagnetics, 2003, Fundamentals of the Physical Theory of Diffraction, 2007; contbr. articles to profl. jours. Recipient USSR State Prize, Moscow, 1990, Leroy Randle Grumman medal for outstanding sci. achievement, N.Y.C., 1991, 20th Century Achievement medal, Cambridge, 1996, Hall of Fame medal, Cambridge, 1996. Fellow IEEE; assoc. fellow AIAA; mem. Electromagnetics Acad. (U.S.), A.S. Popov Sci. Tech. Soc. Radio Engring., Electronics & Telecommunication (Russia). Achievements include origination of the Physical Theory of Diffraction, used for design of American stealth aircrafts and ships; for radar-cross-section calculation, and antenna design.

UHDE, LARRY JACKSON, joint apprentice administrator; b. Marshalltown, Iowa, June 2, 1939; s. Harold Clarence and Rexine Elizabeth (Clemens) U.; m. Linda-Lee Betty Best, Nov. 19, 1960; children: Mark Harold, Brian Raymon. Student, Sacramento City Coll., 1966, Am. River Coll., Sacramento, 1975. Equipment supr. Granite Constrn., Sacramento, 1962-69; truck driver Iowa Wholesale, Marshalltown, Iowa, 1969-70; mgr. Reedy & Essex, Inc., Sacramento, 1970-71; dispatcher Operating Engrs. Local Union 3, Sacramento, 1971-73; tng. coord. Operating Engrs. Joint Apprenticeship Com., Sacramento, 1973-83, apprenticeship div. mgr., 1983-87, adminstr., 1987-95; ret., 1995; instr. asst. advanced transp. tech. Sacremento City Coll., 1996—. Chmn. First Women in Apprenticeship Seminar, 1972, Calif. Apprentice Coun., 1992, chair Blue Ribbon com.; com. mem. Sacramento Gen. Joint Apprenticeship Com., 1973-74; rep. Sacramento Sierra's Bldg. and Constrn. Trades Coun., 1973-75; com. mem. Valley Area Constrn. Opportunity Program, 1974-77; commr. State of Calif. Dept. Indsl. Rels., Calif. Apprenticeship Coun., chmn. 1992; mem. Apprenticeship Adv. Com. Internat. Union Oper. Engrs. Contr: Options; contbr. articles to trade papers. Mgr., v.p. Little League, 1971-75; co-chmn. Fall Festival St. Roberts Ch., 1973-75; v.p. Navy League Youth Program, 1978-81; instr. ARC, 1978-87; counselor United Way 1980—; bd. mem. County CETA Bd., 1981-82; coun. mem. Calif. Balance of State Pvt. Industry Coun., 1982-83, Sacramento Pvt. Industry Coun., 1982-83; coord. Alcholic Recovery Program, 1984-87. With USN, 1956-60. Inducted into Calif. Apprenticeship Hall of Fame, 1996. Mem. Western Apprenticeship Coords. Assn. (statewide dir. 1987—), U.S. Aprenticeship Assn., Sacramento Valley Apprenticeship Tng. Coords. Assn. (rep.), Rancho Murieta County, U.S. Golf Assn., Bing Maloney Golf Club. Democrat. Roman Catholic. Avocations: golf, archery, bowling, hunting, camping.

UHLENHUTH, EBERHARD HENRY, psychiatrist, educator; b. Balt., Sept. 15, 1927; s. Eduard Carl Adolph and Elisabeth (Baier) Uhlenhuth; m. Helen Virginia Lyman, June 20, 1952; children: Kim Lyman, Karen Jane, Eric Rolf. BS in Chemistry, Yale U., 1947; MD, Johns Hopkins U., 1951. Intern Harborview Hosp., Seattle, 1951-52; resident in psychiatry Johns Hopkins Hosp., Balt., 1952-56, asst. psychiatrist in charge outpatient dept., 1956-61, psychiatrist in charge, 1961-62; chief adult psychiatry clinic U. Chgo. Hosps. Clinics, 1968-76; instr. psychiatry Johns Hopkins U., 1956-59, asst. prof., 1959-67, assoc. prof., 1967-68, U. Chgo., 1968-73, prof., 1973-85, acting chmn., 1983-85; prof. psychiatry U. N.Mex., Albuquerque, 1985-97, prof. emeritus, 1997—, Disting. Univ. prof., 2005—, vice chmn. for edn., 1991-94. Cons. in field; mem. clin. psychopharmacology rsch. rev. com. NIMH, 1968-72, mem. treatment devel. and assessment rsch. rev. com., 1987-88; mem. psychopharmacology adv. com. FDA, 1974-78; adv. group to Treatment of Depression Collaborative Rsch. Program, NIMH, 1978-92; study rev. com. Xanax discontinuation program Upjohn Co., 1988-92, Nat. Adv. Coun. on Drug Abuse, NIDA, 1989-92, Coop. Studies Evaluation Com., VA, 1989-92. Mem. editl. bd. Jour. Affective Disorders, 1978—, Psychiatry Rsch., 1979-96, Behavioral Medicine, 1982—, Neuropsychopharmacology, 1992-95, Exptl. and Clin. Psychopharmacology, 1992-99, Depression and Anxiety, 1992—2008; contbr. articles to profl. jours. Recipient Rsch. Career Devel. award USPHS, 1962-68, Rsch. Scientist award, 1976-81. Fellow: Collegium Internat. Neuro-Psychopharmacologicum, Am. Psychopath. Assn., Am. Psychiat. Assn., Am. Coll. Neuropsychopharmacology (pres. 1986); mem.: Psychiat. Rsch. Soc., Balt.-Washington Soc. Psychoanalysis. Office: U NMex Dept Psychiatry MSC09 5030 1 Univ New Mex Albuquerque NM 87131-0001 Home Phone: 505-265-0663; Office Phone: 505-272-8876. Business E-Mail: uhli@unm.edu.

UILKEMA, JOHN K., lawyer; BSE in Mech. Engring., U. Mich., 1957; JD, George Washington U., 1961. Bar: D.C. 1962, Calif. 1963, U.S. Patent and Trademark Office, U.S. Dist. Ct. (all dists.) Calif., U.S. Ct. Appeals (Calif.), U.S. Dist. Ct. (all dists.) D.C., U.S. Ct. Appeals (D.C.), U.S. Ct. Appeals (fed. cir.), U.S. Supreme Ct. Ptnr. Thelen Reid Brown Raysman & Steiner LLP, San Francisco. Mem.: ABA (chair property law sect. 1987—88, ho. dels. 1992—, bd. govs. sect. intellectual property 2002—05). Office: Thelen Reid Brown Raysman & Steiner Ste 1800 101 Second St San Francisco CA 94105 Office Phone: 415-369-7960. Business E-Mail: juilkema@thelen.com.

UKROPINA, JAMES R., lawyer; b. Fresno, Calif., Sept. 10, 1937; s. Robert J. and Persida (Angelich) Ukropina. AB, Stanford U., 1959, MBA, 1961; LL.B., U. So. Calif., 1965. Bar: Calif. 1966. Assoc. firm O'Melveny & Myers, Los Angeles, 1965-72, ptnr., 1972—80, 1992—2000, of counsel Los Angeles, 2001—; exec. v.p., gen. counsel Santa Fe Internat. Corp., Alhambra, Calif., 1980-84, dir., 1981-86; exec. v.p., gen. counsel Pacific Enterprises, Los Angeles, 1984-86, pres. and dir., 1986-89, chmn. bd. and chief exec. officer, 1989-91; chmn., CEO Directions, LLC, 2002—. Bd. dir. Lockheed Martin Corp., Pacific Life Ins. Co., Trust Co. of West Group, Inc., Ctrl. Natural Resources, Keck Found., Internet Brands. Editor in chief So. Calif. Law Rev, 1964-65. Trustee Stanford U., 1991-2000 Mem. ABA, Calif. Bar Assn., Los Angeles County Bar Assn., Annandale Golf Club, Calif. Club, Beta Theta Pi. Office: O'Melveny & Myers 400 S Hope St Los Angeles CA 90071-2899

ULIN, SAMUEL ALEXANDER, computer systems developer; b. Nov. 8, 1955; s. Webster Beattie Ulin and Ann (Fletcher) Rainier; m. Lida Ohan, May 30, 1992. Student, U. Del., 1973-78. Systems design cons. Alpha Ro Inc., Wilmington, Del., 1982-83, Command Computer Svcs., NYC, 1983-84; systems designer DBS Films, Inc., Malvern, Pa., 1984-86; dir. engring. Flight Safety Inc., ISD, Malvern, 1986-87, Irving, Tex., 1987-89; sr. system designer Litigation Scis., Culver City, Calif., 1989-96; v.p. engring. IDEA, Inc., Seattle, 1996—. Designer software for interactive tng. on aircraft sys., 1983, one of first interactive ct. evidence presentation systems used in fed. ct., 1987. Avocations: electronics, stamp and coin collecting, winter sports. Home: 12500 Lithuania Dr Granada Hills CA 91344 Office: Source Photonics 20550 Nordhoff St Chatsworth CA 91311 Business E-Mail: sulin@trialpro.com.

ULLMAN, JEFFREY DAVID, computer scientist, educator; b. NYC, Nov. 22, 1942; s. Seymour and Nedra L. (Hart) Ullman; m. Holly E. Ullman, Nov. 19, 1967; children: Peter, Scott, Jonathan. BS, Columbia U., 1963; PhD, Princeton U., 1966; PhD (hon.), U. Brussels, 1975, U. Paris-Dauphine, 1992. Mem. tech. staff Bell Labs., Murray Hill, NJ, 1966-69, cons., 1969-89; prof. elec. engring., computer sci. Princeton (N.J.) U., 1969-79; prof. computer sci. Stanford (Calif.) U., 1979—2003, prof. emeritus, 2003—; CEO Gradiance Corp., 2003—. Mem. computer sci. adv. panel NSF, 1974—77, mem. info., robotics and intelligent sys. adv. panel, 1986—88; mem. exam. com. computer sci. grad. record exam. Endl. Testing Svc., 1978—86; chmn. doctoral rating com. computer sci. N.Y. State Regents, 1989—93, 1998—99; mem. tech. adv. bd. Google, 1998—, Viquity, 1999—2002, Surromed, 1999—, Whizbang Labs, 1999—2002, Quiq, 1999—2002; adv. bd. World Wide Web Consortium, 1998—99; bd. dirs. Junglee, 1996—98, Kirusa, 2001—03, Enosys software, 2000—01, 2002—03; mem. internat. sci. advisory group Nat. Info. & Comms. Tech., Australia, 2003—; chair Nat. Rsch. Coun. for Nat. Inst. Standards and Tech. Info. Tech. Lab., 2007. Author: (book) Principles of Database and Knowledge-Base Systems, 1988, 1989; author: (with A. V. Aho and J. E. Hopcroft) Data Structures and Algorithms, 1983; author: (with A. V. Aho, M. Lam and R. Sethi) Compilers: Principles, Techniques and Tools, 2006; author: (with A. V. Aho) Foundations of Computer Science, 1992, Elements of ML Programming, 1994, 1998; author: (with J. Widom) A First Course in Database Systems, 1997, 2002, 2008; author: (with H. Garcia-Molina and J. Widom) The Complete Book of Database Systems, 2002; author: (with J. E. Hopcroft and R. Motwani) Intro. to Automata, Languages, and Computation, 2006. Guggenheim fellow, 1989. Fellow: Assn. Computing Machinery (coun. 1978—80, Spl. Interest Group Mgmt. Data Contbns. award 1996, Outstanding Educator award 1998, Knuth prize 2000, Spl. Interest Group Mgmt. Data E.F. Codd Innovations award 2006, E. F. Codd Innovation award 2006); mem.: NAE, Spl. Interest Group Mgmt. Data (vice chmn. 1983—95), Computing Rsch. Assn. (bd. dirs. 1994—2001), Spl. Interest Group Automata and Computability Theory (sec.-treas. 1973—75). Home: 1023 Cathcart Way Palo Alto CA 94305-1048 Office: Stanford U Dept Computer Sci 433 Gates Hall 4A-Wing Stanford CA 94305-9040 E-mail: ullman@gmail.com.

ULLMAN, MYRON EDWARD, III, (MIKE ULLMAN), retail executive; b. Youngstown, Ohio, Nov. 26, 1946; s. Myron Edward Jr. and June (Cunningham) U.; m. Cathy Emmons, June 20, 1969; children: Myron Cayce, Denver Tryan, Peter Brynt, Benjamin Kyrk, Kathryn Kwynn, Madylin Ming Yan. BS in Indsl. Mgmt., U. Cin., 1969; postgrad. Inst. Ednl. Mgmt., Harvard U., 1977. Internat. account mgr. IBM Corp., Cin., 1969-76; v.p. bus. affairs U. Cin., 1976-81; White House fellow The White House, Washington, 1981-82; exec. v.p. Sanger Harris div. Federated Stores, Dallas, 1982-86; mgr. dir., chief oper. officer Wharf Holdings Ltd., Hong Kong, 1986-88; chmn., CEO, dir. R.H. Macy & Co. Inc., NYC, 1988-95; dir., deputy chmn. Federated Dept. Stores, Inc.; chmn., CEO DFS Group Ltd., San Francisco, 1995-98, group chmn., 1999-2000; also bd. dirs.; dir. gen., group mng. dir. LVMH, Louis Vuitton Moet Hennessy, Paris, 1999—2002; chmn. DeBeers-LV, 2000—02; dir., chmn., CEO J.C. Penney Co. Inc., 2004—. Mng. dir. Lane Crawford Ltd., Hong Kong, 1986-88; bd. advisors Gt. Traditions Corp., Cin.; chmn. Omni Hotels, Hampton, N.H., 1988; co-chmn. Global Crossing, Ltd., 2002-04; chmn. bd. dirs. Mercy Ships Internat., 1992-; bd. dirs. Starbuck's Coffee Co., Polo Ralph Lauren, 2004-06, Taubman Ctrs., 2002-04, Kendall Jackson Wine Estates, 2001-04, Lucille Packard Found. Children's Health, 2001-04, Segway LLC, 2003-05. Internat. v.p. U. Cin. Alumni Assn., 1980—; bd. dirs. Nat. Multiple Sclerosis Soc., NYC; bd. dirs. Brunswick Sch., Greenwich, Conn., U. Cin. Found., Lincoln Ctr. Devel., Deafness Rsch. Found., 1997-01, Stanford U. Children's Med. Ctr., 2004-04; chmn. exec. coun. U. Calif. Med. Ctr. Found., San Francisco, 2002-, bd. dirs., 1998—. Mem. White House Fellow Alumni Assn., Econ. Club N.Y.C. (bd. dirs., exec. com.), Nat. Retail Fedn. (chmn., bd. dirs., exec. com. 1993—), Pzena Investment Mgmt. (bd. dirs. 2007-). Republican. Office: JC Penney Corp Inc 6501 Legacy Dr Plano TX 75024-3698 Business E-Mail: mike@meullman.com.

ULLMAN, TRACEY, actress, singer; b. Slough, Eng., Dec. 30, 1959; m. Allan McKeown, 1983; children: Mabel Ellen, John Albert Victor. Student, Itaia Conti Stage Sch., London. Appeared in plays Gigi, Elvis, Grease, The Rocky Horror Show, Four in a Million, 1981 (London Theatre Critics award), The Taming of the Shrew, 1990, The Big Love, (one-woman stage show) 1991; actress: (films) Give My Regards to Broad Street, 1984, Plenty, 1985, Jumpin' Jack Flash, 1986, I Love You To Death, 1990, Household Saints, 1993, Robin Hood: Men in Tights, 1993, I'll Do Anything, 1994, Bullets over Broadway, 1994, Ready to Wear (Prêt-à-Porter), 1994, Everybody Says I Love You, 1996, Panic, 2000, Small Time Crooks, 2000, A Dirty Shame, 2004, (voice only) Corpse Bride, 2005, I Could Never Be Your Woman, 2007, (voice) The Tale of Despereaux, 2008, (TV films) Women of the Night IV, 1995, Once Upon a Mattress, 2004; Brit. TV shows include Three of a Kind, A Kick Up the Eighties, Girls on Top; (TV series) The Tracey Ullman Show, 1987-90 (Emmy award Best Performance, Outstanding Writing, 1990, Golden Globe award Best Actress, 1987), Tracey Takes On, 1996-99 (four Emmys including Outstanding Music, Comedy and Variety Show 1997, Cable Ace award for best comedy variety series 1996), Visible Panty Lines, 2001, Tracey Ullman's State of the Union, 2008-; singer: (albums) You Broke My Heart in Seventeen Places, You Caught Me Out, 1984, Takes on the Hits, 2002. Recipient Brit. Acad. award, 1983, Am. Comedy award, 1988, 90, 91, Emmy award for Best Performance in a Variety/Music Series for "Tracey Ullman Takes on New York", 1994. Office: IFA Talent Agy 8730 W Sunset Blvd Ste 490 Los Angeles CA 90069-2248

ULMER, FRANCES ANN, academic administrator, retired state official; b. Madison, Wis., Feb. 1, 1947; m. Bill Council; children: Amy, Louis. BA in Econs. and Polit. Sci., U. Wis.; JD with honors, Wis. Sch. Law. Polit. advisor Gov. Jay Hammond, Alaska, 1975-81; former mayor City of Juneau, Alaska; mem. Alaska Ho. of Reps., 1986-94, minority leader, 1992-94; lt. gov. State of Alaska, 1995—2002; U.S. rep. to North Pacific Anadramous Fish Commn., 1994—; disting. prof. U. Alaska, Anchorage, 2003—, dir. Inst. Social and Econ. Rsch., 2004—, interim chancellor, 2007—. Office: U Alaska Anchorage Office of Chancellor 3211 Providence Dr, ADM 216 Anchorage AK 99508 Office Phone: 907-786-7710. E-mail: fran.ulmer@uaa.alaska.edu.

ULRICH, PAUL GRAHAM, lawyer, writer, editor; b. Spokane, Wash., Nov. 29, 1938; s. Donald Gunn and Kathryn (Vandercook) U.; m. Kathleen Nelson Smith, July 30, 1982; children: Kathleen Elizabeth Pennington, Marilee Rae Timbrooks, Michael Graham Ulrich. BA with high honors, U. Mont., 1961; JD, Stanford U., 1964. Bar: Calif. 1965, Ariz. 1966, U.S. Ct. Appeals (9th cir.) 1965, U.S. Supreme Ct. 1969. Law clk. judge U.S. Ct. Appeals, 9th Circuit, San Francisco, 1964-65; assoc. Lewis and Roca, Phoenix, 1965-70, ptnr., 1970-85; pres. Paul G. Ulrich P.C., Phoenix, 1985-92, Ulrich, Thompson & Kessler, P.C., Phoenix, 1992-94, Ulrich & Kessler, P.C., Phoenix, 1994-95, Ulrich, Kessler & Anger, P.C., Phoenix, 1995-2000, Ulrich & Anger, P.C., Phoenix, 2000—03, Paul G. Ulrich P.C., 2003—; owner Pathway Enterprises, 1985-91. Judge pro tem divsn. 1, Ariz. Ct. Appeals, Phoenix, 1986; instr. Thunderbird Grad. Sch. Internat. Mgmt., 1968-69, Ariz. State U. Coll. Law, 1970-73, 78, Scottsdale CC, 1975-77, also continuing legal edn. seminars. Author and pub.: Applying Management and Motivation Concepts to Law Offices, 1985; co-editor: Arizona Appellate Handbook, 1978-2000, Working With Legal Assistants, 1980, 81; editor, co-author Future Directions for Law Office Management, 1982, People in the Law Office, 1985-86; co-author, pub.: Arizona Healthcare Professional Liability Handbook, 1992, supplement, 1994, Arizona Healthcare Professional Liability Defense Manual, 1995, Arizona Healthcare Professional Liability Update Newsletter, 1992-99; co-author, editor: Federal Appellate Practice: Ninth Circuit, 1994, 2d edit., 1999, supplement, 2008; contbg. editor Law Office Econs. and Mgmt., 1984-97, Life, Law and the Pursuit of Balance, 1996, 2d edit., 1997; co-author Ariz. Appellate Handbook, 1978-. Mem. Ariz. Supreme Ct. Task Force on Ct. Orgn. and Adminstrn., 1988-89; mem. com. on appellate cts. Ariz. Supreme Ct., 1990-91; bd. visitors Stanford U. Law Sch., 1974-77; adv. com. legal assisting program Phoenix Coll., 1985-95; atty. rep. 9th Cir. Jud. Conf., 1997-2000. With U.S. Army, 1956. Recipient continuing legal edn. award State Bar Ariz., 1978, 86, 90, Harrison Tweed spl. merit award Am. Law Inst./ABA, 1987. Fellow Ariz. Bar Found. (founding 1985—); mem. ABA (chmn. selection and utilization of staff pers. com., econs. of law sect. 1979-81, mem. standing com. legal assts. 1982-86, co-chmn. joint project on appellate handbooks 1983-85, co-chmn. fed. appellate handbook project 1985-88, chmn. com. on liaison with non-lawyers orgns. Econs. of Law Practice sect. 1985-86), Am. Acad. Appellate Lawyers, Am. Law Inst. (life), Am. Judicature Soc. (Spl. Merit citation 1987), Ariz. Bar Assn. (chmn. econs. of law practice com. 1980-81, co-chmn. lower ct. improvement com. 1982-85, co-chmn. Ariz. appellate handbook project 1976-2000), Coll. Law Practice Mgmt., Maricopa County Bar Assn. (bd. dirs. 1994-96), Calif. Bar Assn., Phi Kappa Phi, Phi Alpha Delta, Sigma Phi Epsilon. Democrat. Home and Office: 131 E El Caminito Dr Phoenix AZ 85020-3503 Office Phone: 602-248-9465. Personal E-mail: ulrichpc@aol.com.

ULRICH, PETER HENRY, banker; b. Munich, Nov. 24, 1922; s. Hans George and Hella (Muschweck) U.; m. Carol A. Peek, Oct. 21, 1944; children: Carol Jean Hewes, Patricia Diane (Mrs. Damon Eberhart), Peter James. Student, Northwestern U., 0194—1942, U. Iowa, 1943, Sch. Mortgage Banking, 1954—56. Lic. real estate broker, cert. mortgage banker; cert. rev. appraiser; cert. mortgage underwriter. Escrow officer Security Title Ins. Co., Riverside, Calif., 1946-53; asst. cashier Citizens Nat. Trust & Savs., Riverside, 1953-

57; v.p. Security First Nat. Bank, Riverside, 1957-63; sr. v.p. Bank of Calif. (N.A.), LA, 1963-72; pres. Ban Cal Mortgage Co., 1972-74, Ban Cal Tri-State Mortgage Co., 1974-75; cons., 1975-76; pres., dir. Beneficial Std. Mortgage Co., 1976-88; real estate cons., 1988—. Instr. real estate and bus. San Bernardino Valley Coll., Riverside City Coll., Pasadena City Coll. Pres. Residential Rsch. Com. So. Calif., 1965, Riverside Opera Assn., 1956—59, Riverside Symphony Soc., 1959—61; trustee Idyllwild Arts Found., 1957—, pres., 1970—73, sec., 1986—87; mem. adv. bd. Salvation Army, 1959—, vice chmn., 1971—74, chmn., 1975, Harbor Light Com., 1965—68, 2002—; convocator Calif. Luth. U., 1976—80, 1981—83, regent, 1981—90; v.p. Guild Opera Co., 1991—99; bd. dirs. Lark Ellen Lions Charities, 1994—, pres., 1994—; treas. Opera Buffs, 1983—; mem. Arcadia Beautiful Commn., 1989—95, vice chair, 1991—92, chmn., 1992—93; trustee Calif. Luth. Edn. Found., 1989—2001; v.p. Arcadia Tournament Roses Assn., 1997; mem. Arcadia City Coun., 1995—96; trustee Arcadia Pub. Libr., 1997—2005, chair, 1999, 2005; vol. Arcadia Police Dept., 2002—; v.p. ch. coun. Ch. of the Cross, 2003—04, 2006—; bd. dirs. Arcadia Tournament Roses Assn., Guild Opera Co., Am. Heart Assn. Foothill divsn. chair, 1997—99, South Pasadena-Arcadia Adult Reading Ctrs., 1998—2002, pres., 2002; bd. dirs. Arcadia Coordinating Coun., 2005, 2006; v.p. Arcadia Libr. Found., 2005—. With AUS USAR, 1943—46. Recipient Resolution of Commendation Riverside City Coun., 1963; Resolution of Appreciation LA City Coun., 1968, 1973; named Arcadia Vol. of Yr., 1997. Mem.: Arcadia Human Resources Commn., Arcadia C. of C. (dir. 2004—, chmn. legis. affairs com. 2005—), Assn. Corp. Real Estate Execs. (sec. 1967—71, pres. 1974—75), Inland Empire Mortgage Bankers Assn. (pres. 1962, hon. dir.), So. Calif. Mortgage Bankers Assn. (dir. 1975, 1980—81, v.p. 1982, pres. 1983), Calif. Mortgage Bankers Assn. (sec. 1965, dir. 1972—75, Disting. Svc. award 1997), Nat. Mortgage Bankers Assn. (chmn. Life Ins. Co. com. 1986—87), Lambda Alpha Internat. (historian, dir. 2004—05). Lutheran. Office: 37 E Huntington Dr Arcadia CA 91006-3210 Home: 1420 Santo Domingo Ave Duarte CA 91010-2632 Office Phone: 626-294-1058. Business E-Mail: pulrich@sprintmail.com.

ULRICH, THEODORE ALBERT, lawyer; b. Spokane, Wash., Jan. 1, 1943; s. Herbert Roy and Martha (Hoffman) Ulrich; m. Nancy Allison, May 30, 1966; children: Donald Wayne, Frederick Albert. BS cum laude, U.S. Mcht. Marine Acad., 1965; JD cum laude, Fordham U., 1970; LLM, NYU, 1974. Bar: NY 1971, U.S. Ct. Appeals (2d cir.) 1971, U.S. Supreme Ct. 1974, U.S. Ct. Claims 1977, U.S. Customs Ct. 1978, U.S. Ct. Internat. Trade 1981, U.S. Ct. Appeals (5th cir.) 1988, U.S. Ct. Appeals (DC cir.) 1992, Colo. 1993, U.S. Ct. Appeals (10th cir.) 1994. Mng. clk. U.S. Dept. Justice, NYC, 1968-69, law clk. to fed. dist. judge, 1969-70; assoc. Cadwalader, Wickersham & Taft, NYC, 1970—94, ptnr., 1980-94, Popham, Haik, Schnobrich & Kaufman, Ltd., Denver, 1994-96; pvt. practice law Denver, 1996—. Author: Arbitration of Construction Contracts, V, 1991; co-author: Encyclopedia of International Commercial Litigation, 1991; contbg. author: Marine Engineering Economics and Cost Analysis, 1995; author, editor Fordham Law Rev., 1969. Leader Boy Scouts Am., Nassau County, NY, 1984-94, Denver, 1994—. Capt. USCGR, 1965-86. Mem. ABA, Colo. Bar, Denver Bar, Maritime Law Assn., Am. Soc. Internat. Law, Soc. Naval Archs. and Marine Engrs., U.S. Naval Inst., Am. Arbitration Assn. Home and Office: 4300 E 6th Ave Denver CO 80220-4940 E-mail: tnulrich@verizon.net.

UMBERG, THOMAS JOHN, lawyer; b. Cin., Sept. 25, 1955; s. John H. and Joan (Jansen) U.; m. Robin Bailey; children: Erin, Brett, Tommy. BA cum laude, UCLA, 1977; JD, U. Calif., San Francisco, 1980. Bar: Calif. 1980, U.S. Dist. Ct. (ctr. dist.) Calif. 1981, U.S. Dist. Ct. (so. dist.) Calif. 1986, U.S. Ct. Appeals (9th cir.) 1988. Asst. U.S. atty. Ctrl. Dist. Calif., criminal div., LA, 1987—90; mem. Calif. Assembly, Sacramento, 1990—94, 2004—; ptnr. Morrison & Foerster LLP, Irvine, Calif., 1995—97; dep. dir. White House Office Nat. Drug Control Policy, 1997—2000; mng. ptnr.-Orange County Office Morrison & Foerster LLP, Irvine, Calif., 2000—. Adj. prof. law Southwestern U., 1995—97. Military Prosecutor, U.S. Army, Korea, Italy 1980-1985; col. USAR. Mem.: Calif. Coun. Criminal Justice (mem. 1991—95). Roman Catholic. Office: Morrison & Foerster LLP 19900 MacArthur Blvd Irvine CA 92612-2445 Office Phone: 949-251-7500. Office Fax: 949-251-0900. Business E-Mail: tumberg@mofo.com.

UNDERWOOD, PAUL LESTER, cardiologist; b. Knoxville, Tenn., Mar. 23, 1960; MD, Mayo Med. Sch., 1984. Diplomate Am. Bd. Cardiovascular Disease. Intern Henry Ford Hosp., Detroit, 1984-85; resident internal medicine Mayo Grad. Sch. Medicine, Rochester, Minn., 1985-87; fellow in cardiology Cleve. Clinic, 1990-93; fellow in interventional cardiology Iowa Heart Ctr., Des Moines, 1993; dir. emergency medicine, dir. ICU St. Croix Hosp., U.S. V.I., 1987-90; staff N. Phoenix Heart Ctr., Ariz., 2001—07; dir. rsch. Sonoran Health Specialists-Eclipse Clin. Rsch. Assoc., 2007—. Mem. AMA, Nat. Med. Assn., Assn. Black Cardiologists (former pres.), Am. Coll. Cardiology (councilor), Am. Heart Assn. (bd. dirs. Ariz. affiliate), Soc. for Cardiac Angiography and Interventions. Office: Sonoran Health Specialists Eclipse Clin Rsch Assoc 8414 E Shea Bld Ste 103 Scottsdale AZ 85260 Home: 4727 E Berneil Dr Phoenix AZ 85028-5506 Office Phone: 480-767-3877. Business E-Mail: punderwood@sonoranhealth.com.

UNDERWOOD, ROBERT ANACLETUS, former congressman, university official; b. Tamuning, Guam, July 13, 1948; m. Lorraine Aguilar; 5 children. BA with honors in History, Calif. State U., 1969, MA in History, 1971; cert. edn. adminstrn., U. Guam, 1976; DEd, U. So. Calif., 1987. Loader, sorter United Parcel Svc., LA, 1966-72; tchr. George Washington High Sch., 1972-74; asst. prin. for bus. and student pers. George Washington H.S., 1974-76; asst. and acting prin. Inarajan Jr. H.S., 1976; instr., dir. bilingual bicultural tng. program U. Guam, 1976-81, asst. prof., 1981-83, dir. bilingual edn. assistance for Micronesia project, 1983-88, dean Coll. Edn., 1988-90, acad. v.p., 1990—; mem. del. 103d-107th Congress from Guam, Washington, 1993—2003. Mem. House resources com., armed svcs.; chmn. Asian Pacific Caucus 106th Congress; part-time curriculum writer Guam Bilingual Edn. Project, 1973-76; chmn. Chamorro Lang. Commn., 1979-90. Named Citizen of Yr., Nat. Assn. Bilingual Edn., 1996, Alumnus of Yr. Calif. State U., 1999. Roman Catholic. E-mail: guamtodc@mail.house.gov.

UNDERWOOD, RONALD BRIAN, director, producer; b. Glendale, Calif., Nov. 6, 1953; s. Laurence Joseph and Ella Julia (Green) U.; m. Sandra Joyce Archer, June 8, 1974; children: Larissa, Lana, Lauren. BA in Cinema, U. So. Calif., 1974. Dir. (films) Deer in the Works, 1980, The Mouse and the Motorcycle, 1986, Runaway Ralph, 1988, Tremors, 1990 (also writer), City Slickers, 1991, Heart and Souls, 1993, Speechless, 1994, Mighty Joe Young, 1998, The Adventures of Pluto Nash, 2002, Stealing Sinatra, 2003, In the Mix, 2005, (TV films) The Mouse and the Motorcycle, 1986, Runaway Ralph, 1988, Back When We Were Grownups 2004; assoc. prodr. (films) Crawlspace, 1986. Recipient Peabody award, 1986; Am. Film Inst. fellow, 1975. Office: United Talent Agy 9560 Wilshire Blvd Fl 5 Beverly Hills CA 90212-2400

UNDERWOOD, VERNON O., JR., grocery stores executive; b. 1940; children: Jeff, Chris. BBA, U. So. Calif. With Young's Market Co. LLC, LA, 1955—, pres., 1975—97, CEO, chmn. bd., 1990—. Avocations: golf, bird hunting, travel. Office: Youngs Market Company 14402 Franklin Ave Tustin CA 92780-7013

UNGER, RICHARD WATSON, history professor; b. Huntington, W.Va., Dec. 23, 1942; s. Abraham I. and Marion Patterson U.; 1 child, Emily Patterson. BA, Haverford Coll., Pa., 1963; AM, U. Chgo., 1965; MA, Yale U., 1967, MPhil, 1969, PhD, 1971. Prof. dept. history U. B.C., Vancouver, Canada, 1969—. Author: Dutch Shipbuilding Before 1800, 1978, The Ship in the Medieval Economy, 600-1600, 1980, The Art of Medieval Technology: The Image of Noah the Shipbuilder, 1991, Ships and Shipping in the North Sea and Atlantic, 1400-1600, 1997, A History of Brewing in Holland, 900-1900, Economy, Technology and the State, 2001, Beer in the Middle Ages and the Renaissance, 2004, Britain and Poland Lithuania Contact and Comparision from the Middle Ages to 1795, 2008; editor: Cogs, Caravels and Galleons, 1994; co-editor: War at Sea in the Middle Ages and the Renaissance, 2003, Studies in Medieval and Renaissance History, 1978-95; contbr. articles to profl. jours. Trustee Vancouver Maritime Mus., 1979-83, 97-98. Mem. Medieval Assn. Pacific (pres. 1994-96), Econ. History Soc., Soc. Nautical Rsch. Office: U BC Dept History 1297-1873 East Mall Vancouver BC Canada V6T 1Z1 Business E-Mail: richard.unger@ubc.ca.

UNIS, RICHARD L., judge; b. Portland, Oreg., June 11, 1928; BS, JD, U. Oreg. Bar: Oreg. 1954, U.S. Dist. Ct. Oreg. 1957, U.S. Ct. Appeals (9th cir.) 1960, U.S. Supreme Ct. 1965. Judge Portland Mcpl. Ct., 1968-71, Multnomah County Dist. Ct., 1972-76, presiding judge, 1972-74; former judge Oreg. Cir. Ct. 4th Judicial Dist., 1977-90; former sr. dep. city atty. City of Portland; assoc. justice Oreg. Supreme Ct., Portland, 1990-96; spl. master US Dist. Ct. House, Portland, 1996—2005. Adj. prof. of local govt. law and evidence Lewis & Clark Coll. Northwestern Sch. Law, 1969-76, 77-96; spl. master supr. La.-Pacific Inner-Seal Siding nationwide class action litig.; faculty mem. The Nat. Judicial Coll., 1971-2000; former faculty mem. Am. Acad. Judicial Edn. Author: Procedure and Instructions in Traffic Court Cases, 1970, 101 Questions and Answers on Preliminary Hearings, 1974. Bd. dirs. Oreg. Free from Drug Abuse; mem. Oreg. Adv. Com. on Evidence Law Revision, chmn. subcom., 1974-79. Maj. USAFR, JAGC, ret. Recipient Meritorius Svc. award U. Oregon sch. Law, 1988; named Legal Citizen of Yr. Oreg. Law Related Edn., 1987; inducted into The Nat. Judicial Coll. Hall of Honor, 1988. Mem. Am. Judicature Soc. (bd. dirs. 1975, Herbert Harley Nat. award 1999), Am. Judges Assn., Multnomah Bar Found., Oregon Judicial Conf. (chmn. Oreg. Judicial Coll. 1973-80, legis. com. 1976—, exec. com. of judicial edn. com., judicial conduct com.), N.Am. Judges Assn. (tenure, selection and compensation judges com.), Dist. Ct. Judges of Oreg. (v.p., chmn. edn. com.), Nat. Conf. Spl. Ct. Judges (exec. com.), Oreg. State Bar (judicial adminstrn. com., sec. local govt. com., com. on continuing certification, uniform jury instrn. com., exec. com. criminal law sect., trial practice sect. standards and certification com., past chmn., among others), Oreg. Trial Lawyers Assn. (named Judge of Yr. 1984). Office: 28338 Hist Colum Riv Hwy Troutdale OR 97060-9372 Home Phone: 503-665-9459; Office Phone: 503-669-7286. Personal E-mail: rlugg@comcast.net.

UNKOVIC, NICHOLAS C., lawyer; b. Pitts., 1951; AB magna cum laude, Harvard U., 1973; JD with honors, U. Mich., 1976. Bar: Calif. 1976. Mng. ptnr.-Palo Alto Office Squire, Sanders & Dempsey LLP, mem. mgmt. com. Dir. British Am. Coun. No. Calif., Redem Corp. Named a No. Calif. Super Lawyers, Law & Politics Mag., 2004; named one of Silicon Valley's top corp. lawyers, San Jose Mag. Mem.: ABA (Bus. Law Sect.), State Bar Calif. Fluent in French. Office: Squire Sanders & Dempsey LLP 600 Hansen Way Palo Alto CA 94304-1043 Office Phone: 650-843-3238. Office Fax: 650-843-8777. Business E-Mail: nunkovic@ssd.com.

UNRUH, WILLIAM GEORGE, physics professor, researcher; b. Winnipeg, Man., Can., Aug. 28, 1945; m. Patricia Truman, Apr. 19, 1974; 1 child, Daniel B. BSc, U. Man., Winnipeg, 1967; MA, Princeton U., NJ, 1969, PhD, 1971; DSc (hon.), McMaster U., 2007. Postdoctoral fellow NRC Can., London, Ont., 1971-72; Miller fellow U. Calif., Berkeley, 1973-74; asst. prof. McMaster U., Hamilton, Ont., Canada, 1974-76; asst. prof. to prof. physics U. BC, Vancouver, Canada, 1976—; rsch. fellow Can. Inst. Advanced Rsch., Toronto, Ont., Canada, 1986—, dir. Cosmology Program, 1986-96. Contbr. tech. papers to profl. publs. Recipient Gold medal, BC Sci. Coun., 1991, Killam prize in nat. sci., 1996, medal in Math. & Theoretical Physics, CAP/CRM, 1996; Rutherford Meml. fellow, Royal Soc. Can., 1971, Alfred P. Sloan Rsch. fellow, U. BC, 1978—80, Steacie fellow, Nat. Sci. and Eng. Rsch. Coun., 1984—86, Japan Soc. Promotion Sci. Sr. fellow, Japan, 1986, Vis. fellow, All Souls Coll., Oxford, 2003. Fellow: Royal Soc. of London (Rutherford lectr. 1985), Am. Phys. Soc., Royal Soc. Can. (Rutherford lectr. 1985); mem.: Am. Acad. Arts and Scis. (hon.; fgn.). Office: Univ BC Dept Physics & Astron 6224 Agricultural Rd Vancouver BC Canada V6T 1Z1

UNTERMAN, THOMAS, venture capitalist, lawyer; b. Newport, RI, Oct. 23, 1944; s. Martin D. and Ruth (Marcus) U.; m. Janet M. Mead, Sept. 27, 1980; children: Rebecca, Amy. AB, Princeton U., 1966; JD, U. Chgo., 1969. Bar: Calif. 1970. Assoc. Orrick, Herrington & Sutcliffe, San Francisco, 1969-75, ptnr., 1975-86, Morrison & Foerster, San Francisco, 1986-92; sr. v.p., gen. counsel The Times Mirror Co., LA, 1992-95, sr. v.p., CFO, 1995—, exec. v.p., CFO, 1998-99; mng. ptnr. Rustic Canyon Ventures, Santa Monica, Calif., 2000—. Democrat. Jewish. Office: Rustic Canyon Ventures 2425 Olympic Blvd Ste 6050W Santa Monica CA 90404-4030

UPSON, DONALD V., retired corporate financial executive; b. Hutchinson., Kans., Feb. 8, 1934; s. William Ernest and Luella Beatrice (Hutchison) U.; m. Janis Carol Anderson, Sept. 16, 1956; children: Mark Steven, Brent William. BS, Kans. State U., 1956. C.P.A. With Peat, Marwick, Mitchell & Co., 1956, 60-81, ptnr., 1974-81; exec. v.p., dir. internal audit Del E. Webb Corp., Phoenix, 1981-85; mgr. info. systems Tiernay Turbines Inc., Phoenix, 1986; chief fin. officer Schomac Corp., Tucson, 1986-88; adminstr. U. Ariz., Tucson, 1988-90; pres., chief exec. officer Ariz. Commerce Bank, Tucson, 1990-91; chief fin. officer O'Connor, Cavanagh, Anderson, Westover, Killingsworth & Beshears, P.A., Phoenix, 1991-94; fin. cons., 1995-97; ret., 1997. Pres. Community Orgn. for Drug Abuse, Alcohol and Mental Health Services, Inc., 1977-78; bd. dis. Phoenix council Boy Scouts Am., elder Presbyterian Ch. Served to lt. USAF, 1956-59. Mem. Am. Inst. C.P.A.s, Ariz. Soc. C.P.A.s, Beta Theta Pi (pres. 1955-56) Republican. Home and Office: 1313 E Sheena Dr Phoenix AZ 85022-4485 Personal E-mail: dupson2@cox.net.

UREMOVICH, MICHAEL ELLIOT, transportation company executive; b. Phila., Apr. 23, 1943; s. A. M. and Edythe (Fidcca) U.; m. Carrea S. Cotlow, Aug. 27, 1966. BA, U. Ariz., 1966; MBA, CCNY, 1972; MA, St. Johns Coll. Sr. v.p. mktg. Lee Way Motor Freight, Oklahoma City, 1976-79; prin. Booz, Allen & Hamilton, NYC, 1972-76, 1979-82; v.p. through sr. v.p. mktg. Am. Pres. Lines, Oakland, Calif.; v.p. mktg. So. Pacific Transp.; pres. TSSI; prin. Manalytics Internat., San Francisco; vice-chmn. Pacer Internat., Concord, Calif., 2003—06, chmn., CEO, 2006—. Served with USN, 1961-66. Office: Pacer Internat Ste 1200 2300 Clayton Rd Concord CA 94520

URENA-ALEXIADES, JOSE LUIS, electrical engineer; b. Madrid, Sept. 5, 1949; s. Jose L. and Maria (Alexiades Christodulakis) Urena y Pon. MS in EE, U. Madrid, Spain, 1976; MS in Computer Sci., UCLA, 1978. Rsch. asst. UCLA, 1978; sys. analyst Honeywell Info. Systems, LA, 1978-80; mem. tech. staff Jet Propulsion Lab., Pasadena, Calif., 1980-91; exec. dir. Empresa Nacional de Innovacion S.A., LA, 1991-96; sr. technologist Boeing Satellite Devel. Ctr., LA, 1996—. Contbr. various articles to profl. jours. Two times recipient NASA Group Achievement award. Mem. IEEE, IEEE Computer Soc., IEEE Communications Soc., Assn. for Computer Machinery, World Federalist Assn., Spanish Profl. Am. Inc. Roman Catholic. Avocations: photography, swimming. Office: Boeing Satellite Devel Ctr Mail Stop S50 x366 1700 E Imperial Hwy Los Angeles CA 90245 Home: PO BOX 3522 Idyllwild CA 92549-3522

URI, GEORGE WOLFSOHN, accountant; b. San Francisco, Dec. 8, 1920; s. George Washington and Ruby Uri; m. Pamela O'Keefe, May 15, 1961. AB, Stanford U., 1941, IA, 1943, MBA, 1946; postgrad., U. Leeds, Eng., 1945. CPA, Calif.; CMA, ChFC; Accredited Estate Planner. Mem. acctg., econs. and stats. depts. Shell Oil Co., Inc., San Francisco, 1946—48; ptnr., ret. Irelan, Uri, Mayer & Sheppie; pres. F. Uri & Co., Inc. Instr. acctg. and econs. Golden Gate U., 1949-50. Contbr. articles to profl. jours. Chmn. San Rafael Redevel. Adv. Com., 1977-78, mem., 1978-91, mem. emeritus, 1991—; bd. dirs. San Francisco Planning and Urban Renewal Assn., 1958-60. Served with AUS, 1942-46, to col. Aus. (ret.). Recipient Meritorious Service medal, Sec. of Army, 1978. Mem. AICPA (hon., personal fin. specialist), Calif. Soc. CPA (hon.; sec.-treas. San Francisco chpt. 1956-57, dir. 1961-63, state dir. 1964-66, Forbes medal com. 1968-69, chmn. 1969-71), San Francisco Estate Planning Coun. (dir. 1965-68, Am. Soc. Mil. Comptr., Execs. Assn. San Francisco (pres. 1965-66), Soc. Fin. Profls., Fin. Planning Assn., Commonwealth Club (quar. chmn. 1971), Stanford Alumni Assn. (San Francisco; dir. 1990-99), Army and Navy Club Washington. Office: 1209 Tennessee St San Francisco CA 94107 Personal E-mail: georgeuri@aol.com.

URIE, ALAN T., bank executive; b. Ogden, Utah, Sept. 25, 1957; s. Hurschell G. and E. Mary (Petersen) Urie; m. M. Mae Christensen, July 26, 1980; children: Marcus Timothy, Kristi Mae Harvey, Scott Alan, Catherine Elizabeth, Teresa Janette, Mary Elizabeth. BS, Brigham Young U., 1982; MBA, U. Utah, 1984. National Compliance School Graduate Am. Bankers Assn., 1991. Officer First Security Bank of Utah, N.A., Salt Lake City, 1983—91, asst. v.p., 1991—94, v.p., sr. compliance officer, 1994—2000; v.p. First Security Corp., Salt Lake City, 1996—2000; sr. v.p. Wells Fargo Bank NW, N.A., 2000—, Wells Fargo Bank, N.A., 2004—, Wells Fargo Cmty. Devel. Corp., 2007—. Unit com. mem., leader Boys Scouts Am., South Salt Lake, 1985—; budget adv. bd. Ogden City, Utah, 1986—88; commr., chair South Salt Lake Planning Commn., 1985—86, 1988—95; chmn. Cmty. Affairs Com., South Salt Lake, 1988—90, Gen. Plan Com., South Salt Lake, 1992—96, City Housing Rehab. Loan Com., South Salt Lake, Utah, 2002—; bishop Ch. of Jesus Christ of Latter-day Saints, South Salt Lake, 2003—04, stake presidency mem., 2004—; bd. mem., exec. com. Utah Microenterprise Loan Fund, 2000—, vice chair, 2008—; bd. & exec. com., governance com. Girl Scouts Utah, 2002—08; bd. mem., incorporator South Salt Lake Works, Inc., 2004—; com. mem. Utah Bankers Assn., 1990—2009. Lds Ch. Office: Wells Fargo 299 South Main St Salt Lake City UT 84111-2263

URIOSTE, FRANK J., film editor; Cert. Am. Cinema Editors. Film editor The Mirisch Agy., LA. Films include Whatever Happened to Aunt Alice, The Grissom Gang, Boys in Company C, Fast Break, Loving Couples, Jazz Singer, The Entity, Trenchcoat, Amityville 3-D, Conan II, The Destroyer, Red Sonja, The Hitcher, Robocop (Acad. award nomination), Total Recall, Basic Instinct, Cliffhanger, Tombstone, Terminal Velocity, Cutthroat Island, Executive Decision, Conspiracy Theory, (co-editor) Midway, Hoosiers, Die Hard (Acad. award nomination); prodr.; Beach House, 1995. Address: 1610 Highland Ave Glendale CA 91202-1260

URIS, PATRICIA FIRME, health science association administrator; b. Muskegon, Mich. BSN, U. Colo., 1974, MS in Psychiatric/Mental Health Nursing, 1978, PhD in Nursing, 1993. Staff nurse Colo. Mental Health Inst., Denver, 1984-76; on-call staff Bethesda PsycHealth Sys., Denver, 1977; clin. specialist Pk. E. Comprehensive Cmty. Mental Health Ctr., Denver, 1978; asst. exec. dir. Colo. Nurses Assn., Denver, 1979-80; project co-dir. Western Interstate Commn. Higher Edn., Boulder, Colo., 1980-85; project dir. Western Inst. Nursing/Western Soc. Rsch. Nursing, Boulder, 1987-90, assoc. dir., 1987-90, spl. cons., 1990-94; program devel., mgmt. cons. Arvada, Colo., 1994-95; asst. prof. U. Colo. Health Scis. Ctr., Denver, 1995-99; program adminstr. Bd. Nursing Colo. Dept. Regulatory Agys., Denver, 1999—. Guest lectr. U. Colo. Health Scis. Ctr., 1979-82, 80-83, 94-97, Metro. State Coll., 1979-82; cons. U. Alaska, 1982, Wyo. Dept. Health and Social Svcs., 1982, Utah Dept. Health, 1982; reviewer Appleton-Century-Crofts Pub. Co., 1985, Colo. Dept. Health and Environment, 1996, 97, Nat. Assn. Sch. Nurses, Inc., 1997, HHS, 1997, 98, 99. Cons. Rocky Mountain Ctr. Healthcare Ethics; mem. clin. adv. bd. ONEDAY/The Family AIDS Project, Denver; mem. stds. based edn. com. Arvada W. Sch. Improvement Leadership Team, Jefferson County, Colo. Recipient NIH stipend, 1976-78; Calloway scholar U. Colo. Health Scis. Ctr. Mem. ANA, Am. Psychiatric Nurses Assn., Assn. Child and Adolescent Psychiatric Nurses, Soc. Edn. and Rsch. Psychiatric-Mental Health Nursing, Nat. Assn. Sch. Nurses, Colo. Nurses Assn. (ANA del. 1982, 84, mem. commn. social and legis. concerns 1981-85, chair

1981-83, Virginia S. Paulson award 1981), Colo. Mental Health Assn. (pro bono vol.), Sigma Theta Tau (chpt. bd. dirs. 1993-96, mem. rsch. com. 1995-99, chmn. 1995-96, Henrietta Loughran scholar 1993).

URQUHART, JOHN, medical researcher, educator; b. Pitts., Apr. 24, 1934; s. John and Wilma Nelda (Martin) U.; m. Joan Cooley, Dec. 28, 1957; children: Elizabeth Urquhart Vdovjak, John Christopher (dec. 1965), Robert Malcolm, Thomas Jubal. BA with honors, Rice U., 1955; MD with honors, Harvard U., 1959; D honoris causa, U. Utrecht, 1997. Lic. physician, Calif. Walter B. Cannon fellow in physiology Harvard Med. Sch., Boston, 1956, Josiah Macy, Jr. fellow, 1956-58, 59-61; intern in surgery Mass. Gen. Hosp., 1959-60, asst. resident, 1960-61; investigator Nat. Heart Inst., NIH, Bethesda, Md., 1961-63; asst. prof. physiology U. Pitts. Sch. Medicine, 1963-66, assoc. prof., 1966-68, prof., 1968-70; prof. biomed. engring. U. So. Calif., LA, 1970-71; prin. scientist ALZA Corp., Palo Alto, Calif., 1970-86, dir. biol. scis., 1971-74, pres. rsch. divsn., 1974-78, dir., 1976-78, chief scientist, 1978-82, sr. v.p., 1978-85. Co-founder APREX Corp., Fremont, Calif., pres., 1986-88, dir., 1986-95, chmn., 1988-91, chief scientist, 1988-95; co-founder, chief scientist AARDEX Ltd., Zug, Switzerland, 1995-; vis. prof. pharmacology U. Limburg Sch. Medicine (now Maastricht U.), Maastricht, Netherlands, 1984-85, vis. prof. pharmacoepidemiology, 1986-91, extra ordinary prof. pharmacoepidemiology, 1991-2004, prof. emeritus, 2004-; adj. prof. biopharm. scis. U. Calif., San Francisco, 1984-; dir.'s adv. com. NIH, 1986-88; Boerhaave lectr. U. Leiden, Netherlands, 1991, 94-95, 97; bd. dirs. HBM BioVentures Ltd., Cayman Islands. Co-author: Risk Watch, 1984; contbr. articles to profl. jours.; patentee therapeutic systems for controlled drug delivery and regimen compliance monitoring. Trustee Kettering U. (formerly GMI Engring. and Mgmt. Inst.), Flint, Mich., 1983—. Served with USPHS, 1961-63. Recipient Disting. Alumni award, Rice U., 2002; NIH grantee, 1963-70. Fellow AAAS, Royal Coll. Physicians Edinburgh, Royal Soc. Edinburgh (corr.), Am. Assn. Pharmaceutical Scientists, Internat Soc. Pharmacoepidemiology, Biomed. Engring. Soc. (pres. 1976, Disting. Svc. award 2005); mem. Boylston Med. Soc., Am. Soc. Clin. Pharmacology and Therapeutics, Endocrine Soc., Saturday Morning Club Palo Alto, Am. Physiol. Soc. (Bowditch Lectr. award 1969), Calif. Acad. Medicine, Illuminati Edinburgh. Home and Office: 975 Hamilton Ave Palo Alto CA 94301-2213 E-mail: urquhart@ix.netcom.com.

UTHOFF, MICHAEL, dancer, choreographer, director; b. Santiago, Chile, Nov. 5, 1943; came to U.S., 1962; s. Ernst and Lola (Botka) U.; m. dau., Michelle. Grad. biology, high sch., Chile; dance tng. with Juilliard Sch., 1962-65, Martha Graham, 1962-63, Joffrey Ballet, 1965-68, Sch. Am. Ballet, 1962-64; Laureate in Humanities, St. Joseph Coll., Hartford, Conn. Leading dancer Jose Limon Dance Co., 1964-65, City Center Joffrey Ballet, 1965-68, N.Y.C. Opera, 1968-69; leading dancer, asst. dir. First Chamber Dance Co. N.Y., from 1969; artistic dir. Hartford Ballet Co., 1972-92, Ballet Ariz., 1992—. Mem. faculty Juilliard Sch. Music, N.Y.C., from 1969; guest artist, tchr. Princeton Ballet Soc.; prof. dance SUNY, Purchase, 1972-74; instr. dance and drama movement, Yale U.; works premiered by Compania Nacional de Danzas, Mexico City, 1989; guest choreographer Shanghai Ballet, Republic of China, 1986; led Hartford Ballet on 3-week 11-city tour of Peoples Republic of China by invitation of Shanghai Internat. Culture Assn., 1988, 5-week 9-country tour Latin Am., 1991. Choreographer, dancer-actor film Seafall, 1968; opera prodns. Aida and La Cenerentola, Honolulu, 1972, Conn. Opera Romeo et Juliette, 1989, Pitts. Opera Aida, 1988; choreographer Quartet, City Center Joffrey Ballet, 1968, The Pleasure of Merely Circulating, Juilliard Sch. Music, 1969, Windsong, Reflections, Dusk, Promenade, First Chamber Dance Co., 1969-70, Mozart's Idomeneo for Caramoor Music Festival, 1970, Concerto Grosso for Ballet Clasico 70 of Mexico, also restaged Dusk, 1972, Aves Mirabiles, 1973, Danza a Quattro, 1973, Marosszek Dances, 1973, Duo, 1974, Pastorale, 1974, Brahms Variations, 1974, Autumalal, 1975, Mir Ken Geharget Veren, 1976, Tom Dula, 1976, Unstill Life, 1977, Songs of a Wayfarer, 1977, Ask Not..., 1977, White Mountains Suite, 1978, Bach Cantata, 1978, The Nutcracker, 1979, Romeo and Juliet, 1981, Cachivaches, 1981, Reflections on the Water, 1981, Weeping Willow, 1982, Carmencita Variations, 1982, Hansel and Gretel, 1983, Coppelia, 1986, Speak Easy, 1986, New England Triptych, 1986, Los Copihues, 1988, Petrouchka, 1988, RFD #1, 1989, Classical Symphoniette, 1990, Alice in Wonderland, 1991, Nocturnes, 1991, Sinfonia Danzante, 1991; Nat. Endowment Arts commns. for choreography: Primavera, Minn. Dance Theatre, 1975, Panvezitos, Greater Houston Civic Ballet, 1976, Sonata, The Prodigal Son, Hartford Ballet, 1977, 79. Recipient award for best choreography for Murmurs of the Stream, Chilean Nat. Press, 1983, Critic's Circle Best of Yr. in Arts award, Chile, 1984, Milagno en la Alameda award for Chilean Nat. Women, 1995; grantee various founds. Office: Ballet Ariz 3645 E Indian School Rd Phoenix AZ 85018-5126

UTTAL, WILLIAM R(EICHENSTEIN), psychology and engineering educator, research scientist; b. Mineola, NY, Mar. 24, 1931; s. Joseph and Claire (Reichenstein) U.; m. Michiye Nishimura, Dec. 20, 1954; children: Taneil, Lynet, Lisa. Student, Miami U. Oxford, Ohio, 1947-48; BS in Physics, U. Cin., 1951; PhD in Exptl. Psychology and Biophysics, Ohio State U., 1957. Staff Psychologist, mgr. behavioral sci. group IBM Rsch. Ctr., Yorktown Heights, NY, 1957-63; assoc. prof. U. Mich., Ann Arbor, 1963-68, prof. psychology, 1968-86, rsch. scientist, 1963-86, prof. emeritus, 1986—; grad. affiliate faculty dept. psychology U. Hawaii, 1986-88; rsch. scientist Naval Ocean Systems Ctr.-Hawaii Lab., Kailua, 1985-88; prof., chmn. dept. psychology Ariz. State U., Tempe, 1988—90, prof. dept. indsl. engring., 1992—99, affiliated prof., Dept. of Computer Sci. and Engring., 1993-98, prof. emeritus, 1999—. Vis. prof. Kyoto (Japan) Prefectural Med. U., 1965-66, Sensory Sci. Lab., U. Hawaii, 1968, 73, 2003-08, U. Western Australia, 1970-71, U. Hawaii, 1978-79, 80-81, U. Auckland, 1996, U. Freiburg, 1997, U. Sydney, 1999; pres. Nat. Conf. on On-Line Uses Computers in Psychology, 1974. Author: Real Time Computers: Techniques and Applications in the Psychological Sciences, 1968, Generative Computer Assisted Instruction in Analytic Geometry, 1972, The Psychobiology of Sensory Coding, 1973, Cellular Neurophysiology and Integration: An Interpretive Introduction, 1975, An Autocorrelation Theory of Visual Form Detection, 1975, The Psychobiology of Mind, 1978, A Taxonomy of Visual Processes, 1981, Visual Form Detection in Three Dimensional Space, 1983, Principles of Psychobiology, 1983, The Detection of Nonplanar Surfaces in Visual Space, 1985, The Perception of Dotted Forms, 1987, On Seeing Forms, 1988, The Swimmer: A Computational Model of a Perceptual Motor System, 1992, Toward a New Behaviorism: The Case Against Perceptual Reductionism, 1998, A Computational Model of Vision: The Role of Combination, 1999, The War Between Mentalism and Behaviorism, 2000, The New Phrenology: Limits on the Localization of Cognitive Processes in the Brain, 2001, A Behaviorist Looks at Form Recognition, 2002, Psychomythics, 2003, Dualism, 2004, Neural Theories of Mind, 2005, Human Factors in the Courtroom, 2006, The Immeasurable Mind, 2007, Time, Space and Number in Physics and Psychology, 2008; editor: Readings in Sensory Coding, 1972; assoc. editor Behavioral Rsch. Method and Instrn., 1968—90, Computing: Archives for Electronic Computing, 1963—75, Jour. Exptl. Psychology, Perception and Performance, 1974—79, cons. editor Jour. Exptl. Psychology: Applied, 1994—97; contbr. articles to profl. jours. Served to 2d lt. USAF, 1951-53. USPHS spl. postdoctoral fellow, 1965-66; NIMH research scientist award, 1971-76 Fellow AAAS, APA, Am. Psychol. Soc. (charter), Soc. Exptl. Psychologists (chmn. 1994-95), Ariz. Acad. Sci., Arts & Tech. (founding fellow). Achievements include patents in field. Office: Ariz State U Dept Indsl Engring Tempe AZ 85287-1104 Business E-Mail: aowru@asu.edu.

UTTER, ROBERT FRENCH, dean, retired judge; b. Seattle, June 19, 1930; s. John and Besse (French) Utter; m. Elizabeth J. Stevenson, Dec. 28, 1953; children: Kimberly, Kirk, John. BS, U. Wash., 1952; LLB, 1954. Bar: Wash. 1954. Pros. atty., King County, Wash., 1955-57; individual practice law Seattle, 1957-59; ct. commr. King County Superior Ct., 1959-64, judge, 1964-69, Wash. State Ct. Appeals, 1969-71, Wash. State Supreme Ct., 1971-95, chief justice, 1979-81; ret., 1995; dean of faculty Ctrl. and Eastern European Legal Inst., Prague, Czech Republic, 2001—04, faculty, 2005—. Adj. prof. constl. law U. Puget Sound, 1987—94; cons. CEELI, 1991, 1993—, USIA, 1992; vis. scholar Kyrgystan Judiciary, Kazakhstan, 1993—96, Mongolia, 1997; commentator on Moldovan constitution, 2003; leader comparative law tours; participant internat. confs.; lectr. in field. Editor: books on real property and appellate practice; author: books on state consl. law. Pres., founder Big Brother Assn., Seattle, 1955—67, Job Therapy Inc., 1963—71; mem. exec. com. Conf. Chief Justices, 1979—80, 1981—86; pres. Thurston County Big Bros./Big Sisters, 1984; lectr Soviet Acad. Moscow, 1991; USIA visitor to comment on jud. sys. Latvia, 1992, Kazakhstan, 1993—94; trustee Linfield Coll. Recipient Henry Jackson Disting. Pub. Svc. award, Nat. Wash. Sch. Law, 2000, Warren E. Burger award, Nat. Ctr. for State Cts., 2003, Vol. award, ABA-CEELI Program, 2003; named Alumnus of the Yr., Linfield Coll., 1973, Judge of the Yr., Wash. State Trial Lawyers, 1989, Outstanding Judge, Wash. State Bar Assn., 1990, Seattle-King County Bar Assn., 1992, Outstanding Jurist, 2005, Conder-Faulkner lectr., U. Wash. Sch. Law, 1995, Disting. Alumnus, Sch. Law U. Wash., 1995; Disting. Jud. scholar, U. Ind., 1987. Fellow: Chartered Inst. Arbitrators; mem.: ABA (commentator on proposed constns. of Albania, Bulgaria, Romania, Russia, Lithuania, Azerbaijan, Uzbekistan, Byelarus, Kazakhstan, and Ukraine), Am. Judicature Soc. (sec. 1987—, chmn. bd. dirs., mem. exec. com., Herbert Harley award 1983, Justice award 1998), Order of Coif. Baptist. Personal E-mail: rutter4804@aol.com.

UTZ, SARAH WINIFRED, nursing educator; b. San Diego; d. Frederick R. and Margaret M. (Gibbons) U.; BS, U. Portland, 1943, EdM, 1958; MS, UCLA, 1970; PhD, U. So. Calif., 1979. Clin. instr. Providence Sch. Nursing, Portland, Oreg., 1946-50, edn. dir., 1950-62; edn. dir. Sacred Heart Sch. Nursing, Eugene, Oreg., 1963-67; asst. prof. nursing Calif. State U., L.A., 1969-74, assoc. prof., 1974-81, prof., 1981—, assoc. chmn. dept. nursing, 1982—; cons. in nursing curriculum, 1978—; healthcare cons., 1991—; past chmn. ednl. adminstrs., cons., tchrs. sect. Oreg. Nurses Assn., past pres. Oreg. State Bd. Nursing; mem. rsch. program Western Interstate Commn. on Higher Edn. in Nursing; chmn. liaison com. nursing edn. Articulation Coun. Calif. Author articles and lab manuals. Served with Nurse Corps, USN, 1944-46. HEW grantee, 1970-74, Kellogg Found. grantee, 1974-76, USDHHS grantee, 1987—; R.N., Calif., Oreg. Mem. Am. Nurses Assn., Calif. Nurses Assn. (edn. commr. region 6 1987—, chair edn. interest group region 6, 1987—), Am. Ednl. Rsch. Assn., AAUP, Phi Delta Kappa, Sigma Theta Tau. Formerly editor Oreg. Nurse; reviewer Western Jour. Nursing Rsch. Office: 5151 State University Dr Los Angeles CA 90032-4226

UVA, JOE, broadcast executive; b. 1956; BA, SUNY Albany. Account exec. for CNN Turner Broadcasting Sales, Inc., 1984, v.p. & sales mgr., 1985—90, exec. v.p. sales for CNN/Headline News, 1990—95, pres., Turner Entertainment Group Sales & Mktg., 1996—2001; pres. & CEO OMD Worldwide, NYC, 2002—07; CEO Univision Comm. Inc., 2007—. Bd. dirs. TiVo, Inc., 2004—. Office: Univision Communications Inc Ste 3050 1999 Ave of the Stars Los Angeles CA 90067 Office Phone: 310-556-7665.

UYEHARA, CATHERINE FAY TAKAKO (YAMAUCHI), physiologist, educator, pharmacologist; b. Honolulu, Dec. 20, 1959; d. Thomas Takashi and Eiko Uyehara; m. Alan Hisao Yamauchi, Feb. 17, 1990. BS, Yale U., 1981; PhD in Physiology, U. Hawaii, Honolulu, 1987. Postdoctoral fellow SmithKline Beecham Pharms., King of Prussia, Pa., 1987-89; rsch. pharmacologist Kapiolani Med. Ctr. for Women and Children, Honolulu, 1990-91, dep. chief rschr., 2004—07; chief, dept. clin. investigation, 2007—. Statis. cons. Tripler Army Med. Ctr., Honolulu, 1984-87, 89—, chief rsch. pharmacology, 1991—, dir. collaborative rsch. program, 1995—, dep. chief rsch., 2004-07, mem. grad. faculty in pharmacology, pediatrics, physiology, U. Hawaii John A. Burns Sch. Medicine, 1991—; grad. faculty Interdisciplinary Biomed. Sci. program, 1991—. Contbr. articles to profl. jours. Decorated Med. Merit Order Mil. Mem. Am. Fedn. for Med. Rsch., Am. Physiol. Soc., Am. Heart Assn., Soc. Uniformed Endocrinologists, Endocrine Soc., We. Soc. Pediatric Rsch., N.Y. Acad. Scis., Hawaii Acad. Sci., Sigma Xi. Democrat. Avocations: swimming, diving, crafts, horticulture, music. Office: Dept Clin Investigation 1 Jarrett White Rd Bldg 40 Tamc HI 96859 Office Phone: 808-433-6709.

UYEMOTO, JERRY KAZUMITSU, plant pathologist, educator; b. Fresno, Calif., May 27, 1939; married, 1965; 1 child. BS in Agronomy, U. Calif., Davis, 1962, MS in Plant Pathology, 1964, PhD in Plant Pathology, 1968. Lab. tech. U. Calif., Davis, 1964-66; from asst. to assoc. prof. virology N.Y. State Agrl. Expt. Sta., Cornell U., 1968-77; prof. Kansas State U., Manhattan, 1977-81; sr. staff scientist Advanced Genetic Scis., 1982-84; vis. scientist U. Calif., Davis, 1984-86, rsch. plant pathology, USDA Agrl. Rsch. Svc., 1986—. Recipient Lee M. Hutchins award Am. Phytopath. Soc., 1993. Mem. Assn. Applied Biologists, Am. Phytopath Soc. Achievements include research on a variety of crop plants; research contributions were also made on virus diseases of pome, stone fruit, and annual crop plants; ELISA protocols tested and/or established for serological indexing of ilarviruses in all Prunus tree sources used for scion buds and seeds. Office: UC Davis Dept Plant Path USDA ARS Davis CA 95616

VAAD, GLENN, state legislator; Mem. Dist. 48 Colo. House of Reps., Denver, 2007—. Republican. Office: Colo State Capitol 200 E Colfax Denver CO 80203 Office Phone: 303-866-2943. Business E-Mail: glenn.vaad.house@state.co.us.*

VACANO, JOST, cinematographer; Cinematographer Skouras Agy., Santa Monica, Calif., 1977—. Cinematographer: (films) Soldier of Orange, 1977, Spetters, 1980, Das Boot, 1981, The Neverending Story, 1984, 52 Pick-up, 1986, Robocop, 1987, Rocket Gibraltar, 1988, Total Recall, 1990, Untamed Heart, 1993, Showgirls, 1995, Starship Troopers, 1997, The Hollow Man, 1999.

VACQUIER, VICTOR DIMITRI, biology educator; b. Pitts., July 20, 1940; s. Victor and Vera (Vinogradoff) V.; m. Judith Ellen Payne, July 1, 1973; children: Paul Andre, Marc Christian. AB, San Diego State U., 1963; PhD, U. Calif., Berkeley, 1968. Rsch. asst. U. Calif., Berkeley, 1963-68; rschr. Internat. Lab. Genetics & Biophys., Naples, Italy, 1968-69, Hopkins Marine Sta., Stanford U., Pacific Grove, Calif., 1970-71; asst. rsch. biologist Scripps Inst. Oceanography, U. Calif., La Jolla, 1971-73, assoc. prof. biology, 1978-80, prof., 1980—. Asst. prof. zoology U. Calif.-Davis, 1973-75, assoc. prof., 1975-78. Assoc. editor Gamete Rsch., 1980—, Devel. Biology, 1983—. Mem. Am. Soc. Cell Biology, Soc. Devel. Biology, Internat. Soc. Devel. Biology. Office: U Calif Scripps Instn Oceanography Marine Biology Rsch Divsn La Jolla CA 92093-0202

VAIL, CHARLES DANIEL, veterinarian, consultant; b. Denver, June 11, 1936; s. Allan Paden and Katherine Marie (Phillips) V.; m. Jean Williams Ebsen, June 15, 1963; children: Ellen Marie, David Elston. BS, Colorado A&M, 1958; DVM, Colo. State. U., 1960. Asst. veterinarian Colo. Racing Commn., Littleton, 1958-60; equine practitioner Littleton Large Animal Clinic, 1960—; track veterinarian Centennial Race Track, Littleton, 1962-63. Commr. Colo. Racing Commn., 2007—. Editor-in-chief: Equine Practice, 1986—2000; contbr. articles to profl. jours. Mem. selection com. Outstanding Biology Tchr. award Colo., 1978-80, 88—, Arapahoe Fair Assn., Littleton, 1965-84, gallery disting. grads. Colo. State U. Coll. Vet. Medicine, 1989; chmn. Littleton Rotary Western Heritage Art Fair; bd. dirs. Animal Assistance Found. Denver, 1991-2004, v.p., 1995-96, pres., 1996-97, Western Vet. Conf., 1997-2000, v.p., 2001, pres. elect, 2002, pres., 2003, Friends Littleton Pub. Libr./Mus., 2000-04, Rocky Mountain Stroke Assn., Araphoe C.C. Found., 2004—; mem. devel. coun. Colo. State U., 2002-06; examiner, Clin. Practitionary, 2007-Recipient Honor Alumni award, Coll. Vet. Medicine, Colo. State U., 1991, Meritorious Svc. award, Western Vet. Conf., 2008. Mem. AVMA (publs. com. 1981-87, clin. proficiency examination faculty 2005—), Am. Assn. Equine Practitioners (pres. 1985, dist. life mem.), Colo. Vet. Medicine Assn. (pres. 1980, Veterinarian of Yr. award 1987), Denver Area Vet. Medicine Soc. (pres. 1975), Arapahoe Town and Gown Soc. (v.p. 1999, pres. 2000), Colo. State U. Alumni Assn. (pres. 2001-02), Nottingham Club, Rotary (pres. Littleton 1992-93), Sigma Alpha Epsilon, Omicron Delta Kappa. Home: 5921 S Cherrywood Cir Littleton CO 80121-2465 Office: Littleton Large Animal Clinic 8025 S Santa Fe Dr Littleton CO 80120-4305 Office Phone: 303-794-6359. Office Fax: 303-794-9466. Personal E-mail: cdvm1@yahoo.com.

VAIL, THOMAS PARKER, orthopaedic surgeon; m. Lisa Ann Giannetto. MD, Loyola U., 1985. Diplomate Am. Bd. Orthopaedic Surgery. Prof. orthop. surgery Duke U. Med. Ctr., Durham, NC, 1992—2007; prof. and dept. chmn. orthop. surgery U. Calif., San Francisco, 2007—. Dir. adult reconstructive surgery Duke U. Med. Ctr., Durham. Office: Univ Calif San Francisco MU 320W 500 Parnassus Ave San Francisco CA 94143-0728

VAILAS, ARTHUR C., biomechanics educator; m. Laura Vailas. BS in Exercise Physiology, U. N.H., 1973; PhD in Exercise Physiology, U. Iowa, 1979, postgrad. in Biochem., 1979-82. Asst. prof. dept. kinesiology UCLA, 1982-88, assoc. prof., 1988, U. Wis., Madison, 1988-91, prof., 1991-95, dir. biodynamics lab., 1988-95; vice provost for rsch. and grad. studies U. Houston, 1995, prof., disting. chair biology and biochemistry, 1995, v.p., chancellor, rsch. and intellectual property mgmt., 1998—, prof., mech. engring., Coll. Engring, 2002—, prof., biology and biochemistry, Coll. Natural Sciences and Math., 2002—; vice chancellor U. Houston System; pres. Idaho State U., Pocatello, Idaho, 2006—. Session chair Gordon Rsch. Conf.; mem. life sci. adv. com. NASA, life sci. del. to COSMOS 1887, 2044 Missions; com. chair Musculoskeletal Implementation Group EDO and Countermeasure Sci. Plan; SLS-1 scientist. Contbr. 60 articles to profl. jours. Recipient Rsch. Svc. award NIH, Outstanding Sci. award USSR-NASA; named Disting. Scientist, CSU. Mem. Nat. Rsch. Coun. (mem. NASA com.). Office: Idaho State University Adminstrn Bldg 921 S 8th Ave STOP 8310 Pocatello ID 83209 Office Phone: 208-282-3440. Office Fax: 208-282-4487.

VAILLANT, JEAN-LUC, Internet company executive; Grad., Ecole Nationale Superieure des Telecommunications. Rsch. project leader CNET - France Telecom Rsch., 1992—95; dir. server develop. Sophis, 1995—96; engring. mgr. Fujitsu, 1996—98; dir. tech. Socialnet.com, 1998—2001; dir. software develop. Spotlife Inc., 2001—02; dir. engring. video services Logitech, 2002—03; co-founder LinkedIn Corp., Mountain View, Calif., 2003, v.p. engring., 2003—07, CTO, 2007—. Office: LinkedIn Corp 2029 Stierlin Ct Mountain View CA 94043

VALDEZ, JEFF, broadcast executive, television producer; b. Pueblo, Colo., 1956; married; 2 children. Mobile home maker, janitor, drill bit factory worker, Colo. Springs; owner, stand-up comedian Comedy Corner, Colo. Springs; stand-up comedian, TV writer LA; exec. position Tri-Star TV; founder, chmn. Sí TV, LA, 2004—. Creator Latino Laugh Festival, San Antonio, 1996; apptd. by Pres. Clinton to adv. com. arts John F. Kennedy Ctr. Performing Arts; bd. trustees Am. Mus. Moving Image, 2000. Musician (drummer): Wildfire; prodr.: (TV series) Comedy Compadres, 1993—94, (TV Special) Latino Laugh Festival, 1997; prodr., writer: (TV series) Cafe Ole' with Giselle Fernandez, 1997; Funny is Funny, 1997; exec. prodr.: The Brothers Garcia, 2000, Urban Jungle, 2004, Latino Laugh Festival: The Show, 2004, The Rub, 2004, The Drop, 2004, Across the Hall, 2004, Breakfast, Lunch and Dinner, 2004, Urban Jungle 2: South Ctrl., 2005. Recipient Am. Latino Media Arts award, 1998, Hispanic Achievement award, Hispanic Mag., 1998, Vision award, Latino Entertainment Media Inst., 2000; named one of 100 Most Influential Hispanics, Hispanic Bus., 36 Faces to Watch, LA Times, 1997, 50 Who Matter Now, CNNMoney.com Bus. 2.0, 2006. Office: Sí TV 3030 Andrita St Bldg D Los Angeles CA 90065

VALDEZ, JOSH, health insurance company executive; A, CC AF; BS, Nat. U. Sacramento; MBA, Golden State U.; D in Bus. Adminstn., So. Calif. U. V.p. managed care AltaMed Health Svcs., Calif.; CFO, exec. dir. West Covina Med. Clinic, Eastland Med. Group, Combined Mgmt. Svcs.; regional dir. Fed. Dept. Health and Human Svcs., 2001—04; sr. v.p. Blue Cross Blue Shield, 2004—. Health care adminstr. USAF. Named Man of Yr., Hollenbeck Youth Ctr./Inner-City Games LA, 2005; named one of Top 10 Latinos in Healthcare, LatinoLeaders mag., 2004. Office: Blue Cross Calif 1 WellPoint Way Thousand Oaks CA 91362-5035

VALE, WYLIE W., biochemist; BS, Rice U., 1964; PhD in Physiology & Biochemistry, Baylor U., 1968. Biochemist The Salk Inst., La Jolla, Calif., 1970-78, Clayton Found. Lab. Peptide Biology br. The Salk Inst., La Jolla, 1978—; Helen McLoraine prof. molecular neurobiology Salk Inst. Biol. Studies, pres. Clayton Found. Labs. for Peptide Biology, chmn. faculty; academic co-founder, chief scientific advisor Neurocrine Biosciences, Inc., San Diego, 1992—. Bd. trustees Salk Inst. Biol. Studies; founding bd. scientific & med. advisors Neurocrine Biosciences, Inc., San Diego, 1992—, bd. dirs, 1992; adj. prof. U. Calif. San Diego; elected mem. Inst. of Medicine, 2000. Recipient Fred Conrad Koch award Endocrine Soc., 1997. Mem.: Internat. Soc. Endocrinology (former pres.), Am. Endocrine Soc. (former pres., Fred Conrad Koch award 1997), Inst. Medicine, AAAS, NAS. Office: Salk Inst Biological Sciences PO Box 85800 San Diego CA 92186-5800 also: Neurocrine Biosciences Inc 12790 El Camino Real San Diego CA 92130 E-mail: vale@salk.edu.

VALENTINE, DEAN, film producer; AB, U. Chicago, 1976. Pres. Walt Disney TV/Touchstone TV; pres., CEO United Paramount Network, Los Angeles, 1997—2002; with Europlay Capital Advisors, LLC, 2002—03; pres. First Family Entertainment, Beverly Hills, 2004. Named one of Top 200 Collectors, ARTnews Mag., 2004—08. Avocation: Collector of Comtemporary Art. Office: Dean Valentine 3212 Nebraska Ave Santa Monica CA 90404-4214

VALENTINE, JAMES WILLIAM, paleontologist, educator, writer; b. LA, Nov. 10, 1926; s. Adelbert Cuthbert and Isabel (Davis) V.; m. Grace Evelyn Whysner, Dec. 21, 1957 (div. 1972); children: Anita, Ian; m. Cathryn Alice Campbell, Sept. 10, 1978 (div. 1986); 1 child, Geoffrey; m. Diane Mondragon, Mar. 16, 1987. BA, Phillips U., 1951; MA, UCLA, 1954, PhD, 1958. From asst. prof. to assoc. prof. U. Mo., Columbia, 1958-64; from assoc. prof. to prof. U. Calif., Davis, 1964-77, prof. geol. scis. Santa Barbara, 1977-90, prof. integrative biology Berkeley, 1990-93, prof. emeritus, 1993—. Author: Evolutionary Paleoecology of the Marine Biosphere, 1973, On the Origin of Phyla, 2004; editor: Phanerozoic Diversity, 1985; co-author: Evolution, 1977, Evolving, 1979; contbr. articles to profl. jours. Served with USNR, 1944-46, PTO. Recipient Lapworth medal Palaeontological Assn., 2004; Fulbright rsch. scholar, Australia, 1962-63; Guggenheim fellow Yale U., Oxford U., Eng., 1968-69; Rockefeller Found. scholar in residence, Bellagio, Italy, summer 1974; grantee NSF, NASA. Fellow: AAAS, Paleontol. Soc. (medal 1996), Geol. Soc. Am., Am. Acad. Arts and Scis.; mem.: NAS. Avocation: collecting works of Charles Darwin. Home: 1351 Glendale Ave Berkeley CA 94708-2025 Office: U Calif Dept Integrative Biology Berkeley CA 94720-0001 Office Phone: 510-643-5791. Business E-Mail: jwvsossi@socrates.berkeley.edu.

VALENTINE, JOHN LESTER, state legislator, lawyer; b. Fullerton, Calif., Apr. 26, 1949; s. Robert and Pauline; m. Karen Valentine; 6 children. BS in Acctg. and Econs., Brigham Young U., 1973, JD, 1976. CPA; bar: Utah 1976, US Dist. Ct. Utah, US Ct. Appeals (10th cir.), US Tax Ct., US Supreme Ct. 2002. Atty. Howard, Lewis & Petersen, Provo, Utah, 1976—; mem. Dist. 14 Utah House of Reps., 1988—99, asst. majority whip, 1997—98; mem. Dist. 14 Utah State Senate, 1998—, pres. Instr. probate and estates Utah Valley State Coll.; instr. fin. planning., adj. prof. law Brigham Young U.; chmn. revenue and taxation com. Utah Senate, 1999-2000, vice chmn. exec. appropriations com., judiciary com., pub. edn. subcom., majority whip 2001—; mem. exec offices, cts., corrections and legis. appropriations subcom., Utah House of Reps., 1988-90, capital facilities subcom., 1988-90, retirement com., 1988-90, judiciary com., 1988-92, strategic planning steering com., 1988-90, interim appropriations com., 1988-94, tax. review commn., 1989-98, ethics com., 1990-92, human svcs. and health appropriations subcom., 1990-92, revenue and taxation com., 1988-98, vice chmn. 1990-92; vice chmn. exec. appropriations., 1990-92; chmn. exec. appropriations com., 1992-94, chmn. rules com., 1994-96, higher edn. appropriations com. 1994-96. Mem. adv. bd. Internat. Sr. Games, 1988—; active Blue Ribbon Task Force on Local Govt. Funding, Utah League Cities and Towns, 1990-94, Criminal Sentencing Guidelines Task Force, Utah Judicial Coun., 1990-92, Access to Health Care Task Force, 1990-92, Utah County Sheriff Search and Rescue, Orem Met. Water Bd., Alpine Sch. Dist. Boundary Line Com., 1986-90, Boy Scouts Am.; bd. regents Legis. Adv. Com. UVCC.; mem. exec. bd. Utah Nat. Parks Coun.; mem. adv. coun. Orchard Elem. Sch., Mountainlands Com. an Aging; bd. trustees Utah Opera Co.; judge nat. and local competitions Moot Ct.; voting dist. chmn.; state, county del.; lt. incident command sys. Utah County Sheriff. Recipient Silver Beaver award Boy Scouts Am., Taxpayer Advocate award Utah Taxpayer Assn. Mem. ABA (tax sect.), Utah State Bar, CPA Com., Tax Sect. Specialization Com., Bicentennial Com. Republican. Mem. Lds Ch. Avocation: mountain climbing. Office: Howard Lewis & Petersen 120 E 300 N Provo UT 84606-2907 also: W115 Capitol Complex Salt Lake City UT 84114 Office Phone: 801-373-6345, 801-538-1035. Office Fax: 301-326-1475. Business E-Mail: jvalentine@utahsenate.org.*

VALENTINE, MARK CONRAD, dermatologist; b. Parkersburg, W.Va., Sept. 26, 1948; s. Sestel and Margaret Elaine (Sabolo) V.; m. Elizabeth Michelle Monezis, Apr. 21, 1975; children: Perry Martin, Owen Mark. BA, W.Va. U., 1970; MD, Johns Hopkins U., 1974. Intern, resident U. Hosps. Cleve., 1974-76, resident, 1976-79; dermatologist pvt. practice, Everett, Wash., 1979—. Clin. prof. U. Wash., Seattle, 1979—; active med. staff Providence Everett Gen. Med. Ctr., 1979—. Edit. bd. Jour. of Am. Acad. Dermatology, 1998—2005. Bd. dirs., sec. City Libr. Bd., Mukilteo, Wash., 1994-99; bd. dirs., v.p. Everett Symphony Bd., 1982-85, 2001—2006; bd. dirs. Book Arts Guild, Seattle, 1988-90. Nat. Merit scholar, 1966. Mem. AMA, Am. Acad. Dermatology (adv. coun. 1983-86), Wash. State Dermatol. Assn. (pres.-elect 1996, pres. 1996-97), Seattle Dermatology Soc. (pres. 1985-86), Snohomish County Med. Soc. (bd. dirs. 2001—, pres. 2006), Rotary (Everett), Phi Beta Kappa. Avocations: book collecting, book binding, guitar, piano. Office: 3327 Colby Ave Everett WA 98201-6403 Home Phone: 425-348-6256; Office Phone: 425-258-6767. Personal E-mail: mark1105@aol.com.

VALENTINE-SIBERT, KIMBERLY A., lawyer; b. Lakewood, Calif., Aug. 13, 1967; BA, Golden West Coll.; JD, Western State Univ., 1997. Bar: Calif. 1998, Ariz. Ptnr., elder abuse & malpractice litigation Barbaro & Valentine, Santa Ana, Calif. Named a Rising Star, So. Calif. Super Lawyers, 2006. Mem.: Assn. Trial Lawyers Am., Orange County Trial Lawyers Assn., Consumer Attorneys Calif. Office: Barbaro & Valentine 2d Fl 200 N Main St Santa Ana CA 92701 Office Phone: 714-835-2122. Office Fax: 714-973-4892.

VALERIO BARRAD, CATHERINE M., lawyer; BA, U. Calif., San Diego, 1982; MBA, UCLA, 1984; JD magna cum laude, Northwestern U., 1993. Ba: Calif. 1993, U.S. Ct. Appeals (9th cir.) 1994. Law clk. to Hon. Douglas H. Ginsburg, U.S. Dt. Appeals for D.C. Circuit, Washington, 1993-94; assoc. Sidley & Austin, LA, 1994—. Contbg. author: Federal Appellate Practice Guide, Ninth Circuit, 1994; articles editor Northwestern U. Law Rev., 1992-93; contbr. articles to legal publs. Mem. Order of Coif. Office: Sidley & Austin 555 W 5th St Los Angeles CA 90013-1010 Fax: 213-896-6688. E-mail: cbarrad@sidley.com.

VALLEE, ROY A., electronics executive; b. Southbridge, Mass. married; 2 children. AS in Electronics Tech., Don Bosco Tech. Inst., 1971. Electronics tech. radio products Don Bosco Tech. Inst., 1971—77; field sales rep. Avnet, Inc., Great Neck, NY, 1977, systems bus. mgr. to gen. sales mgr. to gen. mgr. to regional dir. to v.p., pres. Hamilton/Avnet Computer, 1989—90, sr. v.p., dir. worldwide electronics ops., 1990—92, bd. dirs. Phoenix, 1991—, pres., COO, 1992—98, chmn., CEO Phoenix, 1998—. Bd. dirs. Teradyne, Synopsys, Inc.; mem. exec. com. Global Tech. Distbn. Coun. Mem. Govs. Coun. of Innovation and Tech. Named one of Hot 25 Execs., Electronic Buyer's News, 1997, 1999, 2000; named to CRN Industry Hall of Fame, 2007. Office: Avnet Inc 2211 S 47th St Phoenix AZ 85034-6403 Office Phone: 480-643-2000.

VALLERGA, BERNARD A., engineering administrator; BS, U. Calif. Berkeley, 1943, MS, 1948. Materials testing engr. Hershey Inspection Bur., Oakland, Calif., 1946-48; asst. prof. civil engring. U. Calif. Berkeley, 1948-53; mng. engr. Pacific Coast Divsn. Asphalt Inst., San Francisco, 1953-60; v.p. prodn. devel. & mktg. GBO Divsn. Witco Chem. Co., LA, 1960-64; pres. & CEO Material Rsch. & Devel., Inc., Oakland, 1964-72; v.p., mng. prin. Woodward-Clyde Consults, San Francisco-Oakland, 1968-76; pres. B.A. Vallerga, Inc. Consulting Civil Engring., Oakland, 1977—. Chmn. Triaxial Inst. Structural Design Pavements, 1950-52; bd. dirs. Woodward-Clyde Consultants, 1980-82; mem. bd. dirs., v.p. Asphalt Inst., 1962-64; v.p. Design Divsn., Am. Road Builders Assn., 1968-70; chmn. bd. dirs. Woodward Envicon, 1969-72, Subcom. Asphalt Durability, Transp. Rsch. Bd., 1980—; gen. cons. Off Energy Related Inventions, Bur. Stds., Dept. Com., 1980—. Fellow ASCE (mem. Airfield Pavement Com. 1972-79); mem. ASTM (Provost Hubbard award 1989), Internat. Soc. Asphalt Pavements, Assn. Asphalt Paving Technologists (mem. bd. dirs. 1960-62, Recognition award 1988), Nat. Acad. Engring., Sigma Xi. Office: 5881 Balmoral Dr Oakland CA 94619-2438

VALLES, JUDITH, president, former mayor, retired academic administrator; b. San Bernardino, Calif., Dec. 14, 1933; d. Gonzalo and Jovita (Lopez-Torices) V.; m. Chad Bradbury, Sept. 30, 1956 (dec. Sept. 1969); children: Edith Renella, Nohemi Renella, Chad; m. Harry Carl Smith, Oct. 13, 1985. BA in English, Redlands U., Calif., 1956; MA in Spanish Lit., U. Calif., Riverside, 1966; doctorate (hon.), U. Redlands, 2000. Instr. Spanish San Bernardino Valley Coll., Calif., 1963-84, head dept. fgn. lang., 1971-76, chair div. humanities, 1976-81, dean extended day, 1981-83, adminstrv. dean acad. affairs, 1983-87, exec. v.p. acad. and student affairs, 1987-88; pres. Golden West CC, Huntington Beach, Calif., 1988—95; mayor City of San Bernardino, 1998—2006; pres. LA Mission Coll. Mem. adv. com. Police Officers Standards and Tng. Commn., Sacramento, 1991—. Author fgn. lang. annals and sociol. abstracts. Speaker statewide edn. and community orgns., 1988—; bd. dirs. exec. coun. and chief exec. officers Calif. Community Colls., 1990—. Recipient Bishops award for diocese, Outstanding Pub. Svc. award NALEO, 2001; named One of Outstanding Women Orange County YWCA, 1990, Citizen of Achievement LWV, 1989, Woman of Distinction Bus. Press, 1998, Influential Latina of the Yr. Hispanic Lifestyle, 1998, State of Calif. Woman of the Yr., 1999, Humanitarian Yr. Cath. charities, 1999, Citizen Yr. Boy Scouts Am., 1999, Empire Woman Yr. State Assembly, 1999, Outstanding Cmty. Leader, Cmty. Found., 2002, Woman of Yr., State Senate, 2003; inducted into Hall of Fame, San Bernardino Valley Coll. Mem. Women's Roundtable Orange County, Conf. and Visitors Bur., C. of C. (Vanguard), Kiwanis, Charter 100. Avocations: opera, theater, reading, running.

VALONE, KEITH EMERSON, psychologist, psychoanalyst; b. Austin, Tex., Aug. 3, 1953; s. James Floyd and Elizabeth Niles (Emerson) V.; m. Leona Marie Lagace, July 22, 1978; children: Kyle Stephen James, Christienne Marie. BA, U. So. Calif., 1975; MA, U. Ill., 1979, PhD, 1981; PsyD, Inst. Contemporary Psychoanaly, LA, 1995. Lic. psychologist, Calif. Pvt. practice, Pasadena, Calif., 1983—; chief psychology svc. Las Encinas Hosp., Pasadena, 1988; dir. psychology Ingleside Hosp., Rosemead, Calif., 1990-92. Clin. asst. prof. dept. psychology Fuller Theol. Sem., Pasadena, Calif., 1984—85; asst. clin. prof. dept. psychology UCLA, 1984—87; clin. asst. prof. psychiatry and behavioral scis. U. So. Calif. Keck Sch. Medicine, LA, 2006—. Contbr. articles to profl. jours. Mem. APA, Calif. State Psychol. Assn., Phi Beta Kappa. Episcopalian. Office: Ste 321 One W California Blvd Pasadena CA 91105 Office Phone: 626-405-9066. Personal E-mail: kev@valone.com.

VAN ALFEN, NEAL K., plant pathologist; b. Ogden, Utah, July 17, 1943; s. Gerrit Johan and Marguerite (Noorda) Van A. BS, Brigham Young U., 1968, MS, 1969; PhD, U. Calif., Davis, 1972. Asst. plant pathologist Conn. Agr. Exp. Sta., New Haven, Conn., 1972-75; asst. prof. biology Utah State U., Logan, 1975-78, extension plant pathologist, 1975-78, assoc. prof. of biology, 1978-82, prof. of biology and molecular biology/biochem., 1982-90; prof. and head/dept. of plant pathology/microbiology Tex. A&M U., College Station, Tex., 1990-99; dean agrl. and environ. scis. U. Calif., Davis, 1999—. Fellow AAAS, Am. Phytopathol. Soc.; mem. Am. Phytopathol. Soc. (councilor-at-large 1994-97, v.p., pres. 1997-2000), Am. Soc. for Microbiology. Office: U Calif-Davis Coll Agrl and Environ Scis 1 Shields Ave Davis CA 95616-5270 Home Phone: 530-661-2298; Office Phone: 530-752-1605, 530-661-2298. Business E-Mail: nkvanalfen@ucdavis.edu.

VAN ARSDALE, DICK, professional basketball team executive; b. Indpls., Feb. 22, 1943; m. Barbara V.; children: Jill, Jason. AB in economics, Indiana U., 1965. Player New York Knicks (Nat. Basketball Assn.), NYC, 1965-68; with Phoenix Suns, Phoenix, Ariz., 1968-77, color commentator, TV broadcasts, from 1977, interim mgr., 1987, v.p., player personnel, dir. player personnel. Named "Mr. Basketball" of Indiana during high school, NCAA All-American, Indiana U. Office: c/o Phoenix Suns 201 E Jefferson St Phoenix AZ 85004-2412

VAN BRUNT, GARY T., tire dealer company executive; Asst mgr. to mgr., 2d Phoenix store Discount Tire Co. Inc., Scottsdale, Ariz., 1970—77, asst. v.p. Ariz. region, 1977—80, v.p. purchasing, We. region, 1980—85, sr. v.p. purchasing, all regions, 1985—97, exec. v.p. co. ops., 1997—99, CEO, 1999—2004, vice chmn., 2004—. Office: Discount Tire Co Inc 20225 N Scottsdale Rd Scottsdale AZ 85255

VAN BUREN, ABIGAIL (JEANNE PHILLIPS), columnist, educator; b. Mpls., Apr. 10, 1942; d. Morton and Pauline (Friedman) Phillips, (the founder of the Dear Abby advice column in 1956). Student, U. Colo., 1960—62. Writer Dear Abby Radio Show, CBS, 1965—71; columnist Dear Abby, 1987—. Bd. mem. Planned Parenthood of Los Angeles, 1989—90; life-time cons. Group for Advancement of Psychiatry, 1995—; bd. adv. Alzheimers Assn. of Los Angeles, 1996—; bd. mem. Rose and Jay Phillips Found., 1991—, ACLU of So. Calif. Found., 1998—; adv. bd. L.A. Internat. Women's Media Found. Courage in Journalism, 2000—; bd. adv. UCLA Med. Ctr., Ctr. for Rsch. and Training in Humane and Ethical Med. Care (CHEC), 2000—. Bd. advs. Planned Parenthood Fedn. Am., 2004; bd. judges Talbot's Charitable Found. Women's Scholarship Fund, 2006—; mem. White House Commn. Rememberance; bd. dirs. Planned Parenthood of LA, 1989—90, MADD, 2003—, Children's Rights Coun., 2003—; mem. Leadership Coun. Aids Project, LA, 2004; bd. dirs. Nat. Kidney Found., 2004. Recipient Generations of Choice award, Planned Parenthood of L.A., 1999, Minority Organ/Tissue Transplant Edn. Program (MOTTEP) Key of Life award, Howard U., Wash. DC, 2000, award of appreciation, US Gen. Svcs. Adminstrn. Fed. Consumer Info. Ctr., 2000, Star on Hollywood Walk of Fame for Dear Abby Radio Show, 2001, Recognition by the Office of Nat. Drug Control Policy (ONDCP), award from the White House and Substance Abuse and Mental Health Svcs. Adminstrn. for help in launching Nat. Inhalants and Poisons Awareness Week, 2001, Erasing the Stigma Leadership award, Didi Hirsch Mental Health Ctr., 2001, MOTTEP Award of Excellence, 2001, Commendation for Operation Dear Abby and OperationDearAbby.net, Dept. Navy and USMC, 2002, Appreciation for support of the military svc. mems. of the U.S. for Operation Dear Abby and OperationDearAbby.net, Space and Naval Warfare Sys. Ctr. (SPAWAR), 2002, Alzheimer's Assn. Maureen Reagan Advocacy Award, 2003, Appreciation award, Overeaters Anonymous, 2003, Advocacy award, Alzheimer's Assn. L.A., 2003, award of appreciation, US GSA Fed. Citizen Info. Ctr., 2004, Woman of the Yr., Muses, 2007, Straight for Equality award, Parents, Families, Friends of Lesbians Gays, 2007. Mem.: Nat. Adv. Coun. of Alzheimers Assn. Syndicated in the US, Brazil, Mex., Japan, Philippines, Fed. Republic Germany, India, Holland, Denmark, Can., Korea, Thailand, Italy, Hong Kong, Taiwan, Ireland, Saudi Arabia, Greece, France, Dominican Republic, P.R., Costa Rica, US Virgin Islands, Bermuda, China, Kuwait and Guam; published on the Internet at DearAbby.com and OperationDearAbby.net for messages to the military. Office: Phillips-Van Buren Inc 1880 Century Park E Ste 1400 Los Angeles CA 90067

VAN BUSKIRK, RONALD E., lawyer; b. Santa Fe, N. Mex., Oct. 19, 1946; BA, Stanford Univ., 1968; JD, Univ. Mich., 1974. Bar: Calif. 1975, US Dist. Ct. (ea., no., ctrl., so. dist. Calif.), US Ct. Claims, US Ct. Appeals (9th cir.). Assoc. to ptnr. Pillsbury Winthrop Shaw Pittman, San Francisco, 1975—, gen. counsel, chmn. Profl. Responsibility com. Founding mem. Law Firm Gen. Counsel Roundtable; bd. dir. Pacific Legal Found., 1994—, MPC Insurance Ltd., 1995—. Served US Army, 1968—71. Office: Pillsbury Winthrop Shaw Pittman 50 Fremont St San Francisco CA 94105 Office Phone: 415-983-1496. Office Fax: 415-983-1200. Business E-Mail: ronald.vanbuskirk@pillsburylaw.com.

VAN CAMP, BRIAN RALPH, judge; b. Halstead, Kans., Aug. 23, 1940; s. Ralph A. and Mary Margaret (Bragg) Van C.; m. Diane D. Miller, 1992; children: M. Megan, Laurie E. AB, U. Calif., Berkeley, 1962, LLB, 1965. Bar: Calif. 1966. Dep. atty. gen., Calif., 1965-67; agy. atty. Redevel. Agy., City of Sacramento, 1967-70; asst./acting sec. Bus. and Trans. Agy., State of Calif., 1970-71; commr. of corps. State of Calif., Sacramento, 1971-74; partner firm Diepenbrock, Wulff, Plant & Hannegan, Sacramento, 1975-77, Van Camp & Johnson, Sacramento, 1978-90; sr. ptnr. Downey, Brand, Seymour & Rohwer, 1990-97; judge Superior Ct. Calif., Sacramento County, 1997—. Lectr. Calif. Continuing Edn. Bar, Practicing Law Inst., Calif. CPA Soc., Calif. Ctr. for Jud. Edn. and Rsch.; mem. jud. adv. bd. Am. Enterprise Inst./Brookings Jud. Edn. Program, 2007—. Contbr. articles to profl. jours. Mem. Rep. State Ctrl. Com. Calif., 1974-78; mem. electoral coll. Presdl. Elector for State of Calif., 1976; mem. Calif. Health Facilities Fin. Authority, 1985-89; mem. Capital Area Devel. Authority, 1989-97, chmn., 1990-97; mem. Calif. Jud. Coun. Task Force on Quality of Justice, 1998-99, Jud. Coun. Adv. Com. on Civil and Small Claims Law, 2002—, chair subcom. uniform rules, 2004-; bd. dirs. Sacramento Symphony Assn., 1973-85, Sacramento Symphony Found., 1993-2003, Sacramento Area Commerce and Trade Orgn., pres. 1986-87, Sacramento Valley Venture Capital Forum, 1986-90, League to Save Lake Tahoe, 1988-95, Valley Vision, Inc., 1993-97; elder Fremont Presbyn. Ch., 1967-. Recipient Sumner-Mering Meml. award Sacramento U. Calif. Alumni Assn., 1962, Thos. Jefferson award Am. Inst. Pub. Svc., 1994, Excellence in Achievement award Calif. Alumni Assn., 1997; named Outstanding Young Man of Yr., Sacramento Jaycees, 1970, Internat. Young Man of Yr., Active 20-30 Club Internat., 1973, Judge of Yr., Capitol City Trial Lawyers Assn., 2003. Mem. Am. Coll. Bus. Ct. Judges (charter), Boalt Hall Alumni Assn. (bd. dirs. 1991-94), Lincoln Club Sacramento Valley (bd. dirs. 1975-90, pres. 1984-86), U Calif Men's Club (pres. 1968), Sutter Club, Kanadhar Ski Club, Rotary Club Sacramento (pres. 1993-94, Paul Harris Fellow award 1995), Comstock Club (pres. 1976-77). Republican. Presbyterian. Office: 720 9th St Sacramento CA 95814-1302 Office Phone: 916-874-8030. Business E-Mail: vancamp@saccourt.com.

VANCE, GORDON J., state legislator; b. Great Falls, Mont., Dec. 17, 1951; m. Shelley Vance. BA, Mont. State U., 1975. Sales mgr. Bozeman Ford, 1976—84, Team Bozeman, 1995—97; owner car store, 1984—94; gen. mgr. Power Play Motorsports, 1997—2005; mem. Dist. 67 Mont. House of Reps., 2008—. Republican. Office:

Montana House of Representatives PO Box 200400 Helena MT 59620-0400 Mailing: 305 Stillwater Ave Bozeman MT 59718-1917 Home Phone: 406-587-8608; Office Phone: 406-444-4800. Office Fax: 406-444-4825. Personal E-mail: vancehd67@gmail.com.

VAN DAM, HEIMAN, psychoanalyst; b. Leiden, Netherlands; s. Machiel and Rika van D.; m. Barbara C. Strona, Oct. 6, 1945; children: Machiel, Claire Ilena, Rika Rosemary. AB, U. So. Calif., 1942, MD, 1945. Fellow in child psychiatry Pasadena (Calif.) Child Guidance Clinic, 1950; gen. practice psychiatry and psychoanalysis LA, 1951—2006; instr. L.A. Psychoanalytic Inst., LA, 1959—2000, co-chmn. com. on child psychoanalysis, 1960-67, tng. and supervising psychoanalyst, 1972—; supr. child and adolescent psychoanalysis So. Calif. Psychoanalytic Inst., 1986—. Cons. Reiss Davis Child Study Center, 1955-76, Neighborhood Youth Assn., LA, 1964-69; assoc. clin. prof. psychiatry and pediats. UCLA Sch. Medicine, 1960-96, clin. prof. psychiatry and pediats., 1996—; vis. supr. child psychoanalysis San Francisco Psychoanalytic Inst., 1969-79, 2002—, Denver Psychoanalytic Inst., 1972-74; adv. bd. Western State U. Coll. Law, Fullerton, Calif., 1965-83. Corr. editor Arbeits Hefte Kinderanalyse, 1985—2005; contbr. articles to profl. jours. Trustee, edn. com. Center for Early Edn., 1964-92, v.p., 1978-79; bd. dirs. Child Devel. and Psychotherapy Tng. Program, LA, 1975-80, pres., 1975-77; bd. dirs. LA Child Devel. Center, 1977-86, treas., 1978-80; mem. cult clinic Jewish Family Service, L.A., 1978-86; bd. dirs. Lake Arrowhead Crest Estates, 1990-99. Capt. M.C. AUS, 1946-48. Mem. Am. Psychoanalytic Assn. (com. on ethics 1977-80), Assn. Child Psychoanalysis (councillor 1966-69, sec. 1972-74, nominating com. 1978-84, membership com. 1988—2005, Marianne Kris lectr. 1995), Internat. Assn. Infant Psychiatry (co-chmn. program com. 1980-83), Internat. Soc. Adolescent Psychiatry (sci. adv. com. 1988-2004), Phi Beta Kappa. Office: 2864 McConnell Dr Los Angeles CA 90064-4658

VANDAMENT, WILLIAM EUGENE, retired academic administrator; b. Hannibal, Mo., Sept. 6, 1931; s. Alva E. and Ruth Alice (Mahood) V.; m. Margery Vandament, Feb. 2, 1952; children: Jane Louise, Lisa Ann. BA, Quincy Coll., 1952; MS, So. Ill. U., 1953; MS in Psychology, U. Mass., 1963, PhD, 1964; LittD, No. Mich. U., 1997. Psychologist Bacon Clinic, Racine, Wis., 1954-61; NDEA fellow U. Mass., Amherst, 1961-64; asst. prof. SUNY, Binghamton, 1964-69, univ. examiner and dir. instl. research, 1969-73, asst. v.p. planning, instl. research, 1972-76; exec. asst. to pres., dir. budget and resources Ohio State U., Columbus, 1976-79, v.p. fin. and planning, 1979-81; sr. v.p. adminstrn. NYU, NYC, 1981-83; provost, vice chancellor acad. affairs Calif. State U. System, Long Beach, 1983-87; Trustees prof. Calif. State U., Fullerton, 1987-92; pres. No. Mich. U., 1991-97, ret., 1997. Contbr. articles to psychol. jours. and books on higher edn. Office: 2662 E 20th St Apt 310 Signal Hill CA 90755 E-mail: vandament@aol.com.

VAN DAMME, JEAN-CLAUDE (JEAN-CLAUDE VAN VARENBERG), actor; b. Brussels, Oct. 18, 1960; s. Eugene and Eliana Varenberg; m. Maria Rodriguez, 1978 (div. 1984); m. Cynthia Derderian, 1985 (div. 1985); m. Gladys Portgues, 1986 (div. 1992); children: Kristopher, Bianca; m. Darcy LaPier, Feb. 3, 1994 (div. Nov. 1997); 1 child, Nicholas; m. Gladys Portuges, June 25, 1999. Former European karate champion; owner Long Raod Prodns. (also known as 777 Films Corp.). Actor: (films) Monaco Forver, 1984, Rue Barbar, 1984, Breakin', 1984, No Retreat, No Surrender, 1986, Predator, 1987, Bloodsport, 1988, Black Eagle, 1988, Cyborg, 1989, Kickboxer, 1989, Death Warrant, 1990, Lionheart, 1991, Double Impact, 1991, Universal Soldier, 1992, Hard Target, 1993, Time Cop, 1994, Street Fighter, 1994, The Quest, 1995, Sudden Death, 1995, Maximum Risk, 1996, Double Team, 1997, Knock Off, 1998, Legionnaire, 1998, Universal Soldier: The Return, 1999, Replicant, 2001, The Order, 2001, Derailed, 2002, In Hell, 2003, Narco, 2004, Wake of Death, 2004, Second in Command, 2006, The Hard Cops, 2006, Sinay, 2006, Until Death, 2007, The Shepherd: Border Patrol, 2008, JCVD, 2008 Winner Middleweight Championship, European Karate Assn. Office: United Talent Agency # 500 9560 Wilshire Blvd # 500 Beverly Hills CA 90212-2427

VAN DE KAMP, JOHN KALAR, lawyer; b. Pasadena, Calif., Feb. 7, 1936; s. Harry and Georgie (Kalar) Van de K.; m. Andrea Fisher, Mar. 11, 1978; 1 child, Diana. BA, Dartmouth Coll., 1956; JD, Stanford U., 1959. Bar: Calif. 1960. Asst. US atty., LA, 1960—66; US atty., 1966—67; dep. dir. Exec. Office for US Attys., Washington, 1967—68, dir., 1968—69; spl. asst. Pres.'s Commn. on Campus Unrest, 1970; fed. pub. defender LA, 1971—75; dist. atty. LA County, 1975—83; atty. gen. State of Calif., 1983—91; ptnr. Dewey Ballantine, LA, 1991—96, of counsel, 1996—; pres. Thoroughbred Owners, Calif., 1996—2004. Mem. Calif. Dist. Attys. Assn. (pres. 1975-83), Nat. Dist. Attys. Assn. (v.p. 1975-83), Peace Officers Assn. LA County (past pres.), Nat. Assn. Attys. Gen. (exec. com. 1983-91), Conf. Western Attys. Gen. (pres. 1986), State Bar Calif. (bd. govs. 2001-04, pres. 2004-05), Calif. Commn. Fair Adminstrn. of Justice (chair 2006-). Office: Dewey & LeBoeuf LLP 333 So Grand Ave Ste 2600 Los Angeles CA 90071-1530 Office Phone: 213-621-6511. Business E-Mail: jvandekamp@dl.com.

VANDELL, KERRY DEAN, real estate consultant, educator, director, finance educator; b. Biloxi, Miss., Jan. 8, 1947; s. Benedict Sandy and Eleanor Ruby (Lenhart) V.; m. Deborah Ann Lowe, May 16, 1970; children: Colin Buckner, Ashley Elizabeth. BA, MME, Rice U., 1970; M City Planning, Harvard U., 1973; PhD, MIT, 1977. Assoc. engr. Exxon Co., USA, Houston, 1970-71; asst. prof. So. Meth. U., Dallas, 1976-80, assoc. prof., 1980-86, prof., chmn. dept., 1986-89; prof. real estate and urban land econs., chm. dept. U. Wis., Madison, 1989-93, dir. Ctr. for Urban Land Econs. Rsch., 1991—2004, Tiefenthaler chair holder, 1996—2006; exec. dir. Bolz Ctr. Arts Adminstrn., Madison, 2000—05; prof. fin., dir. Ctr. Real Estate Paul Merage Sch. Bus. U. Calif.-Irvine, 2006—. Vis. assoc. prof. Harvard U., Cambridge, Mass., 1985-86; vis. prof. U. Calif., Berkeley, 1988-89, U. Hong Kong, 1997. Mem. editl. bd. Jour. Real Estate Fin. and Econs., 1989—, Land Econs., 1989—, Jour. Property Rsch., 1989-94, Real Estate Econs., 1980—, Internat. Real Estate Rev., 2002—; contbr. numerous articles on mortgage default risk, real estate liquidity, housing market behavior, econs. of architecture, and appraisal theory to profl. jours. Fellow Homer Hoyt Advanced Studies Inst. (faculty 1989—); mem. Urban Land Inst., Am. Real Estate and Urban Econs. Assn. (2nd v.p. 1989, 1st v.p. 1990, pres. 1991, co-editor jour. 1991-96), Asian Real Estate Soc. (bd. dirs. 2002—), Am. Real Estate Soc. Episcopalian. Office: U Calif Irvine Paul Merage Sch Bus Irvine CA 92697 Home: 2658 Victoria Dr Laguna Beach CA 92651 Office Phone: 949-824-1985. Business E-Mail: kvandell@uci.edu.

VANDENBERG, PETER RAY, publishing executive; b. Geneva, Ill., Sept. 8, 1939; s. Don George and Isabel (Frank) Vandenberg; m. Kathryn Stock, June 1973 (div. Apr. 1977). BBA, Miami U., 1962. Creative adminstr. E.F. McDonald Incentive Co., Dayton, Ohio, 1966-73; mfrs.' rep. Denver, 1974-75; mgr. Homestake Condominiums, Vail, Colo., 1975-76; desk clk. Vail Run Resort, 1976-77; sales rep. Colo. West Advt., Vail, 1977-79, pres., 1980-83, Colo. West Publ., Vail, 1983—, casa-sol.com Mexican Vacation Rentals, Puerto Vallarta, Mexico, 1999—. With US Army, 1963—66. Mem.: Sigma Chi. Avocations: sports, music, reading. Business E-Mail: coloradowestpub@yahoo.com.

VAN DEN BERGH, SIDNEY, astronomer; b. Wassenaar, Netherlands, May 20, 1929; emigrated to U.S., 1948; s. Sidney J. and Mieke (van den Berg) vandenB.; m. Paulette Brown; children by previous marriage: Peter, Mieke, Sabine. Student, Leiden U., The Netherlands, 1947-48; AB, Princeton U., 1950; M.Sc., Ohio State U., 1952; Dr. rer. nat., Goettingen U., 1956, DSc (honoris causa), 1995, DSc (honoris causa), 2001. Asst. prof. Perkins Obs., Ohio State U., Columbus, 1956-58; research assoc. Mt. Wilson Obs., Palomar Obs., Pasadena, Calif., 1968-69; prof. astronomy David Dunlap Obs., U. Toronto, Ont., Canada, 1958-77; dir. Dominion Astrophys. Obs., Victoria, B.C., 1977-86; prin. rsch. officer NRC Can., 1977-98, rschr. emeritus, 1998—. Adj. prof. U. Victoria, 1977—. Decorated officer Order of Can. Fellow Royal Soc. London; mem. Am., Royal Astron. Soc. (assoc.), Canadian Astronomy Soc. (sr. v.p. 1988-90, pres. 1990-92). Home: 418 Lands End Rd Sidney BC Canada V8L 5L9 Office Phone: 250-363-0006. Business E-Mail: sidney.vandenbergh@nrl.com, sidney.vandenbergh@nrc.ca.

VAN DEN BERGHE, PIERRE LOUIS, sociologist; b. Lubumbashi, Congo, Jan. 30, 1933; s. Louis and Denise (Caullery) van den B.; m. Irmgard C. Niehuis, Jan. 21, 1956; children: Eric, Oliver, Marc. BA, Stanford U., 1952, MA, 1953; PhD, Harvard U., 1960. Asst. prof. sociology Wesleyan U., Middletown, Conn., 1962-63; asso. prof. sociology SUNY, Buffalo, 1963-65; prof. sociology and anthropology U. Wash., Seattle, 1965-98, prof. emeritus, 1998—. Vis. prof. U. Natal, South Africa, 1960-61, Sorbonne, Paris, 1962, U. Nairobi, Kenya, 1967-68, U. Ibadan, Nigeria, 1968-69, U. Haifa, Israel, 1976, U. New South Wales, Australia, 1982, U. Strasbourg, France, 1985, U. Tuebingen, Germany, 1986, Tel Aviv U., 1988, U. Cape Town, South Africa, 1989, U. Ljubljana, Slovenia, 2005; fellow Advanced Study in Behavioral Scis., Stanford, Calif., 1984-85. Author: 22 books including South Africa, A Study in Conflict, 1965, Race and Racism, 1967, Academic Gamesmanship, 1970, Man in Society, 1978, Human Family Systems, 1979, The Ethnic Phenomenon, 1981, Stranger in Their Midst, 1989, State Violence and Ethnicity, 1990, The Quest for the Other, 1994. Served with M.C. U.S. Army, 1954-56. Mem. Am. Sociol. Assn., Am. Anthrop. Assn., Sociol. Rsch. Assn., Human Behavior and Evolution Soc. Home: 2006 19th Ave E Seattle WA 98112-2902 Office: U Wash Dept Sociology 353340 Seattle WA 98195-3340 Office Phone: 206-543-2051. Business E-Mail: plvdb@u.washington.edu.

VANDEN HEUVEL, KATHLEEN, law librarian; BA, U. Calif., Berkeley, 1981, MLIS, JD, U. Calif., Berkeley, 1986. Libr. Boalt Hall Sch. Law, U. Calif., Berkeley, 1986—, dep. dir. to dir. Law Libr., 1992—. Libr. fellow Townsend Ctr. for Humanities, 1995—96. Office: Law Libr U Calif Berkeley Boalt Hall Sch Law Berkeley CA 94720-7200

VAN DEN HOOGEN, INGRID, information technology executive; BA in Math. and Computer Sci., San Jose State U., Calif. Various software devel. positions GTE Govt. Systems, United Techs., Megatek; with Sun Microsystems, Inc., Santa Clara, Calif., 1987—, head software strategic mktg., sr. v.p. brand, global comm. & integrated mktg. Office: Sun Microsystems Inc 4150 Network Cir Santa Clara CA 95054 Home: PO Box 145 Girdwood AK 99587-0145 Office Phone: 650-960-1300.

VANDER ARK, TOM, foundation administrator; s. Gary; m. Karen Vander Ark. B in mineral engring., Colo. Sch. Mines; MBA, U. Denver. Sr. exec. Pace Membership Warehouse, Inc.; dir. mktg. devel. Cap Gemini Am.; supt. Fed. Way Pub. Schools, Seattle, 1994—99; exec. dir. for edn. Bill & Melinda Gates Found., Seattle, 1999—2006, sr. fellow, 2007—. Office: Bill & Melinda Gates Found PO Box 2350 Seattle WA 98102 Office Phone: 206-709-3100.

VANDERET, ROBERT CHARLES, lawyer; b. Bklyn., Apr. 12, 1947; s. James Gustav and Bernadette Cecelia (Heaney) V.; m. Sharon Kay Brewster, Oct 3, 1970; children: Erin Anne Brewster, Aidan McKenzie Brewster. AB, UCLA, 1969; JD, Stanford U., 1973. Bar: Calif. 1973, U.S. Dist. Ct. (cen. and so. dists.) Calif. 1974, U.S. Ct. Appeals (9th cir.) 1976, N.Y. 1978, U.S. Supreme Ct. 1978, U.S. Dist. Ct. (no. dist.) Calif. 1980, U.S. Dist. Ct. (ea. dist.) Calif. 1981, U.S. Dist. Ct. (so. dist.) N.Y. 1997. Extern law clk. to Justice Tobriner Calif. Supreme Ct., 1972-73; assoc. O'Melveny & Myers, Los Angeles, 1973-80, ptnr., 1980—. Transition aide Chief Justice Rose Bird, Calif. Supreme Ct., 1976. Del. Dem. Nat. Conv., 1968; bd. dirs. Legal Aid Found. L.A., 1978-90, Constn. Rights Found., 1990, Inner City Law Ctr., 1994—; trustee Lawyers Commn. for Civil Rights Under Law, 1993—; vice chancellor Episcopal Diocese of L.A. Mem. ABA (chair media law and defamation torts com. 1991-92), Calif. State Bar (chair, com. on adminstrn. of justice 1996-97), L.A. Bar Assn. (pro bono coun. chair 1993-95). Democrat. Home: 834 Greentree Rd Pacific Palisades CA 90272-3911 Office: O'Melveny & Myers 400 S Hope St Los Angeles CA 90071-2899

VANDERHOEF, LARRY NEIL, academic administrator; b. Perham, Minn., Mar. 20, 1941; s. Wilmar James and Ida Lucille (Wothe) Vanderhoef; m. Rosalie Suzanne Slifka, Aug. 31, 1963; children: Susan Marie, Jonathan Lee. BS, U. Wis., Milw., 1964, MS, 1965; PhD, Purdue U., 1969, Doctorate (hon.), 2000, Inje U. Korea, 2002. Postdoctorate U. Wis., Madison, 1969—70; asst. prof. biology U. Ill., Urbana, 1970-74, assoc. prof., 1974—77, prof., 1977—80, head dept. plant biology, 1977—80; provost Agrl. and Life Scis., U. Md., College Park, 1980—84; exec. vice chancellor U. Calif., Davis, 1984—91, exec. vice chancellor, provost, 1991—94, chancellor, 1994—. Rsch. assoc. U. Wis., 1970—72; vis. investigator Carnegie Inst., 1976—77, Edinburgh (Scotland) U., 1978; cons. in field. Grantee Dimond Travel grantee, 1975, NSF, 1972, 1974, 1976—79, NATO, 1980; fellow, NRC, 1969—70, Eisenhower fellow, 1987. Mem.: AAAS, Nat. Assn. State Univ. and Land Grant Colls. (exec. com. 2000—), Am. Soc. Plant Physiology (bd. editors 1977—82, trustee, exec. com., treas. 1982—88, chmn. bd. trustees 1994—97). Home: 16 College Park Davis CA 95616-3607 Office: U Calif Davis Office Chancellor Davis CA 95616

VAN DER LEEUW, SANDER ERNST, archaeologist, educator; s. Piet Jacob van der Leeuw and Christine Moltzer; m. Anick Gabrielle Coudart, June 23, 2005. PhD, U. Amsterdam, 1976. Rschr. Netherlands Orgn. Pure Rsch., Leiden, 1972—76; lectr. U. Amsterdam, 1976—85, Cambridge U., England, 1985—95; prof. U. Paris I Panthéon-Sorbonne, 1995—2003, Ariz. State U. Sch. Human Evolution & Social Change, Tempe, 2003—, dir., 2003—. Sec.-gen. Coun. for Coordination Humanities and Social Scis., Paris, 2000—02; external prof. Santa Fe Inst., 2000—; dep. dir. Inst. Nat. Scis. of Universe, Paris, 2003—04. Mem. Fyssen Found., Paris, 2000—08, Ariz. Acad. Sci., Tech. and Arts, Phoenix, 2005—08. Fulbright Postdoctoral fellowship, US Govt., 1976—77, Disting. Rsch. fellowship, Ministry Edn., France, 1988, fellowship, Fitzwilliam Coll., Cambridge, 1986—95. Mem.: Inst. U. France (chair, archaeology 2002—07), Royal Netherlands Acad. Arts and Scis. Office: Ariz State Univ PO Box 872402 Tempe AZ 85287-2402

VANDERRYN, JACK, environmental services administrator; b. Groningen, The Netherlands, Apr. 14, 1930; came to U.S., 1939; s. Herman Gabriel and Henrietta S.E. (Hartog) V.; m. Margrit Wolfes, Mar. 18, 1956; children: David, Judith, Amy, Daniel. BA, Lehigh U., 1951, MS, 1952, PhD, 1955. Rsch. and grad. teaching asst. Lehigh U., Bethlehem, Pa., 1952-55; asst. prof. chemistry Va. Poly. Inst., Blacksburg, 1955-58; rsch. participant Oak Ridge (Tenn.) Nat. Lab., 1957; chemist AEC, Oak Ridge, 1958-62, tech. adviser to asst. gen. mgr. R & D, Washington, 1962-67, asst. to gen. mgr., 1971-72, tech. asst. to dir. div. applied tech., 1972-73, chief energy tech. br., div. applied tech., 1973-75; acting dir. div. energy storage Energy Rsch. and Devel. Adminstrn., Washington, 1975, dir. Office Internat. R & D Programs, 1975-77; dir. Office Internat. Programs Dept. Energy, Washington, 1977-82; dir. energy and natural resources AID, Washington, 1982-91; program dir. environment Moriah Fund, Washington, 1991—2003; sr. fellow, environ. and devel. Moriah Fund., 2003—06. Sr. sci. adviser U.S. Mission to Internat. Atomic Energy Agy., Dept. State, Vienna, Austria, 1967-71; lectr. Brookings Instn., 1965-66. Mem., dep. pres., exec. bd. Am. Internat. Sch., Vienna, 1968-71; v.p. Oak Ridge Civic Music Assn., 1959-60; pres. Washington Print Club, 1986-91; pres. Consultative Group on Biodiversity, 1997-2000; bd. dirs. Ctr. for Internat. Environ. Law, 2004—, Forest Stewardship Coun. U.S., 2004-07, Inst. for Conservation Leadership, 2003—, Endangered Species Coalition, 2003—. Home: 207 Park Ave San Carlos CA 94070 Personal E-mail: jackvanderryn@msn.com.

VANDERVEER, TARA, women's college basketball coach; b. Niagara Falls, NY, June 26, 1953; Grad., Ind. U., 1975. Head coach U. Idaho Vandals, 1978—80, Ohio State U. Buckeyes, 1980—85, Stanford U. Cardinal, 1985—. Head coach US Olympic Women's Basketball Team (gold medal), 1996. Author: Shooting From The Outside, 1997. Named Big Ten Coach of Yr., 1984, 1985, Nat. Coach of Yr., 1988, 1989, 1990, Dist. Coach of Yr., 1988, 1989, 1990, Coach of Yr., Pacific-10 Conf., 1989, 1990, 1995, 1997, 2002, 2003, 2004, 2005, 2006, No. Calif. Women's Intercollegiate Coach of Yr., 1988, 1989, 1990, 1992, 1993, USA Basketball Nat. Coach of Yr., 1996, US Olympic Com. Elite Basketball Coach of Yr., 1996; named to Ind. U. Hall of Fame, 1995, Women's Basketball Hall of Fame, 2002, Women's Sports Found. Hall of Fame, Greater Buffalo Hall of Fame. Achievements include coaching the NCAA Women's Basketball Championship winning Stanford University Cardinal, 1990, 92. Avocation: piano. Office: Stanford U Womens Basketball Dept Athletics Arrillaga Family Sports Ctr Stanford CA 94305-6150 Office Phone: 650-723-0284. E-mail: tarahoop@stanford.edu.

VAN DEVENDER, J. PACE, research scientist, science administrator; b. Jackson, Miss., Sept. 12, 1947; m. Nancy Jane Manning, 1971; 3 children. BA in Physics, Vanderbilt U., 1969; MA in Physics, Dartmouth Coll., 1971; PhD in Physics, U. London, 1974. Physicist diagnostics devel. Lawrence Livermore Lab., 1969; mem. tech. staff pulsed power rsch. and devel. Sandia Nat. Labs., Albuquerque, 1974-78, divsn. supr. pulsed power rsch. divsn., 1978-82, dept. mgr. fusion rsch., 1982-84, dir. pulsed power scis., 1984-93, dir. corp. comm., 1993, dir. Nat. Indsl. Alliances Ctr., 1993-95; pres. Prosperity Inst., 1995-98; dir. strategic scis. ctr. Sandia Nat. Labs., Albuquerque, 1998—, chief info. officer, 1998—2002, dir. exec. staff, 2002—03, v.p. sci., tech. and partnerships, chief tech. officer, 2003—. Mem. bd. trust Vanderbilt U., 1969-73. With U.S. Army, 1969-71. Recipient Ernest Orlando Lawrence Meml. award US Dept. Energy, 1991; named one of 100 Most Promising Scientists Under 40, Sci. Digest, 1984; Marshal scholar U. London, 1971-74. Fellow Am. Phys. Soc.; Phi Beta Kappa, Omicron Delta Kappa, Sigma Xi. Office: Sandia Nat Labs MS 0103 PO Box 5800 Albuquerque NM 87185-0103 Office Phone: 505-844-5148. E-mail: jpvande@sandia.gov.

VAN DE WEGE, KEVIN, state legislator; Washington State Representative, District 24, 2007-; member, Agriculture and Natural Resources Committee, Technology, Energy and Communications Committee, 2007-, Washington State Assmbly. Democrat. Office: 316 John L O'Brien Building PO Box 40600 Olympia WA 98504-0600 Office Phone: 360-786-7916.

VAN DRESER, MERTON LAWRENCE, ceramics engineer; b. Des Moines, June 5, 1929; s. Joseph Jerome and Victoria (Love) Van D.; m. Evelyn Lenore Manny, July 12, 1952; children: Peter, Jennifer Sue. BS in Ceramic Engring., Iowa State U., 1951. Tech. supt. Owens-Corning Fiberglas Corp., Kansas City, Mo., 1954-57; rsch. engr. Kaiser Aluminum & Chem. Corp., Milpitas, Calif., 1957-60, rsch. sect. head, 1960-63, lab. mgr., 1963-65, assoc. dir. rsch., 1965-69, dir. refractories rsch. Pleasanton, Calif., 1969-72, dir. non-metallic materials rsch., 1972-83, v.p., dir. rsch. Indsl. Chem. div. and Harshaw/Filtrol Partnership Cleve., 1983-85, dir. bus. devel. Pleasanton, 1985-88, cons., 1988—2003. Mem. adv. bd. dept. ceramic engring. U. Ill., 1974-78; chmn. tech. adv. com. Refractories Inst., 1980-84; mem. nat. materials adv. bd. Nat. Acad. Sci.; mem. Indsl. Rsch. Inst. Contbr. articles to sci. jours.; patentee in field. Sustaining membership chmn. local dist. Boy Scouts Am., 1980; pres. PTA, 1967-68; vol. exec. Pakistan Internat. Exec. Svc. Corps, 1990-91. Aviator C.E., U.S. Army, 1951-54. Recipient Profl. Achievement citation Iowa State U., 1978; named to Lambda Chi Alpha hall of fame, 1996. Fellow: Am. Ceramic Soc. (v.p. 1973—74); mem.: AIME, ASTM (hon.), Metall. Soc., Nat. Inst. Ceramic Engrs., Brit. Ceramic Soc., Masons, Rotary (pres. Pleasanton Club 2002—03, pres. Club Found. 2003—04, Paul Harris fellow), Alpha Tau Zeta (Alumni of Yr. 2006), Keramos (pres. 1976—78, herald 1980—84, Greaves Walker Roll of Honor award). Avocation: flying. Home and Office: 40 Castledown Rd Pleasanton CA 94566-9749

VAN DYCK, WENDY, dancer; b. Tokyo; Student, San Francisco Ballet Sch.; BA in Performing Arts, St. Mary's Coll., 2003. With San Francisco Ballet, 1979—96, prin. dancer, 1987—96, instr., tchr., 1996; co-dir. Lawrence Pech Dance, San Francisco, 1996—. Performances include Forgotten Land, The Sons of Horus, The Wanderer Fantasy, Romeo and Juliet, The Sleeping Beauty, Swan Lake, Concerto in d: Poulenc, Handel-a Celebration, Menuetto, Intimate Voices, Hamlet and Ophelia pas de deux, Connotations, Sunset, Rodin, In the Night, The Dream: pas de deux, La Sylphide, Beauty and the Beast, Variations de Ballet, Nutcracker, The Comfort Zone, Dreams of Harmony, Rodeo, Duo Concertant, Who Cares; performed at Reykjavik Arts Festival, Iceland, 1990, The 88th Conf. of the Internat. Olympic Com., LA, 1984, with Kozlov and Co. Concord Pavilion; guest artist performing role Swan Lake (Act II), San Antonio Ballet, 1985, Giselle, Shreveport (La.) Met. Ballet, 1994; featured in the TV broadcast of Suite by Smuin. Mailing: PO Box 29190 San Francisco CA 94129 Office Phone: 415-308-5881. E-mail: wvandyck@comcast.net.

VAN DYKE, CRAIG, psychiatrist, director; b. Detroit, Oct. 4, 1941; married; two children. BS, U. Wash., 1963, MD, 1967. Asst. prof. psychiatry Yale U., New Haven, Conn., 1974-78; from assoc. to prof. psychiatry U. Calif., San Francisco, 1979-86, prof., chmn. dept. psychiatry, 1994—. Mem. Am. Psychosom. Soc., Internat. Coll. Psychosom. Medicine, Soc. Neurosci., Internat. Neuropsychol. Soc. Office: U Cal San Francisco Langley Porter Psychiatric Inst 401 Parnassus Ave San Francisco CA 94143-0984 E-mail: cvd@lppi.ucsf.edu.

VAN DYKE, MILTON DENMAN, aeronautical engineering educator; b. Chgo., Aug. 1, 1922; s. James Richard and Ruth (Barr) Van D.; m. Sylvia Jean Agard Adams, June 16, 1962; children: Russell B., Eric J., Nina A., Brooke A. and Byron J. and Christopher M. (triplets). BS, Harvard U., 1943; MS, Calif. Inst. Tech., 1947, PhD, 1949. Research engr. NACA, 1943-46, 50-54, 55-58; vis. prof. U. Paris, France, 1958-59; prof. aero. Stanford, 1959—; prof. emeritus, 1992—. Pres. Parabolic Press. Author: Perturbation Methods in Fluid Mechanics, 1964, An Album of Fluid Motion, 1982; editor: Ann. Rev. Fluid Mechanics, 1969-99. Trustee Soc. For Promotion of Sci. and Scholarship, Inc. Served with USNR, 1944-46. Guggenheim and Fulbright fellow, 1954-55 Mem. Am. Acad. Arts and Scis., Nat. Acad. Engring., Am. Phys. Soc., Phi Beta Kappa, Sigma Xi, Sierra Club. Office: Stanford U Div Mechs & Computation Stanford CA 94305-4040

VAN EMBURGH, JOANNE, lawyer; b. Palmyra, NJ, Nov. 18, 1953; d. Earl Henry and Clare (Kemmerle) Van E.; m. Samuel Michael Surloff, July 6, 1993. BA summa cum laude, Catholic U., 1975; JD cum laude, Harvard Law Sch., 1978. Bar: Calif. 1978. Assoc. atty. Agnew Miller & Carlson, LA, 1978-82; ptnr. Sachs & Phelps, LA, 1982-91, Heller, Ehrman, White & McAuliffe, LA, 1991-93; mng. council Toyota Motor Sales, USA, Inc., Torrance, 1993—, asst. gen. coun., 2000—. Mem. ABA. Avocations: reading, cooking, sports. Office Phone: 310-468-4700. Office Fax: 310-468-4052.

VANG, TIMOTHY TENG, religious organization administrator; b. Xieng Khouang, Laos, May 10, 1956; came to U.S., 1976; s. Nao Chai and Mai (Yang) V.; m. Chee Yang, Jan. 1, 1974 (dec. June 1975); m. Lydia Joua Xiong, July 7, 1979; children: Jennifer P., Nathan K., Victor C., Richard M., Tiffany P., Jasmine M. BS in Missions, Cin. Bible Coll., 1984; MDiv in Ch. Ministries, Can. Theol. Sem., Regina, Sask., 1991; DMin in Ch. Leadership, Fuller Theol. Sem., Pasadena, Calif., 1999. Ordained to ministry Ch. of Christ, 1984, Christian and Missionary Alliance, 1986. Machine operator Pellet Co., Green Bay, Wis., 1977-78; mental health worker Inst. Human Design, Oshkosh, Wis., 1978-80; ch. planter Ch. of Christ, Eau Claire, Wis., 1984-86; pastor Boulder (Colo.) Hmong Alliance Ch., 1986-87; dir. Christian edn. Hmong dist. Christian and Missionary Alliance, Brighton, Colo., 1986-87, dist. supt., 1991-96; sr. pastor Sacramento Hmong Alliance, 1997—. Mem. bd. mgrs. Christian and Missionary Alliance, 1994-97; trustee Crown Coll., 1992-96. Organizer Fox Valley Lao/Hmong Assn., Appleton, Wis., 1979. Lt. U.S./Hmong Allied Army, 1971-75. Mem. Christian And Missionary Alliance Ch. Avocations: reading, writing, walking. Office: Sacramento Hmong Alliance Ch 9131 Locust St Elk Grove CA 95624-2017 E-mail: tmtvang@aol.com.

VAN GALDER, VALERIE, marketing executive; b. Chgo. Grad., UCLA. Asst. Rogers & Cowen, 1985—90; v.p. mktg. & publicity Hard Rock Am., 1990—94; head mktg. Fox Searchlight Pictures, 1994—99; exec. v.p. mktg. Sony Screen Gems, 1999—2004; pres. TriStar Pictures, 2004—05; pres. domestic mktg. Columbia TriStar Motion Picture Group, 2005—. Internat. adv. bd. Bermuda Internat. Film Festival, 2005—. Named one of The 100 Most Powerful Women in Entertainment, Hollywood Reporter, 2006, 2007. Mailing: Sony Pres TriStar Pictures 9050 West Washington Blvd Culver City CA 90232

VAN GUNDY, SEYMOUR DEAN, plant pathologist, educator; b. Feb. 24, 1931; s. Robert C. and Margaret (Holloway) Van G.; m. Wilma C. Fanning, June 12, 1954; children: Sue Ann, Richard L. BA, Bowling Green State U., 1953; PhD, U. Wis., 1957. Asst. nematologist U. Calif., Riverside, 1957-63, assoc. prof., 1963-68, prof. nematology and plant pathology, 1968-73, assoc. dean rsch., 1968-70, vice chancellor rsch., 1970-72, chmn. dept. nematology, 1972-84; prof. nematology and plant pathology, assoc. dean rsch. Coll. Natural and Agrl. Scis., 1985-88, acting dean, 1986, interim dean, 1988-90, dean, 1990-93, emeritus dean, prof., 1993—. Former mem. editl. bd. Rev. de Nematologie, Jour. Nematology and Plant Disease; contbr. numerous articles to profl. jours. Grantee, Rockefeller Found., Cancer Rsch., NSF, USDA; NSF fellow, Australia, 1965—66. Fellow AAAS, Am. Phytopathol. Soc., Soc. Nematologists (editor-in-chief 1968-72, v.p. 1972-73, pres. 1973-74, hon. mem. 1997); mem. (hon.) Acad. Scis. Moldova. Home: 1188 Pastern Rd Riverside CA 92506-5619 Office: U Calif Dept Nematology Riverside CA 92521-0001 Personal E-mail: vangundy@hotmail.com.

VAN HOESEN, BETH MARIE, artist, printmaker; b. Boise, Idaho, June 27, 1926; d. Enderse G. and Freda Marie (Soulen) Van H.; m. Mark Adams, Sept. 12, 1953. Student, Escuela Esmaralda, Mexico City, 1945, San Francisco Art Inst., 1946, 47, 51, 52, Fontainbleau Ecole Arts, France, Acad. Julian and Acad., 5Grande Chaumier, Paris, 1948-51; BA, Stanford U., 1948; postgrad., San Francisco State U., 1957-58. One-Woman shows include, De Young Mus., San Francisco, 1959, Achenbach Found., Calif. Palace Legion of Honor, San Francisco, 1961, 74, Santa Barbara (Calif.) Mus., 1963, 74, 76, Oakland (Calif.) Mus., 1980, John Berggruen Gallery, San Francisco, 1981, 83, 85, 88, 91; traveling exhibit Am. Mus. Assn., 1983-85; group shows include, Calif. State Fair, Sacramento, 1951 (award), Library of Congress, Washington, 1956, 57, San Francisco Mus. Modern Art, 70 (award), Boston Mus. Fine Arts, 1959, 60, 62, Pa. Acad. Fine Arts, Phila., 1959, 61, 63, 65, Achenbach Found., 1961 (award), Bklyn. Mus., 1962, 66, 68, 77, Continuing Am. Graphics, Osaka, Japan, 1970, Hawaii Nat. Print. Exhbn., Honolulu, 1980 (award), Oakland Mus., 1975 (award); represented in permanent collections, including, Achenbach Found., San Francisco, Fine Arts Mus., Bklyn. Mus., Mus. Modern Art, N.Y.C., Oakland Mus., San Francisco Mus. Modern Art, Victoria and Albert Mus., (London), Chgo. Art Inst., Cin. Mus., Portland (Oreg.) Art Mus. (Recipient award of Honor, San Francisco Art Commn. 1981); author: Collection of Wonderful Things, 1972, Beth Van Hoesen Creatures, 1987, Beth Van Hoesen Works on Paper, 1995, Beth Van Hoesen Teddy Bears, 2000. Mem. Calif. Soc. Printmakers (award 1993), San Francisco Women Artists. Office: c/o John Berggruen 228 Grant Ave Fl 3D San Francisco CA 94108-4612

VAN HOLDE, KENSAL EDWARD, biochemistry educator; b. Eau Claire, Wis., May 14, 1928; s. Leonard John and Nettie (Hart) Van Holde; m. Barbara Jean Watson, Apr. 11, 1950; children: Patricia, Mary, Stephen, David. BS, U. Wis., 1949, PhD, 1952. Rsch. chemist E.I. du Pont de Nemours & Co., 1952-55; rsch. assoc. U. Wis., 1955-56, asst. prof. Milw., 1956-57; mem. faculty U. Ill., Urbana, 1957-67; prof. dept. biochemistry and biophysics Oreg. State U., Corvallis, 1967, Am. Cancer Soc. rsch. prof., 1977-93, disting. prof., 1988-93, disting. prof. emeritus, 1993—; instr.-in-charge physiology course Marine Biol. Lab., Woods Hole, Mass., 1977-80; mem. research staff Centre des Recherches sur les Macromolecules, Strasbourg, France, 1964-65; mem. study sect. USPHS, 1966-69, 91—; staff Weizmann Inst., Israel, 1981, Lab. Léon Brillouin, Saclay, France, 1989-90. Author: Physical Biochemistry, 1971, Chromatin, 1988; author: (with C. Mathews) Biochemistry, 1989, 3d edit., 2000; author: Principles of Physical Biochemistry, 1998, 2d edit., 2006; editor: Biochmica Biophysica Acta, 1966—68; mem. editl. bd. jours. Biol. Chemistry, 1968—75, 1981—87, 1991—92, assoc. editor, 1992—; assoc. editor Biochemistry, 1973—76, 1982—89; contbr. articles to profl. jours. Trustee Marine Biol. Lab., Woods Hole, 1979—82, 1984—92. NSF sr. postdoctoral fellow, 1964—65, Guggenheim fellow, 1973—74, European Molecular Biology Orgn. fellow, 1975, Humboldt fellow, 2000—01. Fellow: AAAS; mem.: NAS, Am. Acad. Arts and Scis., Biophys. Soc., Am. Soc. Biochemistry and Molecular Biology. Home: 229 NW 32nd St Corvallis OR 97330-5020 Office: Oreg State U Dept Biochemistry Corvallis OR 97331 Office Phone: 541-737-4155.

VANHOLE, WILLIAM REMI, lawyer; b. Denver, June 25, 1948; s. Joseph and Mildred VanHole; m. Gemma VanHole. BS, Colo. State U., 1970; JD, U. Idaho, 1976. Bar: Idaho 1976, U.S. Dist. Ct. Idaho 1976, U.S. Dist. Ct. (ea. dist.) Wis. 1998, U.S. Ct. Appeals (9th cir.) 1983, U.S. Supreme Ct., 2003. Law clk. to judge U.S. Dist. Ct. Idaho, Boise, 1976-78; assoc. Quane, Smith, Howard & Hull, Boise, 1978-81, Langroise, Sullivan & Smylie, Boise, 1981-83; asst. U.S. atty. U.S. Dept. of Justice, Boise, 1983-87; U.S. atty. Dist. of Idaho, 1984-85; assoc. gen. counsel Boise Cascade Corp., 1987—2004, OfficeMax Inc., 2004—. Served with U.S. Army, 1970-72 Mem. Fed. Bar Assn., Idaho Bar Assn., Idaho Assn. Def. Counsel, Def. Rsch. Inst. Republican. Avocations: skiing, fishing, golf. Office: OfficeMax Inc PO Box 50 Boise ID 83728-0050

VAN HOOMISSEN, GEORGE ALBERT, state supreme court justice; b. Portland, Oreg., Mar. 7, 1930; s. Fred J. and Helen F. (Flanagan) Van H.; m. Ruth Madeleine Niedermeyer, June 4, 1960; children: Geroge T., Ruth Anne, Madeleine, Matthew. BBA, U. Portland, 1951; JD, Georgetown U., 1955, LLM in Labor Law, 1957; LLM in Jud. Adminstrn., U. Va., 1986. Bar: D.C. 1955, Oreg. 1956, Tex. 1971, U.S. Dist. Ct. Oreg. 1956, U.S. Ct. Mil. Appeals 1955, U.S. Ct. Customs and Patent Appeals 1955, U.S. Ct. Claims 1955, U.S. Ct. Appeals (9th cir.) 1956, U.S. Ct. Appeals (D.C. cir.) 1955, U.S. Supreme Ct. 1960. Law clk. for Chief Justice Harold J. Warner Oreg. Supreme Ct., 1955-56; Keigwin teaching fellow Georgetown Law Sch., 1956-57; dep. dist. atty. Multnomah County, Portland, 1957-59; pvt. practice Portland, 1959-62; dist. atty. Multnomah County, 1962-71; dean nat. coll. dist. attys., prof. law U. Houston, 1971-73; judge Cir. Ct., Portland, 1973-81, Oreg. Ct. Appeals, Salem, 1981-88; justice Oreg. Supreme Ct., Salem, 1988—2001. Adj. prof. Northwestern Sch. Law, Portland, Willamette U. Sch. Law, Portland State U.; mem. faculty Am. Acad. Judicial Edn., Nat. Judicial Coll.; Keigwin Teaching fellow Georgetown U. Law Sch. Mem. Oreg. Ho. of Reps., Salem, 1959-62, chmn. house jud. com. Ret. col. USMCR. Recipient Disting. Alumnus award U. Portland, 1972. Master Owen M. Panner Am. Inn of Ct.; mem. ABA, Oreg. State Bar, Tex. Bar Assn., Oreg. Law Inst. (bd. dirs.), Arlington Club, Multnomah Athletic Club, Univ. Club. Roman Catholic. Office: Oreg Supreme Ct 2105 SW Elm St Portland OR 97201 Office Phone: 503-228-2202. Personal E-mail: gavanhoomissen@msn.com.

VAN HORNE, JAMES CARTER, economist, educator; b. South Bend, Ind., Aug. 6, 1935; s. Ralph and Helen (McCarter) Van H.; m. Mary A. Roth, Aug. 27, 1960; children: Drew, Stuart, Stephen. AB, De Pauw U., 1957, DSc (hon.), 1986; MBA, Northwestern U., 1961, PhD, 1964. Comml. lending rep. Continental Ill. Nat. Bank, Chgo., 1958-62; prof. fin. Stanford U. Grad. Sch. Bus., 1965-75, A.P. Giannini prof. fin., 1976—2007, assoc. dean, 1973-75, 76-80; dep. asst. sec. Dept. Treasury, 1975-76. Bd. dirs. Montgomery St. Income Securities, 2d Synnex Corp.; commr. workers compensation Rate Making Study Commn., State of Calif., 1990-92. Author: Function and Analysis of Capital Market Rates, 1970, Financial Market Rates and Flows, 2001, Financial Management and Policy, 2002; co-author: Fundamentals of Financial Management, 2005; assoc. editor Jour. Fin. and Quantitative Analysis, 2009, Jour. Fin., 1971—73, Jour. Fixed Income, 1990—. Mem. bd. trustees DePauw U., 1989-96. With AUS, 1957. Mem. Am. Fin. Assn. (past pres., dir.), Western Fin. Assn. (past pres., dir.), Fin. Mgmt. Assn. Home: 2000 Webster St Palo Alto CA 94301-4049 Office: Stanford U Grad Sch Bus Stanford CA 94305

VAN HORNE, R. RICHARD, oil industry and public relations executive; b. Milw., June 7, 1931; s. Ralph Rupert and Edna (Benson) Van H.; m. Elizabeth Whitaker Dixon, July 3, 1954; children— Ann Van Horne Arms, R. Ross, Margaret Van Horne Shuya BBA, U. Wis., 1953. Various positions Anaconda Am. Brass Co., Milw. and Kenosha, Wis., 1955-72, pres., chief exec. officer Waterbury, Conn., 1972-74, Anaconda Aluminum Co., Louisville, 1974-82; sr. v.p. pub. affairs Atlantic Richfield Co., Los Angeles, 1982-85. Bd. visitors Sch. Bus., U. Wis., Madison; mem. U. Wis. Found.; trustee Louisville Cmty. Found. 1st lt. U.S. Army, 1953-55 Sr. fellow Bellarmine Coll. Mem. Mchts. and Mfrs. Assn. (bd. dirs. 1983-85), Am. Petroleum Inst., Nat. Planning Assn. (com. on new Am. realities 1982-84), Bascom Hill Soc., Minocqua Country Club, Sara Bay Country Club. Republican. Episcopalian. Avocations: golf, reading, gardening. Office: Atlantic Richfield Co 515 S Flower St Ste 3700 Los Angeles CA 90071-2201

VAN HORSSEN, CHARLES ARDEN, manufacturing executive; b. Mpls., June 28, 1944; s. Arden Darrel and Margaret E. (Ellingsen) V H.; m. Mary Katherine Van Kempen, Sept. 11, 1967 (div. 1975); children: Lisa, Jackie; m. Mary Ann Pashuta, Aug. 11, 1983; children: Vanessa, Garrett. BSEE, U. Minn., 1966. Design engr. Sperry Univac, Mpls., 1966-68, sr. project engr. Salt Lake City, 1975-80; systems engr. EMR Computer, Mpls., 1968-75; pres. A&B Industries Inc., Phoenix, 1980—99, Axian Tech Inc., Phoenix; pres., CEO Axian Tech, Phoenix, 1999—. Patentee in field. Mem. Ariz. Tooling Machining Assn. (bd. dirs., v.p. 1987-89, pres. 1989-91). Republican. Episcopalian. Office: Axian Tech Inc 21622 N 14th Ave Phoenix AZ 85027-2841 Business E-Mail: van@axiantech.com.

VAN KIRK, JOHN ELLSWORTH, retired cardiologist; b. Dayton, Ohio, Jan. 13, 1942; s. Herman Corwin and Dorothy Louise (Shafer) Van K.; m. Patricia L. Davis, June 19, 1966 (div. Dec. 1982); 1 child, Linnea Gray. BA cum laude, DePauw U., Greencastle, Ind., 1963; BS, Northwestern U., Chgo., 1964, MD with distinction, 1967. Diplomate Am. Bd. Internal Medicine, Am. Bd. Internal Medicine subspecialty in cardiovasc. disease; cert. Nat. Bd. Med. Examiners. Intern Evanston (Ill.) Hosp., 1967-68; staff assoc. Nat. Inst. of Allergy & Infectious Diseases., Bethesda, Md., 1968-70; resident internal medicine U. Mich. Med. Ctr., Ann Arbor, 1970-72, fellow in cardiology, 1972-74, instr. internal medicine, 1973-74; staff cardiologist Mills Meml. Hosp., San Mateo, Calif., 1974—2001, vice-chief medicine, 1977-78, dir. critical care, 1978-96, critical care utilizaton rev., 1988-99, dir. pacemaker clinic, 1976-99; staff cardiologist Mills-Peninsula Hosp., Burlingame, Calif., 1996-99; ret., 1999. Dir. transitional care, 1996—99; mem. courtesy staff Sequoia Hosp., 1984—2001, ret., 1999. Contbr. rsch. articles to profl. jours. Recipient 1st prize in landscaping Residential Estates, State of Calif., 1977. Fellow Am. Coll. Cardiology; mem. AMA (Physician's Recognition award 1968, 72, 75, 77, 80, 82, 85, 87, 89, 93, 97, 2000), Calif. Med. Assn., San Mateo County Med. Soc., Am. Heart Assn., San Mateo County Heart Assn. (bd. dirs. 1975-78, mem. Bay area rsch. com. 1975-76, mem. edn. com. 1975-77, pres.-elect 1976-77, pres. 1977-79), Alpha Omega Alpha. Republican. Mem. United Brethren Ch. Avocations: gardening, computer science, tennis, woodworking, electronics, amateur radio. Home: 235 Amherst Ave San Mateo CA 94402-2201 Personal E-mail: John_VanKirk@msn.com.

VAN LINT, VICTOR ANTON JACOBUS, physicist; b. Samarinda, Indonesia, May 10, 1928; came to U.S., 1937; s. Victor J. and Margaret (DeJager) Van L.; m. M. June Woolhouse, June 10, 1950; children: Lawrence, Kenneth, Linda, Karen. BS, Calif. Inst. Tech., Pasadena, 1950, PhD, 1954. Instr. Princeton (N.J.) U., 1954-55; staff mem. Gen. Atomic, San Diego, 1957-74; physics cons. San Diego, 1974-75; staff mem. Mission Research Corp., San Diego, 1975-82, 83-91; cons., 1991—; spl. asst. to dep. dir. sci. and tech. Def. Nuclear Agy., Washington, 1982-83. Author, editor: Radiation Effects in Electronic Materials, 1976; contbr. articles to profl. jours. Served with U.S. Army, 1955-57. Recipient Pub. Service award NASA, 1981. Fellow IEEE. Republican. Mem. United Ch. of Christ. Home and Office: 1032 Skylark Dr La Jolla CA 92037-7733 Home Phone: 858-454-5978. Business E-Mail: vicvanlint@sbcglobal.net.

VANLUVANEE, DONALD ROBERT, electronics executive; b. Neosho, Mo., July 3, 1944; s. Harry Earl and Joyce Elizabeth (Skillen) VanLuvanee; m. Lynne Marie Hodge; children: Kenneth Richard, Daryl Robert. BSEE, Rensselaer Poly. Inst., 1966, MEEE, 1972. Sr. engr., br. mgr. Tex. Instruments, Dallas, 1972-80; v.p. product design, research and devel. Syntex Dental Products, Valley Forge, Pa., 1980-82; v.p. research and devel. Kulicke and Soffa Industries, Inc., Willow Grove, Pa., 1982, v.p. domestic ops., 1982-84, pres., chief operating officer, 1984—, also bd. dirs. Contbr. articles to profl. jours.; patentee in field. Varsity coach Methacton Ice Hockey Assn., Eagleville, Pa.; head coach, exec. v.p. Colonials of Valley Forge Ice Hockey Assn. Mem. Nat. Assn. Corp. Dirs., Am. Mgmt. Assn., IEEE. Avocations: fishing, model building, guitar, hockey, banjo.

VAN MAERSSEN, OTTO L., aerospace engineer, consulting firm executive; b. Amsterdam, The Netherlands, Mar. 2, 1919; came to U.S., 1946; s. Adolph L. and Maria Wilhelmina (Edelmann) Van M.; m. Hortensia Velasquez, Jan. 7, 1956; children: Maria, Patricia, Veronica, Otto, Robert. BSChemE, U. Mo., Rolla, 1949. Registered profl. engr., Tex., Mo. Petroleum engr. Mobil Oil, Caracas, Venezuela, 1949—51; sr. reservoir engr. Gulf Oil, Ft. Worth and San Tome, Venezuela, 1952—59; acting dept. mgr. Sedco of Argentina, Comodoro Rivadavia, 1960—61; export planning engr. LTV Aerospace and Def., Dallas, 1962—69, R & D adminstr. ground transp. divsn., 1970—74, engr. specialist new bus. programs, 1975—80, mgr. cost and estimating San Francisco and Alaska, 1981—84; owner OLVM Cons. Engrs., Walnut Creek, Calif., 1984—. Cons. LTV Aerospace and Def., Dallas, 1984—. Served with Brit. Army. Intelligence, 1945, Germany. Mem. Soc. Petroleum Engrs. (Legion of Honor), Toastmasters (sec.-treas. Dallas chpt. 1963-64), Pennywise Club (treas. Dallas chpt. 1964-67). Democrat. Roman Catholic. Avocations: travel, photography. Home and Office: OLVM Cons Engrs 1649 Arbutus Dr Walnut Creek CA 94595-1705 Personal E-mail: ottovm@comcast.net.

VAN MOLS, BRIAN, publishing executive; b. LA, July 1, 1931; s. Pierre Matthias and Frieda Carthyll (MacArthur) M.; m. Barbara Jane Rose, Oct. 1, 1953 (dec. 1968); children— Cynthia Lee, Matthew Howard, Brian; m. Nancy Joan Martell, June 11, 1977; children— Thomas Bentley, Cynthia Bentley, Kristi AB in English, Miami U., Oxford, Ohio, 1953. Media supr. McCann-Erickson Inc., 1955-58; salesman Kelly Smith Co., 1959; with sales Million Market Newspaper Inc., 1959-63; sales mgr. Autoproducts Mag., 1964; sr. salesman True Mag., 1965-68, Look Mag., 1969-70; regional advt. dir. Petersen Pub. Co., Los Angeles, 1971-74; pub. Motor Trend, 1982-84; nat. automotive mktg. mgr. Playboy Enterprises, Inc., NYC, 1984-85, nat. sales mgr., 1985—; western advt. dir. Playboy mag., 1985-86; assoc. pub., advt. dir. Cycle World CBS, Inc., Newport Beach, Calif., 1974-81, pub., 1981; v.p., advt. dir. Four Wheeler Mag., Canoga Pk., Calif., 1986-88; v.p., dir. advt. western div. Gen. Media, Inc., 1988-91; v.p., dir. new bus. devel. Paisano Pub., Inc., Agoura Hills, Calif., 1991-92; dir. mktg. Crown Publs., 1993-94; exec. v.p. Voice Mktg. Inc., Thousand Oaks, Calif., 1994, DMR The Reis Co., Tustin, Calif., 1995-96; COO Mesa Exhaust Products, Inc., Costa Mesa, Calif., 1996-97. Mktg. dir. McMullen Argus Pub., Inc., Anaheim, Calif.,

1998-2001. Served with U.S. Army, 1953-55 Mem. Los Angeles Advt. Club, Adcraft Club Detroit, Advt. Sportsmen of N.Y. Republican. Home: 57 St Andrews Cir Durango CO 81301 E-mail: bvanmols@frontier.net.

VAN NATTA, OWEN THOMAS, Internet company executive; b. 1969; m. Jennifer Van Natta. B, U. Calif., Santa Cruz. V.p., worldwide bus. and corp. develop. Amazon.com, 1998—2005; part of the founding team A9.com; COO to chief revenue officer Facebook, 2005—08; CEO Playlist.com, Palo Alto, Calif., 2008—09, MySpace.com, Calif., 2009—. Office: MySpace.com 1223 Wilshire Blvd Ste 402 Santa Monica CA 90403-5400*

VANNIX, CECIL ROBERT, programmer, systems analyst; b. Glendale, Calif., June 14, 1953; s. Cecil H. Jr. and Gloria Jenny (Zappia) V.; married, 1980; children: Robert Jeremy, Leslie Ann. AS in Plant Mgmt., BS in Indsl. Arts, Loma Linda U., 1977; AS in Info. Systems, Ventura City Coll., 1985. Instr. indsl. arts Duarte (Calif.) High Sch., 1977-79, Oxnard (Calif.) High Sch., 1979-81; computer cons. Litton Data Comand Systems, Agoura, Calif., 1976-81, sr. engr. instr., 1981-85; computer cons. McLaughlin Research Corp., Camarillo, Calif., 1976-77, sr. program analyst, 1985-88, Computer Software Analysts, Camarillo, Calif., 1988-90; sr. systems analyst, mgr. S/W systems devel. V.C. Systems, 1990—. Recipient Spl. Achievement award One Way Singers, Glendale, 1975. Mem. Apple PI Computer Club, Litton Computer Club (pres. 1975-76). Republican. Adventist. Avocations: woodworking, automotives, photography, skiing. Home and Office: 2350 Rose Ln Camarillo CA 93012-9024 Personal E-mail: bvannix@iname.com.

VAN SCHOONENBERG, ROBERT G., lawyer, consumer products company executive; b. Madison, Wis., Aug. 18, 1946; s. John W. and Ione (Henning) Schoonenberg. BA, Marquette U., 1968; MBA, U. Wis., 1972; JD, U. Mich., 1974. Bar: Calif. 1975, Fla. 1976. Atty. Gulf Oil Corp., Pitts., 1974-81; v.p., gen. counsel to sr. v.p., gen. counsel, sec. Avery Dennison Corp., Pasadena, Calif., 1981—2004, exec. v.p., gen. counsel, sec., 2004—07, exec. v.p., chief legal officer, sec., 2007—. Judge pro tem Pasadena Mcpl. Ct., 1987-89. Dir., v.p. fin. adminstrn. Am. Cancer Soc., San Gabriel Vally Unit, 1987—; v.p., treas., dir., v.p. investments Pasadena Symphony Assn.; bd. dirs. Pasadena Recreation and Parks Found., 1983-84; mem. Pasadena Citizens Task Force on Crime Control, 1983-84; dir. Boy Scouts, San Gabriel Valley Coun., dir. pub. coun.; bd. dirs. Verugo Hills Hosp. Found.; trustee Southwestern U. Sch. Law. Mem.: Am. Soc. Corp. Secs. (pres., so. Calif. chpt.), Am. Corp. Counsel Assn. (dir.), L.A. County Bar Assn. (past chmn., corp. law dept. sect.). Office: Avery Dennison Corp 150 N Orange Grove Blvd Pasadena CA 91103-3534 Office Phone: 626-304-2000. Office Fax: 626-792-7312. E-mail: rgvs@averydennison.com.

VANSELOW, NEAL ARTHUR, retired academic administrator, internist; b. Milw., Mar. 18, 1932; s. Arthur Frederick and Mildred (Hoffmann) Vanselow; m. Mary Ellen McKenzie, June 20, 1958; children: Julie Ann, Richard Arthur. AB, U. Mich., 1954, MD, 1958, MS, 1963. Diplomate Am. Bd. Internal Medicine, Am. Bd. Allergy and Immunology. Intern Mpls. Gen. Hosp., 1958—59; resident Univ. Hosp., Ann Arbor, Mich., 1959—63; instr. medicine U. Mich., 1963—64, asst. prof., 1964—68, assoc. prof., 1968—72, prof., chmn. dept. postgrad. medicine and health professions edn., 1972—74; dean Coll. Medicine U. Ariz., Tucson, 1974—77; chancellor med. ctr. U. Nebr., Omaha, 1977—82, v.p., 1977—82; v.p. health scis. U. Minn., 1982—89, prof. internal medicine, 1982—89; chancellor Tulane U. Med. Ctr., New Orleans, 1989—94, chancellor emeritus, 1997—; prof. internal medicine Tulane U., New Orleans, 1989—97, prof. internal medicine emeritus, 1997—. Adj. prof. health sys. mgmt. Tulane U., New Orleans, 1993—99, prof. emeritus, 1999—; chmn. Joint Bd. Osteo. and Med. Examiners Ariz., 1974—77; chmn. coun. on Grad. Med. Edn. Dept. Health and Human Svcs., 1986—91; mem. com. on educating dentists for future Inst. Medicine NAS, 1993—95, chairperson com. on future of primary care, 1994—96, co-chairperson com. on U.S. physician supply, 1995—96, scholar in residence, 1994—95, mem. com. to assess occupl. health and safety tng. needs, 1999—2000, chmn. com. on introducing social and behavioral sci. into med. sch. curriculum, 2002—04; chairperson continuing eval. panel Am. Internat. Health Alliance, 2000—01; mem. adv. com. Medschool.com, 2000—01; adj. prof. Sch. Health Adminstrn. and Policy Ariz. State U., 2000—05; mem. spl. emphasis panel NIH, 2005. Panel on interdisciplinary health profl. edn. Nat. League Nursing, 1996—97; exec. com. United Way Midlands, 1980—82, vice-chmn. 1981 campaign; mem. Commn. on Health Professions Pew Charitable Trusts, 1990—92, 1997—99, Commn. on the Future of Med. Edn. U. Calif, 1996—97; mktg. mgmt. governing coun. U. Hosp. Consortium, 1993—95; trustee Meharry Med. Coll., 1996—, chair presdl. search com., 2006; pres., chmn. bd. Am. Friends London Sch. Hygiene and Tropical Medicine, 1998—2002; com. on relationships between medicine and nursing Josiah Macy Jr. Found., 1999—2000; mem. Gov.'s Pan Am. Commn., La., 1991—92; bd. dirs. Devel. Authority for Tucson's Economy, 1975—77, Minn. High Tech. Coun., 1983—86, Minn. Coalition for Health Care Costs, 1983—87, La. Health Care Authority, 1989—90, United Way Greater New Orleans Area, 1992—97; bd. dirs., exec. com. Health Planning Coun. Midlands, Omaha, 1978—82, v.p., 1981—82. Recipient Disting. Alumnus award, U. Mich. Med. Ctr. Alumni Soc., 2007. Fellow: ACP (workgroup on physician workforce and financing med. edn. 1996), Ariz. Acad. Arts, Sci. and Tech. (bd. govs. 2005—, 2005—, founding mem.), Am. Coll. Physician Execs., Am. Acad. Allergy; mem.: Inst. Med. NAS, Soc. Med. Adminstrs., Assn. Acad. Health Ctrs. (bd. dirs. 1983—89, chmn. bd. dirs. 1988), Rio Verde (Ariz.) Cmty. Assn. (bd. dirs. 2000—04), Phi Beta Kappa, Nu Sigma Nu, Beta Theta Pi, Alpha Omega Alpha, Sigma Xi. Home: 18942 E Mountainaire Dr Rio Verde AZ 85263-7093

VAN SICKLE, FREDERICK L., federal judge; b. 1943; m. Jane Bloomquist. BS, U. Wis., 1965; JD, U. Wash., 1968. Ptnr. Clark & Van Sickle, 1970-75; prosecuting atty. Douglas County, Waterville, Wash., 1971-75; judge State of Wash. Superior Ct., Grant and Douglas counties, 1975-79, Cheland and Douglas Counties, Wash., 1979-91, US Dist. Ct. (ea. dist.) Wash., Spokane, 1991—, chief judge, 2000—. Co-chair rural ct. com. Nat. Conf. State Trial Judges, 1987-91. 1st lt. U.S. Army, 1968-70. Mem. Am. Adjudicature Soc., Wash. State Bar Assn., Masons (pres. Badger mountain lodge 1982-83), Scottish Rite, Spokane Rotary, Shriners. Office: US Dist Cts US Courthouse 920 W Riverside Ave Rm 840 PO Box 2209 Spokane WA 99201

VANSICKLE, SHARON DEE, public relations executive; b. Portland, Oreg., Nov. 10, 1955; BA in Mktg. and Journalism, U. Portland, 1976, postgrad., 1977-79. Reporter Willamette Week, Portland, 1976-77; dir. pub. rels. Tektronix, Portland, 1977-83; prin. pub. rels. KVD Pub. Rels., Portland, 1983-98; CEO KVO Pub. Rslc., Portland, 1999—. Chmn. Pinnacle Worldwide, bd. dirs. pub. rels. coun. Vice chair Portland Met. Area Reg. Arts and Culture Coun.; bd. dirs. CPRF, The Oreg. Entrepreneur's Forum, Pres.'s Coun. on Arts & Sci., U. Portland. Mem. Pub. Rels. Soc. Am. (pres. Portland chpt. 1994-95, chair-elect N. Pac. dist., mem. counsilor's acad., bd mem. and chair tech. com. 1999 Spring conf.).

VAN VALKENBURG, EDGAR WALTER, lawyer; b. Seattle, Jan. 8, 1953; s. Edgar Walter and Margaret Catherine (McKenna) Van V.; m. Turid L. Owren, Sept. 29, 1990; children: Ingrid Catherine, Andrew Owren. BA, U. Wash., 1975; JD summa cum laude, Willamette Coll. of Law, 1978; LLM, Columbia U., 1984. Bar: Oreg. 1978, U.S. Dist. Ct. Oreg. 1979, U.S. Ct. Appeals (9th cir.) 1980. Law clk. to assoc. justice Oreg. Supreme Ct., Salem, 1978-79; assoc. Stoel, Rives, Boley, Fraser & Wyse, Portland, Oreg., 1979-82, 84-86; ptnr. Stoel Rives LLP, Portland, Oreg., 1986—; instr. Columbia U., NYC, 1982-84. Bd. dirs. Oreg. Sports Authority; chair Oreg. Econ. and Cmty. Devel. Commn., 2003—. Editor-in-chief: Williamette Law Jour. 1977-78. Bd. dirs., chmn. Multnomah County Legal Aid, 1997-98; bd. dirs. Portland Ctr. Stage, 2004—. Mem. ACLU (pres. Oreg. chpt. 1991-93), Oreg. State Bar (chmn. antitrust sect. 1989-90, mem. Ho. of Dels. 1996-98). Office: Stoel Rives LLP 900 SW 5th Ave Ste 2600 Portland OR 97204-1229

VAN VARENBERG, JEAN-CLAUDE See VAN DAMME, JEAN-CLAUDE

VAN WEELDEN, THOMAS H., former waste industry company executive; b. 1955; With Waste Mgmt.; co-owner hauling co. and 3 landfills, nr. Chgo.; exec. v.p. Allied Waste Industries, Inc., Houston, 1997-97, pres., COO Phoenix, 1992-97, CEO, pres. Scottsdale, Ariz., 1997—, chmn., 1998—2004, also bd. dirs. Bd. dirs. Reid Plastics, Inc. Office: Allied Waste Industries Inc Ste 100 15880 N Greenway Hayden Loop Scottsdale AZ 85260-1649

VAN WYNGARDEN, THOMAS L., lawyer; b. Mar. 16, 1962; BA, UCLA, 1984; JD, U. Calif. Hastings Coll. Law, 1987. Bar: Calif. 1987. Ptnr., litig. practice group Morgan, Lewis & Bockius LLP, Los Angeles. Contbr. articles various profl. jour. Mem.: Defense Research Inst., Civil Trial Lawyers Assn., State Bar Calif.-litig. sect., ABA, L.A. County Bar Assn.-environ. sect. Office: Morgan Lewis & Bockius LLP 300 S Grand Ave 22nd Fl Los Angeles CA 90071-3132 Office Phone: 213-612-2590. Office Fax: 213-612-2501. Business E-Mail: tvanwyngarden@morganlewis.com.

VANYO, BRUCE GORDON, lawyer; b. Cleve., Dec. 4, 1945; BS summa cum laude, Miami U., 1967; JD, Columbia U., 1972. Bar: Calif. 1974. Law clk. to Hon. William Timbers US Ct. Appeals (2nd cir.), 1972-73; ptnr. McCutcheon, Doyle, Brown & Enersen, 1979—84, Wilson, Sonsini, Goodrich & Rosati, Palo Alto, Calif., 1984—2006, co-chair litigation group, 1984—96; ptnr. Kirkland & Ellis LLP, LA, 2006, Katten Muchin Rosenman LLP, LA, 2006—, co-chair securities litig. practice. Prof. securities regulation Hastings Coll. Law, 1983-86; chmn. recent devels. in securities litigation, PLI, 1984-85; chmn. securities litigation prosecution and def. strategies, PLI, 1985, 86, 87; panelist ALI-ABA patent litigation avoidance and successful resolution, 1986. Mng. editor Columbia Law Rev., 1971-72. Named one of 500 Leading Lawyers in Am., Lawdragon, 2005, 100 Most Influential Lawyers, Nat. Law Jour., 2006. Mem. ABA (litigation sect., securities litigation com., corp. counsel com. 1981—), State Bar Calif. (chair adminstrn. of justice com. 1985-86), Bar Assn. San Francisco, Order of Coif. Office: Katten Muchin Rosenman LLP 2029 Century Pk E Ste 2600 Los Angeles CA 90067 E-mail: bruce.vanyo@kattenlaw.com.

VARAIYA, PRAVIN P., electrical engineer; Mem. tech. staff Bell Labs., 1962-63; instr. MIT, Fed. U. Rio de Janeiro; prof. econ. U. Calif., Berkeley, 1975-92, James Fife prof. elec. engring. and computer scis., Nortel Networks disting. prof. elec. engring./computer sci. Dir. Calif. PATH. Mem. editl. bd. Transp. Rsch. Part C, Discrete Event Dynamical Sys: Theory and Applications, Jour. Econ. Dynamics and Control, (Birkhauser series) Progress in Sys. and Control Theory; contbr. numerous articles to profl. jours. Guggenheim fellow; Miller Rsch. prof. Fellow IEEE, Am. Acad. Arts & Sciences; mem. NAE Office: Dept Elec Engring U Calif 271M Cory Hall Berkeley CA 94720 Office Phone: 510-642-5270. Office Fax: 510-642-7815. Business E-Mail: varaiya@eecs.berkeley.edu.

VARAT, JONATHAN D., law educator, dean; b. 1945; BA, U. Pa., Phila., 1967, JD, 1972. Law clk. to judge Walter Mansfield U.S. Ct. Appeals (2d cir.), NYC, 1972-73; law clk. to justice Byron White U.S. Supreme Ct., Washington, 1973-74; assoc. O'Melveny & Myers, Los Angeles, 1974-76; acting prof. UCLA Sch. Law, 1976-81, prof., 1981—, assoc. dean, 1982-83, 91-92, dean, 1998—2003. Co-author: Constitutional Law: Cases and Materials, 2005. Office: UCLA Sch Law PO Box 951476 Los Angeles CA 90095-1476

VARDAVAS, STEPHANIE J., lawyer; b. Balt., Aug. 3, 1956; d. John and Elaine V. BA, Yale U., 1979; JD, Fordham U., 1985. Bar: NY 1986. Exec. trainee Maj. League Baseball Office of Commr., NYC, 1979-80, asst. counsel, 1986—89; mgr. waivers and player records Am. League of Profl. Baseball Clubs, NYC, 1980-85; v.p. legal and bus. affairs ProServ, Inc. (SFX Sports), 1989—97; atty. endorsement and league affairs Nike, Inc., NYC, 1997—. Vol. D'Amours for U.S. Senate, N.H., 1984, Kanjorski for U.S. Ho. of Reps., Pa., 1986, Mark Green for U.S. Senate, N.Y., 1986, Dukakis for Pres., N.Y., 1988, Clinton-Gore, 1992-96, Gore-Lieberman, 2000, Howard Dean for Pres., 2004; pres. Friends of the Multnomah County Libr. Mem.: ABA (forum com. on the entertainment and sports law industries), Sports Lawyers Assn. (bd. dirs. and co-chair tech. com.). Democrat. Greek Orthodox. Avocations: reading, writing, photography, travel. Office: Nike World Headquarters One Bowerman Dr Beaverton OR 97005-6453

VARGA, JEANNE-MARIE, women's healthcare company executive; BS in Med. Tech., Towson State U.; MA in Mgmt. and Supervision, Ctrl. Mich. U. Sr. sci. reviewer Ctr. for Devices and Radiol. Health, FDA, 1980-83; mgr. U.S. regulatory affairs Sorin Biomedica S.P.A., 1983-87; dir. quality assurance and regulatory affairs Baxter Diagnostics, Inc., 1987-92; v.p. worldwide regulatory and quality Sanofi Diagnostics Pasteur, Inc., 1992-98; v.p. regulatory affairs and quality sys. Women First HealthCare, Inc., San Diego, 1998—.

VARGAS, DIANA LISA, television station executive; BA in Mass Media, Hunter Coll., 1983. Acct. exec. Sta. KTTV, LA, 1988-90, sales, 1990-91, local sales mgr., 1991-94, v.p. gen. sales mgr., 1994-97, v.p. gen. mgr., 1997—.

VARGO, RICHARD JOSEPH, accounting educator, writer; BS, Marietta Coll., 1963; MBA, Ohio U., 1965; PhD, U. Wash., 1969. CPA, Calif. Asst. prof. acctg. Sch. Bus. Adminstrn. U. So. Calif., 1968-71; assoc. prof. acctg., chair dept. acctg. Sch. Bus. Adminstrn. Coll. William and Mary, 1971-73; assoc. prof. Coll. Bus. Adminstrn. U. Tex., Arlington, 1973-74, assoc. dean for grad. studies Coll. Bus. Adminstrn., 1974-76, prof. acctg. Coll. Bus. Adminstrn., 1976-81; prof. acctg. Eberhardt Sch. Bus. U. of Pacific, 1981—. Adj. prof. Family Practice and Cmty. Medicine, U. Tex. Southwestern Med. Sch., Dallas, 1977-81; adj. prof. acctg. McGeorge Sch. Law, U. of Pacific, 1982-93; spkr. in field. Author: Effective Church Accounting, 1989; co-author: (with Paul Dierks) Readings in Governmental and Nonprofit Accounting, 1982, (with Lanny Solomon and Larry Walther) Principles of Accounting, 1983, 5th edit., 1996, (with Lanny Solomon and Larry Walther) Financial Accounting, 1985, 4th edit., 1996; contbr. articles to profl. jours. Recipient grant U. Tex. Sys. Organized Rsch. Funds, 1973-74, 75-76, grant U. of Pacific and Kosciuszko Found., 1987, grant Kemper Found., 1989, grant U.S. Dept. Edn. and Rockefeller Bros. Found., 1991. Mem. Beta Alpha Psi (pres. Ohio U. chpt. 1964-65), Beta Gamma Sigma, Phi Kappa Phi. Office: Univ Pacific Eberhardt School Bus Weber Hall Rm 201-13 Stockton CA 95211-0001

VARIAN, HAL RONALD, economics professor; b. Wooster, Ohio, Mar. 18, 1947; s. Max Ronald and Elaine Catherine (Shultzman) V.; m. Carol Johnston, Nov. 1986. S.B., MIT, 1969; MA, U. Calif.-Berkeley, 1973, PhD (NSF fellow), 1973. Asst. prof. econs. MIT, 1973-77; prof. U. Mich., 1977-95, prof. fin., 1983-95, Reuben Kempf prof. econs., 1984-95; prof. sch. bus., dean sch. info. mgmt. and sys. U. Calif., Berkeley, 1995—, Class of 1944 prof., 1996—. Siena chair in econs., U. Siena, Italy, 1990. Author: Microeconomic Analysis, 1978, Intermediate Microeconomics, 1987, Information Rules, 1998; co-editor Am. Econ. Rev., 1987-90. Guggenheim fellow, 1979-80; Fulbright scholar, 1990 Fellow AAAS, Econometric Soc.; mem. Am. Econ. Soc. Office: U Calif Sims 102 South Hl Berkeley CA 94720-0001 Home: 576 Del Amigo Rd Danville CA 94526-3215

VARLEY, HERBERT PAUL, Japanese language and cultural history educator; b. Paterson, NJ, Feb. 8, 1931; s. Herbert Paul and Katharine L. (Norcross) V.; m. Betty Jane Geiskopf, Dec. 24, 1960 BS, Lehigh U., 1952; MA, Columbia U., 1961, PhD, 1964; DHL (hon.), Lehigh U., 1988. Asst. prof. U. Hawaii, Honolulu, 1964-65; asst. prof. dept. East Asian Langs. and Cultures Columbia U., NYC, 1965-69, assoc. prof., 1969-75, prof., 1975-94, prof. emeritus Japanese history, 1994—, chmn. dept. East Asian Langs. and Cultures, 1983-89. Sen Soshitsu XV prof. Japanese cultural history U. Hawaii, spring 1991-93, 94—2004, prof. emeritus, 2004—. Author: The Onin War, 1967, The Samurai, 1970, Imperial Restoration in Medieval Japan, 1971, Japanese Culture, 1973, 4th edit., 2000, A Chronicle of Gods and Sovereigns, 1980, Tea in Japan: Essays on the History of Chanoyu, 1989, Warriors of Japan, As Portrayed in the War Tales, 1994; co-editor Sources of Japanese Tradition, Vol. 1, 2d edit., 2001. Bd. govs. Japanese Cultural Ctr. of Hawaii. Served with U.S. Army, 1952-54, Japan. Recipient Imperial Decoration Govt. Japan, Order of Rising Sun, Gold Rays With Rosette. Mem. Assn. Asian Studies, Japan Soc., Soc. Am. Magicians (pres. local chpt. 1983-84). Avocations: magic, piano. Home: 28 Coppa Rd West Paterson NJ 07424 Business E-Mail: pvarley@hawaii.edu.

VARNER, CARLTON A., lawyer; b. Creston, Iowa, July 14, 1947; BA, U. Iowa, 1969; JD magna cum laude, U. Minn., 1972. Bar: Calif. 1972, DC 1979. Mng. ptnr. Sheppard Mullin Richter & Hampton LLP, LA, 1991—, chmn. exec. com., 1991—98. Spkr. in field. Author: California Antitrust & Unfair Competition Law, 2nd edit., 2001, Old Wine in New Bottles: The Competitor Collaboration Guidelines, 2000. Vice-chair Constitutional Rights Found., 2000—03. Mem.: ABA (chair exemptions & immunities com., antitrust sect. 2002—05), State Bar of Calif. (chair, antitrust sect. 2004), Constl. Rights Found. (v.p.), LA County Bar Assn. (chmn. antitrust sect. 1993—94), Chancery Club of LA. Office: Sheppard Mullin Richter & Hampton LLP 333 S Hope St Fl 48 Los Angeles CA 90071-1406 Office Phone: 213-620-1398.

VARS, JOHN, Internet company executive; b. St. Paul; Grad., U. Wis. Dir. software devel. Preview Travel, Travelocity.com, mgr., lead software engr. internat. partnerships & joint ventures Sydney, 2002—04; co-founder, chief product officer Dogster.com, San Francisco, 2004—, Catster.com, 2004—. Office: Dogster Inc Ste 350 555 DeHaro St San Francisco CA 94107 Office Phone: 415-934-0400. Office Fax: 415-864-6261. E-mail: john@dogster.com.

VARSHAVSKY, ALEXANDER JACOB, molecular biologist, educator; b. Moscow, Nov. 8, 1946; came to U.S., 1977; s. Jacob M. and Mary B. (Zeitlin) V.; m. Vera Bingham, Aug. 30, 1990; children: Roman, Anna, Victoria. BS in Chemistry, Moscow State U., 1970; PhD in Biochemistry, Inst. of Molecular Biology, Moscow, 1973. Rsch. fellow Inst. Molecular Biology, Moscow, 1973—76; asst. prof. dept. biology MIT, Cambridge, 1977-80, assoc. prof. dept. biology, 1980-86, prof. dept. biology, 1986-92; Howard and Gwen Laurie Smits prof. cell biology, divsn. biology Calif. Inst. Tech., Pasadena, 1992—. Vis. fellow Internat. Inst. for Advanced Studies, Kyoto; mem. molecular cytology study sect. NIH. Author more than 150 articles in the field of genetics and biochemistry; holder 14 patents. Recipient Novartis-Drew award, Novartis, 1998, Merit award, NIH, 1998, Gairdner Internat. award (Can.), 1999, Alfred P. Sloan Jr. prize, GM Cancer Rsch. Found., 2000, Lasker award in basic med. rsch., Albert and Mary Lasker Found., 2000, Hoppe-Seyler award, Soc. for Biochemistry and Molecular Biology, Germany, 2000, Merck award, Am. Soc. Biochemistry and Molecular Biology, 2001, Pasarow award in cancer rsch., Pasarow Found., 2001, Wolf prize in medicine, Wolf Found., Israel, 2001, Massry prize, Massry Found., 2001, Max Planck Rsch. prize, Germany, 2001, Horwitz prize, Columbia U., 2001, Wilson medal, Am. Soc. Cell Biology, 2002, Stein & Moore award, Protein Soc., 2005, March of Dimes prize devel. biology, March of Dimes Found., 2006, Gagna and Van Heck prize, Belgium, 2006, Griffuel Cancer Rsch. prize, France, 2006, Schleiden medal, Germany, 2007, Gotham Prize for Cancer Rsch., 2008. Fellow AAAS, Am. Acad. Microbiology, Am. Acad. Arts and Scis.; mem. NAS, Am. Philos. Soc., European Molecular Biology Orgn. (fgn., academia Europaea). Achievements include discoveries in the fields of DNA replication, chromosome structure, ubiquitin system, and intracellular protein turnover. Office: Calif Inst Tech Divsn Biology 1200 East California Blvd Pasadena CA 91125-0001 Office Fax: 626-440-9821. Business E-Mail: avarsh@caltech.edu.

VASA, ROBERT FRANCIS, bishop; b. Lincoln, Nebr., May 7, 1951; MDiv, Dallas Univ., 1976; JCL, Pontifical Gregorian Univ., Rome, 1981. Ordained priest Diocese of Lincoln, 1976, asst. chancellor, vicar gen.; ordained bishop, 2000; bishop Diocese of Baker, Oreg., 2000—. Roman Catholic. Office: Diocese of Baker Chancery Office 911 SE Armour St Bend OR 97708 Office Phone: 541-388-4004. Office Fax: 541-388-2566.

VASCONCELLOS, JOHN, state legislator; b. San Jose, Calif., May 11, 1932; s. John and Teresa (Jacobs) V. BS, Santa Clara U., 1954, LLB, 1959. Bar: Calif. 1960. Assoc. Ruffo & Chadwick, San Jose, 1959; travel sec. Gov. Pat Brown, Sacramento, 1960; mem. Calif. State Legislature, Sacramento, 1966-96, chmn. ways and means com., 1980-96; mem. CA State Senate, 1996—. Chmn. Assembly Dem. Econ. Prosperity Team, Sacramento, 1992—. Author: A Liberating Vision, 1979; developer program Toward a Healthier State. Founder Calif. Task Force to Promote Self Esteem and Personal and Social Responsibility, 1987; mem. Strategic Action Agenda–Toward a Calif./Japan Partnership, 1993. 1st lt. U.S. Army, 1954-56. Named Legislator of the Decade, Calif. C.C. Faculty Assn., 1980, Hi-Tech Legislator of Yr., Am. Electronics Assn., 1983, more than 100 other awards. Avocations: racquetball, reading.

VASKEVITCH, DAVID, computer software company executive; 3 children. BS in Math., Computer Sci., Philosophy, U. Toronto, M in Computer Sci. With Standard Software; owner PlanDesign, Toronto, Canada; with 3Com Corp., Microsoft Corp., Redmond, Wash., 1986—, dir. U.S. mktg., 1986, gen. mgr. enterprise computing, 1993, v.p., distributed applications platform, chief architect, 1998—99, sr. v.p., developer, 1999—2000, sr. v.p. Bus. Applications Divsn., 2000—01, sr. v.p., chief tech. officer Bus. Platform, 2001—. Mem. adv. bd., Live Labs (Rsch. partnership between MSN and Microsoft Rsch.) Microsoft Corp., 2006—. Author: Client/Server Strategies: A Survival Guide for Corporate Re-engineers, 1993. While at the U. Toronto in the 1970's, he invented a typewriter-terminal-based communications messaging network that predated PC-based e-mail systems. Office: Microsoft Corp One Microsoft Way Redmond WA 98052-6399

VASQUEZ, JO ANNE, retired science educator; BS in Biology, No. Ariz. U., 1965, MA in Early Childhood Edn., 1968; PhD in Curriculum and Instrn., Kennedy-Western U., 1999. Assoc. prof. sci. and edn. Ariz. State U.; lead curriculum developer, sci. specialist Mesa Pub. Schs.; profl. devel. cons. Macmillan/McGraw Hill, 2000—; dir. profl. devel., policy, and outreach Ctr. for Rsch. on Edn. in Sci., Math., Engring., and Tech. (CRESMET), Ariz. State U. Writer MacMillan/McGraw-Hill K-6 Sci., 1998—; bd. dirs. Nat. Sci. bd., 2002—; chair elem. sci. tchg. and assessment standards Nat. Bd. Profl. Tchg. Standards; mem. exec. bd. Nat. Acad. Sci. Ctr. for Sci., Math., and Engring. Edn.; former com. chair, reviewer Nat. Sci. Found.; cons. in field. Past pres. adv. bd. Sally Ride's TOYChallenge. Recipient honoree, Nat. Assn. Latino Elected and Apptd. Officials, 2004, Gustave Oahus Elem. Sci. Tchg. award, Robert H. Carleton award, Nat. Sci. Teachers Assn., 2006; named Tchr. Yr., Nat. Environ. Assn. Mem.: Nat. Coun. Elem. Sci. Educators (past pres.), Internat. Coun. Sci. Edn. Orgn. (past pres.), Ariz. Sci. Tchrs. Assn. (past pres.), Nat. Sci. Edn. Leadership Assn. (pres.-elect), Nat. Sci. Tchrs. Assn. (past mem. nat. bd. dirs., elected first Hispanic pres., Disting. Svc. to Sci. Edn. award Search for Excellence in Elem. Sci. Edn. and Supervision). Achievements include first K-12 tchr. apptd. to bd. dirs. NSF Nat. Sci. Bd. Mailing: Arizona State University CRESMET PO BOX 873604 Tempe AZ 85287-3604

VAUGHAN, DIANA, political organization administrator; Vice chmn. Wyo. Rep. Party, chmn., 2008—. Mem. Teton County Rep. Party. Republican. Office: PO Box 9405 Jackson WY 83002 also: Wyo Rep Party PO Box 241 Casper WY 82602-0241 Office Phone: 307-234-9166. Office Fax: 307-473-8640.*

VAUGHN, ISSAC J., lawyer; b. San Francisco, Dec. 12, 1962; BS, Santa Clara U., 1984; attended, Hastings Coll. Law, 1988—89; JD, U. Mich. Law Sch., 1991. Bar: Calif. 1991. Ptnr. Wilson Sonsini Goodrich & Rosati, Palo Alto, Calif. Mem. bd. regents Santa Clara U., 1992—. Named one of Top 20 Lawyers Under 40, Calif. Law Bus., 2001, Am. Top Black Lawyers, Black Enterprise Mag., 2003. Office: Wilson Sonsini Goodrich & Rosati 650 Page Mill Rd Palo Alto CA 94304-1050 Office Phone: 650-493-9300. Business E-Mail: ivaughn@wsgr.com.

VAUGHN, JAMES ENGLISH, JR., neurobiologist; b. Kansas City, Mo., Sept. 17, 1939; s. James English and Sue Katherine (Vaughn); m. Christine Singleton, June 18, 1961; children: Stephanie, Stacey. BA, Westminster Coll., 1961; PhD, UCLA, 1965. Postdoctoral rsch. fellow in brain rsch. U. Edinburgh, Scotland, 1965-66; asst. prof. Boston U. Sch. Medicine, 1966-70; head sect. molecular neuromorphology Beckman Rsch. Inst., City of Hope, Duarte, Calif., 1970—, pres. rsch. staff, 1986, chmn. divsn. neurosci., 1987—2001. Editor (assoc. editor): (Jour.) Jour. Neurocytology, 1978—86; contbr. articles to profl. jours.; mem. editl. bd. (Jour.) Synapse, 1986—, reviewer for Jour. Comparative Neurology, 1974—, Brain Research, 1976—. Recipient Alumni Achievement award, Westminster Coll., 2003; grantee, NSF, 1983—87; fellow Neurosci. Rsch. Program, 1969; rsch. grantee, NIH, 1969—99. Mem.: AAAS, N.Y. Acad. Scis., Internat. Brain Rsch. Orgn., Soc. for Neurosci. (chmn. short course 1977), Am. Assn. Anatomists, Am. Soc. Cell Biology, Sigma Xi.

VAZIRI, NOSRATOLA DABIR, internist, nephrologist, educator; came to U.S., 1969, naturalized, 1977; s. Abbas and Tahera Vaziri. MD, Tehran U., Iran, 1966. Diplomate Am. Bd. Internal Medicine, Am. Bd. Nephrology; cert. hypertension specialist Am. Soc. Hypertension. Intern Cook County Hosp., Chgo., 1969-70; resident Berkshire Med. Ctr., Pittsfield, Mass., 1970-71, Wadsworth VA Med. Ctr., LA, 1971-72, UCLA Med. Ctr., 1972-74; prof. medicine U. Calif.-Irvine, 1979—, prof. physiology and biophysics, 2001—, prof. biol. scis., 2006—, chief nephrology and hypertension divsn., 1977—, dir. hemodialysis unit, 1977-94, vice chmn. dept. medicine, 1982-94, chmn. dept. medicine, 1994-98, chair faculty Coll. Medicine, 2000—02. Sr. assoc. editor: Jour. Spinal Cord Medicine, 1991-2005; mem. editl. bd. Kidney Internat., 2003—, Am. Jour. Nephrology, 1999-02, Nephron, 1999-02, Advancements in Renal Replacement Therapies, 1999-04, Internat. Jour. Artificial Organs, 1990—, Spinal Cord Medicine, 1991-2005, Jour. Renal Nutrition, 2006—; contbr. articles to profl. jours. Mem. sci. adv. coun. Nat. Kidney Found., 1977—. Recipient Golden Apple award, U. Calif. Irvine Coll. Medicine, 1977, Lauds and Laurels award, U. Calif. Irvine Alumni Assn., 1999, Spirit Nephrology award, Nat. Kidney Found., 2002, Athalie Clarke's Outstanding Health Sci. Rschr. award, 2003, Presdl. Lectureship award, Can. Hypertension Soc., Disting. Svc. award, Western Assn. Physicians, 2007. Master: ACP; fellow: Am. Heart Assn. (fellow coun. high blood pressure rsch.); mem.: Am. Soc. Hypertension, Internat. Soc. Nephrology, Assn. Profs. Medicine, Western Assn. Physicians (councilor 2003—05, pres. 2006—07), Am. Paraplegia Soc. (pres. 1992—94, Donald Munro award 2002), Am. Physiol. Soc., Am. Soc. Nephrology, Alpha Omega Alpha. Avocation: gardening. Home: 66 Balboa Cv Newport Beach CA 92663-3226 Office: U Calif Irvine Med Ctr Div Nephrology Dept Medicine 101 The City Dr Orange CA 92868-3201 Business E-Mail: ndvaziri@uci.edu.

VÁZQUEZ, MARTHA ALICIA, federal judge; b. Santa Barbara, Calif., Feb. 21, 1953; d. Remigio and Consuelo Medina Vazquez. BA in Govt., U. Notre Dame, 1975, JD, 1978. Bar: N.Mex. 1979, admitted to practice: US Dist. Ct. (Dist. N.Mex.) 1979. Atty. Pub. Defender's Office, Santa Fe, 1979-81; ptnr. Jones, Snead, Wertheim, Rodriguez & Wentworth, Santa Fe, 1981-93; chief judge U.S. Dist. Ct. N.Mex., Santa Fe, 1993—. Democrat. Roman Catholic. Office: US Courthouse PO Box 2710 Santa Fe NM 87504-2710 Home Phone: 505-231-3810; Office Phone: 505-988-6330. Business E-Mail: vazquezchambers@nmcourt.fed.us.

VEACO, KRISTINA, lawyer; b. Sacramento, Mar. 4, 1948; d. Robert Glenn and Lelia (McCain) V.; 1 child, Nina Katherine. BA, U. Calif., Davis, 1978; JD, Hastings Coll. Law, 1981. Legal adv. to commr. William T. Bagley Calif. Pub. Utilities Commn., San Francisco, 1981-86; sr. counsel Pacific Telesis Group, San Francisco, 1986-94; sr. counsel corp. and securities and pol. law AirTouch Comms., San Francisco, 1994-98; asst. gen. counsel, asst. sec. McKesson Corp., San Francisco, 1999—2006; corp. governance advisor Veaco Group, 2006—. Mem.: NACD, ABA, Soc. Corp. Secs. and Governance Profls. (pres. San Francisco chpt. 2001—02, nat. bd. dirs. 2002—07, pres. Northern Calif. 2008—, mem. adv. com. chpt.), Phi Beta Kappa. Office: 2470 16th Ave San Francisco CA 94116 Office Phone: 415-731-3111. Personal E-mail: kveaco@veacogroup.com.

VEBLEN, JOHN ELVIDGE, lawyer; b. Seattle, Feb. 14, 1944; AB magna cum laude, Harvard U., 1965; BA, MA with first class honors, Oxford U., Eng., 1967; JD, Yale U., 1971. Bar: Wash. 1971, N.Y. 1973. Law clerk U.S. Ct. Appeals (9th cir.), 1971-72; prin. Stoel Rives LLP, Seattle, 1972—. Mem. ABA, Wash. State Bar Assn., Seattle-King County Bar Assn., Phi Beta Kappa. Office: Stoel Rives LLP One Union Sq 600 University St Ste 3600 Seattle WA 98101-4109

VECCHIO, KENNETH SCOTT, engineering educator, department chairman; b. NYC, Feb. 14, 1961; m. Lori Ann Kelly, Feb. 18, 1989. BS, Carnegie-Mellon U., Pitts., 1983; MS, Lehigh U., Bethlehem, Pa., 1985, PhD, 1988. Asst. prof. U. Calif. San Diego, La Jola, 1988—94, assoc. prof., 1994—99, full prof., 1998—2008, dept. chair, Nano Engineering, 2008. Chpt. dir. youth basketball Scripps Ranch NJB, San Diego, 2001—03; youth sports coach Scripps Ranch Soccer, NJB, Little League, San Diego, 1996—2008. Achievements include patents for metallic-intermetallic laminate composites; patents pending for low cost Fe-based bulk metallic glasses; bone substitute materials derived from marine skeletons. Office: Univ CA San Diego-Nanoengineer 9500 Gilman Dr MC-0448 La Jolla CA 92093-0448 Business E-Mail: kvecchio@ucsd.edu.

VEDROS, NEYLAN ANTHONY, microbiologist, educator; b. New Orleans, Oct. 6, 1929; s. Phillip John and Solange Agnes (Melancon) V.; m. Elizabeth Corbett, Apr. 9, 1955; children: Sally Ann, Philippa Jane. BS in Chemistry, La. State U., 1951, MS in Microbiology, 1957; PhD, U. Colo., 1960. Postdoctoral fellow Nat. Inst. Allergy and Infectious Diseases, U. Oreg., Portland, 1960-62; microbiologist Naval Med. Research Inst., Bethesda, Md., 1962-66; research microbiologist Naval Biosci. Lab., Oakland, Calif., 1966-67; assoc. prof. med. microbiology and immunology U. Calif., Berkeley, 1967-72, prof., 1972-91, prof. emeritus, 1991—. Dir. Naval Biosci. Lab., 1968-81; mem. expert panel on bacteriology WHO, 1972-91. Bd. trustees Alameda (Calif.) Library, 1973-78. Served to comdr. M.S.C. USNR, 1952-55, 62-67. Mem.: Internat. Assn. Aquatic Animal Medicine, Internat. Assn. Microbiol. Sci., Am. Soc. Microbiology. Home: 209 Almond Way Healdsburg CA 95448 E-mail: nvedros@earthlink.net.

VEGA, FRANK J., publishing executive; With Gannett Co. Inc., 1978—; asst. to pub., circulation dir. Oakland Tribune; mem. task force to launch USA Today, 1980—82, v.p. circulation, 1982—83; asst. to pres. Mid-Atlantic Regional Newspaper Group, 1983—84; gen. mgr. El Diario-La Prensa, NYC, 1983—84; pub., CEO Cape Publications, Brevard County, Fla., 1984—91; pres. South Regional Newspaper Group, 1985—91; pres., CEO Detroit Newspaper Agy., 1991—2004; pres., pub. San Francisco Chronicle, 2005—. Office: San Francisco Chronicle 901 Mission St San Francisco CA 94103 Office Phone: 415-777-1111.

VEGA, GREGORY A., former prosecutor; b. East Chicago, Ind. BS in Acctg., Ind. U., 1975; JD, Valparaiso U., 1980. Honors program trial atty. Office of Chief Counsel IRS, Chgo.; with U.S. Atty.'s Office for No. Dist. of Ind., 1983-87; asst. U.S. atty. in maj. frauds and econ. crimes unit U.S. Atty.'s Office, San Diego, 1987; U.S. atty. so. dist. Calif., U.S. Dept. Justice, 1999—2001. Instr. Atty. Gen.'s Advocacy Inst., Nat. Inst. Trial Advocacy. Mem. Hispanic Nat. Bar Assn. (past pres. 1997-98), State Bar Calif. (chmn. criminal law adv. commn. 1992-93, bd. legal specialization 1993-96), San Diego County Bar Assn. (jud. evaluation com. 1993), San Diego La Raza Lawyers Assn. (past bd. dirs.). Office: 880 Front St Ste 6293 San Diego CA 92101-8807

VEGHTE, BILL, computer software company executive; married; 2 children. BA with hon. in East Asian Studies, Harvard U. From product mgr. to corp. v.p. Microsoft Corp., Redmond, Wash., 1990—2008, corp. v.p. windows server group, corp. v.p. No. Am., corp. v.p. Windows Bus. Group, 2007—08, sr. v.p. online services & Windows Bus. Group, 2008—. Bd. dir. nPower. Avocations: backcountry skiing, climbing, fishing. Office: One Microsoft Way Redmond WA 98052-6399

VEIGA, JENNIFER L., state legislator; b. Long Beach, Calif., Oct. 10, 1962; BA, U. Colo., 1983; JD with honors, George Wash. U. Nat. Law Ctr., 1987. Atty. Wood, Ris & Hames, PC, Hall & Evans, LLC; mem. Dist. 3 Colo. House of Reps., Denver, 1996—2003; mem. Dist. 31 Colo. State Senate, Denver, 2003—. Capt. Denver Dist. 3 Dem. Com. Mem. Colo. Bar Assn., Colo. Women's Bar Assn. (co-chairwoman task force on gender bias, chairwoman pub. policy com.), West Wash. Pk. Neighborhood Assn. (former dir.). Democrat. Office: Colo State Capitol 200 E Colfax Rm 271 Denver CO 80203 Office Phone: 303-866-4861. Business E-Mail: jennifer.veiga.senate@state.co.us.*

VEINOTT, ARTHUR FALES, JR., university educator; b. Boston, Oct. 12, 1934; m. 1960; children: Elisabeth, Michael; m. 1988. BS, BA, Lehigh U., 1956; D Eng Sc, Columbia U., 1960. From asst. prof. to assoc. prof. indusl. engring. Stanford (Calif.) U., 1962-67, prof. ops. rsch., 1967—, chmn. dept. indsl. engring., 1975-85, prof. mgmt. sci. engring., 1999—. Cons. Rand Corp., 1965, IBM Rsch. Ctr., 1968-69, 89-90; vis. prof. Yale U., 1972-73. Editor Jour. Math. Ops. Rsch., 1974-80. 1st lt. USAF, 1960-62 Guggenheim fellow 1978-79. Fellow Inst. Math. Stats.; mem. Nat. Acad. Engring., Inst. Mgmt. Sci., Ops. Rsch. Soc. Am. Achievements include development of lattice programming, qualitative theory of optimization for predicting the direction of change of optimal decisions resulting from alteration of problem parameters; structure and computation of optimal policies for supply chains and dynamic programs. Office: Stanford U Dept Mgmt Sci Engring Terman 415 Stanford CA 94305-4026

VENKATA, SUBRAHMANYAM SARASWATI, engineering educator, researcher; b. Nellore, Andhra Pradesh, India, June 28, 1942; came to U.S., 1968; s. Ramiah Saraswati and Lakshmi (Alladi) V.; m. Padma Subrahmanyam Mahadevan, Sept. 3, 1971; children: Sridevi Ramakumar, Harish Saraswati. BSEE, Andhra U., Waltair, India, 1963; MSEE, Indian Inst. Tech., Madras, 1965; PhD, U. S.C., 1971. Registered profl. engr., W.Va., Wash. Lectr. in elec. engring. Coimbatore (India) Inst. Tech., 1965-66; planning engr. S.C. Elec. & Gas Co., Columbia, 1969-70; postdoctoral fellow U. S.C., Columbia, 1971; instr. elec. engring. U. Mass., Lowell, 1971-72; asst. prof. W.Va. U., Morgantown, 1972-75, assoc. prof., 1975-79; prof. U. Wash., Seattle, 1979-96; prof., chmn. dept. elec. and computer engring. Iowa State U., Ames, 1996—2002, Palmer chair prof. dept. elec. and computer engring., 2003—04, prof. and chair emeritus, 2004—; dean, disting. univ. prof. Wallace H. Coulter Sch. Engring., Clarkson U., Potsdam, NY, 2004—05; v.p., exec. cons. KEMA, 2005—07; pres. Venkata Cons. Inc., 2007—; prof. U. Wash, Seattle, 2008—. Cons. Puget Sound Energy Co., Bellevue, Wash., 1980-93, GEC/Alsthom, NYC, 1991-92; series editor, bd. dirs. PWS Pub. Co., 1991-98; affiliate prof. U. Wash., Seattle, 1997-07. Author: Introduction of Electrical Energy Devices, 1987; editor, IEEE Transactions on Power Systems, 1998-00, IEEE/PES Rev. Letters, 1999-03, Internat. Jour. Sys.; mem. editl. bd. IEEE/PES/Power and Energy Mag., 2003-; patentee adaptive var compensators, adaptive power quality conditioner, distribution reliability based design software. Advisor Explorers Club, Morgantown, 1976-78; sec. Hindu Temple and Cultural Ctr. Pacific N.W., Seattle, 1990, chmn., 1991, 95; founding chmn. Hindu Temple and Cultural Ctr., Ames, Iowa, 1999—. Recipient W.Va. U. Assocs. award W.Va. U. Found., 1974, 78. Fellow IEEE (editor IEEE Trans. Power Sys. 1998-00, IEEE/PES Rev. Letters 1999-03, Internat. Jour. Sys., mem. editl. bd. IEEE/PES/Power and Energy Mag., 2003-, v.p. publs., 2004-07, Best Paper award 1985, 88, 91, 2005, mem. Conf. Internat. des Grands Reseaux Electriques, IEEE Press for Power Series, 1998—, Outstanding Power Engring. Educator award 1996, chmn. power engring. edn. com. 2000—, Millenneum medal 2000, Power Edn.Com. Disting. Svc. award 2005), Power Engring. Soc. IEEE (v.p. 2004—), Sigma Xi, Tau Beta Pi, Eta Kappa Nu, Rotary. Democrat. Avocations: photography, tennis, ping pong/table tennis. Home and Office: 13224 N Risky Dr Tucson AZ 85755 Office Phone: 520-797-1161, 206-543-2386. Personal E-mail: psvenkata@comcast.net. Business E-Mail: ss.venkata@kema.com.

VENNING, ROBERT STANLEY, lawyer; b. Boise, Idaho, July 24, 1943; s. William Lucas and Corey Elizabeth (Brown) V.; m. Sandra Macdonald, May 9, 1966 (div. 1976); 1 child, Rachel Elizabeth; m. Laura Siegel, Mar. 24, 1979; 1 child, Daniel Rockhill Siegel. AB, Harvard U., 1965; MA, U. Chgo., 1966; LLB, Yale U., 1970. Bar: Calif., U.S. Dist. Ct. (no. dist.) Calif., 1971, U.S. Dist. Ct. (cen. dist.) Calif. 1973, U.S. Ct. Appeals (9th cir.) 1977, U.S. Supreme Ct. 1977, U.S. Ct. Appeals (fed. cir.) 1986, U.S. Ct. Appeals (D.C. cir.) 1987, U.S. Ct. Fed. Claims 1996. Assoc. Heller Ehrman White & McAuliffe (now known as Heller Ehrman LLP), San Francisco, 1970-73, 73-76, ptnr., 1977—, mem. exec. com., 1991-94. Vis. lectr. U. Wash., Seattle, 1973, Boalt Hall Sch. Law, U. Calif., Berkeley, 1982-85, 89, Sch. Bus., Stanford U., 1986-87. Editor Yale Law Jour., 1969-70. Early neutral evaluator U.S. Dist. Ct. (no. dist.) Calif. Alternative Dispute Resolution Program, 1987—, mediator, 2000-. Fellow Am. Bar Found. (life); mem. ABA, San Francisco Bar Assn. (past chair judiciary com.), CPR Inst. for Dispute Resolution, Olympic Club. Office: Heller Ehrman LLP 333 Bush St San Francisco CA 94104-2878 Office Phone: 415-772-6158. Business E-Mail: robert.venning@hellerehrman.com.

VERANT, WILLIAM J., state agency administrator; b. Washington, Dec. 19, 1941; m. Donna M. Verant; children: Bill Jr., Sharon. BSBA, Am. U., Washington, DC. V.p. Fed. Home Mortgage Corp., Calif.; recruited by the Fed. Home Loan Bank Bd. to manage various savings & loan instns. during savings & loan crisis in 1980s; dept. head comml. and multi-family real estate loans/assets Resolution Trust Corp., Newport Beach, Calif.; dir. fin. instns. divsn. N.Mex. Regulation and Licensing Dept., Santa Fe, 1995—, acting dir. securities divsn. Avocation: restoring old cars. Office: NMex Fin Instns Divsn PO Box 25101 Santa Fe NM 87504 Office Phone: 505-476-4885. Office Fax: 505-476-4670. E-mail: william.verant@state.nm.us.

VERBIN, JEFFREY HAROLD, lawyer; b. Chgo., July 28, 1948; s. Marvin Verbin and Eleanor (Chernoff) Cohen; m. Jacqueline Rochelle Lewis, Aug. 23, 1970; children: Matt, Dana, Alexis. BS, U. Ill., 1971; JD, Washington U., St. Louis, 1974. Bar: Ill. 1974, Calif. 1979, Ariz. 1981. With firm Altheimer & Gray, Chgo., 1974-79, Kaufman & Waring, San Diego, 1979-80, O'Connor Cavanagh Anderson Westover Killingsworth & Beshears, Phoenix, 1981—, sr. ptnr.; now mng. shareholder Greenberg Traurig LLP, Phoenix. Co-chair dinner Multiple Sclerosis Soc., Phoenix, 1992; vice chair 39th ann. testimonial dinner NCCJ, Phoenix, 1992; mem. legal and fin. com. Temple Chai, Phoenix, 1991-92. Mem. ABA (comml. fin. svcs., consumer fin. svcs., banking law and savs. instns. coms. of bus. law sect.) Ill. State Bar Assn., State Bar Ariz. chair spl. subcom. of bus. law sect., mem. legis. subcom. of bus. law sect., chair bus. law sect. 1988-89), State Bar Calif., Maricopa County Bar Assn., Order of Coif. Jewish. Avocation:

sports. Office: Greenberg Traurig LLP Ste 700 2375 E Camelback Rd Phoenix AZ 85016-9000 Office Phone: 602-445-8202. Office Fax: 602-445-8100. Business E-Mail: verbinj@gtlaw.com.

VERCAUTEREN, RICHARD FRANK, career officer; b. Manchester, Feb. 9, 1945; s. Louis P. and Janet (Beliveau) V.; m. Gail Anne Settoon, June 3, 1972. BA in Sociology, Providence Coll., 1967; MA in Bus. Mgmt., George Washington U., 1980; MA in Internat. Studies, Georgetown U., 1996. Commd. 2d lt. USMC, 1967, advanced through grades to brig. gen., 1993; platoon comdr. 2d bn., 9th Marines, Vietnam, 1968; comdg. officer Rifle Co., Hawaii, 1971-73; mil. observer UN, Egypt, Israel, Lebanon, 1976-78; comdg. officer Spl. Task Force, S.Am., 1982; aide de camp Marine Forces Atlantic, Norfolk, Va., 1982-84; bn. comdr. 3d bn., 2nd Marines, Camp Lejeune, N.C., 1985-87; regional comdr. Embassy Guards SubSahara Africa, Nairobi, Africa, 1987-90; dep. dir. plans Hdqs., USMC, Washington, 1990-92, dir. plans, 1990-92; comdg. officer 2nd Marine Regiment, Camp Lejeune, 1992-93; comdg. gen. 1st Marine Exped Brigade, Honolulu, 1993-95; dir. stragety and plans Hdqr. USMC, 1995—. Mem. exec. bd. Capitol dist. Boy Scouts Am., Washington, 1991-92; sr. counselor Seminar XXII, MIT, Washington, 1995-96; bd. dirs. Girl Scouts U.S. Decorated Silver Star medal, Legion of Merit, Distinguished Svc. Medal; recipient Holland M. Smith award Navy League, 1982; MIT Ctr. Internat. Tech. Studies fellow in fgn. politics, 1991, fellow in nat. security studies Harvard U., 1995. Mem. Navy League (bd. dirs.), Army-Navy Club (Washington), Oahu Country Club (Honolulu), Plaza Club, Rotary. Avocations: running, golf, skiing, history, travel. Home: PO Box 222 Occoquan VA 22125-0222

VERGER, JOANNE, state legislator; Oregon State Representative, District 47, formerly, member, Coos Bay-North Bend Water Bd, Coos Bay City Coun & Children & Youth Servs Comn, currently; mayor, Coos Bay, currently; Oregon State Representative, District 9, 2003-04; Oregon State Senator, District 5, 2004-.Bd member, Oregon Easter Seal Soc State Bd, United Way & Southwest Oregon Community Col Found, currently; owner, Verger Chrysler, currently. Named One of Oregon 6 Outstanding Women, 93. Democrat. Office: 900 Court St NE S-401 Salem OR 97301 also: 3696 Broadway PMB 344 North Bend OR 97459 Office Phone: 503-986-1705, 541-756-4140. Business E-Mail: sen.joanneverger@state.or.us.

VERHOEVEN, CHARLES K., lawyer; b. 1963; BBA with distinction, U. Iowa, 1985, JD with high distinction, 1988. Assoc. Cravath, Swaine & Moore, NYC, 1988—93; ptnr., head No. Calif. offices Quinn Emanuel et al, Redwood Shores, Calif., 1993—. Mem.: Iowa Law Rev., 1986—87, articles editor:, 1987—88. Named one of Top 20 Lawyers in Calif. Under 40 Yrs. Ol, Calif. Law Bus., Top 30 IP Lawyers, Calif. Daily Jour., 2005, Litigation's Rising Stars, The Am. Lawyer, 2007. Mem.: ABA, Assn. Bar City of New York, State Bar N.Y., State Bar Calif. Office: Quinn Emauel et al 555 Twin Dolphin Dr Ste 560 Redwood City CA 94065 Business E-Mail: charlesverhoeven@quinnemanuel.com.

VERHOEVEN, PAUL, film director; b. Amsterdam, July 18, 1938; m. Martine Verhoeven, Apr. 7, 1967; 3 children. PhD in Maths., Physics, U. Leiden. Dir. (films) Feest, 1963, The Royal Dutch Marine Corps, 1965, Wat Zien Ik, 1971, Turks Fruit, 1973 (Golden Calf award for Best Dutch Film of Century, Netherlands Film Festival, 1999), Keetje Tippel, 1975, Spetters, 1981, The Fourth Man, 1983 (Internat. Critics' award, 1983, Spl. Jury award, 1984), Robocop, 1987 (Best Dir. award, Sitges-Catalonian Internat. Film Festival, 1987, C.S.T. award, Avoriaz Fantastic Film Festival, 1988, Best Dir., Acad. Sci. Fiction, Fantasy & Horror Films, 1988, Readers' Choice award, Kinema Junpo Awards, 1989), Total Recall, 1990, Basic Instinct, 1992, Showgirls, 1995 (Razzie award, 1996), Starship Troopers, 1997, Hollow Man, 2000 (Audience award, Locarno Internat. Film Festival, 2000), (TV series) Hitchhiker, Floris, 1969, (documentary with the Royal Netherlands Navy) Het Korps Mariniers, 1965; dir., co-screenwriter (films) Soldier of Orange, 1979, Flesh and Blood, 1985 (Golden Calf award for Best Dir., Netherlands Film Festival, 1985), dir., prodr. The Black Book, 2006 (Best Internat. Film award, Venice Film Festival, 2006, Golden Calf award for Best Dir., Netherlands Film Festival, 2006, Rembrandt award, 2007, 2008), exec. prod. Hollow Man II, 2006 Recipient Dutch Culture award, Netherlands Film Festival, 1992, Grolsch Film Blvd. award, 2000, Lifetime Achievement award, Amsterdam Fantastic Film Festival, 2002. Office: Care Beth Swofford 9830 Wilshire Blvd Beverly Hills CA 90212-1804

VERKAMP, JOHN, lawyer, state legislator; b. Grand Canyon, Ariz., July 31, 1940; s. Jack and Mary (O'Leary) Verkamp; m. Linda L. Meline, Sept. 14, 1965; children: Melanie, Jay, Gregory. BS in Bus. Adminstrn., U. Ariz., 1962, JD, 1965. Bar: Ariz. 1965, US Ct. Mil. Appeals 1965, US Supreme Ct. 1973. Dep. county atty. Coconino County, Flagstaff, Ariz., 1970—71, county atty., 1981—92; assoc. Mangum, Wall & Stoops, 1972—74; ptnr. VerKamp & Verkamp, 1974—80; assoc. Morgan, Wall, Stoops & Warden, 1993—; mem. gov. bd. Ariz. Pros. Attys. Adv. Coun., Phoenix, 1981—92, chmn., 1985—. Chmn. Coconino County Rep. Com., Flagstaff, 1974—76, Coconino county Legal Aid, 1976—78; vice chmn. Cath. Social Svcs., 1982—83. Served to capt. JAGC US Army, 1965—70, Europe. Mem.: Flagstaff C. of C., Ariz. Assn. Counties (pres. 1989), Sheriffs and County Attys. (Ariz. County Atty. of Yr. 1985, 1987), Ariz. Alliance Police Chiefs, Ariz. County Attys. and Sheriffs Assn. (pres. 1985—86), Nat. Dist. Attys. Assn., Am. Legion. Office: 4774 E Hopi St Phoenix AZ 85044-2021

VERMA, INDER M., biochemist; b. Sangrur, Punjab, India, Nov. 28, 1947; MSc in Biochemistry, Lucknow U., India, 1966; PhD in Biochemistry, Weizmann Inst. Sci., Rehovot, Israel, 1971. From asst. prof. to assoc. prof. Salk Inst., 1974-83; sr. mem. Molecular Biology & Virology Lab, 1983-85; prof. Molecular Biology, 1985-95; prof. Lab. Genetics Salk Inst. for Biol. Sciences, 1995—, Am. Cancer Soc. prof. Molecular Biology. Fellow Jane Coffin Childs Meml. Fund, 1970-73; Reverend Soloman B. Caulker Meml. fellow, 1967-70; adj. assoc. prof. U. Calif. San Diego, 1979-83, adj. prof. Biology, 1983—; March of Dimes Birth Defects Found. Franklin D. Roosevelt Investigator, 1997; mem. Virology Study Sec., 1981-85, elected mem., Inst. of Medicine, 1999. Recipient medal Outstanding Scientist N. Am. Scientists of Indian Origin, 1985-86; merit award NIH, 1987, outstanding investigator award, 1988; bd. trustees Salk Inst., 1989-91 & 94—; mem. acad. coun., 1989—; vchmn. Fac. and Acad. coun., 1989-90 & 94-95; chmn., 1991-92 & 96-97; prof. Molecular Biology, Am. Cancer Soc., 1990; lectr. Purdue U., 1991, Sch. Med. Vanderbilt U., 1992, TATA Meml. Hosp., Bombay, India, 1992, U. Chgo., 1992, Queenstown, New Zealand, 1993, N.Y.U., 1993, Bar-Ilan U., Ramat Gan, Israel, and others. Mem. NAS (councilor, 2006-), Am. Cancer Soc., Third World Acad. Sciences, IOM, Am. Soc. for Gene Therapy (pres. 2000-2001). Office: Salk Inst Biol Studies PO Box 85800 10010 N Torrey Pines Rd San Diego CA 92186-5800 Office Phone: 619-453-4100. Business E-Mail: verma@salk.edu.

VERMEIJ, GEERAT JACOBUS, marine biologist, educator; b. Sappemeer, Groningen, The Netherlands, Sept. 28, 1946; s. J.L. V.; m. Edith Zipser, 1972; 1 child. AB in Biology, Princeton U., 1968; MA in Philosophy, Yale U., 1970, PhD in Biology & Geology, 1971. Zoology instr. U. Md., 1971-72, asst. prof., 1972-74, assoc. prof., 1974-80, prof., 1980-88; prof. dept. geology U. Calif., Davis, 1989—. Author: Biogeography and Adaptation: Patterns of Marine Life, 1978, Evolution and Escalation: An Ecological History of Life, 1987, A Natural History of Shells, 1993. Recipient Guggenheim fellowship, 1975-76, fellowship MacArthur Found., 1992—, Daniel Giraud Elliot Medal, NAS, 2000. Fellow AAAS, Calif. Acad. Scis. Office: U Calif Dept Geology Davis CA 95616

VERNER, MARY, Mayor, Spokane, Washington; 2 children. BA, Davidson Coll.; MS in Environ. Studies, Yale U.; JD, Gonzaga U., 1999. Former Environ. Programs Mgr. Territorial Govt., US VI; former exec. dir. Upper Columbia United Tribes; councilwoman City of Spokane from Dist. 2, 2004—08; mayor City of Spokane, 2008—. Served on City Coun. Fin. Com., City Coun. Pub. Safety Com., City Coun. Pub. Works Com. Bd. mem. Firefighters Pension Bd., Lodging Tax Adv. Bd., Spokane Regional Health Dist. Bd., Spokane County Air Pollution Control Authority, Native Am. Alliance for Policy & Action, Human Rights Commn.; liaison Chase Youth Commn. Teen Adv. Coun. Mem.: Wash. State Bar Assn., Native American Bar Assn., Kiwanis Internat., Experimental Aircraft Assn. Democrat. Office: Spokane City Hall 808 W Spokane Falls Blvd Spokane WA 99201 Office Phone: 509-625-6250. Business E-Mail: mayor@spokanecity.org.*

VERNON, JACK ALLEN, otolaryngology educator, laboratory administrator; b. Kingsport, Tenn., Apr. 6, 1922; s. John Allen and Mary Jane (Peters) Vernon Hefley; m. Betty Jane Dubon, Dec. 12, 1946 (div. 1972); children: Stephen Mark, Victoria Lynn; m. Mary Benson Meikle, Jan. 2, 1973 BA in Psychology, U.Va., 1948, MA in Psychology, 1950, PhD in Psychology, 1952. Instr. psychology Princeton U., N.J., 1952-54, asst. prof. N.J., 1954-60, assoc. prof. N.J., 1960-64, prof. N.J., 1964-66; prof. otolaryngology Oreg. Health Sci. U., Portland, 1966—, also dir. Oreg. Hearing Rsch. Ctr. Author: Inside the Black Room, 1963; editor: Tinnitus, Q&A's, Tinnitus, Treatments and Relief, Mechanisms of Tinnitus; inventor in field. Adv. Office Civil Defense, Washington, 1961-62. Served to 2d lt. USAAF, 1943-44 Recipient Guest of Honor award 1st Internat. Tinnitus Seminar, 1979, Opticon Focus on People award, 2001. Mem. Assn. Rsch. in Otolaryngology (pres. 1973-74), Am. Acad. Ophthalmology and Otolaryngology, Rotary. Democrat. Avocations: woodworking, sailing, skiing, reading. Office: Oreg Hearing Rsch Ctr 3181 SW Sam Jackson Park Rd Portland OR 97201-3011

VERRONE, PATRIC MILLER, lawyer, writer; b. Glendale, NYC, Sept. 29, 1959; s. Pat and Edna (Miller) V.; m. Margaret Maiya Williams, 1989; children: Patric Carroll Williams, Marianne Emma Williams, Theodore Henry Williams. BA, Harvard U., 1981; JD, Boston Coll., 1984. Bar: Fla. 1984, Calif. 1988, US Dist. Ct. (mid. dist.) Fla. 1984, US Dist. Ct. (ctrl. dist.) Calif. 1995, US Ct. Appeals (9th cir.) 1995. Assoc. Allen, Knudsen, Swartz, DeBoest, Rhoads & Edwards, Ft. Myers, Fla., 1984-86; writer The Tonight Show, Burbank, Calif., 1987-90. Adj. prof. Loyola Law Sch., LA, 1998—2000; lectr. U. Calif., LA, 2002—05. Dir., prodr., writer The Civil War-The Lost Episode, 1991; writer: The Larry Sanders Show, 1992—94, The Critic, 1993—95; prodr., writer The Simpsons, 1994—95, 2002—06, Muppets Tonight!, 1995—97 (Emmy award Best Children's Program, 1998), Pinky and the Brain, 1998, Futurama, 1998—2002 (Environ. Media award, 2000, 2003, Writers Guild Am. award nominee, 2004, Emmy nominee, 1999, 2001, 2003, 2004, Writers Guild award nominee, 2004, Emmy award for outstanding animated prog., 2002, Annie award nominee, 2004, Annie award winner, 2007), co-exec. prodr., writer Class of 3000, 2005—, Futurama Movies, 2006—; editor: Harvard Lampoon, 1978—84, Boston Coll. Law Rev., 1983—84, Fla. Bar Jour., 1987—88, LA Lawyer, 1994—2006; issue editor Ann. Entertainment Law Issue, 1995—2006; contbr. articles to profl. jours. including Elysian Fields Quar., White's Guide to Collecting Figures, Frank Sinatra: The Man, The Music, The Legend, Bongo Comics. Bd. dirs. Calif. Confedn. of Arts, 1994-98, Mus. Contemporary Art, 1994-95; trustee Am. Film Inst., 2005—; mem. adv. bd. Hollywood Health and Soc., 2005—. Mem. ABA (vice-chair arts, entertainment and sports law com. 1995-96), Calif. Bar, Calif. Lawyers for Arts, LA County Bar Assn. (sec. barristers exec. com., chmn. artists and the law com., steering com. homeless shelter project, intellectual property and entertainment law sect., state appelate jud. evaluation com., legis. activity com.), Fla. Bar Assn., Assn. Media and Entertainment Counsel (Labor Counsel of Yr. 2006), Writers Guild Am. West (exec. com. animation writers caucus, bd. dirs. 1999-2001, sec., treas., 2001-05, chair organizing com. 2001-05, pres. 2005—, animation writers caucus, Animation Caucus Lifetime Achievement award 2002), Harvard Club Lee County (v.p. 1985-86), Harvard Club So. Calif. Republican. Roman Catholic. Avocations: baseball, history. Home and Office: PO Box 1428 Pacific Palisades CA 90272-1428

VERSCHOOR, THAYER, state legislator; b. Yuma, Ariz., May 16, 1961; m. Carla Verschoor; children: Ryan, Brad, Steve, Lisa, Amy. Student, Mesa Cmty. Coll.; BS in Polit. Sci., Ariz. State U., 1993. Nuc. biol./chemical specialist US Army, 1983—86; asst. nuc. biol./chemical noncommd. officer US Army Reserves, 1986—92; mem. Dist. 22 Ariz. State Senate, 2003—, pres. pro tempore, vice chair healthcare & med. liability reform com. Republican. Office: Ariz State Senate Capitol Complex 1700 W Washington Rm 310 Phoenix AZ 85007 Office Phone: 602-926-4136. Office Fax: 602-417-3220. Business E-Mail: tverscho@azleg.gov.*

VER STEEG, DONNA LORRAINE FRANK, nurse, sociologist, educator; b. Minot, ND, Sept. 23, 1929; d. John Jonas and Pearl H. (Denlinger) Frank; m. Richard W. Ver Steeg, Nov. 22, 1950; children: Juliana, Anne, Richard B. BSN, Stanford, 1951; MSN, U. Calif., San Francisco, 1967; MA in Sociology, UCLA, 1969, PhD in Sociology, 1973. Clin. instr. U. ND Sch. Nursing, 1962-63; USPHS nurse rsch. fellow UCLA, 1969-72, asst. prof. Sch. Nursing, 1973-79, assoc. prof. Sch. Nursing, 1979-94, asst. dean Sch. Nursing, 1979-81, chmn. primary ambulatory care Sch. Nursing, 1976-87, assoc. dean Sch. Nursing, 1983-86, prof. emeritus chair primary care Sch. Nursing, 1994-96, prof. emeritus Sch. Nursing, 1996—; spl. cons., mem. adv. com. on physicians' assts. and nurse practitioner progs. Calif. State Bd. Med. Examiners, 1972-73. Co-prin. investigator PRIMEX Project Family Nurse Practitioners, UCLA Ext., 1974—76; assoc. cons. Calif. Postsecondary Edn. Commn., 1975—76; spl. cons. Calif. Dept. Consumer Affairs, 1978; chair nurse practioner/physician's asst. statewide program planning com. Calif. Area Health Edn. Ctr., 1978—89; mem. Calif. State Legis. Health Policy Forum, 1980—81; accredited visitor Western Assn. Sch. and Coll., 1985; mem. nurse practitioner adv. com. Calif. Bd. RN, 1995—97; mem. Edn. Industry Interface, Info. Devel. Mktg. Sub Com., 1995—99, recruitment, 1999—2001; archivist Calif. Strategic Planning Com. Nursing/Colleagues in Caring Project, 1995—. Contbr. chpts. to profl. books, articles to profl. jours. Recipient Leadership award Calif. Area Health Edn. Ctr. Sys., 1989, Commendation award Calif. State Assembly, 1994; named Outstanding Faculty Mem., UCLA Sch. Nursing, 1982. Fellow Am. Acad. Nursing; mem. AAAS, AAUW, ANA (Calif.) (pres. 1979-81, interim chair 1995-96), Nat. League Nursing, Calif. League Nursing, N.Am. Nursing Diagnosis Assn., Am. Assn. History Nursing, Stanford Nurses Club, Sigma Theta Tau (Alpha Eta chpt. Leadership award Gamma Tau chpt. 1994), Sigma Xi. Home: 708 Swarthmore Ave Pacific Palisades CA 90272-4353 Office: UCLA Sch Nursing Box 956917 Los Angeles CA 90095-6917 Personal E-mail: dversteeg@aol.com. Business E-Mail: dverstee@sonnet.ucla.edu.

VESELY, JEFFREY M., lawyer; b. Glendale, Calif., Feb. 23, 1950; BA, Univ. Calif., Santa Barbara, 1972; JD, San Fernando Valley Univ., 1975; MBA, Golden Gate Univ., 1982. Bar: Calif. 1975, US Supreme Ct. 1980. Ptnr., chmn. Tax practice Pillsbury Winthrop Shaw Pittman, San Francisco. Co-author: Distinctions Between Unitary & Nonunitary Businesses: A Practical Guide, 2001; contbr. articles to profl. jours., chapters to books. Office: Pillsbury Winthrop Shaw Pittman 50 Fremont St San Francisco CA 94105 Office Phone: 415-983-1075. Office Fax: 415-983-1200. Business E-Mail: jeffrey.vesely@pillsburylaw.com.

VESPER, KARL HAMPTON, business and mechanical engineering educator; b. San Marino, Calif., Aug. 12, 1932; s. Karl Conrad and Roxie (Armstrong) V.; m. Joan Frantz, June, 1964; children— Karen, Linda, Holly, Nancy. BS in Mech. Engring, Stanford U., 1955; MS in Mech. Engring, 1965, PhD, 1969; MBA, Harvard U., 1960. Casewriter Harvard Bus. Sch., 1960-61; bus. mgr., mech. engr. Marine Advisers, 1961-62; cons. Dept. State, summer, 1963; dir. Hosmer Machine Co., Contoock, N.H., 1966-67; dir. summer insts. Stanford U., 1966, 67, dir. case devel., research asso., lectr. mech. engring., 1963-69, research asso., NASA faculty fellow in air pollution research design project, summer 1970; editor mech. engring. series McGraw Hill Book Co., NYC, 1966-74; prof. bus. adminstrn., mech. engring. and marine studies U. Wash., Seattle, 1969—, prof. emeritus; Paul T. Babson prof. Babson Coll., 1980-81. Author: How To Write Engineering Cases, 1966, 73, Engineers at Work, 1975, The Entrepreneurial Function, 1977, Entrepreneurship Education, 1985, New Venture Strategies, 1980, rev. edit., 1990, Frontiers of Entrepreneurship Research, 1981-91, Entrepreneurship and National Policy, 1983, New Venture Mechanics, 1993, (with Paul Larson) Washington Entrepreneur's Guide, 1993, New Venture Experience, 1993, rev. edit., 1996; contbr. chpts. to books and articles to profl. jours. Served with USAF, 1955-57. Mem. Am. Inst. for Decision Scis., Acad. Mgmt., Sigma Xi. Home: 3721 47th Pl NE Seattle WA 98105-5224 Office: Hawaii-Hilo Sch Bus and Econs Hilo HI 96720 E-mail: vesper@hawaii.edu.

VEYLANSWAMI, SATGURU BODHINATHA, head of religious order; b. Berkeley, Calif., Oct. 15, 1942; Spiritual studies, Self Realization Fellowship, Vedanta Soc.; studies with Gurudeva. Mgr. Gurudeva's Master Course Corr. Study; v.p. Gurudeva's several nonprofit corps., 1970—; tchr., counsellor younger monks NH; pujari Murugan Temple; sr. adminstrv. positions, tchr. Innersearch Travel-Study progs.; lectr. tours Mauritius, Malaysia, Singapore; lectr. Innersearch Travel Study Progs.; sr. monk Kadavul Hindu Temple; Guru Mahasannidhanam, preceptor of Nandinatha Sampradaya's Kailasa Parampara Kauai's Hindu monastery, 2001—. Devel., arch. Hindu Heritage Endowment, 1993—; creator Kauai Aloha Endowment. Named to 1st Acharya, Gurudeva's Order. Office: Kauai Aadheenam Ashram 107 Kaholalele Rd Kapaa HI 96746-9304

VICKREY, HERTA M., microbiologist; b. San Gregorio, Calif. m. William David Vickrey; children: Ellean H., Carlene L. Smith, Corrine A. Pochop, Arlene A.; m. Robert James Fitzgibbon, Dec. 28, 1979. BA, San Jose State U., 1957; MA, U. Calif., Berkeley, 1963, PhD in Bacteriology and Immunology, 1970. Cert. immunologist, pub. health microbiologist, clin. lab. scientist. Pub. health microbiologist Viral & Rickettsial Diseases Lab., Calif. State Dept. Pub. Health, Berkeley, 1958-60, 61-62, 1964; postgrad. rsch. bacteriologist dept. bacteriology U. Calif., Berkeley, 1963-64; bacteriologist Children's Hosp. Med. Ctr. No. Calif., Oakland, 1958-70; asst. prof. U. Victoria, B.C., Can., 1970-72; rsch. assoc. rsch. dept. Wayne County Gen. Hosp., Wayne, Mich., 1972-83; lab. supr. med. rsch. and edn. U. Mich., Ann Arbor, 1977-83; pub. health lab. dir. Shasta County Pub. Health Svcs., Redding, Calif., 1983-84; sr. pub. health microbiologist Tulare County Pub. Health Lab., Tulare, Calif., 1984—, tech. supr. Visalia, Calif., 1992-93; med. technologist Hillman Health Clin. Lab., Tulare, Calif., 1994-96, clin. lab. scientist, 1996—. Vis. scientist MIT, Cambridge, 1982; organizer, lectr. mycology workshop Tulare County Health Dept. Lab., Visalia, 1988; USPHS trainee U. Calif., Berkeley, 1965, 66. Author: Isolation and Identification of Mycotic Agents, 1987-88; contbr. articles to profl. jours. Fundraiser Battered Women's Shelter, Redding, 1983, Real Opportunities for Youth, Visalia, 1985, 86, Open Gate Ministries, Dinuba, Visalia, 1987-94, 97-99, 2003, Leukemia and Lymphoma Soc., 2003, 04, 05, 06. Fellow NIH, 1966-69, Dr. E.E. Dowdle rsch. fellow, U. Calif., 1969-70; grantee U. Victoria, 1970-72, Med. Rsch. and Edn. and Med. Adminstrn., U. Mich., 1973-83. Mem. No. Calif. Assn. Pub. Health Microbiologists, Calif. Scholarship Soc., Am. Soc. Clin. Pathologists (assoc.), Phi Beta Kappa, Delta Omega, Phi Kappa Phi, Beta Beta Beta. Avocations: biking, hiking, swimming. Home: 3505 W Campus Dr Apt 5 Visalia CA 93277-1869 Office: Tulare County Pub Health Lab 1062 S K St Tulare CA 93274-6421 Office Phone: 559-687-6984.

VICTORINO, LOUIS D., lawyer; b. Lemoore, Calif., May 27, 1945; s. Louis and Mayme (Garcia) V.; m. Kathleen Gilman Berl, June 7, 1975. BA, Stanford U., 1967; JD, UCLA, 1970. DC, Calif. Assoc./ptnr. Pettit & Martin, San Francisco, L.A., 1970-84; ptnr. Seyfarth, Shaw, Fairweather & Geraldson, LA, 1984-88, Pillsbury & Madison, LA, 1988-93, Fried, Frank, Harris, Shriver & Jacobson, LA, 1993—, Sheppard, Mullin, Richter & Hampton, LLP, Washington. Adv. bd. Govt. Contractor, Washington, 1990—; legal advisor Commn. Govt. Procurement, 1971. Co-author: Proving & Pricing Construction Claims, 1990, Government Contractor Briefing Papers Collection, 1987-95, contbr. articles to prof. journs. Mem. ABA (pub.

contract law sect., reg. pres. 1975, editl. bd. Pub. Contract Law Jour. 1991-95), Fed. Bar Assn. (reg. v.p.), Ct. Fed. Claims Bar Assn., Bd. Contract Appeals Bar Assn, adv. bd. Govt. Contractor (federal publications inc.) 1992 - 1999. bd. editors U.C.L.A. Law Review 1968 — 1970. Office: Fried Frank Harris Shrive & Jacobson 725 S Figueroa St Ste 1200 Los Angeles CA 90017-5443 also: Exec Mgmt Grp LLC 1300 I St NW 11 Fl E Washington DC 20005 Office Phone: 202-218-0038, 202-218-0000. Office Fax: 202-218-0020.

VIDALE, JOHN EMILIO, geologist; b. Phila., Mar. 15, 1959; s. Guido Levi and Rosemary (Jacobson) V.; 1 child, Laura. BS, Yale U., 1981; PhD, Calif. Inst. Tech., 1986. Scientist U. Calif., Santa Cruz, 1987-90, U.S. Geol. Survey, Menlo Park, Calif., 1991-95; assoc. prof. UCLA, 1995-99, prof., 1999—, acting dir. Inst. Geophysics and Planetary Physics, 2002—03, interim dir., 2003—04. Editor Bulletin Seismology Soc. Am., 1988-93; contbr. articles to profl. jours. Gilbert fellow U.S. Geol. survey, 1994-95; co-recipient James B. Macelwane Young Investigator medal Am. Geophys. Union, 1994 Fellow Am. Geophys. Union (Macelwane medal 1994). Office: UCLA Dept Earth & Space Sci PO Box 951567 Los Angeles CA 90095-1567 Home: 8726 NE 11th St Bellevue WA 98004-3930 Business E-Mail: vidale@ucla.edu.

VIDOVICH, MARK A., paper products executive; CEO Day Runner, Inc., Irvine, Calif., 1986-2000, chmn. bd. dirs., 2000—.

VIDWANS, SMRUTI JAYANT, microbiologist; b. India; BS in Biology, MIT; PhD in Microbiology, U. Calif., San Francisco, 2001. Amgen rsch. fellow Irvington Inst. Immunological Rsch., 2003; postdoctoral fellow in microbiology and immunology U. Calif., San Francisco, 2004; co-founder Phenotypica. Contbr. articles to profl. jour. Named one of Top 100 Young Innovators, MIT Tech. Review, 2004. Office: U Calif Ctr Bioentrepeneurship 185 Berry St Ste 4603 San Francisco CA 94143-1016

VIEHE, RICHARD B., podiatrist; m. Margaret Viehe; children: Anne, Thomas, Andrew. BS, Cornell U.; MD in Podiatric Medicine, Calif. Coll. Podiatric Medicine, 1971. Resident in podiatry Lincoln Cmty. Hosp., Calif.; staff physician Children's Hosp. of Orange County; Coastal Cmtys. Hosp., Santa Ana; Coll. Hosp., Costa Mesa; Fountain Valley Cmty. Hosp.; Hoag Meml. Presbyn. Hosp., Newport Beach; St. Joseph Hosp., Orange County, & Western Med. Ctr., Santa Ana; pvt. practice Newport Ctr. Podiatry Group, Newport Beach, Calif.; dir. surgical residency Western Medical Center, Santa Ana. Bd. trustee Calif. Coll. of Podiatric Medicine, 1987—; diplomat Am. Bd. of Podiatric Surgery & Am. Bd. of Podiatric Examiners. Fellow: Am. Coll. of Foot & Ankle Surgeons; mem.: Nat. Acad. of Practice, Am. Podiatric Med. Assn. (pres. 2002—03), Orange County Podiatric Med. Assn. (past pres.), Calif. Podiatric Med. Assn. (past pres.), Alpha Gamma Kappa, Pi Delta. Office: Newport Ctr Podiatry Group 1303 Avocado Ave Ste 195 Newport Beach CA 92660

VIGIL, CHARLES J., lawyer; b. Los Alamos, N.Mex, Aug. 24, 1964; s. John Carlos and Catherine Elizabeth (Salazar) V. BBA, U. N.Mex., 1986; JD, U. Mich., 1989. Bar: N.Mex 1989, US Dist. Ct. (Dist. N.Mex) 1989, US Ct. Appeals (10th Cir.) 1989. Atty. Rodey, Dickason, Sloan, Akin & Robb, PA, Albuquerque, 1989—, pres., mng. dir. Articles editor Michigan Jour. of International Law, 1988-89. Co-chmn. N.Mex Commn. on Professionalism, 2005; mem. adv. com. N.Mex Compilation Com.; mem. H. Vearle Payne Am. Inn of Ct., 1999—2002. Mem. ABA (labor law sect., standing com. lawyers' professional liability), Albuquerque Bar Assn., N.Mex State Bar Assn. (pres.-elect 2004, pres. 2005), Nat. Conf. Bar Presidents (exec. coun.) Democrat. Roman Catholic. Office: Rodey Dickason Sloan Akin & Robb PA Ste 2200 201 3rd St NW Albuquerque NM 87103-1888 Office Phone: 505-768-7377. Office Fax: 505-768-7395. Business E-Mail: cvigil@rodey.com.

VIGIL, DANIEL AGUSTIN, academic administrator; b. Denver, Feb. 13, 1947; s. Agustin and Rachel (Naranjo) V.; m. Claudia Cartier. BA in History, U. Colo., Denver, 1978, JD, 1982. Bar: Colo. 1982, U.S. Dist. Ct. Colo. 1983. Project mgr. Math. Policy Rsch., Denver, 1978; law clk. Denver Dist. Ct., 1982-83; ptnr. Vigil and Bley, Denver, 1983-85; asst. dean U. Colo. Coll. Law, Boulder, 1983-89, assoc. dean, 1989—2003; asst. dean U. Denver Coll. Law, 2003—. Apptd. by chief justice of Colo. Supreme Ct. to serve on Colo. Supreme Ct. Ad Hoc Com. on miniority participation in legal profession, 1988-94; adj. prof. U. Colo. Sch. Law; mem. Gov. Colo. Lottery Commn., 1990-97; mem. Colo. Supreme Ct. Hearing Bd., 1998-2002; mem. atty. regulatory adv. com. Colo. Supreme Ct., 2002—; with Colo. Supreme Ct., Judicial Adv. Coun.; vis. law prof. U. Denver Law Coll., 2003—04. Editor (newsletter) Class Action, 1987-88; co-editor (ethics com. column) Colo. Lawyer, 1995-97. Bd. dirs. Legal Aid Soc. Met. Denver, 1986-99, chmn. bd. dirs., 1998-99; past v.p. Colo. Minority Scholarhip Consortium, pres. 1990-91; bd. trustees Colo. Atty.'s Fund for Client Protection, 2001-07; bd. trustees Boulder Bar Found., 2000-04, pres. 2003; mem. Task Force on Cmty. Race Rels., Boulder, 1989-94; past mem. jud. nomination rev. com. U.S. Senator Tim Wirth; chmn. bd. dirs. Colo. Legal Svcs., 2000-. Mem. Colo. Bar Assn. (mem. legal edn. and admissions com. 1989-94, chmn. 1989-91, bd. govs. 1991, 97—), Hispanic Nat. Bar Assn. (chmn. scholarship com. 1990-95), Colo Hispanic Bar Assn. (bd. dirs. 1985-89, pres. 1990, Lifetime Achievement award, 2008), Denver Bar Assn. (joint com. on minorities in the legal profession 1993-95), Boulder County Bar Assn. (ex-officio mem., trustee, 1992-2003), Inns of Ct. (Penfield Tate chpt., 1993-2003), Phi Delta Phi (faculty sponsor) Roman Catholic. Avocations: skiing, cosmology. Home: 2550 Winding River Dr 0-4 Broomfield CO 80020 Office: U Denver Coll Lw 2255 E Evans Ave Denver CO 80208 Office Phone: 303-871-6208. Business E-Mail: dvigil@law.du.edu.

VIGIL, EDWARD, state legislator; m. Evelyn Vigil. Mem. Dist. 62 Colo. House of Reps., 2008—. Democrat. Office: State House 200 E Colfax Denver CO 80203 Office Phone: 303-866-2916. Business E-Mail: edvigil1@gmail.com.*

VIGIL, HENRY P., computer software company executive; BA in Philosophy, Stanford U., MBA. Dir. mktg. desktop applications Microsoft Corp., Redmond, Wash., 1990—95, gen. mgr. interactive TV bus. unit, gen. mgr. internet commerce bus. unit, corp. v.p. consumer strategy & partnerships, sr. v.p. strategy & partnerships, 2006—. Bd. dir. Thomson SA. Founder City Yr. Seattle; mem. bd. adv. Stanford Bus. Sch.; mem. bd. ambassadors Mercy Corps. Office: One Microsoft Way Redmond WA 98052-6399

VIGIL, JEFFREY L., infant and child products manufacturing executive; b. 1954; BS in Acctg., U. Wyo., 1976. Sr. auditor Arthur Andersen & Co., 1976; internal auditor Guaranty Bank and Trust Co., 1979; v.p., treas., contr. Sunnyside Mines, Inc., 1989-90; v.p. fin. Energy Fuels Corp., 1980; v.p. acquisitions Northwestern Growth Corp., Huron, S.D., 1993; v.p. fin. and adminstrn., treas., sec. Koala Corp., Denver, 1996—. Mem. AICP. Office: Unit D 11600 E 53d Ave Denver CO 80239-2312 E-mail: ir@koalabear.com.

VIGIL-GIRON, REBECCA, former state official; b. Taos, N.Mex., Sept. 4, 1954; d. Felix W. and Cecilia (Santistevan) Vigil; 1 child, Andrew R. AA in Elem. Edn., N.Mex. Highlands U., 1978, BA in French, 1991. Sec., project monitor, customer svc. rep. Pub. Svc. Co. N.Mex., 1978-86; sec. state State of N. Mex, Santa Fe, 1987—90, 1999—2006; exec. dir. N.Mex. Commn. Status of Women, 1991; electoral observer UN, Angola, Africa, 1992, Internat. Found. Electoral Sys., Dominican Republic, 1994, Equatorial Guinea, Africa, 1996, Washington, 1996. Participant AMPART, Mex., 1991. Dem. nominee U.S. Ho. Reps., 1990. Named among 100 Most Influential Hispanics in Nation, Hispanic Bus. Mag., 1990; recipient Trio Achievers award S.W. Assn. Student Assistance Programs, 1993, Gov.'s award Outstanding N.Mex. Women, 1994. Mem. Albuquerque Hispano C. of C. (membership rep., sr. sales mktg. rep., corp. rels. coord.) Democrat.

VIGNEAULT, ALAIN, professional hockey coach; b. Quebec City, Can., May 14, 1961; m. Josée Doucet; children: Andréanne, Janie. Player St. Louis Blues, 1981—83; head coach Can. Nat. Jr. Team, 1989-91, Trois-Rivières Draveurs, 1986—87, Hull Olympiques, 1988—92, Beauport Harfangs, 1995—97, Montreal Canadiens, 1997—2000, PEI Rocket, Charlottetown, 2003—05, Manitoba Moose (AHL), 2005—06, Vancouver Canucks, 2006—; asst. coach Ottawa Senators, 1992—95. Recipient Jack Adams Award, 2007. Office: Vancouver Canucks 800 Griffiths Way Vancouver BC Canada V6B 6G1

VILAR, ALBERTO W., investment company executive; b. Cuba, Oct. 4, 1940; BA, Washington and Jefferson Coll., 1962; MBA, Iona Coll., 1969. Co-founder, pres., profile mgr. Amerindo Investment Advisors, San Francisco, 1985—. Active in philanthropic, healthcare, and cultural endeavors; founder Alberto Vilar Global Fellows in the Performing Arts. Roman Catholic. Avocations: art, opera.

VILLABLANCA, JAIME ROLANDO, neuroscientist, medical educator; b. Chillán, Chile, Feb. 1929; arrived in U.S., 1971, naturalized, 1985; s. Ernesto and Teresa (Hernández) V.; m. Guillermina Nieto, Dec. 3, 1955; children: Amparo C., Jaime G., Pablo J., Francis X., Claudio I. Bachelor in Biology, Nat. Inst. Chile, 1946; licentiate medicine, U. Chile, 1953, MD, 1954. Cert. neurophysiologist. Rockefeller Found. postdoctoral fellow in physiology John Hopkins and Harvard Med. Schs., 1959-61; Fogarty internat. rsch. fellow in anatomy UCLA, 1966-68, assoc. research anatomist and psychiatrist, 1971-72; assoc. prof. psychiatry and biobehavioral scis. UCLA Sch. Medicine, 1972-76; prof. psychiatry and biobehavioral scis. UCLA, 1976—2004, prof. neurobiology, 1977—2004, disting. prof. psychiatry and biobehavioral scis., neurobiology, 2004—07, disting. emeritus prof., 2007—. Mem. faculty U. Chile Sch. Medicine, 1954-71, prof. exptl. medicine, 1970-71; vis. prof. neurobiology Cath. U. Chile Sch. Medicine, 1974; cons. in field. Author numerous rsch. papers, book chpts., abstracts; chief regional editor Developmental Brain Dysfunction, 1988-99; editor Internaltional Journal of Developments Neuroscience, 2007-. Decorated Order Francisco de Miranda (Venezuela), 1987; recipient Premio Reina Sofia, Madrid, 1990, Lifetime Achievement award UCLA Sch. Medicine, 2001, Emeritus award Colegio Medico de Chile, 2004; fellow Rockefeller Found., 1959-61, Fogarty Internat. Rsch. fellow NIH, 1966-68; grantee USAF Office Sci. Rsch., 1962-65, Found. Fund Rsch. Psychiatry, 1969-72, USPHS-Nat. Inst. Child Human Devel., 1972-96, USPHS-Nat. Inst. Drug Abuse, 1981-85, USPHS-Nat. Inst. Neurol. Disorders and Stroke, 1988-92, Fgn. Scientist Traveling grant Tokyo Met. Govt., 1995. Mem. AAAS, AAUP, Sleep Rsch. Soc. (Significant Early Contbr. award 2003), Intellectual & Developmental Disabilities Rsch. Ctr., Brain Rsch. Inst., Internat. Brain Rsch. Orgn., Am. Physiol. Soc., Soc. for Neurosci., Assn. Venezolana Padres de Niños Excepcionales, Soc. Child and Adolescent Psychiatry and Neurology (Chile, hon.), Johns Hopkins Med. and Surg. Assn., Sigma Xi. Home: 200 Surfview Dr Pacific Palisades CA 90272-2911 Office: UCLA Dept Psychiatry & Biobehavioral Scis Los Angeles CA 90024-1759 Home Phone: 310-459-2452. Business E-Mail: jvillablanca@mednet.ucla.edu.

VILLAGOMEZ, TIMOTHY P., Lieutenant Governor of the Northern Mariana Islands; b. Sept. 10, 1962; s. Jose T. and Rita P. Villagomez; m. Margaret E. Keene; children: Renaesha, Jose, Rita, Juanita, Timmy, Kinda Rose. BS, San Diego U., 1987. Rep. Dist. 1 Commonwealth No. Mariana Islands Legislature, 2004—06, vice spkr., 2004—06, chmn. Pub. Utilities, Transp., and Comm. Com., 2004—06; lt. gov. Commonwealth No. Mariana Islands, 2006—. Construction & design engr. Commonwealth Utilities Corp., dep. exec. dir., exec. dir., 1994—2002; pacific regulator Micronesia Telecommunications & Cable TV Ops., 1994—2002. Chmn. Gov.'s Declaration Task Force Water State of Emergency, 1995—99, Nat. Rehab. Adv. Coun.; mem. Housing Task Force, 1999—2001, Comml. Devel. & Capital Improvement/Fed. Projects Task Force. Recipient Innovation Award, Nat. Assn. State Facilities, 1998, 1999; named Govt. Businessman of Yr., Saipan C. of C., 2000. Mem.: ASCE, Am. Gen. Contractors, Am. Pub. Power Assn., Pacific Power Assn., Assn. Pacific Island Legislatures (pres. 2004), Jr. Golf Assn. Democrat. Office: Lt Gov Office of Gov Caller Box 10007 Saipan MP 96950 Office Phone: 670-664-8876. Office Fax: 670-664-2311. E-mail: tpvillagomez@itecnmi.com.*

VILLARAIGOSA, ANTONIO RAMON, Mayor, Los Angeles; b. East LA, Jan. 23, 1953; m. Corina Raigosa, 1987 (separated 2007); children: Marisela, Prisila, Antonio Jr., Natilia Fe. BA in History, UCLA, 1977; JD, People's Coll. of Law, 1985. Mem. Calif. State Assembly, 1995—2001, Dem. whip and mem. appropriations and budget coms., majority leader, 1997, speaker, 1998—2001; city councilman, dist. 14 LA City Coun., 2003—05; mayor City of LA, 2005—. Mem. LA Met. Transp. Bd., 1990—94; nat. co-chair Kerry Presdl. Campaign, 2003—04; chair LA City Coun. Transp. Com.; bd. dirs. Met. Transit Authority. Mem. Greater Eastside Voter Registration and Edn. Project, Jobs with Peace, LAUSD Mex. Am. Edn. Commn., L.A. Ctr. for Law and Justice. Recipient Golden Plate award, Acad. Achievement, 2006; named one of 25 Most Influential Hispanics, Time Mag., 2005; disting. fellow at UCLA and U. So. Calif. Achievements include first Latino mayor for LA since Cristobal Aguilar left office in 1872. also: Ste 3200 725 S Figueroa St Los Angeles CA 90017-5432 Office: Office of Mayor City Hall 200 North Spring St Los Angeles CA 90012

VILLAVECES, JAMES WALTER, allergist, immunologist, consultant; b. San Luis Obispo, Calif., Nov. 4, 1933; s. Robert and Solita (Combariza) V. BA, UCLA, 1955; MD (hon.), U. Calif. Med. Sch., 1960. Diplomate Am. Bd. Allergy and Immunology. Intern Sawtelle VA Hosp., LA, 1960-61; preceptorship in adult allergy L.A. County Hosp., LA, 1964-66; fellow in allergy White Meml. CCM, LA, 1966-67; co-chief allergy divsn. Ventura (Calif.) Med. Ctr., 1969—87; practice medicine specializing in allergy-immunology Ventura, 1984—; lectr. wellpoint Calif. AAST, FVIG. Founder botanical weed allergy walks, 1970; cons. in allergy/immunology, Blue Cross, 1991-96; medical invention cons., Inventor Internat., Inc.; inventor, cons. Sprixx: Alcohol-gel Clip on Dispensers, 2001, 3M; mem. Pharmacy and Therapeutics Com., Wellpoint (Blue Cross Calif.) Inc., 1991-96; prodr. Ventura County cities street-tree guide for asthma patients; peer reviewer Blue Cross So. Calif. Wellpoint, 1980, 1994-95; cons., lectr., peer reviewer in field. Writer, prodr., editor films; contbr. articles on biology of pollens and molds of Ventura County to profl. jours.; patentee in field. Bd. dir. Am. Lung Assn., Ventura, 1969-85, pres., 1974, advisor air pollution control com., 1971-74; judge Ventura Sci. Fair, 1970-85; lectr. in field. Recipient commendation County Bd. Suprs., Ventura, 1974; named one of Am.'s Top Physicians Consumers Rsch. Coun. Am., 2003-05. Fellow Am. Acad. Allergy, Asthma, Immunology, Am. Coll. Allergy, Asthma, Immunology; mem. Calif. Soc. Allergy-Immunology, Calif. Med. Assn., Ventura County Med. Assn., Gold Coast Tri-County Allergy Soc. (pres. 1987), CAL Club (hon.), Ventura County Sports Hall of Fame (mem. founding bd.), Mensa. Republican. Achievements include development of infection protection device for hospital and food service establishments. Avocations: writing, photography, lecturing, pistol target shooting, fishing. Home: 928 High Point Dr Ventura CA 93003-1415 Office: Dudley Profl Ctr 4080 Loma Vista Rd Ste M Ventura CA 93003-1811 Office Phone: 805-656-0433. Personal E-mail: allergycare2006@yahoo.com.

VILLICA-A, TAUNYA, corporate financial executive; b. 1972; Co-founder, mng. ptnr. Affinity Fin. Grp. Mem. Ariz. Town Hall; former pres. Kiwanis de Amigos; Cmty. Needs and Preparedness com. chair Am. Red Cross; bd. treasurer Tucson Hispanic Chamber of Commerce; mem. Agua Prieta Shelters. Named one of 40 Under 40, Tucson Bus. Edge, 2006. Office: Affinity Financial Group 5363 E Pima St Tucson AZ 85712 Office Phone: 520-795-3360.

VINCENT, DAVID RIDGELY, financial consultant; b. Detroit, Aug. 9, 1941; s. Charles Ridgely and Charlotte Jane (McCarroll) Vincent; m. Margaret Helen Anderson, Aug. 25, 1962 (div. 1973); children: Sandra Lee, Cheryl Ann; m. Judith Ann Gomez, July 2, 1978; children: Amber, Jesse Joseph Flores(dec.) 1 stepchild, Micheal Flores Jr. BSBA, Calif. State U., Sacramento, 1964; MBA, Calif. State U., Hayward, 1971; PhD, Somerset U., 1991. Cert. mgmt. cons., chartered retirement planning counselor 2008. Sr. ops. analyst Aerojet Gen. Corp., Sacramento, 1960-66; contr. Hexcel Corp., Dublin, Calif., 1966-70; mng. dir. Memorex, Vienna, 1970-74; sales mgr. Ampex World Ops., Friebourg, Switzerland, 1974-76; dir. product mgmt. NCR, Sunnyvale, Calif., 1976-79; v.p. Boole & Babbage Inc., Sunnyvale, 1979-85; gen. mgr. Inst. Info. Mgmt., Sunnyvale Calif., Calif., 1979-85; pres., CEO The Info. Group, Inc., Santa Clara, Calif., 1985—2005; fin. advisor, dist. mgr. Ameriprise Fin. Svcs., Campbell, Calif., 2005—. Author: Perspectives in Information Management, Information Economics, 1983, Handbook of Information Resource Management, 1987, The Information-Based Corporation: Stakeholder Economics and the Technology Investment, 1990, Reengineering Fundamentals: Business Processes and the Global Economy, 1994—96; contbr. articles to profl. jours. Referee emeritus U.S. Soccer Fedn. Mem.: Inst. for Mgmt. Cons., Product Devel. and Mgmt. Assn., Am. Mktg. Assn., Nat. Investor Rels. Inst., Assn. Fin. Profl., World Future Soc., Soc. Competitive Intelligence Profl., Am. Electronics Assn., Nat. Alliance Bus. Econ., Silicon Valley Roundtable, Soc. Info. Mgmt. (treas.), Knights of Columbus (4th degree). Home: 2803 Kalliam Dr Santa Clara CA 95051-6838 Office: Ameriprise Fin Svcs Inc 1919 S Bascom Ave Campbell CA 95008 Office Phone: 408-963-2372. Business E-Mail: david.r.vincent@ampf.com.

VINCENT, DIRK L., lawyer; b. Mar. 24, 1967; BBA, Pacific Lutheran Univ., 1988; JD, Columbia Univ., 1991. Bar: Calif. 1992, Wash. 1992. Law clk. Judge Andrew J. Kleinfeld, US Ct. Appeals Ninth Cir., 1991—92; atty. Gibson, Dunn & Crutcher, LA, 1992—96; co-founder, ptnr., bus. litigation Fairbank & Vincent, LA, 1996—. Adj. prof. Loyola Law Sch., 2001—. Editor (sr., articles): Columbia Bus. Law Rev.; contbr. articles to profl. jours. Recipient Thomas E. Dewey prize; named a Rising Star, So. Calif. Super Lawyers, 2006; Stone Scholar. Mem.: ABA, Assn. Bus. Trial Lawyers, State Bar Calif., LA County Bar Assn. Office: Fairbank Vincent 444 S Flower St Ste 3860 Los Angeles CA 90071-2938 Office Phone: 310-996-5520. Office Fax: 310-996-5530. Business E-Mail: dvincent@fairbankvincent.com.

VINCENT, MARK See DIESEL, VIN

VINCENT, THOMAS JAMES, retired manufacturing executive; b. Balt., Mar. 17, 1934; s. Thomas Alonzo and Helen Geraldine (Cloman) V.; divorced; children: Wayne S. MS, MIT, 1968. Div. gen. mgr. Fairchild Industries, St. Augustine, Fla., 1969-72; pres. T.J. Vincent Properties Ltd., St. Augustine, 1972-75, Pacific Concrete & Rock Co., Honolulu, 1975-77, Ramsey Engring. Co., St. Paul, 1977-80, Kobe Inc., LA, 1980-84, Milchem Inc., Houston, 1984-85, York (Pa.) Internat. Corp., 1985-88, also bd. dirs., cons.; chmn., CEO Hawaii Seafood Growers, Inc., Kahuku, 1990-92. Author: Fairplan, 1962; publ.: In the Name of the Boss Upstairs, The Father Ray Brennan Story, 2004 Founder, pres. Thomas J. Vincent Found. Inc., Kaneohe, Hawaii, 1990—; founder, v.p., treas. Winter Park (Fla.) Family Health Ctr., Inc., 1995—. Named one of Outstanding Young Men in Am., Jaycees, 1965; Alfred P. Sloan fellow MIT, 1967; recipient Rsch. for Progress Achievement award, 1972. Avocations: deep sea fishing, orchid growing. Home and Office: 44-447 Kanoehe Bay Dr Kaneohe HI 96744

VINCENT, VERNE SAINT, protective services official; Chief police Aurora (Colo.) Police Dept., 1995—. Office: Aurora Police Dept 15001 E Alameda Dr Aurora CO 80012-1546

VINCENTI, SHELDON ARNOLD, lawyer, educator; b. Sept. 4, 1938; s. Arnold Joseph and Mae (Burch) Vincenti; children: Matthew Lewis, Amanda Jo. AB, Harvard U., 1960, JD, 1963. Bar: Utah 1963. Sole practice law, Ogden, 1966—67; ptnr. Lowe and Vincenti, Ogden, 1968—70; legis. asst. to U.S. Rep. Gunn McKay, Washington, 1971—72, adminstrv. asst., 1973; prof., assoc. dean U. Idaho Coll. Law, Moscow, 1973—83, dean, prof. law, 1983—95, prof. law,

1995—2006; acad. dean Am. Justice Sch. Law, Paducah, Ky., 2006—. Home: 3285 W Twin Rd Moscow ID 83843-9114 Office: U Idaho Coll Law 6th & Rayburn St Moscow ID 83843

VINCENTI, WALTER GUIDO, aeronautical engineer, emeritus educator; b. Balt., Apr. 20, 1917; s. Guido A. and Agnes (Nicolini) V.; m. Joyce H. Weaver, Sept. 6, 1947; children— Margaret Anna, Marc Guido. AB, Stanford U., 1938, Aero. Engr., 1940. Aero. research scientist NACA, 1940-57; prof. aero. and astronautics and history of tech. Stanford U., 1957-83, prof. emeritus, 1983—. Cons. to industry, 1957—; mem. adv. panel engrng. sec. NSF, 1960-63. Author: (with Charles H. Kruger, Jr.) Introduction to Physical Gas Dynamics, 1965, (with Nathan Rosenberg) The Britannia Bridge, 1978, What Engineers Know and How They Know It, 1990; also papers.; co-editor (with Milton Van Dyke) Annual Review of Fluid Mechanics, 1970-76. Served with USN, 1945-46. Recipient Gold medal Pi Tau Sigma, 1948, Engr.-Historian award ASME, 1997; Rockefeller Pub. Service award, 1956; Guggenheim fellow, 1963 Fellow AIAA; mem. Internat. Acad. Astronautics (corr.), Soc. History Tech. (Usher prize 1984, Leonardo da Vinci medal 1998), Nat. Acad. Engring., Phi Beta Kappa, Sigma Xi, Tau Beta Pi. Home: 555 Byron St #306 Palo Alto CA 94301 Office: Stanford U Stanford CA 94305 Business E-Mail: sts@stanford.edu.

VINCIQUERRA, TONY, broadcast executive; Grad., SUNY. With Times Union, Albany, NY, Sta. WTAE-TV, Pitts.; gen. sales mgr., v.p., sta. mgr. Sta. WBZ-TV, Boston, 1986—93; v.p., gen. mgr. Sta. KYW-TV, Phila.; exec. v.p. CBS TV, 1995—97; group exec. Hearst Corp., 1997; exec. v.p. Hearst-Argyle, 1997—2001, COO, 1999—2001; pres. Fox TV Network, 2001—02; pres., CEO Fox Networks Group, 2002—. Past chmn. Nat. Assn. TV Program Execs.; bd. dirs. Genesis Fund; bd. trustees So. Calif. Pub. Radio. Named one of Most Influential People in the World of Sports, Bus. Week, 2008. Office: FOX Networks Group 10201 W Pico Blvd FNC Bldg 101 5th Fl Los Angeles CA 90035

VINE, NAOMI, museum administrator; b. Seattle; MA and PhD, U. Chgo., 1976; postgrad., Emory U., 1991—. Dir. of edn. Mus. of Contemporary Art, Chgo., 1980-86; chief curator Dayton (Ohio) Art Inst., 1986-88; assoc. dir. High Mus. of Art, Atlanta, 1988; chief exec. ofr., pres. Orange County Mus. of Art, Newport Beach, Calif. Address: Orange Cty Museum of Art 850 San Clemente Dr Newport Beach CA 92660

VINSON, WILLIAM THEODORE, lawyer; BS, USAF Acad., 1965; JD, UCLA, 1969. Bar: Calif. 1970. Judge advocate USAF, 1970-74; trial counsel Phillips Petroleum, San Mateo, Calif., 1974-75; atty. Lockheed Corp., Westlake Village, Calif., 1975-90, v.p., sec., 1990-92, v.p., gen. couns., 92-95; v.p., chief counsel Lockheed Martin Corp., Westlake Village, 1995-98; cons. Lockheed Corp., Westlake Village, 1998; chmn. Siemens Govt. Svcs., Inc., 2001—. Chmn. SAP Govt. Support and Svcs. Inc., 2006—. Bd. dirs. Westminster Free Clinic, 2001—. Office: 5560 E Napoleon Ave Oak Park CA 91377-4746

VIOLA, BILL, artist, writer; b. NYC, Jan. 25, 1951; s. William John and Wynne Viola; m. Kira Perov; children: Blake, Andrei. BFA, Syracuse U., 1973, DFA, 1995, Sch. Art Inst. Chgo., 1997, Calif. Coll. Arts & Crafts, Oakland, 1998, Mass. Coll. Art, 1999, Calif. Inst. of the Arts, Valencia, 2000, U. Sunderland, Eng., 2000. Tech. dir. Art/Tapes/22 Video Studio, Florence, Italy, 1974-76; artist-in-residence Sta. WNET, NYC, 1976-83, WXXI-TV, Rochester, NY, 1979, Sony Corp., Atsugi Labs., Japan, 1980-81, San Diego Zoo, 1984; instr. Calif. Inst. of Arts, Valencia, 1983; represented by James Cohan Gallery, NYC. Solo exhbns. include The Kitchen Ctr., N.Y., 1974, Everson Mus. Art, Syracuse, N.Y., 1975, Mus. Modern Art, N.Y.C., 1979, 87, Whitney Mus. Art, N.Y.C., 1982, Musee d'Art Moderne, Paris, 1983, Mus. Contemporary Art, L.A., 1985, Fukui Prefectural Mus. Art, Fukui City, Japan, 1989, Staditsche Kunsthalle Düsseldorf, 1992, Moderna Musee, Stockholm, 1993, Museo Nacional Centro de Arte Reina Sofia, Madrid, 1993, Musee Cantonal des Beaux-Arts, Lausanne, Switzerland, 1993, Whitechapel Art Gallery, London, 1993, Tel Aviv Mus. Art, 1994, Musée d'Art Contemporain, Montreal, 1993, Centro Cultural/Banco de Brazil, Rio de Janeiro, 1994, 46th Venice Biennale, 1995, Festival d'Automne Paris, 1996, Bill Viola: A 25 Year Survey Exhbn., Whitney Mus. Am. Art, N.Y., travels to Whitney Mus. Am. Art, 1997, L.A. County Mus. Am. Art, 1998, Stedelijk Mus., Amsterdam, 1998, Mus. Pur Moderne Kunst and Shirnkunstalle Dominkankloister, Germany, 1999, San Francisco Mus. Modern Art, 1999, Art Inst. Chgo., 1999-2000, 2KM, Karlsruhe, Germany, 2000, James Cohan Gallery, N.Y., 2000, Anthony d'Offay Gallery, London, 2001, Bill Viola: Going Forth By Day, Deutsche Guggenheim Berlin, 2002; group exhbns. include De Saisset Art Gallery and Mus., Santa Clara, Calif., 1972, Whitney Mus. Am. Art, 1975-87, 89, 93, Stedelijk Mus., Amsterdam, 1984, Carnegie Mus. Art, Pitts., 1988, Kölnischer Kunstverein, Cologne, Germany, 1989, Israel Mus., Jerusalem, 1990, Musée Nat. d'Art Moderne, Ctr. Georges Pompidou, Paris, 1990, Martin Gropius Bau, Berlin, 1991, Mus. Moderne Kunst, Frankfurt, Germany, 1991, Royal Acad., London, 1993, Denver Art Mus., Columbus (Ohio) Art Mus., 1994, Anthony d'Offay Gallery, London, 1995, Mus. Modern Art, N.Y.C., 1995, Tate Gallery, London, 1995, Albright-Knox Art Gallery, 1996, Fabric Workshop, Phila., 1997, MOMA, N.Y., 1999, La Beauté, Found Cartier, 2000, Tate Modern, London, 2000, Nat. Gallery, London, 2000, James Cohan Gallery, NY, 2001; spl. screening film: Dèserts, Vienna, Austria, 1994, WhiteCahpel Art Gallery, London, 2001, 49th Venice Biennale, 2001, Perth Festival, Australia, 2001, Commune di Ferrara, Italy, 2001, Musse d'Art Contemporian de Montreal, Canada, 2001; commns. include The Stopping mind, Mus. Moderne Kunst, Frankfurt, 1991, Nantes Triptych, Dèlegation aux Arts Plastiques, Nantes, France, 1992, Slowly Turning Narrative, Isnt. Comtemporary Art, Phila., Va. Mus. Fine Art, Richmond, 1992, Tiny Deaths, Biennale d'Art Contemporain de Lyon, France, 1993, Dèserts, Konzerthause, Vienna, 1994, 3e Biennale d'Art contemporaire de Lyon, Musèe d'art contemporain, Lyon, France, 1995, Helaba Main Tower, Frankfurt, Germany, 2000, Gotesborgs Musiken, Sweden, 2001, Deserts, Konzerthaus, Vienna, 2001, Deserts, Carnigie Hall, New York, 2001, Deserts, Royal Festival Hall, London, 2001, Deserts, IRCAM, Centre Pomidou Main Hall, Paris, 2001, others; composer: (album) David Tudor-Rainforest IV, 1981; (video) Chott el-Djerid, Anthem, 1983, Hatsu-Yume, 1981, The Reflecting Pool, 1977-79, The Space Between the Teeth, 1976, Bill Viola: Selected Works, 1986, I Do Not Know What It Is I Am Like, 1986, The Passing, 1991, The City of Man, 1989, Nantes Triptych, 1992, Slowly Turning Narritive, 1992, Tiny Deaths, 1993, The Greetings, 1995, The Crossing, 1996, The Quintet of Remembrance, 2000, The Quintet of the Unseen, 2000, The Quintet of the Astonished, The Quintet of the Silent, 2000, Surrender, 2001, Catherine's Room, 2001, Five Angles for the Millenium, 2001, Going Forth By Day, 2002. Japan/U.S. Creative Arts fellow NEA, 1980, Rockefeller Found. Video Artist fellow, 1982, Visual Artist fellow NEA, 1983-89, Guggenheim Meml. Found. fellow, 1985, Intercultural Film/Video fellow Rockefeller Found., 1991; recipient Jury prize U.S. Film and Video Festival, 1982, Grand prize, 1983, Jury prize Video Culture/Can., 1983, Grand prize for video art, 1984, First prize for video art Athens (Ohio) Film/Video Festival, 1984, Maya Deren award Am. Film Inst., 1987, First prize Festival Internat. d'Art Video et des Nouvelles Images Electroniques de Locarno, 1987, John D. and Catherine T. MacArthur Found. award, 1989, Skowhegan medal, 1993, First prize Festival Internat. de Video, Cidade de Vigo, Spain, 1993, Medienkunstpreis, Siemens Kulturprogramm and Zentrum fur Kunst und Medientechnologie, Germany, 1993; scholar-in-residence The Getty Rsch. Inst. for History of Art and Humanities, L.A., 1998. Office: 282 Granada Ave Long Beach CA 90803 E-mail: info@billviola.com.

VIOLETTE, GLENN PHILLIP, transportation engineer; b. Hartford, Conn., Nov. 15, 1950; s. Reginald Joseph and Marielle Theresa (Bernier) B.; m. Susan Linda Begam, May 15, 1988. BSCE, Colo. State U., 1982. Registered profl. engr., Colo. Engring. aide Colo. State Hwy. Dept., Glenwood Springs, Colo., 1974-79, hwy. engr., 1980-82, Loveland, Colo., 1979-80, project engr. Glenwood Canyon, Colo., 1983-97; resident engr. Colo. State Dept. Transp., Craig, 1998—2004, project mgr., 2004—; ret. Guest speaker in field. Contbg. editor, author, photographer publs. in field. Recipient scholarship Fed. Hwy Adminstrn., 1978. Mem. ASCE, Amnesty Internat., Nat. Rifle Assn., Siera Club, Audubon Soc., Nature Conservancy, World Wildlife Fund, Cousteau Soc., Chi Epsilon.

VIRKAR, ANIL V., materials engineer, educator; BTech in Metall. Engring. with honors, Indian Inst. Tech., Bombay, 1967; MS in Engring. Mechanics, La. State U., Baton Rouge, 1969; PhD in Materials Sci., Northwestern U., Evanston, Ill., 1973. Postdoctoral fellow materials sci. & engring. U. Utah, 1973—74, rsch. asst. prof., 1974—76, asst. prof., 1976—79, assoc. prof., 1979—84, prof., 1984—, chair dept. materials sci. & engring., 1998—. Founding mem. Ceramatec, 1976. Contbr. articles to sci. jours., chapters to books. Fellow: Am. Ceramic Soc. (Ross Coffin Purdy award 1993); mem.: Electrochemical Soc., Am. Soc. Metals, NAE. Achievements include patents in field. Office: Dept Materials Sci & Engring U Utah 122 S Central Campus Dr Rm 304 Salt Lake City UT 84112 Office Phone: 801-581-5396. Office Fax: 801-581-4816. E-mail: anil.virkar@m.cc.utah.edu.

VITALE, RUTH ANN, former film company executive; b. Boston, Oct. 20, 1952; d. Joseph J. and Gilda J. (Camuso) V. BA in English, Tufts U., 1974; MS in Journalism, Boston U., 1975. Account exec. Sta. WNAC-TV, Boston, 1976-78, Top Market TV/Post-Newsweek, NYC, 1978-79; v.p., media account exec. McCann Erickson, NYC, 1979-81; mgr. sales ops. Hearst/ABC Video Services, NYC, 1981-82; dir. film acquisition The Movie Channel, NYC, 1982-83; sr. v.p. prodn. Vestron Pictures, Stamford, Conn., 1983-87, ind. producer, 1987-88; sr. v.p. prodn. United Artists/Metro-Goldwyn-Mayer, Inc., Beverly Hills, Calif., 1988—95, Fine Line Features/New Line Cinema Corp., Los Angeles, Calif., 1995—97; co-pres. Paramount Classics, Los Angeles, Calif., 1997—2005; pres. First Look Studios, Inc., Los Angeles, Calif., 2005—07.

VITEK, REG(INALD) A., lawyer; b. Bakersfield, Calif., Apr. 23, 1942; BA, San Diego State Coll., 1964; JD, UCLA, 1967. Bar: Calif. 1967, US Ct. Appeals (2d, 9th cir.), US Supreme Ct. 1976. Ptnr., bus. litigation Seltzer Caplan McMahon Vitek, San Diego. Lectr. Nat. Inst. Trial Advocacy. Mem.: ABA, State Bar Calif., San Diego County Bar Assn., Fed. Bar Assn., Assn. Trial Lawyers Am., San Diego County Trial Lawyers Assn., Assn. Bus. Trial Lawyers (founding mem. San Diego chpt.), Am. Inns of Ct., Louis M. Welsh San Diego chpt. (Master, mem. exec. com.). Office: Seltzer Caplan McMahon Vitek Symphony Towers 750 B St San Diego CA 92101 Office Phone: 858-685-3075. Office Fax: 858-702-6804. Business E-Mail: vitek@scmv.com.

VIZCAINO, JOSE LUIS PIMENTAL, professional baseball coach, retired professional baseball player; b. San Cristobal, Dominican Rep., Mar. 26, 1965; Grad. high sch., Dominican Rep. Infielder LA Dodgers, 1989-90, 1998—2000, spl. asst., 2008—; infielder Chgo. Cubs, 1991-93, NY Mets, 1994-96, Cleve. Indians, 1996, San Francisco Giants, 1997, 2006, NY Yankees, 2000, Houston Astros, 2001—05, St. Louis Cardinals, 2006. Achievements include being a member of the World Series Championship winning New York Yankees, 2000. Office: c/o LA Dodgers Dodger Stadium 1000 Elysian Pk Ave Los Angeles CA 90012-1500

VLAZNY, JOHN GEORGE, archbishop; b. Chgo., Feb. 22, 1937; s. John George and Marie Hattie (Brezina) Vlazny. BA, St. Mary of the Lake Coll., Mundelein, Ill., 1958; STL, Pontifical Gregorian U., Rome, 1962; MA in Classics, U. Mich., 1967; MEd, Loyola U., 1972; LLD (hon.), U. Portland, 1999. Ordained priest Archdiocese of Chgo., 1961, aux. bishop, 1983—87; assoc. pastor St. Paul of the Cross Ch., Park Ridge, Ill., 1962—63, St. Clement Ch., Chgo., 1963—68, St. Aloysius Ch., Chgo., 1968—72, pastor, 1979—81; assoc. pastor St. Sylvester Ch., Chgo., 1972—74, Precious Blood Ch., Chgo., 1974—79; faculty Quigley Prep., North Chgo., Ill., 1963—79, dean of studies, 1969—79; rector Niles Coll., Chgo., 1981—83; ordained bishop, 1983; bishop Diocese of Winona, Minn., 1987—97; archbishop Archdiocese of Portland, 1997—. Pres. Presbyteral Senate, Chgo., 1976—77; mem. Diocesan Clergy Personnel Bd., Chgo., 1981—84, chmn., 1983—84. Bd. dirs. NED, Latino Tng. Ctr., Chgo., 1980—81, Sacred Heart Sch. Theology, Hales Corners, Wis., 1986—, St. Mary's Coll., Winona, 1987—. Mem.: Nat. Conf. Cath. Bishops (various coms. 1983—), Nat. Comms. Found. (bd. dirs. 1990—). Roman Catholic. Avocations: music, running.

VOELZ, DAVID GEORGE, electrical engineer; b. Idaho Falls, Idaho, Feb. 24, 1959; s. George Leo and Emily Jane (Neunast) V.; m. Judi Rae Gore, Aug. 12, 1983. MSEE, U. Ill., 1983, PhD in Elec. Engring., 1987. Rsch. asst. U. Ill., Urbana, 1981-86; electronics engr. Phillips Lab. (formally USAF Weapons Lab.), Kirtland AFB, N.Mex., 1986—. Contbr. articles to Jour. of Geophysical Rsch., Applied Optics, and Optics Letters. Boy scout master Boy Scouts Am., Albuquerque, 1988-90. Recipient, Engineering Excellence award Optical Society of Am., 1995. Fellow Soc. of Photo-Optical Instrumentation Engrs.; mem. IEEE, Optical Soc. Am. Republican. Lutheran. Office: AFRL/DEBS Kirtland AFB NM 87117 Home: 5318 Redman Rd Las Cruces NM 88011-2500

VOGEL, CARL E., communications executive; b. Oct. 18, 1957; BS in Fin. and Acctg., St. Norbert Coll., DePere, Wis. With Jones Intercable, 1983; exec. v.p. EchoStar Comm. Inc., 1994—97; CEO Star Choice Comm., 1998; chmn., CEO Primestar Inc., 1998—99; exec. v.p., COO AT&T Broadband, 1999; sr. v.p. Liberty Media Corp., 1999—2001; pres., CEO Charter Comm. Inc., 2001—05; vice chmn. EchoStar Comm. Corp., 2005—, pres., 2006—. Bd. dirs. C-SPAN, CableLabs, EchoStar Comm. Corp., 2005—. Mem.: Nat. Cable TV Assn. (bd. dirs.). Office: EchoStar Comm Corp 9601 South Meridian Blvd Englewood CO 80112 Office Phone: 303-723-1000.

VOGEL, JEFFREY C., state agency administrator; m. Kathy Vogel; children: Sam, Chase. BS in Acctg., U. Wy., 1983. Acting commr. Wyo. Divsn. Banking, 1996, 2002, dep. banking commr., commr., 2002—. Vice chmn. Mo. Conf. State Bank Suprs., 2005. Office: Wyo Divsn Banking Herschler Bldg 3rd Fl E 122 W 25th St Cheyenne WY 82002 Office Phone: 307-777-7797. Office Fax: 307-777-3555. E-mail: jvogel@wyaudit.state.wy.us.

VOGELSBERG, ROSS TIMM, education educator, researcher; b. Bryn Mawr, Pa., Feb. 23, 1945; s. Robert Wilhelm Vogelsberg and Jean Byram (Fishburn) Blanchard. BS, Colo. State U., 1968; MS, Utah State U., 1974; PhD, U. Ill., 1979. Part-time assoc. Gateways Inc., Ft. Collins, Colo., 1968; master resource tchr. Utah State U., Logan, 1972-74, assoc. dir. project, 1974-77; rsch. assoc. U. Ill., Urbana, 1977-79; project dir., asst. prof. U. Vt., Burlington, 1979-85; project dir., assoc. prof. Temple U., Phila., 1985-94; exec. dir., prof. Rural Inst. Disabilities U. Mont., Missoula, 1995—. Contbr. numerous articles to profl. jours. and chpts. in books. With U.S. Army, 1969-71, ETO. Named one of Outstanding Young Men of Am., U.S. Jaycees, 1982; recipient Svc. award United Cerebral Palsy Pa., 1986. Mem. Assn. for Spl. Edn. Tech., Am. Ednl. Rsch. Assn., Assn. for Persons Analysis, Assn. for Persons with Severe Handicaps, Nat. Soc. for Performance and Instruction, Assn. for the Advancement of Behavior Therapy, Coun. for Exceptional Children, Am. Asns. on Mental Deficiency. Office: U Mont Rural Inst 634 Eddy Ave Missoula MT 59812-0001 Office Phone: 406-243-5467.

VOGT, ERICH WOLFGANG, physicist, academic administrator; b. Steinbach, Man., Can., Nov. 12, 1929; s. Peter Andrew and Susanna (Reimer) V.; m. Barbara Mary Greenfield, Aug. 27, 1952; children: Edith Susan, Elizabeth Mary, David Eric, Jonathan Michael, Robert Jeremy. BS, U. Man., 1951, MS, 1952; PhD, Princeton U., 1955; DSc (hon.), U. Man., 1982, Queen's U., 1984; LLD (hon.), U. Regina, 1986; DSc (hon.), Carleton U., 1988, U. B.C., 1999; LLD (hon.), Simon Fraser U., 1996. Rsch. officer Chalk River (Ont.) Nuclear Labs., 1956-65; prof. physics U. B.C., Vancouver, 1965-95, prof. emeritus, 1995—, assoc. dir. TRIUMF Project, 1968-73, dir. TRIUMF Project, 1981-94, v.p. univ., 1975-81; chmn. Sci. Council B.C., 1978-80. Co-editor: Advances in Nuclear Physics, 1968—; Contbr. articles to profl. jours. Decorated officer Order of Can., Order of BC; recipient Centennial medal of Can., 1967 Fellow Royal Soc. Can., Am. Phys. Soc.; mem. Can. Assn. Physicists (past pres., gold medal for achievement in physics 1988). Office: Triumf 4004 Wesbrook Mall Vancouver BC Canada V6T 2A3 Office Phone: 604-222-1047. Business E-Mail: vogt@triumf.ca.

VOGT, ROCHUS EUGEN, physicist, researcher; b. Neckarelz, Germany, Dec. 21, 1929; came to U.S., 1953; s. Heinrich and Paula (Schaefer) V.; m. Micheline Alice Yvonne Bauduin, Sept. 6, 1958; children: Michele, Nicole. Student, U. Karlsruhe, Germany, 1950-52, U. Heidelberg, 1952-53; SM, U. Chgo., 1957, PhD, 1961. Asst. prof. physics Calif. Inst. Tech., Pasadena, 1962-65, assoc. prof., 1965-70, prof., 1970—2002, R. Stanton Avery disting. svc. prof., 1982—2002, R. Stanton Avery disting. svc. prof. and prof. physics emeritus, 2002—, chmn. faculty, 1975-77, chief scientist Jet Propulsion Lab., 1977-78, chmn. div. physics, math. and astronomy, 1978-83, acting dir. Owens Valley Radio Obs., 1980-81, v.p. and provost, 1983-87. Vis. prof. physics MIT, 1988-94; dir. Caltech/MIT Laser Interferometer Gravitational Wave Observatory Project, 1987-94. Author: Cosmic Rays (in World Book Ency.), 1978, (with R.B. Leighton) Exercises in Introductory Physics, 1969; contbr. articles to profl. jours. Fulbright fellow, 1953-54; recipient Exceptional Sci. Achievement medal NASA, 1981, Profl. Achievement award U. Chgo. Alumni Assn., 1981. Fellow AAAS, A. Phys. Soc. Achievements include research in astrophysics and gravitation. Office: Calif Inst Tech 103-33 1200 E California Blvd Pasadena CA 91125-0001 Home Phone: 626-398-5066; Office Phone: 626-395-3800. Business E-Mail: vogt@caltech.edu.

VOHS, JAMES ARTHUR, health plan administrator; b. Idaho Falls, Idaho, Sept. 26, 1928; s. John Dale and Cliff Lucille (Packer) Vohs; m. Janice Hughes, Sept. 19, 1953 (dec. Oct. 1999); children: Lorraine, Carol, Nancy, Sharla; m. Eileen Galloway, Oct. 8, 2005. BA, U. Calif., Berkeley, 1952; postgrad., Harvard Sch. Bus., 1966. Employed by various Kaiser affiliated orgns., 1952—92; chmn., pres., CEO Kaiser Found. Hosps. and Kaiser Found. Health Plan, INc., Oakland, Calif., 1975—92, chmn. emeritus; chmn. bd. dirs. Holy Names Coll., 1981—92; chmn. Marcus Foster Inst., 1981—. Chmn. Fed. Res. Bank San Francisco, 1991—94. Mem. Oakland Bd. Port Commrs., 1993—96; bd. dirs. Oakland-Alameda County Coliseum Complex, 1986—96, Bay Area Coun., 1985—94, chmn., 1991—92. With US Army, 1946—48. Mem.: Inst. Medicine NAS. Personal E-mail: javohs@sbcglobal.net.

VOIGHT, JERRY D., lawyer; b. Bozeman, Mont., Aug. 21, 1937; children: Janet, Jason. BS in Chem. Engring., Mont. State U., 1959; JD with hons., George Washington U., 1965. Bar: DC 1966, US Supreme Ct. 1969, US Ct. Appeals (Fed. Cir.) 1982, registered: US Patent & Trademark Office. Sr. ptnr. Finnegan, Henderson, Farabow, Garrett & Dunner LLP, Washington, 1972—, mng. ptnr. Palo Alto Office Calif. Contbr. articles to profl. jour. Named one of best lawyers in intellectual property law, Best Lawyers in Am., 2005—06. Mem.: DC Bar Assn., ABA, Am. Intellectual Property Law Assn. Avocations: skiing, collecting wood block prints. Office: Finnegan Henderson Farabow Garrett & Dunner LLP Stanford Rsch Park 700 Hansen Way Palo Alto CA 94304-1016 Office Phone: 650-849-6600. Office Fax: 650-849-6666. Personal E-mail: jerry.voight@finnegan.com.

VOIGHT, JON, actor; b. Yonkers, NY, Dec. 29, 1938; s. Elmer and Barbara (Camp) V.; m. Lauri Peters, 1962 (div. 1967); m. Marcheline Bertrand, Dec. 12, 1971 (div. 1978); children: James Haven, Angelina Jolie. BFA, Cath. U., 1960; studied with, Sanford Meisner and Samantha Harper, NYC. Stage appearances include O Oysters Revue, 1961, The Sound of Music, 1961, A View from the Bridge, 1965, Romeo and Juliet, 1966, The Tempest, 1966, Two Gentlemen of Verona, 1966, That Summer-That Fall, 1967 (Theatre World award

1967), A Streetcar Named Desire, 1973, The Hashish Club, 1975, Hamlet, 1976, The Seagull, 1992; TV appearances include Cimarron Strip, Gunsmoke; films include Fearless Frank, 1967, Hour of the Gun, 1967, Out of It, 1969, Midnight Cowboy, 1969 (Acad. award nom. best actor 1969, NY Critics Circle award 1969, L.A. Film Critics award best actor 1969, BAFTA award most promising newcomer 1969, Golden Globe award most promising newcomer 1969), Catch-22, 1970, The Revolutionary, 1970, Deliverance, 1972, The All American Boy, 1973, Conrack, 1974, The Odessa File, 1974, End of the Game, 1976, Coming Home, 1978 (Acad. Award for Best Actor 1978, Golden Globe award 1978, Cannes Internat. Film festival award 1978, NY Film Critics best actor award 1978, L.A. Film Critics award best actor 1978), The Champ, 1979 (Golden Globe award 1979), Runaway Train, 1985 (Acad. award nominee best actor 1986, London Film Critics award nominee 1986, Golden Globe best actor 1986), Desert Bloom, 1986, Eternity, 1990, The Rainbow Warrior, 1992, Heat, 1995, Mission Impossible, 1996, Rosewood, 1997, Anaconda, 1997, Most Wanted, 1997, The Rainmaker, 1997, U Turn, 1997, I Once Had a Life, 1998, Enemy of the State, 1998, Varsity Blues, 1999, A Dog of Flanders, 1999, Pearl Harbor, 2001, Lara Croft: Tomb Raider, 2001, Zoolander, 2001, Ali, 2001, Holes, 2003, Karate Dog, 2004, The Manchurian Candidate, 2004, Superbabies: Baby Geniuses 2, 2004, National Treasure, 2004, September Dawn, 2006, Transformers, 2007, National Treasure: Book of Secrets, 2007, Pride and Glory, 2008, Four Christmases, 2008; (TV films) Chernobyl: The Final Warning, 1991, The Last of His Tribe, 1992, Convict Cowboys, 1995, Boys Will Be Boys, 1997, Noah's Ark, 1999, Second string, 2002, Jasper, Texas, 2003, The Five People You Meet in Heaven, 2004, Pope John Paul II, 2005; (mini-series) Return to Lonesome Dove, 1993; actor, prodr., co-writer (films) Lookin' To Get Out, 1982, The Fixer, 1998; actor, prodr. (films) Table for Five, 1983, A Tribute to Dustin Hoffman, 1999, Noah's Ark, 1999, Second String, 2000.

VOIGT, BARTON R., state supreme court chief justice; b. Scotland, SD; BA in History, MA in History, U. Wyo., Laramie, JD. Atty., Thermopolis, Wyo.; former Hot Springs County atty.; former county ct. judge Gillette; judge Wyo. Eigth Jud. Dist., Douglas, 1993—2001; justice Wyo. Supreme Ct., 2001—, chief justice, 2006—. Mem. Bd. of Jud. Policy and Adminstrn. Mem.: Wyo. Bar Assn. Office: Wyo Supreme Ct 2301 Capitol Ave Cheyenne WY 82001 Office Phone: 307-777-7573.

VOJTA, PAUL ALAN, mathematics professor; b. Mpls., Sept. 30, 1957; s. Francis J. and Margaret L. V. B in Math., U. Minn., 1978; MA, Harvard U., 1980, PhD, 1983. Instr. Yale U., New Haven, 1983-86; fellow Math. Scis. Rsch. Inst., Berkeley, Calif., 1986-87, Miller Inst. for Basic Rsch., Berkeley, 1987-89; assoc. prof. U. Calif., Berkeley, 1989-92, prof., 1992—. Mem. Inst. for Advanced Study, Princeton, 1989-90, 96-97. Author: Diophantine Approximations and Value Distribution Theory, 1987; editor: Jour. Reine Angew Math., 2004—. Recipient perfect score Internat. Math. Olympiad, 1975. Mem. Am. Math. Soc. (Frank Nelson Cole Number Theory prize 1992), Math. Assn. Am., Phi Beta Kappa, Tau Beta Pi. Avocations: skiing, computers. Office: Univ Calif Dept Math 970 Evans Hall 3840 Berkeley CA 94720-3840

VOLBERDING, PAUL ARTHUR, academic physician; b. Rochester, Minn., Sept. 26, 1949; s. Walter A. and Eldora M. (Prescher) V.; m. Juline Christofferson, June 15, 1971 (div. June 1976); m. Mary M. Cooke, June 6, 1980; children: Alexander, Benjamin, Emily. AB, U. Chgo., 1971; MD, U. Minn., 1975. Resident in internal medicine U. Utah, Salt Lake City, 1975-78; fellow in oncology U. Calif., San Francisco, 1978-81; dir. med. oncology San Francisco Gen. Hosp., 1981—, dir. AIDS program, 1983—; dir. Ctr. for AIDS Rsch. U. Calif., San Francisco, 1988—, prof. medicine, 1990—. Bd. dirs. Dignity Ptnrs. Inc., 1996—; elected mem., Inst. of Medicine, 1999. Editor: Medical Management in AIDS, 1986; editor Jour. of AIDS, 1990—. Fellow ACP, AAAS; mem. Internat. AIDS Soc. (founder, chmn. bd.). Office: U Calif San Francisco San Francisco AIDS Program 995 Potrero Ave San Francisco CA 94110-2859

VOLGY, THOMAS JOHN, political science educator, organization official; b. Budapest, Hungary, Mar. 19, 1946; BA magna cum laude, Oakland U., 1967; MA, U. Minn., 1969, PhD, 1972. Prof. polit. sci. U. Ariz., Tucson; dir. U. Teaching Ctr.; mayor City of Tucson, 1987-91. Exec. dir. Internat. Studies Assn., 1995—; chmn. telecom. com. U. Conf. Mayors, 1988—; Dem. nominee for congress, 1998; cons. H.S. curriculum project Ind. U. Author: Politics in the Trenches, 2001; co-author: The Forgotten Americans, 1992; editor: Exploring Relationships Between Mass Media and Political Culture: The Impact of Television and Music on American Society, 1976; contbr. articles to profl. jours.; producer two TV documentaries for PBS. Mem. Nat. Women's Polit. Caucus Conv., 1983, U.S. Senate Fin. Com., 1985, U.S. Ho. of Reps. Telecomm. Com., 1988—, Polit. Sci. Adminstrn. Com., 1986, Gov.'s Task Force on Women and Poverty, 1986, United Way, 1985-87; bd. dirs. Honors Program, 1981—, U. Teaching Ctr., 1988—, Tucson Urban League, 1981, Ododo Theatre, 1984, So. Ariz. Mental Health Care Ctr., 1987, Nat. Fedn. Local Cable TV Programmers; chmn. Internat. Rels. Caucus, 1981, 86—, Transp. and Telecommunications Com. Nat. League Cities, 1986, 88-91. NDEA scholar, 1964-76; NDEA fellow, 1967-70; recipient Oasis award for oustanding prodn. of local affairs TV programming; named Outstanding Young Am., 1981, Outstanding Naturalized Citizen of Yr., 1980; faculty research grantee U. Ariz., 1972-75, 77-78. Mem. Pima Assn. Govts., Nat. Fedn. Local Cable Programmers. Democrat. Jewish. Office: U Ariz Polit Dept Sci Tucson AZ 85721-0001

VOLPE, PETER ANTHONY, surgeon; b. Columbus, Ohio, Dec. 17, 1936; s. Peter Anthony and Jeanette Katherine (Volz) V.; m. Suzanne Stephens, Sept. 5, 1959; children: John David, Michael Charles; m. Kathleen Ann Townsend, Mar. 28, 1978; 1 child, Mark Christopher; m. Theresa Ann Morse, Aug. 27, 2000. BA cum laude, Ohio State U., 1958, MD summa cum laude, 1961. Diplomate Am. Bd. Surgery, Am. Bd. Colon and Rectal Surgery (pres. 1988). Pvt. practice, San Francisco, 1969—; sr. ptnr. Volpe, Chui, Abel, Yee, Sternberg, San Francisco, 1987—; clin. prof. surgery U. Calif., San Francisco, 1995—. Asst. clin. prof. surgery U. Calif., San Francisco, 1972-95; chmn. dept. surgery St. Mary's Hosp. and Med. Ctr., San Francisco, 1978-90. Contbr. articles to profl. jours. Lt. USN, 1962—64. Fellow ACS (bd. govs. 1988-94), Am. Soc. Colon and Rectal Surgeons (treas. 1985-89, pres. 1990); mem. San Francisco Surg. Soc., San Francisco Med. Soc. Office: Volpe Chiu Abel and Yee Sternberg 3838 California St San Francisco CA 94118-1522 Office Phone: 415-668-0411.

VOLPERT, RICHARD SIDNEY, lawyer; b. Cambridge, Mass., Feb. 16, 1935; s. Samuel Abbot and Julia (Fogel) V.; m. Marcia Flaster, June 11, 1958; children: Barry, Sandy, Linda, Nancy. BA, Amherst Coll., 1956; LL.B. (Stone scholar), Columbia U., 1959. Bar: Calif. bar 1960. Atty. firm O'Melveny & Myers, Los Angeles, 1959-86, ptnr. LA, 1967-86, Skadden, Arps, Slate, Meagher & Flom, LA, 1986-95, Munger, Tolles & Olson, LA, 1995—. Pub. Jewish Jour. of Los Angeles, 1985-87. Editor, chmn.: Los Angeles Bar Jour, 1965, 66, 67, Calif. State Bar Jour, 1972-73. Chmn. cmty. rels. com. Jewish Fedn.-Coun. L.A., 1977-80; bd. dirs. Jewish Fedn.-Coun. Greater L.A., 1976-99, v.p., 1978-81; pres. Los Angeles County Natural History Mus. Found., 1978-84, trustee, 1974—, chair bd. dirs., 1992-97, pres., bd. govs., 1997—; chmn. bd. councilors U. So. Calif. Law Ctr., 1979-85; vice chmn. Nat. Jewish Cmty. Rels. Adv. Coun., 1981-84, mem. exec. com., 1978-85; bd. dirs. U. Judaism, 1973-89, bd. govs., 1973-89; bd. dirs. Valley Beth Shalom, Encino, Calif., 1964-88; mem. capital program major gifts com. Amherst Coll., 1978-86; bd. dirs., mem. exec. com. L.A. Wholesale Produce Market Devel. Corp., 1978-95, v.p., 1981-93, pres. 1993-96; mem. exec. bd. L.A. chpt. Am. Jewish Com., 1967—, pres., 1999-2002, nat bd. govs., 2000-, nat. v.p., 2006-; vice-chmn. Los Angeles County Econ. Devel. Coun., 1978-81; bd. dirs. Jewish Cmty. Found., 1981—, Brandeis-Bardin Inst., 1995-2000, L.A. Chamber Orch., 2002-04; mem. Pacific S.W. regional bd. Anti Defamation League B'nai B'rith, 1964—. Named Man of Year, 1978 Fellow Am. Bar Found.; mem. Los Angeles County Bar Assn. (trustee 1968-70, chmn. real property sect. 1974-75), Los Angeles County Bar Found. (trustee 1977-80, 96-99), Calif. Bar Assn. (com. on adminstrn. justice 1973-76), Am. Coll. Real Estate Lawyers (bd. govs. 1996-99), Anglo-Am. Real Property Inst. (treas. 1995-98), Amherst Club of So. Calif. (dir. 1968-85, pres. 1972-73). Jewish. Home: 16055 Royal Oak Rd Encino CA 91436-3913 Office: Munger Tolles & Olson 355 S Grand Ave 35th Fl Los Angeles CA 90071-1560 Office Phone: 213-683-9101. Business E-Mail: richard.volpert@mto.com.

VON BRANDENSTEIN, PATRIZIA, production designer; Prodn. designer The Mirisch Agy., LA, 1978—. Prodn. designer: (films) Heartland, 1979, Breaking Away, 1979, Ragtime, 1981 (Academy award nomination best art direction 1981), Silkwood, 1983, Amadeus, 1984 (Academy award best art direction 1984), A Chorus Line, 1985, The Money Pit, 1986, No Mercy, 1987, The Untouchables, 1987 (Academy award nomination best art direction 1987), Working Girl, 1988, The Lemon Sisters, 1990, Postcards From the Edge, 1990, Billy Bathgate, 1992, Sneakers, 1992, Leap of Faith, 1993, Six Degrees of Separation, 1993, The Quick and the Dead, 1995, Just Cause, 1995, The People vs. Larry Flynt, 1996, A Simple Plan, 1998, Man on the Moon, 1999, Shaft, 2000, It Runs in the Family, 2002, The Emperor's Club, 2002, Ice Harvest, 2006, All the King's Men, 2006, Goya's Ghosts, 2006; costume designer: (films) Between the Lines, 1977, Saturday Night Fever, 1977, A Little Sex, 1982.

VON DASSANOWSKY, ROBERT, literature and film professor, writer, producer; b. NYC, Jan. 28, 1960; s. Elfi von Dassanowsky. Grad., Am. Acad. Dramatic Arts, Pasadena; BA with honors, UCLA, 1985, MA, 1988, PhD, 1992. Actor, 1975—; asst. prof. German, UCLA, 1992-93; asst. prof. German U. Colo., Colorado Springs, 1993-99, assoc. prof. German and film, 1999—2006, head German studies, 1999—2006, dir. film studies, 1999—, interim chair dept. visual and performing arts, 2000-01, chair dept. langs. and cultures, 2001—06, prof. German and film, 2006—. CEO, prodr. Belvedere Film, LLC, 1999; vis. prof. German UCLA, 2007—08; interim chair dept. langs. & cultures, 2009. Author: (plays) The Birthday of Margot Beck, 1980, Briefly Noted, 1981, Vespers, 1982 (Beverly Hills Theatre Guild award 1984), Tristan in Winter, 1986, Songs of a Wayfarer, 1986, Coda, 1991, (criticism) Phantom Empires: The Novels of A. Lernet-Holenia and the Question of Postimperial Austrian Identity, 1996, Verses of a Marriage, Translation of Poetry Collection by Hans Raimund, 1996, Telegrams from the Metropole: Selected Poetry, 1999, Gale Encyclopedia of Multicultural America, 2nd edit., 2000; contbg. editl. advisor: International Dictionary of Films and Filmmakers, 4th edit., 2001, Mars in Aries, trans. of novel by A. Lernet-Holenia, 2003, Austrian Cinema: A History, 2005; co-editor New Austrian Film, 2009, Hueo Von Hofmannsthal's Der Schnierige: New Approaches, 2009; founding editor Rohwedder: Internat. Jour. Lit. and Art, 1986-93; editor Pen Center mag., 1992-98; contbg. editor Osiris, Rampike, Poetry Salzburg Rev.; mem. editl. bd. Modern Austrian Lit., 1997-01; exec. prodr. The Nightmare Stumbles Past, 2002, Semmelweis, 2001, Wilson Chance, 2005; co-prodr. Epicure, 2002, Believe, 2003; assoc. prodr. The Archduke and Herbert Hinkel, 2009; columnist Celluloid Mag., Austria; editl. adv. bd. Ariadne Press, 1999—; editor U. Press. of South, 2004-; contbr. (European cinema) Greenwood Encyclopedia of World Popular Culture, 2007, dir. Elfi Von Dassanowsky Found. Mem. bd. advisors The Internt. Exptl. Cinema Exposition, Denver Brit. Film Festival, Rockefeller Found. Media Arts Fellowship, 2005-. Recipient Decoration of Honor in Silver, Austria, 2005, Order of the Vitez (Hungary); Cultural grantee City of L.A., 1990, 91, 92; Pres.'s Fund for Humanities grantee U. Colo., 1996, 2001; named Colo. Prof. of Yr., Carnegie Found./Coun. for Advancement and Support of Edn., 2004; recipient Residency award Karolyi Found., France, 1979, Letters, Arts and Scis. Rsch. and Creative Work award U. Colo., 2002, Chancellor's award, 2006 Mem. MLA, PEN USA (bd. dirs. L.A. 1992-99, founder and pres. Colo. chpt. 1994-99 2002-03), PEN Austria, Internat. Lernet-Holenia Soc. (v.p. 1998-2006), Austrian Am. Film Assn. (v.p. 1997—), Austria Mundi (US rep. 2002—), Soc. Cinema and Media Studies, Poets and Writers, Modern Austrian Lit. and Culture Assn. (mem. exec. coun. 2006—09), L.A. Poetry Festival, SAG, Concordia Assn. Journalists and Writers (Austria), Am. Coll. Heraldry (bd. govs. 2000-08), European Acad. Arts and Scis., U.S. Fencing Assn., Constantinian Order St. George, Mensa; fellow Royal Hist. Soc, Europa Nostra Office: U Colo Dept Langs and Cultures Colorado Springs CO 80933-7150 Office Phone: 719-255-3562. E-mail: belvederefilm@yahoo.com.

VONDER HAAR, THOMAS H., meteorology educator; b. Quincy, Ill., Dec. 28, 1942; m. Dee M. Clark, 1980; children: Kim, Kurt, Nicholas, Krista, Matthew. BS, St. Louis U., 1963; MS, U. Wis., 1964, PhD in Meteorology, 1968. Assoc. scientist meteorology Space Sci. & Engring. Ctr. U. Wis., Madison, 1968-70; assoc. prof. meteorology Colo. State U., Ft. Collins, 1970-77, prof. atmospheric sci., 1977—, univ. disting. prof., 1994, head dept. atmospheric sci., 1974-84, acting dean Coll. Engring., 1981-82. Cons. U.S. Army, ITT Aerospace, Sci. and Tech. Corp., World Meteor Orgn. UN, Ball Aerospace Corp., 1969—. Mem. Am. Meteorol. Soc., Sigma Xi. Office: Coop Inst Rsch in Atmosphere Colo State U Fort Collins CO 80523-1375

VON DER HEYDT, JAMES ARNOLD, federal judge; b. Miles City, Mont., July 15, 1919; s. Harry Karl and Alice S. (Arnold) von der H.; m. Verna E. Johnson, May 21, 1952. BA, Albion Coll., 1942; JD, Northwestern U., 1951. Bar: Alaska 1951. Pvt. practice, Nome, Alaska, 1953—59; judge superior ct. Juneau, Alaska, 1959—66; from judge to sr. judge U.S. Dist. Ct. Alaska, 1966—; U.S. commr. Nome, 1951—; U.S. atty. divsn. 2 Dist. Alaska, 1951—53; mem. Alaska Ho. of Reps., 1957—59. Author: Mother Sawtooth's Nome, 1990, Alaska, The Short and Long of It, 2000. Pres. Anchorage Fine Arts Mus. Assn. Recipient Disting. Alumni award Albion Coll., 1995, Professionalism and Ethics award Inn of Ct., 2005. Mem. Alaska Bar Assn. (bd. govs. 1955-59, pres. 1959-60), Am. Judicature Soc., Masons (32d degree), Shriners, Phi Delta Phi, Sigma Nu. Avocations: researching arctic bird life, creative writing, painting. Office: US Dist Ct 222 W 7th Ave Box 40 Anchorage AK 99513-7564 Home Phone: 907-279-4298; Office Phone: 907-677-6254.

VON HIPPEL, PETER HANS, chemistry professor, researcher; b. Goettingen, Germany, Mar. 13, 1931; came to U.S., 1937, naturalized, 1942; s. Arthur Robert and Dagmar (Franck) von H.; m. Josephine Baron Raskind, June 20, 1954; children: David F., James A., Benjamin J. BS, MIT, Cambridge, Mass., 1952; MS, MIT, 1953, PhD, 1955. Phys. biochemist Naval Med. Research Inst., Bethesda, Md., 1956-59; from asst. prof. to assoc. prof. biochemistry Med. Sch. Dartmouth Coll., 1959-67; prof. chemistry, mem. Inst. Molecular Biology U. Oreg., 1967-79, dir. Inst. Molecular Biology, 1969-80, chmn. dept. chemistry, 1980-87; rsch. prof. chemistry Am. Cancer Soc., 1989—. Chmn. biopolymers Gordon Conf., 1968; mem. trustees vis. com. biology dept. MIT, 1973—76; mem. bd. sci. counsellors Nat. Inst. Arthritis, Metabolic and Digestive Diseases NIH, 1974—78, mem. coun. Nat. Inst. Gen. Med. Scis., 1982—86, mem. dir.'s adv. com., 1987—92; bd. dirs. Fedn. Am. Socs. for Exptl. Biology, 1994—98; mem. NIH-CSR panel on boundaries for sci. rev., 1998—2003, mem. joint steering com. for pub. policy, 1998—2005. Mem. editl. bd. Jour. Biol. Chemistry, 1967-73, 76-82, Biochem. Biophys. Acta, 1965-70, Physiol. Revs., 1972-77, Biochemistry, 1977-80, Trends in Biochem. Soc., 1987—, Protein Sci., 1990-95; editor Jour. Molecular Biology, 1986-94; contbr. articles to profl. jours., chpts. to books. Lt. M.S.C. USNR, 1956-59. Recipient Merck award Am. Soc. Biochem. and Molecular Biology, 2000; NSF predoctoral fellow, 1953-55; NIH postdoctoral fellow, 1955-56; NIH sr. fellow, 1959-67; Guggenheim fellow, 1973-74 Fellow: Biophys. Soc., Am. Acad. Arts and Scis.; mem.: AAAS, Am. Philosophic Soc., Fedn. Am. Scientists, Nat. Acad. Scis., Biophys. Soc. (coun. 1970—73, pres. 1973—74), Am. Soc. Biochem. and Molecular Biology, Am. Chem. Soc., Sigma Xi. Home: 1900 Crest Dr Eugene OR 97405-1753 Business E-Mail: petevh@molbio.uoregon.edu.

VON HOFF, DANIEL DOUGLAS, oncologist; b. Oshkosh, Wis., Apr. 29, 1947; BS, Carroll Coll., 1969; MD, Columbia U., 1973. Diplomate Am. Bd. Internal Medicine, Am. Bd. Oncology. Intern in internal medicine U. Calif., San Francisco, 1973-74, resident in internal medicine, 1974-75; med. oncology fellow Nat. Cancer Inst.; mem. faculty medicine U. Tex. Health Sciences Ctr., San Antonio, 1975—99; joined faculty U. Ariz. Health Sciences Center, 1999, prof. medicine, molecular and cell biology, and pathology, dir. Ariz. Cancer Ctr., dir. Cancer Therapeutics Program, 2003; exec. v.p., dir. translational drug devel. divsn., head pancreatic cancer rsch. program Translational Genomics Rsch. Inst. (TGen), Phoenix, 2003, now sr. investigator, dir. translational rsch. Mem. Nat. Cancer Adv. Bd., 2004—, acting chair, 2005—. Recipient Weinberg Award, Dana Farber Cancer Ctr., Harvard Med. Sch., Block Award, Ohio State U., 2003, Frances E. Bull Award, U. Mich. Comprehensive Cancer Ctr. and Divsn. Hematology/Oncology, 2003. Fellow Am. Coll. Physicians; mem. AMA, Am. Assn. Cancer Rsch. (pres. 1999-2000; Richard and Hinda Rosenthal Found. award 1997), Am. Soc. Clin. Oncology. Office: Translational Genomics Rsch Inst Ste 660 445 N 5th St Phoenix AZ 85004

VON REICHBAUER, PETER GRAVES, state senator; b. Seattle, Dec. 30, 1944; s. Ludwig and Marian VonR.; m. Martha Ann Lindberg, June 26, 1983; children: Jeff, Jeremy, Katherine. BA, U. Ala., 1971. Senator State of Wash., Olympia, 1986—; Rep. whip Senate Rep. Caucus, Olympia, 1985—. Treas. St. Francis Community Hosp., Federal Way, Wash., 1986; vice chmn. U.S. Olympics Com., 1986; bd. dirs. Federal Way Boys and Girls Club, 1986. Served to capt. inf. U.S. Army. Mem.: Kiwanis (pres. Federal Way club 1986). Roman Catholic. Office: PO Box 3737 Federal Way WA 98063-3737

VOORHEES, JAMES DAYTON, JR., lawyer; b. Haverford, Pa., Nov. 14, 1917; s. James Dayton Voorhees and Elsa Denison Jameson; m. Mary Margaret Fuller, Sept. 5, 1942 (dec. Apr. 1991); children: J. Dayton III, Susan F. Voorhees-Maxfield, Jane Voorhees Kiss; m. Rosemarie Stewart, Jan. 7, 2004. BA, Yale U., 1940; JD, Harvard U., 1943. Bar: N.H. 1947, Colo. 1948, U.S. Dist. Ct. Colo. 1948, U.S. Ct. Appeals (10th cir.) 1949, U.S. Ct. Appeals (5th cir.) 1956, U.S. Supreme Ct. 1960. Assoc. Johnson & Robertson, Denver, 1947-50; atty. Conoco Inc., Denver, 1950-56; ptnr. Moran, Reidy & Voorhees, Denver, 1956-78, Kutak, Rock & Huie, Denver, 1978-80; ptnr., counsel Davis, Graham & Stubbs, Denver, 1980—. Mem. Denver Bd. Edn., 1965-71, pres. 1967-69. Lt. comdr. USNR, 1941-46, ATO, PTO. Mem.: ABA, Denver Bar Assn., Colo. Bar Assn., University Club, Denver Country Club.

VOORHEES, JOHN LLOYD, columnist; b. DeWitt, Iowa, Aug. 30, 1925; s. Lloyd William and Elsie Irene (Bousselot) V. BA in History, U. Iowa, 1951; BA in Journalism, U. Wash., 1953. Tchr. Oelwein (Iowa) High Sch., 1951-52; columnist Seattle Post-Intelligencer, 1953-71; columnist, critic Seattle Times, 1971-98. With U.S. Army, 1946-48. Democrat.

VOS, HUBERT DANIEL, investor; b. Paris, Aug. 2, 1933; s. Marius and Aline (Porge) V.; m. Susan Hill, Apr. 18, 1958; children: Wendy, James. BA, Institut d'Etudes Politiques, U. Paris, 1954; M in Pub. Adminstrn., Princeton U., 1956. Internal auditor Internat. Packers Ltd., 1957-61, dir. fin., 1962-64; asst. to contr. Monsanto Co., 1964-66, contr. internat. div., 1966-69; v.p. planning and fin. Smith Kline Corp., 1969-72; sr. v.p. fin. Comml. Credit Co., Balt., 1972-74; sr. v.p. fin. and adminstrn., dir. Norton Simon Inc., NYC, 1974-79; sr. v.p. fin., dir. Becton Dickinson and Co., Paramus, NJ, 1979—2004; pres. Stonington Capital Corp., Santa Barbara, Calif., 1984—. Mem. Santa Barbara Mus. Art, Scholarship Found. of Santa Barbara, La Cumbre Golf and Country Club. Home: 800 Via Hierba Santa Barbara CA 93110-2222 Personal E-mail: hubertvos@aol.com.

VOSBECK, ROBERT RANDALL, architect; b. Mankato, Minn., May 18, 1930; s. William Frederick and Gladys (Anderson) V.; m. Phoebe Macklin, June 21, 1953; children: Gretchen, Randy, Heidi, Macklin. BArch, U. Minn., Mpls., 1954. Various archtl. positions, 1956-62; ptnr. Vosbeck-Vosbeck & Assocs., Alexandria, Va., 1962-66, VVKR Partnership, Alexandria, 1966-79; exec. v.p. VVKR Inc.,

1979-82, pres., 1982-88; prin. Vosbeck/DMJM, Washington and Alexandria, Va., 1989-94; v.p. DMJM Arch. and Engring., 1990-94; pvt. practice archtl. cons., 1994—. Mem. Nat. Capital Planning Commn., 1976-81, U.S./USSR Joint Group on Bldg. Design and Constrn., 1974-79; mem. Nat. Park System Adv. Bd., 1984-88. Archtl. works include Pub. Safety Ctr., Alexandria, Va., 1987, Yorktown Visitors Ctr, Va., 1976, Frank Reeves Mcpl. Office Bldg., Washington, 1986, Fed. Bldg., Norfolk, Va., 1979, Jeff Davis Assocs. Office Complex, Arlington, Va., 1991, Westminster Continued Care Retirement Community, Lake Ridge, Va., 1993; author: Design Matters: The Story of VVKR, 2003, A Legacy of Leadership-The Presidents of the American Institute of Architect, 2007. Pres. Alexandria Jaycees, 1960-61; v.p. Va. Jaycees, 1962-63; pres. Alexandria Ch. of Com., 1974-75; bd. dirs. Vail Religious Found., 1995-2008. Engring. officer USMC, 1954-56. Recipient Plaque of Honor, Fedn. Colegios Architects, Republic of Mexico, Alumni Achievement award U. Minn. Coll. Arch., 2001, hon. fellowship Colegios Architects of Spain, Royal Archtl. Inst. Can., Soc. Architects of Mex., AIA Kemper award, 2007, Outstanding Achievement award, U. Minn., 2008; named Outstanding Young Man in Va., 1963, Acadamecian, Internt. Acad. Arch. Fellow AIA (bd. dirs. 1976-78, v.p. 1979-80, pres. 1981), Internat. Union Architects (coun. 1981-87), Nat. Trust Hist. Preservation. Presbyterian. Home and Office: 9064 Ranch River Cir Highlands Ranch CO 80126

VOSEVICH, KATHI ANN, writer, editor; b. St. Louis, Oct. 12, 1957; d. William and Catherine V.; m. James Hughes Meredith, Sept. 6, 1986. AB with honors, St. Louis U., 1980, MA, 1983; PhD, U. Denver, 1988. Tchg. fellow St. Louis U., 1980-83, acad. advising fellow, 1983-84; tchg. fellow U. Denver, 1985-87; prof. ESL BNM Talensch., Uden, Netherlands, 1988-91; instr. English, mentor U. Ga., Athens, 1992-94; vis. asst. prof. Colo. Coll., Colorado Springs, 1994; sr. tech. writer and editor Titan Client/Server Techs., Colorado Springs, 1994-96, head documentation, libr., 1996-97; documentation mgr. Beechwood, Colorado Springs, 1997-98, tech. mgr., 1998-99; tech. writer Microsoft, Redmond, Wash., 1999-2000; documentation and process mgr. Sprint, Denver, 2000; practice and group mgr. e-bus. Sprint Corp., Denver, 2000—02, svc. launch mgr. Mobile Computing Svcs., 2002—03, strategic market mgr., 2003—05, strategic alliances mgr., 2005, lead bus. strategist, 2005—06, sr. comm. mgr., 2006—07; pres. The Dufallu Group, Denver, 2007—, CEO, 2007—; vis. faculty Shorter Coll., 2008—; sr. telecom analyst Faulkner Info., 2008—. Forensic judge USAF Acad., Colo., 1987-88; edn. officer Volkel (The Netherlands) Air Base, 1988-91; instr. English European divsn. U. Md., The Netherlands and Belgium, 1989-91. Author: Customer Care User's Guide, 1996, Interview with Joseph Heller, 1999, Conversations with Joseph Heller in Understanding the Literature of World War II, 1999, Office Update, 1999-2000, Tutoring the Tudors, 2000, Sprint Takes Messaging into the Future, 2003; editor: Subscription Services System Documentation, 1996, Titan Process Documentation, 1994-96; copy editor: Language, Ideas, and American Culture; War, Literature and the Arts; contbr. over 100 electronic texts and articles to profl. jours. Colo. scholar U. Denver, 1985-86, grad. dean scholar, 1988; NEH fellow U. Md., 1994 Mem. MLA, Phi Beta Kappa, Alpha Sigma Nu. Roman Catholic. Avocations: writing, drawing, raising Bernese mountain dogs.

VOTH, ALDEN H., political science professor; b. Goessel, Kans., May 4, 1926; s. John F. and Helena (Hildebrandt) V.; m. Norma E. Jost, Aug. 18, 1956; children: Susan, Thomas. BA, Bethel Coll., 1950; MS in Econs., Iowa State U., Ames, 1953; PhD in Internat. Rels., U. Chgo., 1959. Assoc. prof. polit. sci. Upland (Calif.) Coll., 1960-63; prof. polit. sci. San Jose (Calif.) State U., 1963-65, 67-91, prof. emeritus, 1991—. Vis. prof. polit. sci. Am. U. in Cairo, 1965-67; spkr. in field of crisis in Mid. East. Author: Moscow Abandons Israel, 1980, (with others) The Kissinger Legacy, 1984. Trustee Pomona (Calif.) Valley Am. Assn. UN, 1963; participant China Ednl. Exch., 1996. Am. U. in Cairo Rsch. grantee, 1966; Nat. Coun. on U.S.-Arab Rels. fellow, 1990—. Achievements include Organized four public seminars on the middle east crisis. San Jose, spring, 2005. Home: 1385 Kimberly Dr San Jose CA 95118-1426 Office: San Jose State U One Washington Sq San Jose CA 95192 Office Phone: 408-264-1662. Personal E-mail: ahvoth@aol.com.

VRABECK, KATHY PATTERSON, video game company executive; b. 1963; BA, DePauw U., 1985; MBA, Ind. U., 1989. Sales assoc. Pillsbury Co., Quaker Oats Co., Eli Lilly & Co.; sr. v.p. mktg., gen. mgr. ConAgra Grocery; exec. v.p., global brand mgmt. Activision Inc., 1999—2000, exec. v.p., global pub. & brand mgmt., 2000—03, pres. pub., 2003—06; pres., casual entertainment Electronic Arts, Inc., Redwood City, Calif., 2007—. Bd. dirs. AVP Inc., 2006—. Named one of 100 Most Powerful Women in Entertainment, Hollywood Reporter, 2003, 2004, '25 Up and Coming Media Executives, Bus. Week, 2005, Kelley Sch. Bus. Acad. Alumni Fellows, Ind. U., 2005. Office: Electronic Arts Inc 209 Redwood Shores Pkwy Redwood City CA 94065

VREDEVOE, DONNA LOU, academic administrator, microbiologist, educator, biomedical researcher; BA in Bacteriology, UCLA, 1959, PhD in Microbiology, 1963. USPHS postdoctoral fellow Stanford (Calif.) U., 1963—64; instr. bacteriology UCLA, 1963, postgrad. rsch. immunologist dept. surgery Ctr. Health Scis., 1964-65, asst. rsch. immunologist dept. surgery Ctr. Health Scis., 1964-67, asst. prof. Sch. Nursing, Ctr. Health Scis., 1967-70, assoc. prof., 1970-76; prof. Sch. Nursing, Ctr. Health Scis., 1976—, assoc. dean Sch. Nursing, 1976-78, acting assoc. dean Sch. Nursing, 1985-86, asst. dir. space planning Cancer Ctr., 1976-78, dir. space planning, 1978-90, cons. to lab. nuc. medicine and radiation biology, 1967-80, acting dean Sch. Nursing, 1995-96. Chair acad. senate UCLA, 1999—2000, vice chancellor acad. pers., 2001—06, spl. asst. to chancellor, 2006—07, prof., vice chancellor emerita, 2006—. Contbr. articles to profl. publs. Postdoctoral fellow USPHS, 1963-64; Mabel Wilson Richards scholar UCLA, 1960-61; rsch. grantee Am. Cancer Soc., Calif. Inst. Cancer Rsch., Calif. divsn. Am. Cancer Soc., NIH, USPHS, Am. Nurses Found., Cancer Rsch. Coordinating Com. U. Calif., Dept. Energy, UCLA. Mem Am. Soc. Microbiology, Am. Assn. Immunologists, Am. Assn. Cancer Rsch., Nat. League Nursing (2d v.p. 1979-81), Sigma Xi, Alpha Gamma Sigma, Sigma Theta Tau (nat. hon. mem.). Office: UCLA Sch Nursing 700 Tiverton Ave 3-232 Factor Bldg Box 951702 Los Angeles CA 90095-1702

VUCANOVICH, BARBARA FARRELL, former United States Representative, Nevada; b. Ft. Dix, NJ, June 22, 1921; d. Thomas F. and Ynez (White) Farrell; m. Ken Dillon, Mar. 8, 1950 (dec. 1964); children: Patty Dillon Cafferata, Mike, Ken, Tom, Susan Dillon Anderson; m. George Vucanovich, June 19, 1965 (dec. Dec. 1998). Student, Manhattanville Coll. of Sacred Heart, 1938-39. Owner, operator Welcome Aboard Travel, Reno, 1968-74; Nev. rep. for Senator Paul Laxalt, 1974-82; mem. 98th-104th Congresses from 2d Nev. dist., 1983-96; chmn. appropriations subcom. on military construction; Rep. natl. committeewoman Nev. Rep. Party, 1996-2000. Pres. Nev. Fedn. Republican Women, Reno, 1955-56; former pres. St. Mary's Hosp. Guild, Lawyer's Wives. Mem.: Hidden Valley Country (Reno). Roman Catholic.

VUOTO, ANTHONY (TONY) F., bank executive; BA, Princeton U., NJ; MBA, U. Pa. Wharton Sch. Bus. Pres. consumer lending divsn. Bank One Corp., pres., COO First USA Bank; vice chmn., CFO Providian Fin. Corp., San Francisco, 2002—05; sr. v.p., CFO Card Services Washington Mutual Inc., Seattle, 2005—07, exec. v.p., pres. Card Svcs., 2007—08.*

WAAK, PATRICIA ANN, political organization administrator; b. Muskogee, Okla., Feb. 1, 1943; d. Boxly William and Anne Nell (Smith) Waak; children: Cinira Anne Baldi, Rachel Nell Carter. Student, Tulane U., 1961—62, U. Houston, 1964—65, George Mason U., 1976—77. RN Va. Vol. nurse Peace Corps, Maceio, Brazil, 1966—68; staff nurse U. Wis. Children's Hosp., Madison, 1968—70; dir. counseling Planned Parenthood, Washington, 1973—75; spl. asst. Devel. Support Bur. US Agency for Internat. Devel. (USAID), Washington, 1977—78, assoc. dir. Office of Population, 1978—82, project design team Zimbabwe, 1985, evaluation team Kenya, Uganda, Nigeria, 1987; asst. dir. Columbia U. Ctr. Population and Family Health, NYC, 1982—85; dir. population Nat. Audubon Soc., 1985—2002; chairwoman Colo. Dem. Party, Denver, 2005—. US del. UN Population Commn., 1981—82; cons. Family Planning Internat., 1973, Global Com. of Parliamentarians on Population and Devel., 1984—85; project design team US AID, Zimbabwe, 1985; NGO participant UN Mid-Decade Conf. of Women, Copenhagen, 1981; moderator global population anniversary Peace Corps Conf., 1981; mem. environ. strategy and planning commn. World Conservation Union; lectr. in field. Exec. prodr.: (population videotape) What is the Limit, Sharing the Earth, Finding the Balance, Population and Wildlife; author: Planet Awakening, My Bones are Red. Mem. McGovern-Shriver Presdl. Campaign Staff, 1972; vice chmn. Arlington Dem. Com., 1974; chmn. Arlington Com. on Status of Women, 1975; dep. campaign mgr. Shriver for Pres. Com., 1976; del. Va. Dem. Conv., 1976, 1982. Recipient Population Fellows award, Population Ref. Bur., 1993. Mem.: Women in Def. of Environment, Soc. Internat. Devel., Nat. Women's Polit. Caucus, Assn. for Women in Devel., Nat. Council for Internat. Health (pub. policy com.), Am. Pub. Health Assn. (population sect. coun., com. on women's rights). Democrat. Office: Colorado Dem Party 777 Santa Fe Ave Denver CO 80204 Office Phone: 303-623-4762. Business E-Mail: pwaak@coloradodems.org.*

WACHBRIT, JILL BARRETT, accountant, tax specialist; b. Ventura, Calif., May 27, 1955; d. Preston Everett Barrett and Lois JoAnne (Fondersmith) Batchelder; m. Michael Ian Wachbrit, June 21, 1981; children: Michelle, Tracy. AA, Santa Monica City Coll., 1975; BS, Calif. State U., Northridge, 1979; M in Bus. Taxation, U. So. Calif., 1985. CPA. Supervising sr. tax acct. Peat, Marwick, Mitchell & Co., Century City, Calif., 1979-82; sr. tax analyst Avery Internat., Pasadena, Calif., 1982-83; tax mgr., asst. v.p. First Interstate Leasing, Pasadena, 1983-88; v.p. Security Pacific Corp., LA, 1988-92; tax mgr., acct. El Camino Resources Ltd., Woodland Hills, Calif., 1992-95; tax mgr. Herbalife Internat. of Am., Century City, Calif., 1995-97; dir. tax PMC, Inc., Sun Valley, Calif., 1997—. Republican. Jewish. Avocations: reading, travel, collecting.

WACHS, MARTIN, urban planning educator, author, consultant; b. NYC, June 8, 1941; s. Robert and Doris (Margolis) Wachs; m. Helen Poliner, Aug. 18, 1963; children: Faye Linda, Steven Brett. BCE, CUNY, 1963; MS, Northwestern U., 1965, PhD, 1967. Asst. prof. U. Ill., Chgo., 1967-69, Northwestern U., Evanston, Ill., 1969-71; assoc. prof. urban planning UCLA, 1971-76, prof., 1976-96; dir. U. Calif. Transp. Ctr., 1996-99; prof. civil and environ. engring. and city/regional planning U. Calif., Berkeley, 1996—2005, dir. Inst. Transp. Studies, 1999—2005; dir. transp. space and tech. group RAND Corp., Santa Monica, Calif., 2006—. Vis. disting. prof. Rutgers U., New Brunswick, NJ, 1983—84; mem. exec. com. Transp. Rsch. Bd., 1995—2004, chmn., 2000; vis. fellow Oxford U., England, 1976—77. Author: Transportation for the Elderly: Changing Lifestyles, Changing Needs, 1979, Transportation Planning on Trial, 1996; contbr. articles to profl. jours.; editor: Ethics in Planning, 1984, The Car and the City, 1992. Mem. steering com. LA Parking Mgmt. Study, 1976—78; bd. dirs. LA Commuter Computer, 1978—94; mem. Calif. Commn. Transp. Investment, 1995. Served to capt. Ordnance Corps. US Army, 1967—69. Recipient Pike Johnson award, Transp. Rsch. Bd., 1976, W. N. Carey Disting. Svc. award, 2002, Disting. Tchg. award, UCLA Alumni Assn., 1986, Disting. Planning Educator award, Calif. Planners Found., 1986, Disting. Educator award, Coun. U. Transp. Ctrs., 2003, Disting. Planning Educator award, Assn. Collegiate Schs. Planning, 2006; named Mem. of the Yr., San Francisco chpt. Women's Transp. Seminar, 2006; Guggenheim fellow, 1977, Humanities fellow, Rockefeller Found., 1980, Rsch. lectr., Soc. Sigma Xi, 2004—. Fellow: Am. Inst. Cert. Planners, Am. Coun. Edn.; mem.: ASCE, Inst. Transp. Engrs., Cosmos Club. Jewish. Home: 670 Harbor St #3 Venice CA 90291-5519 Office: RAND Corp Santa Monica CA 90401-3208 Home Phone: 310-306-2080. Business E-Mail: wachs@rand.org.

WACHTEL, ALBERT, writer, educator; b. NYC, Dec. 20, 1939; s. Jacob and Sarah Rose (Kaplansky) W.; m. Sydelle Farber, Mar. 9, 1958; children: Sally Rose, Seth Laurence, Stephanie Allyson, Synthia Laura, Jonathan Benjamin, Jessica Eden, Jacob Ethan. BA, CUNY, 1960; PhD, SUNY, Buffalo, 1968. Instr. SUNY, Buffalo, 1963—66, asst. to dean, 1966—68; asst. prof. U. Calif., Santa Barbara, 1968—74; prof. English, creative writing Pitzer Coll., Claremont (Calif.) Colls., 1974—. Playwright: Paying the Piper, 1968, Prince Hal, 1995; co-editor Modernism: Challenges and Perspectives, 1986; author: The Cracked Looking Glass: James Joyce and the Nightmare of History, 1992; contbr. stories, creative essays to lit. jours., newspapers, and mags. NDEA fellow, 1960-63, fellow Creative Arts Inst., U. Calif., Berkeley, 1970, NEH Summer Inst., Dartmouth Coll., 1987; Danforth Found. assoc., 1978, NEH Seminar, Cornell U., 1998. Jewish. Office: Pitzer Coll Claremont Colls Claremont CA 91711-6101 Office Phone: 909-607-3641. Business E-Mail: awachtel@pitzer.edu.

WADDELL, M. KEITH, consulting company executive; From v.p. to vice chmn., CFO, treas. Robert Half Internat. Inc., Menlo Pk., Calif., 1986—93, treas., 1987—2004, vice chmn., CFO, 1999—2004, vice-chmn., pres., CFO, 2004—. Office: Robert Half International Inc 2884 SandHill Rd Menlo Park CA 94025

WADDINGTON, RAYMOND BRUCE, JR., language educator; b. Santa Barbara, Calif., Sept. 27, 1935; s. Raymond Bruce and Marjorie Gladys (Waddell) W.; m. Linda Gayle Jones, Sept. 7, 1957 (div.); children: Raymond Bruce, Edward Jackson; m. Kathleen Martha Ward, Oct. 11, 1985. BA, Stanford U., 1957; PhD, Rice U., 1963; postdoctoral (Univ. fellow in Humanities), Johns Hopkins U., 1965-66. Instr. English U. Houston, 1961-62; instr. U. Kans., 1962-63, asst. prof., 1963-65; asst. prof. English lit. U. Wis., Madison, 1966-68, assoc. prof., 1968-74, prof., 1974-82; prof. English lit. U. Calif., Davis, 1982—2005. Author: The Mind's Empire, 1974, Aretino's Satyr, 2004, (Italian transl.), 2009; co-editor: The Rhetoric of Renaissance Poetry, 1974, The Age of Milton, 1980, The Expulsion of the Jews, 1994; mem. editl. bd. The Medal, 1991; sr. editor: Sixteenth Century Jour.; editor: Praeger Series on the Early Modern World. Recipient Scaglione prize for Italian Studies, 2005; Huntington Libr. fellow, 1967, 75; Inst. Rsch. in Humanities fellow, 1971-72; Guggenheim fellow, 1972-73; NEH fellow, 1977, 83; Newberry Libr. fellow, 1978; Am. Philos. Soc. grantee, 1965, Gladys Krieble Delmas Found. grantee, 2007. Mem. Renaissance Soc. Am., Milton Soc. Am., Am. Numismatic Soc., 16th Century Soc. and Conf. (pres. 1985), Brit. Art Medal Soc., Logos Club. Home: 39 Pershing Ave Woodland CA 95695-2845 Office: U Calif Dept English Davis CA 95616 E-mail: rbwaddington@ucdavis.edu.

WADDOUPS, CLARK, federal judge; b. Arco, Idaho, Apr. 21, 1946; s. Royal and Veta Lorene (Jones) W.; m. Vickie Lee Tibbitts, Dec. 16, 1967; children: Douglas Clark, Lorene, James Clark, Mary, Amy. Student, Ricks Coll., 1964-65; BA, Brigham Young U., 1970; JD, U. Utah, 1973. Bar: Calif. 1973, Utah 1982. Law clk. to Hon. J. Clifford Wallace US Ct. Appeals (9th cir.), San Diego, 1973-74; assoc. O'Melveny & Myers LLP, LA, 1974-81; ptnr. Kimball, Parr, Waddoups, Brown & Gee, Salt Lake City, 1981—2008; judge US Dist. Ct. Utah, Salt Lake City, 2008—. Office: US District Court District of Utah 350 S Main St Rm 150 Salt Lake City UT 84101 E-mail: utdecf_waddoups@utd.uscourts.gov.*

WADDOUPS, MICHAEL GRANT, state legislator; b. Idaho Falls, Idaho, June 12, 1948; son of Grant E Waddoups & Mary Keith Blattner W; married 1974 to Anna Kay Nield; children: Wendi & Heather. AS in Acctg., Ricks Coll., 1971; BS in Bus. Mgmt., Brigham Young U., 1974. Cert. Property Mgr. Grad. Inst. of Real Estate Mgmt., 1980. Mem. Dist. 39, Utah House of Reps., 1987-96, former mem. Revenue & Taxation Standing Coms., former chmn. Transp. & Pub. Safety Standing Com., former chmn. Transp. & Pub. Safety Appropriation Com., former chmn. Rules Com., former Majority Whip, former mem. Mgmt., Rules, Human Serv & Health Appropriations & Exec Appropriations; mem. Dist. 6, Utah State Senate, 1996-, Senate Pres., chmn. Transp. & Pub. Safety Standing Coms., mem. Revenue & Taxation Standing Coms., co-chmn, Exec Off, Criminal Justice & Legis. Appropriations Coms. Property mgr., Woodbury Corp, 1976-78; corporation property mgr., Commonwealth Mgmt., Ltd, 1978-82; pres., Coop Property Mgmt., Inc, 1982-. Inst Real Estate Mgmt.; Apt Assn. Utah (bd. mem.). Republican. Mormon. Mailing: 2868 W Matterhorn Dr West Jordan UT 84084-5329 Office: W115 Capitol Complex Salt Lake City UT 84114 Home Phone: 801-967-0225; Office Phone: 801-355-1136. Business E-Mail: waddoups@utahsenate.org.*

WADE, GLEN, electrical engineer, educator; b. Ogden, Utah, Mar. 19, 1921; s. Lester Andrew and Nellie (Vanderwerff) W.; m. LaRee Bailey, Mar. 20, 1945; children: Kathleen Ann, RaLee, Lisa Jean, Mary Sue. BS in Elec. Engring, U. Utah, Salt Lake City, 1948, MS, 1949; PhD, Stanford U., Calif., 1954. Research group leader, asso. prof. elec. engring. Stanford U., 1955-60; asso. dir. engring., microwave and power tube div. Raytheon Co., 1960-61, asst gen. mgr. research div., 1961-63; dir. Sch. Elec. Engring., Cornell U., 1963-66, J.P. Levis prof. engring., 1963-66; prof. elec. engring. U. Calif. at Santa Barbara, 1966—. Indsl. advisor U. RI, 1961-63; vis. lectr. Harvard, 1963; cons. to industry, 1956—; vis. prof. Tokyo U., 1971; Fulbright-Hays lectr., Spain, 1972-73; cons. mem. Dept. Def. Adv. Group Electron Devices, 1966-73; Spl. Chair prof. Nat. Taiwan U., 1980-81, internationally renowned fgn. scholar lectureship, 1988; UN vis. prof. Nanjing Inst. Tech., 1986; UN vis. prof. S.E. U. People's Republic of China, 1989, Nat. Com. Sci. and Tech. vis. prof. U. Guanajuato, Mex., 1994—; elected mem. The Electromagnetics Acad., 1990. Editor: Transactions on Electron Devices, 1961-71, IEEE Jour. Quantum Electronics, 1965-68; series editor: Harcourt Brace Jovanovich, 1964—; contbr. articles to profl. jours. U.S. del. Tech. Cooperation Program internat. meeting, 1970. Served with USNR, 1944-46. Recipient ann. award Nat. Electronics Conf., 1959, Outstanding Teaching award Acad. Senate, U. Calif., Santa Barbara, 1977, Prof. of Yr. award U. Calif. at Santa Barbara Mortar Bd. Sr. Honor Soc., 1988, Hon. Chairmanship award Twentieth Acoustical Imaging, 1992, Disting. Alumnus award Engring. Coll. U. Utah, 1998. Fellow IEEE (life; mem. adminstrv. com. profl. group election devices 1960-71, mem. publs. bd., chmn. info. processing com., mem. exec. com. 1971-72, dir. 1971-72, chmn. ednl. activities bd. 1971-72, editor proc. 1977-80, Centennial award 1984, Millennium medal 2000); mem. Am. Phys. Soc., Phi Kappa Phi, Tau Beta Pi, Sigma Xi, Eta Kappa Nu (Outstanding Young Elec. Engr. award 1955) Home: 1098 Golf Rd Santa Barbara CA 93108-2411 Office: Rm 214 Bldg 406 U Calif Santa Barbara CA Office Phone: 805-893-2508. Business E-Mail: wade@ece.ucsb.edu.

WADE, LEROY GROVER, JR., chemistry educator; b. Jacksonville, Fla., Oct. 8, 1947; s. Leroy Grover and Margaret Lena (Stevens) W.; m. Sandra Martinez Kooreny; children: Christine Elizabeth, Jennifer Diane. BA summa cum laude, Rice U., 1969; AM, Harvard U., 1970, PhD, 1974. Resident rsch. fellow Du Pont Corp., Wilmington, Del., 1969; tchg. fellow in chemistry Harvard U., Cambridge, Mass., 1969-74, sr. adviser to freshmen, 1971-74; resident sci. tutor Radcliffe Coll., Cambridge, 1970-74; asst. prof. chemistry Colo. State U., Ft. Collins, 1974-80, assoc. prof., 1980-89; prof. chemistry Whitman Coll., Walla Walla, Wash., 1989—. Author: Annual Reports in Organic Synthesis, 1975-82, 8 vols., Compendium of Organic Synthetic Methods, Vols. III, IV, V, 1977, 80, 84, Organic Chemistry, 1987, 6th edit., 2005; contbr. articles to sci. jours.; reviewer profl. jours., textbooks. Mem. AAAS, Am. Chem. Soc., Am. Acad. Forensic Scis., Phi Beta Kappa (pres. chpt. 1983-84), Sigma Xi. Office: Whitman Coll Chemistry Dept Walla Walla WA 99362 E-mail: wadelg@whitman.edu.

WADHAMS, RICHARD IVORY (DICK WADHAMS), policitcal organization administrator; b. La Junta, Colo., Aug. 26, 1955; s. Victor Frederick and Anna Bell (Goodman) Wadhams; m. Susan Farrell, 1982 (dec.); 2 stepchildren. AA, Otero Jr. Coll., 1975; BA, U. Southern Colo., 1982. Chmn. Bent County Rep. Com., Colo.; staff asst. to US Senator William L. Armstrong, Colo., 1980—83, press sec. re-election com., 1984, press contact, 1985; campaign mgr. US Senator Wayne Allard, Colo., 1996, 2002, Gov. Bill Owens, Colo., 1998, Senator John Thume, SD, 2004; press sec. Senator Conrad Burns, Mont., Gov. Bill Owens, 1999—2001, Senator Wayne Allard; chief of staff US Senator George Allen, 2005—06; chmn. Colo. Rep. Party, 2007—. Mem. YMCA. Mem.: Kiwanis. Republican. Office: Colo Rep Party 5950 S Willow Dr Ste 220 Greenwood Village CO 80111 Business E-Mail: dickwadhams@cologop.org.*

WADLOW, JOAN KRUEGER, retired academic administrator, construction executive; b. LeMars, Iowa, Aug. 21, 1932; d. R. John and Norma I. (Ihle) Krueger; m. Richard R. Wadlow, July 27, 1958; children: Dawn, Kit. BA, U. Nebr., 1953, PhD, 1963; MA, Fletcher Sch. Law and Diplomacy, 1956; cert., Grad. Inst. Internat. Studies, Geneva, 1957. Mem. faculty U. Nebr., Lincoln, 1966-79, prof. polit. scis., 1964-79, assoc. dean Coll. Arts and Scis., 1972-79; prof. polit. scis., dean Coll. Arts and Scis., U. Wyo., Laramie, 1979-84, v.p. acad. affairs, 1984-86; prof. polit. sci., provost U. Okla., Norman, 1986-91; chancellor U. Alaska, Fairbanks, 1991-99. Cons. on fed. grants; bd. dirs. Alaska Sea Life Ctr., Key Bank Alaska; mem. Commn. Colls. N.W. Assn.; pres. Lan Constrn., Inc., 1999-2004. Contbr. articles to profl. jours. Bd. dirs. Nat. Merit Scholarship Corp., 1988-97, Lincoln United Way, 1976-77, Bryan Hosp., Lincoln, 1978-79, Washington Ctr., 1986-99, Key Bank of Alaska, Alaska SeaLife Ctr.; v.p., exec. commr. North Ctrl. Assn., pres., 1991; pres. adv. bd. Lincoln YWCA, 1970-71; mem. def. adv. com. Women in the Svcs., 1987-89; mem. cmty. adv. bd. Alaska Airlines; mem. Univ. Pres.'s Mission to Israel, 1998; mem. bd. dirs. Netarts Oceanside Sanitary Dist., 2002-04. Recipient Mortar Board Tchg. award, 1976, Alumni Scholar Achievement award Rotary Internat., 1998, Alumni Achievement award U. Nebr., 2003; Seacrest Journalism fellow 1953-54, Rotary fellow, 1956-57, fellow Conf. Coop. Man, Lund, Sweden, 1956. Mem. NCAA (divsn. II pres. coun. 1997-99), Internat. Studies Assn. (co-editor Internat. Studies Notes 1978-91), Nat. Assn. State Univs. and Land-Grant Colls. (exec. com. coun. acad. affairs 1989-91, chair internat. affairs counsel 1996-97), Western Assn. Africanists (pres. 1980-82), Assn. Western Univs. (pres. 1993), Coun. Colls. Arts and Scis. (pres. 1983-84), Greater Fairbanks C. of C., Gamma Phi Beta. Republican. Congregationalist. Address: Chancellor Emerita PO Box 246 Oceanside OR 97134-0246 Personal E-mail: wadlow@hughes.net.

WADSWORTH, HAROLD WAYNE, lawyer; b. Logan, Utah, Oct. 12, 1930; s. Harold Maughan and Nellie Grace (Grosjean) W.; m. Laila Anita Ingebrigtsen, Dec. 27, 1957; children: Warren, Kenneth, Jeffrey, Theresa, Erik. BS, Utah State U., 1952; JD with honor, George Washington U., 1959. Bar: D.C. 1959, Utah 1961, U.S. Dist. Ct. Utah 1961, U.S. Ct. Appeals (10th cir.) 1962, U.S. Ct. Appeals (9th cir.) 1978, U.S. Supreme Ct. 1972. Spl. agt. FBI, Atlanta and Macon, 1959-60; assoc. atty., ptnr. Hanson, Wadsworth & Russon, Salt Lake City, 1961-77; ptnr. Watkiss & Campbell, Salt Lake City, 1978-89, Watkiss & Saperstein, Salt Lake City, 1990-91, Ballard, Spahr, Andrews & Ingersoll, Salt Lake City, 1992-95, Jones Waldo Holbrook & McDonough, Salt Lake City, Utah, 1996-98; solo practice atty. Salt Lake City, 1998—. 1st lt. U.S. Army, 1952-54. Republican. Mem. Lds Ch. Avocations: horseback riding, hunting, fishing, opera.

WAFER, THOMAS J., JR., newspaper publisher; Pub. Daily Breeze, Torrance, Calif., 1993—. Office: 5215 Torrance Blvd Torrance CA 90503-4009

WAGGONER, JAMES CLYDE, lawyer; b. Nashville, May 7, 1946; s. Charles Franklin and Alpha (Noah) W.; m. Diane Dusenbery, Aug. 17, 1968; children: Benjamin, Elizabeth. BA, Reed Coll., 1968; JD, U. Oreg., 1974. Bar: Oreg. 1974, U.S. Dist. Ct. Oreg. 1975, U.S. Ct. Appeals (9th cir.) 1980, U.S. Tax Ct. 1979, U.S. Supreme Ct. 1979. Clk. to presiding justice Oreg. Supreme Ct., Salem, 1974-75; assoc. Martin, Bischoff & Templeton, Portland, Oreg., 1975-78, ptnr., 1978-82, Waggoner, Farleigh, Wada, Georgeff & Witt, Portland, 1982-89, Davis Wright Tremaine, Portland, 1990—. Contbr. articles to profl. jours. Fulbright scholar U. London, 1968-69. Mem. ABA, Oreg. Bar Assn., Multnomah Bar Assn., Reed Coll. Alumni Assn. (v.p. 1988, pres. 1989, bd. mgmt.) Alzheimers Assn. of Columbia-Willamette (v.p. 1992, pres. 1993), Order of Coif, Phi Beta Kappa. Democrat. Avocations: woodworking, calligraphy. Office: Davis Wright Tremaine 1300 SW 5th Ave Ste 2300 Portland OR 97201-5682 Home Phone: 503-284-6685; Office Phone: 503-778-5326. Business E-Mail: jimwaggoner@dwt.com.

WAGIE, DAVID A., career military officer; BS in Engring. Scis., USAF Acad., Colorado Springs, 1972; MS, Stanford U., 1973, U. So. Calif., 1977; PhD, Purdue U., 1984. Commd. 2d lt. USAF, 1972, advanced through grades to brigadier gen., 1998; pilot 310th Air Refueling Squadron, Plattsburgh AFB, N.Y., 1974-79; instr. USAF Academy, 1979-81; EC-135 rsch. pilot, dir. test ops. 4952d Test Squadron, Wright-Patterson AFB, Ohio, 1984-85; EC-135 rsch. pilot, dep. chief Aircraft & Avionics Divsn. 4950th Test Wing, Wright-Patterson AFB, Ohio, 1985-86; assoc. prof. Air Command and Staff Coll., 1986-87, USAF Academy, 1987-92, prof., dep. commandant mil. instrn., T-43 pilot, 1992-94, dir. Ctr. Character Devel., T-41 pilot, 1994-96, vice dean faculty, T-41 instr. pilot, 1996-98, dean faculty, T-41 instr. pilot, 1998—.

WAGMEN, LEE H., real estate executive; Degree in Bus., U. Pa., degree in Law. Ptnr. Bryan Cave Law Firm, St. Louis; chmn. Hycel Properties Co.; pres., CEO, TrizecHahn Devel. Corp., San Diego. Office: 5405 Morehouse Dr Ste 200 San Diego CA 92121-4724

WAGNER, CHRISTIAN NIKOLAUS JOHANN, materials engineering educator; b. Saarbrucken-Dudweiler, Germany, Mar. 6, 1927; arrived in U.S., 1959, naturalized, 1969; s. Christian Jakob and Regina (Bungert) W.; m. Rosemarie Anna Mayer, Apr. 5, 1952; children: Thomas Martin, Karla Regine, Petra Susanne. Student, U. Poitiers, France, 1948-49; Licence es Sci., U. Saar, Ger., 1951, Diplom-Ingenieur, 1954, Dr.rer.nat., 1957. Research asst. Inst. fur Metallforschung, Saarbrucken, 1953-54; vis. fellow M.I.T., 1955-56; research asso. Inst. fur Metallforschung, 1957-58; teaching, research asst. U. Saarbrucken, 1959; asst. prof. Yale U., New Haven, Conn., 1959-62, assoc. prof., 1962-70; prof. dept. materials engring. UCLA, 1970-91, prof. emeritus, 1991—, chmn. dept., 1974-79, asst. dean undergrad. studies Sch. Engring. and Applied Sci., 1982-85, acting chmn., 1990-91. Vis. prof. Tech. U., Berlin, 1969, U. Saarbrücken, 1979—80. Contbr. articles to profl. jours. Recipient U.S. Sci. Humboldt award, U. Saarbrucken, 1989—90, 1992. Fellow Am. Soc. Metals Internat.; mem. Am. Crystallographic Assn., Minerals, Metals and Materials Soc. Home: 37621 Golden Pebble Ave Palm Desert CA 92211-1430 Office: UCLA 6532 Boelter HlLos Angeles CA 90095-0001 Personal E-mail: cnjwagner@verizon.net.

WAGNER, DARRYL WILLIAM, lawyer; b. Dixon, Ill., Jan. 14, 1943; s. Earl L. and Lois Mae W.; m. Susan A. Aldrich; children: Peter Alan, Nicholas William. BA, Northwestern U., 1965, JD, 1968. Bar: Ill. 1968, U.S. Dist. Ct. (no. dist.) Ill. 1969, U.S. Ct. Appeals (7th cir.) 1971, Calif. 1982. Sr. counsel Sidley Austin LLP, Chgo., 1969—. Dir. Housing Options for People to Excell, Inc., 1992-94, 96—. Co-author: Illinois Municipal Law: Subdivisions and Subdivisions in Controls, 1978, 81. Mem. ABA, Internat. Assn. Attys. and Execs. in Corp. Real Estate, Ill. State Bar Assn., Chgo. Bar Assn. Presbyterian. Home: 526 A San Ysdidro Rd Santa Barbara CA 93108 Office: Sidley Austin LLP 555 W 5th St Ste 4000 Los Angeles CA 90013-3000 E-mail: dwagner@sidley.com, dwwagnere@ix.netcom.com.

WAGNER, DAVID, computer scientist, educator; b. 1974; AB in Math., Princeton U., NJ, 1995; MS in Computer sci., U. Calif., Berkeley, 1999, PhD in Computer sci., 2000. Asst. prof. to assoc. prof. computer sci. U. Calif., Berkeley, Calif., 1998—. Mem. organizing com. Ctr. Discrete Math. & Theoretical Computer Sci., Rutgers U., Piscataway, NJ; mem. prog. com. Oper. Systems Design & Implementation Symposium, 2004; co-chair IEEE Security & Privacy Conf. Co-author: (numerous sci. publs. including) Cryptoanalysis of the Cellular Encryption Algorithm, 1997, Cryptanalysis of Some Recently-Proposed Multiple Modes of Operation, 1998, TAZ Servers and the Rewebber Network: Enabling Anonymous Publishing on the World Wide Web, 1998, Slide Attacks, 1999, The Boomerang Attack, 1999, Practical Techniques for Searches on Encrypted Data, 2000, Intercepting mobile communications: the insecurity of 802.11, 2001, Securing Wireless and Mobile Networks: Is It Possible?, 2002, Private Circuits: Securing Hardware against Probing Attacks, 2003, Analyzing Internet Voting Security, 2004. Named Best Academic Rschr., Info. Security Mag.; named one of Brilliant 10, Popular Sci. mag., 2002; grantee Sloan Rsch. fellowship. Expert in the field of security, wireless security, sensor network security, cryptography. Discovered flaw in Secure Sockets Layer security tool built into Netscape Navigator (with Ian Goldberg), cryptanalyzed the CMEA algorithm used in cellphones (with Bruce Schneier). Invented new form of cryptanalysis called "slide attack" (with Alex Biryukov). Office: Computer Sci Divsn U Calif Berkeley 629 Soda Hall Berkeley CA 94720-1776

WAGNER, HAROLD A., retired gas industry executive; b. Oakland, Calif., Nov. 12, 1935; s. Harold A. and Lurline Frances (Madsen) Wagner; m. Marcia Kenaston, July 17, 1956; children: Sandra Wagner Boyce, Kristi Wagner Schwiering, Tracey, Eric. BS in Mech. Engring., Stanford U., 1958, SEP, 1982; MBA, Harvard U., 1963. Regional sales mgr. ind. gases U.S. Air Products & Chems., Allentown, Pa., 1963—70; mgr. GM ind. gases U.K.Air Products & Chems., 1970—76; regional sales mgr. GM Ind. Gases Continental Europe, 1976—80, GM Ind. Gases U.S., 1980—81; v.p. sales ind. gases div. FM, 1981—82; v.p. corp. planning Air Products & Chems., 1982—87, v.p. bus. div. chems., 1987—88; pres. AP Europe, 1988—90, exec. v.p., 1990—91, pres., COO, 1991—92, past chmn. pres., CEO; chmn., pres., CEO, dir. Air Products and Chems., 1992—2001, chmn., CEO, dir., ret.; chmn. Agere Systems, 2001—. 1st lt. USAF, 1958—61. Avocations: squash, photography. Home: 4031 Savannah Trl Santa Rosa CA 95404-8897

WAGNER, JOHN LEO, lawyer, retired judge, mediator, arbitrator; b. Ithaca, NY, Mar. 12, 1954; s. Paul Francis and Doris Elizabeth (Hoffschneider) W.; m. Marilyn Modin, June 18, 1987. Student, U. Nebr., 1973-74; BA, U. Okla., 1976, JD, 1979. Bar: Okla. 1980, Calif. 1999, U.S. Dist. Ct. (we. dist.) Okla. 1980, U.S. Dist. Ct. (no. and ea. dists.) Okla. 1981, U.S. Dist. Ct. (ctrl. dist.) Calif. 2000, U.S. Ct. Appeals (10th cir.) 1982. Assoc. Franklin, Harmon & Satterfield Inc., Oklahoma City, 1980-82; ptnr. Franklin, Harmon & Satterfield, Inc., Oklahoma City, 1982; assoc. Kornfeld, Franklin & Phillips, Oklahoma City, 1982-85, ptnr., 1985; magistrate judge U.S. Dist. Ct. No. Dist. Okla., Tulsa, 1985-97; dir. Irell & Manella LLP Alt. Dispute Resolution Ctr., Newport Beach, Calif., 1997—2005. Pres. U. Okla. Coll. Law Assn., 1991-92. Fellow Am. Coll. Civil Trial Mediators, Internat. Acad. Mediators, Fed. Magistrate Judge's Assn. (dir. 10th cir. 1987-89); mem. ABA, 10th Cir. Edn. Com., Okla. Bar Assn., Council Oak Am. Inn of Cts. (pres. 1992-93), Jud. Conf. U.S. (com. ct. adminstrn. and case mgmt. 1992-97), CPR-Georgetown Commn. Ethics and Standards in ADR. Republican. Office: Judicate West ADR 1851 E 1st St Ste 1450 Santa Ana CA 92705 Office Phone: 800-488-8805. Business E-Mail: jwagner@wagneradr.com.

WAGNER, JUDITH BUCK, investment firm executive; b. Altoona, Pa., Sept. 25, 1943; d. Harry Bud and Mary Elizabeth (Rhodes) B.; m. Joseph E. Wagner, Mar. 15, 1980; 1 child, Elizabeth. BA in History, U. Wash., 1965; grad., N.Y. Inst. Fin., 1968. Registered Am. Stock Exch., N.Y. Stock Exch., investment advisor. Security analyst Morgan, olmstead, Kennedy & Gardner, LA, 1968-71, Boettcher & Co., Denver, 1972-75; pres. Wagner Investment Mgmt., Denver, 1975—. Chmn. The Women's Bank, N.A., Denver, 1977-94, organizational group pres., 1975-77; chmn. Equitable Bankshares Colo., Inc., Denver, 1980-94; pres. Equitable Bank of Littleton, Colo., 1985; lectr. Denver U., Metro State, 1975-80. Author: Woman and Money series Colo. Woman Mag., 1976, moderator "Catch 2' Sta. KWGN-TV, 1978-79. Pres. Big Sisters Colo., Denver, 1977-82, bd. dirs., 1972-83; bd. fellows U. Denver, 1985-90; bd. dirs. Red Cross, 1980, Assn. Children's Hosp., 1985, Colo. Health Facilities Authority, 1978-84, Jr. League Cmty. ADv. Com., 1979-82, Bros. Redevel., Inc., 1979-80; mem. agy. rels. com. Mile High United Way, 1978-81, chmn. United Way Venture Way, 1978-81, chmn. United Way Venture Grant com., 1980-81; bd. dirs. Downtown Denver, Inc., 1988-95; bd. dirs., v.p., treas. The Women's Found. Colo., 1987-91; treas., trustee, v.p., Graland Country Day Sch., 1990-97, pres., 1994-97; trustee Denver Rotary Found., 1990-95, Hunt Alternatives Fund, 1992-97; trustee The Colo. Trust, 1998—, chmn., 2003-05; steering com. chair, Ctr. Women's Health Rsch., 2000-07; Major Gifts Com.; co-chair, Planned Parenthood Rocky Capital Campaign. Recipient Making It award Cosmopolitan Mag., 1977, Women on the Go award, Savvy Mag., 1983, Minouri Yasoui award, 1986, Salute Spl. Honoree award, Big Sisters, 1987; named one of the Outstanding Young Women Am., 1979, Woman Who Makes A Difference award Internat. Women's Forum, 1987, Maverick Thinker award Urban Park, 2003; named Disting. Citizen award U. Colo., 2005. Fellow Assn. Investment Mgmt. & Rsch.; mem. Women's Forum Colo. (pres. 1979), Women's Found. Colo., Inc. (bd. dirs. 1986-91), Denver Soc. Security Analysts (bd. dirs. 1976-83, v.p. 1980-81, pres. 1981-82), Colo. Investment Advisors assn., Rotary (treas. Denver chpt. found., pres. 1993-94), Leadership Denver (Outstanding Alumna award 1987), Pi Beta Phi (pres. U. Wash. chpt. 1964-65). Office: Wagner Investment Mgmt Inc Ste 240 3200 Cherry Creek South Dr Denver CO 80209-3245 Office Phone: 303-777-1800.

WAGNER, PATRICIA HAMM, lawyer; b. Gastonia, NC, Feb. 1, 1936; d. Luther Boyd and Mildred Ruth (Wheeler) Hamm; married; children: David Marion, Michael Marion, Laura Marion. AB summa cum laude, Wittenberg U., 1958; JD with distinction, Duke U., 1974. Bar: N.C. 1974, Wash. 1984. Asst. univ. counsel Duke U., Durham, N.C., 1974-75, assoc. univ. counsel health affairs, 1977-80; atty. N.C. Meml. Hosp., 1975-77; assoc. N.C. Atty. Gen. Office, 1975-77, Powe, Porter & Alphin, Durham, 1980-81, prin., 1981-83; assoc. Williams, Kastner & Gibbs, 1984-86, Wickwire, Goldmark & Schorr, 1986-88; spl. counsel Heller, Ehrman, White & McAuliffe, 1988-90, ptnr., 1990—. Arbitrator Am. Arbitration Assn., 1978—; arbitrator, pro tem judge King County Superior Ct., 1986—; tchr. in field. Mem. bd. vis. Law Sch. Duke U., 1992-98; bd. dirs. Seattle Edn. Ctr., 1990-91, Metroctr. YMCA, 1991-94, Cmty. Psychiat. Clinic, Seattle, 1984-86; bd. dirs., sec.-treas. N.C. Found. Alternative Health Programs, Inc., 1982-84; bd. dirs., sec.-treas. N.C. Ctr. Pub. Policy Rsch., 1976-83, vice-chmn., 1977-80; mem. task force on commitment law N.C. Dept. Human Resources, 1978; active Def. Rsch. Inst. 1982-84; bd. dirs. Law Fund, 1992—, v.p., 1993-97, pres., 2000-01; mem. ADR Roundtable, 1996-2001. Fellow Am. Bar Found.; mem. ABA (mem. ho. dels. Seattle-King County Bar Assn. 1991-94, mem. litigation sect.), Am. Soc. Hosp. Attys., Am. Law Inst., Wash. State Bar Assn. (mem. domestic rels. task force 1991-93), Seattle-King Bar Assn. (mem. bd. trustees 1990-93, sec. bd. 1989-90, chair judiciary and cts. com. 1987-89, mem. King County Superior Ct. delay reduction task force 1987-89, mem. gender bias com. 1990-94, chair 1990-91), Wash. Def. Trial Lawyers (chmn. ct. rules and procedures com. 1987, co-editor newsletter 1985-86), Wash. State Soc. Hosp. Attys., Wash. Women Lawyers (treas. 1986, 87). E-mail: pwagner@hewm.com.

WAGNER, PAULA, film company executive; b. Youngstown, Ohio, 1948; m. Robin Wagner (div.); m. Rick Nicita, 1984. BFA in Drama, Carnegie-Mellon U. Agent Creative Artist Agy.; co-founder (with Tom Cruise) Cruise/Wagner Productions, 1993—2006; co-owner (with Tom Cruise) United Artists Entertainment, LLC, 2006—08, CEO, 2006—08. Pres. Dirs. Jury Venice Film Festival; co-chair Hollywood Film Festival. Actress on & off Broadway, (TV miniseries) Loose Change, 1978; co-author: Out of Our Father's House; prodr.: (films) Mission: Impossible, 1996, Without Limits, 1998, Mission: Impossible II, 2000, Vanilla Sky, 2001, The Last Samurai, 2003, Suspect Zero, 2004, Elizabethtown, 2005, Ask the Dust, 2006, Mission: Impossible III, 2006; exec. prodr.: The Others, 2001, Narc, 2002, Shattered Glass, 2003, War of the Worlds, 2005; prodr.: (TV miniseries) Nightmares and Dreamscapes: From the Stories of Stephen King, 2006. Bd. trustees Carnegie-Mellon U.; bd. dir. Nat. Film Preservation Found., Am. Cinematheque, Interlochen Ctr. for the Arts; mem. exec. com. UCLA Sch. Theater, Film and TV. Recipient Women in Hollywood Icon award, Premiere mag., 2001, Excellence in Producing award, Sarasota Film Festival, 2006; co-recipient Nova award for outstanding achievement by new or emerging prodr. in theatrical motion pictures, Producer's Guild, 1997; named a Billion-Dollar Prodr., Daily Variety, 2004; named one of The 100 Most Powerful Women in Entertainment, Hollywood Reporter, 2006, 2007.

WAGNER, ROBERT, actor; b. Detroit, Feb. 10, 1930; m. Natalie Wood, Dec. 28, 1957 (div. Apr. 27, 1962); m. Marion Marshall Donen, July 22, 1963 (div. 1970); 1 child, Kate; m. Natalie Wood, July 16, 1972 (dec. Nov. 29, 1981); 1 child, Courtney, 1 stepdaughter, Natasha Gregson Wagner; m. Jill St. John, May 26, 1990. Actor: (films) The Happy Years, 1950, Halls of Montezuma, 1950, Teresa, 1951, The Frogmen, 1951, Let's Make It Legal, 1951, With a Song in My Heart, 1952, What Price Glory?, 1952, Stars and Stripes Forever, 1952, The Silver Whip, 1953, Titanic, 1953, Beneath the 12-Mile Reef, 1953, Prince Valiant, 1954, Broken Lance, 1954, White Feather, 1955, A Kiss Before Dying, 1956, Between Heaven and Hell, 1956, The Mountain, 1956, The True Story of Jesse James, 1957, Stopover Tokyo, 1957, The Hunters, 1958, In Love and War, 1958, Say One For Me, 1959, All the Fine Young Cannibals, 1960, Sail a Crooked Ship, 1961, The Longest Day, 1962, The War Lover, 1963, The Condemned of Altona, 1962, The Pink Panther, 1963, Harper, 1966, Banning, 1967, The Biggest Bundle of Them All, 1968, Don't Just Stand There!, 1968, Winning, 1969, Madame Sin, 1972, Journey Through Rosebud, 1972, The Towering Inferno, 1974, Midway, 1976, The Concorde...Airport '79, 1979, I Am the Cheese, 1983, Curse of the Pink Panther, 1983, Delirious, 1991, Dragon: The Bruce Lee Story, 1993, Overdrive, 1997, Austin Powers-International Man of Mystery, 1997, Wild Things, 1998, Something to Believe In, 1998, Dill Scallion, 1999, No Vacancy, 1999, Love and Fear, 1999, The Kidnapping of Chris Burden, 1999, Austin Powers: The Spy Who Shagged Me, 1999, Crazy in Alabama, 1999, Forever Fabulous, 2000, Play it to the Bone, 1999, The Calling, 2001, Jungle Juice, 2001, Sol Good, 2001, The Kidnapping of Chris Burden, 2001, Nancy & Frank: A Manhattan Love Story, 2002, Austin Powers in Goldmember, 2002, El Padrino, 2004, Little Victim, 2005, The Wild Stallion, 2006, Hoot, 2006, (voice only) Everyone's Hero, 2006, Man in the Chair, 2007, Netherbeast Incorporated, 2007; (TV movies) How I Spent My Summer Vacation, 1967, City Beneath the Sea, 1971, Crosscurrent, 1971, Perlico-Perlaco, 1971, The Affair, 1973, The Abduction of St. Anne, 1975, Death at Love House, 1976, Cat on a Hot Tin Roof, 1976, Critical List, 1978, To Catch a King, 1984, There Must Be a Pony, 1986, Love Among Thieves, 1987, Indiscreet, 1988, This Gun for Hire, 1991, False Arrest, 1991, Jewels, 1992, Les Audacieux, 1993, Hart to Hart Returns, 1993, Hart to Hart Is Where the Hart Is, 1994, Parallel Lives, 1994, Hart to Hart: Secrets of the Hart, 1995, Dancing in the Dark, 1995, Hart to Hart: Two Harts in 3/4 Time, 1995, Hart to Hart: Harts in High Season, 1996, Hart to Hart: Til Death Do Us Hart, 1996, Fatal Error, 1999, Abzocker, 2000, Rocket's Red Glare, 2000, Becoming Dick, 2000, The Retrievers, 2002, Mystery Woman, 2003, The Fallen Ones, 2005, Category 7: The End of the World, 2005, Making It Legal, 2008, Pretty/Handsome, 2008; (TV series) It Takes a Thief, 1968-1970, Colditz, 1972-74, Switch!, 1975-78, Hart to Hart, 1979-84, Lime St., 1985-87, Hope & Faith, 2003-06, Two and a Half Men, 2007-08; (TV mini-series) Pearl, 1978, Around the World in 80 Days, 1989, Heaven and Hell: North and South, Book III, 1994, The Road to Santiago, 1999; (TV appearances) The 20th Century-Fox Hour, 1955, 1956, The Eleventh Hour, 1963, The Name of the Game, 1970, 1971, Streets of San Francisco, 1972, The HardyBoys/Nancy Drew Mysteries, 1977, Indiscreet, 1988, Saturday Night Live, 1989, Seinfeld, 1990, The Trials of Rosie O'Neill, 1991, 1992, Cybill, 1995,

On the Spot, 2003, Las Vegas, 2006, Boston Legal, 2006, Hustle, 2007; co-author: (with Scott Eyman) Pieces of My Heart: A Life, 2008

WAGNER, WILLIAM GERARD, dean, information scientist, consultant, physicist, investment manager; b. St. Cloud, Minn., Aug. 22, 1936; s. Gerard C. and Mary V. (Cloone) W.; m. Janet Agatha Rowe, Jan. 30, 1968 (div. 1978); children: Mary, Robert, David, Anne; m. Christiane LeGuen, Feb. 21, 1985 (div. 1989); m. Yvonne Naomi Moussette, Dec. 4, 1995. BS, Calif. Inst. Tech., 1958, PhD (NSF fellow, Howard Hughes fellow), 1962. Cons. Rand Corp., Santa Monica, Calif., 1960-65; sr. staff physicist Hughes Research Lab., Malibu, Calif., 1960-69; lectr. physics Calif. Inst. Tech., Pasadena, 1963-65; asst. prof. physics U. Calif. at Irvine, 1965-66; assoc. prof. physics and elec. engring. U. So. Calif., LA, 1966-69, prof. depts. physics and elec. engring., 1969—, dean div. natural scis. and math. Coll. Letters, Arts and Scis., 1973-87, dean interdisciplinary studies and developmental activities, 1987-89, spl. asst. automated record services, 1975-81; founder program in neural, informational & behavioral scis., 1982—. Chmn. bd. Malibu Securities Corp., L.A., 1971—; cons. Janus Mgmt. Corp., L.A., 1970-71, Croesus Capital Corp., L.A., 1971-74, Fin. Horizons Inc., Beverly Hills, Calif., 1971—; allied mem. Pacific Stock Exch., 1974-82; fin. and computer cons. Hollywood Reporter, 1979-81; mem. adv. coun. for emerging engring. techs. NSF, 1987-89; cons. Wagner Tech. Solutions, L.A., 2001—. Contbr. articles on physics to sci. publs. Richard Chase Tolman postdoctoral fellow, 1962—65. Mem.: Am. Phys. Soc., Nat. Assn. Security Dealers, Sigma Xi. Home: 183 Beloit Ave Los Angeles CA 90049-3007 Office: Univ So Calif Hedco Neurosci Bldg Los Angeles CA 90089-2520 Office Phone: 213-740-7839. Business E-Mail: wwagner@usc.edu.

WAGONER, DAVID EVERETT, lawyer, arbitrator; b. Pottstown, Pa., May 16, 1928; s. Claude Brower and Mary Kathryn (Groff) W.; children: Paul R., Colin H., Elon D., Peter B., Dana F.; m. Jean Morton Saunders; children: Constance A., Jennifer L., Melissa J. BA, Yale U., 1950; LLB, U. Pa., 1953. Bar: DC 1953, Pa. 1953, Wash. 1953. Law clk. US Ct. Appeals (3d cir.), Pa., 1955-56; law clk. US Supreme Ct., Washington, 1956-57; ptnr. Perkins & Coie, Seattle, 1957-96. Panel mem. of arbitration forum worldwide including People's Republic of China, B.C. Internat. Comml. Arbitration Ctr., Hong Kong Internat. Arbitration Ctr., London Ct. Internat. Arbitration, AAA's Internat. Ctr. Dispute Resolution. Mem. sch. com. Mcpl. League Seattle and King County, 1958—, chmn., 1962-65; mem. Seattle schs. citizens coms. on equal ednl. opportunity and adult vocat. edn., 1963-64; mem. Nat. Com. Support Pub. Schs.; mem. adv. com. on cmty. colls., to 1965, legislature interim com. on edn., 1964-65; mem. cmty. coll. adv. com. to state supt. pub. instrn., 1965; chmn. edn. com. Forward Thrust, 1968; mem. Univ. Congl. Ch. Coun. Seattle, 1968-70; bd. dirs. Met. YMCA Seattle, 1968; bd. dirs. Seattle Pub. Schs., 1965-73, v.p., 1966-67, 72-73, pres., 1968, 73; trustee Evergreen State Coll. Found., chmn. 1986-87, capitol campaign planning chmn.; trustee Pacific NW Ballet, v.p. 1986. Served to 1st lt. M.C., AUS, 1953-55 Fellow Coll. Comml. Arbitrators, Am. Coll. Trial Lawyers (mem. ethics com., legal ethics com.), Chartered Inst. Arbitrators, Singapore Inst. Arbitrators; mem. ABA (chmn. standing com. fed. jud. improvement, chmn. appellate advocacy com., mem. commn. on separation of powers and jud. independence), Wash. State Bar Assn., Seattle-King County Bar Assn., Acad. Experts, Swiss Arbitration Assn., Nat. Sch. Bds. Assn. (bd. dirs., chmn. coun. Big City bds. edn. 1971-72), English-Speaking Union (v.p. Seattle chpt. 1961-62), Chi Phi. Office: Internat Arbitration Chambers US BankCtr 1420 5th Ave Fl 22 Seattle WA 98101-4087 Home: 1633 Broadmoor Dr E Seattle WA 98112-3747 Office Phone: 206-224-2872. E-mail: email@davidwagoner.com.

WAGONER, DAVID RUSSELL, writer, educator; b. Massillon, Ohio, June 5, 1926; s. Walter Siffert and Ruth (Banyard) W.; m. Patricia Lee Parrott, July 8, 1961 (div. June 1982); m. Robin Heather Seyfried, July 24, 1982; children: Alexandra Dawn, Adrienne Campbell. BA in English, Pa. State U., 1947; MA in English, Ind. U., 1949. Instr. English DePauw U., 1949-50; instr. Pa. State U., 1950-53; asst. prof. U. Wash., 1954-57, assoc. prof., 1958-66, prof., 1966-2000, prof. emeritus, 2000—. Elliston lectr. U. Cin., 1968; editor Poetry NW, 1966-02; poetry editor Princeton U. Press, 1977-81, Mo. Press, 1983— Author: (poetry books) Dry Sun, Dry Wind, 1953, A Place to Stand, 1958, The Nesting Ground, 1963, Staying Alive, 1966, New and Selected Poems, 1969, Working Against Time, 1970, Riverbed, 1972, Sleeping in the Woods, 1974, Collected Poems, 1976, Who Shall Be the Sun?, 1978, In Broken Country, 1979, Landfall, 1981, First Light, 1983, Through the Forest, 1987, Walt Whitman Bathing, 1996, Traveling Light: Collected and New Poems, 1999, The House of Song, 2002, Good Morning and Good Night, 2005; (novels) The Man in the Middle, 1954, Money, Money, Money, 1955, Rock, 1958, The Escape Artist (also film 1982), 1965, Baby, Come on Inside, 1968, Where is My Wandering Boy Tonight?, 1970, The Road to Many a Wonder, 1974, Tracker, 1975, Whole Hog, 1976, The Hanging Garden, 1980; editor: Straw for the Fire: From the Notebooks of Theodore Roethke, 1943-63, 1972. Recipient Morton Dauwen Zabel prize Poetry mag., 1967, Blumenthal-Leviton-Blonder prize, 1974, 2 Fels prizes Coordinating Coun. Lit. Mags., 1975, Tietjens prize, 1977, English-Speaking Union prize, 1980, Sherwood Anderson award, 1980, Union League Prize, 1987, Ruth Lilly Poetry prize, 1991, Levinson prize, 1994, Pacific N.W. Booksellers award, 2000, Arts Fund Lifetime Achievement award, 2007; Guggenheim fellow, 1956, Ford fellow, 1964, Nat. Inst. Arts and Letters grantee, 1967, Nat. Endowment for Arts grantee, 1969 Mem. Acad. Am. Poets (chancellor 1978—2000), Soc. Am. Magicians, Nat. Assn. Blackfeet Indians (asso.) Home: 5416 154th Pl SW Edmonds WA 98026-4348 Office: U Wash PO Box 354330 Seattle WA 98195-4330 E-mail: renogawd@aol.com.

WAGONER, ROBERT VERNON, astrophysicist, educator; b. Teaneck, NJ, Aug. 6, 1938; s. Robert Vernon and Marie Theresa (Clifford) W.; m. Lynne Ray Moses, Sept. 2, 1963 (div. Feb. 1986); children: Alexa Frances, Shannon Stephanie; m. Stephanie Brewster, June 27, 1987. BME, Cornell U., 1961; MS, Stanford U., 1962, PhD, 1965. Rsch. fellow in physics Calif. Inst. Tech., 1965-68, Sherman Fairchild Disting. scholar, 1976; asst. prof. astronomy Cornell U., 1968-71, assoc. prof., 1971-73; assoc. prof. physics Stanford U., 1973-77, prof., 1977—2004, emeritus prof., 2005—. George Ellery Hale disting. vis. prof. U. Chgo., 1978; mem. Com. on Space Astronomy and Astrophysics, 1979-82, theory study panel Space Sci. Bd., 1980-82, physics survey com. NRC, 1983-84; grant selection com. NSERC (Can.), 1990-93; mem., Kavli Inst. Particle Astrophysics Cosmology, 2004-; mem. visitors com. divsn. astron. scis. NSF, 2005 Contbr. articles on theoretical astrophysics and gravitation to profl. jours., mags.; co-author Cosmic Horizons, 1982; patentee in field. Sloan Found. rsch. fellow, 1969-71; Guggenheim Meml. fellow, 1979; grantee NSF, 1973-90, 2000-03, NASA, 1982-99. Fellow Am. Phys. Soc.; mem. Am. Astron. Soc., Internat. Astron. Union, Tau Beta Pi, Phi Kappa Phi Office: Stanford U Dept Physics Stanford CA 94305-4060 Home Phone: 650-493-4241; Office Phone: 650-723-4561. Business E-Mail: wagoner@stanford.edu.

WAGONER, THOMAS H., state legislator; b. Pylesville, Md., Sept. 19, 1942; m to dorothy C Wagoner; children: Dawn & Denise. BA in Tech. Design, Eastern Wash. U., 1966, BA in Edn.; MA in Edn. Adminstrn., U. Alaska, Anchorage, 1980. Alaska State Senator, District Q, 2003-; Member Kenai City coun, 1980-83; Mayor, Kenai City, 1983-86.Owner, Wagoner's Seamless Flooring, 1967-68; Owner, Wagoner's Flooring, 1971-75; Owner, Peninsula Flooring center, 1986-93; Vocat education coordinator, business mgr/budget officer, dean of vocat educ/instrn, Kenai Peninsula Community Col. Rotary; Kenai Chamber of Commerce (past president); Salvation Army (advisor board). Republican. Office: State Capitol Rm 423 Juneau AK 99801-1182 also: Dist Q 145 Main St Loop Ste 226 Kenai AK 99611 Office Phone: 907-465-2828, 907-283-7996. Office Fax: 907-465-4779, 907-283-8127. Business E-Mail: senator_thomas_Wagoner@legis.state.ak.us.*

WAGONFELD, JAMES B., gastroenterologist; b. Bronx, NY, Jan. 30, 1946; m. Judith Wagonfeld; children: Temira Lital, Ariella Lirit. BA, NYU, 1966; MD, U. Health Scis., Chgo., 1970. Diplomate Nat. Bd. Med. Examiners, in internal medicine and gastroenterology Am. Bd. Internal Medicine. Med. intern Duke U. Med. Ctr., Durham, N.C., 1970-71; jr. asst. resident in medicine U. Chgo. Hosps. and Clinics, 1971-72, sr. asst. resident in medicine, 1972-73, NIH fellow in gastroenterology, 1973-75, instr. medicine, 1975-76; asst. prof. medicine U. Oreg. Health Scis. Ctr., Portland, 1976-78; attending physician Portland VA Hosp., 1976-78; pvt. practice Digestive Health Specialists, Tacoma, 1979—93; dir. gastrointestinal study unit Tacoma Gen. Hosp., 1987—; co-dir. gastrointestinal diagnostic nit St. Joseph Hosp. and Health Care Ctr., 1988-90. Cons. FDA panel on rev. of vitamins, minerals, and hematinic drug products, 1974-75. Contbr. articles to profl. jours. Physician Benita Juarez Clinic, Chgo., 1971-73, Cardiac Rehab. Program Tacoma-Pierce County Family YMCA, 1980-84; advisor Portlan dAssn. for Childbirth Edn., 1976-78, RESOLVE, An Advocacy Orgn. for Infertile Couples, 1976-78, Colon Cancer Screening in Sr. Citizens, Multinomah County Pub. Health Dept. and Southwest Wash. Health Dist., 1977-78; scientific advisor Shaw Meml. Lecture series, Oreg. Med. Assn., 1977-78; bd. med. advisors Pacific Northwest Soc. of Gastrointestinal Assts., 1982; trustee Charles Wright Acad., 1984-87, chmn. devel. com., 1985-87, chmn. edn. fund, 1985-86. Recipient NIH rsch. award, 1975-76. Fellow ACP, Am. Coll. Gastroenterology; mem. AMA, Am. Gastroenterologic Assn., Am. Soc. for Gastrointestinal Endoscopy, Pacific Northwest Endoscopy Soc., The Wilderness Med. Soc., Wash. State Med. Assn., Med. Soc. Pierce County, Alpha Omega Alpha. Office: Digestive Health Specialists 3209 S 23d St # 340 Tacoma WA 98405 Office Phone: 206-272-5127.

WAHBE, ROBERT, computer software company executive; Grad., Univ. Calif., Berkeley. Co-founder Colusa Software Inc.; product develop. positions for enterprise develop. tools Microsoft Corp., Redmond, Wash., 1996—2007, corp. v.p. connected systems div., 2007—. Office: Microsoft Corp 1 Microsoft Way Redmond WA 98052-6399

WAINWRIGHT, DAVID STANLEY, patent agent; b. New Haven, May 23, 1955; s. Stanley Dunstan and Lillian (Karelitz) W.;m. Catherine Demetra Kefalas, Aug. 11, 1984; children: Maxwell Stanley Hector, Eric George Alexander. BSc in Physics with 1st class honors, Dalhousie U., Halifax, NS, 1976; MSc in Physics, U. BC, Vancouver, 1979. Registered patent agt., U.S., Can. Model plant supr., scientist, technician Moli Energy Ltd., Maple Ridge, BC, Canada, 1978-84, project leader cell devel., 1984-88, cell devel. mgr., 1988-90, 1990-92, mgr. intellectual property, 1992-98; patent agt. Ballard Power Sys., Burnaby, BC, 1998—2005; sr. patent agent Cardiome Pharma Corp., Vancouver, Canada, 2005—06; IP specialist Questair Techs. Inc., Burnaby, Canada, 2006—. Contbr. articles to profl. jours. Mem. Patent and Trademark Inst. Can. Home: 2585 W 1st Ave Vancouver BC Canada V6K 1G8 Office: Questair Technologies Inc 6961 Russell Ave Burnaby BC Canada V5J 4R8 Office Phone: 604-453-6896. Business E-Mail: wainwright@questairinc.com.

WAINWRIGHT HENBEST, MARGARET A., state representative; b. LA, Aug. 13, 1953; m. Michael Henbest; children: Ryan, Daniel, Kevin. BS in Health Scis., Oreg. U., 1976; MS, Calif. State U., Long Beach, 1984. Pediatric nurse practitioner, pvt. practice, 1984—86; pediatric nurse practitioner, Child Abuse Clinic St. Luke's Regional Med. Ctr., 1991—; asst. prof. nursing Boise State U., 1988—91; state rep. dist. 16A Idaho Ho. of Reps., Boise, 1996—, mem. revenue and taxation com.; mem. CHIPS task force, 1998; chmn. joint legis. oversight com., 2000—; mem. mental health interim com., 1996. Small benefit plan com. Idaho Dept. Commerce, 1994—95. Mem.: ASPAC, ANA, St. Joseph's Home & Sch. Assn. (pres.), Nat. Assn. Pediatric Nurse Practitioners and Assocs., Idaho Nurses Assn. (legis. com. chair nurse practitioner group 1990—), Child Abuse Law Mentors, Mountain States Group (bd. dirs., pres.), Kids Count (bd. dirs.), Discovery Ctr. Idaho (past bd.), Rotary. Democrat. Office: State Capitol PO Box 83720 Boise ID 83720-0038

WAITE, RIC, cinematographer; b. Sheboygan, Wis., July 10, 1933; s. Howard Pierce and Bertha Ann (Pippert) W.; m. Judy Lescher, Apr. 24, 1965; children: Richard R., Burgandy B. Student, U. Colo. Cinematographer: (films) Other Side of the Mountain Part II, 1978, Defiance, 1980, The Long Riders, 1980, Tex, 1982, 48 Hrs., 1982, The Border, 1982, Class, 1983, Footloose, 1984, Red Dawn, 1984, Volunteers, 1985, Summer Rental, 1985, Brewster's Millions, 1985, Cobra, 1986, Adventures in Babysitting, 1987, Great Outdoors, 1989, Marked for Death, 1990, Price of Our Blood, 1990, Out for Justice, 1991, Rapid Fire, 1992, On Deadly Ground, 1994, Truth or Consequences, N.Mex., 1997; (TV) Nakia, 1974, The November Plan, 1976, Nero Wolfe, 1977, Tail Gunner Joe, 1977, The Initiation of Sarah, 1978, And Baby Makes Six, 1979, Revenge of the Stepford Wives, 1980, Baby Comes Home, 1980, Dempsey, 1983, Police Story: Burnout, 1988, Scam, 1993, Last Light, 1993, Andersonville, 1996, Money Plays, 1997, Last Stand at Saber River, 1997, Hope, 1997. 1st lt. USAF, 1951-56. Recipient Emmy award, 1976. Mem. Am. Soc. Cinematographers. Avocations: sailing, flying. Address: Prime Artists Derren Sugar 7650 Topanga Canyon Blvd Canoga Park CA 91304 E-mail: ricwaite@aol.com.

WAITS, THOMAS ALAN, composer, actor, singer; b. Pomona, Calif., Dec. 7, 1949; s. Frank W. and Alma (Johnson) McMurray; m. Kathleen Patricia Brennan, Aug. 10, 1980; children: Kellesimone Wylder, Casey Xavier, Sullivan Blake. Composer 20 albums including Closing Time, 1973, The Heart of Saturday Nite, 1974, Nighthawks at the Diner, 1975, Small Change, 1976, Foreign Affairs, 1978, Blue Valentine, 1979, Heart Attack and Vine, 1980, One From the Heart, 1981, Swordfishtrombones, 1983, Rain Dogs, 1985, Anthology, 1985, Frank's Wild Years, 1987, Big Time, 1988, Bone Machine, 1992, Night on Earth, 1992, The Black Rider, 1993, Beautiful Maladies, 1998, Mule Variations, 1999 (Grammy Award, 1999), Alice, 2002, Blood Money, 2002, Real Gone, 2004, Orphaus, 2006; composer (film scores) One from the Heart, 1983, Streetwise, 1985, Night on Earth, 1991; co-author music and songs (with Kathleen Brennan) for Night on Earth, 1991, End of Violence, 1997, Bunny, 1999, Liberty Heights, 2000, Big Bad Love, 2002, Pollock, 2002, Dead Man Walking, film American Heart; composer songs and music for The Black Rider opera, Hamburg, Germany, 1990; composer songs and music, writer (with Kathleen Brennan) Alice Avant Garde opera, Hamburg, 1992, opera Woyzeck (recipient Italian Drama Critics award for Best Musical, 2003), Copenhagen, 2000; actor (musical) Frank's Wild Years, 1986, (stage play) Demon Wine, 1989; appeared in films Paradise Alley, 1978, The Outsiders, 1983, Rumble Fish, 1983, The Cotton Club, 1984, Down by Law, 1986, Ironweed, 1987, Candy Mountain, 1987, Big Time, 1988, Cold Feet, 1989, The Bearskin, 1991, Queen's Logic, 1991, At Play in the Fields of the Lord, 1991, Bram Stoker's Dracula, 1992, Short Cuts, 1993, Mystery Men, 1999, Coffee & Cigarettes, 2003, Domino, 2003. Recipient Acad. Award nomination Best Song Score for One from the Heart, 1983; Grammy award for best alternative album Bone Machine, 1992, Grammy award for Mule Variations as best contemporary folk music, 2000, Dramalogue award for actor Demon Wine, Danish Theater award for Woyzeck as best musical, 2001. Mem. ASCAP (Founders award for career achievement in songwriting 2001), Musicians Union Local 47, SAG, AFTRA, Motion Picture Acad. Office: Howard Grossman 10880 Wilshire Blvd Ste 1725 Los Angeles CA 90024-4100

WAITT, THEODORE W. (TED WAITT), venture capitalist, former computer company executive; b. Sioux City, Iowa, Jan. 18, 1963; m. Joan Waitt; 4 children. Attended, U. of Iowa; PhD (hon.), U. of SD. Co-founder Gateway Inc., Poway, 1985, pres., 1985—96, 2001—04, CEO, 1993—99, 2001—04, chmn., 1993—2005; founder, chmn., CEO Avalon Capital Group. Founder, chmn. Waitt Family Found., 1993—; chair Waitt Inst. for Historical Discovery, Waitt Inst. for Violence Prevention, Waitt Inst. for Scientific Breakthroughs; trustee Salk Inst., 2005—; chmn., Founding Fathers campaign Family Violence Prevention Fund. Recipient Young Entrepreneur of the Year award, U.S. Small Bus. Assn.; named one of Ten Outstanding Young Americans, U.S. Jr. C. of C., Forbes' Richest Americans, 2005, 2006.

WAITZKIN, HOWARD BRUCE, internist, sociologist, educator; b. Akron, Ohio, Sept. 6, 1945; s. Edward and Dorothy (Lederman) W.; m. Jean Ellis-Sankari, Nov. 12, 2005; 1 stepchild, Daren; 1 child, Sofia. BA summa cum laude, Harvard U., 1966, MA, 1969, MD, PhD, 1972. Diplomate Am. Bd. Internal Medicine, Am. Bd. Geriatric Medicine. Resident in medicine Stanford U. Med. Ctr., Calif., 1972-75, Robert Wood Johnson clin. scholar depts. sociology-medicine Calif., 1973-75; sr. resident in medicine Mass. Gen. Hosp., Boston, 1977-78; assoc. prof. sociology, clin. asst. prof. medicine U. Vt., Burlington, Vt., 1975-77; vis. assoc. prof. health and med. scis. U. Calif., Berkeley, 1978-82, clin. asst. prof. medicine San Francisco, 1978-82; internist La Clínica de la Raza, Oakland, Calif., 1978-82; prof. medicine and social scis. U. Calif., Irvine, 1982-96, chief div. gen. internal medicine and primary care, 1982-90; med. dir. U. Calif.-Irvine-North Orange County Community Clinic, Anaheim, 1982-90; disting. prof. U. N.Mex., 2005—, prof. sociology, family and cmty. medicine, internal medicine and Latin Am. studies, 1997—; sr. fellow Robert Wood Johnson Found. Ctr. Health Policy; internist El Centro Family Health, N.Mex., 2007—. Regional rep., nat. sec. bd. dir. Physicians for Nat. Health Program, Cambridge, Mass., 1989-91; cons. documentary Health Care Across the Border, Nat. Pub. TV, NYC, 1989-90, documentary on US health care system Nat. TV Austria, 1991; cons. BBC, 1992, Pew Health Professions Commn., 1992-94, Assn. Am. Med. Colls., 1992-93, Robert Wood Johnson Found., 1992, Rsch. and Tng. Group in Social Medicine, Santiago, Chile, 1990—, Eisenhower Rural Health Ctr., Idyllwild, Calif., 1995-96, office of pres. breast cancer rsch. initiative U. Calif, 2001, John D. & Catherine T. MacArthur Found., 2004, 09; lectr. med. sociology U. Amsterdam, The Netherlands, 1977; vis. prof. Northwestern U., 1994, U. Ill., Chgo., 1994, U. Wash., 1996, U. N.Mex., 1996, U. Ky., 1996, U. Guadalajara, 1997, 2002, 03, Simon Fraser U., 1997, U. Campinas, Brazil, 1999, Cornell Med. Coll., 1999, U. Utah, 2002, Nat. Inst. Pub. Health, Cuernavaca, Mex., 2003, 06, Robert Wood Johnson Sch. Medicine and Dentistry, NJ, 2003-04, State U. Rio de Jenerio, Brazil, 2008; expert panel on comm. with elderly patients Nat. Inst. Aging, 1997; prin. investigator US Agy. for Healthcare Rsch. and Quality, NIMH, 1991-, Robert Wood Johnson Found., 2003-05, 08-09. Co-author: The Exploitation of Illness in Capitalist Society, 1974; author: The Second Sickness: Contradictions of Capitalist Health Care, 1983, paperback edit., 1986, revised edit., 2000, The Politics of Medical Encounters: How Patients and Doctors Deal with Social Problems, 1991, paperback edit., 1993, At the Front Lines of Medicine: How the Health Care System Alienates Doctors and Mistreats Patients...and What We Can Do About It, 2001, paperback edit., 2004; mem. editl. bd. Internat. Jour. Health Svc., Social Problems, Western Jour. Medicine, Cambio y Salud (Chile), Investigacion en Salud (Mex.), Internat. Jour. Cuban Health and Medicine. Cons. on health policy Jesse Jackson Presdl. Campaign, 1988; bd. dirs., mem. com. on litigation Orange County Pub. Law Ctr., 1990-96. Fellow in ind. study and rsch. NEH, 1984-85, Fulbright fellow, 1983, 88-90, 93-94, sr. fellow NIA, 1989-91, Fogarty Internat. Ctr., NIH, 1994-98, Fulbright New Century Scholar, 2001-02, Guide to Am. Top Physicians, 2002-2008, John Simon Guggenheim Meml. Found. fellow, 2002-03, Jonathan Mann Award for Lifetime Commitment to Pub. Health and Social Justice Issues, N.Mex. Pub. Health Assn., 2003. Fellow ACP, Am. Acad. Physician and Patient, Soc. for Applied Anthropology; mem. APHA, Am. Sociol. Assn. (nat. coun.-at-large med. sociology sect. 1989-92, coord. resolution process concerning nat. health program 1990-91, Leo G. Reeder award for disting. career in medicine and social sci., 1997), Soc. Gen. Internal Medicine, Phi Beta Kappa, Salvador Allende Program Social Medicine (pres. 2006-08). Avocations: music, athletics, gardening, mountain hiking. Office: U NMex Sociology MSC05 3080 Rm 1103 1915 Roma NE Albuquerque NM 87131 Office Phone: 505-277-0860. Business E-Mail: waitzkin@unm.edu.

WAKAMATSU, DON (WILBUR DONALD WAKAMATSU), professional baseball coach; b. Hood River, Oreg., Feb. 22, 1963; m.

Laura Wakamatsu; children: Jacob, Lucas, Jadyn. Attended, Ariz. State U., Tempe. Minor league catcher, 1985—96; catcher Chgo. White Sox, 1991; mgr. Peoria Rookie, Ariz. Summer League, 1997, Class-A High Desert Mavericks, 1997—99, Double-A El Paso, Double-A Erie, Eastern League, 2000; minor league catching coord., roving catching instr. LA Angels, 2001—02; bench coach Tex. Rangers, 2003—06, third base coach, 2007; bench coach Oakland Athletics, 2008; mgr. Seattle Mariners, 2008—. Named Mgr. of Yr., Calif. League, 1998. Achievements include becoming the first Asian-American manager in Major League Baseball history, 2008. Office: Seattle Mariners Safeco Field PO Box 4100 Seattle WA 98134-0100

WAKASHIGE, BENJAMIN TAKA, librarian; b. Paia, Hawaii, Sept. 3, 1947; s. Akio and Asayo (Tagawa) Wakashige; m. Marie Diane Wakashige, Dec. 29, 1969; children: David B.A., Kristen J.A. BA with honors, Western N.Mex. U., 1969; MA in Librarianship, Emporia State U., 1970. Reference libr. Birmingham Southern Coll., Ala., 1972—74; regional libr. blind and physically handicapped Maine State Libr., 1974—75, N.Mex. State Libr., Santa Fe, 1975—77, state libr., 1998—; project dir. Am. Indian Libr. Cultural Ctr. Project, U. N.Mex., Albuquerque, 1979—80; dist. libr. media coord. Zuni Pub. Schs., N.Mex., 1980—82; libr. dir. U. Albuquerque, 1982—85, Albuquerque Acad., 1985. Co-editor (with others): Haiku and Haiga, 1970. With USAR, 1970—72. Mem.: ALA, N.Mex. Adv. Coun. Librs., Greater Albuquerque Libr. Assn., N.Mex. Book League, N.Mex. Libr. Assn. (pres. 1982—83). Democrat. Mem. United Ch. Christ. Office: State Library 1209 Camino Carlos Rey Santa Fe NM 87505

WAKE, DAVID BURTON, biology professor; b. Webster, SD, June 8, 1936; s. Thomas B. and Ina H. (Solem) W.; m. Marvalee Hendricks, June 23, 1962; 1 child, Thomas Andrew BA, Pacific Luth. U., 1958; MS, U. So. Calif., 1960, PhD, 1964. Instr. anatomy and biology U. Chgo., 1964-66, asst. prof. anatomy and biology, 1966-69; assoc. prof. zoology U. Calif., Berkeley, 1969-72, prof., 1972-89, John and Margaret Gompertz prof., 1991-97, prof. integrative biology, 1989—2003, prof. emeritus integrative biology, 2003—, faculty rsch. lectr., 2004, prof. grad. sch., 2005—. Dir. Mus. Vertebrate Zoology U. Calif., Berkeley, 1971-98; curator Herpetology Mus. Vertebrate Zoology, U. Calif., 1969-; vis. Alexander Agassiz prof. Mus. Comparative Zoology, Harvard U., 2002. Author: Biology, 1979; co-editor: Functional Vertebrate Morphology, 1985, Complex Organismal Functions: Integration and Evolution in the Vertebrates, 1989. Recipient Quantrell Tchg. award U. Chgo., 1967, Outstanding Alumnus award Pacific Luth. U., 1979, Joseph Grinnell medal Mus. Vertebrate Zoology, 1998, Henry S. Fitch award Am. Soc. Ichthyologists and Herpetologists, 1999, Joseph Leidy medal Acad. Nat. Sci. Phila., 2006, Berkeley Citation award U. Calif., 2006; grantee NSF, 1965—; Guggenheim fellow, 1982. Fellow AAAS, Am. Acad. Arts and Scis.; mem. NAS, NRC (bd. biology 1986-92), Am. Philos. Soc., Internat. Union for Conservation of Nature and Natural Resources (chair task force on declining amphibian populations 1990-92), Am. Soc. Zoologists (pres. 1992), Am. Soc. Naturalists (pres. 1989), Am. Soc. Ichthyologists and Herpetologists (bd. govs.), Soc. Study Evolution (pres. 1983, editor 1979-81), Soc. Systematic Biology (coun. 1980-84), Herpetologist's League (Disting. Herpetologist 1984). Home: 999 Middlefield Rd Berkeley CA 94708-1509 Home Phone: 510-845-1627. Business E-Mail: wakelab@uclink.berkeley.edu.

WAKE, MARVALEE HENDRICKS, biology professor; b. Orange, Calif., July 31, 1939; d. Marvin Carlton and Velvalee (Borter) H.; m. David B. Wake, June 23, 1962; 1 child, Thomas A. BA, U. So. Calif., 1961, MS, 1964, PhD, 1968. Tchg. asst., instr. U. Ill., Chgo., 1964, asst. prof., 1968—69; lectr. U. Calif., Berkeley, 1969—73, asst. prof., 1973—76, assoc. prof., 1976—80, prof. zoology, 1980—89, chmn. dept. zoology, 1985—89, chmn. dept. integrative biology, 1989—91, 1999—2002, assoc. dean Coll. Letters and Sci., 1975—78, prof. integrative biology, 1989—2003, Chancellor's prof., 1997—2000, prof. of the Grad. Sch., 2004—. Mem. NAS/NRC Bd. on Sustainable Devel., 1995-99, NSF Bio Adv. Commn., 1997-2002; Smithsonian Sci. Commn., 2001-02; adv. bd. Enoyo Life Distinguisher, 2007-.examiner FGGS, Am Mus. Nat. Hist., 2007 Editor, co-editor: Hyman's Comparative Vertebrate Anatomy, 1979, The Origin and Evolution of Larval Forms, 1999, Ecology and Evolution in the Tropics, 2005; co-author: Biology, 1978; contbr. articles to profl. jours. NSF grantee, 1978—; Guggenheim fellow, 1988-89. Fellow: AAAS (chair Biology Sect. G 1998), Calif. Acad. Sci. (trustee 1992—98, hon. trustee 1998—), Am. Acad. Arts and Scis.; mem.: Internat. Soc. Vertebrate Morphology (pres. 2007—), Am. Inst. Biol. Sci. (pres. 2005), World Congress of Herpetology (sec. gen. 1994—97), Internat. Union Biol. Scis. (U.S. nat. com. 1986—2007, chair 1992—95, sec. gen. 1994—2000, pres. 2000—04), Soc. Integrative Comparative Biology (pres. 2001—03), Am. Soc. Ichthyologists and Herpetologists (bd. govs. 1978—, pres. 1984). Office: U Calif Dept Integrative Biology 3060 VLSB Berkeley CA 94720-3140 E-mail: mhwake@socrates.berkeley.edu.

WAKE, NEIL VINCENT, federal judge, lawyer; b. Phoenix, July 2, 1948; s. John Harold and Jewel Frances (Stanton) W.; m. Shari M. Capra, May 10, 1980; children: Aaron Richard, Damon Vincent. BA with high distinction, Ariz. State U., 1971; JD cum laude, Harvard U., 1974. Bar: Ariz. 1974, U.S. Ct. Appeals (9th cir.) 1975, U.S. Ct. Appeals (5th cir.) 1985, U.S. Ct. Appeals (10th cir.) 1984, U.S. Supreme Ct. 1977, Navajo Supreme Ct. 1978. Assoc. Jennings, Strouss & Salmon, Phoenix, 1974-77, ptnr., 1978-82, Beus, Gilbert, Wake & Morrill, Phoenix, 1982-89; pvt. practice Law Offices of Neil Vincent Wake, Phoenix, 1989—94, 1999—2004; ptnr. BryanCave LLP, 1994-98; dist. judge U.S. Dist. Ct. of Ariz., Phoenix, 2004—. Judge pro tem Ariz. Ct. Appeals, 1985, 92; mem. Civil Practice and Procedure Commn., Phoenix, 1983-92, 96-99. Co-author: Arizona Appellate Handbook, 1980, 3d edit., 1997; mem. editl. bd. Ariz. State Bar Jour., 1978-82. Bd. dirs. Community Legal Services, Phoenix, 1976-81. Fellow Am. Acad. Appellate Lawyers; mem. ABA, Maricopa County Bar Assn. Clubs: Plaza (Phoenix). Office: Sandra Day O Connnor US Courthouse 401 W Washington St Phoenix AZ 85003

WAKEFIELD, MARIE A., counselor, educational association administrator; b. Elyria, Ohio, Aug. 9, 1947; stepd. Orville B. and and d. Ethel A. Thomas; m. Charles F. Wakefield, Nov. 13, 1975; children: Paul, Philip, Charlene, Conya. BS in Edn., Cen. State U., Wilberforce, Ohio, 1969; MS, U. Nev., Las Vegas, 1979, adminstrv. endorsement, 1989. Cert. profl. elem. tchr., K-8 counselor, Nev. Elem. tchr. Clark County Sch. Dist., Las Vegas, elem. counselor. Pres. Am. Counseling Assn., Alexandria, Va. Editor parents newsletters. Recipient Outstanding Counseling Edn. award, Dr. Kay P. Carl, John A. Bailey Disting. Profl. award, Profl. Black Women's Rose award. Mem.: ACA (pres.), Assn. Multicultural Counseling Devel., Assn. Adult Devel. Aging (Disting. Svc. award), Western Region Governing Coun., Nev. Counseling Assn., Am. Bus. Womens Assn., Southern Nev. Sch. Counselors Assn., Nat. Self-Esteem Coun. Avocations: piano, reading. Office: 8091 Petunia Flower Way Las Vegas NV 89147 Office Phone: 702-876-5926. Business E-Mail: mawakefield@cox.net.

WALCHER, ALAN ERNEST, lawyer; b. Chgo., Oct. 2, 1949; s. Chester R. and Dorothy E. (Kullgren) W.; children: Dustin Alan, Michael Alan, Christopher Ray. BS, U. Utah, 1971, cert. in internat. rels., 1971, JD, 1974. Bar: Utah 1974, U.S. Dist. Ct. Utah 1974, U.S. Ct. Appeals (10th cir.) 1977, Calif. 1979, U.S. Dist. Ct. (cen. dist.) Calif. 1979, U.S. Ct. Appeals (9th cir.) 1983, U.S. Dist. Ct. (ea., no., and so. dists.) Calif. 1994. Sole practice, Salt Lake City, 1974-79; ptnr. Costello & Walcher, L.A., 1979-85, Walcher & Scheuer, 1985-88, Ford & Harrison, 1988-91, Epstein Becker & Green, 1991-2003; sole practice, 2003-; judge pro tem Los Angeles Mcpl. Ct., 1986-91; dir. Citronia, Inc., Los Angeles, 1979-81. Trial counsel Utah chpt. Common Cause, Salt Lake City, 1978-79. Robert Mukai scholar U. Utah, 1971. Mem. Soc. Bar and Gavel (v.p. 1975-77), ABA, Fed. Bar Assn., Los Angeles County Bar Assn., Century City Bar Assn., Assn. Bus. Trial Lawyers, Phi Delta Phi, Owl and Key. Home: 1050 S Flower St #605 Los Angeles CA 90015 Office Phone: 310-344-6570. Personal E-mail: alan1002@earthlink.net.

WALD, DONNA GENE, advertising executive; b. Peekskill, NY, July 24, 1947; d. David and Blossom (Karlin) W. BA, Rider Coll., 1969; MA, Hunter Coll., 1974. Broadcast traffic rep. SSC&B, Inc., NYC, 1969-74; broadcast buyer J. Walter Thompson, NYC, 1974-78; regional broadcast supr., v.p. Dallas, 1978-81; prof. UCLA, 1984; sr. v.p., account dir. Western Internat. Media, Calif., 1985-95; exec. v.p., regional dir. account svcs., 1995; exec. v.p., dir. account svcs. Pacific region, 1998—2002; sr. v.p., group acct. dir. Inter/Media, Encino, Calif., 2002—. Mem. Advt. Industry Emergency Fund, Hollywood Radio and TV Soc., Assn. Broadcast Execs. of Tex. (bd. dirs. 1979-80, s ec. 1980-81), L.A. Advt. Club (bd. dirs. 1997-98). Home: 14844 Dickens St Apt 106 Sherman Oaks CA 91403-3655 Office: Inter Media 15760 Ventura Blvd 1st Fl Encino CA 91436

WALD, MICHAEL S., law educator; b. 1941; AB, Cornell U., 1963; LLB, Yale U., 1967, MA in Polit. Sci., 1967. Bar: Calif. 1970, DC 1970. Mem. faculty Stanford Law Sch., 1967—, dir. Ctr. for Study of Youth Devel., 1984—87, Jackson Eli Reynolds prof. law, 1990—; atty. Dist. Atty.'s Office, Ventura County, Calif., 1970, Ctr. Law and Social Poliy, Washington, 1970—71, Pub. Defender Svc., 1970—71, Youth Law Ctr., San Francisco, 1971—72. Dep. gen. counsel HHS, 1993—95; exec. dir. Dept. Human Svcs. City and County San Francisco, 1996—97; sr. advisor to pres. Hewlett Found., 2001—03. Co-author: Protecting Abused and Neglected Children, 1988; gen. editor, co-author: Conditions of Children in California, 1989. Recipient Distin. Contbns. to Child Advocacy award, Am. Pyschol. Assn. Divsn. Child, Youth and Family Svcs., 1984, Distin. Contbns. to Protection of Children's Rights award, Nat. Ctr. for Youth Law, 1986; John Simon Guggenheim fellowship, 1982—83. Office: Stanford Law Sch Crown Quadrangle 559 Nathan Abbott Way Stanford CA 94305-8610 Office Phone: 650-723-0322. E-mail: mwald@stanford.edu.

WALD, PETER ALLEN, lawyer; b. 1953; AB magna cum laude, Brown U., 1974; JD magna cum laude, Harvard U., 1977. Bar: Calif. 1979. Law clk. to Hon. James R. Browning US Ct. Appeals (9th cir.), 1977—78; ptnr. Latham & Watkins, LLP, San Francisco, 1996—, global dept. chair, litig. dept. and chair, Bay Area litig. dept. Notes editor Harvard Law Rev., 1977. Named one of Top 10 Trial Lawyers in Am., Nat. Law Jour., 2006. Mem.: Phi Beta Kappa. Office: Latham & Watkins LLP Ste 2000 505 Montgomery St San Francisco CA 94111-2562 Office Phone: 415-395-8006. Office Fax: 415-395-8095. E-mail: peter.wald@lw.com.

WALDEN, DANA, broadcast executive; BA in Comm., U. So. Calif. Formerly with Bender, Goldman & Helper; former v.p. mktg. Arsenio Hall Comm., Paramount; former sr. v.p. media and corp. rels. 20th Century Fox TV, v.p. current programming, 1994—96, former v.p. drama, former sr. v.p. drama, former exec. v.p. drama devel., pres., 1999—, chmn., 2007—. Named one of The 100 Most Powerful Women in Entertainment, Hollywood Reporter, 1999—2007. Mem.: Hollywood Radio and TV Soc. (v.p. 2003—). Office: 20th Century Fox TV 10201 W Pico Blvd Bldg 88 Rm 29 Los Angeles CA 90035

WALDEN, GREG, United States Representative from Oregon; b. The Dalles, Oreg., Jan. 10, 1957; s. Paul Walden; m. Mylene Walden; 1 child. BS in Journalism, U. Oreg., Eugene, 1981. Press sec. Staff of US Rep. Denny Smith of Oreg., 1981—84, chief of staff, 1984—86; owner Columbia Gorge Broadcasters, Inc., The Dalles, 1986—; mem. Oreg. State Ho. Reps., 1989-95, majority leader, 1991-93; mem. Oreg. State Senate, 1995-97, asst. majority leader, 1995-97; mem. US Congress from 2nd Oreg. dist., 1999—, mem. energy and commerce com., vice chmn. oversight and investigations subcommittee, mem. energy independence and global warming com., dep. whip, 2002—. Owner MSW Comm. Bd. dirs., exec. com. Assn. Oreg. Industries; bd. dirs. Oreg. Health Scis. Found. Recipient Benjamin Franklin award, 60+ Assn., Pub. Svc. award, Am. Coll. Nurse-Midwives, Thomas Jefferson award, Food Distbrs. Internat., Disting. Svc. award, Forest Counties Schs. Coalition, Champion award, League Pvt. Property Owners, Congl. Champion award, Nat. Assn. Svc. Conservation Corps, Wheat Adv. award, Nat. Assn. Wheat Growers, Appreciation award, Oreg. Nat. Guard, Sr. Legis. Achievement award, Seniors Coalition, Spirit of Enterprise award, US C. of C., Golden Bulldog award, Watchdog of Treasury; named Outstanding Young Oregonian, Oreg. Jaycees, 1991, Legislator of Yr., Nat. Rep. Legislators Assn., 1993, Agr. Retailers Assn., Ctrl. Oreg. Visitors Assn., Nat. Assn. Home Care, Nat. Rural Health Assn., Oreg. Assn. Home Care, Oreg. Rural Electric Coop. Assn., Safari Club Internat., Oreg. Person of Yr., Dorchester Conf.; named a Hero of Taxpayer, Americans for Tax Reform, Friend of Shareholder, Am. Shareholders Assn., Friend of Pear Industry, N.W. Pear Industry, Friend of Farm Bur., Oreg. Farm Bur. Mem.: Nat. Fedn. Ind. Bus., Hood River C. of C., Elks Club, Rotary Club. Republican. Episcopalian. Office: US House Reps 1210 Longworth House Office Bldg Washington DC 20515 Office Phone: 202-225-6730. Office Fax: 202-225-5774. E-mail: greg.walden@mail.house.gov.

WALDMAN, ANNE LESLEY, poet, performer, editor, publisher, educational administrator; b. Millville, NJ, Apr. 2, 1945; d. John Marvin and Frances (Le Fevre) W.; m. Reed Eyre Bye; 1 son, Ambrose. BA, Bennington Coll., 1966. Dir. The Poetry Project, St. Marks Ch. In-the-Bowery, NYC, 1968-78; dir. Jack Kerouac Sch. of Disembodied Poetics at Naropa Inst., Boulder, Colo., 1974—. Adj. faculty Inst. Am. Indian Arts, Santa Fe; bd. dirs. Com. for Internat. Poetry, Eye and Ear Theatre, N.Y.C.; poet-in-residence with Bob Dylan's Rolling Thunder Rev.; dir. Naropa Study Abroad in Bali, Indonesia, 1998; guest dir. Schule fur Dichtung, Vienna, 1999. Author: (poetry) On the Wing, 1968, O My Life, 1969, Baby Breakdown, 1970, Giant Night, 1970, No Hassles, 1971, Life Notes, 1973, Fast Speaking Woman, 1975, Journals and Dreams, 1976, Shaman, 1977, Countries, 1980, Cabin, 1981, First Baby Poems, 1982, Makeup on Empty Space, 1983, Invention, 1986, Skin Meat Bones, 1986, The Romance Thing, 1987, Blue Mosque, 1988, Helping the Dreamer: New and Selected Poems, 1989, Not a Male Pseudonym, 1990, Lokapala, 1991, Troubairitz, 1993, Iovis: All is Full of Jove, 1993, Kill or Cure, 1994, Iovis II, 1997; editor: Nice To See You: Homage to Ted Berrigan, 1991, The Beat Book, 1996, (anthologies) The World Anthology, 1969, Another World, 1972, Talking Poetics From Naropa Institute vol. 1, 1978, vol. 2, 1979, Out of This World, 1991, (with Andrew Schelling) Disembodied Poetics: Annals of the Jack Kerovac School, 1994, (with Anselm Hollo and Jack Collom) Polemics; translator (with Andrew Schelling) Sons & Daughters of the Buddha, 1996; publisher: anthologies Angel Hair Books, N.Y.C., Full Ct. Press, N.Y.C.; recordings: The Dial-a-Poem Poets Disconnected, Anne Waldman/John Giorno, Fast Speaking Woman, The Nova Convention, Big Ego, Uh-oh Plutonium!, 1982, Crack in My World, 1986, Assorted Singles, 1990; performance videos include Eyes in All Heads, 1990, Live at Naropa, 1991, Battle of the Bards, 1991; featured on nat. pub. radio show All Things Considered, also featured in the poetry documentary Poetry In Motion. Dir. summer writing program Naropa; organizer Surrealist, Objectivist, Feminist, Pan Am. Ecology, Performance Confs., and The Robert Creeley Symposium. Recipient Dylan Thomas Meml. award New Sch., N.Y.C., 1967, Blue Ribbon Am. Film Festival, Nat. Literary Anthology award, 1970; named Heavyweight Champion Poet, 1989, 90; Cultural Artists Program grantee, 1976-77; NEA grantee, 1979-80; recipient Shelley Meml. award, 1996. Mem. PEN Club, Amnesty Internat. Office: c/o Naropa Inst 2130 Arapahoe Ave Boulder CO 80302-6602

WALDO, JAMES CHANDLER, lawyer; b. Seattle, Oct. 23, 1948; s. Burton Chandler and Margaret (Hoar) W.; m. Sharon B. Waldo; children: Sara K., William K., John J. Grad., Whitman Coll., 1970; JD, Willamette U., 1974. Bar: Wash. 1974, U.S. Ct. Appeals (9th cir.) 1976. Exec. asst. Dept. of Labor, Washington, 1974-76; asst. U.S. atty. Justice Dept., Seattle, 1976-79; of counsel ESTEP & LI, Seattle, 1979-80; ptnr. Gordon, Thomas, Honeywell, Malanca, Peterson & Daheim LLP, Seattle, 1981—. Chmn. N.W. Renewable Resources Ctr., Seattle, 1984-97, Wash. State Energy Strategy Com., 1991-93; spl. counsel on Water for Gov., 2001—04. Trustee Western Wash. U., 1981-93. Recipient Outstanding Alumnus of Yr. Whitman Coll., 1994, Dir.'s award Wash. Dept. Fisheries, 1986, Pres.'s award Assn. Wash. Bus., 1988, Outstanding Citizen award Western Assn. Fish & Wildlife Agys., 1987, Merit award, Am. Water Works Assn., 2005. Mem. Am. Water Works Assn. (Award of Merit 2005). Office: Gordon Thomas Honeywell Malanca Peterson & Daheim LLP PO Box 1157 Tacoma WA 98401-1157 Office Phone: 253-620-6541.

WALDORF, GREGORY, Internet company executive, venture capitalist; s. Toby and Bob Waldorf. BA, UCLA; MBA, Stanford U. Co-founder, co-chair devel. com. Startup, East Palo Alto, Calif., 1994; dir. Internet group Pacific Edge Investment Mgmt., Palo Alto; ptnr. Fayaz Sarofim & Co.; gen. ptnr., mgr. W. Coast ops. Charles River Ventures, Palo Alto, 2000; founding investor eHarmony, Pasadena, 2000, CEO, 2006—; co-founder Destination-U, Menlo Park, 2004. Founding mem. Stanford Grad. Sch. Bus. Mgmt. Bd.; bd. overseers Stanford U. Hoover Inst. Mem. SV2, the Silicon Valley Social Venture Fund, 1999—. Office: eHarmony PO Box 60157 Pasadena CA 91116 Office Phone: 626-795-4814.

WALKEN, CHRISTOPHER, actor; b. Astoria, NY, Mar. 31, 1943; s. Paul Walken; m. Georgianne Thon, Jan. 1969. Attended Hofstra U., studied with Wynn Handman, Actors Studio. Stage appearances include Broadway, off-Broadway and regional theatres throughout US and Can.; Broadway debut in J.B, 1959; other stage appearances include Best Foot Forward, West Side Story, Macbeth, The Lion in Winter (Clarence Derwent award 1966), Hamlet, The Rose Tatoo (Theatre World's Most Promising Personality 1966-67), Romeo and Juliet, The Seagull, 2001, The Night Thoreau Spent in Jail (Joseph Jefferson award 1970-71), Kid Champion (Obie award 1975), Miss Julie, Sweet Bird of Youth, Hurlyburly, 1984, Cinders, 1984, A Bill of Divorcement, 1985, Coriolanus, 1988, Othello, 1992, (also playwright) Him, 1995, Mother Courage, 2006; films include The Anderson Tapes, 1971, Next Stop Greenwich Village, The Sentinel, 1977, Roseland, 1977, Annie Hall, 1977, The Deer Hunter, 1978 (NY Film Critics Best Supporting Actor award 1978, Acad. award Best Supporting Actor 1979), Last Embrace, 1979, Dogs of War, 1981, Heavens Gate, 1980, Pennies From Heaven, 1981, The Happiness Cage, 1982, The Dead Zone, 1983, Brainstorm, 1983, A View to a Kill, 1984, At Close Range, 1986, Deadline, 1987, Puss in Boots, 1988, The Milagro Beanfield War, 1988, Biloxi Blues, 1988, Communion, 1989, King of New York, 1990, Homeboy, 1991, The Comfort of Strangers, 1991, McBain, 1991, All American Murder, 1992, Batman Returns, 1992, True Romance, 1993, A Business Affair, 1994, Wayne's World II, 1994, Pulp Fiction, 1994, Search and Destroy, 1995, Nick of Time, 1995, The Addiction, 1995, The Prophecy, 1995, The Funeral, 1996, Basquiat, 1996, The Wild Side, 1996, Things To Do in Denver When You're Dead, 1995, Last Man Standing, 1996, Touch, 1997, Mousehunt, 1997, Excess Baggage, 1997, Suicide Kings, 1997, Antz (voice), 1998, Illuminata, 1998, New Rose Hotel, 1998, The Prophecy II, 1998, Trance, 1998, Sleepy Hollow, 1999, Blast From the Past, 1999, Kiss Toledo Goodbye, 1999, Vendetta, 1999, Scotland PA, 2001, Joe Dirt, 2001, America's Sweethearts, 2001, Chelsea Walls, 2001, The Affair of the Necklace, 2001, Jungle Juice, 2001, Poolhall Junkies, 2002, The Country Bears, 2002, Plots with a View, 2002, Catch Me If You Can, 2002 (Best Actor in Supporting Role, British Acad. Film Award (BAFTA) 2003), Kangaroo Jack, 2003, Gigli, 2003, The Rundown, 2003, Man on Fire, 2004, Envy, 2004, The Stepford Wives, 2004, Around the Bend, 2004, Wedding Crashers, 2005, Domino, 2005, Click, 2006, Man of the Year, 2006, Hairspray, 2007, Balls of Fury, 2007; TV films include Sarah, Plain and Tall, 1991 (Emmy nominee), Skylark, 1993, Scam, 1993; The Opportunists, 1999, The Prophecy III: The Ascent, 1999, Sarah, Plain and Tall: 3, 1999, Julius Caesar, 2002; (TV series) Saturday Night Live (Am. Comedy award 2001), Naked City, 1958, Hawaii Five-O, 1968, Kojak, 1973; (TV mini-series) Julius Caesar, 2002. Recipient Best Supporting Male Performance (True Crime: NYC), Spike TV Video Game awards, 2005, Man of the Yr., Hasty Pudding Theatrical Soc., 2008. Office: c/o Toni Howard Internat Creative Mgmt 10250 Constellation Blvd Los Angeles CA 90067

WALKER, ANN YVONNE, lawyer; b. San Francisco, Sept. 26, 1954; d. C. Richard and Athene (Henderson) Walker. BS with distinction in Math., Stanford U., 1976; JD, Stanford Law Sch., 1979. Bar: Calif. 1979. Assoc. Wilson, Sonsini, Goodrich & Rosati, Palo Alto, Calif., 1979-86, mem., 1986—. Violinist, bd. dirs. Redwood Symphony Orch., 1985—; bd. dirs. Fremont Opera, Inc., 2007—. Named to Best Lawyers in Am., 2006, 2007, Northern Calif. Super Lawyers, Law & Politics Mag., 2004—06. Mem.: ABA (mem. fed. regulation securities com. 1992—, mem. com. lawyer bus. ethics 1993—, mem. standing com. professionalism 1996—99, chair 1997—2001, mem. bus. law sect. publs. bd. 2000—04, mem. bus. law sect. coun. 2001—05, mem. standing com. tech. and info. sys. 2005—), Palo Alto Area Bar Assn., Santa Clara County Bar Assn., Calif. State Bar Assn. (mem. corps. com. 1992—96, chair 1995—96, mem. exec. com. bus. law sect. 1996—, vice chair 1998—99, chair 1999—2000, advisor 2000—05, co-chair coun. state bar sects. 2001—02, advisor emeritus 2005—), Phi Beta Kappa. Office: Wilson Sonsini Goodrich and Rosati 650 Page Mill Rd Palo Alto CA 94304-1050 Office Phone: 650-320-4643. Business E-Mail: awalker@wsgr.com.

WALKER, CARLENE MARTIN, state legislator; b. Sept. 2, 1947; m. Gordon D. Walker; 4 children. BS, Brigham Young U., 1969. Supr. coding & data entry the Wirthlin Group, 1982-86; cons. D.K. Shifflet & Assocs., 1987-88; ptnr., mgr. Covecrest Properties, 1978-99; tech. recruiter Manpower Tech., 1999-2000; mem. Utah State Senate, Salt Lake City, 2001—. Chair, founder Women's Polit. Action Com., chair transp. appropriations. Active AGs Task Force on ID Theft, Capitol Preservation Bd.; bd. dirs. United Way, Salt Lake Convention and Vis. Bur., Hogle Zoo. Republican. Mormon. Office: 4085 E Prospector Dr Salt Lake City UT 84121 Office Phone: 801-773-4599.

WALKER, DAN, former mayor; Mem. Torrance City Coun., 1978—92, 1994—2002; mayor City of Torrance, Calif., 2002—06. Del. South Bay Cities Coun. Govts., L.A. County Sanitation Dist., South Bay Econ. Devel. Partnership; mem. Planning Commn., 1975—77. Mem. L.A. Regional Quality Control Bd.; bd. dirs. Friends of Child Advs.

WALKER, DOUGLAS, computer development company executive; Graduate, Vanderbilt U., 1976. With Western Data Corp., Seattle, 1976-80, Walker, Richer & Quinn, Inc., Seattle, 1980—, now pres., 1989—, CEO. Office: Walker Richer & Quinn Inc 1500 Dexter Ave N Seattle WA 98109-3032

WALKER, FRANCIS JOSEPH, lawyer; b. Aug. 5, 1922; s. John McSweeney and Sarah Veronica (Meechan) W.; m. Julia Corinne O'Brien, Jan. 27, 1951; children: Vincent Paul, Monica Irene Hylton, Jill Marie Nudell, John Michael, Michael Joseph, Thomas More. BA, St. Martin's Coll., 1947; JD, U. Wash., 1950. Bar: Wash. Asst. atty. gen. State of Wash., 1950-51; pvt. practice Olympia, Wash., 1951—. Gen. counsel Wash. Cath. Conf., 1967-76. Lt. (j.g.) USNR, 1943-46; PTO. Home and Office: 2723 Hillside Dr SE Olympia WA 98501-3460 Office Phone: 360-352-2245.

WALKER, FRANKLIN CURTIS, federal agency administrator; b. Sept. 10, 1945; s. Howard and Edna Walker; m. Judy Provins, May 29, 1967; children: Mark, Kathy, Phillip. BS in Biology, N.Mex. State U., 1967. Park ranger White Sands Nat. Monument Nat. Park Svc., 1970-72, park ranger Jefferson Nat. Expansion Meml., 1972-73, park ranger Gulf Islands Nat. Seashore, 1973-77, naturalist south dist. Yellowstone Nat. Park, 1977-80, chief of interpretation Carlsbad Caverns Nat. Park, 1980-85, park supt. Ft. Clatsop Nat. Meml., 1985-90, supt. Nez Perce Nat. Hist. Park Idaho, Oreg., Wash., Mont., 1990-98, supt. Saguaro Nat. Park Tucson, 1998—. 1st lt. U.S. Army, 1967-69. Office: Saguaro Nat Park 3693 S Old Spanish Trl Tucson AZ 85730-5601 Home: 2396 W Beall St Apt 2 Bozeman MT 59718-3104

WALKER, HENRY GILBERT, health care executive, consultant; b. Gowanda, NY, Feb. 16, 1947; s. Henry George and Grace Dayton (Moore) W.; m. Elaine Ruth Darbee, July 18, 1970 (div. Dec. 1979); 1 child, Matthew Case; m. Patricia Ann Andrade, May 14, 1983; children: Michael David, Christopher John. BS in Indsl. Engring., Cornell U., 1969; MBA, U. Chgo., 1975. Evening adminstr. Rush-Presbyn. St.-Luke's Med. Ctr., Chgo., 1973-75; mgmt. cons. Booz, Allen & Hamilton, Chgo., 1975-79; regional adminstr., v.p. S.W. Community Health Service, Albuquerque, 1979-83, adminstr., v.p., 1983-86; exec. v.p. Presbyn. Healthcare Services, Albuquerque, 1986-92; pres., CEO Tucson Med. Ctr., 1992—95, Health Ptnrs. of Ariz., 1995—97, Providence Health System, Seattle, 1997—2004; ptnr. Andrade Walker Consulting, LLC, Bellevue, Wash., 2004—. Bd. dirs. Park Dist., Elmhurst, Ill., 1978, 1979; mem. Dist. III Cmty. Action Com., Albuquerque, 1985; divsn. chmn. United Way of Albuqueque, 1985, 1988. Recipient Hosp. Survey award U. Chgo., 1975, Bachmeyer award U. Chgo., 1975, Outstanding Midshipman award Cornell U., 1969; named one of Emerging Healthcare Leaders, Healthcare Forum, 1985, 86, Healthcares Up and Comers, Modern Healthcare Mag., 1987. Mem.: Healthcare Forum (bd. dirs., chmn.), N.Mex. Hosp. Assn. (chmn. bd. dirs. 1983—85, treas.). Democrat. Presbyterian. Avocations: reading, hiking, skiing.

WALKER, HILL M., educator; Recipient Rsch. award Coun. for Exceptional Children, 1993. Office: U Oregon Ctr Ctr Human Devel 901 E 18th Ave Eugene OR 97403-1354

WALKER, JAMES BRADLEY, academic institution administrator; b. NYC, Apr. 10, 1948; s. James Bradley and Mary Jane (Thayer) W.; m. Virginia Lynn, Apr. 11, 1969; children: Carol Renee, Laura Jane. BS, Calif. Poly. State U., 1975. Comptroller Albuquerque Western Industries, 1975-78; CFO U. N.Mex. Hosp., Albuquerque, 1978-84, Univ. Hosp., Portland, Oreg., 1984-97; v.p. fin. and adminstrn. Oreg. Health Scis. U., Portland, 1992—, exec. v.p., 1998—. Sgt. USAF, 1969-72. Avocations: golf, travel. Office: Oreg Health Scis U Hosp 3181 SW Sam Jackson Park Rd Portland OR 97201-3011

WALKER, JOHN KENT, JR., lawyer; Grad. magna cum laude, Harvard Coll.; grad. with distinction, Stanford Law Sch., 1987. Asst. US atty. US Dept. Justice, San Francisco; sr. counsel AirTouch Comm.; assoc. gen. counsel Netscape, 1998—99; sr. counsel AirTouch Comm.; exec. v.p. Liberate Technologies; dep. gen. counsel eBay Inc.; v.p., gen. counsel Google, 2006—. Office: Google Inc 1600 Amphitheatre Pky Mountain View CA 94043

WALKER, JOHN P., pharmaceutical executive; Pres., CEO Arris Pharm. Corp., South San Francisco; chmn. & CEO Axys Pharms Inc., San Francisco. Office: Axys Pharm Inc 180 Kimball Way South San Francisco CA 94080-6218

WALKER, LORENZO GILES, surgeon, educator; b. Phila., June 29, 1957; s. Manuel Lorenzo and Romaine Yvonne (Smith) W.; m. Yvonne Ruiz; children: Zachary Giles, Benjamin Lee, Cassidy Leigh. BA cum laude, U. Pa., 1978; MD, Harvard U., 1982. Diplomate Am. Bd. Orthopaedic Surgery, Nat. Bd. Med. Examiners; lic. surgeon, Mass., Calif.; cert. added qualification hand surgery, 1993; recertified orthopedic surgery and hand surgery, 2003. Intern in surgery New Eng. Deaconess-Harvard Surg. Svc., Boston, 1982-83, asst. resident in surgery, 1983-84; resident in orthop. surgery Harvard U., Boston, 1985-88; fellow in hand surgery UCLA Med. Sch., 1988-89, asst. clin. prof. orthop. surgery Calif., 1988—, attending physician dept. orthop. Hand Clinic Calif., 1996-98; ptnr. Ventura Orthop. Hand and Sports Med. Group, Calif., 1994-98; solo practice hand surgery, 1998—. Staff physician St. John's Plasant Valley Hosp., Camarillo, Calif., St. John's Regional Med. Ctr., Oxnard, Calif., Cmty. Meml. Hosp., Ventura, Calif.; attending physician, cons. Sepulveda, Calif. VA Hosp.; presenter in field. Cons. reviewer Clin. Orthopaedics and related Rsch., 1990-92; contbr. numerous articles to profl. jours. Vol. Spl. Olympics, Ventura, 1994-96, Direct Relief Internat., Santa Barbara, Calif., 1994-96, Ventura County Rescue Mission, 1994-98. Recipient Cert. of Appreciation, Am. Heart Assn., 1994; UCLA faculty fellow, 1988-89. Mem. Am. Soc. for Surgery of the Hand, Am. Assn. for Hand Surgery, AMA, Calif. Med. Assn., Calif. Orthopaedic Assn., Calif. Ringside Physician, Ventura County Med. Soc., Internat. Soc. Aquatic Medicine, Western Orthopaedic Assn., Orthopaedic Overseas, UCLA Hand Club, Arthroscopy Assn. N.Am., Alpha Epsilon Delta, Onyx Honor Soc., Philomathean Soc. Avocations: photography, scuba diving, sports memorabilia, fishing, travel. Office Phone: 805-485-7764.

WALKER, MICHAEL ANGUS, economist, director; b. Corner Brook, Nfld., Can., Sept. 11, 1945; m. Janet Walker; children: Margot, Joel. BA, St. Francis Xavier U., 1966; MA, U. Western Ont., 1967, PhD, 1971. Instr. U. Western Ont., Canada, 1968—69; with Bank of Can., 1969—72; instr. Carleton U., Canada, 1971; with Fed. Dept. Fin., Canada, 1973—74; exec. dir. The Fraser Inst., Vancouver, B.C., Canada, 1974—2005, sr. fellow, 2005—; pres. The Fraser Inst. Found., 2005—. Bd. dirs. Mancal Corp., The Milton and Rose D. Friedman Found., Canaccord Capital Inc., dir., 2006—. Office: The Fraser Inst 4th Floor 1770 Burrard St Vancouver BC Canada V6J 3G7 Office Phone: 604-688-0221. Business E-Mail: michaelw@fraserinstitute.ca, michael_walker@fraserinstitute.org.

WALKER, PAUL R., lawyer; b. Bronx, NY, Feb. 6, 1945; AB, U. Notre Dame, 1966; LLB, U. Pa., 1969. Bar: N.Y. 1970, Calif. 1972. Former ptnr. Paul, Hastings, Janofsky & Walker, LA; ptnr., chmn. real estate practice group, mem. mgmt. com. & mng. ptnr. LA office Dewey Ballantine LLP, LA. Office: Dewey Ballantine LLP Suite 2600 333 S Grand Ave Los Angeles CA 90071-1530 Office Phone: 213-621-6200. Office Fax: 212-621-6201. Business E-Mail: pwalker@deweyballantine.com.

WALKER, RALPH CLIFFORD, lawyer; b. Bradenton, Fla., Apr. 30, 1938; s. Julius Clifford and Dorothy (Hefner) W.; m. Katherine Marie Christensen, Oct. 10, 1971; children: Laura Elizabeth, Mark Clifford, Tyler Lanier. BA cum laude, Vanderbilt U., 1959; LLB, U. Calif., Berkeley, 1965. Bar: Calif. Ptnr. Orrick Herrington & Sutcliffe, San Francisco, 1965—. Town councilman Town of Ross, Calif., 1970-72.Lt. (j.g.) USN, 1959-62. Mem. ABA, State Bar Calif., San Francisco Bar Assn., University Club (San Francisco, dir. 1986-88, counsel 1983—), Meadow Club (Fairfax, Calif.), Order of Coif. Republican. Presbyterian. Avocations: golf, wine, sports. Office: Orrick Herrington Sutcliffe 405 Howard St Fl 11 San Francisco CA 94105-2680

WALKER, RANDALL H., air transportation executive; b. Boulder City, Nev. m. Terry Walker; 6 children. BS in Acctg. magna cum laude, Brigham Young U. Budget analyst Clark County (Nev.) Mgr.'s Office; bus. mgr. Las Vegas Met. Police Dept.; dep. city mgr. City of Las Vegas; Las Vegas rep. to Nev. State Legislature; asst. county mgr. Clark County, dir. dept. fin.; dep. dir. Clark County Dept. Aviation, now dir. Office: c/o McCarran Internat Airport PO Box 11005 Las Vegas NV 89111-1005

WALKER, RAYMOND JOHN, physicist; b. LA, Oct. 26, 1942; s. Raymond Osmund and Marie Dorothy (Peterman) W. BS, San Diego State U., 1964; MS, UCLA, 1969, PhD, 1973. Rsch. assoc. U. Minn., Mpls., 1973-77; rsch. geophysicist Inst. Geophysics and Planetary Physics UCLA, 1977—, prof. in residence Inst. Geophysics and Planetary Physics and Dept. Earth and Space Sci., 1999—. Mgr. planetary plasma interactions node NASA, 1990-, project scientist planetary data sys., 1992-96, prin. investigator virtual magnetospheric observatory, 2007—; mem. numerous coms. on space physics and the mgmt. of space physics data NRC and NASA. Contbr. articles to profl. jours. Mem. AAAS, Am. Geophys. Union (chair info. tech. com. 1990-92, Edward A. Flinn III award 1996), Am. Astron. Soc. (div. Planetary Sci.). Achievements include research in magnetospheric physics, in planetary magnetospheres, in global magnetohydrodynamic simulation of solar wind-magnetosphere interaction, in data management, in magnetic field modeling. Home: 11053 Tennessee Ave Los Angeles CA 90064-1936 Office: UCLA IGPP 405 Hilgard Ave Los Angeles CA 90095-1567 Home Phone: 310-477-3637; Office Phone: 310-825-7685. Business E-Mail: rwalker@igpp.ucla.edu.

WALKER, RICHARD HUGH, orthopaedic surgeon; b. Elgin, Ill., Jan. 29, 1951; m. Wendy Allen; children: Ashley Elizabeth, Blake Allen, Emily Paige. AB cum laude, Occidental Coll., 1973; MD, U. Chgo., 1977. Diplomate Nat. Bd. Med. Examiners, Am. Bd. Orthopaedic Surgery. Jr. resident in surgery UCLA, 1977-79; jr. resident in orthopaedic surgery Stanford (Calif.) U., 1979-81, sr. resident, 1981-82, chief resident, 1982-83; clin. mem. divsn. orthop. surgery, sect. lower extremity reconstructive surgery Scripps Clinic, La Jolla, Calif., 1983—, co-dir. lower extremity reconstructive surgery fellowship, divsn. orthopaedic surgery, 1989—, assoc. head. divsn. orthopaedic surgery, 1990-97, chmn. dept. surgery, 1998—; v.p. surg. radiol. svcs. Golden Gate U., 2001—. Staff physician dept. surgery Scripps Green Hosp., La Jolla, 1983—; mem. exec. com. Green Hosp. of Scripps Clinic, La Jolla, 1994—2001, chief of staff, 1995—97; Team physician San Diego Padres, 1983—86, team physician, 1995—99; Clin. instr. dept. orthopaedics and rehab. U. Calif., San Diego, 1983—92, asst. clin. prof., 1992—; Mem. bd. dir. Scripps Clinic Med. Group, La Jolla, 1992—, mem. exec. com., 1998—, med. dir. surg. specialties, 1998—2001, mem. joint exec. bd., 1992—93. Cons. reviewer Clin. Orthopaedics and Related Rsch., 1989—, Jour. Bone and Joint Surgery, 1994—; contbr. articles to profl. jours. Mem. AMA, ACS, Am. Acad. Orthopaedic Surgeons, We. Orthopaedic Assn. (program chmn. San Diego chpt. 1994-95, treas. 1995-96, v.p. 1996-97, pres. 1997-98, Resident Paper award 1983), Calif. Orthopaedic Assn., Assn. Arthritic Hip and Knee Surgery (charter mem. 1991), Am. Assn. Hip and Knee Surgeons, Assn. Bone and Joint Surgeons (Nicholas Andry Rsch. award 1997). Office: Scripps Clinic Divsn Orthop Surgery 10666 N Torrey Pines Rd La Jolla CA 92037-1092 Office Phone: 858-554-9882. Business E-Mail: rwalker@scrippsclinic.com.

WALKER, RICHARD K., lawyer; b. Knoxville, Tenn., Oct. 21, 1948; BA with honors, U. Kans., 1970, JD, 1975; student, U. Bonn, Germany; grad. student, U Tübingen, Germany. Bar: Ariz. 1975, D.C. 1977, U.S. Supreme Ct. 1977. Asst. prof. law U. S.C., 1977-81, assoc. prof. law, 1981-82; ptnr. Bishop, Cook, Purcell & Reynolds, Washington, 1981-90, Winston & Strawn, Washington, 1990-93; dir. Streich Lang, Phoenix, 1993-2000; ptnr. Quarles & Brady Streich Lang, Phoenix, 2000—. Bd. trustees Ariz. Theatre Co., 1995-2001, 2004-; bd. dirs. Phoenix Cmty. Alliance, 2001—04. Fulbright Direct Exch. scholar. Mem. ABA, Labor and Employment Law Sec. (mem. equal employment opportunity law com. and devel. of the law under the NLRA com., 1979—), Litigation Sec. (mem. class actions and derivitive suits com. and trial pratice com., 1998—, mem. employment rels. and labor law com., 1979—), Ariz. Assn. Def. Counsel (bd. dirs. 1997-2000). Office: 7047 Greenway Pkway Ste 155 Scottsdale AZ 85254 Office Phone: 602-229-5219, 480-624-2718. E-mail: rwalkerlaw.com@gmail.com.

WALKER, ROGER GEOFFREY, geology educator, consultant; b. London, Mar. 26, 1939; s. Reginald Noel and Edith Annie Walker; m. Gay Parsons, Sept. 18, 1965; children: David John, Susan Elizabeth. BA, Oxford U., Eng., 1961, DPhil in Geology, 1964. NATO postdoctoral fellow in geology Johns Hopkins U., Balt., 1964-66; from asst. to assoc. prof. McMaster U., Hamilton, Ont., Canada, 1966-73, prof. geology, 1973-98, prof. emeritus, 1998—. Tchr. profl. short courses on various aspects of oil exploration in clastic reservoirs, Can., U.S., Brazil, Australia, Japan, Italy, Venezuela, Norway; grant selection com. earth scis. sect. Nat. Scis. and Engring. Rsch. Coun. Can., 1981-84; Judd A. & Cynthia S. Oualline Centennial lectr. U. Tex., Austin, 1986; vis. scientist Denver Rsch. Ctr., Marathon Oil Co., Littleton, Colo., 1973-74, Amoco Can. Petrol Co., Calgary, Alta., 1982; vis. fellow Australian Nat. U., Canberra, 1981; vis. prof. Fed. U. Ouro Preto, Brazil, 1987, 89-91, Fed. U. Rio Grande do Sul, Brazil, 1992; adj. prof. U. Regina, 1997—; pres. Roger Walker Cons., Inc., 1997-2006. Editor: Facies Models, 1979, 3d edit., 1992; contbr. over 140 articles to profl. jours. Recipient oper. and strategic grants Nat. Scis. and Engring. Rsch. Coun. Can., 1966—. Fellow: Royal Soc. Can.; mem.: Internat. Assn. Sedimentologists (Henry Clifton Sorby medal 2002), Can. Assn. Univ. Tchrs., Soc. Sedimentary Geology (Francis J. Pettijohn medal 1997), Soc. Econ. Paleontologists and Mineralogists (hon.; assoc. editor 1970—78, pres. eastern sect. 1975—76, coun. for mineralogy 1979—80), Am. Assn. Petroleum Geologists (Disting. lectr. 1979—80, Disting. Educator award 1999), Can. Soc. Petroleum Geologists (Link award 1983, R.J.W. Douglas Meml. medal 1990), Geol. Assn. Can. (assoc. editor 1977—80, Past Pres.'s medal 1975, Disting. Svc. award 1994, Logan medal 1999). Achievements include research in sedimentary facies analysis, sedimentology of turbidites, quantitative basin analysis, sedimentology of Western Canadian Cretaceous clastic wedge. Home: 83 Scimitar View NW Calgary AB Canada T3L 2B4 Home Phone: 403-208-0210. Personal E-mail: walkerrg@telus.net.

WALKER, RONALD HUGH, retired management consultant; b. Bryan, Tex., July 25, 1937; s. Walter Hugh and Maxine (Tarver) W.; m. Anne Lucille Collins, Aug. 8, 1959; children: Lisa, Marjorie, Lynne. BA, U. Ariz., 1960. With Allstate Ins. Co., Pasadena, Calif., 1964-67, Hudson Co., 1967-69; asst. to sec. interior, 1969-70; founder, 1st dir., staff asst. to Pres. U.S. White House Advance Office, 1970-72; spl. asst. to Pres., 1972-73; dir. Nat. Park Service, Washington, 1973-75; cons. Saudi Arabia, 1975; assoc. dir. World Championship Tennis, 1975-77; pres. Ron Walker & Assocs., Inc., Dallas, 1977-79; sr. ptnr., mng. dir. Korn/Ferry Internat., Washington, 1979—2001; ret., 2000. Bd. dirs., chmn. Guest Svcs. Inc., Mullin Cons., Inc., Vinson & Co.; chmn. NOVAVAX, 1999-2005. Bd. dirs. U.S.S. Arizona Found. and Memorial; mem. Nat. Pk. Svc. Dirs. Coun.; founder, chmn. emeritus Order of Raft, 1972; spl. presdl. del. to Prime Min. Indira Gandhi's funeral New Delhi, 1984; spl. presdl. del. to Games of XXIV Olympiad Seoul, 1988; trustee Nat. Outdoor Leadership Sch., Nat. Fitness Found., Pres.'s Coun. on Phys. Fitness and Sports, 1981—85; bd. dirs. NCAA Found., mem. exec. com., mem. adv. bd.; bd. dirs. Meridian Internat.; mem. Ctr. for Study of Presidency, 1988—95; chmn. Freedom Found. at Valley Forge, 1989—2000; trustee Ford's Theater, Washington; men's chair Project Hope Ann. Ball, 1989, 1990, 1991; chmn. ann. dinner Boys and Girls Clubs Am., 1993; chmn. 50th Presdl. Inauguration, Dedication Richard Nixon Libr., Birthplace, 1990, bd. dirs., 1990; nat. chair Celebrities and Sports for Bush-Quayle; mem. over-site com. U.S. Rowing, 1993; mem. com. Preservation of White House, 1973—75; mem. Nat. Pk. Adv. Bd., 1973—75, Nat. Pk. Found., 1973—75, John F. Kennedy Ctr. for Performing Arts, 1973—75, Friends of Nancy Hanks Ctr.; bd. trustees Mridian House Internat., 1992—; mem. USA Gymnasium Found., 1993—99; trustee U. Ariz. Found.; chair Nat. Pk. Found. Alumni Assn.; bd. dirs Saquaro Nat. Park; mem. adv. bd. Nat. Park Sys., 2004—; vol. Nixon/Agnew Campaign, 1968, transition and inauguration team, 1969; vice chmn., mem. Pres.'s Commn. on Bicentennial U.S. Constn., 1985—88; mem. Coun. for Excellence in Govt., 1988—; mgr., CEO Rep. Nat. Conv., 1984, sr. advisor, 1988, 1992, 1996, 2000, 2004, Bush/Quayle Presdl. Campaign, 1988, Bush/Cheney Presdl. Campaign, 2000, 2004, Bush/Cheney Inauguration; hon. chmn. Cheney Inaugural Activities; coord. v.p. debate Cheney and Lieberman, 2000, Cheney and Edwards, 2004; mem. leadership adv. bd. NCAA; bd. dirs. Grand Teton Nat. Pk. Found., Saquaro Nat. Pk. Found. Capt. US Army, 1961—64. Recipient Disting. Citizen award U. Ariz., 1973, Outstanding Svc. award Dept. Interior, 1975, Centennial Medallion award U. Ariz., 1989, Ellis Island Congl. medal of honor, 1992, Lincoln medal Ford's Theater, 2002. Mem. NCAA (bd. dirs. 1992-2003, exec. com. 1992-2003, adv. bd.), Econs. Club of Washington, Met. Club of Washington, Congl. Country Club, Georgetown Club, City Club of Washington, Univ. Club. of N.Y., Burning Tree Club, Phi Delta Theta (named to Hall of Fame, 1991). Republican. Methodist. Home (Winter): 13535 Placita Montanas de Oro Tucson AZ 85755 E-mail: roadrunnerrhw@aol.com.

WALKER, SAMUEL DAVID, lawyer; b. Madison, Wis., June 21, 1958; s. William Delaney and Suzanne Jamison (Porter) W.; m. Cynthia Fiora Elizabeth Nardini, Aug. 6, 1983; children: John Renato, Samuel Alexander. AB magna cum laude, Duke U., 1980; JD cum laude, Harvard U., 1984. Bar: NC 1984, DC 1992, Colo. 2003, US Supreme Ct., numerous US cts. of appeal and dist. cts. Law clk. to Hon. John D. Butzner Jr. US Ct. Appeals (4th cir.), Richmond, Va., 1984-85; assoc. Robinson, Bradshaw & Hinson, Charlotte, NC, 1985-89; spl. asst. to asst. sec. labor for employment stds. US Dept. Labor, Washington, 1989-90, dep. wage-hour adminstr. and acting wage-hour adminstr., 1990, acting asst. sec. labor for employment stds., 1990-91, dep. asst. sec. labor for employment stds., 1991; dep. asst. sec. edn. for intergovernmental and interagency affairs US Dept. Edn., Washington, 1991-92, acting asst. sec. edn. for intergovernmental and interagency affairs, 1992; of counsel Wiley, Rein & Fielding, Washington, 1992-93, ptnr., 1993—2002; v.p. Coors Brewing Co., Golden, Colo., 2002—05; sr. v.p., global chief legal officer, corp. sec. Molson Coors Brewing Co., Denver, 2005—. Asst. clearance coun. Pres.-elect George W. Bush, 2000—01. Fellow Am. Bar Found.; mem. ABA, Colo. Bar Assn., DC Bar Assn. Avocations: outdoor sports, tennis. Office: Molson Coors Brewing Co 1225 17th St Denver CO 80202 Home: 5330 S Marshall St Littleton CO 80123 Office Phone: 303-277-2164. Office Fax: 303-277-7848. Personal E-mail: samuel.walker@molsoncoors.com.

WALKER, TIMOTHY BLAKE, lawyer, educator; b. Utica, NY, May 21, 1940; s. Harold Blake and Mary Alice (Corder) W.; m. Sandra Blake; children: Kimberlee Corder, Tyler Blake, Kelley Loren. AB magna cum laude, Princeton U., 1962; JD magna cum laude, U. Denver, 1967, MA in Sociology, 1969. Bar: Colo. 1968, Calif. 1969, Ind. 1971. Asst. prof. law U. Pacific, 1968-69; vis. assoc. prof. U. Toledo, 1969-70; assoc. prof. Indpls. Law Sch., Ind. U., 1970-71, U. Denver, 1971-75, prof., 1975-99; prof. emeritus, 1999—; dir. adminstrn. of justice program U. Denver, 1971-78; pvt. practice Denver, 1972-79; of counsel Robert T. Hinds, Jr. & Assocs. PC, Littleton, Colo., 1980-85; ptnr., of counsel Cox, Mustain-Wood, Walker & Schumacher, Littleton, 1985—. Cons., lectr. in field; rsch. on lay representation in adminstrv. agys., Colo., 1975-76. Contbr. articles to profl. jours.; editor: Denver Law Jour., 1966-67; editor-in-chief: Family Law Quar., 1983-92. Mem. Ind. Child Support Commn., 1970-71; pres. Shawnee (Colo.) Water Consumers Assn., 1975-84, 93-95; del. Colo. Rep. Conv., 1978. Colo. Bar Assn. grant, 1975-76. Fellow: Am. Bar Found., Internat. Acad. Matrimonial Lawyers, Am. Sociol. Assn., Am. Acad. Matrimonial Lawyers; mem.: ABA (vice chmn. child custody subcom., sec. Family Law sect. 1992—93, vice chmn., sec. 1993—94, chmn. elect family law sect. 1994—95, chmn. 1995—96, chmn. child custody task force 2000—, alimony, maintenance and support com. 2000—, family sect. del. ho. of dels. 2000—), Colo Trial Lawyers Assn., Ind. Bar Assn., Colo. Bar Assn., Calif. Bar Assn. Presbyterian. also: 6601 S University Blvd Littleton CO 80121-2913 Home Phone: 303-660-9171; Office Phone: 303-730-0067. Personal E-mail: tbwalker10@aol.com.

WALKER, VAUGHN R., federal judge; b. Watseka, Ill., Feb. 27, 1944; s. Vaughn Rosenworth and Catharine (Miles) W. AB, U. Mich., 1966; JD, Stanford U., 1970. Intern economist SEC, Washington, 1966, 68; law clk. to the Hon. Robert J. Kelleher US Dist. Ct. Calif., LA, 1971-72; assoc. atty. Pillsbury Madison & Sutro, San Francisco, 1972-77, ptnr., 1978-90; judge US Dist. Ct. (no. dist.) Calif., San Francisco, 1990—, chief judge, 2004—. Mem. Calif. Law Revision Commn., Palo Alto, 1986-89; bd. advisors Law and Econs. Ctr., George Mason U., 1999—; mem. civil rules adv. com. Jud. Conf. U.S., 2006—. Bd. dirs. Jr. Achievement of Bay Area, San Francisco, 1979-83; bd. dirs. St. Francis Found., San Francisco, 1991-97, 98—, vice chair, 2004-06, chair, 2007—. Woodrow Wilson Found. fellow U. Calif., Berkeley, 1966-67. Fellow Am. Bar Found.; mem. ABA (jud. rep., antitrust sect. 1991-95), Lawyers' Club of San Francisco (pres. 1985-86), Assn. Bus. Trial Lawyers (dir. 1996-98), Am. Law Inst., Am. Saddlebred Horse Assn., San Francisco Mus. Modern Art, Bohemian Club, Olympic Club, Pacific-Union Club. Office: US Dist Ct 450 Golden Gate Ave San Francisco CA 94102-3482

WALKER, VICKI L., state legislator; b. Monroe, Wash., May 29, 1956; m to Steven; children: two. Court reporter, 1983-; Democratic precinct person, 1989-2002; secy-treas & area rep, Cal Young Neighborhood Association, 1990-92; chairwoman Lane Co Democratic Cent Committee, 1992-94; Oregon State Representative, District 41, 1999-2002; Oregon State Senator, District 7, 2003-. Oregon Court Reporters Association. Democrat. Office: 900 Court St NE S-309 Salem OR 97301 Office Phone: 503-986-1707. E-mail: sen.vickiwalker@state.or.us.

WALKER, WALTER FREDERICK, professional basketball team executive; b. Bradford, Pa., July 18, 1954; m. Linda Walker. Diploma, U. Va.; MBA, Stanford U., 1987; BA, U. Va., 1976. Chartered Fin. Analyst. Player Portland (Oreg.) Trail Blazers, 1976-77, Seattle SuperSonics, 1977-82, pres., CEO, 1994—; player Houston Rockets, 1982-84; with Goldman Sachs and Co., San Francisco, 1987-94; prin. Walker Capital, Inc., San Francisco, 1994. Mem. USA gold medal World Univ. Games basketball team, 1973; broadcaster basketball Raycom Network, 1989-94; cons. Seattle SuperSonics, 1994. Bd. dirs. Advanced Digital Info. Corp., Drexler Tech. Corp. Named 1st team Acad. All-Am. U. Va.; named to Pa. State Sports Hall of Fame. Nat. trustee Boys and Girls Clubs of Am. Office: Seattle SuperSonics 351 Elliott Ave W Seattle WA 98119-4101 E-mail: wwalker@sonics-storm.com.

WALKER, WILLIAM O., JR., pediatrician; b. Meridian, Miss., Feb. 27, 1954; s. William Otis and Miriam Wilkerson Walker; m. Patricia Lathrop, June 7, 1975; children: William Lathrop, Kathryn Ryan. MD, Tulane U., New Orleans, 1979. Diplomate Am. Bd. of Pediat., 1984, in Neurodevelopmental Disabilities Am. Bd. of Pediat., 2001, cert. in Developmental Behavioral Pediats. Am. Bd. of Pediat., 2002. Assoc. prof., pediat. U. of Wash. Sch. of Medicine, Seattle, 2001—; dir., develomental behavioral pediat. fellowship Dept. of Pediat., U. of Wash. Sch. of Medicine, Seattle, 2002—. Col. US Army, 1979—2001. Fellow: Am. Acad. of Cerebral Palsy and Devel. Medicine, Am. Acad. of Pediat.; mem.: Child Neurology Soc. Office: Children's Hosp Med Ctr 4800 Sand Point Way NE A7938 Seattle WA 98105 Office Fax: 206-987-3824.

WALKER, WILLIAM TIDD, JR., investment banker; b. Detroit, Sept. 5, 1931; s. William Tidd and Irene (Rhode) W.; m. Patricia Louise Frazier, Sept. 10, 1953; children: Donna Louise, Carol Ann, Sally Lynn, Alyssa Jane. Student, Stanford, 1950. Stockbroker William R. Staats & Co., Los Angeles, 1952-57, sales mgr., 1957-58, syndicate partner, 1958-65; sr. v.p. Glore Forgan, William R. Staats Inc., NYC, 1965-68; partner, exec. com. Lester, Ryons & Co., Los Angeles, 1968; exec. v.p. Bateman Eichler, Hill Richards Inc., Los Angeles, 1969-85. Pres., CEO WTW Inc.; chmn., CEO Walker Assocs.; bd. dirs. Digid, Inc.; chmn. King-Thomason Group, Inc., Stone Mountain Data Ctrs. Inc.; adv. mem. Am. Stock Exch., 1981—; bd. trustee Columbia Coll. Hollywood. With USAF, 1949-52. Mem. Securities Industry Assn. (dir. nat. syndicate com., chmn. Calif. Dist. 10), Pacific Coast Stock Exch. (bd. govs. 1971-72), Investment Bankers Assn. (nat. pub. rels. com. 1966—), Bond Club L.A. (pres. 1973), Calif. Yacht Club, Columbia Coll. Hollywood (trustee). Office: Walker Assocs PO Box 10684 Beverly Hills CA 90213-3684

WALKUP, ROBERT E., Mayor, Tucson; b. Ames, Iowa, Nov. 14, 1936; m. Beth Walkup; 3 children; 2 stepchildren. BS in Indsl. Engring., Iowa State U. Exec. Rockwell Internat., Fairchild Republic; sr. exec. Hughes Aircraft Co.; mayor City of Tuscon, Ariz., 1999—. Chmn. Greater Tucson Econ. Coun.; founder, first chmn. Ariz. Space Commn.; vol. Tucson Cmty. Food Bank; co-founder Pima-Santa Cruz County Sch.-to-Work Program; co-founder El Centro Cultural de las Americas. Capt. U.S. Army. Republican. Avocations: playing guitar, sketching, studying astronomy, restoring antique cars and motorcycles. Office: City Hall 255 W Alameda St Tucson AZ 85701-1362 Fax: 520-791-4213. Business E-Mail: meweb@tucsonaz.gov.*

WALL, DONALD ARTHUR, lawyer; b. Lafayette, Ind., Mar. 17, 1946; s. Dwight Arthur and Myra Virginia (Peavey) W.; m. Cheryn Lynn Heinen, Aug. 29, 1970; children: Sarah Lynn, Michael Donald. BA, Butler U., 1968; JD, Northwestern U., 1971. Bar: Ohio 1971, U.S. Dist. Ct. (no. dist.) Ohio 1973, U.S. Supreme Ct. 1980, Ariz. 1982, U.S. Dist. Ct. (no. dist.) W.Va. 1982, U.S. Ct. Appeals (6th cir.) 1982, U.S. Dist. Ct. Ariz. 1983, U.S. Ct. Appeals (9th and 10th cirs.) 1984, U.S. Ct. Appeals (5th cir.) 1988. Assoc. Squire, Sanders & Dempsey, Cleve., 1971-80, ptnr., 1980-82, Phoenix, 1983—. Spkr. at profl. meetings; program moderator. Contbr. articles to profl. jours. Trustee Ch. of the Saviour Day Ctr., Cleveland Heights, 1979-82; mem. adminstrv. bd. Ch. of Saviour, Cleveland Heights, 1980-83; fin. com. Paradise Valley (Ariz.) United Meth. Ch., 1986-87; bd. dirs., divsn. commr. North Scottsdale (Ariz.) Little League, 1983-92; bd. dirs. Epilepsy Found. N.E. Ohio, 1976-82, pres., 1981-82; bd. dirs. N.E. Cmty. Basketball Assn., 1995-99; bd. visitors U. Ariz. Law Sch., 1996—; bd. mgrs. Scottsdale-Paradise Valley YMCA, 1999—. Mem. ABA (torts and ins. practice and litigation sect., past chmn. r.r. law com., litigation sect.), Def. Rsch. Inst., Ariz. Bar Assn. (labor and trial practice sects.), Maricopa County Bar Assn., Ariz. Assn. Def. Counsel. Methodist. Office: Squire Sanders & Dempsey LLP 40 N Central Ave Ste 2700 Phoenix AZ 85004-4498 E-mail: dwall@ssd.com.

WALL, JAMES EDWARD, telecommunications, petroleum and pharmaceutical executive; b. Santa Barbara, Calif., Nov. 24, 1947; s. Charles Caswell II and Lydia (Sinn) W.; m. Judith Ann Hochman, Aug. 1, 1976. AA, Bakersfield Coll., 1967; BS, Calif. State U., Los Angeles, 1969; MBA, UCLA, 1970; D of Profl. Studies (ABD), Pace U., 1985; PMD, Harvard U. Sch. Bus., 1987. CPA, Calif. Agt. IRS, Los Angeles, 1971-74, agt. service office internat. ops. Washington, 1974-76; mgr. fin. forecasts Am. Ultramar, Ltd., Mt. Kisco, N.Y., 1976-80, treas., 1980-85, v.p., treas., 1985-91; exec. dir. fin. and adminstrn. Ultramar Exploration, London, 1991; v.p., treas. Ultramar Corp., Greenwich, Conn., 1992-94; v.p., corp. treas. ICN Pharms., Costa Mesa, Calif., 1994-95; treas. AirTouch Comms., Inc., San Francisco, 1995-97, treas., controller, 1997-99; CFO Metricom, Inc., San Jose, Calif., 1999—. Chief fin. officer Enstar Corp., Indonesia; mem. bd. mgmt. Unimar Co., 1985-91. Recipient award in acctg. UCLA, 1972, award in gen. bus. mgmt., 1973 Mem. AICPA, Fin. Execs. Inst. (pres. San Francisco chpt. 2000—), UCLA Grad. Sch. Alumni Assn., Harvard U. Bus. Sch. Alumni Assn. Office: Metricom Inc 1 Front St San Francisco CA 94111-5325

WALL, LARRY, computer scientist, web programmer; b. Sept. 27, 1954; m. Gloria Biggar, 1979; children: Heidi, Geneva, Lewis, Aron. Bachelor's Degree, Seattle Pacific U., 1976. With Seagate, NetLabs; programmer NASA Jet Propulsion Lab., Pasadena, Calif., Unisys; rschr., developer O'Reilly & Assocs., Sebastopol, Calif. Co-author: Perl Resource Kit, Programming Perl, Learning Perl. Recipient Free Software award, Free Software Found., 1998. Achievements include creating PERL (Practical Extraction and Report Language) Script. Office: OReilly and Assocs 1005 Gravenstein Hwy North Sebastopol CA 95472 E-mail: larry@wall.org.

WALL, LLOYD L., geological engineer; b. Jerome, Idaho, Feb. 2, 1936; s. Lloyd and Ola (Buck) W.; m. Myrna Bradshaw, Aug. 25, 1954; children: Jeffrey B., Julie, Neil S., Charlene, Gail, Matthew W., Suzzane, Michael L., Connie. AS in Chemistry, Coll. Eastern Utah, 1956; BS in Geology, Brigham Young U., 1958. Registered profl. geoligist Utah, Wyoming. Pres., owner Cons. Geologist, Salt Lake City and Brigham City, 1958—; plant mgr. Thiokol, Brigham City, Utah, 1958-66; mgr. ops. Seakraft, Salt Lake City, 1966-68; mgr. programs Eaton-Kenway, Bountiful, Utah, 1968-76; pres., owner HydraPak, Inc., Salt Lake City, 1976-86; pres. Kolt Mining Co., Salt Lake City, 1979—; owner Lloyd L. Wall & Assocs., Salt Lake City, 1986—; plant mgr. Alcohol Fuels Prodn., 2001—08; process engr. Canole Lamp Co., 2008—. Author: Seal Technology, 1993; developer largest rocket motor vacuum casting system in free world, only high pressure water reclaimation system for solid propellant rocket motors in free world, only acceptable seal mfg. process for NASA Space Shuttle rocket motor. Vol. tchr. Alta Acad., Salt Lake City, 1983—. Served as sgt. N.G., 1954-62. Mem. Geol. Soc. Am., Utah Geol. Assn. Republican. Mem. Lds Ch. Avocations: hunting, fishing, mountain climbing, photography, flying. Home: PO Box 841739 Hildale UT 84784-1739 Office Phone: 435-616-0327.

WALL, M. DANNY, retired finance company executive; BArch, N.D. State U., 1963. Exec. dir. Urban Renewal Agy., Fargo, ND, 1964-71, Salt Lake City Redevel. Agy., 1971-75; dir. legis. Office US Senator Jake Garn, Washington, 1975-78; minority staff dir. Senate Com. Banking, Housing and Urban Affairs, Washington, 1979-80, staff dir., 1980-86, rep. staff dir., 1987; chmn. Fed. Home Loan Bank Bd./Fed. Home Loan Mortgage Corp., Washington, 1987-89; dir. Office Thrift Supervision (formerly Fed. Home Loan Bank Bd.), 1989-90; fin. svcs. cons., 1990—2002; sr. v.p. Dougherty Funding LLC, 1997—2002; chmn, pres. Capmark Bank (formerly GMAC Comml. Mortgage Bank), 2003—07; pres. Morgan Stanley Bank, 2007—09. Home Phone: 801-596-0650. Personal E-mail: alvinadan@aol.com.

WALL, PHIL, information technology executive; B in mech. engring., Imperial Coll., London Univ.; MBA, Brookes Univ., Oxford. Chartered Acct. Fin. mgmt. positions Schlumberger Inc., Equifax Inc.; v.p. fin. internat. fin. ops. First Data Corp., Greenwood Village, Colo., 2002—08, exec. v.p., CFO, 2008—. Office: First Data Corp 6200 S Quebec St Greenwood Village CO 80111

WALLA, CHRIS, musician, music producer; b. Bothell, Wash., Nov. 2, 1975; Founding mem., guitarist, prodr. Death Cab for Cutie, 1997—; founder Hall of Justice Recording, Portland, Oreg., 1997. Musician, prodr. (solo albums) Field Manual, 2008, (Death Cab for Cutie albums) Something About Airplanes, 1999, We Have the Facts and We're Voting Yes, 2000, The Photo Album, 2001, Transatlanticism, 2003, Plans, 2005, Narrow Stairs, 2008, (Death Cab for Cutie songs) I Will Possess Your Heart, 2008 (MTV Video Music award for Best Editing, 2008); prodr.: albums for various artists, including Travis Morrison, The Decemberists, Nada Surf, Tegan and Sara, and Hot Hot Heat. Office: c/o Zeitgeist Artist Mgmt Ste 216 660 W York St San Francisco CA 94110 also: c/o Zeitgeist Artist Mgmt Ste 408 39 W 14th St New York NY 10011 E-mail: info@deathcabforcutie.com.

WALLACE, CANDY, culinary association administrator; Exec. dir. Am. Personal & Pvt. Chef Inst. & Assn., San Diego. Co-author: The Professional Personal Chef: The Business of Doing Business as a Personal Chef, 2007. Mem.: Internat. Assn. Culinary Professionals (Businessperson/Entrepreneur of Yr., Award of Excellence 2003), Women Chefs & Restaurants, Am. Culinary Fedn. (bd. mem. San Diego chpt.), Les Dames d'Escoffier Internat. (bd. mem. San Diego chpt.). Office: Am Personal & Pvt Chef Assn 4572 Delaware St San Diego CA 92116 Business E-Mail: info@personalchef.com.

WALLACE, DOUGLAS C., geneticist, educator; PhD in Microbiology and Human Genetics, Yale U. Prof., dir. Ctr. for Molecular Medicine Emory U. Sch. Medicine, Atlanta, 1990—2002; Donald Bren prof. biol. scis. and molecular medicine U. Calif., Irvine, 2002—; dir. Ctr. for Molecular, Mitochondrial Medicine and Genetics, U. Calif., 2002—. Author of more than 270 rsch. papers published in various jours. including Cell, Science, Nature, Procs. of Nat. Acad. of Scis., New Eng. Jour. Medicine. Recipient Rsch. award for Medical Rsch. in Alzheimer's Disease, Metropolitan Life Found., Pasarow Found. award in Cardiovascular Disease; co-recipient Passano award (with Guiseppi Attardi). Fellow: Am. Acad. Arts and Scis.; mem.: NAS, Am. Soc. Human Genetics (William Allan award 1994). Business E-Mail: dwallace@uci.edu.

WALLACE, HELEN MARGARET, pediatrician, preventive medicine physician, educator; b. Hoosick Falls, NY, Feb. 18, 1913; d. Jonas and Ray (Schweizer) W. AB, Wellesley Coll., 1933; MD, Columbia U., 1937; MPH cum laude, Harvard U., 1943. Diplomate Am. Bd. Pediat., Am. Bd. Preventive Medicine. Intern Bellevue Hosp., NYC, 1938-40; child hygiene physician Conn. Health Dept., 1941-42; successively jr. health officer, health officer, chief maternity and newborn div., dir. bur. for handicapped children NYC Health Dept., 1943-55; prof., dir. dept. pub. health NY Med. Coll., 1955-56; prof. maternal and child health U. Minn. Sch. Pub. Health, 1956-59; chief profl. tng. US Children's Bur., 1959-60, chief child health studies, 1961-62; prof. maternal and child health U. Calif. Sch. Pub. Health, Berkeley, Calif., 1962-80, 99; prof., head divsn. maternal and child health Sch. Pub. Health San Diego State U., Calif., 1980—; Univ. Rsch. lectr. San Diego State U., Calif., 1985—. Cons. WHO numerous locations, including Uganda, The Philippines, Turkey, India, Geneva, Iran, Burma, Sri Lanka, East Africa, Australia, Indonesia, China, Taiwan, 1961—, traveling fellow, 1989—; cons. Hahnemann U., Phila., 1993, Ford Found., Colombia, 1971; UN cons. to Health Bur., Beijing, China, 1987; fellow Aiiku Inst. on Maternal and Child Health, Tokyo, and NIH Inst. Child Health and Human Devel., 1994; dir. Family Planning Project, Zimbabwe, 1984-87; vis. prof. U. Calif., Berkeley, 1999, 00, prof. emeritus, 2000—; mem. adv. com., faculty APHA Com. on Continuing Edn. Author, editor: 20 textbooks; editor (sr.): Health and Social Reform for Families for the 21st Century, 2d edit., 2003, Health and Welfare for Families in the 21st Century, 2003 (award Am. Coll. Nursing, Am. Jour. Nursing); contbr. 335 articles to profl. jours. Mem. coun. on Disabled Children to Media, 1991; dir. San Diego County Infant Mortality Study, 1989—, San Diego Study of Prenatal Care, 1991. Recipient Alumnae Achievement award Wellesley Coll., 1982, U. Minn. award, 1985; Ford Found. study grantee, 1986, 87, 88; fellow World Rehab. Fund, India, 1991-92, Fulbright Found., 1992—, NIH Inst. Child Health and Human Devel., 1994, Aiiku Inst. of Maternal-Child Health, Tokyo, 1994. Fellow: APHA (officer sect., chmn. com. on internat. maternal and child health, mem. faculty and adv. com. maternal and child health program 2000, Martha May Eliot award 1978, award in Internat. Maternal and Child Health 2001), Am. Acad. Pediatrics (Job Smith award 1980); mem.: AMA, Am. Sch. Preventive Medicine, Ambulatory Pediatric Assn., Am. Acad. Cerebral Palsy, Assn. Tchrs. Maternal and Child Health. Home: 850 State St San Diego CA 92101-6046 Office Phone: 619-235-4670.

WALLACE, J. CLIFFORD, federal judge; b. San Diego, Dec. 11, 1928; s. John Franklin and Lillie Isabel (Overing) Wallace; m. Virginia Lee Schlosser, 1957 (dec.); m. Elaine J. Barnes, Apr. 8, 1996 (dec.); m. Dixie Jenee Robison Zenger, Apr. 2, 2001. BA, San Diego State U., 1952; LLB, U. Calif., Berkeley, 1955. Bar: Calif. 1955. With Gray, Cary, Ames & Frye, San Diego, 1955—70; judge US Dist. Ct. (so. dist.), Calif., 1970—72, US Ct. Appeals (9th cir.), San Diego, 1972—96, chief judge, 1991—96, sr. judge, 1996—. Contbr. articles to profl. jours. Stake pres. San Diego East LDS Ch., 1962—67, regional rep., 1967—74, 1977—79. With USN, 1946—49. Recipient Edward J. Devitt Disting. Svc. to Justice award, 2006. Mem.: Inst. Jud. Adminstrn., Am. Bd. Trial Advocates. Mem. Lds Ch. Office: US Ct Appeals 9th Cir 940 Front St Ste 4192 San Diego CA 92101-8918

WALLACE, RICHARD P., computer company executive; BSEE, Univ. Mich.; M engring. mgmt., Santa Clara Univ. Engring. positions Ultratech Stepper, Cypress Semiconductor; mgmt. positions KLA-Tencor Corp., 1988—95, v.p., gen. mgr. Wisard San Jose, Calif., 1995—98, v.p., gen. mgr. Mirage group, 1998—99, group v.p., 1999—2000, exec. v.p., 2000—05, pres., COO, 2005, CEO, 2006—. Office: KLA-Tencor Corp 160 Rio Robles San Jose CA 95134

WALLACE, RUSSELL JOHN, physicist; Rsch. scientist Lawrence Livermore Nat. Lab. Recipient Excellence in Plasma Physics award Am. Phys. Soc., 1995. Office: Lawrence Livermore Nat Lab PO Box 808 Livermore CA 94551-0808

WALLACE, TERRY CHARLES, SR., retired technical administrator, researcher; b. Phoenix, May 18, 1933; s. Terry Milton Wallace and Fair June (Hartman) Wallace Timberlake; m. Yvonne Jeannette Owens, May 21, 1955; children: Terry Charles, Randall James, Timothy Alan, Sheryl Lynn, Janice Marie. BS, Ariz. State U., 1955;

PhD, Iowa State U., 1958. Staff Los Alamos Nat. Lab., 1958-71, dep. group leader, 1971-80, group leader, 1980-83, assoc. divsn. leader, 1983-89, tech. program coord., 1989-91, ret., 1991. Sr. tech. adv. SAIC, Inc., 1994-95; ptnr. Stonewall Enterprises, Los Alamos, 1966-71. Contbr. chpts., articles to profl. jours.; patentee in field. Fundraiser Los Alamos County Republican Party, N.Mex., 1983-84. Served to 1st lt. Chem. Corps, U.S. Army, 1959-61. Mem. Am. Chem. Soc., AAAS, Lab. Retiree Group, Inc. (Los Alamos, treas., bd. dirs. 1995-98), Los Alamos Ret. and Sr. Orgn. (pres., bd. dirs. 1999-2002), Mil. Order World Wars (MG Franklin E. Miles chpt. adj. 1997-99, 2003, treas. 2000-02). Methodist. Home and Office: 1913 Spruce St Los Alamos NM 87544-3041

WALLACH, LESLIE ROTHAUS, architect; b. Pitts., Feb. 4, 1944; s. Albert and Sara F. (Rothaus) W.; m. Susan Rose Berger, June 15, 1969; 1 child, Aaron. BS in Mining Engring., U. Ariz., 1967, BArch, 1974. Registered arch., Ariz.; registered contractor, Ariz. Prin. Line and Space LLC, Tucson, 1978—. Mem. awards jury Sunset mag., 1997, Ariz. Homes of Yr., 1997, L.A. AIA; keynote spkr. various confs. Rep. projects include Ariz. Sonora Desert Mus. Restaurant Complex, Tucson, Elgin Elem. Sch., Ariz., Hillel Student Ctr. U. Ariz., Tucson, Boyce Thompson Southwestern Arborteum Vis. Ctr., Superior, Ariz., San Pedro Riparian Ctr., Sierra Vista, Ariz., Nat. Hist. Trails Ctr., Casper, Wyo., 2002, Vis. Ctr. and Arborteum, Flagstaff, Ariz., 2001, Regional Libr., Phoenix, 2002, Poetry Ctr. for U. Ariz., 2003, New Regional Libr. U. Ariz., Phoenix, 2006; contbr. Sunset Mag., Architecture Mag. and Fine Homebuilding; pub.: Space and Society (Italy), Hinge (Hong Kong), Wallpaper (London); exhibited at U. Ariz., AIA Nat. Conv., Washington, The Dutch Jour., Objekt, 2003; interview and profile pub. in Architecture and Urbanism, 2006. Bd. dirs Tucson Regional Plan, Inc.; pres. Civitas Sonoran (The Environ. Design Coun. of the U. of Ariz. Coll. of Arch.). Recipient Roy P. Drachman Design award, 1982, 85, 93, 2001, Electric League Ariz. Design award, 1987, 88, Gov. Solar Energy award, 1989, Desert Living awards citation, 1991, Ariz. Architect's medal, 1989, Disting. Alumni award U. Ariz., 1998, also 60 additional design awards, including 8 received in 2007, winner $25,000 prize, nat. Endowment of the Arts, 2002, Coll. of Architecture Alumni of Yr., U. Az., 2001, Nat. AIA award, 2008. Fellow AIA (Ariz. Honor award 1989, 92, 96, AIA/ACSA Nat. Design award 1991, Western Mountain region Design award 1992, 96, CA AIA/Phoenix Homes and Gardens Home of the Yr. Honor award 1992, 96, Western Region Silver medal 1996, design award, 2004); mem. SAC AIA (past pres., Design award 1985, 88, 90, 2004-07), Western Mountain Region AIA (named Firm of Yr. 1999), Tex. AIA (jury mem. design awards, 2005—). Achievements include being selected as the architect to design the 300 acre Desert Learning Center Campus and new visitor center in Red Rock Canyon, Nevada. Office: Line and Space 627 E Speedway Blvd Tucson AZ 85705-7433 Office Phone: 520-623-1313. Business E-Mail: studio627@lineandspace.com.

WALLACH, NOLAN R., mathematician, consultant; b. Bklyn., Aug. 3, 1940; s. Morris and Pauline Wallach; m. Barbara Hawkins, Apr. 25, 1965; children: Dana, Pamela. BS, U. Maryland, 1962; MA, Wash. U., St. Louis, Mo., 1963, PhD, 1966. Instr. U. of Calif., Berkeley, 1966—69; asst. prof. math. Rutgers U., New Brunswick, NJ, 1969—70, assoc. prof. math., 1970—72, prof. math., 1972—86, Hermann Weyl prof. math., 1986—89; disting. prof. math. U. Calif.-San Diego, La Jolla, 1989—. Cons. Ctr. for Comm. Rsch., La Jolla, 1995—; mem. Mat. Math. Com., 1985—92. Author: (book) Real Reductive Groups I, II, 1988, Continuous Cohomology, 2d edit., 1999; editor: Mathematics: Theory and Applications, 2001—; co-editor: Annals of Math., 1997—2003. Recipient Sloan fellowship, Alfred Sloan Found., 1972—74, Linback award for rsch. excellence, 1977. Fellow: Am. Acad. Arts and Scis.; mem.: Am. Math. Soc. (mem. edtl. com. 1991—93, editor bull. 1995—98, mem. coun. 1999—2002). Office: U Calif San Diego Dept Math La Jolla CA 92093 Business E-Mail: nwallach@ucsd.edu.

WALLACH, PATRICIA, councilman, retired mayor; b. Chgo. m. Ed Wallach; 3 children. Grad., Pasadena City Coll. Mem. city coun. City of El Monte, Calif., 1990-92, mayor, 1992-99, elected mem. of city coun., 2003—. Ret. tchr.'s aide Mountain View Sch. Dist. Past trustee El Monte Union High Sch. Dist., L.A. County High Sch. for the Arts; amb. of goodwill Zamora, Michoacan, Mex., Marcq-en-Baroeul, France, Yung Kang, Hsiang, Republic of China, Minhang, Peoples Republic of China; bd. dirs. Cmty. Redevel. Agy., El Monte Cmty. Access TV Corp.; del. Foothill Transit. Mem. League of Calif. Cities, San Gabriel Valley Coun. of Govts., Independent Cities Assn., U.S./Mex. Sister Cities Assn., Sister Cities Internat., Women of the Moose, El Monte Women's Club (Women of Yr., 2006, Citizen of Yr., 2008) Office Phone: 626-580-2001.

WALLACH, STEPHEN JOSEPH, cardiologist; b. Bklyn., Dec. 16, 1942; s. Frank and Sylivia B. (Meisel) W.; m. Vicki Wallach, June 30, 1968; children: Jonathan, Rachel. BS in Pharmacy, L.I. U., 1965; MD, U. Okla., 1969. Intern Emory Affiliated, Atlanta, 1960-70, med. resident, 1970-71; gen. med. officer USN, 1971-74; med. resident USN Naval Res. Med. Ctr., Phila., 1974-75, fellow cardiology, 1975-76, mem. staff interstat medicine, 1976-77; asst. prof. John Burns Sch. Medicine, Honolulu, 1977-78; pvt. practice cardiology Queens Med. Ctr., Honolulu, 1978—, chief dept. medicine, 1993-2000, dir. utilization mgmt., dir. inhospital svcs., 1998. Clin. assoc. prof. medicine John A. Burns Sch. Medicine, 1998. Bd. dirs. Am. Heart Assn., Honolulu, 1980-86, pres. Honolulu chpg., 1994-95. Ltd. comdr. USNR, 1971. Fellow Am. Coll. Cardiology; mem. Honolulu County Med. Assn. (pres. 1990-91), Hawaii Med. Assn. (pres. 1991-92), Hawaii Soc. Internal Medicine (pres. 1996—). Jewish. Avocations: movies, hiking, music. Office: Queens Med Ctr 1301 Punchbowl St Ste 206 Honolulu HI 96813-2413

WALLER, MARK, state legislator; b. Macomb, Ill., 1969; m. Jennifer Waller, 1994; children: Truman, Camile. BS in Polit. Sci., So. Ill. U., Edwardsville, 1992; MS in Space Studies, U. ND, 1998; JD, U. Denver Coll. Law, 2003. Dep. dist. atty. Colo. 10th Jud. Dist., Pueblo, 2004—06; pvt. practice Colorado Springs, 2007—; mem. Dist. 15 Colo. House of Reps., Denver, 2009—. Officer USAF, reservist USAFR, 2001—. Republican. Office: Colo State Capitol 200 E Colfax Denver CO 80203 Office Phone: 303-866-5525. Business E-Mail: mark.waller.house@state.co.us.*

WALLER, PETER WILLIAM, public relations executive; b. Kewanee, Ill., Oct. 1, 1926; s. Ellis Julian and Barodel (Gould) Waller; m. Anne-Marie Appelius van Hoboken, Nov. 10, 1950; children: Catherine, Hans. BA with honors, Princeton U., 1949; MA with honors, San Jose State U., 1978. Bur. chief Fairchild Publs., San Francisco, 1953-55; freelance writer Mountain View, Calif., 1956-57; pub. rels. coord. Lockheed Missiles and Space, Sunnyvale, Calif., 1957-64; info. mgr. 1st missions to Jupiter, Saturn, Venus NASA Ames Rsch. Ctr., Mountain View, 1964-83, mgr. pub. info., 1983-95; cons. NASA-Ames Galileo, Lunar Prospector, 1996-97; prodr. space films PacPAW Assoc., 1998—. Speechwriter to pres. Lockheed Missles and Space, 1960—64. Prodr.: (documentaries) Jupiter Odyssey, 1974 (Golden Eagle, 1974); prodr., writer NASA Aero. program, 1984; contbr. articles to profl. jours., encyclopedias. Cons. preservation Lake Tahoe Calif. Resources Agy., Sacramento, 1984. Mem.: No. Calif. Sci. Writers Assn., Sierra Club. Democrat. Congregationalist. Avocations: skiing, travel, architecture, construction, hiking. Home: 3655 La Calle Ct Palo Alto CA 94306-2619 Personal E-mail: pwaller@sbcglobal.net.

WALLERSTEIN, GEORGE, astronomer, educator; b. NYC, Jan. 13, 1930; s. Leo Wallerstein; m. Julie Haynes Lutz, 1998. BA, Brown U., 1951; MS, Calif. Inst. Tech., Pasadena, 1954; PhD, Calif. Inst. Tech., 1958. Postdoctoral rschr. Calif. Inst. Tech., Pasadena, 1957-58; from instr. to assoc. prof. U. Calif., Berkeley, 1958-65; prof. astronomy U. Wash., Seattle, 1965—98, chmn. astronomy, 1965—80, prof. emeritus astronomy, 1998—. Vis. mem. Joint Inst. for Lab. Astrophysicis; vis. scientist Los Alamos Nat. Lab.; bd. dir. Ctr. for Arms Control and Non-Proliferation, Coun. on Econ. Priorities, NAACP Legal Def. Fund, Human Serve. Contbr. articles to Astron. Jour., Astrophys. Jour., Sci. Bd. trustees Brown U., Providence, R.I., 1975-80. Lt. U.S. Navy, 1951-53, Korea. Fellow Royal Astron. Soc., AAAS; mem. Internat. Astron. Union, Astron. Soc. Pacific, Am. Astron. Soc.(former v.p., Henry Norris Russell Lectureship, 2002) Avocations: mountain climbing, skiing, softball. Office: Astronomy Dept 351580 U Wash Seattle WA 98195-0001

WALLIS, ERIC G., lawyer; b. Astoria, NY, Jan. 8, 1950; AB magna cum laude, U. Pacific, 1972; JD, U. Calif., Hasting Coll. of Law, 1975. Bar: Calif. 1975. Ptnr. Reed Smith LLP, Oakland, Calif., 1982—. Editl. assoc. Hastings Law Jour., 1974-75. Mem. ABA (sect. litigation), State Bar Calif., Alameda County Bar Assn. Office: Reed Smith LLP 1999 Harrison St Fl 26 Oakland CA 94612-3520 E-mail: ewallis@reedsmith.com.

WALLOCK, TERRENCE J., lawyer; JD, UCLA, 1970. Bar: Calif. 1971. V.p., gen. counsel Denny's Inc.; sr. v.p., sec., gen. counsel Vons Cos., Arcadia, Calif., 1990—; now sr. v.p., sec., gen. counsel Ralphs Grocery Co., LA, 1990-98, ret., 1998. Office: Ralphs Grocery Co PO Box 54143 Los Angeles CA 90054-0143

WALP, ROBERT M., communications carrier and internet/cable provider executive; b. Charlottesville, Va., 1927; Degree, Calif. Inst. Tech., 1951, degree, 1953. Vice chmn. Gen. Comm., Inc., Anchorage, Alaska. Office: Gen Comm Inc 2550 Denali St Ste 1000 Anchorage AK 99503-2736 Fax: (907) 265-5676.

WALSH, DANIEL FRANCIS, bishop; b. San Francisco, Oct. 2, 1937; Grad., St. Joseph Sem., St. Patrick Sem., Catholic U. Am. Ordained priest Archdiocese of San Francisco, 1963, asst. chancellor, 1970—76, sec. to archbishop, 1976—78, chancellor, 1978—81, vicar gen., 1981—87; assoc. pastor St. Pius, Redwood City, 1963—64; tchr. Serra HS, San Mateo, Calif., 1966—70; ordained bishop, 1981; bishop Diocese of Reno, Nev., 1987—95, Diocese of Las Vegas, 1995—2000, Diocese of Santa Rosa, Calif., 2000—. Roman Catholic. Office: Diocese of Santa Rosa PO Box 1297 Santa Rosa CA 95402 Office Phone: 707-566-3325.

WALSH, DENNY JAY, reporter; b. Omaha, Nov. 23, 1935; s. Gerald Jerome and Muriel (Morton) W.; m. Peggy Marie Moore, Feb. 12, 1966; children from previous marriage: Catherine Camille, Colleen Cecile; 1 son, Sean Joseph. B.J., U. Mo., 1962. Staff writer St. Louis Globe-Democrat, 1961-68; asst. editor Life mag., NYC, 1968-70, assoc. editor, 1970-73; reporter N.Y. Times, 1973-74, Sacramento Bee, 1974—. Served with USMC, 1954-58. Recipient Con Lee Kelliher award St. Louis chpt. Sigma Delta Chi, 1962; award Am. Polit. Sci. Assn., 1963; award Sigma Delta Chi, 1968; Pulitzer prize spl. local reporting, 1969; 1st prize San Francisco Press Club, 1977; Beacon award for lifetime achievement, 1st Amendment Coalition, 2004. Office: Sacramento Bee 21st & Q Sts Sacramento CA 95816 Office Phone: 916-321-1189. Business E-Mail: dwalsh@sacbee.com.

WALSH, DON, engineer, consultant; b. Berkeley, Calif., Nov. 2, 1931; s. J. Don and Marguerite Grace (Van Auker) W.; m. Joan A. Betzmer, Aug. 18, 1962; children: Kelly Drennan, Elizabeth McDonough BS, U.S. Naval Acad., 1954; MS, Tex. A&M U., 1967, PhD, 1968; MA, San Diego State U., 1968. Commd. ensign USN, 1954, advanced through grades to capt., 1974, officer-in-charge Bathyscaph Trieste Trieste, 1959-62, comdr. in USS Bashaw, 1968-69; dir. Inst. Marine and Coastal Studies, prof. ocean engring. U. So. Calif., LA, 1975-83; pres., CEO Internat. Maritime, Inc., 1976—; mng. dir. Deep Ocean Engring., Inc., 1990—2000, also bd. dirs. Dir. Ctr. for Marine Transp. Studies, U. So. Calif., 1980-83, Coastal Resources Ctr., 1990-94; trustee USN Mus. Found., 1989—; mem. Nat. Adv. Com. on Oceans and Atmosphere, 1979-85; bd. govs. Calif. Maritime Acad., 1985-95; pres. Parker Diving, 1989-94. Editor, contbr.: Law of the Sea: Issues in Ocean Resource Management, 1977, Energy and Resources Development of Continental Margins, 1980, Energy and Sea Power: Challenge for the Decade, 1981, Waste Disposal in the Oceans: Minimizing Impact, Maximizing Benefits, 1983; editor Jour. Marine Tech. Soc., 1975-80; mem. editorial bd. U.S. Naval Inst., 1974-75. Bd. dirs. Charles and Anne Lindbergh Found., 1996-2005. Decorated Legion of Merit (2); Woodrow Wilson Internat. Ctr. for Scholars fellow, 1973-74. Fellow Marine Tech. Soc., Acad. Underwater Arts and Scis., Explorers Club (hon. life, bd. dirs. 1994-2000, hon. pres. 2008-, Explorers Medal, 2001); mem. AAAS, Soc. Naval Archs. and Marine Engrs., Am. Soc. Naval Engrs., Navy Inst., Adventurers Club (hon. life), Am. Geog. Soc. (hon. life), Nat. Acad. Engring. Home and Office: Internat Maritime Inc 14758 Sitkum Ln Myrtle Point OR 97458-9726 Personal E-mail: imiwalsh@worldnet.att.net, imiwalsh@mac.com.

WALSH, EDWARD JOSEPH, food products and cosmetics executive; b. Mt. Vernon, NY, Mar. 18, 1932; s. Edward Aloysius and Charlotte Cecilia (Borup) W.; m. Patricia Ann Farrell, Sept. 16, 1961; children: Edward Joseph, Megan Simpson, John, Robert. BBA, Iona Coll., 1953; MBA, NYU, 1958. Sales rep. M & R Dietetic Labs., Columbus, Ohio, 1955-60; with Armour & Co., 1961-71, Greyhound Corp., 1971-87; v.p. toiletries div. Armour Dial Co., Phoenix, 1973-74, exec. v.p., 1975-77; pres., CEO Armour Internat. Co., Phoenix, 1978-84; pres. The Dial Corp. (formerly Armour-Dial Co.), Phoenix, 1984-87, chief exec. officer, 1984-87; pres., chief exec. officer Purex Corp., 1985; chmn., chief exec. officer The Sparta Group Ltd., Scottsdale, Ariz., 1988—2008. Bd. dirs. Nortrust Holding Corp., Phoenix, Matrixx Initiatives, Inc., Phoenix, 2000—07; mem. bd. advisors Brother to Brother Internat., 1988—2001, Universal Tech. Inst., Phoenix, 1996—2004, No. Trust N.A., 2006—. Trustee Scottsdale Meml. Health Found., 1995-98; pres. Mt. Vernon Fire Dept. Mems. Assn., 1960-61. Served with U.S. Army, 1953-55, Germany. Recipient Loftus Lifetime Achievement award, Iona Coll., 2004. Mem. Am. Mgmt. Assn., Nat. Meat Canner Assn. (pres. 1971-72), Cosmetic, Toiletries and Fragrance Assn. (bd. dirs. 1985—87), Nat. Food Processors Assn. (bd. dirs.). Republican. Roman Catholic. Office: The Sparta Group Ltd 6623 N Scottsdale Rd Scottsdale AZ 85250-4421

WALSH, FRANCIS RICHARD, lawyer, arbitrator, educator; b. Newark, Jan. 1, 1924; s. Francis R. Sr. and Loretta Anne (Norton) W.; m. Ethel Anne Walsh, Mar. 12, 1944; 1 child, Jeffrey R. BSBA, Seton Hall U., 1943; JD, Georgetown U., 1948. Prof. Law Sch. Georgetown U., Washington, 1949-51; law clk. to presiding justice U.S. Ct. Appeals (9th cir.), San Francisco, 1948-49; chief broadcast bur. FCC, Washington, 1970-71; pvt. practice San Francisco, 1954-70; prof. law U. San Francisco, 1951-54, 71-74, dean, prof. law, 1957-70; prof. law Hastings Coll. of Law, U. Calif., San Francisco, 1974—. Lt. USNR, 1943—46, PTO. Roman Catholic. Avocations: golf, travel. Home: 28 Spring Rd Kentfield CA 94904 Office: Hastings Coll Law 200 Mcallister St San Francisco CA 94102 Home Phone: 415-461-5723; Office Phone: 415-565-4600.

WALSH, J. MICHAEL, wholesale distribution executive; BS in Indsl. Engring., Tex. Tech U., Lubbock; MBA, Tex. A&M U. Sr. v.p. ops. Core-Mark Holding Co., Inc., 1991—96, sr. v.p. US Distbn., 1996—99, exec. v.p. sales, 1999—2003, pres., CEO, 2003—, bd. dirs., 2004—. Office: Core-Mark Holding Co 395 Oyster Point Blvd Ste 415 South San Francisco CA 94080 Office Phone: 650-589-9445.

WALSH, JAN, library director; MLS, U. Pitts. With Wash. State Libr., Olympia, 1978—, acting state libr., 2002, state libr., 2002—. Mem.: Wash. Libr. Assn., Chief Officers of State Libr. Agys. (Continuing Edn. com., Stats. com.), Libr. Coun. Wash. Office: Wash State Libr Divsn Wash Sec State PO Box 42460 Olympia WA 98504-2460 Office Phone: 360-704-5253. Office Fax: 360-586-7575. E-mail: jwalsh@secstate.wa.gov.

WALSH, JIM, lawyer, former air transportation executive; BA, U. Notre Dame; JD, SUNY, Buffalo. Bar: NY, Fla., Tex., US Ct. Appeals (5th Cir.), US Ct. Appeals (11th Cir.). Atty., bus. law Bond, Schoeneck & King, Syracuse, 1973—79; various positions including v.p. purchasing & inventory control, v.p. law Am. Airlines, Dallas, 1979—91; sr. v.p., gen. counsel, sec. Fairchild Dornier Corp., San Antonio, 1991—2004; sr. v.p., gen. counsel Am. West Holdings, 2004—05, US Airways Group, Inc., Tempe, Ariz., 2005—06.

WALSH, JOAN, editor-in-chief; Freelance writer; with In These Times, Chgo., Santa Barbara News & Review; news editor Salon-.com, San Francisco, 1998—99, v.p. news, 1999—2003, v.p., co-mng. editor, 2003—04, sr. v.p., editorial ops., 2003—04, editor-in-chief, 2005. Office: Salon Media Group 101 Spear St 203 San Francisco CA 94105-1517 Office Phone: 415-645-9200. Business E-Mail: jwalsh@salon.com.

WALSH, JOSEPH FIDLER (JOE WALSH), recording artist, record producer; b. Wichita, Kans., Nov. 20, 1947; s. George William and Helen Alice (Bowen) Walsh; m. Denise Driscoll; 3 children. Student, Kent State U., Ohio. Lead guitarist James Gang, 1968—71; with the Eagles, 1976—, Ringo Starr's All Star Band, 1990; disc jockey WXRK, NY, 1990. Musician (solo): (songs) Walk Away, Funk #49, In the City, Life's Been Good, (albums) Barnstorm, 1972, The Smoker You Drink, the Player You Get, 1973, So, What, 1975, But Seriously Folks, 1978, There Goes the Neighborhood, 1981, You Bought It: You Name It, 1983, The Confessor, 1985, Got Any Gum?, 1987, Ordinary Average Guy, 1991, Songs For A Dying Planet, 1992, Look What I Did, 1995, Little Did he Know..., 1997; musician: (with The James Gang) The James Gang, 1969, The James Gang Rides Again, 1970, (with The Eagles) Hotel California, 1976 (VH1's 100 Greatest Albums, 2001), The Long Run, 1979, Eagles Live, 1980, Hell Freezes Over, 1996 (Am. Music award, Favorite Rock Album, 1996), Long Road Out of Eden, 2007, (songs) Hotel California (Grammy award, Record of Yr., 1978), New Kid in Town (Grammy award, Best Arrangement for Voices, 1980), Heartache Tonight (Grammy award, Best Group Rock Vocal Performance, 1980), How Long (Grammy award, Best Group Vocal Country Performance, 2008), I Dreamed There Was No War, 2007 (Grammy award for Best Pop Instrumental Performance, 2009); actor: (films) The Blues Brothers, 1980; (TV series) The Drew Carey Show, 1998—2001. Recipient Favorite Rock Group award, Am. Music Awards, 1981, 1996, Favorite Adult Contemporary Artist award, 1996, Favorite Rock Album award, 1996; named one of Greatest Artists of Rock & Roll, VH1, 1998, 100 Greatest Artists of All Time, Rolling Stone, 2004; named to Rock & Roll Hall of Fame, 1998. Mem.: Amateur Radio Relay League. Achievements include research in electronic music synthesizers.

WALSH, KATE, actress; b. San Jose, Calif., Oct. 13, 1967; m. Alex Young, Sept. 1, 2007 (separated Nov. 22, 2008). Student, U. Ariz. Actor: (radio plays) Born Guilty; (plays) Moon Under Miami, Troilus and Cressida; (films) Normal Life, 1996, Peppermills, 1997, Night of the Lawyers, 1997, Three Below Zero, 1998, Heaven, 1998, Henry, Portrait of a Serial Killer II, 1998, The Family Man, 2000, Under the Tuscan Sun, 2003, After the Sunset, 2004, Kicking and Screaming, 2005, Inside Out, 2005, Bewitched, 2005, Veritas, Prince of Truth, 2006; (TV series) The Drew Carey Show, 1997—2002, The Mike O'Malley Show, 1999, Turks, 1999, The Norm Show, 2000—01, Mind of a Married Man, 2001, Joint Custody, 2004, Grey's Anatomy, 2005—07 (Outstanding Performance by an Ensemble in a Drama Series, SAG, 2007), Private Practice, 2007—; (TV films) Bobby Cannon, 2005. Mailing: Grey's Anatomy Los Feliz Tower 4th Fl 4151 Prospect Ave Los Angeles CA 90027

WALSH, THOMAS A., production designer; Prodn. designer Doug Apatow Agy., Culver City, Calif., 1980—. Prodn. designer: (IMAX films) Flyers, 1980, Speed, 1984, The Discoverers, 1993, (TV movies) Miss Lonely Hearts, 1981, A Gathering of Old Men, 1986 (Emmy award nomination outstanding art direction 1987), Eugene O'Neill, 1986, War Story: Vietnam, 1988, Without Warning: The James Brady Story, 1990 (Emmy award nomination outstanding art direction 1991), Blindspot, 1992, In Search of Dr. Seuss, 1994, (documentaries) John Huston, 1988, MGM: When the Lion Roars, 1992 (Emmy award outstanding art direction 1993), (feature films) The Handmaid's Tale, 1990, Prayer of the Rollerboys, 1990. Office: Doug Apatow Agency 12049 W Jefferson Blvd #200 Culver City CA 90230-6219

WALSH, WILLIAM DESMOND, investor; b. NYC, Aug. 4, 1930; s. William J. and Catherine Grace (Desmond) W.; m. Mary Jane Gordon, Apr. 5, 1951 (dec. Jan. 18, 2008); children: Deborah, Caroline, Michael, Suzanne, Tara Jane, Peter. BA, Fordham U., 1951; JD, Harvard U., 1955. Bar: NY 1955. Asst. US atty. So. dist. NY, NYC, 1955-58; counsel NY Commn. Investigation, NYC, 1958-61; mgmt. cons. McKinsey & Co., NYC, 1961-67; sr. v.p. Arcata Corp., Menlo Park, Calif., 1967-82; chmn. Sequoia Assocs. LLC, 1982—; pres., CEO Atacra Liquidating Trust, 1982-88. Chmn. bd. dir. Neuroscis. Inst./Scripps, Ameriscape, Inc., Cornelius, Oreg., Creativity Inc., Van Nuys; bd. dir., lead dir. URS Corp., San Francisco; bd. dir. Am. Ireland Fund, Boston. Mem. bd. overseers, chmn. fin. com. Hoover Inst.; co-chmn. dean's adv. bd. Harvard Law Sch.; trustee emeritus Fordham U. Mem. NY State Bar Assn., Harvard Club (NYC and San Francisco), Fordham Club No. Calif., Knights of Malta. Office Phone: 650-321-4346. Office Fax: 650-321-4588.

WALSTON, RODERICK EUGENE, federal official; b. Gooding, Idaho, Dec. 15, 1935; s. Loren R. and Iva M. (Boyer) W.; m. Margaret D. Grandey; children: Gregory Scott W., Valerie Lynne W. AA, Boise Jr. Coll., 1956; BA cum laude, Columbia Coll., 1958; LL.B. scholar, Stanford U., 1961. Bar: Calif. 1961, U.S. Supreme Ct. 1973. Law clk to judge U.S. Ct. Appeals 9th Cir., 1961-62; dep. atty. gen State of Calif., San Francisco, 1963-91, head natural resources sect. 1969-91, chief asst. atty. gen. pub. rights div., 1991-99; spl. dep counsel Kings County, Calif., 1975-76; gen. counsel Metropolitan Water Dist. So. Calif., 2000—02; dep. solicitor U.S. Dept. Interior, 2002—; of counsel Best, Best and Krieger, LLP, Walnut Creek, Calif., 2005. Mem. environ. and natural resources adv. coun. Stanford (Calif.) Law Sch. Contbr. articles to profl. jours.; bd. editors: Stanford Law Rev., 1959-61, Western Natural Resources Litigation Digest, Calif. Water Law and Policy Reporter; spl. editor Jour. of the West. Co-chmn. Idaho campaign against Right-to-Work initiative, 1958; Calif. rep. Western States Water Coun., 1986—; environ. and natural resources adv. coun., Stanford Law Sch. Astor Found. scholar, 1956-58; Nat. Essay Contest winner Nat. Assn. Internat. Rels. Clubs, 1956, Stanford Law Rev. prize, 1961; recipient Best Brief award Nat. Assn. Attys. Gen., 1997, Burton award best article, 2007; named Pub. Lawyer of Yr., Calif. State Bar, 2004, Forensics Hall of Fame, Boise State U., 2009. Mem. ABA (chmn. water resources com. 1988-90, vice chmn. and conf. chmn. 1985-88, 90—, Best Lawyers of America, 2008), Contra Costa County Bar Assn., U.S. Supreme Ct., Hist. Soc., Federalist Soc., World Affairs Coun. No. Calif. Office: Best Best and Krieger LLP 2033 N Main St Walnut Creek CA 94596 Office Phone: 925-977-3304. Business E-Mail: roderick.walston@bbklaw.com.

WALT, MARTIN, physicist, educator; b. West Plains, Mo., June 1, 1926; s. Martin and Dorothy (Mantz) W.; m. Mary Estelle Thompson, Aug. 16, 1950; children: Susan Mary, Stephen Martin, Anne Elizabeth, Patricia Ruth. BS, Calif. Inst. Tech., 1950; MS, U. Wis., 1951, PhD, 1953. Staff mem. Los Alamos Sci. Lab., 1953-56; research scientist, mgr. physics Lockheed Missiles and Space Co., Palo Alto (Calif.) Rsch. Lab., 1956-71, dir. phys. scis., 1971-86, dir. research, 1986-93; cons. prof. Stanford U., 1986—. Mem. adv. com. NRC, NASA, Dept. Def., U. Calif. Lawrence Berkeley Lab. Author 2 books; contbr. articles to sci. jours. Served with USNR, 1944-46. Wis. Research Found. fellow, 1950-51; AEC fellow, 1951-53 Fellow Am. Geophys. Union, Am. Phys. Soc.; mem. Am. Inst. Physics (bd. govs.), Fremont Hills Country Club. Home: 12650 Viscaino Ct Los Altos Hills CA 94022-2517 Office: Stanford U Starlab Packard 352 Stanford CA 94305 Office Phone: 650-723-2690. Business E-Mail: walt@nova.stanford.edu.

WALTER, JOHN C., lawyer, gas industry executive; BA in Econs., U. Colo., Boulder, JD, 1970. Bar: Colo. 1970. Corp. counsel, land mgr. Western Gas Resources, Inc., Denver, 1983—88, v.p., gen. counsel, 1988—94, exec. v.p., gen. counsel, 1994—2000, exec. v.p., gen. counsel, sec., 2001—. Office: Western Gas Resources PO Box 173779 Denver CO 80217-3779

WALTER, PETER, biochemist; b. Berlin; Diploma in Chemistry, Free U. Berlin, 1976; MSc in Organic Chemistry, Vanderbilt U., 1977; PhD in Cell Biology, Rockefeller U., 1981. Prof., chmn. dept. biochemistry & biophysics U. Calif., San Francisco; investigator Howard Hughes Medical Inst. Harvey lectr. Rockefeller U., 1996; Feodor-Lynen lectr. Mosbach Kolloquium, 1998. Co-author: Molecular Biology of the Cell, 2002, Essential Cell Biology, 2003. Recipient Searle Scholar award, 1983, Passano award, 1988, Eli Lilly award, 1988, Alfred P. Sloan award, 1989, Merit award, Nat. Insts. Health, 1990, Wiley Prize biomedical sciences, 2005, Gairdner Found. Internat. award, 2009. Fellow: Am. Acad. Microbiology, Am. Acad. Arts and Scis.; mem.: NAS, European Molecular Biology Orgn. (assoc.). Office: U Calif San Fransisco Dept Biochemistry & Biophysics Genentech Hall N312 600 16th St San Francisco CA 94143-2200 Office Phone: 415-476-5017. Office Fax: 415-476-5233. Business E-Mail: walter@cgl.ucsf.edu.*

WALTERBOS, RENÉ ANTONIUS, astronomer; BA in Astronomy, Physics, U. Leiden, 1979, MS in Astronomy, Physics cum laude, 1982, PhD in Astronomy, 1986. Postdoc. rschr. Inst. Advanced Study, Princeton, N.J., 1986-87, U. Calif., Berkeley, 1987-90; asst. prof. astronomy N.Mex. State U., Las Cruces, 1991-96, head dept., assoc. prof. astronomy, 1996—. Vis. asst. prof. dept. physics U. Calif., Davis, 1989-90. Hubble fellow Space Telescope Sci. Inst., 1990-91; Cottrell scholar Rsch. Corp., 1994. Mem. Internat. Astron. Union, Am. Astron. Soc., Netherlands Astron. Soc., Astron. Soc. Pacific. Achievements include research in structure and evolution of galaxies, properties of the diffuse interstellar medium in galaxies, interaction of massive stars with the interstellar medium in galaxies. Office: New Mex State U Dept Astronomy PO Box 30001 Las Cruces NM 88003-8001

WALTERS, DANIEL L., library director; B, U. Wash., M in Librarianship. With North Ctrl. Regional Libr., Wenatchee, Wash., King County Libr. Sys., Seattle; dir. Spokane Pub. Libr., Wash., Buffalo and Erie County Pub. Libr.; exec. dir. Las Vegas-Clark County Libr. Dist., Nev. Contbr. articles to profl. publs. Mem. exec. com. ARC Inland NW Chpt.; bd. dirs. YMCA, Spokane, Wash. Named Cmty. Person of Yr., Las Vegas Asian C. of C. Mem.: ALA, NY Libr. Assn., Las Vegas Execs. Assn., Wash. Libr. Assn., Nev. Libr. Assn., Online Computer Libr. Ctr., Pub. Libr. Assn. (v.p./pres.-elect 2004). Office: Las Vegas Clark County Libr Dist 833 Las Vegas Blvd N Las Vegas NV 89101 Office Phone: 702-734-7323.

WALTERS, DANIEL RAYMOND, political columnist; b. Hutchinson, Kans., Oct. 10, 1943; s. Howard Duke and Glenna Lucille (Hesse) W.; m. Doris K. Winter, June 16, 1995; children: Danielle, Staci. Mng. editor Hanford (Calif.) Sentinel, 1966-69, Herald News, Klamath Falls, Oreg., 1969-71, Times-Standard, Eureka, Calif., 1971-73; polit. writer and columnist Sacramento (Calif.) Union, 1973-84; polit. columnist, state editor Capitol Bur., Sacramento Bee, 1984—. Author: The New California: Facing the 21st Century, 1986; founding editor Calif. Polit. Almanac, 1989. Office: The Sacramento Bee 925 L St Ste 600 Sacramento CA 95814-3763

WALTERS, MARTHA LEE, state supreme court justice; b. 1951; married; 2 children. JD, U. Ore. Sch. Law, 1977. Pres. Walters, Chanti & Zennache, Eugene, Oreg.; justice Oreg. Supreme Ct., 2006—. Chmn. exec. com. Nat. Conf. Commrs. on Uniform State Laws, 1992—, pres., 2007—. Recipient Pub. Justice award, Oreg. Trial Lawyers Assn., 1998. Mem.: Am. Law Inst., Oreg. Law Comm. Office: Walters Chanti & Zennache 245 E 4th St Eugene OR 97401 Office Phone: 503-986-5668.

WALTERS, MIMI, state legislator; m. David Walters; 4 children. BA in Polit. Sci., UCLA, 1984. California State Assemblywoman, District 73, 2004-08; vchairwoman, Revenue & Tax; member,Aging & Long Term Care, Approp comts, currently. Kidder Peabody & Co, Invest Exec, currently; mem. Dist. 33, Calif. State Senate, 2009-. Republican. Office: Dist 33 24031 El Toro Rd Ste 210 Laguna Hills CA 92653 Office Phone: 949-457-7333. Office Fax: 949-457-7305.

WALTERS, RICHARD FRANCIS, computer science educator; b. Teleajen, Romania, Aug. 30, 1930; s. Ray Pearce and Gertrude (Gravett) W.; m. Shipley Newlin, Aug. 30, 1952; children: Leslie Walters Tuomi, David Todd. BA magna cum laude, Williams Coll., Williamstown, Mass., 1952; MA, U. Wyo., Laramie, 1953; Diplome superieur en scis. naturelles, U. Bordeaux, France, 1955; PhD, Stanford U., Calif., 1957. Geologist Humble Oil and Refining Co., Los Angeles, 1956-60, subsurface geologist Chico, Calif., 1960-63, sr. subsurface geologist New Orleans, 1963-66; sr. research geologist Esso Prodn. Research Co., Houston, 1966-67; lectr. computer sci. U. Calif., Davis, 1967-68, asst. prof. med. edn. and biomed. engirng., 1968-73, assoc. prof. med. edn. and biomed. engring., 1973-78, assoc. prof. community health, 1978-79, prof. community health, 1979-83, prof. elec. and computer engring., 1980-83, prof. divsn. computer sci., 1983—, chair divsn. computer sci., 1983—89, prof. family practice, 1984-96, prof. med. informatics, 1996—; Edward A. Dickson prof. emeritus, 2006—07. Editorial cons. Soc. for Computer Simulations, 1970-76; editorial rev. bd. mem. Jour. of Computer Based Instrn., 1975-89, Med. Informatics, 1977—, MUMPS Users' Group Quarterly, 1981—, Computers in Biology and Medicine, 1982—, MD Computing, 1985-93; contbr. articles to profl. jours. Fellow Am. Geol. Soc., Am. Coll. Med. Informatics; mem. Am. Arbitration Assn. Assn. Computing Machinery (mem. spl. interest group on programming langs. 1980—, 1974—, mem. spl. interest group on mgmt. data base, 1981), MUMPS Users' Group (vice chmn. 1974-75, chmn. 1975-77, 81-83, devel. com. chmn. 1977-79, 80-82, hon. life mem. Europe and Japan), Am. Assn. Med. Systems and Informatics, IEEE (sr.), U. Calif. Davis Emeritus Assn. (pres. 2006-08). Democrat. Episcopalian. Avocation: music. Home: 647 Elmwood Dr Davis CA 95616-3514 Office: U Calif Dept Computer Sci One Shields Ave Davis CA 95616-8562 Office Phone: 530-752-3241. Business E-Mail: walters@cs.ucdavis.edu.

WALTHER, STEVEN T., commissioner, lawyer; b. Reno, Nev., July 18, 1943; m. Diane Walther; children: Natalie, Mario, Wyatt. BA in Russian, U. Notre Dame, 1965; JD, U. Calif., Berkeley, 1968. Bar: Nev. 1968, US Dist. Ct. (Nev.) 1969, Calif. 1969, US Ct. Appeals (9th cir.) 1986, US Supreme Ct. 1991. Ptnr. Walther, Key, Maupin, Oats, Cox & LeGoy, Reno; commr. Fed. Election Commn., Washington, 2006—07, vice chmn., 2008—. Mem. US Commn. on Civil Rights, 1971—; chair Nev. Bd. CLE, 1982—90; panelist US Magistrate Judge Merit Selection Panel, 1990; pres. Western States Bar Conf., 1999—2000; mem. LexiNexis Martindale-Hubbell Legal Adv. Bd., 2001—; pres. Nat. Caucus State Bar Assn., 2002—03; guest lectr. Nat. Jud. Coll., Reno; mem. Nev. State Adv. Com.; chair internat. bus. task force Coll. Bus. Adminstrn., U. Nev., Reno; lectr., presenter on rule of law and human rights issues; mem. Am. Law Inst., mem. consultative group principles and rules of transnational civil procedures, mem. consultative group internat. jurisdiction and judgements. Author: The Globalization of the Rule of Law and Human Rights, 2000. Recipient Awards of Spl. Appreciation, 1991, 1999, Award of Spl. Appreciation, Am. Red Cross, Sierra, Nev. chpt., 1999, Pres. award, Scenic Nev., 2005. Fellow: World Acad. Art and Sci., Am. Bar Found. (chair 2003—04, del. leader, rule of law del. to Russia 2005); mem.: ABA (chair standing com.on world order under law 1993—95, bd. govs. 1995—97, fin. com. 1995—97, ho. del. 1995—97, chair spl. adv. com. on internat. activities 1997—98, mem. Cent. European and Eurasian Law Initiative 1997—98, mem. subcom. on internat. jud. relations 1997—98, rep. to UN 1998—2000, mem. UN and internat. instns. coord. com. 1998—, mem. internat. human rights com. 1999—, mem. Cent. European and Eurasian Law Initiative 2000—01, co-founder 2001, first chair 2001—03, exec. bd. mem. 2001—, coun. mem. 2002—, mem. sect. individual rights and responsibilities, mem. ctr. for human rights, mem. lit. sect., mem. exec. bd., mem. sect. on bus., mem. sect. internat. law), State Bar of Nev. (gov., bd. govs. 1978—91, pres. 1990—91), Human Rights First, Nat. Coun., State Bar of Calif., Washoe County Bar Assn., Am. Inns of Ct. (Bruce R. Thompson chpt.) (master emeritus), Am. Soc. Internat. Law, Nat. Conf. Bar Pres., Inc. (mem. sponsorship com. 1994—95), Nat. Conf. Bar Found. (trustee bd. trustees 2004—), Boalt Hall Alumni Assn., U. Calif. Law Sch. (pres. 2001—02). Democrat. Office: Fed Election Commn 999 E St NW Washington DC 20463

WAN, FREDERIC YUI-MING, mathematician, educator; b. Shanghai, Jan. 7, 1936; arrived in U.S., 1947; s. Wai-Nam and Olga Pearl (Jung) W.; m. Julia Y.S. Chang, Sept. 10, 1960. SB, MIT, 1959, SM, 1963, PhD, 1965. Mem. staff MIT Lincoln Lab., Lexington, 1959—65; instr. math. MIT, Cambridge, 1965—67, asst. prof., 1967—69, assoc. prof., 1969—74; prof. math., dir. Inst. Applied Math. and Stats. U. B.C., Vancouver, 1974—83; prof. applied math. and math. U. Wash., Seattle, 1983—95; prof. math., prof. mech. and aero. engring. U. Calif., Irvine, 1995—. Chmn. Dept. Applied Math. U. Wash., 1984-88, divsn. dean scis. Coll. Arts and Scis., 1988-92; vice chancellor rsch., dean grad. studies U. Calif. Irvine, 1995-2000, faculty athletics rep., 2000-04, dir. math. and computational biology grad. program, 2006—; program dir. divsn. math. sci. NSF, 1986-87, divsn. dir., 1993-94; mem. MIT Ednl. Coun. for B.C. Area Can., 1974-83; trustee NSF Inst. Pure and Applied Math., chmn., 1999-2001; cons. in field Assoc. editor Jour. Applied Mechanics, 1991-95, Can. Applied Math. Quar., Studies in Applied Math., Jour. Dyn. Discrete, Continuous and Impulsive Sys., 1994-97, Natural Resource Modeling 1985-88, Internat. Jour. Solids & Structures, 1996-2005, Jour. Mechanics of Material and Structures, 2005—; contbr. articles to profl. jours. Killam Sr. fellow, 1979; recipient Sloan Found. award, 1973, Phys. Scis. Tchg. Excellence award 2004. Fellow AAAS, ASME; mem. Russian Acad. Natural Scis. (fgn.), Am. Acad. Mechanics (sec. fellows 1984-90, pres. 1993-94), Soc. Indsl. and Applied Math., Can. Applied Math. Soc. (coun. 1980-83, pres. 1983-85, Arthur Beaumont Disting. Svc. award 1991), Am. Math. Soc., Math. Assn. Am., Sigma Xi (pres. U. Calif. Irvine chpt. 2005—) Home: 22 Urey Ct Irvine CA 92612-4077 Office: U Calif Irvine Dept Math Rm 267 MST Bldg Irvine CA 92697-3875 Business E-Mail: fwan@uci.edu.

WANDELL, MORGAN, broadcast executive; b. Feb. 17, 1971; Grad. with honors in Econs., Claremont Coll., Calif., 1993. Writer-prodr. Channel One, pres. programming, 1999—2004; dir. creative affairs Touchstone TV, Burbank, Calif., 1997—99, sr. v.p. drama, 2004—; with Digital Entertainment Network, 1999. Achievements include overseeing the release of the TV shows Grey's Anatomy, Desperate Housewives and Lost and the development of the shows Criminal Minds, Ghost Whisperer, Kyle XY and Ugly Betty. Office: Touchstone TV 500 S Buena Vista St Burbank CA 91521-0001

WANG, CHARLES PING, engineering executive; b. Shanghai, Apr. 25, 1937; came to U.S., 1962; s. Kuan-Ying and Ping-Lu (Ming) W.; m. Lily L. Lee, June 29, 1963. BS, Taiwan U., Republic of China, 1959; MS, Tsinghua U., Singchu, Republic of China, 1961; PhD, Calif. Inst. Tech., 1967. Mem. tech. staff Bellcomm, Washington, 1967-69; research engr. U. San Diego, 1969-74; sr. scientist Aerspace Corp., Los Angeles, 1976-86; pres. Optodyne, Inc., Compton, Calif., 1986—. Adj. prof. U. Calif., San Diego, 1979-90; pres. Chinese-Am. Engr. and Scientists Assn. So. Calif., LA, 1979-81; program chmn. Internation Conf. of Lasers, Shanghai, 1979-80; organizer and session chmn. Lasers Conf., LA, 1981-84, program chmn., Las Vegas, 1985. Editor in chief Series in Laser Tech., 1983-91; contbr. articles to profl. jours. Calif. Inst. Tech. scholar, 1965. Fellow Am. Optical Soc., AIAA (assoc., jour. editor 1981-83). Achievements include invention of discharge excimer laser and laser vector method for 3D volumetric positioning measurement. Office: Optodyne Inc 1180 W Mahalo Pl Compton CA 90220-5443 Office Phone: 310-635-7481. Personal E-mail: optodyne@aol.com.

WANG, DAVID N.K., chemical company executive; PhD in Material Sci., U. Calif., Berkeley. Rschr. Bell Labs., Murray Hill, N.J., 1980; mgr. Worldwide Bus. Ops.; 0; sr. v.p. Applied Materials, Inc., Santa Clara, Calif., 1998—. Office: Applied Materials Inc 3050 Bowers Ave Santa Clara CA 95054-3201

WANG, IGNATIUS CHUNG, bishop; b. Beijing, Feb. 27, 1934; arrived in US, 1974, naturalized; JCD, Urban U., Rome. Ordained priest, Hong Kong, 1959; parish priest, vicar general Diocese of St. George, Grenada, 1962—74; with Archdiocese of San Francisco, 1974—, coord. Chinese Apostolate, 1981; pastor St. Francis of Assisi, San Francisco, 1982—92; named monsignor, 1989; dir. Soc. for the Propagation of the Faith Archdiocese of San Francisco, 1994—2002, chancellor, 1998—2002; ordained bishop, 2003; aux. bishop Archdiocese of San Francisco, 2003—. Roman Catholic. Achievements include first to becoming first US bishop of Asian ancestry. Office: Roman Cath Archdiocese of San Francisco 1 Peter Yorke Way San Francisco CA 94109 Office Phone: 415-614-5500. E-mail: wangi@sfarchdiocese.org.

WANG, JAW-KAI, bioengineering educator; b. Nanjing, Jiangsu, China, Mar. 4, 1932; arrived in U.S., 1955; s. Shuling and Hsi-Ying (Lo) W.; m. Kwang Mei Chow, Sept. 7, 1957 (div. Oct. 1989); children: Angela C.C., Dora C.C., Lawrence C.Y.; m. Bichuan Li, Sept. 25, 1999. BS, Nat. Taiwan U., 1953; MS in Agrl. Engring., Mich. State U., 1956, PhD, 1958. Registered profl. engr., Hawaii. Faculty agrl. engring. dept. U. Hawaii, Honolulu, 1959-93, assoc. prof., chmn. dept. agrl. engring., 1964-68, prof., chmn. dept. agrl. engring., 1968-75, prof. biosys. engring., 1994—2000, prof. molecular bioscis. dept., 2000—02; prof. emeritus U. Hawaii-Manoa, Honolulu, 2004—, dir. Aquaculture Program, 1990-96; spl. asst., Internat. Rsch. Dept., Office of Internat. Cooperation and Devel. U.S. Dept. Agr., 1988; pres. Aquaculture Tech., Inc., 1990—; academic cons. Chinese Acad. Fishery Scis., 2004—, chief sci. advisor, fishery, machinery and instrument rsch. inst., 2004—, chief tech. expert, rsch. inst. fisheries machinery and instrument, 2005—, mem. nat. open lab. for control of aquaculture water quality, 2005—. Co-dir. internat. sci. and edn. coun. USDA; vis. assoc. dir. internat. programs and studies office Nat. Assn. State Univs. and Land-Grant Colls., 1979; vis. prof. Nat. Taiwan U., 1964-65, 2000-01, U. Calif., Davis, 1980; hon. prof. coll. pharmacology Tianjing U., China, 2003; cons. U.S. Army Civilian Adminstrn., Ryukus, Okinawa, 1965, Internat. Rice Rsch. Inst., Philippines, 1971, Pacific Concrete and Rock Co. Ltd., 1974, AID, 1974, Universe Tankships, Del., 1980-81, World Bank, 1981, 82, ABA Internat., 1981-85, Internat. Found. for Agrl. Devel./World Bank, 1981, Rockefeller Found., 1980, Orizaba, Inc., 1983, Agrisys./FAO, 1983, Info. Processing Assocs., 1984, County of Maui, 1984, 85, Dept. of State, 1985, Alexander and Baldwin, 1986; mem. expert panel on agrl. mechanization FAO/UN, 1984-90; sr. fellow East-West Ctr. Food Inst., 1973-74; dir. Info. Sys. and Svcs. Internat., Inc., 1986-90; mem. bd. on agr. and natural resources The Nat. Acads., 2004—; panel mem. Vietnam Edn. Found., 2004-06; acad. cons. Chinese Acad. Fishery Scis., 2004-06; mem. bd. agrl. and natural resources Nat. Acads., 2004-06. Author: Irrigated Rice Production Systems, 1980; editor: Taro-A Review of Colocasia Esculenta and its Potentials, 1983; mem. editl. bd. Aquacultural Engring., 1982—. Recipient Exemplary State Employee award State of Hawaii, 1986, State of Hawaii Disting. Svc. award Office of Gov., 1990. Fellow Am. Soc. Agrl. Engrs. (chmn. Hawaii sect. 1962-63, chmn. grad. instrn. com. 1971-73, various coms., Engr. of Yr. 1976, Tech. Paper award 1978, Kishida Internat. award 1991), Am. Inst. Med. and Biol. Engring.; mem. NAE, Aquaculture Engring. Soc. (pres. 1993-95), Sigma Xi, Gamma Sigma Delta (pres. Hawaii chpt. 1974-75), Pi Mu Epsilon. Office: U Hawaii MBBE Dept 1955 East West Rd Honolulu HI 96822 Home Phone: 808-377-5087; Office Phone: 808-956-8154. Personal E-mail: jawkai@gmail.com. Business E-Mail: jawkai@hawaii.edu.

WANG, LEI, biochemist; b. China; BS in Organic Chemistry, Peking U., 1994, MS in Physical Chemistry, 1997; PhD in Bioorganic Chemistry, U. Calif., Berkeley, 2002. Postdoctoral rschr. biochemistry U. Calif., San Diego, 2002—. Contbr. articles to profl. jour. Recipient Grand prize, Collegiate Inventors Competition, Nat. Inventors Hall Fame, Young Scientist prize, Amersham Biosciences, 2003; named one of Top 100 Young Innovators, MIT Tech. Review, 2004; Merck fellow, Damon Runyon Cancer Rsch. Found., 2002. Office: The Salk Inst 10010 N Torrey Pines Rd La Jolla CA 92037 Business E-Mail: lewang@ucsd.edu.

WANG, SHIH-HO, electrical engineer, educator; b. Kiangsu, China, June 29, 1944; arrived in US, 1968; BEE, Nat. Taiwan U., Taipei, 1967; MEE, U. Calif., Berkeley, 1970, PhD in Elec. Engring., 1971. Asst. prof. elec. engring. U. Colo., Colo. Springs, 1973-76, Boulder, 1976-77; asst. prof. electrical engring. U. Md., College Park, 1977-78, assoc. prof., 1978-84; prof. U. Calif., Davis, 1984—. Cons. Lawrence Livermore (Calif.) Nat. Lab., 1986-88; scientific officer Office Naval Research, Arlington, Va., 1983-84. Assoc. editor Internat. Jour. Robotics and Automation, 1986—90. Served to 2d lt. China Air Force, Taiwan, 1967-68. Mem. IEEE (hon. mention award control systems soc. 1975). Office: Univ Calif Dept Elec Computer Engring Davis CA 95616 Business E-Mail: shwang@ucdavis.edu.

WANG, SUSAN S., manufacturing executive; BA in Acctg., U. Tex.; MBA, U. Conn. CPA, Calif. With Price Waterhouse & Co., NYC; various fin. and acctg. mgmt. positions Xerox Corp., Westvaco Corp.; dir. fin. Solectron Corp., Milpitas, Calif., 1984, v.p. fin., CFO, 1986, sr. v.p., 1990—, also bd. dirs. Mem. adv. bd. YWCA, Santa Clara County; chairperson Fin. Exec. Rsch. Found. Recipient Top Women in Industry award YWCA; named one of San Francisco Bay Area's most powerful corp. women. Mem. AICPA, N.Y. State Soc. CPA, Fin. Execs. Inst. Office: Solectron Corp 777 Gibraltar Dr Milpitas CA 95035-6328

WANG, WILLIAM KAI-SHENG, law educator; b. NYC, Feb. 28, 1946; s. Yuan-Chao and Julia Ying-Ru (Li) W.; m. Kwan Kwan Tan, July 29, 1972; 1 child, Karen You-Chuan. BA, Amherst Coll., Mass., 1967; JD, Yale U., New Haven, Conn., 1971. Bar: Calif. 1972. Asst. to mng. partner Gruss & Co., NYC, 1971-72; asst. prof. law U. San Diego, 1972-74, asso. prof., 1974-77, prof., 1977-81, Hastings Coll. Law, U. Calif., San Francisco, 1981—. Vis. prof. law U. Calif., Davis, 1975—76, Hastings Coll. Law, U. Calif., 1980, UCLA, 1990, Villanova U., 1999, Bklyn. Law Sch., 2000, Leiden (Netherlands) U., 2004; cons. White Ho. Domestic Policy Staff, Washington, 1979; chair investment policy oversight group, bd. participant Law Sch. Admissions Coun.; nat. adjudicatory coun. FINRA, 2007—08, NASD, 2003—07; mem. then chair com. on audit and assn. investment policy Assn. Am. Law Schs., 1995—98. Co-author: Insider Trading, 2d edit., 2008; mem. editl. bd.: Internat. and Comparative Corp. Law Jour.; contbr. articles to newspapers, mags., profl. jours. Mem. State Bar Calif., Am. Law Inst. Home: 455 39th Ave San Francisco CA 94121-1507 Office: U Calif Hastings Coll Law 200 McAllister St San Francisco CA 94102-4978 Office Phone: 415-565-4666. Business E-Mail: wangw@uchastings.edu.

WANG, WILLIAM SHI-YUAN, linguistics educator; b. Shanghai, Aug. 14, 1933; came to U.S., 1948, naturalized, 1960; s. Harper and Lily W.; children: Eugene, Yulun, Yumei, Yusi. AB, Columbia U., 1955; MA, U. Mich., 1956, PhD, 1960. Assoc. prof., chmn. dept. linguistics Ohio State U., Columbus, 1963-65; prof. linguistics U. Calif., Berkeley, 1966—, dir. Project on Linguistic Analysis, 1966—; prof. grad. sch., 1994—. Fellow Center Advanced Studies in Behavioral Scis., 1969-70, 83-84; sr. Fulbright lectr. in, Sweden, 1972, India, 1979 Author: Explorations in Language, 1991; editor: The Lexicon in Phonological Change, 1977, Human Communication, 1982, Language Writing and the Computer, 1986; co-editor: Individual Differences in Language Ability and Language Behavior, 1979; assoc. editor Language, 1967-73; founding editor Jour. Chinese Linguistics, 1973—; contbr. numerous articles to profl. jours. Guggenheim Found. fellow, 1978-79 Mem. Linguistic Soc. Am., Acoustical Soc. Am., Academia Sinica, Internat. Assn. Chinese Linguistics (pres. 1992-93). Office: U Calif 2222 Piedmont Ave Berkeley CA 94720-2170

WANGER, OLIVER WINSTON, federal judge; b. LA, Nov. 27, 1940; m. Lorrie A. Reinhart; children: Guy A., Christopher L., Andrew G., W. Derek, Oliver Winston II. Student, Colo. Sch. Mines, 1958-60; BS, U. So. Calif., 1963; LLB, U. Calif., Berkeley, 1966. Bar: Calif. 1967, US Dist. Ct. (ea. dist.) Calif. 1969, US Tax Ct. 1969, US Dist. Ct. (ctrl. dist.) Calif. 1975, US Dist. Ct. (so. dist.) Calif. 1977, US Dist. Ct. (no. dist.) Calif. 1989, US Ct. Appeals (9th cir.) 1989. Dep. dist. atty. Fresno (Calif.) County Dist. Atty., 1967-69; ptnr. Gallagher, Baker & Manock, Fresno, 1969-74; sr. ptnr. McCormick, Barstow, Sheppard, Wayte & Carruth, Fresno, 1974-91; judge U.S. Dist. Ct. (ea. dist.) Calif., Fresno, 1991—. Adj. prof. Humphreys Coll. Law, Fresno, Calif., 1968—70, San Joaquin Coll. Law, Fresno, 1970—94, dean, 1980—83, chair bd. trustees, pres., 1984—94. Fellow Am. Coll. Trial Lawyers, Internat. Acad. Trial Lawyers; mem. Am. Bd. Trial Advs. (pres. San Joaquin Valley chpt. 1987-89, nat. bd. dirs. 1989-91), Am. Bd. Profl. Liability Attys. (founder, diplomate), Calif. State Bar (mem. exec. com. litigation sect. 1989-92, mem. com. on fed. cts. 1989-90), San Joaquin Valley Am. Inn of Ct. (pres. 1992-93), Beta Gamma Sigma. Office: US Dist Ct 5104 US Courthouse 1130 O St Fresno CA 93721-2201

WANLASS, DENNIS L., manufacturing executive; b. Salt Lake City, Jan. 14, 1949; s. Robert Hancock and Virginia Lee (Swofford) W.; m. Karen Sue Peterson, Nov. 9, 1966; children: Stacey Lee, Stephanie Ann, Dennis Robert, Lindsey Carol, Julie Ann. BS in Acctg., U. Utah, 1970. CPA. Sr. supr. Peat Marwick Mitchell, Salt Lake City, 1970-75; corp. controller Eastman Christensen Co., Salt Lake City, 1975-88; controller Geneva Steel, Vineyard, Utah, 1988-89, v.p., chief fin. officer, 1989—. Bd. dirs., exec. com. Jr. Achievement, Salt Lake City, 1990-91.

WAPNIR, IRENE LEONOR, medical educator; b. Buenos Aires, May 11, 1954; came to U.S., 1963; d. Raul Alberto and Elsa (Michalewicz) W.; m. Ralph Steven Greco; children: Justin Michael, Eric Matthew, Ilana Rose. BA, Goucher Coll., Balt., 1975; MD, U. Autonoma Metropolitana, Mexico City, 1980. Diplomate Am. Bd. Surgery. Intern, resident N.Y. Med. Coll., Bronx, 1980-85; attending physician and asst. prof. surgery Lincoln Hosp.-N.Y. Med. Coll., 1985-87; asst. prof. surgery UMDNJ-Robert Wood Johnson Med. Sch., New Brunswick, 1988-95, chief divsn. comprehensive breast svcs., 1991-93, assoc. prof. clin. surgery, 1995—2000; assoc. prof. surgery Sch. Medicine Stanford (Calif.) U., 2001—. Contbr. articles to profl. jours. Komen Breast Cancer Rsch. grant, Breast Cancer Rsch. Program grant State of Calif.; fellow UMDNJ-Robert Wood Johnson Med. Sch., 1987-88. Office: Stanford Univ Sch Medicine 300 Pasteur Drive Stanford CA 94305 Business E-Mail: wapnir@stanford.edu.

WARBURTON, WENDY, state legislator; b. Malta, Mont., Jan. 17, 1976; BS in Mass Comm., Liberty U., 1998. Pub. rels. assoc. writer/freelance writer Coun. for Exceptional Children, 2002—; mag. editor/comm. coord. Randolph Coll., 2004—06; field staff mgr. Friends of Conrad Burns, 2006; advertiser's adv. Tricia's Trader; mem. Dist. 34 Mont. House of Reps., 2008—. Republican. Christian. Office: Montana House of Representatives PO Box 200400 Helena MT 59620-0400 Mailing: 709 9th St Havre MT 59501-4141 Home Phone: 406-262-3185; Office Phone: 406-444-4800. Office Fax: 406-444-4825. Business E-Mail: wendywarburton@gmail.com.

WARD, CHESTER LAWRENCE, physician, consultant; b. Woodland, Calif., June 8, 1932; s. Benjamin Briggs and Nora Elizabeth Ward; m. Sally Diane Ward, Dec. 10, 1960; children: Katharine, Lynda. BA, U. Calif., Santa Barbara, 1955; MPH, U. Calif., Berkeley, 1966; MD, U. So. Calif., 1962; grad., Indsl. Coll. Armed Forces, 1978. Commd. 2d lt., inf. U.S. Army, 1954, advanced through grades to brig. gen., 1980; surgeon 5th Spl. Forces, Ft. Bragg, NC, Vietnam, 1963-64; chief aviation medicine, preventive medicine and aeromed. consultation service Ft. Rucker, Ala., 1967-68; surgeon Aviation Brigade and USA Vietnam Aviation Medicine Cons., 1968-69; flight surgeon Office of U.S. Army Surgeon Gen., 1970-71; physician The White House, Washington, 1971-75, 76; dir. environ. quality rsch. U.S. Army Med. Rsch. and Devel. Commd., 1975-76; comdr. Womack Cmty. Hosp., 1978—80; surgeon XVIII Airborne Corps, Ft. Bragg, 1978-80; comdr. William Beaumont Army Med. Ctr., El Paso, Tex., 1980-82; med. dir. Union Oil Co., Schaumburg, Ill., 1982-83, dir. domestic medicine LA, 1983-84; exec. dir. continuing med. edn. and clin. prof. emergency medicine U. So. Calif. Sch. Medicine, LA, 1984-85; dir., health officer Dept. Pub. Health, Butte County, Calif., 1985-95; cons., contractor, pvt. practice medicine, 1996—; med. dir. NorCal EMS, 2001—05. Trustee, pres. Oroville Union HS Dist., 1998—2002; chmn. Citizen's Bond Oversight Com., 2003—05; dir. The Estuary Owners' Assn., 2006—08, pres., 2007—08; apptd. by Gov. Wilson Calif. Commn. Emergency Med. Svcs., past commr. Decorated DSM, Legion of Merit (2), Bronze Star, Air medal (5). Fellow: Aerospace Med. Assn., Am. Coll. Preventive Medicine (past regent); mem.: No. Calif. Emergency Med. Svcs. Inc. (governing bd. 1987—2006, dir.), Calif. Med. Assn. (past del.), Butte-Glenn County Med. Soc. (past pres.), Mil. Officers Assn. (past chpt. pres.). Personal E-mail: tvldoc@sbcglobal.net.

WARD, DAVID SCHAD, scriptwriter, film director; b. Providence, Oct. 24, 1947; s. Robert McCollum and Miriam (Schad) W.; children: Joaquin Atwood, Sylvana Soto. BA, Pomona Coll., 1967; M.F.A., UCLA, 1970. Scriptwriter: films include Steelyard Blues, 1971, The Sting, 1973 (Acad. award best original screenplay 1973), The Milagro Beanfield War, 1988, (with Nora Ephron and Jeff Arch) Sleepless in Seattle, 1998 (Academy award nominee Best Original Screenplay 1998), (with John Eskow, Ted Elliott and Terry Rossio) The Mask of Zorro, 2006, (with Phil Sears and Blake T. Evans) Flyboys, 2006; writer, dir. films include Cannery Row, 1981, Major League, 1989, King Ralph, 1991, The Program, 1993, Major League II, 1995, Down Periscope, 1996. Mem.: Acad. Motion Picture Arts and Scis., Dirs. Guild Am. Office: c/o Ben Smith 8942 Wilshire Blvd Beverly Hills CA 90211

WARD, DORIS M., county official; BA in Govt., Ind. U., MS in Edn.; MA in Counseling, San Francisco State U.; PhD in Edn., U. Calif., Berkeley. Tchr. Indpls. Pub. Schs., 1959-67, team leader, supr. tchg. interns, 1967-68; adviser, counselor San Francisco STEP program, 1969-70; coord. curriculum San Mateo County Office of Edn., Redwood City, Calif., 1968-89; mem. bd. govs. San Francisco C.C., 1973-79; mem. bd. suprs. City and County San Francisco, 1980-92, pres. bd. suprs., 1991-92, assessor, recorder, 1992—, elected assessor-recorder, 1996. Adj. assoc. prof. Sch. Edn. Calif. State U., 1969-70, 72-73; advisor to External Masters Degree Program, U. San Francisco, 1972-76; chief cons. Calif. Assembly on regional govt., 1989-92. Contbr. articles to ednl. and polit. jours. Bd. dirs. Nat. Dem. County Officials 1987—, pres. 1994—; mem. Dem. Nat. Com., 1992—, del. 1984, 88, 92, 96 convs. Named Woman of Yr., Zeta Phi Beta, 1984; recipient Disting. Alumni award San Francisco State U., 1993, Disting. Comty. award, U. San Francisco, 1994, Spl. Merit award Sun Reporter Newspaper and numerous other awards for comty. svc. by activist orgns; grantee: NDEA, 1967, 68, Ind. State U., Terre Haute, Ind., Lilly Found., 1967, Rockefeller Found., U. Calif., Berkeley, 1974. Mem. Bay Area Assessors Assn. (sec. 1994, v.p. 95, pres. 96), Calif. Assessors' Assn. (mem. legis. com. 1993, exec. com. 95), Nat. Assn. Counties (bd. dirs. 1989-91, chair human svcs. and edn., 1991-92), Nat. Assn. Black County Officials (bd. dirs. 1987—, regional dir. 1987—), Nat. League of Cities (bd. dirs. 1991-92, vice chair and steering com. Fed. Adminstrn. Intergovtl. Rels. 1990-91), Nat. Black Caucus of Local Elected Officials (bd. dirs. 1987-95), Pi Sigma Alpha, Pi Lambda Theta. Office: City County San Francisco Assessor Recorder Office Rm 190 1 Dr Carlton B Goodlett Pl San Francisco CA 94102-4603

WARD, JOHN JAMES, bishop emeritus; b. LA, Sept. 28, 1920; Student, St. John's Sem., Camarillo, Calif., Catholic U. Am. Ordained priest Archdiocese of LA, 1946, aux. bishop, 1963—96; ordained bishop, 1963. Roman Catholic. Office: Archdiocese LA 3424 Wilshire Blvd Los Angeles CA 90010-2241

WARD, LESLIE ALLYSON, journalist, editor; b. LA, June 3, 1946; d. Harold Gordon and Marilyn Lucille (Dahlstead) W.; m. Robert L. Biggs, 1971 (div. 1977); m. Colman Robert Andrews, May 26, 1979 (div. 1988); m. John P. Lindsay, Oct. 10, 2003. AA, Coll. San Mateo, 1966; BA, UCLA, 1968, MJ, 1971. Reporter, researcher L.A. Bur. Life mag., 1971-72; reporter, news asst. L.A. bur. N.Y. Times, 1973-76; sr. editor New West mag., LA, 1976-78, 79-80; L.A. bur. chief US mag., 1978-79; Sunday style editor L.A. Herald Examiner, 1981-82, editor-in-chief Sunday mags., 1982-83, Olympics editor, 1984, sports editor, 1985-86, sr. writer, 1986; sr. editor L.A. Times Mag., 1988-90; travel editor L.A. Times, 1990—2003. Democrat. Office: LA Times Times Mirror Sq Los Angeles CA 90053

WARD, RONALD R., lawyer; b. Sacramento, June 12, 1947; BA, Calif. State U., 1973; JD, U. Calif., 1976. Bar: Calif. 1977, Wash., U.S. Dist. Ct. Calif. (No. Dist.) 1979, U.S. Dist Ct. (We. Dist.) Wash., U.S. Ct. Appeals (9th cir.). Asst. atty. gen. State of Wash., 1979—82; atty., shareholder Levinson Friedman PS, Seattle, 1982—2005, Jones & Ward, PLLC, Seattle, 2005—. Vol. reading tutor, tchr. asst. Hawthorne Sch., Seattle, mem. parent bd., mem. annual giving steering com.; mem. long-range planning com. Holy Names Acad., Seattle; bd. trustees N.W. Chamber Orch. Recipient President's award, Washington State Trial Lawyers, 2006, Outstanding Plaintiff Trial Lawyer award, Washington Def. Trial Lawyers, 2006; named Super Lawyer, Washington Law & Politics Mag., 2003—; named one of Top 40 Who's Who in Washington Plaintiff's Personal Injury Law, 2006, Top 40 Lawyers, Seattle Mag., 2007. Mem.: ABA (mem. Ho. of Dels. 2004—, mem. commn. for renaissance of idealism in the profession, mem. standing com. on pro bono and pub. svc., Partnership award 2005), Am. Bd. Trial Advocates, Loren Miller Bar Assn., Nat. Bar Assn. (Disting Svc. award 1994), Assn. Trial Lawyers Am., Wash. State Trial Lawyers Assn. (mem. bd. govs. 1989—96, co-chmn. Seattle downtown roundtable 1993—96, v.p. west 1994—96, Spl. Pres. Recognition award 1995), State Bar Calif., Fed. Bar Assn., Wash. State Bar Assn. (mem. bd. govs. 2002—03, pres.-elect 2003—04, pres. 2004—05), King County Bar Assn. Office: Jones & Ward PLLC 1000 Second Ave Ste 4050 Seattle WA 98104-1023 Office Phone: 206-957-1272. Office Fax: 206-957-1275. Business E-Mail: rrw@joneswardlaw.com.

WARDLAW, KIM A. MCLANE, federal judge; b. San Francisco, July 2, 1954; m. William M. Wardlaw Sr., Sept. 8, 1984. Student, Santa Clara U., 1972—73, Foothill C.C., Los Altos Hills, Calif., 1973—74; AB in Comm. summa cum laude, UCLA, 1976, JD with honors, 1979. Bar: Calif., US Dist. Ct. (ctrl. dist.) Calif. 1979, US Dist. Ct. (so. dist.) Calif. 1982, US Dist. Ct. Nev. 1985, US Dist. Ct. (no. dist.) Calif. 1992, US Dist. Ct. Mont. 1993, US Dist. Ct. Minn. 1994, US Dist. Ct. (no. dist.) Ala. 1994, US Dist. Ct. (so. dist.) Miss. 1995, US Supreme Ct. Law clk. US Dist. Ct. Ctrl. Dist. Calif., 1979—80; assoc. O'Melveny and Myers, 1980—87, ptnr., 1987—95; judge US Dist. Ct. Calif., LA, 1995—98, US Ct. Appeals (9th cir.), 1998—. Presdl. transition team Dept. Justice, Washington, 1993; mayoral transition team City of LA, 1995—; bd. govs. UCLA Ctr. for Comm. Policy, 1994—, vice-chair, 1994—; cons. in field. Co-author: The Encyclopedia of the American Constitution, 1986; contbr. articles to profl. jours. Pres. Women Lawyers Pub. Action Grant Found., 1986—87; founding mem. LA Chamber Orch., 1992—; active Legal Def. and Edn. Fund Calif. Leadership Coun., 1993—; active Blue Ribbon of LA Music Ctr., 1993—; del. Dem. Nat. Conv., 1992. Recipient Buddy award, NOW, 1995; named one of Most Prominent Bus. Attys. in LA County, LA Bus. Jour., 1995. Mem.: NOW, ABA, Orgn. Women Execs., Assn. Bus. Trial Lawyers (gov. 1988—), LA County Bar Assn. (trustee 1993—94), Women Lawyers Assn. LA, Calif. Women Lawyers, Mex.-Am. Bar Assn. LA County, Hollywood Womens Polit. Com., Downtown Women Ptnrs., City Club Bunker Hill, Breakfast Club, Chancery Club, Phi Beta Kappa. Office: US Ct Appeals 9th Cir 125 South Grand Ave Pasadena CA 91105

WARE, BILLY, musician; Mem. band BeauSoleil, 1976—. Albums include The Spirit of Cajun Music, 1976, Parlez Nous au Boire, 1984, Louisiana Cajun Music, 1984, Zydeco Gris Gris, 1985, Allons a Lafayette, 1986, Bayou Boogie, 1986, Bayou Cadillac, 1989, Live! From the Left Coast, 1989, Deja Vu, 1990, Cajun Conja, 1991, La Danse de la Vie, 1993, L'Echo, 1994, l'Amour ou la Folie, 1995 (Grammy award for Best Traditional Folk Album, 1997), Arc de Triomphe Two-Step, 1997, Looking Back Tomorrow, 2001, Gitane Cajun, 2004, Live at the 2008 New Orleans Jazz & Heritage Festival (Grammy award for Best Cajun Album, 2009), Live in Louisiana, 2006, Alligator Purse, 2009. Recipient Big Easy Entertainment award for Best Cajun Band, 2005. Office: care Rosebud Agy PO Box 170429 San Francisco CA 94117-0429

WARE, JAMES W., federal judge; b. 1946; BA, Calif. Luth. U., 1969; JD, Stanford U., 1972. Assoc. Blase, Valentine & Klein, Palo Alto, Calif., 1972-77, ptnr., 1977; judge Santa Clara County Superior Ct., U.S. Dist. Ct. (no. dist.) Calif., 1990—. Pro bono East Palo Alto Law Project. Active Am. Leadership Forum; mem. bd. visitors Stanford Law Sch.; active Martin Luther King Papers Project. 2nd lt. USAR, 1969-86. Office: US Dist Cts 280 S 1st St Rm 4150 San Jose CA 95113-3002

WARE, WILLIS HOWARD, computer scientist; b. Atlantic City, Aug. 31, 1920; s. Willis and Ethel (Rosswork) W.; m. Floy Hoffer, Oct. 10, 1943; children— Deborah Susanne Ware Pinson, David Willis, Alison Floy Ware Manoli. BSEE, U. Pa., 1941; MSEE, MIT, 1942; PhD in Elec. Engring, Princeton U., 1951. Research engr. Hazeltine Electronics Corp., Little Neck, N.Y., 1942-46; mem. research staff Inst. Advanced Study, Princeton, N.J., 1946-51, North Am. Aviation, Downey, Calif., 1951-52; mem. corp. research staff, research engr. Rand Corp., Santa Monica, Calif., 1952—. Adj. prof. UCLA Extension Service, 1955-68; first chmn. Am. Fedn. Info. Processing Socs., 1961, 62; chmn. HEW sec.'s Adv. Com. on Automated Personal Data Systems, 1971-73; mem. Privacy Protection Study Commn., 1975-77, vice chmn., 1975-77; mem. numerous other adv. groups, spl. coms. for fed. govt., 1959— Author: Digital Computer Technology and Design, vols. I and II, 1963. Recipient Computers Scis. Man of Yr. award Data Processing Mgmt. Assn., 1975, Exceptional Civilian Svc. medal USAF, 1979, Disting. Svc. award Am. Fedn. Info. Processing Socs., 1986, Nat. Computer Sys. Security award Nat. Computer Sys. Lab./Nat. Computer Security Ctr., 1989, Computer Pioneer award IEEE Computer Soc., 1993, Pioneer award Electronic Frontier Found., 1995, Kristain Beckman award Internat. Fedn. Info. Processing, 1999; named one of Fed. 100 of 1994, Fed. Computer Week. Fellow IEEE (Centennial medal 1984), AAAS, Assn. for Computing Machinery; mem. NAE, AIAA, Sigma Xi, Eta Kappa Nu, Pi Mu Epsilon, Tau Beta Pi. Office: 1700 Main St Santa Monica CA 90401-3208 E-mail: willis@rand.org.

WAREHAM, JOHN L., electronics executive; B in Pharmacy, Creighton U.; MBA, U. Wash. With SmithKline Beecham Corp., Phila., 1968-84, pres. Norden Labs., 1979-84; v.p. diagnostics sys. group Beckman Coulter Inc., Fullerton, Calif., 1984—, pres., COO, 1993-98, pres., CEO, chmn. bd., 1998—. Office: 4300 N Harbor Blvd Fullerton CA 92835-1091

WARFEL, MICHAEL WILLIAM, bishop; b. Elkhart, Ind., Sept. 16, 1948; s. Robert and Josephine (Rumshas) Warfel. Attended, Ind. U.; BA in Philosophy, St. Gregory's Coll. Sem., Cin.; MDiv, Mount St. Mary's Sem. West, 1980; MA in Theology, St. Michael's Coll., Winnoski, Vt., 1990. Ordained priest Archdiocese of Anchorage, 1980; ordained bishop, 1996; bishop Diocese of Juneau, Alaska, 1996—2007; apostolic adminstr. Diocese of Fairbanks, Alaska, 2001—02; bishop Diocese of Great Falls-Billings, Mont., 2007—. With US Army, 1967—71. Mem.: US Conf. Cath. Bishops. Roman Catholic. Avocation: languages. Office: Diocese of Great Falls-Billings Chancery Office 121 23rd St S PO Box 1399 Great Falls MT 59403 Office Phone: 406-727-6683. Office Fax: 406-454-3480.

WARFEL, SUSAN LEIGH, editor; b. LA, Aug. 5, 1959; Ba in Journalism, Sociology, U. So. Calif., LA, 1981. Bus. reporter L.A. Herald Examiner, 1981-83, Investor's Bus. Daily, LA, 1983-88, sr. editor, 1988-96, mng. editor, 1996—. Office: Investor's Bus Daily 12655 Beatrice St Los Angeles CA 90066-7303

WARFIELD, VIRGINIA (GINGER) MCSHANE, mathematics professor; b. Charlottesville, Va., Sept. 30, 1942; m. Bob Warfield, 1964 (dec. 1989); 3 children; m. Rosh Doan, 2005. AB with honors in Math. (cum laude), Bryn Mawr Coll., 1963; MA, Brown Univ., 1965, PhD, 1971. Tchg. asst. Brown Univ., 1964—67; dir., Project SEED Seattle Pub. Schools, 1970—73; part-time lectr., dept., math. Univ. Wash., 1973—83, dir., remedial math. prog., 1982—, full-time lectr., dept. math., 1983—91, sr. lectr., dept. math., 1991—. Conducts Brown Bag Seminars and posting electronic newsletters to expand the discussions Univ. Washington, 1993—; project dir. Preparing Future Faculty Project, 1994—2001; co-private investigator (Co-PI) in three major NSF-funded tchr. enhancement projects: Creating a Cmty. of Math. Learners, Extending the Cmty. of Math. Learners, Grad. Tchg. Fellows in K-12 Edn. (GK-12); co-private investigator (Co-PI) Teaching for the Environment: Active Mathematics on the Olympic Peninsula; creator Washington Teachers of Teachers of Math. Contbr. articles to peer-reviewed jours.; co-author: Discovery Method Algebra, 1993; co-editor: Theory of Situations: Didactique des Mathematiques 1970-1990 (English version), 1997, Théorie des Situations Didactiques (Didactiques des mathématiques 1970-1990, 1998; designer Math 107, Math 120 Math 170 & Math 171 classes. Mem.: Nat. Coun. of Teachers of Math., Assn. pour Rescherche en Didactiques des Math., Math. Assn. Am. (mem. com. on profl. develop. and math. edn.), Nat. Faculty, Assn. for Women in Math. (mem.-at-large, exec. com., chair, edn. com., mem. assn. review group for studying the revisions the NCTM standards, edn. column editor for newsletter, Louise Hay award for Contribution to Math. Edn. 2007), Sigma Xi. Avocations: hiking, palying any bowed instrument that sits on the shoulder (violin, viola, vielle), singing medieval music. Office: Univ Washington Dept Math PDL C-437 Box 354350 Seattle WA 98195-4350 Office Phone: 206-543-7445. Business E-Mail: warfield@math.washington.edu.

WARINER, JEREMY, Olympic track and field athlete; b. Irving, Tex., Jan. 31, 1984; Student, Baylor Univ. Mem. US Olympic Track & Field Team, Athens, Greece, 2004, Beijing, 2008; profl. runner, 2005—. Recipient Gold medal, 400m, 4x400m relay, Athens Olympic Games, 2004, Silver medal, 400m, Gold medal, 4x400m relay, Beijing Olympic Games, 2008, Gold medal, 400m, 4x400m relay, World Championships, 2005, 2007, ESPY award, Best Male Track Athlete, ESPN, 2007; named Mondo Outdoor Track Athlete of Yr., USA Track Coaches Assoc., 2004. Achievements include being NCAA Champion, Indoor 400m, 4x400m relay, Outdoor 400m, 4x400m relay, 2004. Office: c/o USOC 1 Olympic Plaza Colorado Springs CO 80909

WARING, JIM, state legislator; b. Hinsdale, Ill., 1967; BA in Polit. Sci., Northern Ill U., 1990; MA in Polit. Sci., Ariz. State U., 1992, MPA, 1994, PhD in Pub. Adminstrn., 1998. Mem. Dist. 7 Ariz. State Senate, 2003—, chair fin. com., vice-chair pub. safety & human svcs. com. Bd. dirs. Teach for America, 2001—04. Mem.: Am. Soc. Pub. Adminstrn. (pres. 2002—03), Phoenix 100 Rotary Club. Republican. Office: Ariz State Senate Capitol Complex 1700 w Washington Rm 302 Phoenix AZ 85007 Office Phone: 602-926-4916. Fax: 602-417-3250. E-mail: jwaring@azleg.gov.*

WARKENTIEN, MARK, professional sports team executive; m. Maureen Warkentien; children: Kreigh, Aubrie. Grad., Calif. State U., Fullerton, 1976. Coach Riverside City Coll., Saddleback Coll., U. Calif., Irvine, coach women's prog. Riverside; asst. coach Calif. State. U., Fullerton; asst. coach/recruiting coord., asst. athletic dir. UNLV, 1980—91; scout Seattle SuperSonics, 1991—94, Portland Trail Blazers, 1994—95, dir. scouting, 1995—98, asst. gen. mgr., 1998—2003, dir. player pers., 2003—04, Cleve. Cavaliers, 2004—05, interim gen. mgr., 2004—05; dir. player pers. Denver Nuggets, 2005—06, v.p. basketball ops., 2006—. Named NBA Exec. of Yr., 2009. Office: Denver Nuggets 1000 Chopper Cir Denver CO 80204*

WARNECKE, JOHN CARL, architect; b. Oakland, Calif., Feb. 24, 1919; s. Carl I. and Margaret (Esterling) W.; children by previous marriage: John Carl, Rodger Cushing, Margaret Esterling, Frederic Pierce. AB, Stanford U., 1941; MA, Harvard U., 1942. Asso. Miller & Warnecke, architects, 1944-46; prin. John Carl Warnecke, AIA, 1947-58; partner Warnecke & Warnecke, 1954-62; pres., dir. design John Carl Warnecke & Assoc., 1958—. Works include U.S. Naval Acad. Master Plan, Michelson and Chauvenet Halls, Annapolis, Md., U. Calif. at Santa Cruz Master Plan and Library, Lafayette Sq., Washington, Georgetown U. Library, Washington, Kaiser Center for Tech., Pleasanton, Calif.; bldgs., Stanford U., Hawaii State Capitol, Honolulu, Philip A. Hart Senate office bldg., USSR Embassy, Hennepin Govt. Center, Mpls., J.F. Kennedy Meml. Grave, Arlington Nat. Cemetery, Va., Neiman Marcus and Bergdorf Goodman Stores, Logan Airport, Boston, Am. Hosp, Paris, The Sun Co. Hdqrs, Radnor, Pa., King Abdulaziz U. Med. Center, Jedda, Saudi Arabia, Yanbu Town Ctr. Master Plan, Hilton Hotel & Casino, Atlantic City. Mem. Fine Arts Commn., Washington, 1963-67. Recipient Arnold Brunner prize in architecture Nat. Inst. Arts and Letters, 1957; also 70 nat., regional awards for excellence. Fellow AIA; Mem. NAD (assoc., 1958-94, academician, 1994-) Office: 300 Broadway St San Francisco CA 94133-4587 also: 1707 H St NW Ste 1100 Washington DC 20006-3919 also: 462 Broadway New York NY 10013-2618 also: 1180 S Beverly Dr Los Angeles CA 90035-1153 also: Warnecke-Sonoma Vineyard 13427 Chalk Hill Rd Healdsburg CA 95448-9043

WARNER, BRIAN HUGH See MANSON, MARILYN

WARNER, DENNIS ALLAN, psychology professor; b. Idaho Falls, Idaho, Apr. 27, 1940; s. Perry and Marcia E. (Finlayson) W.; m. Charyl Ann DeHart, Dec. 12, 1962; children: Lisa Rae, Sara Michelle, David Perry, Matthew Arie. BS, Brigham Young U., 1964; MS with honors, U. Oreg., 1966, PhD, 1968. Asst. prof. edn. Wash. State U., Pullman, 1968-72, assoc. prof. edn., 1972-78, prof. edn., 1978-85, dir. tchr. edn., 1983-85, prof., chmn. ednl. counseling psychology, 1985-93, interim dir. Partnership Ctr., 1993—94, 2004—06, prof. edn. leadership and counseling psychology, 1994—, assoc. dean Coll. Edn., 1999—2005, exec. assoc. dean Coll. Edn., 2006—, dir. H.S. equivalency program, 2004—. Vis. asst. prof. psychology U. Idaho, Moscow, 1971. Author: Interpreting and Improving Student Test Performance, 1982; contbr. articles to profl. jours. Postdoctoral research assoc. U. Kans., 1976-77. Fellow: APA. Mem. Lds Ch. Home: 645 SW Mies St Pullman WA 99163-2057 Office: Wash State Univ Coll Edn Cleveland Hl Rm 160B Pullman WA 99164-2114 Office Phone: 509-335-1738. Business E-Mail: dawarner@wsu.edu.

WARNER, HAROLD CLAY, JR., banker, investment company executive; b. Knoxville, Tenn., Feb. 24, 1939; s. Harold Clay and Mary Frances (Waters) W.; m. Patricia Alice Rethorst, Sept. 1, 1961; children: Martha Lee, Carol Frances. BS in Econs, U. Tenn., 1961, PhD, 1965. Asst. to pres. First Fed. Savs., Savannah, Ga., 1965-67; v.p. and economist No. Trust Co., Chgo., 1967-73; sr. v.p. and chief economist Crocker Nat. Bank, San Francisco, 1974-79, sr. v.p. liability mgmt., 1979-82; exec. v.p., dir. fixed income mgmt. BA Investment Mgmt. Corp., 1982-84, dir., pres., COO, 1984-86; dir., pres. Montgomery St. Income Securities, Inc., 1984-86; sr. v.p. Bank of Am., San Francisco, 1982-86; chmn. BA Investment Mgmt. Internat., Ltd., 1985-86; pres. Arthur D. Gimbel, Inc., San Mateo, Calif., 1986-87; exec. v.p., chief investment officer Riggs Nat. Bank Washington, 1987-88; chmn. Riggs Investment Mgmt. Corp., 1988-89; sr. v.p., chief economist Bank of Calif., San Francisco, 1989-93; pres., chief investment officer MERUS Capital Mgmt., San Francisco, 1989-93; pres. Govett Asset Mgmt. Co., 1993-95, Govett Fin. Svcs. Ltd., 1993-95; pres., COO Fisher Investments, Inc., Woodside, Calif., 1996; pres. Warner Fiduciary Counsel, LLC, San Francisco, 1997; 1st v.p., sr. dir. portfolio mgmt. Mellon Pvt. Wealth Mgmt., San Francisco, 1998—2007; sr. portfolio mgr., economist Mt. Eden Investment Advisors, San Francisco, 2007—. Lectr. dept. econs. U. Tenn., 1962-63, Grad. Sch. Bus., Loyola U., Chgo., 1969-73; lectr. Pacific Coast Banking Sch., U. Wash., 1978-79; bd. dirs. Children's Hosp. and Rsch. Ctr., 2007—. NDEA fellow, 1961-64 Mem. Burlingame Country Club, Pacific-Union Club, Phi Gamma Delta, Phi Eta Sigma, Beta Gamma Sigma, Omicron Delta Kappa, Phi Kappa Phi. Home: PO Box 2449 Yountville CA 94599-2449 Office: 343 Sansome St Ste 1600 San Francisco CA 94104 Home Phone: 650-347-7809; Office Phone: 415-288-3018. Business E-Mail: hcwarner@mtedeninvest.com.

WARNER, JOHN ARNAN, state supreme court justice; b. Great Falls, Mont., Jan. 22, 1943; s. James Arnan and Cleo (Schaedler) W.; m. Katherine Warner; children: Matthew, Marion, Ann, Jeffrey, Jonathan, Katherine. BA, U. Mont., 1965, LLB, 1967. Bar: Mont. 1967, U.S. Dist. Ct. Mont. 1967, U.S. Ct. Appeals (9th cir.) 1982. Law clk. Mont. Supreme Ct., Helena, Mont., 1967-68; ptnr. Bosch, Kuhr, et al, Havre, Mont., 1968-88; atty. City of Havre, 1984-88; dist. judge 12th Judicial Dist., Mont., 1988—2003; justice Mont. Supreme Ct., 2003—. Former chmn. Supreme Ct. Sentence Review Div.; former mem. Dist. Ct. Council; former chmn. Mont. Jud. Standards Commn.; mem. teaching staff Commn. on Cts. of Limited Jurisdiction; mem. Supreme Ct. Commn. to Review Canons of Jud. Ethics. Past pres. Mont. Swimming, Inc.; past chmn. Hill Top Recovery Bd.; past bd. dirs Mont. AAU; del. Mont. Officials Assn. Mem. ABA, Mont. Bar Assn. (trustee 1980-88, pres. 1987-88, mem. jud. relations com.), 12th Judicial Dist. Bar Assn. (past pres.), Def. Rsch. Inst., Lions (past pres. Havre chpt. swim team). Roman Catholic. Avocations: fishing, hunting, hiking. Office: Mont Supreme Ct Justice Bldg PO Box 203003 Helena MT 59620-3003 Office Phone: 406-444-5494. Business E-Mail: jwarner@mt.gov.

WARNER, JOHN HILLIARD, JR., technical services company executive; b. Santa Monica, Calif., Mar. 2, 1941; s. John Hilliard and Irene Anne (Oliva) W.; m. Helga Magdalena Farrington, Sept. 4, 1961; children: Tania Renee, James Michael BS in Engring. with honors, UCLA, 1963, MS in Engring., 1965, PhD in Engring., 1967. Mem. staff Marquardt Corp., Van Nuys, Calif., 1963; mem. faculty West Coast U., LA, 1969-72; mem. staff TRW Sys. Group, Redondo Beach, Calif., 1967-70, sect. mgr., 1970-73; mem. staff Sci. Applications Internat. Corp., San Diego, 1973-75, asst. v.p., 1975-77, v.p., 1977-80, corp. v.p., 1980-81, sr. v.p., 1981-87, sector v.p., 1987-89, exec. v.p., 1989-96, bd. dirs., 1988—2006, corp. exec. v.p., 1996—2005, chief adminstrv. officer, 2003—06, exec. v.p., 2005—07. Cons. Rand Corp., Santa Monica, 1964—66; bd. dirs. AMSEC LLC, 1997—2007, Mimix Broadband, 2006—08, TREX Enterprises, ICW Group, Cubic Corp.; ptnr. Limestone Ventures. Contbr. articles to profl. jours. Trustee Scripps Health, 2001-06; bd. dirs. Corp. Dirs. Forum, 2001—. AEC fellow, 1963, 66, NSF fellow, 1964, 65. Mem. AIAA, NDIA, Nat. Assn. Corp. Dirs., Healthcare Info. and Mgmt. Sys. Soc., Assn. US Army, Air Force Assn., Armed Forces Commn. and Electronics Assn., Navy League US, La Jolla Chamber Music Soc. (bd. dirs. 1990-97, adv. bd. 1998-2001), San Diego C. of C. (bd. dirs. 2000-04, 07), Calif. C. of C. (bd. dirs. 2000—07), Calif. Bus. Roundtable, Sigma Nu, Tau Beta Pi. Methodist. Avocations: bicycling, golf, fishing, music, travel.

WARNER, KURT (KURTIS EUGENE WARNER), professional football player; b. Burlington, Iowa, June 22, 1971; s. Gene and Sue Warner; m. Brenda Carney Meoni, Oct. 11, 1997; adopted children: Zachary, Jesse children: Elijah, Kade, Jadda, Sierra Rose, Sienna Rae. BA in Comm., No. Ill. U. Quarterback Green Bay Packers, 1994; quaterback Iowa Barnstormers (Arena Football League), 1995—97, Amsterdam Admirals (NFL Europe), 1998, St. Louis Rams, 1998—2004, NY Giants, 2004—05, Ariz. Cardinals, 2005—. Co-author (with Michael Silver): All Things Possible: My Story of Faith, Football and The Miracle Season, 2001. Co-founder First Things First Found., 2000—. Recipient Burt Bell award, Maxwell Football Club, 1999; named Gateway Conf. Offensive Player of Yr., NCAA, 1993, NFL MVP, AP, 1999, 2001, NFL All-Pro, 1999, 2001, Super Bowl XXXIV MVP, NFL, 2000; named to Nat. Football Conf. Pro Bowl Team, 1999—2001, 2008. Christian. Achievements include leading the NFL in: passing touchdowns, 1999, 2001, passer rating, 1999, 2001, passing yards per game, 2000, 2001, passing yards, 2001, pass completions, 2001, others; being a member of Super Bowl XXXIV winning St. Louis Rams, 2000; tying the NFL record with six consecutive 300-yard passing games, 2000; setting the Super Bowl record for passing yards and pass attempts without an interception, 2000. Office: 8701 S Hardy Dr Tempe AZ 85284*

WARNER, PAUL MICHAEL, federal judge, former prosecutor; b. 1952; BA, Brigham Young U., 1973, JD, 1976, MPA, 1984. Atty. judge advocate general's corps USN, 1976—82; asst. atty. gen. State of Utah, Salt Lake City, 1982—83; asst. US atty. Dist. Utah US Dept. Justice, Salt Lake City, 1983—96, US atty., 1996—2006; magistrate judge US Dist. Ct., Salt Lake City, 2006—. With USNR, 1976—82, advanced through ranks to col. Nat. Guard, 1983—, Utah. Office: US Dist Ct 350 S Main St Salt Lake City UT 84101

WARNER, VINCENT W., bishop; Bishop Diocese of Olympia, Seattle, 1990—. Office: Diocese of Olympia PO Box 12126 1551 10th Ave E Seattle WA 98102-4298

WARNOCK, JOHN EDWARD, computer company executive; b. Salt Lake City, Oct. 6, 1940; BS in Math. and Philosophy, U. Utah, 1961, MS in Math., 1964, PhD in Elec. Engring. and Computer Sci., 1969; DSc (hon.), Univ. Utah. With Evans & Sutherland Computer Corp., Computer Scis. Corp., IBM; prin. scientist Xerox Palo Alto Rsch. Ctr., Calif., 1978-81; co-founder, chmn. Adobe Sys., Inc., San Jose, Calif., 1982—, CEO, 1982—2000. Bd. dir. Octavo Corp. Patentee in field; contbr. articles to profl. jours. and industry mags.; spkr. in field. Bd. mem., past chmn. Tech Mus. Innovation; mem. entrepreneurial bd. adv. com. Am. Film Inst. Recipient Computer Achievement award Assn. for Computing Machinery SIGGRAPH, 1989, Tech. Excellence award Nat. Graphics Assn., 1989, ACM Software Sys. award, 1989, Lifetime Achievement award for tech. excellence, PC Mag., 1989, J. Anderson Disting. Achievement award, 1991, Disting. Alumnus award U. Utah, 1995, Cary award Rochester Inst. Tech., 1995, Fellow award, Computer History Mus., 2002; named Entrepreneur of Yr. Ernst & Young, Merril Lynch, Inc., 1991; named to Computer Reseller News Hall of Fame, 1998. Fellow Assn. for Computing Machinery, Am. Acad. Arts & Scis.; mem. NAE, Utah Info. Tech. Assn. Office: Adobe Sys Inc 345 Park Ave San Jose CA 95110-2704

WARREN, CHRISTOPHER CHARLES, electronics executive; b. Helena, Mont., July 27, 1949; s. William Louis and Myrtle Estelle (Moren) W.; m. Danette Marie Geordge, Apr. 21, 1972; 1 child, Jeffrey Scott. Grad. high sch., Helena, 1967. Electrician Supreme Electronics, Helena, 1972-81; v.p., svc. technician Capital Music Inc., Helena, 1981—. State exec. Amusement & Music Operators Assn. Coun. of Affiliated States, Chgo., 1990—. Sgt. USAF, 1968-72, Vietnam. Mem.: Amusement and Music Operators Assn. (bd. dirs. 1992—95, v.p. 1995—2000, sec. 2000—01, treas. 2001—02, 1st v.p. 2002—03, pres. 2003—04, past pres.'s coun. 2004—, Playmeter Mag. Operator of Yr. 2003), Rocky Mountain Elk Found., Ducks Unltd., Mont. Coin Machine Operators Assn. (pres. 1989—91, 1997—99, treas. 2000), Mont. Coin Machine Operators State 8-Ball (chmn.), Valley Nat. 8-Ball Assn. (charter), Internat. Flipper Pinball Assn. (sec./treas. 1991—92, pres. 1993—94), Eagles, Am. Legion, Moose, Vietnam Vets. Am. (life), VFW (life). Avocations: photography, restoring old cars and trucks, hunting, fishing. Home: 8473 Green Meadow Dr Helena MT 59602-8312 Office: Capital Music Inc PO Box 5416 Helena MT 59604-5416 Office Phone: 406-442-7088. E-mail: ccwar@aol.com.

WARREN, DIANE, lyricist; Staff writer Jack White, 1983; founder, owner RealSongs, LA. Author over 100 top ten pop songs including I'll Never Get Over You (Getting Over Me), How Do I Live, I Don't Want to Miss a Thing, If You Asked Me To, Don't Turn Around, Set The Night To Music, I'll Still Love You More, Because You Loved Me (Grammy award, song written specifically for a motion picture or TV, 1996), Rhythm of the Night, Nothing's Gonna Stop Us Now, Unbreak My Heart, Music of My Heart, My First Night With You (Nashville Songwriters Assn. Internat. award, superior creativity in the words and music of a song, 2000), I Will Get There (Nashville Songwriters Assn. Internat. award, superior creativity in the words and music of a song, 2000), There You'll Be, and many others. Hon. com. mem. PETA; founder, David S. Warren Weekly Entertainment Series, Jewish Home for the Aging; donor Wildlife Waystation, 10th Ann. Life Found., The Lange Found. Recipient Songwriter of Yr., Am. Soc. Composers, Authors & Publishers, 1990, 1991, 1993, 1998, 1999, Billboard, George and Ira Gershwin award, outstanding musical achievement, 1998, New Millennium Visionary award, Am. Cinema Awards Found., 1999, Legacy award, Orgn. For the Needs of the Elderly, 1999, Dream Maker's Cir. Award, Dream Found., 2000, Lifetime Achievement award, Bill Gavin Heritage Found., 2000, Angel award, Angels on Earth, 2000, Musician's Adv. award, Am. Soc. Young Musicians, 2001, Telly award, Found. for a Better Life, 2003; named Songwriter of Yr., Nat. Acad. Songwriters, 1996, No. 1 Pop Songwriter of Yr., Am. Songwriter Awards, 1997, Songwriter of Yr., Nashville Songwriters Assn. Internat., 2000; named one of 100 Most Powerful Women in Entertainment, Hollywood Reporter, 2006; named to Songwriters Hall of Fame, 2001, Hollywood Walk of Fame, 2001. Achievements include songs features in over 80 motion pictures. Office: Realsongs 6363 W Sunset Blvd Fl 8 Hollywood CA 90028-7330 Mailing: c/o The Chasen Co 8899 Beverly Blvd Ste 405 West Hollywood CA 90048

WARREN, JAMES RONALD, retired museum director, journalist; b. Goldendale, Wash., May 25, 1925; stepson H.S. W.; m. Gwen Davis, June 25, 1949; children: Gail, Jeffrey. BA, Wash. State U., 1949; MA, U. Wash., 1953, PhD, 1963. Adminstrv. v.p. Seattle Community Coll., 1965-69; pres. Edmonds Community Coll., Lynnwood, Wash., 1969-79; dir. Mus. of History and Industry, Seattle, 1979-89. Lectr. in field. Author history books; columnist Seattle Post Intelligencer, 1979-92, Seattle Times, 1992-96. Served with U.S. Army, 1943-45, ETO, prisoner-of-war, Germany. Mem. VFW, Am. Ex-POW Assn., 42d (Rainbow) Div. Vets., Rotary, also others. Home and Office: 3235 99th Ave NE Bellevue WA 98004-1803 Personal E-mail: jrgwarren@msn.com.

WARREN, KATHERINE VIRGINIA, art gallery director; b. Balt., Aug. 10, 1948; d. Joseph Melvin and Hilda Virginia (Thiele) Heim; m. David Hardy Warren; 1 child, Gabriel Kristopher Coy; 1 stepchild, Michael Jonathan Warren. BA, U. Calif., Riverside, 1976, MA, 1980. Asst. curator Calif. Mus. Photography, Riverside, 1979-80, acting dir., 1980-81, asst. dir., curator of edn., 1981-84; dir. univ. art gallery U. Calif., Riverside, 1980—2003, ret., 2003—. Bd. dirs. Riverside Arts Found., 1980-89, chmn. bd., 1986-88. Marius De Brabant fellow U. Calif., 1977-79. Mem. Am. Assn. Mus., Western Mus. Conf. Office: Sweeney Art Gallery U Calif Riv Side Riverside CA 92521-0001

WARREN, LARRY MICHAEL, clergyman; b. Bonne Terre, Mo., Nov. 25, 1946; s. Orson Wesley and Ruth Margaret (Stine) W.; m. Bonnie Jean Monk Chandler, Apr. 9, 1983; children: Samantha Chandler, John, Abigail Chandler, Anne, Meredith. BA cum laude, Lincoln U., 1969; MDiv with honors, St. Paul Sch. Theology, Kansas City, Mo., 1976; D of Ministry, San Francisco Theol. Sem., 1987. Ordained elder United Meth. Ch., 1978. Pastor Cainsville United Meth. Ch., Mo., 1975-76, Lakelands Parish, Rathdrum, Idaho, 1976-78; assoc. pastor Audubon Pk. United Meth. Ch., Spokane, Wash., 1978-83; pastor Faith United Meth. Ch., Everett, Wash., 1983-90, Tacoma First United Meth. Ch., 1990-95; co-pastor Renton First United Meth. Ch., 1995—2003; pastor Toppenish United Meth. Ch., Wash., 2003—, Summit United Meth. Ch., Wash., 2006—. Adviser Kairos Prison Ministry Wash., Monroe, 1984-92; conf. rep. grad. bd. St. Paul Sch. Theology, Kansas City, 1984, 94-96. Contbr. to col. Dialogue Everett Herald, 1984-88. Adviser DeMolay, Spokane, 1979-81; team mem. Night-Walk, inner-city ministry, Spokane, 1979-82;

coord. Ch. Relief Overseas Project Hunger Walk, Spokane and Everett, 1981, 85; vol. chaplain Gen. Hosp. Everett, 1983-90; trustee Deaconess Children's Svcs., Everett, 1983-88; bd. dirs. Tacoma Cmty. Ho., 2007—. Recipient Legion of Honor DeMolay Internat., 1982. Mem. Fellowship of Reconciliation, North Snohomish County Assn. Chs. (v.p. 1985-89), Pacific N.W. Ann. Conf. Bd. Global Ministries (sec. 1988-92, pres. 1993-97), Renton Ecumenical Assn. Chs. (pres. 1996-98). Democrat. Avocations: reading, travel, stamp collecting/philately, woodworking, coin collecting/numismatics. Office: Summit United Meth Ch 5316 104th St E Tacoma WA 98446 Office Phone: 253-537-6560. Personal E-mail: revlmw@msn.com.

WARREN, NEIL CLARK, Internet company executive, psychologist; b. Iowa, Sept. 18, 1934; m. Marylyn Warren; 3 children. BS in Social Sci., Pepperdine U., 1956; MDiv, Princeton Theological Sem., 1959; PhD in Clin. Psych., U. Chgo., 1967. Asst. prof. Fuller Theological Sem. Grad. Sch. Psych., 1967, dean, 1975—82; pvt. practice Neil Clark Warren & Assocs., 1967—2000; co-founder, chmn. eHarmony, 2000—. Author: Finding the Love of Your Life, 1992, Finding Contentment, 1997, Make Anger Your Ally, 1998, Learning to Live with the Love of Your Life, 1998, The Triumphant Marriage, 1998, God Said It, Don't Sweat It, 1998, Catching the Rhythm of Love, 2000, Falling in Love for All the Right Reasons, 2005; co-author: Love the Life You Live, 2003. Office: eHarmony PO Box 60157 Pasadena CA 91116 Office Phone: 626-795-4814. E-mail: media@neilclarkwarren.com.

WARREN, RICK (RICHARD DUANE WARREN), minister, writer; b. San Jose, Calif., Jan. 28, 1954; s. James Russell and Dorothy Nell (Armstrong) Warren; m. Elizabeth Kay Lewis, June 21, 1975; children: Amy Rebecca, Joshua James, Matthew David. BA, Calif. Bapt. Coll., 1977; MDiv, Southwestern Bapt. Theol. Sem., 1979; D in Ministry, Fuller Theol. Sem., 1989. Youth evangelist Calif. So. Bapt. Convention, Fresno, 1970-74; assoc. pastor First Bapt. Ch., Norwalk, Calif., 1974-76; asst. to pres. Internat. Evangelism Assn., Fort Worth, 1977-79; founding pastor Saddleback Valley Cmty. Ch., Mission Viejo, Calif., 1980—; founder Pastors Web site. Host Civil Forum on the Presidency, Lake Forest, Calif., 2008; keynote speaker Martin Luther King, Jr. Ann. Commemorative Svc., 2009. Author: The Purpose-Driven Church, 1995, Personal Bible Study Methods, 1997, The Power to Change Your Life, 1998, Answers to Life's Difficult Questions, 1999, Planned for God's Pleasure, 2002, The Purpose-Driven Life, 2002 (Gold Medallion award, ECPA Book of Yr., 2003), The Emerging Church, 2003, Daily Inspiration for the Purpose-Driven Life, 2004. Named an Outstanding Preacher, McGregor Found., 1977; named one of 15 World Leaders Who Mattered Most in 2004, TIME mag., The World's Most Influential People, 2005, 2008, America's Top 25 Leaders, US News & World Report, 2005, 15 People Who Make America Great, Newsweek, 2006. Baptist. Office: pastors.com 1 Saddleback Pky Lake Forest CA 92630-8700 also: Saddleback Valley Cmty Ch 24194 Alicia Pky Ste M San Juan Capistrano CA 92691-3927*

WARREN, ROBERT STEPHEN, lawyer; b. Pasadena, Calif., Dec. 9, 1931; s. Harry Ludwig and Maxine Winifred (Hopkins) W.; m. Betty Lou Soden, June 11, 1955 (dec. Sept. 1991); children: Kimberly Ann, Stephen Hopkins; m. Anna Marie Pretzel, Dec. 28, 1993. BA in Econs., U. Southern Calif., 1953, LLB, 1956. Bar: Calif. 1956, Del., U.S. Ct. Appeals (9th cir.), U.S. Dist. Ct. (ctrl. dist.) Calif., U.S. Ct. Mil. Appeals, U.S. Dist. Ct. (so. dist.) Calif., U.S. Dist. Ct. (ea. dist.) Calif., U.S. Dist. Ct. (no. dist.) Calif., U.S. Dist. Ct. Wyo., U.S. Dist. Ct. Colo., U.S. Dist. Ct. (ea. dist.) Wash., U.S. Supreme Ct. From assoc. to ptnr. Gibson, Dunn & Crutcher, LA, 1956, 59—. Contbr. articles to profl. jours.; assoc. editor Southern Calif. Law Rev.; speaker in field. Mem., former chair bd. councilors U. So. Calif. Law Ctr.; past pres., exec. com. mem. Western Justice Ctr. Found. 1st lt. US Army, 1957—59. Recipient Learned Hand award Am. Jewish Com., 1988, Shattuck-Price award Los Angeles County Bar Assn., 1989, Joseph A. Ball award Brennan Ctr. for Justice/NYU, 1997, Trial Lawyer Hall of Fame award Calif. State Bar Assn., 1998. Mem. Am. Coll. Trial Lawyers, Assn. Bus. Trial Lawyers, Order of Coif, City Club on Bunker Hill, Phi Beta Kappa. Republican. Presbyterian. Avocations: hiking, reading, tennis. Office: Gibson Dunn & Crutcher 333 S Grand Ave Ste 4400 Los Angeles CA 90071-3197 Office Phone: 213-229-7326. Business E-Mail: rwarren@gibsondunn.com.

WARREN, TODD, computer software company executive; Product develop. positions through corp. v.p. Microsoft Corp., Redmond, Wash., 1987—, gen. mgr. embedded devices group, 2001, corp. v.p. devices, services & eXperiences group, 2004, corp. v.p. gen. embedded bus., corp. v.p. mobile comm. product group, 2007—. Office: Microsoft Corp 1 Microsoft Way Redmond WA 98052-6399

WARRIOR, DELLA C., academic administrator, art educator; BA in Sociology, Northeastern State U.; MA in Edn., Harvard U. Pres. Inst. Am. Indian Arts, Santa Fe, devel. dir. CEO Otoe-Missouria Tribe, 1989—92; exec. bd. mem. World Indigenous Nations Higher Edn. Consortium; mem. U.S. Pres. Bd. Adv. on Tribal Coll. & U., 2002—.

WARRIOR, PADMASREE Y., computer systems network executive; b. Oct. 22, 1960; m. Mohandas A. Warrior. BSChemE, Indian Inst. Tech., New Delhi, India; MSChemE, Cornell U. Joined Motorola, Inc., Schaumburg, Ill., 1984, v.p., gen. mgr., energy sys. grp., corp. v.p., chief tech. officer, semiconductor products sector, v.p., 1999, corp. officer, 2000, sr. v.p., 2003—05, chief tech. officer, 2003—07, exec. v.p., 2005—07; chief tech. officer Cisco Systems, Inc., San Jose, Calif., 2007—. Gen. mgr. Thoughtbeam, Inc. (subsidiary of Motorola); mem. coun. digital economy Tex. Gov.; mem. rev. panel Tex. Higher Edn. Bd.; dir. Ferro Corp.; mem. exec. bd. CTO Forum. Recipient Women Elevating Sci. and Tech. award, Working Woman Mag., 2001; named one of Top 25 Chief Tech. Officers, InfoWorld mag., 2007, Most Influential Women in Technology, Fast Company, 2009; named to The Women In Tech. Internat. Hall of Fame, 2007. Office: Cisco Systems Inc 170 W Tasman Dr San Jose CA 95134*

WASDEN, LAWRENCE, state attorney general; m. Tracey Wasden; children: Sean, Ashley, Cassidy, Blake. BA, Brigham Young U., 1982; JD, U. Idaho, 1985. Bar: Idaho 1985. Dep. pros. atty. Canyon County, Idaho; dep. atty. gen. Idaho State Tax Commn.; dep. chief of staff State of Idaho, Boise, chief of staff to atty. gen., atty. gen., 2003—. Mem.: Idaho State Bar (founding mem., immediate past chmn. govt. and pub. lawyers sect.). Republican. Office: Office Atty Gen PO Box 83720 700 W Jefferson St Boise ID 83720 Office Phone: 208-334-2400.*

WASHBURN, JON, artistic director; Founder, condr., artistic and exec. dir. Vancouver (B.C., Can.) Chamber Choir, 1971—; condr., artistic dir. Phoenix (Ariz.) Bach Choir, 1992-98. Tchg. resident U. Cin., 1999, Ind. U., 2000, City U. Rio de Janeiro, 2000; guest condr. CBC Vancouver Orch., Masterpiece Ensemble, Phoenix Chamber Orch., Calgary, Edmonton, Nova Scotia, Phoenix and Vancouver Symphony Orchs.; guest condr. Santa Fe Desert Chorale, Estonian Philharmonic Chamber Choir, L.A. Master Chorale, Taipei Philharmonic Chorus, 2000; assoc. composer Can. Music Ctr.; mem. artistic juries Can. Coun.; tchr. in field. Composer, arranger over 80 choral compositions including Rossetti Songs, The Star, A Stephen Foster Medley, Chinese Melodies, Rise!Shine!, Noel Sing We; co-author God's Lamb. Co-recipient Music award Vancouver Awards; recipient Order of Can., 2001, Govt. of Can. Celebration 88 cert. of merit, Queen Elizabeth's Silver and Golden Jubilee medals, 2002, Louis Botto award Chorus Am., 2000, Disting. Svc. award Assn. Can. Choral Condrs., Margaret Hillis award for choral excellence, 1998. Office: Vancouver Chamber Choir 1254 W 7th Ave Vancouver BC Canada V6H 1B6 Office Phone: 604-738-6822. Business E-Mail: jon@vancouverchamberchoir.com. E-mail: info@vancouverchamberchoir.com.

WASHBURN, TED, state legislator; b. White Plains, NY, Apr. 9, 1941; m. Claudia Washburn; children: Raymond, Wendy Houghton, James. Attended, NY State Mcpl. Police Sch., 1963; attended Inservice Tng., NY State Police Acad., 1972; attended, FBI Nat. Acad., 1985. Police officer Bethlehem Police Dept., 1963—67; chief conservation officer NY State Dept. Environ. Conservation Police, 1967—98; com. mem. Precinct 30, 2006—08; mem. Dist. 69 Mont. House of Reps., 2008—. Republican. Christian. Office: Montana House of Representatives PO Box 200400 Helena MT 59620-0400 Mailing: 612 Candlelight Dr Bozeman MT 59718-7255 Home Phone: 406-388-1901; Office Phone: 406-444-4800. Office Fax: 406-444-4825. Business E-Mail: ted@tedwashburn.com.

WASHINGTON, A. EUGENE, medical educator; b. Houston, 1950; MD, U. Calif., San Francisco, 1976. Diplomate Am. Bd. Ob-Gyn., Am. Bd. Gen. Preventive Medicine. Intern USPHS, Staten Island, N.Y., 1976-77; resident Preventive Medicine Harvard U., 1977-79; resident Ob-Gyn. Stanford U., 1986-89; fellow Health Policy Inst. Health PS/U. Calif., San Francisco, 1983-86; prof. Ob-Gyn., Preventive Medicine U. Calif., San Francisco, prof. chair., obstetrics, gynecology, 1989—. Mem. AAAS, APHA, Soc. for Epidemiol. Rsch. Office: U Calif San Francisco PO Box 0132 San Francisco CA 94143-0001

WASHINGTON, DENNIS R., contracting company executive; b. Spokane, Wash., 1934; Equipment operator Guy F. Atkinson Co., Alaska; with King & McLaughlin Construction Co.; founder Washington Construction Co., Missoula, Mont., 1964; chmn., pres., CEO Morrison-Knudsen, 1999; chmn. Washington Group Internat., Inc. (formerly Morrison-Knudsen), Boise, Idaho. Founder Dennis & Phyllis Washington Found., 1998. Recipient Entrepreneurial award, Montana Ambassadors, Moles award outstanding achievement construction, Am. Soc. Civil Engineers, Lewis and Clark Pioneer award, Mont. Acad. Disting. Entrepreneurs, Golden Plate award, Acad. Achievement, Metal of Honor, Nat. Ethnic Coalition Organizations; named one of Forbes' RIchest Americans, 2006. Mem.: Horatio Alger Assn. (Norman Vincent Peale award), Am. Acad. Of Achievement. Office: Washington Group Internat Inc 720 Park Blvd Boise ID 83729 Mailing: The Dennis and Phyllis Washington Found PO Box 16630 Missoula MT 59808-6630 Office Phone: 208-386-5000. Office Fax: 208-386-7186.

WASHINGTON, DENZEL, actor; b. Mt. Vernon, NY, Dec. 28, 1954; s. Denzel and Lynn Washington; m. Pauletta Pearson, June 25, 1983; children: John David, Katia, Malcolm, Olivia. BA in Drama & Journalism, Fordham U., 1977; student, Am. Conservatory Theatre, San Francisco. With NY Shakespeare Festival, Manhattan Theatre Club, New Fed. Theatre. Stage appearances include Coriolanus, 1979, Spell No. 7, The Mighty Gents, Richard III, One Tiger to a Hill, Ceremonies in Old Dark Men, When the Chicken Comes Home to Roost (Audelco award), A Soldier's Play (Obie award 1981), Checkmates, 1988, Split Second, Julius Caesar, 2005; actor: (films) Carbon Copy, 1981, A Soldier's Story, 1981, Power, 1986, Cry Freedom (NAACP Image award, 1987), 1987, For Queen and Country, 1988, The Mighty Quinn, 1989, Glory, 1989 (Golden Globe award 1989, Acad. award for Best Supporting Actor, 1990, NAACP Image award, 1990), Heart Condition, 1990, Mo' Better Blues, 1990, Ricochet, 1991, Mississippi Masala, 1992, Malcolm X, 1992, Much Ado About Nothing, 1993, Philadelphia, 1993, The Pelican Brief, 1993, Crimson Tide, 1995, Virtuosity, 1995, Devil in a Blue Dress, 1995, Courage Under Fire, 1996 (NAACP Image award, 1997), The Preacher's Wife, 1996, Fallen, 1998, He Got Game, 1998, The Siege, 1998, The Bone Collector, 1999, The Hurricane, 2000 (nominee Best Actor Acad. award 2000, Golden Globe award for Best Performance by Actor in Motion Picture Drama 2000), Remember the Titans, 2000, Training Day, 2001 (Acad. award for Best Actor, 2002, nominee Golden Globe award for Best Performance by Actor in Motion Picture Drama 2002), John Q, 2002, Out Of Time, 2003, Man on Fire, 2004, The Manchurian Candidate, 2004, Inside Man, 2006, Déjà Vu, 2006, American Gangster, 2007; actor, dir., prodr. The Antwone Fisher Story, 2002; actor, dir. The Great Debaters, 2007 (Best Picture, African Am. Film Critics Assn., 2007, Outstanding Motion Picture, NAACP Image award, 2008, Outstanding Actor, 2008); actor (TV movies) Wilma, 1977, License to Kill, 1984, The George McKenna Story, 1986; (mini-series) Flesh and Blood, 1979; (TV series) St. Elsewhere, 1982-88; co-author (with Daniel Paisner) A Hand to Guide Me, 2006. Spokesperson Boys and Girls Clubs Am. Recipient Harvard Found. award, 1996, Whitmey M. Young award, L.A. Urban League, 1997, Herbert Hoover Humanitarian award, The Boys & Girls Clubs of America, 2004, Golden Plate award, Acad. Achievement, 2005, Stanley Kubrick Britannia award for Excellence in Film BAFTA/LA Cunard Britannia awards, 2007, Frederick D. Patterson award (with wife Pauletta), United Negro Coll. Fund, 2008; Am. Conservatory Theater scholar; named one of 50 Most Powerful People in Hollywood Premiere mag., 2002-06; named America's Favorite Movie Star, Harris Poll, 2007-08; named to Power 150 Ebony mag., 2008. Avocations: basketball, reading, cooking.

WASHINGTON, JAMES WINSTON, JR., artist, sculptor; b. Gloster, Miss., Nov. 10, 1909; s. James and Lizie (Howard) W.; m. Janie R. Miller, Mar. 29, 1943. Student, Nat. Landscape Inst., 1944-47; D.F.A., Center Urban-Black Studies, 1975. Tchr. summer class N.W. Theol. Union Seattle U., 1988. One man shows U.S.O. Gallery, Little Rock, 1943, Foster-White Gallery, Seattle, 1974, 78, 80, 83, 89 (also at Bellevue Art Mus., 89), Charles and Emma Frye Art Mus., Seattle, 1980, 95, Mus. History and Industry, Seattle, 1981; exhibited in group shows Willard Gallery, N.Y.C., 1960-64, Feingarten Galleries, San Francisco, 1958-59, Grosvenor Gallery, London, Eng., 1964, Lee Nordness Gallery, N.Y.C, 1962 Woodside Gallery, Seattle, 1962-65, Foster-White Gallery, Seattle, 1974, 76, 89, 92, Smithsonian Instn., 1974, San Diego, 1977, others; retrospective exhbn. Bellevue Art Mus., Washington, 1989; represented in permanent collections Seattle, San Francisco, Oakland art museums, Seattle First Nat. Bank, Seattle Pub. Libr. YWCA, Seattle, Meany Jr. H.S., Seattle World's Fair, Expo 70 Osaka, Japan, Whitney Mus. Am. Art, N.Y.C.; commd. sculpture: Bird With Covey, Wash. State Capitol Mus., Olympia, 1983, Obelisk with Phoenix and Esoteric Symbols of Nature in granite, Sheraton Hotel Seattle, 1982, Life Surrounding the Astral Alter, In Matrix, owner T.M. Rosenblume, Charles Z. Smith & Assocs., Seattle, 1986, The Oracle of Truth (6 1/2 ton sculpture) Mt. Zion Bapt. Ch., Seattle, 1987, commd. sculptures King County Arts Commn., 1989, Bailey Gatzent Elem. Sch., Seattle, 1991, Twin Eaglets of the Cosmic Cycle (Quincy Jones), 1993, Fountain of Triumph (Bangasser Assocs. Inc.), 1992-93, Seattle, 1993-94, 94-95, Child in Matrix, 1995, Blunt Tail Owl, 1996, Bunny Rabbit and Robbin, 1996; author book of poetry Poems of Life, 1997 (Internat. Hall of Fame Nat. Soc. Poets). Passover leader Mt. Zion Baptist Ch., Seattle, 1974-87; founder James W. Washington, Jr. and Mrs. Janie Rogella Washington Found. Recipient Spl. Commendation award for many contbns. to artistic heritage of state Gov., 1973, plaque City of Seattle, 1973, plaque Benefit Guild, Inc., 1973, arts service award King County Arts Commn., 1984, cert. of recognition Gov. of Wash., 1984, Editor's Choice award Outstanding Achievement in Poetry Nat. Libr. Poetry, 1993; named to Wash. State Centennial Hall of Honor, Wash. State Hist. Soc., 1984; home and studio designated historic landmark (city and state), 1991; Dr. James W. Washington Jr. and Mrs. Janie Rosella Washington Found. established, 1997. Mem. Internat. Platform Assn., Internat. Soc. Poets (life, awards 1993), Profl. Artists Phila., Masons (33d degree).

WASHINGTON, KERRY, actor; b. Bronx, NY, Jan. 31, 1977; BFA theatre, George Washington Univ., 1998. Actor: (TV films) Magical Make-Over, 1994; (films) Our Song, 2000, 3D, Save the Last Dance, 2001, Lift, 2001, Take the A Train, Bad Company, 2002, United States of Lelan, 2003, The Human Stain, 2003, Sin, 2003, Against the Ropes, 2004, Strip Search, 2004, She Hate Me, 2004, Ray, 2004, Sexual Life, 2005, Mr. & Mrs. Smith, 2005, Fantastic Four, 2005, Wait, 2005, Little Man, 2006, The Last King of Scotland, 2006, The Dead Girl, 2006, I Think I Love My Wife, 2007, Miracle at St. Anna, 2008, Lakeview Terrace, 2008. Nominee Best Female Actress, Ind. Spirit Awards, 2002. Office: c/o Washington Square Arts The Lot Writers Bldg 1041 North Formosa Ave West Hollywood CA 90046

WASHINGTON, WARREN MORTON, meteorologist; b. Portland, Oreg., Aug. 28, 1936; s. Edwin and Dorothy Grace (Morton) W.; m. LaRae Herring, July 30, 1959 (div. Aug. 1975); children: Teri, Kim, Marc (dec.), Tracy; m. Jona Ann, July 3, 1978 (dec. Jan. 1987); m. Mary Elizabeth Washington, Apr., 1995. BS in Physics, Ore. State U., 1958, MS in Meteorology, 1960; PhD in Meteorology, Pa. State U., 1964; degree (hon.), Oreg. State U., 2006. Dir. of climate and global dynamics div. Nat. Center Atmospheric Research, Boulder, Colo., 1978-95; affiliate prof. meteorology oceanography U. Mich. at Ann Arbor, 1968-71; mem. Nat. Adv. Com. for Oceans and Atmospheres, 1978-84. Mem. sec. of energy adv. bd. U.S. Dept. Energy, 1990-93; mem. Nat. Sci. Bd., 1994-2006, chair, 2002-06. Contbr. articles to meteorol. jours. Mem. Boulder Human Rels. Commn., 1969-71; mem. Gov.'s Sci. Adv. Com., 1975-78. Recipient Disting. Alumni award Oreg. State U., 1991, E.B. Lemon Disting. Alumni award Pa. State U., 1991, Le Verrier medal Soc. Meteorol. France, 1995, Bonfils-Stanton Found. award, 2000, Vollum award Reed Coll., 2005; inductee NAS portrait collection African Am. in Sci., Engring., and Medicine, 1997; named Sigma Xi Disting. lectr., 1998-99. Fellow AAAS (bd. dirs.), Am. Meteorol. Soc. (pres. 1994, Anderson award 2000, Charles Brook award 2007); mem. NAE, Am. Philosophy Soc., Am. Geog. Union. Office: PO Box 3000 Boulder CO 80307-3000 Home: 8633 E Iliff Dr Denver CO 80231-3810

WASSER, DENNIS MATTHEW, lawyer; b. Bklyn., Aug. 27, 1942; BA with honors, U. Calif. LA, 1964; JD, U. So. Calif., 1967. Bar: Calif. 1968, cert.: State Bar Calif. Bd. Legal Specialization (specialist in family law). Ptnr. Wasser, Cooperman & Carter, LA. Lectr. in field; co-instr. advanced profl. program family law U. So. Calif., 1989; instr. U. Calif. LA. Contbr. articles to profl. jours. Mem.: ABA, Am. Acad. Matrimonial Lawyers, LA County Bar Assn. (chmn. 1984, mem. exec. com. family law sect. 1978—88), Beverly Hills Bar Assn. (chmn. family law sect. 1978—79). Office: Wasser Cooperman & Carter Ste 1200 One Century Plz 2029 Century Park E Los Angeles CA 90067 Office Phone: 310-277-7117. Office Fax: 310-553-1793.

WASSER, LAURA ALLISON, lawyer; b. LA, May 23, 1968; d. Dennis Wasser. BA, U. Calif. Berkeley, 1991; JD, Loyola Law Sch., 1994. Bar: Calif. 1994. Ptnr. Wasser, Cooperman & Carter, LA. V.p. fin. devel., bd. dirs. Harriet Buhai Ctr. Family Law. Mem.: Calif. State Bar Assn., LA County Bar Assn., Beverly Hills Bar Assn. Office: Wasser Cooperman & Carter Ste 1200 One Century Plz 2029 Century Park E Los Angeles CA 90067 Office Phone: 310-277-7117. Office Fax: 310-553-1793.

WASSERBURG, GERALD JOSEPH, geology and geophysics educator; b. New Brunswick, NJ, Mar. 25, 1927; s. Charles and Sarah (Levine) W.; m. Naomi Z. Orlick, Dec. 21, 1951; children: Charles David, Daniel Morris. Student, Rutgers U., 1946—48; BS in Physics, U. Chgo., 1951, MSc in Geology, 1952, PhD, 1954, DSc (hon.), 1992; D (hon.), Brussels U., 1985, U. Paris, 1986; DSc (hon.), Ariz. State U., 1987, U. Rennes, 1998, U. Turino, Italy, 2000. Rsch. assoc. Inst. Nuc. Studies U. Chgo., 1954-55; asst. prof. Calif. Inst. Tech., Pasadena, 1955-59, assoc. prof., 1959-62, prof. geology and geophysics, 1962-82, John D. MacArthur prof. geology and geophysics, 1982—2001, prof. emeritus, 2001—. Served on Juneau Ice Field Rsch. Project, 1950; cons. Argonne Nat. Lab., Lamont, Ill., 1952-55; former mem. U.S. Nat. Com. for Geochem., com. for Planetary Exploration Study, NRC, adv. coun. Petroleum Rsch. Fund, Am. Chem. Soc.; me. lunar sample analysis planning team (LSAPT) manned Spacecraft Ctr., NASA, Houston, 1968-71, chmn., 1970; lunar sample rev. bd., 1970-72; mem. Facilities Working Group LSAPT, Johnson Space Ctr., 1972-82; mem. sci. working panel for Apollo missions, Johnson Space Ctr., 1971-73; advisor NASA, 1968-88, phys. scis. com., 1971-75, mem. lunar base steering com., 1984; chmn. com. for planetary and lunar exploration, mem. space sci. bd. NAS, 1975-78; chmn. divsn. Geol. and Planetary Scis., Calif. Inst. Tech., 1987-89; vis. prof. U. Kiel, Fed. Republic of Germany, 1960, Harvard U., 1962, U. Bern, Switzerland, 1966, Swiss Fed. Tech. Inst., 1967, Max Planck Inst.,

Mainz and Heidelberg, Fed. Republic of Germany, 1985, others; invited lectr., Vinton Hayes Sr. fellow Harvard U., 1980, Jaeger-Hales lectr. Australian Nat. U., 1980, Harold Jeffreys lectr. Royal Astron. Soc., 1981, Ernst Cloos lectr. Johns Hopkins U., 1984, H.L. Welsh Disting. lectr. U. Toronto, 1986, Danz lectr. U. Wash., 1989, Goldschmidt Centennial lectr. Norwegian Acad. Sci. and Letters, 1989, Lindsay lectr. Goddard Space Flight Ctr., 1996, other lectureshipss; plenary spkr. 125th Anniversary Geol. Soc. Sweden, 1996; 60th Anniversary Symposium spkr. Hebrew U., Jerusalem, 1985, 75th Anniversary Symposium spkr., 2000; Lezione Magistrale, Umbria Libri, Perugia, 2003. Rifleman U.S. Army, 1943-46. Decorated Combat Inf. badge, 2nd Dion Combat Inf. Trymers badge; recipient Group Achievement award NASA, 1969, Exceptional Sci. Achievement award NASA, 1970, Disting. Pub. Svc. medal NASA, 1973, J.F. Kemp medal Columbia U., 1973, Profl. Achievement award U. Chgo. Alumni Assn., 1978, Goldschmidt medal Geochem. Soc., 1978, Disting. Pub. Svc. medal with cluster NASA, 1978, Wollaston medal Geol. Soc. London, 1985, Sr. Scientist award Alexander von Humboldt-Stiftung, 1985, Crafoord prize Royal Swedish Acad. Scis., 1986, Holmes medal, 1987, Regents fellow Smithsonian Inst., Gold medal Royal Astron. Soc., 1991; named Hon. Fgn. fellow European Union Geoscis., 1983. Fellow Am. Acad. Arts and Scis., Geol. Soc. London (hon.), Geol. Soc. Am., Am. Geophys. Union (planetology sect., Harry H. Hess medal 1985, Bowie medal, 2008), Geol. Soc. Am. (life, Arthur L. Day medal 1970), Meteoritical Soc. (pres. 1987-88, Leonard medal 1975), Geochemical Society and the European Assn. for Geochemistry, 1996; mem. Nat. Acad. Scis. (Arthur L. Day prize and lectureship 1981, J. Lawrence Smith medal 1985), Norwegian Acad. Sci. and Letters, Am. Phil. Soc. Achievements include research in geochemistry and geophysics and the application of the methods of chemical physics to problems in the earth scis. Major researches have been the determination of the time scales of nucleosynthesis, connections between the interstellar medium and solar material, the time of the formation of the solar system, the chronology and evolution of the earth, moon and meteorites, the establishment of dating methods using long-lived natural radio-activities, the study of geologic and cosmic processes using nuclear and isotopic effects as a tracer in nature, the origin of natural gases, and the application of thermodynamic methods to geologic systems. Office: Calif Inst Tech Divsn Geol & Planetary Scis Pasadena CA 91125-2500 Business E-Mail: gjw@gps.caltech.edu.

WASSERMAN, ANTHONY IRA, software company executive, educator; b. Bronx, NY, Mar. 1, 1945; s. Joseph K. and Frances (Hirsch) W.; m. Susan Gail Cohen, June 11, 1966; children: Mark, Michelle. AB in Math. and Physics, U. Calif., Berkeley, 1966; MS in Computer Sci., U. Wis., 1967, PhD in Computer Sci., 1970. Prof. med. info. sci. U. Calif., San Francisco, 1973-88; pres., CEO Interactive Devel. Environments, Inc., San Francisco, 1983-93, also chmn. bd. dirs.; pres. Software Methods and Tools, San Francisco, 1997—. Lectr. computer sci. U. Calif., Berkeley, 1971-86, vis. prof., 1996. Editor: Software Development Environments, 1981, Software Design Techniques, 4th edit., 1983, others; contbr. articles to prol. jours. Recipient Silver Core award Internat. Fedn. Info. Processing, 1986. Fellow IEEE, Assn. Computing Machinery (editor-in-chief ACM Computing Surveys 1983-86, Disting. Svc. award 1995). Democrat. Avocations: running, photography. E-mail: twasserman@mindspring.com.

WASSERMAN, BARRY L(EE), architect; b. Cambridge, Mass., May 25, 1935; s. Theodore and Adelaide (Levin) Wasserman; m. Wilma Louise Greenfield, June 21, 1957 (div. 1971); children: Tim Andrew, Andrew Glenn; m. Judith Ella Michalowski, Apr. 22, 1979. BA, Harvard U., 1957, M. Arch., 1960. Registered arch., Calif. Assoc. John S. Bolles Assocs., San Francisco, 1960-69; prin. Wasserman-Herman Assocs., San Francisco, 1969-72; prin., dir. Office Lawrence Halprin U Assocs., San Francisco, 1972-76; dep. state architect State of Calif., Sacramento, 1976-78, state architect, 1978-83; prof. dept. architecture, dir. Inst. Environ. Design, Sch. Environ. Design Calif. State Poly. U., Pomona, 1983-87, chair dept. architecture, Coll. Environ. Design, 1988-96, prof. emeritus, 1997—. Program advisor Fla. A&M U., Tallahassee, 1981—83; adv. com. Interior Design Program Calif. State U., Sacramento, 2004—; bd. dirs. Environ. Coun. Sacramento; design rev. adminstr. Sacramento County, 2006—; cons. in field. Prin. works include Wasserman House, San Rafael, Calif., 1963 (AIA-Sunset Mag. award of Merit, 1965), Anna Waden Libr., San Francisco, 1969 (AIA award of Merit, 1970), Capitol Area Plan, Sacramento, 1977 (Ctrl. Valley chpt. AIA Honor award, 1979); co-author: Ethics and the Practice of Architecture, 2000. Mem. City of Sacramento Planning Commn., 2004—. Recipient awards citation, Prog. Architecture 26th Awards Program, 1979, Octavius Morgan award, Calif. Archs. Bd., 2000. Fellow: AIA (chmn. architecture govt. com. 1979, bd. dirs. environ. coun. Sacramento 2004—). Democrat. Jewish. Home: 6456 Fordham Way Sacramento CA 95831-2218 E-mail: blw2@mindspring.com.

WASSERMAN, CASEY, media company executive; b. 1974; s. Lynne Wasserman; m. Laura Ziffren. BA in Polit. Sci., UCLA, 1996. Founder, chmn., CEO Wasserman Media Group, LLC, 1998—. Owner, Arena Football League team LA Avengers, 1998—; chmn. Arena Football League, 2002—05, mem. exec. com., 2005—. Pres., CEO Wasserman Found.; bd. dirs. NYU, William Jefferson Clinton Presdl. Libr. Found., LA Philharmonic, Jules Stein Eye Inst. Named an Forty Under 40, Sports Bus. Jour.; named one of 25 Most Power Angelenos, LA Bus. Jour., The Most Influential People in the World of Sports, Bus. Week, 2007, 2008; named to Sports Bus. Jour.'s Most Influential List, 2006. Achievements include becoming the youngest owner of a professional sports team at age 24. Office: Wasserman Media Group LLC 12100 W Olympic Blvd Ste 400 Los Angeles CA 90064-1052

WASSERMAN, ROBERT, Mayor, Fremont, California; b. Gary, Ind., Jan. 12, 1934; s. Morris K. and Alice Wasserman; m. Mary Linda Galantin, Sept. 13, 1958; children: Daniel Joseph, Jill Marie. BS Law Enforcement Adminstrn., Calif. State U., 1963; MPA, U. So. Calif., 1975. Chief of police City of San Carlos, Calif., 1969—72, City of Brea and Yorba Linda, Calif., 1972—76, City of Fremont, Calif., 1976—91; councilman Fremont City Council, 1992—2004; mayor Fremont, Calif., 1992—. Chmn. adv. com. Calif. Commn. on Peace Officer Stds. and Tng., 1979—83, mem., Pres.'s Adv. Com. Law Enforcement; cons. to police agys.; Contbr. articles to profl. jours. Bd. mgrs. Fremont-Newark YMCA, 1978—; mem. Internat. Assn. Chiefs of Police, Calif. Peace Officers Assn., 1980—. Served US Army, 1950—52, Korean War. Mem.: Rotary. Democrat. Avocations: sports, reading, travel. Office: City Hall 3300 Capitol Avenue PO Box 5006 Fremont CA 94537 Office Phone: 510-284-4011. Business E-Mail: bwasserman@ci.fremont.ca.us.*

WASSERMAN, STEPHEN IRA, allergist, immunologist, educator; b. LA, Dec. 17, 1942; m. Linda Morgan; children: Matthew, Zachary. BA, Stanford U., 1964; MD, UCLA, 1968. Diplomate Am. Bd. Internal Medicine, Am. Bd. Allergy and Immunology. Intern, resident Peter B. Brigham Hosp., Boston, 1968-70; fellow in allergy, immunology Robert B. Brigham Hosp., Boston, 1972-75; asst. prof. medicine Harvard U., Boston, 1975-79, assoc. prof., 1979, U. Calif.-San Diego, La Jolla, 1979-85, prof., 1985—, chief allergy tng. program Sch. Medicine, 1979-85, chief allergy div. Sch. Medicine, 1985-93, acting chmn. dept. medicine, 1986-88, chmn. dept. medicine, 1988-2000, Helen M. Ranney prof., 1992—2001, chief allergy tng.program Sch. Medicine, 2001—05. Co-dir. allergy sect. Robert B. and Peter B. Brigham Hosps., 1977-79; dir. Am. Bd. Allergy and Immunology; dir. Am. Bd. Internal Medicine., chair, 1999-2000. Contbr. articles to profl. jours. Served to lt. comdr. USPHS, 1970-72, San Francisco. Fellow Am. Acad. Allergy and Immunology (pres. 1997-98); mem. Am. Soc. Clin. Investigation, Assn. Am. Physicians, Am. Assn. Immunologists, Collegium Internationale Allergologicum, Phi Beta Kappa, Alpha Omega Alpha. Office: U Calif San Diego Stein Clin Rsch Bldg Rm 244 9500 Gilman Dr MC 0637 San Diego CA 92093-0637

WASSERMAN, WILLIAM PHILLIP, lawyer; b. LA, Sept. 13, 1945; s. Al and Ceil (Diamond) W.; married; children: Sam, George. BA, U. Calif., Berkeley, 1967; JD, U. Calif., 1970. Bar: Calif. 1971, U.S. Tax Ct. 1971. Ptnr. Ernst & Young LLP, Los Angeles, 1970—. Lectr. in field.; participant in numerous programs, confs., and workshops in field in field. Mem. Editorial adv. bd.: Real Estate Taxation: A Practitioner's Guide, 1984—, Federal Tax Annual: Real Estate, 1982; contbr. numerous articles to profl. jours. Mem. ABA (nat. chmn Tax Sect. com. on real estate problems 1985-87), State Bar Calif., Los Angeles County Bar Assn., Calif. Bd. Legal Specialization (cert. taxation law specialist). Office: Ernst & Young LLP 725 S Figueroa St Los Angeles CA 90017-5524

WASTERLAIN, CLAUDE GUY, neurologist; s. Desire and Simone (De Taeye) W.; m. Anne Marguerite Thomsin, Feb. 28, 1967; 1 child, Jean Michel. Cand. Sci., U. Liege, 1957, MD, 1961; degree in Libr. Sci., Molecular Biology summa cum laude, Free U. Brussels, 1969. Resident Cornell U. Med. Coll., NYC, 1964-67, instr. neurology, 1969-70, asst. prof., 1970-75, assoc. prof., 1975-76, UCLA Sch. Medicine, 1976-79, prof., 1979—2005, vice-chair dept. neurology, 1976—, disting. prof., 2005—; chief neurology svc. VA Med. Ctr., Sepulveda, Calif., 1976—98; chair neurology Greater LA VA Health Care Sys., 1998—. Attending neurologist UCLA Ctr. Health Scis., 1976—. Author, editor: Status Epilepticus, 1984, Neonatal Seizures, 1990, Molecular Neurobiology and Epilepsy, 1992, Progressive Nature of Epileptogenesis, 1996, Status Epilepticus: Mechanism Management, 2006; contbr. articles to med. jours. Recipient N.Y. Neurol. Soc. Young Investigator award, 1965; Rsch. Career Devel. award NIH, 1973-76; William Evans fellow, U. Auckland, New Zealand, 1984; Worldwide AES award for rsch. in epilepsy, 1992; Golden Hammer Tchg. award, 1996; Amb. for Epilepsy, Internat. League Against Epilepsy, 2003; Pierre Gloor award Am. Clin. Neurophysiology Soc., 2006. Fellow Am. Acad. Neurology; mem. Am. Neurol. Assn., Am. Soc. Neurochemistry (coun. mem. 1991-97), Internat. Soc. Neurochemistry, Am. Epilepsy Soc., Royal Soc. Medicine. Avocations: tennis, skiing, jazz, theater. Office: West LA Va Med Ctr 127 11301 Wilshire Blvd Los Angeles CA 90073 Home Phone: 818-368-1116; Office Phone: 310-268-3595. Business E-Mail: wasterla@ucla.edu.

WATANABE, CORINNE KAORU AMEMIYA, judge, state official; b. Wahiawa, Hawaii, Aug. 1, 1950; d. Keiji and Setsuko Amemiya; m. Edwin Tsugio Watanabe, Mar. 8, 1975; children: Traciann Keiko, Brad Natsuo, Lance Yoneo. BA, U. Hawaii, 1971; JD, Baylor U., 1974. Bar: Hawaii 1974. Dep. atty. gen. State of Hawaii, Honolulu, 1974-84, 1st dep. atty. gen., 1984-85, 87-92, atty. gen., 1985-87; assoc. judge Hawaii Intermediate Ct. Appeals, Honolulu, 1992—. Mem. ABA, Hawaii Bar Assn. Office: Hawaii Intermediate Ct Appeals 426 Queen St 2d Fl Honolulu HI 96813

WATANABE, MAMORU, internist, researcher; s. Takazo and Nao W.; m. Marie Watanabe, June 1, 1974; 1 child, David. MD, McGill U., 1957, PhD, 1963. Intern Royal Victoria Hosp., Montreal, 1957—58, resident in medicine, 1958—63; prof. medicine U. Alta., Edmonton, 1967—74, U. Calgary, Alta., 1974—97, head internal medicine Alta., 1974—76, assoc. dean edn. Alta., 1976—80, assoc. dean research Alta., 1980—81, acting dean medicine Alta., 1981—82, dean faculty medicine Alta., 1982—92, prof. emeritus Alta., 1997—. Fellow Royal Coll. Physicians and Surgeons (Can.). Home: 162 Pumpridge Place SW Calgary AB Canada T2V 5E6 Office: U Calgary 3330 Hospital Dr NW Calgary AB Canada T2N 1N4 Office Phone: 403-220-8725. Business E-Mail: watanabe@ucalgary.ca.

WATERMAN, MICHAEL SPENCER, mathematics and biology professor; b. Coquille, Oreg., 1942; s. Ray S. and Bessie E. Waterman; m. Vicki Lynn Buss, 1962 (div. 1977); 1 child, Tracey Lynn BS, Oreg. State U., 1964, MS, 1966; MA, Mich. State U., 1968, PhD, 1969. Assoc. prof. Idaho State U., Pocatello, 1969-75; mem. staff Los Alamos Nat. Lab., 1975-82, cons., 1982—; prof. math. and biology U. So. Calif., LA, 1982—, U. So. Calif. Assocs. Endowed Chair, 1991—. Vis. prof. math. U. Hawaii, Honolulu, 1979-80; vis. prof. structural biology U. Calif., San Francisco, 1982; vis. prof. Mt. Sinai Med. Sch., NYC, 1988; 150th anniversary vis. prof. Chalmers U., 2000; Aisenstadt chair U. Montreal, 2001 Author: Introduction to Computational Biology, 1995; editor: Mathematical Methods for DNA Sequences, Calculating the Secrets of Life, 1995, Genetic Mapping and DNA Sequencing, 1996, Mathematical Support for Molecular Biology, 1999; Annals of Combinatorics, Methodology and Computing in Applied Probability, Genomics, Computational Methods in Science and Technology, Acta Biochimica et Biophysica Sinca; editor-in-chief: Jour. Computational Biology; contbr. articles to profl. jours. Recipient Internat. award, Gardner Found., 2002; grantee, NSF, 1971, 1972, 1975, 1988—, Los Alamos Nat. Lab., 1976, 1981, Sys. Devel. Found., 1982—87, NIH, 1986—99, Sloan Found., 1990—91; fellow, Guggenheim Found., 1995. Fellow AAAS, Am. Acad. Arts and Scis., Inst. Math. Stats.; mem. NAS, French Acad. Sci., Am. Statis. Assn., Soc. Math. Biology, Soc. Indsl. and Applied Math. Office: U So Calif Dept Biol Sci Los Angeles CA 90089-1340

WATERMAN, MIGNON REDFIELD, public relations executive, state legislator; b. Billings, Mont., Oct. 13, 1944; d. Zell Ashley and Mable Erma (Young) Redfield; m. Ronald Fredrick Waterman, Sept. 11, 1965; children: Briar, Kyle. Student, U. Mont., 1963-66. Lobbyist Mont. Assn. Chs., Helena, 1986-90; mem. Mont. Senate, Dist. 26, Helena, 1990—; with pub. rels. dept. Mont. Coun. Tchrs. Math., Helena, 1991-96. Mem. edn., pub. welfare and instns. sub-com. fin. and claims commn. Mont. Senate, rev. oversight com., 1995—, post-secondary policy & budget com., 1995—. Sch. trustee Helena (Mont.) Sch. Dist. 1, 1978-90; bd. dirs. Mont. Hunger Coalition, 1985—; pres. Mont. Sch. Bds. Assn., 1989-90; active Mont. Alliance for Mentally Ill (Mon Ami award 1991). Recipient Marvin Heintz award Mont. Sch. Bds. Assn., 1987, Friends of Edn. award Mont. Assn. Elem. and Middle Sch. Prins., 1989, Child Advocacy award Mont. PTA, 1991, award Mont. Alliance for Mentally Ill, 1991, Outstanding Adv. award Nat. Easter Seals Soc., 1997, Pres.'s award Mont. Assn. Rehab., 1997. Mem. Mont. Sch. Bds. Assn. (Marvin Heintz award 1988, pres.1989-90), Mont. Elem. Sch. Prins., Mont. Parent, Teacher, Student Assn. (child advocacy award 1991). Democrat. Methodist. Home and Office: 530 Hazelgreen Ct Helena MT 59601-5410 Office: Mt State Senate State Capitol Helena MT 59620

WATERS, ALICE L., executive chef, restaurant owner, writer; b. Chatham, NJ, Apr. 28, 1944; 1 child, Fanny. Grad. in French Cultural Studies, U. Calif., Berkeley, 1967; postgrad., Montessori Sch., London; degree (hon.), Mills Coll., Oakland, Calif., 1994. Exec. chef, owner Chez Panisse, Berkeley, Calif., 1971—, Chez Panisse Cafe, Berkeley, Calif., 1980—, Cafe Fanny, Berkeley, Calif., 1984—. Mem. adv. bd. U. Calif., Berkeley; founder, pres. bd. dirs. Martin Luther King Jr. Mid. Sch. Edible Schoolyard; active The Garden Project, San Francisco; spkr. in field of food safety and health; founder, dir. Chez Panisse Found.; internat. gov. Slow Food; vis. dean French Culinary Inst.; hon. trustee Am. Ctr. Food, Wine and the Arts, Napa; bd. mem. San Francisco Ferry Plz. Farmers Market, Land Inst., Nat. Com. for Mothers and Others for Pesticide Limits; advisor Pub. Voice on Food Safety and Health. Author: Chez Panisse Desserts, 1994, Chez Panisse Cooking, 1994, Chez Panisse Menu Cookbook, 1995, Chez Panisse Vegetables, 1996, Chez Panisse Pasta, Pizza, & Calzone, 1996, Fanny at Chez Panisse, 1997, Chez Panisse Café Cookbook, 1999, Chez Panisse Fruit, 2002, The Art of Simple Food, 2007. Recipient Spl. Achievement award, James Beard Found., 1985, Restaurant and Bus. Leadership award, Restaurants and Instns. Mag., 1987, Barbar Boxer Top Ten Women award, 1991, Le Tour du Monde en 80 Toques, Metziner & Varaut, 1991, Nat. Edn. Diplomate award, 1996, John Stanford Heroes award, US Sec. Edn., 1999, Lifetime Achievement award, Bon Appetit Mag., 2000; named Best Chef in America, James Beard Found., 1992, Best Restaurant in America, 1992, Humanitarian of Yr., 1997, Mother of Am. Cooking, NY Times, Best Restaurant in America, Gourmet Mag., 2001; named one of 10 Best Chefs in the World, Cuisine et Vins du France, 1986; named to Calif. Hall of Fame, 2008. Fellow: Am. Acad. Arts & Scis. Office: Chez Panisse 1517 Shattuck Ave Berkeley CA 94709-1598

WATERS, CHARLES R., JR., executive editor; married; 3 children. BA in Liberal Arts, U. Ariz. Editor-pub. Mohave Valley News, Bullhead City, Ariz., 1969-73; editor, pub. The Courier, Prescott, Ariz., 1973-84; profl.-in-residence (vis. asst. prof.) U. Kans., 1984-85; asst. city editor, then night/weekend editor metro-state St. Petersburg (Fla.) Times, 1985-86; asst. mng. editor Reno Gazette-Jour., 1986-87, mng. editor, 1987-89, exec. editor, 1989-90; asst. features editor L.A. Times, 1990-97; exec. editor L.A Times Mag., 1997-98, Fresno Bee, 1998—. Keynote spkr. Nat. Writers Workshop nat. conf., Salt Lake City, 1994; writing and editing cons. Dayton (Ohio) Daily News, 1992; law and media seminar panelist Ford Found., 1980. Trustee William Allen White Found., U. Kans., 1991—; dir. Salvation Army, 1974-84, pres. Prescott adv. bd., 1982, bd. dirs. Reno adv. bd., 1988-90, dir. Fresno adv. bd., 1998—. Nev. State Press Asn. (dir., v.p. 1989-90), Ariz. Press Club (dir., v.p. 1982-84). Office: Fresno Bee 1626 E St Fresno CA 93786-0002

WATERS, LAUGHLIN EDWARD, federal judge; b. LA, Aug. 16, 1914; s. Frank J. and Ida (Bauman) W.; m. Voula Davanis, Aug. 22, 1953; children: Laughlin Edward, Maura Kathleen, Deirdre Mary, Megan Ann, Eileen Brigid. AB, UCLA, 1939; JD, U. So. Calif., 1946. Bar: Calif. 1946. Dep. atty. gen. Calif., Los Angeles, 1946-47; individual practice law Los Angeles, 1947-53; sr. ptnr. Nossaman, Waters, Krueger & Marsh, 1961-76; U.S. atty. So. Dist. Calif., 1953-61; judge U.S. Dist. Ct. (cen. dist.) Calif., 1976—, now sr. judge. Cons. U.S. Dept. State in London, 1970; mem. U.S. Del. to Conf. Environ. Problems in Prague, 1971, White House Conf. on Aging, 1970-71; sr. dist. judge rep. Jud. Coun.; judge Atty Gen.'s Adv. Inst. Mem. Calif. Legislature, 1946-53; vice chmn. Rep. State Ctrl. Com., 1950-51, chmn., 1952-53; bd. dirs. Legal Aid Found., 1954-60; past pres. Cath. Big Brothers. Served as capt. U.S. Army, 1942-46. Decorated Bronze Star with oak leaf cluster, Purple Heart with oak leaf cluster, Combat Inf. badge. Fellow Am. Bar Found., Am. Coll. Trial Lawyers; mem. ABA (chmn. com. on housing and urban devel. 1977-79), Fed. Bar Assn. (founder, past pres.), L.A. County Bar Assn., Am. Judicature Soc., Assn. Bus. Trial Lawyers, U. So. Calif., UCLA Law Assn., Am. Legion, U. So. Calif. Legion Lex, Order Blue Shield, Town Hall, Polish Order Merit Cross with Swords, Hon. Citizen of Chambois, Trun, France, 10th Polish Dragoons (hon.), Soc. Friendly Sons St. Patrick (past pres., Medallion of Merit award), Knights of Malta, Anchor Club, Calif. Club, L.A. Club (past pres.). Roman Catholic.

WATERS, MAXINE, United States Representative from California; b. St. Louis, Aug. 15, 1938; d. Remus and Velma (Moore) Carr; m. Sidney Williams, July 23, 1977; children: Edward, Karen. BA in Sociology, Calif. State U., LA; D (hon.), Spelman Coll., NC Agrl.& Tech. State U., Morgan State U. Vol. coord., tchr. Head Start prog.; mem. Calif. Assembly from dist. 48, 1976—91, US Congress from 35th Calif. dist., 1990—, chief dep. whip, 1990—, mem. house com. fin. svcs., chmn. subcom. housing and cmty. opportunity, mem. subcom. fin. instns. and consumer credit, mem. subcom. oversight and investigations, mem. subcom. domestic and internat. monetary policy, trade, tech., mem. com. on judiciary, subcoms. crime, terrorism, homeland security, immigration, border security and claims. Del. Minority AIDS Initiative, 1998; co-founder Black Women's Forum; mem. Congl. Children's Working Grp., Nat. Devel. & Voting Rights Inst., Progressive Caucus, Nat. Com. Econ. Conversion & Disarmament, Nat. Adv. Com. for Women, 1978—, Dem. Nat. Com., 1980—; chair Congl. Black Caucus, 1997—98; founding mem., chair Out of Iraq Congl. Caucus, 2005—. Founder Free South Africa Movement, Project Build; mem. Calif. Peer Counseling Assn., Nat. Com. Econ. Conversion and Disarmament; founder Maxine Waters Employment Preparation Ctr.; mem. bd. Ctr. Study Sport in Soc., LA Women's Found. Named one of 100 Most Influential Black Americans, Ebony mag., 2006; named to Power 150, 2008. Democrat. Office: US Ho Reps 2344 Rayburn Ho Office Bldg Washington DC 20515-0535 also: 10124 S Broadway Ste 1 Los Angeles CA 90003 Office Phone: 202-225-2201, 323-757-8900. Office Fax: 202-225-7854, 323-757-9506.

WATERS, RAE, state legislator; b. Fort Dix, NJ, June 15, 1956; m. Jim Waters; children: Tommy, Alyssa. BS in Sociology, Northern Ariz. U., 1978. Audio-visual specialist Best Western Hotels, 1979—87; gov. bd. mem. Kyrene Elem. Sch. Dist., 1998—; cmty. columnist Ariz. Republic Newspaper, 2004—06; mem. Dist. 20 Ariz. House of Reps., 2008—. Pres. Kyrene Mcpl. Property Corp., 1997—98. Chmn. Ahwatukee Parenting Group, 1990—92; mem. Kyrene de las Lomas Site Coun., 1995—98, Kyrene Prent Supt. Coun., 1995—98; founder & chmn. Kyrene Citizens for Edn. Fin., 1997; bd. mem. Tchr. Edn. Partnership Commn., 2000—03; mem. Nat. Sch. Bds. Assn. Fed. Rels. Network, 2000—; bd. mem. West Ed, 2006; mem. Maricopa Integrated Health Sys. Blue Ribbon Task Force, 2008. Mem.: Ariz. Sch. Bds. Assn. (Maricopa County dir. 2000—02, officer 2003—05, pres. 2006). Democrat. Catholic. Office: Capitol Complex 1700 W Washington Rm 122 Phoenix AZ 85007-2890 Office Phone: 602-926-5550. Office Fax: 602-417-3120. Business E-Mail: rwaters@azleg.gov.*

WATKINS, CHARLES REYNOLDS, medical equipment company executive; b. San Diego, Oct. 28, 1951; s. Charles R. and Edith A. (Muff) W.; children: Charles Devin, Gregory Michael, Joshua Tomas. BS, Lewis and Clark Coll., 1974; postgrad., U. Portland, 1976. Internat. salesman Hyster Co., Portland, Oreg., 1975-80, Hinds Internat. Corp., Portland, 1980-83; mgr. internat. sales Wade Mfg. Co., Tualatin, Oreg., 1983-84; regional sales mgr. U.S. Surg., Inc., Norwalk, Conn., 1984-86; nat. sales mgr. NeuroCom Internat., Inc., Clackamas, Oreg., 1986-87; pres. Wave Form Systems, Inc., Portland, 1987-98; pres., dir. Wave Form Mfg., Inc., Portland, 1998—; prin. Wave Form Lithotripsy LLC, Portland, 1998—; pres. Wave Form Mfg., Inc., 1998—. Bd. dirs. Portland World Affairs Coun., 1980. Mem. Am. Soc. Laser Medicine and Surgery, Am. Assn. Gynecol. Laparoscopists, Ind. Med. Distbrs. Assn., Portland City Club. Republican. Avocations: flying, photography, travel. Office: Wave Form Sys Inc PO Box 3195 Portland OR 97208-3195 Office Phone: 503-626-2100.

WATKINS, DEAN ALLEN, electronics executive, educator; b. Omaha, Oct. 23, 1922; s. Ernest E. and Pauline (Simpson) W.; m. Bessie Ena Hansen, June 28, 1944; children— Clark Lynn, Alan Scott, Eric Ross. BS, Iowa State Coll., 1944; MS, Calif. Inst. Tech., 1947; PhD, Stanford, 1951. Engr. Collins Radio Co., 1947-48; mem. staff Los Alamos Lab., 1948-49; tech. staff Hughes Research Labs., 1951-53; asso. prof. elec. engring. Stanford, 1953-56; prof., dir. Electron Devices Lab., 1956-64, lectr. elec. engring., 1964-70; co-founder, pres., chief exec. officer, dir. Watkins Johnson Co., Palo Alto, Calif., 1957-67, chmn., chief exec. officer, dir., 1967-80, chmn., dir., 1980-2000. Cons. Dept. Def., 1956-66; mem. White House Sci. Coun., 1988-89. Patentee in field; contbr. articles to profl. jours. Legis. chmn., dir. San Meteo County Sch. Bds. Assn., 1959-69; gov. San Francisco Bay Area Coun., 1966-75; Rep. precinct capt. Portola Valley, 1964; vice chmn. San Mateo County Fin. Com., 1967-69; mem. Calif. Rep. Ctrl. Com., 1964-68; trustee Stanford, 1966-69; regent U. Calif., 1969-96, chmn., 1972-74; mem. governing bd. Sequoia Union H.S. Dist., 1964-68, chmn., 1967-68; mem. governing bd. Portola Valley Sch. Dist., 1958-66; mem. bd. overseers Hoover Instn. on War, Revolution and Peace, Stanford, 1969—, chmn., 1971-73, 85-86; adv. policy commn. Santa Clara County Jr. Achievement; trustee Nat. Security Indsl. Assn., 1965-78. Served from pvt. to 1st lt. C.E., O.R.C. AUS, 1943-46. Fellow IEEE (7th region Achievement award 1957, Frederik Philips award 1981), AAAS; mem. Am. Phys. Soc., Am. Mgmt. Assn., Western Electronic Mfrs. Assn. (chmn. San Francisco coun. 1967, v.p., dir.), Calif. C. of C. (dir. 1965-92, treas. 1978, pres. 1981), Nat. Acad. Engring., Mounted Patrol San Mateo County (spl. dep. sheriff 1960-70), San Mateo County Horseman's Assn., San Benito County Farm Bur., Calif. Cattlemen's Assn., Delta Upsilon. Clubs: Palo Alto (Palo Alto), University (Palo Alto); Shack Riders (San Mateo County); Commonwealth (San Francisco); Rancheros Visitadores.

WATKINS, JOHN FRANCIS, management consultant; b. Alhambra, Calif., May 21, 1925; s. Edward F. and Louise (Ward) W.; divorced; children— Stephen, Katherine, John Francis, William. BSCE, U. Tex., Austin, 1947. With Earle M. Jorgensen Co., Lynwood, Calif., 1947-90, sr. v.p. adminstrn., 1978-90, ret.; owner John F. Watkins Assocs., Pasadena, Calif., 1990—. Pres. bd. Poly. Sch., Pasadena, 1978—80, Holy Family Sch., 1994—2002; adv. bd. mem. Serra H.S., Verbum Dei H.S., Dolores Mission Sch., 1996—; mem. Coll. Sci. and Engring. Coun. Loyola Marymount U., bd. visitors Sch. Edn.; adv. bd. Bishop Mora Salesian H.S., 1994—; mem. Cath. Edn. Found. Archdiocese L.A., 1995—; St. Gabriel pastoral region bd. dirs. Cath. Charities, 1994—; bd. dirs. Boys Republic, Chino Hills, Calif., 1970—, pres., 1977—80; bd. dirs. St. Luke Hosp., Pasadena, 1979—86, chmn. bd., 1982—86; bd. dirs. Econ. Literacy Coun. Calif., 1980—87, Pasadena Mus. of History, 1990—99. Mem. U.S. Navy League (nat. bd. dirs. 1989—, pres. Pasadena coun. 1992-93), Calif. Club, Annandale Golf Club, Serra Club (pres. 1995-97), Valley Club (San Marino, Calif.), Twilight Club (pres. 2002-03). Republican. Roman Catholic. Home and Office: 410 California Ter Pasadena CA 91105-2419 Home Phone: 626-432-4712; Office Phone: 626-432-4712. E-mail: jwatkins@pacificnet.net.

WATKINS, JOHN GOODRICH, psychologist, educator; b. Salmon, Idaho, Mar. 17, 1913; s. John Thomas and Ethel (Goodrich) W.; m. Evelyn Elizabeth Browne, Aug. 21, 1932; m. Doris Wade Tomlinson, June 8, 1946; m. Helen Verner Huth, Dec. 28, 1971; children: John Dean, Jonette Alison, Richard Douglas, Gregory Keith, Rodney Philip, Karen Stroobants, Marvin R. Huth. Student, Coll. Idaho, 1929-30, 31-32; BS, U. Idaho, 1933, MS, 1936; PhD, Columbia U., 1941. Instr. high sch., Idaho, 1933-39; faculty Ithaca Coll., 1940-41; prof. Auburn U., 1941-43; assoc. prof. Wash. State U., 1946-49; chief clin. psychologist U.S. Army Welch Hosp., 1945-46; clin. psychologist VA Hosp., American Lake, Wash., 1949-50; chief clin. psychologist VA Mental Hygiene Clinic, Chgo., 1950-53, VA Hosp., Portland, Oreg., 1953-64; prof. psychology U. Mont., Missoula, 1964-84, prof. emeritus, 1984—, dir. clin. tng., 1964-80. Lectr. numerous univs.; clin. asso. U. Oreg. Med. Sch., 1957; pres. Am. Bd. Examiners in Psychol. Hypnosis, 1960-62. Author: Objective Measurement of Instrumental Performance, 1942, Hypnotherapy of War Neuroses, 1949, General Psychotherapy, 1960, The Therapeutic Self, 1978, (with others) We, The Divided Self, 1982, Hypnotherapeutic Techniques, 1987, rev. edit., 2006, (with others) Hypnoanalytic Techniques, 1992, (with others) Ego States: Theory and Therapy, 1997, Adventures in Human Understanding, 2001, Emotional Resonance, 2005, (with others) Advanced Hypnotherapy: Hypnodynamic Techniques, Routledge, NY, 2007; contbr. articles to profl. jours. Recipient award, Am. Soc. Clin. Hypnosis, 2007. Mem. Internat. Soc. Clin. and Exptl. Hypnosis (co-founder, pres. 1965-67, awards 1960-65), Internat. Soc. Hypnosis (Benjamin Franklin Gold medal award), Soc. Clin. and Exptl. Hypnosis (pres. 1969-71, Morton Prince award), Am. Psychol. Assn. (pres. divsn. 30 1975-76, award 1993), Phi Delta Kappa. Home and Office: 8258 Greenwood Pl Longmont CO 80503 Office Phone: 303-652-6556. Office Fax: 303-652-6525.

WATKINS, STEPHEN EDWARD, accountant, publishing executive; b. Oklahoma City, Sept. 1, 1922; s. Ralph Bushnell and Jane (Howell) W.; m. Suzanne Fowler, Aug. 16, 1976; children— Elizabeth Ann Watkins Racicot, Stephen Edward, Jr. BBA, U. N.Mex., 1944. C.P.A., N.Mex. With Peat, Marwick, Mitchell & Co., 1944-67; pres. The New Mexican daily newspaper, Santa Fe, 1967-78, 90—; pvt. practice pub. acctg. Santa Fe, 1978—. Vestryman Ch. of Holy Faith; trustee St. Vincent Hosp., 1979-85, Orchestra Santa Fe, 1976-82, Hist. Santa Fe Found. (pres. 1990). Mem. AICPA, Sons of Am. Revolution, Rotary. Home: 1325 Don Gaspar Ave Santa Fe NM 87505-4627 Office: 223 E Palace Ave Santa Fe NM 87501-1947

WATSON, ALLISON L., computer software company executive; d. Perry and Mona Lambird; 1 child. BA, Stanford U.; MBA, San Diego State U. With mid-Atlantic sales dist. & East region leadership teams Microsoft Corp., 1993—99, gen. mgr. mid-Atlantic dist., 1999—2001, chief of staff to sr. v.p. of Microsoft Americas, 2001—02, v.p. Worldwide Ptnr. Grp., 2002—06, corp. v.p. Worldwide Ptnr. Grp., 2006—. Named Channel Exec. of Yr., VARBus. Mag., 2004; named one of 10 Worldwide Agenda-Setters, 2006. Office: Microsoft Corp Worldwide Ptnr Group 1 Microsoft Way Redmond WA 98052-6399

WATSON, EMILY, actress; b. London, Jan. 14, 1967; m. Jack Waters, 1995; 1 child, Juliet. Grad., Bristol U. Actress: (films) Breaking the Waves, 1996 (Robert award 1997, N.Y. Film Critics Circle award 1996, Nat. Soc. Film Critics award 1996, L.A. Film Critics Assn. New Generation award 1996, European Film award 1996), Metroland, 1997, The Boxer, 1997, Hilary and Jackie, 1998, The Cradle Will Rock, 1999, Angela's Ashes, 1999, Trixie, 2000, The Luzhin Defence, 2000, Gosford Park, 2001 (SAG award outstanding performance by the cast, 2002), In Search of the Assasin, 2001, Equilibrium, 2002, Punch-Drunk Love, 2002, Red Dragon, 2002, Equilibrium, 2002, Blossoms and Blood, 2003, (voice only) Back to Gaya, 2004, Separate Lies, 2005, (voice only) Corpse Bride, 2005, The Proposition, 2005, Wah-Wah, 2006, Crusade in Jeans, 2006, Miss Potter, 2006, The Water Horse: Legend of the Deep, 2007, Fireflies in the Garden, 2008; (TV films) The Mill on the Floss, 1996, The Life and Death of Peter Sellers, 2004, The Memory Keeper's Daughter, 2008

WATSON, GEORGE W., energy executive; BSEE, Queen's U., Kingston, Can., 1970, MBA in Fin. Mktg., 1972; grad. advanced mgmt. program, Harvard U., 1988. With Can. Imperial Bank Commerce, Toronto; asst. gen. mgr. worldwide, oil and gas divsn. Calgary, 1981; dir. fin. Dome Petroleum, v.p. fin.; v.p., treas. Amoco Can.; pres., CEO Intensity Resources, 1988-90; CFO TransCanada, 1990-93, pres., 1993-99, CEO, 1994-99; ptnr. Northridge Can. Inc., 1999—2002. CEO Critical Control Solutions Corp.; chmn. bd. dirs. Badger Daylighting Inc.; chmn. Zebas Energy Corp., Calgary Olympic Devel. Assn.; bd. dirs. Can. Spirit Resources Corp., Teekay LNG LLP, Repeat Seat Ltd., Recap Energy Inc., Signal Energy Corp. Bd. dirs. Queen's U., TGS N. Am. Real Estate Investment Trust. Address: PO Box 122 Niagara Falls Canada L2E 6S8 Office Phone: 403-705-7510. Business E-Mail: george.watson@criticalcontrol.com. E-mail: georgewwatson@shaw.ca.

WATSON, JOHN S., oil industry executive; b. Calif., Oct. 1956; BA, U. Calif., Davis, 1978; MBA, U. Chgo., 1980. Fin. analyst to various fin. and analytical positions including supervisory positions in the comptroller's fin. and profit analysis groups Chevron Corp., 1980—90, mgr. investor rels., 1990—93; mgr. credit card enterprises Chevron USA Products Co., 1993—95, gen. mgr. strategic planning and quality, 1995—96; pres. Chevron Canada, Ltd., Vancouver, BC, Canada, 1996—98; v.p. strategic planning Chevron Corp., 1998—2001, v.p. fin., CFO, 2001—05, exec. v.p. strategy & devel., 2008—09, vice chmn., 2009—; pres. Chevron Internat. Exploration and Prodn., 2005—08. Merger integration exec. ChevronTexaco, 2001; bd. dirs. Chevron Corp., 2009—. Office: Chevron Corp 6001 Bollinger Canyon Rd San Ramon CA 94583-2324*

WATSON, KAROL ELIZABETH, internist, educator; b. Gary, Ind., Dec. 15, 1963; MD, Harvard Med. Sch., 1989. Cert. Am. Bd. Internal Medicine, 1993, Am. Bd. Internal Medicine, Cardiovascular Disease, 2004. Intern, internal medicine UCLA Sch. Medicine, 1990—91, resident, internal medicine, 1991—92, fellow, cardiology, 1992—97, assoc. prof. medicine; dir., Cholesterol and Lipid Mgmt. Ctr. UCLA CHAMP (Cholesterol, Hypertension, and Atherosclerosis Mgmt. Program); physician, medicine, endocrinology, diabetes and hypertension Gonda Diabetes Ctr. Office: UCLA Med-Cardio Mail Code 167917 Dept Code 1553 Box 951679 BH-307 CHS Los Angeles CA 90095-1679 Office Phone: 310-794-7121. Office Fax: 310-206-9133. Business E-Mail: kwatson@med.net.ucla.edu.*

WATSON, KENNETH MARSHALL, physics professor; b. Des Moines, Sept. 7, 1921; s. Louis Erwin and Irene Nellie (Marshall) W.; m. Elaine Carol Miller, Mar. 30, 1946; children: Ronald M., Mark Louis. BS, Iowa State U., Ames, 1943; PhD, U. Iowa, Iowa City, 1948; ScD (hon.), U. Ind., 1976. Rsch. engr. Naval Rsch. Lab., Washington, 1943-46; staff Inst. Advanced Study Princeton U., 1948-49; rsch. fellow Lawrence Berkeley Lab., Calif., 1949-52, staff Calif., 1957-81; asst. prof. physics U. Ind., Bloomington, 1952-54; assoc. prof. physics U. Wis., Madison, 1954-57; prof. physics U. Calif., Berkeley, 1957-81, prof. oceanography, dir. marine physics lab. San Diego, 1981-93. Cons. Sci. Application Corp., 1981-2004; mem. US Pres.'s Sci. Adv. Com. Panels, 1962-71; adviser Nat. Security Coun., 1972-75; mem. JASON Adv. Panel, 1959-2001; sci. adv. bd. George C. Marshall Inst., 1989—. Author: (with M.L. Goldberger) Collision Theory, 2004; (with J. Welch and J. Bond) Atomic Theory of Gas Dynamics, 1966; (with J. Nutall) Topics in Several Particle Dynamics, 1970; (with Flatté, Munk, Dashen) Sound Transmission Through a Fluctuating Ocean, 1979. Mem.: Nat. Acad. Scis. Home: Unit 2008 8515 Costa Verde Blvd San Diego CA 92122-1150 Office: Univ Calif San Diego 9500 Gilman Dr La Jolla CA 92093-0213 Office Phone: 858-634-6620. Business E-Mail: kmw@ucsd.edu.

WATSON, NOEL G., construction executive; b. Bison, SD, 1936; BSChemE, U. N.D., 1958; postgrad., Colo. Sch. Mines, 1958-60. With AMAX Inc., 1962-65, Jacobs Engring. Group, Pasadena, Calif., 1960-62, 1965—, pres., 1987—2002, CEO, 1992—2006, chmn., 2004—. Office: Jacobs Engineering Group PO Box 7084 1111 S Arroyo Pkwy Pasadena CA 91109

WATSON-BOONE, REBECCA A., dean, researcher, library and information scientist, educator; b. Springfield, Ohio, Mar. 7, 1946; d. Roger S. and Elizabeth Boone; m. Dennis David Ash, 1967 (div. 1975); m. Frederick Kellogg, 1979 (div. 1988); m. Peter G. Watson-Boone, May 26, 1989. Student, Earlham Coll., Richmond, Ind., 1964-67; BA, Case Western Res. U., Cleve., 1968; MLS, U. NC, Chapel Hill, 1971; PhD, U. Wis., Madison, 1995. Asst. reference libr. Princeton U., NJ, 1970-76; head cen. reference dept. U. Ariz., Tucson, 1976-83, assoc. dean Coll. Arts and Scis., 1984-89; co-dir. Placitas Cmty. Libr., N.Mex., 2007—. Loaned exec. Ariz. Bd. Regents, 1988-89; pres. Ctr. for Study of Info. Profls., 1995—2002. Author: Constancy and Change in the Worklife of Research University Librarians, 1998, A Good Match: Library Career Opportunities for Graduates of Liberal Arts Colleges, 2007; contbr. articles to profl. jours. Mem. ALA (div. pres. 1985-86, councilor 1988-92), Assn. Libr. and Info. Sci. Edn., N.Mex. Libr. Assn. Mem. Soc. Of Friends. Office: 30 Camino de la Vina Vieja Placitas NM 87043 Business E-Mail: rebeccawb@comcast.net.

WATT, KENNETH EDMUND FERGUSON, zoology educator; b. Toronto, July 13, 1929; s. William Black Ferguson Watt and Irene Eleanor (Hubbard) Dodd; m. Genevieve Bernice Bendig, Oct. 28, 1955; children: Tanis Jocelyn, Tara Alexis. BA with honor, U. Toronto, 1951; PhD in Zoology, U. Chgo., 1954; LLD, Simon Fraser U., 1970. Biometrician Rsch. div. Dept. Lands and Forests, Ont., Canada, 1954-57; sr. biometrician Can. Dept. Agr., Ottawa, Ont., 1957-60; head, statis. rsch. and svcs. Canadian Dept. Forestry, Ottawa, 1960-63; from assoc. prof. to prof. Dept. Zoology, U. Calif., Davis, 1963-93. Author: Ecology and Resource Management, 1968, Principles of Environmental Sciences, 1973, Understanding the Environment, 1982, Taming the Future, 1991. Recipient Gold medal Entomol. Soc., 1969. Achievements include development of new approach to forecasting future based on exhaustive statistic testing of nonlinear math. equations to long runs of historical data; discovery that change through time in real world systems violates Markov principles. Home: 2916 Quail St Davis CA 95616-5711 Office: U Calif Dept Evolution & Ecology Davis CA 95616 Office Phone: 530-750-3253. Personal E-mail: kenwatt@sbcglobal.net.

WATTENBERG, DAVE, state legislator, rancher; b. Walden, Colo., Apr. 4, 1940; Student, Iowa State U., 1958-60. Rancher, Walden; mem. Colo. State Ho. of Reps., Denver, 1982-84, Colo. State Senate, Denver, 1984—. Chmn. agrl., natural resources and energy com., mem. bus. affairs and labor com., joint legal svcs. com.; bd. dirs. North Park State Bank. Mem. North Park Edn. Edn.; co-chmn. Colo. Gov.'s Roundtable on Hwys. and Transp. Mem. Nat. Cattleman's Assn., Colo. Cattlemen's Assn. Republican. Office: Colo State Senate State Capitol 200 E Colfax Ave Ste 346 Denver CO 80203-1716 Home: 3081 Kendrick St Golden CO 80401-1335

WATTERS, ANN OLIVA, psychologist, educator; d. George Verdelli II and Dorothy Austin Oliva; m. Thomas A. Watters, Aug. 30, 1975; children: Andrew George, Michael Thomas. BA in English, U. Calif., Berkeley, 1974; MA in English Lit., Washington U., St. Louis, 1976; MA in Health Psychology, Calif. Sch. Profl. Psychology, 1997, PhD in Psychology, 1999. Lectr. rhetoric and English Stanford U., Calif., 1987—; pvt. practice clin. psychology San Mateo, Calif., 1999—; asst. clin. prof. psychiatry U. Calif., San Francisco, 2005—. Author, editor: Global Exchange: Reading/Writing in a World Context, 2005; co-author: Creating America: Reading & Writing Arguments, 4th edit., 2005, Writing for Change: A Community Reader. Chair bd. dirs. San Mateo Med. Ctr. Found. Mem.: AAUP, APA, Calif. Psychol. Assn. Office Fax: 650-375-8398. Business E-Mail: watters@stanford.edu.

WATTS, DAVID H., construction company executive; b. Newark, 1938; Grad., Cornell U., 1960. Pres., CEO Ford, Bacon & Davis, Inc, Granite Constrn. Inc., Watsonville, Calif., 1987—2003; chmn. Granite Contrn. Inc., Watsonville, Calif., 1999—. Office: Granite Constrn Inc PO Box 50085 Watsonville CA 95077-5085

WATTS, EMMA, film company executive; Exec. v.p. prodn. 20th Century Fox, co-pres. prodn., 2007—. Named one of The 100 Most Powerful Women in Entertainment, Hollywood Reporter, 2007. Office: 20th Century Fox Film Corp 10201 W Pico Blvd Los Angeles CA 90064 Business E-Mail: emma.watts@fox.com.

WATTS, LINDA SUSAN, humanities educator; BA, U. Del., 1981, MA in History, 1983; MA in Am. Studies, Yale U., 1986, PhD in Am. Studies, 1989. Instr. history and Am. studies U. Del., Newark, 1981—83; instr. English and Am. studies Yale U., New Haven, 1984—86, coord. sr. essays and projects in Am. studies, 1987—89; vis. asst. prof. English, Am. studies, and Afro-Am. studies Wesleyan U., Middletown, Conn., 1989—90; asst. prof. Drake U., Des Moines, 1990—95, asst. prof., assoc. dir. women's studies program, 1992—93, assoc. prof. English, 1995—96, assoc. prof. English, assoc. dean Coll. of Arts and Scis., 1996—99; prof. Am. studies, dir. interdisciplinary arts and scis. program U. Wash., Bothell, 1999—2001, prof. Am. studies, interdisciplinary arts and scis. program, 2001—. Author: Rapture Untold: Gender, Mysticism, and 'The Moment of Recognition' in the Writings of Gertrude Stein, 1996, Gertrude Stein: A Study of the Short Fiction, 1999, Encyclopedia of American Folklore, 2006; contbg. author: The World Is Our Home: Society and Culture in Contemporary Southern Writing; co-author: Social History of the United States: The 1920's, 2008, Social History of the United States: The 1900's, 2008; contbr. articles to profl. jours. HIV/AIDS cmty. edn. instr. ARC, Des Moines, 1992—99, HIV/AIDS instr. trainer, 1996—99; vol. literacy tutor Adult Literacy Ctr., Des Moines, 1998—99; vol. mus. visitor svcs. Experience Music Project, Seattle, 2000—01; vol. AIDS Greater Des Moines, 1992—93, Selfhelp Crafts of the World, Des Moines, 1992—94; vol. curriculum cons., co-instr. Op. Peer Helper, ARC Youth Program, Des Moines, 1993—93; vol. edn. com. mem. AIDS Project of Greater Des Moines, 1993—95; chair HIV/AIDS edn. program com. ARC, Des Moines, 1994—95, vol. mem. HIV/AIDS edn. program com., 1995—99; vol. planning com. mem. World AIDS Day Observance, State of Iowa, Des Moines, 1997—98. Recipient Editor's Choice award for outstanding achievement in poetry, poetry.com, 2000, Open Poetry Competition award, King County Pub. Art Program, State of Wash., 2000, Internat. Poet of Merit award, Internat. Soc. Poets, 2002; named Semi-Finalist N.Am. Open Poetry Contest, Internat. Libr. of Poetry, 2000, Internat. Libr. Poetry, 2001; finalist Women's Studies grant, Woodrow Wilson Found., 1988, Manuscript award, Ill. Nat. Women's Studies Assn., 1990; nominee Poet of Yr., Internat. Soc. Poets, 2001. Mem.: Phi Beta Kappa, Phi Alpha Theta, Phi Kappa Phi. Office: Univ Wash Bothell Box 358511 11136 NE 180th St Bothell WA 98011-8246 Business E-Mail: lwatts@uwb.edu. E-mail: lswatts@u.washington.edu.

WATTS, NAOMI, actress; b. Shoreham, Kent, Eng., Sept. 28, 1968; d. Peter and Myfanwy Watts; 2 children (with Liev Schreiber) Alexander Pete Schreiber, Samuel Kai Schreiber Spl. envoy on HIV/AIDS UN, 2006—. Spokesmodel Angel fragrance by Theirry Mugler, 2008. Actor: (films) For Love Alone, 1986, Flirting, 1991, Matinee, 1993, Wide Sargasso Sea, 1993, Gross Misconduct, 1993, The Custodian, 1993, Tank Girl, 1995, Children of the Corn IV: The Gathering, 1996, Persons Unknown, 1996, Under the Lighthouse Dreaming, 1997, Dangerous Beauty, 1998, A House Divided, 1998, Strange Planet, 2001, Ellie Parker, 2001, Down, 2001, Mulholland Drive, 2001, The Ring, 2002, Plots with a View, 2002, Rabbits, 2002, Ned Kelly, 2003, Le Divorce, 2003, 21 Grams, 2003 (Acad. Award nomination for best actress, 2004, Screen Actors Guild Award nomination for best actress, 2004), We Don't Live Here Anymore, 2004, The Assassination of Richard Nixon, 2004, I Heart Huckabees, 2004, Ellie Parker, 2005, The Ring Two, 2005, Stay, 2005, King Kong, 2005, The Painted Veil, 2006, (voice) Inland Empire, 2006, Eastern Promises, 2007, Funny Games, 2008, The International, 2009; (TV films) Bermuda Triangle, 1996, Timepiece, 1996, The Christmas Wish, 1998, The Hunt for the Unicorn Killer, 1999, The Wyvern Mystery, 2000, The Outsider, 2002; (TV miniseries) Brides of Christ, 1991; (TV series) Home and Away, 1991, Sleepwalkers, 1997. Office: c/o Untitled Entertainment 1801 Century Park E Los Angeles CA 90067

WATTS, OLIVER EDWARD, engineering company executive; b. Hayden, Colo., Sept. 22, 1939; s. Oliver Easton and Vera Irene (Hockett) W.; m. Charla Ann French, Aug. 12, 1962; children: Erik Sean, Oliver Eron, Sherilyn. BS, Colo. State U., 1962. Registered profl. engr., Colo., Calif.; profl. hand surveyor, Colo. Crew chief Colo. State U. Rsch. Found., Ft. Collins, 1962; with Calif. Dept. Water Resources, Gustine and Castaic, 1964-70; land and water engr. CF&I Steel Corp., Pueblo, Colo., 1970-71; engring. dir. United Western Engrs., Colorado Springs, Colo., 1971-76; ptnr. United Planning and Engring Co., Colorado Springs, 1976-79; owner Oliver E. Watts, Cons. Engr., Colorado Springs, 1979—. Dir. edn. local Ch. of Christ, 1969-71, deacon, 1977-87, elder, 1987-96. 1st lt. C.E., AUS, 1962-64. Recipient Individual Achievement award Colo. State U. Coll. Engring., 1981. Fellow ASCE (life; v.p. Colorado Springs br. 1975, pres. 1978); mem. NSPE (pres. Pike's Peak chpt. 1975, sec. Colo. sect. 1976, v.p. 1977, pres. 1978-79, Young Engr. award 1976, Pres.'s award 1979), Cons. Engrs. Coun. Colo. (bd. dirs. 1981-83), Am. Cons. Engrs. Coun., Profl. Land Surveyors Colo., Colo. Engrs. Coun. (del. 1980—), Colo. State U. Alumni Assn. (v.p., dir. Pike's Peak chpt. 1972-76), Lancers, Lambda Chi Alpha. Home: 7195 Dark Horse Pl Colorado Springs CO 80919-1442 Office: 614 Elkton Dr Colorado Springs CO 80907-3514

WAWRYTKO, SANDRA ANN, humanities educator; b. Chgo., Oct. 18, 1951; d. Stanley Andrew Wawrytko and Alyce Valerie Cioch-Wawrytko; m. Charles Wei-hsun Fu, Sept. 29, 1994 (dec. Oct. 15, 1996). BA in Philosophy, Knox Coll., 1972; MA in Philosophy, Washington U., 1975, PhD in Philosophy, 1976. Instr. Washington U., St. Louis, 1973—77; prof. San Diego State U., 1980—. Vis. prof. Chinese Culture U., Yangmingshan, Taiwan, 1984, Fo Guang Buddhist Coll., Kaohsiung, Taiwan, 1990—2007; prin. investigator Lang. Acquisition Rsch. Ctr., San Diego State U., 1994—2003; vis. prof. U. San Diego, 1978—81; founder, exec. dir. Internat. Soc. for Philosophy and Psychotherapy. Author: The Undercurrent of Feminine Philosophy in Eastern and Western Thought, 1981, CRYSTAL: Spectrums of Chinese Culture Through Poetry, 1995; editor: North American Institute of Zen Buddhist Studies, Rethinking the Curriculum: Toward an Integrated Interdisciplinary Education, 1990, The Problem of Evil, 2000, (book series) Asian Thought and Culture, Philosophy and Psychotherapy; co-author: The Buddhist Religion, 1996; narrator: interactive CD-ROM Crystals of Chinese Culture, 2000, author, editor: Saving the Elephant: Asian Encounters with Imperialism, Orientalism, and Gloablization, 2004. Edn. rep. San Diego Sister City Program, Yantai, China, 1985; mem. editl. bd. Jour. Chinese Philosophy; mem. student Fulbright program nat. screening com.; bd. dirs. San Diego Chinese Hist. Soc. and Mus., 2002—; pres., founder Charles Wei-hsun Fu Found., San Diego, 1997—. Recipient Humanities Advancement Poetry Contest award, Humanities Advancement Com., 1983; fellow, Washington. U., 1974—75. Mem.: World Congress of Logotherapy (sec.-gen. 1982—85), Internat. Soc. for Chinese Philosophy (sec., exec. bd. mem. 1990—2003), Phi Beta Delta (governing bd. 2002—06), Phi Beta Kappa (Faculty Lectr. Nu chpt. 2002—03). Avocations: poetry, translating classical Chinese poetry, collecting Asian art and books, creating culinary adventures. Office: San Diego State U Dept Philosophy San Diego CA 92182-0303 E-mail: wawrytko@mail.sdsu.edu.

WAXMAN, ALAN GARLETT, obstetrician/gynecologist, educator; b. Phila., 1946; MD, U. Colo., 1972; MPH, Emory U., 1989. Diplomate Am. Bd. Ob-Gyn. Intern Med. Ctr. VA Hosp., Richmond, Va., 1972-73; resident ob-gyn Colo. Affiliate Hosp.-St. Luke's Hosp., Denver, 1973-76; chief ob-gyn dept. Gallup Indian Med. Ctr., N.Mex., 1980-91; assoc. prof. dept. ob-gyn. U. N.Mex. Sch. of Medicine, Albuquerque, 2000—06, prof., 2006—. Sr. clinician ob-gyn Indian Health Svc., 1994-2000. Fellow Am. Coll. Ob-Gyn; mem. Am. Soc. Colposcopy and Cervical Pathology (com. chmn., resident edn. com., 2006-), N.Mex. Breast and Cervical Cancer Program (adv. coun.), Am. Coll. Ob-Gyn (chmn., 2008-). Office: Univ of New Mexico Dept of OB/Gyn MSC 10-5580 1 Univ of New Mexico Albuquerque NM 87131

WAXMAN, HENRY ARNOLD, United States Representative from California; b. L.A., Sept. 12, 1939; s. Louis and Esther (Silverman) Waxman; m. Janet Kessler, Oct. 17, 1971; children: Michael David, Shia. BA in Polit. Sci, UCLA, 1961, JD, 1964. Bar: Calif. 1965. Practicing atty., 1965—68; mem. Calif. State Assembly, 1969-74, US Congress from 24th Calif. Dist., 1975—93, US Congress from 29th Calif. Dist., 1993—2003, US Congress from 30th Calif. Dist., 2003—; chmn. US House Commerce subcommittee on Health & Environment, 1979-94; ranking minority mem. US House Oversight & Govt. Reform Com., 1997—2007, chmn., 2007—09, US House Energy & Commerce Com., 2009—. Mem. Congl. Children's Working Grp., H. Dem. Steering Com. Pres. Calif. Fedn. Young Dems., 1965—67. Recipient Excellence in Pub. Svc. award, Am. Acad. Pediat., 1983, Pub. Svc. award, Am. Assn. Pub. Health Dentistry, 1985, James Madison award, ALA, 1990, Leadership award, Nat. Gay & Lesbian Task Force, 1991, Leadership in Govt. award, Keystone Ctr., 2001, Health Leadership award, Nat. Orgn. Rare Disorders, 2002, Excellence in Immunization award, Nat. Partnership Immunization, 2002, Nat. Leadership award, Nat. Citizens' Coalition for Nursing Home Reform, 2002, Claude Pepper award, Nat. Inst. Cmty. Based Long-Term Care, 2004, Pub. Svc. award, Internat. Found. Employee Benefit Plans, 2004; named one of The 50 Most Powerful People in DC, GQ mag., 2007. Mem.: Am. Civil Liberties Union, Am. Jewish Congress, Guardians Jewish Home for Aged (Pub. Policy on Aging award 1992), Calif. Bar Assn., B'nai B'rith, Sierra Club, Phi Sigma Alpha. Democrat. Jewish. Office: US Congress 2204 Rayburn Ho Office Bldg Washington DC 20515-0530 also: 8436 W Third St Ste 600 Los Angeles CA 90048 Office Phone: 202-225-3976, 323-651-1040. Office Fax: 202-225-4099, 323-655-0502.*

WAY, E(DWARD) LEONG, pharmacologist, toxicologist, educator; b. Watsonville, Calif., July 10, 1916; s. Leong Man and Lai Har (Shew) Way; m. Madeline Li, Aug. 11, 1944; children: Eric, Linette. BS, U. Calif., Berkeley, 1938, MS, 1940; PhD, U. Calif., San Francisco, 1942. Pharm. chemist Merck & Co., Rahway, NJ, 1942; instr. pharmacology George Washington U., 1943-46, asst. prof., 1946-48; asst. prof. pharmacology U. Calif., San Francisco, 1949-52, assoc. prof., 1952-57, prof., 1957-87, prof. emeritus, 1987—, chmn. dept. pharmacology, 1973-78. USPHS spl. rsch. fellow U. Berne, Switzerland, 1955-56, China Med. Bd. rsch. fellow, vis. prof. U. Hong Kong, 1962-63; Sterling Sullivan disting. vis. prof. Martin Luther King U., 1982; hon. prof. pharmacology and neurosci. Guangzhou Med. Coll., 1987; adv. com. Pharm. Rsch. Mfrs. Assn. Found., 1968-98; mem. coun. Am. Bur. for Med. Advancement in China, 1982; bd. dirs. Li Found., 1970—, pres., 1985-98, bd. dirs. Haight Ashbury Free Clinics, 1986-93; Tsumura prof. neuropsychopharmacology med. sch. Gunma U., Maebashi, Japan, 1989-90; sr. staff fellow Nat. Inst. on Drug Abuse, 1990-91; rschr. on drug metabolism, analgetics, devel. pharmacology, drug tolerance, drug dependence and Chinese materia medica; presenter in field. Editor: New Concepts in Pain, 1967, (with others) Fundamentals of Drug Metabolism and Drug Disposition, 1971, Endogenous and Exogenous Opiate Agonists and Antagonists, 1979; mem. editl. bd. Clin. Pharmacology, Therapeutics, 1975-87, Drug, Alcohol Dependence, 1976-87, Progress in Neuro-Psychopharmacology, 1977-91, Research Communications in Chem. Pathology and Pharmacology, 1978-91, Alcohol and Drug Dependence, 1986-91, Asian Pacific Jour. Pharm., 1985—, Jour. Chinese Medicine, 1993—; contbr. numerous articles and revs. to profl. publs. Recipient Faculty Rsch. Lectr. award, U. Calif., San Francisco, 1974, San Francisco Chinese Hosp. award, 1976, Cultural citation and Gold medal, Ministry of Edn., Republic of China, 1978, Nathan B. Eddy award, Coll. on Problems in Drug Dependence, 1979, Mentorship award, Coll. on Problems in Drug Dependence, San Juan, 2004, Chancellor's award, U. Calif., 1986, Disting. Alumnus award, U. Calif., San Francisco, 1990, Asian Pacific Am. Systemwide Alliance award, 1993, Lifetime Achievement award, Chinese Hist. Soc., 2001, Outstanding Overseas Chinese award, Chinese Cons. Benevolent Assn., Chinese Womens Assn., 2005, Cert. of Honor, Mayor Gavin Newsome, San Francisco, 2005. Fellow Am. Coll. Neuropsychopharmacology (life, emeritus), Am. Coll. Clin. Pharmacology (hon.), Coll. on Problems of Drug Dependence (exec. com. 1978-92, chmn. bd. dirs. 1978-82, Nathan B. Eddy award 1979, Mentorship award 2004); mem. AAAS, Am. Soc. Pharmacology, Exptl. Therapeutics (bd. editors 1957-65, pres. 1976-77, Torald Sollman award 1992), Fedn. Am. Socs. Exptl. Biology (exec. bd. 1975-79, pres. 1977-78), Am. Pharm. Assn. (life, Rsch. Achievement award 1962), AMA, Soc. Aid and Rehab. Drug Addicts (Hong Kong, life), Western Pharmacology Soc. (pres. 1963-64), Japanese Pharm. Soc. (hon.), Coun. Sci. Soc. Pres.' (exec. com. 1979-84, treas. 1980-84), Chinese Pharmacology Soc. (hon.), Academia Sinica (academician), Leory Man Way Found. (founder & pres. 1976-78). Office: Univ Calif Dept Cellular and Molecular Pharmacology U64 PBX 0622 San Francisco CA 94143-0001 Office Phone: 415-476-2722.

WAY, JACOB EDSON, III, museum director; b. Chgo., May 18, 1947; s. Jacob Edson Jr. and Amelia (Evans) W.; m. Jean Ellwood Chappell, Sept. 6, 1969; children: Sarah Chappell Quiroga, Rebecca Stoddard, Jacob Edson IV. BA, Beloit Coll., 1968; MA, U. Toronto, 1971, PhD, 1978; MDiv, Episcopal Theol. Sem. S.W., 2008. From instr. to assoc. prof. Beloit (Wis.) Coll., 1972—85; dir. Logan Mus. Anthropology, Beloit, 1980-85, Wheelwright Mus. Am. Indian, Santa Fe, 1985-89; interim dir. N.Mex. Mus. Natural History, Albuquerque, 1990-91; exec. dir. Space Ctr. Internat. Space Hall of Fame, Alamogordo, N.Mex., 1991-94; dir. N.Mex. Farm and Ranch Heritage Mus., 1994-99; cultural affairs officer State of N.Mex., Santa Fe, 1997—2003; realtor Margo Cutler, Ltd., Santa Fe, 2003—05; rector St. Christopher Episcopal Ch., Lubbock, Tex., 2008—. Evaluator Nat. Park Service, Denver, 1986. Contbr. articles to profl. jours. Mem. Nuke Watch, Beloit, 1983-84; cultural affairs officer State of N.Mex., 1997-2003. Research grants Wis. Humanities Com., 1984, NSF, 1981; grantee Cullister Found., 1978-84; fellow U. Toronto, 1971. Mem. Am. Assn. Mus., Am. Assn. Phys. Anthropology, Can. Assn. for Phys. Anthropology, N.Mex. Assn. Mus. (pres. 1994-96), Soc. Am. Archaeology, Wis. Fedn. Mus. (adv. bd. 1982-85). Avocations: camping, skiing, fishing, reading, horseback riding. Office Phone: 806-799-8208. Personal E-mail: jeway@earthlink.net.

WAYBURN, EDGAR, internist, environmentalist; b. Macon, Ga., Sept. 17, 1906; s. Emanuel and Marian (Voorsanger) W.; m. Cornelia Elliott, Sept. 12, 1947; children: Cynthia, William, Diana, Laurie. AB magna cum laude, U. Ga., 1926; MD cum laude, Harvard U., 1930. Hosp. tng. Columbia-Presbyn. Hosp., NYC, 1931-33; assoc. clin. prof. Stanford (Calif.) U., 1933-65, U. Calif., San Francisco, 1960-76; practice medicine specializing in internal medicine San Francisco, 1933-1985; mem. staff Pacific Presbyn. Med. Ctr., San Francisco, 1959-86, chief endocrine clinic, 1959-72, vice chief staff, 1961-63, hon. staff, 1986—. Editor: Man Medicine and Ecology, 1970, Your Land and Mine, 2004; contbr. articles to profl. and environ. jours. Mem. Sec. of Interior's Adv. Bd. on Nat. Park System, 1979-83, mem. world commn. on protected areas Internat. Union for Conservation Nature and Natural Resources; leader nat. campaigns Alaska Nat. Interest Lands Conservation Act; trustee Pacific Presbyn. Med. Ctr., 1978-86; bd. dirs. Garden Sullivan Hosp., 1965-80; chmn. People For a Golden Gate Nat. Recreation Area, 1971-2005; mem. citizens' adv. commn. Golden Gate Nat. Recreation Area, San Francisco, 1974-2003, leader nat. campaigns, 1955-90; prin. citizen advocate Redwood Nat. Park, 1968, 78; dir. The Antarctica Project, 1993-2003; mem. adv. bd. Pacific Forest Trust; hon. chmn. Tuolomne River Preservation Trust, 1983-1985; prin. adv. Enlargement of Mt. Tamalpais State Pk.; leader campaign to establish Golden Gate Nat. Recreation Area, 1972. Maj. USAF, 1942-46. Recipient Douglas award Nat. Pks. and Conservation Assn., 1987, Leopold award Calif. Nature Conservancy, 1988, Fred Packard award Internat. Union Conservation Nature, 1994, Laureate of Global 500 Roll of Honour award U.N. Environment Programme, 1994, 1st Conservation award Eeotrust, 1994, Albert Schweitzer prize, 1995, Presdl. Medal of Freedom, 1999. Fellow ACP (laureat); mem. AMA, Am. Soc. Internal Medicine, Calif. Med. Assn. (del. 1958-83, Recognition award 1986, Leadership and Quality awards 1986), San Francisco Med. Soc. (pres. 1965, Resolution of Congratulations 1986), Sierra Club (pres. 1961-64, 67-69, John Muir award 1972, hon. pres. 1993—), Sierra Club Found. (dir. 1960-87, pres. 1971-78, hon. pres. 1998—), Fedn. Western Outdoor Clubs (pres. 1953-55). Avocations: exploration, hiking.

WAYLAND, NEWTON HART, conductor; b. Santa Barbara, Calif., Nov. 5, 1940; s. L.C. Newton and Helen Bertha (Hart) W.; m. Judith Anne Curtis, July 3, 1969 (div. 1986). MusB, New Eng. Conservatory Music, 1964, MusM, 1966. Host, composer, performer Sta. WGBH-TV, Boston, 1963-82; pianist, harpsichordist Boston Symphony Orch., 1964-71; music dir. Charles Playhouse, 1965-67; pianist, guest condr., arranger Boston Pops Orch., 1971-74; resident Pops condr. Midwest Pops Orch., South Bend, Ind., 1979-91, Oakland Symphony Orch., Calif., 1980-85, Houston Symphony Orch., 1986-93; prin. Pops condr. Denver Symphony Orch., 1987-89, Vancouver (B.C.) Symphony Orch., 1993—. Guest condr. numerous orchs. U.S. and Canada, 1977—. Recs. include: Music for Zoom (PBS Emmy-winning TV show), 1971-78, Music for Nova (award-winning PBS-TV show), 1972-78, America Swings, 1987, Gershwin Plays Gershwin, 1987, Pop Go the Beatles, 1987, Classical Jukebox, 1988, Stompin' at the Savoy, 1988, Sophisticated Ladies, 1988, A Touch of Fiedler, 1989, Prime Time, 1989; arranger, performer: Jazz Loves Bach, 1968, Fiedler in Rags, 1974; arranger, condr.: Berlin to Broadway with Kurt Weill, 1972; condr. Oedipus Tex (Grammy award 1991); arranger, composer, performer (songs A&M Records) Come On and Zoom, Zoom Tunes. Recipient highest honors New Eng. Conservatory Music, 1974, Chadwick Disting. Achievement medal New Eng. Conservatory Music, 1966. Avocations: hiking, history, theater. Home and Office: 2970 Hidden Valley Ln Santa Barbara CA 93108-1619

WAYMAN, ROBERT PAUL, retired computer company executive; b. Chgo., July 5, 1945; s. Lowell Roger and Dorothy Emma (Francke) Wayman; m. Susan O. Humphrey; children: Jennifer, Allison, Grant, Kirsten, Clayton. BS in Sci. Engring., Northwestern U., Evanston, Ill., 1967, MBA, 1969. Cost acct., Instrument Divsn. Hewlett-Packard Co., Loveland, Colo., 1969—71, mgr. cost accounts, 1971—73, divsn. contr. Palo Alto, Calif., 1973—76, instrument grp. contr., 1976—83, dep. corp. contr., 1981—84, corp. contr., 1984, CFO, 1984—2006, v.p., 1984—87, sr. v.p., 1987—92, exec. v.p., 1992—2006, interim CEO, 2005. Bd. dirs. Hewlett-Packard Co., 1993—2002, 2005—, CNF, Inc., Sybase, Inc.; mem. Policy Coun. of the Tax Found. Dir. Cultural Initiatives of Silicon Valley; mem. adv. bd. Northwestern U. Kellogg Sch. Mgmt. Mem. Fin. Execs. Inst., Coun. Fin. Execs. of the Conf. Bd., Private Sector Coun.

WAYNE, MARVIN ALAN, emergency medicine physician; b. Detroit, Dec. 11, 1943; s. Jack I. and Marian M. (Berk) W.; m. Joan A. Tobin, Dec. 30, 1971; children: Michelle, Dana. MD, U. Mich., 1968. Diplomate Am. Bd. Emergency Medicine. Fellow St. Bartholomew's Hosp., London, 1968, Virginia Mason Hosp., Seattle, 1973-74; resident in surgery U. Colo. Med. Ctr., Denver, 1968-71; pvt. practice Bellingham, Wash., 1974—; staff emergency dept. St. Joseph's Hosp. (merger St. Joseph's Hosp. and St. Luke's Hosp.), Bellingham, Wash., 1974—, vice chmn. dept. emergency medicine, 1980-83, chmn., 1984-86; med. dir. Emergency Med. Svcs., Bellingham, Wash., 1975—; assoc. clin. prof. sch. medicine U. Wash., Seattle, 1986—; asst. clin. prof. Yale U. Sch. of Medicine, New Haven. Vice chmn. emergency med. svcs. com. State of Wash., 1982-83, chmn., 1983-86; med. dir. Med-Flight Helicopter, 1980—, Inst. for Pre-Hosp. Medicine, 1980—; pres. Whatcom County Emergency Med. Svcs. Coun., 1979; med. advisor Mt. Baker Ski Patrol; spkr. nat. and internat. edn. programs; founder, owner Dr. Cookie Inc., Edmonds, Wash., 1985—. Contbr. articles to med. jours. Bd. dirs. YMCA, Bellingham, 1980-84. Maj. M.C., U.S. Army, 1971-73, Vietnam. Recipient Outstanding Achievement award Whatcom County Emergency Med. Svcs. Coun., 1980, Outstanding Ednl. Achievement award Abbott Labs., 1982, Outstanding Advanced Life Support System award State of Wash., 1983, Emergency Med. Svc. rsch. award Wash. Assn. Emergency Med. Technicians and Paramedics, 1983. Fellow Am. Coll. Emergency Physicians (bd. dirs. Wash. chpt. 1977-84, pres. 1978, sci. meetings com. 1984, Outstanding Ednl. Achievement award 1982), Royal Soc. Medicine (Eng.); mem. Wash. State Med. Soc. (emergency med. svc. adv. com. 1978--), Whatcom County Med. Soc., Univ. Assn. for Emergency Medicine, Soc. Critical Care Medicine, Am. Trauma Soc. (founding), Nat. Assn. Emergency Med. Svc. Physicians, Am. Soc. Automotive Medicine, Nat. Assn. Emergency Med. Technicians. Avocations: sailing, windsurfing, skiing, baking. Office: Emergency Med Svcs 1800 Broadway Bellingham WA 98225-3133

WAYTE, ALAN (PAUL), lawyer; b. Huntington Park, Calif., Dec. 30, 1936; s. Paul Henry and Helen Lucille (McCarthy) W.; m. Beverly A. Bruen, Feb. 19, 1959 (div. 1972); children: David Alan, Lawrence Andrew, Marcia Louise; m. Nancy Kelly Wayte, July 5, 1975. AB, Stanford U., 1958, JD, 1960. Bar: Calif. 1961, U.S. Dist. Ct. (so. dist.) Calif. 1961, U.S. Supreme Ct. 1984. Ptnr. Adams, Duque & Hazeltine, LA, 1966-85, Dewey Ballantine, LA, 1985—2004; of counsel DLA Piper LLP, LA, 2004—. Mem. L.A. County Bar Assn. (chmn. real property sect. 1981-82), Am. Coll. Real Estate Lawyers (bd. govs. 1989—, pres. 1994), Am. Coll. Mortgage Attys., Anglo-Am. Real Property Inst. (bd. govs. 1989-91), L.A. Philharm. Assn. (exec. com. bd. dirs. 1973—), Chancery Club, Calif. Club (L.A.), Valley Hunt Club (Pasadena). Office: DLA Piper LLP Suite 2300 550 S Hope St Los Angeles CA 90071 Home Phone: 626-792-8187; Office Phone: 213-330-7734. Office Fax: 213-330-7534. Business E-Mail: alan.wayte@dlapiper.com.

WAZZAN, A(HMED) R(ASSEM) FRANK, engineering educator, dean; b. Lattakia, Syria, Oct. 17, 1935; married, 1959; 3 children. BS, U. Calif., Berkeley, 1959, MS, 1961, PhD in Engring. Sci., 1963. From asst. prof. to assoc. prof. engring. UCLA, 1962-69, prof. engring. and applied sci., 1974—, assoc. dean Henry Samueli Sch. Engring. and Applied Sci., 1981-86, dean Henry Samueli Sch. Engring. and Applied Sci., 1986—2001. Cons. McDonnell Douglas Corp., 1962-71, Lawrence Radiation Lab., 1965-67, Westinghouse Electric Corp., 1974-76, N.Am. Aviation, 1975-78, Rand Corp., 1975—; Honeywell Corp., 1976-78; vis. scholar Electricité de France, Paris, Office of Commr. Atomic Energy, Saclay, France, 1973-79. Reviewer Applied Mech. Rev., 1971-87. Guggenheim fellow, 1966. Fellow Am. Nuclear Soc. Achievements include research in modeling of fuel elements for fast breeder reactor, stability and transition of laminar flows, thermodynamics of solids and of dense gases, and thermal hydraulics of pressurized water reactors. Office: UCLA Henry Samueli Sch Engring Sci Box 951592 6288 Boelter Hall Los Angeles CA 90095-1592

WEAR, BYRON, councilman; Coun. mem. 2nd dist. City of San Diego.

WEATHERLEY-WHITE, ROY CHRISTOPHER ANTHONY, surgeon, consultant; b. Peshawar, India, Dec. 1, 1931; S. Roy and Elfreda (Milward) Boehm, m. Dorian Jeanne Freeman Weatherley-White, Dec. 27, 1961; children: Carl Christopher, Matthew Richard, Larissa Chantal. MA, Cambridge U., 1953; MD, Harvard U., 1958. Surgeon Biomedical Cons., Denver, 1970—; pres. Plastic Surgery Group, Denver, 1992-97. Chmn. Plastic Surgery Rsch. Coun., 1975-76; pres. Rocky Mountain Assn. Plastic Surgeons, 1973-74; v.p. Am. Cleft Palate Assn. Author: Plastic Surgery of the Female Breast, 1982; contbr. over 45 articles to profl. jours. Cons. Colo. Biomedical Venture Ctr., Denver, 1993—; chmn. bd. trustees Colo. Venture Ctrs., 1999—; bd. chairperson Operation Smile, Colo., 2000—. Recipient Rsch. award Am. Soc. Plastic Surgery, 1962, 64. Mem. Harvard Club of N.Y., Oxford-Cambridge Club, Denver Country Club, Denver Athletic Club. Episcopalian. Avocations: flying, skiing, scuba diving, archaeology. Home: 2101 E Hawthorne Pl Denver CO 80206-4116 Office: 2101 E Hawthorne Pl Denver CO 80206-4116

WEATHERUP, ROY GARFIELD, lawyer; b. Annapolis, Md., Apr. 20, 1947; s. Robert Alexander and Kathryn Crites (Hesser) W.; m. Wendy Gaines, Sept. 10, 1977; children: Jennifer, Christine. AB in Polit. Sci., Stanford U., 1968, JD, 1972. Bar: Calif. 1972, U.S. Dist. Ct. 1973, U.S. Ct. Appeals (9th cir.) 1975, U.S. Supreme Ct. 1980. Assoc. Haight, Brown & Bonesteel, LA, Santa Ana, 1972—78, ptnr., 1979—2003, Lewis Brisbois Bisgaard & Smith, LA, 2004—. Judge Moot Ct. UCLA, Loyola U., Pepperdine U.; arbitrator Am. Arbitration Assn.; mem. com. Book Approved Jury Instrns. LA Superior Ct. Mem. ABA, Calif. Acad. Appellate Lawyers, LA County Bar Assn., Town Hall Calif. Republican. Methodist. Home: 17260 Rayen St Northridge CA 91325-2919 Office: Lewis Brisbois Bisgaard & Smith 221 N Figueroa St Los Angeles CA 90012 Home Phone: 818-993-0542; Office Phone: 213-680-5130. E-mail: royweatherup@aol.com.

WEAVER, DAVE, Councilman; m. Linda Weaver; children: Noelani, Danny. BS in Civil Engring., USC, 1963. Cert. RCE. Councilman City of Glendale, Calif., 1997—, mayor, 2000—01, 2006—07. Vice chmn. Glendale Redevelopment Agy.; chmn. Glendale Housing Authority, 1997—98, former vice chmn.; chmn. Redevelopment Agy., 1999—2000, former vice chmn. Mem. Glendale C. of C.; bd. mem. Montrose C. of C.; former pres. LA Fed. Employees Credit Union League, Glendale Homeowners Coordinating Coun., chmn. Hillside Task Force. With Seabees USN, 1964—65, Construction Battalions Hdqs., ret. project mgr. CE US Army. Mem.: Filipino Bus. & Profl. Assn., Hispanic Bus. & Profl. Assn., Glenoaks Canyon Homeowners Assn. (former pres.), Rose Float Assn. (bd. mem., chmn. Dreaming of Roses Fundraiser), Bellarmine-Jefferson High Sch. Sports Booster Club (former pres.), USC Trojan Coaches Club (life), Glendale Cmty. Coll. Alumni Assn. Office: 613 E Broadway Rm 200 Glendale CA 91206 Office Phone: 818-548-4844. Fax: 818-547-6740. E-mail: dweaver@ci.glendale.ca.us.*

WEAVER, DELBERT ALLEN, retired lawyer; b. Shoshone, Idaho, May 28, 1931; s. Arlo Irving and Kate Rosamond (McCarter) W.; m. Jeanne Carol Alford, June 1959; children: Tobin Elizabeth, Michael Andrew, Matthew Stewart, Edward Malcolm. BA, U. Oreg., 1953, LLB, 1956. Bar: Oreg. 1956, U.S. Dist. Ct. Oreg. 1956, U.S. Ct. Appeals (9th cir.) 1968. Ptnr. Weaver & Oram, Eugene, Oreg., 1956-59; dep. atty. City of Portland, Oreg., 1959-68; assoc. Winfree, Latourette, Murphy, et al., Portland, 1968-71; stockbroker Dupont Glore Forgan, Portland, 1971-73; securities examiner corp. div. State of Oreg., Salem, 1973-75, dep. commr. corp. div., 1975-80; pvt. practice Portland, 1980-87; counsel Schwabe, Williamson & Wyatt, Portland, 1987-90, sr. ptnr., 1991-96; pvt. practice Portland, 1996-2000; counsel Dunn, Carney, Portland, 2000—04; ret., 2005. Personal E-mail: dweaver1091@charter.net.

WEAVER, HOWARD C., newspaper executive; b. Anchorage, Oct. 15, 1950; s. Howard Gilbert and Lurlene Eloise (Gamble) W.; m. Alice Laprele Gauchay, July 16, 1970 (div. 1974); m. Barbara Lynn Hodgin, Sept. 16, 1978. BA Johns Hopkins U., 1972, MPhil Cambridge U., 1993. Reporter, staff writer Anchorage Daily News, 1972—76, columnist, 1979—80, mng. editor, 1980—83, editor, 1983—95; editor, owner Alaska Advocate, 1976—79; asst. to pres. McClatchy Newspapers, 1995—97, editor of editl. pages, 1997—2001; v.p. news The McClatchy Co., 2001—. Internat. co-chair Northern News Svc., 1989—94; disting. lectr. journalism U. Alaska, Fairbanks, 1991. Pulitzer Prize juror, 1988, 1989, 1994, 1995, 2002; bd. visitors John S. Knight Fellowship Stanford U.; Pulitzer Prize juror, 2003. Recipient Pulitzer prize, 1976, 1989, Headliner award, Press Club of Atlantic City, 1976, 1989, Gold medal, Investigative Reporters and Editors, 1989, Pub. Svc. award, AP Mng. Editor's Assn., 1976, 1989. Mem.: Investigative Reporters and Editors, Am. Soc. Newspaper Editors, Upper Yukon River Press Club (pres. 1972), Alaska Press Club (bd. dirs. 1972—84), Sigma Delta Chi (Nat. award 1989). Avocations: hockey, travel, opera.

WEAVER, LOIS JEAN, physician, educator; b. Wheeling, W.Va., May 23, 1944; d. Lewis Everett and Ann Weaver. BA, Oberlin Coll., 1966; MD, U. Chgo., 1970. Pulmonary fellow Northwestern U., Evanston, Ill., 1975-77; trauma fellow U. Wash. Harborview Hosp., Seattle, 1977-79, research assoc., instr. medicine, 1979-81, clin. asst. prof. medicine, 1983—; clin. research fellow Virginia Mason Med. Research Ctr., Seattle, 1981-82; mem. med. staff Swedish Hosp., Seattle, 1984-92. Pulmonary cons. Fred Hutchinson Cancer Research Inst., Seattle, 1984-86, regional med. advisor and med. cons., disability quality br. Social Security, Seattle, 1985—. Contbr. sci. articles to profl. jours. La Verne Noyes scholar U. Chgo., 1966; Parker B. Francis fellow Northwestern U., 1975. Mem. AMA, Wash. Lung Assn., Sigma Xi. Avocations: gardening, music. Home: PO Box 2098 Kirkland WA 98083-2098 Office: 701 5th Ave Ste 2900 MIS 105 Seattle WA 98104-7075

WEAVER, MICHAEL JAMES, lawyer; b. Bakersfield, Calif., Feb. 11, 1946; s. Kenneth James and Elsa Hope (Rogers) W.; m. Valerie Scott, Sept. 2, 1966; children: Christopher James, Brett Michael, Karen Ashley. AB, Calif. State U., Long Beach, 1968; JD magna cum laude, U. San Diego, 1973. Bar: Calif., 1973, U.S. Dist. Ct. (so. dist.) Calif. 1973, U.S. Ct. Appeals (9th cir.) 1975, U.S. Supreme Ct. 1977. Law clk. to chief judge U.S. Dist. Ct. (so. dist.) Calif., San Diego, 1973-75; with Latham & Watkins, San Diego. Judge pro tem San Diego Superior Ct.; master of the Bench of the Inn, Am. Inns of Ct., Louis M. Welch chpt.; lectr. Inn of Ct., San Diego, 1981—, Continuing Edn. of Bar, Calif., 1983—, Workshop for Judges U.S. Ct. Appeals (9th cir.), 1990; mem. task force on establishment of bus. cts. sys. Jud. Coun. Calif., 1996-97; adv. com. U.S. Ct. Appeals (9th cir.), 2006—. Editor-in-chief: San Diego Law Rev., 1973; contbr. articles to profl. jours. Bd. dirs., pres. San Diego Kidney Found., 1985-90; bd. dirs. San Diego Aerospace Mus., 1985-97; trustee La Jolla (Calif.) Playhouse, 1990-91. lt. USNR, 1968-74. Fellow Am. Coll. Trial Lawyers; mem. San Diego Assn. Bus. Trial Lawyers (founding mem., bd. govs.), San Diego Def. Lawyers Assn. (dir.), Am. Arbitration Assn., 9th Cir. Jud. Conf. (del. 1987-90, mem. adv. com. 2006—), Calif. Supreme Ct. Hist. Assn. (bd. dirs. 1998—), Safari Club Internat. (San Diego chpt.), San Diego Sportsmen's Club, Coronado Yacht Club. Republican. Presbyterian. Avocations: reading, flying, skiing. Office: Latham & Watkins 600 West Broadway Ste 1800 San Diego CA 92101-8197 Office Phone: 619-238-3012. Business E-Mail: mike.weaver@lw.com.

WEAVER, PAULINE ANNE, lawyer; b. Hornchurch, Eng., Mar. 31, 1949; came to U.S., 1960; d. George Henry and Eunice Mary (Obee) W.; m. Charles Franklin Scribner, Mar. 2, 1974. BA, Memphis State U., 1971, JD, 1979. Bar: Tenn. 1979, Calif. 1980, U.S. Dist. Ct. (no. dist.) Calif. 1980. Law clk. Shelby County Office Pub. Defender, Memphis, 1977-79, Alameda County (Calif.) Office Pub. Defender, Oakland, 1980-82, atty., 1982—. Adj. prof. law John F. Kennedy U., Orinda, Calif. Legal advisor LWV, Fremont, Calif., 1980-83, Parent Info. Network, Fremont, 1979-84, bd. dirs., 1981-84; bd. dirs. Shelter Against Violent Environs., Fremont, 1981—; consumer rep. Alameda County Emergency Med. Care com., 1980-83; mem. Fremont/Newark Philharm. Guild, 1981—; vol. Parole Project, 1984—; vol. tutor Alameda County Adult Literacy Project; past pres. Washington Hosp. Healthcare Found.; bd. dir. Eden Housing. Donnelly J. Hill Meml. scholar Memphis State U. Law Alumni Assn., 1978. Mem. ABA (chmn. domestic violence com. 1984-85, screening subcom., Outstanding State Membership chmn. 1981, Gavel awards, ho. del., bd. gov. 2003-2006), State Bar Calif. (past v.p.), Found. of State Bar Calif. (pres. 2004-), So. Alameda County Bar Assn., Women Lawyers of Alameda County (treas. 1983—), Nat. Women's Polit. Caucus (chmn. 1982-83), Calif. Women Lawyers (past pres.), Nat. Conf. Women's Bar Assn. (past pres.), Alameda County Pub. Defenders Assn., Alameda County Dem. Lawyers Club, Order of Barristers, Alpha Gamma Delta (pres. 1981-83), Delta Theta Phi, Omicron Delta Kappa. Office: Alameda County Public Defender 1401 Lakeside Dr 4th Fl Oakland CA 94612

WEAVER, WILLIAM SCHILDECKER, retired electric power industry executive; b. Pitts., Jan. 15, 1944; s. Charles Henry and Louise (Schildecker) W.; m. Janet Kae Jones, Mar. 7, 1981. BA, Hamilton Coll., 1965; JD, U. Mich., 1968. Bar: Wash. 1968. Assoc. Perkins Coie, Seattle, 1968-74, ptnr., 1975-91; exec. v.p., CFO Puget Sound Power & Light Co., Bellevue, Wash., 1991-97; vice chmn., chmn. unregulated subs. Puget Sound Energy, 1997, pres., COO, 1997, pres., CEO, 1998—2002, chmn., 2001—02, ret. Bd. dirs. Wash. Rsch. Coun., Seattle, 1991-97, chmn., 1995-97; trustee Seattle Repertory Theatre, 1992-95, 99-00, chmn., 2000-02, Corp. Coun. Arts, 1995-02, Pacific Sci. Ctr., 1997-02; bd. dirs. Edison Electric Inst., 1998-02. Mem. ABA, Wash. State Bar Assn., Sovren, The Soc. of Vintage Racing Enthusiasts, Sports Car Club Am., Seattle Yacht Club, Flounder Bay Yacht Club.

WEBB, BRANDON (TYLER WEBB), professional baseball player; b. Ashland, Ky., May 9, 1979; s. Philip and Dreama Webb; m. Alicia Webb; 1 child, Reagan Lucille. Attended, U. Ky., Lexington. Pitcher Ariz. Diamondbacks, 2003—. Founder Brandon Webb K Found., 2005. Recipient Nat. League Cy Young award, 2006; named to Nat. League All-Star Team, MLB, 2006, 2007. Achievements include setting an Arizona Diamondbacks' franchise record with 42 1/3 scoreless innings; leading the National League in: starts, 2004, 2008; wins, 2006, 2008, shutouts, 2006, 2007; innings, 2007; complete games, 2007. Avocation: guitar. Mailing: c/o Arizona Diamondbacks Chase Field 401 E Jefferson St Phoenix AZ 85004

WEBB, H. LAWRENCE, real estate executive; m. Janet Hadley; children: Laura, Emily. Pres. Calif. divsn. John Laing Homes; CEO, WL Homes LLC (merger John Laing Homes and Watt Homes), Irvine, Calif., 1996—. Bd. dirs. Orange County Housing Authority, Interval House. Mem. Nat. Assn. Home Builders (bd. trustees Nat. Sales and Mktg. Coun., inducted into Legends of Mktg. Hall of Fame). Office: WL Homes LLC 895 Dove St Newport Beach CA 92660

WEBB, MAYNARD G., JR., Internet company executive; BA, Fla. Atlantic U. With Thomas Conrad, figgie Internat., IBM; dir., info. tech. Quantum Corp., 1991—95; v.p., CIO Bay Networks Inc., 1995—98; sr. v.p., CIO Gateway, Inc., 1998—99; pres. eBay Techs. Ebay Inc., San Jose, Calif., 1999—2002, COO, 2002—06; CEO LiveOps Inc., Palo Alto, Calif., 2006—. Bd. dir. Hyperion, 2006—.

WEBB, R. CURT, state legislator; b. Lehi, Utah, Oct. 25, 1949; m. Micheale Webb; children: Nathan, David, Suzanne. BA in Bus. Mgmt., Utah State U., 1986. Pres. Cache Title Co., 2001—; mem. Utah House of Reps., 2003—04, mem. Dist. 5, 2007—. Republican. Mormon. Office: W030 State Capitol Complex Salt Lake City UT 84114 Mailing: 233 N Main Logan UT 84321 Home Phone: 435-753-0215; Office Phone: 801-538-1029, 435-753-2467. Office Fax: 801-538-1908. Business E-Mail: curtwebb@utah.gov.

WEBB, VERONICA, fashion model, journalist; b. Detroit, Feb. 25, 1965; d. Leonard Douglas and Marion (Stewart) W.; m. George E. Robb Jr., 2002, 2 children. Student, New Sch. Social Rsch., 1983; signed with, Ford Models, Inc., NYC, 1992—. Contbg. editor, columnist Paper Mag., 1989—; contbg. editor features column Interview Mag., 1990—; spokesmodel Revlon, 1992-96. First featured on cover of Vogue, 1988; appearances incluce (films) Jungle Fever, 1991, Malcolm X, 1992, For Love or Money, 1993, Catwalk, 1995, 54, 1998, Holy Man, 1998, In Too Deep, 1999, The Big Tease, 1999. First African-Am. to receive exclusive cosmetics contract. Mem. Lifebeat (bd. dirs. 1994—). Office: United Talent Agy 9560 Wilshire Blvd Ste 500 Beverly Hills CA 90212

WEBBER, ROBERT, medical researcher; s. I.R. and Fern Webber; m. Diane Faber, Aug. 24, 1968; 1 child, Douglas. BS, U. Calif., Berkeley, 1972; PhD, UCLA Sch. Medicine, 1978. Pres., CEO Rsch. & Diagnostic Antibodies, North Las Vegas, Nev., 1984—, DSX Therapeutics, North Las Vegas, 2005—. Mem.: AAAS, Internat. Order Moose, Protein Soc., Nitric Oxide Soc., Am. Peptide Soc. Avocations: swimming, hiking, travel, cooking. Office: Research & Diagnostic Antibodies 2645 W Cheyenne Ave North Las Vegas NV 89032

WEBEL, CHARLES PETER, human science and psychology educator; b. LA, Dec. 23, 1948; s. James Webel and Jeanne (Herbert). BA, U. Calif., Berkeley, 1969, PhD, 1976; postgrad. in pub. health/social medicine, Harvard U., 1989-91. Chair Ctr. Ednl. Change, Berkeley, 1968-70; filmmaker Nat. Ednl. TV, NYC, 1969-70; lectr. social scis. U. Calif., Berkeley, 1976-78; dir. grad. programs Western Inst. Social Rsch., Berkeley, 1977-78; asst. prof. sociology New Coll., Sarasota, Fla., 1978-79; exec. editor social scis. Columbia U. Press, NYC, 1980-83; asst. prof. philosophy Calif. State U., Chico, 1984-89; teaching fellow gen. edn. Harvard U., Cambridge, Mass., 1990-91; gen. editor scholarly book series Peter Lang Pub., NYC, 1990—. Rsch. assoc. dept. anthropology U. Calif., Berkeley, 1990—94, lectr. Sch. Social Welfare, 2000-01; prof. human sci. and psychology Saybrook Inst., San Francisco, 1990—2001; Fulbright prof. U. Heidelberg, Germany, 2002-03l dir. Ctr. for Peace Studies, prof. social scis. U. Tromso, Norway, 2004-05; UNESCO chair for the philosophy of people U. Castellon, Spain, 2005-06; Fulbright sr. specialist and prof. U. Rome; prof., dir., peace & conflict studies U. NY, Prague, Czech Republic. Author: Terror, Terrorism and the Human Condition, 2006-07; author, editor: Marcuse Critical Theory and The Promise of Utopia, 1988; co-author: Peace and Conflict Studies, 2008; co-editor: Handbook of Peace and Conflict Studies, 2007; filmmaker: Lifestyle, 1969. Organizer Congress Racial Equality, N.Y.C., 1965-66; West Coast sec. Internat. Philosophers for Prevention Nuclear Omnicide, 1985-89. Fulbright scholar Fulbright Commn., Germany, 1971-72; regents fellow U. Calif., Berkeley, 1972-73, dissertation fellow Social Sci. Rsch. Coun., N.Y.C., 1974-76, grad. fellow Harvard U., 1989-91, NEH summer fellow Harvard U., 1986, NEH fellow Cornell U., 1998. Mem. Am. Philos. Assn., Am. Sociol. Assn., Internat. Soc. Polit. Psychology, World Affairs Coun. Avocations: classical music, film, global travel, sports, humor. Personal E-mail: cwebel@aol.com.

WEBER, CHARLES L., electrical engineering educator; b. Dayton, Ohio, Dec. 2, 1937; BSEE, U. Dayton, 1958; MSEE, U. So. Calif., 1960; PhD, UCLA, 1964. Tech. staff Hughes Aircraft Co., Calif., 1958-62; from asst. prof. to prof. elec. engring. U. So. Calif., 1964—. Fellow IEEE. Office: U So Calif Comm Scis Inst Dept Elec Engring Sys Los Angeles CA 90089-2565

WEBER, FRANCIS JOSEPH, archivist, museum director; b. Jan. 22, 1933; s. Frank J. and Katherine E. (Thompson) W. Student, L.A. Coll., 1953, St. Johns Coll., 1955, St. Johns Seminary, 1959, Cath. U. Am., 1962, Am. U., Washington. Ordained priest Roman Cath. Ch., 1959. Archivist Archdiocese L.A., 1962—; prof. history Queen Angels Sem., 1962-72; chaplain St. Catherine Mil. Sch., 1972-75; pastor San Buenaventura Mission, 1975-81; dir. Borromeo Guild, 1984-87; archivist Hist. Mus. Archival Ctr., Mission Hills, Calif. Dir. San Fernando Mission, 1981—. Editor The Tidings, 1990, Hoja Volante, 1984-95, Miniature Book Soc. Newsletter, 1995-97; contbr. articles to profl. jours. Pres. Zamorano Club, 1991-93; sheriff L.A. Corral Westerners, 1995; hist. rev. commn. Diocese of Monterey. Decorated Grand Cross Isabel la Catolica, 1993, Knighthood of The Holy Sepulchre; recipient Commendation award El Pueblo do L.A. State Historic Park, 1970, L.A. County Bd. Supr., 1972, L.A. City Coun., 1981, L.A. County Bd. Supr., 1992, Merit award Rounce and Coffin Club, 1969, 71, 75, 77, 79-80, 84-86, 88, 92-95, Archivist Excellence award Calif. Heritage Preservation Commn., 1995. Fellow Calif. Hist. Soc. (Merit award 1972, 83), Hist. Soc. So. Calif. (bd. dirs.); mem. Assn. Cath. Diocesan Archivists (pres. 1996-97), Santa Barbara Mission Archves (bd. dirs.), Assn. Cath. Diocesan Archives (bd. dirs.). Democrat. Roman Catholic. Office: Hist Mus Archival Ctr 15151 San Fernando Mission Blv Mission Hills CA 91345-1109

WEBER, FRED J., retired state supreme court justice; b. Deer Lodge, Mont., Oct. 6, 1919; s. Victor N. and Dorothy A. (Roberts) W.; m. Phyllis M. Schell, June 2, 1951; children: Anna Marie, Donald J., Mark W., Paul V. BA, U. Mont., 1943, JD, 1947. Bar: Mont. 1947. Atty. Kuhr & Weber, Havre, Mont., 1947-55, Weber, Bosch & Kuhr, and successors, 1956-80; justice Supreme Ct. Mont., Helena, 1981-95. Served to capt. inf. U.S. Army, 1943-46. Fellow Am. Bar Found., Am. Coll. Probate Counsel; mem. ABA, Am. Judicature Soc.

WEBER, LAVERN JOHN, retired marine science administrator, educator; b. Isabel, SD, June 7, 1933; s. Jacob and Irene Rose (Bock) W.; m. Shirley Jean Carlson, June 19, 1959 (div. 1992); children: Timothy L., Peter J., Pamela C., Elizabeth T.; m. Patricia Rae Lewis, Oct. 17, 1992. AAS, Everett Jr. Coll., 1956; BA, Pacific Luth. U., 1958; MS, U. Wash., 1962, PhD, 1964. Instr. U. Wash., Seattle, 1964-67, asst. prof., 1967-69, acting state toxicologist, 1968-69; assoc. prof. Oreg. State U., Corvallis, 1969-75, prof., 1976—, asst. dean grad. sch., 1974-77, dir. Hatfield Marine Sci. Ctr. Newport, 1977—2002, supt. Coastal Oreg. Marine Exptl. Sta., 1989-98, assoc. dean Coll. Agrl. Sci., 1998—. Pres., trustee Newport Pub. Libr., 1991-92, Yaquina Bay Econ. Found., Newport, 1991-92; chmn. Oreg. Coast Aquarium, 1983-95. Recipient Pres. award Newport Rotary, 1984-85. Mem. South Slough Mgmt. Commn., Am. Soc. Pharm. and Exptl. Therapy, West Pharm. Soc., Soc. Toxicology, Soc. Exptl. Biol. Med. (n.w. divsn., pres. 1978, 82, 87), Pacific N.W. Assn. Toxicologists (chair 1985-86, coun. 1991-93), Nat. Assn. Marine Lab. (pres. elect 1998-99, 2000-02), Western Assn. Marine Lab. (pres. 1993). Avocations: woodworking, reading, walking, scuba diving, gardening. E-mail: lavern.weber@oregonstate.edu.

WEBER, MATTHEW GEORGE, lawyer; s. Robert H. and Helena K. Weber; m. Ann Ralston Weber, Aug. 31, 1996; children: Caroline, Lindsey, Thomas. BA magna cum laude, Colo. Coll., Colorade Springs, 1985; JD, Northwestern U. Sch. Law, Evanston, Ill., 1988. Bar: US Dist. Ct., Dist. of Colo., DC Ct. Appeals 1988, US Dist. Ct., DC 1989, Colo. Supreme Ct. 1989, US Ct. Appeals, D.C. Circuit 1989, US Supreme Ct. 1992, US Ct. Appeals, 10th Circuit 1995. Assoc. atty. Dow, Lohnes & Albertson, Washington, 1988—90, Baker & Hostetler, Washington, 1991—94, Hoskin, Farina, Aldrich & Kampf, P.C., Grand Junction, Colo., 1994—99, shareholder, 1999—2003; atty. Holland & Hart, LLP, Denver, 2004—06, ptnr., 2007—. Chair of law day com. Mesa County Bar Assn., Grand Junction, 2002. Author: (68 den. u. l. rev. 57) Media Liability for the Publication of Advertising: When to Kill the Messenger; contbr. (ABA book) Managed Care Litigation. Bd. dirs. Mesa County Chpt. of ARC, Grand Junction, Colo., 1995—96; bd. trustees Mesa County Pub. Libr. Dist., Grand Junction, 1999—2003. Mem.: ABA, Am. Health Lawyers Assn., Denver Bar Assn. Office: Holland & Hart LLP 555 17th St Ste 3200 Denver CO 80202

WEBER, PAULA M., lawyer; b. Washington, Pa., June 6, 1959; BA magna cum laude, Colgate Univ., 1981; JD with high honors, George Washington Univ., 1985. Bar: Calif. 1985. Ptnr., chmn. Employment & Labor practice Pillsbury Winthrop Shaw Pittman, San Francisco. Mem.: Phi Beta Kappa, Order of the Coif. Office: Pillsbury Winthrop Shaw Pittman 50 Fremont St San Francisco CA 94105 Office Phone: 415-983-7488. Office Fax: 415-983-1200. Business E-Mail: paula.weber@pillsburylaw.com.

WEBER, STEPHEN LEWIS, academic administrator; b. Boston, Mar. 17, 1942; s. Lewis F. and Catherine (Warns) W.; m. Susan M. Keim, June 27, 1965; children: Richard, Matthew. BA, Bowling Green State U., 1964; postgrad., U. Colo., 1964-66; PhD, U. Notre Dame, 1969; EdD (hon.), Capital Normal U., China, 1994. Asst. prof. philosophy U. Maine, Orono, 1969—74, assoc. prof., 1974—79, asst. to pres., 1976-79; dean arts and scis. Fairfield U., Conn., 1979-84; v.p. acad. affairs St. Cloud State U., Minn., 1984-88; pres. SUNY Oswego, 1988—96; interim provost SUNY Albany, 1995-96; pres. San Diego State U., 1996—. Contbr. numerous articles on philosophy and acad. adminstrn. to profl. jours. Mem. Commn. on Internat. Edn. and Commn. on Govtl. Rels.; bd. govs. The Peres Ctr. for Peace, San Diego Found.; bd. dirs. San Diego Regional Econ. Devel. Corp.; mem. internat. adv. bd. Found. for the Children of the Californias; bd. dirs. NCAA Divsn. 1 hon. mem. Asia Desk, San Diego Trade Ctr. Named Outstanding Humanities Tchr., U. Maine, 1975. Mem. Am. Philos. Assn., Am. Assn. Higher Edn. Democrat. Avocations: art, woodworking, swimming, boating. Office: San Diego State Univ Office Pres 5500 Campanile Dr San Diego CA 92182-8000 E-mail: presidents.office@sdsu.edu.

WEBER, STEPHEN VANCE, physics researcher; b. Wooster, Ohio, Oct. 31, 1951; s. Dale Sarge and Lucy June (Smith) W.; m. Marie Christensen (dec. 2005), June 21, 1980; children: Erik, Kristina. AB in Physics, Princeton U., 1973; MA in Astronomy, U. Calif., Berkeley, 1974, PhD, 1978. Rsch. fellow Calif. Inst. Tech., Pasadena, 1978-80; asst. prof. Dartmouth Coll., Hanover, NH, 1980-82; rsch. scientist, physicist Lawrence Livermore Nat. Lab., Livermore, Calif., 1982—. Contbr. articles to profl. jours. Mem. Am. Phys. Soc. (excellence in plasma physics award 1995). Achievements include investigations of Rayleigh-Taylor instability and implosions in inertial confinement fusion. Office: Lawrence Livermore Nat Lab L-477 PO Box 808 Livermore CA 94551-0808 Home Phone: 925-447-9114. Business E-Mail: svweber@llnl.gov.

WEBSTER, MICHAEL ANDERSON, experimental psychologist; b. Atlanta, Mar. 24, 1958; s. John Calvin and Evelyn Gayle (Cox) W.; m. Shernaaz Michael Irani, Aug. 6, 1983; children: Anjali Dianne, Menka Linda. Exch. student, Am. U., Cairo, 1978-79; BA in Psychology, U. Calif., San Diego, 1981; MA in Psychology, U. Calif., Berkeley, 1985, PhD in Psychology, 1988. Postdoctoral fellow dept. exptl. psychology U. Cambridge, Eng., 1988-94; assoc. prof. dept. psychology U. Nev., Reno, 1994—. Contbr. articles to profl. jours. NATO fellow NSF, Cambridge U., 1988. Fellow Nat. Eye Inst. (First award 1994); mem. We. Psychol. Assn. (Outstanding Rsch. award 1998), Rocky Mountain Psychol. Assn., Exptl. Psychology Soc. (Eng.), Assn. for Rsch. in Vision and Ophthalmology, Optical Soc. Am. Achievements include research in psychophysical studies of human color vision. Office: Univ Nevada Dept Psychology Reno NV 89557-0001

WEBSTER, PETER JOHN, meteorology educator; b. Cheshire, U.K., May 30, 1942; s. James Robert and Olive W.; children: Benjamin, David. BS, Royal Melbourne Inst. Technol., Australia, 1965; PhD, MIT, 1971. Meteorologist Commn. Bur. Meteorology, 1961-67; postdoctoral fellow UCLA, 1972-73; asst. prof. U. Wash., Seattle, 1973-77; rsch. scientist CSIRO, Melbourne, Australia, 1977-83; adj. prof. Monash U., Melbourne, Australia, 1979-83; prof. Penn State U., University Pk., 1983-91; dir. program in atmospheric and oceanic scis. U. Colo., Boulder, 1991—. Chmn. TOGA Sci. Steering Group, 1986-90, TOGA COARE panel, 1989-95; co-chmn. TOGA COARE Sci. Working Group, 1988-95. Recipient Wilson Rsch. award Penn State U., 1989, Jule G. Charney award Am. Meterol. Soc., 1990, Creativity award NSF, 1990, Alexander von Humboldt Found. award, 1991. Fellow Am. Meteorol. Soc. Office: Univ Colo Prog Atmos & Ocean Scis PO Box 311 Boulder CO 80309-0311

WEBSTER, WILLIAM C., engineering educator; PhD in Naval Arch., U. Calif., Berkeley, 1966. With U. Calif., Berkeley, 1969—, prof., vice provost academic planning and facilities. Contbr. numerous articles to profl. jours. Fellow SNAME (Humboldt fellow, Davidson medal); mem. NAE. Achievements include research in non-linear coupled motions of offshore structures, operations research, shallow water fluid mechanics, steep water waves, wave energy. Office: Office of the Chancellor 222 California Hall MC 1500 Univ of Calif Berkeley CA 94720-1500 E-mail: wwebster@socrates.berkeley.edu.

WEBSTER, WILLIAM G., JR., career military officer; b. Baton Rouge, July 3, 1951; BS, U.S. Mil. Acad., 1974. Commd. 2d lt. U.S. Army, 1974, advanced through grades to lt. gen., 2007, tank co. comdr. Fort Polk, La., 1974—78, ops. and plans officer Seventh Army Combined Arms Tng. Ctr., 1979—82, ops. officer 3-64 Armor, 3d Inf. Divsn. Germany, 1979—82, asst. G-3 and brigade ops. officer 24th Inf. Divsn. Ft. Stewart, Ga., 1984—87, joint staff War Plans Divsn. Washington, 1988—91, comdr. 3d bn., 77th armor in 4th inf. divsn., 1991-93; sr. armor observer contr. Cobra Team Nat. Tng. Ctr., Ft. Irwin, Calif., 1993-94; comdr. 1st brigade, 1st cavalry divsn. Ft. Hood, 1995-97; asst.divsn. comdr. 3d Inf. Divsn., Ft. Stewart, Ga., 1997-98; comdr. Ft. Irwin and Nat. Tng. Ctr., 1998—2000; deployed Ops. Desert Thunder U.S. Army, 1998, Army's dir. tng. Office Dep. Chief of Staff G-3, 2000—01, dep. J-3 U.S. Ctrl. Command Operation Enduring Freedom Afghanistan, 2001—02, dep. comdg. gen. for ops. Third U.S. Army, Combined Forces Land Component Command, Operation Iraqi Freedom Kuwait, 2002—03, Iraq, 2002—03, comdg. gen. 3d Inf. Divsn. Ft. Stewart and Hunter Army Airfield, 2003—06; comdr. Multi-Nat. Divsn. Baghdad, Task Force Baghdad, 2005—06; dir. ops. US No. Command, 2006—07, dep. comdr., 2007—; vice comdr. US Element Am. Aerospace Def. Command (NORAD), Peterson AFB, Colo., 2007—. Decorated Legion of Merit with 4 oak leaf clusters, Air Assault badge, Parachutist badge, Def. Superior Svc. medal, Armed Forces Expeditionary medal; recipient Bronze Star. Office: US No Command 250 Vandenburg Ste B016 Peterson AFB CO 80914

WECKLER, NORA, retired psychology educator, psychotherapist; b. Toronto, Ont., Can., Feb. 16, 1915; d. Bernard and Alice Emily (Heslewood) Loeb; m. Joseph E. Weckler, Oct. 25, 1941 (dec. 1963); children— Linda Ann, David Alan. B.A., U. Toronto, 1937, M.A., 1938, Ph.D., 1941. Lic. psychologist, Calif. Instr. psychology U. Md., College Park, 1942-44; research assoc. U. Chgo., 1944-45; lectr. U. So. Calif., Los Angeles, 1945, 1951-55; from asst. prof. to assoc. prof. Los Angeles State Coll., 1955-58; prof. Calif. State U.-Northridge, 1958-85; pvt. practice psychotherapy, Los Angeles, 1968-2007; adj. prof. Pepperdine U., 1986-88. Mem. Am. Psychol. Assn., Western Psychol. Assn. (sec.-treas. 1980-86, div. pres. 1978-79), Calif. State Psychol. Assn. (conv. co-mgr.; Humanitarian award 1983). Home: 40 Camino Alto #3108 Mill Valley CA 94941

WEDDIG, FRANK O., state legislator; b. West Bend, Wis., Nov. 1, 1944; m. Patricia Weddig. Student, Bethany Coll., Waukesha Vocat. Sch., C.C. Denver, 1971—76. Comml. constrn. electrician, Aurora, Colo.; mem. Colo. State Senate, Denver, 1994-2001, Colo. State Ho. Reps., 2001—04, mem. local govt. com., vets. and mil. affairs. com. Mem. Aurora City Coun., 1981-94, mayor pro tem, 1986-87; bd. dirs. Met. Waste Water Reclamation Dist.; past mem. Aurora Planning and Zoning Commn. With USAF, 1962-66. Mem. NOW, Dem. Leadership Coun., Am. Legion, Common Cause. Democrat. Office: Colo State Ho Reps State Capitol 200 E Colfax Rm 271 Denver CO 80203 also: 15818 E 8th Cir Aurora CO 80011-7304 Fax: 303-360-0462. E-mail: frankweddig@coloradohouse.org.

WEDEPOHL, LEONHARD MARTIN, electrical engineering educator; b. Pretoria, South Africa, Jan. 26, 1933; s. Martin Willie and Liselotte B.M. (Franz) W.; m. Sylvia A.L. St. Jean; children: Martin, Graham. BSc in Engring., Rand U., 1953; PhD, U. Manchester, Eng., 1957. Registered profl. engr., BC. Planning engr. Escom, Johannesburg, 1957-61; mgr. L.M. Ericson, Pretoria, South Africa, 1961-62; sect. leader Reyrolle, Newcastle, England, 1962-64; prof., head dept. Manchester U., 1964-74; dean engring. U. Man., Winnipeg, Canada, 1974-79; dean applied sci. U. BC, Vancouver, Canada, 1979-85, prof. elec. engring., 1985-97, prof. emeritus, 1998—, dean applied sci. emeritus, 1998—. Mem. Sci. Rsch. Coun., London, 1968-74; dir. Man. Hydro, Winnipeg, 1975-79, BC Hydro, Vancouver, 1980-84, BC Sci. Coun., 1982-84; cons. Horizon Robotics, Saskatoon, 1986; chmn. implementation team Sci. Place, Can., 1985; cons. CEPEL, Rio de Janeiro; adv. Man. High Voltage DC Rsch. Ctr.; tech. advisor RTDS Techs., Inc., Winnipeg, 1994—; head protection devel. Rolls Royce Indsl. Power Group, 1995-96; adj. prof. U. Man., 2002-; co-chair Knowledge Cluster, Okanagan Partnership, Kelowna, Can., 2004-; bd. dirs. Okanagan Partnership; co-chair faculty engring. adv. com. UBC-O. Contbr. articles to sci. jours.; patentee in field. Named Hon. Citizen, City of Winnipeg, 1979. Fellow Instn. Elec. Engrs. (premium 1967), Engring. Inst. Can.; mem. Assn. Profl. Engrs. BC. Avocations: music, cross country skiing, hiking. Office: 1511 Chardonnay Pl Westbank BC Canada V4T 2P9 Business E-Mail: wedepohl@shaw.ca.

WEDGEWORTH, ANN, actress; b. Abilene, Tex., Jan. 21, 1935; m. Rip Torn, 1955 (div.); 1 child, Danae; m. Ernest Martin; 1 child, Dianna. Attended, U. Tex.; BA in Drama, So. Methodist U. Actor: (Broadway debut) Make A Million, 1958, (Broadway appearances) Chapter Two (Tony award), Thieves, Blues for Mr. Charlie, The Last Analysis, (off-Broadway appearances) Line, Chapparal, The Crucible, Days and Nights of Beebee Fenstermaker, Ludlow Fair, The Honest to God Shnozzola, A Lie of the Mind, Elba, The Aunts, The Debutante's Ball, (premiers) In the Moonlight Eddie at Pasadena Playhouse, Natural Affection in Pheonix, The Dream in Phila., (toured with nat. cos.) The Sign in Sidney Brustein's Window and Kennedy's Children, (appeared in TV series) Three's Company, The Edge of Night, Another World, Somerset, Filthy Rich, Evening Shade, (TV appearances) All That Glitters, The Equalizer, Roseanne, Bronk, Twilight Zone, Trapper John, M.D.; (TV films) The War Between the Tates, Right to Kill, Cooperstown, Fight for Justice: The Nancy Conn Story, Bogie, A Stranger Waits; (films) Handle With Care (Nat. Soc. Film Critics award), Thieves, Bang the Drum Slowly, Scarecrow, Catamount Killing, Law and Disorder, One Summer Love, Dragon-Fly, Birch Intervals, Soggy Bottom, USA, No Small Affair, Sweet Dreams, The Mens Club, A Tiger's Tale, Made in Heaven, Far North, Miss Firecracker, Green Card, Steel Magnolias, Love and a 45, The Whole Wide World, The Hunter's Moon, Hard Promises, Andy, My Science Project, The Hawk is Dying; (plays) Mother and Child, The Glass Menagerie, Period of Adjustment, Come Blow Your Horn, Goodbye Again, The Tender Trap; TV host Evening at the Improv, A&E.

WEEDEN, NORMAN FRANK, geneticist, educator; b. San Francisco, Calif., Feb. 12, 1948; s. William Frank and Patricia Chubbuck Weeden; m. Catherine Louise Ray, Oct. 6, 1975; children: Alan Matthew, Charles Edward. BS in Chemistry, Stanford U., Menlo Park, Calif., 1969; MS in Biology, Humboldt State U., Arcata, Calif., 1973; PhD in Genetics, U. Calif., Davis, 1981. Prof. Cornell U., Geneva, NY, 1982—99, Mont. State U., Bozeman, 1999—. Disting. vis. prof. South China Inst. Botany, Guangzhou, 1998—99. Editor: Pisum Genetics, 1998; author: (book) A Sierra Nevada Flora, 4th edit. Pres. Weeden Found., NY, NY, 2002—08, bd. dirs., 1993—2008. Recipient Outstanding Svc. award, North Am. Pulse Improvement Assn., 2003. Mem.: Pisum Genetics Assn. (pres. 2000—07). Independent. Achievements include patents for the Matrix Mill, a DNA extraction machine; improved biocontrol agent-Trichoderma harzianum; research in genetic studies in pea, apple, grape, and common bean. Avocations: hiking, botany, swimming, flute, guitar. Office: Dept Plant Sci and Plant Pathology Montana State Univ Bozeman MT 59717 Office Fax: 406-994-7600. Business E-Mail: nweeden@montana.edu.

WEEDIN, JAMES FRANK, biology professor, researcher; b. San Antonio, Tex., Dec. 17, 1949; m. Teresa Faye Johnson, Dec. 30, 1972. AS, San Antonio Coll., Tex., 1969; BA, U. Tex., Austin, 1975; MS, Sul Ross State U., Alpine, Tex., 1976. Prof. C.C. of Aurora, Colo., 1981—, sci. divsn. chair, 1985—93. Bot. cons. Tex. Natural Areas Survey, Austin, 1976—77. Sci. advisor: Chihuahuan Desert Trilogy Film Series, Nat. Edn. TV, 1980; author: (book) Cacti of the Trans-Pecos and Adjacent Areas, 2004 (SW Book award Border Regional Libr. Assn., 2005, Donovan S. Correll award Native Plant Soc. Tex., 2007), (profl. papers) American Jour. Botany, Southwestern Naturalist, Annals of the Mo. Botanical Gardens, (book) Cacti Of Texas - A Field Guide, 2008, Smithsonian Contribution to Botany. Mem. nursing adv. bd. Pickens Tech. Ctr., Aurora, 1982—2006. Recipient Excellence award, U. Tex. Nat. Inst. Staff and Orgnl. Devel., 1991, Master Tchr. award, U. Tex. Nat. Inst. Staff and Faculty Devel., 1991; named Faculty of Yr., C.C. of Aurora, 1990; grantee, U. Tex.-Austin, 1971, Chihuahuan Desert Rsch. Inst., 1975, Cmty. Colls. Colo., 1985. Mem.: Cactus and Succulent Soc. Am. (assoc.), Southwestern Assn. Naturalists (assoc.), Western Interior Paleontol. Soc. (assoc.), Colo. Cactus and Succulent Soc. (assoc.; v.p. 1988—89, grantee 1998, 2006). Avocations: hiking, camping, photography, travel. Home: 1189 Norfolk St Aurora CO 80011 Office: Cmty Coll of Aurora 16000 E CentreTech Pkwy Aurora CO 80011 Office Fax: 303-361-7374. Personal E-mail: weedin@comcast.net. Business E-Mail: jim.weedin@ccaurora.edu.

WEEKS, GERALD, psychologist, educator; b. Morehead City, NC, Nov. 20, 1948; s. Marion G. and Ada (Willis) W. BA in Philosophy and Psychology, East Carolina U., 1971, MA in Gen. Psychology, 1973; PhD in Clin. Psychology, Ga. State U., 1979. Diplomate Am. Bd. Profl. Psychology (pres. 1987-88, bd. dirs. 1982-87), Am. Bd. Family Psychology, Am. Bd. Sexology; cert. marital and family therapist; lic. practicing psychologist, Nev., Pa.; bd. cert. sexologist. Intern in family therapy Harlem Valley Psychiat. Ctr., Wingdale, NY, 1978-79; assoc. prof. psychology U. N.C., Wilmington, 1979-85; dir. tng. Penn Coun. for Relationships, 1985—; clin. asst. prof. psychology Sch. Medicine U. Pa., Phila., 1985-87, clin. assoc. prof., 1988-98; chair, prof. dept. counseling U. Nev.-Las Vegas, 1999—. Pvt. practice Carolina Ob-gyn. Ctr., Wilmington, 1980-85. Author: Paradoxical Therapy, 1982, Treating Couples: The Intersystem Model of the Marriage Council of Philadelphia, 1989, Promoting Change through Paradoxical Therapy, 1991, Paradoxical Psychotherapy: Theory and Practice with Individuals, Couples, and Families, 1982; co-author: (with L. L'Abate) Family Therapy: Basic Concepts and Terms, 1985, (with L. L'Abate) Integrating Sex and Marital Therapy: A Clinicians Guide, 1987, Erectile Dysfunction, 2000, (with N. Gambescia) Couples in Treatment, 1992, rev. edit., 2001, Integrative Solutions: Treating Common Problems in Couple's Therapy, 1995, (with Hof and Trent) Focused Genograms: Intergenerational Assessment of Individuals, Couples and Families, 1999, (with Demaria & Ltof) Hypoactive Sexual Desire, 2002, Treating Infidelity, (with Gambescia and Jenkins) Handbook of Family Therapy, 2003, (with Odell and Methuen) If Only I Had Known: Common Mistakes in Couples Therapy, 2004; contbr. articles to profl. jours. Fellow Am. Assn. Marital and Family Therapy (clin. mem., nat. adv. bd., approved supr.); mem. APA, Acad. Family Psychology, Interpersonal and Social Skills Assn. (founding mem.), Acad. Psychologists in Marital, Sex, and Family Therapy, Am. Assn. of Sex Educators (clin. mem.), Counselors of Therapists. Office: Dept Marriage and Family Therapy PO Box 453045 4505 S Maryland Pky Las Vegas NV 89154-3045 Office Phone: 702-895-1392. Business E-Mail: gerald.weeks@unlv.edu.

WEEKS, JOHN ROBERT, geographer, social studies educator; b. Sacramento, June 1, 1944; s. Robert Louis and Thelma Hope (Evans) W.; m. Deanna Jean Hosea, May 16, 1965; children: John Robert, Gregory, Jennifer. AB, U. Calif., Berkeley, 1966, MA, 1969, PhD, 1972. Asst. prof. sociology Mich. State U., East Lansing, 1971-74, San Diego State U., 1974-78, assoc. prof., 1978-81, prof., 1981-92, prof. geography, 1992—, chmn. dept., 1978-85; adminstrv. dir. Internat. Population Ctr., 1985—; clin. prof. family & preventive medicine U. Calif. Sch. Medicine, San Diego, 1998—. Vis. rsch. demographer U. Calif., Berkeley, 1972; cons. Allied Home Health Assn., 1978-80, Area Agy. on Aging, San Diego, 1979-81, Los Angeles Regional Family Planning Coun., 1986—, East County Econ. Devel. Coun., 1986—, UN Food and Agrl. Orgn., 2002—. Author: Teenage Marriages, 1976, Population, 10th edit., 2008, Aging, 1984, Demography of Islamic Nations, 1988, High Fertility Among Indochinese Refuges, 1989, Demographic Dynamics of the U.S.-Mex. Border, 1992. Grantee USPHS, 1983-84, 87-88, 88-89, 90—, U.S. Adminstrn. on Aging, 1979-80, U.S. Bur. of Census, 1988-89, Andrew W. Mellon Found., 1998-2001, NSF, 2001-04, NICHD, 2004—; trainee USPHS, 1967-71. Mem. Population Assn. Am., Am. Sociol. Assn., Internat. Union for Sci. Study Population, Am. Assn. Geographers. Democrat. Office: San Diego State U Dept Geography San Diego CA 92182 Office Phone: 619-594-8040. E-mail: john.weeks@sdsu.edu.

WEEKS, WILFORD FRANK, retired geophysics educator, glaciologist; b. Champaign, Ill., Jan. 8, 1929; married; 2 children. BS, U. Ill., 1951, MS, 1953; PhD in Geology, U. Chgo., 1956. Geologist mineral deposits br. U.S. Geol. Survey, 1952-55; glaciologist USAF Cambridge Research Ctr., 1955-57; asst. prof. Washington U., St. Louis, 1957-62; adj. prof. earth scis. Dartmouth Coll., Hanover, NH, 1962-85; glaciologist Cold Regions Rsch. and Engring. Lab., Hanover, 1962-89; chief scientist Alaska Synthetic Aperture Radar Facility, Fairbanks, 1986-93; prof. geophysics Geophys. Inst. U. Alaska, Fairbanks, 1986-96. Cons. in field, 1996—; vis. prof. Inst. Low Temperature Sci. Hokkaido U., Sapporo, Japan, 1973; chair Arctic marine sci. USN Postgrad. Sch., Monterey, Calif., 1978-79; mem. earth sys. sci. com. NASA, Washington, 1984-87; advisor U.S. Arctic Rsch. Commn., divsn. polar programs NSF, Washington, 1987-88; chmn. NAS Com. on Cooperation with Russia in Ice Mechanics, 1991-92; mem. environ. task force MEDEA Cons. Group, 1992-2002. Capt. USAF, 1955—57. Recipient Emil Usibelli Prize for Rsch., 1996, U. Ill. Dept. Geology Alumni Achievment award, 1999. Fellow Arctic Inst. N.Am., Am. Geophys. Union; mem. NAE, Internat. Glaciological Soc. (v.p. 1969-72, pres. 1973-75, Seligman Crystal award 1989), Am. Polar Soc. (hon.). Avocations: contrabassist, geophysics. Home and Office: 6533 SW 34th Ave Portland OR 97239-1077 Office Phone: 503-244-1695. E-mail: w-f-weeks@comcast.net.

WEESE, BRUCE ERIC, retired sales executive; b. Chewelah, Wash., Mar. 22, 1942; s. Harry M. and Roberta B. (Carman) Weese; m. Elaine M. Smith, June 18, 1962 (div. July 1972); children: Sandra G., Michael D.; m. Vera B. Reed, Mar. 22, 1975 (div. Aug. 3, 2001); 1 adopted child, Trishele. BA in Edn., Ea. Wash. State U., Cheney, 1964; MBA, Pepperdine U., 1981. Tchr. Grant Joint Union HS Dist., Sacramento, 1964-70; pharm. sales McNeil Labs., San Jose, Calif., 1970-77, Adria Labs., San Francisco, 1977-83, Serono Labs., San Francisco, 1983-84, Boehringer Ingelheim, Santa Rosa, Calif., 1984-91, mgr. govt. affairs western states, 1991-97, area mgr. managed care, 1997-98; pharm. sales rep. Olympia, Wash., 2000—08. Bd. dirs. Russian River Health Ctr., Guerneville, Calif., 1994—95, 1998—, Redwood Empire br. Am. Lung Assn., 1998—. Mem.: Sierra Club, Sequoia Paddlers, United Anglers, Santa Rosa Sailing Club. Democrat. Avocations: kayaking, sailing, fishing. Home: 4013 Grove Rd NW Olympia WA 98502-3766

WEGGE, LEON LOUIS FRANÇOIS, retired economics educator; b. Breendonk, Antwerp, Belgium, June 9, 1933; came to U.S., 1959; s. Petrus Maria and Alberta (De Maeyer) W.; m. Beate Maria Teipel, Nov. 22, 1962; children: Simone, Robert, Elizabeth. B in Thomistical Philosophy, Cath. U. Louvain, Belgium, 1957, Licentiate in Econ. Sci., 1958; PhD in Indsl. Econs., MIT, 1963. Assoc. lectr. U. New S. Wales, Kensington, Australia, 1963-66; prof. econs. U. Calif., Davis, 1966-94, retired, 1994. Vis. prof. U. Bonn, Fed. Republic Germany, 1980-81. Assoc. editor Jour. Internat. Econs., 1971-84; contbr. articles to profl. jours. Rsch. fellow Ctr. for Ops. Rsch. and Econometrics, 1972-73, fellow The Netherlands Inst. for Advanced Study, 1987-88. Mem. Econometric Soc., Am. Statistical Assn. Roman Catholic. Home: 26320 County Rd # 98 Davis CA 95616

WEH, ALLEN EDWARD, aviation executive; b. Salem, Oreg., Nov. 17, 1942; s. Edward and Harriet Ann (Hicklin) W.; m. Rebecca Ann Roberton, July 5, 1968; children: Deborah Susan, Ashley Elizabeth, Brian Roberton. BS, U. N.Mex., 1966, MA, 1973. Asst. to chief adminstrv. officer Bank N.Mex., Albuquerque, 1973; pres. N.Mex. Airways, Inc., Albuquerque, 1974; dep. dir. N.Mex. Indochina Refugee Program, Santa Fe, 1975-76; dir. pub. affairs UNC Mining & Milling Co., Albuquerque, 1977-79; pres., CEO, CSI Aviation Svcs., Inc., Albuquerque, 1979—. Chmn. New Mex. State Republican Party, 2004—08. Bd. dir. N.Mex. Symphony Orch., Albuquerque Conv. and Visitors Bur., 1982; mem. Albuquerque Police Adv. Bd., 1977-78; mem. state fin. com. G.W. Bush for Pres.; co-chmn. N.Mex. Victory, 2000; mem. nat. adv. bd. U. N.Mex. Anderson Sch. Bus.; elected del. GOP Nat. Conv., 2000, 04, 08; chmn. def. bd. Employer Support of the Guard and Res., 2002-03. Capt. USMC, 1966-71, Vietnam; Col. USMCR, 1971-97, active duty, 1990-91, Persian Gulf, 1992-93, Somalia, 2003-04, Iraq. Decorated Silver Star, Legion of Merit, Bronze Star with V device, Purple Heart with two gold stars, Meritorious Svc. medal with gold star, five Air medals. Mem. Marine Corps Res. Assn. (life), Res. Officers Assn. U.S. (life), SCV (life), N.Mex. Retail Assn. (chmn. 1999-2000). Republican. Episcopalian. Office: CSI Aviation Svcs Inc 3700 Rio Grande Blvd NW Albuquerque NM 87107-2876 Office Phone: 505-761-9000.

WEIDNER, JIM, state legislator; b. Yamhill, Oreg., Dec. 28, 1968; married; 4 children. Vibration analyst lumber companies & mills; owner Lago de Chapala restaurant; youth coach; mem. Dist. 24 Oreg. House of Reps., 2008—. Republican. Christian. Office: 900 Court St NE H-387 Salem OR 97301 Office Phone: 503-986-1424. Business E-Mail: rep.jimweidner@state.or.us.

WEIDNER, MARK, environment research executive; b. 1952; MS in Analytical Chemistry, Purdue U., 1976. With Mich. State U., East Lansing, 1976-78; instr. Finnigan Corp., San Jose, Calif., 1978-80; sr. chemist Metro Lab., Seattle, 1980-85; now pres., treas. Analytical Resources, Inc., Seattle, 1985—. Office: Analytical Resources Inc 4611 S 134th Pl #100 Tukwila WA 98168-3212

WEIERS, JAMES P., state legislator; b. Deadwood, SD, Sept. 8, 1953; m. Gina Weiers; 4 children. Pres., CEO BHF Inc.; mem. Dist. 16 Ariz. House of Reps., 1994—2002, mem. Dist. 10, 2004—, former spkr. of the house; senator from Ariz., 2002—04. Active Northside Ch. Christ. Republican. Office: Ariz House Reps Capitol Complex 1700 W Washington Rm 223 Phoenix AZ 85007-2890 Office Phone: 602-926-4173. Office Fax: 602-417-3153. Business E-Mail: jweiers@azleg.gov.*

WEIERS, JERRY P., state legislator; married; 1 child. Founder, owner Weiers Trailer Sales, Phoenix, 1988—; mem. Dist. 12 Ariz. House of Reps., 2005—, chair mil. affairs & pub. safety com., mem. natural resources & rural affairs com., water & energy com. Mem.: Ariz. Elk Soc. (life), Ariz. Desert Bighorn Sheep Soc. (life), Ariz. Antelope Soc. (life). Republican. Mailing: Ariz House Reps Capitol Complex 1700 W Washington Rm 131 Phoenix AZ 85007 Office Phone: 602-926-5894. Office Fax: 602-417-3012 602-417-3012. Business E-Mail: jpweiers@azleg.gov.*

WEIGAND, WILLIAM KENNETH, Bishop Emeritus; b. Bend, Calif., May 23, 1937; s. Harold and Alice Weigand. B in Philosophy, St. Edward's Sem., Kenmore, Wash., 1959; MDiv, St. Thomas Sem., Kenmore, 1963. Ordained priest Diocese of Boise City, Idaho, 1963, chancellor, 1964—68; missionary Cali, Colombia, 1968—78; pastor St. Hubert's Parish, Homedale, Idaho, 1978—80; ordained bishop Diocese of Salt Lake City, 1980, bishop, 1980—93, Diocese of Sacramento, 1993—2008, bishop emeritus Calif., 2008—. Roman Catholic. Office: Diocese Sacramento 2110 Broadway Sacramento CA 95818-2518 Office Phone: 916-733-0200. Office Fax: 916-733-0215.

WEIGEND, GUIDO GUSTAV, geographer, educator; b. Zeltweg, Austria, Jan. 2, 1920; came to U.S., 1939, naturalized, 1943; s. Gustav F. and Paula (Sorgo) W.; m. Areta Kelble, June 26, 1947 (dec. 1993); children: Nina, Cynthia, Kenneth. BS, U. Chgo., 1942, MS, 1946, PhD, 1949. With OSS, 1943-45; with mil. intelligence U.S. War Dept., 1946; instr. geography U. Ill., Chgo., 1946-47; instr. then asst. prof. geography Beloit Coll., 1947-49; asst. prof. geography Rutgers U., 1949-51, assoc. prof., 1951-57, prof., 1957-76, acting dept. chmn., 1951-52, chmn. dept., 1953-67, assoc. dean, 1972-76; dean Coll. Liberal Arts, Prof. geography Ariz. State U., Tempe, 1976-84, prof. geography, 1976-89; ret., 1989. Fulbright lectr. U. Barcelona, 1960-61; vis. prof. geography Columbia U., 1963-67, NYU, 1967, U. Colo., summer 1968, U. Hawaii, summer 1969; liaison rep. Rutgers U. to UN, 1950-52; invited by Chinese Acad. Scis. to visit minority areas in Chinese Cent. Asia, 1988; mem. U.S. nat. com. Internat. Geog. Union, 1951-58, 61-65; chmn. Conf. on Polit. and Social Geography, 1968-69 Author articles, monographs, bulls. for profl. jours.; contbr.: (4th edit.) A Geography of Europe, 1977; geog. editor-in-chief: Odyssey World Atlas, 1966. Bd. adjustment Franklin Twp., N.J., 1959; mem. Highland Park (N.J.) Bd. Edn., 1973-75, v.p., 1975; mem. Ariz. Coun. on Humanities and Pub. Policy, 1976-80; vice chmn. Phoenix Com. on Fgn. Rels., 1976-79, chmn., 1979-81; mem. exec. com. Fedn. Pub. Programs in Humanities, 1977-82; bd. dirs. Coun. Colls. Arts and Scis., 1980-83; commr. N. Cen. Assn. Colls. and Schs., 1976-80, bd. dirs. commn. on instns. of higher edn., 1980-83. Research fellow Office Naval Research, 1952-55, Rutgers Research Council, 1970-71; grantee Social Sci. Research Council, 1956, Ford Found., 1966, Am. Philos. Soc., 1970-71, German Acad. Exchange Service, 1984; Fulbright travel grantee Netherlands, 1970-71. Mem. Assn. Am. Geographers (chmn. N.Y. Met. divsn. 1955-56, editl. bd. 1955-59, mem. coun. 1965-66, chmn. N.Y.-N.J. divsn. 1965-66), Am. Geog. Soc., Phoenix Chamber Mus. Soc. (bd. dirs. 1995-2003, pres. 2000-03), Sigma Xi (pres. Ariz. State U. chpt. 1989-91). Office: Ariz State U Dept Geography Tempe AZ 85287 Home: 7550 N 16th St Apt 3103 Phoenix AZ 85020-4618

WEIHAUPT, JOHN GEORGE, geophysics educator, academic administrator; b. La Crosse, Wis., Mar. 5, 1930; s. John George and Gladys Mae (Ash) W.; m. Audrey Mae Reis, Jan. 28, 1961. Student, St. Norbert Coll., De Pere, Wis., 1948-49; BS, U. Wis., 1952, MS, 1953, U. Wis.-Milw., 1971; PhD, U. Wis., 1973. Exploration geologist Am. Smelting & Refining Co., Nfld., 1953, Anaconda Co., Chile, S.Am., 1956-57; seismologist United Geophys. Corp., 1958; geophysicist Arctic Inst. N.Am., Antarctica, 1958-60, Geophys. and Polar Research Center, U. Wis., Antarctica, 1960-63; dir. participating Coll. and Univ. program, chmn. dept. phys. and biol. sci. U.S. Armed Forces Inst., Dept. Def., 1963-73; assoc. dean for acad. affairs Sch. Sci., Ind. U.-Purdue U., Indpls., 1973-78, prof. geology, 1973-78; asst. dean (Grad. Sch., prof. geoscis. Purdue U.), 1975-78; prof. geology, assoc. acad. v.p., dean grad. studies and research, v.p. Univ. Research Found., San Jose (Calif.) State U., 1978-82; vice chancellor for acad. affairs U. Colo., Denver, 1982-86, prof. geoscis., 1987—. Sci. cons., mem. sci. adv. bd. Holt Reinhart and Winston, Inc., 1967—; sci. editor, cons. McGraw-Hill Co., 1966—; hon. lectr. U. Wis., 1963-73; geol. cons., 1968—; editorial cons. John Wiley & Sons, 1968; editorial adv. bd. Dushkin Pub. Group, 1971— Author: Exploration of the Oceans: An Introduction to Oceanography; mem. editorial bd. Internat. Jour. Interdisciplinary Cycle Research, Leiden; co-discoverer USARP Mountain Range (Arctic Inst. Mountain Range), in Victoria Land, Antarctica, 1960; discoverer Wilkes Land Meteorite Crater, Antarctic. Mem. Capital Community Citizens Assn.; mem. Madison Transp. Study Com., Found. for Internat. Energy Research and Tng.; U.S. com. for UN Univ.; mem. sci. council Internat. Center for Interdisciplinary Cycle Research; mem. Internat. Awareness and Leadership Council; mem. governing bd. Moss Landing Marine Labs.; bd. dirs. San Jose State U. Found. Served as 1st lt. AUS, 1953-55, Korea. Mt. Weihaupt in Antarctica named for him, 1966; recipient Madisonian medal for outstanding community service, 1973; Outstanding Cote Meml. award, 1974; Antarctic medal, 1968 Fellow Geol. Soc. Am., Explorers Club; mem. Antarctican Soc., Nat. Sci. Tchrs. Assn., Am. Geophys. Union, Internat. Council Corr. Edu., Soc. Am. Mil. Engrs., Wis. Alumni Assn., Soc. Study Biol. Rhythms, Internat. Soc. for Chronobiology, Marine Tech. Soc., AAAS, Univ. Indsl. Adv. Council, Am. Council on Edn., Expdn. Polaire France (hon.), Found. for Study Cycles, Assn. Am. Geographers, Nat. Council Univ. Research Adminstrs., Soc. Research Adminstrs., Man-Environ. Communication Center, Internat. Union Geol. Scis., Internat. Geog. Union, Internat. Soc. Study Time, Community Council Pub. TV, Internat. Platform Assn., Ind., Midwest assns. grad. schs., Western Assn. Grad. Schs., Council Grad. Schs. in U.S., Wis. Alumni Assn. of San Francisco, Kiwanis, Carmel Racquet Club (Rinconada), The Ridge at Hiwan (Evergreen, Colo., pres. 1991-93). Achievements include discovery of the Wilkes Land Anomaly and of the USARP Mt. Range in Victoria Land, both in Antarctica; also credited with revision of the discovery date of Antarctic continent by 3 centuries. Home: 30296 Snowbird Ln Evergreen CO 80439-9469 Office: U Colo Campus Box 172 PO Box 173364 Denver CO 80217-3364

WEIHRICH, HEINZ, management educator; b. Germany; came to US, 1959; s. Paul and Anna Weihrich; m. Ursula Weihrich, Aug. 3, 1963. BS, UCLA, 1966, MBA, 1967, PhD, 1973; Dr. (hon.), San Martin de Porres U., Peru, 2000. Assoc. Grad. Sch. Mgmt. UCLA, 1968-73; from asst. to assoc. prof. Ariz. State U., Tempe, 1973-80; prof. global mgmt. and behavioral sci. U. San Francisco, 1980—. Vis. prof. China Europe Internat. Bus. Sch., Shanghai, Grad. Sch. Bus. Adminstrsn., Switzerland, Peking U., Beijing; global mgmt. cons. in field; vis. prof. U. Applied Sci., Ludwigshafen, Germany. Author: Administración una perspectiva global, 1988 (best seller), Administracão Fundamentos da Teoriae da Cienca, Primeiro Volume, 1986, Administracão Organizacão Planejamento e Controle, Segundo Volume, 1987, Administracão Recursos Humanos: Desenvolvimento de Administradores, Terceiro Volume, 1; author: (with Harold Koontz and Cyril O'Donnell) Management, 1980, Japanese, Chinese and Indonesian edits., 1984, Singapore edit., 1985, Indonesian edit., 1986, Philippines edit., Bengali edit., 1989, Taiwan edit., 1985; author: (with Harold Koontz) 9th edit., 1988, Singapore edit., 1988, Chinese edit., 1989, Spanish edit., 1990 (best-seller Spanish speaking world), Korean edit., 1990, Pengurusan (Malaysian) edit., 1991, Czech edit., 1993, Hungarian edit., 1992; author: (with Harold Koontz and Cyril O'Donnell) Management: A Book of Readings, 1980, Essentials of Management, 1982, Taiwan, Philippines, Chinese and India edits., 1986, with Harold Koontz and Cyril O'Donnell: 6th edit., 2004, Chinese edit., Adminstracion Moderna, 1986; author: (with Harold Koontz) Management: A Global Perspective, 1993, Spanish edit., 1993 (best-seller Spanish speaking world), Singapore edit., 1993, Croatian edit., 1995, Chinese, 1998, Measuring Managers--A Double-Barreled Approach, 1981, Manajamen, Jilid 1, 1987, Manajamen, Jilid 2, 1986, Elementos de Administracion, 1983, with Harold Koontz: 6th edit., 2002, 7th edit., 2007, Management Excellence--Productivity through MBO, 1985, Japanese edit., 1990, Greek edit., Produttivita con L' Italian edit., 1987, Administracion, 1985, Management Basiswissen, 1986, Excelencia Administrativa (Mex.), 1987, Chinese edit., 1997, Management: A Global Perspective, internat. edit., 1993, 1993, Administración: Una Perspectiva Global, 1994, 12th edit., 2005 (best seller), Korean edit., 1996, 2006, Croatian edit., 1996, Czech edit., 1996, Elementos de Administracion - Enfoque Internactional, Exta Edicion, 2002; author: (with Harold Koontz & Mark Cannice) Administration - una Perspectiva Global Empresarial, 2008; author: (with George Odiorne and Jack Mendleson) Executive Skills: A Management by Objectives Approach, 1980, with George Odiorne and Jack Mendleson: 6th edit., 2002; author: (with Harold Koontz and A. Ramachandra Aryasri) Principles of Management, 2004; editor (with Jack Mendleson): Management: An MBO Approach, 1978; author (with Harold Koontz): Essentials of Management: Au International Perspective, 7th edit., 2007; contbr. articles to profl. jour. Grantee Am. Mgmt. Assn., 1970. Fellow Internat. Acad. Mgmt., mem. Acad. Mgmt., Assn. Mgmt. Excellence (trustee 1985-87), Assn. Bus. Simulation Exptl. Learning, Acad. Internat. Bus., Beta Gamma Sigma, Sigma Iota Epsilon. Roman Catholic. Office: U San Francisco 2130 Fulton St San Francisco CA 94117-1080

WEIL, ANDREW THOMAS, physician, educator; b. Phila., June 8, 1942; s. Daniel Pythias and Jenny (Silverstein) Weil. BA, Harvard U., 1964, MD, 1968. Intern Mt. Zion Hosp. Med. Ctr., San Francisco, 1968-69; assoc. Harvard Bot. Mus., Cambridge, Mass., 1971-84; fellow Inst. Current World Affairs, NYC, 1971-75; lectr. U. Ariz., Tucson, 1983—96, clin. prof. medicine, founder and dir. program in integrative medicine, 1996—, Lovell-Jones endowed chair integrative rheumatology, 2005—; founder, chmn. Weil Found., Vail, Ariz., Weil Lifestyle, LLC, Phoenix. Dir. integrative health and healing Miraval Resort. Author: Natural Mind, 1972, Marriage of the Sun and Moon, 1980, From Chocolate to Morphine, 1983, Health and Healing, 1984, Natural Health, Natural Medicine, 1990, Spontaneous Healing, 1995, 8 Weeks to Optimum Health, 1997, Eating Well for Optimum Health, 2000, The Healthy Kitchen, 2002, Healthy Aging, 2005, (newsletter) Self-Healing, (website) drweil.com. Served to lt. USPHS, 1969-70. Recipient Inaugural award, Am. Acad. Osteopathy, 2001. Fellow Linnean Soc. London; mem. Am. Acad. Achievement, Sigma Xi. Democrat. Buddhist. Avocation: gardening. Home: 6700 S X9 Ranch Rd Vail AZ 85641-6202 Office: Ariz Health Scis Ctr PO Box 245153 Tucson AZ 85724-5153 also: Weil Found PO Box 922 Vail AZ 85641 Office Phone: 520-647-7865. Personal E-mail: nancy@x9ranch.com.*

WEIL, LEAH, lawyer; b. LA, 1960; m. Fred Schulcz; children: Stephen, Elizabeth. BA, U. Calif., 1982, JD, 1985. Bar: 1985. Assoc. Hill, Wynne, Troop & Meisinger, LA; pvt. practice, 1992—96; various positions including sr. counsel, sr. v.p. legal affairs, dep. gen. counsel Sony Pictures Entertainment, Culver City, Calif., 1996—2001, gen. counsel, 2001—. Office: Sony Pictures Entertainment Inc 10202 W Washington Blvd Culver City CA 90232 Office Phone: 310-244-4000. Office Fax: 310-244-2626.

WEIL, LEONARD, banker; b. 1922; married With U.S. Dept. State, Vienna, Austria, 1946; with Union Bank, Los Angeles, 1946-62; pres., CEO Mfrs. Bank, Los Angeles, 1962-86, pres. emeritus, 1986—. Adj. asst. prof. fin. Anderson Grad. Sch. Mgmt., UCLA (ret.) Trustee UCLA Found.; bd. visitors UCLA Grad. Sch. Mgmt.; past pres. Town Hall; bd. dirs. Braille Inst. Served with U.S. Army, 1943-45 Mem. Calif. Bankers Assn. (bd. dirs., past pres.), Am. Mgmt. Assn., Am. Econs. Assn., Am. Bankers Assn. (past dir.). Office: PO Box 571150 Tarzana CA 91357-1150 Address: 4501 La Barca Pl Tarzana CA 91356-5029 Home Phone: 818-344-3271; Office Phone: 818-344-3183.

WEIL, LOUIS ARTHUR, III, retired newspaper publishing executive; b. Grand Rapids, Mich., Mar. 14, 1941; s. Louis Arthur, Jr. and Kathryn (Halligan) W.; m. Mary Elizabeth Buckingham, Sept. 7, 1963 (div. June 1977); children: Scott Arthur, Christopher Davison, Timothy Buckingham; m. Daryl Hopkins Goss, Jan. 26, 1980. BA in English, Ind. U., 1963; DHL (hon.), Mercy Coll., Grand Valley State U. Various positions Times Herald, Port Huron, Mich., 1966-68; personnel dir., pub. Journal and Courier, Lafayette, Ind., 1968-73; gen. mgr., pub. Gannett Westchester Rockland Newspapers, White Plains, N.Y., 1973-74, pres., gen. mgr., 1974-77, pres., pub., 1977-79; v.p. devel. Gannett Co., Inc., NYC, 1979-83, sr. v.p. planning and devel., 1982-86; chmn., pub. Gannett Westchester Rockland Newspapers, White Plains, 1984-86; pres. The Detroit News, 1986-89, pub., 1987-89; U.S. pub. Time Mag., 1989-91; pub., chief exec. officer, exec. v.p. Ariz. Republic, Phoenix Gazette, Ariz. Bus. Gazette, 1991-96; chmn., pres., CEO Central Newspapers, Inc., Phoenix, 1996-2000. Bd. dirs. Ctrl. Newspapers, Inc., Prudential. Trustee Garvin Sch. Internat. Mgmt. Thunderbird; campaign chmn. Valley of the Sun United Way, 1992; past chmn. Greater Phoenix Leadership; past pres. bd. trustees Phoenix Art Mus. With USN. Office: Louis Weil 5110 N 40th St Ste 244 Phoenix AZ 85018-2151

WEIL, MAX HARRY, internist, cardiologist, educator, researcher; b. Baden, Switzerland, Feb. 9, 1927; arrived in U.S., 1937, naturalized, 1944; s. Marcel and Gretl (Winter) Weil; children: Susan Margot, Carol Juliet. AB, U. Mich., Ann Arbor, 1948; MD, SUNY, NYC, 1952; PhD, U. Minn., Mpls., 1957; DSc (hon.), SUNY Downstate Med. Ctr., 2004. Diplomate Am. Bd. Internal Medicine and Critical Care Medicine, Nat. Bd. Med. Examiners. Intern in internal medicine U. Cin. Med. Ctr., 1952-53; resident U. Minn. Hosps., Heart Hosp., VA Hosp., Mpls., 1953-55; rsch. fellow U. Minn., Mpls., 1955-56; sr. fellow Nat. Heart Inst., Mayo Clinic, Rochester, Minn., 1956-57; chief cardiology City of Hope Med. Ctr., Duarte, Calif., 1957-59; asst. clin. prof. U. So. Calif. Sch. Medicine, LA, 1957-59, asst. prof., 1959-63, assoc. prof., 1963-71, clin. prof., 1971-81; chmn. L.A. Com. on Emergency Med. Svcs., 1968-73; prof., chmn. Dept. Medicine, chief divsn. cardiology Chgo. Med. Sch. U. Health Scis., North Chgo., 1981-91, disting. univ. prof., 1992-94, disting. univ. prof. emeritus Weil Inst. Critical Care Medicine, 1994—. Adj. prof. medicine Northwestern U. Med. Sch., Chgo., 1992—; prof. clin. med. bioengring. U. So. Calif., LA, 1972-91, adj. prof. medicine, 1981-94, clin. prof. anesthesiology, 1995—, rsch. prof. surgery, 1996—; disting. univ. prof. Weil Inst. Critical Care Medicine, Rancho Mirage, Calif., 1995—. Sect. editor Archives Internal Medicine, 1983-86, JAMA, 1969-72; guest editor Am. Jour. Cardiology, 1982, Critical Care Medicine, 1985; mem. editl. bd. Am. Jour. Medicine, 1971-79, Chest, 1980-95, Jour. Circulatory Shock, 1979-92, Clin. Engring. Newsletter, 1980—, Methods of Info. in Medicine, 1977-91, Jour. Clin. Illness, 1986—, Clin. Intensive Care, 1989—; mem. editl. adv. bd. Emergency Medicine, 1978—, Issues in Health Care Tech., 1983-86; assoc. editor Critical Care Medicine, 1973-74, mem. editl. bd., 1973-91, 94-96, sr. editor, 1997; editor-in-chief Acute Care, 1983-90, Jour. Cardiovasc. Pharmacol. Theories, 2003-; contbr. over 1100 articles to profl. jours.; patentee in field. Pres. Temple Brotherhood, Wilshire Blvd. Temple, LA, 1967-68; bd. dirs. Hollywood Presbyn. Med. Ctr., 1976-81, LA chpt. Met. Am. Heart Assn., 1962-67, Chgo. chpt. Met. Am. Heart Assn., 1982-88; active City Health and Med. Welfare Commn., Rancho Mirage, 2002-07. With US Army, 1946-47. Recipient prize in internal medicine SUNY, 1952, Alumni medallion SUNY, 1970; Disting. Svc. award Soc. Critical Care Medicine, 1984; numerous rsch. grants, 1959—; named Disting. Alumni Lectr., 1967, Oscar Schwindetzky Meml. Lectr. Internat. Anesthesia Rsch. Soc., 1978; recipient Lawrence R. Medoff award Chgo. Med. Sch., 1987, Morris L. Parker Rsch. award, 1989, Mission of Mercy award Israeli Nat. Emergency Svcs., 2001; Lilly scholar, 1988-89. Master ACP; fellow Am. Coll. Cardiology (chmn. emergency cardiac care com. 1974-81); master, fellow Am. Coll. Chest Physicians, Am. Coll. Clin. Pharmacology, Am. Coll. Critical Care Medicine (Disting. Investigator award 1990, 96, A.S. Laerdal Lifetime Achievement award 2000, Lifetime Achievement award 2001), Am. Heart Assn. (coun. circulation, coun. basic sci., coun. cardiopulmonary and critical care, coun. clin. cardiology, Dickinson W. Richards Meml. lectureship 1998, Emergency Cardiac Care Lifetime Achievement award 2000), Vet. Emergency Critical Care Soc. (Knowles Meml. lectr. 2002), NY Acad. Sci., Chgo. Soc. Internal Medicine; mem. AMA (sect. editor jour. 1969-72), IEEE, LA County Med. Assn., Am. Physiol. Soc. Am. Soc. Pharmacology and Exptl. Therapeutics, Am. Trauma Soc. (founding mem.), Assn. Computing Machinery, Assn. Am. Med. Colls., Ctrl. Soc. Clin. Rsch., Chgo. Cardiol. Group (sec.-treas. 1986-88, chmn. 1988-90), Chgo. Soc. Internal Medicine, Lake County Heart Assn. (bd. govs. 1983-86), Intensive Care Soc. UK, European Resuscitation Coun., LA Soc. Internal Medicine, Soc. Exptl. Biology and Medicine, Western Soc. Clin. Rsch., Fedn. Am. Socs. Exptl. Biology, Am. Soc. Parenteral and Enteral Nutrition, Nat. Acad. Practice (disting. practitioner), Skull and Dagger, Sigma Xi, Alpha Omega Alpha. Jewish. Avocations: swimming, tennis, photography, American history, philosophy. Office: Weil Inst Critical Care Medicine 35100 Bob Hope Dr Rancho Mirage CA 92270 Office Phone: 760-778-4911. Business E-Mail: weilm@weiliccm.org.

WEIMER, ROBERT JAY, geology educator, energy consultant, civic leader; b. Glendo, Wyo., Sept. 4, 1926; s. John L. and Helen (Mowrey) Weimer; m. Ruth Carol Adams, Sept. 12, 1948; children: Robert Thomas, Loren Edward(dec.), Paul Christner, Carl Scott. BA, U. Wyo., Laramie, 1948, MA, 1949; PhD, Stanford U., Calif., 1953; Deng (hon.), CSM, 2008. Registered profl. engr., Colo. Geologist Union Oil Co. Calif., 1949-54; cons. geologist U.S. and fgn. petroleum exploration, 1954—; prof. geology Colo. Sch. Mines, 1957-83, prof. emeritus, 1983—, Getty prof. geology, 1978-83; vis. prof. U. Colo., 1961, U. Calgary, Can., 1970, Inst. Tech., Bandung, Indonesia, 1975. Fulbright lectr. U. Adelaide, South Australia, 1967; disting. lectr. and continuing edn. lectr. Am. Assn. Petroleum Geologists, Soc. Expl. Geophysicists; ednl. cons. to petroleum cos., 1964—; mem. energy rsch. adv. bd. Dept. Energy, 1985-90, Bd. on Mineral and Energy Resources, Nat. Rsch. Coun., 1988. Editor: Guide to Geology of Colorado, 1960, Symposium on Cretaceous Rocks of Colorado and

Adjacent Area, 1959, Denver Earthquakes, 1968, Fossil Fuel Exploration, 1974, Studies in Colorado Field Geology, 1976, Petroleum System, Denver Basin, 1996. Trustee Colo. Sch. Mines Research Found., 1967-70; pres. Rockland Found., 1982-83; bd. dirs. Foothills Art Ctr., 1997-2002. With USNR, 1944-46. Recipient Disting. Alumnus award U. Wyo., 1982, Mines medal Colo. Sch. Mines, 1984, Brown medal, 1990, Parker medal Am. Inst. Profl. Geologists, 1986, Exemplary Alumni award U. Wyo., 1994, ISEM Hedberg award, 2001, Carla Coleman Conservation award, 2005, Hall of Fame award IPAMS, 2006. Fellow Geol. Soc. Am. (chmn. Rocky Mountain sect. 1966-67, Sloss award 2003), AAAS; mem. Am. Assn. Petroleum Geologists (hon. pres. 1992, Sidney Powers medal 1983, Dist. Educator award 1996), Soc. for Sedimentary Geology (hon., sec.-treas. 1966-67, v.p. 1971, pres. 1972, Twenhofel medal 1995), Colo. Sci. Soc. (hon., pres. 1981), Rocky Mountain Assn. Geologists (hon., pres. 1969, found. bd. 1976-86, Scientist of Yr. 1982, Legend award 2003), Nigerian Mining and Geoscis. Soc. (hon.), Can. Soc. Petroleum Geologists (hon.), Wyo. Geol. Assn. (hon.), Colo. Sch. Mines Alumni Assn. (hon., Coolbaugh award 1996), Am. Geol. Inst. Found. (sec., treas. 1984-88, Legendary Geosci. award 2006-), Geol. Soc. Am. Found. (bd. dirs. 1999-04), Nat. Acad. Engring. (ch. sec. 11 1999), Northwoodside Inc. Land Conservancy Found. (v.p. 1995-96, pres. 1997—, Carla Coleman Conservation award 2005, Arthur Lakes Public Svc. award, 2008), Mt. Vernon Country Club (Golden, bd. dirs. 1956-59, 81-84, pres. 1983-84). Home: RR 3 25853 Mt Vernon Rd Golden CO 80401-9699 Office Phone: 303-526-0247. Business E-Mail: rweimer@mines.edu.

WEINBERG, D. MARK, health insurance company executive; b. Aug. 4, 1952; s. Melvin Weinberg; m. Allyson Weinberg; children: Amanda, Sarah, Tiffany, Sean. BS in Elec. Engring., U. Mo., 1975. Gen. mgr. CTX Products div. Pet, Inc., St. Louis, 1975-81; prin. Touche-Ross and Co., Chgo., 1981-87; exec. v.p. Blue Cross of Calif., Thousand Oaks, 1987-92, Wellpoint Health Networks, Woodland Hills, 1992—. Pres. UNICARE, 1995—02 Contbr. articles to profl. jours. Bd. dirs. NCPFC, Pepperdine Ctr. for the Family, Lightforge Devel. Mem. Conejo Valley C. of C. (bd. dirs.). Address: Wellpoint #1 Wellpoint Way Thousand Oaks CA 91362-3800

WEINBERG, JOHN LEE, federal judge; b. Chgo., Apr. 24, 1941; s. Louis Jr. and Jane Kitz (Goldstein) W.; m. Sarah Kibbee, July 6, 1963; children: Ruth, Leo. BA, Swarthmore Coll., 1962; JD, U. Chgo., 1965. Bar: Ill. 1966, Wash. 1967, U.S. Dist. Ct. (we. dist.) Wash. 1967, U.S. Ct. Appeals (9th cir.) 1967. Law clk. to Hon. Henry L. Burman Ill. Appellate Ct., Chgo., 1965-66; law clk. to Hon. Walter V. Schaefer Ill. Supreme Ct., Chgo., 1966; law clk. to Hon. William T. Beeks U.S. Dist. Ct. Wash., Seattle, 1967-68; atty. Perkins Coie Law Firm, Seattle, 1968-73; magistrate judge U.S. Dist. Ct.; U.S. Magistrate judge Seattle, 1973—2003; ret., 2003; recalled, 2003—. Author: Federal Bail and Detention Handbook, 1988. Mem. ABA, Am. Judicature Soc., Wash. State Bar Assn., Seattle-King County Bar Assn., Fed. Magistrate Judges Assn. (nat. pres. 1982-83). Avocations: sports and physical fitness activities, bridge, jazz piano. Office: US Magistrate Judge 12th Fl United States Courthouse 700 Stewart St Seattle WA 98101 Office Phone: 206-370-8910.

WEINBERG, LEONARD BURTON, political scientist; b. NYC, Nov. 10, 1939; s. Max R. and Rose (Levin) W.; m. Ellen Bach, Aug. 23, 1966 (div.); 1 son, David; m. Sinikka Palomaki, June 4, 1986. BA, Syracuse U., 1961, PhD, 1967; MA, U. Chgo., 1963. Instr. polit. sci. U. Wis., Milw., 1966-67; asst. prof. polit. sci. U. Nev., Reno, 1967-71, assoc. prof., 1971-78, prof., 1978—, chmn. dept., 1979-82. Vis. prof. U. Florence, Italy, 1992. Author: Comparing Public Policies, 1977, After Mussolini, 1979, The Rise and Fall of Italian Terrorism, 1987, Introduction to Political Terrorism, 1989; editor: Political Parties and Terrorist Groups, 1992, Revival of Right-Wing Extremism in the 1990s, 1996, Political Violence and the Democratic Experience. 2000; co-editor: Encounters with the Radical Right, 1992, The Transformation of Italian Communism, 1994, Revival of Right-Wing Extremism in the 1990s, 1997, The Emergence of a Euro-American Radical, 1998. Recipient Fulbright Rsch. award, 1984; Italian Govt. Borsa di Studio, 1965-66; Fulbright grantee, 1965-66, Harry F. Guggenheim grantee, 1995-96. Mem. Am. Polit. Sci. Assn., Internat. Polit. Sci. Assn. (political sociology com.), Conf. Group on Italian Politics of Am. Polit. Sci. Assn., Phi Kappa Phi. Jewish. Office: U Nev Dept Polit Sci Reno NV 89557-0001 Business E-Mail: weinbrl@unr.nevada.edu.

WEINBERG, WILLIAM HENRY, chemical engineer, physicist, educator; b. Columbia, SC, Dec. 5, 1944; s. Ulrich Vivian and Ruth Ann (Duncan) W. BS, U. SC, 1966; PhD in Chem. Engring, U. Calif., Berkeley, 1970; NATO postdoctoral fellow in phys. chemistry, Cambridge U., Eng., 1971. Asst. prof. chem. engring. Calif. Inst. Tech., 1972-74, assoc. prof., 1974-77, prof. chem. engring. and chem. physics, 1977-89, Chevron disting. prof. chem. engring. and chem. physics, 1981-86; prof. chem. engring. and chemistry U. Calif., Santa Barbara, 1989—, assoc. dean Coll. Engring., 1992-96; chief sci. officer Symyx Techs., Santa Clara, Calif., 1996—. Vis. prof. chemistry Harvard U., 1980, U. Pitts., 1987-88, Oxford U., 1991; Alexander von Humboldt Found. fellow U. Munich, 1982; cons. E.I. DuPont Co. Author: (with Van Hove and Chan) Low-Energy Electron Diffraction, 1986; editor 4 books in field; mem. editl. bd. Jour. Applications Surface Sci., 1977-85, Handbook Surfaces and Interfaces, 1978-80, Surface Sci. Reports, 1980—, gen. editor, 1992—, Applied Surface Sci., 1985—, Langmuir, 1990-96, Surface Sci., 1992—, Jour. Combinatorial Chemistry, 1998—; contbr. articles to profl. jours., chpts. to books. Recipient Giuseppe Parravano award Mich. Catalysis Soc., 1989, Disting. Teaching award Coll. of Engring., U. Calif. Santa Barbara, 1995; fellow NSF, 1966-69, Alfred P. Sloan Found., 1976-78, Camille and Henry Dreyfus Found., 1976-81. Fellow AAAS, Am. Phys. Soc. (Nottingham prize 1972), Am. Vacuum Soc.; mem. AIChE (Colburn award 1981), Am. Chem. Soc. (LaMer award 1973, Kendall award 1991, Arthur W. Adamson award 1995), N.Am. Catalysis Soc., Nat. Acad. Engring., Phi Beta Kappa. Office: Symyx Technologies 415 Oakmead Pkwy Sunnyvale CA 94085 Office Phone: 408-764-2000. Business E-Mail: hweinberg@symyx.com.

WEINER, ALLEN SYDNEY, law educator; b. 1963; AB in Social Studies magna cum laude, Harvard U., 1985; JD, Stanford U., 1989. Law clk. to Judge John Steadman US Ct. Appeals DC Cir., 1989—90; atty.-adviser Office of Legal Adviser, US Dept. State, 1990—96, Office Internat. Claims and Investment Disputes, 1990—92, Office Inter-Am. Affairs, 1992—95, Office Politico-Mil. Affairs, 1995—96; attaché US Embassy, The Hague, Netherlands, 1996—98, counselor for legal affairs, 1998—2001; rsch. fellow TMC Asser Inst., The Hague, 2002—03; Warren Christopher prof. practice of internat. law and diplomacy Stanford Law Sch., 2003—07, sr. lectr. internat. law, 2007—. Vis. lectr. faculty law U. Amsterdam, 2001, 02, U. Leiden, 2002; mem. adv. com. Amsterdam-Nyenrode Law Sch., 2001—03. Office: Stanford Law Sch Crown Quadrangle 559 Nathan Abbott Way Stanford CA 94305-8610 Office Phone: 650-724-4818. Business E-Mail: aweiner@stanford.edu.

WEINER, LESLIE PHILIP, neurology educator, researcher; b. Bklyn., Mar. 17, 1936; s. Paul Larry and Sarah (Paris) W.; m. Judith Marilyn Hoffman, Dec. 26, 1959; children: Patrice, Allison, Matthew, Jonathan. BA, Wilkes Coll., 1957; MD, U. Cin., 1961. Diplomate Am. Bd. Psychiatry and Neurology. Intern in medicine SUNY, Syracuse, 1961-62; resident in neurology Johns Hopkins Hosp., Balt., 1962-65, fellow, 1967-69; resident Balt. City Hosp., 1962-63; fellow in virology Slow Virus Lab., Nat. Inst. Neurol and Communicative Disorders-Stroke, NIH, Balt., 1969; asst. prof. neurology Johns Hopkins U., 1969-72, assoc. prof., 1972-75; prof. neurology and microbiology U. So. Calif. Sch. Medicine, LA, 1975—, chmn. dept. neurology, 1979—2003, Richard Angus Grant Sr. chair in neurology, 1987—. Chief neurologist U. So. Calif. Univ. Hosp., 1991-96, mem. bd. govs.; chief neurologist L.A. county-U. So. Calif. Med. Ctr., 1979-94,; chmn. U. So. Calif. Gen. Clin. Res. Ctr., 1994-95; mem. neurosci. tng. study sect. NIH, 1990-93; mem. sci. adv. bd. Hereditary Disease Found., 1992—, chmn., 1994-96; mem. programs rsch. adv. com. Nat. Multiple Sclerosis Soc., 2000-07; cons. in field. Editor: Neural Stem Cells Methods and Protocols, 2007; assoc. editor: Neurobase, 1994-95, Neuronet; mem. editl. bd. Infectious and Geographic Neurol., 1994—; contbr. chpts. to books; contbr. over 150 articles to profl. jours. Chmn. Conn. Stem Cell Peer Review Com., 2007—; bd. dirs. Starbright Found., LA, 1991—99. Capt. M.C. US Army, 1965—67. Grantee, Conrad Hilton Found., 1995—97, Kenneth Norris Found., 1995—, NIH, 1999—, Race to Erase MS Nancy Davis Ctrs. Without Walls, 2000—, McDonald Found., Oxnard Found., Gogian Found., Heron Found. Fellow: Am. Acad. Neurology; mem.: AAAS, Nat. MS Soc. (mem. adv. com. rsch. program 2000—07, grant 2000—), Coalition Advancement Med. Rsch., Assn. Univ. Profs. Neurology, L.A. Acad. Medicine, Johns Hopkins U. Soc. Scholars, Soc. Neurosci., Am. Neurology Assn., Am. Health Assistance Found., Alpha Omega Alpha. Democrat. Jewish. Avocations: collecting books, concerts, plays. Office: RMR 506 2025 Zonal Ave Los Angeles CA 90089 Home Phone: 323-934-0633; Office Phone: 323-442-3020. Office Fax: 323-442-5500. Business E-Mail: lweiner@usc.edu.

WEINER, MICHAEL W., neuroscientist, researcher, educator; BA, Johns Hopkins U., Balt., 1961; MD, SUNY Upstate Med. Ctr., Syracuse, 1965. Diplomate in internal medicine and nephrology Am. Bd. Internal Medicine, 1972. Intern, asst. resident medicine Mt. Sinai Hosp., NYC, 1965—67; clin. fellow metabolism Yale-New Haven Med. Ctr., 1967—68; rsch. fellow Yale U. Sch. Medicine, 1968—70, U. Wis. Inst. Enzyme Rsch., Madison, 1970—72, joint appointment renal sect. dept. medicine, 1970—72, asst. prof., 1972—74; rsch. and edn. assoc. VA, 1971—74, clin. investigator, 1974—77; asst. prof. medicine U. Wis. Sch. Medicine, 1971—74, Stanford U. Sch. Medicine, 1974—80; asst. chief artificial kidney ctr. Palo Alto VA Hosp., Calif., 1974—80; chief metabolism svc. VA Hosp., Madison, 1973—74; assoc. prof. medicine in residence U. Calif., San Francisco, 1980—90, assoc. prof. radiology in residence, 1983—90, assoc. staff mem. Cardiovasc. Rsch. Inst., 1988—93, sr. staff mem. Cardiovasc. Rsch. Inst., 1994, prof. medicine, radiology and psychiatry, 1990—, mem. Alzheimer's Ctr. exec. com., 1994; chief hemodialysis unit San Francisco Vets. Affairs Med. Ctr., 1980—83, sci. dir. Magnetic Resonance Unit, 1985—, dir. Ctr. Imaging of Neurodegenerative Diseases, prin. investigator Neuroscience Ctr. Excellence. Mem. magnetic resonance com. Am. Coll. Radiology, 1989—; mem. sci. rev. bd. Alzheimer's Drug Discovery Found. (formerly Inst. for Study of Aging), 2000—; prin. investigator Alzheimer's Disease Neuroimaging Initiative. Contbr. articles to profl. publs., chapters to books; mem. editl. bd.: Nuc. Magnetic Resonance in Biomedicine, 1988—2003. Recipient Young Investigator award, Am. Coll. Cardiology, 1976, William S. Middleton award, Dept. Vets. Affairs, 2006. Fellow: Internat. Soc. Magnetic Resonance in Medicine (chair com. for affiliated sects. - SMRT 1997—98), Am. Coll. Physicians; mem.: AAAS, AAUP, Western Assn. Physicians, NY Acad. Scis., Radiol. Soc. N.Am. (Editor's Recognition award with Spl. Distinction 1993—95), Soc. Magnetic Resonance Imaging, Soc. Magnetic Resonance in Medicine, Internat. Soc. Magnetic Resonance, Internat. Soc. Artificial Organs, Western Soc. Clin. Investigation, Soc. Exptl. Biology and Medicine, Am. Soc. Pharmacology and Exptl. Therapeutics, Am. Soc. Biol. Chemists, Am. Physiol. Soc., Biophysical Soc., Am. Soc. Artificial Internal Organs, Am. Diabetes Assn., Am. Heart Assn. Coun. on Kidney in Cardiovasc. Disease, Internat. Soc. Nephrology, Am. Soc. Nephrology, Am. Fedn. Clin. Rsch., Bay Area Animal Resonance Club (founder), Mid-West Salt and Water Club, Sigma Xi. Achievements include patents in field. Office: VA Med Ctr MRS Unit 114M 4150 Clement St San Francisco CA 94121 Office Phone: 415-750-2146. Office Fax: 415-668-2864. E-mail: michael.weiner@ucsf.edu.

WEINER, PERRIE M., lawyer; b. Beverly Hills, Calif., 1961; BA summa cum laude, UCLA, 1982; JD, Loyola Law Sch., 1985. Bar: Calif. 1988. Judicial extern Judge Ralph J. Geffen, US Dist. Ct. ctrl. dist. Calif., 1985; law clk. Judge John R. Kronenberg, US Dist. Ct. ctrl. dist. Calif., 1986—87; atty. Brobeck, Phleger & Harrison, 1988—2002; mng. ptnr., internat. co-chmn. securities litig. practice group DLA Piper LLP(US), LA, 2002—. Conf. spkr. in field. Contbr. articles to profl. jours. in field. Recipient Burton award, 2006; named a So. Calif. Super Lawyer, L.A. mag., 2004—09; named one of Calif. Top Mega-Rainmakers, L.A. Daily Jour., 2004—07, Top 10 Securities Litigators in US, Securities Law 360, 2006, 500 Leading Lawyer in America, Law Dragon, 2007, 100 Lawyers, 2008. Mem.: LA County Bar Assn., Phi Beta Kappa. Office: DLA Piper LLP US 1999 Ave of the Stars 4th Fl Los Angeles CA 90067-6022 Office Phone: 310-595-3024. Office Fax: 310-595-3324. Business E-Mail: perrie.weiner@dlapiper.com.

WEINER, PETER H., lawyer; b. NYC, July 10, 1944; BA, Harvard U., 1966; MSc, London Sch. Econs., 1967; LLB, Yale U., 1970. Bar: Calif. 1971. Ptnr. Paul, Hastings, Janofsky & Walker LLP, San Francisco, 1997—, chmn. environ. practice group. Mem. Phi Beta Kappa.

WEINER, SHARON ROSE, public relations executive; d. Mike and Elaine (Feinberg) W.; m. William H. Stryker. BA, Northwestern U., 1965; MBA, U. Hawaii, 1975. Sales rsch. asst. WBBM-TV, Chgo., 1965-66; acct. exec. Pub. Relations Bd., Chgo., 1966-67; pub. relations mgr. Levi Strauss & Co., San Francisco, 1967-73, C. Brewer Co., Honolulu, 1975-76; v.p. Fawcett McDermott Cavanagh Inc., Honolulu, 1976-79; pres., chief exec. officer Stryker Weiner Co., Honolulu, 1979—. Bd. dirs. Hawaii Vis. Bur., Honolulu; v.p. bd. dirs. Aloha coun. Boy Scouts Am. Aloha United Way, Honolulu, Honolulu Symphony. Mem. Pub. Relations Soc. Am. (Gregg W. Perry award 1988), Soc. Am. Travel Writers, Pacific Area Travel Assn., Oahu Country Club, Pacific Club.

WEINGAND, DARLENE ERNA, librarian, educator; b. Oak Park, Ill., Aug. 13, 1937; d. Edward Emil and Erna (Heidenway) W..; m. Wayne Anthony Weston, Sept. 7, 1957 (div. June 1976); children: Kathleen Mary, Lynda Anne, Judith Diane, Barbara Jeanne; m. James Elberling, May 1977 (div. 1980); m. Roger Paul Couture, Apr. 7, 1984. BA in History and English, Elmhurst Coll., 1972; MALS, Rosary Coll., 1973; PhD in Adult Edn./Libr. Sci., U. Minn., 1980. Asst. prof. U. Wis., Madison, 1981-86, assoc. prof., 1986-92, prof., 1992-99, prof. emerita, 1999—, SLIS acting dir., 1991, summer 86, SLIS asst. dir., 1990-94, adminstr. SLIS Continuing Edn. Svcs., 1981-99; adj. prof. and mem. affiliate grad. faculty. U. Hawaii Manoa, Manoa, 1999—2006. Cons. in mktg., continuing edn., libr. futures, info. issues, and mgmt., 1980—; invited mentor Snowbird Leadership Inst., 1990, 92; vis. fellow Curtin U. Tech. Perth, Australia, 1990; Fulbright lectr. U. Iceland, 1988; lectr. 2d World Conf. on Continuing Edn. for Libr. and Info. Sci., Barcelona, 1993, Internat. Fedn. Libr. Assn. Author: Customer Svc. Excellence: A Concise Guide for Librarians, 1997, Future Driven Library Marketing, 1998, Marketing/Planning Library and Information Services, 1999, 4th edit., 2001, Administration of the Small Public Library, 4th edit., 2001, Budgeting and the political Process in Libraries, Simulation Games, 1992 (with others), Connections: Literacy and Cultural Heritage: Lessons from Iceland, 1992, Managing Today's Public Library: Blueprint for Change, 1994, author (with others) Continuing Professional Education and Internat. Fed. of Libr. Assoc.: Past, Present, and a Vision for the Future, 1992; contbr. articles to profl. jours. Recipient excellence award Nat. Univ. Continuing Edn. Assn., 1989, Econ. and Cmty. Devel. award, 1989, outanding achievement in audio applications award Internat. Teleconferencing Assn., 1991, LITA/Libr. Hi-Tech award, 1996, disting. alumna award Dominican U., 1998; Russia project fellow Assn. Libr. and Info. Sci., 1994. Mem. ALA, AAUW, Wis. Assn. for Adult and Continuing Edn. Personal E-mail: weingand@lava.net.

WEINHARDT, J. W., computer company executive; Chmn. bd. dirs., CEO SJW Corp., San Jose, Calif. Office: SJW Corp 374 W Santa Clara St San Jose CA 95113-1502

WEINMAN, GLENN ALAN, lawyer; b. NYC, Dec. 9, 1955; s. Seymour and Iris Rhoda W. BA in Polit. Sci., UCLA, 1978; JD, U. So. Calif., 1981. Bar: Calif. 1981. Assoc. counsel Mitsui Mfrs. Bank, LA, 1981-83; assoc. McKenna, Conner & Cuneo, LA, 1983-85, Stroock, Stroock & Lavan, LA, 1985-87; sr. counsel Buchalter, Nemer, Fields & Younger, LA, 1987-91; ptnr. Keck, Mahin & Cate, LA, 1991-93, Dongell Lawrence Finney LLP, 2006—; sr. v.p., gen. counsel Western Internat. Media Corp., LA, 1993-96; v.p. gen. counsel and human resources, sec. Guess?, Inc., LA, 1996-2000; chief adminstrv. officer Competitive Knowledge, Inc., 2000; v.p., gen. counsel, sec. Luminent, Inc., Chatsworth, Calif., 2000-01; exec. v.p., COO Insolvency Svcs. Group, Woodland Hills, Calif., 2001—03; v.p., gen. counsel, sec. Inter-Con Security Sys., Inc., Pasadena, Calif., 2003—05; ptnr. Dongell Lawrence Finney LLP, 2006—. Mem. ABA (corp. banking and bus. law sect., com. on savs. instns., com. on banking law corp. counsel sect.), Calif. Bar Assn. (bus. law sect., com. fin. instns. 1989-91, com. consumer svcs. 1991-94), LA County Bar Assn. (corp. legal depts. sect., bus. and corps. law sect., subcom. on fin. instns.), Calif. Fashion Assn. (exec. bd. 1997-2000), Am. Apparel Mfrs. Assn. (govt. rels. com. 1997-2000), Legion Lex, U. So. Calif. Law Alumni Assn., Phi Alpha Delta. Avocation: tennis. Office Phone: 213-943-6106. Personal E-mail: gaweinman@aol.com. Business E-Mail: gweinman@dflawyers.com.

WEINSTEIN, GERALD D., dermatology educator; b. NYC, Oct. 13, 1936; m. Marcia Z. Weinstein; children: Jeff, Jon, Debbie. BA, U. Pa., 1957, MD, 1961. Diplomate Am. Bd. Dermatology. Intern Los Angeles County Gen. Hosp., 1961-62; clin. assoc. dermatology br. Nat. Cancer Instn. NIH, Bethesda, Md., 1962-64; resident dept. dermatology U. Miami, Fla., 1964-65; asst. prof. Dept. Dermatology U. Miami, Fla., 1966-71, assoc. prof. Fla., 1971-74, prof. Fla., 1975-79; prof., chmn. dept. dermatology U. Calif., Irvine, 1979—, acting dean Coll. Medicine, 1985-87. Attending staff VA Med. Ctr., Long Beach, Calif., 1979—, UCI Med. Ctr., Orange, Calif., 1979—, St. Joseph Hosp., Orange, 1980—. Contbr. articles to profl. jours., chpts. to books. Recipient Lifetime Achievement award Nat. Psoriasis Found., 1994; co-recipient award for psoriasis rsch. Taub Internat. Meml., 1971; NIH spl. postdoctoral fellow, 1965-67. Mem. Am. Acad. Dermatology (chmn. task force on psoriasis 1986—, bd. dirs. 1984-88). Office: U Calif Irvine Coll Medicine Dept Dermatology C340 Med Scis Bldg 1 Irvine CA 92697-0001

WEINSTEIN, PAULA H., film producer; b. NYC, Nov. 19, 1945; d. Isadore Meyerson and Hannah (Dorner) Weinstein; m. Mark Rosenberg (dec. 1994). Student, Columbia U. Agt. William Morris and ICM, LA, 1973-76; v.p. prodn. Warner Bros., Burbank, Calif., 1976-78; sr. v.p. Twentieth Century Fox, LA, 1978-80; v.p., ptnr. Ladd Co., 1980-81; pres. United Artists Corp., 1981-82; ind. producer, cons. Columbia Pictures, Burbank, Calif., 1983; co-founder Spring Creek Prodns., 1990—. Prodr.: (films) American Flyers, 1985, A Dry White Season, 1989, The Fabulous Baker Boys, 1989, Fearless, 1993, Flesh and Bone, 1993, With Honors, 1994, Something to Talk About, 1995, Analyze This, 1999, Liberty Heights, 1999, The Perfect Storm, 2000, An Everlasting Piece, 2000, Bandits, 2001, Possession, 2002, Analyze That, 2002, Looney Tunes: Back in Action, 2003, Monster-in-Law, 2005, Rumor Has It..., 2005, The Astronaut Farmer, 2006, Blood Diamond, 2006; exec. prodr.: The House of the Spirits, 1993, Deliver Us from Eva, 2003; (TV films) The Rose and the Jackal, 1990, Bejewelled, 1991, Citizen Cohn, 1992, Because Mommy Works, 1994, Truman, 1995, The Cherokee Kid, 1996, First Time Felon, 1997, Cloned, 1997, Giving Up the Ghost, 1998, If You Believe, 1999, Crossed Over, 2002, Iron Jawed Angels, 2004, Recount, 2008 (Primetime Emmy for Outstanding Made for TV Movie, Acad. TV Arts and Scis., 2008); co-exec. prodr. (TV films) Salem Witch Trials, 2002. Democrat. Jewish. Office: Spring Creek Prodns 4000 Warner Blvd Burbank CA 91522-0001

WEINSTEIN, RONALD S., pathologist, educator; b. Schenectady, NY, Nov. 20, 1938; s. H. Edward and Shirley (Diamond) W.; m. Mary Dominica Corabi, July 12, 1964; children: Katherine Eiliesh, John Benjamin. BS, Union Coll., Schenectady, 1960; MD, Tufts U., 1965. Diplomate: Am. Bd. Pathology; 1972. Chemist Marine Biol. Lab., Woods Hole, Mass., 1960-62; intern Mass. Gen. Hosp., Boston, 1965-66, clin. and research fellow, 1965-70, resident in pathology,

1966-70; dir. Mixter Lab., 1966-70; vice chmn. pathology Aerospace Med. Research Labs., Dayton, Ohio, 1970-72; asso. prof. pathology Tufts U., 1972-75; Harriet Blair Borland prof., chmn. dept. pathology Rush Med. Coll. and Rush-Presbyn.-St. Luke's Med. Center, Chgo., 1975-90; prof., head dept. pathology U. Ariz. and U. Med. Ctr., Tucson, 1990—; dir. Ariz. Telemedicine Program, Tucson, 1996—. Teaching fellow Harvard Med. Sch., 1966-70; dir. Central Pathology Lab., Nat. Bladder Cancer Group, 1983-89, mem. editorial bd. Pathology, 1991—, J. Urologic Pathology, 1992—. Mem. editorial bd. Ultrastructural Pathology, 1979—, Human Pathology, 1980—, assoc. editor, 1983-92, mem. editorial bd. Lab. Investigation, 1983—; assoc. editor Advances in Pathology, 1985-91, editor, 1991—; contbr.: articles profl. jours. Served as maj. USAF, 1970-72. Ford Found. fellow, 1959; Congressional intern, 1959; USPHS fellow, 1965-68 Mem.: AMA, Am. Telemed. Assn. (v.p. 2001—), Internat. Coun. Soc. Pathology (v.p. 1992—98, pres. 1998—), Internat. Soc. Urologic Pathology (pres.-elect 1992—94, pres. 1995—96), Chgo. Pathol. Soc. (pres. 1979—80), Assn. Pathology (chmn., sec. treas. 1989—90, v.p. 1998—), U.S. and Can. Acad. Pathology (pres. 1988—89), Internat. Acad. Pathology (councilor 1980—82, internat.councilor 1982—84), Am. Soc. Cell Biology. Office: U Ariz Dept Pathology 1501 N Campbell Ave Tucson AZ 85724-0001

WEINSTOCK, HAROLD, lawyer; b. Stamford, Conn., Nov. 30, 1925; s. Elias and Sarah (Singer) W.; m. Barbara Lans, Aug. 27, 1950; children— Nathaniel, Michael, Philip. BS magna cum laude, N.Y. U., 1947; JD, Harvard, 1950. Bar: Conn. bar 1950, Ill. bar 1950, Calif. bar 1958. Atty. SEC, Washington, 1950-52, IRS, 1952-56; tax atty. Hunt Foods & Industries, Inc., Los Angeles, 1956-58; pvt. practice Beverly Hills, Calif., 1958-71, Los Angeles, 1971—; mem. Weinstock, Manion, Reisman, Shore & Neumann (and predecessor firms), 1958—. Lectr. extension divsn., estate planning courses U. Calif., LA, 1959—86; estate planning and taxation courses Calif. Continuing Edn. of the Bar, 1960-87. Author: Planning An Estate, 4th edit., 2002; contbr. articles to profl. publs. Nat. trustee Union Am. Hebrew Congregations, 1976-79; trustee Jewish Cmty. Found., L.A., 1993-99; adv. bd. Estate Planning Inst. UCLA Law Sch., 1979-92, NYU Inst. on Fed. Taxation, 1986-95. Mem. ABA, Calif. Bar Assn., Beverly Hills Bar Assn. (chmn. probate and trusts com. 1967-68), LA Bar Assn., Beverly Hills Estate Planning Council (pres. 1968-69), Estate Counselors Forum of LA (pres. 1963-64) Jewish (pres. temple 1974-76). Office: Weinstock Manion 1875 Century Park E Fl 15 Los Angeles CA 90067-2501

WEIR, ALEXANDER, JR., chemical engineer, consultant; b. Crossett, Ark., Dec. 19, 1922; s. Alexander and Mary Eloise (Field) W.; m. Florence Forschner, Dec. 28, 1946; children: Alexander III, Carol Jean, Bruce Richard BSChemE, U. Ark., 1943; MChemE, Poly Inst. Bklyn., 1946; PhD, U. Mich., 1954; cert., U. So. Calif. Grad. Sch. Bus. Adminstrn., 1968. Chem. engr. Am. Cyanamid Co., Stamford Rsch. Labs., 1943-47; with U. Mich., 1948-58; rsch. assoc., project supr. Engring. Rsch. Inst., U. Mich., 1948-57; lectr. chem. and metall. engring. dept. U. Mich., 1954-56, asst. prof., 1956-58; cons. Ramo-Woolridge Corp., LA, 1956-57; mem. tech. staff, sect. head, asst. mgr. Ramo-Wooldridge Corp., LA, 1957-60, incharge Atlas Missile Captive test program, 1956-60; tech. adv. to pres. Northrop Corp., Beverly Hills, Calif., 1960-70; prin. scientist for air quality So. Calif. Edison Co., LA, 1970-76, mgr. chem. sys. R & D, 1976-86, chief rsch. scientist, 1986-88; utility cons. Playa Del Rey, Calif., 1988—. Rep. Am. Rocket Soc. to Detroit Nuc. Coun., 1954-57; chmn. session on chem. reactions Nuc. Sci. and Engring. Congress, Cleve., 1955; U.S. del. AGARD (NATO) Combustion Colloquium, Liege, Belgium, 1955; Western U.S. rep. task force on environ. R & D goals Electric Rsch. Coun., 1971; electric utility advisor Electric Power Rsch. Inst., 1974-78, 84-87; industry advisor dept. chemistry and biochemistry Calif. State U., L.A., 1981-88. Author: Two and Three Dimensional Flow of Air through Square-Edged Sonic Orifices, 1954; (with R.B. Morrison and T.C. Anderson) Notes on Combustion, 1955, also some 60 tech. papers; inventor acid rain prevention device used in 5 states. Sea scout leader, Greenwich, Conn., 1944-48, Marina del Rey, Calif., 1965-70; bd. govs., past pres. Civic Union Playa del Rey, chmn. sch., police and fire, nominating, civil def., army liaison coms.; mem. Senate, Westchester YMCA, chmn. Dads sponsoring com., active fundraising; chmn. nominating com. Paseo del Rey Sch. PTA, 1961; mem. LA Mayors Cmty. Adv. Com.; asst. chmn. advancement com., merit badge dean Cantinella dist. LA Area coun. Boy Scouts Am. Recipient Nat. Rsch. Coun. Flue Gas Desulfurization Industrials Scale Reliability award NAS, 1975, Power Environ. Achievement award EPA, 1980, Excellence in Sulfur Dioxide Control award EPA, 1985; named Arkansas Traveler by Gov. Bill Clinton, 1989; Cert. Appreciation, City of LA, 2008. Mem.: AIChE, Am. Geophys. Union, Navy League U.S. (v.p. Palos Verdes peninsula coun. 1961—62), NY Acad. Scis., Sci. Rsch. Soc. Am., Am. Chem. Soc., U.S. Power Squadron (navigator), St. Andrew Soc. So. Calif. (hon. capt. of fleet 1997, mem. bd. govs., chair scholarship com.), Clan Buchanan Soc. Am., Ark. Soc. Children of Am. Revolution (past pres.), Betty Washington Lewis Soc. Children of Am. Revolution (past pres.), Clan MacFarlane Soc., Clan Chattan of the US, Clan Farquharson Assn., Clan Macnachtan Assn., Santa Monica Yacht Club (lifetime hon. cannoneer, chief of protocol, vice chmn. marina mgmt. com.), Sigma Xi, Phi Kappa Phi, Phi Lambda Upsilon, Alpha Chi Sigma, Lambda Chi Alpha. Office: 8229 Billowvista Dr Playa Del Rey CA 90293-7807

WEIR, BRYCE KEITH ALEXANDER, neurosurgeon, neurologist, educator; b. Edinburgh, Apr. 29, 1936; arrived in U.S., 1992, arrived in Can., 2002; s. Ernest John and Marion Weir; m. Mary Lou Lauber, Feb. 25, 1976; children: Leanora, Glyncora, Brocke. BSc, McGill U., Montreal, Que., Can., 1958, MD, CM, 1960, MSc, 1963. Diplomate Am. Bd. Neurol. Surgery, Nat. Bd. Med. Examiners. Intern Montreal Gen. Hosp., 1960-61; resident in neurosurgery Neurological Inst., Montreal, 1962-64, 65-66, NY Neurol. Inst., NYC, 1964—65; neurosurgeon U. Alta., Edmonton, Can., 1967-92, dir. div. neurosurgery, 1982-86, Walter Anderson prof., chmn. dept. surgery, 1986-92; surgeon-in-chief U. Alta. Hosps., 1986-92; Maurice Goldblatt prof. surgery and neurology U. Chgo., 1992—2002, dir. Brain Rsch. Inst., 1993—2001, interim dean biol. scis. divsn. and Pritzker Sch. Medicine, v.p. med. affairs, 2001—02. Past pres. V Internat. Symposium on Cerebral Vasospasm; mem. neurology A study sect. NIH, 1991—93; invited speaker at over 135 profl. meetings; vis. prof. over 68 univs., including Yale U., Cornell U., Columbia U., Duke U., U. Toronto, U. Calif., San Francisco; lectr. in field. Author: Aneurysms Affecting the Nervous System, 1987, Subarachnoid Hemorrhage-Causes and Cures, 1998, Cerebral Vasospasm, 2001; co-editor: Primer on Cerebrovascular Diseases, 1997, Stroke: Pathophysiology, Diagnosis and Management, 4th edit., 2004; mem. editl. bd. Jour. Neurosurgery, chmn. bd, 1993—94, mem. editl. bd. Neurosurgery Quar., Jour. Cerebrovascular Disease, Neurosurgery; contbr. over 275 articles to profl. jours. Named Officer of the Order of Can., 1995. Fellow: ACS, Royal Coll. Surgeons Can., Royal Coll. Surgeons Edinburgh (hon.); mem.: Can. Neurosurg. Soc. (Inaugural Lifetime Achievement award 2006), Interurban Neurosurg. Soc. (chmn.), Nat. Acad. Scis., Inst. Medicine, Japan Neurosurg. Soc. (hon.), Soc. Neurol. Surgeons (Grass gold medal 1992), Am. Acad. Neurol. Surgeons, James. IV Assn. Surgeons, Am. Surg. Assn. Achievements include rsch. in cerebral vasospasm and the surgical management of intracranial aneurysms. Home: 1262 Saturna Dr Parksville BC V9P 2X6 Canada

WEIS, FREDERICK M., academic administrator; m. Mary Fraser Weis; children: Matt, Marianna. Grad., Claremont McKenna Coll., 1965, MBA in Mgmt. and Fin., MA in Higher Edn. Dir. fin. and bus. affairs, treas. Scripps Coll., Claremont, Calif., 1980—82, interim pres., 2007—; v.p., treas. Claremont McKenna Coll., 1982—2002, exec. practitioner in residence, 2003—. Bd. mem. EDFUND, Rancho Cordova, Calif. Contbr. articles to profl. jours. Office: Scripps Coll Office of Pres 1030 Columbia Ave Claremont CA 91711 Office Phone: 909-621-8000.

WEISE, STEVEN O., lawyer; b. LA, Nov. 1, 1949; BA, Yale U., 1971; JD, Boalt Hall Sch. Law, 1974. Bar: Calif. 1974. Shareholder Heller, Ehrman, White & McAuliffe LLP, LA, 1991—. Pres. Fin. Lawyers Conf., 1994; lectr. in field. Contbr. articles to profl. jours. Dir. House Ear Inst., 1975—81, Children's Partnership, 1995—, Inner City Law Ctr., 1996—. Mem.: ABA (mem. coun. bus. law sect. 1998—, chmn. uniform comml. code com. personal property secured transactions 1986—90, advisor uniform comml. code Article 9 drafting com. 1995—98), State Bar Calif. (chmn. exec. com. 1994—95, chmn. uniform comml. code com. 1990—91, mem. permanent editl. bd. uniform comml. code 1998—). Office: 333 S Hope St 39th Fl Los Angeles CA 90071 Office Phone: 213-244-7831. Office Fax: 213-614-1868. Business E-Mail: steve.weise@hellerehrman.com. E-mail: sweise@hewm.com.

WEISEL, THOMAS W., investment company executive; Founder, chmn. & CEO Montgomery Securities, San Francisco, 1978—98, Thomas Weisel Partners, San Francisco, 1999—. Co-author (with Lance Armstrong & Richard Bryant): Capital Instincts: Life As an Entrepreneur, Financier & Athlete, 2003. Trustee Mus. Modern Art, NYC, San Francisco. Office: Thomas Weisel Ptnrs 1 Montgomery St San Francisco CA 94104

WEISER, PAUL DAVID, manufacturing executive; b. NYC, May 30, 1936; s. Irving Julius and Rose (Peckerman) W.; m. Paula Lee Block, June 19, 1960; children: Amy Helen, Deborah Susan. BS in Metallurgy, M.I.T., 1959; LL.B. (editor law rev.), U. Calif., Berkeley, 1963. Bar: Calif. 1963. Assoc. firm Mitchell, Silberberg & Knupp, Los Angeles, 1963-68; sec., gen. counsel Hitachi Koki Imaging Solutions, Inc. (formerly Dataproducts Corp.), 1968—, sr. v.p., sec. Simi Valley, Calif.; chmn. adv. com. shareholder communications SEC, 1981. Contbr. articles legal publns. Served with USAR, 1959-60. Mem. Am. Bar Assn., Am. Soc. Corp. Secs. Jewish. Office: 1757 Tapo Canyon Rd Simi Valley CA 93063-3391

WEISER, TIMOTHY L., athletic director; b. Gt. Bend, Kans., Jan. 30, 1958; 3. Susan Conway; children: Rudy, Melanie. BS in Psychology, Emporia U., Kans., 1981, MS in Counseling, 1982. Admissions counselor Emporia State U., 1982-83; asst. to dir. athletics Wichita (Kans.) State U., 1983-85, asst. dir. athletics, 1985-87, assoc. dir., 1987-88; dir. athletics Austin Peay State U., 1988-93, Ea. Mich. U., 1993-98, Colo. State U., Ft. Collins, 1998—. Office: Colo State U Colo State Athletics Fort Collins CO 80523-0001

WEISS, BOB (ROBERT WILLIAM WEISS), former professional basketball coach; b. Easton, Pa., May 7, 1942; m. Tracy Pritchard. BA, Pennsylvania State U., University Park, PA, 1965. Player Phila. 76er's, 1965-67, Seattle SuperSonics, 1967-68, Milwaukee Bucks, 1968, Chgo. Bulls, 1969-74, Buffalo Braves, 1974-76, Washington Bullets, 1976-77; asst. coach San Diego Clippers, 1977-79, Dallas Mavericks, 1980-86; head coach San Antonio Spurs, 1986-88; asst. coach Orlando Magic, 1989-90; head coach Atlanta Hawks, 1990-93, LA Clippers, 1993—94; asst. coach Seattle SuperSonics, 1994—2005, head coach, 2005—06.

WEISS, CARL, aerospace company executive; b. Bklyn., Dec. 6, 1938; s. Morris Harold and Sonia B. (Botwinick) W.; m. Judith Fellner, Jan. 27, 1963; children: Daniel Oren, Jonathan Michael. BBA, CUNY, 1961, MBA, 1968; postgrad., Harvard U., Boston, 1971. CPA, NY. Acct. Joseph Warren & Co., NYC, 1965-68; asst. contr. Fisher Radio Corp., LI, NY, 1968-69; sr. v.p. Deutsch Relays, Inc., East Northport, NY, 1969-83; owner, exec. v.p. Logical Solutions, Inc., Melville, NY, 1983-92; owner, pres., COO G&H Tech., Inc., Camarillo, Calif., 1992—. Bd. dirs. Deutsch Dagan, Inc. With U.S. Army, 1961-67. Mem. AICPA (future issues com. 1985-88); NY Soc. CPA. Office: G & H Tech Inc 750 W Ventura Blvd Camarillo CA 93010-8382

WEISS, JACK, councilman; m Leslie Kautz; children: two. JD, UCLA. Fgn. policy advisor, Washington; arms control researcher; law clk. US Dist. Ct. Judge Lourdes G. Baird; asst. US atty. LA; lawyer Century City; councilman, Dist. 5 LA City Coun., 2001—, mem. planning & land use mgmt. com., mem. rules and govt. com., vice chair ad hoc stadium com., chair pub. safety com. Sr. fellow Truman Nat. Security Project; founding mem. Cesar E. Chavez Found.; mem. Pacific Coun. on Internat. Policy. Trustee Alternative Living for Aging; chair Santa Monica Bay Restoration Commn.; pres. Santa Monica Bay Watershed Coun.; mem. southwest regional bd. Anti-Defamation League. Recipient award for Public Svc., LA League of Conservation Voters, 2003, Humanitarian award, LA Commn. on Assaults Against Women, 2005; named New Democrat of Week, Democratic Leadership Coun., 2002; named one of 100 New Democrats to Watch, 2003. Mem. Los Angeles Conservancy, Westside Urban Forum, Heal the Bay, LA County Young Democrats, UCLA Law Alumni Assn. (bd. dir.). Office: City Hall 200 N Spring St Rm 440 Los Angeles CA 90012 Office Phone: 213-473-7005. Office Fax: 213-978-2250. Business E-Mail: Councilmember.Weiss@lacity.org.*

WEISS, KENNETH R., newswriter; b. Calif. B in Folklore, U. Calif., Berkeley. Washington corr. NY Times Regional Newspapers; reporter States New Svc., Washington, LA Times, 1990—. Co-recipient John B. Oakes award for Outstanding Environmental Journalism, Columbia U. Grad. Sch. Journalism, 2006, George Polk award for Environmental Reporting, 2006, Walter Sullivan award for Excellence in Sci. Journalism, Am. Geophys. Union, 2007, Pub. Comm. award, Am. Soc. Microbiol., 2007, Print Media award, Am. Inst. Biol. Scis., 2007, Pulitzer Prize for Explanatory Reporting, 2007. Avocation: surfing. Office: LA Times 202 W 1st St Los Angeles CA 90012 E-mail: ken.weiss@latimes.com.

WEISS, MARTIN HARVEY, neurosurgeon, educator; b. Newark, Feb. 2, 1939; s. Max and Rae W.; m. R. Debora Rosenthal, Aug. 20, 1961; children: Brad, Jessica, Elisabeth. AB magna cum laude, Dartmouth Coll., 1960, BMS, 1961; MD, Cornell U., 1963. Diplomate Am. Bd. Neurol. Surgery (bd. dirs. 1983-89, vice chmn. 1987-88, chmn. 1988-89). Intern Univ. Hosps., Cleve., 1963-64, resident in neurosurgery, 1966-70; sr. instr. to asst. prof. neurosurgery Case Western Res. U., 1970-73; asso. prof. neurosurgery U. So. Calif., 1973-76, prof., 1976-78, prof., chmn. dept., 1978—2004, Martin H. Weiss chair in neurol. surgery, 1997—. Chmn. neurology B study sect. NIH; mem. residency rev. com. for neurosurg. Accreditation Commn. for Grad. Med. Edn., 1989—, vice chmn., 1991—93, chmn., 1993—95, mem. appeals coun. in neurosurg., 1995—; vis. prof. U. Mich, 1987; vis. prof. Med. Sch. Harvard U., 1988; vis. prof. U. Wash., 1988, U. Calif., San Francisco, 1994, U. Oreg., 1995, Tufts U., 1996, U. Melbourne, 1996, U. Sydney, 1996, U. Erlangen/Nurnberg, 1999, U. Geneva, 1999, U. Tex., 2004, U. Oreg., 2004, Stanford U., 2005; vis. prof., Bronson Ray lectr. Cornell U., 2005—06; Afrox traveling prof. South African Congress Neurol. Surgeons, 1989; hon. guest Royal Coll. Physicians Endocrine Sect., London, 2001; lectr. in field. Author: Pituitary Diseases, 1980; assoc. editor Bull. L.A. Neurol. Socs., 1976-81, Jour. Clin. Neurosci., 1981—; mem. editl. bd. Neurosurgery, 1979-84, Neurol. Rsch., 1980—, Jour. Neurosurgery, 1987—, chmn., 1995—, assoc. editor, 1996—; editor-in-chief Clin. Neurosurgery, 1980-83, Neuro Sociological Focus, 1996-. Served to capt. USAR, 1964—66, assoc. in gen. surgery USAH, USMA, 1964—66, West Point, NY. Spl. fellow in neurosurgery NIH, 1969-70; recipient Jamieson medal Australasian Neurosurg. Soc., 1996, Pevehouse medal Calif. Assn. Neurol. Surgeons, 2008. Mem. ACS (adv. coun. neurosurgery 1985-88), Soc. Neurol. Surgeons (v.p. 1999, pres.-elect 2000—, pres. 2001-02), Neurosurg. Soc. Am., Am. Acad. Neurol. Surgery (exec. com. 1988-89, v.p. 1992-93, Cushing medal 2005), Rsch. Soc. Neurol. Surgeons, Am. Assn. Neurol. Surgeons (bd. dirs. 1988-91, sec. 1994-97, pres.-elect 1998-99, pres. 1999-00, past pres. 2000-01, Kurze Lectr. 2005, Cushing Medalist, 2005), Congress Neurol. Surgeons (v.p. 1982-83), Western Neurosurg. Soc. (Cloward medal 2006), Neurosurg. Forum, So. Calif. Neurosurg. Soc. (pres. 1983-84), Neurosurgeon Rsch. & Edn. Found. (chmn., exec. com. 2004-), Phi Beta Kappa, Alpha Omega Alpha. Home: 357 Georgian Rd La Canada Flintridge CA 91011-3520 Office: 1200 N State St Los Angeles CA 90033-1029 Home Phone: 818-790-7467; Office Phone: 323-226-7421. Business E-Mail: weiss@usc.edu.

WEISS, NOEL S., epidemiologist; b. Chgo., Mar. 10, 1943; s. Sidney and Dorothy (Bloom) W.; m. Chu Chen, Oct. 12, 1980; children: Jessica, Jeremy. BA, Stanford U., 1965, MD, 1967; MPH, Harvard U., 1969, DrPH, 1971. Epidemiologist Nat. Ctr. for Health Stats., Rockville, Md., 1971-73; prof. U. Washington, Seattle, 1973—; epidemiologist Fred Hutchinson Cancer Rsch. Ctr., Seattle. Author: Clinical Epidemiology: The Study of the Outcome of Illness, 1996. Recipient Rsch. Career Devel. award Nat. Cancer Inst., 1975, Outstanding Investigator award Nat. Cancer Inst., 1985. Mem. Inst. of Medicine, Soc. for Epidemiol. Rsch., Am. Epidemiol. Soc. Democrat. Office: U Wash Sch Pub Health & Cmty Med Dept Epidemiology Box 357236 Seattle WA 98195-7236

WEISS, ROBERT MICHAEL, dermatologist; b. NYC; s. Leonard Seymour and Edith Rose (Levine) W.; 1 child, Michael Louis. Ba, U. Pa., 1970; MD, SUNY, Buffalo, 1974. Diplomate Am. Bd. Dermatology. Intern in internal medicine SUNY, Buffalo, 1974-75, resident in internal medicine, 1975-76, resident in dermatology, 1976-79; pvt. practice in dermatology Las Vegas, Nev., 1979—. Fellow Am. Acad. Dermatology; mem. AMA. Home: 2310 Paseo Del Prado Ste 110 Las Vegas NV 89102-4329

WEISS, ROBERT STEPHEN, medical manufacturing company operating executive; b. Oct. 25, 1946; s. Stephen John and Anna Blanche (Lescinski) W.; m. Marilyn Annette Chesick, Oct. 29, 1970; children: Christopher Robert, Kim Marie, Douglas Paul. BS in Acctg. cum laude, U. Scranton, 1968. CPA, N.Y. Supr. KPMG (formerly Peat, Marwick, Mitchell & Co.), NYC, 1971-76; asst. corp. contr. Cooper Labs., Inc., Parsippany, N.J., 1977-78; group contr. Cooper Vision, Inc., 1980; v.p., corp. contr. Cooper Labs., Palo Alto, Calif., 1981-83, The Cooper Cos., Inc. (formerly CooperVision, Inc.), Palo Alto, Calif., 1984-89; v.p., treas., CFO The Cooper Cos., Inc., Pleasanton, Calif., 1989—2005, sr. v.p., 1992-95, exec. v.p. fin., 1995—2005, COO, 2005—07, CEO, 2007—, pres., 2007—. Bd. dirs. The Cooper Cos., Inc., Pleasanton, Calif, 1996-, Accuray Inc., Sunnyvale, Calif., 2007-. With U.S. Army, 1969-70. Decorated Bronze Star with oak leaf cluster, Army Commendation medal. Mem. AICPA, N.Y. State Soc. CPAs. Office: The Cooper Companies Inc Ste 590 6140 Stoneridge Mall Rd Pleasanton CA 94588 Business E-Mail: rweiss@cooperco.com.

WEISS, SAMUEL, neurobiologist, educator; BSc in Biochemistry, McGill U., Montreal; PhD in Neurobiology, U. Calgary. Postdoctoral fellow Alberta Heritage Found. for Med. Rsch. and Med. Rsch. Coun. Can., 1983—88; asst prof. to prof., Alberta Heritage Found. for med. rsch. scientist, dept. cell biology & anatomy & pharmacology & therapeutics, faculty medicine U. Calgary, 1988—, co-founder, inaugural chair, genes and develop. rsch. group; dir. Hotchkiss Brain Inst. Recipient Alberta Innovation-Growing Brain Cells, Heritage Cmty. Found., 2002, Gairdner Found. Internat. award, 2008; named a Researcher of the Month, Canadians for Health Rsch., 2005. Achievements include discovery of with Fritz Stadeczek discovered the metabotropic glutamate receptor in 1985; adult neural stem cells in mammalian brain and its importance in nerve cell regeneration in 1992; patents in field. Office: Hotchkiss Brain Inst U Calgary 2263 3330 Hospital Dr NW Calgary AB Canada T2N 4N1 Business E-Mail: weiss@ucalgary.ca.*

WEISS, STEPHEN M., lawyer; b. Phila., Mar. 11, 1943; m. Sherry L. Weiss; children: Benjamin, Jessica. BA, U. Ariz., Tucson, 1965, JD, 1968. Bar: Ariz., US Ct. Appeals (9th cir.), US Supreme Ct. 1974. Ptnr. Karp & Weiss P.C., Tucson, 1995—2008, 2008—. Judge pro tempore Pima County Superior Ct., 1981—. Author: (chpt. to book) Domestic Torts, 1989. Mem. Pima County Commn. Trial Ct. Appts., 1985—89, Pima County Commn. Jud. Performance Rev., 1993—95, Supreme Ct. Com. Character and Fitness, 2000—06, co-chair, 2005—06. Named Trial Lawyer of Yr., Trial Lawyers for Pub. Justice, 1994. Mem.: ABA, Ariz. Attys. Criminal Justice, Pima County Bar Assn., State Bar Ariz., Am. Trial Lawyers Assn., Nat. Assn. Criminal

Def. Lawyers, Nat. Conf. Bar Examiners (character and fitness com. 2006—07, state bar criminal law adv. com. 2007—), Fed. Bar Assn. (pres. Tucson chpt. 2001), Morris K. Udall Inn of Ct. (pres. 2002). Office: Karp Weiss PC 3060 N Swan Rd Tucson AZ 85712 Office Phone: 520-325-4200. Office Fax: 520-325-4224. Business E-Mail: sweiss@karpweiss.com.

WEISS, WALTER STANLEY, lawyer; b. Newark, Mar. 12, 1929; s. Jack and Mollie (Orkin) W.; m. Misty M. Moore; children from previous marriage: Jack Stephen, Andrew Scott. AB, Rutgers U., 1949, JD, 1952. Bar: D.C. 1952, N.J. 1956, Calif. 1961. Trial atty. IRS, Phila., Los Angeles, 1957-62; asst. U.S. atty., chief tax div. Los Angeles, 1962-63; ptnr. firm Goodson & Hannam, Los Angeles, 1963-67; mng. ptnr. firm Long & Levit, Los Angeles, 1967-79; ptnr. firm Greenberg & Glusker, Los Angeles, 1979-81, Rosenfeld, Meyer and Susman, Beverly Hills, Calif., 1981-93; prin. Law Office of Walter S. Weiss, LA, 1993—. Judge pro tem L.A. and Santa Monica (Calif.) Mcpl. Cts., 1994—. Contbr. articles to legal jours. Served to capt. JAGC USAF, 1953-56. Named Arbitrator Nat. Assn. Securities Dealers, 1974 Fellow Am. Coll. Trial Lawyers; mem. ABA, Los Angeles County Bar Assn., Beverly Hills Bar Assn. Home: 12349 Ridge Cir Los Angeles CA 90049-1183 Office: 1800 Century Pk E Ste 300 Los Angeles CA 90067 Home Phone: 310-471-4320. E-mail: waltersweiss@gmail.com.

WEISS, WILLIAM HANS, small business owner; b. Spokane, Wash., Feb. 25, 1952; m. Bonnie Weiss; 1 child, Olivia. BA in Human Svcs., Western Wash. U., 1977; MA in Psychology, Goddard Coll., 1980; postgrad., Northwestern Calif. U. Law Sch.; JD, Rutherford U., 2005. Prin. Vocat. Mgmt. Resources, Redmond, Wash., 1980—. Vocat. cons. various cities Social Security Adminstrn.; instr. Western Wash. U., 1990; adj. faculty mem. Seattle Pacific U., 1991; cons. U.S. Dept. Edn. Rehab. Svcs. Adminstrn. Ambassador Sovereign Order of Malta to the Rep. Marshall Islands, 2003—06; consul Republic of Malta, Wash., 2001—. Named Knight of Magistral Grace, Knights of Malta, 1996. Mem.: Internat. Bar Assn. London. Roman Catholic. Office: PO Box 1104 Duvall WA 98019 Office Phone: 425-788-3120. Personal E-mail: consulatewashington@hotmail.com.

WEISSBRODT, ARTHUR S., federal judge; BA, Pa. State U., 1966; JD, Columbia U., 1969. Law clk. to Hon. Edward J. Dimock U.S. Dist. Ct. (so. dist.) N.Y.; apptd. bankruptcy judge no. dist. U.S. Dist. Ct. Calif., 1989. Office: 280 S 1st St Rm 3035 San Jose CA 95113-3010

WEISSMAN, IRVING L., medical researcher; b. Great Falls, Mont., Oct. 21, 1939; married, 1961; 4 children. BS, Mont. State Coll., 1960, DSc (hon.), 1992; MD, Stanford U., 1965. NIH fellow dept. radiology Stanford U., 1965—67, rsch. assoc., 1967—68, from asst. prof. to assoc. prof. dept. pathology, 1969—81; prof. pathology Stanford U. Sch. Medicine, 1981—, Karel & Avice Beekhuis Prof. Cancer Biology, 1987—, prof. devel. biology, 1989—, dir., Inst. of Stem Cell Biology and Regenerative Medicine, 2003—, prof. by courtesy, neurosurgery, prof. by courtesy, biol. sciences. Sr. Dernham fellow Calif. divsn. Am. Cancer Soc., 1969—73; mem. immunobiology study sect. NIH, 1976—80; mem. founding scientific adv. bd. Amgen, 1981—89, DNAX, 1981—92; James McGinnis Meml. lectr. Duke U., 1982; mem. sci. rev. bd. Howard Hughes Med. Inst., 1986; George Feigen Meml. lectr. Stanford U., 1987; Albert Coons Meml. lectr. Harvard U., 1987; Jame Stahlman lectr. Vanderbilt U., 1987; mem. sci. adv. com. Irvington House Inst., 1987; 5th Ann. vis. prof. cancer biology U. Tex. Health Sci. Ctr., 1987; R. E. Smith lectr. U. Tex. Sys. Cancer Ctr., 1988; co-founder SyStemix, Inc., 1988, bd. dirs., 1988—97; mem. founding scientific adv. bd. T-Cell Scis. (now Avant, Inc.), 1988—92; Chauncey D. Leake lectr. U. Calif., 1989; Harvey lectr. Rockefeller U., 1989; Rose Litman lectr., 90; disting. lectr. Western Soc. Clin. Investment, 1990; chmn. U.S.-Japan Immunology Bd., 1992—94; chmn. sci. adv. com. McLaughlin Rsch. Inst., 1992—, trustee, 1992—; bd. govs. Project Inform, 1995—; co-founder Stem-Cells, 1996—, mem. bd. dirs.; co-founder Celltrans (now Cellerant), 2001—; chair scientific adv. bd. Cellerant; spkr. in field. Contbr. articles to profl. publications. Recipient Faculty Rsch. award, Nat. Am. Cancer Soc., 1974—78, Basic Cell Rsch. award, Am. Soc. Cytopathology, Pasarow Award for cancer rsch., 1989, Kaiser Award for Excellence in Preclinical Teaching, Outstanding Investigator Award, NIH, E. Donnall Thomas Award, Am. Soc. Hematology, deVillers Award for Outstanding Achievements in Leukemia Rsch., Leukemia Soc. Am., J. Allyn Taylor Internat. Prize in Medicine, Bass Award, Soc. Neurological Surgeons, Calif. Scientist of Yr., 2002, Elliott Proctor Joslin medal, Am. Diabetes Assn., 2003, Van Bekkum Stem Cell Award, 2003, Disting. Scientist Award, Am. Assn. Cancer Inst., 2003, Alan Cranston Awardee, Alliance for Aging Rsch., 2004, Rabbi Shai Shacknai Mem. Prize in Immunology and Cancer Rsch., Lautenberg Ctr. for Gen. and Tumor Immunology, 2004, medal for Disting. Contributions to Biomedical Rsch., NY Acad. Medicine, 2004; named One of Top 100 Alumni, Mont. State U., 1993, Mont. Conservationist of Yr., Mont. Land Reliance, 1994; scholar, Josiah Macy Found., 1974—75. Fellow: AAAS; mem.: IOM, NAS (steering com. NIOM AIDS panel 1985—86, chair, Panel on Sci. & Med. Aspects of Human Reproductive Cloning, Jessie Stevenson Kovalenko Medal 2004), Inst. Immunology, Am. Assn. Cancer Rsch., Am. Soc. Microbiology, Am. Assn. Pathologists, Am. Assn. Univ. Pathologists, Am. Assn. Immunologists (pres. 1994—95), Am. Acad. Arts and Scis. Achievements include research in phylogeny and developmental biology of cells that make up blood-forming and immune systems; first to isolate, in mice and in man, the blood-forming stem cell; knowledge expected to lead to improved treatment of people with myeloma, lymphoma and breast cancer. Avocations: football, ballet, fly fishing. Office: Stanford U Sch Medicine Dept Pathology B257 Beckman Ctr Stanford CA 94305-5323 E-mail: irv@stanford.edu.

WEISSMANN, PAUL MARTIN, state legislator; b. Denver, June 9, 1964; s. Max Ludwig and Arlene (Bloom) Weissmann; m. Brenda Weissmann. BS, U. Colo., Boulder. Bartender Blue Parrot Restaurant, Louisville, Colo.; bottler Red Gold Bottling, Louisville, 1989—92; mem. Dist. 17 Colo. State Senate, Denver, 1993—96; mem. Dist. 12 Colo. House of Reps., Denver, 2003—, majority leader. Democrat. Jewish. Office: Colo State Capitol 200 E Colfax Rm 271 Denver CO 80203 Office Phone: 303-866-2348. Business E-Mail: reppaul@aol.com.*

WEISWASSER, STEPHEN, electronics executive; b. Detroit, Nov. 21, 1940; BA, Wayne State U.; postgrad., Johns Hopkins U.; JD magna cum laude, Harvard U. Ptnr. Wilmer, Cutler & Pickering; sr. v.p. Capital Cities/ABC, Inc.; pres., CEO Americast, 1995-98; ptnr. Covington & Burling, Washington, 1998-99; exec. v.p., gen. counsel Gemstar Internat. Group Ltd., Pasadena, Calif., 1999—, also bd. dirs. Woodrow Wilson Nat. fellow Johns Hopkins U. Office Fax: 626-792-0257.

WEISZ, RACHEL, actress; b. London, Mar. 7, 1971; 1 child. BA, U. Cambridge, England. Motion picture and TV actress. Actor (films) Death Machine, 1995, Stealing Beauty, 1996, Chain Reaction, 1996, Going All the Way, 1997, Amy Foster, 1997, Land Girls, 1998, I Want You, 1998, Swept From the Sea, 1998, The Mummy, 1999, Sunshine, 1999, Beautiful Creatures, 2001, Enemy at the Gates, 2001, The Mummy Returns, 2001, About a Boy, 2002, The Shape of Things, 2003 (also prodr.), Confidence, 2003, Runaway Jury, 2003, She Died on Canvas, 2003, Envy, 2004, Constantine, 2005, The Constant Gardener, 2005 (Best Performance by an Actress in a Supporting Role in a Motion Picture, Hollywood Fgn. Press Assn., Golden Globe award, 2006, Outstanding Performance by a Female Actor in a Supporting Role, Screen Actors Guild award, 2006, Performance by an Actress in a Supporting Role, Acad. Motion Picture Arts & Sciences, 2006), The Fountain, 2006, Eragon, 2006, My Blueberry Nights, 2007, Fred Claus, 2007, Definitely, Maybe, 2008, The Brothers Bloom, 2009; (TV films) Scarlet and Black, 1993, My Summer with Des, 1998; (plays) Design For Living, 1994, Last Summer, 1999, The Shape of Things, 2001. Office: c/o Ind Talent Group Oxford House 76 Oxford St London W1D 1BS England

WEITHORN, STANLEY STEPHEN, lawyer; b. NYC, Aug. 28, 1924; s. Louis W. and Florence O. (Mandel) W.; m. Corinne J. Breslow, Dec. 26, 1949 (dec. 1987); children: Lois Ann, Michael J.; m. Muriel Casper, Sept. 9, 1990; 1 stepchild, Corey Casper. BSBA, Hofstra U., 1947; JD, NYU Law Sch., 1954, LLM in Taxation, 1956. Bar: N.Y. 1955. Assoc. firm Olwine, Connelly, Chase O'Donnell & Weyher, NYC, 1956—61; ptnr. firm Lewis, McDonald & Varian, NYC, 1961—62; pvt. practice NYC, 1962—63, 1967—68; ptnr. firm Wormser, Koch, Keily & Alessandroni, NYC, 1963—66; sr. ptnr. firm Baer, Marks & Upham (successor to Upham, Meeker & Weithorn), NYC, 1968—88, Epstein, Becker & Green, NYC, 1988—89; sr. counsel Reid & Priest, NYC, 1989—94, Morrison & Foerster, Palo Alto, Calif., 1994—96, Fennemore Craig, Phoenix, 1996—2000, Roberts & Holland, NYC & Scottsdale, 1996—. Spl. prof. law Hofstra U., 1974-78; adj. prof. law U. Miami, Fla., 1975-79; mem. adv. com. U. Miami Law Ctr. Ann. Inst. Estate Planning, 1974-80; coordinator fed. budget and tax policy course nat. policy studies program New Sch. Social Rsch., N.Y.C., 1975; mem. fund raising mgmt. adv. com. Grad. Sch. Mgmt. and Urban professions, New Sch. for Social Rsch., N.Y.C., 1977-84; mem. adv. com. N.Y. U. Inst. on Fed. Taxation, 1980-90; program chmn. Practicing Law Inst. confs., N.Y.C., 1962-78, N.Y. Law Jour. confs., 1980, NYU Inst. on Fed. Taxation confs., 1955-88; tax cons. Pres.'s Com. on Environ. Quality, 1970; lectr. fed. taxation to univ. insts., non-profit org. confs., profl. bus. meetings. Author: Penalty Taxes on Accumulated Earnings and Personal Holding Companies, 1963, Tax Techniques for Foundations and Other Exempt Organizations, 7 vols, 1964, The Accumulated Earnings Tax, 1966; Contbg. editor, mem. adv. bd.: Tax Mgmt, 1959-68; feature columnist: Nat. Law Jour, 1978-79; Contbr. articles to profl. jours. Co-chmn. Port Washington-Manhasset (N.Y.) unit New Dem. Coalition, 1968-69; tax adviser nat. fin. com. McGovern for Pres., 1971-72, mem. N.Y. fin. com., 1971-72; bd. dirs., exec. com. Equal Employment Coun. Inc., N.Y.C., 1968-71; bd. dirs., sec. New Priorities Edn. Fund, 1969-70; bd. dirs., exec. com., sec., co-chmn., pres. Fund for New Priorities in Am., 1969-2004; bd. dirs., treas. Cow Bay Manpower Devel. Corp., Port Washington, 1969-71; bd. dirs., chmn. exec. com., pres. L.I. Pub. Affairs Coun., 1973-78; bd. dirs., pres. Mental Health Assn. Nassau County, N.Y., 1980-85, Herman and Amelia Ehrmann Found., 1977-95; pres. Weithorn and Ehrmann Families Found., 1995—, Am. Soc. Technion, 1992-2000, Social Venture Ptnrs. Ariz., 2003—; bd. dirs. Jewish Family and Children's Svcs., San Francisco; mem. legacy com. United Cerebral Palsy, N.Y.C., 1975-90; bd. dirs. Cmty. Action for Legal Svcs., 1976-78, Frederick and Amelia Schimper Found., 1977-94, Florence Weithorn Warner Found., N.Y.C., 1967-72, N.Y. Fedn. Reform Synagogues, 1973-78, Nat. Coalition for Children's Justice, 1980-90, Am. Inst. for Philanthropic Studies, L.A. and N.Y.C., 1981-92, Nat. Health Coun., 1984-92, Laurent and Alberta Gerschel Found., 1986-96, Interns for Peace, Am.-Israeli Civil Liberties Coalition, 1987-95, Inst. Am. Values, 1987-91, Fund for Human Dignity, 1989-90, Found. Fund, 1986-92, L.I. Cmty. Found., 1989-93, Cancer Prevention Rsch. Inst., 1989-96, Green Seal, 1989-92, New Israel Fund, 1996-2002, Albert L. Schultz Jewish Cmty. Ctr., 1996-2000, Nat. Ctr. Law & Social Justice, 1996-, Am. Jewish World Svc., 2001-, Internat. Edn. and Rsch. Network, 2002-, Heller Family Found., 1994-, Rouhana Family Found., 1990-, Scottsdale Cultural Coun., 2000-, Ariz. State U. Found., 1996-2004, Am. Com. for Weizmann Inst. Sci., 2000-, Piper Fund Proteus Found, 2000-; mem. Emergency Task Force on Juvenile Delinquency Prevention, 1976-79; mem. adv. panel N.Y. chpt. Am. Jewish Com., 1978-80; mem. com. on deferred giving Fedn. Jewish Philanthropies N.Y., 1978-86; mem. legal and tax panel United Jewish Appeal/Fedn. Jewish Philanthropies, N.Y., 1986-91; nat. chair Planned Giving Program, Am. Assocs. Ben-Gurion U. Negev, 1992-2000, mem. exec. com. N.W. region; mem. com. tax policy Nat. Assembly Vol. Health, Social Welfare Orgns. Inc., N.Y.C., 1961-73; mem. com. bequests and legacies Nat. Jewish Hosp., Denver, 1965-78; mem. estate planning com. ARC of Greater N.Y., 1970-98; mem. leadership coun. United Jewish Appeal, N.Y.C., 1966-70; mem. adv. com., project on ch., state and taxation NCCJ, 1980-85; mem. legacy adv. coun. Am. Jewish Congress, N.Y.C., 1968-72; mem. Internat. Coun. on Environ. Law, 1982-92; mem. Pres.'s adv. com. ACLU Found., 1983-2000; chmn. Uptown Tax Discussion Group, 1957-69, Exempt Orgns. Discussion Group, 1973-79, Fresh Meadows Civic Assn., 1961-63; mem. legal activities policy bd. Tax Analysts, 1974—. Served with AUS, 1943-46, ETO. Recipient Allard K. Lowenstein Meml. award Am. Jewish Congress, 1988; honoree Mental Health Assn. Nassau County, N.Y., 1991, Ariz. Citizen Action, 2000, Am. Com. for Weizmann Inst. Sci., 2002, Nat. Gay and Lesbian Task Force, 2003 Fellow Am. Coll. Tax Counsel, Am. Coll. Trust and Estate Counsel; mem. ABA (chmn. subcom. exempt orgns. 1965-69, subcom. charitable contbns. 1971-75), N.Y. State Bar Assn. (exec. com. 1967-69), Assn. of Bar of City of N.Y., Internat. Acad. Estate and Trust Law (exec. coun. 1974-78, 90-96), Univ. Club, Knickerbocker Yacht Club (bd. dirs. 1986-88). Jewish (trustee synagogue 1970-74). Home (Winter): 10040 E Happy Valley Rd Lot 435 Scottsdale AZ 85255 Office: Roberts & Holland LLP 825 8th Ave 37th Fl New York NY 10019 also: 8655 E Via de Ventura G200 Scottsdale AZ 85258 Home: 10040 E Happy Valley Rd Unit 435 Scottsdale AZ 85255-2386 Office Phone: 212-903-8687. Personal E-mail: sweithorn@rhtax.com.

WEITKAMP, WILLIAM GEORGE, retired nuclear physicist; b. Fremont, Nebr., June 22, 1934; s. Alvin Herman and Georgia Ann (Fuhrmeister) W.; m. Audrey Ann Jensen, June 2, 1956; children—Erick, Jay, Gretchen, Laurie. BA, St. Olaf Coll., 1956; MS, U. Wis., 1961, PhD, 1965. Rsch. asst. prof. U. Wash., Seattle, 1965-67; asst. prof. U. Pitts., 1967-68; tech. dir., rsch. prof. Nuclear Physics Lab., U. Wash., Seattle, 1968-95; ret., 1995; rsch. prof. emeritus, 1995—. With USAF, 1956-59. Acad. guest Eidgenossische Technische Hochschule Zurich, Switzerland, 1974-75. Home: 2019 E Louisa St Seattle WA 98112-2207 Office: Univ Wash CENPA Box 354290 Seattle WA 98195-0001 E-mail: weitkamp@u.washington.edu.

WEITZ, BRETT, broadcast executive; b. Feb. 16, 1974; s. Barry Weitz. Prodn. asst. for TV movies; mem. mailroom staff United Talent Agy.; dir. drama devel. Columbia TriStar TV, 2001; with drama dept. 20th Century Fox TV; v.p. creative affairs Fox 21, LA, 2004—. Achievements include working on the TV show North Shore. Office: Fox 21 10201 W Pico Blvd Bldg 88 Los Angeles CA 90035

WEITZEL, MARK P., lawyer; b. 1954; AB with distinction, Stanford U., 1976; MBA, JD, UCLA, 1980. Bar: Calif. 1980, lic.: US Tax Ct., registered: Law Soc. of Eng. & Wales (fng. lawyer). Ptnr. Thelen Reid & Priest LLP, San Francisco, mem. partnership coun. Mem. UCLA Law Rev., 1979—80. Mem.: Order of Coif, Beta Gamma Sigma. Office: Thelen Reid & Priest LLP 101 Second St Ste 1800 San Francisco CA 94105-3601 Office Phone: 415-369-7007. Office Fax: 415-371-1211. Business E-Mail: mweitzel@thelenreid.com.

WEITZMAN, HOWARD L., lawyer, former film company executive; b. LA, Sept. 21, 1939; BS, U. So. Calif., 1962, JD, 1965. Bar: Calif. 1966, U.S. Dist. Ct. (ctrl., ea. and so. dists.) Calif., U.S. Ct. Appeals (9th cir.), U.S. Supreme Ct. 1976, U.S. Ct. Appeals (6th cir.) 1983. Pvt. practice, 1965—86; mng. ptnr. Wyman Bautzer LLP, 1986—91; ptnr., chmn. exec. com. Katten Muchin Zavis & Weitzman, LA, 1991—2001; exec. v.p. corp. ops. Universal Studios (formerly MCA), 1995—98; ptnr. Proskauer Rose LLP, LA, 2001—04, Kinsella Weitzman Iser Kump & Aldisert LLP, Santa Monica, Calif., 2005—. Lectr. U. So. Calif., 1973-83. Recipient Jerry Gielser Memorial award, 1979, 1984. Mem. ABA, L.A. County Bar Assn., Beverly Hill Bar Assn., Foundres Cir. of the Fulfillment Fund Office: Kinsella Weitzman Iser Kump & Aldisert LLP 808 Wilshire Blvd 3rd Fl Santa Monica CA 90401 E-mail: hweitzman@kwikalaw.com.

WELBORN, CARYL BARTELMAN, lawyer; b. Phila., Jan. 29, 1951; d. Raymond C. and Helen Ann Bartelman; m. Lucien Ruby, Apr. 11, 1987. AB, Stanford U., 1972; JD, UCLA, 1976. Bar: Ill. 1976, Calif. 1978. Assoc. Isham Lincoln & Beale, Chgo., 1976—78; from assoc. to ptnr. Morrison & Foerster, San Francisco and L.A., 1978—95; prin. Law Office of Caryl Welborn, 1995—2004; ptnr. DLA Piper US LLP, San Francisco, 2004—. Lectr. real property law. Named Best Lawyers in America. Mem. ABA (chmn. com. on partnerships, real property sect. 1989-93), Am. Coll. Real Estate Lawyers (bd. govs. 1994-2002, pres. 2001), Anglo-Am. Real Property Inst. Office: DLA Piper US LLP 555 Mission St San Francisco CA 94105-2933 Business E-Mail: caryl.welborn@dlapiper.com.

WELBORN, JEFFREY W., state legislator; Mem. Dist. 72 Mont. House of Reps., 2008—. Republican. Office: Montana House of Representatives PO Box 200400 Helena MT 59620-0400 Mailing: 245 Clarks Lookout Rd Dillon MT 59725-8234 Office Phone: 406-444-4800. Office Fax: 406-444-4825.

WELBORN, R. MICHAEL, bank executive; Chmn., CEO Citibank Ariz., CEO, 1996—. Active Greater Phoenix Econ. Coun., Valley of the Sun United Way, Ariz. Bankers Assn. Recipient Torch of Liberty Humanitarian of the Yr. award Anti-Defamation League, 1996. Office: Bank One Ctr 201 N Central Ave Phoenix AZ 85073-0073 Fax: 602-221-4840.

WELCH, ALEX, Internet company executive, application developer; married. BS, Colo. State U. Software engr. Level 3 Comm.; co-founder, CEO Photobucket, Denver, 2003—. Spkr. in field. Finalist Ernst & Young Entrepreneur Of Yr. Award (Rocky Mountain Region), 2007. Office: Photobucket PO Box 13003 Denver CO 80201

WELCH, CAROL MAE, lawyer; b. Oct. 23, 1947; d. Leonard John and LaVerna Helen (Ang) Nyberg; m. Donald Peter Welch, Nov. 23, 1968 (dec. Sept. 1976). BA in Spanish, Wheaton Coll., 1968; JD, U. Denver, 1976. Bar: Colo. 1977, U.S. Dist. Ct. Colo. 1977, U.S. Ct. Appeals (10th cir.) 1977, U.S. Supreme Ct. 1981. Tchr. State Hosp., Dixon, Ill., 1969, Polo Cmty. Schs., Ill., 1969-70; registrar Sch. Nursing Hosp. of U. Pa., Phila., 1970; assoc. Hall & Evans, Denver, 1977-81, ptnr., 1981-92, spec. counsel, 1993-94; mem. Miller & Welch, L.L.C., Denver, 1995—. Mem. Colo. Supreme Ct. Jury Inst., Denver, 1982—; vice chmn. com. on conduct U.S. Dist. Ct., Denver, 1982-83, chmn., 1983-84; lectr. in field. Past pres. Family Tree, Inc. Named to Order St. Ives, U. Denver Coll. Law, 1977. Mem. ABA, Am. Coll. Trial Lawyers (state com.), Internat. Soc. Barristers, Internat. Assn. Def. Counsel, Am. Bd. Trial Advs. (treas. Colo. chpt. 1991-92, pres. 1992-93), Colo. Def. Lawyers Assn. (treas. 1982-83, v.p. 1983-84, pres. 1984-85), Denver Bar Assn., Colo. Bar Assn. (mem. litigation sect. coun. 1987-90), Colo. Bar Found. (trustee 1992—, pres. 1995-97), Def. Rsch. Inst. (chmn. Colo. chpt. 1987-90, regional v.p. 1990-93, bd. dirs. 1993-96), William E. Doyle Inn, The Hundred Club.

WELCH, JASPER ARTHUR, JR., security company executive, consultant; b. Baton Rouge, Jan. 5, 1931; s. Jasper Arthur and Oramay Ballinger (Young) W.; m. Frances Carroll Wright, Mar. 28, 1953 (div. Nov. 1984); children: Jasper Arthur III, Carroll Welch Pawlikowski, Brent Ballinger; m. Jane Ann Alford Tudor, Dec. 31, 1985. BS in Physics, La. State U., 1952; MA in Physics, U. Calif., Berkeley, 1954, PhD in Physics, 1958. Commd. officer 2d lt. USAF, 1952, advanced through grades to maj. gen., 1975; chief analyst Hdqs. USAF, Washington, 1969—71; chief strategic analysis Office Sec. Def., Washington, 1971—74; chief strategic concepts Hdqs. USAF, 1974—75, asst. chief staff for analysis, 1975—79; coord. def. policy NSC, 1979—81; asst. dept. chief staff Hdqs. USAF, 1981—83; ret., 1983. Tech. cons. Jasper Welch Assocs., Santa Fe, 1984—; mem. adv. coun. NASA, Washington, 1985-89; chmn. mil. adv. panel to dir. CIA, Washington, 1986-98; mem. nat. security panel U. Calif., 2000-07. Author: Atomic Theory of Gas Dynamics, 1965; contbr. articles to sci. jours., including Phys. Rev., Strategic Rev. Youth dir. St. Matthews Epis. Ch., Pacific Palisades, Calif., 1969-74, St. Andrews Epis. Ch., Arlington, 1965-68; mem. found. bd. Santa Fe Chamber Music Festival, 1998—2004. Decorated D.S.M. with oak leaf cluster, Legion of merit with two oak leaf clusters. Mem. NAE (found. bd. 1999—2005), Am. Geophys. Union, Am. Phys. Soc., Coun. on Fgn.

Rels. Avocations: music, theater, gardening, hiking, racing sailboats. Office: 2129 Foothills Rd Santa Fe NM 87505

WELCH, LLOYD RICHARD, electrical and communications engineer, educator, consultant; b. Detroit, Sept. 28, 1927; s. Richard C. and Helen (Felt) W.; m. Irene Althea Main, Sept. 12, 1953; children: Pamela Irene Towery, Melinda Ann, Diana Lia Worthington. BS in Math., U. Ill., 1951; PhD in Math., Calif. Inst. Tech., 1958. Mathematician NASA-Jet Propulsion Lab., Pasadena, Calif., 1956-59; staff mathematician Inst. Def. Analyses, Princeton, NJ, 1959-65; prof. elec. engring. U. So. Calif., LA, 1965-99, prof. emeritus, 1999—. Cons. in field of elec. comms Contbr. articles to profl. jours. Served with USN, 1945-49, 51-52 Fellow IEEE (Shannon award Info. Theory Soc. of IEEE 2003); mem. Nat. Acad. Engring., Am. Math. Soc., Math. Assn. Am., Phi Beta Kappa, Sigma Xi, Phi Kappa Phi, Pi Mu Epsilon, Eta Kappa Nu Office: U So Calif Elec Engring Bldg 500A Los Angeles CA 90089-0001 Business E-Mail: welch@usc.edu.

WELCH, S(TEPHEN) ANTHONY, academic administrator, art educator; b. Phila., Apr. 29, 1942; s. Arnold DeMerritt and Mary Scott Welch; m. Hyesoon Kim; children: Nicholas, Bronwen, Emily. Student, U. Munich, Free U. Berlin; BA in German Lit. with honors, Swarthmore Coll., 1965; MA, Harvard U., 1967, PhD History of Art and Architecture, 1972. Lectr. dept. history in art U. Victoria, BC, 1971—72, asst. prof., 1972—75, assoc. prof., 1975—80, prof., 1980—, assoc. dean, 1982—85, Dean of Faculty of Fine Arts, 1985—98, exec. dir. office of internat. affairs, 1998—2003. Vis. prof. U. Minn., U. Wash., U. Chgo.; specialist in Iranian painting, Mughal painting in India, Islamic calligraphy, Sultanate architecture in medieval India, and internat. edn. Author: Shah 'Abbas and the Arts of Isfahan, 1973, Artists for the Shah, 1976, Collection of Islamic Art, Prince Sadruddin Aga Khan, 4 Vols., 1972-78, Calligraphy in the Arts of the Muslim World, 1979, Arts of the Islamic Book, 1982, Treasures of Islam, 1985, Travels and Journal of Ambrosio Bembo, 2006; contbr. articles to scholarly and profl. jours. Office: History in Art Dept Univ Victoria Victoria BC Canada V8W 2Y2 Home Phone: 250-598-3903; Office Phone: 250-721-7942. Business E-Mail: awelch@finearts.uvic.ca.

WELK, RICHARD ANDREW, plastic surgeon; b. Aug. 9, 1956; BS, U. Mich., 1977, MD, 1981. Diplomate Am. Bd. Surgery, Am. Bd. Plastic Surgery. Resident gen. surgery, Grand Rapids, Mich., 1981-86; resident plastic surgery U. Calif., Irvine, 1986-88; plastic surgeon pvt. practice, Kirkland, Wash., 1988-91, Polyclinic, Seattle, 1991—. Mem. Am. Soc. Plastic & Reconstructive Surgery, Am. Soc. Aesthetic Plastic Surgery, Wash. State Med. Assn., Wash. Soc. Plastic Surgeons (pres. 1995-96). Office: Polyclinic 1145 Broadway Seattle WA 98122-4299 Office Phone: 206-860-2317.

WELKER, KARA, agent; b. Mar. 26, 1972; m. Steven Maloney, Apr. 23, 2004. Grad. in Creative Writing, U. Calif., Irvine. With booking dept. Irvine Improv, Calif.; asst. to mgr. Messina/Baker Entertainment Corp., 1994; mgr. 3 Arts Entertainment; ptnr., mgr. Rath-Welker Mgmt.; co-founder Generate, Santa Monica, Calif., 2006—. Exec. prodr.: (TV series) Slice o' Life, 2003, The Barenaked Ladies Variety Show, 2005, The Comedians of Comedy, 2005, Wonder Showzen, 2005; prodr.: Deal, 2005, The Andy Milonakis Show, 2005. Co-founder South Toward Home, Santa Monica, Calif. Office: Generate 1545 26th St Ste 200 Santa Monica CA 90404 E-mail: Kara@generatela.com.

WELLBORN, CHARLES IVEY, strategic planning consultant; b. Houston, Dec. 9, 1941; s. Fred W. and Emily R. (Gladu) W.; m. JD McCausland, Aug. 14, 1965; children: Westly O., Kerry W. Phillips. BA in Econs., U. N.Mex., 1963, JD, 1966; LLM, NYU, 1972. Bar: N.Mex. 1966, U.S. Dist. Ct. N.Mex. 1966. Assoc. Neal & Matkins, Carlsbad, N.Mex., 1966-68, Robinson & Stevens, Albuquerque, 1969-71; ptnr. Schlenker, Parker, Payne & Wellborn, Albuquerque, 1971-76, Parker & Wellborn, Albuquerque, 1976-82, Modrall, Sperling, Roehl, Harris & Sisk, Albuquerque, 1982-95; pres., CEO Sci. & Tech. Corp. at U. N.Mex., Albuquerque, 1995-2000; pres. Wellborn Strategies LLC, Albuquerque, 2000—06. Chmn. N.Mex. Tax Rsch. Inst., 2002—06, N.Mex. Small Bus. Investment Corp., 2003—06. Vice chair U. N.Mex. Found., Inc., 1990—94; mem. Econ. Forum, 1986—2002, chmn., 1995—96; mem. City-County Unification Charter Commn., 2002—03; bd. dirs. N.Mex. Assn. Commerce and Industry, 2003—, N.Mex. Cmty. Capital, 2005—, N.Mex. Symphony Orch., 1988—91, U. N.Mex. Anderson Schs. Mgmt. Found., 1989—94, N.Mex. First, 1989—93, 2000—04, Accion N.Mex., 1995—97, Outpost Performance Space, 2000—04; State N. Mex. Private Equity Investment adv. com., 1991—98; mem. Govs. Prayer Breakfast Com., 1991—2002, chair, 2000—02; bd. dirs. Next Generation Economy Inc., 2002—05, Sci. and Tech. Corp. U. N.Mex., 2000—. Sgt. USAF, 1968—69, Korea. Mem.: ABA (ho. of dels. 1984—91), State Bar N.Mex. (pres. 1982—83), N.Mex. Bar Found. (pres. 1980—82), Albuquerque Bar Assn. (pres. 1977—78). Democrat. Roman Catholic. Office: Wellborn Strategies LLC 3819 La Hacienda Dr NE Albuquerque NM 87110-6115 Office Phone: 505-238-7890.

WELLER, DEBRA ANNE, elementary school educator; AA in Art, St. Petersburg Jr. Coll., 1974; BA in Art Edn., Glassboro State Coll., 1983; MS in Curriculum and Instrn., Nat. U., 1991. Cert. tchr. Profl. storyteller, Mission Viejo, Calif., 1980—; tchr. Capistrano Unified Sch. Dist., San Juan Capistrano, Calif., 1989—; elem. tchg. asst. prin. Bathgate Elem., 1998—, stds. curriculum specialist. Edn. dir. South Coast Storytellers Guild, Costa Mesa, Calif., 1990—; workshop presenter Orange County Dept. Edn., Costa Mesa, 1991—, Imagination Celebration, Irvine, Calif., 1993—; bd. mem. Calif. Kindergarten Assn; parenting instr. Author: (pamphlets) Image-U-Telling Clubs, 1995, Storytelling, the Cornerstone of Literacy, also articles. Adv. Eagles, Boy Scouts Am. Cultural Arts grantee Dana Point (Calif.) Cultural Commn., 1993; City of Mission Viejo grantee, 2003; Arts Orange County Storytelling Inst. grantee, 2005. Mem. NEA, Nat. Storytelling Network (liaison Pacific region), Calif. Tchrs. Assn., Calif. Kindergarten Assn. (bd. dirs., pres.-elect), South Coast Storytellers Guild (pres.), Storytellers Guild (pres. 1995-97, 2003—). Mem. Lds Ch. Avocations: calligraphy, composing, playing banjo, dulcimer and guitar.

WELLER, DIETER M., botanist, researcher; Rsch. scientist IBM Almaden Rsch. Ctr., San Jose, Calif. Recipient Ruth Allen award Am. Phytopathol. Soc., 1997. Office: IBM Almaden Rsch Ctr MSK11-D1 650 Harry Rd San Jose CA 95120-6099 E-mail: dieter@almaden.ibm.com.

WELLER, GUNTER ERNST, geophysics educator; b. Haifa, June 14, 1934; came to U.S., 1968; s. Erich and Nella (Lange) W.; m. Sigrid Beilharz, Apr. 11, 1963; children: Yvette, Kara, Britta. BS, U. Melbourne, Australia, 1962, MS, 1964, PhD, 1968. Meteorologist Bur. Meteorology, Melbourne, 1959-61; glaciologist Australian Antarctic Exps., 1964-67; from asst. prof. to assoc. prof. geophysics Geophys. Inst., U. Alaska, Fairbanks, 1968-72, prof., 1973-98, dep. dir., 1984-86, 90-98; prof. emeritus Geophys. Inst., U. Ala., Fairbanks, 1998—; project dir. NASA-UAF Alaska SAR Facility, Fairbanks, 1983-93. Program mgr. NSF, Washington, 1972-74; pres. Internat. Commn. Polar Meteorology, 1980-83; chmn. polar rsch. bd. NAS, 1985-90, Global Change Steering Com. Sci. com. on Antarctic Rsch., 1988-92; chmn. Global Change Working Group Internat. Arctic Sci. Com., 1990-97; dir. Ctr. for Global Change and Arctic Sys. Rsch., U. Alaska, 1990—; dir. Coop. Inst. Arctic Rsch., 1994—; exec. dir. Arctic Climate Impact Assessment, Arctic Coun., 2000—. Contbr. numerous articles to profl. jours. Recipient Polar medal Govt. Australia, 1969; Mt. Weller named in his honor by Govt. Australia, Antarctica; Weller Bank named in his honor by U.S. Govt., Arctic. Fellow AAAS (exec. sec. arctic divsn. 1982-93), Arctic Inst. N.Am.; mem. Internat. Glaciological Soc., Am. Meteorol. Soc. (chmn. polar meteorology com. 1980-83), Am. Geophys. Union. Home: PO Box 81024 Fairbanks AK 99708-1024 Office: U Alaska Coop Inst Arctic Rsch Fairbanks AK 99775-7740 E-mail: gunter@gi.alaska.edu.

WELLER, STEPHEN G., botanist, educator; BS in Botany with high honors, U. Mich., Ann Arbor, 1971; PhD in Botany, U. Calif., Berkeley, 1975. Asst. prof. U. Ill., Chgo., 1975—81, assoc. prof., 1981—87, U. Calif., Irvine, 1987—92, prof. ecology and evolutionary biology, 1992—. Summer faculty U. Wash., 1975, U. Mich. Biol. Sta., 1981; vis. colleague dept. botany U. Hawaii, 1987; sr. Mellon fellow Smithsonian Instn., 1993—94; McBryde chair Hawaiian plant scis. Nat. Tropical Bot. Garden, 1995—98. Contbr. articles to sci. jours.; assoc. editor: Evolution, 1981—85. Mem.: Soc. Study of Evolution, Soc. Conservation Biology, Am. Soc. Plant Taxonomists, Bot. Soc. Am. (sec. 2006—). Office: Dept Ecology and Evolutionary Biology U Calif Irvine Irvine CA 92697-2525 Office Phone: 949-824-6581. Office Fax: 949-824-2181. E-mail: sgweller@uci.edu.

WELLINS, CORI, literary agent; m. Max Lagao, July 8, 2000. BA in History, UCLA, 1993. Head TV lit. FilmStew Inc.; asst. William Morris Agy., lit. agent, sr. v.p., head TV lit. devel. Actress (films) Arachnophobia, 1990. Named one of The 100 Most Powerful Women in Entertainment, Hollywood Reporter, 2007. Office: William Morris Agy One William Morris Pl Beverly Hills CA 90212

WELLS, CHRISTOPHER BRIAN, lawyer; b. Belleville, Ill., Jan. 23, 1948; s. Frederick Meyers and Ethel Pauline (Morris) W.; m. Gaynelle Vansandt, June 6, 1970; 1 child, Deva Marie. BA in Econs., U. Kans., BS in Bus., 1970, JD, 1973. Enforcement atty. SEC, Seattle, 1977-82; ptnr. Lane, Powell, Spears, Lubersky, LLP, Seattle, 1982—. Capt. U.S. Army, 1973-77. Mem. ABA, Wash. State Bar Assn., King County Trial Lawyers Assn., Wash. Soc. CPA's., Kans. Bar Assn., Securities Industry Assn. (legal and compliance divsn.). Democrat. Office: Lane Powell Spears Lubersky LLP 1420 5th Ave Ste 4100 Seattle WA 98101-2338 E-mail: wellsc@lanepowell.com.

WELLS, GERTRUDE BEVERLY, psychologist; b. Haverhill, Mass., July 14, 1940; d. True Franklyn Wells and Priscilla Eleanor (Browne) Duerstling. BS, SUNY, Fredonia, 1962; MA, Coll. St. Rose, Albany, NY, 1969; PhD, U. Mo., Columbia, 1976; PhD in Clin. Psychology, Fielding Grad. U., Santa Barbara, Calif., 1999. Tchr. speech pathology N.Y. Pub. Schs., Albany and Clifton Park, 1962-70; lectr. SUNY, Albany, 1970-73; asst. prof. Coll. St. Rose, Albany, 1975-77; assoc. prof. U. No. Iowa, Cedar Falls, 1977-78; prof. U. of La., Lafayette, 1978-85; prof., program dir. Calif. State U. Stanislaus, Turlock, 1985-87; prof. comm. Calif. State U., San Francisco, 1987—92; chief exec. officer West Coast Inst., 1992—2000; clin. psychologist, pvt. practice, 2001—. Author: Stuttering Treatment, 1987; contbr. articles to profl. jours. Health svc. provider Nat. Register of Health Svc. in Psychology. Mem.: APA, Calif. Psychol. Assn., Am. Acad. Health Care Providers in Addictive Disorders. Avocations: writing, bicycling, gardening. Office: 16 Joost Ave San Francisco CA 94131 Office Phone: 415-585-5212. Personal E-mail: doctorwells@earthlink.net.

WELLS, GLADYSANN, library director; BA in English, Greensboro Coll., NC, 1970; MLS, SUNY, Albany, 1972. Libr. Empire State Coll., 1972—73; legis. reference libr. N.Y. State Libr., Albany, 1973—78; with Senate Rsch. Svc., 1975—80; libr. Senate Libr., 1978—80; adminstr. N.Y. State Libr., 1980—95; interim dir. N.Y. State Libr. Rsch. Libr., 1995—97; state libr. Ariz. State Libr., 1997—. Editor several books on the economy of the northeast; contbr. articles to profl. jours. Avocations: horseback riding, cross country skiing, hiking, snow shoeing. Office: Ariz State Libr 1700 W Washington Ste 200 Phoenix AZ 85007-2896

WELLS, JAMES ALLEN, biochemist; b. Washington, Apr. 28, 1950; s. Edmund John and Joan (Beans) W.; m. Carol Ann Windsor; children: Julian James Widnsor-Wells, Natalie Hope Windsor-Wells BA in Biochemistry, U. Calif., Berkeley; PhD in Biochemistry, Wash. State U. Postdoctoral researcher Stanford (Calif.) U. Sch. Medicine, 1980-82; scientist Genentech, Inc., South San Francisco, 1982—. Contbr. articles to profl. jours.; patentee in field. Mem. AAAS. Democrat. Home: 65 Otay Ave San Mateo CA 94403-2837 Office: Sunesis Pharmaceuticals Inc 341 Oyster Point Blvd South San Francisco CA 94080

WELLS, KENNETH BROOKS, medical educator, researcher; Prof. psychiatry & biobehavioral scis. UCLA Semel Inst. & Hosp. and Sch. of Medicine; sr. scientist RAND; prin. investigator UCLA/RAND Ctr. for Rsch. Quality in Managed Care. Co-author: Caring for Depression, 1996, Beating Depression: The Journey to Hope, 2002. Recipient Young Investigator Award, Disting. Investigator Award, Acad. Health. Mem.: Am. Psychiatric Assn. (Sr. Health Svc. Rsch. Award), NAS, Inst. Medicine (chair Neuroscience and Behavioral Health Bd.). Address: 1776 Main St Santa Monica CA 90401-3208 Office: UCLA Health Svcs Rsch Ctr 10920 Wilshire Blvd, Ste 300 Los Angeles CA 90024-6505 Office Phone: 310-794-3725. E-mail: kenneth_wells@rand.org.

WELSH, JOHN JOSEPH (JAY), lawyer; m. Rae Terry Welsh; 5 children. B, Hamilton Coll., Clinton, NY, 1962; JD, U. Calif., Berkeley, 1965. Atty. pvt. firms, 1965—91; gen. counsel Jud. Arbitration and Mediation Svcs. (JAMS), Irvine, Calif., 1991—94, mediator, 1995, exec. v.p., gen. counsel. Adj. prof. law U. So. Calif., U. San Francisco; founder JAMS Found., JAMS Inst. Mem.: Internat. Mediation Svcs. Alliance Europe (MEDAL). Avocation: travel. Office: JAMS 1920 Main St at Gillette Ave Ste 300 Irvine CA 92614 Office Phone: 949-224-1810. Office Fax: 949-224-1818. E-mail: jwelsh@jamsadr.com.

WELSOME, EILEEN, journalist, writer; b. NYC, Mar. 12, 1951; d. Richard H. and Jane M. (Garity) Welsome; m. James R. Martin, Aug. 3, 1983. BJ with honors, U. Tex., 1980. Reporter Beaumont (Tex.) Enterprise, 1980—82, San Antonio Light, 1982—83, San Antonio Express-News, 1983—86, Albuquerque Tribune, 1987—94, Westword Newspaper, Denver, 2000—01; observer Tex., 2006—07. Author: The Plutonium Files, 1999 (PEN/Martha Albrand award for first nonfiction, 2000), The General and the Laguer, Little Brown, 2006. Recipient Clarion award, 1989, News Reporting award, Nat. Headliners, 1989, John Hancock award, 1991, Mng. Editors Pub. Svc. award, AP, 1991, 1994, Roy Howard award, 1994, James Aronson award, 1994, Gold Medal award, Investigative Reporters and Editors, 1994, Sigma Delta Chi award, 1994, Investigative Reporting award, Nat. Headliners, 1994, Selden Ring award, 1994, Heywood Broun award, 1994, George Polk award, 1994, Sidney Hillman Found. award, 1994, Pulitzer prize nat. reporting, 1994, PEN/West Lit. award rsch. nonfiction, PEN, 2000; John S. Knight fellow, Stanford U., 1991—92.

WELTER, WILLIAM MICHAEL, marketing and advertising executive; b. Evanston, Ill., Nov. 18, 1946; s. Roy Michael and Frances (DeShields) W.; m. Pamela Bassett, June 11, 1971; children: Barclay, Robert Michael. BS, Mo. Valley Coll., 1966. Account exec. Leo Burnett Co., Inc., Chgo., 1966-74; v.p., account supr. Needham Harper Worldwide, Chgo., 1974-80; v.p. mktg. Wendy's Internat., Inc., Dublin, Ohio, 1981, sr. v.p. mktg., 1981-84, exec. v.p., 1984-87; owner, chief exec. officer Haunty & Welter Advt. Agy., Worthington, Ohio, 1987-91; sr. exec. v.p. mktg. Rax Restaurants Inc., Dublin, 1992; exec. v.p. mktg. Metromedia Steakhouses, Inc., Dayton, 1992-93; sr. v.p. mktg. Metromedia Co., Dayton, 1993-95; exec. v.p., chief mktg. officer Heartland Foods Inc., Dublin, Ohio, 1995-96; exec. v.p. brand mgmt. Late Nite Magic, Inc., Las Vegas, Nev., 1996—99; pres., CEO W.M. Welter & Assocs., Las Vegas, 1996—; pres. Wings West LLC, Las Vegas, 1999—, Buffalo Wild Wings, Inc., Las Vegas, 2001—. Founder Santa's Silent Helpers, Columbus, Ohio, 1985 Mem. Advt. Fedn. Las Vegas, Spanish Trail Country Club. Avocations: golf, fishing. Home: 1517 Angelberry Rd Las Vegas NV 89117-1372 Office: Ste 103 8064 W Sahara Las Vegas NV 89117 Office Phone: 702-304-9292. Fax: 702 360-8379. E-mail: buffalodad@hotmail.com.

WELTS, RICK, professional sports team executive; Student, U. Wash. Dir. pub. rels. Seattle SuperSonics; v.p. Bob Walsh & Assocs., 1979; dir. nat. promotions NBA Properties NBA, NYC, 1982—83, v.p. mktg. NBA Properties, 1983—84, v.p. mktg. and comm. NYC, 1984—88, pres. NBA Properties, 1988—99, exec. v.p., chief mktg. officer, 1996—99; pres. Fox Sports Enterprises, 1999, First In Line; ptnr. ONSPORT, 2001; pres., COO Phoenix Suns, 2002—. Named Co-Marketer of Yr., Brandweek, 1998. Office: Phoenix Suns 201 E Jefferson St Phoenix AZ 85004

WELTY, JOHN DONALD, academic administrator; b. Amboy, Ill., Aug. 24, 1944; s. John Donald and Doris (Donnelly) W.; m. Sharon Welty; children: Anne, Elisabeth, Bryan, Darren, Heather. BS, Western Ill. U., 1965; MA, Mich. State U., 1967; Ed.D., Ind. U., 1974. Asst. v.p. for student affairs SW State U., Marshall, Minn., 1973-74; dir. residences SUNY-Albany, 1974-77, assoc. dean for student affairs, 1977-80; v.p. for student and univ. affairs Indiana U. of Pa., 1980-84, pres., 1984-91, Calif. State U., Fresno, 1991—. Lectr. in field. Contbr. articles to profl. jours. Chair Am. Assn. State Colls. and Univs., Western Assn. Schs. and Colls. Recipient Chancellor's award SUNY, 1977, Chief Exec. Leadership award Coun. for Advancement and Support of Edn., 1999, John Templeton Found. award for leadership in student character devel., 1999. Mem. Fresno Bus. Coun., Fresno Econ. Devel. Commn., Sunnyside Country Club. Lodges: Rotary. Roman Catholic. Office: Calif State U 5241 S Maple Ave Fresno CA 93725-9739 Business E-Mail: johnw@csufresno.edu.

WEN, LEANA S., epidemiologist; b. Shanghai, 1983; d. Ying Sandy Zhang, Xiaolu Wen. BS in Biochemistry, Calif. State Univ., LA; MD, Calif. State Univ., 2007; MSc. student in Global Health, Oxford Univ., 2007—. Appt. mem. Coun. on Grad. Med. Edn. by US Sec. of Health and Human Services. Rhodes Scholar. Mem.: Am. Med. Student Assn. (pres. 2005—06). Achievements include entering college at age 13; Global Health Fellow at WHO, Geneva, Switzerland; DOD David L. Boren Fellow in Rwanda to devel. treatment programs for women who are HIV-positive as the result of genocide-related rape; recipient NIH Fogarty Minority Internat. Rsch. Training Fellowship; an Arnold and Mabel Beckman Found. Rsch. Fellowship; and a Howard Hughes Med. Inst. Biomed. Professional Devel. Scholarship. Home: 6025 Camellia Ave Temple City CA 91780-2068 Personal E-mail: wen.leana@gmail.com. Business E-Mail: wen@wustl.edu.

WENDER, PAUL ANTHONY, chemistry professor; BS, Wilkes Coll., 1969; PhD, Yale U., 1973; PhD (hon.), Wilkes U., 1993. Asst. prof., assoc. prof. Harvard U., 1974-81; prof. chemistry Stanford U., 1981—; Bergstrom prof. chemistry, 1994—. Cons. Eli Lilly & Co., 1980—, lectr. Am. Chem. Soc. Recipient ICI Am. Chem. award Stuart Pharm., merit award NIH, Pfizer rsch. award, 1995. Fellow AAAS; mem. Am. Chem. Soc. (Arthur C. Cope Sholan award 1990, Guenther award, award for creative work in synthetic organic chemistry 1998). Office: Stanford U Mudd Bldg Rm 390 Mail Code 5080 Stanford CA 94305

WENDT, RICHARD L., manufacturing executive; b. 1931; From mgr. frame factory to mgr. ops. Caradco; CEO Jeld-Wen Inc., Klamath Falls, Oreg., 1960—2003, chmn., 2003—. Address: Jeld Wen Inc PO Box 1329 Klamath Falls OR 97601-0268 Office: Jen Weld Inc 401 Harbor Isles Blvd Klamath Falls OR 97601

WENNERSTROM, ARTHUR JOHN, aeronautical engineer; b. NYC, Jan. 11, 1935; s. Albert Eugene and Adele (Trebus) W.; m. Bonita Gay Westenberg, Sept. 6, 1969 (div. Jan. 1989); children: Bjorn Erik, Erika Lindsay; m. Vicki Lynn Merrick, Feb. 17, 1990. BS in Mech. Engring., Duke U., 1956; MS in Aero. Engring., MIT, 1958; DSc of Tech., Swiss Fedn. Inst. Tech., Zurich, 1965. Sr. engr. Aircraft Armaments, Inc., Cockeysville, Md., 1958-59; rsch. engr. Sulzer Bros., Ltd., Winterthur, Switzerland, 1960-62; project engr. No. Rsch. and Engring. Corp., Cambridge, Mass., 1965-67; rsch. leader Air Force Aerospace Rsch. Lab., Dayton, Ohio, 1967-75, Air Force Aero Propulsion Lab., Dayton, 1975-91; dir. NATO Adv. Group for Aerospace R & D, Paris, 1991-94; engring. cons. Hillsborough, NC, 1994-95, Hot Springs Village, Ark., 1995—2003, Henderson, Nev.,

2003—. Mem. tech. adv. com., von Karman Inst. for Fluid Dynamics, Rhode-St-Genese, Belgium, 1988-94, bd. dirs.; lectr. in field. Contbr. articles to profl. jours. 1st lt., USAF, 1962-65. Recipient Cliff Garrett Turbo Machinery award Soc. Automotive Engrs., 1986; named Fed. Profl. Employee of Yr. Dayton C. of C., 1975; fellow Air Force Wright Aeronautical Labs., 1987; named Hon. Prof., Inst. Engring. Thermophysics, Chinese Acad. Scis. and Beijing U. Aeronautics and Astronautics, 1994. Fellow AIAA (assoc. editor 1980-82, Air Breathing Propulsion award 1979), ASME (chmn. turbomachinery com. gas turbine divsn. 1973-75, mem. exec. com. 1977-82, chmn. 1980-81, program chmn. internat. gas turbine conf. 1976, Beijing internat. gas turbine symposium 1985, mem. nat. nominating com. 1985-87, mem. TOPC bd. on rsch. 1985-88, mem.-at-large energy conversion group 1986-88, mem. bd. comm. 1989-91, editor Jour. Engring. for Gas Turbines and Power 1983-88, chmn. bd. editors 1989-91, founder, editor Jour. Turbomachinery 1986-88, mem. internat. adv. com. 1995-96, R. Tom Sawyer award 1993). Achievements include introduction of wide-chord integrally-bladed fan, introduction of swept blading into mil. aircraft turbine engines; 5 patents in field. Home and Office: 363 Marlin Cove Rd Henderson NV 89012-4829 Home Phone: 702-837-1344; Office Phone: 702-837-1344. E-mail: wennco1@cox.net.

WERDEGAR, KATHRYN MICKLE, state supreme court justice; b. San Francisco; d. Benjamin Christie and Kathryn Marie (Clark) Mickle; m. David Werdegar; children: Maurice Clark, Matthew Mickle. Student, Wellesley Coll., 1954—55; AB with honors, U. Calif., Berkeley, 1957; JD with highest distinction, George Washington U., 1962; JD, U. Calif., Berkeley, 1990. Bar: Calif. 1964, U.S. Dist. Ct. (no. dist.) Calif. 1964, U.S. Ct. Appeals (9th cir.) 1964, Calif. Supreme Ct. 1964. Legal asst. civil rights divsn. U.S. Dept. Justice, Washington, 1962—63; rsch. atty., author Calif. State Study Commn. on Mental Retardation, 1963—64; assoc. U. Calif. Ctr. for Study of Law and Soc., Berkeley, 1965—67; spl. cons. State Dept. Mental Health, 1967—68; cons., author Calif. Coll. Trial Judges, 1968—71; dir. criminal law divsn. Calif. Continuing Edn. of Bar, 1971—78; assoc. dean acad. and student affairs, assoc. prof. Sch. Law, U. San Francisco, 1978—81; sr. staff atty. Calif. 1st Dist. Ct. Appeal, 1981—85, Calif. Supreme Ct., 1985—91; assoc. justice Calif. 1st Dist. Ct. Appeal, 1991—94, Calif. Supreme Ct., San Francisco, 1994—. Regents' lectr. U. Calif., Berkeley, 2000. Author: Benchbook: Misdemeanor Procedure, 1971, Misdemeanor Procedure Benchbook rev., 1975, Misdemeanor Procedure Benchbook, 1983; contbr. California Continuing Education of the Bar books; editor: California Criminal Law Practice series, Discovery, 1975, California Uninsured Motorist Practice, 1973, I California Civil Procedure Before Trial, 1977. Recipient 5 Am. Jurisprudence awards, 1960—62, Charles Glover award, George Washington U., 1962, J. William Fulbright award for disting. pub. svc., George Washington U. Law Sch. Alumni Assn., 1996, Excellence in Achievement award, Calif. Alumni Assn., 1996, Roger J. Traynor Appellate Justice of Yr. award, 1996, Justice of Yr. award, Consumer Attys. of Calif., 1998, Citation award, Boalt Hall Sch. Law U. Calif., Berkeley, 2002, Judge Learned Hand Human Rels. award, Am. Jewish Com., 2008. Mem.: Am. Law Inst., Nev./Calif. Women Judges Assn., Calif. Judges Assn., Nat. Assn. Women Judges, Calif. Supreme Ct. Hist. Soc. (bd. dir.), Order of the Coif. Office: Calif Supreme Court 350 McAllister St San Francisco CA 94102-4797 Office Phone: 415-865-7032.

WERNER, TOM, television producer, professional baseball team executive; b. NJ, Apr. 12, 1950; m. Jill Werner; children: Teddy, Carolyn, Amanda. BA, Harvard Univ., 1971. With ABC Television, Inc., 1972-82; co-owner Carsey-Werner Co., Studio City, Calif., 1982—; chmn. San Diego Padres, 1991-94; co-owner Boston Red Sox baseball club, 2002—. Mem. bd. dirs. Old Globe Theatre, Sharp Hospital. Prodr.(co-exec): (TV series) Oh, Madeline, 1983—84, A Different World, 1987—93, Chicken Soup, 1989, Grand, 1990, Davis Rules, 1991, You Bet Your Life, 1992, Frannie's Turn, 1992, Grace Under Fire, 1993—98, She TV, 1994, Cosby, 1996—2000; exec. prodr.: The Cosby Show, 1984 (Emmy awd. Outstanding Comedy Series, 1985), Roseanne, 1988—97, Cybill, 1995—98, 3rd Rock from the Sun, Cosby, 1996—2001, Townies, 1996, Damon, 1998, God, the Devil and Bob, 2000, Normal, Ohio, 2000—01, Grounded for Life, 2001—05, You Don't Know Jack, 2001, The Downer Channel, 2001, That '80s Show, 2002, Whoopi, 2003—04, The Tracy Morgan Show, 2003—04, Game Over, 2004, Good Girls Don't..., 2004; exec. prodr.: (TV series) The Scholar, 2005—; exec. prodr.: (TV films) The Cosby Show: A Look Back, 2002, These Guys, 2003, Grand Union, 2006, Happy Hour, 2006; prodr.: (TV films) The Mayor of Oyster Bay, 2002; exec. prodr.: (films) Let's Go to Prison, 2006. Office: Carsey Werner Prodns 4024 Radford Ave Bldg 3 Studio City CA 91604-2101

WERNER, WILLIAM ARNO, architect; b. San Francisco, Dec. 11, 1937; s. William Arno and Sophie (Menutis) W.; m. Wendy Rolston Wilson, Feb. 3, 1963 (div. Jan. 1983); 1 child, Christa Nichol. BA with honors, Yale U., 1959, BArch, 1962, MArch, 1963. Drafter Serge Chermayeff, Paul Rudolph and Charles Brewer, New Haven, 1961-63; project designer Johnson, Poole & Storm, San Francisco, 1963-64, Leo S. Wou & Assocs., Honolulu, 1965-66, v.p. of design, 1971-72; project architect John Tatom Assocs., Honolulu, 1965-66; sr. designer Skidmore, Owings & Merrill, San Francisco, 1968-71, assoc./project architect, 1972-76; prin. W.A. Werner Assocs., San Francisco, 1976-80; ptnr. Werner & Sullivan, San Francisco, 1980—. Mem. planning commn. City of Sausalito, Calif.; bd. govs. Yale U., New Haven; visitorship in architecture U. Auckland Found., New Zealand, 1994. Prin. works include Alameda Mcpl. Credit Union, Lane Pub. Co., Menlo Park, Calif., Pacific Data Images, Mountain View, Calif., Saga Corp., Menlo Park, Tiffany & Co., Union Square, San Francisco, Somerset Collection, Troy, Mich., Touche Ross & Co., Oakland, U.S. Post Office, San Francisco, (renovations) Fed. Express Co., San Francisco, KD's Grog N' Grocery, San Francisco, Jessie Street Substation, San Francisco, Lakeside Tower Health Ctr./Mt. Zion Hosp., Qantas Bldg, San Francisco, Women's Care, San Francisco, Moon Residence, Dillon Beach, Calif., Shenkar Residence, San Francisco, Tacker Residence, Denver, Lasky Residence, San Francisco, Starring Residence, San Francisco, Whitehead Residence, Monte Rio, Calif., various laboratories, theatres and rsch. facilities, urban design. Recipient Progressive Architecture Design award Jessie St. Substation, 1980, DuPont Co. Design award Touche Ross & Co., 1983, award of Excellence Woodwork Inst. of Calif., 1989, USPS/NEA Nat. Honor award for Design Excellence, 1990, Tucker Design Excellence award Bldg. Stone Inst., Tiffany & Co., 1992. Mem. AIA (San Francisco chpt.), Found. for San Francisco's Architectural Heritage (hon.). Home: 213 Richardson St Sausalito CA 94965-2422 Office: Werner & Sullivan 207 Powell St Ste 800 San Francisco CA 94102-2209

WERNER-JACOBSEN, EMMY ELISABETH, developmental psychologist; b. Eltville, Germany, May 26, 1929; came to U.S., 1952, naturalized, 1962; d. Peter Josef and Liesel (Kunz) W. BS, Johannes Gutenberg U., Germany, 1950; MA, U. Nebr., 1952, PhD, 1955; postgrad., U. Calif., Berkeley, 1953-54. Research asso. Inst. Child Welfare, U. Minn., 1956-59; vis. scientist NIH, 1959-62; asst. prof. to prof. human devel., rsch. child psychologist U. Calif., Davis, 1962-94, rsch. prof., 1995—. Sr. author: The Children of Kauai, 1971, Kauai's Children Come of Age, 1977; author: Cross-Cultural Child Development: A View from the Planet Earth, 1979, Vulnerable, but Invincible, 1982, 3d edit., 1998, Child Care: Kith, Kin and Hired Hands, 1984, Overcoming the Odds, 1992, Pioneer Children on the Journey West, 1995, Reluctant Witnesses: Children's Voices From the Civil War, 1998, Through the Eyes of Innocents: Children Witness World War II, 2000, Unschuldige Zeugen, 2001, Journeys From Childhood to Mid Life: Risk, Resilience and Recovery, 2001, A Conspiracy of Decency: The Rescue of the Danish Jews in World War II, 2002, In Pursuit of Liberty, 2006, Passages to America, 2009; contbr. articles to profl. jours. Recipient Disting. Sci. Contbn. to Child Devel. award, Soc. Rsch. Child Devel., 1999, Dolly Madison Presdl. award for outstanding lifelong contbns. to devel. and wellbeing of children and families, Zero to Three, 1999, Arnold Gesell award, German Soc. Pediat., 2001, award for disting. career contbns. to sci. study of lifespan devel., Soc. for Study of Human Devel., 2005. Fellow: Assn. Psychol. Scis., Soc. Rsch. Child Devel., German Acad. Social Pediats. (hon.). Business E-Mail: eewerner@ucdavis.edu.

WERNICK, SANDRA MARGOT, meeting event planner and public relations executive; b. Tampa, Fla., Sept. 13, 1944; d. Nathan and Sylvia (Bienstock) Rothstein. BA in English, U. Fla., 1966. Tchr. English Miami Beach Sr. HS, 1967; adminstrv. asst. pub. rels. Bozell & Jacobs, Inc., NYC, 1968-69; asst. to dir. pub. rels. Waldorf-Astoria, NYC, 1969-70; dir. advt. and pub. rels. Hyatt on Union Sq., San Francisco, 1974-82; pres. Wernick Mktg. Group, San Francisco, 1982—; exec. dir. Sales and Mktg. Execs. of the Bay Area, 1995-2000; mng. ptnr. The Stanford Group, 1998-99; pres. Auction Magic, San Francisco, 2003—. Bd. dirs. Nat. Kidney Assn., San Francisco, 1985-87; advisor Swords to Plowshares, San Francisco, 1988-89; mem. mktg. com. to bd. Boy Scouts of Greater East Bay, 1995-2000. Recipient Award of Merit, San Francisco Advt. and Cable Car Awards, 1979, Award of Excellence, San Francisco Art Dirs. 1978, Disting. Mktg. award Sales and Mktg. Internat., 1997, awards Am. Hotel and Motel Assn., 1981, 82. Mem. NAFE, Women in Comms. (bd. dirs. 1987-89), Am. Women in Radio and TV (bd. dirs. 1989-90), Pub. Rels. Soc. Am., San Francisco Publicity Club (pres. 1989, awards of excellence 1990, 94, 95-98), Variety Club, Profl. Bus. Women's Assn., Calif. Pacific Med. Ctr. (aux. 1988-95). Democrat. Jewish. Office: 1690 Broadway Ste 705 San Francisco CA 94109-2107 E-mail: sandie@wernickmarketinggroup.com.

WERTHEIM, JOHN V., lawyer, former political organization administrator; b. Santa Fe, Feb. 12, 1968; s. Jerry and Mary Carole Wertheim; m. Bianca Ortiz, Dec. 30, 1994. BA in History, Yale U., 1990; JD, U. N.Mex., 1995. Bar: New Mexico 1997. Fin. analyst, corp. fin. Alex. Brown & Sons, Inc., Balt., 1990-91; N.Mex. dir. Clinton for Pres., 1992; campaign mgr. Bruce King for Gov., Albuquerque, 1994; assoc. atty. The Jones Law Firm, Santa Fe, 1997—2003; mng. dir. Wertheim Doyle & Co., Albuquerque, 1998—2003; ptnr. Jones Snead Wertheim & Wentworth PA, Santa Fe, 2003—. NM Dir. Clinton for Pres. 1992, pres. Young Democrats of New Mexico 1994-96, guest political commentator KANW Public Radio for Ctrl. NM. Dem. Party nominee US Ho. of Reps. 1996, Dem. Candidate 2000 1st Congressional Dist. N.Mex.; former chmn. Dem. Party of N.Mex.; former mem. exec. com. Dem. nat. Com., 2005-07; pres., spkr. Yale Political Union Bd. Dirs., 2007-. 1st. American winner World Debating Championship U. Glasgow Scotland 1990, Pickens Prize for Outstanding Scholarship in African-American History, Yale U. Mem. AAJ, N.Mex. Bar Assn., N.Mex. Trial Lawyers Assn. (bd. dirs., 2007-). Jewish. Avocations: hiking, running, rafting, skiing. Office: Jones, Snead, Wertheim & Wentworth, PA 1800 Old Pecos Trail Santa Fe NM 87505 Office Phone: 505-982-0011. Business E-Mail: johnv@thejonesfirm.com.

WERTHEIM, ROBERT HALLEY, national security consultant; b. Carlsbad, N.Mex., Nov. 9, 1922; s. Joseph and Emma (Vorenberg) W.; m. Barbara Louise Selig, Dec. 26, 1946; children: Joseph Howard, David Andrew. Student, N.Mex. Mil. Inst., 1940-42; BS, U.S. Naval Acad., 1945; MS in Physics, M.I.T., 1954; postgrad., Harvard U., 1969. Commd. ensign U.S. Navy, 1945, advanced through grades to rear adm., 1972; assigned Spl. Projects Office, Washington, 1956-61, Naval Ordnance Test Sta., China Lake, 1961-62, Office Sec. Def., Washington, 1962-65; head Missile br. Strategic Systems Project Office, Washington, 1965-67, dep. tech. dir., 1967-68, tech. dir., 1968-77, dir., 1977-80; sr. v.p. Lockheed Corp., 1981-88; cons. nat. def., 1988—. Emeritus mem. Draper Lab., Inc.; sci. adv. group Dept. Def., Dept. Energy, U.S. Strategic Command; nat. security adv. Lawrence Livermore Nat. Lab. Decorated DSM with cluster, Legion of Merit, Navy Commendation medal, Joint Svc. Commendation medal; recipient Rear Adm. William S. Parsons award Navy League U.S., 1971, Chmn. Joint Chiefs of Staff Disting. Pub. Svc. award, 1996, Sec. of Def. medal, 1996, Disting. Grad. award U.S. Naval Acad., 2005; named Disting. Submariner, Naval Submarine League, 2006; named to Hall of Fame NMMI, 1987. Fellow AIAA, Calif. Coun. Sci. Tech.; mem. Am. Soc. Naval Engrs. (hon. mem., Gold medal 1972), Nat. Acad. Engring., U.S. Naval Inst., Bernardo Heights Country Club, Sigma Xi, Tau Beta Pi. Home: 17705 Devereux Rd San Diego CA 92128-2084 Office: Sci Applications Internat Corp 1074 Thornmint Rd San Diego CA 92127 E-mail: rhwertheim@aol.com.

WESCOTT, WILLIAM BURNHAM, oral maxillofacial pathologist, educator; b. Pendleton, Oreg., Nov. 10, 1922; s. Merton Girard and Josephine (Creasey) W.; m. Barbara L., Dec. 31, 1944 (dec. June 12, 1969); children: William Douglas, Diane Elizabeth; m. Gloria Greer-Collins, Aug. 28, 1989. DMD, U. Oreg., Portland, 1951, MS, 1962. Asst. prof. to assoc. dean admin. U. Oreg. Dental Sch., Portland, 1953-72; co-dir. oral disease rsch. VA, Houston, 1972-75, dir. dental edn. ctr. LA, 1980-85; acting dir. Reg. Med. Edn. Ctr., Birmingham, Ala., 1978-80; chief dental svc. Dept. of Veteran's Affairs, San Francisco, 1985-94; clin. prof. U. Calif., San Francisco, 1994—2006; cons. Northern System of Clinics Dept. Vets. Affairs, 1994—. Dental surgeon, Oreg. Air N.G., Portland, 1954-68; cons. Madigan Army Med. Ctr., Ft. Lewis, W. Va., 1971-74, VA Med. Ctrs., No. Calif., 1985—, prof. pathology Duke U. Med. Sch., 1977-79; cons. U. Med. Ctr., Fresno, 1998—2006; mem. Enloe Hosp. Head and Neck Malignancy Tumor Bd. Contbr. 80 articles to profl. jours. and several chpts. to profl. books; 4 chpts. to books. Dist. chmn. Boys Scouts Am., Portland, 1965-67; bd. dirs. Am. Cancer Soc., Portland, 1964-67; comdr. Veterans Foreign Wars Post 5731, Gridley, Calif., 1994-95, comdr., 1996-98; chmn. Mil. Vets Ct. of Honor Meml., No. Calif., 1997—. With Oreg. N.G., 1938-40; with U.S. Army, 1940-42; lt. col. USAF, 1942-68. Decorated DFC with oak leaf cluster USAF, Oreg. N.G. Merit Svc. Medal, Portland, Fedn. des Anciens Combattants Français medal; named Man of Yr., Gridley C. of C., 2009. Fellow Am. Acad. Oral and Maxillofacial Pathology, Mil. Officers Assn. Am. (sec. 2000—05), Omicron Kappa Upsilon, Sigma Xi. Avocations: woodworking, fishing. Home: 437 Justeson Ave Gridley CA 95948-9434 Office: U Calif Sch Dentistry S 512 San Francisco 3rd & Parnassus San Francisco CA 94143-0424 Office Phone: 415-476-4866. Business E-Mail: wesco83@sbcglobal.net.

WESLING, DONALD TRUMAN, English literature educator; b. Buffalo, May 6, 1939; s. Truman Albert and Helene Marguerite (Bullinger) W.; m. Judith Elaine Dulinawka, July 28, 1961; children: Benjamin, Molly, Natasha. BA, Harvard U., 1960, PhD, 1965; BA, Cambridge U., Eng., 1962. Asst. prof. U. Calif. at San Diego, La Jolla, 1965-67, assoc. prof., 1970-80, prof., 1981—. Lectr. U. Essex, Colchester, Eng., 1967-70. Author: Wordsworth and Landscape, 1970, Chances of Rhyme, 1981, The New Poetries, 1985, The Scissors of Meter, 1996, (with T. Slawek) Literary Voice, 1995, Bakhtin and the Social Moorings of Poetry, 2003, On Literary Emotions, 2008. Office: U Calif Lit # 0410 La Jolla CA 92093 Business E-Mail: dwesling@ucsd.edu.

WESSELKAMPER, SUE, academic administrator; m. Tom Wesselkamper; 2 children. BA History, Govt., Edgecliff Coll.; M Social Work, U. Mich.; PhD Social Welfare, CUNY. Head cmty., social svs. program New River Cmty. Coll.; dir. social work field instrn. program Radford U., Va.; dean sch. arts and scis., assoc. prof. social work Coll. New Rochelle, NY; pres. Chaminade U. Honolulu, 1995—. Author: Enhancing Ethnic Identity Through Cross-Cultural Interaction, An Intercultural Approach to Contemporary Ethnicity, Issues in Implementing Cultural Diversity Content, Role of the Social Worker in Health Planning. Chmn. bd. dirs. Family Svcs. Westchester County, NY; mem. adv. com. Pew Charitable Trust 3d Black Colls. Project on Student Retention; mem. Hawaii Cath. Conf., Hawaii State Network of Am. Coun. on Edn.'s Women Leaders in Higher Edn. Avocations: reading, movies, hiking, travel. Office: Chaminade U of Honolulu 3140 Waialae Ave Honolulu HI 96816

WESSELLS, NORMAN KEITH, biologist, educator, university administrator; b. Jersey City, May 11, 1932; s. Norman Wesley and Grace Mahan Wessells; m. Catherine Pyne Briggs; children: Christopher, Stephen, Philip, Colin, Elizabeth. BS, Yale U., 1954, PhD, 1960. Asst. prof. biology Stanford (Calif.) U., 1962-65, asso. prof., 1965-70, prof., 1971—, chmn. biol. sci., 1972-78; acting dir. Hopkins Marine Sta., 1972-75, asso. dean humanities and scis., 1977-81, dean, 1981-88; prof. biology, provost, v.p. acad. affairs U. Oreg., Eugene, 1988—. Author: (with F. Wilt) Methods in Developmental Biology, 1965, Vertebrates: Adaptations, 1970, Vertebrates: A Laboratory Text, 1976, 81, Tissue Interactions and Development, 1977, Vertebrates; Adaptations; Vertebrates: Physiology, 1979, (with S. Subtelny) The Cell Surface, 1980, (with J. Hopson) Biology, 1988, (with Hopson) Essentials of Biology, 1990. Served with USNR, 1954-56. Am. Cancer Soc. postdoctoral fellow, 1960-62; Am. Cancer Soc. scholar cancer research, 1966-69; Guggenheim fellow, 1976-77 Mem. Soc. Devel. Biology (pres. 1979-80), Am. Soc. Zoologist. Office: U Oreg Office Provost Johnson Hall Eugene OR 97403

WESSLER, MELVIN DEAN, farmer, rancher; b. Dodge City, Kans., Feb. 11, 1932; s. Oscar Lewis and Clara (Reiss) W.; m. Laura Ethel Arbuthnot, Aug. 23, 1951; children: Monty Dean, Charla Cay, Virgil Lewis. Grad. high sch. Farmer, rancher, Springfield, Colo., 1950—. Dir., sec. bd. Springfield Co-op. Sales Co., 1964-80, pres. bd., 1980—; pres. Arkansas Valley Co-op Coun., SE Colo. Area, 1965-87, Colo. Co-op Coun., 1969-72, v.p. 1974, sec. 1980-86; cmty. com. chmn. Baca County, Agr. Stablzn. and Conservation Svc., Springfield, 1961-73, 79—, vice chmn. Baca County Com., 1980-90; mem. spl. com. on grain mktg. Far-Mar-Co; mem. com. for PROMARK, Hutchinson, Kans., 1978. Mem. adv. bd. Denver Bapt. Bible Coll., 1984-89; chmn. bd. dirs. Springfield Cemetery Bd., 1985—; apptd. spl. com. Farmland Industries spl. project Tomorrow, 1987—. Recipient The Colo. Cooperator award Colo. Coop. Coun., 1990. Mem. Colo. Cattlemen's Assn., Colo. Wheat Growers Assn., Southeast Farm Bus. Assn. (bd. dirs. 1991-95), Big Rock Grange (treas. 1964-76, master 1976-82), Southwest Kans. Farm Assn. (dir. 1996—, pres. 1999-2001, v.p. 2007-), Southwest Kans. Farm Bus. Assn. (v.p. 2007-09), Big Rock Grange Master (2006-09). Address: 18363 County Road Pp Springfield CO 81073

WESSLING, ROBERT BRUCE, retired lawyer; b. Chgo., Oct. 8, 1937; s. Robert Euans and Marguerite (Rickert) W.; m. Judith Ann Hanson, Aug. 26, 1961; children: Katherine, Jennifer, Carolyn. BA, DePauw U., 1959; JD, U. Mich., 1962. Bar: U.S. Ct. Appeals (9th cir.) 1965. Assoc. Latham & Watkins, LA, 1962-70, ptnr., 1970-94; ret., 1995. Bd. govs. Fin. Lawyers Conf., Los Angeles, 1974-2000. Mem. World Affairs Coun., L.A.; trustee DePauw U. Mem. Los Angeles Bar Assn., Phi Beta Kappa, Phi Delta Phi, Phi Eta Sigma, Order of Coif. Democrat. Methodist. Avocations: tennis, travel. Personal E-mail: bbwessling@aol.com.

WESSON, HERB J., councilman; b. Cleve. m. Fabian Wesson; children: Douglas, P.J., Herb III, Justin. BA in History, Lincoln U., Pa., 1999. Served as chief of staff LA County Supr. Yvonne Brathwaite Burke; served as chief dep. LA City Councilman Nate Holden; mem. Calif. State Assembly, 1998—2004, served on appropriations, health, utilities, and commerce com., served on bus. and professions com., chair govtl. orgn. com., speaker, 2002—04; councilman, Dist. 10 LA City Coun., 2005—. Mem. Exposition Metro Line Constrn. Authority. Mem. Mid-City C. of C., Culver City C. of C.; former mem. adv. bd. African Cmty. Resource Ctr.; bd. dirs. Martin Luther King, Jr. Gen. Hosp. Found., Second Dist. Edn. Found. Recipient Pub. Svc. award, Greater LA C. of C., Crusader State Leadership award, Calif. Alliance for Pride and Equality, Legis. of Yr. award, Youth Employment Sys., 1999—2000, Pub. Official award, Stonewall Dem. Club, 2000, Legis. of Yr. award, Planned Parenthood LA, 2001, Calif. Assessors' Assn., 2001. Democrat. Office: Dist Office 1819 S Western Ave Los Angeles CA 90006 also: City Hall 200 North Spring St Rm 430 Los Angeles CA 90012 Office Phone: 323-733-8233, 213-473-7010. Office Fax: 323-733-5833, 213-485-9829. Business E-Mail: councilmember.wesson@lacity.org.*

WEST, EDWARD ALAN, retired graphics communications executive; b. LA, Dec. 25, 1928; s. Albert Reginald and Gladys Delia (White) W.; m. Sonya Lea Smith, Jan. 2, 1983; children: Troy A.,

Tamara L.; stepchildren: Debra, Chris, Donna. AA, Fullerton Coll., 1966; student, Cerrotos Coll., 1957, UCLA, 1966-67. Circulation mgr. Huntington Park (Calif.) Signal Newspaper, 1946-52; newspaper web pressman Long Beach (Calif.) Press Telegram, 1955-62; pressman Garden Grove Evening News, 1962—66; gravure web pressman Gravure West, LA, 1966-67; sales engr. Halm Jet Press, Glen Head, N.Y., 1968-70; salesman Polychrome Corp., Glen Head, 1970-74; supr. reprographics Fluor Engring & Construction, Irvine, Calif., 1974-81; dir. reprographics Fluor Arabia, Dhahran, Saudi Arabia, 1981-85, Press Telegram, Long Beach, 1986-97; with Suburban LA Newspaper Group, 1998—2006; ret., 2006. Printing advisor Saddleback C.C., Mission Viejo, Calif., 1979, Mission Viejo, 80. Author: How to Paste up For Graphic Reproduction, 1967. Sgt. USMC, 1952-55, Korea. Decorated UN Svc. medal, Navy commendation medal, Nat. Def. Svc. medal, 3 Battle Stars, Good Conduct, Combat medal Korean Predl. Unit Svc. medal. Mem.: Downey United #220 F & AM, In-Plant Printing Assn. (cert. graphics comm. mgr. 1977, editor newsletter 1977, pres.Orange County chpt. 1979—80, Internat. Man of Yr. award 1980), 1st Marine Divsn. Assn. (life), DemoLay Internat. (50 Yr. Pin), Royal Order of Jesters Ct. 161, Order of Quetzalcoatl #7 (pres. 1994, 1995), Internat. High Twelve 500 (Capistrano pres. 1995, 1996), Knights Templar LA #9 (scottish rite, 50 yr. pin), Masons (50-yr.), Shriners (editor blue and gold unit Legion of Honor El Bekal Ctr. 1989—92, pres. South Coast Shrine club 1991, comdr. Legion of Honor (life) 1992, Shriner of Yr. award 1994, 50 yr. pin), Western Shrine Assn. (comdr. 1996—97, emeritus), Am. Legion, VFW (life). Presbyterian. Home: 198 Monarch Bay Dr Dana Point CA 92629-3437 Office: Suburban LA Newspaper Group 1210 N Azusa Canyon Rd West Covina CA 91790-1003

WEST, JAMES HAROLD, finance company executive; b. San Diego, Oct. 11, 1926; s. Robert Reed and Clara Leona (Moses) W.; m. Norma Jean, 1953 (div.); 1 son, Timothy James; m. Jerel Lynn Smith, Nov. 16, 1976; 1 child, James Nelson. BS, U. So. Calif., 1949. CPA, Calif. Ptnr. McCracken & Co., San Diego, 1950-61; mgr. Ernst & Ernst, San Diego, 1961-64; ptnr. West Turnquist & Schmitt, San Diego, 1964—97, West, Rhode & Roberts, 1997—. Bd. govs. ARC, Washington, 1981-87; pres., bd. dirs. Combined Arts and Edn. Coun., San Diego, 1980-83; pres. Francis Parker Sch., 1988-90; bd. dirs. San Diego Hosp. Assn., 1981-95, 97-2007, San Diegans INc., 1989-92, Mus. Photographic Arts, 1990-92; trustee Calif. Western Sch. Law, 1985-2004; mem. bd. advisors U. So. Calif. Sch. Acctg., 1985-97; treas. San Diego Nat. Sports Tng. Found., 1988-92; mem. acctg. exec. bd. U. San Diego, 1992—. With AUS, 1945-46, PTO. Mem. AICPAs, Calif. Soc. CPAs (bd. dirs. 1963-64), Univ. Club (San Diego), Capital Hill Club (Washington), Masons. Republican. Home: 3311 Lucinda St San Diego CA 92106-2931 Home and Office: 3104 4th Ave San Diego CA 92103-5803 Business E-Mail: jhwest@wrr-cpa.com.

WEST, JOHN BURNARD, physiologist, educator; b. Adelaide, Australia, Dec. 27, 1928; came to U.S., 1969; s. Esmond Frank and Meta Pauline (Spehr) W.; m. Penelope Hall Banks, Oct. 28, 1967; children: Robert Burnard, Joanna Ruth. MB, BChir, Adelaide U., 1951, MD, 1958, DSc, 1980; PhD, London U., 1960; DSc (hon.), U. Barcelona, Spain, 1987, U. Ferrara, Italy, 2004, U. Athens, 2006. Resident Royal Adelaide Hosp., 1952, Hammersmith Hosp., London, 1953-55; physiologist Sir Edmund Hillary's Himalayan Expdn., 1960-61; dir. respiratory rsch. group Postgrad. Med. Sch., London, 1962-67, reader medicine, 1968; disting. prof. medicine and physiology U. Calif., San Diego, 1969—. Leader Am. Med. Rsch. Expdn. to Mt. Everest, 1981; U.S. organizer China-U.S. Conf. on respiratory failure, Nanjing, 1986; mem. life scis. adv. com. NASA, 1985-88, task force sci. uses of space sta., 1984-87, aerospace med. adv. com., 1988-89, chmn. sci. verification com. Spacelab SLS-1, 1983-92, commn. on respiratory physiol. Internat. Union Physiol. Scis., 1985—, commn. on clin. physiol., 1991—, commn. gravitation physiol., 1986—, study sect. NIH, chmn., 1973-75; prin. investigator Spacelabs SLS 1, 2, LMS, Neurolab, 1983—; co-investigator European Spacelabs, D2, Euromir, 1987—; external examiner Nat. U. Singpore, 1995; Wiltshire lectr., London, 1971, Schwidetzky lectr., 1975, Fleischner lectr., 1977, Robertson lectr. Adelaide U., 1978, I.J. Flance lectr. Washington U., 1978, W.A. Smith lectr. Med. Coll. SC, 1982, S. Kronheim lectr. Undersea Med. Soc., 1984, McClement lectr. NYU, 1996, Harry Fritts Jr. Lectr., Stony Brook U., 2007, Moran Campbell Lectr., Brit. Thoracic Soc., 2007. Author: Ventilation/Blood Flow and Gas Exchange, 1965, Respiratory Physiology-The Essentials, 1974, Translations in Respiratory Physiology, 1975, Pulmonary Pathophysiology-The Essentials, 1977, Translations in Respiratory Physiology, 1977, Bioengineering Aspects of the Lung, 1977, Regional Differences in the Lung, 1977, Pulmonary Gas Exchange (2 vols.), 1980, High Altitude Physiology, 1981, High Altitude and Man, 1984, Everest-The Testing Place, 1985, Best and Taylor's Physiological Basis of Medical Practice, 1985, 91, Study Guide for Best and Taylor, 1985, High Altitude Medicine and Physiology, 1989, The Lung: Scientific Foundations, 1991, 2d edit., 1997, Lung Injury, 1992, Respiratory Physiology: People and Ideas, 1996, High Life: A History of High Altitude Physiology and Medicine, 1998; Pulmonary Physiology and Pathology: An Integrated, case-based approach, 2001, Gravity and the Lung, 2001; founder, editor-in-chief High Altitude Medicine and Biology, 2000-. Recipient Ernest Jung prize for medicine, Hamburg, 1977, Presdl. citation Am. Coll. Chest Physicians, 1977, Kaiser Tchg. award 1980; scholar Macy Found., 1974; Jeffries Med. Rsch. award AIAA, 1992. Fellow Royal Coll. Physicians (London), Royal Australasian Coll. Physicians, Royal Geog. Soc. (London), AAAS (med. sci. nominating com. 1987-93, coun. del. sect. med. scis.), Am. Inst. for Med. and Biol. Engring. (founding fellow 1992), Am. Heart Assn. (G.C. Griffith lectr. 1978, D.W. Richards lectr. 1980), Internat. Soc. for Mountain Medicine (pres. 1991-94), Am. Acad. Arts and Scis.; mem. NAS (com. space biology and medicine 1986-90, subcom. on space biology 1984-85, com. advanced space tech. 1992-94, panel on small spacecraft tech. 1994), Am. Assn. Thoracic Surgery (hon.), Nat. Bd. Med. Examiners (physiology test com. 1973-76), Am. Physiol. Soc. (pres. 1984-85, coun. 1981-86, chmn. sect. on history of physiology 1984-92, hist. pubs. adv. com., Reynolds prize for history 1987, Ray Daggs award 1998, Guyton Tchg. award 2002, Julius H. Comroe lectr. 2003), Inst. of Medicine of NAS, Am. Soc. Clin. Investigation, Physiol. Soc. Gt. Britain, Am. Thoracic Soc. (Edward Livingston Trudeau medal 2002), Royal Soc. of Medicine (Hickman medal, 2007), Assn. Am. Physicians, Western Assn. Physicians, Russian Acad. Sci. (elected fgn. mem.), Explorers Club, Fleischner Soc. (pres. 1985), Harveian Soc. (London), Royal Instn. Gt. Britain, Royal Soc. Medicine (London), Hurlingham Club (London), La Jolla Beach & Tennis Club. Home: 9626 Blackgold Rd La Jolla CA 92037-1110 Office: U Calif San Diego Sch Medicine 0623 Dept Medicine La Jolla CA 92093 Office Phone: 858-534-4192. Business E-Mail: jwest@ucsd.edu.

WEST, NATALIE ELSA, lawyer; b. Greenwich, Conn., Mar. 11, 1947; AB, Smith Coll., 1968; JD, U. Calif., Berkeley, 1973. Bar: Calif. 1974. Counsel Calif. Fair Polit. Practices Commn., Sacramento, 1975-79; city atty. City of Berkeley, Calif., 1980-85, City of Novato, Calif., 1985-92, City of Brentwood, Calif., 1994-99; gen. counsel Livermore-Amador Valley Water Mgmt. Agy., 1996—2001; shareholder McDonough, Holland & Allen, Oakland, Calif., 1991—. Lectr. law U. Calif., Berkeley, 2000-01. Pres. city attys. dept. League of Calif. Cities, 1986-87, bd. dirs., 1995-97. Mem. State Bar Calif., Alameda County Bar Assn.

WEST, STEPHEN ALLAN, lawyer; b. Salt Lake City, Mar. 23, 1935; s. Allan Morrell and Ferne (Page) W.; m. Martha Sears, Mar. 21, 1960; children: Stephen Allan, Jr., Page, Adam. JD, U. Utah, Salt Lake City, 1961, BS in Philosophy, 1962. Law clk. to judge US Dist. Ct., Utah, 1961-62; assoc. Marr, Wilkins & Cannon, Salt Lake City, 1962-65, ptnr., 1965-67; atty. Jennings, Strouss, Salmon & Trask, Washington, 1967-68, Marriott Corp., Washington, 1968-71, asst. gen. counsel, 1971-74, v.p. and assoc. gen. counsel, 1974-87, v.p. and dep. gen. counsel, 1987-93; sr. v.p., gen. counsel Marriott Internat., Inc., Washington, 1993-94; pres. Tex. San Antonio Mission Ch. of Jesus Christ of Latter-day Saints, 1995-98, Gen. Authority, 1998—2004. Mem. exec. bd. Interfaith Conf. Met. Washington, 1989-93, vice chmn., 1992-93; mem. exec. bd. Christa McAuliffe Inst. Task Force of Nat. Found. for Improvement Edn.; mem. South Va. U. Nat. Adv. Coun., 2007-, Bringham Young U. Mus. Art Leadership Coun., 2007-, chmn., 2009-; trustee Utah State U. Found., 2007-. Mem. ABA (exec. coun. young lawyers sect. 1964-65), Utah Bar Assn. (exec. com. young lawyers sect. 1962-67), DC Bar Assn., Utah Profl. Rels. Com., U. Utah Alumni Assn. (Disting. Alumni award 1971), Skull and Bones, Owl and Key, Phi Delta Phi, Sigma Chi. Office: 1117 Fox Farm Rd Logan UT 84321 Office Phone: 435-753-4225.

WESTEN, BRODIE CURTIS, JR., (CURT), lawyer; b. Champaign, Ill., Nov. 10, 1960; s. Brodie Curtis and Sarah Jane (Mullen) W.; m. Sue Lynn Heubner, Nov. 21, 1987. BS, Western Ill. U., 1982, MBA, 1983; JD, U. Calif., Berkeley, 1986. Bar: Ill. 1986. Fin. analyst Nat. Credit Union Adminstrn., Washington, 1983; atty. Lord, Bissell & Brook, Chgo., 1986—92; asst. gen. counsel, asst. sec. QualMed (merged with Health Net to form Health Systems Internat. Inc. in 1994), 1992—93, v.p. adminstrn., 1993—94, sr. v.p., gen. counsel, sec., 1994—95, Health Systems Internat. Inc. (merged with Found. Health Corp. to become Found. Health Sytems Inc. in 1997), 1995—97, Found. Health Systems Inc. (changed named to Health Net Inc. in 2000), 1997—2000, Health Net, Inc., Woodland Hills, Calif., 2000—07, sr. v.p., spl. counsel, 2007—. Mem. Colo. Commn. on Coop. Health Care Agreements, 1994—96. Bd. trustees The Children's Burn Found., Sherman Oaks, Calif. Mem. ABA, Ill. Bar Assn., Chgo. Bar Assn. Avocation: golf. Office: Health Net Inc 21650 Oxnard St Woodland Hills CA 91367-4901

WESTER, JOHN CHARLES, bishop; b. San Francisco, Nov. 5, 1950; B in Philosophy, St. Joseph's Coll., Mt. View, Calif.; M, St. Patrick's Coll.; M in Applied Spirituality, U. San Francisco; M in Pastoral Counseling, Holy Names Coll. Ordained priest Archdiocese of San Francisco, 1976, vicar for clergy, 1997-98, aux. bishop, 1998—2007; assoc. pastor St. Raphael Parish, San Rafael, Calif., 1976-79; tchr. Marin Cath. HS, 1979-82, asst. supt. schs., 1979, dir. campus ministry, 1982-84, pres., 1984-86; pastor St. Stephen Parish, San Francisco, 1993-97; ordained bishop, 1998; bishop Diocese of Salt Lake City, 2007—. Roman Catholic. Office: Diocese of Salt Lake City 27 C St Salt Lake City UT 84103 Office Phone: 801-328-8641. Office Fax: 801-328-9680.

WESTERFIELD, PUTNEY, management consulting executive; b. New Haven, Feb. 9, 1930; s. Ray Bert and Mary Beatrice (Putney) W.; m. Anne Montgomery, Apr. 17, 1954; children: Bradford, Geoffrey, Clare. Grad., Choate Sch., 1942-47; BA, Yale, 1951. Co-founder, v.p. Careers, Inc., NYC, 1950-52; mgr. S.E. Asia Swen Publs., Inc., Manila, Philippines, 1952; mem. joint adv. commn. Korea, 1953-54; polit. officer Am. embassy, Saigon, Vietnam, 1955-57; asst. to pub. Time mag., NYC, 1957-59, asst. circulation dir., 1959-61, circulation dir., 1961-66, asst. pub., 1966-68, Life mag., NYC, 1968; pub. Fortune mag., NYC, 1969-73; pres. Chase World Info. Corp., NYC, 1973-75; v.p. Boyden Assocs. Internat., San Francisco, 1976-80, sr. v.p., western mgr., 1980-84, pres., chief exec. officer NYC, 1984-90, San Francisco, 1984—90, mng. dir. NYC, San Francisco, 1990—2005. Bd. dirs. Urban League, N.Y.C., 1969-71, Children's Village, 1968-71, Mediterranean Sch. Found., 1969-71, Nat. Boys Club, 1970-73, U.S. -S. Africa Leaders Exch. Program, 1971-03, Bus. Coun. Internat. Understanding, 1974-76, Yale-China Assn., 1975-78, East Meets West Found., 1991—2007; trustee Choate Sch., Wallingford, Conn., 1967-76, Westover Sch., Middlebury, Conn., 1975-79, Watch Hill Chapel Soc., 1963-77, Assn. Yale Alumni, 1972-75, 80-83. Mem. Burlingame Country Club, Pacific Union Club, Bohemian Club. Home and Office: 10 Greenview Ln Hillsborough CA 94010-6424 E-mail: putneyw@pacbell.net.

WESTERFIELD, RANDOLPH W., finance educator, former dean; BA in Econs., UCLA, 1963, MA in Econs., 1965, PhD in Fin., 1968. Asst. prof. fin. The Wharton Sch., U. Pa., Phila., 1968-73, assoc. prof. fin., 1973-81, sr. rsch. assoc., Rodney L. White Ctr. Fin. Rsch., 1977-88, prof. fin., 1981-88, chair fin. dept., 1986-88; Charles B. Thornton prof. fin., bus. econs. chair U. So. Calif. Sch. Bus. Adminstrn., LA, 1988-93; dean, Robert R. Dockson chair in bus. adminstrn. Marshall Sch. Bus., U. So. Calif., LA, 1993—2004. Bd. dirs. William Lyon Homes, 2000-, Health Mgmt. Assocs. Inc., 2000-, Nicholas Applegate Growth Equity Fund; vis. prof. fin. U. Nova de Lisbon, Portugal, 1981, Stanford U., Palo Alto, Calif., 1981-82, Claremont (Calif.) Grad. Sch., 1983; mem. trust com. Continental Bank, Phila., 1979-88; mem. pension rsch. coun., The Wharton Sch., 1979-88; mem. editl. adv. bd. John Wiley & Sons (Asia) Pte Ltd., 1996; mem. authors adv. coun., Times Mirror-Irwin Co., 1987-97; chmn. Consortium for Grad. Study in Mgmt., 1997; past cons. AT&T, Mobil Oil, UN, U.S. Depts. Labor and Justice. Co-author: (with Stephen A. Ross, Jeffrey Jaffe) Corporate Finance, 1988, 90, 93, 96 (including Can., Australian and internat. edits.), (with Stephen A. Ross, Bradford D. Jordan) Fundamentals of Corporate Finance, 1992, 93, 95, 97 (including South African, Can., Australian, Chinese, Dutch and Spanish edits.), (with Stephen A. Ross, Bradford D. Jordan) Essentials of Corporate Finance, 1996; author monographs; contbr. chpts. to books, numerous articles to profl. jours. and conf. procs.; assoc. editor Fin. Rev., 1985-92. Mem. Nat. Assn. Corp. Bds. (mem. bd. L.A. chpt. 1996). Office: Marshall Sch Bus Adminstrn U So Calif Hoffman Hall 800 701 Exposition Blvd Los Angeles CA 90089-0001

WESTERGREN, TIMOTHY BROOKS, music company executive; b. 1965; BA in Computer Acoustics & Recording Tech., Stanford U., 1988. CEO Nightfly Studios; co-founder Music Genome Project/Savage Beast Technologies, 2000—; founder, chief strategy officer Pandora, 2000—. Composer: (films) The Last Best Sunday, 1999, Now & Then: From Frosh to Seniors, 1999, (ballets) Defying Gravity, 1999. Named a Maverick, Details mag., 2007. Fellow: World Network Found. Office: Pandora 360 22nd St Ste 440 Oakland CA 94612 Office Phone: 510-451-4100. Office Fax: 510-451-4286.

WESTFALL, DAVID PATRICK, academic administrator, educator; b. Harrisville, W.Va., June 9, 1942; s. Creed Simpson and Cecilia Rita (McKay) W.; m. Shirley Anne Spencer, June 27, 1965; children: Timothy David, Alison. AB, Brown U., 1964; MS, W.Va. U., 1966, PhD, 1968. Demonstrator in pharmacology Oxford (Eng.) U., 1968-70; asst. prof. W.Va. U., Morgantown, 1970-73, assoc. prof., 1973-77, prof., 1977-82, U. Nev., Reno, 1982—, chair Sch. Medicine, 1982-97, v.p. acad. affairs, 1996—2001, interim dean Coll. Sci., 2004—. Author chpts. in books; contbr. articles to profl. jours. Mem. Am. Soc. Pharmacology & Exptl. Therapeutics, Western Pharm. Soc. (cons.), Sigma Xi. Avocations: skiing, golf. Office: U Nev Dept Of Pharmacology Reno NV 84537

WESTLAKE, BLAIR, computer software company executive; JD, Whittier Law Sch., 1979. Bar: Calif. Atty. Great Western Fin. Corp., 1979—82, Universal Studios Inc., 1982—85, dir bus. affairs for studio ops., 1985—87, v.p. & sr. v.p. bus. & legal affairs Home Entertainment group, 1987—93, exec. v.p. Home Entertainment group, 1993—96, pres. worldwide pay TV, 1996—97, chmn. TV & Networks group, 1997—2001; corp. exec. v.p. Gemstar-TV Guide Internat., 2001; media cons. to Comcast Corp. & NBC Universal; corp. v.p. media & entertainment group Microsoft Corp., Redmond, Wash., 2004—. Bd. dir. Digital Entertainment Group, ContentGuard Inc., Digital Coast Roundtable. Recipient Alumni award for bus. excellence, Whittier Coll. Sch. Law, 2002, Spl. Founders award, Media & Entertainment Council, 2007. Mem.: Internat. Acad. Television Arts & Sciences (mem. exec. com.), Acad. of Television Arts & Sciences, Acad. of Motion Picture Arts & Sciences, Paley Ctr. for Media, Pacific Council on Internat. Policy. Office: Microsoft Corp 1 Microsoft Way Redmond WA 98052-6399

WESTLY, STEVEN PAUL, venture capitalist; b. LA, Aug. 27, 1956; s. Roy Messell and Sylvia (Snow) Westly Elliott; m. Anita, two children. BA, Stanford U., 1978, MBA, 1983. Program mgr. GTE Sprint, Burlingame, Calif., 1982-85; mng. dir. Bridgemere Capital, San Francisco, 1986-88; pres. Codd & Date Internat., San Jose, Calif., 1988-91; deputy dir. econ. devel. San Jose, Calif., 1991; sr. v.p. eBay; state controller Calif., 2003—06; mng. ptnr. The Westly Group, 2007—. Lectr. Stanford U. Grad. Sch. Bus., 1991-95; bd. dirs. Lane Bros., Menlo Park, Calif. Editor: Energy Efficiency & The Utilities, 1980. Controller Calif. dem. com., 1983-85, no. chair, 1985-87, vice-chmn., 1987-89; mem. Dem. Nat. Com., 1988—; adv. bd. U. San Francisco. Democrat. Presbyterian. Office: The Westly Group 2200 Sand Hill Rd Ste 250 Menlo Park CA 94025-6915

WESTON, BRAD, film company executive; With Lucasfilm; prodr. Columbia Pictures; head acquisitions and devel. Millennium Films, 1997—2000; co-pres. Dimension Films, 2000—05; co-pres. prodn. Paramount Pictures, 2005—07, pres. prodn., 2007—. Office: Paramount Pictures Corp 5555 Melrose Ave West Hollywood CA 90038

WESTON, JANE SARA, plastic surgeon, educator; b. Oceanside, NY, May 21, 1952; m. Jan K. Horn; children: Jonathan Spencer Horn, Jennifer Danielle Horn. MD, Stanford U., 1975-79. Diplomate Am. Bd. Plastic Surgery. Resident gen. surgery Sch. Medicine Stanford (Calif.) U., 1979-82, resident plastic surgery Sch. Medicine, 1982-83; fellow craniofacial surgery Hopital des Enfants Malades, Paris, 1983-84; plastic surgeon Kaiser Permanente Med. Group, San Jose, Calif., 1985-90; pvt. practice Palo Alto, Calif., 1990—. Mem. faculty Stanford U. Med. Sch., 1994-95. Active Leadership Palo Alto, 1993. Fellow ACS; mem. Am. Soc. Plastic and Reconstructive Surgeons (chair women plastic surgeons com. 1993-96, chair ethics com. 1998-99). Avocation: harp. Office: Ste 201 3351 El Camino Real Atherton CA 94027-3802

WESTON, JOHN FREDERICK, business educator, consultant; b. Ft. Wayne, Ind., Feb. 6, 1916; s. David Thomas and Bertha W.; children: Kenneth F., Byron L., Ellen J. BA, U. Chgo., 1937, MBA, 1943, PhD, 1948. Instr. U. Chgo. Sch. Bus., 1940-42, asst. prof., 1947-48; prof. The Anderson Sch. UCLA, 1949—, Cordner prof. The Anderson Sch., 1981-94, prof. emeritus recalled The Anderson Sch., 1986—, dir. rsch. program in competition and bus. policy, 1969—, dir. Ctr. for Managerial Econs. and Pub. Policy, 1983-86. Econ. cons. to pres. Am. Bankers Assn., 1945-46; disting. lecture series U. Okla., 1967, U. Utah, 1972, Miss. State U., 1972, Miami State U., 1975. Author: Scope and Methodology of Finance, 1966, International Managerial Finance, 1972, Impact of Large Firms on U.S. Economy, 1973, Financial Theory and Corporate Policy, 1979, 2d edit., 1983, 3d edit., 1988, Mergers, Restructuring and Corporate Control, 1990, Takeovers, Restructuring and Corporate Governance, 3d edit., 2000, Managerial Finance, 9th edit, 1992; assoc. editor: Jour. of Finance, 1948-55; mem. editorial bd., 1957-59; editorial bd. Bus. Econs., Jour. Fin. Rsch., Managerial and Decision Econs.; manuscript referee Am. Econ. Rev., Rev. of Econs. and Statistics, Engring. Economist, Bus. Econs., Fin. Mgmt. Bd. dirs. Bunker Hill Fund. Served with Ordnance Dept. AUS, 1943-45. Recipient Abramson Scroll award Bus. Econs., 1989-94; McKinsey Found. grantee, 1965-68; GE grantee, 1967; Ford Found. Faculty Rsch. fellow, 1961-62. Fellow Nat. Assn. Bus. Economists; mem. Am. Finance Assn. (pres. 1966, adv. bd. 1967-71), Am. Econ. Assn., Western Econ. Assn. (pres. 1962), Econometric Soc., Am. Statis. Assn., Royal Econ. Soc., Fin. Analysts Soc., Fin. Mgmt. Assn. (pres. 1979-80) Home and Office: UCLA 258 Tavistock Ave Los Angeles CA 90049-3229 Office Phone: 310-472-5110. Business E-Mail: jweston@anderson.ucla.edu.

WESTON, WILLIAM LEE, dermatologist; b. Grand Rapids, Minn., Aug. 13, 1938; s. Eugene and Edith Kathryn (Lee) W.; m. Janet J. Atkinson, June 9, 1964; children: Elizabeth Carol, William Kemp. AB, Whitman Coll., 1960; B in Med. Sci., U. S.D., 1963; MD, U. Colo., 1965. Resident in pediatrics U. Calif., San Francisco, 1967-68; intern, then resident in pediatrics U. Colo., Denver, 1965-67, resident in dermatology, 1970-72, asst. prof. dermatology and pediatrics, 1972-76, prof., 1976—, chmn. dept. dermatology, 1976—. Author: Practical Pediatric Dermatology, 1979, rev. edit., 1985, Color Textbook of Pediatric Dermatology, 1991, rev. edit., 1996; editor-in-chief Current Problems in Dermatology, 1988-93. With AUS, 1968-70. Mem. Soc. Pediatric Dermatology (founder, sec.-treas. 1975-80, pres.

1984-85), Colo. Dermatol. Soc. (pres.), Soc. Investigative Dermatology (bd. dirs.), Am. Acad. Dermatology (bd. dirs.). Methodist. Home: 8550 E Ponderosa Dr Parker CO 80138-8233 Office: 4200 E 9th Ave Denver CO 80220-3706

WESTREICH, BENZION JOSEPH, lawyer; b. NYC, June 2, 1952; s. Osias and Gerda (Gerwitz) W.; m. Joyce M. Mayer, Sept. 13, 1978; children: Jonathan Michael, Daniel Stephan, Zachary Mark. BS summa cum laude, CUNY, 1974, postgrad., 1974-75; JD, Columbia U., 1978. Bar: N.Y. 1979, U.S. Dist. Ct. (ea. and so. dists.) N.Y., Calif. 1988. Assoc. Shearman & Sterling, NYC, 1978-86, ptnr., 1987-88, LA, 1988—, Katten Muchin Zavis Rosenman, LA. Stone scholar Columbia U., 1977, 78. Mem. Phi Beta Kappa. Office: Katten Muchin Zavis Rosenman Ste 2600 2029 Century Park E Los Angeles CA 90067 Office Phone: 310-788-4409, 310-712-8228. E-mail: benny.westreich@kmzr.com.

WESTWOOD, JAMES NICHOLSON, lawyer; b. Portland, Oreg., Dec. 3, 1944; s. Frederick Alton and Catherine (Nicholson) W.; m. Janet Sue Butler, Feb. 23, 1980; children: Laura, David. BA, Portland State U., 1967; JD, Columbia U., 1974. Bar: Oreg. 1974, U.S. Dist. Ct. Oreg. 1974, U.S. Ct. Appeals (9th cir.) 1978, U.S. Ct. Appeals (10th cir.), 2003, U.S. Ct. Appeals (fed. cir.) 1984, U.S. Ct. Appeals (D.C. cir.) 1997, U.S. Supreme Ct. 1981. Assoc. Miller, Anderson, Nash, Yerke & Wiener, Portland, 1974-76, 78-81; asst. to pres. Portland State U., 1976-78; ptnr. Miller, Nash, Wiener, Hager & Carlsen, Portland, 1981-99, Stoel Rives LLP, Portland, 1999—. Recipient Disting. Svc. award Portland State U. Found., 1984, Outstanding Alumni award Portland State U., 1992. Mem. ABA (chmn. forest resources com. 1987-89), Oreg. Bar Assn. (chmn. appellate practice sect. 1996-97, chmn. constnl. law sect. 2006), Am. Acad. Appellate Lawyers, Univ. Club (bd. govs. 1994), Park Blocks Found. (pres. 1999—), CASA for Children (bd. mem. 2006-), City Club (pres. 1991-92). Republican. Unitarian Universalist. Home: 3121 NE Thompson St Portland OR 97212-4908 Office: Stoel Rives LLP 900 SW 5th Ave Ste 2600 Portland OR 97204-1268 Business E-Mail: jnwestwood@stoel.com.

WESTWOOD, MELVIN NEIL, horticulturist, pomologist; b. Hiawatha, Utah, Mar. 25, 1923; s. Neil and Ida (Blake) Westwood; m. Wanda Mae Shields, Oct. 12, 1946; children: Rose Dawn, Nancy Gwen, Robert Melvin, Kathryn Mae. Student, U. Utah, 1948-50; BS in Pomology, Utah State U., 1952; PhD in Pomology, Wash. State U., 1956. Field botanist Utah State U., Logan, 1951-52, supt. Howell Field Sta., 1952-53; rsch. asst. State Coll. Wash., 1953-55; rsch. horticulturist Agrl. Rsch. Svc. USDA, Wenatchee, Wash., 1955-60; assoc. prof. Oreg. State U., Corvallis, 1960-67, prof., 1967-80, prof. emeritus, 1986—; rsch. dir. Nat. Clonal Germplasm Repository, Corvallis, 1980-83, nat. tech. advisor, 1984-86. Author: Deciduous Fruit and Nut Production, 1976, Temperate-Zone Pomology: Physiology and Culture, 1978, 3d edit., 1993, Contract Military Air Transport: From the Ground Up, 1995, Pear Varieties and Species, 1996, The Foods of Lewis and Clark, 2005; author: (with others) Cherry Nutrition, 1966, Pear Rootstocks, 1987, Management and Utilization of Plant Germplasm, 1988, Maintenance and Storage: Clonal Germplasm, 1989, Genetic Resources of Malus, 1991; contbr. articles to profl. jours. With US Air Transport Command, 1943—45, with USAAF, 1946—47. Recipient Hartman Cup award, Oreg. Hort. Soc., 1989, Earl Price Excellence in Rsch. award, Oreg. State U., 1989; grantee, NSF, 1966. Fellow: Am. Soc. Hort. Sci. (mem. pomology sect. 1967—74, chmn. com. environ. quality 1971, mem. publs. com. 1971—74, pres. Western region 1974, bd. dirs. 1974—75, adv. coun. 1974—79, Joseph Harvey Gourley award for Pomology 1958, Stark award for Pomology 1969, Joseph Harvey Gourley award for Pomology 1977, Stark award for Pomology 1977, Outstanding Rschr. award 1986); mem.: AAAS, Am. Pomological Soc. (mem. adbv. bd. 1970—75, mem. exec. bd. 1980—84, Paul Howe Shepard award 1968, 1982, Wilder medal 1980), Am. Soc. Plant Physiologists, Amnesty Internat., UN Assn. USA, Ams. United Separation of Ch. and State, Gamma Sigma Delta, Phi Kappa Phi. Baptist. Achievements include patents for Autumn Blaze ornamental pear; research in Pyrus (pear), Malus (apple) and Prunus (plum, cherry, peach); physiology of rootstock genera. Office: Oreg State U Dept Horticulture Corvallis OR 97331

WETTACK, F. SHELDON, academic administrator; AB, San Jose State U., 1960, MA, 1962; PhD, U. Tex., Austin, 1967. From asst. prof. to prof. Hope Coll., Holland, Mich., 1967-82, dean nat. and social scis., 1974-82; dean faculty arts and scis. U. Richmond, 1982-89; pres. Wabash Coll., Crawfordsville, Ind., 1989-93; v.p., dean of faculty Harvey Mudd Coll., Claremont, Calif., 1993—. Office: Harvey Mudd Coll 301 E 12th St Claremont CA 91711-5901 E-mail: sheldon_wettack@hmc.edu.

WETTAW, JOHN, state legislator, chemistry professor; b. St. Louis, Apr. 17, 1939; BA in Chemistry, So. Ill. U.; PhD in Phys. Chemistry, Mich. State U. NSF post-doctoral rschr. Tex. A&M U.; prof. No. Ariz. U.; mem. Ariz. Ho. of Reps., 1972-92, Ariz. State Senate, 1992—, mem. appropriations com., vice-chmn. judiciary com., chmn. commerce, agr. and natural resources com., chmn. appropriations subcom. on health and welfare, mem. banking, ins. and elections com., mem. joint com. on capital rev., mem. joint legis. budget com., pres. pro tempore. Mem. adv. bd. Grand Canyon Boy Scout Coun. Mem. Kiwanis, No. Ariz. U. Booster Club. Republican. Presbyterian. Address: 1824 Spencer Cir Flagstaff AZ 86004-7301 E-mail: jwettaw@azleg.state.az.us.

WETTERAU, MARK S., food products/distributor executive; m. Virginia Wetterau; children: Stephen, Elizabeth, Olivia. BA, Westminster Coll. With Wetterau Inc., 1980—92; pres., CEO Shop 'n Stop Warehouse Foods, 1988—90; pres. retail & ind. group Wetterau Inc., 1990—91, pres., COO, 1991—92; co-founder, ptnr. Wetterau Assoc., 1992—; pres., CEO Quality Beverage, 1992—98; chmn., CEO, pres. Golden State Foods (of Wetterau Assoc.), Irvine, Calif., 1998—. Chmn. GSF found.; bd. mem. Second Harvest Food Bank of Orange County. Office: Golden State Foods Ste 1100 18301 Von Karman Ave Irvine CA 92612

WETZEL, JODI (JOY LYNN WETZEL), retired history and women's studies educator; b. Salt Lake City, Apr. 5, 1943; d. Richard Coulam and Margaret Elaine (Openshaw) Wood; m. David Nevin Wetzel, June 12, 1967; children: Meredith (dec.), Richard Rawlins. BA in English, U. Utah, 1965, MA in English, 1967; PhD in Am. Studies, U. Minn., 1977. Instr. Am. studies and family social sci. U. Minn., 1973-77, asst. prof. Am. studies and women's studies, 1977-79, asst. to dir. Minn. Women's Ctr., 1973-75, asst. dir., 1975-79; dir. Women's Resource Ctrs. U. Denver, 1980-84, mem. adj. faculty history, 1981-84, dir. Am. studies program, dir. Women's Inst., 1983-84; dir. Women in Curriculum U. Maine, 1985-86, mem. coop. faculty sociology, social work and human devel., 1986; dir. Inst. Women's Studies and Svcs. Met. State Coll. Denver, 1986—, assoc. prof. history, 1986-89, prof. history, 1990—. Speaker, presenter, cons. in field; vis. prof. Am. studies U. Colo., 1985; mem. judges panel nominations rev. Nat. Women's Hall of Fame, Seneca Falls, N.Y., 2002, 03, 04. Co-author: Women's Studies: Thinking Women, 1993; co-editor: Readings Toward Composition, 2d edit., 1969; contbr. articles to profl. publs. Del. at-large Nat. Women's Meeting, Houston, 1977; bd. dirs. Rocky Mountain Women's Inst., 1981-84; treas. Colo. Women's Agenda, 1987-91. U. Utah Dept. English fellow, 1967; U. Minn. fellow, 1978-79; grantee NEH, 1973, NSF, 1981-83, Carnegie Corp., 1988; named to Outstanding Young Women of Am., 1979. Mem. Am. Hist. Assn., Nat. Assn. Women in Edn. (Hilda A. Davis Ednl. Leadership award 1996, Sr. Scholar 1996), Am. Assn. for Higher Edn., Am. Studies Assn., Nat. Women's Studies Assn., Golden Key Nat. Honor Soc. (hon.), Alpha Lambda Delta, Phi Kappa Phi. Office: Met State Coll Den Campus Box 36 PO Box 173362 Denver CO 80217-3362 Personal E-mail: jodiwetzel@comcast.net. Business E-Mail: wetzelj@mscd.edu.

WETZEL, KARL JOSEPH, physics professor, dean; b. Waynesboro, Va., May 29, 1937; s. Mark Ernest and Margaret K. (Jungbluth) W.; m. Barbara Carol Damutz, Aug. 3, 1968; children: Sebastian P., Christopher M. BS in Physics, Georgetown U., 1959; MS in Physics, Yale U., 1960, PhD in Physics, 1965. Physicist Nat. Bur. Standards, Washington, 1959; postdoctoral fellow Inst. Nuclear Physics, Darmstadt, Germany, 1965-67, Argonne (Ill.) Nat. Lab., 1967-69; asst. prof. physics U. Portland, Oreg., 1969-72, assoc. prof. Oreg., 1972-80, prof. Oreg., 1980-2000, prof. emeritus Oreg., 2001—, chmn. sci. dept. Oreg., 1980-86, dean Grad. Sch. Oreg., 1987-98. Cons. in field; adj. prof. State of Oreg. Dept. Continuing Edn., Portland, 1976-96. Contbr. articles to profl. publs. Bd. dirs. Friendly House Ctr., Portland, 1979-82, Choral Arts Ensemble, Portland, 1988-95, 98—. NSF fellow, 1965, 76-77; recipient Pres.' award Oreg. Mus. Sci. and Industry, 1972, Outstanding Advisor award Am. Coll. Test/Nat. Academic Advising Assn., 1984. Mem. Am. Phys. Soc., AAUP. Achievements include first to describe experiments using germanium detectors with neutron-capture gamma-ray spectroscopy; first measurement of Delbrück effect in photon scattering. Office: U Portland 5000 N Willamette Blvd Portland OR 97203-5743

WEXLER, HASKELL, film producer; b. Chgo., 1922; s. Simon Wexler; m. Nancy Ashenhurst (div.); two children; m. Marian Witt (div.); 1 son, Mark; m. Rita Taggart. Ednl. documentaries, Chgo., for eleven years; cinematographer films: The Hoodlum Priest, The Best Man, America America, The Loved One, In the Heat of the Night, Who's Afraid of Virginia Woolf? (Acad. award), The Thomas Crown Affair, American Graffiti, One Flew Over the Cuckoo's Nest, Introduction to the Enemy, Bound for Glory (Acad. award), Coming Home, Colors, Three Fugitives, 1988, Blaze, 1989, Lookin' to Get Out, Matewan, Other People's Money, The Babe, Mulholland Falls, 1995, Rich Man's Wife, 1995, (with others) Days of Heaven, (with others) Rolling Stones-IMAX, The Secret of Roan Inish, Canadian Bacon, Limbo, 1999, HBO 61—, 2001, Silver City, 2004; writer, dir., photographer: Medium Cool, 1969; wrote and directed Latino, 1985; feature documentary Bus Riders Union, Five Days in March, From Wharf Rats to Lords of the Docks, Who Needs Sleep?. Received star on Hollywood's Walk of Fame, 1996. Mem. Acad. Motion Picture Arts and Scis. (bd. govs. cinematographers br.). Personal E-mail: perigol@aol.com.

WEXLER, ROBERT, academic administrator; m. Hannah Wexler. BA summa cum laude, UCLA, MA, PhD, UCLA; MBA, Baruch Coll. Ordained rabbi Jewish Theol. Seminary. Lectr. Near Eastern Studies Princeton U.; prof. Am. Jewish U., LA, 1978—, Colen Disting. Lectr. in Bible, pres., 1992—. Named one of The Top 50 Rabbis in America, Newsweek Mag., 2007. Mem.: Israel Democracy Inst. (exec. com. bd. mem.), World Coun.of Synagogues (exec. com. mem.), Am. Jewish Com. (exec. com. mem.). Office: American Jewish Univ 15600 Mulholland Dr Los Angeles CA 90077-1599 Office Phone: 310-476-9777. Business E-Mail: rwexler@ajula.edu. E-mail: rwexler@uj.edu.

WEYAND, FREDERICK CARLTON, retired career officer; b. Arbuckle, Calif., Sept. 15, 1916; s. Frederick C. W. and Velma Semans (Weyand); m. Lora Arline Langhart, Sept. 20, 1940 (dec. May 2001); m. Mary H. Foster, Nov. 17, 2001; children: Carolyn Ann, Robert Carlton, Nancy Diane. AB, U. Calif.-Berkeley, 1939; LL.D. (hon), U. Akron, 1975. Officer U.S. Army, advanced to gen. chief of staff, 1940-76; sr. v.p. First Hawaiian Bank, Honolulu, 1976-82; trustee Estate of S.M. Damon, Honolulu, 1982—. Bd. dirs. First Hawaiian, Inc., Ltd., First Hawaiian Bank, First Hawaiian Credit Corp. Chmn. ARC, Honolulu, 1982, Hawaiian Open golf Tourney, 1981-82. Decorated D.S.C. U.S. Army, 1967, D.S.M. Army (3), Dept. Def. (1), 1966-76, other U.S. and fgn. mil. decorations. Mem. Am. Def. Preparedness Assn., Assn. U.S. Army, U.S. Strategic Inst. (v.p. 1976—), USAF Assn. Clubs: Waialae Country. Lodges: Masons. Lutheran. Office: SM Damon Estate 999 Bishop St Fl 28 Honolulu HI 96813-4423 Home: 4389 Malia St Apt 317 Honolulu HI 96821-1167 Office Phone: 808-523-9026. Personal E-mail: smdamon@aol.com.

WHALEN, JOHN SYDNEY, management consultant; b. Moncton, NB, Can., Sept. 26, 1934; s. Harry Edward and Sarah Maude (Bourgeois) W.; m. Margaret Joan Carruthers, May 3, 1958; children: Bradley Graham, Elizabeth Ann. Grad., Can. Inst. Chartered Accts., 1959. Chartered acct. Coopers & Lybrand (formerly McDonald, Currie & Co.), St. John, N.B., 1954-63; with Kaiser Services, Oakland, Calif., 1963-75, telecommunications mgr., 1966-69, asst. controller, 1969-70, controller, 1970-74; mgr. corp. acctg. Kaiser Industries Corp., Oakland, 1975; controller Kaiser Engrs., Inc., Oakland, 1975-76, v.p. fin. and adminstm., 1976-82; mgmt. cons., owner Whalen & Assocs., Inc., Alamo, Calif., 1983—. Pres. Round Hill Holdings, Inc., 1993-99. Mem. Commonwealth Club, Rancho Cañada Golf Club. Home: PO Box 709 Alamo CA 94507-0709 Office Phone: 925-820-3506. Personal E-mail: sydwhalen@aol.com.

WHALEN, LUCILLE, retired academic administrator; b. LA, July 26, 1925; d. Edward Cleveland and Mary Lucille (Perrault) W. BA in English, Immaculate Heart Coll., LA, 1949; MSLS, Catholic U. Am., 1955; DLS, Columbia U., 1965. Tchr. elem. and secondary parochial schs., LA, 1945—52; tchr., libr. Conaty Meml. HS, LA, 1950—52; reference/serials libr., instr. in libr. sci. Immaculate Heart Coll., 1955—58; dean Immaculate Heart Coll. (Sch. Libr. Sci.), 1958-60, 65-70; assoc. dean, prof. SUNY, Albany, 1971-78, 84-87, prof. Sch. Info. Sci. and Policy, 1979—84; dean grad. programs, libr. Immaculate Heart Coll. Ctr., LA, 1987—90; ref. libr. (part-time) Glendale CC, 1990—2008. Dir. US Office Edn. Instn. Author, editor (with others): Reference Services in Archives, 1986; author: Human Rights: A Reference Handbook, 1989; author: (with Nina Redman) Human Rights: A Reference Handbook, 2d edit., 1998. Mem. ACLU, Common Cause, Amnesty Internat. Democrat. Roman Catholic. Home: 320 S Gramercy Pl Apt 101 Los Angeles CA 90020-4542 Office: Glendale CC 1500 N Verdugo Rd Glendale CA 91208-2809 Home Phone: 213-383-4046. Personal E-mail: lucillew213@sbcglobal.net.

WHALEY, FRANK, actor; b. Syracuse, NY, July 20, 1963; m. Heather Bucha; children: Buster, Tallulah. Grad., State U. NY. Film appearances include: Ironweed, 1987, Field of Dreams, 1989, Little Monsters, 1989, Born on the Fourth of July, 1989, The Freshman, 1990, JFK, 1991, The Doors, 1991, Career Opportunities, 1991, Back in the U.S.S.R., 1992, A Midnight Clear, 1992, Hoffa, 1992, Swing Kids, 1993, Pulp Fiction, 1994, Swimming With Sharks, 1995, Homage, 1995, Cafe Society, 1995, The Winner, 1996, Broken Arrow, 1996, Retroactive, 1997, Went to Coney Island on a Mission from God: Be Back by Five, 1998, Curtain Call, 1999, Glam, 2001, Pursuit of Happiness, 2001, Chelsea Walls, 2001, A Good Night to Die, 2003, World Trade Center, 2006, The System Within, 2006, The Hottest State, 2006, Crazy Eights, 2006, Vacancy, 2007, Drillbit Taylor, 2008, The Cell 2, 2009; TV films include: Unconquered, 1989, Flying Blind, 1990, To Dance with the White Dog, 1993, Fatal Deception: Mrs. Lee Harvey Oswald, 1993, Dead Man's Gun, 1997, The Wall, 1998, When Trumpets Fade, 1998, Shake, Rattle and Roll: An American Love Story, 1999, Bad News Mr. Swanson, 2001, Sun Gods, 2002, Detective, 2005, Mrs. Harris, 2005, Where There's a Will, 2006, Ruffian, 2007; writer, dir. Joe the King, 1999, The Jimmy Show, 2001, New York City Serenade, 2007; stage appearances include: Tigers Wild, 1986, The Years, 1993; guest appearances include Spenser: For Hire, 1987, Law & Order, 2002, Navy NCIS, 2004, Law & Order: Criminal Intent, 2004, Curb Your Enthusiasm, 2005, Psych, 2006, Boston Legal, 2007, House MD, 2007, Law & Order: Special Victims Unit, 2008, CSI, 2009. Office: Agency for the Performing Arts 405 S Beverly Dr Beverly Hills CA 90212

WHANGER, PHILIP DANIEL, biochemistry and nutrition educator, researcher; b. Lewisburg, W.Va., Aug. 30, 1936; married, 1964; 2 children. BS, Berry Coll., 1959; MS, W.Va. U., 1961; PhD in Nutrition, N.C. State U., 1965. From asst. to assoc. prof. Oreg. State U., Corvallis, 1966-78, prof. nutrition & biochemistry, 1978—. Rsch. assoc. biochemistry Mich. State U., 1965-66; mem. assoc. staff Harvard Med. Sch., 1972-73; vis. scientist Gen. Acad. Exch. Svc., U. Tubingen, 1986, Commonwealth Sci. & Industry Rsch. Orgn., Wembley, Western Australia, Acad. Preventive Medicine, Beijing, 1988. Rsch. fellow NIH, 1966-67, Spl. fellow, 1972; Internat. fellow NSF, 1980-81; Rsch. grantee Oreg. State U., 1968—. Mem. Am. Inst. Nutrition, Am. Soc. Animal Sci., Internat. Bioinorg Scientists, Soc. Environ. Geochemistry and Health. Achievements include research in altered metabolic pathways under selenium deficiency, relationships of vitamin E and selenium in myopathies, biochemical properties of selenium and cadmium metallo-proteins, metabolic pathways for incorporation of selenium into proteins, selenium and gluthathione peroxidise in human blood fractions, selenium deficiencies in primates, selenium intake on human blood and urine fractions. Office: Oreg State U Dept Agrl Chemistry Corvallis OR 97331

WHEELER, DENNIS EARL, mining company executive, lawyer; b. Wallace, Idaho, Dec. 17, 1942; s. Earl L. and Virginia (Rice) W.; m. Jacquline Rae, May 16, 1971; children: Michelle, Maura, Wendy, Brad. BS in Bus., U. Idaho, 1965, JD, 1967. Bar: Idaho 1967. Ptnr. Hull, Hull & Wheeler, Wallace, 1967-78; sr. v.p., gen. counsel Coeur d'Alene (Idaho) Mines Corp., 1978-80, pres., 1980-86, CEO, 1986—, chmn., 1992—. Bd. dirs. Sierra Pacific Resources; vice chmn., dir. Ctr. for Democracy; dir. World Gold Coun., Geneva, 1994—. Pres. Idaho Bd. Edn., 1984-87; founder Jobs Plus, Coeur d'Alene, 1987—; bd. dirs. Ctr. for Democracy, Washington, 1992—, Children's Village, Coeur d'Alene, 1994—, Wildlife Habitat Enhancement Coun., Silver Spring, Md., 1992—, Idaho chpt. Nature Conservancy, Sun Valley, Idaho, 1992—; mem. exec. bd. Boy Scouts Am., Coeur d'Alene, 1994—,=. Recipient Environ. Conservation Disting. Svc. award Soc. for Mining, Metallurgy and Exploration, 1993. Mem. ABA, Idaho Bar Assn., Silver Inst. (pres. 1992-94), Am. Mining Congress (chmn. western bd. govs. 1993—), Elks, Sigma Chi (Significant Sig award 1992). Avocations: fishing, skiing, boating. Office: Coeur D'Alene Mines Corp PO Box 1 Coeur D' Alene ID 83816-0316

WHEELER, JOHN HARVEY, political scientist, writer; b. Waco, Tex., Oct. 17, 1918; m. Norene Burleigh; children: David Carroll, John Harvey III, Mark Jefferson. BA, Ind. U., 1946, MA, 1947; PhD, Harvard U., 1950. Instr. dept. govt., asst. dir. Summer Sch., Harvard U., 1950; asst. prof. Johns Hopkins U., 1950-54; assoc. prof. Washington and Lee U., 1954-56, prof. polit. sci., 1956-60; fellow in residence Ctr. for Study Dem. Instns., 1960-69; program dir., 1970-75; chmn., pres. Inst. Higher Studies, Carpinteria, Calif., 1975—. Martha Boaz rsch. prof. in acad. info. systems U. So. Calif. Libr. Systems, 1986—, Martha Boaz disting. rsch. prof., 1987—; cons. Fund for Republic, 1958-61; adj. prof. New Sch., 1986—, ISIM, 1989—; founder, bd. dirs. The Virtual Acad., 1987; mem. faculty Western Behavioral Scis. Inst., 1990—; mem. BESTnet, Nat. Rsch. and Edn. Network; pres. C-Mode Inst., 1992—; bd. dirs. Silicon Beach Comm. Author: The Conservative Crisis, 1958, (with Eugene Burdick) Fail-Safe, 1962, repub., 1999 (film 1962) asst. exec. prodr., (TV re-make 2000), Democracy in a Revolutionary Era, 1968, The Politics of Revolution, 1971, The Virtual Library, 1987, The Virtual Society, 1988, 2d edit., 1992, Atlantoz 2005, 2002; editor, contbg. author: Beyond Punitive Society, 1973, Structure of Ancient Wisdom, 1983, Bioalgebra of Judgment, 1986, Fundamental Structures Human Reflexion, 1990; editor: (with George Boas) Lattimore, The Scholar, 1953; co-founder, joint chief editor: (with James Danielli) Jour. Social and Biol. Structures, 1973-95; joint editor Goethe's Science, 1986; developed computer-mediated "Freshman Academy", 1993; contbr. articles on constitutionalism and Francis Bacon to profl. jours. Keynote spkr. Subiaco Writing Festival, 2002. Served with AUS, 1941-46. Recipient Mouton Tor award, 2001.

WHEELER, JOHN OLIVER, retired geologist; b. Mussoorie, India, Dec. 19, 1924; s. Edward Oliver and Dorothea Sophie (Danielsen) W.; m. Nora Jean Hughes, May 17, 1952; children: Kathleen Anna Wheeler Hunter, Jennifer Margaret Wheeler Crompton. BASc in Geol. Engring., U. BC, 1947, DSc (hon.), 2000; PhD in Geology, Columbia U., NYC, 1956. Geologist Geol. Survey Can., Ottawa, Ont., 1951-61, Vancouver, BC, 1961-65, rsch. scientist, 1965-70, rsch. mgr. Ottawa, 1970—, chief regional and econ. geology divsn., 1970-73, dep. dir. gen., 1973-79; rsch. scientist Geol. Survey Can. (Cordilleran divsn.), 1979-90, rsch. scientist emeritus, 1990—2006; ret., 2006.

Gen. editor: Geology of Canada, 8 vols., 1989-2006; compiler of regional geol. maps of we. Can., Can. and no. N.Am. and Greenland; contbr. articles to profl. jours.; chpts. to books. Recipient Queen's Silver Jubilee medal, 1977, Can. 125 medal, 1994, Earth Sci. Sector and Dept. awards Nat. Resources Can., 1996, Spl. award of BC-Yukon Chamber of Mines for outstanding contbn. to Can. Cordilleran geology, 2000, Massey medal Royal Can. Geog. Soc., 2002, hon. fellow 2003. Fellow Royal Soc. Can., Geol. Assn. Can. (pres. 1970-71, Logan medal 1983, Disting. fellow 1996), Geol. Soc. Am. (councillor 1971-74), Can. Geosci. Coun. (pres. 1981); mem. Can. Inst. Mining and Metallurgy, Can. Geol. Found. (pres. 1974-79), Can. Alpine Club (hon.), Am. Alpine Club. Anglican.

WHEELER, LARRY RICHARD, accountant; b. Greybull, Wyo., Nov. 30, 1940; s. Richard F. and Olive B. (Fredrickson) Wheeler; m. Patricia C. Marturano, Dec. 3, 1977; children: Anthony, Richard, Teresa, Kara. BS, U. Wyo., 1965. CPA Colo. Staff acct. H. Greger CPA, Ft. Collins, Colo., 1965-66; sr. acct. Lester, Wickham & Draney, Colorado Springs, Colo., 1966-67; acct., contr., treas. J.D. Adams Co., Colorado Springs, 1967-74; ptnr. Wheeler Pierce & Hurd, Inc., Colorado Springs, 1974-80; gen. mgr., v.p. Schneebeck's, Inc., Colorado Springs, 1980-81; prin. L.R. Wheeler & Co., PC, Colorado Springs, 1981-94, pres., 1995—2008, Wheeler & Gilmartin Assocs., PC, Colorado Springs, 1994-95; v.p. Wheeler Ferrante & Co., PC, 2009. Bd. dirs. Schneebeck's Industries, Williams Printing, Inc., Colorado Springs Small Bus. Devel. Ctr. Active U.S. Taekwondo Union; bd. dirs. Domestic Violence Prevention Ctr. Grantee, Paul Stock Found., 1962. Mem.: AICPA, Nat. Assn. Cert. Valuation Analysts, Colo. Soc. CPAs. Office: 317 E San Rafael St Colorado Springs CO 80903-2405 Personal E-mail: lrw1040@aol.com.

WHEELER, MALCOLM EDWARD, lawyer, educator; b. Berkeley, Calif., Nov. 29, 1944; s. Malcolm Ross and Frances Dolores (Kane) W.; m. Donna Marie Stambaugh, July 25, 1981; children: Jessica Ross, M. Connor. SB, MIT, 1966; JD, Stanford U., 1969. Bar: Calif. 1970, Colo. 1992, U.S. Dist. Ct (cen. dist.) Calif. 1970, U.S. Ct. Appeals (9th cir.) 1970, U.S. Ct. Appeals (10th cir.) 1973, U.S. Dist. Ct. (no., so., ea. and cen. dists.) Calif. 1975, U.S. Ct. Appeals (11th cir.) 1987, U.S. Ct. Appeals (D.C. cir.) 1987, U.S. Supreme Ct. 1976, U.S. Ct. Appeals (3d cir.) 1989, (4th cir.) 1992, (8th cir.) 1993, (5th cir.) 1995, (Fed. cir.) 1998. Assoc. Howard, Prim, Smith, Rice & Downs, San Francisco, 1969-71; assoc. prof. law U. Kans., Lawrence, 1971-74; assoc. Hughes Hubbard & Reed, Los Angeles, 1974-77, ptnr., 1977-81, 83-85, cons., 1981-83; ptnr. Skadden, Arps, Slate, Meagher & Flom, Los Angeles, 1985-91; dir. Parcel, Mauro, Hultin & Spaanstra P.C., Denver, 1991-98, Wheeler Trigg & Kennedy, P.C., Denver, 1998—. Vis. prof. U. Iowa, 1978, prof., 1979; prof. U. Kans., Lawrence, 1981-83; chief counsel U.S. Senate Select Com. to Study Law Enforcement Undercover Activities, Washington, 1982-83. Mem. editl. bd. Jour. Products Liability, 1984-90, Fed. Litigation Guide Reporter, 1986-90; contbr. articles to profl. jours. Fellow Am. Coll. Trial Lawyers; mem. ABA, Calif. Bar Assn., Colo. Bar Assn., Am. Law Inst. Home: 100 Humboldt St Denver CO 80218-3932 Office Phone: 303-292-2525. Business E-Mail: wheeler@wtklaw.com.

WHEELER, RALPH MOON M., state legislator, pharmacist; b. American Falls, Idaho, Aug. 10, 1932; s. Ralph Merrill and Monne Mary (Zemo) W.; m. Patricia J. Howard (dec.); children: Vickie D., Michael M., Jodi L.; m. Ann F. Reed, June 19, 1965; children: Clark R., Ryan M. BS, Idaho State U., 1954. Registered pharmacist. Owner Rockland Pharmacy, 1960-88, part-time staff, 1988-90; mem. Idaho Senate, Dist. 35, Boise, 1994—2002; commissioner Power County, 1982-94; mem. Idaho Ho. of Reps., 1973-76; mayor American Falls, Idaho, 1965-72; city councilman, 1957-1965. Pres. Assn. Idaho Cities, Boise, 1971-72, Idaho State Pharmaceutical Assn., 1979-80. Pres. Lion's Club, American Falls, 1962; rep. State Legis. Boise, Idaho, 1972-76; county commr. Power County, American Falls, 1982-94; senator State of Idaho, 1994—, vice chair local govt. and taxation com. Named Pharmacist of Yr., Idaho Pharmaceutical Assn., 1972. Mem. Legislative Chair, Idaho Assoc. of Counties, 1987-90; pres., Idaho Pharmacy Assoc., 1970, pres., Assoc. Idaho Cities, 1971-72, Chamber of Commerce, Lion's Club. Republican. Roman Catholic. Avocations: fly fishing, rafting. Home: 659 Gifford Ave American Falls ID 83211-1315

WHEELER, RAYMOND LOUIS, lawyer; b. Ft. Sill, Okla., Feb. 10, 1945; s. Raymond Louis and Dorothy Marie (Hutcherson) W.; m. Priscilla Wheeler, July 1, 1966 (div. 1982); children: Jennifer, Hilary; m. Cynthia Lee Jackson, July 14, 1984 (div. 1994); children: Matthew Raymond, Madeline Elizabeth; m. Freddie Kay Park, June 10, 1995. BA, U. Tex., 1967; JD, Harvard U., 1970. Bar: Calif. 1972, U.S. Dist. Ct. (no., cen., ea., so. dists.) Calif., U.S. Ct. Appeals (9th cir., 7th cir.), U.S. Ct. Appeals (7th cir.), U.S. Supreme Ct. Law clk. to hon. Irving L. Goldberg U.S. Ct. Appeals 5th cir., 1970-71; assoc. Morrison & Foerster, San Francisco, 1971-76, ptnr., 1976-90, Palo Alto, Calif., 1990—, labor & employment dept. coord. Chmn. labor and employment law dept. Morrison & Foerster, San Francisco, 1984-88, 92—; lectr. labor and EEO law. Exec. editor Harvard Law Rev., 1969-70; editor in chief The Developing Labor Law; mem. nat. adv. bd. Berkeley Jour. Employment and Labor Law, 1980—; contbr. articles to law jours. Fellow Coll. Labor and Employment Lawyers; mem. ABA (chmn. com. on law devel. under labor rels. act 1990-93, coun. mem. sect. labor and employment 1994-02). Republican. Office: Morrison & Foerster LLP 755 Page Mill Rd Palo Alto CA 94304-1018 Office Phone: 650-813-5656. Office Fax: 650-494-0792. Business E-Mail: rwheeler@mofo.com.

WHEELER, STEPHEN FREDERICK, legal administrator; BA in Polit. Sci., Mt. Union Coll., Alliance, Ohio, 1968; MS in Adminstrn. of Justice, Am. U., 1974. Probation officer 19th Dist. Juvenile and Domestic Rels. Ct. Prince William County, Manassas, Va., 1972-75; ct. systems planner Office of Jud. Planning Ky. Jud. Coun., Frankfort, 1975-76; co-dir. Ky. pretrial svcs. Adminstrv. Office of Cts. Ky. Ct. of Justice, Frankfort, 1976-81; ct. adminstr. Jud. Dist. 27A, Gastonia, N.C., 1982-87, Colorado Springs (Colo.) Mcpl. Ct., 1987—2005; ret. Ct. systems cons. Nat. Criminal Justice Collaborative, Sea Island, Ga., 1981-85. E-mail: stvwhlr@cs.com.

WHEELER, STEVEN M., lawyer; b. Evanston, Ill., Jan. 5, 1949; AB, Pricneton U., 1971; JD with distinction, Cornell U., 1974. Bar: Ariz. 1974. Mem. Snell & Wilmer, Phoenix, ptnr., 1980—. Mng. editor Cornell Law Review, 1973-74; contbr. articles to profl. jours. Mem. ABA, Order Coif, Phi Kappa Phi. Office: Snell & Wilmer 1 Arizona Ctr Phoenix AZ 85004-0001

WHEELER, WILLIAM CHAMBERLAIN, JR., retired association administrator, lawyer; b. Bklyn., Feb. 25, 1945; s. William Chamberlain and Helen (Spencer) W. BA, Amherst Coll., 1967; JD, Vanderbilt U., 1970. Bar: Mich. 1979; cert. assn. exec. Assoc. dir. manuscript acquisition Prentice-Hall, Inc., Englewood Cliffs, N.J., 1971-75; asst. dir. dept. law and taxation NYU Sch. Continuing Edn., 1975-77; dir. office continuing legal edn. U. Detroit Sch. Law, 1977-79; sr. rsch. scientist Hwy. Safety Rsch. Inst. U. Mich., 1978-79; cons. Dept. Transp., Washington, 1979-82; exec. dir. Assn. Continuing Legal Edn. Adminstrs., 1983-86; dir. edn. Am. Soc. Safety Engrs., Des Plaines, Ill., 1986-92; exec. v.p. Chgo. Assn. Life Underwriters, 1995-98; prin., CEO ADA Exec. Search, Inc., Chgo., 2000—02. Dir. continuing legal edn. courses and publs., nat. insts. ABA, Chgo., 1982-86; devel. dir. The Living Desert, Palm Desert, Calif., 2002-03; dir. planning and devel. Found. for the Advancement in Rsch. in Medicine, Cathedral City, Calif., 2005—07. Pres. Human Soc. Desrt, 2003—05; co-adminstr. Desert Pride Comm. Ctr., 2006—07; bd. pres. Palm Springs Spiritual Enrichment Ctr., 2004—07; devel. dir. Greater Pride Inc., 2008—. Office: FARM 35741 Paseo Cirulo E Cathedral City CA 92234

WHEELER, WILLIAM ROY, technical advisor; b. Sept. 24, 1923; Sr. tech. advisor KLA-TENCOR, Milpitas, Calif., 1976—. Recipient Albert Nerken award Am. Vacuum Soc., 1996. Office: KLA-TENCOR 1 Technology Dr Milpitas CA 95035-7916

WHELAN, DAVID A., engineering executive; b. Oct. 7, 1954; BA in Physics, U. Calif., San Diego, 1977; MA in Physics, UCLA, 1978, PhD in Physics, 1983. Engring. specialist Northrop Corp., 1983—85; rsch. physicist Lawrence Livermore Nat. Lab., 1985—88; prog. mgr. GM-Hughes Electronics, 1988—94; dir. tactical tech. office Def. Advanced Rsch. Projects Agy., 1995—2001; v.p., chief tech. officer Space and Comm. Boeing Co., 2001—02, v.p. enterprise strategic growth Phantom Works Seal Beach, Calif., 2002—. Mem. sci. adv. bd. USAF. Recipient Sec. of Def. medal, Outstanding Pub. Svc., 1998, Sec. of Def. medal, Outstanding Civil Svc., 2001. Mem.: AIAA, IEEE, Am. Phys. Soc., NAE. Achievements include patents in field. Office: Boeing Phantom Works PO Box 2515 Seal Beach CA 90740 Office Phone: 562-797-2020.

WHELAN, PAUL W., lawyer; b. Auburn, Wash., Dec. 25, 1940; BA, U. Wash., 1962, JD, 1967. Bar: Wash. 1967, US Dist. Ct. Wash. (we. dist.) 1968, US Ct. Appeals (9th cir.) 1972, US Supreme Ct. 1983, US Dist. Ct. Wash. (ea. dist.) 1985, US Claims Ct. 1989. Law clk. Wash. State. Supreme Ct., 1967—68; atty. Strittmatter, Kessler, Whelan, Withey, Coluccio, Seattle. Spkr. in field. Contbr. articles to profl. jours. Mem.: Trial Lawyers Pub. Justice, Fed. Bar Assn., Attys. Info. Exchange Group, Assn. Trial Lawyers Am., Am. Bd. Trial Lawyers (Trial Lawyer of Yr. 2003), Wash. State Trial Lawyers Assn., Wash. State Bar Assn. Avocation: boating. Office: Strittmatter Kessler Whelan Colcuccio 200 Second Ave W Seattle WA 98119-4204 Home Phone: 206-328-9378; Office Phone: 206-448-1777. Business E-Mail: pww@skwc.com.

WHETTEN, JOHN D., food products executive; b. Chgo., June 8, 1940; s. Lester and Kate (Allred) Whetten; m. Becky Pearse; children: Carma, Rebecca, Mary Coza. BS, Brigham Young U., 1965; MBA, U. Calif., Berkeley, 1967. Advt. and mktg. mgr. The Clorox Corp., Oakland, Calif., 1967-79; pres., CEO Challenge Dairy Products, Inc., Dublin, Calif., 1982—; CEO DairyAmerica, Inc., Dublin, Calif., 1995-98. U.S. rep. Internat. Dairy Mktg. and Promotion Ann. Meeting, 1996. Co-chair U.S. Butter Task Force, 1990—97; bd. dirs. Epidermolysis Bullosa Med. Rsch. Found., 1991—, U.S. Dairy Export Coun., 1995—98; mem. nat. steering com. Brigham Young U. Sch. Mgmt., 1992—95; mem. nat. adv. coun. Utah Valley State Coll., 2001—. Recipient Disting. Svc. award, Brigham Young U. Sch. Mgmt., 2005. Mem.: Western Assn. Milk Mktg. Coop. (bd. dirs. 1992—2002, sec. 1994—2002), Barbecue Industry Assn. (dir. 1974—79, pres. 1977—78), Dairy Mktg. Coop. Fedn. (pres. 1992—), Dairy Export Incentive Program Coalition (pres. 1994—), Am. Dairy Products Inst. (bd. dirs. 1982—98, hon. life dir. 1999—, Merit award 2008), Am. Butter Inst. (bd. dirs. 1982—, v.p. 1995—99, pres. 1999—2001, Pres.'s Disting. Svc. award 1991, Spl. Recognition award 2007). Office: Challenge Dairy Products Inc 11875 Dublin Blvd Ste B230 Dublin CA 94568-2818 Business E-Mail: jdw@challengedairy.com.

WHINSTON, ARTHUR LEWIS, lawyer; b. NYC, Feb. 5, 1925; s. Charles Nathaniel and Charlotte (Nalen) W.; m. Melicent Ames Kingsbury, Mar. 19, 1949; children: Ann Kingsbury, James Pierce, Melicent Ames, Louise Ellen, Patricia Kingsbury. B.C.E., Cornell U., 1945; MSE., Princeton U., 1947; JD, N.Y. U., 1957. Bar: N.Y. 1957, Oreg. 1964, U.S. Supreme Ct 1966, U.S. Patent Office 1958, U.S. Ct. Appeals (fed. cir.) 1959; registered profl. engr., N.Y., Oreg. Engr. Chas. N. & Selig Whinston, NYC, 1947-50; lectr. Coll. City N.Y., 1950-51; structures engr. Republic Aviation Corp., Farmingdale, NY, 1951-57; patent lawyer Arthur, Dry & Kalish, 1957-64, Klarquist Sparkman, LLP, 1964—; chmn. Oreg. Bar com. on patent, trademark and copyright law, 1968-69, 77-78, mem. com. unauthorized practice law, 1970-73, chmn., 1972-73, com. on profl. responsibility, 1973-75. Served as ensign, C.E.C., USNR, 1945-46. Recipient Fuertes medal Cornell U. Sch. Civil Engring., 1945 Mem. ABA, Oreg. Bar Assn., N.Y. Bar Assn., Multnomah County Bar Assn., Am. Intellectual Property Law Assn., N.Y. Intellectual Property Law Assn., Oreg. Patent Law Assn. (pres. 1977-78), Profl. Engrs. Oreg. (past state legis. chmn.), Sigma Xi, Chi Epsilon, Phi Kappa Phi. Clubs: Multnomah Athletic. Republican. Office: One World Trade Ctr Ste 1600 Portland OR 97204 Home: 12353 SW Grant Ave Portland OR 97223-5218 Personal E-mail: artmeli@comcast.net.

WHISENHUNT, KEN, professional football coach; b. Atlanta, Feb. 28, 1962; m. Alice Whisenhunt; children: Kenneth Jr., Mary Ashley. BS in Civil Engring., Ga. Tech. U., 1990. Tight end Atlanta Falcons, 1985—88, Washington Redskins, 1990, NY Jets, 1991—92; spl. teams, half backs, & tight ends coach Vanderbilt U., 1995—96; tight ends coach Balt. Ravens, 1997—98; spl. teams coach Cleve. Browns, 1999; tight ends coach NY Jets, 2000, Pitts. Steelers, 2001—03, offensive coord., 2004—06; head coach Ariz. Cardinals, 2007—. Achievements include being a member of Super Bowl XL winning Pittsburgh Steelers, 2006. Office: Ariz Cardinals 8701 S Hardy Dr Tempe AZ 85284

WHISLER, JAMES STEVEN, retired mining executive, lawyer, rancher; b. Centerville, Iowa, Nov. 23, 1954; s. James Thomas and Betty Lou (Clark) W.; m. Ardyce Dawn Christensen, Jan. 20, 1979; children: James Kyle, Kristen Elyse. BS, U. Colo., Boulder, 1975; JD, U. Denver, 1978; MS, Colo. Sch. Mines, 1984, DSc (hon.), 2001; AMP, Harvard Bus. Sch., 1998. Bar: Colo. 1978; CPA, Ariz. Assoc. gen. counsel, sec. We. Nuc., Inc., Denver, 1979—81; exploration counsel Phelps Dodge Corp., NYC, 1981—85, legal and adminstrv. mgr. Phoenix, 1985—87, v.p., gen. counsel, 1987—88, sr. v.p., gen. counsel, 1988—91; pres. Phelps Dodge Mining Co., 1991—98; pres., COO Phelps Dodge Corp., Phoenix, 1997—99, chmn., pres., CEO, 2000—03, chmn., CEO, 2003—07. Bd. dir. Am. West Holdings Corp., 2001—05, Phelps Dodge Corp., 1995—2007, Burlington No. Santa Fe Corp., U.S. Airways Group, Inc., Brunswick Corp., Internat. Paper Corp., 2007—. Mem.: AIME, AICPA, Nat. Cowboy and Western Heritage Mus., Mining and Metall. Soc. Am., Colo. Bar Assn., Soc. Mining Engrs., Mont. Stock Growers' Assn. E-mail: jswhisler@gmail.com.

WHITAKER, JIM, state representative; b. Bremerton, Wash., Sept. 30, 1950; m. Patricia Whitaker; children: Victoria, Christine, Jennifer, Wendy. BS in Journalism, U. Oreg., 1973. Small bus. owner, 1976—; mem Alaska Ho. of Reps., 1998—. Founding mem. Vol. in Policing; mem. Fairbanks City Coun., 1995—98; bd. dirs. Fest. Fairbanks; past bd. dirs. Yukon Quest. Republican. Address: 119 N Cushman St Ste 213 Fairbanks AK 99701-2879

WHITAKER, THOMAS O'HARA, theater educator, director; s. Thomas Russell and Dorothy Whitaker. BA, Oberlin Coll., Ohio, 1975; MFA, Carnegie-Mellon U., Pitts., 1983. Instr. acting Carnegie-Mellon U., Coll. Fine Arts, 1982—83; instr. SW Mo. State U., Springfield, 1983—84; asst. prof. Ind. State U., Terre Haute, 1984—87, U. Tex., Austin, 1987—92, U. Calif., Santa Barbara, 1992—96, assoc. prof., 1996—. Cons. dir., tchr. Conn. Humanities Coun., Hartford, 1980—81; cons. Ctr. Theatre Techniques Edn., Stratford, 1980—81, Comprehensive Arts Program, New Haven, 1980—81; guest artist Oberlin Theater Inst., 1987; tenured dir. Tex. Shakespeare Festival, Kilgore, 1989—; cons. Beijing Inst. World Theater and Film, 2005—; guest prof. Nanjing U., China, 2006—. Musician: (puppet theater) Young Woman's Sorrow, Man is Man, Loot, The Misanthrope, Advice to the Players, Love's Labor's Lost; actor: King Lear; dir.: Tartuffe, Taming of the Shrew; actor: Heartbreak House, (puppet theater) Grey Lady Cantata; dir.: (theater) The Bourgeois Gentleman, Two Gentlement of Verona; dir., dir.: As You Like It; actor: Henry IV, part 1; dir.: Big Love, Arms and the Man, The Merchant of Venice, Life's a Dream, Cyrano de Bergerac, bobrauschenbergamerica Woyzeck Reckless; actor: (film) The Meadow's Green; dir.: (theater) Revel's World of Shakespeare; actor: The Marilyn Project, The Forced Marriage; dir.: Time Play, Misalliance, Fool for Love, Buried Child, Man of La Mancha, 2007. Recipient Boettcher award Directing, Carnegie-Mellon U., 1983; grantee, Conn. Humanities Coun., 1980; scholar, Carnegie-Mellon U., 1982—83. Mem.: Phi Beta Kappa.

WHITE, AL, state legislator; b. Hillsboro, Ill., June 27, 1950; m. Jean White; children: Devin, Jenna. BA in Polit. Sci., We. Ill. U., 1970; M, U. Colo., 1972. Founder RBM Mgmt., Devil's Thumb Ranch & Nordic Ctr., Winter Park Holding, Co., The Summit Ski Shop, Alpine Sun Ski Shop, 1976—84, Golden Spike Ski Shop, 1981—2000, Viking Lodge & Ski Shop, 1988—96; mem. Dist. 56 Colo. House of Reps., Denver, 2000—02; mem. Dist. 8 Colo. State Senate, Denver, 2003—. Bd. sec. Grand County Water & Sanitation Dist.; bd. chmn. Fraser Valley Met. Recreation Dist., Fraser Valley Found. Served with US Army. Mem. LWV, AAUW, PTA, Interfaith Alliance, Northwest Metro C. of C. Republican. Presbyterian. Office: Colo State Capitol 200 E Colfax Rm 271 Denver CO 80203 Office Phone: 303-866-2949. Business E-Mail: al.white.house@state.co.us.*

WHITE, ALVIN MURRAY, mathematics professor, consultant; b. NYC, June 21, 1925; s. Max and Beatrice White; m. Myra Goldstein, Dec. 4, 1946; children: Louis, Michael. BA, Columbia U., 1949; MA, UCLA, 1951; PhD, Stanford U., 1961. Instr. Stanford U., Calif., 1950—54; asst. prof. U. Santa Clara, Calif., 1954—61; postdoctoral fellow U. Wis., Madison, 1961—62; prof. Harvey Mudd Coll., Claremont, Calif., 1962—. Vis. scholar MIT, 1975; initiator-facilitator humanistic math. network of over 2000 mathematicians worldwide; cons. coop. learning tutorial program Claremont Unified Sch. Dist. Editor: Interdisciplinary Teaching, 1981; pub., editor: Humanistic Mathematics Network Jour., Essays on Humanistic Math., Math. Assn. Am., 1993; contbr. articles to profl. jours. Served with USN, 1943-46, PTO. Grantee Fund for Improvement of Post-secondary Edn., Exxon Found. Mem. Am. Math. Soc., Math. Assn. Am., Nat. Coun. Tchrs. Math., Profl. Organizational Developers Network, Fedn. Am. Scientists, AAUP, Sigma Xi. Office: Harvey Mudd Coll 301 E 12th St Claremont CA 91711-5901

WHITE, BETTY, actress, comedienne; b. Oak Park, Ill., Jan. 17, 1922; m. Dick Barker 1945 (div. 1945), m. Lane Allen 1947 (div. 1949), m. Allen Ludden, 1963 (dec. 1981). Student pub. schs., Beverly Hills, Calif. Appearances on radio shows This Is Your FBI, Blondie, The Great Gildersleeve; actress: (TV series) including Hollywood on Television, The Betty White Show, 1954-58, Life With Elizabeth, 1953-55, A Date With The Angels, 1957-58, The Pet Set, 1971, Mary Tyler Moore Show, 1974-77, The Betty White Show, 1977, Mama's Family, 1983-86, The Golden Girls, 1985-92 (Emmy award for best actress 1986), Another World, 1988, The Golden Palace, 1992-93, Maybe This Time, 1995, (TV films) With This Ring, 1978, The Best Place to Be, 1979, Before and After, 1979, Eunice, 1982, Chance of a Lifetime, 1991, The Story of Santa Claus, 1996, A Weekend in the Country, 1996, The Retrievers, 2001, Annie's Point, 2005, (films) Advise and Consent, 1962, Dennis the Menace 2, 1998, Hard Rain, 1998, The Story of Us, 1999, Bringing Down the House, 2003, The Third Wish, 2004; guest appearances include Petticoat Junction, 1969, The Odd Couple, 1972, Fame, 1983, St. Elsewhere, 1985, Who's the Boss, 1985, Matlock, 1987, Empty Nest, 1989, 92, Carol & Company, 1990, Nurses, 1991, Diagnosis Murder, 1994, The Naked Truth, 1995, Suddenly Susan, 1996, (voice) King of the Hill, 1999, 2002, Ally McBeal, 1999, (voice) The Simpsons, 2000, Yes, Dear, 2002, Providence, 2002, That 70s Show, 2002, 03, Everwood, 2003, 04, The Practice, 2004, My Wife and Kids, 2004, Malcolm in the Middle, 2004, (voice) Father of the Pride, 2004, Boston Legal, 2005; frequent celebrity guest on numerous game shows including Hollywood Squares, Match Game; summer stock appearances Guys and Dolls, Take Me Along, The King and I, Who Was That Lady?, Critic's Choice, Bells are Ringing; author (book) Betty White's Pet-Lovers: How Pets Take Care of Us, 1987, Here We Go Again: My Life in Television, 1995; contbr. to forward(book) The Irrepressible Toy Dog, Dr. Fisher's Life on the Ark: Green Alligators, Bushman and Other "Hare Raising" Tales from America's Most Popular Zoo and Around the World, 2004, (preface) The Pets are Wonderful Family Album. Mem. Morris Animal Found., 1976—; zoo commr. Greater LA Zoo, 1998—. Recipient Emmy award NATAS, 1975, 76, 86; LA

Area Emmy award, 1952, Living Legacy award, Women's Internat. Ctr., 1988, star on the Hollywood Walk of Fame; inducted into TV Hall of Fame, 1995; named Amb. to the Animals, Greater LA Zoo, 2006. Mem. AFTRA, Am. Humane Assn., Greater LA Zoo Assn. (dir.). Office: c/o William Morris Agy Betty Fanning 151 S El Camino Dr Beverly Hills CA 90212-2704

WHITE, BEVERLY JANE, retired cytogeneticist; b. Seattle, Oct. 9, 1938; Grad., U. Wash., 1959, MD, 1963. Diplomate Nat. Bd. Med. Examiners, Am. Bd. Pediatrics, Am. Bd. Med. Genetics; lic physician and surgeon, Wash., Calif. Rsch. trainee dept. anatomy Sch. Medicine U. Wash., Seattle, 1960-62, pediatric resident dept. pediatrics, 1967-69; rotating intern Phila. Gen. Hosp., 1963-64; rsch. fellow med. ob-gyn. unit Cardiovascular Rsch. Inst. U. Calif. Med. Ctr., San Francisco, 1964-65; staff fellow lab. biomed. scis. Nat. Inst. Child Health and Human Devel. NIH, Bethesda, Md., 1965-67, sr. staff fellow, attending physician lab. exptl. pathology Nat. Inst. Arthritis, Metabolism and Digestive Diseases, 1969-74, acting chief sect. cytogenetics, 1975-76, rsch. med. officer, attending physician sect. cytogenetics lab. cellular biology and genetics, 1974-86, dir. cytogenetics unit, interinstitute med. genetics program clin. ctr., 1987-95; dir. cytogenetics Corning Clin. Labs., Teterboro, NJ, 1995-96; assoc. med. dir. cytogenetics Nichols Inst.-Quest Diagnostics, San Juan Capistrano, Calif., 1996-97, med. dir. cytogenetics, 1998—2008, med. dir. genetics divsn., 2000—02. Vis. scientist dept. pediat. divsn. genetics U. Wash. Sch. Medicine, 1983-84; intramural cons. NIH, 1975-95; cons. to assoc. editor Jour. Nat. Cancer Inst., 1976; cons. dept. ob-gyn. Naval Hosp., Bethesda, 1988-89; lectr., presenter in field. Recipient Mosby Book award, 1963, Women of Excellence award U. Wash. and Seattle Profl. chpt. Women in Comm., 1959, Reuben award Am. Soc. for Study Sterility, 1963. Fellow Am. Coll. Med. Genetics (founding), Am. Acad. Pediatrics; mem. AMA. Am. Soc. Human Genetics, Assn. Genetic Technologists (program com. 1989).

WHITE, BONNIE YVONNE, management consultant, retired educator; b. Long Beach, Calif., Sept. 4, 1940; d. William Albert and Helen Iris (Harbaugh) W. BS, Brigham Young U., 1962, MS, 1965, EdD in Ednl. Adminstrn., 1976; postgrad., Harvard U., 1987. Tchr. Wilson High Sch., Long Beach, Calif., 1962-63; grad. asst. Brigham Young U., Provo, Utah, 1963-65; instr., dir. West Valley Coll., Saratoga, Calif., 1965-76; instr., evening adminstr. Mission Coll., Santa Clara, Calif., 1976-80; dean gen. edn. Mendocino Coll., Ukiah, Calif., 1980-85; dean instrn. Porterville (Calif.) Coll., 1985-89, dean adminstrv. svc., 1989-93. Rsch. assoc. SAGE Rsch. Internat., Orem, Utah, 1975-99. Mem. AAUW, Faculty Assn. Calif. Cmty. Colls., Calif., Coun. Fine Arts Deans, Assn. Calif. C.C. Adminstrs., Assn. Calif. C.C. Adminstrs. Liberal Arts, Zonta (intern), Soroptimists (intern). Republican. Mem. Lds Ch.

WHITE, BRETT, real estate company executive; BA, U. Calif., Santa Barbara. Sales trainee, indsl. salesperson CB Richard Ellis, LA, 1984—91, sales mgr. San Diego, 1991—2001, mng. dir. Newport Beach LA, 1991—2001, regional mgr. L.A., 1991—2001, pres. brokerage, 1991—2001, chmn. The Ams., 1991—2001, pres., 2001—05, pres., CEO, 2005—, bd. dirs., 1998—, mem. exec. com., 1999—. Bd. dirs. Edison Internat., Southern Calif. Edison. Mem. LA Mus. Contemporary Art, Jr. Achievement. Named Brokerage Exec. of Yr., 2005, Real Estate Industry Exec. of Yr., 2006, Brokerage Exec. of Yr., Comml. Property News, 2006. Office: CB Richard Ellis 11150 Santa Monica Blvd Los Angeles CA 90025 Office Phone: 310-405-8919. Office Fax: 310-405-8950. Business E-Mail: brett.white@cbre.com.

WHITE, CECIL RAY, librarian, consultant; b. Hammond, Ind., Oct. 15, 1937; s. Cecil Valentine and Vesta Ivern (Bradley) W.; m. Frances Ann Gee, Dec. 23, 1960 (div. 1987); children: Timothy Wayne, Stephen Patrick. BS in Edn., So. Ill. U., 1959; postgrad., Syracuse U., 1961; MDiv, Southwestern Bapt. Sem., 1969; MLS, No. Tex. State U., 1970, PhD, 1984. Libr. Herrin (Ill.) H.S., 1964-66; acting reference libr. Southwestern Sem., Ft. Worth, 1968-70, asst. libr., 1970-80; head libr. Golden Gate Bapt. Sem., Mill Valley, Calif., 1980-88, West Oahu Coll., Pearl City, Hawaii, 1988-89; dir. spl. projects North State Coop. Libr. System, Yreka, Calif., 1989-90; dir. libr. St. Patrick's Sem., Menlo Park, Calif., 1990—. Libr. cons. Hist. Commn., So. Bapt. Conv., Nashville, 1983-84, Internat. Bapt. Sem., Prague, Czech Republic, 1996; mem. Thesaurus Com., 1974-84; adv. bd. Cath. Periodical and Lit. Index, 1995—, chair, 1999-2008. Bd. dirs. Hope and Help Ctr., 1986-88, vice chmn., 1987-88. With USAF, 1960—64. Lilly Found. grantee Am. theol. Assn., 1969. Mem. ALA, Am. Theol. Libr. Assn. (coord. cons. svc. 1973-78, program planning com. 1985-88, chmn. 1986-88), Nat. Assn. Profs. Hebrew (archivist 1985—), Assn. Coll. and Rsch. Librs., Cath. Libr. Assn. (mem. exec. bd. 1999-2005, Mary A. Grant Svc. award, 2009), Phi Kappa Phi, Beta Phi Mu. Democrat. Baptist. Home: 229 Rome Place Hayward CA 94544 Office: St Patricks Sem 320 Middlefield Rd Menlo Park CA 94025-3563 Home Phone: 510-429-1955; Office Phone: 650-321-5655. E-mail: cecilrwhite@hotmail.com, stpats@ix.netcom.com.

WHITE, CHARLES R., former mayor; b. Boston; m. Maria White; 4 children. Grad., Riverside CC. Mayor City of Moreno Valley, 1997. Mem. Moreno Valley City Coun., 1996—; mem. So. Calif. Assn. Govt., Regional Coun., Transp. & Comm. Policy Com., Magnetic Levitation Task Force, Growth Visioning Com.; bd. Riverside Transit Agency; mem., chmn. March Joint Powers Commn., 1999, vice chmn., 2001, chmn., 02. Served Planning Commr., Redevelopment Project Area Com., Traffic Safety Adv. Com., Disaster Preparedness Com., Mayor's Drug Task Force; treasurer Friends Moreno Valley Sr. Ctr.; pres. Moreno Valley Elks Lodge; vice comdr. Moreno Valley VFW Post; jr. deacon Moreno Valley Masonic Lodge; pres. Sunnymead Little League; v.p. Sunnymead PTA; co-founder Moreno Valley Youth Fedn. Served USAR. Mem.: Idylwild Am. Legion Post (life). Office: 14177 Frederick St PO Box 88005 Moreno Valley CA 92552

WHITE, CHRISTOPHER TODD, language educator, anthropologist; b. Columbia, Mo., Dec. 7, 1965; s. Eric B. and Barbara K. White; life ptnr. Ryan C. Reiss. BA, U. Nebr., Lincoln, 1990; MA, U. Mo., Kansas City, 1994, U. Nev., Las Vegas, 1998; PhD, U. So. Calif., LA, 2005. Adj. lectr. Rockhurst Coll., Kansas City, Mo., 1994—95; editl. asst. BkMk Press, Kansas City, 1993—95; adj. lectr. English U. Mo., Kansas City, 1993—95; acad. advisor Ednl. Talent Search, Las Vegas, Nev., 1995—96; asst. prof./lectr. U. Nev., Las Vegas, 1996—98; instr. Glendale C.C., Calif., 1998—2003; tchr., rsch. asst. dept. anthropology U. So. Calif., LA, 1998—2005; asst. prof. anthropology SUNY, Brockport, NY, 2005—06; staff anthropologist, Digital Initiatives Unit, U. Rochester, 2007—08; lead ethnographer Colo. State U. Librs., 2007, Rutgers U. Librs., 2009—; vis. asst. prof.,dept sociology & anthropology James Madison U., 2008—. Dir. Homosexual Info. Ctr., LA, 2001—, ONE Inst. and Archives, LA, 2001—02; mem. adv. bd. GLBTQ history website project CUNY, Ctr. Lesbian and Gay Studies, 2008—. Editor: U. Nev.-Las Vegas Jour. Anthropology, 1995—2005, San Dieguito and La Jolla: The Collected Works of Claude N. Warren on the Archaeology af Southern California, 2006; asst. editor Before Stonewell: Activists for Gay and Lesbian Rights in Historical Context, 2002, mem. editl. bd. Collegiate Press, 2002, referee Popular Culture Rev.; columnist: Orange County/Long Beach Blade Mag., 2006—07; author: Pre Gay L.A.: A Social History of the Movement for Homosexual Rights, 2009; contbr. articles to profl. jours. Recipient Patricia Roecio Award in Anthropology, U. Nev.-Las Vegas, 1997, Dissertation Fellowship award, U. So. Calif., 2005; scholar Hal Call Mattachine scholar, Inst. for Study of Human Resources, 2000—01. Mem.: Assn. for Psychol. Anthropology, Homosexual Info. Ctr. (sec.-treas. 2001—), Southwestern Anthropol. Assn., Soc. of Lesbian and Gay Anthropologists (sec.-treas. 1998—2005), Soc. of Linguistic Anthropology, Am. Anthropol. Assn. Democrat. Avocations: camping, book collecting, piano, running, bicycling. Office: James Madison Univ Dept Anthropology Harrisonburg VA 22807 Personal E-mail: ctgrant@mac.com.

WHITE, CONSTANCE BURNHAM, state official; b. Odgen, Utah, July 2, 1954; d. Owen W. and Colleen (Redd) Burnham; m. Wesley Robert White, Mar. 18, 1977. BA in English magna cum laude, U. Utah, 1976, postgrad., 1977, Boston Coll., 1979; JD, Loyola U., 1981. Law clerk Kruse, Landa, Zimmerman & Maycock, Salt Lake City, 1979; law clerk legal dept. Bell & Howell, Lincolnwood, Ill., 1980; clerk, assoc. Parsons, Behle & Latimer, Salt Lake City, 1981-82; assoc. Reynolds, Vance, Deason & Smith, Salt Lake City, 1982-83; chief enforcement sect. Utah Securities Divsn., Salt Lake City, 1984-87, chief licensing sect., 1988, asst. dir., 1989-90; legal counsel Utah Dept. Commerce, Salt Lake City, 1990-92, exec. dir., 1993-95, commr. pub. svc. div., 1995. Mem. Gov.'s Securities Fraud Task Force, 1984; spl. asst. atty. gen., 1986-88; spl. asst. U.S. atty., 1986—. Mem. North Am. Securities Adminstrs. Assn. (vice chair market manipulation com. 1988-89, penny stock/telecom. fraud com. 1989-90, chair uniform examinations com. 1990-92, chair forms revision com. 1992), Utah State Bar (securities adv. com. 1991—, task force on community-based mediation 1991—, chair securities sect. 1992-93). Office: Utah Pub Svc Commn 160 East 300 South Salt Lake City UT 84111

WHITE, DANA, sports association executive; b. Manchester, Conn., 1971; Attended, U. Mass. Founder Dana White Enterprises, Las Vegas, 1992; boxing trainer, group exercise instr.; mgr. of boxers and mixed martial arfts fighters including Tito Ortiz and Chuck Liddell Utimate Fighting Championship (UFC), 2000, pres., 2000—; co-owner Zuffa LLC. Prodr.: (TV series) The Ultimate Fighter, 2005—. Named one of Most Influential People in the World of Sports, Bus. Week, 2008. Office: Zuffa LLC 2960 W Sahara Ste 200 Las Vegas NV 89102

WHITE, DAUN ELOIS, professional society official; b. Winsted, Conn., Feb. 11, 1955; d. Robert Hamilton and Bessie Emma (Land) Daly; m. Stephen Scott White, Feb. 9, 1974; children: Stephen Scott Jr., Derik James. Student, Tri-Community Coll., Covina, Calif., 1974-76; BS in Bus. Adminstrn., U. of Redlands, Calif., 1982. Sec., bookkeeper Century 21 Comml., West Covina, Calif., 1978-80; sec. Century 21 Regional, West Covina, 1980-82; adminstrv. asst. Century 21 Real Estate, Covina, 1982-84, Covina Bd. Realtors, 1984-86; asst. to v.p. acquisitions Occidental Land Rsch., Diamond Bar, Calif., 1986-87; exhibits mgr. Soc. for Advancement Material and Process Engrs., Covina, 1987—91, exec. dir., 1991—2002, Soc. of Hispanic Profl. Engrs., LA, 2003—. Mem. Nat. Assn. Expn. Mgrs., NAFE. Episcopalian. Office: SHPE Inc 5400 E Olympic Blvd Ste 210 Los Angeles CA 90022

WHITE, DAVID L., electronics executive; b. Kansas City, Mo., Apr. 20, 1955; s. Joseph D. and Barbara H. (Gosling) W.; m. Nicole J. Davis, Dec. 18, 1976; children: Christina L., Jennifer M., Trisha D. BS in Physics, Brigham Young U., 1977; MBA, U. Wash., 1979. Applications cons. Burroughs Corp., Seattle, 1978-79; mgr. fin. planning Digital Equipment Corp., Colo. Springs, Colo., 1979-84; corp. controller Zehntel Inc., Walnut Creek, Calif., 1984-89; v.p., corp. controller Conner Peripherals, Inc., San Jose, Calif., 1989; pres., CEO Candescent Tech.; sr. v.p., CFO Asyst Tech.; exec. v.p., CFO Sanmina-SCI Corp., San Jose, Calif., 2004—. Advisor Boy Scouts Am., 1979-92. Named to All Am. Swimming Team, NCAA, 1975. Mem. Fin. Execs. Inst., Am. Prodn. and Inventory Control Soc. Republican. LDS ch. Avocations: swimming, racquetball. Office: Sanmina SCI Corp 2700 N First St San Jose CA 95134

WHITE, DEVON MARKES, professional baseball player; b. Kingston, Jamaica, Dec. 29, 1962; With Calif. Angels, 1981-90, Toronto Blue Jays, 1990-95, Florida Marlins, Miami, 1996—; outfielder Los Angeles Dodgers, 1998—. Player Am. League All Star Team, 1989, 93. Recipient Gold Glove award, 1988-89, 91-94; named Am. League leader put outs by outfielder, 1987, 91-92. Office: Los Angeles Dodgers 1000 Elysian Park Ave Los Angeles CA 90012-1199

WHITE, DOUGLAS JAMES, JR., lawyer; b. NYC, Mar. 20, 1934; s. Douglas James and Margaret (Stillman) W.; m. Denise Beale, May 28, 1960; children: Brian Douglas, James Roderick. BA, U. Oreg., 1955; LLB, Willamette U., 1958. Bar: Oreg. 1958. Law clk. to assoc. justice Oreg. Supreme Ct., Salem, 1958-59; assoc. Schwabe, Williamson & Wyatt (formerly known as Mautz, Souther, Spaulding, Kinsey & Williamson), Portland, Oreg., 1959-69; shareholder, gen. ptnr. Schwabe, Williamson & Wyatt, P.C. (formerly known as Schwabe, Williamson, Wyatt, Moore & Roberts), Portland, Oreg., 1969-79, sr. ptnr., 1979-93; shareholder, 1994—98; ret., 1998; of counsel, 1999—2008. Trustee Jesuit H.S., Beaverton, 1991-94; bd. dirs. St. Vincent de Paul Child Devel. Ctr., Portland, 1979-90, Portland Coun., Soc. St. Vincent de Paul, 1989-92, Portland House of Umoja, 1995—, Friends Sat. Acad., 2006—; bd. dirs., officer Maryville Nursing Home, Beaverton, 1993-99, St. Vincent de Paul Conf. of St. Thomas More, Portland, 1966—; adv. bd. Saturday Acad., Portland, 1982-2005. Mem.: Oreg. State Bar Assn. (real estate and land use sect. exec. com. 1984—85), Flyfisher Club Oreg., Multnomah Athletic Club. Republican. Roman Catholic. Avocations: fly fishing, bridge, walking, hiking, travel. Home: 6725 SW Preslynn Dr Portland OR 97225-2668 Office: Schwabe Williamson & Wyatt 1211 SW 5th Ave Ste 1800 Portland OR 97204-3713 Office Phone: 503-222-9981.

WHITE, DOUGLAS RICHIE, anthropology educator; b. Mpls., Mar. 13, 1942; s. Asher Abbott and Margaret McQuestin (Richie) W.; m. Jayne Chamberlain (div. Feb. 1971); m. Lilyan Amdur Brudner, Mar. 21, 1971; 1 child, Scott Douglas. BA, U. Minn., 1964, MA, 1967, PhD, 1969. Asst. prof. U. Pitts., 1967-72, assoc. prof., 1972-76, U. Calif., Irvine, 1976-79, prof., 1979—. Dep. dir. Lang. Attitudes Rsch. Project, Dublin, 1971—73; vis. prof. U. Tex., Austin, 1974—75, Ecole des Hautes Etudes en Sci. Sociales, Paris, 1999—2002, Inst. Nat. d'Etudes Démographique, 2000; chmn. Linkages: World Devel. Res. Coun., Md., 1986—, pres., Md., 1986—90. Co-editor: Research Methods in Social Networks, 1989, Anthropology of Urban Environments, 1972, Kinship, Networks and Exchange, 1998; founder, gen. editor World Cultures Jour., 1985-90; author sci. software packages; editor Structure and Dynamics Jour.; contbr. articles to profl. jours. Recipient Sr. Disting. U.S. Scientist award, Alexander von Humboldt Stiftung, Bonn, Germany, 1989—91, Bourse de Haute Niveau award, Ministry Rsch. and Tech., Paris, 1992; fellow, Ctr. for Advanced Studies, Western Behavioral Sci. Inst., La Jolla, Calif., 1981—84. Mem. Social Sci. Computing Assn. (pres. elect 1991, pres. 1992.), Santa Fe Inst. (mem. working groups 1999, 2000, 2001, external faculty 2004-). Democrat. Home: 8633 Via Mallorca Unit C La Jolla CA 92037 Office: U Calif School Social Sci Irvine CA 92697-0001 Office Phone: 949-824-5893.

WHITE, EDWARD ALLEN, electronics executive; b. Jan. 1, 1928; s. Joseph and Bessie (Allen) W.; m. Joan Dixon, Dec. 22, 1949 (div. Aug. 1978); children: Leslie Ann Lollar; m. Nancy Rhoads, Oct. 6, 1979. BS, Tufts U., 1947. Vice chmn. White Electronic Designs Corp., Phoenix, 1951—. Pres. Ariz. Digital Corp., Phoenix, 1975—91, Interactive Digital Corp., Phoenix, 1992—. Patentee in field. Bd. dirs. Gov.'s Coun. Children, Youth and Families, Phoenix, 1982-84, Planned Parenthood Fedn. Am., 1984-88; pres., bd. dirs. Planned Parenthood Boltemian Club. Sanfrancisco, Calif., 1984-88; trustee Internat. House, N.Y.C., 1973-75, Tufts U., 1973-83. Recipient Horatio Alger award, 1962. Mem.: World Pres.'s Orgn., Paradise Valley Country Club, Tau Beta Pi. Home: 5786 N Echo Canyon Cir Phoenix AZ 85018-1242 Office: White Electronic Designs Corp 3601 E University Dr Phoenix AZ 85034-7254 Home Phone: 602-840-0704; Office Phone: 602-437-1520 x111. Business E-Mail: ewhite@whiteedc.com.

WHITE, IAN, information technology executive; m. Ellen White; 3 children. Grad. in Elec. Engring., U. Nottingham, Eng.; grad. in Electronic Engring., Derby Tech. Coll., Eng. With Rolls Royce; rsch. & devel. engr. telecom. co.; with Computervision, Sun Microsystems, Inc., 1989—, dir. UK customer svc. ops. & customer edn., dir. UK Installed Base Sales & Sales Support, v.p. Europe, Mid. East and Africa, v.p. Internat. Ams., v.p. Sun Svcs. Ams., sr. v.p. global customer svcs. Office: Sun Microsystems Inc 4150 Network Cir Santa Clara CA 95054 Office Phone: 650-960-1300.

WHITE, JO LYNN, lawyer; Atty. environ. law, Buffalo and Kansas City, Mo.; environ. counsel Allied Waste Industries, Inc., Scottsdale, Ariz., 1997—99, asst. corp. sec., 1999—, dep. gen. counsel, 2003—, v.p., 2005—, acting gen. counsel.

WHITE, JOHN, JR., lawyer; b. St. Louis, Oct. 20, 1943; s. John Aaron and Helen Inez (Stewart) White; children: Dorian, Cameron, Lauren, John Aaron III. BA, U. Nev., 1965; JD, George Washington U., 1968. Bar: DC 1969, Nev. 1969, US Dist. Ct. (DC cir.) 1969, US Supreme Ct. 1979. Atty. City Atty.'s Office, Reno, 1969—74; sole practice Reno, 1974—78; ptnr. White Law Chartered, Reno, 1978—. Adj. prof. in bankruptcy Old Coll. Nev. Sch. Law, 1986—87; lectr. computers and law Nev. State Bar Conv., 1986. Co-author: Nevada Civil Practice Manual, 1986—88. Mem. Gov.'s Commn. on Status People, 1975—78; founder Family Ch. Jesus. With USMC, 1961—68. Mem.: ABA, Washoe County Bar Assn., Am. Bankruptcy Inst., DC Bar Assn., Nev. State Bar Assn., Reno Host Lions (past pres.). Republican. Achievements include pioneer in litigating early cases against Dow Corning and Dow Chemical involving silicone breast implants. Office: White Law Chartered 335 W 1st St Reno NV 89503-5344 Office Fax: 775-322-1228. E-mail: john@whitelawchartered.com.

WHITE, JULIE, actress; b. San Diego, June 4, 1962; d. Edwin and Sue Jane W.; m. Carl Pandel, 1984 (div.); 1 child, Alexandra. Student, Fordham U., Tex. State U. Actress Carsey-Werner Co., CBS-MTM Studios, Studio City, Calif. TV appearances: Grace Under Fire, 1993-97, Six Feet Under, 2001-03, Cavemen, 2007-08, guest appearances on Law & Order: SVU, 2003-07; stage appearances: Dark of the Moon, 1984-85, The Geography of Yearning, 1985-86, Lucky Stiff, 1988, Early One Evening at the Rainbow Bar, Grille, 1989, Largo Desolato, 1990-91, Marathon '91, 1991, The Stick Wife, 1991, Spike Heels, 1992, Money and Friends, 1992-93, Absurd Person Singular, 1992-93, The Heidi Chronicles, 1995, Over Texas, The Family of Mann, Just Say No, Dinner With Friends, 1999, Barbra's Wedding, Bad Dates, Fiction, Marvin's Room, The Little Dog Laughed, 2005 (OBIE award Village Voice 2006, Tony award best performance by a leading actress in a play, 2007), From Up Here, 2008; film appearances: Take Down, 1978, Flypaper, 1997, Say It Isn't So, 2001, Slap Her...She's French, 2002, War of the Worlds, 2005, The Astronaut Farmer, 2007, Transformers, 2007, The Nanny Diaries, 2007, Michael Clayton, 2007.

WHITE, MEG(AN) (MARTHA), musician, vocalist; b. Grosse Pointe, Mich., Dec. 10, 1974; m. John Gillis, 1996 (div. 2000). Drummer, vocalist The White Stripes, 1997—; toured with Pavement and Sleater-Kinney, 1999, 2000. Performer: (albums) The White Stripes, 1999, De Stijl, 2000, White Blood Cells, 2001, Maximum, 2002, Elephant, 2003, Get Behind Me Satan, 2005, Icky Thump, 2007 (Grammy award for Best Alternative Music Album, 2008, Grammy award for Best Duo Rock Performance with Vocals, 2008), (songs) Conquest, 2008 (Best Cinematography, MTV Video Music Awards, 2008); actor: (films) Coffee and Cigarettes, 2003, Cold Mountain, 2003. Office: Monotone Inc 150 S Rodeo Dr # 200 Beverly Hills CA 90212-2408

WHITE, MICHELLE JO, economics professor; b. Washington, 1945; d. Harry L. and Irene Rich; m. Roger Hall Gordon, July 25, 1982. AB, Harvard U., 1967; MSc in Econs., London Sch. Econs., 1968; PhD, Princeton U., 1973. Asst. prof. U. Pa., Phila., 1973-78; from assoc. prof. to prof. NYU, NYC, 1978-83; prof. econs. U. Mich., Ann Arbor, 1984—2001, dir. PhD program in econs., 1992—94, Ann Arbor, 1998—99; prof. econs. U. Calif., San Diego, 2000—. Vis. asst. prof. Yale U., New Haven, 1978; vis. prof. People's U., Beijing, 1986, U. Warsaw, 1990, U. Wis., Madison, 1991, U. Munich, Germany, 1992, 2002, Tilburg U., The Netherlands, 1993, 95, U. Chgo., 1993, Copenhagen Bus. Sch., 1995, Uppsala U., Sweden, 1997, Hebrew U., Israel, 1997, U. Calif. Law Sch. Berkeley, 1999, Harvard Law Sch., 2004; rsch. assoc. Nat. Bur. Econ. Rsch., 2002—; cons. Pension

Benefit Guaranty Corp., Washington, 1987, World Bank, 1999; chmn. adv. com. dept. econs. Princeton U., 1988-90. Editor: The Non-profit Sector in a Three Sector Economy, 1981, Financial Distress and Bankruptcy: Economic Issues, 1997; assoc. editor Jour. Econ. Perspectives, 2004—; contbr. numerous articles to profl. jours. Bd. dirs. Com. on Status of Women in Econs. Profession, 1984-86. Resources for Future fellow, 1972-73; grantee NSF, 1979, 82, 88, 91, 93, 96, 2002, Sloan Found., 1984, Fund for Rsch. in Dispute Resolution, 1989; Fulbright scholar, Poland, 1990. Mem. Am. Econ. Assn., Am. Law and Econ. Assn. (bd. dirs. 1991-92, 2001-04, chair nominating com. 2002, sec.-treas. 2006—07, pres. elect 2007—), Am. Real Estate and Urban Econs. Assn. (bd. dirs. 1992-95), Social Scis. Rsch. Coun. (bd. dirs. 1994-2000, treas. 1996-2000), Midwest Econs. Assn. (1st v.p. 1996-97). Office: U California-San Diego Dept Economics 9500 Gilman Dr La Jolla CA 92093-0508

WHITE, PATRICIA DENISE, law educator, dean; b. Syracuse, NY, July 8, 1949; d. Theodore C. and Kathleen (Cowles) Denise; m. Nicholas P. White, Feb. 20, 1971 (div. 1997); children: Olivia Lawrence, Alexander Cowles; m. James W. Nickel, Sept. 15, 2005. BA, U. Mich., 1971, MA, 1974, JD cum laude, 1974. Bar: D.C. 1975, Mich. 1988, Utah 1995. Assoc. Steptoe & Johnson, Washington, 1975-76; vis. asst. prof. Coll. of Law U. Toledo, 1976-77; assoc. Caplin & Drysdale, Washington, 1977-79; vis. assoc. prof. Law Ctr. Georgetown U., 1979—80, asst. prof., 1980—84, assoc. prof. Law Ctr., 1985-88; vis. prof. Law Sch. U. Mich., Ann Arbor, 1988-94; prof. U. Utah, Salt Lake City, 1994-98; counsel Parsons, Behle and Latimer, Salt Lake City, 1995—98; dean, prof. Sandra Day O'Connor Coll. Law Ariz. State U., 1999—2008; Jack Brown prof. Sandra Day O'Connor Coll. Law, 2008—, dean emeritus, 2008—; spl. counsel Steptoe & Johnson LLP, Wash., 2008—; vis. prof. Georgetown U. Law Ctr., 2008—. Counsel Bodman, Longley and Dahling, Detroit, Ann Arbor, 1990-95. Contbr. articles to profl. jours. Recipient Judge Learned Hand award for Disting. Pub. Svc., Am. Jewish Com., 2009. Fellow: Am. Coll. Tax Coun.; mem.: Mich. Bar Assn., Utah Bar Assn., DC Bar Assn., Law Sch. Admission Coun. (fin. and legal affairs com. 2001—03, chair audit com. 2003—04, chair test devel. and rsch. com. 2005—07), Am. Law Deans Assn. (bd. dirs. 2001—08), Gruter Inst. Law and Behavioral Rsch. (adv. bd. 2001—), Assn. Am. Law Schools. Office: Ariz State Sandra Day O'Connor Coll Law McAllister & Orange Sts PO Box 877906 Tempe AZ 85287-7906 Home Phone: 480-838-6550.

WHITE, RAYMOND LESLIE, geneticist; b. Orlando, Fla., Oct. 23, 1943; s. Lawrence and Marjorie White; m. Joan Palmer Distin, June 1, 1968; children: Juliette, Jeremy. BS in Microbiology, U. Oreg., 1965; PhD in Microbiology, MIT, 1971; postdoctoral studies, Stanford. Rsch. assoc., instr. MIT, Cambridge, 1971-72; postdoctoral fellow Sch. Medicine Stanford U., Calif., 1972-75; asst. prof. Dept. Microbiology U. Mass. Sch. Medicine, Worcester, 1975-78, assoc. prof. Dept. Microbiology, 1978-80; investigator Howard Hughes Med. Inst. U. Utah Med. Ctr., 1980-94; assoc. prof. Dept. Cellular, Viral and Molecular Biology U. Utah Sch. Medicine, 1980-84, co-chmn. Dept. Human Genetics, 1984-94, prof. Dept. Oncological Scis., 1985—; prof. Dept. of Human Genetics U. Utah Sch. of Medicine, 1985—; chmn. Dept. Oncological Scis. U. Utah Sch. Medicine, 1994—, dir. Huntsman Cancer Inst., 1994—2000; chief sci. officer DNA Scis., Inc., Fremont, Calif., 2000—02; dir. Ernest Gallo Clinic & Rsch. Ctr. U. Calif. San Francisco, Emeryville, Calif., 2002—, vice chair, prof. neurology, 2002—. Ad hoc mem. NIH Gen. Med. Sci. Inst. Coun., 1984, mem. NIH study sect., 1979-83. Consulting editor Jour. Clin. Investigation; subject area editor Genomics, 1987-90; contbr. articles to profl. jours. Woodrow Wilson fellow, 1965-66, NIH grad. fellow, 1966-71, Jane Coffins Childs Found. fellow, 1971-75; Nat. Cancer Inst. Cancer Ctr. Support grantee, 1995—; recipient Sword Hope award Am. Cancer Soc., 1995, Lewis S. Rosenstiel award Disting. Work Basic Med. Scis., Brandeis U., 1992, Rosenblatt award for excellence, 1993, Nat. Med. Rsch. award Nat. Health Coun., 1991, Friedrich von Recklinghausen award Nat. Neurofibromatosis Found., 1990, Charles S. Mott prize Gen. Motors Cancer Rsch. Found., 1990, Raymond Bourfine award, Paris, 2002. Mem. NAS, Am. Soc. Human Genetics (Allen Cancer Rsch. award 1989, assoc. editor Cancer Rsch.), Utah Acad. Scis., Inst. Medicine. Achievements include the development of a new technology for mapping and ultimately identifying human genes causing disease and the discovery of fundamental genes and genetic mechanisms important in the inherited and cellular pathways to cancer. Office: Ernest Gallo Clinic & Rsch Ctr Ste 200 5858 Horton St Emeryville CA 94608 Office Phone: 510-985-3102. Office Fax: 510-985-3101. E-mail: rayw@egcrc.net.

WHITE, RICHARD MANNING, electrical engineering educator; b. Denver, Apr. 25, 1930; s. Rolland Manning and Freeda Blanche (Behny) W.; m. Chissie Lee Chamberlain, Feb. 1, 1964 (div. 1975); children: Rolland Kenneth, William Brendan. AB, Harvard U., 1951, AM, 1952, PhD in Applied Physics, 1956. Rsch. assoc. Harvard U., Cambridge, Mass., 1956; mem. tech. staff GE Microwave Lab., Palo Alto, Calif., 1956-63; prof. elec. engring. U. Calif., Berkeley, 1963—2003, Chancellor's prof., 1996-99, prof., graduate sch., 2006—. Chmn. Grad. Group on Sci. and Math. Edn., U. Calif. at Berkeley, 1981-85; co-dir. Berkeley Sensor and Actuator Ctr., 1986—. Co-author: Solar Cells: From Basics to Advanced Systems, Microsensors, 1991, Electrical Engineering Uncovered, 1997, Acoustic Wave Sensors, 1997; editor ElectroTechnology Rev.; patentee in field. Guggenheim fellow, 1968. Fellow AAAS, IEEE (Cledo Brunetto award 1986, Achievement award 1988, Disting. lectr. 1989, Cady award 2000, Rayleigh award 2003); mem. Nat. Acad. Engring., Acoustical Soc. Am., Am. Phys. Soc., Phi Beta Kappa, Sigma Xi. Avocations: photography, hiking, skiing, running, music. Office: U Calif Sensor & Actuator Ctr EECS Dept Ctr Berkeley CA 94720-1774

WHITE, ROBERT C., air transportation executive; b. 1943; Student, Wake Forest U., 1961-65. With Procter & Gamble, Columbus, Ohio, 1971-73; asst. dir. Shreveport (La.) Airport Authority, 1973-75; airport mgr. Gainesville (Fla.) Regional Airport, 1975-78; dep. dir. aviation Jacksonville (Fla.) Port Authority, 1978-80; exec. dir. Peninsula Airport Commn., Newport News, Va., 1980-82; dir./cons. Lockheed Air Terminal, Burbank, Calif., 1982—; exec. dir. Reno Tahoe Internat. Airport, 1988—. With USN, 1966-71. Office: Reno Tahoe Internat Airport PO Box 12490 Reno NV 89510-2490

WHITE, ROBERT JOEL, lawyer; b. Chgo., Nov. 1, 1946; s. Melvin and Margaret (Hoffman) W.; m. Gail Janet Edenson, June 29, 1969 (div. Dec. 1982); m. Penelope K. Bloch, Dec. 22, 1985. BS in Accountancy, U. Ill., 1968; JD, U. Mich., 1972. Bar: Calif. 1972, N.Y. 1985, U.S. Dist. Ct. (ctrl., ea., so. dists.) Calif. 1972, U.S. Ct. Appeals (9th cir.) 1978, U.S. Ct. Appeals (5th cir.) 1983, U.S. Ct. Appeals (6th cir.) 1984, U.S. Supreme Ct. 1977. Staff auditor Haskin & Sells, Chgo., 1968-69; assoc. O'Melveny & Myers, LA, 1972-79, ptnr., 1980—2007, chair reorgn. and restructuring dept., 1986—2001; CEO O'Melvey Cons. LLC, 2001—03; bd. dirs. Image Doc, 2007—, Sytron Holdings Ltd., 2008—. Vis. lectr. U. Mich. Law Sch., Ann Arbor, 1986; lectr. Profl. Edn. Sys., Inc., Dallas, 1987, L.A., 1987, 89, Phoenix, 1990, dir. Syncora Holdings Ltd. and Image Doc USA, Practicing Law Inst., San Francisco and N.Y.C., 1989-93, 2001-, Southwestern Legal Found., Dallas, 1991, UCLA Bankruptcy Inst., 1993, UCLA, 1993; mem. L.A. Productivity Commn., 1993-96. Contbr. articles to profl. jours. Active Constl. Rights Found., 1980—; active Am. Cancer Soc., 1989—, mem. L.A. bd. dirs., 1995—, vice chair, partnership com., 2003-; chair chpt. 11 com. Nat. Bankruptcy Conf., 2004-. Fellow Am. Coll. Brankruptcy; mem. ABA (litig. sect., mem. comml. law and bankruptcy com. 1972—), L.A. County Bar Assn. (comml. law and bankruptcy sect., chmn. fed. cts. com. 1981-82, exec. com. 1982—), Assn. Bus. Trial Lawyers (bd. govs. 1983-85), Fin. Lawyers Conf. (bd. govs. 1986—, pres. 1990-91), Am. Bankruptcy Inst. Avocations: skiing, running, history. Office: O'Melveny & Myers 1999 Ave of Stars Los Angeles CA 90067-6035 Office Phone: 310-246-8485. Business E-Mail: rwhite@omm.com.

WHITE, ROBERT LEE, electrical engineer, educator; b. Plainfield, NJ, Feb. 14, 1927; s. Claude and Ruby Hemsworth Emerson (Levick) W.; m. Phyllis Lillian Arlt, June 14, 1952; children: Lauren A., Kimberly A., Christopher L., Matthew P. BA in Physics, Columbia U., 1949, MA, 1951, PhD, 1954. Assoc. head atomic physics dept. Hughes Rsch. Labs., Malibu, Calif., 1954-61; head magnetics dept. Gen. Tel. and Electronics Rsch. Lab., Palo Alto, Calif., 1961-63; prof. elec. engring., materials sci. and engring. Stanford U., Palo Alto, 1963, chmn. elec. engring. dept., 1981-86, William E. Ayer prof. elec. engring., 1985-88, prof. emeritus, 1988—; exec. dir. The Exploratorium, San Francisco, 1987-89; dir. Inst. Electronics in Medicine, San Francisco, 1973—87, Stanford Ctr. Rsch. on Info. Storage Materials, 1991—2003; initial ltd. ptnr. Mayfield Fund, Mayfield II and Alpha II Fund, Rainbow Co-Investment Ptnrs., Halo Ptnrs.; pres. MacArray, Inc., 2005—. Vis. prof. Tokyo U., 1975, Nat. U. Singapore, 2002; Sony sabbatical chair, 1994; cons. in field. Author: (with K.A. Wickersheim) Magnetism and Magnetic Materials, 1965, Basic Quantum Mechanics, 1967; contbr. numerous articles to profl. jours. With USN, 1945-46. Fellow Guggenheim Oxford U., 1969-70, Canton Hosp., Swiss Fed. Inst. Tech., Zurich, 1977-78, Christensen fellow Oxford U., 1986, IEEE Magnetics Soc. Disting. lectr., 1998. Fellow IEEE, Am. Phys. Soc.; mem. Sigma Xi, Phi Beta Kappa. Home: 450 El Escarpado Stanford CA 94305-8431 Office: Stanford U Dept Material Sci Engr Stanford CA 94305 Office Phone: 650-799-4650. Personal E-mail: rlwhite450@sbcglobal.net.

WHITE, ROBERT MILTON, lawyer; b. Tachikawa AFB, Japan, Oct. 10, 1948; came to U.S., 1948; s. Triggs Reeves and Josephine (Fowler) W. BA, U. N.Mex., 1970; JD, U. Houston, 1973. Bar: N.Mex. 1973, U.S. Dist. Ct. 1973, U.S. Ct. Appeals (10th cir.) 1996, U.S. Supreme Ct. 1996. Ptnr. Levy, White, Ferguson and Grady, Albuquerque, N.Mex., 1973-80, Lastrapes and White, Albuquerque, 1980-83; deputy dir. Dept. of Corrections City of Albuquerque, 1983-86; asst. city atty. City of Albuquerque, 1986-92; pvt. practice Albuquerque, 1992-93; city atty. City of Albuquerque. Bd. dirs. Quote-Unquote, Inc., 1984-89, New Art Connections, 1990—, Internat. Mcpl. Lawyers Assn., 1998—; mem. Hogares, Inc., 1983—, pres., 1990-92; mem. Med. Review Commn. State Bar of N.Mex., 1987. Mem. Albuquerque City Coun., 1979-83, pres. 1983, Nat. League of Cities, Wilmington, Del. (steering com. on transp. and communications), 1981-83, Arthritis Found. 1983-85. Mem. Internat. Mcpl. Lawyers Assn. (bd. dirs. 1998—), State Bar N.Mex. (prof. devel. com. 1994-96, task force on minorities in the bar 1997), N.Mex. Mcpl. Attys. (pres. 1994-95), Order of Barons, Phi Delta Phi. Democrat. Office: PO Box 1293 Albuquerque NM 87103-1293 Home: 1504 Princeton Dr SE Albuquerque NM 87106-3025

WHITE, SHAUN ROGER, Olympic athlete, professional snowboarder, professional skateboarder; b. San Diego, Sept. 3, 1986; s. Kathy and Roger White. Profl. snowboarder Burton Snowboarding team, 1999—; skateboarder Tony Hawk Gigantic Skatepark Tour, 2002; profl. Skateboarder, 2003—; designer The White Collection. Snowboarder US Olympic Team, Torino, Italy, 2006. Actor: (films) The White Album, 2004. Recipient ESPY award, Best Male Action Sports Athlete, ESPN, 2003, 2006, 2008, ESPY award, Best US Olympian, 2006; named Sports-Choice Action Sports, Teen Choice Awards, 2006. Achievements include being the youngest snowboarder to win the US Open Slopestyle Championship, 2004; being the first athlete to compete in both Winter and Summer X Games, 2003; winning the gold medal at Winter X Games, Slopestyle, 2003-2006, Halfpipe, 2003, 2006; winning the gold metal at Summer X Games, Vert, 2005; winning all 5 Grand Prix Superpipes, 2005-2006; winning a gold metal at Torino Olympic Games, Men's Halfpipe, 2006. Office: c/o USSA Box 100 1500 Kearns Blvd Park City UT 84060

WHITE, STANLEY ARCHIBALD, electrical engineer, researcher; b. Providence, Sept. 25, 1931; s. Clarence Archibald White and Lou Ella (Givens) Arford; m. Edda María Castaño-Benítez, June 6, 1956; children: Dianne, Stanley Jr., Paul, John. BSEE, Purdue U., 1957, MSEE, 1959, PhD in Elec. Engring. and Aero. and Engring. Scis., 1965. Registered profl. engr., Ind., Calif. Engr. Rockwell Internat., Anaheim, Calif., 1959-68, mgr., 1968-84, sr. scientist, 1984-90; pres. Signal Processing and Controls Engring. Corp., 1990—2000; pvt. practice San Clemente, Calif., 2000—. Lectr. in elec. engring. U. Calif., 1959-84, adj. prof., 1984-97; cons. and lectr. in field; bd. dirs. Asilomar Signals, Systems and Computers Conf. Corp., 1988-02. Contbr. chpts. to books; contbr. articles to encys. and profl. jours. With USAF, 1951-55. N.Am. Aviation Sci. Engring. fellow, 1963-65; recipient Disting. Lectr. award Nat. Electronics Conf., Chgo., 1973, Engr. of Yr. award Orange County (Calif.) Engring. Coun., 1984, Engr. of Yr. award Rockwell Internat., 1985, Leonardo da Vinci Medallion, 1986, Sci. Achievement award, 1987, Disting. Engring. Alumnus award Purdue U., 1988, Meritorious Inventor's award Rockwell Internat. Corp., 1989, Outstanding Elec. Engr. award Purdue U., 1992, Boeing N.Am. Aviation Top Inventor award, 1998. Fellow AAAS (life), AIAA, IEEE (life; Centennial medal, Millenium medal, chair of ICASSP and ISCAS, Signal Processing Soc. disting. lect. and founding chmn. L.A. coun. chpt., Circuits and Sys. Soc. Tech. Achievement award 1996, Golden Jubilee medal 1999), Inst. for Advancement Engring., N.Y. Acad. Scis. (life); mem. VFW (life), Air Force Assn. (life), Am. Legion (life), Sigma Xi (life; founding pres. Orange County chpt., pres. 1988-00, 05—), Eta Kappa Nu (Paul K. Hudson disting. fellow, internat. dir. emeritus, Vladimir Karapetoff award 2005), Tau Beta Pi. Achievements include 82 US and over 20 foreign patents in field. Avocation: choral music. Office Phone: 949-498-5519. Business E-Mail: stan.white@ieee.org.

WHITE, STEPHEN HALLEY, biophysicist, educator; b. Wewoka, Okla., May 14, 1940; s. James Halley and Gertrude June (Wyatt) W.; m. Buff Ertl, Aug. 20, 1961 (div. 1982); children: Saill, Shell, Storn, Sharr, Skye, Sunde; m. Jackie Marie Dooley, Apr. 14, 1984. BS in Physics, U. Colo., 1963; MS in Physics, U. Wash., 1965, PhD in Physiology and Biophysics, 1969. USPHS postdoctoral fellow biochemistry U. Va., Charlottesville, 1971-72; asst. prof. physiology and biophysics U. Calif., Irvine, 1972-75, assoc. prof. physiology and biophysics, 1975-78, prof. physiology and biophysics, 1978—, vice chmn. physiology and biophysics, 1974-75, chmn. physiology and biophysics, 1977-89. Guest biophysicist Brookhaven Nat. Lab., Upton, L.I., N.Y., 1977-99; mem. NIH BBM study sect., 2005—. Contbr. numerous articles to profl. jours. Served to capt. USAR, 1969-71. Recipient Research Career Devel. award USPHS, 1975-80, Kaiser-Permanente Tchg. award, 1975, 92; fellow Biophysical Soc., 2002; grantee NIH, 1971—, NSF, 1971—. Mem. NSF (adv. panel for molecular biology 1982-85, mem. nat. steering com. advanced neutron source 1992-95), Internat. Union Pure and Applied Biophysics (U.S. nat. com. 1997—2004, chmn. 2000-04), Fedn. Am. Soc. for Exptl. Biology (bd. dirs. 1998-2002), Biophys. Soc. (chmn. membrane biophysics subgroup 1977-78, acting sec., treas. 1979-80, coun. 1981-84, exec. bd. 1981-83, program chmn. 1985, ann. meeting, sec. 1987-95, pres. 1996-97, Disting. Svc. award 1999), Am. Physiol. Soc. (editl. bd. 1981-93, membership com. 1985-86, publ. com. 1987-91), Assn. Chmn. Depts. Physiology (rep. to coun. acad. socs. 1981-82, councilor 1982-83, pres. 1986-87), Soc. Gen. Physiologists (treas. 1985-88), The Protein Soc. (electronic pub. coord. 1993-2007, NIH BBM study section 2005—). Avocations: skiing, cooking, travel. Office: U Calif Dept Physiology & Biophysics Med Sci I-D346 Irvine CA 92697-4560

WHITE, TERRENCE HAROLD, academic administrator, sociologist; b. Ottawa, Ont., Can., Mar. 31, 1943; s. William Harold and Shirley Margaret (Ballantine) W.; m. Susan Elizabeth Hornaday; children: Christine Susan, Julie Pamela. PhD, U. Toronto, 1972. Head dept. sociology and anthropology U. Windsor, Ont., Canada, 1973-75; prof., chmn. dept. sociology U. Alta., Edmonton, Canada, 1975-80, dean faculty of arts, 1980-88; pres. T.H. White Orgn. Rsch. Svcs. Ltd., Edmonton, 1975—2000, Brock U., St. Catharines, Ont., 1988-96, U. Calgary, Alta., 1996—2001, pres. emeritus, prof. bus., 2001—06; dir. corp. affairs and communication Husky Energy, 2006—. Author: Power or Pawns: Boards of Directors, 1978, Human Resource Management, 1979; editor: Introduction to Work Science, 1981, QWL in Canada: Case Studies, 1983. Bd. dirs. Progressive Conservative Assn., Edmonton South, 1976-81, 1st v.p., 1981-85, pres., 1985-87; bd. dirs. Tri-Bach Festival Found., Edmonton, 1981-88, Alta. Ballet Co., 1985-88, Edmonton Conv. and Tourism Authority, Arch Enterprises, 1984-88, Niagara Symphony Soc., YMCA, St. Catharines, 1988-92; chair United Way Campaign St. Catharines, 1992, Fox Found., 1990-96, Can. Summer Games 2001 Bid Com.; bd. dirs. Edmonton Symphony Soc., v.p., 1986-88; bd. govs. U. Alta., 1984-88, Brock U., 1988-96, Ridley Coll., 1990—, Alta. Heritage Found. for Med. Rsch.; active Calgary R & D Authority, 1997; divsn. chair Calgary United Way Campaign, Calgary Econ. Devel. Authority, 1997-2000, McMahon Stadium Soc., Calgary Children's Initiative, Ctr. for Affordable Water and Sanitation; nat. bd. gov.'s Scouts Can., 2003- Recipient Can. 125 Commemorative medal Govt. of Can., Queen's Golden Jubilee medal. Mem. Calgary Petroleum Club, Ranchmen's Club, Rotary (pres. Edmonton South 1981-82), Delta Tau Kappa, Alpha Kappa Delta. Home: Box 68028 28 Crowfoot Terr NW Calgary AB Canada T3G 3N8 Office: U Calgary 2500 University Dr NW Calgary AB Canada T2N 1N4

WHITE, TIMOTHY PETER, academic administrator; b. Buenos Aires, July 9, 1949; came to US, 1957; s. Anthony Robert and Mary (Weston) White; m. Karen N. White; children: Randall Patrick, Timothy Anthony, Alexander John, Logan. Student, Diablo Valley Community Coll., 1966-67; BA magna cum laude, Fresno State U., 1970; MS, Calif. State U., Hayward, 1972; PhD, U. Calif., Berkeley, 1977. Asst. prof. phys. edn. U. Mich., Ann Arbor, 1978-82, assoc. prof., 1982-84, assoc. prof., chmn. dept. kinesiology, 1985-89; rsch. scientist Inst. Gerontology, 1986-91; prof., chmn. U. Mich., Ann Arbor, 1989-91; dept. chmn., prof. dept. human dynamics U. Calif., Berkeley, 1991—2000; provost, exec. v.p. Oreg. State U., 2000—04, interim pres., 2002—03; pres. U. Idaho, 2004—08; chancellor U. Calif., Riverside, 2008—. Editor: (with others) Frontiers of Exercise Biology, 1983; contbr. articles to profl. jours. and chpts. to books on exercise and muscle. Fellow Am. Coll. Sports Medicine (trustee, v.p. 1991—, New Investigator award 1981), Am. Acad. Phys. Edn.; mem. AAAS, AAHPERD, Gerontol. Soc. Am., Am. Physiol. Soc., Sigma Xi, Phi Kappa Phi. Avocations: woodworking, nordic skiing, sailing, swimming, running. Office: U Calif Riverside 4108 Hinderaker Hall 900 University Ave Riverside CA 92521 Office Phone: 951-827-5201. Office Fax: 951-827-3866. E-mail: chancellor@ucr.edu.

WHITE, TONY L., health and medical products executive; BA, We. Carolina U., 1969. Sales rep. Baxter Internat. Inc., 1970-74, dist. mgr., 1974-76, export mgr. Latin Am., 1976-82, v.p. AMPAC, pres. Travenol-Can., 1982-85, pres. Fenwal divsn., 1985-86, pres. scientific products, biomedical divsn., 1986, v.p. diagnostics, 1986-92, exec. vp, 1992-95; chmn., pres., CEO Applied Biosystems Inc. (formerly Applera Corp.), Foster City, Calif., 1995—. With USAR, 1968-74. Office: Applied Biosystems Inc 850 Lincoln Ctr Dr Foster City CA 94404 Office Phone: 650-638-5800, 800-327-3002. Office Fax: 650-638-5998.

WHITESELL, JOHN EDWIN, retired motion picture company executive; b. DuBois, Pa., Feb. 23, 1938; s. Guy Roosevelt and Grace Ethlyn (Brisbin) W.; m. Amy H. Jacobs, June 12, 1960; 1 child, Scott Howard; m. Martha Kathlyn Hall, Sept. 3, 1975; m. Phyllis Doyle, May 8, 1993. BA, Pa. State U., 1962. Asst. mgr. non-theatrical div. Columbia Pictures Corp., NYC, 1963-66; with Warner Bros., Inc., 1966—2003, nat. sales mgr. non-theatrical div. Burbank, Calif., 1968-75, v.p., 1975-76; v.p. internat. sales adminstrn. Warner Bros. Internat. TV Distbn., 1976-2001, cons., 2001—03, ret., 2003. Bd. dirs. Mastermedia Internat. Inc.; past bd. dirs. Found. for Entertainment Programming in Higher Edn.; mem. self-study com. Nat. Entertainment Conf., 1974-75. Served with USNR, 1956-58. Recipient Alumni Fellow award Pa. State U., 2001, Outstanding Alumnus award Pa. State U. DuBois Campus, 1995, Founders award Nat. Entertainment

Conf., 1975. Mem. Nat. Audio-Visual Assn. (motion picture coun. 1973-76, exec. com. film coun. 1969-76, ednl. materials producers coun. 1970-76), Acad. TV Arts and Scis. 1976-80, Nat. Assn. Media Educators (adv. com. 1973-76)

WHITESELL, PATRICK, agent; Previously with Intertalent; agent United Talent Agy.; with Creative Artists Agy., 1995—2000, co-head motion picture talent dept., 2000—01; ptnr. Endeavor Agy., Beverly Hills, Calif., 2001—. Mem. Calif. Film Commn., 2006—. Named one of 50 Most Powerful People in Hollywood, Premiere mag., 2004—06. Office: Endeavor Agy 9601 Wilshire Blvd Beverly Hills CA 90211 Office Phone: 310-248-2000. Office Fax: 310-248-2020.

WHITESIDE, CAROL GORDON, foundation executive; b. Chgo., Dec. 15, 1942; d. Paul George and Helen Louise G.; m. John Gregory Whiteside, Aug. 15, 1964; children: Brian Paul, Derek James. BA, U. Calif., Davis, 1964. Pers. mgr. Emporium Capwell Co., Santa Rosa, 1964-67; pers. asst. Levi Strauss & Co., San Francisco, 1967-69; project leader Interdatum, San Francisco, 1983-88; with City Coun. Modesto, 1983-87; mayor City of Modesto, 1987-91; asst. sec. for intergovtl. rels. The Resources Agy., State of Calif., Sacramento, 1991-93; dir. intergovtl. affairs Gov.'s Office, Sacramento, 1993-97; pres. Great Valley Ctr., Modesto, Calif., 1997—. Bd. dirs. Lincoln Inst. Land Policy. Trustee Modesto City Schs., 1979-83; nat. pres. Rep. Mayors and Local Ofcls., 1990; mem. Sierra Nev. Conservancy Bd., 2005—; chmn. bd. Sierra Health Found. Recipient Lifetime Achievement award League of Calif. Cities, 2002, Excellence in Pub. Svc. award, Fresno Bus. Coun., 2004, Olmstead medal Am. Soc. Landscape Archs., 2007; named Outstanding Woman of Yr. Women's Commn., Stanislaus County, Calif., 1988, Woman of Yr., 27th Assembly Dist., 1991; Toll fellow Coun. of State Govts., 1996, Champion of Am. Dream, Calif. State U., Stanislaus, 2002. Republican. Lutheran. Office: Great Valley Ctr 201 Needham St Modesto CA 95354-0903 Home Phone: 209-521-0485. E-mail: carol@greatvalley.org.

WHITE-THOMSON, IAN LEONARD, retired mining executive; b. Halstead, Eng., May 3, 1936; came to U.S., 1969; s. Walter Norman and Leonore (Turney) W-T.; m. Barbara Montgomery, Nov. 24, 1971. BA with 1st class honors, New Coll., Oxford U., 1960, MA, 1969. Mgmt. trainee Borax Consol. Ltd., London, 1960-61, asst. to sales mgr., 1961-64, asst. to sales dir., 1964; comml. dir. Hardman & Holden Ltd., Manchester, Eng., 1965-67, joint mng. dir., 1967-69; v.p. mktg. dept. U.S. Borax Inc., Los Angeles, 1969-73, exec. v.p. mktg., 1973-88, pres., 1988-98, also dir., chmn., 1996-99; group exec. Pa. Glass Sand Corp., Ottawa Silica Co., U.S. Silica Co., 1985-87; exec. dir. L.A. Opera, 2000—01. Bd. dirs. Canpotex Ltd., chmn. bd., 1974-76. Bd. dirs. Colburn Sch.; bd. dirs. Thornton Sch. U. So. Calif. With Brit. Army, 1954—56. Named Mfr. of Yr., Calif. Mfrs. Assn., 1997. Mem. Can. Potash Prodrs. Assn. (v.p. 1976-77, dir. 1972-77), Chem. Industry Coun. of Calif. (bd. dirs. 1982-85, chmn. 1984), Am. Mining Congress (bd. dirs. 1989), RTZ Borax and Minerals (bd. dirs. 1992, chief exec. 1995-99), Kerr-McGee Corp. (bd. dirs. 1999-2006), Calif. Club (bd. dirs. 2007), Valley Hunt Club. Home: 1897 Braemar Rd Pasadena CA 91103-3712 Personal E-mail: iwhitethom@aol.com.

WHITFORD, BRADLEY, actor; b. Madison, Wis., Oct. 10, 1959; m. Jane Kaczmarek, Aug. 15, 1992; children: Frances, George, Mary. BA, Wesleyan U., 1981. Actor: (plays) Curse of the Starving Class, Three Days of Rain, Measure for Measure, Coriolanus; (Broadway plays) A Few Good Men, 1990—91, Boeing-Boeing, 2008 (Drama Desk award for Outstanding Revival of a Play, 2008); (films) Dead as a Doorman, 1986, Adventures in Babysitting, 1987, Revenge of the Nerds II, 1987, Vital Signs, 1990, Presumed Innocent, 1990, Young Guns II, 1990, Awakenings, 1990, Scent of a Woman, 1992, The Silent Alarm, 1993, RoboCop 3, 1993, My Life, 1993, A Perfect World, 1993, Philadelphia, 1993, The Client, 1994, Cobb, 1994, Billy Madison, 1995, My Fellow Americans, 1996, The Spittin' Image, 1997, The People, 1997, Masterminds, 1997, Red Corner, 1997, Wildly Available, 1999, The Muse, 1999, Bicentennial Man, 1999, Kate & Leopold, 2001, The Sisterhood of the Traveling Pants, 2005, Little Manhattan, 2005; (TV films) C.A.T. Squad, 1986, The Betty Ford Story, 1987, Web of Deception, 1994, Nothing But the Truth, 1995, The Desperate Trail, 1995, In the Line of Duty: Blaze of Glory, 1997, Cloned, 1997, The Sky's on Fire, 1998, Behind the Mask, 1999, Fathers & Sons, 2005; (TV series) NYPD Blue, 1994, The West Wing, 1999—2006, Studio 60 on the Sunset Strip, 2006—07. Co-founder Clothes Off Our Back Found. Office: Endeavor Agy 10th Fl 9601 Wilshire Blvd Beverly Hills CA 90212

WHITFORD, JOSEPH PETER, lawyer; b. NYC, Apr. 30, 1950; BA, Union Coll., 1972; JD, Syracuse U., 1975; LLM in Taxation, George Washington U., 1978. Bar: N.Y. 1976, D.C. 1977, Wash. 1979. Staff atty. divsn. corp. fin. SEC, Washington, 1975-78; assoc. Foster Pepper & Shefelman, Seattle, 1978-83, mem., 1983—. Chmn. bd. dirs. MIT Forum on the Northwest, 1992-93. Office: Foster Pepper & Shefelman PLLC 1111 3rd Ave Ste 3400 Seattle WA 98101-3299

WHITING, ALLEN SUESS, political science educator, writer, consultant; b. Perth Amboy, NJ, Oct. 27, 1926; s. Leo Robert and Viola Allen (Suess) W.; m. Alice Marie Conroy, May 29, 1950; children: Deborah Jean, David Neal, Jeffrey Michael, Jennifer Hollister. BA, Cornell U., 1948; MA, Columbia U., 1950, cert. Russian Inst., 1950, PhD, 1952. Instr. polit. sci. Northwestern U., 1951-53; asst. prof. Mich. State U., East Lansing, 1955-57; social scientist The Rand Corp., Santa Monica, Calif., 1957-61; dir. Office Research and Analysis Far East U.S. Dept. State, Washington, 1962-66; dep. consul gen. Am. Consulate Gen., Hong Kong, 1966-68; prof. polit. sci. U. Mich., Ann Arbor, 1968-82; prof. U. Ariz., Tucson, 1982-93, Regents prof., 1993—, dir. Ctr. for East Asian Studies, 1982-93; cons. U.S. Dept. State, 1968-88; dir. Nat. Com. on U.S.-China Relations, NYC, 1977-94; assoc. The China Council, 1978-88; pres. So. Ariz. China Coun., Tucson, 1983-95. Fellow Woodrow Wilson Ctr., Washington, 1995-96. Author: Soviet Policies in China: 1917-1924, 1954, China Crosses the Yalu, 1968, Chinese Calculus of Deterrence, 1975, Siberian Development and East Asia, 1981, China Eyes Japan, 1989, others; contbr. articles to profl. jours.; spl. commentator McNeill-Lehrer Program; CBS and NBC Spls. on China. Served with U.S. Army, 1945. Social Sci. Rsch. Coun. fellow, 1950, 74-75; Ford Found. fellow, 1953-55; Rockefeller Found. fellow, 1978; Woodrow Wilson Ctr. fellow, 1995-96. Mem. Assn. Asian Studies. Office: U Ariz Dept Polit Sci Tucson AZ 85721-0001 Home: 125 E Canyon View Dr Tucson AZ 85704-5901

WHITLOW, DONNA MAE, daycare and primary school administrator; b. Buffalo, SD, May 23, 1933; d. Carl Axel and Esther Johanna (Wickman) Magnuson; married, June 13, 1953; children: Debra Diane Reasy, Cathleen Denise Corallo, Lisa Mae. Diploma, Eugene Bible Coll., 1956; BA in Religious Edn., Internat. Seminary, 1985, MA, 1986. Corp. sec. various orgns., 1953-56; asst. registrar, prof. child edn. Calif. Open Bible Inst., Pasadena, 1956-57; dir. religious edn. and music, sec. to gen. bd. Jamaica Open Bible Inst., 1958-59; dir. religious edn. and music, sec. to gen. bd. prof. on staff, bus. mgr. Trinidad Open Bible Inst., 1960-65; asst. to full-charge bookkeeper Jennings Strouss Law Firm, 1966-68; dir. religious edn. and music., mem. gen. bd., assoc. pastor Biltmore Bible Christian Ctr., Phoenix, Ariz., 1967—; founder, dir. Biltmore Bible Day Care & Kindergarten, Phoenix, 1977—. Founder bible schs. in South Africa, Argentina, Ctrl. Am., Europe, Caribbean, Singapore, and on every continent. Author: How To Start a Daycare in the Local Church, 1986. Republican. Avocations: water and snow skiing, flying, international travel. Home: 2144 E Lamar Rd Phoenix AZ 85016-1147 Office: Biltmore Bible Christian Ctr 3330 E Camelback Rd Phoenix AZ 85018-2310 Office Phone: 602-956-9266. Personal E-mail: donwhtl@aol.com.

WHITMAN, MEG (MARGARET CUSHING WHITMAN), former Internet company executive; b. LI, NY, Aug. 4, 1956; m. Griffith Rutherford Harsh IV; children: Griff, Will. BA in Economics, Princeton U., 1977; MBA, Harvard U., 1979. Brand asst. Procter & Gamble, 1979—81; v.p. Bain & Co., 1982—89; sr. v.p. mktg. & consumer products divsn. Walt Disney Co, Burbank, Calif., 1989—92; corp. v.p. strategic planning Stride Rite Corp., 1992—93, exec. v.p. Keds divsn., 1993—94, pres. Stride Rite Divsn., 1994—95; pres., CEO Florists' Transworld Delivery (FTD), 1995—97; gen. mgr. preschool divsn. Hasbro Inc., 1997—98; pres., CEO eBay, Inc., San Jose, Calif., 1998—2008; co-chair Republican Victory '08, 2008—. Bd. dirs. eBay, Inc., 1998—2009, Staples Inc., 1999—2008, The Goldman Sachs Group Inc., 2001—02, Procter & Gamble Co., 2003—08, The Gap Inc., 2003—06, DreamWorks Animation SKG, Inc., 2005—08. Bd. trustees Princeton U. Recipient Webby Lifetime Achievement award (eBay), 2007; named Number One on List of Best CEO's, Worth, 2002; named one of 25 Most Powerful Bus. Mgrs., Bus. Week, 2000—, Most Powerful Women in Am. Bus., Fortune mag., 25 Most Powerful People in Bus., 2004, 50 Most Powerful Women in Bus., 2006, 2007, World's 100 Most Influential People, Time Mag., 2004, 2005, 100 Most Powerful Women, Forbes mag., 2005—07, 50 Women to Watch, Wall St. Jour., 2005, 2006, 50 Most Important People on the Web, PC World, 2007. Fellow: Am. Acad. Arts & Scis. Republican. Avocation: fly fishing.*

WHITMORE, BRUCE G., lawyer; BA, Tufts U., 1966; JD, Harvard U., 1969. Bar: N.Y. 1970, Calif. 1973, Pa. 1979. Gen. atty. ARCO Transp. Co., 1985-86; assoc. gen. counsel corp. fin. ARCO, 1986-90; v.p., gen. counsel ARCO Chem. Co., 1990-94; sr. v.p., gen. counsel, corp. sec. Atlantic Richfield Co., LA, 1995-2000. Mem. ABA.

WHITMORE, JON SCOTT, academic administrator, play director; b. Seattle, Mar. 22, 1945; s. Walter James and Eunna (Thody) W.; m. Jennifer Gean Gross, Aug. 17, 1985; children: Ian Scott, Amy Lee. BA in Speech and Theatre, Wash. State U., 1967, MA in Speech and Theatre, 1968; PhD in Dramatic Arts, U. Calif., Santa Barbara, 1974. Instr. theatre Highline Coll., Seattle, 1968-71; grad. asst. U. Calif., Santa Barbara, 1971-74; asst. prof. theatre W.Va. U., Morgantown, 1974-78, assoc. prof., 1978-82, prof., 1979-85, chmn. dept., 1979-84, interim dean, 1984-85; prof., dean faculty arts and letters SUNY, Buffalo, 1985-90; dean Coll. Fine Arts, U. Tex., Austin, 1990-96; provost, prof. theater arts U. Iowa, Iowa City, 1996—2003; pres. Tex. Tech U., Lubbock, 2003—08, San José State U., 2008—. Mem. exec. com. Big XII Athletic Conf., 2006—07. Dir. plays including Suddenly Last Summer, The Miracle Worker, Equus, Romeo and Juliet, Long Days Journey Into Night, The Sea Gull, The Comedy of Errors, The Glass Menagerie, Blithe Spirit, The Tavern, Black Comedy, You're a Good Man Charlie Brown, Vanities, The Effect of Gamma Rays on Man-In-The-Moon Marigolds, Epiphany, Endgame, The Miser, J.B., The Mousetrap, Knapp's Last Tape, Miss Julie, Servant of Two Masters, Before We Were; actor various classical, modern and contemporary plays, and performance pieces; author: Directing Post-modern Theater, 1994, William Saroyan, 1994. Mem. Erie County (N.Y.) Cultural Resources Adv. Bd., 1986-89, long range planning com. Studio Arena Theatre, Buffalo, 1986-90, trustee, 1987-90; mem. coun. fellows Am. Coun. Edn., 1984—; pres. W.Va. Theater Conf., 1978-80, pres.-elect, 1977-78, founding mem., bd. dirs., 1975-81. Recipient ACE Fellow award Am. Council Edn., 1983-84; fellow U. Calif., Santa Barbara, 1973-74, Lilly Found., 1976-77; Maynard Lee Daggy scholar Wash. State U., 1967. Mem. Internat. Coun. Fine Arts Deans, Am. Coun. Arts, Assn. Theatre in Higher Edn. (v.p. adminstrn. 1991—, chmn. nat. conf. planning com. chief adminstrs. program, 1987), Assn. Comm. Adminstrn. (elected to exec. com. 1982-85, chmn. task force theatre adminstrn., 1982-84), Speech Comm. Assn., Coun. Colls. Arts and Scis., Assn. Coll., Univ. and Cmty. Arts Adminstrs., Nat. Assn. State Univs. and Land-Grant Colls. (chair elect commn. arts, 1990-92, chair 1992-93, chair coun. on acad. affairs 2001—). Office: San Jose State U Office of Pres / Tower Hall 207 One Washington Sq San Jose CA 95192-0002 Office Phone: 408-924-1177. E-mail: Jon.Whitmore@sjsu.edu.

WHITNEY, DAVID See MALICK, TERRENCE

WHITNEY, RICHARD K., health products executive; CFO Specialty Laboratories, Inc., 2000—04, bd. dirs., 2004—06, chmn. bd., 2005—06; founder, mng. mem. Whitney Capital, LLC, 2005—; venture ptnr. New Enterprise Assocs., 2006—; CFO DaVita Inc., El Segundo, Calif., 2008—. Office: DaVita Inc 601 Hawaii St El Segundo CA 90245 Office Phone: 310-536-2400. Office Fax: 310-792-8928.

WHITNEY, STAN, marriage and family therapist; b. Wellsboro, Pa., Jan. 15, 1935; m. Ida G. Shoop, Dec. 29, 1960 (div. Jan. 1984); children: Rebecca Whitney Jones, Mark Daniel; m. Gloria Leon LaFleur, Jan. 30, 1988. BA, Jones U., Greenville, SC, 1961, MA, 1962; PhD, ThD, San Antonio Theol. Sem., St. Paul, 1989. Lic. marriage and family therapist Ariz., 1990, Minn., 1989, diplomate Am. Bd. Sexology. Pastoral counselor, Ottawa, Ill., 1964—74; owner Rental Real Estate Co., Ottawa, Ill., 1974—84; pastoral counselor Las Vegas, 1987—92; founder, clin. dir. Hope Counseling Inc., Bullhead City, Ariz., 1992—2002; clinician Mohave Mental Health Clinic, Kingman, Ariz., 1999—2002; clin. dir. Hope Christian Counseling, San Marcos, Calif., 2002—. Exec. bd., cons. Blasingame Found., Dallas, 1987—2002. Mem.: Inst. for Marital and Sexual Therapy, Crisis Care Network, Calif. Assn. Marriage, Family Therapists, Am. Acad. Clin. Family Therapists, Am. Assn. Christian Counselors, Am. Assn. Marriage, Family Therapists. Avocations: computers, books, travel. Office: Christian Counseling Inc PO Box 1718 San Marcos CA 92079

WHITSELL, HELEN JO, lumber executive; b. Portland, Oreg., July 20, 1938; d. Joseph William and Helen (Cornwell) Copeland; m. William A. Whitsell, Sept. 2, 1960; 2 children. BA, U. So. Calif., 1960. With Copeland Lumber Yard Inc., Portland, 1960—, pres., chief exec. officer, 1973-84, chmn., chief exec. officer, 1984—. Office: Copeland Lumber Yards Inc PO Box 80769 Portland OR 97280-1769

WHITTEMORE, ALICE, biostatistician; b. NYC, July 5, 1936; BS, Marymount Manhattan Coll., 1958; MA, Hunter Coll., 1964; PhD in Mathematics, CUNY, 1967. From asst. prof. to assoc. prof. math. Hunter Coll., NYC, 1967-74; adj. assoc. prof. environ. med. N.Y.U., 1974-76, mem. faculty dept. statistics, 1976-87; prof. epidemiology dept. health rsch. and policy Stanford U., Palo Alto, Calif., 1987—. Recipient Sloan Found. rsch. grant, Soc. Ind. and Applied Math. Inst. Math and Soc., 1974-76, Rockefeller Found rsch. grant 1976-77. Mem. NAS Inst. Medicine, AAAS, Soc. Indsl. and Applied Math, Am. Math Soc., Math Assn. Am., Sigma Xi Office: Stanford U Sch Medicine Dept Health Rsch and Policy HBP Redwood Bldg Stanford CA 94305-5092

WHITTEMORE, PAUL BAXTER, psychologist; s. Harry Ballou and Margaret B. Whittemore; m. Jane Moore, Apr. 22, 1995. BA in Religion, Ea. Nazarene Coll., 1970; MDiv., Nazarene Theol. Sem., 1973; MA in Theology, Vanderbilt U., 1975, PhD in Theology, 1978; PhD in Clin. Psychology, U. Tenn., 1987. Cert. in clin. psychology Am. Bd. Profl. Psychology, lic. psychologist Calif. Asst. prof. philosophy Trevecca Nazarene Coll., Nashville, 1973—76; asst. prof. philosophy and religion Point Loma Coll., San Diego, 1976—80; asst. prof. philosophy Mid. Tenn. State U., Murfreesboro, 1980—83; clin. psychology intern LA County/U. So. Calif. Med. Ctr., LA, 1986—87; coord. behavior health ctr. Calif. Med. Ctr., LA, 1987—88; clin. asst. prof. family medicine U. So. Calif. Sch. Medicine, LA, 1988—; pvt. practice Newport Beach, Calif., 1991—. Mem. behavioral sci. faculty Glendale Adventist Family Practice Residency Program, Glendale, Calif., 1989—90; inpatient group therapist Ingleside Hosp., Rosemead, Calif., 1990—92; founder, pres. Date Coach, 1992—2000. Contbr. articles to profl. jours. Recipient Andrew W. Mellon Postdoctoral Faculty Devel. award, Vanderbilt U., 1981. Mem.: AAUP (chpt. v.p. 1982—83), APA, Orange County Psychol. Assn. (bd. dirs. 1996—2001), Calif. Psychol. Assn. (media divsn. sec.-treas. 1997—98), Am. Philos. Assn., Am. Acad. Religion. Achievements include discovery of link between phenylthiocarbamide tasting and depression. Office: 1001 Dove St Ste 145 Newport Beach CA 92660-2123

WHITTEN, CHARLES ALEXANDER, JR., physics professor; b. Harrisburg, Pa., Jan. 20, 1940; s. Charles Alexander and Helen (Shoop) W.; m. Joan Emann, Nov. 20, 1965; 1 son, Charles Alexander III. BS summa cum laude, Yale U., 1961; PhD in Physics, Princeton U., 1966. Rsch. assoc. A.W. Wright Nuclear Structure Lab., Yale U., 1966-68; asst. prof. physics UCLA, 1968-74, assoc. prof., 1974-80, prof., 1980—, vice chmn. physics dept., 1982-86. Vis. scientist Centre d'Etudes Nucléaires de Saclay-Moyenne Energie, France, 1980—81, 1986—87; Vis. prof. U. Sci. and Tech., Hefei, China, 2007. Contbr. articles to profl. jours. Mem. Am. Phys. Soc., Sigma Pi Sigma, Phi Beta Kappa. Home: 9844 Vicar St Los Angeles CA 90034-2719 Office: U Calif Dept Physics Los Angeles CA 90024 Office Phone: 310-825-1691. Business E-Mail: whitten@physics.ucla.edu.

WHITTEN, DAVID GEORGE, chemistry educator; b. Washington, Jan. 25, 1938; s. David Guy and Miriam Deland (Price) W.; m. Jo Wright, July 9, 1960; children: Jenifer Marie, Guy David. AB, Johns Hopkins U., 1959; MA, John Hopkins U., 1961, PhD, 1963. Asst. prof. chemistry U. N.C., Chapel Hill, 1966-70, assoc. prof., 1970-73, prof., 1973-80, M.A. Smith prof., 1980-83; C.E. Kenneth Mees prof. U. Rochester, N.Y., 1983-97, chair dept. chemistry N.Y., 1988-91, 95-97, dir. Ctr. for Photoinduced Charge Transfer N.Y., 1989-95; mem. tech. staff Los Alamos Nat. Lab., 1997-2000; co-founder, chief tech. officer QTL Biosystems, LLC, 2000—; prof. chemistry and biochemistry Ariz. State U., 2000—. Mem. adv. com. for chemistry NSF; cons. Eastman Kodak Co.; Rochester, N.Y. Editor-in-chief, Langmuir, 1998—. Alfred P. Sloan fellow, 1970; John van Geuns fellow, 1973; recipient special U.S. scientist award Alexander von Humboldt Found., 1975; Japan Soc. for Promotion of Sci. fellow, 1982 Mem. AAAS, Am. Chem. Soc. (award in colloid and surface chemistry 1992), Internat. Union of Pure and Applied Chemistry (commn. on photochemistry), Interam. Photochem. Soc. (award 1998). Democrat. Home: 5435 La Colonia Dr NW Albuquerque NM 87120 Office: QTL Biosys LLC 2778 Agua Fria St Bldg C Santa Fe NM 87507 E-mail: whitten@qltbio.com.

WHITTINGHAM, KYLE, college football coach; b. Provo, Utah, Nov. 21, 1959; m. Jamie Daniels; children: Tyler, Melissa, Alex, Kylie. B in Ednl. Psychology, Brigham Young U., Provo, Utah, 1984, M in Athletic Adminstrn., 1987. Linebacker, tng. camp. Denver Broncos, 1982; linebacker Denver Gold, New Orleans Breakers, US Football League, 1983—85; replacement squad LA Rams, 1987; grad. asst. Brigham Young U. Cougars, 1985—86; defensive coord. Coll. Ea. Utah Eagles, 1987; asst. coach Idaho State U. Bengals, 1988—91, defensive coord., 1991—93; defensive line coach U. Utah Utes, 1994, defensive coord., 1995—2004, head football coach, 2004—. Recipient Paul "Bear" Bryant award, Nat. Sportscasters & Sportswriters Assn., 2008; named Mountain West Conf. Co-Defensive Coord. of Yr., Las Vegas Rev. Jour., 2002, Mountain West Coach of Yr., Sporting News, 2008. Office: Univ Utah Athletics Dept 1825 E South Campus Dr Salt Lake City UT 84112-0900*

WHITWORTH, A. LIN, state legislator; b. Inkom, Idaho, Dec. 28, 1933; m. Carol Whitworth; 7 children. Farmer; railroad conductor; mem. Idaho Senate, Dist. 33, Boise, 1994—. Ranking Dem., health and welfare, resources and environment, trasp., and joint legis. coms., mem. oversight com. Bannock county chair, legis. rep., United Transp. Union. Mem. United Transp. Union (local 265), Elks. Democrat. Mem. Lds Ch. Office: State Capitol PO Box 83720 Boise ID 83720-3720

WHORTON, M. DONALD, physician, epidemiologist; b. Las Vegas, N.Mex., Jan. 25, 1943; s. R. H. and Rachel (Siegal) Whorton; m. Diana L. Obrinsky, Apr. 9, 1972; children: Matthew Richard, Laura Elizabeth, Julie Hannah. Student, U.S. Naval Acad., 1961—62; B of Biology, N.Mex. Highlands U., 1964; MD, U. N.Mex., 1968; MPH, Johns Hopkins U., 1973. Intern Boston City Hosp., 1968—69; resident in pathology U. N.Mex., Albuquerque, 1969—71; instr., resident in medicine Balt. City Hosp., 1972—74; instr. Johns Hopkins U., Balt.; assoc. dir. divsn. emergency medicine Balt. City Hosps., 1974—75; clin. asst. prof. divsn. ambulatory and cmty. medicine U. Calif. Sch. Medicine, San Francisco, 1975—77; lectr. U. Calif. Sch.

Pub. Health, San Francisco, 1975—79; med. dir. labor occup. health program Inst. Indsl. Rels., Ctr. for Labor Rsch. and Edn., 1975—79, assoc. clin. prof. occup. medicine, 1979—87; prin. Environ. Health Assocs., Inc., Oakland, 1978—88; v.p. ENSR Health Scis., 1988—94; pvt. practice Alameda, Calif., 1994—2001; with WorkCare, 2001—. Chmn. adv. com. for hazard evaluation svc. and info. system Indsl. Relations Dept., State of Calif., 1979—84; cons. in field; chmn. statewide adv. com. on occupl. and environ. health U. Calif. Ctrs., 1996—. Contbr. articles to profl. jours. Recipient Upjohn Achievement award, 1968; scholar, Robert Wood Johnson Found., 1972—74. Fellow: Am. Coll. Occupl. and Environ. Medicine, Am. Coll. Epidemiology; mem.: APHA, Inst. Medicine NAS, Calif. Med. Assn. (adv. panel on occupl. and environ. medicine), Soc. for Occupl. and Environ. Health, Alpha Omega Alpha. Office: WorkCare 1320 Harbor Bay Pkwy # 115 Alameda CA 94502-6556 Office Phone: 510-748-6900 ext. 201. Personal E-mail: whobrin@lmi.net. Business E-Mail: dwhorton@workcare.com.

WHYBROW, PETER CHARLES, psychiatrist, educator, director, author; b. Hertfordshire, Eng., June 13, 1939; U.S. citizenship, 1975; s. Charles Ernest and Doris Beatrice (Abbott) W.; children: Katherine, Helen Student, U. Coll., London, 1956—59; MB BS, U. Coll., 1962; diploma psychol. medicine, Conjoint Bd., London, 1968; MA (hon.), Dartmouth Coll., 1974, U. Pa., 1994. House officer endocrinology U. Coll. Hosp., 1962, sr. house physician psychiatry, 1963—64; house surgeon St. Helier Hosp., Surrey, England, 1963; house officer pediat. Prince of Wales Hosp., London, 1964; resident psychiatry U. N.C. Hosp., 1965—67, instr., rsch. fellow, 1967—68; mem. sci. staff neuropsychiat. rsch. unit Charshalton, Surrey, 1968—69; dir. residency tng. psychiatry Dartmouth Med. Sch., Hanover, NH, 1969—71, prof. psychiatry, 1970—84, chmn. dept., 1970—78, exec. dean, 1980—83; prof., chmn. dept. psychiatry U. Pa., Phila., 1984—96, Ruth Meltzer prof. psychiatry, 1992; chief psychiatrist Hosp. U. Pa., 1984—96; prof. psychiatry and biobehavioral scis., chmn. dept. psychiatry Sch. Medicine UCLA, 1996—, dir. Semel Inst. for Neurosci. and Human Behavior, 1996—, physician-in-chief Neuropsychiat. Hosp., 1996—, Judson Braun disting. prof. psychiatry, 1999—. Dir. psychiatry Dartmouth Hitchcock Affiliated Hosp., 1970-78; vis. scientist NIMH, 1978-79; cons. VA, 1970—, NIMH, 1972—; chmn. test com. Nat. Bd. Med. Examiners, 1977-84; rschr. psychoendrocrinology Author: Mood Disorders: Toward a New Psychobiology, 1984, The Hibernation Response, 1988, A Mood Apart, 1997, American Mania: When More Is Not Enough, 2005 (Gradiva Book award, Nat. Assn. Advancement Psychoanalysis, 2006); editor: Psychosomatic Medicine, 1977 (Ann. Book award NAMI 2005); mem. editl. bd. Cmty. Psychiatry, Psychiat. Times, Directions in Psychiatry, Neuropsychopharmacology, Depression; contbr. articles to profl. jours Recipient Anclote Manor award psychiat. rsch. U. N.C., 1967, Sr. Investigator award Nat. Alliance for Rsch. into Schizophrenia and Depression, 1989; scholar Josiah Macy Jr. Found., 1978-79; fellow Ctr. Advanced Studies in Behavioral Sci., Stanford, 1993-94; recipient Lifetime Investigator award NDMDA, 1996; decorated Knight of Merit, Sovereign Order of St. John of Jerusalem, 1993; Disting. Prof. U. Calif., 2004 Fellow AAAS, Am. Psychiat. Assn., Royal Coll. Psychiatrists (founder), Am. Coll. Psychiatrists, Ctr. Advanced Study of Behavioral Scis. (hon.), Soc. Psychosomatic Rsch. London (hon.); mem. Am. Assn. Chmn. Depts. Psychiatry (pres. 1977-78), Royal Soc. Medicine, Am. Psychopath Assn., Am. Coll. Neuropsychopharmacology, Soc. Biol. Psychiatry, N.Y. Acad. Scis., Soc. Neurosci., Sigma Xi, Alpha Omega Alpha Office: UCLA Semel Inst Neuroscience & Human Behavior 760 Westwood Plz Los Angeles CA 90095-8353 Office Phone: 310-206-1233. Fax: 310-825-3942. Business E-Mail: pwhybrow@mednet.ucla.edu.

WHYTE, RONALD M., judge; b. 1942; BA in Math., Wesleyan U., 1964; JD, U. So. Calif., 1967. Bar: Calif. 1967, U.S. Dist. Ct. (no. dist.) Calif. 1967, U.S. Dist. Ct. (cen. dist.) Calif. 1968, U.S. Ct. Appeals (9th cir.) 1986. Assoc. Hoge, Fenton Jones & Appel, Inc., San Jose, Calif., 1971-77, mem., 1977-89; judge Superior Ct. State of Calif., 1989-92, U.S. Dist. Ct. (no. dist.) Calif., San Jose, 1992—. Judge pro-tempore Superior Ct. Calif., 1977-89; lectr. Calif. Continuing Edn. of Bar, Rutter Group, Santa Clara Bar Assn., State Bar Calif.; legal counsel Santa CLara County Bar Assn., 1986-89; mem. county select com. Criminal Conflicts Program, 1988. Bd. trustees Santa Clara County Bar Assn., 1978-79, 84-85. Lt. Judge Advocate Gen.'s Corps, USNR, 1968-71. Recipient Judge of Yr. award Santa Clara County Trial Lawyers Assn., 1992, Disting. Svc. award Berkeley Ctr. Law and Tech., 2001; nmaed Fed. Judge of Yr., Santa Clara (Calif.) County Trial Lawyers Assn., 2003. Mem. Calif. Judges Assn., Assn. Bus. Trial Lawyers (bd. govs. 1991-93), Santa Clara Inn of Ct. (exec. com. 1993—), San Francisco Bay area Intellectual Property Inn of Ct. (exec. com. 1994—). Office: US Courthouse 280 S 1st St Rm 2112 San Jose CA 95113-3002

WIATT, JIM (JAMES ANTHONY WIATT), talent agency executive; b. LA, Oct. 18, 1946; s. Norman and Catherine (Sonners) W.; m. Elizabeth Wiatt; children: Isabel, Caroline BA in History & Philosophy, U. So. Calif., 1969. Campaign coord. Tunney for Senate, LA, 1969-71; adminstrv. asst. to Senator John V. Tunney US Senate, LA, 1972-75; agt. FCA, LA, 1976-78; lit. agt. Internat. Creative Mgmt. Inc., LA, 1978-81, motion picture agt., 1981-83, head, motion picture dept., 1983-85, pres., co-CEO, 1985—98; pres., CEO William Morris Agy., Beverly Hills, 1999—. Mem. bd. councilors USC Sch. Cinema-TV; mem. bd. govs. Music Ctr. L.A., Am. Film Inst.; mem. exec. bd. med. scis. UCLA; exec. coun. The Quills; bd. dirs. William Morris Agy. Inc., 2004—. Named one of The 50 Most Powerful People in Hollywood, Premiere mag., 2004—06. Office: The William Morris Agency One William Morris Pl Beverly Hills CA 90212 E-mail: jwiatt@wma.com.*

WICKES, GEORGE, English literature educator, writer; b. Antwerp, Belgium, Jan. 6, 1923; came to U.S., 1923; s. Francis Cogswell and Germaine (Attout) W.; m. Louise Westling, Nov. 8, 1975; children by previous marriage: Gregory, Geoffrey, Madeleine (dec.), Thomas, Jonathan. BA, U. Toronto, Ont., Can., 1944; MA, Columbia U., 1949; PhD, U. Calif., Berkeley, 1954. Asst. sec. Belgian Am. Ednl. Found., NYC, 1947-49; exec. dir. U.S. Ednl. Found. in Belgium, 1952-54; instr. Duke U., Durham, N.C., 1954-57; from asst. prof. to prof. Harvey Mudd Coll. and Claremont Grad. Sch., Calif., 1957-70; prof. English and comparative lit. U. Oreg., Eugene, 1970—, dir. comparative lit., 1974-77, head English dept., 1976-83. Lectr. USIS, Europe, 1969, Africa, 1978, 79; vis. prof. U. Rouen, France, 1970, U. Tübingen, Germany, 1981, U. Heidelberg, Germany, 1996. Editor: Lawrence Durrell and Henry Miller Correspondence, 1963, Henry Miller, Letters to Emil, 1989, Henry Miller and James Laughlin: Selected Letters, 1995; Author: Henry Miller, 1966, Americans in Paris, 1969, The Amazon of Letters, 1976, Memories, 2006: translator: The Memoirs of Frederic Mistral, 1986. With US Army, 1943—46. Fulbright lectr. France, 1962-63, 66, 78; sr. fellow Ctr. for Twentieth Century Studies, U. Wis.-Milw., Milwaukee, 1971, Creative Writing fellow Nat. Endowment Arts, 1973, Camargo fellow, 1991. Mem.: PEN. Office: U Oreg English Dept Eugene OR 97403 Office Phone: 541-346-3938. Business E-Mail: wickes@uoregon.edu.

WICKHAM, DIANNE, nursing administrator; b. Dillon, Mont., Feb. 26, 1952; d. William Byron Wickham and Margaret Dewalt (Lovell) Starkweather. ADN, No. Mont. Coll., 1974; BSN, Mont. State U., 1978, MSN, 1980. RN, Mont. Clin. dir. St. Patrick Hosp., Missoula, Mont., 1980-81; asst. prof. Lewis Clark State Coll., Lewiston, Idaho, 1981-83, Mont. State U., Bozeman, Mont., 1983-86; home health nurse West Mont. Home Health, Helena, 1986-87, dir. clin. svcs., 1987-90; critical care nurse St. James Hosp., Butte, Mont., 1986-87; exec. dir. Mont. State Bd. of Nursing, Helena, 1990—. Mem. long term care com. Gov. Task Force on Aging, Helene, Mont., 1993-95, mem. task force to devel. investigator tng. Nat. Com. of State Bds. Nursing, Chgo., 1993—, mem. adj. faculty Mont. State U., Bozeman, 1993—, cons. in field, 1994—. Judge Soroptomists scholarship award, 1993, JC Penneys Golden Rule award, Helena, 1995. Recipient State award for excellence Am. Acad. Nurses Practitioners, 1994.

WICKIZER, MARY ALICE See BURGESS, MARY

WICKLAND, J. AL, JR., petroleum products and real estate executive; CEO Wickland, to 1995, chmn. emeritus, 1995—. Office: Wickland Corp 3600 American River Dr Ste 145 Sacramento CA 95864-5997 also: PO Box 13648 Sacramento CA 95853-4648

WICKRAMASINGHE, HEMANTHA KUMAR, electrical engineer, physicist; b. Colombo, Sri Lanka, May 31, 1949; naturalized U.S. citizen, 1996; s. Percival Herbert and Therese Elizabeth (Soysa) W.; m. Sophie Marie de La Porte, Nov. 17, 1973; children: Lucille Samantha, Anita Elizabeth. BSc in Electronic Engring., U. London, 1970, PhD in Electronic and Elec. Engring., 1974. Assoc. rsch. asst. dept. electronic and elec. engring. U. Coll. London, 1974-75, lectr. dept. electronic and elec. engring., 1978-83; rsch. assoc. E.L. Ginzton Lab. Stanford (Calif.) U., 1975-78; from mgr. phys. measurements T.J. Watson Rsch. Ctr. to fellow IBM, Yorktown Heights, NY, 1984—2000, fellow T.J. Watson Rsch. Ctr., 2000—, sr. mgr. nanoscale and quantum studies Almaden Rsch. Ctr. San Jose, Calif., 2002—03, sr. mgr. nanoscale sci. and tech., 2003—05, chief tech. officer sci. and tech., 2005—07; Henry Samueli endowed chair, dept. elec. engring. & comuter sci. & dept. biomed. engring. U. Calif., Irvine, 2007—. Cons. Hirst Rsch. Ctr. GE Co., London, 1980-83, U.K. Atomic Energy Authority, Harwell, Eng., 1980-82; adj. prof. Poly. Inst. N.Y., Bklyn., 1985-87; mem. editl. bds. Nanotech., 1991-96, Advances in Nanoscale Physics, electonics and Engring., 1991—, Rev. of Sci. Instruments, 1996—; prof. Editor: Scanned Probe Microscopy, 1992; co-editor: Determining Nanoscale Properties of Materials by Microscopy and Spectroscopy, 1994; contbr. over 150 articles to profl. jours.; holder numerous patents in field. Recipient V.K. Zworykin premium, Inst. Elec. Engrs., 1983, Disting. Corp. Inventor award, Nat. Inventors Hall of Fame, 1998, Morris E. Leeds award, IEEE, 1992, Joseph F. Keithley award, Am. Phys. Soc., 2000; Emeritus fellow, IBM, 2007—. Fellow: IBM, Royal Microscopical Soc., Inst. of Physics, IEEE, Am. Phys. Soc. (centennial spkr. 1999); mem.: Nat. Acad. Engring. Achievements include first introduction of vibrating mode atomic force microscopes, atomic force microscopes into manufacturing lines, first deployment of a magnetic force microscope capable of imaging nanometer scale magnetic properties, work in areas of optics, acoustics, photoacoustics, metrology and scanning probe microscopy. Office: Univ Calif Henry Samueli Sch Engring Dept Elec Engring and Computer Sci 616F Engring Tower Irvine CA 92697 Home Phone: 949-823-9276; Office Phone: 949-824-0378. Personal E-mail: wickla@sbcglobal.net. Business E-Mail: hkwick@uci.edu.

WICKWIRE, PATRICIA JOANNE NELLOR, psychologist, educator; d. William McKinley and Clara Rose (Pautsch) Nellor; m. Robert James Wickwire, Sept. 7, 1957; 1 child, William James. BA cum laude, U. No. Iowa, Cedar Falls, 1951; MA, U. Iowa, Iowa City, 1959; PhD, U. Tex., Austin, 1971; postgrad., U. So. Calif., LA, UCLA, Calif. State U., Long Beach. Lic. ednl. psychologist, marriage and family therapist, Calif.; nat. cert. counselor. Tchr. Ricketts Ind. Schs., Iowa, 1946-48; tchr., counselor Waverly-Shell Rock Ind. Schs., Iowa, 1951-55; reading cons., head dormitory counselor U. Iowa, Iowa City, 1955-57; tchr., sch. psychologist, adminstr. S. Bay Union H.S. Dist., Redondo Beach, Calif., 1962-82, dir. student svcs. and spl. edn. Cons. mgmt. and edn.; pres. Nellor Wickwire Group, 1981—; mem. exec. bd. Calif. Interagy. Mental Health Coun., 1968-72, Beach Cities Symphony Assn., 1970-82; chmn. Friends of Dominguez Hills, Calif., 1981-85. Contbr. articles in field to profl. jours. Pres. Calif. Women's Caucus, 1993-95, 2003-06. Mem. APA, AAUW (exec. bd., chpt. pres. 1962-72), Nat. Career Devel. Assn. (media chair 1992-98), Am. Assn. Career Edn. (pres. 1991—), LA County Dirs. Pupil Svcs. (chmn. 1974-79), LA County Pers. and Guidance Assn. (pres. 1977-78), Assn. Calif. Sch. Adminstrs. (dir. 1977-81), LA County SW Bd. Dist. Adminstrs. for Spl. Edn. (chmn. 1976-81), Calif. Assn. Sch. Psychologists (bd. dirs. 1981-83), Am. Assn. Sch. Adminstrs., Calif. Assn. for Measurement and Evaluation in Guidance (dir. 1981, pres. 1984-85, 98-2000, 04-05), ACA (chmn. Coun. Newsletter Editors 1989-91, mem. com. on women 1989-92, mem. com. on rsch. and knowledge 1994-97, chmn. 1995-97, mem. and chmn. bylaws com. 1998-2001, rep. to joint com. on testing practices 2001-07), Assn. Measurement and Eval. in Guidance (Western regional editor 1985-87, conv. chair 1986, editor 1987-90, exec. bd. dirs. 1987-91, chair position statements and standards 2001—), Calif. Assn. Counseling and Devel. (exec. bd. 1984—, pres. 1988-89, jour. editor 1990-2002), Nat. Assn. for Ind.-Edn. Coop. (bd. dirs. 2002-05), Internat. Career Assn. Network (chair 1985—), Internat. Women's Rev. Bd. (Women's Inner Cir. of Achievement), Calif. Edn. Found. (bd. dirs. 1987—), World Future Soc., Pi Lambda Theta, Alpha Phi Gamma, Psi Chi, Kappa Delta Pi, Sigma Alpha Iota, Phi Delta Kappa. Office: The Nellor Wickwire Group 2900 Amby Pl Hermosa Beach CA 90254-2216 Office Phone: 310-376-7378.

WIDAMAN, GREG, financial executive, accountant; b. St. Louis, 1955; s. Raymond Paul and Louise Agnes Widaman. BS in Bus. and Econs. cum laude, Trinity U., 1978. CPA, Tex. Sr. auditor Arthur Andersen LLP, Houston, 1978-82; sr. cons. Price Waterhouse, Houston, 1983-85; fin. advisor to segment pres. Teledyne, Inc., Century City, Calif., 1985-95; sr. mgr. ops. planning for consumer products ABC Broadcasting/TV The Walt Disney Co., Burbank, Calif., 1995-97; v.p. internal audit and spl. projects Hilton Hotels Corp., Beverly Hills, Calif., 1997—. Cons. Arthur Andersen LLP, Price Waterhouse, Teledyne, Walt Disney Co., Hilton Hotels Corp. Mem. AICPAs, Calif. Soc. CPAs, Christian Bus. Mens com. of U.S.A., World Affairs Coun., MIT/Calif. Tech. Enterprise Forum. Republican. Avocations: white water rafting, water and snow skiing, camping, business, chess. Office: Hilton Hotels Corp World Hdqrs 9336 Civic Center Dr Beverly Hills CA 90210-3604 Home Phone: 310-312-1495; Office Phone: 310-205-4578.

WIDDER, KENNETH JON, pathologist, educator; b. Chgo., Jan. 14, 1953; s. Alan A. and Edith Widder. BS, Carleton Coll., 1974; MD, Northwestern U., Evanston, Ill., 1979. Intern Duke U., Durham, N.C., 1979-80, resident in pathology, 1980-81; asst. clin. prof. pathology U. Calif., San Diego, 1981-84, assoc. clin. prof., 1984—; chmn., chief exec. officer Molecular Biosystems, Inc., San Diego, 1981—. Cons. Eli Lilly & Co., Indpls., 1978-83; mem. adv. com. Congl. Sci. and Tech. Com., Washington, 1986-88. Editor: Methods in Enzymology: Drug and Enzyme Targeting, 1985; patentee in field. Recipient Wiley J. Forbus award N.C. Sco. Pathology, 1981. Mem. AAAS, Am. Soc. Clin. Pathologists, Young Pres. Orgn., Sigma Xi. Office: Santarus Inc 10590 W Ocean Air Dr Ste 200 San Diego CA 92130

WIDYOLAR, SHEILA GAYLE, dermatologist; b. Vancouver, BC, Can., June 11, 1939; d. Walter Herbert and Olive Louise (O'Neal) Roberts; Kithi K. Widyolar, 1960 (div. 1979); 1 child, Keith. BS, Loma Linda U., 1962; MD, Howard U., 1972. Resident U. Calif., Irvine, 1973-76; dermatologist pvt. practice, Laguna Hills, Calif., 1976—. Clin. instr. U. Calif. Sch. Medicine, 1978—86. Chmn. bd. dirs. Opera Pacific, Costa Mesa, Calif., 1996-97. Fellow Am. Acad. Dermatology, Am. Soc. Dermatopathology; mem. AMA, Calif. Med. Assn., Dermatol. Soc. Orange County (pres. 1983), Alpha Omega Alpha. Avocations: music, travel. Office: Ste 403 23911 Calle de Mag Dalena Laguna Hills CA 92653 Office Phone: 949-452-3814.

WIEBE, LEONARD IRVING, pharmacist, educator; b. Swift Current, Sask., Can., Oct. 14, 1941; s. Cornelius C. and Margaret (Teichroeb) W.; m. Grace E. McIntyre, Sept. 5, 1964; children: Glenis, Kirsten, Megan BSP, U. Sask., 1963, MS, 1966; PhD, U. Sydney, Australia, 1970, DSc, 2002; D.Pharm.Sci (hon.), Meiji Pharm. U., Japan, 2002; D.Pharm.Sci, Health Sci. U. Hokkaido, 2003. Pharmacist Swift Current Union Hosp., 1963-64; sessional lectr. U. Sask., Can., 1965-66; asst. prof. U. Alta., Can., 1970-73, assoc. prof., 1973-78, prof., 1978—, dir. Slowpoke Reactor Facility, 1975—89, 2001—02, asst. dean rsch. Can., 1984-87, assoc. dean, 1990-99; prof. dept. exptl. oncology, 1999—; sessional lectr. U. Sydney, Australia, 1973; pres. Internat. Bionucleonics Cons. Lts., 1991—, BioCyDex Inc., 2003—. Rsch. assoc. Cross Cancer Inst., Edmonton, 1978—, Med. Rsch. Coun. Can.; vis. prof. Royal P.A. Hosp., Sydney, 1983-84, Searle vis. profl., 1986; MRC vis. prof., Toronto, 1987; PMAC vis. prof., 1988; McCalla prof. U. Alta, 1993-94; radiopharmacy cons. Australian Atomic Energy Commn., Sydney, 1983-84; mem. MRC standing com. on sci. and rsch., 1995-98; cons. IAEA, 2001, 03; hon. liason prof. Peoples U. Bangladesh. Editor: Liquid Scintillation: Science and Technology, 1976, Advances in Scintillation Counting, 1983; guest editor Jour. of Radioanalytical Chemistry, 1981; editor Internat. Jour. Applied Radiation Instrumentation Sect. A, 1988-90; regional editor Internat. Jour. Nuclear Biology and Medicine, 1992-95; mem. editl. bd. Jour. Pharmacy & Pharm. Sci., Jour. Applied Radiation Isotopes, 1995—. Recipient Janssen-Ortho Rsch. award, 1998, McNeil award, 1988; Commonwealth Univs. Exchange grantee, 1966; Alexander von Humboldt fellow, 1976-79, 82. Mem. Pharm. Bd. of New South Wales, Sask. Pharm. Assn., Soc. Nuclear Medicine, Assn. Faculties of Pharmacy of Can. (McNeil Rsch. award 1988), Can. Radiation Protection Assn., Can. Assn. Radiopharm. Scientists, Am. Pharm. Assn., Am. Assn. Pharm. Sci., Internat. Assn. Radiopharmacy (exec. sec. 1991-95), Can. Assn. Pharm. Scis. (founding), Univ. Club (Edmonton) (pres. 1985). Mem. Mennonite Ch.

WIEDEN, DAN G., advertising executive; b. 1945; m. Bonnie Wieden. BS journalism, Univ Oreg., 1967. With Georgia-Pacific Corp., Portland, Oreg., 1967-72; free-lance writer, 1972-78; with McCann-Erickson, Portland, 1978-80, William Cain, Portland, 1980-82; pres., exec. creative dir. Wieden & Kennedy Internat., Portland, 1982—. Named to Hall of Achievement, Sch. Journalism and Comm., Univ. Oreg., 2000. Office: Wieden & Kennedy Internat LLC 224 NW 13th Ave Portland OR 97209-2953

WIEDOW, CARL PAUL, electromechanical and geophysical instruments company executive; b. Pasadena, Calif., Dec. 3, 1907; s. Carl and Clara Minna (Matthes) W.; m. Mary Maletia Foulks, 1935 (div. Jan. 1946); m. Mary Louise Montesano, Nov. 27, 1947. A.B. in Math., Occidental Coll., 1933; M.S. in Physics, Calif. Inst. Tech., 1945, M.S. in Elec. Engring., 1946; Ph.D. in Elec. Engring., Oreg. State U., 1956. Registered profl. engr., Calif. Assoc. prof. electronics U.S. Naval Postgrad. Sch., Monterey, Calif., 1956-59; design specialist Gen. Dynamics Astronautics, San Diego, 1955-61, Ryan Aerospace div., San Diego, 1961-62; prof., head dept. physics Calif. Western U., San Diego, 1962-66; staff engr. Marine Advisors, La Jolla, Calif., 1966-67; chief of research Humphrey Inc., San Diego, 1967—; cons. engr. Elgin Nat. Watch Co., West Coast Micronics div., 1959-60, Gen. Dynamics Astronautics, San Diego, 1963-64, Havens Industries, San Diego, 1962-64, Solar, San Diego, 1964-66, Anka Industries, Chula Vista, Calif., 1979—. Counselor, judge Sci. Fair, San Diego, 1962—; acad. asst. NSF, 1966-68. Mem. AAUP, Optical Soc. San Diego, Soc. Wireless Pioneers, Quarter Century Wireless Assn., Old Time Communicators, Sigma Xi, Sigma Tau, Sigma Pi Sigma, Pi Mu Epsilon.

WIELECHOWSKI, BILL, state legislator; b. Dec. 7, 1967; m to Laura Wielechowski; children: Willow. BS in Bus. Mgmt./Fin., Seton Hall U., South Orange, NJ, 1985—89; JD, Seton Hall U., 1989—92. Alaska State Senator, District J, 2007-; co-chair, Armed Serv, member, Fish and Game, Transportation and Public Facil, Public Safety, Judiciary, Mil and Vet Affairs, Resources, Transportation Committees, 2007-, Alaska State Senator.attorney, IBEW 1547; designated chair, Alaska Workers' Compensation Bd, 99-2004; hearing officer, Alaska Department of Labor & Workforce Develop, 99-2004, acting chief of adjudications, 2003-04; exec board, Northeast Community Coun, 2001-, vice president & president, formerly; ch, Creekside (Muldoon) Town Center Committee, 2001-06; Mayoral Transition Team Member, 2003; Anchorage Sch District Budget Review Team Member, 2003; Anchorage Planning and Zoning Comn, 2004-06. Spirit of Muldoon, Hometown Hero, 2002; Alaska's Top 40 Under 40, Anchorage Chamber of Commerce & Alaska Jour of Commerce, 2005. Northeast Community Center Bd; Alaska Assoc of Admin Law Judges. Democrat. Avocations: fishing, skiing, Mountain Biking. Office: State Capitol Rm 115 Juneau AK 99801-1182 also: Dist J 716 West 4th Ave

Anchorage AK 99501 Office Phone: 907-465-2435, 907-269-0120. Office Fax: 907-465-2435, 907-269-0122. Business E-Mail: Senator_Bill_Wielechowski@legis.state.ak.us.

WIEMAN, CARL E., physics professor; b. Corvallis, Oreg., Mar. 26, 1951; s. N. Orr and Alison W.; m. Sarah Gilbert. BS, MIT, 1973; PhD, Stanford U., 1977; DS (hon.), U. Chgo., 1997. Asst. rsch. physicist dept. physics U. Mich., Ann Arbor, 1977—79, asst. prof. physics, 1979—84; assoc. prof. physics U. Colo., Boulder, 1984—87, prof., 1987—97, disting. rsch. prof., 1997—; fellow Joint Inst. for Lab. Astrophysics, Boulder, 1985—; prof. Physics and Astronomy Dept. U. BC, Vancouver, 2007—, dir. Carl Wieman Sci. Edn. Initiative (CWSEI), 2007—. Loeb lectr. Harvard U., 1990—91; Rosenthal Meml. lectr. Yale U., 1988, Columbia U., 1988; Cherwell-Simon Meml. lectr. Oxford U., 1999; vis. scholar Phi Beta Kappa, 1999—2000. Recipient Ernest Orlando Lawrence Meml. award, U.S. Dept. Energy, 1993, Einstein medal for laser sci., Soc. Optical and Quantum Electronics, 1995, Fritz London prize for low temperature physics, 1996, Newcomb Cleveland prize, AAAS, 1996, King Faisal Internat. prize for Sci., 1997, Sci. award, Bonfils Stanton Found., 1998, Lorentz medal, Netherlands Royal Acad. Sci., 1998, Benjamin Franklin Medal in Physics, 2000, The Nobel Prize in Physics, 2001, Nat. Sci. Found. Dir. Award for Dist. Teaching Scholars, 2001, U.S. Outstanding Doctoral and Rsch. Univ. Prof., Coun. for Advancement and Support of Edn. & Carnegie Found. for Advancement of Tchg., 2004, U.S. Prof. of Yr., Carnegie Found. for the Advancement of Teaching & the Coun. for Advancement & Support of Edn., 2004, Fellow: Guggenheim, 1990-1991, Hertz Found., 1973-1977, Am. Phys. Soc. (Davisson-Germer prize 1994, Schawlow prize in laser sci. 1998); mem.: NAS, 1995, Am. Physical Soc. (fellow, 1990), Am. Acad. Arts and Sci., 1998, Am. Assn. Physics Tchrs. (Richtmyer lectr. award 1996), Optical Soc. Am. (R.W. Wood prize 1999). Achievements include first to achieve Bose-Einstein condensation, 1995. Office: U BC 2146 Health Sciences Mall Vancouver BC Canada V6T 1Z3 Office Phone: 604-822-1732. E-mail: carl.wieman@phas.ubc.ca.

WIENER, JON, history professor; b. St. Paul, Minn., May 16, 1944; s. Daniel N. and Gladys (Aronsohn) Spratt. BA, Princeton U., 1966; PhD, Harvard U., 1971. Acting asst. prof. UCLA, 1973-74; asst. prof. history U. Calif.-Irvine, 1974-83, prof., 1984—. Plaintiff Freedom of Info. Lawsuit against FBI for John Lennon Files, 1983—. Author: Social Origins of the New South, 1979; Come Together: John Lennon in His Time, 1984, Professors, Politics, and Pop, 1991, Gimme Some Truth: The John Lennon FBI File, 2000, Historians in Trouble, 2005; contbg. editor The Nation mag.; contbr. articles to profl. jours. including The New Republic and New York Times Book Rev. Mem. Am. Hist. Assn., Nat. Book Critics Circle, Orgn. Am. Historians, Liberty Hill Found. (bd. dirs.). E-mail: wiener@uci.edu.

WIENER, VALERIE, state legislator, communications executive, writer; BJ, U. Mo., 1971, MA, 1972, U. Ill., Springfield, 1974; postgrad., McGeorge Sch. Law, 1976—79. Prodr. Checkpoint Sta. KOMU-TV, Columbia, Mo., 1972-73; v.p., owner Broadcast Assocs., Inc., Las Vegas, 1972-86; pub. affairs dir. First Ill. Cable TV, Springfield, 1973-74; editor Ill. State Register, Springfield, 1973-74; prodr. and talent Nev. Realities Sta. KLVX-TV, Las Vegas, 1974-75; account exec. Sta. KBMI (now KFMS), Las Vegas, 1975-79; nat. traffic dir. six radio stas., Las Vegas, Albuquerque and El Paso, Tex., 1979-80; exec. v.p., gen. mgr. Stas. KXKS and KKJY, Albuquerque, 1980-81; exec. adminstr. Stas. KSET AM/FM, KVEG, KFMS and KKJY, 1981-83; press sec., Rep. Harry Reid US House of Reps., Washington, 1983-87; adminstrv. asst. Friends for Harry Reid, Nev., 1986; press sec., Senator Harry Reid US Senate, Washington, 1987-88; owner Wiener Comm. Group, Las Vegas, 1988—; mem., Clark County No. 3 Nev. State Senate, Carson City, 1996—; owner PowerMark Pub., Las Vegas, 1998—. Mem. Nev. Drug Commn., 1997—2000, Nev. Commn. on Aging, 1997—; chair Commn. on Sch. Safety and Jevenile Violence, 1999—2000; mem. Nev. Technol. Crimes Task Force, 2001—03, Nev. Anti-Bullying Task Force, 2001—03, Gov.'s Task Force on Corrections, 2002; chair legis. com. on obesity Nev. State Senate, 2003—06, minority whip, 2001—. Author: Power Communications: Positioning Yourself for High Visibility (Fortune Book Club main selection 1994, Money Book Club selection 1995, Communicator award of distinction 2000), Gang Free: Friendship Choices for Today's Youth, 1995, 2d edit., 1996, The Nesting Syndrome: Grown Children Living at Home, 1997, Winning the War Against Youth Gangs, 1999, Power Positioning: Advancing Yourself as The Expert, 2000 (Nat. awards), PowerMaster HandBook Series, 2000— (eight nat. awards); contbg. writer The Pacesetter, ASAE's Comm. News. Sponsor Futures for Children, Las Vegas, Albuquerque, El Paso, 1979—83; mem. El Paso Exec. Women's Coun., 1981—83, Clark Coun. Sch. Dist. and Bus. Cmty. PAYBAC Spkrs. and Partnership Programs, 1989—, chair legis. com. on juvenile justice, 1999—2000; steering com. Youth Recovery Network, 2001—02; founding mem. Nev. team Action Healthy Kids; media chmn. Gov.'s Coun. Small Bus., 1989—93; vice chmn. Congl. Awards Coun., 1989—93; med. dir. Gov.'s Conf. on Women, 1990; vice chmn. Gov.'s Commn. on Postsecondary Edn., 1992—96; mem. VIP bd. Easter Seals, El Paso, 1982; bd. dirs. BBB So. Nev., 1994—, Pub. Edn. Found., 1997—. Recipient 177 Comm. awards, 1989—, Outstanding Achievement award, Nat. Fedn. Press Women, 1991, Disting. Leader award, Nat. Assn. Cmty. Leadership, 1993, Gold medals in swimming, Nev. Sr. Olympics, 2002—03, 2005—07, Gold medals in fitness and weightlifting, 1998—2003, 2005—07, Walking Silver medal, 2005, Outstanding Women Adv. for Edn. award, Va. Commonwealth U., 2000, Internat. Cmty. Svc. award, Internat. New Thought Alliance, 2001, Winner Nev. 100 Fitness Challenge, Nev. State Legis. Session, 2005, Special Svc. award, Nev. Athletic Trainers Assn., 2007; named Outstanding Vol., United Way, El Paso, 1983, SBA Nev. Small Bus. Media Adv. of Yr., 1992, Nev.'s Disting. Sr. Athlete, 2000, So. Nev. Health Care Policy Hero, 2003, Nev. Legislator of Yr., Soc. Pub. Health Educators, 2004; named one of 27 Healthy Sch. Heroes in U.S., 2002; named to Hall Fame, Leadership Las Vegas, 2006. Mem. Nat. Assn. Women Bus. Owners (media chmn., nat. rep. So. Nev. 1990-91, Nev. Adv. of Yr. award 1992), Nev. Press Women, Nat. Spkrs. Assn., Small Pubs. Assn. N.Am., Dem. Press Secs. Assn., El Paso Assn. Radio Stas., U.S. Senate Staff Club, Las Vegas C. of C. (Circle of Excellence award 1993), Soc. Profl. Journalists. Democrat. Avocations: reading, writing, fitness and weighlifting training and competition, public speaking, community involvement. Office: Nev Senate 401 S Carson St Rm 2132 Carson City NV 89701 Office Phone: 775-684-1422. Business E-Mail: vwiener@sen.state.nv.us.

WIENS, ARTHUR NICHOLAI, psychology professor; b. McPherson, Kans., Sept. 7, 1926; s. Jacob T. and Helen E. (Kroeker) W.; m. Ruth Helen Avery, June 11, 1949; children: Barbara, Bradley, Donald. BA, U. Kans., 1948, MA, 1952; PhD, U. Portland, 1956. Diplomate: Am. Bd. Examiners Profl. Psychology. Clin. psychologist Topeka State Hosp., 1949-53; sr. psychologist outpatient dept. Oreg. State Hosp., Salem, 1954-58, chief psychologist, 1958-61, dir. clin. psychology internship program, 1958-61; clin. instr. U. Oreg. Med. Sch., Portland, 1958-61, asst. prof., 1961-65, assoc. prof., 1965-66; prof. med. psychology, 1966—96; prof. emeritus med. psychology, 1997—. Field assessment officer Peace Corps, 1965; cons. psychologist Portland Ctr. for Hearing and Speech, 1964—67, Dammasch State Hosp., 1967—69, Raleigh Hills Hosp., 1968—84, Oreg. Vocat. Rehab. Divsn., 1973—2001, mem. state adv. com., 1976—93; cons. William Temple Rehab. House, Episcopal Laymen's Mission Soc., 1968—88; chmn. State Oreg. Bd. Social Protection, 1971—84, State of Oreg. Bd. Psychologist Examiners, 1963—66, 1974—77; v.p. bd. dirs. Raleigh Hills Rsch. Found., 1974—80. Contbr. articles to profl. jour. Fellow AAAS, APA (chmn. com. on vis. psychologist program 1972-76, chmn. accreditation com. 1978, mem. task force edn. and credentialing 1979-84); mem. Am. Assn. State Psychology Bd. (pres. 1978-79), Nat. Register Health Svc. Providers in Psychology (bd. dirs. 1985-92, chmn. 1989-92), Profl. Exam. Svc. (bd. dirs. 1982-88, 90-96, chmn. 1986-88), Sigma Xi. Home: 74 Condolea Way Lake Oswego OR 97035-1010 Office: Oreg Health Scis U Portland OR 97201

WIENS, BEVERLY JO, psychology professor; b. Oildale, Calif., Oct. 2, 1947; d. Ernest and Irene Josephine (Klassen) Bartel; m. Gary D. Wiens, Aug. 19, 1967; children: Nicole Marie Wiens Cook, Katie Lyn Wiens. BA, San Jose State U., 1969, MA, 1971, Santa Clara U., 1992; PhD, No. Calif. Grad. U., 2001. Lic. counselor, Calif. Tchr. West Valley Coll., Saratoga, Calif., 1971-76, San Jose (Calif.) City Coll., 1974-75, San Jose State U., 1978; marriage, family therapist Coalition of Counseling Centers, Los Gatos, Calif., 1982-86; assoc. prof. San Jose Bible Coll., 1982-87; prof., dept. chair, counseling psychology San Jose Christian Coll., 1988—2004; dept. chair counseling psychology William Jessup U., Rocklin, Calif., 2004—. Lectr. in field. Mem. Am. Assn. Christian Counselors, Am. Counseling Assn., Calif. Assn. Marital Family Therapists. Republican. Mem. Mennonite Brethren. Office: William Jessup U 333 Sunset Blvd Rocklin CA 95765 Office Phone: 916-577-2261. Business E-Mail: bwiens@jessup.edu.

WIENS, TOM J., state legislator; m Diana Wiens; children: Lauren, Travis, Sarah Faith & Hannah. Precinct committeeman, GOP, member campaign staffs Senator Pete Dominick, President Gerald Ford, & finance comt, Senator Wayne Allard & State Republican Party, formerly; Republican nominee, Colorado State Treasurer, 1978, United States Congressional Colorado 3d Congressional District, 1982; board director, Children's Hosp Res Found; director, Colorado Ski Mus & Hall of Fame, formerly; volunteer police chaplain, formerly; Colorado State Representative, District 45, 2002-04; member Agriculture, Livestock & Natural Res, & Bus Affairs & Labor Committees, Colorado House of Representative, formerly; Colorado State Senator, District 4, 2004-, member, Bus, Labor & Technology, Transportation and Joint Computer Management Committee, currently, Colorado State Senate, owner, operation, Wiens Ranch, Douglas Co, Colorado. Nat Western Stock Show & Rodeo Association; Nat Cutting Horse Association (board director). Republican. Mailing: State Capitol 200 E Colfax Rm 271 Denver CO 80203 Office Phone: 303-866-4869. E-mail: tom@tomwiens.com.

WIESEMAN, KATHERINE C., education educator, consultant; BS in Biology, Coll. William and Mary, Williamsburg, 1979; MA in Ednl. Founds., U. N.Mex., Albuquerque, 1992; PhD, U. Ga., Athens, 1998. Tchg. lic. secondary level sci., social studies, spanish N.Mex, Colo. Prof., tchr. edn. Western State Coll. Colo., Gunnison, 1998—; mid. sch. sci. tchr. Antwerp Internat. Sch., Belgium, Albuquerque Pub. Schs., N.Mex. Consulting, ednl. tech. integration in k-12 classrooms, Varied, 2005—. Contbr. chapters to books. Grantee Mentoring Emphasis for Rural Intern Teachers - U. Mentor, PT3, 2003—07, Collaborative Mentoring for Enhancement Preservice Tchr. Edn., US Dept. Edn., Eisenhower Program Improving Math. and Sci. Instrn. Colo., 2001—03, Bldg. And Reflecting about InterDisciplinary Studies II, 2000—01, Bldg. And Reflecting about InterDisciplinary Studies, 1999—2000. Mem.: NSTA, ASCD, ASTE, NCTM, ASTE (tech. com.), NARST. Office: Western State Coll Teacher Education Program Gunnison CO 81231 Business E-Mail: kwieseman@western.edu.

WIESLER, JAMES BALLARD, retired banker; b. San Diego, July 25, 1927; s. Harry J. and Della B. (Ballard) W.; m. Mary Jane Hall, Oct. 3, 1953; children: Tom, Ann, Larry. BS, U. Colo., 1949; postgrad., Rutgers U., 1962, Advanced Mgmt. Program, Harvard U., 1973. With Bank of Am., NT & SA, 1949-87; v.p., mgr. main office San Jose, Calif., 1964-69; regional v.p. Cen. Coast adminstrn., 1969-74; sr. v.p., head No. European Area office Frankfurt, Fed. Republic of Germany, 1974-78; exec. v.p., head Asia div. Tokyo, 1978-81; exec. v.p., head N.Am. div. Los Angeles, 1981-82; vice chmn., head retail banking San Francisco, 1982-87; ret., 1987. Bd. dirs. Visa USA, Visa Internat., Sci. Applications Internat. Corp.; bd. dirs., chmn. Bank Adminstrn. Inst., 1986-87. Pres. Santa Clara County United Fund, 1969, 70, San Jose C. of C., 1968; fin. chmn. Santa Clara County Reps., 1967-74; bd. dirs. San Diego Armed Svcs., YMCA, Sidney Kimmell Cancer Ctr.; trustee Borrego Cmty. Health Found., 2002-06; trustee, chmn. bd. dirs. Sharp Meml. Hosp.; hon. consul-gen. for Japan, 1990-95. With USN, 1945-46. Mem. San Diego Hosp. Assn. (bd. dirs., treas.), San Diego Zool. Soc., Greater San Diego C. of C. (pres., CEO 1998-99), Bohemian Club, DeAnza Country Club, San Diego Yacht Club. Presbyterian. Home: 605 San Fernando St San Diego CA 92106-3312 Office: Bank Am Nat Trust & Savs 450 B St San Diego CA 92101-8001

WIEST, WILLIAM MARVIN, education educator, psychologist; b. Loveland, Colo., May 8, 1933; s. William Walter and Katherine Elizabeth (Buxman) W.; m. Thelma Lee Bartel, Aug. 18, 1955; children: William Albert, Suzanne Kay, Cynthia May. BA in Psychology summa cum laude, Tabor Coll., 1955; MA, U. Kans., 1957; PhD, U. Calif., Berkeley, 1962. Rsch. asst. psychol. ecology U. Kans., 1955-57; rsch. asst. measurement cooperative behavior in dyads U. Calif., Berkeley, 1958-59; from asst. to assoc. prof. Reed Coll., Portland, Oreg., 1961-74, prof., 1974-95, prof. emeritus, 1995—. Adj. investigator Ctr. Health Rsch., Portland, 1985—; project coord. WHO, Geneva, 1976-84; fgn. travel leader Assiniboine Travel, Winnipeg, Man., Can., 1990-91, Willamette Internat. Travel, Portland, 1993-95; lectr. Fgn. Travel Club, Portland, 1990, 94; vis. scientist Oceanic Inst., Waimanalo, Hawaii, 1967-68; chmn. dept. psychology Reed Coll., Portland, 1973-75, 86; social sci. adv. com. Population Resource Ctr., N.Y.C., 1978—; vis. investigator Health Svcs. Rsch. Ctr., Portland, 1975-76, cons. 1976-80; com. protection human subjects Kaiser Permanente Med. Care Program, Portland, 1978-81; cons. WHO, 1980-81, U.S. Dept. Energy, 1980-83; mem. panel population study sect. HHS. Consulting editor Population and Environment, 1981—; jour. referee Health Psychology, Jour. Social Biology, Jour. Personality and Social Psychology, Memory and Cognition; contbr. articles to profl. jours. Sloan Found. Faculty Rsch. fellow, 1972-73, NSF fellow, 1975-76, USPSH fellow U. Calif., 1957-58, Woodrow Wilson Found. fellow U. Calif., 1960-61. Mem. AAAS, APHA, Am. Hist. Soc. Germans from Russia (conv. spkr. 1991, 97), Germans from Russia Heritage Soc., Am. Psychol. Assn., Population Assn. Am., Phi Beta Kappa, Sigma Xi. Home: 5009 SE 46th Ave Portland OR 97206-5048 Office: Reed Coll Dept Psych SE Woodstock Blvd Portland OR 97202

WIGGINS, PATRICIA A., state legislator; b. Pasadena, Calif., Apr. 19, 1940; m Guy Conner; children: Jim & Steve Silverman (step), three grandchildren. BA, U. Calif., LA, 1977. Aide, assembly woman Valerie Brown, formerly; city counc, Santa Rosa, formerly; California State Assemblywoman, District 7, formerly, member, Rules, Agriculture, Appropriations, Environ Safety & Toxic Materials & Govt Organization Committees, formerly, Select Committees on California Wine, Mental Health & Joint Committee on Rules, formerly, California State Assembly; California State Senator, District 2, 2006-. Democrat. Office: State Capitol Rm 4081 Sacramento CA 95814 also: 710 E St Ste 150 Eureka CA 95501 Mailing: 50 D St Ste 150 Santa Rosa CA 95404 Office Phone: 707-576-2771. Office Fax: 707-576-2773. Business E-Mail: Senator.Wiggins@senate.ca.gov.

WIGGINS, PATRICIA ANN, computer systems analyst, state legislator; b. Pasadena, Calif., Apr. 19, 1940; d. Ralph Curtis and Grace Lucille (Alpeter) W.; m. Yosef Pilch, Aug. 10, 1971 (div. July 1977); m. Guy Reed Conner, Mar. 13, 1983; stepchildren: Stephen Silverman, James Silverman. BA in English, UCLA, 1977. Bookkeeper Europa Motors Ltd., Studio City, Calif., 1959-62, Volvo Imports, North Hollywood, Calif., 1962-64, George Pope Assets, San Francisco, 1964-69; client rels. coord. Property Rsch. Corp., LA, 1969-72; computer systems analyst Sys. Devel. Corp., Santa Monica, Calif., 1977-83, Fireman's Fund Ins., San Rafael, Calif., 1984; computer systems analyst, ptnr. Peer Protocols, Ltd., Costa Mesa, Calif., 1984-89; campaign mgr. Sen. Mike Thompson, Napa, Calif., 1990; field rep. Assemblywoman Valerie Brown, Santa Rosa, Calif., 1992-94; coun. mem. City of Santa Rosa, Calif., 1994—; computer cons. CW Assoc., Santa Rosa, 1990—. Mem. Calif. State Assembly, 1998—. Recipient Vol. Recognition, County of Sonoma, 1996. Mem. NOW, Bus. & Profl. Women, Nat. Women's Polit. Caucus (v.p. 1996), Sonoma Land Trust (bd. mem. 1993-97). Democrat. Avocations: reading, walking. Home: 315 Carrillo St Santa Rosa CA 95401-5111

WIGGS, EUGENE OVERBEY, ophthalmologist, educator; b. Louisville, Apr. 27, 1928; s. Eugene Overbey and Marie Helen (Martin) W.; m. Kathleen; children: Susan, Christopher, Karen, Mark. AB, Johns Hopkins U., 1950; MD, Duke U., 1955. Intern Denver Gen. Hosp., 1955-56; resident in ophthalmology Wilmer Inst. Johns Hopkins Hosp., 1956-59; ophthalmic plastic fellow Byron Smith, MD, NYC, 1969; pvt. practice specializing in oculoplastic surgery Denver, 1961—. Clin. prof. emeritus U. Colo. Med. Ctr.; lectr. ophthalmic plastic surgery various med. ctrs. Contbr. articles to med. jours. With USNR, 1959-61. Mem. Denver Med. Soc., Colo. Med. Soc., Am. Soc. Ophthalmic Plastic and Reconstructive Surgery, Am. Acad. Ophthalmology (svc. award 1982), Colo. Ophthalmology Soc. Republican. Roman Catholic.

WIKSTROM, FRANCIS M., lawyer; b. Missoula, Mont., Aug. 20, 1949; BS, Weber State Univ., 1971; JD, Yale U., 1974. Bar: Utah 1974, US Dist. Ct. Utah 1974, US Ct. Appeals (10th cir.) 1979, US Ct. Appeals (fed. cir.) 2002, US Supreme Ct. 1980. Asst. U.S. atty. U.S. Dist. Ct. Utah, 1979-80, U.S. atty., 1981; mem. Parsons Behle & Latimer, Salt Lake City, 1982—. Mem. Utah State Bar Commn.; former chmn. Utah Judicial Conduct Commn.; chmn. adv. com. on rules civil procedure Utah Supreme Ct.; mem. 10th Cir. Adv. Com.; adj. prof. trial advocacy, U. Utah Coll. Law, 1986-89. Recipient Best Lawyers in Am., Outstanding Lawyer award, Fed. Bar Assn. of Utah, 2002. Fellow Am. Bar Found., Am. Coll. Trial Lawyers; mem. ABA, Salt Lake County Bar Assn. (pres. 1993-94), Am. Inns Ct. II (master bench), Internat. Assn. Def. Counsel. Office: Parsons Behle & Latimer 201 S Main St 1 Utah center Ste 1800 PO Box 45898 Salt Lake City UT 84111-2218 Office Phone: 801-532-1234. Office Fax: 801-536-6111. Business E-Mail: fwikstrom@parsonsbehle.com.

WILBUR, COLBURN SLOAN, foundation consultant, trustee, former executive; b. Palo Alto, Calif., Jan. 20, 1935; s. Blake Colburn and Mary (Sloan) W.; m. Maria Grace Verburg, Sept. 1, 1961; children: Marguerite Louise, Anne Noelle. BA in Polit. Sci., Stanford U., 1956, MBA, 1960. Asst. cashier United Calif. Bank, San Francisco, 1960-65; v.p. Standata, San Francisco, 1965-68; adminstrv. mgr. Tab Products, San Francisco, 1968-69; exec. dir. Sierra Club Found., San Francisco, 1969-76, David and Lucile Packard Found., Los Altos, Calif., 1976—99, CEO, trustee, 1999—; sr. fellow Council on Found., 1999—2000, interim pres., CEO, 2005. Bd. dirs. Colo. Coll., Colorado Springs. Bd. dirs. Philanthropic Ventures Found.; former bd. dirs., mem. adv bd. Global Fund Women, Palo Alto, Calif.; past bd. dirs. Big Bros. San Francisco, Calif. Confederation Arts, Peninsula Grantmakers, Women's Fund Santa Clara; former bd. dirs., pres. Big Bros. Peninsula, North Fork Assn., Peninsula Conservation Ctr.; past bd. dirs., chmn. No. Calif. Grantmakers; bd. dirs., mem. adv. bd. Sierra Club Found., Stanford Theater Found., Palo Alto, U. San Francisco/Inst. Nonprofit Orgn. Mgmt. With U.S. Army, 1957-58. Mem. Commonwealth Club (bd. advisors). Office: David & Lucile Packard Found 300 2nd St Los Altos CA 94022-3694 E-mail: C.Wilbur@packard.org.

WILCOX, DAVID CORNELL, ballet company director; b. LA, May 7, 1951; s. Robert Carlos and Eileen Germaine (Babcock) W.; m. Tami Hirabayashi, Nov. 8, 1989; 1 child, Nicole Marie. Soloist Heidelberg (Germany) Ballet, 1971-72, Nuremberg (Germany) Ballet, 1973-74, Berlin (Germany) Ballet, 1975-78; founder, dir. L.A. Classical Ballet (founded as Long Beach Ballet), Long Beach, Calif., 1981—. Dir. Ballet Arts Ctr., Long Beach, 1981—; asst. prof. Calif. State U., Long Beach, 1984-88; guest faculty Columbia (S.C.) City Ballet, 1991-92. Choreographer various ballets. Mem. Royal Acad. Dancing (assoc.), Dance USA. Avocations: flying, skiing, computer programming. Home: 2630 Faust Ave Long Beach CA 90815-1336 Office: LA Classical Ballet 1122 E Wardlow Rd Long Beach CA 90807-4726

WILCOX, RAND ROGER, psychology professor; b. Niagara Falls, NY, July 6, 1946; s. Howard Clinton and Phyllis Hope (Stevens) W.; m. Karen Lesley Thompson, Apr. 25, 1986; children: Quinn Alexander, Bryce Colin. BA, U. Calif., Santa Barbara, 1968, MA in Math.,

1976, PhD in Ednl. Psychology, 1976. Sr. rsch. assoc. UCLA, 1976-81; prof. psychology U. So. Calif., LA, 1981—. Author: New Statistical Procedures for Social Sciences, 1987, Statistics for Social Sciences, 1996, Robust Estimation and Hypothesis Testing, 1997, 2d edit., 2005, Fundamentals of Modern Statistical Methods, 2001, Applying Contemporary Statistical Techniques, 2003, Basic Statistics Understanding Conventional Methods and Modern Insights, 2009; assoc. editor Psychometrika, Computational Stats. and Data Analysis, Comms. in Stats.; mem. editl. bd. Brit. Jour. Math. and Statis. Psychology, Jour. Math. and Mgmt. Sci., Jour. Edn. in Psychol. Methods; contbr. articles to profl. jours. Recipient T.L. Saaty award Am. Jour. Math. & Mgmt. Scis., 1984. Fellow: Ctr. Excellence Rsch., Royal Statis. Soc., Am. Psychol. Soc.; mem.: Internat. Assn. Statis. Computing, Am. Ednl. Rsch. Assn., Inst. Math. Stats., Am. Statis. Assn., Psychometric Soc. Achievements include research on improved methods for comparing groups and measuring achievement; resistant measures of correlation and regression; substantial gains in power when testing hypotheses. Office: U So Calif Dept Psychology Los Angeles CA 90089-0001 Office Phone: 213-740-2258. Business E-Mail: rwilcox@usc.edu.

WILCOX, RONALD BRUCE, biochemistry educator, researcher; b. Seattle, Sept. 23, 1934; s. Howard Bruce and Edna Jane (McKeown) W.; m. Susan Lenore Folkenberg, May 15, 1937; children: Deanna Marie, Lisa Suzanne. BS, Pacific Union Coll., 1957; PhD, U. Utah, 1962. Research fellow Harvard Med. Sch., Boston, 1962-65; asst. prof. Loma Linda U., Calif., 1965-70, assoc. prof. Calif., 1970-73, prof. biochemistry and microbiology Calif., 1973—, chmn. dept. biochemistry Calif., 1973-83. Mem. gen. plan rev. com. City of Loma Linda, 1981-92; bd. dirs. East Valley United Way, 1990-97. Fellow Danforth Found., St. Louis, 1957; fellow Bank Am. Giannini Found. San Francisco, 1965 Mem. Am. Thyroid Assn., Endocrine Soc. Democrat. Seventh-day Adventist. Home: 25516 Lomas Verdes St Loma Linda CA 92354-2417 Office: Loma Linda U Dept Biochemistry Loma Linda CA 92350-0001 Office Phone: 909-558-1000 x 4527. E-mail: bwilcox@llu.edu.

WILCOX, RYAN D., state legislator; b. Ogden, Utah, Aug. 13; m. Kristen Wilcox; children: Ryder, REagan, Julia. BA in Commercial/ Polit. Sci., Weber State U. Bus. mgr.; mem. Dist. 7 Utah House of Reps., 2009—. Named an Eagle Scout, Boy Scouts of America. Republican. Mormon. Office: W030 State Capitol Complex Salt Lake City UT 84114 Mailing: 1240 Douglas St Ogden UT 84404 Home Phone: 801-334-7787; Office Phone: 801-538-1029. Office Fax: 801-538-1908. Business E-Mail: ryanwilcox@utah.gov.

WILCZYNSKI, JANUSZ S., manufacturing executive, retired physicist; b. Warsaw, May 12, 1929; came to US, 1962; m. Brahna Lauger. Diploma in Indsl. Mechanics, Mining Acad., Cracow, Poland, 1954; MSc in Physics, Jagellonian U., Cracow, Poland, 1957; PhD in Physics and Optics, Imperial Coll. U. London, 1961. Physicist Watson, Ltd., London, 1961-62; rsch. staff mem. T.J. Watson Rsch. Ctr., IBM, Yorktown Heights, NY, 1962-63, mgr. tech. optics, 1963-83, 2d level mgr., 1983-84, sr. mgr., 1984-86, dir., 1986-93; gen. ptnr. Wilc Instruments LLP, 1995. Contbr. over 60 articles to profl. jours. Recipient 13 Invention awards, 1966-98, 7 Outstanding Innovation awards IBM, 1968-91; IBM fellow, 1981. Fellow Optical Soc. Am. (Richardson medal 1988); mem. NAE. Avocation: astronomical optics. Home: PO Box 790 Sandia Park NM 87047-0790 Office Phone: 505-286-8285. Office Fax: 505-286-8272. Personal E-mail: wilczyn@swcp.com.

WILD, NELSON HOPKINS, lawyer; b. Milw., July 16, 1933; s. Henry Goetseels and Virginia Douglas (Weller) W.; m. Joan Ruth Miles, Apr. 12, 1969; children: Mark, Eric; m. Diana Morris, Sept. 7, 2002. AB, Princeton U., 1955; LL.B., U. Wis., 1961. Bar: Wis. 1962, Calif. 1967; cert. specialist in probate, estate planning and trust law State Bar of Calif. Research assoc. Wis. Legis. Council, Madison, 1955-56; assoc. Whyte, Hirschboeck, Minahan, Harding & Harland, Milw., 1961-67, Thelen, Marin, Johnson & Bridges, San Francisco, 1967-70; sole practice law San Francisco, 1970—. Mem. State Bar Calif. Client Trust Fund Commn., 1983, mem. exec. com. conf. dels., 1985-88. Contbr. articles to legal jours. Bd. dirs. Neighborhood Legal Assistance Found., San Francisco, 1974-85, chmn. bd., 1978-81. Served with USAF, 1956-58. Mem. ABA, Calif. Bar Assn., San Francisco Bar Assn., Am. Bar Found., Lawyers of San Francisco Club (gov. 1975, treas. 1981, v.p. 1982, pres.-elect 1983, pres. 1984), Calif. Tennis Club (bd. dirs. 1995-97, pres. 1997). Office: 332 Pine St Ste 710 San Francisco CA 94104-3230 Personal E-mail: nwildlaw@aol.com.

WILDE, THOMAS ANDREW, state legislator, construction executive, writer; b. Mpls., Feb. 11, 1956; m. Melinda Wilde. BA, U. Minn. Mem. Oreg. Legislature, Salem, 1996—, vice chair agr. and natural resources com., mem. pub. affairs com., vice chair rev. com., mem. water and land use com., mem. subcom. on natural resources. Democrat. Home: 9745 SE City View Dr Happy Valley OR 97086-6945 E-mail: wilde.sen@state.or.us.

WILDER, GENE (JERRY SILBERMAN), actor, film director, writer; b. Milw., June 11, 1935; s. William J. and Jeanne (Baer) Silberman; m. Mary Joan Schutz, Oct. 27, 1967 (div. 1974); 1 child, Katharine Anastasia; m. Gilda Radner, 1984 (dec.); m. Karen Boyer, Sept. 8, 1991. BA, U. Iowa, 1955; postgrad., Bristol Old Vic Theatre Sch., 1955-56. Appeared in Broadway play: The Complaisant Lover, 1962 (Clarence Derwent award); appeared in London production of Laughter on the 23rd Floor, 1996; actor: (films) Bonnie and Clyde, 1967, The Producers, 1967 (Acad. award nom. best supporting actor), Start the Revolution Without Me, 1968, Quackser Fortune Has a Cousin in the Bronx, 1969, Willy Wonka and the Chocolate Factory, 1970, Everything You Always Wanted to Know About Sex But Were Afraid to Ask, 1972, Rhinoceros, 1972, Blazing Saddles, 1973, The Little Prince, 1974, Silver Streak, 1976, The Frisco Kid, 1979, Stir Crazy, 1980, Hanky Panky, 1982, See No Evil, Hear No Evil, 1989, Funny About Love, 1990, Another You, 1991; (TV films) Murder in a Small Town, 1999, Alice in Wonderland, 1999, The Lady in Question, 1999; dir., writer, actor: (films) The Adventures of Sherlock Holmes' Smarter Brother, 1975, The World's Greatest Lover, 1977, Sunday Lovers, 1980, The Woman in Red, 1984, Haunted Honeymoon, 1986; actor, co-writer: (films): Young Frankenstein, 1974; actor: (TV appearances) The Defenders, 1962, The DuPont Show of the Week, 1962-63, The Scarecrow, 1972, The Trouble With People, 1973, Marlo Thomas Spl., 1973, Thursday's Games, 1973,The Frank Skinner Show, 1997, Will & Grace, 2002-03 (Emmy award best guest actor 2003); (TV series) Something Wilder, 1994-95; author: Kiss Me Like a Stranger: My Search for Love and Art, 2005, My French Whore, 2006, The Woman Who Wouldn't, 2008 Campaigned with Elaine May and Rene Taylor for Eugene McCarthy, Allard Lowenstein and Paul O'Dwyer, 1968. Served with U.S. Army, 1956-58. Actors Equity Assn., Am. Federation of Television & Radio Artists, DGA, WGA.

WILDS, DANIEL O., health products executive; BA, Calif. State U., LA; MBA, Northwestern U., Evanston, Ill. With Baxter Internat., 1968—92, pres. chemotherapy svc. divsn., pres., COO diagnostic joint venture with Genentech, gen. mgr. Mexico City ops., gen. mgr. Container Devel. Bus. Ctr., dir. strategy devel., v.p. corp. alliances; pres., CEO Medisense, Inc., Adeza Biomed. Corp., 1992—96, Shiloov Biotechnologies (USA) Inc., 1997—98; pres., CEO, dir. Northwest Biotherapeutics, Inc., Boethell, Wash., 1998—.

WILENSKY, HAROLD L., political science professor, sociologist, researcher; b. New Rochelle, NY, Mar. 3, 1923; s. Joseph and Mary Jane (Wainsten) W.; children: Stephen David, Michael Alan, Daniel Lewis. Student, Goddard Coll., 1940-42; AB, Antioch Coll., 1947; MA, U. Chgo., 1949, PhD, 1955. Asst. prof. sociology U. Chgo., 1951-53, asst. prof. indsl. relations, 1953-54; asst. prof. sociology U. Mich., Ann Arbor, 1954-57, assoc. prof., 1957-61, prof., 1961-62, U. Calif., Berkeley, 1963-82, prof. polit. sci., 1982—, research sociologist Inst. Indsl. Relations, 1963—, project dir. Inst. Internat. Studies, 1970-90; project dir. Ctr. for German and European Studies, Berkeley, 1994-96, Inst. Govtl. Studies, 1996—. Mem. rsch. career awards com. Nat. Inst. Mental Health, 1964—67; cons. in field. Author: Industrial Relations: A Guide to Reading and Research, 1954, Intellectuals in Labor Unions: Organizational Pressures on Professional Roles, 1956, Organizational Intelligence: Knowledge and Policy in Government and Industry, 1967, The Welfare State and Equality: Structural and Ideological Roots of Public Expenditures, 1975, The New Corporatism, Centralization, and the Welfare State, 1976, Rich Democracies: Political Economy, Public Policy, and Performance, 2002, (with C.N. Lebeaux) Industrial Society and Social Welfare, 1965, (with others) Comparative Social Policy, 1985, (with L. Turner) Democratic Corporatism and Policy Linkages, 1987; editor: (with C. Arensberg and others) Research in Industrial Human Relations, 1957, (with P.F. Lazarsfeld and W. H. Sewell) The Uses of Sociology, 1967; contbr. articles to profl. jours. Pilot USAAF, 1943—45. Recipient aux. award Social Sci. Rsch. Coun., 1962, Book award McKinsey Found., 1967; fellow Ctr. for Advanced Study in Behavioral Scis., 1956-57, 62-63, German Marshall Fund, 1978-79; Harry A. Millis rsch. awardee U. Chgo., 1950-51. Fellow AAAS; mem. AAUP, Internat. Sociol. Assn., Internat. Polit. Sci. Assn., Indsl. Relations Research Assn. (exec. com. 1965-68), Soc. for Study Social Problems (chmn. editorial com.), Am. Polit. Sci. Assn., Am. Sociol. Assn. (exec. council 1969-72, chmn. com. on info. tech. and privacy 1970-72), Council European Studies (steering com. 1980-83). Democrat. Jewish. Avocations: music, trumpet, skiing. Office: U Calif Dept Polit Sci 1950-210 Barrows Hall Berkeley CA 94720-1902 E-mail: hwilensk@socrates.berkeley.edu.

WILENTZ, AMY, literature educator; b. NYC; d. Robert Nathan Wilentz and Jacqueline Malino; m. Nicholas J. Goldberg; children: Raphael J. Goldberg, Gabriel T. Goldberg, Noah Malino Goldberg. BA, Harvard, Cambridge, Mass., 1976. Contbg. editor Nation Mag., NYC, 1989—; prof. lit. journalism U. Calif., Irvine, 2006—. Author: (non-fiction book) The Rainy Season: Haiti Since Duvalier (Whiting Writers award, 1990), I Feel Earthquakes More Often Than They Happen: Coming to California in the Age of Schwarzenegger, (novel) Martyrs' Crossing (Rosenthal award, 2001); translator: (non-fiction book) In the Parish of the Poor. Office: Univ Calif 410 HIB Irvine CA 92697 Personal E-mail: amywilentz@mac.com. Business E-Mail: awilentz@uci.edu.

WILES, DAVID MCKEEN, chemist; b. Springhill, NS, Can., Dec. 28, 1932; s. Roy McKeen and Olwen Gertrude (Jones) W.; m. Valerie Joan Rowlands, June 8, 1957; children: Gordon Stuart, Sandra Lorraine. BSc with honors, McMaster U., 1954, MSc, 1955; PhD in Chemistry, McGill U., 1957. Rsch. officer chemistry divsn. NRC Can., Ottawa, 1959-66, head textile chemistry sect. chemistry divsn., 1966-75, dir. chemistry divsn., 1975-90; pres. Plastichem Cons., Victoria, B.C., Canada, 1990—. Chmn. Can. High Polymer Forum, 1967—69; v.p. N.Am. Chem. Congress, Mexico City, 1975. Contbr. articles to profl. jours.; mem. editl. adv. bd. numerous profl. jours.; patentee in field. Can. Ramsay Meml. fellow, 1957-59. Fellow Chem. Inst. Can. (chmn. bd. dirs. 1972-74, pres. 1975-76, Dunlop Lectr. award 1981), Royal Soc. Chem. London, Royal Soc. Can.; mem. Am. Chem. Soc. (Polymer Chem. divsn.). Home and Office: 3965 Juan Fuca Terr Victoria BC Canada V8N 5W9 Home Phone: 250-731-0732; Office Phone: 250-721-0732. Personal E-mail: dmwiles@telus.net.

WILETS, LAWRENCE, physicist, educator; b. Oconomowoc, Wis., Jan. 4, 1927; s. Edward and Sophia (Finger) W.; m. Dulcy Elaine Margoles, Dec. 21, 1947; children: Ileen Sue, Edward E., James D.; m. Vivian C. Wolf, Feb. 8, 1976. BS, U. Wis., 1948; MA, Princeton U., 1950, PhD, 1952. Rsch. assoc. Project Matterhorn, Princeton, NJ, 1951-53, U. Calif. Radiation Lab., Livermore, 1953; NSF postdoctoral fellow Inst. Theoretical Physics, Copenhagen, 1953-55; staff mem. Los Alamos (N.Mex.) Sci. Lab., 1955-58; mem. Inst. Advanced Study, Princeton, 1957-58; mem. faculty U. Wash., Seattle, 1958—, prof. physics, 1962-95, prof. emeritus, 1995—. Cons. to pvt. and govt. labs.; vis. prof. Princeton U., 1969, Calif. Inst. Tech., 1971. Author: Theories of Nuclear Fission, 1964, Nontopological Solitons, 1989; contbr. over 180 articles to profl. jours. Del. Dem. Nat. Conv., 1968. NSF sr. fellow Weizmann Inst. Sci., Rehovot, Israel, 1961-62; Nordita prof. and Guggenheim fellow Lund (Sweden) U., Weizmann Inst., 1976—; Sir Thomas Lyle rsch. fellow U. Melbourne, Australia, 1989; recipient Alexander von Humboldt sr. U.S. scientist award, 1983. Fellow Am. Phys. Soc., AAAS; mem. Fedn. Am. Scientists, AAUP (pres. chpt. 1969-70, 73-75, pres. state conf. 1975-76), Explorers Club, Phi Beta Kappa (chpt. pres. 1996-97), Sigma Xi. Achievements include research on theory of nuclear structure and reactions, nuclear fission, atomic structure, atomic collisions, many body problems, subnuclear structure and elementary particles. Office: U Wash Dept Physics PO Box 351560 Seattle WA 98195-1560 Personal E-mail: wilets@comcast.net. Business E-Mail: wilets@u.washington.edu.

WILKE, LEROY, retired church administrator; m. Jane Wilke. Grad., Golden Valley Lutheran Coll.; MA, Minn. State U.; LittD (hon.), Concordia U., 1999. Chaplain's asst. US Army; adminstr., dir. Christian Edn., Mpls., 1969; prof. edn. Concordia Coll., St. Paul, 1976; exec. dir. dist. and congl. svcs. Luth. Ch.-Mo. Synod, St. Louis, 1985—2005. Sec. Karpenko Inst. for Nurturing and Developing Leadership Excellence, 2005—. Lutheran. Office: Kindle 2100 Wadsworth Blvd Lakewood CO 80214-5707 Office Phone: 303-433-3303. Office Fax: 303-433-2280. E-mail: leroy.wilke@lcms.org.

WILKEN, CLAUDIA, judge; b. Mpls., Aug. 17, 1949; BA with honors, Stanford U., 1971; JD, U. Calif., Berkeley, 1975. Bar: Calif. 1975, U.S. Dist. Ct. (no. dist.) Calif. 1975, U.S. Ct. Appeals (9th cir.) 1976, U.S. Supreme Ct. 1981. Asst. fed. pub. defender U.S. Dist. Ct. (no. dist.) Calif., San Francisco, 1975-78, U.S. magistrate judge, 1983-93, dist. judge, 1993—; ptnr. Wilken & Leverett, Berkeley, Calif., 1978-84. Adj. prof. U. Calif., Berkeley, 1978-84; prof. New Coll. Sch. Law, 1980-85; mem. jud. br. com. Jud. Conf. U.S.; past mem. edn. com. Fed. Jud. Ctr.; chair 9th cir. Magistrates Conf., 1987-88; mem. bd. Berkeley H.S. Sch. Site Com., 2004-. Mem. ABA (mem. jud. adminstrn. divsn.), Alameda County Bar Assn. (judge's membership), Nat. Assn. Women Judges, Order of Coif, Phi Beta Kappa. Office: US Dist Ct No Dist 1301 Clay St # 2 Oakland CA 94612-5217

WILKEN, GARY R., state legislator; b. Tacoma, Jan. 24, 1946; m to Susan; children: Matthew, Allison, Karen & Bob. Member, Fairbanks Public Utility Bd, 83-95, Air Force Civilian Advisor Bd, 94-; chairman, Alaska Coun on Econ Education, 84-96, Community Activity Center Task Force, 85-89 & MAPCO Alaska Citizens Advisor Bd, 86-96; co-chmn, Mil Affairs Committee, formerly; member, Alaska Crippled Children Bd, 89-95; member, Long Range Stategic Planning, Alaska Chamber Committee, currently; Alaska State Senator, District O, formerly, member, Finance, Health, Education & Social Serv, State Affairs & Legislature Budget & Audit Committees, currently, Alask State Senate; Alaska State Senator, District E, 2003-.Chairman, Methodist Church Pastor Parish Relations Committee, 94-95; small business owner, currently. News Miner Community Serv Award, 90; Rotarian of Year, 90; Hall of Fame, OSU Sports, 93; Bus Leader of Year, Univ Alaska, Fairbanks, 95. Fairbanks Youth Sports Bd; Fairbanks Youth Sports Found (president, currently); Rotary (president, 87); Chamber of Commerce (chairman, 91-92). Republican. Mailing: State Capitol Rm 518 Juneau AK 99801-1182 Office Phone: 907-465-3709. Fax: 907-465-4714.

WILKENING, LAUREL LYNN, academic administrator, aerospace scientist; b. Richland, Wash., Nov. 23, 1944; d. Marvin Hubert and Ruby Alma Wilkening; m. Godfrey Theodore Sill, May 18, 1974 BA, Reed Coll., Portland, Oreg., 1966; PhD, U. Calif., San Diego, 1970; DSc (hon.), U. Ariz., 1996. From asst. prof. to assoc. prof. U. Ariz., Tucson, 1973—80, dir. Lunar and Planetary Lab., head planetary scis., 1981—83, vice provost, prof. planetary scis., 1983—85, v.p. rsch., dean Grad. Coll., 1985—88; divsn. scientist NASA Hdqrs., Washington, 1980; prof. geol scis., adj. prof. astronomy, provost U. Washington, Seattle, 1988—93; prof. earth system sci., chancellor U. Calif., Irvine, 1993—98. Dir. Rsch. Corp., 1991-2003, Seagate Tech., Inc., 1993-2000, Empire Ranch Found., 1998-2003, 2005—2007; vice chmn. Nat. Commn. on Space, Washington, 1984-86, Adv. Com. on the Future of U.S. Space Program, 1990-91; chair Space Policy Adv. Bd., Nat. Space Coun., 1991-92; co-chmn. primitive bodies mission study team NASA/European Space Agy., 1984-85; chmn. com. rendezvous sci. working group NASA, 1983-85; mem. panel on internat. cooperation and competition in space Congl. Office Tech. Assessment, 1982-83; trustee NASULGC, 1994-97, UCAR, 1988-89, 97-98, Reed Coll., 1992-2002. Editor: Comets, 1982. Recipient trainee, NASA, 1967—70; grantee fellow, U. Calif Regents, 1966—67. Fellow Meteoritical Soc. (councilor 1976-80), Am. Assn. Advanced Sci.; mem. Am. Astron. Soc. (chmn. div. planetary scis. 1984-85), Am. Geophys. Union, AAAS, Planetary Soc. (dir. 1994-2000, v.p. 1997-2000), Phi Beta Kappa. Democrat. Avocations: gardening, camping, swimming.

WILKENS, LENNY (LEONARD RANDOLPH WILKENS JR.), sportscaster, former professional sports team executive, retired professional basketball player; b. Bklyn., Oct. 28, 1937; s. Leonard Randolph Sr. and Henrietta (Cross) W.; m. Marilyn J. Reed, July 28, 1962; children: Leesha Marie, Leonard Randolph III, Jamée McGregor. BS in Econs., Providence Coll., 1960, HHD (hon.), 1980. Profl. basketball player St. Louis Hawks, 1960—68, Seattle SuperSonics, 1968—69, Cleve. Cavaliers, 1972—74; player/coach Seattle SuperSonics, 1969—72, head coach, 1977—85, gen. mgr., 1985—86; head coach Cleve. Cavaliers, 1986—93; vice chmn. Seattle SuperSonics, 2006—07, pres. basketball ops., 2007; counselor Jewish Employment Vocat. Svcs., 1962—63; salesman packaging divsn. Monsanto Co., 1966; player/coach Portland Trail Blazers, 1974—76; head coach Atlanta Hawks, 1993—2000, Toronto Raptors, 2000—03, NY Knicks, 2004—05; color analyst Pac-10 men's basketball FSN, 2004—05, NBA analyst, 2005—06, Seattle SuperSonics color analyst, 2006—. Head coach 4 NBA All-Star Teams, World Champion Basketball Team, 1979, Olympic Basketball Team, 1996, asst. coach, 92. Author: The Lenny Wilkens Story, 1974. Bd. regents Gonzaga U., Spokane; bd. dirs. Seattle Ctr., Big Bros. Seattle, Bellevue Boys Club, Wash., Seattle Opportunities Industrialization Ctr., Seattle U.; co-chmn. UN Internat. Yr. of Child prog., 1979; organizer Lenny Wilkens Celebrity Golf Tournament for Spl. Olympics. 2nd lt. US Army, 1961—62. Named to NBA All-Star Game, 1963-65, 67-71, 73, NIT-NIKE Hall of Fame, 1988, Naismith Meml. Basketball Hall of Fame, 1989 (as a player), 1998 (as a coach); named NBA All-Star Game MVP, 1971, Man of Yr., Boys High Alumni chpt. LA, 1979, Sportsman of Yr., Seattle chpt. City of Hope, 1979, Congl. Black Caucus Coach of Yr., 1979, Continental Basketball Assn. Coach of Yr., 1979, Coach of Yr., Black Pubs. Assn., 1979, NBA Coach of Yr., 1994; named one of NBA's 50 Greatest Players, NBA's Top Ten Coaches, 1997; recipient Whitney Young Jr. award NY Urban League, 1979, Disting. Citizens award Boy Scouts Am., 1980. Achievements include holding record for most career NBA wins. Office: FSN Northwest 3626 156th Ave SE Bellevue WA 98006 Office Phone: 425-641-0104. Office Fax: 425-641-9811.

WILKERSON, GERALD EUGENE, bishop; b. Des Moines, Oct. 21, 1939; Attended, Queen of Angels Sem., San Fernando, Calif., St. John Sem., Camarillo, Calif. Ordained priest, 1965; assoc. pastor Our Lady of Guadalupe, La Habra, Calif., 1965—71, St. Michael, LA, 1971—78, Am. Martyrs, Manhattan Beach, Calif., 1978—82; adminstr. Our Lady of Grace Ch., Encino, Calif., 1982—85, pastor, 1985—97; aux. bishop San Fernando Pastoral Region Archdiocese of LA, 1997—; ordained bishop, 1998. Roman Catholic. Office: 15101 San Fernando Mission Blvd Mission Hills CA 91345-1109

WILKERSON, LUANN, dean, medical educator; BA magna cum laude, Baylor U., 1969; MA in English, U. Tex., 1972; EdD, U. Mass., 1977. Tchg. asst. dept. English U. Tex., Austin, 1970-72; tchr. grade 8 lang. arts Quabbin Regional H.S., Barre, Mass., 1974-75; rsch. asst. Clinic to Improve Univ. Tchg. U. Mass., Amherst, 1974-76, staff assoc., 1976-77; dir. tchg. and media resource ctr., asst. prof. speech and theatre Murray State U., Ky., 1977-80; acting dir., coord. faculty devel. office ednl. devel. and resources Coll. Osteopathic Medicine

Ohio U., Athens, 1980-81; assoc. dir. office curricular affairs, asst. prof. family medicine Med. Coll. Wis., Milw., 1981-83; ednl. specialist ednl. devel. unit Michael Reese Hosp. and Med. Ctr., Chgo., 1983-84; dir. faculty devel. office ednl. devel. Harvard Med. Sch., Boston, 1984-91, lectr. in med. edn., 1988-91; dir. Ctr. for Ednl. Devel. and Rsch. UCLA Sch. Medicine, 1992-99, asst. dean med. edn., 1992-94, assoc. prof. medicine, 1992-95, prof. medicine, 1996—, assoc. dean med. edn., 1995-97, sr. assoc. dean med. edn., 1998—. Mem. editl. bd. Advances in Health Scis. Edn., 1995—, Med. Edn., 1995—, Acad. Medicine, 2001—; reviewer: Acad. Medicine, 1989—, Tchg. and Learning in Medicine, 1990—, Jour. Gen. Internal Medicine, 1988—, Am. Ednl. Rsch. Assn., 1987—, Rsch. Med.Edn. Ann. Conf., 1988—; contbr. articles to profl. jours. and chpts. to books; lectr. in field. Recipient Clinician Tchr. award Calif. Regional Soc. Gen. Internal Medicine, 1995, Excellence in Edn. award UCLA Sch. Medicine, 1998. Mem. Am. Assn. Med. Colls. (mem. rsch. med. edn. com. 1990-93, western chair group on ednl. affairs 1995-97, co-dir. fellowship in med. edn. rsch. 1995-97, convenor spl. interest group on faculty devel. 1997-98, chair group on ednl. affairs 1997—), Am. Ednl. Rsch. Assn., Profl. and Orgnl. Devel. Network (mem. nat. core com. 1977-80, 84-86, exec. dir. 1984-85), Phi Beta Kappa. Office: UCLA Sch Medicine Ctr Ednl Devel & Rsch PO Box 951722 Los Angeles CA 90095-1722 Office Phone: 310-794-7018. E-mail: lwilkerson@mednet.ucla.edu.

WILKIE, DONALD WALTER, retired biologist, aquarium administrator; b. Vancouver, BC, Can., June 20, 1931; s. Otway James Henry and Jessie Margaret (McLeod) W.; m. Patricia Ann Archer, May 18, 1980; children: Linda, Douglas, Susanne. BA, U. B.C., 1960, M.Sc., 1966. Curator Vancouver Pub. Aquarium, 1961-63, Phila. Aquarama, 1963-65; exec. dir. aquarium-mus. Scripps Instn. Oceanography, La Jolla, Calif., 1965-93, exec. dir. emeritus, 1993—; founding dir. Birch Aquarium of Scripps, 1992. Cons. aquarium design, rschg. exhibit content; sci. writer and editor naturalist-marine edn. programs. coach, Scholastic Clay Targets Prog. Author books on aquaria and marine ednl. materials; contbr. numerous articles to profl. jours. Bd. mem. San Diego Shotgun Sports Assn.; pres. UCSD Retirement Assn. 1999-02. Mem. San Diego (Calif.) Zool. Soc. Home: 4548 Cather Ave San Diego CA 92122-2632 Office: U Calif San Diego Scripps Instn Oceanography Libr 9500 Gilman Dr La Jolla CA 92093-0219 E-mail: dwilkie@ucsd.edu, donwilkie1@mac.com.

WILKINS, BURLEIGH TAYLOR, philosophy educator; b. Bridgetown, Va., July 1, 1932; s. Burleigh and Helen Marie (Taylor) W.; children: Brita Taylor, Carla Cowgill, Burleigh William. BA summa cum laude, Duke U., 1952; MA, Harvard U., 1954, Princeton U., 1963, PhD, 1965. Instr. MIT, Cambridge, 1957-60, Princeton U., 1960-61, 63; asst. prof. Rice U., Houston, 1965-66, assoc. prof., 1966-67, U. Calif., Santa Barbara, 1967-68, prof., 1968—. Author: Carl Becker, 1961, The Problem of Burke's Political Philosophy, 1967, Hegel's Philosophy of History, 1974, Has History Any Meaning?, 1978, Terrorism and Collective Responsibility, 1992; editor: The European Convention on Human Rights, 2008. Mem.: Phi Beta Kappa. Office: U Calif Dept Philosophy Santa Barbara CA 93106

WILKINS, CAROLINE HANKE, advocate, political organization worker; b. Corpus Christi, Tex., May 12, 1937; d. Louis Allen and Jean Guckian Hanke; m. B. Hughel Wilkins, 1957; 1 child, Brian Hughel. Student, Tex. Coll. Arts and Industries, 1956—57, Tex. Tech. U., 1957—58; BA, U. Tex., 1961; MA magna cum laude, U. Ams., 1964. Instr. history Oreg. State U., 1967-68; adminstr. Consumer Svcs. divsn. State of Oreg., 1977-80, Wilkins Assocs., 1980—. Mem. PFMC Salmon Adv. subpanel, 1982-86. Author: (with B. H. Wilkins) Implications of the U.S.-Mexican Water Treaty for Interregional Water Transfer, 1968. Mem. Kerr Libr. Bd., Oreg. State U., 1989—95, pres., 1994—95; mem. Corvallis-Benton County Libr. Found., 1991—2001, sec., 1993, v.p., 1994, pres., 1995, mission and goals com. chair, 2000—01; pres. Oreg. State-Corvallis chpt. UNIFEM, 1998—2002; mem. Women and Philanthropy, Oreg. State U. Giving Cir., 2003—07, Oreg. Jud. Fitness and Disability Commn., 2004—, vice chair, 2006, chair, 2007; Dem. precinct committeewoman Benton County, Oreg., 1964—90; publicity chmn. Benton County Gen. Election, 1964; chmn. Get-Out-the-Vote Com., Benton County, 1966; vice chmn. Benton County Dem. Ctrl. Com., 1966—70, 1st Congl. Dist., Oreg., 1966—67, chmn., 1967—68; vice chmn. Dem. Party of Oreg., 1968—69, chmn., 1969—74; mem. exec. com. Western States Dem. Conf., 1970—72; vice chmn. Dem. Nat. Com., 1972—77, mem. arrangements com., 1972, 1976, mem. Dem. Charter Commn., 1973—74, mem., 1972—77, 1985—89, mem. size and composition com., 1987—89, mem. rules com., 1988; mem. ethics commn. Oreg. Govt., 1974—76; del., mem. rules com. Dem. Nat. Conv., 1988; 1st v.p. Nat. Fedn. Dem. Women, 1983—85, pres., 1985—87, parliamentarian, 1993—95, 1999—2001, chair Pres.'s coun., 2001—03, chair by-laws com., 2003—05, parliamentarian, 2005—07, western regional dir., 2005—07; nominating com., 2008—; pres. Oreg. Fedn. Dem. Women, 1997—2001; bd. dirs. Oreg. chpt. US Lighthouse Soc., pres., 1997—98; bd. dirs. Oreg. State U.-Corvallis Symphony, 1998—2001, v.p., 1999—2000, resources com., mem. endowment task force, 2007; bd. dirs. Oreg. State U. Acad. Lifelong Learning, 2003—08. Named Outstanding Mem. Nat. Fedn. Dem. Women, 1992, Woman of Achievement, Oreg. State U. Women's Ctr., 1998. Mem.: Soc. Consumer Affairs Profls., Nat. Assn. Consumer Agy. Adminstrs., Oreg. State U. Folk Club (pres. faculty wives 1989—90, scholarship chair 2000—01, grants com. 2002—03), Zonta Internat. (vice area bd. dirs. dist. 8 1992—94, bd. dist. 8 1994—96, by laws and resolutions chair 1997—98, internat. rels. coord. dist. 8 2000—02, chair dist. 8 nominating com. 2003—06, chair 2005—06, parliamentarian 2006—08, Zonta Internat. Found. bd. dirs. 2007—08, chair devel. com. 2007—08). Office: 3311 NW Roosevelt Dr Corvallis OR 97330-1169

WILKINS, MICHAEL JON, state supreme court justice; b. Murray, Utah, May 13, 1948; s. Jack L. and Mary June (Phillips) W.; m. Diane W. Wilkins, Nov. 9, 1967; children: Jennifer, Stephanie, Bradley J. BS, U. Utah, 1975, JD, 1976; LLM, U. Va., 2001. Bar: Utah 1977, U.S. Dist. Ct. Utah 1977, U.S. Ct. Appeals (10th cir.) 1987, U.S. Supreme Ct. 1986. Mng. ptnr. Wilkins, Oritt & Headman, Salt Lake City, 1989-94; judge Utah Ct. Appeals, 1994—2000; justice Utah Supreme Ct., 2000—, past assoc. chief justice. Mem. Gov.'s Adv. Com. on Corp., Salt Lake City, 1989-94; mem. Utah Supreme Ct. Complex Steering Com., 1993-94; mem. Judiciary Standing Com. on Tech., 1995-2000, chmn., 1995-2000; mem. Legis. Compensation Commn., 1994-95. Trustee Utah Law Related Edn. Project, Inc., Salt Lake City, 1991-95, chmn., 1992-94. 1st lt. U.S. Army, 1968-72. Mem. Lds Ch. Office: Utah Supreme Ct 450 S State St PO Box 140210 Salt Lake City UT 84114-0210

WILKINSON, ALAN HERBERT, nephrologist, educator; b. Johannesburg, July 11, 1948; came to U.S., 1985; s. Raymond C. and Nonie (Levick) W.; m. Angelika A. E. Adami, Dec. 22, 1973; one child: Rebecca Kate Adami. BS in Physiology, Biochemistry, Philosophy, U. Witwatersrand, South Africa, 1969, BS in Biochemistry with honors, 1970, MB, BCh, 1975; cert. health care mgmt., U. Calif., Irvine, 1998. Fellow Royal Coll. Physicians (U.K.), specialist in clin. hypertension. Vis. assoc. Dept. Internal Medicine U. Iowa, Iowa City, 1987-88; assoc. prof. of medicine UCLA Sch. Med., 1988-95, prof. med., 1995—; dir. clin. nephrology UCLA Dept. Med., 1988-93, dir. kidney and pancreas transplantation, 1993—. Contbr. articles to profl. jours. Mem. steering com. Nat. Kidney Found.; mem. U.S. Transplant Games, L.A., 1992; bd. dirs. So. Calif. Renal Disease Coun., 2002-04, med. adv., 2004—. Recipient Exceptional Svc. award Nat. Kidney Found., 1992; Nat. Kidney Found. fellow. Mem. Am. Soc. Transplantation, Internat. Nephrology Soc., Am. Soc. Nephrology. Avocations: ornithology, gardening. Office: UCLA Dept Med 200 Medical Plz Box 951693 Los Angeles CA 90095-1693

WILLARD, H(ARRISON) ROBERT, electrical engineer; b. Seattle, May 31, 1933; s. Harrison Eugene and Florence Linea (Chelquist) Willard. BSEE, U. Wash., 1955, MSEE, 1957, PhD, 1971. Lic. profl. engr., Wash. Staff assoc. Boeing Sci. Rsch. Labs., Seattle, 1959-64; rsch. assoc. U. Wash., 1968-72, sr. engr., rsch. prof. applied physics lab., 1972-81; sr. engr. Boeing Aerospace Co., Seattle, 1981-84; dir. instrumentation and engring. MetriCor Inc. (formerly Tech. Dynamics, Inc.), Redmond, Wash., 1984-92; sr. engr. B.E. Meyers & Co., Inc., Redmond, 1992—. Contbr. articles to profl. jours. With US Army, 1957—59. Mem.: IEEE, Am. Geophys. Union, Sigma Xi, Phi Beta Kappa, Tau Beta Pi. Achievements include patents in field. Office: 14540 NE 91st St Redmond WA 98052-4939

WILLARD-JONES, DONNA C., lawyer; b. Calgary, Alberta, Can., Jan. 19, 1944; m. Douglas E. Jones. BA with honors, U. B.C., 1965, student, 1965-66; JD, U. Oreg., 1970. Bar: Ak. 1970, U.S. Dist. Ct. Ak. 1970, U.S. Ct. Appeals (9th cir.) 1971, U.S. Customs Ct. 1972, U.S. Tax Ct. 1975, U.S. Supreme Ct. 1981. Assoc. Boyko & Walton, 1970-71, Walton & Willard, 1971-73; ptnr. Gruenberg & Willard, 1974, Gruenberg, Willard & Smith, 1974-75, Richmond, Willoughby & Willard, 1976-81, Willoughby & Willard, 1981-89; pvt. practice Anchorage, 1990—. Chmn. fed. adv. group Implementation of Civil Justice Reform Act of 1990, 1991-92; lawyer rep. 9th Cir. Jud. Conf., 1979-80; mem. spl. com. on contempt Ak. Supreme Ct., 1991-92; chmn. Bankruptcy Judge Merit Screening com., 1979; mem. Am. Judicature Soc., 1973-92, Am. Trial Lawyers Assn., 1981-92; bd. dirs. Ak. Legal Svcs. Corp., 1979-80; spkr. in field. Mem. U. B.C. Law Rev.; assoc. editor Oreg. Law Rev.; copy editor Ak. Bar Rag, 1979-84, contbg. editor, 1979-92; annual reviser Probate Counsel, 1972-88. Mem. Anchorage Port Commn., 1987-93, chmn., 1990-93; chmn. Ak. State Officers Compensation Commn., 1986-92; mem. Anchorage Transp. Commn., 1983-87, chmn., 1986-87; vice-chmn. Ak. Code Revision Commn., 1976-78; bd. trustees Ak. Indian Arts, Inc., 1970-92; mem. Chilkat Dancer Ak., 1965—. Recipient Rikli Solo Lifetime Achievement. award, ABA Gen. Pract., 1998. Fellow Am. Bar Found. (life); mem. ABA (ho. dels. 1980-84, 86-96, bd. govs. 1992-96, sec. 1995-96), Nat. Conf. Bar Pres. (exec. coun. 1985-88), Nat. Conf. Bar Founds. (bd. trustees 1983-90), Am. Arbitration Assn., We. States Bar Conf. (pres. 1983-84), Ak. Bar Assn. (Bd. Govs. Disting. Svc. award 1991, bd. govs. 1977-80, pres. 1979-80, pres. 1979-80, numerous coms.), Am. Law Inst. Presbyterian.

WILLES, MARK HINCKLEY, media specialist; b. Salt Lake City, July 16, 1941; s. Joseph Simmons and Ruth (Hinckley) W.; m. Laura Fayone, June 7, 1961; children: Wendy Anne, Susan Kay, Keith Mark, Stephen Joseph, Matthew Bryant. AB, Columbia Coll., 1963, PhD, 1967. Staff banking and currency com. Ho. of Reps., Washington, 1966-67; asst. prof. fin. Wharton Sch. U. Pa., Phila., 1967-69; economist Fed. Res. Bank, Phila., 1967, sr. economist, 1969-70, dir. rsch., 1970-71, v.p., dir. rsch., 1971, 1st v.p., 1971-77; pres. Fed. Res. Bank of Mpls., 1977-80; exec. v.p., chief fin. officer Gen. Mills, Inc., Mpls., 1980-85, pres., COO, 1985-92, vice-chmn., 1992-95; chmn., pres., CEO Times Mirror Co., LA, 1995-2000; pub. L.A. Times, 1997-99; disting. prof. mgmt. Brigham Young U., Provo, Utah, 2000, 2004—; pres. Hawaii Honolulu Mission, Ch. of LDS, 2001—04. Office: Brigham Young Univ 3651 N 100 E Ste 300 Provo UT 84604

WILLETT, ROBERT E., lawyer; b. Glendale, Calif., June 21, 1943; BA, San Fernando Valley State Coll., 1971; JD, U. Calif., Berkeley, 1974. Bar: Calif. 1974, U.S. Supreme Ct. 1987, U.S. Tax Ct. 1988. Lawyer O'Melveny & Myers, LA. Mem. state bar com. for adminstrn. of justice, 1987-90. Assoc. editor Calif. Law Rev., 1972-73, notes and comments editor, 1973-74. Mem. ABA sections on litigation and antitrust, L.A. County Bar Assn. sections on antitrust and litigation (vice chair ct. improvements com. 1985-87). Order of Coif. Office: O'Melveny & Myers LLP 400 S Hope St Los Angeles CA 90071-2899 Office Phone: 213-430-6355. Office Fax: 213-430-6407. Business E-Mail: rwillett@omm.com.

WILLETTE, DONALD CORLISS, pastor; b. Lemmon, SD, June 26, 1941; s. Corliss Noah Willette and Marion Alice (Egland) Allen. BA, St. Mary's Coll./Sem., 1963; MDiv, St. Thomas Sem., Denver, 1984. ordained Roman Catholic priest. Owner, operator Edel Haus Restaurant, Estes Park, Colo., 1975-77; owner, real estate broker Better Homes Gardens, Estes Park, 1977-84; assoc. pastor St. Thomas More, Englewood, Colo., 1984-87, St. Jude Ch., Lakewood, Colo., 1987-88; pastor St. Theresa Ch., Frederick, Colo., 1988-91, St. Louis Ch., Louisville, Colo., 1991—. Founding bd. dirs. Mary's Dream Ltd., Frederick, 1989-92, Migrant Outreach Ministry, Longmont, Colo., 1991-95; tour leader Holy Land Pilgrimages, Jerusalem, 1984-94. With USAF, 1967-73, advanced through grades to col. USAFR, Colo. NG. Mem. Am. Legion (chaplain 1977—), K. of C. (chaplain 1984—), VFW, Elks (chaplain 1979-96, 96—). Avocations: salt water sailing, holy land pilgrimage leader.

WILLHITE, CALVIN CAMPBELL, toxicologist; b. Salt Lake City, Apr. 27, 1952; s. Jed Butler and Carol (Campbell) W. BS, Utah State U., 1974, MS, 1977; PhD, Dartmouth Coll., 1980. Toxicologist USDA, Berkeley, Calif., 1980—85, State of Calif., Berkeley, 1985—. Adj. assoc. prof. toxicology Utah State U., 1984—94; mem. data safety rev. bds. Johns Hopkins Sch. Medicine, 1996; mem. Calif./OSHA Gen. Industry Safety Order PEL Adv. Bd., 1994, 96; mem. com. toxicology NAS, 1998—2005; mem. sci. adv. com. alternative toxicol. methods Nat. Toxicology Program, 2002—05; rev. bd. Nat. Inst. Environ. Health Sci. Ctr. Evaluation Risk Human Reprodn., 2001; devel. toxicity/structure, activity task group Internat. Life Sci. Inst., 2003—; sci. rev. panel Burnham Inst., 2002. Mem. editl. bd.: Toxicology and Applied Pharmacology, 1989—; editor: N.Y. Acad. Scis., 1993, Toxicology, 1996—, Jour. Toxicol. Environ. Health (B), 1997—, Toxicology Letters, 1998—2002, Reproductive Toxicol., 2001—05; contbr. articles on birth defects to profl. jours. Mem. WHO IARC Cancer Prevention Work Group, 1999, European Union/OECD validation regulatory methods ENV/EHS, 2002; commr. City of Novato, Calif., 2000—. Nat. Inst. Child Health and Human Devel. grantee, 1985-92, March of Dimes Birth Defects Found. grantee, 1987-91, Hoffmann LaRoche grantee, 1992-94. Mem. NIH (Health Promotion/Disease Prevention Study sect. 1998), NSF (mem. health effects adv. bd. 1986—), Am. Conf. Govt. Indsl. Hygienists (mem. threshold limit values com. 1989-99), Soc. Toxicology (program com. 1995-99, Frank R. Blood award 1986). Home: 99 Newport Landing Novato CA 94949 Office: State Calif 700 Heinz Ave Berkeley CA 94710-2721 Home Phone: 415-884-2448; Office Phone: 510-540-3766. Personal E-mail: calvinwillhite@hotmail.com.

WILL.I.AM, (WILLIAM JAMES ADAMS JR.), rap artist; b. Mar. 15, 1975; Founding mem. band Atban Klann, 1992—95, band Black Eyed Peas, 1998—. Co-founder i.am clothing, 2001—. Singer, prodr. (Black Eyed Peas albums) Behind the Front, 1998, Bridging the Gap, 2000, Elephunk, 2003, Monkey Business, 2005 (Favorite Rap/Hip-Hop Album, Am. Music Awards, 2006), Maximum Black Eyed Peas, 2005, Renegotiations: The Remixes, 2006, (solo albums) Lost Change, 2001, Must B 21, 2003, Songs About Girls, 2007; singer: (songs) Joints & Jams, 1998, Fallin' Up, 1998, Where is the Love? (feat. Justin Timberlake), 2003, Shut Up, 2003, Hey Mama, 2004 (MTV Video Music Award), Let's Get It Started, 2004 (Grammy, Best Rap Performance, 2005), Don't Phunk with My Heart, 2005 (Grammy award, Best Rap Group Performance, 2006), Don't Lie, 2005, My Humps, 2005 (MTV Video Music award for Best Hip-Hop Video, 2006, Grammy award, Best Group Pop Vocal Performance, 2007), (with Santana) I Am Somebody, 2005, (with Chrisette Michele) Be OK, 2007 (Grammy award, Best Urban/Alternative Performance, 2009), Yes We Can, 2008 (Webby award, Artist of Yr., Internat. Acad. Digital Arts and Scis., 2008, Outstanding Song, Outstanding Music Video, NAACP Image Awards, 2009). Co-founder Peapod Found., LA. Recipient MTV Europe award for Best Pop Act (with Black Eyed Peas), 2004, 2005, Favorite Pop Group & Rap Group, Am. Music Awards, 2005, Favorite Soul/Rhythm & Blues Grp., 2006, Favorite Rap/Hip-Hop Grp., 2006, Webby Artist of Yr., Internat. Acad. Digital Arts and Scis., 2008. Office: iam clothing PO Box 664 Hollywood CA 90078 Office Phone: 323-469-5181, 323-661-1524. Office Fax: 213-856-2712. E-mail: iamclothing@aol.com.

WILLIAMS, A. CODY, councilman; b. Phoenix, Mar. 5, 1960; m. Jeri Williams; children: Alanna, Alan Travis, Cody Jerard. Student, U. Okla.; MBA, Ariz. State U.; postgrad., Harvard U. Diverse workforce specialist and affirmative action officer Intel; v.p., affirmative action officer Security Pac Bank; pres. Alms & Hosanna Consulting Firm; councilman dist. 8 Phoenix City Coun., 1994—; pres., CEO Phoenix Black C. of C., 2002—. Chmn. econ. and downtown subcom., mem. housing and neighborhoods subcom., mem. family and youth subcom. and transportation subcom. Recipient award of recognition for dedicated svcs., Gov.'s African-Am. Adv. Coun., 2004; named one of Most Influential Citizens, The Bus. Jour., 2004; named to State of Ariz. Dem. Hall of Fame, 2003. Avocations: golf, travel. Office: Greater Phoenix Black C of C 201 E Washington St Ste 350 Phoenix AZ 85003 E-mail: cody@phoenixblackchamber.com, teresa@phoenixblackchamber.com.

WILLIAMS, AENEAS DEMETRIUS, professional football player; b. New Orleans, Jan. 29, 1968; Degree in acctg., So. Univ. La., 1990. Cornerback Ariz. Cardinals, Phoenix, 1991. Selected to Pro Bowl, 1994-96; tied for NFL lead in interceptions (9), 1994. Office: c/o Ariz Cardinals PO Box 888 Phoenix AZ 85001-0888

WILLIAMS, ARTHUR COZAD, retired broadcasting executive; b. Forty Fort, Pa., Feb. 12, 1926; s. John Bedford and Emily Irene (Poyck) W.; m. Ann Cale Bragan, Oct. 1, 1955; children: Emily Williams Van Hoorickx, Douglas, Craig. Student, Bucknell U., 1943-44; BA cum laude, U. So. Calif., 1949. Trainee Kaiser Aluminum, 1949; sales Sta. KPMC, 1950-51; v.p., mgr. KFBK and KFBK-FM Radio Stas., Sacramento, 1951-80; with public relations dept. Sacramento Bee, McClatchy Newspapers, 1981-86; ret., 1986. Dir.-treas. Norkal Opportunities, Inc.; pres. Sacramento Bee Credit Union. Served with AUS, 1944-46. Mem. Sigma Delta Chi. Clubs: Rotary, Sutter, Valley Hi Country, Masons, Shriners. Home: 1209 Nevis Ct Sacramento CA 95822-2532 Personal E-mail: artcwilliams@sbcglobal.net.

WILLIAMS, BARRY LAWSON, real estate executive; b. NYC, July 21, 1944; s. Otis Lenzy and Ilza Louise (Berry) W.; m. Adrienne Maria Foster, May 24, 1977; children: Barry C., Jaime, Andrew. AB, Harvard U., 1966, JD, MBA, Harvard U., 1971. Bar: Calif. 1975. Sr. cons. McKinsey & Co., San Francisco, 1971-78; mng. prin. Bechtel Investments Inc., San Francisco, 1979-87; pres. Williams Pacific Ventures Inc., Redwood City, Calif., 1987—. Ptnr. WDG-Ventures, CAC, Redwood City, 1987—; pres. C.N. Flagg Inc., Meriden, Conn., 1988—; bd. dirs. Am. Pres. Co., Oakland, Calif., 1984—, Northwestern Life Ins. Co., Milw., 1987—; chmn. bd. Pacific Presbyn. Med. Ctr., San Francisco, 1980—. Republican. Episcopalian. Avocation: tennis.

WILLIAMS, BART H., lawyer; b. Orleans, France, Oct. 24, 1962; BA, Yale U., 1984, JD, 1987. Bar: Calif. 1988, US Dist. Ct. (ctrl. dist. Calif.) 1988. Assoc. Munger, Tolles & Olson LLP, LA, 1987—91, ptnr., 1994—, co-mng. ptnr., 2004—; asst. US atty. criminal divsn., major frauds sect. Central Dist. Calif., 1991—94. Lawyer del. Ninth Circuit Judicial Conf., 1997—99; mem. bd. trustees Charles R. Drew U. Medicine and Sci.; mem. LA County Bar Assn. Task Force on Criminal Justice System; dep. gen. counsel LA Police Commn. Independent Review Panel; co-chair ABA Lit. Section's Expert Witness Com.; adj. prof. law Loyola Law Sch.; adj. prof. Nat. Inst. Trial Advocacy. Bd. dirs. Alliance Children's Rights. Recipient Potter Stewart prize, Yale Moot Ct. Appeals; named Prosecutor Yr., Internat. Assn. Credit Card Investigators, 1993; named one of Top 20 Lawyers in State of Calif. Under 40 Yrs. Age, Calif. Law Bus. Mag., 2002, 45 Under Forty-Five, Am. Lawyer Mag., 2003, Am. Top Black Lawyers, Black Enterprise Mag., 2003, Calif. Superlawyers, Law & Politics Mag., 2004. Mem.: ABA (mem. task force on ind. counsel act 1997—98, mem. litig. and criminal law sects., chair govt. litig. com. 2000—02), State Bar Calif. Office: Munger Tolles & Olson LLP 355 S Grand Ave 35th Fl Los Angeles CA 90071 Office Phone: 213-683-9295. Office Fax: 213-683-5195. E-mail: Bart.Williams@mto.com.

WILLIAMS, BENJAMIN R., health facility administrator; CIO Horizon/CMS Healthcare Corp., Albuquerque; v.p., info. services & CIO St. Joseph Health Sys., Orange, Calif., 1998, now sr. v.p., strategic innovation & chief info. officer. Spkr. in field. Recipient Innovator of Yr. award., Coll. of Healthcare Info. Mgmt. Executives, 2004. Office: St Joseph Health Sys 500 S Main St Ste 1000 PO Box 14132 Orange CA 92863-1532

WILLIAMS, BENJAMIN V., IV, headmaster, history educator; m. Ginger Williams; children: Ben, Grace, Carson. BA in Am. Studies, Williams Coll.; MA in Am. Civilization, Brown U. With First Boston, NYC; history and English teacher, dir. of development St. Sebastian's Sch., Mass.; dean of middle and upper schools St. John's Sch., Houston, 1993—97; headmaster Cate Sch., Carpinteria, Calif., 1997—. Office: Cate Sch PO Box 5005 Carpinteria CA 93014-5005 Office Phone: 805-684-4127 ext. 200.

WILLIAMS, CARLTON L., communications executive; Pres., CEO Karlkani Infinity Inc., LA, 1989—.

WILLIAMS, CAROL H., advertising executive; b. Chgo. d. Clarence Earl Williams and Betty Jane Norment-Williams; m. Tipkins Hood; children: Tipkins Hood Jr., Carol Hood. Student, Northwestern U. Creative dir., sr. v.p. Leo Burnett Agy., Chgo., 1969—80, Foote-Cone & Belding, San Francisco, 1980—82; prin. owner Carol H. Williams Advt., Inc., Oakland, Calif., 1986—. Active US Dream Acad. Recipient Outstanding Women in Mktg. and Comm. award, Ebony Mag., 2001, Bus. Achievement award, Nat. Coalition 100 Black Women, Inc., 2003, Ad Agy. of Yr., Black Enterprise Mag., 2004; named a Woman to Watch, Advt. Age, 2002; named to Power 150, Ebony mag., 2008. Mem.: NAACP, TEC Internat., Rainbow/PUSH Coalition. Office: Carol H Williams Advertising Inc 555 12th St Ste 1700 Oakland CA 94607-4058

WILLIAMS, CECIL, minister; b. San Angelo, Tex., Sept. 22, 1929; s. Earl Williams; m. Evelyn Robinson, 1982 (dec. 1981); children: Albert, Kim; m. Janice Mirikitani, 1982. BA, Huston-Tillotson U., Austin, 1952; BD, Southern Meth. U., 1955. Chaplain, tchr. Huston-Tillotson U., 1955—59; founder, minister Glide United Meml. Meth. Ch., San Francisco, 1963—. Co-creator Coun. on Religion and Homosexuality, 1964. Author: (Autobiography) I'm Alive, 1980; actor: (films) True Crime, 1999, America's Heart and Soul, 2004, The Pursuit of Happiness, 2006. Named to Power 150, Ebony mag., 2008. Office: Glide Meml United Meth Ch 330 Ellis St San Francisco CA 94102 Office Phone: 415-974-6000.

WILLIAMS, DELWYN CHARLES, telephone company executive; b. Idaho Falls, Idaho, Apr. 27, 1936; s. Charles H. and Vonda (Wood) W.; m. Marlene Grace Nordland, Feb. 29, 1964; children— Stephen, Kirstin, Nicole. BS in Bus., U. Idaho, 1959. C.P.A., Calif. Accountant Peat, Marwick, Mitchell & Co. (C.P.A.s), San Francisco, 1960-65; treas. Dohrmann Instruments Co., Mountain View, Calif., 1965-68; with Continental Telephone Co. of Calif., Bakersfield, 1968-84, controller, 1969-70, v.p., treas., 1970-77, v.p., gen. mgr., 1977-79, pres., 1977-84, also dir.; pres. J.H. Evans, Inc., and subs., 1984-95, CEO, 1995—2001, Via Wireless LLC, 1996—2001. Home: 10052 Oak Branch Cir Carmel CA 93923-8000

WILLIAMS, EVAN, Internet company executive; b. Nebr., Mar. 31, 1972; Web application developer O'Reilly Media, Intel, Hewlett Packard; co-founder, CEO (and developer of Blogger) Pyra Labs (acquired by Google), 1998—2003; head, Blogger Google, 2003—04; co-founder Oden Inc. podcasting (acquired by Sonic Mountain in 2007), 2004, Obvious Corp. (spun off Twitter, Inc.), 2006, Twitter, Inc., San Francisco, 2007, chmn., 2007—08, CEO, 2008—. Named (with Paul Bausch and Meg Hourihan) People of Yr., PC Mag., 2004; named one of 50 Who Matter Now, Business 2.0, 2007, The World's Most Influential People, TIME mag., 2009. Office: Twitter Inc 539 Bryant St Ste 402 San Francisco CA 94107-1269 Office Phone: 866-924-2008.*

WILLIAMS, FORMAN ARTHUR, science engineering educator; b. New Brunswick, NJ, Jan. 12, 1934; s. Forman J. and Alice (Pooley) W.; m. Elsie Vivian Kara, June 15, 1955 (div. 1978); children: F. Gary, Glen A., Nancy L., Susan D., Michael S., Michelle K.; m. Elizabeth Acevedo, Aug. 19, 1978. BSE, Princeton U., 1955; PhD, Calif. Inst. Tech., 1958; Doctorate (hon.), Poly. U. Madrid, 2002. Asst. prof. Harvard U., Cambridge, Mass., 1958-64; prof. U. Calif.-San Diego, 1964-81; Robert H. Goddard prof. Princeton U., NJ, 1981-88; prof. dept. mech. and aerospace engring. U. Calif., San Diego, 1988—, predsidential chair in Energy and Combustion Rsch, 1994—. Adj. prof. Yale U., New Haven, 1997—. Author: Combustion Theory, 1965, 2d edit., 1985; contbr. articles to profl. jours. Fellow NSF, 1962; fellow Guggenheim Found., 1970; recipient U.S. Sr. Scientist award Alexander von Humboldt Found., 1982, Silver medal Combustion Inst., 1978, Bernard Lewis Gold medal Combustion Inst., 1990, Pendray Aerospace Literature award Am. Inst. of Aeronautics and Astronautics, 1993; named Pioneer Rschr. of the 20th Century, Japan Soc. Mech. Engrs., 1995. Fellow AIAA, Am. Phys. Soc.; mem. Combustion Inst., Soc. for Indsl. and Applied Math., Nat. Acad. Engring., Nat. Acad. Engring Mex. (fgn. corr. mem.), Sigma Xi. Home: 8258 Caminito Maritimo La Jolla CA 92037-2204 Office: U Calif San Diego Ctr Energy Rsch 9500 Gilman Dr La Jolla CA 92093-5004 E-mail: faw@ucsd.edu.

WILLIAMS, HAROLD MARVIN, lawyer, retired foundation, academic and federal agency administrator; b. Phila., Jan. 5, 1928; s. Louis W. and Sophie (Fox) W.; m. Nancy Englander; children: Ralph A., Susan J., Derek M. AB, UCLA, 1946; JD, Harvard Law Sch., 1949; postgrad. in law, U. So. Calif., 1955-59; DHL (hon.), Johns Hopkins U., 1987, Occidental Coll., 1997, Calif. State U., 1998. Bar: Calif. 1950. Pvt. practice, LA, 1950, 1953—55; with Hunt Food and Industries Inc., 1955-68, v.p., 1958-60, exec. v.p., 1960-68; gen. mgr. Hunt-Wesson Foods, 1964-66, pres., 1966-68, Hunt Food and Industries Inc., 1968; chmn. bd., fin. com. Norton Simon, 1968—70; prof. mgmt. UCLA, 1970-77; chmn. SEC, Washington, 1977-81; pres., CEO J. Paul Getty Trust, 1981-98, pres. emeritus; of counsel Skadden Arps et al, 1998—. Pres., dir. Special Investments Securities, Inc., 1961—66. Pub. mem. Nat. Advt. Review Bd., 1971—75; trustee Nat. Humanities Ctr., 1987—93; mem. Coun. Fgn. Rels., Com. Econ. Devel., Pres.' Com. Arts, Humanities, 1993—2001, Commn. Econ. Devel. State Calif., 1973—77; energy coord. City of LA, 1973—74; regent U. Calif., 1983—94; commn. rev. master plan higher edn. State Calif., Calif., 1985—87; co chair Calif. Citizens Commn. Higher Edn.; dir. Ethics Resource Ctr.; mem. Commn. Acad. Presidency; co-chmn. Pub. Comm. LA County Govt.; dir. Pub. Policy Inst. Calif., 1995—2003, Calif. Endowment, 1995—2004, Alliance for Coll. Ready Schs., Alliance for Excellent Edn.; chair bd. visitors UCLA Sch. Arts and Arch. 1st lt. AUS, 1951—53, Korea. Decorated Bronze Star. Mem.: State Bar Calif. Office: J Paul Getty Trust 1200 Getty Center Dr Ste 1100 Los Angeles CA 90049-1668 also: Skadden Arps Slate Meagher Flom LLP 300 S Grand Ave Ste 3400 Los Angeles CA 90071 Office Phone: 310-440-6417, 213-687-5370. E-mail: hwilliams@getty.edu.

WILLIAMS, HARRY EDWARD, management consultant; b. Oak Park, Ill., July 20, 1925; s. Harry E. and Mary E.; m. Peggy; 1 child, Jeanne. Student, West Coast U., Los Angeles, 1958-60; BS in Engring., Calif. Coast Coll., Santa Ana, 1975, MBA, 1975; PhD, Golden State U., LA, 1981. Registered profl. engr., Calif. Mgr. Parker Aircraft Co., Los Angeles, 1958-60, Leach Corp., Los Angeles, 1968-69, Litton, Data Systems, Van Nuys, Calif., 1969-72; dir. Electronic Memories, Hawthorne, Calif., 1972-78, Magnavox Co., Torrance, Calif., 1978-80; v.p. Stacoswitch Inc., Costa Mesa, Calif., 1981-87; mgmt. cons., Westminster, Calif., 1987—. Cons. in field. Contbr. articles to profl. jours. With USAAF, 1943-46. Recipient Mgr. of the Yr. award Soc. for Advancement of Mgmt., 1984, Phil Carroll award for outstanding contbns. in field of ops. mgmt., 1985, Profl. Mgr. citation, 1984. Fellow Internat. Acad. Edn. Republican. Methodist. Avocation: target shooting. Office Phone: 714-531-7103. Fax: 714-531-7019. Personal E-mail: heworg@aol.com.

WILLIAMS, HIBBARD EARL, medical educator, physician; b. Utica, NY, Sept. 28, 1932; s. Hibbard G. and Beatrice M. W.; m. Sharon Towne, Sept. 3, 1982; children: Robin, Hans. AB, Cornell U., 1954, MD, 1958. Diplomate Am. Bd. Internal Medicine. Intern Mass. Gen. Hosp., Boston, 1958-59, resident in medicine, 1959-60, 62-64, asst. physician, 1964-65; clin. assoc. Nat. Inst. Arthritis and Metabolic Diseases, NIH, Bethesda, MD, 1960-62; instr. medicine Harvard U., Boston, 1964-65; asst. prof. medicine U. Calif., San Francisco, 1965-68, assoc. prof., 1968-72, prof., 1972-78, chief divsn. med. genetics, 1968-70, vice chmn. dept. medicine, 1970-78; prof., chmn. dept. medicine Cornell U. Med. Coll., NYC, 1978-80; physician-in-chief N.Y. Hosp.-Cornell Med. Ctr., NYC, 1978-80; dean Sch. Medicine U. Calif., Davis, 1980-92, prof. internal medicine, 1980-2000; prof. emeritus, 2000—. Mem. program project com. NIH, Nat. Inst. Arthritis and Metabolic Diseases, 1971-73 Editor med. staff confs. Calif. Medicine, 1966-70; mem. editl. bd. Clin. Rsch., 1968-71, Am. Jour. Medicine, 1978-88; cons. editor Medicine, 1978-86; assoc. editor Metabolism, 1970-80; mem. adv. bd. physiology in medicine New Eng. Jour. Medicine, 1970-75; contbr. articles to med. jours. With USPHS, 1960—62. Recipient Career Devel. award USPHS, 1968; recipient award for excellence in teaching Kaiser Found., 1970, Disting. Faculty award U. Calif. Alumni-Faculty Assn., 1978; John and Mary R. Markle scholar in medicine, 1968 Fellow ACP; mem. AAAS, Am. Soc. Clin. Investigation (sec.-treas. 1974-77), Assn. Am. Physicians, Assn. Am. Med. Colls. (adminstrv. bd., coun. deans 1989-92, exec. coun. 1990-92), Calif. Acad. Medicine (pres. 1984), San Francisco Diabetes Assn. (bd. dirs. 1971-72), Western Assn. Physicians (v.p. 1977-78), Western Soc. Clin. Rsch., Calif. Med. Assn. (chmn. coun. sci. affairs 1990-95, bd. dirs. 1990-95), Calif. Med. Assn. Found. (chmn. bd. dirs. 1997-99), Gianinni Found. (sci. adv. bd. 1990-2000—), St. Francis Yacht Club, Alpha Omega Alph. Office: U Calif Sch Medicine TB150 Davis CA 95616

WILLIAMS, HOWARD RUSSELL, law educator; b. Evansville, Ind., Sept. 26, 1915; s. Clyde Alfred and Grace (Preston) W.; m. Virginia Merle Thompson, Nov. 3, 1942 (dec. Dec. 2000); 1 son, Frederick S.T. AB, Washington U., St. Louis, 1937; LLB, Columbia U., 1940. Bar: N.Y. 1941. With firm Root, Clark, Buckner & Ballantine, NYC, 1940-41; prof. law, asst. dean U. Tex. Law Sch., Austin, 1946-51; prof. law Columbia U. Law Sch., NYC, 1951-63; Dwight prof. Columbia Law Sch., 1959-63; prof. law Stanford U., 1963-85, Stella W. and Ira S. Lillick prof., 1968-82, prof. emeritus, 1982, Robert E. Paradise prof. natural resources, 1983-85, prof. emeritus, 1985—. Oil and gas cons. President's Materials Policy Commn., 1951; mem. Calif. Law Revision Commn., 1971-79, vice chmn., 1976-77, chmn., 1978-79 Author or co-author: Cases on Property, 1954, Cases on Oil and Gas, 1956, 5th edit., 1987, Decedents' Estates and Trusts, 1968, Future Interests, 1970, Oil and Gas Law, 8 vols., 1959-64 (with ann. supplements/rev. 1964-95), abridged edit., 1973, Manual of Oil and Gas Terms, 1957, 11th edit., 2000. Bd. regents Berkeley Bapt. Divinity Sch., 1966-67; trustee Rocky Mountain Mineral Law Found., 1964-66, 68-85. Pvt., maj. US Army, 1941—46. Recipient Clyde O. Martz Tchg. award Rocky Mountain Mineral Law Found., 1994. Mem.: Phi Beta Kappa. Democrat. Home: 360 Everett Ave Apt 4B Palo Alto CA 94301-1422 Office: Stanford U Sch Law Nathan Abbott Way Stanford CA 94305 Office Phone: 650-725-5875.

WILLIAMS, J. D., state controller; b. Malad, Idaho; m. Rosemary Zaugg; 4 daus. MPA, Brigham Young U.; JD, Am. Univ. Bar: Idaho, D.C., several fed. cts.; cert. govt. fin. mgr. Apptd. law clk. D.C. Ct. Appeals; dep. Idaho Atty. Gen. Boise; lawyer Preston, Idaho; mayor City of Preston; appt. auditor State of Idaho, Boise, 1989-94, elected controller, 1994—. Mem. Info. Tech. Res. Coun., Idaho. Past mem. Idaho Law Enforcement Planning Commn., past chmn. Idaho Youth Commn.; past chmn. Preston Sch. Dist. Excellence in Edn. com.; past mem. Idaho Water Resource Bd. Named. Fin. Mgr. of Yr., Idaho. Nat. Assn. State Comptrollers (past pres.), Nat. Assn. State Auditors, Comptrollers and Treasurers (sec. exec. com., Pres.'s award for outstanding svc. in fin. mgmt. to U.S.), Nat. Electronic Commerce Coordinating Coun. (chmn.). Office: Office State Contr State Capital Boise ID 83720-0001

WILLIAMS, J. VERNON, retired lawyer; b. Honolulu, Apr. 26, 1921; s. Urban and W. Amelia (Olson) W.; m. Malvina H. Hitchcock, Oct. 4, 1947 (dec. May 1970); children— Carl H., Karin, Frances E., Scott S.; m. Mary McLellan, Sept. 6, 1980. Student, Phillips Andover Acad., 1937-39; BA cum laude, Amherst Coll., 1943; LL.B., Yale, 1948. Bar: Wash. 1948. Assoc. Riddell, Riddell & Hemphill, 1948-50, ptnr., 1950-95; sr. pin. emeritus Riddell Williams, P.S., Seattle, 1996—. Sec., dir. Airborne Freight Corp., 1968-79, gen. counsel, 1968-96. Chmn. March of Dimes, Seattle, 1954-55; Mem. Mayor's City Charter Rev. Com., 1968-69; chmn. Seattle Bd. Park Commrs., 1966-68; co-chmn. parks and open space com. Forward Thrust, 1966-69; dir. bd. and commrs. br. Nat. Recreation and Parks Assn., 1968-69; chmn. Gov.'s adv. com. Social and Health Services, 1972-75; Bd. dirs. Seattle Met. YMCA, 1965—, pres., 1976-79; trustee Lakeside Sch., 1971-79; mem. alumni council Phillps Andover Acad., 1970-73, Yale Law Sch., 1969-77; chancellor St. Mark's Cathedral, Seattle, 1964-2000. Served with USAAF, 1943-45. Mem. Univ. Club, Seattle Tennis Club, Birnam Wood Golf Club. Home: 2061 43rd Ave E #201 Seattle WA 98112 Office: 4500 1001 4th Ave Plz Seattle WA 98154-1065

WILLIAMS, JAMES FRANKLIN, II, dean, librarian; b. Montgomery, Ala., Jan. 22, 1944; s. James Franklin and Anne (Wester) Williams; m. Madeline McClellan, Jan. 1966 (div. May 1988); 1 child, Madeline Marie; m. Nancy Allen, Aug. 1989; 1 child, Audrey Grace. BA, Morehouse Coll., Atlanta, 1966; MLS, Atlanta U., 1967. Reference libr. Wayne State U. Sci. Libr., Detroit, 1968-69; document delivery libr. Wayne State U. Med. Libr., Detroit, 1969-70, head of reference, 1971-72, dir. med. libr. and regional med. libr. network, 1972-81, regional dir., 1975-82; assoc. dir. of librs. Wayne State U., 1981-88; dean librs. U. Colo., Boulder, 1988—. Bd. regents Nat. Libr. Medicine, Bethesda, Md., 1978—81; pres. Big Twelve Plus Libr. Consortium, 2000; bd. dirs. Coun. Librs. & Info. Resources, Ctr. Rsch. Librs., 1998—, Denver Art Mus., 1997—, pres., 1999—. Mem. editl. bd. Portal: Libraries and the Academy; contbr. articles to profl. jours., chapters to books. Bd. dirs. Educom, 1997—98, Boulder Cmty. Hosp., 2000—. Mem.: ALA (Visionary Leader award 1988, Melvil Dewey medal 2002), Boulder C. of C. (bd. dirs.), Assn. Rsch. Librs. (bd. dirs. 1994-96, 2000-03). Avocations: bicycling, travel, fishing. Office: U Colo Office Dean Librs PO Box 184 Boulder CO 80309-0184 Office Phone: 303-492-7511. Business E-Mail: james.williams@colorado.edu.

WILLIAMS, JOBETH, actress; b. Houston, Dec. 6, 1948; m. John Pasquin, Mar. 14, 1982; children: Nick, Will. Grad., Brown U. Appeared in plays A Coupla White Chicks Sitting Around Talking, 1980, Gardenia, 1982, Idiot's Delight, 1986, Cat on a Hot Tin Roof, 1993; films include Kramer vs. Kramer, 1979, The Dogs of War, 1980, Stir Crazy, 1980, Poltergeist, 1982, Endangered Species, 1982, The Big Chill, 1983, American Dreamer, 1984, Teachers, 1984, Desert Bloom, 1986, Poltergeist II, 1986, Memories of Me, 1988, Welcome Home, 1989, Switch, 1991, Dutch, 1991, Stop! Or My Mom Will Shoot, 1992, Me, Myself and I, 1993, Wyatt Earp, 1994, Parallel Lives, 1994, Little City, 1997, Just Write, 1997, Jungle 2 Jungle, 1997, When Danger Follows You Home, 1997, Justice, 1998, Repossessed, 2002, The Rose Technique, 2002, Into the Fire, 2004, Fever Pitch, 2005, Crazylove, 2005, In the Land of Women, 2007; TV films include Fun and Games, 1980, The Big Black Pill, 1981, Adam, 1983 (Emmy award nominee, Golden Globe award nominee), The Day After, 1983, Kids Don't Tell, 1985, Adam: His Song Continues, 1986, Murder Ordained, 1987, Baby M, 1988 (Emmy award nominee, Golden Globe award nominee), My Name is Bill W., 1989, Child in the Night, 1990, Victim of Love, 1991, Jonathan: The Boy Nobody Wanted, 1992, Sex, Love and Cold Hard Cash, 1993, Chantilly Lace, 1993, Voices from Within, 1994, Lemon Grove, 1994, Parallel Lives, 1994, Voices from Within, 1994, Season of Hope, 1994, Ruby Jean and Joe, 1996, Breaking Through, 1996, It Came From the Sky, 1998, A Chance of Snow, 1998, Justice, 1999, Jackie's Back!, 1999, Trapped in a Purple Haze, 2000, The Ponder Heart, 2001, Homeward Bound, 2002, 14 Hours, 2005, Into the Fire, 2005, Stroller Wars, 2006; TV series include The Guiding Light, 1977-81, Somerset, 1975-76, (voice) Fish Police, 1992, John Grisham's The Client, 1995-96, (voice) Stories from My Childhood, 1998, Payne, 1999; co-exec. prodr.: (TV movie) Bump in the Night, 1991; dir. (films): On Hope, 1994 (Acad. award nominee for Best Live Action Short Film 1995), Winona's Web, 2001.

WILLIAMS, JOHN JAMES, JR., architect; b. Denver, July 13, 1949; s. John James and Virginia Lee (Thompson) W.; m. Mary Serene Morck, July 29, 1972. BArch, U. Colo., 1974. Registered architect, Colo., Calif., Idaho, Va., Utah, N.Mex., Ind., Nebr., Mo., Ga., Ariz., Tex. Project architect Gensler Assoc. Architects, Denver, 1976, Heinzman Assoc. Architects, Boulder, Colo., 1977, EZTH Architects, Boulder, 1978-79; prin. Knudson/Williams PC, Boulder, 1980-82, Faber, Williams & Brown, Boulder, 1982-86, John Williams & Assocs., Denver, 1986-97; John Williams Architecture P.C., 1997—. Panel chmn. U. Colo. World Affairs Conf.; vis. faculty U. Colo. Sch. Architecture and Planning, Coll. Environ. Design, 1986-91; dean's adv. bd. Coll. Arch. and Planning, 2000-04. Author (with others) State of Colorado architect licensing law, 1986. Commr. Downtown Boulder Mall Commn., 1985-88; bd. dirs. U. Colo. Fairway Club, 1986-88; mem. Gov.'s. Natural Hazard Mitigation Coun., State of Colo., 1990. Recipient Tchg. Honorarium, U. Colo. Coll. Architecture and Planning, 1977-80, 88, Excellence in Design and Planning award City of Boulder, 1981-82, Citation for Excellenc, WOOD Inc., 1982, 93, Disting. Profl. Svc. award Coll. Environ. Design U. Colo., 1988, James Sudler Svc. award AIA, Denver, 1998 Mem. AIA (sec. 1988, bd. dirs. Colo. North chpt. 1985-86, chair Colo. govtl. affairs com. 1995-98, Design award 1993, 2001, pres. 1990, sec. Colo. chpt. 1988, ednl. fund Fisher I traveling scholar 1988, state design conf. chair 1991, North chpt. Design award 1993, treas. Denver chpt. 1998, v.p. 1999, pres. edn. Colo. chpt. 2001, Disting. Svc. award Colo. chpt. 2001, Pres. Svc. award, 2004), Architects and Planners of Boulder (v.p. 1982), Nat. Coun. Architect Registration Bd., Nat. Golf Found. (sponsor), Kappa Sigma (chpt. pres. 1970). Avocations: golf, political history, fitness and health. Home: 1031 Turnberry Cir Louisville CO 80027-9594 Office: John Williams Architecture PC 350 Interlocken Blvd Ste 340 Broomfield CO 80021 Office Phone: 303-295-6190. Business E-Mail: johnw@jwarchitecture.com.

WILLIAMS, JOHN TOWNER, composer, conductor; b. LI, NY, Feb. 8, 1932; s. John and Esther Williams; m. Barbara Ruike, 1956 (dec. 1974); children: Jennifer, Mark, Joseph; m. Samantha Winslow, 1980. Student, UCLA; studied with Mario Castelnuovo-Tedesco, Los Angeles; student, Juilliard Sch.; studied with Madame Rosina Lhevinne, NYC; degree (hon.), Berklee Coll. Music, Boston, Northeastern U., Tufts U., U. So. Calif., Boston U., New Eng. Conservatory Music, Providence Coll. Pianist Columbia & Twentieth Century-Fox, 1956—; condr. Boston Pops Orch., 1980—93, laureate condr., 1993—; artist-in-residence Tanglewood Music Ctr., Boston, 1993—94. Guest condr. with orchestras including Cleveland Orch., Denver Symphony, Indianapolis Symphony, London Symphony Orch., Los Angeles Philharmonic, Montreal Orch., Philadelphia Orch., and Toronto Orch. Works include: composer (film scores) I Passed for White, 1960, Because They're Young, 1960, The Secret Ways, 1961, Bachelor Flat, 1962, Diamond Head, 1962, Gidget Goes to Rome, 1963, The Killers, 1964, John Goldfarb, Please Come Home, 1964, None But the Brave, 1965, How to Steal a Million, 1966, The Rare Breed, 1966, Not With My Wife, You Don't, 1966, The Plainsman, 1966, Penelope, 1966, A Guide for the Married Man, 1967, Valley of the Dolls, 1967 (Acad. award nominee), Fitzwilly, 1968, Sergeant Ryker, 1968, The Reivers, 1969 (Acad. award nominee), Daddy's Gone A-Hunting, 1969, Goodbye, Mr. Chips, 1969

(Acad. award nominee), The Story of A Woman, 1970, Fiddler on the Roof, 1971 (Acad. award for musical adaptation 1971), The Cowboys, 1972, The Poseidon Adventure, 1972 (Acad. award nominee), Images, 1972 (Acad. award nominee), Pete 'n' Tillie, 1972, The Paper Chase, 1973, The Long Goodbye, 1973, The Man Who Loved Cat Dancing, 1973, Cinderella Liberty, 1973 (Acad. award nominee), Tom Sawyer, 1973 (Acad. award nominee), Sugarland Express, 1974, Earthquake, 1974, The Towering Inferno, 1974 (Acad. award nominee), Conrack, 1974, Jaws, 1975 (Acad. award, Grammy award, Golden Globe award 1976), The Eiger Sanction, 1976, Family Plot, 1976, Midway, 1976, The Missouri Breaks, 1976, Raggedy Ann and Andy, 1977, Black Sunday, 1977, Star Wars, 1977 (Acad. award, 3 Grammy awards, Golden Globe award 1977), Close Encounters of the Third Kind, 1977 (2 Grammy awards, Acad. award nominee 1978), The Fury, 1978, Jaws II, 1978, Superman, 1978 (2 Grammy awards 1979), Meteor, 1979, Quintet, 1979, Dracula, 1979, "1941", 1979, The Empire Strikes Back, 1980 (2 Grammy awards, Acad. award nominee 1980), Raiders of the Lost Ark, 1981 (Grammy award, Acad. award nominee 1981), Heartbeeps, 1981, E.T., 1982 (Acad. award for best original score, 3 Grammy awards, Golden Globe award 1982), Monsignor, 1982, Yes, Giorgio, 1982 (Acad. award nominee), Superman III, 1983, Return of the Jedi, 1983 (Acad. award nominee), Indiana Jones and the Temple of Doom, 1984 (Acad. award nominee), The River, 1984 (Acad. award nominee), Space Camp, 1986, Emma's War, 1986, The Witches of Eastwick, 1987 (Acad. award nominee), Empire of the Sun, 1987 (Acad. award nominee), Jaws: The Revenge, 1987, Superman IV: The Quest for Peace, 1987, The Secret of My Success, 1987, The Accidental Tourist, 1988 (Acad. award nominee, Indiana Jones and the Last Crusade, 1989 (Acad. award nominee), Always, 1989, Born On The Fourth of July, 1989 (Acad. award nominee), Stanley and Iris, 1990, Presumed Innocent, 1990, Home Alone, 1990 (Acad. award nominee), Hook, 1991 (Acad. award nominee), JFK, 1991 (Acad. award nominee), Far and Away, 1992, Home Alone II, 1992, Jurassic Park, 1993, Schindler's List, 1993 (Acad. award 1993, Grammy award 1994), Sabrina, 1995 (Acad. award nominee for best original score 1996), Nixon, 1995 (Acad. award nominee 1996), Sleepers, 1996, Rosewood, 1997, The Lost World: Jurassic Park, 1997, Seven Years In Tibet, 1997 (Acad. award nominee), Amistad, 1997 (Acad. award nominee), Saving Private Ryan, 1998 (Acad. award nominee, Grammy award 1998), Stepmom, 1998, Star Wars Episode I: The Phantom Menace, 1999, Angela's Ashes, 1999 (Acad. award nominee, Grammy award 2000), The Patriot, 2000 (Acad. award nominee), Artificial Intelligence, 2001 (Acad. award nominee), Harry Potter and The Sorcerer's Stone, 2001 (Acad. award nominee), Minority Report, 2002, Star Wars Episode II: Attack Of The Clones, 2002, Harry Potter: The Chamber Of Secrets, 2002, Catch Me If You Can, 2002 (Acad. award nominee), Harry Potter: The Prisoner Of Azkaban, 2004, The Terminal, 2004, Star Wars Episode III: The Revenge of the Sith, 2005, War of the Worlds, 2005, Memoirs of a Geisha, 2005 (Broadcast Film Assn. award, 2006, Best Original Score-Motion Picture, Hollywood Fgn. Press Assn., Golden Globe award) 2006, Grammy award, 2007), Munich, 2005 (Grammy award, 2007), Indiana Jones and the Kingdom of the Crystal Skull, 2008 (Grammy award, 2009); composer music for songs including:(from Sabrina, lyrics by Alan and Marilyn Bergman) Moonlight, 1995 (Acad. award nominee 1996); composer:(TV programs) Heidi, 1969 (Emmy award), Jane Eyre, 1971 (Emmyaward), Masterpiece Theatre, 1971, Malcolm in the Middle, 2000, Smallville, 2001, (main theme) Jack & Bobby, 2004, others; composer numerous concert pieces and symphonies including Jubilee 350 Fanfare for the Boston Pops, 1980, theme to the 1984 Summer OlympicGames, Liberty Fanfare, 1987; recorded numerous albums with Boston Pops Orch. including Pops in Space, That's Entertainment (Pops on Broadway), Pops on the March, Pops Aroundthe World (Digital Overtures), Aisle Seat, Pops Out of This World, Boston Pops on Stage, America, the Dream Goes On; collaborator: (with Jessye Norman) With A Song in My Heart, Swing, Swing, Swing, Unforgettable; guest condr. major orchs. including London Symphony Orch., Cleve. Orch., Phila. Orch., Toronto Orch., Montreal Orch. Served with USAF, 1952-54. Recipient several gold and platinum records Rec. Industry Assn. Am., Kennedy Ctr. Honors, John F. Kennedy Ctr. Performing Arts, 2004. Composer of over seventy-five film scores. Office: Boston Symphony Orch 301 Mass Ave Boston MA 02115 also: The Gorfaine Schwartz Agency Inc 4111 W Alameda Ave Ste 509 Burbank CA 91505-4171*

WILLIAMS, JOY, writer; b. Chelmsford, Mass., Feb. 11, 1944; d. William Lloyd and Elisabeth (Thomas) Williams; m. Rust Hills; 1 child, Caitlin. MA magna cum laude, Marietta Coll., Ohio, 1963; MFA, U. Iowa, 1965. Rschr., data analyst USN, Siesta Key, Fla., 1967-69; now writer. Vis. instr. U. Houston, 1982, U. Fla., 1983, U. Calif., Irvine, 1984, U. Iowa, 1984, U. Ariz., 1987. Author: State of Grace, 1973, The Changeling, 1978, Taking Care, 1982, Breaking and Entering, 1988, Escapes, 1990, The Quick and the Dead, 2000 (Pulitzer Prize finalist, 2000), Ill Nature: Rants and Reflections on Humanity and Other Animals, 2001 (Rez Short Story award, 2002), The Florida Keys: A History & Guide (10th edit.), 2003, Honored Guest, 2004; contbr. short stories to mags. Recipient Nat. Mag. award for fiction, 1980; NEA grantee, 1973, Guggenheim fellow, 1974. Mem.: AAAL (Harold and Mildred Strauss Livings award 1993), Phi Beta Kappa. Democrat. Office: 1425 E magee Rd Tucson AZ 85718 also: Amanda Urban ICM 40 W 57th St New York NY 10019-4001

WILLIAMS, KENNETH SCOTT, entertainment company executive; b. Tulsa, Okla., Dec. 31, 1955; s. David Vorhees Williams and Mary Louise (Newell) Rose; m. Jann Catherine Wolfe, May 20, 1989; children: Catherine Eloise, Michael Holbrook. BA, Harvard Coll., 1978; MS, Columbia U., 1985. Bank officer Chase Manhattan Bank, NYC, 1978-82; asst. treas. Columbia Pictures Entertainment, NYC, 1982-84, v.p., treas., 1984-89, sr. v.p. fin. and adminstrn. Burbank, Calif., 1990-91; sr. v.p. corp. ops. Sony Pictures Entertainment, Culver City, Calif., 1991-95, exec. v.p., 1995-96; pres. Digital Studio divsn. Sony Pictures Entertainment, 1996-2000, Technicolor Digital Cinema, Burbank, Calif., 2002; pres., CEO Stan Lee Media, Inc., Encino, Calif., 2000—02; COO Ascent Media Group, Santa Monica, Calif., 2002—03, pres., CEO, 2003—06, investment adv. cons., 2007—; CEO Captive Media, Inc., 2007—. Past pres., bd. dirs. L.A. Conservancy; former chmn. Entertainment Tech. Ctr. U. So. Calif.; former trustee U. Calif., Riverside; bd. dirs. L.A. Music Ctr., L.A. Pub. Access TV Channel 36, chmn. bd.; bd. dirs. L.A. Master Chorale; mem. Blue Hill Troupe, NYC, 1979—. Mem. N.Y. Soc. Securities Analysts, Acad. Television Arts and Scis., Fin. Execs. Inst. (v.p.), Acad. Motion Picture Arts & Scis., Digital Coast Roundtable (bd. dirs.), Harvard Club So. Calif. (pres., bd. dirs.), Beta Gamma Sigma. Home: 457 Cuesta Way Los Angeles CA 90077-3434 Personal E-mail: kenneth_s_williams@hotmail.com. Business E-Mail: kwilliam@captivemediainc.com.

WILLIAMS, LAWRENCE ERNEST, physicist; b. Youngstown, Ohio, Nov. 29, 1937; s. William Karapandza and Dorothy (Radulovich) Williams; m. Sonia Bell Bredmeyer; children: Erica, Beverley. BS in Physics, Carnegie-Mellon U., 1959; MS, U. Minn., 1962, PhD, 1965. Asst. prof. physics Western Ill. U., Macomb, 1968-70; asst. prof. radiology U. Minn., Mpls., 1973-78, NIH fellow, 1971-73, assoc. prof., 1978-80; imaging physicist City of Hope, Duarte, Calif., 1980—, prof., 2002—. Adj. assoc. prof. UCLA, 1982-92, adj. prof., 1992—; prof. Eurotech. Rsch. U., Palo Alto, Calif., 1983—; cons. Jet Propulsion Lab, Pasadena, Calif., 1981-84; mem. clin. oncology study sect. NIH, 2000-2003. Co-author: Biophysical Science, rev. 2d edit., 1979; editor Nuclear Medical Physics, 1987, assoc. editor, Med. Physics, 2005—; contbr. articles to med. jours.; patentee, inventor new method of abscess imaging; discoverer excited states in nuclear mass three system, mathematical model of tumor uptake of tracers; developer of a method to evaluate brake radiation doses; patentee, co-discoverer of tumor targeting by liposomes. Treas. United Meth. Ch., West Covina, Calif., 1982-83. Westinghouse Sci. Talent Search scholar, 1955, R.J. Wean scholar, 1957; NSF fellow U. Minn., 1961-62. Fellow Am. Coll. Angiology; mem. Soc. Nuclear Medicine (Gold medal exhibit 1983), Am. Assn. Physicists in Medicine, N.Y. Acad. Scis., Soc. for Computer Applications in Radiology, Sigma Xi. Methodist. Avocations: furniture refinishing, music, sketching. Office: City of Hope Med Ctr 1500 Duarte Rd Duarte CA 91010-3000 Office Phone: 626-359-8111 x 61488. E-mail: lwilliams@coh.org.

WILLIAMS, LEONA RAE, small business owner, consultant; b. Fairfield, Nebr., July 1, 1928; d. Melton M. and Helga D. (Sorensen) Brown; m. Eugene F. Williams, June 6, 1946; 1 child, Dennis D. Grad. high sch., Fairfield. Owner Alice Rae Apparel Shop, Tucson, 1953—96, second location, 1967—96, Green Valley, Ariz., 1976—93, Sun City, Ariz., 1979—96; ret., 1996; owner Boutique on Wheels, 2001—, prin., 2001—. Cons. in field. Sponsor Distributive Edn. Program, 1978-82; coord. fashion shows Am. Cancer Soc., Tucson, 1987, 88, 89. Mem. DAR, Exec. Women's Internat. (chpt. pres. 1994), Mchts. Assn. (pres. 1987-89), Soroptomists, C. of C. Better Bus. Bur., Christian Women. Baptist. Personal E-mail: leonagene@msn.com.

WILLIAMS, LINDA C., lawyer; b. Portsmouth, Va., Apr. 4, 1956; BA with high honors, Univ. Va., 1978, JD, 1982. Bar: Calif. 1984. Law clk. Judge Albert Tate, Jr., US Ct. Appeals (5th cir.), New Orleans; ptnr., head Corp. Securities & Fin. Inst. group Pillsbury Winthrop Shaw Pittman, San Francisco. Instr. Univ. San Francisco Sch. Law. Mem.: Order of the Coif. Office: Pillsbury Winthrop Shaw Pittman 50 Fremont St San Francisco CA 94105 Office Phone: 415-983-7334. Office Fax: 415-983-1200. Business E-Mail: linda.williams@pillsburylaw.com.

WILLIAMS, MARION LESTER, government agency administrator; b. Abilene, Tex., Dec. 1, 1933; s. Martin Lester and Eddie Faye (Wilson) W.; m. Johnnie Dell Ellinger, Dec. 14, 1957; children: Tammy Dawn Cole, Pamela DeAnn Rittenbush. BS, Tex. A&M U., 1956; MS, U. N.Mex., 1967; PhD, Okla. State U., 1971. Test engr. Sandia Nat. Labs., Albuquerque, 1959-61; weapons sys. engr. Naval Weapons Evaluation Facility, Albuquerque, 1961-66; ops. rsch. analyst Joint Chiefs of Staff/Joint Task Force II, Albuquerque, 1966-68; chief reliability div. Field Command DNA, Albuquerque, 1969-71; prin. scientist SHAPE Tech. Ctr., The Hague, Netherlands, 1971-74; chief tech. advisor HQ AF Test & Evaluation Ctr., Albuquerque, 1974-81; chief scientist HQ AF Operational Test & Evaluation Ctr., Albuquerque, 1981-89, tech. dir., 1989—. Vis. adv. com. Okla. State U., Stillwater, 1988—; adv. com. U. N.Mex., Albuquerque, 1985—. Editor T&E Tech. Jour., 1987—; contbr. articles to profl. jour. Sci. advisor N.Mex. Sci. & Tech. Oversigh Com., Albuquerque, 1988; bd. advisors U. N.Mex. Cancer Ctr., 1987—; bd. dirs. Contact Albuquerque, 1986-87. 1st lt. USAF 1956-59. Recipient Presdl. Rank award, 1987, 92. Fellow Mil. Ops. Rsch. Soc. (pres. 1982-83, bd. dir. 1976-81, Wanner award 1991), Internat. Test & Evaluation Ctr. (bd. dirs. 1984-86, 88-90, v.p. 1990, pres. 1992-95), Ops. Rsch. Soc. Am., Tau Beta Pi, Phi Eta Sigma, Alpha Pi Mu, Sigma Tau, Kappa Mu Epsilon. Baptist. Avocations: skiing, computers. Home: 1416 Stagecoach Ln SE Albuquerque NM 87123-4429 Office: HQ AF Operational Test Ctr Kirtland AFB Albuquerque NM 87117-0001 E-mail: mlw505@yahoo.com.

WILLIAMS, MATT(HEW) (DERRICK), former professional baseball player; b. Bishop, Calif., Nov. 28, 1965; Student, U. Nev., Las Vegas. With San Francisco Giants, 1987-96, Cleveland Indians, 1997, Ariz. Diamondbacks, 1998—2003. Player Nat. League All-Star Team, 1990, 94. Recipient Gold Glove award, 1991, 93, 94, Silver Slugger award, 1990, 93-94; named to Sporting News Nat. League All-Star team, 1990, 93-94, Coll. All-Am. team Sporting News, 1986; Nat. League RBI Leader, 1990.

WILLIAMS, MICHAEL ANTHONY, lawyer; b. Mandan, ND, Sept. 14, 1932; s. Melvin Douglas and Lucille Ann (Gavin) Williams; m. Marjorie Ann Harrer, Aug. 25, 1962 (div. 1989); children: Ann Margaret, Douglas Raymond, David Michael; m. Dorothy Ruth Hand, 1989. BA, Coll. of St. Thomas, 1954; LLB, Harvard U., 1959. Bar: Colo. 1959, N.D. 1959, U.S. Dist. Ct. Colo. 1959, U.S. Ct. Appeals (10th cir.) 1959, U.S. Supreme Ct. 1967. Assoc. Sherman & Howard and predecessor Dawson, Nagel, Sherman & Howard, Denver, 1959—65, ptnr., 1965—91; pres. Williams, Youle & Koenigs, P.C., Denver, 1991—2002; prin. Michael A. Williams LLC, Denver, 2002—. Served as 1st lt. USAF, 1955—57. Mem.: ABA, Coll. Comml. Arbitrators, Colo. Bar Assn., Am. Law Inst., Colo. Bar Found., Am. Bd. Trial Advs., Am. Coll. Trial Lawyers. Office: 950 17th St Ste 1800 Denver CO 80202-2811 Office Phone: 303-785-7999. Business E-Mail: mwilliams@wyk.com.

WILLIAMS, MICHELLE, actress; b. Kalispell, Mont., Sept. 9, 1980; d. Larry and Carla; 1 child, Matilda Rose. Actor: (films) Lassie, 1994, Species, 1995, Timemaster, 1995, A Thousand Acres, 1997, Halloween H20: 20 Years Later, 1998, Dick, 1999, But I'm a Cheerleader, 1999, Perfume, 2001, Prozac Nation, 2001, Me Without You, 2001, The United States of Leland, 2003, The Station Agent, 2003, A Hole in One, 2004, Imaginary Heroes, 2004, Land of Plenty, 2004, The Baxter, 2005, Brokeback Mountain, 2005 (Critics Choice award, best supporting actress, Broadcast Film Critics Assn., 2006), The Hawk is Dying, 2006, I'm Not There, 2007, Incendiary, 2008, Deception, 2008, Synecdoche, New York, 2008, Wendy and Lucy, 2008; (TV series) Raising Caines, 1995, Dawson's Creek, 1998—2003; (TV films) My Son Is Innocent, 1996, Killing Mr. Griffin, 1997, If These Walls Could Talk 2, 2000. Named one of 21 Hottest Stars Under 21, Teen People mag., 1999. Avocations: reading, boxing. Office: Creative Artists Agency 2000 Avenue Of The Stars Los Angeles CA 90067-4700

WILLIAMS, MIKEL HOWARD, magistrate judge; b. Lewiston, Idaho, Jan. 2, 1946; m. Lorette Biaggne Williams; children: Dayna, Holly. BA, U. Idaho, LLB, 1969. Bar: Idaho 1969, U.S. Dist. Ct. Idaho 1969, U.S. Ct. Appeals (9th cir.) 1974, U S. Ct. Mil. Appeals 1969, U.S. Supreme Ct. 1969. Asst. U.S. atty. Dist. of Idaho, 1973-77; ptnr. Collins, Manley & Williams, 1977-84; magistrate judge U.S. Dist. Ct., Boise, 1984—. Author in field. Served to lt. col. JAGC, U.S. Army, 1969-93. Rocky Mountain Mineral Law Found. scholar, 1967. Mem. Idaho State Bar. Office: US Dist Ct 550 W Fort St Msc 039 Boise ID 83724-0001

WILLIAMS, NANCY, lawyer; b. Kansas City, Mo., Jan. 2, 1945; BS in Journalism, Northwestern U., 1967; JD magna cum laude, U. Mich., 1980. Bar: Wash. 1981, US Ct. Appeals (9th Cir.), US Dist. Ct. (We. Dist.) Wash., US Dist. Ct. (Ea. Dist.) Wash. Volunteer PeaceCorp, 1967—69; pub. info. officer US Dept. Labor, 1973—78; ptnr. Perkins Coie LLP, Seattle, mem. exec. com., chmn. Labor & Employment Practice Area Seattle Office. Co-editor: Washington Employment Law Letter, 1994—; rev. asst. Equal Employment Law Update, 1996, 1997, 1998; contbg. editor: (rev. asst.) Equal Employment Law Update, 2003—, Employment Discrimination Law, 1996. Mem.: ABA (Labor & Litig. Sect.). Office: Perkins Coie LLP 1201 Third Ave Ste 4800 Seattle WA 98101-3099 Office Phone: 206-359-8473. Office Fax: 206-359-9000. Business E-Mail: nwilliams@perkinscoie.com.

WILLIAMS, NORMA JEAN, lawyer; b. NY, Sept. 19, 1952; d. Arthur Robert and Mildred (McDaniel) Williams; m. Bruce Ephraim Goldstein, Oct. 28, 1989. BA magna cum laude, Wesleyan U., Middletown, Conn., 1974; JD, U. Calif., Berkeley, 1977. Bar: Calif. 1977, US Dist. Ct. (no. dist. Calif.) 1977, US Dist. Ct. (so. dist. Calif.) 1991. Assoc. Crosby, Heafey, Roach & May, Oakland, Calif., 1977-81; assoc. counsel Crocker Nat. Bank, San Francisco, 1981-82; assoc. Berger, Kahn, Shafton & Moss, LA, 1983-84, Brown, Winfield & Canzoneri, LA, 1984-85; ptnr. Williams & Assocs, LA, 1985—98, 2003—; of counsel Arter & Hadol, 1999—2001, Reed Smith, 2001—03. Mem. Urban Land Inst., LA; mem. faculty Practicing Law Inst., NYC. Contbr. articles to profl. jours. Recipient Cert. Appreciation City of LA, 1987. Mem. State Bar Calif. (mem. exec. com. real property law sect. 1990-93, chair real property sect. 1993-96, so. Calif. co-chair fin. sub-sect. real property law sect. 1988-90), LA County Bar Assn. (exec. com. 1993-, chair real property sect., 2006-2007, bd. trustees, 2007-2008), Fin. Lawyers Conf., Am. Coll. Real Estate Lawyers (hon.), Am. Coll. Mortgage Attys. (bd. regents 2004-, legis. com. chair). Office: Williams & Assocs 555 W 5th St Ste 3100 Los Angeles CA 90013 Office Phone: 213-996-8464. Office Fax: 213-947-1799. E-mail: njwilliams@willassoc.com.

WILLIAMS, PAT, former congressman, professor; b. Helena, Mont., Oct. 30, 1937; m. Carol Griffith, 1965; children: Griff, Erin, Whitney. Student, U. Mont., 1956-57, William Jewell U.; BA, U. Denver, 1961; postgrad., Western Mont. Coll.; LLD (hon.), Carroll Coll., Montana Coll. of Mineral Sci. and Tech. Mem. Mont. Ho. of Reps., 1967, 69; exec. dir. Hubert Humphrey Presdl. campaign, Mont., 1968; exec. asst. to US Rep. John Melcher, 1969-71; mem. Gov.'s Employment and Tng. Council, 1972-78, Mont. Legis. Reapportionment Commn., 1973; coord. Mont. Family Edn. Program, 1971—78; co-chmn. Jimmy Carter Presdl. campaign, Mont., 1976; mem. US Congress from 1st Mont. Dist., 1979-96; sr. fellow, regional policy assoc. O'Connor Ctr. for the Rocky Mountain West, Missoula, Mont. Ranking mem. postsecondary edn. subcom; mem. adv. commn. for tribal colleges; Walters Capps meml. lectr., Nat. Fedn. State Humanities Coun., 2001. Coordinator Mont. Family Edn. Program, 1971-78. Served with U.S. Army, 1960-61; Served with Army N.G., 1962-69. Mem. Mont. Fedn. Tchrs. Lodges: Elks, Nat. Assn. Governing Bds. Universities and Colleges (mem. bd. dirs.), Nat. Assn. Job Corps USA Edn. Democrat. Home: 3533 Lincoln Hills Pt Missoula MT 59802-3381 Office: U Montana O Connor Ctr Rocky Mtn W Milw Sta 2nd Fl Missoula MT 59812-0001 Business E-Mail: williams@crmw.org.

WILLIAMS, PATRICIA C., federal judge; Apptd. bankruptcy judge ea. dist. U.S. Dist. Ct. Wash., 1997. Office: 904 W Riverside Ave Ste 304 Spokane WA 99201-1011 Fax: 509-454-5636.

WILLIAMS, PAUL HAMILTON, composer, singer; b. Omaha, Sept. 19, 1940; s. Paul Hamilton and Bertha Mae (Burnside) W.; m. Hilda Keenan Wynn, Apr. 16, 1993. Grad. high sch. Assoc. A & M Records, 1970—; pres. Hobbitron Enterprises, 1973—. Songwriter: (with Roger Nichols) Out in the Country, 1969, Talk it Over in the Morning, 1970, We've Only Just Begun, 1970, (with Craig Doerge) Cried Like A Baby, 1970, (with Jack S. Conrad) Family of Man, 1971, Rainy Days and Mondays, 1971, An Old Fashioned Love Song, 1972, Family of Man, 1972, Let Me Be the One, 1972, (with John Williams) You're So Nice to Be Around, 1973 (Acad. award nomination best song), The Hell of It, 1974, (with Barbara Streisand) Evergreen, 1976 (Acad. award best song, 1976, Golden Globe award 1977, Grammy award 1977), (with Michael Colombier) Wings, 1977, (with Charles Fox) My Fair Share, 1977, (with Kenny Ascher) The Rainbow Connection, 1979; film appearances include The Loved One, 1964, The Chase, 1966, Planet of the Apes, 1967, Watermelon Man, 1970, The Phantom of the Paradise, 1974 (also score 1974, Acad. award nomination best score 1974), Smokey and the Bandit, 1977, The Cheap Detective, 1978, The Muppet Movie, 1979, Stone Cold Dead, 1980, Smokey and the Bandit II, 1980, Smokey and the Bandit III, 1983, The Chill Factor, 1990, The Doors, 1991, A Million to Juan, 1994, Headless Body in Topless Bar, 1995; wrote songs for: The Getaway, 1972, (with John Williams) The Man Who Loved Cat Dancing, 1972, (with Williams) Cinderella Liberty, 1973, (with John Barry) The Day of The Locust, 1975; wrote scores for: (with Ascher) A Star is Born, 1976 (Golden Globe award best score 1976), Bugsy Malone, 1976, One on One, 1977, The End, 1978, (with Ascher) The Muppet Movie, 1979, Agatha, 1979, (with Jerry Goldsmith) The Secret of Nihm, 1982, Ishtar, 1987, The Muppet Christmas Carol, 1992; TV scores include (series) The McLean Stevenson Show, 1976-77, (with Charles Fox) The Love Boat, 1977-86, Sugar Time!, 1977-78, It Takes Two, 1982-83, (movies) No Place to Run, 1972, Emmet Otter's Jug Band Christmas, 1980; numerous TV appearances including 4 NBC Midnight spls; co-host on: numerous TV appearances including Mike Douglas show; actor, voice (TV series) Batman: Gotham Knights, 1997; other TV appearances including, Merv Griffin, Jonathan Winters, others; albums include Simeday Man: Just An Old-Fashioned Love Song, 1971, Life Goes On, 1972, A Little Bit of Love, 1974, Here Comes Inspiration, 1974, Ordinary Fools, 1975, Classics, 1977, A Little on the Windy Side, 1979, Crazy For Loving You, 1981. Co-recipient Best Songwriter Grammy award, 1977. Mem. ASCAP, Nat. Acad. Rec. Arts and Scis. (trustee) Office: 11601

Wilshire Blvd # 2350 Los Angeles CA 90025 also: Tugboat Prodns 4508 Noeline Ave Encino CA 91436-3336 Office: Robert Light Agency PO Box 562 Beverly Hills CA 90213-0562

WILLIAMS, QUENTIN CHRISTOPHER, geophysicist, educator; b. Wilmington, Del., Jan. 1, 1964; s. Ferd Elton and Anne Katherine W.; m. Elise Barbara Knittle, Dec. 19, 1987; children: Byron Frederick, Alanna Katherine, Lynette Barbara, Benjamin Ferd. AB, Princeton U., 1983; PhD, U. Calif., Berkeley, 1988. Rsch. geophysicist Inst. of Tectonics, U. Calif., Santa Cruz, 1988-91; asst. prof. dept. earth sci. U. Calif., Santa Cruz, 1991-95, assoc. prof. dept. earth sci., 1995-99, prof. dept. earth sci., 1999—. Contbr. articles to profl. jours. Presdl. Faculty fellow, 1993-98. Fellow Am. Geophys. Union (Macelwane medal 2000), Mineral. Soc. Am. (award 2000); mem. Am. Phys. Soc. Office: U Calif Santa Cruz Dept Earth Sciences Santa Cruz CA 95064 Business E-Mail: qwilliams@pmc.ucsc.edu.

WILLIAMS, QUINN PATRICK, lawyer; b. Evergreen Park, Ill., May 6, 1951; s. William Albert and Jeanne Marie (Quinlan) Williams; children: Michael Ryan, Mark Reed, Kelly Elizabeth. BBA, U. Wis., 1972; JD, U. Ariz., 1974. Bar: Ariz. 1975, US Dist. Ct. Ariz. 1976, NY 1984. V.p., sec., gen. counsel Combined Comm. Corp., Phoenix, 1975-80; sr. v.p. legal and adminstrn. Swensen's Inc., Phoenix, 1980-86; ptnr. Winston & Strawn, Phoenix, 1985—89, Snell & Wilmer, Phoenix, 1989—2002; shareholder Greenberg Traurig, 2002—; pres. Enterprise network, 2001. Bd. dirs. Ariz. Venture Capital Conf., 1993—2000, Ariz. Tech. Coun., 2001—; co-chmn. Gov.'s Small Bus. Adv. Exec. Coun., 1996—2000; vice-chair Gov. Regulatory Coun., 1995—97; sec. GSPED High Tech. Cluster, 1993—; chair, bd. dirs. Greater Phoenix Econ. Coun., 1996—2000; mem. exec. com. A2Tech Coun., 2002—; mem. Gov.'s Coun. Innovation and Tech., 2003—. With USAR, 1967—73. Mem.: ABA, NY Bar Assn., Maricopa County Bar Assn., State Bar Ariz., Internat. Franchise Assn., Scotsdale C. of C. (bd. dirs. 2003—), Paradise Valley Country Club, Scottsdale Charros. Office: Greenberg Traurig 2375 E Camelback Rd Ste 700 Phoenix AZ 85016-9000 Office Phone: 602-445-8344. Business E-Mail: williamsq@gtlaw.com.

WILLIAMS, RALPH CHESTER, JR., physician, educator; b. Washington, Feb. 17, 1928; s. Ralph Chester and Annie (Perry) W.; m. Mary Elizabeth Adams, June 23, 1951; children: Cathy, Frederick (dec.), John (dec.), Michael, Ann AB with distinction, Cornell U., 1950, MD, 1954; MD (hon.), U. Lund, Sweden, 1991. Diplomate Am. Bd. Internal Medicine. Intern Mass. Gen. Hosp., Boston, 1954-55, asst. resident in internal medicine, 1955-56; resident in internal medicine N.Y. Hosp., 1956-57; chief resident Mass. Gen. Hosp., Boston, 1959-60; guest investigator Rockefeller Inst., NYC, 1961-63; physician in internal medicine and rheumatology, 1963—; assoc. prof. U. Minn., Mpls., 1963-68, prof., 1968-69; prof., chmn. dept. medicine U. N.Mex., Albuquerque, 1969-88; Schott prof. rheumatology and medicine U. Fla., Gainesville, 1988-98; with rheumatology dept. U. N.Mex. Sch. Medicine, Albuquerque, 1998, emeritus prof. medicine, 1998—. Assoc. editor: Jour. Lab. and Clin. Medicine, 1966-69; mem. editl. bd.: Arthritis and Rheumatism, 1968—; contbr. articles to profl. jours. Capt. USAF, 1957—59. Recipient Regents' Meritorious Svc. award, U. N.Mex., 2003. Master Am. Coll. Rheumatology (Gold medal 2004); fellow ACP; mem. Am. Assn. Immunology, Assn. Am. Physicians, Am. Fedn. Clin. Rsch., Am. Soc. Clin. Investigation, Ctrl. Soc. Clin. Rsch., Western Soc. Clin. Investigation, Phi Beta Kappa, Alpha Omega Alpha. Achievements include research in immunologic processes and connective tissue diseases. Home: 624 E Alameda St Apt 13 Santa Fe NM 87501-2293 Office: Ste 400 1650 Hosp Dr Santa Fe NM 87505 Personal E-mail: coolypatch22@cybermesa.com.

WILLIAMS, RICHARD THOMAS, lawyer; b. Evergreen Park, Ill., Jan. 14, 1945; s. Raymond Theodore and Elizabeth Dorothy (Williams) W. AB with honors, Stanford U., 1967, MBA, JD, Stanford U., 1972. Bar: Calif. 1972, U.S. Supreme Ct. 1977. Assoc.,then ptnr. Kadison Pfaelzer Woodard Quinn & Rossi, LA, 1972-87; ptnr. Whitman & Ransom, 1987-93, Whitman, Breed, Abbott & Morgan, LA, 1993-2000, Holland & Knight, LLP, LA, 2000—. Contbg. editor Oil and Gas Analyst, 1978-84. Mem. ABA, L.A. County Bar Assn. Office: Holland & Knight LLP 633 W 5th St Los Angeles CA 90071-2005 Office Phone: 213-896-2410. Business E-Mail: richard.williams@hklaw.com.

WILLIAMS, ROBERT E., lawyer; BA with highest honors, U. Calif., Santa Barbara, 1973; JD, Harvard U., 1976. Bar: Calif. 1976. Ptnr. Fin. and Bankruptcy Practice Group Sheppard, Mullin, Richter & Hampton LLP, LA. Mem.: Am. College of Real Estate Lawyers, Phi Beta Kappa. Office: Sheppard, Mullin, Richter & Hampton LLP 48th Fl 333 S Hope St Los Angeles CA 90071 Office Phone: 213-617-4169. Office Fax: 213-620-1398. Business E-Mail: rwilliams@sheppardmullin.com.

WILLIAMS, ROBERT STONE, protective services official; b. Mathews, Va., Jan. 22, 1952; s. Charles H. and Anne (Stone) W.; m. Danielle Williams, July 1987. AAS, Rowan Tech. Inst., 1972; BS in Fire Protection and Safety Engring, Okla. State U., 1975, MBA, 1976. Adminstrv. specialist Oklahoma City Fire Dept., 1977-79; dep. fire chief Clovis Fire Dept., N.Mex., 1979-82; fire chief Billings Fire Dept., Mont., 1982-88, City of Spokane, Wash., 1988—. Mem. Wash. State Bldg. Code Coun., 1989-94; bd. dirs. Salvation Army, Billings, 1984-85, Am. Heart Internat. Fire Code Inst., 1993-94, 94-95, mem., 1990—. Named Fireperson Yr. Billings Downtown Exchange Club, 1988. Mem. Western Fire Chiefs Assn. (1st v.p. 1984-85, pres. 1985-86), Internat. Assn. Fire Chiefs, Nat. Fire protection Assn., Curry County Jaycees (v.p. 1981-82, Jaycee of Yr. 1982), Billings Jaycees (bd. dirs. 1983-87, v.p. cmty. devel. 1985, Outstanding Jaycee 1983, Disting. Svc. award 1985), Mont. Jaycees (treas. 1986-87, speak-up program mgr. 1986-87, Outstanding Young Montanan award 1985-86). Roman Catholic. Office: Spokane Fire Dept W 44 Riverside Ave Spokane WA 99201-0114

WILLIAMS, ROBERTA GAY, pediatric cardiologist, educator; b. Rocky Mount, NC, Oct. 23, 1941; BS, Duke U., 1963; MD, U. N.C., 1968. Diplomate Am. Bd. Pediats. (mem. com. ofcl. examiners 1985—, bd. dirs. and rep. sub-bd. chmn. com. 1992—, mem. exec. com. 1993—), Am. Bd. Pediatric Cardiology (chmn. 1991-92, cons. 1993). Med.-pediat. intern N.C. Meml. Hosp., Chapel Hill, 1968-69; pediat. resident Columbia Presbyn. Med. Ctr., N.Y., 1969-70; fellow in cardiology Children's Hosp. Med. Ctr., Boston, 1970-73, from asst. in cardiology to assoc. in cardiology, 1973-75, sr. assoc. in cardiology, 1976-82; from instr. pediats. to asst. prof. pediats. Harvard Med. Sch.-Children's Hosp., Boston, 1973-82; assoc. prof. pediats. UCLA Med. Ctr., 1982-86, chief divsn. pediat. cardiology, 1982-95, prof. pediats., 1986-95; chmn. pediat. U. N.C. Sch. Medicine, Chapel Hill, 1995-2000, U. So. Calif., LA, 2000—; v.p. pediat. and acad. affairs Children's Hosp. L.A., 2000—. Attending physician Cardiac Med. Svcs., Children's Hosp. Med. Ctr., Boston, 1974, cardiology cons. Cardiothoracic Surgery Svc., 1974, med. dir. Cardiovasc. Surgery ICU, 1974-79, dir. Cardiac Graphic Lab. and Cost Ctr., 1977-82, mem. com. neonatal ICU, 1978-79, v.p. med. staff, 1980-81; cons. FDA, 1998—; chmn. pediatric cardiac svcs. subcom. N.Y. State Cardiac Adv. Com., 1996—; mem. adv. coun. Nat. Heart, Lung and Blood Inst., 1999—2003; chair pediatric cardiac svcs. com., cardiac adv. com. N.Y. State Dept. Health, 1995—, mem. exec. com. cardiac adv. com., 1995—; seminar leader in field. Mem. editl. bd. Pediat. Cardiology, 1979, Circulation, 1983-91, Am. Jour. Cardiology, 1984-91, Jour. Applied Cardiology, 1985, Clin. Cardiology, 1988, Internat. Jour. Cardiology, 1992-95, Archives of Pediats. and Adolescent Medicine, 1994—; editl. cons. Jour. Am. Coll. Cardiology, 1992-94. Mem. exec. coun. cardiovasc. disease in the young Am. Heart Assn., 1979-85, mem. subcom. congenital cardiac defects, 1980-82, subcom. nominating com., 1982-83; mem. Am. Heart Assn.-Greater L.A. affiliate, 1983—, exec. com. and rsch. com., 1984—, judge young investigator competition, 1984, mem. program com., 1986-90, v.p. med.-exec. com., 1991-92, pres.-elect, 1992-93, and numerous other coms. Fellow Am. Coll. Cardiology (allied health profls. com. 1984-87, mem. physician workforce adv. com. 1988-94, mem. manpower adv. com. 1988—, mem. extramural continuing edn. com. Heart House 1990—, gov. So. Calif. chpt. 1994—, pres. Calif. chpt. 1994—, govt. rels. com., 1998—, trustee 2001-06), Am. Acad. Pediats. (sec. exec. com. sect., mem. com. on fetus and newborn 1985-88, mem. exec. com. sect. on cardiology 1985—, chmn. program com. 1988-89, mem. subcom. Am. Heart Assn. task force on assessment of diagnosis and therapeutic cardiovasc. procedures 1989, chair sect. cardiology 1989, mem. mem. coun. on sects. mgmt. com. 1995—); mem. Soc. for Pediat. Rsch., Am. Pediat. Soc. (dept. chair 1995, exec. com. 1997), Am. Soc. Echocardiography (mem. exec. com. 1975-78, bd. dirs. 1976-80, treas. exec. coun. com. 1981-83, steering com. Future of Pediatric Edn. Task Force, 1996-99, chmn. Future of Pediatric Subsplty. Workgroup, 1996-99. Avocations: photography, hiking. Office: Childrens Hosp LA MS 71 4650 Sunset Blvd Los Angeles CA 90029-2106 Home Phone: 818-952-7193; Office Phone: 323-669-2303. E-mail: rwilliams@chla.usc.edu.

WILLIAMS, ROBIN, actor, comedian; b. Chgo., July 21, 1951; s. Mr. and Mrs. Robert W.; m. Valerie Velardi, June 4, 1978 (div. 1988); 1 child, Zachary; m. Marsha Garces, Apr. 30, 1989 (separated Mar. 21, 2008); children: Zelda, Cody. Attended, Claremont Men's Coll., Marin Coll., Juilliard Sch., NYC. Started as stand-up comedian in San Francisco clubs, including Holy City Zoo, The Boardinghouse; actor: (TV series) Mork and Mindy, 1978-82; (films) Popeye, 1980, The World According to Garp, 1982, The Survivors, 1983, Moscow on the Hudson, 1984, The Best of Times, 1986, Club Paradise, 1986, Seize the Day, 1986, Good Morning Vietnam, 1987 (Golden Globe award 1988, Acad. Award nominee for best actor), The Adventures of Baron Munchausen, 1988, Dead Poets Society, 1989 (Best Actor nomination Golden Globe award, 1994, nominated best actor Acad. award), Cadillac Man, 1990, Awakenings, 1990, Dead Again, 1991, The Fisher King, 1991 (Golden Globe award, Acad. award nominee for best actor 1991), Dead Again, 1991, Hook, 1991, (voice only) Aladdin, 1992 (Spl. Achievement award Hollywood Fgn. Press, Nat. Bd. Rev. 1992), Toys, 1992, Mrs. Doubtfire, 1993 (Golden Globe award for Best Actor in a Musical or Comedy, 1994), Nine Months, 1995, Jumanji, 1995, The BirdCage, 1996, Jack, 1996, The Secret Agent, 1996, Hamlet, 1996, Deconstructing Harry, 1997, Father's Day, 1997, Flubber, 1997, Good Will Hunting, 1997, What Dreams May Come, 1998, Patch Adams, 1998, Bicentennial Man, 1999, Jakob the Liar, 1999, (voice only) A.I.: Artificial Intelligence, 2001, One Hour Photo, 2002, Death to Smoochy, 2002, Insomnia, 2002, The Final Cut, 2004, The House of D, 2004, Noel, 2004, (voice only) Robots, 2005, RV, 2006, The Night Listener, 2006, Man of the Year, 2006, (voice only) Happy Feet, 2006, Night at the Museum, 2006, License to Wed, 2007, August Rush, 2007, World's Greatest Dad, 2009, Shrink, 2009; (TV appearances) Laugh-In, 1977, Eight Is Enough, 1977, America 2-Night, 1978, Happy Days, 1978, '79, Out of the Blue, 1979, Homicide: Life on the Street, 1994, Friends, 1997, L.A. Doctors, 1999, Life with Bonnie, 2003, Law & Order: Special Victims Unit, 2008 (Favorite Scene-Stealing Guest Star, People's Choice Awards, 2009); theatre: Waiting for Godot, 1988; performer: (comedy albums) Reality, What a Concept, 1979 (Grammy award), Throbbing Python of Love, A Night at the Met (Grammy award); host Comic Relief, 1986; (comedy specials) ABC Presents a Royal Gala, 1988 (Emmy award, 1988), Carol, Carl, Whoopi & Robin, 1987 (Emmy award), Robin Williams: Live at the Met, 1986, Robin Williams Live, 1986, Comic Relief, 1986, Young Comedians All Star Reunion, 1988, Robin Williams: Live on Broadway, 2002 (Emmy nomination, Grammy award, 2003); host, Shakespeare: The Animated Tales, 1993 (CableAce Award, Best Entertainment Host) Recipient Golden Apple award Hollywood Women's Press Club, ACE award, Am. Comedy award, 1987, 88, Grammy award for best comedy rec., 1987, Man of Yr. award Hasty Pudding Theatricals, 1989, People's Choice award Favorite Comedy Motion Picture Actor, 1994, ShoWest Conv. award Male Star of Yr., 1994, Cecil B. DeMille award, Hollywood Fgn. Press, 2005, Hollywood Career Achievement award Hollywood Awards, 2006, Favorite Funny Male Star, People's Choice Award, 2007, 2008. Office: 1 Blackfield Dr Ste 409 Belvedere Tiburon CA 94920

WILLIAMS, ROGER STEWART, physician; b. San Diego, Feb. 15, 1941; s. Manley Samuel and Ethelyn Mae W.; children: Roger S., Karen E., David G., Sarah E. MD cum laude, Emory U., 1966. Diplomate Am. Bd. Psychiatry and Neurology. Intern, Grady Hosp., Atlanta, 1966-67. Med. resident Emory U., Atlanta, 1966-68; resident neurology Mass. Gen. Hosp., Boston, 1970-73, assoc. neurologist, 1973-87; assoc. prof. neurology Harvard Med. Sch., Boston, 1977-87; neurologist Billings (Mont.) Clinic, 1987-97; adj. prof. Mont. State U., Bozeman. Contbr. articles to profl. jours. Served to lt. comdr. USN, 1968-70. Kennedy fellow Kennedy Found., Washington, 1973-75; NIMH grantee, Bethesda, Md., 1979-87. Fellow Am. Acad. Neurology; mem. AMA, Mont. Med. Assn., Alpha Omega Alpha.

WILLIAMS, RONALD DEAN, minister, religious organization administrator; b. Decatur, Ill., Oct. 23, 1940; s. Henry Lawrence and Ella Loudica Williams; children: Scott Allan, Mark Lawrence, Derek James; m. Lorretta Ilene Williams, Sept. 1, 2007. BTh, LIFE Bible Coll., LA, 1965; DD, Internat. Ch. Foursquare Gospel, LA, 1992. Ordained to ministry Internat. Ch. Foursquare Gospel, 1966. Pastor Foursquare Gospel Ch., Surrey, Canada, 1965-69, missionary Hong Kong, China, 1969-85; prof. Life Bible Coll., 1985-95; mng. editor Foursquare World Advance, 1993—2002; comm. officer Internat. Ch. Foursquare Gospel, 1988-2000. Bd. dirs. Forsquare Gospel Ch., denominational historian, 2004—07; pres. exec. bd. Internat. Pentecostal Press Assn., Oklahoma City, 1990—98; comm. officer Pentecostal/Charismatic Ch. N.Am., Memphis, 1994—2005; coord. E. Coun. Foursquare Miss., 1979—82. Editor: The Vine and The Branches, 1992; mng. editor: Foursquare World Advance mag., 1985—2002. Coord. 19th Pentecostal World Conf., 2001. With USAF, 1958—61. Avocations: writing, golf, reading, music. Personal E-mail: ron@lifeshighest.com.

WILLIAMS, RONALD OSCAR, mathematician; b. Denver, May 10, 1940; s. Oscar H. and Evelyn J. (Johnson) Williams. BS in Applied Math., U. Colo., Coll. Engring., Boulder, 1964; postgrad., U. Colo., 1968—70, U. Denver, 1975; postgrad. Advanced Tech. Edn. Program, Hughes Aircraft Co., 1980—89; postgrad., George Washington U., DC, 1985; postgrad. Spl. Electronics Course, Lowry AFB, Denver; continuing edn. courses, Gen. Elec. Co., Control Data Corp., NASA, Boulder Police Dept. Computer programmer Apollo Sys. dept. Missile and Space div. Gen. Electric Co., Kennedy Space Ctr., Fla., 1965-67; computer programmer Apollo Sys. dept. Missile and Space divsn. Manned Spacecraft Ctr. (now Johnson Space Ctr.), Houston, 1967—68; computer programmer Grad. Sch. Computing Ctr. and Lab. Atmospheric and Space Physics U. Colo., Boulder, 1968-73; computer programmer analyst Def. Sys. divsn. Sys. Devel. Corp. at Ent AFB, Colorado Springs, Colo., 1974—75, NORAD Cheyenne Mountain Complex, Colorado Springs, 1974—75; engr. def. sys. and command-and-info. sys. Martin Marietta Aerospace (now Lockheed Martin), Denver, 1976—80; sys. engr., def. info. sys. divsn. space and comm. group Hughes Aircraft Co. at Aerospace Data Facility, Buckley AFB, Aurora, Colo., 1980—89; rsch. analyst Math. Rsch. Ctr., Littleton, Colo., 1990—, dir., sr. rsch. mathematician, 1996—. First chair trombonist Wash. Park Elem. Sch. Orch., All-City Elem. Sch. Orch., Merrill Jr. HS Concert Band, Merrill Jr. HS Concert Orch., Merrill Jr. HS German Band, Denver Jr. Police Band, Mile-High Boys' Band, Wells Music Dance Band. Vol. fireman Clear Lake City Fire Dept., Tex., 1968, Harris County Fire Fighters Assn., Tex., 1968; officer Boulder Emergency Squad, 1969-76, rescue squad officer, 1969-76, rescue Self-Contained Underwater Breathing Apparatus diver asst., liaison officer to cadets, 1971, pers. officer, 1971-76, exec. bd., 1971-76, Red Cross Std. First Aid to Injured, Advanced First Aid to Injured, Basic Life Support Cardiopulmonary Resuscitation, EMT, 1973—; charter mem. Assn. Trauma Specialists, Am. Paramedic Assn., Emergency Med. Technician Assn. Colo., Nat. Assn. Trauma Specialists; res. dispatcher A-1 Ambulance, Boulder, 1973-74; spl. police officer Boulder Police Dept., 1970-75; spl. dep. sheriff Boulder County Sheriff's Dept., 1970-71; nat. adv. bd. Am. Security Coun., 1979-91, Coalition of Peace Through Strength, 1979-91. Non-commd. officer USMCR, San Diego, Camp Matthews, Camp Elliott, Camp Pendleton (Camp San Onofre), Twentynine Palms, Camp Wilson, Denver Fed. Ctr., 1958—66. Decorated M1 Rifle Sharpshooter Badge, Basic US Marines Weapons Qualification Badge, Organized Res. medal, Marine Corps League medal, USMC Commemorative medal, Nat. Guard and Res. Commemorative medal, Am. Def. Commemorative medal, Hon. Svc. Commemorative medal, Hon. Discharge; recipient Award of Merit, Boulder Emergency Squad, 1971, 1972, Dedicated Svc. award, 1976, Top Cost Improvement Program award, Hughes Aircraft Co., 1982, Sys. Performance Improvement award, 1982; named to Paul R. Halmos Commemorative Walk, Carriage House Conf. Ctr., Math. Assn. America's Hdqs., Washington. Mem. AAAS, AIAA (sr.), Math. Assn. America, Am. Math Soc., Soc. Indsl. and Applied Math., Math. Study Unit of Am. Topical Assn., Armed Forces Comm. and Electronics Assn., Assn. Old Crows, Nat. Def. Indsl. Assn., Assn. For Intelligence Officers, Nat. Mil. Intelligence Assn., Nat. Cryptologic Mus. Found., Internat. Spy Mus. (Washington), US Naval Cryptologic Vet. Assn., Friends of Bletchley Park, Marine Corps Assn., Marine Corps Heritage Found. (charter mem.), Marine Corps League, Nat. Mus. Marine Corps and Heritage Ctr. (campaign mem.), Air Force Assn., US Naval Inst., Nat. Geog. Soc., Smithsonian Inst., Nat. Space Soc., Soc. Amateur Radio Astronomers, Radio History Soc., Met. Opera Guild, Colo. Pub. Radio (classical music), Rocky Mountain PBS, Colo. Hist. Soc., Hist. Denver, Hist. Boulder, Colorado Railroad Hist. Found, Colorado Railroad Mus., Hawaiian Hist Soc., Nat. Audubon Soc., Audubon Soc. Greater Denver, Denver Bot. Gardens, Denver Mus. Nature and Sci., Denver Zool. Found., Pacific Aviation Mus. Pearl Harbor (founding mem.), Wings Over the Rockies Air & Space Mus., Alumni Assn. U. Colo. Boulder, South High Alumni and Friends Denver, Am. Mensa Ltd., Denver Mile-Hi Mensa, Acoustic Neuroma Assn., Nat. Brain Tumor Soc., Crystal Cathedral Ministries, Sparrows Club, Eagles Club, Summer Ptnr., Year End Ptnr., Swedish Club of Denver. Lutheran.

WILLIAMS, STEPHEN, anthropologist, educator; b. Mpls., Aug. 28, 1926; s. Clyde Garfield and Lois (Simmons) Williams; m. Eunice Ford, Jan. 6, 1962; children: Stephen John, Timothy. BA, Yale U., 1949, PhD, 1954; MA, U. Mich., 1950; MA (hon.), Harvard U., 1962. Asst. anthropology dept. Peabody Mus., Yale U., 1950-52; mem. faculty Harvard U., Cambridge, Mass., 1958—, prof. anthropology, 1967-72, Peabody prof., 1972-93, prof. emeritus, 1993—, chmn. dept., 1967-69; rsch. fellow Peabody Mus., Harvard U., Cambridge, 1954-57, mem. staff, 1954—, dir. mus., 1967-77. Curator N.Am. Archaeology, 1962-93, hon. curator 1993—; dir. rsch. of Peabody Mus.'s Lower Miss. Survey, 1958-93. Author books and articles on N.Am. archaeology, "Fantastic" archaeology and the history of Am. anthropology. Home: 1017 Foothills Trail Santa Fe NM 87505-4537 Office: PO Box 22354 Santa Fe NM 87502-2354 Office Phone: 505-983-8836. Personal E-mail: williamsstephen@msn.com.

WILLIAMS, SUZANNE S., state legislator; b. Okla. City, Feb. 3, 1945; d. Frank and Martha Sanford; m. Ed Williams; children: Todd, Courtney. Educator, learning specialist Cherry Creek Sch. Dist. 5; mem. Dist. 41 Colo. House of Reps., Denver, 1996—2004; mem. Dist. 28 Colo. State Senate, 2004—, majority caucus chair. Mem. Colo. Governor's 2000 Action Plan. Recipient Governor's Award of Excellence, 1985, Insider award Aurora Sentinel, 1994; named Colo. Mother of Yr. Am. Mothers Inc., 1996. Mem.: Cherry Creek Educators' Assn., Am. Home Health Care, Aurora Sister Cities (past pres.), Am. Assn. Univ. Women. Democrat. Protestant. Office: Colo State Capitol 200 E Colfax Denver CO 80203 Office Phone: 303-866-3432. Business E-Mail: suzanne.williams.senate@state.co.us.*

WILLIAMS, TAMBOR, state representative; b. Washington, Mar. 28, 1941; m. Jim Eckersley; 2 children. BA in English and Philosophy, CUNY; MA in Counseling, Western State U.; JD, U. Colo. Atty.; state rep. dist. 50 Colo. Ho. of Reps., Denver, 1996—, mem. appropriations and edn. coms., and joint com. on legis. audit, chair bus. affairs and labor com. Mem.: Colo. Bar Assn., No. Colo. Latino C. of C., Evans C. of C., Greeley/Weld C. of C. Republican. Congregationalist. Avocations: travel, reading, hiking, cooking.

WILLIAMS, TERRIE M., biology professor; MS, PhD, Rutgers U., New Brunswick, NJ. NIH postdoctoral fellow Scripps Instn. Oceanography, 1981—84; Kaiser environ. fellow San Diego Zool. Soc., 1984—86; prof. ecology and evolutionary biology U. Calif., Santa Cruz. Contbr. articles to sci. jours.; author: The Hunter's Breath: On Expedition with the Weddell Seals of the Antarctic. Recipient Women of Discovery, Sea award, Wings WorldQuest, 2007. Office: Ctr Ocean Health U Calif 100 Shaffer Rd Santa Cruz CA 95060 Office Phone: 831-459-5123. Office Fax: 831-459-3383. E-mail: williams@biology.ucsc.edu.

WILLIAMS, THELDA, Councilwoman; Div. comdr. Maricopa County Sheriff's Office Custody Support & Inmate Programs; councilwoman, Dist. 1 Phoenix City Coun., 1989—96, 2008—; interim mayor City of Phoenix, 1994. Chmn. Seniors, Families and Youth com.; mem. Econ., Commerce & Sustainability, Pub. Safety & Veterans coms. Former mem. Aviation Adv. Bd., Transit Commn., Block Watch Oversight Com., Deer Valley Planning Com., Phoenix Planning & Zoning Com., Govs. Commn. to Prevent Violence Against Women, Maricopa County Adult Probation Adv. Bd. Mem.: Women in Local Govt. Assn., Maricopa Assn. Govts. Bd. Office: 200 W Washington St 11th Fl Phoenix AZ 85003 Office Phone: 602-262-7444. Office Fax: 602-534-4793. Business E-Mail: council.district.1@phoenix.gov.*

WILLIAMS, VIC, state legislator; b. Whittier, Calif., Apr. 6, 1963; Mem. Dist. 26 Ariz. House of Reps., 2008—, mem. appropriations com., edn. com., pub. employees, retirement & entitlement reform com. Mem.: Nat. Assn. Social Workers. Republican. Roman Catholic. Office: Ariz House Reps Capitol Complex 1700 W Washington Rm 308 Phoenix AZ 85007 Office Phone: 602-926-5839. Office Fax: 602-417-3026. Business E-Mail: vwilliams@azleg.gov.*

WILLIAMS, WILLIAM COREY, theology educator, consultant; b. Wilkes-Barre, Pa., July 12, 1937; s. Edward Douglas and Elizabeth Irene (Schooley) W.; m. Alma Simmenroth Williams, June 27, 1959; 1 child, Linda. Diploma in Ministerial Studies, NE Bible Inst., 1962; BA in Bibl. Studies, Cen. Bible Coll., 1963, MA in Religion, 1964; MA in Hebrew and Near Ea. Studies, NYU, 1966, PhD in Hebrew Lang. and Lit., 1975; postgrad., Hebrew U., 1977-78, Inst. Holyland Studies, 1986. Ref. libr. Hebraic section Libr. Congress, Washington, 1967-69; prof. Old Testament So. Calif. Coll./Vanguard U., Costa Mesa, 1969—; adj. prof. Old Testament Melodyland Sch. Theology, Anaheim, Calif., 1975-77; vis. prof. Old Testament Fuller Theol. Sem., Pasadena, Calif., 1978-81, 84, Asian Theol. Ctr. Evangelism Missions, Singapore and Sabah, E. Malaysia, 1985, Continental Bible Coll., Saint Pieters-Leeuw, Belgium, 1985, 2000-01, Mattersey Bible Coll., England, 1985, Inst. Holy Land Studies, Jerusalem, 1986, Regent U., 1994. Transl. cons. reviser New Am. Std. Bible, 1969-94; transl. cons. New Internat. Version, 1975-76, New Century Version, 1991, The New Living Translation, 1992-95, New Internat. Version, Reader's Version, 1993-94; transl. cons. editor Internat. Children's Version, 1985-86. Author: (books, tapes) Hebrew I: A Study Guide, 1980, Hebrew II: A Study Guide, 1986, They Spoke From God, 2004; contbr. articles to International Standard Bible Encyclopedia, New International Dictionary of Old Testment Theology and Evangelical Dictionary of Biblical Theology; contbr. articles to profl. jours.; contbr. notes to Spirit Filled Life Study Bible; editor: They Spoke From God, 2004. Nat. Def. Fgn. Lang. fellow NYU, 1964-67; Alumni scholar N.E. Bible Inst., 1960-61; NEH fellow, summer 1992; recipient Disting. Educator's award Assemblies God, 1997. Mem. Soc. Bibl. Lit., Evang. Theol. Soc. (exec. office 1974-77), Inst. Bibl. Rsch., Lockman Found. (hon. mem. bd. dirs 1992-94, mem. edit. bd. 1974-94). Home: 1817 Peninsula Pl Costa Mesa CA 92627-4591 Office: Vanguard U 55 Fair Dr Costa Mesa CA 92626-6520 Business E-Mail: wwilliams@vanguard.edu.

WILLIAMS, WILLIAM K., state representative; b. Ketchikan, Alaska, May 21, 1943; m. Caryl Williams; children: Steve, Mike, Krissy, David, Adam. Former pres. Cape Fox Corp.; mayor Saxman, Alaska; mem. Alaska Ho. of Reps., 1992—; chmn. house resources com., 1993—96; chmn. house transport. com., 1997—98; mem. house fin. com., 1999—2000. Mem. Alaska Native Brotherhood, Saxman Tlingit & Haida, Nat. Conf. State Legis., 1990—2000, We. States Coalition, 1993—96, Saxman City Coun., 1972—92, We. legis. Forestry Task Force, 1993—. Mem.: S.E. Alaska Pres. Assn. (chmn.), So. S.E. Regional Aquaculture Assn. (bd. dirs.), Internat. Longshoremen Warehousemen Union. Republican. Avocations: sports, fishing. Address: 50 Front St Ste 203 Ketchikan AK 99901

WILLIAMS-DERRY, AMY, lawyer; b. NYC, Feb. 19, 1970; BA in Sociology with hon., Brown Univ., 1993; JD, Univ. Va., 1998. Bar: Wash. 1998, US Dist. Ct., Western and Eastern Dist. Wash. 1998, US Ct. Appeals Ninth Circuit 1999. Former litig. assoc. Hillis Clark Martin & Peterson, P.S., Seattle, 1998—2003; assoc. atty. Earth Justice, 2003—05, Keller Rohrback, L.L.P., Seattle, 2005—. Contbr. articles to numerous profl. jours. Named Wash. Rising Star, Super-Lawyer Mag., 2006. Mem.: ABA, King Co. Bar Assn., Wash. Bar Assn. Office: Keller Rohrback LLP Ste 3200 1201 Third Ave Seattle WA 98101-3052

WILLIAMSON, ALAN BACHER, literature educator, poet, writer; b. Chgo., Jan. 24, 1944; s. George and Jehanne (Bacher) W.; m. Anne Winters, Oct. 12, 1968 (div. Feb. 1988); 1 child, Elizabeth Kilner. BA, Haverford Coll., 1964; MA, Harvard U., 1965, PhD, 1969. Asst. prof. U. Va., Charlottesville, 1969-75; Briggs-Copeland lectr. Harvard U., Cambridge, Mass., 1977-80; Fannie Hurst lectr. Brandeis U., Waltham, Mass., 1980-82; prof. English, U. Calif., Davis, 1982—. Poetry panelist Nat. Endowment for Arts, 1989. Author: (criticism) Pity the Monsters, 1974, Introspection and Contemporary Poetry, 1984, Eloquence and Mere Life, 1994, Almost a Girl, 2001, Westernness: A Meditation, 2006, (poetry) Presence, 1983, The Muse of Distance, 1988, Love and the Soul, 1995, Res Publica, 1998, The Pattern More Complicated: New and Selected Poems, 2004. Poetry fellow Nat. Endowment for Arts, 1973; Guggenheim fellow, 1991. Mem. MLA (exec. com. div. on poetry 1987-91). Democrat. Buddhist. Office: U Calif Dept English Davis CA 95616 Business E-Mail: abwilliamson@ucdavis.edu.

WILLIAMSON, CHARLES R., retired energy company executive; PhD in Geology, U. Tex., Austin, 1978. Rsch. assoc. Sci. and Tech. Divsn. Unocal Corp., Brea, Calif., 1977-83, chief exploration geologist U.K., 1983-86; exploration mgr., dir. Unocal Netherlands, The Hague, 1986-89; v.p. exploration Unocal Thailand, Bangkok, 1989-92; v.p. Energy Resources Divsn. Unocal, 1992-94, v.p. planning and info. svcs., 1994-95, v.p. corp. planning and econs., 1995-96, group v.p. internat. opers., 1996-97, group v.p. Asia Opers., 1997-99; exec. v.p. internat. energy ops. Unocal Corp., El Segundo, Calif., 1999—2001; CEO, chmn. Unocal (acquired by Chevron Corp.), 2001—05; exec. v.p., mem. exec. com. Chevron Corp., 2005. Mem. adv. bd. earth seis. dept. Stanford U.; bd. dir. Weyerhaeuser Co., 2004—, lead. dir., 2006—; bd. dir. Talisman Energy Inc., 2006—, PACCAR Inc., 2006—. Mem. Am. Soc. Petroleum Geologists, Soc. Econ. Paleontologists and Mineralogists, Soc. Petroleum Engrs., Internat. Assn. Sedimentologists. Mailing: PACCAR Inc Bd Directors PO Box 1518 Bellevue WA 98009*

WILLIAMSON, CHARLES READY, III, lawyer; b. Boston, Jan. 2, 1944; s. Charles Ready, Jr. and Anne Margaret (Livingstone) Williamson; m. Julie Anne Williamson, Nov. 6, 1971; 1 child, Anne Lucinda. BA, Colgate U., 1965; LLB, Suffolk U., 1968. Bar: Mass. 1968, Oreg. 1970, US Supreme Ct. 1977. Law clk. to Judge Joseph B. Silverio Mass. Land Ct., Boston, 1968—69; VISTA atty., dep. dir. Multnomah county Legal Aid Svc., Portland, 1970—74; assoc. Kell, Alterman & Runstein, 1974—78, 1988—; pvt. practice Portland, 1978—88. Pres. Oreg. Legal Svc. Corp., 1976—77. Contbr. articles in field. Pres. Oreg. Consumer League, 1972—74; mem. Oreg. Bd. Psychologist Examiners, 1973—74; chmn. Oreg. Grad. Sch. Profl. Psychology, Pacific U.; councilor Met. Svc. Dist., 1978—84; treas. Dem. Bus. Forum, 1982—84. Mem.: ABA, Multnomah County Bar Assn., Oreg. Bar Assn. (pres.-elect 2002—03, pres. 2003—04), Portland City Club. Office: Kell Alterman & Runstein 520 SW Yamhill Ste 600 Portland OR 97204-1329

WILLIAMSON, OLIVER EATON, business economics and law professor; m. Dolores Jean (Celeni); children: Scott, Tamara, Karen, Oliver, Dean. BS, Mass. Inst. Tech., 1955; MBA, Stanford U., 1960; PhD, Carnegie Mellon U., 1963; PhD (hon.), Norwegian Sch. Econ. and Bus. Adminstrn., 1986; PhD in Econ. sci. (hon.), Hochschule St. Gallen, Switzerland, 1987, Groningen U., 1989, Turku Sch. Econ. and Bus. Admin, St. Petersburg, Russia, 1996, HEC, Paris, 1997, Copenhagen Bus. Sch., 2000, U. Chile, 2000, Valencia U., 2004, Nice U., 2005. Project. engr. U.S. Govt., 1955-58; asst. prof. econ. U. Calif., Berkeley, Calif., 1963-65; assoc. prof. Pa. State U., Phila., 1965-68, prof., 1968-83, Charles and William L. Day prof. econ. and social sci., 1977-83; Gordon B. Tweedy prof. econ. law and orgn. Yale U., 1983-88; Transam. prof. of bus., econ. and law U. Calif., Berkeley, Calif., 1988-94, Edgar F. Kaiser prof. bus. adminstrn., prof. econ. and law, 1994—2008. Spl. econ. asst. to asst. atty. gen. for antitrust Dept. Justice, 1966—67; dir. Ctr. for Study of Orgnl. Innovation, U. Pa., 1976—83; cons. in field; Thomas Malthus lectr. Hertfordshire U., England, 2006. Author: The Economics of Discretionary Behavior, 1964; Corp. Control and Bus. Behavior, 1970; Markets and Hierarchies, 1975; The Econ. Instn. of Capitalism, 1985; Econ. Orgn., 1986, Antitrust Economics, 1987; The Mechanisms of Governance, 1996; assoc. editor, Bell. Jour. Econ., 1973-74; editor, 1975-82; co-editor Jour. Law, Econ. and Orgn., 1983—2003. Fellow Ctr. for Advanced Study in Behavioral Sci., 1977-78; Guggenheim fellow, 1977-78; Fulbright scholar, 1999; Am. Acad. Arts and Sci. fellow, 1983; recipient Alexander Henderson Award Carnegie-Mellon U., 1962, Alexander von Humboldt Rsch. prize, 1987, Irwin award Acad. Mgmt., 1988, John von Newmann lectr., 1999, H.C. Recktenwald prize in econs., 2004. Fellow Am. Acad. Polit. and Social Sci., Acad. Internat. Bus. (eminent scholar), Indsl. Orgn. Soc. (disting. fellow 2005), Am. Econ. Assn. (v.p. 2000-01, disting. fellow 2007); mem. NAS, Internat. Soc. for New Instnl. Econ. (pres. 1999-2001), Am. Law and Econ. Assn. (pres. 1997-98), Western Econ. Assn. (pres. 1999-2000). Office: Univ Calif Dept Econ Berkeley CA 94720-0001

WILLIS, FRANK ROY, historian, educator; b. Prescot, Lancashire, Eng., July 25, 1930; s. Harry and Gladys Reid (Birchall) W.; children from previous marriage, Jane, Clare, Geoffrey. BA, Cambridge U., Eng., 1952, cert. in edn., 1955, diploma in devel. econs., 1974; PhD, Stanford U., Calif., 1959. Instr. Stanford U., 1959-60; from instr. to assoc. prof. history U. Wash., Seattle, 1960-64; assoc. prof. then prof. U. Calif., Davis, 1964—. Author: The French in Germany, 1962, France, Germany and the New Europe, 1945-1967, 1968, Europe in the Global Age, 1968, Italy Chooses Europe, 1971, Western Civilization: An Urban Perspective, 1973, World Civilizations, 1982, The French Paradox, 1982, Western Civilization: A Brief Introduction, 1987. Fellow, Rockefeller Found., Paris, 1962—63, Guggenheim Found., Rome, 1966—67, Social Scis. Rsch. Coun., Cambridge, 1973—74. Avocation: travel. Office: U Calif Dept History Davis CA 95616

WILLIS, HAROLD WENDT, SR., real estate developer; b. Marion, Ala., Oct. 7, 1927; s. Robert James and Della (Wendt) W.; m. Patsy Gay Bacon, Aug. 2, 1947 (div. Jan. 1975); children: Harold Wendt II, Timothy Gay, April Ann, Brian Tad, Suzanne Gail; m. Vernette Jacobson Osborne, Mar. 30, 1980 (div. 1984); m. Ofelia Alvarez, Sept. 23, 1984; children: Ryan Robert, Samantha Ofelia. Student, Loma Linda U., 1950, San Bernardino Valley Coll. Ptnr. Victoria Guernsey, San Bernardino, Calif., 1950-63, co-pres., 1963-74, pres., 1974—. Pres. Energy Delivery Sys., Food and Fuel, Inc. San Bernardino City water commr., 1964-98, pres. bd. water commrs., 1964-98; bd. councillors Loma Linda U., Calif., 1968-85, pres., 1971-74; active So. Calif. Strider's Relay Team (set indoor Am. and World record in 4x800 1992, sec distance medley relay US and World record for 60 yr. old 1992); pres. So. Calif. Striders Track and Field Club, 2001-02. Ensign, US Mcht. Marine, 1945-46. Mem. Calif. Dairy Industries Assn. (pres. 1963, 64), Liga Internat. (2d v.p. 1978, pres. 1982, 83), Socal Striders Masters Track & Field Club (pres. 2001-02). Seventh-day Adventist (deacon 1950-67). Avocation: pvt. pilot. Office: PO Box 5607 San Bernardino CA 92412-5607 Office Phone: 909-889-0828 ext 303. Personal E-mail: foodnfuel@verizon.net.

WILLIS, JUDY ANN, lawyer; b. Hartford, Conn., July 7, 1949; d. Durward Joseph and Angeline Raphael (Riccardo) Willis. BA, Ctrl. Conn. State U., 1971; postgrad., U. Conn. Law Sch., 1976—77; JD, Boston Coll., 1979. Bar: Mass. 1979, U.S. Dist. Ct. Mass. 1980, Calif. 1990. Sr. atty. H.P. Hood Inc., Charleston, Mass., 1979-83; v.p. law Parker Bros., Beverly, Mass., 1983-89; sr. v.p. bus. affairs Mattel, Inc., El Segundo, Calif., 1989—. Office: Mattel Inc M1-1112 333 Continental Blvd El Segundo CA 90245-5012 E-mail: judy.willis@Mattel.com.

WILLIS, THAYER CHEATHAM, wealth counselor, author; MA, U. Oreg., Eugene; MSW, Portland State U., Oreg. Lic. clin. social worker. Cons. and spkr. wealth planning and mgmt.; spkr. Nat. Assn. Pers. Fin. Advisors Confs., Capital Trust Co. Symposia, Campden Confs., Morgan Stanley Sr. Cons. Confs. Author: Navigating the Dark Side of Wealth: A Life Guide for Inheritors, 2005. Mem.: Nat. Spkrs. Assn., Family Wealth Alliance, Family Firm Inst. Achievements include research in the psychological challenges of wealth; scion of the multi-billion dollar Georgia Pacific Corporation's founding family. Office: 340 Oswego Pointe Dr Ste 205 Lake Oswego OR 97034 Office Phone: 503-636-1179. Office Fax: 503-244-9410.

WILLISCROFT-BARCUS, BEVERLY RUTH, retired lawyer; b. Conrad, Mont., Feb. 24, 1945; d. Paul A. and Gladys L. (Buck) W.; m. Kent J. Barcus, Oct. 1984. BA in Music, So. Calif. Coll., 1967; JD, John F. Kennedy U., 1977. Bar: Calif. 1977. Elem. tchr., Sunnyvale, Calif., 1968-72; legal sec., legal asst. various law firms, 1972-77; assoc. Neil D. Reid, Inc., San Francisco, 1977-79; sole practice Concord, Calif., 1979—2004. Exam. grader Calif. Bar, 1979-2001; real estate broker, 1980-88; tchr. real estate King Coll., Concord, 1979-80; judge pro-tem Mcpl. Ct., 1981-93; mem. Stage Right Drama Group, Concord, Calif., 1999—; lectr. in adoption law. Co-author: Adoption Law in California, Adoption Practice, Procedure and Pitfalls in California; lectr. in field. Bd. dirs. Contra Costa Musical Theatre, Inc., 1978-82, v.p. adminstrn., 1980-81, v.p. prodn., 1981-82; mem. community devel. adv. com. City of Concord, 1981-83, vice chmn., 1982-83, mem. status of women com., 1980-81, mem. redevel. adv. com., 1984-86, planning commnr. 1986-92, chmn., 1990; mem. exec. bd. Mt. Diablo coun. Boy Scouts Am., 1981-85; bd. dirs. Pregnancy Ctrs. Contra Costa County, 1991-2001, chmn., 1993-2000 Mem. Concord C. of C. (bd. dirs., chmn. govt. affairs com. 1981-83, v.p. 1985-87, pres. 1988-89, Bus. Person of Yr. 1986), Calif. State Bar (chmn. adoptions subcom. north, 1994), Contra Costa County Bar Assn., Christian Legal Soc., Todos Santos Bus. and Profl. Women (co-founder, pres. 1983-84, pub. rels. chmn. 1982-83, Woman of Achievement 1980, 81), Soroptimists (fin. sec. 1980-81). Office: PO Box 981 Pittsburg CA 94565-0098

WILLISON, BRUCE GRAY, dean; b. Riverside, Calif., Oct. 16, 1948; s. Walter G. and Dorothy (Phillips) W.; m. Gretchen A. Illig; children: Patrick, Bruce G., Kristen, Jeffery, Geoffrey, Lea. BA in econs., UCLA, 1970; MBA, U. So. Calif., 1973. With Bank of Am., LA, 1973-79; joined First Interstate Bancorp, LA, 1979, dir. mktg., 1981, sr. v.p., mem. mng. com., 1981—82; sr. v.p. trust divsn. First Interstate Bank of Calif., LA, 1982—83, exec. v.p. world banking group, 1983-85; pres., CEO First Interstate Bank Ltd., LA, 1985-86; chmn., CEO First Interstate Bank Oreg., Portland, 1986-91; chmn., pres., CEO First Interstate Bank of Calif., LA, 1991—96; vice chmn. First Interstate Bancorp, LA, 1995—96; pres., COO H.F. Ahmanson and Co., Irwandale, Calif., 1996—99; dean UCLA Anderson Sch. Mgmt., 1999—2006, John E. Anderson chair in mgmt. Bd. dirs. IndyMac Bancorp., Inc., Sun America, Inc., Health Net Inc., 2000—, Homestore, Inc., 2002—. Bd. dirs. United Way of LA, Operation Hope Inc. Served to lt. USN, 1970—72.

WILLNER, ALAN ELI, electrical engineer, educator; b. Bklyn, Nov. 16, 1962; s. Gerald and Sondra (Bernstein) W.; m. Michelle Frida Green, June 25, 1991. BA, Yeshiva U., 1982; MS, Columbia U., 1984, PhD, 1988. Summer tech. staff David Sarnoff Rsch. Ctr., Princeton, NJ, 1983, 84; grad. rsch. asst. dept. elec. engring. Columbia U., NYC, 1984-88; postdoctoral mem. tech. staff AT&T Bell Labs., Holmdel, NJ, 1988-90; mem. tech. staff Bell Comm. Rsch., Red Bank, NJ, 1990-91; prof. U. So. Calif., LA, 1992—, assoc. dir. Ctr. Photonic Tech., 1994—. Head del. Harvard Model UN Yeshiva U., 1982; instr. Columbia U., 1987; rev. panel mem. NSF, Washington, 1992, Washington, 93, Washington, 94, invited optical comm. workshop, 94; chair panel on optical info. and comm., 94; co-chair Conf. on Lasers and Electro-Optics; steering com. and tech. com. mem. Conf. Optical Fiber Comm. Author 1 book; contbr. articles to profl. jours.; editor-in-chief Jour. Lighwave Tech., IEEE Jour. Selected Topics in Quantum Electronics; assoc. editor Jour. Selected Areas in Comm. Mem. faculty adv. bd. U. So. Calif. Hillel Orgn., 1992. Recipient Disting. Lectr. award, IEEE Lasers and Electro-Optics Soc., Armstrong Found. prize, Columbia U., 1984, Best Engring. Tchr. award, USC/TRW, young investigator award, NSF, 1992, Eddy Paper Award, 2001, USL Assoc. Award for Univ. Wide Excellence in Tchg.; grantee NSF, Advanced Rsch. Projects Agy., Packard Found., Powell Found., Ballistic Missile Def. Orgn.; fellow, Semiconductor Rsch. Corp., 1986, Sci. and Engring., David and Lucile Packard Found., 1993, presdl. faculty, NSF, 1994, sr. scholar, Fulbright Found., 1997. Fellow: IEEE, Optical Soc. Am. (symposium organizer ann. mtg. 1992, panel organizer ann. mtg. 1993, symposium organizer ann. mtg. 1995, panel organizer ann. mtg. 1995, program com. for conf. on optical fiber commn. 1996, 1997, program co-chair ann. mtg. 2001, vice chair optical comm. group, tech. council chair-photonics divsn., co-chair sci. and engring. coun., bd. dirs., program co-chair of OSA Annual Mtg., tech. coun. chair photonics divsn.); mem.: IEEE (sr.; editor-in-chief IEEE/OSA Jour. Lightwave Tech.), Soc. Photo-Instrumentation Engring. (program chair telecomm. engring. photonics west 1995, chmn. conf. on emerging techs. for all-optical networks photonics west 1995, program com. for Conf. on Optical Fiber Comm. 1996, conf. program com. components for WDM), IEEE Lasers and Electro-Optics Soc. (chmn. optical comm. subcom. ann. mtg. 1994, bd. govs. 1998—2001, v.p. tech. affairs, mem. optical comm. tech. com., bd. govs., mem. optical networks tech. com., various awards coms., chmn. optical commn. tech. com., awards com. mem. Quantum Electronics, IEEE Fellow, pres.-elect, Disting. Lectr. award), Sigma Xi. Achievements include patents for localized photochemical etching of multilayered semiconductor body, optical star coupler utilizing fiber amplifier tech., and one-to-many simultaneous optical WDM 2-dim. plane interconnections. Home: 9326 Sawyer St Los Angeles CA 90035-4102 Office: U So Calif Dept Elec Engring Eeb 538 Los Angeles CA 90089-0001 Business E-Mail: willner@usc.edu.

WILLOCK, MARCELLE MONICA, retired medical educator; b. Georgetown, Guyana, Mar. 30, 1938; came to U.S. 1954; d. George and Renee W. BA, Coll. New Rochelle, 1958; MD, Howard U., 1962; MA, Columbia U., 1982; MBA, Boston U., 1989. Diplomate Am. Bd. Anesthesiology. Asst. clin. prof. med. ctr. NYU, 1968-72, assoc. clin. prof. med. ctr., 1972-74; asst. prof. clin. anesthesiology Columbia U., NYC, 1978-82; prof. Boston U., 1982, chmn. dept. anesthesiology, 1982—98, asst. provost cmty. affairs, 1998—2002; dean Coll. Medicine Charles R. Drew U., LA, 2002—05; ret., 2005. Sec. The Med. Found., Boston, 1991-94. Contbr. articles to profl. jours. Pres. Louis and Marthe Deveaux Found., Panama, 1965—; trustee Coll. New Rochelle, NY, 1976-82, 2006—. Mem. Am. Soc. Anesthesiologists (del. 1986—, alt. dir. 1990-94, bd. dirs. 1994—, asst. sec. 1999-2001), Mass. Soc. Anesthesiologists (pres. 1988-89), Soc. Acad. Anesthesia Chairs (sec.-treas. 1989-91, pres.-elect 1993-94, pres. 1994—), Alpha Omega Alpha. Roman Catholic. Personal E-mail: mwillock@cdrewu.edu.

WILLOUGHBY, STEPHEN SCHUYLER, mathematics professor; b. Madison, Wis., Sept. 27, 1932; s. Alfred and Elizabeth Frances (Cassell) W.; m. Helen Sali Shapiro, Aug. 29, 1954; children: Wendy

Valentine (Mrs. Peter Gallen), Todd Alan. AB (scholar), Harvard U., 1953, AM in Teaching, 1955; EdD (Clifford Brewster Upton fellow), Columbia U., 1961. Tchr. Newton (Mass.) Pub. Schs., 1954-57, Greenwich (Conn.) Pub. Schs., 1957-59; instr. U. Wis., Madison, 1960-61, asst. prof. math. edn. and math., 1961-65; prof. math. edn. and math. NYU, 1965-87, dir. math. edn. dept., 1967-83, chmn. math., sci. and stats. edn. dept., 1970-80, 86-87, chmn. U. Faculty Coun., 1981-82; prof. math. U. Ariz., Tucson, 1987—2002; prof. emeritus math. and math. edn. NYU, 1987—; prof. emeritus math. U. Ariz., Tucson, 2002—. Mem. nat. bd. advisor Sq. One TV, 1983-94, U.S. Commn. on Math. Instrn., 1984-95, chmn., 1991-95; math. adv. com. Nat. Tchr. Exam. Successor (Praxis), 1989-94; edn. panel New Am. Schs. Devel. Corp., 1991-97; U.S. Nat. rep. Internat. Commn. on Math. Instrn., 1991-95. Author: Contemporary Teaching of Secondary School Mathematics, 1967, Probability and Statistics, 1968, Teaching Mathematics: What Is Basic, 1981, Mathematics Education for a Changing World, 1990, Real Math, 1981, 85, 87, 91, Math: Explorations and Applications, 1998, College Mathematics Through Applications, 1999, The Other End of the Log: Memoirs of an Education Rebel, 2002, SRA Real Math, K-6, 2007 2009; contbr. articles to profl. jours. and encys., chpts. to yearbooks and anthologies. Recipient Leadership in Math. Edn. Lifetime Achievement medal, 1995. Mem. Nat. Coun. Tchrs. Math. (dir. 1968-71, pres. 1982-84), Coun. Sci. Soc. Pres. (chmn. 1988). Home: 5435 E Gleneagles Dr Tucson AZ 85718-1805 Office: U Ariz Dept Math Tucson AZ 85721-0001 Personal E-mail: sswill@comcast.net.

WILLOX, JAMES HUGH, realtor, political organization administrator; b. Cheyenne, Wyo., Feb. 16, 1967; s. James Andrew and Susan Adell W.; m. Tione Marie Johnson, Apr. 8, 1995; children: Bolton, James. BS in Agrl. Econs., U. Wyo., 1989. Intern U.S. Rep. Craig Thomas, Washington, 1990; comml. and farm real estate agt. farm and ranch Horizon Realty; chmn. Republican Party Wyo., 2003—. Chmn. Convers County GOP, Douglas, 1993-99, dist. rep., 1997-98, state GOP vice chmn. 1999-2003; coach Little League Basketball, Douglas, 1991-92. Mem. Local, State, and Nat. FFA (alumni), Local, State, and Nat. Stockgrowers, U. Wyo. Alumni, Moose, Alpha Gamma Rho. Episcopalian. Avocations: politics, reading, basketball refereeing. Home: 630 Poplar Douglas WY 82633 Office: Wyo Republican Party PO Box 241 Casper WY 82601

WILLRICH, MASON, energy industry executive; b. LA, 1933; m. Patricia Rowe, June 11, 1960 (dec. July 1996); m. Wendy Webster, Aug. 30, 1997; children: Christopher, Stephen, Michael, Katharine. BA magna cum laude, Yale U., 1954; JD, U. Calif., Berkeley, 1960. Atty. Pillsbury Madison and Sutro, San Francisco, 1960-62; asst. gen. coun. U.S. Arms Control and Disarmament Agy., 1962-65; assoc. prof. law U. Va., 1965-68, prof. law, 1968-75, John Stennis prof. law, 1975-79; dir. internat. rels. Rockefeller Found., NYC, 1976-79; v.p. Pacific Gas & Electric, San Francisco, 1979-84, sr. v.p., 1984-88, exec. v.p., 1988-89; CEO, pres. PG&E Enterprises, San Francisco, 1989-94; exec. Pacific Gas and Electric Co., San Francisco, 1979-94; chmn. EnergyWorks, 1995-98; ptnr. Nth Power LLC, 1996—2002. Bd. dirs. Goldman Fund. Author: Non-Proliferation Treaty, 1969, Global Politics of Nuclear Energy, 1971, (with T.B. Taylor) Nuclear Theft, 1974, Energy and World Politics, 1975, Administration of Energy Shortages, 1976, (with R.K. Lester) Radioactive Waste Management and Regulation, 1977. Trustee, past chmn. World Affairs Coun. No. Calif.; past chmn. Midland Sch.; trustee Winrock Internat. Guggenheim Meml. fellow, 1973. Mem. Calif. Ind. Sys. Operators (bd. govs.), Phi Beta Kappa, Order of Coif. Office: 38 Dudley Ct Piedmont CA 94611-3442 E-mail: willrichm@aol.com.

WILLS, J. ROBERT, retired academic administrator, theater educator, writer; b. Akron, Ohio, May 5, 1940; s. J. Robert and Helen Elizabeth (Lapham) W.; m. Barbara T. Salisbury, Aug. 4, 1984 (dec. 1998); m. Jeanne Hokin, June 2002. BA, Coll. of Wooster, 1962; MA, U. Ill., 1963; PhD, Case-Western Res. U., 1971; cert. in arts adminstrn, Harvard U., 1976. Instr. to asst. prof., dir. theatre Wittenberg U., Springfield, Ohio, 1963-72; assoc. prof., dir. grad. studies, chmn. dept. theatre U. Ky., Lexington, 1972-77, prof. theatre, dean Coll. Fine Arts, 1977-81; prof. drama, dean Coll. Fine Arts U. Tex., Austin, 1981-89, Effie Marie Cain Regents chair in Fine Arts, 1986-89; provost, prof. theatre Pacific Luth. U., Tacoma, 1989-94; prof. theatre, dean coll. fine arts Ariz. State U., Tempe, 1994—2006; ret. Cons. colls., univs., arts orgns., govt. agencies Author: The Director in a Changing Theatre, 1976, Directing in the Theatre: A Casebook, 1980, rev. edit., 1994; dir. 95 plays; contbr. articles to profl. jours. Bd. dirs. various art orgns., Ky., Tex., Wash., Ariz. Recipient grants public and pvt. agencies. Mem. Nat. Assn. State Univs. and Land-Grant Colls.(chmn. commn. on arts 1981-83), Coun. Fine Arts Deans (exec. com. 1984-89, sec./treas. 1986-89), Univ. and Coll. Theatre Assn. (pres. 1981-82), Assn. for Communication Adminstrn. (pres. 1986-87), Ky. Theatre Assn. (pres. 1976).

WILLS, JOHN ELLIOT, JR., retired historian, writer; b. Urbana, Ill., Aug. 8, 1936; s. John Elliot and George Anne (Hicks) W.; m. Carolin Connell, July 19, 1958; children: Catherine, Christopher John, Jeffrey David, Joanne, Lucinda. BA in Philosophy, U. Ill., 1956; MA in East Asian Studies, Harvard U., 1960, PhD in History and Far Ea. Langs., 1967. History instr. Stanford (Calif.) U., 1964-65, U. So. Calif., LA, 1965-67, asst. prof., 1967-72, assoc. prof., 1972-84, prof., 1984—2004, prof. emeritus, 2004—, acting chair East Asian Langs. and Cultures, 1987-89; dir. East Asian Studies Ctr. USC-UCLA Joint East Asian Studies Ctr., LA, 1990-94. Rsch. abroad in The Netherlands, Taiwan, China, Japan, Macao, Philippines, Indonesia, India, Italy, Spain, Portugal, Eng. Author: Pepper, Guns, and Parleys: The Dutch East India Company and China, 1662-1681, 1974, Embassies and Illusions: Dutch and Portuguese Envoys to K'ang-hsi, 1666-1687, 1984, Mountain of Fame: Portraits in Chinese History, 1994, 1688: A Global History, 2001; co-editor: (with Jonathan D. Spence) From Ming to Ch'ing: Conquest, Region, and Continuity in Seventeenth-Century China, 1979; editor: Eclipsed Entrepots of the Western Pacific: Taiwan and Central Vietnam, 1500-1800, 2002; contbr. articles to profl. jours. Grantee Nat. Acad. Scis., 1985, Am. Coun. Learned Soc., 1979-80; Younger Humanist fellow NEH, 1972-73. Mem. Assn. for Asian Studies, Am. Hist. Assn., Phi Beta Kappa, Phi Kappa Phi (recognition award 1986, 95). Avocation: travel. Home Phone: 626-755-6506. Business E-Mail: jwills@usc.edu.

WILLS, RICHARD H., electronics manufacturing executive; B in Computer Sys., Linfield Coll.; MBA, U. Oreg. Various positions Tektronix, Inc., Beaverton, Oreg., 1979-91, head TDS line, 1991-93, worldwide dir. mktg., 1993-94, v.p., gen. mgr. design svc. and test bus. unit, 1995-97, pres. European ops., 1997-99, pres. measurement bus., 1999-2000, pres., CEO, 2000—, also bd. dirs. With USAF. Office: Tektronix Inc 14200 SW Karl Braun Dr Beaverton OR 97077

WILLSON, MARY FRANCES, ecology researcher, educator; b. Madison, Wis., July 28, 1938; d. Gordon L. and Sarah (Loomans) W.; m. R.A. von Neumann, May 29, 1972 (dec.). BA with honors, Grinnell Coll., 1960; PhD, U. Wash., 1964. Asst. prof. U. Ill., Urbana, 1965-71, assoc. prof., 1971-76, prof. ecology, 1976-90; rsch. ecologist Forestry Scis. Lab., Juneau, Alaska, 1989-99; sci. dir. Great Lakes program Nature Conservancy, 1999-2000. Prin. rsch. scientist, affiliate prof. biology, Inst. Arctic Biology and Sch. Fisheries and Ocean Scis., U. Alaska, Fairbanks-Juneau. Author: Plant Reproductive Ecology, 1983, Vertebrate Natural History, 1984; co-author: Mate Choice in Plants, 1983. Fellow Am. Ornithologists Union; mem. Brit. Ornithologists Union, Soc. for Study Evolution, Am. Soc. Naturalists (hon. mem.), Ecol. Soc. Am., Brit. Ecol. Soc. E-mail: mwillson@gci.net.

WILSKEY, MIKE, marketing professional; b. Seattle; B in Journalism, U. Oreg., 1978. Adv. mgr. Nike, 1984, product line mgr. for cross-tng., internat. advertising mgr., 1990-92, dir. mktg. Asia-Pacific hdqrs., 1993-96, dir. global brand mktg., 1997-98, v.p., dir. global brand mktg., 1998—. Advt. mgr. Gresham Outlook, Valley Observer, 1978-79; mktg. mgr. Oreg. Bus. mag., 1979-80. Office: Nike Inc One Bowerman Dr Beaverton OR 97005

WILSON, ADRIAN (ADRIAN LEMAR WILSON), professional football player; b. High Point, NC, Oct. 12, 1979; m. Alicia Wilson; children: Aubrei Reign, Adrian Jr. Student in parks, recreation and tourism mgmt., NC State U., Raleigh. Strong safety Ariz. Cardinals, 2001—; owner High Point Shoes, Scottsdale, Ariz. Founder Adrian Wilson Found., 2007—. Named to Nat. Football Conf. Pro Bowl Team, NFL, 2006, 2008. Mailing: Ariz Cardinals PO Box 888 Phoenix AZ 85001-0888*

WILSON, BETH A., college official; BA, Calif. State Coll., Sonoma; MBA, Nat. U. Asst. dir. Am. Bus. Coll., 1976-81; scholarship adminstr. Nat. U., 1982-84; v.p. br. ops. Nat. Coll., 1990-91; from exec. dir. bus. sch., group mgr. to v.p. adminstrn. United Edn. and Sofware, 1984-90; exec. dir. Capital Hill campus, then area ops. mgr. Nat. Edn. Ctrs., Inc., 1991-95; ops. dir., regional ops. dir. Corinthian Schs., Inc., Santa Ana, Calif., 1995-97, regional ops. dir. coll. region of Rhodes Colls. divsn., 1997-98, v.p. ops. parent co., 1998—. Office: Corinthian Colls Inc 6 Hutton Centre Dr Ste 400 Santa Ana CA 92707-5764

WILSON, CHANDRA DANETTE, actress; b. Houston, Aug. 27, 1969; children: Joy, Serena, Michael. BFA in Drama, NYU, 1991. Actor: (plays) The Good Times Are Killing Me (Outstanding Debut Performance, Theatre World award), Paper Moon: The Musical, The Family of Mann, Believing, Caroline, or Change (named one of Eight to Watch, Onstage and Behind the Scenes, NY Times, 2004); (Broadway plays) On the Town; (films) Philadelphia, 1993, Lone Star, 1996, Strangers with Candy, 2005; (TV series) Bob Patterson, 2001, Grey's Anatomy, 2005— (Outstanding Performance by a Female Actor in a Drama Series, SAG, 2007, 2007, Best Supporting Actress in Drama Series, NAACP Image awards, 2007, 2008, 2009). Named Favorite Scene Stealing Star, People's Choice Awards, 2008. Mailing: Grey's Anatomy Los Feliz Tower 4th Fl 4151 Prospect Ave Los Angeles CA 90027*

WILSON, DAVID EUGENE, former magistrate judge, lawyer; b. Columbia, SC, Jan. 12, 1940; s. David W. and Emma (Moseley) W.; m. Nancy Ireland, Sept. 5, 1964; children: Amy R., Cara S. BA, U. S.C., 1963, JD, 1966; MA, Boston U., 1971. Bar: Vt. 1972, D.C. 1973, Wash. 1980, U.S. Dist. Ct. Vt. 1972, U.S. Dist. Ct. (we. dist.) Wash. 1976. Asst. atty. gen. State of Vt., Montpelier, 1972-73; asst. U.S. atty. U.S. Dist. Ct. D.C., Washington, 1973-76, U.S. Dist. Ct. (we. dist.) Wash., Seattle, 1976-89, U.S. atty., 1989, asst. U.S. atty., chief criminal div., 1989-92; U.S. magistrate judge Seattle, 1992-2000; ptnr. McKay-Chadwell, 2000—. Mem. faculty Atty. Gen.'s Advocacy Inst., Washington, 1979—, Nat. Inst. Trial Advocacy, Seattle, 1987—. Capt. U.S. Army, 1966-71, col. USAR. Recipient Disting. Community Svc. award B'nai Brith, 1987. Fellow Am. Coll. Trial Lawyers; mem. Fed. Bar Assn., Wash. State Bar, Seattle-King County Bar. Avocations: hunting, fishing, skiing, books. Office: McKay Chadwell PLLC Ste 1601 600 University St Seattle WA 98101-4124

WILSON, DONALD LEE, musician; b. Tacoma, Wash., Feb. 10, 1933; Co-founder, guitarist The Ventures, 1958—. Musician: (albums) Walk Don't Run, 1960, The Ventures, 1961, Another Smash!!!, 1961, The Colorful Ventures, 1961, Twist with the Ventures, 1961, The Ventures Original Four, 1961, Mashed Potatoes & Gravy, 1962, Going to the Ventures' Dance Party!, 1962, The Ventures Play Telstar & The Lonely Bull, 1962, Surfing, 1963, The Ventures Play the Country Classics, 1963, Let's Go!, 1963, Ventures in Space, 1963, The Fabulous Ventures, 1964, The Ventures Knock Me Out!, 1965, The Ventures in Japan, 1965, The Ventures on Stage, 1965, Ventures a Go-Go, 1965, The Ventures' Christmas Album, 1965, Adventures in Paradise, 1965, Where the Action Is!, 1966, The Ventures Play the Batman Theme, 1966, All About the Ventures, 1966, Go with the Ventures!, 1966, Wild Things!, 1966, Guitar Freakout, 1967, Pops in Japan, 1967, Super Psychedelics, 1967, $1,000,000 Weekend, 1967, The Ventures Live, Again!, 1968, Flights of Fantasy, 1968, The Horse, 1968, Underground Fire, 1968, Hawaii Five-O, 1969, Swamp Rock, 1969, Live! The Ventures, 1970, Golden Pops, 1970, The Ventures' 10th Anniversary Album, 1970, New Testament, 1971, Theme from Shaft, 1971, Joy!, 1972, Rock & Roll Forever, 1972, The Ventures Play the Carpenters, 1974, Best of Pops Sounds, 1974, The Jim Croce Songbook, 1974, Now Playing, 1975, Hollywood, 1975, Sunflower '76, 1976, Rocky Road, 1976, TV Themes, 1977, Latin Album, 1979, Chameleon, 1980, 60's Pops, 1981, St. Louis Memory, 1982, The Last Album on Liberty, 1982, NASA 25th Anniversary Commemorative Album, 1983, The Ventures Favorites, 1996, Wild Again, 1997, New Depths, 1998, Plays Southern All Stars, 2001, 60's Rocking Christmas, 2001, Play the Greatest Instrumental Hits, 2002, Christmas Joy, 2002, Ventures Forever, 2004, Summer & Winter, 2004, Space 2001, 2005, Play Seaside Story, 2006. Named to Rock & Roll Hall of Fame, 2008. Office: Taylor Wilson & Assocs Inc PO Box 372021 Reseda CA 91337-2021

WILSON, DOUGLAS FREDERICK, professional sports team executive, retired professional hockey player; b. Ottawa, Ont., Can., July 5, 1957; s. Douglas and Verna Wilson; m. Katherine Ann Kivisto, July 11, 1981; children: Lacey Anne. Defenseman Chgo. Blackhawks, 1977—91, San Jose Sharks, 1991—93, dir. pro devel., 1997—2003, gen. mgr., 2003—; coord. player rels. and bus. devel. NHL Players Assn., 1993—97. Account exec. Coca-Cola, Chgo. Recipient James Norris Meml. Trophy for best NHL defenseman, 1981-82. Avocations: golf, travel. Office: San Jose Sharks 525 W Santa Clara St San Jose CA 95113

WILSON, EDWARD LAWRENCE, engineering company executive, consultant, retired educator; b. Ferndale, Calif., Sept. 5, 1931; s. James Charles and Josephine (Christen) W.; m. Barbara Diane Farrington, July 24, 1960; children— Michael Edward, Teresa Diane AA, Sacramento City Coll., 1952; BS, U. Calif.-Berkeley, 1954, MS, 1958, D.Eng., 1962. Bridge engr. State of Calif., Sacramento, 1953-64; research engr. Aerojet Gen. Corp., Sacramento, 1963-65; from asst. prof. to assoc. prof. U. Calif.-Berkeley, 1965-72, prof. computational methods for structural analysis, 1972-99, prof. emeritus, 1999—; pres. Structural Analysis Programs, Inc., El Cerrito, Calif., 1980—. Dir. BCDC, San Francisco Author numerous papers, reports. Served with U.S. Army, 1955-56; Korea Recipient E.E. Howard award ASCE, 1995. Mem. ASCE, Structural Engring. Assn. No. Calif., Nat. Acad. Engring. Home: 1050 Leneve Pl El Cerrito CA 94530-2750

WILSON, ERIC F.G., information technology executive; BSc with honors, Guelph U. Sr. v.p., chief info. officer Philip Svcs. Corp., Houston, 1997—2000; sr. v.p. operations, chief tech. officer Fusionstorm, San Francisco, 2000—03; sr. v.p., chief info. officer Raley's, West Sacramento, Calif., 2003—. Office: Raleys 500 W Capitol Ave West Sacramento CA 95605

WILSON, GAYLE ANN, civic worker; b. Phoenix, Nov. 24, 1942; d. Clarence Arthur and Charlotte Evelyn (Davison) Edlund; m. Theodore William Graham, Sept. 14, 1963 (div. May 1983); children: Todd Chandler, Philip Edlund; m. Pete Wilson, May 29, 1983. BA, Stanford U., 1965; postgrad., U. San Diego, 1982. First lady State of Calif., Sacramento, 1991-99; bd. directors ARCO, Los Angeles, CA, 1999—. Adv. for early childhood health and improved math. and sci. edn.; bd. dirs. Ctr. for Excellence in Edn., McLean, Va., 1985—, also former chmn.; mem. Jr. League San Diego, 1968—, also past pres.; bd. dirs. Calif. Inst. Tech., Pasadena, 1995—, Children's Inst. Internat., Phoenix House; former spokesperson Access for Infants and Mothers (AIM), Calif. Breast Cancer Initiative, Never Shake a Baby Campaign, Partnership for Responsible Parenting; mem. Calif. Sesquicentennial Commn.; hon. chmn. Calif. Sci. Fair, Calif. 4-H Found., Calif. Perinatal Outreach-BabyCal, Calif. Commn. on Improving Life Through Svc., Keep Calif. Beautiful; hon. co-chmn. Calif. Mentor Initiative; mem. adv. coun. Ct. Apptd. Spl. Advs.; mem. adv. coun. computers in schs. program Detweiler Found.; hon. chmn. bd. dirs. Leland Stanford Mansion Restoration Found.; founding mem. Achievement Rewards for Coll. Scientists; mem. San Diego Park and Recreation Commn., 1980-83; regent Children's Hosp. L.A. Found., 1998—; bd. dirs. Center Theatre Group, L.A., 1998—, ARCO. Recipient Guardian Angel award L.A. ChildShare, 1995, lifetime achievemecnt award Jr. League L.A., 1996. Mem. Phi Beta Kappa. Republican. Avocations: lyric writing, singing, performing, watercolors. Office: 2132 Century Park Ln Apt 301 Los Angeles CA 90067-3320

WILSON, HEATHER ANN, former United States Representative from New Mexico; b. Keene, NH, Dec. 30, 1960; d. George Douglas and Martha Lou (Kernozicky) Wilson; m. Jay Hone; 3 children. BS in Internat. Politics, USAF Acad., Colo., 1982; MPhil in Internat. Rels., U. Oxford, Eng., 1984, PhD in Internat. Rels., 1985. US mission NATO, Brussels, 1987—89; dir. def. policy and arms control NSC, Washington, 1989—91; pres. Keystone Internat., Inc., Albuquerque, 1991—95; cabinet sec. N.Mex. Dept. Children, Youth and Families, Santa Fe, 1992—98; mem. US Congress from 1st N.Mex. dist., 1998—2009, mem. energy and commerce com., mem. permanent select com. on intelligence, ranking mem. tech. and tactical intelligence subcommittee. Adj. prof. U. N.Mex; mem. Def. Adv. Com. on Women in Svcs. Contbr. articles to profl. jours. Capt. USAF, 1982—89. Recipient Hero of the Taxpayer award, Ams. for Tax Reform, 1999, 2002, Spirit of Free Enterprise award, US C. of C., 2000, Guardian of Small Bus. award, Nat. Fedn. Ind. Bus., 2000, Golden Bulldog award, Watchdog of Treasury, 2000, Disting. Cmty. Health Superhero award, Nat. Assn. Cmty. Health Ctrs., Inc., 2005, Javits-Wagner-O'Day Champion award, 2005; named Rhodes scholar, 1982. Mem.: Kiwanis. Republican. Methodist. Avocations: hiking, skiing.*

WILSON, HUGH STEVEN, lawyer; b. Paducah, Ky., Nov. 27, 1947; s. Hugh Gipson and Rebekah (Dunn) W.; m. Clare Maloney, Apr. 28, 1973; children: Zachary Hunter, Samuel Gipson. BS, Ind. U., 1968; JD, U. Chgo., 1971; LLM, Harvard U., 1972. Bar: Calif. 1972, U.S. Dist. Ct. (ctrl. dist.) Calif. 1972, U.S. Dist. Ct. (so. dist.) Calif. 1973, U.S. Ct. Appeals (9th cir.) 1975, U.S. Dist. Ct. (no. dist.) Calif. 1977, U.S. Supreme Ct. 1978, U.S. Dist. Ct. (ea. dist.) 1980. Assoc. Latham & Watkins, LA, 1972-78, ptnr. San Diego, 1978—2004; mng. ptnr. Tennenbaum Capital Ptnrs., LLC, Santa Monica, Calif., 2005—. Recipient Jerome N. Frank prize U. Chgo. Law Sch., 1971. Mem. Calif. Club, Coronado Yacht Club, Order of Coif. Republican. Avocations: literature, zoology. Office: Tennenbaum Capital Ptnrs 2951 28th St Ste 1000 Santa Monica CA 90405 Office Phone: 310-566-1007. E-mail: steve.wilson@tennenbaumcapital.com.

WILSON, IAN ANDREW, molecular biology educator; b. Perth, Scotland, Mar. 22, 1949; BS in Biochemistry, U. Edinburgh, Scotland, 1971; DPhil in Molecular Biology, Oxford U., Eng., 1976; DSc, Oxford U., 2000. Tutor and tchg. asst. in biochemistry Harvard U., 1978-82, rsch. assoc. biochemistry and molecular biology, 1980-82; asst. mem. dept. immunology Scripps Rsch. Inst., La Jolla, Calif., 1982—83, asst. mem. dept. molecular biology, 1983—84, assoc. mem. dept. molecular biology, 1984—90, chmn. structure and chem. affinity group, 1987—, prof., lectr. structural biology and biophysical chem., 1988—, prof. molecular biology, 1991—, prof. Skaggs Inst. Chem. Biology, 1996—. Adj. prof. U. Calif., San Diego, 1998—. Contbr. articles to profl. jours. Recipient Newcomb-Cleve. prize, 1996-97. Fellow: Royal Soc. London; mem.: Acad. Arts and Sci., Am. Chem. Soc., Protein Soc., Brit. Soc. Immunologists, Am. Crystallographic Assn., Am. Assn. Pathologists, Am. Soc. Virologists, Brit. Biophys. Soc. Office: Scripps Rsch Inst BCC206 Dept Molecular Biol 10550 N Torrey Pines Rd La Jolla CA 92037-1000

WILSON, JAMES QUINN, public policy professor; married; 2 children. AB, U. Redlands, 1952; PhD, U. Chgo., 1959; D (hon.), Harvard U., Cambridge, Mass. Henry Lee Shattuck prof. govt. Harvard U., 1961-86; James Collins prof. mgmt., UCLA, 1985-97; Ronald Reagan prof. pub. policy Pepperdine U., Malibu, Calif. Bd. dirs. Police Found., 1971-1993, Am. Enterprise Inst., New Eng. Electric Sys., State Farm Ins, Protection One, RAND Corp., bd. trustees; chmn. coun. academic advisers Am. Enterprise Inst. Author: Negro Politics, 1960, Political Organizations, 1961, Varieties of Police Behavior, 1968, The Amateur Democrat, 1973, The Investigators, 1978, Thinking About Crime, 1983, (with R.J. Herrnstein) Crime and

Human Nature, 1985, (with Roberta Wilson) Watching Fishes, 1985, Bureaucracy: What Government Agencies Do and Why They Do It., 1989, American Government: Institutions and Policies, 1991, The Moral Sense, 1993, On Character, 1994, Moral Judgment, 1997, The Marriage Problem: How Our Culture Has Weakened Families, 2002. Former chmn. Nat. Adv. Coun. Drug Abuse Prevention, Police Found.; former mem. com. on rsch. on law enforcement and the adminstrn. of justice NRC, Pres.'s Fgn. Intelligence Adv. Bd.; former mem. US Atty. Gen.'s Task Force on Violent Crime; former mem. Commn. on Presdl. Scholars, Sloan Commn. on Cable Comms.; former dir. Joint Ctr. for Urban Studies MIT and Harvard. Recipient John Gaus award, 1994. Fellow Am. Acad. Arts and Scis.; mem. Am. Philos. Soc., Am. Polit. Sci. Assn. (pres., 1991-92, James Madison award, Lifetime Achievement award, 2001). Office: Pepperdine Univ Sch Pub Policy 24255 Pacific Coast Hwy Malibu CA 90263-7490

WILSON, JOHN B., clothing company executive; BS in Chem. Engring., Rensselaer Polytechnic Inst.; MBA, Harvard U. Former v.p. Bain & Co.; former sr. v.p. corp. planning Northwest Airlines; exec. v.p., fin. and strategy, CFO Staples, Inc., 1992-96; exec. v.p., chief administrv. officer The Gap, Inc., San Francisco, 1996-98, exec. v.p., COO, 1998—. Office: The Gap Inc 1 Harrison St San Francisco CA 94105-1602

WILSON, JOHN FRANCIS, religious studies educator, archaeologist; b. Springfield, Mo., Nov. 4, 1937; s. Frederick Marion and Jessie Ferrell (Latimer) W.; m. L. Claudette Faulk, June 9, 1961; children: Laura, Amy, Emily. BA, Harding U., Searcy, Ark., 1959; MA, Harding U., Memphis, 1961; PhD, U. Iowa, 1967. Dir. Christian Student Ctr., Springfield, 1959-73; prof. religious studies S.W. Mo. State U., Springfield, 1961-83; prof. of religion, dean Seaver Coll. Arts, Letters and Scis. Pepperdine U., Malibu, Calif., 1983-98; dir. Inst. for the Study of Religion and Archaeology, 1998—. Author: Religion: A Preface, 1982, 2d edit., 1989, Caesarea Phillipi: Banias, The Lost City of Pan, 2004; co-author: Discovering the Bible, 1986, Excavations at Capernaum, 1989; contbr. articles, revs. to profl. publs. Mem. Archaeol. Inst. Am., Am. Schs. of Oriental Rsch., Soc. Bib. Lit., Am. Numismatic Soc., Palestine Exploration Soc. Mem. Ch. of Christ. Office: Pepperdine U Seaver Coll 24255 Pacific Coast Hwy Malibu CA 90263-0002 E-mail: jwilson@pepperdine.edu.

WILSON, JOHN JAMES, federal judge; b. Boston, Dec. 23, 1927; s. John J. and Margaret (Thomas) W.; m. Joan Ellen Bostwick, Sept. 1, 1951 (div. Sept. 1975); children: Jeffrey, John, Julie; m. Elizabeth Brower, Dec. 4, 1975; 1 child, Stephane. AB, Tufts U., 1951; LLB, Stanford U., 1954. Bar: Calif. 1954, Mass. 1954, Oreg. 1982, U.S. Dist. Ct. (no., cen., ea. and so. dists.) Calif., U.S. Dist. Ct. Oreg. Asst. U.S. atty., LA, 1958-60; ptnr. Hill, Farrer & Burrill, LA, 1960-85; bankruptcy judge U.S. Dist. Ct. Calif., San Bernardino, 1985-88, Santa Ana, Calif., 1989-99; ret., 1999. Lt. (j.g.) USN, 1945-50. Seventh Day Adventist. Office: 507 Calle Amigo San Clemente CA 92673-3000 E-mail: j.dub@home.com.

WILSON, JOHN PASLEY, retired law educator; b. Newark, Apr. 7, 1933; s. Richard Henry and Susan Agnes (Pasley) Wilson; m. Elizabeth Ann Reed, Sept. 10, 1955 (div.); children: David Cables, John Pasley, Cicely Reed. AB, Princeton U., 1955; LLB, Harvard U., 1962. Bar: US Dist. Ct. NJ 1962, Mass. 1963, US Dist. Ct. Mass. 1963. Budget examiner Exec. Office of Pres., Bur. of Budget, Washington, 1955-56; assoc. Riker, Danzig, Scherer & Brown, Newark, 1962-63; asst. dean Harvard U. Law Sch., Cambridge, Mass., 1963-67; assoc. dean Boston U. Law Sch., 1968-82; dean Golden Gate U. Sch. Law, San Francisco, 1982-88, prof., 1988—2003, prof. emeritus, 2003—, dean emeritus, 2003—. Vis. prof. dept. health policy and mgmt. Harvard U., 1988; cons. Nat. Commn. Protection Human Subjects Biomedical and Behavioral Rsch.; mem. Mass. Gov.'s Commn. Civil and Legal Rights Developmentally disabled; former chmn. adv. com. Ctr. Cmty. Legal Edn., San Francisco. Author: (book) The Rights of Adolescents in the Mental Health System; contbr. chapters to books, articles to profl. jours. Bd. dirs. Greater Boston Legal Svcs., Chewonki Found.; mem. Health Facilities Appeals Bd., Mass.; assoc. mem. Dem. Town Com., Concord; chmn. Bd. Assessors, Concord; bd. overseers Boston Hosp. Women, past chmn. med. affairs com.; past mem. instl. rev. bd. Calif. Pacific Hosp., San Francisco. Served to lt. (j.g.) USNR, 1956—59. NIMH grantee, 1973. Mem.: Nat. Assn. Securities Dealers (arbitrator). Democrat. Personal E-mail: jwlsn7@comcast.net.

WILSON, L. MICHELLE (MICHELLE WILSON), lawyer, information technology executive; b. Boise, Idaho, Jan. 20, 1963; d. Tom Martin and George Ann Wilson; m., 1 son. BA, Univ. Wash., Seattle, 1985; JD with honors, Univ. Chgo., 1988. Assoc. Perkins Coie, Seattle, 1988—94, ptnr., 1994—99; assoc. gen. counsel Amazon.com Inc., Seattle, 1999—99, v.p., gen. counsel, sec., 1999—2001; sr. v.p. HR, gen. counsel, sec. Amazon.com, Seattle, 2001—03, sr. v.p., gen. counsel, sec., 2003—. Recipient Dow Jones award Wall St. Jour., 1985. Mem. ABA, Washington State Bar Assn., Order of Coif, Phi Beta Kappa, Beta Gamma Sigma. Office: Amazon.com Inc 1200 12th Ave S Ste 1200 Seattle WA 98144-2734 Office Phone: 206-266-1000. Office Fax: 206-266-1821.

WILSON, LESLIE, biochemist, cell biologist, professor; b. Boston, June 29, 1941; s. Samuel Paul Wilson and Lee (Melnicker) Kamerling; m. Carla Helena Van Wingerden, Sept. 9, 1989; children from previous marriage: Sebastian A. Michael, Naomi Beth. BS, Mass. Coll. Pharmacy and Allied Health Scis., 1963; PhD, Tufts U., 1967; postgrad., U. Calif., Berkeley, 1967—69; doctorate honoris causa, U. de la Méditerranée, Marseille, France, 1998. Asst. prof. dept. pharmacology Stanford (Calif.) U. Sch. Medicine, 1969-74; assoc. prof. dept. biol. scis. U. Calif., Santa Barbara, 1975-78, prof. biochemistry, 1979—, chmn. dept. biol. scis., 1987-91, head divsn. molecular, cellular, devel. biol., 1992-93, dir. Alzheimer's Disease Ctr., Neurosci. Rsch. Inst., 2002—. Sci. adv. panel mem. cell and devel. biology Am. Cancer Soc., Atlanta, 1984-88; cons. Eli Lilly & Co., Indpls., 1980-92, Tularik Corp., San Francisco, Amgen Corp., Thousand Oaks, Calif.; cons. Boehringer-Ingelheim, Vienna, 2002—; sci. adv. bd. Mycogenetics, 1990-92, OmniTüra, Inc., Inc., 2001-, Broncus Technologies, Inc., 2003-, Genyous Life Scis., 2001-; co-organizer Internat. Colloquium on the Cytoskeleton and human dis., Marseille, France, 2001; cons. Threshold Pharms., 2006- Editor: Methods in Cell Biology, 1987—; assoc. editor: Biochemistry, 1992—. Bd. dirs. Cancer Ctr., Santa Barbara. Rsch. grantee NIH, 1970—, Am. Cancer Soc., 1986-97, Lilly Rsch. Labs., 1990-2001, Phone-Poulenc-Rover, France, 1998-2001, Pierre Fabre Medicament, Castres, France, 1998-2002, Nereus Pharm., 2003-, Allon Pharms., Bristol- Myers Squibb Mem. AAAS, Am. Soc. Cell Biology (chmn. sci. program 1977), Am. Soc. Biol. Chemistry and Molecular Biology, Am. Soc. Pharmacology and Exptl. Therapeutics, Am. Chem. Soc. Democrat. Office: U Calif Dept Molecular Cellular & Devel Biology Santa Barbara CA 93106 Office Phone: 805-893-2819. E-mail: wilson@lifesci.ucsb.edu.

WILSON, LIZABETH ANNE (BETSY WILSON), dean, library director; b. Waterloo, Iowa, May 21, 1954; d. Martin Lucien and Joanne Hausser Wilson; m. Dean August Pollack, Sept. 1, 1983. BA, Northwestern U., 1972—77; MLS, U. of Ill., 1977—78. Asst. architecture and art libr. U. Ill., 1979—80, asst. undergrad. libr., 1980—86, asst. dir. librs. undergrad. and instrnl. svcs., 1986—92; assoc. dir. librs. for rsch. and instrnl. svcs. U. Wash., Seattle, 1992—2000, dean U. librs., 2001—. Chair of bd. of trustees OCLC, Inc., Dublin, 2003—07; exec. dir. Leopoldo Cicognara Program+, Urbana-Champaign, Ill., 1987—2004; co-founder UWired collaboration at the University of Washington, Digital Futures Alliance. Author (co-author): (journal article) The Bottom Line; contbr. chapters to books, articles. Recipient Margaret E. Monroe Libr. Adult Services award, RUSA/Am. Libr. Assn., 1995, Miriam Dudley Instrn. Libr. award, Assn. Coll. and Rsch. Libraries, 1995, EDUCAUSE Award for Systemic Progress in Tchg. and Learning, 2000. Mem.: Coun. on Libr. Resources (bd. mem. 2007—), Greater Western Libr. Alliance (pres. 2004), Digital Libr. Fedn. (mem. exec. com. 2004—07), OCLC Membs. Coun. (pres. 1999—2000), Assn. Rsch. Librs. (bd. dirs. 2003—06), Instrn. Sect. of ACRL (chair 1990—91), Assn. Coll. and Rsch. Librs. (pres. 2000—01, Excellence in Academic Libr. award 2004, Academic/Rsch. Libr. of Yr. 2007). Office: Dean of Libraries University Washington Box 352900 Seattle WA 98195-2900 Office Fax: 206-685-8727. Business E-Mail: betsyw@u.washington.edu.

WILSON, M. ROY, academic administrator, medical educator; b. Yokohama, Japan, Nov. 28, 1953; BS, Allegheny Coll., 1976; MD, Harvard Med. Sch., 1980; MS in Epidemiology, UCLA, 1990. Diplomate Nat. Bd. Medicine, Am. Bd. Ophthalmology. Intern Harlem Hosp. Ctr., NYC, 1980-81; resident in ophthalmology Mass. Eye & Ear Infirmary/Harvard Med. Sch., Boston, 1981-84, glaucoma, 1984-85; clin. fellow in ophthalmology Harvard Med. Sch., 1980-85, clin. asst. ophthalmology, 1985-86; clin. instr. dept. surgery, Divsn. Ophthalmology Howard U. Sch. Medicine, Washington, 1985-86; asst. prof. ophthalmology UCLA, 1986-91; asst. prof., chief Divsn. Ophthalmology Charles R. Drew U. of Medicine and Sci., LA, 1986-90, assoc. prof., chief Divsn. Ophthalmology, 1991-94, acad. dean, 1993-95, dean, 1995-98, prof., 1994-98, UCLA, 1994-98; dean sch. medicine Creihton U., Omaha, 1998—, interim v.p., 1999-2000, vice pres. health scis., 2001—; pres. Tex. Tech. U. Health Sci. Ctr., Lubbock, 2003—06; chancellor U. Colo at Denver Health Scis. Ctr., 2006—. Asst. in ophthalmology Mass. Eye and Ear Infirmary, 1985-86; cons. ophthalmologist, Victoria Hosp., Castries, St. Lucia, 1985-86; hosp. appointment, UCLA; chief physician Martin Luther King, Jr. Hosp., L.A., 1986—; project dir. Internat. Eye Found., Ministry of Health, 1985-86; biology lab instr., Allegheny coll., 1975; instr. in biochemistry Harvard U. Summer Sch., 1977-78; instr. Harvard Med. Sch., 1980-85, others; cons. and presenter in field; participant coms. in field. Mem. AMA, APHA, Assn. Rsch. in Vision and Ophthalmology, Chandler-Grant Glaucoma Soc., Nat. Med. Assn., Am. Acad. Ophthalmology, Inst. Medicine (elected 2003), Soc. Eye Surgeons Internat. Eye Found., Mass. Eye and Ear Infirmary Alumni Assn., So. Calif. Glaucoma Soc., West Coast Glaucoma Study Club, Assn. Univ. Profs. in Ophthalmology, L.A. Eye Soc., Calif. Med. Assn., Am. Glaucoma Soc., Soc. Epidemiol. Rsch. Office: U Colo at Denver Health Scis Ctr 35 SYS Boulder CO 80309-0035

WILSON, MICHELLE See WILSON, L.

WILSON, MIRIAM GEISENDORFER, retired physician, educator; b. Yakima, Wash., Dec. 3, 1922; d. Emil and Frances Geisendorfer; m. Howard G. Wilson, June 21, 1947; children— Claire, Paula, Geoffrey, Nicola, Marla. BS, U. Wash., Seattle, 1944, MS, 1945; MD, U. Calif., San Francisco, 1950. Mem. faculty U. So. Calif. Sch. Medicine, LA, 1965—, prof. pediatrics, 1969—2004, emeritus prof. pediatrics, 2004—. Office: U So Calif Med Ctr 1129 N State St Rm 1g24 Los Angeles CA 90033-1044

WILSON, MYRON ROBERT, JR., retired psychiatrist; b. Helena, Mont., Sept. 21, 1932; s. Myron Robert, Sr. and Constance Ernestine (Bultman) Wilson. BA, Stanford U., 1954, MD, 1957. Diplomate Am. Bd. Psychiatry and Neurology. Dir. adolescent psychiatry Mayo Clinic, Rochester, Minn., 1965—71; pres., psychiatrist in chief Wilson Ctr., Faribault, Minn., 1971—86, chmn., 1986—90; ret., 1990. Assoc. clin. prof. UCLA, 1985—99. Contbr. articles to profl. jours. Chmn., CEO C. B. Wilson Found., LA, 1972—2006; bd. dirs. Pasadena (Calif.) Symphony Orch. Assn., 1987; vestryman, treas. St. Thomas' Parish, LA, 1993—96. Lt. comdr. USN, 1958—60. Fellow, Mayo Grad. Sch. Medicine, Rochester, 1960—65. Fellow: Internat. Soc. Adolescent Psychiatry (founder, treas. 1985—88, sec. 1985—88, treas. 1988—92), Am. Soc. Adolescent Psychiatry, Am. Psychiat. Assn.; mem.: Order St. John of Jerusalem, Sigma Xi (Mayo Found. chpt.). Episcopalian. Office Phone: 760-325-4956. Personal E-mail: mrobertwilson@aol.com.

WILSON, NANCY LINDA, religious organization administrator; b. Mineola, NY, July 13, 1950; Grad., Allegheny Coll.; student, Boston U.; MDiv, SS, Cyril and Methodius Sem. Ordained to ministry Universal Fellowship of Met. Cmty. Chs. Dist. coord. N.E. dist. Universal Fellowship of Met. Cmty. Chs., clk. bd. of elders Fellowship hdqrs. LA, 1979-86, sr. pastor Met. Comty. Ch., 1986—; vice-moderator UFMCC, LA, 1993—. Bd. trustees Samaritan Inst. Religious Studies; founder, chief ecumenical officer Ecumenical Witness and Ministry; vice chair Progressive Religious Alliance. Author: Our Tribe: Queer Folks, God, Jesus and the Bible, 1995; co-author: Amazing Grace; prodr.: (brochure) Our Story Too. Rockefeller scholar. Office: Met Cmty Ch 8714 Santa Monica Blvd West Hollywood CA 90069-4508

WILSON, OWEN MEREDITH, JR., lawyer, mediator, arbitrator; b. Oakland, Calif., Dec. 22, 1939; s. O. Meredith and Marian Wilson; m. Sandra A. Wilson (div.); children: Ann, Melissa, Jennifer; m. Teddi Anne Wilson; children: Amanda, Lisa. Student, U. Utah, 1957-59; AB, Harvard U., 1961; LLB, U. Minn., 1965. Bar: Oreg. 1965. Ptnr. Lane Powell PC, Portland, Oreg., 1969—2005; prin. Wilson Dispute Resolution, Portland, 2005—. Mem. mediation panel U.S. Dist. Ct., 1986—. Mem. bd. visitors Law Sch. U. Minn., 1990-96. Mem. ABA, Oreg. State Bar Assn., Multnomah Bar Assn. Office: 1211 SW 5th Ave Ste 2950 Portland OR 97204-3158 Home Phone: 503-292-6981; Office Phone: 503-972-5090. Business E-Mail: met@wilsonadr.com.

WILSON, PATRICK JOSEPH, actor; b. Norfolk, Va., July 3, 1973; m. Dagmara Dominczyk, June 18, 2005; 1 child. BFA in drama, Carnegie Mellon U., 1995. Actor: (Broadway plays) The Gershwins' Fascinating Rhythm, 1999, The Full Monty, 2000—01, Oklahoma!, 2002, Barefoot in the Park, 2006, All My Sons, 2008; (films) My Sister's Wedding, 2001, The Alamo, 2004, The Phantom of the Opera, 2004, Hard Candy, 2005, Little Children, 2006 (Young Hollywood award, 2006), Running with Scissors, 2006, Brothers Three: An American Gothic, 2007, Purple Violets, 2007, Evening, 2007, Life in Flight, 2008, Lakeview Terrace, 2008, Passengers, 2008, Watchmen, 2009; (TV miniseries) Angels in America, 2003. Office: c/o Tony Lipp Creative Artists Agency 2000 Avenue of the Stars Los Angeles CA 90067

WILSON, PEGGY, state legislator; b. Anamosa, Iowa, Sept. 8, 1945; m Woody Wilson; children: Tad, Gina and Chris, seven grandchildren. A in Registered Nursing, U. Alaska; AS, Kirkwood Cmty. Coll., 1969—73. Cert. Nationally Cert. Sch. Nurse. Alaska State Representative, District 2, 2001-. EMT, Tok Area Emergency Management Serv, currently; business owner, formerly; milk cow farmer, formerly; sch. nurse Mem. Coun. State Govts., 1990—93; mem. fiscal policy com. Nat. Conf. State Legislatures, 2001—06, mem. women's legis. network, 2003—; mem. Pacific Northwest Econ. Region, 2001—06, Western Legis. Forestry Task Force, 2001—04, Wrangell/Petersburg Resource Adv. Com., 2002—06, Alaska Comprhensive Ctr. Adv. Bd., 2006, Alaska-Can. Electrical Intertie Steering Com., 2006. Mem. Tok Ambulance Squad. Mem.: Bus. and Profl. Women, Rotary Internat., Pilot Internat. (v.p.). Republican. Office: State Capitol Rm 408 Juneau AK 99801-1182 Home Phone: 907-874-3088; Office Phone: 907-465-3824. Office Fax: 907-465-3175. Business E-Mail: Rep_Peggy_Wilson@legis.state.ak.us.*

WILSON, PETE, former Governor of California; b. Lake Forest, Ill., Aug. 23, 1933; s. James Boone and Margaret (Callaghan) W.; m. Betty Robertson (div.); m. Gayle Edlund, May 29, 1983 BA in English Lit., Yale U., 1955; JD, U. Calif., Berkeley, 1962; LL.D., Grove City Coll., 1983, U. Calif., San Diego, 1983, U. San Diego, 1984. Bar: Calif. 1962. Mem. Calif. State Assembly from 76th Dist., Sacramento, 1966-71; mayor City of San Diego, 1971-83; US Senator from Calif., 1983-91; gov. State of Calif., 1991-98; mng. dir. Pacific Capital Group, Beverly Hills, Calif., 1999—2002. Disting. vis. fellow Hoover Inst., Stanford, Calif., 1999—. Author: Drug Abuse as a Legislative Problem, 1968. Trustee Conservation Found.; mem. exec. bd. San Diego County council Boy Scouts Am.; hon. trustee So. Calif. Council Soviet Jews; adv. mem. Urban Land Inst., 1985-86; founding dir. Retinitis Pigmentosa Internat.; hon. dir. Alzheimer's Family Ctr., Inc., 1985; hon. bd. dirs. Shakespeare-San Francisco, 1985 From 2nd lt. to 1st lt. USMC, 1955—58, Hawaii. Recipient Golden Bulldog award, 1984, 85, 86, Guardian of Small Bus. award, 1984, Cuauhtemoc plaque for disting. svc. to farm workers in Calif., 1991, Julius award for outstanding pub. leadership U. So. Calif., 1992, award of appreciation Nat. Head Start, 1992; named Legislator of Yr., League Calif. Cities, 1985, Man of Yr. N.G. Assn. Calif., 1986, Man of Yr. citation U. Calif. Boalt Hall, 1986; ROTC scholar Yale U., 1951-55. Mem. Nat. Mil. Family Assn. (adv. bd.), Phi Delta Phi, Zeta Psi Republican. Episcopalian. Office: Hoover Inst Stanford U 434 Galvez Mall Stanford CA 94305-6010 Office Phone: 650-723-1754. Office Fax: 916-445-4633.

WILSON, RICHARD ALLAN, landscape architect; b. Chgo., Feb. 5, 1927; s. Edgar Allan and Lois Helena (Hearn) W.; m. Lisabet Julie Horchler, May 31, 1958; children: Gary Allan, Carl Bruce. BS, U. Calif., Berkeley, 1952. Engring. draftsman Freeland Evanson & Christenson, San Diego, 1952-53; designer, estimator Blue Pacific Nursery & Landscape Co., San Diego, 1955-59; prin. Richard A. Wilson, FASLA and Assocs., San Diego, 1959—. Sec. Calif. Coun. Landscape Architects, 1982-85; expert witness for law firms, 1983—. Designer Phil Swing Meml. Fountain, 1967. Mem. landscape com. Clairemont Town Coun., San Diego, 1955. With U.S. Army, 1944-46, Korea. Recipient First Pl. award for landscape So. Calif. Expdn., Del Mar, 1963. Fellow Am. Soc. Landscape Architects (del. coun. 1982-85), Am. Inst. Landscape Architects (treas. 1970, 2d v.p. 1971). Republican. Home and Office: 2570 Tokalon Ct San Diego CA 92110-2232

WILSON, ROBERT E., academic administrator; Attended, Culinary Inst. Am. Exec. chef Freedom Plaza, Union Hills Country Club, Club Corp. Am., Del. E. Webb Devel.; chef instr. Scottsdale Culinary Inst., Ariz., 1994—2001, dir. info. technologies Ariz., 1994—2001; pres., co-founder Ariz. Culinary Inst., Scottsdale, 2001—. Office: Arizona Culinary Institute 10585 N 114th St Ste 401 Scottsdale AZ 85259 Office Phone: 866-294-2433.

WILSON, ROBIN SCOTT, retired academic administrator, writer; b. Columbus, Ohio, Sept. 19, 1928; s. John Harold and Helen Louise (Walker) W.; m. Patricia Ann Van Kirk, Jan. 20, 1951; children: Kelpie, Leslie, Kari, Andrew. BA, Ohio State U., 1950; MA, U. Ill., 1951, PhD, 1959. Fgn. intelligence officer CIA, Washington, 1959-67; prof. English Clarion State Coll., Pa., 1967-70; assoc. dir. Com. Instnl. Cooperation, Evanston, Ill., 1970-77; assoc. provost instrn. Ohio State U., Columbus, 1977-80; univ. pres. Calif. State U., Chico, 1980-93, pres. emeritus, 1993—. Author: Those Who Can, 1973, Death By Degrees, 1995, Paragons, 1996; short stories, criticism, articles on edn. Lt. USN, 1953-57. Mem. AAAS, Phi Kappa Phi E-mail: robinwilson@comcast.net.

WILSON, RONALD A., judge; b. 1968; Presiding judge South Tucson City Ct., 2002—. Recipient Rosa Parks Living History Makers award, NAACP, 2006; named 40 Under 40 Tucson Bus. Edge Man of Yr., 2006. Personal E-mail: ronaldawilson@hotmail.com.

WILSON, STEPHEN VICTOR, federal judge; b. Hartford, Conn., Mar. 26, 1942; s. Harry and Rae (Ross) W. BA in Econs., Lehigh U., 1963; JD, Bklyn. Law Sch., 1967; LLM, George Washington U., 1973. Bar: N.Y. 1967, D.C. 1971, Calif. 1972, U.S. Ct. Appeals (9th cir.), U.S. Dist. Ct. (so., cen. and no. dists.) Calif. Trial atty. Tax divsn. U.S. Dept. Justice, 1968-71, asst. U.S. atty. LA, 1971-77, chief spl. prosecutions, 1973-77; ptnr. Hochman, Salkin & Deroy, Beverly Hills, Calif., 1977—85; judge U.S. Dist. Ct. (cen. dist.) Calif., LA, 1985—. Adj. prof. law Loyola U. Law Sch., 1976-79; U.S. Dept. State rep. to govt. W.Ger. on 20th anniversary of Marshall Plan, 1967; del. jud. conf. U.S. Ct. Appeals (9th cir.), 1982-86. Co-editor Tax Crimes--Corporate Liability, BNA Tax Management Series, 1983; contbr. articles to profl. jours. Recipient Spl. Commendation award U.S.

Dept. Justice, 1977. Mem. ABA, L.A. County Bar Assn., Beverly Hills Bar Assn. (chmn. criminal law com.), Fed. Bar Assn. Jewish. Office: US Courthouse 312 N Spring St Ste 217J Los Angeles CA 90012-4704

WILSON, STEVE, museum director; BFA, U. So. Calif.; MFA in acting, Nat. Theatre Conservatory, Denver. Tchr., performing arts chmn. St. Mary's Acad., Colo.; faculty mem. Wolf Theatre Acad. and Stage Eleven; artist-in-residence Cherry Creek and Denver Pub. Sch. Dists., Denver Sch. Arts; exec. artistic dir., acting dir. Mizel Ctr. for Arts and Culture; dir. Wolf Theatre Acad. Office: Mizel Ctr Arts and Culture 350 S Dahlia St Denver CO 80246 Office Phone: 303-316-6363.

WILSON, WARREN SAMUEL, clergyman; b. New Orleans, May 15, 1927; s. Charlie Price and Warnie (Hart) W.; m. Lillie Pearl Harvey, Apr. 10, 1947; 1 child, Barbara LaJoyce. BA, So. U., Baton Rouge, 1950; DDiv, Moody Coll., Chgo., 1952; DDiv (hon.), Trinity Hall Coll. and Sem., Springfield, Ill., 1975. Ordained to ministry Ch. of God in Christ, 1952, crowned bishop, apptd. state bishop, Calif., 1970, chmn. internat. fin. and budget com. Min. St. Bernard St. Church of God in Christ, New Orleans, 1952—60, Fresno (Calif.) Temple Ch. of God in Christ, 1963—; jurisdictional biship Central Valley Ch. of God in Christ, 1970—; internat. fin. chmn. bd. of bishops Ch. of God in Christ, 1974—. Served with USN, 1942-46, PTO. Mem. NAACP (life). Avocations: fishing, boating.

WILSON, WILLIAM (BILL) F., state legislator; b. Great Falls, Mont., Mar. 28, 1961; m to Robin; children: Brittany. Montana State Senator, District 19, 1993-94, District 22, 1995-99, member, Bills & Journals, State Admin, Labor & Employee Relations, Conf, Natural Resources Committees & Select Committee on Const Amendments, formerly, Montana State Senate; member, Montana Boating Advisor Coun, 1995-99; Montana State Representative, District 46, 2003-04, District 22, 2005-, chairman, Ethics Committee, currently, member, Judiciary Committee, currently, Montana House Representative.Laborer, Burlington Northern, 1979, brakeman, 1979-93, conductor, 1982-93, engr, 1994-. United Transportation Union Local 730 (president, 1986-89). Democrat. Mailing: 1305 Second Ave N 3 Great Falls MT 59401-3217 E-mail: bw22@bresnan.net.*

WILSON, WILLIAM HALL, JR., retired telecommunications executive; b. Jan. 25, 1942; s. William Hall and Mary Elizabeth (Wamsley) Wilson; m. Jeri Sue Ishida, Oct. 15, 1976; 1 child, Kauialoahaokalani Rae. BSEE, U. Tenn., Knoxville, 1964; MS in Systems Mgmt., U. So. Calif., LA, 1972. Registered: (patent agt.). Field engr. IBM, Atlanta, 1964—65; engr. Hawaiian Tel. Co., Honolulu, 1969—72, pers. adminstr., 1972—73; mgr. regulatory rels. Hawaiian Tel. Co./GTESC, Honolulu and Washington, 1973—78; dir. reglatory rels. Hawaiian Tel. Co., Honolulu and Washington, 1978—79; dir. systems and procedures GTE Service Co., Lexington, Ky., 1979—84; mgr. govt. comm. GTE Telecom, Inc., Washington, 1984—90; prin. cons. Telecoms. Assocs., McLean, Va., 1990—94; prin. engr. Performance Devel. Corp., Germantown, Md., 1991; patent examiner U.S. Patent and Trademark Office, Washington, 1994—99; electronics engr. FCC, Washington, 1999—2008. Capt. USAF, 1965—69. Mem.: Mensa. Achievements include Nationally rated tournament chess player. Home: 948 Waiakamilo Rd Honolulu HI 96817 Personal E-mail: whwilsonjr@earthlink.net.

WILSON, WILLIAM HARWELL, psychiatrist, educator; b. Memphis, Feb. 6, 1951; s. Joseph Harwell Wilson and Helen Wilson (Cobb) Carruthers; m. Paula Rea, Oct. 18, 1986; children: Rea Xan, Sanford Shepherd. BA, Brown U., 1973; MD, U. Pa., 1981. Diplomate Am. Bd. Psychiatry and Neurology, Nat. Bd. Med. Examiners. Resident in psychiatry U. Wis., Madison, 1981-85; asst. prof. psychiatry U. Pitts. Sch. Medicine, 1985-86, Med. Coll. Pa., Phila., 1986-89, Oreg. Health Scis. U., Portland, 1989—93, asst. dir. pub. psychiatry tng. program, 1989—94, assoc. prof. psychiatry, 1993—2003, prof. psychiatry, 2003—. Dir. prof. edn. unit Dammasch State Hosp., Wilsonville, Oreg., 1989-94; attending psychiatrist Oreg. Health Scis. U. Hosp., 1994—; dir. Inpatient Psychiatric Svc., 2002-. Contbr. numerous articles on treatment of schizophrenia to sci. jours. Grantee NIMH, 1989-93; Recipient of Mental Health award of Excellence, State Oreg. Disting. fellow Am. Psychiat. Assn.; mem. Soc. for Biol. Psychiatry, Psychiatry, World Fedn. Mental Health, Nat. Alliance for Mentally Ill (Exemplary Psychiatrist award 1992, 98), Am. Soc. Clin. Psychopharmacology. Office: Oreg Health Scis U Mail Code UHN-80 3181 SW Sam Jackson Park Rd Portland OR 97239-3011 Office Phone: 503-494-7353. Business E-Mail: wilsonw@ohsu.edu.

WILTON, PETER CAMPBELL, marketing educator; b. Adelaide, SA, Australia, Jan. 28, 1951; came to U.S., 1975; s. Murray and Kathleen (Ratcliffe) W. B in Commerce with hons., U. New South Wales, Sydney, 1972; PhD in Mgmt., Purdue U., 1979. Product mgr. Colgate Palmolive, Sydney, 1973-75; mktg. prof., Hass Sch. of Bus. U. Calif., Berkeley, 1979-87, 92—; COO Myer Pacific Corp., Melbourne, Australia, 1987-90; sr. assoc. Melbourne U., 1990, Sir Donald Hibberd lectr., 1991. Vis. fellow Griffith U., Brisbane, Australia, 1982; vis. assoc. prof. Duke U., Durham, N.C., 1985-86; pres., dir. Applied Mktg. Analysis, Inc., Wilmington, Del., 1987—, Orbis Assocs., San Francisco, 1992—. Contbr. articles to profl. jours. Recipient Mktg. Rsch. Soc. Australia prize, 1973; Australian Govt. fellow, 1975-79; grantee NSF, 1981, 84. Mem. Assn. Pub. Opinion Rsch. (officer 1985), Am. Mktg. Assn. (officer 1982-84), Australian-Am. C. of C. (dir. 1993-95). Avocations: flying, sailing, music, travel. Office: Haas Sch of Bus UCAL Berkeley S 545 Haas Berkeley CA 94720-1900

WIMER, MARK G., healthcare management company executive; BS in Bacteriology, U. Idaho; M of Health Adminstrn., St. Louis U. Pres. skilled nursing facility subs. Sun Healthcare Group, Albuquerque, 1993-97, sr. v.p. inpatient svcs., pres. COO, 1997—. Office: Sun Healthcare Group Inc 101 Sun Ave NE Albuquerque NM 87109-4373

WINBLAD, ANN, investment company executive; BA in Math. and Bus. Adminstrn., U. St. Thomas, St. Paul, Minn., MA in Internat. Econs. and Edn.; LLD (hon.), U. St. Thomas. Systems programmer Fed. Reserve Bank; co-founder Open Systems, Inc., 1976-83; strategic planning cons., IBM, Microsoft, Price Waterhouse, and many start-ups; co-founding ptnr., mng. dir. Hummer Winblad Venture Ptnrs., San Francisco, 1989—. Bd. dirs. Dean & Deluca, Intacct, Market Wire, The Knot, Voltage Security, Arbor Software, Berkeley Systems, Net Perceptions; advisor The Software Forum, San Jose Ctr. for Software Develop., Stanford/MIT Venture Forum. Co-author: Object-Oriented Software, 1990; contbr. articles to profl. publs. Trustee U. St. Thomas, St. Paul, Mich. Office: Hummer Winblad Venture Partners 1 Lombard St Ste 300 San Francisco CA 94111-1130

WINCHESTER, ED, protective services official; Chief of police, Fresno, Calif.

WINDELS, SUE, state legislator; b. Nampa, Idaho, Mar. 11, 1946; m to Carl Otis Windels; children: Derek & Dan. Colorado State Representative, District 27, 1999-2001, member, Education & State Vet & Mil Affairs Committees, formerly, Education & Judiciary Committees, 2001-01, Colorado House Representative; Colorado State Senator, District 19, 2002-, chairwoman, Education Committee, currently, member, State Veterans & Military Affairs, Legislature Coun, Capital Develop, currently, Colorado State Senate. AAUW; LWV; PTA; Interfaith Alliance; Kiwanis Club. Democrat. Christian. Mailing: 13925 W 73rd Ave Arvada CO 80005 Fax: 303-866-4543. E-mail: windels@sni.net; sue.windels.senate@state.co.us.

WINDER, CHARLES L., state legislator; b. Ontario, Oreg., Nov. 21, 1945; s. Henry J. and Dorothy (Bridwell) W.; m. Dianne P. Winder, June 7, 1968; children: Elizabeth Nelson, David C. BA in Polit. Sci., Coll. of Idaho, 1968. Asst. to pres. Makad, Inc., Nampa & Boise, Idaho, 1972-73; v.p. devel. Emkay Devel. Inc., Boise, 1973-79; pres. Winder Devel. Svc. Inc., The Winder Co., Boise, 1979; mem. Dist. 14 Idaho State Senate, Boise, 2008—. Commr. Boise City Planning & Zoning Commn., 1976-81, Ada County Hwy. Dist., Boise, 1981-93; Rep. candidate for Gov. of Idaho, 1994; pres. Jr. Achievement Idaho, Boise, 1989-91; mem. Boise Area Economic Devel. Coun., Boise C. of C., Bible Study Fellowship, Boise City Design & Review/Com., Boise Visions Steering Com.; trustee Coll. of Idaho. Lt. USN, 1968—79. Mem. Nat. Assn. Realtors, Children's Home Soc. Idaho, Ada Planning Assn., Arid Club. Republican. Presbyterian. Avocations: fishing, hunting, photography, reading. Office: Dist 14 5528 North Ebbetts Ave Boise ID 83713 Office Phone: 208-343-2300. Office Fax: 208-389-2088. Business E-Mail: cwinder@senate.idaho.gov.

WINDER, DAVID KENT, judge; b. Salt Lake City, June 8, 1932; s. Edwin Kent and Alma Eliza (Cannon) W.; m. Pamela Martin, June 24, 1955 (dec. 2005); children: Ann, Kay, James. BA, U. Utah, 1955; LLB, Stanford U., 1958. Bar: Utah 1958, Calif. 1958. Assoc. firm Clyde, Mecham & Pratt, Salt Lake City, 1958-66; law clk. to chief justice Utah Supreme Ct., 1958-59; dep. county atty. Salt Lake County, 1959-63, chief dep. dist. atty., 1965-66; asst. U.S. atty. Salt Lake City, 1963-65; partner firm Strong & Hanni, Salt Lake City, 1966-77; judge US Dist. Ct., Salt Lake City, 1977-79, 1979-93, chief judge, 1993-97, sr. judge, 1997—. Examiner Utah Bar Examiners, 1975-79, chmn., 1977-79; mem. jud. resources com., 1998-01. Served with USAF, 1951-52. Mem. Am. Bd. Trial Advocates, Utah State Bar (Judge of Yr. award 1978), Salt Lake County Bar Assn., Calif. State Bar. Democrat. Office: US Dist Ct 110 US Courthouse 350 S Main St Salt Lake City UT 84101-2106

WINDER, ROBERT OWEN, mathematician, computer engineer, geophysicist; b. Boston, Oct. 9, 1934; s. Claude V. and Harriet O. W.; m. Kathleen C. Winder; children by previous marriage: Katherine, Amy. AB, U. Chgo., 1954; BS, U. Mich., 1956; MS, Princeton U., 1958, PhD, 1962; MS, Ariz. State U., 2000. With RCA, 1957-78, group head Princeton and Somerville, NJ, 1969-75, dir. microprocessors, 1975-77, dir. systems, 1977-78; mgr. workstation devel. Exxon Enterprises, Inc., Princeton, 1978-85; v.p. Syntex Computer Systems Inc., Bordentown, NJ, 1985-88; mgr. product engring., Princeton Operation, Intel Corp., 1988-93; mgr. engring. ops. video products div., Intel, Chandler, Ariz., 1993-95. Vis. scholar dept. geol. scis. Ariz. State U., Tempe, 2001—06; active mem. gov. Acad. Village, Tucson, 2007—. Contbr. articles to profl. jours.; patentee in field. NSF fellow, 1956-57; Recipient David Sarnoff award RCA, 1975. Fellow IEEE.

WINE, MARK PHILIP, lawyer; b. Iowa City, Jan. 6, 1949; s. Donald Arthur and Mary Lepha Schneider; m. Carol Jean Sullivan; children: Nicholas Cox, Meredith Kathryn, Callie Ann, Cassidy Mae. AB, Princeton U., 1971; JD, U. Iowa, 1974. Bar: Iowa 1974, Minn. 1976, Calif. 1997, U.S. Dist. Ct. Minn. 1976, U.S. Ct. Appeals (8th cir.) 1976, U.S. Supreme Ct. 1984, U.S. Ct. Appeals (4th cir.) 1985, U.S. Ct. Appeals (7th and Fed. cirs.) 1992, U.S. Ct. Appeals (9th cir.) 1997, U.S. Dist. Ct. (so., no. and ctrl. dists.) Calif. 1997. Law clk. to judge U.S. Ct. Appeals (8th cir.), St. Louis, 1974-76; ptnr. Oppenheimer Wolff & Donnelly, 1976—2002, McDermott, Will & Emery, LA, 2002—08, Orrick Herrington and Sutcliffe, 2008—. Mem. ABA, Internat. Assn. Def. Counsel, Calif. Bar Assn., L.A. Bar Assn., L.A. Intellectual Property Law Assn., Princeton Club So. Calif. Democrat. Avocations: cooking, reading, golf. Home: 6220 E Fox Glen Dr Anaheim CA 92807 Office: Orrick Herrington & Sutcliffe LLP 4 Park Plz Ste 1600 Irvine CA 92614 Office Phone: 949-852-7704. Personal E-mail: mpwineca@sbcglobal.net. Business E-Mail: mwine@orrick.com.

WINFIELD, ARMAND GORDON, retired international plastics consultant, educator; b. Chgo., Dec. 28, 1919; m. Nancy Ethal Ufford, 1946 (div. 1946); m. Lillian Tsukea Kubota, June 8, 1951 (dec. Dec. 1965); m. Barbara Jane La Barge, July 23, 1966 (dec. May 1992); m. Vaclava Ianiuviere, 2002 (div. 2005). Grad., Newark Acad., 1937; BS, Franklin and Marshall Coll., 1941; postgrad., U. N.Mex., 1941—42, Washington U., St. Louis, 1948-50. Undergrad. tchg. fellow Franklin and Marshall Coll., 1939-41; owner Winfield Fine Art in Jewelry, NYC, 1945-48; rsch. dir. Hanley Plastics Co. divsn. Wallace Pencil Co., St. Louis, 1955-57; plastic cons. engr. DeBell & Richardson, Inc., Hazardville, Conn., 1957-64; exec. v.p. Crystopal Ltd., Hazardville, 1963-64; pres., CEO Armand G. Winfield Inc., NYC, West Babylon, NY, 1964—2004, Santa Fe, Albuquerque; mem. faculty Harris Tchrs. Coll., 1950; dept. engring. Washington U., St. Louis, 1956, Yale U., Inst. in Art, 1960-61, Pratt Inst., 1964—70; rsch. prof. mech. engring., dir. tng. and rsch. Inst. for Plastics, U N.Mex., 1993—2004; ret., 2004. Adviser USIA on plastics show to tour USSR, 1960-61; chmn. SPE Traveling Exhibn., Plastics-A New Dimention in Bldg., 1960-62; vis. critic in arch. CCNY, 1968; cons. indsl. design dept., faculty Pratt Inst., Bklyn., 1964-70; instr. prodn. methods, 1968-70; lectr. U. Hartford U. Kans., 1970, U. Ariz., 1978, Calif. Poly. State U., 1980, instr. plastics, U. Mass., Lowell, 1978-82; numerous others; adj. prof. plastics engring. U. Lowell (Mass.), 1978-81; keynote spkr. Acoplásticos conf., Cartagena, Colombia, 1986; conceived and directed the building of 13 installation at N.Y. Worlds Fair, 1962-63; U. N.Mex. del., paper presenter XVIII Pacific Sci. Congress, Beijing, 1995; trustee Plascits Inst. am., Lowell, Mass., 1996-2000; UNIDO expert in newer fibers and composites, India, 1977, cons. glass fibers and composities, Colombia, 1979, low cost housing, India, 1977. Author: The Alexian Brothers, 1951, Merchants Exchange of St. Louis, 1953, Plastics for Architects, Artists and Interior Designers, 1961, 100 Years Young, 1968, co-Author: (with Henry M. Richardson) Plastics-USA, 1961, Inventors Handbook, 1990; contbr. chpts. to books, numerous articles on plastics; monthly column in Display World Mag., 1965-68, Designer Mag., 1971-72, Museum Scope, 1976-77; spl. exhibns. at Smithsonian Inst., Washington, 1988-2003, Cooper Hewitt, N.Y.C., 1993, Mus. Sci. and Industry, London, 1994, Franklin & Marshall Coll. Mus., 1996; patentee on mass-producible process for embedding specimens in acrylics (embedded walkie-talked for U.S. War Dept., 1945; archived in Ctr. for S.W. Rsch., Albuquerque, 1994, Smithsonian Mus. Natural Histroy, 1998, Smithsonian Inst. Nat. Design Mus., 2000, Nat. PlasticsCtr. and Mus., Leominster, Mass., 2004; archive John F. Kennedy Libr. and Mus. Oral History, 2000, Cooper-Hewitt Mus., NYC, contbr. articles to profl. jours.; 7 patents in field. Mem. Vol. in Tech. Assistance, 1983; bd. dirs. Santa Fe Crime Stoppers, 1980-94, chmn., 1986, 87, carnival chmn., 1983, 84. With US Army, 1943—44, WW II. Recipient Santa Fe Crime Stoppers award, 1980-94, Popejoy medal U. N.Mex., 1997; U.S. State Dept. Am. Specialist grantee to USSR, 1961, UNIDO grantee, 1968-79. Fellow Plastics and Rubber Inst. (Eng. 1970), Soc. Plastics Engring., Soc. Plastics Engrs. (sr. mem. emeritus; pres. We. New Eng. sect. 1963-64, v.p. N.Y. sect. 1968-69, chmn. regional tech. conf. 1967, historian ann. tech. conf. 1968; mem. Soc. Advancement Materials and Process Engring. (chpt. chmn. 1986, 87, 94, 95, 96, 97, editor newsletter 1987, 94, 95, spl. status hon. sr. mem. life 1994, chpt. bd. dirs. 1998—); Soc. Plastic Industry, Plastics Pioneers Assn. Home and Office: 6801 Los Volcanes Rd NW Apt A9 Set #1 Albuquerque NM 87121-8408 Office Phone: 505-836-0985.

WINFIELD, DAVE (DAVID MARK WINFIELD), professional sports team executive, sportscaster, retired professional baseball player; b. St. Paul, Oct. 3, 1951; m. Tonya Winfield; children: Arielle Arline, David Mark II. Student, U. Minn.; LLD (hon.), Syracuse U., 1987. Outfielder San Diego Padres, 1973-80, NY Yankees, 1980-90, Calif. Angels, 1990-91, Toronto Blue Jays, 1991-92, Minn. Twins, 1992-94, Cleve. Indians, 1995; commentator Fox Broadcasting Co., Beverly Hills, Calif., 1996—2002; v.p., sr. adv. San Diego Padres, 2002—; analyst, Baseball Tonight ESPN, 2009—. Co-author (with Tom Parker) Winfield: A Player's Life, 1988. Founder David M. Winfield Found. for Underprivileged Youth, 1975—. Recipient Golden Glove award, 1979-80, 1982-85, 1987, Silver Slugger award, 1981-85, 1992, Babe Ruth award, 1992, Branch Rickey award, 1992, Roberto Clemente award, 1994; named Sporting News Am. League Comeback Player of Yr., 1990; named to the Nat. League All-Star Team, 1977-80, Am. League All-Star Team, 1981-88, Sporting News All-Star Team, 1979, 1982-84, 1992, Major League Baseball Hall of Fame, 2001, Coll. Baseball Hall of Fame, 2006. Achievements include member of Major League Baseball World Series Championship winning Toronto Blue Jays, 1992. Office: c/o San Diego Padres PETCO Pk 100 Park Blvd San Diego CA 92101*

WING, THOMAS M., military officer, systems engineer; b. LA, Dec. 8, 1962; s. Wilbur Bill L. and Donna M. Wing; m. Elisa R. Martinez, Aug. 4, 1988; 1 child, Emily Rose. BS in Aerospace Engr., US Naval Acad., Annapolis, Md., 1984; MA, US Naval War Coll., 2008. Lic. USCG cert. master vessels to 1600 GT 1999, 2d mate, unlimited tonnage, all oceans 1999, cert. able seaman, unlimited tonnage, all oceans 1999. Commd. ensign USN, 1984, advanced through grades to CDR, 1999, Divsn. Officer USS Benjamin Stoddert Pearl Harbor, Hawaii, 1985—87, Navigator USS Lynde Mccormick San Diego, 1987—90, instr., curriculum developer Fleet Combat Tng. Ctr., 1990—92, Combat Sys. Officer USS Robert G. Bradley Charleston, SC, 1993—95, Weaps Off Comdesron 23 San Diego, 1995—97, C4 Everett, Wash., 2003—04, liaison officer Joint Theater Air and Ballistic Missile Def. Prince Sultan Air Base, Saudi Arabia, 2003, comusnavcement Manama, Bahrain, 2004—, br. head SPAWAR Sys. Ctr. Pacific, 2006—, CO CNRSW FP/LEPS, 1999—2000. Mem. vestry St. Timothy's Episc. Ch., San Diego, 2002—03. Decorated Combat Action ribbon USN, Civilian Meritorious Svc. award, Joint Svc. Commendation medal. Mem.: Naval war Coll. Fdn. (life), US Naval Acad. Alumni Assn. (life), US Naval Inst. (life), Wing Family Am. (assoc.). Episcopalian. Avocations: sailing, skiing, reading, writing. Office: Space and Naval Warfare Syst Ctr 53560 Hull St San Diego CA 92152-5001 Office Fax: 619-553-6307. Personal E-mail: tmwing@san.rr.com. Business E-Mail: tom.wing@navy.mil.

WINGARD, MATT, state legislator; 1 child, Hunter. BA in Broadcast Journalism, U. Southern Calif. Former TV reporter, Wash.; former aide & legis. admin. Congressman Doc Hastings; former mem. Clackamas Co. Economic Devel. Commn., Portfolio Options Com. Oreg. Pub. Utility Commn.; owner pub. rels. consulting firm, 2002—; mem. Wilsonville C of C, Sherwood C of C; mem. Dist. 26 Oreg. House of Reps., 2008—. Republican. Avocations: fishing, reading, travel, teaching film classes at local library. Office: 900 Court St NE H-474 Salem OR 97301 also: 28356 SW Wagner St Wilsonville OR 97070 Office Phone: 503-986-1426, 503-685-7346. Business E-Mail: rep.mattwingard@state.or.us.

WINGATE, C. KEITH, law educator; b. Darlington, SC, May 12, 1953; s. Clarence L. and Lilly W.; m. Gloria Farley; stepchildren: Brenda, Marvin, Terry and Oliver Champion. BA in Polit. Sci., U. Ill., 1974, JD cum laude, 1978. Bar: Calif., 1978. Assoc. litigation dept. Morrison & Foerster, San Francisco, 1978-80; from asst. to assoc. prof. law U. Calif.-Hastings, San Francisco, 1980-86, prof., 1986—. Dir. Coun. Legal Edn. Opportunity Region I Inst., 1989; vis. prof. law Stanford Law Sch., fall 1990, 94, spring 1998; chair Minority Law Tchrs.' Conf. Com., 1990; mem. acad. assistance work group, 1991; trustee Law Sch. Admission Coun., 1997-2001. Author: (with David I. Levine and William R. Slomanson) Cases and Materials on California Civil Procedure, 1991, (with William R. Slomanson) California Civil Procedure in a Nutshell, 1992, (with Donald L. Doernberg) Federal Courts, Federalism and Separation of Powers, 1994, 2nd edit., 2000. Bd. dirs. Cmty. Housing Devel. Corp., North Richmond, 1990-99. Recipient 10 Outstanding Persons award U. Ill. Black Alumni Assn., 1980; Harno fellow U. Ill., Coll. of Law, 1976. Mem. Assn. Am. Law Schs. (chair sect. minority groups 1990, exec. com. mem. sect. civil proceedure 1991), Charles Houston Bar Assn., Phi Sigma Alpha. Office: U Calif Hastings Coll Law 200 Mcallister St San Francisco CA 94102-4707

WINICK, HERMAN, physicist, educator; b. NYC, June 27, 1932; s. Benjamin and Yetta (Matles) W.; m. Renee Feldman, May 31, 1953; children: Alan Lee, Lisa Frances, Laura Joan. AB, Columbia Coll., 1953; PhD, Columbia U., 1957. Rsch. assoc., instr. U. Rochester, NY, 1957—59; from staff physicist to asst. dir. Cambridge Electron Accelerator Harvard U., Mass., 1959—73; dep. dir. Stanford Synchrotron Radiation Lab. Stanford Linear Accelerator Ctr., Calif.,

1973—96. Rsch. prof. applied physics Stanford U., 1983-97, prof. emeritus, 1998—; chair tech. rev. com. Synchrotron Radiation Rsch. Ctr., Taiwan, 1984-93. Mem. editl. bd. Nuclear Instruments and Methods, 1982-2007; co-editor: Synchrotron Radiation Research, 1980; editor: Synchrotron Radiation Sources: A Primer, 1994. Recipient Humboldt Sr. Scientist award, 1986, Energy Related Tech. award U.S. Dept. Energy, 1987, U.S. Particle Accelerator Sch. prize, 1995, Disting. Assoc. award, U.S. Dept. Energy, 2000, Heinz R. Pagels Human Rights award N.Y. Acad. Scis., 2005. Fellow AAAS, Am. Phys. Soc. (chmn. com. on internat. freedom of scientist 1992, chair Forum on Internat. Physics 2007). Achievements include development of first wiggler and undulator magnets for synchotron radiation research. Home: 853 Tolman Dr Stanford CA 94305-1025 Office: SSRL SLAC 2575 Sand Hill Rd Menlo Park CA 94025-7015 Home Phone: 650-493-1900; Office Phone: 650-926-3155. E-mail: winick@slac.stanford.edu.

WINKLEBY, MARILYN A., medical researcher; BA in Social Sci., Calif. State U., Sacramento, 1968, MA in Clin. Psychology, 1974; MPH in Epidemiology/Biostat, U. Calif., Berkeley, 1983, PhD in Epidemiology, 1986. Project dir. cervical cancer screening study UCLA Sch. Pub. Health, 1974-77; co-prin. investigator Calif. Ctr. Sudden Infant Death Syndrome Risk Factor Study, Sch. Medicine, Dept. Cmty. Health U. Calif., Davis, 1977-81, co-investigator cmty. cardiovascular surveillance program, adj. lectr. Sch. Medicine, Dept. Cmty. Health, 1981-82, project coord. epidemiology unit, stress and hypertension study Dept. Epidemiology Berkeley, 1983-87, rsch. epidemiologist Dept. Behavioral and Devel. Pediat. San Francisco, 1986-91; sr. rsch. scientist/prin. investigator Stanford Ctr. Rsch. in Disease Prevention, Stanford U. Sch. of Medicine, Palo Alto, Calif., 1987—. Epidemiology cons. SIDS Info. and Counseling Project, Dept. Health, State of Calif., Berkeley, 1980-83; founder, dir. Stanford Med. Youth Sci. Program, 1988—; lectr. divsn. health rsch. and policy, dept. medicine Stanford U., 1989—. Contbr. articles to profl. jours. Bd. dirs. Loaves and Fishes Family Kitchen, San Jose, Calif., 1988-92, Mountain View Cmty. Health Clinic, 1992-95. Fellow Am. Heart Assn. (coun. epidemiology 1989, Established Investigator award 1996).

WINKLER, AGNIESZKA M., marketing executive; b. Rome, Feb. 22, 1946; came to U.S., 1953; naturalized, 1959; d. Wojciech A. and Halina Z. (Owsiany) W.; children from previous marriage: children: Renata G. Ritcheson, Dana C Sworakowski; m. Arthur K. Lund. BA, Coll. Holy Name, 1967; MA, San Jose State U., 1971; MBA, U. Santa Clara, 1981. Tchg. asst. San Jose State U., 1968-70; cons. to Ea. European bus. Palo Alto, Calif., 1970-72; pres./founder Commart Communications, Palo Alto, 1973-84; pres./founder, chmn. bd. Winkler Advt., Santa Clara, Calif., 1984—; chmn. bd. SuperCuts, Inc.; chmn., founder TeamToolz, 2000—04, The Winkler Group, 2004—. Bd. dirs. Reno Air, Lifeguard, Lifeguard Life Ins., IP Locks, C200, Inter-tel, Western Folklife Ctr., The Cheesecake Factory Inc., 2007-; exec. com. C200. Author: Warp Speed Branding, 1999. Trustee Santa Clara U., 1991—; trustee O'Connor Found., 1987-93, mem. exec. com., 1988—, mem. Capital Campaign steering com., 1989; mem. nat. adv. bd. Comprehensive Health Enhancement Support System, 1991—; mem. mgmt. west com. A.A.A.A. Agy., 1991—, vice chair no. Calif. coun., 1996—; project dir. Poland Free Enterprise Plan, 1989-92; mem. adv. bd. Normandy France Bus. Devel., 1989-92; mem. bd. regents Holy Names Coll., 1987—; bd. dirs. San Jose Mus. Art, 1987; mem. San Jose Symphony, Gold Baton, 1986; mem. nat. adv. com. Chess, 1991—; dir. Bay Area Coun., 1994—. Recipient CLIO award in Advt., Addy award, others; named to 100 Best Women in Advt., Ad Age, 1988, Best Woman in Advt., AdWeek and McCall's Mag., 1993, one of 100 Best and Brightest Women in Mktg. & Advt., Nat. Assn. Women Bus. Owners, 1996. Mem. Family Svc. Assn. (trustee 1980-82), Am. Assn. Advt. Agys. (agy. mgmt. west com. 1991), Bus. Profl. Advt. Assn., Polish Am. Congress, San Jose Advt. Club, San Francisco Ad Club, Beta Gamma Sigma (hon.), Pi Gamma Mu, Pi Delta Phi (Lester-Tinneman award 1966, Bill Raskob Found. grantee 1965).

WINKLER, HOWARD LESLIE, business, finance, government relations consultant; b. NYC, Aug. 16, 1950; s. Martin and Magda (Stark) W.; m. Robin Lynn Richards, Sept. 12, 1976; 1 child, David Menachem. AA in Mktg., Los Angeles City Coll., 1973, AA in Bus. Data Processing, 1977, AA in Bus. Mgmt., 1981. Sr. cons. Fin. Cons. Inc., Los Angeles, 1972-81; asst. v.p. Merrill Lynch, Inc., Los Angeles, 1981-83; v.p. Drexel, Burnham, Lambert, Inc., Beverly Hills, Calif., 1983-84; pres. Howard Winkler Investments, Beverly Hills, Calif., 1984-90, Landmark Fin. Group, LA, 1990-96. Ptnr. N.W.B. Assocs., L.A., 1988-91; chmn. bd. United Cmty. and Housing Devel. Corp., L.A., 1986-96; bd. mem./sec. United Housing & Cmty. Svcs. Corp., 1995-97; bd. dirs. Earth Products Internat., Inc., Kansas City, Kans., 1992, Fed. Home Loan Bank of San Francisco, 1991-93. Nat. polit. editor B'nai B'rith Messenger, 1986-95. Mem. Calif. Rep. Cent. Com., 1985-93; mem. L.A. County Rep. Cent. Com., 1985-92, chmn. 45th Assembly Dist., 1985-90; mem. Rep. Senatorial Inner Circle, 1986—, Rep. Presdl. Task Force, 1985— (Legion of Merit award 1992); mem. Rep. Eagles, 1988-92; Nat. Rep. Senatorial Com., 1986—, Golden Circle Calif., 1986-92, GOP Platform Planning Com. at Large del., 1992, 96; del. to GOP nat conv., Houston, 1992, San Diego, 1996; Calif. chmn. Jack Kemp for Pres., 1988, mem. nat. steering com. Bush-Quayle '88, 1987, nat. exec. com. Bush-Quayle '92, 1991; mil. adminstrv. supr. CID US Army, 1969-72, SE Asia; legis. and civic action Agudath Israel Calif., 1985—; mem. L.A. County Narcotics and Dangerous Drugs Commn., 1988—, L.A. County Drug Ct. Planning Com., 1996—; trustee, sec.-treas. Minority Health Professions Edn. Found., 1989-94; program chmn. Calif. Lincoln Clubs Polit. Action Com., 1987-88; state co-chmn. Pete Wilson for Gov. Campaign, 1989, John Seymour for Lt. Gov. Campaign, 1989-90; chpt. pres. Calif. Congress of Reps., 1989-93; chmn. Claude Parrish for Bd. of Equalization, 1989-90; founder, dir. Community Rsch. & Info. Ctr., 1986—; mem. fin. com. John Seymour for Senate '92, 1991. Decorated Legion of Merit; recipient Cmty. Svc. award Agudath Israel Calif., 1986, Pres.'s Cmty. Leadership award, 1986, Disting. Cmty. Svc. U.S. Senator Pete Wilson, 1986, Calif. Gov.'s Leadership award, 1986, Cmty. Svc. award U.S. Congresswoman Bobbi Fiedler, 1986, Resolution of Commendation Calif. State Assembly, 1986, Outstanding Cmty. Svc. Commendation Los Angeles County Bd. Suprs., 1986, 90, Outstanding Citizenship award City of Los Angeles, 1986, 90, 94, Cmty. Leadership award Iranian-Jewish Community L.A., 1990, 95, Resolution of Commendation, State of Calif., 1992, Cmty. Svc. Commendation, 1993, Rep. Senatorial Medal of Freedom award, Sentorial Inner Circle, 1994, Commendation L.A. County Bd. Suprs., 1994, 25 Yrs. of Excellent Svc. to the Cmty. award, 1996, Rep. Senatorial Medal of Freedom, 1999. Mem. Calif. Young Reps., Calif. Rep. Assembly, VFW, Jewish War Veterans. Jewish. Avocation: philanthropy. Office: PO Box 480454 Los Angeles CA 90048-1454

WINKLER, LEE B., business consultant; b. Buffalo; s. Jack W. and Caroline (Marienthal) W.; 1 child, James; m. Maria Mal Verde. BS cum laude, NYU, 1945, MS cum laude, 1947. Pres. LBW, Inc. (formerly Winkler Assocs. Ltd.), NYC, Beverly Hills, Calif., 1948—, Winkler Assocs. Ltd., Beverly Hills, Calif., and N.Y.C., 1958—; exec. dir. Global Bus. Mgmt. Inc., Beverly Hills, 1967—. V.p. Bayly Martin & Fay Inc., N.Y.C., 1965-68, John C. Paige & Co., N.Y.C., 1968-71; cons. Albert G. Ruben Co., Beverly Hills, 1971— Served with AUS, 1943-45. Decorated Chevalier Comdr. Order Holy Cross Jerusalem, also Spl. exec. asst., charge d'affaires, 1970; Chevalier Comdr. Sovereign Order Cyprus, 1970 Mem. Nat. Acad. TV Arts and Scis., Nat. Acad. Recording Arts and Scis., Beverly Hills C. of C., Phi Beta Kappa, Beta Gamma Sigma, Mu Gamma Tau, Psi Chi Omega.

WINKLER, MICHAEL, computer company executive; BS in Elec. Engring., Lehigh U.; MBA, Harvard Bus. Sch. Various mgmt. positions Xerox Corp.; v.p., gen. mgr. comp. systems Toshiba Am. Info. Systems, Inc., 1992—95; sr. v.p., group gen. mgr. Compaq Computer Corp. (later acquired by Hewlett-Packard Co.), Houston, 1996—2000, exec. v.p. global bus. units, 2000—01; exec. v.p. global ops. Hewlett-Packard Co., 2001—02, exec. v.p., chief mktg. officer, 2002—. Office: Hewlett-Packard Co 3000 Hanover St Palo Alto CA 94304-1185 Office Phone: 650-857-1501.

WINMILL, B. LYNN, federal judge; m. Judy Jones; 4 children. BA, Idaho State U., 1974; JD, Harvard U., 1977. Atty. Holland and Hart, Denver, 1977-79, Hawley, Troxell, Ennis and Hawley, Pocatello, Idaho, 1984-87; judge Idaho Sixth Jud. Dist. Ct., Pocatello, 1987-95, US Dist. Ct. Idaho, Boise, 1995—, chief judge, 1999—. Adj. prof. law Idaho State Univ., 1991—95. Mem.: Colo. Bar Assn., 6th Dist. Bar Assn., Idaho State Bar Assn. Office: US Dist Ct Idaho US Courthouse 550 W Fort St 6th Fl Boise ID 83724-0001 Office Phone: 208-334-9145. Fax: 208-334-9209.

WINN, STEVEN JAY, critic; b. Phila., Apr. 25, 1951; s. Willis Jay and Lois (Gengelbach) W.; m. Katharine Weber, Sept. 15, 1979 (div. Dec. 1985); m. Sally Ann Noble, July 22, 1989; 1 child, Phoebe Ann. BA, U. Pa., 1973; MA, U. Wash., 1975. Staff writer, editor Seattle Weekly, 1975-79; theater critic San Francisco Chronicle, 1980—2002, arts and culture critic, 2002—. Co-author: Ted Bundy: The Killer Next Door, 1980, Great Performances: A Celebration, 1997; contbr. articles to various publs. Wallace Stegner fellow Stanford U., 1979-80; recipient first prize Excellence in Writing award Am. Assn. of Sunday and Feature Editors, 2002, 2003. Office: San Francisco Chronicle 901 Mission St San Francisco CA 94103-2905 Office Phone: 415-777-8869. E-mail: swinn@sfchronicle.com.

WINNER, KARIN E., editor; b. White Plains, NY, Dec. 27, 1945; BA in Journalism, U. So. Calif. West coast editor Women's Wear Daily, W mag.; features writer San Diego Union (merged with Evening Tribune to become San Diego Union-Tribune, 1991), 1976, asst. editor, 1980—83; exec. editor San Diego Union-Tribune, 1991—95, editor, 1995—. Mem.: Am. Soc. Newspaper Editors, Calif. Soc. Newspaper Editors. Office: San Diego Union-Tribune 350 Camino De La Reina San Diego CA 92108 Mailing: San Diego Union-Tribune PO Box 120191 San Diego CA 92112-0191 Office Phone: 619-293-1201, 619-293-1354, 619-299-3131. E-mail: Karin.winner@uniontrib.com.

WINNINGHAM, MARE, actress; b. Phoenix, May 16, 1959; m. A Martinez (div. 1981); m. William Maple, 1983; children: Riley(dec.), Paddy, Jack, Calla. Appeared in (TV movies and miniseries): The Thorn Birds, 1983, Special Olympics/A Special Kind of Love, 1978, Amber Waves, 1980 (Emmy award 1980), The Women's Room, 1980, Off the Minnesota Strip, 1980, A Few Days in Weasel Creek, 1981, Freedom, 1981, Missing Children: A Mother's Story, 1982, Helen Keller: The Miracle Continues, 1984, Single Bars, Single Women, 1984, Love is Never Silent, 1985 (Emmy award nomination 1986), Who Is Julia?, 1986, A Winner Never Quits, 1986, Eye on the Sparrow, 1991, God Bless the Child, 1988, Turner & Hooch, 1989, Love and Lies, Crossing to Freedom, Fatal Exposure, 1991, She Stood Alone, Those Secrets, Intruders, 1992, Better Off Dead, 1994, The Boys Next Door, 1996, Betrayed by Love, 1994, Letter to My Killer, 1995, George Wallace, 1997, Little Girl Fly Away, 1998, Everything That Rises, 1998, Too Rich: The Secret Life of Doris Duke, 1999, Sally Hemings: An American Scandal, 2000, The Magic of Ordinary Days, 2005; (TV series) Six Feet Under, 2002, Touched by a Angel, 2002, Law & Order:SVU, 2003, Clubhouse, 2004, Grey's Anatomy, 2006-07, Boston Legal, 2007; appeared in (films): One Trick Pony, 1980, Threshold, 1983, St. Elmo's Fire, 1985, Nobody's Fool, 1986, Shy People, 1987, Made in Heaven, 1987, Miracle Mile, 1988, Turner and Hooch, 1989, Hard Promises, 1992, Teresa's Tattoo, Wyatt Earp, 1994, Georgia, 1995 (Acad. award nomination best supporting actress 1995), Bad Day On The Block, 1997, The Adventures of Ociee Nash, 2003, Dandelion, 2004, War Eagle, 2007; sang title song in (film) Freedom, 1981; appeared in (plays) Side Man, 2001, Lessons, 2005, 10 Million Miles, 2007, The Glass Menagerie, 2008; singer (solo album) What Might Be, 1992, Red and Brown, 1996. Office: IFA Talent Agy 8730 W Sunset Blvd Ste 490 Los Angeles CA 90069

WINNOWSKI, THADDEUS RICHARD (TED WINNOWSKI), investment banker, consultant; b. Albany, NY, Feb. 20, 1942; s. Thaddeus Walter and Harriet Frances (Witko) W.; m. Sheila Margaret Neary, June 15, 1968; children: Dona, Paul. BS in Econs., Siena Coll., 1963; postgrad., Rensselaer Poly. Inst., 1968-72. Adminstrv. v.p. Key Bank N.A., Albany, N.Y., 1978-80; pres. Key Bank L.I., Sayville, N.Y., 1980-85; pres., CEO Key Bank Oreg., Woodburn, 1985-86, chmn., CEO Portland, 1986-95, chmn., 1995-97; exec. v.p., group exec. N.W. region Key Corp., Seattle, 1995-97, chmn., CEO, 1996-97; pres., CEO Centennial Bank, Eugene, Oreg., 1998—2002. Mem. adv. bd. Blue Cross/Blue Shield Oreg.; bd. regents U. Portland, 2002-. 1st lt. U.S. Army, 1964-66. Mem. Portland Bus. Alliance (hon. bd. dirs., former chmn.). Roman Catholic. Office Phone: 503-819-8198. Personal E-mail: twinnowski@earthlink.net.

WINOKUR, MARISSA JARET, actress; b. NYC, Feb. 2, 1973; m. Judah Miller, Oct. 7, 2006; 1 child, Zev Isaac Miller. Studied at, Am. Musical and Dramatic Acad. Actor: (plays, Broadway) Grease, 1995, Hairspray, 2002 (Tony award for best actress, 2003), 2005; (plays) Guys and Dolls, Peter Pan, Little Shop of Horrors, Romeo and Juliet, Nunsense II, Grandma Sylvia's Funeral, Hair, Happy Days; (films) Demo Real, 1998, Why Love Doesn't Work, 1999, Never Been Kissed, 1999, American Beauty, 1999, Sleep Easy, Hutch Rimes, 2000, Scary Movie, 2000, Amy's Orgasm, 2001, On Edge, 2001, Now You Know, 2002, Fever Pitch, 2005; (TV films) Beautiful Girl, 2003; co-exec. prodr. (TV films) Beautiful Girl, 2003; actor: (TV films) Ultra, 2006, Fugly, 2007, Betrayals, 2007, (voice): (TV series) Shrek the Halls, 2007, (guest appearances) The Steve Harvey Show, 1998, Felicity, 1999, Dharma & Greg, 1999, 2000, Moesha, 2000, Curb Your Enthusiasm, 2000, Just Shoot Me, 2000, The Ellen Show, 2001, Boston Public, 2001, Stacked, 2005—06. Office Phone: 310-288-5888. Office Fax: 310-288-5868.

WINSLEY, SHIRLEY J., state legislator, insurance agent; b. Fosston, Minn., June 9, 1934; d. Nordin Marvel Miller and Helga Christine Sorby; m. Gordon Perry Winsley, July 19, 1952; children: Alan, Nancy. ABS, Tacoma C.C., 1970; BA, Pacific Luth., 1971. Mem. legis. staff Wash. Senate, Olympia, 1971-75; appraiser Pierce County Assessor, Tacoma, 1971-75; mem. Wash. Ho. of Reps., Olympia, 1974, 77-92; exec. dir. Lakewood (Wash.) Chamber, 1975-76; mem. Wash. Senate, Dist. 28, Olympia, 1993—; ins. agent, family counselor New Tacoma Cemetary & Funeral Home, 1996—; pres. Wash. Senate, Dist. 28, 2003—. Mem., Wash. St. Advisory Council Accrditation of Vocational-Technical Institutes, Wash. St. Historical Soc., Lakewood Sr. Ctr., LEAP. Republican. Lutheran. Home: 1109 Garden Cir Tacoma WA 98466-6218 Office: PO Box 40428 Olympia WA 98504-0428

WINSLOW, DAVID ALLEN, chaplain, retired military officer; b. Dexter, Iowa, July 12, 1944; s. Franklin E. and Inez Maude (McPherson) W.; m. Doribell Rivera Winslow, Jan. 20, 2009; children: Frances, David. BA, So. Nazarene U., 1968; MDiv, Drew U., 1971, STM, 1974; cert. of achievement, Emergency Mgmt. Inst., FEMA, 1997. Ordained to ministry United Meth. Ch. Detroit Annual Conf., 1969; cert. FEMA instr. Clergyman, 1969—; assoc. min. All Sts. Episcopal. Ch., Millington, NJ, 1969-70; asst. min. Marble Collegiate Ch., NYC, 1970-71; min. No. NJ Conf. United Meth. Ch., 1971-75; joined chaplain corps USN, 1974, advanced through grades to lt. comdr., 1980, ret., 1995; chaplain Oak Knoll Naval Med. Ctr., Oakland, Calif., 1993-95; command chaplain USNS Mercy T-AH19, Oakland, 1993—95; disaster cons. Ch. World Svc., Cupertino, Calif., 1997—2001. Chaplain med. assistance team CA-6/nat. disaster med. sys. Contra/Costa County, Calif., 1997—2005; founding mem. Dept. Homeland Security, 2003; salesperson Dept. real estate State of Calif., 2000—. Author: The Utmost for the Highest, 1993, Epiphany: God Still Speaks, 1994, Be Thou My Vision, 1994, Evening Prayers At Sea, 1995, Wiseman Still Adore Him, 1995, God's Power At Work, 1996; (with Walsh) A Year of Promise: Meditations, 1995, editor: The Road to Bethlehem: Advent, 1993, Preparation for Resurrecton: Lent, 1994, God's Promise: Advent, 1994, The Way of the Cross: Lent, 1995; contbr. articles to profl. jours. Bd. dirs. disaster svcs. and family svcs. ARC, Santa Ana, Calif., 1988-91, Child Abuse Prevention Ctr., Orange, Calif., 1990-91; bd. dirs. Santa Clara County Coun. Chs., 1993-94, del., 1995-98; bd. dirs. Salvation Army Adult Rehab. Ctr. Adv. Coun., San Jose, Calif., 1995-2002; bd. dirs. emergency svcs. Santa Clara Valley chpt. ARC, San Jose, 1995-98; bd. dirs. disaster svcs. Interfaith Svc., Inc., San Jose Internat. Airport. Recipient Navy Achievement medal, Navy Commendation medal with Gold Star in lieu of 2nd award, Navy Expeditionary medal, Humanitarian Svc. medal, Battle "E" award, Nat. Def. Svc. medal, sea svc. deployment ribbon with silver star. Fellow Am. Acad. Experts in Traumatic Stress (cert. expert), USN League (hon.), Disabled Am. Vets. (life), Internat. Assn. Civil Aviation Chaplains, Sunrise Exch. Club (chaplain 1989-91), Dick Richards Breakfast Club (chaplain 1988-91), Kiwanis, Masons (life), Ancient Accepted Scottish Rite (32°), Shriners. Avocations: golf, skiing, sailing. Office Phone: 408-858-5983.

WINSLOW, KELLEN BOSWELL, retired professional football player; b. St. Louis, Nov. 5, 1957; s. Homer and Odell W.; m. Katrina McKnight, 1982; children: Kellen Jr. Student, U. Mo., 1974-78. Tight end San Diego Chargers, 1979—87. Commr. Kellen Winslow Flag Football League, San Diego. Named First Team All Pro 1980-1982; named to Am. Football Conf. Pro Bowl Team 1980-83, 87, Pro Football Hall of Fame, 1995, Chargers Hall of Fame.

WINSLOW, MICHAEL T., lawyer, finance company executive; BS, Ind. U., 1976; JD, Northwestern U., 1980. Bar: Oreg. 1980. Staff lawyer Freightliner Corp., 1981-82; asst. gen. counsel, asst. sec. Mercedes-Benz Credit Corp., 1982-86; sr. corp. counsel, asst. sec. Pacificorp Fin. Svcs. (formerly Pacificorp Credit, Inc.), Portland, 1986—95, asst. gen. counsel, chief compliance officer, 1995—2001; v.p., gen. counsel, sec. StanCorp Financial Group, Inc., 2001—. Office: StanCorp Financial Group Inc 1100 SW Sixth Ave Portland OR 97204

WINSLOW, NORMAN ELDON, small business owner; b. Oakland, Calif., Apr. 4, 1938; s. Merton Conrad and Roberta Eilene (Drennen) W.; m. Betty June Cady, Jan. 14, 1962 (div. Aug. 1971); 1 child, Todd Kenelm; m. Ilene Ruth Jackson, Feb. 3, 1979. BS, Fresno State U., Calif., 1959. Asst. mgr. Proctors Jewelers, Fresno, 1959-62; from agt. to dist. mgr. Allstate Ins. Co., Fresno, 1962-69; ins. agt. Fidelity Union Life Ins., Dallas, 1969-71; dist. and zone mgr. 7-Eleven, Inc., Dallas, 1971-78; owner Ser-Vis-Etc. LLC, Fresno, Calif., 1978—. Expert witness, cons. Am. Arbitration/Calif. Superior Cts. Pub./editor FranchiseserviceNews; author: Hands in Your Pockets, 1992; contbr. numerous articles to profl. jours. With USAFNG, 1961-67. Mem. Nat. Coalition of Assn. of 7-11 Franchises (affiliate, mem. adv. bd. 1984-90), Sigma Chi Fraternity (Life). Republican. Methodist. Avocations: gardening, photography, travel, model railroading. Home: 1293 N Fancher Ave Fresno CA 93727 Office: Ser-Vis-Etc LLC PO Box 8444 Fresno CA 93747-8444 Personal E-mail: servisetc@aol.com, eld_02379@aol.com, elru2379@aol.com.

WINSLOW, PAUL DAVID, architect; b. Phoenix, June 12, 1941; s. Fred D. and Thelma E. (Ward) W.; 1 child, Kirk David. BArch, Ariz. State U., 1964. Lic. architect, Ariz., Calif., Nev. Ptnr. The Orcutt/Winslow Partnership, Phoenix, 1972—. Speaker solar energy workshops, Phoenix, 1986-89; adj. prof. Ariz. State U., 1991; mem. profl. adv. coun. Ariz. State U. Coll. Architecture, Tempe, 1970—, bd. dirs. Architecture Found., 1972-76; mem. adv. com. City of Phoenix Bldg. Safety Bd., 1981; mem. adv. bd. Herberger Ctr.; pres. Ariz. State U. Coll. Architecture, Coun. for Design Excellence; bd. dirs. Ctrl. Ariz. Project Assn., Phoenix, 1971-74, Ariz. Ctr. for Law in the Pub. Interest, Phoenix, 1979-86, Phoenix Cmty. Alliance; chmn. Encanto Village Planning Com., Phoenix, 1981-86; chmn. Indian Sch. Citizens adv. com. Ind. Sch. Land Use Planning Team; lectr. on planning Ariz. State U., 1989, city of Presott, Phoenix and Tempe, 1988-89; active Coun. Ednl. Facilities Planners Internat. Mem. Steering Com. on

Re-inventing Neighborhoods Project; chmn. Central and Roosevelt Coalition, 1998-99; chmn. City of Phoenix Neighborhood Initiative Area Steering Com., 1998-99; pres. bd. dirs. Harrington House Internat. Ctr. for Universal Design, 1998-99; pres. bd. dirs. Maryvale Edn. Mall, 1998-99; exec. com. Phoenix Cmty. Alliance. Fellow AIA (bd. dirs. ctrl. Ariz. chpt., also sec., treas., pres.); mem. Ariz. Soc. Architects (bd. dirs. 1970-71, 78-82), Bldg. Owners and Mgrs. Assn. Greater Phoenix (pres. 1989-90, 90-91), Boar Valley Forward Assn. (exec. com. 1994-99), Ariz. Club (Phoenix). Methodist. Home: 5941 E Edgemont Ave Scottsdale AZ 85257 Office: The Orcutt Winslow Partnership 3003 N Central Ave Ste 1600 Phoenix AZ 85012-2908 E-mail: winslow.p@owp.com.

WINSLOW, WALTER WILLIAM, psychiatrist, educator; b. Lacombe, Alta., Can., Nov. 23, 1925; came to U.S., 1959, naturalized, 1964; s. Floyd Raymond and Lily Evangeline (Palmer) W.; m. Barbara Ann Spiker; children: Colleen Denise, Dwight Walter, Barbara Jean, Wendi Jae. BS, La Sierra Coll., 1949; MD, Loma Linda U., 1952. Diplomate: Am. Bd. Psychiatry and Neurology. Intern Vancouver Gen. Hosp., 1952; psychiat. resident Provincial Mental Hosp., Essondale, B.C., 1957-59, Harding Hosp., Worthington, Ohio, 1959-60; instr. dept. psychiatry and indsl. medicine U. Cin., 1960-66, dept. preventive medicine, 1964-66; asst. prof. psychiatry U. N.Mex., Albuquerque, 1966-68, assoc. prof. psychiatry, 1969-74, prof., chmn. dept. psychiatry, 1974-91, dir. mental health programs, 1976-91; med. dir. Charter Hosp. of Albuquerque, 1991-95, Charter-Heights BHS, Albuquerque, 1995—99; ret. Assoc. prof. psychiatry Georgetown U., Washington, 1968-69; dir. bernalillo County Mental Health/Mental Retardation Ctr., 1970-78, 81-91. Author: The History of Psychiatry in New Mexico, 1889-1989, 2005; contbr. articles to profl. jours. Recipient N.Mex. Gov.'s Commendation for 10 yrs. service in mental health, 1979 Fellow Am. Psychiat. Assn. (life, area VII rep. 1981-85, Assembly Speaker's award 1984), Am. Coll. of Psychiatrists (life), Am. Assn. Community Psychiatrists (hon.); mem. AMA, Am. Assn. Psychiatry and the Law, N.Mex. Psychiat. Assn. (pres. 1974-75) Republican.

WINSOR, DAVID JOHN, cost consultant; b. Duluth, Minn., May 27, 1947; s. Alphonse Joseph and Sylvia Mae (Petrich) W.; div. BA in Bus., U. Puget Sound, 1978; M of Mech. Engring., Pacific Western U., 1979. Jr. engr. J.P. Head Mech., Inc., Richland, Wash., 1965-67; estimator, project engr. Subs. of Howard S. Wright Co., Seattle, 1972-75; sr. estimator Massart Co., Seattle, 1975-76; project mgr. Univ. Mechanical, Portland, Oreg., 1976; cons. Kent, Wash., 1976-79; owner Leasair, Federal Way, Wash., 1978-83; pres., owner Expertise Engring. & Cons., Inc., Bellevue, Wash., 1979-82, 90-95; cons. Winsor & Co., Walnut Creek, Calif., 1983—; estimator IDC, Portland, Oreg., 1996-99; cons., 1999—. Cons. NASA, Mountain View, Calif., 1986, Lockheed Missile & Space, Sunnyvale, Calif., 1984-87, The Boeing Co., Seattle, 1979-82. Author: (with others) Current Construction Costs, 1987, 88, 89, Construction Materials Inventory Systems, 1973, 74, Construction Inflation Trends, 1975, 76, 77, 78, 79, 80, 81, Construction Claims and Prevention, 1981, 82. Served to sgt. USAF, 1967-71. Mem. Jaycees (state dir. 1972-73, state chmn. 1973-74). Republican. Roman Catholic. Avocations: flying, golf, gun collecting, classic cars.

WINSTON, GEORGE, solo pianist, guitarist, harmonica player; b. Hart, Mich., 1949; Ind. musician, 1967—; founder Dancing Cat Productions, Santa Cruz, Calif., 1983—. Ten solo piano albums including Ballads and Blues, 1972, Autumn, 1980, Winter Into Spring, 1982, December, 1982, Summer, 1991, Forest, 1994, Linus & Lucy: The Music of Vince Guaraldi, 1996, Plains, 1999, Night Divides the Day--The Music of the Doors, 2002, Montana, A Love Story, 2004; audiobook soundtracks: (with Meryl Streep) The Velveteen Rabbit, 1984, This is America Charlie Brown--Birth of the Constitution, 1988, (with Liv Ullmann) Sadako and the Thousand Paper Cranes Benefit CD, 1995, Remembrance-9/11 Memorial Benefit CD, 2001; prodr., co-prodr. 36 albums of the masters of traditional Hawaiian slack key (finger style) guitar. Office: c/o Dancing Cat Prodns PO Box 4287 Santa Cruz CA 95063-4287 Office Phone: 831-429-5085. E-mail: ml@dancingcat.com.

WINSTONE, RAY, actor; b. London, Eng., Feb. 19, 1957; m. Elaine Winstone, 1979; 3 children. Actor: (films) That Summer, 1979, Scum, 1979, Ladies and Gentlemen, the Fabulous Stains, 1981, Tank Malling, 1989, Ladybird Ladybird, 1994, Yellow, 1996, Masculine Mescaline, 1996, Nil by Mouth, 1997 (Best Performance by Brit. Actor in Ind. Film, Brit. Ind. Film Awards, 1998), Face, 1997, The Sea Change, 1998, Martha, Meet Frank, Daniel and Laurence, 1998, Woundings, 1998, Final Cut, 1998, Five Seconds to Spare, 1999, The War Zone, 1999, Agnes Browne, 1999, Darkness Falls, 1999, Fanny and Elvis, 1999, There's Only One Jimmy Grimble, 2000, Sexy Beast, 2000, Love, Honour and Obey, 2000, Last Orders, 2001 (Best Acting by an Ensemble, Nat. Bd. Review, 2001), The Martins, 2001, Ripley's Game, 2002, Bouncer, 2002, Cold Mountain, 2003, Old Street, 2004, Everything, 2004, King Arthur, 2004, The Magic Roundabout, 2005, The Proposition, 2005 (Best Supporting Actor, San Diego Film Critics Soc. Awards, 2006), (voice) The Chronicles of Narnia: The Lion, the Witch and the Wardrobe, 2005, Breaking and Entering, 2006, The Departed, 2006 (Best Ensemble, Nat. Bd. Review, 2006), (voice) Beowulf, 2007, Indiana Jones and the Kingdom of the Crystal Skull, 2008; exec. prodr.: (films) Brown Paper Bag, 2003, The Cow Thief, 2006; actor: (TV films) Scum, 1977, Love Story: Mr. Right, 1983, Robin Hood and the Sorcerer, 1983, Number One, 1985, Blore M.P., 1989, Absolute Hell, 1991, Black and Blue, 1992, Underbelly, 1992, The Negotiator, 1994, Macbeth on the Estate, 1997, Our Boy, 1997 (Best Actor award, Royal TV Soc., 1999), Births, Marriages and Deaths, 1999, Tube Tales, 1999, Last Christmas, 1999, Tough Love, 2000, Lenny Blue, 2002, Henry VIII, 2003, (voice) Bobby Moore, 2006, All in the Game, 2006; actor, exec. prodr. (TV films) She's Gone, 2004, Sweeney Todd, 2006 (Magnolia award, Shanghai Internat. TV Festival, 2006); actor: (TV series) Fairly Secret Army, 1984, Robin of Sherwood, 1984—86, Father Matthew's Daughter, 1987, Minder, 1984—89, Ghostbusters of East Finchley, 1995, Vincent, 2005—06 (Best Performance by an Actor, Internat. Emmy Awards, 2006). Office: c/o IFA Talent Agy 8730 Sunset Blvd #490 Los Angeles CA 90069

WINTER, DAMON, photographer, photojournalist; b. NY; B in Environ. Sci., Columbia U., NYC. Photographer Newsweek, Magnum Photos, Dallas Morning News; staff photographer LA Times, 2004—07, NY Times, NYC, 2007—. Recipient Nat. Journalism award for photojournalism, Scripps Howard Found., 2006, World Press Photo award, 2007, Pulitzer prize for feature photography, 2009; named Photographer of Yr., Nat. Press Photographers Assn., 2002, Calif. Press Photographer of Yr., 2006; finalist Pulitzer prize for feature photography, 2005. Office: LA Times 202 W 1st St Los Angeles CA 90012 E-mail: dwinfo@damonwinter.com.

WINTER, RALPH D., religious organization administrator, academic administrator; b. 1925; BCE, Calif. Inst. tech., Pasadena; MA in ESL, Columbia U., NYC; BD, Princeton Theol. Sem., NJ; attended, Fuller Theol. Sem., Pasadena; PhD. in Structural Linguistics, Cornell U., Ithaca, NY. Student pastor Lamington Presbyn. Ch., 1953—56; rural devel. specialist Presbyn. Ch., Guatemala, 1956—66; founder, dir. indsl. tng. for Guatemalan Indian pastors Industrias Técnicas, 1958—66; founder, dir. adult edn. ext. program Union Abraham Lincoln, Guatemala, 1961—66; prof. anthropology Landivar U., Guatemala, 1961—66; exec. dir. Asociacion Latinoamericana de Escuelas Teológicas, Norte, 1965—66; prof. hist. devel. of the Christian movement Fuller Theol. Sem., 1966—76, disting. missiologist in residence, 1998—; co-founder, sec.-treas. Am. Soc. of Missiology, 1972—75, pres., 1979—80; founder, gen. dir. Frontier Mission Fellowship, 1976—; gen. dir. US Ctr. for World Mission, 1976—90, dir. inst. internat. studies, 1990—97; pres. William Carey Internat. U., Pasadena, 1977—80, 1990—97, 2000—04, chancellor, 1997—99, 2005—; editor Mission Frontiers Bulletin, 1977—; v.p. Southwest Evang. Missiol. Soc., 1992—99. Founder Inst. the Study of the Origins of Disease, 1999, William Carey Libr., 1969, Presbyn. Frontier Fellowship, 1975, Internat. Soc. Frontier Missiology, 1985; co-founder Assoc. Ch. Mission Committees, 1975; founder Presbyterian Ctr. for Mission Studies, 1973. Named one of 25 Most Influential Evangelicals in America, Time Mag., 2005. Office: William Carey Internat Univ 1539 E Howard St Pasadena CA 91104 Personal E-mail: winter@ralphwinter.org.

WINTERMAN, CRAIG L., lawyer; b. Denver, Oct. 29, 1950; BS, U. Oreg., 1973; JD, Southwestern U., 1976. Bar: Calif. 1977, U.S. Dist. Ct. (cen. dist.) Calif. 1977, U.S. Dist. Ct. (so. and no. dists.) Calif. 1980, U.S. Ct. Appeals (9th cir.) 1980, U.S. Supreme Ct. 1980. Ptnr. Herzfeld & Rubin, LA, 1986—. Mem. State Bar Calif., Assn. So. Calif. Def. Counsel, Assn. Advancement Auto. Medicine, U. Oreg. Alumni Assn. (pres. so. Calif. chpt. 1999-2001). Office: Herzfeld & Rubin 1925 Century Park E Ste 600 Los Angeles CA 90067-2783 E-mail: cwinterman@hrla.net.

WINTERS, BARBARA JO, musician; b. Salt Lake City; d. Louis McClain and Gwendolyn (Bradley) W. AB cum laude, UCLA, 1960, postgrad., 1961, Yale, 1960. Mem. oboe sect. L.A. Philharm., 1961-94, prin. oboist, 1972-94; ret. Clinician oboe, English horn, Oboe d'amore. Recs. movie, TV sound tracks. Avocations: painting, piano. Home: 3529 Coldwater Canyon Ave Studio City CA 91604-4060 Office: 151 S Grand Ave Los Angeles CA 90012-3013

WINTERS, JACKIE F., small business owner, foundation administrator; b. Topeka, Apr. 19, 1937; m. Marc Winters; 4 children. Student, Oreg. State U. Cert. Policy Alternatives Flemming Fellow. Clk. Oreg. Med. Sch., 1959—69; asst. Oreg. Gov. Tom McCall, 1969—79, Oreg. Gov. Vic Atiyeh, 1979—81; owner Jackie's Ribs, 1985—; mem. Oreg. Ho. of Reps., 1998—2002, Oreg. Senate, 2003—. Campaign chair United Way Marion/Polk Counties; active Govs. Task Force on Mental Health, Cmty. Partnership Task Force Oreg. State Fair. Republican. Office: 900 Court St NE S-212 Salem OR 97301 Office Phone: 503-986-1710.

WINTERS, JONATHAN, actor; b. Dayton, Ohio, Nov. 11, 1925; s. Jonathan H. and Alice Kilgore (Rodgers) W.; m. Eileen Ann Schauder, Sept. 11, 1948 (dec. Jan. 11, 2009); children: Jonathan IV, Lucinda Kelley. Student, Kenyon Coll., 1946; B.F.A., Dayton Art Inst., 1950. With radio sta. WING, Dayton, 1949; disc jockey sta. WBNS-TV, Columbus, Ohio, 1950-53. Appeared on: Garry Moore Show, 1954-63, Steve Allen Show, 1954-61, Omnibus, 1954, NBC Comedy Hour, 1956, Jonathan Winters Show, 1956-57, Jack Paar Show, 1963-64, Andy Williams Show, 1966-67, Dean Martin Show, 1966-67, Jonathan Winters Show, CBS-TV, 1968-69, Wacky World of Jonathan Winters, 1972-73; numerous appearances NBC Monitor show, 1963—, Hollywood Squares, 1975—; TV series include Mork & Mindy, 1982-83, Davis Rules, (Emmy award for best supporting actor) 1991-92, 5 spls. Showtime Cable TV; night club appearances, 1953-60; motion picture appearances: It's a Mad, Mad, Mad World, 1963, The Loved One, 1964, The Russians Are Coming, The Russians Are Coming, 1966, Penelope, 1967, The Midnight Oil, 1967, 8 On the Lam, 1967, Oh Dad, Poor Dad, 1968, Viva Max, 1969, The Fish That Saved Pittsburgh, 1979, The Longshot, 1986, Say Yes, 1986, Moon Over Parador, 1988, The Flintstones, 1994, The Shadow, 1994, The Adventures of Rocky and Bullwinkle, 2000, Edward Fudwupper Fibbed Big, 2000, Swing, 2003; rec. artist, Columbia Records.; author: Mouse Breath, Conformity and Other Social Ills, 1965, Winter's Tales, 1987, Hang-Ups, 1990; voice: Arabian Knights, 1995, Santa vs. the Snoman, 1997, also numerous cartoon characters. Served with USMCR, 1943-46, PTO. Named to Comedy Hall of Fame U.S., 1993, Comedy Hall of Fame Can., 1994; recipient Grammy for Comedy Album of Yr., 1996, Mark Twain Prize for Am. Humor, Kennedy Center, 2000.

WINTHROP, JOHN, wines and spirits company executive; b. Salt Lake City, Apr. 20, 1947; children: Grant Gordon, Clayton Hanford. AB cum laude, Yale U., 1969; JD magna cum laude, U. Tex., 1972. Bar: Calif. 1972. Law clk. 9th cir. U.S. Ct. Appeals, LA, 1972-73; conseil juridique Coudert Freres, Paris, 1973-75; v.p. gen. counsel MacDonald Group, Ltd., LA, 1976-82; pres., CEO MacDonald Mgmt. Corp. and MacDonald Group Ltd., LA, 1982-86; pres., chief exec. officer MacDonald Corp. (gen. contractors), LA, 1982-86; chmn., CEO Comstock Mgmt. Co., LA, 1986—; pres., CEO Winthrop Investment Properties, Los Angeles, 1986—; CEO Veritas Imports, LA, 1995—. Bd. dirs. Plus Prods., Tiger's Milk Prods., Irvine, Calif., 1977-80. Contbr. articles to profl. jours. Bd. dirs., sec. L.A. Sheriff's Dept. Found.; bd. dirs. L.A. Opera. Mem. Nat. Eagle Scout Assn. (life), French-Am. C. of C. (bd. dirs. 1982-87), Urban Land Inst., Yale Club N.Y., Calif. Club, The Beach Club, Elizabethan Club, Order of the Coif, Beta Theta Pi. Office: Veritas Imports Penthouse 9460 Wilshire Blvd Beverly Hills CA 90212-2720 E-mail: jwinthrop@veritaswine.com.

WINTHROP, LAWRENCE FREDRICK, judge; b. Apr. 18, 1952; s. Murray and Vauneta (Cardwell) W. BA with honors, Whittier Coll., 1974; JD magna cum laude, Calif. Western Sch., 1977. Bar: Ariz. 1977, Calif. 1977, U.S. Dist. Ct. Ariz. 1977, U.S. Dist. Ct. (so. dist.) Calif. 1981, U.S. Ct. Appeals (9th cir.) 1981, U.S. Dist. Ct. (cen. dist.) Calif. 1983, U.S. Supreme Ct. 1983. Assoc. Snell and Wilmer, Phoenix, 1977—83, ptnr., 1984—93, Doyle, Winthrop, P.C., Phoenix, 1993—2002; judge divsn. one Ariz. Ct. Appeals, Phoenix, 2002—. Judge pro tem Maricopa County Superior Ct., 1987-97; lectr. Ariz. personal injury law and practice and state and local tax law Tax Exec. Inst., Nat. Bus. Inst., Profl. Edn. Systems, Inc., Ariz. Trial Lawyers Assn., Maricopa County Bar. Editor-in-chief: Calif. Western Law Rev., 1976-77. Fellow, Ariz. Found. Legal Svcs. and Edn.(bd. dir. 2005-, pres. 2009-); Charter benefactor, Maricopa County Bar Found.; mem. Ariz. Supreme Ct. Com. on Examinations, 1995-2002; bd. dir. Ariz. Tax Rsch. Assn., 1989-93; bd. dir. Ariz. Assn. Defense Counsel, past. pres. 1988-89; chmn. Valley of Sun Sch. & Habilitation Ctr., 1994-96, bd. dir. 1989-97; mem. Vol. Lawyers' Program, 1980-2002, mem. Bd. Certified Ct. Reporters, Commn. Judicial Conduct, 2009-Mem. Calif. Bar Assn., Ariz. Bar Assn., Am. Bd. Trial Advs., Aspen Valley Golf Club, Lorna Lockwood Inn Ct. (co-pres. 2005-06). Republican. Methodist. Avocations: music, golf. Home: 83 W Cypress St Phoenix AZ 85003 Office: 1501 W Washington St Phoenix AZ 85007 Office Phone: 602-542-1430. Business E-Mail: lwinthrop@appeals.az.gov.

WINTRODE, RALPH CHARLES, lawyer; b. Hollywood, Calif., Dec. 21, 1942; s. Ralph Osborne and Maureen (Kavanagh) W.; m. Leslie Ann O'Rourke, July 2, 1966 (div. Feb. 1994); children: R. Christopher, Patrick L., Ryan B.; m. Denise A. Beetham, Aug. 24, 1999. BS in Acctg., U. So. Calif., 1966, JD, 1967. Bar: Calif. 1967, N.Y. 1984, Japan 1989. From assoc. to ptnr. to of counsel Gibson, Dunn & Crutcher, Tokyo, L.A., Newport Beach and Irvine, Calif., 1967—. Sec. Music Ctr. Los Angeles County, 1986-88; bd. dirs. Coro Found., L.A. County, 1986-87. Mem. Newport Harbor Club, Am. Club Tokyo. Avocations: sailboat racing, auto racing, flying. also: 333 S Grand Ave Ste 4400 Los Angeles CA 90071-1548 Office: Gibson Dunn And Crutcher Llp 3161 Michelson Dr Ste 1200 Irvine CA 92612-4412 E-mail: wintrode@cox.net.

WINTROUB, BRUCE URICH, dermatologist, educator, researcher; b. Milw., Nov. 8, 1943; s. Ernest Bernard and Janet (Zien) W.; m. Marya Kraus, Jan. 20, 1973; children: Annie, Ben, Molly. BA, Amherst Coll., 1965; MD, Washington U., St. Louis, 1969. Diplomate Am. Bd. Internal Medicine, Am. Bd. Dermatology. Intern in medicine Peter Bent Brigham Hosp., Boston, 1969-70, jr. asst. resident in medicine, 1970-71, jr. assoc. in medicine, 1976-80, asst. then attending physician, 1976-81; resident in dermatology Harvard Med. Sch., Boston, 1974-76, instr., 1976-78, asst. prof., 1978-82; assoc. prof. dermatology Sch. Medicine, U. Calif., San Francisco, 1982-85, attending physician med. ctr., 1982—, prof., mem. exec. com. dept. dermatology, 1985-95, 2000—, mem. dean's adv. com., governing bd. continuing med. edn., other coms., 1986-95; chmn. exec. com. dept. dermatology U. Calif., San Francisco, 1985-95, 2000—, exec. vice dean Sch. Medicine, 1995-97, assoc. dean sch. medicine, 1990—95, 2000—04, vice-dean sch. med., 2004—; chief med. officer U. Calif.-San Francisco Stanford Health Care, San Francisco, 1997-99; assoc. dean Sch. Medicine Stanford (Calif.) U., 1997—99; dir. Dermatology Assocs., San Francisco, 1982-85; prof. & chair, dept. dermatology U. Calif.-San Francisco, 1986—95, 1999. Cons. in dermatology Mass. Gen. Hosp., Boston, 1976-82, Beth Israel Hosp. and Children's Hosp. Med. Ctr., Boston, 1978-82, Parker Hill Med. Ctr., Boston, 1980-82; attending physician Robert B. Brigham Hosp. div. Brigham and Women's Hosp., Boston, 1980-81, assoc., 1980-82; chief dermatology svc. Brockton (Mass.) VA Med. Ctr., 1980-82; asst. chief dermatology VA Med. Ctr., San Francisco, 1982-85, mem. space com., 1984-85, dean's adv. com., 1985—, chmn. budget com., 1987—; clin. investigator Nat. Inst. Allergy, Metabolism and Digestive Disease, NIH, 1978; assoc. dean Sch. Medicine Stanford U., 1997—. Author: (with others) Biochemistry of the Acute Allergic Reactions, Fifth International Symposium, 1988; contbr. numerous articles, abstracts to profl. jours. Grantee Clin. fellow and grantee, NIH, 1967—69. Fellow Am. Acad. Dermatology (com. evaluations 1985—, coun. govt. liaison 1987—, congress on tech. plannning commn. 1988—, assoc. editor Dialogues in Dermatology jour. 1982-85, Stellwagon prize 1976); mem. Soc. Investigative Dermatology (chmn. pub. rels. com. 1987-88), Assn. Profs. Dermatology (chmn. program com. 1987—, bd. dirs.), Pacific Dermatol. Assn. (chmn. program com. 1987—), San Francisco Dermatol. Soc., Am. Fedn. Clin. Rsch. (chmn. dermatology program 1988-89), Am. Assn. Immunology, Dystrophic Epidermolysis Bullosa Rsch. Am. (bd. dirs. 1981), Internat. Soc. Dermatology, Internat. Soc. Cutaneous Pharmacology (founding mem.), Am. Soc. Clin. Investigation, Skin Pharmacology Soc., Calif. Med. Soc., San Francisco Med. Soc., Clin. Immunology Soc., Dermatology Found., (bd. dirs., exec. com.), AAAS, Am. Assn. Physicians, Calif. Acad. Medicine, Am. Dermatol. Assn., Sigma Xi, Alpha Omega Alpha. Avocation: golf. Office: Dept Dermatology U Calif San Francisco 1701 Divisadero St Rm 342 San Francisco CA 94143-0316 Office Phone: 415-353-7597. Business E-Mail: wintroub@medsch.ucsf.edu.

WIPKE, W. TODD, chemistry professor; b. Dec. 16, 1940; BS, U. Mo., Columbia, 1962; PhD, U. Calif., Berkeley, 1965. Rsch. chemist Esso Rsch. and Engring. Co., Baton Rouge, 1962; postdoctoral rsch. fellow Harvard U., 1967-69; asst. prof. Princeton U., 1969-75; assoc. prof. chemistry U. Calif., Santa Cruz, 1975-81, prof. chemistry, 1981—2004, rsch. prof. chemistry, 2004—. Founder, sr. v.p. Molecular Design Ltd., San Leandro, Calif., 1978-91; founder, chmn. bd. GluMetrics Inc., 2002-04, dir. 2005-; founder, dir. Leptogen, Inc., 2006—; cons. Ciba-Geigy, Basle, Switzerland, 1978-82, BASF, Ludwigshafen, Fed. Republic Germany, 1974-78, Squibb, Princeton, N.J., 1976-81; adv. EPA, 1984—; mem. sci. adv. bd. Pharmix, Scitegic, Tosk; co-founder Leptogen, 2006. Editor: Computer Representation and Manipulation of Chemical Information, 1973, Computer-Assisted Organic Synthesis, 1977; editor-in-chief: (jour.) Tetrahedron Computer Methodology, 1987-92; editor: Tetrahedron and Tetrahedron Letters, 1987-92; contbr. articles to profl. jours. Capt. US Army, 1966—67. Recipient Eastman Kodak Rsch. award, 1964, Texaco Outstanding Rsch. award, 1962, Alexander von Humboldt Sr. Scientist award, 1987; Merck Career Devel. grantee, 1970; NIH fellow, 1964-65. Mem. Am. Chem. Soc. (assoc., Computers in Chemistry award 1987, St. Charles Found. Alumni award 1996), Assn. Computing Machinery, Chem. Soc., Am. Assn. Artificial Intelligence (charter), Chem. Structure Assn. (charter), Internat. Soc. Study Xenobiotics. Office: U Calif Dept Chemistry Santa Cruz CA 95064

WIRKEN, CHARLES WILLIAM, lawyer; b. Moline, Ill., Aug. 29, 1951; s. Walter William and Elizabeth Claire Wirken; children: Nicole, Michelle. BS, U. Ariz., 1972, JD, 1975. Bar: Ariz. 1975, U.S. Dist. Ct. Ariz. 1976, U.S. Ct. Appeals (9th cir.) 1980, U.S. Ct. Appeals (Fed. cir.) 1985, U.S. Ct. Appeals (10th cir.) 2004, U.S. Supreme Ct. 1980. Assoc. Killian, Legg & Nicholas, Mesa, Ariz., 1975-79; ptnr. Killian, Nicholas, Fischer, Wirken, Cook & Pew, Mesa, 1980-97, Gust Rosenfeld P.L.C., 1997—. Pres. Vol. Lawyers Project, Phoenix, 1981-83; judge pro tem Ariz. Ct. Appeals, 1985-99, Maricopa County

Superior Ct., 1986—; mem. civil study com. Maricopa County Superior Ct., 1984—; bd. dirs. Cmty. Legal Svcs., Phoenix, 1979-82. Exec. v.p. East Valley Partnership, Mesa, 1984; pres. Tri-City Cath. Social Svc., Mesa, 1983, 84; bd. dirs. East Valley Cultural Alliance, Mesa, 1984. Mem. State Bar Ariz. (bd. govs. 1995-06, pres. 2004-05, chair trial practice sect. 2001-02, chair civil practice and procedure com. 2006-07, bd. trustees, client protection fund), Maricopa County Bar Assn. (bd. dirs. 1983-91, pres. 1989-90), East Valley Bar Assn. (pres. 1979-80), Mesa C. of C. (dir. 1980-83, v.p. 1982-83), Rotary (bd. dirs. 1980-89, pres. 1987-88). Democrat. Roman Catholic. Home: 1708 E Knoll St Mesa AZ 85203-2171 Office: Gust Rosenfeld PLC 201 E Washington Ste 800 Phoenix AZ 85004-2327 Home Phone: 480-644-9657; Office Phone: 602-257-7959. Business E-Mail: cwirken@gustlaw.com.

WIRKLER, NORMAN EDWARD, retired architectural, engineering and construction management firm executive; b. Garnavillo, Iowa, Apr. 1, 1937; s. Herbert J. and Irene (Kregel) W.; m. Margaret Anne Gift, Oct. 16, 1959; children: Chris Edward, Scott Norman, Elizabeth Anne. BArch, Iowa State U., 1959. Designer The Durrant Group Inc., Dubuque, Iowa, 1959-64, assoc., 1964-67, prin., 1967-82, pres. Denver, 1982-98; bd. dirs. The Durrant Group, Denver, 1998—, Durant Capital Resources, Denver County, 1993—. Commr., mem. exec. com. Commn. on Accreditation on Corrections, 1985-91; archtl. cons. to Am. Correctional Assn. Standards Program; mem. Am. Correctional Assn. Standards Com., 1992-98; v.p. Garnavillo (Iowa) Bank Corp. Co-author: Design Guide for Secure Adult Correctional Facilities, 1983 Bd. dirs. United Way, Dubuque, 1984. Fellow AIA (pres. Iowa chpt. 1977; mem. nat. com. on arch. for justice 1974—, chmn. 1979; chmn. AIA Ins. Trust 1985-87, mem. Colo. chpt. 1987—); mem. ASTM (detention component standards com. 1982-84), Dubuque C. of C. (legis. com. 1978-83, chmn. 1979; v.p. 1984, exec. com. 1982-85), Iowa State U. Devel. Coun. Club. Republican. Avocations: flying, skiing, jogging, golf, hunting. Office: 3773 Cherry Creek North Dr Ste 1000 Denver CO 80209-3804 E-mail: nwirkler@durrant.com.

WIRT, MICHAEL JAMES, library director; b. Sault Sainte Marie, Mich., Mar. 21, 1947; s. Arthur James and Blanche Marian (Carruth) W.; m. Barbara Ann Hallesy, Aug. 12, 1972; 1 child, Brendan. BA, Mich. State U., 1969; MLS, U. Mich., 1971; postgrad., U. Wash., 1990. Cert. libr., Wash. Acting libr. U. Mich. Ctr. for Rsch. on Econ. Devel., Ann Arbor, 1971-72; instnl. svcs. libr. Spokane County (Wash.) Libr. Dist., 1972-76, asst. dir., 1976-79, acting dir., 1979, dir., 1980—. Mem. adv. com. Partnership for Rural Improvement, Spokane, 1982-85, Wash. State Libr. Planning and Devel. Com., 1984-85, Ea. Wash. U. Young Writers Project Adv. Bd., 1988-89; mem. issues selection com. Citizens League of Greater Spokane, 1991-93, City of Spokane Indian Trail Specific Plan Task force, 1992-95; mem. comm. com. United Way Spokane County, 1994, campaign chair local govt. divsn., 1996. Mem. Wash. Libr. Assn. (2d v.p. 1984-86, dir. 1989-91, pub. rels. com. 1993-2001, chair legis. planning com. 2003—, conf. coord. 2003-05, Merit award 1984, Pres. award 1998), Wash. Libr. Network (rep. Computer Svc. Coun. 1983-86, v.p., treas. State Users Group 1986-87), Am. Libr. Assn. (Pub. Libr. Affiliates Network 1990-93, PLA Bus. Coun. 1990-94, chmn. 1991-94), Spokane Valley C. of C. (local govt. affairs com. 1987-2000, co-chair 1996-98, pub. policy com. 2000-2005, mem. local governance com. 2003-2005, governence com. 2005—), Spokane Regional C. of C. (local govt. com. 1990-94, human svcs. com. 1990-92, chmn. 1991-92, govt. reorgn. task force 1995), Spokane Civic Theatre (bd. dirs. 1996-2001, v.p. 1997-98, 2000, sec. 1998-2000), Inland N.W. Legis. Coalition, Momentum (local govt. strategy com. 1992-94), New Century (govt. collaboration com. 1997-98), Inland N.W. Coun. Librs. (bd. dirs. 1979—, chmn. 1997-98). Office: Spokane County Libr Dist 4322 N Argonne Rd Spokane WA 99212-1853 Office Phone: 509-924-4122. Business E-Mail: mwirt@scld.org.

WIRTH, MICHAEL K. (MIKE WIRTH), oil company executive; b. Oct. 1960; m. Julie Wirth; 4 children. BS, U. Colo. With Chevron Corp., 1982—, design engr., 1982, sr. retail mgr. mktg. Western Ops., 1998—99, gen. mgr. retail mktg., 1999—2000; pres. mktg. Caltex Corp., Singapore, 2000—01; pres. mktg. Asia/Middle East/Africa ChevronTexaco Corp, 2001—04, pres. Global Supply and Trading, 2004—06, exec. v.p. Global Downstream, 2006—. Office: Chevron Hdqs 6001 Bollinger Canyon Rd San Ramon CA 94583*

WIRTHLIN, JOSEPH B., religious organization administrator; b. Salt Lake City, June 11, 1917; s. Joseph L. and Madeline (Bitner) W.; m. Elisa Young Rogers, May 26, 1941; 8 children. Degree in Bus. Adminstrn., U. Utah. Ordained apostle LDS Ch., 1986. Served a mission to Germany, Austria and Switzerland LDS Ch., 1930s, served in stake and ward aux. positions, counselor, bishop to mem. stake presidency, until 1971, 1st counselor Sunday Sch. Gen. Presidency, 1971-75, asst. to coun. of 12 apostles, 1975-76, gen. authority area supr. Europe area, 1975-78, mem. 1st Quorum of Seventy, 1976-86, exec. adminstr. to S.E. area U.S. and Caribbean Islands, 1978-82, mng. dir. Melchizedek Priesthood Com., Relief Soc. and Mil. Rels. Com., 1978-84, exec. adminstr. Brazil, 1982-84, pres. Europe area of ch., 1984-86, mem. presidency of 1st Quorum of Seventy, exec. dir. curriculum dept., editor ch. mags., 1986, apostle, 1986—, mem. missionary exec. coun., gen. welfare svcs. coms., 1986—. Office: LDS Ch Joseph Smith Meml Bldg 47 E North Temple Salt Lake City UT 84150-9704

WIRTHLIN, MILTON ROBERT, JR., periodontist; b. Little Rock, July 13, 1932; s. Milton Robert and Margaret Frances (Clark) W.; m. Joan Krieger, Aug. 1, 1954; children: Michael, Steven, Laurie, David, Aina. DDS, U. Calif., San Francisco, 1956, MS, 1968. Diplomate Am. Bd. Periodontology. Commd. ensign USN, 1955, advanced through grades to capt., 1976, retired, 1985; assoc. prof. U. Pacific, San Francisco, 1985-86; assoc. clin. prof. U. Calif., San Francisco, 1986-96, clin. prof., 1996—, dir. postgrad. periodontology, 1996-99, clin. prof. emeritus, 2000—. Contbr. articles to profl. jours. Asst. scoutmaster Boy Scouts Am., San Bruno, Calif., 1968, com. chmn. Explorer Post, San Francisco, 1981-83; bd. dirs. ARC, Chgo., 1976-81, chair social svc. com., San Francisco, 1981-83. Decorated Meritorious Svc. medal with 2 gold stars; recipient Gabbs prize U. Calif., 1956. Fellow Internat. Coll. Dentists; mem. Am. Dental Assn., Am. Acad. Perdiodontology, Western Soc. Periodontology, Med-Dental Study Guild San Francisco (pres. 1993), Internat. Assn. Dental Rsch., Omicron Kappa Upsilon. Avocations: ho scale model railroading, fly tying, trout fishing, genealogy. Office: U Calif Med Ctr Sch Dentistry San Francisco CA 94143-0762

WIRTHLIN, RICHARD BITNER, researcher; b. Salt Lake City, Mar. 15, 1931; s. Joseph L. and Madeline (Bitner) W.; m. Jeralie Chandler, Nov. 23, 1956; children: Richard L., Mary Ann, J. Mark, Carolyn, Michael, Jill, Susan, John BS, U. Utah, 1956, MA, 1957; PhD, U. Calif.-Berkeley, 1964. Lectr. U. Calif. Med. Ctr., San Francisco, 1960-61; chmn. dept. econs. Brigham Young U., Provo, Utah, 1964-69; ptnr. Merrill-Wirthlin Assocs., Provo, 1964-69; pres., chmn. bd. dirs. Decision/Making/Info., McLean, Va., 1969-84; chmn. bd. dirs., CEO The Wirthlin Group, Salt Lake City, 1987—. Co-author (with Wynton C. Hall): (book) The Greatest Communicator: What Ronald Reagan Taught Me about Politics, Leadership, and Life, 2004. Dir. planning and strategy Reagan/Bush Campaign, 1980, campaign dir. research, planning and policy, 1980-81; dir. planning and evaluation Pres.-Elect Transition Com., 1980-81; cons. to Prime Minister Margaret Thatcher and Brit. Conservative Party, 1989—; bd. dirs. Harris Interactive, 2004—. Recipient Disting. Alumni award U. Utah, 1986, Disting. Alumni Service award Brigham Young U., 1987; named Advt. Man of Yr., Advt. Age, 1981, Pollster of Yr. Polit. Cons., 1981. Mem. Acad. Polit. Sci., Am. Econ. Assn., Am. Mktg. Assn., Am. Assn. Pub. Opinion/Research, Council Survey Research Orgns., Sigma Chi, Omicron Delta Epsilon Republican. Office: 2625 Old Orchard Cir Salt Lake City UT 84121

WIRUM, ANDREA A., lawyer; b. Okla. City, Feb. 24, 1956; BA, Mich. State Univ., 1977; JD, Univ. Calif., Hastings, 1980. CPA 1977; bar: Calif. 1980. Ptnr. Corp. & Securities practice, mem. mng. bd. Pillsbury Winthrop Shaw Pittman, San Francisco. Office: Pillsbury Winthrop Shaw Pittman 50 Fremont St San Francisco CA 94105 Office Phone: 415-983-1735. Office Fax: 415-983-1200. Business E-Mail: andrea.wirum@pillsburylaw.com.

WISE, GEORGE EDWARD, lawyer; b. Chgo., Feb. 26, 1924; s. George E. and Helen L. (Gray) W.; m. Patricia E. Finn, Aug. 3, 1945; children: Erich, Peter, Abbe, Raoul, John. JD, U. Chgo. Bar: Calif. 1949, U.S. Dist. Ct. (no. dist.) Calif. 1948, U.S. Ct. Appeals (9th cir.) 1948, U.S. Dist. Ct. (cen. dist.) 1950, U.S. Supreme CT. 1955. Law clk. Calif. Supreme Ct., 1948-49; sr. ptnr. Wise, Wiezorek, Timmons & Wise, Long Beach, 1949—; of counsel Wise Pearce Yocis & Smith, Long Beach. With USNR, 1943-45. Fellow Am. Coll. Trial Lawyers; mem. ABA, Los Angeles County Bar Assn., Long Beach Bar Assn. (pres. 1970, Atty. of Yr. 1990), Calif. State Bar. Home: 5401 E El Cedral St Long Beach CA 90815-4112 Personal E-mail: georgewise@yahoo.com.

WISE, MARK B., physics professor; b. Montreal, Canada, Nov. 9, 1953; BSc, U. Toronto, 1976, MSc, 1977; PhD, Stanford U., Calif., 1980. Asst. prof. theoretical physics Calif. Inst. Tech., 1982—84, assoc. prof., 1984—85, prof., 1985—92, John A. McCone prof. high energy physics, 1992—. Recipient Loeb lectr., Harvard U., 1998, Sakurai prize, Am. Phys. Soc., 2001; Alfred P. Sloan fellowship, Alfred P. Sloan Found., 1984—86. Fellow: Am. Acad. Arts and Scis.; mem.: NAS, Harvard Soc. Fellows (jr. fellow 1980—83). Office: Calif Inst Tech Particle Theory Group Mail Code 452-48 1200 E California Blvd Pasadena CA 91125 Office Phone: 626-395-6687. Office Fax: 626-568-8473. E-mail: wise@theory.caltech.edu.

WISE, WOODROW WILSON, JR., retired small business owner; b. Alexandria, Va., Mar. 9, 1938; s. Woodrow Wilson Sr. and Helen (Peverill) W.; m. Barbara Jean Hatton, Oct. 6, 1956 (div. 1975); m. Sandra Kay Habitz, Dec. 17, 1983; children: Anthony P., Laura J. Gen. mgr. Alexandria (Va.) Amusement Corp., 1956-73; curator Harold Lloyd Estate, Beverly Hills, Calif., 1973-75; pres. Discount Video Tapes, Inc./Hollywood's Attic, Burbank, Calif., 1975-2000; ret., 2000. Office: Hollywoods Attic PO Box 7122 Burbank CA 91510-7122 Office Phone: 818-244-7904. Business E-Mail: woody@hollywoodsattic.com.

WISEMAN, JANE, broadcast executive; b. Aug. 24, 1971; m. Joe Wiseman. Asst. to head writer of Gen. Hosp. ABC; asst. on Ink CBS; exec. comedy dept. Fox Broadcasting Co., 2000; v.p. comedy devel. NBC Entertainment, Burbank, Calif. Achievements include working on the TV shows Andy Richter Controls the Universe, The Bernie Mac Show, Undeclared, Arrested Development, The Simple Life, Twenty Good Years, 30 Rock and the upcoming The Singles Table. Office: NBC Entertainment 3000 W Alameda Ave Burbank CA 91523

WISNIEWSKI, STEPHEN ADAM, professional football player; b. Rutland, Vt., Apr. 7, 1967; Student, Pa. State U. Offensive guard L.A. Raiders/Oakland Raiders, 1989—. Named All-Pro Team Guard by Sporting News, 1990-93, Coll. All-Am. Team, 1987, 88. Played in Pro Bowl, 1990-91, 93. Home: 36 El Alamo Ct Danville CA 94526-1455

WISTRICH, ANDREW J., federal judge; b. 1951; AB, U. Calif., Berkeley, 1972; JD, U. Chgo., 1976. Law clk. to Hon. Charles Clark U.S. Ct. Appeals (5th cir.), 1976-77; with McCutchen, Doyle, Brown & Enersen, San Francisco, 1978-83, Brown & Bain, Palo Alto, Calif., 1983-94; apptd. magistrate judge cen. dist. U.S. Dist. Ct. Calif., 1994. Office: 255 E Temple St Rm 6100 Los Angeles CA 90012-3332

WITHERS, HUBERT RODNEY, radiotherapist, radiobiologist, educator; b. Queensland, Australia, Sept. 21, 1932; arrived in U.S., 1966; s. Hubert and Gertrude Ethel (Tremayne) W.; m. Janet Macfie, Oct. 9, 1959; 1 child, Genevieve. MB BS, U. Queensland, Brisbane, Australia, 1956; PhD, U. London, 1965, DSc, 1982. Bd. cert. Ednl. Coun. Fgn. Med. Grads. Intern Royal Brisbane and Associated Hosps., 1957; resident in radiotherapy and pathology Queensland Radium Inst. and Royal Brisbane Hosp., 1958-63; U. Queensland Gaggin fellow Gray Lab., Mt. Vernon Hosp., Northwood, Middlesex, England, 1963—65, Royal Brisbane Hosp., 1966; radiotherapist Prince of Wales Hosp., Randwick, Sydney, Australia, 1966; vis. rsch. scientist lab. physiology Nat. Cancer Inst., Bethesda, Md., 1966-68; assoc. prof. radiotherapy sect. exptl. radiotherapy U. Tex. Sys. Cancer Ctr. M.D. Anderson Hosp. & Tumor Inst., Houston, 1968-71, prof. radiotherapy, chief sect. sect. exptl. radiotherapy, 1971-80; prof. dir. exptl. radiation oncology dept. radiation oncology UCLA, 1980-89, 1991—94, prof. vice chair, dir. exptl. radiation oncology dept. radiation oncology, 1991—94, Am. Cancer Sec. Clin. Rsch. prof. dept. radiation oncology, 1992—94, interim dir. Jonsson Comprehensive Cancer Ctr., 1994—95, chmn. radiation oncology, 1994—2005. Assoc. grad. faculty U. Tex., Grad. Sch. Biomed. Scis, Houston, 1969-73, mem. grad. faculty, 1973-80; prof. dept. radiotherapy Med. Sch., U. Tex. Health Sci. Ctr., Houston, U. Tex. Med. Sch., Houston, 1975-80; prof., dir. Inst. Oncology, The Prince of Wales Hosp., U. NSW, Sydney, Australia, 1989-91; mem. com. mortality mil. pers. present-at-atmosphere tests of nuc. weapons Inst. Medicine, 1993-94; mem. radiation effects rsch. bd. NRC, 1993-99; mem. com. neutron dose reporting Internat. Commn. Radiation Units and Measurements, 1982-93, mem. report com. clin. dosimetry for neutrons, 1993-98; mem. task force non-stochastic effects radiation Internat. Com. Radiation Protection, 1980-84, mem. com. 1, 1992-00; mem. radiobiology com. Radiation Therapy Oncology Group, 1979-89, mem. dose-time com., 1980-89, mem. gastroenterology com., 1982-89; fellow Royal Australian Coll. Radiologists Edn. Bd., 1989-91; trustee Am. Bd. Radiology, 1995-04; mem. cancer rsch. coord. com. U. Calif., 1991-97, mem. standing curriculum com. UCLA biomed. physics grad. program, 1993-2007; cons. exptl. radiotherapy U. Tex. Sys. Cancer Ctr., 1980—. Mem. Am. editl. bd.: Internat. Jour. Radiat. Oncol. Biol. Phys., 1982-89, 1991-2007, internat. editl. bd., 1989-91; cons. editor: The European Jour. Cancer, 1990-95; editl. bd. dirs.: Endocurietherapy/Hyperthermia Oncology, 1991—2001, Radiation Oncology Investigations, 1992-2002; assoc. editor: Cancer Rsch., 1993-94, editl. bd. 1995-97. Mem. Kettering selection com. Gen. Motors Cancer Rsch. Found., 1988-89, chmn., 1984, 1989, 1990-94, 2002-04, awards assembly, 1990-94, 2002-04, adv. coun., 1994-2006. Decorated officer Order of Australia, 1998; Named Gilbert H. Fletcher lectr. U. Tex. Sys. Cancer Ctr., 1989, Clifford Ash lectr. Ont. Cancer Inst., Princess Margaret Hosp., 1987, Erskine lectr. Radiol. Soc. N.Am., 1988, Ruvelson lectr. U. Minn., 1988, Milford Schultz lectr. Mass. Gen. Hosp., 1989, Del Regato Found. lectr. Hahnemann U., 1990, Bruce Cain Meml. lectr. New Zealand Soc. Oncology, 1990; recipient Medicine prize Polish Acad. Sci., 1989, Second HS Kaplan Disting. Scientist award Internat. Assn. Radiation Rsch., 1991, Gray medal Internat. Commn. Radiation Units, 1995, U.S. Dept. Energy Fermi award 1997, Radiation Rsch. Soc. Failla award, 1988, Gold medal Royal Australian and N.Z. Coll. Radiologists, 1997, Charles F. Kettering prize GM Cancer Rsch. Found., 1998; Emmanuel van der Schueren medal Belgian Rad One Soc., 2004, Gold medal Gilbert H. Fletcher Soc., 2005, Gold medal Radiol. Soc. N.Am., 2005. Fellow Am. Coll. Radiology, ACS Oncology Group (ethics com. oncology 2002—), Royal Australasian Coll. Radiologists (hon. 1997), Am. Bd. Radiology (bd. cert. therapeutic radiology 1977, Am. Coll. Radiology adv. com. patterns of care study 1988-93, radiation oncology adv. group 1993-98, others, Gold medal 2004), Am. Radium Soc. (credential com. 1986-89, 93-94, treas. 1993-94, pres. 1996-97, others, Janeway medal 1994), Am. Soc. Therapeutic Radiology and Oncology (Gold Medal awards com. 1982, 93, 00, publs. com. 1993-97, vice-chair publs. com., 1996-97, keynote address 1990, Gold medal 1991, Fellow 2006), Nat. Cancer Inst. (ad-hoc rev. coms. 1970—, radiation sudy sect. 1971-75, cons. U.S.-Japan Coop. Study high LET Radiotherapy 1975-77, cancer rsch. emphasis grant rev. com. 1976, clin. cancer ctr. rev. com. 1976-79, toxicology working group 1977-78, reviewer outstanding investigator grants 1984-93, bd. sci. counselors, 1986-88), Nat. Cancer Inst. Can. (adv. com. rsch. 1992-95), Pacific N.W. Radiol. Soc. (hon.), Tex. Radiol. Soc. (hon.), So. Calif. Radiation Oncology Soc. (sec., treas., 1992-94, pres. 1997-98), European Soc. Therapeutic Radiology and Oncology (hon.; Regaud lectr. 2000), Polish Oncology Soc. (hon., Gold medal 2002), Austrian Radiation Oncology Soc. (hon.), Phila. Roentgen Ray Soc. (hon.), Radiation Rsch. Soc. (pres. 1982-83, honors and awards com. 1984-88, ad hoc com. funds utilization 1987-89, adv. com. Radiation Rsch. Jour. 1988-96, Failla awardm 1988). Office: David Geffen Sch Medicine UCLA 10833 Le Conte Ave Los Angeles CA 90095-1714 Business E-Mail: hwithers@mednet.ucla.edu.

WITHERSPOON, REESE (LAURA JEAN REESE WITHERSPOON), actress; b. New Orleans, Mar. 22, 1976; d. John and Betty Witherspoon; m. Ryan Phillippe, June 5, 1999 (div. Oct. 5, 2007); children: Ava Elizabeth, Deacon. Co-owner prodn. co. Type A Films; global amb. Avon cosmetics, 2007—. Actor: (films) The Man in the Moon, 1991, A Far Off Place, 1993, Jack the Bear, 1993, S.F.W., 1994, Freeway, 1996, Fear, 1996, Twilight, 1998, Overnight Delivery, 1998, Pleasantville, 1998, Cruel Intentions, 1999, Election, 1999, Best Laid Plans, 1999, American Psycho, 2000, Little Nicky, 2000, (voice) The Trumpet of the Swan, 2001, Legally Blonde, 2001, The Importance of Being Earnest, 2002, Sweet Home Alabama, 2002, Vanity Fair, 2004, Just Like Heaven, 2005, Walk the Line, 2005 (Best Actress, NY Film Critics Circle, 2005, Boston Soc. Film Critic award, 2005, Broadcast Film Assn., 2006, Nat. Soc. Film Critics award, 2006, Best Performance by an Actress in a Motion Picture-Musical or Comedy, Hollywood Fgn. Press Assn., Golden Globe award, 2006, Outstanding Performance by a Female Actor in a Leading Role, Screen Actors Guild award, 2006, Actress in a Leading Role, British Acad. Film and TV Arts, 2006, Performance by an Actress in a Leading Role, Acad. Motion Picture Arts & Sciences, 2006, Choice Movie Actress: Drama/Action Adventure, Teen Choice awards, 2006), Rendition, 2007, Four Christmases, 2008, (voice) Monsters vs. Aliens, 2009; actor, exec. prodr.: (films) Legally Blonde 2: Red, White & Blonde, 2003; actor, prodr.:(films) Penelope, 2006; actor: (TV films) Wildflower, 1991, Desperate Choices: To Save My Child, 1992; (mini-series) Return to Lonsome Dove, 1993 (TV appearances) Friends, 2000, (voice) King of the Hill, 2000, The Simpsons, 2002 Recipient Catalan Internat. Film Festival Award Best Actress, 1997, Movieline Young Hollywood Award for Breakthrough Performance (Female), 1999, Online Film Critics Soc. Award for Best Actress, 1999, National Soc. of Film Critics Award for Best Actress, 1999; named Favorite Leading Lady, People's Choice Awards, 2006, Favorite Female Movie Star, 2008, 2009, 25 Most Intriguing People, People, 2001, 50 Most Beautiful People, 2002, Favorite Female Film Star, 2004; named one of 100 Most Influential People, Time Mag., 2006, 50 Most Powerful People in Hollywood, Premiere mag., 2006, Women in Entertainment: Power 100, Hollywood Reporter, 2007, The 100 Most Powerful Celebrities, Forbes.com, 2008. Office: Creative Artists Agy 2000 Ave of the Stars Los Angeles CA 90067

WITKIN, JOEL-PETER, photographer, poet; b. Bklyn., Sept. 13, 1939; s. Max and Mary (Pellegrino) W.; 1 child, Kersen Ahanu; m. Barbara Anne Gilbert, 2005. B.F.A., Cooper Union, 1974; M.F.A., U. N.Mex., 1986; student (fellow), Columbia U., 1973-74. Artist in residence Zerybthia Rome, Italy, summer 1996; represented by Galerie Baudoin Lebon, Paris, Catherine Edelman Gallery, Chgo., Silverstein Photography, NYC; artist in residence Berlin, fall 1998, Paris, winter 1998. Lectr. Am. Acad. Rome, 1996, Princeton U., 1997, Camera Work, Berlin, El Escorial, Spain, 1998, Yale U., 2001, Internat. Ctr. Photography, 1999, Moscow Ho. Photography, 2001, Ecole Beaux Arts Superior, Paris, 2005, The Academia, Milano, 2007. Exhibited in Projects Studio One, NYC, 1980, Galerie Texbraun, Paris, 1982, Baudoin Lebon, Paris, 1982, 86, 90, 94, 97, 2000, 02, 04, Kansas Ctiy Art Inst., 1983, Stedelijk Mus., Amsterdam, 1983, Fraenkel Gallery, 1983-84, 87, 91, 93, 95, 97, Pace WildenStein MacGill Gallery, NYC, 1983, 84, 87, 89, 91, 93, 95, 97, San Francisco Mus. Modern Art, 1985, Bklyn. Mus., 1986, Galerie Baudoin Lebon, Paris, 1987, 89, 91, 95, 97, 2000, 02, 04, 07, 08 Centro de Arte Reina Sofia Mus., Madrid, 1988, Palais de Tokyo, Paris, 1989, Fahey/Klein Gallery, LA, 1987, 89, 91, 97, 98, 2005, Mus. Modern Art, Haifa, Israel, 1991, Photo Picture Space Gallery, Osaka, Japan, 1993, 95,

2001, Guggenheim Mus., NYC, 1995, Interkamera, Prague, 1995, Il Castello de Rivoli Mus., Turin, 1995, Encontros de Fotografia, Cuembra, Portugal, 1996, 98, Rencontres de la Photographie, Arles, France, 1996, Taipei Photo Gallery, Taiwan, 1994, 96, 98, Mus. of Fine Arts, Santa Fe, 1998, Wildenstein Gallery, Tokyo, 1998, Pace Wildenstein, LA, 1998, Sternburg Mus., Prauge, 1999, Mesiac Fotographie, Slovakia, 1999, Hotel De Sully, Paris, 2000, Catherine Edelman Gallery, Chgo., 2000, 05, 09, Ricco/Maresca Gallery, NYC, 1997, 99, Athens Sch. Fine Art, 2000, Ctr. Contemporary Art, Honolulu, 2000, Hasted/Hunt Gallery, NYC, 2001, 04, Etherton Gallery, Tucson, 2001, 05, Linda Durham Gallery, Santa Fe, 2005, Stadt Mus., Jena, 2002, Picture Photo Space, Osaka, 2002, Infinito Gallery, Turin, 2002, Galeria Juana de Aizpuru, Madrid, 2003, Photoes Pana, Madrid, 2003, Le Garage Galerie, Toulouse, 2003, ARCO, Madrid, 2004, Gary Tatintsian Gallery, Moscow, 2005, Moscow House Photography, 2005, Witkin Vintage, Hasted/Hunt, NYC, 2006, Café Françoise, Brussels, Paris-Photo, 2006, Chgo. Art Fair, 2007, Cite2000 Internat. des Arts, Paris, 2006, Medici Palace, Seravezza, Italy, 2007, Galleria Ca Di Fra, Milano, 2007, Maison de la Culture de Namur, Belgium, 2007, Luz Bienal de las Artes, Zaragoza, 2007, Paris Photo, 2007, Palazzo Reale, Milano, 2008, Edelman Gallery Chgo., 2008, Silverstein Photography, NYC, 2009, Festival of Nordic Art, Norway, 2009; group shows: Mus. Modern Art, NYC, 1959, San Francisco Mus. Moder Art, 1981, Whitney Biennial, 1985, Palais de Tokyo, Paris, 1986, La Photographie Contemporaine en France, 1996, Foto Masson, Goteberg, Sweden, 1997, Hanlin Museum, So. Korea, 1997, Bogardenkapel, Bruges, 1998, Hayward Gallery, London, 1997, Strasborg Mus. d'Art Moderne et Contemporaine, 1998, The Ansel Adams Ctr., San Francisco, 1999, Camera Work, San Francisco, 1999, The Louvre, Paris, 2000, Museé Bourdelle, Paris, 2000, John Gibson Gallery, NYC, 2000, The High Mus. Art, Ga., 2000, Fotografie Forum, Frankfort, 2001, Nat. Gallery of Can., 2002, Hotel de Sully, Paris, 2002, The Israel Mus., Jerusalem, 2002, The Whitney Mus., NYC, 2002, H. Lunn Collection, Lille, 2003, Photology, Milan, 2003, Akira Ikeda Gallery, Berlin, 2003, Aperture: Photography Past/Forward, NYC, 2003, Nat. Gallery Can., Ottawa, 2004, Yancey Richardson Gallery, NYC, 2004, Ideal And Reality, Museo Morandi, Bologna, Italy, 2004, 08, Guggenheim, Bilbao, 2005, Bruce Silverstein, NYC, 2005, Ctr. D'Art Del'Yonne, 2005, Wessel and O'Connor Fine Art, NYC, 2005, Mus. Contemporary Photography, Chgo., 2005, Cité Internat., Cite International Paris, 2008: "The Book", Paris, 2006, Houston Ctr. for Photography, Silver Retrospective, 2006, "Eye of the Beholder", Richard Avedon collection, 2006, "The Invisible Landscape", Nat. Gallery Can., 2007, Miami Mus., Charles Cowles collection, 2007, Mus. Photography, Bogota, Columbia, 2007, Photo London, Silverstein-Photography, 2007, Terry Etherton Gallery, Tucson, Ariz., 2007, Dalton Gallery, Agnes Scott Coll., Decatur, Ga., (Group Shows) Art & Basel, Miami, 2007, Getty Mus., La., The Nude, 2007, 2nd St. Gallery, Charlottesville, Va., 2008, Bologna Art Fair, 2008, Picasso Mus., Barcelona, 2008, Las Meninas, 2008, Art Basel (Silverstein) 2008, Extraordinary Bodies, The Matter Mus., Pa., 2008,others; represented in permanent collections, Mus. Modern Art, NYC, San Francisco Mus. Modern Art, 1980, Nat. Gallery Art, Washington, Victoria and Albert Mus., London, George Eastman House, NY, Getty Collection, Moder Museet,Stockholm, Sweden, Whitney Mus., NYC, Guggenheim Mus., NYC, Met. Mus., NYC, Tokyo Met.Mus. Photography, 2008, Nat. Gallery Can., Metropolitan Mus. Art, NYC, Phila. Mus. Art, Trouble in Paradise, TVcon Mus. Art, 2009, Aboukrat Gallery, Paris, French Nat. Ctr. Spatial Rsch., 2009, Bestiare Imaginaire, Galleries Baudoin Lebon, Paris, 2009; UBS Bank, Basel, Gianfrknco Composti Collection, Milano; (perm collections): The Hassalblad Found, Sweden, Art Concern, Kortrijk.subject of monographs: Joel-Peter Witkin, 1985, 88-89, 91, 93, 95-96, 98-2003, 06-08, 09; editor: Masterpieces of Medical Photography, 1987, Harms Way, 1994; visual editor: Songs of Experience, 2002, Songs of Innocence, 2003, Songs of Experience and Songs of Innocence, 2004-05, 21st Edits., Bourgeoisie-in-de-Nile, 2006, The History of Hats in Art, NY Times, 2006, Maestro Witkin, Delpire Editeuyr, 2009, Portfolio of Etchings: Landfall Press, Santa Fe, 2007; artist in residence: Paris, 1994, 98, 2000, Rome, 1996, Berlin, 1998, Buenos Aires, 2003, Moscow, 2005., La Photographie Americaine Bibliothe que Nationale de France, 2008, Maccarone Gallery Curaned by Alison Gingas, NYC, Gallerie Hotel La Marcheau-Bastille Paris, 2008, Marietime, Contemporary Art Gallery U. Scnn., 2008; contbr. articles to profl. jours. Served with U.S. Army, 1961-64, Photographer. Decorated Commandeur des Arts et de Lettres (France), 2000; recipient The Augustus Saint Gaudens medal The Cooper Union, 1996, Disting. Alumni award The Cooper Union, 1986, Internat. Ctr. Photography award, 1988, award for N.Y. Times "The Plague Yr.," Soc. Publ. Designers, 2000; Ford Found. grantee, 1977, 78, Nat. Endowment in Photography grantee, 1980, 81, 86, 92; Smithsonian Archives Am. Art award, 2009. Address: 1707 Five Points Rd SW Albuquerque NM 87105-3017 Office Phone: 505-843-6682. Business E-Mail: jwitkin1@comcast.net.

WITT, ALICIA, actress; b. Worcester, Mass., Aug. 21, 1975; d. Robert and Diane W. Home edn. Actress Internat. Creative Mgmt., Beverly Hills, Calif. TV appearances: Cybill, 1995-98, The Disappearance of Vonnie, 1994, Blackout, 1993, Twin Peaks, 1991, Hotel Room, Ally McBeal, 2000, Ring of the Nibelungs, 2004; film appearances: Dune, 1984, Liebestraum, 1991, Bodies, Rest and Motion, 1993, Fun, 1994 (Spl. Jury Recognition award Sundance Film Festival 1994), Four Rooms, 1995, Mr. Holland's Opus, 1995, Citizen Ruth, 1996, The Reef, 1997, Bongwater, 1998, Urban Legend, 1998, (voice) Gen 13, 1998, Cecil B. DeMented, 2000, Playing with Mona Lisa, 2000 (Best Actress award U.S. Comedy Arts Festival 2000), Vanilla Sky, 2001, Ten Tiny Love Stories, 2001, American Girl, 2002, Two Weeks Notice, 2002, The Upside of Anger, 2005, 88 Minutes, 2007; prodr. On the Wise, 2005; actor, prodr. Girls' Lunch, 2004; TV film appearances Ring of the Nibelungs, 2004, Blue Smoke, 2007; TV guest appearances Twin Peaks, 1990, Hotel Room, 1993, The Sopranos, 2000, Ally McBeal, 2000, The Twilight Zone, 2003, (mus. theater) The Gift, 2000; stage appearances Dissonance, 2007. Recipient Spl. Jury Recognition for acting, Sundance Film Festival, 1994, Ind. Spirit Award nomination, 1995. Avocations: listening to big-band recordings, chess, backgammon, bowling. Office: Brillstein-Grey Entertainment 9150 Wilshire Blvd Ste 350 Beverly Hills CA 90212

WITT, DAVID L., curator, writer; b. Kansas City, Mo., Nov. 3, 1951; s. Lloyd Vernon and Dean Witt. BS in Polit. Sci., Kans. State U., 1974; M Liberal Studies, U. Okla., 2000. Naturalist Naish Nature Ctr., Edwardsville, Kans., summers 1967-70; asst. curator Seton Mus., Cimarron, N.Mex., summers 1972-74; curatorial asst. Riley County Hist. Mus., Manhattan, Kans., 1973-74; mus. asst. Millicent Rogers Mus., Taos, N.Mex., 1976-77; curator The Gaspard House Mus., Taos, N.Mex., 1978-79, The Harwood Found., Taos, N.Mex., 1979—2005, Acad. for Love of Learning, Santa Fe, 2005—. Author: The Taos Artists, 1984, Taos Moderns: Art of the New, 1992 (Southwest Book award Border Regional Libr. Assn. 1993), Modernists in Taos from Martin to Dasburg, 2002 (S.W. Book award Border Regional Libr. Assn. 2003, Ralph Emerson Twitchell award N.Mex. Hist. Soc. 2003); co-author: Spirit Ascendant: The Art and Life of Patrociño Barela, 1996 (S.W. Book award Border Regional Libr. Assn. 1997); contbr. Taos Artists and Their Patrons, 1898-1950; contbr. articles to profl. jour. Organizer first N.Mex. Art History Conf., 1986; founder S.W. Art Hist. Coun., 1990. Mem. PEN, Am. Assn. Mus., N.Mex. Assn. Mus. (pres. 1986-88). Home: PO Box 317 Taos NM 87571-0317 Personal E-mail: davidlwitt@cybermesa.com.

WITT, MELVIN SYLVAN, periodical editor, publisher; b. Stockton, Calif., Dec. 25, 1925; s. Arnold and Sarah (Peletz) W.; m. Dorothy Halling, June 17, 1949; children: Ann, Mallory. BS, U. Calif., Berkeley, 1948; JD, U. Calif., San Francisco, 1951. Bar: Calif. 1952. Trial atty. State Compensation Ins. Fund, LA, 1954-57; appellate atty. Calif. Indsl. Accident Commn., San Francisco, 1957-60, trial referee, 1961-64; pvt. practice Berkeley, 1966-68; rsch. atty. Calif. Continuing Edn. of Bar, Berkeley, 1969-75; sec., dep. commr. Calif. Workers' Compensation Appeals Bd., San Francisco, 1964-66, chmn., 1975-80, Calif. Workers' Compensation Adv. Commn. to Calif. State Bar, 1974-75; founder, editor, pub. Calif. Workers' Compensation Reporter, Berkeley, 1973—2007. Adj. prof. law Golden Gate U. Law Sch., San Francisco, 1971—75, 1981, McGeorge Law Sch., U. of Pacific, Sacramento, 1973—75; lectr. U. Calif. Ext., Berkeley, 1961—75. Editor, co-author: California Workers' Compensation Practice, 2nd edit., (Calif. CEB) 1973. With inf., U.S. Army, 1944-46, ETO. Named Pub. Ofcl. of Yr., Calif. Applicants' Attys. Assn., Sacramento, 1980; recipient commendation by resolution Calif. State Legislature, Sacramento, 1981; CAAA scholar, 1999, Lifetime Achievement award, State Bar Calif. Workers' Compensation Sect., 2006. Mem. 78th Inf. Divsn. Vets. Assn. Democrat. Avocation: military history.

WITTE, MARLYS HEARST, internist, educator; b. NYC, 1934; MD, NYU Sch. Medicine, 1960. Intern N.C. Meml. Hosp., Chapel Hill, 1960-61; resident Bellevue Hosp. Ctr., NYC, 1961-63; fellow NYU Hosp., St. Louis, 1965-69; instr. Washington U., St. Louis, 1965-69; prof. surgery U. Ariz., 1969—; attending internist Ariz. Health Sci. Ctr., Tucson, 1965-69, 69—. Mem. AAAS, AMA, Alpha Omega Alpha. Office: U Ariz Coll Medicine PO Box 245063 1501 N Campbell Ave Tucson AZ 85724-0001

WITTE, OWEN NEIL, microbiologist, molecular biologist, educator; b. Bklyn., May 17, 1949; BS, Cornell U., 1971; MD, Stanford U., 1976. Predoctoral fellow Stanford U. Med. Sch., Palo Alto, Calif., 1971-76, MIT Ctr. Cancer Rsch., Cambridge, Mass., 1976-80; asst. prof., Dept. Microbiology, Molecular Genetics UCLA, 1980-82, assoc. prof., Dept. Microbiology, Molecular Genetics, 1982-86, prof., Dept. Microbiology, Molecular Genetics, 1986—, pres.'s chair in devel. immunology, Dept. Microbiology, Molecular Genetics, 1989—, founding dir., Inst. for Stem Cell Biology and Medicine, 2005—; investigator UCLA Howard Hughes Med. Inst., 1986—; prof., microbiology, immunology & molecular genetics UCLA David Geffen Sch. Medicine, 1996—, prof. molecular and med. pharmacology. Adv. bd. mem. Pew Scholars in Biomedical Sci., Damon Runyon Scholars Bd., Lasker Prize Award Jury. Contbr. articles to profl. jours. Am. Cancer Soc. faculty scholar, 1982-87; recipient Faculty award UCLA, 1990, award in basic cancer rsch. Milken Family Med. Found., 1990, Richard and Hinda Rosenthal Found. award Am. Assn. Cancer Rsch., 1991, William Dameshek prize Am. Soc. Hematology, 1993; Outstanding Investigator grantee Nat. Cancer Inst., 50th Anniversary Commemorative award, Leukenia Soc. of Amer., 1999, Warren Alpert Found. prize, 2000, de Villiers Internat. Achievement award, Leukemia and Lymphoma Soc., 2003 Fellow Am. Acad. Arts and Scis., 1996, Am. Acad. Microbiology, 1997; mem. NAS, Inst. Medicine. Office Phone: 310-206-0386. E-mail: owenw@microbio.ucla.edu.

WITTER, DEAN, III, computer company executive; b. NYC, May 27, 1947; s. Dean and Faith (Atkins) W.; m. Rebekah Ann Ferran, June 14, 1969; children: Allison C., Brooks A. BA, Harvard U., 1969; MBA, Stanford U., 1973. Lease underwriter Matrix Leasing Internat., San Francisco, 1973-74, U.S. Leasing Internat., San Francisco, 1974-76; lease mgr. Amdahl Corp., Sunnyvale, Calif., 1976-78, dir. leasing, 1978-81, controller U.S. ops., 1981-83, treas., 1983-89, v.p., 1985-89; Preemptive Techs., Inc., Emeryville, Calif., 1989-90; chief fin. officer Provista Corp., San Jose, Calif., 1990—. Bd. dirs. Zack Electronics, San Francisco. Trustee Dean Witter Found., San Francisco, 1981—, Sorensen Found., San Francisco, 1988—; bd. dirs. Mission Hospice Inc. of San Mateo County. Served with U.S. Army, 1969-71. Mem. Phi Beta Kappa. Republican. Office: 75 Notheatern Blvd Nashua NH 03062-3128

WITTS, SIMON, computer software company executive; m. Karen Witts; children: Peter, Daniel, Hannah. B in math & physics, M in info. tech., Univ. London. Sales mgmt. positions IBM UK Ltd.; enterprise sales mgmt. positions Microsoft Corp., Redmond, Wash., 1993—2003, pres. Microsoft Canada, v.p. sales & mktg. EMEA, corp. v.p. enterprise & ptnr. group, 2003—. Bd. dir. Avanade Inc. Office: Microsoft Corp 1 Microsoft Way Redmond WA 98052-6399

WITWER, JOHN, state legislator; b. Pitts., Dec. 3, 1940; m to Jean. Colorado State Representative, District 25, 98-, member, Appropriations & Finance Committees, currently, Colorado House Representative.Physician, radiologist, pediatric radiologist, 69-. Fellow, America Col Radiology. Republican. Protestant. Address: PO Box 2167 Evergreen CO 80437 Mailing: State Capitol 200 E Colfax Rm 271 Denver CO 80203 Fax: 303-679-0773. E-mail: john.witwer.house@state.co.us.

WITWORTH, CLARK L., sports team executive; CFO Larry H. Miller Group, Murray, Utah. Office: Larry H Miller Group 5650 S State St Murray UT 84107-6131

WOERNER, ROBERT LESTER, landscape architect; b. Rochester, NY, Jan. 31, 1925; s. William John and Loretta Bertha (Hettel) W.; m. Mary Jane Warn, May 12, 1952; children: Jane Marie, Anne Louise. BS, SUNY Coll. Forestry, Syracuse, 1949. Cert. landscape architect, Wash., Idaho. Draftsman N.A., Rotunno Landscape Architects, Syracuse, 1947-49; landscape architect Park Dist., Plan Commn., Yakima, Wash., 1949-50; asst. supt. parks Spokane Park Dept., Spokane, Wash., 1950-56; dir. Denver Bot. Gardens, 1956-58; pvt. practice landscape architect Spokane, 1959-2000; chmn. bd. registration Landscape Architects State of Wash., 1976-78; pres. Council Landscape Archtl. Registration Bds., 1978-79. Mem. Zoning Bd. Adjustment, Spokane, 1983; mem. Urban Design Com., 1983; mem. Capitol Campus Design Adv. Com., 1982-94. Cpl. U.S. Army, 1943-45, ETO. Recipient Indsl. Landscaping Award Am. Assn. Nurserymen, Lincoln Bldg., Spokane, 1966; recipient Cert. of Merit Wash. Water Power, 1967, State Indsl. Landscaping award Wash State Nurserymen's Assn., Wash. Water Power, 1968 Fellow Am. Soc. Landscape Architects (pres. 1979-80, Disting. Svc. award 1976); mem. Kiwanis, Masons. Republican. Roman Catholic.

WOGSLAND, JAMES WILLARD, retired heavy machinery manufacturing executive; b. Devils Lake, ND, Apr. 17, 1931; s. Melvin LeRoy and Mable Bertina (Paulson) W.; m. Marlene Claudia Clark, June 1957; children: Karen Lynn, Steven James. BA in Econs., U. Minn., 1957. Various positions fin. dept. Caterpillar Tractor Co., Peoria, Ill., 1957-64, treas., 1976-81; mgr. fin. Caterpillar Overseas S.A., Geneva, 1965-70, sec.-treas., 1970-76; dir.-pres. Caterpillar Brasil S.A., São Paulo, 1981-87; exec. v.p. Caterpillar, Inc., Peoria, 1989-90, also bd. dirs., vice-chmn., 1990-95; bd. dirs. Ameren Corp., St. Louis, 1997—. Bd. dirs. Ameren Corp., St. Louis. Mem. adv. bd. St. Francis Hosp., Peoria, 1987-95; bd. dirs. Peoria Area Cmty. Found., 1986-92; trustee Eureka Coll., 1987-95; commr. Kootenai County Planning and Zoning Commn., 1997—. Sgt. USAF, 1951-55. Mem. Hayden Lake Golf and Country Club. Republican. Presbyterian. Home: 9675 Easy St Hayden Lake ID 83835-9526

WOHLGENANT, RICHARD GLEN, lawyer, director; b. Porterville, Calif., Dec. 2, 1930; s. Carl Ferdinand and Sara Alice (Moore) W.; m. Teresa Joan Bristow, Dec. 27, 1959; children: Mark Thomas, Tracy Patrice, Timothy James. BA, U. Mont., Missoula, 1952; LL.B., Harvard U., Cambridge, Mass., 1957. Bar: Colo. 1957, U.S. Dist. Ct. Colo. 1957. Assoc. Holme Roberts & Owen LLP, Denver, 1957-62; ptnr./mem. Holme Roberts & Owen, Denver, 1962-99, of counsel, 2000—. Bd. dirs. Adopt-A-Sch., Denver, 1976-80, St. Joseph Found., Denver, 1990-93, Denver Com. Coun. Fgn. Rels., 1988-98, Japanese-Am. Soc. Colo., 1993-98, Rocky Mountain chpt. U.S. Mex. C. of C., 1993-00; bi-nat. bd. U.S./Mex. C. of C., 2000—01; mem. Chamber of the Americas, 2001—03; adv. bd. Human Med. Genetics Prgm., U. Colo. H.S.C., 2000—03; trustee Helen K.and Arthur E. Johnson Found., 2003—, dir. Cordillerm Found, 2002- Mem. ABA, Colo. Bar Assn., Denver Bar Assn., Am. Coll. Real Estate Lawyers, Univ. Club, Law Club, City Club, Cactus Club, Denver Press Club, Mile High Club. Republican. Roman Catholic. Home: 300 Ivy St Denver CO 80220-5855 Office: Holme Roberts & Owen LLP 1700 Lincoln St Denver CO 80203-4500

WOIKE, LYNNE ANN, computer scientist; b. Torrance, Calif., Oct. 20, 1960; d. Stephen J. and Virginia (Ursich) Shane; m. Thomas W. Woike, Feb. 13, 1988; 1 child, Karla. BSc in Computer Sci. cum laude, Calif. State U., Dominguez Hills, 1994. Computer cons. Unocal Oil Co., Wilmington, Calif., 1992-94; x-window/motif software developer Logican Inc., San Pedro, Calif., 1994-95; reticle engr. TRW, Inc., Redondo Beach, Calif., 1982-88, sr. mem. tech. staff product data mgmt. database adminstr., 1995-98, chmn. product data mgmt. change control bd., 1995—98, sr. Unix/NT system adminstr., 1999; tech. lead, subscriber database DIRECTV, Inc., El Segundo, Calif., 1999—2002; computer and network mgr. Northrop Grumman Mission Systems, Redondo Beach, Calif., 2002—. Mem. IEEE, IEEE Computer Sci., Assn. for Computing Machinery (chmn. student chpt. 1993-94), Calif. State U. Sci. Soc. (computer sci. rep. 1993-95). Office: Northrop Grumman Mission Sys One Space Park R5/B180 Redondo Beach CA 90278 Home Phone: 310-831-2181; Office Phone: 310-813-3360. Business E-Mail: lynne.woike@ngc.com.

WOJAHN, R. LORRAINE, retired state senator; b. Tacoma, Sept. 17, 1920; m. Gilbert M. Wojahn (dec.); children: Mark C., Gilbert M. Jr. (dec.). Student, U. Washington, 1938—39. Mem. Wash. State Ho. of Reps., Olympia, 1969-76, Wash. State Senate, Olympia, 1977—2001, ret., 2001. Pres. pro tempore; vice chmn. rules, health and human svcs. com.; mem. labor and commerce, ways and means coms. Bd. dirs. Allenmore Hosp.; trustee Consumer Credit Counseling Svcs., Inc., Tacoma-Pierce County; active, past pres. Eastside Boys and Girls Club, Tacoma-Pierce County; active Wash. State Hist. Soc. Mem.: Alpha Chpt. (hon.), Delta Kappa Gamma (hon.). Democrat.

WOJCICKI, STANLEY GEORGE, physicist, researcher; b. Warsaw, Mar. 30, 1937; came to U.S., 1950; s. Franciszek and Janina (Kozlow) W.; m. Esther Denise Hochman, Nov. 17, 1961; children: Susan Diane, Janet Maia, Anne Elizabeth. AB, Harvard U., 1957; PhD, U. Calif., Berkeley, 1961. Physicist Lawrence Radiation Lab., Berkeley, 1961-66; asst. prof. physics Stanford U., 1966-68, assoc. prof., 1968-74, prof., 1974—, chmn. dept., 1982-85, 2004—07, dep. dir. Superconducting Supercollider Central Design Group, 1984-89; chmn. Stanford Linear Accelerator Center Exptl. Program Adv. Com., 1979-81. Chmn. High Energy Physics Adv. Panel, 1990-96; spokesperson FermiLab Main Injector Neutrine Oscillation Search expt. Assoc. editor Phys. Rev. Letters for Exptl. High Energy Physics, 1978-80. Recipient Alexander von Humboldt Sr. Am. Scientist award, 1981; NSF fellow, 1964-65; Sloan Found. fellow, 1968-72; Guggenheim fellow, 1973-74 Fellow Am. Phys. Soc. Office: Stanford U Varian Physics Bldg 382 Via Pueblo Mall Stanford CA 94305-4060 Office Phone: 650-926-2806. Personal E-mail: sgwojcicki@gmail.com. Business E-Mail: sgweg@slac.stanford.edu.

WOLANER, ROBIN PEGGY, internet and magazine publisher; b. Queens, NY, May 6, 1954; d. David H. and Harriet (Radlow) W.; children: Terry David, Bonnie Lee. BS in Indsl. and Labor Rels., Cornell U., 1975. Sr. editor Viva Mag., NYC, 1975-76; editor Impact Mag., NYC, 1976-77; circulation mgr. Runner's World Mag., Mountain View, Calif., 1977-79; cons. Ladd Assocs., San Francisco, 1979-80; gen. mgr. Mother Jones Mag., San Francisco, 1980-81, pub., 1981-85; founder, pub. Parenting Mag., San Francisco, 1985-91, pres., 1991-92; v.p. Time Pub. Ventures, 1990-96; pres., CEO Sunset Pub. Corp., 1992-95; exec. v.p. CNET, 1997—2002; founder, CEO Tee Bee Del.com, 2006—. Bd. dirs. Working Assets, Tides Found. Author: Naked in the Boardroom: A CEO Bares Her Secrets So You Can Transform Your Career, 2005. Jewish. Home: 124 Jordan Ave San Francisco CA 94118 Personal E-mail: robin_wolaner@yahoo.com.

WOLD, DAVID C., bishop; Bishop of Southwestern Wash. Evang. Luth. Ch. in Am., Tacoma, 1988—. Office: Synod of Southwestern Washington 420 121st St S Tacoma WA 98444-5218

WOLD, JOHN SCHILLER, geologist, former congressman; b. East Orange, NJ, Aug. 31, 1916; s. Peter Irving and Mary (Helff) W.; m. Jane Adele Pearson, Sept. 28, 1946; children: Peter Irving, Priscilla Adele, John Pearson. AB, St. Andrews U., Scotland and Union Coll., Schenectady, 1938; MS, Cornell U., 1939; LLD (hon.), U. Wyo., 1991. Dir. Fedn. Rocky Mountain States, 1966-68; v.p. Rocky

Mountain Oil and Gas Assn., 1967, 68; mem. Wyo. Ho. of Reps., 1957-59; Wyo. Republican candidate for U.S. Senate, 1964, 70; mem. 91st Congress at large from Wyo.; chmn., CEO Wold Trona Co., Inc.; pres., chmn. Wold Talc Co.; ret. Wold Nuclear Co., Wold Mineral Exploration Co., Casper, Wyo.; founding pres. Wyo. Heritage Soc.; founder Central Wyo. Ski Corp. Chmn. Wyo. Natural Gas Pipeline Authority, 1987-91; chmn. bd. Nuclear Exploration and Devel. Corp., Mineral Engring. Co., chmn., CEO Gastech, 2005—. Chmn. Wyo. Rep. Com., 1960-64, Western State Rep. Chmns. Assn., 1963-64; mem. exec. com. Rep. Nat. Com., 1962-64; chmn. Wyo. Rep. State Fin. Com.; Active Little League Baseball, Boy Scouts Am., United Fund, YMCA, Boys Clubs Am.; former pres. bd. trustees Casper Coll.; trustee Union Coll. Served to lt. USNR, World War II. Named Wyo. Man of Yr. AP-UPI, 1968; Wyo. Mineral Man of Yr., 1979, Wyo. Heritage award, 1992, Wyo. Oil/Gas and Mineral Man of 20th Century, Am. Heritage Ctr. of U. Wyo., 1999; named Benefactor of Yr., Nat. Coun. for Resource Devel., 1993. Mem. Wyo. Geol. Assn. (hon. life, pres. 1956), Am. Assn. Petroleum Geologists, Ind. Petroleum Assn. Am., AAAS, Wyo. Mining Assn., Sigma Xi, Alpha Delta Phi. Episcopalian (past vestryman, warden). Home: 1231 W 30th St Casper WY 82601-5372 Office: Mineral Resource Ctr 139 W 2nd St Casper WY 82601-2473 Office Phone: 307-265-7252. Business E-Mail: gastech@woldoil.com.

WOLD, KIMBERLY G., legislative staff member; Grad., Brigham Young U. Pub. affairs program mgr. Phoenix Met. C. of C., 1982-86; asst. dist. dir. U.S. Congressman Jon Kyl, 1987-93, dist. dir., 1993-95; dep. campaign mgr. John Kyl Campaign for U.S. Senate, 1994; dep. state dir. U.S. Sen. John Kyl, 1995-98, state dir., 1998—. Bd. dirs. Drugs Don't Work in Ariz., Maricopa County Victim Compensation Bd.; mem. Gov.'s Commn. on Violence Against Women. Office: Office of Sen Jon Kyl 2200 E Camelback Rd Ste 120 Phoenix AZ 85016-3455 Home: 2423 E Mallory St Mesa AZ 85213-1507*

WOLDT, HAROLD FREDERICK, JR., newspaper publishing executive; b. Atlanta, July 4, 1947; s. Harold Frederick and Dorothy Rose (Lansdowne) W.; m. Lisa Diane Neves; children: Lauren Rae, Katherine Neves, Caroline Neves. BS in Journalism, So. Ill. U., 1969. Classified advt. rep. Chgo. Tribune, 1969-70, classified automobile staff mgr., 1970-72; nat. advt. sales rep. Chgo. Tribune newspapers, NYC, 1972-74, city circulation mgr., 1974-77; nat. circulation mgr. Chgo. Tribune, 1977-80, circulation mgr., 1980-84; v.p., circulation News & Sun Sentinel Co., Ft. Lauderdale, Fla., 1985; circulation dir. Newsday, Inc., Melville, NY, 1986-88, v.p., circulation LI, NY, 1988-94; sr. v.p. circulation Newsday, pres. Distbn. Systems. Am. subs. of Newsday, Inc., 1994-98; v.p. sales circulation mktg. The N.Y. Times, NYC, 1998—2000; dir. circulation Omaha World-Herald; v.p. circulation San Jose Mercury News, Calif., 2001—04, 2006—; sr. v.p. circulation LA Newspaper Group, 2007—, dir. circulation LA Daily News, 2007—. Speaker, participant Am. Press Inst.; bd. dirs. Abilities Health and Rehab. Svcs. (Nat. Ctr. for Disability Svcs.), Albertson, LI, N.Y., 1992-94. Bd. dirs. Robert R. McCormick Boys Club, Chgo., 1980-81; chmn. United Way campaign, Chgo. Tribune, 1980, Omaha World-Herald United Way Campaign, 1999-2000, bd. dir. San Jose Children's Discovery Mus. Calif., Ronald McDonald House Charities of the Bay Area, San Francisco, 2002—. Mem. Am. Pubs. Newspaper Assn. (circulation and readership com. 1988-93), Internat. Circulation Mgrs. Assn. (pres. 1991-92), Alpha Delta Sigma, Tau Kappa Epsilon. Office Phone: 818-713-3101. Personal E-mail: hfwoldt@aol.com. Business E-Mail: harry.woldt@langnews.com.

WOLF, ARTHUR HENRY, museum administrator; b. New Rockford, ND, June 18, 1953; s. Louis Irwin and Vivian Joyce (Grinde) W.; m. Holly M. Chaffee, Oct. 18, 1984. BA in Anthropology, U. Nebr., 1975; MA, U. Ariz., 1977. Lab. asst., acting curator anthropology U. Nebr. State Mus., Lincoln, 1973-75; rsch. asst. Ariz. State Mus., Tucson, 1975-77; curator of collections Sch. Am. Rsch., Santa Fe, 1977-79; dir. Millcent Rogers Mus., Taos, N.Mex., 1979-87, Nev. State Mus. and Hist. Soc., Las Vegas, 1988-92, Mus. of Rockies, Bozeman, Mont., 1992-96; pres. High Desert Mus., Bend, Oreg., 1996—2000; pres. and CEO Mus. of No. Ariz., Flagstaff, 2000—. Speaker in field; cons. Pueblos of Zuni, Picuris, San Ildefonso and Taos. Contbr. articles and revs. to profl. jours. Trustee Kokopelli Archeol. Rsch. Fund, Bozeman, 1992-96; active Mont. Ambs. Recipient Young Alumnus award U. Nebr. Lincoln, 1990. Mem. Am. Assn. Mus. (bd. dirs. 1994—, vis. com. roster 1989—, vice chair 1996-97), Rotary, Assn. Sci. Mus. Dirs. Avocations: travel, reading, music. Office: Wolf Cons 3230 E Flamingo Rd 151 Las Vegas NV 89121 Business E-Mail: wolfconsulting@cox.net.

WOLF, CHARLES, JR., economist, educator; b. NYC, Aug. 1, 1924; s. Charles and Rosalie W.; m. Theresa van de Wint, Mar. 1, 1947; children: Charles Theodore, Timothy van de Wint. BS, Harvard U., Cambridge, Mass., 1943, M.P.A., 1948, PhD in Econs., 1949. Economist, fgn. service officer U.S. Dept. State, 1945-47, 49-53; mem. faculty Cornell U., 1953-54, U. Calif., Berkeley, 1954-55; sr. economist The Rand Corp., Santa Monica, Calif., 1955-67, head econs. dept., 1967-81; dean The Rand Grad. Sch., 1970-97, prof. pub. policy, 1997—, sr. econ. advisor, 1981—, corp. fellow in internat. econs., 1996—; sr. fellow Hoover Inst., 1988—. Bd. dirs. Capital Income Builder Fund, Capital World Growth Fund; lectr. econs. UCLA, 1960-72; mem. adv. bd. ctr. internat. bus. and edn. rsch., UCLA Anderson Grad. Sch. Bus., 1996—. Author: The Costs and Benefits of the Soviet Empire, 1986, Markets or Governments: Choosing Between Imperfect Alternatives, 1989, 2d edit., 1993, Linking Economic Policy and Foreign Policy, 1991, Long-Term Economic and Military Trends: The United States and Asia, 1994-2015, 1995, The Economic Pivot in a Political Context, 1997; co-author: Economic Openness: Many Facets, Many Metrics, 1999, Asian Economic Trends and Their Security Implications, 2000, European Military Prospects, Economic Constraints and the Rapid Reaction Force, 2001, Straddling Economics and Politics: Cross-Cutting Issues, in Asia, the United States and the Global Economy, 2002, Fault Lines in China's Economic Terrain, 2003, North Korean Paradoxes, 2005, The Russian Economy: Progress and Retreat on the Transitional Road, 2006, Modernizing the North Korean System, 2008, Looking Backward and Forward: Policy Issues in the Twenty-first Century, 2008; contbr. articles to profl. jours. Mem. Assn. for Public Policy Analysis and Mgmt. (pres. 1980-81), Am. Econs. Assn., Econometric Soc., Coun. on Fgn. Rels., Pacific Coun. Internat. Policy, Internat. Inst. Strategic Studies London. Clubs: Cosmos (Washington); Riviera Tennis (Los Angeles); Harvard (N.Y.). Office: The Rand Corp 1776 Main St Santa Monica CA 90407-2138 Office Phone: 310-451-6926. Business E-Mail: wolf@rand.org.

WOLF, CYNTHIA TRIBELHORN, librarian, educator; b. Denver, Dec. 12, 1945; adopted d. John Baltazar and Margaret (Kern) Tribelhorn (dec.); m. H.Y. Rassam, Mar. 21, 1969 (div. Jan. 1988); children: Najma Christine, Yousuf John; adopted children: Leonard Joseph Lucero, Lakota E. Narsay Rassam-Lucero, McKinley William Osborn, Kevin Trey, Jackson Andrew Lee, Rachel A., Andrew C.A.; m. Walter Larry Peck, June 21, 1965 (div. Feb. 1967). BA, Colo. State U., 1970; MLS, U. Denver, 1985. Cert. permanent profl. librarian, N.Mex. Elem. tchr. Sacred Heart Sch., Farmington, N.Mex., 1973-78; asst. prof. libr. sci. edn. U. N.Mex., Albuquerque, 1985-91, dir. libr. sci. edn. divsn., 1989-91; pres. Info. Acquisitions, Albuquerque, 1990-99; libr. dir. Southwestern Coll., Santa Fe, 1992-94; mem. youth resources Rio Grande Valley Libr. Sys., Albuquerque, 1994-95, adult reference svc., 1995-98; instr. U. N.Mex., 1998-99; with Albuquerque Pub. Schs., 1998—2003, coach nat. sch. reform policy, 2000—03, rshc. tchr. lit., 2003—. Fine arts resource person for gifted edn. Farmington Pub. Schs., 1979-83; speaker Unofficial Mentorships and Market Rsch., 1992-98. Mem. Farmington Planning and Zoning Commn., 1980-81; bd. dirs. Farmington Mus. Assn., 1983-84; pres. Farmington Symphony League, 1978. Mem. ALA, N.Mex. Library Assn., LWV (bd. dirs. Farmington, 1972-74, 75, pres.). Avocations: mixed media graphics design, market research, creative approaches to personal journals, board game design.

WOLF, DICK (RICHARD A. WOLF), television producer; b. NYC, Dec. 20, 1946; m. Susan Scranton, 1970 (div. 1981); m. Christine Marburg, 1983; 3 children. Student, U. Pa. Exec. producer, pres. Wolf Films, Inc. Copywriter, producer over a dozen campaigns and 100 TV commls., 1969-76; producer, writer (screenplay) Skateboard, 1978, School Ties, 1992; writer, script cons. (TV series) Hill Street Blues, 1985 (Emmy award, Writer's Guild nominations for episode What are Friends For); writer, producer (film) No Man's Land, 1987; writer, producer and actor (film) Masquerade, 1988; writer, exec. producer 4 installments (series TV movies) Gideon Oliver, 1989; writer, creator, exec. producer (series TV movies) Christine Cromwell, 1989-90, (TV series) Nasty Boys, 1990, H.E.L.P., Law & Order, 1990, (Producers Guild Am. shared award Episodic TV 1996, Emmy award Outstanding Drama Series, 1996/97), Mann & Machine, 1992, The Human Factor, 1992, Crime and Punishment, 1993, South Beach, 1993, New York Undercover, 1994, Swift Justice, 1996, Arrest and Trial, 2000, Dragnet, 2003-04; creator, exec. producer (TV series) Feds, 1997, Players; exec. producer (TV series) Law & Order: Special Victims Unit, 1999—, D.C., 2000, Deadline, 2000-01, Law & Order Crime & Punishment, 2002—; exec. prodr., writer Law & Order Criminal Intent, 2001—; prodr. (TV documentary) Twin Towers, 2003; exec. prodr. (TV specials) Tony Bennett: An American Classic, 2006 (Primetime Emmy for Outstanding Variety, Music or Comedy Spl., Acad. TV Arts and Scis., 2007). Recipient Norman Lear Achievement award in TV, Producers Guild Am., 2008. Office: Wolf Films Inc c/o Universal TV 100 Universal City Plz Universal City CA 91608-1002

WOLF, G. VAN VELSOR, JR., lawyer; b. Balt., Feb. 19, 1944; s. G. Van Velsor (dec.) and Alice Roberts (Kimberly) W. (dec.); m. Ann Holmes Kavanagh, May 19, 1984; children: George Van Velsor III, Timothy Kavanagh (dec.), Christopher Kavanagh, Elisabeth Huxley. BA, Yale U., 1966; JD, Vanderbilt U., 1973. Bar: N.Y. 1974, U.S. Dist. Ct. (so. dist.) N.Y. 1974, U.S. Ct. Appeals (2d cir.) 1974, Ariz. 1982, U.S. Dist. Ct. Ariz. 1982, U.S. Ct. Appeals (9th cir.) 1982. Agrl. advisor U.S. Peace Corps., 1966-70; assoc. Milbank, Tweed, Hadley & McCloy, NYC, 1973-75; vis. lectr. law Airlangga U., Surabaya, Indonesia, 1975-76; editor-in-chief Environ. Law Reporter, Washington, 1976-81; assoc. Lewis & Roca, Phoenix, 1981-84, ptnr., 1984-91, Snell & Wilmer, Phoenix, 1991—. Vis. lectr. law U. Ariz., 1990, Vanderbilt U., 1991, U. Md., 1994, Ariz. State U., 1995; cons. Nat. Trust Hist. Preservation, Washington, 1981. Editor: Toxic Substances Control, 1980; editor in chief Environ. Law Reporter 1976-81; contbr. articles to profl. jours. Bd. dirs. Ariz. divsn. Am. Cancer Soc., 1985—96, sec. Ariz. divsn., 1990—92, vice-chmn. Ariz. divsn., 1992—94, chmn. Ariz. divsn., 1994—96, bd. dirs. S.W. divsn., 1996—2003, chmn., 1996—98, nat. bd. dirs., 1999—, bd. dirs. Gt. West divsn., 2003—, bd. dirs., Cancer Action Network, 2002—05, pres. Cancer Action Network, 2003—04, nat. treas., 2004—06, nat. vice chair, 2006—07, chair-elect, 2007—08, nat. chair, 2008—; bd. dirs. Herberger Theatre Ctr., 1998—2006, sec., 2001—03, vice chmn., 2003—04; bd. dirs. Phoenix Little Theatre, 1983—89, chmn., 1985—87. Recipient St. George medal Am. Cancer Soc., 1998 Mem. ABA (vice-chmn. SONREEL commn. state and regional environ. coop. 1995-98, co-chmn. 1998-2000, vice-chmn. environ. audits task force 1998-99, vice-chmn. SONREEL ann. meeting planning com. 1998-99), Assn. of Bar of City of N.Y., Ariz. State Bar Assn. (coun. environ. & nat. res. law sect. 1988-93, chmn. 1991-92, CLE com. 1992-98, chmn. 1997-98), Maricopa County Bar Assn., Ariz. Acad., Union Club N.Y.C., Univ. Club Phoenix, Phoenix Country Club. Office: Snell & Wilmer 400 E Van Buren Phoenix AZ 85004-2202 Office Phone: 602-382-6201. Business E-Mail: vwolf@swlaw.com.

WOLF, HAROLD HERBERT, pharmacy educator; b. Quincy, Mass., Dec. 19, 1934; s. John I. and Bertha F. (Sussman) W.; m. Joan Z. Silverman, Aug. 11, 1957; children: Gary Isaac, David Neal. BS, Mass. Coll. Pharmacy, 1956; PhD, U. Utah, 1961; LLD (hon.), U. Md., 1994. Asst. prof. pharmacology Coll. Pharmacy Ohio State U., 1961-64, assoc. prof., 1964-69, prof., 1969-76, Kimberly prof., 1975-76, chmn. divsn. pharmacology, 1973-76; dean Coll. of Pharmacy, U. Utah, Salt Lake City, 1976-89, prof. pharmacology, 1976—2005, dir. Anticonvulsant Drug Devel. Program, 1989—2002, prof. emeritus, 2005—. Vis. prof. U. Sains Malaysia, 1973-74; mem. Nat. Joint Commn. on Prescription Drug Use, 1976-80; mem. NIH rev. com. Biomed. Rsch. Devel. Grant Program, 1978-79; external examiner U. Malaya, 1978, 92, 96, U. Sains Malaysia, 1980. Contbr. articles in field of ctrl. nervous sys. pharmacology and field of pharm. edn. Recipient Alumni Achievement award Mass. Coll. Pharmacy, 1978, Disting. Faculty award U. Utah, 1989, Rosenblatt prize, 1989, Disting. Alumnus award Coll. Pharmacy, U. Utah, 1991, Weaver prize, 2000. Fellow AAAS, Acad. Pharm. Scis.; mem. Am. Soc. Pharmacology and Exptl. Therapeutics, Am. Pharm. Assn. (task force on edn. 1982-84), Am. Assn. Colls. of Pharmacy (pres. 1977, Disting. Pharmacy Educator award 1988, scholar in residence 1989, chmn. commn. on implementing change in pharmacy edn. 1989-92, 95-96), Am. Soc. Hosp. Pharmacists (commn. on goals 1982-84), Am. Coun. on Pharm. Edn. (bd. dirs. 1985-88), Soc. Neurosci. Jewish. Office: Univ Utah Coll Pharmacy Salt Lake City UT 84112 Business E-Mail: hwolf@hsc.utah.edu.

WOLF, HEATHER, library director; Grad. in Bus. Adminstrn., U. Pacific, Stockton, Calif.; MLS, U. Ariz. Br. mgr., regional br. coord. Maricopa County Libr. Dist., Ariz.; br. mgr., supervisory reference libr. and supervisory libr. collection support svcs. City of Mesa Libr., Ariz., acting dir., 2006, dir., 2006—. Office: City of Mesa Libr 64 E First St Mesa AZ 85201 Office Phone: 480-644-2712. E-mail: heather.wolf@cityofmesa.org.

WOLF, JACK KEIL, electrical engineer, educator; b. Newark, Mar. 14, 1935; s. Joseph and Rosaline Miriam (Keil) W.; m. Toby Katz, Sept. 10, 1955; children: Joseph Martin, Jay Steven, Sarah Keil. BS, U. Pa., 1956; MSE., Princeton, 1957, MA, 1958, PhD, 1960. With R.C.A., Princeton, N.J., 1959-60; asso. prof. N.Y. U., 1963-65; from asso. prof. to prof. elec. engring. Poly. Inst. Bklyn., 1965-73; prof. dept. elec. and computer engring. U. Mass., Amherst, 1973-85, chmn. dept., 1973-75; Stephen O. Rice prof. Ctr. Magnetic Rec. Research, dept. elec. engring. and computer sci. U. Calif.-San Diego, La Jolla, 1985—. Mem. tech. staff Bell Telephone Labs., Murray Hill, N.J., 1968-69; prin. engr. Qualcomm Inc., San Diego, 1985. Editor for coding IEEE Transactions on Information Theory, 1969-72. Served with USAF, 1960-63. NSF sr. postdoctoral fellow, 1971-72; Guggenheim fellow, 1979-80 Fellow AAAS, IEEE (pres. info. theory group 1974, co-recipient info. theory group prize paper award 1975, co-recipient Comm. Soc. prize paper award 1993, Koji Kobayashi medal 1998, Claude Shannon lectr. 2001, Richard W. Hamming medal 2004), Nat. Acad. Engring.; mem. Sigma Xi, Sigma Tau, Eta Kappa Nu, Pi Mu Epsilon, Tau Beta Pi. Achievements include research on information theory, communication theory, computer/communication networks, magnetic recording. Home: 8529 Prestwick Dr La Jolla CA 92037-2025 Office: U Calif San Diego 9500 Gilman Dr La Jolla CA 92093-5004

WOLF, JOSEPH ALBERT, mathematician, educator; b. Chgo., Oct. 18, 1936; s. Albert M. and Goldie (Wikoff) W. BS, U. Chgo., 1956, MS, 1957, PhD, 1959. Mem. Inst. for Advanced Study, Princeton, 1960-62, 65-66; asst. prof. U. Calif., Berkeley, 1962-64, assoc. prof., 1964-66, prof., 1966—94, Miller research prof., 1972-73, 83-84, prof. grad. sch., 1994—; prof. honorario Universidad Nacional de Cordoba, Argentina, 1989. Vis. prof. Rutgers U., 1969-70, Hebrew U., Jerusalem, 1974-76, Tel Aviv U., 1974-76, Harvard U., 1979-80, 86 Author: Spaces of Constant Curvature, 1967, 5th edit., 1984, Unitary Representations on Partially Holomorphic Cohomology Spaces, 1974, Unitary Representations of Maximal Parabolic Subgroups of the Classical Groups, 1976, Classification and Fourier Inversion for Parabolic Subgroups with Square Integrable Nilradical, 1979; (with G. Fels, A.T. Huckleberry) Cycle Spaces of Flag Domains: A Complex Geometric Approach, 2005; Harmonic Analysis on Commutative Spaces, 2007; co-editor, author: Harmonic Analysis and Representations of Semisimple Lie Groups, 1980, The Penrose Transform and Analytic Cohomology in Representation Theory, 1993, Geometry and Representation Theory of Real and P-Adic Grps., 1997, Global Differential Geometry: The Mathematical Legacy of Alfred Gray, 2000; editor Letters in Math. Physics, Jour. of Group Theory in Physics; contbr. articles to profl. jours. Alfred P. Sloan rsch. fellow, 1965-67, NSF fellow, 1959-62; recipient Médaille de l'Université de Liège, 1977, Humboldt prize, 1995. Mem. Am., Swiss Math. Socs. Office: U Calif Dept Math Berkeley CA 94720-3840 Business E-Mail: jawolf@math.berkeley.edu.

WOLF, KELLY J., state representative, contractor; b. Longview, Wash., 1961; Grad., Kenai Ctrl. H.S. Carpenter, contractor; state rep. State of Alaska, 2003—. Republican. Address: PO Box 2416 Kenai AK 99611

WOLF, PATRICIA B., former museum director; Exec. dir. Anchorage Mus. at Rasmuson Ctr. (formerly Anchorage Mus. History and Art), 1989—2007. Steering com. mem. Arctic Studies Ctr. Recipient James Smithson Bicentennial Medal, Smithsonian Instn., 2007.

WOLF, TIMOTHY VAN DE WINT, food products executive; b. Apr. 27, 1953; s. Charles and Theresa Wolf; m. Mary Therese Merritt. BA in Econs. cum laude, Harvard U., 1974; MBA, U. Chgo., 1976. Fin. analyst to sr. fin. analyst Tennant Co., Mpls., 1976-79; mgr. mktg. planning and analysis Electrolux div. Consolidated Food Corp., Stamford, Conn., 1979-80; mgr. bus. planning Pepsi USA, Purchase, NY, 1980-81, mgr. bus. devel. and competitive analysis, 1981-82, dir. bus. planning fountain beverage div., 1982-84; sr. dir. bus. planning Taco Bell Corp., Irvine, Calif., 1984-86; v.p., controller Taco Bell & other sr. fin. mgmt. positions Pepsico, Purchase, NY, 1986—95; CFO Adolph Coors Co. & Coors Brewing Co., 1995—2005; global CFO Molson Coors Brewing Co., Denver, 2005—08; chief integration officer MillerCoors (joint venture), Chgo., 2008—. Bd. dirs. Irvine Med. Ctr. Harvard Coll. scholar, Cambridge, Mass. Mem.: Harvard of So. Calif., U. Calif. Chancellor's (Irvine). Avocations: tennis, skiing, golf, German history, international relations. Office: Molson Coors Brewing Co 1225 17th St Ste 3200 Denver CO 80202

WOLFE, ALLAN, retired physicist; b. Bklyn., Dec. 19, 1942; s. Isidore Irving and Florence (Rosenfeld) W.; m. Marta Elias Boneta, Dec. 30, 1967; 1 child, Daniel Duchaune. BS, Poly. Inst. Bklyn., 1964; MS, U. N.H., 1969, PhD, 1971. Physics chmn. Nasson Coll., Springvale, Maine, 1973-74; prof. physics N.Y.C. Tech. Coll., Bklyn., 1974—2005; ret., 2005. Physicist, visitor AT&T Bell Labs.-Lucent Techs., Murray Hill, N.J., 1977-97; physics rschr. U. L'Aquila, Italy, 1989, Indian Inst. Sci., Bangalore, 1990, Japan Soc. for Promotion Sci., Tokyo, 1990. Contbr. articles to profl. jours. Avocations: chess, jogging, music, Masonry, Japanese, French and Hebrew languages. Address: 720 13th St Boulder CO 80302 Business E-Mail: awolfe@citytech.cuny.edu.

WOLFE, CAMERON WITHGOT, JR., lawyer; b. Oakland, Calif., July 7, 1939; s. Cameron W. and Jean (Brown) W.; m. Frances Evelyn Bishopric, Sept. 2, 1964; children: Brent Everett, Julie Frances, Karen Jean. AB, U. Calif., Berkeley, 1961, JD, 1964. Bar: Calif. 1965, U.S. Dist. Ct. (no. dist.) Calif. 1965, U.S. Ct. Appeals (9th cir.) 1965, U.S. Tax Ct. 1966, U.S. Ct. Claims 1977, U.S. Ct. Appeals (3d cir.) 1980, U.S. Supreme Ct. 1986. Assoc., then ptnr. Orrick, Herrington & Sutcliffe, San Francisco, 1964—. Bd. dirs. Crowley Maritime Corp.; mem. steering com. Western Pension Conf. Pres. League To Save Lake Tahoe, 1979, 80; chmn. League To Save Lake Tahoe Charitable Truste, 1966-91, Piedmont Ednl. Fund Campaign, 1982-83; pres. Piedmont Ednl. Found., 1986-90; bd. dirs. Yosemite Fund, 1993—. With U.S. Army, 1957; with USAR, 1957-65. Mem. ABA (taxation com.), Calif. State Bar, San Francisco Bar Assn., San Francisco Tax Club (pres. 1997-98), Pacific Union Club, Claremont Country Club (Oakland, Calif.), Order of Coif, Phi Beta Kapa. Home: 59 Lakeview Ave Piedmont CA 94611-3514 Office: Orrick Herrington Sutcliffe 405 Howard St Fl 11 San Francisco CA 94105-2680

WOLFE, LAWRENCE J., lawyer; b. 1951; BA, U. Calif. Davis, 1974; JD, U. Wyo, 1980. Asst. atty. gen. Office of Atty. Gen., Wyo., 1980—85, chief nat. resources divsn. Wyo., 1983—85; chair resources dept. Holland & Hart LLP, Cheyenne, Wyo., 2001—06, mng. ptnr., 2007—. Mem.: Cheyenne Rotary Club. Office: Holland & Hart LLP 215 Warren Ave Ste 450 Cheyenne WY 82001-3162 Office Phone: 307-778-4218. Office Fax: 307-778-8175. E-mail: lwolfe@hollandhart.com.

WOLFE, ROBERT A., aerospace executive; BS in Aerospace Engring., MS in Aerospace Engring., Ga. Inst. Tech. With McDonnell Douglas Corp.; sys. integration dir. for the Peacekeeper MIssile Martin Marietta, 1981-84; exec. v.p. govt. and space propulsion bus. Pratt & Whitney, 1990-93, sr. v.p. Ams., exec. v.p. Pratt & Whitney Group, 1994-97; pres. Pratt & Whitney Aircraft divsn. United Techs., 1994-97; pres. Aerojet GenCorp, Inc., Rancho-Cordova, Calif., 1997—, chmn., CEO, 1997—. With USN. Office: PO Box 537012 Sacramento CA 95853-7012

WOLFEN, WERNER F., lawyer; b. Berlin, May 15, 1930; came to U.S., 1939; s. Martin and Ruth Eva (Hamburger) W.; m. Mary Glasier, July 1, 1956; children: Richard, James, Lawrence (dec.). BS, U. Calif., Berkeley, 1950, JD, 1953. Bar: Calif. 1953. Assoc. Irell & Manella, LA, 1953-57, ptnr., 1957-98, sr. ptnr. emeritus, 1999—; pres. Capri Investment Co. LLC, 1999—. Bd. dirs. Calhoun Vision, Inc., Pre-Cash Corp.; bd. visitors UCLA Sch. Arts and Arch., 1995—. Bd. dirs. UCLA Found., 1992-2003; bd. dirs. L.A. Goal, 1994-, pres., 1994-99. Mem. ABA. Democrat. Jewish. Office Phone: 310-203-7521.

WOLFF, GEOFFREY ANSELL, writer, educator, critic; b. LA, Nov. 5, 1937; s. Arthur Saunders III and Rosemary (Loftus) W.; m. Priscilla Bradley Porter, Aug. 21, 1965; children: Nicholas Hinckley, Justin Porter. Grad., Choate Sch., 1955; student, Eastbourne Sch. Art, Eng., 1955-56; BA summa cum laude, Princeton U., 1961; postgrad., Churchill Coll., Cambridge U., Eng., 1963-64. Lectr. in comparative lit. Robert Coll., Istanbul, Turkey, 1961-63; lectr. in Am. civilization Istanbul U., 1962-63; lectr. aesthetics Md. Inst. Coll. Art, 1965-69; vis. lectr. creative arts Princeton (N.J.) U., 1970-71, Ferris prof., 1980, 92; writer-in-residence Brandeis U., Waltham, Mass., 1982-95; prof. English and creative writing U. Calif., Irvine, 1995—. Lectr. English lit. Middlebury (Vt.) Coll., 1976, 78; vis. lectr. Columbia U., N.Y.C., 1979, Brown U., Providence, 1981, 88, Boston U., 1981; mem. policy panel in lit. NEA; book critic Esquire mag., 1979-81; founder Golden Horn lit. mag., 1972; vis. prof. Williams Coll., 1994; dir. program writing, prof. English U. Calif., Irvine, 1995—. Author: Bad Debts, 1969, The Sightseer, 1974, Black Sun, 1976, Inklings, 1978, The Duke of Deception, 1979, Providence, 1986; editor: Best American Essays, 1989, The Final Club, 1990, A Day at the Beach, 1992, The Age of Consent, 1995; book editor Washington Post, 1964-69, Newsweek mag., 1969-71, New Times mag., 1974-79; contbr. to mags. Recipient Award in Lit., Am. Acad. of Arts and Letters, 1994, R.I. Gov.'s Arts award, 1992; Woodrow Wilson fellow, 1961-62, 63-64, Fulbright fellow, 1963-64, Guggenheim fellow, 1972-73, 77-78, NEH sr. fellow, 1974-75, NEA fellow, 1979-80, 86-87, Am. Coun. Learned Socs. fellow, 1983-84, Lila Wallace Writing fellow, 1992. Mem. PEN, Princeton Club (N.Y.C.), Colonial CLub (Princeton), Dunes Club.

WOLFF, HERBERT ERIC, banker, former army officer; b. Cologne, Germany, May 24, 1925; s. Hugo and Juanna Anna (Van Dam) W.; m. Alice (Billy) Rafael, Nov. 13, 1946 (dec. July, 1987); children: Karen (dec. Jan., 1992), Herbert E., Allen R. BA, Rutgers U., 1953; BS, U. Md., 1957; MA, George Washington U., 1962; grad., US Army War Coll., 1962, Harvard U., 1979. Commd. 2nd lt. US Army, 1945, advanced through grades to maj. gen.; served in Fed. Republic of Germany, Greece, Iran, Republic of Korea, Australia, New Guinea, The Phillipines, Japan and Socialist Republic of Vietnam; dep. dir. ops. NSA and Chief CSS, Ft. Meade, Md., 1973—75; dep. corps. comdr. V. Corps US Army, Frankfurt, Germany, 1975-77, comdr. gen. US Army Western Command Hawaii, 1977-81; with First Hawaiian Bank, Honolulu, 1981-2000, sr. v.p., corp. sec., to 2000; hon. consul gen. (Datô) US Pacific region Govt. of Malaysia, Honolulu, 1985—. Author: The Man on Horseback, 1962, The Tenth Principle of War Public Support, 1964, The Military Instructor, 1968. Exec. bd. Aloha coun. Boy Scouts Am.; bd. dirs. USO, Girl Scouts of US, Hawaii, Found. Armed Forces Ctr. Security Studies; vice chmn. March of Dimes; v.p. Hawaii Com. Fgn. Rels.; past pres. Pacific Asian Affairs Coun., Hawaii Army Mus. Soc. Decorated Bronze Star with V and 3 oak leaf clusters, Air medal (24) US Army, Purple Heart, Gallantry Cross with 2 palms, Gallantry Cross with palm and silver star Nat. Order 5th class South Vietnam, Order Nat. Security Merit Choen-Su S. Korea, D.S.M. with oak leaf clusters (2), Silver Star with oak leaf cluster US Army, Legion of Merit with 3 oak leaf clusters, D.F.C., Combat Infantry Badge with two stars, master parachutist, Army aviator; named Citizen of Yr. Fed. Exec. Bd., 1987. Mem. 1st Inf. Divsn. Assn., 1st Cav. Divsn. Assn., Plaza Club (pres., bd. dirs.), Waialae Country Club, Rotary, Phi Kappa Phi. Office: First Hawaiian Ctr 999 Bishop St Honolulu HI 96813-0001 Personal E-mail: generalherbwolff@aol.com.

WOLFF, MANFRED ERNST, chemist, pharmaceutical executive; b. Berlin, Feb. 14, 1930; came to U.S., 1933; s. Adolph Abraham and Kate (Fraenkel) W.; m. Helen S. Scandalis, Aug. 1, 1953 (div. 1971); children: Stephen Andrew, David James, Edward Allen; m. Susan E. Hurbert, Jan. 19, 1973 (div. 1975); m. A. Gloria Johnson, Dec. 25, 1982. BS, U. Calif., Berkeley, 1951, MS, 1953, PhD, 1955. Registered U.S. patent agt. Rsch. fellow U. Va., 1955-57; sr. medicinal chemist Smith, Kline & French Labs., Phila., 1957-60; mem. faculty U. Calif., San Francisco, 1960-82, prof. medicinal chemistry, 1965-82, chmn. dept. pharm. chemistry, 1970-82; dir. discovery rsch. Allergan Labs, Irvine, Calif., 1982-84; v.p. discovery rsch. Allergan Pharms., Irvine, 1984-89; v.p. R & D Immunopharmaceutics Inc., San Diego, 1989-91, sr. v.p. R & D, 1991-95; pres. Intellepharm., Inc., Laguna Beach, Calif., 1997—. Adj. prof. medicinal chemistry U. So. Calif., 1982—; elected mem. U.S. Pharm. Conv. Com. of Revision, 1990—; lectr. Sch. Med. Chemistry Drew U., NJ, 1998-. Editor: Burger's Medicinal Chemistry and Drug Discovery, Vol. 1-5, 5th edit., 1995-97; asst. editor Jour. Medicinal Chemistry, 1968-71; mem. editl. bd. Medicinal Chemistry Rsch., 1991-95, PharmSci., 1999-2004; contbr. articles to profl. jours.; patentee in field. Fellow AAAS, Am Assn. Pharm. Scientists; mem. Am. Chem. Soc. Achievements include discovery of Alphagan and Lumigan medicines for glaucoma, Tazorac medicine for psoriasis, and Thelin medicine for pulmonary arterial hypertension. Office Phone: 949-494-5458. E-mail: drwolff@aol.com.

WOLFF, RONALD KEITH, toxicologist, researcher; b. Brantford, Ont., Can., July 25, 1946; s. Roy Clifford and Agnes Audrey (Stratton) W.; m. Mary Carole Cromien Wolff, Aug. 26, 1972; children: Mark, Sarah, Andrew, Brian. BS, U. Toronto, 1964-68; MS, 1968-69, PhD, 1969-72. Diplomate Am. Bd. Toxicology, 1983. Rsch. assoc. McMaster U., Hamilton, Can., 1973-76; scientist Lovelace Inhalation Toxicology Rsch. Inst., Albuquerque, N.Mex., 1976-88; sr. rsch. scientist Eli Lilly and Co., Greenfield, Ind., 1988—2004; rsch. fellow Nektar Therapeutics, San Carlos, Calif., 2004—. Author: (book chpt.) Comprehensive Treatise on Pulmonary Toxicology, 1992, Comprehensive Toxicology, 1997; contbr. articles to profl. jours. Recipient Frank Blood award Soc. Toxicology, 1989, Thomas T. Mercer joint prize Am. Assn. for Aerosol Rsch. and Internat. Soc. Aerosols in Medicine, 2002. Mem. Am. Assn. for Aerosol Rsch., Internat. Soc. Aerosols in Medicine, Soc. Toxicology, Am. Indsl. Hygiene Assn. Avocations: camping, hiking, hockey. Office: Nektar Therapeutics 201 Industrial Rd Ste 300 San Carlos CA 94070-2396 Office Phone: 650-620-6581. Business E-Mail: rwolff@nektar.com.

WOLFF, SIDNEY CARNE, astronomer, science administrator; b. Sioux City, Iowa, June 6, 1941; d. George Albert and Ethel (Smith) Carne; m. Richard J. Wolff, Aug. 29, 1962 BA, Carleton Coll., 1962, DSc (hon.), 1985; PhD, U. Calif., Berkeley, 1966. Postgrad. research fellow Lick Obs, Santa Cruz, Calif., 1969; asst. astronomer U. Hawaii, Honolulu, 1967-71, assoc. astronomer, 1971-76; astronomer, assoc. dir. Inst. Astronomy, Honolulu, 1976-83, acting dir., 1983-84; dir. Kitt Peak Nat. Obs., Tucson, 1984-87, Nat. Optical Astronomy Observatories, 1987-2001; dir. Gemini Project Gemini 8-Meter Telescopes Project, 1992-94; astronomer, project scientist Large Synoptic Survey Telescope, 2001—04. Pres. SOAR Inc., 1999-2003; project scientist Large Synoptic Survey Telescope, 2002-04. treas. 2005; bd. mem. LSST Corp. Author: The A-Type Stars--Problems and Perspectives, 1983, (with others) Exploration of the Universe, 1987, Realm of the Universe, 1988, Frontiers of Astronomy, 1990, Voyages Through the Universe, 1996, 2nd edit., 2003, Voyages to the Planets, 1999, 2nd edit., 2003, Voyages to the Stars and Galaxies, 1999, 2nd edit., 2003; founding editor: Astronomy Edn. Rev., 2002; contbr. articles to profl. jours. Trustee Carleton Coll., 1989—, chair acad. affairs com., 1995-2005. Rsch. fellow Lick Obs. Santa Cruz, Calif., 1967; recipient Nat. Meritorious Svc. award NSF, 1994. Fellow Royal Astronical Soc.; mem. Astron. Soc. Pacific (pres. 1984-86, bd. dirs. 1979-85), Am. Astron. Soc. (coun. 1983-86, pres.-elect 1991, pres. 1992-94, Edn. prize 2006). Office: Nat Optical Astronomy Obs PO Box 26732 950 N Cherry Ave Tucson AZ 85719-4933 Business E-Mail: swolff@noao.edu.

WOLFF, TOBIAS (TOBIAS JONATHAN ANSELL WOLFF), writer, English professor; b. Birmingham, Ala., June 19, 1945; s. Arthur Saunders and Rosemary (Loftus) Wolff; m. Catherine Dolores Spohn, 1975; children: Michael, Patrick, Mary Elizabeth. BA in English, Hertford Coll., Oxford, Eng., 1972; MA, Stanford U., Calif., 1978; LHD (hon.), Santa Clara U., Calif., 1996. Faculty Goddard Coll., Plainfield, Vt., Ariz. State U., Tempe; prof. Syracuse U., NY, 1980—97; English/creative writing tchr. Stanford U., 1997—, dir. creative writing prog., 2000—02; Ward W. & Priscilla B. Woods prof. Stanford U. Sch. Humanities & Scis. Author: (novels) Ugly Rumours, 1975, The Barracks Thief, 1984 (PEN/Faulkner award for fiction, 1985), Old School, 2003, (short story collections) In the Garden of the North American Martyrs, 1981 (St. Lawrence award for fiction, 1982), Back in the World, 1985, The Night in Question, 1997, Our Story Begins: New and Selected Stories, 2008 (LA Times Book prize, 1989, The Story Prize, 2009), (memoirs) This Boy's Life, 1989, In Pharaoh's Army, 1994 (Esquire-Volvo-Winterstone's award, 1994); editor: Matters of Life and Death: New American Stories, 1983, Best American Short Stories, 1994, The Vintage Book of Contemporary American Short Stories, 1994. Recipient O. Henry award, 1981, 1982, 1985, Rea award for Short Story, 1989, Whiting Writer's award, 1989, Fairfax prize for lit., George Mason U., 2001; grantee Wallace Stegner Fellowship in Creative Writing, Stanford U., 1975, NEA, 1978, 1985, Ariz. Coun. Arts & Humanities, 1980, Guggenheim Found., 1982. Office: Stanford U Dept English Stanford CA 94305-2087 Office Phone: 650-723-0504.*

WOLFGANG, BONNIE ARLENE, musician, bassoonist; b. Caribou, Maine, Sept. 29, 1944; d. Ralph Edison and Arlene Alta (Obetz) W.; m. Eugene Alexander Pridonoff, July 3, 1965 (div. Sept. 1977); children: George Randall, Anton Alexander, Stephan Eugene. MusB, Curtis Inst. Music, Phila., 1967. Soloist Phila. Orch., 1966; soloist with various orchs. U.S., Cen. Am., 1966-75; prin. bassoonist Phoenix Symphony, 1976—, with Woodwind Quintet, 1986—. Home: 9448 N 106th St Scottsdale AZ 85258-6056

WOLFINGER, RAYMOND EDWIN, retired political science professor; b. San Francisco, June 29, 1931; s. Raymond Edwin and Hilda (Holm) W.; m. Barbara Kaye, Aug. 7, 1960; 1 son, Nicholas Holm. AB, U. Calif.-Berkeley, 1951; MA, U. Ill., 1955; PhD, Yale U., 1961. Asst. prof. polit. sci. Stanford U., Calif., 1961—66, assoc. prof., 1966-70, prof., 1970-71, U. Calif., Berkeley, 1971—, Heller prof. polit. sci., 1995—2006; ret., 2006. Dir. U. Calif. Data Archive and Tech. Assistance, 1980-92; chmn. bd. overseers Nat. Election Studies, Ann Arbor, Mich., 1982-86 Author: The Politics of Progress, 1974, (with others) Dynamics of American Politics, 1976, 80, (with Steven J. Rosenstone) Who Votes, 1980, (with others) The Myth of the Independent Voter, 1992; mem. editorial bd. Brit. Jour. Polit. Sci., 1980-84, Am. Polit. Sci. Rev., 1985-88. Bd. dirs. S.W. Voter Rsch. Inst., San Antonio, 1988-96, Consortium of Social Sci. Assns., 1987-93, pres. 1988-90. 1st lt. U.S. Army, 1951-53. Fellow Ctr. for Advanced Study in Behavioral Scis., 1960-61; Guggenheim fellow, 1965; Ford Found. faculty research fellow, 1970-71 Fellow Am. Acad. Arts and Scis. (chair Class III membership com. 1998-99); mem. Am. Polit. Sci. Assn. (sec. 1981-82), AAUP (council 1981-84), Western Polit. Sci. Assn. (v.p. 1988-89, pres. 1989-90). Democrat. Office: Univ Calif Dept Polit Sci Berkeley CA 94720-1950 Business E-Mail: vturnoat@berkeleg.edu.

WOLFMAN, EARL FRANK, JR., surgeon, educator; b. Buffalo, Sept. 14, 1926; s. Earl Frank and Alfreda (Peterson) W.; m. Lois Jeannette Walker, Dec. 28, 1946; children— Nancy Jeannette, David Earl, Carol Anne. BS cum laude, Harvard U., Cambridge, Mass., 1946; MD cum laude, U. Mich., 1950. Diplomate Am. Bd. Surgery. Intern U. Mich., Ann Arbor, 1950-51, asst. resident in surgery, 1951-52, resident in surgery, 1954-55, from jr. clin. instr. surgery to assoc. prof., 1955-66, asst. to dean, 1960-61, asst. dean, 1961-64; practice medicine specializing in surgery, 1957—, Sacramento, 1966—; prof. surgery Sch. Medicine, U. Calif., Davis, 1966—, founding chmn. dept. surgery, 1966-78, founding assoc. dean, 1966-76, mem. staff, chief surg. svcs. Med. Ctr., 1966-78, founding chmn. div. surg. scis., 1966-78. Contbr. articles to profl. jours. Served to lt. M.C. USNR, 1952-54. Fellow ACS; mem. AMA (del. 1987-99), Ctrl. Surg. Soc., Western Surg. Soc., Sacramento Surg. Soc., Pacific Coast Surg. Soc., Frederick A. Coller Surg. Soc., Soc. Surgery Alimentary Tract, Am. Assn. Endocrine Surgeons, Sierra Sacramento Valley Med. Soc., Calif. Med. Assn. (trustee 1991-2000), Am. Soc. Gen. Surgeons. Office: U Calif Davis Sch Medicine Dept Surgery 2221 Stockton Blvd Fl 3 Sacramento CA 95817-2214 Business E-Mail: efwolfman@ucdavis.edu.

WOLFORD, RICHARD G., food products executive; With Dole Foods, 1967—87, pres. packaged foods, 1982—87; CEO HK Acquisition Corp., 1988—96, Del Monte Foods Co., San Francisco, 1997—98, pres., CEO, 1998—2000, chmn., pres., CEO, 2000—. Office: Del Monte Foods Co One Market The Landmark San Francisco CA 94105

WOLFRAM, CHARLES WILLIAM, law educator; b. Cleve., Feb. 28, 1937; s. Carl P. and Dona M. (Minitch) W.; m. Nancy Russell Bass, Dec. 18, 1965; children: Catherine Dana, Peter Russell. AB, Notre Dame U., 1959; LLB, U. Tex., 1962. Bar: D.C. 1962, Minn. 1974. Assoc. Covington & Burling, Washington, 1962-64; mem. FAA Contract Appeals Panel, Washington, 1964-65; asst. prof. law U. Minn., 1965-67, assoc. prof., 1967-70, prof., 1970-81; prof. law Cornell U., Ithaca, N.Y., 1982-84, Charles Frank Reavis Sr. prof. law, 1984-99, Charles Frank Reavis Sr. prof. emeritus, 1999—. Assoc. dean acad. affairs Cornell U., Ithaca, 1986-90, interim dean, 1998-99; vis. prof. U. So. Calif. Law Center, 1976-77. Author: (with J. Morris Clark) Professional Responsibilty: Issues for Minnesota Attorneys, 1976, Modern Legal Ethics, 1986; contbr. chpts. to books, articles to profl. jours. Mem. Am. Law Inst. (chief reporter Restatement of Law Governing Lawyers, 1986- 2000), Order of Coif. Democrat. Office: 2887 College Ave #148 Berkeley CA 94705 Office Phone: 510-841-5542. E-mail: chuwolfram@aol.com.

WOLFRAM, THOMAS, physicist, educator; b. St. Louis, July 27, 1936; s. Ferdinand I. and Audrey H. (Calvert) W.; m. Eleanor Elaine Burger, May 22, 1965; children: Michael, Gregory, Melanie, Susan, Steven. BA, U. Calif., Riverside, 1959, PhD in Physics, 1963; MA in Physics, UCLA, 1960. Engr. Atomics Internat., Canoga Park, Calif., 1960-63; mem. tech. staff N.Am. Aviation Corp. Sci. Ctr., Thousand Oaks, Calif., 1963-68; group leader in solid state physics Rockwell Internat. Sci. Ctr., Thousand Oaks, 1968-72, dir. div. physics and chemistry, 1972-74; prof. physics, chmn. dept. physics and astronomy U. Mo., Columbia, 1974-83; dir. phys. tech. divsn. AMOCO Corp., 1983-87; v.p., gen. mgr. AMOCO Laser Co., 1987-95; bus. cons., 1995—. Cons. in field. Author: The Venture, The Dragon Tamers, Electronic and Optical Properties of d-Band Perovskites; editor: Inelastic Electron Tunneling Spectroscopy, 1978; contbr. articles to profl. jours. Recipient Disting. Prof. award Argonne Univs. Assn., 1977 Fellow: Am. Phys. Soc. Home and Office: 228 Trafalgar Ln San Clemente CA 92672 Personal E-mail: ewolfram@cox.net.

WOLFSON, MARK ALAN, investor, educator, dean; b. Chgo., Sept. 25, 1952; s. Jack and Maribelle (Simen) W.; m. Sheila Rae Aronesti, Aug. 3, 1975; children: Laura Rachel, Charles Michael. BS in Acctg. and Fin., U. Ill., 1973, M in Acctg. Sci., 1974; PhD in Acctg., U. Tex., 1977. Asst. prof. acctg. Stanford (Calif.) U., 1977-81, assoc. prof., 1981-85, prof., 1985-87, Joseph McDonald prof., 1987-92, assoc. dean, 1990-93, Dean Witter prof. acctg. and fin., 1992-96, cons. prof., 2001—; mng. ptnr. Oak Hill Capital Mgmt., 1998—; established Oak Hill Strategic Ptnrs., 1996—, Oak Hill Investment Mgmt., 2000—; prin. Oak Hill REIT Ptnrs., 2004—, Oak Hill Spl. Opportunities Fund, 2004—. Ford Found. vis. assoc. prof. U. Chgo., 1981-82; Thomas Henry Carroll vis. prof. Harvard U., Boston, 1988-89; cons. Fin. Acctg. Stds. Bd., Norwalk, Conn., 1985, 89-92; rsch. assoc. Nat. Bur. Econ. Rsch., Cambridge, Mass., 1988—; steering com. Stanford Inst. Econ. Policy Rsch., 1990-2000, exec. com. 2001—; task force Fed. Home Loan Bank Bd., 1989; bd. dirs. eGain Comm., Fin. Engines, Inc., Accretive Healthcare; mem. investment com. William and Flora Hewlett Found., 2004—. Contbr. numerous articles to profl. jours. Recipient Pomerance prize Chgo. Bd. Options Exch., 1981, Disting. Tchg. award Stanford U., 1990, Notable Contbn. to Lit. award AICPA-Am. Acctg. Assn., 1990, 92, Wildman award, 1991; named Disting. Accountancy Alumnus, U. Ill., 1989. Jewish. Office: Oak Hill Capital 2775 Sand Hill Rd Ste 220 Menlo Park CA 94025-7019

WOLINSKY, LEO C., newspaper editor; BA in Journalism, U. So. Calif., 1972. Journalist, 1972—; staff writer L.A. Times, 1977-86, dep. chief Sacramento bur., 1987-89, city editor, 1990, Calif. polit. editor, 1991, metro editor, asst. mng. editor, 1994-97, mng. editor, 1997-99, 2005—, exec. editor, 2000, dep. mng. editor, 2000—04. Office: Los Angeles Times Times Mirror Sq Los Angeles CA 90053

WOLK, BRUCE ALAN, law educator; b. Bklyn., Mar. 2, 1946; s. Morton and Gertrude W.; m. Lois Gloria Krepliak, June 22, 1968; children: Adam, Daniel. BS, Antioch Coll., 1968; MS, Stanford U., 1972; JD, Harvard U., 1975. Bar: D.C. 1975. Assoc. Hogan & Hartson, Washington, 1975-78; prof. U. Calif. Sch. Law, Davis, 1978—, acting dean, 1990-91, dean, 1993-98. Danforth Found. fellow, 1970-74, NSF fellow, 1970-72, Fulbright sr. research fellow, 1985-86. Mem. ABA, Am. Law Inst. Office: Univ Cal Davis Sch Law King Hall 400 Mrak Hall Dr Davis CA 95616-5201

WOLK, LOIS, state legislator; b. Phila., May 12, 1946; m to Bruce; children: Adam & Dan. BA, Antioch Coll., 1968; MA, Johns Hopkins U., 1971. California State Assemblywoman, District 8, 2002-08; Standing Committee Assignments, Budget, health, Human Serv, natural Resources, Utilities & Commerce, Water, Parks & Wildlife; mem. Dist. 5, Calif. State Senate, 2008-. California Elected Women; charter member, Davis Sci Center Bd; Rotary; Soroptimist; found member, TREE Davis; Univ Retirement Community Found Bd; charter member, YoloBasin Found Bd; founding member, Yolo Land Trust. Democrat. Office: Dist 5 555 Mason St Ste 230 Vacaville CA 95688 Office Phone: 707-454-3808. Office Fax: 707-454-3811.

WOLK, MARTIN, physicist, electrical engineer; b. Long Branch, NJ; 1 child, Brett Martin. BS, George Washington U., 1957, MS, 1968; PhD, U. N.Mex., 1973. Physicist Naval Ordnance Lab., White Oak, Md., 1957—59, Nat. Oceanic Atmospheric Adminstrn., Suitland, Md., 1959—66; solid state physicist Night Vision Lab., Fort Belvoir, Va., 1967—69; rsch. asst. U. N.Mex., Albuquerque, 1969—73; electronics engr. Washington Navy Yard, 1976—83, TRW, Inc., Redondo Beach, Calif., 1983—84; physicist Metrology Engring. Ctr., Pomona, Calif., 1984—85; electronics engr. Naval Aviation Depot North Island, San Diego, 1985—. Cons. Marine Corps Logistics Base, Barstow, Calif., 1985—, Naval Weapons Station, Fallbrook, Calif.,

1987-89, Naval Weapons Support Ctr., Crane, Ind., 1989—. Contbr. articles to Jour. Quantitative Spectroscopy and Radiative Transfer, Monthly Weather Rev., Proceedings of SPIE, Procs. of EUROPTO. Cpl. 11th Airborne Divsn. US Army. Mem.: IEEE, European Optical Soc., Soc. Photo-Optical Instrumentation Engring., Sigma Tau, Sigma Pi Sigma. Achievements include devel. of first Tiros meteorological satellites; rsch. on electron-beam for micro-circuit device fabrication; devel. of electro-optical calibration sys. for the TOW missile sys. optical and night vision sights for the Marine Corps; devel. of visible and infrared spectral radiometric sys. utilizing a Fourier Transform Interferometer spectrometer for primary standards calibration of thermal radiation sources. Home: 740 Eastshore Ter Unit 91 Chula Vista CA 91913-2421 E-mail: martin.wolk@navy.mil.

WOLKOFF, EUGENE ARNOLD, lawyer; b. NYC, June 9, 1932; s. Oscar and Jean (Zablow) W.; m. Judith Gail Edwards, Oct. 15, 1967; children: Mandy, Elana, Alexa, Justine. AB, Bklyn. Coll., 1953; LLB, St. John's U., 1961. Bar: NY 1962, N.Mex. 1994. Practiced in NYC and Santa Fe; mem. Callahan & Wolkoff, NYC, 1965—; gen. counsel BGK Group of Cos. Served to lt. col. USAFR, 1953-75. Mem. ABA, NY State Bar Assn., N.Mex. Bar Assn., Pi Beta Gamma. Office: 330 Garfield St Santa Fe NM 87501-2640 also: 88 Pine St 21st Fl New York NY 10005 Office Phone: 505-992-5100. Business E-Mail: gene@bgkgroup.com.

WOLLENBERG, RICHARD PETER, paper manufacturing company executive; b. Juneau, Alaska, Aug. 1, 1915; s. Harry L. and Gertrude (Arnstein) W.; m. Leone Bonney, Dec. 22, 1940; children: Kenneth Roger, David Arthur, Keith Kermit, Richard Harry, Carol Lynne. BSME, U. Calif., Berkeley, 1936; MBA, Harvard U., 1938; grad., Army Indsl. Coll., 1941; D in Pub. Affairs (hon.), U. Puget Sound, 1977. Prodn. control Bethlehem Ship, Quincy, Mass., 1938-39; with Longview (Wash.) Fibre Co., 1939—, safety engr., asst. chief engr., chief engr., mgr. container operations, 1951-57, v.p., 1953-57, v.p. ops., 1957-60, exec. v.p., 1960-69, pres., 1969-78, pres., chief exec. officer, 1978-85, pres., chief exec. officer, chmn. bd., 1985—2001, chmn. bd. dirs., 2001—. Mem. Wash. State Council for Postsecondary Edn., 1969-79, chmn., 1970-73; mem. western adv. bd. Factory Mutual Ins Co. Trustee Reed Coll., Portland, 1962—, chmn. bd. 1982-90. Served to lt. col. USAAF, 1941-45. Recipient Alumni Achievement award Harvard U., 1994. Mem. NAM (bd. dirs. 1981-86), Pacific Coast Assn. Pulp and Paper Mfrs. (pres. 1981-92), Inst. Paper Sci. and Tech. (trustee), Wash. State Roundtable. Home: 1632 Kessler Blvd Longview WA 98632-3633

WOLPER, DAVID LLOYD, motion picture and television executive; b. NYC, Jan. 11, 1928; s. Irving S. and Anna (Fass) W.; m. Margaret Dawn Richard, May 11, 1958 (div.); children: Mark, Michael, Leslie; m. Gloria Diane Hill, July 11, 1974. Student, Drake U., 1946, U. So. Calif., 1948. V.p., treas. Flamingo Films, TV sales co., 1948-50, v.p. West Coast Ops., 1954-58; chmn., pres. Wolper Prodns., LA, 1958—. Cons., exec. producer Warner Bros., Inc., 1976—. TV prodns. include Race for Space, Making of the President 1960, 64, Biography series, Story of... series, The Yanks are Coming, Berlin: Kaiser to Khrushchev, December 7: Day of Infamy, The American Woman in the 20th Century, Hollywood and The Stars, March of Time Specials, The Rise and Fall of the Third Reich, The Legend of Marilyn Monroe, Four Days in November, Krebiozen and Cancer, National Geographic, Undersea World of Jacques Cousteau, China: Roots of Madness, The Journey of Robert F. Kennedy, Say Goodbye, George Plimpton, Appointment With Destiny, American Heritage, Smithsonian, They've Killed President Lincoln, Sandburg's Lincoln, Primal Man, The First Woman President, Chico and the Man, Get Christie Love, Welcome Back, Kotter!, Collison Course, Roots, Victory at Entebbe, Roots: The Next Generations, Moviola, The Thorn Birds, North and South Books I, II, III, Napoleon and Josephine, Alex Haley's Queen, Men Of The Dragon, Unwed Father, The Morning After; feature films include The Hellstrom Chronicle, Devil's Brigade, The Bridge at Remagen, If It's Tuesday, This Must Be Belgium, Willy Wonka and The Chocolate Factory, Visions of Eight, This is Elvis, Murder in the First, Surviving Picasso, L.A. Confidential; live spl. events include Opening and Closing Ceremonies 1984 Olympic Games, Liberty Weekend July 3-6, 1986. Trustee L.A. County Mus. Art, Am. Film Inst., L.A. Thoracic and Cardiovascular Found., Boys and Girls Clubs Am., U.S. Golf Assn. Found.; bd. dirs. Amateur Athletic Assn. L.A., L.A. Heart Inst., Acad. TV Arts and Scis. Found., So. Calif. Com. for Olympic Games, U. Soc. Calif. Cinema/TV Dept.; bd. govs. Cedars Sinai Med. Ctr.; com. mem. U.S. Olympic Team Benefit; mem. adv. com. Nat. Ctr. Jewish Film. Recipient award for documentaries, San Francisco Internat. Film Festival, 1960, 7 Golden Globe awards, 5 George Foster Peabody awards, Disting. Svc. award, US Jr. C. of C., award, Monte Carlo Internat. Film Festival, 1964, Grand Prix for TV Programs, Cannes Film Festival, 1964, medal of Chevalier, French Nat. Legion of Honor, 1990, Disting. Svc. award, Nat. Assn. Broadcasters, 2007, David L. Wolper Student Documentary Achievement award named in his honor, Internat. Documentary Assn., David L. Wolper Ctr. for Study of Documentary named in his honor, U. So. Calif.; named to TV Hall of Fame, 1988. Mem.: NATAS (50 Emmy awards, 145 Emmy nominations), Caucus for Prodrs., Writers and Dirs., Prodrs. Guild Am. (David L. Wolper Prodr. of Yr. award named in his honor), Acad. Motion Picture Arts and Scis. (Oscar award, 11 Oscar nominations). Office: The David L Wolper Co Inc 617 N Rodeo Dr Beverly Hills CA 90210 Business E-Mail: thewolperletter@msn.com.

WOLTIL, ROBERT D., healthcare management company executive; BS in Acctg. and Finance, U. South Fla. CPA, Fla. Various positions including pres., CEO pharmacy subs. Beverly Enterprises Inc., then CFO; CFO, sr. v.p. fin. svcs. Sun Healthcare Group Inc., Albuquerque, 1996—. Office: Sun Healthcare Group Inc 101 Sun Ave NE Albuquerque NM 87109-4373

WOLYNES, PETER GUY, chemistry researcher, educator; b. Chgo., Apr. 21, 1953; s. Peter and Evelyn Eleanor (Etter) W.; m. Jane Lee Fox, Nov. 26, 1976 (div. 1980); m. Kathleen Cull Bucher, Dec. 22, 1984; children: Margrethe Cull, Eve Cordelia, Julia Jean. AB with highest distinction, Ind. U., 1971; AM, Harvard U., 1972, PhD in Chem. Physics, 1976; DSc (hon.), Ind. U., 1988. Rsch. assoc. MIT, Cambridge, 1975-76; asst. prof., assoc. prof. Harvard U., Cambridge, 1976-80; vis. scientist Max Planck Inst. für Biophysikalische Chemie, Gottingen, Fed. Republic Germany, 1977; assoc. prof. chemistry U. Ill., Urbana, 1980-83, prof. chemistry, 1983-2000, prof. physics, 1985-2000, prof. physics and biophysics, 1989-2000, mem. Ctr. for Advanced Study, 1989-2000; William H. and Janet LyCan prof. chemistry Ctr. for Advanced Study U. Ill., Urbana, 1993-96, Robert Eiszner prof., 1996-2000; prof. chemistry and biochemistry U. Calif., San Diego, 2000—, Francis H.C. Crick prof., 2001—, prof. physics, 2003—. Vis. prof. Inst. for Molecular Sci., Okazaki, Japan, 1982, 87; vis. scientist Inst. for Theoretical Physics, Santa Barbara, Calif., 1987, Ecole normale Supérieure, Paris, 1992; Merski lectr. U. Nebr., 1986; Denkewalter lectr. Loyola U., 1986; Hinshelwood lectr. Oxford U., 1997; Harkins lectr. U. Chgo., 1997; FMC lectr. Princeton U., 1998; Matsen lectr. U. Tex., 2002; Rice lectr. U. NC, 2005; lifson lectr. Weizmann Internat., 2009. Contbr. numerous articles to profl. jours. Sloan fellow, 1981-83, J.S. Guggenheim fellow, 1986-87; Beckman assoc. Ctr. for Advanced Study, Urbana, 1984-85; Fogarty scholar NIH, 1994-98; recipient Hirschfelder prize U. Wis., 2009-. Fellow AAAS, Am. Phys. Soc. (Biol. Physics prize 2004), Am. Acad. Arts and Scis., The Biophys. Soc.; mem. NAS, Am. Chem. Soc. (Pure Chemistry award 1986, Peter Debye award 2000, Edgar Fahs Smith award Phila. sect. 2005), Royal Soc. London(fgn.), German Acad. Sci. Leopoldina, Isreal Chem. Soc. (hon. life mem.), Phi Beta Kappa, Sigma Xi, Phi Lambda Upsilon (Fresenius award 1988), Sigma Pi Sigma, Alpha Chi Sigma. Home: 12737 Sandy Crest Ct San Diego CA 92130-2795 Office: U Calif San Diego Dept Chem and Biochemistry 9500 Gilman Dr MC 0371 La Jolla CA 92093-0371 Home Phone: 858-509-2730; Office Phone: 858-822-4825. Business E-Mail: pwolynes@ucsd.edu.

WOMACK, JAMES ERROL, college president; b. Eugene, Oreg., June 27, 1940; s. John Leon and Dorothy Laverne (Yarbrough) W.; m. Sharron Kay McCullough, June 8, 1963; children: Timothy, Stephen, Joseph, Marilee. BS, N.W. Christian Coll., 1963; M Teaching, Cen. Okla. State U., 1968; postgrad., Pacific Luth. U., 1958-60, U. Oreg., 1960-63, Phillips U., 1966-68, DHum (hon.), 1987. Cert. tchr., Okla., Calif.; cert. fund raising exec.; ordained to ministry Christian Ch. (Disciples of Christ), 1963. Youth min. Lowell (Oreg.) Christian Ch., 1962-63, First Christian Ch., The Dalles, Oreg., 1963-65; youth and edn. min. Putnam City Christian Ch., Oklahoma City, 1965-68; tchr. English and social studies, coach basketball Patterson (Calif.) High Sch., 1968-71; min. youth and edn. Maze Blvd. Christian Ch., Modesto, Calif., 1968-71; dir. devel. Nat. Benevolent Assn. (Colo. Christian Home), Denver, 1976-86; coord. campus activities, coach basketball N.W. Christian Coll., Eugene, 1971-73, dir. planned giving, 1973-76, pres., 1986—. Cons. Luth. Social Svcs. Colo., Denver, 1984-85, Dayton, Ohio, 1986-89, Florence Crittenton Home Svcs., Little Rock, 1985-98; presenter in field. Mem. devel. coun. Woodhaven Learning Ctr.; mem. fin. com. and nurture commn. Cen. Rocky Mountain Region Christian Ch.; chmn. N.W. Oklahoma City Youth Week Activities; trustee N.W. Christian Coll.; active Denver Planned Giving Roundtable; regional bd. dirs. N.W. Regional Ch., Christian Ch. in Kans. Recipient Book Award for Acad. Excellence Christian Bd. of Pub. Mem. Nat. Soc. Fund Raising Execs., Nat. Benevolent Assn. (trustee best of caring fund), Oreg. Ind. Coll. Assn. (mem. exec. com.), Colo. Assn. Fund Raisers (past sec., bd. dirs.), Emerald Empire Fellowship of Christian Athletes (charter mem., sec., bd. dirs.), Ministerial Alliance (chmn. migrant ministries), Rotary (mem. program com. Eugene chpt. 1990), Optimists (bd. dirs. Highland Park chpt.), Civitan, Denver City Club. Avocations: fishing, reading, sports. Office: NW Christian Coll 828 E 11th Ave Eugene OR 97401-3745 Home: 2023 Cedar Ct North Bend OR 97459-2174 E-mail: pres@nwcc.edu.

WOMACK, THOMAS HOUSTON, manufacturing executive; b. Gallatin, Tenn., June 22, 1940; s. Thomas Houston and Jessie (Eckel) Womack; m. Linda Walker, July 20, 1963 (div. Dec. 1989); children: Britton Ryan, Kelley Elizabeth; m. Pamela Ann Reed, Apr. 20, 1991. BSME, Tenn. Tech. U., Cookeville, 1963. Project engr. U.S. Gypsum Co., Jacksonville, Fla., 1963-65; project mgr. Maxwell House Divsn. Gen. Foods Corp., Jacksonville, 1965-68, mfg. mgr. Hoboken, NJ, 1968-71, divsn. ops. planning mgr., 1971-73; industry sales mgr. J.R. Schneider Co., Tiburon, Calif., 1973-79; pres. and CEO Womack Internat., Inc., Mare Island, 1979—; chmn. and CEO Ceramic Microlight Techs., Inc., 1995—; pres. and CEO Micronic Filtration Tech., LLC, 2005—. Mem.: Am. Soc. Chem. Engrs., Soc. Mfg. Engrs., Am. Filtration Soc., Soc. Tribologists and Lubrication Engrs. Achievements include patents in field. Avocation: skiing. Home: 755 Baywood Dr Ste 360 Petaluma CA 94954-5511 Office Phone: 707-562-1000. Office Fax: 707-562-1010. Business E-Mail: womack@womack.com.

WONG, ALFRED YIU-FAI, physics educator; b. Macao, Portugal, Feb. 4, 1937; s. Ka Ku and Wai Fong (Mak) W.; m. Lydia Yun Li, June 19, 1965; children: Alan C., Christopher C. BA in Sci., U. Toronto, 1958, MA, 1959; MSc, U. Ill., 1961; PhD, Princeton U., 1963. Research assoc. Princeton U., 1962-64; asst. prof. physics UCLA, 1964-68, assoc. prof. physics, 1968-72, prof., 1972—. Cons. TRW Systems, Redondo Beach, Calif., 1965-79; bd. dirs. Hipas Observatory, Ark. Contbr. articles to profl. jours. A.P. Sloan fellow UCLA, 1966-67. Fellow Am. Phys. Soc. (Excellence in Plasma Physics award 1985), Sigma Xi, Sigma Pi Sigma. Baptist. Office: UCLA Dept Physics 405 Hilgard Ave Los Angeles CA 90095-9000

WONG, ALICE, lawyer; Grad., U. Calif., Berkeley; JD, Hastings Coll. Law, San Francisco. Dep., homicide unit Dist. Atty., Sacramento. Pub. safety liaison officer Coun. Asian Pacific Islanders Together for Advocacy and Leadership; past bd. pres. My Sister's House women's shelter. Recipient Cmty. Svc. award, Asian Pacific Bar Assn. Sacramento, 2003; named one of Best Lawyers Under 40, Nat. Asian Pacific Am. Bar Assn., 2004. Office: Community Prosecutor Ste 700 901 G St Sacramento CA 95814 Office Phone: 916-874-4978. Office Fax: 916-874-5340. Business E-Mail: alwong@saccounty.net.

WONG, ARNOLD ERIC, chef, restaurant owner; b. San Francisco; Grad., Calif. Culinary Acad. Former bread and pastry chef Silks at the Mandarin Oriental Hotel, San Francisco; former apprentice Masa's, San Francisco; former sous chef Cafe Kati, San Francisco; owner, chef EOS Restaurant and Wine Bar, San Francisco, 1996—. Co-owner Skones Baking Co., San Francisco, The Ashbury Market, San Francisco. Named a Chef of the Yr., San Francisco Chronicle. Office: EOS Restaurant and Wine Bar 901 Cole St San Francisco CA 94117

WONG, BRIAN JET-FEI, surgeon; b. LA, Sept. 23, 1963; s. Richard Toy and Hazel F. (Lue) W. BS, U. So. Calif., 1985; postgrad., Oxford U., 1985-86; MD, Johns Hopkins U., 1990; PhD, U. Amsterdam, 2001. Resident U. Calif., Irvine, 1990-96, clin. instr., 1997-98, asst. prof., 1998—2001, assoc. prof., 2001—06, prof., 2006—07, vice chmn. Rsch. assoc. Beckman Laser Inst., Irvine, 1994—. Recipient Physician Excellence, Orange County Med. Assn.; named one of Best Dr. in USA. Mem. ACS, Biomed. Optical Soc., SPIE, Am. Acad. Facial Plastic Surgery. Avocation: surfing. Office: U Calif Dept Otolaryngology 101 City Dr S # B25r81 Orange CA 92868-3201 Office Phone: 714-456-5753.

WONG, CHI-HUEY, chemistry professor; b. Taiwan, Aug. 13, 1948; came to US, 1979; m. Yieng-Lii, Mar. 26, 1975; children: Heather, Andrew. BS in Chem. and Biochemical Sci., Nat. Taiwan U., 1970, MS in Biochemical Sci., 1977; PhD in Organic Chemistry, MIT, 1982. Asst. rsch. fellow Inst. Biol. Chemistry Academia Sinica, Taipei, Taiwan, 1974-79; postdoctoral fellow Harvard U., 1982—83; asst. prof. chemistry Tex. A&M U., 1983—86, assoc. prof., 1986—87, prof. biochemistry and biophysics Inst. Biosciences and Tech., 1987—89; prof., Ernest W. Hahn chair chemistry Scripps Rsch. Inst., La Jolla, Calif., 1989—, mem. Skaggs Inst. Chem. Biology, 1996—; dir. Genomics Rsch. Ctr. Academia Sinica, Taipei, Taiwan, 2003—. Cons. Dow Chem., 1983—88, W.R. Grace, 1984—87, Miles Lab., 1985—88, G.D. Searle, 1988—90, Amgen, 1991—93, Abbott Labs., 1991—94, Lilly Rsch. Labs., 1991—93, Dow Corning, 1992—94, Mitsubishi Chem. Grp. Sci. and Tech. Rsch. Ctr., Japan, 2005—; sci. adv. Amylin, San Diego, 1989—93, Cytel, 1991—97, Inst. Chemistry, Academia Sinia, 1992—2000, chmn. bd., 1994—2000; sci. adv. Osi Pharm., 1992—98, Affymax, 1992—95, Oncogene Sci., 1993—98, RedCell, 1993—97, ArQule, 1994—95, Inst. Biol. Chemistry, Academia Sinica, 1994—2002, Inst. Molecular and Cell Biology, Nat. U. Singapore, 1994—97, Medinox, Inc., 1996—, Advanced Medicine, Inc., 1997—2000, Kosan Biosciences, 1997—2002, Pharmanex, 1997—, Max-Planck-Inst., Dortmund, Germany, 2000—, Momenta, 2001—03, Diversa, 2001—, Serenex, 2001—, Devel. Ctr. Biotechnology, Taiwan, 2004—; sci. adv., bd. dirs. Indsl. Tech. Rsch. Inst., Taiwan, 2004—; head frontier rsch. prog. glycotechnology Inst. Phys. and Chem. Rsch. (RIKEN), Japan, 1991—99; founder, sci. adv. Combichem, Inc., San Diego, 1994—98; vis. prof. Chem. Ctr. U. Lund, Sweden, 1995—98; corr. rsch. fellow Inst. Biol. Chemistry Academia Sinica, 1996—2002, disting. vis. scholar Inst. Chemistry, 1999—2002; founder, bd. mem., chmn. sci. adv. bd. Optimer Pharms., Inc., San Diego, 1999—; hon. prof. Shanghai Inst. Organic Chemistry, Chinese Acad. Scis., 1999—. Contbr. articles to sci. jours.; mem. editl. bd.: Biocatalysis, 1991—, Carbohydrate Letters, 1995—, Drug Discovery Today, 1996—99, Current Opinion in Chem. Biology, 1998—, Advanced Synthesis and Catalysis, 2000—, editor-in-chief: Bioorganic and Medicinal Chemistry, 1993—, mem. exec. bd. editors: Tetrahedron Publs., 1993—, mem. adv. bd.: Jour. Organic Chemistry, 1993—97, Jour. Chem. Soc., Perkin Trans. 1, 1993—2002, Jour. Am. Chem. Soc., 2005—, Chemistry: An Asian Jour., 2006—; co-author: Enzymes in Synthetic Organic Chemistry, 1994, Combinatorial Chemistry in Biology, 1999, Catalysis from A to Z: A Concise Ency., 1999; author: Carbohydrate-based Drug Discovery, Vols. 1 and 2, 2003. Lt. Taiwan Army, 1970-71. Recipient Searle Scholar award in Biomedical Scis., 1985—88, Presdl. Young Investigator in Chemistry award, NSF, Washington, 1986—91, Arthur C. Cope Scholar award, Am. Chem. Soc., 1993, Divsn. Carbohydrate Chemistry Melville L. Wolfrom award, 1995, Harrison Howe award in Chemistry, 1998, Claude S. Hudson award in Carbohydrate Chemistry, 1999, San Diego Sect. Outstanding Scientist award, 1999, Award for Creative Work in Synthetic Organic Chemistry, 2005, Roy Whistler award, Internat. Carbohydrate Orgn., 1994, Disting. Rsch. Achievement award, Chinese Am. Chem. Soc., 1994, Taiwanese Am. Found. prize in Sci. and Engring., 1997, Internat. Enzyme Engring. award, 1999, Presdl. Green Chemistry Challenge award, 2000. Fellow: AAAS; mem.: NAS, Am. Acad. Arts and Scis., Academia Sinica. Achievements include patents in field. Office: Scripps Rsch Inst Dept Chemistry 10550 N Torrey Pines Rd La Jolla CA 92037-1000 E-mail: wong@scripps.edu.

WONG, DAVID YUE, academic administrator, physics educator; b. Swatow, China, Apr. 16, 1934; came to U.S., 1953; s. Fan and Wen (Tsang) W.; m. Katherine Young, Sept. 3, 1960 (div. Mar. 1988); children: Amy, Eric; m. Elizabeth Elkins, Mar. 26, 1988 BA, Hardin Simmons U., 1954; PhD, U. Md., 1957. Theoretical physicist Lawrence Radiation Lab., U. Calif., Berkeley, 1958-59; asst. prof. physics U. Calif., San Diego, 1960-63, assoc. prof., 1963-67, prof., 1967—, chair dept. physics, 1977-80, provost Warren Coll., 1985-94. Alfred P. Sloan fellow, 1966-68 Mem. Am. Inst. Physics.

WONG, JAMES BOK, economist, chemical engineer, technologist, consultant; b. Canton, China, Dec. 9, 1922; came to U.S., 1938, naturalized, 1962; s. Gen Ham and Chen (Yee) W.; m. Wai Ping Lim, Aug. 3, 1946, (dec.); children: John, Jane Doris, Julia Ann; m. Betty KC Yeow, May 25, 2002. BS summa cum laude in Agr., U. Md., 1949, BS summa cum laude in Chem. Engring., 1950; MS, U. Ill., 1951, PhD, 1954. Rsch. asst. U. Ill., Champaign-Urbana, 1950-53; chem. engr. Std. Oil of Ind., Whiting, 1953-55; process design engr., rsch. engr. Shell Devel. Co., Emeryville, Calif., 1955-61; sr. planning engr., prin. planning engr. Chem. Plastics Group, Dart Industries, Inc. (formerly Rexall Drug & Chem. Co.), LA, 1961-66, supr. planning and econs., 1966-67, mgr. long range planning and econs., 1967, chief economist, 1967-72, dir. econs. and ops. analysis, 1972-78, dir. internat. techs., 1978-81; pres. James B. Wong Assocs., LA, 1981—. Chmn. bd. dirs. United Pacific Bank, 1988—; tech. cons. various corps. Author: Jade Eagle, 2000, Silk Tiger, 2008; contbr. articles to profl. jours. Bd. dirs., pres. Chinese Am. Citizens Alliance Found.; mem. Asian Am. Edn. Commn., 1971-81; grand marshal Chinese Am. Citizens Alliance. Served with USAF, 1943—46. Recipient L.A. Outstanding Vol. Svc. award, 1977. Mem. Am. Chem. Soc., Am. Inst. Chem. Engrs., VFW (vice comdr. 1959), Commodores (named to exec. order 1982), Sigma Xi, Tau Beta Pi, Phi Kappa Phi, Pi Mu Epsilon, Phi Lambda Upsilon, Phi Eta Sigma. Home: 2460 Venus Dr Los Angeles CA 90046-1646 Office Phone: 323-876-4083. Personal E-mail: wjaeagle@aol.com.

WONG, JOE, physical chemist; b. Hong Kong, Aug. 8, 1942; arrived in U.S., 1966; s. Po-lim and Mildred (Tam) W.; m. Mei-Ngan, Dec. 20, 1969; children: Glenn, Christina, Theresa. BSc, U. Tasmania, Australia, 1965, BSc with honors, 1966, DSc, 1986; PhD, Purdue U., 1970. Rsch. chemist Electrolytic Zinc of Australia, Tasmania, 1966; lectr. in phys. chemistry Royal Hobart Coll., Tasmania, 1966; rsch. chemist GE R&D Ctr., Schenectady, N.Y., 1970-86; sr. rsch. chemist Lawrence Livermore Nat. Lab., Calif., 1986—2006. Adj. prof. chemistry SUNY, Albany, 1981-86; cons. prof. Stanford Synchrotron Rad. Lab., 1993—. Author: Glass: Structure by Spectroscopy, 1976; contbr. articles to profl. jours.; 7 patents in field. Sr. fellowship Sci. and Tech. Agy., 1991; recipient Humboldt Rsch. award Humboldt Found., 1991, RD-100 awards, 1990, 91. Fellow Am. Inst. Chemists, Am. Phys. Soc.; mem. AAAS, Am. Chem. Soc., Materials Rsch. Soc., Sigma Xi. Home: 871 El Cerro Blvd Danville CA 94526-2704

WONG, NATHAN DONALD, medicine and epidemiology researcher, educator; b. Downey, Calif., Apr. 18, 1961; s. Donald Wah and Mew Lun (Hee) W.; m. Mia K. Park, July 21, 1996; 1 child, David. BA, Pomona Coll., Claremont, Calif., 1983; MPH, Yale U., New Haven, Conn., 1985, PhD, 1987. Lectr. medicine Yale U., New Haven, 1987; asst. prof. U. Calif., Irvine, 1988—94, assoc. prof.,

1994—2002, dir. heart disease prevention program, dept. medicine, 1991—, prof., 2003—; prof. dept. epidemiology UCLA, 2003—. Prin. investigator Antihypertensive Lipid-Lowering to Prevent Heart Attack Trial and other lipid and cardiovasc. prevention trials, 1994—; co-prin. investigator Women's Health Initiative, 1995—; investigator NIH Multiethnic Study of Atherosclerosis (MESA), Coronary Artery Risk Development in Young Adults, Cardiovascular Health Study, and Epidemiology of Diabetes Interventions and Complications Studies; interviewed for various publs. and programs, including ABC Eyewitness News, L.A. Times, Orange County Register, CBS News, USA Today, N.Y. Times, others; profl. cons. Cedars-Sinai Med. Ctr., 2002—; editor-in-chief textbook Preventive Cardiology, Mcgraw-Hill, 2000, 2d edit, 2005; co-editor (textbook) Metabolic Syndrome and Cardiovascular Disease, 2007. Mem. editl. bd.: Preventive Cardiology, Jour. Cardiovascular Drugs, Jour. Cardiometabolic Risk; contbr. chapters to books, apporx. 150 articles to profl. jours. Mem. Calif. Senate Hearing Panel on Youth Phys. Edn. and Fitness, 1991; chair Calif. Cardiovasc. Disease Prevention Coalition, 1998-99; spkr. numerous internat., nat. and local confs., hosps., and med. spkrs. burs. Rsch. grantee, Bristol Myers-Squibb, Pfizer, Merck. Fellow Am. Coll. Cardiology (membership and credentialing com. 2003—, prevention of cardiovasc. disease com. 2003-04, taskforce 4, 34th Bethesda Conf. 2003), Am. Heart Assn. Coun. on Epidemiology and Prevention. Achievements include research in computed tomography, metabolic syndrome, diabetes, lipids, hypertension, preventive cardiology, coronary and aortic calcium. Avocations: running, hiking, skiing, photography. Office: Heart Disease Prevention Program Sprague Hall 112 Univ Calif Irvine CA 92697-4101 Home Phone: 949-240-2840. Business E-Mail: ndwong@uci.edu.

WONG, STANTON D., lawyer; b. San Francisco, Nov. 4, 1957; AB, Univ. Calif., Berkeley, 1979, MBA, JD, Univ. Calif., Berkeley, 1983. Bar: Calif. 1983. Ptnr., ch-chmn. Securities practice Pillsbury Winthrop Shaw Pittman, San Francisco. Contbr. articles to profl. jours. Office: Pillsbury Winthrop Shaw Pittman 50 Fremont St San Francisco CA 94105 also: 2475 Hanover St Palo Alto CA 94304-1114 Office Phone: 415-983-1790. Office Fax: 415-983-1200. Business E-Mail: stanton.wong@pillsburylaw.com.

WONG, TIMOTHY C., language and literature educator; b. Hong Kong, Jan. 24, 1941; came to U.S., 1951; s. Patrick J. and Rose (Poon) W.; m. Elizabeth Ann Steffens, Dec. 18, 1970; children: Sharon Elizabeth, Rachel Margaret, Laura Katherine. BA, St. Mary's Coll., Moraga, Calif., 1963; MA, U. Hawaii, 1968; PhD, Stanford U., 1975. Vol. U.S. Peace Corps, Thailand, 1963-65; asst. prof. Ariz. State U., Tempe, 1974-79, assoc. prof., 1979-85; resident dir. Coun. on Internat. Ednl. Exchange Peking Univ., China, 1984-85; assoc. prof. Ohio State U., Columbus, 1985-95; prof. Ariz. State U., Tempe, 1995—, dir. Ctr. for Asian Studies, 1995—2002, grad. dir. Asian langs. and civilizations program, 2002—. Author: Wu Ching-tzu, 1978, Stories for Saturday: Twentieth-Century Chinese Popular Fiction, 2003. Mem. Chinese Lang. Tchrs. Assn., Assn. Asian Studies, Am. Oriental Soc. (dir.-at-large 1996-2000, v.p. western br. 2000-01, pres. 2001-03). Democrat. Roman Catholic. Office: Ariz State U Dept Langs and Lits Tempe AZ 85287-0202 Home Phone: 480-705-0316. E-mail: timothy.wong@asu.edu.

WONG-STAAL, FLOSSIE, geneticist, educator; BA, UCLA, 1968, PhD, 1972. Tchg. asst. UCLA, 1969-70, rsch. asst., 1970-72; postdoctoral fellow U. Calif., San Diego, 1972-73; Fogarty fellow Nat. Cancer Inst., Bethesda, Md., 1973-75, vis. assoc., 1975-76, cancer expert, 1976-78, sr. investigator, 1978-81, chief molecular genetics of hematopoietic cells sect., 1982-89; Florence Seeley Riford chair in AIDS rsch., prof. medicine U. Calif. San Diego, La Jolla, 1990—. Vis. prof. Inst. Gen. Pathology, First U. Rome, Italy, 1985. Mem. editl. bd. Gene Analysis Techniques, 1984—, Cancer Letters, 1984-94, Leukemia, 1987—, Cancer Rsch., 1987, AIDS Rsch. and Human Retroviruses (sect. editor), 1987—, DNA and Cell Biology (sect. editor), 1987—, Microbial Pathogenesis, 1987-90, AIDS: An Internat. Jour., 1987—, Internat. Jour. Acquired Immunodeficiency Syndrome, 1988—, Oncogene, 1988—, Jour. Virology, 1990—; contbr. articles to profl. jours. Recipient Outstanding Sci. award Chinese Med. and Health Assn., 1987, The Excellence 2000 award U.S. Pan Asian Am. C. of C. and the Orgn. of Chinese Am. Women, 1991. Mem. Am. Soc. for Virology (charter), Phi Beta Kappa. Office: U Calif San Diego Dept Med 0665 9500 Gilman Dr La Jolla CA 92093-5003

WOO, SHARON Y., healthcare organization executive; b. Honolulu; BA in Music and Math., Mills Coll.; secondary tchg. credential, San Francisco State U. Bd. dirs. Sutter Health Inc., Sacramemto. Trustee Gateway H.S., Golden Gate nat. Parks Assn., Multicultural Alliance, San francisco Ballet, numerous others; chmn. adv. coun. San Francisco Sch. Vols.

WOO, VERNON YING-TSAI, lawyer, real estate developer; b. Honolulu, Aug. 7, 1942; s. William Shu-Bin and Hilda Woo; children: Christopher Shu-Bin, Lia Gay. BA, U. Hawaii, 1964, MA, 1966; JD, Harvard U., 1969. Pres. Woo Kessner Duca & Maki, Honolulu, 1972-87; pvt. practice law Honolulu, 1987—. Judge per diem Honolulu Dist. Family Ct., 1978-84, 1995-2002. Bd. dirs. Boys and Girls Club of Honolulu. 1985-95, pres., 1990-92. Mem.: ABA, Honolulu Bd. Realtors, Hawaii Bar Assn. Home: 2859 Pahoehoe Place Honolulu HI 96817 Office: 201 Merchant St Ste 2302 Honolulu HI 96813 Home Phone: 808-595-3344; Office Phone: 808-529-8822. Personal E-mail: vwoo@hawaii.rr.com.

WOOD, ALEX, state legislator; Washington State Representative, District 3, 1997-, Assistant Minority Whip, currently, vice chairman, Commerce & Labor Committee, currently, member, Select Committee on Environ Health, currently, Transportation Committee, currently, Agriculture & Ecology Committees, formerly, Washington House Representative.Radio & television talk show host, 79-96. Armstrong Award, Columbia Sch Journalism; Vietnam Serv Medal (awarded twice). Soc Prof Journalists. Democrat. Office: State House 437B Legislative Bldg, PO Box 40600 Olympia WA 98504 Mailing: Dist Off Ste 103 1425 N Washington Spokane WA 99201 Office Phone: 360-786-7888, 509-625-5354. E-mail: wood_al@leg.wa.gov.

WOOD, CARL WILLIAM, utilities executive; b. Balt., 1947; m. Anne Patrice Wood, 1973; 2 children. Student, U. Calif., Riverside, 1968. Indsl. electrician Kaiser Steel, 1968—81; nuclear electrician Calif. Edison Co., 1981—86; bus. agent Utility Workers Union Am., Los Alamitos, Calif., 1986—94; sec. Coalition Calif. Utility Employees, 1994—99; nat. deregulation coord. Utility Workers Union Am., Washington, 1997—99; commr. Calif. Pub. Utilities Commn., San Francisco, 1999—. Nat. exec. bd. Utility Workers Union Am., 1987—97; chmn. So. Calif. Gas Workers Coun., 1998—99. Dist. bd. dir. N. County Fire Protection, Fallbrook, Calif., 1994—2000. Office: California PUC 505 Van Ness Ave San Francisco CA 94102 Home Phone: 415-999-0250; Office Phone: 415-703-2440. Business E-Mail: cxw@cpuc.ca.gov.

WOOD, DAVID LEE, entomologist, educator; b. Jan. 8, 1931; BS, SUNY, Syracuse, 1952; PhD, U. Calif., Berkeley, 1960. Lic. forester Calif. Prof. entomology, emeritis dept. Environ. Sci. Policy, Mgmt. U. Calif., Berkeley, 1960—. Lectr., reviewer, cons. in field. Contbr. articles to profl. jours. Recipient Silver medal Swedish Coun. for Forestry and Agril. Rsch., 1983, Founder's award Western Forest Insect Work Conf. 1992. Fellow Entomol. Soc. Can., Entomol. Soc. Am. (Founder's award 1986); mem. AAAS, AIBS, Entomol. Soc. Am., Entomol. Soc. Can., Internat. Soc. Chem. Ecology (Silver medal 2001), Soc. Am. Foresters, Sigma Xi. Home: 26 Hardie Dr Moraga CA 94556-1134 Office: U Calif Divsn Insect Biology 137 Mulford Hall Berkeley CA 94720-3112 Office Phone: 510-642-5538. Business E-Mail: bigwood@nature.berkeley.edu.

WOOD, EVAN RACHEL, actress; b. Raleigh, NC, Sept. 7, 1987; d. Ira David Wood and Sara Lynn Moore. Actor: (films) Digging to China, 1998, Practical Magic, 1998, Detour, 1999, Little Secrets, 2001, S1m0ne, 2002, Thirteen, 2003, The Missing, 2003, Down in the Valley, 2005, Pretty Persuasion, 2005, The Upside of Anger, 2005, (voice only) Asterix and the Vikings, 2006, Shark Bait, 2006, Running with Scissors, 2006, King of California, 2007, In Bloom, 2007, (voice only) Terra, 2007, Across the Universe, 2007, The Life Before Her Eyes, 2007, The Wrestler, 2008; (TV films) In the Best of Families: Marriage, Pride & Madness, 1994, Search for Grace, 1994, A Father for Charlie, 1995, Death in Small Doses, 1995, Get to the Heart: The Barbara Mandrell Story, 1997, Down Will Come Baby, 1999; (TV series) Profiler, 1998—99, Once and Again, 1999—2002, (TV appearances) American Gothic, 1995—98, Touched by an Angel, 2000, The West Wing, 2002, CSI: Crime Scene Investigation, 2003. Office: c/o Toni Howard Internat Creative Mgmt 10250 Constellation Blvd Los Angeles CA 90067

WOOD, GEORGE H., investment executive; b. Kansas City, Mo., Sept. 7, 1946; s. George H. and Helen Lee (Hansen) W. BSBA, U. Mo., 1968, MBA, 1972. Chartered fin. analyst. Securities analyst Kansas City Life Ins. Co., 1972-75, asst. dir. securities, 1975-76; sr. trust officer Commerce Bank of Kansas City, N.A., 1976-79, v.p., fixed income and portfolio group mgr., 1979-80, v.p., mgr. investment dept., 1980-82, sr. v.p., 1982—89, chief investment officer, 1988-90; mng. dir. Merus Capital Mgmt., 1990-94; v.p. Pacific Investment Mgmt. Co. (PIMCO), Newport Beach, Calif., 1994-97, sr. v.p., 1997-99, exec. v.p., 1999-2000; head acct. mgmt. Europe, exec. v.p., mng. dir. PIMCO Asset Mgmt. Co. (divsn. Allianz), Newport Beach, Calif., 2000—01, now external US fixed income & cash equivalent mgr. Past bd. dirs., pres. Young Audiences, Inc.; adv. bd. U. Mo. With AUS, 1969-71. Mem. Inst. Chartered Fin. Analysts (past chmn. curriculum com.), Assn. Investment Mgmt. and Rsch., Fin. Analysts Fedn., San Francisco Soc. Fin. Analysts (bd. dirs.), U. Mo. Alumni Assn., Phi Delta Theta. Office: Pacific Investment Mgmt Co 840 Newport Center Dr Ste 360 PO Box 6430 Newport Beach CA 92658-6430 Business E-Mail: george.wood@pimco.com.

WOOD, JAMES MICHAEL, lawyer; b. Oakland, Calif., Mar. 22, 1948; s. Donald James and Helen Winifred (Reimann) Wood; m. Cynthia Ahart Wood; children from previous marriage: Nathan, Sarah, Ruth 1 stepchild, Alexandra. BA, St. Mary's Coll., 1970; JD, U. San Francisco, 1973. Bar: Calif. 1973, U.S. Dist. Ct. (no., ctrl. and so. dists.) Calif. 1973. Rsch. atty. Alameda County Superior Ct., Oakland, 1973—76; ptnr. Reed Smith LLP, Oakland, 1976—. Presenter profl. confs. Contbr. articles to profl. jours. Chair of bd. dirs. Food and Drug Law Inst., Washington, DC. Recipient Disting. Pro Bono Svc. award, Reed Smith Sean Halpin; named Atty. of Yr., Aids Legal Referral Panel, 2006. Mem.: ABA (litig. sect., health litig. com., litig. products liability com.), Food Drug Law Inst. (bd. dirs., adv. com. 1999—), Nat. Health Lawyers Assn., Am. Acad. Hosp. Attys., Def. Rsch. Inst., Alameda County Bar Assn., No. Calif. Assn. Def. Counsel, State Bar Calif. Office: Reed Smith LLP 1999 Harrison St Ste 2200 Oakland CA 94612-3572 Office Phone: 510-466-6758. Business E-Mail: jmwood@reedsmith.com.

WOOD, JAMES NOWELL, foundation administrator, former museum director; b. Boston, Mar. 20, 1941; s. Charles H. and Helen N. (Nowell) Wood; m. Emese Forizs, Dec. 30, 1966; children: Lenke Hancock, Rebecca Nowell. Diploma, Universita per Stranieri, Perugia, Italy, 1962; BA, Williams Coll., Williamstown, Mass., 1963; MA (Ford Mus. Tng. fellow), NYU, 1966. Asst. to dir. Met. Mus., NYC, 1967-68, asst. curator dept. 20th century art, 1968-70; curator Albright-Knox Art Gallery, Buffalo, 1970-73, assoc. dir., 1973-75; dir. St. Louis Art Mus., 1975-80; pres., dir. Art Inst. Chgo., 1980—2004; pres., CEO J. Paul Getty Trust, LA, 2007—. Vis. com. visual arts U. Chgo., 1980—94; head com. Nat. Endowment Arts; bd. dirs. Pulitzer Found. Arts, 2005—, Sterling and Francine Clark Art Inst., Inst. Fine Arts, NYU, Pulitzer Found. Mem.: Assn. Art Mus. Dirs., Intermuseum Conservation Assn. (past pres.). Office: J Paul Getty Trust 1200 Getty Ctr Dr Los Angeles CA 90049 Office Phone: 310-440-7600. Business E-Mail: jwood@getty.edu.

WOOD, JIM, mayor, Oceanside, California; b. Manchester, NH, Jan. 31, 1948; s. Dwight and Harriet Wood; m. Pam Wood; 3 children. Grad., Mira Costa Coll. Police officer City of Oceanside, Calif., 1971—2002, mayor Calif., 2004—; councilman Oceanside City Coun., Calif., 2002—04. Sr. investigator FBI, NCIS, Secret Service. Mailing: City of Oceanside 300 N Coast Hwy Oceanside CA 92054 Office Phone: 760-435-3029, 760-966-4401. E-mail: jwood@ci.oceanside.ca.us.*

WOOD, KENNETH ARTHUR, retired editor, writer; b. Hastings, Sussex, Eng., Feb. 25, 1926; came to U.S., 1965; s. Arthur Charles and Ellen Mary (Cox) W.; m. Hilda Muriel Harloe, Sept. 13, 1952. Editor Stamp Collector newspaper Van Dahl Publs., Albany, Oreg., 1968—80, editor emeritus, 1980—. Author (ency.) This Is Philately, 1982, (atlas) Where in the World, 1983, Basic Philately, 1984, Post Dates, 1985, Modern World, 1987; author several hundred articles and columns published in the U.K. and U.S.A., 1960—. Served with Brit. Army WW II. Recipient Disting. Philatelist award Northwest Fedn. Stamp Clubs, 1974, Phoenix award Ariz. State Philatelic Hall of Fame, 1979, Disting. Philatelist award Am. Topical Assn., 1979. Fellow Royal Philatelic Soc. (London); mem. Am. Philatelic Soc. (hon. life, Luff award 1987, Hall of Fame Writers Unit, 1984). Avocations: stamp collecting/philately, aviation history, modern history, gardening. Office: 2430 Tudor Way SE Albany OR 97322-5661

WOOD, LINCOLN JACKSON, aerospace engineer; b. Lyons, NY, Sept. 30, 1947; s. William Hulbert and Sarah Brock (Strumsky) Wood. BS with distinction, Cornell U., 1968; MS in Aeronautics and Astronautics, Stanford U., 1969, PhD, 1972. Staff engr. Hughes Aircraft Co., El Segundo, Calif., 1974-77; tech. staff Jet Propulsion Lab. Calif. Inst. Tech., Pasadena, 1977-81, tech. group supr. Jet Propulsion Lab., 1981-89, tech. mgr., 1989-91, dep. tech. sect. mgr., 1991-99, dep. leader Ctr. of Excellence for Deep Space Comm./Nav. Sys., 2000—03, tracking and nav. svc. sys. mgr., deep space mission sys. engring. and ops. programs, 2003—04, program mgr., 2004—. Bechtel instr. engring. Calif. Inst. Tech., Pasadena, 1972—74, lectr. in sys. engring., 1975—76, vis. asst. prof., 1976—78, vis. assoc. prof., 1978—84; cons. in field. Contbr. articles to profl. jours. Bd. dirs. Boys Republic, Chino Hills, Calif., 1991, 1997—2007. Fellow: AIAA (assoc.; assoc. editor Jour. Guidance, Control and Dynamics 1983—89, tech. com. astrodynamics 1985—86, chmn. 1986—88); mem.: AAAS, IEEE (sr.), Am. Astron. Soc. (sr.; assoc. editor Jour. Astron. Scis. 1980—83, space flight mechanics com. 1980—97, gen. chmn. AAS/AIAA Space Flight Mechanics Meeting 1993, chmn. space flight mechanics com. 1993—95), Los Solteros (pres. 1991, 1997—2005), Sigma Xi. Office: Jet Propulsion Lab 4800 Oak Grove Dr Mail Stop 301-150 Pasadena CA 91109 Business E-Mail: lincoln.j.wood@jpl.nasa.gov.

WOOD, LINDA MAY, librarian; b. Ft. Dodge, Iowa, Nov. 6, 1942; d. John Albert and Beth Ida (Riggs) Wiley; m. C. James Wood, Sept. 15, 1964 (div. Oct. 1984). BA, Portland State U., 1964; M in Librarianship, U. Wash., 1965. Reference libr. Multnomah County Libr., Portland, Oreg., 1965-67, br. libr., 1967-72, adminstrv. asst. to libr., 1972-73, asst. libr., asst. dir., 1973-77; asst. city libr. L.A. Pub. Libr., 1977-80; libr. dir. Riverside (Calif.) City and County Pub. Libr., 1980-91; county libr. Alameda County Libr., Fremont, Calif., 1991—. Adminstrv. coun. mem. Bay Area Libr. and Info. Svcs., Oakland, Calif., 1991—. Chair combined charities campaign County of Alameda, Oakland, Calif., 1992; bd. dirs. Inland AIDS project, Riverside, 1990-91; vol. United Way of Inland Valleys, Riverside, 1986-87, Bicentennial Competition on the Constitution, 36th Congl. Dist., Colton, Calif., 1988-90. Mem. ALA (CLA chpt. councilor 1992-95), Calif. Libr. Assn. (pres. 1985, exec. com., ALA chpt. councilor 1992-95), Calif. County Librs. Assn. (pres. 1984), League of Calif. Cities (cmty. svcs. policy com. 1985-90), OCLC Users Coun. (Pacific Network del. 1986-89). Democrat. Avocations: dance, opera, reading. Office: Alameda County Libr 2450 Stevenson Blvd Fremont CA 94538-2326 Home Phone: 510-841-3223; Office Phone: 510-745-1536. E-mail: lwood@aclibrary.org.

WOOD, MARCUS ANDREW, lawyer; b. Mobile, Ala., Jan. 18, 1947; s. George Franklin and Helen Eugenia (Fletcher) W.; m. Sandra Lee Pellonari, July 25, 1971; children: Edward Alan, Melinda Janel. BA cum laude, Vanderbilt U., 1969; JD, Yale U., 1974. Bar: Oreg. 1974, U.S. Dist. Ct. Oreg. 1974, U.S. Ct. Appeals (9th cir.) 1982. Assoc., then ptnr. Rives, Bonihadi & Smith, Portland, Oreg., 1974-78; ptnr. Stoel Rives LLP and predecessor firms, Portland, 1974—. Pres., bd. dirs. Indochinese Refugee Ctr., Portland, 1980, Pacific Ballet Theatre, Portland, 1986-87; bd. dirs. Outside In, Portland, 1989-2006. Lt. USNR, 1969—71. Mem.: ABA, Phi Beta Kappa. Home: 9300 NW Finzer Ct Portland OR 97229-8035 Office: Stoel Rives 900 SW 5th Ave Ste 2300 Portland OR 97204-1229 Home Phone: 503-203-1359. Business E-Mail: mwood@stoel.com.

WOOD, NANCY ELIZABETH, psychologist, educator; d. Donald Sterret and Orne Louise (Erwin) W. BS, Ohio U., 1943, MA, 1947; PhD, Northwestern U., 1952. Prof. Case We. Res. U., Cleve., 1952—60; specialist, expert HEW, Washington, 1960—62; chief rschr. USPHS, Washington, 1962—64; prof. U. So. Calif., LA, 1965—. Learning disabilities cons., 1960-70; assoc. dir. Cleve. Hearing and Speech Ctr., 1952-60; dir. licensing program Brit. Nat. Trust, London. Author: Language Disorders, 1964, Language Development, 1970, Verbal Learning, 1975 (monograph) Auditory Disorders, 1978, Levity, 1980, Stoneskipping, 1989, Bird Cage, 1994, Out of Control, 1999. Pres. faculty senate U. So. Calif., 1987—88. Recipient Outstanding Faculty award, Trojan Fourth Estate, 1982, Pres.' Svc. award, U. So. Calif., 1992. Fellow APA (cert.), AAAS, Am. Speech and Hearing Assn. (legis. coun. 1965-68); mem. Internat. Assn. Scientists. Republican. Methodist. Office: U So Calif University Park Los Angeles CA 90089-0001

WOOD, WILLARD MARK, lawyer; b. Traverse City, Mich., Nov. 30, 1942; s. William Mark and Ebba Forsman Wood; m. Sharon McDermott, June 19, 1965; children: Sean, Pat, Kelly, Ryan, Casey. BA, Santa Clara U., 1964; JD, U. So. Calif., 1967. Bar: Calif., D.C., U.S. Supreme Ct. Judge advocate USMC, Vietnam, 1969-70; ptnr. O'Melveny & Myers, LA, 1971—. Assoc. editor U. So. Calif. Law Review, 1966—67. Capt. USMC, 1967-71, Vietnam. Mem.: DC Bar, LA County Bar Assn., Order of the Coif, ABA, State Bar Calif. (chmn., local disciplinary com.), Phi Delta Phi. Roman Catholic. Office: O'Melveny & Myers 400 S Hope St Ste 1321 Los Angeles CA 90071-2899 Office Phone: 213-430-6220. E-mail: mwood@omm.com.

WOOD, WILLIAM BARRY, III, biologist, educator; b. Balt., Feb. 19, 1938; s. William Barry, Jr. and Mary Lee (Hutchins) W.; m. Marie-Elisabeth Renate Hartisch, June 30, 1961; children: Oliver Hartisch, Christopher Barry. AB, Harvard U., 1959; PhD, Stanford U., 1963. Asst. prof. biology Calif. Inst. Tech., Pasadena, 1965-68, assoc. prof., 1968-69, prof. biology, 1970-77; prof. molecular, cellular and developmental biology U. Colo., Boulder, 1977—, chmn. dept., 1978-83, disting. prof., 2004—. Mem. panel for developmental biology NSF, 1970-72; physiol. chemistry study sect. NIH, 1974-78; mem. com. on sci. and public policy Nat. Acad. Scis., 1979-80; mem. NIH Cellular and Molecular Basis of Disease Rev. Com., 1984-88' mem. bd. sci. edn. Nat Acad. Scis., 2005- Author: (with J. H. Wilson, R.M. Benbow, L.E. Hood) Biochemistry: A Problems Approach, 2d edit., 1981, (with L.E. Hood and J.H. Wilson) Molecular Biology of Eucaryotic Cells, 1975, (with L.E. Hood and I.L. Weissman) Immunology, 1978, (with L.E. Hood, I.L. Weissman and J.H. Wilson) Immunology, 2d edit., 1984, (with L.E. Hood and I.L. Weissman) Concepts in Immunology, 1978; editl. rev. bd. Science, 1984-92; mem. editl. bd. Cell, 1984-87, Developmental Biology, 1995-1999; editor-in-chief, CBE Life Scis. Edn., 2005-; contbr. articles to profl. jours. Recipient U.S. Steel Molecular Biology award, 1969, Alexander von Humboldt Rsch prize, 2004; NIH Rsch. grantee, 1965—, Merit awardee, 1986-96; Guggenheim fellow, 1975-76. Fellow AAAS; mem. Nat. Acad. Scis., Am. Acad. Arts and Scis., Am. Soc. for Cell Biology, Genetics Soc. Am. Soc. for Developmental Biology. Office: Univ Colo Dept MCD Biology 347 UCB Boulder CO 80309

WOOD, WILLIS BOWNE, JR., retired utilities executive; b. Kansas City, Mo., Sept. 15, 1934; s. Willis Bowne Sr. and Mina (Henderson) W.; m. Dixie Gravel, Aug. 31, 1955; children: Bradley, William, Josh. BS in Petroleum Engring., U. Tulsa, 1957; grad. advanced mgmt. prog., Harvard U., 1983. With So. Calif. Gas Co., LA, 1960-74, from v.p. to sr. v.p., 1975-80, exec. v.p., 1983-84; pres., CEO Pacific Lighting Gas Supply Co., LA, 1981-83; from sr. v.p. to chmn., pres., CEO, Pacific Enterprises, LA, 1984-93, chmn., CEO, 1993-98; ret., 1998. Bd. dirs. Automobile Club So. Calif., chmn. bd. dirs., 2005—07, vice chmn., 2007—. Past bd. dirs. LA World Affairs Coun.; past dir., past chmn. bus coun. for Sustainable Energy Future, 1994—; past dir. Pacific Coun. Internat. Affairs; trustee U. So. Calif.; past trustee, past vice-chmn. Harvey Mudd Coll., Claremont, Calif., 1984—2005; trustee emeritus, past chmn. Calif. Med. Ctr. Found., LA, 1983—2002; past trustee, past pres. SW Mus., LA; trustee John and Dora Haynes Found., 1998—. Recipient Disting. Alumni U. Tulsa, 1995; inductee U. Tulsa Engring. Hall of Fame, 2001. Mem. Soc. Petroleum Engrs., Calif. State C. of C. (past bd. dirs.), Am. Automobile Assn. (dir. 1999-2007, chmn. 2002-05), NAM (past bd. dirs.), Calif. Club, Shady Canyon Golf Club. Republican.

WOODALL, DAVID MONROE, engineer, researcher, dean; b. Perryville, Ark., Aug. 2, 1945; m. Linda Carol Page, June 6, 1966; 1 child, Zachary Page. BA, Hendrix Coll., 1967; MS, Columbia U., 1968; PhD, Cornell U., 1976. Registered profl. engr., Idaho. Nuc. engr. Westinghouse Corp., Pitts., 1968-70; asst. prof. U. Rochester, NY, 1974-77, U. N.Mex., Albuquerque, 1977-79, assoc. prof., 1979-83, chair dept., 1980-83, prof., 1984-86; group physics mgr. Idaho Nat. Engring. Lab., Idaho Falls, 1986-92; assoc. dean, dir. rsch. U. Idaho, Moscow, 1992-99, acting dean, 1999; dean coll. sci., engring., math. U. Alaska, Fairbanks, 1999—2003; dir. Ctr. for Nanosensor Tech., 2001—03. Provost & v.p. for academic affairs, Oregon Inst. of Tech., 2003—07, interim pres., 2007-, EAC commr. Accreditation Bd. Engring. Tech., 1990-95, bd. dir., 1997-2003; cons. in field. Contbr. articles to profl. jours. Grantee NSF, DOE, AFOSR, Office Naval Rsch., DMEA, others. Mem. Am. Nuc. Soc. (chpt. chair 1982-83), Am. Soc. Engring. Edn. (divsn. chair 1993, 95, chair engring. rsch. coun., v.p.). Office: Oregon Institute of Technology 3201 Campus Drive Klamath Falls OR 97601 Business E-Mail: david.woodall@oit.edu.

WOODARD, ALFRE, actress; b. Tulsa, Nov. 8, 1953; m. Roderick Spencer, 1983; 2 children. Student, Boston U. Appeared in (films) Remember My Name, 1976, Health, Cross Creek, 1983 (Acad. award nomination), Extremities, 1986, Scrooged, 1988, Mandela, 1988, Miss Firecracker, 1989, Grand Canyon, 1991, The Gun in Betty Lou's Handbag, 1992, Passion Fish, 1992, Heart and Souls, 1993, Rich in Love, 1993, Bopha!, 1993, Blue Chips, 1994, Crooklyn, 1994, How to Make an American Quilt, 1995, Statistically Speaking, 1995, Primal Fear, 1996, A Step Toward Tomorrow, 1996, Stat Trek: First Contact, 1996, Follow Me Home, 1996, Down in the Delta, 1998, Brown Sugar, 1998, Mumford, 1999, What's Cooking, 2000, Love and Basketball, 2000, K-PAX, 2001, Baby of the Family, 2002, (voice) The Wild Thornberrys Movie, 2002, The Singing Detective, 2003, The Core, 2003, Radio, 2003, The Forgotten, 2004, Beauty Shop, 2005, Something New, 2006, The Family That Preys, 2008, (TV series) Tucker's Witch, 1982-83, Sara, 1985, St. Elsewhere, 1985-87, Hill Street Blues (Emmy award for guest appearance in drama series 1984), L.A. Law (Emmy award for guest appearance in drama series 1987), Desperate Housewives (Screen Actors Guild Award for outstanding performance by an ensemble in a comedy series, 2006), 2005-; (TV spls.) For Colored Girls Who Have Considered Suicide/When the Rainbow is Enuf, Trial of the Moke, Words by Heart, (TV films) A Mother's Courage: The Mary Thomas Story, Child Saver, Ambush Murder, Freedom Road, 1979, Sophisticated Gents, 1981, The Killing Floor, Unnatural Causes, 1986, Mandela, 1987, The Child Saver, Sweet Revenge, 1990, Blue Bayou, 1990, Race to Freedom: The Underground Railroad, 1994, Wizard of Oz in Concert, 1995, The Piano Lesson, 1995, Journey to Mars, 1996, Gulliver's Travels, 1996, Member of the Wedding, 1997, Miss Evers' Boys, 1997, Cadillac Desert (miniseries), 1997, Funny Valentines, 1999 (also exec. prodr.), Holiday Heart, 2000, A Wrinkle in Time (miniseries), 2003, The Water is Wide, 2005, others, (plays) For Colored Girls Who Have Considered Suicide, When the Rainbow is Enuf, (off-Broadway plays) A Map of the World, 1985, A Winter's Tale 1989, So Nice They Named Twice, Horatio, What's Cookin', 2000, Love and Basketball, 2000, Dinosaur, 2000. Recipient Emmy awards for guest appearance in drama series, Josephine Premice award for sustained excellence Classical Theatre of Harlem, 2006. Office: Touchstone TV 100 Universal Plz Bldg 2128 Ste G Universal City CA 91608

WOODBRIDGE, JOHN MARSHALL, architect, urban planner; b. NYC, Jan. 26, 1929; s. Frederick James and Catherine (Baldwin) W.; m. Sally Byrne, Aug. 14, 1954 (div. 1975); children: Lawrence F., Pamela B., Diana B. (dec. 2002); m. Carolyn Kizer, Apr. 8, 1975 BA magna cum laude, Amherst Coll., 1951; MFA in Architecture, Princeton U., 1956. Designer John Funk, Arch., San Francisco, 1957-58; designer, assoc. ptnr. Skidmore, Owings & Merrill, San Francisco, 1959-73; staff dir. Pres.'s Adv. Coun. and Pres.'s Temporary Commn. on Pennsylvania Ave., Washington, 1963-65; exec. dir. Pennsylvania Ave. Devel. Corp., Washington, 1973-77. Lectr. architecture U. Calif., Berkeley; vis. prof. U. Oreg., Washington U., St. Louis. Co-author: Buildings of the Bay Area, 1960, A Guide to Architecture in San Francisco and Northern California, 1973, Architecture San Francisco, 1982, San Francisco Architecture, 1992, rev., 2005 Recipient Fed. Design Achievement award Nat. Endowment for Arts, 1988; Fulbright scholar to France, 1951-52. Fellow AIA (emeritus); mem. Nat. Trust Hist. Preservation, Soc. Archtl. Historians, Phi Beta Kappa. Democrat. Episcopalian. Home: 19772 8th St E Sonoma CA 95476-3849

WOODBURY, LAEL JAY, theater educator; b. Fairview, Idaho, July 3, 1927; s. Raymond A. and Wanda (Dawson) W.; m. Margaret Lillian Swenson, Dec. 19, 1949; children: Carolyn Inez (Mrs. Donald Hancock), Shannon Margaret (Mrs. J. Michael Busenbark), Jordan Ray, Lexon Dan. BS, Utah State U., 1952; MA, Brigham Young U., 1953; PhD (Univ. fellow), U. Ill., 1954. Teaching asst. U. Ill., 1953; assoc. prof. Brigham Young U., 1954-61; guest prof. Colo. State Coll., 1962; asst. prof. Bowling Green State U., 1961-62; asso. prof. U. Iowa, 1962-65; producer Ledges Playhouse, Lansing, Mich., 1963-65; prof. speech and dramatics, chmn. dept. Brigham Young U., 1966-70, assoc. dean Coll. Fine Arts and Communications, 1969-73, dean Coll. Fine Arts and Communications, 1973-82. Vis. lectr. abroad; bd. dirs. Eagle Systems Internat.; bd. dir. workshop Fedn. for Asian Cultural Promotion, Republic of China; dir. European study tour. Author: Play Production Handbook, 1959, Mormon Arts, vol. 1, 1972, Mosaic Theatre, 1976, also articles, original dramas; profl. actor PBS and feature films. Chmn. gen. bd. drama com. Young Men's Mut. Improvement Assn., 1958-61; bd. dirs. Repertory Dance Theatre; bd. dirs., chmn. greater ctrl. Utah ARC; chmn. Utah Alliance for Arts Edn.; mem. adv. coun. Utah Arts Festival, Provo City Arts Coun., 2001-; missionary LDS Ch., NYC, 1994. With USN, 1942-46. Recipient Creative Arts award Brigham Young U., 1971, Disting. Alumni award, 1975, Tchr. of Yr. award, 1988, Excellence in Rsch. award, 1992, Disting. Svc. award, 1992, Nat. Arts and Humanities award Nat. Ams. for Arts Orgn., 2006. Mem. Rocky Mountain Theatre Conf. (past pres.), Am. Theatre Assn. (chmn. nat. com. royalties 1972—, mem. fin. com. 1982—), NW Assn. Univs. and Colls. (accrediting officer), Am. Theatre Assn. (v.p. Univ. and Coll. Theatre Assn.), Theta Alpha Phi, Phi Kappa Phi. Home: 1303 Locust Ln Provo UT 84604-3651

WOODEN, JOHN ROBERT, former college basketball coach; b. Martinsville, Ind., Oct. 14, 1910; s. Joshua Hugh and Roxie (Rothrock) W.; m. Nellie C. Riley, Aug. 8, 1932; children: Nancy Anne, James Hugh. BS, Purdue U., 1932; MS, Ind. State U., 1947. Athletic dir., basketball and baseball coach Ind. State Tchrs. Coll., 1946-48; head basketball coach UCLA, 1948-75. Lectr. to colls., coaches, business. Author: Practical Modern Basketball, 1966, They Call Me Coach, 1972; co-author: Wooden--a Lifetime of Reflections and Observations On and Off the Court, 1997, Inch and Miles--Pyramid to Success for Kids, 2004, One on One, 2004; contbr. articles to profl. jours. Served to lt. USNR, 1943-46. Named All-Am. basketball player Purdue U., 1930-32, Coll. Basketball Player Yr., 1932, to All-Time All-Am. Team Helms Athletic Found., 1943, Nat. Basketball Hall of Fame, Springfield (Mass.) Coll., as player, 1960, as coach, 1970, Ind. State Basketball Hall of Fame, 1962, Calif. Father of Yr., 1964, 75, Coach of Yr. U.S. Basketball Writers Assn., 1964, 67, 69, 70, 72, 73, Sportsman of Yr. Sports Illustrated, 1973, GTE Acad. All-Am., 1994, Nat. Collegiate Backetball Hall of Fame, 2006; recipient Whitney Young award Urban League, 1973, 1st ann. Velvet Covered Brick award Layman's Leadership Inst., 1974, 1st ann. Dr. James Naismith Peachbasket award, 1974, Medal of Excellence Bellarmine Coll., 1985, Sportslike Pathfinder award to Hoosier with extraordinary svc. on behalf of Am. youth, 1993, 40 for the Age award Sports Illustrated, 1994, the 1st Frank G. Wells Disney award for role model to youth, 1995, Disting. Am. award Pres. Reagan, 1995, Svc. to Mankind award Lexington Theol. Sem., 1995, NCAA Theodore Roosevelt Sportsman award, 1995, Vince Lombardi award for excellence, 2000, Ind. Legend award, 2000, Presdl. Medal of Freedom, 2003, Pres. Ford award NCAA, 2006; named Basketball Coach of Century, 2000.*

WOODHOUSE, GAY VANDERPOEL, former state attorney general, lawyer; b. Torrington, Wyo., Jan. 8, 1950; d. Wayne Gaylord and Sally (Rouse) Vanderpoel; m. Randy Woodhouse, Nov. 26, 1983; children: Dustin, Houston. BA with honors, U. Wyo., 1972, JD, 1977. Bar: Wyo. 1978, U.S. Dist. Ct. Wyo., U.S. Supreme Ct. Dir. student Legal Svcs., Laramie, Wyo., 1976—77; assoc. Donald Jones Law Offices, Torrington, 1977—78; asst. atty. gen. State of Wyo., Cheyenne, 1978—84, sr. asst. atty. gen., 1984—89, spl. U.S. atty., 1987—89, asst. U.S. atty., 1990—95, chief dept. atty. gen., 1995—98, atty. gen., 1998—2000. Chmn. Wyo. Tel. Consumer Panel, Casper, 1982—86; advisor Cheyenne Halfway House, 1984—93; chmn. Wyo. Silent Witness Initiative Zero Domestic Violence by 2010, 1997, Wyo. Domestic Violence Elimination Coun., 1999—2001; mem. State Bar Commn. First Dist., 2002—05; spl. projects cons. N.Am. Securities Adminstrs. Assn., 1987—89; Chmn. bd. Pathfinder, 1987; S.E. Wyo. Mental Health. Mem.: Wyo. State Bar (pres.-elect 2006—07, pres. 2007—08), Federalist Soc. for Law and Pub.Policy Studies (v.p., Wyo. chpt. 2003—04), Prevent Child Abuse Wyo. (pres. 2004—05), Laramie County Bar Assn., Cheyenne (Wyo.) C. of C., Cheyenne Rotary (bd. dirs.), Toastmasters, Rotary. Republican. Avocations: inline speed skating, stained glass. Office: 123 Capitol Bldg Cheyenne WY 82002-0001 Mailing: PO Box 1888 Cheyenne WY 82003 Office Phone: 307-432-9399. Fax: 307-638-1975. Personal E-mail: gaywoodhouselaw@aol.com. Business E-Mail: Gay@gaywoodhouselaw.com.

WOODLAND, IRWIN FRANCIS, lawyer; b. NYC, Sept. 2, 1922; s. John James and Mary (Hynes) W.; m. Sally Duffy, Sept. 23, 1954; children: Connie, J. Patrick, Stephen, Joseph, William, David, Duffy. BA, Columbia U., 1948; JD, Ohio State U., 1959. Bar: Calif. 1960, Wash., 1991, U.S. Dist. Ct. (cen. dist.) Calif. 1960, U.S. Dist. Ct. (no. dist.) Calif. 1962, U.S. Dist. Ct. (so. dist.) Calif. From assoc. to ptnr. Gibson, Dunn & Crutcher, LA, 1959-88. Bd. dirs. Sunlaw Energy Corp., Vernon, Calif. With USAF, 1942—45, ETO. Mem.: ABA, Wash. State Bar Assn., L.A. Bar Assn., Calif. Bar Assn., Jonathan Club, Phi Delta Phi. Roman Catholic. Address: Gibson Dunn & Crutcher 333 S Grand Ave Ste 4400 Los Angeles CA 90071-1548

WOODLEY, DAVID TIMOTHY, dermatology educator; b. Aug. 11, 1948; s. Raoul Ramos-Mimosa and Marian (Schlueter) W.; m. Christina Paschall Prentice, May 4, 1974; children: David Thatcher, Thomas Colgate, Peter Paschall. AB, Washington U., St. Louis, 1968; MD, U. Mo., 1973. Diplomate Am. Bd. Internal Medicine, Am. Bd. Dermatology, Nat. Bd. Internal Medicine. Intern Beth Israel Med. Ctr., Mt. Sinai Sch. Medicine, N.Y. Hosp., Cornell U. Sch. Medicine, NYC, 1973-74; resident in internal medicine U. Nebr., Omaha, 1974-76; resident in dermatology U. N.C., Chapel Hill, 1976-78, asst. prof. dermatology, 1983-85, assoc. prof. dermatology, 1985-88; prof. medicine, co-chief divsn. dermatology Cornell U. Med. Ctr., NYC, 1988-89; prof., vice chair dept. dermatology Stanford (Calif.) U., 1989-93; prof., chair dept. dermatology Northwestern U., Chgo., 1993-99. Research fellow U. Paris, 1978-80; expert NIH, Bethesda, Md., 1983-89; prof., assoc. chmn. dermatology Stanford U Sch. Medicine, 1989-93; chmn. dermatology Sch. Medicine Northwestern U., 1993-99; prof., chmn. dermatology U. So. Calif., 1999—; mem. study sect. NIH. Contbr. chpts. to books and articles in field to profl. jours. Mem. Potomac Albicore Fleet, Washington, 1982-83, Chapel Hill, 1983—, Jungian Soc. Triangle Area, Chapel Hill, 1983—. Fellow Am. Acad. Dermatology; mem. ACS (assoc.), Dermatology Found., Am. Soc. for Clin. Rsch., Soc. Investigative Dermatology, Assn. Physician Poets, Am. Soc. for Clin. Investigation. Office: U So Calif Keck Sch Medicine Dept Dermatology UC Norris Cancer Ctr Topping Tower 3905 1441 Eastlake Ave Los Angeles CA 90033 Office Phone: 323-865-0983.

WOODLEY, SHAILENE DIANN, actress; b. Simi Valley, Calif., Nov. 15, 1991; d. Loni and Lori Woodley. Actress (TV films) Replacing Dad, 1999, A Place Called Home, 2004, Felicity: An American Girl Adventure, 2005, Once Upon a Mattress, 2005, Final Approach, 2007, (TV series) Crossing Jordan, 2001—04, The O.C., 2003—04, The Secret Life of the American Teenager, 2008, actress (guest appearance) The District, 2001—02, Without a Trace, 2003, Everybody Loves Raymond, 2004, Jack & Bobby, 2004—05, My Name Is Earl, 2006, Close to Home, 2007, CSI: NY, 2007, Cold Case, 2007. Office: c/o Elements Entertainment 1635 North Cahuenga Blvd, 5th Fl Los Angeles CA 90028

WOODRUFF, DIANE CAREY, former academic administrator; b. San Jose, Calif., Dec. 5, 1942; d. Evan Dennis and Dorothy Elizabeth Jelcick; m. D. Thomas Woodruff, July 11, 1998. BA, U. Calif., Berkeley, 1964, EdD, 1979; PhD in Ednl. Adminstrn. and Curriculum and Instruction, U. So. Calif. Asst. supt. State Dept. Edn., Sacramento, 1983; dean Sacramento City Coll., 1983-85; dir. comms. and edn. devel. Los Rios Dist., Sacramento, 1985-88; v.p. Napa Valley Coll., Napa, Calif., 1988-92, supt./pres., 1992; v.p. CC League of Calif., interim pres., CEO; interim chancellor Calif. CC, 2007—08. Author: Motivating and Dissatisfying Factors in a Group Profl. Educators, 1979. Recipient Woman of Yr. award, Calif. Legis., 1996, Leadership Award, Napa Valley Peace Table, 1999, Shirley B. Gordon Internat. Award of Distinction for CC Pres.; named Woman of Distinction in Wine Country, 2000. Mem. Rotary Napa.

WOODRUFF, GENE LOWRY, nuclear engineer, university dean; b. Greenbrier, Ark., May 6, 1934; s. Clarence Oliver and Avie Erscilla (Lowry) W.; m. Marylou Munson, Jan. 29, 1961; children— Gregory John, David Reed BS with honors, U.S. Naval Acad., 1956; MS in Nuclear Engring., MIT, 1963, PhD in Nuclear Engring., 1966. Registered profl. engr., Wash. Asst. prof. nuclear engring. U. Wash., Seattle, 1965-70, assoc. prof., 1970-76, prof., 1976-93, chmn. dept., 1981-84, dir. nuclear engring. labs., 1973-76, dean Grad. Sch., 1984-93, prof. chem. engring. environ. studies, 1989-98, dean emeritus, prof. emeritus, 1998—. Vice-chair, chair-elect Grad. Record Exam., 1991-92, chair, 1992-93; cons. to govt. and industry. Contbr. numerous articles to sci. and tech. jours. Served to lt. USN, 1956-60 Mem. Nat. Soc. Profl. Engrs. (Achievement award 1977), Am. Nuclear Soc. (Achievement award 1977, chmn. honors/awards com. 1981-84, nat. program com. 1971-75, exec. com. fusion div. 1976-80, vice chmn. edn. div. 1983-84, Arthur Holly Compton award 1986), Am. Soc. Engring. Edn., Assn. Grad. Schs. (v.p./pres.-elect 1990-91, pres. 1991-92). Democrat. Home: 2650 S Camano Dr Camano Island WA 98282-6371 E-mail: woodruff@u.washington.edu.

WOODRUFF, KAY HERRIN, pathologist, educator; b. Charlotte, NC, Sept. 22, 1942; d. Herman Keith and Helen Thelma (Tucker) Herrin; m. John T. Lyman, May 3, 1980; children: Robert, Geoffry, Carolyn. BA in Chemistry, Duke U., 1964; MD, Emory U., 1968. Diplomate Am. Bd. Pathology (trustee 1993—, sec. 1998-2000, v.p. 2000-2001, pres. 2001—). Medicine and pediat. intern U. N.C., Chapel Hill, 1968-69, resident in anatomic pathology, 1969-70; chief resident in anatomic pathology, instr. U. Okla., Oklahoma City, 1970-71, fellow in electron microscopy-pulmonary pathology, instr., 1971-72; chief resident in clin. pathology U. Calif., San Francisco, 1972-74, asst. clin. prof. dept. anatomic pathology, 1974-91, assoc. clin. prof., 1991—; chief electron microscopy VA Hosp., San Francisco, 1974-75; pvt. practice, San Pablo, Calif., 1981—. Pres. med. staff Brookside Hosp., San Pablo, 1994, med. dir. Regional Cancer Ctr., 1995-98; assoc. pathologist Children's Hosp., San Francisco, 1979-81, St. Joseph's Hosp., San Francisco, 1977-79; cons. pathologist Lawrence Berkeley (Calif.) Lab., 1974-93; med. dir. Bay Area Tumor Inst. Tissue Network, San Pablo, 1989—; asst. clin. prof. pathology health and med. scis. program U. Calif., Berkeley and U. Calif., San Francisco Joint Med. Program, 1985-91, assoc. clin. prof., 1991—, others. Contbr. articles and abstracts to med. jours. Mem. exec. bd. Richmond (Calif.) Quits Smoking, 1986-90, Bay Area Tumor Inst., Oakland, Calif., 1987—; mem. exec. bd. Contra Costa unit Am. Cancer Soc., Walanut Creek, Calif., 1985-87, mem. profl. edn. com., 1985-90, mem. pub. edn. com., 1985-86, mem. task force on breast health Calif. div., 1992-93; mem. transfusion adv. com. Irwin Meml. Blood Bank, San Francisco, 1977-83; chmn. transfusion adv. com. Alameda Contra County Blood Bank, 1989-92; commr. Calif. Bd. Med. Quality Assurance, 1978-80; pres. Brookside Found., San Pablo, Calif., 1998-2000. Recipient young investigator award Am. Lung Assn., 1975-77; Outstanding Svc. awards Am. Cancer Soc., 1986, 87, Disting. Svc. award, 1988; Disting. Clin. Tchg. award U. Calif., San Francisco and Berkeley Joint Med. Program, 1987, Outstanding Tchg. award, 1988, Excellence in Basic Sci. Instrn. award, 1990, Excellence in Tchr. Clin. Scis. award, 1993; cert. of recognition Cmty. Svc. Richmond, 1989. Mem. AMA, Coll. Am. Pathologists (editl. bd. CAP Today 1986-90, bd. govs. 1990-96, chmn. coun. on practice mgmt. 1994, William Kuhn award for outstanding comm. 1996, Presdl. Medal of Honor 1995, 96), Am. Med. Women's Assn. (exec. bd. 1984-87, regional bd. govs. 1984-87), No. Calif. Women's Med. Assn. (pres. 1982-84), Calif. Soc. Pathologists (bd. dirs. 1988-90), No. Calif. Oncology Group, South Bay Pathology Soc. (pres. 1987), Am. Assn. Blood Banks, Calif. Med. Assn., Alameda-Contra Costa County Med. Soc., Am. Soc. Clin. Pathology, Calif. Pathology Soc. Avocations: classical music, music. Office: Doctors Med Ctr 2000 Vale Rd San Pablo CA 94806-3808

WOODS, DUANE C., waste management executive; b. Spokane, Wash., 1951; BA, U. Wash., Seattle, 1973; JD, U. Puget Sound, Tacoma, Wash., 1980. Bar: Wash. 1980. Asst. sec. State of Wash.; local and state policy and mgmt. positions City of Seattle; ptnr. Heller, Erhman White & McAuliffe and Summit Law Group; v.p., gen. counsel Western Group Waste Mgmt., Inc., Houston, sr. v.p. Western Group. Mem.: Phi Beta Kappa. Office: Waste Mgmt Inc 7025 N Scottsdale Rd Ste 200 Scottsdale AZ 85253 Office Fax: 480-624-8400, 866-863-7960.

WOODS, GRANT, lawyer, former state attorney general; b. Elk City, Okla., May 19, 1954; m. Marlene Galán; children: Austin, Lauren, Cole, Dylan. BA, Occidental Coll., 1976; JD, Ariz. State U., 1979. Atty. gen. State of Ariz., Phoenix, 1990-99; ptnr. Goldstein, McGroder & Woods Ltd., Phoenix, 1999-2000; pvt. practice Phoenix, 2000—; of counsel Leonard, Clancy & McGovern. Founder Mesa Boys and Girls Club. Mem. State Bar Ariz., Ariz. Trial Lawyers Assn. Republican. Office: Grant Woods PC 1726 N 7th St Phoenix AZ 85006-2205*

WOODS, JAMES C., museum director; Dir. Herrett Ctr. Arts and Sci. and Faulkner Planetarium, Twin Falls, Idaho. Office: Coll Southern Idaho Herrett Ctr Arts & Sci 315 Falls Ave Twin Falls ID 83301-3367

WOODS, JAMES STERRETT, toxicologist; b. Lewistown, Pa., Feb. 26, 1940; s. James Sterrett and Jane Smith (Parker) W.; m. Nancy Fugate, Dec. 20, 1969; 1 dau., Erin Elizabeth. AB, Princeton U., 1962; MS, U. Wash., 1968, PhD, 1970; MPH, U. N.C., 1978. Diplomate Am. Bd. Toxicology. Rsch. assoc. dept. pharmacology Yale U. Sch.

Medicine, New Haven, 1970-72; staff fellow environ. toxicology. Nat. Inst. Environ. Health Scis. br. NIH, Research Triangle Park, NC, 1972-75, head biochem. toxicology sect., 1975-77; sr. rsch. leader environ. occupl. health risk evaluation Battelle Ctrs. for Pub. Health Rsch. and Evaluation, Seattle, 1978—2006; prof. U. Wash., Seattle, 1979—. Pres. Am. Bd. Toxicology, 1997-98. Contbr. articles to profl. jours. With USN, 1962-66. Scholar USPHS, 1966-70; Fellow Am. Cancer Soc., 1970-72. Mem. AAAS, Am. Assn. Cancer Rsch., Am. Soc. Pharmacology and Exptl. Therapeutics, Pacific NW Assn. Toxicologists (founding pres.), Soc. Epidemiology Rsch., Soc. Toxicology, Am. Coll. of Epidemiology, Am. Bd. Toxicology (pres. 1997-98). Home: 4525 E Laurel Dr NE Seattle WA 98105-3838 Office: Univ Wash Ste 100 4225 Roosevelt Way NE Seattle WA 98105 Office Phone: 206-685-3443. Business E-Mail: jwoods@u.washington.edu.

WOODS, LAWRENCE MILTON, airline company executive; b. Manderson, Wyo., Apr. 14, 1932; s. Ben Ray and Katherine (Youngman) Woods; m. Joan Frances Van Patten, June 10, 1952; 1 child, Laurie. B.Sc. with honors, U. Wyo., 1953; MA, N.Y. U., 1973, PhD, 1975; LL.D., Wagner Coll., 1973. CPA Colo., Mont.; bar: Mont. 1957. Acct. Peat, Marwick, Mitchell & Co. (C.P.A.'s), Billings, Mont., 1953; supervisory auditor Army Audit Agy., Denver, 1954-56; acct. Mobil Producing Co., Billings, Mont., 1956-59; planning analyst Socony Mobil Oil Co., NYC, 1959-63, planning mgr., 1963-65; v.p. N.Am. divsn. Mobil Oil Corp., NYC, 1966-67, gen. mgr. planning and econs. N.Am. divsn., 1967-69, v.p. N.Am. divsn., 1969-77, exec. v.p. N.Am. divsn., 1977-85, also dir. N.Am. divsn.; pres., CEO, dir. Centennial Airlines, Inc., 1985-87. Bd. dirs., chmn. The Heartland Funds, 2005. Author: Accounting for Capital, Construction and Maintenance Expeditures, 1967, The Wyoming Country Before Statehood, 1971, Sometimes the Books Froze, 1985, Moreton Frewen's Western Adventures, 1986, British Gentlemen in the Wild West, 1989; co-author: Takeover, 1980; editor: Wyoming Biographies, 1991, Wyoming's Big Horn Basin, 1996, Agent R, 2000, John Clay, Jr., 2001, Asa Shinn Mercer, 2003, A Material Witness, 2003, Alex Swan, 2006; contbr. Accountants' Encyclopedia, 1962; editor: Edward Shelley's Journal, 2005. With US Army, 1953—55. Mem.: AICPA, ABA, Mont. Bar Assn. Republican. Lutheran. Office: High Plains Pub Co PO Box 1860 Worland WY 82401-1860

WOODS, NANCY FUGATE, dean, women's health nurse, educator; BS, Wis. State U., 1968; MSN, U. Wash., 1969; PhD, U. N.C., 1978. Staff nurse Sacred Heart Hosp., Wis., 1968, Univ. Hosp., Wis., 1969-70, St. Francis Cabrini Hosp., 1970; nurse clinician Yale-New Haven Hosp., 1970-71; instr. nursing Duke U., Durham, N.C., 1971-72, from instr. to assoc. prof., 1972-78; assoc. prof. physiology U. Wash., Seattle, 1978-82, prof. physiology, 1982-84, chairperson dept. parent and child nursing, 1984-90, prof. dept. parent and child nursing, 1990—, dean Sch. Nursing, 1998—; dir. Ctr. Women's Health Rsch., U. Wash., Seattle, 1989—. Pres. scholar U. Calif., San Francisco, 1985-86. Contbr. articles to profl. jours. Fellow ANA, Am. Acad. Nursing, Inst. Medicare, N.A.S.; mem. AAUP, APHA, Am. Coll. Epidemiology, Soc. Menstrual Cycle Rsch. (v.p. 1981-82, pres. 1983-85), Soc. Advancement Women's Health Rsch. Office: U Wash Sch Nursing PO Box 357260 Seattle WA 98195-7260

WOODS, SANDRA KAY, real estate executive; b. Loveland, Colo., Oct. 11, 1944; d. Ivan H. and florence L. (Betz) Harris; m. Gary A. Woods, June 11, 1967; children: Stephanie Michelle, Michael Harris. BA, U. Colo., 1966, MA, 1967. Personnel mgmt. specialist CSC, Denver, 1967; asst. to regional dir. HEW, Denver, 1968-69; urban renewal rep. HUD, Denver, 1970-73, dir. program analysis, 1974-75, asst. regional dir. cmty. planning and devel., 1976-77, regional dir. fair housing, 1978-79; mgr. ea. facility project Adolph Coors Co., Golden, Colo., 1980, dir. real estate, 1981, v.p. chief environ. health and safety officer, 1982-96, v.p. strategic selling initiatives, 1996—2000; pres. Woods Properties LLP, Golden, 2000—. Mem. Exec. Exch., The White House, 1980. Bd. dirs. Golden Local Devel. Corp., 1981-82; fundraising dir. Coll. Arts and Scis., U. Colo., boulder, 1982-89, U. Colo.found.; mem. exec. bd. NCCJ, Denver, 1982-94; v.p. women in bus. Inc., Denver, 1982-83; mem. steering com. 1984 Yr. for All Denver Women, 1983-84; mem. 10th dist. Denver br. Fed. Res. Bd., 1990-96, chmn. bd., 1995-96; bd. dirs. Nat. Jewish Hosp., 1994—; chmn. Greater Denver Corp., 1991—. Named one of Outstanding Young Women Am., U.S. Jaycees, 1974, 78, Fifty Women to Watch, Businessweek, 1987, 92, Woman of Achievement YWCA, 1988. Mem. Indsl. Devel. Resources Coun. (bd. dirs. 1986-89), Am. Mgmt. Assn., Denver C. of C. (bd. dirs. 1988-96, Disting. Young Exec. award 1974, mem. Leadership Denver, 1976-77), Colo. Women's Forum, Nat. Assn. Office and Indsl. Park Developers (sec. 1988, treas. 1989), Committee of 200 (v.p. 1994-95), Phi Beta Kappa, Pi Alpha Alpha, PEO Club (Loveland). Republican. Presbyterian. E-mail: sandrawoods@qwest.net.

WOODSIDE, D. B. (DAVID BRYAN WOODSIDE), actor; b. Queens, NY, July 25, 1969; BA, SUNY, Albany; MFA, Yale U. Sch. Drama. Actor: (TV series) Murder One, 1996—97, The Division, 2001, Buffy the Vampire Slayer, 2002—03, 24, 2003—07; (TV miniseries) Murder One: Diary of a Serial Killer, 1997; (TV films) The Temptations, 1998, After All, 1999, Flashpoint, 2002, The Law & Mr. Lee, 2003; (films) Scar City, 1998, Romeo Must Die, 2000, More Dogs Than Bones, 2000, Something More, 2003, Easy, 2003; (plays) The Conscientious Objector, 2008; writer, dir., prodr., actor (films) First, 2007.

WOODSOME, EDWIN VALENTINE, JR., lawyer; AB summa cum laude, Holy Cross Coll., 1968; JD magna cum laude, Harvard U., 1971. Bar: Mass. 1972, Calif. 1973, D.C. 1973. Law clk. to Hon. James R. Browning US Ct. Appeals (9th cir.), 1971—72; ptnr. Orrick, Herrington & Sutcliffe LLP, LA, 2003—. Mem.: State Bar Calif., D.C. Bar, ABA (litig. sect., environ. sect., employment sect.), L.A. County Bar Assn. Office: Orrick Herrington & Sutcliffe LLP 777 S Figueroa St Ste 3200 Los Angeles CA 90017 Office Phone: 213-612-2398. Business E-Mail: ewoodsome@orrick.com.

WOODSON, RODERICK KEVIN, sportscaster, football coach, retired professional football player; b. Fort Wayne, Ind., Mar. 10, 1965; Attended, Purdue U., West Lafayette, Ind. Cornerback Pitts. Steelers, 1987—96, San Francisco 49ers, 1997, Balt. Ravens, 1998—2002, Oakland Raiders, 2002—04; ret.; defensive secondary coach Valley Christian Sr. High, Dublin, Calif.; analyst, NFL Total Access NFL Network. Named 1st Team All-Pro, AP, 1989, 1990, 1992—94, 2002, Defensive Player of Yr., 1993; named to Am. Football Conf. Pro Bowl Team, NFL, 1989—94, 1996, 1999—2002, NFL 75th Anniversary All-Time Team, 1994, Pro Football Hall of Fame, 2009. Achievements include leading the NFL in: yards per kick return, 1989; kick off returns, 1991; interceptions, 1999, 2002; member of Super Bowl XXXV winning Baltimore Ravens, 2001. Office: Valley Christian Sr High 7500 Inspiration Dr Dublin CA 94568*

WOODWARD, JACKIE, marketing professional; B in Journalism, U. Mo., Columbia, 1987. Acct. supr. GolinHarris (subs. Interpublic Grp.), 1983—87; gen. mgr. consumer products UltimateBid.com, 2000—01; v.p. global mktg. McDonald's Corp., 2001—06; v.p. media/mktg. svcs. Miller Brewing Co., 2006—08, MillerCoors LLC (merger of Miller and Coors Brewing Cos.), 2008—. Mem.: Media & Entertainment Profls. Office: MillerCoors LLC Hdqs 1225 17th St Denver CO 80202 Office Phone: 303-279-6565. Office Fax: 303-277-5415.

WOODWARD, JOAN B., science association director; BS magna cum laude, U. Mo.; MS in engring. econ. systems, Stanford U.; PhD in mech. engring., U. Calif. With Sandia Nat. Labs., Albuquerque, 1974, dir., Environ. Progs. Ctr., leader material support group, nat. security and weapons progs., mgr., Neutron Generator and Explosives Component Ctr., v.p., Energy, Info., and Infrastructure Tech. Div., currently exec. v.p., dep. dir. Chair lab. mgmt. coun. for Mission and Risk Mgmt. Oversight Sandia Nat. Labs., responsible for ind. assessment of weapons' safety, security, and reliability; bd. mem. Intelligence Sci. Bd (ISB), Congl. Commn. to assess vulnerabilities of US infrastructure to Electromagnetic Pulse; mem. Army Sci. Bd (ASB) study on Force Protection, Defense Sci. Bd. (DSB) study on Homeland Security; co-chair Nat. Reconnaissance Office Bd. (NRO) for Nat. Space Security (NSS); served Nat. Acad. Study on S&T for countering Terrorism. Mem. adv. coun. Kirtland Hon. Comdrs.; mem. bd. adv. Family Security Group, Ctr. for Security Policy; bd. dirs. Bosque Sch., Greater Albuquerque C. of C. Mem.: U. N.Mex Sch. Engring. Bd. of Visitors, U. Mo.-Rolla Dean's Bd. Visitors, N.Mex Women's Forum, Soc. Women Engrs. (life), Phi Kappa Phi. Office: Sandia Nat Labs PO Box 5800, Mail Stop 0102 Albuquerque NM 87185-0102

WOODWARD, LESTER RAY, lawyer; b. Lincoln, Nebr., May 24, 1932; s. Wendell Smith and Mary Elizabeth (Theobald) W.; m. Marianne Martinson, Dec. 27, 1958; children: Victoria L. Woodward Eisele, Richard T., David M., Andrew E. BSBA, U. Nebr., 1953; LLB, Harvard U., 1957; LLD (hon.), Bethany Coll., 1974. Bar: Colo., 1957. Assoc. Davis, Graham & Stubbs, Denver, 1957-59, 60-62, ptnr., 1962—2004, sr. counsel, 2004—. Teaching fellow Sch. Law Harvard U., 1959-60. Bd. dirs. Bethany Coll., Lindsborg, Kans., 1966-74, 87-95, chmn., 1989-92; bd. dirs. Pub. Edn. Coalition, Denver, 1985-92, chmn., 1988-89; mem. Colo. Commn. Higher Edn., Denver, 1977-86, chmn., 1979-81; mem. bd. edn. Denver Pub. Schs., 1999-2005, pres., 2003-05. Mem. ABA, Colo. Bar Assn., Am. Law Inst. Republican. Lutheran. Home: 680 Bellaire St Denver CO 80220-4935 Home Phone: 303-322-8758; Office Phone: 303-892-7392. Business E-Mail: les.woodward@dgslaw.com.

WOODWARD, STEPHEN RICHARD, newspaper reporter; b. Fukuoka City, Japan, July 27, 1953; came to U.S., 1954; s. Leonard Edwin and Etsuko (Okumura) W.; m. Sandra Elizabeth Richardson, Dec. 31, 1979; children: Daniel Joseph, Elizabeth Etsuko. BA in English, Wright State U., 1975; MA in Journalism, U. Mo., 1979. Advt. coordinator Wright State U., Dayton, Ohio, 1976-77; reporter Kansas City (Mo.) Star, 1979-82; assoc. editor then editor Kansas City Bus. Jour., 1982-83; editor then gen. mgr. Portland (Oreg.) Bus. Jour., 1984-86; exec. bus. editor The Hartford (Conn.) Courant, 1986-87; editor San Francisco Bus. Times, 1987-88; bus. editor The Oregonian, Portland, 1989-93, reporter, 1993—. Recipient 1st Place Investigative Reporting award Assn. Area Bus. Publs., 1983, 1st Place Column Writing award Assn. Area Bus. Publs., 1985. Mem. Investigative Reporters and Editors Inc. Avocations: astronomy, chess, creative writing. Office: The Oregonian 1320 SW Broadway Portland OR 97201-3499

WOODWORTH, PATRICIA, museum administrator; BA, U. Md., 1977. With US Dept. Health and Human Services, Washington, Office Mgmt. and Budget, Washington; dir. office planning and budget State of Fla., Tallahassee, 1988—90; dir. dept. mgmt. and budget State of Mich., Lansing, 1990—95; budget dir., policy advisor State of NY, Albany, 1995—98; v.p., CFO U. Chgo., 1998—2002; exec. v.p. fin. and adminstrn., CFO Art Inst. Chgo., 2002—07; v.p., CFO, COO The J. Paul Getty Trusts, LA, 2007—. Particiapant Harvard Program State and Local Execs., 1987. Bd. mem. Nat. Assn. Legis. Fiscal Officers, 1986—87; pres. Midwestern Assn Legis. Fiscal Officers, 1986—87. Recipient Spl. Performance award, Dept. Health and Human Services, 1983, The White House, 1984, 1985; named Floridian the Month, Fla. League Cities, 1988; fellow, Coun. State Govts., 1986. Office: The J Paul Getty Trust 1200 Getty Center Dr Los Angeles CA 90049-1679 Office Phone: 310-440-7300.

WOO HO, DOREEN WOO, bank executive; b. Australia, 1946; m. James Ho; 3 children. BA in East Asian Studies, Smith Coll., 1968; MA in East Asian Studies & Chinese History, Columbia U. Corr. TIME mag., Phnom Penh, Cambodia, 1972—73; with Citibank, 1974—98; pres. consumer credit group Wells Fargo & Co., San Francisco, 1998—, pres. corp. trust services, 2004—. Mem. exec. com. Wells Fargo Diversity Coun. Bd. dirs. San Francisco Opera Assn., 2001—, v.p. treas., exec. com. mem., chair audit com., vice chair dir. & officers com., fin. adv. com.; co-founder Asian Pacific Islander Am. Scholarship Fund; mem. Com. of 100, 2005—. Recipient Fin. Woman of Yr., San Francisco Fin. Women's Assn., 2004; named one of The Bay Area's 100 Most Influential Women, The San Francisco Bus. Times, 2005, The 25 Most Powerful Women in Banking, US Banker mag., 2005—07. Avocation: opera. Office: Wells Fargo & Co 420 Montgomery St San Francisco CA 94163 Mailing: San Francisco Opera Assn 301 Van Ness Ave San Francisco CA 94102

WOOKEY, JOHN, former computer software company executive; b. Seattle; married; 3 children. BS in Econs. and Math., U. Calif., Berkeley, MS in Engring. Scis. Various mgmt. positions Anderson Consulting, Williams & Burrows, Inc.; v.p. devel. Ross Systems, 1987—95; v.p. fin. applications products Oracle Corp., Redwood Shores, Calif., 1995—99, sr. v.p. fin. applications products, 1999—2000, sr. v.p. applications devel., 2000—07.

WOOLEY, JESSICA, state legislator; b. Scottsdale, Ariz., 1968; m. David Henkin; 2 children. BA in Econ., U. Calif., Santa Cruz, 1990; MS in Agrl. & Resource Econ., U. Calif., Berkeley, 1995; JD, U. Calif Boalt Hall Sch. Law, Berkeley, 1997. Atty. Hawaii Legal Aid Soc., 1998—2000; rsch. assoc. U. Hawaii, Manoa, 1999; dep. atty. gen. State of Hawaii, 2000—03; mem. Dist. 47 Hawaii House of Reps., 2008—. Mem. Reserve Adv. Coun. Northwest Hawaiian Islands, 2001—08; steering com. mem. O'ahu Land Trust, 2008. Mem.: Hawaii Bicycling League (bd. mem. 2007—08). Democrat. Office: State Capitol 415 S Beretania St Rm 327 Honolulu HI 96813 Office Phone: 808-586-8540, 808-586-8544. Business E-Mail: repwooley@capitol.hawaii.gov.

WOOLF, MICHAEL E., lawyer; b. Phoenix, Mar. 17, 1949; BS, Ariz. State U., 1971, JD cum laude, 1974. Bar: ariz. 1974. Ptnr. O'Connor, Cavanagh, Anderson, Killingsworth & Beshears, P.A., Phoenix, 1977-99, Mariscal Weeks McIntyre & Friedlander PA, Phoenix, 1999—. Mem. ABA, Maricopa County Bar Assn., State Bar Ariz. Office: Mariscal Weeks McIntyre & Friedlander PA 2901 N Central Ave Ste 200 Phoenix AZ 85012-2705

WOOLFENDEN, JAMES MANNING, nuclear medicine physician, educator; b. LA, Nov. 8, 1942; BA with distinction, Stanford U., 1964; MD, U. Wash., 1968. Diplomate Am. Bd. Nuclear Medicine (chmn. credentials com. 1993-94, vice chmn. exams. com. 1993-95, chmn. exam. com. 1995-96, sec. 1994-96, chmn. 1996-97, life mem.), Nat. Bd. Med. Examiners. Med. intern L.A. County-U. So. Calif. Med. Ctr., 1968-69; med. resident West L.A. VA Med. Ctr., 1969-70; nuclear medicine resident L.A. County-U. So. Calif. Med. Ctr., 1972-74; from asst. prof. radiology to assoc. prof. radiology U. Ariz., Tucson, 1974-84, prof. radiology, 1984—2007, prof. emeritus. Med. staff Univ. Med. Ctr., Tucson, 1974-2007; cons. VA Med. Ctr., 1974-2007; cons. med. staff Tucson Med. Ctr., 1975-2004, Carondelet St. Joseph's Hosp., 1974-98, St. Mary's Hosp., Tucson, 1976-90; mem. Nat. Cancer Inst. site visit team NIH, 1976, mem. NHLB Inst. site visit team NIH, 1976, mem. diagnostic radiology study sect., 1989-97, chmn., 1995-97; med. liaison officer network EPA, 1983-85; cons.-tchg. med. staff Kino Cmty. Hosp., 1984-94; med. officer Clin. Ctr., NIH, Bethesda, 1984-85; mem. Ariz. Cancer Ctr., U. Ariz., 1988—, sr. clin. scientist Univ. Heart Ctr., 1990—; Ariz. bd. regents U. Ariz. Presdl. Search Com., 1990-91; chmn. Ariz. Atomic Energy Commn., 1979-80, Ariz. Radiation Regulatory Hearing Bd., 1981—; bd. dirs. Calif. Radioactive Materials Mgmt. Forum, chmn., 1994-95, Western Forum Edn. in Safe Disposal of Low-Level Radioactive Waste, 1990-2000, vice chmn., 1991-92, chmn., 1992-94. Manuscript reviewer: Noninvasive Med. Imaging, 1983-84, Jour. Nuclear Medicine, 1985—, Investigative Radiology, 1989-94, Archives of Internal Medicine, 1990—; contbr. book chpts.: Diagnostic Nuclear Medicine, 2d edit., 1988, Adjuvant Therapy of Cancer, 1977, Fundamentals of Nuclear Medicine, 1988, others; contbr. articles to profl. jours. Mem. Am. Heart Assn. Coun. on Cardiovasc. Radiology. Maj. U.S. Army, 1970-72, Vietnam. Fellow Am. Coll. Nuc. Physicians (long range planning com. 1981-83, govt. affairs com. 1984-94, exec. com. 1987-91, sec. 1989-91, parliamentarian 1991-95, treas. 1996-98, publs. com. 1993-98, chmn. publs. com. 1993-94, pres.-elect 1998-99, pres. 1999-2000, others); mem. AMA (diagnostic and therapeutic tech. assessment reference panel 1982-98), Am. Nuc. Soc., Soc. Nuc. Medicine (com. on audit 1992-99, trustee 1992-96, ho. dels. 1996-2003, fin. com. 1996-99, bd. dirs. 1997-99, bronze medal for sci. exhibit 1984, bd. dirs., sec.-treas. So. Calif. chpt. 1993-95, pres.-elect 1995-96, pres. 1996-99), Assn. Univ. Radiologists, Ariz. Med. Assn., European Assn. Nuc. Medicine, Pima County Med. Soc., Radiol. Soc. N.Am., Acad. Molecular Imaging, Soc. for Molecular Imaging. Office: Ariz Health Scis Ctr Radiology Rsch 1501 N Campbell Ave Tucson AZ 85724-5067

WOOLHISER, DAVID ARTHUR, hydrologist; b. LaCrosse, Wis., Jan. 21, 1932; s. Algie Duncan and Blanche Lenore (Jasperson) W.; m. Kathryn Brown, Apr. 21, 1957; children: Carl David, Curt Fredric, Lisa Kathryn. BS in Agriculture, U. Wis., Madison, 1955, BSCE, 1955, PhD, 1962; MS, U. Ariz., 1959. Instr. U. Ariz., Tucson, 1955-58; hydraulic engr. Agrl. Rsch. Svc. USDA, Madison, Wis., 1959-61, Columbia, Mo., 1961-63; asst. prof. Cornell U., Ithaca, N.Y., 1963-67; rsch. hydraulic engr. Agrl. Rsch. Svc., Ft. Collins, Colo., 1967-81, Tucson, 1981-91, collaborator, 1991-92. Vis. scientist Inst. Hydrology, Wallingford, Eng., 1977-78; vis. prof. Imperial Coll., London, 1977-78; faculty affiliate Colo. State U., 1967-84; adj. prof. U. Ariz., 1981-92; vis. prof. Va. Poly. Inst. and State U., 1992; sr. rsch. sci. Colo. State U., 1993-94, faculty affiliate, 1994—; vis. prof. U. Córdoba, Spain, 1993-94, 96. Contbr. articles to profl. jours. Recipient disting. svc. citation Coll. Engring. U. Wis., Madison, 1991, Feb. Lab. Consortium award for excellence in tech. transfer, 1998, Ray K. Linsley award Am. Inst. Hydrology, 2000 Fellow Am. Geophys. Union (Robert E. Horton award 1983); mem. NAE, ASCE (Hunter Rouse lectr. 1994, arid lands hydraulic engring. award 1988, Ven Te Chow award 2004). Office: 2833 Sunstone Dr Fort Collins CO 80525 Personal E-mail: woolhiserd@aol.com.

WOOLLATT, PAUL G., financial company executive; COO Downey Fin. Corp., Newport Beach, Calif., 1998—. Office: Downey Fin Corp 3501 Jamboree Rd Newport Beach CA 92660

WOOLLS, ESTHER BLANCHE, library science educator; b. Louisville, Mar. 30, 1935; d. Arthur William and Esther Lennie (Smith) Sutton; m. Donald Paul Woolls, Oct. 21, 1953 (div. Nov. 1982); 1 son, Arthur Paul AB in Fine Arts, Ind. U., 1958, MA in Libr. Sci., 1962, PhD in Libr. Sci., 1973. Elem. libr. Hammond (Ind.) Pub. Schs., 1958-65, libr. coord., 1965-67, Roswell (N.Mex.) Ind. Schs., 1967-70; prof. libr. sci. U. Pitts., 1973-97; prof., dir. Sch. Lib. and Info. Sci. San Jose (Calif.) State U., 1997—2005; consulting editor Librs. Unlimited, Glendale, Calif., 2005—. Exec. dir. Beta Phi Mu, 1981-95. Author: The School Library Media Manager, 1995, 3d edit., 2004, So You're Going to Run a Library, 1995, Ideas for School Library Media Centers, 1996, Whole School Library Handbook, 2004; co-author: Information Literacy, 1999; editor: Continuing Professional Education and IFLA: Past, Present, and a Vision for the Future, 1993, Delivering Lifelong Continuing Professional Education Across Space and Time, 2001. Fulbright scholar, 1995-96; recipient Disting. Svc. award Pa. Sch. Librs. Assn., 1993. Mem. ALA (mem. coun. 1985-89, 95—2003), Am. Assn. Sch. Librs. (bd. dirs. 1983-88, pres. 1993-94, Disting. Svc. award 1997), Pa. Learning Resources Assn. (pres. 1984-85), Internat. Assn. Sch. Librs. (pres. 1998-2001), Internat. Fedn. Libr. Assns. (mem. standing com. sch. librs. sect. 1991-99, sec. Continuing Profl. Edn. Round Table 2000—). Office: Libraries Unlimited 2040 Verdugo Blvd Glendale CA 91208

WOOLRIDGE, ORLANDO, former professional basketball and Olympic coach; Profl. player Chgo. Bulls, 1981, N.J. Nets, L.A. Lakers, 1988-90, Denver Nuggets, Detroit Pistons, Milw. Bucks, Phila. 76ers, 1993-94; asst. coach L.A. Sparks, 1997-98, head coach, 1998-99; asst. coach USA Women's Basketball, 1999—. Cons. L.A.

Sparks. Coach various recreational leagues, asst. girls coach Harvard-Westlake H.S., Studio City, Calif. Office: USA Basketball 5465 Mark Dabling Blvd Colorado Springs CO 80918

WOOLSEY, LYNN C., United States Representative from California; b. Seattle, Nov. 3, 1937; 4 children. Student, U. Wash.; BS, U. San Francisco, 1981. Mgr. human resources Harris Digital Telephone, 1969—80; owner Woolsey Personnel Svs., 1980—92; mem. US Congress from 6th Calif. dist., 1993—, asst. whip, 1993—, mem. edn. & labor com., fgn. affairs com., internat. affairs com., sci. & tech. com. Mem. Petaluma City Coun., 1984—92, vice mayor, 1986, 91; founding mem. Missing & Exploited Children's Caucus; mem. Afterschool Caucus, Child Care Caucus, Congl. Friends of Animals, Congl. Human Rights Caucus, Congl. Task Force Internat. HIV/AIDS, Internat. Workers Rights Caucus, Intelligent Transp. Sys. Caucus, Livable Cmyts. Task Force, Sonoma County Commn. Status of Women; co-chair Congl. Progressive Caucus, Dem. Caucus Task Force Welfare Reform, Edn. Task Force Calif. Delegation Bipartisan Caucus; chair Dem. Caucus Task Force Children & Families. Mem.: NOW, LWV, Sierra Club. Democrat. Office: US Ho Reps 2263 Rayburn Ho Office Bldg Washington DC 20515-0506 Address: Santa Rosa Dist Office Ste 200 1101 Coll Ave Santa Rosa CA 95404 also: San Rafael Dist Office Ste 354 1050 Northgate Dr San Rafael CA 94903 Office Phone: 202-225-5161.

WOOSLEY, ANNE I., cultural organization administrator; Dir. The Amerind Found., Inc., Dragoon, Ariz. Office: The Amerind Found Inc PO Box 400 2100 N Amerind Rd Dragoon AZ 85609

WOOSTER, WARREN S(CRIVER), marine science educator; b. Westfield, Mass., Feb. 20, 1921; s. Harold Abbott and Violet (Scriver) W.; m. Clarissa Pickles, Sept. 13, 1948; children: Susan Wooster Allen, Daniel, Dana. Sc.B., Brown U., 1943; MS, Calif. Inst. Tech., 1947; PhD, UCLA, 1953. From research asst. to prof. Scripps Instn. Oceanography, U. Calif., 1948-73; dir. UNESCO Office Oceanography, 1961-63; dean Rosenstiel Sch. Marine Atmospheric Sci., U. Miami, 1973-76; prof. marine studies and fisheries U. Wash., Seattle, 1976-91, prof. emeritus, 1992, dir. Inst. Marine Studies, 1979-82. Contbr. to books, profl. jours. Served with USNR, 1943-46. Fellow Am. Geophys. Union, Am. Meterol. Soc.; mem. Sigma Xi. Business E-Mail: wooster@u.washington.edu.

WOOTEN, CECIL AARON, retired religious organization administrator; b. Laurel, Miss., June 3, 1924; s. Cecil A. and Alice (Cox) W.; m. Helen Moss, Apr. 4, 1947; children: Michael, Margaret, Martin, Marsha, Mark. BS in Mech. Engring, U. Ala., 1949. With CBI Industries, 1941—83, bd. dirs., 1965-83, mng. dir. CBI Constructors Ltd., London, 1957-62, mgr. Houston sales dist., 1962-64, v.p. engring., 1964—68, v.p., mgr. corp. svcs. Oak Brook, Ill., 1968-69, sr. v.p.-gen. sales mgr., 1969-78; sr. v.p. comml. devel. Chgo. Bridge & Iron Co. (subs. CBI Industries), 1978-79; sr. v.p. corp. adminstrn. CBI Industries, Oak Brook, 1980-83; dir. devel. Christian Family Services, Gainesville, Fla., 1983-86, Denver Ch. of Christ, 1986-88, Boston Ch. of Christ, 1988-92; pres. Internat. Chs. of Christ, Inc., LA, 1994-99; chair Internat. Chs. Christ, LA, 1999—2000, retired, 2002. Bd. dirs. Oak Brook (Ill.) Bank. Former trustee Elmhurst (Ill.) Coll.; former bd. sponsors Good Samaritan Hosp., Downers Grove, Ill. Served to 1st lt. AUS, 1943-46. Mem. ASME, NSPE, Rotary. Personal E-mail: cecilwooten@hotmail.com.

WORLEY, LLOYD DOUGLAS, language educator; b. Lafayette, La., Sept. 11, 1946; s. Albert Stiles and Doris (Christy) W.; m. Maydean Ann Mouton, Apr. 4, 1966; children: Erin Shawn, Albert Stiles II. BA, U. SW La., 1968, MA, 1972; PhD, So. Ill. U., 1979. Ordained priest, Liberal Cath. Ch., 1977, consecrated aux. bishop, 2005. Tchr. Lafayette H.S., 1969-74; vis. asst. prof. dept. English So. Ill. U., Carbondale, 1979-80; asst. prof. dept. English Pa. State U., DuBois, 1980-87; assoc. prof., assoc. dir. composition dept. English U. No. Colo., Greeley, 1987-88, prof. dept. English, 1988—, chair dept. English, 1988—90. Acting dir. Writing Component Ctr. Basic Skills, So. Ill. U., 1980. Editor: Ruthven Literary Bull., 1988-92; contbr. book chpts., articles. Rector Parish of St. Albertus Magnus The Liberal Cath. Ch., 1987-2001, sec-treas. Am. Province; provost Am. Clerical Synod Chpt. The Liberal Cath. Ch., 1991-2001; Sovereign Grand Master, Order of Holy Sepulchre, 1982-; vicar-gen. Decorated Knight Bachelor, 1996, Hereditary Knight of San Luigi, 1996, Knight Cmdr. Order of Merit St. Angilbert, 1993, Prelate Comdr. Order of Noble Companions of Swan, 1993, Grand Chamberlain, 1995, Knight Order of Guadalupe, 1995, Knight Comdr. Justice Sovereign Order St. John, Knight Grand Cross of Bear of Alabona, 1995, Knight Grand Cross Order St. Stanislaus, 1998, Knight Comp. Crown of Alabona, 1998, Knight Grand Cross Order St. John, 1998, Knight Grand Cross Order Sts. Constantine the Great and Helen, Knight Grand Cross of Justice Ordine dei Cavalieri Lauretani, Grand Cross with Collar of Order of Noble Companion of Swan, 2000 Grand Cross of Justice, Sovrano Ordine Militare ed Ospitaliero di S.Maria di Gerusalemme Teutonico di Svevia; created hereditary Baron, Royal and Serene House of Alabona-Ostrogojsk et de Garama, HRSH Prince William I, created Count Palatine of Maxalla, 1996, created Hereditary Duke of Maxalla, 2000. Fellow Philalethes Soc.; mem. ASCD, Internat. Assn. for Fantastic in Arts (divsn. head Am. Lit. 1987-93), Lord Ruthven Assembly (pres. 1988-94, founding pres. emeritus 1994), Conf. Coll. Composition and Commn., Nat. Coun. Tchrs. English, Am. Conf. Irish Studies, Sigma Tau Delta (bd. dirs. 1990-96, high plains regent various states 1992-96, 10-Yr. Outstanding Advisor award 1997), Masons (century lodge #190), Order of DeMolay (chevalier, cross of honor, legion of honor), Knights Holy Sepulchre (Sov. Grand Master), Rose Croix Martinist Order (pres. premier nat. coun.). Democrat. Office: 3620 W 10th B-150 Greeley CO 80634-9655 Home Phone: 970-356-3002; Office Phone: 970-357-2942. Office Fax: 206-350-2268. Business E-Mail: prof@profw.com.

WORTHAM, THOMAS RICHARD, literature and language professor; b. Liberal, Kans., Dec. 5, 1943; s. Tom and Ruth (Cavanaugh) W. AB, Marquette U., 1965; PhD, Ind. U., 1970. From asst. prof. to assoc. prof. UCLA, 1970-82, prof., 1982—, vice-chmn. and dir. undergrad. studies, 1993-97, chmn. dept., 1997—2007. Vis. prof. Am. lit. U. Warsaw, Poland, 1976-77; sr. rsch. fellow Am. Coun. of Learned Socs., 1983-84. Editor: James Russell Lowell's The Biglow Papers: A Critical Edition, 1977, Letters of W. D. Howells, vol. 4, 1892-1901, 1983, The Early Prose Writings of William Dean Howells, 1853-1861, 1990, William Dean Howells' My Mark Twain, 1996, Mark Twain's Chapters From My Autobiography, 1999; asst. editor Nineteenth-Century Fiction, 1971-75, mem. adv. bd., 1976-83, co-editor, 1983-86; co-editor Nineteenth-Century Literature, 1986-95, editor, 1995—; mem. editl. bd. The Collected Works of Ralph Waldo Emerson, 1996—, Am. Documentary Heritage Libr., 1999—. Regent's faculty fellow in the humanities U. Calif., 1971; travel grantee Nat. Endowment for the Humanities, 1985-86, 88-89; grants-in-aid of rsch. Am. Philos. Soc., 1976, 81. Mem. MLA Am. (Norman Foerster prize com. of Am. Lit. sect. 1973, chmn. Pacific coast region, com. on manuscript holdings of Am. Lit. sect. 1972-78, mem. Hubbell prize com. of Am. Lit. sect. 1989-91), Am. Studies Assn., Ralph Waldo Emerson Soc. (bd. dirs. 1992-95), Assn. for Document Editing, Internat. Assn. Univ. Profs. English, Soc. Textual Scholarship. Lutheran. Office: U Calif Dept English 405 Hilgard Ave Los Angeles CA 90095-1530 Office Phone: 310-825-1175. Business E-Mail: wortham@humnet.ucla.edu.

WORTHEN, KEVIN, dean, law educator; AS, Coll. Ea. Utah, 1978; BA summa cum laude, Brigham Young U., 1979, JD summa cum laude, 1982. Law clerk for Judge Malcolm R. Wilkey U.S. Ct. Appeals, Columbia Cir., 1982—83; Judge Byron R. White U.S. Supreme Ct., 1984; atty. Jennings, Strouss & Salmon, Phoenix, 1984—87; Fullbright scholar U. Chile Law Sch., 1994; prof. law Brigham Young U., J. Ruben Clark Law Sch., 1987—, assoc. dean, 1999—2004, dean, 2004—. Chmn. Utah State Constl. Revision Commn. Contbr. articles to law jours. Order of Coif. Mem.: Ariz. State Bar Assn. Office: Brigham Young U J Reuben Clark Sch Law 340 JRCB Provo UT 84602 Office Phone: 801-422-6383. E-mail: worthenk@lawgate.byu.edu.

WORTHINGTON, BRUCE R., lawyer, energy executive; b. 1949; BA in Econs. cum laude, Claremont McKenna Coll.; JD, U. Calif., Davis. Bar: Calif. 1974. Joined law dept. Pacific Gas and Electric Co., 1974, sr. counsel, chief counsel corp., 1991—94, v.p., gen. counsel, 1994—95, sr. v.p., gen. counsel, 1995—97, PG&E Corp., San Francisco, 1997—. Corp. rep. Calif. Minority Counsel Prog. Mem.: ABA (vice chair Sect. Pub. Utility, Comm., and Transp. Law), Calif. Bar Assn., San Francisco Bar Assn.

WOTT, JOHN ARTHUR, retired arboretum and botanical garden executive, horticulture educator; b. Fremont, Ohio, Apr. 10, 1939; s. Arthur Otto Louis and Esther Wilhelmina (Werth) W.; children: Christopher, Timothy, Holly. BS, Ohio State U., 1961; MS, Cornell U., 1966, PhD, 1968. Mem. staff Ohio State Coop. Extension Svc., Bowling Green, 1961-64; rsch. asst. Cornell U., Ithaca, NY, 1964-68; prof. Purdue U., West Lafayette, Ind., 1968-81; prof. Ctr. Urban Horticulture U. Wash., Seattle, 1981—2006, prof. emeritus, 2006—; assoc. dir. Ctr. Urban Horticulture U. Wash., Seattle, 1990-93, acting dir., 2004—05; dir. arboreta Washington Park Arboretum, Seattle, 1993—2005. Writer columns for Nursery Mgmt. Profession, Balls and Burlap, Am. Nurseryman, The Arboretum Found.; contbr. articles to profl. jours. and papers including Nursery Mgr. Profl., Balls and Burlap, Arboreteum Found. Bull., Am. Nurseryman. Mem. Am. Soc. Hort. Sci. (com. chmn. 1967-82), Am. Assn. Bot. Gardens and Arboreta, Internat. Plant Propagators Soc. (internat. pres. 1984, internat. sec.-treas. 1985—2006). Avocations: music, antiques. Office Phone: 206-543-8602. Personal E-mail: jwott10623@aol.com. Business E-Mail: jwott@u.washington.edu.

WOUK, HERMAN, writer; b. NYC, May 27, 1915; s. Abraham Isaac and Esther (Levine) W.; m. Betty Sarah Brown, Dec. 9, 1945; children: Abraham Isaac (dec.), Nathaniel, Joseph. AB with gen. honors, Columbia U., 1934; LHD (hon.), Yeshiva U., 1954; LLD (hon.), Clark U., 1960; LittD (hon.), Am. Internat. Coll., 1979; PhD (hon.), Bar-Ilan U., 1990, Hebrew U., 1997; DLitt (hon), George Washington U., 2001, Trinity Coll., 1998. Writer radio programs for various comedians, NYC, 1935; asst. writer weekly radio scripts comedian Fred Allen, 1936-41. Presdl. cons. to U.S. Treasury, 1941; vis. prof. English Yeshiva U., 1952-57; scholar-in-residence Aspen Inst. Humanistic Studies, 1973-74 Author: (novels) Aurora Dawn, 1947, The City Boy, 1948, Slattery's Hurricane, 1949, The Caine Mutiny, 1951 (Pulitzer Prize award for fiction, 1952), Marjorie Morningstar, 1955, Youngblood Hawke, 1962, Don't Stop the Carnival, 1965, The Winds of War, 1971, War and Remembrance, 1978, Inside, Outside, 1985 (Washingtonian Book award, 1986), The Hope, 1993, The Glory, 1994, A Hole in Texas, 2004, (dramas) The Traitor, 1949, The Caine Mutiny Court-Martial, 1953, (comedy) Nature's Way, 1957, (non-fiction) This is My God, 1959, The Will to Live On, 2000, (screenplays for TV serials) The Winds of War, 1983, War and Remembrance, 1986. Trustee Coll. of V.I., 1961-69; bd. dirs. Washington Nat. Symphony, 1969-71, Kennedy Ctr. Prodns., 1974-75. Exec. officer U.S.S. Southard USNR, 1942-46, PTO. Recipient Richard H. Fox prize, 1934, Columbia U. medal for Excellence, 1952, Alexander Hamilton medal, 1980, U. Calif.-Berkeley medal, 1984, Golden Plate award Am. Acad. Achievement, 1986, USN Meml. Found. 'Lone Sailor' award, 1987, Yad Vashem KaZetnik award, 1990, Bar Ilan U. Guardian of Zion award, 1998, USCD medal U. Calif.-San Diego, 1998. Mem. Naval Res. Assn., Dramatists Guild, Authors Guild, Internat. Platform Assn. (Ralph Waldo Emerson award 1981), PEN Clubs: Bohemian (San Francisco); Cosmos, Metropolitan (Washington); Century Assn. (N.Y.C.). Jewish. Office: care BSW Literary Agy 303 Crestview Dr Palm Springs CA 92264

WOYS, JAMES E., health and medical products executive; B in Acctg., Ariz. State U., Tempe; MBA, Golden Gate U., San Francisco. Cons. Arthur Andersen, 1980—82; Price Waterhouse, 1982—86; dir. corp. fin. & tax Found. Health Corp., 1986—90, v.p., CFO govt. div., 1990—95, sr. v.p. federal services, 1995—98, COO, sr. v.p. Federal services, 1998—99; COO Federal services Health Net, Inc., Woodland Hills, 1999—2001, pres. Federal services, 2001—05, pres. govt. and specialty services, mem. exec. oper. team, 2005—07, interim CFO, 2006—07, COO, 2007—. Office: Health Net Inc 21650 Oxnard St Woodland Hills CA 91367 Office Phone: 818-676-6000.

WOZNIAK, CURTIS S., electronics executive; Various positions in mfg., mktg. and ops. Gen. Motors Corp.; prodn. engring. mgr. Hewlett-Packard Co.; v.p. Desktop Graphics devel. Sun Microsys. Computer Corp., v.p., gen. mgr. Ednl. Products divsn., v.p. engring., v.p. worldwide mktg.; pres., COO Xilinx Inc.; CEO Electroglas Inc., 1996—, also chmn., 1997—. Bd. dirs. SEMI/SEMATECH consortium, Mgmt. Inst. Office: Electroglas Incorporation 5729 Fontanoso Way San Jose CA 95138-1015

WOZNIAK, STEVE (STEPHEN GARY WOZNIAK), computer scientist, philanthropist; b. San Jose, Calif., Aug. 11, 1950; s. Jerry; m. Alice Robertson, 1980 (div.); m. Candice Clark, 1987 (div.); 3 children; m. Suzanne Mulkern, 1990. BS in computer sci. and elec. engring., U. Calif., Berkeley, 1987; DSc (hon.), NC State U., 2004. Designer calculator chips Hewlett-Packard Co., 1976; co-founder Apple Computer, Inc., 1976, v.p. R&D, 1976—81, designer, 1979—81, re-joined as principal, v.p. engring., 1983—85, cons., 1985—; co-founder CL9 - Remote Control Co., pres., 1985—89; founder US Festivals, San Bernardino, Calif., 1983; co-chmn. Axlon, Inc., Sunnyvale, Calif., 1986—; co-founder Wheels of Zeus (wOz), Los Gatos, Calif., 2002, chmn., CEO, 2002—04, chief tech. officer, pres., 2004—06; co-founder, exec. v.p., chief tech. officer Jazz Technologies, Inc. (formerly Acquicor Tech. Inc.), Irvine, Calif., 2006—09; chief scientist Fusion-io, Salt Lake City, 2009—. Bd. dirs. Jacent, Danger, Inc., Acquicor Tech. Inc., 2005—, en2go International Inc., 2008—; Dem. convention del. (Hart), 1984; former tchr. Co-author (with Gina Smith): iWoz: Computer Geek to Cult Icon: how I invented the personal computer, co-founded Apple, and had fun doing it, 2006; performer: Dancing with the Stars, 2009. Founder Elec. Frontier Found.; founding sponsor Tech Museum, Silicon Valley Ballet, Children's Discovery Museum, San Jose, Calif. Recipient Grace Murray Hopper award, Assn. Computing Machinery, 1979, Nat. Medal Tech., presented by Pres. Ronald Reagan, 1985, Fellow award, Computer History Mus., 1997, Heinz Award for Tech., 2000, numerous awards from tech. and cmty. groups; named to Nat. Inventor's Hall of Fame, 2000, Consumer Electronics Hall of Fame, 2004. Mem.: Fremason, Charity Lodge (life). Achievements include invention of the first line of Apple products - the Apple I and II computers; influenced the popular Macintosh computer; supports the Los Gatos School Dist., providing students and teachers with hands-on teaching and donations of state-of-the-art tech. equip; sponsored computers for schs. in USSR through US/USSR Iniative, 1990; youngest Fortune 500 man in 1982 at age 27; involved in charitable activities in field of education. Office: Fusion-io 6350 S 3000 E 6th Fl Salt Lake City UT 84121 Office Phone: 408-358-6030.*

WRAE, NATASHA, lawyer; b. 1971; BS in Molecular and Cell Biology, U. Ariz., 1992; JD, U. Balt., 1999. Lic.: Ariz. 1999, Md. 1999, bar: Ariz. Worked for Mayo Clinic, Rochester, Minn.; atty. Law Office of Natasha Wrae, Tucson, 1999—. Former coach Cholla High Sch. Mock Trial Prog.; head coach U. Ariz. Mock Trial Prog.; vol. judge Tucson 4-H. Named one of 40 Under 40, Tucson Bus. Edge, 2006. Mem.: Am. Mock Trial Assn., Am. Civil. Liberties Union, Nat. Assn. Women Bus. Owners, Nat. Assn. Criminal Def. Lawyers, Ariz. Attorneys for Criminal Justice, ABA, Pima County Bar Assn. Office: Law Office Natasha Wrae Pc 312 S 3rd Ave Tucson AZ 85701-2102 Office Phone: 520-624-4224.

WREDE, ROBERT CLINTON, JR., mathematician, educator; b. Cin., Oct. 19, 1926; s. Robert Clinton and Ruth Ann (Ramsdell) W.; m. Jeanne Snedden, Jan. 29, 1948; children: Scott, Brian, James Clayton. BS, Miami U., Oxford, Ohio, 1949, MA, 1950; postgrad., U. Cin., 1950-51; PhD, Ind. U., 1956. Instr. Miami U., 1950-51; teaching fellow Ind. U., Bloomington, 1951-55; from instr. to assoc. prof. San Jose (Calif.) State U., 1955-63, prof. math., 1963-89, prof. emeritus, 1989—. Cons. rsch. div. IBM, San Jose, 1957-58, Hunter's Point Radiation Lab., San Francisco, 1959. Author: Intro To Vector & Tensor Analysis, 1963, rev. edit., 1972, Schaum's Outlines Advanced Calculus, 2d edit., 2002, Insights into Calculus, 2008, Algebra, 2008, Geometry, 2008, Outlines Advanced 3rd edit., 2009; manuscript cons. John Wiley & Sons, 1961—. Div. leader Urban Coalition, San Jose, 1969—. Pfc. USMC, 1944-45. Mem. AAUP, Math. Assn. Am., Am. Math. Soc., Tensor Soc. (Japan). Home: 132 Wingfoot Ct Aptos CA 95003-5428 Office: Math & Computer Sci Dept San Jose State U 1 Washington Sq San Jose CA 95112-3613 Personal E-mail: robertrio@aol.com.

WRIGHT, ANDREW, English literature educator; b. Columbus, Ohio, June 28, 1923; s. Francis Joseph and Katharine (Timberman) W.; m. Virginia Rosemary Banks, June 27, 1952; children: Matthew Leslie Francis, Emma Stanbery. AB, Harvard U., 1947; MA, Ohio State U., 1948, PhD, 1951. Prof. English lit. U. Calif., San Diego, 1963—, chmn. dept. lit., 1971-74; dir. U. Calif. Study Center, U.K. and Ireland, 1980-82. Vis. prof. U. Queensland, Australia, 1984, Colegio de la Frontera Norte, San Antonio del Mar, Baja, Calif., 1991-92. Author: Jane Austen's Novels: A Study In Structure, 1953, Joyce Cary: A Preface to His Novels, 1958, Henry Fielding: Mask and Feast, 1965, Blake's Job: A Commentary, 1972, Anthony Trollope: Dream and Art, 1983; Fictional Discourse and Historical Space, 1987; contbg. author numerous books, articles to profl. jours., numerous short stories to lit. mags.; editorial bd. Nineteenth Century Fiction, 1964-86. Bd. dirs. Calif. Coun. Humanities, 1983-87. Guggenheim fellow, 1960, 70; Fulbright Sr. Research fellow, 1960-61 Fellow Royal Soc. Lit.; mem. MLA, Jane Austen Soc., Athenaeum (London), Trollope Soc., Santayana Soc., Phi Beta Kappa. Home: 7227 Olivetas Ave La Jolla CA 92037-5335 Office: U Calif San Diego Dept Lit La Jolla CA 92093-0410 Business E-Mail: ahwright@ucsd.edu.

WRIGHT, BAGLEY, venture capitalist, entrepreneur, art collector; m. Virginia Bloedel; children: Merrill, Charles, Robin, Bing. BA, Princeton U., 1946. With Daily Mirror, Newsweek; real estate developer Pentagram Corp., Harbor Properties; chmn Physio Control Corp., 1968—80. Developer Space Needle, Seattle. Named one of Top 200 Collectors, ARTnews Mag., 2004, 2006. Avocation: Collector of Contemporary Art; Japanese Art. Office: 407 Dexter Ave Seattle WA 98109

WRIGHT, CATHIE, state legislator; b. Old Forge, Pa., May 18, 1929; 1 child, Victoria. AA in Acctg., Lackawanna Jr. Coll.; student, U. Scranton. Former mayor and city councilwoman City of Simi Valley; mem. Calif. State Assembly, 1980-92, Calif. State Senate, 1992—2001. Chair Simi Valley Cmty. Devel. Com., Simi Valley Drug Abuse Program; former mem. transp., adv. planning, criminal justice planning bd., animal control com. for Ventura County. Named Woman of Yr., Simi Valley C. of C., 1979, Am. Mothers' Legis. Mother of the Yr., 1985, Outstanding Woman of the Yr., Zonta-Santa Clarita Valley, 1986. Mem. VFW, Las Manitas Aux. Republican.

WRIGHT, CATHY L., museum director; Studied, U. Colo. Boulder; M, U. Denver. Hist. tchr. U. Colo., Colo. Springs; tchr. southwest studies Colo. Coll.; dir., chief cur. Taylor Mus., Colo. Springs Fine Arts Ctr.; dir. Albuquerque Mus. Art and Hist., 2006—. Juror N.Mex State U. Art Gallery Student Exhbn., 2007, Colo. State Fair Fine Arts Exhbn., Pueblo, 2007. Office: Albuquerque Mus Art & Hist 2000 Mountain Rd NW Albuquerque NM 87104 Business E-Mail: clwright@cabq.gov.

WRIGHT, CHATT GRANDISON, academic administrator; b. San Mateo, Calif., Sept. 17, 1941; s. Virgil Tandy and Louise (Jeschien) W.; children from previous marriage: Stephen Brook, Jon David, Shelley Adams; m. Janice Teply, Nov. 28, 1993. Student, U. Calif., Berkeley, 1960-62; BA in Polit. Sci., U. Calif., Davis, 1964; MA in Econs., U. Hawaii, 1968. Instr. econs. U. Hawaii, Honolulu, 1968-70; mgr. corp. planning Telecheck Internat., Inc., Honolulu, 1969—70; economist State of Hawaii, Honolulu, 1970—71; adminstr. manpower

City & County of Honolulu, 1971-72; bus. adminstr., dean. Hawaii Pacific U., Honolulu, 1972-74, v.p., 1974-76, pres., 1976—. Mem. City and County of Honolulu Manpower Area Planning Commn., 1976—82; mem. Mayor's Salary Commn. City and County of Honolulu, 1977—80; mem. Honolulu City Ethics Commn., 1978—84, City and County of Honolulu Labor Market Adv. Coun., 1982—84; bd. dirs. Hawaii Econ. Devel. Corp., 1980—84; trustee Queen's Med. Ctr., Honolulu, 1986—92, Honolulu Armed Svcs. YMCA, 1984—86, Hawaii Maritime Ctr., 1990—92; chmn. bd. trustees Hist. Hawaii Found., 1995—96, trustee, 1990—96; mem. adv. bd. Cancer Rsch. Ctr. Hawaii, 1987; trustee St. Andrew's Priory Sch., 1994—98; bd. dirs. Hawaii Visitors Bur., 1995—97; bd. dir. Downtown Improvement Assn., 1988—96; bd. dirs. Outrigger Duke Kahanamoku Found., 1996—98, Hawaii Opera Theatre, 1997—99; bd. govs. Hawaii Coun. on Econ. Edn., 1998—; trustee Oceanic Inst., 1998—, chmn., 2003—; mem. Hawaii Execs. Coun., 1996—, chmn., 2002, Hawaii Exec. Conf., 2002; bd. govs. Hawaii Med. Libr., 1989—92; mem. adv. bd. Aloha coun. Boy Scouts Am., 1991—2002; trustee Molokai Gen. Hosp., 1991—92; mem. Pacific Asian Affairs Coun., 1998—2001; steering com. Asian Devel. Bank, 2000—. With USN, 1968—70. Recipient Pioneer award Pioneer Fed. Savs. Bank, 1982, Stephen J. Jackstadt award, Hawaii Coun. Econ. Edn., 1998; named Sales Person of Yr., Sales and Mktg. Execs. of Honolulu, 1998; Paul Harris fellow Rotary, 1986; named to Honolulu 100, Honolulu Mag., 2005. Mem.: Hawaii Assn. Ind. Colls. and Univs. (chmn. 1986), Western Coll. Assn. (exec. com. 1989—92), Hawaii Joint Coun. Econ. Edn. (bd. dirs. 1982—88), Nat. Assn. Intercollegiate Athletics (mem. 1985—98, vice chair NAIA coun. of pres. 1994), Assn. Governing Bds. Univs. and Colls., Am. Assn. Higher Edn., Soc. Sci. Assn. (mem. 1994—99), Japan-Am. Soc. Honolulu, Waialae Country Club, Plaza Club (bd. govs. 1992—97), Pacific Club (Honolulu), Outrigger Canoe Club. Republican. Episcopalian. Avocations: hunting, fishing, reading, travel. Office: Hawaii Pacific U Office of Pres 1166 Fort Street Mall Honolulu HI 96813-2708 E-mail: president@hpu.edu.

WRIGHT, DONALD P., retail executive; Sr. v.p. real estate and engring. Safeway, Inc. Office: Safeway Inc 5918 Stoneridge Mall Rd Pleasanton CA 94588 Office Phone: 925-467-3000. Office Fax: 925-467-3323.

WRIGHT, ERNEST MARSHALL, physiologist, consultant; b. Belfast, Ireland, June 8, 1940; came to U.S., 1965; BSc, U. London, 1961, DSc, 1978; PhD, U. Sheffield, Eng., 1964. Research fellow Harvard U., Boston, 1965-66; from asst. prof. to full prof. physiology UCLA Med. Sch., 1967—, chmn. dept. physiology, 1987—2000. Cons. NIH, Bethesda, Md., 1982—, Senator Jacob K. Javits neurosci. investigator, 1985. Fellow: Royal Soc., Biophysical Soc. Office: UCLA Sch Med Dept Physiology 10833 Le Conte Ave Los Angeles CA 90095-1751

WRIGHT, KENNETH BROOKS, lawyer; b. Whittier, Calif., June 5, 1934; s. Albert Harold and Marian (Schwey) W.; m. Sandra Beryl Smith, June 20, 1959; children: Margo Teresa, Daniel Brooks, John Waugh. BA cum laude, Pomona Coll., 1956; JD, Stanford U., 1960. Bar: Calif. 1961, U.S. Supreme Ct. 1979. Assoc., then ptnr. Lawler, Felix & Hall, 1961—77; ptnr. Morgan, Lewis & Bockius, LA, 1978—99, counsel, 1999—2003, ret. ptnr., 2004. Tchg. team leader Nat. Inst. Trial Advocacy, 1978-80; governing com. Calif. Continuing Edn. Bar, 1973-77, chmn., 1975-76; nat. panel arbitrators Am. Arbitration Assn., 1970-91; lectr. ABA Sect. Litig. Nat. Inst., 1979-86; bd. dirs. L.A. Internat. Comml. Arbitration Ctr. Chmn. bd. editors: Am. Bar Jour, 1977-81. Pres. Pomona Coll. Alumni Assn., 1970-71; pres. parent tchr. coun. Campbell Hall Sch., 1973-74, bd. dirs., vice chmn., 1994—; counsel Vol. League San Fernando Valley, 1979-81; chmn. sect. adminstrn. justice Town Hall of Calif., 1970-71; sr. warden Episcopal Ch., 1973-74. Served with U.S. Army, 1956-57. Mem. ABA (dir. programs litig. sect. 1977-81, coun. 1982-88, standing com on comm. 1978-88, chmn. 1987-88, chmn. sect. book pub. com. 1986-89, pres. fellows young lawyers 1985-86, bd. dirs. 1980-89), Internat. Bar Assn., Assn. Bus. Trial Lawyers (chair com. alt. dispute resolution 1991-93, bd. dirs. 1993-96), Am. Law Inst., Am. Bar Found., State Bar Calif. (gov. com. continuing edn. bar 1972-77, chmn. 1975-76), Conf. Barristers (exec. com. 1966-69, 1st v.p. 1969), L.A. County Bar Assn. (com. judiciary 1981-83, chmn. CLE adv. com. 1989-91, vice-chmn. CLE com. 1991-93, bd. dirs. L.A. Lawyers 1989-94), L.A. County Bar Found. (bd. dirs., trustee 1993-99, exec. com. internat. sect. 1996-99), Jonathan Club, Phi Beta Kappa. Republican. Avocations: skiing, tennis. Home: 824 Foothill Ln Ojai CA 93023 Office: Morgan Lewis & Bockius 300 S Grand Ave Los Angeles CA 90071-3109

WRIGHT, MARY ROSE, retired state agency administrator; b. Hartford, Conn., Jan. 12, 1949; d. J. William and Eileen J. (Walsh) Bigoness; m. Roy C. Gunter III, June 24, 1972 (div. Feb. 1988); m. Kenneth Ross Wright, Dec. 1, 1988. BA, Marquette U., 1970; MS, U. Mo., 1972. Prgram analyst State Calif. Dept. Health, Sacramento, 1972-76; tng. ctr. dir. State Calif. Dept. Parks and Recreation, Pacific Grove, 1976-81, visitor svcs. mgr. Monterey, 1981-83, Monterey dist. supr., 1983-92, dep. dir., 1992-93; Monterey dist. supt. Calif. Dept. Parks and Recreation, 1993-99, chief dep. dir. Sacramento, 1999—2002. Hist. preservation commr. City of Monterey, 1984-92. Bd. dirs. Big Sur Health Ctr., 1993—; bd. govs. Santa Lucia Conservancy, 1995-99. Office: Calif Dept Parks and Recreation Chief Dep Dir 1416 9th St Rm 1405 Sacramento CA 95814-5511

WRIGHT, OTIS DALINO, II, judge; b. Tuskegee, Ala., July 7, 1944; BA, Calif. State U., 1976; JD, Southwestern Sch. Law, 1980. Bar: Calif. 1980. Dep. sheriff LA County Sheriff's Dept., 1969—80; dep. dist. atty. Office Atty. Gen., Calif. Dept. Justice, 1980—83; ptnr. Wilson, Elser, Moskowitz, Edelman & Dicker LLP, 1983—2005; judge Superior Ct. Calif., County LA, 2005—07, U.S. Dist. Ct. (ctrl. dist.) Calif., 2007—. With USMC, 1963—69. Office: US Dist Ct 255 E Temple St Los Angeles CA 90012

WRIGHT, PAUL KENNETH, mechanical engineer, educator; b. Watford, Eng., Aug. 24, 1947; came to US, 1979; s. Kenneth Browett and Violet Anne (Woodland) W.; m. Frances June Ody, Oct. 24, 1970 (div. June 1984); children: Samuel, Joseph, Thomas; m. Terry Lee Naylor Schuster, Jan. 1, 1996; stepchildren: Jesse, Jennifer. BSc in Indsl. Metallurgy, U. Birmingham, Eng., 1968, MSc, 1970, PhD in Indsl. Metallurgy, 1971. Consulting engr. dept. sci. and indsl. rsch. Govt. New Zealand, Auckland, 1972—74; sr. lectr. dept. mech. engring. U. Auckland, New Zealand, 1975—79; rsch. assoc. physics Cavendish Lab. U. Cambridge, England, 1978—79; prof. mech. engring. Carnegie Mellon U., Pitts., 1979-87; prof. computer sci., dir. robotics and mfg. rsch. lab. NYU Courant Inst. Math. Scis., NYC, 1987-91; prof. mech. engring. U. Calif., Berkeley, 1991—, A. Martin Berlin prof. and chair mech. engring., 1996—. Mem. mfg. studies bd. NRC, Washington, 1988; co-chair Mgt. Tech. prog. U. Calif., Berkeley, 1995—2005, assoc. dean Coll. Engring., 1999—2005, co-dir. Berkeley Mfg. Inst. and Berkeley Wireless Rsch. Ctr., 1999—, chief scientist Ctr. Info. Tech. Rsch. in Interests of Soc., 2006—. Contbr. articles to sci. jours.; co-author: Manufacturing Intelligence, 1988, Energy Scavenging for Wireless Sensor Networks with Special Focus on Vibrations, 2004; author: 21st Century Manufacturing, 2001. Recipient Bursary award Royal Soc., London, 1978. Mem. ASME (Blackall award 1984), N.Am. Mfg. Rsch. Inst., Am. Computing, NAE. Mem. Ch. Eng. Achievements include patents in field. Avocations: singing jazz, skiing, sports. Office: UC Berkeley 5133 Etcheverry Hall Mailstop 1740 Berkeley CA 94720-1740 Office Phone: 510-642-2527. Office Fax: 510-643-5599. E-mail: pwright@me.berkeley.edu.

WRIGHT, RODERICK D., state legislator; b. Chgo., Ill. 2 children. BA in Urban Studies/City Planning, Pepperdine U. Owner, home and bus. City of Inglewood; field dep. LA City Coun.; liaison LA City Departments of Planning, Personnel, Water & Power, Cmty. Develop.; with the office of LA Mayor Tom Bradley; dist. dir. to Representative Maxine Waters US Congress; mem. Dist. 48 Calif. State Assembly, 1996—2002; mem. Dist. 25 Calif. State Senate, 2008—. Democrat. Office: State Capitol Rm 5064 Sacramento CA 95814 Address: 1 Manchester Blvd Ste 600 Inglewood CA 90301 Office Phone: 916-651-4025, 310-412-0393.*

WRIGHT, VIRGINIA, art collector, curator; m. Bagley Wright; children: Merrill, Charles, Robin, Bing. BA, Barnard Coll., 1951. Asst. Sidney Janis Gallery; trustee Virginia Wright Fund, Seattle Art Mus. Curator Color Field Paintings and Related Abstractions, 2005. Named one of Top 200 Collectors, ARTnews Mag., 2004, 2006. Avocation: Collector of Contemporary Art; Japanese Art.

WRIGHT, WILL, computer game designer; b. Atlanta, Jan. 20, 1960; s. Will Wright, Sr. and Beverlye (Edwards) Wright; m. Joell Jones. Attended, La. State U., La. Tech., The New Sch., Manhattan. Co-founder Maxis Software, Inc.(purchased by Electronic Arts, Inc. in 1997), 1987—97. Designer (computer game) Raid on Bungeling Bay, Broderbund Software, Inc., 1984, SimCity, 1989, SimCity Terrain Editor, Infogrames, 1989, SimCity Enhanced CD ROM, Interplay Entertainment Corp., Maxis Software Inc., 1993, Empire Deluxe Scenarios, New World Computing, Inc., 1993, SimIsle:Missions in the Rainforest, Maxis UK, Ltd., 1995, Seaman, Vivarium Inc., 1999, Psychonauts, Majesco Entertainment Co., 2005, Re-Mission, HopeLab, 2006, The Sims, 2000, The Sims Livin' Large, 2000, Sims Coaster, 2001, Sim Golf, 2001, SimEarth: The Living Planet, Maxis Software, Inc., 1990, SimAnt: The Electronic Art Colony, 1991, RoboSport, 1991, SimLife, 1992, A-Train, 1992, SimCity Classic, 1994, SimFarm, 1993, SimCity 2000 Urban Renewal Kit, 1994, SimTown, 1995, SimTower: The Vertical Empire, 1995, Marble Drop, 1997, SimPark, 1996, SimCopter, 1996, Sim Tunes, 1996, Full Tilt! Pinball, 1996, A-Train Construction Set, Maxis Software Inc., Ocean Software Inc., 1992, SimCity 3000, Electronic Arts, Inc., 1999, The Sims, 2000, SimCity 3000 Unlimited, 2000, The Sims: House Party Expansion Pack, 2001, The Sims: Hot Date Expansion Pack, 2001, The Sims: Unleashed, 2002, The Sims Online, 2002, The Sims (Deluxe Edition), 2002, The Sims: Vacation Expansion Pack, 2002, The Sims: Superstar, 2003, The Sims: Makin Magic, 2003, The Sims: Bustin' Out, 2003, The Sims: Makin Magic Expansion Pack, 2003, Sim City 4 Expansion Pack, 2003, Sim City 4 Rush Hour, 2003, The Urbz: Sims in the City, 2004, SimCity 4, 2004, The Sims: Mega Deluxe, 2004, The Sims 2 University, 2004, The Sims 2: Nightlife, 2005, The Sims 2: Open for Business, 2006, The Sims 2, Electronic Arts, Inc., Maxis Software Inc., 2005, co-designer with Fred Haslam SimCity2000, Maxis Software Inc., 1993. Recipient Lifetime Achievement award, Game Developers Choice awards, 2001, PC Mag., 2005, Vanguard award, Producers Guild of Am., 2007; named one of the most important people in gaming, technology, and entertainment by publications such as, Entertainment Weekly, Time, PC Gamer, Discover and Game Spy; named to Acad. of Interactive Arts and Sciences' Hall of Fame, 2002.

WRIGHTON, NICHOLAS C., research scientist; BA in Biochemistry, MA in Biochemistry, Oxford U.; PhD in Molecular Biology, Nat. Inst. Med. Rsch. Postdoct. researcher DNAX Rsch. Inst., Palo Alto, Calif.; rsch. scientist Affymax, Palo Alto. Recipient Newcomb Cleveland prize AAAS, 1996-97. Achievements include discovery (with others) of EPO mimetics. Office: Affymax Rsch Inst 4001 Miranda Ave Palo Alto CA 94304-1218

WU, DAVID, United States Representative from Oregon; b. Taiwan, Apr. 8, 1955; arrived in US, 1961; m. Michelle Wu; children: Matthew, Sarah. BS, Stanford U., Calif., 1977; student, Harvard Med. Sch.; JD, Yale U., New Haven, 1982. Clk. to fed. judge, Portland, Oreg.; ptnr. Cohen & Wu, Oreg., 1988-98; mem. US Congress from 1st Oreg. dist., 1999—, mem. edn. and labor com., mem. sci. & tech. com., mem. fgn. affairs com., chmn. subcommittee on tech. and innovation, mem. exec. bd. Congl. Asian Pacific Am. Caucus, mem. New Dem. Coalition. Democrat. Office: 620 SW Main Ste 606 Portland OR 97205 Office Phone: 202-225-0855, 503-326-2901. Office Fax: 503-326-5066.

WU, GEORGE H., federal judge; b. NYC, 1950; BA, Pomona Coll., 1972; JD, U. Chgo. Law Sch., 1975. Bar: Calif. 1975. Assoc. Latham & Watkins, 1975—79, LeBoeuf, Lamb, Leiby & MacRae, 1989—91; law clk. Hon. Stanley N. Barnes, US Ct. Appeals (9th cir.), 1976—77, 1979; asst. US atty. US Atty's Office (Ctrl. dist.) Calif., 1982—89, 1991—93; judge LA Mcpl. Ct., 1993—96, LA Superior Ct., 1996—2007, US Dist. Ct. (Ctrl. dist.) Calif., 2007—. Asst. prof. law U. Tenn. Coll. Law, 1979—82. Office: US Dist Ct 312 N Spring St Los Angeles CA 90012

WU, JAMES CHEN-YUAN, aerospace engineering educator; b. Nanking, China, Oct. 5, 1931; came to U.S., 1953, naturalized, 1963; s. Chien Lieh and Cheng-Ling Wu; m. Mei-Ying Chang, Sept. 7, 1957; children— Alberta Yee-Hwa, Norbert Mao-Hwa. Student, Nat. Taiwan U., 1949-52; BS, Gonzaga U., 1954; postgrad., Columbia U., 1954; MS (univ. fellow), U. Ill., 1955, PhD, 1957. Engr. Wah Chang Corp., NYC, 1954; researcher Mass. Inst. Tech. at Cambridge, 1957; asst. prof. Gonzaga U., Spokane, Wash., 1957-59; research specialist Douglas Aircraft Co., 1959-65, group leader, 1960-61, supr., 1961-62, br. chief, 1963-65; prof. aerospace engring. Ga. Inst. Tech., 1965-96; pres. Applied Aero, LLC, 1996—. Cons. N.Am. Aviation Co., Geophys. Tech. Corp., European Atomic Energy Commn., Ispra, Italy, European Atomic Energy Commn. (research center), U.S. Army Research Office, Durham, S.C. Contbr. articles to profl. jours. Chmn. bd. dirs. Chinese-Am. Inst. Recipient profl. achievement award Douglas Aricraft Co., 1963, Outstanding Tchrs. award Gonzaga U., 1959; Asso. fellow Am. Inst. Aeros. and Astronautics Mem. Am. Soc. Engring. Sci. (founding), Soc. Indsl. and Applied Math. (vice-chmn. Pacific N.W. 1958-59), Am. Astron. Soc. (sr.), Am. Phys. Soc., Nat. Assn. Chinese Ams. (pres. Atlanta chpt.), Sigma Xi, Tau Beta Pi, Sigma Alpha Nu. Office: Sch Aerospace Engring Georgia Inst Tech 48365 Avalon Heights Ter Fremont CA 94539-8005

WULBERT, DANIEL ELIOT, mathematician, educator; s. Morris and Anna (Greenberg) W.; children: Kera, Noah. BA, Knox Coll., 1963; MA, U. Tex., Austin, 1964, PhD, 1966. Rsch. assoc. U. Lund, Sweden, 1966-67; asst. prof. U. Wash., Seattle, 1967-73; prof. U. Calif.-San Diego, La Jolla, 1973—, provost Revelle Coll., 2003—. Vis. prof. Northwestern U., Evanston, Ill., 1977. Contbr. articles in field. Office: Provost Bldg Revelle Coll 0321 U Calif San Diego La Jolla CA 92093-0321 Business E-Mail: dwulbert@ucsd.edu.

WUNNICKE, BROOKE, lawyer; b. Dallas, May 9, 1918; d. Rudolph von Falkenstein and Lulu Lenore Brooke; m. James M. Wunnicke, Apr. 11, 1940; (dec. 1977); 1 child, Diane B. BA, Stanford U., 1939; JD, U. Colo., 1945. Bar: Wyo. 1946, Colo. 1969, U.S. Dist. Ct. Wyo. 1947, U.S. Dist. Ct. Colo. 1970, U.S. Supreme Ct. 1958, U.S. Ct. Appeals (10th cir.) 1958. Pvt. practice law, 1946—69; ptnr. Williams & Wunnicke, Cheyenne, Wyo., 1956—69; counsel Calkins, Kramer, Grimshaw & Harring, Denver, 1969—73; chief appellate dep. atty. Dist. Atty's Office, Denver, 1973—86; counsel Hall & Evans L.L.C., Denver, 1986—. Adj. prof. law U. Denver Coll. Law, 1978-97, 1st Frank H. Ricketson Jr. adj. prof., 2003; lectr. Internat. Practicum Inst. Denver, 1976-, lectr. 1978-2003. Author: Ethics Compliance for Business Lawyers, 1987; co-author: Standby Letters of Credit, 1989, Corporate Financial Risk Management, 1992, UCP 500 and Standby Letters of Credit-Special Report, 1994, Standby and Commercial Letters of Credit, 2000, 2009, Annual Supt., Legal Opinion Letters Formbook, 2002, 2009, Annual Supt.; contbr. articles to profl. jours. Pres. Laramie County Bar Assn., Cheyenne, 1967-68; Dir. Cheyenne C. of C., 1965-68 Recipient Outstanding Svc. award, Colo. Dist. Attys. Coun., 1979, 1982, 1986, Disting. Alumni awards, U. Colo. Sch. Law, 1986, 1993, William Lee Knous award, 1997, Lathrop Trailblazer award, Colo. Women's Bar Assn., 1992, Eleanor P. Williams award for Disting. Svc. to Legal Profession, 1997, Potter Lifetime Profl. Svc. award, 1999, Nat. award, Def. Rsch. Inst., 1999, Law Star award, Denver Coll. Law, 2003. Fellow Colo. Bar Found., Am. Bar Found.; mem. ABA, Wyo. State Bar, Denver Bar Assn. (hon. life; trustee 1977-80, award of Merit 2004), Colo. Bar Assn. (hon., life, Award of Merit 1999), Am. Arbitration Assn. (comml. panel), William E. Doyle Inn of Ct. (hon.), Order of Coif, Phi Beta Kappa. Independent. Avocations: reading, writing. Office: Hall & Evans LLC 1125 17th St Ste 600 Denver CO 80202-2037 Office Phone: 303-628-3363. Business E-Mail: wunnickeb@hallevans.com.

WURSTER, CHARLES FREDERICK, environmental scientist, educator; b. Phila., Aug. 1, 1930; s. Charles Frederick and Helen B. Wurster; children: Steven Hadley, Nina F., Erik Frederick. SB, Haverford Coll., 1952; MS, U. Del., 1954; PhD, Stanford U., 1957; DSc (hon.), SUNY, 2009. Rsch. asst. Stanford U., 1954-57; Fulbright fellow Innsbruck, Austria, 1957-58; rsch. chemist Monsanto Rsch. Corp., 1959-62; rsch. assoc. biol. scis. Dartmouth Coll., 1962-65; asst. prof. biol. scis. SUNY, Stony Brook, 1965-70; assoc. prof. environ. scis. Marine Scis. Rsch. Ctr., 1970-94, prof. emeritus, 1994—. Founding trustee, sec., mem. exec. com. Environ. Def. Fund, 1967—; vis. prof. Macquarie U., Sydney, 1988; mem. adminstr.'s pesticide policy adv. com. EPA, 1975—78; leader ecol. tours worldwide. Contbr. articles to profl. publs. Scholar, U. Wash., Seattle. Fellow: AAAS; mem.: Environ. Def. Soc. (New Zealand) (bd. dirs. 1980—), Nat. Pks. Conservation Assn. (trustee 1970—79), Defenders Wildlife (dir. 1975—84, 1987—96). Achievements include research on DDT, PCBs, other chlorinated hydrocarbon effects on phytoplankton, birds; relationship between environmental sciences and public policy; seabird protection; instrumental in banning several insecticides, including DDT, Dieldrin and Aldrin. Address: 644 Hillside Dr E Seattle WA 98112 Office Phone: 206-325-3665. Personal E-mail: cfwurster@yahoo.com.

WÜTHRICH, KURT, molecular biologist, biophysicist, educator; b. Oct. 4, 1938; MS in Chemistry, Physics and Maths., U. Bern, Switzerland, 1962; Eidgenössisches Turn-und Sportlehrerdiplom, U. Basel, Switzerland, 1964, PhD in Chemistry, 1964; D in Chemistry (hon.), U. Siena, Italy, 1997; PhD (hon.), U. Zürich, Switzerland, 1997, Ecole Polytechnique Fédérale, Lausanne, Switzerland, 2001, U. Sheffield, Eng., 2004, U. Valencia, Spain, 2004, King George's Med. U., Lucknow, India, 2005, U. Pecs, Hungary, 2005, Lomonosov State U., Russia, 2006. Postdoctoral tng. U. Basel, U. Calif., Berkeley, Bell Telephone Labs., Murray Hill, N.J., 1964-69; prof. biophysics ETH Zurich, Zürich, Switzerland, 1972—, chmn. dept. biology, 1995-2000; prof. structural biology The Scripps Rsch Inst., La Jolla, 2001—. Mem. coun. Internat. Union Pure and Applied Biophysics, 1975-78, 87-90, sec. gen., 1978-84, v.p., 1984-87; mem. gen. com. Internat. Coun. Sci. Unions, 1980-86, standing com. on free circulation of scientists, 1982-90. Editor Jour. Biomolecular NMR, Quar. Rev. Biophysics, Macromolecular Structures; contbr. articles to profl. jours. Recipient Friedrich Miescher prize Schweizerische Biochemische Gesellschaft, 1974, shield of faculty of medicine Tokyo U., 1983, P. Bruylants medal Cath. U. Louvain, 1986, Stein and Moore award Protein Soc., U.S., 1990, Louisa Gross Horwitz prize Columbia U., 1991, Gilbert N. Lewis medal U. Calif., Berkeley, 1991, Marcel Benoist prize Swiss Confederation, 1992, Disting. Svc. award Miami Winter Symposia, 1993, Prix Louis Jeantet de Médecine, Geneva, 1993, Kaj Linderstrøm-Lang prize Kaj Linderstrøm-Lang Found., Copenhagen, 1996, Eminent Scientist of RIKEN (Tokyo), 1997, Kyoto prize in Advanced Tech., 1998, Guenther Laukien prize Exptl. Nuclear Magnetic Resonance Conf., 1999, Otto Warburg medal Soc. for Biochemistry and Molecular Biology, Germany, 1999, World award M. Gorbatschow Found., 2002, Nobel Prize in Chemistry, 2002; Swiss award, 2002; Fgn. fellow Indian Nat. Sci. Acad.; hon. fellow NAS India. Fellow: AAAS; mem.: U.S. Nat. Acad., World Innovation Found., Schweizerische Akademie der Medizinischen Wissenschaften, Schweizerische Akademie der Technischen Wissenschaften, Acad. Scis. Inst. France, Academia Europea, European Molecular Biology Orgn., Deutsche Akad. der Naturforscher Leopoldina, Indian Biophys. Soc. (hon.), Nuc. Magnetic Resonance Soc. Japan (hon.), Groupement Ampère (hon.), Latvian Acad. Sci. (hon.), European Acad. Arts and Humanities (hon.), Hungarian Acad. Sci. (hon.), Internat. Soc. Magnetic Resonance in Medicine (hon.), Royal Soc. Edinburgh (hon.), Royal Soc. Chemistry (hon.), Swiss Chem. Soc. (hon.), Nat. Magnetic Resonance Soc. India (hon.), Japanese Biochem. Soc. (hon.), Am. Acad. Arts and Scis. (hon.). Office: ETH

Zurich Inst Molecular Biology Biophysics 8093 Zurich Switzerland also: Scripps Rsch Inst Dept Molecular Biology 10550 N Torrey Pines Rd La Jolla CA 92037 Office Phone: +41-44-633-2475.

WWGIACOMINI, GARY T., lawyer; BA, St. Mary's Coll., Calif., 1962; JD, U. Calif. Hastings Coll. of Law, 1965. Ptnr. Hanson Bridgett Marcus Vlahos Rudy LLP. Mem. Marin County Bd. of Supervisors, 1972—96; bd. dirs. Golden Gate Bridge, Highway and Transportation Dist.; coastal commsr., Calif.; mem. San Francisco Bay Conservation and Develop. Commn., Northwest Pacific Railroad Authority, Assn. of Bay Area Govt. Bd. and Local Agy. Formation Commn., Marin Agricultural Land Trust. Bd. dirs. Marconi Conference Ctr. Bd., North Bay Council, Marin Cmty. Found., 2003. Mem.: Marin County Bar Assn., Bar Assn. of San Francisco. Office: Hanson Bridgett 425 Market St San Francisco CA 94105

WYANT, JAMES CLAIR, engineering company executive, educator; b. Morenci, Mich., July 31, 1943; s. Clair William and Idah May (Burroughs) W.; m. Louise Doherty, Nov. 20, 1971; 1 child, Clair Frederick. BS, Case Inst. Tech. (now Case Western Res. U.), 1965; MS in Optics, U. Rochester, 1967, PhD in Optics, 1968. Optical engr. Itek Corp., Lexington, Mass., 1968-74, mgr. optical engring., 1974; lectr. physics Lowell Technol. Inst., Mass., 1969—72, instr. math. and physics, 1970—74; asst. prof. optical scis. U. Ariz., Tucson, 1974—76, assoc. prof., 1976—79, prof., 1979—, prof. elec. and computer engring., 1985—, dir. optical scis., 1999—2005, dean Coll. Optical Scis., 2005—; pres., chmn. bd. dirs. WYKO Corp., Tucson, 1984—97. Vis. prof. U. Rochester, NY, 1983; chmn. Gordon Conf. Holography Plymouth State Coll., NH, 1984; bd. dirs. ILX Lightwave, 1988—, Veeco, 1997—99, Optics 1, 1999—, DMetrix, 2001—; bd. chmn. 4D Tech. Corp., 2002—; vis. prof. Changchun U., 2005—. Editor: Applied Optics and Optical Engineering, vols. VII-X, 1979-80, 83, 87. Fellow Internat. Soc. Optical Engring. (pres. 1986, Gold medal 2003), Optical Soc. Am. (bd. dirs. 1979-81, Tech. Achievement award 1988, Joseph Fraunhofer award 1992, R&D 100 award 1993, Gold medal 2003); mem. Am. Inst. Physics, NAE. Office: Coll Optical Scis U Ariz 1630 E University Blvd Tucson AZ 85721 Office Phone: 520-621-2448. E-mail: Jim.Wyant@Optics.Arizona.Edu.

WYATT, JOSEPH LUCIAN, JR., lawyer, writer; b. Chgo., Feb. 21, 1924; s. Joseph Lucian and Cecile Gertrude (Zadico) W.; m. Marjorie Kathryn Simmons, Apr. 9, 1954; children: Daniel, Linn, Jonathan. AB in English Lit. with honors, Northwestern U., 1947; LLB, Harvard U., 1949. Bar: Calif. 1950, U.S. Dist. Ct. (cen. dist.) Calif. 1950, U.S. Ct. Appeals (9th cir.) 1950, U.S. Tax Ct., U.S. Supreme Ct. 1965. Assoc. firm Brady, Nossaman & Walker, Los Angeles, 1950-58, ptnr. LA, 1958-61; pvt. practice LA, 1961-71; sr. mem. Cooper, Wyatt, Tepper & Plant, P.C., LA, 1971-79; of counsel Beardsley, Hufstedler & Kemble, LA, 1979-81; ptnr. Hufstedler & Kaus, LA, 1981-95; sr. of counsel Morrison & Foerster, LA, 1995—. Mem. faculty Pacific Coast Banking Sch., Seattle, 1963-92, Southwestern Grad. Sch. Banking, 1988-89; advisor Restatement, Trusts 3d, 1988—. Author: Trust Administration and Taxation, 4 vols., 1964—; editor: Trusts and Estates, 1962-74. Lectr. continuing legal edn. programs, Calif. and Tex.; trustee Pacific Oaks Coll. and Children's Sch., 1969-97; counsel, parliamentarian Calif. Democratic party and presdl. conv. dels., 1971—; mem. Calif. State Personnel Bd., 1961-71, v.p., 1963-65, pres., 1965-67; bd trustees Calif. Pub. Employees Retirement System, 1963-71. 1st sgt. USAAF, 1942-45. Fellow Am. Coll. of Trust and Estate Counsel; mem. ABA, Internat. Acad. Estate and Trust Law (treas. 1990-96), Am. Law Inst., Calif. State Bar Assn. (del. state conf. 1956, 62-67), L.A. Bar Assn. (trustee 1956). Democrat. Christian Scientist. Avocations: fishing, composing doggerel. Home: 1119 Armada Dr Pasadena CA 91103-2805 Office Phone: 213-892-5200. E-mail: jwyatt@mofo.com, jwyatt3@charter.net.

WYATT, TOM (JOHN THOMAS WYATT), apparel executive; b. 1955; m. Cheryl F. Wyatt; 2 children. Specialty account sales rep. Vanity Fair Corp., pres. Vanity Fair Intimates, Vanity Fair Coalition, 1995—97; pres. Warnaco Intimate Apparel, NYC, 1997; chmn., CEO Parisian, 1998; pres., CEO Cutter & Buck, Seattle, 2004—06; pres. GapBody Gap Inc., San Francisco, 2006—07, pres. Outlet divsn., 2007—08, pres. Old Navy divsn., 2008—. Bd. mem. Gap Found. Office: Gap Inc 2 Folsom St San Francisco CA 94105

WYDEN, RON(ALD) (LEE), United States Senator from Oregon; b. Wichita, Kans., May 3, 1949; s. Peter and Edith W.; m. Laurie Oseran, Sept. 5, 1978 (div. 1999); 2 children; m. Nancy Bass, Sept. 2005. Student, U. Santa Barbara, 1967-69; AB in Polit. Sci., with distinction, Stanford U., 1971; JD, U. Oreg., 1974. Bar: Oreg. 1975. Campaign aide Senator Wayne Morse, 1972, 74; co-founder, co-dir. Oreg. Gray Panthers, 1974-80; dir. Oreg. Legal Services for Elderly, 1977-79; instr. gerontology U. Oreg., 1976, U. Portland, 1980, Portland State U., 1979; mem. 97th-104th Congresses from 3d Oreg. dist., Washington, 1981-96; US Senator form Oreg., 1996—. Mem. com. fin. US Senate, com. intelligence, com. energy and natural resources, com. budget, spl. com. on aging. Contbr. articles to profl. journals. Mem. Oreg. Environmental Coun. Recipient Service to Oreg. Consumers award Oreg. Consumers League, 1978, Citizen of Yr. award Oreg. Assn. Social Workers, 1979, Significant Service award Multnomah County Area Agy. on Aging, 1980, Philip A. Hart Pubilc Svc. award Consumer Fedn. Am., 1999, Champion of Sci. award, U. Oreg./The Sci. Coalition, 2003; named Young Man of Yr. Oreg. Jr. C. of C., 1980, Senator of Yr. Nat. Assn. Police Orgn., 1997, People of Yr (with Rep. Christopher Cox) PC Computing mag., 1999, Legis. of Yr. Info. Tech. Coun., 2000; named one of 50 Most Important People on the Web, PC World, 2007; named to Legis. Hall of Fame Am. Electronics Assn. Mem. ABA, Iowa Bar Assn., Oreg. Bar Assn. Democrat. Jewish. Office: US Senate 230 Dirksen Senate Office Bldg Washington DC 20510-0001 also: District Office Ste 585 1220 SW 3rd Ave Portland OR 97204 Office Phone: 202-224-5244, 503-326-7525. Office Fax: 202-228-2717. E-mail: senator@wyden.senate.gov.*

WYDICK, RICHARD CREWS, lawyer, educator; b. Pueblo, Colo., Nov. 1, 1937; s. Charles Richard and Alice Wydick; m. Judith Brandli James, 1961; children: William Bruce, Derrick Cameron. BA, Williams Coll., 1959; LL.B., Stanford U., 1962. Bar: Calif. bar 1962. Asso. firm Brobeck, Phleger & Harrison, San Francisco, 1966-71; mem. faculty U. Calif. Law Sch., Davis, 1971—, prof. law, 1975—2003, dean, 1978-80, prof. emeritus, 2003—. Author: Plain English for Lawyers, 5th edit., 2005 Served to capt. USAR, 1962-66. Office: Sch Law U Calif Davis CA 95616

WYLE, FREDERICK S., lawyer; b. Berlin, May 9, 1928; came to U.S., 1939, naturalized, 1944; s. Norbert and Malwina (Mauer) W.; m. Katinka Franz, June 29, 1969; children: Susan Kim, Christopher Anthony, Katherine Anne. BA magna cum laude, Harvard U., 1951, LL.B., 1954. Bar: Mass. 1954, Calif. 1955, N.Y. 1958. Teaching fellow Harvard Law Sch., 1954-55; law clk. U.S. Dist. Ct., No. Dist. Calif., 1955-57; assoc. firm Paul, Weiss, Rifkind, Wharton & Garrison, NYC, 1957-58; pvt. practice San Francisco, 1958-62; spl. asst. def. rep. U.S. del. to NATO, Paris, 1962-63; mem. Policy Planning Council, Dept. State, Washington, 1963-65; dep. asst. sec. def. for European and NATO affairs Dept. Def., Washington, 1966-69; v.p. devel., gen. counsel Schroders, Inc., NYC, 1969-71, atty., cons., 1971-72; chief exec. officer Saturday Rev. Industries, Inc., San Francisco, 1972-76; individual practice law San Francisco, 1976—82. Internat. counsel to Fed. States Micronesia, 1974-82; cons. Rand Corp., Dept. Def., Nuclear Regulatory Commn. Contbr. to: Ency. Brit, 1972, also articles in profl. publs., newspapers. Trustee US Interest Bicycle Club Casino, 1996-99; trustee in bankruptcy Garden City, Inc., 2000-07; liquidating trustee Synthetic Industries, 2000—, Biosurg. Industries, 2000-08: Chpt. 11 trustee Winchester Convalescence Hosp., San Jose, 2008-; negotiator for Gov. of Calif. with Indian tribes re gambling, 2003. With AUS, 1946-47. Mem. Internat. Inst. Strategic Studies, Phi Beta Kappa. Office: 3 Embarcadero Ctr Fl 7 San Francisco CA 94111-4065 Office Phone: 415-788-0781.

WYLE, NOAH, actor; b. Hollywood, Calif., June 4, 1971; m. Tracy Warbin, 2000; children: Owen Strausser, Auden. Artistic prodr. The Blank Theatre Co., LA. Actor: (films) Crooked Hearts, 1991, A Few Good Men, 1992, Swing Kids, 1993, There Goes My Baby, 1994, The Myth of Fingerprints, 1997, Can't Stop Dancing, 1999, Scenes of the Crime, 2001, Enough, 2002, White Oleander, 2002, The Californians, 2004, W., 2008; (TV films) Blind Faith, 1990, Guinevere, 1994, Pirates of Silicon Valley, 1999, Fail Safe, 2000, The Librarian: Quest for the Spear, 2004; (TV series) ER, 1994—2005 (SAG award for outstanding performance by ensemble in drama series, 1998, 1999, TV Guide award for supporting actor of yr. in drama series, 2001); assoc. prodr. Myth of Fingerprints, 1997. Office: The Blank Theatre Co 1301 Lucile Ave Los Angeles CA 90026

WYLIE, RICHARD THORNTON, aerospace engineer; b. Long Beach, Calif., July 11, 1956; s. Howard Hance and Marcella Dart (Metcalf) W. BS, Calif. State Poly. U., Pomona, 1978; MS, U. Calif., Berkeley, 1979. Registered profl. engr., Calif. Engr. Aerocraft Heat Treating, Paramount, Calif., 1991—94, Northrop Grumman Aerospace Sys. (formerly TRW, Inc.), Redondo Beach, Calif., 1980—91, 1994—. Vol. tutor TRW Bootstrap, 1981—91, 1994—2001. Mem. Mensa (scholarship chmn. Harbor area 1995—2004, editor Harbor area newsletter 1996-99). Home: 1005 Kornblum Ave Torrance CA 90503-5113 Home Phone: 310-320-2659; Office Phone: 310-812-2068. Personal E-mail: RTWylie@alum.calberkeley.org.

WYMAN, RICHARD VAUGHN, engineering educator, company executive; b. Painesville, Ohio, Feb. 22, 1927; s. Vaughn Ely and Melinda (Ward) W.; m. Anne Fenton, Dec. 27, 1947; 1 son, William Fenton. BS, Case Western Res. U., 1948; MS, U. Mich., 1949; PhD, U. Ariz., 1974. Registered profl. engr., Nev., Ariz.; registered geologist, Ariz., Calif.; lic. water right surveyor, Nev., cert. minerals appraisor, 1991-. Geologist N.J. Zinc Co., 1949, 52-53, Cerro de Pasco Corp., 1950-52; chief geologist Western Gold & Uranium, Inc., St. George, Utah, 1953-55, gen. supt., 1955-57, v.p., 1957-59; pres. Intermountain Exploration Co., Boulder City, Nev., 1959-93; tunnel supt. Reynolds Electric & Engring. Co., 1961-63, mining engr., 1965-67; asst. mgr. ops. Reynolds Electric and & Engring. Co., 1967-69; constrn. supt. engr. Sunshine Mining Co., 1963-65; lectr. U. Nev., Las Vegas, 1969-73, assoc. prof., 1973-80, dept. chmn., 1976-80, prof., 1980-92, prof. emeritus, 1992—, chmn. dept. civil and mech. engring., 1984-90, chmn. dept. civil and environ. engring., 1990-91. Mineral rep. Ariz. Strip Adv. Bd., 1976-80, U.S.B.L.M.; mem. peer rev. com. Nuclear Waste Site, Dept. Energy, Las Vegas, 1978-82; pres. Ariz. Juno Resources, Boulder City, 1980-87, v.p., 1990-97; pres. Wyman Engring. Cons., 1987—2009; cons. Corp. Andina de Fomento, Caracas, Venezuela, 1977-78; v.p. Comstock Gold, Inc., 1984-93; program evaluator Accreditation Bd. for Engring. and Tech., 1995-2001. Contbr. articles to profl. jours. Sec. Washington County Republican Party, Utah, 1958-60; del. Utah Rep. Conv., 1958-60; scoutmaster Boy Scouts Am., 1959-69; mem. citizens adv. com., tech. adv. com. Clark County Regional Flood Control Dist., 1998-2004. Served with USN, 1944-46. Recipient Order of Engr. award, 2000. Fellow ASCE (life; edn. divsn. 1990, local rep. nat. conv. Las Vegas), Soc. Econ. Geologists (life); mem. AIME/SME (life, chmn. So. Nev. sect. 1971-72, dir. 1968-2002, sec.-treas. 1974-92, chmn. Pacific S.W. Minerals Conf. 1972, gen. chmn. nat. conv. 1980, Disting. Mem. award 1989, Legion of Honor 1999), Assn. Engring. Geologists (dir. S.W. sect. 1989-91), Am. Inst. Minerals Appraisers, Am. Water Works Assn., Nev. Mining Assn. (assoc.), Northwest Mining Assn., Geological Soc. Nev., Assn. Ground Water Scientists and Engrs., Arctic Inst. N.Am. (life), Am. Soc. Engring. Edn., Soc. for History of Discoveries, Am. Philatelic Soc., SAR, Am. Legion, Sigma Xi (pres. Las Vegas sect. 1986-91), Phi Kappa Phi (pres. U. Nev. Las Vegas chpt. 100 1982-83), Sigma Gamma Epsilon, Tau Beta Pi. Congregationalist. Home: 610 Bryant Ct Boulder City NV 89005-3017 Office: Wyman Engring PO Box 60473 Boulder City NV 89006-0473 Home Phone: 702-293-4178.

WYNAR, BOHDAN STEPHEN, retired librarian, writer, editor; b. Lviv, Ukraine, Sept. 7, 1926; came to U.S., 1950, naturalized, 1957; s. John I. and Euphrosina (Doryk) W.; children: Taras, Michael, Roxolana. Diplom-Volkswirt Econs., U. Munich, Germany, 1949, PhD, 1950; MA, U. Denver, 1958. Methods analyst, statistician Tramco Corp., Cleve., 1951-53; freelance journalist Soviet Econs., Cleve., 1954-56; adminstrv. asst. U. Denver Librs., 1958-59, head tech. svcs. div., 1959-62; assoc. prof. Sch. Librarianship, U. Denver, 1962-66; dir. div. libr. edn. State U. Coll., Geneseo, NY, 1966-67, dean Sch. Libr. Sci., prof., 1967-69; pres. Libraries Unlimited Inc., 1969—2002. Author: Soviet Light Industry, 1956, Economic Colonialism, 1958, Ukrainian Industry, 1964, Introduction to Bibliography and Reference Work, 4th edit, 1967, Introduction to Cataloging and Classification, 8th edit, 1992, Major Writings on Soviet Economy, 1966, Library Acquisitions, 2d edit, 1971, Research Methods in Library Science, 1971, Economic Thought in Kievan Rus', 1974; co-author: Comprehensive Bibliography of Cataloging and Classification, 2 vols., 1973, Ukraine: A Bibliographic Guide to English Language Publications, 1990, Independent Ukraine: A Bibliographic Guide to English Language Publications, 1989-99, 2000, Wynar's Introduction to Cataloging and Classification, 2000; editor Ukrainian Quar., 1953-58, Preliminary Checklist of Colorado Bibliography, 1963, Studies in Librarianship, 1963-66, Research Studies in Library Science, 1970—, Best Reference Books, 3d edit., 1985, 4th edit., 1992, Colorado Bibliography, 1980; gen. editor: American Reference Books Ann., 1969-2001; editor: ARBA Guide to Subject Encyclopedias and Dictionaries, 1985, ARBA Guide To Biographical Dictionaries, Reference Books in Paperback, An Annotated Guide, 2d edit., 1976, 3rd edit., 1991, Dictionary of Am. Library Biography, 1978, Ukraine-A Bibliographic Guide to English-Language Publications, 1990, 99, International Writings of Bohdan S. Wynar 1949-1992, 1993, Independent Ukraine, Bibliographic Guide, 2000, My Life-Memoirs-, 2003, Recommended Reference Books for Medium-Sized and Small Libraries, 1981-2001; co-editor, contbr. Ency. Ukraine, 1955—; editor Library Sci. Ann., 1984-90, 98, Libr. Info. Sci. Annual 1984-90, 98—. Bd. dirs., mem. exec. bd. ZAREVO, Inc. Mem. ALA (pres. Ukrainian Congress com. br., Denver 1976), Colo. Library Assn., N.Y. Library Assn., Am. Assn. Advancement Slavic Studies (pres. Ukrainian Research Found. 1976-90), AAUP, Ukranian Hist. Assn. (exec. bd.), Sevčenko Societe Scientifique (Paris), Ukrainian Acad. Arts and Scis. (N.Y.C.).

WYNN, STEVE ALAN (STEPHEN A. WYNN), hotel and gaming company executive; b. New Haven, Conn., Jan. 27, 1942; m. Elaine Paschal, 1963; children: Kevyn, Gillian. BA, U. Pa, 1963. Pres., CEO Best Brands, Inc., 1969-72; chmn., pres., CEO Mirage Resorts Inc. (formerly Golden Nugget Inc.), 1973—2000; mng. mem. Valvino Lamore, LLC, 2000—02; chmn., CEO Wynn Resorts Ltd., 2002—; owner Wynn Las Vegas Resort, 2005—, Wynn Macau, 2006—. Bd. trustees John F. Kennedy Ctr. for Performing Arts, 2006—. Named one of Top 200 Collectors, ARTnews Mag., 2004—08, 100 Most Influential People, Time Mag., 2006, Forbes' Richest Americans, 2003—, World's Richest People, Forbes mag., 2004—, People to Watch in 2007, Sunday Star Ledger. Jewish. Avocation: Collector of French Impressionism; Modern and Contemporary Art. Office: Wynn Resorts Ltd 3145 Las Vegas Blvd S Las Vegas NV 89109

WYNNE, MICHAEL WALTER, former civilian military employee; b. Hillsborough County, Fla., Sept. 4, 1944; s. Edward P. and Dorothy T. Wynne; m. Barbara Ann Hill, July 23, 1966; children: Lisa, Collene, Karen, Laura. BS in Gen. Engring., U.S. Mil. Acad., 1966; MSEE, Air Force Inst. Tech., 1970; MBA in Fin., U. Colo., 1975. Commd. lt. USAF, 1966, advanced through grades to capt., 1969; project engr. Electronics Systems Div., Bedford, Mass., 1966-68; asst. prof. astronautics USAF Acad., Colorado Springs, 1970-73; sec.-treas., v.p. R.A.D. Inc., Colorado Springs, 1973-75; mgr. estimating dept. Ft. Worth div. Gen. Dynamics, 1975-78, mgr. pricing, corp. hdqrs., St. Louis, 1978-82; v.p. contracts, estimating Land Systems div. Gen. Dynamics, Sterling Heights, Mich., 1982-87, v.p. bus. devel., 1987-91; corp.v.p., gen. mgr. Space Systems Div. Gen. Dynamics, San Diego, 1991-92, pres., corp. v.p. Space Systems Div., 1992—94; v.p., gen. mgr. space launch systems Lockheed Martin Astronautics, 1994—97; sr. v.p. for internat. planning & bus. devel. Gen. Dynamics, 1997—99; prin. under sec. acquisition, tech. & logistics US Dept. Def., Washington, 2001—05, under sec. for acquisition, tech. & logistics, 2005, sec. Dept. Air Force, 2005—08. Fellow Nat. Contract Mgmt. Assn. (pres. Detroit chpt. 1983-86), Assn. U.S. Army (pres. Detroit chpt. 1987-89), Am. Def. Preparedness Assn. (pres. Mich. chpt. 1986-87). Roman Catholic. Avocations: golf, skiing.

WYNNE-EDWARDS, HUGH ROBERT, geologist, educator, entrepreneur; b. Montreal, Que., Can., Jan. 19, 1934; s. Vero Copner and Jeannie Campbell (Morris) W.-E.; married Janet Elizabeth McGregor; children from previous marriages: Robin Alexander, Katherine Elizabeth, Renée Elizabeth Lortie, Krista Smyth, Jeannie Elizabeth, Alexander Vernon. BSc with 1st class honors, U. Aberdeen, Scotland, 1955; MA, Queen's U., Kingston, Ont., Can., 1957, PhD, 1959; DSc (hon.), Meml. U., 1975. Registered profl. engr., B.C., 1995. With Geol. Survey Can., 1958-59; lectr. Queen's U., 1968-72, asst. prof., then assoc. prof., 1961-68, prof., head dept. geol. scis., 1968-72; prof., then Cominco prof., head dept. geol. scis. U. B.C., Vancouver, Canada, 1972-77; asst. sec. univ. br. Ministry of State for Sci. and Tech., Ottawa, Canada, 1977-79; sci. dir. Alcan Internat. Ltd., Montreal, 1979-80, v.p. R & D, chief sci. officer, 1980-89; CEO Moli Energy Ltd., Vancouver, 1989-90; pres. Terracy Inc., Vancouver, 1989—; sci. advisor Teck Corp., Vancouver, 1989-91; pres., CEO B.C. Rsch. Inc., Vancouver, 1993-97, exec. chmn., pres., 1997-2000. Chmn. Silvagen Inc., 1996-99; advisor Directorate Mining and Geology, Uttar Pradesh, India, 1964, Grenville project Que. Dept. Natural Resources, 1968-72; vis. prof. U. Aberdeen, 1965-66, U. Witwatersrand, Johannesburg, South Africa, 1972; UN cons., India, 1974; pres. SCITEC, 1977-78; mem. sci. adv. com. CBC, 1980-84; mem. Sci. Coun. Can., 1983-89, Nat. Adv. Bd. on Sci. and Tech., 1987-90 indsl. liaison com. UN Ctr. for Sci. and Tech. in Devel., 1982-84; vice chmn. tech. adv. group Bus. Coun. for Sustainable Devel., Geneva, 1991; mem. Nat. Biotech. Adv. Coun., 1995-98; chmn. Neurosci. Can. Partnership, 1999-2003, Azure Dynamics Inc., 2000-01; pres. Silvagen Holdings Inc., 1999-2000; bd. dirs. Welichem Biotech Inc., chmn., 2000-; bd. dirs. Photon Control Inc. Bd. dirs. Royal Victoria Hosp., Montreal, 1984-89. Decorated officer Order of Can., 1991; recipient Spendiarov prize 24th Internat. Geol. Congress, Montreal, 1972. Fellow Can. Acad. Engring., Royal Soc. Can., World Acad. Arts and Scis.; mem. Can. Rsch. Mgmt. Assn. (vice chmn. 1982-84, chmn. 1984-85, Assn. medal 1987), Univ. Club (Montreal). Mem. United Ch. Canada. Avocations: tennis, skiing, carpentry. Office: Terracy Inc 2030 27th St West Vancouver BC Canada V7V 4L4 Office Phone: 604-926-1191. Business E-Mail: hughwynn@terracy.com.

WYSE, ROGER EARL, physiologist, department chairman; b. Wauseon, Ohio, Apr. 22, 1943; BS in Agr., Ohio State U., 1965; MS, Mich. State U., 1967, PhD in Crop Sci., 1969. Fellow Mich. State U., 1969-70; plant physiologist Agr. Rsch. Svc. USDA, 1970-86; dean of rsch. Cook Coll. Rutgers U., 1986-92; dean, dir. Coll. Agr. and Life Sci. U. Wis., Madison, 1992-98; mng. dir. Burrill & Co., San Francisco, 1998—. Recipient Arthur Flemming award, 1982. Fellow Am. Soc. Agronomy, Crop Sci. Soc. Am.; mem. AAAS, Am. Soc. Plant Physiol. Office: Burrill & Co 1 Embarcadero Ctr Ste 2700 San Francisco CA 94111-3744

YABLONOVITCH, ELI, electrical engineering educator; b. Puch, Austria, Dec. 15, 1946; BSc, McGill U., 1967; AM, Harvard U., 1969, PhD in Applied Physics, 1972. Tchg. fellow Harvard U., 1971—72, asst. prof. applied physics, 1974-76, assoc. prof. applied physics, 1976-79; mem. tech. staff Bell Labs., 1972-74; rsch. assoc., group head Exxon Rsch. Ctr., 1979-84; mem. tech. staff Bellcore, 1984-90, disting. mem. staff, 1990-93, dir. solid state physics rsch., 1991-93; prof. elec. engring. UCLA, 1993—. Chmn. Gordon Conf. on Nonlinear Optics and Lasers, 1979; founder W/PECS Series of Photonic Crystal Internat. Workshops, 1999; Clifford Paterson lectr. Royal Soc. London, 2000; Edison lectr. Notre Dame U., 2004; Anson L. Clark Meml. lectr. U. Tex., 2004; Morris Loeb lectr. Harvard U., 2005; co-founder Eelctronics Inc., Luxtem, Inc., Luminoscent., Inc. A.P.

Sloan fellow, 1978-79; recipient Julius Springer prize in applied physics, 2001. Fellow: IEEE (W. Streifer Sci. Achievement award 1993), Optical Soc. Am. (Adolph Lomb medal 1978, R.W. Wood prize 1996), Am. Physics Soc.; mem.: NAS, NAE. Achievements include research in solar cells, strained-semiconductor lasers, photonic band structure. Office: UCLA Dept Elec Engring 66-147K Engring Bldg IV Los Angeles CA 90095-1594 Business E-Mail: eliy@ee.ucla.edu.

YACKIRA, MICHAEL WILLIAM, electric power industry executive; b. NYC, Aug. 14, 1951; s. Alan Israel and Lillian (Landau) Y.; m. Roberta Guido, July 24, 1977; 3 children BS in Acctg., Herbert H. Lehman Coll., CUNY, 1972. CPA. Sr. acct. Arthur Andersen, NYC, 1972-75; v.p. St. Joe Petroleum, Houston, 1975-83; mgr. fin. analysis U.S. Industries, Stamford, Conn., 1983-84; dir. bus. analysis and research GTE Svc. Corp., Stamford, 1984-85, dir. bus. devel. and analysis, 1985-86, asst. controller budget planning and analysis, 1986-87; v.p. fin. and revenues GTE Fla., Tampa, 1987-88; v.p. fin. and info. mgmt. GTE Info. Svcs., Tampa, 1988-89; v.p. corp. devel. and planning FPL Group, Inc., Juno Beach, Fla., 1989-91; chief planning officer Fla. Power and Light Co., 1990-91; sr. v.p. market and regulatory services, then sr. v.p. CFO Fla. Power & Light Co., Juno Beach, 1991—98; pres. FPL Energy Inc., 1998—2000; v.p., CFO Mars Inc., 2001—02; exec. v.p. strategy & policy NV Energy Inc. (was Sierra Pacific Resources), Las Vegas, Nev., 2003; corp. exec. v.p., CFO NV Energy Inc., Las Vegas, Nev., 2003—07, pres., COO, 2007, pres., CEO, 2007—. Bd. dir. Am. Heart Assn., United Way So. Nev. Office: NV Energy Inc 6226 W Sahara Ave Las Vegas NV 89146 Mailing: NV Energy Inc PO Box 98910 Las Vegas NV 89151-0001

YACOUB, IGNATIUS I., dean; b. Dwar Taha, Syria, Jan. 5, 1937; came to U.S. 1978; s. Immanuel and Martha (Kharma) Y.; m. Mary Haddad, Sept. 14, 1961; children: Hilda, Lena, Emile. AB, Mid. East Coll., Beirut, Lebanon, 1960; MA, Pacific Union Coll., Angwin, Calif., 1964; PhD, Claremont Grad. Sch., Calif., 1976. Dean studies Mid. East Coll., Beirut, 1967-73, 75-78; dir. dept. edn. Afro-Mideast divsn. Seventh-Day Adventist Ch., 1970-73, dir. dept. pub. affairs, 1975-78; prof., chmn. dept. bus. econs. Southwestern Union Coll., Keene, Tex., 1978-80; prof., chmn. dept. bus. and econs. Loma Linda U., Riverside, Calif., 1980-86, founding dean Sch. of Bus. and Mgmt., 1986-90, prof. mgmt., 1995—; founding dean Sch. Bus. and Mgmt., La Sierra U., Riverside, 1990—95; prof. adminstrn. and mgmt. Loma Linda U., Loma Linda, Calif., 1995—. Bd. dirs. Riverside Nat. Bank; bd. advisors City Nat. Bank, 1997—2003. Mem. Exec. 2000 Coun. Riverside Cmty. Hosp. Found., 1991-95. Recipient Gov.'s Appreciation award, Lions Club, Lions Club award, Beirut, cert. Appreciation Exec. 2000 Coun., 1994, 95, Cert. of Appreciation Claremont Grad. Sch. Alumni Coun., 1996, Mentemoreles Univ. Mex., 1992, 94. Mem. Am. Mgmt. Assn., Acad. Mgmt., Soc. for Advancement Mgmt., Greater Riverside C. of C. (Svc. award 1995), Corona C. of C. Seventh-Day Adventist. Home: 2722 Litchfield Dr Riverside CA 92503-6213 Office Phone: 909-558-7148. Personal E-mail: iyacoub@charter.net. Business E-Mail: iyacoub@univ.llu.edu.

YACOVONE, ELLEN ELAINE, banker; b. Aug. 4, 1951; d. Wilfred Elliott and Charlotte Frances (Fox) Drew; m. Richard Daniel Yacovone, June 2, 1979; stepchildren: Christopher Daniel, Kimberly Marie. Student, Broome C.C., 1973-80; cert., Inst. Fin. Edn., Chgo., 1974. Sec. to exec. v.p. Ithaca Savs., NYC, 1968; mortgage clk. Citizens Savs. Bank, 1968-69; with Lincoln Bank, Van Nuys, Calif., 1970-71; asst. bookkeeper Henry's Jewelers, Binghamton, N.Y., 1971-74; teller, br. supt., br. mgr. 1st Fed. Savs., Binghamton, 1974-82, v.p., ctrl. regional sales mgr., 1982-86, dist. sales mgr., 1986-88; br. mgr. Gt. Western Bank, Pensacola, Fla., 1988-89, v.p., regional mgr. San Diego, 1989-95; br. v.p. Washington Mut. Bank (formerly Gateway Ctr.), San Diego, 1995—, Northpark, Calif., 1996—, fin. ctr. mgr. San Diego, Northpark; consumer lending mgr. Calif. Coast Credit Union, 2003. V.p., owner, operator EYE Shirts, 1995—. Vol. Sta. WSKG Pub. TV, Conklin, N.Y., 1974-88, United Way Broome County, Binghamton, 1976-88; mem. Gov.'s Commn. Domestic Violence, Albany, N.Y., 1983-87; mem. Found. State U. Ctr. Binghamton; bd. dirs. Interfaith Shelter Network, San Dieog, 1992-2002, Schs. Success and the San Diego Innovative Preschool Project, 1995-2000, San Diego Urban League, 1995—, Black Econ. Task Force, 1995—. Named Woman of Achievement Broome County Status Women Coun., 1981. Mem. Triple Cities Bus. and Prol. Women (pres. 1979-81, Young Careerist award 1977), Sales and Mktg. Execs., Inst. Fin. Edn. (bd. dirs. 1976-88, pres. 1984-85, winner N.Y. state speech contest 1984), Broome County C. of C., Broome County Bankers Assn. (bd. dirs. 1979-88, pres. 1983-84), Watercolor Soc., Catfish Club. Republican. Methodist. Avocations: exercise, hand painting wearables, woodworking, gardening, needlecrafts. Office: Calif Coast Credit Union PO Box 502080 San Diego CA 92150 Home: 11761 N Joi Dr Oro Valley AZ 85737-8871

YAFFE, BARBARA MARLENE, journalist; b. Montreal, Que., Can., Mar. 4, 1953; d. Allan and Anne (Freedman) Yaffe. Student, McGill U., 1970-73; BA, U. Toronto, 1974; B of Journalism, Carleton U., 1975. Reporter Montreal Gazette, 1975-76, Toronto Globe and Mail, 1976-79, reporter, columnist Halifax, N.S., 1979-81; chief nat. TV news bur. CBC, St. Johns, Nfld., Canada, 1981-84, Edmonton, Alta., Canada, 1983; reporter Toronto Globe and Mail, St. John's, 1984-86; editor Sunday Express, St. John's, 1987-88, Vancouver Sun, 1988-93, columnist, edit. bd. adv., 1993—. Recipient Gov. Gen.'s award, Roland Michener Found., 1977, Commentary award, Jack Webster Found., 2004, Animal Action award, Internat. Fund for Animal Welfare, 2004. Office: c/o Vancouver Sun Ste 1 200 Granville St Vancouver BC Canada V6C 3N3 Office Phone: 604-605-2189. Business E-Mail: byaffe@png.canwest.com.

YAFFE, SUMNER JASON, pediatrician, educator, science administrator; b. Boston, May 9, 1923; s. Henry H. and Ida E. (Fisher) Yaffe; m. Susanne Hecht Goldstein, 2005; children: Steven, Kristine, Jason, Noah, Ian, Zachary. AB, Harvard U., 1945, MA, 1950; MD, U. Vt., 1954. Diplomate Am. Bd. Pediatrics. Rsch. fellow in pharmacology U. Vt. Coll. Medicine, Burlington, 1950—52; intern in pediat. Children's Hosp., Boston, 1954—55, resident, 1955-56; resident in pediatrics St. Mary's Hosp., London, 1956-57; instr. pediatrics Stanford U., Palo Alto, Calif., 1959-60, asst. prof., 1960-63; assoc. prof. pediatrics SUNY-Buffalo, 1963-66, prof., 1966-75, adj. prof. biochem. pharmacology, 1968-75, acting chmn. dept. pediatrics, 1974-75; prof. pediatrics and pharmacology U. Pa., Phila., 1975-81; clin. prof. pediat. Johns Hopkins Hosp., 1986—2001; vis. prof. pediat. UCLA Sch. Medicine, 2001—06; cons. prof. Stanford Med. Ctr., 2006—. Vis. prof. pharmacology Karolinska Inst., Stockholm, 1969—70; dir. Pediat. Renal Clinic, Stanford Med. Ctr., 1960—63; dir. newborn nursery svc. Palo Alto-Stanford Hosp., 1960—63, program dir. Clin. Rsch. Ctr. for Premature Infants, 1962—63; dir. Clin. Rsch. Ctr. for Children Children's Hosp., Buffalo, 1963—70, dir. Poison Control Ctr., 1967—75, dir. divsn. clin. pharmacology, Phila., 1975—81; dir. Ctr. for Rsch. for Mothers and Children Nat. Inst. Child Health and Human Devel., NIH, 1981—2001, program cons., 1963—71, mem. tng. grant com., 1963—65, mem. reproductive biology com., 1965—67; mem. adv. panel on maternal and child health WHO, Geneva, 1970—; liaison rep. drug rsch. bd. NRC, 1971—75, com. on drug dependence, 1972—75, mem. com. on problems of drug safety, 1972—75; mem. adv. panel in pediat. U.S. Pharmacopeia, 1970—, mem. adv. panel in toxicology, 1974—75; cons. Am. Found. for Maternal and Child Health, Inc., 1973—; pres. Maternal and Child Health Rsch. Found., Children's Hosp., 1974—75; Wall Meml. lectr. Children's Hosp., Washington, 1968—; Dr. W.E. Upjohn lectr. Can. Med. Assn., 1974; Louisville pediat. lectr. Sch. Medicine U. Louisville, 1974; William N. Creasy vis. prof. clin. pharmacology SUNY, 1976; advisor Internat. Childbirth Assn. Greater Phila., 1979—83; guest lectr. dept. pediat. Georgetown U. Hosp., Washington, 1988—2001; lectr. in pediat. Johns Hopkins Sch. Medicine, Balt., 1988—2001; mem. Roundtable on Drug Devel., Inst. of Medicine. Author: (book) Clinics in Perinatology, 1974, Drug Assessment: Criteria and Methods, 1979, Pediatric Pharmacology, 1980, Pediatric Pharmacology, 2d edit., 1992; author: (with R. Galinsky) Clinical Therapeutics, 1978; editor (with R. H. Schwartz): Drug and Chemical Risks to the Fetus and Newborn, 1980; editor: (with G. G. Briggs, T. w. Bodendorfer, R. K. Freeman) Drugs in Pregnancy and Lactatin, A Reference Guide to Fetal and Neonatal Risk, 1983, Drugs in Pregnancy and Lactatin, A Reference Guide to Fetal and Neonatal Risk, 2d, edit., 1986, Drugs in Pregnancy and Lactatin, A Reference Guide to Fetal and Neonatal Risk, 4th edit., 1994, Drugs in Pregnancy and Lactatin, A Reference Guide to Fetal and Neonatal Risk, 5th edit., 1998; editor: (with J. V. Aranda) Pediatric Phyarmacology, 2d edit., 1993, Neonatal and Pediatric Pharmacology, 3d edit., 2004; mem. editl. bd.: Pediatric Alert, 1977—, Pharmacology, 1977—, Devel. Pharmacology and Therapeutics, 1979—95, mem. editl. adv. bd.: Drug Therapy, 1979—, cons. editor: Clin. Pharacokinetics, 1977; co-editor: Developmental Pharmacology, 1979—94; contbr. articles to profl. jours. With US Army, 1943—44. Recipient Oscar Hunter award, ASCPT, 2002, Sumner J. Yaffe award, PPAG, 2002; scholar Fulbright, 1956—57. Fellow: Acad. Pharm. Scis.; mem.: AAUP, AMA (com. on drugs 1963—68), Soc. Pediat. Rsch., Perinatal Rsch. Soc., Fedn. Am. Socs. Exptl. Biology, Am. Soc. Pharmacology and Exptl. Therapeutics, Am. Soc. Clin. Pharmacology and Therapeutics (chmn. sect. pediatric pharmacology 1977—83), Am. Pub. Health Assn., Soc. Maternal Fetal Medicine (hon.), Am. Pharmaceutics Assn., Am. Pediat. Soc., Am. Fedn. for Clin. Rsch., Am. Coll. Clin. Pharmacology and Chemotherapy, Am. Acad. Pediat. (chmn. com. drugs 1967—76), Alpha Omega Alpha, Sigma Xi. Personal E-mail: sjyatla@yahoo.com.

YAKATAN, GERALD JOSEPH, pharmaceutical executive; b. Phila., May 20, 1942; s. Nathan and Bella (Resnick) Y.; m. Una Gittleman, Dec. 20, 1964; children: Nicole Blayne, Brook Noel. BS, Temple U., 1963, MS, 1965; PhD, U. Fla., 1971. Asst. prof. U. Tex., Austin, 1971-76, assoc. prof., 1976-80; dir. pharmacokinetics and drug metabolism Warner Lambert Co., Ann Arbor, Mich., 1980-83, v.p. product devel. Morris Plains, N.J., 1983-87; exec. v.p. R & D, Immunetech Pharm., San Diego, 1987-90; founder, pres., CEO Tanabe Rsch. Labs., USA, Inc., San Diego, 1990-95, IriSys R&D, San Diego, 1996—98, chmn., 1998—. Contbr. articles to profl. jours. NIH fellow, 1965-69, NSF fellow, 1964. Fellow Am. Coll. Clin. Pharmacology (hon. regent), Am. Assn. Pharm. Sci., Acad. Pharm. Sci.; mem. U.S. Profl. Tennis Registry, Fla. Blue Key. Democrat. Jewish. Avocations: tennis, reading, travel. Office: Avanir Pharmaceutical 101 Enterprise Ste 300 Aliso Viejo CA 92656-2608

YALAM, ARNOLD ROBERT, allergist, immunologist, consultant; b. NYC, Apr. 11, 1940; s. Herman and Sylvia (Taber) Y.; m. Carol Ann Strocker, June 16, 1964; children: John, Matthew. AB, Johns Hopkins U., 1960; MD, U. Md., Balt., 1964. Diplomate Am. Bd. Internal Medicine, Am. Bd. Allergy and Immunology. Intern Jackson Meml. Hosp., Miami, Fla., 1964-65; resident in internal medicine SUNY Downstate Med. Ctr., Bklyn., 1965-67; fellow Scripps Clinic and Rsch. Found., La Jolla, Calif., 1967-68; cons. allergist and immunologist San Diego, 1970—. Maj. US Army, 1968—70. Fellow Am. Acad. Allergy and Immunoloy; mem. Am. Soc. Addiction Medicine (cert.), San Diego Allergy Soc.

YALAMANCHI, RAMU, Internet company executive; BS in Computer Sci., U. Ill., Urbana-Champaign. Regional sales mgr. AdKnowledge; bus. devel., product mgr. eGroups; co-founder, ptnr. SponsorNet New Media, 1995; founder, CEO hi5 Networks, Inc., 2003—. Office: hi5 Networks, Inc 55 Second St, Ste 300 San Francisco CA 94105 Office Phone: 415-404-6094. Office Fax: 415-704-3482.

YALMAN, ANN, judge, lawyer; b. Boston, June 9, 1948; d. Richard George and Joan (Osterman) Yalman. BA, Antioch Coll., 1970; JD, NYU, 1973. Trial atty. Fla. Rural Legal Svcs., Immokalee, Fla., 1973-74; staff atty. EEO, Atlanta, 1974-76; pvt. practice Santa Fe, 1976—2005; probate judge Santa Fe County, 1999—2005; mcpl. judge Santa Fe, 2006—. Part time U.S. magistrate, N.Mex., 1988—96. Commr. Met. Water Bd., Santa Fe, 1986-88. Mem. N.Mex. Bar Assn. (commr. Santa Fe chpt. 1983-86). Home: 441 Calle La Paz Santa Fe NM 87505-2821 Office: 2511 Camino Entrada Santa Fe NM 87507 Home Phone: 505-983-2615; Office Phone: 505-955-5133. Business E-Mail: ayalman@santa-fenm.gov.

YAMADA, MARIKO, state legislator; b. Denver, Colo., Oct. 23, 1950; m. Janlee Wong, 1984; children: Meilee, Midori. BA in Psychology, U. Colo., Boulder, 1972; MSW, U. Southern Calif., 1974. Asst. dep. co. supr. LA Co., 1975—77; with 1980 Undercount Reduction Campaign US Census Bur., 1977—82; with Office for Civil Rights US Dept. Commerce, 1982—87; EEO, Affirmative Action Officer San Diego Co. Dept. Social Svcs., 1989—94; bd. suprs. Yolo Co., 1999—2003; mem. Dist. 8 Calif. State Assembly, 2008—. Democrat. Avocation: Classic R&B Music. Office: PO Box 942849 Rm 5144 Sacramento CA 94249-0008 also: 555 Mason St Ste 275 Vacaville CA 95688 Office Phone: 916-319-2008, 707-455-8025. Office Fax: 916-319-2108, 707-455-0490.*

YAMAGUCHI, COLLEEN S., lawyer; BBA, U. Hawaii, 1982, MBA, 1985; JD, Georgetown U., 1986. Bar: Wash. 1986. Law firm, Seattle, from 1986; ptnr. Sidley & Austin, LA, 1998—. Assoc. editor Tax Lawyer, 1995-86. Former mem. steering com. Women in Leadership, Wash. Mem. Exec. Devel. Inst., Japanese Am. C. of C. Office: Sidley & Austin 555 W 5th St Los Angeles CA 90013-1010 Fax: 213-896-6600. E-mail: cyamaguc@sidley.com.

YAMAMOTO, JOE, retired psychiatrist, educator; b. LA, Apr. 18, 1924; s. Zenzaburo and Tomie (Yamada) Y.; m. Maria Fujitomi, Sept. 5, 1947; children: Eric Robert, Andrew Jolyon. Student, Los Angeles City Coll., 1941-42, Hamline U., 1943-45; BS, U. Minn., 1946, M.B., 1948, MD, 1949. Asst. prof. dept. psychiatry, neurology, behavioral sci. U. Okla. Med. Center, 1955-58, asst. prof., 1958-60; assoc. prof. dept. psychiatry U. So. Calif. Sch. Medicine, Los Angeles, 1961-69, prof., 1969-77, co-dir. grad. edn. psychiatry, 1963-70; prof. UCLA, 1977-94, emeritus prof., 1994—; dir. Psychiat. Outpatient Clinic, Los Angeles County-U. So. Calif. Med. Center, 1958-77; dir. adult ambulatory care services UCLA Neuropsychiat. Inst., 1977-88, chief Lab. for Cross Cultural Studies; ret. Contbr. articles in field to profl. jours. Served to capt., M.C. U.S. Army, 1953-55. Fellow Am. Psychiat. Assn. (life), Pacific Rim Coll. Psychiatrists, Am. Acad. Psychoanalysis (trustee, mem. exec. com., pres. 1978-79), Am. Coll. Psychiatrists, Am. Orthopsychiat. Assn. (pres.-elect 1993-94, pres. 1994-95, past pres.), Am. Assn. for Social Psychiatry (trustee 1981-84, v.p. 1984-86); mem. So. Calif. Psychoanalytic Inst. and Soc. (pres. 1972-73), Soc. for Study of Culture and Psychiatry, Group for Advancement Psychiatry (bd. dirs. 1992-94), Kappa Phi, Alpha Omega Alpha.

YAMAMOTO, KAORU, emeritus psychology professor; b. Tokyo, Mar. 28, 1932; arrived in U.S., 1959; s. Saburo and Hideko (Watanabe) Y.; m. Etsuko Hamazaki, Apr. 6, 1959 (div. 1986); m. Carol-Lynne Moore, Oct. 4, 1986; children: Keita Carey Moore, Kiyomi Lynne Moore. BS in Engring., U. Tokyo, 1953; MA, U. Minn., 1960, PhD, 1962. Engr. Toppan Printing Co., Tokyo, 1953; engr., rsch. chemist Japan Oxygen Co., Tokyo, 1954-57, 58-59; asst. prof. Kent (Ohio) State U., 1962-65; from asst. to assoc. prof. U. Iowa, Iowa City, 1965-68; prof. Pa. State U., University Park, 1968-72, Ariz. State U., Tempe, 1972-87, U. Colo., Denver, 1987-99, prof. emeritus, 1999—. Vis. prof. U. Minn., Mpls., 1974, Simon Fraser U., Burnaby, B.C., Can., 1984, U.Victoria, B.C., 1985, 86, U. Wash., Seattle, 1987, Zhejiang Normal U., Jinhua, China, 1991; Fulbright lectr. U. Iceland, 1985. Author: The Child and His Image, 1972, Their World, Our World, 1993; author, editor 10 books, including Children and Stress, 2001, Too Clever for Our Own Good, 2007; co-author: Beyond Words, 1988; editor Am. Ednl. Rsch. Jour., 1972-75, Ednl. Forum, 1984-92; contbr. chpts. to books and articles to profl. jours. Recipient Disting. Tchr. award Ariz. State U., 1980; Landsdowne scholar U. Victoria, 1985, Ctr. scholar Ctr. for Rsch. on Ethics and Values Azusa Pacific U., 1998-2000. Fellow: APA; mem.: Motus Humanus. Avocations: winter sports, travel, classical music, reading. Office: 13651 W 54th Ave Arvada CO 80002

YAMAMOTO, KEITH ROBERT, molecular biologist, educator; b. Des Moines, Feb. 4, 1946; BS, Iowa State U., 1968; PhD, Princeton U., 1973. Asst. prof. biochemistry U. Calif., San Francisco, 1976-79, assoc. prof., 1979-83, prof. biochemistry, 1983—2003, vice chmn. dept. biochemistry & biophysics, 1985—94, dir. biochemistry and molecular biology program, 1988—2001, chmn. dept. cellular & molecular pharmacology, 1994—2003, prof. dept. cellular & molecular pharmacology, 1994—; vice dean for rsch. UCSF Sch. Medicine, 2002—03, exec. vice dean, 2002—. Co-author: Gene Wars: Military Control Over the New Genetic Technologies, 1988; co-editor: Transcriptional Regulation, 1992; assoc. editor: Jour. Molecular Biology, 1988—2001; editor: Molecular Biology of the Cell, 1991—2001; editor-in-chief:, 2002—. Testifier hearings on biol. warfare com. on govtl. affairs U.S. Senate, Washington, 1989. Recipient Career Devel. award, NIH, 1977-82, UCSF Disting. Teaching award, 1979-80, Dreyfus Teacher-Scholar award, 1982-86, Gregory Pincus medal Worchester Found. for Exptl. Biology, 1990, Vanderbilt U. Medal of Merit, 1999. Fellow: AAAS; mem.: IOM (elected 2003), NAS, Am. Acad. Arts & Scienees, Am. Acad. Microbiology. Office: UCSF Box 2280 San Francisco CA 94143-2280 Office Phone: 415-476-3128. Office Fax: 415-476-6129. E-mail: yamamoto@cgl.ucsf.edu.

YAMAMOTO, STANLY TOKIO, prosecutor; b. San Jose, Calif., July 22, 1948; s. George and Bettie (Nakamura) Y.; m. Yuri Honda, July 21, 1973; children: Miharu Lesley, Kiyomi Jill. BA, San Jose State U., 1971; JD, Santa Clara U. Sch. Law, 1978. Bar: Calif., 1980, U.S. Dist. Ct. (no. dist.) Calif., 1980, U.S. Dist. Ct. (ea. dist.) Calif., 1983, U.S. Dist. Ct. (ctrl. dist.) Calif., 1993, U.S. Supreme Ct., 1990. Adminstrv. asst. City of Sunnyvale, Calif., 1980-82, dep. city atty. Calif., 1982-84, asst. city atty. Calif., 1984-85, acting city atty. Calif., 1985-87; city atty. City of Modesto, Calif., 1987-92, City of Riverside, Calif., 1992—. Minorities-in-planning intern HUD, 1971-73; adv. Gov.'s Local Govt. Policy Com., 1993. With USAR, 1968-74. Nat. Urban fellow, 1978-79. Mem. League Calif. Cities, Internat. Mcpl. Lawyers. Office: Office of City Atty 3900 Main St Riverside CA 92522-0001

YAMANAKA, SHINYA, stem cell scientist, educator; MD, Kobe U., 1987; PhD, Osaka City U. Grad. Sch., 1993. Resident orthop. surgery Nat. Osaka Hosp., Japan, 1987—89; postdoctoral fellow Gladstone Inst. Cardiovascular Disease, San Francisco, 1993—95, staff rsch. investigator, 1995—96, L.K. Whittier Found. investigator stem cell biology, sr. investigator, 2007—; asst. prof. Osaka City U. Med. Sch., Japan, 1996—99; assoc. prof. Nara Inst. Sci. and Tech., Japan, 1999—2003, prof., 2003—05, Inst. Frontier Med. Scis., Kyoto U., Japan, 2004—; prof. anatomy U. Calif., San Francisco, 2007—. Recipient Gairdner Found. Internat. award, 2009; co-recipient Shaw prize in life sci. and medicine, 2008; named one of The 100 Most Influential People in the World, TIME mag., 2008. Office: Gladstone Inst Cardiovascular Disease 1650 Owens St San Francisco CA 94158 Office Phone: 415-734-2710. Office Fax: 415-355-0960. E-mail: syamanaka@gladstone.ucsf.edu.*

YAMARONE, CHARLES ANTHONY, JR., aerospace engineer, consultant; b. Bronxville, NY, Oct. 30, 1936; s. Charles Anthony and Mildred (La Manna) Y.; m. Catherine MacMullan, May 31, 1957; children: Charles Anthony III, Thomas, Stephen, Mark, James. BSEE, Manhattan Coll., 1958. Design engr. Gen. Precision Inc., Pleasantville, N.Y., 1958-62; engr. supr. Jet Propulsion Lab., Calif. Inst. Tech., Pasadena, 1962-69, sect. mgr., 1969-76, data processing mgr. Topex/Poseidon, 1976-80, project mgr., 1980-96, program mgr. Eart Sci. Flight Projects, 1996—. Recipient Astronautique medal Assn. Aeronautique et Astronautique de France, 1992, medal Ctr. Nat. d'Etudes Spatiales, 1994, Outstanding Leadership medal NASA, 1993. Mem. Am. Geophys. Union, Am. Inst. for Advancement of Science. Office: Jet Propulsion Lab 254686 Topex Project Office 4800 Oak Grove Dr Pasadena CA 91109-8001

YAMASHITA, FRANCIS ISAMI, magistrate judge; b. Hilo, Hawaii, May 14, 1949; s. Yuji and Sadako (Hirayama) Y.; m. Alexa D. M. Fujise, Feb. 26, 1983. BA, Pacific U., 1971; JD, U. Chgo., 1974.

Bar: Hawaii 1974. Law clk. 1st Cir. Ct., Hawaii, 1975-76; dep. pros. atty. City/County of Honolulu, 1976-79, 82-87; assoc. Ikazaki, Devens, Lo, Youth & Nakano, Honolulu, 1979-82; dist. judge State of Hawaii, Honolulu, 1987-92, U.S. magistrate judge, 1992—. Home: 5038 Poola St Honolulu HI 96821-1559

YAMASHITA, KENNETH AKIRA, library administrator, librarian; b. Topaz, Utah, Sept. 11, 1945; s. Susumu and Kiyoko (Kitano) Y. BA, Rutgers U., 1967, MLS, 1972; ArtsD, Simmons Coll., 1982. Reference libr. Montclair Free Pub. Libr., NJ, 1970-73; ext. svcs. libr. Decatur (Ill.) Pub. Libr., 1973-75; asst. to commr. Chgo. Pub. Libr., 1975-78; mktg. rep. Computer Libr. Sys., Inc., Newtonville, Mass., 1978-79; asst. to dir. Mass. Bd. Libr. Commrs., Boston, 1979-81; supervising libr. Stockton (Calif.)-San Joaquin County Pub. Libr., 1982-90, libr. divsn. mgr., 1990—2007; deputy dir., 2008—. Guest lectr. Sch. Libr. Sci., U. Mich., Ann Arbor, 1978; bldg. program and design cons. Stockton-San Joaquin County Public Libr. Lakeland (Fla.) Pub. Libr., Calaveras County (Calif.) Pub. Libr., 1982—; advisor to prof. publs. U. Wis., Madison, Assn. Coll. and Rsch. Librs. Chgo., Calif. State Libr., Sacramento, Gale Pub., Detroit, 1989—; state, fed. grant writer Stockton-San Joaquin County Public Libr., 1990-, Calaveras County Libr., San Andreas, Calif., 1991; mem. rev. com. multi-ethnic recruitment scholarship program Calif. State Libr., 1990, 95; mem. design com. Libr. Staff Edn. Funding Program Calif. State Libr., 1998-01. Assoc. editor: (reference book) Guide to Multicultural Resources, 1995-97; contbr.: Problems in Library Management, 1981, chpts. to books, articles in profl. jours. Sec., bd. dirs. Stockton Shelter for Homeless, 1993-96; mem. diversity awareness team City of Stockton, 1994-98; mem. citizen rev. team United Way San Joaquin County, 1994, 95; participant Leadership Stockton, 1995; co-chair Joint Conf. Librs. of Color, 2006. Asian Studies Com. fellow Ind. U., 1967-69, Carnegie Grant fellow Ind. U., 1969-70, Friends of the Montclair Free Pub. Libr. fellow Rutgers U., 1971, HEA Title II B fellow Simmons Coll., 1979-80. Mem. ALA (chair, adv. com. Office for Libr. Outreach Svcs. 1987-90, councilor 1995-98, 99—, nominating com. 1995, com. on coms. 1997-98, spectrum initiative steering com. 1997—, Equality award, 2007), Asian/Pacific ALA (pres. 1996-97), Calif. Libr. Assn. (coun., assembly mem. 1987-93, pres. pub. libr. sect. 1998), Pub. Libr. Assn. (bd. dirs. & exec. com. 2000-03), Beta Phi Mu. Democrat. Avocations: videos/films, music, aerobics, cooking, travel. Office: Stockton San Joaquin County Pub Libr 605 N El Dorado St Stockton CA 95202-1907 Office Phone: 209-937-8467. E-mail: ken.yamashita@ci.stock.ca.us.

YAMAUCHI, PAUL STEVEN, dermatologist, researcher; PhD, MD, Case We. Res. U., 1991. Med. dir. Clin. Rsch. Specialists, Santa Monica, Calif., 2000—; exec. med. dir. Dermatology Inst. & Skin Care Ctr., Santa Monica, 2004—. Med. lectr., cons. Clin. Rsch. Specialists, Santa Monica, 2000—. Contbr. articles to profl. jours. Recipient Bill Reed Award Lectureship, European Soc. Dermatol. Rsch., 1999, Everett C. Fox Residents and Fellows Award, Am. Acad. Dermatology, 1999, Ronald M. Reisner Award, UCLA Sch. of Medicine, 1998, Paul H. Curtiss, Jr. Musculoskeletal Award, Case We. Res. U., 1993. Fellow: Am. Acad. Dermatologists; mem.: Nat. Psoriasis Found. (corr.). Achievements include research in Clinical research in the development of biologic agents in the treatment of psoriasis and psoriatic arthritis. Key opinion leader in the subject of psoriatic disease; Clinical research in the development of cosmetic procedures for facial rejuvenation. Office: 2001 Santa Monica Blvd Ste 490W Los Angeles CA 90049 Office Fax: 310-829-4150. Business E-Mail: dermatology@earthlink.net.

YAMAYEE, ZIA AHMAD, engineering educator, dean; b. Herat, Afghanistan, Feb. 2, 1948; came to U.S., 1974; s. Sayed and Merjan Ahmad. BSEE, Kabul U., Afghanistan, 1972; MSEE, Purdue U., 1976, PhD, 1978. Registered profl. engr., Calif., Wash. Mem. faculty of engring. Kabul U., 1978; engr. Systems Control, Inc., Palo Alto, Calif., 1979-81; sr. engr. Pacific N.W. Utilities, Portland, Oreg., 1981-83; assoc. prof. elec. engring. Clarkson U., Potsdam, NY, 1983-85; assoc. prof. Gonzaga U., Spokane, 1985-87, dean Sch. Engring., 1988-96; prof., chair elec. engring. dept. U. New Orleans, 1987-88. Part-time rsch. engr. La. Power and Light Co., New Orleans, 1987-88; sr. cons. Engring. and Cons. Svcs., Spokane, 1989-96. Contbr. articles, reports to profl. jours. Bd. dirs. Wash. State Math., Engring. Sci. Achievement, Seattle, 1989-96; mem. Spokane Intercollegiate Rsch. and Tech. Inst. Adv. Coun., 1990-96. NSF grantee. Mem. Am. Soc. Engring. Edn., IEEE (sr.). Office: University of Portland 5000 N Willamette Blvd Portland OR 97203-5798 Office Phone: 503-943-7314. E-mail: yamayee@up.edu.

YAN, MARTIN, celebrity chef; b. Guangzhou, China, 1948; m. Susan Yan; 2 children. Grad., Overseas Inst. Cookery, Hong Kong; BS Food Sci., MS Food Sci., U. Calif., Davis; PhD Culinary Arts (hon.), Johnson & Wales U.; PhD Humane Letters (hon.), Colo. Inst. Art. Product mgr. canning corp., Hong Kong, 1976; mgr, head chef Lee's Garden Restaurant, Alberta, 1977; tchr., Chinese Cooking U. Calif.; founder Yan Can Cook Inc., 1997—, Yan Can Internat. Cooking School, San Francisco. Guest chef-instr. Calif. Culinary Acad., Johnson & Wales U., Culinary Inst. Am., U. San Francisco. Host (TV series) Yan Can Cook, 1978—, Martin Yan's Chinatowns, 2002—, Martin Yan Quick & Easy, 2004—; author: Yan Can Cookbook, 1981, The Joy of Wokking, 1982, Martin Yan, the Chinese Chef, 1985, A Wok For All Seasons, 1988, Everybody's Wokking, 1991, The Well-Seasoned Wok, 1992, Simply Delicious, 1993, A Simple Guide to Chinese Ingredients, 1994, Martin Yan's Culinary Journey Through China, 1995, Martin Yan's Asia, 1997, Martin Yan's Feast, 1998, Chinese Cooking for Dummies, 2000, Martin Yan's Invitation to Chinese Cooking, 2000, Martin Yan's Asian Favorites, 2001, Martin Yan's Chinatown Cooking, 2002, Martin Yan's Quick and Easy, 2004, Martin Yan's China, 2008; guest appearances (TV series) The Today Show, A&E: Top Ten Television Chefs, Cooking Live with Sara Moulton, The Tonight Show, Good Morning America, Q&A Asia, Lo & Co., Howie Mandell Show, Donnie & Marie Show, Mornings on Two, Live with Regis and Kelly, The Dennis Miller Show, Talk Asia (CNN Asia), The Martin Short Show. Recipient Best TV Cooking Show, James Beard Found., 1994, Best TV Food Journalism award, 1996, D'Artagnan Cervena Who's Who of Food and Beverage award, 2001, Single Camera Photography award, Daytime Emmy Awards, 1998, Antonin Careme award, Chef's Assoc. of the Pacific Coast, Courvoisier Leadership award; named Culinary Diplomat, Am. Culinary Fedn. Achievements include design of cookware and kitchen tools; owner of several pan-Asian restaurants, founder and executive chef of Martin Yan's Culinary Arts Center in Shenzhen, China. Office: Yan Can Cook Inc PO Box 4755 Foster City CA 94404 Office Phone: 650-341-0701. Business E-Mail: martin@yancancook.com.

YANCEY, GARY, electronics executive; Pres., CEO Applied Signal Tech., Sunnyvale, Calif. Office: Applied Signal Tech 400 W California Ave Sunnyvale CA 94086-5151

YANG, DEBRA WONG, lawyer, former prosecutor; b. LA, 1959; 3 children. B, Pitzer Coll., 1981; JD, Boston Coll., 1985. Assoc. Haight Dickson Brown & Bonesteel, Santa Monica, Calif., 1985—87, Wildman Harrold Allen & Dixon, Chgo., 1987; law clk. to Dist. Judge Ronald Lew LA, 1988—89; atty. Greenberg Glusker, 1989; judge LA Mcpl. Ct., 1997—2000, LA Superior Ct., 2000—02; US atty. (ctrl. dist.) Calif. US Dept. Justice, LA, 2002—06; ptnr., co-chair crisis mgmt. practice group Gibson, Dunn & Crutcher LLP, LA, 2007—. Adj. prof. U. So. Calif. Law Sch. Former pres. Chinese Am. Mus., LA. Named one of The 50 Most Influential Minority Lawyers in America, Nat Law Jour., 2008. Mem.: Asian Pacific Bar Assn. (Pub. Svc. award 2003), Asian Am. Bar Assn., So. Calif. Chinese Lawyer Assn. Republican. Achievements include first to being the first Asian-American woman to serve as a US Attorney, 2002. Office: Gibson Dunn & Crutcher LLP 333 S Grand Ave Los Angeles CA 90071-3197 Office Phone: 213-229-7472. Office Fax: 213-229-6472. E-mail: dwongyang@gibsondunn.com.

YANG, HENRY T.Y., academic administrator, educator; b. Chungking, China, Nov. 29, 1940; s. Chen Pei and Wei Gen Yang; m. Dilling Tsui, Sept. 2, 1966; children: Maria, Martha. BS, Nat. Taiwan U., 1962, D, 2004; MS, W.Va. U., 1965; PhD, Cornell U., 1968; D (hon.), Purdue U., 1996, Hong Kong U. Sci. and Tech., 2002, City U. Hong Kong, 2005. Structural engr. Gilbert Assocs., Reading, Pa., 1968—69; asst. prof. Sch. Aeros. and Astronautics, Purdue U., West Lafayette, Ind., 1969, assoc. prof., 1972, prof., 1976—94, Neil A. Armstrong Disting. prof. aero. and astronautical engring., 1988—94, sch. head, 1979—84; dean engring. Purdue U., 1984—94; chancellor U. Calif., Santa Barbara, 1994—. Mem. sci. adv. bd. USAF, 1985—89, mem. sci. adv. group aero. sys. divsn., 1986—89; mem. aero. adv. com. NASA, 1985—89; mem. engring. adv. com. NSF, 1988—91; def. sci. bd. DoD (merged with Def. Mfg. Bd.), 1988—91, mem. def. mfg. bd., 1998—99; mem. mechanics bd. vis. ONR, 1990—93; mem. tech. adv. com. Pratt & Whitney, 1993—95; mem. Naval Rsch. Adv. Com., 1996—98; bd. dirs. AlliedSignal, 1996—99, Calif. Coun. Sci. and Technology, 1997—2004; rschr. in field. Contbr. over 160 articles in engring. to profl. jours. Bd. trustees Univs. Rsch. Assn., 2002—; bd. dirs. Axle and Mfg., 2004—. Recipient Twelve Outstanding Tchg. awards, Purdue U., 1970—94, Outstanding Aerospace Engr. award, 1999, Educator of Yr. award, Goleta C. of C., 2002, Pierre Claeyssens award disting. svc., Emmaus Santa Barbara, 2004; named Hon. alumnus, U. Calif. Santa Barbara, 2001, Exec. of Yr., South Coast Bus. and Tech. Awards Dinner, 2004. Fellow: AIAA, Am. Soc. Engring. Edn. (Centennial medal 1993, Benjamin Garver Lamme award, Gold medal 1998); mem.: ASCE, NAE (mem. acad. adv. bd. 1991—94), ASME, Univs. Rsch. Assn., Academia Sinica, Tau Beta Pi. Office: U Calif Santa Barbara Chancellors Office 5221 Cheadle Hall Santa Barbara CA 93106-2030 Office Phone: 805-893-2231. Office Fax: 805-893-8717. Business E-Mail: henry.yang@chancellor.ucsb.edu.

YANG, JERRY, former Internet company executive; b. Taipei, Taiwan, Nov. 6, 1968; married; 1 child. BSEE, MSEE, Stanford U., 1990, PhD studies in Elec. Engring. Co-creator Yahoo! Navigational Guide to the Internet, 1994; co-founder Yahoo!, Inc., Sunnyvale, Calif., 1995, CEO, 2007—09. Bd. dirs. Yahoo! Inc., 1995—, Cisco Systems, Inc., 2000—, Alibaba, 2005—. Co-author (with David Filo, Karen Heyman): (books) Yahoo! Unplugged: your Discovery Guide to the Web, 1995; co-author: (with David Filo, Richard Raucci, Elizabeth Crane) Yahooligans!: Way Cool Web Sites, 1996. Trustee Stanford Univ. Named one of 400 Richest Ams., Forbes mag., 2004, 2005, 2006, 50 Most Important People on the Web, PC World, 2007. Mem.: Com. 100, Phi Kappa Psi. Named company YAHOO!(acronym for Yet Another Hierarchical Officious Oracle).*

YANG, JOSEPH, lawyer; s. Tony Tien-Sheng and Hsiu-Ying Tsai Yang; m. Roxana H. Hwu, 1999; children: Jacqueline O., Russell A. BS, Calif. Inst. Tech., 1986, MS, 1987, PhD, 1991; JD, Stanford U., 1996. Bar: U.S. Patent and Trademark Office 1996, Calif. 1996, U.S. Ct. Appeals (Fed. Cir.) 2002. Engr. TRW Corp., Redondo Beach, Calif., 1986—87; Office Naval Rsch. fellow Calif. Inst. Tech., Pasadena, Calif., 1987—91; rsch. engr. Shell Devel. Co., Houston, 1991—93; tech. advisor Weil, Gotshal & Manges LLP, Menlo Park, Calif., 1994—95; atty. McCutchen, Doyle, Brown & Enersen LLP, Palo Alto, 1995—98; counsel Skadden, Arps, Slate, Meagher & Flom LLP, Palo Alto, 1998—2005; v.p., gen. counsel Cryptography Rsch. Inc., San Francisco, 2005—; founding ptnr. PatentEsque Law Group, LLP, Menlo Park, 2005—. Adj. prof. Sch. Law U. Calif., Berkeley, 1998—99; program chair Practicing Law Inst., NY, 2002—; co-founder intellectual property transactions practice Skadden Arps LLP, Palo Alto; spkr. on intellectual property law. Editor: Advanced Licensing Agreements, 2003—, Advanced Patent Licensing, 2008—; contbr. chapters to books, articles to jours. including The Practical Lawyer, The Licensing Jour., others. Named Outstanding Student in Engring. at Caltech, Inst. for Advancement of Engring., 1986, One of World's Leading IP Strategists, Intellectual Asset Mag., 2009—; fellow, US Office Naval Rsch., 1987—91; scholar, Gen. Motors Corp., 1983—86. Mem.: Assocs. Calif. Inst. Tech. (Pasadena) (ednl. patron 1999—, dir. 2008—), Licensing Execs. Soc., Am. Intellectual Property Law Assn., Calif. Inst. Tech. Alumni Assn. (dir. 1999—2003), Caltech Alumni Assn. (pres. San Francisco chpt. 1999—2003, dir. 2008—). Office: PatentEsque Law Group LLP 2460 Sand Hill Rd Ste 101 Menlo Park CA 94025 Business E-Mail: joe@patentesque.com.

YANG, PEIDONG, material science researcher; b. Suzhou, Jiangsu, China, Aug. 22, 1971; came to US, 1993; s. Xueli and Amei Yang; m. Mei Wang, May 15, 1996. BS in Chemistry, U. Sci. and Tech. of China, Hefei, 1993; MS, Harvard U., 1995, PhD in Chemistry, 1997. Rsch. asst. U. Sci. and Tech. of China, 1989-93, Harvard U., Cambridge, Mass., 1993—99; postdoctoral fellow U. Calif., Santa Barbara, 1997—99, assoc. prof. dept. chemistry, materials sci. and engring. Berkeley, 1999—, dep. dir. Ctr. Integrated Nanomechanical Systems. Chevron Texaco chair chemistry U. Calif., Berkeley, 2003. Assoc. editor: Jour. Am. Chem. Soc. Recipient Zhongzhi Zhang prize, 1992, Presdl. prize, U. Sci. and Tech. of China, 1993, Camille and Henry Dreyfus New Faculty award, 1999, 3M Untenured Faculty award, 2000, Rsch. Innovation award, 2001, Hellman Family Faculty award, 2001, CAREER award, NSF, 2001, Young Investigator award, Alan T. Waterman award, 2007, Arnold and Mabel Beckman Young Investigator award, 2002, Camille Dreyfus Tchr.-Scholar award, 2004, Dupont Young Prof. award, 2004, Julius Springer prize for Applied Physics, 2004; named to TR100, MIT Tech. Rev., 2003; grantee Alfred P. Sloan Rsch. fellowship, 2001. Mem. Am. Chem. Soc. (chmn. nanoscience subdivision, 2003, ExxonMobil Solid State Chemistry award, 2001, Pure Chemistry award, 2005), Materials Rsch. Soc. (Outstanding Young Investigator award, 2004), Am. Phys. Soc. Achievements include invention of metal oxide nanorods and their incorporation into the high temperature superconductor, thus enhancing the critical current density. Office: Dept Chemistry U Calif Berkeley B68 Hildebrand Hall Berkeley CA 94720-1460 Office Phone: 510-643-1545. Office Fax: 510-642-7301. E-mail: p_yang@berkeley.edu.

YANG, ROXANA HWU, lawyer, investor; d. Johnson and Grace Liaw Hwu; m. Joseph Yang; children: Jacqueline, Russell. BSEE, U. Calif., LA, 0199; JD, U. Calif., Berkeley, 1997. Bar: Calif., US Patent and Trademark Office, US Dist. Ct. (no dist.) Calif., US Ct. Appeals (fed. cir.); lic. real estate broker Calif. Atty. Pennie & Edmonds, LLP, Palo Alto, Calif., 1997—2001; prin. Law Office Roxana H. Yang, Los Altos, 2001—05; mng. ptnr. PatentEsque Law Group, LLP, 2005—. Faculty Practising Law Inst., San Francisco, 2002—. Contbr. articles to profl. jours. Ednl. patron Assocs. Calif. Inst. Tech., Pasadena, 1999—2006. Recipient Am. Jury award Torts, Pepperdine U. Sch. Law, Am. Jury award Real Property. Office: PatentEsque Law Group LLP PO Box 400 Los Altos CA 94023 Office Fax: 650-948-0833. Business E-Mail: roxana@patentesque.com.

YANG, YANG, science educator; b. Kaohsiung, Taiwan, Nov. 7, 1958; arrived in U.S., 1985; s. Shun-Wen and Huang-Yin Yang; m. Danmei Lee, May 30, 1987; 1 child, Jonathan Lee Yang. BS in Physics, Nat. Cheng Kung U., 1982; MS in Physics and Applied Physics, U. Mass., 1988, PhD in Physics and Applied, 1992. Rsch. asst. U. Mass., Lowell, 1989-91; rsch. assoc. U. Calif., Riverside, 1991-92; rsch. scientist UNIAX Corp., Santa Barbara, Calif., 1992-96; asst. prof. UCLA, 1997—98, assoc. prof., 1998—2002, prof., 2002—. Contbr. articles to profl. jours. Recipient Prof. Develop. award, U. Mass.-Lowell, 1991, 3M Young Investigator award, 1998, Career award, Nat. Sci. Found., 1998. Mem. Am. Phys. Soc., Material Rsch. Soc. Achievements include 11 patents in field. Office: Dept Materials Sci Engring UCLA 6531 Boelter Hall 405 Hilgard Ave Los Angeles CA 90095-1595 Office Phone: 310-825-4052. Office Fax: 310-825-3665.

YANKOVIC, (WEIRD) AL, singer, satirist; b. Oct. 23, 1959; BArch, Calif. Polytechnic State U. Songs include My Bologna, 1983, Eat It, 1984, I Lost on Jeopardy, 1984, Like a Surgeon, 1985, Yoda, 1985; albums include Weird Al Yankovic, 1983, Weird Al Yankovic in 3-D, 1984, Dare to Be Stupid (Grammy nomination), 1985, (with Wendy Carlos) Peter and the Wolf, 1988; films include UHF, 1989. Office: Close Personal Friends of Al PMB 4018 8033 W Sunset Blvd Los Angeles CA 90046-2427

YANOFSKY, CHARLES, retired biology professor; b. NYC, Apr. 17, 1925; s. Frank and Jennie (Kopatz) Y.; m. Carol Cohen, June 19, 1949, (dec. Dec. 1990); children: Stephen David, Robert Howard, Martin Fred; m. Edna Crawford, Jan. 4, 1992. BS, CCNY, 1948; MS, Yale U., 1950, PhD, 1951, DSc (hon.), 1981, U. Chgo., 1980. Rsch. asst. Yale U., 1951-54; asst. prof. microbiology Western Res. U. Med. Sch., 1954-57; mem. faculty Stanford U., 1958—2000, prof. biology, 1961—2000, Herzstein prof. biology, 1966—2000, prof. emeritus, 2000—; ret. Career investigator Am. Heart Assn., 1969-95. Served with AUS, 1944-46. Recipient Lederle Med. Faculty award, 1957, Eli Lilly award bacteriology, 1959, U.S. Steel Co. award molecular biology, 1964, Howard Taylor Ricketts award U. Chgo., 1966, Albert and Mary Lasker award, 1971, Townsend Harris medal Coll. City N.Y., 1973, Louisa Gross Horwitz prize in biology and biochemistry Columbia U., 1976, V.D. Mattia award Roche Inst., 1982, medal Genetics Soc. Am., 1983, Internat. award Gairdner Found., 1985, named Passano Laureate, Passano Found., 1992; recipient William C. Rose award in biochemistry and molecular biology, 1997, Abbott Lifetime Achievement award Am. Soc. Microbiology, 1998, Nat. medal of Sci., 2003. Mem. NAS (Selman A. Waksman award in microbiology 1972), Am. Acad. Arts and Scis., Genetics Soc. Am. (pres. 1969, Thomas Hunt Morgan medal 1990), Am. Soc. Biol. Chemists (pres. 1984), Royal Soc. (fgn. mem.), Japanese Biochem. Soc. (hon.) Home: 725 Mayfield Ave Stanford CA 94305-1016 Office: Stanford U Dept Of Biological Sci Stanford CA 94305

YARBROUGH, STEVEN B., state legislator; m. Linda Yarbrough, 1968; 3 children. BS in Bus. Adminstrn., Ariz. State U., 1968; JD magna cum laude, Ariz. State U. Coll. Law, 1971. Grad. fellow Univ. adminstrn. Rockefeller Found., 1970—71; adminstr. office student affairs Ariz. State U., 1971—75; bus. law tchr. Mesa Cmty. Coll., 1975—77; practicing atty. Tempe, Chandler, 1975—; ptnr. Yarbrough, Moll & Dunn, Chandler; mem. Dist. 21 Ariz. House of Reps., 2003—, spkr. pro tempore, 2009—, vice-chair rules com., mem. ways & means com. Bd. mem. Valley Christian HS, 1981—2005; exec. dir. Ariz. Christian Sch. Tuition Orgn., 1998—; bd. dirs. Children's Hope Assn., Ariz. State U. Alumni Assn. Republican. Office: Ariz House Reps Capitol Complex 1700 W Washington Rm 218 Phoenix AZ 85007 Office Phone: 602-926-5863. Office Fax: 602-417-3121. Business E-Mail: syarbrou@azleg.gov.*

YARI, BOB, film company executive, producer; b. 1962; Diploma in Cinematography. Owner El Camino Pictures, Bull's Eye Entertainment, Syndicate Films Internat., Bob Yari Prodns., Stratus Film Co., LA. Dir., exec. prodr.: (films) Mind Games, 1989; prodr.: Perfect Fit, 1999, Where the Red Fern Grows, 2003, Employee of the Month, 2004, Agent Cody Banks 2: Destination London, 2004, House of D, 2004, A Love Song for Bobby Long, 2004, Crash, 2004 (Best First Feature, Independent Spirit award, 2006), Haven, 2004, Hostage, 2005; prodr.: (films) Find Me Guilty, 2006; prodr.: (films) Block Party, 2005, The Illusionist, 2006, First Snow, 2006, The Hoax, 2006, Resurrecting the Champ, 2007, Kickin It Old Skool, 2007; exec. prodr.: Agent Cody Banks, 2003, Devil's Pond, 2003, Sueno, 2004, In Enemy Hands, 2004, Laws of Attraction, 2004, Around the Bend, 2004, Thumbsucker, 2005, The Matador, 2005, The Chumscrubber, 2005, The LA Riot Spectacular, 2005, Prime, 2005, Sueno, 2005, Even Money, 2006; exec. prodr.: (films) The Painted Veil, 2006. Named one of 50 Most Powerful People in Hollywood, Premiere mag., 2005. Office: Stratus Film Co 10850 Wilshire Blvd 6th Fl Los Angeles CA 90024 Office Phone: 310-234-8970. Office Fax: 310-234-8975.

YARIV, AMNON, electrical engineering educator, research scientist; b. Tel Aviv, Apr. 13, 1930; arrived in U.S., 1951, naturalized, 1964; s. Shraga and Henya (Davidson) Y.; m. Frances Pokras, Apr. 10, 1972; children: Elizabeth, Dana, Gabriela. BS, U. Calif., Berkeley, 1954, MS, 1956, PhD, 1958. Mem. tech. staff Bell Telephone Labs., 1959-63; dir. laser research Watkins-Johnson Co., 1963-64; mem.

faculty Calif. Inst. Tech., 1964—, Martin Summerfield prof. applied physics, 1966—. Co-founder Xponent, Orbits Corp., Teleris Corp., Inc. Author: Quantum Electronics, 1967, 75, 85, Introduction to Optical Electronics, 1971, 77, 89, Theory and Applications of Quantum Mechanics, Propagation of Light in Crystals. With Israeli Army, 1948—50. Recipient Pender award U. Pa., Harvey prize Technion, Israel, 1992. Fellow IEEE (Quantum Electronics award 1980), Am. Optical Soc. (Ives medal 1986, Esther Beller medal 1998), Am. Acad. Arts and Scis.; mem. NAS, NAE, Am. Phys. Soc. Office: 1201 E California Blvd Pasadena CA 91125-0001 Personal E-mail: azyariv@hotmail.com. Business E-Mail: ziemer@eas.uccs.edu.

YARNELL, MICHAEL ALLAN, mediator, arbitrator, law educator; b. Chgo., Sept. 10, 1944; s. Howard Winfred and Mary Elizabeth (Card) Y.; m. Karen Alice Hockenyos, June 12, 1971 (div. Mar. 1994); children: Sarah Munro, Jacob Rainey; m. Kristina Louise Renshaw, July 17, 1996. BS, Ariz. State U., 1967; JD with honors, U. Ill., 1971; MA, U. Phoenix, 2004. Bar: Ariz. 1971. Ptnr. Streich, Lang, Weeks & Cardon, Phoenix, 1971-91, also bd. dirs.; mem. Myers, Barnes & Jenkins, Phoenix, 1991; judge Maricopa County Superior Ct., Phoenix, 1991—2005, mediator, arbitrator, spl. master, 2005—; adj. prof. U. Canberra Law Sch., Australia, 2004—; assoc. prof. law Phoenix Sch. Law, 2006—. Author: Ins and Outs of Foreclosure, 1981, 13th edit., 2007; projects editor Law Rev. U. Ill. Law Forum, 1970; contbr. articles to profl. jours. Chairperson Phoenix Children's Theatre, 1987; vol. Habitat for Humanity, Adopt-a-Home sponsor; chmn. Legal Cmty. Builds, 1999. 1st lt. US Army, 1971-72, Korea. Fellow Ariz. Bar Found.; mem. ABA, Am. Arbitration Assn. (Roster Neutrals, Comml. Panel), Maricopa Bar Assn., State Bar Ariz. (Outstanding Contbn. to Continuing Legal Edn. award 1988, Com. on Profl. Conduct award 2000), Order of Coif, Lorna Lockwood Inn of Ct. (co-pres. 2000-01), Ariz. Yacht Club (vice comdr. 2000, comdr. 2001-02, staff comdr. 2002-03), Phi Kappa Phi. Republican. Avocations: computers, sailing, white-water rafting. Office: Esplanade Ctr 2415 E Camelback Rd Ste 700 Phoenix AZ 85016 Office Phone: 602-791-3364. Personal E-mail: michael@michaelyarnell.com.

YARRINGTON, PATRICIA E., oil industry executive; b. NJ, Apr. 1956; BA in Polit. Sci., Pomona Coll., Claremont, Calif., 1977; MBA, Northwestern U. Kellogg Sch. Mgmt., Evanston, Ill. With Chevron Corp., 1980—; sr. fin. analyst Chevron USA Inc., 1984—86, mgr. investor relations, 1986; various supervisory positions Chevron Products Co., Chevron U.S.A. Prodn. Co., Chevron Rsch. and Tech. Co.; mgr. credit card enterprises Chevron Products Co., 1995—97, comptr., 1997—98; pres. Chevron Can. Ltd., Vancouver, B.C., Canada, 1998—2000; v.p. strategic planning Chevron Corp., San Ramon, Calif., 2000—01, v.p. policy, govt. & pub. affairs, 2002—, treas., 2007—08, CFO, 2009—. Bd. dirs. Chevron Phillips Chem. Co., ChevronTexaco Found.; mem. econ. adv. coun. Fed. Reserve Bank San Francisco, 2007—08, bd. dirs., 2009—. Office: Chevron Corp 6001 Bollinger Canyon Rd San Ramon CA 94583-2324 Office Phone: 925-842-1000. Office Fax: 925-842-6047.*

YASNYI, ALLAN DAVID, communications company executive; b. New Orleans, June 22, 1942; s. Ben Z. and Bertha R. (Michalove) Y.; m. Susan K. Manders; children: Benjamin Charles, Evelyn Judith, Brian Mallut. BBA, Tulane U., 1964. Free-lance exec. producer, producer, writer, actor, designer TV, motion picture and theatre, 1961-73; producer, performer the Second City; dir. fin. and adminstrn. Quinn Martin Prodns., Hollywood, Calif., 1973-76, v.p. fin., 1976-77, exec. v.p. fin. & corp. planning, 1977; vice chmn., CEO QM Prodn., Beverly Hills, Calif., 1977-78, chmn. bd., CEO, 1978-80; exec. dir. Susan Manders Fine Art, 2002—; pres., CEO The Synapse Comm. Group, Inc., 1981—, ASI Entertainment, 1998-99. Mng. dir. Susan Mandears Fine Art, 2001—; exec. dir., adj. prof. U. So. Calif. Entertainment Tech. Ctr., 1994-99, exec. dir. emeritus, 1999—; participant IC IS Forum, 1990-95; exec. prodr. first live broadcast combining Intelsat, Intersputnik, The Voice of Am., and The Moscow World Radio Svc., 1990; resource guest Aspen Inst. Exec. Seminars, 1990; chmn. bd. dirs. Found. of Global Broadcasting, Washington, 1987-93; nat. adv. bd. DeSantis Ctr. Fla. Atlantic U., 1998-. Trustee Hollywood Arts Coun., 1980-83; exec. v.p., trustee Hollywood Hist. Trust, 1981-91; bd. dirs. Internat. Ctr. Intergative Studies, NYC, 1988-92; bd. dirs. Asthma and Allergy Found. Am., 1981-85. With US Army, 1964-66, Vietnam. Named to Tulane U. Hall of Fame. Mem. Acad. TV Arts and Sci., Inst. Noetic Sci., Hollywood Radio and TV Soc., Hollywood C. of C. (dir., vice chmn. 1978-93), Screen Actors Guild, Assn. Transpersonal Psychology (keynote spkr. 1988). Office: 4132 Fulton Ave Sherman Oaks CA 91423-4340 Office Phone: 818-995-0009. Personal E-mail: yasnyi@aol.com.

YASSIN, ROBERT ALAN, museum director, curator; b. Malden, Mass., May 22, 1941; s. Harold Benjamin and Florence Gertrude (Hoffman) Y.; m. Marilyn Kramer, June 9, 1963; children: Fredric Giles, Aaron David. BA, Dartmouth Coll., 1962; postgrad., Boston U., 1962—63; MA, U. Mich., 1965, postgrad., 1968—70, PhD candidate, 1970; postgrad., Yale U., 1966—68. Asst. to dir. Mus. Art U. Mich., 1965-66, asst. dir., 1970-72, assoc. dir., 1972-73, acting dir., 1973, instr. dept. history of art, 1970-73; co-dir. Joint Program in Mus. Tng., 1970-73; chief curator Indpls. Mus. Art, 1973-75, 87-89, acting dir., 1975, dir., 1975-89; exec. dir. Tucson Mus. Art, 1990—2001, Palos Verdes (Calif.) Art Ctr., 2002—. Adj. prof. Herron Sch. Art Ind. U./Purdue U., 1975-89. Contbr. to mus. publs. Rufus Choate scholar, 1962, Samuel H. Kress Found. fellow, 1968—70, Ford Found. fellow, 1966—68. Mem.: Calif. Assn. Museums, Western Mus. Assn., Nat. Trust Hist. Preservation, Coll. Art Assn. Am., Am. Assn. Museums (bd. dirs. Internat. Coun. Mus. 1986—89). Jewish. Office: Palos Verdes Art Ctr 5504 W Crestridge Rd Rancho Palos Verdes CA 90275 Home: 7321 Marina Pacifica Dr N Long Beach CA 90803-3808 Personal E-mail: rayassin@charter.net. Business E-Mail: byassin@pvartcenter.org.

YATES, ALBERT CARL, academic administrator, chemistry educator; b. Memphis, Tenn., Sept. 29, 1941; s. John Frank and Sadie L. (Shell) Y.; m. Ann Young; children: Steven, Stephanie, Aerin Alessandra, Sara Elizabeth. BS, Memphis State U., 1965; PhD, Ind. U., 1968. Research assoc. U. So. Calif., Los Angeles, 1968-69; prof. chemistry Ind. U., Bloomington, 1969-74; v.p. research, grad. dean U. Cin., 1974-81; exec. v.p., provost, prof. chemistry Washington State U., Pullman, 1981-90; pres. Colo. State U., Fort Collins, 1990—; chancellor Colo. State U. System, Fort Collins, 1990—. Mem. grad. record exam. bd. Princeton (N.J.) U., 1977-81; undergrad. assessment program coun. Ednl. Testing Svc., 1977-81, NRC, 1975-82, Office Edn., HEW, 1978-80; mem. exec. coun. acad. affairs Nat. Assn. State Univs. and Land Grant Colls., 1983-87, Am. Coun. on Edn., 1983-87, nat adv. coun. gen. med. scis. NIH, 1987-90. Contbr. research articles to Jour. Chem. Physics; research articls to Phys. Rev.; research articles to Jour. Physics, Phys. Rev. Letters, Chem. Physics Letters. Served with USN, 1959-62. Recipient univ., state and nat. honors and awards Mem. AAAS, Am. Phys. Soc., Am. Chem. Soc., Sigma Xi, Phi Lambda Upsilon. Home: 1730 Ivy St Denver CO 80220-1428

YATES, DAVID JOHN C., chemist, researcher; b. Stoke-on-Trent, Staffordshire, Eng., Feb. 13, 1927; arrived in US, 1958; s. Eric John and Beatrice Victoria Y.; m. Natalie Chmelnitsky, June 22, 1983 BS with honors, U. Birmingham, UK, 1949; PhD, U. Cambridge, Eng., 1955, Sc.D., 1968. Rsch. physicist Kodak Labs., Wealdstone, London, 1949-50; rsch. chemist Brit. Ceramic Rsch. Assn., Stoke-on-Trent, 1950-51; rsch. assoc. dept. colloid sci. U. Cambridge, 1951-58; lectr. Sch. Mines and dept. chemistry Columbia U., NYC, 1958-60; sr. rsch. fellow Nat. Phys. Lab., Teddington, England, 1960-61; rsch. assoc. corp. labs. Exxon Rsch. and Engring., Annandale, NJ, 1961-86; rsch. prof. dept. of chem. engring. Lafayette Coll., Easton, Pa., 1986-87; rsch. prof. dept. materials sci. Rutgers U., Piscataway, NJ, 1987-88; cons. San Diego, 1988—. Contbr. over 70 articles to profl. jours., chpts. to books; 13 U.S. patents, numerous fgn. patents. Fellow Inst. of Physics (U.K.), Royal Soc. Chemistry (U.K.), N.Y. Catalysis Club (chmn. 1966-67). Clubs: N.Y. Catalysis (chmn. 1965-66). Avocations: photography, bicycling, gliding, travel, sports cars.

YATES, GARY L., marriage and family therapist; b. Washington, Aug. 16, 1944; s. Lewis Edward and Norma Jean (Andruss) Y.; m. Cynthia Ann Pagay, Aug. 16, 1974; children: David, Jonathan, Daniel, Matthew, Nathan. BA, Am. U., 1967; MA, U. No. Colo., 1978. Tchr. St. Anthony's, Kailua, Hawaii, 1970-74, Acad. of Pacific, Honolulu, 1974-79; adminstr. Dept. Pub. Health, San Bernardino, Calif., 1979-81, Charles Drew Sch. of Medicine, LA, 1981-82; assoc. dir. Divsn. of Adolescent Medicine/Children's Hosp., LA, 1982-92; sr. program officer Calif. Wellness Found., Woodland Hills, Calif., 1992-93, program dir., 1993-94, pres., CEO, 1995—. Asst. clin. prof. U. So. Calif., 1988—; bd. dirs. Calif. Wellness Found., Grantmaker in Health, Hispanics in Philanthropy, So. Calif. Assn. Philanthropy, Coun. Found. Contbr. articles to profl. jours.; contbg. author: Multi Agency System of Care, 1990. Mem. L.A. Roundtable for Children, 1988-92, United Way Task Force on AIDS, L.A., 1988-92, San Bernardino Comm. Coun., 1980-82; chmn. Hawaii Sch. Counseling Assn., Honolulu, 1978-79. S(sgt.) U.S. Army, 1968-70. Recipient NACO Achievement award Nat. Assn. U.S. Counties, 1980, 3rd Century award Hollywood Coord. Coun., 1989, Gov.'s Victim's Svc. award Gov. of Calif., 1990, Commendation award Calif. State Senate, 1992, Hispanic Health Leadership award, 1999, L.A. Free Clinic Lenny Somberg award, 1998. Mem. Am. Assn. Humanistic Psychologists, Soc. for Adolescent Medicine, Calif. Assn. Marriage and Family Therapists, Am. Pub. Health Assn. Democrat. Methodist. Avocations: reading, walking. Office: Calif Wellness Found 6320 Canoga Ave Ste 1700 Woodland Hills CA 91367-2565

YATES, HARVEY E., oil industry executive, political organization administrator; Pres. Jalapeno Corp., Albuquerque; chmn. Rep. Party of N.Mex., 2009—. Spkr. in field. Republican. Office: Rep Party of NMex 5150-A San Francisco NE Albuquerque NM 87109 also: Jalapeno Corp 1429 Central Ave NW Albuquerque NM 87104 Office Phone: 505-242-2050, 505-298-3662. Office Fax: 505-292-0755.*

YATES, STEVEN A., curator, artist; b. Chgo., Nov. 14, 1949; s. Thomas A. and Phyllis E. (Wilson) Y.; m. Lynne A. Smith, Aug. 5, 1972; children: Kelsey Victoria, Mackenzie Phyllis. BFA, U. Nebr., 1972; MA, U. N.Mex., 1975, MFA, 1978. Curatorial asst. Sheldon Meml. Art Gallery, 1972-73, U. Art Mus., U. N.Mex., 1973-75; faculty dept. art Claremont (Calif.) Colls. and Pomona, 1976; part-time faculty U. N.Mex., Albuquerque, 1976—, assoc. adj. prof. dept. art and art history, 1994—; curator prints, drawings and photographs Mus. of N.Mex., Santa Fe, 1980-84; curator of photography Mus. Fine Arts, 1985—. Vis. prof. 19th and 20th century photography Santa Fe C.C., 1998-02; vis. specialist in field; instr. U. N.Mex., 1975-78; frequent lectr. and essayist on contemporary and early modern history of photography and rsch. internationally; guest artist Tamarind Inst., Albuquerque, 1988; vis. instr. Pomona Coll., Claremont Coll., Calif., 1976, U. Calif. LA, 1976; lectr., rschr., curator exhbns. internationally. One-man shows include Sheldon Meml. Art Gallery, Lincoln, Nebr., 1978, Gallery A-3, Moscow, 1996, Up and Down Gallery, Kharkov, Ukraine, 1997, U. Nebr., 1997, Mus. Photography, Riga, Latvia, 1998, Gallery A-3 Moscow, 2002; collaborative installation Ctr. for Contemprary Arts, Irving, Tex., 2000; group shows include San Francisco Mus. Modern Art, 1980, 81, 84, 86, 96, Cinema Ctr., Moscow, 1991, St. Petersburg, Russia, 1997, Photographic Icons: Film Form and Montage, A homage to Sergei Eisenstein adn Gustav Klucis, Latvia, 1998, Empires: Russia Past and Present, 1998; represented in permanent collections San Francisco Mus. Modern Art, Sheldon Art Gallery, Mint Mus., Art Mus. U. N.Mex., Ctr. for Creative Photography, Tucson; editor: The Essential Landscape, The New Mexico Photographic Survey, 1985; guest editor spl. issue Contemporary Photography, 1987, El Palacio, 1987, Poetics of Space: A Critical Photographic Anthology, 1995, Betty Hahn: Photography or Maybe Not, 1995, Theatre as Memory: L. Millet, 1999, The Avant-garde Document: A. Macijauskas, 2001, Idea Photographic: After Modernism, 2002, Poéticas del espacia, 2002, Alexander Rodchenko, Modern Photography, Film, and Photomontage, 2003; contbr. essays in field; numerous mus. catalogs and pubs. nationally and internationally. Ford Found. fellow, 1977, Nat. Endowment Arts fellow, 1980; recipient Vreeland award U. Nebr., 1972, Outstanding Alumni Achievement award U. Nebr., 1994; Sr. Fulbright Scholars award USSR, 1991, Russian Fedn., 1995. E-mail: steve.yates@state.nm.us.

YAU, STEPHEN SIK-SANG, computer and information scientist, educator; b. Wusei, Kiangsu, China, Aug. 6, 1935; arrived in US, 1958, naturalized, 1968; BSEE, Nat. Taiwan U., Taipei, 1958; MSEE, U. Ill., Urbana, 1959, PhD, 1961. Asst. prof. elec. engring. Northwestern U., Evanston, Ill., 1961-64, assoc. prof., 1964-68, prof., 1968-88, prof. computer scis., 1970-88, Walter P. Murphy prof. Elec. Engring. and Computer Sci., 1986-88, also chmn. dept. computer scis., 1972-77, chmn. dept. elec. engring. and computer sci., 1977-88; prof. computer and info. sci., chmn. dept. U. Fla., Gainesville, 1988-94; prof. computer sci. and engring. Ariz. State U., Tempe, 1994—, chmn. dept. computer sci. and engring., 1994—2001, dir. Info. Assurance Ctr., 2006—. Conf. chmn. IEEE Computer Conf., Chgo., 1967; gen. chmn. Nat. Computer Conf., Chgo., 1974, First Internat. Computer Software and Applications Conf., Chgo., 1977; Trustee Nat. Electronics Conf., Inc., 1965-68; chmn. organizing com. 11th World Computer Congress, Internat. Fedn. Info. Processing, San Francisco, 1989; gen. co-chmn. Internat. Symposium on Autonomous Decentralized Systems, Japan, 1993, gen. chmn., Phoenix, 1995; conf. co-chair 24th Ann. Internat. Computer Software and Applications Conf., Taipei, 2000. Editor-in-chief Computer mag., 1981-84; assoc. editor Jour. Info. Sci., 1983-99; editor IEEE Trans. on Software Engring., 1988-91; contbr. numerous articles on software engring., distributed and parallel processing systems, computer sci., elec. engring. and related fields to profl. publs.; patentee in field. Recipient Louis E. Levy medal Franklin Inst., 1963, Golden Plate award Am. Acad. Achievement, 1964, The Silver Core award Internat. Fedn. Info. Processing, 1989, Spl. award, 1989, Overseas Outstanding Contributions award, Chinese Computer Fedn., 2006. Fellow IEEE (mem. governing bd. Computer Soc. 1967-76, pres. 1974-75, dir. Inst. 1976-77, chmn. awards com., 1996-97; Richard E. Merwin award Computer Soc. 1981, Centennial medal 1984, Extraordinary Achievement award 1985, Outstanding Contbn. award Computer Sci. Soc. 1985, The Third Millennium medal 2000, Tsutomu Kanai award 2002), AAAS, Franklin Inst.; mem. Assn. for Computing Machinery, Am. Fedn. Info.-Processing Soc. (mem. exec. com. 1974-76, 79-82, dir. 1972-82, chmn. awards com. 1979-82, v.p. 1982-84, pres. 1984-86; chmn. Nat. Computer Conf. Bd. 1982-83, spl. award 1990), Am. Soc. Engring. Edn., Sigma Xi, Tau Beta Pi, Eta Kappa Nu, Pi Mu Epsilon. Office: Ariz State U PO Box 878809 Tempe AZ 85287-8809 Business E-Mail: yau@asu.edu.

YAZDANI, SHAHRAM, pediatrician; b. July 20, 1967; MD, Tulane U. Sch. Medicine, New Orleans, 1995. Cert. Am. Bd. Pediat., 2006. Internship in pediat. UCLA Sch. Medicine, 1995—96, residency in pediat., 1996—98, physician, 1998—, asst. prof. pediat., 1998—, asst. clin. prof. gen. pediat., 1998—. Dir. resident med. edn. UCLA Med. Sch., site dir., 3rd yr. med. sch., mem. ambulatory medicine com., 2001—; med. coord., cons. Madisons Found., 2003—. Mem.: Assn. Pediatric Program Directors. Office: UCLA Children's Health Ctr 200 UCLA Med Plz Ste 265 Los Angeles CA 90095 Office Phone: 310-825-0867. Office Fax: 310-794-5066. Business E-Mail: syazdani@mednet.ucla.edu.

YAZDI, MAHVASH, utilities executive; BS in Indsl. Mgmt., Poly. U., Pomona, Calif.; MBA, U. So. Calif., LA; grad. Mgmt. of Info. Tech. program, Harvard Bus. Sch. With IBM World Trade Corp.; v.p., chief info. officer Hughes Aircraft, 1994; with Edison Internat., Rosemead, Calif., 1997—, sr. v.p. bus. integration, chief info. officer So. Calif. Edison subs., sr. v.p. bus. integration, chief info. officer. Bd. dirs. Columbus Newport Corp.; adv. dir. Lotus Corp., IBM Corp.; mem. So. Calif. Forum of the Trusteeship of the Internat. Women's Forum, 2003. Mem. adv. bd. U. So. Calif. Marshall Sch. Bus.; bd. dirs. Claremont U. Consortium. Office: Edison Internat 2244 Walnut Grove Ave Rosemead CA 91770 Office Phone: 626-302-1212.

YBARRONDO, BRENT, biology professor; PhD, U. Vt., 1993. Prof. biology Adams State Coll., Alamosa, Colo., 1992—, chair. Office: Adams State Coll 208 Edgemont Blvd Alamosa CO 81102 Business E-Mail: baybarro@adams.edu.

YE, JUN, physicist, researcher; b. Shanghai, Nov. 7, 1967; s. Shanxiang Ye and Changhong Fan; m. Ying Zhang, June 22, 1993; 1 child, Shirley Eileen. BS in Applied Physics, U. N.Mex., 1991, MS in Physics, 1991; PhD in Physics, U. Colo., 1997. Postdoctoral rschr. Calif. Inst. Tech., 1997—99; physicist Nat. Inst. Stds. and Tech., 1999—2004, fellow, 2004—; asst. prof. adjoint dept. physics U. Colo., 1999—2003, assoc. prof. adjoint dept. physics, 2004—; assoc. fellow JILA, Nat. Inst. Stds. and Tech., U. Colo., Boulder, 1999—2001, fellow, 2001—. Vis. prof. Inst. Exptl. Physics U. Innsbruck, Austria, 2004; guest prof. East China Normal U., Shanghai, 2004—, Shanghai Jiao Tong U., 2006—. Contbr. articles to sci. jours. Recipient Selection to Frontiers of Engring. Symposium, NAE, 2000, Tech. Rev. Mag.'s TR100 Young Innovator, Tech. Rev. Mag., 2002, Presdl. Early Career award for Scientists and Engrs., US Pres., 2003, Arthur S. Flemming award, US Fed. Govt., 2005, I.I. Ravi prize in Atomic, Molecular and Optical Physics, 2007; grantee Univ. fellowship, U. Colo. Boulder, 1993 - 1994, R.A. Millikan Prize fellowship, Calif. Inst. Tech., 1997 - 1999. Fellow: Optical Soc. Am. (Adolph Lomb medal 1999, William F. Meggers award 2006), Am. Phys. Soc. Achievements include invention of Cavity based ultrasensitive absorption spectroscopy; Phase locking independent ultrafast lasers; research in Highly stabilized lasers for precision measurements; Precision, wide bandwidth optical frequency comb; Cooling and trapping of alkaline earth atoms; Manipulation of cold molecules; patents for Comb generating optical cavity that includes an optical amplifier and an optical modulator; A novel cavity ringdown heterodyne spectroscopy: 1 x 10-10 sensitivity with microwatt light power; patents pending for Sub 10 - femtosecond active synchronization of two passively mode-locked Ti:sapphire oscillators. Office: JILA Nat Inst Standards & Tech U Colo Campus Box 440 Boulder CO 80309-0440 E-mail: ye@jila.colorado.edu.

YEAGER, CAROLINE HALE, writer, retired radiologist, consultant; b. Little Rock, Sept. 5, 1946; d. George Glenn and Crenor Burnelle (Hale) Y.; m. William Berg Singer, July 8, 1978; children: Adina Atkinson Singer, Sarah Rose Singer. BA, Ind. U., Bloomington, 1968; MD, Ind. U., Indpls., 1971. Diplomate Am. Bd. Radiology; med. lic. State of Calif. Intern Good Samaritan Hosp., Los Angeles, 1971-72; resident in radiology King Drew Med. Ctr. UCLA, Los Angeles, 1972-76; dir. radiology Hubert Humphrey Health Ctr., Los Angeles, 1976-77; asst. prof. radiology UCLA, Los Angeles, 1977-84, King Drew Med. Ctr. UCLA, Los Angeles, 1977-85, dir. ultrasound, 1977-84; ptnr. pvt. practice Beverly Breast Ctr., Beverly Hills, Calif., 1984-87; cons. Clarity Communications, Pasadena, Calif., 1981—; pvt. practice radiology Claude Humphrey Health Ctr., 1991-93; dir. sonograms and mammograms Rancho Los Amigos Med. Ctr., 1993-94, ret., 1994. Trustee Assn. Teaching Physicians, L.A., 1976-81; cons. King Drew Med. Ctr., 1984, Gibraltar Savs., 1987, Cal Fed. Inc., 1986, Medical Faculty At Home Professions, 1989—, Mobil Diagnostics, 1991-92, Xerox Corp., 1990-91, Frozen Leopard, Inc., 1990-91; writer gen. med. answers pub. on internet, 1994-. Author: (with others) Infectious Disease, 1978, Anatomy and Physiology for Medical Transcriptionists, 1992; contbr. articles to profl. jours. Trustee U. Synagogue, Los Angeles, 1975-79; mem. Friends of Pasadena Playhouse, 1987-90. Grantee for innovative tng. Nat. Fund for Med. Edn., 1980-81. Mem. Am. Inst. Ultrasound in Medicine, L.A. Radiology Soc. (ultrasound sect.), Nat. Soc. Performance and Instrn. (chmn. conf. Database 1991, publs. L.A. chpt. 1990, info. systems L.A. chpt. 1991, dir. adminstrn. L.A. chpt. 1992, Outstanding Achievement in Performance Improvement award L.A. chpt. 1990, bd. dirs. 1990-93, Pres. award for Outstanding Chpt. 1992, v.p. programs 1993), Stanford Profl. Women L.A. Jewish. Avocations: writing, humor, design. Home and Office: 3520 Yorkshire Rd Pasadena CA 91107-5440 Personal E-mail: doccarrie@earthlink.net.

YEAGER, CHUCK (CHARLES ELWOOD YEAGER), retired air force officer, test pilot; b. Myra, W.Va., Feb. 13, 1923; s. Albert Hal and Susie May (Sizemore) Yeager; m. Glennis Faye Dickhouse (dec. 1990), Feb. 26, 1945; children: Sharon Yeager Flick, Susan F., Donald C., Michael D.; m. Victoria Scott D'Angelo, 2003 Grad., Air Command and Staff Sch., 1952, Air War Coll., 1961; DSc (hon.), W.Va. U., 1948, Marshall U., Huntington, W.Va., 1969; D in Aero. Sci., Salem Coll., W.Va., 1975. Enlisted in USAAF, 1941; advanced through grades to brig. gen. U.S. Air Force, 1969, fighter pilot, ETO, 1943-46, exptl. flight test pilot, 1945-54, various command assignments U.S., Germany, France and Spain, 1954-62; comdr., astronaut tng. Air Force Aerospace Rsch. Pilots Sch.; dir. Space Sch., Edwards AFB, 1960; comdr. 405th Fighter Wing, Seymour Johnson AFB, N.C., 1968-69; vice comdr. 17th Air Force, Ramstein Air Base, Fed. Republic Germany, 1969-71; U.S. def. rep. to Pakistan, 1971-73; spl. asst. to comdr. Air Force Inspection and Safety Ctr., Norton AFB, Calif., 1973, dir. aerospace safety, 1973-75; ret., 1975. Cons. to comdr. Test Pilot Sch., Edwards AFB, 1975—97; presdl. commn. to investigate Challenger accident, 1986; hon. chmn. Duncan Hunter Presdl. Campaign, 2006; spkr. in field. Actor: (films) Smokey and the Bandit II, 1980, The Right Stuff, 1983; (TV movies) Flying Without Fear, 1985; (TV appearances) Goodyear Television Playhouse, 1953, I Dream of Jeannie, 1964; Co-author: (with Leo Janos) Yeager: An Autobiography, 1985, (with Charles Leerhsen) Press On!, 1988, The Quest for Mach One: A First-Person Account of Breaking the Sound Barrier, 1998; featured in: Spaceflight, 1985, Looney Tunes 50th Anniversary, 1986, Realizing 'The Right Stuff,' 2003, The Real Men with 'The Right Stuff,' 2003, Pancho Barnes! A Documentary Film, 2008. Founder Gen. Chuck Yeager Found., Calif., 2002—. Decorated DSM with oak leaf cluster, Silver Star with oak leaf cluster, Legion of Merit with oak leaf cluster, DFC with 2 oak leaf clusters, Bronze star with V device, Air medal with 10 oak leaf clusters, Air Force Commendation medal, Purple Heart; recipient Collier Trophy, 1948, Harmon Internat Trophy, 1958, Congl. medal of Honor, 1976, Presdl. medal of Freedom, 1985; first and youngest mil. pilot inducted into Nat. Aviation Hall of Fame, 1973, inducted to Aerospace Walk of Hon., 1990; promoted to rank of maj. gen. on ret. list, 2005. Achievements include flying in 64 combat missions in World War II, over 120 combat missions in Vietnam; being the first man to fly faster than the speed of sound, Oct. 14, 1947.

YEAGER, KURT ERIC, research and development company executive; b. Cleve., Sept. 11, 1939; s. Joseph Ellsworth and Karolyn Kristine (Pedersen) Y.; m. Rosalie Ann McMillan, Feb. 5, 1960; children: Geoffrey, Phillip; m. Regina Ursula Querfurt, May 12, 1970; 1 dau., Victoria. BA in Chemistry, Kenyon Coll., 1961; postgrad., Ohio State U., 1961-62; MS in Physics, U. Calif., Davis, 1964; MS Wharton Sch. Bus., U. Pa., 1995. Tchg. asst. Ohio State U., 1961-62; officer, program mgr. Air Force Tech. Applications Ctr., Alexandria, Va., 1962-68; assoc. dept. dir. Mitre Corp., McLean, Va., 1968-72; dir. energy rsch. and devel. planning EPA, Washington, 1972-74; dir. fossil power plants dept. Electric Power Rsch. Inst., Palo Alto, Calif., 1974-79, dir. coal combustion systems, 1979-83, v.p. coal combustion systems, 1983-88, v.p. generation and storage, 1988-96, pres., CEO, 1996—2004; founder, pres., CEO, Keyworks, Aptos, Calif., 2004—. Chmn. World Energy Coun. Climate Change Study,2005-07; dir. Galvin Elec. Initiative2005-; Oak Ridge fossil energy adv. bd. Nat. Acad. Engring.; mem. exec. bd. Nat. Coal Coun.; bd. dirs. nat. coalition advanced mfg. US Energy Assn.; bd. dirs. APX Corp., 2005-07; Microfield Corp., 2007- Contbr. articles to profl. jours; Co-author (book) Perfect Power. Pres. No. Va. Youth Football Assn., 1973-74. Capt. USAF, 1962-68, chair Watsonville Airport Adv. Council, 2008 Decorated Air Force Commendation medals (2); recipient Outstanding Svc. award EPA, 1974; named Energy Policy Leader, Sci. Am., 2003. Fellow ASME (rsch. policy bd., trustee com. econ. devel.); mem. AAAS, Am. Chem. Soc., Palo Alto C. of C. Republican. Episcopalian. Office Phone: 831-786-9832. Business E-Mail: kyeager@epri.com.

YEATS, ROBERT SHEPPARD, geologist, educator; b. Miami, Fla., Mar. 30, 1931; s. Robert Sheppard and Carolyn Elizabeth (Rountree) Y.; m. Lillian Eugenia Bowie, Dec. 30, 1952 (dec. Apr. 1991); children: Robert Bowie, David Claude, Stephen Paul, Kenneth James, Sara Elizabeth; m. Angela M. Hayes, Jan. 7, 1993. BA, U. Fla., 1952; MS, U. Wash., 1956, PhD, 1958. Registered geologist, Oreg., Calif., Wash. Geologist, petroleum exploration and prodn. Shell Oil Co., Ventura and L.A., Calif., 1958-67, Shell Devel. Co., Houston, 1967; assoc. prof. geology Ohio U., Athens, 1967-70, prof., 1970-77; prof. geology Oreg. State U., Corvallis, 1977-97, prof. oceanography, 1991-97, prof. emeritus, 1997—, chmn. dept., 1977-85; geologist U.S. Geol. Survey, 1968, 69, 75, Glomar Challenger scientist, 1971, co-chief scientist, 1973-74, 78; mem. Oreg. Bd. Geologist Examiners, 1981-83; chmn. Working Group 1 Internat. Lithosphere Program, 1987-90, chmn. task force group on paleoseismology, 1990-98; chmn. subcom. on Himalayan active faults Internat. Geol. Correlation Program, Project 206, 1984-92; mem. geophysics study com. NRC, 1987-94. Rschr. on Cenozoic tectonics of So. Calif., Oreg., Wash., New Zealand and Himalaya; active faults of Calif. Transverse Ranges, deep-sea drilling in Ea. Pacific; vis. scientist New Zealand Geol. Survey, 1983-84, 99, Geol. Survey of Japan, 1992, Inst. de Phys. du Globe de Paris, 1993, So. Calif. Earthquake Ctr.; sr. cons. Earth Cons. Internat., 1997—, ptnr., 2001—. Author: The Geology of Earthquakes, 1997, Living with Earthquakes in the Pacific Northwest, 1998, 2d edit., 2004, Living with Earthquakes in California-A Survivor's Guide, 2001. Mem. Ojai (Calif.) City Planning Commn., 1961-62, Ojai City Coun., 1962-65. 1st lt. U.S. Army, 1952-54. Named Richard H. Jahns Disting. Lectr. in Engring. Geology, 1995; Ohio U. rsch. fellow, 1973-74; grantee NSF, U.S. Geol. Survey. Fellow AAAS, Geol. Soc. Am. (chmn. structural geology and tectonics divsn. 1984-85, chmn., Cordilleran sect. 1988-89, assoc. editor bull. 1987-89); mem. Am. Assn. Petroleum Geologists (Outstanding Educator award Pacific sect. 1991, Michel T. Halbouty human needs award 1998), Am. Geophys. Union, Seismol. Soc. Am., Earthquake Engring. Rsch. Inst. Home: 1654 NW Crest Pl Corvallis OR 97330-1812 Office: Oreg State U Dept Geoscis Corvallis OR 97331-5506 Office Phone: 541-737-1226. E-mail: yeatsr@geo.oregonstate.edu.

YECIES, LAURA SUSAN, computer software company executive; b. Bklyn., Jan. 12, 1964; d. Allan and Maxine Helen (Kamer) Fried; m. Steven Bruce Yecies, July 8, 1984; children: Derek, Todd, Margot. AB in Govt. magna cum laude, Dartmouth Coll., 1984; MS in Fgn. Svc., Georgetown U., Washington, 1986; MBA, Harvard U., 1988. Ins. analyst Overseas Private Investment Corp., Washington, 1985-86; assoc. corp. fin. Chemical Bank, NYC, 1987; from govt. mktg. specialist to Latin Am. sales mgr. Informix Software, Menlo Park, Calif., 1988-94; dir. mktg. Asia Pacific & L.Am. Copta Corp., Menlo Park, Calif.; v.p. Netscape client product divsn. America Online Inc.; gen. mgr. mail divsn. Yahoo Inc.; v.p., gen. mgr. consumer & small bus. divsn. Check Point Software Technologies; CEO Sharpcast Inc., San Mateo, Calif., 2008—. Lectr. internat. mktg. Santa Clara U., 1991; bd. dirs. Sharpcast Inc., 2008- Mem. World Affairs Coun., Phi Beta Kappa. Democrat. Avocations: violin, theater. Office: Sharpcast Inc 2121 S El Camino Real 6th Fl San Mateo CA 94403*

YEE, ALFRED ALPHONSE, structural engineer, consultant; b. Honolulu, Aug. 5, 1925; s. Yun Sau and Kam Ngo (Lum) Y.; m. Janice Ching (div.); children: Lailan, Mark, Eric, Malcolm, Ian; m. Elizabeth Wong, June 24, 1975; children: Suling, Trevor, I'Ling. BSCE, Rose Hulman Inst. Tech., 1948, Dr. of Engring. (hon.), 1976; MEng in Structures, Yale U., 1949. Registered profl. engr., Hawaii, Calif., Guam, Tex., Minn., No. Marianas Islands. With civil engring. dept. Dept. Pub. Works, Terr. of Hawaii, Honolulu, 1949-51; structural engr. 14th Naval Dist., Pearl Harbor, Hawaii, 1951-54; pvt. practice structural engring. cons. Honolulu, 1954-55; structural engring. cons. Park & Yee Ltd., Honolulu, 1955-60; pres. Alfred A. Yee & Assocs. Inc., Honolulu, 1960-82; v.p., tech. adminstr. Alfred. A. Yee div. Leo A. Daly, Honolulu, 1982-89; pres. Applied Tech. Corp., Honolulu, 1984—. Patentee in concrete tech., land and sea structures; contbr. articles to profl. jours. Served with U.S. Army, 1946-47. Named Engr. of Yr., Hawaii Soc. Profl. Engrs., 1969, one of Men Who Made Marks in 1970, Honolulu, 1970. Mem. ASCE (hon.), NSPE, CASE, ACEC, NAE, Am. Concrete Inst. (hon.), Post-Tensioning Inst., Precast-Prestressed Concrete Inst. (PCI medal of honor award 1997), Prestressed Concrete Inst. (State of Art award 1991), Structural Engrs. Assn. Hawaii, Yale Sci. and Engring. Assn. (Martin P. Korn award 1965, Robert J. Lyman award 1984), Singapore Concrete Inst. Avocations: golf, swimming. Office: 1217 Palolo Ave Honolulu HI 96816-2525 E-mail: atc@lava.net.

YEE, FLORENCE, library director; Mgr. Pearl City Bookmobile, Hawaii Kai Pub. Libr.; br. mgr. Kaimuki Pub. Libr.; acting dir. Hawaii State Libr., Honolulu, 2003—04, dir., 2004—, Hawaii State Libr. for Blind and Physically Handicapped, Honolulu, 2004—. Mem. Congresswoman Patsy T. Mink Commn. Mem.: Hawaii Libr. Assn. Office: Hawaii State Libr 478 S King St Honolulu HI 96813-2901 Office Phone: 808-586-3555. Office Fax: 808-733-8426.

YEE, LELAND Y., state legislator; b. China; 4 children. BA, U. Calif., Berkeley, 1970; MA, San Francisco State U., 1972; PhD in Child Psychology, U. Hawaii, 1975. Pres. Bd. Edn. City of San Francisco, 1988-96, mem. Bd. Suprs., 1996—2002; mem. Calif. State Assembly, 2002—06, speaker pro tempore, 2004—06; asst. pres. pro tempore Calif. State Senate, 2007—, mem. Dist. 8 Calif., 2007—. Pres. Nat. Asian Pacific Am. Caucus of State Legislators, 2004—. Address: San Francisco State Bldg 455 Golden Gate Ave Ste 14200 San Francisco CA 94102 Office: State Capitol Rm 4074 Sacramento CA 95814 Address: 400 S El Camino Rd Ste 630 San Mateo CA 94402 Office Phone: 916-651-4008. Business E-Mail: senator.yee@senate.ca.gov.*

YEH, RAYMOND WEI-HWA, architect, educator; b. Shanghai, Feb. 25, 1942; came to U.S., 1958, naturalized, 1976; s. Herbert Hwan-Ching and Joyce Bo-Ding (Kwan) Y.; m. Hsiao-Yen Chen, Sept. 16, 1967; children— Bryant Po Yung, Clement Chung-Yung, Emily Su-Yung. BA, U. Oreg., 1965, B.Arch., 1967; M.Arch., U. Minn., 1969. Cert. Nat. Coun. Archtl. Registration Bds.; registered architect, Tex., Okla., Calif., Hawaii. Draftsman, designer various archtl. firms, 1965-68; design arch. Ellerbe Architects, St. Paul, 1968-70; v.p., dir. design Sorey, Hill, Binnicker, Oklahoma City, 1973-74; prin. arch. Raymond W.H. Yeh & Assos., Norman, Okla., 1974-80; asst. prof. to prof. U. Okla., Norman, 1970-79; head dept. architecture, prof. Calif. Poly. State U., San Luis Obispo, 1979-83; dean Coll. Architecture U. Okla., Norman, 1983-92; prin. arch. W.H. Raymond Yeh, Norman, 1983-93; dean sch. architecture U. Hawaii at Manoa, Honolulu, 1992—2007, prof., 2008—; prin. arch. Yeh Studio, 2007—. Profl. adviser Neighborhood Conservation and Devel. Center, Oklahoma City, 1977 79 Works include: St. Thomas More U. Parish and Student Center, Norman, Summit Ridge Center Retirement Community, Harrah, Okla., (recipient Nat. Design award Guild Religious Architecture 1978). Nat. Endowment for Arts fellow, 1978-79 Fellow AIA (dir., pres. Okla. chpt. 1986, design awards, nat. com. chmn. 1989); mem. Calif. Coun. Archtl. Edn. (dir., pres. 1982-83), Okla. Found. for Architecture (founding chair bd. 1989-90), Asian Soc. Okla. (award of Excellence 1992), Asia Pacific Ctr. for Arch. (founding bd. dirs. 1996). Presbyterian. Office: U Hawaii Manoa Sch Architecture Honolulu HI 96822 Business E-Mail: ray@yehstudio.com.

YEH, WILLIAM WEN-GONG, civil engineering educator; b. Szechwan, China, Dec. 5, 1938; s. Kai-Ming and Der-Chao (Hu) Y.; m. Jennie Pao, Mar. 25, 1967; children: Michael, Bobby. BSC.E., Nat. Cheng-Kung U., Taiwan, 1961; MSC.E., N.Mex. State U., 1964; PhD in Civil Engring., Stanford U., 1967. Acting asst. prof. Stanford U., 1967; asst. research engr. UCLA, 1967-69, asst. prof. civil engring., 1969-73, assoc. prof., 1973-77, prof., 1977—, chmn. dept., 1985-88. Cons. Office of Hydrology, UNESCO, Paris, 1974, Jet Propulsion Lab., Pasadena, Calif., 1975-78, U.S. Bur. Reclamation, Phoenix, 1977-81, Dept. Water and Power, São Paulo, Brazil, 1981—, Rockwell Internat., 1983-88, U.S. AID, 1987-91, Met. Water Dist. of So. Calif., 1989—. Contbr. numerous articles to scholarly jours. Recipient Disting. Faculty award UCLA Engring. Alumni Assn., 1975; recipient Engring. Found. Fellowship award United Engring. Trustees, 1981, Centennial Disting. Alum award N.Mex. State U., 1996, Warren A. Hall medal, U. Coun. Water Resources, 1999, numerous research grants including NSF, 1967—. Fellow Am. Geophys. Union (Robert E. Horton award 1989), ASCE (hon., editor Jour. Water Resources Planning and Mgmt. 1988-93, Julian Hinds award 1994); mem. Am. Water Resources Assn. Home: 822 Hanley Ave Los Angeles CA 90049-1914 Office: U Calif 5732 B BH 405 Hilgard Ave Los Angeles CA 90095-9000

YELLEN, JANET LOUISE, bank executive; b. Bklyn., Aug. 13, 1946; d. Julius and Anna Ruth (Blumenthal) Yellen; m. George Arthur Akerlof, July 8, 1978; 1 child, Robert Joseph. BA in Econs. summa cum laude, Brown U., Providence, 1967; PhD, Yale U., New Haven, 1971; LLD (hon.), Brown U., 1998; LHD (hon.), Bard Coll., 2000. Asst. prof. econs. Harvard U., Cambridge, Mass., 1971-76; lectr. London Sch. Econs. and Polit. Sci., Washington, 1978-80; asst. prof. econs. Sch. Bus. Adminstrn., U. Calif., Berkeley, 1980-82, assoc. prof., 1982-85, prof. Haas Sch. Bus., 1985—, Bernard T. Rocca Jr. prof. internat. bus. and trade, 1992—, Eugene E. and Catherine M. Trefethem prof. bus., 1999—; cons. div. internat. fin., Fed. Res. Sys., Washington, 1974-75, economist trade and fin. studies sect., 1977-78, mem., 1994-97; chair, Coun. Econ. Advisors Exec. Office of the Pres., Washington, 1997-99; pres., CEO Fed. Res. Bank San Francisco, 2004—. Mem. adv. panel in econs. NSF, 1977—78, 1991—92, com. visitors, econs. prog., 1996, 2004; adv. bd. Women's Econ. Round Table, 1999—, Ctr. Internat. Polit. Economy, 1999—, Jerome Levy Econs. Inst., 2002—, Calif. Assembly Select Com. on Asian Trade, 2003; bd. dirs. Economists Allied for Arms Reduction, 2002—, Delta Dental Calif., 2003—; mem. amb. adv. coun. for Marshall Scholarships, 1996—, OECD, High-Level Sustainable Devel. Group, 1999—2001, NAS Panel, Ensuring Best Presidential Sci. and Tech. Appointments, 2000; chair Pres. Interagency Com. on Women's Bus. Enterprise, 1997—99, Econ. Policy Com. Orgn. for Econ. Coop. and Devel., 1997—99; rsch. fellow MIT, Cambridge, 1974; cons. Congl. Budget Office, 1975—76, mem. panel econ. advisers, 1993—94; rsch. affiliate Yale U., 1976; fellow Yale Corp., 2000—; rsch. assoc. Nat. Bureau Econ. Rsch., 1999—; prin. investigator Russell Sage Found. Grant on Sustainable Employment, 2000; sr. adviser Macroeconomic Advisers, 2003—; mem. Brookings Panel on Econ. Activity, 1987—88, 1990—91, sr. adviser, 1989—94, adv. bd., 1999—; Yrjö Jahnsson Found. lectr. on macroecon. theory, Helsinki, 1977—78; mem. Coun. on Fgn. Rels, 1976—81. Author (with Arrow and Shavell): The Limits of the Market in Resource Allocation, 1977; assoc. editor Jour. Econ. Perspectives, 1987—91; contbr. articles to profl. jours. Recipient Maria & Sidney Rolfe award for Nat. Econ. Svc., Women's Econ. Round Table, 1997, Wilbur Lucius Cross Medal, Yale U., 1997; named one of 50 Women to Watch, Wall St. Jour., 2005; grantee NSF, 1975—77, 1990—94; fellow, 1967—71; Hon. Woodrow Wilson fellow, 1967, Guggenheim fellow, 1986—87. Fellow: Am. Acad. Arts & Scis.; mem.: Western Econ. Assn. (pres. 2003—04), Am. Econ. Assn. (adv. com. to pres. 1986—87, nominating com. 1988—90), Phi Beta Kappa. Office: Fed Res Bank San Francisco PO Box 7702 San Francisco CA 94105-7702 Office Phone: 415-974-2000.*

YEN, DAVID WEI-LUEN, information technology executive; b. Chang-hwa, Republic of China, Sept. 24, 1951; came to US, 1975. s. Te-Maw and Shoon-hwa (Luh) Y.; m. Grace Shau-Ling Jen, Jan. 9, 1977; children: Irene, Christine. BSEE, Nat. Taiwan U., Taipei, 1973; MS in Elec. and Computer Engring., U. Ill., Urbana-Champaign, 1977, PhD in Elec. and Computer Engring., 1980. Sr. mem. tech. staff TRW, Inc., Sunnyvale, Calif., 1980-82; mfg. automation position IBM Rsch., San Jose, Calif., 1982-84; co-founder, dir. hardware devel. Cydrome, Inc., Milpitas, Calif., 1984—88; with Sun Microsystems, Inc., Santa Clara, Calif., 1988—, v.p., gen. mgr. enterprise systems, integrated products, enterprise server products and enterprise server engring., exec. v.p. processor and network products, exec. v.p. scalable systems, head storage group, exec. v.p. microelectronics. Mem. IEEE (sec. computer standards com. 1983-84), Eta Kappa Nu, Phi Kappa Phi. Achievements include patents in field. Office: Sun Microsystems Inc 4150 Network Cir Santa Clara CA 95054 Office Phone: 650-960-1300.

YEN, TEH FU, civil and environmental engineering educator; b. Kun-Ming, China, Jan. 9, 1927; came to U.S., 1949; s. Kwang Pu and Ren (Liu) Y.; m. Shiao-Ping Siao, May 30, 1959 BS, Cen. China U., 1947; MS, W.Va. U., 1953; PhD, Va. Poly. Inst. and State U., 1956; PhD (hon.), Pepperdine U., 1982, Internat. U. Dubna, Russia, 1996, All Russian Petroleum Exploration Inst., St. Petersburg, Russia, 1999. Sr. research chemist Good Yr. Tire & Rubber Co., Akron, 1955-59; fellow Mellon Inst., Pitts., 1959-65; sr. fellow Carnegie-Mellon U., Pitts., 1965-68; assoc. prof. Calif. State U., Los Angeles, 1968-69, U. So. Calif., 1969-80, prof. civil engring. and environ. engring., 1980—. Hon. prof. Shanghai U. Sci. and Tech., 1986, U. Petroleum, Beijing, 1987, Daqing Petroleum Inst., 1992; cons. Universal Oil Products, 1968-76, Chevron Oil Field Rsch. Co., 1966-75, Finnigan Corp., 1976-77, GE, 1977-80, United Techs., 1978-79, TRW Inc., 1982-83, Exxon, 1981-82, DuPont, 1985-88, Min. Petroleum, Beijing, 1982—, Biogas Rsch. Inst.-UN, Chengdu, 1991. Author: numerous tech. books; contbr. articles articles to profl. jours. Recipient Disting. Svc. award Tau Beta Pi, 1974, Imperial Crown Gold medal, Iran, 1976, Achievement award Chinese Engring. and Sci. Assocs. So. Calif., 1977, award Phi Kappa Phi, 1982, Outstanding Contbn. honor Pi Epsilon Tau, 1984, Svc. award Republic of Honduras, 1989, award in Petroleum Chem. Am. Chem. Soc., 1994, Kapitsa Gold medal Russian Fedn., 1995. Fellow Chem. Soc., Inst. Petroleum, Am. Inst. Chemists; mem. Am. Chem. Soc. (life; bd. dirs. 1993, councillor, founder and chmn. geochemistry divsn. 1979-81, Chinese Acad. Scis. (standing com.), Acad. Scis. Russian Fedn. (academician, fgn. mem.), Assn. Environmental Engring. and Sci. Profs. Office: U So Calif KAP 224A Viterby Sch Engring 3620 S Vermont Ave Los Angeles CA 90089-2531 Office Phone: 213-740-0586. Business E-Mail: tfyen@usc.edu.

YEN, WEN-HSIUNG, language and music professional, educator; b. Tainan, Taiwan, June 26, 1934; came to U.S., 1969; m. Yuan-yuan Yen, Jan. 6, 1961; children: Tin-ju, Tin-jen, Tin-Tao. BA, Nat. Taiwan Normal U., 1960; MA, UCLA, 1971; PhD in Music, World U., 1988; Candidate Philosophy in Ethnomusicology, UCLA, 1995; cultural doctorate philosophy of music, The World Univ., 1988. Instr. Nat. Taichung Tchr. Coll., 1961-62; prof. Chinese Culture U., Taipei, 1964-69; lectr. West L.A. C.C., 1978-82; founder Chinese Culture Sch. L.A., 1976—. Grad. tchg. asst. U. Md., 1982-83; instr. L.A. City Coll., 1983—, Calif. State U. L.A., 1984—, Pasadena City Coll., 1989—; prof. Chinese Santa Monica (Calif.) Coll., 1986—, Calif. State U. Northridge, 1986—; founder Wen Yen Piano Studio, 1972—; founder, dir. Chinese Mus. Orch. So. Calif., 1974—; founder, pres. Chinese- Amer. Musicians Assn. of So. Calif., 1990—; co-chair Conf. Students of Chinese Lang. and Culture; Chinese lang. instrn. course designer, instr. All Seasons Children's Learning Ctr., 2001—; music dir. Soc. Confucian Studies Am., 2004—; dir. bd. Chinese Studies Ctr., Calif. State U., LA, Party Potridge Club LA, 2009-. Musician: musical compositions include Collection of Works by Mr. Yen, 1969, (recordings) Art Songs and Chinese Folk Songs, 1982, Ode To My Home Land, 1992, Taiwanese Folk Songs Suite; musician: (Opera) Taiwanese Gezaix Suite; musician: Mother Earth-Found-Season: Spring, Summer, Autumn and Winter, 1997, Song of 911; author: Taiwan Folk Songs, 1967, vol. 2, 1969, A Collection of Wen-hsiung Yen's Songs, 1968, vol. 2, 1987, vol. 3, 2000 (award Fedn. Overseas Assns., 2000, 2002); translator: Achievement and Methodology for Comparative Musicology, 1968, Chinese Musical Culture and Folk Songs, 1989, Silk and Bamboo Expresses Emotion and Meaning, 2000, Ethnomusicology Series, 2002; composer: 100 songs and instrumental music; exhibitor traditional Chinese musical instruments and publs., Chinese Culture Ctr., 1995, 1996, Arcadia Pub. Libr., 1999; musician: East and West Music Concert, 2004, Concert for Traditional Music and New Performing Arts, 2006; organizer concerts, contbr. articles to profl. jours.; musician: (performer) Taiwanese Cultural Festival, 2008; Photographer (exhibitions) Chinese Calligraphy Painting Soc. Bd. dirs. So. Calif. Coun. Chinese Sch., 1998—; bd. dirs. Chinese Studies Ctr., Calif. State U., L.A., 1990—; conductor Chinese Music Orch. So. Calif., 1974-; prodr. Chinese Art and Culture

Festival, 1990-2003; sustaining mem. Rep. Nat. Com., 2002; advisor Lu Mei Tong Xin Hui Taiwanese Am. Assn., 2003—. Recipient 30 Yrs. Outstanding Tchr. award, Overseas Chinese Affairs Commn., Taiwan, 2006, World Chinese Writer Assn., Taipei, 2008, award, Chinese Art & Literary Assn., 2009. Mem.: Northern Am. Chinese Writers Assn. So. Calif. (v.p. 2000, pres. 2008), Fedn. Overseas Chinese Assns. (bd. dirs. (hon.) 2002), So. Calif. Coun. Chinese Schs. (chmn. exec. com.), Chinese Am. PTA So. Calif. (supr. 1985—), Taiwan Benevloent Assn. Calif. (v.p. 1986, pres. 1987—89, bd. dirs.), Taiwan Benevolent Assn. Am. (bd. dirs.), Alumni Assn. Chinese Culture U. So. Calif., Soc. Asian Music (founder, pres.), Internat. Coun. Traditional Music, Coll. Music Soc., Soc. Ethnomusicology, Chinese Performing Arts Assn. of Am. (bd. dirs.), Chinese Choral Soc. So. Calif. (music dir.), Chinese-Am. Musicians Assn. So Calif. (pres.). Avocations: walking, ping pong/table tennis, tai chi chuan. Office: Chinese Culture Sch 615 Las Tunas Dr Ste B Arcadia CA 91007-8469 Office Phone: 626-447-3823. Personal E-mail: wenhyen2000@yahoo.com.

YEO, RON, architect; b. LA, June 17, 1933; s. Clayton Erik and Rose G. (Westman) Y.; m. Birgitta S. Bergkvist, Sept. 29, 1962; children: Erik Elov, Katarina Kristina. B.Arch., U. So. Calif., 1959. Draftsman Montierth & Strickland (Architects), Long Beach, Calif., 1958-61; designer Gosta Edberg S.A.R. Arkitekt, Stockholm, 1962; partner Strickland & Yeo, Architects, Garden Grove, Calif., 1962-63; pres. Ron Yeo, Architect, Inc., Corona del Mar, Calif., 1963—. Cons., lectr. in field. Archtl. works include Garden Grove Civic and Cmty. Ctr., 1966, Hall Sculpture Studio, 1966, Garden Grove Cultural Ctr., 1978, Gem Theater, 1979, Festival Amphitheatre, 1983, Los Coyotes Paleontol. Interpretive Ctr., 1986, Calif. State U. Fullerton Alumni House, 1997, O'Neill Regional Pk. Nature Ctr., 1998, Upper Newport Bay Interpretive Ctr., 2000, Point Vicente Interpretive Ctr., 2006, Back Bay Sci. Ctr., 2007, Stough Canyon Nature Ctr., 2000, Quon residence, 2005. Mem. Orange County Planning Commn., 1972-73, 1975-76; chmn. Housing and Community Devel. Task Force, 1978, Orange County Fire Protection Planning Task Force, City of Newport Beach City Arts Commn., 1970-72; pres. Orange County Arts Alliance, 1980-81; gen. plan advisory com. Newport Beach, 2002-06. Fellow AIA; mem. Green Bldg. Coun., Internat. Conf. Bldg. Ofcls., Nat. Assn. for Interpretation (founding), Constrn. Specification Inst. Democrat. Office: Ron Yeo FAIA Architect Inc 500 Jasmine Ave Corona Del Mar CA 92625-2308

YEOH, MICHELLE, actress; b. Ipoh, Perak, Malaysia, Aug. 6, 1962; m. Dickson Poon, 1988 (div. 1992). BA, Royal Acad. of Dance. Owner prodn. co. Mythical Fiims. Actor: (films) Owl vs. Dumbo, 1984, My Lucky Stars 2: Twinkle Twinkle Lucky Stars, 1985, In the Line of Duty, 1986, Dynamite Fighters, 1987, Easy Money, 1987, Supercop, 1992, Butterfly Sword, 1993, Executioners, 1993, Holy Weapon, 1993, Supercop 2, 1993, Eastern Three Heros, 1993, The Tai-Chi Master, 1993, Wing Chun, 1994, Shaolin Popey 2: Messy Temple, 1994, Wonder Seven, 1994, The Stunt Woman, 1996, The Soong Sisters, 1997, Tomorrow Never Dies, 1997, Moonlight Express, 1999, Crouching Tiger, Hidden Dragon, 2000, Memoirs of a Geisha, 2005, Fearless, 2006, Sunshine, 2007, Far North, 2007, Purple Mountain, 2008, The Children of Huang Shi, 2008, The Mummy: Tomb of the Dragon Emperor, 2008, Babylon A.D., 2008; actor, exec. prodr.: The Touch, 2002; Silver Hawk, 2004; singer: (CD single) Love Quite Like a Comet, 1993. Recipient Asian Media award, Asian Am. Internat. Film Festival, 1998, Asian Film award, MTV Asia Awards, 2004, Knight of the Legion of Honor, Govt. of France, 2007; named Miss Malaysia, 1983. Office: c/o UTA 9560 Wilshire Blvd 516 Beverly Hills CA 90212

YEOMANS, DONALD KEITH, astronomer; b. Rochester, NY, May 3, 1942; s. George E. and Jessie Y.; m. Laurie Robyn Ernst, June 20, 1970; children: Sarah, Keith. BA, Middlebury Coll., Vt., 1964; MS, U. Md., 1967, PhD, 1970. Supr. Computer Scis. Corp., Silver Spring, Md., 1973-76; sr. rsch. astronomer Jet Propulsion Lab., Pasadena, Calif., 1976-92, supr., 1992—. Discipline specialist Internat. Halley Watch, 1982-89; sci. investigator NASA Comet Mission, 1987-91, Near-Earth Asteroid Rendezvous Mission, 1994-2001, Multi-Comet Flyby Mission, 1997-2002, Comet Impact Mission, 1999-2006; project scientist for asteroid sample return mission, 1998—; mgr. NASA Near-Earth Object Program Office, 1998-. Author: Comet Halley: Once in a Lifetime, 1985, The Distant Planets, 1989, Comets: A Chronological History of Observation, Science, Myth, and Folklore, 1991. Recipient Space Achievement award AIAA, 1985, Exceptional Svc. medal NASA, 1986, Achievement award Middlebury Coll. Alumni, 1987; named NASA/JPL Sr. Rsch. Scientist, 1993. Mem.: Am. Astron. Soc. (chair divsn. planetary scis. 1999—2000, chair hist. astronomy divsn. 2005—06). Democrat. Presbyterian. Avocations: tennis, history of astronomy. Office: Jet Propulsion Lab #301-150 4800 Oak Grove Dr Pasadena CA 91109-8001 Office Phone: 818-354-2127. Business E-Mail: donald.k.yeomans@jpl.nasa.gov.

YERXA, RON, film producer; Grad., Stanford U., Calif. Journalist, HS tchr., East LA; story analyst Time-Life Films; exec. CBS, Sovereign Films; co-founder Bona Fide Prodns., 1993—. Exec. prodr.: (films) Jack the Bear, 1993, I Am Trying to Break Your Heart, 2002; (TV films) The Spree, 1998; prodr.: (films) King of the Hill, 1993, Election, 1999, The Wood, 1999, Pumpkin, 2002, Cold Mountain, 2003, The Ice Harvest, 2005, Bee Season, 2005, Little Miss Sunshine, 2006, Little Children, 2006. Office: Bona Fide Prodns Ste 804 8899 Beverly Blvd Los Angeles CA 90048

YESTADT, JAMES FRANCIS, music director, conductor; b. Harrisburg, Pa., Nov. 24, 1921; s. Frederic John and Emelie Josephine (Speer) Y.; m. Victoria Ann Turco; children: Gregory James, Frederic John II, James Francis Jr. MusB, Lebanon Valley Conservatory Music, Pa., 1947; MA in Music, Columbia U., 1952; postgrad., New Sch. Music, Pa.; cert. in performance, Lucerne (Switzerland) Conservatory, 1962. Assoc. music prof. Xavier U., New Orleans, 1947-58; music dir., condr. New Orleans Summer Pops, 1954-58; resident condr. New Orleans Philharm. Symphony Orch., 1960-63; condr., dir. Transylvania Symphony Orch., Brevard, N.C., 1963-66; music dir., condr. Mobile (Ala.) Symphony Orch., 1965-71; dir. orchestral studies U. So. Miss., Hattiesburg, 1971-76; music dir., condr. Baton Rouge Symphony Orch., 1976-82; dir. orchestral studies La. State U., Baton Rouge, 1976-88; music dir., condr. Sun Cities Symphony of the West Valley, Sun City, Ariz., 1988—. Dir., condr. Mobile Opera Co., 1966-82; guest condr. Jackson (Miss.) Symphony Orch., 1986, Zurich Radio Orch., Orquesta Sinfonica de castillia y Leon, Spain, New Orleans Opera, numerous festivals, U.S., Europe. Numerous TV appearances and radio shows Served with U.S. Army, 1942-46, ETO. Mem. Music Educators Nat. Conf. (Performance award 1984), Coll. Music Soc., Am. Symphony Orch. League. Office: Sun Cities Symphony PO Box 1417 Sun City AZ 85372-1417

YGLESIAS, KENNETH DALE, college president; b. Tampa, Fla. s. Jose and Julia Yglesias; m. Donna Carmen Belli, Nov., 1977. BA, U. South Fla., 1969; MA, Western Carolina U., 1973; EdD, U. So. Calif., 1977. Cert. tchr., Calif., Fla. Tchr., coach pub. schs., Tampa, 1969-73; tchr., dept. chmn. Am. Sch. Madrid, 1973-76; fgn. svc. officer USIA, Washington and Tel Aviv, 1977-79; assoc. prof. Pepperdine U., LA, 1979-83; prof., dir. El Camino Coll., Torrance, Calif., 1981-83; adminstrv. dean Coastline Coll., Fountain Valley, Calif., 1983-88; v.p. Coast C.C. Dist., Costa Mesa, Calif., 1988-95; pres. Golden West Coll., Huntington Beach, Calif., 1995—2004; chancellor Coast Cmty. Coll. Dist., Costa Mesa, Calif., 2004—. Contbr. articles to profl. jours. Bd. dirs. C.C.'s for Internat. Devel., 1988-94, Orange County Marine Inst., Costa Mesa, 1990-93, United Way Orange County, Santa Ana, Calif., 1991-94. Mem. Am. Assn. for Higher Edn. (Hispanic caucus), Assn. Calif. C.C. Adminstrs., Phi Delta Kappa. Democrat. Roman Catholic. Avocations: basketball fan, walking. Office: Golden West Coll PO Box 2748 Huntington Beach CA 92647-0748

YIH, MAE DUNN, state legislator; b. Shanghai, May 24, 1928; d. Chung Woo and Fung Wen (Feng) Dunn; m. Stephen W.H. Yih, 1953; children: Donald, Daniel. BA, Barnard Coll., 1951; postgrad., Columbia U., 1951-52. Asst. to bursar Barnard Coll., NYC, 1952-54; mem. Oreg. Ho. Reps. from 36th dist., 1977-83, Oreg. Senate from 19th dist., 1983—. Mem. Clover Ridge Elem. Sch. Bd., Albany, Oreg., 1969-78, Albany Union H.S. Bd., 1975-79; mem. Joint Legis. Ways and Means Com., Senate Transp. Com., 1999, Senate pres. protemore, 1993. Episcopalian. Home: 34465 Yih Ln NE Albany OR 97322-9557 Office: Oreg Senate S 307 State Capitol Salem OR 97310-0001

YILMA, TILAHUN DANIEL, virologist, veterinarian, educator, researcher; b. Bulki, Gemugofa, Ethiopia, Dec. 15, 1943; parents Wolde-Ab Yilma and Getenesh Negewo. BS in Vet. Sci., U. Calif., Davis, 1968, DVM, 1970, PhD in Microbiology, 1977. Head vet. scv. Min. Agr., Harar, Ethiopia, 1970-71; lectr. UNDP/FAO of the UN Sch. for Animal Health Assts., DebreZeit, Ethiopia, 1971-72; rsch. assoc. USDA, Greenport, N.Y., 1977-79; asst. prof. vet. microbiology, pathology Wash. State U., Pullman, 1980-85, assoc. prof. vet. microbiology, pathology, 1985-86; prof. virology U. Calif., Davis, 1986—, dir. Internat. Lab. Molecular Biology for Tropical Disease Agents. Patentee in field. Recipient Ciba-Geigy prize Ciba-Geigy Ltd., 1990, Beecham award, 1988. Mem.: NAS. Office: U Calif Sch Vet Medicine 2079A Haring Hall Davis CA 95616 Business E-Mail: tdvilma@ucdavis.edu.

YOCAM, DELBERT WAYNE, retired software products company executive; b. Long Beach, Calif., Dec. 24, 1943; s. Royal Delbert and Mary Rose (Gross) Y.; m. Janet McVeigh, June 13, 1965; children—Eric Wayne, Christian Jeremy, Elizabeth Janelle. BA in Bus. Adminstrn., Calif. State U.-Fullerton, 1966; MBA, Calif. State U., Long Beach, 1971. Mktg.-supply changeover coordinator Automotive Assembly div. Ford Motor Co., Dearborn, Mich., 1966-72; prodn. control mgr. Control Data Corp., Hawthorne, Calif., 1972-74; prodn. and material control mgr. Bourns Inc., Riverside, Calif., 1974-76; corp. material mgr. Computer Automation Inc., Irvine, Calif., 1976-78; prodn. planning mgr. central staff Cannon Electric div. ITT, World hdqrs., Santa Ana, Calif., 1978-79; exec. v.p., COO Apple Computer, Inc., Cupertino, Calif., 1979-91; pres., COO, dir. Textronix Inc., Wilsonville, Oreg., 1992-95; chmn., CEO Borland Internat., Inc./Inprise Corp., Scotts Valley, Calif., 1996-2000, ret., 2000. Mem. faculty Cypress Coll., Calif., 1972-79; bd. dirs. Adobe Sys Inc., San Jose, Calif., Softricity, Inc., Boston; vice chmn. Tech. Ctr. Innovation, San Jose, Calif., 1989-90. Mem. Am. Electronics Assn. (nat. bd. dirs. 1988-89), Control Data Corp. Mgmt. Assn. (co-founder 1974), L.A. County Heart Assn. (active 1966). E-mail: yocam@aol.com.

YOHALEM, HARRY MORTON, lawyer; b. Phila., Jan. 21, 1943; s. Morton Eugene and Florence (Mishnun) Y.; m. Martha Caroline Remy, June 9, 1967; children: Seth, Mark. BA with honors, U. Wis., 1965; JD cum laude, Columbia U., 1969, M in Internat. Affairs, 1969. Bar: NY 1969, DC 1981, Calif. 1992, U.S. Supreme Ct. 1985. Assoc. Shearman & Sterling, NYC, 1969-71; asst. counsel to gov. State of NY, Albany, 1971-73, counsel office planning svcs., 1973-75; asst. gen. counsel FEA, Washington, 1975-77; mem. staff White House Energy Policy and Planning Office, Washington, 1977; dep. gen. counsel for legal svcs. Dept. Energy, Washington, 1978-80, dep. under sec., 1980-81; ptnr. Rogers & Wells, Washington, 1981-91; gen. counsel Calif. Inst. Tech., Pasadena, 1991—. Editor comments Columbia Jour. Transnat. Law, 1967-68, rsch. editor, 1968-69. Prin. Coun. for Excellence in Govt., Washington, 1990—; pres. Opera Bel Canto, Washington, 1984-87; mem. Lawyers Com. for Arts, Washington, 1981-88; bd. visitors dept. English U. Wis., 1999-2007. Harlan Fiske Stone scholar Columbia U., 1967, 69. Mem.: Athenaeum, Phi Kappa Phi. Home: 702 E California Blvd Pasadena CA 91106 Office: Calif Inst Tech Mail Code 108-31 1200 E California Blvd Pasadena CA 91125 Business E-Mail: harry.yohalem@caltech.edu.

YOO, JOHN CHOON, law educator, former federal agency administrator; b. Seoul, South Korea, June 10, 1967; s. John H. and Sook (Hee) Y. BA in History, Harvard U., 1989; JD, Yale U., 1992. Bar: Pa. 1993, U.S. Dist. Ct. (9th cir.) 1997. Law clk. to Judge Laurence Silberman US Ct. Appeals (D.C. cir.), Washington, 1992-93; law clk. to Justice Clarence Thomas US Supreme Ct., Washington, 1994-95; gen. counsel US Senate Judiciary Com., Washington, 1995-96; prof. law Boalt Hall Sch. Law, Berkeley, Calif., 1993-94, 96—; dir. Internat. Legal Studies Program, Boalt Hall Sch. Law, Berkeley, Calif., 1999—2001; dep. asst. atty. gen., Office Legal Counsel US Dept. Justice, Washington, 2001—03. Visiting scholar Am. Enterprise Inst.; visiting prof. U. Chgo., Free U. of Amsterdam, 1998; Fletcher Jones Disting. vis. prof. law Chapman U. Sch. Law, 2008—09. Author: The Powers of War and Peace: The Constitution and Fgn. Affairs After 9/11, 2005, War by Other Means: An Insider's Account of the War on Terror, 2006. Recipient Paul M. Bator award, Federalist Soc. for Law & Pub. Policy. Fellow: Soc. of Historians of Am. Foreign Relations, Rockefeller Found., Coun. on Fgn. Rels.; mem.: Berkeley Jour. of Internat. Law, Nat. Constitution Ctr., The Federalist Soc. Office: Boalt Hall Sch Law U Calif Berkeley 890 Simon Hall Berkeley CA 94720-0001 E-mail: yoo@law.berkeley.edu.*

YORK, GARY ALAN, lawyer; b. Glendale, Calif., Aug. 29, 1943; m. Lois York, 1987; 1 child, Jonathan Alan. BA, Pomona Coll., 1965; LLB, Stanford U., 1968. Bar: Calif. 1969. Ptnr. Dewey Ballantine, LA, 1985-95, Buchalter, Nemer, Fields & Younger, LA, 1995-98, Le Boeuf, Lamb, Greene & MacRae, LA, 1998—2002, Baker & Hostetler, LA, 2002—07. Instr. law sch. UCLA, 1968-69. Bd. editors Stanford Law review, 1966-68. Mem. ABA (chmn. real estate fin. com., real property probate and trust sect. 1987-89, chmn. usury com. 1992-93), L.A. County Bar Assn. (chmn. real estate fin. sect. 1993-96, exec. com. 1995—), State Bar of Calif., Am. Coll. Real Estate Lawyers, Am. Coll. Mortgage Attys.

YORK, HERBERT FRANK, university official; b. Rochester, NY, Nov. 24, 1921; s. Herbert Frank and Nellie Elizabeth (Lang) Y.; m. Sybil Dunford, Sept. 28, 1947; children: David Winters, Rachel, Cynthia. AB, U. Rochester, 1942, MS, 1943; PhD, U. Calif., Berkeley, 1949; DSc (hon.), Case Inst. Tech., 1960; LL.D., U. San Diego, 1964, Claremont Grad. Sch., 1974. Physicist Radiation Lab., U. Calif., Berkeley, 1943-58, assoc. dir., 1954-58; asst. prof. physics dept. U. Calif., Berkeley, 1951-54, assoc. prof., 1954-59, prof., 1959-61; dir. Lawrence Radiation Lab., Livermore, 1952-58; chief scientist Advanced Rsch. Project Agy., U.S. Dept. Def., 1958; dir. advanced rsch. projects divsn. Inst. for Def. Analyses, 1958; dir. def. rsch. and engring. Office Sec. Def., 1958-61; chancellor U. Calif.-San Diego, 1961—64, acting chancellor, 1970—72, prof. physics, 1964—88, prof. emeritus, 1988—, chmn. dept. physics, 1968-69, dean grad. studies, 1969-70, dir. program on sci., tech. and pub. affairs, 1972-88; dir. Inst. Global Conflict and Cooperation, 1983-88, dir. emeritus, 1988—. Amb. Comprehensive Test Ban Negotiations, 1979-81; trustee Aerospace Corp., Inglewood, Calif., 1961-87; mem. Pres.'s Sci. Adv. Com., 1957-58, 64-68, vice chmn., 1965-67; trustee Inst. def. Analysis, 1963-96; gen. adv. com. ACDA, 1962-69; mem. Def. Sci. Bd., 1977-81; spl. rep. of sec. def. at space arms control talks, 1978-79; mem. task force future nat. labs. Sec. Emergy, 1994-95; cons. Stockholm Internat. Peach Rsch. Inst.; rschr. in application atomic energy to nat. def. problems of arms control and disarmament, elem. particles. Author: Race to Oblivion, 1970, Arms Control, 1973, The Advisors, 1976, Making Weapons, Talking Peace, 1987, Does Strategic Defense Breed Offense?, 1987, (with Sanford Lakoff) A Shield in the Sky, 1989, Arms and the Physicist, 1994; also numerous articles on arms or disarmament; bd. dirs. Bull. Atomic Scientists. Trustee Bishop's Sch., La Jolla, Calif., 1963-65. Recipient E.O. Lawrence award AEC, 1962, Vannevan Bush award, 2000, Clark Kerr award, 2000, Enrico Fermi award, 2000; Guggenheim fellow, 1972. Fellow AAAS, Am. Phys. Soc. (forum on physics and soc. award 1976, Leo Szilard award 1994), Am. Acad. Arts and Sci.; mem. Fedn. Am. Scientists (chmn. 1970-71, exec. com. 1969-76, 95-2000, pub. svc. award 1992), Pugwash Movement 1969—, Phi Beta Kappa, Sigma Xi. Office Phone: 858-459-1776. Business E-Mail: hyork@uscd.edu.

YORK, JAMES ORISON, retired real estate executive; b. Brush, Colo., June 27, 1927; s. M. Orison and Marie L. (Kibble) Y.; m. Janice Marie Sjoberg, Aug. 1, 1959; children: Douglas James, Robert Orison. Student, U. Calif., Berkeley, 1945—46; BA cum laude, U. Wash., 1949. Tchg. fellow U. Wash., Seattle, 1950-52; econ. rsch. analyst Larry Smith & Co. Real Estate, Seattle, 1953-60, ptrn., 1960-66, pres. San Francisco, 1966-71; pres., chief exec. officer R.H. Macy Properties, NYC, also sr. v.p. planning and devel., dir. R.H. Macy & Co., Inc., 1971-88; chmn. James York Assocs. (real estate and venture capital), 1988—2008. Dir. emeritus UBP Properties, Inc.; chmn., N.Y.C. retail div. Am. Cancer Soc. Contbg. author: Shopping Towns-USA, 1960. Trustee ICSC Ednl. and Rsch. Found. With USNR, 1945-47. Recipient Disting. Alumnus award Econs. U. Wash., 1989. Fellow Phi Beta Kappa; mem. Am. Soc. Real Estate Counselors, Urban Land Inst., Internat. Real Estate Fedn., Internat. Coun. Shopping Ctrs., Olympic Club (San Francisco); Am. Yacht Club (Rye, N.Y.), Corinthian Yacht Club (Seattle), Union League (N.Y.C.), KM, Order St. John, Wash. Athletic Club (Seattle), Royal Victoria (B.C.) Yacht Club, Lambda Alpha. Home: 4 Riverstone Laguna Niguel CA 92677-5309 also: Sunrise Country Club 6 Malaga Dr Rancho Mirage CA 92270-3820 Personal E-mail: jysail@aol.com.

YORK, MICHAEL (MICHAEL YORK-JOHNSON), actor; b. Fulmer, Eng., Mar. 27, 1942; s. Joseph Gwynne and Florence Edith (Chown) Johnson; m. Patricia McCallum, Mar. 27, 1968. MA, Oxford U., Eng., 1964; DFA (hon.), U. SC. Profl. debut with Dundee Repertory Theatre, Scotland, 1964; mem. Nat. Theatre Co., London, 1965-66; TV film or miniseries appearances include: Much Ado About Nothing, The Forsyte Saga, Rebel in the Grave, True Patriot, Jesus of Nazareth, 1977, A Man Called Intrepid, 1979, The Phantom of the Opera, 1983, The Master of Ballantrae, 1984, Space, 1985, The Far Country, 1985, Are You My Mother, 1986, Ponce de Leon, 1987, Till We Meet Again, 1989, The Road to Avonlea, 1991, Gardens of the World, 1993; The Four Minute Mile, The Lady and the Highway Man, 1988, The Heat of the Day, 1988, The Hunt for Stolen War Treasure, 1989, The Night of the Fox, 1990, The Magic Paintbrush, 1993, David Copperfield's Christmas, 1994, Teklab, 1994, Fall From Grace, 1994, Not of This Earth, 1995, Duel of Hearts, September, 1995, A Young Connecticut Yankee in King Arthur's Court, 1995, A Knight in Camelot, (TV series) Knots Landing, 1987, SeaQuest, 1995, The Naked Truth, 1995, Babylon 5, 1995, The Ring, 1996, Un Coup De Baguette Magique, True Women, 1997, Sliders, 1997, The Magnificat, 1997, the Long way home, 1997, A Christmas Carol, 1997, The Search for Nazi Gold, 1998, The Ripper 1998, Dead Man's Gun, 1998, Perfect Little Angels, 1998, The Haunting of Hell House, 2000, The Lot, 2000, Founding Fathers, 2002, Liberty's Kids, 2002, Curb Your Enthusiasm, 2002, Founding Brothers, 2002, La Femme Musketeer, 2004, Icon, 2005, The Simpsons, 2006, Law and Order: Criminal Intent, 2006; stage appearances include: Any Just Cause, 1967, Hamlet, 1970, Broadway prodns. of Outcry, 1973, Ring Round the Moon, 1975, Bent, 1980, Cyrano de Bergerac, 1981, Whisper in the Mind, 1990, The Crucible, 1991, Someone Who'll Watch Over Me, 1993, Nora, 1993, Ira Gershwin at 100, 1996, Enoch Arden, 2003, Russian David...Soviet Goliath, 2004, Peer Gynt, 2005, Shadows and Voices, 2005, Amadeus, 2006, Camelot, 2007, Strauss Meets Frankenstein 2008; appeared in motion pictures including: The Taming of the Shrew, 1966, Accident, 1966, Red and Blue, 1967, Smashing Time, 1967, Romeo and Juliet, 1967, The Strange Affair, 1967, The Guru, 1968, Alfred the Great, 1968, Justine, 1969, Something for Everyone, 1969, Zeppelin, 1970, La Poudre D'Escampette, 1971, Cabaret, 1971, England Made Me, 1971, Lost Horizon, 1972, The Three Musketeers, 1973, Murder on the Orient Express, 1974, Great Expectations, 1974, Conduct Unbecoming, 1974, The Four Musketeers, 1975, Logan's Run, 1976, Seven Nights in Japan, The Last Remake of Beau Geste, 1977, The Island of Dr. Moreau, 1977, Fedora, 1977, The Riddle of the Sands, 1978, Final Assignment, 1980, The White Lions, Success is the Best Revenge, Perfect Little Angels, 1998, Dawn, 1985, Vengeance, 1986, The Secret of the Sahara, 1987, Imbalances, 1987, Lethal Obsession, 1987, Midnight Cop, 1988, The Return of the Musketeers, 1989, The Long Shadow, 1991, Eline Vere, 1991, Wide Sargasso Sea, 1991, Rochade, 1991, Discretion Assured,

Shadow of a Kiss, 1993, Gospa, 1994, Goodbye America, Austin Powers, Dark Planet, The Treat, 1997, Wrongfully Accused, 1998, One Hell of a Guy, 1998, Lovers and Liars, 1998, The Ghostly Rental, 1999, Austin Powers: The Spy Who Shagged Me, 1999, The Omega Code, 1999, Borstal Boy, 2000, Megiddo, 2001, Austin Powers in Goldmember, 2002, Moscow Heat, 2004; radio performances The Dark Tower, 1977, (Peabody award), A Matter of Honor, 1986, Babbitt, 1987, The Crucible, 1988, Are You Now, UTZ, 1989, McTeague, 1992, Make and Break, 1993; recs. include: Mere Christianity, 1982, Anna Karenina, 1985, Don Quixote, 1986, The King Must Die, 1988, British Rock: The First Wave, UTZ, 1989, The Modigliani Scandal, 1989, The Mummy, 1989, Candide, 1989, The Vampire Lestat, 1989, The Berlin Stories, 1990, The Remains of the Day, 1990, City of Joy, 1991, Beyond Love, 1991, Memories, Dreams, Reflections, 1991, A Poet's Bible, 1992, Einstein's Dreams, 1993, Accidentally on Purpose, 1993, The English Patient, 1993, Fortune's Favorite, 1993, The Three Musketeers, 1993, Paradise Lost, 1993, The Bookof Psalms, 1994, The Book of Virtues, 1994, The MagicPaw-Paw, 1994; (recs.) The Rubaiyat of Omar Khayyam, 1995, Aesop's Fables, 1995, The Poetry of Edgar Allen Poe, 1995, The Hunting of the Snark, Caesar's Women, 1996, Treasure Island, 1996, (Grammy nomination) The Wind in the Willows, 1996, Rose, 1996, Daily Word, 1997, Les Miserables, 1998, Caesar, 1998, Brave New World, 1998, Titanic Hearings, 1998, The Fencing Master, 1999 (Audie award), Rikki Tikki Tavi, 1999, King Rat, 1999, Going Home: Jesus and Buddha, 2000, The Lion, The Witch and The Wardrobe, 2000, A Shakespearean Actor Prepares, 2002, The Theory of Everything, 2003, Creating True Peace, 2003, The Bounty, 2003, Goodbye to Berlin, 2004, The Final Solution, 2004, For the Time Being: Advent, 2005, Jane Goodall's Message of Peace, How Do I Love Thee?, 2006, Peter And The Wolf, 2007, Word of Promise, Audio Bible, 2007, Inspiration for Today, 2008; author: The Courage of Conviction, 1985, Voices of Survival, 1987; author: Accidentally on Purpose, 1992, A Shakespearean Actor Prepares, 2000, Dispatches From Armageddon, 2002, Are My Blinkers Showing?, 2005. Chmn. Calif. Youth Theatre. Decorated officer Order Brit. Empire, chevalier Nat. Order Arts and Letters (France). Avocations: travel, music, art. Office: Peter Strain & Associate 5455 Wilshire Blvd # 1812 Los Angeles CA 90036 Office Phone: 323-525-3391.

YORK, THEODORE ROBERT, retired consulting company executive; b. Mitchel Field, NY, May 4, 1926; s. Theodore and Helen (Zierak) York; BS, U.S. Mil. Acad., 1950; MBA, George Washington U., 1964; MPA, Nat. U., 1984. Commd. 2d lt. USAF, 1950, advanced through grades to col., 1970, ret., 1974; pres. T. R. York Cons., Fairfax, Va., 1974-79, T. R. Cons., San Diego, 1979-85; dir. Software Productivity Consortium, Herndon, Va., 1985-90; pres. ULTRA-PLECS Intelligent Bldgs., Sandy, Utah, 1991—2002, ret., 2002. Decorated DFC, Air medal (5), Meritorius Svc. medal, Joint Svcs. Commendation medal, Air Force Commendation medal (5). Mem. Masons, Shriners. Avocations: computers, electronics. Personal E-mail: tedusma50@hotmail.com.

YORKE, THOM (THOMAS EDWARD YORKE), singer; b. Wellingborough, England, Oct. 7, 1968; children: Noah, Agnes. Student in English and Art, Exeter U., Eng. Guitarist Flickernoise; orderly; singer, guitarist Radiohead, 1992—. Singer, musician (albums with Radiohead) Pablo Honey, 1993, The Bends, 1995, Ok Computer, 1997 (Grammy award, Best Alternative Music Performance, 1998), (albums with Radiohead albums) Kid A, 2000 (Grammy award, Best Alternative Music Performance, 2001), (albums with Radiohead) Amnesiac, 2001, Hail to the Thief, 2003, In Rainbows, 2007 (Grammy award, Best Alternative Music Album, 2009), (solo albums) The Eraser, 2006. Named one of The 100 Most Influential People in the World, TIME mag., 2008. Office: Capital Records 1750 North Vine St 10th Floor Hollywood CA 90028 also: Chrysalis Music Group The Chrysalis Building Bramley Rd London W10 6SP England*

YORN, RICK, talent agent; b. 1968; Ptnr. Artists Mgmt. Group (acquired by The Firm), Beverly Hills, Calif., 2000—02; co-chmn. The Firm, Beverly Hills, Calif., 2002—. Prodr.: (films) Sidewalks of New York, 2001, You Stupid Man, 2002; exec. prodr.: Gangs of New York, 2002, The Aviator, 2004; exec. cons. (TV series) The Fighting Fitzgeralds, 2001. Office: The Firm 6th Fl 9465 Wilshire Blvd Beverly Hills CA 90212 Office Phone: 310-860-8000. Office Fax: 310-860-8100.

YOST, DAN, telecommunications industry executive; BSEE, MBA, So. Meth. U., Dallas. Sr. mgmt. position NETCOM Online Comm., MetroCel Cellular, Inc., McCaw Cellular Comm., AT&T Wireless; pres., COO Allegiance Telecom, Inc., Dallas; exec. v.p. product & IT Qwest Comm. Internat., Inc., Denver, 2004—08, exec. v.p. for Mass Markets Orgn. (MMO), 2008—. Bd. dirs. ACE Cash Express. Office: Qwest Comm Internat Inc 1801 California St Denver CO 80202 Office Phone: 303-992-1400. Office Fax: 303-896-8515.

YOST, NICHOLAS CHURCHILL, lawyer; b. Washington, Aug. 15, 1938; s. Charles Woodruff and Irene Ravitch (Oldakowska) Yost; m. Sandra Moore Rennie; children: Robert, Scott, Daniel. AB in Pub. & Internat. Affairs, Princeton U., 1960; LLB, U. Calif., Berkeley, 1963. Bar: Calif., 1964, US Supreme Ct., 1972, DC, 1978. Dep. atty. gen. adminstrv. law Calif. Dept. Justice, 1965-69; counsel Calif. State Environ. Quality Study Coun., 1969-71; dep. atty. gen. in charge environ. unit Calif. Dept. Justice, 1971-77; gen. counsel Coun. Environ. Quality, Exec. Office of Pres., Washington, 1977-81; vis. scholar Environ. Law Inst., Washington, 1981-82; sr. atty. Ctr. for Law in Pub. Interest, Washington, 1982-85; ptnr. Dickstein, Shapiro & Morin, Washington, 1985-94, Sonnenschein Nath & Rosenthal, San Francisco, 1994—. US dir. Law and Adminstrn. Project under US-USSR environ. agreement, 1977—81; dir. Pres.'s Task Force on Global Resources and Environment, 1980—81; mem US Del. to UN Conf. on Environment and Devel., Rio de Janeiro, 1992; mem. & subcom. chair Calif. EPA Blue Ribbon Commn. on a Unified Environ. Statute, 1994; NEPA counsel Presidio Trust. Contbr. articles to profl. journals Capt. US Army, 1963—65. Recipient Nat. Environ. Quality Award, Natural Resources Coun. Am., 1996. Mem. ABA (chmn. standing com. on environ. law 1989-91), State Bar Calif. (chmn. com. on environ. 1975-76), DC Bar Assn. (co-chmn. environ., energy and natural resources sect. 1985-86, 88-89), Environ. Law Inst. (bd. dirs. 1986-92), UN Assn. LA (v.p. 1969-71), UN Assn. Wash. (bd. dirs. 1987-93). Office: Sonnenschein Nath & Rosenthal LLP 26th Fl 525 Market St San Francisco CA 94105 Home Phone: 415-543-1031; Office Phone: 415-882-2440. Office Fax: 415-882-0300. Business E-Mail: nyost@sonnenschein.com.

YOUD, T. LESLIE, retired civil engineer; b. Spanish Fork, Utah, Apr. 2, 1938; s. Thomas Leslie and Mary (Evans) Y.; m. Denice Porter, June 26, 1962; children: Verlin, Lance, Melinda, Thomas, Emily. BS, Brigham Young U., 1964; PhD, Iowa State U., 1967. Rsch. civil engr. U.S. Geological Survey, Menlo Park, Calif., 1967-84; prof. Brigham Young U., Provo, Utah, 1984—2003; ret., 2004. Recipient Maeser Rsch. award Brigham Young U., 1991, Utah Engring. Educator of Yr., 1995, ASCE H. Bolton Seed medal, 2002. Mem. NAE, ASCE (hon.), Internat. Soc. for Soil Mechanics and Fnd. Engring., Earthquake Engring. Rsch. Inst.(hon.) Mem. Lds Ch. Achievements include development of techniques for mapping earthquake induced liquefaction hazard and techniques for estimating earthquake induced laterial spread displacements; inventor system for coupling accelerometers into bore hole casings. Home: 1132 E 1010 N Orem UT 84097-4306 Office: Brigham Young U Dept Civil Engring Provo UT 84602 Office Phone: 801-422-6327. E-mail: tyoud@byu.edu.

YOUMANS, JAMES, set designer; Set designer: The Wash, The American Plan, The Colorado Catechism, Sincerely Forever, Jersey City, Romance in Hard Times, A Mom's Life, Tales of the Lost Formicans, Gus and Al, Wolfman, (Broadway plays) Swinging on a Star, 1995, Gypsy, 2008, West Side Story, 2009. Office: Mark Taper Forum 5905 Wilshire Blvd Los Angeles CA 90036-4504

YOUMANS, JULIAN RAY, neurosurgeon, educator; b. Baxley, Ga., Jan. 2, 1928; s. John Edward and Jennie Lou (Milton) Y.; children—Reed Nesbit, John Edward, Julian Milton. BS, Emory U., 1949, MD, 1952; MS, U. Mich., 1955, PhD, 1957. Diplomate: Am. Bd. Neurol. Surgery. Intern U. Mich. Hosp., Ann Arbor, 1952-53, resident in neurol. surgery, 1953-55, 56-58; fellow in neurology U. London, 1955-56; asst. prof. neurosurgery U. Miss., 1959-62, assoc. prof., 1962-63, Med. U. S.C., 1963-65, prof., 1965-67, chief div. neurosurgery, 1963-67; prof. U. Calif., Davis, 1967-91; prof. emeritus, 1991—; chmn. dept. neurosurgery U. Calif., 1967-82. Cons. USAF, U.S. VA, NRC. Editor: Neurological Surgery, 1973; contbr. articles to profl. jours. No. vice chmn. Republican State Central Com. of Calif., 1979-81. Served with U.S. Navy, 1944-46. Mem. ACS (bd. govs. 1972-78), Congress of Neurol. Surgeons (exec. com. 1967-70), Am. Acad. Neurology, Am. Assn. Neurol. Surgeons, Am. Assn. Surgery of Trauma, Pan-Pacific Surg. Assn., Western Neurosurg. Soc., Neurosurg. Soc. Am., Soc. Neurol. Surgeons, Soc. Univ. Neurosurgeons, N. Pacific Soc. Neurology and Psychiatry, Royal Soc. Medicine, Am. Trauma Soc., U.S. C. of C., Bohemian Club, Rotary. Republican. Episcopalian. Office Phone: 530-756-6018.

YOUNG, ANDRE RAMELLE See DR. DRE

YOUNG, BRYANT COLBY, professional football player; b. Chicago Heights, Ill., Jan. 27, 1972; Student, Notre Dame U. Defensive tackle San Francisco 49ers, 1994—. Named to Pro Bowl, 1996. Office: care San Francisco 49ers 4949 Centennial Blvd Santa Clara CA 95054-1229

YOUNG, BRYANT LLEWELLYN, lawyer; b. Rockford, Ill., Mar. 9, 1948; s. Llewellyn Anker and Florence Ruth Y. AB, Cornell U., 1970; JD, Stanford U., 1974. Bar: Calif. 1974, Nev. 1975, D.C. 1979. Law clk. U.S. Dist. Ct. (no. dist.) Calif., San Francisco, 1974-75; assoc. Dinkelspiel, Pelavin, Steefel & Levitt, San Francisco, 1975-77; White House fellow, spl. asst. to sec. HUD, Washington, 1977-78, spl. asst. to sec., 1978-79; gen. mgr. to acting gen. mgr. New Cmty. Devel. Corp., 1979-80; mgmt. cons. AVCO Corp., 1980; spl. asst. to chmn. bd., CEO U.S. Synthetic Fuels Corp., Washington, 1980-81, project dir., 1981; pres. Trident Mgmt. Corp., San Francisco, 1981-87; of counsel Pelavin, Norberg, Harlick & Beck, San Francisco, 1981-82, ptnr., 1982-87; mng. ptnr. bus. sect. Carroll, Burdick & McDonough, San Francisco, 1987-90; founding ptnr. Young, Vogl & Harlick, San Francisco, 1990-93, Young, Vogl, Harlick, Wilson & Simpson, LLP, San Francisco, 1993-99; pres. Young Enterprises, Inc., 1995—2004; mgr. SRY Industries LLC, 1997—, KML Hospitality Industries LLC, 1997—, Nev. Nugget LLC, 2004—; ptnr. Young Vogl LLP, 1999—2001; prin. Law Offices of Bryant L. Young, 2002—. Dir. The Whitman Inst. Pub. affairs com. San Francisco Aid Retarded Citizens, Inc., 1977; U.S. co-chmn. New Towns Working Group, U.S.-USSR Agreement on Cooperation in Field of Housing and Other Constrn., 1979-80; treas., bd. dirs. White House Fellows Found., 1980-84; prin. Coun. Excellence in Govt., Washington, 1986-94; adv. com. Nat. Multi-Housing Coun., 1987-92; mem. Ross Sch. Found., 1994-97, sec., 1995-97; bd. dirs. Marin AIDS Project, 1996-97, sec., 1997; trustee Ross Sch., 1997-2003, pres. 2002-2003. Mem. ABA (real property, trust and probate law sects. 1975-96), White House Fellows Assn. (chmn. ann. meeting 1979, del. China 1980), Marin County Sch. Bds. Assn., Am. Field Svc. Returnees Assn., Can.-Am. C. of C. No. Calif. (v.p., bd. dirs. 1992), Chile-Calif. Found. (exec. com., bd. dirs. 1993-96). Office: 44 Montgomery St ste 3350 San Francisco CA 94104-4602 Office Phone: 415-291-1970. E-mail: bly@ebzlaw.net.

YOUNG, DONALD ALLEN, writer, consultant; b. Columbus, Ohio, June 11, 1931; s. Clyde Allen and Helen Edith (Johnston) Y.; m. Rosemary Buchholz, Feb. 26, 1955 (div. Nov. 1976); children: Kent Allen, Kelly Ann; m. Marjorie Claire Kirkel, Aug. 20, 1977; stepchildren: Jo Alene, Andrea Lynn, Beth Ellen. Student, Ohio State U., 1949-51, Columbia Coll., 1952, North Cen. Coll., Naperville, Ill., 1956, Coll. DuPage, 1978. Editor various newspapers, mags., Detroit, Chgo., Columbus, 1946-63, 1973-74, 1978-79; v.p. Frydenlund Assocs., Chgo., 1963; pub. rels. mgr. info. sys. divsn. Gen. Electric Co., Phoenix, 1963-70; publs. dir. Data Processing Mgmt. Assn., Park Ridge, Ill., 1970-72; pub. rels. mgr. Addressograph-Multigraph Corp., Arlington Heights, Ill., 1975-76; acct. exec. John Ripley & Assocs., Glenview, Ill., 1977-78; edtl. dir. Radiology/Nuc. Medicine mag., Des Plaines, Ill., 1979-81; pres. Young Byrum Inc., Hinsdale, Ill., 1982-83; writer, cons. Tucson, 1983—. Cons. in field; sports reporter, Copley newspapers, 1975-83; mem. adv. coun. Oakton C.C., 1970-75. Author: (books) Principles of Automatic Data Processing, 1965, Data Processing, 1967, Rate Yourself as a Mgr., 1985, Nobody Gets Rich Working for Somebody Else, 1987, 1993, 2001, Adventure Guide to Iceland, 2008, Rate Your Exec. Potential, 1988, 2001, If They Can.You Can, 1989, The Entrepreneurial Family, 1990, How to Export, 1990, Women in Balance, 1991, Sleep Disorders: America's Hidden Nightmare, 1992, Small Bus. Troubleshooter, 1994, 2000, Crime Wave: Am. Needs a New Get-Tough Policy, 1996, Popcorn Publications, 1996, Adventure Guide to So. Calif., 1997, Romantic Weekends: America's S.W., 1998, Adventure Guide to the Pacific N.W., 1998, Momentum: How to Get It-How to Keep It, 1999, Don't Get Mad-Get Rich, 1999, Walking Places in Wash. D.C., 2000, 100 Ways to Bring Out Your Best, 2002, Louisiana, An Adventurer's Guide, 2004. Arbitrator Better Bus. Bur., Tucson, 1987-92; docent Ariz. Sonora Desert Mus., 1988-92, Tucson/Pima Arts Coun., 1993-94. With USAF, 1952-56. Recipient Jesse Neal award Assn. of Bus. Pub., 1959, 61, Silver Anvil award Pub. Rels. Soc. of Am., 1976. Mem. Publicity Club of Chgo. (pres. 1978-79). Soc. Southwestern Authors (pres. 1992), Glen Ellyn (Ill.) Jaycees (bd. dirs., SPOKE award 1959, Outstanding Jaycee 1960), Young Reps. Club (v.p. 1960). Avocations: photography, travel, hiking, fishing. Home: 4866 N Territory Loop Tucson AZ 85750-5948 Personal E-mail: mardon01@comcast.net.

YOUNG, DONALD E., United States Representative from Alaska; b. Meridian, Calif., June 9, 1933; m. Lula Fredson; children: Joni, Dawn. AA, Yuba Jr. Coll., 1952; BA., Chico State Coll., Calif., 1958. Former educator, river boat capt.; mem. Fort Yukon City Council, 6 years, mayor, 4 years; mem. Alaska Ho. of Reps., 1966-70, Alaska Senate, 1970-73, U.S. Congress from Alaska, 1973—; now ranking mem. transp. & infrastructure com., chmn. resources com., steering com., homeland sec. com. Served in 41st Tank bn. US Army, 1955—57. Republican. Episcopalian. Office: US Ho Reps 2111 Rayburn Ho Office Bldg Washington DC 20515 Office Phone: 202-225-5765. Office Fax: 202-225-0425.

YOUNG, DOUGLAS REA, lawyer; b. LA, July 21, 1948; s. James Douglas and Dorothy Belle (Rea) Y.; m. Terry Forrest, Jan. 19, 1974; 1 child, Megann Forrest BA cum laude, Yale U., 1971; JD, U. Calif., Berkeley, 1976. Bar: Calif., 1976, US Dist. Ct. (no. dist.) Calif. 1976, US Ct. Appeals (6th and 9th cirs.) 1977, US Dist. Ct. (ctrl. dist.) Calif. 1979, US Dist. Ct. Hawaii, US Dist. Ct. (so. dist.) Calif., US Supreme Ct. 1982; cert. specialist in appellate law. Law clk. U.S. Dist. Ct. (no. dist.) Calif., San Francisco, 1976—77; assoc. Farella, Braun & Martel LLP, San Francisco, 1977—82, ptnr., 1983—. Spl. master US Dist. Ct. (no. dist.) Calif., 1977-78, 88, 96, 2000; mem. Criminal Justice Act Def. Panel no. dist. Calif.; mem. faculty Calif. Continuing Edn. of Bar, Berkeley, 1982—, Nat. Inst. Trial Advocacy, Berkeley, 1984—, Practicing Law Inst., 1988—; adj. prof. Hastings Coll. Advocacy, 1985—; vis. lectr. law Boalt Hall/U. Calif., Berkeley, 1986; judge pro tem San Francisco Mcpl. Ct., 1984-05, San Francisco Superior Ct., 1990—. Author: (with Purver and Davis) California Trial Handbook, ed edit., (with Hon. Richard Byrne, Purver and Davis), 3d edit., (with Purver, Davis and Kerper) The Trial Lawyers Book, (with Hon. Eugene Lynch, Taylor, Purver and Davis) California Negotiation and Settlement Handbook; contbr. articles to profl. jours Bd. dirs. Berkeley Law Found., 1977-78, chmn., 1978-79; bd. dirs. San Francisco Legal Aid Soc., pres., 1993—; bd. dirs. Pub. Interest Clearinghouse, San Francisco, chmn., 1987—, treas., 1988—; chmn. Attys. Task Force for Children, Legal Svcs. for Children, 1987—; mem. State Bar Appellate Law Adv. Commn., 1994— Recipient Appreciation award Berkeley Law Found., 1983, Criminal Justice Achievement award Criminal Trial Lawyers Assn. No. Calif., 2002; named a No. Calif. Super Lawyer San Francisco mag., 2004-05, Top Ten Super Lawyer San Francisco mag., 2005-06. Fellow ABA (Pro Bono Pub. award 1992), Am. Coll. Trial Lawyers, Am. Acad. Appellate Lawyers; mem. San Francisco Bar Assn. (founding chmn. litig. sect. 1988-89, award of appreciation 1989, bd. dirs. 1990-91, pres. 2001), Calif. Acad. Appellate Lawyers, McFetridge Am. Inn of Ct. (master), Lawyers Club San Francisco. Democrat. Office: Farella Braun & Martel 235 Montgomery St Ste 3000 San Francisco CA 94104-2902 Office Phone: 415-954-4438. Business E-Mail: dyoung@fbm.com.

YOUNG, ERNEST D., national historic site official; Park ranger, law enforcement officer, mus. curator Pu'ukahola Nat. Hist. Site, Kawaihae, Hawaii, also lead interpretive park ranger, in charge Visitor Ctr. Mailing: 62-3601 Kawaihae Rd Kamuela HI 96743

YOUNG, FRANK NOLAN, JR., commercial building contracting company executive; b. Tacoma, Feb. 26, 1941; s. Frank N. and Antoinette (Mahncke) Y.; m. Susan E. Bayley, Aug. 13, 1965; children: Sandra Susanne, Frank Nolan III. BA in Bus. and Fin., U. Wash., 1963. V.p. Strand Inc., Bellevue, Wash., 1966-73; chmn., treas., CEO, dir. Gall Landau Young Constrn. Co. Inc., Bellevue, 1973—; v.p., sec., dir. Cascade Structures, Kirkland, Wash., 1972—. Mem. Assoc. Gen. Contractors (pres. Seattle 1985, trustee 1968—, nat. dir.). Republican. Episcopalian. Clubs: Lakes, TAS Ski Found. (pres. 1983-84), Overlake Golf and Country, Seattle Yacht (trustee, 1992-95). Lodges: Elks, Masons, Shriners, Royal Order Jesters (impresario 1983-89). Home: 2929 81st Pl SE Unit P Mercer Island WA 98040-3044 Office: Gall Landau Young PO Box 6728 Bellevue WA 98008-0728

YOUNG, HOWARD THOMAS, foreign language educator; b. Cumberland, Md., Mar. 24, 1926; s. Samuel Phillip and Sarah Emmaline (Frederick) Y.; m. Carol Osborne, Oct. 5, 1949 (div. 1966); children: Laurie Margaret, Jennifer Anne; m. Edra Lee Airheart, May 23, 1981; 1 child, Timothy Howard. BS summa cum laude, Columbia U., NYC, 1950, MA, 1952, PhD, 1954. Lectr. Columbia U., NYC, 1950-54; asst. prof. Romance langs. Pomona Coll., Claremont, Calif., 1954-60, assoc. prof., 1960-66, Smith prof. Romance langs., 1966-98, prof. emeritus, 1998—. Vis. prof. Middlebury Program in Spain, Madrid, 1986-87, U. Zaragoza, 1967-68, Columbia U., summer 2000; chief reader Spanish AP Ednl. Testing Svc., Princeton, 1975-78, chmn. Spanish lang. devel. commn., 1976-79; mem. fgn. lang. adv. commn. Coll. Bd., NYC, 1980-83; mem. West Coast selection commn. Mellon Fellowships for Humanities, Princeton, 1984-86, European selection com., 1987, 90; trans. cons. Smithsonian Inst. Author: The Victorious Expression, 1964, Juan Ramón Jiménez, 1967, The Line in the Margin, 1980; editor: T.S. Eliot and Hispanic Modernity, 1995; contbr. London Times Higher Edn. Supplement; contbr. numerous articles and book revs. to profl. jours. Dir. NEH summer seminar for Sch. tchrs., 1993. Served with USNR, 1944-46, ETO. Fellow Del Amo Found., 1960-61, NEH, 1975, 89-90; Fulbright fellow; 1967-68; Rockefeller Study Ctr. scholar, 1976. Mem. MLA, Assn. Tchrs. Spanish and Portuguese, Am. Comparative Lit. Assn., Acad. Am. Poets, Assn. Lit. Scholars and Critics. Home: 447 W Redlands Ave Claremont CA 91711-1638 Office: Pomona Coll Romance Lang Dept 550 Harvard Ave Claremont CA 91711-6380 Home Phone: 909-625-2841. Business E-Mail: HTYoung@pomona.edu.

YOUNG, JACQUELINE EURN HAI, former state legislator, consultant; b. Honolulu, May 20, 1934; d. Paul Bai and Martha (Cho) Y.; m. Harry Valentine Daniels, Dec. 25, 1954 (div. 1978); children: Paula, Harry, Nani, Laura; m. Daniel Anderson, Sept. 25, 1978 (div. 1984); m. Everett Kleinjans, Sept. 4, 1988 (div. 1998). BS in Speech Pathology, Audiology, U. Hawaii, 1969; MS in Edn., Spl. Edn., Old Dominion U., 1972; advanced cert., Loyola Coll., 1977; PhD in Communication, Women's Studies, Union Inst., 1989. Dir. dept. speech and hearing Md. Sch. for the Blind, Balt., 1975-77; dir. deaf-blind project Easter Seal Soc. Oahu, Hawaii, 1977-78; project dir. equal ednl. opportunity programs Hawaii State Dept. Edn.,

Honolulu, 1978-85, state ednl. specialist, 1978-90; state rep. dist. 20 Hawaii State Legislature, Honolulu, 1990-92, state rep. dist. 51, 1992-94; vice-speaker Hawaii Ho. of Reps., Honolulu. Apptd. to U.S. Dept. Def. Adv. Commn. on Women in the Svc.; cons. spl. edn. U.S. Dept. Edn., dept. edn. Guam, Am. Samoa, Ponape, Palau, Marshall Islands, 1977-85; cons. to orgns. on issues relating to workplace diversity; adj. prof. commn., anthopology, mgmt. Hawaii Pacific U.; chief staff officer Am. Cancer Soc. Hawaii Pacific, 2004—. TV writer, host, producer, 1992—. 1st v.p. Nat. Women's Polit. Caucus, 1988-90; chair Hawaii Women's Polit. Caucus, 1987-89; bd. dirs. YWCA Oahu, Kalihi Palama Immigrant Svc. Ctr., Hawaii Dem. Movement, Family Peace Ctr.; appointee Honolulu County Com. on the Status of Women, 1986-87; founding bd. dirs. Windward Spouse Abuse Shelter, 1993—; campaign dir. Protect Our Constn., 1998; trustee St. Louis Sch., 1997-99; mem. nat. adv. coun. ACLU, 2004; nat. bd. dirs. Hawaiian Am. Coalition; mem. Asian and Pacific Islander Am. Health Assn.; mem. Hawaii State Adv. Com. on Civil Rights. Recipient Outstanding Woman Leader award YWCA of Oahu, 1994, Pres.'s award Union Inst., 1993, Fellow of the Pacific award Hawaii-Pacific U., 1993, Headliner award Honolulu chpt. Women in Commn., 1993, Korean Am. Alliance Washington Spl. Recognition award, 1998, Hawaii Women Lawyers Disting. Svc. award, 1999, Disting. Equity Adv. award Hawaii chpt. Nat. Coalition for Sex Equity in Edn., 1998, NEA Mary Hatwood Futrell for advancing women's rights award, 1999, Friend of Social Work award Hawaii chpt. NASW, 1998, Allan Saunders award Hawaii chpt. ACLU, 1999, Light of the Orient award Korean Am. Found., 2006; named one of Extraordinary Women Hawaii, Found. Hawaii Women's History, 2001.

YOUNG, JAMES W., biotechnology company executive; BS in Chemistry, Fordham U.; PhD in Organic Chemistry, Cornell U. Sr. v.p. rsch. & devel. ALZA Crop.; pres. pharms. divsn. Affymax; sr. v.p., gen. mgr. pharms. divsn. Sepracor Corp.; CEO, dir. Sunesis Pharms., Inc., South San Francisco, 2000—. Office: Sunesis Pharmaceuticals 395 Oyster Point Blvd Ste 400 South San Francisco CA 94080-1995

YOUNG, JERRY WAYNE, college president; b. Newbern, Tenn., Apr. 14, 1938; s. William Wesson and Elvaura (Jones) Y.; m. Linda F. Yoder; 1 child, Jeffrey W. BS, U. Utah, 1961; MA, Ariz. State U., 1968; PhD, Kent State U., 1973. Commd. 2d lt. USMC, 1960, advance through grades to maj., 1968; instr. U. Utah, Salt Lake City, 1960-61; tchr., coach Yuma (Ariz.) High Sch., 1963-66; dir. student activities Cuyahoya Community Coll., Cleve., 1967-69; coord. student union Kent (Ohio) State U., 1969-70; dean students Allegany Community Coll., Cumberland, Md., 1971-77; dean Clark City Community Coll., Las Vegas, 1977-83; pres. Centralia (Wash.) Coll., 1983-86, Chaffey Coll., Rancho Cucamonga, Calif., 1986—2001. Contbr. articles to profl. jours. Bd. dirs. Baldy View United Way, Ontario, Calif., 1990—. Recipient Master Tchr. award Tempe Elem. Dist., 1967; Harvard U. Inst. for Edn. Mgmt. grantee, 1988. Mem. Am. Assn. Community and Jr. Colls., Assn. Calif. Coll. Adminstrs., Am. Assn. Univ. Adminstrs., Calif. Community Coll. Chief Exec. Officers, Rancho Cucamonga C. of C. (v.p. 1990—), Inland Empire Indsl. Rsch. Assn. (pres. 1990—), Western Region Accreditation Assn. (accreditation evaluator 1987—) Northwest Region Accreditation Assn. (accreditation evaluator 1980—). Avocations: jogging, camping, reading, writing, photography. Office: Chaffey Cmty Coll Office Pres 5885 Haven Ave Rancho Cucamonga CA 91737-3002

YOUNG, JONI J., finance educator, researcher; b. Pana, Ill., June 25, 1958; d. M. Deon and Wilma J. Young; m. Tony Cebuhar, May 30, 1987. BS in Fin., U. Ill., Champaign, 1979, MS in Accountancy, 1981, PhD in Accountancy, 1991. CPA N.Mex Soc. Auditor Arthur Andersen and Co., Chigo., 1981—85; prof. acctg. Temple U., Phila., 1991—92, U. N.Mex, Albuquerque, 1992—, dept. chair acctg., 2007—. Contbr. articles to profl. jours. on acctg. Bd. mem. YDI, Inc., Albuquerque, 2002—04. Recipient Faculty Achievement Recognition, U. N.Mex, 2004; Doctoral fellowship, AICPA, 1985, KPMG, 1987, Deloitte and Touche, 1989. Fellow: Am. Accountign Assn.; mem.: Soc. Acctg. Historians. Independent. Avocations: yoga, quilting, reading. Office: Anderson Sch Management msc05 3090 1 Univ New Mexico Albuquerque NM 87106 Business E-Mail: young@mgt.unm.edu.

YOUNG, LAI-SANG, mathematician, educator; b. Hong Kong, 1952; BS, U. Wisconsin, 1973; MA, U. Berkeley, 1976, PhD, 1978. Prof. Northwestern U., 1978, U. Warwick, England, 1979—80, Michigan State U., 1980; prof. math. UCLA, 1981; visiting prof. Math. Sci. Rsch. Inst., Berkeley, 1983—84, U. Bielefeld, Germany, 1985—86, Inst. Advanced Study, Princeton, 1989; prof. math. NYU, Courant Inst. Math. Sci., NYC. Recipient Ruth Lyttle Math. prize Am. Math. Soc., 1993, Guggenheim Fellowship, 1997-98. Fellow: Am. Acad. Arts & Sci.

YOUNG, LAWRENCE, electrical engineering educator; b. Hull, Eng., July 5, 1925; arrived in Can., 1955; naturalized, 1972; s. Herbert and Dora Y.; m. Margaret Elisabeth Jane, Jan. 5, 1951. BA, Cambridge U., Eng., 1946, PhD, 1950, ScD, 1963. Asst. lectr. Imperial Coll., London, 1952-55; mem. research staff B.C. Research Council, 1955-63; assoc. prof. U. B.C., Vancouver, 1963-65, prof. dept. elec. engring., 1965-90, prof. emeritus, 1990—. Author: Anodic Oxide Films, 1961; contbr. articles to profl. jours. Recipient Callinan award Dielectrics div. Electrochemical Soc., 1983, Can. Electrochem. Gold medal, 1990. Fellow IEEE, Royal Soc. Can., Electrochem. Soc. Office: U BC Dept Elec and Computer Engring Vancouver BC Canada V6T 1W5

YOUNG, LIONEL WESLEY, radiologist; b. New Orleans, Mar. 14, 1932; s. Charles Henry and Ethel Elsie (Johnson) Y.; m. Florence Inez Brown, June 24, 1957; children: Tina Inez, Lionel Thomas, Owen Christopher. BS in Biology, St. Benedict's Coll., Atchison, Kans., 1953; MD, Howard U., 1957. Diplomate Am. Bd. Radiology. Intern Detroit Receiving Hosp., Wayne State Univ. Coll. of Medicine, 1957-58; resident Strong Meml. Hosp., U. Rochester (N.Y.) Med. Ctr., 1958-61; pediatric radiologist, assoc. prof. radiology and pediatrics U. Rochester Med. Ctr., 1965-75; prof. radiology and pediatrics U. Pitts., 1975-86; dir. radiology and pediatrics Children's Hosp. of Pitts., 1980-86; chmn. radiology Children's Hosp. Med. Ctr. of Akron (Ohio), 1986-91, Children's Hosp. and Northeastern Ohio U. Coll. Medicine, Rootstown, 1987-91; dir. Divsn. Pediat. Radiology Loma Linda (Calif.) U. Med. Ctr. and Children's Hosp., 1991—. Pres. Akron Pediatric Radiologists, 1986—. Lt. comdr. USN, 1961-63. Mem. Am. Coll. Radiology (mem. coun., steering com.), Soc. for Pediatric Radiology. Democrat. Roman Catholic. Avocation: music. Office: Divsn Pediatric Radiology Loma Linda U Childrens Hosp 11234 Anderson St Loma Linda CA 92354-2804 Home Phone: 909-335-8735; Office Phone: 909-824-4281. E-mail: lwyoung@ahs.llumc.edu.

YOUNG, LOWELL SUNG-YI, health facility administrator, medical educator; b. Honolulu, Dec. 5, 1938; AB, Princeton U., 1960; MD, Harvard U., 1964. Di;omate Am. Bd. Internal Medicine with subspecialty in infectious diseases. Intern, jr. asst. resident, sr. asst. resident med. divsn. Bellevue Hosp. and Meml. Hosp., NYC, 1964-67; fellow in medicine Cornell U. Med. Coll., 1965-67; epidemic intelligence officer bacterial diseases br. Nat. Communicable Disease Ctr., Atlanta, 1967-69, chief spl. pathogens sect., 1968-69; spl. postdoctoral rsch. fellow Nat. Inst. Allergy and Infectious Diseases, 1969-70; rsch. fellow in medicine Meml. Hosp./Cornell U. Med. Coll., 1969-70; clin. asst. physicisn infectious disease svc. dept. medicine Meml. Hosp., 1970-72, assoc. dir. microbiology lab., 1971-72; instr. in medicine Cornell U. Med. Coll., 1970-72; chief divsn. infectious disease Calif. Pacific Med. Ctr., San Francisco, 1985-99; asst. clinician Sloan-Kettering Inst. for Cancer Rsch., 1971-72; dir. Kuzell Inst., San Francisco, 1985—; asst., assoc. prof. med. UCLA, 1972—85. Adj. prof. pharmacy U. of Pacific, San Francisco, 1989-95; mem. microbiology and invectious diseases adv. com. Nat. Inst. Allergy and Infectious Diseases, 1981-85, mem. allergy and immunology rsch. com., 1975-79; mem. adv. coun. Nat. Infectious diseases, 1996-2000; mem. staff Calif. Pacific Med. Ctr., Mt. Zion Hosp. and Med. Ctr., U. Calif., San Francisco. Mem. editl. bd. Antomicrobial Agts. and Chemotherapy, Infection and Immunity; contbr. numerous articles to profl. jours., chpts. to books. Recipient Alexander D. Langmuir prize Epidemic Intelligence Svc., 1970, Garrod medal Brit. Soc., 1992. Fellow ACP (mem. med. self-assessment com.), Infectious Diseases Soc. Am. (councillor 1983-85); mem. Am. Soc. for Clin. Investigation, Am. Fedn. for Clin. Rsch., Am. Soc. for Microbiology, Western Soc. for Clin. Rsch., Internat. Immunocompromised Host Soc., Brit. Soc. Antimicrobial Chemotherapy. Office: Kuzell Inst 2200 Webster St Ste 305 San Francisco CA 94115-1821 Office Phone: 415-600-1734. Business E-Mail: younglx@sutterhealth.org.

YOUNG, MARC D., lawyer; BA in Econs. and Polit. Sci., U. Utah, 1986, JD, 1991. Bar: Calif. 1993. Law clk. to Hon. David K. Winder U.S. Dist. Ct., Dist. UT, 1992; joined Morrison & Foerster, LA, 1993, ptnr., co-chmn. real estate practice group. Mem.: State Bar Calif., ABA, L.A. County Bar Assn. Office: Morrison & Foerster LLP 555 West Fifth St Ste 3500 Los Angeles CA 90013-1024 Office Phone: 212-892-5659. Office Fax: 212-892-5454. Business E-Mail: myoung@mofo.com.

YOUNG, MICHAEL KENT, academic administrator, law educator; b. Sacramento, Nov. 4, 1949; s. Vance Lynn and Ethelyn M. (Sowards) Young; m. Suzan Kay Stewart, June 1, 1972; children: Stewart, Kathryn, Andrew. BA summa cum laude, Brigham Young U., Provo, Utah, 1973; JD magna cum laude, Harvard U., Cambridge, Mass., 1976. Bar: Calif. 1976, NY 1985. Law clk. to Justice Benjamin Kaplan, Supreme Jud. Ct. Mass., Boston, 1976—77; law clk. to Justice William H. Rehnquist U.S. Supreme Ct., Washington, 1977—78; assoc. prof., prof., Fuyo prof. Japanese law Columbia U., NYC, 1978—98, dir. Program Internat. Human Rights and Religious Liberties, 1995—98; dir. Ctr. Japanese Legal Studies and Ctr. for Korean Legal Studies, NYC, 1985—98; dean, Lobingier prof. comparative law and jurisprudence George Washington U. Sch. of Law, Washington, 1998—2004; dep. legal advisor U.S. Dept. State, Washington, 1989—91, dep. under sec. for econ. affairs, 1991—93, amb. for trade and environ. affairs, 1992—93; pres. and prof. law U. Utah, Salt Lake City, 2004—. Mem. US Commn. on Internat. Religious Freedom, 1998—2005, chair, 2001—02, 2002—03, vice chair, 2002—03; vis. scholar law faculty U. Tokyo, 1978—80, 1983; vis. prof. Waseda U., 1989; chmn. bd. advisors Japan Soc., 1996—98; counsel select subcom. on arms transfers to Bosnia US Ho. of Reps., 1996; mem. steering com. Law Profs. for Dole, 1996; mem. com. on internat. jud. rels. US Jud. Conf., 1999—2005; mem. Brown v. Bd. Edn. 50th Anniversary Commemoration Com.; chair NAFTA labor agreement adv. com. Dept. of Labor; mem. trade and environ. policy adv. com. US Trade Rep. Office, 2003—. Author: Fundamentals of U.S. Trade Law, 2001, Japanese Law in Context, 2001, International Environmental Law: Cases, Materials and Problems, 2007. Bd. visitors USAF Acad., 2000—02; bd. govs. East West Ctr.; bd. dirs. Salt Lake C. of C., Envision Utah, Alliance for Unity, Herbert I. and Elsa B. Michael Found., The Craig H. Neilsen Found., Magnet Bank, tanner lectrs. human Vvlues. Recipient Disting. Contbns. to Human Rights award, Ctr. for Internat. Religious Freedom, Brigham Young U., 2005, Excellence in Edn. award, Utah Hispanic C. of C., Excellence in Ethics award, Utah Valley State U., 2005, Internat. Humanitarian award, Pub. Affairs Office, LDS Ch., 2006, Disting. Svc. award, J. Reuben Clark Soc., 2006, The Helping Hand award, Utah Youth Village, 2006, award of Merit and Knighthood Order St. Michael of the Wing, 2007, US Chaina Collaboration Leadership award, Chines Assn. Sci. Tech., 2008, Disting. Svc. award, Brigham Young U., 2008; named Communicator of Yr., Publs. Soc. Am. and Internat. Assn. Bus. Communicators, Internat. Leader of Yr., World Trade Assn., 2008; POSCO Rsch. Inst. fellow, 1995—98, Japan Found. fellow, 1979—80, Fulbright fellow, 1983—84. Fellow: Am. Bar Found.; mem.: Coun. Fgn. Rels. Mem. Lds Ch. Avocations: skiing, scuba diving, photography. Home: 1480 Military Way Salt Lake City UT 84103 Office: U Utah 201 S President's Cir Rm 203 Salt Lake City UT 84112 Office Phone: 801-581-5701. Business E-Mail: president@utah.edu.

YOUNG, STEVEN RAY, lawyer; b. Hollywood, Calif., June 30, 1954; s. Troy Raymond and Faye Evelyn (Murray) Young; m. Solange Young; children: Conrad, Courtney, Corine, Crystal. BA, U. Utah, 1977; JD, Pepperdine U. Sch. Law, Malibu, Calif., 1980. Bar: Calif. 1980, Wash. 1991, US Dist. Ct. (no., ctrl. and so. dists.) Calif., US Ct. Appeals (9th cir.). Assoc. Voss & Cook LLP, Newport Beach, Calif., 1980-85, Munns, Kefford, Hoffman, Hunt & Throckmorton, Newport Beach, Calif., 1985-87, ptnr., 1987-89, Cummings & Young, Newport Beach, Calif., 1989-93, Young, Amundsen & Dial, Newport Beach, Calif., 1993—97; pvt. practice civil justice atty., 1997—. Exec. bd. mem. Calif. Dem. Party, 2005—, v.p. Bus. & Profl. Caucus, 2006—. Mem.: ABA, Peter Elliott Inns of Ct. (pres.), Wash. State Bar Assn., Calif. Bar Assn., Internat. Brotherhood Elec. Workers (Local 441), Los Amigos, Dana Point Lighthouse Soc., Sons of Am. Legion. Democrat. Mem. Lds Ch. Mailing: Campaign Address 101 Pacifica Ste 100 Irvine CA 92618 Office Phone: 949-338-4459. Office Fax: 949-788-3999.

YOUNG, TONY, councilman; b. Madrid; s. James and Jeanne Young; m. Jacqueline Young. Grad. in Socio-econs., Howard U.; attended, U. San Diego. Intern Congressman Jim Bates; legis. aide to San Diego County Supr. Leon Williams; chief of staff to City Councilman Charles L. Lewis III; councilman, Dist. 4 San Diego City Coun., 2005—, co-chmn. City-County Reinvestment Task Force, vice chair Com. Pub. Safety and Neighborhood Svcs., chmn. Com. on Budget and Fin. Tchr. O'Farrell Middle Sch., San Diego, Muirlands Middle Sch., San Diego. Democrat. Office: 202 C St MS 10A San Diego CA 92101 also: 415 Euclid Ave San Diego CA 92102 Office Phone: 619-236-6644. Office Fax: 619-236-7273. E-mail: anthonyyoung@sandiego.gov.*

YOUNG, WILLIAM D., chemical engineer; BS in Chem. Engring., Purdue U., D. in Engring. (hon.), 2000; MBA, Ind. U. Various positions in prodn. and process engring. Eli Lilly and Co.; various positions Genentech, Inc., 1980-99, COO; CEO, chmn. of bd. ViroLogic, Inc., San Francisco, 1999—. Mem. NAE. Office: ViroLogic Inc 345 Oyster Point Blvd South San Francisco CA 94080-1913

YOUNGBAUER, STEVEN R., state legislator, lawyer; b. Alma, Wis., Feb. 25, 1950; m. Echo Youngbauer; 1 child. BA, Winona State Coll., 1974; JD, U. Wyo., 1982. Bar: Wyo. Pvt. practice, 1982-86; gen. coun., atty., 1987-90; mgr. land, atty., 1990—; mem. Wyo. Senate, Dist. 23, Cheyenne, 1998—. Mem. Wyo. Environ. Quality Coun. (chairperson), Wyo. State Bar Assn., Wyo. Mining Assn., Wyo. Tax Payers Assn. Republican. Roman Catholic. E-mail: youngbauer@vcn.com.

YOUNGER, LAURIE, broadcast executive; BA in Comm., Queens Coll.; MBA, UCLA, 1983. Former dir. bus. affairs 20th Century Fox; dir. bus. affairs network TV divsn. The Walt Disney Co., 1985—86, v.p. bus. affairs, 1986—90; sr. v.p. bus. affairs and adminstrn. Walt Disney TV and Telecomm.; sr. v.p. ABC, Inc., 1996—98, sr. v.p., CFO, 1998—2003, exec. v.p., CFO, 2003—; exec. v.p. ABC TV Distbn., 2000—03; pres. Buena Vista Worldwide TV, 2003—. Named one of 100 Most Powerful Women in Hollywood, Hollywood Reporter, 2003, 2004, 2005, 2006. Office: ABC Inc 500 S Buena Vista St Burbank CA 91521-4775

YOUNGJOHNS, ROBERT H., computer software company executive; married. MA in Physics and Philosophy with honors, Oriel Coll., Oxford Univ. Various engring. and mgmt. roles IBM, 1980—95; v.p. Sun Microsystems, England, 1995—98; v.p. sales & mktg. Sun Microsystems Europe Middle East and Africa, 1998—2002; exec. v.p. global sales ops. Sun Microsystems, 2002—04, exec. v.p. strategic devel. and Sun financing Santa Clara, Calif., 2004—05; pres., CEO Callidus Software Inc., 2005—07; corp. v.p., pres. No. Am. sales & mktg. Microsoft Corp., Redmond, Wash., 2007—. Bd. dir. Callidus Software Inc., 2005—. Office: Microsoft Corp 1 Microsoft Way Redmond WA 98052-6399*

YOUNG WRIGHT, NANCY, state legislator; b. N.Mex. m. Allen Wright; children: Erin, Kelsey. BA in Journalism, N.Mex. State U. Bd. mem. Amphitheater Unified Sch. Dist., 1997—2007, pres., 2002—04; mem. Dist. 26 Ariz. House of Reps., 2008—, mem. edn. com., water & energy com. Exec. dir. Southern Ariz. ArtsReach Writing Program, 2004—07; past pres. Oro Valley Neighborhood Coalition. Vol. Animal Rescue Found., 2007—. Democrat. Office: Ariz House Reps Capitol Complex 1700 W Washington Rm 329 Phoenix AZ 85007 Office Phone: 602-926-3398. Office Fax: 602-417-3126. Business E-Mail: nyoungwright@azleg.gov.*

YOUPA, DONALD GEORGE, broadcast executive; b. NJ; BA in Polit. Sci., Rutgers U., 1959. Exec. dir., v.p. Sears-Roebuck Found., Chgo.; v.p. devel. KCET, LA, 1978-80, sr. v.p. mktg. and devel., 1980-87, exec. v.p., 1987-94, exec. v.p., COO, 1994—. Office: KCET 4401 Sunset Blvd Los Angeles CA 90027-6090 E-mail: dyoupa@kcet.org.

YOUSEF, FATHI SALAAMA, communications educator, management consultant; b. Cairo, Jan. 2, 1934; arrived in U.S., 1968, naturalized, 1973; s. Salaama and Rose (Tadros) Yousef; m. Marjan Lowies El-Faizy, June 24, 1994. BA, Ain Shams U., Cairo, 1955; MA, U. Minn., 1970, PhD, 1972. Svc. ctr. supt. Shell Oil Co., Cairo, 1955-61; indsl., mgmt. tng. instr. ARAMCO, Dhahran, Saudi Arabia, 1961-68; tchg. assoc. U. Minn., Mpls., 1968-72; comm. studies prof. emeritus Calif. State U., Long Beach, 1972—. With orgn. and indsl. engring. dept. ARAMCO, 1978—80. Co-author: An Introduction to Intercultural Communication, 1975, 1985; contbr. Grantee, NSF, 1981, 1982, 1983. Mem.: Assn. Egyptian Am. Scholars. Democrat. Office: Calif State U Dept Comm Studies Long Beach CA 90840 Business E-Mail: fyousef@csulb.edu.

YSURSA, BEN T., Secretary of State, Idaho; b. Boise, Idaho, June 10, 1949; m. Penny Ysursa; children: Shawn Del, Matthew, Andrew. BA, Gonzaga U., 1971; JD, St. Louis U. Law Sch., 1974. Bar: Idaho 1974. Dep. sec. state State of Idaho, Boise, 1974—76, chief dep., 1976—2002, sec. state, 2002—. Mem. Basque Ctr., St. John's Parish; pres. Adh County Lincoln Day, 1990. Recipient Boyd Martin award, Assn. Idaho Cities, Outstanding Adminstr., Idaho Rep. Party, 1992. Mem.: Reagan-Bush Idaho Com. (treas. 1984), NHSS (secs. state 2003), Idaho State Bar Assn. Republican. Roman Catholic. Office: Office Sec State Rm 203 700 W Jefferson Boise ID 83720-0080 Office Phone: 208-334-2300. Office Fax: 208-334-2282. E-mail: bysursa@idsos.state.id.us.

YU, BIN, statistician, educator; BS in Math, Peking U., 1984; MA in Stats., U. Calif. Berkeley, 1987, PhD of Stats., 1990. Asst. prof. U. Wis. Madison, 1990—92; asst. prof., assoc. prof. U. Calif. Berkeley, 1993—2000, prof., 2001—. Postdoctoral fellow MSRI, Berkeley, 1991; vis. asst. prof. Yale U., New Haven, 1993; mem. tech. staff Bell Labs. Lucent, Murray Hill, NJ, 1997—2000. Guest editor spl. issue Statistica Sinica, 2001, IEEE Signal Processing; contbr. articles to profl. jours. Grantee, Army Rsch. Office, 1991, 1994, 1998, 2001, 2004, 2005, NSF, 1994, 1998, 2001, 2004, 2006; Guggenheim fellow, 2006. Fellow: AAAS, IEEE, Am. Stats. Assn., Inst. Math. Stats. Achievements include patents for lossless coding and data network tomography. Avocations: reading, walking, swimming, movies. Office: Univ Calif Berkeley 367 Evans Hall #3860 Berkeley CA 94720

YU, JEN, medical educator; b. Taipei, Taiwan, Jan. 23, 1943; came to U.S., 1969; s. Chin Chuan and Shiu Lan (Lin) Y.; m. Janet Chen, June 16, 1973; children: Benjamin, Christopher. MD, Nat. Taiwan U., 1968; PhD in Physiology, U. Pa., 1972. Diplomate Am. Bd. Phys. Medicine and Rehab. Intern Phila. Gen. Hosp., 1972-73; resident in phys. medicine and rehab. Hosps. of U. Pa., 1973-75; asst. prof. dept. phys. medicine and rehab. U. Pa. Sch. Medicine, Phila., 1975-76, U. Tex. Health Sci. Ctr., San Antonio, 1976-79, assoc. prof., 1979-81; prof. dept. phys. medicine and rehab. U. Calif. Irvine Coll. Medicine, 1981-82, prof., chmn. dept. phys. medicine and rehab., 1982—. Contbr. articles to profl. jours. Mem. Am. Acad. Phys. Medicine and Rehab., Am. Congress Rehab. Medicine, Assn. Acad. Physiatrists,

Am. Assn. Anatomists, Soc. for Neurosci. Office: U Calif Irvine Med Ctr Dept Phys Medicine & Rehab 101 The City Dr Orange CA 92868-3201 Home Phone: 949-856-3264; Office Phone: 714-456-6504. Business E-Mail: jyu@uci.edu.

YU, JOHN SUN, neurosurgeon, immunologist; b. Seoul, Republic of Korea, Sept. 11, 1963; s. Victor Seung Jae Yu, Grace Eun Duk Yu; m. Helena Yoon; children: Jeffrey, Lauren. BA, BS, Stanford U., 1985; MD, Harvard U., 1990, MS in Genetics, 1990. Diplomate Am. Bd. Neurol. Surgery. Resident in neurosurgery Mass. Gen. Hosp., Boston, 1997; neurosurgeon Cedars-Sinai Med. Ctr., LA, 1997—, co-dir. Comprehensive Brain Tumor Program, 1997—; med. dir. Gamma Knife, 2006—; chmn., chief sci. officer Immunocellular Therapeutics Ltd., Woodland Hills, Calif., 2006—; dir. surg. neuro-oncology Cedars-Sinai Med. Ctr., LA, 2007—. Editor: Current Stem Cell Rsch. and Therapy; contbr. articles to Lancet, Cancer Rsch., Human Gene Therapy, others.; patent for differentiation of whole bone marrow cells into neural progenitor cells, 2001. Recipient Acad. award, Am. Acad. Neurol. Surgery, 1998, Betty Lea Stone award, Am. Cancer Soc., 1986, Preuss Resident Rsch. award, AANS and CNS, 1995, Mahaley Clin. Rsch. award, 2005; grantee, NIH, 2001—. Mem.: Am Assn. Neurol. Surgeons (tumor sect.). Office: Cedars-Sinai Neurosurg Inst 8631 W Third St Ste 800E Los Angeles CA Office Phone: 310-423-7900. Business E-Mail: yuj@cshs.org.

YU, SUSAN C(HUNG-MI), lawyer; BA, U. Calif., Berkeley, 1996; JD cum laude, Syracuse U., 1998. Bar: Calif. 1998. Ptnr. Collins, Mesereau, Reddock & Yu, LLP, LA, 1998—. Vol. St. James' Ch., First A.M.E. Ch. legal clinic; mem. panel of judges for annual student speech competition LA Olympic Lion's Club, 2000—. Dana Hinman Scholar. Mem.: ABA, Century City Bar Assn., Asian Pacific Am. Bar Assn., LA County Bar Assn., Justinian Hon. Law Soc. Office: Collins, Mesereau, Reddock & Yu LLP 1875 Century Park E 7th Fl Los Angeles CA 90067 Office Phone: 310-284-3120. Office Fax: 310-861-1007. E-mail: yu@cmrylaw.com.

YUAN, ROBIN TSU-WANG, plastic surgeon; b. Boston, July 2, 1954; s. Robert Hsun-Piao and Grace I. (Chen) Y. AB, Harvard U., 1974, MD, 1978. Diplomate Am. Bd. Plastic Surgery. Resident in gen. surgery UCLA Med. Ctr., 1978-80, Cedars-Sinai Med. Ctr., LA, 1980-81, 83-84; resident in plastic surgery U. Miami (Fla.)-Jackson Meml. Hosp., 1985-87; pvt. practice LA, 1987—. Clin. instr. divsn. plastic surgery UCLA, 1987-98, asst. clin. prof., 1998—; vice-chief divsn. plastic surgery Cedars-Sinai Med. Ctr., LA, 1991—; pres., CEO, founder Family of Independent Reconstructive Surgery Teams, 1990—, pres. Millard Soc., 2003. Author: Cheer Up...You're Only Half Dead!, Reflections at Mid-Life, 1996; contbr. numerous articles to med. jours. Mem. Am. Soc. Plastic and Reconstructive Surgery, Am. Cleft Palate Assn., Calif. Med. Assn. (del.), LA County Med. Assn. (bd. govs. dist. 1), Phi Lambda (co-mgr. 1991—). Avocations: tennis, skiing, golf, creative writing, violin. Office: 462 N Linden Dr Ste 236 Beverly Hills CA 90212 Office Phone: 310-385-8425. Personal E-mail: robinpbhps@aol.com.

YUE, AGNES KAU-WAH, otolaryngologist; b. Shanghai, Peoples Republic China, Dec. 1, 1947; arrived in US, 1967; d. Chen Kia and Nee Yuan; m. Gerald Kumata, Sept. 25, 1982; children: Julie, Allison, Benjamin. BA, Wellesley Coll., 1970; MD, Med. Coll. Pa., 1974; postgrad., Yale U., 1974-78. Intern Yale-New Haven Hosp., 1974-75, resident, 1975-78; fellow U. Tex. M.D. Anderson Cancer Ctr., Houston, 1978-79; asst. prof. U. Wash., Seattle, 1979-82; physician Pacific Med. Ctr., Seattle, 1979-90; pvt. practice Seattle, 1991—. Fellow Am. Acad. Otolaryngology; mem. Northwest Acad. Otolaryngology. Avocations: sailing, opera, cooking. Office: 1801 NW Market St Ste 410 Seattle WA 98107-3909 Office Phone: 206-782-1090.

YUE, ALFRED SHUI-CHOH, metallurgical engineer, consultant; b. China, Nov. 12, 1920; s. Choy Noon-woo and Sze Man-hun (Tom) Yue; m. Virginia Chin-wen Tang, May 21, 1944; children: Mary, Raymond Yuan, John, Ling Tsao, David, Nancy Chang. BS, Chao-tung U., 1942; MS, Ill. Inst. Tech., 1950; PhD, Purdue U., 1956. Assoc. engr. Taiwan Aluminum Co., 1942-47; instr. Purdue U., 1952-56; research engr. Dow Chem. Co., Midland, Mich., 1956-62; sr. mem. Lockheed, Palo Alto Rsch. Lab., 1962-69; from prof. engring. and applied sci. to cons. UCLA, LA, 1969—. Hon. prof. Xian Jiao-tong U., China, 1980. Sec.-gen. Chinese Culture Assn. U.S., 1967; bd. dirs. Chinese scholar to U.S. Fellow: AIAA (assoc.); mem.: AIME, Materials Rsch. Soc., Am. Soc. Metals, Sigma Xi, Phi Tau Phi (pres. 1978—82), Tau Beta Pia, Sigma Pi Sigma.

YUGLER, RICHARD S., lawyer; b. Passaic, NJ, Sept. 5, 1955; s. Abram and Audrey (DuBester) Y.; m. A. Christine Tarpey, Mar. 8, 1986; children Simon and Susannah. BA, Syracuse U., 1977; JD, Lewis & Clark Coll., Portland, 1980. Bar: Oreg. 1980, Washington 2002, Oreg. Supreme Ct., Washington Supreme Ct., US Supreme Ct. (Dist. Oreg.) 1981, US Ct. Appeals (9th Cir.) 1982, US Ct. Appeals (Fed. Cir.) 1985, US Supreme Ct. 1983. Assoc. Merten & Saltviet, Portland, 1980-83, Merten & Fink, Portland, 1983-85; pvt. practice, Portland, 1985-86, 89—; ptnr. Redden, McGaughey, Yugler & Jack, Portland, 1986-87, Merten & Yugler, Portland, 1987-89; barrister Am. Inn at Ct., Portland, 1987—; ptnr. Landye Bennett Blumstein LLP, Portland, Oreg. Arbitrator, settlement panelist Multnomah County Cts. & Pvt. UMI Panels. Author: Child Care Task Force Committee Report, 1987. Bd. dirs., officer New Rose Theatre, 1986-89; mem. Dizziness & Balance Disorder Assn., Family Head Injury support Group, 1989, child care task force City Club of Portland, 1985-87, author com. report, 1987. Mem. ABA (young lawyers sect.), Nat. Bar Assn., Oreg. Trial Lawyers Assn. (membership com.), Assn. Trial Lawyers Am., Multnomah Bar Assn. (sec. 1990, continuing legal edn. com. 1988, bd. dirs. reorgn. task force 1989, chmn. com. Bicentennial of U.S. Constn. 1987, award of merit 1986-87), Oreg. State Bar Assn. (local profl. responsibility com. 1989, pres.-elect 2006), Lewis and Clark Alumni Assn. (pub. rels. com. 1987), City Club of Portland (child care task force 1985-87). Avocations: squash, golf, running, skiing. Office: Landye Bennett Blumstein LLP Ste 3500 1300 SW 5th Ave Portland OR 97201 Office Phone: 503-224-4100. Office Fax: 503-224-4133. E-mail: ryugler@landye-bennett.com.

YUILLE, ALAN LODDON, physicist, researcher; BA in Math. with hons., Cambridge U., Eng., 1976, PhD in Applied Math., Physics, 1986. Rsch. assoc. Harvard U., Cambridge, Mass., 1986-88, asst. prof., 1988-92, assoc. prof., 1992-96; sr. rsch. scientist Smith-Kettlewell Eye Rsch. Inst., San Francisco, 1995—. Vis. scientist MIT, Cambridge, 1982-83, affiliate, 1986-88, Isaac Newton Inst. Math., Cambridge, 1993; lectr. Harvard U., Cambridge, 1986-87; Fesler-Lambert vis. prof. U. Minn., 1992; presenter in field. Author: (chpt.) Computer Vision: Theory and Industrial Applications, 1986, The Handbook of Brain Theory and Neural Networks, 1994; co-author: (chpt.) Image Understanding, 1985, 87, The Neuron as a Computational Unit, 1989, An Invitation to Cognitive Science, Vol. 2, 1990, Advances in Control Networks and Large-Scale Parallel-Distributed Processing Models, 1991, Computational Models of Visual Processing, 1991Active Vision, 1992, Bayesian Approaches to Perception, 1994, DIMACS: Partitioning Data Sest, 1994, Artificial Neural Networks with Applications in Speech and Vision, 1994; contbr. articles to Neural Computation, Neural Networks, Vision Rsch., Jour. Complexity, Jour. Optical Soc. Am., Jour. Math. Imaging Vision, Pattern Analysis Machine Intelligence, Jour. Theoretical Biology, Biological Cybernetics, Internat. Jour. Robotic Vision, Internat. Jour. Computer Image, Nature, Jour. Cognitive Neurosci., Neural Computation; editor Jour. Math. Imaging Vision. NATO fellow, 1981-82; Trinity Coll. scholar, 1974-78; recipient Rouse Ball prize, 1974-77, Raleigh Rsch. prize, 1979.

YUKAWA, SUMIO, engineering consultant, researcher; b. Seattle; BS, MS, U. Mich., PhD in Metall. Engring., 1954. With GE; cons. Boulder. With U.S. Army, 1944-47. Mem. ASME (Pressuve Vessel and Piping award 1998). Achievements include research on materials for steam and gas turbines and nuclear energy equipment. Home: 330 Cheshire Ct Colorado Springs CO 80906-7664

YUND, MARY ALICE, biotechnology consultant; b. Xenia, Ohio, Feb. 12, 1943; d. John Edward and Ethel Louise Stallard; m. E. William Yund, June 11, 1966. BA, Knox Coll., 1965; PhD, Harvard U., 1970. Asst. rsch. geneticist U. Calif., Berkeley, 1975-88; pvt. practice cons. Berkeley, 1988-97; biotech. cons. Tech. Forecasters, Inc., Alameda, Calif., 1997—. Mem. devel. biology adv. panel NSF, Washington, 1983-87; vis. scientist NSF/ CSIRO U.S./ Australia Coop. Sci. Progam, North Ryde, Australia, 1980; co-chair women in Biosci. Conf., Stanford, Calif., 1993; organizer sci. seminar series and confs. in field. Contbr. articles, revs. to profl. jours., chpts. to books. Cons., counselor Bay Area Biosci. Ctr., Oakland, Calif., 1992—. Rsch. grantee NSF, NIH, 1975-86. Mem. AAAS, Genetics Soc. Am., Soc. for Developmental Biology, Am. Soc. Zoologists, Assn. for Women in Sci. (chpt. officer 1991—), Phi Beta Kappa, Sigma Xi. Achievements include first identification and characterization of ecdysteroid receptors. Office: 723 Woodhaven Rd Berkeley CA 94708-1540

YUST, DAVID E., artist, educator; b. Wichita, Kans., Apr. 3, 1939; s. Earl and Truly Yust; m. Joan G. Dalby, Mar. 13, 1966; children: Erin L., Joel C. BFA, U. Kans., Lawrence, 1963; MFA, U. Oreg., Eugene, 1969. Prof. Colo. State U., Ft. Collins, 1965—. One-man shows include Denver Art Mus., 1976, Wichita Art Mus., Kans., 1979, Wichita Ctr. for the Arts, 1998, Rourke Art Mus., Moorehead, Minn., 2003, Ft. Collins Mus. Contemporary Art, Colo., 2003, Plus Gallery, Denver, 2006, Arvada Ctr., Arvada, 2008, Art in Embassies Program, US Dept. State, Zagreb, Croatia, 2003—06, Manama, Bahrain, 2008—, Colorado Abstract, Ctr. Visual Art, Denver, 2009. Bd. dirs. Denver Art Mus., 1998—, D.A.M. Contemporaries, 1998—. Recipient Afkey award, Alliance for Contemporary Art, Colo., 2000, John Stern Disting. Prof. award, Colo. State U., 2004; named Art Educator of Yr., Colo. Art Edn. Assn., 2003, Nat. Art Edn. Assn., Pacific Region, 2004. Office: Colo State U Fort Collins CO 80523 Office Phone: 970-491-6774, 970-491-5478. Business E-Mail: davyust@lamar.colostate.edu.

ZABLE, WALTER JOSEPH, electronic products manufacturing company executive; b. Los Angeles, 1915. B.S., Coll. William and Mary, 1937; M.S. in Physics and Math., U. Fla., 1939. Electronics engr. Newport News Shipyard & Drydock Co., 1940-43; sr. devel. engr., Sperry Gyroscope Co., 1944-47; prior 1951 ITT Fed. Telecommunications Labs., Flight Research Co., Gen. Dynamics Corp., Convair div.; with Cubic Corp., San Diego, 1951—, chmn. bd., pres., chief exec. officer, also dir.; dir. First Nat. Bank. Mem. Nat. Assn. Mfrs. (dir.). Office: Cubic Corp 9333 Balboa Ave PO Box 85587 San Diego CA 92186-5587

ZACCARIA, ADRIAN, utilities executive; b. 1944; BS, US Mcht. Marine Acad., 1966. Engr. Raytheon Co., Lexington, Mass., 1967-68, Gen. Dynamics Corp., Falls Ch., Va., 1968-71; with Bechtel Grp., Inc., San Francisco, 1974—, pres., COO, 1996—. Bd. trustees US Mcht. Marine Acad. Mem.: NAE. Office: Bechtel Grp Inc 50 Beale St San Francisco CA 94105-1895 Office Phone: 415-768-1234.

ZACCHINO, NARDA, newspaper editor; b. San Diego, 1947; BA in english lit., UCLA. Assoc. editor L.A. Times, Calif. Office: Los Angeles Times Times Mirror Sq Los Angeles CA 90053

ZAHARIA, ERIC STAFFORD, health facility administrator; b. Pomona, Calif., Aug. 24, 1948; s. Edgar A. and Dorothy (Stafford) Zaharia; m. Caryle Koentz, Dec. 23, 1967; children: Tye W., Tieg A. BA, Pomona Coll., 1970; MEd, U. Ariz.-Tucson, 1973; PhD, George Peabody Coll., 1978. Mental retardation worker Ariz. Tng. Program, Tucson, 1970-71, unit dir., 1971-73; dir. residential svcs. Willmar State Hosp., (Minn.), 1973-76; rsch. asst. Inst. on Mental Retardation and Intellectual Devel., Nashville, 1976-78; dir. mental retardation program svcs. Dept. Mental Health/Mental Retardation, State of Tenn., Nashville, 1978-79; dir. Caswell Ctr., Kinston, N.C., 1979-86; program adminstr. Colo. Divsn. of Devel. Disabilities, Denver, 1986-90; dir. Utah divsn. Svcs. for People with Disabilities, Salt Lake City, 1990-95; ind. cons. Park City, Utah, 1995-2000; dir. Ariz. Divsn. Devel. Disabilities, Phoenix, 2000—. Mem. adj. faculty East Carolina U., Greenville, 1979—86; bd. dirs. Neuse Enterprises Inc., Kinston. Chmn. Big Bros./Sisters Kinston Inc., 1980—83; mem. N.C. Coalition for Cmty. Svc., 1982—85. Mem.: Assn. Retarded Citizens, Nat. Assn. Supts., Am. Assn. Mental Retardation, Kinston C. of C. (bd. dirs. 1983—86), Pub. Residential Facilities. Home: 8086 N Painted Feather Dr Tucson AZ 85743-7419

ZAHN, STEVE, actor; b. Marshall, Minn., Nov. 13, 1967; m. Robyn Peterman, July 16, 1994; children: Henry James, Audrey. PhD in Fine Arts (hon.), Norther Ky. U., 2007. Co-founder Malaparte theater co. Actor: (TV films) First Love, Fatal Love, 1991, Subway Stories: Tales from the Underground, 1997, Speak, 2004; (films) Rain Without Thunder, 1992, Reality Bites, 1994, Crimson Tide, 1995, Race the Sun, 1996, SubUrbia, 1996, The Object of My Affection, 1998, Out of Sight, 1998, Safe Men, 1998, You've Got Mail, 1998, Happy, Texas, 1999 (Spl. Jury prize, Sundance Film Festival, 1999, Ind. Spirit award for Best Supporting Male, 2000), Forces of Nature, 1999, Freak Talks About Sex, 1999, (voice) Stuart Little, 1999, Hamlet, 2000, Chain of Fools, 2000, Saving Silverman, 2001, (voice) Dr. Dolittle 2, 2001, Joy Ride, 2001, Chelsea Walls, 2001, Riding in Cars with Boys, 2001, (voice) Stuart Little 2, 2002, National Security, 2003, Daddy Day Care, 2003, Shattered Glass, 2003, Employee of the Month, 2004, Sahara, 2005, Bandidas, 2006, Rescue Dawn, 2006, Sunshine Cleaning, 2008, Strange Wilderness, 2008; actor, actor: (films) The Great Buck Howard, 2008; (TV series) Picture Window, 1994, Liberty! The American Revolution, 1997; (TV miniseries) From the Earth to the Moon, 1998, Comanche Moon, 2008. Avocations: fly fishing, guitar. Office: Endeavor Agy 9601 Wilshire Blvd 3rd fl Beverly Hills CA 90212

ZAILLIAN, STEVEN, screenwriter, director; b. Fresno, Calif., Jan. 30, 1953; BA, San Francisco State U., 1975. Scripts include: The Falcon and the Snowman, 1985, Awakenings, 1990 (Acad. award nominee for best adapted screenplay, 1990), Jack the Bear, 1993, Schindler's List, 1993 (Acad. award best adapted screenplay 1993), Mission: Impossible, 1996, Hannibal, 2001, The Interpreter, 2005; co-writer (with Donald Stewart and John Milius) Clear and Present Danger, 1994; scriptwriter, dir.: Searching for Bobby Fisher, 1993, A Civil Action, 1998; co-writer: Gangs of New York (nominee Acad. Award Best Original Screenplay, 2002), American Gangster, 2007; scriptwriter, dir., exec. prodr.: A Civil Action, 1998; scriptwriter, dir., prodr.: All the King's Men, 2006

ZAITZ, LESLIE LEE, reporter; b. St. Helens, Oreg., June 23, 1955; s. Clarence and Joanne (Kness) Z.; m. Julie Grenz, Feb. 24, 1981 (div. Aug. 1986); children: Grant, Dain; m. Scotta Callister, Oct. 16, 1987. Student, U. Oreg., 1974-75, Portland State U., Oreg., 1975-76. Reporter Springfield News, Oreg., 1974-76, The Oregonian, Portland, Oreg., 1976-87, now sr. investigative reporter; pres. Wheatland Pub. Corp., Keizer, Oreg., 1987; pub. Keizertimes, Keizer, Oreg., 1987. Author: (reference book) Paper Trail, 1981; pub. South Salem Times, Salem, Oreg., 1988. Mem. Keizer Bus. Retention and Devel. Commn., 1988; bd. dirs. Salem (Oreg.) chpt. ARC, 1989. Recipient Bruce Baer Award, 1978, 1981, 1999, 2001; co-recipient George Polk award for Nat. Reporting, 2006. Mem. Investigative Reporters and Editors, Oreg. Newspaper Pubs. Assn., Salem C. of C. (bd. dirs. 1989). Democrat. Office: The Oregonian 1320 SW Broadway Portland OR 97201 Office Phone: 503-585-0985. E-mail: leszaitz@news.oregonian.com.

ZAKHEIM, IRVING LEE, gift import company executive; b. LA, Dec. 4, 1948; s. Benjamin David and Louise Victoria (deMayo) Z.; m. Angela Rae Long, Feb. 29, 1988; chidlren: Sara Rose, Robert Joseph, Mary Louise, Benjamin Charles. BA, Calif. State U., Northridge, 1972. Profl. baseball player Chgo. White Sox, 1971-73; ins. agt. Equitable Life, LA, 1973-75; pres., CEO Zak Designs, Inc., LA, 1976—, also chmn. bd., 1976—; pres. Patchwork Creations, Angeles City, Philippines, 1976-83. Mem. L.A. C. of C., L.A. City C. of C., Spokane Area C. of C., Indland N.W. World Trade Coun., Nat. Housewares Mfrs. Assn., Juvenile Products Mfrs. Assn., Nat. Bath, Bed and Linen Assn., Nat. Assn. Catalog Showroom Mfrs. Avocations: golf, tennis, running. Office: PO Box 19188 Spokane WA 99219-9188

ZAKHOR, AVIDEH, engineering educator, consultant; PhD, MIT, Cambridge, 1987. Prof. U. Calif., Berkeley, 1988—. Recipient Henry Ford Engring. award, Ford found., 1983, Presdl. Young Investigator award, Pres. George Herbert Walker Bush, 1990, Young Investigator award, Office Naval Rsch., 1992, Best paper award, IEEE, 1997, 1999, 2002, 2007, Prize, Okawa Found., 2004. Office: Univ California 507 Cory Hall Berkeley CA 94720

ZALAVRAS, CHARALAMPOS, orthopedic surgeon; arrived in U.S., 2000; s. Georgios Zalavras and Maria Zalavra. Attended, Aristoteleion U. Med. Sch., Greece, 1991; PhD, U. Ioannina, Greece, 2000. Cert. orthop. surgeon Ministry of Health, Greece, European Union, physician's cert. of registration Med. Bd. Calif. Resident dept. orthop. surgery U. Ioannina, Ioannina, Greece, 1996—2000; from clin. rsch. fellow to assoc. prof. Dept. Orthop. Surgery U. So. Calif., LA, 2000—06, assoc. prof. Dept. Orthop. Surgery, 2006—. Recipient Best Scientific Work award, Balkan Congress Orthops., 1997, Best Resident, Fellow Paper award, Arthroscopy Assn. No. Am., 2002, Marshall Urist Young Investigator award, Assn. Bone and Joint Surgeons, 2003. Mem.: ACS, Muscuooskeletal Infection Soc. N.Am. (v.p.), Hellenic Soc. for Reconstructive Microsurgery, Hellenic Soc. for Surgery of Hand, Hellenic Assn. Orthop. Surgery and Traumatology, European Soc. Sports Traumatology, Knee Surgery and Arthroscopy, Western Orthop. Assn. Office Fax: 323-226-4051. Business E-Mail: zalavras@usc.edu.

ZALL, PAUL MAXWELL, language educator, consultant; m. Elisabeth Weisz, June 21, 1948; children: Jonathan, Barnaby, Andrew. BA, Swarthmore Coll., 1948; AM, Harvard U., 1950, PhD, 1951. Teaching fellow Harvard U., 1950-51; instr. Cornell U., 1951-55, U. Oreg., 1955-56; research editor Boeing Co., 1956-57; asst. prof. Calif. State Coll., Los Angeles, 1957-61, asso. prof., 1961-64, prof. English, 1964-86; research scholar, cons. to library docents Huntington Library, San Marino, Calif., 1986-96; acting chmn. dept. Calif. State Coll., 1969-71. Cons. in report writing, proposal preparation and brochures to industry and govt. agys., 1957-99. Author: Elements of Technical Report Writing, 1962, Hundred Merry Tales, 1963, Nest of Ninnies, 1970, Weakly Blast, 1960-85, Literary Criticism of William Wordsworth, 1966, (with John Durham) Plain Style, 1967, Simple Cobler of Aggawam in America, 1969; (with J.R. Trevor) Proverb to Poem, 1970, Selected Satires of Peter Pindar, 1971, Comical Spirit of Seventy Six, 1976, (with Leonard Franco) Practical Writing, 1978, Ben Franklin Laughing, 1980; (with J.A.L. Lemay) Autobiography of Benjamin Franklin, 1981; Norton Critical Edition of Franklin's Autobiography, 1986, Abe Lincoln Laughing, 1983, 95; (with E. Birdsall) Descriptive Sketches, 1984, Mark Twain Laughing, 1985, Being Here, 1987, George Washington Laughing, 1989, Franklin's Autobiography: Model Life, 1989, Founding Mothers, 1991, Becoming American, 1993, 98, Lincoln's Legacy, 1994, Wit and Wisdom of the Founding Fathers, 1996, Blue and Gray Laughing, 1996, Lincoln on Lincoln, 1999, 2003, Dolley Madison, 2001, Franklin on Franklin, 2001, Jefferson on Jefferson, 2002, Washington on Washington, 2003, Adams on Adams, 2004, Benjamin Franklin's Humor, 2005, Lincoln's Legacy of Laughter, 2007. Pres. Friends of South Pasadena Library, 1967-70. Served with USAAF, 1942-45, ETO. Recipient Outstanding Prof. award, 1965; grantee, John Carter Brown Libr., Huntington Libr., 1993; fellow, Am. Philos. Soc., 1964, 1966, Huntington Libr., 1993. Home: 2040 Amherst Dr South Pasadena CA 91030-3906 Office: Huntington Libr San Marino CA 91108 Fax: 626-449-5720. E-mail: pzall9@hotmail.com.

ZALLER, JOHN RAYMOND, political science professor; BA in History, U. Calif., San Diego, 1971; MA in Polit. Sci., U. Calif., Berkeley, 1976, PhD in Polit. Sci., 1984. Reporter Orange Coast Daily

Pilot, 1972—74; asst. prof., dept. politics Princeton U., NJ, 1984—86; prof., dept. polit. sci. UCLA, 1986—. Author: The American Ethos: Public Attitudes Toward Capitalism and Democracy, 1984, The Nature and Origins of Mass Opinion, 1992 (APSA award, 1994, Warren Miller prize, 2000, Doris Graber prize, 2001, Book prize, Am. Assn. Pub. Opinion Rsch., 2002); co-author (with M. Cohen, D. Karol, H. Noel): The Party Decides: Presidential Nominations Before and After Reform, 2008; mem. editl. bd.: Pub. Opinion Quar., Polit. Behavior, Jour. Politics, Am. Polit. Sci. Rev., assoc. editor:, 2007—; contbr. articles to profl. jours., chapters to books. Grantee, NSF, 1992—95, Social Sci. Rsch. Coun.; Regents fellow, U. Calif. Berkeley, 1982—83, Guggenheim fellow, 1992—93, fellow, Ctr. Advanced Study in the Behavioral Sciences, 1993—94. Fellow: Am. Acad. Arts and Scis. Office: UCLA Dept Polit Sci 4289 Bunche Hall Box 951472 Los Angeles CA 90095-1472 Office Phone: 310-825-7527. Office Fax: 310-825-0778. Business E-Mail: zaller@ucla.edu.*

ZALUTSKY, MORTON HERMAN, lawyer; b. Schenectady, Mar. 8, 1935; s. Albert and Gertrude (Daffner) Z.; m. Audrey Englebardt, June 16, 1957; children: Jane, Diane, Samuel BA, Yale U., 1957; JD, U. Chgo., 1960. Bar: Oreg. 1961. Law clk. to presiding judge Oreg. Supreme Ct., 1960-61; assoc. Hart, Davidson, Veazie & Hanlon, 1961-63, Veatch & Lovett, 1963-64, Morrison, Bailey, Dunn, Cohen & Miller, 1964-69; prin. Morton H. Zalutsky, P.C., 1970-76; ptnr. Dahl, Zalutsky, Nichols & Hinson, 1977-79, Zalutsky & Klarquist, P.C., Portland, Oreg., 1980-85, Zalutsky, Klarquist & Johnson, Inc., Portland, 1985-94; Zalutsky & Klarquist, P.C., Portland, 1994—. Instr. Portland State U., 1961-64, Northwestern Sch. of Law, 1969-70; assoc. prof. U. Miami Law Sch.; lectr. Practising Law Inst., 1971—, Oreg. State Bar Continuing Legal Edn. Program, 1970, Am. Law Inst.-ABA Continuing Legal Edn. Program, 1973—, 34th, 37th NYU ann. insts. fed. taxation, So. Fed. Tax Inst., U. Miami Inst. Estate Planning, Southwestern Legal Found., Internat. Foun. Employee Benefit Plans, others; dir. A-E-F-C Pension Plan, 1994-99, chmn., 1989-99. Author: (with others) The Professional Corporation in Oregon, 1970, 82; contbg. author: The Dentist and the Law, 3d edit.; editor-in-chief: Matthew Bender's Federal Tax Service, 1987-90; contbr. articles to profl. jours. Mem. vis. com. U. Chgo. Law Sch., 1986-88. Mem. ABA (vice chair profl. svcs. 1987-89, mem. coun. tax sect. 1985-87, spl. coord. 1980-85), Am. Law Inst., Am. Bar Retirement Assn. (trustee, bd. dirs., vice chair 1990-91, chair 1991-92), Am. Coll. Employee Benefits Coun. (charter mem.), Am. Coll. Tax Coun. (charter mem.), Multnomah County Bar Assn., Am. Tax Lawyers (charter mem.), Oreg. Estate Planning Coun. Jewish. Home: 3118 SW Fairmount Blvd Portland OR 97201-1466 Office: 215 SW Washington St Fl 3 Portland OR 97204-2636 Office Phone: 503-248-0300. E-mail: mort@erisalaw.com.

ZAME, WILLIAM R., economist, mathematician, educator; b. Long Beach, NY, Nov. 4, 1945; s. Herbert and Miriam Zame; m. Linda Susan Goettina, Nov. 24, 1997; m. Elaine Bennett, 1989 (dec. 1995). BS, Calif. Inst. Tech., Pasadena, 1965; MS, Tulane U., 1967, PhD, 1970. Instr. Rice U., Houston, 1970—72; asst prof. math. SUNY, Buffalo, 1972—76; assoc. prof. math. Tulane U., New Orleans, 1975—78, SUNY, Buffalo, 1976—81, prof. math., 1981—91; prof. math. and econs. Johns Hopkins U., Balt., 1991—94, UCLA, 1994—. Assoc. editor Jour. Math. Econs., 1988—, Jour. Econ. Theory, 1990—, Econometrica, 1998—; mem. com. on status of women in the econs. profn., 1997—99; co-organizer profl. confs. including Exptl. Econs., Calif. Inst. Tech./UCLA, 1999, Econometric Soc. Summer Mtgs., 2002; vis. prof. Inst. Advanced Study, U. Wash., Inst. Math. and its Applications, Math. Scis. Rsch. Inst., Inst. Mittag-Leffler, U. Copenhagen, Va. Poly. Inst., U. Calif., Berkeley. Contbr. articles to profl. jours., chapters to books. Grantee NSF, 1970—88, 1988—; Guggenheim fellow, 2004—05. Fellow: Econometric Soc. (program com. summer mtgs. 1991, 1997, program co-chair summer mtgs. 2002). Office: UCLA Dept Econs 405 Hilgard Ave Los Angeles CA 90095-9000

ZANETTI, TERESA A., state legislator; b. Columbus, Ga., Jan. 20, 1958; m. Gregory Zanetti; children: Daniel, Michael. BA, Harvard U., 1979; MA, St. John's Coll., 1987. Test adminstr. Army Edn. Ctrs., Augsburg, Germany, 1982—85; bur. chief N.Mex. State Dept. Regulation and Licensing, 1989—90; faculty Albuquerque Acad., 1990—97; columnist Albuquerque Tribune, 2000—02; state rep. dist. 15 N.Mex. Ho. of Reps., Santa Fe, 2002—. Mem. N.Mex. State. Bd. Edn., 2001—02; v.p. Laguna Edn. Found., 2006—. Named Rookie of the Yr., Greater Albuquerque C. of C., 2002; Coe fellow, Stanford U., 1995. Republican.

ZANJANI, ESMAIL D., medical educator, research scientist; b. Rasht, Iran, Dec. 23, 1938; came to U.S., 1959; s. Hussayn D. and Sakineh (Shadkan) Z.; m. Sally Springmeyer, 1963; children: Don, Mariah, George. BA, NYU, 1964, MS, 1966, PhD in Exptl. Hematology, 1969. Asst. prof. medicine Mt. Sinai Sch. Medicine, NYC, 1970-72, asst. prof. physics, 1970-77; organizing chmn. dept. physics Imperial Med. Ctr. Iran, 1976-79, organizing dean basic scis., 1976-79; dir. bone marrow tissue culture diagnostic unit, rsch. physics VA Med. Ctr., Mpls., 1977-87, rsch. career scientist to sr. rsch. career scientist Reno, 1979—; prof. dept. physics, dept. medicine U. Minn. Sch. Medicine, Mpls., 1977-87; adj. prof. medicine and physiology U. Nev. Sch. Medicine, Reno, 1987—2002, prof. dept. animal biotechnology, Coll. Agr., Biotechnology and Natural Resources, 2002—, dir., Stem Cell and Exptl. Hematology Lab., chair, dept. animal biotechnology. Mem., hematology study sect. NIH, 1998—2002. Author: (with M. Tavassoli and J.L. Ascensao) Regulation of Erythropoiesis, 1988, (with M. Tavassoli, J.L. Ascensao, N.G. Abraham and A.S. Levine) Molecular Biology of Hemopoiesis, 1988, (with J.L. Ascensao, M. Tavassoli, F.R. MacKintosh and A.S. Levine) Molecular Biology of Erythropoiesis, 1989; mem. editl. bd. Stem Cell, 1980-83, Blood, 1983-88, Jour. Cell Cloning, 1983-91, Jour. Pathobiology, 1991-; mem. editl. bd. Exptl. Hematology, 1984-87, assoc. editor, 1998, editor-in-chief, 2003; assoc. editor, Jour. of Hematology and Stem Cell Rsch., 2000; bd. reviewers Jour. Lab. Clin. Medicine, 1991—; contbr. chpts. to over 40 books; contbr. several articles to profl. jours.; contbr. chapters to books. Recipient Jay F. Krakaur award, Gladys Mateyko award for excellence in biology; grants NIH, M.E.R.I.T. award, Nat. Heart, Lung, and Blood Inst., NIH, 1997. Mem. Internat. Soc. Exptl. Hematology (coun., pres., 2001, editor), Am. Soc. Hematology, Am. Fedn. Clin. Rsch., Ctrl. Soc. Clin. Rsch., European Hematology Soc., Am. Soc. of Gene Therapy, Sigma Xi (award). Achievements include leading a team of scientists that have created the first human-sheep chimera, which has the body of a sheep and half human organs. Home: 4360 Slide Mountain Cir Reno NV 89511-9530 Office: VA Med Ctr 151B 1000 Locust St Reno NV 89502-2597 also: Dept Animal Biotechnology Univ Nev Mail Stop 202 Fleischmann Agr Office 103 1664 N Virginia St Reno NV 89557 Office Phone: 775-784-7737. Office Fax: 775-784-7736. Business E-Mail: ezanjani@cabnr.unr.edu, Zanjani@scs.unr.edu.

ZANUCK, RICHARD DARRYL, motion picture company executive; b. Beverly Hills, Calif., Dec. 13, 1934; s. Darryl F. and Virginia (Fox) Z.; m. Lili Gentle; children: Virginia, Janet; m. Linda Harrison, Oct. 26, 1969; children: Harrison Richard, Dean Francis; m. Lili Fini, Sept. 23, 1978. Grad., Harvard Mil. Acad., 1952; BA, Stanford, 1956. Story, prodn. asst. Darryl F. Zanuck Prodns., 1956, v.p., 1956-62; president's prodn. rep. 20th Century-Fox Studios, Beverly Hills, 1962-63, v.p. charge prodn., 1963-69, pres., 1969-71, dir., 1966-71; founder, pres., owner Zanuck Co., Beverly Hills, 1989—. Chmn. 20th Century-Fox Television, Inc.; sr. exec. v.p. Warner Bros., Inc., 1971-72; co-founder, pres. Zanuck/Brown Co., 1972-88. Producer: The Sting, 1973 (Acad. award), The Sugarland Express, 1974, Jaws, 1975, Jaws 2, 1978, The Island, 1980, Neighbors, 1982, The Verdict, 1983, Cocoon, 1985, Cocoon, the Return, 1988, Driving Miss Daisy, 1989 (Acad. award, Irving G. Thalberg award 1991), Rush, 1991, Rich in Love, 1992, Mulholland Falls, 1996, Deep Impact, 1998, True Crime, 1999, Rules of Engagement, 1999, Planet of the Apes, 2000, Road to Perdition, 2001, Big Fish, 2003; prodr. Acad. Award Show, 2000. Nat. chmn. Fibrosis Assn., 1966-68; mem. organizing com. 1984 Olympics; trustee Harvard Sch. 2d lt. U.S. Army. Named Producer of Yr., Nat. Assn. Theatre Owners, 1974, '85, Producers Guild Am., 1989; recipient Irving Thalberg award, 1991, Lifetime Achievement award, Producers Guild Am., 1993. Mem. Acad. Motion Picture Arts and Scis. (bd. govs.), Screen Producers Guild, Phi Gamma Delta. Office: Zanuck Co 9465 Wilshire Blvd Ste 930 Beverly Hills CA 90212-2608

ZAPEL, ARTHUR LEWIS, book publishing executive; b. Chgo., 1921; m. Janet Michel (dec.); children: Linda (dec.), Mark, Theodore, Michelle; m. Cynthia Rogers Pisor, 1986; stepchildren: Dawn, Anthony. BA in English, U. Wis., 1946. Writer, prodr. Westinghouse Radio Stas.; film writer Galbreath Studios, Ft. Wayne; creative dir. Kling Studios, Chgo., 1952-54; writer, prodr. TV commls. J. Walter Thompson Advt., Chgo., 1954-73, v.p. TV and radio prodn., 1954-73; founder, pres. Arthur Meriwether, Inc., 1973-83; pres. Meriwether Pub. Ltd., 1969-90, chmn., 1990-97. Pres. Westcliffe (Colo.) Ctr. for the Arts. Author: Sweet Uncertainty, 2001; illustrator: 'Twas the Night Before, The Jabberwock mystery; created game A Can of Squirms; wrote plays and musical comedy scripts for ednl. use in schs. and chs.; supr. editing and prodn. 2500 plays and musicals, 1970-99; exec. editor 210 books on theater skills for secular and religious use. Founding pres. Art Students League of Colorado Springs, 1992; past pres. Colo. Springs Symphony Coun.; past bd. dirs. Colorado Springs Opera Festival. Recipient numerous awards Freedoms Found., Valley Forge, Art Dirs. Club N.Y., Art Dirs. Chgo., Hollywood Advt., 1960-67, Gold Records Radio Ad Bur., 1959-60, XV Festival Internat. Du Film Publicitaire Venise, 1968, Gold Camera award U.S. Indsl. Film Festival, 1983, Dukane award, 1983, Gold award Houston Internat. Film Festival, 1984, 2d pl. award Best New Fiction, Colo. Ind. Publishers Assoc., 2002. Office: Meriwether Pub Ltd 885 Elkton Dr Colorado Springs CO 80907-3576

ZAPOLSKY, DAVID A., lawyer; JD, Boalt Hall Sch. Law, Berkeley, Calif. Former litig. ptnr. Dorsey & Whitney and Bogle & Gates Law Firm; v.p., assoc. gen. counsel litig. and regulatory matters Amazon-.com, Seattle, 1999—2006, exec. v.p., gen. counsel, 2006—. Office: Amazon.com Ste 1200 1200 12th Ave So Seattle WA 98144-2734

ZAPPE, JOHN PAUL, city editor, newspaper executive, educator; b. NYC, July 30, 1952; s. John Paul and Carolyn (Pikor) Z. BA, Marist Coll., 1978; JD, Syracuse U., NY, 1978. Reporter Poughkeepsie Jour., 1973-75, Nev. State Jour., Reno, 1979-80; prin. Am. Media Bold, Oakland, Calif., 1981-83; reporter Press-Telegram, Long Beach, Calif., 1983-88, city editor, 1988-97, webmaster PT Connect, 1995-97, mgr. new media, 1997-98; dir. new media Riverside (Calif.) Press-Enterprise, 1998-2000; v.p. new media L.A. Newspaper Group, Woodland Hills, Calif., 2000—03; prin. Zappe Media Svcs., 2003—; dir. bus. devel. Classified Intelligence, sr. analyst. Tchr. Syracuse U., 1976-78, Calif. State U., 1985-87, U. So. Calif., 2003—04; prin. Am. Media Bold, 1981-83. Chmn. Local 69 Newspaper Guild, Long Beach, 1984-87. Mem. NAA New Media Fedn., Belgian Tervuren Club of Southern Calif. (pres.), Sierra Club (mem. exec. com. Long Beach group, LA chpt.), S. Coast Agility Team (dir.) Office Phone: 562-252-0686. Business E-Mail: zappemedia@gmail.com.

ZARANKA, WILLIAM F., academic administrator, author; b. Elizabeth, NJ, Dec. 22, 1944; s. William A. and Anne M. (Paulauska) Z.; m. Ruth Annalea Falchero; children: Jacob, Philip. BA, Upsala Coll., 1966; MA, Purdue U., 1968; PhD, U. Denver, 1974. Instr. Purdue U., West Lafayette, Ind., summer 1969; asst. prof. U. Pa., Phila., 1975-78; teaching fellow U. Denver, 1969-71, instr. English, 1969-71, 74-75, asst. prof., dir. creative writing, 1978-84, dean arts and humanities, 1984-89, provost, 1989—2001, prof. English, 2001—. Author: The Branx X Anthology of Poetry, 1981, The Brand X Anthology of Fiction, 1983, (poetry) A Mirror Driven through Nature, 1981, Blessing, 1986. Fellow Breadd Loaf Writers Conf., 1981. Roman Catholic. Avocation: astronomy. Office: U Denver Office of Provost 2199 S University Blvd Denver CO 80210-4711

ZARE, RICHARD NEIL, chemistry professor; b. Cleve., Nov. 19, 1939; s. Milton and Dorothy (Amdur) Zare; m. Susan Leigh (Shively), Apr. 20, 1963; children: Bethany Jean, Bonnie Sue, Rachel Amdur. BA, Harvard U., 1961, PhD, 1964; post grad., U. Calif., Berkeley, 1961—63; DS (hon.), U. Ariz., 1990, Northwestern U., 1993, ETH, Zürich, 1993, Columbia U., 2000, State U. West Ga., 2001; DP (hon.), Uppsala U., Sweden, 2000; PhD (hon.), U. York, 2001, Hunan U., 2002, U. Paul Sabatier, 2003. Postdoctoral fellow Harvard U., 1964; rsch. assoc. Joint Inst. for Lab. Astrophysics, 1964—65; asst. prof., chemistry MIT, 1965—66; asst. prof., dept. physics and astrophysics U. Colo., 1966—68, assoc. prof. physics, astrophysics, chemistry, 1968—69; prof. chemistry Columbia U., 1969—77, Higgins prof. natural sci., 1975—77; prof. Stanford U., 1977—, Shell, disting. prof. chemistry, 1980—85, Marguerite Blake Wilbur prof., natural sci., 1987—, prof., physics, 1992—, Howard Hughes Med. Inst. prof., 2006—. Cons. Aeronomy Lab, NOAA, 1966—77; radio standards physics divsn. Nat. Bur. Std., 1968—77, Lawrence Livermore Lab., U. Calif., 1974—, SRI, Internat., 1974—, Los Alamos Sci. Lab., U. Calif., 1975—; fellow adj. Joint Inst. Lab. Astrophysics, U. Colo.; sci. adv. com. IBM, 1977—92; chmn. commn. on phys., scis., and math applications Nat. Rsch. Coun., 1992—95; chmn. bd. dir. Ann. Rev., Inc., 1995—. Contbr. articles to profl. jour.; editor: Chem. Physics Letters, 1982—85. Recipient Fresenius award, Phi Lambda Upsilon, 1974, Michael Polanyi medal, 1979, Nat. Medal Sci., 1983, Spectroscopy Soc. Pitts. award, 1983, Michelson-Morley award, Case Inst. Tech., Case Western Res. U., 1986, ISCO award for significant contbn. to instrumentation for biochemical separations, 1990, Bing Fellowship Tchg. award, 1996, Eastern Analytical Symposium award, 1997, Exceptional Sci. Achievement award, NASA, 1997, Space award Aviation Week and Space Tech., 1997, Disting. Svc. award, Nat. Sci. Bd., 1998, Centennial medal, Harvard U., Welch award, 1999, Wolf prize in chemistry, Wolf Found., Israel, 2005, Chandler medal, Columbia U., 2005, Pupin medal, 2005, Oesper award, U. Cin., 2006; named Calif. Scientist of Yr., 1997; fellow Alfred P. Sloan fellow, 1967—69, Non-resident fellow, Joint Inst. for Lab. Astrophysics, 1970—, Christensen fellow, St. Catherine's Coll. Oxford U., 1982, Stanford U., 1984—86. Fellow: AAAS, Inst. of Physics, Royal Soc. Chemistry (hon. Faraday medal 2001), Calif. Acad. Sci. (hon.); mem.: NAS (coun. mem., Chem. Sci. award 1991), European Acad. Scis., Chinese Acad. Scis. (fgn.), Swedish Acad. Scis. (fgn.), Royal Soc. London (fgn.), Chem. Soc. London, World Jewish Acad. Scis. (hon.), Am. Philos. Soc., Am. Chem. Soc. (Harrison Howe award 1985, Remsen award 1985, Kirkwood award 1986, Willard Gibbs medal 1990, Peter Debye award in phys. chemistry 1991, Linus Pauling medal 1993, Dannie-Heineman prize 1993, Harvey prize 1993, Analytical Chemistry Divsn. award in chem. instrumentation 1995, Analytical Chemistry award 1998, G.M. Kosalapoff award 1998, E. Bright Wilson award in spectroscopy 1999, Nobel Laureate Signature award 2000, Charles Lathrop Parsons award 2001, Madison Marshall award 2001, James Flack Norris award for outstanding achievement in the tchg. of chemistry 2004, Nichols medal NY sect. 2004, George C. Pimentel award 2008), Am. Phys. Soc. (Earle K. Plyler prize 1981, Irving Langmuir Prize 1985, Arthur L. Schawlow prize in laser sci. 2000), Am. Acad. Arts and Scis., Phi Beta Delta. Achievements include research in laser chemistry and chem. physics. Office: Stanford U Dept Chemistry Stanford CA 94305-5080 Office Phone: 650-723-3062. Business E-Mail: rnz@stanford.edu.

ZARELLI, JOSEPH, state legislator; m to Tani; children: four daughters, two grandchildren. Washington State Senator, District 18, 95-, member, Education & Ways & Means Committees, currently, vice chairman, Human Serv & Corrections Committees, currently, Washington State Senate.Owner investigation & security consultant firm, currently; foster parent, Clark Co, 86-. America Soc Indust Security Columbia River Chap. Republican. Christian. Address: Vancouver WA Mailing: State Senate 205 Irv Newhouse Bldg, PO Box 40418 Olympia WA 98504-0482 Office Phone: 360-786-7634; 800-562-6000. Fax: 360-786-7173. E-mail: zarelli_jo@leg.wa.gov.

ZAREM, HARVEY ALAN, plastic surgeon; b. Savannah, Ga., Feb. 13, 1932; s. Harry A. and Rose (Gold) Z.; m. Beth McCanghey, July 11, 1981; children: Harold, Allison, Melissa, Kathryn, Michael, Robert. BA, Yale U., 1953; MD, Columbia U. Coll. Physicians and Surgeons, 1957. Diplomate Am. Bd. Surgery, Am. Bd. Plastic Surgery; lic. physician, Md., Ill., Calif. Intern, surgery Johns Hopkins Hosp., Balt., 1957-58, resident, plastic surgery, 1964-66; rsch. fellow Peter Bent Brigham Hosp., Boston, 1958-59, asst. resident, surgery, 1959-61; resident, surgery then chief resident Boston City Hosp., 1961-63; postdoctoral fellow NYU, NYC, 1963-64; from asst. prof. to assoc. prof. surgery U. Chgo., 1966-73; head, sect. plastic surgery U. Chgo. Hosp. and Clinics; prof. surgery U. Calif., LA, 1973-87, prof. emeritus, 1987—, chief, divsn. plastic and reconstructive surgery, 1973—87; mem. med. staff Pacific Surgicenter, Santa Monica, Calif., 1987—. Physician Sepulveda (Calif.) VA Hosp., 1974—; mem. med. staff St. Johns Hosp., Santa Monica, Calif., 1987—, Santa Monica Hosp., 1988—; vis. prof. So. Ill. U., 1983, Lackaland AFB, 1986, Creighton U., 1987, Comesa, Milan, 1989, Baylor Coll. Medicine, 1990; Kazanjian vis. prof. Mass. Gen. Hosp., 1986, 88; cons. and presenter in field; cons. plastic surgery, Wadsworth VA Hosp., LA; surgeon, Extreme Makeover, ABC TV, 2003-. Contbr. numerous articles to profl. jours. Grantee NIH, 1964-75, NIH, 1967-72, Sheldon and Carol Appel Family Found., 1982—, Chantal Pharms., 1983-84, Mentor Corp./Heyer-Schulte Products, 1985—, Michael Jackson Burn Found., 1986-87. Fellow ACS; mem. AMA, Am. Soc. Plastic Reconstructive Sugeons, Inc., Am. Burn Assn., Am. Cleft Palat Assn., Am. Assn. Plastic Surgeons (trustee 1987, 1989), Am. Soc. Aesthetic Plastic Surgery, Inc., Am. Assn. Hand Surgery, Am. Assn. Surgery of Trauma, Calif. Med. Asssn., Calif. Soc. Plastic Surgeons, New Eng. Soc. Plastic Surgeons (hon.), L.A. County Med. Assn., Johns Hopkins Med. and Surg. Soc., Plastic Surgery Rsch. Coun., Soc. Head and Neck Surgeons (sr.), Soc. U. Surgeons, Lipoplasty Soc. N.Am., Bay Surgical Soc., N.W. Soc. Plastic Surgeons (hon.), Calif. Plastic Surgeon Assn. (pres.), Calif. Yacht Club, Beverly Hills Country Club, (bd. dirs.). Office: Pacific Surgicenter 1301 20th St Ste 470 Santa Monica CA 90404-2082 Home Phone: 310-474-3904; Office Phone: 310-315-0222. Business E-Mail: hzarem@ucla.edu, drzarem@drzarem.com.

ZARGES, THOMAS H., engineering executive; Degree in Engring., Va. Mil. Inst. V.p. bus. devel. United Engrs. & Constructors, 1990; pres., CEO power and indsl./mfg. divsns. Washington Group, 1991; sr. exec. v.p. ops. Washington Group Internat., Boise, Idaho, 2002—. Office: Washington Group Internat PO Box 73 Boise ID 83729

ZARINS, CHRISTOPHER KRISTAPS, surgeon, educator; b. Tukums, Latvia, Dec. 2, 1943; came to U.S., 1946; s. Richard A. and Maria (Rozenbergs) Z.; m. Zinta Zarins, July 8, 1967; children: Daina, Sascha, Karina. BA, Lehigh U., 1964; MD, Johns Hopkins U., 1968. Surgery residency U. Mich., Ann Arbor, 1968-74; asst. prof. surgery U. Chgo., 1976-79, assoc. prof. surgery, 1979-82, prof. surgery, 1983-93, chief of vascular surgery, 1978-93; prof. surgery Stanford (Calif.) U., 1993—, chmn. divsn. vascular surgery, 1993—2005, acting chmn. dept. of surgery, 1995-97. Author: Essays In Surgery, 1986, Atlas of Vascular Surgery, 1988; editor Jour. of Surg. Rsch., 1982-95; contbr. articles to profl. jours. Pres. Latvian Med. Found., Boston, 1991. Lt. comdr. USN, 1974-76. Grantee NIH, NSF. Mem. Am. Surg. Soc., Soc. for Clin. Surgery, Soc. for Vascular Surgery (pres. 1998-99), Internat. Soc. for Cardiovascular Surgery, Soc. of Univ. Surgeons, Latvian Nat. Acad. of Scis., Latvian Vascular Surg. Soc. (pres. 1989), Soc. for Vascular Surgery (pres. 1998-99). Avocations: triathlons, skiing. Office: Stanford U Med Ctr Divsn Vascular Surgery 300 Pasteur Dr # H3642 Stanford CA 94304-2203 Office Phone: 650-725-7830.

ZARO, BRAD A., research and development company executive, biologist; b. San Jose, Calif., Dec. 4, 1949; s. Raymond J. and Irene R. Z.; children: Amy C., Kristen E. BA in Zoology, San Jose State U., 1974, MA in Biology, 1981. Chemist, Dept. Drug Metabolism Syntex Rsch., Inc., Palo Alto, Calif., 1976-78, chemist II, Dept. Drug Metabolism, 1978-81, chemist III, Dept. Drug Metabolism, 1981-84, clin. rsch. assoc. I, Inst. of Clin. Medicine, 1984-85, clin. rsch. assoc.

II, Inst. of Clin. Medicine, 1985-87, sen. clin. rsch. assoc., Inst. of Clin. Medicine, 1985-87; sen. clin. rsch. assoc. Triton Biosciences, Inc., Alameda, Calif., 1988, mgr. clin. trials, 1988; pres., CEO Clinimetrics Rsch. Assoc., Inc., San Jose, 1988—. Contbr. articles to scholarly jours. Mem. AAAS, Am. Coll. Clin. Pharmacology, Am. Soc. Pharmacognosy, Assn. Clin. Rsch. Profls., Drug Info. Assn. Democrat. Roman Catholic. Avocations: scuba diving, skiing, flying. Home: 5681 Morningside Dr San Jose CA 95138-2229

ZAWACKI, BRUCE EDWIN, surgeon, educator, ethicist; b. Northampton, Mass., Dec. 6, 1935; BS, Coll. of Holy Cross, 1957; MD, Harvard U., 1961; MA, U. So. Calif., 1986. Diplomate Am. Bd. Surgery. Intern in surgery Mass. Gen. Hosp., 1961—62, resident in surgery, 1962—65; vis. scholar in trauma surgery Birmingham Accident Hosp., Birmingham, England, 1966; resident in surgery Mass. Gen. Hosp., 1967; gen. surgeon So. Calif. Permanente Med. Group, Panorama City, 1969-71; dir. burn ctr. L.A. County and U. So. Calif. Med. Ctr., LA, 1971-98; assoc. prof. surgery U. So. Calif. Sch. Medicine, LA, 1975-98, assoc. prof. emeritus, 1998—; assoc. prof. religion U. So. Calif. Sch. Religion, LA, 1992-98; assoc. for edn. Pacific Ctr. for Health Policy and Ethics, 1997—; adj. assoc. prof. religion U. So. Calif., 2001—02. Contbr. articles to profl. jours. Served to maj. U.S. Army, 1967-68. Mem. Am. Burn Assn. (2d v.p., bd. trustees 1992-93; Harvey Stuart Allen Disting. Svc. award 1996), Am. Soc. Bioethics and Humanities, L.A. Surg. Soc., Internat. Soc. for Burn Injuries. Achievements include first to describe the natural history of reversible burn injury, the independence of burn hypermetabolism from evaporative water loss and an autonomous role for burn patients without precedent for survival.

ZDURIENCIK, JACK, professional sports team executive; m. Debbie Zduriencik. BEd, Calif. State U.; MA in Phys. Edn., Austin Peay U. Area scout NY Mets, 1983—89, advance scout, 1986, 1988, scouting cross-checker, 1990, 1994—95, minor league ops. dir., 1996—97, spl. asst. to the gen. mgr., 1998; dir. scouting Pitts. Pirates, 1991—93; dir. internat. scouting, spl. asst. to the gen. mgr. LA Dodgers, 1998; spl. asst. to the gen. mgr., dir. amateur scouting Milw. Brewers, 1999—2008; gen. mgr. Seattle Mariners, 2008—. Named Maj. League Exec. of Yr., Baseball America, 2007. Achievements include being the first ever non-general manager to be named Major League Baseball's Executive of the Year, 2007. Office: Seattle Mariners PO Box 4100 Seattle WA 98104

ZEBROSKI, EDWIN LEOPOLD, risk management consultant; b. Chgo., Apr. 1, 1921; s. Peter Paul and Sophie (Rydz) Z.; m. Gisela Karin Rudolph, Sept. 6, 1969; children: Lars, Zoe, Susan, Peggy. BS, U. Chgo., 1941; PhD, U. Calif., Berkeley, 1947. Registered prof. engr., Calif. Project engr. Gen. Electric Co., Schenectady, N.Y., 1947-53, mgr. devel. engring. San Jose, Calif., 1958-73; mgr. engring. SRI Internat., Menlo Park, Calif., 1954-58, dir. systems and materials dept., 1974-79; dir. nuclear safety analysis ctr. EPRI, Palo Alto, Calif., 1979-81; v.p. engring. INPO, Atlanta, 1981-83; chief nuclear scientist EPRI, 1982—88; dir. risk mgmt. svcs. APTECH Engring. Svcs., Sunnyvale, Calif., 1988-97; safety and risk mgmt. advisor Oak Ridge Nat. Lab., 1997—2000, DOE-Sandia Nat. Lab., 2000—04. Vis. prof. Purdue U., Lafayette, Ind., 1977-78; cons. OTA, Washington, 1980, 82-83, Dept. Energy, Washington, 1985-90, panels Nat. Rsch. Coun., 1990—, Electricite de France, 1986-87, Dept. Interior, Washington, 1987-89, EPRI, Palo Alto, 1988-98, Acad. Sci., USSR, 1987, Karlsruhe Lab., Germany, 1988; mem. commn. engring. edn. NRC, Washington, 1970-73; mem. NAS-NRC Panel on Decision-Making in Govt. Agy., 1997-98; mem. NAS-NRC Panel on High Level Waste R&D, 2001; mem. NAE Panel on Countering Terrorism, 2002—03. Contbr. chpts. to books, numerous articles to profl. jours.; patentee in field. Pres. bd. dirs. Unitarian Ch., Palo Alto, 2005—06; bd. dirs. Stevenson House, Palo Alto, 2003—07. Recipient Charles A. Coffin award Gen. Electric Co., Schenectady, 1954, Edward Teller award, 2002. Fellow AAAS, Am. Nuclear Soc. (bd. exec. com. 1969-71), Am. Inst. Chemists; mem. NAE (chmn. energy com. 1984-86, chmn. mem. com. 1986-87, policy com. 1995-96), Am. Phys. Soc., Soc. for Risk Analysis. Avocations: safety and risk management, public sector decision processes, music, writing. Business E-Mail: edzeb1@comcast.net.

ZEECK, DAVID A., newspaper editor; m. Valarie S. Zeeck; children: Phillip, Michael. BJ, U. Mo., 1973; MBA, Rockhurst Coll. Various positions The Kans. City Star, 1974—94; exec. editor The News Tribune, Tacoma, 1994—. Instr. in field. Mem.: Am. Assn. Newspaper Editors (bd. dirs., pres. 2006—07). Presbyn. Office: The News Tribune 1950 South St Tacoma WA 98405 Mailing: PO Box 11000 Tacoma WA 98411 E-mail: david.zeeck@mail.tribnet.com.

ZEFF, OPHELIA HOPE, lawyer; b. Oak Park, Ill., Aug. 19, 1934; d. Bernard Allen and Esther (Levinsohn) Gurvis; m. David Zeff, Dec. 29, 1957 (div. 1983); children: Sally Lyn Zeff Propper, Betsy Zeff Russell, Ellen, Adam; m. John Canterbury Davis, Sept. 18, 1987. BA, Calif. State U., 1956; JD, U. Pacific, 1975. Bar: Calif. 1975. Reporter Placerville (Calif.) Mountain Dem., 1956-57, Salinas Californian, 1957-59; corr. Modesto (Calif.) Bee, 1962-64; atty. ALRB, Sacramento, 1975-76, Yolo County Counsel, Woodland, Calif., 1976-78, Law Office of O.H. Zeff, Woodland, 1978-85; employee rels. officer Yolo County, 1985-87; ptnr. Littler, Mendelson, Fastiff, Tichy & Mathiason, Sacramento, 1987-98, Atkinson, Andelson, Loya, Ruud & Romo, Sacramento, 1998—. Mem. Vallejo (Calif.) Sch. Bd., 1971-74, pres., 1974; mem. Woodland Libr. Bd., 1982; v.p. LWV, Vallejo, 1972; mem. LWV, Sacramento, 1987—. Recipient Am. Jurisprudence Lawyer Coop. Pub., 1974. Mem. Sacramento County Bar, Sacramento Women Lawyers, Indsl. Rels. Assn. No. Calif., Traynor Soc. (life). Democrat. Jewish. Avocations: hiking, skiing, bicycling, reading, travel.

ZEHR, CLYDE JAMES, religious organization administrator; b. Valley Ctr., Kans., Oct. 4, 1934; s. John Wesley and Anna Mae (Carithers) Z.; m. Leona Mae Zehr, Nov. 23, 1957; children: Karen Elaine, Mark Wesley. BS, U. Kans., 1957; ThM, Western Evang. Sem., Portland, Oreg., 1961; MBA, Seattle U., 1976. Ordained to ministry Evang. Meth. Ch., 1961. Structural engr. Boeing Co., Seattle, 1957-59; pastor Rockwood Evang. Meth. Ch., Portland, 1961-63; missionary OMS Internat., Seoul, Republic of Korea, 1964-80; dir. Christian Leadership Seminars, Kent, Wash., 1980-82; supt. N.W. dist. Evang. Meth. Ch., Kent, 1982-86, gen. supt. Wichita, Kans., 1986-94, N.W. dist. supt. Seattle, 1995—. Author: Study Notes on Leadership, 1982, The Innovator/Administrator Conflict, 1986, Focus on Effectiveness, 1990. Republican. Office: Evang Meth Ch NW Dist Office PO Box 75673 Seattle WA 98125-0673

ZEHR, CONNIE, sculptor, art educator; b. Ohio, 1938; BFA, Ohio State U. Artist Occidental Coll., 1977; visiting artist Calif. State U. Fullerton, 1978—80, Claremont Grad. Sch., 1981, UCLA, 1981, U. Calif. Irvine, 1981—82; prof. Claremont Grad. Sch., 1982—, chairperson dept. art. One-woman shows include Newspace, L.A., Calif., 2002, Harris Art Gallery, U. LaVerne, Calif., 1998, Weingart Gallery, Occidental Coll., 1991, Santa Monica (Calif.) Coll. Art Gallery Santa Monica (Calif.) Coll., 1989, West Gallery, Claremont Coll. Grad. Sch., 1988, Taipei (Taiwan) Fine Arts Mus., 1987, Calif. State U., Fullerton, Calif., Barnsdall Mcpl. Art Gallery, L.A., Calif. Mural Project Claremont Cmty. Found., 1999; Transit Ctr. Art Com. City Claremont, 1992; Visual Art Com. Claremont Cmty. Found., 1991—; Art Selection Panel for Grand Hope Park Cmty. Redevel. Agency, LA, 1986; Process Oriented Design Santa Ana Calif., 1987. Grantee Individual Artist Grant, Nat. Endowment Arts, 1975, Landmark Project, Art Collaboration, 1984, Individual Artist Grant, 1986, Mentor Grant, Lorser Feitelson & Helen Lundeberg-Feitelson Arts Found., 1987. Office: Art Dept Claremont Grad U 251 East 10th St Claremont CA 91711 Office Phone: 909-607-9292.

ZEIGER, ROBERT S., allergist; b. Bklyn., July 31, 1942; s. Murray and Mildred Z.; m. Karen P. Zeiger, June 25, 1967; children: Joanna, Laurie. BA with honors, Tulane U., 1963; MD, PhD, SUNY, Bklyn., 1969. Diplomate Am. Bd. Pediatrics, Am. Bd. Allergy-Immunology. Intern pediatrics Harriet Lane Johns Hopkins Hosp., Balt., 1969-70; staff assoc. NIH, Bethesda, Md., 1970-72; resident pediatrics Boston Children's Hosp., 1972-73, allergy fellow, 1973-75; instr. Harvard Med. Sch., Boston, 1975-76; chief of allergy Kaiser Permanent, San Diego, 1976—; clin. assoc. prof. U. Calif., San Diego, 1980-87, clin. prof., 1987—. Editorial bd. Family Practice Survey, 1983-85, Jour. Allergy Clin. Immunology, 1985-91, Pediatric Allergy Immunology Jour., 1990—; author: Nasal Manifestations of Systemic Diseases, 1990; contbr. articles to profl. jours. Lt. comdr. USPHS, 1970-72. Phizer Honor scholar Phizer Corp., 1967-69, Charles A. Janeway scholar Harvard U., 1975; Hood Found. grantee, 1975-77. Fellow Am. Acad. Pediatrics, Am. Acad. Allergy Clin. Immunology (Travel award 1975), Phi Beta Kappa, Alpha Omega Alpha. Democrat. Avocations: tennis, travel, golf, films. Office: Kaiser Permanente 7060 Clairemont Mesa Blvd San Diego CA 92111-1003 also: U Calif San Diego Dept Pediat 9500 Gilman Dr La Jolla CA 92093-0833

ZEITLIN, HERBERT ZAKARY, college administrator, educational consultant, writer; b. NYC, Jan. 14; s. Leonard and Martha Josephine (Soff) Zeitlin; m. Eugenia F. Pawlik, July 3, 1949; children: Mark Clyde, Joyce Therese Zeitlin Harris, Ann Victoria, Clare Katherine. BS, NYU, 1947, MA, 1949; EdD, Stanford U., 1956. Tchr. Mepham HS, Bellmore, NY, 1946—47, Nassau County Vocat. Edn. Extension Bd., Mineola, NY; electronics instr., adj. faculty Mephan CC; tchr., counselor, dir. testing Phoenix Union HS and Coll. Dist.; dean eve. coll., prin. high sch. Antelope Valley Union HS and Coll. Dist., Lancaster, Calif.; dean instrn. Southwestern Coll., Chula Vista, Calif.; pres., supt., cons. Triton Coll., River Grove, Ill., 1964—79; dean, pres. West LA Coll., 1976-80; pres. Trident Cons., LA, mgmt. cons., 1976—; adj. faculty Ariz. State U., Flagstaff, No. Ill. U., DeKalb, U. Calif., Santa Barbara. Author: Turbulent Birth of Triton College, 2001, Corruption: How to Fight It and Win, 2004, What Makes A Teacher Great?, 2007; editor: in field. Pres. Antelope Valley Breeze & Sage, Bon Vivant Homeowners Assn.; mayor Upper Woodland Hills, Calif. With USAAF, 1942—46. Recipient Spl. commendation, Chgo. Tribune, Richard Ogilvie, former Gov. Ill., Spl. Achievement award for visionary accomplishment, Ill. Sch. Adminstrs. Assn.; named Adminstr. of the Yr., Triton Coll. Faculty Assn., 1974, Most Influential Educator in Ill., Chgo. Sun Times. Mem.: Ariz. State Vocat. Assn. (pres.), Ariz. Vocat. Guidance Assn. (pres.), Maywood Ill. Rotary (pres.), Antelope Valley Rotary (pres.). Mailing: Trident Cons PO Box 571412 Tarzana CA 91357 Home: 20124 Phaeton Dr Woodland Hills CA 91364 Home Phone: 818-884-7819. Personal E-mail: herbertzzeitlin@aol.com.

ZEITLIN, MARILYN AUDREY, former museum director; b. Newark, July 14, 1941; d. Sidney M. and Theresa (Feigenblatt) Litchfield; widowed; children: Charles C. Sweedler, Milo Sweedler. Student, Vanderbilt U., 1963-65; AB in Humanities, Harvard U., 1966, MA in Teaching of English, 1967; postgrad., Cornell U., 1971-74. Dir. Ctr. Gallery, Bucknell U., Lewisburg, Pa., 1975-78; Freedman Gallery, Albright Coll., Reading, Pa., 1978-81; Anderson Gallery, Va. Commonwealth U., Richmond, 1981-87; curator, acting co-dir. Contemporary Arts Mus., Houston, 1987-90; exec. dir. Washington Projects for the Arts, 1990-92; dir. Univ. Art Mus., Ariz. State U., Tempe, 1992—2007. Juror Dallas Mus. of Arts, McKnight Awards, Mpls.; grant evaluator IMS; grant evaluator, panelist NEH; lectr., cons. in field. Editor, contbr. essays to art publs. Bd. dirs. Cultural Alliance Washington Samuel H. Kress fellow, 1972-73. Mem. Assn. Coll. and Univ. Mus. and Galleries (v.p. 1986-88), Am. Assn. Mus., Coll. Art Assn. (U.S. commr. Venice Biennale 1995). Office: Ariz State U Art Mus PO Box 872911 Tempe AZ 85287-2911 Office Phone: 480-965-2787. Business E-Mail: marilyn.zeitlin@asu.edu.

ZEITLIN, MAURICE, sociology educator; b. Detroit, Feb. 24, 1935; s. Albert J. and Rose (Goldberg) Zeitlin; m. Marilyn Geller, Mar. 1, 1959; children: Michelle, Carla, Erica. BA cum laude, Wayne State U., 1957; MA, U. Calif., Berkeley, 1960, PhD, 1964. Instr. anthropology and sociology Princeton (N.J.) U., 1961-64; rsch. assoc. Ctr. Internat. Studies, 1962-64; from asst. prof. to assoc. prof. sociology U. Wis., Madison, 1964—70, prof., 1970-77; dir. Ctr. Social Orgn., 1974-76; disting. prof. sociology UCLA, 1977—, rsch. assoc. Inst. Inds. Rels. Vis. prof. polit. sci. and sociology Hebrew U., Jerusalem, 1971—72. Author (with R. Scheer): Cuba: An American Tragedy, 1963, 1964, Revolutionary Politics and the Cuban Working Class, 1967, 1970, The Civil Wars in Chile, 1984; author: (with R. E. Ratcliff) Landlords and Capitalists, 1988, The Large Corporation and Contemporary Classes, 1989; author: (with J. Stepan-Norris) Talking Union, 1996, Left Out: Reds and America's Industrial Unions, 2003; Latin Am. editor: Ramparts mag., 1967—73, editor-in-chief: Political Power and Social Theory, 1980—90; mem. editl. adv. bd. Progressive mag., 1985—96; editor (with J. Petras): Latin America: Reform or Revolution?, 1968, American Society, Inc., 1970, 1977, Father Camilo Torres: Revolutionary Writings, 1972, Classes, Class Conflict, and the State, 1980, How Mighty a Force?, 1983, Insurgent Workers: The Origins of Industrial Unionism, 1987. Chmn. Madison Citizens for a Vote on Vietnam, 1967—68, Am. Com. for Chile, 1973—75; mem. exec. bd. U.S. Com. Justice to Latin Am. Polit. Prisoners, 1977—84; mem. exec. com. Calif. Campaign for Econ. Democracy, 1983—86. Recipient Project Censored award, Top Censored Story, 1981; co-recipient Inaugural Disting. Publ. award in Labor Studies, Soc. for Study Social Problems, 1996; named to Ten Best Censored Stories list, 1978; Ford Found. fellow, 1965—67, 1970—71, Guggenheim fellow, 1981—82, NSF grantee, 1981, 1982, 1998. Mem.: Internat. Sociol. Assn. (mem. editl. bd. 1977—81), Am. Sociol. Assn. (mem. governing coun. 1977—80, co-recipient Disting. Contbn. Scholarship award in Polit. Sociology 1992, 1996, 2002, The 2004 Max Weber award for an Outstanding Book Published Over the Past Three Years in Orgns., Occupations and Work). Democrat. Jewish. Office: UCLA Dept Sociology 264 Haines Hall Los Angeles CA 90095-1551 Office Phone: 310-825-3968. Business E-Mail: zeitlin@soc.ucla.edu.

ZEKMAN, TERRI MARGARET, graphic designer; b. Chgo., Sept. 13, 1950; d. Theodore Nathan and Lois (Bernstein) Z.; m. Alan Daniels, Apr. 12, 1980; children: Jesse Logan, Dakota Caitlin. BFA, Washington U., St. Louis, 1971; postgrad, Art Inst. Chgo., 1974-75. Graphic designer (on retainer) greeting cards and related products Recycled Paper Products Co., Chgo., 1970—, Jillson Roberts, Inc., Calif.; apprenticed graphic designer Helmuth, Obata & Kassabaum, St. Louis, 1970-71; graphic designer Container Corp., Chgo., 1971; graphic designer, art dir., photographer Cuerden Advt. Design, Denver, 1971-74; art dir. D'Arcy, McManus & Masius Advt., Chgo., 1975-76; freelance graphic designer Chgo., 1976-77; art dir. Garfield Linn Advt., Chgo., 1977-78; graphic designer Keiser Design Group, Van Noy & Co., Los Angeles, 1978-79; owner and operator graphic design studio Los Angeles, 1979—. Art and photography tchr. Ctr. for Early Edn., L.A., 1996—, Buckley Sch., Sherman Oaks, 1996—; 3d grade tchr. asst., 1999—. Recipient cert. of merit St. Louis Outdoor Poster Contest, 1970, Denver Art Dirs. Club, 1973 Personal E-mail: redzek50@aol.com.

ZELENOK, DAVID STEPHEN, city official; BSCE, U.S. Air Force Acad., 1977; MS in Engring., U. Tex., 1980. Civil engr. USAF, Washington, San Antonio, Austin; mem. faculty dept. civil engring. U.S. Air Force Acad.; county hwy. mgr. Pa. Dept. Transp.; city engr. Wichita Falls, Tex.; st. supt. City of Colorado Springs, Colo., 1987-90, dir. transp., 1990—96, dir. pub. works, 1996—.

ZELENY, DENNIS, food products executive; b. Blkyn., Dec. 9, 1955; s. Stanly and Olga (Freida) Z. BS, Cornell U., 1977; MBS, Columbia U., 1985. With labor rels. adminstrn. Parker Pen Co., Janesville, Wis., 1977-78; rep. employee rels. Pepsi-Cola Co., NYC, 1978-79, mgr. area employee rels. Detroit, 1979-81, mgr. div. employee rels., 1981-83, N.J., 1983-85, dir. personnel Purchase, N.Y., 1985-88; v.p. employee rels. Pepsi-Cola West, Irvine, Calif., 1988—. Mem. Am. Mktg. Assn., Am. Soc. Personnel Adminstrs. Avocations: running, piano, reading, sports. Office: Pepsi-Cola Co 2600 Michelson Dr Irvine CA 92612-1550

ZELIBOR, THOMAS E., career officer; b. Chgo. BS in Oceanography, U.S. Naval Acad., 1976. Commd. ensign USN, advanced through ranks to rear adm.; various assignments to comdr. air wing USS Dwight D. Eisenhower, 1995; comdr. Naval Space Command, 1998-2001; radm., COMCARGRU THREE USN, 2001. Decorated Def. Superior Svc. medal, Legion of Merit, Disting. Svc. medal, Disting. Flying Cross with Combat V, Meritorious Svc. medal, three Strike/Flight Air medal (two with Combat V), Air medal (with Combat V), three Navy Commendation meds (two with Combat V), two Navy Achievement medals.

ZELIGER, BERNARD I., retired dean, orthopedic surgeon; LHD (hon.), Touro U., 2003. Orthopedic surgeon, Pa.; provost and dean Touro U. Coll. Osteo. Medicine, Vallejo, Calif., 1995—2002, chief acad. officer; pres. Full Cir. Found., Las Vegas, 2003—. Sr. examiner Am. Osteopathic Bd. Orthopedic Surgery, v.p. bd. dirs. Named Physician of Yr., Cmty. Gen. Hosp., Harrisburg, Pa., 1987, Man of Yr., Ctrl. Pa. March of Dimes, 1990. Mem.: Am. Coll. Osteopathic Surgeons (pres.), Am. Osteopathic Acad. Orthopedics (pres., Knotty Cane award 1986).

ZELIKOW, HOWARD MONROE, management and financial consultant; b. Bklyn., Apr. 17, 1934; s. Herman and Mae (Rebell) Z.; m. Doris Brown, June 10, 1956 (div. Aug. 1987); children: Lori Ann Zelikow Florio, Daniel M.; m. Marcie Peskin Rosenblum, Dec. 12, 1987. BA, Dartmouth Coll., 1955; MBA, Amost Tuck Sch., 1956. Acct. Ernst & Ernst, NYC, 1956-61; controller Kratter Corp., NYC, 1961-64; mgr. J.H. Cohn, CPAs, Newark, 1964-65; ptnr. Zelikow & Rebell CPAs, NYC, 1965-70; v.p. Oxbow Constrn. Corp., Port Washington, N.Y., 1970-76; exec. v.p., treas., chief fin. officer Progressive Ins. Cos., Mayfield Village, Ohio, 1976-87; prin. ZKA Assocs., Cleve., 1987-96; ptnr., mng. dir. Kayne Anderson Investment Mgmt., LA, 1988—. Trustee Village of Great Neck Estates, Great Neck, N.Y., 1975-76. Mem. Hillcrest Club, Phi Beta Kappa. Jewish. Home: 10114 Empyrean Way Los Angeles CA 90067-3830 Office: Kayne Anderson Investment Mgmt 1800 Avenue Of The Stars Los Angeles CA 90067-4212 Business E-Mail: hzelikow@kayne.com.

ZELLERBACH, WILLIAM JOSEPH, retired paper company executive; b. San Francisco, Sept. 15, 1920; s. Harold Lionel and Doris (Joseph) Z.; m. Margery Haber, Feb. 25, 1946; children: John William, Thomas Harold, Charles Ralph, Nancy. BS, Wharton Sch., U. Pa., 1942; grad., Advanced Mgmt. Program, Harvard U., 1958. With Crown Zellerbach Corp. and subs., 1946-85; officer, dir. Crown Zellerbach Corp., 1960-85. Mem gen. adv. com. fgn. assistance programs AID, 1965-68; chmn. bd. Zellerbach Family Found. Served as lt. USNR, 1942-46. Mem. Nat. Paper trade Assn. (pres. 1970) Clubs: Villa Taverna (San Francisco), Presidio Golf (San Francisco), Pacific Union (San Francisco), Commonwealth (San Francisco); Peninsula Country (San Mateo, Calif.). Office: 575 Market St Ste 2950 San Francisco CA 94105

ZELMANOWITZ, JULIUS MARTIN, mathematics professor, academic administrator; b. NYC, Feb. 20, 1941; s. Morris and Tillie (Holtz) Z.; m. Joan R. Traubel, June 24, 1962; 1 child, Dawn Michèle. AB, Harvard U., 1962; MS, U. Wis., 1963, PhD, 1966. From asst. prof. to assoc. prof. U. Calif., Santa Barbara, 1966—77, prof. math., 1977—2006, assoc. vice chancellor acad. affairs, 1985-87, assoc. vice chancellor acad. personnel, 1988-98; assoc. prof. Carnegie-Mellon U., Pitts., 1970-71; interim vice provost acad. initiatives U. Calif., 1999-2000, v.p. acad. initiatives, 2000—06, sr. vice provost acad. programs, 2005; dep. dir. Math. Sci. Rsch. Inst., Berkeley, Calif., 2006—08. Vis. asst. prof. UCLA, 1969—70, vis. assoc. prof., 1973—74; vis. prof. U. Rome, 1977, McGill U., Montreal, Que., Canada, 1982—83, 1987—88, U. Munich, 1983, 88, U. Calif., Berkeley, 2006—. Contbr. articles to profl. jours. Sr. rsch. grantee Italian Nat. Rsch. Coun., Rome, 1977, Palermo, 1988; named Milw. Prof. of Maths. The Technion, Haifa, Israel, 1979; Fulbright sr. fellow, Munich, 1983. Mem. Am. Math. Soc., Math. Assn. Am. Home: 2369 Century Hl Los Angeles CA 90067-3527 Office Phone: 510-643-6040. Business E-Mail: julius@math.ucsb.edu, jz@msri.org.

ZELON, LAURIE DEE, judge; b. Durham, NC, Nov. 15, 1952; d. Irving and Doris Miriam (Baker) Z.; m. David L. George, Dec. 30, 1979; children: Jeremy, Daniel. BA in English with distinction, Cornell U., 1974; JD, Harvard U., 1977. Bar: Calif. 1977, US Ct. Appeals (9th cir.) 1978, US Supreme Ct. 1989. Assoc. Beardsley, Hufstedler & Kemble, LA, 1977-81, Hufstedler, Miller, Carlson & Beardsley, LA, 1981-82, ptnr., 1983-88, Hufstedler, Miller, Kaus & Beardsley, LA, 1988-90, Hufstedler, Kaus & Ettinger, LA, 1990-91, Morrison & Foerster, LA, 1991-2000; judge LA Superior Ct., 2000—03; assoc. justice Calif. Ct. Appeal, LA, 2003—. Contbg. author: West's California Litigation Forms: Civil Procedure Before Trial, 1996; editor-in-chief Harvard Civil Rights and Civil Liberties Law Rev., 1976-77 Bd. dirs. NY Civil Liberties Union, 1973-74. Mem. ABA (chmn. young lawyers divsn. pro bono project 1981-83, delivery and pro bono projects com. 1983-85, subgrant competition-subgrant monitoring project 1985-86, chair standing com. on lawyers pub. svc. responsibility 1987-90, chair law firm pro bono project 1989-91, standing com. legal aid and indigent defendants 1991-97, chmn. 1993-97, mem. ho. dels. 1993—, state del. 1998-2006, commn. on ethics 2000 1997-2002, bd. govs. 2006—), Calif. Bar Assn. (bd. dirs. appellate project 1995-2000, chair commn. on access to justice 1997-99), LA County Bar Assn. (trustee 1989-91, v.p. 1992-93, sr. v.p. 1993-94, pres.-elect 1994-95, pres. 1995-96, fed. cts. and practices com. 1984-93, vice chmn. 1987-88, chmn. 1988-89, chmn. judiciary com. 1991-92, chmn. real estate litigation subsect. 1991-92), Women Lawyers Assn. LA, Calif. Women Lawyers Assn. Democrat. Office: Calif Ct of Appeal 2d Appellate Dist 300 S Spring St Los Angeles CA 90013 Business E-Mail: laurie.zelon@jud.ca.gov.

ZEMPLENYI, TIBOR KAROL, cardiologist, educator; b. Part Lupča, Czechoslovakia, July 16, 1916; came to U.S., 1968, naturalized, 1974; s. David Dezider and Irene (Pollak) Z.; m. Hana Bendová, Aug. 13, 1952; 1 son, Jan. MD, Charles U., Prague, Czechoslovakia, 1946, Docent Habilit., 1966; CSc. (PhD), Czechoslovak Acad. Sci., 1960, DSc., 1964. Clin. asst. with dept medicine Prague Motol Clinic and Charles U., 1946-52; head atherosclerosis rsch. Inst. for Cardiovascular Rsch., Prague, 1952-68; assoc. prof. medicine Charles U., 1966-68, U. So. Calif., LA, 1969-75, prof., 1975-92, prof. emeritus, 1992—. Attending physician L.A. County- U.So. Calif. Med. Ctr. Author: Enzyme Biochemistry of the Arterial Wall, 1968; editl. bd. Atherosclerosis, 1962-75, Cor et Vasa, 1993—; adv. bd. Advances in Lipid Rsch., 1963-66; contbr. articles to numerous profl. jours. WHO fellow for study in Sweden and Gt. Britain, 1959. Fellow Am. Heart Assn., Am. Coll. Cardiology; mem. Western Soc. for Clin. Rsch., Longevity Assn. (mem. sci. bd.), European Atherosclerosis Group, Italian Soc. for Atherosclerosis (hon.). Office: 3400 Loadstone Dr Sherman Oaks CA 91403-4512

ZENEV, IRENE LOUISE, museum curator; b. Albuquerque, Nov. 18, 1948; d. Stanley D. and Louise Marie (Risler) Z.; 1 child, Carson M. Bell. BA, U. N.Mex., 1971. Dir. Umpqua Valley Arts Assn., Roseburg, Oreg., 1978-82; edn. coord. Douglas County Mus., Roseburg, 1985-86, curator history, 1986-98; exhibits curator Benton County Mus., Philomath, Oreg., 1998—2006; editor Dispatch newsletter Oreg. Mus. Assn., 1995-98. Pubs. rschr. Oreg. Mus. Assn., Portland, 1989-92; exec. dir., Benton County Hist. Soc. and Mus., 2007-. Reviewer The Roseburg News-Review, 1989-93. Chmn. Douglas County Oreg. Trail Sesquicentennial Celebration Com., 1991-93; mem. Oreg. Coun. for Humanities, 1997-2000, sec. bd., 1998-2000; bd. dirs. Oreg. Mus. Assn., 2002-06, v.p., 2002-2004, pres., 2004-06; bd. dirs. Western Mus. Assn., 2005-06; mem. Oreg. Heritage Commn., 2007-, commr. Mem. Registrar's Com. Western Region (Oreg. state rep. 1995-99), Mus. Assessment Program Peer Reviewer. Home: PO Box 964 Philomath OR 97370 Office Phone: 541-929-6230 ext. 102. Business E-Mail: irene@bentoncountymuseum.org.

ZERBE, KATHRYN JANE, psychiatrist; b. Harrisburg, Pa., Oct. 17, 1951; d. Grover Franklin and Ethel (Schreckengaust) Z. BS with BA equivalent cum laude, Duke U., Durham, NC, 1973; MD, Temple U., Phila., 1978. Diplomate Am. Bd. Psychiatry. Resident Karl Menninger Sch. Psychiatry, Topeka, 1982, dean, dir. edn. and rsch., 1992-97; staff psychiatrist Menninger Found., Topeka, 1982-2001; v.p. edn. and rsch. The Menninger Clinic, Topeka, 1993-97, prof., 1997-2001, Jack Aron chair in psychiat. edn., 1997-2001, apptd. tng. and supr. analyst, 1995—; prof. psychiatry, prof. ob-gyn. Oreg. Health Scis. Univ., Portland, 2001—; dir. behavioral medicine dept. Oreg. Health Scis. U., Portland, 2001—06; dir. outpatient clinic Oreg. Health Scis. Univ., Portland, 2003—, vice chair for psychotherapy, 2003—; tng. and supr. analyst Oreg. Psychoanalytic Inst., 2002—. Instr. numerous seminars and courses. Author: The Body Betrayed: Women, Eating Disorders and Treatment, 1993, Women's Mental Health in Primary Care, 1999, Eating Disorders for Ob-Gyns, 2007, (book) Integrated Tretment of Eating Disorder, 2008, numerous articles profl. rsch. papers; editor: Womens Mental Health: Primary Care Clinics, 2001; assoc. editor:, 1996—98; editor: Bull. of Menninger Clinic, 1998; mem. editl. bd.: Eating Disorders Rev., Eating Disorders: The Jour. of Treatment and Prevention Postgrad. Medicine; editor (sect.): Current Women's Health; contbr. book revs. and articles to profl. jours. Probation officer Juvenile divsn. Dauphin County, Pa., 1973. Recipient Ann. Laughlin Merit award The Nat. Psychiat. Endowment Fund, 1982, Outstanding Paper of Profl. Programs award The Menninger Found. Alumni Assn., 1982, Writing award Topeka Inst. for Psychoanalysis, 1985, 90, Mentorship award, 1997, Women Helping Women award, 1995, Tchr. of Yr. award Psychiatry Residents, 1988, 96, 99, 03, 05, 06; named one of Outstanding Young Women in Am., 1986, 88, Portland's Top Drs., 2007; Seeley fellow, 1979-82; Hilde Bruch lectureship, 1996. Fellow Am. Psychiat. Assn. (Alexandra Symonds award 2005, Edith Sabshin award 2007); mem. AMA, Am. Coll. Psychiatrists, Am. Med. Women's Assn., Oreg. Med. Assn., Oreg. Psychiat. Assn., Sigma Xi, Alpha Omega Alpha. Avocations: writing, reading, art history, travel. Office: Oreg Health and Scis U Adult Psychiatry 3181 SW Sam Jackson Park Rd Portland OR 97239-3098 Office Phone: 503-295-9909. Personal E-mail: kzbone@comcast.net. Business E-Mail: zerbek@ohsu.edu.

ZERELLA, JOSEPH T., retired pediatric surgeon; b. Youngstown, Ohio, Mar. 7, 1941; s. Atilio and Ann (Capuzello) Z.; m. Diana Isabelle Talbot, Aug. 5, 1967; children: Ann, Michael, Mark. BS, Northwestern U., 1962, MD, 1966. Diplomate Am. Bd. Surgery, Am. Bd. Pediatric Surgery. Intern Med. Coll. Wis., Milw., 1966-67, resident in surgery, 1967-68, 70-73; tng. fellow in pediatric surgery Children's Hosp. Med. Ctr., Cin., 1973-75; staff pediatric surgeon Phoenix Children's Hosp., 1975—; pvt. practice medicine, specializing in pediatric surgery Phoenix, 1975—. Mem. staff Good Samaritan Hosp., Phoenix, 1975—, sect. chief pediatric surgery, 1979—; mem. staff St. Joseph's Hosp., Phoenix, 1975—, sect. chief pediatric surgery, 1980—. Contbr. articles to profl. jours. Capt. USAR, 1968—70. Fellow ACS, Am. Acad. Pediatrics, Am. Pediatric Surg. Assn., Pacific Assn. Pediatric Surgeons. Roman Catholic. Mailing: 8426 N 15th Dr Phoenix AZ 85021 E-mail: dzerella@aol.com.

ZETTEL, LAURA A., psychology professor, researcher; b. Warren, Mich., Feb. 29, 1976; d. Richard J. and Donna Zettel. BA, U. Mich., Ann Arbor, 1997; PhD, U. Calif., Irvine, 2004. Rschr. U. Mich., Ann Arbor, 1997—98; instr. and rschr. U. Calif., Irvine, 1998—2005; prof. Calif. State U., Fullerton, Calif., 2005—. Tchg. asst. cons. U. Calif., Irvine, 2002—04; adj. faculty Soka U. Am., Aliso Viejo, Calif., 2004. Named Most Promising Future Faculty Mem., U. Calif. Irvine, 2004; grantee, Anthony Marchionne Found., 2003; fellow, U. Calif. Irvine, 2004. Mem.: APA, Gerontol. Soc. Am. Avocations: travel, reading, tennis. Office: Psychology Dept CSUF PO Box 6846 Fullerton CA 92834-6846 Home: Po Box 3965 Fullerton CA 92834-3965 Business E-Mail: lzettel@fullerton.edu.

ZEWAIL, AHMED HASSAN, chemistry and physics educator, consultant, editor; b. Damanhour, Egypt, Feb. 26, 1946; arrived in U.S., 1969, naturalized, 1982; s. Hassan A. Zewail and Rawhia Dar; m. Dema Zewail; children: Maha, Amani, Nabeel, Hani. BS, Alexandria U., Egypt, 1967, MS, 1969; PhD, U. Pa., 1974; MA (hon.), Oxford U., 1991; DSc (hon.), Am. U., Cairo, 1993, Katholieke U., Leuven, Belgium, U. Pa., U. Lausanne, Switzerland, 1997; DU (hon.), Swinburne U., Australia, 1999; HDA Sc (hon.), Arab Acad. for Sci. and Tech., Egypt, 1999, Alexandria U., 1999; DSc (hon.), U. New Brunswick, Canada, 2000; DHC (hon.), U. Rome, Italy, 2000, U. de Liège, Belgium, 2000. Teaching asst. U. Pa., Phila., 1969—70; IBM fellow U. Calif., Berkeley, 1974—76; asst. prof. chem. physics Calif. Inst. Tech., Pasadena, 1976—78, assoc. prof., 1978—82, prof., 1982—89, Linus Pauling prof. chem. physics, 1990—94, Linus Pauling prof. chemistry and prof. physics, 1995—, dir. NSF Lab. for Molecular Scis., 1996—. Cons. Xerox Corp., Webster, NY, 1977—80, ARCO Solar, Inc., Calif., 1978—81. Editor Laser Chemistry, 1980—85, Jour. Phys. Chemistry, 1985—90, Chem. Physics Letters, 1991—; editor: International Series Monographs on Chemistry, 1992—, Advances in Laser Spectroscopy, 1977—, 1978—, Photochemistry and Photobiology, 1983—, Ultrafast Phenomena, 1990—, 1993—, 1994—, The Chemical Bond: Structure and Dynamics, 1992, Femtochemistry-Ultrafst Dynamics of the Chemical Bond, 1994; contbr. numerous articles to sci. jours., patentee in solar energy field. Recipient Tchr.-Scholar award, Dreyfus Found., 1979—85, Alexander von Humboldt Sr. U.S. Scientist award, 1983, John Simon Guggenheim Meml. Found. award, 1987, King Faisal Internat. prize in sci., 1989, NASA award, 1991, 1st AMM Achievement award, 1991, Nobel Laureate Signature award, 1992, Carl Zeiss award, Cairo U. Medal and Shield of Honor, 1992, U. Qatar medal, 1993, Wolf prize in chemistry, Wolf Found., Israel, 1993, Niles award of honor Bonner Chemiepreis, Germany, 1994, Order of Merit first class, Egypt, 1995, Coll. de France medal Leonardo Da Vinci award of excellence, France, 1995, J.G. Kirwood medal, Yale U., 1996, Beijing U. medal, 1996, Robert A. Welch award in chemistry, 1997, Pitts. Spectroscopy award, 1997, Benjamin Franklin medal, 1999, Paul Karrer Gold medal, Zurich, 1999, Roentgen prize, Germany, 1999, E.O. Lawrence award, U.S. Govt., 1999, Merski award, U. Nebr., 1999, Nobel prize in Chemistry, 1999, Egypt Postage Stamp with portrait issued, 1999, Grand Collar of the Nile, Highest Award, 2000, Order of Zayed, United Arab Emirates, 2000, Ahmed Zewail fellow established, U. Pa., 2000, Order of Cedar, Lebanon, 2000, Order of ISESCO 1st class, Saudi Arabia, 2000, Order of merit, Tunisia, 2000, Insignia Pontifical Acad., Vatican, 2000, Albert Einstein World Award of Sci., 2006. Mem.: NAS (Chem. Scis. award 1996), AAAS, Third World Acad. Scis., European Acad. Arts, Scis. and Humanities, Royal Danish Acad. Scis. and Letters, Pontifical Acad. Sci., Am. Phys. Soc. (Herbert P. Broida prize 1995), Am. Philos. Soc., Am. Chem. Soc. (Buck-Whitney medal 1985, Harrison-Howe award 1989, Hoechst prize 1990, Peter Debye award 1997, Linus Pauling medal 1997, 1st E.B. Wilson award 1997, William H. Nichols award 1998, Richard C. Tolman medal 1998), Am. Acad. Arts and Scis. (Royal Netherlands Acad. Arts and Scis. medal 1993), Sigma Xi (Earle K. Plyler prize 1993, Wolf prize 1993). Office: Arthur Amos Noyes Lab of Chem Physics Calif Inst Tech MC 127-72 1200 E California Blvd Pasadena CA 91125 Business E-Mail: zewail@caltech.edu.

ZHANG, DU, engineering educator; b. Nanjing, Jiangsu, China; arrived in U.S., 1984; s. Wen-Tang Zhang and Xue-Wen Yu; m. Meiliu Lu; 1 child, Bryan. BS, Nanjing U., 1977, MS, 1982; PhD, U. of Ill., 1987. Lectr. Nanjing U., 1977—80, 1982—84; rschr. U. of Ill., Chgo., 1984—87; asst. prof. Calif. State U., Sacramento, 1987—89, assoc. prof., 1989—93, prof., 1993—, dept. assoc. chair, 1996—97, dept. grad. coord., 1997—98, dept. chair, 2004—. Mem. program com. various internat. confs., 1991—2006. Editor: (book) Machine Learning Applications in Software Engineering, Advances in Machine Learning Applications in Software Engineering; assoc. editor: Internat. Jour. Artificial Intelligence Tools, 2003—, guest editor: Internat. Jour. Software Engring. and Knowledge Engring., 2004, Software Quality Jour., 2005, Internat. Jour. Cognitive Informatics and Natural Intelligence, 2007, mem. editl. bd.:, 2005—; contbr. articles to prof. jours. and tech. reports in field, chapters to books. Recipient Chancellor's Student Svc. award, U. of Ill., 1986, Student Leadership Recognition award, U. of Ill. Alumni Assn., 1987, Nat. award, U.S. Achievement Acad., 1987, Outstanding Scholar award, Coll. of Engring., Calif. State U., Sacramento, 1998, 2004, Meritorious Performance award, Calif. State U., Sacramento, 1989, 1996. Mem.: ACM, IEEE (sr.; program chair 15th internat. conf. tools with artificial intelligence 2003, vice-program chair internat. conf. tools artificial intelligence 2003, gen. chair 16th internat. conf. tools with artificial intelligence 2004, internat. symposium on bioinformatics and bioengring. 2004, program co-chair internat. conf. info. reuse and integration 2004—06, 4th internat. conf. cognitive informatics 2005, program co-chair internat. conf. cognitive informatics 2005, 2007—08, SMC tech. com. on knowledge acquisition in intelligent sys., program co-chair internat. conf. software and knowledge engring. 2007—08), IEEE Computer Soc. (tech. coun. on software engring., multimedia computing com.), Upsilon Pi Epsilon, Phi Beta Delta. Achievements include research in A high-level Petri net model for definite clause logic programs; ZCZOS, a distributed operating system; Pr/T net model for planning; Pr/T net model for parallel query processing in deductive databases; Theory And Verification Methods For Knowledge Bases; Machine Learning Applications In Software Engineering. Avocations: travel, sports. Office: Calif State U 6000 J St Sacramento CA 95819-6021

ZHANG, HONG, engineering company executive, educator, inventor; s. Hong Zhang and Hong; m. Fangqiu Sun; children: Perryn S. Chang, Helen S. Chang. BS, Tsinghua U., Beijing, 1994; PhD in Mech. Engring., U. Pa., Phila., 2000. Assoc. prof. Rowan U., Glassboro, NJ, 2000—; CEO AA Rotating Apparatus Corp., Metuchen, NJ, 2004—. Founder Confucian and Horace Mann Acad. Edn. and Culture Corp., Hayward, Calif., 2008—. Achievements include design of lighter than air flying robot system; robotic testing and surveillance system for shallow to medium depth water; invention of an omnidirectional display system; gaming apparatus and system with remote controlled vehicle; patents for an integrated computer display console; interactive mobile aqua probing and surveillance system; a splash proof pot lid; patents pending for design of a totally enclosed no-lubricant gear speed reducer; a easy-gripping and expandable computer mouse; research in nonlinear visual servo control for an under-actuated mobile robot and motion planning for multiple robots; founding of an online language teaching and culture development company. Avocation: writing. Business E-Mail: hozhangg@gmail.com.

ZHANG, JINSHU, lawyer; b. Chengdu, China, July 11, 1959; m. Yuan Fu; 1 child, Jonathan R. BA, Beijing U., 1982; MA, U. Hawaii, 1989, UCLA, 1990; JD, U. Calif., Berkeley, 1993. Bar: Calif. 1993, (U.S. Ct. Appeals, 9th cir.), Calif. (U.S. Dist. Ct., ctrl. dist.). Ptnr. Jones Day, L.A., 1996—99; ptnr. head China practice Greenberg Traurig, LLP, L.A., 2000—08; ptnr. Reed Smith LLP, L.A., 2008—. Advisor, exec. com., internat. sect. State Bar Calif., L.A. Mem.: Calif. State Bar Assn. (adv. exec. com. internat. law sect.). Office: Reed Smith LLP 355 S Grand Ave Ste 2900 Los Angeles CA 90071 E-mail: jzhang@reedsmith.com.

ZHANG, YA-QIN, computer software company executive; b. Taiyuan, China, Jan. 7, 1966; came to U.S., 1986; s. Jung-Fang Bi; m. Jenny Jian Wang, Apr. 28, 1989; 1 child, Sophie W. Zhang. BS, U. Sci. and Tech. China, Hefei, 1983, MS, 1985; PhD in elec. engring., George Washington U., 1989. Mem. tech. staff Contel Corp., Chantilly, Va., 1990-91; sr. mem. tech. staff GTE Corp., Waltham, Mass., 1990-95; dir. multimedia tech. of lab. Sarnoff Corp., Princeton, NJ, 1995—99; asst. mng. dir., mng. dir. Microsoft Rsch. Asia, 1999—2004; corp. v.p. mobile & embedded devices Microsoft Corp., Redmond, Wash., 2004—07, corp. v.p., rsch. & develop. in China, 2007—. Guest editor SPIE, 1996. Editor 8 books, 1995—; contbr. over 150 articles to profl. jours. and internat. confs. Coun. chair Ind. Fedn. Chinese Students and Scholars, 1989. Fellow IEEE (sr.; Indsl. Pioneer award; guest editor tech. jour. 1995, mem. editorial bd. Computer Press 1997, editor-in-chief Circuits & Systems for Video Technology 1997); mem. ISD, ITU, Eta Kappa Nu (Outstanding Young Elec. Engr. award 1997, Engr. of Yr. 1997). Achievements include the building of several products in videophone, digital TV and satellite communications; patentee in field. Office: Microsoft Corp 1 Microsoft Way Redmond WA 98052-6399

ZIADEH, FARHAT J., Middle Eastern studies educator; b. Ramallah, Palestine, Apr. 8, 1917; s. Jacob and Nimeh Farah Z.; m. Suad Salem, July 24, 1949; children— Shireen, Susan, Rhonda, Deena, Reema. BA, Am. U., Beirut, 1937; LL.B., U. London, 1940. Bar: Barrister-at-law Lincoln's Inn 1946. Instr. Princeton U., 1943-45, lectr. Oriental studies, 1948-54, asst. prof., 1954-58, asso. prof., 1958-66; magistrate Govt. of Palestine, 1947-48; editor Voice of Am., USIA, 1950-54; prof. U. Wash., Seattle, 1966—, prof., chmn. dept. Near Eastern lang. and lit., 1970-82, dir. Ctr. Arabic Study Abroad, 1983-89. Adj. prof. U. Wash. Law Sch., 1978-87, prof. emeritus, 1987— Author: Reader in Modern Literary Arabic, 1964, Lawyers, The Rule of Law and Liberalism in Modern Egypt, 1968, Property Law in the Arab World, 1979; contbr. articles to profl. jours. Mem. Middle East Studies Assn. (pres. 1979-80), Am. Oriental Soc. (past pres. western br.), Am. Research Center in Egypt (past bd. govs., exec. com.), Am. Assn. Tchrs. Arabic (past pres.) Eastern Orthodox. Office: Univ Wash Mid Eastern Studies Dept Seattle WA 98195-0001 Home Phone: 206-523-2093; Office Phone: 206-543-4959. E-mail: farhat@u.washington.edu.

ZIDICH, JOHN M., publishing executive; b. San Francisco, 1954; m. Pam Zidich; children: Katie, Ali. Circulation dist. mgr. to advt. and sales mgmt. positions The Record (Gannett Newspapers), Stockton, Calif., 1977—90; retail advt. mgr. Reno Gazette-Jour., Nev., 1990—2000, pres., pub., 2000—01; exec. v.p. Ariz. Republic, Phoenix, 2001—04, pres., COO, 2004—05, CEO, pub., 2005—. Bd. dir. Banner Health Found., Greater Phoenix C. of C., Phoenix Suns Charities. Mem.: Ariz. Sports Found. Avocations: cooking, golf, entertaining. Office: Arizona Republic 200 E Van Buren St PO Box 1950 Phoenix AZ 85001 Office Phone: 602-444-8000.

ZIEGAUS, ALAN JAMES, public relations executive; b. Bremerton, Wash., May 8, 1948; s. Alan Moon and Dorothy (Lamont) Z.; m. Constance Jean Carver, 1972; children: Jennifer, Ashley. BJ, San Diego State U., 1970. Staff writer San Diego Tribune, 1972-77; exec. asst. San Diego City Council, 1977-78; v.p. Gable Agy., San Diego, 1978-80; pres. Stoorza, Ziegaus & Metzger, San Diego, 1980-2000. Mem. planning com. County San Diego, 1980-82; mem. sewage task force City of San Diego, 1986-88, civil svc. com., 1992—; trustee armed forces YMCA, San Diego, 1984—. Recipient Best Investigative Series award AP, 1975. Mem. San Diego Press Club (Best News Story award 1973). Office: Stoorza Ziegaus & Metzger 225 Broadway Fl 18 San Diego CA 92101-5005 Home: 11343 Breckenridge Way San Diego CA 92131-2953

ZIEGLER, JACK (JACK DENMORE), cartoonist; b. NYC, July 13, 1942; s. John Denmore and Kathleen Miriam (Clark) Z.; m. Jean Ann Rice, Apr. 20, 1968 (div. 1995); children: Jessica, Benjamin, Maxwell; m. Kelli Joseph, Aug. 1996. BA in Comm. Arts, Fordham U., 1964. Free-lance cartoonist, NYC, 1972—; cartoonist The New Yorker, NYC, 1974—. Author: Hamburger Madness, 1978, Filthy Little Things, 1981, Marital Blitz, 1987, Celebrity Cartoons of the Rich and Famous, 1987, Worst Case Scenarios, 1990, Mr. Knocky, 1993, The Essential Jack Ziegler, 2000, How's The Squid?, 2004, Olive Or Twist?, 2005, You Had Me at Bow Wow, 2006; illustrator: (children's books) Lily of the Forest, 1987, Flying Boy, 1988, Annie's Pet, 1989, Eli and the Dimplemeyers, 1994 (adult books) Waiting Games, 1983, The Joy of Stress, 1984, That's Incurable!, 1984, Modern Superstitions, 1985, The No-Sex Handbook, 1990, There'll Be a Slight Delay, 1991, Byte Me!, 1996, Fictoids, 2005. Democrat. Personal E-mail: jkziegler@sbcglobal.net.

ZIEGLER, R. W., JR., lawyer, consultant; b. Pitts. children: Caroline, Gretchen, Jeremy, Benjamin, Phoebe, Polly. Student, Carnegie Mellon, U. Pitts.; JD, Duquesne U., 1972. Bar: Pa. 1972, Calif. 1981, U.S. Ct. Appeals (3d cir.) 1977, U.S. Dist. Ct. (we. dist.) Pa. 1972, U.S. Supreme Ct. 1977, U.S. Tax Ct. 1978, Calif. 1982, U.S. Dist. Ct. (no. dist.) Calif. 1982, U.S. Ct. Appeals (9th cir.) 1982. Ptnr. Ziegler & Ombres, Pitts., 1973-79; pres. Ziegler Ross Inc., San Francisco,

1979—2007, Ziegler Consultants, 2007—. Lectr. for Bar Assns. Author: Law Practice Management; editor: Law Office Guide in Computing. Mem. ABA, Am. Mgmt. Assn., Pa. State Bar Assn., Calif. State Bar Assn., Assn. of Legal Admin., Young Presidents' Org., Am. Assn. of Law Librarians., San Francisco Bar Assn. Office: 1559B Sloat Blvd Ste 200 San Francisco CA 94132 Office Phone: 415-682-4944.

ZIELINSKI, MELISSA L., museum director; BS, Coll. William and Mary, 1978; MS, N.C. State U., 1983. Park svc. ranger, interpreter Cape Hatteras Nat. Seashore, Buxton, N.C., 1980, 81; exhibits intern N.C. Mus. Natural Scis., Raleigh, 1980-81, 81-82, asst. curator pub. programs, 1984-92; vol. svcs. coord. N.C. State U., 1981-82, 82-83, lab. instr. vertebrate zoology lab., 1983; naturalist Durant Nature Park Raleigh (N.C.) Parks and Recreation Dept., 1983-84; mus. educator Humboldt State U. Natural History Mus., Arcata, Calif., 1992-93, dir., 1993—. Co-author, editor, illustrator vertebrate zoology lab. text, 1983-84. Sch. edn. program dir. Friends of the Dunes The Nature Conservancy, Arcata, Calif., 1993-94, mem. Mem. Am. Mus. Natural History, Nat. Assn. Interpretation, Nat. Marine Educators Assn., Guild of Natural Sci. Illustrators, Nat. Audubon Soc. Home: 1363 Mill Creek Rd Mckinleyville CA 95519-4448 Office: Humboldt State U Natural History Mus 1315 G St Arcata CA 95521-5820

ZIEMANN, GEORGE PATRICK, bishop emeritus; b. Pasadena, Calif., Sept. 13, 1941; Attended, Our Lady of the Angels Sem., San Fernando, Calif., 1959—61; BA, MA, St. John's Sem., Camarillo, Calif.; MS in Edn., Mt. St. Mary's Coll., LA. Ordained priest Archdiocese of LA, 1967; assoc. pastor St. Matthias Parish, Huntington Park, Calif., 1967—71; tchr. of religion Mater Dei HS, Santa Ana, Calif., 1971—74; vice rector, dean of studies Our Lady Queen of Angels Sem., Mission Hills, Calif., 1974—87; aux. bishop Archdiocese of LA, 1986—92; ordained bishop, 1987; bishop Diocese of Santa Rosa, Calif., 1992—99, bishop emeritus, 1999—. Episcopal advisor Nat. Assn. Cath. Chaplains, Region XI, Nat. Assn. Diocesan Dirs. of Campus Ministry, Nat. Cath. Cemetery Conf., Nat. Conf. Catechetical Leadership. Roman Catholic. Office: Diocese Of Santa Rosa Roman Catholic 329 10th St PO Box 1297 Santa Rosa CA 95402-1297

ZIEMER, RODGER EDMUND, electrical engineering educator, consultant; b. Sargeant, Minn., Aug. 22, 1937; s. Arnold Edmund and Ruth Ann (Rush) Z.; m. Sandra Lorann Person, June 23, 1960; children: Mark Edmund, Amy Lorann, Norma Jean, Sandra Lynn. BS, U. Minn., 1960, MS, 1962, PhD, 1965. Registered profl. engr., Mo. Research asst. U. Minn., Mpls., 1960-62, research assoc., 1962; prof. elec. engring. U. Mo., Rolla, 1968-83, U. Colo., Colorado Springs, 1984—, chmn. dept. elec. engring., 1984-93; program dir. comms. rsch. NSF, 1998-2001. Cons. Emerson Electric Co., St. Louis, 1972-84, Mid-Am. Regional Coun., Kansas City, Mo., 1974, Motorola, Inc., Scottsdale, Ariz., 1980-84, Martin Marietta, Orlando, 1980-81, TRW, Colorado Springs, summer, 1985, Sperry, Phoenix, 1986, Pericle Communications, summer, 1994, Motorola, Schaumburg, 1995, Scottsdale, 1996, Arlington Heights, 1997. Author: Principles of Communications, 1976, Principles of Communications, 2d edit., 1985, Principles of Communications, 3d edit., 1990, Principles of Communications, 4th edit., 1995, Principles of Communications, 5th edit., 2002, Signals and Systems, 1983, Signals and Systems, 2d edit., 1989, Signals and Systems, 3d edit., 1993, Signals and Systems, 4th edit., 1998, Digital Communications and Spread Spectrum Systems, 1985, Introduction to Digital Communication, 1992, Introduction to Digital Communication, 2d edit., 2001, Introduction to Spread Spectrum Communications, 1995, Elements of Engineering Probability and Statistics, 1997; editor: IEEE Jour. on Selected Areas in Comms., 1989, 1992, 1995, IEEE Comm. Mag., 1991. Served to capt. USAF, 1965-68. Scholar Western Electric, 1957-59; trainee NASA, 1962-65. Fellow IEEE (life; Third Millenium award 2000); mem. Am. Soc. Engring. Edn., Armed Forces Comms. and Electronics Assn., Sigma Xi, Tau Beta Pi, Eta Kappa Nu. Lutheran. Home: 8315 Pilot Ct Colorado Springs CO 80920-4412 Office: Univ Colo PO Box 7150 Colorado Springs CO 80933-7150 Home Phone: 719-590-7859; Office Phone: 719-262-3350. Business E-Mail: ziemer@eas.uccs.edu.

ZIERING, WILLIAM MARK, lawyer; b. New Britain, Conn., Feb. 4, 1931; s. Jacob Max and Esther (Freedman) Z.; m. Harriet Koskoff, Aug. 20, 1958 (div. Sept. 1993); 1 son, Benjamin. BA, Yale U., 1952; JD, Harvard U., 1955. Bar: Conn. 1955, Calif. 1962. Assoc. Koskoff & McMahon, Plainville, Conn., 1959-60; sr. trial atty. SEC, San Francisco, 1960-65; pvt. practice law San Francisco, 1965—; ptnr. Bremer & Ziering, 1972-77. Instr. Golden Gate U. Law Sch., San Francisco, 1968-75 Vice pres., bd. dirs. Calif. League Handicapped, 1972—. Served to comdr. USNR, 1955-58. Mem. ABA, Calif. Bar Assn., San Francisco Bar Assn. (past chmn. securities, corps. and banking), Navy League (dir.) Clubs: Commonwealth. Home: 440 Davis Ct Apt 620 San Francisco CA 94111-2418 Office Phone: 415-982-4581. Personal E-mail: wmziering@sbcglobal.net.

ZIFFREN, KENNETH, lawyer; b. Chgo., June 24, 1940; BA, Northwestern U., 1962; JD, UCLA, 1965. Bar: Calif. 1967. Law clerk to Chief Justice Warren, 1965—66; ptnr. Ziffren Brittenham LLP, LA. Mem.: ABA, L.A. Copyright Soc., Beverly Hills Bar Assn., L.A. County Bar Assn. (pres. 1977—78), State Bar Calif. Office: Ziffren Brittenham LLP 1801 Century Park W Los Angeles CA 90067-6406

ZIL, J. S., forensic specialist, psychiatrist, educator; b. Chgo. s. Stephen Vincent and Marillyn Charlotte (Jackson) Z.; 1 child, Charlene-Elena. BS magna cum laude, U. Redlands, 1969; MD, U. Calif., San Diego, 1973; MPH, Yale U., 1977; JD with honors, Jefferson Coll., 1985. Med. clk. Clinica de Casa de Todos, Tijuana, Mexico, 1968—70; intern, resident in psychiatry and neurology U. Ariz., 1973-75; fellow in psychiatry, advanced fellow in social, cmty. and forensic psychiatry, Yale faculty cons. to Conn. State Dept. Corrections, 1975-77; instr. psychiatry Yale U., 1976-77; instr. physiology U. Mass., 1976-77; unit chief inpatient and Day Hosp., Conn. Mental Health Ctr., Yale-New Haven Hosp., 1975—77; asst. prof. psychiatry U. Calif., San Francisco, 1977-82, assoc. prof. psychiatry and internal medicine, 1982—86, vice-chmn. dept. psychiatry, 1983-86; prof. natural sci. Calif. State U., 1985-87; assoc. prof. bioengring. and internal medicine U. Calif., Berkeley, San Francisco, 1982-92, clin. faculty Davis, 1991-99, legis. liaison Ctrl. Office, 1988—; med. dir. Sierra Vista Hosp., U. Southern Calif., 2003—07, dir. postgrad. tng., 2003—, dir. ethics program, 2007—. Chief psychiatry and neurology VA Med. Ctr., Calif., 1977—86; prin. investigator Sleep Rsch. and Physiology Lab., 1980—86; chmn. dept. psychiatry and neurology U. Calif., San Francisco, Ctrl. San Joaquin Valley Med. Edn. Program and Affiliated Hosps. and Clinics, 1983—86; chief psychiatrist State Calif. Dept. Corrections, 1986—89, chief forensic Psychiatrist, 1986—2003; chmn. State of Calif. Inter-Agy. Tech. Adv. Com. on Mentally Ill Inmates & Parolees, 1986—92; mem. med. adv. com. Calif. State Pers. Bd., 1986—95; apptd. councilor Calif. State Mental Health Plan, 1988—93; cons. Nat. Inst. Corrections, 1992—94; invited faculty contbr. and editor Am. Coll. Psychiatrist's Resident in Tng. Exam, 1981—86; commr. physician's adv. bd. Pres. Commn. on Bus., U.S. Ho. of Reps., 2002—. Author: Suicide Prevention handbook, 1987, 8th edit., 2007, The Case of the Sleepwalking Rapist, 1992, Mentally Disordered Criminal Offenders, 5 vols., 1989, 2nd edit., 1992; contbg. author The Measurement Mandate: On the Road to Performance Improvement in Health Care, 1993, Psychiatric Services in Jails and Prisons, 2nd edit., 2000, assoc. editor Corrective and Social Psychiatry Jour., 1978—97; co-editor: Corrective and Social Psychiatry Jour., 1997—2005; editor-in-chief:, 2005—; referee Corrective and Social Psychiatry Jour., 1980—, reviewer, 1981—; contbr. articles to profl. jours. Nat. Merit scholar, 1965; recipient Nat. Recognition award Bank of Am., 1965, Julian Lee Roberts award U. Redlands, 1969, Kendall award Internat. Symposium in Biochemistry Rsch., 1970, Campus-Wide Profl. Achievement award U. Redlands, 1994, U. Calif., 1995-1996. Fellow Royal Soc. Health (disting. life), Am. Assn. Social Psychiatry; mem. AAUP, APHA, Am. Psychiat. Assn., Am. Assn. Mental Health Profls. in Corrections (nat. pres. 2002—), Nat. Coun. on Crime and Delinquency, Calif. Scholarship Fedn. (past pres.), Delta Alpha, Alpha Epsilon Delta. Office: PO Box 160208 Sacramento CA 95816-0208 Office Phone: 916-326-0478. Personal E-mail: salmonbend@aol.com.

ZILLMER, JOHN J., waste management administrator; MBA, Kellogg Graduate School Northwestern Univ. Mgmt. Aramark Corp., pres. food and support services group, exec. vice-pres.; chmn. bd. and CEO Allied Waste Industries, 2005—. Mem. bd. dir. United Stations Directors, Inc. Office: Allied Waste Industries 18500 N Allied Way Phoenix AZ 85054 Office Phone: 480-627-2700.

ZILLY, THOMAS SAMUEL, federal judge; b. Detroit, Jan. 1, 1935; s. George Samuel and Bernice M. (McWhinney) Z.; divorced; children: John, Peter, Paul, Luke; m. Jane Greller Noland, Oct. 8, 1988; stepchildren: Allison Noland, Jennifer Noland. BA, U. Mich., 1956; LLD, Cornell U., 1962. Bar: Wash. 1962, U.S. Ct. Appeals (9th cir.) 1962, U.S. Supreme Ct. 1976. Ptnr. Lane, Powell, Moss & Miller, Seattle, 1962-88; dist. judge U.S. Dist. Ct. (we. dist.) Wash., Seattle, 1988—. Judge pro tem Seattle Mcpl. Ct., 1972-80; mem. adv. com. bankruptcy rules U.S. Judicial Conf., 1998—; chair adv. com. U.S. Jud. Conf., 2004-2007. Contbr. articles to profl. jours. Mem. Cen. Area Sch. Council, Seattle, 1969-70; scoutmaster Thunderbird Dist. council Boy Scouts Am. Seattle, 1976-84; bd. dirs. East Madison YMCA. Served to lt. (j.g.) USN, 1956-59. Recipient Tuahku Dist. Service to Youth award Boy Scouts Am., 1983. Mem. ABA, Wash. State Bar Assn., Seattle-King County Bar Assn. (treas. 1979-80, trustee 1980-83, sec. 1983-84, 2d v.p. 1984-85, 1st v.p. 1985-86, pres. 1986-87). Office: US Dist Ct 700 Stewart St Ste 15229 Seattle WA 98101

ZIMBARDO, PHILIP GEORGE, psychologist, educator, writer; b. NYC, Mar. 23, 1933; s. George and Margaret (Bisicchia) Z.; m. Christina Maslach, Aug. 10, 1972; children: Zara, Tanya; 1 son by previous marriage, Adam. AB, Bklyn. Coll., 1954; MS, Yale U., 1955, PhD, 1959; D (hon.), U. Peru, 1996; LHD in Clin. Psychology, Pacific Grad. Sch. Psychology, 1996, D (hon.), 1997, Nat. U. of San Martin, 1996, Nat. U. Peru, Thessaloneki, Greece, 1997, Aristotle U., 1998. Asst. prof. psychology Yale U., New Haven, 1959-61, NYU, NYC, 1961-67; vis. assoc. prof. psychology Columbia U., NYC, 1967-68; prof. psychology Stanford (Calif.) U., 1968—; prof. Naval Post Grad. Sch., Monterey, 2002—, Pacific Grad. Sch. Psychology, 2006—; dir. Ctr. Interdisciplinary Policy, Edn., Rsch. in Terrorism, 2006—. Pres. P.G. Zimbardo, Inc., San Francisco; sr. project advisor Exploratorium, 1993; host, writer, gen. acad. advisor PBS-TV series Discovering Psychology, 1987, 2001; cons. NBC. Author: Cognitive Control of Motivation, 1969, Canvassing for Peace, 1970, Psychology and Life, 18th edit., 2007, Shyness, What It Is, What To Do About It, 1977, Influencing Attitudes and Changing Behavior, rev. edit., 1977, The Shyness Workbook, 1979, A Parent's Guide to the Shy Child, 1981, reprinted, 1999, The Psychology of Attitude Change and Social Influence, 1991, Core Concepts in Psychology, 6th edit., 2008, The Lucifer Effect, 2007, The Time Paradox, 2008. Ctr. for Advanced Study of Behavioral Scis. fellow, 1971; recipient Peace medal Tokyo Police Dept., 1972, City Medal of Honor, Salamanca, Spain, Disting. Tchr. award Am. Psychol. Found., 1975, award Havel Found., 2005. Fellow APA (pres. 2002, Presdl. citation Discovery Psychology series 1994, Tchg. award 1999); mem. Am. Psychol. Soc., AAUP, Internat. Congress Psychology, Western Psychol. Assn. (pres. 1985, 2001), Ea. Psychol. Assn., Calif. Psychol. Assn. (Disting. Contbn. to Rsch. award 1978), Soc. for Psychol. Study of Social Issues, Coun. Sci. Soc. Pres. (chair 2005), Sigma Xi, Phi Beta Kappa, Psi Chi. Roman Catholic. Office: Stanford U Psychology Dept Stanford CA 94305 Home Phone: 415-776-4748. Office Fax: 415-673-2294. Business E-Mail: zim@stanford.edu.

ZIMENT, IRWIN, medical educator; b. Eng., 1936; MB BChir, Cambridge U., 1961. Intern, resident, England, 1961-64, USA, 1964-65; resident Bronx Mcpl. Hosp. Ctr., 1965-66; dir. respiratory therpay Harbor Gen. Hosp., Torrance, Calif., 1968-75; chief medicine Olive View-UCLA Med. Ctr., 1975—2001, med. dir., 1994-97; prof. medicine UCLA Sch. Medicine, 1980—2001, prof. emeritus clin. medicine, 2002—. Contbr. articles to profl. jours. Trustee Chest Found., 2000—. Infectious Disease fellow Wadsworth VA Hosp., L.A., 1966-68. Mem. Am. Thoracic Soc. (clin. problems assembly chmn. 1981-82, resp. bd. med. advisors 1986-90), Am. Coll. Chest Physicians (mem. editl. bd. 1997-2000), Nat. Assn. Med. Dir. Respiratory Care (founding mem., vice pres. 1978, treas. 1979-81, bd. dirs. 1983-89, 98—), Calif Thoracic Soc. (pres. 1980-81, various coms. 1970-85), L.A. Lung Assn. (various coms. 1969-86). Office: Olive View UCLA Med Ctr Dept Med Rm 2B 182 14445 Olive View Dr Sylmar CA 91342-1437

ZIMET, CARL NORMAN, psychologist, educator; b. Vienna, June 3, 1925; came to U.S., 1943, naturalized, 1945; s. Leon and Gisela (Kosser) Z.; m. Sara F. Goodman, June 4, 1950; children: Andrew, Gregory. BA, Cornell U., 1949; PhD, Syracuse U., 1953; postdoctoral fellow, Stanford U., 1953-55. Diplomate in clin. psychology Am. Bd. Profl. Psychology (trustee 1966-74). Instr., then asst. prof. psychology and psychiatry Yale U., 1955-63; mem. faculty U. Colo. Med. Center, 1963—, prof. clin. psychology, 1965—2007, head div., 1963—2006, prof. emeritus, 2007—. Mem. Colo. Bd. Psychol. Examiners, 1966-72, Colo. Mental Health Planning Commn., 1964-66; mem. acad. adv. com. John F. Kennedy Child Devel. Center, U. Colo., 1966-68; chmn. Council for Nat. Register of Health Service Providers in Psychology, 1975-85, pres., mem. exec. bd. div. psychotherapy, 1970-89; chair exec. com. Assn. Psychol. Internship Ctrs., 1988-91. Bd. editors: Jour. Clin. Psychology, 1962-91, Jour. Clin. and Cons. Psychology, 1964-73, Psychotherapy, 1967—, Profl. Psychology, 1969-75. With USNR, 1943-46. Recipient Disting. Service award Colo. Psychol. Assn., 1976 Fellow: APA (coun. reps. 1969—72, 1973—76, bd. dirs. 1985—88, Disting. award for profl. contbn., div. psychotherapy and div. clin. psychology 1987), Soc. Personality Assessment (pres. 1975—76, 1975—76, chair gen. psychol. svcs. 1987—97, bd. dirs.); mem.: Med. Sch. Profs. Psychology (pres. 1992—94, bd. dirs. 2004—06), Denver Psychoanalytic (trustee 1968—71), Am. Acad. Clin. Psychology (pres. 1993—2001). Home: 400 E 3rd Ave # 901 Denver CO 80203 Office Phone: 303-315-8611. Business E-Mail: carl.zimet@uchsc.edu.

ZIMMER, GEORGE A., men's apparel executive; b. NYC, Nov. 21, 1948; s. Robert Zimmer; m. Lorri Zimmer; 4 children. BA in Econ., Washington U., St. Louis, 1970. Founder The Men's Wearhouse Inc., Houston, 1973, chmn., pres., 1974—91, chmn., pres., CEO, 1991—97, chmn., CEO, 1997—. Bd. dir. Apollo Group Inc., 2006—. Bd. dirs. Inst. Noetic Sciences. Office: The Mens Wearhouse 40650 Encyclopedia Cir Fremont CA 94538-2453 also: 5803 Glenmont Dr Houston TX 77081

ZIMMER, LARRY WILLIAM, JR., sports announcer; b. New Orleans, Nov. 13, 1935; s. Lawrence W. Sr. and Theodora (Ahrens) Z.; m. Dawn M. Caillouet, June 4, 1955 (div. June 1972); children: Larry III, Tracey; m. Brigitte Bastian, Nov. 17, 1972. Student, La. State U., 1953-55; BJ, U. Mo., 1957. Sports dir. KFRU Radio, Columbia, Mo., 1960-66; asst. mgr. programming WAAM Radio, Ann Arbor, Mich., 1966-71; broadcaster football, basketball Mich., 1966-70; sportscaster, sports dir. KOA Radio, Denver, 1971—; broadcaster Denver Broncos Football, 1971-96; broadcaster football, basketball U. Colo. Buffaloes, 1971—; broadcaster Denver Rockets, 1972-74. Adj. prof. journalism U. Colo., 2001—. Author: Stadium Stories--The Denver Broncoes, 2004. Bd. mem. Colo. Ski Mus. and Hall of Fame, Vail, 1981-2000, Opera Colo., Denver, 1985—, Colo. chap. Nat. Football Found; former mem. adv. bd. Jefferson Co. Youth Advocacy Ctr. 1st lt. US Army, 1958-60. Named Colo. Sportscaster of the Yr., Nat. Sportscasters and Sportswriters Assn., Salisbury, NC, 1988, 90, 91, 2001, 02, Broadcaster of the Yr., Colo. Broadcaster's Assn., Denver, 1995; recipient Powerade award for best radio/TV sports story of yr. Nat. Sportscasters and Sportswriters Assn., 2000. Avocations: skiing, walking, opera. Office: KOA Radio 72 Paradise Rd Golden CO 80401 Business E-Mail: larryzimmer@clearchannel.com.

ZIMMERER, KATHY LOUISE, museum director; b. Whittier, Calif., Dec. 9, 1951; BA cum laude, U. Calif., Berkeley, 1974; MA, Williams Coll., 1976. From tour guide to curatorial asst. Sterling and Francine Clark Inst., Williamstown, Mass., 1975-76; spl. asst. dept. modern art L.A. County Mus. Art, 1976-77; mus. edn. fellow Fine Arts Mus. San Francisco, 1977-78; dir. coll. art gallery SUNY, New Paltz, 1978-80; cons. in field, 1980-81; dir. univ. art gallery Calif. State U., Dominguez Hills, 1982—. Project dir. Painted Light: California Impressionist Paintings from the Gardena H.S./L.A. Unified Sch. Dist., 1996—. Mem. Internat. Assn. Art Critics, Art Table. Office: Univ Art Gallery Calif State U 1000 E Victoria St Carson CA 90747-0001 Home Phone: 562-421-1743; Office Phone: 310-243-3334. E-mail: kzimmerer@csudh.edu.

ZIMMERMAN, BERNARD, judge; b. Munich, Bavaria, Fed. Republic Germany, May 31, 1946; came to U.S., 1949; s. Sam and Roza Z.; m. Grace L. Suarez, Oct. 23, 1976; children: Elizabeth, Adam, David, Dara Bylah. AB, U. Rochester, 1967; JD, U. Chgo., 1970. Bar: Calif. 1971, La. 1971, U.S. Supreme Ct. 1975, U.S. Dist. Ct. (no., ea., cen. and so. dists.) Calif., U.S. Dist. Ct. (ea. dist.) La., U.S. Ct. Appeals (9th cir.). Law. clk. chief judge U.S. Dist. Ct. (ea. dist.) La., New Orleans, 1970-71; asst. prof. law La. State U., Baton Rouge, 1971-72; ptnr. Pillsbury, Madison & Sutro, San Francisco, 1972-95; legal cons. 3d Constnl. Conv. Commonwealth of the No. Mariana Islands, Northern Mariana Islands, 1995; U.S. magistrate judge U.S. Dist. Ct. (no. dist.) Calif., 1995—. Dep. pub. defender City of San Francisco, 1975; arbitrator U.S. Dist. Ct., San Francisco, AAA; judge pro tem San Francisco Superior and Mcpl. Cts. Bd. dirs., mem. exec. com. San Francisco Lawyers' Com. on Urban Affairs, 1984-95, treas., 1987; mem. regional bd. Anti-Defamation League, 1989-95. Mem. Phi Beta Kappa. Clubs: Olympic (San Francisco). Office: 450 Golden Gate Ave San Francisco CA 94102-3661 Office Phone: 415-522-4093.

ZIMMERMAN, CHRIS, professional sports team executive; BA in Econs. and Mass Comm., U. Vermont; MBA, Babson Coll. Sr. v.p. Saatchi and Saatchi Advertising, NYC; USA advertising dir. Nike Brand; joined Nike Golf USA, 1998, gen. mgr.; pres., CEO Nike Bauer Hockey Inc., 2003—06, Canucks Sports & Entertainment; pres., CEO, alt. gov. Vancouver Canucks, 2006—. Former asst. hockey coach Babson College. Bd. mem. Canucks for Kids Fund, Special Olympics BC. Office: Vancouver Canucks 800 Griffiths Way Vancouver BC V6B 6G1 Canada

ZIMMERMAN, GAIL MARIE, medical foundation executive; b. Ft. Wayne, Ind., June 23, 1945; d. Albert Douglas and Aina Dorothy (Johnson) Z. BA, U. Puget Sound, 1967. Intelligence analyst CIA, Washington, 1970-72; rsch. asst. Arthur Young & Co., Portland, Oreg., 1972-74; emergency med. service planner Marion-Polk-Yamhill Counties, Salem, Oreg., 1975-76; health cons. Freedman Assocs., Portland, Oreg., 1976-77; legis. asst. U.S. Senator Bob Packwood, Portland, Oreg., 1977-78; pres., CEO Nat. Psoriasis Found., Portland, 1979—. Mem. dermatology panel U.S. Parmacopoeial Conv., 1985-94; lay rep. Nat. Inst. Arthritis, Musculoskeletal and Skin Disease, NIH, 1990-94. Founding bd. dirs. Nat. Abortion Rights Action League, Portland, 1977; pres. bd. dirs. Oreg. Common Cause, Portland, 1977-78 Mem.: Internat. Fedn. Psoriasis Assn. (chair 1995—2001, vice chair 2001—). Avocations: tennis, flute. Office: Nat Psoriasis Found 6600 SW 92nd Ave Ste 300 Portland OR 97223-7195 Home Phone: 503-635-7698; Office Phone: 503-546-8366. Business E-Mail: gzimmerman@psoriasis.org.

ZIMMERMAN, GARY A(LAN), chemistry educator, academic administrator, profl. genealogists; b. Seattle, Oct. 19, 1938; s. Philo Ralph and Nellie Evelyn (Heritage) Z.; m. Leslie Anne Ryder, June 25, 1960 (div. Mar. 1987); children: Teresa Jean, Thomas Edward; m. Marie Claire Markham Hudgins, Feb. 20, 1988 (div. Jan 1994) m. Michele Genthon, May 20, 1995 BS with honors, Calif. Inst. Tech., 1960; PhD, U. Wis., 1964. Faculty Seattle U., 1964-88, prof., 1976-88, dean sci. and engring., 1973-79, acad. v.p., 1980-81, exec. v.p., 1981-87; provost, chief oper. officer Antioch U. Seattle, Seattle, 1988—99; pres. Fiske Genealogy Libr., 1998—. Bd. dirs. Pacific Sci.

Ctr. Found., 1985-91. Mem. Bellevue (Wash.) City Council, 1974-80, mayor, 1978-80; chmn. coun. Municipality Met. Seattle, 1980-90; chmn. King County Solid Waste Mgmt. Bd., 1978-80; bd. dirs. Chief Seattle coun. Boy Scouts Am., 1979—; governing coun. Pacific Hosp. Preservation Devel. Authority, 1997-, chair 2006-. Recipient Pres.'s award Nat. Def. Transp. Assn., 1981; NIH fellow, 1961-64; Woodrow Wilson fellow, 1960-61 Fellow AAAS; mem. AAUP, Am. Assn. Clin. Chemistry (bd. dirs. 1977-84, pres.-elect 1982, pres. 1983), Am. Chem. Soc., Pioneer Assn. Wash. (historian 1987-89, 2003-, pres. 1989-90, past pres. 1990-92, treas. 1992-2009), Bellevue C. of C. (bd. dirs. 1978-88), Bellevue Rotary Club (pres. 2007-2008). Home: 3900 112th Ave NE Bellevue WA 98004-7772 Office: Fiske Genealogy Libr 1644 43rd Ave E Seattle WA 98112-3222 Office Phone: 206-328-2716. Business E-Mail: gzim@fiskelibrary.org.

ZIMMERMAN, GARY J., utilities association executive; b. Chgo., 1960; B, U. Colo., Boulder, 1982; MBA, U. Denver, 1984. Intern Office of Senator William L. Armstrong US Senate; with Unisource Worldwide; group v.p. south ctrl. US xpedx; COO WebTransport, 2000; v.p. bus. ops. Denver Ops. Ctr. 180 Connect, Inc.; exec. v.p. Arabian Horse Assn., 2006—08; exec. dir. Am. Water Works Assn., 2008—. Office: Am Water Works Assn 6666 W Quincy Ave Denver CO 80235-3011 Office Phone: 303-794-7711. Office Fax: 303-347-0804.

ZIMMERMAN, MICHAEL DAVID, lawyer; b. Chgo., Oct. 21, 1943; s. Elizabeth Porter; m. Lynne Mariani (dec. 1994); children: Evangeline Albright, Alessandra Mariani, Morgan Elisabeth; m. Diane Hamilton, 1998. BS, U. Utah, 1966, JD, 1969, LLD (hon.), 2001. Bar: Calif. 1971, Utah 1978. Law clk. to Chief Justice Warren Earl Burger U.S. Supreme Ct., Washington, 1969-70; assoc. O'Melveny & Myers, LA, 1970-76; assoc. prof. law U. Utah, 1976-78, adj. prof. law, 1978-84, 89-93; of counsel Kruse, Landa, Zimmerman & Maycock, Salt Lake City, 1978-80; spl. counsel Gov. of Utah, Salt Lake City, 1978-80; ptnr. Watkiss & Campbell, Salt Lake City, 1980-84; assoc. justice Supreme Ct. Utah, Salt Lake City, 1984-93, 98-00, chief justice, 1994-98; atty., mediator, arbitrator, ptnr. Snell & Wilmer, Salt Lake City, 2000—. Co-moderator Justice Soc. Program of Snowbird Inst. for Arts and Humanities, 1991, 92, 93, 94, 95, 97, 98; moderator, Tanner lecture panel dept. philosophy U. Utah, 1994; faculty Judging Sci. Program Duke U., 1992, 93; bd. dirs. Conf. of Chief Justices, 1995-98. Note editor: Utah Law Rev., 1968-69; contbr. numerous articles to legal publs. Mem. Project 2000, Coalition for Utah's Future, 1985—96; trustee Hubert and Eliza B. Michael Found., 1994—98; bd. dirs. Rowland-Hall St. Mark's Sch., 1995—2002; bd. assoc. Utah Mus. Natural History Found., 1997—; bd. dirs. Summit Inst. for Arts and Humanities, 1989—2002, chair, 2002—; bd. dirs. Hansen Planetarium, 1997—2001, Snowbird Inst. for Arts and Humanities, 1989—98, Deer Valley Inst. for Arts and Humanities, 1996—98, Kanzeon Zen Ctr., 1999—, chair, 2000—; bd. dirs. Utah Coun. on Conflict Resolution, 1999—2005, chair, 1999—2005; bd. dirs. Pvt. Adjudication Ctr.; mem. Duke U., 2000—02; co-dir. Registry of Ind. Sci. and Tech. Advisors, Duke U., 2000—02; chair Utah Jud. Coun. Task Force on Racial and Ethnic Fairness in the Jud. Sys., 1996—2000. Recipient Excellence in Ethics Award, Ctr. for Study of Ethics, 1994, Disting. Svc. Award Utah State Bar, 1998, Individual Achievement Award Downtown Alliance, 1997, The Peter W. Billings, Sr. American Arbitration Assoc. Outstanding Dispute Resolution Svc. Award, 1997, Humanitarian award, Nat. Conf. for Cmty. and Justice, 2005; named Utah State Bar Appellate Ct. Judge of Yr., 1998. Fellow: Am. Bar Found.; mem.: Am. Acad. Appellate Lawyers, Gov. Radiation Exposure Study Mgmt. Com., Ririe-Woodbury Dance Co. (exec. bd. 1982—84), U.S. Dept. of Energy Dose Assessment Adv. Group of the Off-Site Radiation Exposure Reconstruction Project (Utah citizen rep. 1980—84), Utah Legal Svc. Corp. (Bd. of Trustees 1985—87, 2002—), U. Utah Master of Pub. Adminstrn. Program Practitioners' Adv. Com. (mem 1985—89), U.S. Vet. Adminstrn. Adv. Com. on Environ. Hazards (e.g., agent orange, nuclear radiation 1985—89), Nat. Endowment for the Humanities Scholar in Residence at Utah Valley Cmty. Coll. (Orem, Utah 1990), Order of Coif, Am. Judicature Soc. (bd. dirs. 1995—2001), Am. Inns of Ct. VII, Utah Jud. Coun. (supreme ct. rep. 1986—91, chair 1994—98), Jud. Conf. U.S. (adv. com. civil rules 1985—91), Salt Lake County Bar Assn., Utah Bar Assn., Am. Law Inst., ABA (faculty mem. appellate judges' seminar 1993), Phi Kappa Phi. Office: Snell & Wilmer 15 West South Temple Ste 1200 Salt Lake City UT 84101 Office Phone: 801-257-1964. E-mail: mzimmerman@swlaw.com.

ZIMMERMAN, WILLIAM ROBERT, entrepreneur, engineering based manufacturing company executive; b. Cleve., May 11, 1927; s. Irving and Ella (Berger) Z.; m. Nancy Owen, 1963 (div. 1970); 1 child, Amanda; m. Eileen Samuelson, Nov. 11, 1979. BS, MIT, 1948, MS, 1949. Cons. Kurt Salmon Assocs., Washington, 1949-50, A.T. Kearney and Co., Chgo., 1950-52; mill mgr. Am. Envelope Co., West Carrollton, Ohio, 1952-56; exec. v.p. Avery Internat., Pasadena, Calif., 1956-67; pres. Swedlow, Inc., Garden Grove, Calif., 1967-73, Monogram Industries, Inc., Santa Monica, Calif., 1973-78. Bd. dirs. Life Script, Orange, Calif., Adept Techs., Los Alamos, OSO Techs., Rancho Cucamonga, Calif., Monitor Products, Inc., Oceanside, Calif., Summa Industries, Fullerton, Calif. Pres. coun. Boy Scouts Am., Painesville, Ohio, 1957-62; exec. com. Jr. Achievement So. Calif., L.A., 1975-77; trustee Los Angeles County Mus. Nat. History, 1987-97, Harvey Mudd Coll., Claremont, Calif., 1983—. Mem.: Calif. (Los Angeles); Valley Hunt, Annendale (Pasadena). Republican. Avocations: tennis, jogging, golf. Office: Zimmerman Holdings Inc 790 Huntington Cir Pasadena CA 91106-4510

ZIMMERMANN, JOHN PAUL, plastic surgeon; b. Milw., Mar. 9, 1945; s. Paul August and Edith Josephine (Tutsch) Z.; m. Bianca Maria Schaldach, June 13, 1970; children: Veronica, Jean-Paul. BS in Biology, Chemistry, Marquette U., 1966; MD, Med. Coll. Wis., 1970. Diplomate Am Bd. Plastic Surgery. Internship surgery Stanford U. Sch. of Medicine, Calif., 1970-71, residency in gen. surgery, plastic & reconstructive surgery Calif., 1974-79; flight surgeon USAF, 1971-73; fellowship head & neck surgery Roswell Park Meml. Cancer Inst., Buffalo, N.Y., 1977; pvt. practice Napa, Calif., 1979—. Dir. Aesthetic Surgery Ctr. of Napa Valley, Calif., 1993—; clinical asst. prof. of plastic surgery Stanford U. Sch. of Medicine, Calif., 1993—; bd. dirs. Interplast, Palo Alto, Calif. (pres., bd. dirs. 1991-94, chmn. bd. dirs. 1994-95). Mem. Am. Soc. Plastic Surgeons, Am. Soc. Aesthetic Plastic Surgeons, Lipoplasty Soc., Calif. Soc. Plastic Surgeons (bd. dirs.), Calif. Med. Assn., Napa County Med. Assn. Republican. Roman Catholic. Avocations: sailing, golf. Office: Plastic Reconstructive Surgery Ctr 3443 Villa Ln Ste 10 Napa CA 94558-6417

ZIMRING, FRANKLIN E., lawyer, educator; b. 1942; BA, Wayne State U., 1963; JD, U. Chgo., 1967. Bar: Calif. 1968. Asst. prof. U. Chgo., 1967-69, assoc. prof., 1969-72, prof., 1972-85; co-dir. Ctr. for Studies in Criminal Justice, 1973-75, dir., 1975-86; prof. law dir. Earl Warren Legal Inst., U. Calif., Berkeley, 1985—2002. Author: (with Newton) Firearms and Violence in American Life, 1969; The Changing Legal World of Adolescence, 1982; (with Hawkins): Deterrence, 1973, Capital Punishment and the American Agenda, 1986, The Scale of Imprisonment, 1991, The Search for Rational Drug Control, 1992, Crime is Not the Problem, 1997, American Youth Violence, 1998, Punishment and Democracy, 2001, The Contradictions of American Capital Punishment, 2003, An American Travesty, 2004, American Juvenile Justice, 2005, The Great American Crime Decline, 2007. Mem. Am. Acad. Arts and Scis. Office: U Calif Earl Warren Legal Inst Boalt Hall Berkeley CA 94720 Business E-Mail: zimring@law.berkeley.edu.

ZINE, DENNIS P., councilman; b. LA; children: Chris, Eric. Mem. LA Police Dept., sgt., reserve officer, 2001—; councilman, Dist. 3 LA City Coun., 1997—, chmn. personnel com., vice chmn. info tech. and gen. svc. com., mem. public safety & transp. com., vice chair audits and govtl. efficiency com., mem. rules and govt. com., mem. edn. and neighborhoods com., mem. exec. employee rels. com. Bd. dir. LA Police Protective League; LA representative on public safety & crime prevention steering com. Nat. League of Cities; vice chmn. Charter Reform Commn., 1997; dir. Ind. Cities Assn.; bd. dir. League of Calif. Cities; chair Nat. Immigration Task Force; commr. LA County Jud. Procedures Commn.; pres. Executives of the LA Jewish Home for the Aging, 2006. Founder People Organizing a Safe, Secure Environment; bd. dir. West Valley YMCA. Office: City Hall 200 N Spring St Rm 450 Los Angeles CA 90012 also: Dist Office 19040 Vanowen St Reseda CA 91335 Office Phone: 213-473-7003, 818-756-8848. Office Fax: 213-485-8988, 818-756-9179. E-mail: councilmember.zine@lacity.org.*

ZINGG, PAUL JOSEPH, academic administrator; b. Newark, July 22, 1947; s. Carl William Zingg and Dolores Lucking Dulebohn. BA in History, Belmont Abbey Coll., Belmont, NC, 1968; MA in History, U. Richmond, Va., 1969; PhD in History, U. Ga., 1974. Chair and asst. prof., dept. of history and polit. sci. St. Bernard's Coll., Cullman, Ala., 1975-77; dean, academic affairs Daniel Hale Williams U., Chgo., 1977-78; adj asst./assoc. prof., dept. of Am. civilization U. Pa., Phila., 1978—86, asst. dean, academic affairs, Coll. of Arts and Sciences, 1978—79, vice dean, undergraduate studies and admissions, Coll. of Arts and Sciences, 1979—83, Am. Coun. on Edn. Fellow in Academic Adminstrn. and spl. asst. to the pres., 1983—84, exec. asst. to pres., 1984—86; cons. U. Calif., Berkeley, 1986; dean liberal arts and prof., dept. of history St. Mary's Coll., Moraga, Calif., 1986-93; prof., dept. of history Calif. Poly. State U., San Luis Obispo, Calif., 1993—2003, dean liberal arts, 1993-95, provost and acad. v.p., 1995—2003; pres. Calif. State U., Chico, 2004—. Vis. instr. history Ga. Coll., Milledgeville, 1971; cons., contbr. on exhibits Oakland Mus., 1992-94, Calif. Hist. Soc., 2004, PBS-TV documentary film Baseball, 1991-93; editorial cons. U. Nebr. Press, 1994—, U. Ill. Press, 1995-, others. Author: Pride of the Palestra, 1987, Harry Hooper, 1887-1974: An American Baseball Life, 1993, Runs, Hits and and Era: The Pacific Coast League, 1903-1958, 1994, 2nd edit., 1996, A Good Round: A Journey Through the Landscapes and Memory of Golf, 1999, The Moraine Country Club 1930-2005, An Ensersid Odyssey: In Search of the Gods of Golf and Ireland, 2008; co-author: Through Foreign Eyes, 1982; editor, co-author: The Academic Penn, 1986; editor, contbr.: The Sporting Image: Readings in American Sport History; editor: In Search of the American National Character, 1984; contbr. numerous articles to profl. jours. Mem. Calif. Hist. Soc., 2000—; charter mem., Calif. Coun., Oakland Mus., 1995—. NEH summer fellow, 1975, summer rsch. grant, 1989, Ctr. for Internat. Study and Rsch. fellow, 1980-82, Am. Coun. on Edn. fellow, 1983-84; U. Pa. Rsch. Found. awards, 1983-85, faculty mem. of the yr., 1984, grantee St. Mary's Coll., 1987, 90, 91, 93, alumni faculty scholarship award, 1992. Mem. Orgn. Am. Historians, Soc. for History Edn., N.Am. Soc. for Study of Sport, Am. Studies Assn., Soc. for Am. Baseball Rsch., Am. Coun. on Edn., Assn. Am. Colls. and Univs., Am. Assn. Higher Edn., Nat. Assn. State Univs. and Land-Grant Colls., Rotary Club, Merion Golf Club, Butte Creek Country Club, Canyon Oaks Country Club, Phi Alpha Theta, Phi Beta Delta. Avocations: golf, labrador retrievers, baseball. Office: Calif State U 400 W First St Chico CA 95928-0155 Office Phone: 530-898-5201. E-mail: pzingg@csuchico.edu.

ZINKE, RYAN K., state legislator; b. Bozeman, Mont., Nov. 1, 1961; m. Lolita Charlotte Zinke; children: Jennifer, Wolf, Konrad. BS in Geology, U. Oreg., 1984; MBA in Fin., Nat. U., 1991; MS in Global Leadership, U. San Diego, 2004. Mission comdr. SEAL Team Six, 1992; ground force comdr. Joint Special Ops. Command, 1996; comdr. Joint Task Force, Bosnia, 1999, Kosovo, 2001; exec. officer SEAL Tng. Ctr., 2003; dep. comdr. CJSOTF-AP Spl. Forces, Iraq, 2004; dir. Naval Spl. Warfare Tech., 2006; pres./CEO CDI, 2008; pres. Great Northern Peace Pk. Found., 2008; mem. Dist. 2 Mont. State Senate, 2008—. Republican. Lutheran. Office: Montana Senate PO Box 200500 Helena MT 59620-0500 Mailing: 409 W 2nd St Whitefish MT 59937-3010 Home Phone: 406-862-0823; Office Phone: 406-444-4800. Office Fax: 406-444-4875. Business E-Mail: ryan@zinkeforsenate.com.

ZINN, GEORGE, computer software company executive; b. Detroit, Mich. AB, Bowdoin Coll.; MBA, Univ. Wash. Fin. analysis & mgmt. positions Microsoft Corp., Redmond, Wash., 1996—2004, asst. treas., CFO intellectual property & licensing div., corp. v.p., treas., 2004—. Named one of Top 40 Fin. Profl. Under 40, Treasury & Risk Mgmt. Mag. Office: Microsoft Corp 1 Microsoft Way Redmond WA 98052-6399

ZINSER, ELISABETH ANN, former academic administrator; b. Meadville, Pa., Feb. 20, 1940; d. Merle and Fae Zinser. BS, Stanford U., 1964; MS, U. Calif., San Francisco, 1966, MIT, 1982; PhD, U. Calif., Berkeley, 1972. Nurse VA Hosp., Palo Alto, Calif., 1964-65, San Francisco, 1969-70; instr. Sch. Nursing U. Calif., San Francisco, 1966-69; pre-doctoral fellow Nat. Inst. Health, Edn. and Welfare, 1971-72; adminstr. Sch. Medicine U. Wash., Seattle, 1972-75, Coun. Higher Edn., State of Ky., 1975-77; prof., dean. Coll. Nursing U. N.D., Grand Forks, 1977-83; vice chancellor acad. affairs U. N.C., Greensboro, 1983-89; pres. Gallaudet U., Washington, 1988, U. Idaho, Moscow, 1989-95; chancellor U. Ky., Lexington, 1995—2001; pres. So. Oreg. Univ., Ashland, 2001—06. Bd. dir. Assoc. Am. Coll. & Univ., 1999—, Am. Council Edn., Nat Assoc. State Univ. & Land Grant Coll.; bd. mem. Ctr. on Academic Integrity; past chmn. Commn. Outreach & Tech. Transfer. Primary author: (with others) Contemporary Issues in Higher Education, 1985, Higher Education Research, 1988; spkr. in field. Mem. Oreg. Women's Forum; bd. mem. Ashland C. of C., Oreg. Shakespeare Festival, Crater Lake Nat. Park Trust. Leadership fellow Bush Found., 1981-82.

ZIPPIN, CALVIN, epidemiologist, educator; b. Albany, NY, July 17, 1926; s. Samuel and Jennie (Perkel) Z.; m. Patricia Jayne Schubert, Feb. 9, 1964; children: David Benjamin, Jennifer Dorothy. AB magna cum laude, SUNY, Albany, 1947; ScD, Johns Hopkins U., Balt., 1953. Rsch. asst. Sterling-Winthrop Rsch. Inst., Rensselaer, NY, 1947-50, Johns Hopkins U., Balt., 1950—53; instr. biostats. Sch. Pub. Health, U. Calif., Berkeley, 1953-55; asst. to full rsch. biostatistician Sch. Medicine U. Calif., San Francisco, 1955-67, asst. prof. preventive medicine, 1958-60; post doctoral fellow London Sch. Hygiene and Tropical Medicine, 1964-65; prof. epidemiology U. Calif., San Francisco, 1967-91, prof. emeritus, 1991—. Vis. assoc. prof. stats. Stanford U., 1962; adv. WHO, 1969—; vis rsch. worker Middlesex Hosp. Med. Sch., London, 1975; com. mem. Am. Cancer Soc. and Nat. Cancer Inst., 1956—; faculty adviser Regional Cancer Centre, Trivandrum, India, 1983—; cons., lectr., vis. prof. in field. Co-author book, book chpts.; author or co-author papers primarily on biometry and epidemiology of cancer; editl. advisor Jour. Stats. in Medicine, 1981-86. Mem., alt. mem. Dem. Ctrl. Com., Marin County, Calif., 1987-96. Recipient Disting. Alumnus award SUNY, Albany, 1969, Lifetime Achievement and Leadership award Nat. Cancer Inst., 2003, also awards, fellowships and grants for work in cancer biometry and epidemiology. Fellow Am. Statis. Assn., Am. Coll. Epidemiology, Royal Statis. Soc. Gt. Britain; mem. Biometric Soc. (mem. internat. coun. 1978-81, pres. Western N.Am. region 1979-80), Calif. Cancer Registrars Assn. (hon.), Internat. Assn. Cancer Registries (hon.), B'nai B'rith (pres. Golden Gate lodge 1970-71, pres. Greater San Francisco unit 21 2003-06, internat. bd. govs. 2005—07, greater San Francisco Man of Yr., 2009), Phi Beta Kappa, Sigma Xi, Delta Omega. Office: Univ Calif Dept Epidemiology and Biostats San Francisco CA 94107 Office Phone: 415-514-8000. Business E-Mail: calvin.zippin@ucsf.edu.

ZIRIN, HAROLD, astronomer, educator; b. Boston, Oct. 7, 1929; s. Jack and Anna Zirin; m. Mary Noble Fleming, Apr. 20, 1957; children: Daniel Meyer, Dana Mary. AB, Harvard U., 1950, AM, 1951, PhD, 1952. Asst. phys. scientist RAND Corp., 1952-53; lectr. Harvard, 1953-55; research staff High Altitude Obs., Boulder, Colo., 1955-64; prof. astrophysics Calif. Inst. Tech., 1964-98, prof. emeritus, 1998—; staff mem. Hale Obs., 1964-80; chief astronomer Big Bear Solar Obs., 1969-80, dir., 1980-97; Disting. Rsch. Prof. N.J. Inst. Tech., 1996—. U.S.- USSR exchange scientist, 1960-61; vis. prof. Coll. de France, 1986, Japan Soc. P. Sci., 1992. Author: The Solar Atmosphere, 1966, Astrophysics of the Sun, 1987; co-translator: Five Billion Vodka Bottles to the Moon, 1991; adv. editor: Soviet Astronomy, 1965-69; editor Magnetic and Velocity Fields of Solar Active Regions. Trustee Polique Canyon Assn., 1977-90. Agassiz fellow, 1951-52; Sloan fellow, 1958-60; Guggenheim fellow, 1960-61 Mem. Am. Astron. Soc., Internat. Astron. Union, AURA (dir. 1977-83) Office: Calif Inst Tech 264 33 Pasadena CA 91125-0001 Home: 842 E Villa St Apt 357 Pasadena CA 91101-1211 E-mail: hz@caltech.edu.

ZIRKLE, LEWIS GREER, orthopedist; b. Pittsfield, Mass., July 23, 1940; s. Lewis Greer and Vivian (Shaw) Z.; m. Sara K. Zirkle, Aug. 24, 1963; children: Elizabeth, Molly, Julie. BS, Davidson Coll., 1962; MD, Duke U., 1966. Intern Duke U. Hosp., 1966-67, resident, 1968-73, U.S. Army, Shriner's Hosp., 1967-68; pvt. practice Richland, Wash., 1973—. Chmn. program in Vietnam, Orthopedics Overseas, 1992—; bd. dirs., pres. S.E. Asia helmet program, Surg. Implant Generations Network. Contbr. articles to profl. jours. Maj. U.S. Army, 1968-73. Recipient Kiwanis World Svc. medal, 1997; named Vol. of Yr., Orthopedics Overseas. Mem.: Am. Bd. Orthop. Surgery, Am. Acad. Orthop. Surgery, Piedmont Soc., Am. Orthop. Assn. Presbyterian. Avocations: reading, sports. Home: 2548 Harris Ave Richland WA 99352-1638 Office: NW Orthopedics 875 Swift Blvd Richland WA 99352-3592 Office Phone: 509-946-1654. E-mail: lgzirkle@sign-post.org.

ZISCHKE, MICHAEL HERMAN, lawyer; b. Yokahama, Japan, Dec. 30, 1954; s. Peter H. and Alice Marian (Oliver) Z.; children: Julia Carol, Jessica Marian; m. Nadin Sponamore, Sept. 30, 2006. BA magna cum laude, Dartmouth Coll., 1977; JD, U. Calif., Berkeley, 1982. Bar: Calif. 1982. Legis. asst. Congressman Bob Carr, Washington, 1977-79; assoc. Miller, Starr & Regalia, Oakland, Calif., 1982-87, McCutchen, Doyle, Brown & Enersen, Walnut Creek, Calif., 1987-91, counsel, 1991-93; ptnr. Landels Ripley & Diamond LLP, San Francisco, 1993—2000, Morrison & Foerster LLP, San Francisco, 2000—06, co-chmn. land use and environ. law practice group, 2003—06; ptnr. Cox Castle & Nicholson, LLP, 2007—. Lectr. land use issues U. Calif. Extension, 1988—, U. Calif. Davis Sch. Law, 1993—2001, U. Southern Calif. Law Sch., 1995—2006. Co-author: Land Use Initiatives and Referenda in California, 1990, Practice Pursuant to the California Environmental Quality Act, 1993, 2d edit., 2008; contbr. articles to profl. jours. Dir. Boys & Girls Clubs Oakland, 1988-2000, Child Care Law Ctr., 1998-2008. Mem. ABA, Calif. State Bar Assn. (exec. com. environ. law sect., 1995-2004), Calif. Bldg. Industry Assn. (select com. on industry litigation), Bar Assn. San Francisco. Democrat. Episcopalian. Office Phone: 415-262-5109.

ZITO, BARRY, professional baseball player; b. Las Vegas, Nev., May 13, 1978; Student, U. Calif., Santa Barbara, Pierce Jr. Coll., U. So. Calif. Pitcher Oakland Athletics, 2000—06, San Francisco Giants, 2006—. Recipient Am. League Cy Young award, 2002; named to, Am. League All-Star team, 2002, 2003. Achievements include has appeared on TV shows including JAG, Arli$$, and the Chris Isaak Show; led American League in Wins, 2002. Office: Pac bell Park 24 Willie Mays Plz San Francisco CA 94107

ZIVE, GREGG WILLIAM, judge; b. Chgo., Aug. 9, 1945; s. Simon Louis and Betty Jane (Hansen) Z.; m. Franny Alice Forsman, Sept. 3, 1966; 1 child, Joshua Carleton; m. Lu Ann Zive, June 9, 1974; 1 child, Dana Mary. BA in Journalism, U. Nev., 1967; JD magna cum laude, U. Notre Dame, 1973. Bar: Calif. 1973, Nev. 1976, U.S. Ct. Appeals (9th cir.), U.S. Supreme Ct. Assoc. Gray, Cary, Ames & Frye, San Diego, 1973-75, Breen, Young, Whitehead & Hoy, Reno, 1975-76; ptnr. Hale Lane, Peek, Dennison & Howard, Reno, 1977-90, Lionel, Sawyer & Collins, Reno, 1990-92, Bible, Hoy, Trachok, Wadhams & Zive, 1992-95; U.S. bankruptcy judge Dist. Nev., 1995—. Lectr. bus. law U. Nev., 1977-80. Note and comment editor Notre Dame, 1972-73; contbr. articles to profl. jours. Bd. dirs. Washoe Youth Found., 1977-91, Jr. Achievement; commr. Washoe County Parks, 1988-95, chmn., 1990; trustee U. Nev., Reno Found., 1986-94, trustee emeritus, 1994—, chmn., 1993, exec. bd., 1991-96; bd. dirs. YMCA Sierra, 1989-95; mem. univ. legis. rels. com., 1986-95; dir. Friends of

Libr., 1995-2003, v.p., 1998; mem. adv. com. Sparks Redevelopment Authority, 1992-94; trustee Access to Justice Found., 1998-2004, Endowment for Edn., 2004-. 1st lt. U.S. Army, 1968-70. Mem. Calif. Bar Assn., State Nev. Bar Assn. (law related edn. com.), San Diego County Bar Assn., Washoe County Bar Assn. (exec. bd. 1987-93, pres. 1992-93), Nat. Conf. Bankruptcy Judges (bd. govs. 1998-2001), Am. Bankruptcy Inst., Master Inns Ct. (emeritus), Bruce Thompson Chpt., Am. Judicature Soc., Vol. Lawyers Washoe County (bd. dirs. 1991), Washoe Legal Svc. (bd. dirs. 1992-95, pres. 1995), U. Nev. Alumni Assn. (coun. 1981-87, pres. 1986-87), Univ. Club (dir., past pres.). Home Phone: 775-828-2729; Office Phone: 775-784-5017. Business E-Mail: gregg_zive@nvb.us.courts.gov.

ZLATOFF-MIRSKY, EVERETT IGOR, violinist; b. Evanston, Ill., Dec. 29, 1937; s. Alexander Igor and Evelyn Ola (Hill) Z.-M.; m. Janet Dalbey, Jan. 28, 1976; children from previous marriage— Tania, Laura. B.Mus., Chgo. Mus. Coll., Roosevelt U., 1960, M.Mus., 1961. Mem. faculty dept. music Roosevelt U., Chgo., 1961-66. Founding mem., violinist, violist Music of the Baroque, 1971-2003. Violinist orch. Lyric Opera of Chgo., 1974-2003; concert master, pers. mgr., 1974-2003, violinst, violist, Contemporary Chamber Players U. Chog., 1964-82, solo violinist, Bach Soc., 1966-83; violist, violinist, Lexington String Quartet, 1966-81; rec. artist numerous recs., radio-TV and films; solo violinist appearing throughout U.S. Recipient Olive Ditson award Franklin Honor Soc., 1961 Mem. Nat. Acad. Rec. Arts and Scis. Republican. Roman Catholic. Home: 1600 Old Pecos Trail Santa Fe NM 87505 E-mail: jdzm@aol.com.

ZOBELL, CHARLES W., newspaper managing editor; b. Provo, Utah, Mar. 17, 1950; m. Marilyn M. Earl, May 5, 1978; children: David, Rebecca. BA in Comm., Brigham Young U., 1974. Reporter Las Vegas Rev.-Jour., 1975-78; dir. Office Intergovtl. Rels. City of Las Vegas, 1978-80; city editor Las Vegas Rev.-Jour., 1980-92, mng. editor, 1992—. Vol. rep. Mormon Ch., Argentina, 2 yrs. Office: Las Vegas Review Jour Donrey Med Grp PO Box 70 1111 W Bonanza Rd Las Vegas NV 89125

ZOE, RACHEL (RACHEL ZOE ROSENZWEIG), fashion stylist; b. NYC, Sept. 1, 1971; m. Rodger Berman. Grad., George Washington U., 1993. With YM Mag.; fashion stylist for various celebrities including Cameron Diaz, Kate Beckinsale, Jennifer Garner, Paris Hilton, Keira Knightley; fashion stylist to Nicole Richie, 2004—06. TV appearances The Simple Life, 2006, Project Runway, 2006; exec. prodr.: (TV series) The Rachel Zoe Project, 2008—.

ZOHN, MARTIN STEVEN, lawyer; b. Denver, Oct. 22, 1947; s. William and Alice Zohn; m. Carol Falender, June 6, 1980; children: David Joseph, Daniel Robert. BA, Ind. U., 1969; JD, Harvard U., 1972. Bar: Calif. 1972, Ind. 1973, US Ct. Claims 1980, US Supreme Ct. 1980, US Ct. Appeals (9th cir.) 1981. Assoc. Cadick, Burns, Duck & Neighbors, Indpls., 1972-77, ptnr., 1977-80, Pacht, Ross, Warne, Bernhard & Sears, Inc., LA, 1980-86, Shea & Gould, LA, 1986-89, Proskauer Rose LLP, LA, 1989—. Pres. Indpls. Settlements, Inc., 1977-79. Bd. dirs. Pub. Counsel, 2001—, treas., 05, sec., 06, vice chair, 07. Mem. Fin. Lawyers Conf. (mem. bd. govs. 2007, sec. 2008), LA County Bar Assn. (exec. com. prejudgment remedies sect. 1985-92, exec. com. bankruptcy sect. 2001—), Beverly Hills Bar Assn. (exec. com. bus. law sect. 1985-92, exec. com. bankruptcy sect. 2003—), Phi Beta Kappa. Office Phone: 310-284-5648. Business E-Mail: mzohn@proskauer.com.

ZOOK, JOHN EDWIN, surgeon; b. Tabor, Iowa, Oct. 3, 1924; s. Abram Eyster Zook and Eunice (Francis) Brenneman; m. Jeanne Pierson, Sept. 7, 1952; children: Rebecca Clair, Daniel John, Paul Michael. BA, Lewis and Clark Coll., 1950; MD, U. Oreg., 1954. Cert. in tropical medicine Antwerp Sch. Tropical Medicine, Belgium, 1956, diplomate Am. Bd. Surgery. Intern Emanuel Hosp., Portland, Oreg., 1954—55; dir. med. activities Africa Intermennonite Mission, Republic of the Congo, 1961—65, surgeon, 1969—77; resident surgery Good Samaritan Hosp., Portland, 1965—69; pvt. practice medicine specializing in gen. surgery Portland, 1977—2005; chief staff Mt. Hood Med. Ctr., 1982; exchange physician China Ednl. Exchange Program, Chungquin Med. Coll., 1984—90; chief staff Woodland Pk. Hosp., 1989. Mem. bd. dirs., 1988—91. Ednl. missionary Unevangelized Tribes Mission, Republic of the Congo, 1943—46; med. missionary Congo Inland Mission, 1955—65; v.p. Mennonite Men of Mennonite Ch., 1982—. Fellow: ACS; mem.: Portland Surg. Soc., Internat. Coll. Surgeons (Oreg. regent 1980—84, v.p. 1985). Republican. Office: E Portland Surg Clinic 25500 SE Stark St Gresham OR 97030 Home Phone: 503-257-5190. Personal E-mail: jeannezook123@msn.com.

ZSCHAU, ED, former congressman; b. Omaha, Jan. 6, 1940; s. Ernest and Alice Fay Z.; m. JoAnn Weidmann. AB cum laude in Philosophy, Princeton U., 1961; MBA, Stanford U., 1963, MS in Statistics, 1964, PhD in Bus. Adminstrn., 1967. Asst. prof. Stanford U., 1963-68; vis. asst. prof. Harvard Bus. Sch., 1967-68; founder & CEO System Industries, 1968-82; mem. 98th and 99th Congress from 12th Dist. Calif., 1982—86; gen. ptnr. Brentwood Assocs, LA, 1987—88; chmn. & CEO Censtor Corp., 1988—93; gen. mgr. IBM Storage Systems Div., 1993—95; founder & chmn. emeritus Tech. Museum of Innovation, San Jose, Calif., 1990—. Co-chmn. Pres. Reagan's Bus. Adv. Panel, 1980; mem. Pres. Reagan's Task Force on Entrepreneurship and Innovation, 1980; del. White House Conf. on Small Bus., 1980; chmn. bd. San Francisco Bay Area High Tech. Sci. Ctr., 1983. Named Bus. Leader of Yr. Santa Clara Country Bus. Mag., 1978 Mem. Am. Electronics Assn. (dir. 1974-79), Am. Council Capital Formation (dir. 1979-80) Republican. Mailing: PO Box 7391 Menlo Park CA 94026-7391

ZSCHAU, MARILYN, singer; b. Chgo., Feb. 9, 1944; d. Edwin Arthur Eugene and Helen Elizabeth (Kelly) Z.; m. Frans Baars, Sept. 2005. BA in Radio, TV and Motion Pictures, U. N.C., 1959; grad., Juilliard Sch. Music, 1965; studied opera theatre with Christopher West, studied voice with Florence Page Kimball, studied with John Lester. Toured with Met. Nat. Co., 1965-66; debut, Vienna Volksoper, in Die Tote Stadt, 1967, Vienna Staatsoper, in Ariadne auf Naxos, 1971; with N.Y.C. Opera in La Fanciulla del West, 1978; debut Royal Opera, covent Garden in La Boheme, 1982, Met. Opera, in La Boheme, 1985, La Scala, in Die Frau ohne Schatten, 1986; has toured and sung in many countries including S.Am., Japan, and Australia. Office: 4245 Wilshire Blvd Oakland CA 94602-3549 Home Phone: 510-336-9269; Office Phone: 510-484-7742. E-mail: marilynzschau@yahoo.com.

ZSIGMOND, VILMOS, cinematographer, film director; b. Szeged, Hungary, June 16, 1930; came to U.S., 1957, naturalized, 1962; s. Vilmos and Bozena (Illichmann) Z.; children: Julia, Susi. MA, U. Film and Theater Arts, Budapest, Hungary, 1955. Free-lance cinematographer for numerous commls., also ednl., documentary and low-budget feature films, 1965-71; now dir., cinematographer on commls. (winner several nat. and internat. awards); feature films, 1971-; films include McCabe and Mrs. Miller, 1971; Images, 1972, Deliverance, 1972, The Long Goodbye, 1973, Scarecrow, 1973, Cinderella Liberty, 1973, The Sugarland Express, 1974, Obsession, 1976, Close Encounters of the Third Kind, 1977 (Acad. award 1977), The Last Waltz, 1978, The Rose, 1978, The Deerhunter, 1978 (Acad. award nomination and Brit. Acad. award), Heavens Gate, 1979, The Border, 1980, Blow Out, 1980, Jinxed, 1981, Table for Five, 1982, The River, 1983 (Acad. award nomination), No Small Affair, 1984, Real Genius, 1985, Witches of Eastwick, 1986, Journey to Spirit Island, 1988, Fatman and Little Boy, 1989, Two Jakes, 1989, Bonfire of the Vanities, 1990, Stalin, 1991 (CableAce award, Direction of Photography and/or Lighting Direction in a Dramatic/Theatrical Special/Movie or Miniseries, ASC award, Emmy award), Sliver, 1992; dir. The Long Shadow, 1992, Intersection, 1993, Maverick, 1993, The Crossing Guard, 1994, Assassins, 1995, The Ghost and the Darkness, 1996 (ASC Award nomination), Fantasy for a New Age, 1997, Playing By Heart, 1998, The Body, 1999, The Mists of Avalon, 2000, Life as a House, 2001, (opera film) Bánk Bán, 2002, Jersey Girl, 2003, Melinda and Melinda, 2004, The Black Dahlia, 2005. Recipient lifetime achievement award Worldfest, Flagstaff, 1998. Mem. Acad. Motion Picture Arts and Scis., Dirs. Guild, Am. Soc. Cinematographers (lifetime achievement award 1998). Home Phone: 310-305-8258; Office Phone: 818-753-6300. Personal E-mail: vilmoszsigmond@hotmail.com. Business E-Mail: patty@themackagency.net.

ZUBRIN, JAY ROSS, surgeon; b. Phila., June 11, 1936; BS, Dickinson Coll., 1959; MD, Temple U., 1963. Diplomate Am. Bd. Surgery. Intern San Francisco Gen. Hosp., 1963-64; resident in gen. surgery U. Calif. Med. Ctr., 1964-69; pvt. practice; chief of staff Hoag Meml. Hosp. Presbyn., Newport Beach, Calif. Mem. ACS, AMA, Calif. Med Assn., Orange County Med. Assn. (pres. 2005-06). Office: Ste 601 351 Hospital Rd Newport Beach CA 92663-3500 Office Phone: 949-548-2264. Office Fax: 949-650-3606. Business E-Mail: JZubrin@hoaghospital.org.

ZUCKER, JEFFREY A., broadcast executive; b. Homestead, Fla., Apr. 9, 1965; m. Caryn Stephanie Nathanson, 1996; children: Andrew, Elizabeth, Peter. BA in Am. History, Harvard Coll., 1986. Rschr., 1988 Olympic Games, Seoul, Korea NBC Sports, 1986—88; field prodr. NBC News, 1989; exec. prodr. Today, 1992—93, Now with Tom Brokaw and Katie Couric, NBC Nightly News with Tom Brokaw, 1993, Today, 1994—2000; pres. NBC Entertainment, 2000—03, NBC Entertainment, News and Cable Group, 2003—05; CEO NBC Universal TV, 2005—07; pres., CEO NBC Universal, 2007—. Exec. prodr.: (news segments) Russian coup, 1991, Persian Gulf War, 1991, 1993 and 1997 presdl. inaugurations, the bombing of Centennial Olympic Pk., 1996, 1996 and 2000 polit. conventions, Decision 2000; writer: The Games of the XXIV Olympiad (Emmy award, outstanding writing, 1988); supervising prodr.: "Senator Edward Kennedy" Today (Emmy award, outstanding interview, 1991); exec. prodr.: "California Fire" Now with Tom Brokaw and Katie Couric (Emmy award, outstanding coverage of a single breaking news story, 1993), "Tragedy in Rwanda" Now with Tom Brokaw and Katie Couric (Emmy award, outstanding background/analysis of a single current story, 1994), "The Brain" Now with Tom Brokaw and Katie Couric (Emmy award, outstanding informational or cultural program, 1994). Jewish. Office: NBC 3000 W Alameda Ave Burbank CA 91523-0002 also: NBC Universal 52nd Fl 30 Rockefeller Plz New York NY 10112*

ZUCKERBERG, MARK ELLIOT, Internet company executive, entrepreneur, programmer; b. Dobbs Ferry, NY, May 14, 1984; Attended, Harvard U. Co-founder, CEO Facebook, Inc., Palo Alto, Calif., 2004—. Named Media Achiever of Yr., Campaign Media Awards, 2007, Most Influential Person in High Tech. Industry, Agenda Setters, 2007, Best Start-up CEO, CrunchBase, 2007; named one of 50 Who Matter Now, Business 2.0, 2006, The 100 Most Influential People in the World, TIME mag., 2008, Top 25 Web Celebs, Forbes mag., 2007; named to 50 Most Interesting List, Creativity mag., 2008. Achievements include development of one of the most widely used networking websites among college and high school students throughout the US, Canada and Europe; being the youngest ever self-made billionaire. Office: Facebook Inc 156 University Ave Ste 300 Palo Alto CA 94301-1631

ZUICHES, JAMES JOSEPH, sociologist, educator; b. Eau Claire, Wis., Mar. 24, 1943; s. William Homer and Bronnie Monica (Stich) Z.; m. Carol Ann Kurilo, Aug. 19, 1967; children:; James Daniel, Joseph Kurilo. BA in Philosophy, U. Portland, 1967; MS in Sociology, U. Wis., 1969, PhD in Sociology, 1973. Instr., asst. prof., assoc. prof. sociology Mich. State U., East Lansing, 1971-82, prof., 1982; assoc. program dir. in sociology NSF, Washington, 1979-80, program dir. in sociology, 1980-82; assoc. dir. rsch. Cornell U., Ithaca, N.Y., 1982-86; assoc. dean Coll. Agr. and Home Econs., Wash. State U., Pullman, 1986-94, dir. Agrl. Rsch. Ctr., 1986-94; program dir. food sys. and rural devel. W.K. Kellogg Found., Battle Creek, Mich., 1994-95; dean Coll. Agr. and Home Econs. Wash. State U., Pullman, 1995—2003, prof. Dept. Cmty. and Rural Sociology, 1986—. Mem. adv. subcom. NSF, 1977-79; sci. adv. com. USDA Nat. Rsch. Initiative, Washington, 1992-93; com. on future land grant univ. bd. on agr., NRC, Washington, 1994-96; pub. Wash. Land and People Mag., 1987-92; mem. Bd. Natural Resources, Wash. State, 1995-2003. Co-editor: The Demography of Rural Life, 1993; contbr. articles to profl. jours. Pres., bd. dirs. Edgewood Village Children's Ctr., East Lansing, 1978-79. Recipient sustained superior performance award NSF, 1981; rsch. grantee NIMH, 1973, ERDA, 1978. Fellow AAAS; mem. Rural Sociol. Soc. (pres. 1992-93, editor 50th Anniversary Rsch. Series, 5 vols. 1988-93), Am. Sociol. Assn., Population Assn. Am. Roman Catholic. Avocations: skiing, swimming, hiking, reading. Office Phone: 509-335-8540.

ZUKER, CHARLES S., neuroscientist, biology professor; PhD, MIT. Investigator Howard Hughes Medical Inst.; prof. biology & neurosciences U. Calif., San Diego, 1986—. Scientific advisor Avalon Ventures; scientific co-founder Aurora Biosciences, 1995, Senomyx, Inc., 1999; mem. scientific adv. bd. Ambit Biosciences, CMEA Ventures. Recipient Alcon award, AAAS, 1999, Gogan award, 2000; fellow, Jane Coffin, U. Calif. Berkeley, Whitaker Health Scis. Found., MIT. Mem.: Am. Acad. Arts and Scis., Nat. Acad. Scis.

ZUMWALT, ROGER CARL, hospital administrator, healthcare consultant; b. Eugene, Oreg., Oct. 26, 1943; s. Robert Walter and Jean Elaine (Adams) Z.; children: Kathryn Nicole Zumwalt DeWeber, Timothy Robert Zumwalt. Student, Boise State U., 1963—65; BA, We. Oreg. U., 1969; postgrad., U. Iowa, 1969—71; MA cum laude, Oreg. State U., 1973. Adminstr. Coulee Cmty. Hosp., Grand Coulee, Wash., 1973-75; exec. dir. Eastmoreland Hosp., Portland, Oreg., 1975—81, Cmty. Hosp., Grand Junction, Colo., 1981-97; pres., healthcare cons. accreditation Zumwalt Consulting, Salem, Oreg., 1997—; dir. adminstrv. svcs. divsn. SAIF Corp., Salem, 1998—2008. Chmn., bd. dirs. Alphabet House Pediat. Rehab. and Edn., 1998—2000, Castle Rock Med. Group, Inc., Denver, 1998—2003; part owner, chmn. bd. dirs. Castle Rock Med. Ctr., Colo., 1998—, N.W. Okla. Regional Med. Ctr. Cherokee, 2000; spkr. numerous local and nat. presentations, subjects including healthcare, hosp. mktg./success/costs, 1981—97; guest lectr. Mesa State Coll., 1992—98, Colo. Christian Coll., 1996—98. Newspaper columnist, 1973-75; contbr. articles, presentations to profl. publs. Commr. Multnomah County Health Care Commn., Portland, Oreg., 1978-81; health cons. Grant County Housing Auth., Grand Coulee, 1974-75; mem. pk. bd. City of Tigard, Oreg., 1976-78; caucus rep. Mesa County Rep. Party, Grand Junction, 1988; mem. adv. com., pres.'s office Mesa State Coll., Grand Junction, 1989; bd. dirs. Hospice of Grand Valley, Grand Junction, 1992-97, mem. devel. com., 1993-97, vice chmn. bd. dirs., 1994-97; bd. dirs. Grand Valley Hospice, 1992-96; com. mem. Salem Coalition on Youth Literacy, 2000—. Fellow Coll. Osteo. Healthcare Execs. (bd. dirs. 1985-88, pres. 1987, examiner 1989—, Disting. Svc. award 1989); mem. Am. Osteo. Healthcare Assn. (bd. dirs. 1987-98, treas. 1992-93, 1st v.p. 1994-95, 2d v.p. 1993-94, vice chairperson 1994-95, chmn. 1996-97, chairperson 1997-98, past chmn. 1998), Am. Osteo. Assn. (ex-officio mem. bd. dirs. 1996), Bur. Healthcare Facilities Accreditation (v.p. 1994, advisor 1995-98, accreditation cons. 1995—, accreditation surveyer 1978—, accreditation survey instr. 1994—), Joint Commn. on Am. Healthcare Orgn. (task force on small and rural hosps. 1994-98), Colo. Hosp. Assn. (bd. dirs. 1987-92), Mountain States Vol. Hosp. Assn. (bd. dirs. 1984-98, exec. com. 1991-98, v.p. 1993, vice chmn. bd. dirs. 1992-98), We. Coll. Ind. Practice Assn. (Medicine Mauls Measles com., fin. com. 1991-92), We. Colo. Health Care Alliance (bd. dirs. 1989-94, v.p. 1992, chmn. bd. dirs. 1993), Mesa County Mental Health Assn. (bd. dirs. 1988-89, 91-92), Grand Junction C. of C. (bd. dirs. 1991-93), Rotary (Grand Coolee, Wash. 1973-75, Portland 1975-81, Grand Junction 1981-98, Salem 1998—, chmn. fund raising com. 2000-01, bd. dirs. 2001-02), Western Oreg. U. Alumni Assn. (bd. dirs. 2006—, v.p. bd. dirs. 2006-07, pres.-elect 2007-08, pres., 2008-), Masons, Shriners (pres. Grand Junction club 1989, bd. dirs. El Jebel 1986-90, 1st v.p. Western Colo. club 1989, pres. 1990-91), KC. Republican. Roman Catholic. Avocations: golf, camping, fishing, travel. Home and Office: 592 Meadowbrook Ln Stayton OR 97383-1465 E-mail: rogzum@netzero.net.

ZUMWALT, ROSS EUGENE, forensic pathologist, educator; b. Goodrich, Mich., July 18, 1943; s. Paul Lawrence and Lila Ann (Birky) Z.; m. Theresa Ann Schar, Sept. 12, 1970 (div. Apr. 1988); children: Christopher Todd, Tenley Ann; m. Cheryl Lynn Willman, Sept. 4, 1988; 1 child, David Willman Zumwalt. BA, Wabash Coll., 1967; MD, U. Ill., 1971. Diplomate in anat. and forensic pathology Am. Bd. Pathology. Intern, resident in pathology Mary Bassett Hosp., Cooperstown, NY, 1971-73; resident in anat. and forensic pathology Southwestern Med. Sch., Dallas, 1973-76; asst. med. examiner Dallas County, Dallas, 1974-76; staff pathologist, dir. labs. Naval Regional Med. Ctr., Camp Lejeune, NC, 1976-78; dep. coroner Cuyahoga County, Cleve., 1978-80, Hamilton County, Cin., 1980-86; assoc. prof. pathology U. Cin. Sch. Medicine, 1980-86; prof. pathology U. N.Mex. Sch. Medicine, Albuquerque, 1987—; chief med. investigator Office of Med. Investigator, Albuquerque, 1991—; pres. Am. Bd. of Pathology, Tampa, 2000—01. Trustee Am. Bd. Pathology, Tampa, Fla., 1993-2004. Lt. comdr. USN, 1976-78. Fellow Am. Acad. Forensic Scis., Coll. Am. Pathologists; mem. AMA, Nat. Assn. Med. Examiners (bd. dirs. 1984-96, pres. 1995-96), Am. Soc. Clin. Pathologists, Am. and Can. Acad. Pathologists. Avocation: golf. Home Phone: 505-344-7480; Office Phone: 505-272-0710. Business E-Mail: rzumwalt@salud.unm.edu.

ZUNGER, ALEX, research scientist; BSc, MSc, Tel Aviv U., PhD in chemical physics, 1976. Post doctoral Northwestern U., 1975—77; IBM fellow U. of Calif., 1977—78; prin. scientist Nat. Renewable Energy Lab., 1984—91, inst. rsch. fellow, 1991—. Founder and head Nat. Renewable Energy Lab., Solid State Theory Group, 1978—; adj. prof. physics U. of Colo. at Boulder. Contbr. 400 jour. pubs. including over 85 in phys. rev. letters and rapid comm. Recipient John Bardeen award, 2001, Annesur Rahman award, Am. Physical Soc., 2001, DOE-BES award for sustained rsch. in solid state physics, 1997, Outstanding achievement award, IBM fellowship, 1980; named the 39th most cited physicist out of more than 500,000 physicists examined, Inst. of Sci. Info. Office: Nat Renewable Energy Lab Mail Stop 3213 OfficeSERF/W1009 Ctr 5900 1617 Cole Blvd Golden CO 80401

ZURZOLO, VINCENT P., federal judge; b. 1956; BA, U. Calif., San Diego, 1978; JD, U. Calif., Davis, 1982. With Greenberg, Glusker, Fields, Claman & Machtinger, LA; apptd. bankruptcy judge cen. dist. U.S. Dist. Ct. Calif., 1988. Mem. ABA, Nat. Conf. Bankruptcy Judges, Fin. Lawyers Conf., L.A. County Bar Assn. (bankruptcy com. of comml. law and bankruptcy sect.). Office: 1360 Roybal Federal Bldg 255 E Temple St Los Angeles CA 90012-3334

ZUSSY, NANCY LOUISE, librarian; b. Tampa, Fla., Mar. 4, 1947; d. John David and Patsy Ruth (Stone) Roche; m. R. Mark Allen, Dec. 20, 1986. BA in Edn., U. Fla., 1969; MLS, U. So. Fla., 1977, MS in Pub. Mgmt., 1980. Cert. librarian, Wash. Ednl. evaluator State of Ga., Atlanta, 1969-70; media specialist DeKalb County Schs., Decatur, Ga., 1970-71; researcher Ga. State Libr., Atlanta, 1971; asst. to dir. reference Clearwater (Fla.) Pub. Libr., 1972-78, dir. librs., 1978-81; dep. state libr. Wash. State Libr., Olympia, 1981-86, state libr., 1986—2002; owner Nancy Zussy Allen Massage Therapy, 2003—. Chmn. Consortium Automated Librs., Olympia, 1982-97; cons. various pub. librs., Wash. and other U.S. states, Uzbekistan, Russia, 1981—; exec. officer Wash. Libr. Network, 1986-90; v.p. WLN (non-profit orgn.), 1990-93. Contbr. articles to profl. jours. Treas. Thurston-Mason Community Mental Health Bd., Olympia, 1983-85, bd. dirs., 1982-85; mem. race com. Seafair Hydroplane Race, Seattle, 1986—, mem. milk carton derby team, 1994—, announcer, prodr. air show; co-chair Pub. Info. Access Policy Task Force, 1995-96; mem. Gov.'s Work Group on Comml. Access to Govt. Electronic Records, 1996-97; mem. K-20 Telecomms. Oversight and Policy Com., 1996-2002. Mem. ALA, Assn. Specialized and Coop. Libr. Agys. (legis.

com. 1983-86, chmn. 1985-87, vice chmn. state libr. agys. sect. 1985-86, chmn. 1986-87, chmn. govt. affairs com. Libr. Adminstrn. and Mgmt. Assn., 1986-87), Freedom To Read Found. (bd. dirs. 1987-91), Chief Officers of State Libr. Agys. (bd. dirs.-at-large 1987-90, v.p., pres.-elect 1990-92, pres. 1992-94), Wash. Libr. Assn. (co-founder legis. planning com. 1982-2002, fed. rels. coord. 1984-2002), Fla. Libr. Assn. (legis. and planning com. 1978-81), Pacific N.W. Libr. Assn., Rotary (bd. dirs. 1995-96), Phi Kappa Phi, Phi Beta Mu. Avocations: hiking, barbershop quartets, boating, cross country skiing. Office: Nancy Zussy Allen Massage Th 2639 Parkmont Ln SW Ste A2 Olympia WA 98502-1165

ZWEIFEL, DONALD EDWIN, editor, lobbyist, consultant; b. LA, Nov. 30, 1940; s. Robert Fredrick and Eugenia Bedford (White) Z.; m. Donna Jean Croslin; 1 son, Phillip Matthew. Student, Orange Coast Coll., 1963-67, 90-92, U. Calif., Irvine, 1968-70, Western State U. Coll. Law, 1973, Irvine U. Coll. Law, 1974-75, Rancho Santiago Jr. Coll., 1988, Chapman U., 1993—97; grad., Aviation Ground Sch., 1990; student, USAF Air U., 1994—95, USAF Air. U., 2000—01. Cert. student pilot, registered lobbyist Calif. State Legislature. Devel. tech. Hughes Aircraft, Newport Beach, Calif., 1963-64; co-founder, station mgr. Sta. KUCI-FM, Irvine, Calif., 1970; owner, mgr. Zweifel Jaguar Car Sales and Svc., Santa Ana, Calif., 1975-76; pres. Zweifel & Assocs. Inc., Santa Ana, 1977-86, Zweifel South Coast Exotic Cars, Orange, Calif., 1987-96, ret., 1996; assoc. editor, cons. Compliance News Pub. Co., Long Beach, Calif., 1998—. Mem. small bus. coun. CalTrans, 2000—; legis. com., small bus. adv. coun. Calif. Dept. Gen. Svcs., 2005—; environ. air and water quality com. Associated Gen. Contractors, 2007—, mem. Regulatory and Environ. Task Force, Calif., 2007—. Co-author: Challenge 2000, Regaining the America's Cup, 1996; editor: (coll. textbook) The Dream Is Alive, Space Flight and Operations In Earth Orbit. Vol. emergency coord. emergency mgmt. divsn. Orange County Fire Authority, 1985-87, Navy Relief Soc., 1993, 1st. lt. CAP Squadron 88 Group VII, 1993-95, sr. programs officer, 1993-94, asst. transp. officer Calif. Wing Hdqrs., 1994-95, Group VII Facilities officer, 1994-95, 2000-02, squadron pers. officer, 1993-95, 2000-02, Calif. wing rep. to Orange County Vol. Orgns. Active in Disaster, ARC, 1994-95, Calif. wing vol. Office Emergency Svcs., Calif., 1994-96, 2000-21, grad. Squadron Leadership Sch., 1993, Wing Supply Officers Sch., 1995, squadron safety officer, pub. affairs officer, asst. aerospace edn. officer, 1998-2001; program coord. Young Astronaut Coun., 1989-90; cadet CAP, USAF aux., Long Beach, Calif., 1953-59; mem. Orange County Homeless Issues Taskforce, 1994-95, 1997-2000, Orange County Homeless Svc. Providers for the Reuse of Marine Corps Air Sta., Tustin, Calif., 1994-95; legis. com. Orange County Vets. Adv. Coun., 1998-2006; chmn. tech. rev. subcom. Marine Corps Air Sta., El Toro, Calif., 1998-2001; apptd. to CalEPA DTSC Adv. Group Mil. Base Closure, 1995-99, CalEPA Dept. Toxic Substances Control Adv. Group pro-bono cons., Orange County Citizen's Adv. Commn. and El Toro Local Redevel. Authority, 1996-2001; vol. mediator Victim-Offender Reconciliation program, 1995-96; restoration adv. bd. MCAS Tustin, 1994—, co-chair, 2003—; restoration adv. bd. MCAS, El Toro, Calif., 1994—; active Freedom Com. of Orange County; cmty. emergency response team City of Placentia, 2003—; homeless vets. com. United Vets. Orgn. Orange County; fed. advocate for Disabled Veteran Bus. Enterprise, 2004; dir. Orange County Walk of Honor, 1998 With U.S. Army Nat. Guard, 1958—59. Recipient 6 certs. achievement Fed. Emergency Mgmt. Agy., 1989-96, 2 certs. appreciation CAP, 2 certs commendation, 1994, cert. appreciation Southwest Divsn. Naval Facilities Engring. Commd., 2000, Meritorious Svc. award, Calif. State Assembly Restoration Adv. Bd. Assemblyman John Campbell, 2001. Mem. Air Force Assn. (vice-chmn. civilian recruitment Calif. state membership com. 1988-91, v.p. govt. rels. Calif. 2006—, v.p. membership, Gen. Doolittle chpt. bd. dirs. 1987-89, 90-92, dir. Gen. Jimmy Doolittle chpt. 2005—, Exceptional Svc. award Gen. Jimmy Doolittle chpt. 1988, 91, Calif. Meritorious Svc. award 1988, v.p. membership Gen. Curtis E. LeMay Orange County chpt. 2000-02, 2004), Calif. Assn. for Aerospace Edn. (fellow), Marine Corps Hist. Found. (life), Aerospace Edn. Found. (Gen. Jimmy Doolittle fellow 1988, Gen. Ira Eaker fellow 1989, Pres.'s award 1988), US Naval Inst., AIAA (Cert. of Appreciation 1989, LA chpt. hist. com. 1989), Gulf & Vietnam Vets. Strategic Studies Archives (cons., co-founder 1983—, dir.), Marine Corps League (assoc., capt. Heinsey detachment 2000-02), Confederate Air Force (col.1989), AmVets (nat. jr. coord. com. 2003-05, Calif. jr. coord. 2003-04, 2d vice comdr. dist. II, Dept. Calif 2003-04, 1st vice comdr. dist. 2004-05, 2d vice-comdr. post 18 2006—, So. Calif. JROTC awards coord. 2007—), Masons, Saddleback Master Chorale of Orange County. Avocations: sailing, travel, flying. Personal E-mail: dzweifel@sbcglobal.net.

ZWERDLING, ALEX, language educator; b. Breslau, Germany, June 21, 1932; came to U.S., 1941, naturalized, 1946; s. Norbert and Fanni (Alt) Z.; m. Florence Goldberg, Mar. 23, 1969; 1 son, Antony Daniel. BA, Cornell U., 1953; postgrad. (Fulbright scholar), U. Munich, Germany, 1953-54; MA, Princeton U., 1956, PhD, 1960. Instr. English Swarthmore Coll., 1957-61; asst. prof. English U. Calif., Berkeley, 1961-67, asso. prof., 1967-73, prof., 1973-86, prof. English Berkeley, 1988—, chmn. grad. studies, 1985-86; univ. prof. George Washington U., 1986-88. Vis. prof. Northwestern U., 1977; dir. edn. abroad program U. Calif., London, 1996-98; mem. advanced placement exam. com. Ednl. Testing Svc., 1975-79; mem. fellowship panel Nat. Endowment for Humanities, 1977-82, 84-87, Nat. Humanities Ctr., 1989-90; fellow Ctr. for Advanced Study in Behavioral Scis., 1964-65. Author: Yeats and the Heroic Ideal, 1965, Orwell and the Left, 1974, Virginia Woolf and the Real World, 1986, Improvised Europeans: American Literary Expatriates and the Siege of London, 1998; mem. adv. com. PMLA, 1978-82. Recipient Berkeley citation U. Calif., Berkeley, 2003; Am. Coun. Learned Socs. fellow, 1964-65; NEH fellow, 1973-74; Guggenheim fellow, 1977-78; Woodrow Wilson Ctr. fellow, 1991-92, fellow Nat. Humanities Ctr., 1992-93. Mem. MLA (chmn. 20th Century Brit. lit. div. 1969-70, 85-86). Office: U Calif Dept English Berkeley CA 94720-1030

ZWOYER, EUGENE MILTON, retired consulting engineering executive; b. Plainfield, NJ, Sept. 8, 1926; s. Paul Ellsworth and Marie Susan (Britt) Z.; m. Dorothy Lucille Seward, Feb. 23, 1946; children: Gregory, Jeffrey, Douglas. Student, U. Notre Dame, 1944, Mo. Valley Coll., 1944-45; BS, U. N.Mex., 1947; MS, Ill. Inst. Tech., 1949; PhD, U. Ill., 1953. Mem. faculty U. N.Mex., Albuquerque, 1948-71, prof. civil engring., dir. Eric Wang Civil Engring. Rsch. Facility, 1961-70; rsch. assoc. U. Ill., Urbana, 1951-53; owner, cons. engr. Eugene Zwoyer & Assocs., Albuquerque, 1954-72; exec. dir., sec. ASCE, NYC, 1972-82; pres. Am. Assn. Engring. Socs., NYC, 1982-84; exec. v.p. T.Y. Lin Internat., San Francisco, 1984-86, pres., 1986-89; owner Eugene Zwoyer Cons. Engr., 1989—2002; COO, treas. Polar Molecular Corp., Saginaw, Mich., 1990, exec. v.p., 1991-92; ret., 2002. Trustee Small Bus. Research Corp., 1976-80; trustee Engring. Info., Inc., 1981-84; internat. trustee People-to-People Internat. 1974-86; v.p. World Fedn. Engring. Orgns., 1982-85. Served to lt. (j.g.) USN, 1944-46. Named Outstanding Engr. of Yr. Albuquerque chpt. N.Mex Soc. Profl. Engrs., 1969, One Who Served the Best Interests of the Constrn. Industry, Engring. News Record, 1980; recipient Disting. Alumnus award the Civil Engring. Alumni Assn. at U. Ill., 1979, Disting. Alumnus award Engring. Coll. Alumni Assn., U. N.Mex., 1982, Can.-Am. Civil Engring. Amity award Am. Soc. Civil Engrs., 1988, Award for Outstanding Profl. Contbns. and Leadership Coll. Engring. U. N.Mex., 1989 Mem. AAAS, ASCE (dist. bd. dirs. 1968-71), NSPE, AFTRA, Am. Soc. Engring. Edn., Nat. Acad. Code Adminstrn. (trustee, mem. exec. com. 1973-79), Engrs. Joint Coun. (bd. dirs. 1978-79), Engring. Soc. Commn. on Energy (bd. dirs. 1977-82), Sigma Xi, Sigma Tau, Chi Epsilon. Home: 6363 Christie Ave Apt 1326 Emeryville CA 94608-1940 E-mail: eugenezwoyer@comcast.net.

ZYGOCKI, RHONDA I., oil industry executive; b. St. John's, Nfld., Can., July 1957; B. in Civil Engring., Meml. U. Nfld., 1980. Petroleum engr. Chevron Can. Resources, Calgary, gen. mgr. strategic bus. svcs., 1993—94, CFO, 1997—99; profit ctr. mgr. Chevron USA Prodn. Co., Houston, 1994—97; mgr. strategic planning Chevron Corp., San Ramon, Calif., 1999—2000, adv. to bd. chmn., 2000—01, v.p. health, environment & safety, 2003—07, corp. v.p. policy, govt. & pub. affairs, 2007—; mng. dir. ChevronTexaco Australia Pty. Ltd., Perth, 2001—03. Bd. dirs. Internat. Petroleum Industry Environ. Conservation Assn., Internat. Assn. Oil & Gas. Bd. dirs. Engrs. Without Borders, Tiger Woods Learning Ctr. Office: Chevron Corp 6001 Bollinger Canyon Rd San Ramon CA 94583-2324

ZYSMAN, JOHN ADLER, political scientist, educator; b. Omaha, Mar. 23, 1946; s. Evelyn Zysman; m. Victoria Rehn; 1 child, Lara. PhD of Polit. Sci., MIT, Boston, MA, 1973; BA, Harvard Coll., 1968. Lectr. Dept. Polit. Sci. MIT, Boston, 1973—74; asst. prof. Dept. Polit. Sci. U. Calif.-Berkeley, 1974—82, assoc. prof. Dept. Polit. Sci., 1982—87, prof. Dept. Polit. Sci., 1987—; co-dir. Berkeley Roundtable on Internat. Economy, 1982—. Office: BRIE / Univ of California 2234 Piedmont Avenue Berkeley CA 94720-2322 Office Phone: 510-642-3067. Office Fax: 510-643-6617. Business E-Mail: johnz@socrates.berkeley.edu.

'rofessional Index

Chong, Richard David *architect*
Christopher, James Walker *architect, educator*
Miller, William Charles *architect, educator*

WASHINGTON

Mount Vernon
Hall, David Ramsay *architect*
Klein, Henry *architect*

Redmond
Sowder, Robert Robertson *architect*

Seattle
Bain, William James, Jr. *architect*
Bosworth, Thomas Lawrence *architect, retired educator*
Buursma, William F. *architect*
Jacobson, Phillip Lee *architect, educator*
Johnston, Norman John *retired architecture educator*
Jonassen, James O. *architect*
Jones, Grant Richard *landscape architect*
King, Indle Gifford *industrial designer, educator*
Kolb, Keith Robert *architect, educator*
Kundig, Tom *architect*
Lovett, Wendell Harper *architect, educator*
Malcolm, Garold Dean *architect*
Meyer, C. Richard *architect*
Miles, Don Clifford *architect*
Moudon, Anne Vernez *urban design educator*
Olson, James William Park *architect*
Piven, Peter Anthony *architect, management consultant*
Thomas, John Val *architect*

Tacoma
Liddle, Alan Curtis *retired architect*

CANADA

BRITISH COLUMBIA

Vancouver
Erickson, Arthur Charles *architect*

ADDRESS UNPUBLISHED

Blair, Frederick David *interior designer*
Bobrow, Michael Lawrence *architect*
Brotman, David Joel *architectural firm executive, consultant*
Dermanis, Paul Raymond *architect*
Feldhamer, Thelma Leah *retired architect*
Gerou, Phillip Howard *architect*
Hastings, L(ois) Jane *architect, educator*
Henderson, John Drews *architect*
Hinshaw, Mark Larson *architect, urban planner*
Hooper, Roger Fellowes *retired architect*
Mc Sheffrey, Gerald Rainey *architect, educator, city planner, author*
Moore, Richard Alan *landscape architect*
Naidorf, Louis Murray *architect*
Odermatt, Robert Allen *architect*
Peters, Robert Woolsey *retired architect*
Siefer, Stuart B. *architect*
Strong, Annsley Chapman *interior designer, volunteer*
Thiel, Philip *retired design educator*
Thistlethwaite, David Richard *architect*
Tomasi, Donald Charles *architect*
Woerner, Robert Lester *landscape architect*

ARTS: LITERARY *See also* COMMUNICATIONS MEDIA

UNITED STATES

ALASKA

Anchorage
Strohmeyer, John *writer, retired editor*
Thomas, Lowell, Jr. *writer, retired military officer, state senator*

ARIZONA

Phoenix
Ellison, Cyril Lee *literary agent, retired publishing executive*

Tempe
Raby, William Louis *writer, consultant*

Tucson
Williams, Joy *writer*
Young, Donald Allen *writer, consultant*

CALIFORNIA

Alamo
Reed, John Theodore *writer*

Aromas
Fleischman, Paul *children's author*

Atascadero
Locke, Virginia Otis *writer*

Berkeley
Hass, Robert Louis *poet, literature educator*
Katzen, Mollie *writer*
Masumoto, David Mas *writer, farmer*
Pollan, Michael *author, journalist, professor*

Beverly Hills
Apatow, Judd *scriptwriter, television and film producer*
Ball, Alan *screenwriter*
Black, Shane *screenwriter*
Chase, David (David DeCaesare) *scriptwriter, television director and producer*
Greenberg, Richard *playwright*
Groening, Matthew (Abram) *writer, cartoonist*
Kaufman, Charlie *scriptwriter*
Mandel, Babaloo *scriptwriter*
Mendelsohn, Daniel *writer, humanities professor*
Roth, Eric *screenwriter*
Schulian, John (Nielsen Schulian) *screenwriter, author*
Shanley, John Patrick *playwright, screenwriter*
Slade, Bernard *playwright*
Steinem, Gloria *writer, editor, advocate*
Ward, David Schad *scriptwriter, film director*
Wellins, Cori *literary agent*

Claremont
Wachtel, Albert *writer, educator*

Cromberg
Kolb, Ken Lloyd *writer*

Davis
Major, Clarence Lee *writer, painter, poet, educator*
McPherson, Sandra Jean *poet, educator*

Del Mar
Morton, Frederic *author*

Greenbrae
Carrel, Annette Felder *writer*

Hayward
Robinson, Curtis John *writer, educator, marketing professional, consultant*

Hillsborough
Atwood, Mary Sanford *writer*

Julian
Rice, Earle, Jr., (Earle Wilmont Rice Jr.) *writer*

La Jolla
Antin, David *poet, critic*

Lodi
Schulz, Laura Janet *writer, retired executive secretary*

Los Angeles
Daniels, Gregory Martin *screenwriter*
Gilroy, Tony *scriptwriter, film director*
Haggis, Paul Edward *scriptwriter, television producer, television director*
Highwater, Jamake *writer, educator*
Horta, Silvio *scriptwriter*
Jenkins, Tamara *scriptwriter, film director*
Koepp, David *screenwriter*
Lettich, Sheldon Bernard *director, screenwriter*
Manelli, Donald Dean *scriptwriter, film and television producer*
Meyers, Nancy Jane *screenwriter, producer, director*
Noguchi, Thomas Tsunetomi *writer, pathologist*
Sedaris, Amy *writer, actress*
Shagan, Steve *scriptwriter, film producer*
Shapiro, Mel *playwright, educator, theater director*
Steel, Ronald Lewis *writer, historian, educator*

Mendocino
Feehan, Christine *writer*

Newport Beach
Koontz, Dean Ray *writer*

Oakland
Foley, Jack (John Wayne Harold Foley) *poet, writer, editor-in-chief*
Kivel, Paul *writer*

Palm Springs
Wouk, Herman *writer*

Pasadena
Yeager, Caroline Hale *writer, retired radiologist, consultant*

Penngrove
Haslam, Gerald William *writer, educator*

Petaluma
Pronzini, Bill John (William Pronzini) *writer*
Spiegelman, Art *writer, cartoonist*

Playa Del Rey
McNeill, Daniel Richard *writer*

Pomona
Mezey, Robert *poet*

Rancho Santa Margarita
Shusterman, Neal Douglas *writer, scriptwriter*

San Diego
Doig, Ivan *writer*
Lederer, Richard Henry *writer, educator, columnist*
Mahdavi, Kamal B. (K. B. M.) *writer, researcher*

San Francisco
Rusher, William Allen *writer, commentator, columnist*

San Jose
Singh, Loren Chan *writer, educator*

San Rafael
Turner, William Weyand *writer*

Santa Barbara
Canfield, Jack *writer, speaker, trainer*
Poynter, Dan *author, publisher, speaker*

Santa Monica
Scott, Jill *poet, musician*

Stanford
Conquest, Robert (George Robert Acworth Conquest) *writer, historian, poet*
Djerassi, Carl *writer, retired chemistry professor*
Steele, Shelby *writer, educator*
Wolff, Tobias (Tobias Jonathan Ansell Wolff) *writer, English professor*

COLORADO

Boulder
Waldman, Anne Lesley *poet, performer, editor, publisher, educational administrator*

Crestone
Calloway, Larry *writer*

Denver
Dallas, Sandra *writer*
Ducker, Bruce *writer, lawyer*
MacGregor, George Lescher, Jr. *freelance/self-employed writer*
Nemiro, Beverly Mirium Anderson *author, educator*

IDAHO

Boise
Skurzynski, Gloria Joan *writer*

Sun Valley
Briley, John Richard *writer*

MONTANA

Bonner
Smith, Annick *writer*

Missoula
Haines, John Meade *poet, translator, writer*

NEW MEXICO

Albuquerque
Anaya, Rudolfo *writer, educator*
Priem, Richard Gregory *writer, executive*

Ranchos De Taos
Dickey, Robert Preston *writer, educator, poet*

Santa Fe
Momaday, Navarre Scott *writer, poet*

NEW YORK

New York
Balogh, Mary *writer*
Earling, Debra Magpie *writer, educator*
Hamilton, Laurell Kaye *writer*
Krantz, Judith Tarcher *novelist*
Murphy, Patrice Ann (Pat Murphy) *writer*

OREGON

Newport
Kennedy, Richard Jerome *writer*

Portland
Hoffman, Alice *writer*

UTAH

Salt Lake City
Osherow, Jacqueline Sue *poet, English language educator*

WASHINGTON

Kirkland
Szablya, Helen Mary *writer, language educator*

La Conner
Robbins, Thomas Eugene *writer*

Lynnwood
Bear, Gregory Dale *writer, illustrator*

Sammamish
Trask, Robert Riley Chauncey *writer, educa foundation administrator*

Seattle
Gardiner, John Jacob *writer, educator, philosopher*
Kenney, Richard Laurence *poet, English language educator*
Wagoner, David Russell *writer, educator*

Tacoma
Maynard, Steven Harry *writer*

Vashon
Cushman, Karen Lipski *writer*

WYOMING

Laramie
Boresi, Arthur Peter *writer, educator*

CANADA

BRITISH COLUMBIA

Vancouver
Bowering, George Harry *writer, consultant, language educator*
Cohen, Leonard (Norman Cohen) *poet, wri musician*
Tolle, Eckhart *writer*

ADDRESS UNPUBLISHED

Alinder, Mary Street *writer, educator*
Avery, Stephen Neal *playwright, writer*
Baird, Alan C. *screenwriter*
Bass, Ronald *screenwriter*
Bochco, Steven *screenwriter, television pro*
Bower, Janet Esther *writer, educator*
Burke, Jan Helene *writer*
Coonts, Stephen Paul *writer*
Cussler, Clive Eric *author*
Darabont, Frank *screenwriter, director*
David, Larry *television scriptwriter and producer, actor*
Davis, J. Alan *writer, film and television producer*
Egan, Timothy K. *writer, journalist*
Eglee, Charles Hamilton *scriptwriter, film television producer*
Farrelly, Bobby (Robert Leo Rarrelly Jr.) *scriptwriter, film director and producer*
Farrelly, Peter John *screenwriter*
Fraser, Kathleen Joy *poet, creative writing professor*
Fritz, Ethel Mae Hendrickson *writer*
Ganz, Lowell *scriptwriter, television produ*
Goldman, William *writer, scriptwriter*
Gray, Thomas Stephen *writer*
Haas, Charlie *screenwriter*
Herman, George Adam *writer, literature educator*
Hicks, David Earl *writer*
Kingston, Maxine Hong *writer, educator*
Larson, Erik *writer*
Lippard, Lucy Rowland *writer, educator, c curator*
Lopez, Barry Holstun *writer*
Madsen, Susan Arrington *writer*
Mazursky, Paul *screenwriter, theatrical dir and producer*
Mc Cann, Cecile Nelken *writer, artist*
McGee, Harold James *writer*
Mc Intyre, Vonda Neel *writer*
Medoff, Mark Howard *playwright, scriptw*
Miller, Carole Ann Lyons *writer, editor, publisher, marketing executive*
Mitchell, Laura Remson *public policy ana writer*
Mogel, Leonard Henry *writer*
Morrow, Barry Nelson *screenwriter, produ*
Parke, Marilyn Neils *writer*
Phillips, Jill Meta *writer, critic, astrologer*
Proulx, (Edna) Annie *writer*
Rubin, Bruce Joel *screenwriter, director, producer*
Rutsala, Vern A. *poet, writer, language edu*
Sackett, Susan Deanna *writer*
Salat, Cristina *writer*
Schenkkan, Robert Frederic *playwright, screenwriter*
Shepard, Sam (Samuel Shepard Rogers) *playwright, actor*
Shindler, Merrill Karsh *writer, radio perso*
Silverman, Treva *scriptwriter, television producer, consultant*
Tarn, Nathaniel *poet, educator, translator*
Vosevich, Kathi Ann *writer, editor*
Wolff, Geoffrey Ansell *writer, educator, cr*

Carolla, Adam *actor, radio personality, film producer, scriptwriter*
Carrey, Jim *actor*
Cates, Gilbert *television and film producer, theater director*
Cee-Lo, (Thomas DeCarlo Callaway) *singer*
Charles, Ray *musician, composer, lyricist, arranger, conductor*
Cheadle, Donald Frank *actor*
Clark, Dick *performer, producer*
Craig, Daniel *actor*
Craig, Sidney Richard *theatrical agent*
Crawford, Chace *actor*
Crockett, Donald Harold *composer, music educator*
Cruz, Penélope *actress*
D'Accone, Frank Anthony *music educator*
Daly, Timothy *actor*
Dane, Eric *actor*
Delson, Brad Phillip *musician*
Del Toro, Benicio *actor*
Dempsey, Patrick *actor*
Dennehy, Brian *actor*
De Palma, Brian Russell *film director*
Dillon, Kevin *actor*
Donaldson, Roger *film director, film producer*
Dr. Dre, (Andre Ramelle Young) *rap musician, record producer*
DuMont, James Kelton, Jr. *actor, theater producer*
Duritz, Adam *musician*
Eckhart, Aaron *actor*
Efron, Zac *actor, singer*
Elrod, Lu *music professor emerita, actress*
Farrell, David Michael *musician*
Farrell, Joseph *film producer and company executive, financial analyst*
Feinstein, Michael Jay *singer, pianist, musicologist, actor*
Ferrera, America Georgine *actress*
Firth, Colin Andrew *actor*
Flanagan, Fionnula Manon *actress, writer, theater director*
Fleischmann, Ernest Martin *performing arts executive, consultant*
Foley, James *film director*
Forte, Will (Orville Willis Forte IV) *actor, scriptwriter*
Gaviola, Karen Z. *television director*
Gere, Richard *actor*
Gugino, Carla *actress*
Hahn, Joseph *disc jockey, video director*
Hanks, Tom *actor, film producer, director*
Hardison, Kadeem *actor*
Harper, Hill (Frank Harper) *actor*
Harrelson, Woody *actor*
Hart, Mary *television talk show host*
Hartke, Stephen Paul *composer, educator*
Henley, Don *singer, drummer, songwriter*
Henson, Taraji Penda *actress*
Hill, Michael J. *film editor*
Hirsch, Judd *actor*
Hoffman, Philip Seymour *actor*
Horovitz, Adam Keefe (Adrock, King Ad-Rock) *musician*
Howard, Toni *talent agency executive*
Hurd, Gale Anne *film producer*
Hurt, William *actor*
Ice Cube, (O'Shea Jackson) *rap artist, actor*
Ice-T, (Tracy Marrow) *rap artist, actor*
Ireland, Kathy *actress, apparel designer*
Jackman, Hugh *actor*
Jackson, Joshua Carter *actor*
Jewel, (Jewel Kilcher) *folk singer, songwriter*
Jones, Sir Tom (Thomas Jones Woodward) *singer*
Kelley, David E. *producer, writer*
Keyes, Cheryl L. *musician, educator*
Koules, Oren D. *film producer, professional sports team executive*
Kyles, Cedric Antonio (Cedric the Entertainer) *comedian, actor*
Landers, Audrey *actress, singer*
Lauridsen, Morten Johannes *composer, music educator*
LeBeau, Mary Delle *dancer, educator, writer*
Liman, Doug *film director, film producer*
Linkletter, Arthur Gordon *radio and television broadcaster*
Lopez, George *actor, comedian*
Lopez, Jennifer *actress, singer, dancer*
Lovato, Demi (Demetria Devonne Lovato) *actress*
Lunden, Joan *television personality*
Maldonado, Gregory Matthew *music director, educator*
Malkovich, John *actor*
Malone, Nancy *actress*
Manheim, Camryn *television and film actress*
McQueen, Justice Ellis (L. Q. Jones) *actor, television director*
Medak, Peter *film director*
Murphy, Eddie *actor, comedian*
Murphy, (Frances) Elaine *musician, harpist, flutist*
Murray, Chad Michael *actor*
Neuwirth, Bebe (Beatrice Neuwirth) *dancer, actress*
Newhart, Bob (George Robert Newhart) *entertainer*
Nicholson, Jack *actor*
Nielsen, Leslie *actor*
O'Brien, Pat *television personality*
O'Connell, Taaffe Cannon *actress, publishing executive*
O'Hurley, John *actor*
O'Neal, Tatum *actress*
Osment, Haley Joel *actor*
Owen, Clive *actor*
Paltrow, Gwyneth *actress*
Perez, Rosie *actress*
Pickens, James T., Jr. *actor*
Pinto, Freida *actress*
Piven, Jeremy *actor*
Pompeo, Ellen *actress*
Pressly, Jaime Elizabeth *actress*
Pullman, Bill *actor*
Ratzenberger, John Deszo *actor, writer, film director*
Reinhold, Judge (Edward Ernest Reinhold Jr.) *actor*
Richie, Nicole *television personality*
Rickles, Donald Jay *comedian, actor*
Roberts, Julia Fiona *actress*
Rock, Chris *actor, comedian*
Rodriguez, (Mayte) Michelle *actress*
Rohrer, Susan Earley *film producer, director, scriptwriter*
Rourke, Mickey (Philip Andre Rourke Jr.) *actor*
Schlesinger, Adam *musician*
Schwartzman, Jason Francesco *actor, musician*
Selleck, Tom *actor*
Serkis, Andy *actor*
Sher, Stacey M. *film and television producer*
Shyamalan, M. Night (Manoj Nelliyattu Shyamalan) *film director*
Smiley, Tavis *television talk show host, writer*
Snyder, Zack *film director*
Sobieski, Leelee (Liliane Rudabet Gloria Eslveta Sobieski) *actress*
Stahl, Nick *actor*
Stevenson, Robert Murrell *music educator*
Streep, Meryl (Mary Louise Streep) *actress*
Streisand, Barbra Joan *singer, actress, film director*
Swofford, Beth *agent*
Todd, Beverly *actress*
Tomlin, Lily *actress*
Ullman, Tracey *actress, singer*
Waits, Thomas Alan *composer, actor, singer*
Walken, Christopher *actor*
Walsh, Kate *actress*
Watts, Naomi *actress*
Williams, Michelle *actress*
Williams, Paul Hamilton *composer, singer*
Wilson, Chandra Danette *actress*
Wilson, Patrick Joseph *actor*
Winningham, Mare *actress*
Winstone, Ray *actor*
Winters, Barbara Jo *musician*
Witherspoon, Reese (Laura Jean Reese Witherspoon) *actress*
Wood, Evan Rachel *actress*
Woodley, Shailene Diann *actress*
Wyle, Noah *actor*
Yankovic, (Weird) Al *singer, satirist*
Yerxa, Ron *film producer*
York, Michael (Michael York-Johnson) *actor*

Malibu
Herschensohn, Bruce *film director, scriptwriter*

Marina Del Rey
Milsome, Douglas *cinematographer*

Mendocino
Eckert, Rinde *composer, librettist*

Menlo Park
Baez, Joan Chandos *vocalist*

Newport Beach
Steinberg, Leigh William *sports agent*

North Hollywood
English, Diane *television producer, writer, communications executive*
Sacco, Tony *cinematographer, television director, film director*
Smothers, Tom *actor, singer*
Taravella, Rosie *actress*

Oakland
DeFazio, Lynette Stevens *dancer, choreographer, violinist, actress, educator*
Zschau, Marilyn *singer*

Palm Springs
Greene, Shecky *entertainer*

Pasadena
Hicklin, Ronald Lee *music production company executive*
Horak, Jan-Christopher *filmmaker, educator, curator*
Pinsky, Drew (David Drew Pinsky) *television personality, psychotherapist*

Pleasanton
Goddard, John Wesley *cable television company executive*

Rancho Palos Verdes
Steiner, Frances Josephine *conductor, musician, educator*

Reseda
Edwards, Nokie *musician*
Wilson, Donald Lee *musician*

Rialto
Robertson, Carey Jane *musician, educator*

Sacramento
Nice, Carter *conductor*

San Diego
Campbell, Ian David *opera company director*
Flettner, Marianne *opera administrator*
Noel, Craig *performing arts company executive, producer*
O'Brien, Jack George *artistic director*

San Dimas
Peters, Joseph Donald *filmmaker*

San Francisco
Alesi, Tommy *musician*
Breaux, Jimmy *musician*
Brevig, Eric *special effects expert, executive*
Burtt, Ben *sound designer, director, editor*
Caniparoli, Val William *choreographer, dancer*
Doucet, David *musician*
Doucet, Michael *musician, songwriter*
Eilenberg, Lawrence Ira *theater educator, artistic director*
Emunah, Renee *drama therapist, professor*
Getty, Gordon Peter *composer, philanthropist*
Gibbard, Ben *singer, musician*
Gockley, David (Richard David Gockley) *opera company director*
Goode, Joe *performing company executive*
Hastings, Edward Walton *theater director*
King, Alonzo *artistic director, choreographer*
Kitundu, Walter *sound artist, instrument designer, composer*
Knoll, John *visual effects supervisor*
Lau, Jenny Kwok Wah *theater educator, consultant, film educator*
LeBlanc, Tina *dancer*
LeGarie, Warren *sports agent*
Muren, Dennis E. *special effects expert*
Pippin, Donald Ferrell *musician, director, conductor*
Rosenberg, Pamela *opera director, conductor*
Runnicles, Donald *conductor*
Shorenstein Hays, Carole *theater producer*
Talbot, Stephen Henderson *television producer, documentary filmmaker, writer*
Tomasson, Helgi *dancer, choreographer, company executive*
Van Dyck, Wendy *dancer*
Walla, Chris *musician, music producer*
Ware, Billy *musician*

San Jose
Dalis, Irene *mezzo soprano, performing arts association administrator*
Nahat, Dennis F. *performing company executive, choreographer*
Near, Timothy *theater director*

San Marcos
Houk, Benjamin Noah *performing company executive, choreographer*

San Rafael
Lucas, George Walton, Jr. *film director, producer, scriptwriter*
Sheldon, Gary *conductor, music director*

Santa Barbara
Feigin, Joel *composer, educator*
Wayland, Newton Hart *conductor*

Santa Clarita
Feldman Nebenzahl, Bernardo *composer, educator*

Santa Cruz
Martinez, Alma R. *actress, theater director, educator*
Winston, George *solo pianist, guitarist, harmonica player*

Santa Monica
Bruckheimer, Jerry Leon *producer*
Cameron, James *film director, screenwriter, producer*
Cole, Gary Michael *actor*
Cornell, Chris (Christopher John Cornell) *singer, musician*
Eminem, (Marshall Mathers III) *rap artist*
Ferrell, Conchata Galen *actress, performing arts educator*
Hannigan, Alyson *actress*
Louis-Dreyfus, Julia *actress*
Manson, Marilyn (Brian Hugh Warner) *singer, musician*
McGinley, John C. *actor*
Meester, Leighton (Leighton Marissa Claire Meester) *actress*
Seyfried, Amanda Louise *actress*
Shannon, Molly Helen *actress*
Summer, Donna (La Donna Adrian Gaines) *singer, songwriter, actress*
Suschitzky, Peter *cinematographer*
Tamblyn, Amber Rose *actress*
Valentine, Dean *film producer*
Welker, Kara *agent*

Santa Ynez
Harris, Richard A. *film editor*

Sherman Oaks
Beck, Glenn *radio personality*
Elfman, Danny *composer*
Fogerty, John Cameron *musician, composer*
Karras, Alex *actor, retired professional football player*
Schlessinger, Laura *radio talk show host*
Tesh, John *television talk show host, musician*

Stanford
Cohen, Albert *musician, educator*

Smith, Anna Deavere *actress, playwright, educator*

Stevenson Ranch
Ernst, Donald William *producer*
Krainin, Julian Arthur *film director, produc cinematographer, writer*

Studio City
Barrett, Dorothy *performing company exec*
Duffield, Thomas Andrew *art director, production designer*
King, Carole (Carole Klein) *lyricist, singer*
Smart, Jean *actress*
Werner, Tom *television producer, professio baseball team executive*

Tarzana
Richman, Peter Mark *actor, painter, film producer*

Toluca Lake
Nunez, Oscar *actor*

Tujunga
Loehwing, Lord Rudi Charles *film produce director, publicist, radio broadcasting executive, journalist*

Universal City
Denton, James *actor*
Leno, Jay (James Douglas Muir Leno) *talk host, comedian, writer*
Scott, Seann William *actor*
Sheridan, Nicollette *actress*
Spielberg, Steven Allan *film director, prod*
Wolf, Dick (Richard A. Wolf) *television producer*
Woodard, Alfre *actress*

Valley Center
Camp, Joseph Shelton, Jr. *film producer, director, writer*

Valley Village
Barkin, Elaine Radoff *composer*

Van Nuys
Morgan, Lanny *musician*

Ventura
Newton-John, Olivia *singer, actress*

West Hollywood
Cage, Nicolas (Nicolas Coppola) *actor*
Cole, Natalie Maria *singer*
Foster, Jodie (Alicia Christian Foster) *actr film director, producer*
Friendly, David T. *film executive, producer*
Goodwin, Ginnifer *actress*
Harper, Robert *actor*
Holloway, Josh *actor*
Jackson, Randy *music producer, television personality, musician*
Jaglom, Henry David *actor, director, write*
Presley, Priscilla (Pricilla Ann Wagner, Pri Beaulieu Presley) *actress*
Romijn, Rebecca *actress, model*
Rose, Axl (William Bruce Bailey, W. Axl *singer*
Ryan, Amy *actress*
Stein, Ben (Benjamin Jeremy Stein) *televi personality, writer, lawyer, economist*
Stein, Chris *musician*
Tarantino, Quentin Jerome *film director, scriptwriter*
Tomei, Marisa *actress*
Washington, Kerry *actor*

COLORADO

Boulder
Boydston, James Christopher *composer*
Fink, Robert Russell *music educator and theorist, retired dean*
Kuchar, Theodore *conductor, academic administrator, musician*
Sable, Barbara Kinsey *retired music educ*
Sarson, John Christopher *television produ director, writer*
Symons, James Martin *theater and dance educator*

Colorado Springs
Scott, Stephen *composer, musician, educa*

Denver
Allen, Keith W. *actor, singer, songwriter*
Boggs, Gil *principal ballet dancer*
Fredmann, Martin *ballet company artistic director, educator, choreographer*
Kahane, Jeffrey *conductor, pianist, music director*

GEORGIA

Duluth
Moss, Shad Gregory (Bow Wow, Lil' Bo Wow) *rap artist*

HAWAII

Honolulu
Cazimero, Robert *musician*

.HO

no Falls
ccolo, John *conductor, music director*

atello
ge, Thom Ritter *conductor, composer*

.INOIS

cago
rson, Carly *singer, former Olympic gymnast*

SSACHUSETTS

ton
ıams, John Towner *composer, conductor*

m
les, Mavis *singer*

CHIGAN

Arbor
ı, Geri A. *composer, pianist*

NNESOTA

t Paul
egan, Nicholas *music director*

SSOURI

t Louis
Kay, Charles *opera company director*

NTANA

at Falls
son, Gordon James *performing company*
ecutive, conductor

VADA

son City
, David *conductor, arranger, composer*

Vegas
y, Virko *composer, conductor, pianist*
o, Joseph Armand *music director, pianist,*
mposer, orchestrator
ns, Clarence *musician*
Benjamin Stuart *television producer,*
ector
s, Jerry (Joseph Levitch) *comedian*

o
els, Ronald Dale *conductor*

V MEXICO

uquerque
s, Bill (James William Evans) *dance*
ofessor, academic administrator,
oreographer
roa, Guillermo *conductor*

ta Fe
es, Richard *former opera company director*
, Chris *composer*
ky, Steven Alan *musician, classical music*
ecutive
nstein, Bernard *orchestra conductor*
es, Molly *performing company executive,*
nposer
ff-Mirsky, Everett Igor *violinist*

V YORK

oklyn
er, Allegra Fuller *dancer, film director,*
ucator

York
o, Lorraine *actress*
iro, Robert *actor, film producer and*
ector, restaurant owner
Cent, (Curtis James Jackson) *rap artist*
, Deborah Ann *singer*
horn, Michael W. *television producer,*
ertainment company executive
, Alicia (Alicia Augello Cook) *singer*
arlane, Seth Woodbury *television producer,*
iptwriter
Chris *actor*
ins, Tim (Timothy Francis Robbins) *actor,*
n director

.AHOMA

a
lle, Patti (Patricia Louise Holte) *singer,*
ertainer

OREGON

Ashland
Hirschfeld, Gerald Joseph *cinematographer*
Rauch, Bill *performing company executive, theater director*
Shaw, Arthur E. *conductor*

Central Point
Savage, Michael (Michael Alan Weiner) *radio personality, commentator*

Eugene
Bailey, Exine Margaret Anderson *soprano, educator*
Benson, Joan *musician, educator*
Riley, Grannan *performing company executive*

Forest Grove
Burch-Pesses, Thomas Michael *music educator*

Portland
Berentsen, Kurtis George *music educator, conductor*
Hartmann, Thom *radio personality, political commentator, writer*
Kalmar, Carlos *conductor, music director*
Love, Edith Holmes *theater producer*
Ryberg, William A. *orchestra executive*
Stowell, Christopher R. *performing company executive, choreographer, retired dancer*

UTAH

Montezuma Creek
Schaefer, Kim *music educator*

Park City
Becker, William Watters *theater producer*

Provo
Randle, Cammon C. *filmmaker*
Woodbury, Lael Jay *theater educator*

Salt Lake City
Andrews, Donald L. *performing arts company executive*
Grant, Raymond Thomas *arts administrator*
Morey, Charles Leonard III *theatrical director, playwright*

WASHINGTON

Bremerton
Cottrell-Adkins, Leone *opera company director*

Clarkston
Torgerson, Linda Belle *music educator*

Poulsbo
Forbes, David Craig *musician*

Seattle
Anang, Amma Cecilia *dance company administrator*
Boal, Peter Cadbury *performing company executive*
Brock, Isaac *musician*
Graney, Pat *choreographer*
Grohl, Dave (David Eric Grohl) *musician*
Jenkins, Speight *opera company director, writer*
Russell, Francia *retired ballet director, educator*
Stowell, Kent *retired ballet director*
Thomas, Karen P. *composer, conductor*

Walla Walla
Simon, Nancy Lynn *performing arts educator, director*

Woodinville
Sanders, Richard Kinard *actor*

CANADA

ALBERTA

Calgary
Monk, Allan James *baritone*
Raeburn, Andrew Harvey *performing arts consultant*

BRITISH COLUMBIA

Vancouver
Krall, Diana *musician, singer*
Lavigne, Avril *singer*
McLachlan, Sarah *musician, composer*
Murray, Anne *singer*
Washburn, Jon *artistic director*

ENGLAND

London
Beckham, Victoria Caroline *singer, apparel designer*
Weisz, Rachel *actress*

FRANCE

Paris
Deneuve, Catherine (Catherine Dorleac) *actress*

ADDRESS UNPUBLISHED

Anderson, Gillian Leigh *actress*
Anderson, Pam (Pamela Denise Anderson) *actress*
Applegate, Christina *actress*
Apted, Michael David *film director*
Avary, Roger Roberts (Frank Brauner) *film director, producer, writer*
Baerwald, Susan Grad *television broadcasting company executive, producer*
Bailey, Robert C. *opera company executive*
Baker, Anita *singer*
Bank, Roy J. *television producer*
Banner, Bob *television producer, director*
Beatty, Warren *actor, film director, film producer*
Bello, Maria Elana *actress*
Benton, Robert *film director, screenwriter*
Berg, Peter *actor*
Bergen, Candice *actress, writer, photojournalist*
Bernhard, Sandra *actress, comedienne, singer*
Bigelow, Michael *film director, visual effects expert*
Bissell, James Dougal III *motion picture production designer*
Blaine, David (David Blaine White) *magician*
Blige, Mary Jane *singer*
Bluemer, Bevan *acrobatics company executive*
Bonet, Lisa (Lilakoi Moon, Lisa Michelle Boney) *actress*
Borgnine, Ernest *actor*
Brady, Mary Rolfes *music educator*
Braff, Zach *actor, director, scriptwriter*
Bridges, Jeff *actor*
Brosnan, Peter Lawrence *documentary filmmaker*
Brown, Bryan *actor*
Burns, Edward J., Jr. *actor, film director*
Calman, Craig David *actor, writer*
Carter, Scott *television producer*
Cattrall, Kim *actress*
Chávez, Denise Elia *performance writer, actress*
Cher, (Cherilyn Sarkisian) *singer, actress*
Clarkson, Kelly Brianne *singer*
Close, Glenn *actress*
Columbus, Chris J. *film director, screenwriter*
Condon, Tom (Thomas Joseph Condon) *sports agent, retired professional football player*
Connery, Sir Sean (Thomas Sean Connery) *actor*
Corman, Eugene Harold (Gene Corman) *motion picture producer*
Cosby, Bill *actor, television producer*
Cromwell, James *actor*
Crosby, Norman Lawrence *comedian*
Cullum, John *actor, singer*
Cunningham, Ron *choreographer, artistic director*
Dale, Jim *actor*
Demme, Jonathan *director, producer, writer*
Diamond, Neil Leslie *singer, composer*
Dolenz, Mickey (George Michael Dolenz, Mickey Braddock) *entertainer, actor, television producer*
Douglas, Kirk (Issur Danielovitch) *actor*
Durning, Charles *actor*
Englund, Robert *actor, director, producer*
Falco, Edie *actress*
Foster, Lawrence *concert and opera conductor*
Foster, Mary Christine *film producer, writer*
Frot-Coutaz, Cecile *television producer*
Fullenwider, Nancy Vrana *composer, dancer, musician, educator*
Gabler, Lee *talent agency executive*
Gandolfini, James *actor*
Garner, Jennifer Anne *actress*
Garofalo, Janeane *actress, comedienne*
Garrett, Brad *actor, comedian*
Getty, Balthazar *actor*
Gibson, Mel *actor, film director and producer*
Goen, Bob *television show host*
Graham, Bill *opera company director*
Griffin, Jean (Alva Jean Griffin) *entertainer*
Guttenberg, Steve *actor*
Hawkins, Oliver Taylor (Taylor Hawkins) *musician*
Heche, Anne (Anne Celeste Heche) *actress*
Henderson, Florence *actress, singer*
Holman, Bill *composer*
Hsu-Li, Magdalen *singer, poet, painter*
Hunt, Helen (Helen Elizabeth Hunt) *actress*
Hurley, Elizabeth (Liz Hurley) *actress, model*
Jackson, Janet *singer, dancer*
Jackson, Victoria Lynn *actress, comedienne*
Jacobus, Arthur *dance company administrator*
Janis, Conrad *actor, musician, art dealer*
Jones, Shirley *actress, singer*
Kaminski, Janusz Zygmunt *cinematographer*
Kaylan, Howard Lawrence *musical entertainer, screenwriter, composer*
Keith, Toby (Toby Keith Covel) *country singer, songwriter, producer*
Kellman, Barnet Kramer *film, stage and television director*
Kerns, Joanna de Varona *actress, writer, director*
Kinnear, Greg *actor, film producer*
Knowles, William Leroy (Bill Knowles) *television news producer, journalism educator*
Kramer, Remi Thomas *film director*
Kudrow, Lisa (Marie Diane) *actress*
LaBeouf, Shia *actor*
Lachey, Nick (Nicholas Scott Lachey) *singer, actor*
Ladd, Diane *actress, writer, film director, producer*
Lane, Nathan (Joseph Lane) *actor*
LaPaglia, Anthony *actor*
Levy, Eugene *actor, film director, screenwriter*
Lewis, George *music educator*
Lightfoot, William Carl *performing arts association executive, symphony musician*
Lithgow, John Arthur *actor*
Little Richard, (Richard Wayne Penniman) *musician, lyricist, minister*
Lovett, Richard *talent agency executive*
Madden, John Philip *motion picture director, actor*
Madonna, (Madonna Louise Veronica Ciccone) *singer, actress, producer*
Madsen, Virginia *actress*
Malick, Terrence (David Whitney II) *film director*
Marshall, Peter *actor, singer, game show host*
Martin, Andrea Louise *actress, comedienne, writer*
McFarlane, Seth Woodbury *television producer, animator*
Meyerink, Victoria Paige *film producer, actress*
Miguel, Luis *musician*
Mirisch, Lawrence Alan *motion picture agent*
Moore, Demi (Demi Guynes, Demetria Gene Guynes) *actress*
Mortensen, Viggo *actor, writer*
Myerson, Alan *television director, film director*
Neary, Patricia Elinor *ballet director*
Neblett, Carol *soprano*
Neeson, Liam *actor*
Nichols, Mike *stage and film director*
Nobert, Frances *music educator*
O'Boyle, Maureen *television show host*
O'Donnell, Rosie *television personality, actress, comedienne*
O'Hara, Catherine *actress, comedienne*
Phillips, Michelle Gilliam *actress, writer*
Poster, Steven B. *cinematographer, photographer, publisher, digital imaging consultant*
Prince, Faith *actress, singer*
Ptak, John *talent agent*
Queally, Hylda *agent*
Rapaport, Michael *actor*
Reeves, Keanu *actor*
Richie, Lionel B., Jr. *singer, lyricist, theater producer*
Richmond, Rocsan *television executive producer, investigative reporter, small business owner*
Robertson, Cliff *actor, writer, director*
Robinson, Rich *musician*
Rodriguez, Jai *television personality*
Rodriguez, Robert *filmmaker*
Roseanne, (Roseanne Barr) *actress, comedienne, television producer, writer*
Rosenberg, Philip *production designer*
Russell, Kurt *actor*
St. John, Kristoff *actor*
Sajak, Pat *television game show host*
Sargent, Joseph Daniel *motion picture and television director*
Sarsgaard, Peter *actor*
Schallert, William Joseph *actor*
Schneider, Rob *actor*
Schuur, Diane Joan *vocalist*
Schwimmer, David *actor*
Seale, John Clement *director, cinematographer*
Seinfeld, Jerry *comedian, actor, television producer, scriptwriter*
Sewell, Rufus *actor*
Shandling, Garry *comedian, scriptwriter, actor*
Sheen, Martin (Ramon Estevez) *actor*
Sheindlin, Judith (Judge Judy) *television personality, judge*
Shepherd, Cybill Lynne *actress, singer*
Shields, Brooke Christa Camille *actress, model*
Shiflett, Chris *musician*
Silvestri, Alan Anthony *film composer*
Smith, Irby Jay *film producer*
Smith, Phyllis *actress*
Snyder, David L. *film production designer*
Spurlock, Morgan *television producer, film producer*
Stallone, Sylvester Gardenzio *actor, film director, scriptwriter, producer*
Stanek, Alan Edward *retired music educator, performing arts association administrator*
Stern, James D. *film and theater producer*
Stone, Oliver *film director, producer, scriptwriter*
Stone, Sharon *actress*
Summers, Cathleen *film producer*
Sutherland, Donald *actor*
Tiano, Anthony Steven *television producer, publishing executive*
Vacano, Jost *cinematographer*
Voight, Jon *actor*
Von Brandenstein, Patrizia *production designer*
Wagner, Robert *actor*
Walsh, Joseph Fidler (Joe Walsh) *recording artist, record producer*
Washington, Denzel *actor*
Watson, Emily *actress*
Wedgeworth, Ann *actress*
Wexler, Haskell *film producer*
Whitaker, Thomas O'Hara *theater educator, director*
White, Julie *actress*
Wilder, Gene (Jerry Silberman) *actor, film director, writer*
Williams, JoBeth *actress*
Winokur, Marissa Jaret *actress*
Winters, Jonathan *actor*
Woodside, D. B. (David Bryan Woodside) *actor*

Zsigmond, Vilmos *cinematographer, film director*

ARTS: VISUAL

UNITED STATES

ALASKA

Cordova
Bugbee-Jackson, Joan *sculptor, educator*

ARIZONA

Prescott Valley
Decil, Stella Walters (Del Decil) *artist*

Tucson
Koerber, Erica *photographer*

CALIFORNIA

Arcadia
Danziger, Louis *graphic designer, educator*

Arcata
Land-Weber, Ellen *photography professor*

Berkeley
Genn, Nancy *artist*
Hartman, Robert Leroy *artist, educator*
Kasten, Karl Albert *artist, printmaker, educator*
Miyasaki, George Joji *artist*
Simpson, David William *artist, educator*

Beverly Hills
Ferretti, Dante *display designer*

Bolinas
Okamura, Arthur Shinji *artist, educator*

Carmel
Jacobs, Ralph, Jr. *artist*

Carson
Hirsch, Gilah Yelin *artist, writer*

Claremont
Benjamin, Karl Stanley *artist, educator*
Blizzard, Alan *artist*
Dunye, Cheryl *artist, filmmaker*
Lachowicz, Rachel *artist, educator*
Rankaitis, Susan *artist*
Zehr, Connie *sculptor, art educator*

Concord
Broadbent, Amalia Sayo Castillo *graphic arts designer*

La Jolla
Jensen, Henrik Wann *computer graphics designer, educator*
Silva, Ernest R. *visual arts educator, artist*

Larkspur
Napoles, Veronica *graphic designer, consultant*

Long Beach
Oviatt, Larry Andrew *retired art educator*
Viola, Bill *artist, writer*

Los Angeles
Caroompas, Carole Jean *artist, educator*
Curran, Darryl Joseph *photographer, educator*
Fairey, Shepard *printmaker*
Hamilton, Patricia Rose *art dealer*
Hockney, David *artist*
Ketchum, Robert Glenn *photographer, print maker*
Lhuillier, (Diane) Monique *apparel designer*
Loomis, Rick *photographer*
Park, Lee (Lee Parklee) *artist*
Rodriguez, Katy *apparel designer*
Sanditz, Lisa *painter*
Stone, George *artist, educator*
Winter, Damon *photographer, photojournalist*
Youmans, James *set designer*

Mckinleyville
Berry, Glenn *artist, educator*

Mendocino
de la Fuente, Lawrence Edward *artist*

Monrovia
Dobay, Susan Vilma *artist*

Morgan Hill
Freimark, Robert (Bob Freimark) *artist*

Novato
McNamara, John Stephen *artist, educator*

Oakland
Gonzalez, Arthur Padilla *artist, educator*
Rath, Alan T. *sculptor*
Saunders, Raymond Jennings *artist, educator*
Thompson, Mark Lee *art educator, sculptor*

Pacific Grove
Elinson, Henry David *artist, language educator*

Palm Springs
Carnase, Thomas Paul *graphics designer, consultant*

Pasadena
Pashgian, Margaret Helen *artist*

Phelan
Erwin, Joan Lenore *artist, educator*

Piedmont
Mayeri, Beverly *artist, ceramic sculptor, educator*

Sacramento
Allan, William George *artist, educator*

San Diego
Nelson, Kadir *illustrator, artist*

San Francisco
Beall, Dennis Ray *artist, educator*
Bechtle, Robert Alan *artist, educator*
Benton, Fletcher *sculptor*
Chin, Sue Soone Marian (Suchin Chin) *artist, photojournalist*
DeSoto, Lewis Damien *artist, educator*
Dickinson, Eleanor Creekmore *artist, educator*
Goldstine, Stephen Joseph *art educator*
Hershman, Lynn Lester *artist*
Martin, Fred *artist, academic administrator*
McClintock, Jessica *fashion designer*
Monteith, Matthew *photographer*
Petersen, Roland *artist, printmaker*
Piccolo, Richard Andrew *artist, educator*
Stermer, Dugald Robert *designer, writer, illustrator, consultant*
Toney, Anita Karen *printmaker*
Trujillo, Marc *painter*
Van Hoesen, Beth Marie *artist, printmaker*

San Jose
Barone, Angela Maria *artist, researcher*
Estabrook, Reed *artist, educator*

San Juan Bautista
Nutzle, Futzie (Bruce John Kleinsmith) *artist, writer, animator*

San Luis Obispo
Dickerson, Colleen Bernice Patton *artist, educator*

San Pedro
Parkhurst, Violet Kinney *artist*

Santa Barbara
Eguchi, Yasu *artist*

Santa Monica
Craig, Stuart N. *film production designer*
Giannulli, Mossimo *designer, apparel business executive*

Sausalito
Kuhlman, Walter Egel *artist, educator*

South Pasadena
Askin, Walter Miller *artist, educator*

Stanford
Corn, Wanda Marie *fine arts educator*

Studio City
Leonard, Herman *photographer*

Topanga
Millar, Robert *artist*

Valencia
Kersels, Martin *conceptual artist*

Venice
Garabedian, Charles *artist*

West Hollywood
Barker, Clive *artist, film director and producer, scriptwriter*

COLORADO

Aspen
Fischl, Eric *artist*

Boulder
Chong, Albert Valentine *artist, educator*
Matthews, Eugene Edward *artist*

Denver
Enright, Cynthia Lee *illustrator*

Fort Collins
Jacobs, Peter Alan *artist, educator*
Yust, David E. *artist, educator*

Lake George
Norman, John Barstow, Jr. *graphics designer, educator*

Loveland
Bierbaum, Janith Marie *artist*

IDAHO

Coeur D' Alene
Clabby, Michael *computer graphics designer, educator*

MASSACHUSETTS

Chatham
Reid, Charles Clark *artist*

MONTANA

Livingston
Chatham, Russell *artist*

Missoula
Rippon, Thomas Michael *art educator, artist*

NEVADA

Las Vegas
Martinez, Adriana *photographer*

Reno
Boyle, (Charles) Keith *artist, educator*
Goin, Peter Jackson *art educator*

NEW MEXICO

Albuquerque
Barry, Steve *sculptor, educator*
Keating, David *photographer*
Leesman, Beverly Jean *artist, critic, writer, educator*
Qualley, Charles Albert *art educator*
Radebaugh, Alan Paine *artist*
Witkin, Joel-Peter *photographer, poet*

Corrales
Eaton, Pauline *artist, educator*

Santa Fe
Clift, William Brooks III *photographer*
Peña, Amado Maurilio, Jr. *artist, curator, lecturer*

NEW YORK

New York
Baldessari, John Anthony *artist*
Mutu, Wangechi *collage artist, painter*
Ruscha, Edward *artist*

OREGON

Ashland
Hay, Richard Laurence *theater set designer*

Cannon Beach
Greaver, Harry *artist*

Hillsboro
Hurley, Bruce Palmer *artist*

Newport
Gilhooly, David James III *artist*

Portland
Lorenz, Nancy *artist*
Ramsby, Mark Delivan *lighting designer, consultant*

WASHINGTON

Bainbridge Island
Carlson, Robert Michael *artist*

Battle Ground
Hansen, James Lee *sculptor*

Kent
Pierce, Danny Parcel *artist, educator*

Olympia
Haseltine, James Lewis *artist, consultant*

Seattle
Berger, Paul Eric *artist, photographer*
De Alessi, Ross Alan *lighting designer*
Feldman, Roger Lawrence *artist, educator*
Gardiner, T(homas) Michael *artist*
Garvens, Ellen Jo *artist, educator*
Govedare, Philip Bainbridge *artist, educator*
Lundin, Norman Kent *artist, educator*
Spafford, Michael Charles *artist*
Stearns, Susan Tracey *lighting design company executive, lawyer*

Spokane
Mobley, Karen Ruth *art director*

WYOMING

Cody
Jackson, Harry Andrew *artist*

Laramie
Reif, (Frank) David *artist, educator*

CANADA

BRITISH COLUMBIA

Salt Spring Island
Raginsky, Nina *artist*

Vancouver
Bonifacho, Bratsa *artist*

Victoria
Harvey, Donald *artist, educator*

SASKATCHEWAN

Saskatoon
Bornstein, Eli *artist, sculptor*

ADDRESS UNPUBLISHED

Antreasian, Garo Zareh *artist, lithographer, educator*
Barrow, Thomas Francis *artist, educator*
Bateman, Robert McLellan *artist*
Bell, Larry Stuart *artist*
Butler, Leslie Ann *artist, writer, editor*
Butterfield, Deborah Kay *sculptor*
Campbell, Demarest Lindsay *artist, writer, interior designer*
Casanova, Aldo John *sculptor*
Chihuly, Dale Patrick *artist*
Cobb, Virginia Horton *artist, educator*
Condon, Brody Kiel *computer graphics de*
Cox, Pat *artist*
Dill, Laddie John *artist*
Dominguez, Eddie *artist*
Ferreira, Armando Thomas *sculptor, educa*
Ford, Tom *apparel designer and executive*
Gold, Betty Virginia *artist*
Hammond, Harmony *artist, educator*
Hanson, Janice Crawford *artist, financial a*
Howard, David E. *artist*
Judge, Mike *animator*
Lefranc, Margaret (Margaret Schoonover) *illustrator, editor, writer*
Loquasto, Santo *theatrical set designer*
Maraldo, Ushana *multimedia designer, arti photographer, writer*
Misrach, Richard Laurence *photographer*
Nagatani, Patrick Allan Ryoichi *artist, art educator*
Neri, Manuel *sculptor, educator*
Nichols, Iris Jean *retired illustrator*
Pederson, Con *animator*
Raciti, Cherie *artist*
Scott, Deborah L. *costume designer*
Sharp, Anne Catherine *artist, educator*
Shiershke, Nancy Fay *artist, educator, pro manager*
Summers, Carol *artist*
Turner, Bonese Collins *artist, educator*
Tyler, Richard *fashion designer*
Washington, James Winston, Jr. *artist, scu*
Wright, Virginia *art collector, curator*
Zekman, Terri Margaret *graphic designer*
Zoe, Rachel (Rachel Zoe Rosenzweig) *fas stylist*

ASSOCIATIONS AND ORGANIZATIONS *See als specific fields*

UNITED STATES

ALASKA

Anchorage
Higgins, Patti Carolyn *political organizati administrator*
Jones, Jewel *social services administrator*
Ruedrich, Randy *political organization administrator*

ARIZONA

Cottonwood
Groseta, Andy (Peter Andrew Groseta) *lob*

Dragoon
Woosley, Anne I. *cultural organization administrator*

Glendale
Lloyd, Llyn Allan *association executive*

Phoenix
McCain, Cindy (Cindy Lou Hensley McC *philanthropist, wholesale distribution executive*
Mohraz, Judy Jolley *foundation administr*
Pederson, Jim *political party official*
Pullen, Randy *political organization administrator*
Swartz, Jack *retired chamber of commerce executive*

scott
ey, Daniel Edward *foundation lministrator, educator*

ttsdale
bson, Frank Joel *cultural organization lministrator*
leara, Sara *non-profit organization executive*

son
zales, Sarah *women's organization director*
d, Marcia *civic worker*
ner, Rome *social services administrator*
y, Stephanie Lemme *hospital organization lministrator*
nillo, Alba *community educator*
Ethan *non-profit organization executive*
as, Josh *non-profit organization director*
pe, Jason M. *non-profit organization rector*
ll, John Albert *organization executive, nsultant*

LIFORNIA

ersfield
ta, Dolores Clara (Dolores Fernández) *labor ion administrator*

keley
n, David *nonprofit organization lministrator*
rs, Miles Alvin *educational association lministrator, researcher*

erly Hills
anson, Howard F., Jr. *philanthropist*
is, Sidney *motion picture association ecutive, film company executive*

bank
linson, Joseph Eli *foundation administrator, wyer*

oga Park
rer, Marion Irvine *cultural administrator*

mel Valley
kel, Peter Timothy *arts administrator, lucator*

remont
nedy, Brian T. *think-tank executive*

ver City
el, Paul Arthur *fundraising management ecutive, consultant*

eryville
oet, Edward E. *retired foundation lministrator, former biochemicals company ecutive, former dean*

ino
s, Audrey Menein *not-for-profit developer*

sno
avonian, Gerald S. *political organization lministrator*

ine
anson, Roberta *philanthropist*
on, Kenneth Ray *professional association lministrator*

ne
iguez, Arturo Salvador *labor union official*

atfield
n, Joan Kurley *retired not-for-profit ndraiser*

Jolla
dow, Jeffrey *think-tank executive, former nbassador*

Altos
on, Carol S. *foundation administrator, wyer*
ur, Colburn Sloan *foundation consultant, ustee, former executive*

Angeles
rado, Pablo *day laborer organizer, migrant rights activist*
, Walter S. *think-tank executive*
d, Eli *foundation administrator, art llector*
, Robert Anthony *international relief ganization, former professional sports team d film company executive*
iano, Neil Gerard *civil rights organization ecutive, former mayor*
andez, Antonia *foundation administrator, wyer*
ley, F(rancis) Haynes, Jr. *foundation ecutive, lawyer*
k, James Curtis, II, *cultural organization ministrator*
ow, Deborah *foundation administrator*
tti, Alfred Kendall *organization executive*
ell, James Lawrence *educational association ministrator, museum director, geologist*
itt, Jean *not-for-profit organization ecutive*
, Robert K. *foundation administrator, ysician*
White, Daun Elois *professional society official*
Wilson, Gayle Ann *civic worker*
Wood, James Nowell *foundation administrator, former museum director*

Los Gatos
Allan, Lionel M. *director for-profit and non-profit companies, Legal and Business Advisor*

Menlo Park
Altman, Drew E. *foundation executive*
Pallotti, Marianne Marguerite *foundation administrator*
Smith, Marshall Savidge *foundation executive*

Mill Valley
Burke, Kathleen J. *foundation administrator*

Modesto
Whiteside, Carol Gordon *foundation executive*

Mountain View
Bills, Robert Howard *political party executive*

Newbury Park
McCune, Sara Miller *foundation executive, publisher*

Novato
Peters, Thomas *foundation administrator*

Oakland
Alexander, Stewart A. *political organization worker*
Miller, Maurice Lim *cultural organization administrator*
Pendleton, Othniel Alsop *fundraiser, clergyman*

Pacific Palisades
Hubbs, Donald Harvey *foundation executive*

Palm Springs
Ellsworth, Frank L. *not-for-profit executive*

Palo Alto
Moore, Kenneth G. *foundation administrator, former manufacturing executive*
Moore, Steven E. *foundation administrator*
Nichols, William Ford, Jr. *foundation, health science association administrator, educator*
Skoll, Jeffrey S. *philanthropist, former internet company executive*

Pasadena
Ellner, Carolyn Lipton *non-profit organization executive, dean, consultant*
Staehle, Robert L. *foundation executive*

Redwood City
Postel, Mitchell Paul *association administrator*

Richmond
Hawkins, Robert B. *think-tank executive*

Riverside
Peterson, Arthur Laverne *foundation administrator*

Ross
Giovinco, Joseph *non profit agency administrator, writer*

Sacramento
Nehring, Ron *political organization administrator*
Torres, Art *former political organization administrator, former state legislator*

San Diego
Grosser, T.J. *not-for-profit fundraiser*
McBrayer, Sandra L. *educational director, homeless outreach educator*
Swanson, Mary Catherine *educational association administrator*
Wallace, Candy *culinary association administrator*

San Francisco
Bereuter, Douglas Kent *foundation administrator, former congressman*
Bitterman, Mary Gayle Foley *foundation executive*
Burton, John L. *political organization administrator, retired state legislator*
Canales, James Earl, Jr. *foundation president*
Dachs, Lauren Bechtel *non-profit organization executive*
Eastham, Thomas *retired foundation administrator*
Fisher, Robert Morton *foundation and academic administrator*
Freedman, Marc *think-tank executive*
Fuller, William P. *foundation administrator*
Gimon, Juliette *foundation administrator, volunteer*
Goldman, Richard N. *foundation administrator*
Guillermo, Tessie *foundation administrator*
Guttentag, Lucas *advocate, lawyer*
Johnson, Chalmers *educational association administrator, retired political science professor*
LaRiva, Gloria *labor union administrator, advocate*
Lehane, Christopher S. *political consultant*
Mattern, Douglas James *think-tank executive*
Mitchell, Theodore Reed *educational association administrator, former academic administrator*
Nee, D.Y. Bob *think tank executive, engineering consultant*
Newirth, Richard Scott *cultural organization administrator*
Pipes, Sally C. *think-tank executive*
Tripp, Alan H. *educational association administrator, consultant*

San Jose
Hutton, Carole Leigh *not-for-profit executive, former newspaper editor*

San Luis Obispo
Jamieson, James Bradshaw *foundation administrator*

Santa Barbara
Rehm, Susan J. *social services professional*

Santa Clarita
Boyer, Carl III *not-for-profit developer, retired mayor, municipal official*

Santa Monica
Abarbanel, Gail *social services administrator, educator*
Klowden, Michael Louis *think-tank executive*
Milken, Michael R. *think-tank executive, philanthropist*
Rich, Michael David *think-tank executive, lawyer*
Thomson, James Alan *think-tank executive*

Sonoma
Collins, Dennis Arthur *retired foundation administrator*

Stanford
Bryk, Anthony S. *educational association administrator*
Lyman, Richard Wall *foundation and academic administrator, historian*
Raisian, John *think-tank executive, economist*
Seelig, Tina L. *entrepeneurship program director, educator*
Shulman, Lee S. *former educational association administrator*

Stinson Beach
Metz, Mary Seawell *retired foundation and academic administrator*

Studio City
Frumkin, Simon *political organization worker, writer*

Universal City
Gumpel, Glenn J. *association executive*

Woodside
Blum, Richard Hosmer Adams *foundation administrator, educator, writer*

COLORADO

Boulder
Hess, John Warren *professional society administrator*
Sanders, Lucinda (Lucy Sanders) *information technology organization executive*

Centennial
Lessey, Samuel Kenric, Jr. *foundation administrator*

Colorado Springs
Killian, George Ernest *retired educational association administrator*

Denver
Childears, Linda *foundation administrator*
Chu, Roderick Gong-Wah *educational association administrator*
Hogan, Curtis Jule *labor union administrator, industrial relations specialist, consultant*
Ibarra, Irene M. *foundation administrator*
Nelson, Bernard William *foundation executive, educator, physician*
Schrenk, Gary Dale *foundation executive*
Waak, Patricia Ann *political organization administrator*
Zimmerman, Gary J. *utilities association executive*

Englewood
Neiser, Brent Allen *foundation executive, public affairs and personal finance speaker, consultant*

Greenwood Village
Wadhams, Richard Ivory (Dick Wadhams) *policitcal organization administrator*

Loveland
Rodman, Alpine C. *arts and crafts company executive, photographer*

DISTRICT OF COLUMBIA

Washington
Echaveste, Maria *lobbyist, former federal official*
Hansen, Christopher W. *trade association administrator*
Hansen, Jennie Chin *association executive*
Harris, Leslie *think-tank executive, lawyer*
Stonesifer, Patty (Patricia Q. Stonesifer) *former foundation administrator*

HAWAII

Honolulu
Lee, Willes K. *political organization administrator*
Morrison, Charles Edward *think-tank executive*
Robinson, Robert Blacque *foundation administrator*
Schatz, Brian E. *political organization administrator, environmentalist, former state legislator*
Schoenke, Marilyn Leilani *foundation administrator*

Volcano
Nicholson, Marilyn Lee *arts administrator*

IDAHO

Boise
Olson, A. Craig *foundation administrator, former retail executive*
Semanko, Norman M. *political organization administrator*

MONTANA

Billings
Sample, Joseph Scanlon *foundation executive*

Cut Bank
Johnson, Liane *political organization administrator*

Missoula
Kemmis, Daniel Orra *cultural organization administrator, author*

NEVADA

Carson City
Ayres, Janice Ruth *social services administrator*

Henderson
Freyd, William Pattinson *not-for-profit fundraiser, director*

Incline Village
Johnston, Bernard Fox *foundation executive, writer*

Las Vegas
Lieberman, Sam *political organization administrator*
Lowden, Sue *political organization administrator*
Martin, Myron Gregory *foundation administrator*
Segerblom, Sharon B. *social services administrator*

Reno
Mason, John E. *political association executive*

NEW MEXICO

Albuquerque
Cole, Terri Lynn *organization administrator*

OREGON

Ashland
Kreisman, Arthur *higher education consultant, retired humanities educator*

Corvallis
Wilkins, Caroline Hanke *advocate, political organization worker*

Portland
Collins, Maribeth Wilson *retired foundation administrator*
Edmunson, James L. *political organization administrator*
Hudson, Jerry E. *foundation administrator*
Johnson, David J. *educational association administrator*
Rooks, Charles S. *foundation administrator*
Smith, Meredith Wood *political organization administrator*
Tiernan, Bob (Robert Tiernan) *political organization administrator, former state legislator*

Salem
Corcoran, Anthony Austin *union organizer, state senator*

TEXAS

Dallas
Lane, John Rodger *art association administrator, retired museum director*

UTAH

Bountiful
Burningham, Kim Richard *educational association administrator, former state legislator*

Salt Lake City
Evans, Max Jay *historical society administrator*
Holbrook, Meghan Zanolli *fundraiser, public relations specialist, political organization chairman*
Holland, Wayne, Jr. *political organization administrator*
Julander, Paula Foil *retired foundation administrator*

WASHINGTON

Olympia
Berendt, Paul *political organization worker*
Olson, Steven Stanley *social service executive*

Redmond
Andrew, Jane Hayes *non-profit organization executive*

Seattle
Bell, William C. *foundation administrator*
Chapman, Bruce Kerry *institute executive*
Davidson, Robert William *not-for-profit executive*
Esser, Luke *political organization administrator*
Friedman, Alexander Stephen *foundation administrator, investment banker*
Gates, Melinda French *foundation administrator*
Green, Joshua III *foundation administrator, retired bank executive*
Jacobs, Deborah L. *foundation administrator, former library director*
Jones, Allan *medical research organization executive*
Mathews, Sylvia Mary *foundation administrator*
Petry, Don D. *educational association administrator*
Raikes, Jeffrey Scott *foundation administrator, former computer software company executive*
Vander Ark, Tom *foundation administrator*

Spokane
Falkner, James George, Sr. *foundation executive*

Tacoma
Graybill, David Wesley *chamber of commerce executive*

WYOMING

Jackson
Vaughan, Diana *political organization administrator*

TERRITORIES OF THE UNITED STATES

AMERICAN SAMOA

Pago Pago
Schuster, Su'a Carl *political organization administrator, bishop*

CANADA

ALBERTA

Calgary
Hume, James Borden *foundation administrator, director*
Roberts, John Peter Lee *cultural advisor, administrator, educator, writer*

CAMBODIA

Phnom Penh
Mam, Somaly *advocate*

ADDRESS UNPUBLISHED

Anderson, Ned, Sr. *Apache tribal official*
Baker, William Morris *cultural organization administrator*
Becerra, Rosina Madeline *social welfare educator*
Boal, Dean *retired arts center administrator, educator*
Chassman, Leonard Fredric *retired labor union administrator*
Conran, James Michael *consumer advocate, public policy consultant*
Dale, Deborah *foundation executive*
Day, Vance D. *former political organization administrator, lawyer*
Garner, Carlene Ann *not-for-profit fundraiser, consultant*
Gilbert, Melissa *former actors guild executive, actress*
Hammer, Susan W. *educational foundation executive, former mayor*
Hawkins, Brian Lee *former educational association administrator*
Hernández, Sandra R. *foundation administrator*
Himes, Diane Adele *buyer, fundraiser, actress, lobbyist*
Johnson, Deborah Lorraine *not-for-profit executive, consultant*
Kipke, Michele Diane *education and social services administrator, former hospital director*
Lansing, Sherry Lee *foundation administrator, former film company executive*
Makepeace, Mary Lou *foundation administrator, former mayor*
Miller, Harriet Sanders *former art center director*
Munitz, Barry A. *former foundation administrator*
Peck, Robert David *educational foundation administrator*
Pisano, A. Robert *former actors guild executive, former film company executive*
Quehl, Gary Howard *educational association administrator, consultant*
Ramo, Virginia M. Smith *civic worker*
Rice, Susan F. *fundraising consultant*
Ross, Charlotte Pack *social services administrator*
Showalter, Marilyn Grace *trade association administrator, director*
Stoval, Linda *political coach, consultant*
Swig, Roselyne Chroman *community consultant*
Toms, Justine Willis *educational organization executive*
Uhde, Larry Jackson *joint apprentice administrator*

ATHLETICS

UNITED STATES

ARIZONA

Glendale
Doan, Shane *professional hockey player*
Gretzky, Wayne Douglas *professional hockey coach, retired professional hockey player*
Jovanovski, Ed *professional hockey player*
Maloney, Don *professional sports team executive, retired professional hockey player*
Porter, Kevin *professional hockey player*

Phoenix
Barbosa, Leandro Mateus *professional basketball player*
Bidwill, William V. *professional sports team executive*
Boldin, Anquan *professional football player*
Byrnes, Eric James *professional baseball player, radio, television personality*
Fitzgerald, Larry Darnell, Jr. *professional football player*
Gentry, Alvin *professional basketball coach*
Gibson, Kirk Harold *professional baseball coach, retired professional baseball player*
Graves, Rod *professional sports team executive*
Hinch, A.J. (Andrew Jay Hinch) *professional baseball coach*
Kerr, Steve (Stephen Douglas Kerr) *professional sports team executive, retired professional basketball player*
Leinart, Matthew Stephen *professional football player*
Lemieux, Claude *professional hockey player, professional sports team executive*
Miller, Christopher James *professional football coach, retired professional football player*
Nash, Steve *professional basketball player*
O'Neal, Shaquille Rashaun *professional basketball player*
Pitman, Jim *professional sports team executive*
Sarver, Robert G. *professional sports team owner*
Stoudemire, Amare Carsares *professional basketball player*
Taurasi, Diana Lurena *professional basketball player*
Van Arsdale, Dick *professional basketball team executive*
Webb, Brandon (Tyler Webb) *professional baseball player*
Welts, Rick *professional sports team executive*
Williams, Aeneas Demetrius *professional football player*
Wilson, Adrian (Adrian Lemar Wilson) *professional football player*

Scottsdale
Ogilvy, Geoff *professional golfer*

Tempe
Erickson, Dennis *college football coach, former professional football coach*
Grimm, Russ *professional football coach, retired professional football player*
Sendek, Herb *men's college basketball coach*
Snyder, Lester M. *sports association executive*
Turner Thorne, Charli *women's college basketball coach*
Warner, Kurt (Kurtis Eugene Warner) *professional football player*
Whisenhunt, Ken *professional football coach*

Tucson
Bonvicini, Joan M. *women's college basketball coach*
Kearney, Joseph Laurence *retired athletic conference administrator*
Miller, Sean *men's college basketball coach*
Stoops, Mike *college football coach*

CALIFORNIA

Alameda
Asomugha, Nnamdi *professional football player*
Cable, Thomas Lee (Tom Cable) *professional football coach*
Davis, Al (Allen Davis) *professional football team executive*
Garcia, Jeff (Jeffrey Jason Garcia) *professional football player*
Lechler, Shane (Edward Shane Lechler) *professional football player*
McFadden, Darren *professional football player*
Russell, JaMarcus *professional football player*

Aliso Viejo
Cohen, Sasha (Alexandra Pauline Cohen) *ice skater*

Anaheim
Abreu, Bobby (Bob Kelly Abreu) *professional baseball player*
Carlyle, Randy *professional hockey coach, retired professional hockey player*
Figgins, Chone (Desmond DeChone Figgins) *professional baseball player*
Fuentes, Brian Christopher *professional baseball player*
Getzlaf, Ryan *professional hockey player*
Giguere, Jean-Sebastien *professional hockey player*
Guerrero, Vladimir Alvino *professional baseball player*
Hedican, Bret *professional hockey player*
Hunter, Torii Kedar *professional baseball player*
Moreno, Arturo (Arte Moreno) *professional sports team executive, former advertising executive*
Murray, Bob (Robert Frederick Murray) *professional sports team executive, former professional hockey player*
Niedermayer, Scott *professional hockey player*
Pronger, Chris *professional hockey player*
Pronger, Sean James *coach, former professional hockey player*
Schulman, Michael *professional sports team executive, lawyer*
Selanne, Teemu *professional hockey player*

Beaumont
Addis, Thomas Homer III *professional golfer*

Berkeley
Montgomery, Mike *men's college basketball coach*
Tedford, Jeff *college football coach*

Beverly Hills
Johnson, Magic (Earvin Johnson Jr.) *professional sports team and development company executive, retired professional basketball player*

Camarillo
Bryan, Bob Charles *professional tennis player*

Carson
Arena, Bruce *professional soccer coach*

Danville
Behring, Kenneth E. *professional sports team owner*
Wisniewski, Stephen Adam *professional football player*

El Segundo
Bryant, Kobe *professional basketball player*
Buss, Jerry (Gerald Hatten Buss) *professional sports team owner*
Bynum, Andrew *professional basketball player*
Gasol, Pau *professional basketball player*
Kupchak, Mitchell *professional sports team executive, retired professional basketball player*
Milton-Jones, DeLisha *professional basketball player*
Odom, Lamar Joseph *professional basketball player*

La Jolla
Bavasi, Peter Joseph *sports management executive*

La Verne
Mosley, Shane *boxer*

Long Beach
Monson, Dan *men's college basketball coach*

Los Angeles
Brown, Dustin *professional hockey player*
Caldwell, Nikki *women's college basketball coach*
Camby, Marcus D. *professional basketball player*
Carroll, Pete *college football coach*
Colletti, Ned Louis, Jr. *professional sports executive*
Cooper, Michael Jerome *professional baske coach, former professional basketball pla*
Dalis, Peter T. *athletic director*
Davis, Baron *professional basketball player*
Dunleavy, Mike (Michael Joseph Dunleavy *professional basketball coach*
Floyd, Tim *men's college basketball coach, former professional basketball coach*
Furcal, Rafael *professional baseball player*
Garciaparra, Nomar (Anthony Nomar Garciaparra) *professional baseball player*
Hamilton, Scott Scovell *professional figure skater, former Olympic athlete*
Hopkins, Bernard *professional boxer*
Howland, Ben *men's college basketball coa*
Hudson, Orlando Thill *professional baseba player*
Jackson, Philip Douglas *professional baske coach*
Kopitar, Anze *professional hockey player*
Lasorda, Tommy (Thomas Charles Lasorda *retired professional baseball team manag*
Lavin, Stephen Michael *university basketba coach*
Leiweke, Timothy *sports executive, marketi professional*
Leslie, Lisa DeShaun *professional basketba player*
Lombardi, Dean *professional sports team executive*
Maloney, Kristen *gymnast*
Ng, Kim (Kimberly J. Ng) *professional spo team executive*
Parker, Candace Nicole *professional basket player*
Robitaille, Luc *sports team executive, retire professional hockey player*
Roeser, Andy *professional sports team exec*
Scates, Allen Edward *coach*
Sherfy, Bradley Lloyd *professional golfer*
Torre, Joe (Joseph Paul Torre) *professional baseball team manager*
Vizcaino, Jose Luis Pimental *professional baseball coach, retired professional base player*
White, Devon Markes *professional basebal player*

Moraga
Bennett, Randy *men's college basketball co*

Northridge
Jumonville, Felix Joseph, Jr. *physical educa educator, real estate company officer*

Oakland
Cabrera, Orlando Luis *professional basebal player*
Chavez, Eric *professional baseball player*
Cohan, Christopher J. *professional sports te owner*
Cowens, David William (Dave Cowens) *professional basketball coach and retired player, insurance executive*
Crawford, Aaron Jamal (Jamal Crawford) *professional basketball player*
Croshere, Austin *professional basketball pla*
Ellis, Monta *professional basketball player*
Geren, Bob (Robert Peter Geren) *professior baseball manager*
Giambi, Jason Gilbert *professional basebal player*
Harris, Larry *professional basketball coach*
Holliday, Matt *professional baseball player*
Mullin, Christopher Paul *professional sport team executive, retired professional bask player*
Nelson, Donald Arvid (Nellie Nelson) *professional basketball coach*
Rowell, Robert *professional sports team executive*
Schott, Stephen C. *professional sports team executive*
Starks, John Levell *professional basketball player*
Thomas, Frank Edward *professional basebo player*

Playa Del Rey
Lewis, Carl (Frederick Carlton Lewis) *Oly track and field athlete*

Sacramento
Abdur-Rahim, Shareef (Julius Shareef Abdul-Rahim) *professional basketball co retired professional basketball player*
Boucek, Jenny *professional basketball coac*
Carril, Pete (Peter J. Carril) *professional basketball consultant*
Fox, Ned *professional sports team owner*
Griffith, Yolanda Evette *professional basket player*
Lawson, Kara *professional basketball playe*
Maloof, Gavin Patrick *professional sports t executive*
Maloof, Joseph *professional sports team ov*
Martin, Darrick David *professional basketb player*
Nocioni, Andres Marcelo *professional bask player*
Petrie, Geoffrey Michael *professional sport team executive, retired professional bask player*
Reynolds, Jerry Owen *professional sports t executive*

ias, John *professional sports team executive*

Diego
, Bud (Harry Ralston Black) *professional eball manager*
nds, Jim (James Patrick Edmonds) *fessional baseball player*
, Antonio *professional football player*
alez, Adrian *professional baseball player*
r, Charlie (Charles Joiner Jr.) *professional tball coach, retired professional football yer*
man, Shawne DeAndre *professional tball player*
ad, Jeff *professional sports team executive*
s, Philip *professional football player*
, A.J. *professional sports team executive*
nson, LaDainian *professional football yer*
r, Norv(al) (Eugene) *professional football ich*
eld, Dave (David Mark Winfield) *fessional sports team executive, rtscaster, retired professional baseball yer*

Francisco
y, Bruce *professional baseball team nager*
, Will (William Nuschler Clark Jr.) *fessional sports team administrator, retired fessional baseball player*
on, Randy (Randall David Johnson) *fessional baseball player*
wan, Peter Alden *professional sports team l retail executive*
Robert Allen (Robb Nen) *retired fessional baseball player*
tti, David Allen (Dave Righetti) *fessional baseball coach, retired fessional baseball player*
n, Brian R. *professional baseball team cutive*
Barry *professional baseball player*

Jose
, Rob *professional hockey player*
, Dan *professional hockey player*
son, John, Jr. *professional sports team cutive*
au, Patrick *professional hockey player*
kov, Evgeni *professional hockey player*
ick, Jeremy *professional hockey player*
nton, Joe *professional hockey player*
n, Douglas Frederick *professional sports m executive, retired professional hockey yer*

a Clara
h, Andrew Bruce *professional sports team cutive*
oughan, Scot G. *professional sports team cutive*
etary, Mike *professional football coach, red professional football player*
, Alex (Alexander Doug Smith) *fessional football player*
g, Bryant Colby *professional football yer*

ford
sby, Bob *athletic director*
ins, Johnny Earl, Jr. *men's college sketball coach*
sbeck, Harold Irving *professional sports m owner, management educator*
ugh, Jim (James Joseph Harbaugh) *college tball coach, retired professional football yer*
erveer, Tara *women's college basketball ich*

kton
hy, Jeremiah T. *professional sports team, nstruction executive*

a
, Tony *professional skateboarder*

nut Creek
ck, C. Wiles, Jr. *athletic official*
en, Thomas Carter *college athletics nference commissioner*

dland Hills
aila *professional boxer*

ORADO

der
s, Charles Merrill *sports association cutive, consultant*

rado Springs
k, Nicole *professional figure skater*
Bryan Ezra *Olympic track and field athlete*
gelo, Jerry John *professional sports team cutive*
hlin, Natalie *Olympic swimmer*

Cutone, Kathaleen Kelly *athletic representative, figure skater and former judge*
Kwan, Michelle Wing *professional figure skater*
Murray, Ty *professional rodeo cowboy*
Ogrean, David William *sports association executive*
Scherr, James Edwin *sports association executive*
Wariner, Jeremy *Olympic track and field athlete*
Woolridge, Orlando *former professional basketball and Olympic coach*

Denver
Anthony, Carmelo *professional basketball player*
Baylor, Don Edward *professional baseball coach, retired professional baseball player*
Beuerlein, Steve Taylor *professional football player*
Billups, Chauncey *professional basketball player*
Chapman, Rex *professional sports team executive, retired professional basketball player*
Foote, Adam *professional hockey player*
Hejduk, Milan *professional hockey player*
Helton, Todd *professional baseball player*
Hurdle, Clint (Clinton Merrick Hurdle) *professional baseball manager, former professional baseball player*
Issel, Daniel Paul *sports team executive, former professional basketball coach*
Karl, George *professional basketball coach*
Knight, Greg *professional sports team executive*
Lacroix, Pierre *professional sports team executive*
Sakic, Joe (Joseph Steve) *professional hockey player*
Street, Huston Lowell *professional baseball player*
Tulowitzki, Troy Trevor *professional baseball player*
Warkentien, Mark *professional sports team executive*

Englewood
Bailey, Champ *professional football player*
Beake, John *professional football team executive*
Bowlen, Pat (Patrick Dennis Bowlen) *professional sports team and holding company executive, lawyer*
Dawkins, Brian Patrick *professional football player*
Jordan, LaMont *professional football player*
McDaniels, Josh *professional football coach*
Nolan, Mike *professional football coach*
Orton, Kyle *professional football player*

Fort Collins
Weiser, Timothy L. *athletic director*

Greenwood Village
Elway, John Albert *professional sports team executive, retired professional football player*

IDAHO

Boise
Petersen, Chris *college football coach*

ILLINOIS

Lake Forest
Cutler, Jay *professional football player*

NEVADA

Las Vegas
Kruger, Lon *men's college basketball coach*
White, Dana *sports association executive*

NEW MEXICO

Albuquerque
Alford, Steve (Steven Todd Alford) *men's college basketball coach*

OREGON

Corvallis
Riley, Michael *college football coach*
Robinson, Craig *men's college basketball coach*

Eugene
Bellotti, Mike *college football coach*
Kent, Ernie *men's college basketball coach*
Sisley, Becky Lynn *physical education educator*

Portland
Aldridge, LaMarcus Nurae *professional basketball player*
Glanville, Jerry *college football coach, former professional football coach*
Golub, Mike *professional sports team executive*
Levi, Alexis *professional sports team executive, owner, agent*

McMillan, Nathaniel (Nate McMillan) *professional basketball coach*
Miller, Larry G. *professional sports team executive*
Oden, Greg *professional basketball player*
Pritchard, Kevin *professional sports team executive*
Roy, Brandon Dawayne *professional basketball player*

UTAH

Murray
Witworth, Clark L. *sports team executive*

Park City
Kelly, Thomas J. *sports association executive*
White, Shaun Roger *Olympic athlete, professional snowboarder, professional skateboarder*

Provo
Mendenhall, Bronco *college football coach*
Rose, Dave *men's college basketball coach*

Salt Lake City
Boozer, Carlos Austin, Jr. *professional basketball player*
Boylen, Jim *men's college basketball coach*
Howells, R. Tim *professional sports team executive*
O'Connor, Kevin *professional sports team executive*
Okur, Mehmet *professional basketball player*
Sloan, Jerry (Gerald Eugene Sloan) *professional basketball coach*
Whittingham, Kyle *college football coach*

Sandy
Rigby, Randy *professional sports team executive*

West Jordan
Azzi, Jennifer L. *personal trainer, retired professional basketball player*

WASHINGTON

Bellevue
Ellis, John W. *professional baseball team and utilities executive*

Kirkland
Brown, Chadwick Everett *professional football player*

Pullman
Bennett, Dick *college basketball coach*
Bone, Ken *men's college basketball coach*

Renton
Holmgren, Mike (Michael George Holmgren) *professional football coach*
Houshmandzadeh, T.J. (Touraj Houshmandzadeh) *professional football player*
Leiweke, Tod *professional sports team executive*
Mora, Jim (James Lawrence Mora) *professional football coach*
Ruskell, Tim *professional sports team executive*

Seattle
Allen, Paul Gardner *professional sports team and computer company executive*
Armstrong, Charles G. *professional baseball executive, lawyer*
Bird, Sue (Suzanne Brigit Bird) *professional basketball player*
Griffey, Ken, Jr., (George Kenneth Griffey Jr.) *professional baseball player*
Hasselbeck, Matt *professional football player*
Jackson, Lauren *professional basketball player*
Johjima, Kenji *professional baseball player*
Jones, Julius Andre Maurice *professional football player*
Lawton, Matt *professional baseball player*
Romar, Lorenzo *men's college basketball coach*
Stottlemyre, Mel (Melvin Leon Stottlemyre Sr.) *professional baseball coach, former professional baseball player*
Suzuki, Ichiro *professional baseball player*
Wakamatsu, Don (Wilbur Donald Wakamatsu) *professional baseball coach*
Walker, Walter Frederick *professional basketball team executive*
Zduriencik, Jack *professional sports team executive*

Spokane
Ueberroth, Peter Victor *sports association executive*

WYOMING

Newcastle
Engle, Kathleen Faye *elementary education educator*

CANADA

ALBERTA

Calgary
Hotchkiss, Harley N. *professional hockey team owner, oil industry executive*
Iginla, Jarome *professional hockey player*
Jokinen, Olli *professional hockey player*
Keenan, Mike (Micheal Edward Keenan) *professional hockey coach, former professional sports team executive*
Kiprusoff, Miikka *professional hockey player*
Sutter, Darryl John *professional sports team executive, former professional hockey coach*

Edmonton
Lowe, Kevin Hugh *professional sports team executive, former hockey player and coach*
Moreau, Ethan *professional hockey player*
Souray, Sheldon *professional hockey player*

BRITISH COLUMBIA

Vancouver
Demitra, Pavol *professional hockey player*
Gillis, Mike (Michael David Gillis) *professional sports team executive, retired professional hockey player*
Luongo, Roberto *professional hockey player*
Sedin, Henrik *professional hockey player*
Vigneault, Alain *professional hockey coach*
Zimmerman, Chris *professional sports team executive*

ADDRESS UNPUBLISHED

Alderson, Sandy (Richard Lynn Alderson) *former professional sports team executive*
Alexander, Shaun *professional football player*
Allen, Larry Christopher *retired professional football player*
Alou, Felipe Rojas *former professional baseball team manager*
Barton, Gregory Mark *Olympic athlete*
Baylor, Elgin Gay *former professional sports team executive, retired professional basketball player*
Bonds, Barry (Lamar) *former professional baseball player*
Bourque, Ray *retired professional hockey player*
Bowness, Rick (Richard Gary Bowness) *professional athletics coach*
Bravo, Paul *professional soccer player*
Brenly, Bob *professional sports team executive, broadcaster*
Crawford, Marc *former professional hockey coach*
Deadmarsh, Adam *former professional hockey player*
Dilfer, Trent *professional football player*
Forsberg, Peter *professional hockey player*
Goodman, Jim *former professional sports team executive*
Granato, Catherine (Cammi Granato) *former olympic athlete, sports association executive*
Harman, Jennifer (Jennifer Harman-Traniello) *professional poker player*
Hebert, Guy *professional hockey player*
Hill, Bob (Robert G. Hill) *former professional basketball coach*
Hollandsworth, Todd Mathew *professional baseball player*
Lipinski, Tara Kristen *retired professional figure skater*
Little, (William) Grady *former professional baseball coach, team manager*
MacTavish, Craig *former professional hockey coach, retired professional hockey player*
Malone, Kevin *sports team executive*
Musselman, Eric *former professional basketball coach*
Olson, Lute (Robert Luther Olson) *retired men's college basketball coach*
Patterson, Steve *former professional sports team executive*
Rice, Jerry Lee *retired professional football player*
Schottenheimer, Marty (Martin Edward Scottenheimer) *former professional football coach*
Shanahan, Mike (Michael Edward Shanahan) *former professional football coach*
Sharman, William *professional basketball team executive*
Shell, Art (Arthur Shell Jr.) *former professional football coach*
Timms, Michele *retired professional basketball player*
Tobin, Vincent Michael *professional football coach, former sports team executive*
Weiss, Bob (Robert William Weiss) *former professional basketball coach*
Williams, Matt(hew) (Derrick) *former professional baseball player*

Winslow, Kellen Boswell *retired professional football player*
Wooden, John Robert *former college basketball coach*

BUSINESS *See* FINANCE: INDUSTRY

COMMUNICATIONS *See* COMMUNICATIONS MEDIA; INDUSTRY: SERVICE

COMMUNICATIONS MEDIA *See also* ARTS: LITERARY

UNITED STATES

ALASKA

Anchorage
Cowell, Fuller A. *newspaper publisher*
Tobin, William Joseph *newspaper editor*

ARIZONA

Fountain Hills
Kinderwater, Joseph C. (Jack Kinderwater) *publishing company executive*

Gilbert
Kenney, Thomas Frederick *retired broadcast executive*

Marana
Steckler, Larry *publishing executive, writer*

Phoenix
Benson, Stephen R. *editorial cartoonist*
Breland, Sandy Ann *broadcast executive, director*
Early, Robert Joseph *magazine editor*
Edens, Gary Denton *broadcast executive*
Grafe, Warren Blair *broadcast executive*
Leach, John F. *editor, director, journalist, educator*
Lovely, Randy *editor-in-chief*
Miller, William *broadcast executive*
Moyer, Alan Dean *retired newspaper editor*
Stahl, Richard G. C. *journalist, editor*
Weil, Louis Arthur III *retired newspaper publishing executive*
Zidich, John M. *publishing executive*

Scottsdale
Johnson, Micah William *television newscaster, director*
Joseph, Gregory Nelson *media critic, writer, actor, advocate*

Tempe
Allen, Charles Raymond *television station executive*

Tucson
Allvin, Paul G. *communications educator*
Martin, June Johnson Caldwell *journalist*

CALIFORNIA

Agoura Hills
Fabregas, J. Robert *retail appearel executive*
Teresi, Joseph *publishing executive*

Alhambra
Duke, Donald Norman *publishing executive*

Alpine
Greenberg, Byron Stanley *newspaper and business executive, consultant*

Alta Loma
Straka, Laszlo Richard *retired publishing consultant*

Arcadia
Belnap, David F. *journalist*

Bakersfield
Beene, Richard Stuart *newspaper editor*

Belvedere Tiburon
Kramer, Lawrence Stephen *journalist*
Rosenthal, Robert Jon *newspaper editor, journalist*

Berkeley
Bagdikian, Ben Haig *journalist, educator*
Clark, James Henry *publishing company executive*
Lesser, Wendy *editor, writer, consultant*
Susskind, Teresa Gabriel *publishing executive*

Beverly Hills
Bradshaw, Terry (Terry Paxton Bradshaw) *sports announcer, former professional football player*
Corwin, Stanley Joel *book publisher*
Davis, Jonathan, Jr. *broadcast executive*
Friedman, Robert Lee *film company executive*
Gabler, Elizabeth Brand *film company executive*
Gerber, William Norman *motion picture executive*
Grazer, Brian *film company executive*
Heller, Paul Michael *film company executive, producer*
Hill, David *broadcast executive*
Lond, Harley Weldon *editor, publishing executive*
Minnillo, Vanessa Joy *news correspondent*
Rapino, Michael *music company executive*
Schneider, Charles Ivan *newspaper executive*
Stern, Leonard Bernard *television and motion picture production company executive*
Strauss, Ricky *film company executive, producer*
Wolper, David Lloyd *motion picture and television executive*
Zanuck, Richard Darryl *motion picture company executive*

Brea
Hewitt, Hugh *editor, writer, radio talk show host*

Brisbane
Daniels, Caroline *publishing executive*

Burbank
Berwick, Frances *broadcast executive*
Bird, Andy *film company executive*
Cohen, Polly *film company executive*
Cook, Richard W. (Dick Cook) *film company executive*
Downey, Susan *film company executive*
Fleishman, Susan Nahley *entertainment company executive*
Gregorian, Lisa *broadcast executive*
Hansen, Libby *broadcast executive*
Hashe, Janis Helene *editor*
Horn, Alan F. *film company executive*
Iger, Bob (Robert Allen Iger) *entertainment company executive*
Janollari, David *television broadcasting executive, cable and television producer*
Kaye, Jhani *radio station executive, television producer and director*
Kroll, Sue (Susan A. Kroll) *film company executive*
Kwan-Rubinek, Veronika *broadcast executive*
Liss, Walter C., Jr. *television station executive*
Marinelli, Janice *broadcast executive*
McLoughlin, Hilary Estey *broadcast executive*
McPherson, Stephen *broadcast executive*
Meyer, Barry Michael *motion picture executive*
Robertson, Richard Trafton *entertainment company executive*
Robinov, Jeff (Jeffrey Stephen Robinov) *film company executive*
Ross, Rich *broadcast executive*
Roth, Peter *broadcast executive*
Shuler, Dennis W. *entertainment company executive*
Sklar, Marty (Martin A. Sklar) *entertainment company executive*
Staggs, Thomas O. *entertainment company executive*
Sweeney, Anne M. *cable television company executive*
Tarrant, Alison *broadcast company executive*
Wandell, Morgan *broadcast executive*
Wiseman, Jane *broadcast executive*
Younger, Laurie *broadcast executive*
Zucker, Jeffrey A. *broadcast executive*

Burlingame
Mendelson, Lee M. *film company executive, producer, director, writer*

Camarillo
DePatie, David Hudson *motion picture company executive*
Doebler, Paul Dickerson *publishing management executive*
Howry, Joe R. *newspaper editor*

Carlsbad
Howard, Robert Staples *newspaper publisher*

Carmel
Mollman, John Peter *publishing executive*

Chatsworth
Faerber, Charles N. *editor*

Culver City
Bishop, David *entertainment company executive*
Feingold, Benjamin S. *broadcast executive*
Fischer, Bradley J. *film company executive*
Lynton, Michael *film company executive*
Milano, Adam *film company executive*
Pascal, Amy Beth *film company executive*

Daly City
Batlin, Robert Alfred *retired newspaper editor*

Del Mar
Faludi, Susan C. *journalist, scholarly writer*
Kaye, Peter Frederic *columnist*
Marcus, Larry David *broadcast executive*

Dublin
Woodson, Roderick Kevin *sportscaster, football coach, retired professional football player*

El Cajon
Russell, Anne M. *editor-in-chief*

El Segundo
Carey, Chase (Charles G.) *broadcast executive*
Churchill, Bruce B. *broadcast executive*
Doyle, Patrick T. *broadcast executive*
Guyardo, Paul *broadcast company executive*
Palkovic, Michael W. *broadcast executive*
Pontual, Romulo *broadcast executive*

Emeryville
Catmull, Edwin Earl *film company executive, computer graphics engineer*
Lasseter, John Alan *film company executive, computer animator*
Mather, Ann *film company executive*
Roth, Joe *motion picture company executive*

Encino
Altschul, David Edwin *record company executive, lawyer*
Pearl, Mariane (Mariane van Neyenhoff Pearl) *journalist, filmmaker*

Fall River Mills
Caldwell, Walter Edward *editor, small business owner*

Frazier Park
Nelson, Harry *journalist, medical writer*

Fresno
Morales, Hugo *broadcast executive*
Waters, Charles R., Jr. *executive editor*

Glendale
Enrico, Roger A. *film company executive, retired food and beverage company executive*
Katzenberg, Jeffrey *film company executive*
MacDonald, Laurie *film company executive*
Parkes, Walter F. *film company executive*
Snider, Stacey *film company executive*

Happy Camp
Brown, Barbara Black *publishing company executive*

Hollywood
Perth, Rod *network entertainment executive*
Salzman, David Elliot *entertainment industry executive*

Huntington Beach
De Massa, Jessie G. *media specialist*
Garofalo, David P. *publishing executive, former mayor*

Inglewood
Sludikoff, Stanley Robert *publisher, writer*

Irvine
Horne, Terry *publishing executive*
Lesonsky, Rieva *editor-in-chief*
Power, Francis William *newspaper publisher*
Siegel, Barry *journalist, writer, literature educator*

La Canada
Paniccia, Patricia Lynn *journalist, writer, lawyer, educator*

La Jolla
Copley, David C. *publishing executive*
Freedman, Jonathan Borwick *journalist, writer, educator*
Hall, TennieBee M. *editor*
Harris, T. George *editor*
Morgan, Neil *editor, journalist, writer*
Pfeiffer, Phyllis Kramer *publishing executive*
Ramirez, Michael P. *editorial cartoonist*

Long Beach
Adler, Jeffrey D. *media consultant, management consultant*
Ruszkiewicz, Carolyn Mae *newspaper editor*
Yousef, Fathi Salaama *communications educator, management consultant*

Los Angeles
Archerd, Army (Armand A. Archerd) *columnist, retired commentator*
Arthur, John M. *editor*
Bart, Peter Benton *editor, film producer, writer*
Bernstein, William *film company executive*
Berry, Stephen Joseph *reporter*
Boyle, Barbara Dorman *film company executive*
Boyter, Cale *film company executive*
Bryson, Louise Henry *retired broadcast executive*
Cannon, Reuben *casting company executive, film producer*
Charen, Mona *columnist*
Chavez, Michael Robinson *photojournalist*
Clarke, Peter *communications and health educator*
Cole, K.C. *journalist, writer*
Corrao, Lauren *broadcast executive*
Darling, Juanita Marie *correspondent*
Delugach, Albert Lawrence *journalist*
de Passe, Suzanne *record company executive*
Dolan, Mary Anne *journalist, columnist*
Dwyre, William Patrick *journalist*
Field, Ted (Frederick) *film company and recording industry executive*
Fields, Robin *reporter*
Findley, John Allen, Jr. *publishing executive*
Firstenberg, Jean Picker *retired film institu executive*
Flanigan, James J(oseph) *journalist*
Freer, Randy *broadcast executive*
Gazzale, Bob *film institute executive*
Gianopulos, Jim *film company executive*
Goldwyn, John *film company executive*
Goren, Edward Gerald (Ed Goren) *broadc executive*
Gross, Larry Paul *communications educat*
Hacken, Carla *film company executive*
Hartenstein, Eddy W. *publishing executive, former electronics executive*
Hefner, Hugh Marston *editor-in-chief*
Hicks, Christopher *music company executi*
Hofmeister, Sallie Ann *editor*
Israel, David *journalist, scriptwriter, film producer*
Jacobson, Sidney *editor*
Johnson, John Malcolm, Jr. *reporter*
Jones, Quincy *producer, composer, arrang conductor, trumpeter*
Kleiner, Arnold Joel *television station exe*
Klunder, Jack D. *publishing executive*
Knapp, Cleon Talboys *publishing executive*
Kraft, Scott Corey *news correspondent*
Kristof, Kathy M. *journalist*
Larrubia, Evelyn *reporter*
Lazarus, David *journalist*
Lazarus, Mell *cartoonist*
Lee, Kwan Min *communications educator, consultant*
Lee, Stan (Stanley Martin Lieber) *cartoon publisher, writer*
Leonard, Jack *reporter*
Levin, Harvey Robert *reporter, television producer, lawyer*
Levine, Jesse E. *publishing executive*
Levine, Pamela *film company executive*
Levinsohn, Peter *film company executive*
Lipstone, Howard Harold *television produ executive*
Litewka, Albert Bernard *entertainment exe*
Lopez, Steve *journalist*
Lowenthal, Abraham Frederic *internationa relations educator*
Lozano, Monica Cecilia *publishing executi*
Maharaj, Davan R. *editor*
Maltin, Leonard *commentator, writer*
Mann, Wesley F. *editor, writer, reporter*
Martin, Roland S. *journalist, former editor*
Mashariki, Zola B. *film company executive*
Miles, Jack (John Russiano) *journalist, ed*
Muchnic, Suzanne *art writer, educator, lec*
Murphy, Philip Edward *broadcast executiv*
Newcombe, Richard Sumner *newspaper syndicate executive*
Newton, Jim *editor*
Parent, Mary Campbell *film company exec*
Parisi, Paula Elizabeth *writer, photographe editor*
Parks, Michael Christopher *journalist, edu*
Paul, Charles S. *motion picture and televis company executive*
Piller, Charles Leon *journalist*
Plate, Thomas Gordon *columnist, educator*
Ramos, Jorge *newscaster*
Rawitch, Robert Joe *journalist, educator*
Rice, Peter *broadcast executive*
Rosenberg, Howard Anthony *journalist*
Rosenzweig, Richard Stuart *publishing cor executive*
Rothman, Tom (Thomas Edgar Rothman) *company executive*
Rush, Herman E. *television executive*
Salmon, Beth Ann *magazine editor-in-chie*
Saltzman, Joseph *journalist, educator, tele producer*
Sarnoff, Thomas Warren *television executi*
Saylor, Mark Julian *newspaper editor*
Scully, Vincent Edward *sports broadcaster*
Shuster, Alvin *journalist, reporter*
Singleton, Joan Vietor *publishing executive writer, film producer*
Sipchen, Bob *reporter*
Sloan, Harry Evans *film company executiv*
Sloan, L. Lawrence *publishing executive*
Smith, Gordon E. *publishing executive*
Stanton, Russ W. *editor-in-chief*
Steele, Bruce Carl *magazine editor*
Tellem, Nancy Reiss *broadcast executive*
Thompson, Anne Kathleen *entertainment journalist*
Tulsky, Fredric Neal *journalist*
Uva, Joe *broadcast executive*
Valdez, Jeff *broadcast executive, television producer*
Van Buren, Abigail (Jeanne Phillips) *colun educator*
Vinciquerra, Tony *broadcast executive*
Walden, Dana *broadcast executive*
Ward, Leslie Allyson *journalist, editor*
Warfel, Susan Leigh *editor*
Wasserman, Casey *media company executi*
Watts, Emma *film company executive*
Weiss, Kenneth R. *newswriter*
Weitz, Brett *broadcast executive*
Williams, Kenneth Scott *entertainment cor executive*
Wolinsky, Leo C. *newspaper editor*
Yari, Bob *film company executive, produce*
Youpa, Donald George *broadcast executiv*
Zacchino, Narda *newspaper editor*

Los Gatos
Hastings, Reed (Wilmot Reed Hastings Jr. *rental company executive, former educa association administrator*

nhattan Beach
el, David *entertainment company executive*

ina Del Rey
neim, Richard David *broadcast executive, ector*

nlo Park
, Michael Graves *publishing executive*
n, Kevin J. *publishing executive, media nner*
s, Leonard C. *media executive*

nterey
stein, Kenneth F. *entertainment and blishing company executive*

wport Beach
, Paul John *magazine editor*

dand
nan, Jane A. *publishing executive*
ge, Donald Warner *online columnist and tor, freelance writer*
nney, Judson Thad *broadcast executive*
g, Peter *editor, writer*
ergren, Timothy Brooks *music company ecutive*

anside
, Marilyn Mohr *columnist*

fic Grove
ile, James Michael *communications ucator, writer*

fica
David Macaulay *journalist, consultant*
, Kevin *editor*

n Desert
g, Henry Faithful *editor, consultant, rnalist, poet*

n Springs
d, James Wilson *publishing consultant*
s, Michelle M. *publishing executive*
, Zane Boyd *editor, publisher*

Alto
gan, John C. (Bud Colligan) *multimedia npany executive*
ns, Samuel *publishing executive*

Robles
n, Benjamin Andrew *retired journalist*

wood City
Ronnie (Ronald Mandel Lott) *retired fessional football player*

rside
s, Etta (Jamesetta Hawkins) *recording artist*
sky, Robert Lawrence *journalist*

ing Hills Estates
d, Paul Francis *cartoonist*

ramento
Cheryl Elbright *publishing executive*
on, Glenda Maria *newswriter*
strom, Marjie *editor*
, Gary B. *publishing company executive*
er, Maria Owings *former news respondent*
Melanie *editor-in-chief*
n, Denny Jay *reporter*
rs, Daniel Raymond *political columnist*
ams, Arthur Cozad *retired broadcasting ecutive*

Helena
ra, Antonia *editor, writer*

Diego
an, Larry A. *entertainment company ecutive, producer, director*
, Stephen P. *editorial cartoonist*
nan, Julian Mortimer *broadcasting npany executive, consultant*
Lee Ann *reporter, newscaster*
, Herbert George *newspaper editor*
Robert Campbell, II, *publishing executive*
s, Robert Lawrence *art critic, historian*
n, Edward J. *broadcasting company cutive*
, Peter A. *columnist*
one, Gary P. (Pike) *newspaper tor-in-chief, cartoonist*
, Paul Joseph *retired broadcasting cutive*
r, Karin E. *editor*

Francisco
, Joseph A. *television station executive*
rson, Chris W. *editor-in-chief*
lle, John *journalist, educator, writer, repreneur*
nfield, Arthur John *music critic, writer*
stein, Phil *publishing executive*
e, Ward III *editor*
ron, Heather Anne *publishing executive*
n, Dwight Allan *columnist, writer*
, Marilyn *journalist*
, Sandy *journalist*
son, Keay *newswriter*
y, Glenn Ernest, Jr. *sportswriter*
na, Julius Carl *journalist*

Eaton, Jerry *television executive*
Falk, Steven B. *newspaper publishing executive*
Fifer, Sally Jo *broadcast executive, editor*
Fox, Mitchell B. *publishing executive*
Fox, Steve *editor-in-chief*
Garchik, Leah Lieberman *journalist*
German, William *newspaper editor*
Gonzales, Richard Steven *broadcast executive*
Graysmith, Robert *political cartoonist, author*
Hamilton, Joan Nice *editor-in-chief*
Klein, Marc S. *editor, publishing executive*
Lara, Adair *columnist, writer*
McCracken, Harry *journalist*
McEvoy, Nion Tucker *editor*
Meyer, Thomas James *editorial cartoonist*
Perlman, David *journalist*
Rennie, I. Drummond *periodical editor, medical educator*
Roffman, Howard *motion picture company executive*
Rosenheim, Daniel Edward *journalist, television news director*
Rubenstein, Steven Paul *newspaper columnist*
Russell, Sabin *newswriter*
Ryan, Joan *columnist*
Sansweet, Stephen Jay *journalist, writer, marketing executive*
Saunders, Debra J. *columnist*
Schwarz, Glenn Vernon *newspaper editor*
Sias, John B. *former multi-media company executive, newspaper publisher, publishing executive*
Smith, Patrick (Patrick Santosuosso) *columnist, pilot*
Vega, Frank J. *publishing executive*
Walsh, Joan *editor-in-chief*
Winn, Steven Jay *critic*
Wolaner, Robin Peggy *internet and magazine publisher*

San Jose
Butler, David J. *newspaper editor*
Carey, Peter Kevin *reporter*
Elder, Robert Laurie *newspaper editor*
Harris, Jay Terrence *communications educator*
Mendoza, Martha *reporter*
Migielicz, Geralyn *photojournalist*
Ridder, P(aul) Anthony *newspaper company executive*
Riggs, George E. *newspaper publishing executive*
Rockstroh, Dennis John *journalist*
Trousdale, Stephen Richard *newspaper editor*
Tully, Mac *publishing executive*

San Rafael
Morgan, Michael Brewster *publishing executive*

Santa Ana
Brusic, Ken *editor-in-chief*
Katz, Tonnie *newspaper editor*
Treshie, R. David *former newspaper publishing executive*

Santa Barbara
Ackerman, Marshall *publishing executive*
Brantingham, Barney *journalist, writer*
Brilliant, Ashleigh Ellwood *cartoonist, writer*
Dubroff, Henry Allen *editor, journalist, entrepreneur*
Peck, Abraham *editor, media consultant, educator*
Roberts, Jerry *newspaper editor*
Segal, Helene Rose *periodical editor*
Tapper, Joan Judith *magazine editor*

Santa Monica
Alpert, Herb *composer, recording artist, producer, painter*
Berman, Gail *former film company executive, media company executive*
Feltheimer, Jon *entertainment company executive*
Friedman, Robert Glenn *film company executive*
Huffington, Arianna *columnist, writer, editor*
Iovine, Jimmy *recording industry executive*
Mancuso, Frank G. *entertainment and communications company executive*
McCreary, Lori L. *film company executive*
Morgan, Dave *editor*
Morgenstern, Joe *film critic*
Palen, Tim *film company executive*
Rifkin, Arnold *film company executive*
Sacchi, John *film company executive*
Slater, Mary Jo *former broadcasting executive, casting director*
Stern, Sandra *film company executive*

Santa Rosa
Person, Evert Bertil *retired newspaper and radio executive*
Swofford, Robert Lee *editor, journalist*

Sebastopol
O'Reilly, Tim *computer book publishing company executive, open sourcer advocate*

Sherman Oaks
Drudge, Matt (Matthew Nathan Drudge) *journalist, celebrity blogger*

Sonoma
Beckmann, Jon Michael *publishing company executive*

Stanford
Roberts, Donald Frank, Jr. *communications educator*

Torrance
Adelsman, Jean (Harriette Adelsman) *newspaper editor*
Wafer, Thomas J., Jr. *newspaper publisher*

Universal City
Baker, Bridget *broadcast executive*
Bromstad, Angela *broadcast executive*
Langley, Donna *film company executive*
Linde, David *film company executive*
Lowe, Kristin *film company executive*
Madison, Paula *broadcast executive*
Menendez, Belinda *broadcast executive*
Meyer, Ron *film company executive*
Rocco, Nikki *film company executive*
Shmuger, Marc *film company executive*
Silverman, Ben *broadcast executive, television producer*
Stuber, Scott *film company executive*

Valley Springs
Anema-Garten, Durlynn C. *communications educator, counseling administrator, writer*

Ventura
Kirman, Charles Gary *photojournalist*

Walnut Creek
Mott, Frederick B., Jr. *publishing executive*

West Hollywood
Grey, Brad *film company executive*
Huntsberry, Frederick D. *film company executive*
Lesher, John *film company executive*
Powell, Amy Ruth *film company executive*
Schwartz, Robin *broadcast executive*
Weston, Brad *film company executive*

Woodland Hills
DeWitt, Barbara Jane *journalist*
Harris, Barbara S. *publishing executive, editor-in-chief*
Latona, Valerie Ann *editor-in-chief*
Lund, Robert W. *newspaper editor*
McCluggage, Kerry *film and television executive*
Murphy, Irene Helen *publishing executive*

COLORADO

Aspen
Hayes, Mary Eshbaugh *editor, writer*

Boulder
Bull, James Robert *publishing executive*
El Mallakh, Dorothea Hendry *editor, publishing executive*
Rienner, Lynne Carol *publishing executive*

Colorado Springs
Mansfield, Roger Leo *astronomy and space publisher*
Zapel, Arthur Lewis *book publishing executive*

Denver
Bates, James Robert *newspaper editor*
Britton, Dennis A. *former newspaper editor, executive*
Chavez, Jeanette *editor*
Clark, Gary R. *newspaper editor*
Cohen, Andrew *news analyst, lawyer*
Cubbison, Christopher Allen *newspaper editor*
Dance, Francis Esburn Xavier *communication educator*
Drake, Sylvie (Jurras) *theater critic*
Giffin, Glenn Orlando, II, *music critic, writer, newspaper editor*
Kern, Jerome H. *consulting firm executive*
Moore, Gregory L. *editor*
Morgese, James N. *broadcast executive*
Price, Kathleen McCormick *editor, writer*
Rockford, Marv *television executive*
Rothman, Paul A. *publishing executive*
Saltz, Howard Joel *newspaper editor*
Scudder, Richard B. *newspaper executive*
Sheeler, Jim *journalist, educator*
Simone, Robert M. *broadcast executive*
Singleton, William Dean *publishing executive*

Durango
Van Mols, Brian *publishing executive*

Evergreen
Dobbs, Gregory Allan *journalist*

Fort Collins
May, Stephen James *communications educator, writer*

Georgetown
Stern, Mort(imer) P(hillip) *communications educator, editor, reporter, consultant*

Golden
Baron, Robert Charles *publishing executive*
Zimmer, Larry William, Jr. *sports announcer*

Highlands Ranch
Harris, Douglas Clay *retired newspaper executive*

Paonia
Ring, Ray *editor*

Pueblo
Rawlings, Robert Hoag *newspaper publisher*

HAWAII

Honolulu
Flanagan, John Michael *editor, publisher*
Gatti, Jim *editor*
Keyes, Saundra Elise *newspaper editor*
Simonds, John Edward *retired newspaper editor*

Kaneohe
Jellinek, Roger *editor*

IDAHO

Boise
Boren, Robert Reed *communications educator*
Gowler, Vicki Sue *editor-in-chief*
McLuskie, Ed *communications educator*

Idaho Falls
Harris, Darryl Wayne *publishing executive*

Sandpoint
Bowne, Martha Hoke *editor, consultant*

KANSAS

Wichita
Lilly, George David *broadcasting executive*

MONTANA

Bigfork
Blumberg, Nathan(iel) Bernard *journalist, educator, writer and publisher*

Billings
Svee, Gary Duane *newspaper editor, writer, journalist*

NEVADA

Henderson
Kelley, Michael John *newspaper editor*

Las Vegas
Berghel, Hal L. *columnist, inventor, consultant, lecturer, educator*
Norman, Jean Reid *journalist*
Scherf, Dietmar *publishing executive, artist, minister*
Tash, Martin Elias *publishing company executive*
Zobell, Charles W. *newspaper managing editor*

Reno
Hengstler, Gary Ardell *publisher, editor, lawyer*
McKibben, Ryan Timothy *newspaper executive*

NEW MEXICO

Albuquerque
Hadas, Elizabeth Chamberlayne *editor*
Lang, Thompson Hughes *publishing executive*
Moskos, Harry *columnist, editor*

Raton
Carroll, William *publishing company executive*

Santa Fe
Bowman, Jon Robert *magazine editor, film critic*
Burns, Scott *columnist*
Dirks, Lee Edward *newspaper executive*
Lichtenberg, Maggie Klee *publishing executive*
Stieber, Tamar *journalist*

Silver City
Fryxell, David Allen *publishing executive*

NEW YORK

New York
Gaspin, Jeffrey M. *broadcast executive*
Karlgaard, Rich *publishing executive*

OREGON

Albany
Wood, Kenneth Arthur *retired editor, writer*

Canby
Jarvey, Paulette Sue *publishing executive*

Corvallis
Hall, Don Alan *editor, writer*

Eugene
Baker, Alton Fletcher III *editor, publishing executive*
Bassett, Carol Ann *journalism educator, writer*
Sherriffs, Ronald Everett *communication and film educator*
Tykeson, Donald Erwin *broadcast executive*

Medford
Atkinson, Perry *broadcast executive, former political organization administrator*

Portland
Bhatia, Peter K. *editor, journalist*
Bunza, Linda Hathaway *editor, writer, composer, director*

Graves, Earl William, Jr. *journalist*
Hooker, Elaine Norton *news executive*
Johnston, Richard C. *newspaper editor*
Johnston, Virginia Evelyn *retired editor*
Kosseff, Jeff *reporter, news correspondent*
Mapes, Jeffrey Robert *journalist*
Rowe, Sandra Mims *editor*
Stickel, Frederick A. *publishing executive*
Woodward, Stephen Richard *newspaper reporter*
Zaitz, Leslie Lee *reporter*

Salem
Mainwaring, William Lewis *publishing company executive, author*

UTAH

Park City
Gallivan, John William *retired publishing executive*

Provo
Bartlett, Leonard Lee *retired communications educator, advertising executive*
Hughes, (Robert) John *journalist, educator*
Willes, Mark Hinckley *media specialist*

Salt Lake City
Anderson, Arthur Salzner *publishing company and marketing executive*
Beecham, William R. *newspaper editor*
Brown, Carolyn Smith *communications educator, consultant*
Conway, Nancy Ann *newspaper editor*
Fehr, John William *newspaper editor*
Hatch, George Clinton *television executive*
Sillars, Malcolm O. *communications educator*

WASHINGTON

Bellevue
Dolgen, Jonathan L. *former motion picture company executive, investor*
Wilkens, Lenny (Leonard Randolph Wilkens Jr.) *sportscaster, former professional sports team executive, retired professional basketball player*

Bellingham
Meals, Pamela F. *publishing executive*

Blaine
Miller, Ronald *journalist, critic*

Edmonds
Owen, John *retired newspaper editor*

Port Angeles
Brewer, John Charles *journalist*

Pullman
Haarsager, Dennis Lee *broadcast executive*

Redmond
Boyle, Alan *editor*

Seattle
Blethen, Frank A. *newspaper publisher*
Boardman, David *editor*
Bruner, Nancy J. *publishing executive*
Buckner, Philip Franklin *newspaper publisher*
Bunting, Kenneth Freeman *newspaper editor*
Cochran, Wendell Albert *science editor*
Crumb, R. (Robert Dennis Crumb) *cartoonist*
Domke, David S. *communications educator*
Ellegood, Donald Russell *publishing executive*
Fancher, Michael Reilly *editor, publishing executive*
Godden, Jean W. *columnist*
Gwinn, Mary Ann *editor*
Hartl, John George *film critic*
Henderson, Paul III *journalist, private investigator*
Hills, Regina J. *journalist*
Lacitis, Erik *journalist*
MacLeod, Alex *newspaper editor*
Medved, Michael *film critic, author, talk show host*
Nash, Cynthia Jeanne *journalist*
Parks, Michael James *editor*
Pascal, Naomi Brenner *editor-at-large, publishing executive*
Sizemore, Herman Mason, Jr. *newspaper executive*
Soden, John P. *publishing executive*
Stanton, Michael John *newspaper editor*
Turner, Wallace L. *reporter*

Spokane
Cowles, William Stacey *newspaper publisher*
Kafentzis, John Charles *journalist, educator*
Kunkel, Richard Lester *public radio executive*
Steele, Karen Dorn *journalist*

Tacoma
Mladenich, Ronald E. *publishing executive*
Zeeck, David A. *newspaper editor*

Vancouver
Middlewood, Martin Eugene *writer, consultant*

CANADA

ALBERTA

Edmonton
Hughes, Linda J. *newspaper publisher*

BRITISH COLUMBIA

Vancouver
Yaffe, Barbara Marlene *journalist*

ADDRESS UNPUBLISHED

Ambrose, Daniel Michael *publishing executive*
Anders, George Charles *journalist, writer*
Anderson, N. Christian III *former newspaper publisher*
Avnet, Jonathan Michael *motion picture company executive, film director*
Bandow, Douglas Leighton *editor, columnist, consultant*
Barber, Gary *motion picture company executive*
Bernheimer, Martin *music critic*
Bierstedt, Peter Richard *entertainment industry consultant, lawyer*
Blackstock, Joseph Robinson *newspaper editor*
Brogliatti, Barbara Spencer *retired television and motion picture executive, consultant*
Bryant, Thomas Lee *retired magazine editor*
Buhler, Jill Lorie *editor, writer*
Calley, John *former motion picture company executive, film producer*
Cardone, Bonnie Jean *freelance/self-employed photojournalist*
Carlson, Gary R. *publishing executive*
Carlson, Stacy C. *former motion picture association executive*
Churgin, Amy *former publishing executive*
Clark, Peter Bruce *retired publishing executive*
Crabbs, Roger Alan *publishing executive, director, small business owner, military officer, educator*
Curtin, David Stephen *newswriter*
Davis, Donald Alan *news correspondent, author*
De Line, Donald *former film company executive*
Dietrich, William Alan *reporter, writer*
Disney, Roy Edward *broadcasting company executive*
Doctor, Kenneth Jay *digital content consultant*
Duncan, David Ewing *editor, writer*
Dwan, Dennis Edwin *broadcast executive, photographer*
Ellis, Robert Harry *retired broadcast executive, academic administrator*
Endicott, William F. *journalist*
Engdahl, Todd Philip *editor*
Esposito, Joseph John *publishing company executive*
Ewell, Miranda Juan *journalist*
Farnsworth, Elizabeth *broadcast journalist*
Fenwick, James Henry *editor, writer, columnist*
Feola, Louis *broadcast executive*
Fox, John *film company executive*
Frauenfelder, Mark *editor-in-chief, blogger, illustrator*
Gates, Susan Inez *magazine publisher*
Geffen, David Lawrence *film company executive*
Geiger, Beth C. *freelance/self-employed journalist*
Geller, Glenn *broadcast executive*
Gilbert, Richard *broadcast executive*
Gill, Libby *television executive*
Glickman, Daniel Robert *motion picture association executive, former United States Secretary of Agriculture*
Grushow, Sandy *broadcast executive*
Haile, L. John, Jr. *journalist, publishing executive*
Hammer, Bonnie *broadcast executive*
Harbert, Ted (Edward W. Harbert III) *broadcast executive*
Heaphy, Janis Besler *retired publishing executive*
Hiller, David Dean *former publishing executive*
Hiltzik, Michael *journalist*
James, Bruce Richard *publishing executive*
Jensen, Jack Michael *publishing executive*
Johnson, Carol Ann *editor*
Johnson, William Potter *publishing executive, director*
Jones, Leonade Diane *media publishing company executive*
Joseph, Michael Thomas *broadcast consultant*
Kadin, Heather *broadcast executive*
Kellner, Jamie *broadcast executive*
Kennedy, Kevin Curtis *sports commentator, former professional baseball team manager*
Kiel, Jeff E. *former publishing executive*
Kinsley, Michael E. *newspaper columnist*
Kramer, Donovan Mershon, Sr. *newspaper publisher*
Laird, Jere Don *news reporter*
Levin, Robert Barry *motion picture company executive*
Lewis, Thomasine Elizabeth *magazine editor-in-chief*
Lieberfarb, Warren N. *digital media pioneer*
Lloyd, Michael Jeffrey *recording producer*
Maharidge, Dale Dimitro *journalist, educator, writer*
Main, Robert Gail *communications educator, training services executive, television and film producer, retired military officer*
Malott, Adele Renee *editor*
Manning, Richard Dale *writer*
McFarling, Usha Lee *journalist*
McGurk, Christopher Jamie *film company executive*
McLaughlin, Leighton Bates, II, *retired journalist, reporter, educator*
McManus, Patrick Francis *editor, educator, writer*
McRee, Lisa *television host, producer*
Mechanic, William M. *former television and motion picture industry executive*
Melody, Michael Edward *publishing company executive*
Mestres, Ricardo A. III *film company executive*
Might, Thomas Owen *newspaper company executive*
Minor, Halsey *multimedia company executive*
Murphy, Kim *newspaper bureau chief*
Neufeld, Mace *film company executive*
Nijhuis, Michelle *freelance journalist*
Oppedahl, John Frederick *newspaper publisher, executive*
O'Shea, James E. *former editor-in-chief*
Osterhaus, William Eric *broadcast executive*
Perenchio, Andrew Jerrold *film and television executive*
Perry, Michael C. *theatre publisher, educator*
Pope, Katherine Collins *former broadcast executive*
Rasor, Dina Lynn *journalist, private investigator*
Read, Richard Eaton *newspaper reporter*
Rinearson, Peter Mark *journalist, writer, software executive*
Rodrigue, George P. *newspaper executive*
Rodriguez, Rick *former executive editor*
Rosett, Daniel J. *film company executive*
Sands, Rick (Richard Sands) *former film company executive*
Sardella, Edward Joseph *television news anchor*
Satz, Louis K. *publishing executive*
Shaevitz, Geoff *film company executive*
Shaw, Eleanor Jane *newspaper editor*
Shaye, Robert Kenneth *film company executive*
Smith, Martin Bernhard *retired journalist*
Tata, Giovanni *publishing executive*
Taylor, George Frederick *newspaper publisher, editor*
Twigg-Smith, Thurston *newspaper publisher*
Vandenberg, Peter Ray *publishing executive*
Vargas, Diana Lisa *television station executive*
Vitale, Ruth Ann *former film company executive*
Voorhees, John Lloyd *columnist*
Wagner, Paula *film company executive*
Weaver, Howard C. *newspaper executive*
Welsome, Eileen *journalist, writer*
Whitesell, John Edwin *retired motion picture company executive*
Witt, Melvin Sylvan *periodical editor, publisher*
Woldt, Harold Frederick, Jr. *newspaper publishing executive*
Zappe, John Paul *city editor, newspaper executive, educator*
Ziegler, Jack (Jack Denmore) *cartoonist*
Zweifel, Donald Edwin *editor, lobbyist, consultant*

EDUCATION *See also* specific fields for postsecondary education

UNITED STATES

ALASKA

Anchorage
Byrd, Milton Bruce *academic administrator*
Comeau, Carol Smith *school system administrator*
Ennis, William Lee *physics educator*
North, Douglas McKay *academic administrator*
Sandberg, Arlene *elementary school educator*
Ulmer, Frances Ann *academic administrator, retired state official*

Chiniak
Griffin, Elaine B. *educator*

Dillingham
Bouker, Ina B. *elementary school educator*

Fairbanks
Doran, Timothy Patrick *academic administrator*
Hamilton, Mark R. *academic administrator*
Jones, Stephen B. *academic administrator*
Lind, Marshall L. *academic administrator*

Juneau
Pugh, John Robert *academic administrator, educator, retired state official*
Sampson, Roger *school system administrator*

ARIZONA

Flagstaff
Haeger, John Denis *academic administrator*

Glendale
Altersitz, Janet Kinahan *principal*
Cole, James W. *dean*

Green Valley
Turner, Harold Edward *retired education educator*

Mesa
Christiansen, Larry K. *college president*
Dillenberg, Jack *dean*

Phoenix
Coor, Lattie Finch *university president*
Horne, Thomas Charles *school system administrator*
Morris, Erdie L. *dean, medical educator*
Noone, Laura Palmer *academic administra lawyer*
Palacios, Christina *academic administrator*
Pepicello, William J. *academic administrat*
Sperling, John Glen *education company executive, educator*
Whitlow, Donna Mae *daycare and primary school administrator*

Prescott
Rheinish, Robert Kent *university administr*

Rio Verde
Vanselow, Neal Arthur *retired academic administrator, internist*

Scottsdale
Hill, Louis Allen, Jr. *retired dean, civil eng consultant*
Stone, Alan Jay *retired academic administ*
Wilson, Robert E. *academic administrator*

Sierra Vista
Adams, Frank *adult education educator, consultant*

Tempe
Arredondo, Patricia *academic administrato psychology professor*
Crow, Michael M. *academic administrator*
Mittelstaedt, Robert E., Jr. *dean*
Thor, Linda M. *college president*

Tucson
Bootman, J. Lyle *pharmacy educator*
Brennan, Carrie *principal*
Carney, Kevin *principal*
Cate, Rodney Michael *academic administr*
Janes, Raena *private school educator*
Kaltenbach, C(arl) Colin *dean, educator*
Likins, Peter William *retired academic administrator*
Massaro, Toni Marie *dean, law educator*
Pfeuffer, Roger *school system administrato*
Popson, Lucy (Maria D. Popson) *elementa school educator*
Shelton, Robert Neal *academic administra physics professor, researcher*
Stoffle, Carla Joy *university library dean*

CALIFORNIA

Alameda
Carter, Roberta Eccleston *counseling administrator*

Alhambra
Suzuki, Bob H. *retired academic administ*

Aptos
Bohn, Ralph Carl *educational consultant*

Arcadia
Baltz, Patricia Ann (Pann) *retired elementa school educator*
Matsuura, Kenneth Ray *counseling administrator*

Arcata
McCrone, Alistair William *retired academi administrator*

Azusa
Felix, Richard E. *academic administrator*
Liegler, Rosemary Menke *dean*

Bakersfield
Hefner, John *principal*

Berkeley
Bender, Richard *dean, architect, educator*
Birgeneau, Robert Joseph *academic administrator, physicist, researcher*
Crandall, Keith C. *dean*
diSessa, Andrea A. *education educator*
Doyle, Fiona Mary *dean, metallurgical en educator*
Freedman, Sarah Warshauer *education edu*
Gray, Paul Russell *academic administrator electrical engineering educator*
Heathcock, Clayton Howell *chemistry edu researcher*
Linn, Marcia Cyrog *education educator*
Maurer, Stephen Mark *academic program director*
Miles, Raymond Edward *retired dean, organizational behavior and industrial relations educator*
Pearson, P. David *dean*
Ralston, Lenore Dale *academic policy and program analyst*
Raphael, Steven P. *dean, political science professor*
Roychowdhury, Jaijeet *professor*

ll, Orville *former dean*
tell, Stephen Michael *dean, health services searcher*

bank
l, Jacqueline Powers *academic lministrator*
sen, Kenneth Ray *academic administrator*

narillo
ett, Kenneth Lee *superintendent*
, Richard R. *academic administrator*

itola
son, Kingsbury Temple *educational and ancial consultant*

pinteria
iams, Benjamin V., IV, *headmaster, history ucator*

co
g, Paul Joseph *academic administrator*

us Heights
ke, Herman Ernest Frederick, Jr. *retired ementary school educator, consultant*

remont
ander, John David, Jr. *college administrator*
loro, Anthony Frank *dean*
1, Pamela Brooks *academic administrator*
hner, Charles Taylor *educator*
e, Maria Margaret *academic administrator, gineering and computer science educator*
uire, John David *academic administrator, ucator, writer*
by, David William *academic administrator, emistry professor*
dera Trombley, Laura Elise *academic lministrator, literature educator*
ey, Peter William *former academic lministrator*
ss, Jon Calvert *retired academic ministrator*
, Frederick M. *academic administrator*
ack, F. Sheldon *academic administrator*

ver City
well-Brogdon, Florence Morency *school stem administrator, educational consultant*

is
n, Delaine Andree *education educator*
chbacher, Rex Robert *dean, law educator*
ey, Robert Herschel *dean*
o, John W. *university librarian*
erhoef, Larry Neil *academic administrator*

mond Bar
eño, Eugene Timothy *elementary education ucator, principal*

ondido
ers, Adrian Lionel *retired educational nsultant*

field
orian, Donald George *retired academic ministrator*

nont
roff, Jerry *secondary school educator*

sno
ni, Ronald Walter *retired history educator*
, John Michael *provost*
art, Deborah Claire *dean*
y, John Donald *academic administrator*

erton
oghue, Mildred Ransdorf *education educator*
lon, Milton Andrew *academic administrator*
h, Ephraim Philip *academic administrator*

ndale
len, Lucille *retired academic administrator*

eta
hart, Thomas Eugene *retired academic ministrator, engineering educator*

ward
Norma S. *academic administrator*

tington Beach
sias, Kenneth Dale *college president*

ne
Rafael Luis *dean, engineering educator*
rio, Thomas Charles *dean*
nerinsky, Erwin *dean, law educator*
e, Michael V. *academic administrator, hthalmologist, educator*
cher, Everly Borah *academic administrator, partment chairman*
off, Gerald J. *university librarian*
son, Jack Walter *retired academic ministrator*
ano, Andrew J. *dean, finance educator*

Jolla
son, Richard Chatham *academic ministrator, cognitive scientist*
ner, David Allen *academic administrator, dical educator*
nee, Webster K. *director*
, Marye Anne *academic administrator*

Frieman, Edward Allan *academic administrator, educator*
Gabay, Janis T. *literature and language educator*
Lee, Jerry Carlton *university administrator*
Schottlaender, Brian E.C. *university librarian*
Sullivan, Robert S. *college dean*

La Verne
Morgan, Stephen Charles *academic administrator*

Lodi
Reinold, Christy Diane *school counselor, consultant*

Loma Linda
Goodacre, Charles J. *dean, educator*
King, Helen Emori *dean, nursing educator*
Kyle, James Lewis *dean, physician*

Long Beach
Alexander, F. King *academic administrator*
Lathrop, Irvin Tunis *retired dean*
Lauda, Donald Paul *retired dean*
Reed, Charles Bass *chief academic administrator*

Los Angeles
Armstrong, Lloyd, Jr. *academic administrator, physics professor*
Astin, Alexander William *education educator*
Bernstein, Leslie *academic administrator, biostatistician, epidemiologist*
Bice, Scott Haas *dean, law educator*
Brewer, David L. III *school system administrator, retired military officer*
Dewey, Donald Odell *dean, academic administrator*
Ghez, Andrea Mia *astronomy and physics educator*
Gilliam, Franklin D., Jr. *dean, political science professor*
Gothold, Stuart Eugene *school system administrator, education educator*
Hayes, Robert Mayo *dean, library and information scientist, educator*
Henderson, Brian Edmond *dean, physician, educator*
Hoi, Samuel Chuen-Tsung *academic administrator*
Hubbard, John Randolph *retired academic administrator, diplomat*
Inocencio, E. Bing *college president*
Kelly, James J. *dean, social work educator*
Kleingartner, Archie *dean, educator, academic administrator*
Knott, Jack H. *dean, political science professor*
Levey, Gerald Saul *dean, internist, educator*
Lieber, David Lee *university president*
Lim, Larry Kay *university official*
Lynch, Beverly Pfeifer *education and information studies educator*
Mandel, Joseph David *academic administrator, lawyer*
McKinney, Virginia Elaine Zuccaro *educational administrator*
Moriuchi, K. Derek *secondary school educator*
Nakanishi, Don Toshiaki *Asian American studies educator, writer*
Needleman, Jack *education educator, researcher*
Park, No-Hee *dean, academic administrator*
Rasmussen, Robert Kenneth *dean, law educator*
Rodes, David Stuart *college program director*
Sample, Steven Browning *academic administrator*
Schill, Michael H. *dean, law educator*
Shideler, Ross Patrick *literature and language educator, writer, translator, poet*
Silverman, Leonard M. *dean, electrical engineering educator*
Skotheim, Robert Allen *academic administrator, educator*
Slavkin, Harold Charles *dean, biologist*
Torres-Gil, Fernando M. *academic administrator*
Vredevoe, Donna Lou *academic administrator, microbiologist, educator, biomedical researcher*
Wagner, William Gerard *dean, information scientist, consultant, physicist, investment manager*
Wazzan, A(hmed) R(assem) Frank *engineering educator, dean*
Wexler, Robert *academic administrator*
Wilkerson, LuAnn *dean, medical educator*

Lynwood
Sitomer, Alan Lawrence *literature and language educator*

Malibu
Benton, Andrew Keith *academic administrator, lawyer*
Phillips, Ronald Frank *academic administrator*
Starr, Kenneth Winston *dean, lawyer*

Merced
Tomlinson-Keasey, Carol Ann *academic administrator*

Mill Valley
Mac Intyre, Donald John *college president*

Modesto
Price, Robert William *school superintendent, consultant*

Monterey Park
Moreno, Ernest H. *college president*

Napa
Stauffer, Thomas Michael *university president*

Northridge
Curzon, Susan Carol *academic administrator*
Mitchell, James Andrew *education educator*

Oakland
Diaz, Sharon *education administrator*
Gomes, Wayne Reginald *academic administrator*
Greer, Sandra Charlene *academic administrator, chemistry professor*
Holmgren, Janet L. *academic administrator*
Rippel, Clarence W. *academic administrator*

Ojai
Mulligan, Michael K. *headmaster*

Orange
Doti, James L. *academic administrator*
Hamilton, Harry Lemuel, Jr. *academic administrator, science educator*
Kraft, Arthur *dean*

Pacific Palisades
Georges, Robert Augustus *retired folklore and mythology educator, researcher, writer*

Palm Desert
Heydman, Abby Maria *academic administrator*

Palo Alto
Pizzo, Philip A. *dean, pediatrician, educator*

Pasadena
Arnold, Frances Hamilton *chemistry educator*
Becker, Christopher *educator, chef*
Chameau, Jean-Lou *academic administrator*
Douglas, Kimberly *university librarian*
Hoffmann, Michael R. *dean, environmental science educator*
Lingenfelter, Sherwood Galen *academic administrator, retired anthropologist*
Stolper, Edward Manin *secondary school educator*

Playa Del Rey
Baker, Robert M.L., Jr. *academic administrator, research scientist*

Pleasant Hill
Edelstein, Mark Gerson *college president*

Pomona
Dishman, Rose Marie Rice *academic administrator, researcher*
Trotter, F(rederick) Thomas *retired academic administrator*

Rancho Cucamonga
Young, Jerry Wayne *college president*

Rancho Palos Verdes
McFadden, Thomas *former academic administrator*
Petak, William John *systems management educator*

Redlands
Appleton, James Robert *academic administrator, educator*

Riverside
Boldt, William Gregory *academic administrator, consultant*
Geraty, Lawrence Thomas *academic administrator, archaeologist, educator*
Hendrick, Irving Guilford *education educator*
Jackson, Ruth Moore *university librarian*
White, Timothy Peter *academic administrator*
Yacoub, Ignatius I. *dean*

Rohnert Park
Babula, William *dean, writer*

Sacramento
Drummond, Marshall Edward (Mark) *academic administrator*
Gerth, Donald Rogers *retired university president, educator*
Harris, Robert M. *college president*
Nakano, George Sakaye *principal*
O'Connell, Jack T. *school system administrator*
Parker, Elizabeth Rindskopf *dean, law educator*
Reed-Graham, Lois L. *counseling administrator, writer, management consultant*
Scott, Jack Alan *academic administrator, former state senator*
Silva, Joseph, Jr. *dean, medical educator*
Smith, Marie B. *college president*
Stuart, David R. *academic administrator*
Trzyna, Thaddeus Charles *academic institution administrator*

San Diego
Brody, William Ralph *academic administrator, radiologist, educator*
Castruita, Rudy *school system administrator*
Cohn, Carl A. *school system administrator*
Donley, Dennis Lee *school librarian*
Feinberg, Lawrence Bernard *dean, psychologist*
Hays, Garry D. *academic administrator*
Lyons, Mary E. *academic administrator*
Mayer, George Roy *education educator*
Meno, Lionel R. *academic administrator*
Rodriguez, Daniel B. *dean, law educator*
Weber, Stephen Lewis *academic administrator*

San Dimas
Cameron, Judith Lynne *secondary school educator*
Mori, Allen Anthony *retired academic administrator*

San Francisco
Abbott, Richard Lee *physician*
Bratton, Christopher Alan *academic administrator, videographer, art educator*
Clifford, Geraldine Joncich *retired education educator*
Corrigan, Robert Anthony *academic administrator*
Dracup, Kathleen Anne *dean, nursing educator*
Dugoni, Arthur A. *dean emeritus, orthodontics educator*
Dullea, Charles W. *university chancellor emeritus, priest*
Kane, Mary Kay *academic administrator, law educator*
Kessler, David Aaron *dean, medical educator, former federal agency administrator*
Kleinberg, David Lewis *education administrator*
Kozloff, Lloyd M. *dean, microbiologist, educator*
Lo Schiavo, John Joseph *academic administrator*
Murdoch, Colin *academic administrator*
Privett, Stephen A. *academic administrator, priest*
Sakamoto, Katsuyuki *retired academic administrator, psychologist, educator*
Stephens, Elisa *college president*
Subbiondo, Joseph L. *academic administrator*

San Jose
Alire, Camila A. *dean emerita, librarian, educator*
Haycock, Kenneth Roy *academic administrator, educator, consultant*
Iglesias, Don *school system administrator*
Okerlund, Arlene Naylor *academic administrator, writer*
Whitmore, Jon Scott *academic administrator, play director*

San Luis Obispo
Baker, Warren J(oseph) *university president*

San Marcos
Lilly, Martin Stephen *retired university dean*

San Rafael
Fink, Joseph Richard *academic administrator*

Santa Ana
Moore, David Gene *academic administrator*
Wilson, Beth A. *college official*

Santa Barbara
Boyan, Norman J. *retired education educator*
Gallo, Marta Irene *retired literature and language educator*
Lucas, Gene *academic administrator*
O'Dowd, Donald Davy *retired university president*
Sinsheimer, Robert Louis *retired academic administrator, educator*
Yang, Henry T.Y. *academic administrator, educator*

Santa Clara
Locatelli, Paul Leo *academic administrator*
Polden, Donald *dean, law educator*
Shoup, Terry Emerson *dean, engineering educator*

Santa Clarita
Lavine, Steven David *academic administrator*

Santa Cruz
Blumenthal, George *academic administrator, astronomy and astrophysics professor*
Steel, Virginia (Ginny Steel) *university librarian*

Santa Monica
Soloff, Laura J. *academic administrator*

Saratoga
Barna, Lillian Carattini *school system administrator*
Houston, Elizabeth Reece Manasco *correctional education consultant*

Scotts Valley
Chace, William Murdough *former university administrator, literature educator*

Seaside
Anderson, David Louis *academic administrator, history professor*
Kadushin, Karen Donna *dean*

Signal Hill
Vandament, William Eugene *retired academic administrator*

Silverado
Mamer, James Michael *secondary school educator*

South Pasadena
Fuller, Kathy J. *special education educator, consultant, researcher*
Parks, Debora Ann *retired principal*

Stanford
Anderson, Theodore Wilbur *statistics educator*
Boaler, Jo *education educator*
Bridges, Edwin Maxwell *education educator*
Darling-Hammond, Linda *education professor*
Eisner, Elliot W. *education educator*
Etchemendy, John *academic administrator, educator*
Evers, Williamson Moore (Bill Evers) *education policy analyst, former federal agency administrator*
Hennessy, John L. *academic administrator*
Joss, Robert L. *dean*
Kamil, Michael *education educator*
Kays, William Morrow *academic administrator, mechanical engineer*
Kirst, Michael Weile *education educator, researcher*
Kramer, Larry *dean, lawyer, educator*
Laughlin, Robert B. *academic administrator, physics professor*
Naimark, Norman M. *academic administrator*
Palm, Charles Gilman *academic administrator*
Riggs, Henry Earle *academic administrator, engineering educator*
Spence, Andrew Michael *former dean, finance educator*
Stone, William Edward *academic administrator, consultant*
Strober, Myra Hoffenberg *education educator, consultant*
Veinott, Arthur Fales, Jr. *university educator*

Stockton
Blodgett, Elsie Grace *elementary school educator, small business owner, property manager*
DeRicco, Lawrence Albert *retired college president*
DeRosa, Donald V. *academic administrator*
Sorby, Donald Lloyd *retired dean*

Tarzana
Zeitlin, Herbert Zakary *college administrator, educational consultant, writer*

Torrance
Kuc, Joseph A. *research scientist*
Roney, Raymond G. *dean, educator, writer*

Valley Center
Arciniega, Tomas Abel *university president*

Ventura
Renger, Marilyn Hanson *elementary school educator*

Walnut Creek
Fielding, Elizabeth Brown *education educator*
Lilly, Luella Jean *retired academic administrator*
Merrill, Richard James *retired educational director*

Weimar
Kerschner, Lee R(onald) *academic administrator, political scientist, educator*

Whittier
Cruz, Denis J. *elementary school educator*

Yucaipa
Gomez, Louis Salazar *college president*

COLORADO

Aurora
Hartenbach, David Lawrence *school system administrator*

Bayfield
Horton, Frank Elba *academic administrator, geographer, educator*

Berthoud
Kubik, Timothy Robert White *director, history educator*

Beulah
Anderson, Ronald Delaine *education educator*

Boulder
Borko, Hilda *education educator*
Buechner, John C. *academic administrator*
Dilley, Barbara Jean *college administrator, choreographer, educator*
Landesman, Howard M. *retired academic administrator*
Peterson, G. P. (Bud Peterson) *academic administrator*
Williams, James Franklin, II, *dean, librarian*
Wilson, M. Roy *academic administrator, medical educator*

Colorado Springs
Celeste, Richard F. *academic administrator, retired ambassador, Former Governor, Ohio*
Martin, Jeryl (Jill Martin) *principal*
Shockley-Zalabak, Pamela Sue *academic administrator*

Denver
Benson, Bruce Davey *academic administrator, oil and gas company executive*
Byyny, Richard Lee *former academic administrator, physician, educator*
Coombe, Bob (Robert D.) *academic administrator*
Hecox, Morris B. *academic administrator*
Jordan, Stephen M. *academic administrator*
Kourlis, Rebecca Love *director, former state supreme court justice*
Matkowski, Bette *academic administrator*
Moloney, William J. *school system administrator*
Ritchie, Daniel Lee *former academic administrator*
Vigil, Daniel Agustin *academic administrator*
Yates, Albert Carl *academic administrator, chemistry educator*
Zaranka, William F. *academic administrator, author*

Estes Park
Ryder, Susan R. *elementary school educator*

Fort Collins
Baldwin, Lionel Vernon *retired university president*
Fotsch, Dan Robert *retired elementary school educator*
Harper, Judson Morse *retired university administrator, consultant, educator*
Penley, Larry Edward *academic administrator, finance educator*
Perryman, Lance *dean*

Golden
Bickart, Theodore Albert *university president emeritus*
Klug, John Joseph *secondary school educator, director*
Scoggins, M. W. (Bill Scoggins) *academic administrator*
Shea, Dion Warren Joseph *academic administrator, fundraiser*
Truly, Richard H. *academic and federal agency administrator, retired pilot*

Greeley
Duff, William Leroy, Jr. *retired dean, finance educator*

Gunnison
Wieseman, Katherine C. *education educator, consultant*

Littleton
Bosworth, Bruce Leighton *school administrator, educator, consultant*
Grounds, Vernon Carl *seminary administrator*
Rothenberg, Harvey David *educational administrator*

Louisville
Bravo, Adele *elementary school educator*

Nederland
Lutz, Frank Wenzel *education administration educator*

Thornton
Johnson, Michael *principal*

U S A F Academy
Regni, John F. *academic administrator, career military officer*

Westminster
Hartman, Susan P(atrice) *adult education administrator*

DISTRICT OF COLUMBIA

Washington
Mohrman, Kathryn J. *academic administrator*

HAWAII

Ewa Beach
Awakuni, Gail *principal*

Hilo
Pezzuto, John Michael *dean, pharmacology educator*
Tseng, Rose *academic administrator*

Honolulu
Englert, Peter *academic administrator, director*
Gee, Chuck Yim *dean*
Hamamoto, Patricia *school system administrator, educator*
King, Arthur R., Jr. *education educator, researcher*
Konan, Denise *academic administrator, economics professor*
LaBelle, Thomas Jeffrey *research executive, academic administrator*
McClain, David Stanley *academic administrator, business and management professor*
Mortimer, Kenneth P. *retired academic administrator*
Muranaka, Jami *biology educator*
Perkins, Frank Overton *academic administrator, marine biologist*
Soifer, Aviam *dean, law educator*
Wesselkamper, Sue *academic administrator*
Wright, Chatt Grandison *academic administrator*

Kailua Kona
Diama, Benjamin *retired secondary school educator, composer, writer*

Laie
Shumway, Eric Brandon *academic administrator*

Pearl City
Awakuni, Gene I. *academic administrator, psychologist*

IDAHO

American Falls
Jensen, Randy *principal*

Boise
Andrus, Cecil Dale *academic administrator, former United States Secretary of the Interior*
Kaupins, Gundars Egons *education educator*
Kohn, Matthew J. *education educator, researcher*
Luna, Thomas *school system administrator*
Maloof, Giles Wilson *academic administrator, educator, author*
Ruch, Charles P. *academic administrator*

Caldwell
Hendren, Robert Lee, Jr. *academic administrator*
Hoover, Robert Allan *university president*

Lewiston
Thomas, Dene Kay *academic administrator, educator*

Moscow
Daley-Laursen, Steven B. *academic administrator, dean, environmental scientist, educator*
Hatch, Charles R. *dean*

Nampa
Hagood, Richard A. *academic administrator, educator*

Parma
Sharkey, (John) Mick *biology educator*

Pocatello
Sagness, Richard Lee *education educator, former academic dean*
Smith, Elaine E. *school system administrator*

Rexburg
Clark, Kim Bryce *academic administrator*

Twin Falls
Gentry, James Robert *education educator*
Graves, Karen Lee *counselor*

MAINE

Bar Harbor
Krevans, Julius Richard *academic administrator, internist*

MASSACHUSETTS

Cambridge
Edley, Christopher Fairchild, Jr. *dean, law educator*

MONTANA

Billings
Mace, Michael R. *academic administrator, real estate development consultant, mortgage executive*
Park, Janie C. *provost*
Sexton, Ronald P. *academic administrator*

Bozeman
Acord, Lea *dean*
Gamble, Geoffrey *academic administrator*

Butte
Gilmore, W. Franklin (Frank) *academic administrator*

Dillon
Storey, Richard D. *academic administrator, biology professor*

Havre
Capdeville, Alex *academic administrator*

Helena
Crofts, Richard A. *academic administrator*
Stearns, Sheila MacDonald *academic administrator*

Lewistown
Edwards, Linda L. *former elementary education educator*

Missoula
Brown, Perry Joe *dean*
Dennison, George Marshel *academic administrator*
Vogelsberg, Ross Timm *education educator, researcher*

Montana City
Shaver, James Porter *retired education educator, dean*

Whitefish
Carmichael, Gary Alan Alan *social studies educator*

NEVADA

Carson City
Rheault, Keith W. *school system administra*

Henderson
Maryanski, Fred J. *academic administrator*
Teemant, Melanie J. *middle school educato*

Incline Village
Large, Larry Denton *academic administrato*

Las Vegas
Cram, Brian Manning *school system administrator*
Ferrillo, Patrick J., Jr. *dean, endodontist*
Hair, Kittie Ellen *retired secondary school educator*
Hall, Gene E. *education educator*
Harter, Carol Clancey *academic administra English language educator*

Minden
Tyndall, Gaye Lynn *secondary school educ*

Reno
Ceppos, Jerry (Jerome Merle Ceppos) *dean former newspaper editor*
Dietrich, Dean Forbes *academic administra*
Glick, Milton Don *academic administrator, chemist*
McCarty-Puhl, J-Petrina *chemistry educator*
McFarlane, Stephen C. *dean, researcher*
Perry, Jean Louise *academic administrator*
Westfall, David Patrick *academic administr educator*

NEW MEXICO

Albuquerque
Garcia, F. Chris *academic administrator, political scientist, educator*
Graff, Pat Stuever *secondary school educat*
Harris, David W. *academic administrator*
Lattman, Laurence Harold *retired academic administrator*
Schmidly, David J. *academic administrator, biology professor*

Dulce
Tiong, Tamra A. *elementary school educatc*

Hobbs
Dill, Gary A. *academic administrator*

Las Cruces
Conroy, William B. *retired university administrator*
Thayer, Michael J. *secondary school educa*

Las Vegas
Fries, James A. *academic administrator*

Los Alamos
Benjamin, Susan Selton *elementary school educator*

Placitas
Watson-Boone, Rebecca A. *dean, research library and information scientist, educat*

Portales
Byrnes, Lawrence William *dean*
Frost, Everett Lloyd *academic administrato anthropologist*
Gamble, Steven G. *academic administrator*

Santa Fe
Cerny, Charlene Ann *director*
Garcia, Veronica *school system administra*

Socorro
Lopez, Daniel Heraldo *academic administr*

Taos
Garcia, Christine *academic administrator, educator, researcher*

NORTH CAROLINA

Hendersonville
Evans, Anthony Howard *retired university president*

OREGON

Ashland
Cullinan, Mary Patricia *academic administ literature and language professor*

Beaverton
Duncan, Richard Fredrick, Jr. *retired secon school educator, consultant*

Corvallis
Arnold, Roy Gary *academic administrator*
Byrne, John Vincent *educational consultan*
Davis, John Rowland *academic administra*

Eugene
Cox, Joseph William *former academic administrator, education educator*
Frohnmayer, David Braden *academic administrator*

ENGINEERING

UNITED STATES

ARIZONA

Mesa
Rummel, Robert Wiland *aeronautical engineer, writer*

Paradise Valley
Ratkowski, Donald J. *mechanical engineer, consultant*
Russell, Paul Edgar *electrical engineering educator*

Phoenix
Freyermuth, Clifford L. *structural engineering consultant*

Prescott
Bieniawski, Zdzislaw Tadeusz Richard *engineering educator, writer, consultant*
Kahne, Stephen James *systems engineering educator, engineering company executive, academic administrator*

Scottsdale
Cazier, Barry James *electrical engineer, software developer*
Gookin, Thomas Allen Jaudon *civil engineer*
Kiehn, Mogens Hans *aviation engineer, consultant*

Tempe
Balanis, Constantine Apostle *electrical engineering educator*
Berman, Neil Sheldon *retired chemical engineering professor*
Carpenter, Ray Warren *engineering educator, materials engineer*
Ferry, David Keane *electrical engineering educator*
Guilbeau, Eric J. *biomedical and electrical engineer, educator*
Karády, George György *electrical engineering educator, consultant*
Mahajan, Subhash *electronic materials educator*
Schroder, Dieter Karl *electrical engineering educator*
Shah, Jami J. *mechanical engineering educator, researcher*

Tucson
Hiskey, J. Brent *metallurgical engineer, educator*
Kerwin, William James *electrical engineering educator, consultant*
Kohloss, Frederick Henry *retired engineer*
Mense, Allan Tate *research and development engineering executive*
Peterson, Thomas W. *engineering educator*
Slack, Donald Carl *agricultural engineer, educator*
Smerdon, Ernest Thomas *engineering educator*
Venkata, Subrahmanyam Saraswati *engineering educator, researcher*
Wyant, James Clair *engineering company executive, educator*

CALIFORNIA

Alameda
Brown, Stephen Lawrence *environmental consultant*

Aliso Viejo
Steuert, Douglas Michael *engineering and construction management company executive*

Arcadia
Carroll, William Jerome *civil engineer*
Trussell, R(obert) Rhodes *environmental engineer*

Arroyo Grande
Hoffmann, Jon Arnold *retired aeronautical engineer*

Atherton
Morel-Seytoux, Hubert Jean *civil engineer, educator*

Auburn
Aro, Glenn Scott *environmental and safety executive*

Berkeley
Baldwin, Gary Lee *electronics engineer, educator*
Bea, Robert G. *civil engineering educator*
Berger, Stanley Allan *mechanical and biomechanical engineering educator*
Birdsall, Charles Kennedy *electrical engineer*
Blanch, Harvey Warren *chemical engineering educator*
Bogy, David B(eauregard) *mechanical engineering educator*
Brodersen, Robert W. *engineering educator*
Cairns, Elton James *chemical engineering professor, consultant*
Chopra, Anil Kumar *civil engineering educator*
Chua, Leon O. *electrical engineering and computer science educator*
Derenzo, Stephen E. *electrical engineering and computer science educator, researcher*
Desoer, Charles Auguste *electrical engineer*
Dornfeld, David Alan *engineering educator*
Dubon, Oscar D., Jr. *engineering educator*
Fenves, Gregory L. *engineering educator*
Filippou, Filip C. *engineering educator*
Finnie, Iain *mechanical engineer, educator*
Fuerstenau, Douglas Winston *mineral engineering educator*
Garrison, William Louis *civil engineering educator*
Grossman, Lawrence Morton *nuclear engineering educator*
Hsu, Chieh Su *applied mechanics engineering educator, researcher*
Hu, Chenming *engineering educator*
Javey, Ali *engineering educator*
Kastenberg, William Edward *engineering professor, former academic administrator*
Katz, Randy H. *electrical engineering, computer sciences educator*
King, Cary Judson III *chemical engineer, educator, academic administrator*
Kuh, Ernest Shiu-Jen *electrical engineering educator*
Leitmann, George *mechanical engineer, educator*
Lewis, Edwin Reynolds *biomedical engineering educator, academic administrator*
Lieberman, Michael A. *electrical engineer, educator*
Liepmann, Dorian *engineering educator*
Ma, Fai *mechanical engineering educator*
Mc Niven, Hugh Donald *engineering science educator, earthquake engineering researcher*
Messerschmitt, David Gavin *engineering educator*
Monismith, Carl Leroy *civil engineering educator*
Muller, Richard Stephen *electrical engineer, educator*
Neureuther, Andrew R. *engineering educator*
Newman, John Scott *chemical engineer, educator*
Oldham, William George *electrical engineering and computer science educator*
Ott, David Michael *engineering company executive*
Pagni, Patrick John *mechanical engineering science educator, safety engineer, researcher*
Pigford, Thomas Harrington *nuclear engineering educator*
Pister, Karl Stark *engineering educator*
Polak, Elijah *engineering educator, computer scientist*
Popov, Egor Paul *retired engineering educator*
Prausnitz, John Michael *chemical engineer, educator*
Sastry, Sosale Shankara *electrical engineer, computer scientist, dean, educator*
Schwarz, Steven Emanuel *electrical engineering educator, administrator*
Smith, Otto J. M. *electrical engineering educator*
Varaiya, Pravin P. *electrical engineer*
Webster, William C. *engineering educator*
White, Richard Manning *electrical engineering educator*
Wright, Paul Kenneth *mechanical engineer, educator*
Zakhor, Avideh *engineering educator, consultant*

Brentwood
Rawson, Eric Gordon *optical engineer*

Campbell
Levy, Salomon *mechanical engineer*
Ross, Hugh Courtney *electrical engineer*

Carmichael
Throner, Guy Charles, Jr. *aerospace engineering executive, scientist, inventor, consultant*

Chico
Allen, Charles William *mechanical engineer, educator*
Roth, Ronald Lee *engineering educator*

Claremont
Dym, Clive Lionel *engineering educator*
Molinder, John Irving *engineering educator, consultant*
Monson, James Edward *electrical engineer, educator*
Phillips, John Richard *engineering educator*
Tanenbaum, Basil Samuel *engineering educator*

Clovis
Brahma, Chandra Sekhar *civil engineering educator*

Compton
Wang, Charles Ping *engineering executive*

Costa Mesa
Carpenter, Frank Charles, Jr. *electronics engineer*

Culver City
Mann, Michael Martin *engineering executive*

Cupertino
Haskell, Barry Geoffry *computer engineer, researcher*

Davis
Akesson, Norman Berndt *agricultural engineer, emeritus educator*
Beadle, Charles Wilson *retired mechanical engineering educator*
Bower, Robert W. *electrical engineer*
Chancellor, William Joseph *agricultural engineering educator*
Cheney, James Addison *civil engineering educator*
Dorf, Richard Carl *electrical engineering and management educator*
Gates, Bruce Clark *chemical engineer, educator*
Krener, Arthur J. *systems engineering educator*
Larock, Bruce Edward *civil engineering educator*
Laub, Alan John *engineering educator*
Lavernia, Enrique Jose *materials science and engineering educator, dean*
Levy, Bernard C. *electrical engineer, educator*
Wang, Shih-Ho *electrical engineer, educator*

El Cerrito
Wilson, Edward Lawrence *engineering company executive, consultant, retired educator*

El Segundo
Chang, I-Shih *aerospace engineer*
Mende, Howard Shigeharu *mechanical engineer*

Emeryville
Kavanaugh, Michael C. *environmental engineer*
Zwoyer, Eugene Milton *retired consulting engineering executive*

Encinitas
Deets, Dwain Aaron *retired aerospace technology executive*

Encino
Friedman, George Jerry *aerospace engineering executive*
Knuth, Eldon Luverne *engineering educator*

Fairfield
Edson, William Alden *retired electrical engineer, researcher*

Folsom
Ettlich, William F. *electrical engineer*

Fremont
Chen, Wai-Kai *electrical engineering and computer science educator, consultant*
Engelbart, Douglas C. *engineering executive*
Wu, James Chen-Yuan *aerospace engineering educator*

Glendale
Dallas, Saterios (Sam Dallas) *aerospace engineer, researcher, consultant*

Greenbrae
Elder, Rex Alfred *civil engineer*

Hacienda Heights
Love, Daniel Joseph *consulting engineer*

Irvine
Alexopoulos, Nicolaos George *electrical engineer, educator, dean*
Ang, Alfredo Hua-Sing *civil engineering educator*
Chelapati, Chunduri Venkata *civil engineering educator*
Liebeck, Robert H. *aerospace engineer*
Samueli, Henry *electrical engineer, educator, professional sports team executive*
Sirignano, William Alfonso *aerospace and mechanical engineer, educator*
Sklansky, Jack *electrical and computer engineering educator, researcher*
Stubberud, Allen Roger *electrical engineering educator*
Ting, Albert Chia *biomedical engineer, researcher*
Wickramasinghe, Hemantha Kumar *electrical engineer, physicist*

La Canada Flintridge
Price, Humphrey Wallace *aerospace engineer*

La Crescenta
Otoshi, Tom Yasuo *electrical engineer, consultant*

La Jolla
Asbeck, Peter Michael *engineering educator*
Chang, William Shen Chie *electrical engineering educator*
Chien, Shu *physiology and bioengineering educator*
Fung, Yuan-Cheng Bertram *bioengineering educator, writer*
Goddard, Joe Dean *chemical engineering educator, researcher*
Levy, Ralph *engineering executive, consultant*
Marzullo, Keith *computer science and engineering educator*
Milstein, Laurence Bennett *electrical engineering educator, researcher*
Penner, Stanford Sol *engineering educator*
Rudee, Mervyn Lea *engineering educator, researcher*
Rudolph, Walter Paul *engineering research company executive*
Schmid-Schoenbein, Geert Wilfried *biomedical engineer, educator*
Sung, Kuo-Li Paul *bioengineering educator*
Vecchio, Kenneth Scott *engineering educator, department chairman*
Williams, Forman Arthur *science engineering educator*
Wolf, Jack Keil *electrical engineer, educator*

Laguna Hills
Hammond, R. Philip *chemical engineer*

Livermore
Christensen, Richard Monson *mechanical and materials engineer*
Goodwin, Bruce T. *engineer*
Hallquist, John O. *engineering company executive*
Johnson, Roy Ragnar *electrical engineer, researcher*
King, Ray John *electrical engineering educ engineering company executive*

Lompoc
Means, James Andrew *retired engineer*

Long Beach
Dillon, Michael Earl *mechanical engineerin executive, educator*
Kumar, Rajendra *electrical engineering edu*
Philpott, Lindsey *civil engineer, researcher, educator*

Los Altos Hills
Sharpe, Roland Leonard *structural engineer consultant*

Los Angeles
Abidi, Asad Ali *electrical engineer, educato*
Breuer, Melvin Allen *electrical engineering educator*
Bucy, Richard Snowden *aerospace engineer and mathematics educator, consultant*
Chang, Jane P. *chemical engineering educa*
Cheng, Tsen-Chung *electrical engineering educator*
Chui, Chi On *electrical engineer, educator*
Crombie, Douglass Darnill *aerospace communications system engineer*
Danziger, Bruce Edward *structural engineer*
Dhir, Vijay K. *engineering educator*
Dorman, Albert A. *engineering executive, consultant, architect*
Hovanessian, Shahen Alexander *electrical engineer, educator, consultant*
Itoh, Tatsuo *engineering educator*
Ju, Jiann-Wen (Woody Ju) *mechanics educa researcher*
King-Ning, Tu *materials science and engineering educator*
Klinger, Allen *engineering educator*
Kuehl, Hans Henry *electrical engineering educator*
MacKenzie, John Douglas *engineering edu*
Marmarelis, Vasilis Zissis *engineering educ writer, consultant*
Masri, Sami F(aiz) *civil and mechanical engineering educator, consultant*
Maxworthy, Tony *mechanical and aerospac engineering educator*
Mendel, Jerry Marc *electrical engineering educator*
Muntz, Eric Phillip *aerospace and mechani engineering educator, consultant*
Newman, Richard G. *engineering company executive*
Nikias, Chrysostomos L. (Max Nikias) *engineering educator*
Nobe, Ken *chemical engineering professor*
Ozcan, Aydogan *electrical engineer, educat*
Perrine, Richard Leroy *environmental engin educator*
Ramo, Simon *retired engineering executive*
Reed, Irving Stoy *electrical engineer*
Rubinstein, Moshe Fajwel *engineering edu*
Safonov, Michael George *electrical enginee educator, consultant*
Scholtz, Robert Arno *electrical engineering educator*
Settles, F. Stan, Jr. *engineering educator, manufacturing executive*
Shinozuka, Masanobu *civil engineer, educa*
Speyer, Jason Lee *aeronautical engineer, educator*
Stenstrom, Michael Knudson *civil engineer educator*
Strong, Pamela Kay *material and process engineer*
Udwadia, Firdaus Erach *engineering educa consultant*
Urena-Alexiades, Jose Luis *electrical engin*
Wagner, Christian Nikolaus Johann *materia engineering educator*
Weber, Charles L. *electrical engineering educator*
Welch, Lloyd Richard *electrical and communications engineer, educator, cons*
Willner, Alan Eli *electrical engineer, educa*
Yablonovitch, Eli *electrical engineering educator*
Yeh, William Wen-Gong *civil engineering educator*
Yen, Teh Fu *civil and environmental engine educator*

Menlo Park
George, Dileep *electrical engineer*
Honey, Richard Churchill *retired electrical engineer*
Levenson, Milton *chemical engineer, consu*
McCarthy, Roger Lee *mechanical engineer*
Montague, L. David *aerospace engineer*

Milpitas
Nanis, Leonard *engineering educator, cons*

Moffett Field
Kerr, Andrew W. *aerodynamics researcher*
Luna, Bernadette *mechanical engineer*
McCroskey, William James *retired aeronau engineer*
Statler, Irving Carl *aerospace engineer*

aarch Beach
;herty, Elmer Lloyd, Jr. *retired chemical gineering professor, consultant*

arovia
ards, Kenneth Neil *chemical engineering ecutive*

aterey
r, Jon Terry *computer engineering educator, searcher*
), Paul James *retired mechanical gineering educator, consultant, researcher, an*
kaya, Turgut *mechanical engineering ucator*

antain View
land, Albert Smiley *electrical engineer, earcher*
son, Conor Deane *mechanical engineer*

'ark
, Haresh Chandulal *civil engineering ucator*

'port Coast
am, Charles Ferdinand *electrical engineer*

th Tustin
, William Evans *aerospace engineer, gineering company executive, consultant*

thridge
shaw, Richard Rotherwood *engineering ecutive*
oo, Robert James *engineering service npany executive*

ato
gue, Robert Brophy *retired nuclear gineer*

dand
en, Joseph *structural engineering educator*
rga, Bernard A. *engineering administrator*

nge
sees, James Eugene *engineering executive, nsultant*

ada
rt, Jerome B. *consulting environmental gineer*

a Desert
und, Richard Frank *research and technical cutive*

Alto
Celeste Volz *aerospace engineer*
;e, Philip Gibson, Jr. *mechanical and rospace engineering educator*
Wan Hee *engineering educator*
:, Calvin Forrest *engineering educator*
'er, Ronald William *electrical engineering ucator*
r, John Joseph *nuclear engineer, researcher*

s Verdes Estates
Jorg Emil *electrical engineer*

adena
r, Curtis A. *engineering executive*
inridge, James Bernard *optical scientist*
es, William Bruce *electrical engineer, ucator, researcher*
Richard A. *aerospace engineer*
k, Fred Ellsworth Clow *engineering and sics professor*
, Mark E. *chemical engineering educator*
s, Michelle *electrical engineer, educator*
i, Charles *aerospace engineer*
n, Richard Charles *chemical engineering ucator*
las, George R. *chemical engineering ucator*
l, Roy Walter *engineering educator*
William E. *engineering and construction npany executive*
rt, Robert S(aul) *optical engineer*
ang, Hans Georg *aeronautical engineering cator, science administrator*
Wilfred Dean *mechanical engineer, ucator*
ngs, Paul Christian *civil engineering cator, academic administrator*
ss, Wolfgang Gustav *engineering educator*
ield, Julia Ann *chemical engineering cator*
Ericson John *environmental engineering ence educator, consultant*
ing, Robert M. *aerospace engineer*
e, Frank E(arl) *engineering educator*
n, Craig Lee *engineering company cutive*
ebrook, Robert David *electronics educator*
aead, Brian K. *aerospace engineer*
ay, Richard M. *engineering educator*
ps, Robert *engineering educator, researcher*
len, Fredric *civil engineering educator, nsultant*
ani, Tomasso P. *engineer*
co, Anatol *aeronautical engineer*
sky, Rolf Heinrich *mechanical engineer*
ld, John Hersh *chemical engineering fessor*
, Lincoln Jackson *aerospace engineer*

Yamarone, Charles Anthony, Jr. *aerospace engineer, consultant*
Yariv, Amnon *electrical engineering educator, research scientist*

Pinole
Emmanuel, Jorge Agustin *chemical engineer, environmental consultant*

Playa Del Rey
Weir, Alexander, Jr. *chemical engineer, consultant*

Pleasanton
Van Dreser, Merton Lawrence *ceramics engineer*

Pomona
Nise, Norman S. *engineering educator*
Teague, Lavette Cox, Jr. *systems educator, consultant*

Richmond
Moehle, Jack P. *civil engineer, engineering executive*

Riverside
Balandin, Alexander A. *electrical engineer, educator*
Beni, Gerardo *electrical engineer, educator*
Hackwood, Susan *electrical and computer engineering educator*

Sacramento
Lathi, Bhagawandas Pannalal *retired electrical engineering educator*
Zhang, Du *engineering educator*

San Diego
Basso, Robert J. *manufacturing engineer, inventor*
Brown, Alan J. *electrical engineer*
Cater, Jack Ernest *acoustical engineer, researcher*
Chang, Daniel Haiming *engineering executive*
Conly, John Franklin *retired engineering educator*
Crook, Sean Paul *aerospace systems division director*
Dahlberg, Kenneth C. *engineering executive*
Davenport, Roger Lee *research engineer*
Dean, Richard Anthony *mechanical engineering executive*
Friedman, Arthur Daniel *electrical engineer, computer scientist, investment company executive, educator*
Gupta, Madhu Sudan *electrical engineering educator*
Katz, Joseph *aerospace engineer, educator*
Lieber, Richard Louis *biomedical engineering scientist, educator*
Mehrabadi, Morteza M. *engineer, researcher, educator*
Paget, John Arthur *mechanical engineer*
Plotkin, Allen *aerospace engineer, educator*
Slate, John Butler *biomedical engineer*

San Francisco
Abramson, Norman *retired engineering educator, electronics executive*
Bechtel, Riley Peart *engineering company executive*
Bechtel, Stephen Davison, Jr. *retired engineering company executive*
Dolby, Ray Milton *electrical engineer, company executive*
Hotchkiss, Ralf David *engineer, educator*
Keller, Edward Lowell *electrical engineer, educator*
Koffel, Martin M. *engineering company executive*
Tang, Man-Chung *civil engineer, company executive*

San Jose
Chamberlin, Donald Dean *computer engineer*
Contos, Paul Anthony *engineer, investment consultant*
Dennison, Ronald Walton *engineer*
Markle, David A. *optical engineer*

San Marcos
Purdy, Alan Harris *biomedical engineer*

San Pedro
McCarty, Frederick Briggs *electrical engineer, consultant*
Simmons, William *retired aerospace engineer, research and development company executive*

San Rafael
Douglas, James *construction engineering educator*

Santa Ana
Amoroso, Frank *retired communication system engineer, consultant*

Santa Barbara
Chmelka, Bradley Floyd *chemical engineering educator*
Coldren, Larry Allen *electrical engineering educator, consultant*
Fredrickson, Glenn Harold *chemical engineering and materials educator*
Hu, Evelyn Lynn *electrical and computer engineering educator*
Kokotovic, Petar V. *electrical and computer engineering educator*
Kramer, Edward John *materials engineering educator*
Kroemer, Herbert *electrical engineering educator*
Lange, Frederick F. *materials engineer, educator*
Lawrance, Charles Holway *retired civil and sanitary engineer*
Lick, Wilbert James *mechanical engineering educator*
Mitra, Sanjit Kumar *electrical and computer engineering educator*
Nakamura, Shuji *engineering educator*
Odette, G. Robert *mechanical and environmental engineering educator*
Sensiper, Samuel *electrical engineer*
Tirrell, Matthew V. *engineering educator*
Wade, Glen *electrical engineer, educator*

Santa Clara
Chan, Shu-Park *electrical engineering educator*
Diffie, Whitfield (Whit) *computer and communications engineer*
Parden, Robert James *engineering educator, management consultant*
Roknaldin, Farzam *mechanical engineer, educator*

Santa Cruz
Kang, Sung-Mo (Steve Kang) *electrical engineering educator*
Langdon, Glen George, Jr. *electrical engineer*

Santa Monica
Gritton, Eugene Charles *nuclear engineer, director*
Kayton, Myron *engineering company executive*
Kummer, Wolfgang H. *electrical engineer*
Sherman, Zachary *civil engineer, aerospace engineer, consultant*

Santa Rosa
Apfel, Joseph H. *optical engineer, research scientist*

Seal Beach
Whelan, David A. *engineering executive*

South Pasadena
Kopp, Eugene Howard *communications and electrical engineer, consultant*

South San Francisco
Hull, Cordell William *engineering, construction, and project management executive, investor*
Tananbaum, James *medical engineering company executive*
Young, William D. *chemical engineer*

Stanford
Aziz, Khalid *petroleum engineering educator*
Boahen, Kwabena *bioengineering educator*
Boudart, Michel *chemical engineer, consultant, educator*
Cannon, Robert Hamilton, Jr. *aerospace engineering educator*
Cox, Donald Clyde *electrical engineering educator*
Eshleman, Von Russel *electrical engineering educator, aerospace scientist*
Fan, Shanhui *engineering educator*
Franklin, Gene Farthing *engineering educator, consultant*
Gibbons, James Franklin *electrical engineering educator*
Goodman, Joseph Wilfred *electrical engineering educator*
Gray, Robert Molten *electrical engineering educator*
Hesselink, Lambertus *electrical engineering and physics educator*
Hewett, Thomas Avery *petroleum engineer, educator*
Horowitz, Mark A. *electrical engineering and computer science educator*
Howard, H. Taylor *electrical engineer, educator*
Howard, Ronald A. *systems engineer, educator*
Inan, Umran Savas *electrical engineering educator, researcher*
Jameson, Antony *aerospace engineering educator*
Journel, André G. *petroleum engineering educator*
Kailath, Thomas *electrical engineer, educator*
Kane, Thomas Reif *engineering educator*
Kelley, David M. *mechanical engineer, educator*
Khosla, Chaitan S. *chemical engineer*
Kino, Gordon Stanley *electrical engineering educator*
Kitanidis, Peter K. *engineering educator*
Levitt, Raymond Elliot *civil engineer, educator*
Linvill, John Grimes *engineering educator*
Macovski, Albert *electrical engineer, educator*
McCarty, Perry Lee *civil and environmental engineering educator*
Meng, Teresa H. *electrical engineer, educator*
Mitchell, Reginald Eugene *mechanical engineering educator*
Orr, Franklin Mattes, Jr. *petroleum engineering educator*
Ortolano, Leonard *civil engineering educator, water resources planner*
Parkinson, Bradford Wells *astronautical engineer, educator*
Paté-Cornell, Marie-Elisabeth Lucienne *engineering educator*
Pease, Roger Fabian Wedgwood *electrical engineering educator*
Perry, William James *engineering educator, former United States Secretary of Defense*
Plummer, James D. *electrical engineering educator, dean*
Roberts, Paul V. *civil and environmental engineering educator*
Roth, Bernard *mechanical engineering educator, researcher*
Saraswat, Krishna *electrical engineering educator*
Siegman, Anthony Edward *electrical engineer, educator*
Springer, George Stephen *mechanical engineering educator*
Steele, Charles Richard *biomedical and mechanical engineering educator*
Street, Robert Lynnwood *civil, mechanical and environmental engineer*
Stuart, Andrew Mark *mechanical engineering educator*
Swartz, James R. *chemical engineer, educator*
Sweeney, James Lee *engineering educator*
Tyler, George Leonard *electrical engineering educator*
Van Dyke, Milton Denman *aeronautical engineering educator*
Vincenti, Walter Guido *aeronautical engineer, emeritus educator*
White, Robert Lee *electrical engineer, educator*

Studio City
Delnik, Alexander *engineering executive, consultant*

Sunnyvale
Petersen, Kurt Edward *electrical engineer, researcher, entrepreneur*
Weinberg, William Henry *chemical engineer, physicist, educator*

Tarzana
Hansen, Robert Clinton *electrical engineer, consultant*

Thousand Oaks
Marshall, David B. *structural ceramics professional*

Torrance
Robbins, James Edward *electrical engineer*
Wylie, Richard Thornton *aerospace engineer*

Ukiah
MacDonald, Norval *safety engineer*

Ventura
Gaynor, Joseph *chemical engineer, management consultant*

Walnut Creek
Hanson, Robert Duane *engineering educator*
Van Maerssen, Otto L. *aerospace engineer, consulting firm executive*

Whittier
Stahl, James F. *engineer*

Yorba Linda
Porcello, Leonard Joseph *engineering research and development executive*

COLORADO

Aurora
Schloss, Kristy Anne *engineering company executive*

Boulder
Amadei, Bernard Paul *civil engineer, not-for-profit developer, educator*
Anseth, Kristi S. *tissue engineer, educator*
Avery, Susan Kathryn *electrical engineering educator, researcher*
Barnes, Frank Stephenson *electrical engineer, educator*
Born, George Henry *aerospace engineer, educator*
Carlson, Lawrence Evan *mechanical engineering educator*
Corotis, Ross Barry *civil engineer, educator, academic administrator*
Datta, Subhendu K. *mechanical engineer, educator*
Hanna, William Johnson *electrical engineering educator*
Hauser, Ray Louis *engineer, researcher, entrepreneur*
Hill, David Allan *electrical engineer*
Joy, Edward Bennett *electrical engineer, educator, consultant*
McGuire, Robin K. *engineering company executive*
Mikulas, Martin M., Jr. *aerospace engineer, educator*
Reitsema, Harold James *aerospace engineer*
Sani, Robert LeRoy *chemical engineering professor*
Smith, Ernest Ketcham *electrical engineer*
Snyder, Howard Arthur *aerospace engineering educator, consultant*
Sullivan, Jacquelyn F. *engineering education program administrator*
Timmerhaus, Klaus Dieter *chemical engineering professor*

Broomfield
Boulos, Paul Fares *civil and environmental engineer*
Bressler, Marcus Nathan *engineer, consultant*

Donze, Jerry Lynn *electrical engineer*

Colorado Springs
Watts, Oliver Edward *engineering company executive*
Yukawa, Sumio *engineering consultant, researcher*
Ziemer, Rodger Edmund *electrical engineering educator, consultant*

Denver
Aaron, M. Robert *electrical engineer*
Chamberlain, Adrian Ramond *transportation engineer*
McCandless, Bruce, II, *aerospace engineer, retired astronaut*
Reshotko, Eli *aerospace engineer, educator*

Durango
Langoni, Richard Allen *retired civil engineer*

Englewood
Peterson, Ralph Randall *engineering executive*
Schirmer, Howard August, Jr. *civil engineer*

Estes Park
Ojalvo, Morris *civil engineer, educator*

Fort Collins
Abt, Steven R. *civil engineer, educator*
Boyd, Landis Lee *agricultural engineer, educator*
Garvey, Daniel Cyril *mechanical engineer*
Grigg, Neil S. *civil engineering educator*
Kaufman, Harold Richard *mechanical engineer, physics educator*
Matthies, Frederick John *civil and environmental engineer*
Richardson, Everett Vern *hydraulic engineer, educator, administrator, consultant*
Roesner, Larry August *civil engineer*
Shackelford, Charles Duane *civil engineering educator, researcher*

Golden
Gosink, Joan P. *retired engineering educator*
Loomis, Christopher Knapp *metallurgical engineer*

Greenwood Village
Arvizu, Dan Eliab *mechanical engineer*

Lakewood
Barrett, Michael Henry *civil engineer*

Longmont
Nordgren, Ronald Paul *retired engineering educator, researcher*

Loveland
Fleischer, Gerald Albert *industrial engineer, educator*

Parker
Grant, Paul *chemical engineer, real estate broker, lawyer*

Westminster
Dalesio, Wesley Charles *former aerospace educator*

HAWAII

Hilo
Vesper, Karl Hampton *business and mechanical engineering educator*

Honolulu
Chen, Wai-Fah *civil engineering educator*
Chiu, Arthur Nang Lick *engineering educator, consultant*
Cox, Richard Horton *civil engineering executive*
Hamada, Harold Seichi *civil engineer, educator*
Koide, Frank Takayuki *electrical engineering educator*
Sato, Richard Michio *consulting engineering company executive*
Wang, Jaw-Kai *bioengineering educator*
Yee, Alfred Alphonse *structural engineer, consultant*

IDAHO

Boise
Cory, Wallace Newell *retired civil engineer*
Durcan, Mark D. *engineering executive*
Zarges, Thomas H. *engineering executive*

Idaho Falls
Daniher, John M. *retired engineer*
Riemke, Richard Allan *nuclear engineer*
Sackett, John Irvin *nuclear engineer*

Moscow
DeShazer, James Arthur *biological engineer, educator, research administrator*

Pocatello
Jacobsen, Richard T. *mechanical engineering educator*

MONTANA

Bozeman
Cokelet, Giles Roy *biomedical engineering educator*
McLeod, Bruce Royal *electrical engineering educator, consultant*
Sanks, Robert Leland *environmental engineer, retired educator*
Stanislao, Joseph *engineering educator, consultant*

Pony
Anderson, Richard Ernest *agricultural engineer, consultant, rancher*

NEVADA

Boulder City
Wyman, Richard Vaughn *engineering educator, company executive*

Henderson
Wennerstrom, Arthur John *aeronautical engineer*

Incline Village
Thompson, David Alfred *industrial engineer*

Las Vegas
Boehm, Robert Foty *mechanical engineer, educator, researcher*
Culp, Gordon Louis *consulting engineer, management consultant*
Herzlich, Harold J. *chemical engineer*
Messenger, George Clement *engineering executive, consultant*
Neumann, Edward Schreiber *transportation engineering educator*

Reno
Batchman, Theodore Earl *electrical engineering educator, researcher*
Fuerstenau, M(aurice) C(lark) *metallurgical engineer*
Haupt, Randy Larry *electrical engineering educator*
Kleppe, John Arthur *electrical engineer, educator, company executive*
Tsoulfanidis, Nicholas *engineering educator, dean*

NEW MEXICO

Albuquerque
Baum, Carl Edward *electrical engineer, researcher*
Brinker, Charles Jeffrey *chemistry and chemical engineering educator*
Datye, Abhaya Krishna *chemical and nuclear engineer, educator*
Dorato, Peter *electrical and computer engineering educator*
Haddad, Edward Raouf *civil engineer, consultant*
Hall, Jerome William *research engineering educator*
Karni, Shlomo *retired engineering and religious studies professor*

Belen
Toliver, Lee *mechanical engineer*

Cerrillos
Lutz, Raymond Price *retired industrial engineer, educator*

Kirtland AFB
Voelz, David George *electrical engineer*

Los Alamos
Dudziak, Donald John *nuclear engineer, educator*

OREGON

Corvallis
Byers, William D. *engineering executive*
Engelbrecht, Rudolf *electrical engineering educator*
Marple, Stanley Lawrence, Jr. *electrical engineer, researcher*
Temes, Gabor Charles *electrical engineering educator*

Florence
Ericksen, Jerald Laverne *retired science engineering educator*

Klamath Falls
Woodall, David Monroe *engineer, researcher, dean*

Lake Oswego
Kovtynovich, Dan *geotechnical engineer, civil engineer, scientist*

Myrtle Point
Walsh, Don *engineer, consultant*

Portland
Yamayee, Zia Ahmad *engineering educator, dean*

UTAH

Brigham City
Krejci, Robert Henry *aerospace engineer*

Logan
Bowles, David Stanley *engineering educator, consultant*
Clyde, Calvin Geary *civil engineer, educator*
Hargreaves, George Henry *civil and agricultural engineer, researcher*
Keller, Jack *agricultural engineering educator, consultant*

Manti
Funk, William Henry *retired environmental engineering educator*

North Logan
Allen, Dell K. *industrial engineer*

Provo
Jackson, James F. *nuclear engineer, educator*
Jensen, Michael Allen *engineering educator*
Merritt, LaVere Barrus *engineering educator, civil engineer*
Smoot, Leon Douglas *chemical engineer, educator, retired dean*
Youd, T. Leslie *retired civil engineer*

Salt Lake City
DeVries, Kenneth Lawrence *mechanical engineer, educator*
Gandhi, Om Parkash *electrical engineer*
Ghosh, Sambhunath (Sam) *environmental engineer, educator*
Olsen, Donald Bert *biomedical engineer, experimental surgeon, research facility director*
Pariseau, William G. *mining engineer, educator*
Pershing, David Walter *chemical engineering educator, researcher*
Sandquist, Gary Marlin *engineering educator, researcher, consultant, writer, military officer*
Sohn, Hong Yong *chemical and metallurgical engineer, educator*
Stringfellow, Gerald B. *engineering educator*
Virkar, Anil V. *materials engineer, educator*

WASHINGTON

Anacortes
Pratt, David Terry *engineering consultant*

Bellingham
Jansen, Robert Bruce *consulting civil engineer*

Black Diamond
Morris, David John *mining engineer, consultant, mining executive*

Brush Prairie
Edlich, Richard French *biomedical engineer, educator*

Camano Island
Woodruff, Gene Lowry *nuclear engineer, university dean*

Dupont
Pettit, Ghery St. John *electronics engineer*

Issaquah
Evans, Ersel Arthur *engineering executive, consultant*

Kenmore
Guy, Arthur William *electrical engineering educator, researcher*

Mukilteo
Bohn, Dennis Allen *engineering executive*

Olympia
Sesonske, Alexander *nuclear and chemical engineer*

Pullman
Crowe, Clayton T. *engineering educator*
Stock, David Earl *mechanical engineering educator*

Redmond
Willard, H(arrison) Robert *electrical engineer*

Seattle
Bowen, Jewell Ray *chemical engineering professor*
Davis, Earl James *chemical engineering professor emeritus*
Finlayson, Bruce Alan *retired chemical engineering professor*
Galloway, Patricia Denese *civil engineer*
Gilbert, Paul H. *engineering executive, consultant*
Hoffman, Allan Sachs *chemical engineer, educator*
Ishimaru, Akira *electrical engineering educator*
Kapur, Kailash Chander *industrial engineering educator*
Kevorkian, Jirair *aeronautics and astronautics engineering educator*
Kobayashi, Albert Satoshi *mechanical engineering educator*
Lauritzen, Peter Owen *electrical engineering educator*
Lidstrom, Mary E. *chemical engineering and microbiology professor*
Liu, Chen-Ching *electrical engineering educator*
Mc Feron, Dean Earl *mechanical engineer, educator*
Raese, David Senna *aerospace and mass properties engineer, consultant*
Raisbeck, James David *engineering compa executive*
Schmidt, Peter Gustav *marine engineer*
Sleicher, Charles Albert *chemical engineer*
Spindel, Robert Charles *electrical enginee educator*
Sutter, Joseph F. *aeronautical engineer, consultant, retired air transportation exe*

WYOMING

Casper
Hinchey, Bruce Alan *environmental engine company executive, state legislator, state legislator*

Laramie
Rechard, Paul Albert *retired civil engineer, company executive, consultant*

CANADA

ALBERTA

Calgary
Malik, Om Parkash *electrical engineering educator, researcher*
McDaniel, Roderick Rogers *petroleum eng consultant*

Edmonton
Lock, Gerald Seymour Hunter *retired mechanical engineering educator*
McDougall, John Roland *civil engineer*
Offenberger, Allan Anthony *retired electric engineering educator*
Otto, Fred Douglas *chemical engineering professor*
Smith, Daniel Walter *engineering educator*

BRITISH COLUMBIA

Lake Country
Muggeridge, Derek Brian *engineering exec consultant*

Vancouver
Grace, John Ross *chemical engineering ed*
Salcudean, Martha Eva *mechanical engine educator*
Young, Lawrence *electrical engineering educator*

Victoria
Antoniou, Andreas *electrical engineering educator*

Westbank
Wedepohl, Leonhard Martin *electrical engineering educator*

SASKATCHEWAN

Regina
Mollard, John Douglas *engineering and ge executive*

ADDRESS UNPUBLISHED

Ballhaus, William Francis, Jr. *former aero industry executive, engineer*
Ballhaus, William Louis *engineering exec*
Bershad, Neil Jeremy *electrical engineerin educator*
Bose, Anjan *electrical engineering educat academic administrator*
Brown, Steven Harry *engineering executiv*
Burchard, John Kenneth *retired chemical engineer*
Carlson, Robert Codner *industrial enginee educator*
Carnesale, Albert *engineering educator, fo academic administrator*
Cathey, Wade Thomas *electrical engineeri educator*
Chapman, Gary T. *aeronautical engineer, educator*
Charwat, Andrew Franciszek *engineering educator*
Chen, Shoei-Sheng *retired mechanical eng*
Cheng, Wan-Lee *mechanical engineer, edu*
Chizeck, Howard Jay *engineering educato*
Crouch, Peter E. *engineering educator*
Crowley, Joseph Michael *electrical engine educator*
Daly, Donald F. *retired engineering compa executive*
Der Torossian, Papken *engineering executi*
de Soto, Simon *mechanical engineer*
Eaton, George Wesley, Jr. *petroleum engin oil company executive*
Ellington, James Willard *retired mechanic engineer*
Ettinger, Harry Joseph *retired industrial h engineer, consultant*
Gentry, Donald William *engineering execu mining engineer*

ıardt, Heinz Adolf August *retired aircraft sign engineer*
nnon, Gary LeRoy *civil engineering ucator*
ington, Roger Fuller *electrical engineering ucator, retired*
John H. *communications engineer*
pner, David William *mechanical gineering educator*
ies, Robin *computer engineer*
son, Noel Lars *biomedical engineer*
dar, Charles Bell *mechanical engineer, gineering executive*
man, Irving *retired engineering educator*
mi, Hossein *petroleum engineer*
, Donald Evan *electrical engineering ucator, dean*
ht, Patricia Marie *biomedical engineer, nsultant*
se, Keith Winston *engineering company ecutive*
h, Frank *research engineer, consultant*
rence, Kristine Guerra *project engineer*
Young King *biomedical engineering ucator*
berger, David Gilbert *electrical engineer, ucator*
, Richard Godfrey *environmental gineering educator*
x, Robert James *chemical engineer, ucator*
in, J(ohn) Edward *architectural engineer*
on, John Latimer *engineering executive*
aram, Kartikeya *electrical engineer, ucator*
loskey, Thomas Henry *mechanical engineer, nsultant*
uire, Michael John *environmental engineer*
ner, Kenneth Martin *electrical engineer, nsultant*
gan, James John *environmental engineering ucator*
gan, Jeff Scott *research engineer*
hin, Konstantin K. *electrical engineer*
nan, Norris Stanley *electrical engineer*
en, Jakob *computer interface engineer*
er, Buddy Dennis *biomedical engineer, ucator*
er, Donald Sherwood *engineering educator, onomist, cost estimator, management nsultant*
, Clayton Olaf *engineering educator*
er, Junior DeVere (Bob Seader) *retired emical engineering professor*
e, Frieder *structural engineer, educator*
k, Maurice Edwin *aerospace engineer, nsultant*
an, James Michael *retired research gineer*
, Dragoslav D. *engineering educator, searcher*
r, Carson William *retired electrical gineer*
tte, Glenn Phillip *transportation engineer*
e, Stanley Archibald *electrical engineer, searcher*
Alfred Shui-Choh *metallurgical engineer, nsultant*
g, Hong *engineering company executive, ucator, inventor*

ANCE: BANKING SERVICES
See also FINANCE: INVESTMENT SERVICES

UNITED STATES

SKA

horage
y, Daniel Hon *bank executive*
uson, Edward Bernard *banker*

ZONA

enix
n, Michael Carl *bank executive*
tein, Charles Bruce *investment banker, ucation company executive*
on, Barbara Jo *bank executive*
rdson, Judy McEwen *investment banker, nsultant*
orn, R. Michael *bank executive*

tsdale
eld, Ernest *bank executive, consultant*
ard, George Edmund *bank executive, credit nager, marketing professional*

son
ey, Gilbert Francis *retired bank executive*
sel, Hunter *mortgage company executive*

IFORNIA

ura Hills
nd, Stanford L. *mortgage company ecutive*

Arcadia
Ulrich, Peter Henry *banker*

Beverly Hills
Benter, George H., Jr. *banker*
Goldsmith, Bram *banker*
Israel, Richard Stanley *investment banker*
Walker, William Tidd, Jr. *investment banker*

Burbank
Miller, Clifford Albert *merchant banker*

Calabasas
Desoer, Barbara Jean *mortgage company executive*

Carmel
Dobey, James Kenneth *banker*

Costa Mesa
Giannini, Valerio Louis *investment banker*

Fresno
Smith, Richard Howard *banker*

Goleta
Nahra, Lynda J. *bank executive*

Irvine
Kuhn, Robert Lawrence *investment banker, corporate financier, strategist, writer*

La Jolla
Bower, Christopher James *investment banker*

La Mesa
Schmidt, James Craig *retired bank, savings and loan association executive*

Lafayette
Dethero, J. Hambright *banker*

Laguna Hills
Pelton, Harold Marcel *mortgage broker*

Lake Arrowhead
Fitzgerald, John Charles, Jr. *investment banker*

Long Beach
Hancock, John Walker III *banker*

Los Angeles
Badie, Ronald Peter *banker*
Barren, Bruce Willard (HRH The Duke de Serres) *merchant banker*
Cho, Eung-Rae (Brian) *bank executive*
Kang, Alvin *bank executive*
Kim, Min Jung *bank executive*
Min, Soo Bong *bank executive*
Riordan, George Nickerson *investment banker*

Malibu
DeMieri, Joseph L. *retired bank executive*

Menlo Park
Roberts, George R. *investment banker*
Schmidt, Chauncey Everett *banker, director*

Newport Beach
Frederick, Dolliver H. *investment banker*
Matzdorff, James Arthur *investment banker, internet marketing professional*
Prince, Thomas E. *bank executive*
Woollatt, Paul G. *financial company executive*

Oakland
Judd, James Thurston *savings and loan executive*

Ontario
Myers, Christopher D. *bank executive*

Orinda
Trowbridge, Thomas, Jr. *mortgage company executive*

Pasadena
Freeman, Ralph Carter *investment banker, management consultant*
Ng, Dominic *bank executive*
Patton, Richard Weston *retired mortgage company executive*

Redding
Morrison, Gregg Scott *executive*

San Diego
Reinhard, Christopher John *merchant banker, venture capitalist, biotechnologist, director*
Wiesler, James Ballard *retired banker*
Yacovone, Ellen Elaine *banker*

San Francisco
Atkins, Howard Ian *bank executive*
August-deWilde, Katherine *banker*
Bee, Robert Norman *banker*
Boutros, George F. *investment banker*
Callahan, Patricia R. *bank executive*
Demarest, David Franklin, Jr. *banker, retired government official*
Gillette, Frankie Jacobs *retired savings and loan association executive, federal agency administrator, social worker*
Hoyt, David A. *bank executive*
Kovacevich, Richard Marco (Dick Kovacevich) *bank executive*
Liu, Peter *bank executive*
Loughlin, Michael J. *bank executive*
Luikart, John Ford *investment banker*
MacMillen, Lisa Bechtler *bank executive*
Matthews, Gilbert Elliott *investment banker*
McGettigan, Charles Carroll, Jr. *investment banker*
McGrath, Don John *bank executive*
Modjtabai, Avid *bank executive*
Oman, Mark C. *bank executive*
Ostler, Clyde W. *banker*
Stumpf, John Gerard *bank executive*
Tolstedt, Carrie L. *bank executive*
Warner, Harold Clay, Jr. *banker, investment company executive*
Woo Ho, Doreen Woo *bank executive*
Yellen, Janet Louise *bank executive*

San Jose
Hall, Robert Emmett, Jr. *investment banker, realtor*

San Mateo
Douglass, Donald Robert *banker*

San Rafael
Djordjevich, Miroslav-Michael *bank executive*
Payne, David L. *bank executive*

Santa Ana
Piszel, Anthony S. (Buddy Piszel) *mortgage company executive*

Santa Barbara
Tilton, David Lloyd *savings and loan association executive*

Santa Clara
Kamm, Barbara B. *bank executive*

Santa Monica
Heimbuch, Babette E. *bank executive*
Rampino, Louis J. *bank executive*

Santa Rosa
Meekins, Deborah *bank executive*

Sherman Oaks
Keys, Scott *bank executive*

Tarzana
Weil, Leonard *banker*

COLORADO

Colorado Springs
Olin, Kent Oliver *banker*

Denver
Grant, William West III *banker*
Malone, Robert Joseph *retired bank executive*
Nicholson, Will Faust, Jr. *bank executive*

Englewood
Rosser, Edwin Michael *mortgage company executive*

Greenwood Village
Imhoff, Walter Francis *retired investment banker*
Sims, Douglas D. *bank executive*

Lakewood
Fugate, Ivan Dee *banker*
Orullian, B. LaRae *retired bank executive*

Vail
Hoover, Gary Lynn *retired banker*

HAWAII

Honolulu
Dods, Walter Arthur, Jr. *bank executive*
Hoag, John Arthur *retired bank executive*
Johnson, Lawrence M. *retired bank executive*
Landon, Allan R. *bank executive*
Midkiff, Robert Richards *trust company, finance company executive, consultant*
Tanoue, Donna A. *bank executive, former federal agency administrator*
Wolff, Herbert Eric *banker, former army officer*

IDAHO

Ketchum
McElhinny, Wilson Dunbar *banker*

Twin Falls
Eaton, Curtis Howarth *banker, lawyer*

NEVADA

Las Vegas
Troidl, Richard John *banker*

Logandale
Smiley, Robert William, Jr. *investment banker*

NEW MEXICO

Santa Fe
Dreisbach, John Gustave *investment banker*

NORTH CAROLINA

Pinehurst
Rhody, Ronald Edward *bank, communications executive*

OREGON

Bend
Moss, Patricia L. *bank executive*

Lake Oswego
McKay, Laura L. *bank executive, consultant*

Portland
Hayward, Lani *bank executive*

UTAH

Ogden
Browning, Roderick Hanson *banker*

Park City
Montgomery, James Fischer *savings and loan association executive*

Saint George
Beesley, H(orace) Brent *bank executive*

Salt Lake City
Chillingworth, Lori *bank executive*
Eccles, Spencer Fox *banker, director*
Simmons, Harris H. *bank executive*
Speer, Susan H. *bank executive*
Urie, Alan T. *bank executive*

WASHINGTON

Coupeville
Piercy, Gordon Clayton *bank executive, educator*

Everett
Nelson, Carol Kobuke *bank executive*

Renton
Longbrake, William Arthur *bank executive*

Seattle
Andrew, Lucius Archibald David III *bank executive*
Arnold, Robert Morris *banker*
Bley, John L. *financial executive*
Campbell, Robert Hedgcock *investment banker, lawyer*
Faulstich, James R. *retired bank executive*
Riccobono, Richard M. *bank executive, former federal administrator*
Rice, Norman B. *bank executive, former mayor*
Rotella, Stephen J. *former bank executive*

Spokane
Horton, Susan Pittman *bank executive*
Stanley, Heidi B. *bank executive*

Tacoma
Anderson, Lynn L. *bank executive*
Dressel, Melanie J. *bank executive*

Walla Walla
Purcell, Cynthia D. *bank executive*

WYOMING

Cheyenne
Knight, Robert Edward *bank executive, educator*

ADDRESS UNPUBLISHED

Casey, Thomas W. *former bank executive*
Clark, Raymond Oakes *banker*
Cockrum, William Monroe III *investment banker, educator*
Creighton, Norman P. *bank executive*
Dean, John Wesley III *investment banker, former federal official*
Fetters, Norman Craig, II, *retired banker*
Gilchrist, James Beardslee *banker*
Gouw, Julia Suryapranata *bank executive*
Horvath, Debora D. *bank executive*
Keir, Gerald Janes *banker*
Kettell, Russell Willard *former bank executive*
Killinger, Kerry Kent *retired bank executive*
Lawer, Betsy *banker, small business owner, vintner, director*
Lenard, Michael Barry *merchant banker, lawyer*
Mathis, Daniel R. *banking officer*
Mozilo, Angelo R. *retired mortgage company executive*
Ott, Jason E. *banker*
Perry, Michael W. *former bank executive*
Rank, Larry Gene *retired bank executive*
Romero-Rainey, Rebeca *bank executive*
Sohn, Sung Won *former bank executive*
Stephenson, Herman Howard *retired banker*
Trafton, Stephen J. *bank executive*
Vuoto, Anthony (Tony) F. *bank executive*

Winnowski, Thaddeus Richard (Ted Winnowski) *investment banker, consultant*

FINANCE: FINANCIAL SERVICES

UNITED STATES

ARIZONA

Flagstaff
Everett, Judith *merchandising educator*

Phoenix
Castleberry, W. Thomas *financial company executive*
Hathaway, Peter S. *corporate financial executive*
Lemon, Leslie Gene *retired diversified financial services company executive, lawyer*
Scozzari, Albert *portfolio manager, inventor*
Upson, Donald V. *retired corporate financial executive*

Scottsdale
Breyne, Matthew M. *finance company executive*
Marszowski, Bruno A. *finance company executive*

Sun City West
Douglass, Eva Rose *retired accountant*

Surprise
Miller, James Rumrill III *finance educator*

Tempe
Pany, Kurt Joseph *finance educator, consultant*
Poe, Jerry B. *financial educator*

Tucson
Adelstone, Jeffrey Alan *accountant, tax law specialist, educator*
Elger, William Robert, Jr. *accountant*
Hellon, Michael Thomas *tax specialist, political organization worker*
Márquez-Peterson, Lea *business broker*
Villica-a, Taunya *corporate financial executive*

Wickenburg
Daniel, James Richard *accountant, corporate financial executive*

CALIFORNIA

Atherton
Barker, Robert Jeffery *financial executive*

Berkeley
Staubus, George Joseph *finance educator*

Beverly Hills
Widaman, Greg *financial executive, accountant*

Brea
Mc Intyre, James A. *diversified financial services executive*
Oh, Tai Keun *business educator, consultant*

Burbank
Murphy, Peter E. *corporate financial executive*

Calabasas
Garcia, Carlos M. *financial services company executive*
Goldfield, Emily Dawson *finance company executive, artist*
Sieracki, Eric P. *diversified financial services company executive*

Camarillo
Smith, David Michael *financial planner*

Campbell
Vincent, David Ridgely *financial consultant*

Carlsbad
Gillis, Christine Diest-Lorgion *retired certified financial planner, stockbroker*
Steele, Charles Glen *retired accountant*

Carmel
Bonfield, Andrew Joseph *tax practitioner*

Dana Point
Kesselhaut, Arthur Melvyn *financial consultant*

El Segundo
Rotherham, Thomas G. *diversified financial services company executive*

Encino
Dor, Yoram *accountant*

Foster City
Coghlan, John Philip *corporate financial executive*
Pollitt, Byron H., Jr. *finance company executive, former retail executive*

Fountain Valley
Penderghast, Thomas Frederick *business educator*

Fresno
Tellier, Richard Davis *management educator*

Hayward
McKenzie, Brian Bruce *finance educator*
Randisi, Elaine Marie *accountant, educator, writer*

Huntington Beach
Strutzel, Jod Christopher *escrow company executive*

Irvine
Callé, Craig R.L. *finance company executive*
Cole, Robert K. *diversified financial services company executive*
Feldstein, Paul Joseph *management educator*
Parnes, Andrew H. *financial executive*

La Canada Flintridge
Chavez, Albert Blas *financial executive*

Lincoln
Patten, Thomas Henry, Jr. *retired educator, personnel director*

Livermore
Bronson, Joseph R. *manufacturing company executive*

Los Altos
Scifres, Donald Ray *finance company executive*

Los Angeles
Allen, Sharon *accounting firm executive*
Anderson, John Edward *diversified holding company executive, lawyer*
Barkley, Joseph Richard *controller*
Borsting, Jack Raymond *business administration educator*
Brown, Kathleen *diversified financial services company executive*
Garrison, P. Gregory *diversified financial services company executive*
Leach, Anthony Raymond *financial executive*
Lowy, Peter *corporate financial executive*
McGagh, William Gilbert *financial consultant*
Mock, Theodore Jaye *finance educator*
Mosich, Anelis Nick *accountant, writer, educator, consultant*
Ramer, Lawrence Jerome *corporation executive*
Resnick, Lynda *corporate financial executive*
Tuttle, Rick *city controller*
Udvar-Hazy, Steven F. *leasing company financial executive*
Westerfield, Randolph W. *finance educator, former dean*
Weston, John Frederick *business educator, consultant*

Los Gatos
McLaughlin, Glen *financial services company executive*

Menlo Park
Scholes, Myron S. *financier, former law and finance educator*

Mill Valley
Bull, George E. III *finance company executive*
Mumford, Christopher Greene *corporate financial executive*

Newport Beach
Cote, Brian E. *financial executive*
Haussmann, Trudy Diane *financial planner*
Wood, George H. *investment executive*

North Hollywood
Boulanger, Donald Richard *financial services executive*

Oceanside
Taverna, Rodney Elward *financial services company executive*

Oxnard
Jones, Craig Robert *financial executive*

Palo Alto
Horngren, Charles Thomas *finance educator*

Pasadena
Babayans, Emil *financial planner*
Hirschmann, James William III *diversified financial services company executive*
Norton, Karen Ann *accountant*

Pleasanton
Call, John G. *corporate financial executive*
Edwards, Robert L. *corporate financial executive*

Redlands
Pick, James Block *business professor, writer*

Sacramento
Dear, Joseph Albert *pension fund administrator*
Marzion, Kenneth W. *pension fund administrator*
Palmer, William Joseph *accountant*
Stausboll, Anne *pension fund administrator*

Salinas
Mehta, Siddarth N. *credit services company executive*

San Diego
Goldstein, Rey *accountant*
Jeub, Michael Leonard *financial consultant*
Markowitz, Harry Max *finance and economics educator*
Riedy, Mark Joseph *finance educator*
Sopp, Mark W. *corporate financial executive*
Stambaugh, Larry G. *strategic business consultant*
West, James Harold *finance company executive*

San Francisco
Bauch, Thomas Jay *financial consultant, retired lawyer, apparel executive*
Dawson, Peter A. *corporate financial executive*
Gebler, David B. *finance company executive*
Grubb, Edgar Harold *financial services industrial executive*
James, George Barker, II, *financial executive*
Lynn, Evadna Saywell *investment analyst*
Paterson, Richard Denis *corporate financial executive*
Saunders, Joseph W. *finance company executive*
Simini, Joseph Peter *accountant, financial consultant, writer, former educator*
Sonneborn, William Charles *diversified financial services company executive*
Uri, George Wolfsohn *accountant*
Weihrich, Heinz *management educator*

San Jose
Ceran, Jennifer Ellen *treasurer*
Effren, Gary Ross *financial executive*
Holland, David K. *treasurer*
Jiang, William Yuying *business educator, consultant, researcher*

San Marcos
Kagan, Stephen Bruce (Sandy Kagan) *corporate financial executive*
Melcher, Trini Urtuzuastegui *retired finance educator*

San Mateo
Hopkins, Cecilia Ann *business educator*
Johnson, Charles Bartlett *corporate financial executive*
Johnson, Gregory Eugene *diversified financial services company executive*
Johnson, Rupert Harris, Jr. *diversified financial services company executive*

Santa Ana
Kennedy, Parker S. *finance company executive*

Santa Clara
Dillon, Adrian T. *financial executive*
Paisley, Christopher B. *business educator*

Santa Monica
Markoff, Steven C. *finance company executive*

Stanford
Beaver, William Henry *accounting educator*
Holloway, Charles Arthur *public and private management educator*
McDonald, John Gregory *financial investment educator*
Montgomery, David Bruce *marketing educator*
Pfeffer, Jeffrey *business educator*

Stockton
Plovnick, Mark Stephen *business educator*
Post, Gerald V. *business educator*
Taylor, Francis Michael *auditor, municipal official*
Vargo, Richard Joseph *accounting educator, writer*

Sunnyvale
Rivet, Robert J. *semiconductor company executive*

Tarzana
Firestone, Morton H. *finance company executive*

Vista
Ferguson, Margaret Ann *tax specialist, consultant*

West Hollywood
Santillan, Antonio *financial company executive*

West Sacramento
Anderson, William Wallace *financial executive*

Westlake Village
Detterman, Robert Linwood *financial planner*

Woodland Hills
Tuthill, Walter Warren *accountant, management consultant*

COLORADO

Boulder
Baughn, William Hubert *former business educator and academic administrator*
Melicher, Ronald William *finance educator*
Stanton, William John, Jr. *marketing educator, author*

Broomfield
Seabrook, Raymond J. *corporate financial executive*

Colorado Springs
Wheeler, Larry Richard *accountant*

Denver
Herz, Leonard *financial consultant*
O'Toole, James Joseph *business educator*

Englewood
Flowers, David J. *corporate financial exec*

Fort Collins
Hendrick, Ronald Lynn *controller*
Johnson, Mildred I. *retired business educat*

Highlands Ranch
Townsend, James Douglas *chief financial o accountant*

Lakewood
Hadley, Marlin LeRoy *financial planner, consultant*

Longmont
Sandler, Thomas R. *accountant, director*

Nederland
Thomas, Daniel Foley *retired diversified financial services company executive*

Wheat Ridge
Leino, Deanna Rose *business educator*

HAWAII

Hilo
Kojima, Sheri S. *high school business educ*

Honolulu
Betts, James William, Jr. *financial analyst, consultant*
Hook, Ralph Clifford, Jr. *business educator*

IDAHO

Boise
Ingram, Cecil D. *accountant, state legislat*

MASSACHUSETTS

Cambridge
Chatterjee, Sharmila *marketing educator*

MONTANA

Billings
Stapleton, Corey *financial planner*

Bozeman
Davis, Nicholas Homans Clark *finance com executive*

Great Falls
Christiaens, Chris (Bernard Francis) *financ analyst, state legislator*

NEBRASKA

Omaha
Carrica, Jean Leon *business educator*
Munger, Charles T. *diversified company executive*

NEVADA

Las Vegas
Bass, Charles Morris *financial and systems consultant*
Chatfield, Robert Evans *finance professor, college administrator*
Parry, Clint *business coaching executive*

NEW MEXICO

Albuquerque
Young, Joni J. *finance educator, researcher*

Las Cruces
Constantini, Louis O. *financial consultant, stockbroker*
Peterson, Robin Tucker *marketing educato*

Santa Fe
Thornburg, Garrett, Jr. *finance company executive*
Watkins, Stephen Edward *accountant, pub executive*

OREGON

Eugene
Miner, John Burnham *industrial relations educator, writer*

Newport
Sonnier, Patricia Bennett *business manage educator*

:land
:h, Samuel Henry *diversified financial* *:vices company executive*
:rson, Eric Robert *finance executive, film* *:oducer*

:AH

:m
:, H(arold) Keith *retired business* *:anagement educator, marketing consultant*

: Lake City
:y, Rodney Howard *diversified financial* *:vices and broadcast company executive,* *:ired academic administrator, federal official*
:s, Glen Ray *retired diversified management* *:rvices company executive*
:son, Auston Gilbert III *auditor*
:on, Roger Hugh *corporate financial* *:ecutive, educator, consultant*

:SHINGTON

:ngham
:, Steven Charles *business administration* *:ucator, consultant*

:kland
:son, Warren Wade *business administration* *:ucator*

:ttle
:r, Roland Jerald *finance educator*
:tt, Robert Lee *financial company executive*
:ly, Dwight Douglas *finance director*
:, George James III *financial services* *:mpany executive*
:Lachlan, Douglas Lee *marketing educator*
:tak, Tom *corporate financial executive*
:npson, Richard *financial executive*

:kane
:on, Robert Lyle *accounting firm executive*
:eron, Alex Brian *accountant, educator*

CANADA

:TISH COLUMBIA

:couver
:essich, Richard Victor (Alvarus) *business* *:ministration researcher*

FRANCE

:tainebleau
:er, Philip M. *management science educator,* *:iter*

ADDRESS UNPUBLISHED

:ya, Richard Alfred, Jr. *financial consultant*
:eson, Sue Hart *business educator*
:nan, Winfield Scott *finance educator*
:nan, Ciaran Brendan *accountant, oil* *:dustry executive*
:ey, Marcia B. *corporate financial executive*
:n, William Alan *finance educator,* *:anagement consultant, writer*
:akos, Christos Michael *retired internet* *:ancial services company executive*
:i, Mathew G. *financial consultant and* *:thor*
:ey, Dolores Florence *retired corporate* *:easurer, finance company executive*
:r, John Edson, II, *finance company* *:ecutive, consultant, investment advisor*
:klin, William Emery *international business* *:ucator*
:man, Tully Michael *finance company* *:ecutive*
:k, Carolyn Jean *financial consultant, retired* *:dge*
:, Leonard William *accounting educator*
:r, Robert *financial executive, economist*
:inger, Frank Casper *retired diversified* *:ancial services company executive*
:son, Ernest Charles *financial executive*
:ucci, Samuel H. *financial executive*
:son, Suzanne Nora *retired diversified* *:ancial services company executive, lawyer*
:n, Mark Allan *financial executive*
:e, Nicholas G. *retired finance company* *:ecutive*
:er, Gary Andrew *portfolio manager*
:ore, Kimberly S. *financial services* *:ecutive*
:, Thomas W. *treasurer manufacturing* *:mpany*
:ard, William Robert *retired operations* *:anagement educator*
:n, Ronald Isaac *financial executive*
:er, Alan Carhart *finance company executive*
:vasan, Venkataraman *marketing and* *:anagement educator*
:cill, James McNeill *retired finance educator*
:ill, Dennis Carothers *corporate financial* *:ecutive*

Stewart, Richard Alfred *business executive*
Stockholm, Charles M. *diversified financial services company executive*
Tornese, Judith M. *financial institution executive*
Turner, Henry Brown *finance company executive, director*
Wachbrit, Jill Barrett *accountant, tax specialist*
Wall, M. Danny *retired finance company executive*

FINANCE: INSURANCE

UNITED STATES

ALABAMA

Birmingham
Galbraith, John Robert *insurance company executive*

ARIZONA

Paradise Valley
Tyner, Neal Edward *retired insurance company executive*

Sun City
Reynolds, John Francis *insurance company executive*

CALIFORNIA

Camarillo
Schweizer, Edward Sowers *insurance agency owner*

Encino
Parrott, Dennis Beecher *retired insurance industry executive*

Irvine
Matros, Richard K. *insurance company executive*

Los Angeles
Houston, Ivan James *insurance company executive*
Johnson, E. Eric *insurance company executive*
Joseph, George *insurance company executive*
Tirador, Gabriel *insurance company executive*

Newark
Gupta, Anju *risk management consultant*

Newport Beach
Cheever, Sharon Ann *insurance company executive, lawyer*
Gerken, Walter Bland *insurance company executive*
Morris, James T. *insurance company executive*
Tran, Khanh T. *insurance company executive*

Rancho Cordova
Alenius, John Todd *retired insurance executive*

San Francisco
Lamberson, John Roger *insurance company executive*
Martinez, Belinda *health insurance company executive*

San Rafael
Keegan, Jane Ann *insurance executive, consultant*

Santa Ana
Gilmore, Dennis J. *insurance company executive*
McMahon, Frank V. *insurance company executive*

Santa Barbara
Evans, Thomas Edgar, Jr. *title insurance agency executive*
Stone, Patrick F. *insurance company executive*

Santa Monica
Schaeffer, Leonard David *health insurance company executive*

Santa Rosa
Farrell, Thomas Joseph *insurance company executive, consultant*

Thousand Oaks
Valdez, Josh *health insurance company executive*
Weinberg, D. Mark *health insurance company executive*

Woodland Hills
Clarey, Patricia T. *health insurance company executive, former state official*

COLORADO

Fort Collins
Schendel, Winfried George *insurance company executive*

Littleton
Rotherham, Larry Charles *insurance executive*

FLORIDA

Jacksonville
Foley, William Patrick, II, *insurance company executive*

IDAHO

Idaho Falls
Dunstan, Larry Kenneth *endowment director*

MONTANA

Whitefish
Hemp, Ralph Clyde *retired reinsurance company executive, consultant, arbitrator, umpire*

OREGON

Depoe Bay
Lang, George Frank *insurance company executive, lawyer, consultant*

Portland
Parsons, Eric E. *insurance company executive*

WASHINGTON

Mountlake Terrace
Dyer, Philip E. *insurance company executive*

Seattle
Armstrong, Mary M. *insurance company executive*
Eigsti, Roger Harry *retired insurance company executive*
Kari, Ross *insurance company executive*
Koster, John Frederick *insurance executive*

Woodland
Hansen, Walter Eugene *insurance executive*

WYOMING

Cheyenne
Moore, Dan Sterling *insurance executive, sales trainer*

ADDRESS UNPUBLISHED

Becker, JoAnn Elizabeth *retired insurance company executive*
Borda, Richard Joseph *retired insurance company executive*
Conroy, Thomas Francis *insurance company consultant*
Dackow, Orest Taras *insurance company executive*
Delaney, William Francis, Jr. *reinsurance broker*
Fibiger, John Andrew *life insurance company executive*
Herman, Joan Elizabeth *retired health insurance company executive*
Metcalf, Wayne C. III *retired insurance company executive*
Newman, Steven Harvey *insurance company executive, director*
Sutton, Thomas C. *retired insurance company executive*
Zebroski, Edwin Leopold *risk management consultant*

FINANCE: INVESTMENT SERVICES

UNITED STATES

ALASKA

Anchorage
Hickel, Walter Joseph *retired investment company executive, foundation administrator, former United States Secretary of the Interior*
Jay, Christopher Edward *stockbroker*

ARIZONA

Phoenix
Stern, Richard David *investment company executive*

Scottsdale
Getz, Bert Atwater *investment company executive*
Mc Gill, Archie Joseph *venture capitalist*

Tubac
Schuyler, Robert Len *investment company executive*

Tucson
Lomicka, William Henry *investor*

CALIFORNIA

Arcadia
Berkus, David William *venture capitalist*

Atherton
Sollman, George Henry *venture capitalist*

Benicia
Szabo, Peter John *investment company executive, mining engineer, financial planner, lawyer*

Beverly Hills
Covitz, Carl D. *investment company executive, federal and state official*
Eisner, Michael Dammann *investment and former entertainment company executive*
Evans, Louise *investor, retired psychologist*
Gambrell, Thomas Ross *investor, retired physician, surgeon*
Gores, Tom T. *investment company executive*
Kerkorian, Kirk *investor, former motion picture company executive, consultant*

Carmel
Hamilton, Beverly Lannquist *investment executive*

Foster City
Krikorian, Blake *entrepreneur, consumer electronics company executive*

Fremont
Grant, Alan J. *business executive, educator*

Fresno
Dauer, Donald Dean *investment company executive*

Granada Hills
Drew, Paul S. *entrepreneur*

La Jolla
Conn, Robert William *venture capital investor*

Lake Sherwood
Mann, Nancy Louise (Nancy Louise Robbins) *entrepreneur*

Los Altos
Carsten, Jack Craig *venture capitalist*

Los Angeles
Angeloff, Dann Valentino *brokerage house executive*
Barrack, Thomas J., Jr. *real estate investor, lawyer*
Hurwitz, Lawrence Neal *investment banking company executive*
Johnson, Jeffrey M. *private equity company executive, former publishing executive*
Larkin, Thomas Ernest, Jr. *investment management company executive*
Latzer, Richard Neal *investment company executive*
Nogales, Luis Guerrero *investment company executive*
Saban, Haim *investment company executive, television producer*

Menlo Park
Balkanski, Alexandre *investment company executive*
Byers, Brook *venture capitalist, investor*
Compton, Kevin R. *venture capitalist, professional sports team executive*
Doerr, John (L. John Doerr III) *venture capitalist*
Fenton, Noel John *venture capitalist*
Giancarlo, Charles H. *investment company executive, former computer systems network executive*
Gordon, William Bingham (Bing Gordon) *venture capitalist, former software marketing executive*
Joy, Bill (William Nelson Joy) *venture capitalist, former computer software company executive*
Khosla, Vinod *investment company executive*
Kramlich, C(harles) Richard (Dick) *venture capitalist*
LaPorte, Kathleen Darken *venture capitalist*
Lynch, Charles Allen *investment company executive, director*
Marquardt, David F. *venture capitalist*
Perkins, Tom (Thomas James Perkins) *venture capital company executive*
Westly, Steven Paul *venture capitalist*
Wolfson, Mark Alan *investor, educator, dean*

Napa
Strock, David Randolph *brokerage house executive*

Newport Beach
Arnott, Robert Douglas *investment company executive*
El-Erian, Mohamed A. *investment company executive*
Gross, Bill (William H. Gross) *investment company executive, financial analyst*

North Hills
Iacocca, Lee (Lido Anthony) *venture capitalist, retired automotive executive*

Orange
Tuggle, Francis Douglas *entrepreneur, consultant, management educator, scientist*

Palo Alto
Avis, Gregory M. *venture capitalist*
Breyer, Jim (James William Breyer) *venture capitalist*
Kawasaki, Guy *venture capitalist, investment banker, entrepreneur*
Sculley, John *investment company executive, former computer company executive*

Pasadena
Fredericks, Ward Arthur *venture capitalist*
Zimmerman, William Robert *entrepreneur, engineering based manufacturing company executive*

Pinedale
Falcone, Patricia Jeanne Lalim *investor, foundation administrator*

Sacramento
Ailman, Christopher J. *investment company executive*

San Diego
Brandes, Charles H. *investment company executive*
Dunn, David Joseph *investment company executive*

San Francisco
Bettinger, Walter W., II, *investment company executive*
Buckner, John Knowles *investor*
Casnocha, Benedict T. *entrepreneur*
Dachs, Alan Mark *investment company executive*
Draper, William Henry III *venture capitalist*
Gund, George III *financier, professional sports team executive*
Hagenbuch, John Jacob *investor*
Hazen, Paul Mandeville *private equity firm executive, retired bank executive*
Hellman, F(rederick) Warren *investor*
Levine, Alison *entrepreneur, leadership development consultant, adventurer*
Martinetto, Joseph R. *investment company executive*
Mullin, Hadley (Mary Hadley Mullin) *private equity firm executive*
Pfau, George Harold, Jr. *investment advisor*
Pottruck, David Steven *private equity firm executive*
Quattrone, Frank P. *investment company executive*
Rock, Arthur *venture capitalist*
Schwab, Charles Robert, Jr., (Chuck Schwab) *investment company executive*
Shansby, John Gary *investor*
Siebel, Kenneth *investment advisor*
Steyer, Thomas Fahr *investment company executive*
Thiel, Peter Andreas *hedge fund manager*
Weisel, Thomas W. *investment company executive*
Winblad, Ann *investment company executive*

Santa Ana
Martinez, Rueben *entrepreneur*

Santa Barbara
Bartlett, James Lowell III *investment company executive*
Emmeluth, Bruce Palmer *investment company executive, venture capitalist*
Orfalea, Paul James *investment company executive, former printing company executive*
Vos, Hubert Daniel *investor*

Santa Monica
Shahani, Sudhin *entrepreneur, Internet company executive*
Tennenbaum, Michael Ernest *investor*
Unterman, Thomas *venture capitalist, lawyer*

Saratoga
Horn, Christian Friedrich *venture capital company executive*

Sausalito
Amelio, Gilbert Frank *venture capitalist, information technology executive*
Apatoff, Michael John *entrepreneur*

Simi Valley
Sproles, Kevin *entrepreneur, Internet company executive*

Sonoma
Gardner, James Harkins *venture capitalist*

Sunnyvale
Rubin, Gary Andrew *entrepreneur, computer engineer*

Thousand Oaks
Gregory, Calvin *real estate investor*

Woodland Hills
Feiman, Thomas E. *investment company executive*

COLORADO

Boulder
Shaykin, Leonard P. *investor*

Denver
Black, Gary D. *investment company executive*
Case, Steve (Stephen M.) *healthcare investment company executive, former media and entertainment company executive*
Eppler, Jerome Cannon *investment advisor*
Scheid, Steven L. *investment company executive*
Wagner, Judith Buck *investment firm executive*

Grand Junction
Skogen, Haven Sherman *investment company executive*

HAWAII

Honolulu
Haight, Warren Gazzam *investor*
Lee, Lorrin L. *internet marketing entrepreneur, architect, writer*

NEVADA

Boulder City
Stephenson, Arthur Emmet, Jr. *investment company executive*

Incline Village
Johnson, James Arnold *venture capitalist*

Las Vegas
Kelly, Sean *entrepreneur*
Root, Wayne Allyn *entrepreneur, television producer, writer*

Sparks
Holder, Harold Douglas, Sr. *investor, hotel executive*

OREGON

Portland
Arthur, Michael Elbert *financial advisor, lawyer*
Cohen, Stuart F. *investment company executive*
Coleman, Debi (Deborah Ann) *investment and former computer company executive*
Milton, Catherine Higgs *entrepreneur*
Paulson, Chester Leon Frederick *brokerage house executive*
Rutherford, William Drake *investment executive*
Stott, Peter Walter *investment company executive*

UTAH

Salt Lake City
Ballard, Melvin Russell, Jr. *investment executive, church official*
Meldrum, Peter Durkee *venture capitalist, biotechnology company executive*
Peterson, Joel C. *investment company executive*

WASHINGTON

Bellevue
Connors, John G. *venture capitalist, former computer software company executive*

Kirkland
Ryles, Gerald Fay *investor, finance company executive*

Port Townsend
Jones, John Wesley *entrepreneur*

Redmond
Christie, Doug (Douglas Dale Christie) *entrepreneur, former professional basketball player*

Seattle
Heath, Richard Raymond *retired investment company executive*
McAleer, William Harrison *technology venture capitalist*
McCaw, John Elroy, Jr. *investment company executive, professional sports team executive*
Ruckelshaus, William Doyle *investment company executive, former federal agency administrator*
Wright, Bagley *venture capitalist, entrepreneur, art collector*

Sequim
Kretschmer, Keith Hughes *investor*

WYOMING

Jackson
Trauner, Gary *entrepreneur*

CANADA

ALBERTA

Calgary
Cumming, Thomas Alexander *brokerage house executive*

BRITISH COLUMBIA

Vancouver
Aquilini, Francesco *investment company executive, professional sports team executive*
Saunders, Peter Paul *investor*

ADDRESS UNPUBLISHED

Allen, Donald Vail *investment company executive, pianist*
Amos, Wally (Famous Amos) *entrepreneur*
Berkley, Stephen M. *entrepreneur, investor*
Daie, Jaleh *investment company executive*
De Lutis, Donald Conse *investment advisor, consultant*
Dunn, Richard Joseph *retired investment advisor*
Gordy, Berry *entrepreneur, film producer, recording industry executive*
Greber, Robert Martin *retired financial investments executive*
Greene, Frank Sullivan, Jr. *investment company executive*
Griego, Linda *entrepreneur*
Holte, Debra Leah *investment company executive, financial analyst*
Hurt, William Holman *investment management company executive*
Jerrytone, Samuel Joseph *financial property broker*
Kazi, Sumaya *entrepreneur*
Leahy, T. Liam *business development and technology investor*
Level, Leon Jules *investor, director*
Linde, Ronald Keith *investor*
Morgenroth, Earl Eugene *entrepreneur*
Nilsson, A. Kenneth *investor*
Pacholski, Richard Francis *securities trader, financial consultant*
Paup, Martin Arnold *securities and real estate investor*
Reilly, William Kane *investment company executive, preservationist, former federal agency administrator*
Scher, Laura Susan *financial company executive*
Shriram, K. Ram *investment company executive*
Stephens, Donald R(ichards) *investor*
Vilar, Alberto W. *investment company executive*
Waitt, Theodore W. (Ted Waitt) *venture capitalist, former computer company executive*
Walsh, William Desmond *investor*

GOVERNMENT: AGENCY ADMINISTRATION

UNITED STATES

ALASKA

Anchorage
Burke, Marianne King *state agency administrator, finance executive, consultant*
Udland, Duane S. *protective services official*

Juneau
Davis, Mark R. *state agency administrator*

ARIZONA

Glendale
Dobrotka, David Allen *protective services official*
Goforth, Nathan Dan *retired protective services official*

Mesa
Nielson, Theo Gilbert *protective services official, university official*

Peoria
Strope, Michael Lee *protective services official*

Phoenix
Chavez, Nelba R. *state and former federal agency administrator*
Gerard, Susan E. *state agency administrator, former state senator*
Harris, Jack F. *police chief*
Karnas, Fred G., Jr. *poverty and homeless specialist*
North, Warren James *government official*
Rotellini, Felecia A. *state agency administrator*
Travous, Kenneth E. *state agency administrator*

Tucson
Casper, Wayne Arthur *city official, educator*
Walker, Franklin Curtis *federal agency administrator*

CALIFORNIA

Bakersfield
Bernard, Alexander *protective services offi*

Berkeley
Butler, Daschel E. *protective services offici*

Beverly Hills
Snowden, David L. *protective services offi*

Edwards AFB
Meske, Sandy *government agency adminis*

El Monte
Clayton, Wayne Charles *protective services official, educator*

Fremont
Steckler, Craig Theodore *protective service official*

La Jolla
Petersen, Richard Herman *federal agency administrator, aeronautical engineer*

Los Angeles
Bratton, Bill (William Joseph Bratton) *poli chief*
Itabashi, Hideo Henry *coroner, pathologist, educator, consultant*

Pasadena
Parker, Robert Allan Ridley *federal agency administrator, astronaut*

Sacramento
Bornstein, Julie Ilene *state agency adminis*
Campbell, Tom *state agency administrator, former congressman*
Helmick, D.O. *protective services official*
Kelley, Michael A. *state agency administra*
Marin, Rosario *state agency administrator, former federal agency administrator*
Wright, Mary Rose *retired state agency administrator*
Zil, J. S. *forensic specialist, psychiatrist, educator*

San Diego
Lansdowne, William M. *police chief*
Osby, Robert Edward *protective services o*

San Francisco
Fujii, Sharon M. *federal agency administra*
Tarnoff, Peter *federal agency administrator, consultant*

Santa Monica
Poe, Robert George, Jr. *state official, management and finance consultant*
Timmer, Barbara *state agency administrato*

Stockton
Ratto, Douglas C. *protective services offici*

Yuba City
Doscher, Richard John *protective services*

COLORADO

Aurora
Vincent, Verne Saint *protective services offi*

Colorado Springs
Kramer, Lorne C. *protective services offici*

Denver
Adkins, Jeanne M. *state agency administra*
Fulkerson, Richard J. *state agency adminis*
Gonzales, Richard L. *protective services off*
Mathews, Laurie A. *state agency administr*
Mencer, Sue (Constance Suzanne Mencer) *former federal agency administrator*

Eldorado Springs
Lovins, L. Hunter *public policy institute executive, consultant, educator*

Englewood
McGraw, Jack Wilson *federal agency administrator*

Golden
Stewart, Frank Maurice, Jr. *federal agency administrator*

Longmont
Kaminsky, Glenn Francis *business owner, r protective services official*

HAWAII

Hickam AFB
Trapp, Lansford E. *air force officer*

Hilo
Carvalho, Wayne G. *protective services offi*

Honolulu
Chapman, Duane Lee (Dog Chapman) *bail enforcement agent, television personality*
Griffin, Dominic B. III *state agency administrator*
Nagata, Rolston H. *state agency administra*
Tagomori, Howard H. *protective services o*

AHO

se
Gavin M. *state agency administrator*
man, Gregory Erwin *state agency dministrator*
s, Donna Marilyn *state agency dministrator, former legislator*
h, Marsha H. *state agency administrator, wyer*
sugi, Patrick A. *state agency administrator*

ho Falls
alch, Ann *federal agency administrator, rmer state senator*

NTANA

ena
dwin, Annie M. *state agency administrator*
ger, Doug J. *state agency administrator*

VADA

son City
rson, Mary L. *state agency official*

Vegas
drup, Steven W. *state agency administrator*
ino, Mario H. *protective services official*

th Las Vegas
hand, Russell David, II, *retired protective rvices official*

o
n, John Alfred *federal agency administrator*

W MEXICO

uquerque
errez, Sidney M. *federal agency ministrator*
toya, Patricia T. *federal agency ministrator*
iams, Marion Lester *government agency ministrator*

ta Fe
son, Eric B. *police chief*
, Robin Dozier *state agency administrator*
rs, Jerry L. *federal agency administrator*
nt, William J. *state agency administrator*

EGON

tland
sen, Reginald B. *protective services official*

m
s, Walter E. *protective services official*
an, David C. *state agency administrator*

AH

vo
er, Gregory M. *protective services official*

Lake City
, G. Edward *state agency administrator*
r, Bruce Douglas *federal agency ministrator, educator, writer*
s, Mildred Thomas *state agency ministrator, educator*

SHINGTON

Wenatchee
ey, Robert John *retired federal agency fessional*

npia
, Scott *state agency administrator*

tle
alis, Richard F. *federal agency ministrator*

im
ey, James Robert *government official, rnational affairs scholar*

ane
ell, G. Ronald *protective services official*
ms, Robert Stone *protective services cial*

OMING

enne
r, Steve *state agency administrator*
errera, Juan Abran (Age) *federal judicial urity official*
Jeffrey C. *state agency administrator*

ADDRESS UNPUBLISHED

an, Rodney Lee *federal agency ministrator*
Anderson, Wayne Carl *global public affairs officer, retired corporate financial executive*
Bishop, C. Diane *state agency administrator, educator*
Bowman, Jeffrey R. *former fire chief*
Brubaker, Crawford Francis, Jr. *federal agency administrator, aerospace scientist, consultant*
Bustamante, Tommy A. *protective services official*
Carmona, Richard Henry *former Surgeon General of the United States*
Gifford, Raymond L. *state agency administrator*
Gold, Rick L. *water resources consultant*
Guay, Gordon Hay *federal agency administrator, marketing educator, consultant*
Hedrick, Basil Calvin *state agency administrator, ethnohistorian, educator, museum and multicultural institutions consultant*
Howell, Helen *state agency administrator*
Keegan, Lisa Graham *state agency administrator*
Larson, Jo Ann *government agency administrator*
Lovejoy, Lynda M. *former state agency administrator, state legislator*
Patino, Douglas Xavier *academic foundation and government agency administrator*
Perock, Wayne R. *state agency administrator*
Shuman, Thomas Alan *protective services official, consultant*
Silva, Robert Owen *retired protective service official*
Stamper, Norman Harvey *former police chief*
Tritten, James John *retired federal agency administrator*
Troncoso, Jose Gerardo *protective services official*
Winchester, Ed *protective services official*

GOVERNMENT: EXECUTIVE ADMINISTRATION

UNITED STATES

ALASKA

Anchorage
Parnell, Sean *Lieutenant Governor of Alaska, former state legislator, lawyer*

Fairbanks
Murkowski, Frank Hughes *former Governor of Alaska*
Smith, Robert London, Sr. *commissioner, retired air force officer, political scientist, educator*

Juneau
Burnett, Jerry *state treasurer*
Galvin, Patrick *Commissioner Department Revenue, Alaska*
Palin, Sarah Heath *Governor of Alaska*
Svobodny, Richard A. *state attorney general*

ARIZONA

Chandler
Dunn, Boyd W. *mayor, Chandler, Arizona, lawyer*

Gilbert
Berman, Steven *Mayor, Gilbert, Arizona*

Glendale
Scruggs, Elaine M. *Mayor, Glendale, Arizona*

Marana
Davidson, Gilbert *city manager*

Mesa
Brown, Wayne J. *former mayor*
Hawker, Keno *former mayor, trucking company executive*
Smith, Scott *Mayor, Mesa, Arizona, business, financial and legal consultant*

Phoenix
Bennett, Kenneth R. *state official, former state senator*
Brewer, Jan (Janice Kay Brewer) *Governor of Arizona*
Goddard, Terry *state attorney general*
Gordon, Phillip Bruce *Mayor, Phoenix*
Lyons, Lionel Dale *city official*
Martin, Dean *state treasurer*
Miel, Vicky Ann *city official*
Pierce, Gary L. *Arizona Corp Commissioner*

Scottsdale
Lane, W. James *Mayor, Scottsdale, Ariz., airline executive, CPA*
Quayle, Dan (James Danforth Quayle) *former Vice President of the United States*
Quayle, Marilyn Tucker *wife of former United States Vice President, lawyer*

Sun Lakes
Sharpless, Joseph Benjamin *retired county official*

Tempe
Hallman, Hugh *Mayor, Tempe, Arizona*

Tucson
Garza, Elizeo *director solid waste management, Tucson*
Meyerson, Ronald L. *city official*
Miller, Elizabeth Rodriguez *city official*
Walkup, Robert E. *Mayor, Tucson*

CALIFORNIA

Anaheim
Pringle, Curt *Mayor, Anaheim, California*

Bakersfield
Hall, Harvey L. *Mayor, Bakersfield, California, medical transportation company executive*
Mosby, Dorothea Susan *retired municipal official*

Chula Vista
Cox, Cheryl *Mayor, Chula Vista, California*
Padilla, Stephen *former mayor*

Corona
Nolan, Steve *Mayor, Corona, California*

Coronado
Hostler, Charles Warren *retired ambassador, international affairs consultant*

Felicity
Istel, Jacques Andre *Mayor, Felicity, California*

Fontana
Nuaimi, Mark N. *Mayor, Fontana, California*

Fremont
Lydon, Daniel T. *city official*
Wasserman, Robert *Mayor, Fremont, California*

Fresno
Autry, Alan *Former Mayor, Fresno, California, film company executive, actor, former professional football player*
Swearengin, Ashley *Mayor, Fresno, California*

Garden Grove
Dalton, William J. *Mayor, Garden Grove, California*

Glendale
Drayman, John *Mayor, Glendale, California*

Huntington Beach
Bohr, Keith *Mayor, Huntington Beach, California*

Irvine
Agran, Larry *mayor, lawyer*
Kang, Sukhee *Mayor, Irvine, California*
Krom, Beth *former Mayor, Irvine, California*

Livermore
Brown, Cathie *city official*

Long Beach
Burroughs, Gary L. *city official*
Foster, Robert G. (Bob Foster) *Mayor, Long Beach, California*

Los Angeles
Adelman, Andrew A. *city manager*
Antonovich, Michael Dennis *county official*
Fielding, Jonathan Evan *county health department administrator, pediatrician*
Fong, Matthew Kipling *state official*
Howe, Con Edward *city manager*
Jeff, Gloria Jean *city official*
Molina, Gloria *municipal official*
Nodal, Adolfo V. *city manager*
Smith, Ann Delorise *municipal official*
Toman, Mary Ann *federal official*
Villaraigosa, Antonio Ramon *Mayor, Los Angeles*

March Air Force Base
Stewart, Richard A. *former mayor*

Menlo Park
Lane, Laurence William, Jr. *retired ambassador, publisher*

Modesto
Ridenour, Jim *Mayor, Modesto, California*

Moreno Valley
Batey, William H., II, *Mayor, Moreno Valley, California*
White, Charles R. *former mayor*

Oakland
Dellums, Ronald Vernie *Mayor, Oakland, California, retired congressman*
Heminger, Steve *city official*

Oceanside
Lyon, Richard *retired mayor, military officer*
Wood, Jim *mayor, Oceanside, California*

Ontario
Leon, Paul S. *Mayor, Ontario, California*
Ovitt, Gary C. *mayor*

Oxnard
Holden, Thomas E. *Mayor, Oxnard, California*

Pasadena
Bogaard, William Joseph *mayor, lawyer, educator*

Pomona
Rothman, Elliott *Mayor, Pomona, California*

Rancho Cucamonga
Kurth, Donald James, Jr. *Mayor, Rancho Cucamonga, California, medical educator*

Redlands
Hanson, Gerald Warner *retired county official*

Richmond
Corbin, Rosemary MacGowan *former mayor*

Riverside
Loveridge, Ronald Oliver *Mayor, Riverside, California*

Sacramento
Bowen, Debra Lynn *Secretary of State, California, former state legislator*
Brown, Jerry, Jr., (Edmund Gerald Brown Jr.) *state attorney general, former mayor, governor*
Bustamante, Cruz M. *former lieutenant governor*
Chick, Laura Newman *state official, former city official*
Friery, Thomas P. *city treasurer*
Garamendi, John R. *Lieutenant Governor of California, former state legislator*
Hunter, Patricia Rae (Tricia Hunter) *state official*
Johnson, Kevin Maurice *Mayor, Sacramento, retired professional basketball player*
Lockyer, Bill (William Lockyer) *state treasurer*
Nichols, Mary D. *state official, former federal agency administrator*
Schwarzenegger, Arnold Alois *Governor of California*

San Bernardino
Morris, Patrick J. *Mayor, San Bernardino, California*

San Diego
Golding, Susan G. *former mayor*
Jacob, Dianne *county official*
Sanders, Jerry *Mayor, San Diego, former social services executive*

San Francisco
Achtenberg, Roberta *former federal official*
Frank, Anthony Melchior *federal official, former financial executive*
Hewitt, Conrad W. *former commissioner, accountant*
Islambouly, Hagar Abdel-Hamid *consul general*
Newsom, Gavin Christopher *mayor, San Francisco*
Ward, Doris M. *county official*

San Jose
Dando, Pat *city official*
McHugh, Peter *mayor*
Reed, Charles Rufus (Chuck Reed) *Mayor, San Jose, California, lawyer*

Santa Ana
Pulido, Miguel Angel *Mayor, Santa Ana, California*

Santa Monica
Aaron, David L. *diplomat, author*

Santa Rosa
Gorin, Susan *Mayor, Santa Rosa, California*

Solana Beach
Gildred, Theodore E. *former diplomat, real estate developer*

Stanford
Wilson, Pete *former Governor of California*

Stockton
Chavez, Edward *Mayor, Stockton, California, protective services official*
Giottonini, James B. *city official*
Johnston, Ann *Mayor, Stockton, California*
Meissner, Helen Gong *municipal official*
Pinkerton, Steven James *city official*

Valencia
Ferry, Frank *mayor, Santa Clarita, California, principal*

Walnut Creek
Walston, Roderick Eugene *federal official*

West Covina
Manners, Nancy *retired mayor*

Yuba City
Kemmerly, Jack Dale *retired state official*

COLORADO

Aurora
Nicholas, Thomas Peter *municipal official*
Sheffield, Nancy *city agency administrator*
Tauer, Ed *Mayor, Aurora, Colorado*

Colorado Springs
Rivera, Lionel *Mayor, Colorado Springs, Colorado*

Denver
Brown, Keith Lapham *retired ambassador*

Buescher, Bernard A. (Bernie Buescher) *state official, air transportation executive*
Cohen-Vader, Cheryl Denise *municipal official*
Frontera, Michael P. *municipal official*
Gallagher, Dennis Joseph *municipal official, state senator, educator*
Hickenlooper, John W. *Mayor, Denver*
Kennedy, Cary *state treasurer*
O'Brien, Barbara *Lieutenant Governor of Colorado*
Ritter, Bill (August William Ritter Jr.) *Governor of Colorado, former prosecutor*
Rowe, Tina L. *government official*
Skaggs, David Evans *state official, former congressman*
Suthers, John William *state attorney general*

Englewood
Kourlis, Thomas A. *state commissioner*

DISTRICT OF COLUMBIA

Washington
Walther, Steven T. *commissioner, lawyer*

HAWAII

Camp H M Smith
Twining, Charles Haile *ambassador*

Hilo
Kenoi, William P. *Mayor, Hilo, Hawaii*

Honolulu
Aiona, James R., Jr. *Lieutenant Governor of Hawaii*
Bennett, Mark J. *state attorney general*
Bronster, Margery S. *retired state attorney general, lawyer*
Hannemann, Mufi *Mayor, Honolulu*
Kawamura, Georgina K. *state treasurer, finance company executive*
Lingle, Linda *Governor of Hawaii*
Marks, Robert Arthur *lawyer, attorney general*

Mililani
Cayetano, Benjamin Jerome *former governor, former state senator and representative*

IDAHO

Boise
Benham, James H. *state official*
Bieter, David H. *Mayor, Boise, Idaho*
Crane, Ron G. *state treasurer*
Kustra, Robert W. (Bob Kustra) *former state official, academic administrator*
Little, Brad *Lieutenant Governor of Idaho, former state legislator*
Otter, Butch (C. L. Otter, Clement Leroy Otter) *Governor of Idaho, former United States Representative from Idaho*
Terteling-Payne, Carolyn Ann *city official*
Wasden, Lawrence *state attorney general*
Williams, J. D. *state controller*
Ysursa, Ben T. *Secretary of State, Idaho*

Soda Springs
Clark, Trent L. *government public affairs manager*

MICHIGAN

Ann Arbor
Ford, Betty Ann (Elizabeth Ann Ford) *former First Lady of the United States, health facility executive*

MONTANA

Billings
Larsen, Richard Lee *city manager, consultant, retired mayor, arbitrator*

Butte
Martz, Judy Helen *former governor*

Clancy
Ekanger, Laurie *retired state official, consultant*

Helena
Bohlinger, John C. *Lieutenant Governor of Montana, former state legislator*
Bullock, Steve *state attorney general*
Jergeson, Greg *Public Service Commissioner, Montana*
McCulloch, Linda Harman *state official, former school system administrator*
Mood, Doug *Commissioner, Montana Public Serv Comn*
O'Keefe, Mark David *state official*
Schweitzer, Brian *Governor of Montana*
Toole, Kenneth R., Jr. *Public Svc Commissioner, Montana*

Missoula
Brown, Bob (Robert Joseph Brown) *former state official*

NEVADA

Carson City
Gibbons, Jim (James Arthur Gibbons) *Governor of Nevada, former United States Representative from Nevada*
Krolicki, Brian Keith *Lieutenant Governor of Nevada, former state official, state legislator*
Marshall, Kate *state treasurer*
Masto, Catherine Marie Cortez *state attorney general, former county official*
Miller, Ross James *secretary of state*

Henderson
Gibson, James B. *mayor, Henderson, Nevada*
McKinney, Sally Vitkus *state official*

Las Vegas
Goodman, Oscar Baylin *Mayor, Las Vegas, lawyer*
List, Robert Frank *former Governor of Nevada*

North Las Vegas
Montandon, Michael *Mayor, North Las Vegas, Nevada*

Reno
Cafferata, Patricia Dillon *state official*
Cashell, Robert A. (Bob Cashell) *Mayor, Reno, Nevada, former lieutenant governor, business executive*

NEW MEXICO

Albuquerque
Cargo, David Francis *former Governor of New Mexico*
Carruthers, Garrey Edward *former governor of New Mexico, academic administrator*
Chavez, Martin Joseph *Mayor, Albuquerque, lawyer*
Darnell, Ray D. *city official*
Kotchian, Sarah Bruff *municipal official*
Madrid, Patricia A. *former state attorney general*
Sedillo, Orlando Delano *city official*

Clovis
Bradley, Walter D. *lieutenant governor, real estate broker*

Los Alamos
Gonzales, Stephanie *state official*

Santa Fe
Coss, David *mayor*
Dasenbrock, Reed Way *state official, former academic administrator, literature educator*
Denish, Diane D. *Lieutenant Governor of New Mexico*
Herrera, Mary E. *Secretary of State, New Mexico*
King, Gary K. *state attorney general*
Lewis, James Beliven *state treasurer*
Montoya, Michael A. *state official, accountant*
Richardson, Bill (William Blaine Richardson III) *Governor of New Mexico, former United States Secretary of Energy*

OREGON

Eugene
Bascom, Ruth F. *retired mayor*
Torrey, James D. *mayor, communications executive, consultant*

Portland
Adams, Sam *Mayor, Portland, Oregon*
Church-Gaultier, Lorene Kemmerer *retired government official*
Katz, Vera *former mayor, college administrator, state legislator*
Lake, Joseph Edward *ambassador*
Myers, Hardy *former state attorney general*

Salem
Brown, Kate *state official, former state legislator*
Kroger, John Richard *state attorney general, former prosecutor, law educator*
Kulongoski, Ted (Theodore Ralph Kulongoski) *Governor of Oregon, former state supreme court justice*
Taylor, Janet R. *Mayor, Salem, Oregon*

UTAH

Ogden
Evans, Keith Edward *government official, researcher*

Salt Lake City
Allen, Ronald Carl *commissioner, artist, consultant, former state senator, computer company executive*
Anderson, Ross Carl *Mayor, Salt Lake City, Utah, lawyer, human rights advocate*
Becker, Ralph Elihu, Jr. *Mayor, Salt Lake City, Utah*
Herbert, Gary Richard *Lieutenant Governor of Utah*
Huntsman, Jon Meade, Jr. *Governor of Utah, former federal agency administrator*
Shurtleff, Mark L. *state attorney general*

Stephens, Martin R. *state official*
White, Constance Burnham *state official*

WASHINGTON

Olympia
Gregoire, Christine O'Grady *Governor of Washington, former state attorney general*
McKenna, Rob *state attorney general, former councilman*
Owen, Bradley Scott *Lieutenant Governor of Washington*
Reed, Sam *Secretary of State, Washington*
Sutherland, Douglass B. *former mayor, tent and awning company executive*

Renton
Lowry, Michael E. *former governor, former congressman*

Seattle
Covington, Germaine Ward *municipal agency administrator*
Diers, James Alan *municipal official*
Gardner, Booth *former governor*
Johnson, Darryl Norman *former ambassador*
Nickels, Greg *Mayor, Seattle*
Plough, Alonzo L. *city health department administrator*
Rosellini, Albert D. *former governor*

Spokane
Greenwood, Collette P. *municipal official, finance officer*
Pfister, Terri *city official*
Verner, Mary *Mayor, Spokane, Washington*

Sumas
Hemry, Larry Harold *former federal agency official, writer, inventor*

Tacoma
Baarsma, Bill *Mayor, Tacoma*
Luttropp, Peter C. *city official*

Vancouver
Pollard, Royce *Mayor, Vancouver, Washington*

WYOMING

Cheyenne
Freudenthal, Dave (David D. Freudenthal) *Governor of Wyoming*
Geringer, James E. *former governor*
Maxfield, Max R. *Secretary of State, Wyoming*
Rodekohr, Diane E. *state official*
Woodhouse, Gay Vanderpoel *former state attorney general, lawyer*

Evanston
Harris, Mark W. *former mayor, lawyer*

Laramie
Dickman, Francois Moussiegt *former foreign service officer, educator*

TERRITORIES OF THE UNITED STATES

AMERICAN SAMOA

Pago Pago
Ripley, Afa, Jr., (Fepulea'i A. Ripley Jr.) *attorney general*
Sunia, Aitofele Toese F. *Lieutenant Governor of American Samoa*
Tulafono, Togiola T.A. *Governor of American Samoa*

GUAM

Hagatna
Camacho, Felix Perez *Governor of Guam*
Cruz, Michael W. *Lieutenant Governor of Guam, surgeon*
Limtiaco, Alicia Garrido *state attorney general, former prosecutor*

NORTHERN MARIANA ISLANDS

Saipan
Baka, Gregory *acting attorney general*
Fitial, Benigno Repeki *Governor of Northern Mariana Islands*
Villagomez, Timothy P. *Lieutenant Governor of the Northern Mariana Islands*

CANADA

BRITISH COLUMBIA

Vancouver
Austin, Jacob (Jack Austin) *retired Canadian government official*

SASKATCHEWAN

Saskatoon
Blakeney, Allan Emrys *Canadian governme official, lawyer, educator*

ADDRESS UNPUBLISHED

Alter, Edward T. *former state treasurer*
Ash, Roy Lawrence *former federal official*
Babauta, Juan Nekai *former governor*
Baca, Jim *mayor*
Barnhart, Arthur L. *state official*
Bayless, Betsey *state official*
Bettenhausen, Matthew Robert *state official lawyer*
Boardman, Connie *former mayor, biologist, educator*
Botelho, Bruce Manuel *mayor, retired state attorney general*
Bradbury, Bill (William Chapman Bradbury *former state official*
Broadwater, Bruce A. *mayor*
Brown, Pamela S. *former attorney general*
Brown, Willie Lewis, Jr. *former mayor, sta legislator, lawyer*
Cenarrusa, Pete T. *retired state official*
Chanos, George J. *former state attorney ge*
Clayton, Raymond Edward *municipal offici*
Colberg, Talis James *former state attorney general*
Coop, Frederick Robert *retired city manage*
Cooper, Roberta *former mayor*
Dennis, Gigi (Ginette E. Dennis) *former st official*
Dunford, David Joseph *foreign service offi ambassador*
Edwards, Randall *former state treasurer*
Eliot, Theodore Lyman, Jr. *former ambass consultant*
Fenstersheib, Martin *city health departmen administrator*
Foxley, Cecelia Harrison *commissioner*
Gardom, Garde Basil *former lieutenant gov of British Columbia*
Gonzales, Ron *mayor, former county super*
Graham, Janet C. *former state attorney ger*
Guinn, Kenny C. (Kenneth Carroll Guinn) *former governor*
Harris, Jeremy *former mayor*
Hawkins, James Victor *former state officia*
Hett, Joan Margaret *ecological consultant*
Hill, Harry David *city official, human reso professional*
Hodgkins, Francis Irving (Butch Hodgkins *retired county official*
Holmes, Genta Hawkins *former diplomat*
Huddle, Franklin Pierce, Jr. *diplomat*
Hull, Jane Dee *former governor, state legis*
Hunt, Lorraine T. *former lieutenant govern*
Johnson, Brad *former state official*
Johnson, Gary Earl *former governor*
Jones, Bill *former state official, rancher*
Jones, Jan Laverty *former mayor*
Keegan, John Charles *former mayor, retire military officer, former state legislator*
Knowles, Tony (Anthony Carroll Knowles *former governor*
Leman, Loren Dwight *former lieutenant governor, civil engineer*
McKeachnie, Gayle F. *former lieutenant governor*
McMurdo, C(harles) Gregory *state official, lawyer*
McPherson, Bruce A. *former state official, former state legislator*
Meyer, Joseph B. *state treasurer*
Miller, George *former mayor*
Morris, Sharon Hutson *city manager*
Murphy, Michael Joseph *former state trea*
Norton, Jane Ellen Bergman (Jane Bergma *former lieutenant governor*
O'Neill, Beverly Lewis *former mayor, coll president*
Pearce, Drue *federal official, former state legislator*
Perkins, Jan *municipal official*
Powers, John T., Jr. *former mayor*
Price, John *former ambassador*
Price, Robert Otis *former mayor*
Reagan, Nancy Davis (Anne Francis Robb *former First Lady of the United States, volunteer*
Renkes, Gregg D. *former state attorney g*
Ricks, Mark G. *former lieutenant governo senator*
Rimsza, Skip *former mayor*
Riordan, Richard J. *former state official, f mayor*
Rudin, Anne *retired mayor, nursing educa*
Schoettler, Gail Sinton *former ambassado*
Shelley, Kevin Francis *former state officia*
Smith, Sarah Jane (Sally Smith) *mayor*
Swihart, James W., Jr. *diplomat*
Symington, J. Fife III *former governor, pc consultant*
Tambs, Lewis Arthur *diplomat, historian, educator*
Tauer, Paul E. *mayor, educator*
Valles, Judith *president, former mayor, ret academic administrator*
Vigil-Giron, Rebecca *former state official*
Walker, Dan *former mayor*
Zelenok, David Stephen *city official*

OVERNMENT: LEGISLATIVE ADMINISTRATION

UNITED STATES

ASKA

chorage
gich, Mark P. *United States Senator from Alaska, former mayor*
nde, Con *state legislator*
wdery, John J. *state legislator*
ogan, Mike *state legislator*
gmon, Bryce *state legislator*
s, Johnny *state legislator*
nze, Cheryll Boren *state representative*
ffman, Lyman F. *state legislator*
lmes, Lindsey S. *state legislator*
Guire, Lesil *state legislator*
yer, Kevin *state legislator*
rgulewski, Arliss *state legislator*

gle River
son, Fred *state legislator*
llips, Randy *state legislator, marketing professional*

irbanks
, Hugh *state representative*
tenberg, David *state legislator*
omas, Joseph James, Jr. *state legislator*
itaker, Jim *state representative*

neau
sterman, Alan *state legislator*
enault, Charles (Mike Chenault) *state legislator*
sna, Sharon *state legislator*
ghill, John B. *state legislator*
wford, Harry *state legislator*
hlstrom, Nancy *state legislator*
vis, Bettye Jean *state legislator*
on, Kim *state legislator*
nch, Hollis *state legislator*
to, Carl *state legislator*
ris, John *state legislator*
vker, Mike *state legislator*
nsley, William Lynn (Willie Hensley) *state senator, corporate executive*
m, James A. *state representative*
Paskvan *state legislator*
ansen, Kyle *state legislator*
le, Reggie *state legislator*
ler, Wes *state legislator*
ly, Timothy Donahue *former state legislator*
ttula, Beth *state legislator*
okesh, Albert M. *state legislator*
n, Bob *state legislator*
ckie, Jerry *state legislator, small business owner*
ett, Charisse E. *state legislator*
on, Donald *state legislator*
on, Kurt *state legislator*
uels, Ralph *state legislator*
ton, Paul *state legislator*
vens, Gary *state legislator*
tze, Bill *state legislator*
k, Chris S. *state legislator*
goner, Thomas H. *state legislator*
lechowski, Bill *state legislator*
ken, Gary R. *state legislator*
son, Peggy *state legislator*

nai
f, Kelly J. *state representative, contractor*

chikan
iams, William K. *state representative*

me
er, Richard *state legislator*

rth Pole
es, Jeannette Adeline *state legislator, accountant, small business owner*
rriault, Gene *state legislator*

silla
en, Lyda *state legislator*
ek, Beverly *state representative*

angell
or, Robin L. *state legislator, lawyer*

IZONA

gstaff
aw, John *state legislator, chemistry professor*

sa
ers, Russell W. *state legislator, sculptor, painter*

enix
ser, Edward *state legislator*
ud, Paula *state legislator*
ns, Kirk *state legislator*
rre, Amanda *state legislator*
n, Carolyn S. *state legislator*
n, Sylvia Tenney *state legislator*
Alvarez, Manuel V. *state legislator*
Antenori, Frank R. *state legislator*
Ash, Cecil P. *state legislator*
Baier, Maria *Councilwoman*
Barnes, Ray *state legislator*
Barto, Nancy K. *state legislator*
Bedford, Olivia Cajero *state legislator*
Bee, Timothy S. *state legislator*
Biggs, Andy *state legislator*
Blanchard, Jay S. *state senator*
Bradley, David T. *state legislator*
Brown, Jack A. *state legislator, rancher, real estate broker*
Burges, Judy M. *state legislator*
Burns, Robert *state legislator*
Burton Cahill, Meg *state legislator*
Campbell, Chad *state legislator*
Campbell, Cloves C., Jr. *state legislator*
Chabin, Tom *state legislator*
Cheuvront, Kenneth David *state legislator*
Court, Steve *state legislator*
Crandall, Rich *state legislator*
Crump, Sam *state legislator*
Daniels, Lori S. *state legislator, insurance agent*
Deschene, Christopher C. *state legislator*
DiCiccio, Sal *Councilman*
Driggs, Adam *state legislator*
Farley, Steve *state legislator*
Fleming, Patricia V. *state legislator*
Freestone, Thomas Lawrence *state legislator*
Garcia, Jorge Luis *state legislator*
Garcia, Martha *state legislator*
Goodale, Doris *state legislator*
Gorman, Pamela *state legislator*
Gould, Ronald M. *state legislator*
Gowan, David *state legislator*
Grace, Sue *state legislator*
Gray, Charles Dale (Chuck Gray) *state legislator*
Gray, Linda J. *state legislator*
Hale, Albert A. *state legislator*
Harper, Jack W. *state legislator*
Heinz, Matthew G. *state legislator*
Hendrix, Laurin *state legislator*
Huppenthal, John *state legislator*
Johnson, Michael *councilman*
Jones, Russell L. *state legislator*
Kavanagh, John *state legislator*
Konopnicki, Bill *state legislator, small business owner*
Kyl, Jon Llewellyn *United States Senator from Arizona*
Landrum-Taylor, Leah N. *state legislator*
Leff, Barbara *state legislator*
Lesko, Debbie *state legislator*
Lopes, Phil *state legislator*
Lopez, Linda *state legislator*
Lujan, David M. *state legislator*
Mattox, Claude *councilman*
McComish, John *state legislator*
McCune-Davis, Debbie *state legislator*
McGuire, Barbara G. *state legislator*
Melvin, Albert A. *state legislator*
Meyer, Eric *state legislator*
Meza, Robert *state legislator*
Miranda, Ben *state legislator*
Miranda, Richard *state legislator*
Montenegro, Steve B. *state legislator*
Murphy, Richard (Rick) A. *state legislator*
Neely, Peggy *councilwoman*
Nelson, John B. *state legislator*
Nichols, Warde V. *state legislator*
Nowakowski, Michael *Councilman*
Pancrazi, Lynne *state legislator*
Paton, Jonathan L. *state legislator*
Patterson, Daniel *state legislator*
Pearce, Russell *state legislator*
Pierce, Steve *state legislator*
Pratt, Frank *state legislator*
Quelland, Doug *state legislator*
Reagan, Michele *state legislator*
Rios, Rebecca Angela *state legislator*
Salmon, Matt *Former United States Representative, Arizona, communications executive*
Schapira, David *state legislator*
Seel, Carl E. *state legislator*
Siebert, Dave *City Councilman, Phoenix, Arizona*
Simplot, Tom *Councilman*
Sinema, Kyrsten *state legislator*
Solomon, Ruth *state legislator, educational association administrator*
Tibshraeny, Jay *state legislator*
Tobin, Andrew Michael *state legislator*
Tovar, Anna *state legislator*
Verschoor, Thayer *state legislator*
Waring, Jim *state legislator*
Waters, Rae *state legislator*
Weiers, James P. *state legislator*
Weiers, Jerry P. *state legislator*
Williams, A. Cody *councilman*
Williams, Thelda *Councilwoman*
Williams, Vic *state legislator*
Wold, Kimberly G. *legislative staff member*
Yarbrough, Steven B. *state legislator*
Young Wright, Nancy *state legislator*

Tucson
Bartlett, David Carson *state legislator*
Bee, Keith A. *state legislator*

Window Rock
Henderson, James, Jr. *state legislator, political organization worker, consultant*
Jackson, Jack C. *state legislator, rancher*

CALIFORNIA

Alamo
Baker, William P. (Bill Baker) *former congressman*

Anaheim
Solorio, Jose *state legislator*

Arroyo Grande
Lagomarsino, Robert John *former congressman*

Brea
Duvall, Michael D. *state legislator*

Chula Vista
Peace, Steve *state legislator*

Concord
DeSaulnier, Mark *state legislator*

Costa Mesa
Tran, Van *state legislator*

El Cajon
Anderson, Joel *state legislator*

Fresno
Arambula, Juan *state legislator*

Glendale
Krekorian, Paul *state legislator*
Moorhead, Carlos J. *former congressman*
Weaver, Dave *Councilman*

Hanford
Gilmore, Danny D. *state legislator*

Huntington Beach
Coerper, Gil *Councilman, Huntington Beach, California*
Silva, Jim *state legislator*

Imperial Beach
Shaffer, Raymond C. *state legislator*

Inglewood
Price, Curren D. *state legislator*

Laguna Hills
Walters, Mimi *state legislator*

Larkspur
Bosco, Douglas H. *former Congressman, lawyer*

Long Beach
Lowenthal, Bonnie *state legislator*

Los Altos
Ruskin, Ira *state legislator*

Los Angeles
Bass, Karen *state legislator*
Cardenas, Tony *councilman*
Davis, Mike *state legislator*
de Leon, Kevin *state legislator*
Feuer, Michael *state legislator*
Greuel, Wendy *councilwoman*
Hahn, Janice *councilwoman*
Huizar, Jose *councilman*
LaBonge, Tom *councilman*
Parks, Bernard *councilman*
Pavley, Fran J. *state legislator*
Perry, Jan *Councilwoman*
Reyes, Ed P. *councilman*
Rosendahl, Bill *councilman*
Smith, Greig Louis *councilman*
Weiss, Jack *councilman*
Wesson, Herb J. *councilman*
Zine, Dennis P. *councilman*

Martinez
Canciamilla, Joseph *state legislator*
Torlakson, Tom *state legislator*

Menlo Park
Zschau, Ed *former congressman*

Monterey
Browder, John Glen *former congressman, educator*

Mountain View
Fong, Paul *state legislator*

Norwalk
Mendoza, Tony *state legislator*

Pacoima
Alarcón, Richard *councilman*

Palm Desert
Benoit, John J. *state legislator*
Kelley, David G. *state senator*

Pomona
Torres, Norma *state legislator*

Rancho Cucamonga
Emmerson, Bill *state legislator*

Redondo Beach
Oropeza, Jenny *state legislator*

Redwood City
Sher, Byron D. *state legislator, law educator*

Rialto
Carter, Wilmer Amina *state legislator*

Riverside
Nestande, Brian *state legislator*

Roseville
Gaines, Ted *state legislator*
Leslie, Tim (Robert Leslie) *state legislator*

Sacramento
Aanestad, Sam *state legislator*
Ashburn, Roy *state legislator*
Berryhill, Bill *state legislator*
Blakeslee, Sam *state legislator*
Block, Marty *state legislator*
Brulte, James L. *state legislator*
Buchanan, Joan *state legislator*
Chavez, Edward L. *councilman, mayor*
Chesbro, Wesley *state legislator*
Chu, Judy May *assemblywoman*
Cogdill, David *state legislator*
Conway, Connie *state legislator*
Corbett, Ellen M. *state legislator*
Figueroa, Liz *former state senator*
Fletcher, Nathan *state legislator*
Fuentes, Felipe *state legislator*
Furutani, Warren T. *state legislator*
Goldberg, Jackie *councilwoman*
Hagman, Curt *state legislator*
Hall, Isadore III *state legislator*
Hancock, Loni *state legislator*
Harkey, Diane L. *state legislator*
Hill, Jerry *state legislator*
Huber, Alyson *state legislator*
Hughes, Teresa P. *state legislator*
Johnston, Patrick *state senator*
Jones, Dave *state legislator*
Knight, Steve *state legislator*
Kuehl, Sheila James *state board member*
Laird, John *state legislator*
Lewis, John R. *state legislator*
Logue, Dan R. *state legislator*
Ma, Fiona *state legislator*
Machado, Michael *state legislator*
Maldonado, Abel *state legislator*
Miller, Jeff *state legislator*
Morrow, Bill *state legislator*
Mountjoy, Richard *state legislator*
Nakanishi, Alan *state legislator*
Nielsen, James Wiley *state legislator*
Oller, Thomas R. *state senator*
Ortiz, Deborah V. *state legislator*
Perez, John A *state legislator*
Perez, Manuel V. *state legislator*
Rainey, Richard K. *state legislator*
Romero, Gloria *state legislator*
Samuelian, Steven Neil *state legislator*
Skinner, Nancy *state legislator*
Steinberg, Darrell S. *state legislator*
Torrico, Alberto *state legislator*
Wiggins, Patricia A. *state legislator*
Wright, Roderick D. *state legislator*
Yamada, Mariko *state legislator*
Yee, Leland Y. *state legislator*

Salinas
Cabellero, Anna M. *state legislator*

San Diego
Atkins, Toni *former councilwoman*
DeMaio, Carl *councilman*
Emerald, Marti *councilwomen, reporter*
Faulconer, Kevin *councilman*
Frye, Donna *councilwoman*
Gloria, Todd *councilman*
Hueso, Ben *councilman*
Kehoe, Christine T. *state legislator*
Lightner, Sherri *councilwoman, mechanical engineer*
Young, Tony *councilman*

San Francisco
Alioto-Pier, Michela *city supervisor*
Ammiano, Tom *state legislator*
Avalos, John *city supervisor*
Campos, David *city supervisor, lawyer*
Chiu, David *city supervisor, lawyer*
Chu, Carmen *city supervisor*
Daly, Chris *city supervisor*
Dufty, Bevan *city supervisor*
Elsbernd, Sean R. *city supervisor*
Mar, Eric Lee *city supervisor, college professor*
Maxwell, Sophenia (Sophie) *city supervisor*
Mirkarimi, Ross *city supervisor*

San Jose
Alquist, Elaine Kontominas *state legislator*
Beall, Jim T., Jr. *state legislator*
Campos, Nora *Councilwoman*
Chirco, Judy *Councilwoman*
Chu, Kansen *councilman*
Constant, Pete *councilman*
Herrera, Rose A. *councilwoman*
Kalra, Ash *councilman*
Liccardo, Sam T. *councilman*
Nguyen, Madison *councilwoman*
Oliverio, Pierluigi *councilman*
Pyle, Nancy *Councilwoman*

Santa Ana
Correa, Lou *state legislator*
Seymour, John *former senator*

Santa Barbara
Jackson, Hannah Beth *former state legislator*

Santa Cruz
Monning, William W. *state legislator*

Santa Maria
Seastrand, Andrea H. *former congresswoman, state agency administrator*

Saratoga
Konnyu, Ernest Leslie *former congressman*

Stockton
Singleton, Marvin Ayers *state legislator, otolaryngologist*

Vacaville
Wolk, Lois *state legislator*

Van Nuys
Hertzberg, Robert M. *former state legislator*

West Covina
Torres, Esteban Edward *former congressman, trade association administrator*

Westlake Village
Strickland, Audra *state legislator*

Woodland Hills
Brownley, Julia *state legislator*

Yucaipa
Cook, Paul J. *state legislator*

COLORADO

Arvada
Windels, Sue *state legislator*

Boulder
McNulty, Frank *state legislator*

Colorado Springs
Lamborn, Douglas L. *United States Representative from Colorado*
May, Ronny (Ron) Joe *state legislator*

Denver
Acree, Cindy *state legislator*
Anderson, Norma V. *state legislator*
Apuan, Dennis *state legislator*
Bacon, Robert L. *state legislator*
Baumgardner, Randy *state legislator*
Benefield, Debbie *state legislator*
Borodkin, Alice *state legislator*
Boyd, Betty Ann *state legislator*
Brophy, Greg *state legislator*
Butcher, Dorothy B. *state legislator*
Cadman, Bill Lee *state legislator*
Carroll, Morgan *state legislator*
Carroll, Terrance D. *state legislator, lawyer*
Casso, Edward E. *state legislator*
Cerbo, Michael P. *state legislator*
Clapp, Lauri *state representative*
Coleman, Fran Natividad *state representative*
Court, Lois *state legislator*
Curry, Kathleen E. *state legislator*
Dicks, Patricia K. *legislative staff member*
Faatz, Jeanne Ryan *councilwoman*
Feeley, Michael F. *state legislator*
Ferrandino, Mark *state legislator*
Fischer, Randy *state legislator*
Fitz-Gerald, Joan *state legislator*
Foster, Joyce *state legislator*
Frangas, K. Jerry *state legislator*
Gagliardi, Sara *state legislator*
Garcia, Michael *state legislator*
Gardner, Bob B. *state legislator*
Gardner, Cory *state legislator*
Gerou, Cheri *state legislator*
Gibbs, Dan *state legislator*
Gordon, Kenneth Marshall *state legislator*
Green, Gwyn M. *state legislator*
Groff, Peter *state legislator*
Grossman, Dan *state senator*
Hagedorn, Robert (Bob), Jr. *state legislator*
Harvey, Ted *state legislator*
Heath, S. Rollie, Jr. *state legislator*
Hernandez, Robert Michael *state legislator, software engineer*
Hillman, Mark D. *state legislator*
Hodge, Mary Ann *state legislator*
Hudak, Evie *state legislator*
Hullinghorst, Dickey Lee *state legislator*
Isgar, Jim *state legislator*
Jahn, Cheri *state legislator*
Judd, Joel Stanton *state legislator, lawyer*
Kefalas, John Michael *state legislator*
Keller, Maryanne (Moe Keller) *state legislator*
Kerr, Andrew (Andy Kerr) *state legislator*
Kerr, James (Jim Kerr) *state legislator*
Kester, Kenneth *state legislator*
King, Keith C. *state senator*
King, Steve *state legislator*
Kopp, Mike *state legislator*
Labuda, Jeanne *state legislator*
Lambert, Kent *state legislator*
Levy, Claire *state legislator*
Linkhart, Doug(las) D. *state legislator*
Liston, Larry G. *state legislator*
Looper, Marsha *state legislator*
Lundberg, Kevin *state legislator*
Massey, Thomas W. *state legislator*
May, Mike *state legislator*
McCann, Elizabeth Harrison *state legislator, lawyer*
McCluskey, Bob R. *state representative*
McElhany, Andrew (Andy) *state legislator*
McFadyen, Liane (Buffie McFadyen) *state legislator*
McGihon, Anne Lee *state legislator, lawyer*
McKinley, Wes *state legislator*
Meiklejohn, Alvin J., Jr. *state legislator, lawyer, accountant*
Merrifield, Michael *state legislator*
Middleton, Karen *state legislator*
Miklosi, Joe *state legislator*
Mitchell, Shawn *state legislator*
Morse, John P. *state legislator*
Murray, Carole R. *state legislator*
Newell, Linda *state legislator*
Nichol, Alice J. *state legislator*
Nikkel, B.J. *state legislator*
Owen, David Turner *state legislator, owner, operator*
Pace, Sal *state legislator*
Penry, Joshua P. *state legislator*
Pommer, John (Jack Pommer) *state legislator*
Priola, Kevin *state legislator*
Renfroe, Scott *state legislator*
Rice, Joe *state legislator*
Riesberg, James L. *state legislator*
Roberts, Ellen *state legislator*
Romanoff, Andrew *state legislator*
Romer, Chris *state legislator*
Rose, Ray *state legislator*
Sandoval, Paula E. *state legislator*
Scanlan, Christine *state legislator*
Schafer, Sue *state legislator*
Scheffel, Mark *state legislator*
Schultheis, David C. *state legislator*
Schwartz, Gail S. *state legislator*
Shaffer, Brandon *state legislator*
Solano, Judith Anne *state legislator*
Sonnenberg, Jerry *state legislator*
Spence, Nancy *state legislator*
Stafford, Debbie *state legislator*
Stephens, Amy *state legislator*
Summers, Ken *state legislator*
Takis, Stephanie *state legislator*
Tanner, Gloria Travis *state legislator*
Tapia, Abel J. *state legislator*
Tate, Penfield *state senator*
Teck, Ronald Jay *state legislator*
Thiebaut, William *state legislator, lawyer*
Tipton, Scott *state legislator*
Tochtrop, Lois Anne *state legislator*
Todd, Nancy Janann *state legislator*
Tupa, Ron *state legislator*
Vaad, Glenn *state legislator*
Veiga, Jennifer L. *state legislator*
Vigil, Edward *state legislator*
Waller, Mark *state legislator*
Wattenberg, Dave *state legislator, rancher*
Weddig, Frank O. *state legislator*
Weissmann, Paul Martin *state legislator*
White, Al *state legislator*
Wiens, Tom J. *state legislator*
Williams, Suzanne S. *state legislator*
Witwer, John *state legislator*

Englewood
Blickensderfer, Charles Thomas (Tom) *state legislator, lawyer*

Fort Collins
Schaffer, Robert W. (Bob Schaffer) *former congressman*

Grand Junction
Bishop, Tilman Malcolm *state legislator*
Bradford, Laura Kay *state legislator, small business owner*

Lakewood
Armstrong, William L. *former senator*

Loveland
Marostica, Don *state legislator*

Steamboat Springs
Taylor, Jack *state legislator*

Westminster
Udall, Mark *United States Senator from Colorado*

DISTRICT OF COLUMBIA

Washington
Abercrombie, Neil *United States Representative from Hawaii*
Akaka, Daniel Kahikina *United States Senator from Hawaii*
Baca, Joe *United States Representative from California*
Baird, Brian N. *United States Representative from Washington*
Barrasso, John Anthony *United States Senator from Wyoming, orthopedic surgeon*
Baucus, Max Sieben *United States Senator from Montana*
Becerra, Xavier *United States Representative from California, lawyer*
Bennet, Michael Farrand *United States Senator from Colorado*
Bennett, Robert F. *United States Senator from Utah*
Berkley, Shelley (Rochelle Levine Berkley) *United States Representative from Nevada, lawyer*
Berman, Howard Lawrence *United States Representative from California, lawyer*
Bilbray, Brian Patrick *United States Representative from California*
Bingaman, Jeff (Jesse Francis Bingaman Jr.) *United States Senator from New Mexico*
Bishop, Robert *United States Representative from Utah*
Bono Mack, Mary Whitaker *United States Representative from California*
Bordallo, Madeleine Zeien (Mrs. Ricardo Jerome Bordallo) *Delegate to United States House Representative from Guam*
Boxer, Barbara *United States Senator from California*
Calvert, Ken *United States Representative from California*
Cantwell, Maria E. *United States Senator from Washington*
Capps, Lois Ragnhild Grimsrud *United States Representative from California, former school nurse*
Cardoza, Dennis A. *United States Representative from California*
Chaffetz, Jason *United States Representative from Utah, former corporate communications executive*
Coffman, Mike (Michael H. Coffman) *United States Representative from Colorado, former state official*
Costa, Jim *United States Representative from California*
Crapo, Michael Dean *United States Senator from Idaho, former congressman, lawyer*
Davis, Susan A. *United States Representative from California*
DeFazio, Peter Anthony *United States Representative from Oregon*
De Gette, Diana Louise *United States Representative from Colorado, lawyer*
Dicks, Norman De Valois *United States Representative from Washington*
Dreier, David Timothy *United States Representative from California*
Ensign, John Eric *United States Senator from Nevada, former United States Representative from Nevada*
Enzi, Michael Bradley *United States Senator from Wyoming, accountant*
Eshoo, Anna Georges *United States Representative from California*
Farr, Sam *United States Representative from California*
Feinstein, Dianne *United States Senator from California*
Filner, Bob (Robert Filner) *United States Representative from California*
Flake, Jeff *United States Representative from Arizona*
Franks, Trent *United States Representative from Arizona*
Gallegly, Elton William *United States Representative from California*
Giffords, Gabrielle *United States Representative from Arizona, former state senator*
Grijalva, Raul *United States Representative from Arizona*
Hansen, James Vear *former congressman*
Harman, Jane *United States Representative from California*
Hastings, Doc (Richard Norman Hastings) *United States Representative from Washington*
Hatch, Orrin Grant *United States Senator from Utah*
Heinrich, Martin T. *United States Representative from New Mexico*
Herger, Walter William, Jr. *United States Representative from California*
Hersh, Sarah A. *legislative staff member*
Heyrend, Alyson L. *legislative staff member*
Honda, Michael M. (Mike Honda) *United States Representative from California*
Hunter, Duncan Duane *United States Representative from California, military officer*
Inouye, Daniel Ken *United States Senator from Hawaii*
Inslee, Jay Robert *United States Representative from Washington*
Issa, Darrell E. *United States Representative from California*
Kirkpatrick, Ann L. *United States Representative from Arizona, lawyer*
Larsen, Richard Ray (Rick Larsen) *United States Representative from Washington*
Lee, Barbara Jean *United States Representative from California*
Lewis, Charles Jeremy (Jerry Lewis) *United States Representative from California*
Lofgren, Zoe *United States Representative from California*
Lujan, Ben Ray, Jr. *United States Representative from New Mexico, former state official*
Lummis, Cynthia Marie *United States Representative from Wyoming, former state official, lawyer*
Lungren, Daniel Edward *United States Representative from California, former state attorney general*
Markey, Betsy (Elizabeth Helen Markey) *United States Representative from Colorado*
Marter, Ben *legislative staff member*
Matheson, James David (Jim) *United States Representative from Utah*
Matsui, Doris Okada *United States Representative from California*
McCain, John (John Sidney McCain III) *United States Senator from Arizona*
McCarthy, Kevin *United States Representative from California, former state legislator*
McClintock, Tom (Thomas Miller McClintock II) *United States Representative from California, former state senator*
McDermott, James A. *United States Representative from Washington, psychiatrist*
McKeon, Howard Phillip (Buck McKeon) *United States Representative from Californ*
McMorris-Rodgers, Cathy *United States Representative from Washington*
McNerney, Jerry (Gerald M. McNerney) *Uni States Representative from California, engineer*
Miller, Gary G. *United States Representative from California*
Miller, George III *United States Representati from California*
Minnick, Walter Clifford *United States Representative from Idaho, former buildin materials company executive*
Mitchell, Harry E. *United States Representat from Arizona, former state legislator*
Murkowski, Lisa Ann *United States Senator from Alaska*
Murray, Patty (Patricia Lynn Murray) *United States Senator from Washington*
Napolitano, Grace Flores *United States Representative from California*
Nunes, Devin *United States Representative f California*
Pastor, Edward *United States Representative from Arizona*
Pelosi, Nancy Patricia *United States Representative from California*
Perlmutter, Ed (Edwin George Perlmutter) *United States Representative from Colora former state legislator, lawyer*
Polis, Jared Schutz *United States Representa from Colorado, entrepreneur, philanthropi*
Radanovich, George P. *United States Representative from California*
Rehberg, Dennis R. *United States Represent from Montana*
Reichert, David G. (Dave Reichert) *United States Representative from Washington*
Reid, Harry Mason *United States Senator fr Nevada*
Richardson, Laura A. *United States Representative from California*
Risch, Jim (James Elroy Risch) *United State Senator from Idaho, former Governor of Idaho*
Rohrabacher, Dana T. *United States Representative from California*
Roybal-Allard, Lucille *United States Representative from California*
Royce, Ed (Edward Randall Royce) *United States Representative from California*
Saavedra, Maura *legislative staff member*
Salazar, John Tony *United States Representa from Colorado*
Sánchez, Linda T. *United States Representat from California*
Sanchez, Loretta *United States Representati from California*
Schiff, Adam Bennett *United States Representative from California, lawyer*
Schrader, Kurt *United States Representative Oregon, former state senator*
Shadegg, John Barden *United States Representative from Arizona*
Sherman, Bradley James *United States Representative from California*
Simpson, Michael K. *United States Representative from Idaho*
Smith, Adam *United States Representative f Washington*
Speier, Jackie (Karen Lorraine Jacqueline Speier) *United States Representative from California, former state senator*
Stark, Fortney Hillman (Pete Stark) *United States Representative from California*
Tauscher, Ellen O'Kane *United States Representative from California*
Teague, Harry *United States Representative New Mexico*
Tester, Jon(athan) *United States Senator fro Montana, former state legislator, farmer*
Thompson, Mike (C. Michael Thompson) *U States Representative from California*
Titus, Alice Costandina (Dina Titus) *United States Representative from Nevada, forme state legislator*
Udall, Thomas S. (Tom) *United States Sena from New Mexico*
Walden, Greg *United States Representative Oregon*
Waters, Maxine *United States Representati from California*
Waxman, Henry Arnold *United States Representative from California*
Woolsey, Lynn C. *United States Representa from California*
Wyden, Ron(ald) (Lee) *United States Senat from Oregon*
Young, Donald E. *United States Representa from Alaska*

HAWAII

Hilo
Chang, Jerry Leslie *state legislator*

Honolulu
Aquino, Henry J. C. *state legislator*
Cachola, Romy Munoz *state legislator*
Chumbley, Avery B. *state legislator*
Chun, Jonathan J. *state legislator*
Coffman, Denny *state legislator*
Fasi, Frank Francis *state legislator*
Gabbard, Mike (Gerald Mike Gabbard) *sta legislator*
Galuteria, Brickwood *state legislator*

Starr, Charles *state legislator, farmer, contractor*
Tomei, Carolyn *state legislator*
Verger, Joanne *state legislator*
Walker, Vicki L. *state legislator*
Weidner, Jim *state legislator*
Wingard, Matt *state legislator*
Yih, Mae Dunn *state legislator*

Troutdale
Minnis, John Martin *state legislator, protective services official*

UTAH

Brigham City
Knudson, Peter C. *state legislator*

Clearfield
Minson, Dixie L. *legislative staff member*

Corinne
Ferry, Miles Yeoman *state legislator*

Highland
Peterson, Craig Anton *state legislator*

Hooper
Hull, Joseph L. *state legislator*

Kaysville
Steele, David H. *state legislator*

Logan
Hillyard, Lyle William *state legislator*

Midvale
Mansell, L. Alma *state legislator*

Ogden
Allen, D. Edgar *state legislator*
Gladwell, David L. *state legislator*
Montgomery, Robert F. *state legislator, retired surgeon, rancher*

Orem
Hellewell, Parley G. *state legislator*

Payson
Muhlestein, Robert M. *state senator*

Provo
Valentine, John Lester *state legislator, lawyer*

Riverton
Evans, R. Mont *state legislator*

Salt Lake City
Black, Wilford Rex, Jr. *state legislator*
Carnahan, Orville Darrell *state legislator, academic administrator*
Chavez-Houck, Rebecca *state legislator*
Davis, Gene *state legislator*
Duckworth, Susan *state legislator*
Evans, Beverly Ann *state legislator, school system administrator*
Garn, Edwin Jacob (Jake Garn) *former senator*
Greenwood, Richard A. *state legislator, protective services official*
Hinkins, David P. *state legislator*
Jenkins, Scott K. *state legislator*
Liljenquist, Daniel R. *state legislator*
Mayne, Karen *state legislator*
Moore, Annette B. *aide*
Okerlund, Ralph *state legislator*
Poulton, L. Steven *state legislator*
Powell, Kraig *state legislator*
Seegmiller, F. Jay *state legislator*
Shepherd, Karen *former congresswoman*
Suazo, Pete *state legislator*
Tempest, Richard Blackett *state senator, general contractor*
Waddoups, Michael Grant *state legislator*
Walker, Carlene Martin *state legislator*
Webb, R. Curt *state legislator*
Wilcox, Ryan D. *state legislator*

Syracuse
Spencer, Terry R. *state legislator, lawyer*

Veyo
Jones, Lorin V. *state senator*

West Valley City
Peterson, Millie M. *state senator*

WASHINGTON

Coupeville
Smith, Norma *state legislator*

Federal Way
von Reichbauer, Peter Graves *state senator*

Lake Stevens
Quigley, Kevin Walsh *state legislator, lawyer*

Olympia
Alexander, Gary C. *state legislator*
Angel, Jan *state legislator*
Bauer, Albert *state legislator*
Becker, Randi *state legislator*
Benton, Donald Mark *state legislator, political organization chairman*
Carlson, Don M. *state senator*
Deccio, Alexander A. *state legislator*
Eddy, Deborah H. *state legislator*
Eide, Tracey J. *state legislator*
Fairley, Darlene *state legislator*
Finn, Fred *state legislator*
Franklin, Rosa *state legislator*
Fraser, Karen *state legislator*
Goodman, Roger Elliot *state legislator, lawyer, state agency director*
Grant-Herriot, Laura *state legislator*
Hale, Patricia S. *state legislator*
Hargrove, James (Jim) E. *state legislator*
Haugen, Mary Margaret *state legislator*
Herrera, Jaime *state legislator*
Hewitt, Mike *state legislator*
Hope, Mike *state legislator*
Horn, James A. *state legislator*
Jacobsen, Ken *state legislator*
Johnson, Norm *state legislator*
Kastama, Jim *state legislator*
Kline, Adam *state legislator*
Klippert, Brad *state legislator*
Kohl-Welles, Jeanne E. *state legislator*
Liias, Marko *state legislator*
Long, Jeanine Hundley *state legislator*
Maxwell, Marcie *state legislator*
McAuliffe, Rosemary *state legislator*
McCaslin, Bob *state legislator*
McDonald, Daniel Robert *state legislator*
Morton, Harry B (Bob) *state legislator*
Nelson, Sharon *state legislator*
Parker, Kevin *state legislator*
Parlette, Linda Evans *state legislator*
Prentice, Margarita *state legislator*
Probst, Tim *state legislator*
Quall, Dave *state legislator*
Ranker, Kevin *state legislator*
Rasmussen, Marilyn *state legislator*
Regala, Debbie *state legislator*
Roach, Pam *state legislator*
Rockefeller, Phil *state legislator*
Ross, Charles R. *state legislator*
Santos, Sharon Tomiko *state legislator*
Schmick, Joe *state legislator*
Schoesler, Mark Gerald *state legislator*
Sheahan, Larry L. *state legislator, lawyer*
Sheldon, Betti L. *state legislator*
Shin, Paull Hobom *state legislator, investment company executive*
Stevens, Val *state legislator*
Swecker, Dan *state legislator*
Taylor, David *state legislator*
Van de Wege, Kevin *state legislator*
Winsley, Shirley J. *state legislator, insurance agent*
Wood, Alex *state legislator*
Zarelli, Joseph *state legislator*

Port Angeles
Kessler, Lynn Elizabeth *state legislator*

Renton
Thomas, Brian Chester *retired state legislator, engineer*

Seattle
Chopp, Frank V. *state legislator*
Evans, Daniel Jackson *former senator, management consultant*
Pedersen, Jamie D. *state legislator, lawyer*

Spanaway
Campbell, Thomas J. *state legislator, chiropractor*

Spokane
Brown, Lisa J. *state legislator*

Sunnyside
Honeyford, Jim *state legislator*

University Place
Kelley, Troy Xavier *state legislator, lawyer*

WYOMING

Casper
Fagan, Tucker *legislative staff member, former state agency administrator*
Hawks, Bill *state legislator, oil industry executive*

Cheyenne
Anderson, James *state legislator*
Cohee, Roy G. *state legislator*
Decaria, Ken *state legislator*
Devin, Irene K. *state legislator, nurse*
Erb, Richard A. *state legislator, real estate company executive*
Esquibel, Floyd Amarante *state legislator*
Gilmore, Mike *state legislator*
Harris, Mark O. *state legislator*
Hines, John J. *state legislator*
Hunnicutt, Rick *state legislator*
Johnson, Wayne Harold *state legislator*
Kunz, April Brimmer *state legislator, lawyer*
McKim, Robert *state legislator*
Meuli, Larry *state representative*
Moniz, Glenn *state legislator*
Patton, John *state legislator*
Pedersen, Bryan *state legislator*
Reese, Paul Wayne *state representative*
Schiffer, John C. *state legislator*
Simpson, Colin M. *state legislator*

Gillette
Gilbertz, Larry E. *former state legislator, entrepreneur*
Lubnau, Thomas Edwin, II, *state legislator, lawyer*

Jackson
Jorgensen, Peter M. *state legislator*

Lagrange
Meier, Curt *state legislator*

Laramie
Hansen, Matilda *former state legislator*
Maxfield, Peter Charles *state legislator, lawyer, educator*

Riverton
Bebout, Eli Daniel *state legislator*

Sheridan
Landon, Jack D., Jr. *state legislator*

TERRITORIES OF THE UNITED STATES

NORTHERN MARIANA ISLANDS

Saipan
Benavente, Diego Tenorio *territorial legislator, former lieutenant governor*

ADDRESS UNPUBLISHED

Allard, Wayne (Alan Wayne Allard) *retired US Senator from Colorado, veterinarian*
Arzberger, Gus *state legislator, retired farmer, rancher*
Barr, Scott *state legislator*
Beauprez, Bob (Robert L. Beauprez) *former congressman*
Beyer, Casey K. *legislative staff member*
Bilbray, James Hubert *Former United States Representative from Nevada, lawyer, consultant*
Blackham, Leonard Moyle *state legislator*
Bundgaard, Scott *state legislator*
Burns, Brenda *state senator*
Cannon, Christopher Black *former United States Representative from Utah, lawyer*
Case, Edward Espenett *former United States Representative from Hawaii, lawyer*
Cirillo, Edward J. *state legislator, retired financial planner*
Close, Betsy L. *state representative*
Cook, Merrill A. *former congressman, explosives industry executive*
Craig, Larry Edwin *former United States Senator from Idaho, congressman*
Cramer, Chuckie *legislative staff member*
Crippen, Bruce D. *former state legislator, real estate manager*
Cubin, Barbara Lynn *former United States Representative from Wyoming*
Cummiskey, Chris *state legislator*
Domenici, (Pete) Vichi *retired United States Senator from New Mexico*
Dornan, Robert Kenneth *former congressman*
Dymally, Mervyn Malcolm *retired state legislator*
Epps, Mary Ellen *state legislator*
Evans, John *state legislator, lawyer, educator*
Fox, Galen W. *state representative*
Gentile, Liz *state legislator*
Greene, Enid *former United States Representative from Utah*
Hart, Gary *former United States Senator from Colorado, lawyer*
Hartley, Mary *state legislator*
Hatfield, Mark Odom *former senator*
Hayden, Cedric L. *former state legislator, dentist*
Hayworth, J.D. (John David Jr.) *former congressman*
Hefley, Joel Maurice *former congressman*
Hill, Richard Allan (Rick Hill) *former congressman*
Hooley, Darlene Kay Olson *former United States Representative from Oregon*
Hunter, Duncan Lee *retired United States Representative from California*
Ipsen, Grant Ruel *state legislator, insurance and investments professional*
Kolbe, Jim (James Thomas Kolbe) *former United States Representative, Arizona*
Larson, Mark R. *former state legislator*
Lincoln, Georgianna *state legislator*
Longville, John *state legislator*
Lopez, Joe Eddie *state legislator*
Maloof, Phillip J. *state legislator*
Marshall, Rosemary *former state representative*
Martinez, Matthew Gilbert *former congressman*
Matsunaka, Stanley T. *former state legislator*
McCormack, Mike *former congressman*
Morgan, Carl, Jr. *state representative*
Oakland, Suzanne N.J. Chun *state legislator*
O'Connell, Mary Ann *state legislator, small business owner*
Ose, Douglas *former congressman*
Packard, Ronald C. *former congressman*
Pascoe, Patricia Hill *former state legislator*
Pettis-Roberson, Shirley McCumber *Former US Repr, Calif*
Pombo, Richard William *former congressman, rancher, farmer*
Powers, Ray Lloyd *former state senator, dairy farmer, rancher*
Renzi, Rick (Richard George Renzi) *forme United States Representative from Arizor*
Rossi, Dino J. *former state legislator*
Sali, Bill (William Thomas Sali) *former U States Representative from Idaho*
Sheldon, Timothy M. *state legislator*
Shields, Frank W. *state legislator*
Smith, Tom *state legislator, military officer*
Sorensen, Sheila *state legislator*
Stallings, Valerie Aileen *retired councilwon consultant*
Stengel, Joseph P. *former state legislator*
Stevens, Ben *former state legislator*
Stevens, Ted (Theodore Fulton Stevens) *fo United States Senator from Alaska*
Stonington, Emily S. *state legislator*
Tancredo, Tom (Thomas Gerard Tancredo) *retired United States Representative from Colorado*
Tebedo, MaryAnne *state legislator*
Thompson, Jill Lynette Long *former congressman*
Tipton, Harry Basil, Jr. *state legislator, phy*
Torgerson, John *state senator*
Underwood, Robert Anacletus *former congressman, university official*
Vasconcellos, John *state legislator*
Vucanovich, Barbara Farrell *former United States Representative, Nevada*
Wallach, Patricia *councilman, retired mayo*
Wear, Byron *councilman*
Williams, Tambor *state representative*
Wilson, Heather Ann *former United States Representative from New Mexico*
Wojahn, R. Lorraine *retired state senator*
Wright, Cathie *state legislator*
Young, Jacqueline Eurn Hai *former state legislator, consultant*
Youngbauer, Steven R. *state legislator, law*
Zanetti, Teresa A. *state legislator*

HEALTHCARE: DENTISTR

UNITED STATES

ARIZONA

Tucson
Hawke, Robert Francis *dentist*
Nadler, George L. *orthodontist*

CALIFORNIA

Beverly Hills
Sands, Kevin B. *cosmetic dentist*

Loma Linda
Feller, Ralph Paul *dentist, educator*

Los Angeles
Dorfman, William M. (Bill Dorfman) *denti*
Dummett, Clifton Orrin *dentist, educator*

Manteca
Tonn, Elverne Meryl *pediatric dentist, dent benefits consultant, forensic odontologist*

Monterey Park
Sekiguchi, Eugene *dentist*

Northridge
Logan, Lee Robert *orthodontist, departmen chairman*

Pasadena
Mc Carthy, Frank Martin *oral surgeon, edu*

San Francisco
Braham, Raymond L. *pediatric dentistry educator*
Greenspan, Deborah *dental educator*
Olsen, Steven Kent *dentist*
Wescott, William Burnham *oral maxillofac pathologist, educator*
Wirthlin, Milton Robert, Jr. *periodontist*

COLORADO

Boulder
Schaffer, Joel Lance *dentist*

Littleton
Patterson, Daniel William *retired dentist*

HAWAII

Honolulu
Nishimura, Pete Hideo *oral surgeon*

NEVADA

Las Vegas
Rawson, Raymond D. *dentist, state legislat*

EGON

nts Pass
erson, Gordon Sutherland *periodontist*

SHINGTON

levue
, Roy Christopher *periodontist, scientist, lucator*

rett
er, William Donald *orthodontist*

ttle
rkin, Samuel Franklin *dentist, educator, ychologist*
ing, Susan Weller *dental educator, atomist*
ender, Lars Gösta *dental educator*
or, Rhys *dentist*

OMING

per
n, Michael Ray *dentist*

CANADA

BERTA

monton
aly, Tarek H. *orthodontist, biomedical gineer*

ADDRESS UNPUBLISHED

feld, Ronald Elwood *retired dental lucator*
nan, David Jay *orthodontist*
man, Jerry Irwin *retired dental educator*
brun, Ernest *oral biology and riodontology educator*

HEALTHCARE: HEALTH SERVICES

UNITED STATES

ZONA

a
s, Don A. *healthcare company executive*

enix
s, James Cecil *hospital administrator*
er, Kenneth Lloyd, Jr. *health system ministrator, retired military officer*
r, Steven Lawrence *health facility ministrator*

tsdale
n, Frederick Lee *health facility ministrator*
rs, Marlene O. *retired hospital ministrator*

ona
rton, Marianne Rose *occupational therapist*

son
ss, Ernest Peter *healthcare facility ministrator, planner, professor public health*
oshire, Donald Gray *hospital executive*
kins, Emil *chiropractor*
ia, Eric Stafford *health facility ministrator*

IFORNIA

mbra
ineau, Michael R. *healthcare educator, earcher*

dia
rson, Holly Geis *health facility ministrator, educator, commentator*

eley
ll, Mina J. *lab administrator, biochemist*
n, Jay Martin *optometrist, research entist, educator*
rt, Neil Robin *social work educator, writer, sultant*
r, Harold D. *public health administrator, mmunications specialist, educator*
f, Joyce Cohen *public health service cer, educator*
David Malcolm *family planning specialist, cator*

ank
orn, Terry O. *health facility administrator*

Claremont
Martin, Jay Herbert *psychoanalyst, literature professor, political science professor*

Costa Mesa
Graff, Cynthia Stamper *health facility administrator*

Cypress
Scott, Gregory W. *health care company executive*

Davis
Fowler, William Mayo, Jr. *rehabilitation medicine physician*
Lewis, Jonathan *health care association administrator*
Schneeman, Barbara Olds *nutritionist, educator*
Stern, Judith Schneider *nutritionist, researcher, educator*
Turnlund, Judith Rae *nutritionist*

Irvine
Jones, Joie Pierce *acoustician, writer, educator*

La Jolla
Hazzard, Mary Elizabeth *nursing educator*

Laguna Beach
Arnold, John David *management counselor*

Los Angeles
Andersen, Ronald Max *health services researcher, educator*
Ash, Lawrence Robert *public health educator*
Boswell, James Douglas *medical research executive*
Cohn, Daniel Howard *laboratory director*
Cordova, Richard D. *hospital administrator*
de la Rocha, Castulo *health services executive*
Epstein, Marsha Ann *public health service officer, physician*
Haughton, James Gray *health facility administrator, consultant*
Horowitz, Ben *health facility administrator*
McCabe, Edward R. B. *hospital administrator, educator, physician*
Noce, Walter William, Jr. *hospital administrator*
Priselac, Thomas M. *health facility executive, educator*
Roberts, Robert Winston *social worker, educator, dean*
Rosenthal, J. Thomas *hospital administrator, medical educator*
Stoughton, W. Vickery *healthcare executive*
Territo, Mary C. *health facility administrator, hematologist, educator*
Thompson, Judith Kastrup *nursing researcher*
Utz, Sarah Winifred *nursing educator*
van Dam, Heiman *psychoanalyst*
Ver Steeg, Donna Lorraine Frank *nurse, sociologist, educator*

Malibu
Palacio, June Rose Payne *nutritional science educator*

Marysville
Myers, Elmer *psychiatric social worker*

Menlo Park
Holmquest, Donald Lee *health organization director, nuclear medicine physician, lawyer, retired aerospace engineer*

Mill Valley
Chater, Shirley *health educator*

Moraga
Allen, Richard Garrett *healthcare educator*

Moreno Valley
Hadfield, Tomi Senger *hospital administrator*

Morro Bay
LaLanne, Jack (François Henri LaLanne) *physical fitness specialist, entrepreneur*

Mount Shasta
Mariner, William Martin *chiropractor*

Mountain View
Dwork, Cynthia *researcher*

Newport Beach
Stephens, Michael Dean *hospital administrator*

North Hills
Burton, Paul Floyd *retired social worker*

Oakland
Bouska Lee, Carla Ann *nursing and healthcare educator*
Carpenter, Kenneth John *retired nutrition educator*
Crane, Robert Meredith *health facility administrator*
Hafey, Joseph Michael *health association executive*
Howatt, Sister Helen Clare *human services administrator, director, retired school librarian*
King, Janet Carlson *nutrition educator, researcher*
Miller, Barry *researcher, psychologist*
Sargent, Arlene Anne *nursing educator*

Orange
Brown, Lillian Eriksen *retired nursing administrator, consultant*

Williams, Benjamin R. *health facility administrator*

Oxnard
Herlinger, Daniel Robert *hospital administrator*
Lopez, Manuel M. *optometrist, former mayor*

Palo Alto
Skeff, Kelley Michael *health facility administrator*

Pasadena
Nackel, John George *health venture capital executive*

Roseville
Ammon, Donald R. *hospital administrator*

San Diego
Covert, Michael Henri *healthcare facility administrator*
Lewis, Shirley Jeane *retired therapist, educator*
Norling, Richard Arthur *healthcare executive*
Rosen, Peter *health facility administrator, emergency physician, educator*
Schmidt, Terry L. *healthcare executive*
Springer, Wayne Richard *healthcare system official, research biochemist*

San Francisco
Auerback, Sandra Jean *social worker*
Eckstrom, John *health facility administrator*
Green, Robert Leonard *hospital management company executive*
Harrington, Charlene Ann *sociology and health policy educator*
Laret, Mark R. *health facility executive*
Mahley, Robert W. *health facility administrator*
Sahatjian, Manik *retired nurse, retired psychologist*
Sheiner, Lewis B. *pharmacist, educator*
Speidel, John Joseph *public health professional, educator*
Stone, Norman Clement *psychologist, foundation administrator*
Young, Lowell Sung-yi *health facility administrator, medical educator*

San Jose
Lu, Nancy Chao *nutrition and food science educator*

San Marcos
Whitney, Stan *marriage and family therapist*

San Mateo
Hoops, Alan R. *health care company executive*

San Rafael
Friesecke, Raymond Francis *health company executive, president*

Santa Ana
Folick, Jeffrey M. *healthcare systems company executive*
Schub, Craig S. *health science association administrator*

Santa Monica
Brook, Robert Henry *public health service officer, internist, educator*

Saratoga
Greenleaf, John Edward *human research consultant*

Sausalito
Sonkin, Daniel Jay *marriage and family therapist, writer*

Sherman Oaks
Krueger, Kenneth John *nutritionist, educator*

Sonoma
Markey, William Alan *health facility administrator, consultant*

Stanford
Henriksen, Thomas Hollinger *researcher*
Marsh, Martha H. *hospital administrator*
Mc Namara, Joseph Donald *researcher, retired protective services official*

Thousand Oaks
Emerson, Alton Calvin *retired physical therapist*

Victorville
McGulpin, Elizabeth Jane *nurse*

Westlake Village
Dimitriadis, Andre C. *health care executive*

Woodland Hills
Pettit, John W. *health facility administrator*
Yates, Gary L. *marriage and family therapist*

Woodside
Potter, Myrtle Stephens *healthcare consulting company executive, retired pharmaceutical executive*

COLORADO

Buena Vista
Herb, Edmund Michael *optometrist, educator*

Colorado Springs
Cameron, Paul Drummond *health facility administrator*

Denver
Jennett, Shirley Shimmick *health facility administrator*
Kohnen, Kerry *hospital administrator*
Taussig, Lynn Max *healthcare administrator, pulmonologist, pediatrician, educator*

Fort Collins
Savage, Eldon Paul *retired environmental health educator*
Tyler, Gail Madeleine *nurse*

Lakewood
Johnson, Ramey Kayes *community health nurse*

Meeker
Omer, Robert Wendell *hospital administrator*

HAWAII

Honolulu
Cadman, Edwin Clarence *health facility administrator, retired educator*
Fischer, Joel *social work educator*
Lum, Jean Loui Jin *nursing educator*

Kaneohe
Au, Whitlow W.L. *acoustician*

NEVADA

Las Vegas
Emerson, Shirley *retired professor counseling*
Francis, Timothy Duane *chiropractor*
Israel, Joan *social worker*
MacDonald, Erin E. *healthcare company executive*
Marlon, Anthony M. *healthcare company executive, cardiologist*
Wakefield, Marie A. *counselor, educational association administrator*

Reno
Graham, Denis David *marriage and family therapist, educational consultant*
Pinson, Larry Lee *pharmacist, state agency administrator*

NEW MEXICO

Albuquerque
Mateju, Joseph Frank *hospital administrator*
Spinella, Judy Lynn *health facility administrator*

Santa Fe
Melnick, Alice Jean (AJ Melnick) *counselor*

Truth Or Consequences
Rush, Domenica Marie *health facilities administrator*

OREGON

Corvallis
Oldfield, James Edmund *retired nutrition educator*

Eugene
Hamren, Nancy Van Brasch *office manager*

Lake Oswego
Willis, Thayer Cheatham *wealth counselor, author*

Pendleton
Smiley, Richard Wayne *researcher*

Portland
Giffin, Sandra Lee *nursing administrator*
Goldfarb, Timothy Moore *hospital administrator*
Greenlick, Merwyn Ronald *health services researcher*
Kaplan, Mark S. *healthcare educator*
King, John G. *health service administrator*
Pfeifer, Larry Alan *public health service coordinator*
Rooks, Judith Pence *nurse midwife, consultant*
Tetz, Karen Bonnie *nurse, educator*

Stayton
Zumwalt, Roger Carl *hospital administrator, healthcare consultant*

TEXAS

Austin
Schneider, Thomas Richard *hospital administrator*

Dallas
Focht, Michael Harrison *health care industry executive*

UTAH

Salt Lake City
Gamble, Shawna *marriage and family therapist, psychologist*

Melton, Arthur Richard *public health administrator*
Wirthlin, Richard Bitner *researcher*

WASHINGTON

Bellevue
Edwards, Kirk Lewis *medical services company executive*

Olympia
Inverso, Marlene Joy *optometrist*

Seattle
Barnard, Kathryn Elaine *nursing educator, researcher*
Dorpat, Theodore Lorenz *psychoanalyst*
Hansen, Thomas Nanastad *hospital administrator, pediatrician*
Hansten, Philip Douglas *pharmacist, educator*
Johnston, William Frederick *emergency services administrator*
Katz, Treuman P. *health facility administrator*
McDonald, Michael Lee *health facility administrator, retired military officer*
Monsen, Elaine Ranker *nutritionist, educator, editor*
Perkin, Gordon Wesley *international health executive*
Peterson, Jane White *nursing educator, anthropologist*
Sellick, Kathleen A. *hospital administrator*

Spokane
Robinson, Herbert Henry III *psychotherapist, educator*

Tacoma
Larson Bonck, Maureen Inez *rehabilitation consultant*

Walla Walla
Cooper, Sarah Jean *nursing educator*

Wenatchee
Reilly, Joan *nursing educator*

WYOMING

Bondurant
Ellwood, Paul Murdock, Jr. *health policy analyst, consultant*

Cheyenne
Dale, Marcia Lyn *nursing educator*

Laramie
Schatz, Mona Claire Struhsaker *social worker, educator, consultant, researcher*

Wilson
Hall, Zach Winter *former scientist and research administrator*

CANADA

ALBERTA

Edmonton
Fields, Anthony Lindsay Austin *health facility administrator, oncologist, educator*

ADDRESS UNPUBLISHED

Aehlert, Barbara June *health facility administrator*
Anderson, Dorothy Fisher *retired social worker, psychotherapist*
Binnie, Nancy Catherine *retired nurse, educator*
Blumberg, Mark Stuart *health service researcher, scientist, director*
Brokaw, Meredith A. *women's health care company director*
Brown, Barbara June *hospital and nursing administrator*
Callison, Nancy Fowler *nurse administrator*
Casey, Nancy J. *women's healthcare company executive*
Christiansen, David K. *health facility administrator*
Clayton, Paul Douglas *health care administrator*
Crawford, Debra P. *women's healthcare company executive*
Crawford, Randi *health facility administrator*
Culton, Paul Melvin *retired counselor, educational administrator, professor, interpreter*
De Antoni, Edward Paul *retired lab administrator*
DeLapp, Tina Davis *retired nursing educator*
Dubé, Susan E. *women's healthcare company executive*
Essex, Lauren S. *women's health care company executive*
Ewell, Charles Muse *health care industry executive, consultant, publisher, educator*
Fehr, Lola Mae *health facility administrator*
Gengler, Sue Wong *health educator, consultant, speaker, trainer*
Godager, Jane Ann *retired social worker*
Grobstein, Ruth H. *health facility administrator*
Hays, Patrick Gregory *healthcare executive*
Healy, Sonya Ainslie *retired health facility administrator*
Higgins, Ruth Ann *social worker, family therapist*
Hinton, James H. *healthcare services administrator*
Hofmann, Paul Bernard *healthcare consultant*
Howard, Mark J. *hospital administrator*
Johnson, Wendy S. *women's healthcare company executive*
Kerr, Frederick Hohmann *retired health facility and academic administrator*
King, Sheldon Selig *health facility administrator, educator*
Latta, George Haworth III *neonatal/perinatal nurse practitioner*
Lofton, Kevin Eugene *medical facility administrator*
MacPherson, Shirley *clinical therapist*
Marquardt, Terry Tyrone *optometrist*
Martin, Julie *women's healthcare company executive*
Michel, Mary Ann Kedzuf *retired nursing educator*
Mikel, Thomas Kelly, Jr. *laboratory administrator*
Nisbet, Toma A. *nursing administrator*
Norbeck, Jane S. *retired nursing educator*
Phanstiel, Howard G. *managed healthcare company executive*
Poe, Laura *nursing educator, administrator*
Preszler, Sharon Marie *psychiatric home health nurse*
Rindone, Joseph Patrick *clinical pharmacist, educator*
Robinson, Gail Patricia *retired mental health counselor*
Scala, James *health facility administrator, consultant, writer*
Schnabel, Gary A. *health facility administrator, director*
Simonson, Susan Kay *social worker*
Smith, Leslie Roper *hospital and health facility administrator*
Steele, Dale F. *women's healthcare company executive*
Stickles, Bonnie Jean *retired nurse*
Suber, Robin Hall *former medical and surgical nurse*
Uris, Patricia Firme *health science association administrator*
Varga, Jeanne-Marie *women's healthcare company executive*
Vohs, James Arthur *health plan administrator*
Walker, Henry Gilbert *health care executive, consultant*
Wickham, Dianne *nursing administrator*
Wiebe, Leonard Irving *pharmacist, educator*
Woo, Sharon Y. *healthcare organization executive*

HEALTHCARE: MEDICINE

UNITED STATES

ALASKA

Anchorage
Christensen, Ronald E. *physician*
Harvey, Elinor B. *child psychiatrist*

Valdez
Todd, Kathleen Gail *physician*

ARIZONA

Gilbert
Labovitz, Earl A. *allergist*

Glendale
Teague, Robert Cole *physician*

Green Valley
Bachman, David Christian *orthopedic surgeon*
Ford, Neville F. *clinical pharmacologist*
Moser, Robert Harlan *internist, educator, writer*

Mesa
Bunchman, Herbert Harry, II, *plastic surgeon*
Hagen, Nicholas Stewart *medical educator, consultant*

Phoenix
Ammon, John Richard *anesthesiologist*
Borel, James David *anesthesiologist*
Chambliss, Linda R. *obstetrician, consultant*
Charlton, John Kipp *pediatrician*
Goldberg, Morris *internist*
Heppell, Jacques Philippe *surgeon, educator*
Lovett, William Lee *surgeon*
Mulligan, David Cobourn *medical educator*
Reed, Wallace Allison *anesthesiologist*
Stern, Stanley *psychiatrist*
Swafford, Leslie Eugene *physician assistant, consultant*
Von Hoff, Daniel Douglas *oncologist*
Zerella, Joseph T. *retired pediatric surgeon*

Scottsdale
Harrison, Nedra Joyce *surgeon*
Hecht, Frederick *pediatrician, medical geneticist, writer, editor*
Kail, Konrad *physician*
Khandheria, Bijoy K. *cardiologist*
Kinney, Carolyn *physician*
Lewis, John Christopher *allergist*
Orford, Robert Raymond *physician, consultant*
Reznick, Richard Howard *pediatrician*
Roarke, Michael Charles *medical educator, nuclear medicine physician*
Sanderson, David R. *physician*
Shors, Clayton Marion *retired cardiologist*
Tajik, A(bdul) J(amil) *cardiologist, educator*
Underwood, Paul Lester *cardiologist*

Sedona
Metzner, Richard Joel *psychiatrist, psychopharmacologist, educator*

Tempe
Anand, Suresh Chandra *physician*
Schneller, Eugene Stewart *health administration and policy educator*

Tucson
Ablin, Richard Joel *immunologist, educator*
Addis, Ilana Beth *obstetrician*
Adler, Kenneth Gordon *physician*
Alberts, David Samuel *physician, pharmacologist, educator*
Alpert, Joseph Stephen *cardiologist, educator*
Anderson, Dayna *medical researcher*
Ben-Asher, M. David *physician*
Corrigan, James John, Jr. *pediatrician, dean, educator*
Dalen, James Eugene *cardiologist, educator*
Ewy, Gordon Allen *cardiologist, researcher, educator*
Goldfarb, Robert Paul *neurological surgeon*
Graham, Anna Regina *pathologist, educator*
Harris, David Thomas *immunology educator*
Hattery, Robert Ralph *radiologist, educator*
Hess, Richard Neal *plastic surgeon*
Levenson, Alan Ira *psychiatrist, physician, educator*
Marcus, Frank Isadore *cardiologist, educator*
Martin, Loren Winston *allergist*
Meislin, Harvey Warren *emergency healthcare physician, professional society administrator*
Morgan, Wayne Joseph *medical educator, medical association administrator*
Rogers, Lee Frank *radiologist*
Russell, Findlay Ewing *physician*
Sibley, William Austin *neurologist, educator*
Weil, Andrew Thomas *physician, educator*
Weinstein, Ronald S. *pathologist, educator*
Witte, Marlys Hearst *internist, educator*
Woolfenden, James Manning *nuclear medicine physician, educator*

Yuma
Anderson, John Albert *physician*

CALIFORNIA

Agoura Hills
deCiutiis, Alfred Charles Maria *oncologist, television producer*

Alameda
Chen, Arthur *physician, hospital administrator*
Whorton, M. Donald *physician, epidemiologist*

Arroyo Grande
Grisez, James Louis *physician, plastic surgeon*

Atherton
Weston, Jane Sara *plastic surgeon, educator*

Auburn
Henrikson, Donald Merle *forensic pathologist*

Bakersfield
Prunes, Fernando *plastic surgeon, educator*

Bellflower
Henry, Harold M. *obstetrician, gynecologist, maternal-fetal medicine*
Maples, Karen Elizabeth *obstetrician, gynecologist*

Belmont
Ellis, Eldon Eugene *retired surgeon*

Belvedere Tiburon
Fishman, Robert Allen *retired neurologist, educator, department chair*
Hoffman, Julien Ivor Ellis *pediatrician, cardiologist, educator*

Berkeley
Budinger, Thomas Francis *radiologist, educator*
Grossman, Elmer Roy *pediatrician*
Tempelis, Constantine Harry *immunologist, educator*
Troxel, David B. *pathologist*

Beverly Hills
Amron, David M. *dermatologist*
Fisher, (Donald) Garth *plastic surgeon*
Karpman, Harold Lew *cardiologist, educator, writer*
Marshak, Harry *plastic surgeon*
Moelleken, Brent Roderick Wilfred *plastic surgeon*
Ryan, Frank Harry *plastic surgeon*
Semel, George Herbert *plastic surgeon*
Yuan, Robin Tsu-Wang *plastic surgeon*

Borrego Springs
Strong, John Oliver *plastic surgeon, educat*

Burbank
Renner, Andrew Ihor *surgeon*

Burlingame
Rosenfield, Lorne King *plastic surgeon*

Canyon Lake
Sparks, Dale Boyd *allergist, health facility administrator*

Carlsbad
Bennett, C. Frank *molecular pharmacologis*
Chopra, Deepak *preventive medicine physic writer*
Kizer, Kenneth Wayne *physician, executive, educator*

Cathedral City
Gaede, James Ernest *physician, educator*

Cerritos
Lee, Jhemon Hom *physician*

Chula Vista
Cohen, Elaine Helena *pediatrician, cardiol educator*

Corona Del Mar
Tobis, Jerome Sanford *physician*

Culver City
Rose, Margarete Erika *pathologist*

Dana Point
Fisher, Delbert Arthur *pediatric endocrinol educator, retired health facility administr*

Davis
Cardiff, Robert Darrell *pathology educator*
Gardner, Murray Briggs *pathologist, educa*
Halsted, Charles Hopkinson *internist*
Jensen, Hanne Margrete *pathologist, educa*
Overstreet, James Wilkins *obstetrics and gynecology educator, administrator*
Plopper, Charles George *anatomist, cell bi*
Rhode, Edward Albert *veterinary medicine educator, veterinary cardiologist*
Richman, David Paul *neurologist, educator researcher*
Williams, Hibbard Earl *medical educator, physician*

Del Mar
Judd, Lewis Lund *psychiatrist, educator*

Downey
Perry, Jacquelin *orthopedist, surgeon*

Duarte
Figlin, Robert Alan *hematologist, oncologi*

El Dorado Hills
Sparks, Robert Dean *medical administrato gastroenterologist*

El Macero
Stowell, Robert Eugene *pathologist, retire educator*

Emeryville
Fields, Howard Lincoln *neurologist, physiologist, educator*

Encino
Lesavoy, Malcolm Alan *plastic surgeon*

Fairfield
Chapman, Ronald William *physician, coun official*

Fontana
Resch, Charlotte Susanna *plastic surgeon*

Fountain Valley
Kieu, Quynh Dinh *pediatrician, not-for-pr developer*

Fremont
Steinmetz, Seymour *pediatrician*

Fresno
Leigh, Hoyle *psychiatrist, educator, writer*
Thompson, Leonard Russell *pediatrician*

Fullerton
Aston, Edward Ernest, IV, *dermatologist*
Sugarman, Michael *physician, rheumatolo*

Grass Valley
Ely, Parry Haines *dermatologist, educator*

Greenbrae
Parnell, Francis William, Jr. *otolaryngolog*

Gualala
Ring, Alice Ruth Bishop *retired preventive medicine physician*

Hillsborough
Curd, John Gary *physician, scientist*

Inglewood
Dorr, Lawrence Douglas *orthopedic surge*

ne
denberg, Richard Myron *radiologist, ysician, educator*
rge, Kattunilathu Oommen *physician, ucator*
bell, Floyd Allan *internist, educator*
, Moon Hyun *endocrinologist, educator*
di, Ricardo *neurobiologist*
ioglu, Orhan *radiologist, educator*
ligan, Edward James *retired obstetrician, necologist, educator*
nstein, Gerald D. *dermatology educator*
g, Nathan Donald *medicine and idemiology researcher, educator*

ul
vood, Ivan Richmond *retired pediatric lmonologist*

tfield
nan, Donald Frederick *physician*

Crescenta
ardi, Vincent Michael *pediatrician, educator, trepreneur*

Jolla
nson, John William *hematologist*
ey, David Nelson *pathology educator, dean, ademic administrator*
tz, Roland C. *nephrologist, educator*
vn, Stuart I. *ophthalmologist, educator*
ell, Ruth Marie *medical educator, academic lministrator*
ssio, Donald John *internist, neurologist, ucator*
sdale, Joel Edward *psychiatry educator*
ngton, Thomas S. *pathologist, molecular d vascular biologist, educator*
and, Cedric Frank *epidemiologist, educator*
Gordon N. *medical educator*
mb, Beatrice Alexandra *physician, medical searcher*
z, Robert William *retired dermatologist*
burger, Robert N. *pediatrician, educator, nsultant*
nann, Alan Frederick *biomedical researcher, ucator*
ier, Anthony Adam *pediatrician, educator*
r, Adrian Michael *physician*
s, Kenneth Lyons *pediatrician, birth defects searcher*
Kay, Dianne Brenda *nephrologist*
doza, Stanley Atran *pediatric nephrologist, ucator*
ssa, A. R. *surgeon, educator*
mura, Robert Motoharu *pathologist*
an, William Leo *pediatrician, educator*
tone, Michael Beauregard Alan *munologist, educator*
ler, Harold E. *psychologist, educator*
den, Carole Ann *clinical pathologist, ucator*
l, John C. *physician, researcher*
nfeld, Michael Geoffrey *medical educator*
eider, Gerald L. *plastic surgeon*
oley, Robert T. *medical educator*
ren, Stephen Linner *oncologist*
er, Robert *plastic surgeon*
h, Richard Alan *neurologist, medical sociation administrator*
gelberg, Hans Leonhard *medical educator*
berg, Daniel *preventive medicine physician, ucator*
Eng Meng *immunologist, biomedical searcher*
, David *oncologist, researcher*
npson, Charlotte Ellis *pediatrician, ucator, writer*
er, Richard Hugh *orthopaedic surgeon*

Mirada
ger, Charles *dermatologist*

Quinta
n, Roy Macbeth *retired obstetrician, ucator*

una Beach
Ronald Jeffrey *dermatologist, pathologist*

una Hills
di, Stephen John *physician*
volar, Sheila Gayle *dermatologist*

coln
g, Vernon *retired surgeon, military officer*

rmore
rd, James Pickett *internist, educator*

na Linda
y, Leonard Lee *surgeon*
ens, Berel Lyn *physician, academic and alth facility administrator*
dstater, Murray Everett *physiatrist*
Brian Stanley *pathologist, educator*
, Philip J. *medical educator*
in, Charlotte Joan *cardiologist, educator*
esty, Robert Alan *plastic surgeon*
Gerald Arthur *nuclear radiologist*
rado, Josep G. *nuclear medicine physician, earcher*
ouk, Anees Jacob *surgeon*
rts, Walter Herbert Beatty *anatomist, ucator*
, James Munro *radiation oncologist*

Strother, Allen *biochemical pharmacologist, researcher*
Young, Lionel Wesley *radiologist*

Long Beach
Molina, Joseph Mario (Mario Molina) *medical administrator*

Los Angeles
Alkon, Ellen Skillen *physician*
Anderson, Gail V. *obstetrician, gynecologist*
Ansell, Benjamin Jesse *physician*
Apt, Leonard *pediatric ophthalmologist*
Apuzzo, Michael Lawrence John *neurological surgeon*
Aronowitz, Joel Alan *plastic and reconstructive surgeon*
Barrett, Cynthia Townsend *neonatologist*
Beart, Robert W., Jr. *colon and rectal surgeon, educator*
Becker, Donald Paul *surgeon, neurosurgeon*
Berman, David Albert *pharmacologist, educator*
Bernstein, Sol *cardiologist, educator*
Blahd, William Henry *nuclear medicine physician, director*
Bluestone, David Allan *pediatrician*
Bondareff, William *psychiatrist, educator*
Borenstein, Daniel Bernard *psychiatrist, educator*
Braunstein, Glenn David *physician, educator*
Caprioli, Joseph *ophthalmologist*
Casillas, Jacqueline Nieto *hematologist, oncologist, educator*
Chandor, Stebbins Bryant *pathologist*
Cherry, James Donald *pediatrician*
Chopra, Inder Jit *endocrinologist*
Cicciarelli, James Carl *immunology educator*
Clemente, Carmine Domenic *anatomist, educator*
Coates, Thomas Duane *pediatrician, hematologist, educator*
Coates, Thomas J. *medical association administrator*
Cooper, Edwin Lowell *anatomy educator*
Davidson, Ezra C., Jr. *obstetrician, gynecologist, academic administrator, educator*
Detels, Roger *epidemiologist, retired dean*
Diamond, Jason Brett *head, neck and facial plastic surgeon*
Edgerton, Bradford Wheatly *plastic surgeon*
Enstrom, James Eugene *epidemiologist*
Ettenger, Robert Bruce *physician, pediatric nephrologist*
Fahey, John Leslie *immunologist*
Feig, Stephen Arthur *pediatrician, hematologist, oncologist, educator*
Fleming, Arthur Wallace *physician, surgeon*
Fodor, Peter Bela *plastic surgeon, educator*
Fogelman, Alan Marcus *internist*
Fowler, Vincent R. *dermatologist*
Francis, Charles K. *medical educator*
Frasier, S. Douglas *medical educator*
Gale, Robert Peter *physician, scientist, researcher*
Geller, Kenneth Allen *otolaryngologist*
Geller, Stephen Arthur *pathologist, educator*
Gewertz, Bruce Labe *surgeon, educator*
Giannotta, Steven Louis *neurosurgery educator*
Gorney, Roderic *psychiatrist, educator*
Grody, Wayne William *physician, educator*
Guze, Phyllis Arlene *internist, educator, academic administrator*
Haywood, L. Julian *cardiologist, educator*
Herrmann, Christian, Jr. *medical educator*
Hirsch, Anthony Terry *physician*
Holland, Gary Norman *ophthalmologist, educator*
Hollander, Daniel *gastroenterologist, educator*
Horwitz, David A. *rheumatologist, educator*
House, John William *otolaryngologist*
Ignarro, Louis J. *pharmacology educator*
Jadvar, Hossein *nuclear radiologist, biomedical engineer*
Jalali, Behnaz *psychiatrist, educator*
Jelliffe, Roger Woodham *cardiologist, pharmacologist*
Johnson, Cage Saul *hematologist, educator*
Jones, Peter Anthony *medical research administrator*
Kahn, Fredrick Henry *retired internist*
Kamil, Elaine Scheiner *pediatric nephrologist, educator*
Kar, Saibal *cardiologist*
Karlan, Beth Young *obstrician-gynecologist*
Katz, Roger *pediatrician, allergist, immunologist, educator*
Kelly, Arthur Paul *physician*
Kim, Kwang-Jin *medical educator*
Kleeman, Charles Richard *nephrologist, educator, researcher*
Klitzner, Thomas S. *pediatric cardiologist*
Koch, Richard *retired pediatrician, educator*
Korsch, Barbara M. *pediatrician*
Lazareff, Jorge Antonio *neurosurgeon, researcher*
Lewis, Charles Edwin *epidemiologist, educator*
Liberman, Robert Paul *psychiatry educator, researcher, writer*
Lim, David Jong-Jai *otolaryngology educator, researcher*
Maloney, Robert Keller *ophthalmologist, medical educator*
Martinez, Miguel Acevedo *urologist, consultant, lecturer*
McFadden, P. Michael *physician, surgeon*
Miller, Lee Todd *pediatrician, educator*
Miller, Timothy Alden *plastic and reconstructive surgeon*
Mishell, Daniel R., Jr. *obstetrician, gynecologist, educator*
Mondino, Bartly J. *ophthalmologist*
Morgan, Elizabeth *plastic surgeon*
Moxley, John Howard III *internist*
Murphree, A. Linn *ophthalmologist*
Neufeld, Naomi Das *endocrinologist*
Newman, Anita Nadine *surgeon*
Nezami, Elahe *medical educator*
Nissenson, Allen Richard *physician, educator*
Noble, Ernest Pascal *pharmacologist, biochemist, educator, psychiatrist*
Oppenheim, William L. *pediatric orthopedist*
Parmelee, Arthur Hawley, Jr. *pediatric medical educator*
Paulson, Richard John *obstetrician, gynecologist, educator*
Perloff, Joseph Kayle *cardiologist, educator*
Pi, Edmond Hsin-Tung *psychiatry educator*
Pike, Malcolm Cecil *preventive medicine educator*
Rao, Narsing A. *ophthalmologist, pathologist, educator*
Rimoin, David Lawrence *medical geneticist*
Ritvo, Edward Ross *psychiatrist*
Rotter, Jerome Israel *medical geneticist*
Roven, Alfred Nathan *surgeon*
Rubin, Robert Terry *psychiatrist, researcher, educator*
Ryan, Stephen Joseph, Jr. *ophthalmologist, educator*
Salusky, Isidro B. *pediatric nephrologist, educator*
Scheibel, Arnold Bernard *psychiatrist, educator, research director*
Schelbert, Heinrich Ruediger *nuclear medicine physician*
Schneider, Edward Lewis *medicine educator, research administrator*
Shah, Prediman K. *cardiologist, educator*
Shemin, Richard Jay *cardiothoracic surgeon, educator*
Sherman, Randolph *plastic and reconstructive surgeon, educator*
Siegel, Michael Elliot *nuclear medicine physician, educator*
Spencer, Carole A. *medical association administrator, educator*
Stiehm, E. Richard *pediatrician, educator*
Straatsma, Bradley Ralph *ophthalmologist, educator*
Tabachnick, Norman Donald *psychiatrist, educator*
Tachdjian, Raffi *pediatrician*
Takahashi, Masato *pediatric cardiologist, educator*
Tolo, Vernon Thorpe *orthopedist, educator*
Trento, Alfredo A. *thoracic surgeon, educator*
Wasterlain, Claude Guy *neurologist*
Watson, Karol Elizabeth *internist, educator*
Weiner, Leslie Philip *neurology educator, researcher*
Weiss, Martin Harvey *neurosurgeon, educator*
Wells, Kenneth Brooks *medical educator, researcher*
Whybrow, Peter Charles *psychiatrist, educator, director, author*
Wilkinson, Alan Herbert *nephrologist, educator*
Williams, Roberta Gay *pediatric cardiologist, educator*
Wilson, Miriam Geisendorfer *retired physician, educator*
Withers, Hubert Rodney *radiotherapist, radiobiologist, educator*
Woodley, David Timothy *dermatology educator*
Yamauchi, Paul Steven *dermatologist, researcher*
Yazdani, Shahram *pediatrician*
Yu, John Sun *neurosurgeon, immunologist*

Lower Lake
Hodgkin, John E. *pulmonologist*

Menlo Park
Harris, Edward Day, Jr. *physician*
Hoffman, Thomas Edward *dermatologist*
Hubert, Helen Betty *epidemiologist*
Kovachy, Edward Miklos, Jr. *psychiatrist, consultant*

Milpitas
Chiu, Peter Yee-Chew *physician*

Monrovia
Comings, David Edward *medical geneticist*

Monterey
Black, Robert Lincoln *pediatrician, educator*
Lehr, Jeffrey Marvin *immunologist, allergist*

Mountain View
Abel, Elizabeth Ann *dermatologist*
Brilliant, Larry (Lawrence Brent Brilliant) *preventive medicine physician, entrepreneur*

Napa
Zimmermann, John Paul *plastic surgeon*

Newhall
Stein, Karl N. *plastic and reconstructive surgeon*

Newport Beach
Chiu, John Tang *physician*
Connolly, John Earle *surgeon, educator*
Daniel, Rollin Kimball *plastic surgeon*
Lambros, Val (Vasilios S. Lambros II) *plastic surgeon*
Paul, Malcolm David *plastic and reconstructive surgeon*

Shamoun, John Milam *plastic surgeon*
Solmer, Richard *surgeon*
Viehe, Richard B. *podiatrist*
Zubrin, Jay Ross *surgeon*

Oakland
Benton-Hardy, Lisa Renee *psychiatrist, educator*
Der, David F. *family practice physician, retired general surgeon*
Gruber, Ronald P. *plastic surgeon, researcher*

Oceanside
Curtin, Thomas Lee *ophthalmologist*

Orange
Berman, Michael Leonard *gynecologic oncologist*
Crumley, Roger Lee *surgeon, educator, otolaryngologist*
DiSaia, Philip John *obstetrician, gynecologist, radiology educator*
Fisher, Mark Jay *neurologist, neuroscientist, educator*
Lott, Ira Totz *pediatric neurologist*
Morgan, Beverly Carver *pediatrician, educator*
Mosier, Harry David, Jr. *physician, educator*
Rowen, Marshall *radiologist*
Vaziri, Nosratola Dabir *internist, nephrologist, educator*
Wong, Brian Jet-Fei *surgeon*
Yu, Jen *medical educator*

Pacific Palisades
Beck, John Christian *physician, educator*
Claes, Daniel John *physician*
Daniels, John R. *oncologist, educator*
Love, Susan Margaret *surgeon, educator, writer*
Rachelefsky, Gary Stuart *medical educator*

Palm Springs
Kern, Donald Michael *internist*

Palo Alto
Adamson, Geoffrey David *reproductive endocrinologist, surgeon*
Babb, Richard Rankin *gastroenterologist, educator*
Bensch, Klaus George *pathology educator*
Blessing-Moore, Joann Catherine *allergist, pulmonologist*
Britton, M(elvin) C(reed), Jr. *rheumatologist*
Chen, Stephen Shi-hua *pathologist, biochemist*
Commons, George W. *plastic surgeon*
Cooke, John P. *cardiologist, educator, researcher*
Dafoe, Donald Cameron *surgeon, educator*
Dement, William Charles *medical researcher, educator*
Desai, Kavin Hirendra *pediatrician*
Fries, James Franklin *internal medicine educator*
Galel, Susan Alpert *transfusion medicine physician*
Goldstein, Mary Kane *physician*
Harkonen, Wesley Scott *physician, pharmaceutical company executive*
Hays, Marguerite Thompson *nuclear medicine physician, educator*
Hentz, Vincent R. *surgeon*
Holman, Halsted Reid *physician, educator*
Linna, Timo Juhani *immunologist, researcher, educator*
Litt, Iris Figarsky *pediatrics educator*
Michie, Sara H. *pathologist, educator*
Mitchell, Beverly Shriver *hematologist, oncologist, educator*
Needleman, Philip *cardiologist, pharmacologist*
Peng, Stanford Lee-Yu *physician*
Rasgon, Natalie Luzina *psychiatry and behavioral sciences professor, director*
Schendel, Stephen Alfred *surgeon, educator*
Schrier, Stanley Leonard *hematologist, educator*
Schurman, David Jay *orthopedic surgeon, educator*
Shuer, Lawrence Mendel *neurosurgery educator*
Strober, Samuel *immunologist, educator*
Sunshine, Philip *pediatrician*
Tune, Bruce Malcolm *pediatrics educator, renal toxicologist*
Urquhart, John *medical researcher, educator*

Palos Verdes Estates
Myhre, Byron Arnold *pathologist, educator*

Palos Verdes Peninsula
Narasimhan, Padma Mandyam *physician*
Thomas, Claudewell Sidney *psychiatrist, educator*

Panorama City
Bass, Harold Neal *pediatrician, medical geneticist*
Fleisher, Arthur A., II, *physician*
Sue, Michael Alvin *allergist*

Pasadena
Buchwald, Jed Zachary *environmental health researcher, science history educator*
Glovsky, Myron Michael *medical educator*
Harvey, Joseph Paul, Jr. *orthopedist, educator*
Mathies, Allen Wray, Jr. *former pediatrician, hospital administrator*
Opel, William *medical research administrator*
Puliafito, Carmen Anthony *ophthalmologist, healthcare executive*
Shaw, Anthony *pediatric surgeon, retired educator*

Pinole
Naughton, James Lee *internist*

Pleasanton
Hisaka, Eric Toru *plastic surgeon*

Portola Valley
Fogarty, Thomas James *surgery educator*

Poway
Kruggel, John Louis *plastic surgeon*

Rancho Mirage
Chuang, Tsu-Yi *dermatologist, epidemiologist, educator*
Cone, Lawrence Arthur *medical educator*
Weil, Max Harry *internist, cardiologist, educator, researcher*

Rancho Santa Fe
Carr, David Turner *physician*
Nadler, Henry Louis *pediatrician, educator, geneticist*

Redding
Renard, Ronald Lee *allergist*

Redlands
Skoog, William Arthur *retired oncologist*

Redondo Beach
Grollman, Julius Harry, Jr. *cardiovascular and interventional radiologist*

Redwood City
Marton, Laurence Jay *pathologist, researcher, educator*

Richmond
Arnon, Stephen Soulé *physician, research scientist*
Duhl, Leonard J. *psychiatrist, educator*

Riverside
Bricker, Neal S. *physician, educator*
Childs, Donald Richard *pediatric endocrinologist*
Green, Dolores L. *medical association administrator*
Linaweaver, Walter Ellsworth, Jr. *physician*

Sacramento
Achtel, Robert Andrew *pediatric cardiologist, educator*
Bogren, Hugo Gunnar *radiology educator*
Chapman, Michael William *orthopedist, educator*
Hales, Robert Ernest *psychiatrist, educator*
Jackson, Richard Joseph *epidemiologist, educator, pediatrician, preventive medicine physician*
Leong, Albin B. *pediatric pulmonologist, allergist, educator*
Lilla, James A. *plastic surgeon*
Lim, Alan Young *plastic surgeon*
Low, Reginald Inman *cardiologist*
Lynch, Peter John *retired dermatologist*
Nagy, Stephen Mears, Jr. *physician, allergist*
Rab, George T. *pediatric orthopedic surgeon*
Rounds, Barbara Lynn *psychiatrist*
Stevenson, Thomas Ray *plastic surgeon*
Styne, Dennis Michael *physician, educator*
Tung, Prabhas *plastic surgeon*
Wolfman, Earl Frank, Jr. *surgeon, educator*

San Bernardino
De Haas, David Dana *emergency physician*
Gorenberg, Alan Eugene *physician*

San Bruno
Bradley, Charles William *podiatrist, educator*

San Clemente
Kim, Edward William *ophthalmic surgeon*

San Diego
Batey, Sharyn Rebecca *medical writer*
Bloom, Floyd Elliott *internist, neuroscientist*
DeMaria, Anthony Nicholas *cardiologist, educator*
Ebbeling, William Leonard *physician*
Friedman, Paul Jay *retired radiologist*
Hayden, Stephen R. *emergency physician, educator*
Horgan, Santiago *surgeon*
Jacoby, Irving *physician*
Jamieson, Stuart William *surgeon, educator*
Jeste, Dilip Vishwanath *psychiatrist, researcher*
Kahn, Bruce S. *obstetrician, gynecologist*
Kaplan, George Willard *urologist*
Leopold, George Robert *radiologist*
O'Malley, Edward *psychiatrist, consultant*
Parthemore, Jacqueline Gail *internist, educator, hospital administrator*
Ray, Albert *physician, educator*
Reid, Robert Tilden *medical association administrator, internist*
Resnik, Robert *medical educator*
Roizen, Michael F. *anesthesiologist, medical educator, writer*
Ross, John, Jr. *cardiologist, educator*
Schmidt, Joseph David *urologist*
Wallace, Helen Margaret *pediatrician, preventive medicine physician, educator*
Wasserman, Stephen Ira *allergist, immunologist, educator*
Widder, Kenneth Jon *pathologist, educator*
Zeiger, Robert S. *allergist*

San Francisco
Abbas, Abul K. *pathologist, educator*
Amend, William John Conrad, Jr. *physician, educator*
Ascher, Nancy Louise *surgeon*
Bainton, Dorothy Ford *pathologist, educator*
Barondes, Samuel Herbert *psychiatrist, educator*
Becker, David Kenneth *pediatrician, educator*
Behrens, M. Kathleen *medical researcher*
Beinfield, Harriet *medical association administrator*
Benet, Leslie Zachary *pharmacologist, educator*
Bernstein, Harold Seth *pediatric cardiologist, molecular geneticist*
Boles, Roger *otolaryngologist*
Bourne, Henry R. *pharmacology professor, department chairman, researcher*
Bradford, David S. *surgeon*
Brotman, Martin *gastroenterologist*
Brown, Donald Malcolm *plastic surgeon*
Buncke, Gregory M. *plastic surgeon*
Capozzi, Angelo *surgeon*
Chatterjee, Kanu *cardiologist, educator*
Clever, Linda Hawes *physician*
Cobbs, Price Mashaw *social psychiatrist*
Cooper, Allen David *medical researcher, educator*
Crawford, Michael Howard *cardiologist, educator, researcher*
Dawson, Chandler Robert *ophthalmologist, educator*
Diab, Mohammad *orthopedic surgeon*
Engleman, Ephraim Philip *rheumatologist*
Epstein, Charles Joseph *pediatrician, geneticist, biochemist, educator*
Epstein, John Howard *dermatologist*
Erskine, John Morse *surgeon*
Farmer, Diana Lee *pediatric surgeon*
Fielder, David R. *medical research administrator*
Foster, Elyse *cardiologist, educator*
Foster-Barber, Audrey Elizabeth *neurologist, educator*
Frick, Oscar Lionel *pediatrician, educator*
Frieden, Ilona Josephine *pediatric dermatologist*
Friedman, Gary *plastic surgeon*
Ganem, Donald E. *immunologist*
Gellin, Gerald Alan *dermatologist*
Goldschlager, Nora Fox *internist, cardiologist, educator*
Goode, Erica Tucker *internist*
Gooding, Charles Arthur *radiologist, physician, educator*
Gooding, Gretchen Ann Wagner *physician, educator*
Goosby, Eric Paul *epidemiologist*
Greene, Warner Craig *medical educator, administrator*
Greenspan, Francis S. *physician*
Greenspan, John S. *dental and medical educator, researcher, academic administrator*
Greenspan, Louise Catherine *pediatrician*
Grossman, William *medical researcher, educator*
Grumbach, Melvin Malcolm *pediatrician, educator*
Hauser, Stephen L. *medical educator*
Havel, Richard Joseph *physician, educator*
Heyman, Melvin Bernard *pediatric gastroenterologist*
Higashida, Randall Takeo *radiologist, neurosurgeon, medical educator*
Hinman, Frank, Jr. *urologist, educator*
Hoffman, William Yanes *plastic surgeon, educator*
Hoskins, H. Dunbar *ophthalmologist, medical association administrator*
Humphreys, Michael Harrington *internist, researcher*
Ikeda, Clyde Junichi *plastic and reconstructive surgeon*
Jablons, David M. *surgeon, educator*
Jaffe, Robert Benton *obstetrician, gynecologist, endocrinologist*
Jampolis, Melina Beth *internist, physician nutrition specialist*
Jonsen, Albert R(upert) *medical ethics educator*
Kan, Yuet Wai *hematologist, educator*
Kenyon, Cynthia J. *medical researcher*
King, Talmadge E. *physician*
Koda-Kimble, Mary Anne *pharmacologist, educator, dean*
Koo, John Ying Ming *psychiatrist, dermatologist*
Leake, Patricia Ann *medical educator, researcher*
Lee, Philip Randolph *medical educator*
Levy, Jay A. *medical educator*
Lo, Bernard *medical educator*
Low, Randall *internist, cardiologist*
Lucia, Marilyn Reed *physician*
Mason, Dean Towle *cardiologist*
Mathias, Robert S. *pediatric nephrologist*
McAninch, Jack Weldon *urological surgeon, educator*
McNamara, Margaret M. *pediatrician*
Miller, Ronald D. *medical educator, researcher*
Murray, John Frederic *cardiologist, educator*
Mustacchi, Piero *preventive medicine physician, educator*
Ousterhout, Douglas Kenneth *plastic surgeon*
Owsley, John Quincy, IV, *plastic surgeon, educator*
Perkins, Herbert Asa *hematologist, educator*
Petrakis, Nicholas Louis *epidemiologist, medical researcher, educator*
Phillips, Theodore Locke *radiologist, educator*
Ptacek, Louis John *medical educator, medical researcher*
Rabow, Michael Warren *physician, educator*
Raffin, Thomas Alfred *physician, educator, venture capitalist*
Reijo Pera, Renee A. *reproductive science director, educator*
Resneck, Jack Selwyn, Jr. *dermatologist, medical educator*
Ristow, Brunno *plastic surgeon*
Rudolph, Abraham Morris *pediatrician, educator*
Rutherford, George Williams III *preventive medicine physician*
Schmidt, Robert Milton *preventive medicine physician, educator, medical association administrator*
Schrock, Theodore R. *surgeon*
Schroeder, Steven Alfred *medical educator*
Seebach, Lydia Marie *physician*
Shaw, Richard Eugene *cardiovascular researcher*
Sherr, Elliott Harold *neurologist, researcher*
Shinefield, Henry Robert *pediatrician*
Smith, David Elvin *physician*
Smith, Lloyd Hollingsworth *physician*
Soifer, Scott Jay *pediatrician*
Spivey, Bruce E. *ophthalmologist, educator, health facility administrator*
Stamper, Robert Lewis *ophthalmologist, educator*
Taekman, Michael Seymour *neurological surgeon*
Terr, Lenore Cagen *psychiatrist, writer*
Vail, Thomas Parker *orthopaedic surgeon*
Van Dyke, Craig *psychiatrist, director*
Volberding, Paul Arthur *academic physician*
Volpe, Peter Anthony *surgeon*
Washington, A. Eugene *medical educator*
Way, E(dward) Leong *pharmacologist, toxicologist, educator*
Wintroub, Bruce Urich *dermatologist, educator, researcher*
Zippin, Calvin *epidemiologist, educator*

San Jose
Lippe, Philipp Maria *neurosurgeon, academic administrator, educator*
Nguyen, Thinh Van *internist*

San Luis Obispo
Cotter, John Burley *ophthalmologist*
Pinkel, Donald Paul *pediatrician*

San Marino
Sadun, Alfredo Arrigo *neuro-ophthalmologist, scientist, educator*

San Mateo
Chabra, Anand *public health physician, epidemiologist*
Van Kirk, John Ellsworth *retired cardiologist*

San Pablo
Woodruff, Kay Herrin *pathologist, educator*

San Rafael
Ramirez, Archimedes *neurosurgeon, educator*

San Ramon
Litman, Robert Barry *physician, writer, television and radio commentator*

Sanger
Patton, Jack Thomas *family practice physician*

Santa Ana
Myers, Marilyn Gladys *pediatric hematologist, oncologist*

Santa Barbara
Bischel, Margaret DeMeritt *physician, consultant*
Fisher, Steven Kay *neurobiology educator*
Formby, Bent Clark *immunologist*
Jovanovic, Lois *medical researcher*
Klakeg, Clayton Harold *retired cardiologist*
Kohn, Roger Alan *surgeon*
Liebhaber, Myron I. *allergist*
Mathews, Barbara Edith *gynecologist*
Prager, Elliot David *surgeon, educator*
Riemenschneider, Paul Arthur *retired physician, retired radiologist*
Shackman, Daniel Robert *psychiatrist*

Santa Cruz
Shorenstein, Rosalind Greenberg *internist*

Santa Monica
Carr, Ruth Margaret *plastic surgeon*
Hoefflin, Steven M. *plastic surgeon*
Kawamoto, Henry Katsumi, Jr. *plastic surgeon*
McGuire, Michael Francis *plastic surgeon*
O'Connor, Edward Joseph *neurologist*
Resnick, Jeffrey I. *plastic surgeon*
Schultz, Victor M. *physician*
Singer, Frederick Raphael *medical researcher*
Stern, Walter Eugene *neurosurgeon, educator*
Teitelbaum, Steven *plastic surgeon*
Tompkins, Ronald K. *retired surgeon, educator*
Zarem, Harvey Alan *plastic surgeon*

Santa Rosa
Bozdech, Marek Jiri *physician, educator*
McAvoy, John Martin *plastic surgeon*

Scotts Valley
Pletsch, Marie Eleanor *plastic surgeon*

Sherman Oaks
Handel, Neal *plastic surgeon, researcher, educator*
Zemplenyi, Tibor Karol *cardiologist, educator*

South San Francisco
Dixit, Vishva M. *pathology educator*
Humphrey, Patrick Paul *pharmacologist*
Hurst, Deborah *pediatric hematologist*

Stanford
Abrams, Herbert LeRoy *radiologist, educat*
Arber, Daniel Alan *hematologist, pathologis*
Blaschke, Terrence Francis *medicine and molecular pharmacology educator*
Blau, Helen Margaret *pharmacology educa*
Brown, J. Martin *oncologist, educator*
Butcher, Eugene Corning *pathologist, scien educator*
Carlson, Robert Wells *internist, educator*
Chase, Robert Arthur *surgeon, educator*
Cohen, Harvey Joel *pediatric hematology a oncology educator*
Donaldson, Sarah Susan *radiologist*
Egbert, Peter Roy *ophthalmologist, educato*
Farquhar, John William *physician, educator*
Fee, Willard Edward, Jr. *otolaryngologist*
Fire, Andrew Z. *pathologist, geneticist, edu*
Fisher, George Albert, Jr. *internist, oncolog*
Friedman, Gary David *epidemiologist*
Garber, Alan Michael *internist, educator, economist*
Glazer, Gary Mark *radiology educator*
Goodman, Stuart B. *medical educator*
Greenberg, Harry B. *gastroenterologist, edı*
Hanley, Frank Louis *surgeon, educator*
Henderson, Victor Warren *behavioral and geriatric neurologist, epidemiologist, researcher, educator*
Hlatky, Mark Andrew *cardiologist, research*
Horwitz, Ralph Irving *internist, epidemiolo educator, former dean*
Hunt, Sharon Ann *cardiologist*
Jacobs, Charlotte De Croes *oncologist, edu*
Jardetzky, Oleg *retired medical educator, researcher*
Kay, Mark Allan *medical educator*
Kraemer, Helena Antoinette Chmura *psych educator*
Leibel, Steven Arnold *oncologist*
Levy, Ronald *medical educator, researcher*
Malenka, Robert C. *psychiatrist, educator*
Mansour, Tag Eldin *pharmacologist, educa*
Mark, James B. D. *surgeon, educator*
Marmor, Michael Franklin *ophthalmologist, educator*
McDevitt, Hugh O'Neill *immunologist, edu*
McDougall, Iain Ross *nuclear medicine educator*
McQuillen, Michael Paul *neurologist, educ*
Miller, D. Craig *cardiovascular surgeon*
Owens, Douglas K. *physician, researcher*
Polan, Mary Lake *obstetrics and gynecolog educator*
Powers, Rebecca Ann *psychiatrist, health f administrator*
Reitz, Bruce Arnold *cardiac surgeon, educ*
Robbins, Robert Clayton *surgeon*
Rosenberg, Saul Allen *oncologist, educator*
Rubenstein, Edward *physician, educator*
Schatzberg, Alan Frederic *psychiatrist, researcher*
Shortliffe, Linda Marie Dairiki *urology edu researcher*
Stamey, Thomas Alexander *urologist, educ*
Wapnir, Irene Leonor *medical educator*
Weissman, Irving L. *medical researcher*
Zarins, Christopher Kristaps *surgeon, educ*

Stockton
Matuszak, Alice Jean Boyer *pharmacy edu*

Sylmar
Corry, Dalila Boudjellal *internist, educator*
Ziment, Irwin *medical educator*

Temple City
Wen, Leana S. *epidemiologist*

Templeton
Abernathy, Shields B. *allergist, immunolog internist*

Thousand Oaks
Eisenberg, Paul Richard *cardiologist, consu educator*
Farshidi, Ardeshir B. *cardiologist, educator*
Pakula, Anita Susan *dermatologist*
Scott, Mary Celine *pharmacologist*
Solomon, David Harris *geriatrician, educa*

Torrance
Algra, Ronald James *dermatologist*
Brass, Eric Paul *internal medicine and pharmacology educator, academic administrator*
Budoff, Matthew Jay *cardiologist*
Emmanouilides, George Christos *physician educator*
Isenberg, Sherwin Jay *pediatric ophthalmo*
Katz, Ronald Lewis *physician, educator*
Mehringer, Charles Mark *medical educator*
Stabile, Bruce Edward *surgeon*
Swerdloff, Ronald S. *physician, educator, researcher*
Tanaka, Kouichi Robert *hematologist, educ*

Ukiah
McClintock, Richard Polson *dermatologist*

Ventura
Villaveces, James Walter *allergist, immuno consultant*

alnut Creek
son, Jay Wilmer *pathologist, educator*
ien, Morris Frank *retired medical administrator, physician, consultant, researcher*

st Hills
, James Michael *orthopedic surgeon*

stminster
ng, Khanh Vinh Quoc *nephrologist, researcher*

ittier
kett, David Clinton *physician*

LORADO

vada
choff, Theodore Carl *infectious disease physician, epidemiologist*
rier, Robert William *physician, educator*

rora
aglia, Frederick Camillo *physician*
n, Paul A., Jr. *oncologist, educator*
rchill, Mair Elisa Annabelle *medical educator*
wford, E. David *urologist, surgeon, researcher*
nessey, Paul Vincent *pediatrics and pharmacology educator, researcher*
ston, Richard Boles, Jr. *pediatrician, educator, biomedical researcher*
s, M. Douglas, Jr. *pediatrician, educator*
py, Michael Steven *pediatrics educator*
a, Audrey Hart *physician*
ff, Donald Wilfred *pediatrician, educator*
re, James H(enry) *psychiatrist*

ulder
k, S. Allan *physician, educator*

non City
r, Gary Alan *physician*

orado Springs
ord, Marilyn Joyce *emergency physician, consultant*
erville, James Jasper *pediatrician*
ms, William Wallace *physician*
l, Harold Wade *retired medical association administrator, military officer*

nver
urso, Frank Joseph *physician, educator*
pbell, David Neil *physician, educator*
ton, Mack Louis *surgeon, educator*
aran, John Howard *plastic and reconstructive surgeon*
rello, Charles A. *medical educator*
ow, Patricia Anne *internist, health facility executive*
tz, Loren Eugene *dermatologist, pathologist, medical association administrator*
vlee, Glenn P(age) *anesthesiologist, educator, director*
vson, Clifford Russell *internist*
er, Myles Stuert *surgeon*
is, Robert Adron *pharmacologist*
in, Robert J. *plastic surgeon, educator*
ng, Linda Chen *plastic surgeon*
er, Richard Joseph *physician, dermatologist*
an, Michael Dee *medical educator*
k, Bruce William *otolaryngologist, educator*
son, Candice Elaine Brown *pediatrician, educator*
annon, Elizabeth Anne *neonatologist, hospital administrator*
gman, Richard David *pediatrician, academic administrator, educator*
gsley, Pauline Royal *psychiatrist*
en, Gary Loy *physician, researcher*
rus, Jeremy A. *psychiatrist*
g, Donald Y. M. *pediatric allergist*
enfeld, JoAnn *physician, educator*
ck, Marvin Jay *ophthalmologist*
kovchick, Vincent J. *surgeon*
ack, Philippa Charlotte *immunologist, researcher*
in, Richard Jay *medical educator*
re, Ernest Eugene, Jr. *surgeon, educator*
ns, Douglas K. *psychiatrist, educator*
, Thomas Lee *internist, educator*
rantz, Marvin *thoracic surgeon*
, David William *physician, educator, researcher*
er, William Gerald *cardiac surgeon*
ne, John Edward *internist, educator*
nwasser, Lanny Jeffrey *allergist, immunologist*
dell, Sidney *preventive medicine physician, educator, department chairman*
m, Carol Ann *obstetrician, gynecologist*
mark, Kurt R. *medical educator, researcher*
nsky, Eva Borska *pediatrician, geneticist, educator*
er, Stanley James *pediatrics and pharmacology educator*
therley-White, Roy Christopher Anthony *surgeon, consultant*
on, William Lee *dermatologist*

lewood
, Clifford Alan *pediatric endocrinologist*
e, David Maurice *plastic surgeon*

Fort Collins
Benjamin, Stephen Alfred *pathologist, department chairman, educator, researcher*
Reif, John Steven *epidemiologist, veterinarian*
Roehrig, John T. *immunologist, educator*

Golden
Johnson, Mark Bernarr *preventive medicine physician*

Grand Junction
Janson, Richard Anthony *plastic surgeon*

Greeley
Cook, Donald Evan *pediatrician, educator*
Schneider, Carole M. *medical educator, director*

Greenwood Village
Grainger, John R. *medical association administrator*

Vail
Bevan, William Arnold, Jr. *emergency physician*
Philippon, Marc Joseph *orthopaedic surgeon*

Wheat Ridge
Fleischaker, Gordon Henry, Jr. *pediatrician*
Hashimoto, Christine L. *physician*

HAWAII

Honolulu
Chesne, Edward Leonard *physician*
Curb, Jess David *medical educator, researcher*
Fitz-Patrick, David *endocrinologist, educator*
Flowers, Robert Swaim *medical educator, surgeon*
Goldstein, Sir Norman *dermatologist*
Ho, Reginald Chi Shing *medical educator*
Ishii, Clyde Hideo *plastic surgeon*
Kane, Thomas Jay III *surgeon, educator*
Lau, H. Lorrin *obstetrician, gynecologist*
Lee, Yeu-Tsu Margaret *surgeon, educator*
McCarthy, Laurence James *physician, pathologist*
Oda, Yoshio *physician, internist*
Parsa, Fereydoun Don *plastic surgeon*
Schatz, Irwin Jacob *cardiologist, educator*
Sharma, Santosh Devraj *obstetrician, gynecologist, educator*
Sia, Calvin Chia Jung *pediatrician*
Wallach, Stephen Joseph *cardiologist*

Lahaina
Percy, Helen Sylvia *physician*

Mililani
Gardner, Sheryl Paige *gynecologist*

Waikoloa
Copman, Louis *radiologist*

IDAHO

Idaho Falls
Lee, Glenn Richard *medical association administrator, educator*

Post Falls
Riggs, Jack Timothy *emergency physician, retired lieutenant governor*

Sandpoint
Bird, Forrest M. *retired medical inventor*

MASSACHUSETTS

Cambridge
O'Shea, Erin K. *biomedical researcher*

MONTANA

Big Sky
Strickler, Jeffrey Harold *pediatrician*

Billings
Knapp, Howard Raymond *internist, clinical pharmacologist*

Bozeman
Pardue, A. Michael *retired plastic and reconstructive surgeon*
Quinn, Mark T. *medical educator*

Helena
Reynolds, James Francis, Jr. *physician*

Whitefish
Miller, Ronald Alfred *family physician*

NEVADA

Las Vegas
McCann, Biff (Raymond Biff McCann) *plastic surgeon*
Moritz, Timothy Bovie *psychiatrist*
Speck, Eugene Lewis *internist*
Weiss, Robert Michael *dermatologist*

North Las Vegas
Webber, Robert *medical researcher*

Reno
Bray, Timothy J. *orthopedist, surgeon*
Small, Elisabeth Chan *psychiatrist, educator*
Zanjani, Esmail D. *medical educator, research scientist*

NEW MEXICO

Alamogordo
Ashdown, Franklin Donald *physician, composer*

Albuquerque
Baack, Bret Rolyn *plastic surgeon*
Chang, Barbara Karen *medical educator, director*
Chilton, Lance Alix *pediatrician*
Gordon, Larry Jean *sanitarian, environmental health consultant*
Heffron, Warren A. *physician, educator*
Hudson, Patrick A. *plastic surgeon*
Knospe, William Herbert *medical educator*
Lindeman, Robert Dean *medical educator, researcher, consultant*
Mason, William vanHorn *dermatologist*
McCarthy, Denis M. *medical educator*
Napolitano, Leonard Michael *anatomist, university administrator*
Omer, George Elbert, Jr. *retired orthopaedic surgeon, educator*
Saland, Linda Carol *anatomist, neuroscientist, educator*
Strasburger, Victor C. *pediatrician*
Uhlenhuth, Eberhard Henry *psychiatrist, educator*
Waitzkin, Howard Bruce *internist, sociologist, educator*
Waxman, Alan Garlett *obstetrician/gynecologist, educator*
Wimer, Mark G. *healthcare management company executive*

Farmington
Neidhart, James Allen *oncologist, educator*

Las Cruces
Jacobs, Kent Frederick *dermatologist*

Los Alamos
Smith, Fredrica Emrich *rheumatologist, internist*

Portales
Goodwin, Martin Brune *retired radiologist*

Santa Fe
Alfidi, Ralph Joseph *retired radiologist, educator, researcher, administrator*
Kingsmore, Stephen Francis *physician, research scientist*
Williams, Ralph Chester, Jr. *physician, educator*

Tesuque
Bornstein, Paul *medical educator, biochemist*

OREGON

Corvallis
Baird, William McKenzie *chemical carcinogenesis researcher, biochemistry professor*

Eugene
Jewell, Mark Laurence *plastic surgeon*
Loescher, Richard Alvin *retired gastroenterologist*
Roe, Thomas Leroy Willis *retired pediatrician*

Gresham
Zook, John Edwin *surgeon*

Klamath Falls
Bohnen, Robert Frank *hematologist, oncologist, educator*
Novak, James F. *physician*

Lake Oswego
Hutchens, Tyra Thornton *pathologist, educator*
Julien, Robert Michael *anesthesiologist, writer*

Medford
Shekhar, Stephen S. *obstetrician, gynecologist*

Portland
Baker, Diane R.H. *dermatologist*
Barry, John Maynard *urologist*
Bennett, William Michael *internist, educator, nephrologist*
Bloom, Joseph D. *psychiatrist, medical educator*
Campbell, John Richard *pediatric surgeon*
Casey, Daniel E. *psychiatrist, educator*
Connor, William Elliott *internist, educator*
Druker, Brian Jay *medical educator, researcher*
Fraunfelder, Frederick Theodore *ophthalmologist, educator*
Greer, Monte Arnold *endocrinologist, educator*
Hedges, Jerris *medical educator, health services researcher*
Jacob, Stanley Wallace *surgeon, educator*
Kendall, John Walker, Jr. *internist, researcher, dean*
Kitzhaber, John Albert *emergency physician, former governor*
Layman, Charles Donald *plastic surgeon*
MacArthur, Carol Jeanne *pediatric otolaryngology educator*
Mozena, John Daniel *podiatrist*
Palmer, Earl A. *ophthalmologist, educator*
Patterson, James Randolph *physician*
Scott, John D. *pharmacologist*
Sussman, Michael David *orthopedic surgeon*
Sutherland, Donald Wood *retired cardiologist*
Taylor, Robert Brown *physician, educator, writer*
Vernon, Jack Allen *otolaryngology educator, laboratory administrator*
Wilson, William Harwell *psychiatrist, educator*
Zerbe, Kathryn Jane *psychiatrist*
Zimmerman, Gail Marie *medical foundation executive*

UTAH

Mapleton
Hillyard, Ira William *retired pharmacologist, educator*

Park City
Cooley, Vernon Jackman *orthopedic surgeon*

Provo
Hwang, Chun *cardiologist*

Salt Lake City
Betz, A. Lorris *pediatrician, educator*
Capecchi, Mario Renato *genetics educator*
Carey, John Clayton *pediatrician, educator, medical geneticist*
Dolcourt, John (Jack) Lawrence *pediatrician*
Foster, Carol Marvel *pediatric endocrinologist*
Fujinami, Robert Shin *pathologist, researcher*
Gleich, Gerald Joseph *immunologist, researcher, educator*
Goldstein, Michael L. *neurologist*
Grosser, Bernard Irving *psychiatrist, educator*
Lyon, Joseph Lynn *physician, medical educator*
Meyers, Rebecka Louise *pediatric general surgeon*
Moser, Royce, Jr. *preventive medicine physician, educator*
Nelson, Russell Marion *surgeon, educator*
Petersen, Finn Bo *oncologist, educator*
Shipman, Jean Pugh *medical librarian*
Stanford, Joseph Barney *medical educator, physician*
Tani, Lloyd Yasuo *pediatrician, educator*
Thomas, David Snow *plastic surgeon*
Wolf, Harold Herbert *pharmacy educator*

Vernal
Tyus, Harold Maurice *ichthyologist*

VIRGINIA

Mc Lean
Rippen, Helga Edith *pharmaceutical company administrator*

WASHINGTON

Bellevue
Coe, Robert Campbell *retired surgeon*
Phillips, Zaiga Alksnis *pediatrician*
Shifrin, Donald Lee *pediatrician*

Bellingham
Howe, Warren Billings *physician*
James, Helen Ann *plastic surgeon*
Wayne, Marvin Alan *emergency medicine physician*

Burien
Risse, Guenter Bernhard *physician, historian, educator*

Centralia
Miller, James McCalmont *pediatrician*

Clyde Hill
Condon, Robert Edward *surgeon, educator, consultant*

Coupeville
Mayhew, Eric George *medical researcher, educator, consultant*

Everett
Valentine, Mark Conrad *dermatologist*

Friday Harbor
Geyman, John Payne *physician, educator*

Issaquah
Barchet, Stephen *obstetrician, gynecologist, retired military officer*

Kent
O'Bara, Kenneth J. *physician*

Kirkland
Barto, Deborah Ann *physician*
Dundas, Dennis Franklin *plastic surgeon*

Lakewood
Pliskow, Vita Sari *anesthesiologist*

Liberty Lake
Mielke, Clarence Harold, Jr. *hematologist*

Mercer Island
Dunner, David Louis *medical educator*

Mountlake Terrace
Baxter, Richard Alan *plastic surgeon, educator*

Olympia
Fisher, Nancy Louise *pediatrician, geneticist, retired nurse*

Port Angeles
Andrew, Louise Briggs *emergency physician, medical legal consultant*

Richland
Bair, William J. *retired radiobiologist*
Zirkle, Lewis Greer *orthopedist*

Seattle
Aldea, Gabriel S. *cardiothoracic surgeon, educator*
Andrews, Robert Goff *pediatrician, educator*
Ansell, Julian S. *urologist, educator*
Appelbaum, Frederick Ray *oncologist*
Berkowitz, Bobbie *medical educator*
Bevan, Michael J. *immunologist, educator, researcher*
Bowden, Douglas McHose *neuropsychiatric scientist, neuroinformaticist*
Boyko, Edward John *internist, medical researcher*
Buck, Linda B. *medical educator*
Catterall, William A. *pharmacology, neurobiology educator*
Chatard, Peter Ralph Noel, Jr. *aesthetic plastic surgeon*
Clowes, Alexander Whitehill *surgeon, educator*
Corey, Lawrence *medical educator*
Cullen, Bruce F. *anesthesiologist*
Dale, David C. *physician, educator*
Dawson, Patricia Lucille *surgeon*
Day, Robert Winsor *preventive medicine physician, researcher*
Eddy, Allison *nephrologist, educator*
Eyre, David R. *orthopedics educator*
Fine, James Stephen *physician*
Gassner, Holger Guenther *surgeon, consultant*
Giblett, Eloise Rosalie *retired hematologist*
Given, Douglass Bruce *physician*
Gralow, Julie Ruth *physician*
Guntheroth, Warren Gaden *pediatrician, educator*
Guralnick, Michael J. *medical research administrator*
Hazzard, William Russell *geriatrician, educator*
Hellström, Ingegerd *medical researcher*
Holmes, King Kennard *medical educator*
Hornbein, Thomas Frederic *anesthesiologist*
Hudson, Leonard Dean *physician*
Kahn, Steven Emanuel *medical educator*
Kalina, Robert Edward *ophthalmologist, educator*
Kimball, Harry Raymond *medical association administrator, educator*
Klebanoff, Seymour Joseph *medical educator*
Kraft, George Howard *physician, educator*
Krohn, Kenneth Albert *radiologist, educator*
Larrabee, Wayne Fox, Jr. *facial plastic surgeon*
Larson, Eric B. *medical educator, director, internist*
Maier, Ronald Vitt *surgeon, educator*
Martin, Thomas Reed *medical educator, medical association administrator*
Matsen, Frederick Albert III *orthopedic educator*
McClure, R. Dale *physician*
Moore, Daniel Charles *retired anesthesiologist*
Motulsky, Arno Gunther *internist, geneticist, educator*
Neligan, Peter C. *plastic surgeon, educator*
Nelson, James Alonzo *radiologist, educator*
O'Brien, Kevin D. *medical educator*
Ostrow, Jay Donald *gastroenterology educator, researcher*
Pagon, Roberta Anderson *pediatrician, educator*
Palmer, Jerry Philip *medical educator, researcher, internist*
Perrin, Edward Burton *biomedical researcher, public health educator*
Phillips, William Robert *physician*
Ravenholt, Reimert Thorolf *epidemiologist, researcher*
Ritchie, James L. *cardiologist*
Rivara, Frederick Peter *pediatrician, educator*
Rose, Eric *physician, consultant*
Rosenblatt, Roger Alan *physician, educator*
Shepard, Thomas Hill *physician, educator*
Sidbury, Robert *pediatrician*
Simon, Gregory E. *psychiatrist, researcher*
Stanford, Janet Lee *physician, epidemiologist*
Stapleton, F. Bruder *pediatric nephrologist, academic administrator*
Stenchever, Morton Albert *obstetrician, gynecologist*
Stolov, Walter Charles *medicine physiatrist, educator*
Su, Judy Ya Hwa Lin *pharmacologist*
Swanson, Phillip Dean *neurologist*
Thirlby, Richard Coller *surgeon*
Thomas, Edward Donnall *internist, hematologist, retired medical educator*
Todaro, George Joseph *pathologist, researcher*
Walker, William O., Jr. *pediatrician*
Weaver, Lois Jean *physician, educator*
Weiss, Noel S. *epidemiologist*
Welk, Richard Andrew *plastic surgeon*
Yue, Agnes Kau-Wah *otolaryngologist*

Sequim
Jenden, Donald James *pharmacologist, educator*

Spokane
Cohen, Arnold Norman *gastroenterologist*
Lee, Hi Young *physician, acupuncturist*

Tacoma
Flemming, Stanley Lalit Kumar *physician, mayor, state legislator*
Wagonfeld, James B. *gastroenterologist*

Vancouver
Lenfant, Claude Jean-Marie *physician, director*

Wenatchee
Gotthold, William Eugene *emergency physician*
Primm, Richard Kirby *physician*

Woodinville
Couser, William Griffith *nephrologist, academic administrator, educator*

WYOMING

Buffalo
Fehir, Kim Michele *oncologist, hematologist*

Casper
Bennion, Scott Desmond *physician*
Prypchan, Lida D. *psychiatrist*
Scaling, Sam T. *obstetrician, gynecologist*

CANADA

ALBERTA

Calgary
Smith, Eldon *cardiologist, physiologist, educator*

Edmonton
Christian, Ralph Gordon *veterinary pathologist, agriculturalist, consultant, researcher*
Halloran, Philip Francis *nephrologist, immunologist*

BRITISH COLUMBIA

Parksville
Weir, Bryce Keith Alexander *neurosurgeon, neurologist, educator*

Vancouver
Baird, Patricia Ann *physician, educator*
Doyle, Patrick John *otolaryngologist, department chairman*
Eaves, Allen Charles Edward *hematologist, health facility administrator*
Friedman, Sydney M. *anatomist, educator, medical researcher*
Hardwick, David Francis *pathologist*
Levy, Julia *immunology educator, researcher*
Ling, Victor *oncologist, educator*
McGeer, Edith Graef *retired neurological science educator*
Riedel, Bernard Edward *retired pharmaceutical sciences educator*
Schaller, Jane Green *pediatrician*
Slonecker, Charles Edward *anatomist, medical educator, writer*
Mizgala, Henry F. *physician, consultant, retired medical educator*

ADDRESS UNPUBLISHED

Abildskov, J. A. *cardiologist, educator*
Abrams, Arthur Jay *retired physician*
Abrams, Fredrick Ralph *physician, clinical ethicist*
Achauer, Bruce Michael *plastic surgeon*
Alfaro, Felix Benjamin *retired physician*
Amylon, Michael David *physician, educator*
Appenzeller, Otto *neurologist, researcher*
Badgley, Theodore McBride *retired psychiatrist, neurologist*
Barbo, Dorothy Marie *obstetrician, gynecologist, educator*
Barricks, Michael Eli *retinal surgeon*
Baxter, John Darling *internist, endocrinologist, educator, health facility administrator*
Benfield, John Richard *surgeon, educator*
Berg, Alfred Oren *epidemiology and family practice medicine educator*
Berman, Jennifer R. *urologist*
Berthelsdorf, Siegfried *retired psychiatrist*
Brandon, Kathryn Elizabeth Beck *pediatrician*
Brega, Kerry Elizabeth *physician, researcher*
Briggs, Burton A. *medical educator*
Brown, James W. *gastroenterologist*
Buist, Neil Robertson MacKenzie *pediatric educator, medical association administrator*
Buncke, Harry J. *retired plastic surgeon, educator*
Burket, John McVey *retired dermatologist*
Carroll, Karen Colleen *pathologist, infectious diseases specialist*
Carson, Dennis A. *immunologist, researcher, cancer biologist*
Castellino, Ronald Augustus Dietrich *radiologist, educator*
Castro, Maria Graciela *medical educator, geneticist, researcher*
Chesney, Margaret A. *medical educator, researcher*
Chiu, Dorothy *retired pediatrician*
Cleaver, James Edward *radiologist, educator*
Clement, Douglas Bruce *medical educator*
Cobb, John Candler *medical educator*
Coppolillo, Henry Peter *psychiatrist*
Dann, Francis Joseph *dermatologist, educator*
Date, Elaine Satomi *physiatrist, educator*
Davidson, Mayer B. *endocrinologist, educator, researcher*
Davis, Roy Kim *otolaryngologist, retired health facility administrator*
Dennis, Karen Marie *plastic surgeon*
Edwards, Bruce George *retired ophthalmologist, military officer*
Fortmann, Stephen Paul *medical educator, researcher, epidemiologist*
Friedmann, Theodore *physician*
Gale, Arnold David *pediatric neurologist, consultant*
Gibbs, Ronald Steven *obstetrician, gynecologist, educator*
Glassheim, Jeffrey Wayne *allergist, immunologist, pediatrician*
Goldberg, Mark Arthur *neurologist*
Goldstein, Avram *pharmacology educator*
Gonick, Harvey Craig *nephrologist, educator*
Grillo-López, Antonio J. *physician*
Hammar, Sherrel Leyton *medical educator*
Harrigan, Rosanne Carol *medical educator*
Heiner, Douglas Cragun *pediatrician, educator, immunologist, allergist*
Henney, Christopher Scot *immunologist*
Herzberger, Eugene E. *retired neurosurgeon*
Hinshaw, David B., Jr. *radiologist*
Ho, Ralph Tinghan *radiologist*
Hood, William Boyd, Jr. *cardiologist, educator*
Iserson, Kenneth Victor *bioethicist, writer, medical educator*
Jacobson, Eugene Donald *medical educator, academic administrator, researcher*
Jaffe, Charles J. *allergist*
Jaouen, Richard Matthie *plastic surgeon*
Jarvik, Gail Pairitz *medical geneticist*
Kaback, Michael *medical educator*
Kaplan, Selna L. *medical educator*
Kaplowitz, Neil *gastroenterologist, educator*
Keller, Roberta Lynn *physician, researcher*
Kirkpatrick, Charles Harvey *immunologist, researcher*
Kline, Frank Menefee *psychiatrist*
Knobloch, Ferdinand J. *psychiatrist, educator*
Koller, Loren D. *veterinary medicine educator*
Kramer, Richard Jay *gastroenterologist, educator*
Levin, Jack *physician, biomedical investigator, educator*
Lieberman, Abraham Nathan *physician, medical administrator*
Lowen, Robert Marshall *plastic surgeon*
Mace, John Weldon *pediatrician*
Mala, Theodore Anthony *physician, consultant*
Malcolm, Dawn Grace *family physician*
Mankoff, David Abraham *nuclear medicine physician*
Martin, George Monroe *pathologist, gerontologist, educator*
Martino, Silvana *osteopath, medical oncologist*
McAnelly, Robert D. *physiatrist*
McGrath, Mary Helena *plastic surgeon, educator*
Mellinkoff, Sherman Mussoff *medical educator*
Merkin, Albert Charles *pediatrician, allergist*
Miller, Jack David R. *radiologist, physician, educator*
Millikan, Clark Harold *physician*
Modny, Cynthia Jean *dermatologist*
Motto, Jerome Arthur *psychiatrist, educator*
Nelson, William Rankin *retired surgeon, educator*
Nguyen, Khanh Gia *medical educator*
Olefsky, Jerrold M. *medical educator, researcher*
Padian, Nancy *medical educator, epidemiologist*
Pallin, Samuel Lear *ophthalmologist, educator, medical director*
Parker, John William *retired pathology educator*
Parkin, James Lamar *retired otolaryngologist, educator*
Patchin, Rebecca J. *anesthesiologist, educator, administrator*
Payne, Anita Hart *reproductive endocrinologist, researcher*
Prinz, Patricia A. *retired psychiatry educator, researcher*
Prusiner, Stanley Ben *neurologist, biochemist, virologist, educator*
Ranney, Helen Margaret *retired internist, hematologist, educator*
Rebhun, Joseph *allergist, immunologist, medical educator*
Ren, Xing Jian *physician*
Rewcastle, Neill Barry *neuropathologist*
Schauf, Victoria *pediatrician, educator*
Schenker, Marc Benet *preventive medicine physician, medical educator, department chairman*
Scherger, Joseph Edward *family physician, educator*
Schiff, Martin *physician, surgeon*
Sewell, Robert Dalton *pediatrician*
Shabot, Myron Michael *critical care educator*
Sher, Paul Phillip *pathologist*
Shohet, Stephen Byron *medical educator*
Siegel, Sheldon C. *pediatrician, immunologist, allergist*
Simmons, Geoffrey Stuart *physician, educator, writer*
Smith, Josef Riley *retired internist*
Smith, Sherwood Paul *plastic surgeon*
Soeldner, John Stuart *physician, educator*
Sokol, Ronald Jay *pediatric gastroenterologist, researcher*
Steckel, Richard J. *retired radiologist, educator, academic administrator*
Stringham, Renée *physician*
Terry, Robert Davis *neuropathologist, educa*
Thompson, Dennis Peters *plastic surgeon*
Tourtellotte, Wallace William *neurologist, educator*
Twigg, Nancy L. *nursing association administrator*
Walker, Lorenzo Giles *surgeon, educator*
Ward, Chester Lawrence *physician, consulta*
Wayburn, Edgar *internist, environmentalist*
Wiggs, Eugene Overbey *ophthalmologist, educator*
Williams, Roger Stewart *neurologist*
Willock, Marcelle Monica *retired medical educator*
Wilson, Myron Robert, Jr. *retired psychiatri*
Winkleby, Marilyn A. *medical researcher*
Winslow, Walter William *psychiatrist, educa*
Yaffe, Sumner Jason *pediatrician, educator, science administrator*
Yalam, Arnold Robert *allergist, immunologi consultant*
Yamamoto, Joe *retired psychiatrist, educato*
Youmans, Julian Ray *neurosurgeon, educato*
Zalavras, Charalampos *orthopedic surgeon*
Zawacki, Bruce Edwin *surgeon, educator, ethicist*
Zumwalt, Ross Eugene *forensic pathologist, educator*

HUMANITIES: LIBERAL STUDIES

UNITED STATES

ALABAMA

Mobile
Steadman, John Marcellus III *retired langua educator*

ALASKA

Anchorage
Crawford, Ronald Merritt *history and geog educator*

Fairbanks
Krauss, Michael Edward *linguist*

ARIZONA

Phoenix
Cristiano, Marilyn Jean *speech communicat educator*

Scottsdale
Land, George Ainsworth *philosopher, consu writer*

Tempe
Green, Monica H. *history professor*
Honegger, Gitta *language educator*
Iverson, Peter James *historian, educator*
MacKinnon, Stephen R. *Asian studies administrator, educator*
Wong, Timothy C. *language and literature educator*

Tucson
Dinnerstein, Leonard *historian, educator*
Kleese, William Carl *genealogy research consultant, financial services representat*
Rabuck, Donna Fontanarose *English writin educator*
Schulz, Renate Adele *German studies and second language acquisition educator*

CALIFORNIA

Arcadia
Yen, Wen-Hsiung *language and music professional, educator*

Bakersfield
Flachmann, Michael Charles *English langu educator*
Kegley, Jacquelyn Ann *philosophy educato*
Meyers, Christopher *humanities educator, consultant*

Berkeley
Alter, Robert Bernard *literature educator, c*
Anderson, William Scovil *classics educato*
Bronstein, Arthur J. *linguistics educator*
Chihara, Charles Seiyo *philosophy educato*
Costa, Gustavo *Italian studies scholar*
Crews, Frederick Campbell *humanities edu writer*
Gallagher, M. Catherine *English literature educator*
Herr, Richard *history professor*
Kay, Paul de Young *linguist*
Kerman, Joseph Wilfred *musicologist, criti*
Lakoff, George *linguistics professor*
Litwack, Leon Frank *historian, retired edu*
Long, Anthony Arthur *classics educator*
Mavroudi, Maria *philologist, educator*

ddlekauff, Robert Lawrence *historian, educator, academic administrator*
gler, Michael Nicholas *peace and conflict studies educator*
tridge, Loren Wayne *art historian, educator*
uch, Irmengard *linguist, educator*
effler, Samuel *philosophy educator*
aley, Raphael *history professor*
z, Peter Howard *art historian, educator*
annon, Thomas Frederic *German language educator*
zkine, Yuri *history professor*
ane, Thomas O. *speech educator*
cy, Robert (Edward) *literature and language professor, translator*
ng, William Shi-Yuan *linguistics educator*
erdling, Alex *language educator*

rlsbad
istman, Albert Bernard *historian*

rmel
ng, Kyung Cho *Korean history specialist, writer, educator*

ico
ore, Brooke Noel *philosophy educator*

aremont
as, Jay David *philosopher, consultant, linguist, educator*
ns, Richard Dean *historian, educator, writer*
vis, Nathaniel *humanities educator*
tmar, Kevin John Hoffmann *literature and language professor, department chairman*
gren, Charles Augustin *historian, educator*
caulay, Ronald Kerr Steven *linguistics educator, retired dean*
Kirahan, Richard Duncan *classics and philosophy educator*
ss, Myra Ellen (Myra Moss Rolle) *philosophy educator*
ney, Thomas Clive *retired English language educator*
h, John King *philosopher, educator*
tag, Frederick Earl *philosophy educator*
ng, Howard Thomas *foreign language educator*

ma
akonstantino, Stacy *language educator*

vis
dgett, Harriet *retired language educator*
den, John Olin *English literature educator, writer*
man, Michael Jerome *humanities educator*
dington, Raymond Bruce, Jr. *language educator*
liamson, Alan Bacher *literature educator, poet, writer*
is, Frank Roy *historian, educator*

sno
ymjian, Dickran *art historian, educator*

llerton
klund, Nancy Basler *history professor*

ndale
Grassi, Leonard *art historian, educator*

ass Valley
hkiss, Bill *author, educator*

ine
d, Carolyn Patricia *history professor*
k, Michael Phillip *English educator*
man, William John *language educator, academic administrator*
dy, Penelope Jo *philosopher, educator*
, Vicki Lynn *history professor, department chairman*
on, Dana Ferrin *classics educator*
ntz, Amy *literature educator*

Jolla
stein, Michael Alan *history educator*
, Julia S. *linguist, educator, dean*
Michael Graham *historian, educator*
acker, Ronald Wayne *linguistics educator*
r, Seth *literature professor, writer*
Donald, Marianne *classicist*
son, Frederick Arlan *philosophy educator*
kes, Naomi *science historian*
ing, Donald Truman *English literature educator*
ght, Andrew *English literature educator*

g Beach
yen, Huong Tran *former elementary and secondary language educator, former district office administrator*

Angeles
, Michael John Bridgman *language educator*
rs, Edward Alter *history professor*
, Ehrhard *Germanic languages and literature educator*
shaw, Murray Charles *musicologist, educator, composer*
n, S(tephen) Marshall *philosophy educator*
dson, Herbert Alan *Near Eastern languages and cultures educator*
, Andrew Roy *philologist, educator*
, Peter Solomon *art historian, curator, critic*

Friedlander, Saul *historian, educator*
Hovannisian, Richard G. *historian, educator*
Hundley, Norris Cecil, Jr. *historian, educator*
Keenan, Edward L. *linguist, educator*
Kelly, Henry Ansgar *language educator*
Kolve, V. A. *English literature educator*
Laird, David *humanities educator emeritus*
Levine, Philip *classics educator*
Mellor, Ronald John *history professor*
Rouse, Richard Hunter *historian, educator*
Schaefer, William David *language educator*
Silverman, Debora Leah *history professor*
Stockwell, Robert Paul *linguist, educator*
Tangherlini, Timothy R. *literature educator*
Troy, Nancy J. *art history educator*
Wortham, Thomas Richard *literature and language professor*

Malibu
Larson, Edward John *history and law professor*
Marshall, Donald Glenn *English language and literature educator*

Menlo Park
Bales, Royal Eugene *retired philosophy educator*

Merced
Amussen, Susan Dwyer *history professor*
Hallman, Max O. *humanities and philosophy professor, director*

Newport Beach
Mc Culloch, Samuel Clyde *history professor*

Northridge
Omatsu, Glenn *Asian American studies professor*

Pacific Palisades
Perloff, Marjorie Gabrielle *literature educator*

Palos Verdes Peninsula
Alkon, Paul Kent *language educator*

Pasadena
Kousser, J(oseph) Morgan *historian, educator*
Mandel, Oscar *literature and language professor, writer*

Portola Valley
Carnochan, Walter Bliss *retired humanities educator*

Riverside
Fagundo, Ana Maria *language educator*
Ross, Delmer Gerrard *historian, educator*
Snyder, Henry Leonard *historian, educator, writer*

Sacramento
Carr, Gerald Francis *language educator*
Meindl, Robert James *language educator, poet*

San Diego
Alcosser, Sandra Beth *English language educator, writer*
González-Trujillo, César Augusto *Chicano studies educator, writer*
Wawrytko, Sandra Ann *humanities educator*

San Francisco
Cherny, Robert Wallace *historian, educator*
Costa-Zalessow, Natalia *foreign language educator*
Needleman, Jacob *philosophy educator, writer*
Stump, David James *philosopher, educator*

San Marino
Zall, Paul Maxwell *language educator, consultant*

Santa Barbara
Abbott, Horace Porter *English literature educator*
Chafe, Wallace LeSeur *linguist, educator*
Crawford, Donald Wesley *philosophy educator, university official*
Fingarette, Herbert *philosopher, educator*
Fleming, Brice Noel *retired philosophy educator*
Gunn, Giles Buckingham *language, religious studies and global and international studies educator*
Hoffmeister, Gerhart *German language educator*
Lim, Shirley Geok Lin *language educator*
Mahlendorf, Ursula Renate *literature educator*
McGee, James Sears *historian, educator*
Rose, Mark Allen *humanities educator*
Russell, Jeffrey Burton *historian, educator*
Wilkins, Burleigh Taylor *philosophy educator*

Santa Cruz
Stevens, Stanley David *historian, researcher, retired librarian, archivist*

Santa Monica
See, Carolyn *English language educator, writer, book critic*

Sherman Oaks
Howe, Daniel Walker *historian, educator*

Stanford
Baker, Keith Michael *history professor*
Dekker, George Gilbert *literature professor, writer, former academic administrator*
Duus, Peter *retired historian*
Felstiner, John *literature educator, translator*
Gelpi, Albert Joseph *language educator, department chairman, critic*

Jollimore, Troy *philosophy professor, poet*
Kennedy, David Michael *historian, educator*
Loftis, John (Clyde), Jr. *language educator*
Lohnes, Walter F. W. *German language and literature educator*
Martin, Richard Peter *classics educator, consultant*
Moravcsik, Julius Matthew *philosophy educator*
Newman-Gordon, Pauline *French language and literature educator*
Orgel, Stephen Kitay *language educator*
Perry, John Richard *philosophy educator*
Robinson, Paul Arnold *historian, educator, writer*
Saller, Richard Paul *classics educator*
Sheehan, James John *historian, educator*
Stansky, Peter David Lyman *historian, writer, retired professor*
Traugott, Elizabeth Closs *linguist, educator, researcher*

Stockton
Krise, Thomas Warren *academic administrator, literature and language professor, retired military officer*
Limbaugh, Ronald Hadley *retired historian, cultural organization administrator*

Torrance
Anderson, Marilyn Wheeler *English language educator*

COLORADO

Boulder
Engel, Barbara Alpern *history professor*
Hill, Boyd H., Jr. *medieval history educator*
Limerick, Patricia Nelson *history professor*
Rood, David S. *linguistics educator*
Taylor, Allan Ross *linguist, educator*

Colorado Springs
Barton, Ruth *retired language educator*
Cramer, Owen Carver *classics educator, department chairman*
Stavig, Mark Luther *language educator*
von Dassanowsky, Robert *literature and film professor, writer, producer*

Denver
Hassrick, Peter Heyl *art historian, educator*
Wetzel, Jodi (Joy Lynn Wetzel) *retired history and women's studies educator*

Golden
Sneed, Joseph Donald *philosophy educator, writer*

Grand Junction
Fay, Abbott Eastman *history professor*

Greeley
Worley, Lloyd Douglas *language educator*

Highlands Ranch
Cherno, Melvin *humanities educator*

Pueblo
Farwell, Hermon Waldo, Jr. *parliamentarian and speech educator*

HAWAII

Honolulu
Aung-Thwin, Michael Arthur *history educator*
Ball, Robert Jerome *classics educator*
Bender, Byron Wilbur *linguistics educator*
Dyen, Isidore *linguistic scientist, educator*
Jordan, Amos Azariah, Jr. *foreign affairs educator, retired military officer*
Rapson, Richard L. *history professor*
Schweizer, Niklaus R. *German educator*

MONTANA

Missoula
Kittredge, William Alfred *humanities educator*

NEVADA

Reno
Glotfelty, Cheryll *literature and language professor*

NEW JERSEY

West Paterson
Varley, Herbert Paul *Japanese language and cultural history educator*

NEW MEXICO

Albuquerque
Davies, Thomas Mockett, Jr. *history professor*
Hutton, Paul Andrew *historian, educator, writer*

Los Lunas
Melzer, Richard Anthony *historian, educator*

Santa Fe
Maehl, William Henry *historian, academic administrator, consultant*

OREGON

Eugene
Pascal, C(ecil) Bennett *classics educator*
Wickes, George *English literature educator, writer*

Keizer
Dmytryshyn, Basil *historian, educator*

Port Orford
Drinnon, Richard *retired historian*

Portland
Beckham, Stephen Dow *history educator*
Brashier, Kenneth E. *humanities educator*
Eifler, Karen Elizabeth *language educator*
Englert, Walter George *classics and humanities educator*
Faller, Thompson Mason *philosophy educator*
Steinman, Lisa Malinowski *English literature educator, writer*

UTAH

Provo
Lyon, James Karl *German language educator*
Peer, Larry Howard *literature educator*
Skinner, Andrew Charles *history professor, writer*

VIRGINIA

Charlottesville
Daugherty, Leo *literature and language educator*

Harrisonburg
Gelfand, Howard Michael *history professor*
White, Christopher Todd *language educator, anthropologist*

WASHINGTON

Bellevue
Ellison, Herbert Jay *retired historian, educator*

Bothell
Watts, Linda Susan *humanities educator*

Burien
Burgess, Charles Orville *history professor*

Cheney
Steiner, Henry-York *English language and literature educator*

Lake Forest Park
Adams, Hazard Simeon *retired language educator, writer*

Olympia
Coontz, Stephanie Jean *history professor, writer*

Seattle
Bozarth, George S. *historian, musicologist, musician*
Butow, Robert Joseph Charles *historian, educator*
Coburn, Robert Craig *philosopher, educator*
Coldewey, John Christopher *English literature educator*
Fine, Arthur I. *philosopher, educator*
Gerstenberger, Donna Lorine *humanities educator*
Harmon, Daniel Patrick *classics educator*
Heer, Nicholas Lawson *language educator*
Jones, Edward Louis *historian, educator*
Keyt, David *philosophy and classics educator*
Korg, Jacob *English literature educator*
Pressly, Thomas James *history professor*
Pyle, Kenneth Birger *historian, educator*
Sun, Yilin *language educator*
Ziadeh, Farhat J. *Middle Eastern studies educator*

Spokane
Carriker, Robert Charles *history professor*

Walla Walla
Edwards, Glenn Thomas *history educator*

WYOMING

Cody
Garry, James B. *historian, naturalist, storyteller, writer*
Price, B. Byron *historian*

Laramie
Chisum, Emmett Dewain *historian, researcher, archaeologist*

Powell
Myers, Rex Charles *historian, educator, retired dean*

CANADA

ALBERTA

Edmonton
Demers, Patricia A. *English literature professor*

BRITISH COLUMBIA

Burnaby
Kitchen, John Martin *historian, educator*

Vancouver
Bentley, Thomas Roy *retired language educator, writer*
Conway, John S. *history professor*
Newmeyer, Frederick Jaret *linguist, educator*
Overmyer, Daniel Lee *humanities educator*
Pacheco-Ransanz, Arsenio *language educator, historian, educator*
Unger, Richard Watson *history professor*

ADDRESS UNPUBLISHED

Attebery, Louie Wayne *language educator*
Batts, Michael Stanley *retired language educator*
Bosmajian, Haig Aram *speech communication educator*
Brack, O. M., Jr. *language educator*
Bremer, Ronald Allan *genealogist, editor*
Bush, Sarah Lillian *retired historian*
Clark, Eve Vivienne *linguist, educator*
Ellis, John Martin *German literature educator*
Elsbree, Langdon *English language educator*
Felstiner, Mary Lowenthal *retired history professor*
Forster, Merlin Henry *foreign languages educator, writer, researcher*
Gillespie, Gerald Ernest Paul *comparative literature educator, writer*
Hadda, Janet Ruth *language educator, lay psychoanalyst*
Kari, Daven Michael *English and religious studies professor*
Karlinsky, Simon *language educator, writer*
Karlstrom, Paul Johnson *art historian*
Kravitz, Ellen King *musicologist, educator*
Kultermann, Udo *architectural and art historian, educator, writer*
Leonard, Glen Milton *historian*
Lisio, Donald John *historian, educator*
Marcus, Karen Melissa *language educator*
Mathews, E. Anne Jones *retired library educator, academic administrator*
McMaster, Juliet Sylvia *English language educator*
Newmark, Leonard Daniel *linguistics educator*
Nix, Nancy Jean *librarian, designer*
Riasanovsky, Nicholas Valentine *retired historian, educator*
Rolle, Andrew *historian, writer*
Saint-Jacques, Bernard *linguistics educator*
Schwartz, Leon *foreign language educator*
Topik, Steven Curtis *historian, educator*
Toulmin, Stephen Edelston *humanities educator*
Wiener, Jon *history professor*
Wills, John Elliot, Jr. *retired historian, writer*

HUMANITIES: LIBRARIES

UNITED STATES

ALASKA

Anchorage
Keller, Karen A. *library director*

Juneau
Schorr, Alan Edward *librarian, publishing executive*

ARIZONA

Chandler
Brown, Brenda *library director*

Glendale
Caltabiano, Anne *library director*

Lake Havasu City
Mahan, James E. *archivist, educator*

Mesa
Schneider, Rebecca *librarian*
Wolf, Heather *library director*

Phoenix
Garvey, Toni *library director*
Wells, GladysAnn *library director*

Scottsdale
Hamilton, Rita *library director*

Tempe
Metros, Mary Teresa *librarian*

Tucson
Griffen, Agnes Marthe *retired library administrator*
Ledeboer, Nancy *library director*

CALIFORNIA

Alhambra
Birch, Tobeylynn *librarian*

Anaheim
Miller, Jean Ruth *retired librarian*
Stone, Carol *library director*

Bakersfield
Duquette, Diane Rhea *library director*

Berkeley
Buckland, Michael Keeble *librarian, educator*
Harlan, Robert Dale *library and information scientist, educator, academic administrator*
Leonard, Thomas C. *librarian, dean*
Minudri, Regina Ursula *librarian, consultant*

Chula Vista
Palmer, David J. *library director, municipal official*

Davis
Grossman, George Stefan *library director, law educator*
Sharrow, Marilyn Jane *library administrator*

Fremont
Hofacket, Jean *library director*
Wood, Linda May *librarian*

Fresno
Bosch Cobb, Karen *library director*

Fullerton
Ayala, John L. *retired librarian, dean*

Glendale
Hunt-Coffey, Nancy *library director*
Michelson, Lillian *librarian, researcher*
Woolls, Esther Blanche *library science educator*

Huntington Beach
Hayden, Ron L. *library director*

La Jolla
Mirsky, Phyllis Simon *librarian*

Long Beach
Schmidt, Eleanore *library director*

Los Angeles
Bates, Marcia Jeanne *information scientist educator*
Brecht, Albert Odell *library and information technology administrator*
Chang, Henry C. *library administrator*
Ciccone, Amy Navratil *art librarian*
Cuadra, Carlos Albert *library and information scientist, consultant*
Custen, Barbara S. *library director*
Gilman, Nelson Jay *library director*
Patron, Susan Hall *librarian, writer*
Quinlan, Catherine *library director*
Richardson, John Vinson, Jr. *library and information science professor*
Starr, Kevin *librarian, educator*

Menlo Park
White, Cecil Ray *librarian, consultant*

Mission Hills
Weber, Francis Joseph *archivist, museum director*

Modesto
Czopek, Vanessa *library director*

Monterey
Reneker, Maxine Hohman *librarian*

Northridge
Duran, Karin Jeanine *librarian*

Oakland
Green, David Edward *retired librarian, priest, translator*
Hafter, Ruth Anne *library director, educator*
Martinez, Carmen Lorena *library director*

Oceanside
Lange, Clifford Elmer *retired librarian*

Pollock Pines
Rickard, Margaret Lynn *library director, consultant*

Redlands
Burgess, Larry Eugene *library director, historian, educator*

Sacramento
Gold, Anne Marie *library director*
Killian, Richard M. *library director*

San Bernardino
Burgess, Michael (Robert Reginald) *librarian, writer*
Roop, Ophelia Georgiev *library director*

San Diego
Dyer, Charles Richard *law library director, educator*
Sannwald, William Walter *librarian*
Sauer, David Andrew *librarian, writer*
Schon, Isabel *library science specialist, educator*

San Francisco
Herrera, Luis *library director*

San Jose
Light, Jane Ellen *library director*
Schmidt, Cyril James *librarian*

San Luis Obispo
Dowell, David Ray *library administrator*

San Marcos
Ciurczak, Alexis *librarian*

San Marino
Robertson, Mary Louise *archivist, historian*

San Mateo
Johnson, Victoria L. *library director*

Santa Ana
Adams, John M. *library director*
Richard, Robert John *library director*

Santa Barbara
Johnson, Brenda L. *university librarian*
Keator, Carol Lynne *library director*

Santa Clara
Hopkinson, Shirley Lois *library and information scientist, educator*

Santa Monica
Levin, Barry Raymond *rare book dealer, film producer*

Sebastopol
Sabsay, David *library director, consultant*

Stanford
Derksen, Charlotte Ruth Meynink *librarian*
Keller, Michael Alan *librarian, musicologist*

Stockton
Rencher, Natalie R. *library director*
Yamashita, Kenneth Akira *library administrator, librarian*

Thousand Oaks
Brogden, Stephen Richard *library director*

Ventura
Kreissman, Starrett *librarian*

Yorba Linda
Naftali, Timothy J. *library director, historian, educator, writer*

COLORADO

Boulder
Bintliff, Barbara Ann *library director, law educator*
O'Brien, Elmer John *librarian, educator*

Canon City
Cochran, Susan Mills *research librarian*

Colorado Springs
Miller, Paula J. *library director*

Denver
Amore, Shirley C. *library director*
Garcia, June Marie *librarian*
Hainer, Eugene *state librarian*
Turner, Marcellus *library director*

Edwards
Chambers, Joan Louise *retired librarian, dean*

Grand Junction
Bragdon, Lynn Lyon *library administrator*

Lakewood
Knott, William Alan *library director*

Louisville
Maddock, Jerome Torrence *library and information scientist*

HAWAII

Hilo
Golian-Lui, Linda Marie *librarian*

Honolulu
Flynn, Joan Mayhew *librarian*
Mochida, Paula T. *library director*
Yee, Florence *library director*

IDAHO

Boise
Bolles, Charles Avery *librarian*
Joslin, Ann *state librarian*

Moscow
Force, Ronald Wayne *retired librarian*

MONTANA

Billings
Cochran, William Michael *librarian*

Helena
Fitzpatrick, Lois Ann *library administrator*
Staffeldt, Darlene Maria Preble *library direct*

NEVADA

Carson City
Jones, Sara Sue Fisher *librarian*
Rocha, Guy Louis *archivist, consultant, historian*

Henderson
Fay, Thomas F. *library director*

Las Vegas
Walters, Daniel L. *library director*

Reno
Cummings, Nancy *library director*
Hunsberger, Charles Wesley *library director*

NEW MEXICO

Albuquerque
Clarke, Julia L. *library director*
Freeman, Patricia Elizabeth *multi-media specialist, educational consultant*

Carlsbad
Regan Gossage, Muriel *librarian*

Santa Fe
Akeroyd, Richard G., Jr. *library director*
Wakashige, Benjamin Taka *librarian*

OREGON

Corvallis
Landers, Teresa Price *librarian*

Eugene
Edwards, Ralph M. *librarian*

Portland
Morgan, James Earl *librarian, administrator*

Salem
Oberg, Larry Reynold *librarian*
Scheppke, Jim *library director*
Turnbaugh, Roy Carroll *archivist*

UTAH

Orem
Hall, Blaine Hill *retired librarian*

Provo
Jensen, Richard Dennis *librarian*
Olsen, Randy J. *university librarian*

Salt Lake City
Morris, Donna Jones *library director*
Morrison, David Lee *librarian, educator*

Springville
Gillum, Gary Paul *retired librarian*

WASHINGTON

Issaquah
Ptacek, William H. *library director*

Olympia
Walsh, Jan *library director*
Zussy, Nancy Louise *librarian*

Seattle
Blase, Nancy Gross *librarian*
Boylan, Merle Nelson *librarian, educator*
Hildreth, Susan *library director*
Mason, Marilyn Gell *retired library administrator, writer, consultant*
Pearl, Nancy Linn *librarian*
Stroup, Elizabeth Faye *librarian*

Spokane
Burr, Robert Lyndon *information services specialist*
Bynagle, Hans Edward *library director, philosophy educator*
George, Aubrey Westmoreland *library direc*
Wirt, Michael James *library director*

WYOMING

Cheyenne
Boughton, Lesley D. *library director*

CANADA

ALBERTA

Lethbridge
Rand, Duncan Dawson *retired librarian*

ITISH COLUMBIA

toria
ards, Vincent Philip Haslewood *librarian*

SKATCHEWAN

gina
ell, Trevor John David *archivist*

katoon
nedy, Marjorie Ellen *librarian*

ADDRESS UNPUBLISHED

erson, Herschel Vincent *retired librarian*
erson, Rachael Keller (Rachael Keller) *tired library director*
er, Zachary Moshe *librarian*
am, Keith M. *librarian, educator, dministrator*
on, Allan Judge *retired librarian*
nan, Michael Joseph *retired library director, ucator*
ld, Martha Bernice *retired librarian*
or, Dorothy Deborah *retired librarian*
eman, Marian Isabel *librarian, educator*
nes, Fontayne *retired library director*
en, Kathleen Mary *retired librarian*
ins, Darrell Lee *librarian*
enberg, John Kenneth *retired librarian*
rop, Ann *retired librarian, educator*
Pali Jae *retired librarian, writer*
nhardt, Thomas Wilburn *librarian, library rector*
ell, Virginia Lee *retired librarian*
Donald, Alan Hugh *academic administrator*
nalko, James Paul *library association dministrator*
lty, Susan Louise *archivist*
n, Amy *library director*
son, Roger Lee *library director*
k, Marilyn Anne *retired librarian, piano acher*
nael, Molly (Mary E. Raphael) *retired brary director*
esinger, Deborah Lee *retired librarian*
osser, Anne Griffin *librarian*
l, Patricia Poldervaart *retired librarian, nsultant*
r, Anna *retired library director*
ngand, Darlene Erna *librarian, educator*
f, Cynthia Tribelhorn *librarian, educator*
ar, Bohdan Stephen *retired librarian, writer, litor*

HUMANITIES: MUSEUMS

UNITED STATES

ASKA

rbanks
itis, Aldona Claire *museum director, art storian*

IZONA

bee
avson, Carrie *museum director*

gstaff
nig, Robert Glass *museum director*
Michael J. *museum director*

ndale
stead, Sheila Louise *art gallery owner*

en Valley
, Harlan Gilbert *national park perintendent, business executive*

sa
l, Tray C. *museum director*

enix
nger, James K. *museum director*
nan, Michael Dennis *museum director*
nan, Roger Wayne *museum director*

ttsdale
entz, Cassandra *curator*

npe
in, Marilyn Audrey *former museum director*

son
y, Richard Halbert *museum director*
in, Charles Allan *museum director, artist*
, James Edward *retired museum director, nsultant*

LIFORNIA

ata
y, Stephen Fairchild *retired museum rector, ornithologist, birding tour guide*
Zielinski, Melissa L. *museum director*

Bakersfield
Enriquez, Carola Rupert *museum director*
Meyer, Charles G. *museum director*

Berkeley
Benedict, Burton *retired museum director, anthropologist*
Day, Lucille Lang *museum administrator, educator, writer*
Grossman, Bonnie *art gallery director*

Bodega Bay
Cohen, Daniel Morris *museum administrator, marine biologist, researcher*

Caliente
de Fonville, Paul Bliss *monument and library administrator*

Carlsbad
Nosanow, Barbara Shissler *museum director, curator*

Carson
Zimmerer, Kathy Louise *museum director*

Claremont
Moreno, William A. *museum director*

Culver City
Coolidge, Matthew *curator*

Death Valley
Martin, Richard H. *national park service executive*

Escondido
Killmar, Lawrence E. *animal park curator*

Fresno
Monaghan, Kathleen M. *art museum director*

La Jolla
Armstrong, Elizabeth Neilson *curator*
Beebe, Mary Livingstone *curator*
Davies, Hugh Marlais *museum director*

Long Beach
Nelson, Harold Bernhard *museum director*

Los Angeles
Barron, Stephanie *curator*
Brand, Michael *museum director*
Byrnes, James Bernard *museum director, consultant*
Hirano, Irene Ann Yasutake *museum director*
Holo, Selma Reuben *museum director, educator*
Hooks, Rosie Lee *museum director, actor, filmmaker*
Hopkins, Henry Tyler *museum director, art educator*
King, Duane Harold *museum administrator*
Naef, Weston John *retired museum curator*
Philbin, Ann *art facility director*
Pisano, Jane G. *museum administrator*
Rudolph, Jeffrey N. *museum director*
Strick, Jeremy *curator, museum director*
Woodworth, Patricia *museum administrator*

Los Olivos
Knowles, Elizabeth Pringle *museum director*

Newport Beach
Vine, Naomi *museum administrator*

Northridge
Lewis, Louise Miller *gallery director, art history educator*

Palm Springs
Nash, Steven Alan *museum director, curator, art historian*
Stearns, Robert Leland *curator*

Rancho Palos Verdes
Yassin, Robert Alan *museum director, curator*

Riverside
Esparza, Richard R. *museum director*
Green, Jonathan William *museum director, educator, artist, writer*
Warren, Katherine Virginia *art gallery director*

Sacramento
Jones, Lial A. *museum director*

San Diego
Cartwright, Derrick *museum director*
Hager, Michael W. *museum director*
Longenecker, Martha W. *museum director*
Ollman, Arthur Lee *museum director, photographer*
Sidner, Robert Brown *museum director*
Spencer, Ted M. *museum director*
Teagle, Rachel *museum director*

San Francisco
Becker, Stephen Arnold *museum administrator*
Benezra, Neal *museum director, curator*
Buchanan, John Edward, Jr. *museum director*
Farrington, Gregory C. *museum director, former academic administrator*
Leviton, Alan Edward *curator*
O'Neill, Brian *national recreation area administrator*
Rinder, Lawrence R. *museum director, curator*
Ross, David A. *art museum director*

San Jose
Hernandez, Jo Farb *museum director, consultant*
Krane, Susan *museum director, curator*
Norberg, Deborah Dorsey *museum administrator*

San Marino
Murdoch, John *museum director*

Santa Ana
Keller, Peter Charles *museum director, mineralogist*

Santa Barbara
Feinberg, Larry J. *museum director, curator*
Karpeles, David *museum director*

Santa Clara
Schapp, Rebecca Maria *museum director*

Stanford
Seligman, Thomas Knowles *museum administrator*

The Sea Ranch
Baas, Jacquelynn *museum director, art historian*

Yosemite National Park
Bates, Craig Dana *curator, ethnographer, government official*
Forgang, David M. *curator*

COLORADO

Alma
Swanson, Erik Christian *museum director*

Colorado Springs
LeMieux, Linda Dailey *museum director*

Denver
Downey, Tom *museum director, former lawyer*
Heinrich, Christoph *curator*
Sharp, Lewis Inman *museum director, curator*
Wilson, Steve *museum director*

Grand Junction
Bradley, William Steven *art museum director*

Parker
Smartt, Richard A. *museum director*

HAWAII

Fort Shafter
Fairfull, Thomas McDonald *museum director*

Honolulu
Ellis, George Richard *museum administrator*

Kaneohe
Lagoria, Georgianna Marie *curator, writer, editor, visual art consultant*

IDAHO

Boise
Swanson, Kenneth J. *museum administrator*

Coeur D' Alene
Dahlgren, Dorothy *museum director*

Pocatello
Jackson, Allen Keith *retired museum administrator*

Twin Falls
Woods, James C. *museum director*

MONTANA

Billings
Peterson, Robyn Gayle *museum director*

Deer Lodge
McWright, Michael J. *historic site administrator*

Missoula
Brown, Robert Munro *museum director*
Millin, Laura Jeanne *museum director*

NEVADA

Carson City
Barmore, James Gilbert *museum director, curator*

Las Vegas
Herridge, Elizabeth *museum director*
Lewis, Oli Parepa *curator*
Lumpkin, Libby *museum director*
Wolf, Arthur Henry *museum administrator*

NEW MEXICO

Alamogordo
House, George Michael *museum curator*

Albuquerque
Bawden, Garth Lawry *museum director*
Moore, James C. *museum director*
Solimon, Ronald James (Ron Soliman) *museum administrator*
Wright, Cathy L. *museum director*

Hobbs
Smith, Calvin Bruce *museum director*

Roswell
Rufe, Laurie J. *museum director*

Ruidoso Downs
Eldredge, Bruce Beard *museum director*

Santa Fe
Ice, Joyce *museum director*

Taos
Witt, David L. *curator, writer*

OREGON

Milwaukie
Eichinger, Marilynne Katzen *museum administrator*

Philomath
Zenev, Irene Louise *museum curator*

Portland
Stueber, Nancy *museum director*

Salem
Olbrantz, John Paul *museum director, art historian*

UTAH

Provo
Gray, Campbell *museum director*

Salt Lake City
George, Sarah B. *museum director*
Olsen, Steven Lloyd *museum administrator, educator*

WASHINGTON

Bellevue
Warren, James Ronald *retired museum director, journalist*

Bellingham
Clark-Langager, Sarah Ann *curator, academic administrator*

Redmond
Sobey, Edwin J. C. *museum director, oceanographer, consultant*

Seattle
Bufano, Ralph A. *retired museum executive*
Callan, Josi Irene *museum director*
Chew, Ron Alpha *museum director*
Garfield, Leonard *museum director*
Gates, Mimi Gardner *museum director*

Spokane
Rooney, Marsha *curator, museum staff member*

Tacoma
Close, Timothy (John Timothy Close) *museum director*

Yakima
Baule, John Alvin *museum director, consultant*

WYOMING

Devils Tower
Cartwright, Chas *national monument administrator*

Laramie
Breithaupt, Brent Henry *museum curator*
Moldenhauer, Susan *museum director, curator*

CANADA

ALBERTA

Canmore
Janes, Robert Roy *museum director, archaeologist, editor, consultant*

BRITISH COLUMBIA

Victoria
Finlay, James Campbell *retired museum director*

ADDRESS UNPUBLISHED

Andrews, Richard Otis *former art gallery director, curator*
Bettison, Cynthia Ann *museum director, archaeologist*
Consey, Kevin Edward *museum administrator*
Douglas, Diane Miriam *museum director*

Ebie, William D. *retired museum director*
Glad, Suzanne Lockley *retired museum director*
Glenn, Constance White *art museum director, educator, consultant*
Greaves, James Louis *art conservator*
Gribbon, Deborah *museum director*
Grinell, Sheila *museum director, consultant*
Houlihan, Patrick Thomas *museum director*
Kelm, Bonnie G. *art museum director, appraiser, educator, consultant*
Klobe, Tom *retired art gallery director*
López, Eugenio Alonso *art gallery owner, food products executive*
Lorenz, Marianne *curator*
Mason, James Albert *retired museum director, former university dean*
Pal, Pratapaditya *curator*
Payton, Cydney *museum director, curator*
Petersen, Martin Eugene *curator*
Rich, Andrea Louise *former museum administrator*
Roseman, Kim *gallery director*
Sanchez-Kennedy, Maria *museum director*
Sano, Emily Joy *former museum director*
Sauvey, Raymond Andrew *museum director*
Schumacher, Henry Jerold *museum director, retired military officer*
Segger, Martin Joseph *museum director, educator, art historian*
Shimoda, Jerry Yasutaka *retired national historic park manager*
Towe, A. Ruth *retired museum director*
Way, Jacob Edson III *museum director*
Wolf, Patricia B. *former museum director*
Yates, Steven A. *curator, artist*

INDUSTRY: MANUFACTURING
See also **FINANCE: FINANCIAL SERVICES**

UNITED STATES

ALASKA

Haines
Kaufman, David Graham *construction executive*

ARIZONA

Avondale
Rosztoczy, Ferenc Erno *construction and agricultural machinery executive*

Chandler
Elliott, Lee Ann *company executive, former government official*
Kim, James Joo-Jin *electronics company executive*

Gilbert
Earnhardt, Hal J. III *automotive executive*

Phoenix
Carter, Ronald Martin, Sr. *pharmaceutical executive*
Church, Steve *electronics executive*
Follette, William Albert *electronics company executive*
Giedt, Bruce Alan *paper company executive*
Giltner, Phil (F. Phillips Giltner III) *food distributing executive*
Hamada, Rick *electronics executive*
Kamins, Edward *electronics executive*
Mondry, Lawrence N. *automotive executive*
Phillips, Steve *electronics executive*
Pulatie, David L. *metal products executive*
Sadowski, Raymond *electronics executive*
Stegmayer, Joseph Henry *housing industry executive*
Vallee, Roy A. *electronics executive*
Van Horssen, Charles Arden *manufacturing executive*
White, Edward Allen *electronics executive*

Scottsdale
Dion, Philip Joseph *consumer products and services executive, real estate and construction company executive*
Farley, James Newton *retired manufacturing executive, electrical engineer*
Freedman, Stanley Marvin *manufacturing executive*
Howard, William Gates, Jr. *electronics company executive*
Rethore, Bernard Gabriel *manufacturing and mining company executive, consultant*
Van Brunt, Gary T. *tire dealer company executive*
Walsh, Edward Joseph *food products and cosmetics executive*

Tucson
Finley, Dorothy Hunt *beverage distribution company executive*
Francesconi, Louise L. *defense equipment manufacturing company executive*
Meeker, Robert Eldon *retired manufacturing company executive*
Repp, Page W., Jr. *construction executive*

CALIFORNIA

Agoura Hills
Deitchle, Gerald Wayne *restaurant company executive*

Aliso Viejo
Morrison, Patricia B. *former electronics executive*
Pearson, J. Michael *pharmaceutical executive*
Yakatan, Gerald Joseph *pharmaceutical executive*

Anaheim
Palfenier, David *food products executive*

Atherton
Goodman, Sam Richard *electronics executive*

Berkeley
Castello, John L. *pharmaceutical executive*

Beverly Hills
Kardashian, Kim (Kimberly Noel Kardashian) *apparel retailer, television personality*
Winthrop, John *wines and spirits company executive*

Burbank
Adams, William B. *chemical company executive*
Gelwix, Max D. *chemical company executive*
Joseff, Joan Castle *manufacturing executive*
Raulinaitis, Pranas Algis *electronics executive, consultant*

Calabasas
Dreier, R. Chad (Robert Chad Dreier) *construction and mortgage company executive*
Sperber, Burton S. *construction executive*

Camarillo
Cleary, Thomas Charles *technology company executive*
Weiss, Carl *aerospace company executive*

Carlsbad
Baker, Donna M. *research and development company executive, lawyer*
Crooke, Stanley Thomas *pharmaceutical executive*
Hammes, Michael Noel *automotive company executive*

Carmel Valley
Kasson, James Matthews *electronics executive*

Carson
Berenato, Joseph C. *manufacturing executive*
Heiser, James S. *manufacturing executive*

Chatsworth
Bhartia, Prakash *defense research management executive, educator*

Coachella
Barker, Douglas P. *food products executive*

Coronado
Sack, Edgar Albert *electronics company executive*

Costa Mesa
Hazewinkel, Van *manufacturing executive*
Laidlaw, Victor D. *construction executive*

Culver City
Leve, Alan Donald *electronics executive*

Cupertino
Mathias, Leslie Michael *electronic manufacturing company executive*
Sobrato, John A. *construction executive*

Cypress
Bowlus, Brad A. *health care company executive*
Schembri, David Charles *automotive company executive*

Davis
Bennett, Alan B. *research and development company executive, educator*

Del Mar
Cooper, Martin *electronics company executive*
Mulford, Rand Perry *health products executive, consultant*

Delano
Caratan, Anton G. *food products executive*

Dublin
Whetten, John D. *food products executive*

El Segundo
Thiry, Kent J. *health products executive*
Whitney, Richard K. *health products executive*

Emeryville
Goldstein, Jack *biopharmaceutical executive, microbiologist*
O'Dea, Patrick J. *food products executive*
Renton, Hollings C. *health products executive*

Encinitas
Bartok, Michelle *cosmetic company executive*

Escalon
Barton, Gerald Lee *farming company executive*

Foothill Ranch
Baden, Colin *apparel executive*
La Duc, John *manufacturing executive*

Foster City
Denny, James M. *pharmaceutical and former retail executive*
Martin, John C. *pharmaceutical company executive*
Perry, Mark L. *medical products executive*
Rabbat, Guy *electronics executive, consultant*
White, Tony L. *health and medical products executive*

Fremont
Alsborg, Thomas C. *electronics executive*
Bagley, James W. *semiconductor equipment company executive*
Blair, Robert L. *technology company executive*
Chan, Fred S.L. *electronics company executive*
Chuang, Kevin *electronics manufacturing executive*
Conlisk, Raimon L. *high technology management consulting executive*
Guire, Ronald W. *electronics company executive*
Huang, Robert T. *electronics executive*
Murai, Kevin M. *electronics executive*
Newberry, Stephen G. *semiconductor equipment company executive*
Polk, Dennis *electronics executive*
Rusch, Thomas William *manufacturing executive*
Shah, Ajay *electronics executive*
Zimmer, George A. *men's apparel executive*

Fullerton
Garrett, Scott T. *medical products executive*
Miller, Arnold *electronics executive*
Wareham, John L. *electronics executive*

Glendale
Harris, John J. *food products executive*

Glendora
Cahn, David Stephen *cement company executive*

Greenfield
Munoz, John Joseph *retired transportation company executive*

Hillsborough
Keller, John Francis *retired food products executive, mayor*
Schapiro, George A. *electronics executive*

Hollywood
Parks, Robert Myers *appliance manufacturing company executive*

Huntington Beach
McKnight, Robert B., Jr. *sporting goods manufacturing executive*

Irvine
Alspach, Philip Halliday *manufacturing executive*
Click, James H. *automotive executive*
Fisker, Henrik *automobile designer and company executive*
McGregor, Scott A. *electronics company executive*
Mussey, Joseph Arthur *health and medical product executive*
Olson, Gene L. *food products executive*
Peterson, Jeffrey V. *construction executive*
Pyott, David Edmund Ian *pharmaceutical executive*
Salesky, William Jeffrey *corporate executive*
Wetterau, Mark S. *food products/distributor executive*
Zeleny, Dennis *food products executive*

La Jolla
Snyder, Evan *stem cell biologist, neuroscientist, physician, educator*

Lafayette
Romanowski, Bill (William Thomas Romanowski) *nutrition company executive, retired professional football player, actor*

Lake Forest
Higby, Lawrence M. *medical products executive*

Lompoc
Bongiorno, James William *electronics executive*

Long Beach
Kanner, Edwin Benjamin *electrical manufacturing company executive*

Los Alamitos
Caplan, Karen B. *food products executive*

Los Angeles
Adler, Fred Peter *retired electronics company executive*
Aroesty, Sidney A. *medical diagnostic manufacturing company executive*
Campanella, Yvette Lynn *cosmetics executive*
Charney, Dov *apparel executive*
Gerstell, A. Frederick *manufacturing executive*
Golleher, George *food company executive*
Hannah, David H. *metal products executive*
Hollinger, William R. *construction executive*
Jones, Jerve Maldwyn *construction company executive*
Karges, William A. III *food company executive*
Marciano, Maurice *apparel executive*
Marciano, Paul L. *apparel executive*
Mezger, Jeffrey T. *construction executive*
Murdock, David H. *food products executive*
Perkins, William Clinton *manufacturing executive*
Resnick, Stewart Allen *diversified company executive*
Tamkin, S. Jerome *manufacturing executive consultant*

Malibu
Berman, Stephen G. *toy manufacturing exe*

Mckinleyville
Thueson, David Orel *pharmaceutical execu researcher, writer, educator*

Menlo Park
Carlson, Curtis R. *electronics research indu executive*
Halperin, Robert Milton *retired electrical machinery company executive*
Marks, Michael E. *electronics executive*
Moos, Walter Hamilton *pharmaceutical cor executive*
Okarma, Thomas Bernard *biotechnology company executive*
Reed, Kathleen Rand *manufacturer, market consultant, sociologist*
Saifer, Mark Gary Pierce *pharmaceutical executive*
Taft, David Dakin *chemicals executive*

Milpitas
Forsyth, G. Fred *electronics executive*
Hasler, William Albert *electronics executive*
Stephens, Bob *electronics executive*
Swanson, Robert H., Jr. *electronics executi*
Wang, Susan S. *manufacturing executive*

Mission Viejo
Sganga, John B. *retired furniture holding company executive*

Monterey
Meyers, Gerald A. *metal products executive*

Mountain View
Reidel, Arthur *health products executive, semiconductor company executive*

Newport Beach
Johnson, William Stanley *metal distributior company executive*
Lerner, Sandy *cosmetics executive*
Lyon, William, Sr. *construction executive*
Mohajer, Dineh *cosmetics company executi*
Siegel, David M. *construction executive*

Oakland
Heinrich, Daniel J. *chemicals executive*
Kahn, Timothy F. *food products company executive*
Kane, Jacqueline P. *chemical company exec*

Oceanside
Montgomery, Michael Davis *research and development company executive, real est investor*

Palo Alto
Balzhiser, Richard Earl *research and development company executive*
Bennett, Alan Jerome *electronics executive, physicist*
Guertin, Timothy E. *medical products exec*
Kung, Frank F. *biotechnology and life scier investor, venture capitalist*
Sager, Philip Travis *pharmaceutical executi cardiologist, researcher*
Smith, Julie Ann *pharmaceutical executive*
Staprans, Armand *electronics executive*
Sweitzer, Michael Cook *healthcare product executive*

Palos Verdes Estates
Mackenbach, Frederick W. *welding produc manufacturing company executive*

Pasadena
Bishop, Robert Calvin *pharmaceutical com executive*
Davidson, Robert C., Jr. *manufacturing exe*
Hunter, Milton *construction company exec retired career military officer*
Kresa, Kent *manufacturing executive, retir aerospace executive*
Marlen, James S. *chemical, plastics and bu materials manufacturing company execu*
McNulty, James F. *construction company executive*
Smith, Howard Russell *manufacturing exec director*
Watson, Noel G. *construction executive*

Petaluma
Womack, Thomas Houston *manufacturing executive*

Placerville
Magelitz, Larry L. *construction company executive*
Sundgren, Donald E. *construction executive*

Playa Del Rey
Mishelevich, David Jacob *medical product executive*

asanton
d, David F. *food products executive*
ng, David T. *food products executive*
ick, Neil Francis *retired medical products wholesale executive*
ss, Robert Stephen *medical manufacturing company operating executive*

nona
wn, Ronald G. *automotive company executive*
arty, Charles J. *automotive executive*

way
nhart, Douglas Edward *construction company executive*

ncho Cordova
chetti, David J. *manufacturing executive*

ncho Mirage
enbaum, James Richard *liquor distributing company executive, real estate developer*

ncho Santa Fe
, Eugene Lee *retired pharmaceutical executive*

dding
nerson, Archie Aldis (Red Emmerson, A.A. mmerson) *sawmill owner*

londo Beach
iwada, Reynold Shigeru *electronics executive*

lwood City
nson, Edward J. *electronics corporation and ancial executive*
nser, George, Jr. *electronics executive*
ler, Peter Cole *construction company executive*
sants, John F. *electronics executive*

hmond
nan, Paul E. *pharmaceutical company executive*

Vista
rnoff, Daniel Lester *pharmaceutical executive, consultant*

erside
h, Elden Leroy *recreational vehicle and anufactured housing company executive*

ramento
cigaluppi, Roger John *agricultural products executive*

nas
ivel, Joe G. *food products executive*
or, Steven Bruce *agriculture company executive*

Anselmo
verini, John Edward *construction company executive*

Bernardino
h, Phillip J. *food products executive*

Carlos
, Ted W. *biotechnology company executive*
ack, Betty Gillespie *retired health care rvices executive*

Clemente
, Earnest Hubert, Jr. *tool company executive*

Diego
ne, Brian Kiernan *pet food and supplies mpany executive*
s, Richard B. *pharmaceutical executive*
zler, Jay D. *pharmaceutical executive*
s, Alan James *pharmaceutical executive, armacologist*
r, Paul Victor *pharmaceutical executive*
ica, Joseph A. *pharmaceutical executive*
, Robert E. *manufacturing executive*
Gene Wells *industrial executive*
os, Alexander Gus *construction and ofessional sports team executive*
, Harry Williams *aircraft propulsion system mpany executive*
, Walter Joseph *electronic products anufacturing company executive*

Francisco
rson, R. John *apparel executive*
obell, Jeffrey C. *health products executive*
mergren, John H. *health products executive*
kins, Trip *electronics executive*
n, Paul C. *health products executive*
n, Simon *apparel executive*
rgan, Kevin M. *retail apparel company executive*
, David William *research executive*
oney, David L. *former pharmaceutical olesale and healthcare management mpany executive*
n, Terence D. *food products executive*
or, Robert E. *building materials company ecutive, lawyer*
rs, David L. *food products executive*
n, Marc E. *health products executive*
Rogers, T. Gary *apparel company executive, former food products company executive*
Seelenfreund, Alan *retired pharmaceutical company executive*
Simmons, Sabrina L. *apparel executive*
Slipsager, Henrik C. *building services company executive*
Spratt, Randall N. *healthcare services and information technology executive*
Thacher, Carter Pomeroy *diversified manufacturing company executive*
Tully, Herbert Bullard *chemical manufacturing executive*
Wilson, John B. *clothing company executive*
Wolford, Richard G. *food products executive*
Wyatt, Tom (John Thomas Wyatt) *apparel executive*
Zellerbach, William Joseph *retired paper company executive*

San Jose
Ackel, Rick R. *electronics manufacturing executive*
Bell, W. Donald *electronics executive*
Faggin, Federico *electronics executive*
Fry, David *electronics executive*
Fry, John C. *electronics executive*
Hill, Richard S. *manufacturing executive*
Pausa, Clements Edward *electronics company executive*
Perlegos, George *electronics executive*
Rodgers, T(hurman) J. *semiconductor company executive*
Rosendin, Raymond Joseph *electrical contracting company executive*
Rostoker, Michael David *retired micro-electronics company executive*
Schroeder, Kenneth L. *electronics executive*
Simon, Ralph E. *electronics executive*
Sola, Jure *electronics executive*
Steinberg, Charles Allan *electronics manufacturing company executive*
White, David L. *electronics executive*
Wozniak, Curtis S. *electronics executive*
Zaro, Brad A. *research and development company executive, biologist*

San Mateo
Kennedy, W(ilbert) Keith, Jr. *retired electronics executive, transportation executive*

San Pedro
Hamai, James Yutaka *manufacturing executive*

San Rafael
Parker, Pam *apparel manufacturing company executive*

San Ramon
Bruns, George H. *electronics executive*
Cosmez, Mark H., II, *electronics executive*
Mariotta, Claudio *electronics executive*
Stabbert, Frederick Joseph *paper company executive*

Santa Ana
Baumgartner, Anton Edward *automotive sales professional*
Falstrup, Asger *electronics executive*

Santa Barbara
Prindle, William Roscoe *retired glass company executive*

Santa Clara
Barrett, Craig R. *electronics company executive*
Barrett, Ronald W. *biopharmaceutical executive*
Davis, George S. *manufacturing executive*
Fodor, Stephen P. A. *chemical company executive*
Grove, Andrew Steven *electronics executive*
Halla, Brian L. *electronics executive*
Huang, Jen-Hsun *electronics executive*
Larson, William *electronics executive*
Lee, Jimmy S.M. *electronic executive*
Logan, Mark Byron *optics corporation executive*
Maloney, Sean M. *electronics company executive*
Moore, Gordon E. *electronics executive, researcher*
Morgan, James C. *retired manufacturing executive*
Murray, Patricia *electronics company executive*
Otellini, Paul S. *electronics company executive*
Pinto, Mark R. *manufacturing executive*
Solomon, Darlene J.S. *electronics executive*
Splinter, Michael R. *manufacturing executive*
Sullivan, William P. *electronics executive*
Wang, David N.K. *chemical company executive*

Santa Maria
Ferini, Robert Pat *agricultural products company executive*

Santa Monica
Rosensweig, Daniel L. *video gaming company executive*

Santa Paula
Dillard, Michael L. *food products company executive*

Saratoga
Houston, Joseph Brantley, Jr. *optical instrument company executive*
Rollo, F. David *healthcare company executive, cardiologist*

Sebastopol
Graham, Howard Holmes *winemaker, restaurant manager, small business owner, retired financial executive*

Simi Valley
Weiser, Paul David *manufacturing executive*

South San Francisco
Brewer, Richard B. *biotechnology company executive*
Desmond-Hellmann, Susan *medical products manufacturing executive*
Walker, John P. *pharmaceutical executive*
Young, James W. *biotechnology company executive*

Stanford
Elliott, David Duncan III *science company executive*
Miller, William Frederick *research and development company executive, educator, financial consultant*

Sun Valley
Kamins, Philip E. *diversified manufacturing company executive*

Sunnyvale
Bachman, Brian Richard *former electronics executive*
Barnes, W. Michael *electronics executive*
Bowman, A. Blaine *electronics executive*
Brachman, Ron *research and development company executive*
Burkett, Marvin D. *electronics executive*
Doluca, Tunc *electronics executive*
Gutshall, Thomas L. *clinical diagnostics company executive*
Lewis, John Clark, Jr. *retired manufacturing company executive*
McCollam, Craig A. *manufacturing executive*
Smith, Lonnie Max *diversified industries executive*
Yancey, Gary *electronics executive*

Sylmar
Tutor, Ronald N. *construction executive*

Thousand Oaks
Birren, James Emmett *research and development company executive*
Bonanni, Fabrizio *medical products executive*
Bradway, Robert *medical products executive*
Hanagan, Thomas James *medical products executive*
McNamee, Brian *medical products executive*
Morrow, George J. *medical products executive*
Perlmutter, Roger *medical products executive*
Sharer, Kevin W. *medical products executive*

Torrance
Edelbrock, O. Victor *automotive part manufacturing executive*
Ismail, Alexandre *diversified technology and manufacturing company executive*
Mendel, John W. *automotive executive*
Thompson, Jeffrey L. *automotive parts manufacturing executive*

Tustin
Hester, Norman Eric *chemical company technical executive, chemist*
Legere, Edward J. *health products executive*

Upland
Goodman, John M. *construction executive*

Valencia
House, David L. *electronics components company executive*
Mann, Alfred *pharmaceutical executive*

Ventura
Barber, Jerry Randel *retired medical device company executive*

Walnut
Shontere, James G. *construction executive*

Watsonville
Barton, William E. *construction company executive*
Costanzo, Patrick M. *construction executive*
Doney, William G. *construction executive*
Watts, David H. *construction company executive*

Westlake Village
Colburn, Keith W. *electronics executive*
DeLorenzo, David A. *food products executive*
Lullo, Thomas A. *electronics executive*

Woodland Hills
Brandenberg, Frank G. *electronics executive*
Brown, Michael R. *former defense industry executive*
Capezza, Joseph C. *health insurance company executive*
Frame, Larry A. *electronics executive*
Gellert, Jay M. *health and medical products executive*
Greaves, Roger F. *health and medical products executive*
Mayhew, Karin D. *health and medical products executive*
Scheff, Jonathan H. *health and medical products executive*
Sivori, John P. *health and medical products executive*
Woys, James E. *health and medical products executive*

Woodside
Gates, Milo Sedgwick *retired construction company executive*

COLORADO

Berthoud
Abbott, David L. *agricultural products executive*

Boulder
Clark, Melvin Eugene *chemical company executive*
Crane, Lansing E. *paper company executive*

Broomfield
Hayes, John A. *packaging company executive*
Hoover, R. David *packaging company executive*
Marcy, Charles Frederick *food company executive*

Carbondale
Mattis, Louis Price *pharmaceutical and consumer products company executive*

Centennial
Reese, Monte Nelson *agricultural association executive*

Colorado Springs
Cimino, Jay *automotive company executive*

Denver
Alvarado, Linda G. *construction executive*
Henry, Charles L. (Jerry) *manufacturing executive*
Leprino, James G. *food products executive*
Livingston, Johnston Redmond *manufacturing executive*
Marcum, Walter Phillip *manufacturing executive*
Mizel, Larry A. *housing construction company executive*
Nields, Morgan Wesson *medical supply company executive*
Swinburn, Peter *brewery company executive*
Wolf, Timothy Van de Wint *food products executive*

Golden
Coors, Peter Hanson *brewery company executive*

Greeley
Carrico, Stephen J. *construction company executive*
Morgensen, Jerry Lynn *construction company executive*

Lone Tree
Bauer, Randy Mark *management training firm executive*

Niwot
Duerden, John H. *apparel executive*

Wellington
Grant, Lewis O. *agricultural products executive, meteorology educator*

FLORIDA

Clearwater
Newman, Francis A. *medical device company executive*

Englewood
Richard, Edward H. *manufacturing executive, retired municipal official*

West Palm Beach
Tollenaere, Lawrence Robert *retired industrial products company executive*

Winter Park
Merrill, Harvie Martin *retired manufacturing executive*

GEORGIA

Atlanta
Mattia, Thomas Gerard *beverage company executive*

HAWAII

Honolulu
Goth, Harvey L. *construction company executive*
Schuler, James K. *construction executive*

Kaneohe
Vincent, Thomas James *retired manufacturing executive*

IDAHO

Boise
Appleton, Steven R. *electronics executive*
Foster, Ronald C. *electronics executive*
Groce, Augustus Ben *paper company executive*

Hanks, Stephen Grant *construction executive, lawyer*
Harad, George Jay *retired manufacturing executive*
Hawkins, Jay L. *electronics executive*
Hlobik, Lawrence S. *agricultural products executive*
Lewis, Roderic W. *electronics executive, lawyer*
Miller, Jon Hamilton *forest products company executive*
Simplot, Scott R. *diversified food products company executive*
Washington, Dennis R. *contracting company executive*

Hayden Lake
Wogsland, James Willard *retired heavy machinery manufacturing executive*

MONTANA

Big Sky
Ryan, Raymond D. *retired steel and insurance company executive*

Bozeman
Minton, Dwight Church *manufacturing executive*

Great Falls
Semenza, Dirk A. *metal fabrication executive*
Sletten, John Robert *construction company executive*

Helena
Warren, Christopher Charles *electronics executive*

NEVADA

Boulder City
Johnsen, Ken C. *steel products company executive*

Henderson
Fiore, Nicholas Francis *metal products executive*

Las Vegas
Adcock, Corey J. *construction executive*
Strahan, Julia Celestine *electronics company executive*

Reno
Jacobson, Raymond Earl *electronics executive*

NEW MEXICO

Albuquerque
Friberg, George Joseph *electronics company executive, entrepreneur*
King, James Nedwed *construction company executive, lawyer*
Roberts, Dennis William *construction executive*
Winfield, Armand Gordon *retired international plastics consultant, educator*
Woltil, Robert D. *healthcare management company executive*

Los Alamos
Gregg, Charles Thornton *research and development company executive, molecular biologist, researcher*

Sandia Park
Wilczynski, Janusz S. *manufacturing executive, retired physicist*

Santa Fe
Odell, John H. *construction executive*
Robinson, Charles Wesley *boat design company executive*

NEW YORK

New York
Denmark, Bernhardt *manufacturing executive*

OREGON

Beaverton
Bird, Lewis L. III *apparel executive*
Blair, Donald W. *apparel executive*
Clarke, Thomas E. *apparel executive*
Denson, Charles D. *apparel executive*
DeStefano, Gary M. *apparel executive*
Edwards, Trevor *apparel executive*
Jackson, Jeanne Pellegren *apparel executive, former investment company executive*
Knight, Philip Hampson *apparel executive*
Parker, Mark G. *apparel executive*
Slade, Colin L. *electronics manufacturing executive*
Wills, Richard H. *electronics manufacturing executive*

Bend
Babcock, Walter Christian, Jr. *membrane company executive*

Hillsboro
Barnes, Keith Lee *electronics executive*

Klamath Falls
Wendt, Richard L. *manufacturing executive*

Medford
De Boer, Sidney B. *automotive executive*
Heimann, M.L. (Dick Heimann) *auto dealership executive*

Odell
Garcia, David *agricultural products executive*
Girardelli, Ronald K. *food products executive*

Portland
Carter, John D. *metal products executive*
Cassard, Christopher D. *lumber company executive*
Donegan, Mark *metal products executive*
Larsson, William Dean *metal products executive*
Pamplin, Robert Boisseau, Sr. *retired textile manufacturing executive*
Pamplin, Robert Boisseau, Jr. *manufacturing company executive, minister, writer*
Watkins, Charles Reynolds *medical equipment company executive*
Whitsell, Helen Jo *lumber executive*

Springfield
Detlefsen, William David, Jr. *chemicals executive*

SOUTH DAKOTA

Rapid City
Daughenbaugh, Randall Jay *retired chemical company executive, consultant*

TEXAS

Austin
Beyer, Richard Michael *manufacturing executive*

UTAH

Heber City
Day, Gerald W. *wholesale grocery company executive*

Saint George
Bangerter, Norman Howard *building contractor, developer, former governor, Former Governor, Utah*

Salt Lake City
Dew, Bill *construction executive*
Esplin, J. Kimo *chemicals executive*
Gregory, Herold La Mar *chemical company administrator*
Hankins, Anthony P. *chemicals executive*
Hembree, James D. *retired chemical company executive*
Horan, John J. *pharmaceutical company executive*
Hulme, Paul G. *chemicals executive*
Huntsman, Jon Meade, Sr. *chemicals company executive*
Huntsman, Peter R. *chemicals executive*
Keenan, Thomas J. *chemicals executive*
Kern, Michael J. *chemicals executive*
Ninow, Kevin J. *chemicals executive*
Oyler, James Russell, Jr. *manufacturing executive*
Ridd, Brian V. *chemicals executive*
Stanutz, Donald J. *chemicals executive*
Stitley, James Walter, Jr. *food manufacturing executive*

Sandy
Bland, Dorothy Ann *construction executive, real estate agent*

Vineyard
Brown, Birchel S. *steel products company executive*
Cannon, Joseph A. *steel products company executive, political party official*

WASHINGTON

Bellevue
Cardillo, James G. *automotive executive*
Cremin, Robert W. *manufacturing executive*
Gangl, Kenneth R. *automotive executive*
Lepore, Dawn Gould *Internet pharmaceutical company executive*
Pigott, Charles McGee *transportation equipment manufacturing executive*
Pigott, Mark C. *automotive executive*
Plimpton, Thomas E. *automotive executive*
Tembreull, Michael A. *automotive executive*
Young, Frank Nolan, Jr. *commercial building contracting company executive*

Bellingham
Henley, Dale C. *grocery company executive*

Bothell
Stein, Michael A. *pharmaceutical executive*

Coupeville
Thom, Richard David *retired electronics executive*

Eastsound
Anders, William Alison *aerospace and defense manufacturing executive*

Everett
Helsell, Robert M. *construction executive*

Federal Way
Bedient, Patricia M. *paper company executive*
Corbin, William R. *wood products executive*
Fulton, Daniel S. *paper company executive*
Hogans, Mack L. *paper company executive*
Rogel, Steven R. *paper company executive*

Kent
Hebeler, Henry Koester *retired electronics executive, aerospace engineer*

Lake Tapps
Huck, Larry Ralph *manufacturing executive, sales consultant*

Longview
Wollenberg, Richard Peter *paper manufacturing company executive*

Manson
Stager, Donald K. *retired construction company executive*

Mill Creek
Lowber, Stephen Scott *financial executive*

Mountlake Terrace
Kallshian, Jan *electronics manufacturing company executive*
Thompson, David C. *electronics manufacturing company executive*

Redmond
Fils-Aime, Reggie *electronics executive*
Hatlen, Joel S. *electronics manufacturing executive*
Lombard, George *electronics company executive*
Panke, Helmut *retired automotive executive*

Seattle
Albrecht, Richard Raymond *retired manufacturing executive, lawyer*
Behnke, Carl Gilbert *beverage franchise executive*
Bundrant, Charles H. *food products executive*
Casey, M. Michael *food products executive*
Denson, Nikkole E. *beverage company executive, film producer*
Friend, Stephen H. *biotechnology company executive*
Gillis, Steven *biotechnology company executive*
Holley, Rick R. *lumber company executive*
Kilpatrick, John Aaron *construction and development company executive*
Lincoln, Howard *manufacturing company and sports team executive*
Schoenfeld, Walter Edwin *manufacturing executive*

Spokane
Siegel, Louis Pendleton *retired forest products executive*
Tarr, Gregory L. *health and medical products company executive*

Tacoma
Tash, Graham Andrew, Jr. *automobile retail company executive*

Tukwila
Harnish, John J. *manufacturing executive*

Vancouver
Berglund, Carl Neil *electronics company executive*

WISCONSIN

Milwaukee
Hanson, John Nils *industrial high technology manufacturing company executive*

WYOMING

Wilson
Gordon, Stephen Maurice *manufacturing company executive, rancher*

CANADA

ALBERTA

Calgary
Holman, J(ohn) Leonard *retired manufacturing corporation executive*
Lipton, Jeffrey Marc *chemicals executive*

Edmonton
Katz, Daryl A. *pharmaceutical executive, entrepreneur, professional sports team executive*

SASKATCHEWAN

Regina
Phillips, Roger *retired steel company execut*

ADDRESS UNPUBLISHED

Abbe, Charles J. *manufacturing executive*
Anderegg, Karen Klok *business executive*
Asura, John F. *paper company executive*
Bender, John C. *paper company executive*
Bennett, Paul Grover *agribusiness executive*
Bos, John Arthur *retired aircraft manufactu executive*
Brann, Alton Joseph *manufacturing executi*
Bres, Philip Wayne *automotive executive*
Casamento, Charles Joseph *pharmaceutical industry executive*
Chao, Allen Y. *pharmaceutical executive*
Chaykin, Robert Leroy *manufacturing and marketing executive*
Chiplin, John *medical company executive*
Chu, James *electronics executive*
Coors, Jeffrey H. *technology manufacturing executive*
Coors, William K. *retired brewery company executive*
DeLustro, Frank Anthony *biomedical comp executive, research immunologist*
Derbes, Daniel William *manufacturing exec*
Dickerson, Gary E. *former electronics exec*
Dinkel, John George *automotive executive, consultant*
Ehrhorn, Richard William *electronics execu*
Engle, Steven B. *biotechnology company executive*
Evans, Barton, Jr. *retired analytical instrum company executive*
Fenton, Dennis Michael *retired medical pro executive*
Fogg, Richard Lloyd *food products executi*
Fritz, Rene Eugene *manufacturing executive*
Garruto, John Anthony *cosmetics executive*
Gaynor, C.W. *paper company executive*
George, Robert D. *technology corporation executive*
Glover, James Todd *manufacturing executiv*
Graber, William Raymond *former pharmaceutical executive*
Granchelli, Ralph S. *company executive*
Gurney, Daniel Sexton *race car manufactu company and racing team executive*
Haas, Robert Douglas *retired apparel comp executive*
Halle, Bruce T. *automotive products compa executive*
Hamilton, Darden Cole *construction management company executive*
Hammann, Gregg C. *fitness equipment exec*
Hanson, Larry Keith *plastics company exec*
Hanson, Richard E. *retired paper company executive*
Hausman, Arthur Herbert *electronics comp executive*
Heiner, Dennis Grant *manufacturing execut*
Herbert, Gavin Shearer *health care product company executive*
Hind, Harry William *pharmaceutical comp executive*
Hirai, Kazuo (Kaz) *electronics executive*
Hirsch, Horst Eberhard *metal products exec consultant*
Hitchcock, Frederick E., Jr., (Fritz) *automo company executive*
Hixson, Harry F., Jr. *health products execu*
Hume, Frederick Raymond *electronics exec*
Ingle, M(orton) Blakeman *chemicals execu*
Inouye, Michael K. *medical products comp executive*
Jackson, Hunter *health products executive*
Jenkins, Maynard L., Jr. *automotive executi*
Johnston, Lawrence R. (Larry Johnston) *re food products executive*
Kaiser, Glen David *construction company executive*
Kaplan, Jerry (S. Jerrold Kaplan) *former electronics company executive*
Kavli, Fred *retired manufacturing and engineering executive, physicist*
Kern, Irving John *retired food company executive*
Kiely, W. Leo, III, (Leo Kiely) *retired brev company executive*
Laney, Michael L. *manufacturing executive*
Lehrer, Steven *health products executive*
Littman, Irving *forest products company executive*
Lombard, Kenneth T. *beverage and music company executive*
Madden, Richard Blaine *forest products executive*
Mahoney, Gerald Francis *manufacturing executive*
Malone, James Richard *manufacturing exe*
Marineau, Philip Albert *apparel executive*
Matthews, William *health products executi*
McEachern, Alexander *electronics executiv*
McKennon, Keith Robert *chemical compar executive*
Meyer, Jerome J. *diversified technology company executive*
Midgett, Leon A. *manufacturing executive*
Moretti, August Joseph *pharmaceutical executive, lawyer*
Nanula, Richard D. *former heath products company executive*

holas, Henry Thompson III *former electronics company executive*
kerson, Guy Robert *lumber company executive*
liucci, Riccardo *pharmaceutical executive*
ole, Henry Joe, Jr. *business executive*
e, Pamela J. *former health products executive*
att, Kedar Davis, Jr. *research and development company executive*
eney, Susan O. *paper company executive*
ath, Stephen D. *retired pharmaceutical company executive*
h, Duane J. *pharmaceutical executive*
ate, Robert Emile *drug and cosmetic consultant*
uhsler, Helmut *biotechnology company executive*
il, Larraine Diane *materials company executive*
aw, Jane Elizabeth *retired pharmaceutical company executive*
ith, Charles Conard *refractory company executive*
ith, Orin C. *retired beverage service company executive*
vens, Paul Irving *manufacturing executive*
ver, Wilbur G., Jr. *manufacturing executive*
livan, G. Craig *household products executive*
gart, Richard J. *retired paper company executive*
omas-Graham, Pamela *apparel executive*
omsen, Carl *electronics company executive*
njack, Thomas J. *lumber company executive*
ner, Andrew L. *healthcare management company executive*
Luvanee, Donald Robert *electronics executive*
alass, Dennis L. *manufacturing executive*
kins, Dean Allen *electronics executive, educator*
swasser, Stephen *electronics executive*
dow, Carl Paul *electromechanical and geophysical instruments company executive*
ds, Daniel O. *health products executive*
ger, Kurt Eric *research and development company executive*

INDUSTRY: SERVICE

UNITED STATES

ASKA

chorage
vber, John M. *communications executive*

neau
g, Robert Wilson *public relations specialist*

IZONA

ve Creek
eilly, Thomas Eugene *retired human resources consultant*

andler
nello-McCay, Rosanne *sales executive*

gstaff
ns, Ronald Allen *lodging chain executive*

een Valley
an, James Thomas *communications executive*

sa
phy, Edward Francis *sales executive*

nds Park
, Sydney *public relations executive*

vson
arty, Christopher Joseph *management and financial consultant*

oenix
in, Albert Sterling *business management consultant*
berg, Harley *marketing professional*
, Donald Alan *data processing executive*
rich, Mark L. *corporate communications director*
er, Donald W. *waste management executive*
ner, John J. *waste management administrator*

scott
ner, Robert Arthur *private investigator*

ttsdale
ada, Nobuo *chef*
r, James Edward *hotel executive, lawyer*
anovich, Norma JoAnne *training services executive*
onnell, William Thomas *management consultant*
ck, James Martin *communications executive, writer, entrepreneur*
Weelden, Thomas H. *former waste industry company executive*
ds, Duane C. *waste management executive*

Sun City West
Stevens, George Richard *business consultant, public information officer*

Surprise
Baum, Phyllis Gardner *retired travel management consultant*

Tempe
Garvin, Sam Scott *marketing executive*
Laybourne, Stanley *computer technology company executive*

Tucson
Barton, Stanley Faulkner *retired management consultant*
Click, Carrie *public relations executive*
Cooper, Corinne *communications consultant, lawyer*
Eberhardt, Marty Lampert *botanical garden administrator*
Kennedy, Lydia *human resources specialist*
Pedersen, Arlene *web design company executive*
Walker, Ronald Hugh *retired management consultant*

CALIFORNIA

Agoura Hills
Gressak, Anthony Raymond, Jr. *sales executive*

Alameda
Blackmore, Peter *computer company executive*
Potash, Jeremy Warner *public relations executive*

Alamo
Whalen, John Sydney *management consultant*

Aliso Viejo
Blum, Scott Allen *Internet company executive*
Grigsby, Frederick J., Jr. *human resources executive*
Grover, Neel *Internet company executive*
Harder, Wendy Wetzel *communications executive*

Alviso
Rogers, Thomas Sydney *communications company executive*
Sordello, Steve *communications executive*

Anaheim
Miller, Mark A. *information technology training executive*

Aptos
Trounstine, Philip John *communications consultant*

Arcadia
Jemelian, John Nazar *management consultant*

Atherton
Baran, Paul *computer executive*

Bakersfield
Gallagher, Joseph Francis *marketing executive*

Belvedere Tiburon
Eckstut, Michael Kauder *management consultant*

Berkeley
Waters, Alice L. *executive chef, restaurant owner, writer*
Wilton, Peter Campbell *marketing educator*

Beverly Hills
Berger, Adam *Internet company executive*
Hefter, Lee *chef*
Hilton, (William) Barron *hotel executive*
Huckestein, Dieter H. *hotel company executive*
Nassetta, Christopher J. *hotel executive*
Richman, Keith *communications executive*
Riess, Gordon Sanderson *management consultant*

Burbank
Caouette, David Paul *public relations executive*
Cheng, Albert *communications executive*
Cohen, Valerie A. *entertainment company executive*
Garner, Scott *communications executive*
Kantor, Susan *marketing executive*

Camarillo
Cobb, Roy Lampkin, Jr. *retired computer sciences corporation executive*

Cambria
Morse, Richard Jay *human resources and organizational development specialist, consultant*

Campbell
Battista, Richard *chef, educator*

Carlsbad
Lambert, James L. *data storage systems company executive*

Carmel
Smith, Gordon Paul *management consultant*

Carpinteria
Adizes, Ichak *management consultant, writer*
Morgan, Alfred Vance *management consulting company executive*

Puzder, Andrew F. *food service executive, lawyer*

Claremont
Hawkins, Gregory J. *consumer products company executive*

Compton
Beauchamp, Patrick L. *distributing company executive*

Concord
Travers, Judith Lynnette *human resources executive*

Corona Del Mar
O'Brien, John William, Jr. *management consultant*

Corte Madera
Mindel, Laurence Brisker *restauranteur*
Tate, John William *consumer products company executive, former food products executive*

Culver City
Boonshaft, Hope Judith *public relations executive*
Holt, Dennis F. *media buying company executive*
Van Galder, Valerie *marketing executive*

Cupertino
Cook, Timothy D. *computer company executive*
Cooperman, Daniel *computer company executive, lawyer*
Fadell, Tony (Anthony M. Fadell) *computer company executive*
Jobs, Steve (Steven Paul Jobs) *computer company executive*
Johnson, Ron *computer company executive*
Oppenheimer, Peter *computer company executive*
Papermaster, Mark D. *computer company executive*
Schiller, Philip W. *computer company executive*

Dana Point
Mardian, Robert Charles, Jr. *restaurateur*

Dublin
Chen, John S. *computer company executive*

El Dorado Hills
Davies, William Ralph *service executive*

El Segundo
DeBuck, Donald G. *computer company executive*
Eckert, Robert A. *consumer products company executive*
Farr, Kevin M. *consumer products executive*
Gieselman, Jon *advertising executive*
Kilpatrick, Frank Stanton *marketing executive*
Laphen, Michael W. *computer services company executive*
Shanks, Eric *communications executive*

Encino
Dennis, David L. *management consultant*
Wald, Donna Gene *advertising executive*

Escondido
Mogul, Leslie Anne *business development and marketing consultant*

Foster City
Miller, Jon Philip *marketing professional, pharmaceutical executive*
Yan, Martin *celebrity chef*

Fremont
Sanchez, Marla Rena *communications executive*

Fresno
Ganulin, Judy *public relations professional*
Levy, Joseph William *department stores executive*

Fullerton
Sheridan, Christopher Frederick *human resources executive*

Glendale
Dohring, Doug *marketing executive*
Margol, Irving *personnel consultant*

Granite Bay
Holtz, Sara *marketing consultant*

Healdsburg
Keane, Douglas *chef*

Hillsborough
Westerfield, Putney *management consulting executive*

Hollywood
Batt, Anthony *Internet company executive*
Goldman, Tyler *Internet company executive, lawyer*

Irvine
Leber, Mike *advertising executive*
Owens, David *food service executive, marketing professional*
Poole, Christopher K. *arbitration services company executive*
Robino, David J. *computer company executive*
Rollans, James O. *service company executive*

Sherwood, Rod(erick) III *computer company executive*
Snyder, Rick (Richard D. Snyder) *computer company executive*

Jackson
Halvorson, Frank Elsworth *sales executive*

Kentfield
Edgar, James Macmillan, Jr. *management consultant*

La Jolla
Bardwick, Judith Marcia *management consultant*

La Quinta
Peden, Lynn Ellen *marketing executive*

Laguna Niguel
Greenberg, Lenore *public relations professional*

Lake Forest
Coyne, John F. *computer company executive*
Earhart, Donald Marion *management consultant, health care company executive*
Hopp, Terry A. *computer company executive*
Massengill, Matthew H. *computer company executive*
Shakeel, Arif *computer company executive*

Larkspur
Denton, Charles Mandaville *corporate communications specialist, journalist*

Long Beach
Nussbaum, Luther James *computer company executive*

Los Angeles
Bloch, Paul *public relations executive*
Bohle, Sue *public relations executive*
Bollenbach, Stephen Frasier *retired hotel executive*
Cecere, Domenico *homebuilding company executive*
Chernin, Peter F. *multimedia company executive*
Clow, Lee *advertising agency executive*
Coleman Smith, Salaam *communications executive*
Coots, Laurie *advertising executive*
Crosby, Peter Alan *management consultant*
Dayton, Sky *telecommunications company executive*
Dotolo, Vinny *chef*
Eiserman, Rick *marketing executive*
Emerson, Barry D. *computer company executive*
Faber, George Donald *retired communications executive*
Feldman, Robert C. (Bob) *public relations executive*
Feniger, Susan *chef, television personality, writer*
Geoffrion, Arthur Minot *management scientist*
Gottfried, Ira Sidney *management consulting executive*
Hansen, Alexander E. *advertising agency executive*
Hartsough, Gayla Anne Kraetsch *management consultant*
Hatamiya, Lon Shoso *consultant, former state official*
Hateley, J. Michael *human resources executive*
Helper, Lee *strategic business marketing and marketing communications consultant*
Hill, Bonnie Guiton *consulting company executive*
Hirshberg, Eric *advertising executive*
Hopkins, Michael *communications executive*
Hutton, Fiona S. *communications executive*
Kessler, Robert Allen *retired data processing executive*
Kleiman, Evan *chef*
Kline, Richard Stephen *communications and public affairs executive*
Kozberg, Joanne Corday *public affairs consultant*
Levine, Michael *public relations executive, author, television and radio personality*
Logan, Nancy Jane *broadcast sales and marketing executive*
Mamer, John William *business educator*
Marianella, Vincenzo *bartender*
Milliken, Mary Sue *chef, television personality, writer*
Nadler, Gerald *management consultant, educator*
Nazarian, Sam *hotel executive, film producer*
Peel, Mark *chef, restaurant owner*
Rice, Regina Kelly *marketing executive*
Schultz, Louis Michael *advertising agency executive*
Sella, Tony *marketing executive*
Shook, Jon *chef*
Silverton, Nancy *chef*
Sitrick, Michael Steven *public relations executive*
Small, Stacy H. *luxury travel company executive, former magazine editor*
Spindler, Paul *communications executive, consultant*
Spofford, Robert Houston *advertising agency executive*
Tardio, Thomas A. *public relations executive*
Tinsley, Jeffrey *Internet company executive*
Winkler, Howard Leslie *business, finance, government relations consultant*
Zelikow, Howard Monroe *management and financial consultant*

Malibu
Tellem, Susan Mary *public relations executive*

Manhattan Beach
Deutsch, Barry Joseph *consulting and management development company executive*

Marina Del Rey
Gold, Carol Sapin *international management consultant, speaker, writer*
Jeffrey, John Orval *Internet company executive, lawyer*

Menlo Park
Eslambolchi, Hossein *communications executive*
Kvamme, Mark D. *marketing professional*
Lanzone, Jim *Internet company executive*
Messmer, Harold Maximilian, Jr., (Max Messmer) *consulting company executive*
Ramsay, Michael *communications company executive*
Richards, Stephen C. *corporate development executive*
Waddell, M. Keith *consulting company executive*

Mill Valley
Hargrave, Sarah Quesenberry *consulting company and training executive*

Milpitas
Corrigan, Wilfred J. *computer company executive*
Harari, Eli *computer company executive*
Levy, Kenneth *retired computer company executive*
Simson, Claudine *computer company executive*
Talwalkar, Abhi Y. (Abhijit Y. Talwalkar) *computer company executive*

Morgan Hill
McGuire, Thomas Roger *distribution company executive*

Moss Beach
Glauthier, T. J. *management consultant*

Mountain View
Brown, Shona L. *Internet company executive*
Campbell, William V. *computer company executive*
Cook, Scott David *computer software company executive*
de Geus, Aart J. *computer software company executive*
Edsell, Patrick L. *computer company executive*
Engeström, Jyri *Internet company executive*
Golub, Ben *Internet company executive*
Hayes, Dotty (Dorothy Damon Hayes) *computer software company executive*
Hoffman, Reid *Internet company executive*
Huang, Kai *computer game company executive*
Koponen, Petteri *Internet company executive*
Lewin, Dan'l *computer software company executive*
Masonis, Todd *Internet company executive*
Nye, Dan *Internet company executive*
Qureishi, A. Salam *computer company executive*
Ring, Cameron *Internet company executive*
Roper, William Alford, Jr. *Internet company executive*
Vaillant, Jean-Luc *Internet company executive*

Napa
Fox, Jeremy *chef*

Newport Beach
Dougherty, Raleigh Gordon *manufacturer representative*
Hancock, Ellen Marie *communications executive*
Lipson, Melvin Alan *technology and business management consultant*
Shonk, Albert Davenport, Jr. *advertising executive*

Northridge
Stark, Martin J. *international management consultant*

Oakland
Knauss, Donald R. *consumer products company executive*
Lebda, Douglas R. *Internet company executive*
Stetler, Russell Dearnley, Jr. *investigator*
Williams, Carol H. *advertising executive*

Ojai
Allen, David Ratcliff *management consultant, writer*
Martel, Lisa *food service executive*

Orange
Jay, David Jakubowicz *management consultant*

Pacific Palisades
Humphreys, Robert Lee *advertising executive*

Palm Springs
Arnold, Stanley Norman *management consultant, educator*
Scott, Walter, Jr. *business consultant*

Palo Alto
Banerjee, Prith *computer company executive, computer engineering professor*
Bianchini, Gina L. *Internet company executive*
Bocian, Peter *computer company executive*
Bradley, (R.) Todd *communications and computer company executive*
Dower, William J. *research company executive*
Flaxman, Jon E. *computer company executive*
Fruchterman, James Robert, Jr. *computer company and not-for-profit executive*
Grantham, Donald *computer company executive, former computer systems network executive*
Hurd, Mark Vincent *computer company executive*
Joshi, Vyomesh I. *computer company executive*
Lesjak, Catherine A. *computer company executive*
Lyons, Cathy *computer company executive*
Maritz, Paul *computer software company executive*
Mendenhall, Michael *computer company executive*
Moskovitz, Dustin Aaron *Internet company executive, entrepreneur, application developer*
Mott, Randy (Randall D. Mott) *computer company executive*
Neale-May, Donovan *marketing executive*
Perez de Alonso, Marcela *human resources specialist, information technology executive*
Renfro, John M. *human resources specialist*
Robison, Shane V. *computer company executive*
Sandberg, Sheryl Kara *Internet company executive*
Spohn, Nor Rae *computer company executive*
Ticknor, Carolyn M. *computer company executive*
Waller, Peter William *public relations executive*
Winkler, Michael *computer company executive*
Zuckerberg, Mark Elliot *Internet company executive, entrepreneur, programmer*

Pasadena
Caine, Stephen Howard *data processing executive*
Caldwell, Kim A. *company executive*
Hernandez, Enrique, Jr., (Rick Hernandez) *security firm executive*
Kaplan, Gary *executive recruiter*
O'Bryant, Daniel R. *consumer products company executive*
Scarborough, Dean A. *consumer product company executive*
Steiner, Greg *Internet company executive*
Waldorf, Gregory *Internet company executive, venture capitalist*
Warren, Neil Clark *Internet company executive, psychologist*
Watkins, John Francis *management consultant*

Petaluma
Guadarrama, Belinda *computer company executive*

Pleasanton
Burd, Steven A. *food service executive*
Dietz, Diane M. *marketing executive*
Gordon, Robert Allen, Jr. *food service executive, lawyer*
Jackson, Russell M. *food service executive*
Plaisance, Melissa C. *consumer products company executive*

Rancho Palos Verdes
Douglass, Craig Bruce *computer technology executive*

Rancho Santa Fe
Baker, Charles Lynn *management consultant*
Matthews, Leonard Sarver *advertising and marketing executive*

Redlands
Rankin, Alex C. *management executive*

Redwood City
O'Brien, Sean *chef*
Stone, Herbert Allen *management consultant*

Riverside
O'Reilly, Patrick James *public relations executive*

Rutherford
Staglin, Garen Kent *computer company executive, venture capitalist*

Sacramento
McElroy, Leo Francis *communications consultant, journalist*
Schmidt, Steve (Stephen E. Schmidt) *public relations executive*
Swatt, Stephen Benton *communications executive, consultant*

Saint Helena
Sone, Hiro *chef, restaurant owner, writer*

Salinas
Jeffries, Russell Morden *communications company official*

San Bruno
Chen, Steve Shih *Internet company executive*
Grove, Steve *Internet company executive*

San Carlos
Vanderryn, Jack *environmental services administrator*

San Clemente
Konney, Paul Edward *health products executive, lawyer*

San Diego
Adams, Loretta *marketing executive*
Comrie, Sandra Melton *human resource executive*
Epstein, Daniel J. *management consultant*
Gilbertson, Oswald Irving *marketing executive*
Jacobs, Irwin Mark *communications executive*
Jacobs, Paul E. *communications company executive*
Jagoda, Barry Lionel *communications executive, writer*
Lang, Linda A. *food service executive*
Myers, James M. *pet products executive*
Nelson, Craig Alan *management consultant*
North, Robert L. *computer software executive*
Nugent, Robert J., Jr. *fast food company executive*
Padovani, Roberto *communications executive*
Rosenberg, Donald Jay *communications company executive, lawyer*
Wertheim, Robert Halley *national security consultant*
Ziegaus, Alan James *public relations executive*

San Francisco
Adelson, Jay Steven *Internet company executive*
Appleman, Nate *chef*
Bancel, Marilyn *fund raising management consultant*
Benioff, Marc *Internet company executive*
Bernstein, Gerald William *management consultant, researcher*
Birch, Michael *Internet company executive, application developer*
Butenhoff, Susan Grace *public relations executive*
Caldwell, Dalton *Internet company executive, application developer*
Carpenter, Steven A. *Internet company executive*
Clark, Richard Ward *management consultant*
Coburn, Lawrence *Internet company executive*
Conway, Craig A. *retired computer company executive*
Crawford, Carol Anne *marketing professional*
des Jardins, Traci *chef, restaurant owner*
Dorman, David W. *management consultant, former telecommunications industry executive*
Doumani, Lissa *chef*
Freeman, Matt *advertising executive*
Garg, Akash *Internet company executive*
Goodby, Jeffrey *advertising agency executive*
Gordon, Judith *communications consultant, writer*
Hernandez, Aileen C(larke) *urban consultant*
Hickerson, Glenn Lindsey *leasing company executive*
Holmes, Irvin R., Jr. *marketing professional*
Keller, Hubert *chef, restaurant owner*
Kertzman, Mitchell E. *former software company executive, venture capitalist*
Kroenert, Rob *Internet company executive, marketing professional*
Kunz, Heidi *healthcare company executive*
LaTour, Thomas W. *hotel executive*
Leondakis, Niki Anna *food service executive*
Lindstrom, Kent J. *Internet company executive*
McEvoy, Nan Tucker *publishing company executive, olive rancher*
Murphy, Kathleen Anne Foley *marketing communications executive*
Nash, Jill *communications executive*
Newmark, Craig Alexander *Internet company executive*
Owades, Ruth Markowitz *marketing company executive*
Pearce, William D. *marketing executive*
Pritzker, John A. *leisure services executive*
Prueitt, Elisabeth *pastry chef*
Reed, Doug *Internet company executive*
Rheingold, Ted *Internet company executive*
Saeger, Rebecca *advertising executive*
Schleier-Smith, Johann *Internet company executive*
Shorenstein, Douglas W. *corporate executive*
Silverstein, Richard *advertising agency executive*
Stoll, Craig *chef*
Stoppelman, Jeremy *Internet company executive, entrepreneur*
Torme, Margaret Anne *public relations executive, management consultant*
Tseng, Greg *Internet company executive*
Vars, John *Internet company executive*
Wernick, Sandra Margot *meeting event planner and public relations executive*
Williams, Evan *Internet company executive*
Wong, Arnold Eric *chef, restaurant owner*
Yalamanchi, Ramu *Internet company executive*

San Jose
Bengier, Gary T. *online company executive*
Bingham, H. Raymond *computer software company executive*
Bostrom, Susan L. *marketing executive*
Calderoni, Frank A. *computer company executive*
Carey, Matt *Internet company executive*
Carter, Larry R. *computer company executive*
Chellam, Kris *data processing executive*
Compton, Charles (Kip) *communications executive*
DCamp, Kathryn Acker *human resources executive*
Donahoe, John Joseph, II, *Internet company executive*
Elfrink, Wim *computer company executive*
Feld, Donald H. *network consultant*
Jordan, Jeff *Internet company executive*
Justice, Richard J. *computer company executive*
Linton, Mike *marketing executive*
Liu, Derek *Internet company executive*
Lynch, Kevin *computer software company executive, application developer*
Norrington, Lorrie M. *Internet company executive*
Omidyar, Pierre M. *Internet company execut*
Oshman, M. Kenneth *computer company executive*
Pond, Randy *computer company executive*
Roberts, George P. *computer company execu*
Roelandts, Willem P. *data processing execut*
Schaller, Anthony Josef *technology managen executive*
Sherman, Craig *Internet company executive*
Silverman, Josh *communications executive*
Swan, Robert H. *Internet company executive*
Tewksbury, Ted (Theodore L. Tewksbury III *communications executive*
Thompson, Scott *Internet company executive*
Wallace, Richard P. *computer company exec*
Warnock, John Edward *computer company executive*
Weinhardt, J. W. *computer company executi*

San Mateo
Helfert, Erich Anton *management consultant writer, educator*
Yecies, Laura Susan *computer software com executive*

San Rafael
Bass, Carl *computer software company exec*
Evenhuis, Henk J. *research company executi*
Finkelstein, James Arthur *management consultant*
Kennedy, James Waite *management consulta writer*

San Ramon
Laymon, Joe W. *human resources specialist*

Santa Barbara
Emmons, Robert John *corporate executive,*
McKee, Kathryn Dian Grant *human resourc consultant*

Santa Clara
Bhagat, Nancy *marketing executive*
Bryant, Andy D. *computer company executi*
Couillaud, Bernard J. *executive*
Culbertson, Leslie S. *computer company executive*
Estrin, Judith *computer company executive*
Franz, Thomas R. *computer company execu*
Halloran, Jean M. *human resources speciali*
Hutcheson, Jerry Dee *manufacturing compa executive*
Lin, Frank C. *computer company executive*
MacDonald, Donald J. *marketing executive*
Morris, Michael H. *computer company exec*
Morris, Sandra K. *computer company execu*
Parker, Gerhard H. *communications professi*
Perlmutter, David (Dadi) *computer company executive*
Pimentel, Albert A. (Rocky Pimentel) *comp software company executive*
Pollace, Pamela L. *public relations executiv*
Rudolph, Ronald Alvin *human resources specialist*
Scott, Edward William, Jr. *computer compa executive*
Smith, Stacy J. *computer company executive*
Sodhani, Arvind *computer company executi*

Santa Fe Springs
Hammond, Judy McLain *business services executive*

Santa Monica
Bachrach, Charles Lewis *advertising agency executive*
Berman, Jeff *Internet company executive*
Blankley, Tony *public relations executive, columnist, radio personality*
Mancuso, Vince *advertising executive*
Ovitz, Michael S. *communications executive*
Patel, Chandra Kumar Naranbhai *communications executive, educator, entrepreneur, researcher*
Postaer, Larry *advertising executive*
Rice, Donald Blessing *corporate executive, former federal official*
Rubin, Gerrold Robert *advertising executive*
Ryan, Jane Frances *corporate communicatic executive*
Van Natta, Owen Thomas *Internet company executive*

Santa Rosa
Schudel, Hansjoerg *international business consultant*

Scotts Valley
Luczo, Stephen James *computer hardware company executive*
Park, Chong S. *computer company executiv*
Pope, Charles C. *computer hardware compa executive*

Sherman Oaks
Cook, Paul Maxwell *technology company executive*
Lindgren, Timothy Joseph *supply company executive*
Yasnyi, Allan David *communications comp executive*

SOUTH CAROLINA

Charleston
Martin, Thomas Rhodes *communications executive, writer, educator*

UTAH

Farmington
Freed, Peter Quentin *amusement park executive*

Heber City
McLean, Hugh Angus *management consultant*

Park City
Milner, Harold William *hotel executive*

Provo
Herrera, Shirley Mae *personnel and security executive*

Salt Lake City
Covey, Stephen Merrill Richards *business consultant, speaker, author*
Howell, Scott Newell *computer company executive, state legislator, state legislator*
Johnson, Jon L. *advertising executive*
Smith, Hyrum Wayne *management executive*
Thomas, David G. *advertising executive*

Sandy
Phillips, Ted Ray *advertising executive*

WASHINGTON

Bellevue
Giuliani, David *personal care products company executive*
Khosrowshahi, Dara *travel company executive*
Ladd, James Roger *international business executive, consultant*
McReynolds, Neil Lawrence *management consultant*
Myhrvold, Nathan P. *technology executive*
Otterholt, Barry L. *technology management consultant*

Federal Way
Dooley, James H. *product company executive*
Muzyka-McGuire, Amy *marketing professional, nutritionist, consultant*

Gig Harbor
Stover, Miles Ronald *management consultant*

Issaquah
Matthews, John *human resources specialist, wholesale distribution executive*

Kent
Cheung, John B. *research and development executive*

Kirkland
Evans, Robert Vincent *sales and marketing executive*

Medina
Dagnon, James Bernard *human resources executive*

Olympia
Marcelynas, Richard Chadwick *management consultant*
Weese, Bruce Eric *retired sales executive*

Port Ludlow
Krugman, Stanley Lee *international management consultant*

Redmond
Abu-Hadba, Walid *computer software company executive*
Allard, J. *computer software company executive*
Anderson, Nancy J. *computer software company executive, lawyer*
Ayala, Orlando *computer software company executive*
Bach, Robert J. (Robbie Bach) *computer software company executive*
Ballmer, Steven Anthony *computer software company executive*
Béjar, Martha *computer software company executive*
Belfiore, Joe *computer software company executive*
Berkowitz, Steven *computer software company executive*
Brod, Frank H. *computer software company executive, accountant*
Brooks, Brad *computer software company executive*
Brummel, Lisa E. *computer software company executive*
Burt, Thomas William *computer software company executive, lawyer*
Capossela, Chris *computer software company executive*
Charney, Scott *computer software company executive, lawyer*
Chrapaty, Debra J. *computer software company executive*
Cohen, Larry *computer software company executive*
Crozier, Alain *computer software company executive*
DelBene, Kurt *computer software company executive*
Delman, Michael *computer software company executive*
DeVaan, Jon S. *computer software company executive*
Dunaway, Cammie *marketing executive*
Elliott, Gerri *computer software company executive*
Elop, Stephen A. *computer software company executive*
Fathi, Ben *computer software company executive*
Flessner, Paul *computer software company executive*
Gates, Bill (William Henry Gates III) *computer software company executive*
George, Grant *computer software company executive*
Gibbons, Tom *computer software company executive*
Gounares, Alexander *computer software company executive*
Guggenheimer, Steve *computer software company executive*
Guthrie, Scott *computer software company executive*
Hey, Tony *computer software company executive*
Ho, Roz *computer software company executive*
Hogan, Kathleen *computer software company executive*
Huston, Darren *computer software company executive*
Jha, Rajesh K. *computer software company executive*
Jones, Chris *computer software company executive*
Kaigler, Denise M. *marketing executive*
Kelly, Bob *computer software company executive*
Khaki, Jawad *computer software company executive*
KIm, Shane *computer software company executive*
Klein, Peter *computer software company executive*
Koch, Mitchell L. *computer software company executive*
Kummert, Ted *computer software company executive*
Larson-Green, Julie *computer software company executive*
Leblond, Antoine *computer software company executive*
Lees, Andrew *computer software company executive*
Levin, Lewis *computer software company executive*
Lichtman, Moshe *computer software company executive*
Liddell, Christopher P. *computer software company executive*
Liffick, Steve *computer software company executive*
Lu, Qi *computer software company executive*
MacDonald, Brian *computer software company executive*
Martinez, Maria *computer software company executive*
Mathews, Mich *computer company executive*
Mattrick, Donald A. *computer software company executive*
Matz, Joseph S. *computer software company executive*
McAniff, Richard *computer software company executive*
Mehdi, Yusuf *computer software company executive*
Minervino, Jim *computer software company executive*
Mitchell, William H. *computer software company executive*
Moberg, Jens Winther *computer software company executive*
Mount, Mindy (Melinda J. Mount) *computer software company executive*
Muglia, Bob (Robert L. Muglia) *computer software company executive*
Mundie, Craig James *computer software company executive*
Nadella, Satya *computer software company executive*
Nash, Mike *computer software company executive*
Nelson, Kimberly Terese *computer software company executive, former federal agency administrator*
Neupert, Peter *computer software company executive*
Ozzie, Ray (Raymond E. Ozzie) *computer software company executive*
Pall, Gurdeep Singh *computer software company executive*
Parthasarathy, Sanjay *computer software company executive*
Passman, Pamela S. *computer software company executive*
Peracca, Alain *computer software company executive*
Phelps, Marshall C., Jr. *computer software company executive*
Poole, Will *computer software company executive, information technology executive*
Rashid, Richard F. *computer software company executive*
Rodriguez, Enrique *computer software company executive*
Rosini, Eduardo B. *computer software company executive*
Roskill, Jon *computer software company executive*
Rudder, Eric D. *computer company executive, information technology executive*
Schappert, John Conrad *computer software company executive*
Schiro, Steve *computer software company executive*
Scott, Tony *computer software company executive*
Sheldon, Jeanne *computer software company executive*
Shirley, Jon Anthony *former computer software company executive*
Sinofsky, Steven J. *computer software company executive*
Smith, Bradford Lee *computer software company executive, lawyer*
Snapp, Mary E. *computer software company executive, lawyer*
Somasegar, Sivarama Kichenane *computer software company executive*
Teper, Jeffrey Allen *computer software company executive*
Thompson, Rick *computer software company executive*
Tobey, Brian *computer software company executive*
Treadwell, David *computer software company executive*
Turner, Kevin (B. Kevin Turner) *computer software company executive*
Vaskevitch, David *computer software company executive*
Veghte, Bill *computer software company executive*
Vigil, Henry P. *computer software company executive*
Wahbe, Robert *computer software company executive*
Warren, Todd *computer software company executive*
Watson, Allison L. *computer software company executive*
Westlake, Blair *computer software company executive*
Witts, Simon *computer software company executive*
Youngjohns, Robert H. *computer software company executive*
Zhang, Ya-Qin *computer software company executive*
Zinn, George *computer software company executive*

Renton
Pugh, Donald E. *industry executive*

Seattle
Barton, Richard N. *computer company executive*
Beren, Steve *Internet marketing professional*
Bianco, James A. *research and development executive*
Coles, Martin *beverage service company executive*
Davenport, Terry Dean *beverage service company executive, marketing executive*
Dederer, Michael Eugene *retired public relations executive*
Dillon, Matthew *chef*
Duryee, David Anthony *management consultant*
Elgin, Ron Alan *advertising executive*
Eller, Marlin *security firm executive*
Gass, Michelle Petkers *beverage service company executive, marketing executive*
Glaser, Robert *communications executive*
Hough, John Dennis *public relations executive*
Howell, R. Scott *industry executive*
Komen, Richard B. *food service executive*
Kraft, Donald Bowman *advertising agency executive*
MacDonald, Andrew Stephen *management consulting firm executive*
McAndrews, Brian Patrick *computer software company executive*
Miyata, Keijiro *culinary arts educator*
Patton, Jody *management company executive*
Roberts, Harry *beverage service company executive, marketing executive*
Sasenick, Joseph Anthony *health care company executive*
Schultz, Howard D. *beverage service company executive*
Stowell, Ethan *chef*
Walker, Douglas *computer development company executive*

Spokane
Chamberlain, Barbara Kaye *communications executive*
Geraghty, John Vincent *public relations consultant*
Klawitter, Ronald F. *computer company executive*
Oehlke, Jack W. *computer company executive*

Vancouver
Ogden, Valeria Munson *management consultant, state representative*

Woodinville
Love, Keith Sinclair *communications executive*

WYOMING

Fort Laramie
Mack, James A. *parks director*

Yellowstone National Park
Lewis, Suzanne *parks director*

CANADA

BRITISH COLUMBIA

Kelowna
Merrifield, Lane *Internet company executive*
Priebe, Lance *Internet company executive, application developer*

Vancouver
Campbell, Bruce Alan *corporate coach*

Victoria
Nuttall, Richard Norris *management consult physician*

FRANCE

Paris
Courtois, Jean-Philippe *computer software company executive*

ADDRESS UNPUBLISHED

Abrams, Jonathan *Internet company executi*
Allan, James S. *sales professional*
Allen, A. William, III, (Bill) *food service executive*
Allen, Barry K. *communications executive, human resources specialist*
Allen, Louis Alexander *management consul*
Anderson, Herbert W. *consumer products company executive*
Anderson, Paul Irving *management executiv*
Anderson, Tom *former Internet company executive*
Anschutz, Philip F. *communications and professional sports team executive*
Bacas, Andrew R. *data processing executive*
Barger, William James *management consult educator*
Becerra, Octavio *corporate executive chef*
Bell, Jeff *former computer software market executive*
Bennett, Stephen M. *former computer softw company executive*
Biondi, Frank J., Jr. *entertainment company executive*
Bishop, Robert R. *computer company execu*
Bishop, William Peter *management consult rancher, musician*
Blaine, Davis Robert *valuation consultant, investment banker*
Blau, Elizabeth Anne *restaurant executive*
Bloom, Gary L. *data processing executive*
Bohannon, Robert H. *diversified services company executive*
Bonnie, Shelby W. *Internet company execu*
Bow, Stephen Tyler, Jr. *business executive*
Boyd, Dean Weldon *management consultan*
Braden, George Walter, II, *sales executive*
Brady, Donna Elizabeth *sales, marketing an performing company executive*
Burns, Michael Joseph *operations and sales-marketing executive*
Cantor, Alan Bruce *management consultant application developer*
Carter, Dennis Lee *marketing professional*
Chakrin, Lewis M. *consumer products com executive*
Chamberlain, William Edwin, Jr. *managem consultant*
Chun, Jennifer *communications executive*
Claflin, Bruce L. *software company executi*
Clark, Jim *communications executive*
Cook, Brian R. *corporate professional*
Cooke, John F. *entertainment company exe*
Cotsen, Lloyd E. *retired consumer products company executive*
Crosson, John Albert *advertising executive*
Cunningham, Andrea Lee *public relations executive*
Daniels, Richard Martin *public relations executive*
David, Clive *events executive*
Davis, Megan J. *consulting firm executive*
Dean, Leslie Alan (Cap Dean) *internationa economic, social and political developme consultant, interagency and defense anal*
Decker, Susan Lynne *former Internet comp executive*
DePinto, David J. *public relations executive*
Devenuti, Rick (Richard R. Devenuti) *form computer software company executive*
deWilde, David Michael *management consultant, lawyer, finance company exec retired recruiter*
DeWolfe, Christopher T. *former Internet company executive*
Doan, Mary Frances *advertising executive*
Dobler, Donald William *retired procuremen materials executive, dean*
Donald, James Lloyd (Jim Donald) *former beverage service company executive*
Dowie, Ian James *management consultant*
Duncan, James Daniel *paper distribution company executive*
Eastham, John D. *marketing executive*

on, Donna R. *business executive*
ly, David Maxon *health policy and*
nanagement advisor
vards, Susan M. *hotel executive*
stein, Clifford Jay *advertising executive*
imore, George Wiley *management consultant*
ner, Louis McLane, Jr. *management*
consultant
gg, Norman Lee *retired advertising executive*
res, Candace *special events director*
dericks, Dale Edward *communications*
company executive
chke, Charles M. *computer company*
executive
bertson, Robert G. *computer company*
executive
eckman, Alan Jay *Internet company*
executive
no, Steven J. *technical communications*
product company executive
dall, Jackson Wallace, Jr. *restaurant*
company executive
ene, Alvin *management consultant*
ndal, Mary Ann *former sales professional*
ta, Anoop *computer software company*
executive
ni, Mohan *communications company*
executive
naford, Peter Dor *public relations executive,*
writer
ka, Catherine M. *Internet company executive*
ris, Robert Norman *advertising executive,*
educator
sdorfer, Gary Lee *management consultant*
es, Janet Gray *retired management*
consultant, mayor
ard, Robert Culver, Jr. *retired hotel executive*
kmann, Richard J. *sporting goods company*
executive
fman, Lou *public relations executive,*
educator, writer
nes, Gregg *communications executive*
zman, D. Keith *management consultant,*
record company executive
aldahl, Todd *computer software company*
executive
eycutt, Van B. *retired computer services*
company executive
vard, Gary Scott *communications executive*
well, Kevin L. *hotel executive*
ley, Chad Meredith *Internet company*
executive
aye, Wayne Ryo *computer company executive*
son, Phillip Ellis *marketing executive, writer*
en, Rodney H. *hotel executive*
ason, Laymon, Jr. *management analyst*
an, Jeffrey Guy *marketing professional,*
consultant
ensen, Blake J. *former Internet company*
executive
ur, Amit *former Internet company executive*
llis, John Peter *computer company executive,*
lawyer
m, Jawed *Internet company executive,*
application developer
y, James S. *personal care industry executive*
nedy, Debra Joyce *marketing professional*
gle, Timothy K. *communications executive*
pman, Richard H. (Dick Lampman) *former*
computer company executive
ni, Terry (Joseph Terrence Lanni) *retired*
hotel corporation executive
dge, Robert James *marketing research*
executive
Richard Kenneth *software company*
executive
pert, Philip *advertising executive, writer,*
news correspondent
rmore, Ann Martinelli *computer company*
executive
ch, Daniel C. *multimedia executive*
kezich, Ron *computer software company*
executive
schullat, Robert W. *former consumer*
products company executive
sik, George A. *packaging executive*
er, Allan *public relations executive,*
consultant
land, Maria U. *Internet company executive*
ris, Arlene Myers *marketing professional*
rison, David Fred *communications executive*
n, Carol Holladay *retired park and*
recreation director
lan, Julie Anne Carroll *management*
consultant
ri, Paul Celestin *communications executive*
rien, David Peter *corporate director*
yrne, Michael *retired management*
consultant
n, Dale C. *public relations executive*
, Simone *public relations executive*
a, Harry Joel *retired international affairs*
executive, consultant
ti, Kathy Ann *sales professional*
, Michael S. *computer software company*
executive
rson, Dennis Joseph *retired management*
consultant
m, Len *communications executive*
son, Joe *computer software company*
executive
h, Stephen Jon *public relations executive*
ll, Dennis D. *retired computer company*
executive
Frank W. III *computer company executive*
, Wolfgang *chef*
ll, Steven Richard *international*
management consultant, engineer, economist

Railsback, Sherrie Lee *management consultant,*
educator
Reisman, Judith Ann Gelernter *media*
communications executive, educator
Reyes, Gregory L. *former communications*
executive
Rice, Rod W. *corporate executive*
Rose, (Robert) Kevin *Internet company*
executive, blogger
Saywell, William George Gabriel *business*
development and management consultant
Scaglione, Cecil Frank *marketing, publishing*
executive
Scanlon, John M. *fiber optics company executive*
Scherman, Carol E. *human resources*
professional
Seale, Robert McMillan *office services company*
executive
Semel, Terry S. *retired Internet company*
executive
Smith, Edwin P. *security studies center director,*
career officer
Smith, Milton Ray *computer company executive,*
lawyer
Smith, Thomas Winston *cotton marketing*
executive
Smyth, Cornelius Edmonston *retired hotel*
executive
Sollender, Joel David *management consultant,*
financial executive, accountant
Srivastava, Amitabh *computer software company*
executive
Stedman, John Addis *management consultant*
Stelmar, Wayne J. *building company executive*
Stevens, Berton Louis, Jr. *data processing*
executive
Stewart, Kirk T. *public relations executive*
Sudarsky, Jerry M. *industrialist*
Swette, Brian T. *online company executive*
Tatum, Jackie *former parks and recreation*
manager, municipal official
Thompson, Craig Snover *corporate*
communications executive
Thompson, David M. *computer software*
company executive
Thornton, Felicia D. *food service company*
executive
Tillinghast, Charles Carpenter III *retired*
marketing company executive
VanSickle, Sharon Dee *public relations executive*
Vidovich, Mark A. *paper products executive*
Warner, John Hilliard, Jr. *technical services*
company executive
Wasserman, Anthony Ira *software company*
executive, educator
Wayman, Robert Paul *retired computer company*
executive
Webb, Maynard G., Jr. *Internet company*
executive
Weiner, Sharon Rose *public relations executive*
White, Bonnie Yvonne *management consultant,*
retired educator
Whitman, Meg (Margaret Cushing Whitman)
former Internet company executive
Williams, Carlton L. *communications executive*
Williams, Harry Edward *management consultant*
Winkler, Agnieszka M. *marketing executive*
Winkler, Lee B. *business consultant*
Winsor, David John *cost consultant*
Yang, Jerry *former Internet company executive*
Yocam, Delbert Wayne *retired software products*
company executive
York, Theodore Robert *retired consulting*
company executive

INDUSTRY: TRADE

UNITED STATES

ALASKA

Anchorage
Schnell, Roger Thomas *small business owner,*
retired state official, military officer

Denali National Park
Swenson, Richard Allen *business owner, animal*
trainer

ARIZONA

Chandler
Basha, Edward N., Jr. *grocery chain owner*

Phoenix
Francis, Philip L. *retail executive*
Steckler, Phyllis Betty *business owner*

CALIFORNIA

Aliso Viejo
Purdy, Alan MacGregor *financial executive*

Burbank
Wise, Woodrow Wilson, Jr. *retired small*
business owner

Burlingame
Kircher, Matt *retail executive*

Moldaw, Stuart G. *venture capitalist, retail*
clothing stores executive

Cathedral City
Jackman, Robert Alan *retail executive*

City Of Commerce
Lynch, Martin Andrew *retail company executive*
Martin, Richard J. *food wholesale executive*
Plamann, Alfred A. *wholesale distribution*
executive

Fresno
Winslow, Norman Eldon *small business owner*

Indian Wells
Biagi, Richard Charles *retail executive, real*
estate consultant

Los Angeles
Hawley, Philip Metschan *retired retail executive,*
management consultant
Roeder, Richard Kenneth *business owner, lawyer*
Sinay, Joseph *retail executive*

Manhattan Beach
King, Sharon Marie *consulting company*
executive

Modesto
Piccinini, Robert M. (Bob Piccinini) *grocery*
store chain executive

Newport Beach
Peets, Terry R. *retail executive*

Pleasanton
Balmuth, Michael A. *retail executive*
Everette, Bruce L. *retail executive*
Ferber, Norman Alan *retail executive*
Renda, Larree M. *retail executive*
Shachmut, Kenneth Michael *retail executive*
Stern, David R. *retail executive*
Tidwell, Jerry *retail executive*
Wright, Donald P. *retail executive*

San Bernardino
Brown, Jack H. *supermarket company executive*

San Francisco
Calhoun, John Joseph (Jack) *retail executive*
Fisher, Donald G. *retail executive*
Fisher, Doris *retail executive*
Fisher, Robert J. *retail executive*
Folkman, David H. *retail, wholesale and*
consumer products consultant
Hansen, Marka *retail executive*
Lenk, Edward C. (Toby) *retail executive*
Lester, W. Howard *retail executive*
McCollam, Sharon L. *retail executive*
Murphy, Glenn T. *retail executive*
Peck, Art *retail executive*
Sage-Gavin, Eva Marie *retail executive*
Tasooji, Michael B. *retail executive*

Signal Hill
Jarc, Frank Robert *retail executive*

South San Francisco
Mertens, Lynne G. *retail executive*
Walsh, J. Michael *wholesale distribution*
executive

Tustin
Underwood, Vernon O., Jr. *grocery stores*
executive

Walnut Creek
Brown, William E. *retail executive*
Bryant, Warren F. *retail executive*

West Sacramento
Teel, Joyce Raley *retail executive*

COLORADO

Colorado Springs
Noyes, Richard Hall *bookseller*

Denver
Newberry, Elizabeth Carter *greenhouse and*
floral company owner
Schwartz, Jeffrey H. *distribution facilities*
executive
Vigil, Jeffrey L. *infant and child products*
manufacturing executive

Englewood
Lubetkin, Alvin Nat *sporting goods retail*
company executive
Morton, John Douglas *retail executive*

Vail
Jones, Jeffrey W. *retail executive*

IDAHO

Boise
Herbert, Kathy J. *retail executive*
Long, William D. *grocery store executive*

MONTANA

Billings
Mason, Paul *small business owner, lighting*
designer

NEW MEXICO

Albuquerque
East, Daniel K. *small business owner*

Las Cruces
Johansson, Voleen *gun shop ownner*

OREGON

Bend
Lemas, Noah *small business owner*

Burns
Timms, Eugene Dale *wholesale business owner,*
state senator

Klamath Falls
Pastega, Richard Louis *retired retail specialist*

Medford
De Boer, Jeffrey B. *auto dealership executive*

Myrtle Creek
Shirtcliff, John Delzell *business owner, oil*
jobber

Salem
Winters, Jackie F. *small business owner,*
foundation administrator

TEXAS

Plano
Ullman, Myron Edward, III, (Mike Ullman)
retail executive

UTAH

Salt Lake City
Fields, Debbi (Debra Fields Rose) *cookie*
franchise executive

WASHINGTON

Bellevue
Fiske, Neil S. *retail executive*

Bellingham
Cole, Craig W. *grocery chain executive*

Duvall
Weiss, William Hans *small business owner*

Issaquah
Brotman, Jeffrey H. *wholesale distribution*
executive
DiCerchio, Richard D. *wholesale distribution*
executive
Galanti, Richard A. *wholesale business executive*
Sinegal, James D. *wholesale distribution*
executive

Seattle
Bridge, Herbert Marvin *retail executive*
Cottle, Gail Ann *retail executive*
Fix, Wilbur James *department store executive*
Koppel, Michael G. *retail executive*
Moriguchi, Tomio *gift and grocery store*
executive
Nordstrom, Blake W. *retail executive*
Nordstrom, Bruce A. *department store executive*
Nordstrom, John N. *department store executive*

Spokane
Zakheim, Irving Lee *gift import company*
executive

Yakima
Newland, Ruth Laura *small business owner*

WYOMING

Jackson
Law, Clarene Alta *small business owner, state*
legislator

ADDRESS UNPUBLISHED

Barth, David Keck *retired wholesale distribution*
executive, consultant
Bersell, Sean Devlin *trade association executive*
Blum, Gerald Henry *retired retail executive*
Busch, Joyce Ida *small business owner*
Chevalier, Paul Edward *retired retail executive,*
lawyer
DeBerry, Donna *retail executive*
Delaney, Marnie Patricia *retail executive*
Donley, Russell Lee III *small business owner,*
former state legislator
Finnigan, Robert Emmet *retired small business*
owner
Garrard, William Robert *radio station owner*
Goldman, Gerald Hillis *beverage distribution*
company executive
Greenstein, Merle Edward *import/export*
company executive
Gust, Anne Baldwin *former retail apparel*
company executive
Ming, Jenny J. *former retail executive*

Pressler, Paul S. *former retail executive*
Ritchey, Samuel Donley, Jr. *retired retail executive*
Rodman, Sue A. *wholesale company executive, artist, writer*
Schwartz, Stephan Andrew *entrepreneur, writer*
Shapiro, Marc Robert *retail executive*
Stewart, Thomas J. *wholesale distribution executive*
Williams, Leona Rae *small business owner, consultant*

INDUSTRY: TRANSPORTATION

UNITED STATES

ALASKA

Anchorage
Bowers, Paul D. *transportation company executive*
Sullivan, George Murray *transportation executive, consultant, retired mayor*

Fairbanks
Ruff, Doyle C. *airport manager*

ARIZONA

Grand Canyon
Bryant, Leland Marshal *business and nonprofit executive*

Phoenix
Gillette, Robert J. *aerospace transportation executive*
Knight, Gary J. *transportation executive*
Knight, Kevin P. *transportation executive*
Moyes, Jerry C. *transportation executive, professional sports team executive*
Peru, Ramey (Ramiro G. Peru) *transportation executive*

Tempe
Kerr, Derek J. *transportation executive*
Kirby, J. Scott *air transportation executive*
Lakefield, Bruce R. *air transportation executive*
Parker, Doug (William Douglas Parker, W. Douglas Parker) *air transportation executive*

CALIFORNIA

Concord
Orris, Donald C. *freight transportation executive*
Uremovich, Michael Elliot *transportation company executive*

El Segundo
Hunt, Brian L. *program manager*
Musk, Elon *aerospace transportation executive*

Irvine
Lorimer, Mark W. *transportation company executive*

La Jolla
Drake, Hudson Billings *aerospace and electronics executive*

La Palma
Knowles, Marie L. *transportation executive*

Los Angeles
Bruce, William A. *airport executive*
Bush, Wesley G. *aerospace transportation executive*
Lovett, Wayne J. *air transportation executive, lawyer*
Mager, Artur *retired aerospace executive*
Mall, William John, Jr. *aerospace transportation executive, retired military officer*
Myers, Albert F. *aerospace executive*
Palmer, James F. *aerospace transportation executive*
Sugar, Ronald D. *aerospace transportation company executive*

Los Osos
Moore, Walter Dengel *rapid transit system professional*

Mojave
Melvill, Michael W. *aircraft company executive, experimental test pilot*
Searfoss, Richard A. *aerospace transportation executive, retired astronaut*

Oakland
Andrasick, James Stephen *transportation executive*
Rhein, Timothy J. *retired transportation company executive*

Ontario
Drinkwater, Peter Loftus *airport executive*

Palo Alto
Berry, Robert Emanuel *aerospace company executive*

Ramona
Hoffman, Wayne Melvin *retired airline official*

Rancho Santa Fe
Arledge, Charles Stone *former aerospace executive, entrepreneur*

Sacramento
Acree, G. Hardy *airport executive*
Wolfe, Robert A. *aerospace executive*

San Diego
Butterfield, Alexander Porter *air transportation executive, former federal official*
Mc Kinnon, Clinton Dan *aerospace transportation executive*

San Francisco
Foret, Mickey Phillip *retired air transportation executive*
Royer, Kathleen Rose *pilot*

San Jose
Tonseth, Ralph G. *airport executive*

San Mateo
Detter, Gerald L. *transportation executive*
Pileggi, Jennifer Wendy *transportation services executive*
Stotlar, Douglas W. *transportation executive*

San Pedro
Keller, Larry Alan *water transportation executive*

Saratoga
Reagan, Joseph Bernard *retired aerospace executive, management consultant*

COLORADO

Broomfield
Bobrick, Steven Aaron *transportation executive*

Denver
McMorris, Jerry *transportation company, sports team executive*
Meurlin, Keith W. *airport manager*

HAWAII

Honolulu
Doane, W. Allen *water transportation executive*

IDAHO

Boise
Ilett, Frank, Jr. *trucking executive, educator*

NEVADA

Las Vegas
Walker, Randall H. *air transportation executive*

Reno
Horton, Gary Bruce *transportation company executive*
Shoen, Edward Joseph *transportation and insurance companies executive*
White, Robert C. *air transportation executive*

NEW MEXICO

Albuquerque
Figueroa, Francisco Armando *aerospace defence executive, chief financial officer*
Weh, Allen Edward *aviation executive*

Holloman AFB
Klause, Klaus J. *aircraft company executive*

Las Cruces
Borman, Frank *former astronaut, laser patent company executive*

OREGON

Eugene
Toolson, Kay *transportation executive*

Mcminnville
Lane, Larry K. *air industry service executive*

West Linn
Brockley, John P. *airport terminal executive*

UTAH

North Salt Lake
Bouley, Joseph Richard *pilot*

Orem
Snow, Marlon O. *trucking executive, state agency administrator*

Saint George
Atkin, Jerry C. *air transportation executive*

WASHINGTON

Seattle
Ayer, William S. *air transportation executive*
Beighle, Douglas Paul *aerospace transportation executive*
Bezos, Jeffrey Preston *mail order services company executive*
Brazier, Robert G. *transportation executive*
Carson, Scott E. *aerospace transportation executive*
Cella, John J. *freight company executive*
Delavar, Michael *pilot*
Dickenson, Larry *aerospace transportation executive*
Freudenberger, Kent W. *freight company executive*
Gates, R. Jordan *delivery service executive*
Kelly, John F. *air transportation executive*
Knox, Venerria L. *transportation executive*
Rose, Peter J. *delivery service executive*
Smith, F. D. (Ricky Smith) *rail transporation executive*

Spokane
Ueberroth, John A. *air transportation executive*

WYOMING

Worland
Woods, Lawrence Milton *airline company executive*

CANADA

ALBERTA

Calgary
Durfy, Sean *air transportation executive*

ADDRESS UNPUBLISHED

Aldrin, Buzz *retired astronaut*
Blake, Patrick H. *trucking executive*
Brand, Vance Devoe *astronaut, director*
Cook, Stephen Champlin *retired shipping company executive*
Gasich, Welko Elton *retired aerospace defense executive, management consultant*
Guinasso, Victor *delivery service executive*
Gulcher, Robert Harry *aerospace transportation executive*
Johnson, Robert D. *aerospace transportation executive*
Kennard, Lydia H. *former airport terminal executive*
McCarty, Shirley Carolyn *retired aerospace executive*
McConnel, Richard Appleton *aerospace company official*
O'Brien, Raymond Francis *transportation executive*
Rivkind, Perry Abbot *federal railroad agency administrator*
Savitz, Maxine Lazarus *retired aerospace transportation executive*
Solomon, John Davis *aviation executive*
Sullenberger (Sully), Chesley Burnett III *pilot, airline safety consulting company executive*

INDUSTRY: UTILITIES, ENERGY, RESOURCES

UNITED STATES

ALASKA

Anchorage
Duncan, Ronald A. *telecommunications company executive*
Walp, Robert M. *communications carrier and internet/cable provider executive*

Fairbanks
Beistline, Earl Hoover *mining consultant*

ARIZONA

Phoenix
Adkerson, Richard C. *mining executive*
Huffman, Edgar Joseph *oil industry executive*
Post, William Joseph *utility executive*
Quirk, Kathleen L. *mining executive*

Scottsdale
Birkelbach, Albert Ottmar *retired oil industry executive*

Show Low
Pershing, Robert George *retired telecommunications industry executive*

Tempe
Hickson, Robin Julian *mining company executive*

Tucson
Jamison, Harrison Clyde *retired oil compan[y] executive*
Kissinger, Karen G. *energy executive*
Nelson, Dennis R. *energy executive*
Peeler, Stuart Thorne *oil industry executive, consultant*
Peters, Charles William *nuclear energy indu[stry] executive*

CALIFORNIA

Alameda
Lu, Hong Liang *telecommunications industr[y] executive*

Carmel
Williams, Delwyn Charles *telephone compa[ny] executive*

Folsom
Regan, William Joseph, Jr. *energy company executive*

Los Angeles
Chazen, Stephen I. *oil industry executive*
Foley, John V. *water company executive*
Irani, Ray R. *oil, gas and chemical compan[y] executive*
Lienert, James M. *oil industry executive*
Mandles, Martinn Heroe *facility services company executive*
Van Horne, R. Richard *oil industry and pub[lic] relations executive*

Martinez
Meyer, Jarold Alan *oil company research executive*

Mill Valley
Premo, Paul Mark *oil industry executive*

Mountain View
Koopmans, Chris *telecommunications indus[try] executive*

Newport Beach
Mercer, D. Scott *telecommunications indust[ry] executive*

Oxnard
Casey, Mary A. *telecommunications compa[ny] executive*
Enos, Kelly D. *telecommunications compan[y] financial executive*

Pacific Palisades
Mulryan, Henry Trist *mining executive, consultant*

Palo Alto
Agassi, Shai *alternative energy company executive, former application developer*
Cohen, Karl Paley *nuclear energy consulta[nt]*
Loewenstein, Walter Bernard *nuclear energ[y] industry executive*

Palos Verdes Peninsula
Christie, Hans Frederick *retired utilities executive*

Pasadena
White-Thomson, Ian Leonard *retired minin[g] executive*

Piedmont
Willrich, Mason *energy industry executive*

Rosemead
Craver, Theodore F., Jr. *utilities and energy executive*
Featherstone, Diane L. *utilities executive*
Fohrer, Alan J. *utilities company executive*
Gault, Polly L. *utilities executive*
House, Cecil R. *utilities executive*
Parsky, Barbara J. *utilities executive*
Scilacci, W. James, Jr. *utilities executive*
Yazdi, Mahvash *utilities executive*

Sacramento
Wickland, J. Al, Jr. *petroleum products and [real] estate executive*

San Diego
Altman, Steven R. *telecommunications exe[cutive]*
Felsinger, Donald E. *utilities corporation executive*
Guiles, Edwin A. *utilities company executiv[e]*
Hutcheson, S. Douglas *telecommunications industry executive*
Nickell, Robert E. *electric power industry executive*
Schmale, Neal E. *utilities company executi[ve]*
Snell, Mark A. *utilities executive*
Thornley, Anthony S. *telecommunications company executive*

San Francisco
Barcon, Barbara L. *utilities executive*
Darbee, Peter A. *utilities executive*
Dickinson, Wade *oil industry executive, ed[ucator]*
Goldstein, David Baird *energy executive, physicist*
Harvey, Kent M. *utilities executive*
Iribe, P. Chrisman *utilities executive*
Johns, Christopher P. *utilities executive*
McFadden, Nancy Elizabeth *utilities execu[tive]*

gley, Philip J. *retired telecommunications industry executive*
enberg, Rand L. *utilities executive*
on, John R. *utilities executive*
oul, John Allan *retired utilities executive*
l, James Edward *telecommunications, petroleum and pharmaceutical executive*
od, Carl William *utilities executive*
caria, Adrian *utilities executive*

n Jose
co, Jack A. *energy executive*
hrie, Laura D. *energy executive, human resources specialist*

n Mateo
n, Sam L. *telephone company executive*

n Ramon
be, Lydia I. *oil industry executive*
hancourt, John E. *oil industry executive*
ber, Pierre R. *oil industry executive*
s, John D. *oil industry executive*
nphrey, Mark A. *oil industry executive*
kland, George L. *oil industry executive*
Donald, John W. *oil industry executive*
Reilly, David J. *oil industry executive*
or, Jay R. *oil industry executive*
uttish, Thomas R. *oil industry executive*
gele, Paul K. *oil industry executive*
lor, Charles A. (Chuck Taylor) *oil industry executive*
son, John S. *oil industry executive*
th, Michael K. (Mike Wirth) *oil company executive*
rington, Patricia E. *oil industry executive*
gocki, Rhonda I. *oil industry executive*

nta Ana
rance, Dale R. *oil company executive*

nta Barbara
Duffie, Malcolm *oil industry executive*

nta Rosa
gner, Harold A. *retired gas industry executive*

otts Valley
man, Donald E. *telecommunications industry executive*

uth Pasadena
nell, Michael Hartman *mining executive*

nnyvale
on, James (Jim Olson) *telecommunications industry executive*

estwood
l, Wonhee *telecommunications industry executive*

LORADO

oomfield
el, Sunit *telecommunications industry executive*

nver
derson, Donald H. *energy executive*
nbre, Ronald C. *mining executive*
nfort, Stephanie Georges *telecommunications industry executive*
l, Larry Dean *utilities executive, lawyer*
milton, Frederic Crawford *oil company executive*
ger, Paula *telecommunications industry executive*
son, Randall J. *energy executive*
vis, Jerome A. *petroleum company executive, investment banker*
cey, William Blackmore *oil industry executive*
gg, Jimmy W. *gas industry executive*
eller, Edward A. *telecommunications industry executive*
rman, John Edward *petroleum landman*
ebaert, Richard C. *retired telecommunications industry executive*
Brien, Richard T. *mining executive*
Connor, Thomas C. *energy executive*
hards, Thomas E. *telecommunications industry executive*
hardson, John W. *telecommunications industry executive*
key, Laura L. *telecommunications industry executive*
lor, Teresa *telecommunications industry executive*
ompson, Lohren Matthew *oil company executive*
mton, Roland *telecommunications industry executive*
gemba, Robert D. *telecommunications industry executive*
eblood, Harry Albert, Jr. *oil industry executive*
t, Dan *telecommunications industry executive*

rango
rston, William Richardson *oil and gas industry executive, geologist*

glewood
nett, Robert R. *telecommunications company executive*
leyer, William T. *cable company executive*

Loveland
Bierbaum, J. Armin *petroleum company executive, consultant*

HAWAII

Honolulu
Lau, Constance H. (Connie Lau) *electric power industry executive*
Wilson, William Hall, Jr. *retired telecommunications executive*

IDAHO

Coeur D' Alene
Wheeler, Dennis Earl *mining company executive, lawyer*

MONTANA

Billings
Reed, Kenneth G. *petroleum company executive*

NEBRASKA

Omaha
Scott, Walter, Jr. *telecommunications industry executive*

NEVADA

Las Vegas
Shaw, Jeffrey William *gas industry executive*
Yackira, Michael William *electric power industry executive*

Reno
Gundersen, Wayne Campbell *energy executive, consultant*
Leclerc, Robert L. *mining company executive*

Winnemucca
Hesse, Martha O. *gas industry executive*

NEW MEXICO

Albuquerque
Robinson, Charles Paul *nuclear energy industry executive, diplomat*
Sterba, Jeffry E. *energy executive*
Yates, Harvey E. *oil industry executive, political organization administrator*

High Rolls Mountain Park
Ellison, Luther Frederick *oil industry executive*

Roswell
Anderson, Donald Bernard *oil industry executive*

OREGON

Beaverton
Timmins, Timothy A. *telecommunications industry executive*

Lake Oswego
Lorenzini, Paul Gilbert *electric power industry executive*

Newport
Morrow, James Thomas *energy executive*

Portland
Jungers, Francis *oil consultant*
Reiten, Richard G. *natural gas industry executive*

UTAH

Ogden
Adams, J. Phillip *oil industry executive*

Salt Lake City
Barlow, Charles *oil company executive*
Cash, Roy Don *retired gas and petroleum company executive*
Holding, R(obert) Earl *oil industry executive*
Rattie, Keith O. *gas industry executive*

WASHINGTON

Bellevue
Post, Denny Marie *telecommunications industry executive, marketing professional*
Reynolds, Stephen Philip *utility company executive*
Williamson, Charles R. *retired energy company executive*

Spokane
Eliassen, Jon Eric *retired corporate financial and utilities executive*
Ely, Gary G. *utilities company executive*
Meyer, David J. *energy executive, lawyer*

Tacoma
Temple, Thomas C. *oil company executive*

WYOMING

Casper
Stroock, Thomas Frank *oil and gas company executive*

Rock Springs
Kauchich, John Steven *oil and gas company executive*

CANADA

ALBERTA

Calgary
Anderson, J.C. *oil and gas industry executive, rancher*
Daniel, Patrick D. *energy executive*
Haskayne, Richard Francis *retired petroleum company executive*
Maier, Gerald James *gas industry executive*
McKinnon, F(rancis) A(rthur) Richard *utilities executive*
Meyers, Kevin O. *oil industry executive*
Southern, Nancy C. *utilities executive*

Red Deer
Donald, Jack C. *gas industry executive*

BRITISH COLUMBIA

Vancouver
Keevil, Norman B. *mining executive*

Winfield
Horton, William Russell *retired utilities executive*

Niagara Falls
Watson, George W. *energy executive*

ADDRESS UNPUBLISHED

Arlidge, John Walter *retired utilities executive*
Bodensteiner, Lisa M. *former utilities executive, lawyer*
Bruce, James Edmund *retired utilities executive*
Bryson, John E. *retired utilities executive*
Bushey, Richard Kenneth *utility executive*
Butler, Jack Fairchild *electric power industry executive*
Childers, Charles Eugene *mining company executive*
Clevenger, Jeffrey Griswold *mining company executive*
Conger, Harry Milton *mining company executive*
Cullen, James G. *telecommunications industry executive*
Dea, Peter Allen *gas industry executive, geologist*
Derr, Kenneth Tindall *retired oil industry executive*
Dietler, Cortlandt S. *oil industry executive*
Duque, Henry McArthur *utilities executive, consultant*
Fagin, David Kyle *mining executive*
Fisher, Thomas E. *energy company executive*
Frisbee, Don Calvin *retired utilities executive*
Glynn, Robert D., Jr. *former electric power and gas industry executive*
Higgins, Walter M. III *retired electric power industry executive*
Holliger, Fredric Lee *oil industry executive*
Huffman, James Thomas William *oil industry executive*
Imle, John F., Jr. *oil company executive*
Land, Kenneth Dean *test and balance agency executive, consultant*
Lassonde, Pierre *retired mining executive*
Losse, John William, Jr. *mining company executive*
May, Robert P. *retired energy executive*
Mc Carthy, Walter John, Jr. *retired utilities executive*
McDaniel, Thomas R. *retired utilities executive*
Middleton, James Arthur *oil and gas company executive*
Murdy, Wayne William *retired mining executive*
Noski, Charles H. *former telecommunications executive*
Ornasa, John *retired utilities executive*
Rendu, Jean-Michel Marie *mining executive*
Roberts, Lawrence Gilman *telecommunications industry executive*
Sanders, Charles Franklin *energy executive, consultant*
Senty, James A. *energy executive*
Shoup, Andrew James, Jr. *retired oil industry executive*
Smith, Gordon Ray *utilities executive*
Snider, Timothy R. *retired mining executive*
Soregaroli, A(rthur) E(arl) *mining executive, geologist*
Taylor, Leslie George *mining and finance company executive*
Thompson, Jack Edward *mining company executive*
Travis, Vance Kenneth *petroleum business executive*
Weaver, William Schildecker *retired electric power industry executive*

Whisler, James Steven *retired mining executive, lawyer, rancher*
Wood, Willis Bowne, Jr. *retired utilities executive*

INFORMATION TECHNOLOGY
See also **SCIENCE: MATHEMATICS AND COMPUTER SCIENCE**

UNITED STATES

ARIZONA

Scottsdale
Stott, Brian *software company executive, consultant*

Tempe
Crown, Eric J. *information systems executive*
Crown, Timothy A. *information technology executive*
Fennessy, Richard A. *information technology executive*

CALIFORNIA

Aliso Viejo
Dutile, Robert Arthur *information technology manager*

Berkeley
Karp, Richard Manning *computer science educator*
Séquin, Carlo H. *computer science educator*

Costa Mesa
Cox, Fred B. *software company executive*

Culver City
Berland, James Fred *software company executive*

Cupertino
Bregman, Mark *information technology executive*
Clyde, Robert Allan *computer software engineer*
Ive, Jonathan *information technology executive, product designer*
Nielsen, Tod *information technology executive*
Serlet, Bertrand *information technology executive*
Tamaddon, Sina *information technology executive*
Thompson, John Wendell *information technology executive*

Cypress
Romero, Tony *information technology executive*

El Segundo
Cooper, Milton E. *computer science company professional*

Foster City
Milligan, John F. *information technology executive*

Glen Ellen
Hurlbert, Roger William *information technology executive*

Irvine
Morhaime, Mike *video game company executive*

Lafayette
Lewis, Sheldon Noah *technology consultant*

Los Altos
Esber, Edward Michael, Jr. *software company executive*

Los Angeles
Boehm, Barry William *computer science educator*
Hwang, John Dzen *information systems educator*

Martinez
Tong, Siu Wing *computer programmer*

Menlo Park
Bechtolsheim, Andy (Andreas von Bechtolsheim) *information technology executive*
Hewlett, Walter B. *application developer*
Mangiola, Mark *information technology executive*
Murphy, Matt *information technology executive*

Modesto
Kushar, Kent *information technology executive*

Moffett Field
Davies, Carol B. *computer programmer, researcher*

Mountain View
Baker, Mitchell *computer software developer, foundation administrator*
Brin, Sergey Mihailovich *information technology executive*

Cerf, Vinton Gray *information technology executive*
Coughran, William M., Jr. *information technology executive, researcher*
Denzel, Nora Manley *information technology executive*
Drummond, David C. *information technology executive, lawyer*
Eustace, Alan *information technology executive*
Gillis, Edwin *information technology executive*
Hughes, Gregory *information technology executive*
Kamangar, Salar *information technology executive*
Kordestani, Omid *information technology executive*
Mayer, Marissa Ann *information technology executive*
Page, Larry (Lawrence E. Page) *information technology executive*
Pichette, Patrick *information technology company executive*
Rosenberg, Jonathan *information technology executive*
Rubin, Andrew E. (Andrew E. Rubin) *technology product developer*
Schmidt, Eric Emerson *information technology executive*

Oakland
Safka, Jim *information technology executive, investment services company executive*

Pasadena
Chandy, K. Mani *computer science educator*

Redwood City
Block, Keith *computer software company executive*
Kurian, Thomas *computer software company executive*
Lee, V. Paul *entertainment software company executive*
Phillips, Charles E., Jr. *computer software company executive*
Polese, Kim *software company executive*
Probst, Lawrence F. III *interactive software/gaming executive*
Riccitiello, John S. *interactive software/gaming executive, venture capitalist*
Rottler, Juergen *computer software company executive*
Rozwat, Charles *computer software company executive*
Vrabeck, Kathy Patterson *video game company executive*

Redwood Shores
Catz, Safra A. *computer software company executive*
Ellison, Larry (Lawrence Joseph Ellison) *computer software company executive*
Epstein, Jeffrey Emanuel *computer software company executive*
Henley, Jeffrey O. *computer software company executive*

Sacramento
Hummel, John *information technology executive*

San Diego
Jones, Ronald H. *computer information systems executive*
Legrand, Shawn Pierre *enterprise support services manager*
Pottenger, Mark McClelland *computer programmer*
Rastetter, William H. *biotechnology company executive*
Short, Jay Milton *biotechnology company executive*
Tom, Lawrence *technology executive*

San Francisco
Ben-Horin, Daniel *information technology executive*
Buckmaster, Jim *online community bulletin board company executive*
Dodge, Geoffrey A. *information technology executive, former publishing executive*
Dorsey, Jack *software architect*
Hirschmann, Peter *video game company executive*
Kapor, Mitchell David *application developer, foundation administrator*
Kingdon, Mark *computer software company executive*
Rosedale, Philip E. *computer software company executive*
Stone, Issac (Biz Stone) *application developer, consultant*
Torvalds, Linus Benedict *application developer*
Trott, Mena *application developer*

San Jose
Belluzzo, Rick E. (Richard) *information technology and former computer software company executive*
Chambers, John Thomas *computer systems network executive*
Chandler, Mark D. *computer systems network executive, lawyer*
Chizen, Bruce R. *computer software company executive*
Chuang, Alfred Sze *information technology executive*
Emmett, Brian *software developer*
Fishback, Dennis *information technology executive*
Helleboid, Olivier *information technology executive*
Ill, Charles III *information technology executive*
Loiacono, John P. *information technology executive*
Meltzer, Cliff *information technology executive*
Morgridge, John P. *computer systems network executive*
Narayen, Shantanu *computer software company executive*
Ratzlaff, Cordell R. *application developer*
Warrior, Padmasree Y. *computer systems network executive*

San Mateo
Herscher, Penny *information technology executive*

San Rafael
Hughes, Louis Ralph *information technology executive*

Santa Ana
Boyd, Larry C. *information technology executive*
Humes, William D. *information technology executive*
Monié, Alain *information technology executive*
Salem, Karen E. *information technology executive*
Spierkel, Gregory M. *information technology executive*

Santa Barbara
Boehm, Eric Hartzell *information technology executive*

Santa Clara
Benson, Jon H. *information technology executive*
Beveridge, Crawford W. *information technology executive*
Bryant, Diane M. *information technology executive*
Bucklin, Christine B. *information technology executive*
Fowler, John *information technology executive*
Gadre, Anil *information technology executive*
Green, Rich *information technology executive*
Harris, David M. *information technology executive*
Heel, Joe *information technology executive*
Lehman, Michael Evans *information technology executive*
MacGowan, Bill *information technology executive*
McNealy, Scott Glenn *information technology executive*
Miller, Dan *information technology executive*
Murdock, Ian *information technology executive*
Papadopoulos, Gregory Michael *information technology executive*
Schwartz, Jonathan Ian *information technology executive*
Sutphin, Brian *information technology executive*
Tremblay, Marc *information technology executive*
Van Den Hoogen, Ingrid *information technology executive*
White, Ian *information technology executive*
Yen, David Wei-Luen *information technology executive*

South Pasadena
Hsieh, Ming *information technology executive*

South San Francisco
Ryan, Tom *reporting applications platform company executive*

Stanford
Feigenbaum, Edward Albert *retired computer science educator*

Sunnyvale
Balogh, Aristotle N. *information technology executive*
Benhamou, Eric A. *information technology company executive*
Calderoni, Robert M. *software company executive*
de Ruiz, Hector J. *information technology executive*
Hawkins, Jeff *information technology company executive*
Johnson, Kevin *information technology executive, former computer software company executive*
Kispert, John H. *information technology executive*
Kriens, Scott Gregory *information technology executive*
Maresca, Joseph William, Jr. *technology executive, physical oceanographer*
McCoy, Thomas M. *information technology executive*
Meyer, Dirk (Derrick R. Meyer) *information technology executive*
Ruiz, Hector de Jesus *information technology executive*
Sanders, W. J. III *information technology executive*

West Sacramento
Wilson, Eric F.G. *information technology executive*

Westlake Village
Borenstein, Lorna M. *information technology executive*

Woodland Hills
Brooks, Robert Eugene *decision support software designer*
Stratton, Gregory Alexander *application developer, director, mayor*

COLORADO

Boulder
Kenney, Belinda Jill Forseman *information technology executive*

Broomfield
Martin, Patrick J. *technology company executive*

Denver
Allen, Richard *computer software executive*
Rodriguez, Juan Alfonso *information technology executive*
Smith, Derrin Ray *information systems company executive*

Greenwood Village
Capellas, Michael D. *information technology executive*
DeRodes, Robert P. *information technology executive*
Wall, Phil *information technology executive*

HAWAII

Honolulu
Sekine, Deborah Keiko *systems analyst, programmer*

IDAHO

Boise
Mahoney, James E. *information technology executive*

NEVADA

Las Vegas
Stanley, Tim *information technology executive*

Reno
Matthews, Thomas J. *game company executive*

NEW MEXICO

Albuquerque
Orman, John Leo *software engineer, writer*
Wellborn, Charles Ivey *strategic planning consultant*

NEW YORK

New York
Roedel, Richard W. *video game developing company executive*

TEXAS

Dallas
Beer, James A. *information technology executive, former air transportation executive*

UTAH

Provo
Kitto, Franklin Curtis *computer systems specialist*

Salt Lake City
Mendenhall, Robert W. *education technology executive*

VIRGINIA

Arlington
Cofoni, Paul Michael *information technology executive*

WASHINGTON

Mercer Island
Herres, Phillip Benjamin *computer software executive*

Oak Harbor
Meaux, Alan Douglas *facilities technician, artist*

Redmond
Burgum, Doug *software company executive*
Cutler, David Neil, Sr. *software engineer*
Tatarinov, Kirill *computer software industry expert*

Seattle
Lazowska, Edward Delano *computer science educator*
Mayo, Robert N. *computer science researcher*
Simonyi, Charles *software engineer*

Spokane
Ballinger, Charles Kenneth *information specialist*

WISCONSIN

Brookfield
Jones, Richard K. *information technology executive*

WYOMING

Cheyenne
Looplock, Paul *computer technician*

CANADA

ALBERTA

Edmonton
Davis, Wayne Alton *computer science educa*

ADDRESS UNPUBLISHED

Allchin, Jim *information technology executiv*
Anderson, Christine Marlene *software engine*
Anderson, Donald Lloyd *weapon systems consultant*
Andreessen, Marc Lowell *software company executive, internet innovator*
Berry, Richard Lewis *information technology manager, writer, magazine editor, lecturer, programmer*
Caldwell, Nanci *former computer software company executive*
Dalzell, Rick *information technology executi*
Drexler, Jerome *technology company executi*
Duffield, David A. *application developer, for computer software company executive*
Foster, Kent B. *retired information technolog executive*
Frei, Brent R. *computer software executive*
Fuller, Dale L. *software security company executive*
Greene, Diane B. *information technology executive*
Hariton, Lorraine Jill *information technology executive*
Hemann, Raymond Glenn *research company executive*
Howard, H. William *information technology executive*
Howe, Bill *information technology executive*
Lee, Bryan *information technology executive*
Lyons, Susanne D. *information technology executive*
McCaffrey, Cindy *information technology executive*
Mullarkey, Maureen T. *former game compan executive*
Nazem, Farzad *information technology execu*
Peterson, Marissa T. *former computer system network executive*
Reyes, George *retired information technolog executive*
Rohde, James Vincent *software systems com executive*
Satterwhite, R. Scott *technology company executive*
Shaheen, George T. *former computer softwar company executive*
Siebel, Thomas M. *software company execut*
Tevanian, Avadis, Jr. *information technology executive*
Thompson, Kenneth *software engineer*
Wookey, John *former computer software company executive*

INTERNET *See* INFORMATIO TECHNOLOGY

LAW: JUDICIAL ADMINISTRATION

UNITED STATES

ALASKA

Anchorage
Burgess, Timothy M. *federal judge, former prosecutor*
Eastaugh, Robert L. *state supreme court just*
Fabe, Dana Anderson *state supreme court ch justice*
Fitzgerald, James Michael *federal judge*
Holland, H. Russel *federal judge*
Sedwick, John W. *federal judge*
von der Heydt, James Arnold *federal judge*

Fairbanks
Kleinfeld, Andrew J. *federal judge*

neau
peneti, Walter L. *state supreme court justice*
isten, Morgan *state supreme court justice*

IZONA

oenix
lerson, Lawrence Ohaco *federal judge, awyer*
es, W. Scott *state supreme court justice*
ch, Rebecca White *state supreme court ustice, lawyer*
omfield, Robert Cameron *federal judge*
by, William Cameron, Jr. *federal judge*
roll, Earl Hamblin *federal judge*
e, Charles G., II, *federal judge*
nes, Francis Pendleton III *judge*
vkins, Michael Daly *federal judge*
ks, Bethany Gribben *judge, lawyer*
witz, Andrew D. *state supreme court justice*
es, Charles E. *retired state supreme court hief justice*
tone, Frederick J. *judge*
Clennen, Crane *judge*
Gregor, Ruth Van Roekel *state supreme court hief justice*
Namee, Stephen M. *federal judge*
enblatt, Paul Gerhardt *judge*
n, Michael D. *state supreme court justice*
roeder, Mary Murphy *federal judge*
er, Roslyn Olson *federal judge*
erman, Barry G. *federal judge*
nd, Roger Gordon *federal judge*
ke, Neil Vincent *federal judge, lawyer*
throp, Lawrence Fredrick *judge*

cson
mmer, J. William, Jr. *judge, lawyer*
lar, James M. *federal judge*
l, John McCarthy *judge*

ma
in, Jay R. *federal judge*

LIFORNIA

reka
d, Larry B. *federal judge*

esno
k, Dennis L. *judge*
le, Robert Everett *federal judge*
cker, Myron Donovan *federal judge*
ian, Brett J. *federal judge*
i, Anthony W. *judge*
Neill, Lawrence Joseph *federal judge*
nger, Oliver Winston *federal judge*

s Angeles
art, Alan M. *judge*
rcón, Arthur Lawrence *federal judge*
er, Valerie L. *federal judge*
ck, Robert N. *federal judge*
ford, Samuel Lawrence *federal judge*
roll, Ellen A. *judge, lawyer*
pman, Rosalyn M. *federal judge*
vez, Victor Edwin *judge*
lins, Audrey B. *judge*
ry, Daniel Arthur *judge*
ierrez, Philip S. *federal judge*
ter, Terry Julius, Jr. *federal judge*
hberger, William Foster *lawyer*
Lance Allan *judge*
nson, Earl, Jr. *judge, author*
leher, Robert Joseph *judge*
ler, William D. *federal judge*
g, George H. *judge*
s, J. Spencer *federal judge*
v, Ronald. S. W *federal judge*
nella, Nora Margaret *judge*
rshall, Consuelo Bland *federal judge*
Mahon, James W. *federal magistrate judge*
sk, Richard Mitchell *judge*
elzer, Mariana R. *federal judge*
l, Manuel Lawrence *federal judge*
ssell, Barry *federal judge*
phens, Albert Lee, Jr. *federal judge*
asugi, Robert Mitsuhiro *federal judge*
lin, Robert J. *judge*
son, Stephen Victor *federal judge*
trich, Andrew J. *federal judge*
ght, Otis Dalino, II, *judge*
, George H. *federal judge*
on, Laurie Dee *judge*
zolo, Vincent P. *federal judge*

endocino
sterson, William A. *retired judge*

kland
nstrong, Saundra Brown *federal judge*
zil, Wayne D. *federal judge*
en, Edward D. *federal bankruptcy judge*
sen, D. Lowell *federal judge*
vsome, Randall Jackson *judge*
aikovsky, Leslie J. *federal judge*
ken, Claudia *judge*

sadena
chever, Robert *federal judge*
nandez, Ferdinand Francis *federal judge*
ner, Raymond Corley *federal judge*
dwin, Alfred Theodore *federal judge*
, Cynthia Holcomb *federal judge*
zinski, Alex *federal judge*
son, Dorothy Wright *federal judge*
Paez, Richard A. *federal judge*
Rymer, Pamela Ann *federal judge*
Tashima, Atsushi Wallace *federal judge*
Wardlaw, Kim A. McLane *federal judge*

Ramona
Marquez, Alfredo C. *federal judge*

Riverside
Goldberg, Mitchel R. *federal judge*
Jury, Meredith A. *federal judge*
Larson, Stephen G. *federal judge*
Naugle, David N. *federal judge*
Phillips, Virginia A. *judge*

Sacramento
Burrell, Garland E., Jr. *federal judge*
Callahan, Consuelo Maria *federal judge*
Damrell, Frank C., Jr. *judge*
Garcia, Edward J. *federal judge*
Karlton, Lawrence K. *federal judge*
Klein, Christopher M. *federal judge*
McManus, Michael S. *federal judge*
Mendez, John Anthony *federal judge*
Moulds, John F. *judge*
Nowinski, Peter A. *federal judge*
Russell, David E. *judge*
Van Camp, Brian Ralph *judge*

San Clemente
Wilson, John James *federal judge*

San Diego
Aaron, Cynthia G. *judge*
Adler, Louise DeCarl *judge*
Anello, Michael M. *federal judge*
Bowie, Peter Wentworth *judge, educator*
Brewster, Rudi Milton *judge*
Enright, William Benner *judge*
Gonzalez, Irma Elsa *federal judge*
Hargrove, John James *bankruptcy judge*
Harutunian, Albert T(heodore) III *judge*
Huff, Marilyn L. *federal judge*
Jones, Napoleon A., Jr. *federal judge*
McKeown, Mary Margaret *federal judge*
Moskowitz, Barry T. *judge*
Porter, Louisa S. *federal judge*
Thompson, David Renwick *federal judge*
Thompson, Gordon, Jr. *federal judge*
Turrentine, Howard Boyd *federal judge*
Wallace, J. Clifford *federal judge*

San Francisco
Alsup, William *judge*
Baxter, Marvin Ray *state supreme court justice*
Bea, Carlos Tiburcio *federal judge*
Berzon, Marsha S. *federal judge*
Breyer, Charles Roberts *judge, lawyer*
Browning, James Robert *federal judge*
Carlson, Thomas Edward *judge*
Chesney, Maxine M. *judge*
Chin, Ming W. *state supreme court justice*
Conti, Samuel *federal judge*
Corrigan, Carol A. *state supreme court justice*
Fletcher, William A. *federal judge, educator*
George, Ronald M. *state supreme court chief justice*
Haerle, Paul Raymond *judge*
Henderson, Thelton Eugene *federal judge*
Illston, Susan Y. *federal judge*
Jarvis, Donald Bertram *judge*
Kennard, Joyce L. *state supreme court justice*
Kline, John Anthony *judge*
Moreno, Carlos R. *state supreme court justice*
Noonan, John T., Jr. *federal judge, educator*
Patel, Marilyn Hall *judge*
Robertson, Armand James, II, *judge*
Schwarzer, William W. *federal judge*
Walker, Vaughn R. *federal judge*
Werdegar, Kathryn Mickle *state supreme court justice*
Zimmerman, Bernard *judge*

San Jose
Fogel, Jeremy Don *judge*
Grube, James R. *federal judge*
Infante, Edward A. *federal judge*
Panelli, Edward Alexander *retired state supreme court justice*
Ware, James W. *federal judge*
Weissbrodt, Arthur S. *federal judge*
Whyte, Ronald M. *judge*

San Marino
Mortimer, Wendell Reed, Jr. *retired judge*

Santa Ana
Carter, David O. *judge*
Guilford, Andrew John *federal judge*
Ryan, John Edward *federal judge*
Stotler, Alicemarie Huber *federal judge*

Santa Barbara
Aldisert, Ruggero John *federal judge*

Studio City
Gold, Arnold Henry *judge*
Lasarow, William Julius *retired federal judge*

Susanville
Kellison, Craig M. *federal judge*

Woodland Hills
Greenwald, Arthur M. *federal judge*
Mund, Geraldine *judge*
Pregerson, Harry *federal judge*

COLORADO

Black Hawk
Rodgers, Frederic Barker *judge*

Denver
Abram, Donald Eugene *retired federal judge*
Arguello, Christine Marie *federal judge*
Babcock, Lewis Thornton *federal judge*
Bender, Michael Lee *state supreme court justice*
Brimmer, Philip A. *federal judge*
Coats, Nathan B. *state supreme court justice*
Daniel, Wiley Young *federal judge*
Ebel, David M. *federal judge*
Eid, Allison Hartwell *state supreme court justice*
Felter, Edwin Lester, Jr. *judge*
Gorsuch, Neil McGill *federal judge, lawyer*
Hobbs, Gregory James, Jr. *state supreme court justice*
Kane, John Lawrence, Jr. *judge*
Kirshbaum, Howard M. *retired judge*
Krieger, Marcia Smith *federal judge*
Lucero, Carlos *federal judge*
Martinez, Alex J. *state supreme court justice*
Matheson, Charles E. *federal judge*
Matsch, Richard P. *judge*
McWilliams, Robert Hugh *federal judge*
Miller, Walker David *federal judge*
Mullarkey, Mary J. *state supreme court chief justice*
Porfilio, John Carbone *federal judge*
Rice, Nancy E. *state supreme court justice*
Rovira, Luis Dario *state supreme court justice*
Schlatter, O. Edward *judge*
Stacy, Richard A. *judge*
Tymkovich, Timothy Michael *federal judge*

Golden
Jackson, Richard Brooke *judge*

Littleton
Erickson, William Hurt *retired state supreme court justice*

Westminster
Scott, Gregory Kellam *former state supreme court justice, lawyer*

HAWAII

Honolulu
Acoba, Simeon Rivera, Jr. *state supreme court justice, educator*
Clifton, Richard Randall *federal judge*
Duffy, James Earl, Jr. *state supreme court justice*
Ezra, David Alan *federal judge*
Gillmor, Helen *federal judge*
King, Samuel Pailthorpe *federal judge*
Klein, Robert Gordon *former state supreme court justice*
Kurren, Barry M. *federal judge*
Moon, Ronald T.Y. *state supreme court chief justice*
Nakayama, Paula Aiko *state supreme court justice*
Recktenwald, Mark E. *state supreme court justice*
Watanabe, Corinne Kaoru Amemiya *judge, state official*
Yamashita, Francis Isami *magistrate judge*

IDAHO

Boise
Boyle, Larry Monroe *federal judge*
Burdick, Roger S. *state supreme court justice*
Eismann, Daniel T. *state supreme court chief justice*
Horton, Joel D. *state supreme court justice*
Jones, James Thomas *state supreme court justice, former state attorney general*
Jones, Warren Eugene *state supreme court justice*
Lodge, Edward James *federal judge*
McDevitt, Charles Francis *retired judge, lawyer*
Nelson, Thomas G. *federal judge*
Trott, Stephen Spangler *federal judge*
Williams, Mikel Howard *magistrate judge*
Winmill, B. Lynn *federal judge*

Pocatello
Smith, Norman Randy *federal judge*

KANSAS

Lawrence
Briscoe, Mary Beck *federal judge*

MONTANA

Billings
Fagg, Russell *judge, lawyer*
Shanstrom, Jack D. *federal judge*
Thomas, Sidney R. *federal judge*

Glendive
McDonough, Russell Charles *retired state supreme court justice*

Helena
Cotter, Patricia O'Brien *state supreme court justice*
Harrison, John Conway *retired state supreme court justice*
Leaphart, W. William *state supreme court justice*
McGrath, Mike *state supreme court chief justice, former state attorney general*
Morris, Brian *state supreme court justice*
Nelson, James C *state supreme court justice*
Rice, Jim *state supreme court justice*
Warner, John Arnan *state supreme court justice*

Missoula
Erickson, Leif B. *federal judge*
Molloy, Donald William *federal judge, lawyer*

Polson
Turnage, Jean Allen *retired state supreme court chief justice*

NEVADA

Carson City
Cherry, Michael A. *state supreme court justice*
Gibbons, Mark *state supreme court justice*
Hardesty, James W. *state supreme court chief justice*
Parraguirre, Ronald David *state supreme court justice*
Saitta, Nancy M. *state supreme court justice*
Springer, Charles Edward *retired judge*

Las Vegas
Becker, Nancy Anne *former state supreme court justice*
Bybee, Jay Scott *federal judge, former federal agency administrator*
Douglas, Michael Lawrence *state supreme court justice*
Hunt, Roger Lee *federal judge*
Johnston, Robert Jake *federal magistrate judge*
Pro, Philip Martin *judge*
Rawlinson, Johnnie Blakeney *federal judge*
Steffen, Thomas Lee *retired judge, lawyer*

Reno
Brunetti, Melvin T. *federal judge*
Goldwater, Bert M. *federal judge*
Hug, Procter Ralph, Jr. *federal judge*
McKibben, Howard D. *federal judge*
McQuaid, Robert A., Jr. *federal judge*
Reed, Edward Cornelius, Jr. *federal judge*
Sandoval, Brian Edward *federal judge, former state attorney general*

NEW MEXICO

Albuquerque
Conway, John E. *federal judge*
Franchini, Gene Edward *state supreme court justice*
Garcia, Lorenzo F. *federal judge*
Hansen, Curtis LeRoy *federal judge*
Parker, James Aubrey *federal judge*
Puglisi, Richard Lawrence *federal judge*
Svet, Don J. *federal judge*

Clovis
Tharp, Fred C., Jr. *federal judge, lawyer*

Gallup
Ionta, Robert W. *federal judge, lawyer*

Las Cruces
Galvan, Joe H. *federal judge*
Smith, Leslie C. *federal judge*

Santa Fe
Black, Bruce D. *judge*
Chavez, Edward L. *state supreme court chief justice*
Kelly, Paul Joseph, Jr. *federal judge*
Maes, Petra Jimenez *state supreme court justice*
Serna, Patricio *state supreme court justice*
Vázquez, Martha Alicia *federal judge*
Yalman, Ann *judge, lawyer*

OREGON

Eugene
Coffin, Thomas M. *federal magistrate judge*
Hogan, Michael R(obert) *judge*
Radcliffe, Albert E. *judge*
Walters, Martha Lee *state supreme court justice*

Medford
Cooney, John P. *judge*
Panner, Owen M. *federal judge*

Pendleton
Bloom, Stephen Michael *magistrate judge, lawyer*

Portland
Beatty, John Cabeen, Jr. *judge*
Dunn, Randall Lawson *judge*
Graber, Susan P. *federal judge*
Haggerty, Ancer Lee *federal judge*
Jones, Robert Edward *federal judge*
Leavy, Edward *federal judge*
Marsh, Malcolm F. *federal judge*
O'Scannlain, Diarmuid Fionntain *federal judge*
Redden, James Anthony *federal judge*
Riggs, R. William *retired state supreme court justice*
Skopil, Otto Richard, Jr. *federal judge*
Sullivan, Donal D. *federal judge*

Van Hoomissen, George Albert *state supreme court justice*

Salem
Balmer, Thomas Ancil *state supreme court justice*
De Muniz, Paul J. *state supreme court chief justice*
Durham, Robert Donald, Jr. *state supreme court justice*
Gillette, W. Michael *state supreme court justice*
Kistler, Rives *state supreme court justice*
Linde, Hans Arthur *state supreme court justice*
Linder, Virginia Lynn *state supreme court justice*
Peterson, Edwin J. *retired judge, mediator, educator*

Troutdale
Unis, Richard L. *judge*

UTAH

Monticello
Redd, F. Bennion *federal magistrate*

Park City
Kaufman, Roger Wayne *retired judge*

Salt Lake City
Anderson, Stephen Hale *federal judge*
Benson, Dee Vance *federal judge*
Clark, Glen Edward *judge*
Durham, Christine Meaders *state supreme court chief justice*
Greene, John Thomas *judge*
Jenkins, Bruce Sterling *federal judge*
McConnell, Michael W. *federal judge, law educator*
McKay, Monroe Gunn *federal judge*
Murphy, Michael R. *federal judge*
Nehring, Ronald E. *state supreme court justice*
Nuffer, David O. *judge*
Parrish, Jill Niederhauser *state supreme court justice*
Sam, David *federal judge*
Waddoups, Clark *federal judge*
Warner, Paul Michael *federal judge, former prosecutor*
Wilkins, Michael Jon *state supreme court justice*
Winder, David Kent *judge*

WASHINGTON

Olympia
Alexander, Gerry L. *state supreme court chief justice*
Chambers, Thomas Jefferson *state supreme court justice*
Fairhurst, Mary E. *state supreme court justice*
Guy, Richard P. *retired state supreme court justice*
Johnson, Charles William *state supreme court justice*
Johnson, James Martin *state supreme court justice, lawyer*
Madsen, Barbara A. *state supreme court justice*
Owens, Susan *state supreme court justice*
Sanders, Richard Browning *state supreme court justice*
Smith, Charles Z. *retired state supreme court justice*

Seattle
Brandt, Philip H. *federal judge*
Coughenour, John Clare *federal judge*
Dimmick, Carolyn Reaber *federal judge*
Fletcher, Betty Binns *federal judge*
Glover, Thomas T. *federal judge*
Gould, Ronald Murray *federal judge*
Mc Govern, Walter T. *federal judge*
Overstreet, Karen A. *federal bankruptcy judge*
Steiner, Samuel J. *judge*
Tallman, Richard C. *federal judge, lawyer*
Weinberg, John Lee *federal judge*
Wilson, David Eugene *former magistrate judge, lawyer*
Zilly, Thomas Samuel *federal judge*

Spokane
Imbrogno, Cynthia *judge*
Nielsen, William Fremming *federal judge*
Quackenbush, Justin Lowe *federal judge*
Van Sickle, Frederick L. *federal judge*
Williams, Patricia C. *federal judge*

Tacoma
Arnold, J. Kelley *United States magistrate judge*
Bryan, Robert J. *federal judge*

Tukwila
Talmadge, Philip Albert *retired judge, state senator*

Yakima
Suko, Lonny Ray *judge*

WYOMING

Casper
Downes, William F. *federal judge*

Cheyenne
Brimmer, Clarence Addison *federal judge*
Brorby, Wade *federal judge*
Burke, E. James *state supreme court justice, lawyer*
Golden, T. Michael *state supreme court justice*
Hill, William U. *state supreme court justice, former state attorney general*
Johnson, Alan Bond *federal judge*
Kite, Marilyn S. *state supreme court justice, lawyer*
McNiff, Peter J. *federal judge*
Taylor, William Al *state supreme court justice*
Voigt, Barton R. *state supreme court chief justice*

Green River
Marty, Lawrence A. *magistrate*

Jackson
Bommer, Timothy J. *magistrate judge, lawyer*

Lander
Gist, Richard D. *federal judge*

Powell
Patrick, H. Hunter *retired judge, lawyer*

Sheridan
Connor, Robert W., Jr. *federal judge*

Yellowstone National Park
Cole, Stephen E. *magistrate judge*

CANADA

ALBERTA

Calgary
Major, John Charles *judge*

SASKATCHEWAN

Regina
Bayda, Edward Dmytro *retired chief justice*

ADDRESS UNPUBLISHED

Aiken, Ann L. *federal judge*
Allred, Clark B. *judge*
Anderson, Carl West *retired judge*
Baca, Joseph Francis *retired judge*
Baird, Lourdes G. *federal judge*
Barr, James Norman *retired federal judge*
Barrett, James Emmett *federal judge*
Bedsworth, William W. *judge*
Beezer, Robert Renaut *federal judge*
Boren, Roger W. *judge*
Bosson, Richard Campbell *state supreme court justice*
Boulden, Judith Ann *judge*
Bridge, Bobbe Jean *former state supreme court justice*
Brooks, Ruben B. *judge*
Bryner, Alexander O. *former state supreme court justice*
Burke, Edmond Wayne *retired judge, lawyer*
Carson, Wallace Preston, Jr. *retired state supreme court justice*
Coan, Patricia A. *retired judge*
Compton, Allen T. *retired state supreme court justice*
Dela Cruz, Jose Santos *retired commonwealth supreme court justice*
Farris, Jerome *federal judge*
Frye, Helen Jackson *federal judge*
Gray, Karla Marie *retired state supreme court chief justice*
Hagen, David Warner *retired judge*
Heen, Walter Meheula *retired judge, former political party executive*
Holmes, Dallas Scott *judge, educator*
Ireland, Faith *retired state supreme court justice, lawyer*
Kidwell, Wayne L. *retired state supreme court justice*
Legge, Charles Alexander *federal judge*
Levinson, Steven Henry *retired state supreme court justice*
Low, Harry William *judge*
Manglona, Ramona V. *judge, former attorney general*
Matthews, Warren Wayne *retired state supreme court justice*
Maupin, A. William *retired state supreme court chief justice*
McKee, Roger Curtis *retired federal judge*
Moore, Daniel Alton, Jr. *retired state supreme court justice*
Myers, Robert David *judge*
Nottingham, Edward Willis, Jr. *former federal judge*
Reinhardt, Stephen Roy *federal judge*
Robart, James Louis *federal judge, lawyer*
Rose, Robert Edgar *retired state supreme court justice*
Rosenblum, Ellen F. *judge*
Schroeder, Gerald Frank *retired state supreme court justice*
Shearing, Miriam *retired state supreme court chief justice*
Shubb, William Barnet *judge*
Stewart, Isaac Daniel, Jr. *retired state supreme court justice*
Tevrizian, Dickran M., Jr. *judge*
Trout, Linda Copple *former state supreme court justice*
Waters, Laughlin Edward *federal judge*
Weber, Fred J. *retired state supreme court justice*
Wilson, Ronald A. *judge*
Zive, Gregg William *judge*

LAW: LAW PRACTICE AND ADMINISTRATION

UNITED STATES

ALASKA

Anchorage
Berkowitz, Ethan A. *lawyer, former state representative*
Brown, Keith E. *lawyer*
Cantor, James Elliot *lawyer*
Claman, Matthew W. *lawyer, acting Mayor, Anchorage*
De Lisio, Stephen Scott *lawyer, director, pastor*
Edwards, George Kent *lawyer*
Grahame, Heather H. *lawyer*
Greenstein, Marla Nan *lawyer*
Katcher, Jonathon A. *lawyer*
Kendall-Miller, Heather *lawyer*
Langworthy, Robert H. *law educator*
Loeffler, Karen Louise *prosecutor*
Oesting, David W. *lawyer*
Reeves, James N. *lawyer*
Roberts, John Derham *lawyer*
Serdahely, Douglas J. *lawyer, former state judge*

Fairbanks
Tiemessen, John J. *lawyer*

Juneau
Cole, Charles Edward *lawyer, state attorney general*
Collins, Patricia A. *lawyer, judge*
Rozell, William Barclay *lawyer*

Kodiak
Jamin, Matthew Daniel *lawyer, judge*

ARIZONA

Fountain Hills
Berg, Madelaine R. *lawyer*

Kingman
Basinger, Richard Lee *lawyer*

Phoenix
Allen, Robert Eugene Barton *lawyer*
Alsentzer, William James, Jr. *lawyer*
Bain, C. Randall *lawyer*
Baker, William Dunlap *lawyer*
Bakker, Thomas Gordon *lawyer*
Begam, Robert George *lawyer*
Betts, Janet Gniadek *lawyer*
Birk, David R. *lawyer, electronics executive*
Bivens, Donald Wayne *lawyer, political organization administrator*
Blanchard, Charles Alan *lawyer, retired state senator*
Bodney, David Jeremy *lawyer*
Burke, Timothy John *lawyer*
Cohen, Jon Stephan *lawyer*
Colburn, Donald D. *lawyer*
Cole, George Thomas *lawyer*
Colton, Sterling David (David Colton) *lawyer*
Comus, Louis Francis, Jr. *lawyer*
Cooledge, Richard Calvin *lawyer*
Coppersmith, Sam *lawyer, former congressman*
Cowley, Samuel C. *lawyer, transportation services executive*
Crockett, Clyll Webb *lawyer*
Crozier, Scott A. *lawyer*
Davies, David George *lawyer, educator*
Dawson, John Joseph *lawyer*
Derdenger, Patrick *lawyer*
Derouin, James Gilbert *lawyer*
Donovan, Timothy R. *lawyer*
Dunipace, Ian Douglas *lawyer*
Ehmann, Anthony Valentine *lawyer*
Everroad, John David *lawyer*
Fellows, Gerald Lee *lawyer*
Fenzl, Terry Earle *lawyer*
Fine, Charles Leon *lawyer*
Gaffney, Donald Lee *lawyer*
Gaffney, John T. *lawyer*
Gallagher, Michael L. *lawyer*
Gilbert, Donald Roy *lawyer*
Goldstein, Stuart Wolf *lawyer*
Griller, Gordon Moore *legal association administrator, consultant*
Grimwood, Helen Perry *lawyer*
Haga, David L. *lawyer*
Halpern, Barry David *lawyer*
Hammond, Larry Austin *lawyer*
Harrison, Mark I. *lawyer*
Hayden, William Robert *lawyer*
Hicks, William Albert III *lawyer*
Hirsch, Steven A. *lawyer*
Hochuli, Edward G. *lawyer*
Hoecker, Thomas Ralph *lawyer*
Howard, William Matthew *arbitrator, lawye writer*
Hoxie, Joel P. *lawyer*
Humetewa, Diane J. *prosecutor*
Huntwork, James Roden *lawyer*
James, Charles E., Jr. *lawyer*
Jirauch, Charles W. *lawyer*
Johnson, Christopher D. *lawyer*
Kant, Robert S. *lawyer*
Knoller, Guy David *lawyer*
Kreutzberg, David W. *lawyer*
Kurn, Neal *lawyer*
Loftin, Nancy Carol *lawyer, utilities executi*
Lubin, Stanley *lawyer*
Martori, Joseph Peter *lawyer*
Mast, Gregory Lewis *lawyer*
May, Bruce Barnett *lawyer*
McMillan, Lee Richards, II, *lawyer, mining executive*
Meschkow, Jordan M. *lawyer*
Nadeau, Mark Allen *lawyer*
Olsen, Alfred Jon *lawyer*
Placenti, Frank Michael *lawyer*
Platt, Warren E. *lawyer*
Rathwell, Peter John *lawyer*
Refo, Patricia Lee *lawyer*
Rethore, Bernard M. *lawyer*
Rivera, Jose de Jesus *lawyer*
Rose, Scott A. *lawyer*
Rosenfeld, Lawrence J. (Larry) *lawyer*
Ross, Richard Frederick *lawyer*
Rudolph, Gilbert Lawrence *lawyer*
Salerno, Thomas James *lawyer*
Savage, Stephen Michael *lawyer, departmen chairman*
Sherk, Kenneth John *lawyer*
Silverman, Alan Henry *lawyer*
Stahl, Louis A. *lawyer*
Storey, Norman C. *lawyer*
Stuart, Gary Lester *lawyer*
Tennen, Leslie Irwin *lawyer, consultant*
Thomas, Andrew P. *prosecutor*
Thompson, Terence William *lawyer*
Ulrich, Paul Graham *lawyer, writer, editor*
Verbin, Jeffrey Harold *lawyer*
Verkamp, John *lawyer, state legislator*
Wall, Donald Arthur *lawyer*
Wheeler, Steven M. *lawyer*
Williams, Quinn Patrick *lawyer*
Wirken, Charles William *lawyer*
Wolf, G. Van Velsor, Jr. *lawyer*
Woods, Grant *lawyer, former state attorney general*
Woolf, Michael E. *lawyer*
Yarnell, Michael Allan *mediator, arbitrator, educator*

Scottsdale
Calise, Nicholas James *lawyer*
Hermann, Robert John *lawyer*
Inman, William Peter *lawyer*
Krupp, Clarence William *lawyer, health faci administrator*
Lord, Robert James *lawyer*
Lowry, Edward Francis, Jr. *lawyer*
Marks, Merton E. *lawyer, international arbitrator, mediator, consultant*
Nielsen, Greg Ross *lawyer*
Peshkin, Samuel David *retired lawyer*
Walker, Richard K. *lawyer*

Surprise
Fennelly, Jane Corey *lawyer*

Tempe
Andrews, Steven R. *lawyer*
Jennings, Marianne Moody *lawyer, educator*
Johnson, Stephen L. *lawyer, transportation executive*
Marchant, Gary Elvin *lawyer*
Matheson, Alan Adams *law educator*
Rogers, Mark Nicholl *lawyer*
Spritzer, Ralph Simon *lawyer, educator*
White, Patricia Denise *law educator, dean*

Tucson
Amhowitz, Harris J. *lawyer, educator*
Blackman, Lee L. *lawyer*
Boswell, Susan G. *lawyer*
Chiorazzi, Michael Gerard *law librarian, educator*
Cohen, Gary J. *lawyer*
Coker, Mich *lawyer*
Dobbs, Dan Byron *lawyer, educator*
Farhang, Ali J. *lawyer*
Feldman, Stanley George *lawyer*
Froman, Sandra Sue *lawyer*
Gantz, David Alfred *law educator, academic administrator*
Grand, Richard D. *lawyer*
Kimble, William Earle *lawyer*
Kozolchyk, Boris *law educator, consultant*
Kuklin, Susan Beverly *lawyer, librarian, educator*
Kuykendall, Gregory John *lawyer*
Mc Donald, John Richard *lawyer*
Meehan, Michael Joseph *lawyer*
Morrow, James Franklin *lawyer*
O'Leary, Thomas Michael *lawyer*
Pace, Thomas M. *lawyer*
Petersen, Frederick J. *lawyer*
Robinson, Bernard Leo *lawyer*
Rose, Carol Marguerite *law educator*
Samet, Dee-Dee *lawyer*
Schorr, S. L. *lawyer*
Simmons, Sarah R. *lawyer*
Strong, John William *lawyer, educator*
Tindall, Robert Emmett *lawyer, educator*

Chung, Tong Soo *lawyer*
Clark, R(ufus) Bradbury *lawyer, director*
Cochran, Steve *lawyer*
Cohen, Cynthia Marylyn *lawyer*
Cole, William Louis *lawyer*
Collier, Charles Arthur, Jr. *lawyer*
Collins, Michael K. *lawyer*
Conley, Mark A. *lawyer*
Cook, Melanie K. *lawyer*
Cooley, Steve *prosecutor*
Cooper, Robert E. *lawyer*
Coupe, James Warnick *lawyer*
Coyne, Joseph Francis, Jr. *lawyer*
Crabtree-Ireland, Duncan *lawyer*
D'Angelo Melby, Donna Marie *lawyer*
Daniels, John Peter *lawyer*
Darby, G(eorge) Harrison *lawyer*
Darden, Christopher Allen *lawyer, writer*
Daum, John F. *lawyer*
Davis, Gray (Joseph Graham Davis) *lawyer, former governor*
De Brier, Donald Paul *lawyer, oil industry executive*
DeCarlo, John T. *lawyer*
de Castro, Hugo Daniel *lawyer*
Decker, Richard Jeffrey *lawyer*
Delgadillo, Rockard J. (Rocky Delgadillo) *lawyer*
Demoff, Marvin Alan *lawyer*
Denham, Robert Edwin *lawyer*
Diamond, Stanley Jay *lawyer*
Diaz, Maria G. *lawyer*
Dienes, Louis Robert *lawyer*
Dixon, Patrick Richard *prosecutor*
Dodd, Jan Eve *lawyer*
Donovan, John Arthur *lawyer*
Douglas, Joel Bruce *lawyer*
Drooyan, Richard E. *lawyer*
Drummy, Kathleen H. *lawyer*
Dudziak, Mary Louise *law educator*
Dunham, Scott H. *lawyer*
Eatman, Louis Perkins *lawyer*
Edelman, Scott Alan *lawyer*
Eley, Hunter R. *lawyer*
Ellingsen, Richard D. *lawyer*
Evans, Gregory Hinojosa *lawyer*
Fairbank, Robert Harold *lawyer*
Farmer, Robert Lindsay *lawyer*
Fein, Ronald Lawrence *lawyer*
Feldman, Larry Robert *lawyer*
Feldman, Lewis G. *lawyer*
Fenning, Lisa Hill *lawyer, mediator, retired judge*
Feo, Edwin F. *lawyer*
Fields, Bertram Harris *lawyer*
Fields, Henry Michael *lawyer*
Finkel, Evan *lawyer*
Finnegan, Michael J. *lawyer*
Flagel, Mark Alan *lawyer*
Follick, Edwin Duane *law educator, dean, chiropractor*
Frackman, Russell Jay *lawyer*
Fragner, Matthew Charles *lawyer*
Francis, Merrill Richard *lawyer*
Freier, Elliot G. *lawyer*
Friedman, Alan E. *lawyer*
Frimmer, Paul Norman *lawyer*
Futami, Norman *lawyer*
Gallo, Jon Joseph *lawyer*
Garbacz, Gregory A. *lawyer*
Garrett, Elizabeth *law educator, academic administrator*
Gebb, Sheldon Alexander *lawyer*
Geragos, Mark John *lawyer*
Gest, Howard David *lawyer*
Girard, Robert David *lawyer*
Glaser, Patricia L. *lawyer*
Glazer, Michael *lawyer*
Golay, Frank H., Jr. *lawyer*
Goldman, Allan Bailey *lawyer*
Goldman, Benjamin Edward *lawyer*
Goldman, Donald Aaron *lawyer*
Goldman, Joel A. *lawyer*
Goldman, Ronald L.M. *lawyer*
Goo, Valerie M. *lawyer*
Goodman, Max A. *lawyer, educator*
Gordon, David Eliot *lawyer*
Gorman, Joseph Gregory, Jr. *lawyer*
Goss, Kent *lawyer*
Graves, Anna Marie *lawyer*
Green, William Porter *lawyer*
Greenberg, Gordon Alan *lawyer*
Griffey, Linda Boyd *lawyer*
Grobe, Charles Stephen *lawyer, accountant*
Gross, Allen Jeffrey *lawyer*
Gross, Ariela Julie *law educator*
Grosz, Philip J. *lawyer*
Gurfein, Peter J. *lawyer*
Halberstadter, David *lawyer*
Halkett, Alan Neilson *lawyer*
Halm, Howard Lee *lawyer*
Handler, Joel F. *law educator*
Handzlik, Jan Lawrence *lawyer*
Hansell, Dean *lawyer*
Hanson, John J. *retired lawyer*
Harkness, Nancy P. *lawyer*
Havel, Richard W. *lawyer*
Haviland, Peter L. *lawyer*
Hayutin, David Lionel *lawyer*
Heinke, Rex S. *lawyer*
Heller, Philip *lawyer*
Hellow, John R. *lawyer*
Hemminger, Pamela Lynn *lawyer*
Herman, Stephen Charles *lawyer*
Heyler, Grover Ross *retired lawyer*
Hieronymus, Edward Whittlesey *retired lawyer*
Hight, B. Boyd *retired lawyer*
Hirsch, Barry L. *lawyer*
Holliday, Thomas Edgar *lawyer*
Holscher, Mark Charles *lawyer*
Holtzman, Robert Arthur *lawyer*
Hooper, Patric *lawyer*
Hufstedler, Seth Martin *lawyer*
Hufstedler, Shirley Mount *lawyer, former United States Secretary of Education*
Husar, Linda S. *lawyer*
Hyman, Milton Bernard *lawyer*
Hyman, Ursula H. *lawyer*
Iredale, Nancy Louise *lawyer*
Irving, Paul Howard *lawyer*
Irwin, Philip Donnan *lawyer*
Jackson, Alan Jay *prosecutor*
Jansen, Allan W. *lawyer*
Joaquin, Linton *lawyer*
Johnson, Channing D. *lawyer*
Johnson, Jonathan Edwin, II, *lawyer*
Johnstone, Kathryn I. *lawyer*
Jordan, Martha B. *lawyer*
Jordan, Robert Leon *lawyer, educator*
Juo, James *lawyer*
Kalyvas, James R. *lawyer*
Kanoff, Mary Ellen *lawyer*
Kaplan, Mark Vincent *lawyer*
Karst, Kenneth Leslie *law educator*
Katz, Jason Lawrence *lawyer, insurance company executive*
Katzenstein, Andrew M. *lawyer*
Kesselman, David W. *lawyer*
Khan, Amman A. *lawyer*
Kieffer, George David *lawyer*
Kiley, Anne Campbell *lawyer*
Kim, Sabrina S. *lawyer*
Kirwan, R. DeWitt (Kyle) *lawyer*
Klein, Eric A. *lawyer*
Kleinberg, Marvin H. *lawyer*
Klinger, Marilyn Sydney *lawyer*
Krupka, Robert George *lawyer*
Kuechle, John Merrill *lawyer*
Kupietzky, Moshe Joseph *lawyer*
Kwoh, Stewart *lawyer, cultural organization administrator*
Lack, Walter J. *lawyer*
Lambert, Thomas P. *lawyer*
Langa, Brian D. *lawyer*
Langan, Kenneth J. *lawyer*
Langberg, Barry Benson *lawyer*
Lappen, Chester I. *lawyer*
Latham, Joseph Al, Jr. *lawyer*
Lauchengco, Jose Yujuico, Jr. *lawyer*
Lawler, Jean Marie *lawyer*
Layne, Jonathan K. *lawyer*
Leanse, Thomas J. *lawyer*
Le Berthon, Adam *lawyer*
Leibow, Ronald Louis *lawyer*
Le Sage, Bernard E. *lawyer*
Lesser, Joan L. *lawyer*
Letwin, Leon *law educator*
Leung, Frankie Fook-Lun *lawyer*
Levine, C. Bruce *lawyer*
Levine, Jerome L. *lawyer*
Levine, Meldon Edises *lawyer, Former United States Representative, California*
Levyn, Thomas Stanley *lawyer, former mayor*
Lewis, Cynthia *law librarian*
Lichter, Linda *lawyer*
Lindholm, Dwight Henry *lawyer*
Ling, Robert M., Jr. *lawyer, consumer products company executive*
Lipsig, Ethan *lawyer*
Litvack, Mark D. *lawyer*
Logan, Ben H. III *lawyer*
Long, Gregory Alan *lawyer*
Lubitz, Stuart *lawyer*
Lui, Elwood *lawyer*
Lundy, Robert W., Jr. *lawyer*
MacLaughlin, Francis Joseph *lawyer*
Maeder, Gary William *lawyer*
Mancino, Douglas Michael *lawyer*
Marmaro, Marc *lawyer*
Marmorstein, Victoria E. *lawyer*
Marshall-Daniels, Meryl *mediator, executive coach*
Martinez, Vilma Socorro *lawyer*
Mason, Cheryl White *lawyer*
Mayorkas, Alejandro *lawyer, former prosecutor*
McAniff, Edward John *lawyer*
McCarty, David J. *lawyer*
McDermott, John E. *lawyer*
McKnight, Frederick L. *lawyer*
McLane, Frederick Berg *lawyer*
McNevin, Christopher J. *lawyer*
Meer, Jon Douglas *lawyer*
Meisinger, Louis M. *lawyer*
Melby, Donna D. *lawyer*
Mesereau, Thomas Arthur, Jr. *lawyer*
Metzger, Robert Streicher *lawyer*
Meyer, Bruce D. *lawyer*
Meyer, Catherine Dieffenbach *lawyer*
Meyer, Michael Edwin *lawyer*
Midler, Laurence H. (Larry) *lawyer, real estate company executive*
Millard, Neal Steven *lawyer, educator*
Miller, Milton Allen *lawyer*
Miller, Robert A., Jr. *lawyer*
Mintz, Marshall Gary *lawyer*
Modabber, Zia F. *lawyer*
Molleur, Richard Raymond *lawyer*
Moor, Carl H. *lawyer*
Morrissey, J. Richard *lawyer*
Moskowitz, Joel Steven *lawyer*
Mulcahy, Benjamin R. *lawyer*
Mullen, John H. *lawyer*
Murray, Anthony *lawyer*
Neely, Sally Schultz *lawyer*
Neiter, Gerald Irving *lawyer*
Newman, David Wheeler *lawyer*
Newman, Michael Rodney *lawyer*
Nicholas, William Richard *lawyer*
Niles, John Gilbert *lawyer*
Nocas, Andrew James *lawyer*
Nochimson, David *lawyer*
Norris, William Albert *lawyer, mediator, retired judge*
Oberstein, Norman S. *lawyer*
O'Brien, Robert Charles *lawyer*
O'Connell, Kevin *lawyer*
O'Donnell, Pierce Henry *lawyer*
Oh, Angela E. *lawyer*
O'Leary, Prentice Lee *retired lawyer*
Oliver, Dale Hugh *lawyer*
Olsen, Frances Elisabeth *law educator, theorist*
Olson, Ronald Leroy *lawyer*
Oppenheim, Charles B. *lawyer*
Oppenheimer, Randy (Mark Randall Oppenheimer) *lawyer*
Ordin, Andrea Sheridan *lawyer*
Ostroff, Peter I. *lawyer*
Owen, Michael Lee *lawyer*
Owens, James Franklin *lawyer*
Pachino, Barton P. *lawyer*
Palmer, Robert L. *lawyer*
Panish, Brian Joseph *lawyer*
Papiano, Neil Leo *lawyer*
Parsky, Gerald Lawrence *lawyer*
Pascotto, Alvaro *lawyer*
Pasich, Kirk Alan *lawyer*
Pedersen, Norman A. *lawyer*
Perlis, Michael Fredrick *lawyer*
Perron, Edward Adrian *lawyer*
Perry, Ralph Barton III *lawyer*
Peters, Aulana Louise *lawyer, former government agency commissioner*
Peters, Richard T. *lawyer*
Peters, William James *lawyer*
Peterson, Kurt C. *lawyer*
Peterson, Linda S. *lawyer*
Petrocelli, Daniel M. *lawyer*
Petroff, Laura R. *lawyer*
Phillips, Stacy D. *lawyer*
Pircher, Leo Joseph *lawyer, director*
Piuze, Michael Joseph *lawyer*
Porter, John E. *lawyer*
Porter, Verna Louise *lawyer*
Posner, Harriet S. *lawyer*
Power, John Bruce *lawyer*
Preonas, George Elias *lawyer*
Presant, Sanford Calvin *lawyer, educator, writer, tax specialist*
Price, William Charlie *lawyer*
Pugsley, Robert Adrian *law educator*
Quicksilver, William Todd *lawyer*
Quinn, John J. *lawyer*
Rabinovitz, Joel *lawyer, educator*
Racine, Scott H. *lawyer*
Raeder, Myrna Sharon *lawyer, educator*
Rakow, Jay *lawyer, film company executive*
Ramsey, Jerry A. *lawyer*
Rappeport, Ira J. *lawyer*
Rath, Howard Grant, Jr. *lawyer*
Ray, Gilbert T. *lawyer*
Re, Donald Maurice *lawyer*
Reddick, C.N. (Frank)lin III *lawyer*
Reeves, Barbara Ann *lawyer*
Reid, E. Lewis *lawyer*
Reisman, Ellen Kelly *lawyer*
Renwick, Edward S. *lawyer*
Ressler, Alison S. *lawyer*
Reyes Robbins, Ann Marie *lawyer, researcher, educator, former magistrate judge*
Richards, Eric Albert Stephan *lawyer*
Richland, Kent Lewis *lawyer*
Riff, Lawrence P. *lawyer*
Rishwain, James Michael, Jr. *lawyer*
Roberts, Virgil Patrick *lawyer, judge*
Robertson, Hugh Duff *lawyer*
Rodriguez, Denise Rios *lawyer*
Rosenthal, Sol *lawyer*
Rosett, Arthur Irwin *lawyer, educator*
Ross, Bruce Shields *lawyer*
Rothenberg, Alan I. *lawyer, professional sports association executive*
Rustand, Kay *lawyer*
Ruthberg, Miles N. *lawyer*
Sacks, Robert A. *lawyer*
Sager, Kelli L. *lawyer*
Samuels, Mark A. *lawyer*
Saxe, Deborah Crandall *lawyer*
Schindler, David J. *lawyer*
Schwartz, Robert M. *lawyer*
Scoular, Robert Frank *lawyer*
Shacter, David Mervyn *lawyer*
Shapiro, Marvin Seymour *lawyer*
Shapiro, Robert *lawyer*
Shartin, Stacy D. *lawyer*
Sheehan, Lawrence James *lawyer*
Sheller, John Willard *lawyer*
Sherrell, John Bradford *lawyer*
Sherwood, Arthur Lawrence *lawyer*
Shiba, Wendy C. *lawyer*
Shockro, Michael J. *lawyer*
Shortz, Richard Alan *lawyer*
Shultz, John David *lawyer*
Siegel, Clark Byron *lawyer*
Siegel, Robert (Bob) A. *lawyer*
Silbergeld, Arthur F. *lawyer*
Silva, Clarice F. (Clarice F. Chavira-Sliva) *lawyer*
Simmons, Richard J. *lawyer*
Sloan, Sheldon Harold *lawyer*
Smith, Derek E. *lawyer*
Smith, Gregory R. *lawyer*
Snider, Darryl *lawyer*
Spitzer, Matthew Laurence *law educator*
Stamm, Alan *lawyer*
Starrett, Lucinda *lawyer*
Stashower, Arthur L. *lawyer*
Stein, Laurence Jay *lawyer*
Stein, Sheryl E. *lawyer*
Stinehart, William, Jr. *retired lawyer*
Stone, Gregory Paul *lawyer*
Stone, Lawrence Maurice *lawyer, educator*
Stout, Lynn Andrea *law educator*
Strickland, Julia B. *lawyer*
Sullivan, Peter Meredith *lawyer*
Sweeney, Paul W., Jr. *lawyer*
Taggart, Jennifer T. *lawyer*
Takesh, Fahi *lawyer*
Tarr, Ralph William *lawyer, former federal government official*
Taylor, Minna *lawyer*
Teele, Cynthia Lombard *lawyer*
Tepstein, Daniel C. *lawyer*
Thomas, Geoffrey L. *lawyer*
Thoren-Peden, Deborah Suzanne *lawyer*
Thorpe, Gogory B. *lawyer*
Title, Gail Migdal *lawyer*
Tobisman, Stuart Paul *lawyer*
Treister, George Marvin *lawyer*
Trygstad, Lawrence Benson *lawyer*
Ukropina, James R. *lawyer*
Valerio Barrad, Catherine M. *lawyer*
Van de Kamp, John Kalar *lawyer*
Vanderet, Robert Charles *lawyer*
Van Wyngarden, Thomas L. *lawyer*
Vanyo, Bruce Gordon *lawyer*
Varat, Jonathan D. *law educator, dean*
Varner, Carlton A. *lawyer*
Victorino, Louis D. *lawyer*
Vincent, Dirk L. *lawyer*
Volpert, Richard Sidney *lawyer*
Wagner, Darryl William *lawyer*
Walcher, Alan Ernest *lawyer*
Walker, Paul R. *lawyer*
Wallock, Terrence J. *lawyer*
Warren, Robert Stephen *lawyer*
Wasser, Dennis Matthew *lawyer*
Wasser, Laura Allison *lawyer*
Wasserman, William Phillip *lawyer*
Wayte, Alan (Paul) *lawyer*
Weatherup, Roy Garfield *lawyer*
Weiner, Perrie M. *lawyer*
Weinstock, Harold *lawyer*
Weise, Steven O. *lawyer*
Weiss, Walter Stanley *lawyer*
Westreich, Benzion Joseph *lawyer*
White, Robert Joel *lawyer*
Willett, Robert E. *lawyer*
Williams, Bart H. *lawyer*
Williams, Harold Marvin *lawyer, retired foundation, academic and federal agency administrator*
Williams, Norma Jean *lawyer*
Williams, Richard Thomas *lawyer*
Williams, Robert E. *lawyer*
Winterman, Craig L. *lawyer*
Wood, Willard Mark *lawyer*
Woodland, Irwin Francis *lawyer*
Woodsome, Edwin Valentine, Jr. *lawyer*
Wright, Kenneth Brooks *lawyer*
Yamaguchi, Colleen S. *lawyer*
Yang, Debra Wong *lawyer, former prosecut*
Young, Marc D. *lawyer*
Yu, Susan C(hung-Mi) *lawyer*
Zhang, Jinshu *lawyer*
Ziffren, Kenneth *lawyer*

Malibu

Davenport, David *lawyer, educator, academ administrator*
Factor, Max III *arbitrator, mediator*
Kmiec, Douglas William *law educator, colu*
Nelson, Grant Steel *law educator*

Manhattan Beach

Mandel, Martin Louis *lawyer*

Marina Del Rey

Orr, Ronald Stewart *lawyer*
Schulman, Robert S. *lawyer*

Menlo Park

Brest, Paul A. *law educator, foundation administrator*
Chao, Howard H. *lawyer*
Charlson, Michael Lloyd *lawyer*
Denenberg, Alan F. *lawyer*
Fisher, Ora T. *lawyer*
Haslam, Robert Thomas III *lawyer*
Hearst, William Randolph III *lawyer, forme newspaper publisher*
Hermle, Lynne C. *lawyer*
Hockett, Christopher Burch *lawyer*
Karel, Steven *lawyer*
Kaufman, Christopher Lee *lawyer*
Kelly, Daniel Grady, Jr. *lawyer*
Kennelly, Dennis L. *lawyer*
Kirk, Cassius Lamb, Jr. *retired lawyer, inve*
Madison, James Raymond *lawyer*
Mendelson, Alan Charles *lawyer*
Mummery, Daniel R. *lawyer*
Yang, Joseph *lawyer*

Mill Valley

Cole, Richard Charles *lawyer*
Schwartzbach, M. Gerald *lawyer*

Milpitas

DuChene, Todd Michael *lawyer*
Fawcett, Matthew Knowlton *lawyer*

Mission Viejo

Sessions, Don David *lawyer*

desto
Allister, Kirk W. *lawyer*
ens, Jack Byron *lawyer*

nterey
is, Craig Alphin *lawyer, manufacturing company executive*

untain View
idson, Gordon Kirby *lawyer*
nell, Laura A. *lawyer*
st, David L. *lawyer*
w, George Martin *lawyer, writer*
h, Horace Lyons *lawyer*
ahow, Lynn Harold *lawyer*
ker, John Kent, Jr. *lawyer*

pa
mas, William Scott *lawyer*

wport Beach
kin, Scott David *lawyer*
k, Thomas P., Jr. *lawyer*
rie, Robert Emil *retired lawyer*
dstein, Michael Gerald *lawyer, director*
an, Nancy Margaret *lawyer*
ron, J. Jay *lawyer*
ston, John Charles *lawyer*
ar, Richard William, Jr. *lawyer*
e, Stephen Phillip *lawyer*
lips, Layn R. *lawyer*
napp, Roger Herbert *lawyer, consultant*
ger, Gary James *lawyer*

rth Hollywood
is, Edmond Ray *lawyer*

rthridge
quist, Lisa A. *lawyer*

vato
dreas, Christopher Eric *lawyer*
in, James Patrick *lawyer*

k Park
son, William Theodore *lawyer*

kland
n, Jeffrey Michael *lawyer*
y, Phillip Samuel *lawyer*
ant, Arthur H. *lawyer*
kley, Mike Clifford *lawyer*
ies, Colleen T. *lawyer*
ning, Jayne Elizabeth *lawyer*
el, Carolyn E. *lawyer*
nson, Kenneth F. *lawyer*
n, Steven M. *lawyer*
er, Thomas Robbins *lawyer, publisher*
nby, William Albert *lawyer, arbitrator, ediator*
inson, Charles Furlonge *lawyer*
n, Laura *lawyer, consumer products company ecutive*
tman, William Ellsworth *lawyer*
lis, Eric G. *lawyer*
ver, Pauline Anne *lawyer*
od, James Michael *lawyer*

nda
og, John A. *lawyer*
f, Andrew Joseph *lawyer, transportation and ilities executive*

ific Palisades
, Charles Griffin *lawyer, real estate and orporate financial company executive*
ery, Thomas Long *lawyer, administrator*
lla, Stanley *lawyer*
one, Patric Miller *lawyer, writer*

m Desert
hard, Herbert Ashley *lawyer*

o Alto
ams, William F. *lawyer*
arez, Fred *lawyer*
n, Frederick David *lawyer*
us, Brian J. *lawyer*
on, Lee F. *lawyer*
ner, Steven E. *lawyer*
lley, Donald Edward *lawyer*
ham, Samuel Townsend Jack III *lawyer*
ng, Carmen *lawyer*
nas, Charles N. *lawyer, computer company ecutive*
nis, C. Cabell, Jr. *lawyer*
an, Richard Elliot *lawyer*
pton, Charles (Chris) T. *lawyer*
vford, Roy Edgington III *lawyer*
ningham, Brian C. *lawyer, corporate ecutive*
chy, Craig Edward *lawyer*
Calvo, Jorge A. *lawyer*
er, John Charles *lawyer*
man, Boris *lawyer*
m, Keith Avery *lawyer*
is, Jean Burke *lawyer*
, John A. *lawyer*
ush, David Malcolm *lawyer*
her, James C. *lawyer*
on, Virginia Lee *lawyer*
nan, Maureen J. *lawyer*
o, Joseph A. *lawyer*
g, Joseph F. *lawyer*
st, David W. *lawyer*
kley, Robert Craig *lawyer*
ox, Frank S. *lawyer*
k, Jonathan S., Sr. *lawyer*

Holston, Michael Joseph *lawyer, computer company executive*
Ivey, Thomas J. *lawyer*
Jackson, Cynthia L. *lawyer*
King, Kenton J. *lawyer*
Kleinberg, James P. *lawyer*
Korman, Martin *lawyer*
Laurie, Ronald Sheldon *lawyer*
Massey, Henry P., Jr. *lawyer*
McCall, Jennifer Jordan *lawyer*
McGlynn, J. Casey *lawyer*
Michels, Dirk *lawyer*
Miller, Scott D. *lawyer*
Monroy, Gladys H. *lawyer*
Neal, Stephen Cassidy *lawyer*
Newcombe, George Michael *lawyer*
Nuchi, Lior O. *lawyer*
O'Brien, Bradford Carl *lawyer*
Park, Marina H. *lawyer*
Petkanics, Donna M. *lawyer*
Radcliffe, Mark Flohn *lawyer*
Randall, Jeffrey G. *lawyer*
Robinson, Walter J. III *lawyer*
Roos, John Victor *lawyer*
Salmon, Denis R. *lawyer*
Smith, Glenn A. *lawyer*
Smith, Gregory C. *lawyer*
Sonsini, Larry W. *lawyer*
Sullivan, Dennis C. *lawyer*
Taylor, Barry E. *lawyer*
Tiffany, Joseph Raymond, II, *lawyer*
Unkovic, Nicholas C. *lawyer*
Vaughn, Issac J. *lawyer*
Voight, Jerry D. *lawyer*
Walker, Ann Yvonne *lawyer*
Wheeler, Raymond Louis *lawyer*

Palos Verdes Estates
DeLuce, Richard David *lawyer*

Pasadena
Calleton, Theodore Edward *lawyer, educator*
D'Angelo, Robert William *lawyer*
Graubart, Jeffrey Lowell *lawyer*
Haight, James Theron *lawyer*
Hunt, Gordon *lawyer*
Kleinpeter, Amy E. Clark *lawyer*
Logan, Francis Dummer *retired lawyer*
Markley, William C. *lawyer*
Miller, Susan Calabrese *lawyer, consumer products company executive*
Mueth, Joseph Edward *lawyer*
Myers, R(alph) Chandler *lawyer*
Silverstein, Robert P. *lawyer*
Solis, Carlos *lawyer*
Sullivan, William Francis *lawyer*
van Schoonenberg, Robert G. *lawyer, consumer products company executive*
Wyatt, Joseph Lucian, Jr. *lawyer, writer*
Yohalem, Harry Morton *lawyer*

Petaluma
Archer, Richard Joseph *lawyer*

Pittsburg
Williscroft-Barcus, Beverly Ruth *retired lawyer*

Pleasanton
Askanas, Mark S. *lawyer*
Fine, Marjorie Lynn *lawyer*
Oder, Kenneth William *lawyer*

Point Richmond
Edginton, John Arthur *lawyer*

Pope Valley
Johnson, Reverdy *lawyer*

Portola Valley
Nycum, Susan Hubbell *lawyer*
Olson, Walter Gilbert *lawyer*
Tight, Dexter Corwin *lawyer*

Rancho Mirage
Pierno, Anthony Robert *lawyer*

Rancho Palos Verdes
Haile, Lawrence Barclay *lawyer*
Schimmenti, John Joseph *lawyer*

Redondo Beach
Neely, Alexis *lawyer*

Redwood City
Barkan, David M. *lawyer*
Bell, Frank Ouray, Jr. *lawyer*
Bene, Steven G. *lawyer, game systems company executive*
Daley, Dorian Estelle *lawyer, computer software company executive*
Gunderson, Robert Vernon, Jr. *lawyer*
Linzner, Joel *lawyer*
Millard, Richard Steven *lawyer*
Powers, Matthew Douglas *lawyer*
Sullivan, Kathleen Marie *lawyer, law educator*
Verhoeven, Charles K. *lawyer*

Richmond
Jenkins, Everett Wilbur, Jr. *lawyer, writer, historian*

Riverside
Carney, Jane W. *lawyer*
Heiting, James Otto *lawyer*
Lear, William H. *lawyer*
McGill, Leonard John *lawyer*
Yamamoto, Stanly Tokio *prosecutor*

Rosemead
Adler, Robert L. *lawyer, utilities executive*

Sacramento
Blake, D. Steven *lawyer*
Brown, Lawrence George *prosecutor*
Burton, Randall James *lawyer*
Costigan, Richard III *lawyer*
Day, James McAdam, Jr. *lawyer*
Fait, Glenn A. *lawyer, educator*
Friedman, Morton Lee *retired lawyer*
Goode, Barry Paul *lawyer*
Haynes, Raymond Neal, Jr. *lawyer, state legislator*
Hoffelt, Richard H. *lawyer*
Kelso, J(ohn) Clark *law educator, consultant*
Lesch, Barry M. *lawyer*
Scott, McGregor W. *lawyer, former prosecutor*
Stevens, Charles J. *lawyer, former prosecutor*
Twiss, Robert Manning *prosecutor*
Wong, Alice *lawyer*

Saint Helena
Seavey, William Arthur *lawyer, vintner*

San Bernardino
Prince, Timothy Peter *lawyer*
Stout, Dennis Lee *prosecutor*

San Carlos
Lee, John Jin *lawyer*

San Diego
acovelle, John A. *lawyer*
Adelman, Marc D. *lawyer*
Andreos, George Phillip *lawyer*
Bell, Robert Jeffrey *lawyer*
Boggs, William S. *lawyer*
Bowen, R. William *lawyer*
Brooks, John White *lawyer*
Brownlie, Robert William *lawyer*
Buzunis, Constantine Dino *lawyer*
Chaudhri, Javade *lawyer, utilities executive*
Cohn, Marjorie F. *law educator, legal association administrator*
Corbett, Luke Robinson *lawyer*
Damoose, George Lynn *lawyer*
Danis, Mark Wilmot *lawyer*
Dollarhide, Mary C. *lawyer*
Dorne, David J. *lawyer*
Eigner, William Whitling *lawyer*
Forbes, Brian L. *lawyer*
Gartman, John E. *lawyer*
Gerber, Robert Scott *lawyer*
Haile, Lisa A. *lawyer*
Heidrich, Robert Wesley *lawyer*
Hewitt, Karen Peckham *prosecutor*
Hofflund, Paul *retired lawyer*
Insogna, Anthony M. *lawyer*
Klinedinst, John David *lawyer*
Lam, Carol Chien-Hua *lawyer*
Lathrop, Mitchell Lee *lawyer*
McClellan, Craig Rene *lawyer*
McGinnis, Robert E. *lawyer*
McMahon, Gerald Lawrence *lawyer*
Mebane, Julie S. *lawyer*
Mittermiller, James Joseph *lawyer*
Morris, Grant Harold *law educator*
Morris, Sandra Joan *lawyer*
Nicholas, Blair *lawyer*
O'Malley, James Terence (Terry) *lawyer*
Payne, Margaret Anne *lawyer*
Peters, Scott *lawyer, former councilman*
Plourd, Christopher John *lawyer, consultant*
Pray, Ralph Marble III *lawyer*
Pugh, Richard Crawford *lawyer, educator*
Rains, Cameron Jay *lawyer*
Rehmus, Charles Martin *arbitrator*
Rice, Thomas Hilary (Speedy Rice) *lawyer*
Robbins, Darren J. *lawyer*
Root, George Lincoln, Jr. *lawyer*
St. George, William Ross *lawyer, retired naval officer, consultant*
Schoville, Dennis A(rnold) *lawyer*
Scott, Douglas Edward *lawyer*
Shepherd, Bruce P. *lawyer*
Shippey, Sandra Lee *lawyer*
Smith, Steven Ray *law educator*
Snyder, David Richard *lawyer*
Swinton, Stephen P. *lawyer*
Vega, Gregory A. *former prosecutor*
Vitek, Reg(inald) A. *lawyer*
Weaver, Michael James *lawyer*

San Francisco
Abbott, Barry Alexander *lawyer*
Alderman, William Fields *lawyer*
Alexis, Geraldine M. *lawyer*
Alioto, Angela Mia *lawyer*
Allecta, Julie *lawyer*
Allen, Jose R. *lawyer*
Anderson, Edward Virgil *lawyer*
Arbuthnot, Robert Murray *lawyer*
Atkinson, Gordon C. *lawyer*
Auwers, Linda S. *lawyer*
Bancroft, James Ramsey *lawyer*
Banks, Michelle *lawyer, retail executive*
Barbagelata, Robert Dominic *lawyer*
Barber, James P. *lawyer*
Baxter, Ralph H., Jr. *lawyer*
Baysinger, Kara *lawyer*
Bedford, Daniel Ross *lawyer*
Benvenutti, Peter J. *lawyer*
Bettinger, Michael John *lawyer*
Bleich, Jeffrey Laurence *lawyer, educator*
Blohm, Kenneth E. *lawyer*
Blum, Robert M. *lawyer*
Bomse, Stephen V. *lawyer*
Bookin, Daniel Henry *lawyer*
Booth, Forrest *lawyer*
Borowsky, Philip *lawyer*
Boughey, James Dennis *lawyer*
Boven, Douglas George *lawyer*
Brandel, Roland Eric *lawyer*
Briscoe, John *lawyer*
Brosnahan, James Jerome *lawyer*
Brown, Donald Wesley *lawyer*
Brown, Geoffrey Francis *public defender, lawyer*
Brown, Walter Francis, Jr. *lawyer*
Bruen, James A. *lawyer*
Burden, James Ewers *lawyer*
Burns, Brian Patrick *lawyer*
Bushnell, Roderick Paul *lawyer*
Cabraser, Elizabeth Joan *lawyer*
Campbell, Scott Robert *lawyer, former food products executive*
Canady, Richard Warren *lawyer*
Carlson, John Earl *lawyer*
Cartmell, Nathaniel Madison III *lawyer*
Chao, Cedric C. *lawyer*
Clopton, Karen Valentia *lawyer, president civil services commission*
Clowes, John Howard *lawyer*
Coffin, Judy Sue *lawyer*
Coleman, Thomas Young *lawyer*
Collas, Juan Garduño, Jr. *lawyer*
Collins, Mary Ann *lawyer*
Coombe, George William, Jr. *lawyer, retired bank executive*
Corash, Michèle B. *lawyer*
Corcoran, Maureen Elizabeth *lawyer, director*
Cowan, Stephen A. *lawyer*
Cranston, Mary Bailey *lawyer*
Cregan, Nora C. *lawyer*
Cumming, George Anderson, Jr. *lawyer*
Curran, Mary *lawyer*
Czachor, Bruce *lawyer, consultant*
Danoff, Eric Michael *lawyer*
Davis, Roger Lewis *lawyer*
Dell, Robert Michael *lawyer*
DeMuro, Paul Robert *lawyer*
Diamond, Philip Ernest *lawyer*
Diekmann, Gilmore Frederick, Jr. *lawyer*
Dolan, Brendan G. *lawyer*
Dolinko, Robert A. *lawyer*
Dubreuil, Francis W. *lawyer*
Dunne, Kevin Joseph *lawyer*
Durie, Daralyn J. *lawyer*
Dwyer, Carrie Elizabeth *lawyer, investment company executive*
Edmonson, Tracy K. *lawyer*
Edwards, Robin Morse *lawyer*
Elliott, Scott D. *lawyer*
Epsen, Robert A. *lawyer*
Ericson, Bruce Alan *lawyer*
Eth, Jordan David *lawyer*
Falk, Jerome B., Jr. *lawyer*
Feldman, Robert Paul *lawyer*
Finberg, James Michael *lawyer*
Fink, Scott Alan *lawyer*
Fogel, Paul David *lawyer*
Fohrman, Burton H. *lawyer*
Folberg, Harold Jay *lawyer, educator, dean, mediator*
Fong, Kevin Murray *lawyer*
Foster, David Scott *lawyer*
Friedman, K. Bruce *lawyer*
Friese, Robert Charles *lawyer*
Garvey, Joanne Marie *lawyer*
Getto, Ernest John *lawyer*
Gillette, Patricia K. *lawyer*
Gonzalez, Matt *lawyer*
Goodwin, David B. *lawyer*
Gowdy, Franklin Brockway *lawyer*
Graff, Joan Messing *lawyer*
Gresham, Zane Oliver *lawyer*
Gruel, Steven Francis *lawyer*
Guggenhime, Richard Johnson *lawyer*
Gwire, William *lawyer*
Haas, Raymond P. *lawyer*
Haber, Scott R. *lawyer*
Hane, Laurie S. *lawyer*
Harris, Kamala D. *prosecutor*
Hasson, Kirke Michael *lawyer*
Hazard, Geoffrey Cornell, Jr. *law educator*
Hecker, Peter S. *lawyer*
Heilbron, David Michael *lawyer, arbitrator, mediator*
Hendrick, James T. *lawyer*
Henson, Ray David *law educator, consultant*
Hernandez, Gary A. *lawyer*
Hernandez, Jennifer Lynn *lawyer*
Herrera, Dennis J. *lawyer*
Hewlett, Clothilde *lawyer*
Higgins, Daniel B. *lawyer*
Hinman, Harvey DeForest *lawyer*
Hirsch, (William) Reece *lawyer*
Hisert, George Arthur *lawyer*
Hofmann, John Richard, Jr. *retired lawyer*
Holden, Frederick Douglass, Jr. *lawyer*
Hosie, Spencer *lawyer*
Hoxie, Timothy Gordon *lawyer*
Hubbell, Robert B. *lawyer*
Hudner, Philip *lawyer, rancher*
Huhs, John I. *lawyer*
Hunt, James L. *lawyer*
Jacobs, Seth Alan *lawyer*
Jaffe, Seth Roth *lawyer, retail executive*
Jahn, Paul E. *lawyer*
Jay, Lee P. (Leslie Jay) *lawyer*
Johnson, Stephen Patrick Howard *lawyer*
Joseph, Allan Jay *lawyer*
Jung, David Joseph *law educator*
Juster, Kenneth Ian *lawyer*
Kallstrom, D. Ward *lawyer*
Karchmer, Scott D. *lawyer*

Keker, John Watkins *lawyer*
Kelly, J. Michael *lawyer*
Kennedy, Raoul Dion *lawyer*
Kern, Brad D. *lawyer*
Kern, John McDougall *lawyer*
Knapp, Charles Lincoln *law educator*
Knebel, Jack Gillen *lawyer*
Knutzen, Martha Lorraine *lawyer*
Koeppel, John A. *lawyer*
Kozloff, Theodore J. *lawyer*
Krevans, Rachel *lawyer*
Kuhl, Paul Beach *lawyer*
Lane, Fielding H. *retired lawyer*
Lane, Nathan III *lawyer*
Larrabee, Matthew Lloyd *lawyer*
Larson, John William *lawyer*
Lee, Richard Diebold *lawyer, educator*
Leonard, Geoffrey Porter *lawyer*
Leshy, John David *lawyer, solicitor, educator*
Levie, Mark Robert *lawyer*
Levin, Barry Steven *lawyer*
Levit, Victor Bert *lawyer, foreign representative, civic worker*
Lieff, Robert Lawrence *lawyer*
Livermore, Samuel Morgan *lawyer*
Livsey, Robert Callister *lawyer*
Londen, Jack W. *lawyer*
Lopes, James Louis *lawyer*
Lowell, Frederick K. *lawyer*
Lowenthal, Steven R. *lawyer*
Lyons, James Elliott *lawyer*
Malkin, Joseph M. *lawyer*
Maly, Michael Kip *lawyer*
Mann, Bruce Alan *lawyer, investment banking executive*
Marcus, Richard Leon *lawyer, educator*
Markham, Jesse William, Jr. *lawyer*
Marshall, Patrick C. *lawyer*
Marshall, Raymond Charles *lawyer*
Martel, John Sheldon *lawyer, writer, musician*
Masters, Joseph *lawyer, engineering company executive*
Mattes, Martin Anthony *lawyer*
McDevitt, Ray Edward *lawyer*
McElhinny, Harold John *lawyer*
McGuckin, John Hugh, Jr. *lawyer*
McKeon, Jami Wintz *lawyer*
Mc Laughlin, Jerome Michael *lawyer, shipping company executive*
McNally, Thomas Charles III *lawyer*
Miller, Ann G. *lawyer*
Miller, William Napier Cripps *lawyer*
Minnick, Malcolm David *lawyer*
Morrissey, John Carroll, Sr. *lawyer*
Murphy, Michael Thomas *lawyer*
Murray, Kathleen Anne *lawyer*
Musfelt, Duane Clark *lawyer*
Myers, Peter Scott *lawyer*
Nellis, Noel W. *lawyer*
Odgers, Richard William *lawyer*
Offer, Stuart Jay *lawyer*
Olson, Robert Howard *lawyer*
Palmer, Venrice Romito *lawyer, educator*
Park, Hyun *lawyer, utilities executive*
Park, Roger Cook *law educator*
Parrish, Jenni *law librarian, educator*
Paxton, Jay L. *lawyer*
Penskar, Mark Howard *lawyer*
Pickett, Donn Philip *lawyer*
Piels, William B. *lawyer*
Plishner, Michael Jon *lawyer*
Pope, Marcia L. *lawyer*
Popofsky, Melvin Laurence *lawyer*
Potter, James G. *lawyer, food products executive*
Preuss, Charles Frederick *lawyer*
Pringle, Paul C. *lawyer*
Pringle, Robert Bernard *lawyer*
Radlo, Edward John *lawyer, mathematician*
Ragan, Charles Ransom *lawyer*
Reding, John Anthony, Jr. *lawyer*
Reese, John Robert *lawyer*
Rembe, Toni *lawyer, director*
Renfrew, Charles Byron *lawyer*
Renne, Paul A. *lawyer*
Rice, Denis Timlin *lawyer*
Richards, Norman Blanchard *lawyer*
Riley, William L. *lawyer*
Robinson, Ralph W. *lawyer*
Roethe, James Norton *lawyer*
Rogan, Richard A. *lawyer*
Roger, Kent M. *lawyer*
Roosevelt, Michael A. *lawyer*
Rosenfeld, Robert A. *lawyer*
Ross, Jeffrey S. *lawyer*
Rowland, John Arthur *lawyer*
Rubin, Michael *lawyer*
Russoniello, Joseph Pascal *prosecutor, lawyer*
Ryan, Kevin Vincent *lawyer, former prosecutor*
Sanders, Joel Steven *lawyer*
Sanger, Priya Seshachari *lawyer*
Savage, Mark Randall *lawyer*
Sax, Paul J. *lawyer*
Schaffer, Jeffrey L. *lawyer*
Schenkkan, Dirk McKenzie *lawyer*
Schlinkert, William Joseph *lawyer*
Seabolt, Richard L. *lawyer*
Seegal, John Franklin *lawyer*
Seeger, Laureen E. *lawyer, health products executive*
Seff, James M. *lawyer*
Seneker, Carl James, II, (Kim) *lawyer*
Shenk, George H. *lawyer*
Shepherd, John Michael *lawyer*
Shiffman, Michael A. *lawyer*
Shostak, Linda E. *lawyer*
Shwarts, Robert S. *lawyer*
Singer, Allen Morris *lawyer*
Siniscalco, Gary Richard *lawyer*
Skaggs, Sanford Merle *lawyer*
Smegal, Thomas Frank, Jr. *lawyer*
Smith, Brian D. *lawyer*
Snow, Tower Charles, Jr. *lawyer*
Snyder, Darin W. *lawyer*
Sparks, Thomas E., Jr. *lawyer*
Staring, Graydon Shaw *lawyer*
Steel, Michael J. *lawyer*
Steer, Reginald David *lawyer*
Steskal, Christopher James *lawyer, former prosecutor*
Stewart, Terry *lawyer*
Story, Joan H. *lawyer*
Street, Paul Shipley *lawyer*
Stromberg, Ross Ernest *lawyer*
Strother, James M. *lawyer*
Studley, Jamienne Shayne *lawyer, educator*
Sugarman, Myron George *lawyer*
Sugarman, Paul William *lawyer*
Sullivan, Robert Edward *lawyer*
Taylor, William James (Zak) *lawyer*
Thompson, Patrick S. *lawyer*
Thompson, Robert Charles *lawyer*
Thornton, Charles Victor *lawyer*
Uilkema, John K. *lawyer*
Van Buskirk, Ronald E. *lawyer*
Veaco, Kristina *lawyer*
Venning, Robert Stanley *lawyer*
Vesely, Jeffrey M. *lawyer*
Wald, Peter Allen *lawyer*
Walker, Ralph Clifford *lawyer*
Walsh, Francis Richard *lawyer, arbitrator, educator*
Wang, William Kai-Sheng *law educator*
Weber, Paula M. *lawyer*
Weitzel, Mark P. *lawyer*
Welborn, Caryl Bartelman *lawyer*
Wild, Nelson Hopkins *lawyer*
Williams, Linda C. *lawyer*
Wingate, C. Keith *law educator*
Wirum, Andrea A. *lawyer*
Wolfe, Cameron Withgot, Jr. *lawyer*
Wong, Stanton D. *lawyer*
wwGiacomini, Gary T. *lawyer*
Wyle, Frederick S. *lawyer*
Yost, Nicholas Churchill *lawyer*
Young, Bryant Llewellyn *lawyer*
Young, Douglas Rea *lawyer*
Ziegler, R. W., Jr. *lawyer, consultant*
Ziering, William Mark *lawyer*

San Jose
Denver, Thomas HR *lawyer*
Emmer, Maurice Stanley *lawyer*
Gallo, Joan Rosenberg *lawyer*
Greenstein, Martin Richard *lawyer*
Jackman, Steven H. *lawyer, electronics executive*
Jacobson, Michael R. *lawyer, Internet company executive*
Kennedy, George Wendell *prosecutor*
Mitchell, David Walker *lawyer*
Nissly, Kenneth L. *lawyer*
Towery, James E. *lawyer*
Tyler, Michael Robert *lawyer*

San Marino
Galbraith, James Marshall *lawyer, corporate executive*
Tomich, Lillian *lawyer*

San Mateo
Grill, Lawrence J. *lawyer, accountant, bank executive*
Schmoller, Eberhard G. H. *retired lawyer*
Simpson, Murray L. *lawyer*
Tyle, Craig S. *lawyer, investment company executive*

San Rafael
Chilvers, Robert Merritt *lawyer*
Drexler, Kenneth *lawyer*

San Ramon
Garten, David Burton *lawyer*
Haynes, William James, II, *lawyer*
James, Charles Albert *lawyer, oil industry executive*

Santa Ana
Aitken, Christopher R. *lawyer*
Aitken, Wylie A. *lawyer*
Callahan, Daniel J. *lawyer*
Capizzi, Michael Robert *lawyer, former prosecutor*
DeGiorgio, Kenneth D. *lawyer, insurance company executive*
Digorgio, Kenneth *lawyer*
Fay-Schmidt, Patricia Ann *paralegal*
Konowiecki, Joseph Samuel *lawyer, health facility administrator*
Mei, Tom Y. K. *lawyer*
Schroeder, Michael John *lawyer*
Storer, Maryruth *law librarian*
Valentine-Sibert, Kimberly A. *lawyer*
Wagner, John Leo *lawyer, retired judge, mediator, arbitrator*

Santa Barbara
Braun, David A(dlai) *lawyer*
Cappello, A. Barry *lawyer*
Carlson, Arthur W. *lawyer*
Elliott, Warren G. *lawyer*
Herman, James Edward *lawyer*
Schley, Michael Dodson *lawyer*
Sneddon, Thomas William, Jr. *prosecutor*

Santa Clara
Clark, John M. III *lawyer*
Dillon, Michael A. (Mike) *lawyer, information technology executive*
Glancy, Dorothy Jean *lawyer, educator*
Hsieh, Marina Cing *lawyer, educator*
Ludgus, Nancy Lucke *lawyer*
Nordlund, Donald Craig *lawyer, electronics executive*
Sewell, D. Bruce (Bruce Sewell, Durward Bruce Sewell) *lawyer*
Simon, James Lowell *lawyer*
Sweeney, Joseph J. *lawyer, manufacturing executive*

Santa Clarita
Kotler, Richard Lee *lawyer*

Santa Fe Springs
Oxman, (Ricky) Brian *lawyer*

Santa Monica
Amos, Reed C. *lawyer*
Chapman Holley, Shawn Snider *lawyer*
Cooper, Jay Leslie *lawyer*
Cron, Steven Michael *lawyer*
Dombek, Curtis Michael *lawyer*
Garner, Donald K. *lawyer*
Geiser, Thomas Christopher *lawyer, insurance company executive*
Grossman, Marshall Bruce *lawyer*
Hinerfeld, Robert Elliot *lawyer*
Loo, Thomas S. *lawyer*
McMillan, M. Sean *lawyer*
Modisett, Jeffrey A. *lawyer, former state attorney general*
Preble, Laurence George *lawyer*
Shaw, Nina L. *lawyer*
Soodik, Lynn *lawyer*
Tunney, John Varick *lawyer, former United States Senator from California*
Weitzman, Howard L. *lawyer, former film company executive*
Wilson, Hugh Steven *lawyer*

Santa Rosa
Goldberg, Steven Murray *lawyer*
Handelman, Albert G. *lawyer*

Sausalito
Gordon, Robert Eugene *lawyer*

Scotts Valley
Heller, Edward P. III *lawyer*
Hudson, William L. *lawyer, electronics executive*

Sherman Oaks
Genga, John Michael *lawyer*
Joyce, Stephen Michael *lawyer*
Park, Susan *lawyer*

Sonoma
Metzler, Roger James, Jr. *lawyer*

Stanford
Alexander, Janet Cooper *law educator*
Babcock, Barbara Allen *lawyer, educator*
Barton, John Hays *law educator*
Casper, Gerhard *law educator, retired academic administrator*
Cohen, William *law educator*
Craswell, Richard *law educator*
Ehrlich, Thomas *law educator*
Ford, Richard Thompson *law educator*
Franklin, Marc Adam *law educator*
Friedman, Lawrence M. *law educator*
Goldstein, Paul *lawyer, educator*
Gould, William Benjamin, IV, *law educator*
Greely, Henry T. (Hank) *law educator*
Grey, Thomas C. *law educator*
Grundfest, Joseph Alexander *law and business educator*
Heller, Thomas Charles *law educator*
Karlan, Pamela Susan *law educator*
Kelman, Mark Gregory *law educator*
Klausner, Michael David *law educator*
Lemley, Mark Alan *law educator*
Lessig, L. Lawrence III *law educator, writer*
Lomio, J. Paul *law librarian, researcher*
Martinez, Jenny S. *lawyer*
Polinsky, A. Mitchell *law and economics educator*
Rabin, Robert L. *law educator*
Rhode, Deborah Lynn *law educator*
Scott, Kenneth Eugene *lawyer, educator*
Sofaer, Abraham David *lawyer, former federal judge, educator, consultant*
Srikantiah, Jayashri *law educator*
Thompson, Buzz (Barton H. Jr.) *law educator*
Wald, Michael S. *law educator*
Weiner, Allen Sydney *law educator*
Williams, Howard Russell *law educator*

Sunnyvale
Callahan, Michael John *lawyer*
Doyle, Mary E. *lawyer*

Tarzana
Bardach, Sheldon Gilbert *lawyer*

Thousand Oaks
Gentile, Joseph F. *lawyer, educator*
Scott, David J. *lawyer, medical products executive*

Tiburon
Tobin, James Michael *lawyer*

Torrance
Carlson, Terrance L. *lawyer, aerospace transportation executive*
Hahn, Elliott Julius *lawyer*
Kaufman, Sanford Paul *lawyer*

Van Nuys
Arabian, Armand *arbitrator, mediator, lawye*
Brown, Charles Gailey *lawyer, retired state attorney general*
McLain, Christopher M. *lawyer*

Vista
Hennenhoefer, James A. *lawyer*

Walnut
McKee, Catherine Lynch *lawyer, educator*

Walnut Creek
Garrett, James Joseph *lawyer*
Ginsburg, Gerald J. *lawyer, management consultant*
Hanschen, Peter Walter *lawyer*
Miller, Eugene H. *lawyer*
Nord, Paul Elliott *lawyer, accountant*
Pagter, Carl Richard *lawyer*
Rainey, William Joel *lawyer*

Watsonville
Futch, Michael *lawyer, construction executi*

West Hollywood
Margolin, Bruce M. *lawyer*

Westlake Village
Carter, C. Michael *lawyer*
Strote, Joel Richard *lawyer*

Woodland Hills
Adreani, Michael B. *lawyer*
Even, Randolph M. *lawyer*
Lin, Lawrence Shuh Liang *lawyer*
Tiano, Linda V. *lawyer, insurance company executive*
Westen, Brodie Curtis, Jr., (Curt) *lawyer*

Yorba Linda
McCune, Brenda L. *lawyer*

COLORADO

Boulder
Bruff, Harold Hastings *law educator, former dean*
Corbridge, James Noel, Jr. *law educator*
Deaktor, Darryl Barnett *lawyer*
Dubofsky, Jean Eberhart *lawyer, retired stat supreme court justice*
Echohawk, John Ernest *lawyer*
Fiflis, Ted James *lawyer, educator*
Flowers, William Harold, Jr. *lawyer*
Getches, David Harding *lawyer, educator, d*
Madden, Alice Donnelly *lawyer*
Mills, A(lvin) J(ackson), Jr., (Jack) *lawyer*
Moses, Raphael Jacob *lawyer*
Peterson, Courtland Harry *law educator*
Porzak, Glenn E. *lawyer*
Roberts, William R. *lawyer*
Stevens, Glenn H. *lawyer*

Broomfield
Baker, Charles E. *lawyer*

Colorado Springs
Kubida, William Joseph *lawyer*
Nussbaum, Leonard Martin *lawyer*
Sargent, Walter Harriman, II, *lawyer*

Denver
Aisenberg, Bennett S. *lawyer*
Aro, Edwin Packard *lawyer*
Arundel, James D. *lawyer*
Austin, H(arry) Gregory *lawyer*
Baer, Richard N. *lawyer, telecommunication industry executive*
Bain, Donald Knight *lawyer*
Banks, Britt D. *lawyer*
Bartlit, Fred Holcomb, Jr. *lawyer*
Beatty, Michael L. *lawyer*
Belitz, Paul Edward *lawyer*
Benson, Robert Eugene *lawyer*
Benton, Auburn Edgar *lawyer*
Berry, Robert Worth *lawyer, retired military officer, educator*
Blair, Andrew Lane, Jr. *lawyer, educator*
Blitz, Stephen M. *lawyer*
Bluher, John H. *lawyer, diversified financial services company executive*
Brega, Charles Franklin *lawyer*
Briggs, Steve Clement *lawyer*
Bronesky, Joseph J. *lawyer*
Burke, Kenneth John *lawyer*
Butler, David *lawyer*
Cain, Douglas Mylchreest *lawyer*
Carlson, Erik B. *lawyer*
Carr, James Francis *lawyer*
Carrigan, Jim R. *arbitrator, mediator, retire judge*
Carver, Craig R. *lawyer*
Cassidy, Samuel H. *lawyer, humanities educ*
Cheroutes, Michael Louis *lawyer*
Clark, Phillip R. *lawyer*
Cooper, Billy J. *lawyer*
Cooper, Paul Douglas *lawyer*
Cope, Thomas Field *lawyer*
Dauer, Edward Arnold *law educator*
Davis, R. Steven *lawyer, telecommunication industry executive*
Dean, James Benwell *lawyer*

npsey, Stanley (Howard Stanley Dempsey) *awyer, mining and investment company xecutive*
vine, Sharon Jean *lawyer*
ver, Michael J. *lawyer*
, Troy A. *lawyer, former prosecutor*
ff, J(ohn) Eric *lawyer*
sman, Frank *lawyer*
ber, Steven W. *lawyer*
therstone, Bruce Alan *lawyer*
egan, Cole *lawyer*
orge, Russell Lloyd *lawyer, former state egislator*
msley, Sean C. *lawyer*
ldon, Harold Alan *lawyer*
ris, Dale Ray *lawyer, arbitrator, mediator*
tley, James Edward *lawyer*
wley, Robert Cross *lawyer*
ndrix, Lynn Parker *lawyer*
agland, Donald Wright *lawyer*
dges, Joseph Gilluly, Jr. *lawyer*
ffman, Daniel Steven *lawyer, educator*
me, Richard Phillips *lawyer*
pfenbeck, George Martin, Jr. *lawyer*
itsma, Peter C. *lawyer*
sband, John Michael *lawyer*
in, R. Robert *lawyer*
obs, Paul Alan *lawyer*
es, Peter F. *lawyer*
es, Richard Michael *lawyer*
in, Edwin Sam *lawyer*
ler, Glen Elven, Jr. *lawyer*
g, James M. *lawyer*
tzele, John Alfred *lawyer*
endl, Cathy Stricklin *lawyer*
nm, Richard Douglas *lawyer, former governor*
one, William J. *lawyer, former prosecutor*
man, Eileen R. *lawyer*
y, Mark Ray *lawyer*
w, Andrew M. *lawyer*
w, John Wayland *lawyer*
ns, James M. *lawyer*
ckey, Pamela Robillard *lawyer*
ldonado, Kirk Francis *lawyer*
Cabe, John L. *lawyer*
rker, Steven Joseph *lawyer*
yer, Frederick G. *lawyer*
ller, Gale Timothy *lawyer*
ller, Robert Nolen *lawyer*
ye, John Edward *lawyer*
rane, William Edward *lawyer*
wcom, Jennings Jay *lawyer, director*
Brien, Kevin E. *lawyer*
nan, Lee R. *lawyer*
mer, David Gilbert *lawyer*
ers, Stephen C. *lawyer*
ros, Raymond Louis, Jr. *lawyer*
umbus, Gary M. *lawyer*
ner, Larry S. *lawyer, educator*
chnow, James R. *lawyer*
ail, Beverly J. *lawyer*
iat, Gerald M. *lawyer*
h, Robert Stephen *lawyer*
sema, Fredric A. *lawyer*
nuels, Donald L. *lawyer*
well, Donald Ray *lawyer, performing company executive*
a, Kevin Michael *lawyer*
pherd, John Frederic *lawyer*
efel, David Simon *lawyer*
ton, Raymond L., Jr. *lawyer*
omasch, Roger Paul *lawyer*
uff, Michael *lawyer*
ich, Theodore Albert *lawyer*
lker, Samuel David *lawyer*
lter, John C. *lawyer, gas industry executive*
ber, Matthew George *lawyer*
eeler, Malcolm Edward *lawyer, educator*
liams, Michael Anthony *lawyer*
hlgenant, Richard Glen *lawyer, director*
odward, Lester Ray *lawyer*
nnicke, Brooke *lawyer*

glewood
tt, Stephen M. *lawyer, retired entertainment company executive*
Muth, Laurence Wheeler, Jr. *lawyer, utilities executive*
ris, Robert W. *lawyer*
rkowski, Elizabeth M. *lawyer*
skowitz, David K. *lawyer*
ncer, Margaret Gilliam *lawyer*
abe, Charles Y. *lawyer*

rt Collins
wartz, Allen R. *lawyer*

lden
erts, Celia Anne *lawyer*
erger, Carl Frederick *lawyer*
pel, David Benjamin *lawyer*
llipson, Donald E. *lawyer*

eenwood Village
ney, David R. *lawyer, information technology executive*
, Robert Alan *lawyer*
nsey, John Arthur *lawyer*
lapbach, David *lawyer*

ward
pkins, Donald J. *retired lawyer*

kewood
nphrey, Charles Edward, Jr. *lawyer*
yer, Lynn Nix *lawyer*

Littleton
Walker, Timothy Blake *lawyer, educator*

Lone Tree
Spelts, Richard John *lawyer*

Longmont
Manka, Ronald Eugene *lawyer*

Louisville
Raymond, Dorothy Gill *lawyer*

Loveland
Clark, Roger Earl *lawyer*

Norwood
Reagan, Harry Edwin III *lawyer*

Pueblo
Humes, James Calhoun *lawyer, communications consultant, writer, educator*

Rocky Ford
Mendenhall, Harry Barton *lawyer*

Westminster
Gilmore, Timothy Jonathan *paralegal, consultant*

Windsor
Downey, Arthur Harold, Jr. *lawyer, mediator*

DISTRICT OF COLUMBIA

Washington
Cobb, Ty *lawyer*
Kroener, William Frederick III *lawyer*
Moring, John Frederick *lawyer*

FLORIDA

Jacksonville
Eklund, Carl Andrew *lawyer*

HAWAII

Honolulu
Akiba, Lorraine Hiroko *lawyer*
Akinaka, Asa Masayoshi *lawyer*
Ariyoshi, George Ryoichi *lawyer, business consultant, former governor*
Callies, David Lee *lawyer, educator*
Carson, Ellen Godbey *lawyer*
Case, James Hebard *lawyer*
Char, Vernon Fook Leong *lawyer*
Cowan, Stuart Marshall *lawyer*
Devens, Paul *retired lawyer*
Devlin, Patricia *lawyer*
Dreher, Nicholas C. *lawyer*
Gay, E(mil) Laurence *lawyer*
Gelber, Don Jeffrey *lawyer*
Geshell, Richard Steven *lawyer*
Godbey, Robert Carson *lawyer*
Hart, Brook *lawyer*
Hazlett, Mark A. *lawyer*
Hipp, Kenneth Byron *lawyer*
Jaffe, Edward A. *lawyer*
Katayama, Robert Nobuichi *retired lawyer*
Kawachika, James Akio *lawyer*
Kim, Gregory Robert *lawyer, entrepreneur*
Kubo, Edward Hachiro, Jr. *prosecutor*
Lacy, John Robert *lawyer*
Larsen, David Coburn *lawyer, educator*
Lee, Dale W. *lawyer*
Lilly, Michael Alexander *lawyer, writer*
Mau-Shimizu, Patricia Ann *lawyer*
Miller, Clifford Joel *lawyer*
Miller, Richard Sherwin *law educator*
Morry, G. Richard *retired lawyer*
Okinaga, Lawrence Shoji *lawyer*
Potts, Dennis Walker *lawyer*
Reber, David James *lawyer*
Roth, Randall W. *lawyer*
Sia, Jeffrey H.K. *lawyer*
Starshak, James L. *lawyer*
Turbin, Richard *lawyer*
Woo, Vernon Ying-Tsai *lawyer, real estate developer*

Kula
Rohlfing, Frederick William *lawyer, retired judge, political scientist*

Wailuku
Goldsmith, Stephen Ernest *lawyer*
Luna, B. Martin *lawyer*

IDAHO

Boise
Barber, Phillip Mark *lawyer*
Burke, Cameron S. *legal association administrator*
Geston, Mark Symington *lawyer*
Holleran, John W. *lawyer*
Hunter, Forrest Walker *lawyer*
Leroy, David Henry *lawyer*
McGown, John, Jr. *lawyer*
Minnich, Diane Kay *legal association administrator*
Moss, Thomas E. *prosecutor*
Myers, William Gerry III *lawyer*
Park, William Anthony (Tony Park) *lawyer*
Parry, Richard D. *lawyer, construction executive*
Richardson, Betty H. *lawyer, former prosecutor*
Shurtliff, Marvin Karl *lawyer*
Silak, Cathy R. *lawyer, former state supreme court justice*
VanHole, William Remi *lawyer*

Caldwell
Kerrick, David Ellsworth *lawyer*

Coeur D' Alene
Ormsby, Michael Charles *lawyer*

Hailey
Roark, Keith (R. Keith Roark) *lawyer, political organization administrator*

Moscow
Vincenti, Sheldon Arnold *lawyer, educator*

Pocatello
EchoHawk, Larry *lawyer, former state attorney general*

Twin Falls
Sinclair, James Walter *lawyer*
Sudweeks, Jay Dean *lawyer*

ILLINOIS

Oak Park
Sengpiehl, Paul Marvin *lawyer, retired state official*

MASSACHUSETTS

Boston
Loder, John Mark *lawyer*

MICHIGAN

Troy
Pearce, Harry Jonathan *lawyer, manufacturing executive*

MONTANA

Billings
Cromley, Brent Reed *lawyer, state senator*
Gallinger, Lorraine D. *prosecutor*
Mercer, William W. *prosecutor*
Towe, Thomas Edward *lawyer*

Bozeman
Buckley, Daniel P. *lawyer*
Conover, Richard Corrill *lawyer*
Pape, Rebecca Hogan *lawyer*

Butte
McCarthy, Bernard Francis *lawyer*
Peterson, John Leonard *lawyer, judge*

Great Falls
Doherty, Steve *lawyer, state legislator*
Haddon, Sam Ellis *lawyer*

Havre
Marisuen, Keith A. *lawyer*

Helena
Hunt, William Edward, Sr. *lawyer, retired state supreme court justice*
Meadows, Judith Adams *law librarian, educator*

Missoula
Manning, John Willard *lawyer*

Wilsall
Adams, Dirk Standley *lawyer*

NEVADA

Carson City
McCarthy, Ann Price *lawyer*

Elko
Puccinelli, Andrew James *lawyer*

Las Vegas
Arum, Robert *lawyer, sports events promoter*
Bernhard, Peter C. *lawyer, state agency administrator*
Bersi, Ann *lawyer*
Brammell, Stephen Harrison *lawyer*
Bridges, B. Ried *lawyer*
Brower, Gregory A. *prosecutor, lawyer*
Bryan, Richard H. *lawyer, educator, former senator, Former United States Senator, Nevada*
Chesnoff, David Zeltner *lawyer*
Collins, Frank Edwin *lawyer*
Consul, Vincent A. *lawyer*
Faiss, Robert Dean *lawyer*
Gentile, Dominic P. *lawyer*
Havemann, Michael R. *legal administration*
Hilbrecht, Norman Ty *lawyer*
Jacobs, Gary N. *lawyer, hotel executive*
James, Mark A. *lawyer, former state legislator*
James, Phyllis A. *lawyer*
Kennedy, Dennis L. *lawyer*
Landau, Yvette E. *lawyer, resort company executive*
Larson, Brian A. *lawyer*
Miller, Robert Joseph *lawyer, former governor*
Moss, Gary Curtis *lawyer*
Oshins, Steven Jeffrey *lawyer*
Pray, Donald Eugene *lawyer*
Rapoport, Nancy B. *law educator*
Sheets, Thomas R. *lawyer, gas industry executive*
Solomon, Jack Avrum, Jr. *lawyer, automotive executive, art dealer*
Solomon, Mark A. *lawyer*

Reno
Bell, Robert Cecil *lawyer*
Hibbs, Loyal Robert *lawyer*
Hill, Earl McColl *lawyer*
Hunterton, C. Stanley *lawyer*
Johnson, David D. *lawyer, game company executive*
Kaleta, Paul J. *lawyer, utilities executive*
Pagni, Albert Frank *lawyer*
White, John, Jr. *lawyer*

NEW MEXICO

Albuquerque
Bardacke, Paul *lawyer*
Bergman, Barbara E. *law educator*
Caruso, Mark John *lawyer*
Colón, Brian S. *lawyer, political organization administrator*
Deloria, Philip S. (Sam) *lawyer*
Fouratt, Gregory J. *prosecutor*
Franse, R. Nelson *lawyer*
Goldberg, Catherine T. *lawyer*
Hart, Frederick Michael *law educator*
Hewes, Jonathan William *lawyer*
Hollander, Nancy *lawyer*
Kelly, John J. *lawyer, former prosecutor*
Lasater, W(illiam) Robert, Jr. *lawyer*
Martz, Clyde Ollen *retired lawyer*
Miller, Ranne B. *lawyer*
Murphy, Robert F. *lawyer*
Neerken, Julie P. *lawyer*
O'Brien, Daniel J. *lawyer*
Ortiz, Patrick T. *lawyer*
Paster, Janice Dubinsky *lawyer, former state legislator, state legislator*
Ricco, Edward Robert *lawyer*
Robb, John Donald, Jr. *lawyer*
Roehl, Jerrald J. *lawyer*
St. John, Robert M. *lawyer*
Salazar, John Paul *lawyer*
Sisk, Daniel Arthur *lawyer*
Slade, Lynn *lawyer*
Thompson, Rufus E. *lawyer*
Thornton, J. Duke *lawyer*
Throckmorton, Rex Denton *lawyer*
Vigil, Charles J. *lawyer*
White, Robert Milton *lawyer*

Bayard
Foy, Thomas Paul *lawyer, retired state legislator, bank executive*

Corrales
Arkin, Michael Barry *lawyer, arbitrator, writer*

Las Cruces
Lutz, William Lan *lawyer*

Roswell
Kraft, Richard Lee *lawyer*

Santa Fe
Adams, Mark Kildee *lawyer*
Brannen, Jeffrey Richard *lawyer*
Burton, John Paul (Jack Burton) *lawyer*
Dodds, Robert James III *lawyer*
McClaugherty, Joe L. *lawyer, educator*
Pound, John Bennett *lawyer*
Scheuer, Ralph H. *lawyer*
Wertheim, John V. *lawyer, former political organization administrator*
Wolkoff, Eugene Arnold *lawyer*

Socorro
Bejnar, Thaddeus Putnam *law librarian*

NEW YORK

New York
Haffner, F. Kinsey *lawyer*
Johnson, David J., Jr. *lawyer*
Kiekhofer, William Henry *lawyer*
Weithorn, Stanley Stephen *lawyer*

OREGON

Ashland
Sawyer, Sandra McCommas *lawyer, former judge*

Beaverton
Carter, James C. *lawyer, apparel executive*
Mc Cray, Ronald David *lawyer, apparel executive*
Stewart, Lindsay D. *lawyer, apparel executive*
Vardavas, Stephanie J. *lawyer*

Central Point
Richardson, Dennis Michael *lawyer, educator*

Corvallis
Frohnmayer, John Edward *lawyer, writer*

Dayton
Anderson, Herbert Hatfield *lawyer, farmer*

Eugene
Aldave, Barbara Bader *lawyer, educator*
Hildreth, Richard G. *lawyer, educator*
Jacobson, Jon L. *law educator*
McCrea, Shaun S. *lawyer*
Scoles, Eugene Francis *lawyer, educator*

Keizer
Stevens, Sharon Cox *lawyer*

Lake Oswego
Byczynski, Edward Frank *lawyer, corporate financial executive*

Lincoln City
Arant, Eugene Wesley *lawyer*

Medford
Carter, William G. *lawyer*

Newport
Strever, Kevin Kirk *lawyer*

Portland
Abravanel, Allan Ray *lawyer*
Brenneman, Delbert Jay *lawyer*
Brown, David W. *lawyer*
Cable, John Franklin *lawyer*
Cook, Nena *lawyer*
Crowell, John B., Jr. *lawyer, former government official*
Culpepper, David Charles *lawyer*
Curtis, Michael *lawyer*
Deering, Thomas Phillips *retired lawyer*
English, Stephen Francis *lawyer*
Epstein, Edward Louis *lawyer*
Ernst, David A. *lawyer*
Feuerstein, Howard M. *lawyer*
Foley, Ridgway Knight, Jr. *lawyer, writer*
Franzke, Richard Albert *lawyer*
Froebe, Gerald Allen *lawyer*
Glasgow, William Jacob *lawyer, venture capitalist, business executive*
Goe, Douglas E. *lawyer*
Greene, Herbert Bruce *lawyer, investor, entrepreneur*
Harnden, Edwin A. *lawyer*
Hart, John Edward *lawyer*
Hinkle, Charles Frederick *lawyer, educator*
Hirshon, Robert Edward *lawyer*
Houser, Douglas Guy *lawyer*
Immergut, Karin J. *prosecutor*
Jarvis, Peter R. *lawyer*
Jensen, J. Alan *lawyer*
Johansen, Judith A. *lawyer*
Johnson, Alexander Charles *lawyer, electrical engineer*
Johnson, Mark Andrew *lawyer*
Jolles, Bernard *lawyer*
Josephson, Richard Carl *lawyer*
Kanter, Stephen *lawyer, educator, dean*
Kester, Randall Blair *lawyer*
Knoll, James Lewis *lawyer*
Larpenteur, James Albert, Jr. *retired lawyer*
Lewis, Charles S. III *lawyer*
Livingston, Louis Bayer *lawyer*
Love, William Edward *lawyer*
Luedtke, Roger A. *lawyer*
Lusky, John Anderson *lawyer*
Maloney, Robert E., Jr. *lawyer*
Margolin, Phillip Michael *lawyer*
Menashe, Albert Alan *lawyer*
Miller, William Richey, Jr. *lawyer*
Mowe, Gregory Robert *lawyer*
Nicolai, Thomas R. *lawyer*
Norby, Mark Alan *lawyer*
Nunn, Robert Warne *lawyer*
Olson, Kristine *prosecutor*
Paulus, Norma Jean Petersen *lawyer*
Purcell, John F. *lawyer*
Rawlinson, Dennis Patrick *lawyer*
Richardson, Campbell *retired lawyer*
Richter, Peter Christian *lawyer*
Rosen, Steven O. *lawyer*
Rosenbaum, Lois Omenn *lawyer*
Rubin, Bruce Alan *lawyer*
Ryan, John Duncan *lawyer*
Sand, Thomas Charles *lawyer*
Schreck, George Charles *lawyer*
Schuster, Philip Frederick, II, *lawyer, writer, educator*
Shellan, Ronald A. *lawyer*
Simpson, Robert Glenn *lawyer*
Stewart, Milton Roy *lawyer*
Stone, Richard James *lawyer*
Sullivan, Edward Joseph *lawyer*
Tomlinson, William M. *lawyer*
Tucker, Roy W. *lawyer*
Van Valkenburg, Edgar Walter *lawyer*
Waggoner, James Clyde *lawyer*
Westwood, James Nicholson *lawyer*
Whinston, Arthur Lewis *lawyer*
White, Douglas James, Jr. *lawyer*
Williamson, Charles Ready III *lawyer*
Wilson, Owen Meredith, Jr. *lawyer, mediator, arbitrator*
Winslow, Michael T. *lawyer, finance company executive*
Wood, Marcus Andrew *lawyer*
Yugler, Richard S. *lawyer*
Zalutsky, Morton Herman *lawyer*

Salem
Abrams, Marc *lawyer, political organization worker*
Breen, Richard F., Jr. *law librarian, educator*
Brown, Eden Rose *lawyer*
Clark, David Scott *law educator, consultant*
Haselton, Rick Thomas *lawyer*
Mannix, Kevin Leese *lawyer*
Swaim, Michael E. *lawyer, former mayor*

UTAH

Logan
Daines, N. George *lawyer*
Jenkins, James C. *lawyer*
West, Stephen Allan *lawyer*

Orem
Schofield, Anthony Wayne *lawyer*

Provo
Hansen, H. Reese *law educator, former dean*
Staheli, Kory D. *law librarian*
Thomas, David Albert *law educator, director*

Salt Lake City
Adams, Joseph Keith *lawyer*
Anderson, Kent Taylor *lawyer*
Baldwin, John *legal association administrator, lawyer*
Baucom, Sidney George *lawyer*
Berman, Daniel Lewis *lawyer*
Bird, David R. *lawyer*
Brown, Charles R. *lawyer*
Buchi, Mark Keith *lawyer*
Cassell, Paul George *law educator, former federal judge*
Christensen, Harold Graham *lawyer*
Christensen, Ray Richards *lawyer*
Clark, Scott H. *lawyer*
Cornaby, Kay Sterling *lawyer, retired state senator*
Curtis, D. Jay *lawyer*
Curtis, LeGrand R., Jr. *lawyer*
Firmage, Edwin Brown *lawyer, educator*
Haslam, Dennis V. *lawyer, former professional sports team executive*
Holtkamp, James Arnold *lawyer, educator*
Kirkham, John Spencer *lawyer, director*
Leta, David Edward *lawyer*
Livsey, Herbert C. *lawyer*
Manning, Brent V. *lawyer*
Matheson, Scott Milne, Jr. *law educator*
Matsumori, Douglas *lawyer*
McCoy, Harry E., II, *lawyer*
McDermott, Kathleen E. *lawyer, corporate executive*
Mock, Henry Byron *lawyer, writer, consultant*
Mooney, Jerome Henri *lawyer*
Moore, James R. *lawyer*
Oaks, Dallin Harris *lawyer, church official*
Prince, William B. *lawyer*
Reeder, F. Robert *lawyer*
Scruggs, Samuel D. *lawyer, chemicals executive*
Shea, Patrick A. *lawyer*
Smith, Janet Hugie *lawyer*
Sorenson, Stephen Jay *lawyer*
Threedy, Debora Lynn *law educator*
Tolman, Brett L. *prosecutor*
Wikstrom, Francis M. *lawyer*
Zimmerman, Michael David *lawyer*

South Jordan
Larson, Bryan Alan *lawyer*

Vernal
Judd, Dennis L. *lawyer*

VIRGINIA

Richmond
Effel, Laura *lawyer*

Roanoke
Steele, (Margaret) Anita Martin *law librarian, educator*

WASHINGTON

Anacortes
Cavanaugh, Michael Everett *lawyer, arbitrator, mediator*

Bellevue
Anderson, David Coryell *lawyer, automotive executive*
Kari, Donald G. *lawyer*
O'Connor, Jennifer L. *lawyer, energy executive*
Sebris, Robert, Jr. *lawyer*
Sweeney, David Brian *lawyer*

Bellingham
Packer, Mark Barry *lawyer, financial consultant, foundation official*

Bothell
Gustafson, Alice Fairleigh *lawyer*

Everett
Ostergaard, Joni Hammersla *lawyer*

Federal Way
McDade, Sandy D. *lawyer, paper company executive*

Gig Harbor
Thompson, Ronald Edward *lawyer*

Hoquiam
Kessler, Keith Leon *lawyer*

Issaquah
Benoliel, Joel *lawyer*

Kennewick
Fearing, George B. *lawyer*

Mercer Island
Anderson, Peter MacArthur *retired lawyer*
Medved, Robert Allen *lawyer*
Sandler, Michael David *lawyer*

Olympia
Isaki, Lucy Power Slyngstad *lawyer*
Walker, Francis Joseph *lawyer*

Port Angeles
Taylor, S. Brooke *lawyer*

Pullman
Savage, David William *lawyer*

Seattle
Alkire, John D. *lawyer, arbitrator, mediator*
Alvord, Chase *lawyer*
Andreasen, Steven W. *lawyer*
Andrews, J. David *lawyer*
Aspaas, Jennifer *lawyer*
Batalov, Leo *lawyer*
Birk, Ian *lawyer*
Birmingham, Richard Joseph *lawyer*
Black, W. L. Rivers III *lawyer*
Blair, M. Wayne *lawyer*
Blais, Robert Howard *lawyer*
Blom, Daniel Charles *lawyer, investor, retired insurance company executive*
Blumenfeld, Charles Raban *lawyer*
Boeder, Thomas L. *lawyer*
Boggs, Paula Elaine *lawyer, beverage service company executive*
Bridge, Jonathan Joseph *lawyer, retail executive*
Bridgman, Geoff *lawyer*
Burkhart, William Henry *lawyer*
Carletti, Christopher M. *lawyer*
Carr, Thomas A. *lawyer*
Chapman, Fay L. *lawyer, bank executive*
Char, Patricia Helen *lawyer*
Chicoine, Nicole Mooney *lawyer*
Chong, Arthur *lawyer*
Claflin, Arthur Cary *lawyer*
Clinton, Richard M. *lawyer*
Comfort, Robert Dennis *lawyer*
Cross, Bruce Michael *lawyer*
Cullen, Jack Joseph *lawyer*
Cunningham, Janis Ann *lawyer*
Cunningham, Joel Dean *lawyer*
Davis, John MacDougall *lawyer*
Dial, Ellen Conedera *lawyer*
Dillow, John David *lawyer*
Dong, Nelson G. *lawyer*
Dotten, Michael Chester *lawyer*
Ellis, James Reed *retired lawyer*
Emory, Meade *lawyer*
Farr, Ross *lawyer*
Fischer, Thomas Covell *law educator, consultant, writer*
Fisher, Jeffrey L. *lawyer*
Foster, Susan Eileen *lawyer*
Gaffney, Joseph M. *lawyer*
Gandara, Daniel *lawyer*
Gerrard, Keith *lawyer*
Giles, Robert Edward, Jr. *lawyer*
Gittinger, D. Wayne *lawyer*
Glover, Karen Elaine *lawyer*
Goeltz, Thomas A. *lawyer*
Gores, Thomas C. *lawyer*
Gorton, Slade (Thomas Slade Gorton III) *lawyer, lobbyist, former senator*
Gradel, James D. *lawyer*
Graham, Stephen Michael *lawyer*
Gray, Marvin Lee, Jr. *lawyer*
Green, William L. *lawyer*
Haman, Raymond William *retired lawyer*
Hamilton, Steven G. *lawyer*
Hansen, Wayne W. *lawyer*
Hermsen, James R. *lawyer*
Hill, G. Richard *lawyer*
Hilpert, Edward Theodore, Jr. *retired lawyer*
Hoffman, Mark Frederick *lawyer*
Holtan, Ramer B., Jr. *lawyer*
Hopp, Richard A. *lawyer*
Huff, Gary D. *lawyer*
Huston, John Charles *law educator*
Hutcheson, Mark Andrew *lawyer*
Israel, Allen D. *lawyer*
Jackson, Dillon Edward *lawyer*
Jackson, Dylan E. *lawyer*
Jaffe, Robert Stanley *lawyer*
Johnson, Bruce Edward Humble *lawyer*
Judson, C(harles) James (Jim Judson) *lawyer*
Kane, Alan Henry *lawyer*
Kane, Christopher *lawyer*
Kaplan, Robert David *lawyer*
Katz, Charles J., Jr. *lawyer*
Keegan, John E. *lawyer*
Kellogg, Kenyon P. *lawyer*
Kelly, Kevin Francis *lawyer*
King, Jeffrey J. *lawyer*
Klein, Otto George III *lawyer*
Knight, W. H., Jr., (Joe Knight) *law educator, former dean*
Koehler, Reginald Stafford III *lawyer*
Koh, Steve Y. *lawyer*
Kraft, James Allen *lawyer*
Kusunose, Taro *lawyer*
Landefeld, Stewart M. *lawyer*
Leitzell, Terry Lee *lawyer*
Lemly, Thomas Adger *lawyer*
Lisbakken, James Robert *lawyer*
Loveless, Keith *lawyer, air transportation executive*
Manning, J. Richard *lawyer*
Marshall, Toby *lawyer*
McCann, Richard Eugene *lawyer*
McKay, John *law educator, former prosecut*
McKay, Michael Dennis *lawyer*
Mussehl, Robert Clarence *lawyer*
Nellermoe, Leslie Carol *lawyer*
Nelson, Christina Gerrish *lawyer*
Neukom, William H. *lawyer*
Niemi, Janice *retired lawyer, state legislator, judge*
Noble, Phillip D. *lawyer*
Nunn, Todd L. *lawyer*
O'Brien, Kristiana *lawyer*
Oehler, Richard William *lawyer*
Olsen, Harold Fremont *lawyer*
Osenbaugh, Kimberly W. *lawyer*
Palmer, Douglas S., Jr. *lawyer*
Parris, Mark S. *lawyer, professional athletes consultant*
Parsons, A. Peter *lawyer*
Petrie, Gregory Steven *lawyer*
Pettigrew, Edward W. *lawyer*
Pflaumer, Katrina C. *lawyer*
Prentke, Richard Ottesen *lawyer*
Price, John R. *lawyer, educator*
Pritchard, Llewelyn George *lawyer*
Pym, Bruce Michael *lawyer*
Redman, Eric *lawyer*
Reynvaan, Michael Thomas *lawyer*
Rieke, Paul Victor *lawyer*
Ritter, Daniel Benjamin *lawyer*
Robbins, Stephen J. M. *lawyer*
Robinson, Jeffery P. *lawyer*
Rosenthal, Gabriel *lawyer*
Rummage, Stephen Michael *lawyer*
Samiljan, Katriana *lawyer*
Sandman, Irvin W(illis) *lawyer*
Schneider, Harry H., Jr. *lawyer*
Schultheis, Patrick Joseph *lawyer*
Schwab, Evan Lynn *lawyer*
Schwartz, Irwin H. *lawyer*
Scott, Rachel E. *lawyer*
Smith, Scott A. *lawyer*
Soltys, John Joseph *lawyer*
Spellman, John Dennis *lawyer, former gover of Washington, Former Governor, Washin*
Spitzer, Hugh D. *lawyer*
Squires, William Randolph III *lawyer*
Steel, John Murray *lawyer*
Steers, George W. *lawyer*
Stokke, Diane Rees *lawyer*
Takenaka, Toshiko *lawyer, educator*
Terwilliger, Molly *lawyer*
Thorne, David W. *lawyer*
Thorson, Lee A. *lawyer*
Treiger, Irwin Louis *lawyer*
Tune, James Fulcher *lawyer*
Veblen, John Elvidge *lawyer*
Wagoner, David Everett *lawyer, arbitrator*
Ward, Ronald R. *lawyer*
Wells, Christopher Brian *lawyer*
Whelan, Paul W. *lawyer*
Whitford, Joseph Peter *lawyer*
Williams, J. Vernon *retired lawyer*
Williams, Nancy *lawyer*
Williams-Derry, Amy *lawyer*
Wilson, L. Michelle (Michelle Wilson) *lawy information technology executive*
Zapolsky, David A. *lawyer*

Snohomish
Ellis, Stephen Charles *lawyer*

Spokane
Connelly, James P. *prosecutor*
Eymann, Richard Charles *lawyer*
Koegen, Roy Jerome *lawyer*
McDevitt, James A. *prosecutor, lawyer*

Tacoma
Defebaugh, James E., IV, *lawyer*
Gordon, Joseph Harold *lawyer*
Holt, William E. *lawyer, managing partner*
Miller, Judson Frederick *lawyer, retired mili officer*
Waldo, James Chandler *lawyer*

Tukwila
Fitzpatrick, Thomas Mark *lawyer*

Vancouver
Kleweno, Gilbert H. *lawyer*

Wenatchee
Bastian, Stanley A. *lawyer*
Foreman, Dale Melvin *lawyer, state official*

WYOMING

Buffalo
Kirven, Timothy J. *lawyer*

Casper
Durham, Harry Blaine III *lawyer*
Sullivan, Michael John *lawyer, former ambassador*

Cheyenne
Crank, Patrick J. *lawyer, former state attorn general*

udenthal, Steven Franklin *lawyer, political rganization worker*
nes, John Grier *lawyer, state legislator*
ma, Jack D. *lawyer*
sonetti, Thomas L. *lawyer, former federal gency administrator*
ight, John Blain *lawyer*
lfe, Lawrence J. *lawyer*

dy
pson, Alan Kooi *lawyer, former senator*

ckson
uster, Robert Parks *lawyer*
nce, Gerry (Gerald Leonard Spence) *lawyer, writer*

ramie
ney, Lisa Frances *lawyer*
er, Warren A. *lawyer*

verton
ard, NettaBell *lawyer*

eridan
ey, Rex Odell *lawyer, state senator*

RRITORIES OF THE UNITED STATES

JAM

gatna
ck, Frederick A. *prosecutor*

ORTHERN MARIANA ISLANDS

ipan
adas, Leonardo M. *prosecutor*

CANADA

BERTA

lgary
ghes, Margaret Eileen *law educator, retired ean*
gheed, Peter *lawyer, former Canadian remier*
ottom, David T. *lawyer, energy executive*

ITISH COLUMBIA

rnaby
nwright, David Stanley *patent agent*

ncouver
ikett, Tony *mediator, negotiator, writer*
erson, Leslie Raymond *barrister*

SKATCHEWAN

gina
cKay, Harold Hugh *lawyer*

skatoon
Daniel Russell *law educator, academic dministrator*

ADDRESS UNPUBLISHED

ott, Charles Favour *lawyer*
amson, Leslie Hope *lawyer*
ily, Rima J. *lawyer*
xander, George Jonathon *lawyer, educator, ean*
n, Terrence R. *lawyer*
ley, William Thompson *lawyer*
ken, Gordon Morris *law educator*
kensen, John Reser *lawyer*
kins, Ann O'Neil *lawyer, former computer ompany executive*
eville, Philip Frederick *lawyer*
civengo, Cathy Ann *lawyer*
ing, Ray Gilbert *lawyer, educator*
wley, Peter David *corporate director, investor*
den, Daniel G. *former prosecutor*
nes, Stephen D. *lawyer*
enstein, Mark A. *lawyer*
l, Phillip L. *retired lawyer*
cher, Harold Irving *retired lawyer*
knight, Lon (J.A. Bouknight Jr.) *lawyer, etired utilities executive*
ver, Allan Maxwell *lawyer*
d, William Sprott *lawyer*
wer, Roy Edward *lawyer*
gden, John *lawyer*
thers, Lynda Lee *lawyer*
cieri, Shirley H. *lawyer*
erdick, Kim H. *lawyer, petroleum executive*
dy, Robert Charles *former prosecutor*
dge, Richard James, Jr. *lawyer*
ce, William Thomas *lawyer, educator*
, Richard *lawyer*
h, William Merritt *retired lawyer*
lera, Louis Edward *law educator, former deral official*

Carmichael, David Richard *lawyer, retired insurance company executive*
Castro, Raul Hector *lawyer, Former Governor, Arizona, ambassador*
Charlton, Paul K. *former prosecutor, lawyer*
Cheatham, Robert William *retired lawyer*
Clark, Karen Heath *lawyer*
Clark, William Patrick, Jr. *lawyer, former United States Secretary of the Interior*
Cobb, Miles Alan *retired lawyer*
Codon, Dennis P. *lawyer*
Commander, Eugene R. *lawyer*
Conner, Lindsay Andrew *lawyer*
Conte, Mario G., Jr. *lawyer*
Copeland, Robert Glenn *lawyer*
Curtis, John Joseph *lawyer, writer*
Dailey, Dianne K. *lawyer*
Danner, Bryant Craig *lawyer*
Daughton, Donald *lawyer*
Dolan, Andrew Kevin *retired lawyer*
Dolan, Peter Brown *lawyer*
Doody, Gregory L. *lawyer, former energy executive*
Dowdy, Robert Alan *retired lawyer, director*
Doyle, David C. *lawyer*
Dunlap, F. Thomas, Jr. *lawyer, retired electronics executive*
Edwards, Richard Alan *retired lawyer*
English, Stephen Raymond *lawyer*
Erichsen, Peter Christian
Etra, Donald *lawyer*
Faal, Edi M. O. *lawyer*
Faber, Michael Warren *lawyer*
Feller, Lloyd Harris *lawyer*
Fisher, Lawrence N. *lawyer, engineering and construction management company executive*
Flanagan, Norman Patrick *lawyer*
Franklin, Michael Harold *arbitrator, lawyer, consultant*
Frost, Sterling Newell *arbitrator, mediator, management consultant*
Gardiner, Lester Raymond, Jr. *retired lawyer*
Gill, Margaret Gaskins *lawyer*
Goldberg, David Theo *law educator, writer*
Gomez, Larry *former prosecutor*
Gordley, James Russell *law educator*
Gould, David *lawyer*
Granneman, Vernon Henry *lawyer*
Gray, Jan Charles *lawyer, business owner*
Gray, Patricia Joyce *retired legal association administrator*
Green, Carol H. *consultant, retired lawyer, journalist, educator*
Gross, Lawrence Alan *lawyer*
Guild, Clark Joseph, Jr. *lawyer*
Hackett, Robert John *lawyer*
Hall, Paul J. *lawyer*
Halleck, Charles White *lawyer, photographer, former judge*
Hammond, George Charles *lawyer*
Handler, Carole Enid *lawyer, city planner*
Harris, Richard Eugene Vassau *lawyer*
Hebert, William N. *lawyer*
Hedberg, Steven Michael *lawyer*
Heinen, Nancy Regina *lawyer, former computer company executive*
Hendrickson, D. John *lawyer*
Heng, Donald James, Jr. *lawyer*
Heppe, Karol Virginia *lawyer, educator*
Herringer, Maryellen Cattani *lawyer*
Holbrook, Connie C. *lawyer*
Honeystein, Karl *lawyer, media specialist*
Hornick, Robert Newton *lawyer, educator*
Howard, Nancy E. *lawyer*
Hudson, Eliot R. *lawyer*
Hunter, William Dennis *lawyer*
Hybl, William Joseph *lawyer, foundation administrator*
Iamele, Richard Thomas *retired law librarian*
Iglesias, David Claudio *former prosecutor*
Irwin, William Rankin *retired lawyer*
Jamison, Daniel Oliver *lawyer*
Jensen, Robert Trygve *retired lawyer*
Johnston, James R. *lawyer*
Jolley, R. Gardner *lawyer*
Jones, J. Sorton *lawyer*
Jonsen, Eric Richard *lawyer*
June, Roy Ethiel *lawyer*
Kallgren, Edward Eugene *lawyer*
Kaplan, Barry Martin *lawyer*
Keatinge, Robert Reed *lawyer*
Kennedy, Thomas J. *lawyer*
Kienitz, LaDonna Trapp *lawyer, librarian, municipal official*
Killeen, Michael John *lawyer*
Kippur, Merrie Margolin *lawyer*
Klafter, Cary Ira *lawyer*
Knecht, James Herbert *retired lawyer*
Kreger, Brian Frederick *lawyer*
Kuhrau, Edward W. *retired lawyer*
Kunowski, Herbert Peter *lawyer*
Lackland, John *lawyer, nurseryman*
Lanahan, Daniel Joseph *lawyer*
Landis, Gregory P. *lawyer*
Landreth, Kathryn E. *lawyer*
Lathrope, Daniel John *law educator*
Lewis, Donald Clyde *lawyer*
Libbin, Anne Edna *lawyer*
Liebeler, Susan Wittenberg *lawyer*
Lightstone, Ronald *lawyer*
Linde, Maxine Helen *lawyer, corporate financial executive, investor*
Lupin, Louis Martin *lawyer*
Lyon, Bruce Arnold *lawyer, educator*
Mabey, Ralph R. *lawyer*
Manos, Christopher Lawrence *lawyer, mediator*
Matteucci, Sherry Scheel *former prosecutor*
Maulding, Barry Clifford *lawyer, director*

McCarthy, J. Thomas *lawyer, educator*
Mc Cormack, Francis Xavier *lawyer, former oil company executive*
McCormick, Homer L., Jr. *lawyer*
McDougall, Roderick Gregory *lawyer*
McGrath, David M. *lawyer*
McIntosh, Terrie Tuckett *lawyer*
McKenzie, Curtis David *lawyer*
McManus, Richard Philip *lawyer, agricultural products executive*
Menhall, Dalton Winn *lawyer, insurance executive, professional association administrator*
Merritt, Nancy-Jo *lawyer*
Meyerson, Ivan D. *lawyer, former corporate financial executive*
Michael, Mark Dixwell *lawyer*
Michaelson, Jon *lawyer*
Mitchell, Briane Nelson *lawyer*
Moloney, Stephen Michael *lawyer*
Morie, G. Glen *lawyer, manufacturing executive*
Moya, Patrick Robert *lawyer*
Mudd, John O. *lawyer*
Nanda, Ved Prakash *law educator, director, academic administrator*
Natcher, Stephen Darlington *retired lawyer, electronics executive*
Nathanson, Paul S. *lawyer, educator*
Nekritz, Edward Steven *lawyer*
Newman, Carol L. *lawyer*
Ockey, Ronald J. *lawyer*
O'Connor, Paul Daniel *lawyer*
O'Dowd, Sarah A. *lawyer*
O'Keefe, Edward Franklin *lawyer*
O'Rourke, C. Larry *lawyer*
Ostrovsky, Lawrence Zelig *lawyer*
Parks, Patricia Jean *lawyer*
Parode, Ann *lawyer*
Partida, Gilbert A. *lawyer*
Partridge, Bruce James *lawyer, educator, writer, parliamentarian*
Petty, George Oliver *retired lawyer*
Phair, Joseph Baschon *lawyer*
Pollard, Henry *arbitrator, mediator*
Press, Anthony L. *lawyer*
Reveal, Ernest Ira III *retired lawyer*
Rew, Lawrence Boyd *lawyer*
Richardson, Charles H. *lawyer*
Richey, Mary Ellen *lawyer*
Roman, Stan G. *lawyer*
Rosky, Burton Seymour *lawyer*
Roster, Michael *lawyer*
Rounsaville, Guy, Jr. *lawyer*
Salomon, Darrell Joseph *lawyer*
Sattler, Bruce Weimer *lawyer*
Sawdei, Milan A. *lawyer*
Sax, Joseph Lawrence *lawyer, educator*
Schaller, Gordon A. *lawyer*
Schenk, Lynn *lawyer, former congresswoman*
Schmidt, Karl A. *lawyer*
Schuchard, Robert L. *lawyer*
Schulman, Alan *lawyer*
Schwartz, Bernard Julian *lawyer*
Scott, Michael Dennis *lawyer*
Seeger, Leinaala Robinson *law librarian, educator*
Segel, Karen Lynn Joseph *lawyer, tax specialist*
Shanahan, Lauri M. *lawyer, former retail executive*
Shanks, Patricia L. *lawyer*
Sidran, Mark Harris *lawyer*
Smith, Kerry Clark *lawyer*
Sochynsky, Yaroslav *lawyer, arbitrator, mediator*
Sokol, Jan D. *lawyer*
Sparks, John Edward *lawyer*
Springer, Paul David *lawyer, film company executive*
Stephens, Shand Scott *lawyer*
Sterrett, James Kelley, II, *lawyer*
Stiska, John Charles *lawyer*
Stone, Gary Leon *retired lawyer*
Stratton, Richard James *lawyer*
Swanson, Victoria Clare Heldman *lawyer*
Taylor, Robert P. *lawyer*
Taylor, Ruth Anne *lawyer*
Tingle, James O'Malley *retired lawyer*
Trimble, Phillip Richard *law educator*
Trost, Glenn W. *lawyer*
Van Emburgh, Joanne *lawyer*
Voorhees, James Dayton, Jr. *lawyer*
Wadsworth, Harold Wayne *lawyer*
Wagner, Patricia Hamm *lawyer*
Walsh, Jim *lawyer, former air transportation executive*
Weaver, Delbert Allen *retired lawyer*
Weiner, Peter H. *lawyer*
Weinman, Glenn Alan *lawyer*
Welch, Carol Mae *lawyer*
Wessling, Robert Bruce *retired lawyer*
West, Natalie Elsa *lawyer*
Wheeler, Stephen Frederick *legal administrator*
White, Jo Lynn *lawyer*
Whitmore, Bruce G. *lawyer*
Willard-Jones, Donna C. *lawyer*
Wilson, John Pasley *retired law educator*
Wolfen, Werner F. *lawyer*
Worthington, Bruce R. *lawyer, energy executive*
York, Gary Alan *lawyer*
Zeff, Ophelia Hope *lawyer*
Zischke, Michael Herman *lawyer*

Zohn, Martin Steven *lawyer*

MEDICINE *See* HEALTHCARE: MEDICINE

MILITARY

UNITED STATES

ALASKA

Anchorage
Gamble, Patrick K. *retired military officer, rail transportation executive*

Elmendorf AFB
Case, Thomas R. *career officer*

ARIZONA

Prescott
Schaeffer, Reiner Horst *military officer, foreign language professional*

Scottsdale
Coffinger, Maralin Katharyne *retired career officer, consultant*

Yuma
Hudson, John Irvin *retired career officer*

CALIFORNIA

El Segundo
Hamel, Michael A. *career officer*

La Jolla
Counts, Stanley Thomas *retired military officer, retired electronics executive*
Greer, Howard Earl *retired career officer*

Long Beach
Higginson, John *retired career officer*

Monterey
Matthews, David Fort *career officer*
Oliver, Daniel T. *military education administrator, career officer, retired*
Schrady, David Alan *civilian military employee, educator*

Newport Beach
Pace, Peter *retired military officer, management consultant*

San Diego
Contreras, Thomas J., Jr. *career officer*
Darmstandler, Harry Max *retired military officer*
Stone, Thomas Edward *defense contractor, retired career officer*
Wing, Thomas M. *military officer, systems engineer*

COLORADO

Colorado Springs
Caruana, Patrick Peter *retired military officer*
McFann, Maurice L., Jr. *career officer*
Renuart, Victor Eugene, Jr., (Gene Renuart) *career military officer*
Sawyer, Thomas William *career officer*

Dillon
Dugan, Michael Joseph *former career officer, health agency executive*

Monument
Rokke, Ervin Jerome *military officer, academic administrator*

Peterson AFB
Webster, William G., Jr. *career military officer*

U S A F Academy
Lorenz, Stephen R. *career officer*
Merchant, P. Glenn, Jr. *military officer, physician*

Westcliffe
Hollingsworth, Bobby G. *career officer*

Woodland Park
Stewart, Robert Lee *retired career officer, astronaut*

HAWAII

Camp H M Smith
Keating, Timothy J. *career military officer*

Hickam AFB
Heflebower, Charles R. *career officer*

Honolulu
Hays, Ronald Jackson *career officer*
Pollock, Gale Susan *career military officer*
Weyand, Frederick Carlton *retired career officer*

IDAHO

Boise
Clemins, Archie Ray *career officer*

NEW MEXICO

Albuquerque
Flournoy, John Charles, Sr. *retired civilian military employee, officer*

Cedar Crest
Sheppard, Jack W. *retired career officer*

Santa Fe
Sumner, Gordon, Jr. *retired military officer*

OREGON

Portland
Feichtinger, Mark R. *career officer*

UTAH

Hill AFB
Bergren, Scott C. *career officer*

VIRGINIA

Dumfries
Avrit, Richard Calvin *defense consultant, career officer*

Fairfax Station
Lewis, Fred Parker *career officer*

Occoquan
Vercauteren, Richard Frank *career officer*

WASHINGTON

Anacortes
Higgins, Robert (Walter) *career naval officer, physician*

Kirkland
Shelley, Marke R. *career officer*

Lynnwood
Jenes, Theodore George, Jr. *retired military officer*

ADDRESS UNPUBLISHED

Allery, Kenneth Edward *career officer*
Antanitus, David J. *career officer*
Beard, Timothy R *career officer*
Bowen, James Thomas *career officer*
Brautigan, Roger L. *reserve career officer*
Bryan, James D. *career officer*
Carter, William George III *career officer*
Chandler, Carrol H. (Howie Chandler) *career military officer*
Cooning, Craig R. *career officer*
Davis, Harley Cleo *retired military officer*
Eberhart, Ralph E. *retired military officer*
Ellison, David R. *career officer*
Fargo, Thomas Boulton *retired career military officer*
Forgan, David Waller *retired career officer*
Gardner, Emerson N., Jr. *military officer*
Geraci, Richard V. *military officer, government agency administrator*
Goslin, Thomas B. *career officer*
Holmes, Michael L. *career officer*
Jackson, James T. *career officer*
Marlow, Edward A. *former army officer*
Mullen, William Joseph III *retired career army officer*
O'Berry, Carl Gerald *former military officer, electrical engineer*
Radzik, Albin F. *federal analyst, military consultant*
Rees, Raymond F. *military officer*
Sams, John B., Jr. *career officer*
Slaght, Kenneth D. *career officer*
Smith, Zannie O. *retired career officer*
Snyder, Daniel James *military career officer*
Thomas, John D., Jr. *career officer*
Thompson, Joseph Stanton *career officer*
Wagie, David A. *career military officer*
Wynne, Michael Walter *former civilian military employee*
Yeager, Chuck (Charles Elwood Yeager) *retired air force officer, test pilot*
Zelibor, Thomas E. *career officer*

REAL ESTATE

UNITED STATES

ALASKA

Anchorage
Hofseth, Pauline C. *realtor*

ARIZONA

Cortaro
Fossland, Joeann Jones *real estate company executive*

Phoenix
De Michele, O. Mark *real estate company executive*
Hanneman, LeRoy C., Jr. *real estate executive*
Lewis, Orme, Jr. *real estate company executive, land use adviser*

Prescott
Masotti, Louis Henry *real estate educator, consultant*

Scottsdale
Gleason, John H. *real estate development company executive*
Grogan, James J. *real estate company executive*
Mariucci, Anne L. *real estate development company executive*
Mickus, Donald V. *real estate development corporation executive*
Roach, Charles T. *real estate company executive*
Schweikert, David *real estate agent, former state legislator*
Spencer, John Andrew *real estate development corporation executive*

Tempe
Kim, Joochul *urban planner, educator*
Schrader, William P. *organization executive, farmer*

Tucson
Swihart, H. Gregg *real estate company executive*

CALIFORNIA

Aptos
Nicholson, Joseph Bruce *real estate developer*

Belvedere Tiburon
Caselli, Virgil P. *real estate executive*

Beverly Hills
Bergman, Nancy Palm *real estate investment company executive*
Tamkin, Curtis Sloane *real estate development company executive*

Carmel
Didion, James J. *real estate company executive*

City Of Industry
Roski, Edward P., Jr. *real estate developer, professional sports team executive*

Healdsburg
Brunner, Howard William *professional land surveyor*

Hesperia
Previtti, James P. *real estate executive*

Irvine
Chronley, James Andrew *real estate executive*
Sabin, Gary B. *real estate executive*
Stack, Geoffrey Lawrence *real estate developer*
Staky, Richard *real estate development company executive*
Vandell, Kerry Dean *real estate consultant, educator, director, finance educator*

La Jolla
Foley, L(ewis) Michael *real estate company officer*

Laguna Beach
Hanauer, Joe Franklin *real estate company officer*

Laguna Niguel
York, James Orison *retired real estate executive*

Long Beach
McGann, John Milton *real estate executive*

Los Angeles
Green, Richard E. *real estate company executive*
Linsk, Michael Stephen *real estate company executive*
Maguire, Robert Francis III *retired real estate company executive*
Nelson, James Augustus, II, *real estate company executive, architect*
Sterling, Donald T. *real estate mogul, professional sports team owner*
Sulentic, Robert E. *real estate company executive*
White, Brett *real estate company executive*

Lynwood
Dove, Donald Augustine *city planner, educator*

Newport Beach
Bren, Donald L. *real estate company executive*
Gilchrist, Richard Irwin *real estate developer*
Kenney, William John, Jr. *real estate developer*
Matteucci, Dominick Vincent *real estate developer*
Turner, Jana L. *real estate company executive*
Webb, H. Lawrence *real estate executive*

Palmdale
Anderson, R(obert) Gregg *real estate company executive*

Palo Alto
Klein, Robert Nicholas, II, *real estate developer*

Pebble Beach
Getreu, Sanford *retired city planner*

Playa Del Rey
Schoenfeld, Lawrence Jon *real estate developer*

Rancho Palos Verdes
Allbee, Sandra Moll *real estate broker*

Rohnert Park
Burger, Eugene J. *property manager*

San Bernardino
Willis, Harold Wendt, Sr. *real estate developer*

San Diego
Mc Comic, Robert Barry *real estate company executive, lawyer*
Wagmen, Lee H. *real estate executive*

San Francisco
Bracken, Thomas Robert James *real estate investment executive*
Freund, Fredric S. *real estate broker and manager*
Shorenstein, Walter Herbert *commercial real estate development company executive*

San Jose
Rothblatt, Donald Noah *urban and regional planner, educator*

San Rafael
Roulac, Stephen E. *real estate consultant*

Santa Barbara
Arnold, Michael Neal *real property appraiser, consultant*

Santa Monica
Anderson, Dana K. *real estate company executive*
Wachs, Martin *urban planning educator, author, consultant*

Saratoga
Santana, Ronny *real estate agent, small business owner*

Valencia
Cusamano, Gary M. *real estate executive*
Dierckman, Thomas E. *land use planner*
Lee, Thomas L. *real estate executive*
Mork, Stuart R. *land and farming company executive*
Schmidt, Stephen C. *real estate developer*

Valley Village
Bishop, Kathryn Elizabeth *realtor, film producer, writer*

Vista
Cavanaugh, Kenneth Clinton *retired real estate consultant*

COLORADO

Aurora
Lochmiller, Kurtis L. *real estate entrepreneur*

Centennial
Reece, Paris G. *real estate company executive*

Denver
Considine, Terry *real estate company executive*
Kroenke, E. Stanley *real estate developer, professional sports team owner*
Mandarich, David D. *real estate corporation executive*

Grand Junction
Nelson, Paul William *real estate broker*

Vail
Kelton, Arthur Marvin, Jr. *real estate developer*

HAWAII

Honolulu
Jones, Michael T. *real estate development executive*
Jones, Pamela S. *real estate development executive*
Oyler, David L. *real estate development executive*

IDAHO

Idaho Falls
Thorsen, Nancy Dain *retired real estate bro*

NEVADA

Lake Tahoe
Chase, Shari *real estate company executive, broker*

Las Vegas
Jabara, Michael Dean *real estate developer, former technology entrepreneur*
Maravich, Mary Louise *realtor*
Pulliam, Francine Sarno *real estate broker, developer*

NEW MEXICO

Albuquerque
Stahl, Jack Leland *real estate company exec*

NEW YORK

New York
Swig, Kent M. *real estate company executiv*

OREGON

Portland
Dickinson, Janet Mae Webster *relocation consulting executive*
Packard, Robert Goodale III *urban planner*

Springfield
Davis, George Donald *executive land use po consultant*

UTAH

Salt Lake City
Frazier, G. Rex *real estate executive*

WASHINGTON

Bellevue
Scott, J. Lennox *real estate company execut*

Federal Way
McMichael, J(ack) Richard *real estate devel*
Nitta, Jeffrey W. *real estate executive*

Rollingbay
Morris, Donald Charles *real estate company executive*

Seattle
Kirk, Judd *real estate development executive*
Kruse, Shari *real estate agent*
Sasaki, Tsutomu (Tom Sasaki) *eco products trading company executive*

Spokane
Covey, Michael J. *forest products and real e executive*

WYOMING

Casper
Willox, James Hugh *realtor, political organization administrator*

CANADA

BRITISH COLUMBIA

Vancouver
Evans, John deCourcey *real estate company officer*

Victoria
Barrie, Len *real estate developer, profession sports team executive*

ADDRESS UNPUBLISHED

Bartlett, Arthur Eugene *real estate company executive*
Dickey, Robert Marvin (Rick Dickey) *prope manager*
Fetterly, Lynn Lawrence *real estate broker manager*
Fischer, Michael Ludwig *environmental executive*
Fredericks, Patricia Ann *real estate executiv*
Furlotti, Alexander Amato *real estate and investment company executive*

es, John Stanley *urban development xecutive*
hamed, Joseph, Sr. *real estate broker, eveloper, farmer*
llin, Stan *real estate company executive*
kratz, Frank D. *real estate company xecutive*
ling, Michael Frederick *supermarket ompany, real estate executive*
ley, Stuart McKinnon *real estate consultant*
ers, Robert Scot *real estate developer*
ahl, Stanley Frederick *real estate developer*
liams, Barry Lawson *real estate executive*
ods, Sandra Kay *real estate executive*

RELIGION

UNITED STATES

ASKA

chorage
wietz, Roger L. *archbishop*

IZONA

ncan
ts, Eugene Thomas *minister, secondary ducation educator*

oenix
enkel, Barbara Ann *minister, nurse, social vorker*

ottsdale
rnton, John S., IV, *retired bishop*

n City
nilton, Ronald Ray *minister*

cson
anas, Gerald Frederick *bishop*

LIFORNIA

aheim
yen, Tai Anh *minister*

ascadero
es, Kathryn Cherie *pastor*

ldwin Park
skill, James Lawrence *minister*

rstow
es, Nathaniel B., Jr. *bishop*

rkeley
ner, Michael *rabbi*
dge, Lewis Seymour *theologian, educator, niversity dean*

adbury
npbell, Robert Charles *minister, theology tudies educator*

rlingame
ing, William Edwin *bishop*

marillo
erson, Stuart W. *religious raido broadcaster*

stro Valley
rrison, Glenn Leslie *minister*

aremont
w, William Waldo, Jr. *bishop*
cheman, Clark Arthur *philosophy and eligious studies educator*
ders, James Alvin *retired minister, retired eligious studies educator*

sta Mesa
liams, William Corey *theology educator, onsultant*

k Grove
g, Timothy Teng *religious organization dministrator*

untain Valley
stein, Stephen Jan *rabbi*

esno
nbock, John Thomas *bishop*

llerton
n, Sang Koo *pastor, educator*

ke Forest
rren, Rick (Richard Duane Warren) *minister, riter*

ncaster
nner, George Cyril, Jr. *minister, educational dministrator*

mita
toris, Joseph Martin *bishop emeritus*

Los Angeles
Anderson, Robert Marshall *retired bishop*
Berg, Philip *religious organization administrator*
Blake, Charles E. *minister, bishop*
Borsch, Frederick Houk *bishop*
Boyd, Malcolm *minister, writer*
Breuer, Stephen Ernest *religious organization administrator, consultant*
Chedid, John George *bishop emeritus*
Clark, Edward *bishop*
Finley, Mordecai *rabbi*
Fitzgerald, Tikhon (Lee R. H. Fitzgerald) *bishop*
Freehling, Allen Isaac *rabbi*
Levy, Naomi *rabbi*
Mahony, Roger Michael *cardinal, archbishop*
Mc Pherson, Rolf Kennedy *clergyman, religious organization administrator*
Ogilvie, Lloyd John *clergyman*
Phillips, Keith Wendall *minister*
Salazar, Alexander *bishop*
Shaheen, Robert Joseph *bishop*
Solis, Oscar Azarcon *bishop*
Ward, John James *bishop emeritus*

Malibu
Wilson, John Francis *religious studies educator, archaeologist*

Menlo Park
DuMaine, R. Pierre *bishop emeritus*

Mission Hills
Wilkerson, Gerald Eugene *bishop*

Monterey
Garcia, Richard John *bishop*
Ryan, Sylvester Donovan *bishop emeritus*
Shimpfky, Richard Lester *bishop*

Oakland
Cordileone, Salvatore Joseph *bishop*
Jakubowsky, Frank Raymond *religious writer*

Orange
Brown, Tod David *bishop*
Luong, Dominic *bishop*
McFarland, Norman Francis *bishop*

Palm Desert
Ponder, Catherine *clergywoman*

Palm Springs
Jones, Milton Wakefield *publisher*

Pasadena
Winter, Ralph D. *religious organization administrator, academic administrator*

Portola Valley
Garsh, Thomas Burton *publisher*

Reedley
Dick, Henry Henry *minister*

Sacramento
Madera Uribe, Jose de Jesus *bishop emeritus*
Quinn, Francis Anthony *bishop emeritus*
Soto, Jaime *bishop*
Weigand, William Kenneth *Bishop Emeritus*

San Bernardino
Barnes, Gerald Richard *bishop*
Burgess, Mary Alice (Mary Alice Wickizer) *publisher*
Del Riego, Rutilio J. *bishop*

San Diego
Brom, Robert Henry *bishop*
Chavez, Gilbert Espinoza *bishop emeritus*
Downing, David Charles *retired minister*
Hughes, Gethin B. *bishop*
Mathes, James R. *bishop*
Scorgie, Glen Given *religious studies educator*

San Francisco
Brickner, David *religious organization administrator, consultant*
Brown, Amos Cleophilus *minister*
Justice, William J. *bishop*
Kelly, James Anthony *priest*
Kushner, Lawrence *rabbi*
Niederauer, George H. *archbishop*
Rosen, Moishe *religious organization founder*
Wang, Ignatius Chung *bishop*
Williams, Cecil *minister*

San Jose
Edmonds, Charles Henry *retired publisher*

Santa Barbara
Curry, Thomas John *bishop*

Santa Clara
McGrath, Patrick Joseph *bishop*

Santa Rosa
Walsh, Daniel Francis *bishop*
Ziemann, George Patrick *bishop emeritus*

Seaside
Hamilton, W. W. *religious organization administrator*

Sonora
Chandler, Edwin Russell *clergyman, writer*
Jones, Georgia Ann *publisher*

Stockton
Blaire, Stephen Edward *bishop*
Null, Paul Bryan *minister*

Studio City
Meenan, Alan John *clergyman, theology studies educator*

Sun Valley
Stitzinger, James Franklin *religious studies educator, library director*

Tustin
Crouch, Paul Franklin *minister, religious organization administrator*

West Hollywood
Wilson, Nancy Linda *religious organization administrator*

COLORADO

Colorado Springs
Dobson, James Clayton *evangelist, psychologist, author*
Hanifen, Richard Charles Patrick *bishop emeritus*
Loux, Gordon Dale *philanthropic consultant*
Sheridan, Michael John *bishop*

Denver
Chaput, Charles J. *archbishop*
Hayes, Edward Lee *religious organization administrator*
Murphy, Sister Lillian *sister, not-for-profit organization executive*
Sheeran, Michael John Leo *priest, academic administrator*

Dillon
Follett, Robert John Richard *publisher*

Fort Collins
Rolston, Holmes III *theology studies educator, philosopher*

Lakewood
Wilke, LeRoy *retired church administrator*

Pueblo
Tafoya, Arthur Nicholas *bishop*

HAWAII

Honolulu
Fisch, Michael J. *publisher*
Merrifield, Donald Paul *ministries coordinator*
Silva, Clarence Richard *bishop*

Kapaa
Veylanswami, Satguru Bodhinatha *head of religious order*

IDAHO

Boise
Driscoll, Michael Patrick *bishop*

MONTANA

Billings
Barnea, Uri N. *rabbi, conductor, musician*

Great Falls
Warfel, Michael William *bishop*

Helena
Jones, Charles Irving *bishop*
Thomas, George Leo *bishop*

NEBRASKA

Bellevue
Milone, Anthony Michael *bishop emeritus*

NEVADA

Las Vegas
Bishop, Leo Kenneth *clergyman, educator*

Minden
Jackson, John Jay *clergyman*

NEW MEXICO

Albuquerque
Sheehan, Michael Jarboe *archbishop*

OREGON

Bend
Connolly, Thomas Joseph *bishop emeritus*
Vasa, Robert Francis *bishop*

Dallas
Calkins, Loren Gene *religious organization administrator, pastor*

Eugene
Sanders, Jack Thomas *religious studies educator*

Portland
Beauchamp, E(dward) William *priest, lawyer, university administrator, management educator*
Steiner, Kenneth Donald *bishop*

UTAH

Salt Lake City
Eyring, Henry Bennion *head of religious order*
Holland, Jeffrey R. *religious organization administrator*
Monson, Thomas Spencer *religious organization administrator, retired publishing executive*
Packer, Boyd K. *church official*
Perry, L. Tom *religious organization administrator, merchant*
Scott, Richard G. *religious organization administrator*
Smith, Eldred Gee *church leader*
Wester, John Charles *bishop*
Wirthlin, Joseph B. *religious organization administrator*

WASHINGTON

Bellevue
Berkley, James Donald *clergyman*

Des Moines
Tuell, Jack Marvin *retired bishop*

Seattle
Brunett, Alexander Joseph *archbishop*
Hunthausen, Raymond Gerhardt *archbishop emeritus*
Tyson, Joseph Jude *bishop*
Warner, Vincent W. *bishop*
Zehr, Clyde James *religious organization administrator*

Spokane
Edwards, James Robert *minister, educator*
Skylstad, William Stephen *bishop*

Tacoma
Warren, Larry Michael *clergyman*
Wold, David C. *bishop*

Vancouver
Congdon, Roger Douglass *theology studies educator, minister*
Crews, William Odell, Jr. *religious organization administrator*

Yakima
Sevilla, Carlos Arthur *bishop*

WYOMING

Cheyenne
Hart, Joseph Hubert *bishop emeritus*

INDIA

Kollum
Devi, Amritanandamayi (Sri Mata Amritanandamayi Devi, Amma) *spiritual leader*

ADDRESS UNPUBLISHED

Allison, Andrew Marvin *church administrator*
Berenbaum, Michael Gary *theology educator*
Bigger, Darold F. *religious studies educator*
Booth, John Nicholls *minister, writer, photographer*
Bubar, Joseph Bedell, Jr. *pastor*
Cook, Tony Michael *church administrator, legislative staff member*
Cummins, John Stephen *bishop emeritus*
Emerson, R. Clark *priest*
Estep, John Hayes *religious organization administrator, clergyman*
Fleming, Carolyn Elizabeth *religious organization administrator, interior designer*
Flynt, Larry Claxton, Jr. *publisher*
Hammond, Charles Ainley *clergyman*
Hurley, Francis T. *archbishop emeritus*
Jaoudi, Maria M. *religious studies and humanities educator*
Koran, Dennis Howard *publisher*
Ladehoff, Robert Louis *bishop*
Lapin, Daniel *rabbi*
Meier, George Karl III *minister, lawyer*
Messer, Donald Edward *theology educator, administrator*
Milligan, Sister Mary *theology studies educator, consultant*
Owen-Towle, Carolyn Sheets *clergywoman*
Peck, Paul Lachlan *minister*
Pelotte, Donald Edmond *bishop*
Plomp, Teunis (Tony Plomp) *minister*
Probasco, Calvin Henry Charles *clergyman, college administrator*
Straling, Phillip Francis *bishop emeritus*
Swanson, Paul Rubert *minister*
Vlazny, John George *archbishop*

Willette, Donald Corliss *pastor*
Williams, Ronald Dean *minister, religious organization administrator*
Wilson, Warren Samuel *clergyman*
Winslow, David Allen *chaplain, retired military officer*
Wooten, Cecil Aaron *retired religious organization administrator*

SCIENCE: LIFE SCIENCE

UNITED STATES

ALASKA

Fairbanks
Chapin, F. Stuart III *ecologist*
Kessel, Brina *ornithologist, educator, researcher*

ARIZONA

Flagstaff
Cortner, Hanna Joan *retired political scientist, researcher*
Price, Peter Wilfrid *ecology educator, researcher*

Glendale
Collins, Richard Francis *microbiologist, educator*

Litchfield Park
Ollson, Mickey Louis *zoo owner*

Maricopa
Kimball, Bruce Arnold *soil scientist*

Payson
Stephenson, Larry Kirk *geography educator, financial planner*

Phoenix
Bolin, Vernon Spencer *microbiologist, consultant*

Scottsdale
Magness, Rhonda Ann *retired microbiologist*

Surprise
Steffan, Wallace Allan *entomologist, educator, museum director*

Tempe
Curtiss, Roy III *life sciences professor*
Hölldobler, Berthold Karl *zoologist*
Poste, George Henry *biology professor, former pharmaceutical company executive*
Uttal, William R(eichenstein) *psychology and engineering educator, research scientist*
Vasquez, Jo Anne *retired science educator*

Tucson
Brusca, Richard Charles *biologist, researcher, educator*
Enquist, Brian Joseph *ecologist, educator*
Foster, Kennith Earl *life sciences educator*
Gerba, Charles Peter *microbiologist, educator*
Haynes, Caleb Vance, Jr. *geology and archaeology educator*
Hubbard, William Bogel *planetary sciences educator*
Macys, Sonja *science association director*
Moran, Nancy A. *ecologist, educator*
Titley, Spencer Rowe *geology educator*

Wikieup
Brattstrom, Bayard Holmes *biology professor*

CALIFORNIA

Agoura Hills
Fox, Stuart Ira *physiologist*

Alameda
Earle, Sylvia Alice *research biologist, oceanographer*

Albany
Schwimmer, Sigmund *food enzymologist*

Arcata
Black, Jeffrey M. *professor (wildlife)*

Atherton
Coleman, Robert Griffin *geology educator*

Berkeley
Anderson, John Richard *entomologist, educator*
Baldwin, Bruce Gregg *botany educator, researcher*
Barrett, Reginald Haughton *wildlife management educator*
Berkner, Klaus Hans *laboratory administrator, physicist*
Bern, Howard Alan *biologist, researcher, science educator*
Botchan, Michael R. *molecular biologist, biochemist*
Burnside, Mary Beth *biology professor, researcher*
Casida, John Edward *toxicology and entomology professor*
Chapela, Ignacio H. *biologist, researcher*
Chen, Lu *neurobiologist, biology professor*
Cline, Thomas Warren *geneticist, educator*
Cooper, William Secord *information science educator*
Diamond, Marian Cleeves *neuroscientist, educator*
Doudna, Jennifer A. *molecular biologist, educator*
Eisen, Michael B. *research scientist, educator*
Fung, Inez Y. *science educator*
Harris, Eva *molecular biology educator*
King, Nicole *molecular biologist, educator*
Koehl, Mimi R. *integrative biology professor*
Levine, Mark David *science administrator, director*
Levine, Michael Steven *science educator*
Lidicker, William Zander, Jr. *zoologist, educator*
Lipps, Jere Henry *biology and geology professor*
Manga, Michael *earth science educator, geophysicist*
Marletta, Michael A. *biochemistry educator, researcher*
Oster, George F. *molecular biologist, environmental scientist*
Patek, Sheila N. *biologist, educator*
Rine, Jasper *geneticist, educator*
Schachman, Howard Kapnek *molecular biologist, educator*
Schekman, Randy W. *molecular biology administrator, biochemist*
Scott, Eugenie Carol *science foundation director, anthropologist*
Shu, Frank Hsia-San *astronomy educator, researcher, writer*
Sobel, Noam *science educator*
Spear, Robert Clinton *environmental health educator, consultant*
Teeguarden, Dennis Earl *forest economist, educator*
Wake, David Burton *biology professor*
Wake, Marvalee Hendricks *biology professor*
Willhite, Calvin Campbell *toxicologist*
Wood, David Lee *entomologist, educator*
Yund, Mary Alice *biotechnology consultant*

Bodega Bay
Clegg, James Standish *physiologist, biochemist, educator*

Chico
Ediger, Robert Ike *botanist, educator*

Cupertino
Cheeseman, Douglas Taylor, Jr. *wildlife tour executive, photographer, educator*

Davis
Addicott, Fredrick Taylor *botanist*
Ardans, Alexander Andrew *veterinarian, educator, lab administrator*
Baldwin, Ransom Leland *animal science educator*
Barbour, Michael G(eorge) *botanist, educator, ecologist, consultant*
Barthold, Stephen W. *veterinarian*
Baskin, Ronald Joseph *biophysicist educator, dean*
Bruening, George E. *virologist*
Colvin, Harry Walter, Jr. *physiology educator*
Day, Howard Wilman *geology educator*
Enders, Allen Coffin *anatomy educator*
Epstein, Emanuel *plant physiologist*
Gilbertson, Robert Leonard *plant pathology educator*
Greenwood, M. R. C. *biologist, nutrition educator, former academic administrator*
Hedrick, Jerry Leo *biochemistry and biophysics educator*
Hendrickx, Andrew George *research physiologist*
Hess, Charles Edward *environmental horticulture educator*
Jones, Edward George *neuroscientist, educator*
Kado, Clarence Isao *molecular biologist*
Kirkpatrick, Bruce Charles *plant pathology educator*
Kuhl, Tonya L. *science educator*
Lucas, William John *science educator*
Luciw, Paul A. *molecular virologist, educator*
Meyer, Margaret Eleanor *retired microbiologist*
Moyle, Peter Briggs *marine biologist, educator*
Mukherjee, Amiya K. *metallurgy and materials science educator*
Murphy, Terence Martin *biology professor*
Qualset, Calvin O. *agronomist, educator*
Rappaport, Lawrence *plant physiology and horticulture educator*
Ronald, Pamela C. *plant pathologist, educator*
Rost, Thomas Lowell *retired botany educator*
Roth, John Roger *geneticist, biology educator*
Savageau, Michael Antonio *science educator, engineering educator*
Schoener, Thomas William *ecologist, educator*
Sillman, Arnold Joel *physiologist, educator*
Steffey, Eugene Paul *veterinary medicine educator*
Turcotte, Donald Lawson *geophysical sciences educator*
Uyemoto, Jerry Kazumitsu *plant pathologist, educator*
Van Alfen, Neal K. *plant pathologist*
Vermeij, Geerat Jacobus *marine biologist, educator*
Watt, Kenneth Edmund Ferguson *zoology educator*
Yilma, Tilahun Daniel *virologist, veterinarian, educator, researcher*

Del Mar
Farquhar, Marilyn Gist *cell biologist, pathologist, educator*

Emeryville
Chien, David Ying *biotechnologist, epidemiologist*
Houghton, Michael *geneticist*
White, Raymond Leslie *geneticist*

Encinitas
Duval, Julian J. *arboretum administrator*
Hale, David Fredrick *biotechnology executive*

Fullerton
Jones, Claris Eugene, Jr. *botanist, educator*

Grass Valley
Suri, Jasjit S. *research scientist*

Healdsburg
Vedros, Neylan Anthony *microbiologist, educator*

Hopland
Jones, Milton Bennion *retired agronomist*

Irvine
Allen, Douglas D. *horticulture and products company executive*
Ayala, Francisco José *geneticist, educator*
Carew, Thomas James *neuroscientist, educator*
Clegg, Michael Tran *genetics educator, researcher*
Gardiner, David M. *biologist, educator*
Lenhoff, Howard Maer *biological sciences educator, academic administrator*
Ribak, Charles Eric *neuroscientist, educator*
Simmon, Vincent Fowler *biotechnology executive*
Stanbridge, Eric John *biology professor*
Thigpen, Stephen P. *horticulture products company executive*
Weller, Stephen G. *botanist, educator*

La Jolla
Baldridge, Kim *science educator*
Brenner, Sydney *molecular biologist, researcher*
Brooks, Charles Lee III *computational biophysicist, educator*
Chrispeels, Maarten Jan *biology professor*
Evans, Ronald M. *microbiologist, educator*
Gilbert, James Freeman *geophysics educator*
Gleeson, Joseph *science educator*
Guillemin, Roger C.L. *physiologist, academic administrator*
Helinski, Donald Raymond *biologist, educator*
Hirsch, Jorge E. *science educator*
Hunter, Tony (Anthony Rex) *molecular biologist, educator*
Ideker, Trey *computational and molecular biologist*
Kooyman, Gerald Lee *physiologist, researcher*
Rahman, Yueh-Erh *biologist*
Richman, Douglas Daniel *medical virologist, educator, internist*
Schroeder, Julian Ivan *biology professor*
Sherman, Irwin William *biological sciences educator, academic administrator*
Sorge, Joseph Anthony *molecular biologist*
Thomas, Charles Allen, Jr. *molecular biologist, educator*
Vacquier, Victor Dimitri *biology educator*
West, John Burnard *physiologist, educator*
Wilkie, Donald Walter *retired biologist, aquarium administrator*
Wilson, Ian Andrew *molecular biology educator*
Wong-Staal, Flossie *geneticist, educator*

Loma Linda
Longo, Lawrence Daniel *physiologist, obstetrician, gynecologist, educator*
Taylor, Barry Llewellyn *microbiologist, educator*

Long Beach
Schubel, Jerry Robert *marine scientist educator, dean*

Los Alamitos
Aberman, Harold Mark *veterinarian*

Los Angeles
Agnew, John A. *science educator*
Arbib, Michael Anthony *neuroscientist, educator, computer scientist*
Baker, Robert Frank *molecular biologist, educator*
Banerjee, Utpal *biology professor, research scientist*
Bok, Dean *cell biologist, educator*
Boles, Richard Gregory *clinical geneticist, researcher*
Bottjer, David John *earth science and biology educator*
Chen, Irvin Shao Yu *microbiologist, educator*
Craft, Cheryl Mae *neurobiologist, anatomist, researcher*
De Robertis, Edward M. F. *research scientist, educator*
Diamond, Jared Mason *biologist, writer*
Eisenberg, David Samuel *molecular biologist, educator*
Finch, Caleb Ellicott *neurobiologist, educator*
Finegold, Sydney Martin *microbiology educator*
Fischer, Alfred George *geology educator*
Gasson, Judith C. *research scientist*
Gibson, Arthur Charles *biologist, educator*
Gilman, John Joseph *research scientist*
Goldberg, Robert B. *molecular biologist, educator*
Gordon, Malcolm Stephen *biology professor*
Greenberger, Martin *biotechnologist, inform scientist, educator*
Grinnell, Alan Dale *neuroscientist, educator*
Ljubimov, Alexander V. *molecular biologist, biologist, researcher*
Melnick, Michael *geneticist, educator*
Orme, Antony Ronald *geography educator*
Schopf, James William *paleobiologist, researcher, educator*
Sonnenschein, Ralph Robert *physiologist*
Szego, Clara Marian *cell biologist, educator*
Taylor, Charles Ellett *biologist, educator*
Thompson, Paul Matthew *neuroscientist*
Tobin, Allan Joshua *biologist*
Villablanca, Jaime Rolando *neuroscientist, medical educator*
Wright, Ernest Marshall *physiologist, consul*
Yang, Yang *science educator*

Madera
Curry, Cynthia J. R. *geneticist*

Malibu
Davis, Stephen Darrel *biology professor, researcher*

Marina Del Rey
Rizzo, Albert Skip *research scientist, educat*

Menlo Park
Jorgensen, Paul J. *research company executi*

Moffett Field
Dalton, Bonnie *life science administrator*
Gundy-Burlet, Karen *research scientist*
Harper, Lynn D. *biologist*
Kittel, Peter *research scientist*
Lissauer, Jack Jonathan *astronomy educator*

Monrovia
Kimnach, Myron William *botanist, horticult*

Monterey
Packard, Julie *aquarium administrator*
Packard Burnett, Nancy *biologist*

Moss Landing
Stephens, Robert *horticulturist*

Mountain View
Cox, David R. *geneticist, educator*

Northridge
Allen, Larry Glenn *biology professor, department chairman*

Oakland
Ames, Bruce Nathan *biochemisty and molec biology professor*
Collins, James Francis *toxicologist*
Foley, Sylvester Robert, Jr. *science administrator, retired military officer*
Parrott, Joel J. *zoo director*

Pacific Grove
Somero, George Nicholls *biology educator*

Palm Desert
Sausman, Karen *zoological park administrat*

Palo Alto
Anderson, Charles Arthur *retired science administrator*
Ernst, Wallace Gary *geology educator, dean*
Johnson, Noble Marshall *research scientist*
Tsien, Richard Winyu *biology professor*
Wrighton, Nicholas C. *research scientist*

Parlier
Michailides, Themis J. *plant pathology educ*

Pasadena
Anderson, David J. *biology professor*
Baltimore, David *microbiologist, educator, former academic administrator*
Davidson, Eric Harris *molecular and developmental biologist, educator*
Dickinson, Michael Hughes *physiologist, biotechnologist*
Goldreich, Peter Martin *astrophysics and planetary physics educator*
Helou, George *science administrator, educat*
Ingersoll, Andrew Perry *planetary science educator*
Konishi, Masakazu *neuroscientist, educator*
Meyerowitz, Elliot Martin *biology professor*
Owen, Ray David *biology professor*
Revel, Jean-Paul *biology professor*
Shaw, R. Daniel *anthropology professor*
Steidel, Charles C. *astronomy educator*
Tirrell, David A. *research scientist, educator*
Varshavsky, Alexander Jacob *molecular biologist, educator*
Wasserburg, Gerald Joseph *geology and geophysics educator*
Zewail, Ahmed Hassan *chemistry and physic educator, consultant, editor*

Quincy
Hall, Anthony Elmitt *agriculturist, physiolog*

Richmond
Beall, Frank Carroll *science director and educator*

verside
:ley-Serres, Julia N. *geneticist, educator*
:tnicki-Garcia, Salomon *microbiologist, educator*
:strand, Norman Carl *plant genetics, conservation and evolution educator*
:en, Harry Western, II, *geology and geophysics educator*
Hughen, Alan *geneticist, educator*
:llar, Jocelyn G. *entomologist, educator*
:e, Albert Lee *soil science educator, researcher*
Gundy, Seymour Dean *plant pathologist, educator*

cramento
:oze, Thomas Franklin *toxicologist*

n Carlos
:lff, Ronald Keith *toxicologist, researcher*

n Diego
:right, Thomas D. *science foundation director, educator, researcher*
:hibald, James David *biology educator, paleontologist*
:tus, Raymond Thomas *neuroscientist, writer, pharmaceutical executive*
:nstein, Sanford Irwin *biology professor*
:ler, Charles Linford *zoo executive director emeritus, former development director*
:an, James Michael, Jr. *zoological park administrator*
:becco, Renato *biologist, educator*
:er, Joseph R. *plant molecular and cellular biologist*
:hart, Walter *molecular biologist, educator*
:ge, Fred H. *neuroscientist, educator*
:is, Arthur *geography educator*
:nemann, Stephen F. *molecular neurobiologist educator*
:han, Chandra *research biochemistry educator*
:ers, Douglas George *zoological society administrator*
:rault, Jacques *biology professor*
:aechter, Moselio *microbiology educator*
:nowski, Terrence Joseph *science educator*
:lor, Tony S. *research scientist*

n Francisco
:erts, Bruce Michael *cell biologist, former foundation administrator*
:lerson, David E. *zoological park administrator*
:ckburn, Elizabeth Helen *molecular biologist*
:lt, David Scott *neuroscience and physiology educator*
:ments, John Allen *physiologist*
:jardin, Dennis E. *plant pathologist, educator*
:, Su *science educator*
:neman, Donald *parasitology and tropical medicine educator*
:berger, Stephen G. *physiologist, educator*
:ndra, York T. *geology educator*
:quez-Magaña, Leticia Maria *biology professor*
Cormick, Frank *research scientist*
:ler, Walter Luther *scientist, pediatrician, educator*
:, Renee Reijo *biology professor*
:ston, Henry James III *neurobiologist, anatomist, educator*
:dall, Janet Ann *biology professor, researcher*
:wans, Smruti Jayant *microbiologist*
:ner, Michael W. *neuroscientist, researcher, educator*
:e, Roger Earl *physiologist, department chairman*
:amoto, Keith Robert *molecular biologist, educator*

Jose
:ler, Dieter M. *botanist, researcher*

Marcos
:ath, Robert Gordon *botanist, educator*

Mateo
:per-Smith, Jeffrey Paul *botanic garden administrator*

ta Barbara
:ash, Lawrence *science history educator*
:stman, Arthur Castner, Jr. *science advisor, consultant*
:well, John C(hambers) *geology educator, researcher*
:ne, Thomas *geology educator*
:doch, William Wilson *ecologist, educator*
:neider, Edward Lee *botanist, researcher*
:ker, Shirley Lois Cotter *botanist, educator*

ta Cruz
:key, Harry Douglas *information and computer science educator*
:genheim, Jean Harmon *biologist, educator*
:Thorne *geosciences educator*
:er, Robert Carmi, Jr. *microbiology educator, university administrator*
:iams, Terrie M. *biology professor*

ta Monica
:eson, Melvin Erwin *management sciences company executive, educator*

th San Francisco
Ann L. *biotechnology company executive*
:nthal, Arnon *science association director*

Scheller, Richard H. *physiologist, science educator*

Stanford
Baylor, Denis Aristide *neuroscientist, educator*
Blandford, Roger David *science educator*
Briggs, Winslow Russell *plant biologist, educator*
Brown, Patrick O. *molecular biologist, educator*
Byers, Tom H. *management science and engineering educator*
Campbell, Allan McCulloch *bacteriology educator*
Cohen, Stanley Norman *geneticist, educator*
Cork, Linda Katherine *veterinary pathologist, educator*
Daily, Gretchen Cara *ecologist, environmental services administrator*
Davis, Mark M. *microbiologist, educator*
Davis, Ronald Wayne *genetics researcher, biochemistry educator*
Dirzo, Rodolfo *biologist, educator, researcher*
Ehrlich, Anne Howland *research biologist*
Ehrlich, Paul Ralph *biology professor*
Falkow, Stanley *microbiologist, educator*
Fang, Guowei *science educator*
Francke, Uta *geneticist, educator*
Grossman, Arthur R. *science educator, researcher*
Hanawalt, Philip Courtland *biology professor, researcher*
Long, Sharon Rugel *molecular biologist, educator*
Moore, Tirin *neuroscientist, educator*
Scott, Matthew Peter *biology educator*
Shapiro, Lucy *molecular biology educator*
Shatz, Carla J. *biology professor, researcher*
Shooter, Eric Manvers *retired neurobiology professor, consultant*
Simoni, Robert D. *biology educator*
Spudich, James A. *biology professor*
Sturrock, Peter Andrew *space science and astrophysics educator*
Theriot, Julie *microbiologist, medical educator*
Yanofsky, Charles *retired biology professor*

Stockton
McNeal, Dale William, Jr. *biological sciences educator*

Sunnyvale
Larrick, James William *science administrator*

The Sea Ranch
Hayflick, Leonard *cell biologist, biogerontologist, microbiologist, educator, writer*

Tulare
Vickrey, Herta M. *microbiologist*

Ukiah
Sandmeyer, E. E. *toxicologist, consultant*

Vacaville
Erwin, Robert Lester *biotechnology company executive*

Walnut
Shannon, Cynthia Jean *biology professor*

COLORADO

Alamosa
Ybarrondo, Brent *biology professor*

Aurora
Neville, Margaret Cobb *physiologist, educator*
Pfenninger, Karl H. *cell biology and neuroscience educator*
Weedin, James Frank *biology professor, researcher*

Boulder
Armstrong, David Michael *biology professor*
Breed, Michael Dallam *biology professor*
Conti, Peter Selby *astronomy educator*
De Fries, John Clarence *behavioral genetics educator, researcher*
Dubin, Mark William *neuroscientist, educator, academic administrator*
Fifkova, Eva *behavioral neuroscience educator*
Hanley, Howard James Mason *research scientist*
Knoelker, Michael T.F. *science observatory director*
Mc Intosh, J(ohn) Richard *retired biologist, educator*
Meier, Mark Frederick *research scientist, educator, artist, small business owner*
Mitchell, Joan LaVerne *research scientist*
Prescott, David Marshall *biology professor*
Roble, Raymond Gerald *science administrator*
Serafin, Robert Joseph *science center administrator, electrical engineer*
Snow, Theodore Peck *astrophysics educator*
Southwick, Charles Henry *zoologist, educator*
Staehelin, Lucas Andrew *cell biology professor emeritus*
Tans, Pieter P. *research scientist*
Thomas, Gary Edward *science educator, researcher*
Tolbert, Margaret A. *geochemistry educator*
Wood, William Barry III *biologist, educator*

Brush
Gabriel, Donald Eugene *science educator*

Carbondale
Cowgill, Ursula Moser *biologist, educator, environmental consultant*

Colorado Springs
Bybee, Rodger Wayne *science administrator*
Comes, Robert George *research scientist*
Engfer, Susan Marvel *zoological park executive*

Denver
Kappler, John W. *microbiology educator*

Fort Collins
Fausch, Kurt Daniel *fisheries ecologist, educator*
Follett, Ronald Francis *soil scientist*
Halvorson, Ardell David *soil scientist, researcher*
Keim, Wayne Franklin *retired agronomist, geneticist*
Mortvedt, John Jacob *soil scientist, researcher*
Niswender, Gordon Dean *physiologist, educator*
Paul, Eldor Alvin *agriculture, ecology educator*
Peterson, Gary Andrew *agronomics researcher*
Quick, James S. *geneticist, plant breeder*
Roos, Eric Eugene *plant physiologist*
Seidel, George Elias, Jr. *zoology educator*
Smith, Ralph Earl *virologist*

Golden
Bettinghaus, Erwin Paul *research scientist*
Weimer, Robert Jay *geology educator, energy consultant, civic leader*
Zunger, Alex *research scientist*

Littleton
Vail, Charles Daniel *veterinarian, consultant*

Longmont
Dierks, Richard Ernest *veterinarian, academic administrator*

Loveland
Grieve, Robert Burton *parasitologist, educator*

HAWAII

Aiea
Munechika, Ken Kenji *research center administrator*

Hilo
Crosby, Michael P. *science administrator*

Honolulu
Donlon, Timothy A. *cytogeneticist*
Fok, Agnes Kwan *retired cell biologist, educator*
Fujioka, Roger Sadao *microbiologist, researcher*
Gubler, Duane J. *virologist, educator, researcher*
Kamemoto, Fred Isamu *retired zoologist*
Mandel, Morton *molecular biologist*
Sagawa, Yoneo *horticulturist, educator*

Kailua
Shank, Charles Vernon *science administrator, educator, physicist*

Kamuela
Young, Ernest D. *national historic site official*

Kame
Uyehara, Catherine Fay Takako (Yamauchi) *physiologist, educator, pharmacologist*

IDAHO

Boise
Morgan, Barbara R. *science educator, former astronaut*

Moscow
Scott, James Michael *research biologist*

Pocatello
Vailas, Arthur C. *biomechanics educator*

Sagle
Carlson, James Roy *animal science educator*

Sun Valley
Ring, Terry William *company executive, environmentalist*

MONTANA

Arlee
MacFarland, Craig George *natural resource management professional*

Bozeman
Costerton, John William Fisher *microbiologist*
Lavin, Matthew T. *horticultural educator*
Patten, Duncan Theunissen *ecologist educator*
Weeden, Norman Frank *geneticist, educator*

Butte
Peoples, Donald R. *research scientist*

Helena
Johnson, John Philip *geneticist, researcher*

Missoula
Brewer, Carol A. *biology professor*
Craighead, John Johnson *wildlife biologist*

Thomas, Jack Ward *retired wildlife biologist, educator*

NEVADA

Reno
Gifford, Gerald Frederic *retired science educator*

NEW MEXICO

Albuquerque
Henderson, Rogene Faulkner *toxicologist, researcher*
Hsi, David Ching Heng *plant pathologist, geneticist, educator*
Woodward, Joan B. *science association director*

Los Alamos
Anastasio, Michael R. *science administrator*
Wallace, Terry Charles, Sr. *retired technical administrator, researcher*

Santa Fe
Moore, Jay Winston *director cytogenetics laboratory*
Smith, Philip Meek *science administrator, consultant*

NEW YORK

New York
Goodman, Corey Scott *neuroscientist, biotechnologist, educator*

OREGON

Corvallis
Chambers, Kenton Lee *botany educator*
Frakes, Rodney Vance *plant geneticist, educator*
Johnson, Kenneth Bjorn *botanist, plant pathologist, educator*
Loper, Joyce E. *plant pathologist, educator*
Morita, Richard Yukio *microbiology and oceanography educator*
Poinar, George Orlo, Jr. *entomologist, science educator*
Stone, Jeffrey Kyle *mycologist, educator*
Westwood, Melvin Neil *horticulturist, pomologist*

Eugene
Matthews, Brian W. *molecular biology educator*
Stahl, Franklin William *biology educator*
Wessells, Norman Keith *biologist, educator, university administrator*

Florence
Marble, Duane Francis *geography educator, researcher*

Mcminnville
Roberts, Michael Foster *biology professor*

Pendleton
Klepper, Elizabeth Lee *retired physiologist*

Portland
Bhagwan, Sudhir *computer industry and research executive, consultant*
Khalil, Mohammad Aslam Khan *environmental science, engineering and physics educator*
Lendaris, George Gregory *systems science educator*
Machida, Curtis A. *research molecular neurobiologist, molecular virologist, oral biologist, educator*
Spencer, Peter Simner *neurotoxicologist*

Prineville
Geisen, Michael *science educator*

Talent
MacMillen, Richard Edward *biological sciences educator, researcher*

Wilsonville
Gordon, John Charles *forestry educator*

UTAH

Logan
Aust, Steven Douglas *biochemistry, biotechnology and toxicology educator*
Dobrowolski, James Phillip *agriculturist, educator*
Malechek, John Charles *ecology and range science educator*
Rashid, Kamal A. *university administrator, research educator*
Rasmussen, Harry Paul *horticulture and landscape educator*
Shultz, Leila McReynolds *botanist, educator*

Oakley
Silverstone, Leon Martin *neuroscientist, cardiologist, educator, research scientist*

Provo
Crookston, R. Kent *agronomy educator*
McArthur, Eldon Durant *geneticist, researcher*
Smith, H(oward) Duane *zoology educator*

Salt Lake City
Beckerle, Mary C. *cell biologist, educator*
Johnson, Stephen Charles *exercise physiology and sport science educator*
McAllister, James Patterson, II, *research scientist, educator*
Opitz, John Marius *clinical geneticist, pediatrician*

WASHINGTON

Bellingham
Ross, June Rosa Pitt *biologist, educator*

Eatonville
Geddes, Gary Lee *wildlife park director*

Lopez Island
Brownstein, Barbara Lavin *geneticist, educator, director*

Pullman
Carrington, James C. *botanist, educator*
Hosick, Howard Lawrence *cell biology professor, academic administrator*

Richland
Chikalla, Thomas David *retired science facility administrator*

Seattle
Bassingthwaighte, James Bucklin *physiologist, educator, medical researcher*
Beyers, William Bjorn *geography educator*
Boersma, P. Dee *conservation biologist, educator*
Buffington, John Douglas *ecologist*
Byers, Peter H. *geneticist*
Charlson, Robert Jay *atmospheric sciences educator*
Creager, Joe Scott *geology and oceanography educator*
Daniel, Thomas L. *zoology educator*
Disteche, Christine M. *geneticist*
Evans, Charles Albert *microbiology educator*
Felsenstein, Joseph *science educator*
Fidel, Raya *information science educator*
Gottschling, Daniel E. *molecular research biologist*
Greenberg, E. Peter *microbiologist*
Hartmann, Dennis Lee *atmospheric science educator*
Hartwell, Leland Harrison (Lee Hartwell) *geneticist, educator*
Hellström, Karl Erik *science educator, researcher*
Hendrickson, Anita Elizabeth *biology professor*
Hille, Bertil *physiology educator*
Hood, Leroy Edward *molecular biologist, educator*
Kenny, George Edward *pathobiology educator*
King, Ivan Robert *astronomy educator*
King, Mary-Claire *geneticist, educator*
Kirby, Ronald Eugene *fish and wildlife research administrator*
Kirschner, Marc Alan *neuroscientist*
Klinger, Terrie *science educator*
Kohn, Alan J. *zoology educator*
Kruckeberg, Arthur Rice *botanist, educator*
Kuhl, Patricia K. *science educator*
Nester, Eugene William *microbiology educator*
Olstad, Roger Gale *science educator*
Orians, Gordon Howell *biology professor*
Senczuk, Anna Maria *cell biologist, researcher*
Smith, Orville Auverne *physiology educator*
Stahl, David A. *microbiologist, educator*
Stuart, Kenneth D. *plant research administrator, microbiologist*
Towne, David L. *zoological park administrator*
Woods, James Sterrett *toxicologist*

Sequim
Karr, James Richard *ecologist, educator, research director*

Veradale
Keating, Eugene Kneeland *animal scientist, educator*

Wenatchee
Elfving, Don C. *horticulturist, educator*
Schrader, Lawrence Edwin *plant physiologist, educator*

WYOMING

Jackson
Cox, Paul Alan *ethnobotanist, educator*

Laramie
Lewis, Randolph Vance *molecular biologist, researcher*

CANADA

ALBERTA

Calgary
Johnson, Edward Arnold *ecologist, educator*
Jones, Geoffrey Melvill *physiology research educator*
Walker, Roger Geoffrey *geology educator, consultant*
Weiss, Samuel *neurobiologist, educator*

Edmonton
Babiuk, Lorne Alan *virologist, immunologist, researcher*
Cossins, Edwin Albert *biology professor, academic administrator*
Gough, Denis Ian *geophysics educator*
Stelck, Charles Richard *geology educator*

Lethbridge
Cho, Hyun Ju *retired veterinary research scientist*

BRITISH COLUMBIA

Bamfield
Druehl, Louis Dix *biology professor*

Sidney
Bigelow, Margaret Elizabeth Barr (M.E. Barr) *retired botany educator*
Kendrick, William Bryce *biologist, consultant, editor, writer*

Vancouver
Donaldson, Edward Mossop *research scientist, marine biologist, consultant*
Jones, David Robert *retired zoology educator*
Lindsey, Casimir Charles *zoologist, educator*
McNeill, John Hugh *pharmaceutical sciences educator*
Newman, Murray Arthur *aquarium administrator*
Phillips, Anthony George *neurobiology researcher*
Rennie, Paul Steven *research scientist, surgeon*
Schluter, Dolph A. *biologist, educator*
Shaw, Michael *biologist, educator*
Sinclair, Alastair James *geology educator*

Victoria
Turpin, David Howard *biologist, educator, academic administrator*

White Rock
Phillips, John Edward *zoologist, educator*

SASKATCHEWAN

Saskatoon
Huang, Pan Ming *soil science educator*

SWITZERLAND

Zurich
Wüthrich, Kurt *molecular biologist, biophysicist, educator*

ADDRESS UNPUBLISHED

Ares, Manuel, Jr. *biology professor, researcher*
Atkin, J Myron *science educator*
Barham, Warren Sandusky *horticulturist*
Baselt, Randall Clint *toxicologist*
Block, Barbara Ann *biology professor*
Bryant, Peter James *biologist, educator*
Bucalo, Louis Randall *biotechnology executive*
Burnham, Clifford Wayne *geology educator, director*
Burton, Lawrence DeVere *agriculturist, educator*
Carter, Bruce L.A. *biotechnologist, director*
Case, Ted Joseph *biologist, educator*
Chang, Susan Marina *neuroscientist*
Coughlin, Shaun R. *research scientist*
Coyle, Marie Bridget *retired microbiologist, lab administrator*
Epel, David *biologist, educator*
Erwin, Donald Carroll *plant pathology educator*
Farkas, Daniel Frederick *food science and technology educator*
Garon, Claude Francis *laboratory administrator, researcher*
Gennaro, Antonio L. *biology professor*
Gerritsen, Mary Ellen *vascular and cell biologist*
Gillette, Nancy E. *entomologist, researcher*
Goldstein, Walter Elliott *biotechnology executive*
Grey, Robert Dean *biology professor, former academic administrator*
Harlin, Marilyn Miler *marine botany educator, researcher, consultant*
Hauptmann, Randal Mark *biotechnologist*
Hemmingsen, Barbara Bruff *retired microbiologist*
Herz, Michael Joseph *marine environmental scientist*
Hildebrand, Verna Lee *human ecology educator*
Johnson, Stephen Walter *veterinarian*
Jones, Richard Hunn *biostatistician, researcher, educator*
Kartha, Kutty Krishnan *plant pathologist*
Klausner, Richard Daniel *cell biologist, researcher*
Kolb, James A. *science foundation director, writer*
Mansfield, Elaine Schultz *molecular geneticist, automation specialist*
McClellan, Roger Orville *toxicologist*
McGraw, Donald Jesse *biologist, science historian, writer*
Moll, Russell Addison *aquatic ecologist, science administrator*
Nanos, George Peter, Jr. *former science administrator, military officer, physicist*
Nikaido, Hiroshi *microbiologist*
Nybakken, James Willard *marine biology educator*
Purves, William Kirkwood *biologist, educator*
Quail, Peter Hugh *biologist, educator*
Roeller, Herbert Alfred *biology professor*
Rogers, Jack David *plant pathologist, educator*
Schuh, Antonius *biotechnology company executive*
Simon, Melvin I. *molecular biologist, educator*
Sloan, Anne Elizabeth *food scientist, writer*
Sonntag, Bernard H. *agronomist, researcher, public information officer*
Sparling, Mary Lee *biology professor*
Stamps, Judy A. *retired biology professor*
Stark, Nellie May *forester, ecologist, educator*
Stickney, Robert Roy *fisheries educator*
Sullivan, Woodruff Turner III *astronomy educator, research scientist*
Talmage, David Wilson *retired microbiologist, educator, dean*
Thrasher, Jack Dwayne *toxicologist, researcher, consultant*
Vaughn, James English, Jr. *neurobiologist*
Wallace, Douglas C. *geneticist, educator*
Weber, Lavern John *retired marine science administrator, educator*
White, Beverly Jane *retired cytogeneticist*
Willson, Mary Frances *ecology researcher, educator*
Witte, Owen Neil *microbiologist, molecular biologist, educator*
Wooster, Warren S(criver) *marine science educator*
Wott, John Arthur *retired arboretum and botanical garden executive, horticulture educator*
Zuker, Charles S. *neuroscientist, biology professor*

SCIENCE: MATHEMATICS AND COMPUTER SCIENCE *See also* INFORMATION TECHNOLOGY

UNITED STATES

ARIZONA

Tempe
Smith, Harvey Alvin *mathematics professor, consultant*
Yau, Stephen Sik-sang *computer and information scientist, educator*

Tucson
Willoughby, Stephen Schuyler *mathematics professor*

CALIFORNIA

Berkeley
Arveson, William Barnes *mathematics professor*
Bailey, David H. *computer scientist*
Bajcsy, Ruzena Kucerova *computer science educator*
Bergman, George Mark *mathematician, educator*
Berlekamp, Elwyn Ralph *mathematics professor*
Bickel, Peter John *statistician, retired educator*
Borcherds, Richard Ewen *mathematics professor*
Brewer, Eric A. *computer science educator*
Chorin, Alexandre Joel *mathematician, educator*
Colella, Philip *mathematician*
Demmel, James W. *computer science educator*
Eisenbud, David *mathematics professor*
Graham, Susan Lois *computer scientist, consultant*
Jones, Vaughan Frederick Randal *mathematician, educator*
McKusick, Marshall Kirk *computer scientist*
Osserman, Robert *mathematician, educator, writer*
Patterson, David Andrew *computer scientist, educator, consultant*
Schoenfeld, Alan Henry *mathematics education professor, researcher*
Simon, Horst D. *computer scientist*
Smith, Alan Jay *computer science educator, consultant*
Tarter, Michael Ernest *biostatistician, educator*
Vojta, Paul Alan *mathematics professor*
Wagner, David *computer scientist, educator*
Wolf, Joseph Albert *mathematician, educator*
Yu, Bin *statistician, educator*

Camarillo
Vannix, Cecil Robert *programmer, systems analyst*

Carson
Kowalski, Kazimierz *computer science educator, researcher*

Chatsworth
Ulin, Samuel Alexander *computer systems developer*

Claremont
Coleman, Courtney Stafford *mathematician, educator*
Grabiner, Judith Victor *mathematics professo*
Grabiner, Sandy *mathematics professor*
Henriksen, Melvin *mathematician, educator*
Myhre, Janet *statistician, educator, consulta*
Pippenger, Nicholas John *mathematician, Computer Scientist Researcher Educator*
White, Alvin Murray *mathematics professor, consultant*

Danville
Lowery, Lawrence Frank *mathematic scienc and computer educator*

Davis
Müller, Hans-Georg *statistician*
Olsson, Ronald Arthur *computer science educator*
Walters, Richard Francis *computer science educator*

Elk Grove
McDavid, Douglas Warren *executive researc consultant*

Glendale
Kay, Alan C. *computer scientist, nonprofit organization executive*

Irvine
Hoffman, Donald David *cognitive and comp science educator*
Saari, Donald Gene *mathematician, departm chairman, economist*
Wan, Frederic Yui-Ming *mathematician, educator*

La Jolla
Freedman, Michael Hartley *mathematician, educator, researcher*
Graham, Ronald Lewis *mathematician*
Halkin, Hubert *mathematics professor, researcher*
Terras, Audrey Anne *mathematics professor*
Wallach, Nolan R. *mathematician, consulta*
Wulbert, Daniel Eliot *mathematician, educa*

Los Angeles
Adleman, Leonard M. *computer scientist, educator*
Afifi, Abdelmonem A. *biostatistics educator, dean*
Bekey, George Albert *computer scientist, educator*
Chen, Tony F. *mathematics professor, dean*
Estrin, Gerald *computer scientist, engineerin educator, academic administrator*
Golomb, Solomon Wolf *mathematician, electrical engineer, director, educator*
Gordon, Basil *retired mathematics professor*
Kleinrock, Leonard *computer scientist*
Pearl, Judea *computer scientist, educator*
Port, Sidney Charles *mathematician, educat*
Roberts, Paul Harry *mathematics professor*
Tao, Terence Chi-Shen *mathematics profess*
Waterman, Michael Spencer *mathematics an biology professor*
Zelmanowitz, Julius Martin *mathematics professor, academic administrator*

Marina Del Rey
Swartout, William R. *mathematician, educa director*

Menlo Park
Neumann, Peter Gabriel *computer scientist*
Sutherland, Ivan E. *computer scientist*

Milpitas
Wheeler, William Roy *technical advisor*

Monterey
Brown, Gerald G. *operations research spec educator*
Denning, Peter James *computer scientist, engineer*

Moss Landing
Lange, Lester Henry *mathematics professor*

Mountain View
Buchheit, Paul *computer programmer, entrepreneur*
Lamport, Leslie B. *computer scientist*

Palo Alto
Green, Cordell *computer scientist, educator*

Pasadena
Franklin, Joel Nicholas *mathematician, edu*
Knowles, James Kenyon *applied mathemati educator*
Marsden, Jerrold Eldon *mathematician, edu engineer*
Mead, Carver Andress *computer science educator emeritus*

Pomona
Bernau, Simon John *mathematics professor*

Portola Valley
Kuo, Franklin F. *computer scientist, electric engineer*

Redondo Beach
Woike, Lynne Ann *computer scientist*

Redwood City
Kolarov, Krasimir Dobromirov *computer scientist, researcher*

iverside
tliff, Louis Jackson, Jr. *mathematics professor*

an Diego
rgin, George Hans *computer scientist, educator*
les, Alfred Washington *mathematics professor, consultant*
lland, Michael James *computer services administrator*
lamon, Peter *mathematics professor, researcher*

n Francisco
ll, C. Gordon *computer architect and engineer, entrepreneur, researcher*
use, Allan Baird *mathematician, computer scientist, educator*
ung, Kason Kai Ching *computer specialist*

n Jose
apman, John *computer scientist*
well, Martin Edward *computer scientist*
ede, Robert Clinton, Jr. *mathematician, educator*

nta Barbara
nsen, Eugene Carlyle *mathematician, educator*
nc, Henryk *mathematics professor*
nons, Stephen *mathematics professor, researcher*

nta Clara
sling, James *computer scientist, web programmer*

nta Monica
re, Willis Howard *computer scientist*

nta Rosa
es, Raleigh Stanton, Jr. *retired mathematics professor, academic administrator*
ggins, Patricia Ann *computer systems analyst, state legislator*

bastopol
ll, Larry *computer scientist, web programmer*

anford
on, Bradley *statistician, educator*
nrahan, Patrick M. *computer scientist*
ller, Joseph Bishop *mathematician, educator*
uth, Donald Ervin *computer sciences educator*
ler, Daphne *computer scientist*
stein, Donald Samuel *mathematician, educator*
oin, Karl Cooper *mathematics educator*
oen, Richard Melvin *mathematics professor, researcher*
un, Sebastian Burkhard *computer science educator, researcher*
man, Jeffrey David *computer scientist, educator*
ittemore, Alice *biostatistician*

ousand Oaks
Fattah, Yousri M. *computer scientist*

rrance
nanov, Volodymyr Alexeevich *computer science educator, researcher, computer science educator, researcher*

stlake Village
nson, John Backus *computer scientist, retired data processing executive*

LORADO

ulder
kin, Gregory *mathematician*
ver, Fred William *information scientist, director, educator*
narchi, David Edward *retired information science educator*
ielski, Jan *retired mathematics professor*

lorado Springs
mons, George Finlay *retired mathematics professor*

nver
er, Gary Raymond *biostatistician*
ne, Stanley E. *mathematics professor*

t Collins
erson, Charles William *computer science educator*
lke, Paul William, Jr. *statistician, consultant*

ayette
ling, Thomas Allan *retired mathematics professor*

STRICT OF COLUMBIA

shington
man, Peter A. *dean*

HAWAII

Hilo
Gersting, Judith Lee *computer scientist, educator, researcher*

Honolulu
Swanson, Richard William *retired statistician*

IDAHO

Moscow
Bobisud, Larry Eugene *mathematics professor*

NEVADA

Las Vegas
Blattner, Meera McCuaig *computer scientist, educator*
Marcella, Joseph *information scientist*

Reno
Kleinfeld, Erwin *mathematician, educator*
Lowndes, David Alan *retired programmer analyst, application developer*

Yerington
Price, Thomas Munro *computer consultant, retired*

NEW MEXICO

Albuquerque
Bell, Stoughton *computer scientist, mathematician, educator*

Belen
Gutjahr, Allan Leo *mathematics educator, researcher*

Las Cruces
Salamanca-Riba, Susana Alicia *mathematics professor*
Selden, Annie *mathematics professor*

Santa Fe
Kellner, Richard George *mathematician, computer scientist*

NORTH CAROLINA

Durham
Bryant, Robert Leamon *mathematics educator*

OREGON

Eugene
Andrews, Fred Charles *mathematics professor*

Portland
Ahuja, Jagdish Chand *mathematics professor*
Bleiler, Steven A. *mathematician*
Maier, David Eugene *computer science educator*

Salem
Baker, Edwin Stuart *retired computer consultant*

Wilsonville
Skiens, William Eugene *electrical interconnect systems scientist, polymer engineer*

UTAH

Orem
Moore, Hal G. *retired mathematician, educator*

Salt Lake City
Horn, Susan Dadakis *statistician, educator*
Trapa, Peter Engel *mathematics professor*
Wozniak, Steve (Stephen Gary Wozniak) *computer scientist, philanthropist*

WASHINGTON

Eastsound
de Boor, Carl-Wilhelm R. *mathematician*

Kenmore
Sobolewski, John Stephen *computer scientist, director, consultant*

Kennewick
Cochran, James Alan *emeritus mathematics professor, department chairman, dean*

Pullman
Hildebrandt, Darlene Myers *retired information scientist*
Kallaher, Michael Joseph *mathematics professor*

Redmond
Blinn, James F. *computer scientist*
Smith, Burton Jordan *computer designer*

Seattle
Breslow, Norman Edward *biostatistics educator, researcher*
Criminale, William Oliver, Jr. *applied mathematics professor*
Kalet, Ira Joseph *medical computer scientist*
Lee, John Marshall *mathematics professor*
Mason, Robert McSpadden *information scientist, educator, dean*
Michael, Ernest Arthur *mathematics professor*
O'Malley, Robert Edmund, Jr. *mathematics professor*
Segal, Jack *mathematics professor*
Warfield, Virginia (Ginger) McShane *mathematics professor*

CANADA

BRITISH COLUMBIA

Vancouver
Boyd, David William *mathematician, educator*
Clark, Colin Whitcomb *mathematics professor*
Feldman, Joel Shalom *mathematician*
Granirer, Edmond Ernest *mathematician, educator*
Sion, Maurice *mathematics professor*

Victoria
Manning, Eric *computer scientist, educator, dean, researcher*

SASKATCHEWAN

Regina
Symes, Lawrence Richard *computer science educator, university dean*

ADDRESS UNPUBLISHED

Bailar, Barbara Ann *retired statistician*
Basch, Reva *information services company executive*
Bollapragada, Ramesh *information scientist, educator*
Borwein, Jonathan Michael *mathematics professor*
Chang, Mei-Chu *mathematics professor*
Chui, Charles K. *mathematics professor*
Gray, James N. *computer scientist*
Hoppensteadt, Frank Charles *mathematician, educator, dean*
Johnstone, Iain Murray *statistician, educator, consultant*
Mints, Grigori Efroim *mathematics specialist*
Natsuyama, Harriet Hatsune Kagiwada *mathematician, educator*
Oliver, Nuria Maria *computer science researcher*
Riffenburgh, Robert Harry *biostatistician, researcher*
Rosen, Judah Ben *computer scientist*
Selinger, Patricia Griffiths *computer science professional*
Suppes, Patrick *statistician, philosopher, psychologist, educator*
Williams, Ronald Oscar *mathematician*
Winder, Robert Owen *mathematician, computer engineer, geophysicist*
Wright, Will *computer game designer*
Young, Lai-Sang *mathematician, educator*

SCIENCE: PHYSICAL SCIENCE

UNITED STATES

ALASKA

Fairbanks
Dorman, Craig Emery *oceanographer, academic administrator*
Eichelberger, John Charles *volcanologist, educator*
Fathauer, Theodore Frederick *meteorologist*
Roederer, Juan Gualterio *retired physics professor*
Weller, Gunter Ernst *geophysics educator*

ARIZONA

Amado
Criswell, Stephen *astronomer*

Chandler
Meieran, Eugene Stuart *materials scientist*

Flagstaff
Eastwood, Kathleen DeGioia *physics and astronomy professor*
Millis, Robert Lowell *astronomer, science observatory director*
Shoemaker, Carolyn Spellman *planetary astronomer*

Green Valley
Bates, Charles Carpenter *oceanographer*

Oro Valley
Swalin, Richard Arthur *scientist, company executive*

Rio Rico
Lowell, J(ames) David *geological consultant, cattle rancher*

Tempe
Bauer, Ernst Georg *physicist, researcher*
Goronkin, Herbert *physicist*
Juvet, Richard Spalding, Jr. *chemistry professor*
Moore, Carleton Bryant *geochemistry educator*
Pettit, George Robert *chemist, educator, cancer researcher*
Starrfield, Sumner Grosby *astrophysics educator, researcher*

Tucson
Angel, James Roger Prior *astronomer*
Barrett, Bruce Richard *physics professor*
Bloembergen, Nicolaas *physicist, researcher*
Broadfoot, Albert Lyle *physicist*
Campbell, Mary Kathryn *chemistry professor*
Crawford, David L. *astronomer*
De Young, David Spencer *astrophysicist, educator*
Drake, Michael J. *meteoriticist, planetary scientist, educator*
Dunn, Floyd *biophysics and biomedical engineering professor*
Falco, Charles Maurice *physicist, researcher*
Fan, Xiaohui *astrophysicist, educator*
Foltz, Craig B. *astronomer, educator*
Girardeau, Marvin Denham *physics professor*
Green, Richard Frederick *astronomer*
Hall, Henry Kingston, Jr. *chemistry professor*
Hartmann, William Kenneth *astronomy scientist*
Hill, Henry Allen *physicist, researcher*
Hoffmann, William Frederick *astronomer*
Hunten, Donald Mount *planetary scientist, educator*
Jannuzi, Buell T. *astronomer*
Johnson, Robert Bruce *hydrologist*
Karkoschka, Erich *planetary science researcher, writer*
Kennicutt, Robert Charles, Jr. *astronomer*
Kessler, John Otto *physicist, researcher*
Krider, E. Philip *atmospheric scientist, educator*
Lunine, Jonathan Irving *astronomer, educator*
Macleod, Hugh Angus McIntosh *optical science educator, physicist, consultant*
Marcialis, Robert Louis *planetary astronomer*
McEwen, Alfred Sherman *planetary geologist*
Mould, Jeremy Richard *astronomer*
Neugebauer, Marcia *physicist, researcher*
Neuman, Shlomo P. *hydrologist, educator*
Powers, Linda Sue *biophysicist, educator, biomedical engineer*
Prewitt, Charles Thompson *geochemist*
Roemer, Elizabeth *retired astronomer, educator*
Scotti, James Vernon *astronomer*
Sprague, Ann Louise *aerospace scientist*
Strittmatter, Peter Albert *astronomer, educator*
Tifft, William Grant *retired physics professor, scientist*
Wolff, Sidney Carne *astronomer, science administrator*

CALIFORNIA

Alhambra
Huang, Jia-Sheng Jack *optics scientist, researcher*

Atherton
Fried, John H. *chemist*
Gill, Stephen Paschall *retired physicist, mathematician*

Bakersfield
Dorer, Fred Harold *retired chemistry educator*

Berkeley
Alivisatos, Armand Paul *chemist, educator*
Alper, Mark D. *biochemist*
Attwood, David Thomas *physicist, researcher*
Barnett, R(alph) Michael *theoretical physicist, educational agency administrator*
Benson, Sally M. *atmospheric scientist*
Bergman, Robert George *chemist, educator*
Berry, William Benjamin Newell *geologist, educator, former museum administrator*
Bertozzi, Carolyn R. *chemistry professor*
Bousso, Raphael *physicist, educator*
Bragg, Robert Henry *physicist, researcher*
Bustamante, Carlos J. *biophysicist, educator*
Calendar, Richard Lane *biochemistry educator*
Carmichael, Ian Stuart Edward *geologist, educator*
Cerny, Joseph III *chemistry professor, retired dean, director*
Chew, Geoffrey Foucar *physicist*
Clarke, John *physics professor*
Cohen, Marvin Lou *physics professor*
Cuffey, Kurt M. *geophysicist, geochemist, educator*
Dynes, Robert C. *physics professor, former academic administrator*
Ellman, Jonathon Anthony *chemist*
Filippenko, Alexei Vladimir *astrophysicist, educator*
Fleming, Graham Richard *chemistry educator*
Fowler, Thomas Kenneth *physicist*
Fréchet, Jean *chemistry professor*
Freedman, Stuart Jay *nuclear science educator*
Gaillard, Mary Katharine *physicist, educator*
Glaser, Donald Arthur *physicist*
Goldhaber, Gerson *astrophysicist, researcher*
Hahn, Erwin Louis *physicist, researcher*

Haller, Eugene Ernest *materials scientist, educator*
Halpern, Martin Brent *physics professor*
Hearst, John Eugene *retired chemistry professor, consultant, researcher*
Heiles, Carl Eugene *astronomer, educator*
Hoffman, Darleane Christian *chemistry professor*
Jeanloz, Raymond *geophysics educator*
Keasling, Jay D. *chemistry professor, research scientist*
Kerth, Leroy T. *physics professor*
Kirz, Janos *physicist*
Kittel, Charles *physicist, educator emeritus*
Klein, Spencer Robert *physicist*
Klinman, Judith Pollock *biochemist, educator*
Leemans, Wim Pieter *physicist*
Lester, William Alexander, Jr. *chemist, educator*
Lin, Robert Peichung *physicist, educator, researcher*
Linn, Stuart Michael *biochemist, educator*
Ma, Chung-Pei Michelle *astronomer, educator*
Mandelstam, Stanley *physicist*
Marcy, Geoffrey W. *astronomer, physicist, educator*
Markowitz, Samuel Solomon *chemistry professor*
McKee, Christopher Fulton *physicist, astronomer, educator*
Miller, William Hughes *theoretical chemist, educator*
Moore, C. Bradley *chemistry professor*
Morris, John William, Jr. *metallurgy educator*
Murayama, Hitoshi *physicist, educator*
Nygren, David Robert *physicist, researcher*
Pavlath, Attila Endre *chemist, researcher*
Perlmutter, Saul *astrophysicist, educator*
Perry, Dale Lynn *chemist*
Pines, Alexander *chemistry educator, researcher, consultant*
Rasmussen, John Oscar *nuclear research scientist*
Raymond, Kenneth Norman *chemistry professor, researcher*
Ritchie, Robert Oliver *materials science educator, department chairman*
Rosenblatt, Gerd Matthew *chemist*
Saykally, Richard James *chemistry professor*
Sessler, Andrew Marienhoff *physicist*
Shapiro, Marjorie D. *physics professor*
Shugart, Howard Alan *physicist, researcher*
Smith, Kirk Robert *environmental health sciences educator, researcher*
Smoot, George Fitzgerald III *astrophysicist*
Somorjai, Gabor Arpad *chemist, educator*
Spinrad, Hyron *astronomer*
Stacy, Angelica M. *chemistry educator*
Steiner, Herbert Max *physics professor*
Strauss, Herbert Leopold *chemistry professor*
Streitwieser, Andrew, Jr. *retired chemistry professor*
Strovink, Mark William *physics professor*
Thomas, Gareth *metallurgy educator*
Thompson, Anthony Wayne *metallurgist, educator, consultant*
Tjian, Robert Tse Nan *biochemistry educator, biology and virology researcher*
Townes, Charles Hard *physics professor*
Trilling, George Henry *physicist, researcher*
Valentine, James William *paleontologist, educator, writer*
Yang, Peidong *material science researcher*

Chico
Mejia, Barbara Oviedo *retired chemistry professor*

Chino
Koestel, Mark Alfred *geologist, photographer*

Chula Vista
Wolk, Martin *physicist, electrical engineer*

Claremont
Helliwell, Thomas McCaffree *physicist, researcher*
Pinnell, Robert Peyton *chemistry educator*

Corona Del Mar
Britten, Roy John *biophysicist*

Costa Mesa
Faridi, Abbas M. *physics professor*

Danville
Wong, Joe *physical chemist*

Davis
Black, Arthur Leo *biochemistry educator*
Cahill, Thomas Andrew *physicist, researcher*
Conn, Eric Edward *plant biochemist*
Jungerman, John Albert *physics professor*
Liu, Kai *physics professor*
Troy, Frederic Arthur, II, *medical biochemistry professor*

Duarte
Williams, Lawrence Ernest *physicist*

El Dorado Hills
Bartlett, Robert Watkins *metallurgist, educator, consultant*

Fresno
Gump, Barry Hemphill *chemistry and food science educator*
Kauffman, George Bernard *chemistry professor*

Fullerton
Shapiro, Mark Howard *physicist, educator, dean*

Gardena
Martin, Melissa Carol *radiological physicist*

Goleta
Clarke, Peter J. *physicist, technology executive*

Irvine
Bander, Myron *physics professor, dean*
Benford, Gregory Albert *physicist, writer*
Bradshaw, Ralph Alden *biochemistry educator*
Cho, Zang Hee *physics professor*
Clark, Bruce Robert *geologist, consultant*
Dzyaloshinskii, Igor Ekhielievich *physicist*
Maradudin, Alexei A. *physics professor*
McLaughlin, Calvin Sturgis *biochemistry professor*
Nomura, Masayasu *biological chemistry professor*
Nowick, Arthur Stanley *metallurgy and materials science educator*
Nowick, James S. *chemistry educator*
Overman, Larry Eugene *chemistry educator*
Phalen, Robert Franklynn *environmental scientist*
Randerson, James T. *geophysicist, educator*
Rose, Irwin A. (Ernie) *biochemist, educator*
Rowland, Frank Sherwood *chemistry professor*
Rynn, Nathan *physics professor, consultant*
White, Stephen Halley *biophysicist, educator*

La Canada Flintridge
Baines, Kevin Hays *astronomer, planetary scientist*

La Jolla
Abarbanel, Henry Don Isaac *physicist, academic administrator*
Andre, Michael Paul *physicist, educator*
Arnold, James Richard *chemist, educator*
Asmus, John Fredrich *physicist*
Backus, George Edward *theoretical geophysicist*
Baran, Phil S. *chemistry professor*
Benson, Andrew Alm *biochemistry educator*
Berger, Wolfgang H. *oceanographer, educator, geologist*
Boger, Dale L. *chemistry professor*
Branscomb, Lewis McAdory *physicist, researcher*
Burbidge, E. Margaret *astronomer, educator*
Burbidge, Geoffrey *astrophysicist, educator*
Cobble, James Wikle *chemistry professor*
Continetti, Robert E. *chemistry professor*
Cox, Charles Shipley *oceanography researcher, educator*
Crutzen, Paul Josef *research meteorologist, chemist*
Dennis, Edward Alan *chemistry and biochemistry professor*
Dixon, Jack Edward *biological chemistry professor, consultant*
Driscoll, Charles Frederick *physicist, educator*
Edelman, Gerald Maurice *biochemist, neuroscientist, educator*
Feher, George *biophysicist, educator*
Haymet, Anthony Douglas-John *research scientist, chemistry educator*
Itano, Harvey Akio *biochemistry educator*
Janda, Kim D. *chemist, educator*
Joyce, Gerald Francis *biochemist, educator*
Kadonaga, James Takuro *biochemist*
Kearns, David Richard *chemistry professor*
Kennel, Charles Frederick *atmospheric physics professor, academic administrator, government official*
Kolodner, Richard David *biochemist, educator, director*
Lal, Devendra *nuclear geophysics educator*
Lerner, Richard Alan *chemistry educator, scientist*
Maple, M. Brian *physics professor*
Marti, Kurt *chemistry professor*
McCammon, James Andrew *chemistry professor*
McIlwain, Carl Edwin *physicist*
Molina, Mario Jose *physical chemist, educator*
Munk, Walter Heinrich *geophysics educator*
Nicolaou, Kyriacos Costa (K. C. Nicolaou) *chemistry professor*
Orcutt, John Arthur *geophysicist, researcher*
Patton, Stuart *biochemist, educator*
Peterson, Laurence E. *physics educator*
Ride, Sally Kristen *physics professor, research scientist, retired astronaut*
Rotenberg, Manuel *physics professor*
Sandwell, David *geophysicist, educator*
Schimmel, Paul Reinhard *biochemist, biophysicist, educator*
Sclater, John George *geophysics educator*
Sham, Lu Jeu *physics professor, physicist*
Sharpless, K. Barry *chemist, educator*
Shuler, Kurt Egon *chemist, educator*
Siegel, Jay Steven *chemistry educator*
Somerville, Richard Chapin James *atmospheric scientist, educator*
Tsien, Roger Yonchien *chemist, cell biologist*
Van Lint, Victor Anton Jacobus *physicist*
Wang, Lei *biochemist*
Watson, Kenneth Marshall *physics professor*
Wolynes, Peter Guy *chemistry researcher, educator*
Wong, Chi-Huey *chemistry professor*

Laguna Hills
Rossiter, Bryant William *chemistry consultant*

Livermore
Alder, Berni Julian *physicist, researcher*
Cauble, Robert C. *research scientist*
Celliers, Peter H. *physicist*
Collins, Gilbert Wilson *physicist*
Cook, Robert Crossland *chemist, researcher*
Haan, Steven William *physics researcher*
Hooper, Edwin Bickford *physicist*
Kidder, Ray Edward *physicist, consultant*
Kirkwood, Robert Keith *applied physicist*
Leith, Cecil Eldon *retired physicist*
Lindl, John D. *physicist*
Murray, Cherry Ann *physicist, researcher*
Nuckolls, John Hopkins *physicist, researcher*
Remington, Bruce A. *physics researcher*
Sack, Seymour *nuclear scientist*
Santer, Benjamin David *atmospheric scientist*
Shotts, Wayne J. *nuclear scientist, federal agency administrator*
Spiller, Eberhard Adolf *physicist, researcher*
Tarter, Curtis Bruce *physicist, science administrator*
Wallace, Russell John *physicist*
Weber, Stephen Vance *physics researcher*

Loma Linda
Wilcox, Ronald Bruce *biochemistry educator, researcher*

Long Beach
Bauer, Roger Duane *chemistry professor, consultant*

Los Altos
Fraknoi, Andrew *astronomer, educator*
Hahn, Harold Thomas *physical chemist, chemical engineer*

Los Angeles
Benson, Sidney William *chemistry researcher*
Bhaumik, Mani Lal *physicist*
Boyer, Paul Delos *biochemist, educator*
Braginsky, Stanislav Iosifovich *physicist, geophysicist, researcher*
Campbell, Kenneth Eugene, Jr. *vertebrate paleontologist, ornithologist*
Chapman, Orville Lamar *chemist, educator*
Chester, Marvin *physics educator*
Clarke, Steven Gerard *chemistry professor*
Coleman, Charles Clyde *physicist, educator*
Coleman, Paul Jerome, Jr. *physicist, researcher*
Cornwall, John Michael *physics professor, consultant*
Coroniti, Ferdinand Vincent *physics and astronomy professor*
Dows, David Alan *chemistry professor*
Ganas, Perry Spiros *physicist*
Gutierrez, Carlos G. *chemistry professor*
Hall, Clarence Albert, Jr. *geologist, educator*
Houk, Kendall Newcomb *chemistry professor*
Igo, George Jerome *physics professor*
Ingersoll, Raymond Vail *geologist, educator*
Jordan, Thomas Hillman *geophysicist, educator*
Joshi, Chandrashekhar Janardan *physics educator*
Jung, Michael Ernest *chemistry educator*
Kaesz, Herbert David *chemistry educator*
Kaplan, Isaac Raymond *chemistry professor*
Keilis-Borok, Vladimir Isaackovich *geophysicist*
Kivelson, Margaret Galland *physicist*
Knopoff, Leon *geophysics educator*
Koga, Rokutaro (Rocky Koga) *physicist*
Kostoulas, Ioannis Georgiou *physicist, consultant*
Krupp, Edwin Charles *astronomer*
Levine, Raphael David *chemistry professor*
Lieber, Michael Randall *biochemist, educator*
Markland, Francis Swaby, Jr. *biochemist, educator*
Neelin, J. David *meteorologist, educator*
Neufeld, Elizabeth Fondal *biochemist, educator*
Nimni, Marcel Ephraim *biochemistry educator*
Olah, George Andrew *chemist, educator*
Onak, Thomas Philip *chemistry educator*
Paulson, Donald Robert *chemistry professor*
Reiss, Howard *chemistry professor*
Roberts, Sidney *biological chemist*
Scott, Robert Lane *chemist, educator*
Smith, Emil L. *biochemist, educator*
Stanton, Robert James, Jr. *geologist, educator*
Stellwagen, Robert Harwood *biochemistry professor*
Taylor, Howard S. *chemistry and physics educator, researcher*
Thorne, Richard Mansergh *physicist*
Trimble, Stanley Wayne *hydrologist*
Vidale, John Emilio *geologist*
Walker, Raymond John *physicist*
Whitten, Charles Alexander, Jr. *physics professor*
Wong, Alfred Yiu-fai *physics educator*

Malibu
Margerum, J(ohn) David *chemist, researcher*
Pepper, David M. *scientist, educator*

Menlo Park
Allen, Matthew Arnold *physicist*
Bernstein, Lawrence R. *inorganic chemist, pharmaceutical chemist*
Brodsky, Stanley Jerome *physics educator, consultant*
Bukry, John David *geologist*
Carr, Michael Harold *geologist*
Crosley, David Risdon *chemical physicist*
Dieterich, James H. *geologist*
Dorfan, Jonathan Mannie *physicist, researcher*
Drell, Persis Sydney *physicist*
Drell, Sidney David *physicist, arms control and national security specialist*
Lachenbruch, Arthur Herold *geophysicist, researcher*
Penzias, Arno Allan *astrophysicist, information scientist, researcher*
Richter, Burton *physicist, educator*
Taylor, Richard Edward *physicist, researcher*
Winick, Herman *physicist, educator*

Mission Viejo
Glasky, Alvin Jerald *retired medical research scientist*

Moffett Field
Heere, Karen R. *astrophysicist*

Monrovia
Andary, Thomas Joseph *biochemist, research*

Monterey
Collins, Curtis Allan *oceanographer*
Turner, Robert Elwood *physicist*

Morgan Hill
Kuster, Robert Kenneth *semi-retired scientist*

Moss Landing
Brewer, Peter George *ocean geochemist*
Clague, David A. *geologist*
Coale, Kenneth Hamilton *biogeochemist, educator*

Mountain View
Drake, Frank Donald *radio astronomer, educ*

Murrieta
Lake, Bruce Meno *physicist*

Northridge
Smathers, James Burton *medical physicist, educator*

Oakland
Brust, David *physicist*
Linford, Rulon Kesler *physicist, electrical engineer*

Oroville
Sincoff, Steven Lawrence *chemistry educator*

Pacific Grove
Lindstrom, Kris Peter *environmental consult*

Palo Alto
Eng, Lawrence Fook *biochemistry educator, neurochemist*
Herring, (William) Conyers *retired physicist, educator*
Huberman, Bernardo A. *physicist*
Levinthal, Elliott Charles *physicist, research*
Martin, Robert Bruce *chemistry professor*
Palmer, Robert Brian *physicist*
Perl, Martin Lewis *physicist, educator, chem engineer*
Sleep, Norman H. *geophysics educator*
Street, Robert A. *research physicist*
Title, Alan M. *astrophysicist*

Pasadena
Ahrens, Thomas J. *geophysicist*
Albee, Arden Leroy *geologist, educator*
Allen, Clarence Roderic *geologist, educator*
Anderson, Don Lynn *geophysicist*
Anson, Fred Colvig *chemistry educator*
Asimow, Paul D. *geophysicist, educator*
Baldeschwieler, John Dickson *chemist, educ*
Barish, Barry C. *physics professor, researche*
Barnes, Charles Andrew *physicist, researche*
Beauchamp, Jesse Lee (Jack Beauchamp) *chemistry professor*
Beer, Reinhard *atmospheric scientist*
Bejczy, Antal Károly *research scientist and facility administrator*
Bercaw, John Edward *chemistry educator, consultant*
Boehm, Felix Hans *physicist, researcher*
Buratti, Bonnie J. *aerospace scientist*
Chahine, Moustafa Toufic *atmospheric scien*
Chan, Sunney Ignatius *retired chemistry educator*
Cohen, Marshall Harris *astronomer, educato*
Crisp, David *atmospheric physicist, research scientist*
Cutri, Roc Michael *research scientist*
Dervan, Peter Brendan *chemistry professor*
Dougherty, Dennis A. *chemistry educator*
Dressler, Alan Michael *astronomer*
Duxbury, Thomas *planetary scientist*
Farley, Kenneth A. *geochemist, educator*
Frautschi, Steven Clark *physicist, researcher*
Freedman, Wendy Laurel *astronomer, educa director*
Fu, Lee-Lueng *oceanographer*
Golombek, Matthew Philip *research scientis planetary geologist*
Goodstein, David Louis *physics professor*
Gray, Harry Barkus *chemistry professor*
Grotzinger, John Peter *paleontologist, educa*
Grubbs, Robert Howard *chemistry professor*
Gurnis, Michael Christopher *geological scie educator*
Heath, James R. *chemistry educator*
Heindl, Clifford Joseph *physicist, researcher*
Helmberger, Donald Vincent *geophysical educator, researcher*
Hitlin, David George *physicist, researcher*
Johnson, William Lewis *materials scientist, educator*
Kamionkowski, Marc Paul *astrophysicist, educator*
Kanamori, Hiroo *geophysicist, professor emeritus*

taev, Alexei *physics and computer science professor*
nge, Andrew E. *astrophysicist*
wis, Nathan Saul *chemistry professor*
pes, Rosaly Mutel Crocce *astronomer, planetary geologist*
arcus, Rudolph Arthur *chemist, educator*
atijevic, Jacob R. *aerospace scientist*
ayo, Stephen L. *biochemist*
cGill, Thomas Conley *physics educator*
c Koy, Basil Vincent Charles *theoretical chemist, educator*
anich, Mario Enrique *research scientist, electronics executive*
inney, E. Sterl III *astrophysicist*
litzer, Hugh David *physicist, educator*
eskill, John Phillip *physics professor*
berts, John D. *chemist, educator*
ndage, Allan Rex *astronomer*
rgent, Wallace Leslie William *astronomer, educator*
hmidt, Maarten *astronomy educator*
hwarz, John Henry *theoretical physicist, educator*
kanina, Zdenek *astronomer*
ith, Edward John *geophysicist, physicist*
ilker, Linda Joyce *aerospace scientist*
evenson, David John *planetary scientist, educator*
one, Edward C. *physicist, researcher*
orne, Kip Stephen *physicist, researcher*
nbrello, Thomas Anthony, Jr. *physics professor*
gt, Rochus Eugen *physicist, researcher*
se, Mark B. *physics professor*
omans, Donald Keith *astronomer*
in, Harold *astronomer, educator*

easanton
llings, Charles Henry *retired physicist*

mona
llack, Wayne Ross *nutritional biochemist, toxicologist, food scientist*

dondo Beach
ster, John Stuart, Jr. *physicist, former defense industry executive*

verside
oenstein, Dallas Leroy *chemistry professor*

cramento
dy, James Aaron *medical physics professor*
senfeld, Arthur H. *physics professor, researcher*

n Carlos
hmann, George Blatz *genetic engineering company executive*

n Clemente
lfram, Thomas *physicist, educator*

n Diego
ator, Charles Robert *biochemistry professor*
ou, Kuo-Chen *biophysical chemist*
stil, Russell Gordon *geologist, educator*
, Lang Li *nuclear scientist, physicist*
rgan, Mark Quenten *astrophysics educator*
cus, Howard J. *geologist, engineer, educator*
eour, Elie Alexis *biophysicist, researcher, historian*
nbaugh, Ronald Dennis *physicist, researcher*
it, Edward J. *research physicist*
e, Wylie W. *biochemist*
na, Inder M. *biochemist*

n Francisco
rd, David A. *biochemistry and biophysics educator*
erman, Boris William *physicist, educator, academic administrator*
lingame, Alma Lyman *chemist, educator*
sman, Marvin *biochemist*
f, Lloyd Sterling *earthquake geologist*
en, Fred Ehrenkranz *biophysics professor*
isi, Joseph L. *biochemist, educator*
dsky, Gerold Morton *biochemistry professor*
es, Thomas Larry *chemistry professor*
as, David *biochemist*
y, Regis Baker *biochemistry and biophysics educator*
shall, Grayson William, Jr. *materials scientist, biomedical engineer, health sciences educator, dentist*
Andrej *chemistry professor*
er, Peter *biochemist*
anaka, Shinya *stem cell scientist, educator*

n Jose
ord, M. George *physicist, research administrator*
ill, Patrick James *physics professor, environmental scientist*
Hiroshi *chemist, researcher*
Chris P. *research physicist*
in, Stuart Stephen Papworth *materials scientist, physicist*

Luis Obispo
meister, David Walter *physicist*

ta Barbara
rs, Guenter *physicist, researcher*
ater, Tanya Maria *marine geophysicist, educator*
chalom, David Daniel *physics professor*
Bowers, Michael Thomas *chemistry professor*
Bruice, Thomas C. *chemist, educator*
Buratto, Steven K. *chemistry educator*
Caldwell, David Orville *physics professor*
Dudziak, Walter Francis *physicist*
Fisher, Matthew P. A. *physicist*
Ford, Peter C. *chemistry professor*
Gossard, Arthur Charles *physicist, researcher*
Gross, David Jonathan *physicist*
Gutsche, Steven Lyle *physicist*
Heeger, Alan Jay *physicist, educator*
Hubbard, Arthur Thornton *chemist, educator*
Kohn, Walter *physicist, retired educator*
Langer, James Stephen *physicist, researcher*
Luyendyk, Bruce Peter *geophysicist, educator, academic administrator*
Macdonald, Ken Craig *geophysicist*
Morse, Daniel E. *biochemistry educator, science administrator*
Peale, Stanton Jerrold *physics educator*
Pilgeram, Laurence Oscar *biochemist*
Scalapino, Douglas James *physics educator*
Wilson, Leslie *biochemist, cell biologist, professor*

Santa Clara
Dafforn, Geoffrey Alan *biochemist*
Hayn, Carl Hugo *physics professor, priest*
Lee, Chan-Yun *physicist, process engineer, educator*

Santa Cruz
Bunnett, Joseph Frederick *chemist, educator*
Faber, Sandra Moore *astronomer, educator*
Griggs, Gary Bruce *oceanographer, geologist, educator, director*
Kraft, Robert Paul *astronomer, educator*
Margon, Bruce Henry *astrophysicist, educator*
Miller, Joseph S. *astronomy researcher*
Nelson, Jerry Earl *astrophysics educator*
Silver, Mary Wilcox *oceanography educator*
Williams, Quentin Christopher *geophysicist, educator*
Wipke, W. Todd *chemistry professor*

Santa Monica
Intriligator, Devrie Shapiro *physicist*

Santa Rosa
Banks, Peter Morgan *physics professor*

Sherman Oaks
Caren, Robert Poston *aerospace scientist*

South San Francisco
Martin, David William, Jr. *biomedical research company executive, educator*
Wells, James Allen *biochemist*

Stanford
Archer, Cristina Lozej *research scientist*
Baldwin, Robert Lesh *biochemist, educator*
Berg, Paul *biochemist, educator*
Bienenstock, Arthur Irwin *physicist, educator, federal official*
Block, Steven Michael *biophysicist, educator*
Boxer, Steven G. *physical chemistry educator*
Brauman, John I. *chemist, educator*
Bravman, John Cole *materials scientist, educator*
Brunger, Axel Thomas *biophysicist, researcher, educator*
Bube, Richard Howard *retired materials scientist, educator*
Byer, Robert Louis *applied physics educator, university dean*
Collman, James Paddock *chemistry professor*
Fayer, Michael David *chemist, educator*
Fejer, Martin M. *physics professor*
Fetter, Alexander Lees *theoretical physicist, educator*
Harbaugh, John Warvelle *geologist, educator*
Harrison, Walter Ashley *physicist, researcher*
Kennedy, Donald *environmental scientist, educator, editor*
Keren, Kinneret *biophysicist*
Kool, Eric T. *chemist, educator*
Kornberg, Roger David *biochemist, structural biologist*
Kovach, Robert Louis *geophysics educator*
Lehman, I(srael) Robert *biochemist, educator*
Little, William Arthur *physicist, researcher*
Matson, Pamela Anne *environmental scientist, science educator*
Moerner, William Esco *physical chemist, educator*
Osheroff, Douglas Dean *physics professor, researcher*
Quake, Stephen R. *physics professor, researcher*
Ross, John *physical chemist, educator*
Rossing, Thomas D. *physics professor*
Solomon, Edward Ira *chemistry professor, researcher*
Stryer, Lubert *biochemist, educator*
Susskind, Leonard *physicist, educator*
Thompson, George Albert *geophysicist, educator*
Trost, Barry Martin *chemist, educator*
Wagoner, Robert Vernon *astrophysicist, educator*
Walt, Martin *physicist, educator*
Wender, Paul Anthony *chemistry professor*
Wojcicki, Stanley George *physicist, researcher*
Zare, Richard Neil *chemistry professor*

Sunnyvale
Armistead, Robert Ashby, Jr. *scientific research company executive*
Chang, William Zhi-Ming *research scientist*
Gozani, Tsahi *nuclear physicist*

Toluca Lake
Litwack, Gerald *biochemistry researcher, educator, administrator*

Torrance
Rogers, Howard H. *retired chemist*

COLORADO

Arvada
Mullineaux, Donal Ray *geologist*

Boulder
Albritton, Daniel Lee *atmospheric scientist*
Anderson, Dana Z. *physics educator*
Bartlett, David Farnham *physics professor*
Begelman, Mitchell Craig *astrophysicist, educator, writer*
Canup, Robin M. *astrophysicist, science administrator*
Chappell, Charles Franklin *meteorologist, consultant*
Clark, Alan Fred *physicist*
Clark, Noel A. *physics professor*
Cornell, Eric Allin *physics professor*
Cumalat, John *physics professor*
DePuy, Charles Herbert *chemist, educator*
Dryer, Murray *physicist, educator*
Faller, James Elliot *physicist, researcher*
Ferguson, Eldon Earl *retired physicist*
Fleming, Rex James *meteorologist*
Garstang, Roy Henry *astrophysicist, educator*
Gosling, John Thomas *space plasma physicist, researcher*
Hall, John Lewis *physicist, researcher*
Hermann, Allen Max *physics professor*
Hildner, Ernest Gotthold III *solar physicist, researcher, administrator*
Holzer, Thomas E. *physicist*
Jin, Deborah *physicist, educator*
Kapteyn, Henry Cornelius *physics professor, engineering educator*
Killeen, Timothy Laurence *aerospace scientist, science administrator*
King, Edward Louis *retired chemistry professor*
LeMone, Margaret Anne *atmospheric scientist*
Leone, Stephen Robert *chemical physicist, educator*
Lineberger, William Carl *chemistry professor*
Low, Boon Chye *physicist*
Mahlman, Jerry David *retired meteorologist*
McCray, Richard Alan *astrophysicist, educator*
Miller, Harold William *nuclear geochemist*
Nam, Sae Woo *physicist*
Peterson, Roy Jerome *physicist, educator*
Phelps, Arthur Van Rensselaer *physicist, consultant*
Ravishankara, Akkihebal R. *chemist*
Robinson, Peter *retired paleontology educator, consultant*
Roellig, Leonard Oscar *physics professor*
Schneider, Nicholas McCord *planetary scientist, educator, textbook author*
Tatarskii, Valerian Il'Ich *physics researcher*
Trenberth, Kevin Edward *atmospheric scientist*
Truce, William Everett *chemist, educator*
Washington, Warren Morton *meteorologist*
Webster, Peter John *meteorology educator*
Wolfe, Allan *retired physicist*
Ye, Jun *physicist, researcher*

Denver
Cobban, William Aubrey *paleontologist*
Eaton, Gareth Richard *chemistry professor, dean*
Foster, Norman Holland *geologist*
McCord, Joe Milton *biochemist, educator*
Neumann, Herschel *retired physics professor*
Ormes, Jonathan Fairfield *astrophysicist, researcher, educator*
Smith, Dwight Morrell *chemistry professor, academic administrator*
Stedman, Donald Hugh *chemist, educator*
Weihaupt, John George *geophysics educator, academic administrator*

Fort Collins
Bamburg, James Robert *biochemistry professor*
Fixman, Marshall *chemist, educator*
Gray, William Mason *meteorologist, atmospheric science educator*
Ladanyi, Branka Maria *chemist, educator*
Thompson, David W.J. *atmospheric scientist, educator*
Thurai, Merhala *research scientist*
Vonder Haar, Thomas H. *meteorology educator*
Woolhiser, David Arthur *hydrologist*

Golden
DeSanto, John A. *physicist, educator, mathematics professor*
Duke, Michael B. *aerospace scientist*
Edwards, Glen R. *metallurgist*
Hamilton, Warren Bell *geologist, geophysicist, educator, researcher*
Kennedy, George Hunt *chemistry educator*
Krauss, George *metallurgist*
Landon, Susan Melinda *petroleum geologist*
Tilton, John Elvin *mineral economics educator*
Trefny, John Ulric *retired college president*

Highlands Ranch
Brierley, James Alan *biohydrometallurgy consultant*

Lone Tree
Spisak, John Francis *corporation executive*

HAWAII

Hawaii National Park
Swanson, Donald Alan *geologist*

Hilo
Griep, David Michael *astronomical scientist, researcher*

Honolulu
Bercovici, David Anthony Leonardo *geophysics educator, researcher*
Hawke, Bernard Ray *planetary scientist, researcher*
Herbig, George Howard *astronomer, educator*
Hey, Richard Noble *marine geophysicist*
Ihrig, Judson La Moure *chemist*
Karl, David Michael *oceanographer, educator*
Keil, Klaus *geology educator, consultant*
Khan, Mohammad Asad *geophysics educator, retired minister, former senator of Pakistan*
Kong, Laura S. L. *geophysicist*
Miller, Joyce Ellen *oceanographer, hydrographer*
Seff, Karl *zeolite chemist, chemistry educator*
Sharma, Shiv Kumar *geophysicist*

Kihei
Borchers, Robert Reece *physicist, science administrator*

IDAHO

Idaho Falls
Alldredge, Leroy Romney *retired geophysicist*

Moscow
Bitterwolf, Thomas Edwin *chemistry educator*
Miller, Maynard Malcolm *geologist, educator, geoscience institute director, former state legislator*
Shreeve, Jean'ne Marie *chemist, educator*

MASSACHUSETTS

Cambridge
Hernquist, Lars Eric *astronomer, educator*

MONTANA

Bozeman
Grieco, Paul Anthony *chemistry professor*
Horner, John Robert *paleontologist, researcher, curator*
Jacobsen, Jeffrey Scott *environmental scientist*
Lapeyre, Gerald J. *physics educator, researcher*
Mertz, Edwin Theodore *retired biochemist, emeritus educator*
Schmidt, Victor Hugo *physics professor, researcher*

NEVADA

Henderson
Anspaugh, Lynn Richard *research biophysicist*
Trivelpiece, Alvin William *physicist, educator, consultant*

Las Vegas
Barth, Delbert Sylvester *environmental studies educator*

Reno
Livermore, John S. *geologist*
Price, Jonathan G. *geologist*
Taranik, James Vladimir *geologist, educator*

NEW MEXICO

Albuquerque
Campana, Michael Emerson *hydrogeology and hydrology educator, researcher*
Emin, David *physicist*
Loehman, Ronald Ernest *materials scientist*
Loftfield, Robert Berner *biochemistry professor*
Lucas, Spencer G. *paleontologist, curator, director*
Van Devender, J. Pace *research scientist, science administrator*

Las Cruces
Kemp, John Daniel *biochemist, educator*
Walterbos, René Antonius *astronomer*

Los Alamos
Becker, Stephen A. *physicist*
Brown, Lowell Severt *physicist, researcher*
Engelhardt, Albert George *physicist*
George, Timothy G. *metallurgist*
Gibson, Benjamin Franklin *physicist*
Johnson, Mikkel Borlaug *physicist*
Judd, O'Dean P. *physicist*
Keller, Richard Allen *chemist*
Kim, Ki-Yong *physicist*
Korber, Bette Tina Marie *chemist*
Kubas, Gregory Joseph *research chemist*
Mead, William Charles *physicist*
Mihalas, Dimitri Manuel *astrophysicist, educator*
Mitchell, Terence Edward *materials scientist*
Pack, Russell T. *retired theoretical chemist*
Picraux, Samuel Thomas *physicist, researcher*

Press, William Henry *physicist, computer scientist*
Reynders, John Van Wicheren *computational physicist*
Rosen, Louis *physicist*
Selden, Robert Wentworth *physicist, consultant*
Smith, James Lawrence *research physicist*
Swift, Gregory *physicist*
Terrell, (Nelson) James *physicist*
Thompson, Joe D. *physicist*

Los Lunas
Seiler, Fritz Arnold *physicist*

Santa Fe
Cheetham, Alan Herbert *paleontologist*
Cowan, George Arthur *chemist, bank executive, director*
Fisher, Robert Alan *laser physicist*
Gell-Mann, Murray *theoretical physicist, educator*
Giovanielli, Damon Vincent *physicist, consultant*
Hammer, Charles F. *retired chemistry professor*
Hirt, Cyril William *physicist*
Lee, David Mallin *physicist*
Whitten, David George *chemistry educator*

Socorro
Chapin, Charles E. *geologist, mineralogist*

Sunspot
Altrock, Richard Charles *astrophysicist*
Keil, Stephen Lesley *astrophysicist*

OREGON

Albany
Dooley, George Joseph III *metallurgist*

Ashland
Abrahams, Sidney Cyril *physicist, crystallographer*
Espinoza, Edgard O'Niel *forensic chemist*
Goddard, Kenneth William *forensic scientist, writer*

Beaverton
Pankow, James F. *environmental science and engineering educator*

Corvallis
Dalrymple, Gary Brent *research geologist*
Drake, Charles Whitney *physicist*
Holman, Robert Alan *oceanography educator*
Mathews, Christopher King *biochemist, educator*
Thomas, Thomas Darrah *chemistry educator*
Van Holde, Kensal Edward *biochemistry educator*
Whanger, Philip Daniel *biochemistry and nutrition educator, researcher*
Yeats, Robert Sheppard *geologist, educator*

Eugene
Crasemann, Bernd *physicist, researcher*
Deshpande, Nilendra Ganesh *physics professor*
Donnelly, Russell James *physicist, educator*
Griffith, Osbie Hayes *retired chemistry professor*
Hutchison, James E. *chemistry educator*
Maurer, Robert Distler *retired industrial physicist*
Mazo, Robert Marc *retired chemistry professor*
Peticolas, Warner Leland *retired physical chemistry educator*
Retallack, Gregory John *geologist, educator*
Richmond, Geraldine Lee *chemist, educator*
von Hippel, Peter Hans *chemistry professor, researcher*

Portland
Gard, Gary Lee *chemistry professor, researcher*
Mooers, Christopher Northrup Kennard *physical oceanographer, educator*
Weeks, Wilford Frank *retired geophysics educator, glaciologist*
Wetzel, Karl Joseph *physics professor, dean*

TEXAS

Houston
Spudis, Paul D. *geologist*

UTAH

Hildale
Wall, Lloyd L. *geological engineer*

Logan
Scouten, William Henry *chemistry educator, academic administrator*
Steed, Allan J. *physical science research administrator*

Provo
Henderson, Douglas James *physicist, chemist, educator, researcher*
Izatt, Reed M. *chemistry researcher*

Salt Lake City
Allison, Merle Lee *geologist*
Dick, Bertram Gale, Jr. *physics professor*
Kim, Sung Wan *chemistry professor*
Miller, Jan Dean *metallurgy educator*
Miller, Joel Steven *inorganic and organic materials chemist, educator*
Poulter, Charles Dale *chemist, educator, consultant*
Stang, Peter John *organic chemist*
Straight, Richard Coleman *photobiologist, natural philosopher*

Sandy
Kenison, Lynn T. *chemist*

WASHINGTON

Bellevue
Delisi, Donald Paul *geophysicist*

Bellingham
Cox, David Jackson *biochemistry professor*

Edmonds
Galster, Richard W. *engineering geologist*

Ellensburg
Rosell, Sharon Lynn *physics and chemistry professor*

Friday Harbor
Agosta, William Carleton *chemist, educator*

Indianola
Gutsche, Carl David *chemistry professor*

Lakewood
Harding, Karen Elaine *chemistry professor, department chairman*

Manchester
Fearon, Lee Charles *chemist*

Redmond
Meshii, Masahiro *materials science educator*

Richland
Bevelacqua, Joseph John *physicist, researcher*
Fruchter, Jonathan Sewell *research scientist, geochemist*
Kathren, Ronald Laurence *health physicist*
Moore, Emmett Burris, Jr. *physical chemist, educator*

Seattle
Andersen, Niels Hjorth *chemistry professor, biophysicist, consultant, researcher*
Atwater, Brian F. *geologist, educator*
Baum, William Alvin *astronomer, educator*
Bernard, Eddie Nolan *oceanographer*
Bichsel, Hans *physicist, consultant, researcher*
Bodansky, David *physicist, researcher*
Borden, Weston Thatcher *chemistry professor*
Brown, Robert Alan *geophysicist, educator*
Brownlee, Donald Eugene, II, *astronomer, educator*
Cahn, John Werner *metallurgist, educator*
Campbell, Charles Taylor *chemistry educator*
Christian, Gary D. *chemistry professor*
Christiansen, Walter Henry *aerospace scientist, educator*
Cramer, John Gleason, Jr. *experimental physicist, educator*
Davidson, Ernest Roy *chemist, educator*
Davie, Earl Warren *biochemistry educator*
Deming, Jody Wheeler *oceanography educator*
El-Moslimany, Ann Paxton *paleoecologist, educator, writer*
Engel, Thomas Walter *chemistry professor*
Evans, Bernard William *geologist, educator*
Fischer, Edmond Henri *biochemistry educator*
Floss, Heinz G. *chemistry professor, researcher*
Fortson, Edward Norval *physics educator*
Gouterman, Martin Paul *chemistry educator*
Halver, John Emil *nutritional biochemist*
Heath, George Ross *oceanographer*
Henley, Ernest Mark *physics professor, retired dean*
Hogan, Craig J. *astronomer, educator*
Krebs, Edwin Gerhard *biochemistry educator*
Kwiram, Alvin L. *retired chemistry professor, academic administrator*
Lubatti, Henry Joseph *physicist, researcher*
Mallory, V(irgil) Standish *geologist, educator*
Olmstead, Marjorie Ann *physics professor*
Porter, Stephen Cummings *geologist, educator*
Rabinovitch, Benton Seymour *chemist, educator emeritus*
Reinhardt, William Parker *chemical physicist, educator*
Rhines, Peter Broomell *oceanographer, atmospheric scientist*
Stern, Edward Abraham *physics professor*
Thouless, David James *retired physicist, educator*
Wallerstein, George *astronomer, educator*
Weitkamp, William George *retired nuclear physicist*
Wilets, Lawrence *physicist, educator*
Wurster, Charles Frederick *environmental scientist, educator*

Shelton
Satchler, George Raymond *physicist, researcher*

Spokane
Crosby, Glenn Arthur *chemistry professor*

Tukwila
Weidner, Mark *environment research executive*

Walla Walla
Wade, Leroy Grover, Jr. *chemistry educator*

WYOMING

Casper
Wold, John Schiller *geologist, former congressman*

Laramie
Borgman, Leon E. *geologist*
Johnson, Paul E. *astronomer, educator*
Meyer, Edmond Gerald *retired chemistry professor, energy scientist, academic administrator*
Roark, Terry Paul *astronomer, educator*

CANADA

ALBERTA

Calgary
Campbell, Finley Alexander *geologist, consultant*
Milone, Eugene Frank *astronomer, educator*
Sreenivasan, Sreenivasa Ranga *physicist, researcher*

Edmonton
Harris, Walter Edgar *chemistry professor*
Kay, Cyril Max *biochemist, educator*
Rostoker, Gordon *physicist, researcher*
Rutter, Nathaniel Westlund *geologist, educator*

BRITISH COLUMBIA

Burnaby
Arrott, Anthony Schuyler *physics educator*

Delta
Russell, Richard Doncaster *geophysics educator, academic administrator*

Sidney
van den Bergh, Sidney *astronomer*

Vancouver
Hardy, Walter Newbold *physics professor, researcher*
Ozier, Irving *physicist, researcher*
Unruh, William George *physics professor, researcher*
Vogt, Erich Wolfgang *physicist, academic administrator*
Wieman, Carl E. *physics professor*

Victoria
Batten, Alan Henry *astronomer*
Best, Melvyn Edward *geophysicist*
Hutchings, John Barrie *astronomer, researcher*
Israel, Werner *physicist, educator*
Morton, Donald Charles *astronomer*
Wiles, David McKeen *chemist*

West Vancouver
Wynne-Edwards, Hugh Robert *geologist, educator, entrepreneur*

SASKATCHEWAN

Saskatoon
Kerrich, Robert *geologist, educator*

ADDRESS UNPUBLISHED

Akasofu, Syun-Ichi *geophysicist, educator*
Baldwin, George Curriden *physicist, researcher*
Ball, Lawrence *retired physical scientist*
Behrendt, John Charles *geophysicist, researcher, writer*
Birnbaum, Milton *laser physicist, educator, researcher*
Bouquet, Francis Lester *physicist*
Boyer, Herbert Wayne *retired biochemist, biotechnology company executive*
Browne, John Charles *physicist, researcher, lab administrator*
Cahn, Robert Nathan *physicist*
Campbell, Mary Stinecipher *retired chemist*
Chamberlin, Michael John *retired biochemistry professor*
Chappell, Willard Ray *physics educator, environmental scientist*
Chemla, Daniel S. *physics educator*
Christoffersen, Ralph Earl *chemist, researcher, director*
Cramer, James Dale *physicist, scientific company executive*
Currie, Philip John *research paleontologist, educator, museum curator*
Dehmelt, Hans Georg *retired physicist*
Dixon, Gordon Henry *biochemist, educator*
Doi, Roy Hiroshi *retired biochemist, educator*
Doolittle, Russell Francis *biochemist, educator*
Dugar, Sundeep *chemist*
Dunn, Arnold Samuel *biochemistry educator*
Dunn, Bruce Sidney *materials scientist, educator*
Eck, Robert Edwin *retired physicist*
Flinn, Paul Anthony *materials scientist*
Flory, Curt Alan *research physicist*
Gardner, Wilford Robert *physicist, researcher*
Garmany, Catharine Doremus *astronomer*
Haisch, Bernard Michael *astronomer, researcher*
Hakkila, Eero Arnold *retired nuclear safegua technology chemist*
Hawker, Craig J. *research scientist*
Ho, Chih-Ming *physicist, researcher*
Horton, Robert Carlton *geologist*
Howard, Robert Franklin *observatory administrator, astronomer*
Hulet, Ervin Kenneth *retired nuclear chemist*
Huynh, My Hang Vo *energetic materials che*
Hwang, Cordelia Jong *retired chemist*
Ingle, James Chesney, Jr. *geology educator*
Inlow, Rush Osborne *chemist*
Jackson, Kenneth Arthur *physicist, researche*
Johnson, Arthur William, Jr. *retired research scientist*
Jones, Thornton Keith *chemist, researcher*
Joselyn, Jo Ann *space scientist*
Kahn, Steven Michael *astrophysicist, educato*
Kanes, William Henry *geology educator, research center administrator*
Karplus, Paul Andrew *biochemistry educator*
Kedes, Laurence Herbert *biochemistry profes physician, researcher*
Kustin, Kenneth *chemist*
Levenson, Marc David *optics and lasers specialist, editor*
Lillegraven, Jason Arthur *retired paleontolog educator*
Louie, Steven Gwon Sheng *physics professor researcher*
MacCracken, Michael Calvin *atmospheric scientist*
Malins, Donald Clive *biochemist, researcher*
McMillan, Paul Francis *chemistry educator*
McTague, John Paul *materials scientist, educator, chemist, researcher*
Morse, Joseph Grant *chemistry educator*
Moss, Joel M. *physicist*
Mullis, Kary Banks *biochemist*
Nacht, Sergio *biochemist*
Norcross, David Warren *physicist, researche*
Noyes, Henry Pierre *physicist*
Olsen, Clifford Wayne *retired physical chem consultant*
O'Neil, Thomas Michael *physicist, researche*
Pettit, Erin *glaciologist*
Phelps, Michael Edward *biophysics professo*
Portis, Alan Mark *physicist, researcher*
Proctor, Richard James *geologist, consultant*
Quinn, Helen Rhoda Arnold *physicist*
Ragent, Boris *physicist*
Raleigh, Cecil Baring *geophysicist*
Rhyne, James Jennings *condensed matter physicist*
Richards, Paul Linford *physics educator, researcher*
Robertson, Robert Graham Hamish *physicist*
Rosenkilde, Carl Edward *retired physicist*
Rychnovsky, Scott Douglas *chemist, educato*
Schellman, John A. *chemistry professor*
Schock, Robert Norman *geophysicist*
Sharon, Timothy Michael *physicist*
Sheffield, Richard Lee *physicist*
Shirley, David Arthur *chemistry professor, science administrator*
Sinha, Sunil Kumar *physicist*
Solomon, Susan *atmospheric chemist*
Somerville, Christopher Roland *biochemist, educator*
Stanley, Steven Mitchell *paleontologist, edu*
Stern, Robin Lauri *medical physicist*
Sydansk, Robert Dunn *chemist, petroleum engineer*
Tabazadeh, Azadeh *environmental scientist, researcher*
Taylor, Hugh Pettingill, Jr. *geologist, educat*
Tedford, Charles Franklin *biophysicist*
Thiemens, Mark H. *chemistry professor*
Ufimtsev, Pyotr Yakovlevich *physicist, elect engineer, educator*
Wheeler, John Oliver *retired geologist*
Wolff, Manfred Ernst *chemist, pharmaceutic executive*
Yates, David John C. *chemist, researcher*
Yuille, Alan Loddon *physicist, researcher*

SOCIAL SCIENCE

UNITED STATES

ARIZONA

Apache Junction
Kizziar, Janet Wright *psychologist, writer, lecturer*

Phoenix
Cheifetz, Lorna Gale *psychologist*

Scottsdale
Baker, Edward Martin *engineering and industrial psychologist*
O'Brien, John Conway *economist, educator writer*

Tempe
Balling, Robert C., Jr. *geography educator*
Denhardt, Robert B. *political science profe director*
Gordon, Leonard *social sciences educator*
Guinouard, Donald Edgar *psychologist*
Hechter, Michael Norman *sociologist*

hanson, Donald Carl *physical anthropologist*
elnick, Rob *research administrator*
'Neil, Michael Joseph *opinion survey executive, marketing research consultant*
escott, Edward C. *economist, educator*
owley, Beverley Davies *sociologist*
ackton, Frank Joseph *public affairs educator*
mon, Sheldon Weiss *political science professor*
nith, V. Kerry *economics professor*
n der Leeuw, Sander Ernst *archaeologist, educator*
eigend, Guido Gustav *geographer, educator*

ucson
xinn, George Harold *rural sociology educator*
ock, Michael Kent *economics and law professor, former government official*
eiger, Ronald Louis *social sciences educator*
arke, James Weston *emeritus political science professor, writer*
ne, Robert Stacy *researcher, consultant*
ll, Jane H. *anthropologist, educator*
rwood, Laurie *psychologist, artist*
arshall, Robert Herman *retired economics professor*
hwebel, Milton *psychologist, educator*
nith, David Wayne *retired psychologist, educator*
ren, David *archaeologist, educator, writer, filmmaker*
ni, William Arthur *anthropologist, educator*
ompson, Raymond Harris *retired anthropologist, educator*
lgy, Thomas John *political science educator, organization official*
hiting, Allen Suess *political science educator, writer, consultant*

ALIFORNIA

naheim
bar, Alfred Julian *retired economic consultant, investor, educator*

rkeley
elman, Irma Glicman *economics professor*
erlof, George Arthur *economics professor*
adeff, David Albert *economics professor*
erbach, Alan Jeffrey *economist, educator*
umrind, Diana *research psychologist*
llah, Robert Neelly *sociologist, educator*
andes, Stanley Howard *anthropology educator, writer*
eslauer, George William *political science educator*
eit, Earl Frank *economist, educator*
llier, David *political science professor*
lson, Elizabeth Florence *anthropologist*
ster, Troy *sociology educator*
lman, Lauren B. *sociologist, law educator*
bert, Richard Joseph *economics professor*
nn, Evelyn Nakano *social sciences educator*
fter, Ervin R. *psychology educator*
kansson, Nils Hemming *economist, educator*
sen, Arthur Robert *psychologist, educator*
ce, Rosemary Alexandria *anthropology educator, department chairman*
abel, Jerome Bernard *sociologist, educator*
ler, Theodore Edwin *retired economics professor*
ch, Patrick Vinton *anthropology educator, archaeologist*
, Ronald Demos *demographer, economist, educator*
isel, Sherman Joseph *economist, educator*
slach, Christina *psychology professor*
Fadden, Daniel Little *economist, educator*
ir, William Ker, Jr. *political science professor*
ler, Laura *anthropologist, educator*
gaard, Richard Bruce *economist, educator, consultant*
gley, John Michael *economist, educator*
sser, Gordon C(lyde) *agricultural and resource economics educator*
ch, Michael *economics professor*
ch, Robert Bernard *political economics educator, former United States Secretary of Labor*
enzweig, Mark Richard *psychologist, neuroscientist, educator*
ch, Vincent M. *anthropologist, educator*
tchmer, Suzanne Andersen *economics professor*
lensky, Eugene *economics professor*
oway, Frank Jones *social sciences educator, historian*
on, Laura D'Andrea *economics professor, former dean*
an, Hal Ronald *economics professor*
nsky, Harold L. *political science professor, sociologist, researcher*
iamson, Oliver Eaton *business economics and law professor*
finger, Raymond Edwin *retired political science professor*
nan, John Adler *political scientist, educator*

son
er, Beverly Blazey *psychologist, educator*

co
all, Scott Grant *sociologist, educator, academic administrator*
h, Valene Lucy *anthropologist, educator*

remont
k, Gordon Carl *economist, educator*

Burdekin, Richard Charles Keighley *economics professor*
Csikszentmihalyi, Mihaly *psychology professor*
Jaffa, Harry Victor *political philosophy educator emeritus*
Lasswell, Marcia Lee *psychologist, educator*
Leeb, Charles Samuel *psychologist*
Lipman-Blumen, Jean *public policy and organizational behavior educator*
Pachon, Harry Peter *politics educator*
Rossum, Ralph Arthur *political science professor*

Corona Del Mar
Davis, Arthur David *psychology educator, musician*

Davis
Cohen, Lawrence Edward *sociologist, educator, criminologist*
Groth, Alexander Jacob *political science professor*
Mason, William A(lvin) *psychologist, educator, researcher*
McHenry, Henry Malcolm *anthropologist, educator*
Musolf, Lloyd Daryl *political science professor, educational association administrator*
Owings, Donald Henry *psychologist, educator*
Skinner, G(eorge) William *anthropologist, educator*
Smith, Michael Peter *social sciences educator, researcher*
Spindler, George Dearborn *anthropologist, educator, writer*
Sumner, Daniel Alan *economist, educator*
Wegge, Leon Louis François *retired economics educator*

Eureka
Bowker, Lee Harrington *sociologist, educator, writer*

Fresno
Dackawich, S. John *sociology educator, academic administrator*
O'Connor, Kevin John *psychologist, educator*

Fullerton
Segal, Nancy Lee *psychology professor, researcher*
Zettel, Laura A. *psychology professor, researcher*

Hayward
Meyer, Ann Jane *human development educator*

Hermosa Beach
Wickwire, Patricia Joanne Nellor *psychologist, educator*

Hollywood
Fisher, Joel Marshall *political scientist, educator, wine consultant*

Irvine
Aigner, Dennis John *economics professor, consultant*
Burton, Michael Ladd *anthropology educator*
Danziger, James Norris *political science professor*
Duncan, Greg John *economics researcher*
Freeman, Linton Clarke *sociologist, educator*
Greenberger, Ellen *psychologist, educator*
Huff, C(larence) Ronald *sociologist, criminologist, educator*
Luce, R. Duncan (Robert Duncan Luce) *psychology professor*
Margolis, Julius *economics professor*
Mc Gaugh, James Lafayette *psychobiologist*
Schonfeld, William Rost *political science professor*
Sperling, George *psychologist, educator*
Treas, Judith Kay *sociology educator*
White, Douglas Richie *anthropology educator*

Kenwood
Podboy, John Watts *clinical, forensic psychologist*

La Jolla
Cain, William Stanley *experimental psychologist, educator, researcher*
Fantino, Edmund *psychology professor*
Farson, Richard Evans *psychologist*
Fowler, James H. *political science professor*
Fowler, Raymond Dalton *psychologist, educator*
Granger, Clive William John (Sir Clive Granger) *retired economist*
Harris, Philip Robert *management and space psychologist*
Jacobson, Gary Charles *political science professor*
Mandler, George *psychologist, educator*
Mandler, Jean Matter *psychologist, educator*
Pratt, George Janes, Jr. *psychologist author*
Schneider, Benjamin *psychology professor, consultant*
Scull, Andrew T. *sociologist, educator*
Smith, Peter Hopkinson *political scientist, consultant, writer*
Spiro, Melford Elliot *anthropology educator*
Starr, Ross Marc *economist, educator*
White, Michelle Jo *economics professor*

La Quinta
Hoston, Germaine Annette *political science professor*

Long Beach
Baber, Walter Franklin *political science professor*

Los Angeles
Allen, Walter Recharde *sociology educator*
Álvarez, Rodolfo *sociology educator, consultant*
Anawalt, Patricia Rieff *anthropologist, researcher*
Anderson, Austin Gilman *economics research company consultant*
Aoki, Masanao *economics professor*
Arnold, Jeanne Eloise *anthropologist, educator*
Basch, Darlene Chakin *clinical social worker*
Bennett, Charles Franklin, Jr. *biogeographer, educator*
Cerrell, Joseph Robert *political scientist, public relations consultant*
Champagne, Duane Willard *sociology educator*
Clark, Burton Robert *sociologist, educator*
Currie, Janet M. *economics professor*
Damasio, Antonio R. *psychology and neurology professor, researcher*
Damasio, Hanna *psychology and neuroscience professor, researcher*
Darby, Michael Rucker *economist, educator*
Dekmejian, Richard Hrair *political science professor*
Dr. Phil, (Phillip Calvin McGraw) *psychologist, television personality*
Duranti, Alessandro *anthropology professor*
Ellickson, Bryan Carl *economics professor*
Fanselow, Michael Scott *psychology professor*
Hadfield, Gillian Kereldena *economist, law educator*
Intriligator, Michael David *economist, educator*
Irwin, Michael Ray *psychology professor, researcher*
Kaplan, Robert Malcolm *health researcher, educator*
Klein, Benjamin *economics professor, consultant*
La Force, James Clayburn, Jr. *economist, educator*
Malamuth, Neil Moshe *psychology and communication educator*
Nelson, Howard Joseph *geographer, educator*
O'Neil, Harold Francis *psychologist, educator*
Pagden, Anthony Robin *political science professor, historian, writer*
Phinney, Jean Swift *psychology professor*
Raven, Bertram H(erbert) *psychology professor*
Read, Dwight *anthropologist, researcher*
Scott, Allen John *public policy and geography educator*
Sears, David O'Keefe *psychology professor*
Seeman, Melvin *sociologist, educator*
Shearer, Derek Nocross *political science professor, diplomat, academic administrator*
Taylor, Shelley E. *psychology researcher, educator*
Telles, Cynthia Ann *psychologist*
Thompson, Richard Frederick *psychologist, neuroscientist, educator*
Turner, Ralph Herbert *sociologist, educator*
Wilcox, Rand Roger *psychology professor*
Wong, James Bok *economist, chemical engineer, technologist, consultant*
Wood, Nancy Elizabeth *psychologist, educator*
Zaller, John Raymond *political science professor*
Zame, William R. *economist, mathematician, educator*
Zeitlin, Maurice *sociology educator*

Malibu
Wilson, James Quinn *public policy professor*

Mckinleyville
Emenhiser, JeDon Allen *retired political science professor, dean*

Mill Valley
Weckler, Nora *retired psychology educator, psychotherapist*

Modesto
Berry, John Charles *psychologist, academic administrator*

Newport Beach
Whittemore, Paul Baxter *psychologist*

North Hollywood
Totton, Carl Allen, II, *psychologist*

Northridge
Mitchell, Rie Rogers *psychologist, counselor, educator*
Reagan, Janet Thompson *psychologist, educator*

Novato
Criswell, Eleanor Camp *psychologist*

Oakland
Nebelkopf, Ethan *psychologist*
Theroux, David Jon *economist, educator, research and development company executive*

Orange
Smith, Vernon Lomax *economist, educator*

Pacific Palisades
Hoffenberg, Marvin *retired political science professor*
Longaker, Richard Pancoast *retired political science professor, academic administrator*

Palo Alto
Card, Stuart Kent *psychologist, researcher*
Flanagan, Robert Joseph *economics professor*
Moos, Rudolf H. *psychologist, researcher*
Ricardo-Campbell, Rita *retired economist educator*
Scitovsky, Anne Aickelin *economist, researcher*

Pasadena
Balswick, Jack Orville *social science educator*
Davis, Lance Edwin *economics professor*
Dimitrius, Jo-Ellan *trial consultant*
Ledyard, John Odell *economics professor, consultant*
Munger, Edwin Stanton *political geography educator*
Palfrey, Thomas Rossman *economics professor, political science professor*
Plott, Charles Raymond *economics educator*
Scudder, Thayer *anthropologist, educator*
Valone, Keith Emerson *psychologist, psychoanalyst*

Portola Valley
March, James Gardner *social sciences educator*

Redwood City
Beutler, Larry Edward *psychologist, educator*
Calvin, Allen David *psychologist, educator*

Riverside
Calfee, Robert Chilton *psychologist, educator*
Deolalikar, Anil B. *economics professor, researcher*
Griffin, Keith Broadwell *retired economics professor*
Petrinovich, Lewis Franklin *psychologist, educator*
Rosenthal, Robert *psychology professor*
Turk, Austin Theodore *social studies educator*

Rocklin
Wiens, Beverly Jo *psychology professor*

Rolling Hills Estates
Castor, Wilbur (Webb) Wright *futurist, writer, consultant, playwright, actor*

Sacramento
Covin, David L. *retired political science professor*
Nation, Joseph Edward *public policy analyst, researcher*
Newland, Chester Albert *public administration educator*

San Diego
Gazell, James Albert *public administration educator*
Lane, Sylvia *economist, educator*
Madhavan, Murugappa Chettiar *economics professor*
Robinson-Zañartu, Carol A. *psychology professor, department chairman*
Stoessinger, John George *political science professor*
Weeks, John Robert *geographer, social studies educator*

San Francisco
Doupe, Allison Jane *psychaitry and physiology educator*
Estes, Carroll Lynn *sociologist, educator*
Gamson, Joshua Paul *sociology educator, writer*
Gemello, John Michael *economics professor, consultant, academic administrator*
Hare, Julia *educational psychologist, author, consultant*
Jamison, Dean Tecumseh *economist*
Krippner, Stanley Curtis *psychologist*
Kwan, Simon H. *financial economist, researcher*
Marston, Michael *economist, consultant*
Rice, Dorothy Pechman *medical economist*
Soh, Chunghee Sarah *anthropology educator*
Wells, Gertrude Beverly *psychologist*

San Jose
Danopoulos, Constantine P. *political science professor*
McDowell, Jennifer *sociologist, composer, playwright*
Pellegrini, Robert J. *psychology educator*
Voth, Alden H. *political science professor*

San Luis Obispo
Fisher, Eric O'Neill *economist*

San Rafael
Tosti, Donald Thomas *psychologist, consultant*

Santa Barbara
Comanor, William S. *economist, educator*
Cosmides, Leda *cognitive psychologist, educator*
Davidson, Roger H(arry) *political science professor*
Eckstein, Miguel P. *psychology professor*
Erasmus, Charles John *anthropologist, educator*
Goodchild, Michael Frank *geographer, educator*
Gravitz, Herbert L. *clinical psychologist, writer*
Jochim, Michael Allan *archaeologist*
Kendler, Howard H(arvard) *psychologist, educator*
Mayer, Richard Edwin *psychology professor*

Santa Clara
Foldvary, Fred Emanuel *economist, educator*
Gilbert, Lucia Albino *psychology professor*

Santa Cruz
Cheung, Yin-Wong *economics professor*

Crosby, Faye Jacqueline *psychology professor, writer*
Pratkanis, Anthony Richard *social psychologist, educator*

Santa Monica
Kurtzman, Joel Allan *economist*
Reville, Robert T. *economist*
Smith, James Patrick *economist*
Stiehm, Judith Hicks *political scientist*
Wolf, Charles, Jr. *economist, educator*

Sonora
Clarke, Paula Katherine *anthropologist, researcher, social studies educator*

Stanford
Abramovitz, Moses *economist, educator*
Amemiya, Takeshi *economist, statistician*
Anderson, Martin Carl *economist*
Arrow, Kenneth Joseph *economist, educator*
Bandura, Albert *psychologist, educator*
Boskin, Michael Jay *economics professor*
Bulow, Jeremy Israel *economist*
Bunzel, John Harvey *political science professor*
Carlsmith, James Merrill *psychologist, educator*
Carstensen, Laura Lee *psychology professor*
Damon, William Van Buren *developmental psychologist, educator, writer*
Diamond, Larry *political scientist*
Enthoven, Alain Charles *economist, educator*
Fetterman, David Mark *anthropologist, educator, evaluator*
Fuchs, Victor Robert *economist, educator*
Granovetter, Mark *sociology educator*
Hall, Robert Ernest *economics professor*
Harris, Donald J. *economics educator*
Hickman, Bert George, Jr. *economist, educator*
Holloway, David James *political science educator*
Howell, James Edwin *economist, educator*
Inkeles, Alex *sociology educator*
Johnston, Bruce Foster *economics professor*
Krasner, Stephen David *political science educator, former federal agency administrator*
Kreps, David Marc *economist, educator*
Krumboltz, John Dwight *psychologist, educator*
Kurz, Mordecai *economics professor*
Laitin, David Dennis *political science professor*
Lazear, Edward Paul *economics professor*
Lepper, Mark Roger *psychologist, educator*
Lewis, John Wilson *political science professor*
Maccoby, Eleanor Emmons *psychology professor*
Martin, Joanne *social sciences educator*
McClelland, James Lloyd *psychologist, educator, cognitive neuroscientist*
Mc Lure, Charles E., Jr. *economist, consultant*
Meier, Gerald Marvin *economics professor*
Milgrom, Paul Robert *economics educator*
Moore, Thomas Gale *economist, educator*
Noll, Roger Gordon *economist, educator*
Oyer, Paul *economist*
Rice, Condoleezza *political science professor, former United States Secretary of State*
Roberts, Donald John *economics, business professor, consultant*
Romer, Paul Michael *economics professor*
Shultz, George Pratt *economics professor, former United States Secretary of State*
Sowell, Thomas *economist, syndicated columnist*
Steele, Claude Mason *psychology professor*
Taylor, John Brian *economist, educator*
Van Horne, James Carter *economist, educator*
Zimbardo, Philip George *psychologist, educator, writer*

Trabuco Canyon
Addy, Jo Alison Phears *economist*

Turlock
Ahlem, Lloyd Harold *psychologist*

Walnut Creek
Berson, David William *economist*

COLORADO

Arvada
Yamamoto, Kaoru *emeritus psychology professor*

Aspen
Manosevitz, Martin *psychologist*

Boulder
Borysenko, Joan *psychologist, biologist*
Bourne, Lyle Eugene, Jr. *psychology professor*
Greenberg, Edward Seymour *political science professor*
Greene, David Lee *physical anthropologist, educator*
Healy, Alice Fenvessy *psychology professor, researcher*
Jessor, Richard *psychologist, educator, director*
Kintsch, Walter *retired psychology professor*
Menken, Jane Ava *demographer, educator*

Castle Rock
Hendrick, Hal Wilmans *human factors educator*

Colorado Springs
Farrer, Claire Anne Rafferty *anthropologist, educator*

Denver
Beresford, Thomas Patrick *psychology professor, alcohol/drug abuse services professional*
Guy, Mary Ellen Johnston *political science professor*
Moorcroft, William Herbert *retired bio-psychologist, educator, researcher*
Nelson, Sarah Milledge *archaeology educator*
Zimet, Carl Norman *psychologist, educator*

Fort Collins
Bennett, Thomas LeRoy, Jr. *clinical neuropsychology educator*
Berry, Kenneth J. *sociology educator*
Suinn, Richard Michael *psychologist*

Golden
Petrick, Alfred, Jr. *economist, educator*

Gunnison
Drake, Roger Allan *psychology professor, neuroscience researcher*

Littleton
Lohman, Loretta Cecelia *social scientist, consultant*

Longmont
Watkins, John Goodrich *psychologist, educator*

Nederland
Sutton, Philip D(ietrich) *psychologist, educator*

Pine
Jones, David Milton *economist, educator*

DISTRICT OF COLUMBIA

Washington
Cain, Bruce Edward *political science professor, consultant*

HAWAII

Honolulu
Bitterman, Morton Edward *psychologist, educator*
Cho, Lee-Jay *social scientist, demographer*
Fullmer, Daniel Warren *former psychologist, educator*
Mark, Shelley Muin *economist, educator*
Pedersen, Paul Bodholdt *psychologist, educator*
Shay, Roshani Cari *political science professor and healthcare professional*
Suh, Dae-Sook *political science professor*

IDAHO

Boise
Overgaard, Willard Michele *retired political scientist*

Caldwell
Angresano, James *political economics professor*

Pocatello
Piland, Neill Finnes *health services economist, researcher, educator*

Sandpoint
Glock, Charles Young *retired sociologist, writer*

Sun Valley
Stewart, John Todd *economist, consultant*

MONTANA

Bozeman
Gray, Philip Howard *former psychologist, writer, educator*
Spencer, Robert C. *retired political science educator*

Miles City
Gerber, Robin *history and social sciences educator*

Missoula
Lopach, James Joseph *political science professor*
McKeown, Ashley *biological anthropologist, educator*
Power, Thomas Michael *economist, educator*

NEVADA

Ely
Alderman, Minnis Amelia *psychologist, educator, small business owner*

Las Vegas
Goodall, Leonard Edwin *public administration educator*
Perlman, Seth Joseph *political risk analyst*
Weeks, Gerald *psychologist, educator*

Reno
Chapman, Samuel Greeley *political science professor, criminologist*
Crowley, Joseph Neil *political science professor, former academic administrator*
Derby, Jill Talbot *anthropologist, educator, consultant*
Hayes, Steven Charles *psychologist, educator*
Haynes, Gary Anthony *archaeologist*
Lemire, David Stephen *school psychologist, educator*
Webster, Michael Anderson *experimental psychologist*
Weinberg, Leonard Burton *political scientist*

NEW MEXICO

Albuquerque
Condie, Carol Joy *anthropologist, science administrator*
Harris, Fred R. *political scientist, educator, former United States Senator from Oklahoma*
Lamphere, Louise *anthropology and women's studies educator*
McCrady, Barbara Sachs *psychologist, educator*
Schwerin, Karl Henry *anthropology educator, researcher*

Corrales
Adams, James Frederick *psychologist, academic administrator, educator*
Elliott, Charles Harold *clinical psychologist*

Las Vegas
Riley, Carroll Lavern *anthropology educator*

Santa Fe
Williams, Stephen *anthropologist, educator*

Silver City
Lopez, Linda Carol *social sciences educator*

OREGON

Corvallis
Castle, Emery Neal *economist, educator*
Gillis, John Simon *retired psychologist, educator*
Ray, Edward John *economics professor, academic administrator*

Eugene
Aikens, C(lyde) Melvin *anthropologist, educator, archaeologist*
Davis, Richard Malone *economics professor*
Freyd, Jennifer Joy *psychology professor*
Khang, Chulsoon *economics professor*
Kimble, Daniel Porter *psychology educator*
Littman, Richard Anton *psychologist, educator*

Newberg
Adams, Wayne Verdun *pediatric psychologist, educator*

Portland
Harter, Lafayette George, Jr. *retired economics professor*
Kristof, Ladis Kris Donabed *political scientist, writer*
Matarazzo, Joseph Dominic *psychologist, educator*
Wiens, Arthur Nicholai *psychology professor*

UTAH

Boulder
Gove, Walter R. *sociology educator*

Logan
Fifield, Marvin G. *psychologist, educator*
Roberts, Richard N. *psychologist*

Ogden
Amsel, Eric David *psychology professor*

Provo
Bahr, Howard Miner *sociologist, educator*
Brown, Ralph Browning *sociologist, educator*
Fry, Earl Howard *political scientist, educator*
Hawkins, Alan J. *family life educator, researcher*
Kunz, Phillip Ray *sociologist, educator*
Pope, C. Arden III *economics professor*
Porter, Blaine Robert Milton *sociology professor, psychology professor*

Salt Lake City
Benjamin, Lorna Smith *psychologist*
Bilginsoy, Cihan *economics professor*
Harpending, Henry Cosad *anthropologist, educator*
Kumpfer, Karol Linda *research psychologist*
Lease, Ronald Charles *financial economics educator*

WASHINGTON

Bellingham
Burdge, Rabel James *sociology educator*

Ellensburg
Jacobs, Robert Cooper *political scientist, consultant*

Friday Harbor
MacGinitie, Walter Harold *psychologist, educator*

La Conner
Knopf, Kenyon Alfred *economist, educator*

Pullman
McSweeney, Frances Kaye *psychology professor*
Rawlins, V. Lane *economics professor, retired academic administrator*
Warner, Dennis Allan *psychology professor*

Seattle
Borgatta, Edgar F. *sociologist, educator*
Chirot, Daniel *sociology and international studies educator*
Fiedler, Fred Edward *retired organizational psychology educator, consultant*
Gross, Edward *retired sociologist*
Hirschman, Charles, Jr. *sociologist, educator*
MacDonald, Don *psychology educator*
Morrill, Richard Leland *geographer, educator*
Olson, David John *political science professor*
Patrick, Donald Lee *sociologist, educator*
Plotnick, Robert David *economic consultant, educator*
Sarason, Irwin G. *psychology professor*
Schaie, K(laus) Warner *human development a psychology educator*
Schwartz, Pepper Judith *sociologist, educator*
Turnovsky, Stephen John *economics professor*
van den Berghe, Pierre Louis *sociologist*

Spokane
May, Richard B. *psychology professor*

University Place
Bourgaize, Robert G. *economist*

Vancouver
Archer, Stephen Hunt *economist, educator*

WYOMING

Laramie
Allen, John Logan *retired geographer*
Chai, Winberg *political science professor, foundation administrator*
Crocker, Thomas Dunstan *economics profess*
Gill, George Wilhelm *retired anthropologist*
Rothfuss, Christopher J. *political science professor*
Tschirhart, John Thomas *economist, educator*

Powell
Brophy, Dennis Richard *psychology and philosophy professor, academic administra minister*

CANADA

ALBERTA

Calgary
Stebbins, Robert Alan *sociology educator*

Edmonton
Freeman, Milton Malcolm Roland *anthropol educator*

Saint Albert
Randhawa, Bikkar Singh *retired psychologis educator*

BRITISH COLUMBIA

Burnaby
Brantingham, Paul Jeffrey *criminologist, educator*
Kimura, Doreen *psychology professor, researcher*

Vancouver
Cynader, Max Sigmund *psychology and physiology professor, researcher*
Holsti, Kalevi Jacque *political scientist, department chairman*
Kesselman, Jonathan Rhys *economics profes public policy researcher*
Laponce, Jean A. *political scientist, educato*
Marchak, Maureen Patricia *anthropology an sociology educator, academic administrat*
Shearer, Ronald Alexander *economics profes*
Suedfeld, Peter *psychologist, educator*
Tees, Richard Chisholm *psychology profess emeritus*
Walker, Michael Angus *economist, director*

Victoria
Copes, Parzival *economist, researcher*

ADDRESS UNPUBLISHED

Anderson, Duane *anthropologist*
Attiyeh, Richard Eugene *economics profess*
Babcock-Lumish, Terry Lynne *economic geographer*
Beck, Colleen Marguerite *archaeologist*
Bergin, Allen Eric *clinical psychologist, educator*
Bonnell, Victoria Eileen *sociologist, educat*
Burns, Marcelline *retired psychologist, researcher*
Carlson, Roger David *psychologist, educat minister*
Churchill, Ward LeRoy *social sciences edu advocate*
Cohen, Malcolm Martin *psychologist, resea*
Davis, James Allan *gerontologist, educator*